106TH EDITION

BURKE'S
PEERAGE
&
BARONETAGE

Photograph by Karsh of Ottawa, 1985, © Camera Press, London

HM The Queen

BURKE'S PEERAGE & BARONETAGE

106TH EDITION

EDITOR-IN-CHIEF
CHARLES MOSLEY

VOLUME II
LANSDOWNE–ZOUCHE

To 'This royal throne of kings, this scepter'd isle'

BURKE'S PEERAGE & BARONETAGE

Morris Genealogical Books SA
owners of
Burke's Peerage (Genealogical Books) Ltd

Published by
Burke's Peerage (Genealogical Books) Ltd
7 rue du Bugnon
1299 Crans
Switzerland

Tel: +4122 776 5109
Fax: +4122 776 0889
Editorial email: CMosley@compuserve.com

ISBN 2-940085-02-1

Distributed by
Morris Genealogical Books SA
c/o RotoVision SA
Sheridan House
112–116 Western Road
Hove BN3 1DD
UK

Tel: (+44) 1273 716026
Fax: (+44) 1273 727269
email: brianm@rotovision.com

Published for libraries worldwide by
Fitzroy Dearborn Publishers
919 North Michigan Avenue
Chicago
Illinois 60611
USA

Tel: (+1) 312 587 0131
Fax: (+1) 312 587 1049

310 Regent Street
London
W1R 5AJ
England

Tel: (+44) 171 636 6627
Fax: (+44) 171 636 6982

ISBN 1-57958-083-1

Burke's logo designed by Clive Spring, Brighton, England
Technical support, design, layout and preparation by Bookcraft Ltd, Stroud, England
Production by Provision Pte Ltd, Singapore
Printed and bound in Hong Kong

Publisher's Preface

Brian Morris

This 106th edition of *Burke's Peerage & Baronetage* is the first since 1970, that is, for 29 years. Indeed in purely editorial terms the gap is more like 30 years. In the pre-computer era of the late 1960s it was necessary to finish the editorial process much further in advance of publication, too soon to include many members of peerage or baronetage families born about then. In genealogical terms that amounts to roughly two 'lost' generations. The newly born children of 1970 have now grown up and begotten their own children. With the publication of the 106th edition it is possible to include them. Perhaps up to half the living persons in *Burke's Peerage & Baronetage* have never featured in it before.

The new edition is the result of five years' unremitting toil by a full-time editorial team of eleven. They have been supplemented by seven outside researchers, copy editors and proof-readers, who in turn have been backed up by the services of distinguished consultants in such specialised fields as Celtic family history, heraldry and peerage law. Still further information has been obtained through the goodwill, diligence and generosity with their time of members of the two and a half thousand or so families who feature in *Burke's Peerage & Baronetage* and to whom we have sent proofs of their entries.

Sir Bernard Burke, one of the former editors of *Burke's Peerage & Baronetage*, was in addition the author of a book entitled the *Vicissitudes of Families*. The historic reference book he gave his name to has undergone its own vicissitudes. In 1980 there was an incomplete reissue of the 105th edition. Since the mid-1980s its authority and prestige have been exploited for crudely commercial ends by persons displaying minimal concern for scholarship or indeed serious genealogical publishing generally. It cannot be stated too emphatically that such persons have nothing whatever to do directly with this publication, *Burke's Peerage & Baronetage*.

Since the purchase by Morris Genealogical Books SA in 1989 of Burke's Peerage (Genealogical Books) Ltd (the copyright holder of *Burke's Peerage & Baronetage*), both I as publisher and the Editor-in-Chief, Charles Mosley, have been dedicated to restoring the good name and scholarly content of this cornerstone of British publishing. Though it is a reference work, indeed a major one, *Burke's Peerage & Baronetage* is much more. It amounts to a narrative of the leading families in these islands and shows how they have played a formative role in shaping the civilisation of the entire English-speaking world. In that context it complements *American Presidential Families*, the other major work published by Morris Genealogical Books, which traces the remarkable number of links between the first families of the United States and those in *Burke's Peerage & Baronetage*.

The 106th edition contains many innovations and improvements. The following are particularly worth noting:

- The larger format and change of typeface to enhance legibility and ease of use.

- The inclusion of many more titles following the proliferation of life peers, continuing additions to the hereditary peerage and baronetage, however small, and historic titles brought out of abeyance or dormancy.

- The inclusion of many more collateral branches, particularly where they are related to other families in *Burke's Peerage & Baronetage*. We now include for the first time since their titles became extinct figures of national importance such as Pitt the Elder, Pitt the Younger and Lord Palmerston.

- Details of political and court appointments of peers and baronets, both living and dead.

- An index of living people which extends to over 200 pages and includes some 100,000 names.

- A description and history of leading family seats.

- An account of previous creations of identically named titles. As this work covers over 1,000 years of history, many titles have been created several times and cross-references in other articles to a given title do not necessarily signify the present one. Where such is the case it is now made clear.

- The inclusion of nearly 30,000 addresses of living people, together with their correct form of written address.

- Translations of family mottoes.

- The inclusion of much new and revised Celtic genealogy.

- Thorough consultation of advances in scholarship over the last century, and correction of many past errors.

As with any work, particularly of this magnitude, inaccuracies and omissions may occur. The *Burke's Peerage & Baronetage* editorial staff are only human; so too are our correspondents, who sometimes compose letters containing genealogical information that is illegible, exaggerated or internally inconsistent. We have even at times received contradictory information from different members of the same family. Unfortunately, the urgency of meeting our editorial schedule has not always permitted us to clarify matters. We fully intend to correct any such errors in future editions, and our readers are cordially invited to inform us of any changes or additions which should be incorporated.

ACKNOWLEDGEMENTS

The publisher wishes to thank all those people whose dedication and hard work have made this 106th edition possible: Charles Mosley, Editor-in-Chief, whose knowledge of the subject and attention to detail are equal to none; Lt-Cdr Peter Hinton MBE, Maj James Johnston and Roger Powell, senior editors; Tricia Badham, Sandra Banbury, Mary Banks, Carol Glover, Anne Griffiths, Helen Major, Bawn O'Beirne-Ranelagh, Debbie Postlethwaite and Judy Robson, junior editors and researchers; the outside experts Sir Crispin Agnew of Lochnaw, Rothesay Herald of Arms; Max Craven, of the Derbyshire Record Office; Frederick Hogarth; Cecil Humphery-Smith, of the Institute of Heraldic and Genealogical Studies; Sir Malcolm Innes of Edingight, Lord Lyon King of Arms; Charles Lysaght; Kenneth Nicholls, Statutory Lecturer, University College Cork; Len Nicol and Ted Sparrow of Fileset, who put the text of the 105th edition of *Burke's Peerage and Baronetage* into computer files; Dr Michael Siddons, Wales Herald Extraordinary; the staff of the House of Lords Library; Mr P C Thompson of the King's School, Worcester; Peter Townend, former editor of *Burke's Peerage & Baronetage*; and Thomas Woodcock, Norroy and Ulster King of Arms.

Thanks also to Bookcraft Ltd, who have made the production of such a massive work technically possible: John Button who, as project manager, oversaw each stage of the process; Katy Elphinstone who redrew the coats of arms; Caroline Sheldrick who undertook the bulk of the indexing; Jessica Standing and Kim Wilkins who organised the mailing of proofs; Mary Barton, Jessica Bale and Philippa Morgan who were responsible for incorporating thousands of additions and amendments; and Posy Gosling, for final proofreading.

Contents

Volume I

The following list includes courtesy titles (for a definition of which *see* Glossary). Not all such titles are currently in use, but they have been so historically and could be again. They are shown here in upper and lower case with a cross-reference (e.g. Aberdour, Lord, *see* MORTON) to the substantive title. Since all title holders are listed here they do not appear in the Index as well, unless they are mentioned in an entirely different article through a connection by marriage.

VOLUME II

Contents

READER'S GUIDE

INDENTATION AND ENUMERATION

The traditional *Burke's Peerage & Baronetage* arrangement of showing successive generations by indenting each one a further space to the right has been adhered to. In previous editions the first generation was marked in bold arabic numerals and the second one in regular arabic numerals. It was then found that the distinction between the two sorts was not visible enough. Accordingly the present edition has regular arabic numerals for the first generation followed by arabic numerals in brackets for the second one. Thereafter the 1a, 1b, 1c, formula is followed for successive generations exactly as in past editions, thus:

GEORGE VI; had issue:
1 ELIZABETH II etc
2 Margaret; *m* 1st Earl of Snowdon and has:
  (1) David etc
  (1) Sarah; *m* Daniel Chatto and has:
    1a Samuel

PLUS SIGNS AND ASTERISKS

All living people, except former spouses deprived by divorce of continued membership of the family under discussion, are marked with either a plus sign (+, in previous editions a diamond) or an asterisk. Those with a plus sign are usually in remainder (*see* Glossary for definition) to the main title whose holder's family is the subject of the article. Sometimes such persons are only in remainder to a subsidiary title, such as a baronetcy conferred before the peerage came into existence. In that case the situation is explained, usually in biographical details concerning the ancestor from whom their branch of the family descends. Living people marked with an asterisk are not in remainder to any of the titles being dealt with. (In the following example the 'titles being dealt with' should be regarded as those appertaining to the Crown or Heir Apparent, for the Earl of St Andrews *is* in remainder to his father's Dukedom of Kent, though not to the Crown and its associated titles; unfortunately no other sufficiently well-known example exists.) Thus:

GEORGE V; had, with other issue:
1 EDWARD VIII etc
2 GEORGE VI
3 GEORGE, 1st DUKE OF KENT; had issue:
  (1) +EDWARD etc, 2nd DUKE OF KENT; *m* etc and has:
    1a *GEORGE etc, *Earl of St Andrews*; *m* 1988 *Sylvana Tomaselli [since he married a Catholic he is no longer in line to the throne, though his children are] and has:
      1b +Edward, *Lord Downpatrick*
      1b +Marina-Charlotte
      2b +Sophia

The current holder of a title, whether appearing in the **Lineage** section or at the head of the entire article, is not given either a + or a * sign as he (or she) cannot be in remainder to his/her own title yet at the same time can hardly be said to be *not* in remainder.

MALES AND FEMALES, ORDER OF LISTING

Because the majority of hereditary titles can descend only to males, sons continue to be listed before daughters. For a historical overview of how this situation arose, for all that it is nowadays considered indefensible by apostles of sexual equality, *see* in particular the Thomas Woodcock article. Where fathers-in-law are mentioned as being 'of' a place this should be taken to refer to the domicile at the time of his child's marriage (unless he is a Scottish chieftan or laird, when no comma will be found between his surname and his territorial designation). The purpose here is to facilitate further genealogical research. Where two people are each a member of a family in *Burke's Peerage & Baronetage* their children are usually listed in one article only, and a cross-reference to them is given in the other article. The choice of the family in which to list the children is dictated by which title those children are in remainder to, if any.

CADET LINES

In previous editions the second and subsequent marriages of a founder of a cadet (junior) line of a family were unidentified by either a numeral or a name, *i.e.*, the narrative continued, sometimes after more than a page of descendants of the progenitor by his first wife, 'He *m* 2ndly etc'. It was thus not clear who 'He' was. The new system continues the numeral — 1, (2), 3a or whatever — plus '(cont.)' to indicate continuity.

DATING

Dates between the beginning of January and the end of March for years before the mid-18th century are often given in the form 1594/5. That is because until the English calendar reform of the years 1750–53 the year was calculated as beginning in spring, as it still does where the tax year is concerned, and the drastically out-of-synchronisation Julian Calendar was still in force. Unfortunately it has not always been possible to ascertain which side of a single date the overlap occurred, *i.e.*, whether, when one comes across an event said to have taken place in February 1546, that means 1545/6 or 1546/7.

The position is complicated by the fact that in the Catholic countries of Europe a major revision of the Calendar was undertaken as far back as 1582 by POPE GREGORY XIII, hence the modern calendar being called the Gregorian one. But the Protestant countries, out of reluctance to countenance a system of Romish origins, took longer to accept it. And even in Catholic Europe not all countries followed suit immediately. The territories under the Spanish Crown, that is to say Spain proper and southern Italy, also Portugal, converted their calendars in March 1582, along with Rome and the papal states. France delayed until nine months later, the Catholic states of Germany (roughly southern and southwestern Germany) until the next year. The Protestant states of Germany only changed over in 1700. Scotland was a century and a half in advance of England, adopting 1 January as New Year's Day from 1600. Thus for not much under two centuries (and right up till the Revolution in the case of Russia) what were called Old Style and New Style dating systems existed side by side. They were at various times 10 or 11 days apart.

TYPOGRAPHY OF TITLES

Extant titles are in bold type except for generations in which they were held *de jure* (by right, as opposed to being officially recognised) when they are in regular capitals, thus:

1d THEOPHILUS HENRY HASTINGS, *de jure* 11th EARL OF HUNTINGDON according to the decision of the Ho Lords 1819 which recognised his nephew as Earl; etc
2d George; *d* 6 Feb 1802, having had, with two er sons:
  1e Francis; *b* 1770; *d* 1776
  2e Henry; *b* 1774; *d* 1796
  3e Ferdinando; *b* 1776; *d* 1801
  4e HANS FRANCIS, **12th Earl**

Extinct, dormant or abeyant titles (*see* respectively Glossary and Thomas Woodcock article for definitions) held by cadet branches of the family which is the subject of the article are always printed in regular capitals, however many generations they may have been extant in their time, for example:

4e HANS FRANCIS, **12th Earl**
  3d Ferdinando; *d* in his 14th year
2a Walter Hastings; Mil Kt Windsor; *d* 1672
  3a Sir RICHARD HASTINGS, 1st and last Bt; *dsp* 1666/8, when the btcy expired

Where a female member of the family dealt with marries a peer or baronet his title is in initial capital letters then lower case:

FRANCIS HASTINGS, **16th Earl of Huntingdon**; *m* 1st and had:
1 *Moorea; *m* 1st 22 June 1957 (*divorce* 1966), as his 2nd w, Woodrow Wyatt, later Baron Wyatt of Weeford (*d* 7 Dec 1997) etc

Heads of state, including Popes and OLIVER CROMWELL, are in capitals, as are heirs to a title, whether apparent (*e.g.*, an eldest son) or presumptive (*e.g.*, a childless title-holder's next younger brother, who may subsequently be displaced on the title-holder's begetting a son). When the holder of a baronetcy who is the subject of the article is created a peer, or when a holder of a lesser peerage is promoted to a higher one, his lesser titles should be taken to have survived but to have been submerged in his chief title, thus:

Sir GERARD's bro,
Sir Joshua Vanneck, 2nd Bt, and **1st Baron Huntingfield of Heveningham Hall**; had issue:
1 JOSHUA VANNECK, **2nd Baron Huntingfield of Heveningham Hall**
2 Gerard etc

In some cases a title of higher rank was held in the past by the predecessor of the present peer but this has become extinct. In cross-references in other articles to such cases it has been found easiest for the general reader to mention the title by which the current peer is known because that is the name of the article itself. It may nonetheless have been of lower rank than the title, now extinct, which the peer of former times would ultimately have held. Thus in the article CHICHESTER, E, the cross-reference against the husband of Catherine, daughter of The Rt Hon Henry Pelham, is to the 9th Earl of Lincoln, a title which still exists, rather than to the 2nd Duke of Newcastle-under-Line [*sic*], a title which does not. Where a specific title has expired but others continued, the text says so.

It may be objected (and indeed has been already by one correspondent writing in to our editorial offices) that a personage is always referred to by the highest title he achieves in his lifetime. That is not the case, however. The 18th-century Prime Minister Lord North is usually so known, rather than as Earl of Guilford. The early 19th-century statesman Lord Castlereagh succeeded in the last year of his life to the Marquessate of Londonderry (*qv*) but virtually no serious history book calls him anything other than Castlereagh.

ABBREVIATIONS

To save space, certain abbreviated forms have been used which refer to specific cases although they could have other applications. For example, Newcastle the city (the context will always make it plain when this rather than the dukedom is being referred to) should be taken as referring to Newcastle-upon-Tyne and Legion of Honour (or Legn Hon) to the French order of that name. Where one of the other geographical Newcastles is meant, *e.g.*, -under-Lyme, or the Belgian Legion of Honour, the text says so.

SUBSIDIARY TITLES

Where a peer holds more than one title the chief of them is listed first in capital letters and the others follow. Some, with two or more peerages of the same rank, may nevertheless use fewer than the total. The Duke of Richmond and Gordon, for instance, is also Duke of Lennox (as well as holder of a French

dukedom) but chooses to be known by his first two dukedoms only. Others hold nearly identically worded titles, in which case the version preferred by the peer or the senior of the two (*see* for example ROSSMORE) is placed first in capital letters. A distinction is drawn in the headings of, and cross-references to, articles between a multiple title which is in fact a single such (for example ABERDEEN AND TEMAIR, that being the full designation of the Marquessate) and one that is not, for example BUCCLEUCH and QUEENSBERRY, which consists of two separate dukedoms. In the first case the AND is upper case; in the second, lower case.

TITLE-HOLDERS' PREFERENCES

The holder's preference as to title when he holds two or more of the same rank may vary from generation to generation. Thus Lord Stanley of Alderley, who is also Lord Sheffield (*i.e.*, he posseses two baronies of equal rank), chooses to be known principally as the former. But his predecessor in the titles preferred to be known principally as Lord Sheffield.

Other peers who prefer to use only one of their titles, although possessing another of equal rank, include Lord Egremont and Lord Oaksey, hence the listing of them in *Burke's Peerage & Baronetage* as 'EGREMONT, LECONFIELD and', and 'OAKSEY, TREVETHIN and', a wording which on the face of it may appear eccentric as flouting alphabetical order but which is faithful to the personal taste of the individual who is the principal subject of the article.

NOMENCLATURE OF TITLES

It will be noticed that the full recital of a peer's title is not necessarily the same as the version on the heading or the version the peer in question chooses to be known by. For example, the former of the two earldoms held by the Earl of Cork and Orrery was in the original letters patent of 1620 drafted in the form 'Earl of the County of Corke'. The final 'e' of 'Corke' was subsequently dropped and the version used today is 'Earl of Cork'. In 1620 the distinction between a county and a town, even a county town, was still significant in a title of honour. An earldom, for instance, that took its name from a county was more prestigious than one that took its name from a town or other entity, this being a dim memory of the early Middle Ages when an earl was necessarily earl of a county only. Today the distinction has become meaningless.

The initial paragraph of any given article, that is to say the recital of all the current peer's titles, gives the full wording of them in the version that appears to have been used in the drawing up of the original letters patent or writ of summons (*see* Glossary). Even here obvious errors abound, some dating back to the drawing up of the original document. Examples survive of preternaturally garbled Anglo-Norman French or dog Latin, to say nothing of abbreviations which may have had a perfectly clear meaning in the house style of the medieval chancellery but which have had to be patiently construed since. Accordingly the occasional modification to the original has been ventured upon by subsequent transcribers.

Similar considerations apply to mottoes. It has been our intention to provide a translation that makes sense. This is not always possible, for example because the motto has become garbled over the centuries, or was composed by a person with an imperfect grasp of the language it is in. It is not even clear that every motto was actually composed by an individual as opposed to evolving through a process of family tradition passed down orally from generation to generation. Thus the interpretation of many mottoes must remain a matter of debate.

As to the wording of the title, the version given is that which as far as can be ascertained is the one preferred by the peer or peeress for everyday use; this is reflected in the wording of the heading. (The recital of a peer's names in round brackets after the listing of the peerages in bold sometimes takes the form 'Sir

John Smith Bt' if he possesses a baronetcy as well; it is thus always the form of wording he would be known by if he possessed no peerage or were to renounce his present ones.)

CORRECT FORM OF EPISTOLARY ADDRESS

The use of square brackets for every living person in *Burke's Peerage & Baronetage* for whom we have an address allows any reader to write to the person featured without fear of committing a solecism. The letters after a person's name in square brackets are confined to decorations or appointments emanating from the Crown. Academic and professional qualifications have been excluded from the square brackets because they are strictly speaking of institutional rather than national provenance. They do feature in the subject's career details, however.

FAMILY NAMES AND INDIVIDUAL STYLE OF ADDRESS

The surname of the peer as given inside round brackets following the recital of all his titles is presumed to be that of other members of the family in the male line unless stated otherwise. Where another version has been adopted (usually the original surname with another surname grafted on to it to make a 'double-barrelled' one) it is spelled out in capital letters in the case of the founder of the specific branch of the family and its adoption by all his descendants is then to be presumed. Where a title or major descent of a family is through a female line, the presumed change of surname on the marriage of an heiress is marked by giving her forenames in capitals and her maiden name in lower case, but her husband (or rather the husband through whom she transmits the relevant descent if she marries more than once) is treated the other way round.

In practice things may well be more complex. Examples are the article DENBIGH and DESMOND, where one branch of the family have for at least two centuries spelled their surnames Fielding whereas the main branch prefers Feilding, although the exact moment at which this divergence took place is impossible to pinpoint. Then again, in the enormous family of the Barons ASHTOWN, although one branch predominantly uses the surname Chenevix-Trench or Chenevix Trench (for variations in use of hyphens *see* the next paragraph), not all that branch's members do. In still other families the original surname may be extended by the regular but never quite formalised addition of one of the 'family' forenames (*e.g.*, Price and Rose Price or Beresford and De la Poer Beresford).

In previous generations major changes of surname tended to be officially recorded, either by the granting of royal licences or, latterly, the use of deed poll. Stress is laid upon the phrases 'tended' and 'tends'. Pontificating about trends in family history for periods before the last century and a half, when some degree of homogeneity began to occur, is extremely rash. The knitting of different ethnic groups with different customs into a single nation state took place over eons. Indeed the entity called the United Kingdom only dates from 1800. Standardised spelling, particularly of names, is even more recent. In older editions of *Burke's Peerage & Baronetage* forenames were hyphenated ('Mary-Alice', 'Charles-Edward') and the 'Mac-/Mc' prefix in the case of Scottish or Irish families called, say, MacGregor or McCarthy, was elided to 'M'Gregor' or 'M'Carthy'. They are not now. Accordingly the sort of notion that is sometimes advanced, *e.g.*, in the case of the Fielding/Feilding example quoted above, *viz.*, that the change from 'ei' to 'ie' came about because Henry Fielding the novelist was the first member of the family sufficiently educated to be able to spell, misses the point. It presupposes in 18th-century England (a) a conscious desire to match a family name (Feilding/Fielding) to a common noun (field); (b) standardised spelling of that common noun; (c) a steady and widespread awareness of the difference between the 'ie' and 'ei' versions in

the first place, whereas many documents that survive from that era, even those drafted by educated persons, may contain two different spellings of the same word indifferently juxtaposed within a single paragraph.

Today change of nomenclature tends to be more casual, at any rate in its manner as opposed to its motivation. A look at the motivation behind such changes throws light on why there are such variations. It may be part of a process of enhanced political consciousness, the classic example being the evolution of 'Anthony Wedgwood Benn' to 'Tony Benn'. Some women who retain their maiden names following marriage do so from a sense of burgeoning feminism, others from a wish to maintain a professional identity formed earlier in life.

Among forms of address we have been asked to insert in square brackets along with an address for a woman are 'The Hon Ms. —' and in the case of a peer's daughter divorced from a French Count and now domiciled in Monaco 'The Hon Mme Jane Binks', where 'Jane' was her forename and 'Binks' her maiden name. These examples, though less unorthodox than they may seem on first appearance ('The Honourable Mr Binks', for instance, was perfectly *en règle* during the Regency), are cited to demonstrate how the doctrine of 'empowerment' motivates people to impose their own private code of correct form on the pre-existing one.

The change of nomenclature is neither one-way nor simultaneous along all fronts, to use a military term. Members of a peerage family may use several versions of their name, one for the workplace, another for social life. Being christened Lyulph Ydwallo Odin Nestor Egbert Lyonel Toedmag Hugh Saxon Esa Cromwell Orma Nevill Dysart Plantagenet Tollemache-Tollemache would today be a definite career handicap. A hundred years ago such mannerist strings of vocables were more widely accepted. Even in social life it is not unknown for people to use several aliases, depending on the social stratum of their companions of the moment. Nor is the development recent. HENRY V, whether in his Prince Hal phase or as King on the eve of Agincourt, is a classic example of what one might call the Haroun al-Raschid syndrome. Incognitos were much used by QUEEN VICTORIA and EDWARD VII when travelling as private individuals. The DUKE OF EDINBURGH in our own day has changed his name several times throughout a long and distinguished career.

Where a baronet changes his name the two (or more) versions are printed in regular (*i.e.* non-bold) capital letters, though the recital of the actual title (*e.g.*, **5th Bt**) remains in bold. For example:

Sir SIGMUND NEUMANN later NEWMAN (deed poll 9 March 1936), **1st Bt**

Some children take their mother's surname (such cases include the aforesaid DUKE OF EDINBURGH's children). Others, born out of wedlock, take their biological father's surname, even if their mother has married someone else. Still other children, born in wedlock, may take the surname of a subsequent husband of their mother's (the best known case of this is Bill Clinton, born William Jefferson Blythe). In all these cases that surname is shown in capital letters after their forenames.

The problems connected with changes of nomenclature mentioned above are not confined to surnames. The Earl of Rosse, for instance, is known by those Irish neighbours and friends fortunate enough to be on first name terms with him as Brendan (his fourth of five such) but by his English relatives as William (his first of five such).

The hyphenation of surnames is equally hard to give a definitive ruling on. Its presence or absence can arouse strong contending passions in members of a single family. In some cases, Leslie(-)Melville for instance, the family name of the Earls of Leven and Melville, earlier generations appear to have favoured the hyphen, latter ones by and large not. But in the case of at least one other Scottish family two brothers use different versions at this very moment, one hyphenated and the other not, and each, together with his adherents among his other relatives, insists that his is the 'correct' version.

GLOSSARY

This glossary is designed to help readers understand terms used in *Burke's Peerage & Baronetage*. It does not purport to have wider application, for instance to general or specialist law, so that terms such as **writ** are dealt with only insofar as they refer to titles of honour, nor to foreign countries, so that **impeachment**, for instance, is not discussed in its US context. Words in **bold** type occurring in any given article have an entry of their own, for which *see*, especially since observations on one topic frequently have reference to one or more of the others.

abeyance: *see* Thomas Woodcock article.

attainder: in **peerage** (1) matters, a primarily political means, now obsolete, of enforcing the sovereign's punitive will in a manner which bypassed the usual judicial system. Being political, the vehicle was parliamentary, hence the phrase 'Bill' and (if the Bill was passed) 'Act' of attainder. The practice was formally introduced in England in 1459, although similar operations involving the stripping of an overmighty subject of his lands and/or titles had of course been carried out by Kings for many centuries previously. Attainder was abolished in 1879, although the last Act of Attainder had been passed many years earlier, against Lord Edward FitzGerald (*see* LEINSTER, D) following his participation in the 1798 Uprising in Ireland.

Attainder was an especially favourite method of the Tudor monarchs for eliminating possible rivals for the throne (whether actual or potential) while incurring the least possible risk of an acquittal. For instance, the rules of evidence admissible in an ordinary law court were either restricted to whatever might lead to a conviction or suspended altogether. An attainted person was said to be corrupted in blood, whereby neither he nor his descendants could ordinarily inherit either a title of honour or property. If the attainted person was already the holder of the title or property these were forfeited.

Attainders could be and were reversed, sometimes as much as several centuries later, but as with the imposition of the attainder itself only by an Act of Parliament. Individuals, even if by now deceased, who had in the meantime descended from an attainted person holding a **peerage** (1) dignity such that they would have subsequently inherited that dignity had it not been for the attainder were sometimes retrospectively restored. But sometimes only the living person who would at the moment of the passing of the Act of Restoration have been entitled to the dignity was restored (and of course from then on that person's successors in the title). It depended on the wording of the Act of Parliament.

baron: holder of lowest rank of dignity, called a barony, in the **peerage** (2) of England, Great Britain, Ireland or United Kingdom (but almost never of Scotland, for which *see* **lord**). A related term is the now obsolescent 'baronage', meaning either the collective noun for the order of barons or a reference book dealing with them.

In early medieval society in England a baron was a man who held land directly from a sovereign. The sovereign was not necessarily the king. He might be a Count Palatine, for instance the Earl of Chester, or a Palatine Bishop, for instance that of Durham (*see* VERNON, B. for an example of a holder of baronial rank in such circumstances), both of whom at that time wielded massively devolved powers because of the important positions of their domains on the borders with Wales and Scotland respectively. But on a national scale barons comprised not just the body of men who were later to become barons in the sense of holders of a **peerage** (1) title of that rank but also every **earl**, or strictly speaking every such

earl as held land directly from the King (which in practice amounted to all of them), for an **earl** at that time was primarily an official rather than a nobleman who possessed a personal dignity with a certain rank in the **peerage**.

The term baron later came to be applied to the more important magnates, that is to say those who were issued by the Crown with a **writ of summons** to the councils of the realm that developed into Parliament, specifically its Upper House. Since the heirs of such magnates tended to be of similar substance the practice grew up fitfully of repeating a **writ of summons** to a man's son, grandson and so on, though this was not invariably done and the consensus of scholarly opinion nowadays is that the creation of a specifically hereditary **peerage** (1) was not intended by the issue in early times of such a **writ**.

The wording of a **writ** was predominantly to a *dominus*, or **lord** in Latin. That is how the custom arose of addressing or referring to all peers below the rank of **duke**, but particularly those of baronial rank, as 'Lord Blank' (or in print as 'The Lord Blank' or 'The Rt Hon The Lord Blank' in ascending degrees of formality), hence also the *Burke's Peerage & Baronetage* policy of putting the word 'Baron' in parentheses in such cases. Indeed to refer in the third person to any baron in the **peerage** (2) of England, Great Britain, Ireland, Scotland or the United Kingdom as 'Baron Blank' rather than 'Lord Blank' is a solecism, though most female holders of a barony (but not Scottish lordships of Parliament) seem to prefer to be both addressed and referred to in the third person as 'Baroness Blank', while holders of a barony in foreign nobilities should invariably be addressed and referred to as 'Baron Blank'.

From the late 14th century a baron might also be so created by **letters patent**, that is to say by the King's express wish. His qualification for the rank of baron did not now depend on the extent of his lands or the degree of sovereignty wielded by the person he held them from, only by his favour with the monarch. Later, **letters patent** took over almost entirely from **writs of summons** as a mode of creating titles. From roughly the 18th century on, the monarch tended to be supplanted as chief mover in the award of baronies, indeed all titles of honour, by politicians, principally the prime minister, though the monarch could and did protest in private (but often to no avail) at what he or she considered unsuitable choices. The monarch retained the right of nominating his or her own choice of persons for ennoblement but this was sparingly exercised. Nevertheless the official 'fount of honour' remains the Crown.

A baron's wife should be referred to in print as 'Lady Blank', 'The Lady Blank' or 'The Rt Hon The Lady Blank' in ascending order of formality and a baron's divorced wife as 'Jane Lady Blank'. A baron's children are addressed on an envelope as 'The Hon [short for 'Honourable' and sometimes still, if in rather old fashioned style, only partly shortened to Hon.ble] Adam/Eve Binks' (where Binks is the name of the family holding the barony of, *e.g.*, Blank). They have no special form of address in direct speech. A baron would normally be addressed to his face as 'Lord Blank', his wife, whether current or divorced, and widow as 'Lady Blank'. Some peers and peeresses do not use the prefix Rt Hon on the grounds that it more properly belongs to Privy Counsellors: Lady Grimthorpe is one such among wives of barons. The form of second person address 'My Lord'/'My Lady', formerly in use even by those who felt themselves the social equal (or even the social superior) of the holder of the barony or his wife/former wife/widow, would now tend to be used only by domestic servants (if any), estate workers (if any), tenants (if any) and tradesmen in a small way of business.

In Ireland the term barony could have three meanings: (1) a title of honour; (2) an administrative unit of territory, smaller than a county, roughly equivalent to a hundred in England; (3) a feudal status involving the administration of local law courts and imposition of certain dues. The last of these was roughly equivalent to the original meaning attached to barons in early medieval England in that they usually appertained to land holdings held 'in chief'; in short, other, lesser holdings, were held from them. A feudal barony might be, but was not necessarily, co-terminous with an administrative one. A few feudal baronies developed into peerages of Parliament, notably Delvin (see WESTMEATH, E), and thus, confusingly, became baronies in the sense of (1). The rest tended to be used in an increasingly honorific sense, though they were not passed on when the territorial holdings with which they had once been associated changed ownership. The market in Irish baronies that has grown up in the late-20th century appears therefore to rest on a confusion over the three meanings of the term.

In Scotland the term baron means broadly a holder of a feudal territorial entity. He had originally to hold his territorial barony directly of the Crown and to have been at some point, either *ab initio* or by the later erecting of his lands into a barony, endowed with jurisdictional powers in civil and criminal cases. As in England a distinction developed between lesser barons and greater ones. Unlike in England this was codified in a law, passed in 1428. The greater baron continued to attend Parliament and developed into the holder of a peerage called a **lord** of Parliament. This came about since barony was a type of land tenure; a large agglomeration of lands held *in baroniam* could result in the holder being recognised as of higher rank, that is to say a **lord** of Parliament, and on a still more extensive scale as an **earl**. A very few lordships of Parliament have been created in the Scottish **peerage** involving the wording 'baron' and it has sometimes been argued that the Barony of Renfrew which is one of the PRINCE OF WALES's Scottish titles is one such by virtue of a law of 1469 settling it on the eldest son of the King of Scots or by virtue of the union of English and Scottish crowns in 1603. Another school argues that it is fundamentally a territorial designation, still subsidiary to the Dukedom of Rothesay.

Barons of the Exchequer were judges who presided in certain types of revenue litigation. They were abolished in 1875.

baronet: holder of a hereditary title of honour called a baronetcy. This title is unique to the kingdoms of the British Isles that since the 17th century have at different times merged to form the United Kingdom. The collective name for baronets is baronetage, though this can also mean a reference book listing holders of baronetcies (e.g., *Burke's Peerage & Baronetage*). The order of baronets was invented by JAMES I to raise money. Nominally this was for the upkeep of military forces in Ireland, hence the badge of the Red Hand of Ulster featuring as a baronet's device (except in the case of Nova Scotia creations (see below), where the saltire (see Heraldic Glossary) of Ulster was used instead). At the same time the Red Hand is not invariably shown in a baronet's coat of arms. It was made clear at the time that no order should henceforth be called into existence that was of equal or higher degree than the baronetage yet beneath the lowest rank of peerage.

Many baronets have subsequently been created peers, but the order is wholly distinct from both the knightage (see **knight**) and the **peerage** (2) as can be shown by the fact that the 1st and last Lord Barrett of Newburgh was made a baronet after being created a peer. Baronets were originally given the right to be knighted, which would make no sense if they were merely, as is sometimes wrongly asserted, hereditary knights. They also once had the right to have their eldest sons knighted on the latter attaining their majority, a privilege which was bestowed by JAMES I in 1616 after candidates dried up following his ruling that baronets' precedence should be lower than that of barons' younger sons but which was rescinded by GEORGE IV in 1827.

Nevertheless as late as 1842 Sir Richard Broun, 8th Bt (qv), who did not succeed to his father's baronetcy till 1844, started calling himself Sir Richard Broun on the grounds that the right

of a baronet's heir apparent to be knighted had not lapsed, though the Lord Chancellor of the day had declined to bring him before QUEEN VICTORIA to be dubbed when he had petitioned for the honour back in 1836. Broun had two years previous even to that occasion tried to get the order to which his father belonged granted certain privileges, among them the right of all baronets to wear a neck badge, one that had been extended back in 1629, but to Nova Scotia baronets only. Although Broun has been widely ridiculed (by no one more than Disraeli, who put him in *Sybil* as the absurd Sir Vavasour Firebrace), his campaign was not wholly unsuccessful. In 1854 Sir John Kingston James, who was to succeed his father as 2nd Baronet 15 years later (see 1970 edn JAMES, Bt), was knighted, specifically as a baronet's eldest son. In 1874, Ludlow, eldest son of Sir James Cotter, 4th Bt (qv), was knighted on coming of age. (He predeceased his father by 20 years, dying unmarried in 1882.) But when in 1895 Claude, the eldest son of Sir Claude de Crespigny, 4th Bt (see 1949 edn), petitioned to be knighted he was turned down. Lastly, in 1929 Broun won his most significant, if posthumous, victory when all baronets were accorded their own neck badge.

The baronetage of England dates from 22 May 1611, that of Ireland from the following 30 September, that of Nova Scotia or Scotland (so called in the former case because the moneys raised were supposed to go towards establishing the colony of Nova Scotia in North America and applicants received a land grant there; the grants were stopped in 1638) from 28 May 1625, that of Great Britain following the Union of English and Scottish Parliaments in 1707 and that of the United Kingdom following the Union of Parliaments of Great Britain and Ireland in 1801. Nearly all baronetcies are heritable by and through males only. The exceptions are a handful in the baronetage of Nova Scotia, for example the one held (but not used) by the Labour MP Tam Dalyell (qv). There is no mechanism for formally renouncing a baronetcy in the way there is for a **peerage** (1).

In the 19th century the custom grew up of conferring baronetcies on distinguished men who were deemed by Victorian convention not quite worthy of a peerage, usually because of their calling rather than because of lack of wealth. Engineers were one group frequently so honoured. The other chief group was members of the medical profession, whereas lawyers, who were also members of a profession, tended to be honoured, where they were honoured at all, with peerages. It also became the custom to confer a baronetcy on Lord Mayors of London. The last person so honoured was Sir Ralph Perring in 1963.

An Official Roll of the Baronetage is kept up by the Home Office. Anyone who wishes to be officially recognised as a baronet must prove his succession, as with peers. A royal warrant of 8 February 1910 decreed that no person should be received as a baronet or addressed or mentioned by that title in any civil or military commission, letters patent or any other official document unless his name figured on the Official Roll. But in practice it may take years for a claim to be recognised, even supposing a claim is pursued. Yet the potential new baronet may not even wish to take up the title, either through a reluctance to incur expenditure or through lack of interest. Accordingly, most books of reference, including *Burke's Peerage & Baronetage*, treat the successor, where clearly indicated, as having established his claim. For example, by the end of 1995 no claim had been made regarding the baronetcy of FitzGerald of Geraldine Place, although the most recent officially recognised holder of the title, the 2nd baronet, had died 38 years previously. Meanwhile his second but eldest surviving son and non-official successor as 3rd baronet had died in 1988. Yet the line of inheritance was perfectly obvious. It was just that both the putative 3rd and 4th baronets were Catholic priests. They were also probably citizens of the Republic of Ireland and may well have deemed it inappropriate to make a claim. They nonetheless appeared as holders of the baronetcy in books of reference. Where the succession is not obvious the baronetcy may have fallen into a state of **dormancy**.

The Standing Council of the Baronetage, founded as the Honourable Society of the Baronetage in 1898 to protest against the declaration granting sons of life peers superior precedence the year before but renamed in 1903, promotes the interests of the order, in particular by helping claimants.

A baronet is addressed on an envelope as 'Sir John Blank, Bart [or 'Bt', both forms being short for Baronet]', his wife as 'Lady Blank'. The prefix 'Sir' (also used for a **knight**) derives from the Latin comparative adjective *senior*, i.e., older or of higher rank. A baronetess, i.e., the female holder of a baronetcy, is addressed on an envelope as 'Dame Anne Blank, Btess'. The form of address in direct speech to a baronet called Sir John Blank is 'Sir John', to his wife 'Lady Blank' and to a baronetess called Dame Anne Blank 'Dame Anne'. Husbands of baronetesses and children of baronets or baronetesses have no special form of address.

Blue, Admiral (of) the: forerunner of modern Rear-Admiral; a commanding officer of one of three squadrons, the other two being the Red and White, into which the Royal Naval fleets were divided under a system in force between the 17th and 19th centuries. The Admiral of the Red was the senior and commanded from the centre of the Fleet. The Admiral of the White commanded from in front and that of the Blue from the rear.

courtesy title: strictly speaking any honorific prefix, whether 'Hon', 'Lady' etc, extended by custom to the near relative of a peer. (For such lesser prefixes, *see* the individual articles **baron**, **duke**, **earl**, **marquess**, **viscount**.) It is here proposed to concentrate on the major ones. Many a holder of a **peerage** (1), especially if of senior rank such as an **earl**, **marquess** or **duke**, has more than one title. He usually 'lends' one of his lesser titles to his eldest son and sometimes one to the latter's eldest son as well. Thus the eldest surviving son and heir of the Duke of Marlborough (*qv*) is called Marquess of Blandford and the latter's son is called Earl of Sunderland, the two titles being among the Duke's lesser substantive ones. Such 'loans' are called courtesy titles since their bearers are not substantive peers but only commoners in a relationship of expectancy to their father's (or grandfather's) genuine peerages, and although they may be addressed as titled personages it is by courtesy. The lesser title so 'lent' may not necessarily exist, or if it does may not necessarily be one of the substantive peer's actual titles, for example the Barony of Clinton on past occasions in the case of the Earldom of Lincoln, though at present the eldest son of the latter does not use it precisely because it is not a title held by the immediate family. Again, on the death of the 10th Earl of Huntingdon (*qv*) in 1789 his subsidiary titles passed to his sister but the Earldom passed to a cousin, who became 11th Earl. The 12th Earl's eldest son was known by courtesy as Lord Hastings till he succeeded to the Earldom, even though neither of the two Baronies of that name were held by his branch of the family. And his son, the future 14th Earl, was known by courtesy as Viscount Hastings although that title had not only never been held by the family at all but had never even existed. It is customary to refer in writing to a courtesy **marquess**, **earl** or **viscount**, **baron** or **lord**, as 'Marquess of Blandford', 'Earl of Sunderland', etc, without the preceding definite article ('The'). In the body of *Burke's Peerage & Baronetage* courtesy titles are printed in italics.

custos rotulorum: a Latin phrase meaning 'keeper of the rolls' and referring to an honorific post, often associated with the Lord Lieutenant of a county.

decreet: Scottish term meaning judgment in a court of law.

dormancy: state of suspension of a title of honour. A **peerage** (1) or baronetcy is said to be dormant when it has not yet been established who the current holder is, if any. The process of establishing the rightful holder of the title may take centuries, depending on the vigour and wealth of interested parties. Unlike **abeyance**, with which it is often confused (*see* Thomas Woodcock article), there is no time limit on the process whereby dormancies may be terminated.

dowager: theoretically any widow possessed of a dower, or life interest in part of her deceased husband's property, but by extension and in modern practice the widow of (1) a **baron**; (2) a **baronet**; (3) a **duke**; (4) an **earl**; (5) a **marquess** or (6) a **viscount**. If the new holder of the title has not married and there are no other widows of previous title holders in the family, the widow's style of address does not change from what it was when her husband was alive. But since hereditary titles may pass through several hands over a relatively short period, for instance during a war, there may be more than one dowager associated with that title at any one time. The senior dowager, i.e., the one who has first become a dowager, is addressed or referred to as (1) 'The Dowager Lady Blank'/'The Rt Hon The Dowager Lady Blank'/'Jane Lady Blank'/'The Rt Hon Jane Lady Blank'; (2) 'Dowager Lady Blank' [note the absence of any definite article]/'Jane Lady Blank'; (3) 'The Dowager Duchess of Blank'/'Her Grace The Dowager Duchess of Blank'/'Jane Duchess of Blank'/'Her Grace Jane Duchess of Blank'; (4) 'The Dowager Countess (of) Blank'/'The Rt Hon The Dowager Countess (of) Blank'/'Jane Countess (of) Blank'/'The Rt Hon Jane Countess (of) Blank'; (5) 'The Dowager Marchioness (of) Blank'/'The Most Hon The Dowager Marchioness (of) Blank'/'Jane Marchioness (of) Blank'/'The Most Hon Jane Marchioness (of) Blank'; and (6) 'The Dowager Viscountess (of) Blank'/'The Rt Hon The Dowager Viscountess (of) Blank'/'Jane Viscountess (of) Blank'/'The Rt Hon Jane Viscountess (of) Blank'. Junior dowagers may only use the form featuring their forename. The use of 'Rt Hon' etc is in each case the more formal version.

The state of dowagerhood is taken to imply that the current holder of the title following the dowager's bereavement will, if he has not already done so, take to himself a wife and that the latter will become the 'reigning' baroness, baronet's wife, duchess etc. For that reason it makes no sense to speak of the widow of a **knight** or **life peer** as 'dowager' since on the knight's or life peer's death the title becomes extinct. The earliest use of the word in conjunction with a specific title appears to have been for CATHERINE OF ARAGON on her surviving her first husband ARTHUR, when she was called 'Princess Dowager' till she married her brother-in-law the future HENRY VIII. At that time, owing to low life expectancy, a dowager was often a young woman, even a girl. It was only in later centuries, when life expectancy rose substantially, that its association with advanced age began. In modern times that association has caused many widows of peers or of baronets to reject the style of address 'Dowager' and adhere to 'Jane Lady Blank' etc instead.

duke: holder of highest rank of dignity in **peerage** (2), called a dukedom. The female equivalent is duchess. The word derives from the Latin *dux*, a military leader or general under the Roman Empire as early as the 2nd century AD who was usually appointed to command troops in a specific campaign. In later centuries he tended to be put in charge of a border region as the equivalent of the modern General Officer Commanding. Similar officials existed in the Merovingian and Carolingian Empires of a few hundred years later. As royal power declined in the 10th century dukes acquired more independence. Meanwhile a class of non-official military leaders developed and where they managed to establish themselves as independent sovereign rulers they kept the title duke as opposed to king. The Dukes of Normandy constitute the example most relevant to English history.

It is often said that the title duke was unknown in England till it was conferred on the Black Prince in 1337, but Kings from WILLIAM I (THE CONQUEROR) down to EDWARD III from the moment of his accession styled themselves Duke of Normandy, Duke of the Normans or Duke of Aquitaine as well as being known by their regal titles. Sixty years later RICHARD II made up for lost time, as it were, when he created five dukedoms in a single day. This is still the record for peerage creations combining both profusion and eminence of rank. He had already created a life dukedom, that of Ireland, conferring it on his close friend the 9th Earl of Oxford (*see* SAINT ALBANS). In Scotland the first dukedom, that of Rothesay (*see* ROYAL FAMILY, section PRINCE OF WALES), was created in 1398.

Those on whom dukedoms were conferred were always close blood relatives of the sovereign till the 16th century, and even then the first wholly non-royal creation, Charles Brandon, made Duke of Suffolk in 1514, was HENRY VIII's brother-in-law. By the latter half of ELIZABETH I's reign a series of Acts of **attainder** had totally eliminated dukedoms from the English peerage. The order revived in the 17th and 18th centuries and during the latter period there were at one time 50 extant, though held by only 40 persons, more than has ever been the case since. Dukedoms by now had tended to become the crowning glory for very rich noblemen who controlled several seats in the House of Commons. Two notable exceptions were those of Marlborough and Wellington, awarded for military success and therefore closer in spirit to the original purpose of a *dux* or duke.

Among those who are reliably reported to have refused dukedoms are the 3rd Marquess of Lansdowne (*qv*), Disraeli (*see* 1881 edn BEACONSFIELD, E), following his diplomatic triumph at the Congress of Berlin, and Sir Winston Churchill (*see* MARLBOROUGH) on his retirement from the premiership in 1955. On the last occasion Buckingham Palace is said to have declared to Sir Jock Colville (*see* COLVILLE OF CULROSS), Churchill's Principal Private Secretary, that no dukedoms would ever again be conferred on non-royals but that the offer would be made to Churchill on the understanding that he was certain to turn it down.

A duke is addressed or referred to formally as 'Your/His Grace' and addressed less formally as 'Duke'. For his eldest son's style of address *see* **courtesy title**. His younger sons and all daughters are referred to as '(The) Lord John Manners/(The) Lady Diana Manners' (*see* **earl** for discussion of the definite article before 'Lord'/'Lady'). A duchess is addressed or referred to formally as 'Your/Her Grace' but a duke's divorced wife should not be, though the late Margaret Duchess of Argyll (the correct way of referring to a divorced wife of a duke) campaigned doggedly to retain the prefix.

A related expression, the Dukeries, describes an area of Nottinghamshire rich in estates or mansions that have historically belonged to dukes: Clumber House (Dukes of Newcastle; *see* LINCOLN, E), Thoresby House (Dukes of Kingston; *see* KINGSTON, preliminary remarks, also 1953 edn MANVERS, E), Welbeck Abbey (Dukes of Portland; *see* PORTLAND, E), Worksop Manor (Dukes of Norfolk; *qv*).

earl: holder of third highest rank of dignity in the **peerage** (2), called an earldom. The word derives from the Norse *jarl* or *earl* (*see also* CAITHNESS) via the Anglo-Saxon *eorl* and is the sole **peerage** (2) rank not to have a latinate etymology. For a discussion of earls in the immediate pre-Conquest era and for two or three centuries afterwards, both in England and Scotland, *see* in particular the articles BUCHAN, NORTHUMBERLAND, RUTLAND and WINCHESTER. *See also* **baron**. The earl in the first few centuries after the Conquest, being still chiefly an official, was granted the 'third penny', or a slice of the revenue accruing from fees for cases brought in the county court of the shire over which he presided. From the later Middle Ages (*see* section on earlier creations of Earldom of March in WEMYSS and MARCH) the practice grew up of creating earldoms named after non-county entities, sometimes even families, *e.g.*, Earl Ferrers or Earl Fortescue (note that in such cases the 'of' is omitted).

An earl is referred to on paper or addressed on an envelope as 'The Earl (of) Blank' or 'The Rt Hon The Earl (of) Blank' in ascending order of formality, though a few such, notably the Earl of Mar and Kellie and the Earl of Scarbrough (*qqv*), prefer not to be addressed as 'The Rt Hon' at all on the grounds that the prefix more properly belongs to Privy Counsellors. In a social context 'Lord Blank' rather than 'The Earl (of) Blank' is considered preferable, though if the precise rank of the person referred to needs to be indicated the latter is the only way out. When addressing an earl in the second person 'Lord Blank' will suffice.

An earl's wife is called a countess, reflecting his notional equivalence in rank to the continental count. The same rules of address apply to her as to him, the word 'Countess' being substituted for 'Earl', and where divorced wives of earls are concerned the form of address is as with the divorced wives of a **baron** except that the words 'Countess (of)' replace 'Lady'. For an earl's eldest son *see* **courtesy title**. An earl's younger son(s) is/are addressed as for a baron's son. An earl's daughter is addressed as 'Lady Jane Binks', where 'Jane' is her forename and 'Binks' her surname, whether maiden or married. The practice has revived in recent years of adding a 'The' to 'Lady' when referring to her in the third person (also to 'Lord' where he is a duke's or marquess's younger son). It emanates from Court Circles but is deprecated by some members of the College of Arms. This is on the understandable grounds that it not only encroaches on the definite article which more properly pertains to a full peer but also implicitly places in an inferior position not just the eldest son and heir of an **earl**, **marquess** or **duke** since he has no 'The' to his **courtesy title** but a Prince or Princess who is not a child of the sovereign since they too are not accorded a 'The'. But the practice may well commend itself inasmuch as it presumably has the sanction of the Crown.

Earldoms have for the last 200 years been traditionally granted to former Prime Ministers, though neither exclusively nor invariably so.

extinct: state of demise of title, when all possible heirs under the terms of the **remainder** with which it was originally granted have died out. *See also* **abeyant** and **dormant**.

heir of entail/tailzie: he (or she) who inherits under the terms of an entail.

heir general: senior descendant of original grantee of title regardless of sex, whether of the heir himself/herself or the line by which he/she is so placed in relationship to the grantee.

heir male: he who may inherit a title or titles by virtue of being the senior male-line kinsman of the grantee.

heir male and of provision: in Scottish law, he who inherits as heir male general, that is, not just a direct descendant but the descendant of a brother or ascendant, such as an uncle, great-uncle or cousin (provided the relationship is through the male line).

heir male of the body: as immediately above, but directly descended from the original grantee.

ilk: Scottish term meaning 'of the same name'. Hence a Chief called 'MacQuern of that Ilk' is identical with 'MacQuern of MacQuern'.

impeachment: prosecution before House of Lords as judges, House of Commons being the accuser. Unlike **attainder** it follows judicial rules. Thus the defence can call witnesses. On the other hand sentencing does not necessarily follow a verdict of guilty but only if the House of Commons favours it. The latter body can thereby in effect also pardon the defendant. The earliest impeachment known was that of the 3rd/4th Lord (Baron) Latimer (of Corby) in 1376 (*see* LATYMER), whose association with JOHN OF GAUNT had made him unpopular, and was a milestone in the rising power of the House of Commons, as was the frequent use of impeachment in the 17th century. The last impeachment was that of the 1st Viscount Melville (*qv*) of Melville in 1806.

knight: person who holds a title of honour called a knighthood, almost invariably conferred for the grantee's lifetime only. (Holders of three hereditary knighthoods of feudal origin have long existed in Ireland: the Knight of Glin, or the Black Knight (*see* WAKEFIELD), the Knight of Kerry, or the Green Knight (*see* FitzGERALD, Bt, of Valencia), and the White Knight, a member of the FitzGibbon family, among whom a claimant to the title apparently exists although it has been **dormant** for many years.) A knight is usually referred to in the third person as 'Sir John Smith', where John is his sole or preferred forename and Smith his surname. A somewhat more familiar variant (and one which can be used in direct speech as well) is 'Sir John'. The hereditary Knights already mentioned are not so addressed or referred to. The Knight of Glin is addressed formerly in the second person as 'Knight' (his wife as 'Madam FitzGerald') and colloquially referred to in the third person as 'The Knight'. The Knight of Kerry, being a **baronet**, is addressed in the same way as with other members of that order. The title of White Knight, being dormant, has no form of address, though should the claimant be successful the Knight of Glin's form of address as 'The Knight' would presumably have to be modified since it would not be clear which of the two was being referred to. Honorary knighthoods awarded to foreign nationals, such as Bob Geldof or various former US Presidents, do not carry with them the right of the grantee to be called 'Sir', nor do knighthoods awarded to those in holy orders. The wife of a knight is addressed as 'Lady Smith' (*not* 'Lady Jane Smith' unless the daughter of a **duke**, **earl** or **marquess**). If her husband falls into one of the categories just mentioned as not being called 'Sir' she remains 'Mrs' (or 'Ms').

The style 'Sir Smith' is considered a solecism, though not uncommon among people whose first language is other than English, the error probably arising from a literal translation of the form Chevalier plus a surname, as in the Chevalier St George or the Chevalier Bayard. The French word *chevalier*, as also *ritter* (cognate with 'rider') in German, suggests an equestrian origin for knights, and certainly the class of *equites* (literally 'horsemen') in Ancient Rome, who ranked just below senators, are usually translated as 'knights'. Moreover Sir Richard Broun in his propagandising on behalf of the privileges he held were possessed by **baronet**s spoke of them as *equites aurati* ('gilded knights'), presumably on the grounds of their similar form of address ('Sir John Smith'), even though a **baronet** is not a knight. The Anglo-Saxon word *cniht* from which the term is derived meant originally a youth or subordinate fighting man, however, and later a confidential servant. The Anglo-Saxons did not fight on horseback, so that the knighting of his infant grandson ATHELSTAN by KING ALFRED in the 890s, apparently the earliest known instance of its kind in England, should probably be seen as a primarily religious ceremony. The ritual nature of investiture with knighthood, now obsolete, should not be overlooked. The keeping of a vigil on the eve of admission to knighthood persisted for some centuries, as did a cleansing ceremony by bathing, hence ultimately the Order of the Bath. As late as the 19th century the writer Thomas Love Peacock attacked the award of a knighthood, which he insisted was still an exclusively Christian institution, on a Parsee and two members of the Jewish faith.

But in England from the Norman Conquest knighthood was predominantly military in character. The **baron** would grant some of his lands as a knight's fee to a subtenant who in return had to serve on campaign under his feudal superior, though only for a fixed term. At that time the dubbing of a knight, that is to say the brief resting of the sword on the shoulder of the person so honoured, could be carried out by the feudal superior. The knighting of men, particularly on military service, by commanding officers persisted for many centuries and was the origin of the term knight banneret, where the grantee's pennon was clipped as a mark of distinction. Meanwhile, as the system of land tenure by military service became increasingly replaced by money payments, the holder of a knight's fee increasingly failed to get himself knighted. As early as 1247 it was decreed that all freeholders with an annual income of 40 shillings (roughly £50,000 in late-1990s terms) should present themselves for dubbing as knights. Meanwhile those who did get themselves knighted tended more and more to make of it a species of coming-of-age rite of passage. And so evolved the landless knight, the precursor of the knight bachelor.

A knight in recent times has held his title in one of several chivalric orders, *e.g.*, the Garter, Thistle, St Patrick, Bath, Star of India, St Michael and St George, Indian Empire, Royal Victorian Order or Order of the British Empire, or as a knight bache-lor (for the ramifications of all of which *see* the essay on Precedence). Since nowadays a knight can only have been created such in his own lifetime and of his own volition it would be absurd for the possibility of renunciation to exist. In earlier centuries, when persons of sufficient distinction were sometimes fined for refusing to take up knighthood (the possession of which imposed in turn various obligations), it was a different matter.

lady: general honorific designation for wife of a **lord** (of which word it is the female version), **baronet** or **knight**. Alternatively the substantive title of the female holder of (1) a Scottish lordship of Parliament, (2) **barony**. Also used as an honorific prefix before the forename and surname of the daughter of a **duke**, **marquess** or **earl** (*see* also **courtesy title**).

letters patent: official documents, so called from their being 'patent', that is to say open or unsealed, issued under the Great Seal and containing various pronouncements by the sovereign. Increasingly since the late 14th century the means of creating a **peer** or **baronet**.

life peer: member of the House of Lords appointed to it for the rest of his/her natural life. Life peerages were conferred as early as the 14th century, and in several different ranks of the **peerage** (2), but for the most part, especially when on women (usually royal mistresses), did not carry the right to a seat in the legislature. From 1958 on that situation has changed and life membership of the House of Lords has since then been the principal condition under which additions to it are made. A life peer nowadays is invariably of the rank of **baron**.

limitation: *see* **remainder**.

lord: a general term denoting a dignity. It may be hereditary, in which case it is specifically applied to a lord of Parliament in the **peerage** (2) of Scotland and colloquially or loosely to a male who holds the title of **baron**, **earl**, **marquess** or **viscount**, either substantively or as a **courtesy title**. (A **duke** is not usually so referred to, although it might be argued that inasmuch as he has usually been a member of the House of Lords he is a lord by virtue of his being a duke.) It may be appointive and for the grantee's life only or a fixed term, such as is the case with a **life peer**, law lord (a high-ranking appellate judge) or bishop with a seat in the House of Lords. Not every lord, even one with a seat in the House of Lords, is a **peer**. Bishops, for instance, are spiritual lords. On the other hand every **peer** is a lord. The Lord Advocate and Lord Chancellor are high-ranking politically appointed lawyers. The Lord Chamberlain, Lord High Almoner, Lord High Commissioner to the General Assembly of the Church of Scotland, Lord Steward and some Lords-in-Waiting are Court appointments. The Lord Chancellor, Lord President of the Council and Lord Privy Seal are senior Government ministers. The Lord Great Chamberlain is the holder of a hereditary ceremonial post concerned with the sovereign's attendance at Parliament and great state occasions such as the lying in state of a recently deceased sovereign and the coronation of the new one. The post is shared in alternate reigns by the Marquess of Cholmondeley (*qv*), the present incumbent, and representatives of the Marquess of Lincolnshire (*see* CARRINGTON) and Earl of Ancaster (*see* WILLOUGHBY DE ERESBY). The Lord High Constable and Lord High Steward hold ceremonial offices nowadays filled only for the single day of a coronation. The Lord High Constable of Scotland holds a hereditary post passed down with the Earldom of Erroll (*qv*). Politically appointed Lords-in-Waiting are Government whips. A lord of the manor was previously a person with certain powers of jurisdiction and the right to collect feudal dues in the administrative unit called a manor but is now often little more than the possessor of some documents relating to a place name and at the most a few residual minor property rights, though confusion in the popular mind between the various categories of lord has lent the term in recent years a factitious importance and encouraged the commercial exchange of such documents.

marquess/marquis: holder of second highest rank of dignity in **peerage** (2), called a marquessate. The term is said to derive from the term march, a border area, whose custodian was of high rank as early as Carolingian times. The first marquess in the English peerage was created in 1385 (*see* SAINT ALBANS, **Lineage (of de Vere)**). The spelling marquis is preferred by some holders of that title, usually Scottish and in particular the Duke of Roxburghe (*qv*). In such cases it is said to recall the historic links between Scotland and France, the French word for marquess being of course *marquis*.

As with an **earl**, a marquess's title may derive from a place name, in which case it carries an 'of', or be a personal one, such as 'Conyngham', in which case it does not. A marquess is addressed or referred to as 'The Marquess (of) Blank' or 'The Most Hon The Marquess (of) Blank' in ascending order of formality. His wife is addressed or referred to as 'The Marchioness (of) Blank' or 'The Most Hon The Marchioness (of) Blank'. For his eldest son and heir *see* **courtesy title**. His younger sons and all daughters are addressed as for those of a **duke**. Marquessates were often awarded to Viceroys of India.

peerage: (1) a type of title of honour; (2) a collective term for persons, called peers, who possess certain titles of honour; (3) a reference work listing persons holding one or more (1) who make up (2). Where (1) is concerned, the reader should bear in mind that not all titles of honour are peerages (*see* for instance **baronet** and **knight**). Those that are comprise the ranks of **duke**, **marquess**, **earl**, **viscount** and **baron** in that order of descending relative seniority.

The term peerage derives from the Latin word for equal (*par*) and to the extent that all peers with seats in the House of Lords have tended to be summoned to it irrespective of their relative rank, importance or wealth, the term still has some relevance. But not every holder of a peerage (1) is summoned to the House of Lords. Minors are not, for instance, nor are Irish peers (for the complex reasons why in the latter case, *see* Charles Lysaght essay). Between 1707 and 1963 Scottish peers elected representatives from among themselves to sit in the House of Lords, hence the term 'rep S peer' in individual family articles in the main body of this work. As this work was going to press it seemed likely that most holders of a hereditary peerage (1) would shortly cease to be allowed to sit and vote in the House of Lords.

The institution of a peerage (2) as a body of notional equals, sometimes even the equal of the King in the extent of land they held, existed in mainland Europe long before the development of the House of Lords offshore. Under CHARLEMAGNE in the 9th century and in Flanders and France some two or three centuries later bodies of great nobles existed to whom historians have given the name peerage (2). In Scotland an early form of national peerage (2) is said by some scholars to have existed in the shape of the *mormaers* (*see* BUCHAN, preliminary remarks). But the main ones in the British Isles have historically been those of (a) England, which existed from early times till the Union of English and Scottish Parliaments in 1707; (b) Scotland, which ditto, (c) Ireland, which existed from the Middle Ages for the most part till the Union of Parliaments of Great Britain and Ireland in 1801 but to which further additions were made afterwards (*see* Charles Lysaght essay); (d) Great Britain, which existed from the above-mentioned Union of English and Scottish Parliaments till the 1801 Union, also above-mentioned; and (e) the United Kingdom, in which nearly every creation since 1801 has been made.

Someone possessing a title in the peerage (2) of England is not necessarily an Englishman by birth as opposed to a Scot, Irishman etc. Nor has he even necessarily always been English by birth as opposed to naturalisation. The same goes for the other national categories of peer. Piers de Gaveston, a Gascon, was created Earl of Cornwall in the peerage of England in 1308. The Duke of Schomberg, so created in the Irish peerage in 1689, was born at Heidelberg of a German father and an English mother. He could have been created a Duke in the peerage of England, indeed was naturalised as an Englishman a few weeks before his ennoblement. The peerage of England comprises all peers created by sovereigns of England up to 1707. From 1603 to 1707 sovereigns of England and sovereigns of Scotland were the same person, though the kingdoms themselves were still separate, and continued to create titles in the peerages of both kingdoms. The peerage of Scotland comprises all peers created by Kings or Queens of Scots up to 1707. Again, not all such grantees were necessarily Scottish. The Viscountcy of Falkland, for instance, now the oldest in the Scottish peerage (2), was originally conferred on an Englishman.

For a discussion of the principal examples of peerage (3), *see* the Introduction.

Red, Admiral (of) the: forerunner of modern Admiral; *see* also **Blue, Admiral (of) the**

regality: in Scotland, jurisdiction over an area of landed estate granted by the Crown or the landed estate over which the jurisdiction was so granted.

remainder: terms under which a hereditary title of honour may be transmitted, thus anyone in remainder to a title is a potential inheritor of it. An alternative expression is **limitation**. For an exhaustive account of the various kinds of remainder *see* Thomas Woodcock essay.

retour: in Scotland, a jury's decision as to who is the rightful heir.

sasine: the holding of land, originally by virtue of having been presented with constituent elements of that land, *viz*, earth and stone.

viscount: holder of the second lowest rank of **peerage** (1), called a viscounty or viscountcy. The word derives from the Latin *vice-comes*, or deputy to a *comes* (early equivalent of count), and in the British Isles was in early times used to refer to the Sheriff of a county, the **earl** (Anglo-Saxon equivalent of a count) of that county being then its chief administrative officer, appointed by the Crown. The Latin term *vicecomitatu*, meaning a sheriffdom, was used in Scottish legal documents until quite recently. Viscount only began to be used as a peerage honour in the 15th century, and is in fact the most recent addition to the ranks of the **peerage** (2). The first viscountcy was conferred in February 1439/40 on the 6th Lord (Baron) Beaumont (*see* BEAUMONT, Bt), who thus became Viscount Beaumont. Unlike viscounts in the English peerage, those in the Scottish peerage, the first of whom was Fentoun, so created in 1606, were known as 'Viscount of Blank', even where 'Blank' was a family name rather than a place. The only one still to use this form would appear to be the Viscount of Arbuthnott. For observations on the level of distinction considered as meriting a viscountcy in the 19th and 20th centuries *see* the appropriate passage in the Introduction. *Mutatis mutandis*, a viscount, his wife, widow and children are addressed or referred to as for a **baron**.

White, Admiral of the: forerunner of modern Vice-Admiral; *see* also **Blue, Admiral (of) the**

writ/writ of summons: instrument for calling an individual to the councils of the realm that developed into Parliament and later to the Upper House of Parliament itself. From the early 16th century the issuing of writs of summons as a means of creating peers declined, being replaced increasingly by **letters patent**. It is still used for accelerated promotions, however, that is to say the method of calling up the heir to a peerage by the name of one of his father's subsidiary titles. The most recent such instance was the case of Lord Cecil of Essendon, formerly (and colloquially still) known as Viscount Cranborne, eldest son and heir of the Marquess of Salisbury (*qv*). Occasionally as late as the 17th century a writ of summons was issued to a peer's eldest son calling him up to the House of Lords in the name of a **barony** his father did not in fact possess. Such a case was that of Strange (*qv*) in 1628. It became a doctrine, as decided in a legal judgment of 1736, that such 'mistaken' writs had the effect of creating a fresh peerage.

HERALDIC GLOSSARY

Heraldry evolved in 12th-century Western Europe, probably in response to the growing difficulty of recognising men in armour as that armour became heavier and more enveloping. At Hastings, when a rumour spread among the Normans that WILLIAM I (THE CONQUEROR) had been killed, he had only to tilt his helmet back as he rode among them for all to see that he was alive. Two hundred years later such a feat would have required considerable exertion and the help of a squire. Knights could by now only distinguish one another by devices on their shields or on the surcoats worn over their armour. Noblemen's devices were used by their followers as badges on their own shields and coats, and in the feudal army men were accustomed to muster under the banner of their lord, which was marked with his coat of arms. Crests, which were also distinguishing marks, came later.

Heraldic devices became hereditary as first the son then the more remote descendants of the original feudal lord retained the original device so as to guide their followers in battle. The devices outlived the use of armour, however, and by the 17th century were being widely used in non-military ways. By now the granting and use of coats of arms in England had come under the supervision of a body of heralds called the College of Arms, which had been set up under royal authority in 1483. In Scotland the Lyon Office, later Lord Lyon Office, supervised the use of arms.

It is probable that arms were not originally granted by anyone, but were assumed by various person as and when they pleased. Thus from time to time two or more people might be using the same device. In the Scrope-Grosvenor case in the late 14th century, when Lord Scrope challenged the right of Sir Robert Grosvenor to use the same coat of arms that he did himself, the duplication was accidental. Indeed a third person mentioned as using those arms was a Cornish knight called Carminow.

This celebrated case was only finally settled by the King himself, who found for Scrope. By now the Crown was assuming jurisdiction over the use of arms. A century later this had become firmly established, and since then it has been heraldic law that arms can only be borne in accordance with the rules made by the heralds under royal authority. Unfortunately, the forum for prosecuting illicit assumptions of arms in England, the Court of Chivalry, is obsolescent, despite a brief revival in the early 1950s. In Scotland the Court of the Lord Lyon has more teeth and still enforces laws against the irregular or illicit assumption of arms.

Note: for the convenience of the ordinary reader the word 'colour' in definitions is almost always to be understood as having its everyday meaning rather than the restricted one it has in heraldic language, where it is only one of three basic types of **tincture**. On the very few occasions it is used in this specialised sense it is set in **bold** type, as are all other terms given their own entry.

---

abased or **abaisé**	used of an **ordinary** borne below its usual position
abatement	one of the nine marks of degradation of coat armour
accollé (*see* **gorged**)	
accosted	side by side
accrued	grown to maturity
achievement	a fully **marshall**ed coat of arms
acorned	bearing acorns
addorsed	placed back to back, used especially of wings lying close to a creature's back
affrontée	full-faced
Agnus Dei	a lamb bearing a cross with a halo round its head
aislé	winged
alant or **aland**	a mastiff with short ears
allerion	an eagle without beak or feet
ambulant (*see* **passant**)	
amethyst	a semi-precious stone, formerly used to express **purpure**
ancient	a small flag on the stern of a ship
ancred or **anchored**	used of cross whose four tips resemble anchor flukes
annulet	a ring
antique crown (*see* **eastern crown**)	
appaumé	a hand open, with fingers and thumb at full length
argent (arg.)	the **metal** silver, shown as white in heraldic illustration
armed	used to describe all birds of prey whose talons and beaks are coloured differently from their bodies, also quadrupeds so variegated
arraché (*see* **erased**)	
arrondie	rounded
assis (*see* **sejant**)	
attired	applied to the horns of animals of the deer species instead of **armed**
attires	the horns of a buck
azure (az.)	blue
badge	decorative device identifying a family, often borne by retainers, *e.g.*, on livery. It is not strictly speaking part of a heraldic **achievement** and is therefore not included in the illustrations of arms in this book. Indeed it is only included in this glossary at all because of popular misapprehension as to its status. (For a similar misapprehension *see* also **crest**)
baillond	used of a lion holding a staff in its mouth
banded	encircled with a band or riband
bar	a horizontal division occupying one fifth of the shield
barbed	(from the French word *barbe*) the leaves surrounding a full-blown rose are called barbs, hence the phrase 'a rose gu. barbed etc'
barnacles	instruments used by farriers to curb horses
baron and femme, per	the **impalement** of the arms of husband and wife
bars gemel	two **bars** or **barrulets** placed parallel to each other, 'gemel' deriving from the Italian *gemelli*, twins
barrulet	diminutive of **bar**
barry/barruly	used of a **field** or **charge** divided by horizontal lines
base	the lower part of a shield
basilisk	a monster, like a **wyvern** or **cockatrice** but with a dragon's head at the end of its tail
basnet/basinet	a helmet
baton	(from the French *baston*, a staff or cudgel) a shape like a truncheon, generally a mark of bastardy. Unlike a **bend** it is **couped**, or cut short of the shield's edges
battled arrondie	denotes that a battlement is rounded at the top
battled-imbattled	one battlement on another
beaked (*see* **armed**)	
bearing	applicable to any single **charge** or heraldic device
beaver (*see* **visor**)	
bend	a division of a shield formed by two diagonal lines from the **dexter chief** to the **sinister base**
bendlet	half-size diminutive of **bend**
bend sinister	a **bend** issuing from the **sinister chief**
bendy	used of a **field** or **charge** divided diagonally into four or more even-numbered parts
bezant	a Byzantine gold coin, represented as a round flat piece of gold without impress
bezanté	**semée** of **bezants**
billets	rectangles
billeté	**semée** of **billets**
bird-bolt	a small blunt-headed arrow
blazon	rules under which coats of arms are drawn up; also, as a verb, to describe a coat of arms in correct heraldic language

bordure	a uniform edge to a shield, occupying one fifth of the **field**
botonnée	used of a cross whose tips resemble **trefoils**
bouget (*see* **water-bouget**)	
bowed	embowed or arched
braced (*see* **interlaced**)	
breys (*see* **barnacles**)	
brimsey	a gad-fly
brassarts/ brassets	armour for the elbows and arms
burgonet	a steel cap worn in battle
cabossed/ caboshed	used of a full-faced animal head cut off just above the neck
cabrée, effray or **salient**	used of a horse rising on its hind legs
cadency	used of younger sons or descent from a junior branch of the family
caduceus	a wand with two snakes entwined round it
caltrap, galtrap or **chevaltrap**	an iron weapon used to wound horses' hooves, its spikes being positioned so that however it lies on the ground one will always point upwards
Calvary or **passion cross**	a cross with three steps
canting arms	arms which include a punning allusion to the name of the bearer
canton	corner division occupying one third of the **chief**
cartouche	an oval, formerly used to show armorials of Popes and other clerics
cap of maintenance or **dignity**, or **chapeau**	headgear of crimson velvet **doubled** ermine
caparison	the trappings of a warhorse
carbuncle (*see* **escarbuncle**)	
casque	a helmet
castle	shown in heraldry as two towers at either end of a wall, the latter embattled and with a gateway
cat-a-mountain	a wild cat, always drawn **guardant**
celestial crown	an **eastern** or **antique crown** with a star on each point
cercellée (*see* **recercellée**)	
chain-shot	bullets linked by a chain
chamber piece	a short piece of artillery without a gun carriage (*see* **mortar**)
chapeau (*see* **cap of maintenance**)	
chaplet	a garland of flowers and leaves
charge	a figure or device on a shield
charged	used of a **field** or **ordinaries** with a device on them
chaussé	shod
chequy or **checky**	used of a **field** covered with small squares of alternate **tinctures**
chevron	a division of a shield shaped like the lower half of a **saltire** and occupying one third or one fifth of the area, according to whether it is charged or not
chevronel	half-size diminutive of **chevron**
chief	the upper third of a shield
chimera	a monster with a woman's face, a lion's mane and legs, a goat's body and a dragon's tail
cinquefoil	a five-petalled flower
civic wreath or **crown**	a garland of oak leaves and acorns
clarion or **claricord**	a rest for a lance
clenched	used of a closed hand
closet	diminutive of **bar**
cockatrice	a monster with a bird's wings and legs and a snake's tail
colour	in its specialised heraldic meaning, one of three types of **tincture**
combatant	fighting or **rampant** face to face
company and compony counter-compony	used of an **ordinary** made up of one (**compony**) or two (**counter-compony**) rows of alternate squares of **metals** and **colours**
confronté	facing each other
conjoined	joined together
conjoined in lure	used of two wings joined together, their tips downwards
contourné	used of an animal facing to the **sinister**
corbie	a raven
corded	an **ordinary** or **charge** bound with cords
cotised or **cottised**	(in French a *bande diminuée qui cotoye un autre bande*) a diminutive of the **bend**, a quarter of its breadth and one half of the width of the **bendlet**, generally borne in couples with a **bend** or **charge** between them. Two together are termed **cotises**, but when one is on each side of the **fess** or **bend** they are usually termed a **bend** or **fess** cotised
couchant	used of an animal lying down

couché	used of a shield suspended by one corner from a belt
counter-changed	used of a **field** divided by a **bend** or other **ordinary** in which the **charges** in each section are of the **colour** or **metal** of the **field** of the other section
counter-embowed	bent with the elbow to the **sinister** or bent in a reverse direction
counterflory	a **tressure flory** in which the alternate **fleurs-de-lys** are reversed
counter-potent	one of the heraldic **furs** in which the heads of the T-shaped sections are juxtaposed (*see* **potent**)
counter-vair	differs from **vair** in that the rows of shields are arranged **base** against **base** and point against point
couped	term used when the head or limb of an animal or any other **charge** is cut off by an even line
couple-close	a diminutive of the **chevron** and often borne with it as the **cotise** is borne with the **bend**; it contains a quarter of the **chevron** and is always borne in pairs
courant	running
coward	used of an animal when drawn with its tail between its legs
cramp	a piece of iron turned up at each end, usually borne in pairs
crampet, crampit, chape or **batterolle**	the steel mounting at the bottom of a scabbard
crenellée (*see* **embattled**)	
crescent	differs from the **increscent** and the **decrescent** in having its horns turned towards the **chief** of the shield
crest	heraldic device originally borne on top of a helmet, particularly in tournaments, but latterly used to decorate signet rings, cutlery, plate, crockery etc. as a mark of ownership by a family. Frequently misused nowadays to mean **achievement**, or the entire coat of arms rather than just a part of it.
crined	used to describe the beard or hair when different in colour from the body
cronel	the iron head of a tilting-spear
crozier	the staff of a prelate
crusily	used when the **field** or **charge** is strewn with crosses
cubit arm	an arm with the hand attached, **couped** at the elbow
cuisses	armour covering the thighs and knees
dancettée	(in French *danché* and *dentellé*) is applied to lines whose teeth or indents are larger and wider than those of a line **indented**
debruised	used when an **ordinary** or **subordinary** is placed over an animal or **charge** (*see* **surmounted**)
dechaussé (*see* **dismembered**)	
decked	used when the feathers of a bird are trimmed at the edges with a small line of a different colour from the rest of the body
decrescent	a half moon, having the horns towards the **sinister**
defamed	without a tail
degreed or **degraded**	having degrees or steps at the end
dejected	anything thrown down, *e.g.* 'a **garb** dejected.'
delve or **delf**	one of the nine marks of **abatement**, resembling a square clod of earth
demi	half, the top half being understood when no other is mentioned
despectant	used of animals looking downwards
developed	unfurled, as in flying colours
dexter	the right-hand side of a shield viewed from the position of the person holding it
dimidiated	divided in two equal parts
disclosed, expanded or **expansed**	an alternative to **displayed**, used of tame birds
dismembered	used of a **charge** cut into pieces, which are set a small distance apart but preserve the original form
displayed	a bird of prey with its wings expanded
disponed	arranged
distilling	letting blood
dormant	sleeping; differs from **couchant** in that the head is lowered
doubled	with the lining turned up around the edge
double-queued	having two tails
drapeau	a flag
drawing-iron	an instrument used by wire-drawers
ducal coronet or **crest coronet**	a coronet composed of four leaves of equal height above the rim
duciper	a **cap of maintenance**
eastern crown	the crown worn by Jewish kings
eft (*see* **newt**)	
eightfoil or **huitfoil**	an eight-petalled flower
elevated	used of birds' wings when open and upright
embattled or **imbattled**	used of buildings having battlements
embowed	bent or bowed

embrued	having drops of blood upon or falling from it
enaluron	eight birds placed in the border
endorse	a quarter-size diminutive of the **pale**
endorsed (*see* **addorsed**)	
enfield	a monster with a fox's head, an elephant's chest, a horse's mane, an eagle's forelegs, a greyhound's body and hind legs and a lion's tail
enfiled	pierced by the blade of a weapon
Englishman's head	used in Welsh **blazons** to mark feats in the struggle against the English
engould	used of a **charge** whose ends enter an animal's mouth
engrailed	a scalloped partition line with the spikes outwards
enhanced	an **ordinary** placed higher than its usual position
enmanche (*see* **manche**)	
ensigned	a **charge** with another above it
entoyre	a border charged with eight inanimate **charges**
enurney	a border charged with eight animals
environné	surrounded
enwrapped	folded round
epaulier	armour for the shoulders
equipped	used of a horse with all its trappings
eradicated	uprooted, as of trees or plants
erased	torn from the body, with jagged edges
erect	upright
ermine (**erm.**)	white **fur** with black spots
ermines	black **fur** with white spots
erminois	gold **fur** with black spots
escallop-shell	a pilgrim's badge
escarbuncle	a precious stone, shown as eight sceptres issuing from a central **annulet**
escutcheon of pretence	the shield on which a man bears his wife's arms if she is an heiress. It is borne in the centre of his own shield and is usually of the same shape
esquierre	a bearing similar to the gyron (*see* **gyronny**), but extending across the whole shield
estoile	a star, usually of six wavy points; when an estoile has more than six points they are alternately straight and wavy
evett or **lizard**	a small animal like a crocodile, usually shown **vert**, used in the arms of some Irish families
expanded or **expansed**	displayed
falchion	a broadsword
fan	the instrument by which chaff is blown away
feathered	used of arrows whose flights are a different colour from the shafts; also called **flighted**
fer-de-moline	the iron fixed in the centre of a millstone, holding it up and guiding its motion; also called a **millrind**, **inkmoline** or **inke-de-moline**
fer-de-fourchette	used of a cross or **saltire** whose tips end with a forked iron
femau or **fermaile**	a belt buckle
fess	a division of a shield formed by two lines drawn horizontally and occupying one third of it
fess point	the centre of the shield
fesswise	placed like a fess
feuil-de-scie	a **pale** or **fess** indented on one side with teeth like the edge of a saw
field	the entire surface of the shield upon which the **charges** or **bearings** are depicted
figured	used of a **charge** shown with a human face, such as the sun
file (*see* **label**)	
fillet	a diminutive of the **chief**
fimbriated	bordered or hemmed with a different colour
firme	used of a cross **patée** extending to both sides of a shield
fireball	a grenade with flames issuing from the top
fire beacon (*see* **beacon**)	
fitchée	pointed at the end
flanches or **flaunches**	divisions on both sides of a shield formed by the segment of a circle drawn from the **chief** to the **base**
fleur-de-lys	the flower of the lily, having three leaves instead of nature's five
flexed	bent or bowed
flory, fleury, flurty or **floretty**	flowered with **fleurs-de-lys**
flotant	floating
flouretté	the same as **fleury**
flower of the flag	the same as **fleur-de-lys**
foliated	leaved
fountain	a **roundle barry wavy** of six **arg.** and **az.**
fourchée	forked at the end
fracted	broken
fraise	a strawberry leaf
fresnée	used of an animal rearing on its hind legs
fret	a **saltire** and a **mascle** interlaced
fretty	a **field** covered with **conjoined frets**
fructed	bearing fruit
fur	a pattern, constituting part of an achievement, based on the appearance of animal pelts; *see* for example **ermine** and **vair**.
furnant	emitting smoke
furnished	used of a horse when caparisoned, or of a stag to refer to its **attires**
fusil	an elongated lozenge
fusilly	covered with **fusils**
gad-bee	a dun fly
gads	plates of steel or iron
galley (*see* **lymphad**)	
galtrap (*see* **caltrap**)	
gamb	(from the French *jambe*) the foreleg of an animal; when **couped** or **erased** near the middle joint it is only a paw
garb	a sheaf of any kind of grain; when other than wheat the kind must be stated
gardant (*see* **guardant**)	
gardebras	the elbow-piece of a suit of armour
garde-visure	a vizor
garnished	decorated
gaze	applied to a beast of the chase when looking full front. See **guardant** for other animals in this posture
gemel (*see* **bars gemel**)	
genet	a small animal like a fox
gillyflower, July flower	a blood-red carnation
giron (*see* **gyronny**)	
givers (*see* **guiuré**)	
gliding	used of snakes when moving **fessways**
glory	a series of rays issuing from a **charge** or ordinary
gobony (*see* **compony**)	
golpe	a purple **roundle**
gonfannon	a banner
gordian knot	double **annulets** linked to each other and to one in the centre
gyronny	
gore or **gusset**	two curved lines, one from the **sinister chief** point the other from the **base** middle point, meeting in an acute angle at the **fess** point
gorge or **gurge**	a **water-bouget**
gorged	encircled round the throat
gorges	a whirlpool
gorget	armour for the chest
goutte	a drop
gouttée (*see* **guttée**)	
gradient	used of a tortoise when shown walking
greave	armour for the legs
grice	a young wild boar
grieces	steps on which crosses may be placed (*see* **Calvary**)
griffin or **gryphon**	a monster with the upper half an eagle and the lower half a lion
griffin-male	a **griffin** without wings but with large ears
grittic	used of a **field** made up equally of **metal** and **colour**
guardant	full-faced; *see* also **gaze**
guidon or **pennon**	a flag
guiuré, givers, or gringolé	(from *guivris*, viper) used of **charges** which end in serpent's heads
gules (**gu.**)	red
gun shot or **gun stone**	a black **roundle**
guttée or **gutty**	(from the Latin *gutta*, drop) sprinkled with drops (*gouttes*)
guttée d'eau	sprinkled with water
guttée de larmes	sprinkled with tears
guttée de poix	sprinkled with pitch
guttée de sang	sprinkled with blood
guttée d'huile or **guttée d'olive**	sprinkled with drops of green oil
guttée d'or	sprinkled with gold
guttée reversed	inverted drops
guze	a red **roundle**
gyronny	the division of a shield by cross and **saltire** in six to twelve even-numbered parts
habergeon	a short coat of mail without sleeves
habited	clothed; the same as **vested**
halbert	a pole-axe
halcyon	a kingfisher

half-spear	a spear with a short handle
harpy	a mythical bird with a woman's face, neck and breasts, and a vulture's body and legs
harpoon	a salmon or eel-spear
hart	a stag more than seven years old
harvest-fly	a butterfly
hatchment	(corruption of **achievement**) the coat of arms of a dead person, put up on the front of the house then taken and displayed in the local church
hauberk	a twisted coat of mail
hauriant or **haurient**	used of a fish when upright, as if putting its head above water to take in air
haussé or **enhanced**	used of a **chevron** or **fess** when higher than its usual position
hawk's jesses	leather thongs fastening the bells attached to a hawk's legs
hawk's lure	a falconer's decoy of two wings joined with their tips downwards and fastened to a line and ring
hay-fork (*see* **shake-fork**)	
heads	usually have their posture stated: **affrontée** when in profile, **guardant** when full-faced and **regardant** when looking backwards; 'head' on its own implies in profile
healme or **casque**	a helmet
hem break or **hackle**	an instrument for bruising hemp
herison	a hedgehog
hill or **hillock**	used when only one hill is intended; if more than one the correct term is hillocks or molehills
hilted	used of the handle of a sword
hind	a female stag, generally **blazon**ed **trippant**
hirondelle	a swallow
honourable ordinaries	used of nine basic heraldic charges: **chief**, **fess**, **pale**, **bend**, **bend sinister**, **bar**, cross, **saltire** and **chevron**
hooded	used of a human face when the head-dress is of a different colour from the face; or of a bird of prey when it has a hood over its head
hoofed	used to describe the colour of the hooves of an animal when different from the colour of the animal itself; cloven-footed animals are said to be **unguled**
horned	used to describe the colour of the horns of an animal when different from the colour of the animal itself (*see* **attired**)
huit-foil (*see* **eightfoil**)	
humet or **humetté**	used of an **ordinary** when its tips do not reach the sides of the shield
hunting-horn, **cornet** or **buglehorn**	a semicircular horn; when the belt is of another colour it is called **stringed** of that colour
hurst	a group of trees
hurt	a blue **roundle**
hurtée or **hurty**	**semée** of **hurts**
hydra	a many-headed dragon
imbattled (*see* **embattled**)	
imbowed (*see* **embowed**)	
imbrued or **imbued** (*see* **embrued**)	
impalement/ impaling	two coats of arms side by side on the same shield
incensed or **incensan**	used of angry animals with fire issuing from their mouths and ears
increment or **increscent**	used when a crescent is shown with the horns towards the **dexter**
indented	a serrated line, like **dancettée** but with smaller notches
Indian or **Assyrian goat**	a goat with bent horns and ears like those of a **talbot**
indorsed or **endorsed** (*see* **addorsed**)	
inescutcheon	a small shield borne as a **charge** on another, usually indicating marriage with an heir or co-heir
inflamed	burning in flames
infula	a tiara
ink moline (*see* **fer-de-moline**)	
in lure	two wings joined with the tips downward
in pride	used of a peacock or turkey cock with its tail spread out
in splendour	the sun surrounded by rays
inter	between
interlaced	linked together
invected	like **engrailed** but with the spikes pointing inwards
invexed	arched
iron ring	a tool used by wire-drawers
issuant	rising or coming out of; when an animal is **blazon**ed as such only the upper half is shown
jamb or **jambe** (*see* **gamb**)	
jellop or **jowlop**	a cock's comb
jessant	shooting forth as vegetables spring forth; half the **charge** only is depicted when **blazon**ed jessant

jessant-de-lys	a **fleur-de-lys** in a leopard's mouth
jesses	the leather thongs that fasten the bells to the legs of a hawk
joinant (*see* **conjoined**)	
jupon	a surcoat
knowed (*see* **nowed**)	
label or **lambel**	a piece of silk or linen with three pendants, usually used as a mark of **cadency**
lambrequin (*see* **mantle**)	
langued	used when an animal's tongue is of a different colour from its body
lattice, tirlace, trellée	a trellis whose pieces are nailed together at the crossings
laurel	an emblem of victory and triumph
laver	a cutter or ploughshare
legged or **membered**	used when the legs of an animal or bird are of a different colour from its body
leopard	French heralds used to call the lion **passant guardant** a leopard, and the royal lions of England were at one time so **blazon**ed
leopard's faces	a phrase used when no part of the neck appears and the posture is full-faced; when **erased** or **couped** at the neck in profile the word 'head' is used instead
lever	a cormorant
leveret	a young hare
lined	the inside lining of a piece of clothing when differently coloured from the outside; also used of chains and ropes fixed to the collars of animals
lioncel or **lionel**	a young lion
lion dragon	a monster with the upper half a lion and the lower half a dragon
Lion of England	sometimes used for a lion **rampant guardant**
lion poisson or **sea lion**	a monster resembling a lion in the upper half and a fish in the lower, with webbed feet
listen	the scroll or ribbon on which the motto is inscribed
lodged	used of beasts of the chase when lying on the ground
lopped or **snagged**	cut so as to show the thickness
lozenge	a diamond-shaped **charge**
lozengy	covered with **lozenge**s
lucy or **luce**	a pike (fish)
luna	the moon
lure or **leure** (*see* **hawk's lure**)	
lymphad or **galley**	a ship with one mast and many oars
maiden's head	the head and neck of a woman **couped** below the breast, the head wreathed with roses and crowned with an **eastern crown**
mail	protective clothing made of small close rings, linked together as if woven and shown as being like fish scales
mailed	clothed in mail
main	a hand
maintenance (*see* **cap of maintenance**)	
manche or **maunche**	a sleeve with long hanging ends
maned	used of an animal when the mane is of a different colour from the body
mantelle or **chappe**	used when the two upper angles to the **field** are cut off by two lines issuing from the middle **chief** point to either side of the shield, forming two triangles of a different colour from the field, as if a mantle were thrown over it and the ends drawn back
man-tiger	a monster with a lion's body, the head and face of an old man and horns like an ox
mantle or **lambrequin**	the cloak on which achievements are painted
mantlings	ornamented foliage-work for adorning helmets in painting armorial **bearings**
marined	used of any monster with the lower body like a fish
marine wolf	a seal
marshal	to arrange **charges**, **ordinaries** etc in correct order on a coat of arms
martlet or **merion**	a mythical bird shaped like a martin with feathers in place of its legs, the mark of a fourth son
mascle	a hollowed-out **lozenge**
masculy	covered with **mascle**s
masoned, masony or **maşçonné**	used when the **field**, **charge** or **crest** is divided like a wall by lines of a given colour
membered (*see* **legged**)	
meslé	mingled
metal	one of the basic types of **tincture** or colour used in heraldry: white and yellow, for instance, are described not as themselves but as **argent** and **or** (silver and gold)
millpick	an instrument used by millers and millwrights to dress millstones

millrind (*see* fer-de-moline)	
modilion, cotoose or scroll	the foliage ornament of a pillar
mooted or moulted (*see* eradicated)	
morion	a steel cap or helmet prevalent particularly in the 16th century, its upper half curving downwards, its edges curving upwards
morné or mortné	(French 'stillborn') a lion rampant without tongue, teeth or claws
morse	a sea-lion
mort	a skull, usually placed on the hatchment of the last of a family
mortier	a cap of state
mound	(French *monde*, Latin *mundus*, the world) a globe encircled with a horizontal band of diamonds and other precious stones, from the upper edge of which springs a similarly studded semicircular band, and having on the top a cross; the mound forms part of the regalia of an emperor or king
mount	when the bottom or base of the shield is represented as a field, and curved
mourned	blunted
mullet	the rowel of a spur, in English heraldry with five straight points and in French heraldry with six
mullet pierced	a mullet with a hole in the centre, allowing the colour on which it is borne to appear through it
muraillé	walled
mural crown	a circle of gold, crenellated like a battlement
murrey	blood-coloured
muschetors or mushetours	the black tail of the ermine, but without the three spots used to depict ermine
naiant or natant	swimming, used of fish when drawn horizontally
naissant	rising or coming out of
narcissus	a flower of six petals, each resembling a cinquefoil
naval crown	a crown composed of ships' sterns and sails arranged alternately
nebulée or nebuly	a line of partition like a dove-tail joint with the corners rounded
nerved	used of leaves and plants whose veins are a different colour from the rest
nislée or nyllée	slender, narrow or reduced almost to nothing
nowed	tied in a knot
ogress (*see* pellet)	
ombré	shadowed
ondé (*see* undée)	
opinicus	a winged monster with a lion's body, an eagle's head and neck and a short tail like a camel's
oppressed (*see* debruised)	
or	the metal gold, shown as yellow in heraldic illustration
orange	a tawny roundle
organ rest (*see* rest)	
orle	a diminutive of the bordure but not attached to the outside of the shield; charges so arranged are in orle
orlé	bordered
over all	when a charge or ordinary is placed over other bearings; surmounted, debruised and oppressed are similar terms
overt	used of bird's wings when open
pale	a band placed vertically in the middle of a shield
pall or paile	an archiepiscopal vestment of white lamb's wool, formed in heraldry by half a pale issuing from the base meeting in the fess point half a saltire issuing from the dexter and sinister chief to form a letter Y
pallet	a diminution of the pale
palisado	a crown composed of palisade-shaped points
palisse	a division of the field in the form of piles reaching from top to bottom, representing the palisades before a fortification
paly	divided into an equal number of pieces of alternate colours by perpendicular partition lines; the number of divisions must be specified: paly of six, of eight, etc
paly-bendy	pales cut by diagonal partition lines
palmer's staff	(French *bourdon*) a pilgrim's staff
papilone	a field divided into variegated specks like those on a butterfly, but ranged like the scales of a fish
park pales	palings depicted close to each other, with pointed tops
pascuant or pasquant	used of animals when grazing
Paschal or Holy Lamb	a lamb passant arg. carrying the banner of St George
passant	used of an animal in a walking position
passant guardant	used of an animal walking with its head full-face
Passion Cross (*see* Calvary Cross)	
passant reguardant	walking, but looking back
passant repassant	used when animals are shown walking past each other in opposite directions

Pater Noster or Nostré	a cross composed of beads
pa(t)té	(French *patte*, paw) splayed towards the end, as a paw is
pattes	paws
pavement	depicted like masonry
pavilion	an oblong tent with a projecting entrance
pean	a fur with gold spots on a black ground
peel	a tool used for drawing bread from the oven
pegasus	a horse with wings
pelican	always shown pecking her breast so that it bleeds; when feeding her young in this manner she is said to be 'in her piety'
pellet or ogress	a black roundle
pelletty or pellettée	semée of pellets
penner and ink horn	a case for holding pens and ink
pennon	a pointed or swallow-tailed flag
permoncel or pencil	a small streamer or flag
penny-yard	a small coin
per	used to show how a shield, ordinary or charge is divided by any of the partition lines, as per bend, per pale etc
petronel	a pistol
pheon	the head of a dart or arrow
pierced	used when an ordinary or charge is perforated; the shape should be specified — square, round etc
piety (*see* pelican)	
pile	a wedge issuing from the chief and tapering towards the base
pilgrim's scrip	a wallet or pouch
plate	a silver or white roundle
playing tables	backgammon tables
plenitude	a full moon
plié	used of a bird when its wings are folded
ployé	bowed and bent
plummet	a plumb line
poing	a closed hand
pomme	a green roundle (plural pomels)
popinjay	a small green parrot with red beak and legs
portant	used of a cross that is not erect but placed across the shield as if being carried on the shoulder
posé (*see* statant)	
pot	a steel hat
potent	a crutch; also a fur composed of crutch- or T-shaped divisions
potenté	a line of division formed by crutch-shaped figures
pouldron	armour for the shoulder
pounce	the talons of a bird of prey
powdered	*see* semée
pride (*see* in pride)	
proper/ppr.	used of objects when shown in their natural colours
purfled, trimmed or garnished	used of the studs and rims of armour when they are a different colour from the armour itself
purflew or purfled	used of a border of fur shaped like vair; when of one row it is termed purflewed, when of two, counter-purflewed
purpure	purple
python	a winged serpent
quarterly	used of a shield divided into four equal sections by vertical and horizontal lines
quatrefoil	a four-leaved grass
queue	tail
queue-fourchée (*see* double queued)	
quintain	a tilting post
quise, à la	at the thigh (French *à la cuisse*)
radiant, rayonned, rayonnant, rayoneé	used to express any ordinary or charge edged with glittering rays, like the sun
raguly	like embattled, but with the protuberances set obliquely
ramé	a French term for branched or attired
rampant	used of an animal standing on its hind legs
rampant sejant	used of a lion when sitting with the forelegs raised
rangé	arranged in order
raping	used of animals devouring their prey
razed (*see* erased)	
rays	when round the sun they are 16 in number, when round an estoile nine; they are shown alternately straight and wavy
rearing	used of a horse when standing on the hind legs with the forelegs raised
rebated	when the point of a weapon or part of a cross is broken off
reboundant	used of a lion's tail when it forms the letter 'S' with the point outwards

rebus	used of an **achievement** whose **charges** allude to the name of the bearer, *e.g.* castles for Castleton
recercellée	used of a cross whose ends are slightly forked and curled back
reclinant	bending backwards
reflexed or **reflected**	curved or turned round, as the chain from the collar of a beast thrown over its back
regardant	looking behind or backwards
reindeer	in heraldry, a stag with double **attires**
remora	a snake
removed	implies that the **ordinary** has fallen or become removed from its proper position
rencontre (*see* **cabossed**)	
renverse	when anything is set with its head downwards or contrary to its natural way or turned upside down
rere mouse	a bat
respectant or **respecting**	used of animals when placed face to face
reserved	contrary to the usual position
rests, clarions or **clavichords**	the rest for a lance; by some authorities called musical instruments, they bear a resemblance to a fluted bracket
retorted	used of snakes when intertwined
reversed	turned upside down
riband or **ribbon**	an eighth part of a **bend**, of which it is a diminutive
rising	used of birds when preparing to take flight
rompu or **rompé**	broken
rose	always represented as full-blown with the petals expanded, **seeded** in the middle, and backed by five green barbs or leaves. When an heraldic rose is red it must be **blazon**ed **gu.** not **ppr.**; a rose is termed '**barbed** and **seeded** ppr.' when the barbs are green and the seeds yellow
roundels/roundles	round **charges**, flat when of **metal** and spherical when of **colour**; they change their names according to their **tinctures** (*see* under individual names)
rousant	the same as **rising**
rustre	a **lozenge** pierced; similar to a **mascle** but with a round instead of a diamond-shaped hole
sable (sa.)	black
sacre or **saker**	a falcon with a grey head, blue feet and legs and a dark brown back; also a small cannon
sagittarius	a creature half man and half horse shooting with a bow and arrow
salamander	a mythical animal whose natural habitat is fire; it is shown green, surrounded with flames
salient	the posture of an animal leaping on its prey
salmon spear	the same as a **harpoon**
saltant	used of a squirrel, cat, weasel, rat etc when springing forward
saltire	an 'X'-shaped cross
saltirewise	in the position of a **saltire**
sanglier	a wild boar
sanguine	blood-coloured (*see* also **murrey**)
sanglant	bloody, torn off or erased
sarcellée	cut through in the middle
satyr	a creature with a lion's tail, the ears and horns of an antelope and the face of a man
scallop	a type of shell
scarpe	a diminutive of the **bend sinister**, representing a shoulder-belt or officer's scarf
scintillant	sparkling
scrip (*see* **pilgrim's scrip**)	
sea dog	a creature like a **talbot** but with a beaver's tail, a scalloped fin down the back from head to tail, scaled body, legs and tail and webbed feet
sea lion	a monster with a lion's body and a fish's tail
sea pie	a dark brown water fowl with a red head and white neck and wings
seax	a scimitar with a semi-circular notch on the back of the blade
seeded	used of the seeds of roses, lilies etc when of a different colour from the flower itself
segreant	used of the **griffin** when erect with wings **addorsed**
sejant or **segeant**	sitting
sejant addorsed	used when two animals are sitting back to back
semée	used when a **field**, **crest** or **supporter** is scattered with minor **charges**, *e.g.* **crescents**, **mullets** or **fleurs-de-lys**; *see* also **powdered**
seraph's head	a child's head between three pairs of wings, two in **chief**, two in **fess** and two in **base**
sexfoil	a grass or flower with six leaves, in form like a **cinquefoil**
shack-bolt	a fetter put on the wrists or ankles of prisoners
shafted	used to denote that a spear-head has a handle
shake-fork	like the **pall**, but not touching the edges of the shield, and with a point at each end like the **pile**
shambrough	a ship
shapewined	in a curved line
sheaf (*see* **garb**)	
side	a portion of the shield cut off by a perpendicular line
single	the tail of a deer
sinister	the left side of the shield (*see* **dexter**)
sinister chief	the left side of the chief
sinople	green
siren or **syren**	a mermaid
skean	a short sword or dagger
slashed	sleeves of garments cut open lengthways, the gashes filled in with puffing of another colour
slay, slea or **reed**	an instrument used by weavers
slipped	having a stalk, shown as torn from the original stem
spancelled or **fettered**	used of a horse that has the fore and hind legs fettered by fetter locks fastened to the end of a stick
spear-head imbrued	with the point bloody
speed, at	used of a stag when running
sperver	a tent
sphinx	a monster with a lion's body, the wings of an eagle and the head and breasts of a woman
spindle (*see* **fusil**)	a spade
splendour	a term for the sun when represented with a human face and emitting rays
sruttle	a winnowing fan or basket
starved (*see* **estoile**)	stripped of leaves, etc
statant	standing
staves	walking sticks used by pilgrims
subordinaries	class of **charges** next in importance to the **honourable ordinaries** (*qv*), comprising the **canton**, **inescutcheon**, **gyron**, **orle**, **tressure**, **lozenge**, **mascle**, **rustre**, **fusil**, **fret**, **flanch**, **bordure**, **pile**, **label**, **billet** and **flasque**
subverted	reversed, turned upside down
sufflue	rest or clarion
super charge	one figure **charge**d or borne upon another
supporters	figures placed on either side of a shield
surcoat	a loose, light coat worn over armour
surgeant	rising
surmounted	where one **charge** is placed over another
surtout or **sur-le-tout**	used of a small shield placed on the centre of a larger one
syke (*see* **fountain**)	
tabard	the surcoat embroidered with the Sovereign's arms and worn by heralds
talbot	a hunting dog with thick snout and hanging ears
targant, torgant or **torqued**	bending and rebending like the letter 'S'
target	a round buckler or shield
tasces or **tasses**	armour which covers the thighs
tau	a cross with no upper vertical arm
tenne or **tawney**	orange
terras	the representation of a piece of ground at the bottom of the **base**, generally shown green
tiara or **triple crown**	a cap or helmet of golden cloth, from which hang two pendants, embroidered and fringed at the ends, **semée** of crosses of gold. The cap is enclosed by three marquess's coronets and on the top is a mound of gold with a cross of the same material
tiercé	used when the shield is divided into three equal parts of different colours
timbre	signifies the helmet when placed over the arms in a complete **achievement**
tincture	colour in heraldic illustration; there are three basic types: colours (all unpatterned colours that are not **metals**), **metals** (such as **argent** or **or**) and **furs**
tirret	manacles or handcuffs
toison d'or	a golden fleece, or the Holy Lamb
torqued	wreathed
torse	the wreath on which the crest is placed
torteau	a red **roundle**
tortillé	**nowed** or **wreathed**
tourné (*see* **reguardant**)	
tower	triple-towered; when the word 'tower' is used in **blazon** without any further description it should be shown without the three small turrets rising from the battlements
transmuted	counterchanged
transpierced	pierced through
traversed	turned to the **sinister** side of the shield
treflée	used of a cross whose arms end in three semicircles, each representing the **trefoil**; a **bend** treflée has **trefoils** issuing from the side
trefoil	a three-leaved grass

treille or **trellise**   latticed; differs from **fretty** in that the pieces do not interlace under and over but cross over each other and are nailed at the joints

tressure   the half-size diminutive of the **orle**

tressure flory   a **tressure** having **fleurs-de-lys** placed at intervals round it

tressure flory counter-flory   a **tressure flory** in which the alternate **fleurs-de-lys** point to the centre of the **field**

trian aspect   showing three-quarters of the body

tricorporate   when the bodies of three animals are shown issuing from the **dexter**, **sinister** and **base** points of the shield, meeting joined to one head in the centre

trien   three

trippant   used of beasts of the chase as **passant** is to beasts of prey, shown with one foot up as if trotting; counter-trippant is when two beasts are tripping past each other in opposite directions

triumphal crown or **garland**   composed of laurel

trononée or **demembrée**   used of cross or other **bearing** which is dismembered but so arranged that the pieces retain the original form of the bearing

true lovers' knot   a double knot made with two bows on each side, interlacing each other and with two ends: snakes are sometimes twisted in this form

umbraced (*see* **vambraced**)

umbrated or **adumbrated**   shadowed

undée, ondée or **undy**   wavy

unguled   used of animals' hooves when they are coloured differently from the body

urchin   a hedgehog

uriant   used of a fish when shown with the head downwards and the tail erect

urvant or **urved**   turned or bowed upwards

vair or **vaire**   a **fur** shown as rows of small shields, alternately reversed

vallary crown   a gold circlet surmounted by flat, pointed strips

vambrace   armour for the arm

vambraced   used when the arm is completely covered with armour

vamplate   a gauntlet

vamplet   a broad pan of steel attached to the lower part of a tilting-spear to protect the hand

vannet   the **escallop** when shown without the ears

verblée   a hunting-horn edged with **metal** of a different colour

verdoy   a border charged with eight flowers, leaves or fruit, *e.g.* 'a **border gu.**, verdoy of oak leaves or'

vert   green

verted or **reverted**   same as **flexed** or **reflexed**

verules or **ferrals**   several rings, one within another, with the same centre

vested   clothed

vigilant   used of a cat when watching for prey

vol   two wings of an eagle displayed and **conjoined**

volant   flying

voided   used of a **charge** with the middle cut out so that the **field** is seen through it

voiders   a diminutive of **flanch**

vorant or **engoulant**   devouring

vulned   wounded so that blood appears

wallet (*see* **pilgrim's scrip**)

watching (*see* **vigilant**)

water bouget   a vessel to carry water

wavy (*see* **undée**)   a line of partition formed like waves

weare, weir or **dam**   in **fess**, is made with stakes and osier twigs interwoven as a fence against water

welt or **edge**   a narrow border to an **ordinary** or **charge**

wings conjoined   wings expanded, elevated and united at the bottom (*see* **lure**)

woodman   wild man or savage

wound   a purple **roundle** (*see* **golpe**)

wreath   a garland or chaplet; the wreath upon which the **crest** is usually borne is composed of two bands of silk twisted together

wyvern   a monster with the wings and upper part of a dragon and the lower part of a snake

ABBREVIATIONS

A

AA	Anti-aircraft; Automobile Association; Architectural Association; Augustinians of the Assumption
AAA	Amateur Athletics Association; American Accounting Association
AAAC	Australian Army Air Corps
AAAL	American Academy of Arts and Letters
AAAS	American Association for the Advancement of Science
AAC	Army Air Corps
AACCA	Associate, Association of Certified and Corporate Accountants
AACE	Association for Adult and Continuing Education
AADip	Architectural Association Diploma
A&AEE	Aeroplane and Armament Experimental Establishment
AAF	Auxiliary Air Force
AAFCE	Allied Air Forces in Central Europe
AAG	Assistant Adjutant-General
AAI	Associate, Chartered Auctioneers' and Estate Agents' Institute
AAIL	American Academy and Institute of Arts and Letters
AAM	Association of Assistant Mistresses in Secondary Schools
AAMC	Australian Army Medical Corps
AA&QMG	Assistant Adjutant and Quartermaster-General
AAPS	Aquatic and Atmospheric Physical Sciences
AAS	American Astronomical Society
AASA	Associate, Australian Society of Accountants
AASC	Australian Army Service Corps
AATSE	Australian Academy of Technological Sciences and Engineering
AAUQ	Associate in Accountancy, University of Queensland
AB	Bachelor of Arts (US); able-bodied seaman
ABA	Amateur Boxing Association; Antiquarian Booksellers' Association; American Bar Association
ABC	Australian Broadcasting Commission; American Broadcasting Companies; Amateur Boxing Club; Associate, Birmingham Conservatoire
ABCA	Army Bureau of Current Affairs
ABCC	Association of British Chambers of Commerce
ABCFM	American Board of Commissioners for Foreign Missions
ABI	Association of British Insurers
ABIA	Associate, Bankers' Institute of Australasia
ABINZ	Associate, Bankers' Institute of New Zealand
ABIS	Association of Burglary Insurance Surveyors
ABM	Advisory Board of Ministry
ABNM	American Board of Nuclear Medicine
Abp/Archbp	Archbishop
ABP	Associated British Ports
ABPsS	Associate, British Psychological Society
ABRC	Advisory Board for the Research Councils
ABS	Associate, Building Societies' Institute
ABSA	Association for Business Sponsorship of the Arts
ABSI	Associate, Boot and Shoe Institution
ABSM	Associate, Birmingham and Midland Institute School of Music
ABTA	Association of British Travel Agents
ABTAPL	Association of British Theological and Philosophical Libraries
AC	Companion, Order of Australia; Ante Christum (before Christ)
ACA	Associate, Institute of Chartered Accountants
Acad	Academy
ACARD	Advisory Council for Applied Research and Development
ACAS	Advisory, Conciliation and Arbitration Service; Assistant Chief of the Air Staff
ACBSI	Associate, Chartered Building Societies Institute
ACC	Association of County Councils; Anglican Consultative Council
ACCA	Associate, Chartered Association of Certified Accountants
ACCEL	American College of Cardiology Extended Learning
ACCM	Advisory Council for the Church's Ministry
ACCS	Associate, Corporation of Secretaries (formerly of Certified Secretaries)
ACDP	Australian Committee of Directors and Principals

A/Cdre	Air Commodore
ACDS	Assistant Chief of Defence Staff
ACE	Association of Consulting Engineers; Member, Association of Conference Executives
ACF	Army Cadet Force
ACFA	Army Cadet Force Association
ACFAS	Association Canadienne-Française pour l'Avancement des Sciences
ACFHE	Association of Colleges for Further and Higher Education
ACG	Assistant Chaplain-General
ACGI	Associate, City and Guilds of London Institute
ACGS	Assistant Chief of the General Staff
ACIArb	Associate, Chartered Institute of Arbitrators
ACIB	Associate, Chartered Institute of Bankers
ACII	Associate, Chartered Insurance Institute
ACIS	Associate, Institute of Chartered Secretaries and Administrators (formerly Chartered Institute of Secretaries)
ACIT	Associate, Chartered Institute of Transport
ACLS	American Council of Learned Societies
ACM	Association of Computing Machinery
ACMA	Associate, Chartered Institute of Management Accountants (formerly Institute of Cost and Management Accountants)
ACNS	Assistant Chief of Naval Staff
ACommA	Associate, Society of Commercial Accountants
ACORD	Advisory Committee on Research and Development
ACOS	Assistant Chief of Staff
ACOST	Advisory Council on Science and Technology
ACP	Association of Clinical Pathologists; Associate, College of Preceptors; African/Caribbean/Pacific
ACPO	Association of Chief Police Officers
ACRE	Action with Rural Communities in England
ACS	American Chemical Society; Additional Curates Society
ACSEA	Allied Command South East Asia
ACSM	Associate, Camborne School of Mines
ACT	Australian Capital Territory; Australian College of Theology; Associate, College of Technology; Association of Corporate Treasurers
Actg	Acting
ACTT	Association of Cinematograph, Television and Allied Technicians
ACTU	Australian Council of Trade Unions
ACU	Association of Commonwealth Universities
ACWA	Associate, Institute of Cost and Works Accountants
AD	Dame of the Order of Australia: Anno Domini (in the year of the Lord); Air Defence
ADAS	Agricultural Development and Advisory Service
ADB	Asian Development Bank; Associate of the Drama Board (Education)
ADB/F	African Development Bank/Fund
ADC	Aide-de-Camp
ADC(P)	Personal Aide-de-Camp to The Sovereign
ADCM	Archbishop of Canterbury's Diploma in Church Music
AD Corps	Army Dental Corps
Addl	Additional
ADEME	Assistant Director Electrical and Mechanical Engineering
ADFManc	Art and Design Fellow, Manchester
ADFW	Assistant Director of Fortifications and Works
ADGB	Air Defence of Great Britain
ADGMS	Assistant Director-General of Medical Services
ADH	Assistant Director of Hygiene
Adj	Adjutant
ADJAG	Assistant Deputy Judge Advocate General
ADK	Order of Ahli Darjah Kinabalu
ADM	Advanced Diploma in Midwifery
Admin	Administration
Adml	Admiral
Admlty	Admiralty
ADMS	Assistant Director of Medical Services
ADOS	Assistant Director of Ordnance Services
ADP	Automatic Data Processing
ADPA	Associate Diploma of Public Administration

ADS&T	Assistant Director of Supplies and Transport
ADVS	Assistant Director of Veterinary Services
advsr/y	adviser/advisory
ADWE&M	Assistant Director of Works, Electrical and Mechanical
AE	Air Efficiency Award
AEA	Atomic Energy Authority; Air Efficiency Award
AEAF	Allied Expeditionary Air Force
AEC	Agriculture Executive Council; Army Educational Corps; Atomic Energy Commission
AECMA	Association Européenne des Constructeurs de Matériel Aérospatial
AEE	Atomic Energy Establishment
AEEU	Amalgamated Engineering and Electrical Union
AEF	Amalgamated Union of Engineering and Foundry Workers; American Expeditionary Forces
AEGIS	Aid for the Elderly in Government Institutions
AEI	Associated Electrical Industries
AEM	Air Efficiency Medal
AER	Army Emergency Reserve
AERE	Atomic Energy Research Establishment (Harwell)
AEU	Amalgamated Engineering Union
AFA	Amateur Football Alliance
AFAIAA	Associate Fellow, American Institute of Aeronautics and Astronautics
AFASIC	Association for All Speech Impaired Children
AFB	Air Force Base
AFBPsS	Associate Fellow, British Psychological Society
AFC	Air Force Cross; Association Football Club
AfC	Association for Colleges
AFCAI	Associate Fellow, Canadian Aeronautical Institute
AFCEA	Armed Forces Communications and Electronics Association
AFCENT	Allied Forces in Central Europe
AFD	Doctor of Fine Arts (US)
AFDS	Air Fighting Development Squadron
AFF	Agriculture, Fisheries and Food (see also MAFF)
Affrs	Affairs
AFHQ	Allied Force Headquarters
AFI	American Film Institute
AFIA	Associate, Federal Institute of Accountants (Australia)
AFIAP	Artiste, Fédération Internationale de l'Art Photographique
AFIAS	Associate Fellow, Institute of Aeronautical Sciences (US)
AFICD	Associate Fellow, Institute of Civil Defence
AFIMA	Associate Fellow, Institute of Mathematics and its Applications
AFM	Air Force Medal
AFNORTH	Allied Forces in Northern Europe
AFOM	Associate, Faculty of Occupational Medicine
AFRAeS	Associate Fellow, Royal Aeronautical Society
AFRC	Agricultural and Food Research Council
AFV	Armoured Fighting Vehicles
Ag	Agricultural
AG	Attorney-General
AGAC	American Guild of Authors and Composers
AGARD	Advisory Group for Aerospace Research and Development
AGC	Adjutant General's Corps
AGH	Australian General Hospital
AGI	Artistes Graphiques Internationaux; Associate, Institute of Certificated Grocers
AGR	Advanced Gas-cooled Reactor
AGRA	Army Group Royal Artillery; Association of Genealogists and Record Agents
AGSM	Associate, Guildhall School of Music and Drama; Australian Graduate School of Management
Agy	Agency
AHA	Area Health Authority; American Hospitals Association; Associate, Institute of Health Service Administrators
AHA(T)	Area Health Authority (Teaching)
AHQ	Army Headquarters
AHSM	Associate, Institute of Health Services Management
AH-WC	Associate, Heriot-Watt College, Edinburgh
AIA	Associate, Institute of Actuaries; American Institute of Architects; Association of International Artists
AIAA	American Institute of Aeronautics and Astronautics
AIAgrE	Associate, Institution of Agricultural Engineers
AIAL	Associate Member, International Institute of Arts and Letters
AIArb	Associate, Institute of Arbitrators
AIAS	Associate, Incorporated Association of Architects and Surveyors
AIB	Associate, Institute of Bankers
AIBD	Associate, Institute of British Decorators
AIBP	Associate, Institute of British Photographers
AIBScot	Associate, Institute of Bankers in Scotland

AIC	Agricultural Improvement Council; Associate, Institute of Chemistry
AICA	Associate Member, Commonwealth Institute of Accountants; Association Internationale des Critiques d'Art
AICC	All-India Congress Committee
AICE	Associate, Institution of Civil Engineers
AIChE	American Institute of Chemical Engineers
AICPA	American Institute of Certified Public Accountants
AICS	Associate, Institute of Chartered Shipbrokers
AICTA	Associate, Imperial College of Tropical Agriculture
AIDS	Acquired Immune Deficiency Syndrome
AIE	Associate, Institute of Education
AIEE	Associate, Institution of Electrical Engineers
AIF	Australian Imperial Forces
AIFireE	Associate, Institution of Fire Engineers
AIG	Adjutant-Inspector-General
AIH	Associate, Institute of Housing
AIHort	Associate, Institute of Horticulture
AIIA	Associate, Insurance Institute of America; Associate, Indian Institute of Architects
AIIMR	Associate, Institute of Investment Management and Research
AIInfSc	Associate, Institute of Information Scientists
AIIRA	Associate, International Industrial Relations Association
AIL	Associate, Institute of Linguists
AILA	Associate, Institute of Landscape Architects
AILocoE	Associate, Institute of Locomotive Engineers
AIM	Associate, Institution of Metallurgists; Australian Institute of Management
AIMarE	Associate, Institute of Marine Engineers
AIMC	Associate, Institute of Management Consultants
AIME	American Institute of Mechanical Engineers
AIMgt	Associate, Institute of Management
AIMSW	Associate, Institute of Medical Social Work
AInstM	Associate Member, Institute of Marketing
AInstP	Associate, Institute of Physics
AInstPI	Associate, Institute of Patentees and Inventors
AIP	Association of Independent Producers
AIPR	Associate, Institute of Public Relations
AIProdE	Associate, Institution of Production Engineers
AIQS	Associate Member, Institute of Quantity Surveyors
AIRTE	Associate, Institute of Road Transport Engineers
AIRTO	Association of Independent Research and Technology Organizations
AIS	Associate, Institute of Statisticians
AISA	Associate, Incorporated Secretaries' Association
AIStructE	Associate, Institution of Structural Engineers
AITI	Associate, Institute of Translators and Interpreters
AITP	Associate, Institute of Town Planners, India
AJAG	Assistant Judge Advocate General
AJEX	Association of Jewish Ex-Service Men and Women
AK	Knight, Order of Australia; Alaska
AKC	Associate, King's College London
AL	Alabama
ALA	Associate, Library Association; Association of London Authorities
ALAA	Associate, Library Association of Australia
ALAI	Associate, Library Association of Ireland
ALAM	Associate, London Academy of Music and Dramatic Art
ALCD	Associate, London College of Divinity
ALCM	Associate, London College of Music
ALCS	Authors Lending and Copyright Society
ALFSEA	Allied Land Forces South-East Asia
ALI	Argyll Light Infantry; Associate, Landscape Institute
ALICE	Autistic and Language Impaired Children's Education
ALLC	Association for Literary and Linguistic Computing
ALP	Australian Labor Party
ALPSP	Association of Learned and Professional Society Publishers
ALS	Associate, Linnean Society
ALVA	Association of Leading Visitor Attractions
AM	Albert Medal; Member, Order of Australia; Master of Arts (US); Alpes Maritimes
AMA	Association of Metropolitan Authorities; Assistant Masters Association; Associate, Museums Association; Australian Medical Association
AMARC	Associated Marine and Related Charities
Amb	Ambassador
AMBDA	Associate Member, British Dyslexia Association
AMBIM	Associate Member, British Institute of Management
AMBritIRE	Associate Member, British Institution of Radio Engineers
AMC	Association of Municipal Corporations
AMCST	Associate, Manchester College of Science and Technology
AMCT	Associate, Manchester College of Technology

AME	Association of Municipal Engineers
AMEME	Association of Mining Electrical and Mechanical Engineers
AMet	Associate of Metallurgy
AMF	Australian Military Forces
AMGOT	Allied Military Government of Occupied Territory
AMIAE	Associate Member, Institution of Automobile Engineers
AMIAgrE	Associate Member, Institution of Agricultural Engineers
AMIBF	Associate Member, Institute of British Foundrymen
AMICE	Associate Member, Institution of Civil Engineers
AMIChemE	Associate Member, Institution of Chemical Engineers
AMIE(Aust)	Associate Member, Institution of Engineers, Australia
AMIE(Ind)	Associate Member, Institution of Engineers, India
AMIED	Associate Member, Institution of Engineering Designers
AMIEE	Associate Member, Institution of Electrical Engineers
AMIERE	Associate Member, Institution of Electronic and Radio Engineers
AMIH	Associate Member, Institute of Housing
AMIMechE	Associate Member, Institution of Mechanical Engineers
AMIMinE	Associate Member, Institution of Mining Engineers
AMIMM	Associate Member, Institution of Mining and Metallurgy
AMInstBE	Associate Member, Institution of British Engineers
AMInstCE	Associate Member, Institution of Civil Engineers
AmInstEE	American Institute of Electrical Engineers
AMInstR	Associate Member, Institute of Refrigeration
AMInstT	Associate Member, Institute of Transport
AMInstTA	Associate Member, Institute of Traffic Administration
AMINucE	Associate Member, Institution of Nuclear Engineers
AMIRSE	Associate Member, Institute of Railway Signalling Engineers
AMIStructE	Associate Member, Institution of Structural Engineers
AMMA	Assistant Masters and Mistresses Association
AMN	Ahli Mangku Negara (Malaysia)
AMNZIE	Associate Member New Zealand Institute of Engineers
AMP	Advanced Management Program; Air Member for Personnel
AMRC	Association of Medical Research Charities
AMRINA	Associate Member, Royal Institution of Naval Architects
AMS	Assistant Military Secretary; Army Medical Services
AMSO	Air Member for Supply and Organisation
AMTE	Admiralty Marine Technology Establishment
AMTRI	Advanced Manufacturing Technology Research Institute
ANA	Associate National Academician (US)
ANAF	Arab Non-Arab Friendship
ANC	African National Congress
ANECInst	Associate, NE Coast Institution of Engineers and Shipbuilders
ANGAU	Australian New Guinea Administrative Unit
Anon	Anonymously
ANU	Australian National University
ANZAAS	Australian and New Zealand Association for the Advancement of Science
Anzac	Australian and New Zealand Army Corps
AO	Officer, Order of Australia; Air Officer
AOA	Air Officer in charge of Administration
AOC	Air Officer Commanding
AOC-in-C	Air Officer Commanding-in-Chief
AOD	Army Ordnance Department
AOER	Army Officers Emergency Reserve
APA	American Psychiatric Association
APACS	Association of Payment and Clearing Systems
APCK	Association for Promoting Christian Knowledge, Church of Ireland
APD	Army Pay Department
APEX	Association of Professional, Executive, Clerical and Computer Staff
APHA	American Public Health Association
APIS	Army Photographic Intelligence Service
APM	Assistant Provost Marshal
APMI	Associate, Pensions Management Institute
apptd	appointed
APR	Accredited Public Relations Practitioner
APS	Aborigines Protection Society; American Physical Society
APsSI	Associate, Psychological Society of Ireland
APSW	Association of Psychiatric Social Workers
APT&C	Administrative, Professional, Technical and Clerical
APTC	Army Physical Training Corps
AQ	Administration and Quartering
AQG/AQMG	Assistant Quartermaster-General
AR	Associated Rediffusion (Television); Arkansas
ARA	Associate, Royal Academy
ARACI	Associate, Royal Australian Chemical Institute
ARAD	Associate, Royal Academy of Dancing
ARAeS	Associate, Royal Aeronautical Society

ARAgS	Associate, Royal Agricultural Societies (i.e., of England, Scotland and Wales)
ARAIA	Associate, Royal Australian Institute of Architects
ARAM	Associate, Royal Academy of Music
ARAS	Associate, Royal Astronomical Society
ARBA	Associate, Royal Society of British Artists
ARBC	Associate, Royal British Colonial Society of Artists
ARBS	Associate, Royal Society of British Sculptors
ARC	Architects' Registration Council; Agricultural Research Council; Aeronautical Research Council
ARCA	Associate, Royal College of Art; Associate, Royal Canadian Academy
ARCamA	Associate, Royal Cambrian Academy of Art
ARCE	Academical Rank of Civil Engineer
ARCIC	Anglican-Roman Catholic International Commission
ARCM	Associate, Royal College of Music
ARCO	Associate, Royal College of Organists
ARCO(CHM)	Associate, Royal College of Organists with Diploma in Choir Training
ARCPsych	Associate Member, Royal College of Psychiatrists
ARCS	Associate, Royal College of Science
ARCST	Associate, Royal College of Science and Technology (Glasgow)
ARCUK	Architects' Registration Council of the United Kingdom
ARCVS	Associate, Royal College of Veterinary Surgeons
ARE	Associate, Royal Society of Painter-Printmakers (formerly of Painter-Etchers and Engravers); Arab Republic of Egypt; Admiralty Research Establishment
AREINZ	Associate, Real Estate Institute, New Zealand
ARELS	Association of Recognised English Language Schools
ARIAS	Associate, Royal Incorporation of Architects in Scotland
ARIBA	Associate, Royal Institute of British Architects
ARIC	Associate, Royal Institute of Chemistry
ARICS	Professional Associate, Royal Institution of Chartered Surveyors
ARINA	Associate, Royal Institution of Naval Architects
ARLT	Association for the Reform of Latin Teaching
ARMS	Associate, Royal Society of Miniature Painters
ARP	Air Raid Precautions
ARPS	Associate, Royal Photographic Society
ARR	Association of Radiation Research
ARRC	Associate, Royal Red Cross
ARSA	Associate, Royal Scottish Academy
ARSC	Association of Recorded Sound Collections
ARSCM	Associate, Royal School of Church Music
ARSM	Associate, Royal School of Mines
ARTC	Associate, Royal Technical College (Glasgow)
ARVIA	Associate, Royal Victoria Institute of Architects
ARWA	Associate, Royal West of England Academy
ARWS	Associate, Royal Society of Painters in Water-Colours
ASA	Associate Member, Society of Actuaries; Associate of Society of Actuaries (US); Australian Society of Accountants; Army Sailing Association; Advertising Standards Authority
ASAA	Associate, Society of Incorporated Accountants and Auditors
ASAI	Associate, Society of Architectural Illustrators
ASAM	Associate, Society of Art Masters
ASBAH	Association for Spina Bifida and Hydrocephalus
ASC	Administrative Staff College, Henley; Army Service Corps
ASCA	Associate, Society of Company and Commercial Accountants
ASCAB	Armed Services Consultant Approval Board
ASCAP	American Society of Composers, Authors and Publishers
ASCE	American Society of Civil Engineers
ASCHB	Association for Study of Conservation of Historic Buildings
AScW	Association of Scientific Workers
ASD	Armament Supply Department
ASE	Amalgamated Society of Engineers; Association for Science Education
ASEAN	Association of South East Asian Nations
ASEE	American Society for Engineering Education
ASH	Action on Smoking and Health
ASIA(Ed)	Associate, Society of Industrial Artists (Education)
ASIAD	Associate, Society of Industrial Artists and Designers
ASLE	American Society of Lubrication Engineers
ASLEF	Associated Society of Locomotive Engineers and Firemen
ASLIB/Aslib	Association for Information Management (formerly Association of Special Libraries and Information Bureaux)
ASM	Association of Senior Members
ASME	American Society of Mechanical Engineers; Association for the Study of Medical Education
ASO	Air Staff Officer
ASSC	Accounting Standards Steering Committee

ASSET	Association of Supervisory Staffs, Executives and Technicians
Assist	Assistant
Assoc	Association
AssocISI	Associate, Iron and Steel Institute
AssocMCT	Associateship of Manchester College of Technology
AssocMIAeE	Associate Member, Institution of Aeronautical Engineers
AssocRINA	Associate, Royal Institution of Naval Architects
AssocSc	Associate in Science
Assur	Assurance
ASTA	Association of Short Circuit Testing Authorities
ASTC	Administrative Service Training Course
ASTMS	Association of Scientific, Technical and Managerial Staffs
AS&TS of SA	Associated Scientific and Technical Societies of South Africa
ASVU	Army Security Vetting Unit
ASWDU	Air Sea Warfare Development Unit
ASWE	Admiralty Surface Weapons Establishment
ATA	Air Transport Auxiliary
ATAE	Association of Tutors in Adult Education
ATAF	Allied Tactical Air Force
ATC	Air Training Corps; Art Teacher's Certificate
ATCDE	Association of Teachers in Colleges and Departments of Education
ATCL	Associate, Trinity College of Music, London
ATD	Art Teacher's Diploma

ATI	Associate, Textile Institute
ATL	Association of Teachers and Lecturers
ATO	Ammunition Technical Officer
ATPL (A)or(H)	Airline Transport Pilot's Licence (Aeroplanes), or (Helicopters)
ATS	Auxiliary Territorial Service
attd	attached
ATTI	Association of Teachers in Technical Institutions
ATV	Association TeleVision
AUA	American Urological Association
AUCAS	Association of University Clinical Academic Staff
AUEW	Amalgamated Union of Engineering Workers
AUS	Army of the United States
AUT	Association of University Teachers
Aux	Auxiliary
AVCC	Australian Vice-Chancellors' Committee
AVCM	Associate, Victoria College of Music
AVD	Army Veterinary Department
Ave	Avenue
AVLA	Audio Visual Language Association
AVR	Army Volunteer Reserve
AWA	Anglian Water Authority
AWAS	Australian Womens' Army Service
AWO	Association of Water Officers
AWRE	Atomic Weapons Research Establishment
AZ	Arizona

B

b	born
B	Baron
BA	Bachelor of Arts; British Airways
BAA	British Airports Authority
BAAB	British Amateur Athletic Board
BAAL	British Association for Applied Linguistics
BAAS	British Association for the Advancement of Science
BAB	British Airways Board
BAC	British Aircraft Corporation
BACM	British Association of Colliery Management
BACUP	British Association of Cancer United Patients
BAe	British Aerospace
BAED	Bachelor of Arts in Environmental Design
BAFO	British Air Forces of Occupation
BAFPA	British Association of Fitness Promotion Agencies
BAFTA	British Academy of Film and Television Arts
BAG	Business Art Galleries
BAgrSc	Bachelor of Agricultural Science
BAI	Baccalarius in Arte Ingeniaria (Bachelor of Engineering)
BAIE	British Association of Industrial Editors
BALPA	British Air Line Pilots' Association
BAO	Bachelor of Art of Obstetrics
BAOMS	British Association of Oral and Maxillo-Facial Surgeons
BAOR	British Army of the Rhine (formerly on the Rhine)
BAOS	British Association of Oral Surgeons
BAppSc(MT)	Bachelor of Applied Science (Medical Technology)
bapt	baptised
BARB	Broadcasters' Audience Research Board
BARC	British Automobile Racing Club
BArch	Bachelor of Architecture
BAS	Bachelor in Agricultural Science
BASc	Bachelor of Applied Science
BASCA	British Academy of Songwriters, Composers and Authors
BASEEFA	British Approvals Service for Electrical Equipment in Flammable Atmospheres
BASW	British Association of Social Workers
BBA	British Bankers' Association; Bachelor of Business Administration
BBB of C	British Boxing Board of Control
BBC	British Broadcasting Corporation
BB&CIRly	Bombay, Baroda and Central India Railway
BBFC	British Board of Film Classification
BBM	Bintang Bakti Masharakat (Public Service Star) (Singapore)
BBS	Bachelor of Business Studies
BBSRC	Biotechnology and Biosciences Research Council
BC	Before Christ; British Columbia; Borough Council
BCAR	British Civil Airworthiness Requirements
BCC	British Council of Churches
BCE	Bachelor of Civil Engineering; Before the Christian Era
BCh/BChir	Bachelor of Surgery

BChD	Bachelor of Dental Surgery
BCIA	British Clothing Industries Association
BCL	Bachelor of Civil Law
BCMF	Bible Churchmen's Missionary Society
BCMF	British Ceramic Manufacturers' Federation
BCOF	British Commonwealth Occupation Force
BCom/BComm	Bachelor of Commerce
BComSc	Bachelor of Commercial Science
BCPC	British Crop Protection Council
BCS	Bengal Civil Service; British Computer Society
BCSA	British Constructional Steelwork Association
BCURA	British Coal Utilization Research Association
BCYC	British Corinthian Yacht Club
BD	Bachelor of Divinity
Bd	Board
BDA	British Dental Association; British Deaf Association; British Dyslexia Association
Bdcasting	Broadcasting
Bde	Brigade
BDQ	Bachelor of Divinity Qualifying
Bdrs	Borderers
BDS	Bachelor of Dental Surgery
BDSc	Bachelor of Dental Science
BE	Bachelor of Engineering; British Element
BE&A	Bachelor of Engineering and Architecture (Malta)
BEA	British East Africa; British European Airways; British Epilepsy Association
BEAMA	Federation of British Electrotechnical and Allied Manufacturers' Associations (formerly British Electrical and Allied Manufacturers' Association)
BEAS	British Educational Administration Society
BEc	Bachelor of Economics
BEC	Business Education Council
BECTU	Broadcasting, Entertainment, Cinematograph and Theatre Union
BEd	Bachelor of Education
Beds	Bedfordshire
BEE	Bachelor of Electrical Engineering
BEF	British Expeditionary Force; British Equestrian Federation
BEM	British Empire Medal
BEMAS	British Education Management and Administration Society
BEME	Brigade Electrical and Mechanical Engineer
BEng	Bachelor of Engineering
BEO	Base Engineer Officer
Berks	Berkshire
BESO	British Executive Service Overseas
BEVA	British Equine Veterinary Association
B&FBS	British and Foreign Bible Society
BFI	British Film Institute
BFMIRA	British Food Manufacturing Industries Research Association

BFPO	British Forces Post Office
BFSS	British Field Sports Society
BFWG	British Federation of Women Graduates
BGS	Brigadier General Staff
BHA	British Hospitality Association
BHF	British Heart Foundation
BHL	Bachelor of Hebrew Letters
BHRA	British Hydromechanics Research Association
BHRCA	British Hotels, Restaurants and Caterers' Association
BHS	British Horse Society
BIBA	British Insurance Brokers' Association
BIBRA	British Industrial Biological Research Association
BICC	British Insulated Callender's Cables
BICERA	British Internal Combustion Engine Research Association
BICERI	British Internal Combustion Engine Research Institute
BICSc	British Institute of Cleaning Science
BIEC	British Invisible Exports Council
BIEE	British Institute of Energy Economics
BIF	British Industries Fair
BIFU	Banking Insurance and Finance Union
BIIBA	British Insurance and Investment Brokers' Association
BIM	British Institute of Management
BIR	British Institute of Radiology
BIS	Bank for International Settlements
BISF	British Iron and Steel Federation
BISFA	British Industrial and Scientific Film Association
BISPA	British Independent Steel Producers Association
BISRA	British Iron and Steel Research Association
BJ	Bachelor of Journalism
BJSM	British Joint Services Mission
BKSTS	British Kinematograph, Sound and Television Society
BL	Bachelor of Law; British Library
BLA	British Liberation Army
Bldg Soc	Building Society
BLDSA	British Long Distance Swimming Association
BLE	Brotherhood of Locomotive Engineers; Bachelor of Land Economy
BLegS	Bachelor of Legal Studies
BLESMA	British Limbless Ex-Servicemen's Association
BLitt	Bachelor of Letters
Blvd	Boulevard
BM	British Museum; Bachelor of Medicine; British Monomark
BMA	British Medical Association
BMedSci	Bachelor of Medical Science
BMEO	British Middle East Office
BMet	Bachelor of Metallurgy
BMEWS	Ballistic Missile Early Warning System
BMG	British Military Government
BMH	British Military Hospital
BMilSc	Bachelor of Military Science
BMJ	British Medical Journal
BMM	British Military Mission
BMR	Bureau of Mineral Resources
BMRA	Brigade Major Royal Artillery
Bn	Battalion
BNAF	British North Africa Force
BNC	Brasenose College (Oxford)
BNEC	British National Export Council
BNF	British National Formulary
BNFL	British Nuclear Fuels Ltd
BNOC	British National Oil Corporation; British National Opera Company
BNP	Banque Nationale de Paris
BNSc	Bachelor of Nursing Science
BNSC	British National Space Centre
BOAC	British Overseas Airways Corporation
BomCS	Bombay Civil Service
BOT	Board of Trade
BOTB	British Overseas Trade Board
BOU	British Ornithologists' Union
Bp	Bishop
BPA	British Paediatric Association

BPG	Broadcasting Press Guild
BPharm	Bachelor of Pharmacy
BPIF	British Printing Industries Federation
BPMF	British Postgraduate Medical Federation
BPsS	British Psychological Society
Br/br	British; Branch; branch
BR	British Rail
BRA	British Rheumatism and Arthritis Association
BRB	British Railways Board
BRC(S)	British Red Cross Society
BRE	Building Research Establishment
Brig	Brigadier
Brig-Gen	Brigadier-General
BritIRE	British Institution of Radio Engineers
BRNC	Britannia Royal Naval College
bro	brother
BRS	British Road Services
BRurSc	Bachelor of Rural Science
BS	Bachelor of Surgery; Bachelor of Science; British Standard
BSA	Bachelor of Scientific Agriculture; Birmingham Small Arms; Building Societies' Association
BSAA	British South American Airways
BSAP	British South Africa Police
BSAS	British Society of Animal Science
BSc	Bachelor of Science
BSC	British Steel Corporation; Bengal Staff Corps
BScA, BScAgr	Bachelor of Science in Agriculture
BSc(Dent)	Bachelor of Science in Dentistry
BSc(Est Man)	Bachelor of Science in Estate Management
BScN/BSN	Bachelor of Science in Nursing
BScSoc/BSocSc	Bachelor of Social Sciences
BSE	Bachelor of Science in Engineering (US)
BSES	British Schools Exploring Society
BSF	British Salonica Force
BSFA	British Science Fiction Association
BSI	British Standards Institution
BSIA	British Security Industry Association
BSJA	British Show Jumping Association
BSME	Bachelor of Science in Mechanical Engineering; British Society of Magazine Editors
BSNS	Bachelor of Naval Science
BSRA	British Ship Research Association
BSS	Bachelor of Science (Social Science)
BST	Bachelor of Sacred Theology
BSurv	Bachelor of Surveying
BT	Bachelor of Teaching; British Telecommunications
Bt	Baronet
BTA	British Tourist Authority (formerly British Travel Association)
BTC	British Transport Commission
BTCV	British Trust for Conservation Volunteers
BTDB	British Transport Docks Board
BTEC	Business and Technology (formerly Technician) Education Council
BTh	Bachelor of Theology
BTP	Bachelor of Town Planning
Btss	Baronetess
BUAS	British Universities Association of Slavists
Bucks	Buckinghamshire
BUGB	Baptist Union of Great Britain
BUPA	British United Provident Association
bur	buried
BURA	British Urban Regeneration Association
BV	Besloten Vennootschap
BVA	British Veterinary Association
BVetMed	Bachelor of Veterinary Medicine
BVI	British Virgin Islands
BVM	Blessed Virgin Mary
BVMS	Bachelor of Veterinary Medicine and Surgery
BVSc	Bachelor of Veterinary Science
BWI	British West Indies
BWM	British War Medal

C

c	*circa* ('around', of dates)
C	Conservative
CA	County Alderman; Chartered Accountant (Scotland and Canada); California
CAA	Civil Aviation Authority
CAABU	Council for the Advancement of Arab and British Understanding
CAAV	(Member of) Central Association of Agricultural Valuers
CAB	Citizens' Advice Bureau; Centre for Agricultural and Biosciences (formerly Commonwealth Agricultural Bureau)
CACTM	Central Advisory Council of Training for the Ministry
CAER	Conservative Action for Electoral Reform
CAFOD	Catholic Fund for Overseas Development
CALE	Canadian Army Liaison Executive
Calif	California
CAM	Communications, Advertising and Marketing
Cambs	Cambridgeshire
CAMC	Canadian Army Medical Corps
CAMRA	Campaign for Real Ale
CAMS	Certificate of Advanced Musical Study
CAMW	Central Association for Mental Welfare
Cantab	*Cantabrigiensis* (of Cambridge)
Cantuar	*Cantuariensis* (of Canterbury)
Capt	Captain
CARD	Campaign against Racial Discrimination
Cards	Cardiganshire
CARE	Cottage and Rural Enterprises
CARICOM	Caribbean Community
CARIFTA	Caribbean Free Trade Area
Carmarths	Carmarthenshire
CAS	Chief of the Air Staff
CASI	Canadian Aeronautics and Space Institute
CAT	College of Advanced Technology; Countryside Around Towns
CATE	Council for the Accreditation of Teacher Education
Cav	Cavalry
CAWU	Clerical and Administrative Workers' Union
CB	Companion, Order of the Bath; County Borough
CBC	County Borough Council
CBCO	Central Board for Conscientious Objectors
CBE	Commander, Order of the British Empire
CBI	Confederation of British Industry
CBIM	Companion, British Institute of Management
CBiol	Chartered Biologist
CBNS	Commander British Navy Staff
CBS	Columbia Broadcasting System; Confraternity of the Blessed Sacrament
CBSA	Clay Bird Shooting Association
CBSJ	Chartered Building Societies Institute
CBSO	City of Birmingham Symphony Orchestra
CC	Companion, Order of Canada; City Council; County Council(lor); Cricket Club; Cycling Club; County Court
CCAB	Consultative Committee of Accountancy Bodies
CCAHC	Central Council for Agricultural and Horticultural Co-operation
CCBE	Commission Consultative des Barreaux de la Communauté Européenne
CCBI	Council of Churches for Britain and Ireland
CCC	Corpus Christi College; Central Criminal Court; County Cricket Club
CCE	Chartered Civil Engineer
CCF	Combined Cadet Force
CCFM	Combined Cadet Forces Medal
CCG	Control Commission Germany
CCH	Cacique's Crown of Honour, Order of Service of Guyana
CChem	Chartered Chemist
CCHMS	Central Committee for Hospital Medical Services
CCIA	Commission of Churches on International Affairs
CCIS	Command Control Information System
CCJ	Council of Christians and Jews
CCPR	Central Council of Physical Recreation
CCRA	Commander Corps of Royal Artillery
CCRE	Commander Corps of Royal Engineers
CCREME	Commander Corps of Royal Electrical and Mechanical Engineers
CCRSigs	Commander Corps of Royal Signals
CCS	Casualty Clearing Station; Ceylon Civil Service; Countryside Commission for Scotland
CCSU	Council of Civil Service Unions
CCTA	Commission de Coopération Technique pour l'Afrique
CCTS	Combat Crew Training Squadron
CD	Canadian Forces Decoration; Commander, Order of Distinction (Jamaica); Civil Defence
CDA	Co-operative Development Agency
CDEE	Chemical Defence Experimental Establishment
CDipAF	Certified Diploma in Accounting and Finance
Cdr	Commander
CDRA	Committee of Directors of Research Associations
Cdre	Commodore
CDS	Chief of the Defence Staff
CDU	Christlich-Demokratische Union
CE	Civil Engineer
C of E	Church of England
CEA	Central Electricity Authority
CEC	Commission of the European Communities
CECD	Confédération Européenne du Commerce de Détail
CECG	Consumers in European Community Group
CEDEP	Centre Européen d'Education Permanente
CEE	Communauté Economique Européen
CEED	Centre for Economic and Environmental Development
CEF	Canadian Expeditionary Force
CEFIC	Conseil Européen des Fédérations de l'Industrie Chimique
CEGB	Central Electricity Generating Board
CEI	Council of Engineering Institutions
CEIR	Corporation for Economic and Industrial Research
CEM	Council of European Municipalities
CEMA	Council for the Encouragement of Music and Arts
CEMR	Council of European Municipalities and Regions
CEMS	Church of England Men's Society
CEN	Comité Européen de Normalisation
CENELEC	European Committee for Electrotechnical Standardization
CEng	Chartered Engineer
Centl	Central
Cento	Central Treaty Organisation
CEO	Chief Executive Officer
CEPT	Conférence Européenne des Postes et des Télécommunications
CERL	Central Electricity Research Laboratories
CERN	Organisation (formerly Centre) Européenne pour la Recherche Nucléaire
Cert	Certificate
CERT	Charities Effectiveness Review Trust
CertCPE	Certificate in Clinical Pastoral Education
Cert Ed	Certificate of Education
CertITP	Certificate of International Teachers' Program (Harvard)
CEST	Centre for Exploitation of Science and Technology
CET	Council for Educational Technology
CETS	Church of England Temperance Society
CF	Chaplain to the Forces; Companion, Order of Fiji
CFA	Canadian Field Artillery
CFE	Central Fighter Establishment; College of Further Education
CFM	Cadet Forces Medal
CFR	Commander, Order of the Federal Republic of Nigeria
CFS	Central Flying School
C&G	City and Guilds of London Institute
CGA	Community of the Glorious Ascension; Country Gentlemen's Association
CGeol	Chartered Geologist
CGH	Order of the Golden Heart of Kenya (1st class)
CGIA	Insignia Award of City and Guilds of London Institute
CGLI	City and Guilds of London Institute
CGM	Conspicuous Gallantry Medal
CGRM	Commandant-General Royal Marines
CGS	Chief of the General Staff
Ch/ch	Chief/chief; Church
CH	Companion of Honour
CHAR	Campaign for the Homeless and Rootless
ChB	Bachelor of Surgery (Chirurgy)
CHB	Companion of Honour of Barbados
CHC	Community Health Council
Ch Ch	Christ Church
CHE	Campaign for Homosexual Equality
ChLJ	Chaplain, Order of St Lazarus of Jerusalem
Chllr	Chancellor
chm	chairman/chairwoman
ChM	Master of Surgery
CHM	Chevalier of Honour and Merit (Haiti)

1

CHN	Community of the Holy Name
CHSC	Central Health Services Council
ChStJ	Chaplain, Most Venerable Order of the Hospital of St John of Jerusalem
CI	Imperial Order of the Crown of India; Channel Islands
CIA	Chemical Industries Association; Central Intelligence Agency
CIAD	Central Institute of Art and Design
CIAgrE	Companion, Institution of Agricultural Engineers
CIAL	Corresponding Member, International Institute of Arts and Letters
CIArb	Chartered Institute of Arbitrators
CIB	Chartered Institute of Bankers
CIBS	Chartered Institution of Building Services
CIBSE	Chartered Institution of Building Services Engineers
CIC	Chemical Institute of Canada
CICB	Criminal Injuries Compensation Board
CICHE	Committee for International Co-operation in Higher Education
CICI	Confederation of Information Communication Industries
CID	Criminal Investigation Department
CIDEC	Conseil International pour le Développement du Cuivre
CIE	Companion, Order of the Indian Empire; Confédération Internationale des Etudiants
CIFRS	Comité International de la Rayonne et des Fibres Synthétiques
CIGasE	Companion, Institution of Gas Engineers
CIGRE	Conférence Internationale des Grands Réseaux Electriques
CIGS	Chief of the Imperial General Staff
CIIA	Canadian Institute of International Affairs
CIL	*Corpus inscriptionum latinarum* (body of Latin writings)
CIM	China Inland Mission
CIMA	Chartered Institute of Management Accountants
CIMarE	Companion, Institute of Marine Engineers
CIMEMME	Companion, Institution of Mining Electrical and Mining Mechanical Engineers
CIMgt	Companion, Institute of Management
CIMGTechE	Companion, Institution of Mechanical and General Technician Engineers
C-in-C	Commander-in-Chief
CINCHAN	Allied Commander-in-Chief Channel
CIOB	Chartered Institute of Building
CIPD	Companion, Institute of Personnel and Development
CIPFA	Chartered Institute of Public Finance and Accountancy
CIPL	Comité International Permanent des Linguistes
CIPM	Companion, Institute of Personnel Management
CIR	Commission on Industrial Relations
CIRES	Co-operative Institute for Research in Environmental Sciences
CIRIA	Construction Industry Research and Information Association
CIRP	Collège Internationale pour Recherche et Production
CIS	Institute of Chartered Secretaries and Administrators (formerly Chartered Institute of Secretaries); Command Control Communications and Information Systems; Commonwealth of Independent States
CISAC	Confédération Internationale des Sociétés d'Auteurs et Compositeurs; Centre for International Security and Arms Control
CIT	Chartered Institute of Transport; California Institute of Technology
CITB	Construction Industry Training Board
CIU	Club and Institute Union
CIV	City Imperial Volunteers
Civ	Civil
CJ	Chief Justice
CJC	Companions of Jesus Christ
CJM	Congregation of Jesus and Mary (Eudist Fathers)
Cl	Class; Close
CL	Commander, Order of Leopold
CLA	Country Landowners' Association
CIEx	Companion, Institute of Export
CLIC	Cancer and Leukemia in Children
CLIP	Common Law Institute of Intellectual Property
CLit	Companion of Literature (Royal Society of Literature Award)
CLJ	Commander, Order of St Lazarus of Jerusalem
CLP	Constituency Labour Party
CLRAE	Congress (formerly Conference) of Local and Regional Authorities of Europe
CLY	City of London Yeomanry
CM	Member, Order of Canada; Congregation of the Mission (Vincentians); Master in Surgery; Certificated Master; Canadian Militia

CMA	Canadian Medical Association; Cost and Management Accountant (NZ)
CMAC	Catholic Marriage Advisory Council
CMath	Chartered Mathematician
CMB	Central Midwives' Board
CMC	Certified Management Consultant
Cmd	Command (*e.g.*, Southern Command)
cmded	commanded
cmdg	commanding
Cmdt	Commandant
CMet	Chartered Meteorologist
CMF	Commonwealth Military Forces; Central Mediterranean Force
CMG	Companion, Order of St Michael and St George
CMLJ	Commander of Merit, Order of St Lazarus of Jerusalem
CMO	Chief Medical Officer
CMP	Corps of Military Police
CMS	Church Missionary Society
CMS	Church Mission (formerly Church Missionary) Society; Certificate in Management Studies
CMT	Chaconia Medal of Trinidad
CMZS	Corresponding Member, Zoological Society
CNAA	Council for National Academic Awards
Cncl	Council
Cncllr	Councillor
CND	Campaign for Nuclear Disarmament
CNI	Companion, Nautical Institute
CNIM	Commander, Order of Military Merit (Canada)
CNO	Chief of Naval Operations
CNR	Canadian National Railways
CNRS	Centre National de la Recherche Scientifique
Co	County; Company
c/o	care of
CO	Commanding Officer; Commonwealth Office (after Aug 1966); Colonial Office (before Aug 1966): Conscientious Objector; Colorado
CODEST	Committee for the Development of European Science and Technology
COHSE	Confederation of Health Service Employees
COI	Central Office of Information
CoID	Council of Industrial Design (now Design Council)
Col	Colonel
Coll	College; Collegiate
Colo	Colorado
COMEC	Council of the Military Education Committees of the Universities of the UK
COMET	Committee for Middle East Trade
Commn	Commission
commnd	commissioned
Commr	Commissioner
CompAMEME	Companion, Association of Mining Electrical and Mechanical Engineers
CompICE	Companion, Institution of Civil Engineers
CompIEE	Companion, Institution of Electrical Engineers
CompIERE	Companion, Institution of Electronic and Radio Engineers
CompIGasE	Companion, Institution of Gas Engineers
CompIWES	Companion, Institution of Water Engineers and Scientists
CompIMechE	Companion, Institution of Mechanical Engineers
CompOR	Companion, Operational Research Society
CompTI	Companion of the Textile Institute
CON	Commander, Order of the Niger
Conf	Conference
Conn	Connecticut
Const	Constitutional
Co-op	Co-operative
COPA	Comité des Organisations Professionels Agricoles de la CEE
COPEC	Conference of Politics, Economics and Christianity
COPUS	Committee on the Public Understanding of Science
Corp	Corporation
Corresp Memb	Corresponding Member
COS	Chief of Staff; Charity Organization Society
COSA	Colliery Officials and Staffs Association
CoSIRA	Council for Small Industries in Rural Areas
COSLA	Convention of Scottish Local Authorities
COSPAR	Committee on Space Research
COSSAC	Chief of Staff to Supreme Allied Commander
COTC	Canadian Officers' Training Corps
CP	Central Provinces; Cape Province; Congregation of the Passion; Communist Party
CPA	Commonwealth Parliamentary Association; Chartered Patent Agent; Certified Public Accountant (Canada)
CPAG	Child Poverty Action Group
CPAS	Church Pastoral Aid Society

CPC	Conservative Political Centre
CPCH	College of Paediatrics and Child Health
CPEng	Chartered Professional Engineer (of Institution of Engineers of Australia)
CPFA	Member or Associate, Chartered Institute of Public Finance and Accountancy
CPhys	Chartered Physicist
CPL	Chief Personnel and Logistics
Cpl	Corporal
CPM	Colonial Police Medal
CPR	Canadian Pacific Railway
CPRE	Council for the Protection of Rural England
CPRS	Central Policy Review Staff
CPRW	Campaign for the Protection of Rural Wales
CPS	Crown Prosecution Service
CPSA	Civil and Public Services Association; Church of the Province of South Africa
CPSU	Communist Party of the Soviet Union
CPsychol	Chartered Psychologist
CPU	Commonwealth Press Union
CQSW	Certificate of Qualification in Social Work
cr	created/creation
CR	Community of the Resurrection
CRA	Commander, Royal Artillery
CRAC	Careers Research and Advisory Centre
CRAeS	Companion, Royal Aeronautical Society
CRAG	Clinical Resources and Audit Group
CRASC	Commander, Royal Army Service Corps
CRC	Cancer Research Campaign; Community Relations Council
CRCP(C)	Certificant, Royal College of Physicians of Canada
CRE	Commander, Royal Engineers; Commission for Racial Equality; Commercial Relations and Exports
CREME	Commander, Royal Electrical and Mechanical Engineers
Cres	Crescent
CRMP	Corps of Royal Military Police
CRNCM	Companion, Royal Northern College of Music
CRO	Commonwealth Relations Office
CS	Civil Service; Clerk to the Signet
CSA	Confederate States of America; Child Support Agency
CSAB	Civil Service Appeal Board
CSB	Bachelor of Christian Science
CSC	Conspicuous Service Cross; Congregation of the Holy Cross
CSCA	Civil Service Clerical Association
CSCE	Conference on Security and Co-operation in Europe
CSD	Civil Service Department; Co-operative Secretaries Diploma; Chartered Society of Designers
CSDE	Central Servicing Development Establishment
CSEU	Confederation of Shipbuilding and Engineering Unions
CSG	Companion, Order of the Star of Ghana; Company of the Servants of God
CSI	Companion, Order of the Star of India
CSIR	Commonwealth Council for Scientific and Industrial Research
CSIRO	Commonwealth Scientific and Industrial Research Organization (Australia)
CSM	Company Sergeant-Major
CSO	Chief Scientific Officer; Chief Signal Officer; Chief Staff Officer; Central Statistical Office
CSP	Chartered Society of Physiotherapists; Civil Service of Pakistan
CSS	Companion, Star of Sarawak; Council for Science and Society
CSSB	Civil Service Selection Board
CSSR	Congregation of the Most Holy Redeemer (Redemptorist Order)
Cstat	Chartered Statistician
CSTI	Council of Science and Technology Institutes
CStJ	Commander, Most Venerable Order of the Hospital of St John of Jerusalem
CSU	Christlich-Soziale Union in Bayern
CSV	Community Service Volunteers
CSW	Certificate in Social Work
CT	Connecticut
Ct	Court
CTA	Chaplain Territorial Army
CTB	College of Teachers of the Blind
CTC	Cyclists' Touring Club; Commando Training Centre; City Training College
Ctee	Committee
CText	Chartered Textile Technologist
CTR(Harwell)	Controlled Thermonuclear Research
CU	Cambridge University
CUAC	Cambridge University Athletic Club
CUAFC	Cambridge University Association Football Club
CUBC	Cambridge University Boat Club
CUCC	Cambridge University Cricket Club
CUF	Common University Fund
CUHC	Cambridge University Hockey Club
CUMS	Cambridge University Musical Society
CUNY	City University of New York
CUP	Cambridge University Press
CURUFC	Cambridge University Rugby Union Football Club
cv	*curriculum vitae*
CV	Cross of Valour (Canada)
CVCP	Committee of Vice-Chancellors and Principals of the Universities of the United Kingdom
CVO	Commander, Royal Victorian Order
CVS	Council for Voluntary Service
CVSNA	Council of Voluntary Service National Association
CWA	Crime Writers Association
CWGC	Commonwealth War Graves Commission
Cwlth	Commonwealth
CWS	Co-operative Wholesale Society
CWU	Communication Workers Union

D

d	died
D	Duke
DA	Dame of St Andrew, Order of Barbados; Diploma in Anaesthesia; Diploma in Art
DAAG	Deputy Assistant Adjutant-General
DAA&QMG	Deputy Assistant Adjutant and Quartermaster-General
DAC	Development Assistance Committee; Diocesan Advisory Committee
DACG	Deputy Assistant Chaplain-General
DAD	Deputy Assistant Director
D&AD	Designers and Art Directors Association
DAdmin	Doctor of Administration
DADMS	Deputy Assistant Director of Medical Services
DADOS	Deputy Assistant Director of Ordnance Services
DADQ	Deputy Assistant Director of Quartering
DADST	Deputy Assistant Director of Supplies and Transport
DAEd	Diploma in Art Education
DAG	Deputy Adjutant-General
DAgr	Doctor of Agriculture
DAgrFor	Doctor of Agriculture and Forestry
DAMS	Deputy Assistant Military Secretary
DAppSc	Doctor of Applied Science
DA&QMG	Deputy Adjutant and Quartermaster-General
DArch	Doctor of Architecture
DArt(s)	Doctor of Art(s)
das	died on active service
DASc	Doctor in Agricultural Sciences
DATA	Draughtsmen's and Allied Technicians' Association
DATEC	Art and Design Committee, Technician Education Council
dau	daughter
DBA	Doctor of Business Administration
DBE	Dame Commander, Order of the British Empire
DC	District Commissioner; District Council; District of Columbia
DCAe	Diploma of College of Aeronautics
DCAS	Deputy Chief of the Air Staff
DCB	Dame Commander, Order of the Bath
DCC	Diploma of Chelsea College
DCCH	Diploma in Community Child Health
DCDS	Deputy Chief of Defence Staff
DCE	Diploma of a College of Education
DCG	Deputy Chaplain-General
DCGRM	Department of the Commandant General Royal Marines
DCGS	Deputy Chief of the General Staff
DCH	Diploma in Child Health
DCh	Doctor of Surgery
DCIGS	Deputy Chief of the Imperial General Staff
DCL	Doctor of Civil Law

DCLI	Duke of Cornwall's Light Infantry
DCLJ	Dame Commander, Order of St Lazarus of Jerusalem
DCM	Distinguished Conduct Medal
DCMG	Dame Commander, Order of St Michael and St George
DCMHE	Diploma of Contents and Methods in Health Education
DCnL	Doctor of Canon Law
DCO	Duke of Cambridge's Own
DComm	Doctor of Commerce
DCP	Diploma in Clinical Pathology; Diploma in Conservation of Paintings
DCS	Deputy Chief of Staff; Doctor of Commercial Sciences
DCSO	Deputy Chief Scientific Officer
DCT	Doctor of Christian Theology
DCVO	Dame Commander, Royal Victorian Order
DD	Doctor of Divinity
DDes	Doctor of Design
DDGAMS	Deputy Director General, Army Medical Services
DDH	Diploma in Dental Health
DDL	Deputy Director of Labour
DDME	Deputy Director of Mechanical Engineering
DDMI	Deputy Director of Military Intelligence
DDMO	Deputy Director of Military Operations
DDMS	Deputy Director of Medical Services
DDMT	Deputy Director of Military Training
DDNI	Deputy Director of Naval Intelligence
DDO	Diploma in Dental Orthopaedics
DDPH	Diploma in Dental Public Health
DDPR	Deputy Director of Public Relations
DDPS	Deputy Director of Personal Services
DDR	Deutsche Demokratische Republik
DDRA	Deputy Director Royal Artillery
DDS	Doctor of Dental Surgery; Director of Dental Services
DDSc	Doctor of Dental Science
DDSD	Deputy Director Staff Duties
DDSM	Defense Distinguished Service Medal
DDST	Deputy Director of Supplies and Transport
DDWE&M	Deputy Director of Works, Electrical and Mechanical
DE	Doctor of Engineering; Delaware
DEA	Department of Economic Affairs
decd	deceased
DEconSc	Doctor of Economic Science
DEd	Doctor of Education
Def	Defence
Deleg	Delegate
Delegn	Delegation
DEME	Directorate of Electrical and Mechanical Engineering
DEMS	Defensively Equipped Merchant Ships
DenD	Docteur en Droit
DEng	Doctor of Engineering
DenM	Docteur en Médicine
DEOVR	Duke of Edinburgh's Own Volunteer Rifles
Dep/dep	Deputy/deputy
DEP	Department of Employment and Productivity; European Progressive Democrats
Dept/Deptl	Department/Departmental
DERA	Defence Evaluation and Research Agency
Derbys	Derbyshire
DèS/DèsSc	Docteur ès sciences
DES	Department of Education and Science
DèsL	Docteur ès lettres
DesRCA	Designer of the Royal College of Art
Devpt	Development
DFA	Doctor of Fine Arts
DFAS	Decorative and Fine Art Society
DFC	Distinguished Flying Cross
DFE	Department for Education
DFEE	Department for Education and Employment
DFH	Diploma of Faraday House
DFLS	Day Fighter Leaders' School
DFM	Distinguished Flying Medal
DG	Director General
DGAA	Distressed Gentlefolks Aid Association
DGAMS	Director-General Army Medical Services
DGEME	Director General Electrical and Mechanical Engineering
DGLP(A)	Director General Logistic Policy (Army)
DGMS	Director-General of Medical Services
DGMT	Director-General of Military Training
DGMW	Director-General of Military Works
DGNPS	Director-General of Naval Personal Services
DGP	Director-General of Personnel
DGPS	Director-General of Personal Services

DGS	Diploma in Graduate Studies
DGStJ	Dame of Grace, Order of St John of Jerusalem
DGU	Doctor of Griffith University
DH	Doctor of Humanities
DHA	District Health Authority
Dhc	*Doctor honoris causa*
DHEW	Department of Health Education and Welfare (US)
DHL	Doctor of Humane Letters; Doctor of Hebrew Literature
DHM	Dean Hole Medal
DHMSA	Diploma in the History of Medicine (Society of Apothecaries)
DHQ	District Headquarters
DHSS	Department of Health and Social Security
DHum	Doctor of Humanities
DHumLit	Doctor of Humane Letters
DIAS	Dublin Institute of Advanced Sciences
DIC	Diploma of the Imperial College
DICTA	Diploma of Imperial College of Tropical Agriculture
DIG	Deputy Inspector-General
DIH	Diploma in Industrial Health
DIMP	Daijah Indera Mahkota Pahang
DIntLaw	Diploma in International Law
Dip	Diploma; Diplomatic
DipAA	Diploma in Applied Art
DipAD	Diploma in Art and Design
DipAe	Diploma in Aeronautics
DipArch	Diploma in Architecture
DipASE	Diploma in Advanced Study of Education, College of Preceptors
DipAvMed	Diploma of Aviation Medicine, Royal College of Physicians
DipBA	Diploma in Business Administration
DipBS	Diploma in Fine Art, Byam Shaw School
DipCAM	Diploma in Communications, Advertising and Marketing of CAM Foundation
DipCC	Diploma of the Central College
DipCD	Diploma in Civic Design
DipCE	Diploma in Civil Engineering
DipEcon	Diploma in Economics
DipEd	Diploma in Education
DipEE	Diploma in Electrical Engineenng
DipEI	Diploma in Electronics
DipESL	Diploma in English as a Second Language
DipEth	Diploma in Ethnology
DipFD	Diploma in Funeral Directing
DipFE	Diploma in Further Education
DipFM	Diploma in Forensic Medicine
DipGSM	Diploma in Music, Guildhall School of Music and Drama
DipHA	Diploma in Hospital Administration
DipHSM	Diploma in Health Services Management
DipHum	Diploma in Humanities
DipLA	Diploma in Landscape Architecture
DipLib	Diploma of Librarianship
DipM	Diploma in Marketing
DipN	Diploma in Nursing
DipNEC	Diploma of Northampton Engineering College
DipPA	Diploma of Practitioners in Advertising
DipPSA	Diploma in Public Service Administration
DipREM	Diploma in Rural Estate Management
DipSMS	Diploma in School Management Studies
DipSoc	Diploma in Sociology
DipTA	Diploma in Tropical Agriculture
DipT&CP	Diploma in Town and Country Planning
DipTh	Diploma in Theology
DipTMHA	Diploma in Training and Further Education of Mentally Handicapped Adults
DipTP	Diploma in Town Planning
DipTPT	Diploma in Theory and Practice of Teaching
Dir/dir	Director/director
DIS	Diploma in Industrial Studies
Dist	District
DistTP	Distinction in Town Planning
DIur	Doctor of Law
div	divorced
Div	Division
Div Test	Divinity Testimonium (of Trinity College, Dublin)
Divnl	Division(al)
DJAG	Deputy Judge Advocate General
DJPD	Dato Jasa Purba Di-Raja Negeri Sembilan (Malaysia)
DJStJ	Dame of Justice, Order of St John of Jerusalem
DJur	*Doctor Juris* (Doctor of Law)
DK	Most Esteemed Family Order (Brunei)
DL	Deputy Lieutenant

DLC	Diploma of Loughborough College
DLES	Doctor of Letters in Economic Studies
DLI	Durham Light Infantry
DLit/DLitt	Doctor of Literature; Doctor of Letters
DLittS	Doctor of Sacred Letters
DLJ	Dame of Grace, Order of St Lazarus of Jerusalem
DLO	Diploma in Laryngology and Otology
DM	Doctor of Medicine
DMA	Diploma in Municipal Administration
DMD	Doctor of Medical Dentistry (Australia)
DME	Director of Mechanical Engineering
DMet	Doctor of Metallurgy
DMI	Director of Military Intelligence
DMin	Doctor of Ministry
DMiss	Doctor of Missiology
DMJ	Diploma in Medical Jurisprudence
DMJ(Path)	Diploma in Medical Jurisprudence (Pathology)
DMLJ	Dame of Merit, Order of St Lazarus of Jerusalem
DMO	Director of Military Operations
DMR	Diploma in Medical Radiology
DMRD	Diploma in Medical Radiological Diagnosis
DMRE	Diploma in Medical Radiology and Electrology
DMRT	Diploma in Medical Radio-Therapy
DMS	Director of Medical Services; Decoration for Meritorious Service (South Africa); Diploma in Management Studies
DMSc	Doctor of Medical Science
DMSSB	Direct Mail Services Standards Board
DMT	Director of Military Training
DMus	Doctor of Music
DMW	Dame, St Michael of the Wing (Portugal)
DN	Diploma in Nursing
DNB	Dictionary of National Biography
DNE	Director of Naval Equipment
DNH	Department of National Heritage
DNI	Director of Naval Intelligence
DO	Diploma in Ophthalmology; Diploma in Osteopathy
DOAE	Defence Operational Analysis Establishment
DObstRCOG	Diploma of Royal College of Obstetricians and Gynaecologists
DOC	District Officer Commanding
DocEng	Doctor of Engineering
DoE	Department of the Environment
DoH	Department of Health
DoI	Department of Industry
DOL	Doctor of Oriental Learning
Dom	*Dominus* (Lord)
DOMS	Diploma in Ophthalmic Medicine and Surgery
DOR	Director of Operational Requirements
DOrthRCS	Diploma in Orthodontics, Royal College of Surgeons
DOS	Director of Ordnance Services; Doctor of Ocular Science
DP	Data Processing
DPA	Diploma in Public Administration; Discharged Prisoners' Aid; Doctor of Public Administration
DPD	Diploma in Public Dentistry
DPEc	Doctor of Political Economy
DPed	Doctor of Pedagogy
DPh/DPhil	Doctor of Philosophy
DPH	Diploma in Public Health
DPharm	Doctor of Pharmacy
DPhilMed	Diploma in Philosophy of Medicine
DPhysMed	Diploma in Physical Medicine
DPLG	Diplômé par le Gouvernement
DPM	Diploma in Psychological Medicine
DPMS	Dato Paduka Mahkota Selangor (Malaysia)
DPP	Director of Public Prosecutions
DPR	Director of Public Relations
DPS	Director of Postal Services; Director of Personal Services; Doctor of Public Service
DPSA	Diploma in Public and Social Administration
DPSE	Diploma in Professional Studies in Education
DPsych	Doctor of Psychology
DQMG	Deputy Quartermaster-General
Dr	Doctor
Dr ing	Doctor of Engineering
Dr jur	Doctor of Laws
Dr rer nat	Doctor of Natural Science
Dr rer pol	Doctor of Political Science
DRA	Defence Research Agency
DRAC	Director Royal Armoured Corps
DrArch	Doctor of Architecture
DRC	Diploma of Royal College of Science and Technology, Glasgow
DRCOG	Diploma of Royal College of Obstetricians and Gynaecologists
DRD	Diploma in Restorative Dentistry
DrŒcPol	*Doctor Œconomiæ Politiæ* (Doctor of Political Economy)
DRS	Diploma in Religious Studies
DRSAMD	Diploma of the Royal Scottish Academy of Music and Drama
DS	Directing Staff; Doctor of Science
DSA	Diploma in Social Administration
DSAC	Defence Scientific Advisory Council
DSAO	Diplomatic Service Administration Office
DSc (SocSci)	Doctor of Science in Social Science
DSC	Distinguished Service Cross
DSc	Doctor of Science
DScA	Docteur en sciences agricoles
DSCHE	Diploma of the Scottish Council for Health Education
DScMil	Doctor of Military Science
DSD	Director Staff Duties
DSF	Director Special Forces
DSIR	Department of Scientific and Industrial Research
DSL	Doctor of Sacred Letters
DSLJ	Dato Seri Laila Jasa (Brunei)
DSM	Distinguished Service Medal
DSNB	Dato Setia Negara Brunei
DSNS	Dato Setia Negeri Sembilan (Malaysia)
DSO	Distinguished Service Order
DSocSc	Doctor of Social Science
dsp	*decessit sine prole* (died without issue)
dspl	*decessit sine prole legitima* (died without legitimate issue)
dspm	*decessit sine prole mascula* (died without male issue)
dspml	*decessit sine prole mascula legitima* (died without legitimate male issue)
dspms	*decessit sine prole mascula superstite* (died without surviving male issue)
dsps	*decessit sine prole superstite* (died without surviving issue)
DSP	Director of Selection of Personnel; Docteur en sciences politiques (Montreal)
Dss	Deaconess
DSS	Department of Social Security; Doctor of Sacred Scripture
DSSc	Doctor of Social Science
DST	Director of Supplies and Transport
DStJ	Dame of Grace, Most Venerable Order of the Hospital of St John of Jerusalem; Dame of Justice, Most Venerable Order of the Hospital of St John of Jerusalem
DTA	Diploma in Tropical Agriculture
DTD	Dekoratie voor Trouwe Dienst (Decoration for Devoted Service)
DTech	Doctor of Technology
DTh/DTheol	Doctor of Theology
DTH	Diploma in Tropical Hygiene
DThPT	Diploma in Theory and Practice of Teaching
DTI	Department of Trade and Industry
DTM&H	Diploma in Tropical Medicine and Hygiene
DU/DUniv	Honorary Doctor of the University
Dunelm	*Dunelmensis* (of Durham)
DUP	Democratic Unionist Party; Docteur de l'Université de Paris
DVA	Diploma of Veterinary Anaesthesia
Dve	Drive
DVH	Diploma in Veterinary Hygiene
DVLA	Driver and Vehicle Licensing Authority
DVLC	Driver and Vehicle Licensing Centre
DVM	Doctor of Veterinary Medicine
DVMS/DVM&S	Doctor of Veterinary Medicine and Surgery
dvm	*decessit vita matris* (died in the lifetime of the mother)
dvp	*decessit vita patris* (died in the lifetime of the father)
DVR	Diploma in Veterinary Radiology
DVSc	Doctor of Veterinary Science
DVSM	Diploma in Veterinary State Medicine

E

E	East; Earl; England, used usually of titles of honour created in the peerage or baronetage of England
EAA	Edinburgh Architectural Association
EACR	European Association for Cancer Research
EAGA	Energy Action Grants Agency
EAHY	European Architectural Heritage Year
EAP	East Africa Protectorate
EAW	Electrical Association for Women
EBC	English Benedictine Congregation
Ebor	*Eboracensis* (of York)
EBRD	European Bank for Reconstruction and Development
EBU	European Broadcasting Union
Ec	Economic
EC	Etoile de Courage (Canada); European Community; European Commission; Emergency Commission
ECA	Economic Co-operation Administration; Economic Commission for Africa
ECAFE	Economic Commission for Asia and the Far East
ECCTIS	Education Courses and Credit Transfer Information Systems
ECE	Economic Commission for Europe
ECGD	Export Credits Guarantee Department
ECLA	Economic Commission for Latin America
ECLAC	United Nations Economic Commission for Latin America and the Caribbean
ECOVAST	European Council for the Village and Small Town
ECSC	European Coal and Steel Community
ECU	English Church Union
ed	edited; editor
ED	Efficiency Decoration; Doctor of Engineering (US); European Democrat
EdB	Bachelor of Education
EDC	Economic Development Committee
EdD	Doctor of Education
EDF	European Development Fund
EDG	European Democratic Group; Employment Department Group
Edin	Edinburgh
edn	edition
EDP	Executive Development Programme
EdS	Specialist in Education
edtl	editorial
educ	educated
Educn	Education
EEC	European Economic Community
EEF	Engineering Employers' Federation; Egyptian Expeditionary Force
EEIBA	Electrical and Electronic Industries Benevolent Association
EETPU	Electrical Electronic Telecommunication & Plumbing Union
EETS	Early English Text Society
EFCE	European Federation of Chemical Engineering
EFTA	European Free Trade Association
eh	ehrenhalber (honorary)
EI	East Indian; East Indies
EIA	Engineering Industries Association
EIB	European Investment Bank
EICS	East India Company's Service
EIS	Educational Institute of Scotland
EISCAT	European Incoherent Scatter Association
EIU	Economist Intelligence Unit
ELBS	English Language Book Society
ELSE	European Life Science Editors
ELT	English Language Teaching
EM	Edward Medal
EMBL	European Molecular Biology Laboratory
EMBO	European Molecular Biology Organisation
EMP	Electro Magnetic Pulse; Executive Management Program Diploma
EMS	Emergency Medical Service
Engr/engr	engineer
Engrg	Engineering
ENO	English National Opera
ENSA	Entertainments National Service Association
ENT	Ear Nose and Throat
EO	Executive Officer
EOC	Equal Opportunities Commission
EOPH	Examined Officer of Public Health
EORTC	European Organisation for Research on Treatment of Cancer
EP	European Parliament
EPP	European People's Party
EPSRC	Engineering and Physical Sciences Research Council
ER	East Riding; Eastern Region (British Railways)
er	elder
ERA	Electrical Research Association
ERC	Electronics Research Council
ERD	Emergency Reserve Decoration (Army)
ESA	European Space Agency
ESCAP	Economic and Social Commission for Asia and the Pacific
ESF	European Science Foundation
ESL	English as a Second Language
Esq	Esquire
ESRC	Economic and Social Research Council; Electricity Supply Research Council
ESRO	European Space Research Organization
est	eldest
ESTA	European Sciences and Technology Assembly
Estab/s	Establishment/s
ESU	English-Speaking Union
ETA	Engineering Training Authority
ETH	Eidgenössische Technische Hochschule
ETUC	European Trade Union Confederation
ETUCE	European Trade Union Committee for Education
EU	European Union
EUDISED	European Documentation and Information Service for Education
Euratom	European Atomic Energy Community
EurBiol	European Biologist
EurChem	European Chemist
EurIng	European Engineer
EUROM	European Federation for Optics and Precision Mechanics
EUW	European Union of Women
eV	eingetragener Verein
exec	executive
Expdn(y)	Expedition(ary)
Extrdy	Extraordinary

F

f	father
FA	Football Association
FAA	Fellow, Australian Academy of Science; Fleet Air Arm
FAAAI	Fellow, American Association for Artificial Intelligence
FAAAS	Fellow, American Association for the Advancement of Science
FAAO	Fellow, American Academy of Optometry
FAAP	Fellow, American Academy of Pediatrics
FAARM	Fellow, American Academy of Reproductive Medicine
FAAV	Fellow, Association of Agricultural Valuers
FAAVCT	Fellow, American Academy of Veterinary and Comparative Toxicology
FABE	Fellow, Association of Building Engineers
FACC	Fellow, American College of Cardiology
FACCA	Fellow, Association of Certified and Corporate Accountants
FACCP	Fellow, American College of Chest Physicians
FACD	Fellow, American College of Dentistry
FACDS	Fellow, Australian College of Dental Surgeons
FACE	Fellow, Australian College of Education
FACerS	Fellow, American Ceramic Society
FACHSE	Fellow, Australian College of Health Service Executives
FACI	Fellow, Australian Chemical Institute
FACMA	Fellow, Australian College of Medical Administrators
FACMG	Fellow, American College of Medicinal Genetics
FACOG	Fellow, American College of Obstetricians and Gynaecologists
FACOM	Fellow, Australian College of Occupational Medicine
FACP	Fellow, American College of Physicians
FACR	Fellow, American College of Radiology
FACRM	Fellow, Australian College of Rehabilitation Medicine

FACS	Fellow, American College of Surgeons
FACVT	Fellow, American College of Veterinary Toxicology
FADM	Fellow, Academy of Dental Materials
FADO	Fellow, Association of Dispensing Opticians
FAeSI	Fellow, Aeronautical Society of India
FAFPHM	Fellow, Australian Faculty of Public Health Medicine
FAGO	Fellowship in Australia in Obstetrics and Gynaecology
FAGS	Fellow, American Geographical Society
FAHA	Fellow, Australian Academy of the Humanities
FAI	Fellow, Chartered Auctioneers' and Estate Agents' Institute; Fédération Aéronautique Internationale
FAIA	Fellow, American Institute of Architects
FAIAA	Fellow, American Institute of Aeronautics and Astronautics
FAIAS	Fellow, Australian Institute of Agricultural Science
FAIB	Fellow, Australian Institute of Bankers
FAIBiol	Fellow, Australian Institute of Biology
FAICD	Fellow, Australian Institute of Company Directors
FAIE	Fellow, Australian Institute of Energy
FAIEx	Fellow, Australian Institute of Export
FAIFST	Fellow, Australian Institute of Food Science and Technology
FAII	Fellow, Australian Insurance Institute
FAIM	Fellow, Australian Institute of Management
FAIP	Fellow, Australian Institute of Physics
FAMA	Fellow, Australian Medical Association
FAMI	Fellow, Australian Marketing Institute
FAmNucSoc	Fellow, American Nuclear Society
FAMS	Fellow, Ancient Monuments Society
FANY	First Aid Nursing Yeomanry
FANZCA	Fellow, Australian and New Zealand College of Anaesthetists
FANZCP	Fellow, Australian and New Zealand College of Psychiatrists
FAO	Food and Agriculture Organization of the United Nations
FAOrthA	Fellow, Australian Orthopaedic Association
FAPA	Fellow, American Psychiatric Association
FAPHA	Fellow, American Public Health Association
FAPI	Fellow, Australian Planning Institute
FAPM	Fellow, Association of Project Managers
FAPS	Fellow, American Phytopathological Society
FArborA	Fellow, Aboricultural Association
FARE	Federation of Alcoholic Rehabilitation Establishments
FARELF	Far East Land Forces
FAS	Fellow, Antiquarian Society; Fellow, Nigerian Academy of Science; Funding Agency for Schools
FASA	Fellow, Australian Society of Accountants
FASCE	Fellow, American Society of Civil Engineers
fase	fascicule
FASI	Fellow, Architects' and Surveyors' Institute
FASME	Fellow, American Society of Mechanical Engineers
FASPOG	Fellow, Australian Society for Psychosomatic Obstetrics and Gynaecology
FASSA	Fellow, Academy of the Social Sciences in Australia
FAusIMM	Fellow, Australasian Institute of Mining and Metallurgy
FAustCOG	Fellow, Australian College of Obstetricians and Gynaecologists
FBA	Fellow, British Academy; Federation of British Artists
FBCartS	Fellow, British Cartographic Society
FBCO	Fellow, British College of Optometrists (formerly of Ophthalmic Opticians (Optometrists))
FBCS	Fellow, British Computer Society
FBEC(S)	Fellow, Business Education Council (Scotland)
FBES	Fellow, Biological Engineering Society
FBHA	Fellow, British Hospitality Association
FBHI	Fellow, British Horological Institute; Fellow, British Horticultural Institute
FBHS	Fellow, British Horse Society
FBI	Federation of British Industries; Federal Bureau of Investigation
FBIA	Fellow, Bankers' Institute of Australasia
FBIAT	Fellow, British Institute of Architectural Technicians
FBIBA	Fellow, British Insurance Brokers' Association
FBID	Fellow, British Institute of Interior Design
FBIIBA	Fellow, British Insurance and Investment Brokers' Association
FBIM	Fellow, British Institute of Management
FBINZ	Fellow, Bankers' Institute of New Zealand
FBIPP	Fellow, British Institute of Professional Photography
FBIRA	Fellow, British Institute of Regulatory Affairs
FBIS	Fellow, British Interplanetary Society
FBKS	Fellow, British Kinematograph Society
FBKSTS	Fellow, British Kinematograph, Sound and Television Society
FBOA	Fellow, British Optical Association
FBOU	Fellow, British Ornithologists' Union
FBPICS	Fellow, British Production and Inventory Control Society
FBPsS	Fellow, British Psychological Society
FBritIRE	Fellow, British Institution of Radio Engineers (later FIERE)
FBS	Fellow, Building Societies Institute (later FCBSI)
FBSI	Fellow, Boot and Shoe Institution
FBSM	Fellow, Birmingham School of Music
FC	Football Club
FCA	Fellow, Institute of Chartered Accountants; Fellow, Institute of Chartered Accountants in Australia; Fellow, New Zealand Society of Accountants; Federation of Canadian Artists
FCAI	Fellow, New Zealand Institute of Cost Accountants; Fellow, Canadian Aeronautical Institute
FCAM	Fellow, CAM Foundation
FCAnaes	Fellow, College of Anaesthetists
FCASI	Fellow, Canadian Aeronautics and Space Institute
FCBSI	Fellow, Chartered Building Societies Institute
FCCA	Fellow, Chartered Association of Certified Accountants
FCCEA	Fellow, Commonwealth Council for Educational Administration
FCCS	Fellow, Corporation of Secretaries (formerly of Certified Secretaries)
FCCT	Fellow, Canadian College of Teachers
FCEC	Federation of Civil Engineering Contractors
FCFI	Fellow, Clothing and Footwear Institute
FCGI	Fellow, City and Guilds of London Institute
FCGP	Fellow, College of General Practitioners
FCH	Fellow, Coopers Hill College
FChS	Fellow, Society of Chiropodists
FCI	Fellow, Institute of Commerce
FCIA	Fellow, Corporation of Insurance Agents
FCIArb	Fellow, Chartered Institute of Arbitrators
FCIB	Fellow, Corporation of Insurance Brokers; Fellow, Chartered Institute of Bankers
FCIBS	Fellow, Chartered Institution of Building Services; Fellow, Chartered Institute of Bankers in Scotland
FCIBSE	Fellow, Chartered Institution of Building Services Engineers
FCIC	Fellow, Chemical Institute of Canada (formerly Canadian Institute of Chemistry)
FCIEH	Fellow, Chartered Institute of Environmental Health
FCIH	Fellow, Chartered Institute of Housing
FCII	Fellow, Chartered Insurance Institute
FCIJ	Fellow, Chartered Institute of Journalists
FCILA	Fellow, Chartered Institute of Loss Adjusters
FCIM	Fellow, Chartered Institute of Marketing; Fellow, Institute of Corporate Managers (Australia)
FCIOB	Fellow, Chartered Institute of Building
FCIPA	Fellow, Chartered Institute of Patent Agents
FCIPS	Fellow, Chartered Institute of Purchasing and Supply
FCIS	Fellow, Institute of Chartered Secretaries and Administrators (formerly Chartered Institute of Secretaries)
FCISA	Fellow, Chartered Institute of Secretaries and Administrators (Australia)
FCIT	Fellow, Chartered Institute of Transport
FCIWEM	Fellow, Chartered Institution of Water and Environmental Management
FCM	Faculty of Community Medicine
FCMA	Fellow, Chartered Institute of Management Accountants (formerly Institute of Cost and Management Accountants)
FCMSA	Fellow, College of Medicine of South Africa
FCNA	Fellow, College of Nursing, Australia
FCO	Foreign and Commonwealth Office
FCOG(SA)	Fellow, South African College of Obstetrics and Gynaecology
FCollH	Fellow, College of Handicraft
FCollP	Fellow, College of Preceptors
FCommA	Fellow, Society of Commercial Accountants
FCOphth	Fellow, College of Ophthalmologists
FCOptom	Fellow, College of Optometrists
FCP	Fellow, College of Preceptors
FCP(SoAf)	Fellow, College of Physicians, South Africa
FCPA	Fellow, Australian Society of Certified Practising Accountants; Fellow, Canadian Psychological Association
FCPath	Fellow, College of Pathologists
FCPCH	Fellow, College of Paediatrics and Child Health
FCPS	Fellow, College of Physicians and Surgeons
FCPS (Pak)	Fellow, College of Physicians and Surgeons of Pakistan
FCPSO(SoAf)	Fellow, College of Physicians and Surgeons and Obstetricians, South Africa
FCRA	Fellow, College of Radiologists of Australia
FCS	Federation of Conservative Students
FCS/FChemSoc	Fellow, Chemical Society

FCSD	Fellow, Chartered Society of Designers
FCSHK	Fellow, College of Surgeons of Hong Kong
FCSLT	Fellow, College of Speech and Language Therapists
FCSP	Fellow, Chartered Society of Physiotherapy
FCSSA	Fellow, College of Surgeons, South Africa
FCSSL	Fellow, College of Surgeons of Sri Lanka
FCST	Fellow, College of Speech Therapists
FCT	Federal Capital Territory; Fellow, Association of Corporate Treasurers
FCTB	Fellow, College of Teachers of the Blind
FCU	Fighter Control Unit
FCWA	Fellow, Institute of Costs and Works Accountants
FDA	Association of First Division Civil Servants
FDF	Food and Drink Federation
FDI	Fédération Dentaire Internationale
FDP	Freie Demokratische Partei
FDS	Fellow in Dental Surgery
FDSRCPSGlas	Fellow in Dental Surgery, Royal College of Physicians and Surgeons of Glasgow
FDSRCS	Fellow in Dental Surgery, Royal College of Surgeons of England
FDSRCSE	Fellow in Dental Surgery, Royal College of Surgeons of Edinburgh
FE	Far East
FEAF	Far East Air Force
FEANI	Fédération Européenne d'Associations Nationales d'Ingénieurs
FEBS	Federation of European Biochemical Societies
FECI	Fellow, Institute of Employment Consultants
Fedn	Federation
FEE	Fédération des Expertes Comptables Européens
FEEC/FEFCE	Further Education Funding Council for England
FEF	Far East Fleet
FEI	Fédération Equestre Internationale
FEIDCT	Fellow, Educational Institute of Design Craft and Technology
FEIS	Fellow, Educational Institute of Scotland
FELCO	Federation of English Language Course Opportunities
Fell	Fellow
FEng	Fellow, Royal Academy (formerly Fellowship) of Engineering
FES	Fellow, Entomological Society; Fellow, Ethnological Society
FESC	Fellow, European Society of Cardiology
FF	Fianna Fáil; Field Force
FFA	Fellow, Faculty of Actuaries (in Scotland); Fellow, Institute of Financial Accountants
FFA(SA)	Fellow, Faculty of Anaesthetists (South Africa)
FFAEM	Fellow, Faculty of Accident and Emergency Medicine
FFARACS	Fellow, Faculty of Anaesthetists, Royal Australasian College of Surgeons
FFARCS	Fellow, Faculty of Anaesthetists, Royal College of Surgeons of England
FFARCSI	Fellow, Faculty of Anaesthetists, Royal College of Surgeons in Ireland
FFAS	Fellow, Faculty of Architects and Surveyors, London
FFB	Fellow, Faculty of Building
FFCM	Fellow, Faculty of Community Medicine
FFCMI	Fellow, Faculty of Community Medicine of Ireland
FFDRCSI	Fellow, Faculty of Dentistry, Royal College of Surgeons in Ireland
FFF	Free French Forces
FFFP	Fellow, Faculty of Family Planning of the Royal College of Obstetricians and Gynaecologists
FFHC	Freedom from Hunger Campaign
FFHom	Fellow, Faculty of Homoeopathy
FFI	French Forces of the Interior; Finance for Industry
FFOM	Fellow, Faculty of Occupational Medicine
FFOMI	Fellow, Faculty of Occupational Medicine of Ireland
FFPath, RCPI	Fellow, Faculty of Pathologists of the Royal College of Physicians of Ireland
FFPHM	Fellow, Faculty of Public Health Medicine
FFPHMI	Fellow, Faculty of Public Health Medicine of Ireland
FFPM	Fellow, Faculty of Pharmaceutical Medicine
FFPS	Fauna and Flora Preservation Society
FFR	Fellow, Faculty of Radiologists
FG	Fine Gael
FGA	Fellow, Gemmological Association
FGCL	Fellow, Goldsmiths' College, London
FGCM	Fellow, Guild of Church Musicians
FGDS	Fédération de la Gauche Démocratique et Socialiste
FGGE	Fellow, Guild of Glass Engineers
FGI	Fellow, Institute of Certificated Grocers
F and GP	Finance and General Purposes
FGS	Fellow, Geological Society

FGSM	Fellow, Guildhall School of Music and Drama
FGSM(MT)	Fellow, Guildhall School of Music and Drama (Music Therapy)
FHA	Fellow, Institute of Health Service Administrators (formerly Hospital Administrators)
FHAS	Fellow, Highland and Agricultural Society of Scotland
FHCIMA	Fellow, Hotel Catering and Institutional Management Association
FHFS	Fellow, Human Factors Society
FHKIE	Fellow, Hong Kong Institution of Engineers
FHMAAAS	Foreign Honorary Member, American Academy of Arts and Sciences
FHS	Fellow, Heraldry Society; Forces Help Society and Lord Roberts Workshops
FHSA	Family Health Services Authority
FHSM	Fellow, Institute of Health Services Management
FH-WC	Fellow, Heriot-Watt College (now University), Edinburgh
FIA	Fellow, Institute of Actuaries
FIAA	Fellow, Institute of Actuaries of Australia
FIAA&S	Fellow, Incorporated Association of Architects and Surveyors
FIAAS	Fellow, Institute of Australian Agricultural Science
FIAgrE	Fellow, Institution of Agricultural Engineers
FIAgrM	Fellow, Institute of Agricultural Management
FIAI	Fellow, Institute of Industrial and Commercial Accountants
FIAL	Fellow, International Institute of Arts and Letters
FIAM	Fellow, International Academy of Management
FIAP	Fellow, Institution of Analysts and Programmers
FIArb	Fellow, Institute of Arbitrators
FIArbA	Fellow, Institute of Arbitrators of Australia
FIAS	Fellow, Institute of Aeronautical Sciences (US)
FIASc	Fellow, Indian Academy of Sciences
FIAWS	Fellow, International Academy of Wood Sciences
FIB	Fellow, Institute of Bankers
FIBA	Fellow, Institute of Business Administration, Australia
FIBD	Fellow, Institute of British Decorators
FIBiol	Fellow, Institute of Biology
FIBiotech	Fellow, Institute for Biotechnical Studies
FIBMS	Fellow, Institute of Biomedical Sciences
FIBP	Fellow, Institute of British Photographers
FIBScot	Fellow, Institute of Bankers in Scotland
FIC	Fellow, Institute of Chemistry; Fellow, Imperial College, London
FICA	Fellow, Commonwealth Institute of Accountants; Fellow, Institute of Chartered Accountants in England and Wales
FICAI	Fellow, Institute of Chartered Accountants in Ireland
FICD	Fellow, Institute of Civil Defence; Fellow, Indian College of Dentists; Fellow, International College of Dentists
FICDDS	Fellow, Institute of Civil Defence and Disaster Studies
FICE	Fellow, Institution of Civil Engineers
FICeram	Fellow, Institute of Ceramics
FICFM	Fellow, Institute of Charity Fundraising Managers
FICFor	Fellow, Institute of Chartered Foresters
FIChemE	Fellow, Institution of Chemical Engineers
FICI	Fellow, Institute of Chemistry of Ireland; Fellow, International Colonial Institute
FICM	Fellow, Institute of Credit Management
FICMA	Fellow, Institute of Cost and Management Accountants
FICorrST	Fellow, Institution of Corrosion Science and Technology
FICS	Fellow, Institute of Chartered Shipbrokers; Fellow, International College of Surgeons
FICT	Fellow, Institute of Concrete Technologists
FICW	Fellow, Institute of Clerks of Works of Great Britain
FIDA	Fellow, Institute of Directors, Australia
FIDCA	Fellow, Industrial Design Council of Australia
FIDE	Fédération Internationale des Echecs; Fellow, Institute of Design Engineers; Fédération Internationale pour le Droit Européen
FIDEM	Fédération Internationale de la Médaille
FIEAust	Fellow, Institution of Engineers, Australia
FIEC	Fellow, Institute of Employment Consultants
FIED	Fellow, Institution of Engineering Designers
FIEE	Fellow, Institution of Electrical Engineers
FIEEE	Fellow, Institute of Electrical and Electronics Engineers (NY)
FIEHK	Fellow, Institution of Engineering, Hong Kong
FIEI	Fellow, Institution of Engineering Inspection; Fellow, Institution of Engineers of Ireland
FIEIE	Fellow, Institution of Electronics and Electrical Incorporated Engineers
FIEJ	Fédération Internationale des Editeurs de Journaux et Publications
FIElecIE	Fellow, Institution of Electronic Incorporated Engineers
FIERE	Fellow, Institution of Electronic and Radio Engineers

FIES	Fellow, Illuminating Engineering Society; Fellow, Institution of Engineers and Shipbuilders, Scotland
FIET	Fédération Internationale des Employés, Techniciens et Cadres
FIEx	Fellow, Institute of Export
FIExpE	Fellow, Institute of Explosives Engineers
FIFA	Fédération Internationale de Football Association
FIFF	Fellow, Institute of Freight Forwarders
FIFireE	Fellow, Institution of Fire Engineers
FIFM	Fellow, Institute of Fisheries Management
FIFor	Fellow, Institute of Foresters
FIFST	Fellow, Institute of Food Science and Technology
FIGasE	Fellow, Institution of Gas Engineers
FIGCM	Fellow, Incorporated Guild of Church Musicians
FIGD	Fellow, Institute of Grocery Distribution
FIGO	International Federation of Gynaecology and Obstetrics
FIH	Fellow, Institute of Housing; Fellow, Institute of the Horse
FIHE	Fellow, Institute of Health Education
FIHM	Fellow, Institute of Housing Managers
FIHort	Fellow, Institute of Horticulture
FIHospE	Fellow, Institute of Hospital Engineering
FIHT	Fellow, Institution of Highways and Transportation
FIHVE	Fellow, Institution of Heating and Ventilating Engineers
FIIA	Fellow, Institute of Industrial Administration; Fellow, Institute of Internal Auditors
FIIB	Fellow, International Institute of Biotechnology
FIIC	Fellow, International Institute for Conservation of Historic and Artistic Works
FIIDA	Fellow, International Interior Design Association
FIIM	Fellow, Institution of Industrial Managers
FIInfSc	Fellow, Institute of Information Scientists
FIInst	Fellow, Imperial Institute
FIIP	Fellow, Institute of Incorporated Photographers
FIIPC	Fellow, India International Photographic Council
FIIPE	Fellow, Indian Institution of Production Engineers
Fil Hed	Filosofie Hedersdoktor
FIL	Fellow, Institute of Linguists
FILA	Fellow, Institute of Landscape Architects
FILDM	Fellow, Institute of Logistics and Distribution Management
FilDr	Doctor of Philosophy
FILLM	Fédération Internationale des Langues et Littératures Modernes
FIllumES	Fellow, Illuminating Engineering Society
FILog	Fellow, Institute of Logistics
FIM	Fellow, Institute of Materials (formerly Institution of Metallurgists, then Institute of Metals)
FIMA	Fellow, Institute of Mathematics and its Applications
FIMarE	Fellow, Institute of Marine Engineers
FIMatM	Fellow, Institute of Materials Management
FIMBRA	Financial Intermediaries, Managers and Brokers Regulatory Association
FIMC	Fellow, Institute of Management Consultants
FIMCB	Fellow, International Management Centre from Buckingham
FIMechE	Fellow, Institution of Mechanical Engineers
FIMfgE	Fellow, Institution of Manufacturing Engineers
FIMFT	Fellow, Institute of Maxillo-facial Technology
FIMgt	Fellow, Institute of Management
FIMGTechE	Fellow, Institution of Mechanical and General Technician Engineers
FIMH	Fellow, Institute of Materials Handling (later FIMatM); Fellow Institute of Military History
FIMI	Fellow, Institute of the Motor Industry
FIMinE	Fellow, Institution of Mining Engineers
FIMIT	Fellow, Institute of Musical Instrument Technology
FIMLS	Fellow, Institute of Medical Laboratory Sciences
FIMLT	Fellow, Institute of Medical Laboratory Technology (later FIMLS)
FIMM	Fellow, Institution of Mining and Metallurgy
FIMMA	Fellow, Institute of Metals and Materials Australasia
FIMS	Fellow, Institute of Mathematical Statistics
FIMT	Fellow, Institute of the Motor Trade
FIMTA	Fellow, Institute of Municipal Treasurers and Accountants
FIMunE	Fellow, Institution of Municipal Engineers
Fin/fin	Financial/financial
FIN	Fellow, Institute of Navigation
FINA	Fédération Internationale de Natation Amateur
FInstAM	Fellow, Institute of Administrative Management
FInstArb(NZ)	Fellow, Institute of Arbitrators of New Zealand
FInstB	Fellow, Institution of Buyers
FInstBiol	Fellow, Institute of Biology
FInstD	Fellow, Institute of Directors
FInstE	Fellow, Institute of Energy
FInstEnvSci	Fellow, Institute of Environmental Sciences
FInstF	Fellow, Institute of Fuel
FInstFF	Fellow, Institute of Freight Forwarders Ltd
FInstHE	Fellow, Institution of Highways Engineers
FInstLEx	Fellow, Institute of Legal Executives
FInstM	Fellow, Institute of Meat; Fellow, Institute of Marketing
FInstMC	Fellow, Institute of Measurement and Control
FInstMet	Fellow, Institute of Metals
FInstMSM	Fellow, Institute of Marketing and Sales Management
FInstNDT	Fellow, Institute of Non-Destructive Testing
FInstP	Fellow, Institute of Physics
FInstPet	Fellow, Institute of Petroleum
FInstPI	Fellow, Institute of Patentees and Inventors
FInstPS	Fellow, Institute of Purchasing and Supply
FInstSM	Fellow, Institute of Sales Management
FInstSMM	Fellow, Institute of Sales and Marketing Management
FInstW	Fellow, Institute of Welding
FINucE	Fellow, Institution of Nuclear Engineers
FIOA	Fellow, Institute of Acoustics
FIOB	Fellow, Institute of Building
FIOH	Fellow, Institute of Occupational Hygiene
FIOM	Fellow, Institute of Office Management
FIOP	Fellow, Institute of Printing
FIOSH	Fellow, Institute of Occupational Safety and Health
FIP	Fellow, Australian Institute of Petroleum
FIPA	Fellow, Institute of Practitioners in Advertising
FIPD	Fellow, Institute of Personnel and Development
FIPDM	Fellow, Institute of Physical Distribution Management (later FILDM)
FIPEMB	Fellow, Institution of Physics and Engineering in Medicine and Biology
FIPENZ	Fellow, Institution of Professional Engineers, New Zealand
FIPG	Fellow, Institute of Professional Goldsmiths
FIPHE	Fellow, Institution of Public Health Engineers
FIPlantE	Fellow, Institute of Plant Engineers
FIPM	Fellow, Institute of Personnel Management
FIPR	Fellow, Institute of Public Relations
FIProdE	Fellow, Institution of Production Engineers
FIQ	Fellow, Institute of Quarrying
FIQA	Fellow, Institute of Quality Assurance
FIQS	Fellow, Institute of Quantity Surveyors
FIRA	Furniture Industry Research Association
FIRA(Ind)	Fellow, Institute of Railway Auditors and Accountants (India)
FIRE(Aust)	Fellow, Institution of Radio Engineers (Australia)
FIREE(Aust)	Fellow, Institution of Radio and Electronics Engineers (Australia)
FIRI	Fellow, Institution of the Rubber Industry (later FPRI)
FIRM	Fellow, Institute of Risk Management
FIRSE	Fellow, Institute of Railway Signalling Engineers
FIRTE	Fellow, Institute of Road Transport Engineers
FIS	Fellow, Institute of Statisticians
FISA	Fellow, Incorporated Secretaries' Association; Fédération Internationale des Sociétés d'Aviron
FISE	Fellow, Institution of Sales Engineers; Fellow, Institution of Sanitary Engineers
FISITA	Fédération Internationale des Sociétés d'Ingénieurs des Techniques de l'Automobile
FISM	Fellow, Institute of Supervisory Managers
FISOB	Fellow, Incorporated Society of Organ Builders
FISP	Fédération Internationale des Sociétés de Philosophie
FIST	Fellow, Institute of Science Technology
FISTC	Fellow, Institute of Scientific and Technical Communicators
FISTD	Fellow, Imperial Society of Teachers of Dancing
FIStructE	Fellow, Institution of Structural Engineers
FISW	Fellow, Institute of Social Work
FITD	Fellow, Institute of Training and Development
FITE	Fellow, Institution of Electrical and Electronics Technician Engineers
FIW	Fellow, Welding Institute
FIWE	Fellow, Institution of Water Engineers
FIWEM	Fellow, Institution of Water and Environmental Management
FIWES	Fellow, Institution of Water Engineers and Scientists
FIWM	Fellow, Institution of Works Managers
FIWPC	Fellow, Institute of Water Pollution Control
FIWSc	Fellow, Institute of Wood Science
FIWSP	Fellow, Institute of Work Study Practitioners
FJIE	Fellow, Junior Institution of Engineers
FJL	Fellow, Institute of Journalists
FKC	Fellow, King's College London
FKCHMS	Fellow, King's College Hospital Medical School

fl	*floruit* (flourished)
FL/Fla	Florida
FLA	Fellow, Library Association
FLAI	Fellow, Library Association of Ireland
FLAS	Fellow, Chartered Land Agents' Society
FLCM	Fellow, London College of Music
FLHS	Fellow, London Historical Society
FLI	Fellow, Landscape Institute
FLIA	Fellow, Life Insurance Association
FLS	Fellow, Linnean Society
Flt	Flight
F/Lt	Flight Lieutenant
FM	Field-Marshal
FMA	Fellow, Museums Association
FMAAT	Fellow Member, Association of Accounting Technicians
FMANZ	Fellow, Medical Association of New Zealand
FMES	Fellow, Minerals Engineering Society
FMF	Fiji Military Forces
FMI	Foundation for Manufacturing and Industry
FMS	Federated Malay States; Fellow, Medical Society; Fellow, Institute of Management Services
FMSA	Fellow, Mineralogical Society of America
FNA	Fellow, Indian National Science Academy
FNAEA	Fellow, National Association of Estate Agents
FNCO	Fleet Naval Constructor Officer
Fndn	Foundation
fndr	founder
FNECInst	Fellow, North East Coast Institution of Engineers and Shipbuilders
FNI	Fellow, Nautical Institute; Fellow, National Institute of Sciences in India
FNIA	Fellow, Nigerian Institute of Architects
FNM	Free National Movement
FNZEI	Fellow, New Zealand Educational Institute
FNZIA	Fellow, New Zealand Institute of Architects
FNZIAS	Fellow, New Zealand Institute of Agricultural Science
FNZIC	Fellow, New Zealand Institute of Chemistry
FNZIE	Fellow, New Zealand Institution of Engineers
FNZIM	Fellow, New Zealand Institute of Management
FNZPsS	Fellow, New Zealand Psychological Society
FO	Foreign Office; Field Officer; Flying Officer
F/O	Flying Officer
FODA	Fellow, Overseas Doctors' Association
FODC	Franciscan Order of the Divine Compassion
FOIC	Flag Officer in charge
FOMI	Faculty of Occupational Medicine of Ireland
FONA	Flag Officer, Naval Aviation
FONAC	Flag Officer Naval Air Command
For	Foreign
FOR	Fellowship of Operational Research
For Affrs	Foreign Affairs
FOREST	Freedom Organisation for the Right to Enjoy Smoking Tobacco
FOX	Futures and Options Exchange
FPA	Family Planning Association
FPC	Family Practitioner Committee
FPEA	Fellow, Physical Education Association
FPHM	Faculty of Public Health Medicine
FPhS	Fellow, Philosophical Society of England
FPhysS	Fellow, Physical Society
FPI	Fellow, Plastics Institute (later FPRI)
FPIA	Fellow, Plastics Institute of Australia
FPMI	Fellow, Pensions Management Institute
FPRI	Fellow, Plastics and Rubber Institute
FPS	Fellow, Pharmaceutical Society; Fauna Preservation Society
FRA	Fellow, Royal Academy
FRACDS	Fellow, Royal Australian College of Dental Surgeons
FRACGP	Fellow, Royal Australian College of General Practitioners
FRACI	Fellow, Royal Australian Chemical Institute
FRACMA	Fellow, Royal Australian College of Medical Administrators
FRACO	Fellow, Royal Australian College of Ophthalmologists
FRACOG	Fellow, Royal Australian College of Obstetricians and Gynaecologists
FRACP	Fellow, Royal Australasian College of Physicians
FRACR	Fellow, Royal Australasian College of Radiologists
FRACS	Fellow, Royal Australasian College of Surgeons
FRAD	Fellow, Royal Academy of Dancing
FRAeS	Fellow, Royal Aeronautical Society
FRAgS	Fellow, Royal Agricultural Societies (of England, Scotland and Wales)
FRAHS	Fellow, Royal Australian Historical Society

FRAI	Fellow, Royal Anthropological Institute of Great Britain and Ireland
FRAIA	Fellow, Royal Australian Institute of Architects
FRAIB	Fellow, Royal Australian Institute of Building
FRAIC	Fellow, Royal Architectural Institute of Canada
FRAIPA	Fellow, Royal Australian Institute of Public Administration
FRAM	Fellow, Royal Academy of Music
FRAME	Fund for the Replacement of Animals in Medical Experiments
FRANZCP	Fellow, Royal Australian and New Zealand College of Psychiatrists
FRAPI	Fellow, Royal Australian Planning Institute
FRAS	Fellow, Royal Astronomical Society; Fellow, Royal Asiatic Society
FRASB	Fellow, Royal Asiatic Society of Bengal
FRASE	Fellow, Royal Agricultural Society of England
FRAstS	Fellow, Royal Astronomical Society
FRBS	Fellow, Royal Society of British Sculptors; Fellow, Royal Botanic Society
FRCA	Fellow, Royal College of Art; Fellow, Royal College of Anaesthetists
FRCCO	Fellow, Royal Canadian College of Organists
FRCD(Can)	Fellow, Royal College of Dentists of Canada
FRCGP	Fellow, Royal College of General Practitioners
FRCM	Fellow, Royal College of Music
FRCN	Fellow, Royal College of Nursing
FRCO	Fellow, Royal College of Organists
FRCO(CHM)	Fellow, Royal College of Organists with Diploma in Choir Training
FRCOG	Fellow, Royal College of Obstetricians and Gynaecologists
FRCOphth	Fellow, Royal College of Ophthalmologists
FRCP	Fellow, Royal College of Physicians, London
FRCPA	Fellow, Royal College of Pathologists of Australasia
FRCPath	Fellow, Royal College of Pathologists
FRCP(C)	Fellow, Royal College of Physicians of Canada
FRCPE/FRCPEd	Fellow, Royal College of Physicians, Edinburgh
FRCPI	Fellow, Royal College of Physicians of Ireland
FRCP&S (Canada)	Fellow, Royal College of Physicians and Surgeons of Canada
FRCPsych	Fellow, Royal College of Psychiatrists
FRCR	Fellow, Royal College of Radiologists
FRCS	Fellow, Royal College of Surgeons of England
FRCSCan	Fellow, Royal College of Surgeons of Canada
FRCSE/FRCSEd	Fellow, Royal College of Surgeons of Edinburgh
FRCSGlas	Fellow, Royal College of Physicians and Surgeons of Glasgow
FRCSI	Fellow, Royal College of Surgeons in Ireland
FRCSoc	Fellow, Royal Commonwealth Society
FRCUS	Fellow, Royal College of University Surgeons (Denmark)
FRCVS	Fellow, Royal College of Veterinary Surgeons
FREconS	Fellow, Royal Economic Society
FREI	Fellow, Real Estate Institute (Australia)
FRES	Fellow, Royal Entomological Society of London
FRFPSG	Fellow, Royal Faculty of Physicians and Surgeons, Glasgow
FRG	Federal Republic of Germany
FRGS	Fellow, Royal Geographical Society
FRGSA	Fellow, Royal Geographical Society of Australasia
FRHistS	Fellow, Royal Historical Society
FRHS	Fellow, Royal Horticultural Society
FRHSV	Fellow, Royal Historical Society of Victoria
FRIAS	Fellow, Royal Incorporation of Architects of Scotland; Royal Institute for the Advancement of Science
FRIBA	Fellow, Royal Institute of British Architects
FRIC	Fellow, Royal Institute of Chemistry
FRICS	Fellow, Royal Institution of Chartered Surveyors
FRIH	Fellow, Royal Institute of Horticulture (NZ)
FRIN	Fellow, Royal Institute of Navigation
FRINA	Fellow, Royal Institution of Naval Architects
FRIPA	Fellow, Royal Institute of Public Administration
FRIPHH	Fellow, Royal Institute of Public Health and Hygiene
FRMCM	Fellow, Royal Manchester College of Music
FRMedSoc	Fellow, Royal Medical Society
FRMetS	Fellow, Royal Meteorological Society
FRMIA	Fellow, Retail Management Institute of Australia
FRMS	Fellow, Royal Microscopical Society
FRNCM	Fellow, Royal Northern College of Music
FRNS	Fellow, Royal Numismatic Society
FRPharmS	Fellow, Royal Pharmaceutical Society
FRPS	Fellow, Royal Photographic Society
FRPSL	Fellow, Royal Philatelic Society, London
FRS	Fellow, Royal Society
FRS(Can)	Fellow, Royal Society of Canada (also a Fellow of the Royal Society of Chemistry)

FRSA	Fellow, Royal Society of Arts
FRSAI	Fellow, Royal Society of Antiquaries of Ireland
FRSAMD	Fellow, Royal Scottish Academy of Music and Drama
FRSanI	Fellow, Royal Sanitary Institute
FRSC	Fellow, Royal Society of Canada; Fellow, Royal Society of Chemistry
FRSC (UK)	Fellow, Royal Society of Chemistry (used when a person is also a Fellow of the Royal Society of Canada)
FRSCM	Hon Fellow, Royal School of Church Music
FRSE	Fellow, Royal Society of Edinburgh
FRSGS	Fellow, Royal Scottish Geographical Society
FRSH	Fellow, Royal Society for the Promotion of Health
FRSL	Fellow, Royal Society of Literature
FRSM/FRSocMed	Fellow, Royal Society of Medicine
FRSNZ	Fellow, Royal Society of New Zealand
FRSSAf	Fellow, Royal Society of South Africa
FRST	Fellow, Royal Society of Teachers
FRSTM&H	Fellow, Royal Society of Tropical Medicine and Hygiene
FRTPI	Fellow, Royal Town Planning Institute
FRTS	Fellow, Royal Television Society
FRVA	Fellow, Rating and Valuation Association
FRVC	Fellow, Royal Veterinary College
FRVIA	Fellow, Royal Victorian Institute of Architects
FRZSScot	Fellow, Royal Zoological Society of Scotland
FS	Field Security
FSA	Fellow, Society of Arts; Fellow, Society of Antiquaries
FSAA	Fellow, Society of Incorporated Accountants and Auditors
FSAE	Fellow, Society of Automotive Engineers; Fellow, Society of Art Education
FSAI	Fellow, Society of Architectural Illustrators
FSAIEE	Fellow, South African Institute of Electrical Engineers
FSAM	Fellow, Society of Art Masters
FSArc	Fellow, Society of Architects (merged with RIBA 1952)
FSaRS	Fellow, Safety and Reliability Society
FSAScot	Fellow, Society of Antiquaries of Scotland
FSASM	Fellow, South Australian School of Mines
FSBI	Fellow, Savings Banks Institute
fsc	Foreign Staff College
FSCA	Fellow, Society of Company and Commercial Accountants
FScotvec	Fellow, Scottish Vocational Education Council
FSCRE	Fellow, Scottish Council for Research in Education
FSDC	Fellow, Society of Dyers and Colourists
FSE	Fellow, Society of Engineers
FSG	Fellow, Society of Genealogists
FSGT	Fellow, Society of Glass Technology
FSI	Fellow, Chartered Surveyors' Institution; Fellow, Securities Institute
FSIA	Fellow, Securities Institute of Australia
FSIAD	Fellow, Society of Industrial Artists and Designers
FSLAET	Fellow, Society of Licensed Aircraft Engineers and Technologists
FSLCOG	Fellow, Sri Lankan College of Obstetrics and Gynaecology
FSLTC	Fellow, Society of Leather Technologists and Chemists
FSMA	Fellow, Incorporated Sales Managers' Association (later FInstMSM, then FInstM)
FSMC	Freeman of the Spectacle-Makers' Company
FSME	Fellow, Society of Manufacturing Engineers
FSMPTE	Fellow, Society of Motion Picture and Television Engineers (US)
FSNAD	Fellow, Society of Numismatic Artists and Designers
FSNAME	Fellow, American Society of Naval Architects and Marine Engineers
FSRHE	Fellow, Society for Research into Higher Education
FSRP	Fellow, Society for Radiological Protection
FSS	Fellow, Royal Statistical Society
FSTD	Fellow, Society of Typographic Designers
FSVA	Fellow, Incorporated Society of Valuers and Auctioneers
FT	*Financial Times*
FTAT	Furniture, Timber and Allied Trades Union
FTC	Flying Training Command, Full Technological Certificate, City and Guilds of London Institute
FTCD	Fellow, Trinity College, Dublin
FTCL	Fellow, Trinity College of Music, London
FTI	Fellow, Textile Institute
FTII	Fellow, Chartered Institute (formerly Incorporated Institute, then Institute) of Taxation
FTMA	Fellow, Telecommunications Managers Association
FTP	Fellow, Thames Polytechnic
FTS	Fellow, Australian Academy of Technological Sciences and Engineering; Flying Training School; Fellow, Tourism Society
FTSC	Fellow, Tonic Sol-fa College
FTSE	Fellow, Australian Academy of Technological Sciences and Engineering
FUCUA	Federation of University Conservative and Unionist Associations
FUMDS	Fellow, United Medical and Dental Schools
FUMIST	Fellow, University of Manchester Institute of Science and Technology
Fus	Fusiliers
FVRDE	Fighting Vehicles Research and Development Establishment
FWAAS	Fellow, World Academy of Arts and Sciences
FWACP	Fellow, West African College of Physicians
FWCMD	Fellow, Welsh College of Music and Drama
FWeldI	Fellow, Welding Institute
FWSOM	Fellow, Institute of Practitioners in Work Study, Organisation and Method
FZS	Fellow, Zoological Society
FZSScot	Fellow, Zoological Society of Scotland

G

GA	Geologists' Association; Gaelic Athletic (Club); Georgia
GAI	Guild of Architectural Ironmongers
GAP	Gap Activity Projects
GAPAN	Guild of Air Pilots and Air Navigators
GATT	General Agreement on Tariffs and Trade
GB	Great Britain, used chiefly of creations of titles of honour of
GBA	Governing Bodies Association
GBE	Knight or Dame Grand Cross, Order of the British Empire
GBGSA	Governing Bodies of Girls' Schools Association (formerly Association of Governing Bodies of Girls' Public Schools)
GBSM	Graduate, Birmingham and Midland Institute School of Music
GC	George Cross
G/Capt	Group Captain
GCB	Knight/Dame Grand Cross of the Order of the Bath
GCBS	General Council of British Shipping
GCFR	Grand Commander, Order of the Federal Republic of Nigeria
GCH	Knight Grand Cross, Hanoverian Order
GCHQ	Government Communications Headquarters
GCIE	Knight Grand Commander, Order of the Indian Empire
GCLJ	Grand Cross, St Lazarus of Jerusalem
GCLM	Grand Commander, Order of the Legion of Merit of Rhodesia
GCM	Gold Crown of Merit (Barbados)
GCMG	Knight or Dame Grand Cross, Order of St Michael and St George
GCON	Grand Cross, Order of the Niger
GCSE	General Certificate of Secondary Education
GCSG	Knight Grand Cross, Order of St Gregory the Great
GCSI	Knight Grand Commander of the Order of the Star of India
GCSJ	Knight Grand Cross of Justice, Order of St John of Jerusalem (Knights Hospitaller)
GCSL	Grand Cross, Order of St Lucia
GCStJ	Bailiff or Dame Grand Cross, Most Venerable Order of the Hospital of St John of Jerusalem
GCVO	Knight or Dame Grand Cross, Royal Victorian Order
gdau	grand-daughter
Gd(s)	Guard(s)
GDBA	Guide Dogs for the Blind Association
GDC	General Dental Council
Gdn(s)	Garden(s)
GDR	German Democratic Republic
Gen	General
GER	Great Eastern Railway
Ges	Gesellschaft
gf	grandfather
GFD	Geophysical Fluid Dynamics
GFS	Girls' Friendly Society
ggdau	great-grand-daughter
ggf	great-grandfather
gggf	great-great-grandfather
ggggf	great-great-great-grandfather
gggggf	great-great-great-great-grandfather, etc
gggs	great-great-grandson, etc
ggmother	great-grandmother

ggs	great-grandson
GGSM	Graduate in Music, Guildhall School of Music and Drama
GHQ	General Headquarters
Gib	Gibraltar
GIMechE	Graduate, Institution of Mechanical Engineers
GL	Grand Lodge
GLAA	Greater London Arts Association
GLAB	Greater London Arts Board
GLC	Greater London Council
Glos	Gloucestershire
GM	George Medal; Grand Medal (Ghana)
GMB	(Union for) General, Municipal, Boilermakers
GMBATU	General, Municipal, Boilermakers and Allied Trades Union
GmbH	Gesellschaft mit beschränkter Haftung
GMC	General Medical Council; Guild of Memorial Craftsmen; General Management Course (Henley)
GMIE	Grand Master, Order of the Indian Empire
GMSI	Grand Master, Order of the Star of India
GMWU	General and Municipal Workers' Union
gn	great-nephew/-niece
GNC	General Nursing Council
Gns	Guineas
GOC	General Officer Commanding
GOC-in-C	General Officer Commanding-in-Chief
GOE	General Ordination Examination
Govr	Governor
Govt	Government
Gp/gp	Group/group
GP	General Practitioner; Grand Prix
GPDST	Girls' Public Day School Trust
GPMU	Graphical, Paper and Media Union
GPO	General Post Office
GQG	Grand Quartier Général
Gr	Greek
GR	General Reconaissance
Gren	Grenadier
GRSM	Graduate, Royal Schools of Music
gs	grandson
GS	General Staff; Grammar School
GSA	Girls' Schools Association
GSM	General Service Medal; (Member of) Guildhall School of Music and Drama
GSMD	Guildhall School of Music and Drama
GSO	General Staff Officer
Gt	Great
GTCL	Graduate, Trinity College of Music
GTS	General Theological Seminary (New York)
GUI	Golfing Union of Ireland
GWR	Great Western Railway

H

HA	Historical Association; Health Authority
HAA	Heavy Anti-Aircraft
HAC	Honourable Artillery Company
HACAS	Housing Association Consultancy and Advisory Service
Hants	Hampshire
HARCVS	Honorary Associate, Royal College of Veterinary Surgeons
Harv	Harvard
HAT	Housing Action Trust
HBM	His/Her Britannic Majesty (Majesty's); Humming Bird Gold Medal (Trinidad)
HC	High Commissioner
H of C	House of Commons
HCEG	Honourable Company of Edinburgh Golfers
HCF	Honorary Chaplain to the Forces
HCIMA	Hotel, Catering and Institutional Management Association
HCO	Higher Clerical Officer
HCSC	Higher Command and Staff Course
HDA	Hawkesbury Diploma in Agriculture (Australia)
HDD	Higher Dental Diploma
HDFA	Higher Diploma in Fine Art
HDipEd	Higher Diploma in Education
HE	His/Her Excellency; His Eminence
HEA	Health Education Authority
HEC	Ecole des Hautes Etudes Commerciales; Higher Education Corporation
HEFCE	Higher Education Funding Council for England
HEFCW	Higher Education Funding Council for Wales
HEH	His/Her Exalted Highness
HEIC	Honourable East India Company
HEICS	Honourable East India Company's Service
HEO	Higher Executive Officer
HEQC	Higher Education Quality Council
Herefs	Herefordshire
Herts	Hertfordshire
HF	Home Fleet
HFARA	Honorary Foreign Associate, Royal Academy
HFEA	Human Fertilisation and Embryology Authority
HFRA	Honorary Foreign Member, Royal Academy
HG	Home Guard
HGTAC	Home Grown Timber Advisory Committee
HH	His/Her Highness; His Holiness; Member, Hesketh Hubbard Art Society
HHA	Historic Houses Association
HHD	Doctor of Humanities (US)
HI	Hawaii
Highrs	Highlanders
HIH	His/Her Imperial Highness
HIllH	His/Her Illustrious Highness
HIM	His/Her Imperial Majesty
HJ	Hilal-e-Jurat (Pakistan)
HKIA	Hong Kong Institute of Architects
HKIPM	Hung Kong Institute of Personnel Management
HLD	Doctor of Humane Letters
Hldgs	Holdings
HLI	Highland Light Infantry
HM	His/Her Majesty
HMA	Head Masters' Association
HMAS	His/Her Majesty's Australian Ship
HMC	Headmasters' and Headmistresses' (formerly Headmasters') Conference; Hospital Management Committee
HMCIC	His/Her Majesty's Chief Inspector of Constabulary
HMCS	His/Her Majesty's Canadian Ship
HMHS	His/Her Majesty's Hospital Ship
HMI	His/Her Majesty's Inspector
HMIED	Honorary Member, Institute of Engineering Designers
HMMTB	His/Her Majesty's Motor Torpedo Boat
HMNZS	His/Her Majesty's New Zealand Ship
HMOCS	His/Her Majesty's Overseas Civil Service
HMS	His/Her Majesty's Ship
HMSO	His/Her Majesty's Stationery Office
HNC	Higher National Certificate
HND	Higher National Diploma
Ho	House
Ho Lds	House of Lords
Hon	Honourable; Honorary
Hons	Honours
Hosp	Hospital
HPk	Hilal-e-Pakistan
HQ	Headquarters
HQA	Hilali-Quaid-i-Azam (Pakistan)
HRCA	Honorary Royal Cambrian Academician
HRE	Holy Roman Empire
HRGI	Honorary Member, The Royal Glasgow Institute of the Fine Arts
HRH	His/Her Royal Highness
HRHA	Honorary Member, Royal Hibernian Academy
HRI	Honorary Member, Royal Institute of Painters in Water Colours
HROI	Honorary Member, Royal Institute of Oil Painters
HRSA	Honorary Member, Royal Scottish Academy
HRSW	Honorary Member, Royal Scottish Water Colour Society
HS	High School
HSC	Health and Safety Commission
HSE	Health and Safety Executive
HSH	His/Her Serene Highness
Hts	Heights
Hum	Humanity, Humanities (Classics)
Hunts	Huntingdonshire
Hus	Hussars
husb	husband
HVCert	Health Visitor's Certificate
Hy	Heavy

I

I	Island; Ireland, used chiefly of creations of titles of honour of; 'The First' in a sequence of I, II, III etc
IA	Indian Army; Iowa
IAAF	International Amateur Athletic Federation
IAC	Indian Armoured Corps; Institute of Amateur Cinematographers
IACP	International Association of Chiefs of Police
IACR	Institute of Arable Crops Research
IADB	Inter American Development Bank
IADR	International Association for Dental Research
IAEA	International Atomic Energy Agency
IAF	Indian Air Force; Indian Auxiliary Force
IAHM	Incorporated Association of Headmasters
IAM	Institute of Advanced Motorists; Institute of Aviation Medicine
IAMAS	International Association of Meteorology and Atmospheric Sciences
IAMC	Indian Army Medical Corps
IAMTACT	Institute of Advanced Machine Tool and Control Technology
IAO	Incorporated Association of Organists
IAOC	Indian Army Ordnance Corps
IAPS	Incorporated Association of Preparatory Schools
IAPSO	International Association for the Physical Sciences of the Oceans
IARO	Indian Army Reserve of Officers
IAS	Indian Administrative Service; Institute for Advanced Studies; International Academy of Science
IASC	International Arctic Science Committee
IASS	International Association for Scandinavian Studies
IATA	International Air Transport Association
IATUL	International Association of Technological University Libraries
IAU	International Astronomical Union
IAWPRC	International Association on Water Pollution Research and or Control
ibid	ibidem (in the same place)
IBA	Independent Broadcasting Authority; International Bar Association
IBCA	International Braille Chess Association
IBG	Institute of British Geographers
IBRD	International Bank for Reconstruction and Development (World Bank)
IBRO	International Bank Research Organisation; International Brain Research Organisation
IBTE	Institution of British Telecommunications Engineers
i/c	in charge; in command
ICA	Institute of Contemporary Arts; Institute of Chartered Accountants in England and Wales
ICAA	Invalid Children's Aid Association
ICAEW	Institute of Chartered Accountants in England and Wales
ICAI	Institute of Chartered Accountants in Ireland
ICAO	International Civil Aviation Organization
ICBP	International Council for Bird Preservation
ICBS	Irish Christian Brothers' School
ICC	International Chamber of Commerce
ICCA	International Council for Commercial Arbitration
ICCROM	International Centre for Conservation at Rome
ICD	Iuris Canonici Doctor (Doctor of Canon Law); Independence Commemorative Decoration (Rhodesia)
ICE	Institution of Civil Engineers
ICED	International Council for Educational Development
ICEF	International Federation of Chemical, Energy and General Workers' Unions
ICES	International Council for the Exploration of the Sea
ICF	International Federation of Chemical and General Workers' Unions
ICFC	Industrial and Commercial Finance Corporation
ICFTU	International Confederation of Free Trade Unions
ICHCA	International Cargo Handling Co-ordination Association
IChemE	Institution of Chemical Engineers
ICI	Imperial Chemical Industries
ICJ	International Commission of Jurists
ICL	International Computers Ltd
ICM	International Confederation of Midwives
ICMA	Institute of Cost and Management Accountants
ICME	International Commission for Mathematical Education
ICOM	International Council of Museums
ICOMOS	International Council of Monuments and Sites
ICorrST	Institution of Corrosion Science and Technology
ICPO	International Criminal Police Organization (Interpol)
ICRC	International Committee of the Red Cross
ICRF	Imperial Cancer Research Fund
ICS	Indian Civil Service
ICSA	Institute of Chartered Secretaries and Administrators
ICSD	International Council for Scientific Development
ICSID	International Council of Societies of Industrial Design; International Centre for Settlement of Investment Disputes
ICSS	International Committee for the Sociology of Sport
ICSTIS	Independent Committee for Supervision of Telephone Information Services
ICSTM	Imperial College of Science, Technology and Medicine, London
ICSU	International Council of Scientific Unions
ICT	International Computers and Tabulators Ltd
ID	Independence Decoration (Rhodesia); Idaho
IDA	International Development Association
IDB	Internal Drainage Board; Industrial Development Board
idc	completed a course at, or served for a year on the Staff of, the Imperial Defence College
IDC	Imperial Defence College; Inter-Diocesan Certificate
IDRC	International Development Research Centre
IDS	Institute of Development Studies; Industry Department for Scotland
IEA	Institute of Economic Affairs
IEC	International Electrotechnical Commission
IEE	Institution of Electrical Engineers
IEEE	Institute of Electrical and Electronics Engineers (NY)
IEEIE	Institution of Electrical and Electronics Incorporated Engineers
IEETE	Institution of Electrical and Electronics Technician Engineers
IEI	Institution of Engineers of Ireland
IEIE	Institution of Electronics and Electrical Incorporated Engineers
IEME	Inspectorate of Electrical and Mechanical Engineering
IEng	Incorporated Engineer
IERE	Institution of Electronic and Radio Engineers
IES	Indian Educational Service; Institution of Engineers and Shipbuilders in Scotland; International Electron Paramagnetic Resonance Society
IExpE	Institute of Explosives Engineers
IFAC	International Federation of Automatic Control
IFAD	International Fund for Agricultural Development (UNO)
IFAW	International Fund for Animal Welfare
IFBWW	International Federation of Building Woodworkers
IFC	International Finance Corporation
IFIAS	International Federation of Institutes of Advanced Study
IFIP	International Federation for Information Processing
IFL	International Friendship League
IFLA	International Federation of Library Associations
IFORS	International Federation of Operational Research Societies
IFPI	International Federation of the Phonographic Industry
IFRA	World Press Research Association
IFS	Irish Free State; Indian Forest Service
IG	Instructor in Gunnery
IGasE	Institution of Gas Engineers
IGPP	Institute of Geophysics and Planetary Physics
IGS	Independent Grammar School
IGU	International Geographical Union; International Gas Union
IHA	Institute of Health Service Administrators
IHospE	Institute of Hospital Engineering
IHSM	Institute of Health Services Management
IHVE	Institution of Heating and Ventilating Engineers (later CIBS)
IILS	International Institute for Labour Studies
IIM	Institution of Industrial Managers
IIMR	Institute of Investment Management and Research
IIMT	International Institute for the Management of Technology
IInfSc	Institute of Information Scientists
IIS	International Institute of Sociology
IISI	International Iron and Steel Institute
IISS	International Institute of Strategic Studies
IIT	Indian Institute of Technology
IL/Ill	Illinois
ILA	International Law Association
ILEA	Inner London Education Authority
ILEC	Inner London Education Committee
IIExE	Institution of Incorporated Executive Engineers

ILO	International Labour Office; International Labour Organisation
ILP	Independent Labour Party
ILR	Independent Local Radio; International Labour Review
IM	Individual Merit
IMO	International Maritime Organization
IMA	International Music Association; Institute of Mathematics and its Applications
IMCB	International Management Centre from Buckingham
IMCO	Inter-Governmental Maritime Consultative Organization
IME	Institute of Medical Ethics
IMEA	Incorporated Municipal Electrical Association
IMechE	Institution of Mechanical Engineers
IMechIE	Institution of Mechanical Incorporated Engineers
IMEDE	Institut pour l'Etude des Méthodes de Direction de l'Entreprise
IMF	International Monetary Fund
IMGTechE	Institution of Mechanical and General Technician Engineers
IMinE	Institution of Mining Engineers
IMM	Institution of Mining and Metallurgy
IMMLEP	Immunology of Leprosy
IMMTS	Indian Mercantile Marine Training Ship
Imp	Imperial
IMRO	Investment Management Regulatory Organisation
IMS	Indian Medical Service; Institute of Management Services; International Military Staff
IMTA	Institute of Municipal Treasurers and Accountants
IMU	International Mathematical Union
IMunE	Institution of Municipal Engineers (now amalgamated with Institution of Civil Engineers)
IN	Indian Navy; Indiana
INASFMH	International Sports Association for People with Mental Handicap
Inc	Incorporated
INCA	International Newspaper Colour Association
Incog	Incognito
Ind	Independent
Industs	Industries
Inf	Infantry; Information
INFORM	Information Network Focus on New Religious Movements
INSA	Indian National Science Academy
INSEA	International Society for Education through Art
INSEAD/Insead	Institut Européen d'Administration des Affaires
Inspr	Inspector
Inst	Institute; Institution
InstBE	Institution of British Engineers
Instr	Instructor
InstSMM	Institute of Sales and Marketing Management
InstT	Institute of Transport
insur	insurance
Internat	International
Intell	Intelligence
INTELSAT	International Telecommunications Satellite Organisation
IOB	Institute of Banking
IOC	International Olympic Committee; Intergovernmental Oceanographic Commission
IOCD	International Organisation for Chemical Science in Development
IOD	Institute of Directors
IODE	Imperial Order of the Daughters of the Empire
IOGT	International Order of Good Templars
IoM	Isle of Man
IOM	Indian Order of Merit
IOOF	Independent Order of Odd-fellows
IOP	Institute of Painters in Oil Colours
IOTA	(Fellow of) Institute of Transport Administration
IoW	Isle of Wight
IPA	International Publishers' Association
IPCS	Institution of Professional Civil Servants
IPFA	Member or Associate, Chartered Institute of Public Finance and Accountancy
IPHE	Institution of Public Health Engineers
IPI	International Press Institute; Institute of Patentees and Inventors
IPlantE	Institution of Plant Engineers
IPM	Institute of Personnel Management
IPPA	Independent Programme Producers' Association; International Planned Parenthood Federation
IPPR	Institute for Public Policy Research
IPPS	Institute of Physics and The Physical Society
IProdE	Institution of Production Engineers

IPS	Indian Police Service; Indian Political Service; Institute of Purchasing and Supply
IPU	Inter-Parliamentary Union
IRA	Irish Republican Army
IRAD	Institute for Research on Animal Diseases
IRC	Industrial Reorganization Corporation; Interdisciplinary Research Centre
IRCAM	Institute for Research and Co-ordination in Acoustics and Music
IRCert	Industrial Relations Certificate
IREE(Aust)	Institution of Radio and Electronics Engineers (Australia)
IRI	Institution of the Rubber Industry
IRO	International Refugee Organization
IRPA	International Radiation Protection Association
IRRV	(Fellow/Member of) Institute of Revenues, Rating and Valuation
IRTE	Institute of Road Transport Engineers
Is	Island(s)
IS	International Society of Sculptors, Painters and Gravers
ISBA	Incorporated Society of British Advertisers
ISC	Imperial Service College, Haileybury; Indian Staff Corps
ISCM	International Society for Contemporary Music
ISCO	Independent Schools Careers Organisation
ISE	Indian Service of Engineers
ISI	International Statistical Institute
ISIS	Independent Schools Information Service
ISJC	Independent Schools Joint Council
ISM	Incorporated Society of Musicians
ISMAR	International Society of Magnetic Resonance
ISME	International Society for Musical Education
ISMRC	Inter-Services Metallurgical Research Council
ISO	Imperial Service Order; International Organization for Standardization
ISSA	International Social Security Association
ISSTIP	International Society for Study of Tension in Performance
ISTC	Iron and Steel Trades Confederation; Institute of Scientific and Technical Communicators
ISTD	Imperial Society of Teachers of Dancing
IStructE	Institution of Structural Engineers
It/Ital	Italian
IT	Information Technology; Indian Territory (US)
ITA	Independent Television Authority (later IBA)
ITAB	Information Technology Advisory Board
ITB	Industry Training Board
ITC	International Trade Centre; Independent Television Commission
ITCA	Independent Television Association (formerly Independent Television Companies Association Ltd)
ITDG	Intermediate Technology Development Group
ITEME	Institution of Technician Engineers in Mechanical Engineering
ITF	International Transport Workers' Federation
ITN	Independent Television News
ITO	International Trade Organization
ITU	International Telecommunication Union
ITV	Independent Television
ITVA	International Television Association
IUA	International Union of Architects
IUB	International Union of Biochemistry
IUBMB	International Union of Biochemistry and Molecular Biology
IUC	Inter-University Council for Higher Education Overseas
IUCN	World Conservation Union (formerly International Union for the Conservation of Nature and Natural Resources)
IUCW	International Union for Child Welfare
IUGS	International Union of Geological Sciences
IUHPS	International Union of the History and Philosophy of Science
IULA	International Union of Local Authorities
IUP	Association of Independent Unionist Peers
IUPAC	International Union of Pure and Applied Chemistry
IUPAP	International Union of Pure and Applied Physics
IUPC	Inter-University and Polytechnic Council for Higher Education Overseas
IUPS	International Union of Physiological Sciences
IUTAM	International Union of Theoretical and Applied Mechanics
IVF	In-vitro Fertilisation
IVS	International Voluntary Service
IWA	Inland Waterways Association
IWEM	Institution of Water and Environmental Management
IWES	Institution of Water Engineers and Scientists (later IWEM)
IWGC	Imperial War Graves Commission
IWM	Institution of Works Managers
IWO	Institution of Water Officers

IWPC	Institute of Water Pollution Control (later IWEM)
IWS	International Wool Secretariat
IWSA	International Water Supply Association
IWSOM	Institute of Practitioners in Work Study Organisation and Methods
IWSP	Institute of Work Study Practitioners
IY	Imperial Yeomanry
IYRU	International Yacht Racing Union
IZ	I Zingari

J

JA	Judge Advocate
JACT	Joint Association of Classical Teachers
JAG	Judge Advocate General
Jas	James
JCB	*Juris Canonici* (or *Civilis*) *Baccalaureus* (Bachelor of Canon (or Civil) Law)
JCD	*Juris Canonici* (or *Civilis*) Doctor (Doctor of Canon (or Civil) Law)
JCI	Junior Chamber International
JCL	*Juris Canonici* (or *Civilis*) *Licentiatus* (Licentiate in Canon (or Civil) Law)
JCO	Joint Consultative Organisation
JCR	Junior Common Room
JCS	Journal of the Chemical Society
JD	Doctor of Jurisprudence
JDipMA	Joint Diploma in Management Accounting Services
JG	Junior Grade
JInstE	Junior Institution of Engineers
jl(s)	journal(s)
JMB	Joint Matriculation Board
JMN	Johan Mangku Negara (Malaysia)
JMOTS	Joint Maritime Operational Training Staff
jnlst	journalist
Jno/Joh	John
JP	Justice of the Peace
Jr	Junior
jsc	qualified at a Junior Staff Course, or the equivalent, 1942–46
JSD	Doctor of Juristic Science
jsdc	completed a course at Joint Service Defence College
JSDC	Joint Service Defence College
JSLS	Joint Services Liaison Staff
JSM	Johan Setia Mahkota (Malaysia)
JSPS	Japan Society for the Promotion of Science
jssc	completed a course at Joint Services Staff College
JSSC	Joint Services Staff College
jt/jtly	joint, jointly
JUD	*Juris Utriusque Doctor* (Doctor of Both Laws (Canon and Civil))
JWS/jws	Joint Warfare Staff

K

k	killed
ka	killed in action
KA	Knight of St Andrew, Order of Barbados
Kans	Kansas
KAR	King's African Rifles
kas	killed on active service
KB	Knight of the Bath; Knight Bachelor; Knight Banneret
KBE	Knight Commander, Order of the British Empire
KC	King's Counsel
KCB	Knight Commander, Order of the Bath
KCC	Commander, Order of the Crown, Belgium and Congo Free State
KCH	King's College Hospital; Knight Commander, Hanoverian Order
KCHS	Knight Commander, Order of the Holy Sepulchre
KCIE	Knight Commander, Order of the Indian Empire
KCL	King's College London
KCLJ	Knight Commander, Order of St Lazarus of Jerusalem
KCMG	Knight Commander, Order of St Michael and St George
KCSA	Knight Commander, Military Order of the Collar of St Agatha of Paternò
KCSG	Knight Commander, Order of St Gregory the Great
KCSHS	Knight Commander with Star, Order of the Holy Sepulchre
KCSI	Knight Commander, Order of the Star of India
KCSJ/KCStJ	Knight Commander, Order of St John of Jerusalem (Knights Hospitaller)
KCSS	Knight Commander, Order of St Silvester
KCVO	Knight Commander, Royal Victorian Order
KCVSA	King's Commendation for Valuable Services in the Air
KDG	King's Dragoon Guards
KEH	King Edward's Horse
KEO	King Edward's Own
KG	Knight, Order of the Garter
KGCSS	Knight Grand Cross, Order of St Silvester
KGO	King George's Own
KGStJ	Knight of Grace, Order of St John of Jerusalem
KH	Knight, Hanoverian Order
KHC	Honorary Chaplain to the King
KHDS	Honorary Dental Surgeon to the King
KHNS	Honorary Nursing Sister to the King
KHP	Honorary Physician to the King
KHS	Honorary Surgeon to the King; Knight, Order of the Holy Sepulchre
K-i-H	Kaisar-i-Hind
KJStJ	Knight of Justice, Order of St John of Jerusalem
KLJ	Knight, Order of St Lazarus of Jerusalem
KM	Knight of Malta
KORR	King's Own Royal Regiment
KOSB	King's Own Scottish Borderers
KOYLI	King's Own Yorkshire Light Infantry
KP	Knight, Order of St Patrick
KPM	King's Police Medal
KRH	King's Royal Hussars
KRRC	King's Royal Rifle Corps
KS	King's Scholar; Kansas
KSC	Knight of St Columba
KSG	Knight, Order of St Gregory the Great
KSJ	Knight, Order of St John of Jerusalem (Knights Hospitaller)
KSLI	King's Shropshire Light Infantry
KSS	Knight, Order of St Silvester
KStJ	Knight, Most Venerable Order of the Hospital of St John of Jerusalem
KStJ(A)	Associate Knight of Justice, Most Venerable Order of the Hospital of St John of Jerusalem
Kt	Knight
KT	Knight, Order of the Thistle
ktd	knighted
KY	Kentucky

L

L	(Scottish) Lord of Parliament
LA	Los Angeles; Library Association; Literate in Arts; Liverpool Academy; Louisiana
LAA	Light Anti-Aircraft
Lab	Labour
LAC	London Athletic Club
LACSAB	Local Authorities Conditions of Service Advisory Board
LAE	London Association of Engineers
LAMDA	London Academy of Music and Dramatic Art
LAMSAC	Local Authorities' Management Services and Computer Committee
LAMTPI	Legal Associate Member, Town Planning Institute

Lancs	Lancashire
LAPADA	London and Provincial Antique Dealers' Association
LARSP	Language Assessment, Remediation and Screening Procedure
LAUTRO	Life Assurance and Unit Trust Regulatory Organisation
LBC	London Broadcasting Company; London Borough Council
LBHI	Licentiate, British Horological Institute
LC	Cross of Leo
L of C	Library of Congress; Lines of Communication
LCAD	London Certificate in Art and Design (University of London)
LCC	London County Council (later GLC)
LCh	Licentiate in Surgery
LCJ	Lord Chief Justice
LCL	Licentiate of Canon Law
LCP	Licentiate, College of Preceptors
LCSP	London and Counties Society of Physiologists
LCST	Licentiate, College of Speech Therapists
LD	Liberal and Democratic; Licentiate in Divinity
Ld	Lord (*e.g.*, of the Manor)
LDDC	London Docklands Development Corporation
LDiv	Licentiate in Divinity
Ld Lt	Lord-Lieutenant
Ldr	Leader
LDS	Licentiate in Dental Surgery
LDV	Local Defence Volunteers
Ldy	Lady (*e.g.*, -in-Waiting)
LEA	Local Education Authority
LEDU	Local Enterprise Development Unit
Legn Hon	Legion of Honour
Leics	Leicestershire
LEP	Local Ecumenical Project
LEPRA	British Leprosy Relief Association
LèsL	Licencié ès Lettres
LG	Lady Companion, Order of the Garter
LGSM	Licentiate, Guildhall School of Music and Drama
LGStJ	Lady of Grace, Order of St John of Jerusalem
LGTB	Local Government Training Board
LH	Light Horse
LHD	*Literarum Humaniorum Doctor* (Doctor of Literature)
LHSM	Licentiate, Institute of Health Services Management
LI	Light Infantry; Long Island
Lib	Liberal
Lib Dem	Liberal Democrat
LIBA	Lloyd's Insurance Brokers' Association
LIBER	Ligue des Bibliothèques Européennes de Recherche
Lic	Licence
LicMed	Licentiate in Medicine
LIFFE	London International Financial Futures and Options Exchange
Lincs	Lincolnshire
LIOB	Licentiate, Institute of Building
Lit	Literature; Literary
Lit Hum	*Literae Humaniores* (Classics)
Lit	Literary
LittD	Doctor of Literature; Doctor of Letters
LJ	Lord Justice
LJStJ	Lady of Justice, Order of St John of Jerusalem
LLA	Lady Literate in Arts
LLB	Bachelor of Laws
LLC	Limited Liability Company
LLCM	Licentiate, London College of Music
LLD	Doctor of Laws
LLL	Licentiate in Laws
LLM	Master of Laws
LM	Licentiate in Midwifery
LMBC	Lady Margaret Boat Club
LMC	Local Medical Committee
LMCC	Licentiate, Medical Council of Canada
LMed	Licentiate in Medicine
LMH	Lady Margaret Hall, Oxford
LMR	London Midland Region (BR)
LMRTPI	Legal Member, Royal Town Planning Institute
LMS	London, Midland and Scottish Railway; London Missionary Society
LMSR	London Midland and Scottish Railway
LMSSA	Licentiate in Medicine and Surgery, Society of Apothecaries
LNat	Liberal National
LNER	London and North Eastern Railway
LNWR	London and North West Railway
LOB	Location of Offices Bureau
LP	Life Peer; Limited Partnership
LPh	Licentiate in Philosophy
LPO	London Philharmonic Orchestra
LPTB	London Passenger Transport Board
LRAD	Licentiate, Royal Academy of Dancing
LRAM	Licentiate, Royal Academy of Music
LRB	London Rifle Brigade
LRCP	Licentiate, Royal College of Physicians, London
LRCPE	Licentiate, Royal College of Physicians, Edinburgh
LRCPI	Licentiate, Royal College of Physicians of Ireland
LRCPSGlas	Licentiate, Royal College of Physicians and Surgeons of Glasgow
LRCS	Licentiate, Royal College of Surgeons of England
LRCSE	Licentiate, Royal College of Surgeons, Edinburgh
LRCSI	Licentiate, Royal College of Surgeons in Ireland
LRFPS(G)	Licentiate, Royal Faculty of Physicians and Surgeons, Glasgow
LRIBA	Licentiate, Royal Institute of British Architects
LRPS	Licentiate, Royal Photographic Society
LRSM	Licentiate, Royal Schools of Music
LRT	London Regional Transport
LSA	Licentiate, Society of Apothecaries; Licence in Agricultural Sciences
LSE	London School of Economics and Political Science
LSHTM	London School of Hygiene and Tropical Medicine
LSO	London Symphony Orchestra
LSWR	London and South-Western Railway
Lt	Lieutenant
LT	London Transport; Licentiate in Teaching
LTA	Lawn Tennis Association
LTB	London Transport Board
Lt-Cdr	Lieutenant-Commander
LTCL	Licentiate, Trinity College of Music, London
Lt-Col	Lieutenant-Colonel
Ltcy	Lieutenancy
Ltd	Limited
LTE	London Transport Executive
Lt-Gen	Lieutenant-General
LTh	Licentiate in Theology
LUOTC	London University Officers' Training Corps
LVO	Lieutenant, Royal Victorian Order (formerly MVO (Fourth Class))
LWT	London Weekend Television

M

m	married
M	Marquess; Middle; Monsieur
MA	Master of Arts; Military Assistant; Massachusetts
M&A	Mergers and Acquisitions
MAA	Manufacturers' Agents Association of Great Britain
MAAF	Mediterranean Allied Air Forces
MAAT	Member, Association of Accounting Technicians
MACE	Member, Australian College of Education; Member, Association of Conference Executives
MACI	Member, American Concrete Institute
MACM	Member, Association of Computing Machines
MACS	Member, American Chemical Society
MADO	Member, Association of Dispensing Opticians
MAE	Member, Academia Europaea
MAEE	Marine Aircraft Experimental Establishment
MAF	Ministry of Agriculture and Fisheries
MAFF	Ministry of Agriculture, Fisheries and Food
MAHL	Master of Arts in Hebrew Letters
MAI	*Magister in Arte Ingeniaria* (Master of Engineering)
MAIAA	Member, American Institute of Aeronautics and Astronautics
MAICE	Member, American Institute of Consulting Engineers
MAIChE	Member, American Institute of Chemical Engineers
Maj	Major
Maj-Gen	Major-General
MALD	Master of Arts in Law and Diplomacy
Man	Manitoba
MAO	Master of Obstetric Art
MAOT	Member, Association of Occupational Therapists
MAOU	Member, American Ornithologists' Union

MAP	Ministry of Aircraft Production
MAPsS	Member, Australian Psychological Society
MARAC	Member, Australasian Register of Agricultural Consultants
MArch	Master of Architecture
MASAE	Member, American Society of Agricultural Engineers
MASc	Master of Applied Science
MASC	Member, Australian Society of Calligraphers
MASCE	Member, American Society of Civil Engineers
MASME	Member, American Society of Mechanical Engineers
Mass	Massachusetts
MAT	Master of Arts and Teaching (US)
Math	Mathematics; Mathematical
MATh	Master of Arts in Theology
MATSA	Managerial Administrative Technical Staff Association
MAusIMM	Member, Australasian Institute of Mining and Metallurgy
MB	Medal of Bravery (Canada); Bachelor of Medicine
MBA	Master of Business Administration
MBASW	Member, British Association of Social Workers
MBC	Metropolitan/Municipal Borough Council
MBCS	Member, British Computer Society
MBE	Member, Order of the British Empire
MBES	Member, Biological Engineering Society
MBFR	Mutual and Balanced Force Reductions (negotiations)
MBHI	Member, British Horological Institute
MBIFD	Member, British Institute of Funeral Directors
MBIM	Member, British Institute of Management
MBKS	Member, British Kinematograph Society
MBKSTS	Member, British Kinematograph, Sound and Television Society
MBOU	Member, British Ornithologists' Union
MBPICS	Member, British Production and Inventory Control Society
MBritIRE	Member, British Institution of Radio Engineers
MBS	Member, Building Societies Institute
MBSc	Master of Business Science
MC	Military Cross; Missionaries of Charity
MCAM	Member, CAM Foundation
MCB	Master in Clinical Biochemistry
MCBSI	Member, Chartered Building Societies Institute
MCC	Marylebone Cricket Club; Metropolitan County Council
MCCDRCS	Member in Clinical Community Dentistry, Royal College of Surgeons
MCD	Master of Civic Design
MCE	Master of Civil Engineering
MCFP	Member, College of Family Physicians (Canada)
MCGI	Member, City and Guilds of London Institute
MCh/MChir	Master of Surgery
MChE	Master of Chemical Engineering
MChemA	Master in Chemical Analysis
MChOrth	Master of Orthopaedic Surgery
MCIBS	Member, Chartered Institution of Building Services
MCIBSE	Member, Chartered Institution of Building Services Engineers
MCIH	Member, Chartered Institute of Housing
MCIM	Member, Chartered Institute of Marketing
MCIOB	Member, Chartered Institute of Building
M.CIRP	Member, International Institution for Production Engineering Research
MCIS	Member, Institute of Chartered Secretaries and Administrators
MCIT	Member, Chartered Institute of Transport
MCIWEM	Member, Chartered Institution of Water and Environmental Management
MCL	Master in Civil Law
MCMES	Member, Civil and Mechanical Engineers' Society
MCom	Master of Commerce
MConsE	Member, Association of Consulting Engineers
MConsEl	Member, Association of Consulting Engineers of Ireland
MCOphth	Member, College of Ophthalmologists
MCP	Member of Colonial Parliament; Master of City Planning (US)
MCPA	Member, College of Pathologists of Australia
MCPath	Member, College of Pathologists
MCPP	Member, College of Pharmacy Practice
MCPS	Member, College of Physicians and Surgeons
MCS	Madras Civil Service; Malayan Civil Service
MCSD	Member, Chartered Society of Designers
MCSEE	Member, Canadian Society of Electrical Engineers
MCSP	Member, Chartered Society of Physiotherapy
MCST	Member, College of Speech Therapists
MCT	Member, Association of Corporate Treasurers
md	managing director
MD	Doctor of Medicine; Military District; Maryland
MDC	Metropolitan District Council
MDes	Master of Design
MDiv	Master of Divinity
MDS	Master of Dental Surgery
MDSc	Master of Dental Science
ME	Mining Engineer; Middle East; Master of Engineering; Maine
MEAF	Middle East Air Force
MEc	Master of Economics
MEC	Member of Executive Council; Middle East Command
MECAS	Middle East Centre for Arab Studies
Mech	Mechanics; Mechanical
MECI	Member, Institute of Employment Consultants
MEd	Master of Education
Med	Medical
MEF	Middle East Force
MEIC	Member, Engineering Institute of Canada
MELF	Middle East Land Forces
Memb/memb	Member/member
Meml	Memorial
Mencap	Royal Society for Mentally Handicapped Children and Adults
MEng	Master of Engineering
MEO	Marine Engineering Officer
MEP	Member of the European Parliament
MESc	Master of Engineering Science
MetR	Metropolitan Railway
Metsoc	Metals Society
MEXE	Military Engineering Experimental Establishment
MF	Master of Forestry
MFA	Master of Fine Arts
MFC	Mastership in Food Control
MFCM	Member, Faculty of Community Medicine
MFGB	Miners' Federation of Great Britain
MFH	Master of Foxhounds
MFHom	Member, Faculty of Homeopathy
MFOM	Member, Faculty of Occupational Medicine
MFPaed	Member, Faculty of Paediatrics, Royal College of Physicians of Ireland
MFPHM	Member, Faculty of Public Health Medicine
mfr	manufacturer
MG	Machine Gun
MGA	Major General in charge of Administration
MGC	Machine Gun Corps
MGDSRCS	Member in General Dental Surgery, Royal College of Surgeons
MGGS	Major-General, General Staff
MGI	Member, Institute of Certificated Grocers
MGM	Metro-Goldwyn-Mayer
MGO	Master General of the Ordnance; Master of Gynaecology and Obstetrics
Mgr	Monsignor
MHA	Member of House of Assembly
MHCIMA	Member, Hotel Catering and Institutional Management Association
MHK	Member of the House of Keys
MHort(RHS)	Master of Horticulture, Royal Horticultural Society
MHR	Member of the House of Representatives
MHRA	Modern Humanities Research Association
MHRF	Mental Health Research Fund
MHSM	Member, Institute of Health Services Management
MI	Military Intelligence; Michigan
MIAeE	Member, Institute of Aeronautical Engineers
MIAgrE	Member, Institution of Agricultural Engineers
MIAM	Member, Institute of Administrative Management
MIAS	Member, Institute of Aeronautical Science (US)
MIBC	Member, Institute of Business Counsellors
MIBF	Member, Institute of British Foundrymen
MIBiol	Member, Institute of Biology
MIBritE	Member, Institution of British Engineers
MIB(Scot)	Member, Institute of Bankers in Scotland
MICE	Member, Institution of Civil Engineers
MICEI	Member, Institution of Civil Engineers of Ireland
MICFor	Member, Institute of Chartered Foresters
Mich	Michigan
MIChemE	Member, Institution of Chemical Engineers
MICM	Member, Institute of Credit Management
MICorrST	Member, Institution of Corrosion Science and Technology
MICS	Member, Institute of Chartered Shipbrokers
Middx	Middlesex
MIDI	Member, Institute of Design of Ireland

MIDPM	Member, Institute of Data Processing Management
MIE	Member Institution of Engineers
MIE(Aust)	Member, Institution of Engineers, Australia
MIE(Ind)	Member, Institution of Engineers, India
MIED	Member, Institution of Engineering Designers
MIEE	Member, Institution of Electrical Engineers
MIEEE	Member, Institute of Electrical and Electronics Engineers (NY)
MIEEM	Member, Institute of Ecology and Environmental Management
MIEI	Member, Institute of Engineering Inspection
MIEIE	Member, Institution of Electronics and Electrical Incorporated Engineers
MIEMgt	Member, Institute of Environmental Management
MIEnvSc	Member, Institute of Environmental Science
MIERE	Member, Institution of Electronic and Radio Engineers
MIES	Member, Institution of Engineers and Shipbuilders, Scotland
MIET	Member, Institute of Engineers and Technicians
MIExpE	Member, Institute of Explosives Engineers
MIFA	Member, Institute of Field Archaeologists
MIFF	Member, Institute of Freight Forwarders
MIFireE	Member, Institution of Fire Engineers
MIFM	Member, Institute of Fisheries Management
MIFor	Member, Institute of Foresters
MIGasE	Member, Institution of Gas Engineers
MIGeol	Member, Institution of Geologists
MIH	Member, Institute of Housing
MIHM	Member, Institute of Housing Managers (later MIH)
MIHort	Member, Institute of Horticulture
MIHT	Member, Institution of Highways and Transportation
MIHVE	Member, Institution of Heating and Ventilating Engineers (later MCIBS)
MIIA	Member, Institute of Industrial Administration (later FBIM)
MIIM	Member, Institute of Industrial Managers
MIInfSc	Member, Institute of Information Sciences
Mil	Military; Militia
MIL	Member, Institute of Linguists
MILGA	Member, Institute of Local Government Administrators
MILocoE	Member, Institution of Locomotive Engineers
MILog	Member, Institute of Logistics
MIM	Member, Institute of Metals (formerly Institution of Metallurgists)
MIMarE	Member, Institute of Marine Engineers
MIMC	Member, Institute of Management Consultants
MIMechE	Member, Institution of Mechanical Engineers
MIMEMME	Member, Institution of Mining Electrical and Mining Mechanical Engineers
MIMgt	Member, Institute of Management
MIMGTechE	Member, Institution of Mechanical and General Technician Engineers
MIMI	Member, Institute of the Motor Industry
MIMinE	Member, Institution of Mining Engineers
MIMM	Member, Institution of Mining and Metallurgy
MIMunE	Member, Institution of Municipal Engineers
Min	Minister; Ministry
MIN	Member, Institute of Navigation
Minn	Minnesota
MInstAM	Member, Institute of Administrative Management
MInstBE	Member, Institution of British Engineers
MInstCE	Member, Institution of Civil Engineers
MInstD	Member, Institute of Directors
MInstE	Member, Institute of Energy
MInstEnvSci	Member, Institute of Environmental Sciences
MInstF	Member, Institute of Fuel
MInstHE	Member, Institution of Highway Engineers
MInstM	Member, Institute of Marketing
MInstMC	Member, Institute of Measurement and Control
MInstME	Member, Institution of Mining Engineers
MInstMet	Member, Institute of Metals
MInstP	Member, Institute of Physics
MInstPet	Member, Institute of Petroleum
MInstPI	Member, Institute of Patentees and Inventors
MInstPkg	Member, Institute of Packaging
MInstPS	Member. Institute of Purchasing and Supply
MInstR	Member. Institute of Refrigeration
MInstRA	Member, Institute of Registered Architects
MInstT	Member, Institute of Transport
MInstTM	Member, Institute of Travel Managers in Industry and Commerce
MInstW	Member, Institute of Welding
MInstWM	Member, Institute of Wastes Management
MINucE	Member, Institution of Nuclear Engineers
MIOA	Member, Institute of Acoustics
MIOB	Member, Institute of Building
MIOM	Member, Institute of Office Management
MIOSH	Member, Institution of Occupational Safety and Health
MIPA	Member, Institute of Practitioners in Advertising
MIPD	Member, Institute of Personnel and Development
MIPlantE	Member, Institution of Plant Engineers
MIPM	Member, Institute of Personnel Management
MIPR	Member, Institute of Public Relations
MIProdE	Member, Institution of Production Engineers
MIQ	Member, Institute of Quarrying
MIQA	Member, Institute of Quality Assurance
MIRE	Member, Institution of Radio Engineers (later MIERE)
MIREE(Aust)	Member, Institution of Radio and Electronics Engineers (Australia)
MIRO	Mineral Industry Research Organisation
MIRT	Member, Institute of Reprographic Technicians
MIRTE	Member, Institute of Road Transport Engineers
MIS	Member, Institute of Statisticians
MIS(India)	Member, Institution of Surveyors of India
MISI	Member, Iron and Steel Institute (later part of Metals Society)
MIStructE	Member, Institution of Structural Engineers
MIT	Massachusetts Institute of Technology
MITA	Member, Industrial Transport Association
MITD	Member, Institute of Training and Development
MITE	Member, Institution of Electrical and Electronics Technician Engineers
MITI	Member, Institute of Translation and Interpreting
MITT	Member, Institute of Travel and Tourism
MIWE	Member, Institution of Water Engineers
MIWEM	Member, Institution of Water and Environmental Management
MIWES	Member, Institution of Water Engineers and Scientists
MIWM	Member, Institution of Works Managers
MIWPC	Member, Institute of Water Pollution Control
MIWSP	Member, Institute of Work Study Practitioners
MJA	Medical Journalists Association
MJI	Member, Institute of Journalists
MJIE	Member, Junior Institution of Engineers
MJS	Member, Japan Society
MJur	*Magister Juris* (Master of Law)
ML	Licentiate in Medicine; Master of Laws
MLA	Member of Legislative Assembly; Modern Language Association; Master in Landscape Architecture
MLC	Member of Legislative Council
MLCOM	Member, London College of Osteopathic Medicine
MIEx	Member, Institute of Export
MLitt	Master of Letters
Mlle	Mademoiselle
MLM	Member, Order of the Legion of Merit (Rhodesia)
MLO	Military Liaison Officer
MLR	Modern Language Review
MM	Military Medal; Merchant Marine
MMA	Metropolitan Museum of Art
MMB	Milk Marketing Board
MMD	Movement for Multi-Party Democracy
Mme	Madame
MME	Master of Mining Engineering
MMechE	Master of Mechanical Engineering
MMet	Master of Metallurgy
MMGI	Member, Mining, Geological and Metallurgical Institute of India
MMin	Master of Ministry
MMM	Member, Order of Military Merit (Canada)
MMS	Member, Institute of Management Services
MMSA	Master of Midwifery, Society of Apothecaries
MN	Merchant Navy; Minnesota
MNAS	Member, National Academy of Sciences (US)
MND	Motor Neurone Disease
MNECInst	Member, North East Coast Institution of Engineers and Shipbuilders
MNI	Member, Nautical Institute
MNSE	Member, Nigerian Society of Engineers
MNZIS	Member, New Zealand Institute of Surveyors
MNZPI	Member, New Zealand Planning Institute
MO	Medical Officer; Military Operations; Missouri
MOD	Ministry of Defence
Mods	Moderations (Oxford)
MOF	Ministry of Food
MOH	Medical Officer(s) of Health
MOI	Ministry of Information

MOMI	Museum of the Moving Image
Mon	Monmouthshire
MOP	Ministry of Power
MOrthRCS	Member in Orthodontics, Royal College of Surgeons
MoS	Ministry of Supply
Most Rev	Most Reverend
MoT	Ministry of Transport
MOV	Member, Order of Volta (Ghana)
MP	Member of Parliament
MPA	Master of Public Administration; Member, Parliamentary Assembly, Northern Ireland
MPBW	Ministry of Public Building and Works
MPH	Master of Public Health
MPIA	Master of Public and International Affairs
MPMI	Member, Property Management Institute
MPO	Management and Personnel Office
MPP	Member, Provincial Parliament
MPRISA	Member, Public Relations Institute of South Africa
MPS	Member, Pharmaceutical Society
MR	Master of the Rolls; Municipal Reform
MRAC	Member, Royal Agricultural College
MRACP	Member, Royal Australasian College of Physicians
MRACS	Member, Royal Australasian College of Surgeons
MRAeS	Member, Royal Aeronautical Society
MRAIC	Member, Royal Architectural Institute of Canada
MRAS	Member, Royal Asiatic Society
MRC-LMB	Medical Research Council Laboratory of Molecular Biology
MRC	Medical Research Council
MRCA	Multi-Role Combat Aircraft
MRCGP	Member, Royal College of General Practitioners
MRCOG	Member, Royal College of Obstetricians and Gynaecologists
MRCOphth	Member, Royal College of Ophthalmologists
MRCP	Member, Royal College of Physicians, London
MRCPA	Member, Royal College of Pathologists of Australia
MRCPath	Member, Royal College of Pathologists
MRCPE	Member, Royal College of Physicians, Edinburgh
MRCPGlas	Member, Royal College of Physicians and Surgeons of Glasgow
MRCPI	Member, Royal College of Physicians of Ireland
MRCPsych	Member, Royal College of Psychiatrists
MRCS	Member, Royal College of Surgeons of England
MRCSE	Member, Royal College of Surgeons of Edinburgh
MRCSI	Member, Royal College of Surgeons in Ireland
MRCVS	Member, Royal College of Veterinary Surgeons
MRE	Master of Religious Education
MRES/MREmpS	Member, Royal Empire Society
MRHS	Member, Royal Horticultural Society
MRI	Member, Royal Institution
MRIA	Member, Royal Irish Academy
MRIAI	Member, Royal Institute of the Architects of Ireland
MRIC	Member, Royal Institute of Chemistry
MRIN	Member, Royal Institute of Navigation
MRINA	Member, Royal Institution of Naval Architects
MRO	Member, Register of Osteopaths
MRPharmS	Member, Royal Pharmaceutical Society
MRSanI	Member, Royal Sanitary Institute
MRSC	Member, Royal Society of Chemistry
MRSH	Member, Royal Society for the Promotion of Health
MRSL	Member, Order of the Republic of Sierra Leone
MRSM	Member, Royal Society of Medicine
MRST	Member, Royal Society of Teachers
MRTPI	Member, Royal Town Planning Institute
MRurSc	Master of Rural Science
MRUSI	Member, Royal United Service Institution
MRVA	Member, Rating and Valuation Association
MS, MSS	Manuscript, Manuscripts
MS	Master of Surgery; Master of Science (US); Mississippi
MSA	Master of Science, Agriculture (US); Mineralogical Society of America
MSAAIE	Member, Southern African Association of Industrial Editors
MSAE	Member, Society of Automotive Engineeers (US)
MSAICE	Member, South African Institution of Civil Engineers
MSAInstMM	Member, South African Institute of Mining and Metallurgy
MSAutE	Member, Society of Automobile Engineers
MSC	Manpower Services Commission; Missionaries of the Sacred Heart; Madras Staff Corps
MSc	Master of Science
MSD	Meritorious Service Decoration (Fiji)
MSE	Master of Science in Engineering (US)
MScD	Master of Dental Science
MSF	(Union for) Manufacturing, Science, Finance
MSH	Master of Stag Hounds
MSI	Member, Securities Institute
MSIAD	Member, Society of Industrial Artists and Designers
MSINZ	Member, Surveyors' Institute of New Zealand
MSIT	Member, Society of Instrument Technology
MSM	Meritorious Service Medal; Madras Sappers and Miners
MSN	Master of Science in Nursing
MSocIS	Member, Société des Ingénieurs et Scientifiques de France
MSocSc	Master of Social Sciences
MSocWork	Master of Social Work
MSR	Member, Society of Radiographers
MS&R	Merchant Shipbuilding and Repairs
MSW	Master, Social Work/Welfare
MSt	Master of Studies
MSTD	Member, Society of Typographic Designers
MT	Mechanical Transport; Montana
Mt	Mount, Mountain
MTA	Music Trades Association
MTAI	Member, Institute of Travel Agents
MTB	Motor Torpedo Boat
MTCA	Ministry of Transport and Civil Aviation
MTD	Midwife Teachers' Diploma
MTech	Master of Technology
MTEFL	Master in the Teaching of English as a Foreign or Second Language
MTh	Master of Theology
MTIA	Metal Trades Industry Association
MTIRA	Machine Tool Industry Research Association
MTPI	Member, Town Planning Institute
MTS	Master of Theological Studies
MUniv	Honorary Master of the University
MusB	Bachelor of Music
MusD	Doctor of Music
MusM	Master of Music
MV	Merchant Vessel; Motor Vessel (naval)
MVEE	Military Vehicles and Engineering Establishment
MVO	Member, Royal Victorian Order
MVSc	Master of Veterinary Science
MW	Master of Wine
MWA	Mystery Writers of America
MWeldI	Member, Welding Institute
MWSOM	Member, Institute of Practitioners in Work Study Organisation and Methods

N

n	nephew/niece
N	Nationalist; Navigating Duties; North
NA	National Academician (America)
NAACP	National Association for the Advancement of Colored People
NAAFI	Navy, Army and Air Force Institutes
NAAS	National Agricultural Advisory Service
NAB	National Advisory Body for Public Sector Higher Education
NABC	National Association of Boys' Clubs
NAC	National Agriculture Centre
NACAB	National Association of Citizens' Advice Bureaux
NACCB	National Accreditation Council for Certification Bodies
NACETT	National Advisory Council for Education and Training Targets
NACF	National Art-Collections Fund
NACRO	National Association for the Care and Resettlement of Offenders
NADFAS	National Association of Decorative and Fine Arts Societies
NAE	National Academy of Engineering
NAEW	Nato Airborn Early Warning
NAHA	National Association of Health Authorities
NAHAT	National Association of Health Authorities and Trusts
NALGO/Nalgo	National and Local Government Officers' Association
NAMAS	National Measurement and Accreditation Service
NAMCW	National Association for Maternal and Child Welfare
NAMH	MIND (National Association for Mental Health)
NAMMA	NATO MRCA Management Agency
NAPAG	National Academies Policy Advisory Group
NAPT	National Association for the Prevention of Tuberculosis

NARM	National Association of Recording Merchandisers (US)
NAS/UWT	National Association of Schoolmasters/Union of Women Teachers
NAS	National Academy of Sciences
NASA	National Aeronautics and Space Administration (US)
NASDIM	National Association of Security Dealers and Investment Managers (later FIMBRA)
Nat/l	National
Nat Sci	Natural Sciences
NATCS	National Air Traffic Control Services
NATFHE	National Association of Teachers in Further and Higher Education (combining ATCDE and ATTI)
Natl	Natural
NATLAS	National Testing Laboratory Accreditation Scheme
NATO	North Atlantic Treaty Organisation
NATS	National Air Traffic Services
NATSOPA	National Society of Operative Printers, Graphical and Media Personnel (formerly of Operative Printers and Assistants)
NAYC	Youth Clubs UK (formerly National Association of Youth Clubs)
NB	New Brunswick; Nebraska
NBA	North British Academy
NBC	National Book Council (later NBL); National Broadcasting Company (US)
NBL	National Book League
NBPI	National Board for Prices and Incomes
NC	National Certificate; North Carolina
NCA	National Certificate of Agriculture
NCARB	National Council of Architectural Registration Boards
NCB	National Coal Board
NCC	National Computing Centre; Nature Conservancy Council; National Consumer Council
NCCE	Nature Conservancy Council for England (English Nature)
NCCI	National Committee for Commonwealth Immigrants
NCCL	National Council for Civil Liberties
NCD	National Capital District, Papua New Guinea
NCDAD	National Council for Diplomas in Art and Design
NCEA	National Council for Educational Awards
NCET	National Council for Educational Technology
NCH	National Children's Homes
NCLC	National Council of Labour Colleges
NCOPF	National Council for One Parent Families
NCSE	National Council for Special Education
NCSS	National Council of Social Service
NCTA	National Community Television Association (US)
NCTJ	National Council for the Training of Journalists
NCU	National Cyclists' Union
NCVCCO	National Council of Voluntary Child Care Organisations
NCVO	National Council for Voluntary Organisations
NCVQ	National Council for Vocational Qualifications
ND	North Dakota
NDA	National Diploma in Agriculture
NDD	National Diploma in Dairying; National Diploma in Design
NDH	National Diploma in Horticulture
NDIC	National Defence Industries Council
NDP	New Democratic Party
NDTA	National Defense Transportation Association (US)
NE	North-east
NEAB	Northern Examinations and Assessment Board
NEAC	New English Art Club
NEAF	Near East Air Force
NEARELF	Near East Land Forces
NEB	National Enterprise Board
NEBSS	National Examinations Board for Supervisory Studies
NEC	National Executive Committee
NECCTA	National Education Closed Circuit Television Association
NECInst	North East Coast Institution of Engineers and Shipbuilders
NEDC	National Economic Development Council; North East Development Council
NEDO	National Economic Development Office
NEH	National Endowment for the Humanities
NEL	National Engineering Laboratory
NERC	Natural Environment Research Council
NFC	National Freight Consortium (formerly Corporation, then Company)
NFCG	National Federation of Consumer Groups
NFER	National Foundation for Educational Research
NFHA	National Federation of Housing Associations
NFMS	National Federation of Music Societies
NFS	National Fire Service
NFSH	National Federation of Spiritual Healers
NFT	National Film Theatre
NFU	National Farmers' Union

NFWI	National Federation of Women's Institutes
NGO	Non-Governmental Organisation(s)
NGTE	National Gas Turbine Establishment
NH	New Hampshire
NHBC	National House-Building Council
NHS	National Health Service
NI	Northern Ireland; Native Infantry
NIAB	National Institute of Agricultural Botany
NIACRO	Northern Ireland Association for the Care and Resettlement of Offenders
NIAE	National Institute of Agricultural Engineering
NIAID	National Institute of Allergy and Infectious Diseases
NICEC	National Institute for Careers Education and Counselling
NICG	Nationalised Industries Chairmen's Group
NICS	Northern Ireland Civil Service
NID	Naval Intelligence Division; National Institute for the Deaf; Northern Ireland District; National Institute of Design (India)
NIESR	National Institute of Economic and Social Research
NIH	National Institutes of Health (US)
NIHCA	Northern Ireland Hotels and Caterers Association
NII	Nuclear Installations Inspectorate
NILP	Northern Ireland Labour Party
NIMR	National Institute for Medical Research
NISTRO	Northern Ireland Science and Technology Regional Organisation
NJ	New Jersey
NLCS	North London Collegiate School
NLF	National Liberal Federation
NLYL	National League of Young Liberals
NM	New Mexico
NMR	Nuclear Magnetic Resonance
NNMA	Nigerian National Merit Award
NNOM	Nigerian National Order of Merit
Northants	Northamptonshire
NOTB	National Ophthalmic Treatment Board
Notts	Nottinghamshire
NP	Notary Public
NPA	Newspaper Publishers' Association
NPFA	National Playing Fields Association
NPk	Nishan-e-Pakistan
NPL	National Physical Laboratory
nr	near
NR	North Riding
NRA	National Rifle Association; National Recovery Administration (US); National Rivers Authority
NRAO	National Radio Astronomy Observatory
NRCC	National Research Council of Canada
NRD	National Registered Designer
NRDC	National Research Development Corporation
NRPB	National Radiological Protection Board
NRR	Northern Rhodesia Regiment
ns	Graduate of Royal Naval Staff College, Greenwich
NS	Nova Scotia, *i.e.*, Scotland, where creations of Baronets are concerned; New Style in the Calendar (in Great Britain since 1750–53); National Society; National Service
NSA	National Skating Association
NSAIV	Distinguished Order of Shaheed Ali (Maldives)
NSF	National Science Foundation (US)
NSM	Non-Stipendiary Minister
NSMHC	National Society for Mentally Handicapped Children
NSPCC	National Society for the Prevention of Cruelty to Children
NSQT	National Society for Quality through Teamwork
NSRA	National Small-bore Rifle Association
N/SSF	Novice, Society of St Francis
NSTC	Nova Scotia Technical College
NSW	New South Wales
NT	New Testament; Northern Territory (Australia); National Theatre; National Trust
NTDA	National Trade Development Association
NT&SA	National Trust and Savings Association
NTUC	National Trades Union Congress
NUAAW	National Union of Agricultural and Allied Workers
NUBE	National Union of Bank Employees
NUFLAT	National Union of Footwear Leather and Allied Trades
NUGMW	National Union of General and Municipal Workers (later GMBATU)
NUHKW	National Union of Hosiery and Knitwear Workers
NUI	National University of Ireland
NUJ	National Union of Journalists
NUJMB	Northern Universities Joint Matriculation Board
NUKFAT	National Union of Knitwear, Footwear and Apparel Trades
NUM	National Union of Mineworkers

NUMAST	National Union of Marine, Aviation and Shipping Transport Officers
NUPE	National Union of Public Employees
NUR	National Union of Railwaymen
NUS	National Union of Students
NUT	National Union of Teachers
NUTG	National Union of Townswomen's Guilds
NUTN	National Union of Trained Nurses
NUU	New University of Ulster
NV	Nevada
NVQ	National Vocational Qualification
NW	North-west
NWC	National Water Council
NWF	North West Frontier
NWFP	North-West Frontier Province
NWP	North-Western Province
NWT	North-Western Territories
NY	New York
NYC	New York City
NYO	National Youth Orchestra
NZ	New Zealand
NZEF	New Zealand Expeditionary Force
NZIA	New Zealand Institute of Architects
NZRSA	New Zealand Retired Services Association

O

O	Ohio (USA)
OA	Officier d'Académie
OAM	Medal of the Order of Australia
OAS	Organization of American States; On Active Service
OASC	Officer Aircrew Selection Centre
OAU	Organisation for African Unity
OB	Order of Barbados
OBC	Order of British Columbia
OBE	Officer, Order of the British Empire
OBI	Order of British India
OC	Officer Commanding; Order of Canada (equivalent to former award SM)
OCA	Old Comrades Association
OCC	Order of the Caribbean Community
OCDS	Overseas College of Defence Studies (Canada)
OCF	Officiating Chaplain to the Forces
OCS	Officer Candidates School
OCSS	Oxford and Cambridge Shakespeare Society
OCTU	Officer Cadet Training Unit
OCU	Operational Conversion Unit
OD	Officer, Order of Distinction (Jamaica)
ODA	Overseas Development Administration
ODI	Overseas Development Institute
ODM	Ministry of Overseas Development
ODSM	Order of Diplomatic Service Merit (Lesotho)
OE	Order of Excellence (Guyana)
O & E	Operations and Engineers (US)
OEA	Old Etonian Association; Overseas Education Association
OECD	Organization for Economic Co-operation and Development
OED	Oxford English Dictionary
OEEC	Organization for European Economic Co-operation
OF	Order of the Founder, Salvation Army
OFEMA	Office Française d'Exportation de Matériel Aéronautique
OFFER	Office of Electricity Regulation
Offr	Officer
OFM	Order of Friars Minor (Franciscans)
OFMCap	Order of Friars Minor Capuchin (Franciscans)
OFMConv	Order of Friars Minor Conventual (Franciscans)
OFR	Order of the Federal Republic of Nigeria
OFS	Orange Free State
OFSTED	Office for Standards in Education
OFT	Office of Fair Trading
Oftel	Office of Telecommunications
OGS	Oratory of the Good Shepherd
OH	Ohio
OHMS	On His/Her Majesty's Service
O i/c	Officer in charge
OJ	Order of Jamaica
OK	Oklahoma
OL	Officer, Order of Leopold; Order of the Leopard (Lesotho)
OLJ	Officer, Order of St Lazarus of Jerusalem
OLM	Officer, Legion of Merit (Rhodesia)
OM	Order of Merit
O & M	organisation and method
OMCS	Office of the Minister for the Civil Service
OMI	Oblate of Mary Immaculate
OMM	Officer, Order of Military Merit (Canada)
ON	Order of the Nation (Jamaica)
OND	Ordinary National Diploma
Ont	Ontario
ONZ	Order of New Zealand
O & O	Oriental and Occidental Steamship Co.
OON	Officer, Order of the Niger
OOnt	Order of Ontario
OP	*Ordinis Praedicatorum* (of the Order of Preachers (Dominican)); Observation Post
op(s)	operation(s)
Opcon	Operational Control
OPCS	Office of Population Censuses and Surveys
Oppn	Opposition
OPSS	Office of Public Service and Science
OQ	Officer, National Order of Quebec
OR	Order of Rorima (Guyana); Operational Research; Oregon
ORC	Orange River Colony
ORGALIME	Organisme de Liaison des Industries Métalliques Européennes
ORL	Otorhinolaryngology
ORS	Operational Research Society
ORSA	Operations Research Society of America
ORSL	Order of the Republic of Sierra Leone
ORT	Organization for Rehabilitation through Training
ORTF	Office de la Radiodiffusion et Télévision Française
OSA	Order of St Augustine (Augustinian); Ontario Society of Artists
OSB	Order of St Benedict (Benedictine)
osc	Graduate of Overseas Staff College
OSCE	Organisation for Security and Co-operation in Europe
OSFC	Franciscan (Capuchin) Order
O/Sig	Ordinary Signalman
OSNC	Orient Steam Navigation Co.
OSRD	Office of Scientific Research and Development
OSS	Office of Strategic Services
OST	Office of Science and Technology
OStJ	(Officer of the) Order of St John of Jerusalem
OStJ	Officer, Most Venerable Order of the Hospital of St John of Jerusalem
OSUK	Ophthalmological Society of the United Kingdom
OT	Old Testament
OTC	Officers' Training Corps
OTL	Officer, Order of Toussaint L'Ouverture (Haiti)
OTU	Operational Training Unit
OTWSA	Ou-Testamentiese Werkgemeenskap in Suider-Afrika
OU	Open University
OUAC	Oxford University Athletic Club
OUAFC	Oxford University Association Football Club
OUBC	Oxford University Boat Club
OUCC	Oxford University Cricket Club
OUDS	Oxford University Dramatic Society
OUP	Oxford University Press; Official Unionist Party
OURC	Oxford University Rifle Club
OURFC	Oxford University Rugby Football Club
OURT	Order of the United Republic of Tanzania
Oxon	Oxfordshire; *Oxoniensis* (of Oxford)

P

p	page
pa	*per annum* (a year)
PA	Pakistan Army; Personal Assistant; Pennsylvania
PAA	President, Australian Academy of Science
pac	passed the final examination of the Advanced Class, The Military College of Science
PACE	Protestant and Catholic Encounter
PAg	Professional Agronomist
PAO	Prince Albert's Own
Parl(y)	Parliament(ary)
PASI	Professional Associate, Chartered Surveyors' Institution
PBMA	President of the British Medical Association
PBS	Public Broadcasting Service
PC	Privy Council/Counsellor; Police Constable; Perpetual Curate; Peace Commissioner (Ireland); Progressive Conservative (Canada)
PCC	Parochial Church Council
PCE/PGCE	Postgraduate Certificate of Education
PCEF	Polytechnic and Colleges Employers' Forum
PCFC	Polytechnics and Colleges Funding Council
PCL	Polytechnic of Central London
PCMO	Principal Colonial Medical Officer
PdD	Doctor of Pedagogy (US)
Pde	Parade
PDG	Président Directeur Général
PDR	People's Democratic Republic
PDRA	post doctoral research assistant
PDSA	People's Dispensary for Sick Animals
PDTC	Professional Dancer's Training Course Diploma
PE	Procurement Executive
PEI	Prince Edward Island
Pembs	Pembrokeshire
PEN	Poets, Playwrights, Editors, Essayists, Novelists (Club)
PEng	Registered Professional Engineer (Canada); Member, Society of Professional Engineers
Penn	Pennsylvania
PEP	Political and Economic Planning
PER	Professional and Executive Recruitment
Perm	Permanent
PEST	Pressure for Economic and Social Toryism
PETRAS	Polytechnic Educational Technology Resources Advisory Service
PF	Procurator-Fiscal
PFA	Professional Footballers' Association
pfc	Graduate of RAF Flying College
PFE	Program for Executives
PGA	Professional Golfers' Association
PH	Presidential Order of Honour (Botswana)
PHAB	Physically Handicapped and Able-Bodied
PhB	Bachelor of Philosophy
PhC	Pharmaceutical Chemist
PhD	Doctor of Philosophy
Phil	Philology, Philological; Philosophy, Philosophical
PhL	Licentiate of Philosophy
PHLS	Public Health Laboratory Service
PhM	Master of Philosophy (USA)
PhmB	Bachelor of Pharmacy
Phys	Physical
PIA	Personal Investment Authority
PIARC	Permanent International Association of Road Congresses
PIB	Prices and Incomes Board (later NBPI)
PICAO	Provisional International Civil Aviation Organization
PIRA	Paper Industries Research Association
PITCOM	Parliamentary Information Technology Committee
PJG	Pingat Jasa Gemilang (Singapore)
PJK	Pingkat Jasa Kebaktian (Malaysia)
Pk	Park
Pl	Place; Plural
PLA	Port of London Authority
PLC/plc	public limited company
Plen	Plenipotentiary
PLI	President, Landscape Institute
PLP	Parliamentary Labour Party; Progressive Liberal Party (Bahamas)
PLR	Public Lending Right
PM	Prime Minister
PMA	Personal Military Assistant
PMC	Personnel Management Centre

PMD	Program for Management Development
PMG	Postmaster-General
PMN	Panglima Mangku Negara (Malaysia)
PMO	Principal Medical Officer
PMRAFNS	Princess Mary's Royal Air Force Nursing Service
PMS	Presidential Order of Meritorious Service (Botswana); President, Miniature Society
PNBS	Panglima Negara Bintang Sarawak
Pncpl	Principal
PNEU	Parents' National Educational Union
PNG	Papua New Guinea
PNP	People's National Party
PO	Post Office
P/O	Pilot Officer
P&O	Peninsular and Oriental Steamship Company
POB	Presidential Order of Botswana
Poly	Polytechnic
POMEF	Political Office Middle East Force
Pop	Population
POUNC	Post Office Users' National Council
POW	Prisoner of War; Prince of Wales's
pp	pages
PP	Parish Priest; Past President
PPA	Periodical Publishers Association
PPARC	Particle Physics and Astronomy Research Council
PPCLI	Princess Patricia's Canadian Light Infantry
PPDF	Parti Populaire pour la Démocratie Française
PPE	Philosophy, Politics and Economics
PPInstHE	Past President, Institution of Highway Engineers
PPIStructE	Past President, Institution of Structural Engineers
PPITB	Printing and Publishing Industry Training Board
PPP	Private Patients Plan
PPRA	Past President, Royal Academy
PPRBA	Past President, Royal Society of British Artists
PPRBS	Past President, Royal Society of British Sculptors
PPRE	Past President, Royal Society of Painter-Printmakers (formerly of Painter-Etchers and Engravers)
PPRIBA	Past President, Royal Institute of British Architects
PPROI	Past President, Royal Institute of Oil Painters
PPRP	Past President, Royal Society of Portrait Painters
PPRTPI	Past President, Royal Town Planning Institute
PPRWA	Past President, Royal Watercolour Association
PPS	Parliamentary Private Secretary
PPSIAD	Past President, Society of Industrial Artists and Designers
PQ	Province of Quebec
PR	Public Relations; Parti républicain
PRA	President, Royal Academy
PRAS	President, Royal Agricultural Society
PRBA	President, Royal Society of British Artists
PRBS	President, Royal Society of British Sculptors
PRCS	President, Royal College of Surgeons
PRE	President, Royal Society of Painter-Printmakers (formerly of Painter-Etchers and Engravers)
Preb	Prebendary
PrEng	Professional Engineer
Pres	President
PRHA	President, Royal Hibernian Academy
PRI	President, Royal Institute of Painters in Water Colours; Plastics and Rubber Institute
PRIA	President, Royal Irish Academy
PRIAS	President, Royal Incorporation of Architects in Scotland
PRISA	Public Relations Institute of South Africa
Priv	Private
pro tem	*pro tempore* (for the time being)
PRO NED	Promotion of Non-Executive Directors
PRO	Public Relations Officer, Public Records Office
Proc	Proctor; Proceedings
Prof	Professor; Professional
PROI	President, Royal Institute of Oil Painters
PRORM	Pay and Records Office, Royal Marines
Prov	Provost, Provincial
Prox	*Proximo* (next)
Prox acc	*Proxime accessit* (next in order of merit to the winner)
PRS	President, Royal Society; Performing Right Society Ltd
PRSA	President, Royal Scottish Academy
PRSE	President, Royal Society of Edinburgh
PRSH	President, Royal Society for the Promotion of Health
PRSM	President, Royal Society of Medicine

PRSW	President, Royal Scottish Water Colour Society	PSOE	Partido Socialista Obrero Español
PRUAA	President, Royal Ulster Academy of Arts	PSSC	Personal Social Services Council
PRWA	President, Royal West of England Academy	PTA	Passenger Transport Authority; Parent-Teacher Association
PRWS	President, Royal Society of Painters in Water Colours	PTE	Passenger Transport Executive
ps	passed School of Instruction (of Officers)	Pte	Private
PS	Pastel Society; Paddle Steamer	ptnr	partner
psa	Graduate of RAF Staff College	ptsc	passed Technical Staff College
PSA	Property Services Agency; Petty Sessions Area	Pty	Proprietary (used of Australian and some other countries' businesses)
psc	Graduate of Staff College		
PSD	Petty Sessional Division; Social Democratic Party (Portugal)	Publicns	Publications
PSGB	Pharmaceutical Society of Great Britain	PUP	People's United Party
PSI	Policy Studies Institute	PVSM	Pararn Vishishc Seva Medal (India)
PSIAD	President, Society of Industrial Artists and Designers	PWD	Public Works Department
psm	Certificate of Royal Military School of Music	PWE	Political Welfare Executive
PSM	Panglima Setia Mahkota (Malaysia)	PWO	Prince of Wales's Own
PSMA	President, Society of Marine Artists	PWR	Pressurized Water Reactor
PSNC	Pacific Steam Navigation Company	PYBT	Prince's Youth Business Trust
PSO	Principal Scientific Officer; Personal Staff Officer		

Q

Q	Queen	QMAAC	Queen Mary's Army Auxiliary Corps
QAIMNS	Queen Alexandra's Imperial Military Nursing Service	QMC	Queen Mary College, London
QALAS	Qualified Associate, Chartered Land Agents' Society	QMG	Quartermaster-General
QARANC	Queen Alexandra's Royal Army Nursing Corps	QMW	Queen Mary and Westfield College, London
QARNNS	Queen Alexandra's Royal Naval Nursing Service	QO	Qualified Officer; Queen's Own
QBD	Queen's Bench Division	QOOH	Queen's Own Oxfordshire Hussars
QC	Queen's Counsel	Q(ops)	Quartering (operations)
QCVSA	Queen's Commendation for Valuable Service in the Air	QOY	Queen's Own Yeomanry
QEH	Queen Elizabeth Hall	QPM	Queen's Police Medal
QEO	Queen Elizabeth's Own	Qr	Quarter
QFSM	Queen's Fire Service Medal for Distinguished Service	QRIH	Queen's Royal Irish Hussars
QGM	Queen's Gallantry Medal	QRV	Qualified Valuer, Real Estate Institute of New South Wales
QHC	Honorary Chaplain to the Queen	QS	Quarter Sessions; Quantity Surveying
QHDS	Honorary Dental Surgeon to the Queen	qs	RAF graduates of the Military or Naval Staff College
QHNS	Honorary Nursing Sister to the Queen	QSM	Queen's Service Medal (NZ)
QHP	Honorary Physician to the Queen	QSO	Queen's Service Order (NZ)
QHS	Honorary Surgeon to the Queen	QUB	Queen's University, Belfast
Qld	Queensland	qv	quod vide (which see)
Qly	Quarterly	QWI	Qualified Weapons Instructor

R

(R)	Reserve	RAIA	Royal Australian Institute of Architects
RA	Royal Academician; Royal (Regiment of) Artillery	RAIC	Royal Architectural Institute of Canada
RAA	Regional Arts Association; Royal Australian Artillery	RAM	(Member of) Royal Academy of Music
RAAF	Royal Australian Air Force	RAMC	Royal Army Medical Corps
RAAMC	Royal Australian Army Medical Corps	RAN	Royal Australian Navy
RABI	Royal Agricultural Benevolent Institution	RANR	Royal Australian Naval Reserve
RAC	Royal Automobile Club; Royal Agricultural College; Royal Armoured Corps	RANVR	Royal Australian Naval Volunteer Reserve
		RAOC	Royal Army Ordnance Corps
RACDS	Royal Australian College of Dental Surgeons	RAPC	Royal Army Pay Corps
RACGP	Royal Australian College of General Practitioners	RARDE	Royal Armament Research and Development Establishment
RAChD	Royal Army Chaplains' Department	RARO	Regular Army Reserve of Officers
RACI	Royal Australian Chemical Institute	RAS	Royal Astronomical Society; Royal Asiatic Society; Recruitment and Assessment Services
RACO	Royal Australian College of Ophthalmologists		
RACOG	Royal Australian College of Obstetricians and Gynaecologists	RASC	Royal Army Service Corps
		RASE	Royal Agricultural Society of England
RACP	Royal Australasian College of Physicians	RAuxAF	Royal Auxiliary Air Force
RACS	Royal Australasian College of Surgeons; Royal Arsenal Co-operative Society	RAVC	Royal Army Veterinary Corps
		RB	Rifle Brigade
RADA	Royal Academy of Dramatic Art	RBA	Member, Royal Society of British Artists
RADAR	Royal Association for Disability and Rehabilitation	RBC	Royal British Colonial Society of Artists
RADC	Royal Army Dental Corps	RBK&C	Royal Borough of Kensington and Chelsea
R-Adml	Rear Admiral	RBL	Royal British Legion
RADIUS	Religious Drama Society of Great Britain	RBS	Royal Society of British Sculptors
RAE	Royal Australian Engineers; Royal Aerospace Establishment (formerly Royal Aircraft Establishment)	RBSA	(Member of) Royal Birmingham Society of Artists
		RBY	Royal Bucks Yeomanry
RAEC	Royal Army Educational Corps	RC	Roman Catholic
RAeS	Royal Aeronautical Society	RCA	Member, Royal Canadian Academy of Arts; Royal College of Art; (Member of) Royal Cambrian Academy
RAF	Royal Air Force		
RAFA	Royal Air Force Association	RCAC	Royal Canadian Armoured Corps
RAFO	Reserve of Air Force Officers	RCAF	Royal Canadian Air Force
RAFRO	Royal Air Force Reserve of Officers	RCamA	Member, Royal Cambrian Academy
RAFVR	Royal Air Force Volunteer Reserve	RCAS	Royal Central Asian Society
RAI	Royal Anthropological Institute of Great Britain and Ireland; Radio Audizioni Italiane	RCDS	Royal College of Defence Studies

RCEME	Royal Canadian Electrical and Mechanical Engineers
RCGP	Royal College of General Practitioners
RCHA	Royal Canadian Horse Artillery
RCHM	Royal Commission on Historical Monuments
RCM	(Member of) Royal College of Music
RCN	Royal Canadian Navy; Royal College of Nursing
RCNC	Royal Corps of Naval Constructors
RCNR	Royal Canadian Naval Reserve
RCNVR	Royal Canadian Naval Volunteer Reserve
RCO	Royal College of Organists
RCOG	Royal College of Obstetricians and Gynaecologists
RCP	Royal College of Physicians, London
RCPath	Royal College of Pathologists
RCPE/RCPEd	Royal College of Physicians, Edinburgh
RCPI	Royal College of Physicians of Ireland
RCPSG	Royal College of Physicians and Surgeons of Glasgow
RCPsych	Royal College of Psychiatrists
RCR	Royal College of Radiologists
RCS	Royal College of Surgeons of England; Royal Corps of Signals; Royal College of Science
RCSE/RCSEd	Royal College of Surgeons of Edinburgh
RCSI	Royal College of Surgeons in Ireland
RCT	Royal Corps of Transport
RCVS	Royal College of Veterinary Science; Royal College of Veterinary Surgeons
Rd	Road
RD	Rural Dean; Royal Naval and Royal Marine Forces Reserve Decoration
R&D	Research and Development
RDA	Royal Defence Academy
RDC	Rural District Council
RDF	Royal Dublin Fusiliers
RDI	Royal Designer for Industry (Royal Society of Arts)
RDS	Royal Dublin Society
RE	Royal Engineers; Fellow, Royal Society of Painter-Printmakers (formerly of Painter-Etchers and Engravers); Religious Education
REACH	Retired Executives Action Clearing House
recd	received
REconS	Royal Economic Society
Regnl	Regional
Regt	Regiment
rels	relations
REME	Royal Electrical and Mechanical Engineers
Renfrews	Renfrewshire
REngDes	Registered Engineering Designer
REOWS	Royal Engineers Officers' Widows' Society
Rep/rep	Representative/representative
REPC	Regional Economic Planning Council
RERO	Royal Engineers Reserve of Officers
Res	Resigned; Reserve; Resident; Research
RES	Royal Empire Society
ret	retired
RETI	Association of Traditional Industrial Regions
Rev	Reverend; Review
RFA	Royal Field Artillery; Royal Fleet Auxiliary
RFC	Royal Flying Corps; Rugby Football Club
RFD	Reserve Force Decoration
RFH	Royal Festival Hall
RFN	Registered Fever Nurse
RFPS(G)	Royal Faculty of Physicians and Surgeons, Glasgow
RFR	Rassemblement des Français pour la République
RFU	Rugby Football Union
RGA	Royal Garrison Artillery
RGI	Royal Glasgow Institute of the Fine Arts
RGJ	Royal Green Jackets
RGN	Registered General Nurse
RGS	Royal Geographical Society
RGSA	Royal Geographical Society of Australasia
RHA	Royal Hibernian Academy; Royal Horse Artillery; Regional Health Authority
RHAS	Royal Highland and Agricultural Society of Scotland
RHB	Regional Hospital Board
RHBNC	Royal Holloway and Bedford New College, London
RHC	Royal Holloway College, London
RHF	Royal Highland Fusiliers
RHG	Royal Horse Guards
RHistS	Royal Historical Society
RHQ	Regional Headquarters
RHR	Royal Highland Regiment
RHS	Royal Horticultural Society; Royal Humane Society
RHV	Royal Health Visitor
RI	(Member of) Royal Institute of Painters in Water Colours; Rhode Island
RIA	Royal Irish Academy
RIAI	Royal Institute of the Architects of Ireland
RIAM	Royal Irish Academy of Music
RIAMC	Royal Indian Army Medical Corps
RIAS	Royal Incorporation of Architects in Scotland
RIASC	Royal Indian Army Service Corps
RIBA	(Member of) Royal Institute of British Architects
RIBI	Rotary International in Great Britain and Ireland
RIC	Royal Irish Constabulary; Royal Institute of Chemistry
RICS	Royal Institution of Chartered Surveyors
RIE	Royal Indian Engineering (College)
RIF	Royal Inniskilling Fusiliers
RIIA	Royal Institute of International Affairs
RILEM	Réunion internationale des laboratoires d'essais et de recherches sur les matériaux et les constructions
RIM	Royal Indian Marines
RIN	Royal Indian Navy
RINA	Royal Institution of Naval Architects
RINVR	Royal Indian Naval Volunteer Reserve
RIPA	Royal Institute of Public Administration
RIPH&H	Royal Institute of Public Health and Hygiene
RIrF	Royal Irish Fusiliers
RLC	Royal Logistic Corps
Rlrd(s)	Railroad(s)
RLSS	Royal Life Saving Society
Rlwy	Railway
RM	Royal Marines; Resident Magistrate; Registered Midwife
RMA	Royal Marine Artillery; Royal Military Academy, Sandhurst
RMB	Rural Mail Base
RMC	Royal Military College
RMC	Royal Military College Sandhurst
RMCM	(Member of) Royal Manchester College of Music
RMCS	Royal Military College of Science
RMedSoc	Royal Medical Society, Edinburgh
RMetS	Royal Meteorological Society
RMFVR	Royal Marine Forces Volunteer Reserve
RMIT	Royal Melbourne Institute of Technology
RMLI	Royal Marine Light Infantry
RMN	Registered Mental Nurse
RMO	Resident Medical Officer(s)
RMP	Royal Military Police
RMPA	Royal Medico-Psychological Association
RMS	Royal Microscopical Society; Royal Mail Steamer; Royal Society of Miniature Painters
RMT	Rail, Maritime and Transport Union
RN	Royal Navy; Royal Naval; Registered Nurse
RNAS	Royal Naval Air Service
RNAY	Royal Naval Aircraft Yard
RNC	Royal Naval College
RNCM	(Member of) Royal Northern College of Music
RND	Royal Naval Division
RNEC	Royal Naval Engineering College
RNIB	Royal National Institute for the Blind
RNID	Royal National Institute for Deaf People (formerly Royal National Institute for the Deaf)
RNLI	Royal National Lifeboat Institution
RNLO	Royal Naval Liaison Officer
RNR	Royal Naval Reserve
RNS	Royal Numismatic Society
RNSA	Royal Naval Sailing Association
RNSC	Royal Naval Staff College
RNT	Registered Nurse Tutor; Royal National Theatre
RNTNEH	Royal National Throat, Nose and Ear Hospital
RNVR	Royal Naval Volunteer Reserve
RNVSR	Royal Naval Volunteer Supplementary Reserve
RNXS	Royal Naval Auxiliary Service
RNZAC	Royal New Zealand Armoured Corps
RNZAF	Royal New Zealand Air Force
RNZIR	Royal New Zealand Infantry Regiment
RNZN	Royal New Zealand Navy
RNZNVR	Royal New Zealand Naval Volunteer Reserve
R of O	Reserve of Officers
ROC	Royal Observer Corps
ROF	Royal Ordnance Factories
ROI	Member, Royal Institute of Oil Painters
RoSPA	Royal Society for the Prevention of Accidents
Roy	Royal
RP	Member, Royal Society of Portrait Painters
RPC	Royal Pioneer Corps
RPE	Rocket Propulsion Establishment

RPMS	Royal Postgraduate Medical School
RPO	Royal Philharmonic Orchestra
RPR	Rassemblement pour la République
RPS	Royal Photographic Society
RPSGB	Royal Pharmaceutical Society of Great Britain
RRC	Royal Red Cross
RRE	Royal Radar Establishment
RRF	Royal Regiment of Fusiliers
RRS	Royal Research Ship
RSA	Royal Scottish Academician; Royal Society of Arts; Republic of South Africa
RSAA	Royal Society for Asian Affairs
RSAF	Royal Small Arms Factory
RSAI	Royal Society of Antiquaries of Ireland
RSAMD	Royal Scottish Academy of Music and Drama
RSanI	Royal Sanitary Institute
RSAS	Royal Surgical Aid Society
RSC	Royal Society of Canada; Royal Society of Chemistry; Royal Shakespeare Company
RSCM	Royal School of Church Music
RSCN	Registered Sick Children's Nurse
RSE	Royal Society of Edinburgh
RSF	Royal Scots Fusiliers
RSFSR	Russian Soviet Federated Socialist Republic
RSGS	Royal Scottish Geographical Society
RSH	Royal Society for the Promotion of Health
RSL	Royal Society of Literature; Returned Services League of Australia
RSM/RSocMed	Royal Society of Medicine
RSM	Royal School of Mines
RSMA	Royal Society of Marine Artists
RSME	Royal School of Military Engineering
RSMHCA	Royal Society for Mentally Handicapped Children and Adults
RSNC	Royal Society for Nature Conservation
RSO	Rural Sub-Office; Railway Sub-Office; Resident Surgical Officer
RSPB	Royal Society for Protection of Birds
RSPCA	Royal Society for Prevention of Cruelty to Animals

RSPP	Royal Society of Portrait Painters
RSRE	Royal Signals and Radar Establishment
RSSAf	Royal Society of South Africa
RSSAILA	Returned Sailors, Soldiers and Airmen's Imperial League of Australia
RSSPCC	Royal Scottish Society for Prevention of Cruelty to Children
RSTM&H	Royal Society of Tropical Medicine and Hygiene
RSUA	Royal Society of Ulster Architects
RSV	Revised Standard Version
RSW	Member, Royal Scottish Society of Painters in Water Colours
Rt Hon	Right Honourable
Rt Rev	Right Reverend
RTC	Royal Transport Corps
RTE	Radio Telefis Eireann
RTL	Radio-Télévision Luxembourg
RTO	Railway Transport Officer
RTPI	Royal Town Planning Institute
RTR	Royal Tank Regiment
RTS	Religious Tract Society; Royal Toxophilite Society; Royal Television Society
RTYC	Royal Thames Yacht Club
RU	Rugby Union
RUC	Royal Ulster Constabulary
RUI	Royal University of Ireland
RUKBA	Royal United Kingdom Beneficent Association
RUR	Royal Ulster Regiment
RURAL	Society for the Responsible Use of Resources in Agriculture and on the Land
RUSI	Royal United Services Institute for Defence Studies (formerly Royal United Service Institution)
RVC	Royal Veterinary College
RWA/RWEA	(Member of) Royal West of England Academy
RWAFF	Royal West African Frontier Force
RWF	Royal Welch Fusiliers
RWS	(Member of) Royal Society of Painters in Water Colours
RYA	Royal Yachting Association
RYS	Royal Yacht Squadron
RZSScot	Royal Zoological Society of Scotland

S

s	son
s	succeeded
S	Saint; Scotland (of creation in peerage of); South
(S)	(in Navy) Paymaster; Scotland
SA	South Australia; South Africa; Société Anonyme
SAAF	South African Air Force
SABC	South African Broadcasting Corporation
sac	qualified at small arms technical long course
SAC	Scientific Advisory Committee
SACEUR	Supreme Allied Commander Europe
SACIF	Sociedad Anónima Commercial Industrial Financiera
SACLANT	Supreme Allied Commander Atlantic
SACRO	Scottish Association for the Care and Resettlement of Offenders
SACSEA	Supreme Allied Command, SE Asia
SA de CV	Sociedad Anónima de Capital Variable
SADF	Sudanese Auxiliary Defence Force
SADG	Société des Architectes Diplômés par le Gouvernement
SAE	Society of Automobile Engineers (US)
SAInstMM	South African Institute of Mining and Metallurgy
Salop	Shropshire
SAMC	South African Medical Corps
SARL	Société à Responsabilité Limitée
Sarum	Salisbury
SAS	Special Air Service
Sask	Saskatchewan
SASO	Senior Air Staff Officer
SAT	Senior Member, Association of Accounting Technicians
SATB	Soprano, Alto, Tenor, Bass
SATRO	Science and Technology Regional Organisation
SB	Bachelor of Science (US)
SBAA	Sovereign Base Areas Administration
SBAC	Society of British Aerospace Companies (formerly Society of British Aircraft Constructors)
SBS	Special Boat Service
SBStJ	Serving Brother, Most Venerable Order of the Hospital of St John of Jerusalem

SC	Senior Counsel (Eire and some other countries' equivalent to QC)
SC	Star of Courage (Canada); Senior Counsel; South Carolina
sc	student at the Staff College
SCA	Society of Catholic Apostolate (Pallottine Fathers); Société en Commandité par Actions
SCAA	School Curriculum and Assessment Authority
SCAO	Senior Civil Affairs Officer
SCAPA	Society for Checking the Abuses of Public Advertising
SCAR	Scientific Committee for Antarctic Research
ScD	Doctor of Science
SCDC	Schools Curriculum Development Committee
SCF	Senior Chaplain to the Forces; Save the Children Fund
Sch	School
SCI	Society of Chemical Industry
SCIS	Scottish Council of Independent Schools
SCL	Student in Civil Law
SCM	State Certified Midwife; Student Christian Movement
SCONUL	Standing Conference of National and University Libraries
Scot	Scotland; Scottish
ScotBIC	Scottish Business in the Community
SCOTMEG	Scottish Management Efficiency Group
SCOTVEC	Scottish Vocational Education Council
SD	Staff Duties; South Dakota
SDA	Social Democratic Alliance; Scottish Diploma in Agriculture; Scottish Development Agency
SDB	Salesian of Don Bosco
SDF	Sudan Defence Force; Social Democratic Federation
SDI	Strategic Defence Initiative
SDLP	Social Democratic and Labour Party
SDP	Social Democratic Party
SE	South East
SEAC	South-East Asia Command
SEALF	South-East Asia Land Forces
SEATO	South-East Asia Treaty Organization
Sec	Secretary
SEC	Security Exchange Commission
SED	Scottish Education Department

SEE	Society of Environmental Engineers
SEFI	European Society for Engineering Education
SEN	State Enrolled Nurse
SEPM	Society of Economic Palaeontologists and Mineralogists
SERC	Science and Engineering Research Council
SERT	Society of Electronic and Radio Technicians
Serv(s)	Service(s)
SESO	Senior Equipment Staff Officer
SFA	Securities and Futures Authority
SFInstE	Senior Fellow, Institute of Energy
SFInstF	Senior Fellow, Institute of Fuel
SFTA	Society of Film and Television Arts
SFTCD	Senior Fellow, Trinity College Dublin
SGA	Member, Society of Graphic Art
SGBI	Schoolmistresses' and Governesses' Benevolent Institution
Sgt	Sergeant
SHA	Secondary Heads Association; Special Health Authority
SHAC	London Housing Aid Centre
SHAEF	Supreme Headquarters, Allied Expeditionary Force
SHAPE	Supreme Headquarters, Allied Powers, Europe
SHEFC	Scottish Higher Education Funding Council
SHHD	Scottish Home and Health Department
SH&MA	Scottish Horse and Motormen's Association
SIAD	Society of Industrial Artists and Designers
SIAM	Society of Industrial and Applied Mathematics (US)
SIB	Shipbuilding Industry Board; Securities and Investments Board
SICAV	Société d'Investissement à Capital Variable
SICOT	Société Internationale de Chirurgie Orthopédique et de Traumatologie
SID	Society for International Development
SIESO	Society of Industrial and Emergency Services Officers
SIMA	Scientific Instrument Manufacturers' Association of Great Britain
SIME	Security Intelligence Middle East
SIMG	Societas Internationalis Medicinae Generalis
SinDrs	Doctor of Chinese
SIROT	Société Internationale pour Recherche en Orthopédie et Traumatologie
sis	sister
SIS	Secret Intelligence Service
SITA	Société Internationale de Télécommunications Aéronautiques
SITPRO	Simpler Trade Procedures Board (formerly Simplification of International Trade Procedures)
SJ	Society of Jesus (Jesuits)
SJAB	St John Ambulance Brigade
SJD	Doctor of Juristic Science
SJJ	Setia Jubli Perak Tuanku Ja'afar
SKGB	Ski Club of Great Britain
SL	Serjeant-at-Law; Sociedad Limitada
SLA	Special Libraries Association
SLAC	Stanford Linear Accelerator Centre
SLAET	Society of Licensed Aircraft Engineers and Technologists
SLAS	Society for Latin-American Studies
SLD	Social and Liberal Democrats
S/Ldr	Squadron Leader
SLG	Community of Sisters of the Love of God
SLP	Scottish Labour Party
slr	solicitor
SM	Medal of Service (Canada); Master of Science; Officer qualified for Submarine Duties
SMA	Society of Marine Artists
SMB	Setia Mahkota Brunei
SME	School of Military Engineering
SMHO	Sovereign Military Hospitaller Order (Malta)
SMIEE	Senior Member, Institute of Electrical and Electronics Engineers (New York)
SMIRE	Senior Member, Institute of Radio Engineers (New York)
SMMT	Society of Motor Manufacturers and Traders Ltd
SMN	Seri Maharaja Mangku Negara (Malaysia)
SMO	Senior Medical Officer; Sovereign Military Order
SMP	Senior Managers' Program
SMPTE	Society of Motion Picture and Television Engineers (US)
SMRTB	Ship and Marine Requirements Technology Board
SNAME	Society of Naval Architects and Marine Engineers (US)
SNCF	Société Nationale des Chemins de Fer Français
SND	Sisters of Notre Dame
SNH	Scottish Natural Heritage
SNP	Scottish National Party
SNR	Society for Nautical Research
SNTS	Society for New Testament Studies

SO	Staff Officer; Scientific Officer; Symphony Orchestra
SOAS	School of Oriental and African Studies
Soc	Society
SocCE(France)	Société des Ingénieurs Civils de France
Soc & Lib Dem	Social and Liberal Democrats
SODEPAX	Committee on Society, Development and Peace
SOE	Special Operations Executive
SOGAT	Society of Graphical and Allied Trades
SOLACE	Society of Local Authority Chief Executives
SOLT	Society of London Theatre
Som	Somerset
SOM	Society of Occupational Medicine
SOSc	Society of Ordained Scientists
SOTS	Society for Old Testament Study
Sov	Sovereign
sowc	Senior Officers' War Course
sp	*sine prole* (without issue)
SP	Self-Propelled (Anti-Tank Regiment)
SpA	Società per Azioni
SPAB	Society for the Protection of Ancient Buildings
SPARKS	Sport Aiding Medical Research for Children
SPCA	Society for the Prevention of Cruelty to Animals
SPCK	Society for Promoting Christian Knowledge
SPCM	Dadah Seri Paduka Cura Si Manja Kim (Malaysia)
SPD	Salisbury Plain District; Sozialdemokratische Partei Deutschlands
SPDK	Seri Panglima Darjal Kinabalu
SPG	Society for the Propagation of the Gospel
SPk	Sitara-e-Pakistan
SPMB	Seri Paduka Makhota Brunei
SPMK	Darjah Kebasaran Seri Paduka Mahkota Kelantan (Malaysia)
SPMO	Senior Principal Medical Officer
SPNC	Society for the Promotion of Nature Conservation
SPNM	Society for the Promotion of New Music
SPR	Society for Psychical Research
SPRC	Society for Prevention and Relief of Cancer
sprl	société de personnes à responsabilité limitée
SPSO	Senior Principal Scientific Officer
SPTL	Society of Public Teachers of Law
SPUC	Society for the Protection of the Unborn Child
Sq	Square
sq	staff qualified
SQA	Sitara-i-Quaid-i-Azam (Pakistan)
Sqdn	Squadron
Sr	Señor
Sr/sr	senior
SR	Special Reserve; Southern Railway; Southern Region (BR)
SRC	Science Research Council; Students' Representative Council
SRCh	State Registered Chiropodist
SRHE	Society for Research into Higher Education
SRIS	Science Reference Information Service
SRN	State Registered Nurse
SRNA	Shipbuilders and Repairers National Association
SRO	Supplementary Reserve of Officers; Self-Regulatory Organisation
SRP	State Registered Physiotherapist
SRY	Sherwood Rangers Yeomanry
SS	Saints; Straits Settlements; Steamship
SSA	Society of Scottish Artists
SSAC	Social Security Advisory Committee
SSAFA/SS&AFA	Soldiers', Sailors' and Airmen's Families Association
SSBN	Nuclear Submarine, Ballistic
SSC	Solicitor before Supreme Court (Scotland); Sculptors Society of Canada; Societas Sanctae Crucis (Society of the Holy Cross); Short Service Commission
SSEB	South of Scotland Electricity Board
SSEES	School of Slavonic and East European Studies
SSF	Society of St Francis
SSJE	Society of St John the Evangelist
SSM	Society of the Sacred Mission; Seri Setia Mahkota (Malaysia)
SSO	Senior Supply Officer; Senior Scientific Officer
SSR	Soviet Socialist Republic
SSRC	Social Science Research Council
SSSI	Site of Special Scientific Interest
SSStJ	Serving Sister, Most Venerable Order of the Hospital of St John of Jerusalem
St	Street; Saint
STA	Sail Training Association
Staffs	Staffordshire

STB	*Sacrae Theologiae Baccalaureus* (Bachelor of Sacred Theology)
STC	Senior Training Corps
STD	*Sacrae Theologiae Doctor* (Doctor of Sacred Theology)
STh	Scholar in Theology
Stip	Stipend; Stipendiary
STL	*Sacrae Theologiae Lector* (Reader or a Professor of Sacred Theology)
STM	*Sacrae Theologiae Magister* (Master of Sacred Theology)
STP	*Sacrae Theologiae Professor* (Professor of Divinity, old form of DD)
STRIVE	Society for Preservation of Rural Industries and Village Enterprises
STSO	Senior Technical Staff Officer

STV	Scottish Television
Sub-Lt	Sub-Lieutenant
SUNY	State University of New York
Supp Res	Supplementary Reserve (of Officers)
Supt	Superintendent
Surgn	Surgeon
surv	surviving
SW	South-west
SWET	Society of West End Theatre
SWIA	Society of Wildlife Artists
SWPA	South West Pacific Area
SWRB	Sadler's Wells Royal Ballet

T

T	Telephone; Territorial
T/	Temporary rank, *e.g.*,T/Capt (Temporary Captain)
T&AFA	Territorial and Auxiliary Forces Association
T&AVR	Territorial and Army Volunteer Reserve
TA	Telegraphic Address; Territorial Army
TAA	Territorial Army Association
TAF	Tactical Air Force
TANS	Territorial Army Nursing Service
TANU	Tanganyika African National Union
TAR	Territorial Army Reserve
TARO	Territorial Army Reserve of Officers
TAS	Torpedo and Anti Submarine Course
TASS	Technical, Administrative and Supervisory Section of AUEW
TAVRA/TA&VRA	Territorial Auxiliary and Volunteer Reserve Association
Tbnl	Tribunal
TC	Order of the Trinity Cross (Trinidad and Tobago)
TCCB	Test and County Cricket Board
TCD	Trinity College, Dublin (University of Dublin, Trinity College)
TCF	Temporary Chaplain to the Forces
TCPA	Town and Country Planning Association
TD	Territorial Decoration; Territorial Efficiency Decoration; Efficiency Decoration (T&AVR) (from April 1967); Teachta Dala (Member of the Dáil, Eire)
TDD	Tubercular Diseases Diploma
TE	Technical Engineer
TEAC	Technical Educational Advisory Council
TEC	Technician Education Council; Training and Enterprise Council
Tech	Technical
TEFL	Teaching English as a Foreign Language
TEFLA	Teaching English as a Foreign Language to Adults
TEM	Territorial Efficiency Medal
TEMA	Telecommunication Engineering and Manufacturing Association
temp	in the time of; temporary
TEng(CEI)	Technician Engineer
Tenn	Tennessee
TeolD	Doctor of Theology
TES	*Times Educational Supplement*
TESL	Teaching English as a Second Language
TESOL	Teaching English to Speakers of Other Languages
TET	Teacher of Electrotherapy
Tex	Texas
TF	Territorial Force
TFA	Territorial Forces Association

TFR	Territorial Force Reserve
TFTS	Tactical Fighter Training Squadron
TGEW	Timber Growers England and Wales Ltd
TGO	Timber Growers' Organisation
TGWU	Transport and General Workers' Union
ThD	Doctor of Theology
THED	Transvaal Higher Education Diploma
THELEP	Therapy of Leprosy
THES	*Times Higher Education Supplement*
ThL	Theological Licentiate
ThSchol	Scholar in Theology
TIMS	The Institute of Management Sciences
TLS	*Times Literary Supplement*
TM	Their Majesties
TMMG	Teacher of Massage and Medical Gymnastics
TN	Tennessee
TNC	Theatres National Committee
TOSD	Tertiary Order of St Dominic
TP	Transvaal Province
TPI	Town Planning Institute
Tport	Transport
Trans/trans	Translation; Translated
Transf	Transferred
TRC	Thames Rowing Club
TRE	Telecommunications Research Establishment (later RRE)
Treas	Treasurer
Trg	Training
TRH	Their Royal Highnesses
TRIC	Television and Radio Industries Club
Trin	Trinity
TRRL	Transport and Road Research Laboratory
TS	Training Ship
TSB	Trustee Savings Bank
tsc	passed a Territorial Army Course in Staff Duties
TSD	Tertiary of St Dominic
TSSA	Transport Salaried Staffs' Association
Tst	Trust
Tstee/tstee	Trustee/trustee
TUC	Trades Union Congress
TULV	Trade Unions for a Labour Victory
TUS	Trade Union Side
TV	Television
TVEI	Technical and Vocational Education Initiative
TWA	Thames Water Authority
TX	Texas
TYC	Thames Yacht Club

U

U	Unionist; University
UACE	Universities Association for Continuing Education
UAE	United Arab Emirates
UAR	United Arab Republic
UAU	Universities Athletic Union
UBC	University of British Columbia
UBI	Understanding British Industry
UC	University College
UCAS	Universities and Colleges Admissions Service
UCCA	Universities Central Council on Admissions

UCCF	Universities and Colleges Christian Fellowship of Evangelical Unions
UCE	University of Central England
UCET	Universities Council for Education of Teachers
UCH	University College Hospital (London)
UCL	University College London (University)
UCLA	University of California at Los Angeles
UCLES	University of Cambridge Local Examinations Syndicate
UCMSM	University College and Middlesex School of Medicine
UCNS	Universities' Council for Non-academic Staff
UCNW	University College of North Wales

UCRN	University College of Rhodesia and Nyasaland
UCS	University College School
UCSD	University of California at San Diego
UCW	University College of Wales; Union of Communication Workers
UDC	Urban District Council; Urban Development Corporation
UDF	Union Defence Force; Union Démocratique Française
UDR	Ulster Defence Regiment; Union Démocrates pour la Vème République
UDSR	Union Démocratique et Socialiste de la Résistance
UE	United Empire Loyalist (Canada)
UEA	University of East Anglia
UED	University Education Diploma
UEFA	Union of European Football Associations
UF	United Free Church
UFAW	Universities Federation for Animal Welfare
UFC	Universities' Funding Council
UGC	University Grants Committee (later UFC)
UIAA	Union Internationale des Associations d'Alpinisme
UICC	Union Internationale contre le Cancer
UIE	Union Internationale des Etudiants
UISPP	Union Internationale des Sciences Préhistoriques et Protohistoriques
UITP	International Union of Public Transport
UJD	*Utriusque Juris Doctor* (Doctor of both Laws, Doctor of Canon and Civil Law)
UK	United Kingdom of Great Britain and Ireland 1801–1922; United Kingdom of Great Britain and Northern Ireland 1922–; used chiefly of peerage and baronetage creations of
UKAC	United Kingdom Automation Council
UKAEA	United Kingdom Atomic Energy Authority
UKCC	United Kingdom Central Council for Nursing, Midwifery and Health Visiting
UKCIS	United Kingdom Chemical Information Service
UKERNA	United Kingdom Education and Research Networking Association
UKIAS	United Kingdom Immigrants' Advisory Service
UKISC	United Kingdom Industrial Space Committee
UKLF	United Kingdom Land Forces
UKMF(L)	United Kingdom Military Forces (Land)
UKMIS	United Kingdom Mission
UKOOA	United Kingdom Offshore Operators Association
UKPIA	United Kingdom Petroleum Industry Association Ltd
UKSC	United Kingdom Support Command
UKSLS	United Kingdom Services Liaison Staff
ULCI	Union of Lancashire and Cheshire Institutes
ULPS	Union of Liberal and Progressive Synagogues
UMDS	United Medical and Dental Schools
UMIST	University of Manchester Institute of Science and Technology
UN	United Nations
UNA	United Nations Association
unc	uncle
UNCAST	United Nations Conference on the Applications of Science and Technology
UNCIO	United Nations Conference on International Organisation
UNCITRAL	United Nations Commission on International Trade Law
UNCSTD	United Nations Conference on Science and Technology for Development
UNCTAD/Unctad	United Nations Commission for Trade and Development
UNDP	United Nations Development Programme
UNDRO	United Nations Disaster Relief Organisation
UNECA	United Nations Economic Commission for Asia

UNEP	United Nations Environment Programme
UNESCO/Unesco	United Nations Educational, Scientific and Cultural Organisation
UNFAO	United Nations Food and Agriculture Organisation
UNFICYP	United Nations Force in Cyprus
UNHCR	United Nations High Commissioner for Refugees
UNICE	Union des Industries de la Communauté Européenne
UNICEF/Unicef	United Nations Children's Fund (formerly United Nations International Children's Emergency Fund)
UNIDO	United Nations Industrial Development Organisation
UNIDROIT	Institut International pour l'Unification du Droit Privé
UNIFEM	United Nations Development Fund for Women
UNIFIL	United Nations Interim Force in Lebanon
UNIPEDE	Union Internationale des Producteurs et Distributeurs d'Energie Electrique
UNISIST	Universal System for Information in Science and Technology
UNITAR	United Nations Institute of Training and Research
Univ	University College (Oxford)
unm	unmarried
UNO	United Nations Organization
UNRRA	United Nations Relief and Rehabilitation Administration
UNRWA	United Nations Relief and Works Agency
UNSCOB	United Nations Special Commission on the Balkans
UP	United Provinces; Uttar Pradesh; United Presbyterian
UPGC	University and Polytechnic Grants Committee
UPNI	Unionist Party of Northern Ireland
UPU	Universal Postal Union
UPUP	Ulster Popular Unionist Party
URC	United Reformed Church
URSI	Union Radio-Scientifique Internationale
US(A)	United States (of America)
USAAF	United States Army Air Force
USAF	United States Air Force
USAID	United States Agency for International Development
USAR	United States Army Reserve
USC	University of Southern California
USDAW	Union of Shop Distributive and Allied Workers
U-Sec	Under Secretary
USM	Unlisted Securities Market
USMA	United States Military Academy
USMC	United States Marine Corps
USN	United States Navy
USNR	United States Naval Reserve
USPG	United Society for the Propagation of the Gospel
USPHS	United States Public Health Service
USPS	United States Postal Service
USR	Universities' Statistical Record
USS	United States Ship
USSR	Union of Soviet Socialist Republics
USVI	United States Virgin Islands
UT	Utah
UTC	University Training Corps
Utd	United
UU	Ulster Unionist
UUUC	United Ulster Unionist Coalition
UUUP	United Ulster Unionist Party
UWCC	University of Wales College of Cardiff
UWE	University of the West of England
UWIST	University of Wales Institute of Science and Technology
UWT	Union of Women Teachers

V

v	*versus* (against)
V	Five (Roman numerals); Version; Vicar; Viscount; Vice
V-	Vice-
VA	Lady, Royal Order of Victoria and Albert
VA/Va	Virginia
V&A	Victoria and Albert Museum
VAD	Voluntary Aid Detachment
VAT	Value Added Tax
VC	Victoria Cross; Voluntary Controlled
VCAS	Vice-Chief of the Air Staff
VCDS	Vice-Chief of the Defence Staff
VCGS	Vice-Chief of the General Staff
VCNS	Vice-Chief of the Naval Staff

VD	Royal Naval Volunteer Reserve Officers' Decoration (later VRD); Volunteer Officers' Decoration; Victorian Decoration
VDC	Volunteer Defence Corps
Ven	Venerable
Vet	Veterinary
VG	Vicar-General
VHS	Honorary Surgeon to Viceroy of India
VIC	Victoria Institute of Colleges
vm	*vita matris* (in the lifetime of the mother)
VM	Victory Medal
VMH	Victoria Medal of Honour (Royal Horticultural Society)
Vol	Volume; Volunteer
Voly	Voluntary
vp	*vita patris* (in the lifetime of the father)

VPP	Volunteer Political Party
VPRP	Vice-President, Royal Society of Portrait Painters
VPRS	Vice-President, Royal Society
VQMG	Vice-Quartermaster-General

VR	*Victoria Regina* (Queen Victoria); Volunteer Reserve
VRD	Royal Naval Volunteer Reserve Officers' Decoration
VSO	Voluntary Service Overseas
VT/Vt	Vermont
VUP	Vanguard Unionist Party

W

w	wife
W	West
WA	Western Australia; Washington
WAAF	Women's Auxiliary Air Force (later WRAF)
WAOS	Welsh Agricultural Organisations Society
Warwicks	Warwickshire
Wash	Washington State
WCC	World Council of Churches
W/Cdr	Wing Commander
WCMD	Welsh College of Music and Drama
WDA	Welsh Development Agency
WEA	Workers' Educational Association; Royal West of England Academy
WES/PNEU	Worldwide Education Service of Parents' National Educational Union
WEU	Western European Union
WFSW	World Federation of Scientific Workers
WFTU	World Federation of Trade Unions
WhF	Whitworth Fellow
WHO	World Health Organization
WhSch	Whitworth Scholar
WI	West Indies; Women's Institute; Wisconsin
Wilts	Wiltshire
WIPO	World Intellectual Property Organization
Wis	Wisconsin
WJEC	Welsh Joint Education Committee

WLA	Women's Land Army
WLD	Women Liberal Democrats
WLF	Women's Liberal Federation
Wm	William
WMO	World Meteorological Organization
WNO	Welsh National Opera
WO	War Office; Warrant Officer
Worcs	Worcestershire
WOSB	War Office Selection Board
WR	West Riding; Western Region (British Railways)
WRAC	Women's Royal Army Corps
WRAF	Women's Royal Air Force
WRANS	Women's Royal Australian Naval Service
WRNS	Women's Royal Naval Service
WRVS	Women's Royal Voluntary Service
WS	Writer to the Signet
WSAVA	World Small Animal Veterinary Association
WSPA	World Society for the Protection of Animals
WSPU	Women's Social and Political Union
WUS	World University Service
WV	West Virginia
WVS	Women's Voluntary Services
WW	World War
WWF	World Wide Fund for Nature (formerly World Wildlife Fund)
WY	Wyoming

X

X	Ten (Roman numerals)

Y

YC	Young Conservative; Yeomanry Cavalry
YCNAC	Young Conservatives National Advisory Committee
Yeo	Yeomanry
YES	Youth Enterprise Scheme
YHA	Youth Hostels Association
YMCA	Young Men's Christian Association
YOI	Young Offenders Institute
Yorks	Yorkshire

YPTES	Young People's Trust for Endangered Species
yr	younger
yrs	years
yst	youngest
YTS	Youth Training Scheme
YVFF	Young Volunteer Force Foundation
YWCA	Young Women's Christian Association

Z

ZANU	Zimbabwe African National Union

ZAPU	Zimbabwe African People's Union

Surnames of Peerage Families

Where the surname and title are identical, or where the latter is no more than an elaboration of the former (*e.g.* 'Jenkins' and 'Jenkins of Hillhead'), it has been thought unnecessary to include it in this listing. Surnames given are those in use by one or more male-line branches of the family holding the peerage, and are subject to minor variations, such as the inclusion or exclusion of a hyphen, among individual members of that family.

(I) In Alphabetical Order of Peerage

ABERCONWAY . . . . McLaren	BRIDPORT . . . . Hood	CRANWORTH . . . . Gurdon
ABERCORN . . . . Hamilton	BRISTOL . . . . Hervey	CRATHORNE . . . . Dugdale
ABERDARE . . . . Bruce	BROCKET . . . . Nall-Cain	CRAWFORD and BALCARRES . . . . Lindsay
ABERDEEN AND TEMAIR . . . . . Gordon	BROOKEBOROUGH . . . . Brooke	CRAWSHAW . . . . Brooks
ABERGAVENNY . . . . Nevill	BROUGHAM AND VAUX . . . . Brougham	CRICKHOWELL . . . . Edwards
ABINGER . . . . Scarlett	BROUGHSHANE . . . . Davison	CROHAM . . . . Allen
ACTON . . . . Lyon-Dalberg-Acton	BROWNLOW . . . . Cust	CROMARTIE . . . . Mackenzie
ADDINGTON . . . . Hubbard	BRUNTISFIELD . . . . Warrender	CROMER . . . . Baring
AILESBURY . . . . Brudenell-Bruce	BUCCLEUCH AND	CROMWELL . . . . Bewicke-Copley
AILSA . . . . Kennedy	QUEENSBERRY . . Montagu(-)Douglas(-)Scott	CULLEN OF ASHBOURNE . . . . . Cokayne
AIRLIE . . . . Ogilvy	BUCHAN . . . . Erskine	DACRE . . . . Douglas-Home
ALANBROOKE . . . . Brooke	BUCKINGHAMSHIRE . . . . Hobart-Hampden	DACRE OF GLANTON . . . . . Trevor-Roper
ALBEMARLE . . . . Keppel	BURGH . . . . Leith	DALHOUSIE . . . . Ramsay
ALDENHAM and HUNSDON OF	BURNHAM . . . . Lawson	DARCY DE KNAYTH . . . . Ingrams
HUNSDON . . . . Gibbs	BURTON . . . . Baillie	DARESBURY . . . . Greenall
ALDINGTON . . . . Low	BUTE . . . . Crichton-Stuart	DARNLEY . . . . Bligh
ALLENDALE . . . . Beaumont	BUXTON OF ALSA . . . . Buxton	DARTMOUTH . . . . Legge
ALTRINCHAM . . . . Grigg	CAITHNESS . . . . Sinclair	DARWEN . . . . Davies
ALVINGHAM . . . . Yerburgh	CALDECOTE . . . . Inskip	DAVENTRY . . . . . . FitzRoy-Newdegate
AMHERST OF HACKNEY . . . . Cecil	CALEDON . . . . Alexander	DEAN OF THORNTON-LE-FYLDE . . McDowall
AMPTHILL . . . . Russell	CALVERLEY . . . . Muff	DECIES . . . . Beresford, De la Poer Beresford,
AMWELL . . . . Montague	CAMDEN . . . . Pratt	Horsley-Beresford
ANGLESEY . . . . Paget	CAMOYS . . . . Stonor	DE CLIFFORD . . . . Russell
ANNALY . . . . White	CAMROSE . . . . Berry	DE FREYNE . . . . French
ANNANDALE AND	CARBERY . . . . Evans-Freke	DELAMERE . . . . Cholmondeley
HARTFELL . . . Hope(-)Johnstone, Johnstone	CAREW . . . . Conolly-Carew	DE LA WARR . . . . Sackville
ANTRIM . . . . McDonnell	CARLISLE . . . . Howard	DE L'ISLE . . . . Sidney
ARGYLL . . . . Campbell	CARNARVON . . . . Herbert	DE MAULEY . . . . Ponsonby
ARRAN . . . . Gore	CARNOCK . . . . Nicolson	DENBIGH and DESMOND . . Feilding, Fielding
ASHBOURNE . . . . Gibson	CARRICK . . . . Butler	DENHAM . . . . Bowyer
ASHBROOK . . . . Flower	CARRINGTON . . . . Carington	DERAMORE . . . . . De Yarburgh-Bateson
ASHBURTON . . . . Baring	CASTLE STEWART . . . . Stuart	DE RAMSEY . . . . Fellowes
ASHCOMBE . . . . Cubitt	CASTLEMAINE . . . . Handcock	DERBY . . . . Stanley
ASHTOWN . . . Chenevix(-)Trench, Trench	CAVAN . . . . Lambart	DE ROS . . . . Maxwell
ATHOLL . . . . Murray	CAWDOR . . . . Campbell	DERWENT . . . . Vanden-Bempde-Johnstone
AUCKLAND . . . . Eden	CHALFONT . . . . Gwynne Jones	DE SAUMAREZ . . . . Saumarez
AVEBURY . . . . Lubbock	CHANDOS . . . . Lyttelton	DE VESCI . . . . Vesey
AYLESFORD . . . . Finch-Knightley	CHARLEMONT . . . . Caulfeild	DEVON . . . . Courtenay
BALFOUR OF BURLEIGH . . . . . . Bruce	CHELMSFORD . . . . Thesiger	DEVONPORT . . . . Kearley
BANGOR . . . . Ward	CHESHAM . . . . Cavendish	DEVONSHIRE . . . . Cavendish
BARNARD . . . . Vane	CHICHESTER . . . . Pelham	DILHORNE . . . . . . Manningham-Buller
BASING . . . . Sclater-Booth	CHILSTON . . . . Akers-Douglas	DONEGALL . . . . Chichester
BATH . . . . Thynn, Thynne	CHURCHILL . . . . Spencer	DONERAILE . . . . St Leger
BEARSTED . . . . Samuel	CHURSTON . . . . Yarde-Buller	DONOUGHMORE . . . . . Hely-Hutchinson
BEAUFORT . . . . Somerset	CLANCARTY . . . . Le Poer Trench	DOWNE . . . . Dawnay
BEAVERBROOK . . . . Aitken	CLANMORRIS . . . . Bingham	DOWNSHIRE . . . . Hill
BEDFORD . . . . Russell	CLANWILLIAM . . . . Meade	DROGHEDA . . . . Moore
BELHAVEN AND STENTON . . . . Hamilton	CLARENDON . . . . Villiers	DUCIE . . . . Moreton
BELLWIN . . . . Bellow	CLEDWYN OF PENRHOS . . . . . Hughes	DUDLEY, Baroness . . . . Hamilton, Wallace
BELMORE . . . . Lowry-Corry	CLINTON . . . . . Fane, Fane Trefusis	DUDLEY, Earl of . . . . Ward
BELPER . . . . Strutt	CLITHEROE . . . . Assheton	DUFFERIN AND CLANEBOYE . . . Blackwood
BELSTEAD . . . . Ganzoni	CLWYD . . . . Roberts	DULVERTON . . . . Wills
BERKELEY . . . . Gueterbock	CLYDESMUIR . . . . Colville	DUNALLEY . . . . Prittie
BERNERS . . . . Kirkham, Pollock	COBBOLD . . . . Lytton Cobbold	DUNBOYNE . . . . Butler
BESSBOROUGH . . . . Ponsonby	COBHAM . . . . Lyttelton	DUNDEE . . . . Scrymgeour,
BICESTER . . . . Smith	COLERAINE . . . . Law	Scrymgeour(-)Wedderburn
BIDDULPH . . . Biddulph, Maitland-Biddulph	COLGRAIN . . . . Campbell	DUNDONALD . . . . Cochrane
BLAKENHAM . . . . Hare	COLWYN . . . . Smith	DUNLEATH . . . . Mulholland
BLEDISLOE . . . . Bathurst	COLYTON . . . . Hopkinson	DUNMORE . . . . Murray
BOLINGBROKE and SAINT JOHN . . . St John	COMBERMERE . . . . . Stapleton-Cotton	DUNRAVEN AND
BOLTON . . . . Orde-Powlett	CONGLETON . . . . Parnell	MOUNT-EARL . . . . . . Wyndham-Quin
BOSTON . . . . Irby	CORK and ORRERY . . . . Boyle	DUNROSSIL . . . . Morrison
BOYD OF MERTON . . . . . Lennox-Boyd	COTTENHAM . . . . Pepys	DUNSANY . . . . Plunkett
BOYNE . . . . Hamilton-Russell	COTTESLOE . . . . Fremantle	DURHAM . . . . Lambton
BRABAZON OF TARA . . . . Moore-Brabazon	COURTOWN . . . Stopford, Stopford-Sackville	DYNEVOR . . . . Rhys
BRABOURNE . . . . Knatchbull	COWDRAY . . . . Pearson	DYSART . . . . . . Grant of Rothiemurchus,
BRADFORD . . . . Bridgeman	COWLEY . . . . Wellesley	Greaves, Tollemache
BRAYBROOKE . . . . Neville	CRAIGAVON . . . . Craig	EBURY . . . . Grosvenor
BRAYE . . . . Aubrey-Fletcher	CRAIGMYLE . . . . Shaw	EDINBURGH . . . . Mountbatten
BRENTFORD . . . . Joynson-Hicks	CRANBROOK . . . . Gathorne-Hardy	EFFINGHAM . . . . Howard

(II) IN ALPHABETICAL ORDER OF SURNAME

LANSDOWNE

Arms: Quarterly, 1st and 4th, ermine on a bend azure a magnetic needle pointing at a polar star or (for PETTY); 2nd and 3rd, argent a saltire gules, a chief ermine (for FitzMAURICE). **Crests:** 1 A beehive beset with bees diversely volante proper, 2 A centaur drawing a bow and arrow proper, the part from the waist argent. **Supporters:** Two pegasi ermine, bridled, crined, winged and unguled or, each charged on the shoulder with a fleur-de-lys azure. **Motto:** *Virtute non verbis* ('By courage, not words'). **Creations:** B. (by prescription) (I) 1295 (Kerry and Lixnaw), V. and E. (I) 17 Jan 1722/3 (Clanmaurice and Kerry respectively), B. and V. (I) 7 Oct 1751 (Dunkeron and Fitzmaurice respectively), E. (I) 6 June 1753 (Shelburne), B. (GB) 20 May 1760 (Wycombe), M., E. and V. (GB) 6 Dec 1784 (Lansdowne, Wycombe of Chepping Wycombe and Calne and Calston respectively).

THE 8TH MARQUESS OF LANSDOWNE, Co Somerset, **Earl of Kerry**, **Earl of Shelburne**, Co Wexford, **Earl Wycombe of Chepping Wycombe**, Co Buckingham, **Viscount Clanmaurice**, **Viscount Fitzmaurice**, **Viscount Calne and Calston**, Co Wilts, **Baron of Kerry** and **Lixnaw**, **Baron Dunkeron**, and **Lord Wycombe, Baron of Chipping Wycombe**, Co Buckingham (George John Charles Mercer Nairne Petty-FitzMaurice, PC (1964), JP (Perthshire 1950), DL (Wilts 1952)) [The Most Hon The Marquess of Lansdowne PC JP DL, Meikleour House, Perthshire PH2 6EA]; *b* 27 Nov 1912 (HM GEORGE V stood sponsor); *s* cousin 1944; *educ* Eton and Ch Ch Oxford; Maj RSG, formerly 2nd Lt Scottish Horse (TA), WW II (Croix de Guerre), Ld in Waiting 1957–58, Jt Parly U-Sec FO 1958–62, Min State Cwlth and Colonial Affrs 1962–64, UK alternate Rep Cncl Europe and WEU 1957 and 1958, chm: Victoria League 1946–89, Malaysian Inter-Govtl Ctee 1963, Franco-Br Soc 1972–83; memb Exec Ctee Nat Art Collections Fund 1973–, Sec Jr Unionist League E Scotland 1939, Pres: Wessex Provincial Area Nat Union C and U Assocs 1959–63, Franco-Scottish Soc, Officers' Families Fund; Priv Sec to Br Amb Paris 1944, memb Roy Co Archers, Prime Warden Fishmongers' Co 1967–68, Cdr Legn Hon 1979; *m* 1st 18 March 1938 Barbara (*d* 17 Feb 1965), dau of Harold Stuart Chase, of Santa Barbara, California, by Gertrude Boyer, and has had:

1 +CHARLES MAURICE, *Earl of Shelburne*, DL (Wilts 1990) [Earl of Shelburne DL, Bowood House, Calne, Wilts SN11 0LZ]; *b* 21 Feb 1941; *educ* Eton; Page of Hon to HM THE QUEEN 1956–57, late Kenya Regt, Lt Roy Wilts Yeo (TA) and Wessex Yeo, fought (C) Coventry NE 1979, memb: Wilts CC 1970–85, SW Ec Planning Cncl 1972–77, Historic Buildings and Monuments Commn 1983–89, Prince's Cncl 1990–; Pres: Wilts Playing Fields Assoc 1965–74, Wilts Assoc Boys and Youth Clubs 1976–, Chm Calne & Chippenham RDC 1972–73 and N Wilts DC 1973–76, HHA 1988–93 (Dep Pres 1986–88); *m* 1st 9 Oct 1965 (*divorce* 1987) Lady Frances Helen Mary Eliot, only dau of 9th Earl of Saint Germans (*qv*); *m* 2nd 1987 *Fiona Mary, dau of Donald Merritt, and by his 1st w has:

  (1) +Simon Henry George, *Viscount Calne and Calstone*; *b* 24 Nov 1970

  (2) +William Nicholas Charles; *b* 25 Sept 1973

  (1) *Arabella Helen Mary; *b* 30 Aug 1966; *m* 1993 *Rupert W H Unwin, yr s of Martin I H Unwin, of Shipton Moyne, Glos, and has:

    1a *Abrahm [*sic*] Arthur George; *b* 15 Nov 1996

  (2) *Rachel Barbara Violet; *b* 30 Jan 1968; *m* 1991 *James William Richard Spickernell (*see* LEICESTER, E) and has:

    1a *Benjamin Thomas Richard; *b* 15 Sept 1994

    2a *Frederick Charles William; *b* 16 Oct 1996

2 +Robert Harold [The Lord Robert Mercer Nairne Petty-Fitzmaurice, The Old Manse, Kinclaven, by Stanley, Perth]; *b* 16 Feb 1947; *educ* Gordonstoun, Kent U (BA 1969), Washington U (MBA 1971, PhD); FBIM; *m* 1 Nov 1972 *Jane Elizabeth, only dau of Lord Douglas Claude Alexander Gordon (*see* HUNTLY, M), and has:

  (1) +Samuel George; *b* 1976

  (2) +Joseph Douglas; *b* 1980

  (1) *Emily Jane; *b* 3 Aug 1974

1 Caroline Margaret; *b* 8 Jan 1939; *d* unm 27 Sept 1956

2 *Georgina Elizabeth; *b* 10 Jan 1950; *m* 1st 1974 (*divorce* 1980) Guy Hamilton; *m* 2nd *Robert Eric Miller and by her 1st husb has:

  (1) *Josiah Stirling; *b* 1975

  (2) *Emma Carissa; *b* 1977

The 8th MARQUESS *m* 2nd 1969 (*divorce* 1978) Hon Selina Polly Dawson Eccles, only dau of 1st Viscount Eccles (*qv*) and formerly w of Robin Andrew Duthac Carnegie (*see* SOUTHESK, E); *m* 3rd 1978 Gillian Ann (*d* 1982), dau of Alured Morgan; *m* 4th 12 July 1995 *Penelope Eve, dau of Cdr George Francis Norton Bradford, RN, formerly w of David Rolt and widow of Hon John Astor (*see* ASTOR OF HEVER, B)

Lansdown, previous creation: George Granville, nephew of John, Earl of Bath (*see* BATH, M, preliminary remarks), was created Baron Lansdown of Biddeford [*sic*], in the Co of Devon, on New Year's day 1711/2. His grandfather Sir Bevil Granville had been killed in battle during the Civil War in 1643 at Lansdown Hill, near Bath, just as he was defeating the Parliamentary army under Sir William Waller, hence George's choice of title. The new Lord Lansdown of Biddeford was suspected of Jacobitism and imprisoned in the Tower of London for nearly a year and a half about the time of the 1715 Uprising. He was indeed created titular Duke of Albemarle by the Old Pretender, James III, so there were clearly some grounds for the authorities' suspicions. He died in January 1734/5, when the title expired. His wife Mary was widow of Thomas Thynne, of the Marquess of Bath's family.

Lord Lansdown of Biddeford's uncle, the Earl of Bath mentioned above, had as a subsidiary title that of Viscount Granville of Lansdown. His great-granddaughter was the Lady Sophia Carteret who married the 1st Marquess of Lansdowne of the current creation, hence the latter's choice of title when promoted to a marquessate.

Lineage: ROBERT FitzMAURICE (*see* LEINSTER, D); held lands in Tipperkevin, Co Kildare, and seems to have had a grant of the cantred (administrative unit akin to a shire hundred) of Otornas and Oflannon, Co Kerry, which formed the basis of the later territory of Clanmaurice; had:

1 Gerald fitz Robert; *d* between 1252 and 1262, leaving:

  (1)Agatha; *m* David de St Michael, feudal Baron of Reban, Co Kildare

  (2) Mabel; *m* James de Bermingham, feudal Ld of Tethmoy

2 Thomas fitz Robert (Sir); ktd by 1261; seems to have been granted the Kerry lands by his bro Gerald towards the end of the latter's life; already held Malahiff and other lands in Kerry; fndr Franciscan Friary of Ardfert; had, with a dau (Nesta):

  (1) MAURICE Fitz THOMAS, **1st Baron of Kerry** and **Lixnaw** (I), *cr* apparently by a sitting in Parl 1295; *m* 1st Ellen, dau and heiress of William fitz Elias, with whom he got Listowel and other lands in the cantred of Altry, Co Kerry; *m* 2nd Sibyl — and *d* on or after 14 April 1305, leaving by her a s (Gerald) and by his 1st w, with two yr sons (Peter/Piers, ancestor of the PIERSEs of Co Kerry; Robert):

    1a NICHOLAS Fitz MAURICE, **2nd Baron of Kerry** and **Lixnaw**; ktd 1312; allegedly *m* Slany, dau of Connor O'Brien, Prince of Thomond (*see* INCHIQUIN, B), and *d* 1317, leaving:

      1b William; *k* Dermod *Og* ('The Younger'), Chief of the MacCarthys, in court before the Judge of Assize at Tralee, Co Kerry, 1325, for which blinded but not executed, though his lands were forfeited

      2b MAURICE Fitz NICHOLAS, **3rd Baron of Kerry** and **Lixnaw**; captured by Maurice, 1st Earl of Desmond, and sentenced to death (being starved) in prison at Castle Island, Co Kerry, 16 Aug 1339; *m* Honora, dau of O'Connor, of Kerry, and had a s (David, *dsp* & *vp*)

      3b JOHN, **4th Baron**

      1b Aveline; *m* her cousin Maurice fitz Thomas, Earl of Desmond

The 3rd BARON's bro,

JOHN Fitz NICHOLAS, **4th Baron of Kerry** and **Lixnaw**; styled 'Lord of Kerry' 1345; apparently ktd by 1374; had the family estates restored; *m* 1st his cousin Honora/Margaret, dau of O'Brien of Thomond, and had issue; *m* 2nd Elinor, dau of Gerald fitz Pierce, and had two sons (Garrett/Gerald, ancestor of the FitzMAURICEs of Duagh; Robert); his s by his 1st w:

MAURICE Fitz JOHN FITZ NICHOLAS, **5th Baron of Kerry** and **Lixnaw**; *m* 1st *c* 1355 Elizabeth (*d* 27 July 1364), dau of David de Caunton, and had a s (John, *dsp* & *vp* *c* Jan 1364/5); *m* 2nd his cousin Joan fitz Maurice and *d* allegedly in 1398, having by her had, with other issue:

PATRICK Fitz MAURICE Fitz JOHN or FitzMAURICE (this surname seems to have been adopted about now), **6th Baron of Kerry** and **Lixnaw**, also called 'The Bearded'; composed a quarrel May 1421 with his cousin James FitzGerald, Earl of Desmond, over certain rights in Kerry, the agreement on the whole favouring the Earl; *m* *c* 27 March 1422 his cousin Catherine, dau of Teig MacCarthy *Mor* ('The Great' or 'The Elder'), and had, with a yr s (Edmond, *k* 1446):

THOMAS FitzMAURICE, **7th Baron of Kerry** and **Lixnaw**, also called 'The Stammerer'; *m* *c* 21 Oct 1447 his cousin Anore/Honora, dau of James Geraldine, Earl of Desmond, and *d* after 1479, having had, with two yr sons (Robert, ancestor of the FitzMAURICEs of Ardglas and Tubrid; John, apptd Abbot of Rattoo 1488) and a dau (Mary, *m* her cousin Thomas, Knight of Glin, and had issue):

EDMOND FitzMAURICE, **8th Baron of Kerry** and **Lixnaw**; *m* *More*, dau of Connor O'Connor, of Kerry, and *d* 1510, having had, with a yr s (Gerald, *m* *Joan, dau of the Knight of Glin, and had, with an er s (John, *dsp*), Richard, who *m* Una, dau of Gerald *Og* Stack, and was f of Gerald, living 1597, who *m* Ellen, dau of Connor MacAuliffe, and had two sons, Richard and Edmond):

EDMOND FitzMAURICE, **9th Baron of Kerry** and **Lixnaw**; attended the Dublin Parl which proclaimed HENRY VIII KING OF IRELAND June 1541 and signed the report to the KING; *m* 1st Una, dau of Teig MacMahon, of Corcavasey, in Thomond, and had issue; *m* 2nd Amy (by whom he had no issue), dau of Turlogh Mac-I-Brien-Ara and widow of 10th Earl of Desmond, and *d* while attending the next session of Parl at Limerick Nov 1541, leaving by his 1st w:

1 Edmond; *m* a dau of Dermod O'Connor Kerry and *dvp* *c* 1540, leaving a dau (*m* Dermod macTeig MacCarthy, of Molahiff)

2 PATRICK FitzMAURICE, **10th Baron of Kerry** and **Lixnaw**; *m* Slany (*m* 2nd Sir Donald O'Brien, of Dough), dau of 1st Earl of Thomond (*see* INCHIQUIN, B), and *d c* 1543, about a year after his f, leaving:

(1) EDMOND FitzMAURICE, **11th Baron of Kerry** and **Lixnaw**; *d* young a year after his f 1544

(2) THOMAS FitzMAURICE, **12th Baron of Kerry** and **Lixnaw**; *d* young 1545 a month after his bro

3 GERALD FitzMAURICE, **13th Baron of Kerry** and **Lixnaw**, called 'The Redhaired'; *m* 1550 Julia (*m* 2nd Cormac McCarthy Reagh, of Carbery), dau of Cormac *Og* MacCarthy, of Muskerry, and was *k* 1545 two months after succeeding his n

4 THOMAS FitzMAURICE, **14th Baron of Kerry** and **Lixnaw**, PC (I); *b c* 1520; soldier in Imperial armies Italy till *c* 1545, when *s* bro; confirmed in possession as Baron of Lacksnaway (Lixnaw) by QUEEN MARY 23 Oct 1553; ktd 1567; rebelled against ELIZABETH I 1583–85; *m* 1st Lady Margaret FitzGerald (*d* 1563), dau of James Fitz John FitzGerald, Earl of Desmond, by his 2nd w Móre, dau of Maolrony O'Carroll, and had:

(1) PATRICK, **15th Baron**

(2) Edmund; went to Spain and was living 1631; had a dau (Mary, *m* Teige MacCarthy, of Cosmange)

(3) Robert; *k* Isles of Arran, leaving a s (Gerald, Ch Cdr under PHILIP III OF SPAIN)

(1) Joan; *m* 3rd Earl of Thomond (*see* INCHIQUIN, B)

4 (cont.) The **14th Baron** *m* 2nd (repudiated her 1580 so he could *m* the widow of James FitzMaurice, but may have remarried her) Finola/Penelope, dau of Sir Donal O'Brien, bro of 3rd Earl of Thomond (*see* INCHIQUIN, B); *m* 3rd Catherine (*d* 1582), dau of Teig MacCarthy *Mor*, er bro of Donal, 1st Earl of Clancare, and *d* 16 Dec 1590, having had no issue by them

His est s,

PATRICK FitzMAURICE, **15th Baron of Kerry** and **Lixnaw**; *b c* 1541; *m* Jane Roche, dau of David, 5th Lord Roche of Fermoy (*see* FERMOY, B, preliminary remarks), and had:

1 THOMAS, **16th Baron**

2 Gerald; Capt in Spanish serv; *d* Louvain Sept 1632

3 Maurice; *m* 1st Honora, dau of Teig MacMahon, of W Corcavaskin, and had:

(1) Elizabeth; *m* Owen MacCarthy, of Drishane

3 (cont.) Maurice FitzMaurice *m* 2nd Eleanor, dau of Thomas FitzGerald, of Ballygleaghan (now Holly Park), Co Limerick, and by her had:

(1) Gerald; Capt; *m* Katherine, dau of John Pierse, of Ballymacaquim, and had a s (Gerald, *d* Denmark 1673)

(2) Thomas; Capt in Tangier; *m* Eleanor, dau of Florence MacCarthy, s of MacCarthy *Mor*, and had a s (William) and a dau (Eleanor)

(1) Eleanor; *m* Capt John Hussey

4 Robert

1 Joan; *m* Donal O'Sullivan *Mor*, of Dunkerron, Co Kerry, Chief of his name

The 15th BARON *d* 12 Aug 1600; his est son,

THOMAS FitzMAURICE, **16th Baron of Kerry** and **Lixnaw**; *b* 1574; pardoned for his and his f's rebellion 1603, his estates restored him 1604, restoration confirmed 1612; *m* 1st *c* 1594 Lady Honora O'Brien (*d* 1600), dau of 3rd Earl of Thomond (*see* INCHIQUIN, B), and had, with other issue:

1 PATRICK, **17th Baron**

1 Joan; *m* George FitzHarris, of Clonodfoy, Co Limerick

The **16th Baron** *m* 2nd 1615 Gille/Julia Power, dau of 4th Baron Le Power and Coroghmore (*see* WATERFORD, M), and by her had:

2 Edmund, of Galey, Co Kerry; Col; *m* Ellena McCarthy, dau of 1st Viscount Muskerry (*qv*, preliminary remarks) of the 1628 *cr*, and had:

(1) Thomas; *m* Eleanor/Elena, dau of Dermot MaccCarthy, of Ballea, Co Cork

3 Garrett; Col; *m* Lady Lucia Touchet, dau of 2nd Earl of Castlehaven (*see* 1970 edn AUDLEY, B), and *d* 16 Dec 1662, leaving:

(1) Richard; Capuchin friar as Fr Cyprian, Pncpl of the Order 1689

(1) Eleanor; *m* Sir Turlough MacMahon, Bt, and *dsp*

(2) Katherine; *m* 1st James Barry; *m* 2nd Capt John Stevenson

4 Richard; Col; *ka* Battle of Newbury 1644

5 Thomas; *m* Ellen, dau of David, Viscount Roche of Fermoy (*see* FERMOY, B, preliminary remarks), and widow of 1st Viscount Muskerry of the 1628 *cr*, and *dsp*

6 Robert; Col; *d* unm 1680

2 Katherine; *m* John FitzGerald, 12th Knight of Kerry (*see* FitzGERALD, Bt, of Valencia)

3 Margaret; *m* 1st Walter Bermingham, of Dunfert, Co Kildare; *m* 2nd by 1654 2nd Lord Bourke, Baron of Brittas; *m* 3rd Col Charles O'More, of Ballina, Co Kildare, and *d* 13 June 1638

4 Mary; *m* 1st Maj-Gen Patrick Purcell (executed under Commonwealth 1652), of Croagh, Co Limerick; *m* 2nd James Butler, of Kilmoyler, Co Tipperary

The 16th BARON *d* 3 June 1630; his est s,

PATRICK FitzMAURICE, **17th Baron of Kerry** and **Lixnaw**; *b* 1595; brought up a Protestant; *m* by March 1617/8 Honora, dau of Sir Edmond FitzGerald, of Ballymaloe and Cloyne, Co Cork, and had, with an est s (*dvp*) and four other daus:

1 WILLIAM, **18th Baron**

2 Raymond; *m* 1st Anne (*d* March 1681), dau of 1st Baron Barry of Santry, and had two sons (the er, Thomas, being of Gortacrossane, Co Kerry); *m* 2nd Elizabeth, dau of Henry Kenny, MP, of Kenny's Hall, Co Wexford, and *d* 5 July 1713

1 Honora; *m* William Fenton

2 Jane; *m* as his 2nd w Thomas Leigh, s of 1st Baron Leigh of Stoneleigh (*see* LEIGH, B), and had issue; *m* 2nd Richard Giffard; *m* 3rd — Bagot

3 Elizabeth; *m* 1st Thomas Amory, Victualler Navy; *m* 2nd Charles O'Connor Kerry and *d* 13 Sept 1733 aged 83

4 Mary; *m* Sir Ignatius White, Bt, *cr* Marquis d'Abbeville in France, Eng Amb The Hague 1686–88

---

5 Margaret; *m* 29 March 1660, as his 3rd w, 4th Baron Teynham (*qv*)

The 17th BARON was *bur* 5 Jan 1660/1; his est s,

WILLIAM FitzMAURICE, **18th Baron of Kerry** and **Lixnaw**; *b* 1633; fought for JAMES II Battle of the Boyne 1690 and went with JAMES to France afterwards; *m c* 1665 Constance, dau of William Long, wineseller, of the Rose Tavern, Covent Gdn, London, and had, with two daus:

1 THOMAS, **1st Earl**

2 William, of Gallane, Co Kerry; Col; *m* Deborah, dau of Sir John Brookes, Bt, and *d* 1710, leaving:

(1) John, of Springfield Castle, Co Limerick; *m* his cousin Anne, dau of Hon James FitzMaurice, of Kilmihill (*see* below); and had:

1a John, of Springfield Castle; had:

1b Anne; *m* 1st Baron Muskerry (*qv*)

(1) Mary; *m* her cousin **1st Earl of Shelburne** and had issue (*see* below)

(2) Elizabeth; *m* Josiah Hort, Archbp Tuam

3 James, of Kilmihill; Capt; *m* Catherine, dau and heiress of William Harman, of Dublin, and had:

(1) Harman; *m* Margaret, dau of Gamaliel Fitzgerald

(1) Anne; *m* 1st 1720 John Odell, of Bolderoghy; *m* 2nd 1732 her cousin John FitzMaurice (*see* above)

1 Honora; *m* Sir William Piers, Bt, of Tristernagh

2 Constance; *m* John Odell, of Ballingarry, Co Limerick

The 18th BARON *d* March 1696/7; his est s,

THOMAS FitzMAURICE, **1st Earl of Kerry**, so *cr* 17 Jan 1722/3, as also VISCOUNT CLANMAURICE (both I), PC (I by April 1711); *b* 1668; made his peace with WILLIAM III; MP (I Parl) Co Kerry 1692–93 and 1695–97; *m* 14 Jan 1692/3 Anne (*d* Nov 1737), only dau of Sir William Petty, MD, FRS, Oxford Prof of Anatomy 1651, by Elizabeth (*cr* BARONESS SHELBURNE for life 13 Dec 1688; *d* Feb 1708), widow of Sir Michael Fenton, Bt, of Mitchelstown, Co Cork, and dau of Sir Hardress Waller, of Castletown, Co Limerick, and sis of (a) 1st and last Baron Shelburne of the 1688 *cr* and (b) 1st and last Earl of Shelburne of the 1719 *cr* (*see* CORK and ORRERY, E), and *d* 16 March 1741, having had, with three other sons (*dvp*):

1 WILLIAM FitzMAURICE, **2nd Earl of Kerry**, PC (I 1746); *bapt* 2 March 1694/5; Col Coldstream Gds, Govr Ross Castle, Co Kerry, 1721, Govr Co Kerry 1746, Ld Lt Co Kerry; *m* 1st 1730 Elizabeth (*dsp* 29 Feb 1736), dau of — Moss and widow of — Leeson; *m* 2nd 29 June 1738 Lady Gertrude Lambart (*m* 2nd 7 July 1750 James Tilson, of Pallis, King's Co, and *d* Oct 1775), dau of 4th Earl of Cavan (*qv*), and *d* 4 April 1747, having had by her:

(1) FRANCIS THOMAS FitzMAURICE, **3rd Earl of Kerry**; *b* 9 Sept 1740; *m c* 18 March 1768 Anastacia (*d* 9 April 1799), divorced w of Charles Daly, of Loughrea, Co Galway, and dau and coheir of Peter Daly, of Quansbury, Co Galway, and *dsp* 4 July 1818

(1) Anna Maria; *m* 10 June 1764 Maurice FitzGerald, Knight of Kerry (*see* FitzGERALD, Bt, of Valentia)

2 JOHN FitzMAURICE later PETTY (on inheriting 1741 estates of his maternal uncle 1st and last Earl of Shelburne of the 1719 *cr*), **1st Earl of Shelburne**, Co Wexford, so *cr* 6 June 1753, as also earlier 7 Oct 1751 BARON DUNKERON and VISCOUNT FITZMAURICE (all I); also 20 May 1760 LORD WYCOMBE, BARON OF CHEPPING WYCOMBE, Co Buckingham (GB), PC (I 8 Feb 1753/4); *b* 1706; *educ* Westminster and Middle Temple; Sheriff Co Kerry 1732, MP (Whig I Parl) Co Kerry 1743–51, Govr Co Kerry 1754, MP (GB Parl) Chipping Wycombe 1754–60; *m* 16 Feb 1734 his 1st cousin Mary, dau of Hon William FitzMaurice, of Gallane, Co Kerry (*see* above), and *d* 14 May 1761, having had:

(1) WILLIAM FitzMAURICE later PETTY, **2nd Earl of Shelburne** and **1st Marquess of Lansdowne**, Co Somerset, so *cr* 6 Dec 1784, as also EARL WYCOMBE OF CHEPPING WYCOMBE, Co Buckingham, and VISCOUNT CALNE AND CALSTON, Co Wilts (all GB), KG (1782), PC (1763); *b* 2 May 1737; joined Army 1757, Gen 1783, MP Chipping Wycombe 1760–61, First Ld Trade April–Dec 1763, Sec State for the South 1766–68, For Sec March–July 1782, PM 1782–83; *m* 1st 3 Feb 1765 Lady Sophia Carteret (*d* 5 Jan 1771), dau of John, Earl Granville, and had:

1a JOHN HENRY PETTY, **2nd Marquess of Lansdowne**; *b* 6 Dec 1765; MP (Whig) Chipping Wycombe 1786–1802; *m* 27 May 1805 Mary Arabella (*d* 24 April 1833), widow of (Sir) Duke Gifford, self-styled Baronet, of Castle Jordan, Co Meath, and dau of Rev Hinton Maddock, and *dsp* 15 Nov 1809

(1) (cont.) The **1st Marquess** *m* 2nd 19 July 1779 Lady Louisa Fitzpatrick (*d* 7 Aug 1789), dau of 1st Earl of Upper Ossory, and *d* 7 May 1805, having by her had, with a dau (Louisa, *d* young):

2a HENRY PETTY later PETTY-FitzMAURICE (1818), **3rd Marquess of Lansdowne** and **4th Earl of Kerry** (as which s cousin 1818), KG (1836), PC (1806); *b* 2 July 1780; *educ* Westminster, Edinburgh and Trin Coll Cambridge; MP (Whig) Calne 1802–06, Cambridge U 1806–07 and Camelford 1807–09, Chllr Exchequer 1806–07, Home Sec 1827–28, Ld Pres Cncl 1830–34, 1835–41 and 1846–52 and in Cabinet without office 1852–58, Ld Lt Wilts 1827–63, FRS 1811, Ld Rector Glasgow U 1827–31; *m* 30 March 1808 Lady Louisa Emma Fox-Strangways (*d* 3 April 1851), 5th dau of 2nd Earl of Ilchester (*qv*), and had:

1b William Thomas, *Earl of Kerry*, MP; *b* 30 March 1811; *m* 18 March 1834 Lady Augusta Lavinia Priscilla Ponsonby (*m* 2nd 2 April 1845 Hon Charles Alexander Gore and *d* 19 Nov 1904, leaving issue (*see* ARRAN, E)), 2nd dau of 4th Earl of Bessborough (*qv*), and *dvp* 21 Aug 1836, leaving:

1c Mary Caroline; *m* 4 Oct 1860 Lt-Gen Rt Hon Sir Percy Egerton Herbert, PC, KCB, MP (*d* 7 Oct 1876), and *d* 17 Sept 1927, having had issue (*see* POWIS, E)

2b HENRY, **4th Marquess**

1b Louisa; *m* 10 Feb 1845 Hon James Kenneth Howard, and *d* 12 June 1906, leaving issue (*see* SUFFOLK and BERKSHIRE, E)

(2) Thomas, of Llewenny Hall, Denbighs; *m* 21 Dec 1777 Mary, Countess of Orkney in her own right, and *d* 28 Oct 1793, leaving issue (*see* ORKNEY, E)

1 Elizabeth Anne; *m* Dec 1712 1st Baron Branden (*see* 1832 edn) and *d* 17 Dec 1757

2 Arabella; *m* Arthur Denny (*see* DENNY, Bt, of Castlemoyle)

3 Charlotte; *m* Sir John Conway Colthurst, 1st Bt (*qv*)

The 3rd MARQUESS *d* 31 Jan 1863; his only surv son,

HENRY PETTY-FitzMAURICE, **4th Marquess of Lansdowne**, KG (1864); *b* 7 Jan 1816; *educ* Westminster and Trin Coll Cambridge; MP (Lib) Calne 1837–56, a Ld Treasury 1847–48, chm GWR, called up to Ho Lds 11 July 1856 *vp* in f's Barony of Wycombe, Parly U-Sec For Affrs 1856–58; *m* 1st 18 Aug 1840 Lady Georgina Herbert (*dsp* 28 Feb 1841), dau of 11th Earl of Pembroke and (7th Earl of) Montgomery (*qv*); *m* 2nd 1 Nov 1843 Emily Jane Mercer Elphinstone de Flahault, Lady Nairne in her own right (*see* MERSEY, V), and had:

1 HENRY CHARLES KEITH, **5th Marquess**

2 EDMOND GEORGE PETTY-FitzMAURICE, 1st and last BARON FitzMAURICE, of Leigh, Wilts (UK), so *cr* 9 Jan 1906; *b* 19 June 1846; MA Cantab, barrister Lincoln's Inn, MP Calne 1868–85 and N Wilts 1898–1905, Br Rep Commn reorganisation European Provinces of Turkey and Crete under Berlin Treaty 1880–81, 2nd Br Plen London Conf Navigation Danube 1883, Boundary Commr Local Govt Act 1887, 1st Br Plen London Conf on African Sleeping Sickness 1907–08, Parly U-Sec For Affrs 1882–85 and 1905–08, Chllr Duchy Lancaster 1908–09, author: *The Lives* of Earl Granville, Sir William Petty and the Earl of Shelburne, and other works, FBA, Hon DLitt Bristol; *m* 23 Nov 1889 (*anulled* 1894) Caroline, dau of W J FitzGerald, of Litchfield, Conn., and *dsp* 21 June 1935, when the 1906 Barony expired

1 Emily Louisa Anne; *m* 2 June 1886 Col Hon Everard Charles Digby, Gren Gds, and *d* 2 Dec 1939, leaving issue (*see* DIGBY, B)

The 4th MARQUESS *d* 5 July 1866; his er son,

HENRY CHARLES KEITH PETTY-FitzMAURICE, **5th Marquess of Lansdowne**, KG (1894), GCSI (1888), GCIE (1888), GCMG (1884), PC (1895); *b* 14 Jan 1845; *educ* Eton (Fell 1880–83) and Balliol Coll Oxford; a Ld Treasury (Lib) 1868–72, Parly U-Sec: War 1872–74, India 1880; Govr Gen Canada 1883–88, Viceroy India 1888–94, Sec State: War 1895–1900, For Affrs 1900–05 and Min Without Portfolio 1915–16, Hon Col Roy Wilts Yeo, MA, Hon DCL Oxon, Hon LLD McGill, Cantab and Leeds U, Ld Lt Wilts 1896–1920, Tstee Nat Gallery, Chm Cncl BRCS 1915–20, Chllr Order St Michael and St George 1917–20, Roy Victorian Chain; *m* 8 Nov 1869 Lady Maud Evelyn Hamilton (*d* 21 Oct 1932), dau of 1st Duke of Abercorn (*qv*), and *d* 3 June 1927, having had:

1 HENRY WILLIAM EDMOND PETTY-FitzMAURICE, **6th Marquess of Lansdowne**, DSO, MVO (1905), DL (Co Kerry); *b* 14 Jan 1872; *educ* Eton and Balliol Coll Oxford; MP (U) W Derbys 1908–18, Lt-Col Res of Offrs Irish Gds, formerly Lt Gren Gds, Boer War 1899–1900 and WW I, FSA, Kt Cdr Charles III Spain and Legn Hon; *m* 16 Feb 1904 Elizabeth Caroline, JP (1943), CC (1943–45) Wilts (*m* 2nd 14 Feb 1940 Lord Colum Crichton-Stuart, 3rd s of 3rd Marquess of Bute (*qv*), and *d* 25 March 1964), only dau of Sir Edward Stanley Hope, KCB (*see* LINLITHGOW, M), and *d* 5 March 1936, having had:

(1) Henry Maurice John, *Earl of Kerry*; *b* 7 Oct 1913; *d* 12 Sept 1933

(2) CHARLES HOPE PETTY-FitzMAURICE, **7th Marquess of Lansdowne**; *b* 9 Jan 1917; *educ* Eton and Balliol Coll Oxford (BA 1938); Capt Roy Wilts Yeo WW I 1939–44 (wounded); *ka* Italy 20 Aug 1944

(3) Edward Norman; Lt Irish Gds WW II; *b* 28 July 1922; *educ* Eton and Balliol Coll Oxford; *ka* 11 Aug 1944

(1) KATHERINE EVELYN CONSTANCE, *s* bro as LADY NAIRNE (*see* MERSEY, V) in her own right

(2) *Elizabeth Mary [The Lady Elizabeth Lambton, The Old Rectory, Calstone Wellington, Calne, Wilts]; *b* 16 March 1927; *m* 27 June 1950 *Maj Charles William Lambton and has issue (*see* DURHAM, E)

2 Charles George Francis PETTY-FitzMAURICE later MERCER NAIRNE PETTY-FitzMAURICE (1 Jan 1914), MVO, of Meikleour and Tullybeagles, Perthshire, and Aldie, Kinross-shire; Maj 1st Dragoons, Equerry in Ordinary to HM GEORGE V when PRINCE OF WALES 1909–10, Equerry 1910–14, ADC to FM Earl Roberts Boer War 1899–1900, served WW I; *b* 12 Feb 1874; *m* 20 Jan 1909 Lady Violet Mary Elliot Murray-Kynynmound (*m* 2nd 28 Aug 1916 1st Baron Astor of Hever (*qv*) and *d* 3 Jan 1965), yst dau of 4th Earl of Minto (*qv*), and was *ka* 30 Oct 1914, leaving:

(1) GEORGE JOHN CHARLES MERCER NAIRNE later NAIRNE PETTY-FitzMAURICE (decree of Lord Lyon 1947), **8th and present Marquess of Lansdowne**

(1) *(Mary) Margaret Elizabeth [The Lady Margaret Myddelton, Chirk Castle, nr Wrexham, N Wales]; *b* 6 Feb 1910 (HM QUEEN MARY stood sponsor); granted 1946 rank of marquess's dau; *m* 27 July 1931 Lt-Col Ririd Myddelton, MVO, DL, Coldstream Gds (*d* 1988), s of Col Robert Edward Myddelton, TD, JP, DL, of Chirk Castle, and has:

1a *David Foulk [David Myddelton Esq, New Hall, Chirk, Wrexham LL14 5AD]; Capt late Coldstream Gds, High Sheriff Clwyd 1980; *b* 25 May 1932; *educ* Eton; *m* 1st 5 Jan 1965 (*divorce* 1969) Anne, only dau of Charles Frederick Ratcliffe-Brotherton, JP, of Kirkham Abbey, Yorks, and has:

1b *Guy Charles; *b* 17 Jan 1966

1a (cont.) David Myddelton *m* 2nd 1970 *Christine Serena Cherry, dau of Arthur Malcolm Morris, OBE, Dept External Affrs, Canberra, Australia, and by her has:

2b *Mark Ririd; *b* 1973

1b *Sian Moyra; *b* 1971

2a *Hugh Robert [Hugh Myddelton Esq, 139 Holland Park Ave, London W11]; *b* 17 Oct 1938; *educ* Eton; late Coldstream Gds; *m* 27 July 1967 *Hon Sarah Cecily Allsopp, only dau of 5th Baron Hindlip (*qv*), and has:

1b *Alexander Ririd Henry; *b* 7 March 1969

1b *Claerwen Georgina Margaret; *b* 1972; *m* 19 Oct 1996 *John H S Maclean, er s of Rev Kenneth Maclean

1a *Fiona Violet, LVO (1980); Ldy-in-Waiting to HRH PRINCESS MARGARET, COUNTESS OF SNOWDON 1960; *b* 24 Sept 1934; *m* 22 July 1963 Capt Alistair Sturgis Aird and has issue (*see* AIRD, Bt)

1 Evelyn Emily Mary, GCVO (1937), JP (Derbys), DJStJ, Hon LLD Leeds; *b* 27 Aug 1870; Mistress Robes to HM QUEEN MARY 1910–53; *m* 30 July 1892 9th Duke of Devonshire (*qv*) and *d* 2 April 1960, leaving issue

---

2 Beatrix Frances, GBE (1919); DGStJ; *b* 25 March 1877; *m* 1st 16 Oct 1897 6th Marquess of Waterford (*d* 1 Dec 1911) and had issue; *m* 2nd 19 Aug 1918 12th Duke of Saint Albans (*qv*) and *d* 5 Aug 1953

LARCOM

Arms: Argent on a mount a hawthorn bush proper, in chief an eagle displayed gules. **Crest:** On a cap of maintenance azure doubled ermine a martlet sable, a fleur-de-lys in its beak or. **Motto:** *Le Roy, la loy* ('The King, the law'). **Creation:** Bt. (UK) 24 Dec 1868.

SIR (CHARLES) CHRISTOPHER ROYDE LARCOM, 5TH BT [Sir Christopher Larcom Bt, 8 The Postern, Barbican, Wood St, London EC2Y 8BJ; 4 Village Cay Marina, PO Box 145, Road Town, Tortola, British Virgin Islands]; *b* 11 Sept 1926; *s f* 1967; *educ* Radley and Clare Coll Cambridge (Wrangler 1947, BA 1947, MA 1951); Lt RN 1947–50; ACA (1954), FCA 1965; memb Lond Stock Exchange 1959–86 (memb Cncl 1970–80), ptnr Grieveson Grant & Co 1960 (ret 1986); *m* 8 Sept 1956 *Barbara Elizabeth, dau of Balfour Bowen, of Eton Lodge, Highwood, Essex, and has:

1 *Mary Elizabeth; *b* 15 Feb 1957; *m* 6 Aug 1983 *Joseph William Arnold, s of J Arnold

2 *Jane Catherine; *b* 4 June 1958; *m* 1988 *Andrew J Edyvean, s of L A Edyvean, of Urchfont, Wilts, and has:

(1) *Charlotte Louise; *b* 1994

3 *Julia Dorothy; *b* 6 Feb 1961; *m* 2 Oct 1982 *John Dyer, est s of Michael Dyer, of Clare House, Great Broxted, Essex, and has:

(1) *Benjamin Charles; *b* 1985

(1) *Sophie Claire; *b* 1984

4 *Anna Balfour; *b* 11 Sept 1962

Lineage: THOMAS LARCOM, of Whippingham, IoW; *b* 1708; settled Alverstoke, Hants; *m* 1731 and *d* 1784, leaving an only s:

THOMAS LARCOM; *b* 15 Dec 1732; *m* Charity Banton and *d* 12 Feb 1768, leaving:

1 Thomas; 1st Lt under Howe (*qv*) Battle of Glorious First of June 1798, made Cdr aboard the *Queen Charlotte* on the morning of the victory; Flag-Capt to Adml Sir Thomas Graves in Newfoundland, cmded the *Russell*, 74 (guns), in Lord Bridport (*qv*)'s action in the W Indies; *d unm* 1804

2 JOSEPH

1 Anne; *d unm*

The 2nd son,

JOSEPH LARCOM; Capt RN; promoted after Glorious First of June 1798; involved in quelling mutiny at The Nore; Post-Capt cmdg the *Hind*, 32, serving W Indies, Bermuda and Nova Scotia; cmded a sqdn off Egypt; Resident Naval Commr Malta; *m* 13 March 1792 Ann, dau of William Hollis, of Laverstoke, and was *bur* Gibraltar 1818, leaving:

1 Joseph Paffard Dickson; *b* 14 Sept 1795; Capt RN; *m* 17 Sept 1844 Westmorland Jane (*d* 20 March 1906), dau of Adml George McKinley, and *dsp* 1 Nov 1850

2 THOMAS AISKEW (Sir), **1st Bt**

1 Mary Anne; *m* 23 Jan 1813 Gen Montagu Burrows (*d* 23 Feb 1848) and *d* 16 April 1832, leaving issue

2 Elizabeth

3 Harriet; *d unm* 8 March 1886

The yr son,

Sir Thomas Aiskew Larcom, 1st Bt (UK), so *cr* 24 Dec 1868, KCB (1860), PC (I 1868); *b* 22 April 1801; 2nd Lt RE 1820, Maj-Gen 1858; i/c Ordnance Survey Office Dublin 1828, Commr Public Works Ireland 1846, U-Sec State Ireland, LLD, FRS; *m* 1 March 1840 Georgina (*d* 15 Dec 1898), only dau of Lt-Gen Sir George D'Aguilar, KCB, and had:

1 George; *b* 10 Dec 1840; ICS, political agent Jungeera, nr Bombay; *d* 16 June 1878

2 Thomas Henry; *b* 7 April 1842; Cdr RN; *d* 14 Aug 1877

3 CHARLES (Sir), **2nd Bt**

4 Arthur, CB; *b* 9 Nov 1847; *educ* Oriel Coll Oxford (MA); barrister; Oriental Sec Teheran 1879–81, Actg 3rd Sec Tokyo 1884–87, Sr Clerk FO 1899–1910; *m* 30 July 1884 Sophie (*d* 8 Sept 1913), dau of Alexander Perceval, of Temple House, Co Sligo, and *d* 19 March 1924

1 Georgina Frances; *m* 7 Aug 1873 Col Edward St John Griffiths, JP, 19th Regt (*d* 7 July 1923), of Upton House, Nursling, Hants, yr s of John Rogers Griffiths, of Pilton, Devon, and *d* 11 July 1914, leaving issue

Sir THOMAS *d* 15 June 1879; his est son,

Sir Charles Larcom, 2nd Bt; *b* 2 Dec 1843; Lt-Col RA, Assist Mil Sec to Govr and C-in-C Malta 1885; *m* 29 Dec 1881 Jeanie (*d* 18 Dec 1937), dau of Alexander Perceval, of Temple House, Co Sligo, and *d* 28 March 1892, leaving:

1 **Sir Thomas Perceval Larcom, 3rd Bt**, DSO (1918); *b* 5 Oct 1882; *educ* Eton and RMC Sandhurst; Maj RHA, Bde-Maj 1916, Staff Offr RA 10th Corps 1917 WW I (despatches), ret 1928, WW II Lt-Col HG, FRGS; *d* unm 30 Oct 1950

2 PHILIP (Sir), **4th Bt**

3 Charles Arthur Aiskew, DSO (1941); *b* 13 April 1891; Cdre RN, dir Naval Air Div Admlty WW II; *m* 26 Oct 1935 Joan Peveril Ward, er dau of Sir Reginald Ward Edward Lane Poole, KCVO, of Bucklers Wood, Beaulieu, Hants, and *dsp* 18 Aug 1964

The 3rd Bt's brother,

Sir Philip Larcom, 4th Bt; *b* 13 Sept 1887; *educ* Cheltenham; Lt RNVR; *m* 18 Dec 1920 Aileen Monica Royde, yr dau of Rev Arthur George Colbeck, Rector Hasketon, Suffolk, and *d* 19 July 1967, leaving:

1 Sir (CHARLES) CHRISTOPHER ROYDE LARCOM, **5th and present Bt**

1 *Monica Rosemary Georgina [Mrs William Walrond, 7 Old House Cl, Church Rd, London SW19]; *b* 1 Dec 1921; *m* 7 March 1942 *William Eric Walrond, s of Robert Dudley Walrond, of Putney, and has:

(1) *Patricia Mary; *b* 8 Sept 1943

(2) *Anne Carol; *b* 27 July 1947

(3) *Christine Diana; *b* 27 Jan 1953

LATHAM, Baron

Arms: Per fess gules and chequy or and sable, a fess barry wavy argent and azure, in chief a seax fesswise, point to the sinister, cutting edge upwards proper, pommel and hilt of the second, ensigned with a saxon crown also of the second. **Crest:** Two spurs, one in bend the other in bend sinister, rowels upwards or, straps sable with buckles gold. **Supporters:** On either side a horse sable, charged on the shoulder with a plate and gorged with a mural coronet with a chain reflexed over the back or. **Motto:** *Bene est tentare* ('It is good to try'). **Creation:** B. (UK) 16 Jan 1942.

THE 2ND BARON LATHAM, of Hendon, Co Middlesex (Dominic Charles Latham) [The Rt Hon The Lord Latham, PO Box 355, Kensington, NSW 2033, Australia]; *b* 20 Sept 1954; *s* gf 1970; *educ* NSW U (BEng 1977, MEngSc 1981); civil engr Electricity Commn of NSW 1979–88, structural engr Rankine & Hill Consulting Engrs 1988–91, sr structural engr Gerard Barry Assocs 1992–, social dancing teacher 1993–

Lineage: GEORGE LATHAM, of Norwich; *b* 1852; *m* Sarah *née* Mason (*d* 21 July 1933 aged 77) and *d* 28 Dec 1929, leaving:

CHARLES LATHAM, **1st Baron Latham**, of Hendon, Co Middlesex (UK), so *cr* 16 Jan 1942 JP (Middx 1945); *b* 26 Dec 1888; *educ* elementary sch Norwich; Roy Sussex Regt WW I, certified accountant, FACCA, FCIS, Ld Lt Middx 1945–56, Pres Nat Union Clerks 1915, memb Public Works Loan Bd 1930–46, memb Economy ('May') Ctee apptd by Chllr Exchequer 1931, memb London and Home Cos: Jt Electricity Bd 1928–34, Traffic Advisory Ctee 1934–46, former memb Hendon UDC and Alderman Hendon Borough 1926–34, memb Exec Ctee London Lab Pty 1915–16 and 1934–42 (Treasurer 1942–47), Alderman LCC 1928–34 and 1946–47, LCC rep S Hackney 1934–46 (chm Fin Ctee LCC 1934–40, CD and Gen Purposes Ctee 1940–46, Ldr LCC 1940–47), dir Earls Ct, memb Bd LPTB 1935–47, chm London Tport Exec 1947–53, memb Metropolitan Water Bd and chm Fin Ctee, memb Standing Advsy Ctee, v-pres Building Socs Assoc 1949–70, KStJ, Offr Legn Hon; *m* 1st 14 June 1913 (*divorce* 1957) Maya Helen (*d* 1978), dau of Louis George Allman, of Hendon; *m* 2nd 28 March 1957 Sylvia May (*d* 1985), dau

of Alexander Newmark, of London, and widow of Alexander Kennard, and *d* 31 March 1970, having by his 1st w had:

1 Francis Charles Allman; *b* 24 Jan 1917; *educ* Dauntsey's; Maj IA (Warwicks Yeo and RASC) WW II; *m* 1st July 1942 Margaret (*d* 28 Jan 1944), dau of Ernest Fuller, of Maidstone; *m* 2nd Aug 1944 (*divorce* 1950) Eleanor Roma, dau of Isadore Roseman; *m* 3rd 1951 Gabrielle Monica (*d* 1987), dau of Dr S M O'Riordan, and *d* Nov 1959, leaving:

(1) DOMINIC CHARLES LATHAM, **2nd and present Baron Latham**

(2) +ANTHONY; *b* 20 Sept 1954; heir presumptive

1 *Barbara Wendy (Maia); *b* 7 Jan 1920; *educ* Hendon Coll; WAAF WW II; *m* 1st 17 April 1941 (*divorce* 1945) Capt Denis Charles Wildish, RASC, s of Charles Albert Wildish; *m* 2nd 26 Oct 1946 (*divorce* 1951) Peter Anthony Charles Kurt Bruckmann, er s of Kurt Bruckmann, of Cookham Dean; *m* 3rd 1966 *Malcolm Blundell Cole-Fontayn, slr, and by her 2nd husb has:

(1) *Karen Francesca; *b* 1948

2 *Jean Helen [The Hon Mrs Dykes, 78 Sackville Rd, Hove, Sussex]; *b* 17 July 1921; *educ* Hendon Coll; WRNS WW II; *m* 1st 22 Aug 1945 (*divorce* 1961) S/Ldr Ronald Gellatly, RNZAF, s of Capt Thomas William Gellatly, of Montucka, Nelson, NZ, and has issue; *m* 2nd 17 June 1970 *James Oswald Dykes, of Lagos, and by her 1st husb has:

(1) *Paul; *b* 1946

3 *Diana Dorothy; *b* 18 Sept 1925; *educ* N London Collegiate Sch and Bradford Jr Coll, Boston, Mass.; *m* 19– *— Barringer

LATHAM, Bt

Arms: Gules an eagle displayed or between two bezants in fess, on a chief of the second a cross moline sable between two roses of the field. **Crest:** An eagle, wings elevated, inverted and addorsed or, resting the dexter claw on a torteau and charged on the wing with a cross as in the arms. **Motto:** *Fortuna et labore* ('By good luck and hard work'). **Creation:** Bt. (UK) 24 May 1919.

SIR RICHARD THOMAS PAUL LATHAM, 3RD BT, of Crow Clump, Walton-upon-Thames, Surrey [Sir Richard Latham Bt, 2125 Birnam Wood Drive, Santa Barbara, CA 93108, USA]; *b* 15 April 1934; *s* f 1955; *educ* Eton and Trin Coll Cambridge (BA 1957, MA 1962); late Lt Queen's Own Worcs Hus (TA); *m* 6 Dec 1958 *Marie-Louise Patricia, er dau of Frederic Hooper Russell, of Vancouver, and has:

1 *Nicola Patricia; *b* 27 Oct 1959; *m* 1986 *Colin David Jones, of Vancouver

2 *Alison; *b* 17 Jan 1965; *m* 1989 *Gary William Schild, of W Vancouver

Lineage: SAMUEL LATHAM, of Manchester; had:

Sir Thomas Paul Latham, 1st Bt (UK), so *cr* 24 May 1919; *b* 19 June 1855; dir Courtaulds; *m* 1888 Florence Clara (*d* 12 Dec 1950), Order Mercy, dau of William Henry Walley, of Manchester, and *d* 26 Oct 1931, leaving:

1 **Sir (Herbert) Paul Latham, 2nd Bt**; *b* 22 April 1905; *educ* Eton and Magdalen Coll Oxford; MP (C) Scarborough and Whitby 1931–41, memb LCC 1928–34; *m* 29 June 1933 (*divorce* 1943) Lady Patricia Doreen Moore (*d* 3 March 1947), only dau of 10th Earl of Drogheda (*qv*), and *d* 24 July 1955, leaving:

(1) Sir RICHARD THOMAS PAUL LATHAM, **3rd and present Bt**

1 Violet Irene; *b* 8 Dec 1895; *m* 15 June 1920 (*divorce* 1926) Cuthbert Francis Hamilton (*d* 27 Sept 1938), er s of Rev Francis Chetwode Hamilton, of Charlton Manor, Knaresborough

2 Audrey Clara Lilian; *b* 4 April 1899; *m* 1st 12 July 1921 (*divorce* 1928) Sir Henry Ralph Stanley Birkin, 3rd Bt (*qv*) and had issue; *m* 2nd 5 July 1928 Lt-Col Lord Edward Hay (*k* by enemy action 18 June 1944), s of 10th Marquess of Tweeddale (*qv*), and had further issue; *m* 3rd 28 Feb 1948 (*divorce* 1952) Hon Niall Greville Chaplin, yr s of 2nd Viscount Chaplin (see 1970 edn); *m* 4th 12 Dec 1952 Maj-Gen Sir Stewart Graham Menzies, KCB, KCMG, DSO, MC, Life Gds (*d* 29 May 1968), s of John Graham Menzies

LATYMER

ESSE QUAM VIDERI

Arms: Quarterly, 1st and 4th, argent a stag's head erased gules, between the attires a pheon azure, the whole within a bordure embattled of the last charged with four buckles or (for COUTTS); 2nd and 3rd, or on a pile azure ten besants, four, three, two and one, on a chief ermine a long passant of the second (for MONEY). **Crests:** 1 A man from the middle upwards shooting an arrow from a bow all proper (for COUTTS), 2 A besant between two wings azure, each semée de lys or. **Supporters:** On either side a griffin or. **Badge:** A griffin segreant or, beaked and membered azure and armed argent. **Motto:** *Esse quam videri* ('To be rather than to seem'). **Creation:** B. (E) 25 Feb 1431/2.

THE 8TH BARON LATYMER (Hugo Nevill Money-Coutts) [The Rt Hon The Lord Latymer, Vivero Hortus, Santa Maria, Mallorca, Spain]; *b* 1 March 1926; *s f* 1987; *educ* Eton; ACA, late Lt Gren Gds; *m* 1st 28 July 1951 (*divorce* 1965) Hon Penelope Ann Clare, yr dau of Baroness Emmet of Amberley (*see* RENNELL, B), and has:

1 +CRISPIN JAMES ALAN NEVILL [The Hon Crispin Money-Coutts, c/o Coutts & Co, 440 Strand, London WC2R 0QS]; *b* 8 March 1955; *educ* Eton and Keble Coll Oxford (BA, rowing blue 1975); head internat private banking Coutts & Co, dir Manek Investment Management Ltd 1997–; *m* 1st 4 March 1978 Hon Lucy Rose, yst dau of Baron Deedes (LP, *qv*); *m* 2nd 2 Aug 1995 *Shaunagh Anne Henrietta, dau of (George Silver) Oliver Annesley Colthurst (*see* COLTHURST, Bt) and formerly w of Thomas Peter William Heneage (*see* MORTON, E), and by his 1st w has:

  (1) +Drummond William Thomas; *b* 11 May 1986

  (1) +Sophia Patience; *b* 1985

  (2) +Evelyn Rose; *b* 1988

2 +Giles Thomas Nevill; *b* 2 May 1957; *educ* Eton and Oriel College Oxford

1 +Clare Louise [The Hon Mrs Edmonds, Buscott Farm, Ashcott, Somerset]; *b* 1 Dec 1952; *m* 12 Sept 1978 *John Stephen Courtenay Edmonds, s of John Courtenay Edmonds, of Upper Quinton, Stratford-upon-Avon

The 8th BARON *m* 2nd 16 Oct 1965 *Jinty Ann, 2nd dau of Peter George Calvert, of Kensington, and by her has:

3 +Henry Eugene; *b* 26 Aug 1967; *educ* Eton

2 +Vera Dulcie Harriet; *b* 24 Feb 1972; *educ* Bryanston

3 +Fanny Clara Maria; *b* 22 Dec 1973; *educ* Bryanston

Lineage: WILLIAM le LATIMER (*i.e.*, interpreter; *see* SAINT DAVIDS, V, **Lineage (of Philipps)**, for a similar instance of a surname deriving from a linguistic skill; here the 'le' was later corrupted to 'de' in the mistaken belief that Latimer was a place) of Scampston, E R Yorks; Sheriff Yorks July 1254–60 and 1266–67; ktd by 1262; *d* by 22 Nov 1268, leaving:

1 WILLIAM le LATIMER, 1st LORD (Baron) LATIMER (of Corby), aparently *cr* by writ of summons 1290 to an assembly deemed by later (though not the very latest) doctrine to have been a Parl, though the first recorded writ dates from 29 Dec 1299; saw action at English defeat by Scots of Stirling 1297 and English victory over Scots of Falkirk 1298; Keeper Berwick 1300, participating Siege of Carlaverock June 1300; *m c* 1268 Alice, er dau and coheir of Walter Ledet, whereby he acquired Corby, Northants, with other extensive possessions, and *d* 5 Dec 1304, leaving:

  (1) WILLIAM le LATIMER, 1st/2nd LORD (Baron) LATIMER (of Corby), so *cr* by writ of summons to Parl 6 Feb 1298/9 (*i.e.*, nearly a year prior to the first recorded writ of summons to his f, though the latter may have been summoned even earlier; *see* above); *b c* 1276; fought at English defeat by Scots of Bannockburn 1314, when captured and held at Bothwell till ransomed some eight months after the battle; fought for EDWARD II Battle of Boroughbridge 16 March 1321/2 against the rebellious Thomas, Earl of Lancaster, though one of the latter's supporters till *c* 1318; Keeper York Jan 1322/2; envoy to negotiate peace with Scotland 1324; *m* 1st by 20 April 1295 (*divorce* by 22 July 1312) Lucy, yr dau and coheir of Sir Robert de Thweng, and had issue; *m* 2nd by 18 Aug 1314 Sibyl, dau of Sir Richard de Fourneaux and widow of William de Huntingfield, and *d* by 23 July 1317, leaving by her a s (Thomas); his s by his 1st w:

1a WILLIAM le LATIMER, 2nd/3rd LORD (Baron) LATIMER (of Corby); *b c* 1301; ktd by 1328; *m* Elizabeth, dau of 1st Lord (Baron) Botetourt, and *d* by 2 Nov 1335, leaving:

1b WILLIAM le LATIMER, 3rd/4th LORD (Baron) LATIMER (of Corby), KG (1362); *b* 29 March 1329/30; fought in 1st Div Battle of Crécy 1346; ktd by 1351, Lt and Capt Gen Gascony 1359, Steward Household 1369 and perhaps now or later became Chamberlain, Constable Dover Castle and Warden Cinque Ports 1372; *m* by 1353 Elizabeth, possibly dau of Edmund FitzAlan, Earl of Arundel (*see* NORFOLK, D), and *dspm* 28 May 1381, leaving:

1c ELIZABETH Latimer, *de jure* BARONESS LATIMER (of Corby) in her own right according to later doctrine; *b c* 1356; *m* 1st by 9 Oct 1381, as his 2nd w, John de NEVILL(E), 3rd Lord (Baron) Neville (of Raby) (*see* ABERGAVENNY, M), and had:

1d JOHN NEVILL(E), 5th/6th LORD (Baron) LATIMER (of Corby); settled most of his lands on his Nevill(e) half-bro, the 1st Earl of Westmorland (*see* ABERGAVENNY, M, also below) to the exclusion of his full sister Elizabeth's son, even though many of these lands came to him through their mother; *dsp* 1430

1d Elizabeth; *m* Sir Thomas de WILLOUGHBY, 3rd s of 1st Lord (Baron) Willoughby de Eresby (*qv*), apparently by his 2nd w, and had:

1e JOHN WILLOUGHBY, *de jure* 6th/7th LORD (Baron) LATIMER (of Corby), though never called to Parl; *b c* 1400; *m* Jane Welby and *d* 24 Feb 1436/7, leaving:

1f JOHN WILLOUGHBY, *de jure* 7th/8th LORD (Baron) LATIMER (of Corby), though never called to Parl, JP (1453); *b c* 1421; Sheriff Dorset 1455–56, ktd 1461; *m* by 4 March 1444/5 Anne, dau of Edmund Cheyney, of Bro(o)k(e), Wilts, and Ottery, Devon, and *d* by Aug 1477, leaving:

1g ROBERT WILLOUGHBY, 1st LORD (Baron) WILLOUGHBY DE BROKE (*qv*) and *de jure* 8th/9th LORD (Baron) LATIMER (of Corby), as which petitioned to be recognised following writs of summons to Parl to him and the **1st Lord** (Baron) **Latymer** (*see* below) 12 Aug 1491; the latter's counsel argued that ROBERT's ancestor's Barony of Latimer (of Corby) could not descend to heirs general (*i.e.*, could not include females and their issue) since it was created by writ — a doctrine in total contradiction to the one prevailing since the 17th century

1c (cont.) BARONESS LATIMER (of Corby) *m* 2nd, as his 3rd w, 4th Lord (Baron) Willoughby de Eresby (*qv*) and *d* 5 Nov 1395, leaving:

1d Margaret; thought to have *dsp* or *unm* by 1430

2 John; *m* his er bro's w's sis Christian, dau and coheir of Walter Ledet, and *d* by 12 Dec 1282, leaving:

  (1) THOMAS le LATIMER, 1st LORD (Baron) LATIMER (of Braybrook, Northants) (E), so *cr* according to later doctrine by writ of summons Parl 29 Dec 1299 (though neither he nor his descendants were called to subsequent Parls), also of Wardon; *b c* 1270; *m* by July 1297 Lora, dau of Henry de Hastings, and *d* by 2 Feb 1333/4, leaving:

1a WARIN le LATIMER, *de jure* 2nd LORD (Baron) LATIMER (of Braybrook); *b c* 1300; fought for EDWARD II Battle of Boroughbridge (*see* above against 2nd LORD (Baron) LATIMER (of Corby)); *m* by 1328 Catherine, dau of John, Lord (Baron) La Warre (*see* DE LA WARR, E), and *d* of bubonic plague 13 Aug 1349, leaving:

1b JOHN le LATIMER, *de jure* 3rd LORD (Baron) LATIMER (of Braybrook); *b c* 1334; *m* Maud and *dsp* or *dsps c* Dec 1356

2b WARIN le LATIMER, *de jure* 4th LORD (Baron) LATIMER (of Braybrook); *b c* 1341; *d* apparently *unm* by Jan 1361/2

3b THOMAS le LATIMER, *de jure* 5th LORD (Baron) LATIMER (of Braybrook); *b c* 1341; ktd by 1365, MP Northants Jan 1376/7 and 1378, prominent Lollard 1382–95; *m* between Aug 1360 and 14 April 1366 Anne, widow of John Beysin, of Ashley, Staffs, and *dsp* 14 Sept 1401

4b EDWARD LATIMER, *de jure* 6th LORD (Baron) LATIMER; *b c* 1346; *m* Margaret — and *dsp* 31 Jan 1410/1

1b Elizabeth; *m* Thomas GRIFFIN and had:

1c Richard; *m* Anne Chamberlain and *d* by 1411, leaving:

1d JOHN GRIFFIN, *de jure* 7th LORD (Baron) LATIMER (of Braybrook); *b c* 1381; *m* Elizabeth — and *dsp* 1 Feb 1444/5

2d Nicholas; *m* Margaret, dau of Sir John Pilkington, and had, with an er s (John, thought to have *dsp* by 1445):

1e NICHOLAS GRIFFIN, *de jure* 8th LORD (Baron) LATIMER (of Braybrook), JP; *b* 5 June 1426; Sheriff Northants 1473; *m* 1st Catherine, dau of Richard Curzon; *m* 2nd — Roos; *m* 3rd Marina, dau and heir of John Belers, of Eye Kettleby, Leics, and widow of Sir Thomas Green, of Green's Norton, and *d* 6 June 1482, leaving by his 1st w:

1f JOHN GRIFFIN, *de jure* 9th LORD (Baron) LATIMER (of Braybrook); *b c* 1454; *m* by 20 July 1473 Emmote, dau of Richard Wheathill, of Calais, and *d* 26 Sept 1485, leaving, with three other sons (George; David; Richard):

1g NICHOLAS GRIFFIN, *de jure* 10th LORD (Baron) LATIMER (of Braybrook), KB (1501), JP (Northants 1502, 1504); *b c* 1476; Sheriff Northants 1504; *m* 1st Anne, dau of Sir Thomas Throckmorton; *m* 2nd Alice, dau of John Thornburgh, and *d* 15 May 1509, leaving:

1h THOMAS GRIFFIN, *de jure* 11th LORD (Baron) LATIMER (of Braybrook), JP (Northants 1532–44); *b c* 1496; *educ* Lincoln's Inn 1509; ktd by 1533, Sheriff Northants 1534; *m* Jane, yr dau of Richard Newton, of Court of Wick in Yatton, Somerset, and *dspms* 27 Aug 1566, having had:

1i Rice; *educ* Lincoln's Inn; *m* Elizabeth, dau of Sir Thomas Brudenell, of Dean (Deene), Northants (*see* AILESBURY, M), and was *k vp* during Ket's Rebellion at Norwich 1549, leaving:

1j MARY Griffin, *de jure* BARONESS LATIMER (of Braybrook) in her own right according to later doctrine; *b c* 1546; *m* Sir Thomas MARKHAM, yr s of John Markham by his 3rd w Anne Strelley, and had, with between five and 11 other sons and apparently four daus:

1k Griffin (Sir); *ktd* 1591; attainted for treason 1603, leaving either no issue or two daus, when either the Barony of Latimer (of Braybrook) fell into abeyance between his daus (subject to the attainder) or it passed (again subject to the attainder) to his next est bro and any issue of the latter

2h Edward; ancestor of the Barons Griffin and Braybrooke (*qv*)

1g Mary; *m* 8th Lord (Baron) Audley (*see* 1970 edn) and had issue

JOHN NEVILL(E), 5th/6th LORD (Baron) LATIMER (of Corby)'s half-bro,

RALPH de NEVILL(E), 1st EARL OF WESTMORLAND of the 1397 *cr*; had (by his 2nd w) a 10th s:

GEORGE NEVILL(E), **1st Lord** (Baron) **Latymer** (E), so *cr* by writ of summons 25 Feb 1431/2, PC (1439); *ktd* 1426; went mad by 11 June 1451, but remained only intermittently so since he went on being called to Parl for another 18 years; thought to have supported the Lancastrian party; *m* Feb 1436/7 Elizabeth (*d* by 2 Oct 1480), dau and in her issue coheir of Richard Beauchamp, Earl of Warwick (*see* WARWICK, BROOKE and, E), and had:

1 Henry (Sir); *m* Joanna, dau of 1st Lord (Baron) Berners (*qv*), and *dvp* 26 July 1469, being *k* at the Battle of Edgcote, nr Banbury (defeat of the Woodville faction among the Yorkists by the Warwick ('the Kingmaker') faction), leaving:

(1) RICHARD, **2nd Lord**

(2) Thomas, of Malvern, Worcs, and Shenstone, Staffs; living 1540; had issue

(1) Joane; *m* Sir James Ratcliffe

2 Thomas, of Shenstone, Staffs

1 Jane

2 Katherine; *m* 1st Oliver Dudley (*d* 1480) and had issue; *m* 2nd Sir James Ratcliffe (*dsp*), s of Sir John Ratcliffe, KG

The gs,

RICHARD NEVILL(E), **2nd Lord** (Baron) **Latymer**, KB (Jan 1477/8); *b* 1468; cmded troops Battle of Stoke 1487 against Lambert Simnel's followers, also helped suppress Perkin Warbeck's followers 1496; fought Battle of Flodden 1513; *m* 1st *c* 1490 Anne, dau of Sir Humphrey Stafford, of Grafton, Worcs, and had, with other issue:

1 JOHN, **3rd Lord**

2 William, of Penwyn; *b* 15 July 1497; *m* Elizabeth, dau of Sir Giles Greville; their issue died out 1631

3 Thomas, of Piggot's Hardley, Essex; *b* 24 Dec 1502; *m* Mary, dau and coheir of Sir Thomas Teye, of Mark's Teye, and *d* 28 Oct 1544, having had issue

4 Marmaduke, of Mark's Teye; *b* 1506; *m* Elizabeth, dau and coheir of Sir Thomas Teye, of Mark's Teye, and *d* 28 May 1545, having had issue

1 Margaret; *b* 9 March 1494; *m* Edward Willoughby (*dvp*), son and heir of 2nd Lord (Baron) Willoughby de Broke (*qv*), and had issue (*see also* WARWICK, BROOKE and, E)

2 Dorothy; *b* 29 March 1496; *m* Sir John Dawnay (*d* 2 March 1553), of Cowick, Yorks, and had issue (*see* DOWNE, V)

3 Elizabeth; *b* 28 April 1500; *m* Sir Christopher Danby, of Farnley, Yorks, and had issue

4 Susannah; *b* 28 April 1501; *m* Richard Norton and had issue (*see* GRANTLEY, B)

The **2nd Lord** *m* 2nd *c* 5 July 1522 Margaret, widow of Sir James Strangwishe, and *d* 12–28 Dec 1530

His est son,

JOHN NEVILL(E), **3rd Lord** (Barpon) **Latymer**, JP (N R Yorks 1530); *b* 17 Nov 1493; *ktd* 1513, MP Yorks 1529; participated 1536 in Pilgrimage of Grace but later claimed it was under duress and was pardoned, despite being among the leaders deputed to negotiate with the King's forces sent to suppress it; *m* 1st Dorothy (*d* 7 Feb 1526/7), sis and coheir of 14th Earl of Oxford (*see* SAINT ALBANS, D), and had:

1 JOHN, **4th Lord**

1 Margaret; living 1542

The **3rd Lord** *m* 2nd 20 July 1528 Elizabeth (*dsp*), dau of Sir Edward Musgrave; *m* 3rd 1533 Katharine (*m* 3rd 12 July 1543, as her 3rd of four husbs, HENRY VIII; *see* BURGH, B), dau of Sir Thomas Parr, of Kendal, and *d* 2 March 1542/3, having by her had no surv dau

His only son,

JOHN NEVILL(E), **4th Lord** (Baron) **Latymer**; *b c* 1520; served French and Scottish campaigns 1544 and 1545 respectively, *ktd* 1545; *m c* 1545 Lady Lucy Somerset (*d* 23 Feb 1582/3), dau of 2nd Earl of Worcester (*see* BEAUFORT, D), and *dspm* 22 April 1577, when the Barony fell into abeyance between his four daus:

1 Katherine; *m* 1st by 25 Jan 1561/2 2nd Earl of Northumberland of the 1557 *cr* (*see* NORTHUMBERLAND, D); *m* 2nd 1588 Francis Fitton (*dsp* 17 June 1608), of Binfield, and *d c* Dec 1587, leaving issue

2 Dorothy; *m* 27 Nov 1564 1st Earl of Exeter (*see* EXETER, M) and *d* 23 March 1608, leaving issue

3 LUCY

4 Elizabeth; *m* 1st Sir John Danvers (*d* 10 Dec 1594), of Dauntsey, Wilts, and had issue (*see* OSBORN, Bt); *m* 2nd Sir Edmund Carey, of Moulton Park, ancestor of the Barons Hunsdon of Hunsdon of the Jan 1558/9 *cr* (*see* ALDENHAM and HUNSDON OF HUNSDON, B, preliminary remarks), and was *bur* 24 June 1630

The 3rd dau,

LUCY Nevill(e); *m* Sir William CORNWALLIS (*see* CORNWALLIS, B) and *d* 30 April 1608, having had:

1 FRANCES

2 Elizabeth; *m* 1st 1592 Sir William Sandys; *m* 2nd 11 May 1630, as his 2nd w, 1st Viscount Lumley of Waterford (*see* SCARBROUGH, E) and *dsp*, *bur* 2 Feb 1657/8

3 Cornelia; *m* Sir Richard Fermor (*see* HESKETH, B), and had issue

4 Anne; *m* 13 Nov 1610 7th Earl of Argyll (*see* ARGYLL, D) and had issue

The est dau,

FRANCES Cornwallis; *m* Sir Edmond WITHIPOLE (*ktd* Jan 1599/1600; *d* 6 Nov 1619) and *d* Sept 1625, leaving:

Sir WILLIAM WITHIPOLE, of Christ Church, Ipswich, Suffolk; *ktd* 1617; *m* 25 April 1621 Jane, widow of Henry Ratcliffe, Viscount FitzWalter (*dvp* 20 Nov 1620, *see* FITZWALTER, B), and dau and coheir of Sir Michael Stanhope, of Sudbury, Suffolk, and *d* 11 Aug 1645, having had, with an only s (Edmund, *d* in infancy, *bur* 3 March 1634):

ELIZABETH Withipole; *m* 6 June 1642 6th VISCOUNT HEREFORD (*qv*) and was *bur* 27 Jan 1669, having had, with a s and er dau (both *d* young):

FRANCES Devereux; *b* 1659; *m* (licence 12 July 1679), as his 1st w, 4th VISCOUNT TRACY OF RATHCOOLE (*see* SUDELEY, B), and *d* 20 March 1687, having had:

ELIZABETH Tracy; *b* 19 March 1679/80; *m* 1st 11 Nov 1704 Robert BURDETT, of Bramcote, Warwicks (*dvp* 6 Jan 1716), son and heir of Sir Robert Burdett, 3rd Bt, and had a surv s and eight daus; *m* 2nd Robert Holden (*d* 17 June 1746), of Aston, Derbys, and *d* 27 May 1747; her s by her 1st husb:

Sir ROBERT BURDETT, 4th Bt; *b* posthumously 28 May 1716; *educ* New Coll Oxford; DCL, MP Tamworth 1748–68; *m* 1st 6 Nov 1739 Elizabeth (*d* 24 Aug 1747), only dau of Sir Charles Sedley, Bt; *m* 2nd 17 July 1753 Caroline (*dsp* 10 Nov 1769), widow of Sir Henry Harpur, 5th Bt, and dau of 2nd Duke of Rutland (*qv*), and *d* 15 Feb 1797, having by his 1st w had an only surv s:

FRANCIS BURDETT; *b* 22 April 1743; *m* 30 Dec 1766 Eleanor (*d* 30 May 1783), dau and coheir of William Jones, of Ramsbury Manor, Wilts, and *dvp* 3 Feb 1794, leaving, with other issue (*see* 1949 edn BURDETT, Bt, of Bramcote):

Sir FRANCIS BURDETT, 5th Bt; *b* 25 Jan 1770; *educ* Westminster and Ch Ch Oxford; MP (Radical) Boroughbridge 1796–1802, Middx 1802–04 (election declared void) and 1806–06 (election again declared void), Westminster 1807–37 and (C) N Wilts 1837–44; *b* 25 Jan 1770; *m* 5 Aug 1793 Sophia (*d* 12 Jan 1844), yst dau and coheir of Thomas Coutts, of The Strand, London, banker, and *d* 23 Jan 1844, having had:

1 Sir ROBERT BURDETT, 6th Bt; Col, High Sheriff Derbys 1848; *b* 26 April 1796; *d unm* 7 June 1880

1 Sophia; *bapt* 2 Aug 1794; *m* 23 Oct 1833 Hon Robert Otway Cave (*dvm* 29 Nov 1844), of Stanford Hall, Leics, er surv s of Henry Otway by Sarah, Baroness Braye (*qv*) in her own right, and *dsp* 20 Dec 1849

2 Susannah; *bapt* 4 Jan 1801; *m* 29 Nov 1830 John Trevanion Purnell Bettesworth Trevanion (*d* 9 March 1840), of Caerhays, Cornwall, and *dsp* 17 May 1886

3 Joanna Frances; *d unm* 4 April 1862

4 CLARA MARIA Coutts, of Stodham Park, Hants; *m* 28 April 1850, as his 2nd w, Rev James Drummond MONEY later MONEY-COUTTS (roy licence 20 Sept 1880; he *d* 20 April 1875), Rector Sternfield, Suffolk, and *d* 22 Dec 1899, leaving:

(1) FRANCIS BURDETT THOMAS, **5th Lord**

5 ANGELA GEORGINA Burdett, 1st and last BARONESS BURDETT-COUTTS (UK), so *cr* 9 June 1871; *b* 21 April 1814; *m* 12 Feb 1881 William Lehman Ashmead BARTLETT later BURDETT-COUTTS (roy licence 29 May 1882), MP Westminster, s of Ellis Bartlett, of Plymouth, Mass., and *dsp* 30 Dec 1906, when the Barony expired

The Rev JAMES and Mrs MONEY-COUTTS's s,

FRANCIS BURDETT THOMAS MONEY later MONEY-COUTTS (roy licence 1880) later still COUTTS-NEVILL (roy licence for himself only 1914), **5th Baron Latymer** (to which barony declared coheir by Ho Lds resolution 15 July 1912, abeyance terminated and he called to Ho Lds by writ 11 Feb 1913); *b* 18 Sept 1852; MA, LLM Cambridge; versifier; *m* 15 April 1875 Edith Ellen (*d* following an accident 28 April 1942), est dau of Charles Churchill, of Weybridge Park, Surrey, and had:

1 HUGH BURDETT, **6th Baron**

1 Clara Burdett; *educ* LMH Oxford; *m* 7 March 1905 Rev Melville Watson Patterson (*d* 19 Jan 1944), Fell and Sr Tutor Trin Coll Oxford, 3rd s of William Patterson, of Birkenhead, and *d* 8 Jan 1969 aged 91, leaving:

(1) +Rosamund Margaret; *b* 1905; *m* 1934 Selwyn Duruz (*d* 1976)

(2) +Joan Elizabeth; *b* 1908; *m* 1st 1931 (*divorce* 1937) Sebastian Max Alexander Myer Clement Salaman (*d* 1976); *m* 2nd 1947 *Raymond Coxon, IG, and by her 1st husb has:

1a +Clement Francis [Clement Salaman Esq, 5 Second Ave, London SW14 8QF]; *b* 1932; *m* 1961 *Juliet Nicholson

2a +Frederick Nicholas Paul [Frederick Salaman Esq, Flat 6, 62 Elm Park Gdns, London SW10]; *b* 1936; *educ* Radley and Trin Coll Oxford; *m* 1st 1960 (*divorce* 1974) Elisabeth Cecily, dau of Frances Sclater, of Bunces Farm, Newick, Sussex, and has:

1b +Sophia; *b* 1963

2b +Charlotte; *b* 1966

2a (cont.) Frederick Salaman *m* 2nd 1983 *Lyndsay Margaret, dau of James Meiklejohn, of Wise Lane, Mill Hill, and by her has:

3b +Rose Clementine; *b* 1983

4b +Phoebe Joy; *b* 1987

(3) +Lindsay Marion [Mrs Humphrey Lynch, 19 Eastfield Court, Church St, Faringdon, Oxon]; *b* 1918; *m* 1939 *Humphrey Gilbert Bohun Lynch and has:

1a +Francis Nicholas [Francis Lynch Esq, Hadley, Wootton Rivers, Marlborough, Wilts]; *b* 1944; *educ* Merton Coll Oxford; *m* 1st 1965 (*divorce* 1974) Amanda Underwood; *m* 2nd 1983 *Susan, dau of Eric Wright, of Hawaii, and by her has:

1b +Hugh Arthur; *b* 1991

1a +Alison Harriet; *b* 1955

2 Eleanora Burdett; *m* 15 Sept 1917 Eric Walter Carr, er s of Walter Carr, and *dsp* 13 March 1966

3 Joan Burdett; *m* 3 Oct 1905 (*divorce* 1941) Lt-Col James Arundel Nixon, DSO, King's Own Regt (*d* 16 Nov 1950), s of Maj-Gen Arundel James Nixon, RA, and *d* 21 June 1968 aged 87, having had:

(1) Arundel James; *b* 1907; *m* 1st 1930 (*divorce* 1940) Edna Duffy and had:

1a +Peter; *b* 1934; lives in Australia

(1) (cont.) Arundel Nixon *m* 2nd 1941 Paloma Margaret (*m* 2nd 1951 Geoffrey Thomas Luke, of Victoria, Australia, and *d* 1980), and *d* 1949, leaving by her:

2a +David Guy [David Nixon-Luke Esq, 22 Lambert Rd, Toorak, Victoria 3142, Australia]; *b* 1945; *m* 1970 *Charryce Laleen Yolanna, yst dau of Montague Neville Lea, of NSW, and has:

1b +Guy Jaeger Evans Arundel; *b* 1976

2b +Jordan Geoffrey Bradshaw; *b* 1982

3b +Reece David Valmont; *b* 1986

1a +Nikki [Mrs Nikki Martin, 96 Bendigo St, E Richmond, Victoria, Australia]; *b* 1942; *m* 1961 (*divorce* 1982) Robert William Martin and has:

1b +James Patrick; *b* 1965

1b +Sarah Jane; *b* 1963

(2) +Guy John [Guy Nixon Esq, 47 Mount Row, St Peter Port, Guernsey GY1 1NU]; *b* 1909; *educ* Eton and Pembroke Coll Cambridge (BA); AIB; *m* 1st 1933 Barbara Helen (*d* 1991), yr dau of Francis William Whitbourn Morgan; *m* 2nd 1992 *Mrs Michelle James, dau of James Frederick Carey, of Guernsey, and by his 1st w has:

1a +Sara; *b* 1933; *m* 1959 *John Gordon Mathias and has:

1b +Jeremy; *b* 1963

1b +Penelope; *b* 1960

4 Margaret Burdett; *m* 8 June 1907 Francis Churchill Still (*d* 14 Dec 1937), slr, Capt RGA, only s of Ernest Robert Still, of Leatherhead, Surrey, and *d* 18 Dec 1948, leaving:

(1) Robert; *b* 1910; *m* 1944 *Elizabeth Eleanor [Mrs Robert Still, Bucklebury Lodge, Bucklebury, Berks RG7 6PB], dau of S K Westman, FRCS, of Harley St, W1, and *d* 1971, having had:

1a +Susan; *b* 1945; *m* 1965 *R C R Chesters, of Winchester and has:

1b +William; *b* 1971

1b +Celia; *b* 1973

2a +Anthea; *b* 1947; *m* 1974 *Michael Dillon, of Oxford, and has:

1b +Simon; *b* 1975

2b +Timothy; *b* 1983

3b +David; *b* 1985

1b +Ruth; *b* 1977

3a +Katherine; *b* 1949; *m* 1971 *Peter Hyde, of Hove, and has:

1b +Robert; *b* 1972

2b +David; *b* 1981

3b +Jonathan; *b* 1990

1b +Elizabeth; *b* 1983

4a +Claudia; *b* 1954; *m* 1977 (*divorce* 1987) Lucian W M Camp, of Hampstead

(1) +Ursula Margaret; *b* 1913; *m* 1935 *Archibald Bury and lives in Australia

The 5th BARON *d* 8 June 1923; his only son,

HUGH BURDETT MONEY-COUTTS, **6th Baron Latymer**, TD, JP (Devon and Hants); *b* 13 Aug 1876; *educ* Radley and New Coll Oxford (BA 1900); Capt Roy N Devon Hus WW I 1915–17 Gallipoli and Egypt; *m* 11 June 1900 Hester Frances (*d* 1 Feb 1961), 4th dau of Maj-Gen John Cecil Russell, CVO, and had:

1 THOMAS BURDETT, **7th Baron**

2 Alexander Burdett, OBE (1946); Lt-Col Roy Scots Fus WW II, Master Tobacco Pipe-Makers' and Tobacco-Blenders' Co 1964–65; *b* 11 Dec 1902; *educ* Eton and New Coll Oxford; *m* 24 June 1930 Mary Elspeth (*d* 14 April 1990), er dau of Sir Reginald Arthur Hobhouse, 5th Bt (*qv*), and *d* 21 Jan 1994, having had:

(1) +David Burdett (Sir), KCVO (1991) [Sir David Money-Coutts KCVO, Magpie House, Peppard Common, nr Henley-on-Thames, Oxon RG9 5JG]; *b* 19 July 1931; *educ* Eton and New Coll Oxford; Capt Roy Glos Hus (TA) 1951–67, joined Coutts & Co 1954 (dir 1958–96, md 1970–86, chm 1976–93), dir M & G Gp plc 1987–97 (chm 1991–97); *m* 17 May 1958 *Helen Penelope June Utten, dau of Cdr Killingworth Richard Utten Todd, RIN, by Helen St Bride, er dau of Rev Archibald William Douglas, MA (*see* MORTON, E), and has:

1a +Ben(jamin) Burdett [Benjamin Money-Coutts Esq, Overbury Ct, Old Odiham Rd, Alton, Hants GU34 4BX]; *b* 18 July 1961; corporate fin dir Charterhouse Tilney; *m* 7 Nov 1987 *Patricia Anne, est dau of Dr Carl Trepagnier, of Houston, Texas, and has:

1b +Christopher Burdett; *b* 1 Nov 1990

2b +Zachary Alexander; *b* 13 March 1994

1b +Cecily Anne; *b* 23 July 1992

1a +Harriet St Bride [Mrs Martin Pottinger, Mount Pleasant Cottage, Upottery, Devon EX14 9PF]; *b* 3 April 1959; *m* 1st 6 Oct 1979 (*divorce* 1985) Charles Spencer Chetwode Ram, yst s of Maj Henry Stopford Chetwode Ram, RE; *m* 2nd 30 Sept 1985 *Martin Neil Pottinger, yr s of Peter Henry Jameson Pottinger, of Corstorphine, Edinburgh, and by him has:

1b +William Jameson; *b* 19 Nov 1985

2b +Thomas George; *b* 6 Jan 1989

3b +Robin David; *b* 21 Sept 1990

1b +Flora St Bride; *b* 25 April 1987

2a +Laura Isabella [Mrs Jamie Corrie, Foxley, Peppard Common, Henley-on-Thames RG9 5LB]; *b* 28 Sept 1965; *m* 20 June 1987 *P Jamie Corrie, er s of Peter Corrie, of Corner House, Peppard Common, Oxon, and has:

1b +Joshua Richard; *b* 24 March 1992

1b +Lucinda Mary; *b* 12 Oct 1994

2 (cont.) Lt-Col the Hon Alexander and Mrs Money-Coutts also adopted:

*Elizabeth [Mrs George Weber, Scotsgrove House, Thame, Oxon OX9 3RU]; *b* 30 April 1948; *m* 3 May 1969 *George Weber (see WILLIAMS, Bt, of Bridehead) and has issue

*Sarah; *b* 2 Aug 1950

3 Godfrey Burdett; Maj RE WW II (despatches); *b* 18 March 1905; *educ* Eton; *m* 1 June 1931 Anne Cecilia (*d* 13 April 1969), only dau of Hon Wilfrid James (see NORTHBOURNE, B), and *d* 1979, leaving:

(1) +Julia Jane [Mrs Christopher Thomasson, Somerton Castle, Boothby Graffoe, Lincs LN5 0LI]; *b* 17 June 1933; *m* 1st 14 July 1951 (*divorce* 1968) Capt Richard John Fisher Turner, RN, only s of G/Capt E F Turner of Limavady, Co Londonderry; *m* 2nd 1991 *Christopher Thomasson and by her 1st husb has:

1a +Antony Robin Fisher; *b* 4 Oct 1952; *m* 1973 *Barbara Maeve, dau of Harry Stokes, of Guildford, Surrey, and has:

1b +Barnaby Adam Fisher; *b* 1978

2b +Adam Benedict; *b* 1982

2a +Simon John Fisher; *b* 21 Nov 1954

3a +James Michael Fisher; *b* 19 Dec 1956; *m* 1983 *Linda Richardson

1 Mercy Burdett; BRC Mission Greece and Mediterranean WW II, dir Br Sch Khania; *b* 16 April 1910; *educ* LMH Oxford (MA); *m* 15 May 1947 *Michael Seiradhakis [Michael Seiradhakis, Ethnikis, Symfiliosis 39, GR 57019, Perea, Greece], s of John Seiradhakis, of Crete, and *d* 1993, leaving:

(1) +John Hugh [John Seiradhakis Esq, Ethnikis, Symfiliosis 39, GR 57019, Perea, Greece]; *b* 5 March 1948; *m* 1978 *Benedicta Teppe and has:

1a +Michael; *b* Feb 1981

1a +Elena; *b* 1 July 1979

(1) +Sophia Hester [Mrs Charalambos Papoutsakis, 9 Georgiadi Street, 71305 Heraklion, Crete, Greece]; *b* 7 April 1949; *m* 1st 1974 (*divorce* 1978, resumed maiden name) George Pinderis; *m* 2nd 1985 *Charalambos Papoutsakis

The 6th BARON *d* 23 Nov 1949; his est son,

THOMAS BURDETT MONEY-COUTTS, **7th Baron Latymer**; *b* 6 Aug 1901; *educ* Radley and Trin Coll Oxford (MA); chm London Ctee Ottoman Bank, Investment Tst Corp, Claverhouse Investment Tst, Robert Fleming Investment Tst; dir: Coutts and Co, Nat Prov Bank, N Atlantic Securities Corp (ret 1972), memb Cncl Foreign Bondholders, v-chm Middx Hosp, OStJ; *m* 8 Jan 1925 Patience Margaret (*d* 7 Aug 1972), dau of William Courtenay Thompson, and *d* 24 May 1987, leaving:

1 HUGO NEVILL MONEY-COUTTS, **8th and present Baron Latymer**

1 +Joanna Harriet Nevill [The Hon Mrs Langlais, PO Box 113, N Hartland, VT 05052, USA]; *b* 19 April 1928; *m* 12 Jan 1951 *Pierre H C Langlais, only s of Z Langlais, of Quebec City, and has:

(1) +Eric; *b* 8 Jan 1952

(1) +Nicole; *b* 15 Jan 1953

(2) +Louise; *b* March 1954

(3) +Odette *b* 1961

(4) +Jacqueline; *b* 1962

2 +Susan Margaret Nevill [The Hon Mrs Dipple, Nether Walstead, Lindfield, Sussex RH16 2QJ]; *b* 16 May 1933; *m* 1st 26 July 1956 (*divorce* 1965) Michael John Turner, QC (Sir Michael from 1985), yr s of Theodore Francis Turner, QC, of New York (see 1956 edn SCHUSTER, B), and has:

(1) +Mark Christopher; *b* 27 Jan 1959; *educ* Radley; *m* 1985 *Michele — andhas issue

(1) +Louise Margaret Ruth [Mrs Michael Crouch, Stepaside Cottage, Aldingbourne, W Sussex PO20 6UB]; *b* 22 May 1960; *m* 1993 *Michael H Crouch, s of Henry Crouch, of Walton-on-Thames, Surrey, and has:

1a +Abigail Margaret Alison; *b* 18 Sept 1993

2a +Emily Susan Rebecca; *b* 23 March 1995

2 (cont.) The Hon Mrs Susan Turner *m* 2nd 4 Nov 1965 *Ian Alexander Keith Dipple, s of Keith Dipple, and by him has:

(2) +Alexandra Margaret; *b* 9 Jan 1967

(3) +Joanna Shannon; *b* 5 June 1968

LAUDERDALE

Arms: Or a lion rampant gu., couped at all his joints of the field, within the royal tressure az., in a dexter canton arg. a saltire az., surmounted of an inescutcheon or, charged with a lion rampant within a double tressure flory counterflory gu., behind the shield on staffs in saltire ppr. two representations of the Cross of St Andrew, fringed or, ropes and tassles of the last (Insignia of Office of Bearer Scottish Flag). **Crest:** A lion sejant affrontée gu., ducally crowned ppr. or, holding in the dexter paw a sword of the last, hilted and pommeled or, and in the sinister a fleur-de-lys az. **Supporters:** Two eagles, wings expanded, ppr. **Motto:** *Consilio et animis* ('By wisdom and courage'). **Creations:** L. (S) 17 May 1590; V. (S) 2 April 1616; L., V. and E. (S) 14 March 1624; Bt. (NS) 1680.

THE 17TH EARL OF LAUDERDALE, **Viscount of Lauderdale**, **Viscount Maitland**, **Lord (Maitland of) Thirlestane**, **Lord Thirlestane and Boltoun** and a **Baronet** (Sir Patrick Francis Maitland, Bt) [The Rt Hon The Earl of Lauderdale, 10 Ovington Sq, London SW3 1LH; 12 St Vincent St, Edinburgh]; *b* 17 March 1911; *s* bro 1968, also as Hereditary Bearer Nat Flag of Scotland (by decree of Ld Lyon King of Arms 1952, overturning various previous judgements) and Ch of Clan Maitland; *educ* Lancing and BNC Oxford (BA 1933); FO 1943–45; MP (U, but Ind C May-Dec 1957) Lanark 1951–59, consultant ec geography, industl consultant, late ed and manager *Fleet Street Letter Service* and agency for political and diplomatic news, ed *Whitehall Letter*, Special Balkans and Danubian Correspondent *The Times* 1939–41, *Washington News Chronical* 1941, war correspondent Pacific, Australia, NZ, *News Chronicle* 1941–43, fndr and chm Expanding Cwlth Gp HC 1955–59, chm Sub-Ctee Energy Tport and Res, Ho Lds Select Ctee EEC Affrs 1974–79, V-Chm & Co-Fndr Parly Gp Energy Studies 1980–, dir Elf Petroleum (UK), memb Coll Guardians Nat Shrine Our Lady of Walsingham Norfolk 1955– (Guardian Emeritus 1982–), Pres Ch Union 1956–61, FRGS; author: *European Dateline* (1945) and *Task for Giants* (1959); *m* 20 July 1936 *Stanka, er dau of Prof Milivoje Lozanitch, of Belgrade, and has:

1 +IAN, *Viscount Maitland* [The Master of Lauderdale, Viscount Maitland, 150 Tachbrook St, London SW1V 2NE]; *b* 4 Nov 1937; *educ* Radley and BNC Oxford (MA 1965); Lt RNR 1963–73, production mktg manager De La Rue Instruments 1968–70, investment analyst Hedderwick Borthwick & Co 1970–74, Nat Westminster Bank 1974–95, regnl manager Maghreb 1986, ME and N Africa 1989, Sr Regnl Manager Africa and Middle East 1991; dir Maitland Consultancy Servs 1995–; memb Roy Co Archers 1986–; *m* 27 April 1963 *Ann Paule, dau of Geoffrey Clarke, of Dolphin Sq, London SW1, and has:

(1) +John Douglas, *Master of Maitland* [The Master of Maitland, 21 Claverley Grove, London N2 2DG]; *b* 29 May 1965; *educ* Emanuel Coll Battersea

(1) *Sarah Caroline [The Hon Sarah Maitland Parks, Vintner's Lodge, Warborough Rd, Shillingford, Oxon OX10 7SA]; *b* 26 March 1964; *educ* St Paul's Girls' Sch and Trevelyan Coll Durham (BA); *m* 1988 *Stuart G Parks, s of K Parks, of Wargrave, Berks

2 +Sydney Milivoje Patrick [The Rev and Hon Sydney Maitland, 14 Kersland St, Glasgow G12 8BL]; *b* 23 June 1951; *educ* Eton, Edinburgh (BSc) and Strathclyde (Dip TP); ordained Scottish Episcopal Church 1987, late town planner; *m* 7 June 1974 *(Dorothy) Eileen, dau of Reginald Bedell, of Lanarks

1 *(Helen) Olga [The Lady Olga Hay, 21 Cloudesley St, London NI]; *b* 23 May 1944; *educ* Sch of St Mary and St Anne Abbots Bromley and French Lycée London; jnlst; MP (C) Sutton and Cheam (as Lady Olga Maitland) 1992–97, Pres Def and Security Forum; *m* 19 April 1969 *Robin William Patrick Hamilton Hay, LLB, Crown Court Recorder, s of William Reginald Hay, of Nottingham, and has:

(1) *Alastair Patrick Hamilton; *b* 18 Aug 1972; *educ* Edinburgh U

(2) *Fergus William Hamilton; *b* 22 April 1981

(1) *Camilla Charlotte Hamilton; *b* 24 June 1975; *educ* Exeter U

2 *(Caroline Charlotte) Militsa [The Lady Militsa Maitland, 12 St Vincent St, Edinburgh EH3 6SH]; *b* 18 Nov 1946; *educ* London U (BA); Br Assoc for Counselling Accredited Counsellor 1996

Lineage: THOMAS de MATALAN(T); of Anglo-Norman origin; settled in Berwicks *temp* WILLIAM I (THE LION) (reigned 1165–1214); alleged ancestor of:

Sir RICHARD MAITLAND; *m* Avicia, dau and heiress of Thomas de Thirlestane, who brought him that property (which he successfully defended against an English army under EDWARD I), and had:

WILLIAM MAITLAND, of Thirlestane; living *c* 1258; *d c* 1293, had:

Sir ROBERT MAITLAND, of Thirlestane, also of Lethington, which he acquired from Sir John Gifford of Yester (*see* TWEEDDALE, M) and which was confirmed to him by roy charter 1345; *m* —, sis of Sir Robert Keith, Gt Marischal of Scotland (*see* KINTORE, E), and was *ka* Battle of Neville's Cross 17 Oct 1346, leaving:

JOHN MAITLAND, of Thirlestane and Lethington; *m* Agnes, sis of 9th Earl of Dunbar/March (*see* DUNBAR, Bt, of Mochrum), and *d c* 1395, leaving:

Sir ROBERT MAITLAND, of Thirlestane and Lethington; *b c* 1369; *m* Marion Abernethy (*m* 2nd Sir John Scrymgeour, *see* DUNDEE, E), and had, with other issue:

WILLIAM MAITLAND, of Thirlestane and Lethington; *m* Margaret Wardlaw and *d c* 1471, having had:

JOHN MAITLAND, of Thirlestane and Lethington; *b* 18 Aug 1464; *m* apparently a dau of the Laird of Dundas and may have *dvp*, leaving:

WILLIAM MAITLAND, of Lethington and Thirlestane, to which *s* young, Duncan of Dundas being his guardian; had sasine of Thirlestane 1477; *m* Martha, dau of 2nd Lord Seton (*see* EGLINTON and WINTON, E), and was *k* Flodden 1513, leaving, with other issue:

Sir RICHARD MAITLAND, of Lethington (the castle of which was burned by the English 1549; it was presumably restored by 1571, when on his er son's going to join supporters of MARY QUEEN OF SCOTS in Edinburgh Castle it was taken by the Regent's followers and held by them till Feb 1583/4) and Thirlestane, PC (S 1561); *b* 1496; *educ* St Andrews and Paris; had roy charter of lands of Blyth 1537; Ld of Session as Lord Lethington 1561–84; author of a history of the SETONS and compiler of an important collection of early Scottish poems (many of which he wrote himself); *m* Mary, dau of Sir Thomas Cransto(u)n of Crosbie, and *d* 20 March 1585/6, having had:

1 William, of Lethington, PC 1561; *b c* 1528; *educ* St Andrews; Envoy England and France Feb and March 1557/8 respectively; England again Nov 1559–Feb 1559/60 and again Sept 1561, and again May-July 1562, again Feb 1562/3, again April 1564, also France April-June 1563; Speaker S Parl 1560; Pncpl Sec to MARY QUEEN OF SCOTS 1561 onwards, to whom he long stayed faithful even after her political eclipse, becoming head of her supporters who held out in Edinburgh Castle 1571–73; probably connived at murders of both Rizzio and Darnley and may have been instrumental in arranging latter; *m* 1st Janet Menteith (*dsp*); *m* 2nd 6 Jan 1567 Mary, dau of Malcolm, 3rd Lord Fleming, and *d* a prisoner of the English at Leith 9 June 1573, having had:

(1) James; turned RC and possibly on that account was barred from inheriting Lethington and Thirlestane by his gf; *m* Agnes Maxwell and *d c* 1625, leaving, with two daus:

1a Richard; he or descendants of his (or perhaps of his sisters) were living in France 1682

(1) Margaret; *m* as his 1st w 1st Earl of Roxburghe and had issue (*see* ROXBURGHE, D)

2 JOHN, **1st Lord**

3 Thomas; *b c* 1550; *educ* St Andrews and Paris; versifier, jurist and political writer; *d* 1572

1 Helen; *m* Sir John Cockburn of Clerkington

2 Margaret; *m* William Douglas of Whittinghame

3 Mary; *m* Alexander lauder of Hatton

4 Isabel; *m* James Heriot of Trabroun

The 2nd s,

Sir JOHN MAITLAND, **1st Lord (Maitland of) Thirlestane** (S), so *cr* 17 May 1590, PC (S Jan 1567/8–Oct 1569 and 1583); *b c* 1545; *educ* St Andrews and in France; Keeper Privy Seal Scotland 1567, Ld of Session 1568–71 and 1581–87, ktd 1584, Sec State 1584–91, Ld Chllr (S) 1587–95; *m c* 16 Jan 1582/3 Jean, only dau and heiress of 4th Lord Fleming (*see* ABERCORN, D, and HUNTLY, M), and *d* 3 Oct 1595, leaving:

JOHN MAITLAND, **1st Earl of Lauderdale**, so *cr* 14 March 1624 , as also VISCOUNT MAITLAND and LORD THIRLESTANE AND BOLTOUN as also earlier 2 April 1616 VISCOUNT OF LAUDERDALE (all S), with remainder to heirs male and successors in the Lordship of Thirlestane; Commr: for Plantation of Kirks 1617 and 1621, of Parl 1621 and Taxes 1634; Ld of Session 1618–26 and Extrdy Ld 1626–28; Pres S Parl 1644–Jan 1644/5; *m* by 18 June 1610 Lady Isabel Seton (*d* 2 Nov 1638), dau of 1st Earl of Dunfermline (*see* EGLINTON and WINTON, E), and *d* 18 Jan 1645, having had, with 13 other children (of whom only one other *s* and a dau survived their *f*):

1 JOHN MAITLAND, **2nd Earl of Lauderdale** and 1st and last DUKE OF LAUDERDALE AND MARQUESS OF MARCH, EARL OF LAUDERDALE, VISCOUNT MAITLAND, LORD THIRLESTANE, MUSSELBURGH AND BOLTOUN (all S), so *cr* 26 May 1672, also 1st and last EARL OF GUILFORD, Co Surrey, and BARON PETERSHAM, Co Surrey (both E), so *cr* 25 June 1674, KG (1672), PC (S Jan 1660/1, E 1679); *b* 24 May 1616; Covenanter by 1643, supported CHARLES II 1650, captured by English Battle of Worcester 1651 and held in Tower London and other prisons 1650–59; Gentleman Bedchamber 1660–73, Sec State Scotland 1661–80, Extrdy Ld of Session 1661–82, Commr S Treasury 1667–82, High Commr S Parl 1669–74, Pres Cncl in Scotland 1672–81, virtually ruling Scotland singlehanded 1662–80 (when he fell from favour and was sacked) and one of the members of CHARLES II's inner circle of advsrs known as the CABAL (the L of which stood for Lauderdale); since he was without sons he procured a regrant of his then honours 16 Sept 1667 with remainder to his dau Mary but with power to rescind the arrangement, a power he invoked 1675 (apparently at the prompting of his 2nd w, Mary's stepmother, who was alleged to have been OLIVER CROMWELL's mistress at one time), changing the remainder back to its original destination of heirs male; *m* 1st *c* Aug-Sept 1632 Anne (*d* 1671), 2nd dau of 1st Earl of Home (*qv*), and had:

(1) Mary; *m* 4 Dec 1666 2nd Marquess of Tweeddale (*qv*)

1 (cont.) The **2nd Earl** *m* 2nd 17 Feb 1671/2 Elizabeth, Countess of Dysart (*qv*) in her own right, and *dspm* 24 Aug 1682, when the titles *cr* 1672 and 1674 expired

2 CHARLES MAITLAND, **3rd Earl of Lauderdale**, PC (S 1661–82 and 1686); MP Midlothian 1669–72; a Ld of Session as Lord Halton 1670–82; granted hereditary post of Roy Standard Bearer of Scotland following death 1668 of 1st Earl of Dundee (*qv*), though this subject to various conflicting claims and decisions in following centuries, culminating in the Lord Lyon Office decree of 1952 (*see* above); Capt-Gen the Mint 1660–82, Treasurer Depute 1672; *m* 18 Nov 1652 Elizabeth, dau and coheir of Richard Lauder of Hatton, Co Edinburgh, and *d* 9 June 1691, having had, with three other sons (including William, 6th s, *m* 1st Christian Makgill, self-styled Vicountess of Oxfurd (*see* OXFURD, V), *m* 2nd Margaret Walker and *d* 1724) and two daus:

(1) RICHARD MAITLAND, **4th Earl of Lauderdale**, PC (S 1678); *b* 20 June 1653; MP Midlothian 1678, Ld Justice Gen 1681–84, Gen the Mint 1685–89, Commr Treasury 1687–89; as an RC and Jacobite who went with JAMES II and VII to St Germain after 1689 was outlawed 23 July 1694; *m* 1 July 1678 Anne (*m* 2nd 6th Earl of Moray (*qv*) and *d* 18 Sept 1734), 2nd dau of 9th Earl of Argyll (*see* ARGYLL, D), and *dsp* 1695

(2) **Sir John Maitland, 1st Bt** (NS), so *cr* 18 Nov 1680, and **5th Earl of Lauderdale**, PC (S 1688/9); *b c* 1655; advocate 1679, Ld of Session as Lord Ravelrig then as Lord Halton, MP Midlothian 1685–86 and 1689–96, Col Edinburgh Militia; *m c* 1680 Lady Margaret Cunningham (*d* 12 May 1742), only child of 10th Earl of Glencairn (*see* CUNINGHAME, Bt), and *d* 30 Aug 1710, having had, with other issue:

1a James, *Viscount Maitland*; *b c* 1680; *m c* 31 Aug 1702 Jean (*d* 11 Feb 1747), dau of John, Earl of Sutherland (*qv*), and *dvp* & *spm* 1709, having had:

1b Jane; *m* (contract 8 Sept 1726) Sir James Fergusson, 2nd Bt, of Kilkerran (*qv*), and had issue

2a CHARLES, **6th Earl**

3a Alexander; had:

1b Barbara; *m* 1st Sir Edward Gibson, 2nd Bt (*see* GIBSON-CRAIG-CARMICHAEL, Bt); *m* 2nd Helenus Halkerston of Rathillet and *d* 19 June 1782

The 5th EARL's est surv son,

CHARLES MAITLAND, **6th Earl of Lauderdale**; *b c* 1688; fought as Offr Battle of Sheriffmuir 1715 (presumably against the Jacobites), Ld Lt and Sheriff Midlothian, Capt-Gen the Mint; rep S peer 1741–44; *m* 15 July 1710 Lady Elizabeth Ogilvy (*d* 24 Sept 1778), dau of 1st Earl of Seafield (*qv*), and *d* 15 July 1744, having had, with other issue:

1 JAMES MAITLAND, **7th Earl of Lauderdale**; *b* 23 Jan 1718; Lt-Col 1745–65, rep S peer 1747–61 and 1782–84; *m* 24 April 1749 Mary (*d* 20 July 1789), dau and coheir of Sir Thomas Lombe, Alderman London, and *d* 17 Aug 1789, having had, with other issue:

(1) Valdave Charles Lauder, *Viscount Maitland*; *b* 14 Dec 1752; *d* 5 Sept 1754

(2) JAMES MAITLAND, **8th Earl of Lauderdale**, KT (1821), PC (1806 and 1826); *b* 26 Jan 1759; *educ* Edinburgh High Sch, Trin Coll Oxford and Edinburgh, Glasgow and Paris Us; advocate 1780, MP Newport Cornwall 1790–96 and Malmesbury 1784–89, rep S peer 1790–96; *cr* 22 Feb 1806 BARON LAUDERDALE OF THIRLESTANE, Co Berwick (UK), Keeper Gt Seal Scotland 1806–07; *m* 15 Aug 1782 Eleanor (*d* 16 Sept 1856), only dau and heiress of Anthony Todd, and *d* 15 Sept 1839, having had, with other issue:

1a JAMES MAITLAND, **9th Earl of Lauderdale**; *b* 12 May 1784; *educ* Eton and Edinburgh U; MP (Whig) Camelford 1806–07, Richmond 1818–20 and (Tory) Appleby 1826–32, Ld Lt Berwicks 1841–60; *d* unm 22 Aug 1860

2a ANTHONY MAITLAND, **10th Earl of Lauderdale**, GCB (1862, KCB 1832, CB 1816), KCMG (1820); *b* 10 June 1785; Adml the Red 1862, MP (Whig) Haddington Burghs 1813–18 and (Tory) Berwicks 1826–32, Naval ADC to WILLIAM IV 1830–37 and HM QUEEN VICTORIA 1837–41; *d* unm 22 March 1863, when the UK Barony expired

1a Eleanor; *m* 1815 James Balfour, of Whittinghame, Berwicks (*see* BALFOUR, E), and *d* 23 May 1869, having had issue

2a Julian Jane; *m* 1823 Sir John Warrender, 5th Bt, and *d* 19 May 1827, leaving issue (*see* BRUNTISFIELD, B)

(3) Thomas (Sir), GCB, PC; Lt-Gen, Govr Malta and Ionian Islands; *d* 1824

(4) William Mordaunt; Gen; *m* 1st Mary, dau of Rev Richard Orpen, of Killowen, and widow of John Travers, of Co Cork; *m* 2nd 5 June 1819 Jane (*d* 5 Sept 1854), dau of Rev Thomas Walker and widow of Dalhousie Watherstone, and *d* 24 June 1841, leaving by his 1st w:

1a THOMAS MAITLAND, **11th Earl of Lauderdale**, GCB (1873, KCB 1865, CB 1841); *b* 3 Feb 1803; RN: joined 1816, Lt 1823, Cdr 1827, Capt 1837, ktd 1843, Capt Gunnery Sch Portsmouth 1854–57, Cdr Pacific Fleet 1860–62, Adml 1868, First Naval ADC to HM QUEEN VICTORIA 1866–73; rep S peer 1867–78; Kt of King Charles III of Spain (awarded for his cmdg off coast of Spain in Civil War 1836–37); *m* 7 Feb 1828 Amelia (*d* 18 Feb 1890), 3rd dau of William Young, of Rio de Janeiro, and *d* 1 Sept 1878, having had:

1b Thomas Mordaunt; *b* 1838; *d* 7 Aug 1844

1b Isabel Anne; *d* 3 May 1854

2b Mary Jane; *m* 7 Jan 1868 12th Earl of Meath (*qv*) and *d* 4 Nov 1918, leaving issue

3b Alice Charlotte; *d* 30 Jan 1883

(1) Hannah Charlotte; *m* 18 April 1785 7th Marquess of Tweeddale (*qv*) and *d* 8 May 1804, leaving issue

(2) Jane; *m* 1st Samuel Long, bro of Lord Farnborough (1st *cr*); *m* 2nd 5 Nov 1808 Sir William Houstoun, 1st Bt, GCB, and *d* 1 June 1833, leaving issue (*see* HOUSTON-BOSWALL, Bt)

2 Charles MAITLAND later BARCLAY-MAITLAND; *m* 1st Isabel (*d* 23 Oct 1761), dau and heiress of Sir Alexander Barclay of Towie, and had, with four daus:

(1) Charles, of Tillicoultry; *m* 15 Sept 1786 Elizabeth Mary Hale and *d* 1816, leaving:

1a Charles (Rev); *b* 4 Nov 1789; Rector Little Longford, Wilts; *m* 6 Sept 1810 Anne, dau of Thomas Knott, of Stockland, and *d* Dec 1844, having had:

1b Charles; *b* 12 May 1821; *d* 1822

2b CHARLES BARCLAY-MAITLAND, **12th Earl of Lauderdale**; *b* 29 Sept 1822; *d* unm 13 Aug 1884 after being struck by lightning on Braidshaw Rigg Moor, nr Lauder

1b Maria Anne; *m* 9 Jan 1840 Rev James Hardwicke Dyer (*d* 14 Nov 1871) and *d* 22 June 1845, leaving issue

(2) Alexander; Lt 100th Regt; *m* Margaret Cooper and *d* 1794, having had a s and dau

2 (cont.) Charles BARCLAY-MAITLAND *m* 2nd April 1765 —, dau of Patrick Haldane of Gleneagles; *m* 3rd 11 Feb 1768 Janet (*d* 6 Nov 1799), yst dau of Sir Thomas Moncreiffe of that Ilk, 2nd Bt (*see* ERROLL, E), and *d* 28 Nov 1795

3 Richard; *b* 10 Feb 1724; joined Army 1743, Capt 1759, present taking of Quebec 1759, DAG Forces Quebec 1760 and N America 1764, Col 1772; *m* 11 July at New York Mary McAdam (*d* 10 Jan 1787) and *d* 13 July 1772 (two days after his marriage), leaving:

(1) Richard; *b* 1768; Capt Durham Fencibles; *m* 26 Feb 1789 Harriot (*m* 2nd 12 May 1804 Powles Harrison and *d* June 1845), dau of John Bower, of Scorton, and *dsp* 17 March 1802

(2) Patrick, of Kilmaron Castle, Fife; *b* 1770 before his parents' marriage but legitimated by it *ex post facto* according to Scottish law in a decision of the Ho Lds Privileges Ctee 1885; ptnr John Palmer & Co, Calcutta bankers; *m* 28 Feb 1807 Anne, dau of Colthurst Bateman, and *d* 29 Jan 1821, leaving:

1a Frederick Colthurst; *b* 1 Jan 1808; Maj-Gen IA; *m* 29 Aug 1837 Anne Deering (*d* 24 March 1887), dau of Stephen Williams, and *d* 3 Aug 1876, having had:

1b FREDERICK HENRY, **13th Earl**

2b George Thomas; *b* 23 Dec 1841; Lt-Col BSC, granted rank of earl's yr s 29 Aug 1885, memb Roy Co Archers; *d* unm 23 Sept 1910

1b Ellen; *d* unm 1852

2a Patrick John; *b* 12 May 1816; *m* 1838 Laura (*d* 1849), dau of H Robarts, of Peckham Rye, and *d* 1886, having had:

1b Frederick; *b* 1846

1b Charlotte; *b* 1839

2b Laura; *b* 1842; *m* C Ross

1a Eliza; *b* 22 Dec 1808; *m* 6 Feb 1827 William Morris Reade, of Rossennona, Co Kilkenny, and *d* 3 Sept 1884

(3) John; *b* 1771; Adml; *m* 1st 22 April 1799 Elizabeth, dau of Archibald Ogilvie of Inchmartine; *m* 2nd 8 Jan 1820 his er bro's sis-in-law Dora, dau of Colthurst Bateman and widow of George Augustus Simson, and *dsp* 20 Oct 1836

(4) James; *b* 1772; Lt-Col 75th Regt; *k* Siege of Bhurtpore 9 Jan 1805

4 Sir ALEXANDER MAITLAND, 1st Bt, *qv*

5 Frederick Lewis, of Rankeillour; *b* 19 June 1730; Capt RN; *m* 27 Aug 1767 Margaret (*d* April 1825), only dau of James Dick and heir of line of Rankeillour (*see* OXFURD, V), and *d* 16 Dec 1786, leaving, with three daus:

(1) Charles; *b* 26 Dec 1769; 17th Light Dragoons; *m* 26 Aug 1794 Mary (*d* 11 June 1824), dau of David Johnston, and *d* 1820, leaving, with other issue:

1a David MAITLAND later MAITLAND MAKGILL CRICHTON (of Rankeillour); *b* 4 March 1801; heir of line through his paternal grandmother to the Crichton Viscounts Frendraught; *m* 1st 7 Aug 1827 Eleanor Julian (*d* Jan 1833), 2nd dau of Thomas Hog of Newliston, and had, with other issue:

1b Charles Julian, of Rankeillour; *b* 15 May 1828; *m* 24 Dec 1851 Anna Campbell (*m* 2nd 8 June 1871 Edward Everard Rushworth, CMG, DCL, Lt Govr Jamaica, and *d* 6 Aug 1907), est dau of Lt James N Jarvis, RN, Colonial Sec and memb Supreme Cncl Tobago, and *d* 22 Jan 1858, having had, with other issue:

1c David, of Rankeillour; *b* 24 March 1854; 78th Highrs; *m* 9 Dec 1875 Emily (*d* 14 July 1933), dau of Charles Drummond Bailey, of Charlton Musgrove, Somerset, and *d* 25 Dec 1889, leaving:

1d Charles Julian; *b* 5 Sept 1880; 10th Bn Gordon Highrs, Lt 3rd Bn Seaforth Highrs, memb Roy Co Archers; *m* 15 Feb 1902 Sybil Twynihoe (*d* 1984), dau of Twynihoe William Erie, Master Supreme Court, and was *ka* 25 Sept 1915, having had:

1e David; *b* 15 Jan, *d* 12 Feb 1903

2e Charles Frederick Andrew; *b* 3 April 1907; *educ* Trin Coll Cambridge (BA); Lt Black Watch (SR); *d* 28 Sept 1938

3e Douglas; *b* 24 April 1909; *educ* Winchester; Maj Gordon Highrs WW II (wounded); *m* 24 Oct 1936 Sybil Frederica Coore (*d* 1992), only dau of Frederick Lechmere Paton, JP, of Newent, Glos, and *d* 5 April 1968, leaving:

1f Charles; *b* 25 July 1942; *educ* Winchester; recognised by Lord Lyon Office as Ch Clan Crichton 1980; *m* 16 Jan 1971 *Isla Susan [Mrs Charles Maitland Makgill Crichton, Monzie Castle, Crieff, Perthshire], dau of Matthew Frederick Gloag, of Bonhard House, Perthshire, and *d* 1992, leaving:

1g +David; *b* 11 Sept 1972

1f *Veronica Ann [Mrs Ian Dickinson, The Manor House, Riding Mill, Northumberland NE44 6HW]; *b* 13 Nov 1938; *m* 1978 Ian Joicy Dickinson (*d* 13 Dec 1996)

1e Mary Sylvia; *b* 2 July 1905; *d* 1 July 1994

2e *Rosemary Julian [Mrs James Musker, 37 Clareville Grove, London SW7 5AU]; *b* posthumously 5 Dec 1915; *m* 8 June 1940 F/Lt James Herbert Lonsdale Musker, RAFVR, 7th Hus (*d* 16 Aug 1966), er s of Maj Herbert Musker, OBE, of Rushford Hall, Thetford, Norfolk, and has:

1f *Juliet Alexandra Sarah [Mrs William Barry, 12 Kensington Pk Mews, London W11; Malthouse Farmhouse, Manningford Abbots, Wilts SN9 6HY]; *b* 22 Aug 1941; *m* 21 May 1965 *William Edward Barry and has issue (*see* BARRY, Bt)

2d James Henry; *b* 19 May 1885; Lt-Cdr RN, Assoc of King's Coll U London; *m* 28 Jan 1908 Emily Christina (*d* 1972), 2nd dau of Hugh

Weir-MacColl, of Appin, Argyll, and Newlands, S Africa, and d 1948, leaving:

1e David Hugh, DSO (1942), DSC; b 11 Oct 1910; Cdr RN WW II (wounded, despatches three times), Cdr Dannebrog Denmark, Polish Naval Citation, Fell Inst Linguists, Chm Assoc Unit Tst Managers 1974

1e *Alice Mary Emily; b 16 Feb 1914; m 30 June 1937 Vernon Charles Chambers (d 1983), yr s of Robert Anstey Chambers, and has:

1f *Virginia; b 16 April 1942; m 10 Feb 1968 (George) Digby MacDougall Dodd (d 1987), 3rd s of Maj Sir John Samuel Dodd, of Jersey, and has:

1g *Julian Crichton; b 1973

1g *Tamsin Serena Georgina; b 1971

2f *Vanessa [Mrs James Fleischman, Portland House, Rt 1/217A, Caledonia, MN 55921, USA; Portland House, 45 Dresden Rd, London N19 3BG]; b 5 June 1946; m 1977 *James Alan Fleischmann, MB, BCh, MRCP (UK), MRCGP, DCH, DRCOG, and has:

1g *James Maitland; b 1985

1g *Diana Maitland; b 1982

1d Anna Campbell Margaret Emily; m 17 Oct 1907 Rev Henry Gibbon (d 1947) and d 7 April 1954, leaving issue

2d Evelyn Bertie Charlotte; m 1 June 1905 Hon Kenelm Pleydell-Bouverie, 6th s of 4th Earl of Radnor (qv), and d 24 March 1936, leaving issue

3d Mary Scott; m 1 Feb 1902 Maj Robert Edward Fitzmayer Wemyss, RFA, s of Gen H Manley Wemyss, CB, and d 21 Jan 1923, leaving issue

1c Anna Charles; m 28 April 1887 Thomas Henry Yorke Trotter (d 11 March 1934), barrister, MusD, MA Oxon, and d 28 March 1943, leaving issue

1b Mary Stuart; m 1 May 1849 V-Adml Philip Horatio Townsend Somerville (d 12 May 1881) and d 1 June 1895, leaving issue

1a (cont.) David MAITLAND MAKGILL CRICHTON m 2nd 2 Dec 1834 Esther (d 19 Oct 1892), dau of Andrew Coventry, LLD, of Shanwell, and d 11 July 1851, having by her had:

2b David MAITLAND MAKGILL CRICHTON later MAKGILL CRICHTON MAITLAND (1884); b 20 Aug 1841; Maj-Gen Gren Gds; m 29 Oct 1873 Lady Margaret Pleydell-Bouverie (d 5 Jan 1924), 2nd dau of 4th Earl of Radnor (qv), and d 2 Jan 1907, leaving:

1c Coventry, JP (Rutland); b 3 Feb 1877; Cdr RN, Boer War and WW I; m 12 Nov 1902 Alice Mary (d 20 Oct 1965), 2nd dau of Col Charles Birch-Reynardson, of Holywell Hall, Stamford, Lincs, and d 20 Oct 1958, leaving:

1d Henry David, OBE (1945); b 21 Dec 1904; educ Eton; Col REME WW II (despatches), Offr US Legn Merit; m 1st 3 June 1930 (divorce 1949) Barbara Ellen, only dau of Brig-Gen Sir George Ayscough Armytage, 7th Bt (qv), and had:

1e *Judith Elizabeth [Mrs Anthony Houssemayne du Boulay, Langford Farm, Sydling St Nicholas, Dorset DT2 9NP]; b 28 July 1933; m 29 July 1965 *Anthony John Houssemayne du Boulay, yst s of Capt Charles John Houssemayne du Boulay, RN, of Exton Ho, Exton, Hants

2e *Sarah Barbara [Sga Francesco Boscu, via Monti 11, Varallo, Pombia, Italy]; b 5 April 1936; m 1st 10 July 1958 Count Alessandro Monneret de Villard, only s of Count Piero Monneret de Villard by Baroness Olga von Rosen, of Milan; m 2nd 1984 *Francesco Boscu and by her 1st husb has:

1f *Raffaella Augusta Barbara; b 9 Oct 1961

2f *Xenia Olga Anastasia; b 15 May 1965

3f *Tatiana; b 1970

1d (cont.) Col Henry Makgill Crichton Maitland m 2nd 14 March 1949 Audrey Estelle Ljufling (m 3rd 1982 Maurice J C Allom (d 1995), of Dene Park, Tonbridge, Kent and d 2 Aug 1994), dau of Henry John Hyde-Johnson and widow of Lt (A) Peter Thorp Eckersley, JP, MP, RNVR, and d 14 Oct 1970

1d Jean; b 12 Sept 1907; m 18 Sept 1935 A/Cdre James Silvester, CBE (d 5 Jan 1956), RAF, yst s of Henry Silvester, of Oldbury, Worcs, and d 1989, leaving issue

2c Frederick Lewis, DSO (1918); b 7 March 1878; educ Eton; Lt-Col Gordon Highrs, T/Lt-Col cmdg Serv Bn Roy Welch Fus 1916 and 2nd Bn Gordon Highrs 1917–18, Boer War (severely wounded), WW I (despatches), Serbian Order White Eagle 4th Cl with swords; m 21 Feb 1921 Amy Anne Charlotte (d 26 May 1927), dau of Stuart Duckett, of Russelltown Park, Carlow, and widow of Brig-Gen Louis Murray Phillpotts, CMG, DSO, and dsp 12 Nov 1949

3c Mark Edward, CVO (1952), DSO (1917), JP (Oxon 1919, Wilts 1929), DL (Wilts 1932); b 4 July 1882; educ Eton; Col Gren Gds, Boer War, WW I (wounded, despatches, Croix de Guerre), WW II as Lt-Col cmdg Gren Gds 1939–41, memb Roy Co Archers and Gentlemen-at-Arms 1928–52; m 15 Oct 1924 Patience Irene Fleetwood (d 23 April 1974), 2nd dau of Sir John Michael Fleetwood Fuller, 1st Bt (qv), and d 30 Jan 1972, leaving:

1d +John David [Maj John Makgill Crichton Maitland, Daluaine, Rhynie, Huntly, Aberdeenshire AB54 4NA]; b 10 Sept 1925; educ Eton; Maj Gren Gds 1945; Ld Lt Renfrewshire 1980–94 (DL 1962); m 1st 12 June 1954 Jean Patricia (d 1984), only child of Maj-Gen Sir Michael O'Moore Creagh, KBE, MC (see McGRIGOR, Bt); m 2nd 1987 *Mary Ann Vere, only dau of Maj Charles Herbert Harberton Eales (see OGILVY, Bt) and widow of Capt James Quintin Penn Curzon (see HOWE, E) and by his 1st w has:

1e +Mark Archibald [Mark Makgill Crichton Maitland Esq, 44 Cloncurry St, London SW6]; b 19 March 1955; educ Eton; m 1987 *Judith Mainwaring, er dau of H G Turner, of Nottingham, and has:

1f +Archie David; b 1988

2f +Nicholas Hugh; b 1990

1e *Mary Elizabeth [Mrs Roy North, Woolmer Cottage, Willingham Green, Suffolk CB8 0SN]; b 19 July 1962; m 1993 *Roy North, s of K North, of Horncastle, Lincs

2d +Mark Michael [Maj Mark Makgill Crichton Maitland Esq, 2 Grosvenor Crescent, Edinburgh EH12 5EP]; b 19 May 1928; educ Eton; Maj (ret) Gordon Highrs

1d Irene Margaret; b 21 April 1927; m 12 Dec 1953 (divorce 1986) Maj Michael Christopher Alfred Codrington (see CODRINGTON, Bt, of Dodington (1876)), and d 1994, leaving issue

1c Mary Esther; b 26 Sept 1875; d unm 8 July 1961

2c Margaret; b 6 Oct 1885

3b Andrew Coventry; b 20 June 1845; dir Standard and Chartered Banking Gp 1872; m 19 Sept 1878 Katherine Charlotte (d 24 Nov 1941), est dau of Sir Edward Hulse, 5th Bt (qv), and d 29 July 1925, leaving:

1c David Edward; b 25 June 1879; educ Harrow; Lt-Col QO Cameron Highrs; m 15 April 1909 Phyllis (d 1982), dau of Claude Arthur Cuthbert, of Bryn Garth, Herefs, and d 17 Dec 1952, having had:

1d Andrew James (Sir); b 28 Dec 1910; educ Wellington; 1st Punjab Regt IA 1941–45, Col 1944–45, Dep Dir Movements QMG Branch GHQ India 1944–45; chm Employers' Side Nat Jt Cncl Port Tport Ind and Nat Assoc Port Employers 1958–65, Arbitrator Police Cncl 1966, V-Chm PLA, md P&O Steam Navigation Co, chm Overseas Containers Ltd, dir Julian S Hodge & Co, Staflex Internat, dir Kamunting Tin Dredging 1974; ktd 1963; m 24 July 1948 Isabel (d 19 June 1997), dau of Andrew Joseph McGill, of Sydney, NSW, and widow of John Eric Bain, and d 29 Oct 1995

2d David; b 13 July 1914; 2nd Lt Roy Northumberland Fus WW II; das (drowned) March 1941

3d +Edward M, OBE (1948, MBE 1945) [Maj-Gen Edward Maitland-Makgill-Crichton OBE, 211 Braid Rd, Edinburgh EH10 6HT]; b 23 Nov 1916; educ Bedford Sch and RMC Sandhurst; Maj-Gen, QO Cameron Highrs WW II (wounded, despatches), GOC 51st (Highland) Div Dist 1956–68, ret 1968; m 4 April 1951 *Sheila Margaret, yr dau of William Rowland Hibbins, and has:

1e +David Edward; b 18 Jan 1952; educ Bedford Sch; Maj QO Highrs; m 1979 *Sheena Anne, dau of Alexander Dougal Callander, of Coldon, Stirlingshire, and has:

1f +Andrew Alexander; b 1 Aug 1986

1f *Amanda Clare; b 21 May 1984

2e +(Andrew) James; b 10 Sept 1953; educ Bedford Sch and RMA Sandhurst; Lt-Col The Highrs 1974; m 1977 *Karen Gail, dau of Derek Charles Smith, and has:

1f +William Roderick; b 22 Aug 1979

2f +Edward Thomas; b 19 Aug 1982

3f +Thomas James; b 13 Aug 1986

1f *Eila Victoria; b 1 Jan 1990

3e +Charles William; b 19 May 1961; educ Strathallan and RMA Sandhurst; Capt (ret) Black Watch

1d Jean Beatrice; b 28 Dec 1912; m 1st 18 April 1933 (divorce 1946) 2nd Baron Morris (qv) and had issue; m 2nd 6 April 1946 Baron Salmon (LP) and d 1989

2d *(Katherine) Grizel [Mrs Russell Barton, 2322 Clover St, Rochester, NY 14618, USA]; b 7 April 1930; m 24 July 1954 *Russell William Andrew Charles Barton, MB, MRCP, DPM, s of Charles William Barton, and has:

1e *Karen Elizabeth; b 24 May 1956

2e *Sarah Muriel; b 23 March 1958

2c Henry Coventry, CB (1937), CMG (1919), DSO (1916); b 29 June 1880; educ Charterhouse; Col Roy Scots Fus, ADC to HM GEORGE V 1934–37, cmdg 1st Bn Roy Scots Fus 1928, Brig, AA and QMG Gibraltar 1931, T/Brig and Cdr 14th Inf Bde 1933–37, Hon Brig 1937, Boer War (severely wounded), WW I (wounded, despatches), WW II 1939–41 as Area Cdr, Legn Hon; m 21 Oct 1911 Dorothy Margaret (d 1979), dau of Sir Walter Thorburn, DL, MP, and d 29 Sept 1953, having had:

1d Hamilton Ian; b 5 April 1918; Lt Roy Scots Fus WW II; ka June 1940

1d *Diana Elizabeth Katherine, TD [Miss Diana Maitland Makgill Crichton TD, Hedge Cottage, Kingston Deverill, nr Warminster, Wilts]; b 25 April 1916

3c Andrew Gavin, DSO (1917), MC; b 3 July 1881; educ Charterhouse and Oriel Coll Oxford; Lt-Col 5th Bn Cameron Highrs WW I (despatches); d unm 5 Sept 1956

4c Charles Lewis; b 16 Oct 1883; Lt-Cdr RN, served China 1900 and WW I (despatches), Russian Order St Stanislas; d 7 Oct 1921

5c James Richard; b 5 June 1885; Cdr RN, WWs I and II; d unm 1 Dec 1943

6c John Denys; b 15 Dec 1897; Lt Black Watch WW I (severely wounded); m 24 Jan 1930 Denise (m 2nd 7 Dec 1932 (divorce 1943) Douglas S Fraser and d 1984, having resumed her 1st husb's name), dau of J H Crosby, of Johannesburg, and d 28 Oct 1931, leaving:

1d +Michael John [Michael Maitland Crichton Makgill Esq, Candy Cottage, PO Box 177, Rivonia 2128, Johannesburg, S Africa]; b 25 April 1931; educ Rhodes U (BA 1952), Witwatersrand U (LLB 1954) and Oriel Coll Oxford; m 23 April 1958 *Euphemia Daphne Joan, dau of Albert Edward Hopkins, of Durban, and has:

1e +Anthony John; b 5 Feb 1960

1e *Philippa Anne; b 15 March 1965

1c (Eleanor) Esmé; *m* 14 Oct 1908 Hakewill Tresyllian Williams (*d* 2 April 1929), JP, DL, of Churchill Court, Kidderminster, Worcs, s of Henry Williams, of Rockingham Hall, Hagley, and *d* 4 Feb 1967, leaving issue

2c Kathleen Esther; *m* 17 Sept 1919 Sidney Gobourn, s of G Gobourn, and had:

  1d *Peter Charles Crichton; *b* 1924; Maj RCT, late Cameron Highrs, WW II (wounded); *m* 1953 *Elizabeth Barbara, dau of Rev D Foster, ACF, and has:

    1e *Andrew Denis Crichton; *b* 1960

    2e *Guy Crichton; *b* 1964

    1e *Catherine Elizabeth Crichton; *b* 1962

  2d *Edward David Crichton; *b* 1927; WW II with Roy Fus; *m* July 1955 *Shirley Ann Davis Lloyd and has:

    1e *Timothy Richard Crichton; *b* 1958

    1e *Felicity Mary; *b* 1961

3c Norah Grizel; *m* 14 July 1908 Maj Charles Noel Lyall, RA (*d* 12 April 1942), s of George Lyall, MP, and *d* 23 Dec 1977, leaving:

  1d *Ronald Crichton; *b* 18 Oct 1912; *educ* Canford; Hants Regt and RAOC WW II

  2d *Charles Leslie; *b* 10 June 1919; *educ* Charterhouse and Worcester Coll Oxford; *m* 5 July 1969 *Marjorie Yvonne Josèphe, dau of Joseph Marie Alexandre de Burlet, formerly of Nivelle, Belgium

  1d Marjorie Cecil; *b* 18 April 1909; ATS 1939–47

  2d *Barbara Kathleen; *b* 25 Feb 1911; *m* 20 April 1940 Wilfred Danvers Brinton, DM, FRCP, 2nd s of Hubert Brinton, of London, and has:

    1e *Veronica Ruth; *b* 24 Aug 1946; *m* 29 Sept 1978 *Ian Dickinson

    2e *Margaret Danvers; *b* 15 May 1949

4c Margaret Nona

5c Muriel Christian; *m* 16 July 1913 Aldred Clement Rowden (*d* 30 Dec 1935), Registrar Corp of Sons of Clergy, only s of A W Rowden, KC, and had:

  1d *Maurice Edward Aldred; *b* 1918; Capt 60th Regt WW II (wounded)

  2d Cecil William Aldred; *b* 1921; Lt 60th Regt; *d* unm 1952

  1d Diana Hope; Sector Offr WAAF WW II (despatches, Croix de Guerre with star); executed Natzweiler Camp 1944

6c Vera Helen; *m* 21 Jan 1915 Richard Chetwynd-Stapylton and *d* 25 April 1959, leaving issue (*see* CHETWYND, V)

2b Esther Frederica; *m* 25 March 1865 Capt Augutus Chetham Strode, CB, RN (*d* 10 March 1874), and had issue

2a Lewis; *b* 12 April 1812; R-Adml; *m* 1st 12 Dec 1841 Henrietta Louisa (*d* Jan 1868), dau of Hon Sir John Henry Newbolt, Ch Justice Madras, and had:

  1b Charles; *b* 13 Dec 1848; *d* Nov 1849

2a (cont.) Lewis Maitland *m* 2nd 24 March 1869 Mary (*d* 10 Feb 1911), 2nd dau of Archibald F Allan, and *d* 25 Feb 1876, having by her had:

  2b Frederick Lewis; *b* 18 July 1874; *m* 6 Aug 1896 Constance Zeila (*d* 23 April 1960), dau of Andrew Dewar Durie, MD, and *d* 9 Feb 1915, having had:

    1c Frederick Lewis; *b* 7 Nov 1898, *d* 1898

    2c Henry Lewis; *b* 11 March, *d* 3 Oct 1901

    3c David Randolph, VRD; *b* 15 Feb 1902; *educ* Trin Coll Glenalmond and Edinburgh U (MB ChB, FRCP); DMR (D), Surgn Lt-Cdr RNVR WW II; *m* 24 Nov 1930 *Barbara Mary Carnegie, only dau of Edward Henry Wemyss, of Kirkton, Fife, and *d* 3 April 1995, leaving:

      1d David Lewis; *b* 27 March 1932; *m* 1st 29 April 1961 Anna Mary Smith (*d* 1968), ward of J de R Kent, of East Molesey, Surrey, and had:

        1e +Lewis Randolph; *b* 1962

        2e +Niall David (twin); *b* 1962

        3e +Angus Charles; *b* 1964

      1d (cont.) David Maitland *m* 2nd *Jennifer Mary, dau of W O Davis, of Isle of Soay, Inverness-shire, and *d* 15 May 1995, leaving by her:

        1e *Sarah Mary; *b* 1971

      2d +Henry Christopher [Henry Maitland Esq, Grange of Lindores, Newburgh, Cupar Fife KY14 6JN]; *b* 4 March 1935; *educ* Trin Coll Glenalmond; *m* 19 Oct 1968 *Charlotte Mary Ross, dau of Rae Tod, of S Oswald Rd, Edinburgh, and widow of Lt J W Harvey, RN, and has:

        1e +Christopher Ross; *b* 13 Oct 1969

        2e +Gavin Edward; *b* 1976

        1e *Barbara Anne; *b* 1972

        2e *Mary Flora (twin with Gavin); *b* 1976

      1d *Mary [Mrs Peter Wang, Lawhead Loch, W Calder, Midlothian EH55 8LW]; *b* 31 July 1939; *m* 10 Feb 1962 *Peter Laurtiz Wang, s of Sigurd Wang, of Boreland House, Lockerbie, Dumfriesshire, and has:

        1e *Mark Sigurd Maitland [Mark Wang Esq, 25 Calder Rd, Bellsquarry, W Lothian EH54 9AA]; *b* 9 May 1963; *m* 29 May 1993 *Jayne Chantry and has:

          1f *Markus Edward; *b* 31 May 1994

          2f *Magnus Henry; *b* 12 Oct 1996

        2e *Patrick David [Patrick Wang Esq, Rudaki Prospekt 83, Penjikent, Tajikistan 735500]; *b* 4 March 1965; *m* 3 July 1994 *Carol Scott and has:

          1f *Lawrence Scott; *b* 15 June 1996

        3e *Robert Magnus [Robert Wang Esq, 11 Rose Court, Easher Park Dve, Edinburgh EH4 6JR]; *b* 20 July 1969

1b Mary Agnes; *m* 1st 1903 (*annulled* 1904) Rev W M Tocher (*d* 1927); *m* 2nd 13 July 1907 Hugh Miller, WS, and *d* 1943

2b Anna Louise; *m* 29 Aug 1893 Rev C H Titterton, BD (*d* 1958) and *d* 6 Sept 1914, leaving issue

(2) James MAITLAND later MAITLAND-HERIOT, WS; *b* 11 Sept 1774; *m* 31 Dec 1813 Margaret (*d* 28 Jan 1869), dau of William Dalgleish, of Scotscraig, and *d* 26 April 1848, having had, with other issue:

1a Frederick Lewis, JP, DL Fife; *b* 6 Feb 1818; *educ* Edinburgh Acad; Hon Sheriff Substitute Fife 1862–81, Advocate 1839, Advocate-Depute 1857 and 1859–62; *m* 3 Oct 1848 Martha (*d* 28 July 1904), 2nd dau of Sir Andrew Agnew, 7th Bt, of Lochnaw (*qv*), and *d* 7 March 1881, leaving:

  1b Andrew Agnew, JP (Fife); *b* 3 April 1851; *educ* Edinburgh Acad; memb Roy Co Archers; *m* 1st 15 Oct 1884 (*divorce* 1886) Annie Colquhoun (*d* 28 Aug 1929), only dau of Neil Colquhoun Campbell, of Barnhill; *m* 2nd 22 Feb 1887 Gertrude (*d* 21 April 1921), dau of Theophilus Hamilton, and *d* 30 April 1930, leaving by her:

    1c Frederick Lewis; *b* 3 May 1889; *m* 3 June 1919 Mabel Mary (*d* 7 Dec 1962), dau of James Keenan, of Rosario, Argentina, and *d* 8 Oct 1953, leaving:

      1d *Pamela Gertrude [Mrs Christopher Boothby, 26 Cwrt Deri, Heol-y-Felin, Rhiwbina, Cardiff CF4 6JB]; *b* 15 Jan 1921; *m* 25 May 1940 Maj Christopher Evelyn Boothby (*see* BOOTHBY, Bt), and has issue

      2d *Jean Ursula [Mrs John Adams, 82 Beaufort Mansions, Beaufort St, London SW3 5AF]; *b* 28 June 1923; *m* 1st 15 Jan 1944 (*divorce* 1952) Capt Alan Seaforth Cox, yst s of Charles Edward Cox, of Staffs, and has:

        1e *Andrew Frederick Seaforth [Andrew Cox Esq, 8 Morpeth Mansions, Morpeth Terrace, London SW1]; *b* 1945; *m* 1st 1964 (*divorce* 1976) Carol Ilott and has:

          1f *Oliver; *b* 1967

          1f *Emma; *b* 1964

          2f *Zoe; *b* 1969

        1e (cont.) Andrew Cox *m* 2nd 1978 *Tricia Harley and by her has:

          2f *Toby; *b* 1974

          3f *Charlie; *b* 1982

      2d (cont.) Mrs Jean Cox *m* 2nd 23 July 1955 John Griffith Adams (*d* 1978), s of Thomas James Adams, of Narberth, Pembs, and by him has:

        2e *Sebastian Thomas Maitland; *b* 1961

    1c Mary Gertrude; *b* 7 Sept 1887; *d* unm 25 Dec 1967

  2b Frederick; *b* 14 Sept 1852; *educ* Edinburgh Acad; *m* 6 Jan 1882 Emily Macaulay (*d* 24 Sept 1918), dau of Charles Pelly (*see* PELLY, Bt), and *d* 31 Aug 1925, having had:

    1c Frank de Courcy; *b* 1882; *educ* Rugby; *m* 1st 4 Jan 1912 Marguerita Mary (*d* 13 Oct 1935), dau of George Duncan Logan, MD, and had:

      1d Ian de Courcy; *b* 2 Oct 1912; *d* unm 6 Oct 1934

      1d *Jean [Mrs Henry Martin, Guardizabal 1619, Montevideo, Uruguay]; *b* 30 Oct 1915; *m* 12 Dec 1935 Henry Ranald Martin OBE (*d* 1979), s of Lt-Col Martin Martin, of Isle of Skye, and has:

        1e *Ian Duncan [Ian Martin Esq, PO Box 546, Asunción, Paraguay]; *b* 8 Jan 1937; *m* 12 Dec 1961 *June Hope Castleton, of Montevideo, and has:

          1f *Angus Ian; *b* 1973

          2f *Patrick Duncan Ian; *b* 1975

          1f *Virginia Jean; *b* 1963

          2f *Anthea Lorraine; *b* 1966

          3f *Andrea June; *b* 1968

        2e *Norman [Norman Martin Esq, Estancia Chica, Radial Conchillas, Dept Colonia, Uruguay]; *b* 21 Oct 1941; *m* 28 Aug 1965 *Jacqueline Ann Booth, of Los Cerros de San Juan, Uruguay, and has:

          1f *Ian Ranald Calvert; *b* 20 Aug 1966

          2f *Alastair Reginald; *b* 6 Sept 1968

          3f *Nicholas Andrew; *b* 1970

          4f *Anthony Norman; *b* 1974

        3e *Donald de Courcy [Donald de Courcy Martin Esq, Apartado 9, Valencia, Venezuela]; *b* 23 Oct 1943; *m* 28 Feb 1969 *Elizabeth Mary, dau of James Christie, CBE, of Montevideo, and has:

          1f *Angus Donald; *b* 1973

          2f *Kenneth James; *b* 1976

          1f *Veronica Ann; *b* 1971

          2f *Fiona Jean; *b* 1976

        4e *Adrian Ranald; *b* 10 May 1953

    1c (cont.) Frank Maitland-Heriot *m* 2nd 27 June 1939 *Marion Mercier Moore, of Hillsborough, Calif., and *d* 25 Aug 1957

    2c (Charles) Adrian, DSC; *b* 1886; Capt RAF WW I; *m* 27 Feb 1919 Dorothy Mary Margaret (*d* 1979), dau of A Egerton-Savory, and *d* 26 July 1950, having had:

      1d Francis Reginald; *b* 9 Jan 1920; F/Lt RAF WW II; *kas* 1 July 1945

      1d *Audrey Enid [Mrs John Rogerson, 95 Ridgmount Gdns, London WC1E 7AZ]; *b* 8 Sept 1921; WAAF WW II; *m* 1972 *John Rogerson

    3c Frederick Melville; *b* 1888; *educ* Rugby; *m* 5 March 1925 Madeline Janette (*d* 8 March 1954), dau of Alexander Rigaud Wilson-Wood, of Timsbury Manor, and *d* 31 Aug 1951, having had:

      1d Michael Hugo; *b* 27 July 1926; *d* 5 Feb 1929

    4c George Vivian; *b* 1891; *educ* Rugby; *m* 27 Feb 1919 Marjorie Kathleen (*d* 1983), 2nd dau of Edward J Silcock, MICE, of Leeds, and *d* 1979, leaving:

      1d +Torrance [Torrance Maitland-Heriot Esq, Galvez 1423 D°2, Rosario, Argentina]; *b* 15 Jan 1920; *educ* Lancing; WW II in RAF (wounded); *m* 3 Oct 1947 Elda Carmen (*d* 1963), dau of John Stevenson Pearson, of Argentina, and has:

        1e +Edward John Stevenson; *b* 8 April 1950; *educ* The Grange Sch, Santiago, Chile; *m* 197– *Leonore —

2d +Frederick Euan; b 1 Dec 1924; Fleet Air Arm 1944–45; m 1954 *Vera Margaret, yst dau of Gavin Greig Watson, of Tigre, Argentina

3d Nigel Hugh; b 3 Oct 1926; educ The Grange Sch, Santiago; RAC 1944–47; m 1953 Beryl Frances (d 1989), er dau of Jack Richard Anderson, and d 1991, leaving:

  1e +Christopher John; b 5 May 1955; m 1980 *Maria Elena Cristina Cocco and has:

    1f *Leonardo Nicholas; b 1984

    2f *Pablo Alexander; b 1986

    1f *Veronica Natalia; b 1982

  1e *Elizabeth Veronica [Sra Ernesto Bernardo Sarli, Dr Chabrillon 50, 3200 Concordia, Entre Rios, Argentina]; b 2 Feb 1959; m 1993 *Ernesto Bernardo Sarli

1d *Clare Antoinette; b 10 March 1922; WAAF 1941–46; m 1980 *Oscar Cividiño

5c Edward Errol, DSC; b 1892; educ Rugby; RNAS WW I 1916–18; m 1st 1949 (divorce 1955) Jytte Grun; m 2nd 1956 *Beatrice Constance, er dau of Henry Campbell-Orde (see CAMPBELL-ORDE, Bt) and widow of Rodney Whittard Doherty, and dsp 13 Sept 1964

6c Ralph Lionel, MC and bar (1917); b 1895; WW I with RFA (wounded twice, despatches); m 1 Oct 1927 Helen Moira (m 2nd 8 Dec 1937 George A Scott and d 1985, having had further issue), dau of Harry Hugh Jeffries, of Fisherton, Argentina, and d 12 March 1935, leaving:

  1d +Ralph Desmond [Ralph Maitland-Heriot Esq, CC 26, Villa La Angostura 8407, Provincia Neuquin, Argentina]; b 18 Feb 1930; educ The Grange Sch, Santiago; m 1st 30 April 1955 Annelise Moira (d 19–), est dau of Eric Atkinson, of Hurlingham, Buenos Aires; m 2nd 19– *Patricia Chiswell, dau of — Bradbury, and by his 1st w has:

    1e +Richard Patrick [Mr Richard Maitland-Heriot Esq, Juan de Garay 1051, 1686 Hurlingham Prov, Buenos Aires, Argentina]; b 5 Feb 1956; orthopaedic surgn; m 19–

    2e +Timothy James; b 7 Sept 1958; m 19–

    1e *Rosalind Elizabeth; b 23 April 1962; m 19–

  1d *Pamela Avril [Mrs Anthony Oliviera, 9 Grasmere Ave, London SW15]; b 1 Oct 1928; m 6 Dec 1952 Anthony Benjamin Oliviera (d 1983), MB, BS, FRCS, only s of Graeme Oliviera, of Yarmouth, IoW, and has:

    1e *David Benjamin Graeme [David Oliviera Esq, 62 Coombe Lane West, Kingston-on-Thames, Surrey]; b 11 Sept 1955; educ Stowe and Cambridge U (MRCP, PhD); Prof Renal Medicine St George's Hosp Tooting; m 1984 *Patricia Margaret, dau of G/Capt John Edward Ffrancon Williams, CBE, and has:

      1f *Benjamin Anthony; b 1985

      2f *Samuel John; b 1987

      1f *Amelia Sophie; b 1988

    1e *Lynette Moira [S/Ldr Lynette Reid, Stable Lodge, Middleton Stoney, Oxon]; b 9 March 1957; S/Ldr RAF; m 1992 *S/Ldr Jonathan PQ Reid, s of Sir John Reid

7c Gerald Ian, MC, ED; b 1898; educ Sedbergh; WW I with 1st Div Artillery (gassed), Lt-Col cmdg Calcutta Light Horse (AFI) 1935–39, WW II attd RAC India 1940–47; m 5 April 1921 *Paula Elsie Barbara [Mrs Gerald Maitland-Heriot, Constantia Hill Farm, Belair Dve, Constantia, CP, S Africa], dau of Cuthbert Henry Gordon, of India, and d 1987, leaving:

  1d *Celia [Mrs Robert Hanbury, Drumstinchall, Dalbeattie, Kirkcudbrightshire]; b 29 June 1934; m 28 Oct 1961 *Robert Edmund Scott Hanbury, er s of Capt Robert Francis Hanbury, JP, and has:

    1e *Roland William Edmund; b 4 Sept 1964; educ Eton; m 1993 *Heather Gail, dau of Douglas Adams, of Dunmurry, Co Antrim

    1e *Melanie Rhona; b 5 April 1967

1c Alba Illeene; b 13 Aug 1884; m 8 March 1910 Horace John Hale and d 196–, leaving issue

2c Kathleen Enid; b 1902; m 1924 Henry A Cowan (d 1956) and d 14 Feb 1956, leaving issue

3b John de Courcy; b 1 July 1854; d 16 June 1855

4b William (Sir), KBE (1928, CBE 1930), JP; b 26 April 1856; educ HMS Britannia, Edinburgh Acad and Edinburgh U; Chm Dumfries and Galloway War Pensions Ctee, Mil Rep Dumfriesshire CO Tbnl 1914–19, memb Scottish Advsy Cncl to Min Pensions, Educnl Commn Scotland; m 1st 27 Dec 1883 Grace Gilroy (d 14 March 1898), 3rd dau of David W Bowman, of The Beech, Broughty Ferry, and had:

  1c Kate Grace; m 29 Oct 1908 Robert George Dashwood Thomas (d 12 May 1950), s of Col Charles D Thomas, Coldstream Gds, and d 14 July 1968, leaving issue

4b (cont.) Sir William m 2nd 25 April 1902 Alice Harley (d 11 Oct 1937), 3rd dau of John Bruce, JP, of Barmoor Castle, Northumberland, and widow of George Walmsley Hodgson, of Bonaly Tower, Midlothian, and d 21 July 1932

5b Francis Douglas; b 26 Jan 1860; educ Edinburgh Acad; m 17 Oct 1916 Margaret Louisa (d 23 Sept 1956), yst dau of Lt-Col H D Maitland, IA, and d 13 April 1937

6b Gerald; b 28 Oct 1868; d 2 Nov 1900

1b Madeline; m 1st 19 Jan 1881 Alexander Cunningham Boothby and had issue (see BOOTHBY, Bt); m 2nd 1890 Alexander Rigaud Wilson Wood (d 24 April 1934), of Timsbury Manor, Romsey, Hants, and d 27 Dec 1930, leaving further issue

2b Gertrude Margaret; m 19 Jan 1881 James Home Rigg (d 9 Jan 1927), of Downfield and Tarvit, Cupar, Fife, s of Patrick Rigg by Margaret, est dau of John Waugh Brougham (see BROUGHAM AND VAUX, B), and d 22 Feb 1946, leaving issue

3b Elizabeth Carnegie; m 8 Nov 1889 Sir Alexander Sharp Bethune, 9th Bt (qv), and d 16 March 1935, leaving issue

4b Mary Victoria; m 12 Aug 1896 Frederick Henry Christian (d 8 March 1947), JP, of Midlington, Droxford, Hants, and d 26 Aug 1959, leaving issue

2a William HERIOT-MAITLAND later HERIOT-MAITLAND-DOUGALL, of Scotscraig, Tayport, Fife (previously owned by his maternal gf William Dalgeish, JP, DL (Fife)); b 3 July 1819; V-Adml; Col cmdg Fife and Stirling Vol Artillery, Tay Submarine Mines; m 18 Dec 1851 Elizabeth Kinnear (d 16 April 1900), est dau and heiress of William Stark Dougall, of Scotscraig, Fife, and d 7 March 1890, leaving:

  1b William, of Scotscraig, Fife, JP, DL; b 12 Oct 1852; Cdr RN; m 20 May 1886 Charlotte Isabella (d 1953), dau of Capt Frederick King (see LOVELACE, E), and d 3 June 1916, having had:

    1c Arnold; b 29 June 1887; Capt RN; m 8 Dec 1937 Violet Frances (d 25 June 1974), yst dau of F J Parson, and dsp

    2c Wilmot Edward, DSO (1914), MC; b 1 Dec 1890; educ Charterhouse; Col RA WW I (wounded, despatches), ADC to HM GEORGE VI 1941–45; m 1st 24 July 1930 Mary Louisa (d 3 Aug 1959), er dau of Capt Arthur Schreiber, of Brooks Hall, Ipswich, and had:

      1d +Colin [Lt-Cdr Colin Maitland-Dougall RN, Dowhill, Kelty, Fife KY4 0HZ]; b 2 Dec 1933; educ RNC Dartmouth; m 10 Oct 1964 *Philippa Blackstone, dau of Cdr Garnet Henry Wise, RN, of Titchfield, Hants, and has:

        1e +Frederick Andrew; b 9 June 1973

      1d *Eve Diana [Mrs Diana Hunter, The Priest's House, Sutton Montis, Yeovil, Somerset BA22 7HE]; b 15 Sept 1936; m 1st 23 May 1959 (divorce 1977) Maj Arthur John French, RIR, est s of Lt-Col George Arthur French, OBE, of Newbay, Co Wexford, by his 1st w Katherine Lorne, er dau of Brig-Gen James Dalgleish Heriot-Maitland, CMG, DSO (see below); m 2nd 1977 (divorce 1993) Desmond Saville Hunter and by her 1st husb has:

        1e *Miles Arthur Maitland [Miles French Esq, The Priest's House, Sutton Montis, Yeovil, Somerset]; b 12 March 1961; educ Wellington; m 1991 *Anne Rosemary Maurice, er dau of Sir Charles Boscawen Frederick, 10th Bt (qv), and has:

          1f *Raphael Maitland; b 20 April 1994

          1f *Naomi Hilda; b 26 July 1992

        2e *Dominick George Maitland; b 17 Nov 1970; by *Kirsty Innes has:

          1f *Joseph Miles French; b 6 July 1996

        1e *Amelia Mary Katherine; b 30 March 1963

    2c (cont.) Col Wilmot Heriot-Maitland-Dougall m 2nd 20 Oct 1960 *Hilda, dau of G C Wardle, of Leek, Staffs, and widow of Lt-Col Robert John Halkett Baddeley, MC, and d 1972

    3c Kenneth; b 7 Jan 1893; d 6 May 1894

    1c Marjorie; d unm 3 Jan 1914

    2c Ethel Clare; b 1898; m 1954 Capt Evelyn Twysden Wickham, OBE, RN, of Rokeby Lodge, Bathford, Somerset, and d 1983

  2b Frederick Heriot; b 17 Jan 1854; m 5 April 1880 Elizabeth (d 29 Dec 1904), dau of John D Hopkins, of Savannah, Ga., and d 21 Oct 1916, having had:

    1c William; b 19 Jan 1884; d 31 May 1885

    1c Edith; b 16 May 1882; m 1st Nov 1906 (divorce 1910) Stephen Phipps, of Hudson, Wisc.; m 2nd April 1921 George Greenwood Share (d 1 Dec 1959), of London, and dsp 26 Aug 1969

    2c Bessie; b 2 Feb, d 17 Nov 1881

  3b James St Leger; b 17 Jan 1867; m 29 March 1894 Winifred McKinstry (d 2 Feb 1954), dau of Alfred Marchmont Watson, MD, and d 11 May 1940, having had:

    1c William McKinstry; b 14 March 1895; Sub-Lt RCN; das 12 March 1918

    2c Hamish Kinnear; b 4 April 1898; WW I as Cpl 103rd Bn CEF; ka 9 April 1917

  1b Mary Catherine; d 12 July 1919

3a James Makgill MAITLAND-HERIOT later HERIOT-MAITLAND (Sir), KCB; b 14 June 1837; Maj-Gen RE; m 1st 28 Nov 1872 Frances Lorne Mary (d 14 Sept 1876), dau of Gen Sir John Campbell, KCSI, and had:

  1b James Dalgleish, CMG (1916), DSO (1900), JP and DL (Perthshire); b 21 Jan 1874; educ Wellington; Col Rifle Bde, Hon Brig-Gen 1922, Boer War (severely wounded, despatches), WW I (despatches); m 3 Aug 1903 Mary Turner (d 11 March 1937), 2nd dau of de jure 9th Earl of Dundee (qv), and d 18 Jan 1958, leaving:

    1c Richard Ogilvy, JP (Perthshire 1940) DL (1963); b 20 Jan 1913; educ Winchester and Trin Coll Cambridge; Capt Black Watch (TA) WW II, ADC to GOC-in-C Scottish Cmd 1944 and C-in-C Norway 1945, memb Roy Co Archers, King Haakon VII of Norway Liberty Medal; m 3 July 1935 *Patricia [Mrs Richard Heriot-Maitland, Woodlands Lodge, Errol, Perthshire], er dau of Lt-Col Cecil Bevis, OBE, JP, and d 1972, leaving:

      1d +Lewis Dalgleish, TD [Lewis Heriot-Maitland Esq TD, Errol Park, Perthshire]; b 15 July 1943; educ Winchester; m 14 Nov 1976 *Prudence Jane, dau of J R B Norris, of Canberra, Australia, and has:

        1e +James Richard; b 21 Sept 1978

        1e *Lucia Jane; b 1981

        2e *Eliza; b 20 June 1983

        3e *A dau; b 1985

      2d +Patrick Richard [Patrick Heriot-Maitland Esq, Fossoway Lodge, Kinross, Perthshire]; b 23 April 1947; educ Wellington; m 8 July 1978 *Marilyn, dau of R S Grant, of St Petersburgh, Fla., and has:

        1e +Charles; b 1980

        1e *Katherine; b 28 Jan 1983

        2e *Joanna; b 1985

        3e *Alexandra; b 1989

      1d *(Mary) Lorne; b 16 April 1945

1c Katherine Lorne; *b* 15 Dec 1904; *m* 20 April 1933 Lt-Col George Arthur French, OBE, RIF, er *s* of Col George Arthur French, CMG, of Newbay, Wexford, and *d* 3 Dec 1954, leaving issue

2c Joan Margaret, JP (Argyll 1960); *b* 14 April 1909; *d* 21 Jan 1995

2b John Campbell; *b* 21 Jan 1874; Capt and Brevet Maj Scots Gds Boer War; *d* 28 Oct 1934

3a (cont.) Sir James Heriot-Maitland *m* 2nd 4 Oct 1882 Jessie Stewart (*m* 2nd 14 Dec 1903 the Prince of Formosa and *d* 1905), dau of Capt George Hutchings, RN, and *d* 26 Aug 1902

1a Isabella Louisa; *m* 20 Nov 1850 Capt Henry King, RN, and *d* 15 April 1853, leaving issue (*see* LOVELACE, E)

2a Charlotte Mary; *m* 25 April 1854 Capt Frederick King and *d* 14 Aug 1927, having had issue (*see* LOVELACE, E)

(3) Frederick Lewis (Sir), KCB, of Lindores House, Fife; *b* 1776; R-Adml; *m* April 1804 Catherine (*d* 6 March 1865), dau of Daniel Conner, of Bally Bricken, Co Cork, and *dsp* 30 Dec 1839

6 Patrick, of Freugh; *b* 10 April 1734; *m* 24 Sept 1774 Jane Maitland, Dowager Countess of Rothes (*qv*), and *d* 19 May 1797, leaving:

(1) John, of Balgreggan; *m* 5 July 1803 Jane (*d* 21 Feb 1872), dau of Sir William Maxwell, 4th Bt, of Monreith (*qv*), and *d* 20 May 1811, leaving, with other issue:

1a Patrick, of Freugh and Balgreggan, Wigtownshire, JP and DL; *b* 26 July 1804; *m* 23 Oct 1844 Matilda Frances Harriet (*d* 27 March 1894), 5th dau of James Buchanan, of Craigend Castle, Stirling, by Lady Janet, est dau of 12th Earl of Caithness (*qv*), and *d* 8 April 1859, having had a dau and three sons (*d* unm)

2a John; *b* 9 July 1807; Lt-Gen RA; *m* 11 July 1849 Arabella Jane (*d* 19 Jan 1876), dau of Rev Joseph Wright, and *d* 16 March 1881, having had, with other issue:

1b Elphinstone Vans Agnew, of Freugh and Balgreggan; *b* 27 Feb 1856; *m* 15 Nov 1887 Lucy (*m* 2nd 1904 Alexander Francis and *d* Dec 1953), dau of Maj-Gen Henry Bower, Madras Army, and *d* 13 Feb 1904, leaving:

1c Catherine Georgiana Alice; *b* 30 Aug 1888; *d* unm 1 Sept 1969

2b William Alexander Murray; *b* 11 Feb 1859; *d* unm

3b Patrick Lauderdale; *b* 24 June 1862; *m* 16 Aug 1904 Julia Elizabeth (*d* 10 March 1953), dau of George May of Cleveland, Ohio, and *d* 9 Sept 1939, leaving:

1c +Lawrence Lauderdale [Lawrence Maitland Esq, 24 Coopersfield, Debenham, Suffolk IP14 6QR]; *b* 30 June 1905; *educ* Ackworth Sch and Sheffield U; Maj Res Offrs Gordon Highrs WW II; engr

1b Eglantine Henrietta Keith; *b* 1864; *m* 5 Sept 1893 George Hardyman, MB, FRCS, of Perrymead Court, Bath, and *d* 19 July 1930, leaving issue

The 12th EARL's cousin,

FREDERICK HENRY MAITLAND, **13th Earl of Lauderdale**, DL (Haddington); *b* 16 Dec 1840; rep S peer 1888–1918, Ld Lt Berwicks 1889–1901, Lt-Col Bengal Staff Corps, formerly 8th and 4th Hus, served For Dept Govt India 1869–89, Capt Lothian and Berwicks Yeo Cav; *m* 1st 28 Nov 1864 Charlotte Sarah (*d* Sept 1879), dau of Lt-Col B W A Sleigh, 77th Regt, and had:

1 FREDERICK COLIN MAITLAND, **14th Earl of Lauderdale**, OBE (1919), JP and DL (Berwicks); *b* 12 April 1868; rep S peer, Ensign Roy Co Archers, Hon Col 11th (HAC and City London Yeo) Bde RHA (TA), Hon Col cmdg City of London (Rough Riders) Yeo, Hon Lt-Col Scots Gds and RSG, T/Lt-Col 23rd Bn Roy Fus 1914–16 (wounded), Lt-Col cmdg 3rd Garrison Bn Northumberland Fus 1916, Assist Dir Aux Forces Army HQ Staff 1903–08, memb Gentlemen-at-Arms, Imp Yeo Boer War (medal with four clasps, despatches); *m* 16 April 1890 Gwendoline Lucy (*d* 30 Jan 1929), dau of Judge R Vaughan Williams, of Bodlonfa, Flints, and *d* 14 Sept 1931, leaving:

(1) IAN COLIN MAITLAND, **15th Earl of Lauderdale**, DL (Berwickshire); *b* 30 Jan 1891; Capt 3rd Bn QO Cameron Highrs, ADC to Ld Lt Ireland 1916, Staff Lt 1917; Min Shipping 1918–19, Hon Maj 1932 and 1945, WW II, rep S peer 1931–45, memb Roy Co Archers, Hon Pres Corp of Accountants 1931–45; *m* 11 Nov 1912 Ethel Mary (Ivy) (*d* 11 Dec 1970), er dau of James Jardine Bell-Irving, of Makerstoun, Kelso, and *dspms* 17 Feb 1953, having had:

1a Ivor Colin James, *Viscount Maitland*; *b* 29 Aug 1915; Lt Lothians and Border Yeo WW II; *m* 29 Oct 1936 *Helena Ruth, OStJ [Helena Viscountess Maitland, Park House, Makerstoun, Roxburghshire TD5 7PA; Flat E, 34 Cadogan Sq, London SW1X 0JL], yr dau of Col Sir Herbert Charles Perrott, 6th Bt (*see* 1921 edn), and was *ka* N Africa 18 Jan 1943, leaving:

1b *Mary Helena; *b* 23 Oct 1938; granted with sisters 28 Oct 1953 rank of earl's daus; *m* 9 April 1958 4th Baron Biddulph (*qv*) and has issue

2b *Anne Priscilla [The Lady Anne Eyston, Mapledurham House, Reading RG4 7TR]; *b* 4 May 1940; *m* 6 Feb 1968 *John Joseph Eyston, yr s of Thomas More Eyston, JP, of Hendred House, Berks, and has:

1c *Edward Thomas Ivor; *b* 1 April 1969; *m* 22 Feb 1997 *Alexandra, dau of Frederick Grounds, of March, Cambs

1c *Katherine Agnes Mary; *b* 19 May 1970

2c *Mary Amicia Helena; *b* 3 Nov 1972

3b *Elizabeth Sylvia [The Lady Elizabeth Maitland, 11 Boundary Cl, Woodstock, Oxon OX20 1LR]; *b* posthumously 12 May 1943

1a Sylvia Gwendoline Eva; *b* 22 Sept 1913; *m* 3 June 1937 6th Baron Carew (*qv*) and *d* 1991, having had issue

2 Sydney George William (Rev), JP (Berwicks); *b* 12 Dec 1869; *educ* Westminster and Trin Coll Cambridge (MA); Rector Ingestre Staffs 1927–37, Lt 3rd Bn Roy Scots Fus; *m* 11 April 1899 Ella Frances (*d* 28 Feb 1949), dau of Rev James Richards, Vicar St Peter's, Rochdale, and *d* 21 Aug 1946, leaving:

(1) Rev ALFRED SYDNEY FREDERICK MAITLAND, **16th Earl of Lauderdale**; *b* 17 April 1904; *educ* Westminster and Sidney Sussex Coll Cambridge (BA 1925, MA 1938); Priest i/c St John's W Worthing 1939–51, Vicar 1951–53, Curate All Saints Woodham Woking 1953–56, Rector Catsfield Sussex 1957–60 (ret); *m* 1st 6 Aug 1938 Norah Mary (*d* 3 Nov 1938), dau of William Henry La Touche; *m* 2nd 4 June 1940 Irene Alice May, dau of Rev Charles Percy Shipton, of Halsham, Yorks, and *dsp* 27 Nov 1968

(2) PATRICK FRANCIS, **17th and present Earl**

---

(1) *(Ella) Mary; *b* 24 Aug 1906; granted 28 Oct 1953 rank of earl's dau; *m* 5 Sept 1932 John Alder Cripps Blumer, Educn Dept Tanganyika Territory, 3rd s of Dr F Milnes Blumer, of The Mount, Stafford, and has:

1a *Anthony John Maitland; *b* 13 Jan 1936; *educ* Malvern; Lt RA; *m* 29 Sept 1962 *Mary Erica, er dau of Dr E J C Bockett, of Farnborough, Hants, and has:

1b *Robert John Maitland; *b* 1 Nov 1963

2b *Patrick Neil James; *b* 2 Nov 1965

1b *Elizabeth Mary; *b* 8 Nov 1968

2a *Peter William [Peter Blumer Esq, c/o EMI Europe, AMGH, 5 Kolu 41, Maarweg 149, Germany]; *b* 6 Oct 1942; *educ* Malvern and St Andrews U

3a *Christopher James Frederick, [Christopher Blumer Esq, c/o 19 Queens Rd, Cheltenham, Glos GL50 2LT]; *b* 3 Feb 1947; *educ* Malvern and Leeds U

1a *Phoebe Mary; *b* 9 June 1933; *m* 12 Oct 1960 *Ralph Hornblower, Jr, yr s of Ralph Hornblower, of Plymouth, Mass., and has:

1b *John Greenwood; *b* 6 Oct 1961

2b *David Maitland; *b* 29 Sept 1963

3b *James Wainwright; *b* 29 Sept 1963

2a *Philippa Sydney Isabel [Mrs James Bell, c/o 19 Queen's Rd, Cheltenham, Glos GL50 2LR]; *b* 30 May 1945; *m* 13 Sept 1973 *James C Bell, er s of A C Bell, of Stourbridge

3 Alfred Henry; *b* 9 Dec 1872; Maj QO Cameron Highrs, Sudan 1898, Atbara and Omdurman (medal with two clasps and Khedive's Star), Boer War (medal with five clasps), WW I; *m* 5 Jan 1905 Edith (*d* 27 March 1963), yst dau of Sanford George Treweeke Scobell, of Redmarley, Glos, and was *ka* Sept 1914, leaving:

(1) Edith Charlotte; *b* 15 Nov 1905; *m* 28 June 1930 Lt-Col Humphrey Ion Bradshaw, Gordon Highrs, of Banbridge, Co Down, and *d* 12 May 1951, leaving issue

(2) Nora Beatrice; *b* 4 Oct 1907; *m* 4 July 1935 S/Ldr Peter Yorke, OBE, RAFVR, 2nd s of John Cecil Yorke, JP, of Halton Place, Hellifield, Yorks, and had issue

1 Nora; *m* 24 Oct 1899 Sir William Fitzherbert, 7th Bt (*qv*), and *dsp* 19 April 1958

The **13th Earl** *m* 2nd 1883 Ada Twyford (*d* 14 Sept 1931), dau of Rev Henry Trail Simpson, Rector Adel, Yorks, and *d* 1 Sept 1924, having by her had:

2 Ada Marian; *m* 1st 12 Dec 1905 Capt Sir Ralph Henry Sacheverel Wilmot, 6th Bt (*d* of wounds recd on active serv 14 Jan 1918), and had issue; *m* 2nd 21 June 1921 Arnold Nield, s of John Nield, of Warrington, Lancs, and *d* 16 April 1971

LAURIE

Arms: Sable a cup argent with a garland between two laurel branches, all issuing out of the same vert. **Crest:** Two branches of laurel in saltire proper. **Motto:** *Virtus semper viridis* ('Virtue is always flourishing'). **Creation:** Bt. (UK) 15 March 1834.

SIR (ROBERT) BAYLEY EMILIUS LAURIE, 7TH BT, of Bedford Square, Middlesex [Sir Bayley Laurie Bt, The Old Rectory, Little Tey, Essex CO6 1JA]; *b* 8 March 1931; *s* f 1983; *educ* Eton; 1st Bn Seaforth Highrs 1949–51, Capt Seaforth Highrs (TA) 1951–67, memb Lloyd's 1955, ch exec C T Bowring U/A 1974–83, chm Bowring Members Agy 1983; *m* 14 Sept 1968 *Laurelie Meriol Winifrida, er dau of Sir Reginald Lawrence William Williams, 7th Bt, of Bodelwyddan (*qv*), and has:

1 *Clare Meriol; *b* 1974

2 *Serena Catherine; *b* 1976

Lineage (of Bayley): PHILIPPE de BAILLEUL later BAYLEY; migrated from the Spanish Netherlands to England in the 17th century to escape persecution (presumably as a Protestant); bought Willow Hall, Thorney, nr Peterborough; had:

DANIEL BAYLEY; had:

ISAAC BAYLEY, of Chesterton, Hunts; *m* 4 April 1732 Orme (*d* 27 March 1766), est dau of Henry Bigland, of Frolesworth, Leics, of a branch of the BIGLANDs of Bigland, Lancs, and had:

1 Edward (Rev), DD; Rector Courtenhall, Northants; *m* thrice and *d* 1813, leaving issue

2 JOHN

3 Charles, of Peterborough; *m* Cordelia, dau of Samuel Taylor, of Peterborough, and had issue

4 Henry, of Uppingham; *m* Elizabeth, dau of John Sly, of Stand Ground, Hunts, and had issue

5 Isaac, of Market Harborough, Leics; *m* 1st Mary, only child of Rev George Widowson, and had:

  (1) Isaac; Capt 72 Regt; *b* 25 May 1766; *m* 5 Sept 1793 Isabella Fenton, dau of Gen Stewart, and had issue

5 (cont.) Isaac Bayley *m* 2nd 25 May 1772 Mary (*d* 26 April 1785), dau of Edward Bigland, and *d* 9 July 1786, leaving issue

ISAAC BAYLEY *d* Aug 1751; his 2nd son,

JOHN BAYLEY, of Elton, Northants; *m* Sarah (*d* 25 Oct 1801), dau and heir of White Kennett, Preb Peterborough (s of Dr White Kennett, Bp Peterborough), and *d* 22 Oct 1790, leaving a 2nd s:

Sir John Bayley, 1st Bt (UK), so *cr* 15 March 1834; *b* 3 Aug 1763; Judge King's Bench, Baron Exchequer; ktd 1808; *m* 20 May 1790 Elizabeth (*d* 23 Jan 1837), yst dau of John Markett, of Meopham Court, Kent, and had:

1 JOHN EDWARD GEORGE (Sir), **2nd Bt**

2 Kennett Champain (Rev); Rector Copford, Essex; *b* 13 Oct 1798; *m* 23 June 1831 Charlotte (*d* 27 Aug 1860), est dau of James Drake Brockman, of Beachborough, Kent, and *d* 2 June 1861, having had:

  (1) John; Maj 7th Hus; *b* 22 Sept 1833; *m* 9 June 1863 Juliana Mary Georgiana (*d* 3 Feb 1926), only dau of Rev Thomas Charles Hyde Leaver, Rector Rockhampton, Glos, and *dsp* 18 Feb 1880

  (2) George; Col 1st Bn E Surrey Regt; *b* 27 Jan 1837; *d* unm 26 Feb 1907

  (3) Kennett, of Sevenoaks, Inchicore, Co Dublin; *b* 31 Oct 1838; *m* 2 Aug 1864 Louisa Jane (*d* 4 April 1900), dau of Rev William Bowling, and *d* 24 June 1911, leaving:

    1a Kennett Champain; slr Durham; *b* 23 Aug 1873; *m* 20 Nov 1902 Norah Kathleen (*d* 25 Feb 1963), only dau of Capt Henry William Roberts, 98th Regt, of Hollingside, Durham, and *d* 23 Feb 1935, leaving:

      1b Kennett, CB (1953), CBE (1945, OBE 1940); *b* 8 Nov 1903; *educ* Rugby and RMA Woolwich; Maj-Gen Oxon and Bucks LI Burma 1930–32 and WW II (despatches), ADC to HM GEORGE VI 1949, Ch Staff Br Forces Egypt 1949–51, Dir Personnel Admin War Office 1951–55, Dir Boys' Trg War Office 1955–57; *d* unm 29 March 1967

      2b John Maurice, DSC (1940); Cdr RN served WW II (despatches); *b* 8 Jan 1905; *educ* Rugby; *m* 6 April 1935 *Mary Boyd, dau of Frederick Marmaduke Osborn, of Sheffield, and *d* 2 Nov 1995, leaving:

        1c +Michael John (Rev) [The Rev Michael Bayley, 27 Meadow Bank Ave, Sheffield S7 1PB]; *b* 9 Nov 1936; *educ* Rugby and Corpus Christi Coll Cambridge (BA 1959); PhD Sheffield; *m* 26 Oct 1963 *Ruth Fleur Annette, dau of John Jones, of Calverley, and has:

          1d +Robin Kennett; *b* 2 July 1966

          2d +Andrew John; *b* 23 Sept 1968

          1d *Jill Ruth; *b* 27 Sept 1964; *m* 1987 *Hugh Bowden, s of Rev Dr J S Bowden, of Highgate, and has:

            1e *Isabel Ruth; *b* 27 May 1994

            2e *Clare Harriet; *b* 22 June 1997

          2d *Emma Susan; *b* 1970

        2c Kennett Ian; Capt RGJ; *b* 7 March 1941; *educ* Bradfield and RMA Sandhurst; *m* 25 Sept 1965 Helen Julia (*d* 12 April 1994), dau of Patrick Dudley Benjafield, of Shalford, Surrey, and *d* 12 June 1996, leaving:

          1d +Benjamin George Robson; *b* 4 May 1967; *m* July 1993 *Sarah Dawson

          1d *Sarah Mary Helen; *b* 13 May 1969

        3c +Peter Charles; *b* 22 Sept 1943; *educ* Durham; *m* 1980 *Catherine Anne, dau of Dr J Dunclee, of Saskatoon, Canada, and has:

          1d +Jonathan; *b* 27 Jan 1986

          1d *Ellen Elizabeth; *b* 24 April 1989

    1b Ethel Meverall; *b* 9 May 1906; *m* 27 Dec 1928 Hon John Roche, er s of Baron Roche (LP; *see* 1956 edn), and had issue

    2a Francis Edmund; BA Cantab; *b* 5 July 1878; *d* unm 26 Oct 1943

    3a Arthur George, CBE (1919), DSO (1916); *b* 5 July 1878; Col Oxon and Bucks LI Boer War 1899–1902 (two medals, five clasps), Col Gen Staff WW I (despatches), NWF India (medal 1930); *m* 20 Nov 1923 Katherine May Frederica (*d* 31 Aug 1952), only child of Brig-Gen Francis Alexander Fortescue, CB, CMG (*see* FORTESCUE, E), and *d* 1 March 1949, leaving:

      1b *Elizabeth Frances Mary Louise [Mrs James Moffett, 26B Elm Park Rd, London SW3]; *b* 1924; *m* 1st 24 July 1946 (*divorce* 1953) Maj John David Nicholas Retallack, Welsh Gds, est s of Col Charles Retallack; *m* 2nd 15 Dec 1953, as his 2nd w, Francis Trelawny Williams (*d* 1977), er s of Henry Harcourt Williams, JP, of Pencalenick, St Clements, Truro; *m* 3rd 1983 *James Andrew Moffett, Lt-Cdr USNR, and by her 2nd husb has:

        1c *Trelawny Michael [Trelawny Williams Esq, 11 Ashchurch Park Villas, London W12 9SP]; *b* 19 June 1957; *m* 1994 *Olivia Rosemary, dau of Cdr Axel Mortensen, of Oxton, Notts, and has:

          1d *Amber May; *b* 22 April 1996

    1a Louisa; *m* 2 Feb 1891 George Alexander (*d* 2 Nov 1930), barrister, of Wimbledon Park, London, s of John Alexander, MP, of Milford, Co Carlow, and *d* 27 Oct 1941, leaving issue

    2a Eleanor Charlotte; *m* 6 Nov 1889 Albany Hawke Charlesworth (*d* 1914), of Grinton Lodge, Richmond, Yorks, and *d* 11 Dec 1941, having had issue

    3a Ethel; *m* 22 April 1896 Maj John Alexander, of Milford Ho, Co Carlow, 1st Dragoon Gds, and *d* 1916, leaving issue

    4a Evelyn; *m* 1898 Rev Lewis Westmacott (*d* 1949), Hon Canon Gloucester, and *d* 27 Sept 1961, leaving issue

  (1) Charlotte; *m* 2 April 1861 Rev C A Baynes (*d* 1881), Vicar Binley, Leics, and *d* 9 Dec 1899, leaving issue

3 Francis; barrister, Judge Westminster County Court; *b* 6 Feb 1803; *m* 1st 31 Aug 1830 Elizabeth (*d* 8 April 1838), est dau of Alexander Macdonald, of Westminster; *m* 2nd 17 April 1854 Charlotte (*d* Dec 1873), dau of Frederic Roulet, and *d* 1893, having by his 1st w had:

  (1) John Arthur; Maj 52nd LI; *b* 1831; *m* 5 June 1853 Elizabeth (*d* 6 May 1915), dau of Samuel Sterling, of Belfast, and *dsp* 4 Feb 1903

  (1) Louisa Frances; *m* 4 June 1867 Rev Sir George Henry Cornewall, 5th Bt (*d* 25 Sept 1908; *see* 1959 edn), of Moccas Court, Herefs, and *d* 2 Feb 1900, leaving issue

1 Marianne; *m* 22 June 1826 Rev Henry Clissold (*d* 1 Jan 1867) and *d* 24 April 1858, leaving issue

2 Lucy; *d* unm July 1820

3 Elizabeth Magdalene; *d* unm 26 Feb 1878

Sir JOHN *d* 10 Oct 1841; his est son,

Sir John Edward George Bayley, 2nd Bt, barrister; *b* 23 Dec 1793; *m* 1st 27 June 1822 Charlotte Mary (*d* 2 Aug 1854), 2nd dau of John Minet Fector (*see* below); *m* 2nd 18 Aug 1855 Selina (*d* 15 Jan 1865), dau of Col Marlay, and had by his 1st w:

1 (JOHN ROBERT LAURIE) EMILIUS (Sir), **3rd Bt**

2 Lyttelton Holyoake (Sir); *b* 6 May 1827; barrister Middle Temple 1850, Attorney-Gen, MLC and MLA NSW 1859, Advocate-Gen and MLC Bombay 1866–69, High Court Judge Bombay 1869–95, Lt-Col cmdg Bombay Vol Rifle Corps, Hon ADC to Viceroy India; *m* 12 May 1852 Isabella (*d* 9 April 1860), dau of Anthony Mactier, of Durris Ho, Kincardineshire, and *d* 4 Aug 1910, having had, with a dau (*d* unm):

  (1) Stanhope Lyttelton Fector; barrister; *b* 9 March 1858; *m* 1st 1891 Emilie Ann (*d* Feb 1910), widow of James Baillie Watson; *m* 2nd 28 Aug 1917 Edith (*d* 1 Nov 1924), yst dau of William Robson, of Hollingside, Durham, and *dsp* Italy 27 April 1934

  (2) Vernon Batthyany Fector; slr 1885; *b* 28 March 1860; *m* 11 Oct 1894 Mary Frederica (*d* 17 June 1949), dau of Maj-Gen Alexander Clark-Kennedy, and *d* 3 June 1920, leaving:

    1a Frederica Mary Isabel; *b* 30 Oct 1897; *m* 3 Feb 1920 Henry Theodore Warren Oswell, Malayan CS (*d* 18 Aug 1970), er s of Cdr Thomas John Oswell, RN of Holmbury St Mary, Surrey, and had issue

  (1) Isabel Constance; *m* 6 Oct 1880 John McAdam Gladstone (*d* 19 Aug 1884) and *d* 1923, leaving issue

Sir JOHN *d* 23 Dec 1871; his er son,

Rev Sir (JOHN ROBERT LAURIE) EMILIUS BAYLEY later LAURIE of Maxwelton (roy licence 26 Feb 1887 on inheriting Maxwelton), **3rd Bt**; *b* 16 May 1823; BD, Vicar Woburn 1843–56 and St John's, Paddington 1867–88, Rector St George's Bloomsbury 1856–67; *m* 1 Feb 1855 Marianne Sophia (*d* 22 June 1903), 3rd dau of Edward Royd Rice, MP, of Dane Court, Kent, and *d* 4 Dec 1917, having had:

1 **Sir Claude Villiers Emilius Laurie, 4th Bt**, CB, DSO; *b* 25 Nov 1855; *educ* Trin Coll Cambridge (MA); barrister Inner Temple, Lt-Col and Hon Col cmdg 3rd Bn KOSB 1905–10, Lt-Col 2nd/5th Bn 1914–16; *d* unm 19 Feb 1930

2 WILFRID EMILIUS (Sir), **5th Bt**

3 Cecil Emilius, JP Dumfriesshire; *b* 4 Jan 1862; *m* 23 Oct 1900 Helen Janet Douglas (*d* 1 April 1919), est dau of Robert Douglas Campbell, RN, bro of 1st Baron Blythswood (*see* 1940 edn), and *d* 30 Jan 1919, leaving:

  (1) Douglas Claude Emilius; *b* 12 Nov 1902; *d* unm 18 Aug 1957

  (2) Archibald Montagu; *b* 5 July 1904; *d* unm 28 May 1984

  (3) Ronald Edward; Maj KOSB WW II; *b* 16 Jan 1911; *m* 19 July 1941 Rosemary Lilian (*d* 8 Oct 1995), er dau of John Gauld Fullerton, and *d* 29 Dec 1952, leaving:

    1a +ANDREW RONALD EMILIUS [Andrew Laurie Esq, 7 St Oswalds Rd, Hexham, Northumberland NE46 2HF]; *b* 20 Oct 1944; heir presumptive; *m* 11 April 1970 *Sarah Anne, est dau of C D Patterson, of Hexham, and has:

      1b +John Christopher Emilius; *b* 12 June 1971; *m* 7 Aug 1993 *Lucie Françoise Géraldine, dau of J Wackermann, of Lunéville

      2b +Michael James Edward; *b* 17 Aug 1973

    1a *Rosemary Helen [Mrs David McMullan, 2 Lostock Ave, Poynton, Cheshire SK12 1DR]; *b* 3 Dec 1942; *m* 20 Aug 1966 *David Frederick McMullan, 2nd s of H W McMullan, OBE, of Dorchester Park, Belfast, and has:

      1b *Andrew David Sean; *b* 7 Jan 1970; *m* 15 April 1997 *Anne, er dau of D O'Kearney-Flynn, of Buttevant, Co Cork

  (1) Alice Helen; *b* 12 Sept 1901; *m* 1 Oct 1935 Norman Edward Feasey, yst s of George Feasey, and *dsp* 25 Feb 1987

  (2) Cassandra Gladys; *b* 26 Sept 1905; *d* unm 12 Oct 1994

  (3) Olive Cecil; *b* 11 Jan 1907; *m* 6 Aug 1930 Victor Edward Reinganum and *d* 18 April 1942, leaving issue

  (4) Margaret (Meg) May; *b* 13 Jan 1908; *m* 30 April 1934 Lt-Col Sir Reginald Douglas Henry Houldsworth, 4th Bt (*qv*), and *d* 1 Aug 1995, leaving issue

  (5) Frances Muriel; *b* 18 July 1909; *m* 3 Feb 1938 Rev James Bruce Harington Evans, Rector St Marylebone (*d* 1958), er s of Rev James Lachlan Evans, and *d* 25 Sept 1979, leaving:

    1a *Anthony James Cecil; *b* 20 May 1940

    1a *Judith Frances; *b* 8 Nov 1946

  (6) *Christina Eve [Mrs Kenneth McCall, Barbuie, Moniaive, Dumfriesshire]; *b* 24 Dec 1912; *m* 28 July 1938 Kenneth Murray McCall (*d* 1987), only s of Maj William McCall, of Caitloch, Moniaive, and has:

    1a *David James; *b* 1941; *m* 1971 *Evelyn Lucy, dau of Thomas McCosh, of Pitcon, Dalry, Ayrshire, and has:

      1b *Philippa; *b* 1973

      2b *Sarah Christina; *b* 1978

      3b *Emma Elizabeth; *b* 1982

    2a *William Kenneth; *b* 1944; *m* 1971 *Hon Gillian Patricia Denman, dau of 5th Baron Denman (*qv*), and has:

      1b *Hamish Spencer Murray; *b* 15 Sept 1972

      2b *Andrew Robert Calum; *b* 19 June 1981

1b *Fiona Jane; *b* 11 Feb 1975

1a *Patricia Helen [Mrs Timothy Hughes, Fanville Head Farm, Hook Norton, Oxon]; *b* 1942; *m* 1970 *Timothy Morgan Hughes and has:

  1b *Charles Edward Kenneth; *b* 1971

  1b *Davina Jane; *b* 1973

  2b *Iona Caroline; *b* 1978

2a *Joan [Mrs JohnCamp Farm, Farmington, Northleach, Glos]; *b* 1948; *m* 1969 *Capt John James Dean Barrow and has:

  1b *Richard Raymond; *b* 1971

  1b *Georgina Rachael; *b* 1975

(7) *Elizabeth Janet; *b* 13 April 1915; *m* 1st 21 Feb 1948 (*divorce* 1960) Francis Evelyn Tarik Marshall (*d* 6 Feb 1970), only s of George Vincent Tarik Marshall, of Hong Kong; *m* 2nd 2 April 1960 Maj Francis Dudley Rose, RE (AER) (*d* 1968), er s of James Rose, of Lough, Lincs, and by her 1st husb has:

  1a *Julian Emilius Harold; *b* 23 Nov 1950; *educ* Charterhouse

  1a *Janet Phillipa Ann; *b* 1948

4 Arthur Emilius; *b* 13 May 1866; *d* 2 Sept 1874

1 Blanche Alice May; *m* 15 April 1879 Rev David Anderson (*d* 1916), Preb St Paul's, and *d* 1945, leaving issue

The 4th Bt's bro,

Sir Wilfred Emilius Laurie, 5th Bt; *b* 1 June 1859; *educ* Trin Coll Cambridge (LLB); barrister; *m* 2 June 1890 Marian Isabel (*d* 25 Jan 1950), 2nd dau of John Stirling of Fairburn, DL, and had:

1 JOHN EMILIUS (Sir), **6th Bt**

2 Wilfrid Walter; Capt 3rd Bn KOSB WW I; *b* 18 Oct 1897; *ka* 19 May 1917

1 Sylvia Marian; *d* unm 12 Aug 1967

2 Evelyn Mary; *m* 24 July 1923 Col Noel Edward Baxter (*d* 29 March 1950), s of John Henry Baxter, JP, of Gilston, Fife, and *d* 9 May 1974, having had three sons and a dau

3 Jean Winifred; *m* 3 July 1948 Ronald Schofield (*d* 1964), only s of G A Schofield, of Barton Mills, Mildenhall, Suffolk

4 Eila Isabel; *m* 17 Oct 1928 R-Adml James Uchtred Farie, CMG (*d* 17 Sept 1957), s of Col G Farie, HLI

Sir WILFRED *d* 15 Dec 1936; his only surv son,

Sir John Emilius Laurie, 6th Bt, CBE (1940), DSO (1916) and bar (1919), JP and DL Dumfriesshire; *b* 12 Aug 1892; *educ* Eton and RMC Sandhurst; commd Seaforth Highrs 1912, WW I (despatches, Chev Legn Hon), cmded 6th (Morayshire) Bn and 2nd Bn 1934–38, Tientsin Area 1939–40, 157th Inf Bde and 52nd (Lowland) Div 1940–42, Combined Ops Trg Centre Inverary 1943–45 WW II (despatches), ret 1945, Col Seaforth Highrs 1947–57, Hon Maj-Gen; *m* 2 Nov 1922 Evelyn Clare Gardner (*d* 1987), dau of Lt-Col Lionel James Richardson-Gardner, 14th Hus, and *d* 10 Jan 1983, leaving:

1 Sir ROBERT BAYLEY EMILIUS LAURIE, **7th and present Bt**

1 *Rosemary Evelyn Anne [Mrs Robin Moodie, Hill House, Penton Mewsey, nr Andover, Hants]; *b* 3 Jan 1924; *m* 11 Jan 1949 Cdr Robin Henry Ramsay Moodie, RN (*d* 1994), only s of Edwin Ramsay Moodie, of Ghyll Manor, Rusper, Sussex, and has had:

  (1) *John Ramsay; *b* 28 Jan 1955; *educ* Eton; *m* 1989 *Caroline Mary Hughes and has:

    1a *Sam Ramsay; *b* 1991

    1a *Iona Vive; *b* 1993

  (2) *Edward Robin [Edward Moodie Esq, Hill House, Penton Mewsey, Hants]; *b* 1 Nov 1956; *educ* Eton; *m* 1993 *Patricia Fitzgerald

  (1) Elizabeth Vive; *b* 15 April 1959; *d* 21 Aug 1961

2 *Marian Clare [The Rt Hon The Lady Laing of Dunphail, High Meadows, Windsor Rd, Gerrard's Cross, Bucks SL9 8ST]; *b* 3 July 1927; *m* 1 April 1950 *Baron Laing of Dunphail (*qv*) and has issue

Lineage (of Laurie): STEPHEN LAURIE, of Dumfries; bought 1611 the Maxwelton and other estates from Sir Robert Gordon of Lochinvar; *m* Marion, dau of John Corsane, MP Dumfries, by Janet, dau of Lord Maxwell, and *d* 14 Dec 1637, having had, with two daus (Janet, *m* 8 Feb 1620 John Irving, 1st of Friars Carse and 2nd of Irving, JP, Provost Dumfries, and had issue; Agnes):

JOHN LAURIE of Maxwelton; Covenanter, hence fined £3,600 for nonconformity; *m* 1631 Agnes, dau of Sir William Grierson of Lag (*see* GRIERSON, Bt), and *d* 1672, having had, with four yr sons and two daus:

Sir ROBERT LAURIE, 1st Bt (NS), so *cr* 27 March 1685, of Maxwelton; *m* 1st Mary, dau of Sir Robert Dalzell, Bt, of Glenae, and had three daus (Mary, *m* James Grierson of Capenoch (*see* GRIERSON, Bt); Catherine; Agnes, *m* Robert Gordon); *m* 2nd 27 July 1674 Jean, dau of Walter Riddell of Minto, and *d* April 1698, having by her had:

1 Sir ROBERT LAURIE, 2nd Bt; *k* in a fall from his horse 1702

2 WALTER (Sir), 3rd Bt

3 John; Col the Gds

4 Catherine; *m* Walter Riddell of Friershaw Glenriddell (*see* RIDDELL, Bt)

5 Violet; *m* — Corbet

6 Susan; *m* — Gordon

7 Anna, the 'Annie Laurie' of the ballad; *b* 16 Dec 1682; *m* 1709 Alexander Fergusson of Cragdarroch, MP, and *d* May 1764

The 2nd Bt's next bro,

Sir WALTER LAURIE, 3rd Bt; *m* 1st 1708 Jean, dau of Sir John Patrick Nisbet of Dean, and had a s and dau (Agnes, *d* an infant); *m* 2nd Henrietta, dau of Sir Robert Grierson, 1st Bt (*qv*), and *d* 23 Nov 1731, having by her had two other sons (Walter; William); his s by his 1st w:

Sir ROBERT LAURIE, 4th Bt; MP Dumfries 1738–41; *m* 4 Feb 1733 Christian (*d* 21 Aug 1755), dau of Charles Erskine of Alva, 3rd s of Sir Charles Erskine, 1st Bt (*see* ROSSLYN, E), and *d* 28 April 1779, having had, with five daus:

Gen Sir ROBERT LAURIE, 5th Bt; Kt Marshal of Scotland 1785–1804; Gen, Col 8th Dragoons, MP Dumfriesshire 1774–1804; *b* c 1748; *m* 1st 18 July 1763 Mary Elizabeth, dau of 5th Lord Ruthven of Freeland (*see* CARLISLE, E); *m* 2nd 14

April 1778 Judith (*d* 14 Jan 1824), dau of Capt Hatley and widow of Robert Wollaston, and *d* 10 Sept 1804, having by his 1st w had:

1 Sir ROBERT LAURIE, 6th and last Bt, of Maxwelton, KCB; *b* 25 May 1764; Adml; *m* Mary Hope and *dsp* 7 Jan 1848, when the btcy expired

1 Anne Wortley Montagu; *b* 13 June 1771; *m* 22 Feb 1794 John Minet Fector, of Kearsney Abbey, and had, with other issue:

  (1) John Minet FECTOR later LAURIE (1848); *m* 1841 Isabella, dau of Maj Gen John Murray, CB, and *dsp* 24 Feb 1868

  (1) Charlotte; *b* 1801; *m* 27 June 1822 **Sir John Edward George Bayley, 2nd Bt**, and had issue (*see* above)

LAWES

Pour la Foi

Arms: Quarterly, 1st and 4th, argent three bendlets gules, on a chief sable a barrulet dancettée or (for WITTEWRONGE); 2nd and 3rd, or two flaunches azure, on a chief nebuly of the last three estoiles of the first (for LAWES). **Crests:** 1 A Saracen's head affrontée and couped below the shoulders proper, wreathed about the temples and tied in a bow or and gules, 2 On a mount vert the trunk of a tree fesswise eradicated and sprouting to the dexter, surmounted by an ermine passant proper. **Motto:** *Pour la foi* ('For the faith'). **Creation:** Bt. (UK) 9 May 1882.

SIR JOHN MICHAEL BENNET LAWES, 5TH BT, of Rothamsted, Co Hertford [Sir John Lawes Bt, c/o Barclays Bank plc, PO Box 55, Lymington, Hants SO41 9WF]; *b* 24 Oct 1932; *s f* 1979; *educ* Elizabeth Coll, Guernsey

Lineage: THOMAS BENNET; *m* Elizabeth, dau of James Wittewronge, of Rothamsted, Herts, Recorder St Albans (s of Sir John Wittewronge, 1st Bt (*cr* 2 May 1692, extinct 13 Jan 1771), by his 2nd wife Elizabeth, dau of Timothy Middleton, of Stansted Mountfichet, Essex), and was gf of:

1 John BENNET, JP; inherited Rothamsted from his cousin Thomas Wittewronge, the last of his line (*d* unm 1763), and *dsp*

1 MARY Bennet; *m* Thomas LAWES and had:

  (1) John Bennet, of Rothamsted, Herts, DL; *m* Aug 1812 Marianne, dau of John Sherman, of Drayton, Oxon, by Margaret (dau of James Johnstone and widow of Rev David George Knox), and had:

    1a JOHN BENNET (Sir), **1st Bt**

    1a Marianne; *m* 30 Oct 1834 Charles Thomas Warde, of Clopton, Warwicks (*d* 6 May 1865)

    2a Emily Catherine; *m* 9 Oct 1845 Lewis Mathias (*d* 13 Oct 1882), of Lamphey Court, Pembs, and *d* 1877 leaving issue

JOHN LAWES *d* 22 Oct 1822; his only son,

Sir John Bennet Lawes, 1st Bt (UK), so *cr* 19 May 1882, of Rothamsted, JP; *b* 28 Dec 1814; DSc Cambridge; FRS; *m* 28 Dec 1842 Caroline (*d* 29 Nov 1895), yst dau of Andrew Fountaine, of Narford Hall, Norfolk, and had:

1 CHARLES BENNET (Sir), **2nd Bt**

1 Caroline; *m* 25 Aug 1870 Walter Pennington Creyke (*d* 21 Jan 1892), est s of Ven — Creyke, of Bolton Percy, Yorks, and *d* 8 Sept 1946, leaving issue

Sir JOHN *d* 31 Aug 1900; his only son,

Sir CHARLES BENNET LAWES later LAWES-WITTEWRONGE (roy licence 18 April 1902 with arms), **2nd Bt**; *b* 3 Oct 1843; BSc Cambridge; sculptor; *m* 8 April 1869 Marie Amelie Rose (Amy) (*d* 13 Aug 1928), est dau of Charles George Fountaine, and *d* 6 Oct 1911, having had, with a dau:

Sir John Bennet Lawes-Wittewronge, 3rd Bt; *b* 28 July 1872; *m* 1897 Helena Ramsey (*d* 10 Jan 1961), dau of Henry Ramsey Cox, of Folkestone, Kent, and had:

1 JOHN CLAUD (Sir), **4th Bt**

2 Sydney Vernon; *b* 1906; *m* 1929 (*divorce* 1933) Esmé, dau of E A Biddulph, of Roseville, NSW, and *dsp* 15 Aug 1955

1 Caroline Adelaide; *m* 1928 (*divorce* 1951) Richard K E Woodhouse, BE, AMIE (Aust), only s of Prof — Woodhouse, Sydney U, and *d* 24 June 1954, having adopted a s (*d* accidently at sch 1954)

2 Sylvia; *m* 1927 Victor Kinsella MD, ChM (Sydney U), FRCS, and *d* 1967, leaving two sons and a dau

Sir JOHN *d* 8 Sept 1931; his er son,

Sir JOHN CLAUD BENNET LAWES-WITTEWRONGE later LAWES (deed poll 30 Oct 1951), **4th Bt**; *b* 9 Sept 1898; *educ* Blundell's; 2nd Lt RFA (SR) WW I; *m* 1st 5 June 1928 Kathleen Marjorie Livingstone (*d* 23 May 1938), er dau of Gerald Tylston Hodgson, of Tullimaar, Perranarworthal, Cornwall, and had:

1 Sir JOHN MICHAEL BENNET LAWES, **5th and present Bt**

Sir JOHN *m* 2nd 26 Oct 1938 Naomi Constance Helen (*d* 5 Aug 1996), yst dau of Lancelot Wykeham Badnall, of Kensington, and *d* 9 Dec 1979, leaving by her:

1 *Janet Caroline [Mrs John Berney-Ficklin, 35 Gibralter Dve, Palm Desert, CA 92260, USA]; *b* 24 Dec 1940; *m* 18 July 1964 *John Christopher Berney-Ficklin, only s of Alexander Tennent Mackintosh Berney-Ficklin, OBE, MC, of La Haye du Puits, Castel, Guernsey, and has:

91) *Todd Alexander; *b* 29 Nov 1975

(1) *Karen Lawes; *b* 21 March 1973

LAWRENCE, Baron

Arms: Erm. on a cross raguly gu. an eastern crown or, on a chief az. two swords in saltire ppr., pommels and hilts gold, between as many leopard's faces arg. **Crest:** Out of an eastern crown or a cubit arm entwined by a wreath of laurel and holding a dagger, all ppr. **Supporters:** Dexter, an officer of the Guide Cavalry (Irregulars) of the Pathan tribe in the province of Peshawar, habited and accoutred ppr.; sinister, an officer of the Sikh Irregular Cavalry, also habited and accoutred ppr. **Motto:** Be ready. **Creations:** Bt. (UK) 16 Aug 1858, B. (UK) 3 April 1869.

THE 5TH BARON LAWRENCE OF THE PUNJAUB AND OF GRATELY, Co Southampton, and a **Baronet** (Sir David John Downer Lawrence, Bt) [The Rt Hon The Lord Lawrence, c/o Bird and Bird, 90 Fetter Lane, London EC4A 1JP]; *b* 4 Sept 1937; *s f* 1968; *educ* Bradfield

Lineage: ALEXANDER LAWRENCE (*see* LAWRENCE, Bt, of Lucknow); had a 6th (but 4th noticed) s:

Sir John Laird Mair Lawrence, 1st Bt (with thanks of Parl and £2,000 p.a. from East India Co for having helped suppress Indian Mutiny), and **1st Baron Lawrence of the Punjaub and of Grately**, Co Southampton (both UK), so *cr* 16 Aug 1858 and 3 April 1869 respectively, GCB (1857, KCB 1856), GCSI (1866, KSI 1861), PC (1859); *b* 4 March 1811; *educ* Free GS Londonderry, Wraxall Coll nr Bath and Haileybury; joined Bengal CS 1829, assist to Ch Commr Delhi 1831, Magistrate and Collector Delhi 1831837, Settlement Offr Ettawah 1838, Commr Sutlej 1848 and Punjab 1852–58, Lt-Govr Punjab 1859, memb Supreme Cncl India 1858–63, Viceroy 1863–68, Chm London Sch Bd 1870–73; *m* 26 Aug 1841 Harriette Katherine, CI (*d* 28 Dec 1917), dau of Rev Richard Hamilton, Rector Culdaff, Co Donegal, and had:

1 JOHN HAMILTON, **2nd Baron**

2 Henry Arnold; *b* 17 March 1848; *m* 6 May 1879 Constance Charlotte (*d* 8 April 1929), est surv dau of Rev George Irving Davies, Rector Kelsale, Suffolk, and *d* 16 April 1902, having had:

(1) A son; *b* and *d* 21 Sept 1883

(2) John Dalhousie; *b* 2 Aug 1887; *d* 2 June 1900

(3) Malcolm Eyton; Lt 6th Bn KRRC; *b* 10 March 1889, *ka* 10 Jan 1915

(4) Christopher Hal; 2nd Lt KRRC; *b* 11 Nov 1893, *ka* 13 Oct 1914

(1) Constance Letitia; *b* 26 Jan 1881; *m* 3 Nov 1921 Brian Halsey Tyrwhitt-Drake (*d* 11 July 1949), only s of Hon Montague Tyrwhitt-Drake, of Victoria, BC, and *d* 28 July 1949, leaving issue

(2) Phyllis May; *b* 4 May 1882; *m* 16 Jan 1906 Rev John Arthur Thomas (*d* 27 Oct 1954), Rector Westcote, Glos, s of W Thomas, of Wrexham, and *d* 17 Dec 1956, leaving issue

(3) Mary Paolina; *b* 26 Jan 1886; *m* 14 Sept 1921 Sir Thomas St Quintin Hill, KCMG, OBE, only s of R A St Quintin Hill, and *d* 22 Oct 1963, leaving issue

3 CHARLES NAPIER LAWRENCE, 1st and last BARON LAWRENCE OF KINGSGATE, of Holland House, Kingsgate, Co Kent (UK), so *cr* 23 July 1923; *b* 27 May 1855; *educ* Marlborough; chm: LNWR 1921–24 (dir 1884), chm LMSR 1923–24, Antofagasta and Bolivia Rlway, N Br and Mercantile Assur, Roy Commn Insur Acts 1925–26; *m* 22 June 1881 Catherine, only dau of Frederick

Wiggin Sumner, of New York, and n of James Gerard, US Amb UK, and *dsp* 17 Dec 1927, when the title expired

4 Herbert Alexander (Sir), GCB; *b* 8 Aug 1861; Gen and CGS Br Armies France 1918–19, Hon Col 65th (Manch) AA Bde RA (TA), Col Manchester Regt and 17th/21st Lancers, Lt-Col and Hon Col cmdg King's Colonials, Boer War 1899–1902 (despatches twice, brevet, Queen's medal with six clasps and King's medal with two clasps) and WW I, Serbian Order Karageorge 2nd Cl with swords, Grand Cordon Leopold of Belgium and Croix de Guerre Belgium, US DSM, Grand Offr Mil Order Avis Portugal, Grand Cross Star Romania, Grand Offr Legn Hon and Croix de Guerre, Order Rising Sun Japan 1st Cl, Hon DCL Oxon, Hon LLD St Andrews; *m* 26 April 1892 Hon Isabel Mary Mills (LCC) (*d* 30 March 1941), dau of 1st Baron Hillingdon (*see* 1970 edn), and *d* 17 Jan 1943, having had:

(1) Oliver John; *b* 5 Aug 1893; *ka* 25 May 1915

(2) Michael Charles, Lt PO Rifles, T/Capt Coldstream Gds WW I; *b* 6 Oct 1894; *d* 19 of wounds recd in action 18 Sept 1916

(1) Elizabeth Barbara Peace, JP; *b* 18 May 1902; *m* 1 June 1923 Maj Desmond Abel Smith, MC (*d* 26 July 1974), est s of Eustace Abel Smith, of Longhills, Lincs, and had:

1a *John Lawrence; *b* 9 April 1934; *educ* Eton

1a *June Isabel; *b* 3 May 1924

2a Aileen Mary; *b* 29 Nov 1925; *m* 20 Feb 1947 Maj William James Bodington, DFC, The Cameronians (Scottish Rifles), s of Surgn-Capt P J Bodington, RHG, and *d* 13 April 1959, leaving issue

3a *Elizabeth Ann; *b* 30 Aug 1929; *m* 12 Aug 1961 Lt Col Denis Herbert Arthur Lewey, Coldstream Gds, only s of Sir Arthur Werner Lewey, of Haben Ho, Petersfield, Hants, and has:

1b *Richard Arthur Justin; *b* 18 Aug 1964

2b *Christopher Guy Desmond; *b* 25 Sept 1966

1b *Clare Katharine Peace; *b* 25 Sept 1966

4a *Catherine Clare; *b* 1 May 1938

1 Catherine Letitia; *m* 28 Jan 1868 Col William Lowndes Randall, IA (*d* 13 April 1911), 4th s of Archdeacon — Randall, and *d* 22 April 1931, leaving issue

2 Harriette Emily; *m* 28 July 1877 Sir Henry Stewart Cunningham, KCIE, yst s of Rev J W Cunningham, and *d* 8 July 1918, leaving issue

3 Alice Margaret; *m* 14 July 1870 Rev Launcelot Charles Walford (*d* 2 July 1936) and *d* 3 May 1944, leaving issue

4 Mary Emma, OBE (1918); *m* 27 Feb 1872 Francis William Buxton and *d* 21 Feb 1939, having had issue (*see* BUXTON, Bt)

5 Edith; *d* unm 24 Feb 1861

6 Maude Agnes, DBE (1926), Dir Women's Estabs Treasury, Ch Woman Inspr Bd Educn; *d* unm 11 Jan 1933

The 1st BARON *d* 27 June 1879; his est son,

JOHN HAMILTON LAWRENCE, **2nd Baron Lawrence of the Punjaub and of Grately**, JP Middx, DL Bucks; *b* 1 Oct 1846; *educ* Trin Coll Cambridge (BA); barrister, Capt Herts Yeo Cav, Ld-in-Waiting 1895–1905, Grand Cross Order Frederick of Wurttemberg with crown 1904; *m* 22 Aug 1872 Mary Caroline Douglas (*d* 16 Nov 1938), only child of Richard Campbell, of Auchinbreck, Argyllshire, and *d* 22 Aug 1913, having had, with an er s (*d* in infancy) and a dau (*d* unm):

ALEXANDER GRAHAM LAWRENCE, **3rd Baron Lawrence of the Punjaub and of Grately**, JP and DL (Middx); *b* 29 March 1878; *educ* Eton and Worcester Coll Oxford; Capt 3rd Bn Beds and Herts Regt, 3rd King's (Liverpool) Regt and Maj 11th (Co of London) Bn The London Regt; *m* 1st 12 Nov 1907 Dorothy Helen, CBE (1920) (*d* 1 Feb 1935), dau of Anthony Pemberton Hobson, of Greenford; *m* 2nd 3 Sept 1936 Jessie (*d* 29 Dec 1936), dau of Col Byron Gordon Daniels and widow of William Frederic Lawrence, JP, of Cowesfield House, Wilts; *m* 3rd 29 June 1938 Catherine Louisa (*d* 24 Oct 1965), dau of Charles Fernihough, of Staffs, and widow of William Burnet Craigie, of S Kensington and Argentina, and by his 1st w had:

1 JOHN ANTHONY EDWARD, **4th Baron**

1 *Catherine Dorina Mary [The Hon Catherine Lawrence, W Wittering Nursing Home, West Wittering, Sussex]; *b* 1910

2 Sara Honora Angel; *b* 1912

3 Dinah Felicity Forster; *d* 21 Dec 1918

4 Mary Letitia; *b* 1919; *m* 6 Jan 1951 Douglas Lionel Woodhouse, AAPSW, only s of Alfred Jeffrey Woodhouse, of Chiswick, and *d* April 1958, leaving issue

5 *Nona Georgette; *b* 1922; *m* 8 Feb 1945 W/Cdr Vincent George Byrne, RAF (*d* 1978), yst s of James Byrne, of Malahide Co Dublin, and has had:

(1) Nicholas John Joseph; *b* 1946; *m* 1968 *Catherine Penelope [Mrs Nicholas Byrne, Wincombe Cottage, Donhead St Mary, Dorset], dau of Douglas Smith, and *d* 30 July 1994, leaving:

1a *Kirstie Mary Kate; *b* 1969; *m* 1997 *—

2a *Tara Mary Fiona; *b* 1971

3a *Fiona Georgina Mary; *b* 1976

(2) *James Vincent [James Byrne Esq, Hawkyard House, Chipping Norton, Oxon]; *b* 1950; MD, FRCS, FRCR; *m* 1975 *Juliet Elizabeth Anson, dau of John Bailey, and has:

1a *Thomas Vincent Lawrence; *b* 1979

2a *George Henry St Clare; *b* 1981

3a *Henry Charles Mogeridge; *b* 1985

1a *Rowena Catherine Anson; *b* 1977

(3) *(Vincent) Patrick [Patrick Byrne Esq, 17 Birchland Ave, London SW12 8ND]; *b* 1952; *m* 1989 *Mary Gabriel, 2nd dau of Sir James Napier Finnie McEwen, 2nd Bt (*qv*), and has:

1a *Elliot James; *b* 1991

2a *John Joseph; *b* 1995

1a *Rosanna Clare; *b* 1993

(4) *Dominic Lawrence; *b* 1959; MD MRCOG; *m* 1990 *Susan Amanda, BSc, MRCOG, dau of Capt Richard Bates, RN, of Winchester, and has:

1a *Katharine Letitia; *b* 1992

(5) *Rory Shaun [Rory Byrne Esq, 30 West Hill Rd, London SW18]; *b* 1961; *m* 1988 *Andrea Carina, dau of Peter Riediker, of Zurich, and has:

1a *Edward Alexander; b 1990

2a *Christian Rory; b 1992

1a *Jessica Katherine; b 1989

(1) *Teresa Marie [Mrs Robin Wickham, Maynards Farm, Matfield, Kent TN12 7PL]; b 1947; m 1968 *Robin Herbert Wickham and has:

1a *Simon James Wykeham; b 1969

2a *Patrick David Wykeham; b 1972

(2) *Clare Mary Anne [Mrs Tass Whittaker, Mayfield, Habbin Hill, Rogate, Hants GU31 5HN]; b 1955; m 1981 *Tass Whittaker and has:

1a *Lara Nona Jane; b 1983

2a *Amy Marie Clare; b 1986

3a *Eleanor Charlotte; b 1988

(3) *Fiona Rosaleen Mary; b 1957; m 9 April 1983 *Robert J Rolls, s of Thomas Rolls, of W Sussex, and has:

1a *Giles Thomas Alexander; b 1984

1a *Annabel India Sarah; b 1986

2a *Sophie Amelia Lucy; b 1988

The 3rd BARON d 24 June 1947; his only son,

JOHN ANTHONY EDWARD LAWRENCE, **4th Baron Lawrence of the Punjaub and of Grately**; b 16 Oct 1908; educ Haileybury; Lt 8th Bn Middx Regt (TA); m 1st 8 Aug 1936 (divorce 1947) Margaret Jean, only child of Arthur Downer, of Rotherfield, Kent; m 2nd 16 Oct 1948 *Joan Alice Mildred (m 2nd 1969 John Eddison (d 1989)), only dau of Col Arthur John Lewer, OBE, DL, JP, of Bonchurch, IoW, and d 8 Oct 1968, having by his 1st w had:

DAVID JOHN DOWNER LAWRENCE, **5th and present Baron Lawrence of the Punjaub and of Grately**

LAWRENCE, Bt, of Ealing Park

Arms: Ermine a cross raguly gules, in the 1st and 4th quarters a serpent nowed proper. **Crest:** A griffin's head couped argent, in front thereof a serpent nowed proper. **Motto:** *Mente et labore* ('By mind and work'). **Creation:** Bt. (UK) 30 April 1867.

SIR WILLIAM FETTIPLACE LAWRENCE, 5TH BT, of Ealing Park, Middlesex [Sir William Lawrence, The Knoll, Walcote, Warwicks B49 6LZ]; b 23 Aug 1954; s f 1986; educ King Edward VI Sch Stratford-on-Avon; memb: Stratford-on-Avon DC 1982– (chm 1990–91), S Warwicks Gen Hosps NHS Tst 1993–, Heart of England Tourist Bd 1989– (chm 1991–); dir S Warwicks Business Ptnrship 1995–, memb Ct Birmingham U 1990–, govr Roy Shakespeare Theatre 1991–, chm Midland Music Festivals 1996–

Lineage: WILLIAM LAWRENCE; m 1716 Anne (d 1755), dau of Rev Charles Stafford, Fell Magdalen Coll Oxford, by Elizabeth Fettiplace (dau of Charles Fettiplace, JP, of Earl's Court, Upper Lambourn, Berks, himself s of Sir Edmund Fettiplace, of Childrey), and d 1739, leaving:

WILLIAM FETTIPLACE LAWRENCE, of Burford, Oxon; b 1723; m Barbara Jenner Lane (d 1758) and d 1778, leaving:

WILLIAM LAWRENCE, of Cirencester, Glos; b 11 Sept 1753; m 9 April 1778 Judith (d 24 Feb 1839), 2nd dau of William Wood, of Tetbury, Glos, and had, with other issue:

1 WILLIAM (Sir), **1st Bt**

2 Charles, of The Querns, Cirencester; b 21 March 1794; m 26 May 1818 Lydia, yst dau of Devereux Bowly, of Chesterton Ho, Cirencester, and d 5 July 1881, having had issue

1 Susanna; m 6 Dec 1814 George Bevir (d 21 March 1846) and d 21 Jan 1849, leaving issue

2 Mary; m 24 Sept 1814 Stephen Wilkins (dsp 17 Jan 1828) and d 30 April 1815

3 Judith; m 7 July 1812 Rev Henry Cripps and had issue (see PARMOOR, B)

WILLIAM LAWRENCE d 19 Feb 1837; his est son,

Sir William Lawrence, 1st Bt (UK), so cr 30 April 1867, of Ealing Park, Middx; b 16 July 1783; educ Elmore Court School, Glos; surgn to and lecturer surgery St

Bartholomew's Hosp, twice Pres Coll Surgeons; Serjeant-Surgn to HM QUEEN VICTORIA 1857, FRS 1813 (later V-Pres), corresponding memb Institut de France; m 14 Aug 1823 Louisa (d 14 Aug 1855), yst dau of John Trevor Senior, of Broughton Ho, Aylesbury, Bucks, and d 5 July 1867, having had, with an er s (d young) and three daus (d unm):

Sir (James John) Trevor Lawrence, 2nd Bt, KCVO, JP Surrey; b 30 Dec 1831; PRHS 1884–1913, Treas St Bartholomew's Hosp 1892–1904, MP Mid-Surrey 1875–85 and S E Surrey 1885–92, KGStJ, FRGS; m 6 Oct 1869 Elizabeth (d 18 March 1916), only child of John Mathew, of Burford, Dorking, and had:

1 WILLIAM MATTHEW TREVOR (Sir), **3rd Bt**

2 Aubrey Trevor, MBE, KC (1927); b 15 Jan 1875; educ Ch Ch Oxford (MA); barrister Inner Temple, Chllr Dioceses: Sheffield 1914, Worcester 1920, Peterborough 1922, Southwell 1922, Winchester 1924, Leicester 1927 and Portsmouth 1927; with Min Munitions 1915–19; m 8 June 1901 Constance Emily Fanning (d 9 July 1957), dau of Joseph McGaw, of Kooba, NSW, and Mickleham Downs, Dorking, and d 23 March 1930, leaving:

(1) John Trevor; b 18 Jan 1908; educ Shrewsbury and Ch Ch Oxford; d unm 2 May 1963

(2) +PETER STAFFORD HAYDEN [Peter Lawrence Esq, Simeons, Little Milton, Oxford OX44 7QE]; b 9 Feb 1913; heir presumptive; educ Eton and Ch Ch Oxford (BA 1935, MA 1945); assist master Eton 1936–77, housemaster 1951–68, T/Lt-Cdr (Special Br) RNVR as Radar Offr WW II (despatches); m 10 Aug 1940 *Helena Frances, 2nd dau of Hon George William Lyttelton (see COBHAM, V), and has:

1a +Aubrey Lyttelton Simon; b 22 Sept 1942; educ Eton and Ch Ch Oxford (BA 1964, MA 1968); m 24 April 1984 *Danielle de Froidmont and has:

1b +Thomas Lyttelton de Froidmont; b 12 April 1985

2a +Robin Peter Charles; b 29 Oct 1950; educ Eton

1a *Pamela Jane; b 10 April 1945; educ N Foreland Lodge and UCL (BA 1970, PGCE 1978); m 17 Dec 1981 *Stuart Wooler and has:

1b *Harry Peter Lawrence; b 3 Sept 1988

1b *Alice Honor Lawrence; b 15 May 1982

2a *Anthea Mary; b 6 June 1947; educ N Foreland Lodge and London U (BEd); m 20 Dec 1980 *Clinton Cavers

3a *Jemima Rachel; b 24 Jan 1956; educ Wycombe Abbey and Roy Northern Coll of Music (GMus); m 9 Sept 1978 *Joseph Severs Taylor and has:

1b *Oscar George; b 27 June 1987

2b *Rowan Joseph; b 16 Nov 1988

3b *Bryn Hugh; b 29 Sept 1990

1b *Ivy Rosanna; b 10 June 1985

4a *Susanna Lucy; b 26 Feb 1958; educ Lord Williams's Sch Thame and Leeds U (MB, ChB 1981)

(1) Ruth Christian, JP; b 14 June 1904; m 15 Dec 1934 Philip Olaf Buxton, JP (see BUXTON, Bt), and d 31 March 1976, leaving issue

3 Harold John; b 15, d 17 Feb 1876

4 Charles Trevor, OBE (1926); b 18 Sept 1879; Maj Hants Regt Boer War (medal, three clasps), with Nigeria Regt 1901–05 (despatches) and 1917–18, raised Nigeria Land Contingent 1914 (despatches), Commr Nigeria Br Emp Exhibn 1923–25 Adminr Lagos, MEC 1932; m 7 March 1916 Adeliza (d 1950), dau of Maj-Gen Sir John Fretcheville Dykes Donnelly, KCB, RE, and dsp 10 April 1953

5 A son; b and d 15 April 1883

1 Bessie Mary; m 17 June 1911 Henry Rottenburg, MIEE, 2nd s of Paul Rottenburg, of Holmhurst, Glasgow, and d 11 March 1944, leaving issue

Sir TREVOR d 22 Dec 1913; his est son,

Sir William Matthew Trevor Lawrence, 3rd Bt, JP Surrey; b 17 Sept 1870; FSA, BA Oxon, PhD Berlin, Almoner St Bartholomew's Hosp, Offr du Mérite Agricole, Victoria Medal of Honour Horticulture, V-Pres Iris Soc, Pres: Alpine Garden Soc, Cactus and Succulent Soc of GB, Embroiderers' Guild; Examiner Bd Educn 1902–22, Treas RHS 1923–23, Sec POW Info Bureau 1914–15, Admlty War Staff 1915; m 24 Feb 1908 (Bertha) Iris Eyre, Dep Pres Surrey BRCS, chm POW and Welfare Dept Surrey WW II, Victoria Medal Horticulture (d 16 June 1955), yst dau of Brig-Gen Eyre Macdonnell Stewart Crabbe, CB, and had:

1 WILLIAM (Sir), **4th Bt**

2 Roger Fettiplace; Capt RA WW II; b 19 Aug 1919; shot by the Germans after escaping from a POW Camp in Italy 15 Jan 1944

1 Mary Barbara; b 26 Feb 1909; m 9 Sept 1933 His Hon Judge Alfred Alexander Gordon Clark (d 25 Aug 1958), 3rd s of Henry Herbert Gordon Clark, of Mickleham Hall, Surrey, and d 17 Sept 1975, leaving:

(1) *Charles Philip Gordon (Rev); b 25 May 1936; educ Eton, Worcester Coll Oxford (BA 1959, MA 1963) and Cuddesdon Coll; Chaplain Tonbridge Sch 1965–68, Rector Keston 1968; m 20 Feb 1965 *Thalia Elizabeth, dau of Cdr Frederick William Fitzjohn Oldham, OBE, RNVR, of Providence, Copthorne, Sussex, and has:

1a *Sophia Jane; b 25 Aug 1967

(1) *Alexandra Mary Gordon; b 30 July 1938; educ Courtauld Inst London U (BA 1960); m 20 July 1963 *Hugo Martin Wedgwood, est s of Sir John Hamilton Wedgwood, 2nd Bt, TD (qv), and has issue

(2) *Cecilia Mary Gordon; b 26 March 1944; educ LMH Oxford (BA 1965)

2 Elizabeth Anne; b 9 June 1910; m 13 Nov 1937 F/O Clement Nelson Swann, RAF (d 11 Aug 1938), 2nd s of Ernest E Swann, of Douglas, IoM, and had:

(1) *Clemency Anne Rosemary; b posthumously 28 Jan 1939; m 1962 *Michael Selby Gray and has issue

3 Naomi; b 8 July 1915; m 1st 9 Sept 1939 Richard Peppercorn Duckham (d 6 April 1957), only s of Sir Arthur Duckham; m 2nd 13 July 1957 F/Lt Vivian James, RAF, yr s of Jenkin James, of Port Talbot, Glam, and had:

(1) *Siriol Anne; b 17 Jan 1960

Sir WILLIAM d 4 Jan 1934; his er son,

Sir William Lawrence, 4th Bt, FRHS; b 14 July 1913; educ Bradfield; Maj E Surrey Regt WW II, seconded AFV Div Min Supply, sr exec Wilmot Breeden Ltd,

Pres W Warwicks Scout Cncl, V-Pres Stratford-on-Avon & S Warwicks C Assoc; *m* 1st 20 Jan 1940 (*divorce* 1945) Zoë, yst dau of Henry Stedham Stanley Pether, of Grazeley Ho, Iffley, Oxon; *m* 2nd 10 July 1945 *Pamela Mary [Lady Lawrence, The Knoll, Walcote, Warwicks B49 6LZ], late FANY, yr dau of James Edgar Gordon, of Cheshire, and *d* 1986, having by her had:

1 Sir WILLIAM FETTIPLACE LAWRENCE, **5th and present Bt**

1 *Lavinia Margaret [Mrs Julian Seymour, Waterdale House, E Knoyle, Salisbury, Wilts]; *b* 13 April 1947; *m* 1971 *Julien Conway Seymour and has issue (*see* HERTFORD, M)

2 *Caroyln Mary [Mrs Carolyn Evelyn, Hookers Place, Bentworth, Hants GU34 5RB]; *b* 26 Aug 1949; *m* 15 April 1972 (*divorce* 1990) Nicholas Peter Evelyn, yr s of Maj Peter Evelyn, Gren Gds, and has:

  (1) *Rupert Peter; *b* 1973
  (2) *James Nicholas; *b* 1976

LAWRENCE, Bt, of Lucknow

Arms: Erm. on a cross raguly gu. an eastern crown or, on a chief az. two swords in saltire ppr., pommels and hilts gold, between as many leopard's faces arg. **Crest:** Out of an eastern crown or a cubit arm entwined by a wreath of laurel and holding a dagger, all ppr. **Motto:** Never give in. **Creation:** Bt. (UK) 10 Aug 1858.

SIR JOHN WALDEMAR LAWRENCE, 6TH BT, of Lucknow, OBE (1945) [Sir John Lawrence Bt OBE, 1 Maishes Cottages, Northstoke, Bath BA1 9AT]; *b* 27 May 1907; *s* bro 1967; *educ* Eton and New Coll Oxford (MA); PA to Dir German Jewish Aid Ctee 1938–39, European Intell Offr and European Servs Organiser BBC 1939–42, Press Attaché Moscow 1942–45, freelance writer 1946, ed *Frontier* 1958–75, author: *A History of Russia* (1960), *Russians Observed* (1969), *Lawrence of Lucknow* (1990), chm: Keston Coll 1969–83 (pres 1984–), GB-USSR Assoc 1970–85; Offr Order Orange Nassau 1950; *m* 1st 7 Dec 1948 Jacynth Mary (*d* 1987), dau of Rev Francis George Ellerton and formerly w of (a) Guy Douglas Hamilton Warrack and (b) Michael Donaldson-Hudson; *m* 2nd 1988 *Audrey Viola, widow of John Woodiwiss.

Lineage: ALEXANDER LAWRENCE (*s* of William Lawrence, of Portrush, Co Antrim, by Amelia Fleming, of Portrush); *b* 7 Nov 1764; Lt-Col, Govr Upnor Castle; *m* 5 May 1797 Catherine Letitia (*d* 30 April 1846), dau of Rev George Knox, Rector Lifford, and had, with other issue:

1 Alexander William; *b* 1 July 1803; Maj-Gen, Col 2nd Madras Light Cav; *m* 31 March 1828 Rosanna Lyster and *d* 21 Feb 1868, having had a s (*d* 1852)

2 George St Patrick (Sir), KCSI, CB; *b* 17 March 1804; Lt-Gen, Lt-Col BSC; *m* 3 April 1830 Charlotte Isabella (*d* 12 May 1878), dau of John Browne, Surgn-Gen Bengal, and *d* 16 Nov 1884, leaving issue

3 HENRY MONTGOMERY

4 JOHN LAIRD MAIR LAWRENCE, *cr* BARON LAWRENCE OF THE PUNJAUB AND OF GRATELY (*qv*)

5 Richard Charles, CB, Gen BSC; *b* 26 Oct 1817; *m* 30 March 1839 Ellen (*d* 23 Jan 1900), dau of Col William Youngson, EIC Madras Estab, of Bowscar, Cumberland, and *d* 1896, leaving issue

1 Letitia Catherine; *m* 1837 Rev Henry Horace Hayes (*d* 1853), Vicar N Stoke, and *d* 1865

2 Honoria Angelina; *m* Oct 1831 Col Nathaniel Dunbar Barton, Bengal Army, and *d* 27 Sept 1889

3 Marianne Amelia; *m* 6 July 1835 James Fogo Bernard, of Clifton, Bristol, MD, and had issue

4 Marcia Eliza; *m* 1837 Abraham Goodall, Inspr-Gen Hosps, IA, and *d* 8 March 1883

ALEXANDER LAWRENCE *d* 7 May 1835; his 3rd son,

Sir Henry Montgomery Lawrence, KCB 1848 (CB 1846); *b* Ceylon 28 June 1806; joined Bengal Artillery 1821, served Burma, Kabul and Sutlej Campaigns, Br Resident: Nepal 1843 and Lahore 1846, Lt-Col 1846, Govr-Gen's Agent NWF, Gen, Ch Commr Govt of Punjab on its annexation 1849, Govr-Gen's Agent Rajputana 1853, Ch Commr Oudh 1857, organised defence of Lucknow Indian Mutiny 1857; essayist, author: *The Adventures of an Officer in Runjeet Singh's*

Service; *m* 21 Aug 1837 Honoria (*d* 16 Jan 1854), dau of Rev George Marshall, of Carndonagh, Co Donegal, and *d* in the Residency, Lucknow, 4 July of wounds from a shell 2 July 1857, having had:

1 **Sir Alexander Hutchinson Lawrence, 1st Bt** (UK), so *cr* 10 Aug 1858 in consideration of his f's servs, with remainder in default of heirs male of his own body to his bro; *b* 1838; *m* 28 Aug 1862 Alice Eacy (*m* 2nd 10 Oct 1871 Sir George Young, 3rd Bt, of Formosa Place (*qv*), and *d* 22 Aug 1922), dau of Evory Kennedy, MD, of Queensberry Place, London, and Belgard, Co Dublin, and was accidentally *k* 27 Aug 1864 by the collapse of a bridge on the Tibet Rd in India, leaving:

  (1) **Sir Henry Hayes Lawrence, 2nd Bt**, JP Co Dublin, High Sheriff 1891; *b* 26 Feb 1864; *m* 10 Nov 1890 Victoria Margaret (*m* 2nd 16 Nov 1904 Rev James Berkeley Bristow and *d* 18 Dec 1951), 2nd dau of Theodore Walrond, CB, of Maidenhead and Bayswater, and *d* 27 Oct 1898, leaving:

    1a Norah Margaret; *b* 16 Dec 1891; *d* unm 1966
    2a Alice Henrietta; Kaisar-i-Hind Gold Medal, MFHom 1957; *b* 6 May 1895; *educ* Cheltenham Ladies' Coll, LMH Oxford (MA 1923) and Roy Free Med Sch for Women London (MRCS, LRCP 1948); *m* 18 Dec 1922 Sir Hopetoun Gabriel Stokes, KCIE, CSI, MEC, Madras (*d* 10 Nov 1951), s of Sir Henry Stokes, KCSI, and *d* 7 Jan 1975
    3a Margaret Eacy; *b* 8 Sept 1896; *m* 16 Aug 1921 Lt-Col Richard Eldred Hindson, RWF (*d* 15 Sept 1966), est s of Rev John Hutchinson Hindson, and *d* 2 May 1966, leaving issue

2 HENRY WALDEMAR (Sir), **3rd Bt**

1 Letitia; *d* an infant, Aug 1842

2 Honoria Letitia; *m* 9 Aug 1873 Henry George Hart (*d* 12 Jan 1921), Headmaster Sedbergh Sch, and *d* 18 Dec 1923

The 2nd Bt's unc,

Sir Henry Waldemar Lawrence, 3rd Bt, JP London and Surrey; *b* 24 Jan 1845; *educ* Cambridge (BA); barrister and Sub Treas Inner Temple; *m* 10 July 1873 Emily Mary (*d* 14 Sept 1925), dau of Sir George Burdett L'Estrange, and *d* 3 June 1908, having had, with two daus (*d* young or unm):

Sir Alexander Waldemar Lawrence, 4th Bt, JP Somerset; *b* 18 May 1874; *educ* New Coll Oxford (MA); Assist Slr Treasury 1917–24, Ch Assist Slr 1924–26, Hon Memb ABA; *m* 13 Aug 1904 Anne Elizabeth Le Poer (*d* 17 Oct 1950), only child of Henry Le Poer Wynne, Foreign Sec to Govt India, and *d* 1939, leaving:

1 **Sir Henry Eustace Waldemar Lawrence, 5th Bt**; *b* 10 July 1905; *d* unm 29 Dec 1967

2 Sir JOHN WALDEMAR LAWRENCE, **6th and present Bt**

3 +GEORGE ALEXANDER WALDEMAR [George Lawrence Esq, Brockham End, nr Bath, Somerset]; *b* 22 Sept 1910; heir presumptive; *educ* Eton and Trin Coll Cambridge (BA); *m* 10 June 1949 *Olga, dau of Peter Schilovsky, late Govr Kostroma, Russia, and has:

  (1) +Henry Peter; *b* 2 April 1952; *educ* Eton; *m* 1979 *Penelope Maureen Nunan and has:
    1a +Christopher Cosmo; *b* 1979
    1a *Isabelle Olga Jane; *b* 1984
  (1) *Natalia Honoria; *b* 6 Jan 1951; *m* 1980 *Mehrdad Shokoohy
  (2) *Catherine Letitia; *b* 4 June 1953; *m* 1976 *Stephen James Paul Todd and has:
    1a *Peter James; *b* 1982
    1a *Helen Anna; *b* 1979

LAWRENCE, Bt, of Sloane Gardens

Arms: Ermine an escarbuncle or, surmounted by a lotus flower proper, on a chief arched gules a dragon passant or. **Crest:** A cubit arm, vested gules, cuffed ermine, holding in the hand a plane leaf proper and charged on the sleeve with a trefoil slipped or. **Supporters:** On either side a heron holding in the beak a sprig of plane fructed proper. **Motto:** *Gwaith gyda gobaith* ('Work with hope'). **Creation:** Bt. (UK) 13 July 1906.

SIR DAVID ROLAND WALTER LAWRENCE, 3RD BT, of Sloane Gardens, Chelsea [Sir David Lawrence Bt, 28 High Town Rd, Maidenhead, Berks SL6 1PB]; *b* 8 May 1929; *s f* 1950; *educ* Radley and RMC Sandhurst; Capt Coldstream Gds Malaya 1949–50; *m* 31 Jan 1955 *Audrey, yr dau of Brig Desmond Young, MC, IA, and formerly w of 11th Duke of Leeds (*see* 1963 edn)

Lineage: GEORGE LAWRENCE, of Trevella, Llangwm, Mon, JP (Mon); *b* 3 Aug 1805; *m* 1st Mary Geach and had issue; *m* 2nd 31

March 1844 Catharine (*d* 3 Nov 1901), dau of Edward Lewis, of Wenvoe, Glam, and *d* 6 March 1896, having by her had:

Sir Walter Roper Lawrence, 1st Bt (UK), so *cr* 13 July 1906, GCIE (1906), GCVO (1918), CB (1917); *b* 9 Feb 1857; memb Cncl India 1907–09, served ICS 1877–97, Under Sec and Officiating Sec Indian Govt 1887–89, Settlement Commr Kashmir 1889–95, Agent in Ch to Duke of Bedford 1895–98, Priv Sec to Viceroy India 1898–1903, Ch of Staff to HRH THE PRINCE OF WALES (later HM GEORGE V) Indian tour 1905–06, T/Col Army 1914, Hon Col 1918, T/Maj-Gen (special appt) 1919, KGStJ, Pres Union Jack Club, v-pres King Edward VII Sanatorium; *m* 18 March 1885 Lilian Gertrude (*d* 18 Dec 1929), dau of John Gwynne James, of Aylstone Hill, Herefs, and *d* 25 May 1940, leaving:

1 (PERCY) ROLAND BRADFORD (Sir), **2nd Bt**

2 (Henry Walter) Neville; *b* 26 Oct 1891; *educ* Wellington and Balliol Coll Oxford; Capt Res Offrs Coldstream Gds WW I (twice wounded); High Sheriff Surrey 1949; *m* 27 April 1933 Sarah (*d* 21 Feb 1947), dau of Nicholas Murray Butler, of New York, and *d* 24 May 1959, leaving:

  (1) +(Walter Nicholas) Murray [Murray Lawrence Esq, Grey Walls, Hook Heath Rd, Woking, Surrey GU22 0QD]; *b* 8 Feb 1935; *educ* Winchester and Trin Coll Oxford; *m* 29 April 1961 *Sally Louise, est dau of Lt Col Alleyn Becher O'Dwyer, and has:

    1a *Sarah Louise; *b* 26 Dec 1962; *m* 1st 26 April 1986 Andrew Crawley (*d* 10 Sept 1988) and has:

      1b *Charles Murray; *b* 17 March 1987

      1b *Jessica Mary; *b* 10 Nov 1988

    1a (cont.) Mrs Andrew Crawley *m* 2nd 16 July 1995 *Hank Slack and has by him:

      2b *Lucy Catherine; *b* 27 April 1996

    2a *Catherine Jane Lawrence; *b* 24 Nov 1964; *m* 1 Feb 1992 *Rupert Elliott and has:

      1b *Hector Edmund Murray; *b* 16 Nov 1996

      1b *Eliza Harriet Rosemary; *b* 29 Aug 1994

The 1st Bt's er son,

Sir (Percy) Roland Bradford Lawrence, 2nd Bt, MC; *b* 9 April 1886; *educ* Eton and RMC Sandhurst, Lt-Col Res Offrs Coldstream Gds WW I (despatches twice); *m* 3 Oct 1925 Susan, 3rd dau of Sir Charles Stewart Addis, KCMG, LLD, of Woodside, Frant, Sussex, and *d* 16 May 1950, having had:

1 Sir DAVID ROLAND WALTER LAWRENCE, **3rd and present Bt**

2 A son; *b* and *d* 18 Aug 1936

3 +CLIVE WYNDHAM [Clive Lawrence Esq, Woodside, Frant, nr Tunbridge Wells, Kent TN3 9HW]; *b* 6 Oct 1939; heir presumptive; *educ* Gordonstoun; Lt Coldstream Gds 1959–64; *m* 22 June 1966 *Sophie Annabel, yr dau of Ian Hervey Stuart Black, of The Old Manse, Balfron, Stirlingshire, and has:

  (1) +James Wyndham Stuart; *b* 25 Dec 1970

  (2) +Simon Roland Stuart; *b* 1973

  (3) +Hugo Hervey Stuart; *b* 1975

1 *Jean Jacqueline [Mrs Harold Quitman, Rookley Farmhouse, Upper Somborne, Hants]; *b* 18 June 1926; *m* 2 Sept 1950 *Harold Channing Quitman, only s of E A Quitman, of Kensington, and has:

  (1) *Jeremy Roland Channing; *b* 5 June 1953

  (1) *Annabel Susan Maude; *b* 6 Dec 1951

2 *Susan Louise; *b* 21 Jan 1944; *m* 1966 *Norman Gardner, of Montreal, and has:

  (1) *Suzanne Vanessa; *b* 1965

  (2) *Amanda Sarah; *b* 1968

LAWRENCE-JONES

Arms: Azure on a fess or three grenades fired proper; in chief a castle and over it the word 'Netherlands' in letters of gold, and in base a lion couchant argent. **Crest:** In front of a castle argent a lion couchant or, gorged with a wreath of laurel and pendant therefrom an escutcheon gules charged with a representation of the Badajoz medal as in the arms. **Motto:** *Marte et arte* ('By war and art'). **Creation:** Bt. (UK) 30 Sept 1831.

SIR CHRISTOPHER LAWRENCE-JONES, 6TH BT, of Cranmer Hall, Norfolk; *b* 19 Jan 1940; *s unc* 1969; *educ* Sherborne, Gonville and Caius Coll Cambridge (MA 1964), and St Thomas's Hosp (MB, BChir 1964); Ld Manor Fakenham, Norfolk, DIH Eng 1968, FFOM 1987, FRCP 1991, Med Advsr BP, Ch MO ICI Gp, chm Medichem, Pres Occupational Med Section Roy Soc of Medicine, memb Management Ctee Br Occupnl Health Research Fndn 1991–94; *m* 3 Feb 1967 *Gail, dau of Cecil Arthur Pittar, FRCS, of Auckland, NZ, and has:

  1 +MARK CHRISTOPHER; *b* 28 Dec 1968

  2 +John Alexander; *b* 23 Jan 1971

Lineage: DAVID JONES (s of Daniel Jones, of Sunny Hill, by Jane, dau and heiress of William Williams, of Garrig Vechan, Carmarths); *b* 1678; *m* 1702 Mary, dau and heiress of Robert Sheldrake, of Fakenham, moved there and *d* 1759, leaving, with a yr s (Daniel, bought the Cranmer Hall estate 1751):

JOHN JONES; *b* 1705; *m* 1732 Elizabeth, only child of Rev Francis Wace, Rector Blakeney, Norfolk, by Elizabeth, dau and coheir of Rev Clement Heigham, of Barrow, Suffolk, Rector Sculthorpe, and *d* 1769, leaving, with other issue:

JOHN JONES; *b* 18 Nov 1751; Offr 29th Foot; *m* 1780 Mary (*d* 1816), dau of John Roberts, of Languard Fort, and had, with other issue:

1 JOHN THOMAS (Sir), **1st Bt**

2 George Mathew; *b* 1785; Capt RN; *d* at Malta 1831

3 William Daniel; *b* 3 July 1787; Maj-Gen RA; *m* 18 Feb 1828 Elizabeth (*d* 12 March 1859), dau of George Smith, of Nottingham, and *d* 20 May 1857, having had issue

4 Henry Taylor; *b* 5 Feb 1790; *m* 23 Oct 1828 Caroline Munster (*d* 4 June 1858), dau of Lt-Gen Wulff, RA, and widow of Sir Richard Hardinge, 1st Bt (*qv*), and *d* 6 June 1860, having had issue

5 Harry David (Sir), GCB; *b* 14 March 1792; served Walcheren Expdn 1809, Peninsula War (medal with five clasps) and New Orleans Campaign 1814–15; Lt-Gen and Col cmdg RE, Govr Sandhurst, cmded land forces capture Bomarsund 1854, Cmdg Engr Siege Sebastopol Feb–8 Sept 1855; *m* 1824 Charlotte (*d* 16 Oct 1880), dau of Rev Thomas Hornsby, and *d* 4 Aug 1866, having had issue

1 Eliza Heigham Wace; *m* 22 July 1822 Maj George Wilkes Uhett, RA (*d* 1825), of Cheltenham, Glos, yst s of Rev Preb Thomas Uhett, and had issue

JOHN JONES *d* 1806, his est son,

Sir John Thomas Jones, 1st Bt (UK), so *cr* 30 Sept 1831, KCB; *b* 1783; Maj-Gen RE, ADC to HM QUEEN VICTORIA; *m* 20 April 1816 Catherine Maria (*d* 1 Dec 1859), dau of Effingham Lawrence, and *d* 26 Feb 1843, having had:

1 **Sir Lawrence Jones, 2nd Bt;** *b* 10 Jan 1817; murdered by brigands Macri, Turkey, 7 Nov 1845

2 WILLOUGHBY (Sir), **3rd Bt**

3 Herbert Walsingham (Rev); *b* 10 Oct 1826; MA; Rector Sculthorpe, Norfolk, Hon Canon Norwich; *m* 23 April 1850 Catherine Rachel, 2nd dau of Daniel Gurney, of N Runcton, Norfolk, and *d* 9 Feb 1889, having had:

(1) Bertram; *b* 18 May 1862; *d* 1868

1 Emily Florence; *m* 27 Dec 1849 William Franks (*d* 1879), of Woodhill, Herts, and *d* 1891, leaving issue

The 2nd Bt's bro,

Sir Willoughby Jones, 3rd Bt, JP and DL; *b* 24 Nov 1820; Norfolk: Chm QS, High Sheriff 1851; *m* 15 April 1856 his cousin Emily (*d* 23 June 1917), dau of Henry Taylor Jones, and had:

1 LAWRENCE JOHN (Sir), **4th Bt**

2 Herbert Edward (Rt Rev); *b* 6 April 1861; MA, DD, Cambridge; Bp Suffragan Lewes 1914–20, Hon Canon St Albans 1909, examining Chaplain to Bp St Albans 1912–14; *m* 18 July 1888 Madeline Long (*d* 18 May 1928), dau of Edward Long Fox, MD, FRCP, of Clifton, and *d* 19 Feb 1920, leaving:

(1) Edward Lawrence; *b* 7 Aug 1891; *educ* Eton and Balliol Coll Oxford; *m* 1st 1915 (*divorce* 1922) Kathleen Nairne, dau of William Cumin Scott, of Blackheath; *m* 2nd 15 Dec 1923 Mary Senior, yst dau of James Rowland Williams, of Kew Park, Montpelier, Jamaica, and *dsp* Aug 1948

(1) Violet Madeleine

3 Willoughby; Lt Norfolk Regt; *b* 18 May 1864; *d* in Burma 1889

4 Harry Daniel; *b* 6 Aug 1868; *d* 30 Aug 1869

1 Mary Florence; *d* unm 31 Jan 1956 aged 97

2 Catherine; *d* unm 26 Nov 1879

3 Gertrude Isabel; *m* 4 Aug 1898 Edward Fuller-Maitland, of Wood Rising, Rye, Sussex, yst s of Thomas Fuller-Maitland, and *d* 1 March 1941

4 Maud Emily; *d* unm 23 March 1931

Sir WILLOUGHBY *d* 21 Aug 1884; his est son,

Sir Lawrence John Jones, 4th Bt, JP (Norfolk 1882–1938); *b* 16 Aug 1857; *educ* Eton and Trin Coll Cambridge (BA 1880, MA 1883); barrister Inner Temple 1882; Capt 3rd Vol Bn Norfolk Regt; *m* 1st 13 April 1882 Evelyn Mary (*d* 17 July 1912), dau of James Johnstone Bevan, of Northgate Ho, Bury St Edmunds; *m* 2nd 2 March 1916 Paula (*d* 23 Feb 1956), dau of Francis Joseph Schuster, of S Kensington, and *d* 21 Oct 1954, having by his 1st w had:

1 Willoughby John; *b* 19 March 1884; *d* 11 Aug 1898

2 **Sir Lawrence Evelyn Jones, 5th Bt**, MC (1918), TD, of Cranmer Hall, Norfolk; *b* 5 April 1885; *educ* Eton and Balliol Coll Oxford; FRSL; barrister Inner Temple 1909; Maj Beds Yeo, WW I (wounded, POW); with Herbert Wagg, merchant bankers; author: *A la Carte, A Victorian Boyhood, Edwardian Youth, Georgian Afternoon*; *m* 23 Nov 1912 Lady Evelyn Alice Grey (*d* 15 April 1971), dau of 4th Earl Grey (*qv*), and *d* 6 Sept 1969, having had:

(1) *Nancy Lawrence [Mrs David Morse, The Old Vicarage, Wooler, Northumberland]; *b* 7 Oct 1913; *m* 12 Nov 1941 David Vivian Morse, MA, FRCS, LRCP (*d* 1993), yr s of Francis Alfred Vivian Morse, slr, of Upper Cowden, Five Acres, Sussex, and had:

1a *Jonathan Patrick; *b* 7 Oct 1942; *educ* Eton and Balliol Coll Oxford

2a *Oliver James; *b* 14 March 1949; *educ* Eton

1a *Annabel Harriet; *b* 27 Sept 1944; *educ* Cranborne Chase and Sussex U; *m* 1972 *Alexander Urquhart and has two daus

(2) Dinah Evelyn Lawrence; *b* 11 June 1916; *d* unm 25 Dec 1942

(3) Delia Vera Lawrence; *b* 27 Aug 1920; *d* 10 April 1927

(4) *Vivien Lawrence [Mrs Simon Asquith, 44 Gilpin Ave, London SW14 8QY]; *b* 30 Aug 1923; *m* 1 Oct 1942 Simon Anthony Roland Asquith (*see* OXFORD AND ASQUITH, E) and has issue

(5) *Lavinia Lawrence [Mrs Frank Monaco, 28 Radnor Walk, London SW3 4 BN]; *b* 21 July 1925; *m* 25 Oct 1980 *Frank John Monaco

3 Bertram Edward; *b* 1 Oct 1886; Cdr RN (emergency list); *m* 1st 13 Feb 1913 (*divorce* 1938) Gwendolen Mary, only child of Herbert Goodall, and had a s (*b* and *d* 20 Dec 1928); *m* 2nd 16 Nov 1938 Margaret Louise, est dau of Geoffrey Montague Cookson, of Howes Eype Farm, Bridport, Dorset, and *d* 16 April 1958, having by her had:

(2) Sir CHRISTOPHER JONES later LAWRENCE-JONES (deed poll 6 Feb 1969), **6th and present Bt**

4 Maurice Herbert (Rev); *b* 8 Dec 1888; BA Cambridge; *d* 8 Sept 1915

1 Hester Catherine; *d* unm 1 Nov 1918

2 Rachel Margaret Lawrence

LAWSON

Arms: Per chevron argent and or a chevron invected sable, plain cotised vert, between two martlets in chief of the third and a trefoil slipped in base of the fourth. **Crest:** Between two arms embowed proper, holding a sun in splendour, a trefoil as in the arms, the whole surmounted by a rainbow, also proper. **Motto:** *Surge et fulge* ('Arise, and shine forth'). **Creation:** Bt. (UK) 12 July 1900.

SIR JOHN CHARLES ARTHUR DIGBY LAWSON, 3RD BT, DSO (1943), MC (1940), of Weetwood Grange, W Riding of Yorks [Col Sir John Lawson Bt DSO MC, Hillmore Cottage, Bishops Hull Rd, Bishops Hull, Somerset TA1 5ER]; *b* 24 Oct 1912; *s* f 9 Feb 1959; *educ* Stowe and RMC Sandhurst; commissioned 11th Hus 1933, served Palestine 1936–37, Transjordan Frontier Force 1938, W Desert 1940–43 (despatches twice), Armoured Advsr to Gen Patton N Africa 1943, Staff Coll 1943, US Marines Staff Coll 1944, Special Liaison Offr to Gen Montgomery NW Europe 1944, US Legn Merit, cmded Inns of Court Regt 1945–47, ret 1947, Hon Col 11th (PAO) Hus 1965–69, Col Roy Hus (PWO) 1969–73; chm Fairbairn Lawson Ltd, Leeds, and all subsidiary cos 1968–79, memb cncl Leeds U 1972–79; *m* 1st 17 March 1945 (*divorce* 1949) Rose (*d* 29 Dec 1972), only child of Lt David Cecil Bingham (*see* LUCAN, E), widow of P/O William M L Fiske III and previously w of 7th Earl of Warwick (*see* WARWICK, BROOKE and, E); *m* 2nd 22 Dec 1954 Tresilla Ann Elinor (*d* 1985), est dau of Maj Eric Tremayne Buller-Leyborne-Popham, MC, of Robin Hood Ho, Little Gaddesden, Herts, and formerly w of John Garland de Pret-Roose, and by her has:

1 +CHARLES JOHN PATRICK [Charles Lawson Esq, Heckwood, Sampford Spiney, Devon PL20 6LU]; *b* 19 May 1959; *educ* Harrow, Leeds U and RAC Cirencester; ARICS, dir Jackson-Stops and Staff, Exeter; *m* 18 Sept 1987 *Lady Caroline Lowther, 3rd dau of 7th Earl of Lonsdale (*qv*), and has:

(1) +Jack William Tremayne; *b* 6 Dec 1989

(2) +Thomas Charles Lancelot; *b* 5 May 1992

(3) +Ralph Hugh Arthur; *b* 7 Sept 1995

(1) *Tess; *b* 30 Aug 1988

Lineage: SAMUEL LAWSON; MP Leeds NE 1837; served apprenticeship Murray and Woods, of Holbeck, Leeds (who made the Blenkinsop locomotive — the first engine to run commercially in England, carrying coal 1812); started own business as maker of flax-spinning machinery 1802, granted patent 1834 for operating fallers by a screw or thread which remained an essential fundamental principle in textile industry for over a century; Poor Law Guardian 1859; *d* 13 Dec 1866, leaving:

JOHN LAWSON, of Bramhope Manor, nr Leeds, Yorks; *b* 28 Dec 1805; *m* 30 May 1835 Sarah (*d* 8 April 1883), dau of John James Baker, of York, and *d* 2 Jan 1883, leaving:

Sir Arthur Tredgold Lawson, 1st Bt (UK), so *cr* 12 July 1900, JP (N and W Rs Yorks and Leeds), of Weetwood Grange, W RidingYorks; *b* 8 Feb 1844; chm: Fairbairn Lawson Combe Barbour Ltd, dir *Yorkshire Post* and GER; Chev Legn Hon; *m* 25 June 1879 Louise Frederica Edith Auguste (*d* 20 June 1939), dau of John Stacpoole O'Brien, of Tanderagee, Co Armagh, and Ennis, Co Clare, and *d* 1 June 1915, leaving:

1 DIGBY (Sir), **2nd Bt**

2 Arthur Bertram, DSO and bar (1918); *b* 18 Dec 1882; Capt and Brevet Maj (Actg Lt-Col) 11th Hus, GSO(2) 1917, T/Lt-Col Glos Regt WW I (despatches, brevet), Order St Stanislas Russia 3rd Cl with Swords; *ka* 24 June 1918

1 Olive Louise; *m* 14 April 1921 Capt Raymond George Wavell-Paxton, Coldstream Gds (*d* 31 March 1948), only surv s of Col Arthur Henry Wavell (*see* 1953 edn WAVELL, E), and *d* 23 Oct 1951, leaving:

(1) *Phoebe Louise [Mrs Derek Grant, Carters Lodge, Handcross, W Sussex RH17 6AA]; *b* 12 May 1925; *m* 24 July 1954 *His Honour Derek Aldwin Grant, DSO, QC, Circuit Judge 1969–84, s of Charles Frederick Grant, CSI, ICS, and has:

1a *Oliver Wavell; *b* 18 Aug 1955; *m* 17 July 1993 *Susanna Margit White

1a *Melanie Jane; *b* 8 Jan 1960; *m* 26 June 1982 *Jonathan Cartwright

2a *Angela Mary; *b* 9 May 1961

3a *Alison Louise; *b* 15 Dec 1965

The er s,

Sir Digby Lawson, 2nd Bt, TD, JP (Somerset); *b* 3 Sept 1880; *educ* Winchester and Trin Hall Cambridge (BA 1902); Capt 19th Hus, Maj Yorkshire Hus Yeo (TAR), WW I (despatches), Pres Summary Courts BAOR 1919–26; dir: Fairbairn Lawson Combe Barbour Ltd, of Leeds and Belfast, and Urquhart Lindsay and Robertson Orchar Ltd, of Dundee; *m* 1st 8 Dec 1909 (*divorce* 1920) Iris Mary (*d* May 1940), er dau of Hon Eustace Robert Southwell Fitzgerald (*see* 1889 edn FITZGERALD OF KILMARNOCK, B), and had:

1 +Sir JOHN CHARLES ARTHUR DIGBY LAWSON, **3rd and present Bt**

2 +Patrick William [Patrick Lawson Esq, St Mary's House, Langford, nr Bristol, Somerset]; *b* 9 April 1914; *educ* Nautical Coll Pangbourne; *m* 24 June 1939 *Jean Mary, er dau of Col Sydney Ernest Smith, CBE, of Stuckeridge, Oakford, Devon, and has:

(1) +Nicholas Patrick David [Nicholas Lawson Esq, Morestead, Windlesham Rd, Chobham, Surrey]; *b* 17 July 1940; *educ* Sherborne; *m* 1st 15 Sept 1962 (*divorce* 1970) Anne Somerville de Laval, only dau of S/Ldr Guy de Laval Harvie, and has:

1a +Julian Alexander Nicholas; *b* 5 Sept 1963

1a *Rebecca de Laval; *b* 22 April 1965

(1) (cont.) Nicholas Lawson *m* 2nd 1971 *Jill, dau of Clifford Wendover Beeson, and by her has:

2a +Rupert Christopher David; *b* 1972

(2) +Timothy James [Timothy Lawson Esq, Bourn Lodge, Bourn, Cambs CB3 7SX]; *b* 15 May 1942; *educ* Sherborne and RAC Cirencester; FRICS; *m* 18 Sept 1965 *Elizabeth, yr dau of John White, of Green Close, Poulton, Glos, and has:

1a +Mark James; *b* 13 Jan 1968

2a +Simon Alexander; *b* 4 Feb 1970

3a +Peter John; *b* 20 Sept 1974

(3) +(Michael) Shaun [Shaun Lawson Esq, Great House Farm, Lynwick St, Rudgwick, Sussex]; *b* 6 Sept 1945; *educ* Sherborne; *m* 1970 *Jane Hamilton and has:

1a +James Patrick; *b* 1972

2a +Richard Shaun; *b* 1973

3a +Henry John; *b* 1978

1 *Daphne Olive [Mrs Richard Cely Trevilian, Midelney Manor, Drayton, nr Langport, Somerset]; *b* 26 Sept 1910; *m* 27 July 1936 *Maj Richard Edwin Fearing Cely Trevilian, TD, DL, s of Maj Maurice Fearing Cely Trevilian, JP, DL, of Midelney Manor, and has:

(1) *John Maurice Richard; *b* 25 Sept 1948; *educ* Repton and Aix-en-Provence; *m* 1971 *Penelope, yst dau of Raymond Hodgson, and has:

1a *Thomas Richard John; *b* 1976

1a *Alice Mary; *b* 1974

(1) *Jane Mary [Mrs Adam Kwiatkowski, Piazza Castello 24, Milan, Italy]; *b* 1 Jan 1938; *m* 18 June 1962 *Adam Stanislaus Kwiatkowski, yr s of Michael Kwiatkowski, of Lens, France, and has:

1a *Damian Michael Richard; *b* 14 April 1965

1a *Sophia Helena; *b* 20 Feb 1963; *m* 1984 *Nicholas James Prestige

(2) *Susanna Rose [Mrs Ewan Hilleary, 197 Pottle St, Horningsham, Wilts BA12 7LX]; *b* 12 Oct 1939; ARCM 1960; *m* 1st 14 July 1962 (*divorce* 1970) Jeremy Gwynne Pilcher, late Gren Gds, er s of Lt-Col William Spelman Pilcher, DSO, and has:

1a *Jonathan Swaine Trevilian; *b* 2 Feb 1965

1a *Katharine Alexandra; *b* 22 Aug 1963; *m* 1991 *Charles Rupert Hunter and has:

1b *Sam Alexander; *b* 23 Oct 1992

1b *Lily Rose; *b* 3 April 1995

2a *Charlotte Serena; *b* 22 Aug 1963; *m* 1992 *James Paul Gilfred Studholme, yr s of Sir Paul Henry William Studholme, 2nd Bt (*qv*) and has issue

(2) (cont.) Mrs Susanna Pilcher *m* 2nd 1972 *Ewan Iain MacLeod Hilleary and has:

2a *Angus Ewan MacLeod; *b* 1977

(3) *Teresa Melliscent; *b* 6 Dec 1946; *m* 8 Nov 1969 *Edward Anthony Dawson, only s of E W Dawson, of The Old Rectory, Idmiston, nr Salisbury, Wilts, and has:

1a *Edward Finch; *b* 1971

1a *Hannah Dinah; *b* 1974

Sir Digby *m* 2nd 2 Nov 1922 Hon Victoria Frances Maud (*d* 10 Jan 1931), dau of Col James Evan Bruce Baillie, MVO, of Dochfour, and Baroness Burton (*see* BURTON, B), and by her had:

3 James Alexander Bertram; *b* 10 Oct 1923; *educ* Winchester; Lt (A) RN WW II; *d unm* 18 June 1946 as result of aeroplane accident in Pacific off Sydney

4 Arthur Simon Albert; *b* 23 Feb 1925; *educ* Winchester; served 1st Roy Dragoons WW II, Lt 11th (PAO) Hus 1947–48; Lt-Col, late cmdg N Somerset Yeo; *m* 1st 2 May 1953 (*divorce* 1961) Virginia Elizabeth Grace, dau of Maj William Steel Huddleston, RHA, and had:

(1) +Piers James; *b* 14 March 1957; Capt Roy Hus (PWO); *m* 1985 *Belinda, est dau of R Garnham, and has:

1a +Bertram Digby Alexander; *b* 1991

1a *Arabella Harriet; *b* 1987

2a *Phoebe Elizabeth Grace; *b* 1989

4 (cont.) Arthur Lawson *m* 2nd 7 April 1961 (*divorce* 1986) Alison Deirdre, er dau of Lt-Col Ian Stuart Balmain, 15th/19th Hus, of Sigwells, Sherborne, Dorset, and by her had:

(1) *Frances Lisa Victoria; *b* 16 May 1962

(2) *Louise Christian; *b* 16 May 1963; *m* 1992 *Michael Gatcombe

(3) *Clare Alison; *b* 11 Aug 1968; *m* 1989 *David Burnett and has:

1a *Aaron; *b* 1991

1a *Rebecca; *b* 1990

4 (cont.) Arthur Lawson *m* 3rd 1987 *Magdalen Cecilia, er dau of Lt-Col Francis Carey Boylan, MBE, and widow of John Staniland, and *d* 31 Oct 1995

Sir Digby *m* 3rd 20 Feb 1933 Ruth Mary (*d* 5 May 1961), 2nd dau of Thomas Wallis Gimson, of Fenton, Staffs, and *d* 9 Feb 1959, having by her had:

5 +Simon Digby; *b* 9 Sept 1945; *educ* Sherborne, London U (BA) and Oxford (MLitt, DPhil); *m* 3 June 1972 *Georgina Mary, dau of S/Ldr J C G Sarll, DFC, of Coldharbour, Dorking, Surrey, and has:

(1) +Thomas Digby; *b* 1975

(1) *Daisy Alexandra Ruth; *b* 1983

LAWSON OF BLABY

Creation: B. (LP, UK) 1992.

THE BARON LAWSON OF BLABY, of Newnham, Co Northants (Nigel Lawson, PC 1981) [The Rt Hon The Lord Lawson of Blaby PC, House of Lords, London SW1A 0PW]; *b* 11 March 1932; *educ* Westminster and Ch Ch Oxford (BA 1954, Hon student 1996); Sub-Lt RNVR 1954–56; editorial staff *Financial Times* 1956–60; city ed *Sunday Telegraph* 1961–63; Special Assist to PM 1963–64; jnlst and broadcaster 1965 and 1970–72; ed *The Spectator* 1966–70; Fell Nuffield Coll Oxford 1972–73; v-chm C Political Centre Nat Advsy Ctee 1972–75; Special Political Advsr C HQ 1973–74; MP (C) Blaby 1974–92, Oppn Whip 1976–77, Oppn Spokesman Treasury and Ec Affairs 1977–79, Fin Sec Treasury 1979–81, Energy Sec 1981–83, Chllr Exchequer 1983–1989; dir: Barclays Bank 1990–, GPA Gp 1990–93; Pres Br Inst of Energy Ecs 1995–; memb Bd Dirs Inst Internat Ec Washington 1991; Chm: Coningsby Club 1963–64, Central Europe Trust 1990–, CAIB Emerging Russia Fund 1997; memb Internat Advsy Bd: Creditanstalt Bankverein 1991–, Total SA 1994–; author: *The Power Game* (with Jock Bruce-Gardyne, 1976), *The View from No. 11* (1992) and *The Nigel Lawson Diet Book* (with Thérèse Lawson, 1993); *m* 1st 1955 (*divorce* 1980) Vanessa Mary Addison (*d* 1985), 2nd dau of Felix Addison Salmon, of Ham Common, Surrey, and has had:

1 *Dominic Ralph Campden; *b* 1956; *educ* Westminster and Ch Ch Oxford; ed *The Spectator* 1990–95, *Sunday Telegraph* 1995–; author; *m* 1st 1982 Jane Fiona, dau of David Christopher Wastell Whytehead, of W Dulwich; *m* 2nd 1991 *Hon Rosamond Mary Monckton, only dau of 2nd Viscount Monckton of Brenchley (*qv*), and by her has had:

(1) *Savannah Vanessa Lucia; *b* 1992

(2) Natalia

(3) *Domenica Marianna Tertia; *b* 1 June 1995

2 *Thomas Nigel Maclear; *b* 1976; *educ* Eton and Ch Ch Oxford

1 *Nigella Lucy; *b* 1960; *educ* Godolphin & Latymer and LMH Oxford; jnlst and broadcaster; *m* 1992 *John Diamond and has:

(1) *Bruno Paul Nigel; *b* 1996

(1) *Cosima Thomasina; *b* 1993

2 Thomasina Posy; *b* 1961; *m* 1985 *Ivan Hill and *d* 1993

3 *Horatia Holly; *b* 1966; *m* 1997 *Hon Inigo Thomas, er s of Lord Thomas of Swynnerton (*qv*)

BARON LAWSON OF BLABY *m* 2nd 1980 *Thérèse Mary, dau of Henry Charles Maclear Bate, of Putney, and has:

4 *Emily Hero; *b* 1981

Lineage: RALPH LAWSON; *m* Joan Elisabeth Davis and had, with a dau, Diana, an only s:

NIGEL, *cr* a **Baron**

LAWSON-TANCRED

Arms: Arg. a chevron between three escallops gu. **Crest:** An olive tree fructed ppr. **Motto:** *Aimez Dieu* ('Love God').
Creation: Bt. (E) 17 Nov 1662.

SIR HENRY LAWSON-TANCRED, 10TH BT, of Boroughbridge, Co York, JP (W R Yorks 1967) [Sir Henry Lawson-Tancred Bt JP, Aldborough Manor, Boroughbridge, Yorks YO5 9EP]; *b* 12 Feb 1924; *s f* 1945; *educ* Stowe and Jesus Coll Cambridge; F/O RAFVR WW II 1942–45; *m* 1st 26 July 1950 Jean Veronica (*d* 1 Nov 1970), yst dau of Gerald Robert Foster, JP, of Stockeld Pk, Wetherby, Yorks (*see* OGILVY, Bt), and has:

1 +ANDREW PETER [Andrew Lawson-Tancred Esq, 13 Musgrave Cres, London SW6 4PT]; *b* 18 Feb 1952; *educ* Eton and Leeds U; barrister Middle Temple 1977

2 +Rupert Thomas; *b* 26 Nov 1953; *educ* Gordonstoun

3 +James Gilchrist Henry; *b* 25 Aug 1956; *educ* Trin Coll Glenalmond and RMA Sandhurst

4 +Gerald Nicholas; *b* 24 Oct 1961; *educ* Trin Coll Glenalmond

5 +Alastair David Piers; *b* 15 Nov 1964; *educ* Bootham Sch, York; *m* 1993 *Virginia C, only dau of Col Joseph Hordern, OBE, of Radwinter, Essex, and has:

  (1) *Georgina Mary Christina; *b* 3 Oct 1997

1 *Finella Mary; *b* 9 Jan 1959; *m* 1991 *Nicholas S Orr, yr s of George Alistair Orr, of Mountgreenan, Ayrshire, and has:

  (1) *James Charles Tancred; *b* 29 July 1995

  (1) *Rosamond ('Rosie') Anne Jane; *b* 1993

Sir HENRY *m* 2nd *Mrs Susan Dorothy Marie-Gabrielle Drummond, dau of Sir Kenelm Cayley, 10th Bt (*qv*)

Lineage: RICHARD TANKARD, of Boroughbridge, Yorks; *m* Adela Bussye and had an er s:

WILLIAM TANCKARD; *m* Preciosa, dau of Gilbert Basset and had an est s:

HERBERT TANCKARD; *m* Margery, dau of Hugh Staveley, and had:

WILLIAM TANCKARD; owned estates at Boroughbridge, Aldborough, Minskip, Rowcliff and elsewhere in Yorks; Steward Knaresborough Forest to Richard, Earl of Cornwall (2nd s of KING JOHN), *temp* HENRY III; *m* Tessania, dau of Oliver Aldborough, and had an est s:

JOHN TANCKARD; *m* Margery, dau of Sir Ralph Babthorpe, and had an est s:

WILLIAM TANCKARD; Judge Hants Assizes 1371–76; *m* Annabella, dau of Sir Thomas Ros, of Youlton, and had an est s:

WILLIAM TANCKARD; *m* Margaret, dau of Sir Thomas de la River, of Bransby, and had:

HUGH TANCKARD; *m* Dionisia, dau of Henry Southill, and had:

WILLIAM TANCKARD; *m* Alice, dau of Sir Richard Aldborough, and had an est s:

WILLIAM TANCKARD; *m* 1st Margaret, dau of John Slingsby, of Scriven, Yorks; *m* 2nd Ellinor, dau of Thomas Mountford, of Hackforth, and by her had, with a yr s (Richard, Recorder York 1509–18, *m* Jane, dau of William Barker, and was ancestor of the TANCREDs of Pannall):

HUGH TANCKARD; *m* Anne, dau of John Slingsby, of Scriven, and had an est s:

WILLIAM TANCKARD; Recorder York 1537–73, MP Boroughbridge 1553; *m* Anne, dau of John Pulleyne, of Killinghall, and had, with other issue, including a yr s (Ralph, *m* Mary, dau and sole heiress of William Lawson, of Cramlington, and was ancestor of the TANCREDs of Arden, Yorks):

THOMAS TANCRED; *m* Jane, dau and coheir of Bernard Paver, of Brampton, through whom he acquired that estate, and had, with other issue:

1 William, of Boroughbridge; *m* Joan, dau of Ralph, and sis and coheir of Thomas Basforth, of Thormanby, and *d* 1597

2 THOMAS

3 Charles, of Whixley; *m* Barbara, dau of William Wyvill, of Osgarby, and was ancestor of the TANCREDs of Whixley

1 Elizabeth; *m* Henry Blenkensop, of Holbech Hall, and had issue

2 Catherine; *m* Henry Norton and had issue

3 Isabel; *m* 1st Christopher Readshaw; *m* 2nd Dr Lee, of York, and had issue

4 Frances; *m* Lancelot Lancaster, of Stockbridge, Westmorland

The est surv son,

THOMAS TANCRED, of Boroughbridge; *m* Anne, dau of Sir Edward Fitton, of Cheshire, and *d* Feb 1626/7, leaving:

Sir Thomas Tancred, 1st Bt (E), so *cr* 17 Nov 1662, of Boroughbridge; *m* Frances (*bur* 27 April 1655), dau and coheir of Christopher Maltby, of Cottingham, and was *bur* 19 Aug 1663, leaving an only s:

Sir William Tancred, 2nd Bt; *m* 1st Dorothy (*bur* 30 July 1660), dau and coheir of Robert Wilde, of Hunton, and had a dau (Elizabeth, *m* Christopher Percehay, of Ryton); *m* 2nd 1663 Elizabeth (*bur* 9 Sept 1681), dau of Charles Waldegrave, of Stanning Hall, Norfolk, 2nd s of Sir Edward Waldegrave, 1st Bt (*see* WALDEGRAVE, E), and by her had, with three other sons:

1 THOMAS (Sir), **3rd Bt**

2 Charles; *m* Mary, dau of S Walpole, and left issue

3 Waldegrave; *m* Aletheia, dau of Sir Edward Blackett, 2nd Bt, and *dsp*

Sir WILLIAM was *bur* 22 Aug 1703; his est surv son,

Sir Thomas Tancred, 3rd Bt; *b* 1665; *m* 1712 Elizabeth (*bur* 21 Dec 1753), of William Messenger, of Fountains Abbey, Yorks, and was *bur* 27 Aug 1744, having had, with other issue (including a dau Henrietta Maria, *m* 1st William Ingleby, of Raventofts, and 2nd Nicholas Wogan, of Rathcoffy) an only surv s:

Sir Thomas Tancred, 4th Bt; *m* 1740 Judith (*d* 1781), dau of Peter Dalton, of Grenanstown, Co Tipperary, and *d* 30 May 1759, having had, with other issue, including two yr sons (William; Charles, in the Army) and a dau (Barbara, *m* Thomas Taylor, of Cornay, Co Durham, and *d* 21 March 1817):

Sir Thomas Tancred, 5th Bt; DCL; barrister; *m* 7 Oct 1776 Penelope (*d* 21 April 1837), dau of Thomas Assheton Smith, of Bowdon, Cheshire, and *d* 3 Aug 1784, having had, with a yr s (William, RN; *d* West Indies 1799):

Sir Thomas Tancred, 6th Bt; *b* 24 July 1780; *m* 25 April 1805 Harriet Lucy (*d* 16 June 1864), yst dau of Rev Offley Crewe, of Muxton, Staffs, and had, with a dau (*d* unm):

1 THOMAS (Sir), **7th Bt**

2 Henry John; *b* 8 April 1816; Chllr NZ U, MLC NZ; *m* 3 July 1857 Georgiana (*d* 10 Jan 1913), dau of Lt-Col Matthew Richmond, CB, of Nelson, NZ, and *dsp*

3 William (Ven); Archdeacon Launceston, Tasmania; Vicar Kilmersdon, Bath; *b* 6 Aug 1818; *m* Henrietta, dau of Maj Shaw, and *dsp* 22 May 1864

1 Susan; *m* 2 Jan 1849 Rev Thomas Clarke Whitehead and *d* 23 March 1910, leaving issue. He *d* 28 April 1873

Sir THOMAS *d* 29 Aug 1844; his est son,

Sir Thomas Tancred, 7th Bt, MA Oxon, Fell Merton Coll 1832–40; *b* 16 Aug 1808; *m* 16 April 1839 Jane (*d* 16 Nov 1901), 3rd dau of Prideaux John Selby, DL, JP, of Twizell Ho, Northumberland, and The Mote, Tonbridge, Kent, and had, with another s (*d* young) and dau (*d* unm):

1 THOMAS SELBY (Sir), **8th Bt**

2 Prideaux Francis; *b* 2 Feb 1850; *dsp* 6 Dec 1911

3 Clement William; *b* 16 Sept 1853; *m* 16 July 1878 Alice Maude (*d* 7 June 1944), 3rd dau of Oswald Bloxsome, formerly of The Rangers, Sydney, NSW, and *d* 4 Oct 1888, leaving:

  (1) Christopher Humphrey, OBE (1922), F/Lt RAF; *b* 11 May 1888; *educ* Westminster; *m* 1st 27 March 1915 (*divorce* 1923) Gladys Winifred Carrington, dau of Walter Robert Chandler; *m* 2nd 26 April 1927 (*divorce* 1938) Agnes Mary, dau of Samuel Henry Slater, CMG, CIE, ICS, and by her had:

    1a Anthony Christopher; *b* 1 July 1930; *educ* Eton; *d* 7 Oct 1995

  (1) (cont.) Christopher Tancred *m* 3rd 1 July 1938 (*divorce* in Egypt 1943) Priscilla Noel Cecilia, est of John Arthur Barclay, of New York; *m* 4th 11 March 1944 *Sadika [Mrs Christopher Tancred, 21 Lexham Gdns, London W8 5JJ], dau of Radwan Khalil Miligui, of Cairo, and *d* 20 Sept 1971

  (1) Irene Maude; *m* 1906 her cousin Harry Bradford Tancred Hawkins and had issue. He *d* 17 March 1959

  (2) Esmé Isabelle; *m* 1909 (*divorce*) Francis Deardon Roscoe and had issue

4 Seymer Mitford; *b* 21 April 1856; *m* 4 June 1896 Charlotte Dorothea (*d* 12 Feb 1955), dau of William Gillespie Dickson, LLD, Sheriff-Pncpl Lanarks, Procurer and Advocate-Gen Mauritius, and *d* 21 Nov 1929, having had:

  (1) Seymer Thomas; *b* and *d* 5 June 1898

  (1) Mary Tytler; *m* 30 May 1918 Harold John Ridger, Paymaster-Lt RNR, 2nd s of C M Ridger, and *d* 16 Jan 1966, leaving issue. He *d* 10 Jan 1955

  (2) Margaret Selby; *m* 26 July 1927 Rev Canon Crewe Chetwode Hamilton (*d* 8 Feb 1969), 5th s of Rev Charles Chetwode Hamilton, Rector Broome, Worcs, and had:

    1a *Guy Tancred; MB, BS 1957; *b* 26 Sept 1931; *m* 1957 *Elizabeth Georgia Arnold, dau of Alfred George Nelson Jones, and has:

      1b *Simon John Chetwode; *b* 28 Feb 1959

      2b *Thomas Guy; *b* 11 July 1965

      1b *Julia Elizabeth; *b* 4 Sept 1961

      2b *Sarah Katherine; *b* 21 Jan 1963

5 Harry George; *b* 24 Dec 1858; *m* 1st 19 April 1881 Emily Alicia de Courcy (*d* 1 April 1907), er dau of Maj Slingsby Bell, of Napier, NZ, and had:

  (1) Bertram Selby; served WWs I and II; *b* 19 April 1895; *m* 19 Sept 1924 Elsa, dau of A V Sims, of NZ, and *d* 31 March 1965, leaving:

    1a +Rex Selby Assheton [Rex Tancred Esq, 12B Oleander Pl, Bell Block, New Plymouth, New Zealand]; WW II 1943–46 in RNZAF; *b* 21 July 1925; *m* 25 Sept 1948 *Shirley Edith, dau of H Box, of NZ, and has:

      1b +Philip Rex; *b* 3 May 1952

      1b *Linda Joanna; *b* 17 April 1954; *m* 1972 *Allan John Brooking, s of Frederick John Brooking, of New Plymouth, and has:

        1c *Daniel John; *b* 1976

        1c *Jemma Claire; *b* 1977

2c *Talia Louise; b 1979

2b *Susan Shirley [Mrs Stephan Kerr, King Rd, RD6, Inglewood, New Zealand]; b 28 Aug 1955; m 1975 *Stephen Thomas Kerr, s of Kelvyn Thomas Kerr, of New Plymouth, and has:

    1c *Alisha Maree; b 1981

    2c *Rachel Lee; b 1983

2a +Lyle Ashley [Lyle Tancred Esq, 205 Frankley Rd, New Plymouth, New Zealand]; b 21 July 1933; m 11 April 1959 *Beverley Ethel, dau of Nelson Howard Bishop, of New Plymouth, and has:

    1b +Stephen Ashley; b 9 Feb 1962

1a *Elwyn Elsa; b 9 Nov 1927; m 1954 *Archibald James Gamble and adopted:

    *Craig Anthony; b 16 Oct 1965

(1) Vera Elphinstone; m — Wilmshurst, and d 29 Dec 1956

(2) Cecil Mountstuart; b 1884; m 8 April 1907; d 19–, leaving issue:

    1a Emmie; b 1908

(3) Valerie Waldegrave Mitford; m A Thomas and d 25 Oct 1958, leaving issue

(4) Zillah Selby; b 1893; m 1915 Raymond F M Atkinson and had:

    1a *Veronica Selby [Mrs Gary Gorsline, 4304 Jeffries Ave, Burbank, CA 91505 USA]; b 29 Nov 1915; m 23 Sept 1943 *Gary Elmer Gorsline and has:

       1b *Victoria Elizabeth Selby [Mrs David Maske, 7550 Coldwater Canyon, N Hollywood, CA 91605, USA]; b 11 May 1945; m 1963 *David Wayne Maske and has:

          1c *Michael Andrew [Michael Maske, 6489 Hope St, Simi Valley, CA 93063, USA]; b 1964

          2c *Douglas Adam [Douglas Maske, 2374 Timber Lane Circle, Simi Valley, CA 93063, USA]; b 1965; m 1988 *Jennifer Ellen Weyand and has:

            1d *Kirstie Adrianna; b 1991

          1c *Julie Michelle; b 1970; m 1992 *Andi Costin Gorgescu and has:

            1d *Christopher David; b 1992

5 (cont.) Harry Tancred m 2nd 22 June 1908 Rosie Elphinstone, widow of Henry A Warren, manager Bank of NZ, and yr dau of Maj Slingsby Bell (see above), and d 22 April 1940

1 Lucy Sybil; m 28 Feb 1807 Robert Samuel Hawkins, of Dunedin, NZ, and d 10 July 1933, leaving issue. He d 1915

2 Edith Jane; m 13 Jan 1875 George Phipps Williams, MInstCE, of Christchurch, Canterbury, NZ, 2nd s of Joshua Strange Williams, QC, of Lincoln's Inn, and d 8 Nov 1911, leaving issue

3 Bertha Eveline; m 23 Oct 1878 William Fownes Somerville, yr s of James Curtis Somerville, DL, of Dinder Ho, Somerset, and d 20 Feb 1952, having had issue. He d 15 Jan 1910

Sir THOMAS d 7 Oct 1880; his est son,

Sir Thomas Selby Tancred, 8th Bt, CE; b 1 Oct 1840; m 1 May 1866 Mary Harriet (d 26 May 1918), 2nd dau of Col George Willoughby Hemans, and had:

1 THOMAS SELBY (Sir), **9th Bt**

2 Francis Willoughby; b 21 Feb 1874; d 25 Nov 1925

1 Felicia Harriet; m 3 Aug 1905 Francis Murray, of Notting Hill, yr s of Francis Murray, of S Kensington, and d his widow 8 July 1938

2 Gwendoline Sybil; b 19 Oct 1868; d unm 8 Feb 1959

3 Edith Mary; d unm 30 Jan 1957

4 Constance Anne; m 2 Aug 1910 Alfred Robert Warren, est s of Alfred Warren, of S Kensington, and d 21 Aug 1964 aged 88, leaving issue. He d 2 Dec 1922

Sir THOMAS d 11 April 1910; his er son,

Sir THOMAS SELBY TANCRED later LAWSON-TANCRED (deed poll Nov 1914), **9th Bt**, JP WR Yorks; Maj Centl India Horse IA, served Miranzai Expdn 1891 (medal with clasp) and WW I 1914; b 14 May 1870; m 25 April 1912 Margery Elinor, JP WR Yorks (d 5 June 1961), er dau and coheir of Andrew Sherlock Lawson, DL, JP, of Aldborough Manor, Yorks (see 1970 edn LAWSON, Bt, of Knavesmire), and d 15 Dec 1945, having had:

1 Andrew Thomas; F/Lt RAF WW II; b 10 Aug 1914; educ Winchester; ka over Germany 14/15 Jan 1944

2 Sir HENRY LAWSON-TANCRED, **10th and present Bt**

3 +Christopher (Rev) [The Rev Christopher Lawson-Tancred, 3 Minterne Ho, Minterne Magna, Dorset DT2 7AX]; b 12 Feb 1924; educ Stowe and Trin Coll Cambridge; barrister Lincoln's Inn 1950, F/O RAFVR WW II 1942–45, Deacon Chichester Diocese 1965, Priest 1966; m 2 Feb 1951 *Cerise Eyre Campbell, er dau of Sir Hugh Eyre Campbell Beaver, KBE, of Luxford, Crowborough, Sussex, and has:

    (1) +Hugh Christopher; b 10 Oct 1955; educ Eton; m 1993 *Emily C A R, dau of James Macaskie, of Yarlington, Somerset, and has:

       1a *Josephine Rose; b 1993

    (1) *Cerise Elinor; b 14 May 1952; m 1988 *David Holmes, MRCVS, s of Dudley Holmes, and has:

       1a *Finella Harriet Rachel; b 1991

    (2) *Olivia Eyre [Mrs Richard Bourne, Petvins Cottage, Haselbury Plucknet, Somerset]; b 28 Feb 1957; m 1986 *Richard L Bourne, Cdr RN, s of Leonard Richard Thomas Bourne, and has:

       1a *Simon Richard; b 1989

       2a *Nicholas Hugh; b 1992

1 Elinor Mary; b 10 March 1913

2 *Pauline [Mrs Douglas Nicholson, Cocken House, Plawsworth, nr Chester-le-Street, Co Durham]; b 6 Oct 1916; m 30 April 1937 (Frank) Douglas Nicholson, TD, JP, DL (d 1984), s of Sir Frank Nicholson, CBE, of Southill, Chester-le-Street, and has:

    (1) *Paul Douglas (Sir) [Sir Paul Nicholson, Quarry Hill, Brancepeth, Co Durham DH7 8DW]; b 7 March 1938; educ Harrow and Clare Coll Cambridge; late Lt Coldstream Gds, chm Vaux Group plc 1976–, High Sheriff Co Durham 1980, ktd 1993, Ld Lt Co Durham 1997– (DL 1980–97); m 18 July 1970

*Sarah, yst dau of Col Sir Edmund Castell Bacon, 13th and 14th Bt, KG (qv), and has:

    1a *Lucy; b 1972

(2) *Nigel Frank; b 15 June 1940; educ Harrow and Clare Coll Cambridge; m 1982 *Mrs S A Barnes, of Durban

(3) *Andrew; b 5 Nov 1945; educ Harrow; m 1972 *Angela, dau of V-Adml Denis Bryan Harvey Wildish, CB, and has:

    1a *Rosemary; b 1975

    2a *Caroline; b 1976

(4) *Mark Thomas; b 22 Nov 1950; educ Harrow; m 1996 *Lucille Cutler

(5) *Frank; b 11 Feb 1954; educ Harrow; m 1986 *Lavinia Margaret Grace, dau of Nigel John Ivo Stourton, OBE (see MOWBRAY, SEGRAVE and STOURTON, B), and has:

    1a *Simon Douglas; b 1989

    2a *Hugo Frank; b 1991

    3a *Edward Ivo; b 1994

LAYTON

Creation: B. (UK) 16 Jan 1947.

THE 3RD BARON LAYTON, of Danehill, Co Sussex (Geoffrey Michael Layton) [The Rt Hon The Lord Layton, House of Lords, London SW1A 0PW]; b 18 July 1947; s f 1989; educ St Paul's, Stanford U and U of S California; m 1st 4 Jan 1969 (divorce 1970) Viviane, yst dau of François P Cracco, of Louvain, Belgium; m 2nd 1989 *Caroline Jane, dau of William Thomas Mason, of Fairford, Glos, and formerly w of Adml Spyros Soulis, of Athens

Lineage: THOMAS LAYTON, of Pirbright, Surrey; had:

ALFRED JOHN LAYTON, of The Chalet, Fulham Park Rd, SW; b Jan 1849; m 25 Dec 1880 Mary, FRCO (d Sept 1929), yst dau of Walter Johnson, schoolmaster, and had:

1 WALTER THOMAS, **1st Baron**

2 Wilfred; d Feb 1969

3 Gilbert Clemens

1 Margaret; m 1st F C Walker (ka 1915) and had issue; m 2nd 1944 A G Walker (d 1965) and d 13 April 1966

ALFRED LAYTON d June 1934; his est son,

WALTER THOMAS LAYTON, **1st Baron Layton**, of Danehill, Co Sussex (UK), so cr 16 Jan 1947, CH (1919), CBE (1917); b 15 March 1884; educ King's Coll Sch London, Westminster City Sch, UCL (BA 1904) and Trin Coll Cambridge (BA 1907, MA 1911); Fell Gonville and Caius Coll Cambridge 1909–14, lecturer economics Cambridge 1912, Newmarch Lecturer UCL 1909–12, memb Munitions Cncl 1917–18, ed Economist 1922–28, ktd 1930, memb Consultative Ec Ctee League Nations, dir Ec and Fin Section League Nations, chm: News Chronicle 1930–50, The Star 1936–50, Economist 1944–63 (dep chm 1964–66), dir Nat Fedn Iron and Steel Mfrs, Dir-Gen Programmes Min Supply 1940–42, Chm Exec Ctee Min Supply 1941–42, Ch Advsr Programmes and Planning Min Production 1942–43, Head Jt War Production Staff 1942–43, v-chm Daily News Ltd, dir Nat Mutual Assur Soc, v-pres C Assembly Cncl Europe 1949–57, Dep Ldr Libs Ho Lds 1952–55, memb ITA 1954–56, dir Tyne-Tees TV Co 1958–61, Hon Fell Gonville and Caius Coll Cambridge, Fell UCL, Hon LLD: Columbia U, New York 1933, Melbourne 1943; author: An Introduction to the Study of Prices, Relation of Capital and Labour, Dorothy — A Memoir of Lady Layton; Legn Hon, Orders Crown Italy, St Maurice and St Lazarus Italy and St Stanislas Russia; m 2 April 1910 Eleanor Dorothea (d 18 March 1959), dau of Francis Beresford Plumptre Osmaston, of Limpsfield, Surrey, and had:

1 MICHAEL JOHN, **2nd Baron**

2 +DAVID, MBE (1946) [The Hon David Layton MBE, 69 Devonshire Rd, London SE 3LX]; b 5 July 1914; heir presumptive; educ Gresham's and Trin Coll Cambridge (BA), Lt-Col RE WW II, NCB 1946, md Incomes Data Servs 1966; m 1st 5 April 1939 (divorce 1972) Elizabeth, RIBA 1964, dau of Rev Robert Miller Gray, of Hampstead; m 2nd 1972 *Joy Parkinson and by his 1st w has:

    (1) +Jonathan Francis [Jonathan Layton Esq, 2 Amroth Cl, Horniman Ave, London SE23]; engr; b 16 Feb 1942; educ Bryanston; m 1971 *Julia Goodwin and has:

       1a +Jeremy; b 1978

       2a +Robert; b 1982

       1a *Jessica; b 1974

    (2) +Mark Oliver [Mark Layton Esq, 24 Leaside Ave, London N10 3BU]; with Br Aluminium; b 22 June 1944, educ Bryanston and Reading U; m *Penelope Hamilton

    (1) *Hilary Ruth; b 13 July 1947, educ Durham U

3 +Christopher Walter [The Hon Christopher Layton, Grimstone Manor, Jordan Lane, Horrabridge, Devon PL20 7QY]; b 31 Dec 1929; educ Oundle and King's Coll Cambridge; Intell Corps 1948–49, ec and industl jnlst, fndr memb Grimstone Community 1990; m 1st 8 July 1952 (divorce1957) Anneliese Margaret, dau of Joachim von Thadden, of Hanover, and has:

    (1) +John Stephen; b 11 Jan 1955

    (1) *Diana; b 11 June 1953

3 (cont.) The Hon Christopher Layton m 2nd 15 April 1961 (divorce 1995) Margaret Ann, dau of Leslie Moon, of Molesey, Surrey, and by her has had:

    (2) Eleanor Rachel; b 6 Sept 1963; d 1985

    (3) *Sarah Jean; b 7 Dec 1964

    (4) *Lesley Claire; b 1971

3 (cont.) The Hon Christopher Layton m 3rd 1995 *Wendy Daniels, dau of Kenneth Bartlett, of Hemel Hempstead, and by her has:

    (5) *A dau; b 19–

1 Margaret Dorothea; *b* 13 March 1911; *educ* Newnham Coll Cambridge (MA); *m* 20 Dec 1939 *Alfred Geiringer, chm Commercial Servs, Reuters, er son of Wilhelm Geiringer, of Vienna, and *d* 5 July 1962, leaving issue

2 *Jean Mary [The Hon Mrs Eisler, Syskon Cottage, 2 Millfield Lane, London N6 6JD]; *b* 14 April 1916; consultant music therapist, Nardoff Robbins Music Therapy Centre London; ARCM, VRMT; *m* 12 June 1944 Paul Eisler (*d* 15 Aug 1966), yr s of Ernst Eisler, of Prague, and has:

  (1) *John; *b* 12 June 1946; *educ* Prague U (BArch 1969); Assoc Ptnr R Meyer, New York 1995–; *m* 1977 *Eva Tlustá, of Prague, and has:

    1a *Martin; *b* 1977

    2a *Mark; *b* 1980

  (2) *Ivan; *b* 14 Sept 1948; *educ* Prague and New Coll Oxford; Sr Lecturer Inst Psychiatry London; Chm Inst Family Therapy; *m* 1971 *Zuzana Tibenslea, of Bratislava, Slovakia, and has:

    1a *Philip; *b* 1973

    1a *Lucinka; *b* 1976

3 *Olive Shirley [The Hon Mrs Gellhorn, 33 Leinster Ave, London SW14 7JW]; actress, opera singer; *b* 18 Dec 1918; *m* 18 May 1943 *Peter Gellhorn, FGSM, conductor, s of Dr Alfred Gellhorn, architect, and has:

  (1) *Martin Oliver; *b* 28 Aug 1945; *educ* Westminster; *m* 7 June 1969 (*divorce* 1976) Susanna Elizabeth, yst dau of Dr Thomas Gladstone, MB, BS, of Ilkeston, Derbys, and has:

    1a *Catherine; *b* 1969

  (2) *Philip Nicholas; *b* 30 Jan 1951; *educ* Westminster

  (1) *Mary Ann; *b* 5 May 1959

  (2) *Barbara Dorothea; *b* 14 Nov 1960

4 *(Elizabeth) Ruth Frances [The Hon Mrs Ruth Pegna, 2 Farmington, Cheltenham, Glos GL54 3NQ]; Intell Serv ATS WW II 1942–45; *b* 27 April 1923; *m* 25 Nov 1944 (*divorce* 1965) Edward William Guttieres Pegna, s of Frederick Guttieres Pegna, of Alexandria, and has had:

  (1) *Robin Arnold; *b* 5 Sept 1945; *educ* Bryanston and King's Coll Cambridge; *m* 1968 *Catherine Bridget Gray, dau of John Henderson, of Greenwood, Frant, Sussex, and has:

    1a *Jonathan; *b* 1982

    1a *Catherine; *b* 1973

    2a *Alice; *b* 1976

  (2) *Christopher John; *b* 28 May 1956

  (1) Alison Dorothea Hélène; *b* 7 Feb 1948; *d* 1966

  (2) *Shirley Elizabeth; *b* 29 Oct 1951

The 1st BARON *d* 14 Feb 1966; his est son,

MICHAEL JOHN LAYTON, **2nd Baron Layton**, of Danehill, Co Sussex; *b* 28 Sept 1912; *educ* St Paul's and Gonville and Caius Coll Cambridge (BA Mech, MA); CEng, FIMechE, FIM; works manager Ibbotson Bros 1939–43, manager Armoured Car Factories Rootes Gp 1943–46; Industry Div Br CCG Berlin 1946–48; head Internat Rels Br Iron and Steel Fedn 1948–55, Guest Keen Iron and Steel Co Ltd 1955–56, Sales Controller The Steel Co of Wales 1956, dir 1960, assist md mktg 1965, md 1967, exec bd memb BSC 1967–77, dir: *News Chronicle* 1955–60, *Economist* 1973–89, pres Br Shippers' Cncl 1974–89, dir Wolff Steel Hldgs 1977–89; *m* 31 Jan 1938 Dorothy (*d* 1994), dau of Albert Luther Cross, of Rugby, and *d* 1989, leaving:

1 GEOFFREY MICHAEL LAYTON, **3rd and present Baron Layton**

1 *Deanna Christian [The Hon Mrs Jennings, Barn Ridge, 18 High Trees Rd, Reigate, Surrey RH2 7EJ]; MB, BS Lond 1963, MRCS Eng, LRCP Lond 1963; *b* 19 Oct 1938; *m* 19 Dec 1964 *Melvin Calverley Jennings, MB, BS, FRCS, LRCP, yst s of Calverley Middlemiss Jennings, FRCS, of 23 Park Rd, Cheam, Surrey, and has:

  (1) *Andrew Melvin; *b* 1965

  (2) *Simon; *b* 1967

  (3) *Robert; *b* 1970

LEA

Arms: Or a fess indented between in chief two lions passant gules and in base on a rock a beaver statant proper, charged with five ermine spots and holding in the mouth a sprig of willow, slipped vert. **Crest:** On a mound vert in front of a demi-heraldic antelope argent, horned, maned, tufted and unguled or, supporting with his forelegs a birdbolt palewise of the last, three pheons in fess sable.
Motto: *Semper fidelis* ('Always faithful').
Creation: Bt. (UK) 6 Oct 1892.

SIR THOMAS WILLIAM LEA, 5TH BT, of The Larches, Co Worcester, and Sea Grove, Dawlish, Devon; *b* 6 Sept 1973; *s f* 1990; *educ* Uppingham

Lineage: THOMAS LEA, of Kidderminster, Worcs; *b* 1588; *m* Jane — and *d* 1675, leaving an est s:

THOMAS LEA, of Kidderminster; *b* 1619; *m* 1st Margaret — and had issue, including an er s (Thomas, *b* 1646); *m* 2nd Elizabeth — and *d* Dec 1689, having by her had a s (Jonathan, ancestor of the LEAs of Netherton and Far Forest); his yr s by his 1st w:

STEPHEN LEA, of Kidderminster; *b* 1651; *m* 18 Aug 1676 Margaret Callow and *d* 1716, leaving a 2nd s:

JOHN LEA, of Kidderminster; *b* 1679; *m* 6 Jan 1703/4 Elizabeth Cooper and *d* Oct 1726, leaving:

JOHN LEA, of Kidderminster; *b* 1708; *m* Esther Lane and *d* 1777, leaving:

FRANCIS LEA, of Kidderminster; *b* 31 Dec 1733; *m* Hannah — (*d* 20 April 1815) and *d* 22 Feb 1805, leaving, with other issue, including a s (Thomas, *b* 1771):

ELIZABETH Lea; *b* 4 Dec 1768; *m* 12 April 1792 William BUTCHER (*d* 12 Jan 1832) and *d* 17 Dec 1818, leaving:

GEORGE BUTCHER later LEA (roy licence 27 March 1834 on becoming heir to his maternal unc Thomas), of The Larches, Kidderminster; *b* 31 July 1796; *m* 20 Oct 1831 Emma (*d* 5 March 1862), dau and coheiress of George Harris, of Oaklands, Glos, and had:

1 THOMAS (Sir), **1st Bt**

2 George Harris, JP, DL (Herefs); *b* 2 April 1842; *educ* Cambridge (MA); Co Ct Judge (Herefs, Salop); *m* 1st 29 Nov 1864 Mary (*d* 25 Sept 1867), dau of E Futvoye, and had issue; *m* 2nd 25 Feb 1873 Marion (*d* 29 Nov 1901), dau of C Bushell, and *d* 3 May 1915, having had further issue

1 Emma; *m* Basil Woodd Smith and *d* 1870

2 Linnie; *m* June 1860 James A Crowther and *d* 1896

3 Annie; *m* 19 Dec 1872 Francis Young and *d* 1886

GEORGE LEA *d* 2 Sept 1859; his est son,

Sir Thomas Lea, 1st Bt (UK), so *cr* 6 Oct 1892, JP (Worcs), of The Larches, Co Worcester, and Sea Grove, Devon; *b* 17 Jan 1841; MP Kidderminster 1868–74, Co Donegal 1879–85 and S Londonderry 1886–1900; *m* 20 Jan 1864 Louey (*d* 28 Sept 1910), dau of William Birch, of Barton-under-Needwood, Staffs, and had:

1 THOMAS SYDNEY (Sir), **2nd Bt**

2 Percy Harris (Rev); *b* 6 Jan 1872; *educ* Charterhouse and Trin Coll Cambridge (BA 1894); Vicar St Peter's S Tottenham 1930–42; *m* 30 Sept 1896 Katherine Ellen Margaret (*d* 1941), dau of Rev R A Gent, and *d* 8 June 1957, leaving:

  (1) George Francis Percival; *b* 8 April 1901; *educ* Westminster and Trin Coll Cambridge (BA 1923); *m* 3 Nov 1934 Maria (*d* 1987), dau of Wilhelm Schultz, of Vienna, and *d* 1987, leaving:

    1a +Francis William Peter [Francis Lea Esq, 34 Radnor Rd, Weybridge, Surrey KT13 8JU]; *b* 21 June 1944; *educ* Hill Sch Pottstown, Pa., and Brown U, RI, USA; *m* 1977 *Audrey Christine, dau of Maurice Davison, of Cuckfield, Sussex

  (2) Hugh Christopher; *b* 7 Feb 1904; *educ* Westminster and Wadham Coll Oxford (BA 1929); *m* 4 July 1935 Mary Susannah (*d* 8 Nov 1966), er dau of Arthur Blomfield Jackson, FRIBA, and *d* Oct 1967

1 Florence Louey; *b* 22 Sept 1873; *m* 13 June 1900 Vivian Edward Young (*d* 12 Jan 1956), of Shaftesbury Ho, Woking, s of Francis Young, and *d* 11 Oct 1962, leaving issue

Sir THOMAS *d* 9 Jan 1902; his er son,

Sir (Thomas) Sydney Lea, 2nd Bt, JP (Worcs); *b* 28 Jan 1867; *educ* Clare Coll Cambridge (MA, LLB); *m* 5 Sept 1896 Mary Ophelia (*d* 17 Jan 1933), est dau of Robert Woodward, of Arley Castle, Bewdley, Worcs, and had:

1 THOMAS CLAUDE HARRIS (Sir), **3rd Bt**

2 Robert Francis Gore, OBE (1942); *b* 22 Jan 1906; *educ* Lancing and Clare Coll Cambridge (BA 1927, MA 1934); W/Cdr AAF WW II (despatches); *m* 1st 5 March 1936 Valerie Josephine (*d* following an accident 15 March 1948), er dau of Sir James Henry Domville, 5th Bt (*qv*), and had:

(1) *Annabel Ophelia Clare [Mrs Simon Ricketts, 69 Fentiman Rd, London SW8 1LH]; *b* 19 Aug 1945; *m* 1973 *Simon Henry Martin Ricketts and has:

(1) *Theo; *b* 1975

(1) *Catriona; *b* 1977

2 (cont.) Robert Lea *m* 2nd 3 May 1956 *Susan [Mrs Robert Lea, Le Clos du Chemin, St Peter, Jersey, CI, yr dau of John Eric Greenwood, of the Priory of Lady St Mary, Wareham, Dorset, and *d* 1994, having by her had:

(1) +(Francis) Rupert Chad [Rupert Lea Esq, Duxford Mill, Cambs CB2 4PT]; *b* 2 Nov 1957; *educ* Eton; *m* 1987 *Hon Susan Kinnaird, dau of 13th Lord Kinnaird (*see* 1970 edn)

3 John Sydney Birch; *b* 15 May 1911; *educ* St Edward's Sch Oxford; *m* 21 Aug 1954 *Elisabeth Edith Maunsell [Mrs John Lea, Kemerton Hosue, Crowle, Worcs], only dau of Lt-Col Philip Victor Willingham Gell, of Hopton Hall, Wirksworth, Derbys, and *d* 1984, leaving:

(1) +Richard John Philip [Richard Lea Esq, 158 Feltsham Rd, London SW15 1DP]; *b* 5 Aug 1957; *educ* Stowe; *m* 1990 *Jane Hopkins

(1) *Sarah Caroline Aileen [Mrs Peter Sankey, Cranmere, Worfield, Salop WV15 5LP]; *b* 18 March 1956; *m* 1st 1986 Robin GREENSHIELDS, later DAVENPORT GREENSHIELDS (*d* 1990), of Davenport Ho, Worfield, and has:

1a *William John Peter; *b* 1989

(1) (cont.) Mrs Robin Greenshields *m* 2nd 1991 *Peter William Richard Sankey (*see* MILBURN, Bt) and has further issue

1 Mary Truda; *b* 15 Nov 1904; *m* 29 Jan 1954 Cyril Reginald Egerton (*see* SUTHERLAND, D) and *dsp* 27 Sept 1982

Sir SYDNEY *d* 18 Nov 1946; his est s,

Sir Thomas Claude Harris Lea, 3rd Bt; *b* 13 April 1901; *educ* Lancing and Clare Coll Cambridge (BA, LLB 1923); Cdr RNVR WW II (despatches); *m* 1st 3 Dec 1924 Barbara Katherine, OBE, JP (Worcs), MA Cambridge (*d* 12 June 1945), chm WLA Worcs, memb Co War Ag Exec Ctee, dau of Albert Julian Pell, JP, DL, of Wilburton Manor, Isle of Ely; *m* 2nd 30 June 1950 *Diana Silva [Diana Lady Lea, Harp House, Lower Broad St, Ludlow, Salop], only dau of James Howard Thompson, MIME, of Coton Hall, Bridgnorth, Salop, and formerly w of Capt Guy William Banner-Martin, IA, and by his 1st w had:

1 (THOMAS) JULIAN LEA (Sir), **4th Bt**

1 Barbara Mary; *b* 6 Sept 1925; *m* 24 Nov 1951 *James Blackley Hague Goble [James Goble Esq, Court Farm, Upton Snodsbury, Worcs WR7 4NN], only s of Leslie Herbert Goble, CMG, of The Pound Ho, Brabourne, Lees, Kent, and *d* 1986, leaving:

(1) *Timothy James Lea; *b* 26 April 1957; *educ* Marlborough, Corpus Christi Coll Cambridge (MA) and RMA Sandhurst; Lt-Col AAC; *m* 11 Feb 1989 *Catherine M, dau of Henry Dolan, and has:

1a *James Henry Lea; *b* 1995

1a *Alice Mary Lea; *b* 1993

(2) *Jonathan Julian; *b* 19 July 1961; *educ* Marlborough and Exeter U (BSc); *m* 3 Sept 1994 *Hélène, dau of Comte de Garets, and has:

1a *Thomas Xavier Kemlin; *b* 1997

1a *Mary Solange Lea; *b* 1996

2 *Rosemary [Miss Rosemary Lea, 1245 Park Ave, New York, NY 10128,USA]; *b* 27 June 1927

3 *Philippa Margaret [Mrs Orlando Kenyon-Slaney, Bachelors Cottage, High Halden, Kent TN26 3JD]; *b* 20 April 1929; *m* 25 May 1960 *Orlando Michael Philip Kenyon-Slaney (*see* KENYON, B) and has issue

4 *Lavinia Ann [Mrs Andrew Marsden-Smedley, The Glebe House, Bayton, nr Kidderminster, Worcs]; *b* 3 Dec 1932; *m* 30 April 1960 *Andrew Bethell Marsden-Smedley, yr s of Cdr John Bertram Aubrey Marsden-Smedley, RN, and has:

(1) *Robert Andrew; *b* 9 Jan 1962; *m* 1996 *Claudia V M, yr dau of Wyndham Knight, of Hants

(2) *William Bethell; *b* 30 March 1964; *m* 1991 *Alexandra G B, er dau of John Kirkland, of Essex

Sir THOMAS *d* 26 Sept 1985; his est son,

Sir (Thomas) Julian Lea, 4th Bt; *b* 18 Nov 1934; Lt RN; *m* 13 June 1970 *Gerry Valerie, only dau of Capt Gibson C Fahnestock, USAF, and Mrs David Knightly, of Dilton, Brockenhurst, Hants, and *d* 19 Oct 1990, having had:

1 Sir THOMAS WILLIAM LEA, **5th and present Bt**

2 +ALEXANDER JULIAN; *b* 28 Oct 1978; heir presumptive; *educ* Oakham

3 +Oliver David Pell; *b* 3 June 1983

1 *Rebecca Barbara; *b* 15 Jan 1972

2 *Henrietta Katherine; *b* 31 Dec 1976; *d* 18 Sept 1989

LEATHERS

Arms: Azure a lymphad, sails set or, flags flying to the dexter gules, on a chief of the second three lozenges sable. **Crest:** A lozenge sable in front of two anchors in saltire or. **Supporters:** Dexter, a sea lion; sinister, a sea horse argent; each gorged with a collar of lozenges conjoined sable. **Motto:** *Dum spiro servo* ('While I breathe, I serve'). **Creations:** B. (UK) 19 May 1941, V. (UK) 18 Jan 1954.

THE 3RD VISCOUNT LEATHERS and **Baron Leathers**, of Purfleet, Co Essex (Christopher Graeme Leathers, JP (Clwyd 1993)) [The Rt Hon The Viscount Leathers JP, Lime Cottage, High St, Burwash, E Sussex TW19 7EL]; *b* 31 Aug 1941; *s f* 1996; *educ* Rugby and OU (BA); MIM, MICS; Wm Cory & Son Ltd 1961–84, Mostyn Docks Ltd 1984–86, shipping consultant 1986–88, Dept Trade 1988–; Liveryman Shipwrights Co, Freeman Watermen's and Lightermen's Co; Trin Ho Sub-Commr Pilotage 1984; *m* 27 June 1964 *Maria Philomena, yr dau of Michael Merriman, of Charlestown, Co Mayo, and has:

1 +JAMES FREDERICK; *b* 27 May 1969; *educ* Rugby and Corpus Christi Coll Cambridge (MA)

1 *Melissa Maria; *b* 22 April 1966; *educ* Homell Sch Handaft and Leeds U (MSc); *m* 21 May 1994 *Timothy James Wesley, only s of Reginald Wesley, of Stallingborough, Lincs

Lineage: ROBERT LEATHERS, of Stowmarket, Suffolk; *m* Emily — and had:

FREDERICK JAMES LEATHERS, **1st Viscount Leathers**, of Purfleet, Co Essex, so *cr* 18 Jan 1954, as also earlier 19 May 1941 BARON LEATHERS, of Purfleet, Co Essex (both UK), CH (1943), PC (1941); *b* 21 Nov 1883; advsr Min Shipping on coal 1940, Min War Tport May 1941–Aug 1945, UK rep Combined Shipping Adjustment Bd 1942–45, Sec State Co-ordination Tport, Fuel and Power Oct 1951, Hon LLD Birmingham and Leeds U, underwriting memb Lloyd's, Warden Shipwrights's Co, Pres Inst Shipbrokers, MIT, MIPT, Hon MINA; *m* 1 June 1907 Emily Ethel (*d* 30 Dec 1971), dau of Henry Baxter, of Southend, Essex, and had:

1 FREDERICK ALAN, **2nd Viscount**

2 +Leslie John [The Hon Leslie Leathers, Middleton Park, Middleton Stoney, Oxon OX6 8SQ; 14 Seymour Place, Odiham, Hants RG29 1AY]; *b* 25 Nov 1911; *educ* Brighton Coll; slr 1935, Maj WW II, memb Cncl London Chamber Commerce 1961–, Gen Commr Taxes 1961–, dir Mann, George and Co, underwriting memb Lloyd's; *m* 1 June 1937 *(Elizabeth) Stella, only dau of Thomas Stanley Nash, of Sidcup, and has:

(1) +Michael John Nash [Michael Leathers Esq, Oldhams, Foxhill, W Sussex GU28 9NU]; *b* 18 March 1938; *educ* Radley; underwriting memb Lloyd's; *m* 27 Oct 1962 *Shelley Matthews, only dau of Keith Westwood Marten, JP, of Gedgrave Hall, Orford, Suffolk, and has:

1a +Simon Michael John; *b* 11 Jan 1964

2a +Sean Patrick James; *b* 5 Feb 1966

3a +Richard Anthony; *b* 11 March 1968

4a +Benjamin Matthew; *b* 1971

5a +Nicholas Paul Tarquin; *b* 1974

(2) +David Frederick James [David Leathers Esq, 14 Holmead Rd, London SW6 2JG]; *b* 11 Dec 1942; *educ* Rugby; *m* 27 July 1968 *Amanda Elizabeth Ann, er dau of Lt-Col Arthur Vyvyan Denton, of Dial House, Lower Bourne, Surrey, by Patricia Elizabeth Mary, er dau of Claude Frances Strickland, CIE (*see* STRICKLAND-CONSTABLE, Bt), and has:

1a +Jonathan James; *b* 11 April 1974

2a +Andrew Thomas; *b* 18 June 1975

(1) *Rosemary Elizabeth [Mrs Winfried Bischoff, 28 Bloomfield Terrace, London SW1W 8PQ]; *b* 11 Oct 1945; *m* 8 Jan 1972 *Win(fried) Franz Wilhelm Bischoff, chm Schroders plc, est s of Paul H Bischoff, of Düsseldorf, and has:

1a *Christopher William; *b* 1973

2a *Charles Francis; *b* 1975

1 *Audrey Mary [The Hon Mrs Evans, 29 Crittles Court, Townlands Rd, Wadhurst, E Sussex TN5 6BY]; *b* 21 Dec 1915; *m* 7 July 1938 Edward Noel Evans (*d* 12 Feb 1964), s of Edward William Evans, and has:

(1) *Richard Edward Craig [Richard Evans Esq, 10 St Anns Villas, London W11]; b 8 Feb 1945; educ Haileybury; m 1973 *Jillian Sonia, dau of H W Reid, of The Manse, Royston, Herts, and has:

     1a *Charles Noel Edward; b 1975

     1a *Hilary Jane; b 1977

     2a *Melissa Kate b 1981

(2) Peter James; b 4 Nov 1946; educ Haileybury; m 19– *Lynne, dau of James Irving Cosgrove and widow of Desmond Hawe, and d 1988, leaving:

     1a *Katie Samantha; b 1982

     2a *Jessica Jane; b 1984

(1) *Jacqueline Mary [Mrs Michael Hind, Ravensdale Farm, Faitcrouch Lane, Wadhurst, E Sussex TN5 6PT]; b 29 Dec 1940; m 1st 28 April 1961 (divorce 1969) Barrington Hugh Lawes, yr s of T Lawes, and has:

     1a *Nicholas Hugh; b 27 Nov 1962; m 1987 *Julie, dau of Sir Noel Edward Vivian Short, MBE, MC

     1a *Suzanna Jane; b 27 June 1964

(1) (cont.) Mrs Jacqueline Lawes m 2nd 1 March 1969 *Michael Hind and by him has:

     2a *Sally Louise; b 1970

The 1st VISCOUNT d 19 March 1965; his est son,

     FREDERICK ALAN LEATHERS, **2nd Viscount Leathers**; b 4 April 1908; educ Brighton Coll and Emmanuel Coll Cambridge (BA 1929, MA 1931); FICS, memb: Baltic Exchange, Shipwrights' Co, Watermen's and Lightermen's Co and Inst of Petroleum, underwriting memb Lloyd's, chm Wm Cory and Son Ltd (dir 1929–72), Cory Mann George Ltd (dir 1929–72), Cory Ship Towage Ltd (dir 1941–72), dir Nat West Bank; m 1st 22 June 1940 (divorce 1983) Elspeth Graeme (d 1985), yr dau of Sir Thomas Alexander Stewart, KCSI, KCIE; m 2nd 6 April 1983 *Mrs Lorna M Barnett [The Rt Hon The Dowager Viscountess Leathers, Huntsmore, Shackleford, Surrey GU8 6AN], dau of A K Marshall and widow of A A C Barnett, and d 21 Jan 1996, having by his 1st w had:

1 CHRISTOPHER GRAEME LEATHERS, **3rd and present Viscount Leathers**

2 +Jeremy Baxter [The Hon Jeremy Leathers, c/o Stocksigns Ltd, 43 Ormside Way, Redhill, Surrey RH1 2LG]; b 11 April 1946; educ Rugby and Trin Coll Dublin (BA 1969); m 28 June 1969 *Fiona Lesley, yr dau of George Stanhope Pitt, of Rowbarns Manor, East Horsley, Surrey, and has:

     (1) +Luke Alexander; b 17 Feb 1974; educ Salford U (BA 1997)

     (1) *Tara Charlotte; b 14 June 1972; educ Manchester U (BA)

     (2) *Fern Griselda; b 2 Feb 1979

1 *Anne Catherine [The Hon Mrs Centner, Suite 159, Postnet X18, Roudebosch 7701, S Africa]; b 1 Jan 1944; educ Benenden; m 1st Dec 1975 (divorce 1975) Michael Brookstone; m 2nd Jan 1977 *Arthur Sydney Centner, only s of Harry Centner, of Johannesburg, and has:

     (1) *Lucy Emma; b 21 Nov 1977

2 *Deborah Elspeth [The Hon Mrs Pitt, 6 Bassingham Rd, London SW18 3AG]; b 23 Oct 1947; educ OU (BA); m 1st July 1966 (divorce 1970) Thomas Richard Chadbon, er s of Thomas William Chadbon, of Rushmere, The Ave, Chichester, Sussex, and has:

     (1) *Dominic Thomas; b 8 Dec 1966; educ UEA (BA)

     (2) *Nicholas Richard; b 30 Sept 1968

2 (cont.) The Hon Mrs Deborah Chadbon m 2nd 12 Dec 1980 *Richard William Pitt, yst s of G S Pitt, and by him has:

     (1) *Isabelle; b 1981

LECHMERE

CHRISTUS · PELICANO

Arms: Gules a fess or, in chief two pelicans vulning themselves of the last. **Crest:** A pelican azure vulning herself proper. **Motto:** Christus pelicano ('Christ in the pelican'). **Creation:** Bt. (UK) 10 Dec 1818.

SIR BERWICK HUNGERFORD LECHMERE, 6TH BT, of The Rhydd, Worcestershire, JP (Worcs 1966) [Sir Berwick Lechmere Bt JP, Church End House, Hanley Castle, Worcs WR8 0BL]; b 21 Sept 1917; s f 1965; educ Charterhouse and Magdalene Coll Cambridge; FRICS, CStJ]; High Sheriff 1962, V-Lt Hereford and Worcester 1977 (DL Worcs 1972–74, Hereford and Worcester 1974–77); m 1st 24 May

1952 (annulled 1954) Susan Adele Mary, only child of Cdr George Henry Maunsell-Smyth, RN, of Mangersbury, Stow-on-the-Wold, Glos; m 2nd 17 Nov 1954 *Norah Garrett, est dau of Lt-Col Christopher Garrett Elkington, DSO, DL, of The Moat Ho, Cutnall Green, Worcs

Lineage: The Severn End estate (formerly called Lechmere's Place or Lechmere's Field), Hanley Castle, Worcs, was in the LECHMEREs' hands by the Domesday Survey 1086

JOHN LECHMERE, of Lechmere's Place; had:

RICHARD LECHMERE; living temp HENRY VI; m Joan, coheir of John Whitmore, of Hanley, and had:

THOMAS LECHMERE, of Hanley; m Alianore/Eleanor, dau of Humphrey Frere, of Blankets, Worcs, and had, with a yr s (Roger, of Fownhope, Herefs; a descendant of whom left Fownhope to Sir NICHOLAS LECHMERE; see below):

RICHARD LECHMERE; m 11 Aug 1541 Margery (d 30 Oct 1573), dau and coheir of Thomas Rocke, of Ripple, and d 23 March 1568, leaving:

EDMUND LECHMERE; b 1550; m July 1575 Anne (d Jan 1620), dau of Henry Dingley, of Charlton, Worcs, by Mary, dau of Sir Edward Nevill(e) (see ABERGAVENNY, M), and d 1616, leaving:

EDMUND LECHMERE; b 19 June 1577; barrister Middle Temple; m 1st— Blackwall (dsp), of Abingdon, Berks; m 2nd June 1610 Margaret (d 14 March 1634), dau of Sir Nicolas Overbury, of Bourton, Glos, and by her had, with other issue:

1 Richard; b June 1611; dsp 7 Aug 1632

2 NICHOLAS

3 Edmund; b Aug 1623; Parly Capt of Foot Civil War; d unm 4 Feb 1646

4 Thomas; of Totteridge, Herts; bapt 25 Jan 1616; d 11 March 1669, leaving, with other issue:

     (1) Thomas; m Dec 1677 Jane Blagrave

     (2) Nicholas; London merchant; m Judith, only dau of John Corbett, of Alston, Salop, and had:

         1a Richard, of Sutton Hall, London, living 1738; had:

             1b Nicholas (Rev); Preb Winchester; d 1770

     (3) Richard, of Newborne Hall, Suffolk

1 Anne; bapt 27 Nov 1615; m 8 Aug 1634 Thomas Russell, yr s of Sir Thomas Russell, of Strensham, Worcs

2 Mary; m Nicolas Short

3 Margaret; bapt 18 Jan 1620; m Edmond Neale, of London, and had issue

4 Elizabeth; m 1643 Gabriel Yonge, of Chobham, Surrey, and d 5 Jan 1686

5 Jane; m 9 April 1654 William Parsons, of Tewkesbury, and d 1694

EDMUND LECHMERE d 31 July 1650; his 2nd son,

Sir NICHOLAS LECHMERE; b Sept 1613; bequeathed the Fownhope estate, Herefs, by his cousin (see above); barrister Middle Temple 1641, MP Bewdley, Baron of the Exchequer; m 12 Nov 1642 Penelope (d 3 June 1690), dau of Sir Edwin Sandys, of Northborne, Kent, by Katherine, dau of Sir Richard Bulkeley, of Beaumaris, and had, with other issue:

1 Edwin; b 1 April 1646; d unm

2 EDMUND

3 Sandys, of Fownhope; b 23 Aug 1651; m Joanna, dau of Robert Clarke and widow of John Holmes, and d 1694, leaving issue

1 Letitia; b 19 Jan 1644; d unm 7 Oct 1669

2 Penelope; b 29 July 1647; m 27 Sept 1664 Ralph Taylor, MA, of Welland, Worcs, and d 29 May 1710

3 Isabella; b 21 Aug 1655; m 9 July 1678 Richard Barneby, of Brockhampton, Herefs

4 Mary; b 29 Nov 1656; m 23 April 1685 Higham Coke, of Suckley, Worcs, and d 21 April 1689

Sir NICHOLAS d 30 April 1701; his 2nd son,

EDMUND LECHMERE, of Severn End; b 5 Nov 1648; m 7 Aug 1673 Lucy (d 9 Nov 1729), dau of Sir Anthony Hungerford, of Farley Castle, Somerset, and had:

1 ANTHONY

2 NICHOLAS LECHMERE, 1st and last BARON LECHMERE OF EVESHAM, Co Worcester (GB), so cr 4 Sept 1721, PC (1718), QC (1708); b 5 Aug 1675; barrister Middle Temple, MP (Whig) Appleby 1708–10, Cockermouth 1710–17 and Tewkesbury 1717–21, Slr Gen 1714–15, Chllr Duchy Lancaster 1717–27, Attorney-Gen 1718–20; m 1719 Lady Elizabeth Howard (m 2nd Sir Thomas Robinson, of Rokeby, Yorks, and d 1739), est dau of 3rd Earl of Carlisle (qv), and dsp 18 June 1727, when the Barony expired

3 Edmund; b 22 April 1677; Capt RN; ka fighting French War of Spanish Succession 15 Jan 1703

4 William; b 21 July 1678; d unm 26 Sept 1725

5 Thomas; b 18 June 1683; Surveyor-Gen Customs N America; m Anne, dau of Govr Winthrop, of Connecticut, and d 4 June 1765, leaving, with other issue:

     (1) Richard; m Mary Phipps, gdau of Sir William Phipps, Govr Massachusetts, and had:

         1a Thomas; memb cncl Bombay; m Mary Hughes and dsp

         1a Anne; m John Coore, of Firby Hall, Yorks, and had issue

         2a Mary; m James Russell and had issue

         3a Elizabeth; m Samuel Worrall, of Over, Glos, and had issue

6 Richard, of Wick, Worcs; b 25 Jan 1686; m Elizabeth Corfield, widow of Thomas Swift, of Slaughters Ct, Powicke, Worcs, and d 7 Jan 1775, leaving:

     (1) William, of Steeple Aston, Oxon; V-Adml; m 31 Oct 1787 Elizabeth (d 1827), dau of Sir John Dashwood-King, 3rd Bt, of West Wycombe (qv), and d 12 Dec 1815, leaving:

         1a Charles; Capt RN; d 1822

         2a John, of Hill Ho, Steeple Aston, Oxon; Cdr RN; m 24 Feb 1823 Anna Maria, 2nd dau of Hon Andrew Foley, MP (see FOLEY, B), and d 1866, leaving issue

         3a Richard; d 1875, leaving issue

         1a Lucy; m Richard Parkinson, of Kinnersley Castle, Herefs, and d 1834, leaving issue

2a Mary; *b* 2 April 1791; *m* 4 Oct 1814 2nd Baron De Saumarez (*qv*) and *d* 12 May 1849, leaving issue

3a Elizabeth; *m* C Monro and *d* 1874

4a Caroline Amelia; inherited Steeple Aston; *m* 10 Sept 1844 Maj Arthur Ogle, 2nd s of Rev John Savile Ogle, DD, and had issue

5a Augusta; *b* 9 June 1810; *m* 1836 James Moncrieff Melville, of Hanley, Corstorphine, Edinburgh, and *d* 1836, leaving issue

(2) Nicholas; *d* on his estate in Jamaica

(1) Lucy; *m* Col Thompkins, of Weston Turville Ho, Bucks

(2) Elizabeth; *m* Thomas Tudor, of Garth, Montgomeryshire, and had issue

1 Lucy; *b* 11 Nov 1679; *m* 8 June 1699 Henry Biggs, of Benthall, Salop, and *d* 26 June 1758

2 Penelope; *b* 21 Dec 1680; *m* 20 Nov 1701 William Scudamore, of Kentchurch, Herefs, and *d* 1737

EDMUND LECHMERE *d* 1703; his est son,

ANTHONY LECHMERE, of Severn End; *b* 1674; MP Hanley Castle; *m* Anne dau of Thomas Foley, MP (*see* FOLEY, B), and *d* 8 Feb 1720, leaving:

1 Edmund, of Severn End; *b* 4 April 1710; MP Worcester 1734; *m* 1st 12 Oct 1732 Elizabeth (*d* 13 Sept 1762), dau and heiress of Sir Blundel Charlton, Bt, of Ludford, Salop, and had:

(1) Nicholas LECHMERE later CHARLTON-LECHMERE (on inheriting estates of his unc Sir Blundel Charlton, Bt), of Ludford, Salop; *b* 18 Dec 1733; Col Worcs Militia; *m* Susannah, dau of Jesson Case, of Powicke, Worcs, and *d* 1807, leaving:

1a Edmund; *d* unm

1a Francis; *d* unm; the Severn End estate was sold 1830

(2) Edmund; *b* 8 Sept 1747; barrister, MP Worcester 1774; *dsp* & *vp* Nov 1798

1 (cont.) Edmund Lechmere *m* 2nd 4 June 1765 Elizabeth, dau of Rev John Whitmore, Vicar Lechlade, Glos, and *d* April 1805, having by her had:

(3) **Sir Anthony Lechmere, 1st Bt** (UK), so *cr* 10 Dec 1818, of The Rhyd, Hanley; *b* 2 Nov 1766; *m* 1st 15 May 1787 Mary (*d* 3 Dec 1820), dau and heiress of Joseph Berwick, of Hallow Park, Worcs, and had, with four daus:

1a EDMUND HUNGERFORD (Sir), **2nd Bt**

2a Anthony Berwick; *b* 28 May 1802; MA, Hon Canon Worcester, RD, Vicar Welland and Hanley Castle; *m* 11 Oct 1842 Emily Mary (*d* 18 March 1869), est dau of Sir Harry Verelst Darell, 2nd Bt (*qv*), and *dsp* 8 Oct 1788

1a Eliza Anne; *b* 11 Aug 1789; *m* 14 Feb 1847 Samuel Wall, of Worthy Pk, Hants, and *d* 26 Dec 1875

2a Emma Catherine; *b* 20 May 1809; *m* 9 Aug 1852 Cdr William Candler (*d* 8 April 1865), of Malvern Link, Worcs, and *d* 22 Nov 1885

(3) (cont.) **Sir Anthony** *m* 2nd 8 Sept 1823 Eleanor (*d* 20 Aug 1857), dau of Bayley Villiers, of Gloucester, and *d* 25 March 1849, leaving by her:

3a William Henry; *b* 15 Oct 1825; *d* unm 25 March 1857

The est son,

Sir Edmund Hungerford Lechmere, 2nd Bt; *b* 25 May 1792; *m* 1819 Maria Clara (*d* 29 Jan 1865), Maid-of-Honour to HM QUEEN VICTORIA, dau of Hon David Murray (*see* ELIBANK, L), and had:

1 EDMUND ANTHONY HARLEY (Sir), **3rd Bt**

1 Mary Clara Elizabeth; *m* 4 Aug 1842 Evelyn Philip Shirley and *d* 25 Aug 1894, leaving issue (*see* FERRERS, E)

2 Louisa Augusta; *m* 17 July 1858 Lambert Louis, Count d'Arras (*d* 1893), of St Valerie, Picardy, and *d* 31 Oct 1906

Sir EDMUND *d* 2 April 1856; his only son,

Sir Edmund Anthony Harley Lechmere, 3rd Bt; *b* 8 Dec 1826; High Sheriff Worcs 1862, MP: Tewkesbury 1866–68, W Worcester 1878–85, Bewdley 1885–92 and S Worcester 1892–94, KStJ and Kt Medjidie 1st Cl; *m* 30 Sept 1858 Louisa Katherine (*d* 15 Aug 1904), only surv child of John Haigh, of Whitwell Hall, Yorks, and had:

1 Reginald Hungerford; *b* 14 Jan, *d* 1 March 1864

2 EDMUND ARTHUR (Sir), **4th Bt**

3 Anthony Hungerford, JP, DL (Worcs); *b* 15 July 1868; *educ* Charterhouse; KGStJ, Capt attd Worcester Regt; *m* 15 Jan 1920 Cecily Mary, OStJ (*d* 5 April 1964), only surv dau of Rev Charles Bridges, of Bredenbury Rectory, Herefs, and widow of William George Lupton of The Green, Bromyard, Herefs, and *d* 29 Aug 1954, leaving:

(1) +REGINALD ANTHONY HUNGERFORD [Reginald Lechmere Esq, Primeswell, Evendine Lane, Colwall, nr Malvern, Worcs WR13 6DT]; *b* 24 Dec 1920; heir presumptive; *educ* Charterhouse and Trin Hall Cambridge; Capt 5th Roy Inniskilling Dragoon Gds WW II, antiquarian and rare book-dealer; *m* 28 Aug 1956 *Anne Jennifer, 2nd dau of Alfred Camille Dind, of Orbe, Switzerland, and has:

1a +Nicholas Anthony Hungerford [Nicholas Lechmere Esq, Severn End, Hanley Castle, Worcs]; *b* 24 April 1960; *m* 1991 *Caroline Jane, yr dau of Lt-Col Gerald Patrick Gahan, of Tisbury, Wilts, and has:

1b +Freddie Patrick Hungerford; *b* 9 Dec 1992

1b *Charlotte Grace Elise; *b* 17 Jan 1995

2a +Adam Francis; *b* 28 Nov 1962; *m* 24 April 1993 *Rosalind, 3rd dau of Rt Rev P H E Goodrich, and has:

1b *Susannah Phoebe; *b* 13 June 1997

3a +Mark Edmond Dind; *b* 7 Sept 1966; *m* 22 May 1995 *Maureen, 2nd dau of John Thomas Ryan, of Detroit, and has:

1b +Thomas Reginald Dind; *b* 7 Nov 1996

1a *Jennifer Sarah; *b* 1 Feb 1959; has:

1b *Samuel Joseph Lechmere Bryan; *b* 3 April 1990

4 Joscelyne Alban; *b* 19 Dec 1871; *educ* Winchester; *m* 9 May 1907 Lily (*d* 1 July 1963), only dau of John Cassavetti, of Myr Hall, Torquay, S Devon, and *dsp* 14 Jan 1962

5 Nicholas George Berwick; *b* 20 Sept 1881; Lt Scots Gds, Esq OStJ; *m* 23 June 1904 Mary Katharine (*dsp* 26 July 1910), only dau of Maj John Pegg, formerly of Repton Mount, Basingstoke, and was *ka* 17 Oct 1915

1 Alice Mary; *d* an infant Dec 1862

2 Katherine Mary; *b* 28 Feb 1875; *d* unm 16 Oct 1961

Sir EDMUND *d* 18 Dec 1894; his est surv son,

Sir Edmund Arthur Lechmere, 4th Bt, JP, DL (Worcs); patron livings of Hanley Castle and Eldersfield, Worcs; *b* 21 Sept 1865; *m* 1st 1885 Alice, dau of Edward Samuels, of Canterbury, NZ; *m* 2nd 1 March 1897 Katherine (*d* 11 Dec 1955), dau of Edward Peyton Wright, of Brunswick Sq, London W, and *d* 21 May 1937, leaving by his 1st w:

Sir Ronald Berwick Hungerford Lechmere, 5th Bt, JP, DL (Worcs); *b* 16 May 1886; *educ* Charterhouse; Capt 5th Dragoon Gds, Adj 1st Res Regt of Cav WW I 1914–15 (wounded); *m* 7 Aug 1915 Constance Marguerite, dau of Lt-Col Charles Wigram Long, RA, and *d* 22 Feb 1965, having had:

1 Edmund Charles; *b* 13 Aug 1916; *d* 19 July 1935

1 Sir BERWICK HUNGERFORD LECHMERE, **6th and present Bt**

1 *Joan Penelope Alice; *b* 27 August 1919

LEEDS

Arms: Arg. a fess gu. between three eagles displayed sa., a bordure wavy of the second. **Crest:** A staff raguly fessways vert, thereon a cock gu., wings expanded, combed, wattled, beaked and legged or, the whole debruised by a bendlet sinister erm. **Motto:** *Vigilate!* ('Watch ye!'). **Creation:** Bt. (UK) 31 Dec 1812.

SIR CHRISTOPHER ANTHONY LEEDS, 8TH BT, of Croxton Park, Co Cambridge [Sir Christopher Leeds Bt, 7 rue de Turique, 54000 Nancy, France; 6 Hurlingham Lodge, 14 Manor Rd, Eastcliffe, Bournemouth BH1 3EY]; *b* 31 Aug 1935; *s* cousin 1983; *educ* King's Sch Bruton, LSE (BSc (Econ) 1958) and U of S Calif (MA 1966); assist master: Merchant Taylors 1966–68, Christ's Hosp 1972–75, Stowe 1978–81, publisher 1975–78, sr lecturer U of Nancy II 1982–; *m* 1974 (*divorce* 1981) Elaine Joyce, dau of S/Ldr Cornelius Harold Albert Mullins

Lineage: Sir George William Leeds, 1st Bt (UK), so *cr* 31 Dec 1812, of Croxton Park, Co Cambridge; *b* 11 Nov 1773; Equerry to THE DUKE OF SUSSEX; *m* 1st 5 Jan 1797 Maria (*d* 1 May 1817), dau of Rev William Sanderson, of Morpeth, and had, with other issue:

1 JOSEPH EDWARD (Sir), **2nd Bt**

2 George; *b* 20 Feb 1807; *m* 1st 1886 Henrietta Elizabeth (*d* 1838), dau of Henry Heyward; *m* 2nd 9 May 1850 Anne, 2nd dau of Thomas Dumayne Place, of Ffrwd Vale, Glam, and *d* 7 Jan 1864, having by her had:

(1) William Howard (Rev); *b* 1853; *m* 1886 Ethel Beatrice (*d* 12 March 1937), dau of Charles Henry Perkins, of the Admlty, and *d* 1893, leaving:

1a Mary Faith; *m* 5 April 1917 V-Adml Sir John Anthony Vere Morse, KBE, CB, DSO (*d* road accident S Rhodesia 7 May 1960), s of Sydney Morse, of Kensington, and *d* 7 Jan 1968, having had:

1b Clyde Anthony; *b* 1919; *ka* Battle of River Plate serving in HMS *Exeter* 13 Dec 1939

1b *Jane Antonia Unity; *b* 1918; *m* 1941 *James Bruce Douglas, BM, BCh, BSc, and has:

1c *Charles William

1c *Amelia Harriet

2a *Gabriel Frances

(1) Emily; *d* 25 June 1922

(2) Florence Mary; *d* unm

1 Elizabeth; *m* 29 July 1819 Rev Robert Elliott Graham, Rector Ludivan, Cornwall, and *d* April 1844

2 Anne; *m* 19 Aug 1823 V-Adml Sir William Augustus Montagu, CB, KCH, and *d* his widow 30 Sept 1864

Sir George *m* 2nd 31 July 1819 Eleanor, 2nd dau of Owsley Rowley, and by her had:

3 Augustus Frederick, of Barfield, Ryde; *b* 11 May 1820; *m* 17 June 1851 Anna Maria Frances (*d* 8 Dept 1904), dau of Rev James Anthony Savage, of Sussex Sq, Brighton, and n of Sir James Brooke, and *d* 18 June 1888, leaving:

(1) Augustus Rowley Brooke, Capt 4th Vol Bn Hants Regt; *b* 15 May 1852; *m* 1st 14 July 1881 (*divorce* 1885) Antoinette Anne, dau of Gen Sir John Cheape,

GCB; m 2nd May 1888 Amy Vaughan (d 9 Oct 1935), dau of Rev John George Jones, Rector Hurstmonceux, and d 20 April 1922, having by his 1st w had:

1a John de Cerwick; Army Lt WW I, subject for *The Pilgrim Soldier* by John Watkins; b 5 Jan 1894; ka 3 Sept 1916

4 Edward Montagu; b 4 March 1824; m 21 Jan 1854 Jessie (d 31 March 1916), dau of Thomas Spears, of Kirkcaldy, and d 19 Dec 1878, leaving:

(1) Oglander George Montagu; b 2 March 1857; educ Clare Coll Cambridge (BA); m 8 Oct 1885 Louise Mabel, dau of Thomas de Stanton Lord, and d 1 May 1937

(2) Edward Ernest; b 1 May 1859; m 1884 Emma Seddon (d 26 Aug 1939), dau of S Seddon Walbank, MD, of Duluth, Minn., and d 1919, leaving:

1a Jessie Louisa; b 1886; m 19– Fitzgerald Moore

2a Kate Frances; b 1887; m 19– Philip Seddon Mellor

(3) Thomas Louis, CMG (1918); DSO (1916), Lt-Col 59 Scinde Rifles IA WW I (despatches); b 25 July 1869; m 14 April 1904 Clara Guion (d 1940), dau of Lt-Col Henry S Kilbourne, US Army, and d 8 July 1926, leaving:

1a *Sylvia Guion [Mrs Douglas Ward-Campbell, 37 Church Sq Mansions, Harrogate, Yorks HG1 4SP]; b 2 Oct 1914; m 12 Jan 1943 Douglas Ian Ward-Campbell (d 1976), s of Baron Hanno von Schiiking, of Majorca, and has:

1b *Iain Gordon Leeds [Iain Ward-Campbell Esq, 12 Rossett Green Lane, Harrogate, Yorks HG2 9LJ]; b 25 July 1944; educ Marlborough and Trin Coll Cambridge (MA), FCA; m 1966 *Christine Mary, dau of Dr Bernard Clive Nicholson, of Harrogate, and has:

1c *Robert Iain Nicol; b 1969; m 1993 *Diane Jennifer Martin

2c *Gordon James; b 1970; m 1995 *Catherine Clare Veltman

3c *David Leeds; b 1975

4c *Andrew Douglas Clive; b 1979

5c *John Alexander; b 1981

1c *Mary Sylvia Frances; b 1973

2b *Nicholas Carlton Guion [Nicholas Ward-Campbell Esq, 47 Brewster Place, Cambridge, Ontario, Canada]; b 10 Aug 1947; educ Marlborough; m 1973 Dorothee Anastasia (d 1996), only dau of Wasyl Pikula, of Cambridge, Ontario, and has:

1c *Belinda Maria Sylvia; b 1977

2c *Kimberley Meghann Leeds; b 1979

3 Louisa; m 27 Nov 1845 Sir Henry Oglander, 7th and last Bt, DL (d 1874), of Nunwell and Parnham, and dsp 22 April 1894

Sir GEORGE d 19 July 1838; his est son,

Sir Joseph Edward Leeds, 2nd Bt; b 31 Oct 1798; m 9 Sept 1822 Marian (d 14 Feb 1883 aged 79), only dau of William Thomas Stretton, and d 13 May 1862, having had:

1 **Sir Edward Leeds, 3rd Bt**, Col IA; b 26 May 1825; m 1st 15 June 1848 Emily Anne (d 11 Oct 1849), only dau of Maj Charles Boulton, HEICS, and had:

(1) **Sir George Augustus Leeds, 4th Bt**; b 2 Aug 1849; m 26 Dec 1871 Carolin Amelia (d 27 Aug 1897), dau of James Page, and dsp 27 Dec 1894

1 (cont.) **Sir Edward** m 2nd 21 Jan 1854 Fanny (d 15 Sept 1919), only dau of Maj-Gen Henry Templer, HEICS, and d 16 Feb 1876, having by her had:

(2) **Sir Edward Templer Leeds, 5th Bt**; b 11 Oct 1859; m 24 April 1906 Charlotte Augusta (d 10 Oct 1931), dau of Rev Edward Crow, and dsp 31 May 1924

(1) Fanny Edouine Ada; m 1 Dec 1882 George Falconer Taylor, India Forest Dept, and d 30 Aug 1908

(2) Evelyn Marian; d unm 18 July 1927

(3) Emily; m 1st 24 June 1880 (divorce 1901) Sir Richard Morris Dane, KCIE (d 13 Feb 1940); m 2nd 1902 Col George Mowat Duff, CIE (d 29 Dec 1935), and d 30 Aug 1928, leaving issue

(4) Ethel May; m 17 Jan 1894 Henry William Spurway and d 1934, leaving issue

(5) Violet; m 15 Oct 1890 Lt-Col William Hatton Hildebrand, IA (d 28 March 1926), and d 9 March 1938, having had issue

(6) Mildred Eleanor; d unm Dec 1947

2 Henry; b 28 Aug 1827; m 1st 25 March 1854 Anna Dorothea (d May 1858), 2nd dau of Rev J E H Simpson, of Drumsnatt Rectory, Co Monaghan, and had:

(1) Joseph Edward Henry (Very Rev), BD; Dean of Salina, Kansas; b 2 Dec 1857; m 1881 (divorce 1891) Elizabeth Massey, dau of Richard Quin, JP, of Firgrove Ho, Innishannon, Co Cork, and d 10 March 1907, leaving:

1a Marion Adelaide Lucy; b 1882

2a Lilian Anna Marian; b 1884; m 1907 H Davison

2 (cont.) Henry Leeds m 2nd 28 Aug 1860 Adelaide Louisa (d c 1910), dau of William Davis, and d 12 Feb 1892, having by her had:

(2) William Henry Arthur St John; ICS; Commr Meiktila and Segaing, Burma; b 3 March 1864; m 15 March 1898 Edith Mabel (d April 1957, having m 2nd 5 Oct 1920 John Hugh McNeale, Indian Police (d 1956) and d April 1957), dau of Maj-Gen Jackson Muspratt Muspratt-Williams, and d 22 Aug 1917, leaving:

1a **Sir Reginald Arthur St John Leeds, 6th Bt**, DL (Devon 1964); High Sheriff 1952–53; b 13 May 1899; educ RNCs Osborne and Dartmouth, Cdr RN, F/O RAF, WW I, WW II as Naval Liaison Offr Fighter Cmd, memb London Stock Exchange 1928–69; m 22 Nov 1926 Winnaretta, only dau of Paris Eugene Singer, of Paris, and d 18 Jan 1970, leaving:

1b **Sir George Graham Mortimer Leeds, 7th Bt**; b 21 Aug 1927; educ Eton; Capt Gren Gds, memb London Stock Exchange; m 1 June 1954 (divorce 1965) Nicola, 3rd dau of Douglas Robertson McBean, MC, and d 1983, leaving:

1c *Miranda Noel Winnaretta [Mrs Maxim Mackay-James, Higher Wynford House, Wynford Eagle, Dorset DT2 0ET]; b 17 July 1956; educ Cranborne Chase and Durham U; gardener; m 1980 *Dr Maxim Alexander Mackay-James, yr s of Lt-Cdr P M Mackay-James, of Florida, and has:

1d *Thomas George Peter; b 1984

2d *Archie Alexander; b 1986

2c Anthea Jane; b 27 Feb 1958; d Indonesia 1989

3c *Harriet Annabelle; b 13 March 1962; m 1983 *Maj Richard John Carrow, RGJ, only s of David Carrow, and has:

1d *Anthony; b 19–

2d *Hugh David; b 1991

1d *Rozel Anthea (twin); b 1991

1b *Rhodanthe Winnaretta [Mrs Gerald Selous, Langley Grange, Langley, Norfolk NR14 6BL]; b 1 April 1929; m 1st 26 April 1952 Capt Ronald David Hutton, MC, RE (d 1984), yr s of Charles Inglis Hutton, of Harwell, Berks; m 2nd 1991 *Cdr Gerald M B Selous, OBE, VRD, JP, and by her 1st husb has:

1c *Matthew Charles Arthur [Matthew Hutton Esq, Broom Farm, Chedgrave, Norwich NR14 6BQ]; b 10 Sept 1953; educ Eton and Ch Ch Oxford (MA); slr, tax consultant and farmer; m 1984 *Anne Elizabeth Caroline, er dau of Leslie Leppard, of Axminster, Devon, and has:

1d *David Thomas Charles; b 1988

1d *Victoria Emily Louise; b 1986

2d *Alexandra Charlotte Kate; b 1990

1c *Deborah Helen [Mrs Charles Stebbings, 21 Highbury Terrace, London N5 1UP]; b 7 Sept 1955; educ Benenden and York U; jnlst; m 1984 *Charles David Sandys Stebbings, s of David Stebbings, and has:

1d *Archie David; b 1987

2d *Frederick Mortimer Lincolne; b 1996

1d *Romily Paris; b 1989

2d *Eleanor Clemency; b 1993

2c *(Cecilia) Paris [Mrs Nigel Back, Washingford House, Cooks Rd, Bergh Apton, Norwich NR15 1AA]; b 7 Sept 1955; educ Bedgebury Park; schoolteacher; m 1982 *Nigel Quarles Back, FCA, and has:

1d *Charles; b 1986

1d *Emma; b 1984

2d *Katherine; b 1988

3c *Louisa Winn [Mrs Matthias Sauerbruch, 74 Ledbury Rd, London W11]; b 21 Nov 1957; educ Benenden, Bristol U and AA; architect; m 1991 *Matthias Sauerbruch

2a Geoffrey Hugh Anthony; Maj RTR, Lt KSLI, WW II 1939–42 (wounded); b 23 Sept 1911; m 1st 25 Aug 1934 Yolande Thérèse (d 24 Oct 1944), dau of James Alexander Mitchell; m 2nd 17 Sept 1945 *Florence Theresa, dau of Arthur Marshall Longfield, and d 27 Sept 1962, leaving by his 1st w:

1b Sir CHRISTOPHER ANTHONY LEEDS, **8th and present Bt**

1a Rosamond Edith Lilian; b 15 Dec 1900; m 7 Dec 1922 Maj Douglas Stewart Davison, DSO, 2nd Lancers, IA (d 19 Nov 1929), er s of Maj-Gen Kenneth Stewart Davison, CB, and has:

1b *Nigel St John, DMus Edin 1961, FRCO, Lecturer Music Bristol U, Conductor Bristol Opera Co; b 1 Dec 1929; educ Wellington and Peterhouse Cambridge (MA, MusB 1954); m 1st 21 Aug 1965 Kirstine Grahame, est dau of Graham William Churchill Meikle; m 2nd 1997 *Bridget (Biddy) Tait, dau of — Murray, and by his 1st w has:

1c *Robert Metcalfe; b 3 Dec 1966

1c *Anna Churchill; b 31 May 1968

1b *Stella Stewart; b 15 Oct 1923; m 18 May 1946 Surgn Lt-Cdr Maurice Gerald Low, VRD, MB, ChB, RNVR, s of Dr Alexander Petrie Low, of Dundee, and has:

1c *Donald Andrew; b 26 Oct 1948; educ Trin Coll Glenalmond

2c *Hamish Stewart; b 17 April 1960

1c *Fiona Penelope; b 3 May 1947

2c *Catriona Rosamond Jean; b 21 March 1951

2b *Alison Daphne; b 15 Oct 1923; m 29 Aug 1959 *John Clement Ball, BSc, MD, CM, RCA, and has:

1c *John Clement; b 13 Aug 1960

1c *Rosamond Eleanor; b 8 Aug 1962

(3) Lionel Nelson, Lt ISC; b 4 Feb 1867; dsp

(4) Edward Adderley Oglander, Br V-Consul Liége 1904–06, Lt 1st Bn Welsh Regt; b 24 Nov 1869; m 1895 —, dau of R F Vevers, of Hereford, and d 24 Sept 1923, leaving:

1a *Vera Mary; b 1898

(5) Charles George Stretton; MB Edinburgh; b 24 July 1875; m March 1905 Louisa Christian (m 2nd 28 Oct 1921 Archibald Clark (d 2 Jan 1936); m 3rd 16 April 1943 John McLinden (d 29 June 1960) and d 27 Jan 1960), only dau of James Barker Duncan, WS, of Edinburgh, and d 31 May 1909, leaving:

1a Charles Rupert Duncan; MB, ChB Edinburgh 1928, FRCS Ed 1937, DOMS Lond; b Dec 1905; m 1st 14 April 1938 Belinda Elizabeth, BSc, MB, BCh, BAO, FRCSE (d 30 Dec 1953), er dau of John Nesbitt, of Portumna, Co Galway; m 2nd 2 Feb 1954 Muriel, 3rd dau of John Paton Wilson, of Edinburgh, and d 26 Oct 1966

1a *Lilian Margaret; DA Edin Coll Art, Lecturer Art Coll Domestic Science Edinburgh 1936; b 19 Jan 1908

3 William Montagu; Lt 50th Regt; b 20 July 1832; m 24 Dec 1854 Emma (d 26 June 1918), est dau of Henry Hildyard, and d 31 March 1899, leaving:

(1) William Henry Montagu; Hon Lt 1st Vol Bn Welsh Regt, Extra Queen's Messenger, High Sheriff Pembs 1920; b 6 Dec 1858; m 28 April 1892 Mary (d 21 July 1956), er dau of James Fyfe Jamieson, of S Kensington, and d 11 Jan 1947, having had:

1a Roland; Lt-Cdr RN; b 1893; m 22 April 1925 (divorce 1930) Betty Nora, yst dau of C P Dawson, of Shanghai, and d 28 March 1933

2a Aubrey; b 4 Aug 1903; m 11 Feb 1933 Barbara (d 1994), only child of J Travis, of Lightcliffe, Yorks, and d 1992, leaving:

1b +ANTONY HILDYARD; b 15 Dec 1937; heir presumptive; m 1966 (divorce 1973) Elizabeth Helen Cornell, of Toronto

2b +Sharman; b 25 June 1953

1b *Sally Gillian; b 21 May 1936; m 31 May 1961 *John Arthur Nation, BSc, PhD, only s of Arthur John Nation, of Somerset, and has:

1c *Philip David Oliver; b 1962

2c *Robert James Anthony; b 1964

(2) Joseph Edward Montagu; *b* 15 July 1864; *m* 1st 2 April 1902 Kathleen Leigh Manners (*d* 1921), est dau of John Leigh Goldie McCarthy, MD, of Ontario; *m* 2nd 15 Nov 1929 Agnes Irwin, only dau of Richard Thomas Lancefield, of Ontario, and *d* 22 Aug 1940

(3) Charles Frederic Augustus; *b* 10 June 1868; *m* 4 March 1902 Mildred Katharine Mary (*d* 26 Jan 1938), 3rd dau of Denham Robinson, of Hampton Wick, and *d* 29 July 1951, leaving:

1a Charles Hildyard Denham; *b* 12 Dec 1902; *m* 17 Aug 1940 *Merran Elizabeth, RD [Mrs Charles Leeds, PO Box 927, Claresholm, Alberta T0L 0T0, Canada], dau of John Hilary Drew, of Kitscoty, Alberta, and *d* 1975, leaving:

1b +John Charles Hildyard, BSc Civil Eng (1965) [John Leeds Esq, 408 Ranch Estates Bay, NW Calgary, Alberta T3G 1T6, Canada]; *b* 25 Dec 1941; *m* 26 June 1965 *Eileen Rose, dau of Joseph Francis Shalka, of Fort Kent, Alberta, and has:

1c +Michael John Hildyard; *b* 1975; BSc Mech Eng

1c *Diane Katherine; *b* 26 Aug 1967; BEd, MEd; *m* 1992 *Rodney Orr, BEd

2c *Brenda Merran; *b* 1971; BSc (1991), LLB (1995); barrister

2b +Charles Eric Montagu [Charles Leeds Esq, Box 927, Claresholm, Alberta T0L 0T0, Canada]; *b* 26 Jan 1945; Surt Dipl, rancher on original Leeds ranch (bought 1887); *m* 1971 *Patricia Marlene, dau of Irwin E Brown, of Stavely, Alberta, and has:

1c +Montagu Charles; *b* 1975; Chem Tech Dipl 1995

2c +Shayne Irwin; *b* 1977; Automotive Tech Dipl 1997

3c +Cameron Wesley; *b* 1981

3b +James Douglas Logie [James Leeds Esq, Box 42, Claresholm, Alberta T0L 0T0, Canada]; *b* 6 Oct 1948; rancher on original Leeds ranch; *m* 1972 *Irene Mary, dau of J A Hughes, of Longview, Alberta, and has:

1c +Anthony Hildyard; *b* 1975; Automotive Tech Dipl 1995

2c +Christopher James (twin); *b* 1975; Livestock Prod Tech Dipl 1995

3c +Mark Douglas; *b* 1983

1c *Paula Marie; *b* 1978

1b *Helen Merran [Ms Helen Leeds, 9 Glenlawn Ave, Winnipeg Mau R2M 0X6]; *b* 20 April 1951; BSc Pharmacy; staff pharmacist Winnipeg Hosps

2a Eric Edward; *b* 1907; *m* 22 Nov 1934 Freda Foster, of Claresholm, Alberta, and *d* 1994, having had:

1b *Jacqueline May; *b* 4 Nov 1935; *m* 1955 *Raleigh Robert Hugh Tatham and has:

1c *Roderick Hugh; *b* 1958

1c *Catherine Ann; *b* 1956

2c *Carolyn Jill; *b* 1960

3c *Susan Margaret; *b* 1963

1a Marjorie Mary Mildred [Mrs Henry Sharples, Box 401, Claresholm, Alberta, Canada]; *b* 7 May 1904; *m* 9 April 1935 *Henry Sharples (*d* 1972), s of Charles Sharples, of Claresholm, and has:

1b *Mildred Joanne [Mrs Anthony Perlich, Box 1057, Lethbridge, Alberta T1J 4A2, Canada]; *b* 8 June 1939; *m* 1962 *Anthony Perlich and has:

1c *David Anthony; *b* 1969

1c *Jeanine Marie; *b* 1971

2c *Nancy Joan; *b* 1978

2b *Carol Barbara [Mrs Terence Henker, Box 202, Claresholm, Alberta T0L 0T0, Canada]; *b* 21 Sept 1940; *m* 1st 1960 (*divorce* 1973) Donald Charles Stewart; *m* 2nd 1973 *Terence Willard Henker and by her 1st husb has:

1c *Donald Charles Henry; *b* 1964; *m* 1994 *Whitney Camille Conrad

1c *Barbara Joan; *b* 1962; *m* 1990 *Paulin Larochelle and has:

1d *Geoffrey Donald; *b* 1993

2c *Patricia Marjorie; *b* 1967

3b *Kathleen Marjorie [Mrs Kenneth Tratch, 2217 27th St South, Lethbridge, Alberta T1K 2T1, Canada]; *b* 17 Jan 1943; *m* 1966 *Kenneth Eugene Tratch and has:

1c *Robert Kenneth; *b* 1971

1c *Carole Anne; *b* 1967; *m* 1989 *Vaughn Sterenberg

2c *Karen Kathleen; *b* 1968; *m* 1994 *Dennis Hoffman

4b *Judith Susan [Mrs Helmut Meckelborg, RR8-22-16, Lethbridge, Alberta T1J 4P4, Canada]; *b* 9 April 1945; *m* 1966 *Helmut Charles Meckelborg and has:

1c *Douglas Charles; *b* 16 April 1969

2c *James Joseph; *b* 6 March 1970

1c *Susan Kathleen; *b* 19 Sept 1967; *m* 1st 1989 (*divorce* 1993) Brian Ostrander and has:

1d *Robyn Johanna; *b* 9 Aug 1991

1c (cont.) Mrs Susan Ostrander *m* 2nd 1994 *Jason Lynn Taylor, of Calgary, and has by him:

1d *Kyle Charles; *b* 18 June 1997

2d *Lauren Alberta; *b* 17 April 1994

(1) Lilian Emma; *m* 27 Dec 1882 Lt-Col Frederick Henry John Birch, RA (*d* 30 Nov 1911)

(2) Lucy Helen Grace; *m* 6 July 1886 David Evan Stephens, of Parc-yr-Onen, Carmarths, and had issue

(3) Frederica Katherine; *m* 1894 Col Alexander Egerton Dallas, CMG, OBE, IA (*d* 16 May 1949), and *d* 3 May 1945, leaving issue

(4) Eleanor Constance Mabel; *d* unm 2 April 1950

4 Joseph Robert; Lt RMA; *b* 19 April 1838; *dsp* 19 Nov 1870

5 George Lewis; Lt 37th Foot; *b* 19 Nov 1845; *m* 5 Aug 1873 Lucy Anne (*d* 9 May 1927), yst dau of Mashiter Helme, of Brighton, and *d* 12 Jan 1900, leaving:

(1) Mashiter; *b* 9 Jan 1883; *m* 1st 20 Dec 1911 (*divorce* 1922) Iris Wilhelmina, dau of Wilhelm Anton Hasbach, Prof Political Economy; *m* 2nd 29 Sept 1927

Grace Grant, yst dau of Frederick Grant Potter, of New York, and *d* 11 Nov 1937, having by his 1st w had:

1a +Joseph Mashiter; *b* 10 Aug 1912

(1) Sylvia Catherine; *m* 29 June 1912 Charles Courtenay Cumming (*d* 1922), s of Adml Sir Arthur Cumming, KCB, and *d* 2 April 1950

1 Marian Elizabeth; *m* 22 April 1848 Edmund James CRADOCK formerly ADDERLEY (*d* 14 May 1903), of Knighton, Leics, bro of 1st Baron Norton (*qv*), and *d* 16 Oct 1882, leaving issue

2 Eleanor Charlotte Berkeley; *m* 29 April 1854 Charles Stansfeld Rawson (*d* 2 June 1863), of Glanhancoye, and *d* 20 July 1904

3 Frederica Charlotte; *d* 17 June 1876

4 Georgina; *d* 13 Sept 1874

5 Emily Catherine; *m* 21 Aug 1866 William Frederick March Phillips (*d* 27 Sept 1901), s of Rev Edward Thomas March Phillipps, Rector Hathern, Leics, and *dsp* 25 March 1915

LEES of Blackrock

Arms: Azure a fess chequy argent and sable, between six cross-crosslets fitchée, three in the chief and three in the nombril points or, and three billets, two in the honour and one in the base points, of the second. **Crest:** A dexter hand couped above the wrist and erect proper, grasping a crescent or. **Mottoes:** 1 *Exegi* ('I have accomplished'), 2 An honest man's the noblest work of God. **Creation:** Bt. (UK) 30 June 1804.

SIR THOMAS HARCOURT IVOR LEES, 8TH BT, of Black Rock, Co Dublin [Sir Thomas Lees Bt, c/o Fosseys, The Street, Slinfold, W Sussex RH13 7RS]; *b* 6 Nov 1941; *s f* 1963

Lineage: ADAM LEES, of Cumnock, Ayrshire, had:

Sir John Lees, 1st Bt (UK), so *cr* 30 June 1804; served Army Germany under Marquess of Granby (*see* RUTLAND, D); Priv Sec to Ld Lt Ireland; Usher Black Rod, Sec-at-War and Sec to PO Ireland; *m* 20 Oct 1766 Mary, est dau of Robert Cathcart, of Glandusk, Ayrshire, and had:

1 HARCOURT (Sir), **2nd Bt**

2 John Cathcart; *b* 21 Oct 1777; barrister; *m* 4 Feb 1800 Mary, sis of Sir Robert Shaw, 1st Bt (*qv*), and *d* Sept 1858, having had, with other issue:

(1) Cathcart; MD; *b* 26 Feb 1811; *m* 24 May 1843 Elinor (*d* 1883), 2nd dau of Isaac Matthew d'Olier, of Booterstown, Co Dublin, and *d* 16 Dec 1861, leaving:

1a Robert Shaw; *b* 23 March 1844; *m* 6 Feb 1883 Anna Magdalena, dau of Ven Alexander Stewart, Archdeacon Ross, Co Cork, and *d* 1904, having had:

1b Madeleine Elinor; *m* 1918 Henry William Crosthwait

2b Mabel Caroline; *d* 1891

2a Isaac d'Olier; *b* 3 April 1850; *d* 1887

3a John Cathcart; *b* 18 Oct 1854; *m* 18 Aug 1886 Helen Campbell (*d* 1948), dau of John Rutherfoord d'Olier, of Herbert Ho, Booterstown, and *d* 6 Feb 1922, having had:

1b John Rutherfoord LEES later D'OLIER-LEES (deed poll 1952); MInstCE, 2nd Lt RE; *b* 17 Sept 1887; *educ* St Paul's and UCL; *m* 16 Aug 1923 Margery (*d* 1975), er dau of Thomas H Scott, of Sunderland, and *d* 1972, leaving:

1c +JOHN CATHCART [John d'Olier-Lees Esq, The Cottage, 58 Southampton Rd, Ringwood, Hants BH24 1JD]; *b* 12 Nov 1927; heir presumptive; *educ* Claysmore and OTC Bangalore; commissioned Border Regt India, seconded E Lancs Regt, 21st SAS Regt (Artists Rifles) TA 1953–66; *m* 26 Jan 1957 *Wendy Garrold, yr dau of Brian Garrold Groom, and has:

1d +Trevor John Cathcart; *b* 7 Jan 1961; *m* 1992 *Susan Ciabrello

2d +James Scott Lewis; *b* 30 April 1963

2c +Edmund Campbell [Edmund d'Olier-Lees Esq, Lapley Farmhouse, Coaley, Dursley, Glos]; *b* 10 June 1929; FCA; *m* 23 April 1960 *Hilary Vernon, only dau of John Gilbert Harbord, of Englefield Green, Surrey, and has:

1d +Robert Arthur Campbell; *b* 17 Aug 1963
1d *Caroline Margery; *b* 3 March 1961; *m* 1990 *Richard James Dean and has:
1e *Edward James; *b* 1992
2d *Deborah Helen; *b* 25 March 1962
3c Thomas Rutherfoord; *b* 18 April 1931; *m* 17 Sept 1960 *Anne Elizabeth, er dau of William Simpson Dalgetty, MB, ChB, of Edinburgh, and *d* 19 Nov 1984, leaving:
1d +Guy Rutherford; *b* 4 May 1962
2d +Mark Angus; *b* 25 Oct 1964
1d *Catherine Anne; *b* 1966
2d *Julia Elizabeth; *b* 1968
1c *Elizabeth d'Olier [Mrs Geoffrey Martin, Flagstones, 1 Brattlewood, Kent TN13 1QS]; *b* 27 Feb 1925; *m* 18 Aug 1956 *Geoffrey John Martin, s of Frederick John Holt Martin, and has:
1d *Timothy John Hoit [Timothy Martin Esq, 6 Coronet Court, North Rocks, NSW 2151, Australia]; *b* 1 Jan 1958; *m* 1984 *Merryn Blacklock and has:
1e *Thomas Geoffrey Hoit; *b* 1986
1e *Lisa Adele Martin; *b* 1984
2e *Catherine Lee; *b* 1989
2d *Robin Geoffrey; *b* 31 July 1959
2c *Helen Campbell [Miss Helen d'Olier-Lees, 15 Whittingstall Rd, London SW6]; *b* 8 June 1926
1b Helen Campbell; *m* 28 July 1926 John Richard Matthew, MICE, Capt RE (*d* 1953), yst s of James Matthew, of Perth and Montevideo, and had:
1c *Helen Mary d'Olier; *b* 19 March 1929; *educ* London U (MA)
2b Elinor Maivie; *d* 8 Nov 1918
1a Margaret Elinor; *d* unm 1 May 1924
2a Mary Emily; *d* unm 16 May 1928
(1) Eliza; *m* 27 Oct 1836 Rev John Lees (*see below*) and *dsp*
(2) Mary Jane; *m* 27 Oct 1857 Henry Watson (*d* 16 June 1876), s of John Watson, of Ballydarton, Co Carlow
3 Townshend; *b* 3 Aug 1779; *d* unm
4 Edward Smith (Sir); *b* 3 Aug 1781; ktd by GEORGE IV on his visit to Ireland 1821, Sec to PO Ireland and Scotland till 1845; *m* 1821 — (*d* 17 May 1853), yst dau of Capt Clarke, 40th Regt, and *dsp* 24 Sept 1846
5 William Eden; *b* 5 Aug 1784; Surveyor-Gen Irish PO; *m* 1810 Sophia Cornelia (*d* 17 June 1869), dau and coheir of Maj-Gen Cornelius Helden, of Ballinlough, Co Longford, and *d* 24 Dec 1856, leaving, with four daus:
(1) John; *b* 1813; *dsp* 1864
(2) Edward; *b* 17 March 1814; *m* 18 Aug 1840 Mary Harriet (*d* 7 Nov 1875), dau of Lt-Col Western, Govr Lagos, and *d* 30 Nov 1862, leaving, with other issue:
1a Harcourt; *b* 25 Nov 1843; *m* 7 June 1867 Mary Massy (*d* 1 April 1914), est dau of Joseph Burke, of The Lodge, Templemore, Co Tipperary, and *d* 4 Nov 1938, having had:
1b Harcourt Edward; *b* 1884; *m* 1961 Eileen, widow of Edward Byron de Lacy
1b Fanny Isabel, *d* 14 Nov 1868
2b Kathleen Western; *m* 28 Dec 1909 William Joseph Kelly, s of William Ferguson Kelly
3b Ethel Sophia Hariet Western
1a Anna Gifford; *m* 22 July 1879 Byron de Lacy (predeceased her in America), s of Francis de Lacy, Pleading Offr Exchequer Ct, Dublin, and *d* 1 July 1927, leaving issue
2a Emily Mary Armit; *m* 1881 Henry Warburton Hodgetts, S Australia CS, and had issue
6 Thomas Orde; *b* 30 June 1788; *m* 1811 Charity, dau of William Armit, of Dublin, and had:
(1) John (Rev); *b* 1814; Rector Annadown, Co Galway; *m* 1st 27 Oct 1836 Eliza (*dsp*), dau of John Cathcart Lees (*see above*); *m* 2nd 14 April 1845 Lady Louisa Hastings (*d* 7 Feb 1868), dau of 11th Earl of Huntingdon (*qv*), and *d* 6 April 1871, having by her had:
1a Thomas Orde Hastings, JP (Northants); *b* 22 Feb 1846; *educ* Trin Coll Dublin (MA); barrister, RIC, Ch Constable Northants and IoW to 1898; *m* 24 Aug 1871 Grace (*d* 24 Aug 1935), only dau and heiress of Joshua Wigly Bateman, Sec Duchy Cornwall, and *d* 30 Sept 1924, having had:
1b Edmund Hastings Harcourt; Capt Border Regt; *b* 21 Dec 1875; *ka* 28 Oct 1914
2b Thomas Orde Hans, OBE (1919), AFC; *b* 23 May 1877; Prof Peers Coll Japan, Lt-Col RMLI and RAF WW I; *m* 1st 14 Oct 1902 Rhoda Isabel (*d* 23 July 1930), dau of P Musgrove, widow of R Lovat Fraser, and had:
1c *Grace Isabel Renée; *m* 1st 25 Nov 1932 (*divorce* 1942) Sir Alfred Jules Ayer, FBA, s of Jules Luis Cyprien Ayer, and has issue; *m* 2nd 1961 *Stuart Newton Hampshire, FBA, s of G N Hampshire
2b (cont.) Thomas Lees *m* 2nd 1932 *Ellaline Hisako and *d* 1958, leaving by her:
2c *Daphne Orde Louise; *b* 11 Dec 1936
1b Mabel Louise; *m* 6 July 1902 Col Maximilian St Leger Simon, CBE, RE, s of Maximilian Frank Simon, CMG, MD (*d* 5 Jan 1951), Pncpl MO Straits Settlements, and had issue
1a Ellen; *m* 13 March 1866 Maj-Gen Thomas Scovell Charles Bigge, CB (*d* 14 May 1914), of The Lye Ho, Bricket Wood, St Albans, and *d* 12 June 1928, leaving issue
(2) Henry; Maj 28th Regt; *b* 30 Nov 1816; *m* 28 Oct 1848 Eliza Maria (*d* 19 Aug 1881), dau of Daniel McKay, of Dublin, and *d* 10 Jan 1878, leaving:
1a Henry Rowland John; *b* 21 April 1852; *m* 3 Feb 1878 Isabella (*d* 17 Feb 1902), dau of Capt Hardie, of Granton, and *d* 1889
1b Henry Orde Macallister; Capt Merchant Serv; *b* 10 April 1880; *m* 1902 Marion Paul Scott (*d* 1951) and *d* 12 June 1933, leaving:

1c Henry Orde Westwater; *b* 14 Jan 1903; *m* 28 Aug 1944 Dorothea Joan, dau of John Evans
1c Dorothy Ann; *b* 10 Oct 1904; *m* 15 Dec 1943 her bro's bro-in-law Robert William Nicholson Evans, slr, s of John Evans, and had:
1d *Morag Pauline; *b* 29 Jan 1945
2d *Dorothea Ann Joan [Mrs Charles Heaney, 2 The Crescent, Lucan, Co Dublin, Ireland]; *b* 31 Oct 1946; *m* 26 Aug 1967 *Charles David Edward Heaney, s of James Frederick Heaney, of Glasnevin, Dublin, and has:
1e *Rebecca Ann; *b* 7 March 1968
2b Charles Harcourt; *b* 16 Dec 1881; Inland Revenue Dept Dundee; *m* 27 June 1914 Isabella, dau of Adam J Gillies, of Edinburgh
1b Mabel Augusta; *b* 1878; *m* Thomas Traill and had issue
1a Louisa Maria; *m* 28 Oct 1872 Edward John Ottley and *dsp* 1893
2a Augusta; *m* 11 Aug 1869 Maj Matthew Charles Brodie Macalister, of Crubasdale, and *d* 1898, leaving issue
3a Cerise Antoinette
(3) William Armit; *b* 9 Sept 1827; *m* 1st 11 Sept 1846 Sophia (*d* 12 Jan 1859), dau of Rev John Rowley, LLD, Preb Ch Ch Dublin; *m* 2nd 6 Feb 1861 Mary Louisa (*dsp* 4 Jan 1898), dau of John Hamilton, of The Grove, and *d* 11 Oct 1885, having by his 1st w had:
1a Hastings Rowley; *b* 4 Jan 1850; Lt RN; *m* 4 April 1877 Hilda Maude, dau of Robert Gunter (*see* 1970 edn GUNTER, Bt), and *d* 11 Oct 1883, leaving:
1b Nora Maude; *m* 15 Oct 1910 Maj John Weddall Nelson, DSO (*d* 25 Dec 1935), Roy W Kent Regt, and had issue
2b Gladys Noel Sophia; *m* 8 Sept 1908 Capt Frederick George Ross, RASC (*d* 18 July 1937), and had issue
1a Mary Cerise; *m* 31 July 1867 John Henry Darley (*d* 1883), of Ferney, Stillorgan, Dublin, and *d* 24 May 1934, leaving issue
2a Fanny Isabella; *m* 30 July 1868 Col William Benjamin Digby, of Ballinacurra, Co Westmeath, and *d* 7 May 1872
3a Mary Armit; *m* 1st 24 Nov 1869 William MacGeough Bond (*d* 1896), of Moy, Co Armagh, and had issue; *m* 2nd 30 July 1903 Maj-Gen Beauchamp John Colclough Doran, CB, Roy Irish Regt, and *d* 11 Aug 1932
4a Emma; *m* 17 Nov 1874 John T Crosthwait (*d* 1889), of Clonskeagh, Co Dublin, and *d* 19 Jan 1931, having had issue
5a Georgina; *d* unm
6a Sophie; *m* 1st 1893 William Charles Kingsbury Wilde (*d* 1899) and had issue; *m* 2nd 20 Oct 1900 Alexander Louis Teixeira de Mattos (*d* 5 Dec 1921), Sec War Trade Intell Dept, and *d* 7 Oct 1922
(1) Charlotte; *m* Rev George Sydney Smith, DD (*d* Sept 1875)
(2) Georgina; *m* 1st 12 Aug 1847 James Graves (*d* 28 Oct 1852); *m* 2nd 29 May 1860 Thomas Williams
(3) Diana
1 Charlotte; *d* unm

Sir JOHN *d* Sept 1811; his est son,
Rev Sir Harcourt Lees, 2nd Bt; *b* 29 Nov 1776; Rector Killany; *m* Oct 1812 Sophia (*d* 11 Aug 1874) dau of Col Thomas Lyster, of Grange, Co Roscommon, and had, with three other daus (*d* unm):
1 JOHN (Sir), **3rd Bt**
2 George Cholmondeley; 61st Regt; *m* 1st 1840 Georgina (*d* 1843), yst dau of Maj George Colclough, 33rd Regt; *m* 2nd 1886 Antoinette (*d* 22 May 1919), yst dau of Benjamin Louis du Guè, of Lausanne, and *d* 15 March 1896, leaving by his 1st w:
(1) Alice; *d* unm 28 May 1925
3 Thomas Ellis Bridgeman; Maj IA; *b* 1818; *m* 10 March 1857 Janet Edmestone, dau of Capt William Balfour, RN, of Trenaby, and widow of Capt Edward Stanley, 57 Regt, and *dsp* 19 Sept 1865
4 William Nassau; *b* 1826; LLD, Maj-Gen IA and Persian Interpreter to Indian Govt; *d* unm 9 March 1889
1 Mary; *m* 1833 John Meiklam (*d* 20 May 1882), of Gladswood, Berwicks, and *d* 7 Aug 1895, leaving issue

Sir HARCOURT *d* 7 March 1852; his est son,
Sir John Lees, 3rd Bt; *b* 31 Dec 1816; *m* 29 May 1839 Maria Charlotte (*d* 3 Jan 1881), only dau of Edward Richard Sullivan (*see* SULLIVAN, Bt), and had:
1 HARCOURT JAMES (Sir), **4th Bt**
2 Arthur Richard; *b* 18 July 1842; Col 2nd Bn York and Lancaster Regt; *m* 1st 19 Dec 1866 Amy (*d* 10 Jan 1867), 2nd dau of Henry Morgan Godwin; *m* 2nd 28 Sept 1880 Annie Russel (*m* 2nd Rev Spencer Henry Harrison), dau of F G Gilbert, of Scarborough, and *d* 15 Sept 1887, leaving by her:
(1) John Arnold; *b* 31 May 1886; Lt-Cdr RN; *m* 21 Oct 1913 Katherine, er dau of James Gibbons, and was lost in HMS *Monmouth* in action off Chile 1 Nov 1914
3 James Lillyman Martell; *b* 11 June 1845; *m* 29 June 1869 Emily (*m* 2nd 19 Dec 1871 Clement Upperton), yr dau of John Brady, MD, MP Letrim, and *d* 11 Dec 1870
1 Bellina Alicia Maria; *d* 26 Jan 1858
2 Nora Frances Sophia; *m* 22 Nov 1876 Clarence Pigou and *d* 26 Jan 1902, leaving issue
3 Mary Charlotte Cooke; *d* 8 May 1935
4 Hester Elizabeth Ida; *d* unm 12 May 1928

Sir JOHN *d* 19 June 1892; his est son,
Sir Harcourt James Lees, 4th Bt; *b* 24 April 1840; Lt 60th Rifles; *m* 1st 8 Nov 1860 (*divorce* 1872) Charlotte Anne, dau of William McTaggart, and had:
1 John Caldwell; *b* 9 July 1861; *m* 1891 Emma Elizabeth, dau of T Eden and *dsp* 6 Aug 1908
2 **Sir Arthur Henry James Lees, 5th Bt**; FRES; *b* 18 Jan 1863; *m* 4 Oct 1927 Helen Agnes Marion, dau of Charles C Chittick, of Belle Vue, Nevis, BWI, and widow of Thomas Orr Gibb, and *d* 10 March 1949, leaving:
(1) *Mary Helen [Mrs David Hahn, 3 Valsayn Avenue, Valsayn Park, Curepe, Trinidad, WI]; *b* 3 July 1928; *m* 1949 David Stuart Hahn and has:

1a *Stuart Arthur; b 5 Oct 1949

2a *Harold Daniel; b 16 Sept 1953

3 Herbert William; b 3 Feb 1864; d 29 July 1888

4 Edwin Leslie; b 22 Nov 1866; m 1900 Annie (d 1961) dau of Jabez Charlton, of Southall, Middx, and d Jan 1937, leaving:

(1) Charlotte Anne Dorothy; b 1901

(2) Kathleen Mary; b 1903; m 2 Aug 1937 Frederick Joseph Excell and d 1 Nov 1965

(3) Margaret Monica Lauré; b 1908; m 26 July 1936 Arthur John Porter and had issue

(4) *Geraldine Barbara Elizabeth; b 1910

(5) *Josephine Edwina Agnes; b 1917; m Jan 1940 Edmund Ross Spencer (d 1942)

5 Lionel Walter; b 11 March 1868; m 1891 Antonia, dau of Antonio Pereira, of Buenos Aires, and d 1898, having had:

(1) Arthur Florence; d young

1 Laura Marie; b 20 April 1865; d unm 5 Dec 1948

2 Eva Janet; b 1 May 1869; m 31 July 1902 Lt-Col John Plomer Bliss (d 1941), 2nd W India Regt, and d 9 Sept 1954, leaving issue

Sir Harcourt m 2nd 9 Dec 1872 (divorce 1887) Harriet Ellen Constance, 2nd dau of Henry Morgan Howard; m 3rd 20 June 1899 Louise Hayes, of USA (m 2nd 26 Nov 1925 George R Snowden) and d 23 March 1917, having by his 2nd w had:

6 Cecil Harcourt Folder, Capt; b 20 June 1873; m 1st Nellie Hayes (d 1903) and had:

(1) Constance Lilian; b 1900; m 1920 Ernest Wilson (d 1963) and had:

1a *Douglas Ernest; b 1921

2a *Leslie Erroll; b 1924

1a *Cynthia Esther; b 1927; m 1st 1949 (divorce 1954) Howard Raymond Comins; m 2nd 1959 *Raymond Allison and has:

1b *Lee Constance; b 1962

1b *Wendy Edith (twin); b 1962

6 (cont.) Capt Cecil Lees m 2nd 1905 Frances Louisa Wegg (d 1913); m 3rd 1917 Jeannie King (d 1967), dau of George Paterson, of Edinburgh, and was k Dublin 29 March 1921, leaving by his 2nd w:

(2) Katherine Phyllis; b 190–; m 1927 Thomas Ferguson Tate

(3) Stella; b 1908; m 1938 John Henry Flack and had issue

(4) *Esmé Frances [Mrs Esmé James, PO Box 1849, Durban, Natal, S Africa]; b 1910; m 1938 (divorce 1946) George Franklin James and has:

1a *Veronica Anne [Mrs James Gorden, 29 Quentin Smythe Rd, Kloof, Natal, S Africa]; b 1939; m 1963 *James Anthony Gorden and has:

1b *Michael James Lockhart; b 1965

1b *Melissa Anne Helga; b 1967

2b *Nicola Barbara Janetta; b 1969

3b *Gilliam Sarah Esme; b 1972

7 JEAN MARIE IVOR (Sir), **6th Bt**

3 Constance Harcourt; b 13 Aug 1876; m Arthur Owen

4 Norah Mary; b 8 Oct 1877; m George Henry Croft

The 5th Bt's half-bro,

Sir Jean Marie Ivor Lees, 6th Bt; b 31 March 1875; educ Paul's Sch; Boer War 1899–1902, Capt WW I; m 1st 1898 Beatrice Nora Mary (d 1927), dau of Edward Edwin Davis, of Kingston-on-Thames; m 2nd 1927 Gladys Isobel (d 10 Aug 1971 aged 86), dau of Frederick William Bull, of Basset, Hants, and by his 1st w had:

1 CHARLES ARCHIBALD EDWARD IVOR (Sir), **7th Bt**

1 Constance Lilian Norah; b 1900; m 1923 Henry George Knight and had:

(1) *Janet Norah Rosemary [Mrs Alan Chisholm, Fosseys, The Street, Slinfold, Sussex]; b 19 July 1928; m 1975 *Alan Chisholm, BSc, CEng, FICE

Sir JEAN d 2 April 1957; his son,

Sir Charles Archibald Edward Ivor Lees, 7th Bt; b 6 March 1902; educ Canada; Capt RASC WW II; m 1924 Lily, dau of Arthur Williams, of Manchester, and d Jan 1963, having had:

1 Sir THOMAS HARCOURT LEES, **8th and present Bt**

1 Norah Doreen; b 1924; k by enemy action 1940

LEES of Longdendale

Arms: Sable two bars argent, on a chief of the last a garb or, between two roses gules, barbed and seeded proper. **Crest:** Upon a rock proper a lion rampant gules supporting a flagstaff proper, flowing therefrom a banner sable charged with a garb or. **Motto:** *Perge sed caute* ('Go on, but cautiously'). **Creation:** Bt. (UK) 2 March 1937.

SIR (WILLIAM) ANTONY CLARE LEES, 3RD BT, of Longdendale in the County Palatine of Chester; b 14 June 1935; s f 1976; educ Eton and Magdalene Coll Cambridge (BA 1956, MA); m 1986 *Joanna Olive Crane

Lineage: JOHN LEES; b 1793; d 10 Nov 1847, leaving:

WILLIAM LEES, of Birkdale, Lancs; b 17 Oct 1840; m Emma (d 3 March 1902), dau of Dr William Clare, and d 9 June 1916, leaving:

Sir (William) Clare Lees, 1st Bt (UK), so cr 2 March 1937, OBE (1920), JP (Cheshire); b 9 Dec 1874; educ Leys Sch Cambridge; LLD, CStJ, chm Bleachers Assoc, dep-chm: Lloyd's Packing Warehouses, Martins Bank (chm Manchester Bd), chm Phoenix Assur (Manchester Bd), dir Manchester Ship Canal Co, v-pres Ct Arbitration Internat Chamber Commerce and FBI, Govr Manchester U, Dep Ch Exec Offr War Dept (Cotton Textiles) 1917–19, Commercial Advsr to Br Delegation Internat Conf Customs Formalities League Nations 1923, Pres Manchester Chamber Commerce 1922–24, Manchester Statistical Soc 1925, Assoc Br Chambers Commerce 1931–32, Textile Inst 1933 and Manchester and Dist Bankers' Inst 1939–42, chm Lancs Ctee on Indian Trade Rels, memb BOT Advy Cncl 1924–27 and 1931–33, Balfour Ctee 1924–29, Br Ec Mission to S America 1929, chm Textile Mission India 1933, memb Weir Conf War Damage 1939, ktd 1924; m 29 Jan 1901 Kathleen (d 23 June 1967 aged 91), dau of John Nickson, of Liverpool, and d 26 May 1951, leaving:

1 **Sir (William) Hereward Clare Lees, 2nd Bt**; b 6 March 1904; educ Leys Sch; dir Bleachers Assoc 1935–67 and Dist Bd Martins Bank 1959–69; m 5 July 1930 Dorothy Gertrude (d 5 June 1996), dau of Francis Alexander Lauder, and d 20 April 1976, leaving:

(1) Sir (WILLIAM) ANTONY CLARE LEES, **3rd and present Bt**

(1) *Jennifer Dorothy Clare [Mrs John Wallinger, Beechlands Farmhouse, Newick, Sussex BN8 4RX]; b 6 Feb 1932; m 19 Sept 1953 *John Ben Arnold Wallinger, only s of Lt-Col Ernest Arnold Wallinger, DSO, RA, and Mrs Julian Grande, of the Tower House, Cuckfield, Sussex, and has:

1a *John Christopher Arnold; b 20 Dec 1956

2a *Timothy Hereward Arnold; b 23 Feb 1959

1a *Vanessa Jennifer Clare; b 12 Aug 1962

1 *Enid Clare; b 1901

LEES of
South Lytchett Manor

Arms: Per chevron dovetailed argent and gules, in chief two mill-rinds sable, and in base an owl of the first. **Crest:** A mill-rind fesswise sable, thereon an owl argent. **Motto:** Without haste, without rest. **Creation:** Bt. (UK) 13 Feb 1897.

SIR THOMAS EDWARD LEES, 4TH BT, of South Lytchett Manor, Lytchett Minster, Dorset, JP (Dorset 1951) [Sir Thomas Lees Bt JP, Post Green, Lytchett Minster, Dorset BH16 6AP]; b 31 Jan 1925; s f 1955; educ Eton and Magdalene Coll Cambridge (BA Ag); RAF WW II (wounded), CC Dorset 1952–74, High Sheriff 1960, chm: Lytchett Minister Gospel Film Assoc, Post Green Community Tst; memb Gen Synod C of E 1970–90, Hon DLitt Bournemouth 1992; m 12 March 1949 Faith Justin (d 4 Sept 1996), only dau of George Gaston Jessiman, OBE, of Swaynes Living, Gt Durnford, Wilts, and has:

  1 +CHRISTOPHER JAMES, TD [Christopher Lees Esq TD, Race Farm, Lytchett Minster, Dorset BH16 6BB]; b 4 Nov 1952; educ Eton, Edinburgh U (BSc 1976) and Bournemouth and Poole Coll of Art and Design (BTEC); Roy Wessex Yeo; m 1st 1977 (divorce 1988) Jennifer, dau of John Wyllie, of Newton Stewart, Wigtownshire; m 2nd 1989 *Clare, dau of Austen Young, FRCS, of Sheffield and Ynyslas, and by her has:

    (1) +John Austen; b 15 Feb 1992
    (2) +Edward Quintus; b 13 March 1997
    (1) *Gabriel Jane; b 3 Aug 1990
    (2) *Rosamund Patricia; ba 26 Feb 1994
    (3) *Mary Faith; b 26 Aug 1995

  1 *Sarah Margaret; b 3 April 1951; m 1979 *John Marcus Omond and has:

    (1) *Marcus James Mucha; b 1979
    (2) *Andrew Simon Mucha; b 1981
    (1) *Tamsin; b 1984

  2 *Bridget Selina [Mrs Martin Green, Kitchermans, Huntick Rd, Lytchett Minster, Dorset]; b 3 Oct 1954; m 1976 *Martin Christopher Green and has:

    (1) *Thomas Andrew; b 1978
    (1) *Alice Hannah; b 1981

  3 *Elizabeth Jane; b 26 March 1957; m 1991 *Colin Bierton and has:

    (1) *Michael; b 1992
    (2) *Joshua; b 1995

Lineage: DANIEL LEES, of Greenfield, Lancs; m Betty Lee and had:

JOHN LEES, of Mount Pleasant, Oldham, Lancs; b Dec 1759; m 12 April 1784 Sarah, dau of John Lees, of Oldham, by Sarah Winterbottom, and d 18 May 1828, leaving, with other issue:

JAMES LEES, of Green Bank, Glodwick, Oldham; b 19 July 1794; m 1st 2 Sept 1819 Charlotte (d 5 June 1856), dau of Thomas Evans, of Staley Bank, Ashton-under-Lyne; m 2nd 22 Dec 1857 Mary Anne, dau of Joseph Stodart, of Carlisle; m 3rd 1866 Martha, dau of T Bowman, and had by his 1st w, with other issue:

THOMAS EVANS LEES, of Hathershaw and Woodfield, Oldham, JP, DL (Lancs); b 2 July 1829; educ Eton: Lt-Col 31st Lancs Rifle Volunteers; m 15 Sept 1858 Bernarda Maria Elisa, only dau of Elliot Bay Turnbull, of Puebla, Mexico, and had, with other issue (d young):

  1 ELLIOTT (Sir), **1st Bt**
  1 Bernarda Gracia; m 26 April 1892 Percival John Browne, CB (d 27 July 1909, lost in the Waratah, nr Cape of Good Hope), Lt 1st Roy Dragoons, Col 7th Bn Imp Yeo, and d 17 Nov 1948, having had issue
  2 Eveline Jane Alfreda; m 30 Oct 1889 Col Laurence Parke, Durham LI (d 30 Nov 1929), and d 1 May 1961 aged 89, leaving issue
  3 Florence Elizabeth; b 14 Oct 1873; d unm 1935
  4 Catherine Percy; m 7 Feb 1899 Maj-Gen Sir Oliver Stewart Wood Nugent, KCB, DSO (d 31 May 1926), s of Maj-Gen St George Mervyn Nugent, of Ferren Connell, Co Cavan, and had issue

  5 Mary Dorothea; b 29 Dec 1876; m 20 Oct 1897 Henry Redhead Kindersley (d 14 Aug 1942), barrister, 5th s of Edward Leigh Kindersley-Porcher, JP, of Clyffe, Dorset, and d 27 May 1957, leaving issue

THOMAS LEES d 13 Jan 1879; his est son,

  Sir Elliott Lees, 1st Bt (UK), so cr 13 Feb 1897, DSO, TD, JP, of South Lytchett Manor, Lytchett Minster, Dorset; b 23 Oct 1860; educ Eton and Ch Ch Oxford (MA 1889); MP (C) Oldham 1886–92 and Birkenhead 1894–1906, Hon Capt, Maj and Hon Lt-Col Dorset (QO) Yeo, Imp Yeo Boer War 1900 (medal with five clasps, despatches twice); m 26 July 1882 Florence (d 22 Oct 1917), 4th dau of Patrick Keith, of S Kensington, and d 16 Oct 1908, having had:

  1 **Sir Thomas Evans Keith Lees, 2nd Bt;** b 11 April 1886; educ Ch Ch Oxford (BA); Lt Dorset Yeo, 15th Hus, ADC to Govr NS Wales 1912, cmded 2nd S Midland Mounted Bde 1915; m 16 Sept 1913 Benita Blanche (m 2nd 7 Dec 1929 1st Viscount Alanbrooke (qv) and was k in a car crash 4 May 1968, leaving issue), est dau of Sir Harold Pelly, 4th Bt (qv), and d 24 Aug 1915 of wounds recd in action in the Dardanelles
  2 JOHN VICTOR ELLIOTT (Sir), **3rd Bt**
  3 Bernard Percy Turnbull, MC; Capt Dorset Yeo; b 7 Sept 1891; m 2 June 1919 Mary (d 1980), only dau of Col Philip John Joseph Radcliffe, CMG (see RADCLIFFE, Bt), and d 2 Sept 1922, leaving:

    (1) Michael; b 17 May 1921; educ Ampleforth; Capt QO Dorset Yeo WW II (severely wounded); author The Rape of Serbia (1990); m 16 Aug 1944 *Gwendolen [Mrs Michael Lees, Portman Place, Blandford Forum, Dorset], er dau of Edgar Stanley Johnson, of Meadowside, Twickenham, and d 23 March 1993, leaving:

      1a *Christine Mary [Mrs Antonio Bueno, 12 Canning Place Mews, London W8]; b 12 June 1946; barrister Inner Temple; m 22 July 1966 *Antonio de Padua José Maria Bueno, s of Antonio de Padua Bueno, of S Kensington, and has:

        1b *Nicola Anna Christina; b 20 July 1967; m 26 Sept 1992 *Jonathan Richard Brill
        2b *Julia Catherine Mary; b 1972
        3b *Emily Antonia Mercedes; b 1988
      2a *Michèle Anne; b 12 Nov 1954; has:
        1b *Samuel; b 6 Jan 1986

    (1) Dolores; b 20 April 1920; Lt French Army WW II (French Croix de Guerre); m 18 April 1953 *Cdr Harry Selby Bennett, RN, UK Naval and Mil Attaché Caracas, s of Mr Justice Cecil Harry Andrew Bennett, QC, and d Nov 1992, leaving:

      1a *James Sebastian Selby; b 14 June 1954; educ Eton
      2a *Bruce Dominic Selby; b 13 July 1958

    (2) *Bernadette Mary [Mrs Robin Lyon, Lot 9, Wilderness Rd, Prevelly, W Australia 6285]; b posthumously 11 April 1923; 3rd Offr WRNS WW II; Master Applied Psychology, Clinical and Educnl 1981, Murdoch U, W Australia; m 1st 3 July 1943 F/Lt Richard Osborne Curtis, RAFVR (ka 20 Jan 1944), 2nd s of Maj Gen Henry Curtis, CB, DSO, MC, of Trokes Coppice, Lytchett Minster, Dorset; m 2nd 3 Nov 1956 Lt-Col (Gordon) Robin Kingston Lyon, OBE, 3rd Carabiniers, and by him has:

      1a *Kim Philip; b 15 Jan 1960

  1 Florence Mary Bernarda; b 2 Jan 1885; m 11 Aug 1914 Hon James Willim Best, OBE, yst s of 5th Baron Wynford (qv), and d 3 Dec 1961, leaving issue
  2 Gracia Katharine Hope; b 10 Jan 1890; d 27 July 1909, lost in the Waratah nr Cape of Good Hope
  3 Eleanor Juliet Anne; b 8 July 1894; m 15 Feb 1919 Capt Eustace Howard Marsden, RIN (d 13 May 1959), s of John Hudson Marsden, and had issue
  4 Alice Irene Dieudonnée; b 2 May 1902; m 19 Sept 1929 Lt-Col Gerald Stewart Oxley, MC, 60th Rifles (d 23 Dec 1960), er s of John Stewart Oxley, CBE, of Monks, Balcombe, Sussex, and had issue
  5 Margaret Alfreda; b 11 Aug 1903; d 26 Nov 1918

The 2nd Bt's bro,
  Sir John Victor Elliot Lees, 3rd Bt, DSO, MC, DL; b 11 Dec 1887; memb Gentlemen-at-Arms 1938–51, Lt-Col and Brevet Col 4th Bn Dorset Regt, Lt-Col Res of Offrs KRRC, Col TA 1932, served WWs I (severely wounded, despatches, Croix de Guerre) and II (OC 5th Bn Dorset Regt); m 30 Dec 1915 Madeline Annie Pamela (d 28 July 1967), producer Lytchett Minster Gospel Films, 2nd dau of Sir Harold Pelly, 4th Bt (qv), and d 16 April 1955, having had:

  1 James; b 3 March 1920; Capt 60th Rifles and Special Boat Service WW II; d of wounds Dalmatia 11 March 1945
  2 Sir THOMAS EDWARD LEES, **4th and present Bt**
  1 Katharine Margaret; b 29 Aug 1918; m 4 March 1944 F/O Gerald Henry Rawlinson, RAFVR (d 1975), yr s of Alfred Rawlinson, of Westminster, and d 1994, leaving:

    (1) *Carol Margaret; b 21 Nov 1945; m 1st 15 Sept 1967 (divorce 1969) Robert Lionel Simmons and has:

      1a *Rebecca Margaret; b 23 July 1968
    (1) (cont.) Mrs Carol Simmons m 2nd 1973 *Edward Welstead and by him has:
      1a *Alexander; b 1978

  2 *Rosamund Elizabeth [Mrs Dominic Conway, 720 Lonsdale Rd, Ottawa, Ontario, Canada]; b 16 Aug 1921; m 16 Oct 1943 Prof Dominick John Conway, MD, FRCP, RAFVR (d 1989), Prof of Paediatrics Ottawa U, s of James Conway, of S Rhodesia, and has:

    (1) *James Robin; b 1945
    (2) *Oliver Patrick; b 1951
    (1) *Bryony May; b 1946
    (2) *Dawn Madeline; b 1948
    (3) *Alison Elizabeth; b 1949
    (4) *Diana Rosemary; b 1956
    (5) *Florentia Anne; b 1959
    (6) *Emily Rosamund; b 1960

  3 *(Benita) Anne [Mrs John Barkworth, 1 Sackville St, Winterborne Kingston, Dorset]; b 22 Feb 1923; m 23 April 1949 *Col John Anthony Sandbach

Barkworth, 3rd Carabiniers, est s of Maj Julian Sandbach Barkworth, RA, and has:

(1) *Anthony Julian Sandbach; *b* 1955; *m* 1985 *Catherine, dau of Bruce Barnard, of NZ

(1) *Primrose Madeline; *b* 1951

(2) *Clare Helena; *b* 1953

4 *Jane Madeline [Mrs Jane Brian, Jarvis, Lytchett Minster, Dorset]; *b* 10 Nov 1926; *m* 1st 28 Feb 1946 (*divorce* 1962) S/Ldr Simon Hugh Kevill-Davies (*d* 21 March 1975), RAF, only s of Capt Hugh Somerset Kevill-Davies; *m* 2nd 18 Nov 1966 (*divorce* 1971) Michael Vaughan Brian, DSc, s of Percy Brian, MSc, of Hall Green, Birmingham, and by her 1st husb has:

(1) *Hugh John; *b* 8 June 1948; *educ* Malvern and Magdalene Coll Cambridge

(1) *Sheila Anne; *b* 1 March 1950; *m* 1979 (*divorce* 1997) Patric Morrissey

(2) *Benita Jane; *b* 28 Aug 1954; *m* 1985 *Thomas Francis Coningham Denny (*see* DENNY, Bt, of Castle Moyle)

5 Mary Gabriel; *b* 31 Oct 1928; *d* unm 22 July 1961

LEESE

Arms: Gules a fess embattled counter-embattled between in chief two falcons belled or and in base a hand erect couped at the wrist, holding a dagger in pale proper, pommel and hilt gold.
Crest: A falcon belled or, supporting with the dexter claw a flagstaff proper, headed and tasselled or, therefrom to the dexter a banner gules, charged with a dagger in pale proper, pommel and hilt gold.
Motto: *Vita cara carior libertas* ('Life is dear, liberty dearer').
Creation: Bt. (UK) 15 July 1908.

SIR JOHN HENRY VERNON LEESE, 5TH BT; *b* 7 Aug 1901; *s* first cousin 1979

Lineage: JOSEPH LEESE, of Dunham Massey, Cheshire, and Southport, Lancs; *b* 13 Feb 1815; *m* 28 Aug 1842 Frances Susan (*d* 3 Aug 1890), dau of John Scurr, of Montevideo and Liverpool, and *d* 28 April 1906, leaving a 2nd s:

Sir Joseph Francis Leese, 1st Bt (UK), so *cr* 15 July 1908, QC (1891), of Send Holme, Send, Surrey, JP (Manchester and Surrey); *b* 28 Feb 1845; *educ* Cambridge and London U (BA 1864); Capt 3rd Roy Lancaster Militia; barrister Inner Temple 1868, MP (Lib) Accrington 1892–1910, Recorder Manchester 1893–1914, ktd 1895, Bencher Inner Temple 1899; *m* 20 Nov 1867 Mary Constance (*d* 31 Jan 1928), only child of William Hargreaves, of Broad Oak, Accrington, Lancs, and Send Holme, Woking, Surrey, and *d* 29 July 1914, leaving:

1 **Sir William Hargreaves Leese, 2nd Bt**, JP (Herts); *b* 24 Aug 1868; *educ* Winchester and Trin Hall Cambridge (BA 1890); barrister Inner Temple 1893, slr 1906; *m* 12 Dec 1893 Violet Mary (*d* 15 Nov 1947), dau of Albert George Sandeman, of Presdales, Herts, and *d* 17 Jan 1937, leaving:

(1) **Sir Oliver William Hargreaves, 3rd Bt**, KCB (1943), CBE (1940), DSO (1916), JP (1949), DL (1947) (both Salop); *b* 27 Oct 1894; *educ* Eton; Lt-Gen Coldstream Gds, WW I (wounded, despatches), WW II (despatches), cmdg 15th (Scottish) Div 1941, Gds Armoured Div 1941–42, 30th Corps 1942, 8th Army 1943, C-in-C Allied Land Forces SE Asia 1944–45, GOC-in-C Eastern Cmd 1945–46, ret 1946; Hon Col Salop Yeo RAC (TA) 1947, Midland Area Patron Br Legion 1950, Lt Tower London 1954–57, High Sheriff Salop 1958, Pres: CCFA 1954, Warwicks Co Cricket Club 1959, Br Legion 1961, Salop Co Cricket Club 1961, MCC 1965, Cricket Soc 1969, OEA 1946 (Chm 1964); dir Securicor, Cdr US Legn Merit and Legn Hon, Croix de Guerre, Grand Cordon Nichan Iftikhar and Order Virtuti Militari of Poland; *m* 18 Jan 1933 Margaret Alice (*d* 30 April 1964), only dau of Cuthbert Leicester-Warren (*see* LEIGHTON, Bt), and *dsp* 22 Jan 1978

(2) Peter Albert; *b* 10 July 1905; *educ* Eton; Capt Coldstream Gds; *m* 14 April 1937 Rosamond Betty (*m* 2nd 6 Jan 1948 Alan James Peech, of High House, Blyth, Worksop, er s of Albert O Peech), yr dau of Lt-Col Geoffrey Dugdale, MC, JP, of Rosemount, Kingsland, Salop, and *dsp* 20 Sept 1943

(3) **Sir Alexander William Leese, 4th Bt**; *b* 27 Sept 1900; *educ* Eton; Capt SR Coldstream Gds WW II (invalided 1941); *d* unm 30 July 1979

(1) Betty Violet Mary; *b* 28 Sept 1899; *m* 27 Oct 1925 Robert Hamlyn Mervyn Drake, 2nd s of Bernard Mervyn Drake, of Copyhold, Cuckfield, Sussex, and *d* 17 May 1958, leaving issue

2 Vernon Francis, OBE (1918); *b* 20 Feb 1870; *m* 31 Oct 1900 Edythe Gwendoline (*d* 15 Oct 1929), dau of Charles Frederick Stevenson, of Exmouth, Devon, and *d* 3 Aug 1927, leaving:

(1) Sir JOHN HENRY VERNON LEESE, **5th and present Bt**

(2) Frederick Joseph; *b* 13 Jan 1914

(1) Margaret Gwendoline; *b* 2 Feb 1907

3 Neville, DSO (1917), OBE (1919); *b* 23 March 1872; *educ* Winchester; Lt-Col RASC, Boer War 1900–02, WW I (despatches); *m* 1893 Matildau, dau of J Saunders, and *d* 1948, having had:

(1) Robin; *d* young

(1) Cicely Violet; *m* 1921 Leonard Hay Mottram and had:

1a *Peter Hay; *b* 1922; RASC WW II

2a *Joe Neville; *b* 1927; Lt-Col Australian Regular Army, RTC, Dorset Regt; *m* 1st 1954 (*divorce* 1977) June Patricia Mary, only child of Lt-Col C F Garfit, IMS, of Spain; *m* 2nd 1978 *Moira Livingstone, only dau of William Finnie, of Canberra, and by his 1st w has:

1b *Richard Neville Garfit; *b* 1957

2b *David Leonard Garfit; *b* 1963

1a *Pamela Mary; *b* 1924

(2) Rosemary; *d* young

(3) Mary Aurelia Neville; *m* 1928 John Frederick Fawcett and had:

1a *Joan Mary; *b* 1928

2a *Rosemary Ann; *b* 1938

(4) Joyce Alice Noreen; *m* 1936 William Eric Oldnall and had:

1a *William Neville Russell; *b* 1943

1a *Felicity Ann Russell; *b* 1937

2a *Tessa Mary Russell; *b* 1939

4 Theodore; *b* 9 June 1874; *d* unm 25 Dec 1916

5 Cecil Mellor; *b* 24 March 1876; *m* 21 June 1916 Jessie (*d* May 1969), dau of G E Tournay, of Deal, and *d* 28 Dec 1921, leaving:

(1) Lincoln; *b* 3 Dec 1917; Capt Gloucester Regt WW II; *ka* Oct 1943

6 Clive, MBE (1918); *b* 24 April 1885; WW I as Maj RASC; *m* 20 April 1916 Dorothy (*d* 19 May 1949), dau of Alfred Dickson, of Chester, and *d* 9 Nov 1932, leaving:

(1) *Cynthia Hilary; *b* 19 March 1919; Lt-Col WRAC

1 Constance Alice; *b* 10 April 1878; *m* 11 Sept 1907 Lt-Col Sidney Robert Gordon Kendall, CBE, IA (*d* 19 March 1959), s of Surgn-Gen Henry Kendall, Army Med Dept, and *d* April 1964, leaving issue

2 Dorothy Violet; *b* 26 Nov 1883; *m* 11 April 1907 Leonard Curtis Rawlence (*d* 7 Dec 1957), of Weybridge, s of James Edward Rawlence, of The Chantry, Wilton, Salisbury, and *d* 28 April 1942, leaving issue

Le FLEMING

Arms: Gules a fret argent. **Crest:** A serpent nowed, holding in his mouth a garland of olive and vine, all proper. **Motto:** *Pax, copia, sapientia* ('Peace, plenty, wisdom'). **Creation:** Bt. (E) 4 Oct 1705.

SIR DAVID KELLAND Le FLEMING, 13TH BT, of Rydal, Co Westmorland [Sir David le Fleming Bt, 147 Stanford St, Ashhurst, Manawatu, New Zealand]; *b* 12 Jan 1976; *s* f 1995; *educ* Queen Elizabeth Coll Palmerston N and Wairarapa Polytech Coll

Lineage: Sir MICHAEL FLAMENG, FLANDRENSIS (*i.e.*, 'Flemish' in Latin) or FURNES (derived from property owned by the family at Furness, Lancs); *fl* 1127; ancestor of:

Sir THOMAS FLEMING; ktd by 1409; *m* Isabel, one of four daus and coheirs of Sir John Lancaster, who brought the feudal Lordship of Rydal to her husb's family, and was ancestor of:

Sir DANIEL FLEMING, of Rydal Hall, Cumberland; *b* 24 July 1633; *educ* Queen's Coll Oxford and Gray's Inn; MP Cockermouth 1685–87, High Sheriff Cumberland 1660, ktd 1681, antiquary; *m* 27 Aug 1655 Barbara (*d* 13 April 1675), est dau of Sir Henry Fletcher, 1st Bt, of Hutton, Cumberland, and *d* 25 March 1701, having had, with six other sons:

1 Sir William Fleming, 1st Bt (GB), so *cr* 4 Oct 1705, with remainder, in default of male issue, to the male descendants of his f, of Rydal Hall; *b* 15 March 1656; MP Westmorland 1696–98, 1698–1700 and 1704–05; Commr Excise 1698; *m* 1 Aug 1723 Dorothy (*d* 31 March 1757), dau of Thomas Rowlandson, of Kendal, and *dspm* 29 Aug 1736, having had:

(1) Dorothy; *m* 19 June 1746 Edward Wilson, of Dallam Tower, and had issue (*see* BROMLEY, Bt)

(2) Barbara; *m* Edward Parker, of Browsholme, Yorks

(3) Catherine; *m* 6 July 1755 Sir Peter LEICESTER formerly BYRNE, 4th Bt, of Nether-Tabley (*see* 1967 edn), and *d* 8 Dec 1786, leaving issue

2 Rt Rev Sir George Fleming, 2nd Bt; *b c* 1670; *educ* St Edmund's Hall Oxford; Vicar: Aspatria, Cumberland, 1695 and Kirkland 1703; Rector: Stanwix 1703, Salkeld 1705, Ullesby, Cumberland, 1719 and Grasmere 1729; Carlisle: Canon 1701, Archdeacon 1705, Dean 1727, Bp 1735–47, LLD Feb 1726/7; *m* 28 Oct 1708 Catherine (*d* 1 May 1736), dau of Robert Jefferson, of Carlisle, and *d* 2 July 1747, having had, with two daus (*d* young):

(1) William (Ven); *b* 10 Aug 1709; *educ* Queen's Coll Oxford; DCL, Archdeacon Carlisle 1734–43; *m* 27 Dec 1739 Dorothy, dau of Daniel Wilson, of Dalham Tower, Westmorland (*see* BROMLEY, Bt), and *dvp* 12 March 1742, leaving:

1a Catherine; *m* 9 Jan 1742 Thomas Ayscough

(1) Mary; *m* Humphrey Senhouse, of Netherhall

(2) Catherine; *m* Joseph Dacre Appleby, of Kirklington

(3) Mildred; *m* Edward Stanley, of Ponsonby Hall, Cumberland

3 Michael; Maj, MP Westmorland 1707–08; *m* Dorothy Benson and had:

(1) **Sir William Fleming, 3rd Bt**; Ensign Howard's Foot, Sheriff Cumberland 1754–55, MP Cumberland 1756–57; *m* 1745 Elizabeth (*d* 22 April 1788), dau of Christopher Petty or Petyt, of Skipton-in-Craven, Yorks, and *d* 31 March 1757, having had, with other issue:

1a **Sir Michael le Fleming, 4th Bt**; *b* 10 Dec 1748; High Sheriff Northumberland 1770, MP Westmorland 1774–1806, Lt-Col Cumberland Militia 1779–1806; *m* 23 Nov 1782 Lady Diana Howard (*d* 20 June 1816), only dau and heiress of 14th Earl of Suffolk and (7th Earl of) Berkshire (*qv*), and *d* 19 May 1806, leaving:

1b Anne Frederica Elizabeth; *b* 1784; *m* 4 Feb 1807 her cousin **Sir Daniel Fleming, 5th Bt** (*see* below)

1a Barbara; *m* Edward Parker, of Brownholme, Yorks, and *d* 23 April 1813

2a Elizabeth; *m* 20 Dec 1731 Andrew Hudleston (*d* 2 Feb 1822), of Hutton John, and *d* 23 Aug 1830, leaving issue

3a Dorothy; *m* 12 Aug 1774 George Edward Stanley, of Ponsonby Hall, Cumberland, and *d* 1786, having had issue

(1) Susan; *m* Michael Knott, of Rydal

4 Roger (Rev); Vicar Brigham; *m* Margaret Moorhouse (*d* 24 May 1749) and *d* 1736, leaving an only s:

(1) Daniel, of Whitehaven; *m* Mary, dau of Joseph Dixon, of Whitehaven, and had, with other issue:

1a Roger, of Whitehaven; *m* Isabella, dau of William Hicks, of Whitehaven, and had, with another s and two daus:

1b **Sir Daniel Fleming, 5th Bt**; *b c* 1785; *m* 4 Feb 1807 his cousin, Anne Frederica Elizabeth (*d* 5 April 1861), dau of **Sir Michael le Fleming, 4th Bt**, and *dsp* 1821

2b RICHARD (Sir), **6th Bt**

5 Fletcher, of Rayrigg and Belfield, Westmorland, whose descendants died out in the male line

The 5th Bt's bro,

Rev Sir Richard Fleming, 6th Bt; *b* 4 Nov 1791; *educ* Trin Hall Cambridge (MA); Rector Grasmere and Windermere, Westmorland, and Bowness, Cumberland; *m* 6 Sept 1825 Sarah, 3rd dau of W B Bradshaw, of Halton Hall, Lancs, and *d* 3rd April 1857, leaving:

1 Sir MICHAEL FLEMING later LE FLEMING, **7th Bt**; *b* 6 April 1828; *m* 1853 Mary (*d* 1903), yst dau of Capt Boddie, Russian Imp Navy, and *d* 1883, leaving:

(1) **Sir Andrew Fleming Hudleston Le Fleming, 8th Bt**; *b* 1855; *m* 1895 Jeanette, dau of Roderick Fraser, of Glen Lovat, Seacliff, Otago, NZ, and *dsp* 20 Oct 1925

(1) Isabella Emily; *m* 1876 George Alfred Birndon, of Kaiapoi, N Canterbury, NZ

2 William; *b* 18 Oct 1832; *m* 1858 Mary (*d* 2 Sept 1880), est dau of Thomas Wilson, of High Wray, Windermere, and *d* March 1906, having had:

(1) WILLIAM HUDLESTON (Sir), **9th Bt**

(2) Richard Thomas; *b* 6 Jan 1863; *m* 7 Oct 1891 Emma Louisa (*d* 1935), dau of Edward Jones, of Christchurch, and *d* 29 April 1955, leaving:

1a Richard Henry Edward; *b* 1892; *m* 1918 Mabel Gladys, dau of Henry Parslow, and *d* 1960, leaving:

1b +Albert Edward [Albert le Fleming Esq, 3 Kauri St, Inglewood, Taranaki, New Zealand]; *b* 1923; RNZAF WW II; *m* 1946 *Eileen Ellen, dau of John Moffet, and has:

1c +Richard John [Richard le Fleming Esq, Old Te Kuite Rd, Otorohanga, New Zealand]; *b* 1953; *m* 1976 *Yvonne Lenare, dau of Owen Butler, and has:

1d +Nathan John; *b* 1978

2d +Jared Paul; *b* 1980

3d +Daniel Richard; *b* 1985

1c *Judith Merle [Mrs Paul Scown, Durham Rd, RD8 Inglewood, Taranaki, New Zealand]; *b* 1949; *m* 1967 *Paul Eric Scown and has:

1d *Darren Matthew; *b* 1967

1d *Kylie Jane; *b* 1971; *m* 1998 *Murray Owen Cameron

1b *Noala Doris [Mrs Raymond Petersen, 15 Murdoch St, Hawera, New Zealand]; *b* 9 Nov 1920; *m* 25 March 1942 *Raymond Petersen and has:

1c *Janice Margaret [Mrs Ross Canty, 66 Colins St, Hawera, New Zealand]; *b* 25 Aug 1945; *m* 23 Aug 1965 *Ross William Canty

2c *Fay Maralyn [Mrs Maxwell Paton, 4 Sabys Rd, Christchurch 8003, New Zealand]; *b* 26 Aug 1948; *m* 9 Nov 1968 *Maxwell Edward Paton

1a Elizabeth Louisa; *b* 5 Dec 1893; *m* 1st 1910 Walter Willis (*d* 19–) and had issue; *m* 2nd Emile Oscar Jayet (*d* 1955) and by him had issue; *m* 3rd 1964 Lionel H Grafton (*d* 1966)

(1) Elizabeth Diana; *m* 16 July 1903 John Green, s of James Fleming Green, and *dsp* 1916

1 Elizabeth Sarah Anne Bradshaw; *m* 8 Oct 1857 James Carter Shepherd, MRCS, of Ambleside, and *d* 1896, leaving issue

2 Isabella Maria; *m* 1861 Edmund Henry Ensor, of Rollesby, Norfolk, and Canterbury, NZ (*d* 1894), and had issue

The 8th Bt's cousin,

Sir William Hudleston le Fleming, 9th Bt, JP (NZ); *b* 26 May 1861; *m* 2 Nov 1885 Martha (*d* 26 April 1944), dau of John Kelland, of Cruwys Morchard, Devon, and had, with other issue:

1 William Kelland; *b* 11 Oct 1887; NZ Rifles WW I; *das* 1918

2 FRANK THOMAS (Sir), **10th Bt**

3 Stanley Hudleston, JP; *b* 20 March 1898; chm Waimate West CC, memb S Taranaki Power Bd; *m* 1925 Isabel Christina, dau of William Mackay, of Gore, Otago, NZ, and had:

(1) +Eoin Stanley; *b* 30 May 1926

1 Maud; *b* 28 Oct 1886; *m* 1919 John Green, of New Plymouth, NZ, and *d* 1 July 1941, leaving issue

2 Eliza Ann; *b* 26 April 1892

3 Fanny Lindsay; *b* 24 March 1896

Sir WILLIAM *d* 31 Oct 1945; his est surv son,

Sir Frank Thomas le Fleming, 10th Bt; *b* 27 Dec 1888; NZ Forces WW I; *m* 24 March 1921 Isabella Annie Fraser, dau of James Craig, of Taranaki, NZ, and *d* July 1971, leaving:

1 WILLIAM KELLAND (Sir), **11th Bt**

2 +Gordon Halsey [Gordon Fleming Esq, 78 Ngatai St, Manaia, Taranaki, New Zealand]; *b* 18 Nov 1925; *m* 1962 *Lorna Marjorie, dau of R F Trim, of Trimoana, NZ, and has:

(1) +Mark Ronald Feltham; *b* 1965

(2) +Roderick Gordon Hudleston; *b* 1970

(1) *Ruth Maree; *b* 1963

(2) *Helen Lorna; *b* 1964

(3) *Alison Halsey; *b* 1967

3 +Lindsay Craig [Lindsay Fleming Esq, 31 Whakapaki St, PO Box 8, Urenui, New Zealand]; *b* 10 March 1927; *m* 1955 *Jean Irene, dau of F G Campbell, of Pateon, NZ, and has:

(1) +John Fraser; *b* 1958

(2) +Hugh Vincent; *b* 1959

(1) *Frances Mary; *b* 1956

(2) *Annette Isabel; *b* 1963

(3) *Louise Joy; *b* 1969

The 10th Bt's est son,

Sir William Kelland le Fleming, 11th Bt; *b* 27 April 1922; *m* 28 April 1948 *Noveen Avis, dau of C C Sharpe, of Rukuhia, NZ, and *d* 1988, leaving:

1 **Sir Quentin John le Fleming, 12th Bt**; *b* 27 June 1949; proprietor Palmerston North Taxis Ltd 1982–95; *m* 1971 *Judith Ann [Lady le Fleming, 147 Stanford St, Ashhurst, Manawatu, New Zealand], dau of C J Peck, JP, of Ashhurst, and *d* 14 March 1995, leaving:

(1) Sir DAVID KELLAND le FLEMING, **13th and present Bt**

(2) +ANDREW JOHN; *b* 1979; heir presumptive

(1) *Josephine Kay; *b* 1973

2 +Peter Douglas; *b* 1958

3 +Murray Kelland; *b* 1960

4 +A son

1 *Rosemary Lynette; *b* 13 Oct 1951; *m* 1975 *Howard Asplin and has:

(1) *Steven; *b* 1977

(2) *Blair; *b* 1979

(3) *Neil; *b* 1982

2 *Elaine Dawn; *b* 12 June 1953; *m* 1980 *John Buchanan and has:

(1) *Timothy; *b* 1983

(2) *Richard; *b* 1986

3 *Marie Louise; *b* 1955

4 *Vicki Karin; *b* 1964; *m* 1989 *Roger Whitmore

LEGARD

Arms: Arg. on a bend between six mullets, pierced gu., a cross-patée or. **Crest:** A greyhound passant or, collared sa., studded arg. **Motto:** *Per crucem ad stellas* ('By the cross to heaven'). **Creation:** Bt. (E) 29 Dec 1660.

SIR CHARLES THOMAS LEGARD, 15TH BT, of Ganton, Co York [Sir Charles Legard Bt, Scampston Hall, Malton, N Yorks YO17 8NG]; *b* 26 Oct 1938; *s f* 1984; *educ* Eton; *m* 1st 24 Nov 1962 Elizabeth, only dau of John M Guthrie, of High House, E Ayton, Scarborough, Yorks, and has:

1 +CHRISTOPHER JOHN CHARLES [Christopher Legard Esq, Grizzlefield House, Felixkirk Rd, Thirsk, N Yorks YO7 2ED]; *b* 19 April 1964; *educ* Eton; *m* 1986 *Miranda M, dau of Maj Fane Travers Gaffney (*see* FEILDEN, Bt), and has:

(1) +Benjamin Fane John; *b* 12 May 1995

2 +Edward Thomas [Edward Legard Esq, Manor House, Whitwell-on-the-Hill, Yorks YO9 7JJ]; *b* 19 Nov 1966; *educ* Eton; *m* 1993 *Lucy F, est dau of Ivone Peter Kirkpatrick, of Donhead St Andrew, Dorset, and has:

(1) +Oliver Robert; *b* 3 July 1995

(1) *Celia Mary; *b* 12 Dec 1996

1 *Louise Elizabeth; *b* 24 May 1969

Sir CHARLES *m* 2nd 1987 *Caroline Sarah, dau of Maj Arthur Ralph Kingsley Weston, of Howlet Hall, Sleights, Whitby, Yorks

Lineage: RALPH LEGARD, of Anlaby, Yorks; *m* Isabel, dau of Sir Piers Hildyard, of Wynstead, and had, with other issue:

JOHN LEGARD, of Ganton, E R Yorks; *m* Margaret, dau of Robert Franke, of London, and had:

JOHN LEGARD, of Ganton; living 1612; *m* Elizabeth (*d* 21 June 1627), dau of Sir William Mallory, of Studley, Yorks, and *d* 1643, having had, with other issue:

JOHN LEGARD; *b* 1606; *m* Mary, dau and heiress of Sir John Dawnay (*see* DOWNE, V), and *dvp*, having had, with other issue:

Sir John Legard, 1st Bt (E), so *cr* 29 Dec 1660 (following his early support for the Restoration), of Ganton; *b* 1631; MP Scarborough 1660; *m* 1st 18 Oct 1655 Grace (*d* 1658), 3rd dau of 1st Earl of Holdernesse (*see* DARCY DE KNAYTH, B), and had a dau; *m* 2nd 12 Aug 1658 Frances, est dau and coheir of Sir Thomas Widdrington, Serjeant-at-law, and *d* 1678, leaving by her, with other issue:

1 JOHN (Sir), **2nd Bt**

1 Dorothy; *m* 29 May 1690 Thomas Grimston, of Grimston and York, and had:

(1) Thomas; *b* 26 Sept 1702; *m* 16 Oct 1722 Jane, dau and coheir of John Close, of Richmond, N R Yorks, and *d* 22 Oct 1751, having had:

1a John; *b* 17 Feb 1724/5; *m* 12 March 1753 his cousin Jane, dau of **Sir Thomas Legard, 4th Bt**, and had, with other issue:

1b Thomas; *b* 9 Dec 1753; *m* 19 Feb 1780 Frances, dau of **Sir Digby Legard, 5th Bt**, and *d* 2 May 1821, having had, with other issue:

1c Charles, JP, DL Yorks; *b* 2 July 1791; *educ* Harrow and Trin Coll Cambridge; *m* 10 Nov 1823 Jane, dau of Very Rev Thomas Trench (*see* ASHTOWN, B), and *d* 21 March 1859, leaving issue

1b Jane; *m* her cousin Lt-Col George Legard (*see* below) and *dsp*

The 1st Bt's s,

Sir John Legard, 2nd Bt; *bapt* 16 June 1659; *m* 1st 1682 Elizabeth (*d* 1695), dau of Leonard Wastell, of Bolton, and had issue; *m* 2nd 1695 Dorothy (*d* 11 July 1739), dau of Sir William Cayley, 2nd Bt, of Brompton (*qv*), and *d* 5 May 1715, leaving by her, with other issue:

1 **Sir John Legard, 3rd Bt**; *d unm* 14 April 1719

2 **Sir Thomas Legard, 4th Bt**; *m* 1726/7 hs cousin Frances (*bur* 4 May 1736), dau and coheir of John Digby (*see* DIGBY, B), and had, with other issue:

(1) DIGBY (Sir), **5th Bt**

(1) Jane; *m* her cousin John Grimston and had issue (*see* above)

Sir THOMAS *d* May 1735; his only son,

Sir Digby Legard, 5th Bt; *m* Aug 1755 Jane (*d* 15 Sept 1811), 3rd dau and eventual coheir of George Cartwright, of Ossington, Notts, and *d* 4 Feb 1773, leaving:

1 **Sir John Legard, 6th Bt**; *m* 22 June 1782 Jane (*d* 19 Dec 1833), dau of Henry Aston, of Aston, Cheshire, and *dsp* 16 July 1807

2 THOMAS (Sir), **7th Bt**

3 George; Lt-Col; *m* his cousin Jane, dau of John Grimston, of Grimston Garth (*see* above), and *dsp*

4 William (Rev); Vicar Ganton; *m* 7 Feb 1803 Cecilia Elizabeth (*d* 31 Dec 1854), dau of James Oldershaw, MD, of Stamford, and *d* 1 Feb 1826, leaving, with two daus (*d* unm):

(1) James Anlaby; Capt RN; *b* 13 Oct 1805; *m* 6 May 1845 Katherine (*d* 11 March 1887), dau of Sir George Cayley, 6th Bt (*qv*), and widow of Henry Ralph Beaumont (*see* ALLENDALE, V), and *d* 25 June 1869, leaving:

1a James Digby (Sir), KCB, JP (N and E R Yorks), DL (N R Yorks); *b* 12 July 1846; Col cmdg: N R Vol Regt, E Yorks Inf Vol Bde and Yorks RFA (res), Capt RA, psc, served Zulu War 1879 (despatches); *m* 30 Aug 1877 Julia Helen (*d* 4 Dec 1950 aged 100), 2nd dau of Alfred Arkwright, of Wirksworth, Derbys, and *d* 16 Sept 1935, having had:

1b Alfred Digby, CBE (1919); Lt-Col, Brevet Col KRRC; *b* 19 June 1878; *m* 19 Aug 1902 Winifred (*m* 2nd 3 June 1947, as his 2nd w, Maj-Gen George Henry Addison, CB, CMG, DSO (*d* 5 Feb 1964), and *d* 1962), only dau of Col Sir William George Morris, KCMG, CB, RE, and *d* 15 Aug 1939, leaving:

1c Katherine Emily Winifred; *b* 6 June 1903; *m* 23 Dec 1940 Capt Charles Barsdorf, of Dinard, France, and *dsp* 26 July 1949

2c Ursula Rebecca Julia; *b* 14 Aug 1904; *m* 21 April 1934 Capt Lionel G Thomas, RE (*d* 4 July 1936), and *d* 26 Dec 1957, leaving issue

3c *Diana [Mrs John Wheeler, Bockingfold, nr Marden, Kent TN12 9PH]; *b* 8 Feb 1918; *m* 22 April 1950 *John Percival Wheeler and has:

1d *Michael John; *b* 20 Sept 1952; *educ* Lancing

1d *Bridget Diana; *b* 31 Oct 1954; *m* 1983 *Michael Wood, s of Brig R B P Wood, of Leverstock Green, Herts, and has:

1e *Patrick Michael Oliver; *b* 1991

1e *Rebecca Diana; *b* 1989

2b George Percy; Lt RN; *b* 15 Aug 1879; *m* 2 Aug 1905 Andolie Susannah (*d* 1 Jan 1955), er dau of Percy F Luck, of Stockholm, and *d* 14 Feb 1921, leaving:

1c Charles Percy Digby; *b* 17 June 1906; *educ* Cheltenham; Lt-Col 5th Roy Inniskilling Dragoon Gds WW II; *m* 5 June 1934 Gertrude Kate (*d* 8 April 1969), yst dau of Arthur Thomson, of Wimbledon and Java, and *d* 1980, leaving:

1d *Sarah Anthea; *b* 10 June 1939; *m* 15 Jan 1966 *Capt Malcolm James Sherwin, QOH, and has:

1e *Simon Patrick; *b* 8 Sept 1967

1e *Amanda Kate; *b* 25 Feb 1969

2d *(Dinah) Annabel [Mrs Annabel Holt, Stearsby Hagg Farm, Stearsby, Yorks]; *b* 25 June 1941; *m* 25 July 1964 (*divorce* 1984) James Harrison Holt, only s of Lt-Col Vernon Harrison Holt, MC, JP, DL, by Elizabeth Kathleen, yr dau of Sir Philip Bealby Reckitt, 3rd Bt, OBE (*see* 1940 edn), and has:

1e *Philip James Harrison; *b* 13 July 1965; *m* 1990 *M Jane R, est dau of Ewan Harper, of Titchmarsh, Northants

2e *Michael Vernon Charles; *b* 11 Nov 1966

1e *Elizabeth Rebecca; *b* 24 March 1969

3d *Lavinia Anlaby; *b* 4 July 1944; *m* 1982 *Robin George Newman (*see* CLARENDON, E)

2c James Frederick; Lt RA; *b* 1 Aug 1907; *educ* Trin Coll Cambridge (MA); *d* 3 July 1934

1c Vendela Susan Esther; *b* 26 Jan 1911; *m* 4 July 1938 (*divorce* 1947) Maj Colin Clement Geoffrey Milward, Northumberland Fus (*ka* Korea 3 Jan 1951), s of Maj-Gen Sir Clement Arthur Milward, KCIE, CB, CBE, DSO, and had:

1d *Gervase Colin; *b* 14 April 1944

1d *Susan Mary; *b* 17 May 1939

3b Richard Anlaby, Lt Yorks Art; *b* 10 Nov 1880; *educ* Eton; *m* 19 June 1929 Dorice (*d* 1976), yr dau of Harold Ostler, of Hull, and *d* 8 May 1973, leaving:

1c +Richard Digby [Richard Legard Esq, Apartado 110, Garrucha 04630, Almeria, Spain]; *b* 6 April 1930; *educ* Stowe; *m* 1st Aug 1966 (*divorce* 1975) Mrs Jean H Dodd, of York; *m* 2nd 1985 *Joan Frances Hall, dau of Francis Johnson Flynn, and by his 1st w has:

1d +James Richard Anlaby; *b* 1 July 1967; *educ* Worksop and RMA Sandhurst

4b Thomas Francis; twin; *b* 1885; *d* 2 Nov 1933

5b Reginald John; Lt 2nd Bn W Yorks Regt; *b* 26 Sept 1893; *d* 9 May 1915 of wounds recd in action

1b Helen Mary Alice; *m* 26 April 1921 Seymour Garstin Harvey (*d* 12 Aug 1953) and *d* Oct 1959

2b Evelyn Elizabeth Catherine (twin with Thomas); *m* 28 July 1910 Capt George Archibald Maxwell (*d* car crash 18 May 1969) and *d* 9 March 1970, leaving:

1c *Jean Helen; *b* 6 Dec 1912; *m* 22 Aug 1939 *Col Ian Hugh Trevor Baldwin, RA, and has:

1d *Martin Trevor Maxwell; Lt RA; *b* 22 June 1943; *educ* Tonbridge and RMA Sandhurst

2d *Anthony Ian Maxwell; *b* 14 April 1949; *educ* Winchester and York U

3d *George William Robert; *b* 17 Feb 1955; *educ* Winchester and York U

1d *Christina Helen; *b* 23 April 1945

3b Edith Victoria; *m* 23 April 1913 Roger John Kinloch Barber-Starkey (*d* 13 April 1963), 3rd s of William Joseph Starkey Barber-Starkey, JP, of Alderham Park, Bridgnorth, Salop, and *d* 7 Sept 1959, leaving issue

4b Pauline Octavia; m 30 Sept 1936 Col Henry Halford Dawes, OBE, Roy E Kent Yeo (d 17 Feb 1940), yst s of Sir Edwyn Sandys Dawes, KCMG, JP, of Mount Ephraim, Kent, and dsp 20 Dec 1969 aged 77

2a Allayne Beaumont, 60th Rifles; b 14 April 1847; m 1880 Mary Adelaide (d 18 Jan 1933), dau of T Buckley, of Detroit, and d 27 Jan 1933, leaving:

1b Adrienne Catherine; b 1882; m 1913 Gabriel Noel Dyer (d 1918) and had:

1c Catherine Adelaide Anne; b 1914; m 1st 23 June 1939 (divorce 1954) Capt John Henry Mark Fane, MBE, Green Howards (see CLINTON, B); m 2nd 2 March 1957 *Charles John Crossley (see SOMERLEYTON, B)

2b Mary Olive; d unm Jan 1937

(2) William Barnabas; Col Bengal Army; b 27 Dec 1809; m 11 Dec 1845 Ann Maria, 3rd dau of Robert Onebye Walker, and d 27 Jan 1890, leaving:

1a Edith Cecilia; d unm

2a Evelyn Mary; m 1886 William J Gillett (d 1917), of Ashley House, Shalford, Surrey, and dsp Jan 1948

(3) Frederick (Rev); d 26 June 1897

(1) Isabel; m 3 Nov 1842 William Chester (dsp 4 Aug 1855; see BAGOT, B) and d 1887

5 Digby, of Watton Abbey, Yorks; b 1766; m 11 Dec 1797 Frances, 3rd dau of Ralph Creyke, of Marton, Yorks, and had, with daus:

(1) George, of Westhorpe House, Scarborough; b 10 June 1802; m 23 June 1828 Anne Elizabeth (d 1887), est dau and coheir of Francis Ramsden Hawksworth, of Barmbro' Grange, Doncaster, and d 31 Oct 1882, leaving, with a dau (d unm):

1a Francis Digby (Rev); Rector Stokesley, Northallerton; b 13 March 1829; m 18 April 1872 Jane (d 22 March 1875), dau of Adml Frederick Edward Vernon Harcourt (see VERNON, B), and d 10 Nov 1874, leaving:

1b D'Arcy, CMG (1919), DSO (1918); b 5 June 1873; Col 17th Lancers, Hon Brig-Gen 1924, Boer War 1900–02, WW I (despatches, Legn Hon); m 19 Nov 1908; m 19 Nov 1908 Lady Edith Margaret Emily Mary Foljambe (d 3 Nov 1962), est dau of 1st Earl of Liverpool (qv), and d 9 March 1953, leaving:

1c Robert Francis, RD; WW II as Capt RA (despatches 1945); b 16 Oct 1909; educ Shrewsbury; d unm 23 Nov 1983

2c +Antony Ronald, MBE (1940) [Maj Antony Legard MBE, Fairway, Station Rd, Delamere, Cheshire CN8 2HZ]; b 17 Jan 1912; educ Winchester and Trin Coll Oxford (BA); Maj RE WW II; with ICI; m 28 May 1946 *Maud, er dau of Clifford Schwabe, of Cuddington Grange, Northwich, and has:

1d +Simon Littledale [Simon Legard Esq, Codd Hall, Common Rd, S Cave, Brough, E Yorks HU15 2EA]; b 20 Oct 1947; m 6 Oct 1971 *Heather Ann, est dau of Frederick Temperton, of Hessle and has:

1e +Richard Simon; b 21 Nov 1976

1e *Helen Louise; b 26 Dec 1974

2d +David Antony; b 10 May 1953

1d *Diana May; b 28 April 1950

3c +Peter Herbert [Peter Legard Esq, 11 Glan Aber Park, Chester CH4 8LE]; b 1 Nov 1917; educ Shrewsbury and Edinburgh U (BSc); with Forestry Commn, Lt Lanarks Yeo; m 31 Jan 1959 *Brenda Valerie, only dau of Lt-Col Stanley Kidd, TD, DL, and has:

1d +Jonathan Antony (Jonathan Legard Esq, 9 Bridgman Rd, London W4 5BA]; b 17 July 1961; m 28 Sept 1996 *Kate, dau of W/Cdr Christopher Chacksfield

1d *Edith Veronica Jane; b 8 Nov 1964

1b Marcia; m 21 Jan 1902 Rev Arthur Crosbie Blunt (d Oct 1952), Vicar Gargrave-on-Craven, Yorks, s of Rev Canon Blunt, and d 27 Nov 1923, leaving issue

2a John Hawksworth; b 30 April 1838; m 26 April 1873 Frances, dau of Rev Slingsby Duncombe Shafton and widow of Maj Coates, and d 1906, leaving:

1b George Shafto; Capt Durham LI; b 8 Feb 1874; d 24 Sept 1924

2b Ralph Hawksworth; Capt 2nd Bn DLI; b 29 July 1875; ka 9 Aug 1915

3a Albert George; Ch Inspr Schs Wales; b 31 May 1845; m 7 Jan 1875 Anna Mildreda (d 29 Dec 1920), dau of Matthew R Bigge, of Islip Grange, Northants, and d 18 Feb 1922

1a Anna Everilda; m 9 Feb 1871 Charles Granby Burke (d 15 May 1898), Master Common Pleas Ireland, and dsp 3 Jan 1909

2a Agnes Lucy; m 19 Jan 1860 Rev Charles Pierrepont Peach (d 1886), Vicar Appleton-le-Street, Malton, and d 9 April 1910, leaving issue

(2) Digby Charles (Rev); b 29 May 1815; m 6 Oct 1846 Henrietta Isabella (d 1897), dau of Rev Francis Simpson, and d 3 July 1851, leaving:

1a Digby Charles; b 1 July 1851; m 19 Aug 1880 Eleanor Clementina (d 13 April 1835), dau of Rev David Bruce, Canon Durham, and d 16 Feb 1924, having had, with another s and two daus (d young):

1b George Bruce; Capt Roy W Kent Regt WW I (despatches); b 7 March 1885; ka 27 Oct 1914

2b Charles (Rev), MC (1916); b 9 June 1887; educ Cheltenham and New Coll Oxford; Capt Lincs Regt and ADC Personal Staff WW I, Rector Burghclere with Newtown Berks 1937–1958; m 23 July 1918 Ethel Gertrude (d 25 Aug 1973), dau of Rev George Strickland Marriott, and d 15 Aug 1976, having had:

1c (George) Hugo Digby, MBE (1943); Lt-Cdr RN WW II; b 26 Feb 1920; educ RNC Dartmouth; m 30 March 1944 *Eve Lilian (m 2nd 10 Sept 1973 Guy Hughes) [Mrs Guy Hughes, Yew Tree Plat, Winchelsea, Sussex TN36 4EN], dau of Capt Francis Howard, DSC, RN, and d 17 June 1966, leaving:

1d +Robin Hugo Charles [Robin Legard Esq, 53 Harwood Rd, London SW6]; b 17 Jan 1945; educ Milton Abbey and Selwyn Coll Cambridge (BA)

1d *Joanna Frances [Miss Joanna Legard, 19 Rankeillor St, Edinburgh]; b 17 Oct 1948; educ Exeter U

2d *Hilary Jane; b 14 Jan 1951

2c +John Bruce [John Legard Esq, 75 Holland Park, London W11]; b 24 Nov 1924; educ Cheltenham

3b Roger Alexander; Lt Lincs Yeo WW I; b 15 June 1891; educ Radley; d unm 29 Jan 1972

4b Geoffrey Philip; Lt Northumberland Fus; b 11 Oct 1892; ka 8 May 1915

1b Muriel Dundas

1a Francis Anne; d 24 June 1880

2a Mary; m 28 Aug 1873 James Goulton Constable, of Walcot Hall, Scunthorpe, Lincs, and d 4 Jan 1920, leaving issue

(1) Jane; m Ven Robert Isaac Wilberforce (d 3 Feb 1857) and d 1853

(2) Frances; d unm

(3) Agnes; m 14 April 1832 Thomas Marshall (d 20 March 1838) and d 3 Jan 1868

6 Richard; Collector Customs Jamaica; dsp

1 Jane; m — Smith, of Sunderlandwick, Yorks

2 Frances; m her cousin Thomas Grimston (see above), of Grimston Garth, Yorks, and d 1827, leaving issue

3 Henrietta Charlotte; m — Smith, of York

Sir JOHN's yr bro,

Sir Thomas Legard, 7th Bt; Cdr RN; bapt 5 Dec 1762; m 26 Dec 1802 Sarah Bishop (d 26 Jan 1814) and d 5 July 1830, leaving:

1 **Sir Thomas Digby Legard, 8th Bt**; b 30 May 1803; m 31 May 1832 Hon Frances Duncombe (d 15 June 1881), dau of 1st Baron Feversham (qv), and d 10 Dec 1860, leaving:

(1) **Sir Francis Digby Legard, 9th Bt**; b 8 May 1833; d unm Maderia 5 Jan 1865

(2) **Sir Darcy Widdrington Legard, 10th Bt**; b 10 Dec 1843; d unm Rome 12 April 1866

(3) **Sir Charles Legard, 11th Bt**, JP, DL; b 2 April 1846; Chm Yorks E R CC, MP Scarborough 1874–80; m 30 April 1878 Frances Emily (d 18 May 1940), yr dau of Francis Alexander Hamilton, of Brent Lodge, Finchley, Middx, and dsp 6 Dec 1901

(1) Caroline Jane; m 18 April 1865 William Henry Fife (d 24 Feb 1874), of Lee Hall, Northumberland, and d 6 Oct 1906, leaving issue

2 Henry Willoughby; Offr 9th Lancers; b 1805; m 26 Oct 1839 Charlotte Henrietta (d 25 Jan 1844), sis of 8th Baron Middleton (qv), and d 21 Nov 1845, leaving:

(1) **Sir Algernon Willoughby Legard, 12th Bt**; b 14 Oct 1842; m 27 July 1872 Alicia Egerton (d 21 May 1939), yst dau of Rev George William Brooks, Rector Gt Hampden, Bucks, and dsp 6 Sept 1923

(2) Cecil Henry (Rev); LLM; Rector Cottesbrooke Northants 1887–1914; b 28 Nov 1843; educ Magdalene Coll Cambridge (MA); m 29 April 1873 Emily Mary (d 12 May 1915), dau of James Hall, of Scorboro Hall, Yorks, and d 20 Feb 1918, leaving:

1a DIGBY ALGERNON (Sir), **13th Bt**

1a Gertrude Cassandra; b 8 Nov 1879; m 23 June 1909 Henry Percival Cross (d 4 May 1912), yr s of James Percival Cross, of Catthorpe Towers, Leics, and d 9 Aug 1943

1 Matilda; m 26 Oct 1829 Robert Alexander, of Lincoln's Inn, QC, FRS, FAS

2 Harriet; m 14 Aug 1820 E N Alexander, FAS, of Heathfield, Halifax

3 Catherine; d 8 Dec 1889 aged 83

The 12th Bt's nephew,

Sir Digby Algernon Hall Legard, 13th Bt; b 7 Dec 1876; educ Eton and Magdalene Coll Cambridge (BA 1899); m 2 June 1904 Georgina Blanche Elaine (d 20 Nov 1952), 2nd dau of William Joseph Starkey Barber-Starkey, of Darley Dale, and had:

1 THOMAS DIGBY (Sir), **14th Bt**

2 John D'Arcy; b 2 May 1908

3 William Ernest; F/O RAF WW II; b 24 July 1911; m 29 Sept 1939 *Alice (m 2nd 27 Nov 1943 Col Basil Perry Beale, OBE, MC, DL (d 29 Nov 1967)) [Mrs Basil Beale, Appleton House, Appleton-le-Street, Malton, Yorks], yst dau of Hon George Ellis Vestey (see VESTEY, B), and was ka 1 June 1940, leaving:

(1) *Anne [Mrs Harry Seymour, PO Box 311, De Funiak Springs, Fla., USA]; b posthumously 15 Sept 1940; m 1st 19– Francis Curtis Luckow and has:

1a *William Frank; b 1962

1a *Laura; b 1963

(1) (cont.) Mrs Luckow m 2nd 1965 *Harry Seymour and by him has:

2a *Donna Anne; m 1992 *Michael Whiteside and has:

1b *Siena Katherine Seymour; b 1993

1 Cassandra Rosamond Elaine; m 1st 26 July 1939 Capt Charles Paul Cuthbert Cayley, RE, and had issue (see CAYLEY, Bt); m 2nd 24 Aug 1946 John Heseltine Sarginson (d 1972) and d 1989, leaving further issue

Sir DIGBY d 5 Jan 1961; his er surv son,

Sir Thomas Digby Legard, 14th Bt; b 16 Oct 1905; educ Lancing and Magdalene Coll Cambridge; Capt RA; m 3 Sept 1935 Mary Helen, er dau of Lt-Col Edmund George Savile L'Estrange Malone, JP, and d 27 March 1984, leaving:

1 Sir CHARLES THOMAS LEGARD, **15th and present Bt**

2 +William Robert [William Legard Esq, Lowthorpe Lodge, Lowthorpe, Driffield, Yorks]; b 31 Oct 1943; educ Eton and RAC Cirencester; m 1st 30 Sept 1967 (divorce 1974) Sally Ann, dau of W H Craig, of Clatto Hill, Fife; m 2nd 1978 *Helen, only dau of R G Le-Pine, of Little Driffield, E Yorks, and by her has:

(1) *Arabella Mary Elaine; b 16 July 1978

(2) *Victoria Helen; b 1980

3 +James Digby [James Legard Esq, Mill Farm, Scampston, Malton, N Yorks]; b 17 June 1946; educ Eton; m 5 Aug 1969 *(Daphne) Jane, est dau of Denison Hayton West, of Belgrave Lodge, Belgrave, nr Chester, and has:

(1) +Thomas James St Quintin; b 13 Nov 1971; educ St Edward's Oxford, and RAC Cirencester

(1) *Sophie Jane; b 1 July 1973

LEICESTER

PRUDENS QUI PATIENS

Arms: Per pale gu. and az. three eagles displayed arg. **Crest:** On a chapeau az. doubled erm. an ostrich arg., holding in its mouth a horseshoe or. **Supporters:** On either side an ostrich arg., the dexter gorged with a ducal coronet per pale gu. and az., lines reflexed over the back of the first; the sinister gorged with a like coronet, per pale az. and gu., the line reflexed over the back az. **Motto:** *Prudens qui patiens* ('He is prudent who is patient'). **Creation:** V. and E. (UK) 12 Aug 1837.

THE 7TH EARL OF LEICESTER OF HOLKHAM, Co Norfolk, and **Viscount Coke** (Edward (Eddy) Douglas Coke, DL (Norfolk)) [The Rt Hon The Earl of Leicester DL, Holkham Hall, Wells-next-the Sea, Norfolk NR23 1AB]; *b* 6 May 1936; *s f* 1994; *educ* St Andrew's Coll, Grahamstown, S Africa; *m* 1st 28 April 1962 (*divorce* 1985) Valeria Phyllis, est dau of Leonard A Potter, of Harlyn, Home Farm, Northchurch, Herts, and has:

  1 +THOMAS EDWARD, *Viscount Coke; b* 6 July 1965; *educ* Eton and Manchester U (BA); late Page of Hon to HM THE QUEEN, served Scots Gds 1987–93, Equerry to HRH THE DUKE OF KENT 1991–93; *m* 21 Dec 1996 *Polly M, yst dau of David Whateley, of Dorset

  2 +Rupert Henry John; *b* 1975

  1 *Laura Jane Elizabeth; *b* 14 March 1968; *m* 1993 *Jonathan Paul, er s of Alastair Paul, of Edinburgh, and Mrs Jonathan Woollatt, of Honiton, Devon

The 7th EARL *m* 2nd 1986 *Sarah, dau of Noel Henry Boys Forde, of Wells-next-the-Sea, Norfolk, and formerly w of Colin Graham Ramsey de Chair

Leicester, Earldom of: Robert de Beaumont, a companion in arms of WILLIAM I (THE CONQUEROR) at Hastings, was granted after the Conquest much land in the Midlands of England, but most of it was in Warwickshire rather than Leicestershire. Indeed his younger brother became Earl of Warwick (*qv*). Robert also held territory in Normandy and is usually referred to as Count of Meulan. He was a leading political figure in the reigns of WILLIAM II and HENRY I and on the death of one Ives de Grandmesnil in the First Crusade, the funds for campaigning in which Ives had raised from Robert on the security of his estates, came into full possession of them, including a sizeable part of Leicester. The rest of the town was later granted him by HENRY I and it is possible that he became Earl of Leicester. His son, another Robert, certainly called himself Earl of Leicester. The 3rd Earl of this creation, yet another Robert, rebelled against HENRY II and the town of Leicester was captured and set fire to by the King in 1173, although the castle itself was not taken. The 3rd Earl was later captured by HENRY II, however, and the King then pulled the castle down.

The 4th Earl, who was also the fourth named Robert, accompanied RICHARD I on the Third Crusade but accomplished a smooth transfer of loyalty to JOHN on the latter's succession in 1199. On his death without issue in 1204 the elder of his two sisters and coheirs, Amice, began calling herself Countess of Leicester. Her first husband was Simon de Montfort, feudal Lord of Montfort (roughly halfway between Paris and Chartres) and Rochefort, and her son by him, another Simon de Montfort, was being regarded as Earl of Leicester by the years 1205 or 1206, shortly after the death of his maternal uncle, the 4th Earl of whatever creation had occurred in about 1102. The new de Montfort Earl led the victorious crusade against the Albigensian heretics in southern France and carved out for himself a substantial territory in the Toulouse-Carcassonne area, hanging, burning and in one case entombing down a well his opponents as he went and arrogating to himself the titles of the more important heretics, such as Duke of Narbonne, Marquis of Provence, Count of Toulouse and Vicomte of Albi. He was killed in 1218 while besieging Toulouse, hit by a well-aimed stone launched from a mangonel within the city.

It is his son who was the famous Simon de Montfort Earl of Leicester of the mid-13th-century struggle by the Barons against HENRY III. Yet prior to that the famous Simon was one of the closest confidants of the King, marrying his sister Eleanor, being appointed Viceroy in Gascony and being invested in 1239 officially as Earl of Leicester. He was also invested with plenary powers in dealing on behalf of HENRY III with the Pope. After Civil War had broken out between himself and the Barons on one side and the King's party on the other, and in particular after his victory over the King at the battle of Lewes in 1264, he for a time

more or less ruled England, though matters were nominally under HENRY's direction and the so-called Parliament of 1265 was summoned by legal forms. With his defeat and death at HENRY's hands at the Battle of Evesham in 1265 this whole magnificent ascendancy collapsed.

A few months after Evesham HENRY III bestowed the Earldom of Leicester on his youngest son Edmund Crouchback. The 2nd Earl of this 1265 creation, Thomas of Brotherton, was the leader of the revolt against EDWARD II in 1321/2, being better known as Earl of Lancaster. With the death in March 1360/1 of the 4th Earl of Leicester of this creation (Henry of Grosmont, for the last ten years of his life Duke of Lancaster as well), the male line of what for want of a better term one may call the 'Plantagenet' holders of the title ceased. But Henry of Grosmont's mad son-in-law William, Count of Hainault, Holland, Zeeland and Friesland and Duke of Bavaria, was known in England as Earl of Leicester from late March 1360/1 till his wife's death from plague just over a year later, whereupon the title passed to her sister's husband John of Gaunt, better known as Duke of Lancaster and founder of the Lancastrian line of contenders for the throne. John of Gaunt's son Henry, who later became HENRY IV, held the Earldom of Leicester as one of his minor titles but on his usurping the throne it merged with the crown.

The Earldom of Leicester was revived in 1564 for Robert Dudley, son of the Duke of Northumberland who had dominated the last years of EDWARD VI's reign. The creation took place chiefly, it would seem, because he was viewed as a possible husband for MARY QUEEN OF SCOTS (whom he was later to sit in trial upon). He was in high favour with ELIZABETH I already, however. Indeed the real mystery in his elevation to the peerage is why he was created Earl of Leicester when it seems to have been one of the few counties in which he had not been granted tracts of land by the Queen. It is this Earl of Leicester whose wife Amy Robsart is popularly supposed to have been done away with to facilitate her husband's marriage with ELIZABETH, being found dead at the bottom of the stairs at Cumnor Place, Oxfordshire, on the morning of 8 Sept 1560. On Dudley's death without legitimate issue in 1588 the Earldom expired. The title was again revived, thirty years later, in favour of Sir Robert Sydney (*see* DE L'ISLE, V), but expired in 1743. In between the first Coke-held Earldom of Leicester (*see* below) and the second and current one, the title was conferred on George Townshend, of the family of the Marquesses Townshend (*qv*), being held by him and his son between 1784 and 1855. The current Earldom, popularly thought of as being 'of Leicester', thus overlapped with another title of that name by 18 years, hence the full designation of the current Earldom as 'of Leicester of Holkham'.

Lineage: ROBERT COKE, of E Ruston, Norfolk; *m* Agnes, dau and heiress of Robert Crispying, of Happisburgh, and had:

JOHN COKE, of Sparham, Norfolk; *m* Alice, dau and coheir of William Folcard, of Sparham, Norfolk, and had:

ROBERT COKE, of Sparham; *m* Anne Wodehouse, of Waxham, and had:
  1 ROBERT
  2 Thomas, of Hackford, Norfolk; *m* Joan — (*m* 2nd Henry Messenger) and *d* 1561, leaving:
    (1) George, of Hackford; *d* unm 7 Feb 1609/10, leaving Hackford to his half-bro Augustine Messenger, ancestor of the COLLYERs of Hackford Hall
    (2) Henry; *dsp*

The er son,
  ROBERT COKE, of Mileham; *b* 1513; *m* 1543 Winifred, dau of William Knightley, attorney, of Norwich, and had, with a dau (Elizabeth, *m* as his 2nd w Richard Osborne; *see* OSBORN, Bt):

Sir EDWARD COKE, PC (to 1621, when dismissed); *b* 1549; the celebrated lawyer; Recorder Coventry and Norwich, MP Norfolk and (1628 Buckingham) , Speaker H of C; Slr-Gen 1592, Attorney Gen 1593, ktd 1603, Ch Justice Common Pleas 1606, Ch Justice King's Bench 1613; champion of Parly rights, for which imprisoned Tower London 1621; proposed and framed Petition of Right 1628; author: *Commentary on the Tenures of Littleton* (*see* CHANDOS, V); *m* 1st Bridget, dau and coheir of John Paston, of Huntingfield Hall, Suffolk, 3rd s of Sir William Paston, of Paston, and had, with three other children (*d* young):
  1 Robert (Sir); *b* 1586; *m* Theophila, dau of Thomas, Lord Berkeley (*qv*), and *dsp* 19 July 1653
  2 Arthur; *m* Elizabeth (*d* 14 Nov 1627), dau and heiress of Sir George Walgrave, of Hitcham, Norfolk, and *d* 6 Dec 1629, leaving four daus
  3 John, of Holkham, Norfolk, *m* Merial, dau and heiress of Anthony Wheatley, s of William Wheatley, Prothonotary Common Pleas, and had, with six er sons and seven daus:
    (1) John, of Holkham, *d* unm and was *s* by his cousin Robert Coke, of Thorington, Suffolk (*see* below)
  4 HENRY
  5 Clement, of Langford, Derbys; *m* Sarah, dau and coheir of Alexander Reddish, of Reddish, Lancs, by the dau and coheir of Robert Langley, of Agecroft, and *d* 23 May 1629, having had, with another s and two daus:
    (1) Sir EDWARD COKE, 1st Bt (E, so *cr* 30 Dec 1611, of Langford; *m* 1644 Catherine, dau and coheir of Sir William Dyer, and *d* by 1669, having had, with three daus:
      1a Sir ROBERT COKE, 2nd Bt; MP Derbys; *bapt* 29 April 1645; *m* Sarah Barker (*bur* 13 Feb 1685)
      2a Sir EDWARD COKE, 3rd and last Bt; *bapt* 6 Oct 1646; *m* Catherine (*bur* 13 Dec 1688) and *dsp* 26 Aug 1727, when the btcy expired
  1 Anne; *m* 11 Sept 1601 Ralph Sadleir, of Standon, Herts
  2 Bridget; *m* 1st William Barney, s of Sir Thomas Barney; *m* 2nd William Skinner, s and heir of Sir Vincent Skinner

Sir EDWARD *m* 2nd Lady Elizabeth, widow of Sir William Hatton and dau of 1st Earl of Exeter (*see* EXETER, M), and *d* 3 Sept 1633, having by her had two daus

His 5th (but 4th here noticed) son by his 1st w,
  HENRY COKE, of Thorington; *m* Margaret, dau and heiress of Richard Lovelace, of Kingsdown, Kent, and had, with three yr sons:

RICHARD COKE, of Thorington; *m* Mary, dau of Sir John Rous, 1st Bt, of Henham Hall, Suffolk (*see* STRADBROKE, E), and had an only s:

ROBERT COKE, of Thorington, and later Holkham, which he inherited from his cousin John (see above); m Lady Anne Osborne, dau of 1st Duke of Leeds (see 1963 edn), and d 16 Jan 1678/9, leaving an only s:

EDWARD COKE, of Holkham; m c 1696 Cary (d 4 Aug 1707), dau of Sir John Newton, 3rd Bt, of Barr's Court, Glos, and d 13 April 1707, having had:

1 THOMAS COKE, 1st EARL OF LEICESTER, so cr 9 May 1744, as also VISCOUNT COKE OF HOLKHAM, Co Norfolk, and earlier 28 May 1728 BARON LOVEL OF MINSTER LOVEL, Co Oxford (all GB), KB (1725); b 17 June 1697; educ Turin U; MP (Whig) Norfolk 1722–28, Jt PMG 1733–March 1745 and May 1745–58 and PMG March-May 1745 and 1758–59; m 3 July 1718 Lady Margaret Tufton, 4th dau and coheir of 6th Earl of Thanet (see DE CLIFFORD), and dsps 20 April 1759, when his titles expired, having had an only s:

(1) Edward, Viscount Coke; b 2 Feb 1718/9; educ Ch Ch Oxford; MP (Whig) Norfolk 1741–47 and Harwich 1747–53; m 1 April 1747 Lady Mary Campbell (d 30 Sept 1811), dau and coheir of 2nd Duke of Argyll (qv), but dvp 1753

2 Edward, of Langford, Derbys; d unm Aug 1733

3 Robert, of Langford; V-Chamberlain to QUEEN ANNE; m 13 June 1733 Lady Jane Holt, de jure Baroness Wharton (qv) and dsp 1750

1 Cary; m 1716 Sir Marmaduke Wyvill, 6th Bt (dsp 27 Dec 1754), of Constable Burton, Yorks, and d 11 June 1734

2 Anne; m Philip Roberts, Maj 2nd Horse Gds, and had, with five yr sons and a dau:

(1) Wenman ROBERTS later COKE, of Longford, Derbys, and Holkham; m 2nd Elizabeth (d 1810), dau of George CHAMBERLAYNE later DENTON, of Hillesden, Bucks, and had:

1a THOMAS WILLIAM, 1st Earl

2a Edward, of Longford; m 1792 Grace, dau of William Colhoun, of Wrotham, Norfolk, and had issue (see VERNON, B)

1a Margaret; m 21 Dec 1760 Sir Henry Hunloke, 4th Bt (d 15 Nov 1804), and d 22 Jan 1821, leaving issue

2a Elizabeth; m 7 July 1774 1st Baron Sherborne (d 22 May 1820, see 1970 edn) and d 17 Dec 1824, leaving issue

WENMAN COKE d 11 April 1776; his er son,

THOMAS WILLIAM, 1st Earl of Leicester of Holkham, Co Norfolk, so cr 12 Aug 1837, as also VISCOUNT COKE (both UK), allegedly succumbing from sheer fatigue after seven prior offers by six different Prime Ministers to the doctrine that a peerage be conferred on the first commoner in England (which he was in point of acreage owned); b 6 May 1754; educ Eton; MP Norfolk 1776–84, 1790–1807 and 1807–32 and Derby Feb-April; an important agricultural improver; m 1st 5 Oct 1775 Jane (d 2 June 1800), sis of 1st Baron Sherborne (see 1970 edn), and had:

1 Jane Elizabeth; m 1st 21 June 1796 Charles, Viscount Andover (dsp 11 Jan 1800; see SUFFOLK and BERKSHIRE, E); m 2nd 17 April 1806 Adml Sir Henry Digby, KCB (d 19 Aug 1842), and d 29 April 1843

2 Anne Margaret; m 15 Sept 1794 1st Viscount Anson (d 31 July 1818) and d 23 May 1843, leaving issue (see LICHFIELD, E)

3 Elizabeth Wilhelmina; m 5 Dec 1822 John Spencer Stanhope (d 7 Nov 1873), of Cannon Hall, Yorks, and d 30 Oct 1873

The 1st Earl m 2nd 26 Feb 1822 Lady Anne Amelia Keppel (m 2nd 25 Oct 1843 Rt Hon Edward ('Bear') Ellice, MP, and d 22 July 1844), dau of 4th Earl of Albemarle (qv), and by her had:

1 THOMAS WILLIAM, 2nd Earl

2 Edward Keppel; Capt Scots Fus Gds, MP W Norfolk 1847–52; b 20 Aug 1824; m 5 Aug 1851 Hon Diana Agar Ellis (d 18 July 1890), sis of 2nd Viscount Clifden (see 1970 edn), and dsp 26 May 1889

3 Henry John, of Longford Hall, Brailsford, Derbys, RN; b 3 Jan 1827; m 22 July 1861 Lady Katharine Grey Egerton (d 28 Jan 1920), Woman of the Bedchamber to HM QUEEN MARY, 2nd dau of 2nd Earl of Wilton, GCH (qv), and d 12 Nov 1916, having had:

(1) Clement; Lt Scots Gds; b 26 April 1862; d unm 2 Dec 1901

(2) Reginald Grey; Lt Scots Gds, Imp Yeo S Africa 1901–02; b 10 July 1864; m 1st 2 April 1892 Elizabeth Wilson; m 2nd 21 April 1892 (divorce 1908) Phyllis Susan (d 29 March 1939), dau of Francis William Bott, of Somersall, Derbys; m 3rd 1909 Galia (d 9 Dec 1947), dau of Prof Michael Hambourg, of Clifton Gardens, W, and d 8 Feb 1930, having by her had:

1a +Henry; b 12 Aug 1912; m 8 Feb 1934 *Erica Joyce, dau of Gerald E Rattigan and gdau of Lady Rattigan, and has:

1b +Basil; patient at Netherae Hospital, Coulsdon, Surrey; b 21 Oct 1935

1a Sylvia Katharine; b 4 Jan 1910; m 1st 26 June 1936 (divorce1947) George Basil Stafford (d 6 July 1955), BSc, AIC, FGS, s of George Stafford; m 2nd 29 March 1947 Percival Rupert Christopher Wren, s of Percival Christopher Wren, and d 5 April 1969

2a *Stella [Mrs John Ryan, 43 Westminster Court, St Stephens Hill, St Albans, Herts]; b Dec 1910; m 1931 *John Michael Ryan and has issue

(1) Sybil Mary; m 15 Feb 1887 Maj-Gen Sir Charles Crutchley, KCB, KCVO, Scots Gds (d 1 Dec 1920), and d 16 Aug 1939, having had issue

4 Wenman Clarence Walpole; Lt-Col Scots Fus Gurds, MP E Norfolk 1858–65; served Crimea, Sardinian Order Valour, Kt Medjidie; b 13 July 1828; d unm 10 Jan 1907

4 Margaret Sophia; m 1 May 1849 Sir Archibald Keppel Macdonald, 3rd Bt (see BOSVILLE MACDONALD, Bt), and dsp 4 Nov 1868

The 1st EARL d 30 June 1842; his est son,

THOMAS WILLIAM COKE, 2nd Earl of Leicester of Holkham, KG (1873); Norfolk: JP, DL, Ld Lt and custos rotulorum 1846–1906, Keeper Privy Seal to HRH THE PRINCE OF WALES 1866–1901; b 26 Dec 1822; m 1st 20 April 1843 Juliana (d 21 April 1870), est dau of Samuel Charles Whitbread, of Cardington, Beds, and had, with three other sons (d young):

1 THOMAS WILLIAM, 3rd Earl

2 Wenman; Lt-Col Rifle Bde, ADC to C-in-C Army 1895–1900, served Afghanistan 1879 (medal); b 20 Nov 1855; d unm 30 May 1931

---

1 Julia; m 26 April 1864 7th Viscount Powerscourt (qv) and d 7 Aug 1931, leaving issue

2 Anne; m 16 Jan 1874 Lt-Col Edmund Manningham Buller (see DILHORNE, V) and d 23 Jan 1876, leaving issue

3 Gertrude; m 5 April 1866 7th Earl of Dunmore (qv) and d 28 Nov 1943, leaving issue

4 Mary, CBE (1920); m 18 Dec 1879 6th Earl of Dartmouth (qv) and d 28 Dec 1929, leaving issue

5 Winifred; m 2 Sept 1873 4th Earl of Leitrim (d 5 April 1892; see 1953 edn) and d 22 March 1940, leaving issue

6 Margaret; m 2 May 1874 2nd Baron Belper (qv) and d 2 Aug 1922, leaving issue

7 Mildred; m 5 Nov 1878 3rd Earl of Lichfield (qv) and d 12 May 1941, leaving issue

The 2nd Earl m 2nd 26 Aug 1875 Hon Georgina Caroline Cavendish (d 26 Feb 1937), est dau of 2nd Baron Chesham (qv), and by her had:

3 Richard, DL Norfolk; Maj Scots Gds, Boer War 1899–1902 and WW I (wounded twice); b 20 Aug 1876; educ Eton and Trin Coll Cambridge; m 1st 1 Dec 1907 (divorce1927) Hon Doreen O'Brien (d 10 June 1960), yst dau of 14th Baron Inchiquin (qv), and had:

(1) +Richard Lovel, DSO (1945), MC, ERD (1992), DL (Norfolk 1977) [Maj Richard Coke DSO MC ERD DL, Weasenham Hall, King's Lynn, Norfolk PE32 2SN]; Maj Scots Gds Italy WW II, High Sheriff Norfolk 1981; b 3 April 1918; educ Stowe and RAC Cirencester; m 28 April 1951 Molly (d 12 April 1997), yr dau of Walter Townshend Fletcher, of Dorchester, and has had:

1a +Richard Townshend, Lt Scots Gds; b 1 Feb 1954; educ Radley; m 19 Nov 1996 *Carrie-Lee, dau of Neil Early, of New York, and Mrs Lee Ashby, of Santa Monica, Calif.

2a +(Edward) Justin; b 16 April 1961; educ Gresham's and RAC Cirencester; m 1 June 1996 *Suzannah Elizabeth Olivia, only dau of Lt-Col Paul Long, OBE, of Assington Green, Suffolk, and Mrs Kerry Long, of Anmer, Norfolk

1a Diana Caroline; b 11 Jan 1953; m 9 Jan 1975 *20th Earl of Caithness (qv) and d by her own hand 8 Jan 1994, leaving issue

(1) Nell; b 8 Jan 1910; m 17 Dec 1936 as his 1st w, James Hilton Luddington, s of James Little Luddington, JP of Wallington Hall, Norfolk, and d 1 March 1960, leaving issue

(2) Moira; b 24 Aug 1911; d unm 15 Nov 1945

(3) *Hersey [Mrs Peter Marsham, Waterloo Cottage, Gayton, King's Lynn, Norfolk]; b 20 March 1915; m 18 July 1946 Lt-Col Peter William Marsham, MBE (see ROMNEY, E), and has issue

(4) *Bridget Doreen; b 24 Feb 1924; m 1st 18 Dec 1943 (divorce 1953) Capt Thomas Richard Edwards-Moss (see EDWARDS-MOSS, Bt) and has issue; m 2nd 3 June 1953 *2nd Baron Rathcavan (qv) and has further issue

3 (cont.) Maj Richard Coke m 2nd 19 July 1932 Elizabeth Vera Catherine Alice (d 1988), dau of Louis Leopold Martial Baynard de Beaumont (see O'HAGAN, B), and d 14 June 1964, having by her had:

(2) +Henry Francis [Henry Coke Esq, 4 Dormy House, Brancaster, King's Lynn, Norfolk PE31 8DT]; b 1 March 1938; educ Gresham's; m 1st 8 June 1966 (divorce 1971) (Marie Christina) Rosalind, 2nd dau of Robert Watson McCrone, of Pitliver, by Dunfermline, Fife, and has had:

1a A son; b 2 July, d 12 July 1970

1a *Nicola Katherine; b 17 Sept 1967

2a *Sarah Victoria Dayas; b 4 Sept 1971

(2) (cont.) Henry Coke m 2nd 1976 (divorce 1993) Margaret Victoria Louise, dau of Patrick Brodie, of Horley, Surrey, and by her has:

3a *Georgina Sarah Brodie; b 1979

4a *Camilla Anne Brodie; b 1980

(5) *(Mildred Jeanne) Carolyn [Mrs Carolyn Harms, 41 Christchurch Hill, London NW3 1LA]; b 26 Feb 1934; m 30 Sept 1966 (divorce 1971) David Stephen Harms, s of Donald Harms, of Rowlands Castle, Hants, and has:

1a *Hera; b 1956; m 1991 *Derek Dale Peterson, est s of Dale Gunnar Peterson, of Belleview, Florida, and has:

1b *Jacob Gunnar; b 24 Feb 1994

1b *Jaclyn Elise; b 29 May 1997

2a *Jane Mary; b 25 May 1968

(6) *Elizabeth Charmian [Mrs Richard Spickernell, Bincknoll House, Wootton Bassett, Wilts SN4 8QR]; b 18 Aug 1935; educ Bedford Coll Lond (BA 1957); m 13 Feb 1960 *Richard Francis Spickernell, only s of John Edwin Spickernell (see BOOTHBY, Bt), and has:

1a *Godfrey John Wenman; b 11 Jan 1962

2a *James William Richard; b 10 April 1965; m 1991 *Lady Rachel Barbara Violet Petty-FitzMaurice (see LANSDOWNE, M)

4 Edward, DSO, MC; Lt-Col 5th Bn Rifle Bde, Mil Attaché, Boer War 1900–02 and WW I (despatches twice, wounded twice); b 17 Oct 1879; d unm 4 Sept 1944

5 John Spencer (Hon Sir), KCVO (1953, CVO 1946); Maj Scots Gds, Boer War 1902 and WW I, Extra Gentleman Usher to HM GEORGE VI and Equerry to HM QUEEN MARY 1938–53; b 30 Sept 1880; m 15 Jan 1907 Hon Dorothy Olive (d 22 Dec 1937), only child of 1st Viscount Burnham (see BURNHAM, B), and d 23 Dec 1957, leaving:

(1) Gerald Edward, CBE (1967), JP (Hants 1952); Lt-Col Scots Gds WW II, Treas Bridewell Roy Hosp 1946–90, dir RTZ and S G Warburg, Govr BBC 1961–66; b 25 Oct 1907; educ Eton and New Coll Oxford; m 2 Sept 1939 Patricia (d 8 Aug 1995), est dau of Rt Hon Sir Alexander George Montagu Cadogan, OM, GCMG, KCB (see CADOGAN, E), and d 1990, having had:

1a +John Alexander; b 15 June 1946; educ Eton; m 1980 (divorce 1987) Karen Johnson

2a Michael Gerald; b 29 March 1949; educ Eton; d unm 1 July 1972

3a +David Edward; b 22 April 1951; educ Eton, UEA and Manchester U; m 1973 *Karen Phillips and has:

1b +Michael Alexander; b 1979

1b *Charis Hester; b 1975

1a *Lavinia Mary [Mrs Peter Wilson, Vale Court, Colerne, Chippenham, Wilts SN14 8EL]; *b* 20 Sept 1944 (HM QUEEN MARY stood sponsor); *m* 8 April 1967 *Peter Raymond Wilson, 2nd s of Raymond Clive Wilson, of The Beacon, Penn, Bucks, and has:

1b *Nicholas Peter; *b* 10 June 1971

2b *Andrew Michael; *b* 5 Sept 1974

2b *Miranda Mary; *b* 27 July 1969

(1) *Rosemary Olive; *b* 18 Nov 1910; *m* 4 March 1935 3rd Baron Hamilton of Dalzell (*qv*) and has issue

(2) Celia Dorothy; *b* 3 July 1919; *m* 30 May 1942 *Capt Stamp Godfrey Brooksbank [Capt Stamp Brooksbank, 3 N Oak Lodge, Lythe Hill Pk, Haslemere, Surrey GU27 3T7], Coldstream Gds (*m* 2nd 17 Dec 1996 *Mrs Pauline Elizabeth Harrington) (*see* BROOKSBANK, Bt), and *d* 6 June 1996, leaving issue

6 Reginald, DSO; Capt Scots Gds (SR), barrister Inner Temple 1908, served WW I (despatches), Special Commr Income Tax; *b* 10 Nov 1883; *educ* Oxford U (BA); *m* 17 July 1924 Katherine (*d* 9 Nov 1977), dau of Hon Edward Alan Dudley Ryder (*see* HARROWBY, E), and *d* 30 April 1969, leaving:

(1) *Mary Margaret [Miss Mary Coke, 76 Abercrombie St, London SW11 2JD]; *b* 25 April 1925

(2) *Katharine Vera [Mrs Peter Cator, The Barns, Condicote, Glos GL54 1ES]; *b* 27 July 1927; *m* 23 Jan 1951 *Peter John Cator, only s of Sir Geoffrey Cator, CMG (*see* MOSTYN, B), and has:

1a *Charles Henry [Charles Cator Esq, 5 Halsey St, London SW3 2QH]; *b* 1 Oct 1952; *educ* Eton and Bristol U; dep chm Christie's Europe

1a *Caroline Sarah [Mrs Piers de la Force, 8 Lindore Rd, London SW11 1HJ]; *b* 5 July 1954; *m* 1985 *Piers H de la Force, yr s of Martin de la Force, of Montevideo, and Mrs Falaise de la Force, of 3 Herbert Cres, SW1, and has:

1b *James Edward; *b* 1987

1b *Alexandra Eloise; *b* 1989

7 Lovell William; Cdr RN (emergency list), served WWs I and II; *b* 19 Aug 1893; *d* unm 18 March 1966

1 Mabel, MBE (1920); (*m* 8 Aug 1929, as his 2nd w, James Little Luddington (*d* 8 Sept 1935), of Wallington Hall, King's Lynn, est s of James Luddington, of Littleport, Cambs, and *dsp* 29 Jan 1967

The 2nd EARL *d* 24 Jan 1909; his est son,

THOMAS WILLIAM COKE, **3rd Earl of Leicester of Holkham**, GCVO, CMG, TD; ADC to TM EDWARD VII 1903–10 and GEORGE V 1910, Ld Lt and custos rotulorum Norfolk 1906–29, Pres Norfolk TAA 1908–29, Col Scots Gds and POW's Own Norfolk Artillery, Hon Col 4th Bn Norfolk Regt, Egypt 1882, Suakin 1885, Boer War 1902–05 (despatches); *b* 20 July 1848; *m* 26 Aug 1879 Hon Alice Emily White, DBE (*d* 24 April 1936), 2nd dau of 2nd Baron Annaly (*qv*), and *d* 19 Nov 1941, leaving:

1 THOMAS WILLIAM COKE, **4th Earl of Leicester of Holkham**, JP Norfolk, Ld Lt Norfolk 1944–49; *b* 9 July 1880; *educ* Eton; Maj Scots Gds, ADC Personal Staff 1917–18, Boer War 1902 and WWI, KStJ; *m* 2 Dec 1905 Marion Gertrude (*d* 23 Nov 1955), 4th dau of Col Hon Walter Rodolph Trefusis, CB (*see* CLINTON, B), and *d* 21 Aug 1949, leaving:

(1) THOMAS WILLIAM EDWARD COKE, **5th Earl of Leicester of Holkham**, MVO (4th Cl 1937), DL (Norfolk 1944); *b* 16 May 1908 (HM EDWARD VII stood sponsor); *educ* Eton and RMC Sandhurst; Maj Scots Gds, Hon Col 1st Cadet Bn Roy Norfolk Regt, Equerry to HRH THE DUKE OF YORK 1934–37, Extra Equerry to TM GEORGE VI 1937–52 and THE QUEEN 1952, WW II: ADC to C-in-C Middle East 1941, cmded 4th Bn Norfolk HG 1952–56, pres: Norfolk CLA 1958–61, Roy Norfolk Ag Assoc 1958; local dir Roy Insur Co, govr Gresham's 1967, Roy Order George I Greece 1963; *m* 1 Oct 1931 Lady Elizabeth Mary Yorke, only child of 8th Earl of Hardwicke (*qv*), and *d* 3 Sept 1976, leaving:

1a *Anne Veronica, LVO 1991 [The Rt Hon The Lady Glenconner LVO, Flat 2, 19 Holland Park, London W11; East End Farm, Burnham Thorpe, King's Lynn, Norfolk PE31 8HW; Beau Estate, Soufriere, St Lucia, WI]; *b* 16 July 1932; train bearer to HM THE QUEEN Coronation 1953, Extra Lady-in-Waiting to HRH THE PRINCESS MARGARET, COUNTESS OF SNOWDON 1971–, pres: Nat Assoc for Maternal and Child Welfare 1985, SOS 1979–83; *m* 21 April 1956 *3rd Baron Glenconner (*qv*) and has issue

2a *Carey Elizabeth [The Lady Carey Basset, Quarles, Wells-next-the-Sea, Norfolk NR23 1RY]; *b* 5 May 1934; *m* 30 April 1960 *Bryan Roland Basset, CBE, only surv s of Ronald Lambert Basset (*see* DARTMOUTH, E), and has:

1b *David Francis; *b* 21 Dec 1961

2b *Michael James; *b* 30 July 1963

3b *James Bryan; *b* 3 April 1968

3a *Sarah Marion [The Lady Sarah Walter, Westwood, Balthayock, by Perth]; *b* 23 July 1944; *m* 27 June 1970 *Maj David F W Walter, s of Reginald Walter, of Balthayock, and has:

1b *Nicholas Robert; *b* 1972

2b *James George; *b* 1975

(2) David Arthur, DFC; *b* 4 Dec 1915 (HRH THE DUKE OF WINDSOR stood sponsor); *educ* Eton and Trin Coll Cambridge (BA 1937); F/Lt RAFVR WW II 1939–41; *k* on air operations in Libya 9 Dec 1941

(1) Angela Mary; *b* 6 Nov; *d* Dec 1906

(2) *Silvia Beatrice, JP (Norfolk 1950) [The Lady Silvia Combe JP, The Manor House, Burnham Thrope, King's Lynn, Norfolk]; *b* 19 Oct 1909; *m* 15 Oct 1932 Capt Simon Harvey Combe, MC, Irish Gds (*d* 1 April 1965), 2nd s of Maj Boyce Combe, JP, of Great Holt, Farnham, Surrey, and has:

1a *Robin Harvey [Robin Combe Esq, Bayfield Hall, Holt, Norfolk]; late Lt RN; *b* 2 Jan 1934; *m* 21 Jan 1960 *Olga, dau of R J Wise, of Bridgend, Glamorgan, and has:

1b *Roger Mark Harvey; *b* 29 Dec 1960

2b *Simon Reginald [Simon Combe Esq, 4 Brandlehow Rd, London SW15 2ED]; *b* 23 Feb 1962; *m* 1992 *Elizabeth A, dau of John Knight, of Spratton, Northampton

1b *Carey Romaine; *b* 2 Dec 1964

2b *Silvia; *b* 1967

1a *Rowena Marion; *b* 9 Aug 1935; *m* 27 April 1963 (*divorce* 1983) Jocelyn Roland Rupert Geoffrey Feilding and has issue (*see* DENBIGH and DESMOND, E)

(3) Katharine Mary; Woman of the Bedchamber to HM QUEEN ELIZABETH THE QUEEN MOTHER May 1961–June 1963; *b* 7 March 1920; *m* 2 July 1940 *Maj Thomas Cockayne Harvey, CVO, DSO, Scots Gds, Priv Sec to HM THE QUEEN (now QUEEN ELIZABETH THE QUEEN MOTHER) 1946–51, Extra Gentleman Usher to TM GEORGE VI 1951 and THE QUEEN 1952, yr s of Col John Harvey, of Ringstead Bury, Norfolk, and had:

1a *David Vincent; late Scots Gds, memb London Stock Exchange; *b* 12 Sept 1941; *educ* Radley; *m* 12 April 1969 *Kathleen, yst dau of Henry Blaise, of Brussels

1a *Caroline Susan; *b* 21 Sept 1943

2a *Juliet Mary Elizabeth; *b* 27 Nov 1946; *m* 15 May 1969 *Maurizio Grana, only child of Angelo Grana, of Rome

2 Arthur George; attd RNVR, RHG, Midshipman RN; *b* 6 April 1882; *m* 10 May 1906 Phyllis Hermione, MBE (*m* 2nd 15 Oct 1925 Maj-Gen Sir Richard Granville Howard-Vyse, KCMG, DSO, DL (*d* 5 Dec 1962), of Stoke Pl, Slough, and *d* 22 Sept 1976), only dau of Francis Saxham Elwes Drury, of Pont St, SW, and was *ka* Dardanelles 22 May 1915, leaving:

(1) ANTHONY LOUIS LOVEL, **6th Earl**

(1) Diana Merial; *b* 7 Nov 1907; granted rank of earl's dau 1977; *m* 30 July 1930 (*divorce* 1938) Trevor Moorhouse (*d* 1975), only s of Maj S Moorhouse, and *d* 13 Nov 1996, leaving:

1a *Carolyn [Mrs Emil Landau, PO Box 1238, Houston Cove Lane, Damariscotta, ME 04543, USA]; *b* 1935; *m* 1961 *Emil Landau and has:

1b *Alexander James; *b* 1969

3 Roger, AFC, JP and DL Norfolk; Cdr RN, S/Ldr RAF, served WWs I (despatches) and II; *b* 28 Dec 1886; *d* unm 14 Oct 1960

1 Marjory Alice; *m* 27 April 1910 Lt-Col Sir North Victor Cecil Dalrymple-Hamilton, KCVO, CB (*see* STAIR, E) and *d* 24 Dec 1946

2 Alexandra Marie Bridget; *m* 17 July 1917 9th Earl of Airlie (*qv*) and had issue

The 5th EARL's cousin,

ANTHONY LOUIS LOVEL COKE, **6th Earl of Leicester of Holkham**; RAF WWII; *b* 11 Sept 1909; *m* 1st 11 Sept 1934 (*divorce* 1947) Moyra Joan (*d* 1987), dau of Douglas Crossley, and had:

1 EDWARD DOUGLAS COKE, **7th and present Earl of Leicester of Holkham**

2 +Wenman John [The Hon Wenman Coke, Peterstone Priory, Wells-next-the-Sea, Norfolk NR23 1RR]; *b* 24 May 1940; *educ* St Andrew's Coll Grahamstown; *m* 1969 *Carolyn Mary, er dau of D Steuart Redler, of Cape Town, and has:

(1) +Anthony Stuart; *b* 1969

(2) +Richard Oliver; *b* 1975

(1) +Rosalind Elizabeth; *b* 1971

1 *Almary Bridget [The Lady Almary Ivens-Ferraz, Splashy Fen, PO Box 186, Underberg 3257, Natal, S Africa]; *b* 18 June 1939; *educ* Rhodes U, Grahamstown; *m* 20 July 1963 *Peter Ivens-Ferraz, BA, LLB, s of Austin Ivens-Ferraz, of Transkei, and has:

(1) *Robyn Ann; *b* 30 Jan 1964

(2) *Bronwen Mary; *b* 24 May 1965

(3) *Penelope Kate; *b* 16 Feb 1967

(4) *Caitlin Tessa; *b* 1970

The **6th Earl** *m* 2nd 1947 Vera (*d* 1984), dau of Herbert William Haigh, of Durham; *m* 3rd 1985 *Elizabeth Hope Smith [The Rt Hon The Dowager Countess of Leicester, Hillhead, PO Box 544, Plettenberg Bay 6600, CP S Africa], dau of Clifford Arthur Johnstone, of Cape Province, and *d* 1994

Seat: Holkham Hall, Wells-next-the-Sea, Norfolk. The Lord Leicester responsible for Holkham was not a holder of the extant title but the 1st and last Earl of the 1744 creation. He had come into his Norfolk properties in 1707 when aged only ten but did not start building Holkham till 1735. Nevertheless he had given the subject of his new house much thought. He was studying classical architecture and the fine arts in their native habitat as early as 1712 when in Italy on the Grand Tour, carting back to England many of the more portable pieces such as statuary or pictures. And in East Anglia itself he had begun sheltering the site of his intended mansion from the harsh North Sea winds by planting trees from 1720 on. Yet there was delay both in starting and completing the actual construction. Indeed the latter was only accomplished five years after Leicester's death in 1759. This is due partly to the effort being a collaborative one. Leicester himself was a highly active patron: he insisted on approving, and sometimes amending, each detail of the plans. Then there was the active participation of a fellow Whig nobleman, the Earl of Burlington (*see* CORK and ORRERY, E). In fact William Kent, the official architect, who had met Leicester in Italy through Burlington, was only one of four knowledgeable intelligences involved, the last being Matthew Brettingham, who first assisted Kent then took over as superintending architect after the latter's death in 1748.

The principal material, a dun brick, is unlovely, but was deliberately chosen as the nearest simulacrum manageable locally to that used by Andrea Palladio for so many of his villas in the hinterland of Venice (though it is worth noting that Palladio had intended a number of them to be of stone). Even in Italy such dwellings were only used in high summer and Holkham's sheer monumental grandeur, hardly cosy at the best of times, is made doubly forbidding by the vast flatness of the Norfolk landscape and the over-ventilated coastal location. If the upper classes had a hard time of it at Holkham, the lower ones were not let off lightly either: the cramped nature of the servants' quarters meant footmen were obliged to sleep four to a bed. Even the famous Marble Hall (something of a misnomer since the ionic pillars are alabaster), though an effective shelter from the elements, has a chill atmosphere. It tends nowadays to be likened to a pagan temple and certainly the pillars and frieze are copied from the Temple of Fortuna Virilis in Rome. But there are still those who, more profanely, compare it to a waterless public bath, as the 18th-century agriculturalist and social and political writer Arthur Young seems to have been the first to do.

But to expect a sybaritic atmosphere in the main part of Holkham is to misunderstand Lord Leicester's purpose. The principal rooms were for state occasions. These comprised the Dining Room, Sculpture Gallery (based on the one at Chiswick House, Lord Burlington's unassisted creation, only larger), the Saloon, Landscape Room (so-called because of its marvellous Claude and Poussin scenic paintings) and the Great Apartment, a suite in itself. It was the four wings that were to be for everyday use. One was for the immediate family (though even here the Library, for instance, is among the most exquisite rooms in the whole house), another for guests, a third for culinary purposes and the fourth, the private chapel, for spiritual ones.

Holkham's durability is beyond doubt. As recently as the late 1980s virtually nothing either in the essential fabric or the interior embellishments such as gilding and velvet wall paper had had to be renovated since the mid-18th century, the dry climate of northeast Norfolk perhaps helping as preservative. What has helped even more is the good sense of subsequent Lords Leicester in knowing well when to leave alone (other than the north portico and orangery, the contribution of the 2nd Earl).

LEIGH, Baron

Arms: Gu. a cross engrailed arg., in the first quarter a lozenge of the second. **Crest:** A unicorn's head, erased arg., armed and crined or. **Supporters:** On either side a unicorn, armed, maned, tufted and unguled or, gorged with a ducal coronet gu., pendant therefrom an escutcheon charged with the arms of BRYDGES (arg. a cross sa., thereon a leopard's face or). **Motto:** *Tout vient de Dieu* ('All comes from God'). **Creation:** B. (UK) 11 May 1839.

THE 5TH BARON LEIGH OF STONELEIGH, Co Warwick (John Piers Leigh) [The Rt Hon The Lord Leigh, House of Lords, London SW1A 0PW]; *b* 11 Sept 1935; *s f* 1979; *educ* Eton, Oriel Coll Oxford and London U; *m* 1st 27 April 1957 (*divorce* 1974) Cecilia Poppy, yst dau of Robert Cecil Jackson, of Redlynch, Wilts, and Mrs Balch, and has had:

1 +CHRISTOPHER DUDLEY PIERS [The Hon Christopher Leigh, Fern Farm, Adlestrop, Moreton-in-Marsh, Glos GL56 0YL]; *b* 20 Oct 1960; *educ* Eton and RAC Cirencester; *m* 1990 *Sophy-Ann, dau of Richard Burrows, of The Old Hall, Groby, Leics, and has:

  (1) +Rupert Dudley; *b* 21 Feb 1994
  (1) *Lucy Alexandra; *b* 2 Nov 1995
1 Jane Katherine; *b* 20 and *d* 22 Jan 1959
2 *Camilla Anne; *b* 2 Aug 1962

The 5th BARON *m* 2nd 1976 (*divorce* 1982) Susan, yst dau of John Reginald Cleave, of Whitnash, Leamington Spa, and by her has:

2 +Piers Henry John; *b* 20 March 1979; *educ* Eton

The 5th BARON *m* 3rd 1982 *Lea, only dau of Col Harry Noël Havelock Wild, OBE, and formerly w of Lt-Col Brian Gustavus Hamilton-Russell (see BOYNE, V)

Lineage: HAMON de LEIGH; held half the Manor of High Leigh, Cheshire *temp* HENRY II (see also GREY, B); ggf of:

RICHARD de LEIGH, of High Leigh; had:

AGNES; *m* 1st Richard de Lymm and had a s (Thomas, took mother's name); *m* 2nd William de Hawardyn; *m* 3rd William Venables and by him had:

JOHN LEIGH (took mother's name), of Booths, Cheshire; *m* 1st Ellen, dau of Richard Dent, of Cheshire, and had a s (John, ancestor of the LEIGHs of Booths); *m* 2nd Ellen, dau of Thomas Corona, of Adlington, and had:

ROBERT LEIGH, of Adlington; *m* 1st by 1330 Sybil, dau of Henry de Honford or Hanford, of Hanford, Cheshire, and had a s (Robert, ancestor of the LEIGHs of Adlington); *m* 2nd Maud, dau and heiress of Adam de Norley, and by her had:

Sir PIERS LEIGH, of Lymm, Cheshire; bore the Black Prince's standard Battle of Crécy 1346, where he captured the Count de Tancarville; *m* 1388 Margaret, widow of Sir John Savage, of Clifton, Kent, and dau and heiress of Sir Thomas Dammery, of Bradley, a leading participant at Crécy, and was executed at Chester 1399 as a supporter of the deposed RICHARD II, leaving, with an er s (Peter (Sir), KB, *k* Battle of Agincourt 24 Oct 1415, ancestor of the LEIGHs of Lymm):

JOHN LEIGH; *m* Alice, dau and heir of John Alcock, of Ridge, who brought him the Manor of Ridge, and had, with another s (Roger, ancestor of the LEIGHs of Ridge):

RICHARD LEIGH, of Rushall; had:

ROGER LEIGH, of Rushall and Wellington, Salop; had, with an er s (William, ancestor of the LEIGHs of Rushall):

Sir THOMAS LEIGH, JP (Salop 1536); *b c* 1504; merchant of the Staple (a restrictive trade group dealing in wool); Mercers' Co: Freeman 1526, Warden 1544 and 1552, Master 1554, 1558 and 1564; City of London: Alderman 1552, Sheriff 1555, Ld Mayor 1558, ktd 1558, memb Merchant Adventurers' Co; *m* by 13 March 1536 Alice (*d* 1603), dau and heiress of John Barker *alias* Coverall or Coverdale, of Wolverton, Salop, and n and pncpl heir of Sir Rowland Hill, a rich Alderman (who had bought the former Cistercian religious house of Stoneleigh Abbey, Warwicks, from the executors of Charles Brandon, Duke of Suffolk, to whom it had been granted shortly after the Dissolution of the Monasteries 1538; the LEIGHs lived at Stoneleigh, which was added to *c* 1600 and hugely enlarged and remodelled to Francis Smith's designs 1714–26, till 1993), and *d* 17 Nov 1571, leaving:

1 Rowland, of Adlestrop, Glos, and Longborough, Warwicks; *m* 1st Margery, dau of Thomas Lowe, of London, and had a dau (Elizabeth, *m* 1st — Hanmer and 2nd — Broughton); *m* 2nd Catherine, dau of Sir Richard Berkeley, of Stoke Giffard, Glos, and *d* in or after 1596, having by her had, with two daus, an only surv s:

(1) William, of Adlestrop and Longborough; *b c* 1586; *m* Elizabeth, dau of Sir William Whorwood, of Sandwell Castle, Staffs, and *d* 1632, leaving:

1a William, of Adlestrop and Longborough; *m* Joanna, dau of Thomas Pury, and *d* 17 June 1690, leaving, with three er sons (*d* young):

1b Theophilus, of Adlestrop and Longborough; *m* 1st Elizabeth, dau and sole heiress of Sir William Craven, of Lenchwick, Worcs, and had issue (*d* young or unm); *m* 2nd 1689 Mary Brydges (*d* 13 June 1703), dau of 8th Baron Chandos of Sudeley (see CHANDOS, V, preliminary remarks, also TEMPLE OF STOWE, E), and *d* 10 Feb 1724/5, having by her had, with five yr sons and two other daus:

1c William, of Adlestrop and Longborough; *b* 3 Nov 1691; *m* Mary (*d* 10 July 1756), dau of Robert Lord, of York Buildings, and *d* 9 Dec 1757, having had, with other issue:

1d James, of Adlestrop and Longborough; *bapt* 7 July 1724; *m* 10 March 1755 Lady Caroline Brydges, est dau of 2nd Duke of Chandos (see TEMPLE OF STOWE, E) by his 1st w Mary (see KINLOSS, L), and *d* 31 March 1774, leaving:

1e James Henry, of Adlestrop and Longborough, and later of Stoneleigh (which he inherited on the death of the 5th and last BARON LEIGH OF STONELEIGH's sis Mary 2 July 1806; see below); *b* 8 Feb 1765; *m* 8 Dec 1786 Julia Judith (*d* 8 Feb 1843), est dau of 7th Baron Saye and Sele (*qv*), and had:

1f CHANDOS, **1st Baron**

1f Julia; *m* 1836 Gen Henry Robert Colvile, DL (*d* 1 Nov 1875), of Kempsey Ho, Worcester, and *dsp* 21 Jan 1871

2f Caroline Eliza; *m* 27 June 1822 Sir James Buller East, 2nd Bt, MP (see 1878 edn), and *dsp* 7 April 1870

3f Mary; *m* 2 July 1817 Frederick Charles Acton Colvile (*d* 2 Feb 1872), Capt 3rd Foot Gds, of Barton Ho, Warwicks, and *d* 6 June 1871, leaving issue

4f Augusta Elizabeth; *m* 15 May 1827 Grenville Charles Lennox Berkeley (see BERKELEY, B) and *d* 4 May 1877, leaving issue

1d Cassandra; *m* 8 Sept 1739 Sir Edward Turner, 2nd Bt (see PAGE-TURNER, Bt), and *d* 18 Oct 1770, having had issue

1c Emma; *m* Peter Waldo, DD

2c Cassandra; *m* Thomas Wright

3c Maria; *m* Sir Hungerford Hoskyns, 4th Bt (*qv*)

4c Anne; *m* her next er sister's bro-in-law Rev John HOSKYNS later HOSKYNS-ABRAHALL, Bt) and had issue

2 Sir THOMAS LEIGH, 1st Bt (E), so *cr* 29 June 1611, of Stoneleigh; Sheriff Warwicks 1581–82, ktd by 1595; *m c* 1570 Katharine (*d* 1639), 4th dau of Sir John Spencer (see MARLBOROUGH, D), and *d* 1 Feb 1625/6, having had, with other issue:

(1) John (Sir); *m* 1st Ursula, dau of Sir Christopher Hoddesdon, of Leighton Buzzard, Beds; *m* 2nd Anna, dau of Sir Anthony Cope, Bt, of Hanwell, Oxon (see 1970 edn), and *dvp* having by her had a s (John) and by his 1st w:

1a Sir THOMAS LEIGH, 2nd Bt, and 1st BARON LEIGH OF STONELEIGH, Co Warwick (E), so *cr* 1 July 1643, JP (Warwicks); *b* 1595; *educ* Magdalen Coll Oxford; MP Warwicks 1628–29, High Sheriff Warwicks 1636–37; royalist Civil War (played host to CHARLES I at Stoneleigh after Coventry had denied him entry), hence fined £4,895 (over £166,000 in late–1990s terms); *m* 11 Nov 1610 Mary, dau and coheiress of Sir Thomas Egerton (see GREY EGERTON, Bt), and *d* 22 Feb 1671, having had, with other issue:

1b Thomas; *b c* 1616; *educ* Cambridge; royalist Civil War, MP Staffs 1661–62; *m* 1st allegedly Anne, dau of Richard Bingham, of Lambeth, and had a dau (Jane, *m* 2nd Jane, dau of 17th Baron of Kerry and Lixnaw (see LANSDOWNE, M), and *dvp* 1662, leaving by her, with other issue:

1c THOMAS LEIGH, 2nd BARON LEIGH OF STONELEIGH; *bapt* 17 June 1652; *educ* Ch Ch Oxford; *m* 1st April 1669 Elizabeth (*dsp* July 1678), dau of Richard Brown, of Shingleton in Chart, Kent; *m* 2nd 25 Oct 1679 Eleanor Watson, est dau of 2nd Baron Rockingham, and *d* 12 Nov 1710, having by her had, with other issue (including Eleanor, *m* Hon Thomas Verney; see WILLOUGHBY DE BROKE, B):

1d EDWARD LEIGH, 3rd BARON LEIGH OF STONELEIGH; *b* 13 Jan 1683/4; *educ* Balliol Coll Oxford; *m* 11 Sept 1705 Mary, dau of Thomas Holbech, of Fillongley, Warwicks, and *d* 9 March 1737/8, leaving, with other issue:

1e THOMAS LEIGH, 4th BARON LEIGH OF STONELEIGH; *bapt* 29 April 1713; *educ* Balliol Coll Oxford; *m* 1st *c* 1736 Maria Rebecca, sis of 5th Baron Craven of Hampstead Marshall (see CRAVEN, E), and had, with three other sons (*d* young) and several daus (*d* unm):

1f EDWARD LEIGH, 5th and last BARON LEIGH OF STONELEIGH; b 1 March 1742; educ Oriel Coll Oxford; High Steward Oxford U 1767–86; d unm 4 June 1786, having been certified insane since 1774, when his titles expired

1e (cont.) The 4th BARON m 2nd Dec 1747 Catherine, dau of Rowland BERKELEY formerly GREEN, of Cotheridge, Worcs, and d 30 Nov 1749, leaving by her:

    1f Anne; m Andrew Hacket

2c Charles; m 1st Anne, dau of Sir Edward Littleton, of Pillaton, Staffs (see HATHERTON, B) and widow of Sir Thomas Holt (e), 1st Bt; m 2nd — and had by his 1st w:

    1d Alicia; b c 1661; m 3 Sept 1678, as his 1st w, 1st Baron Altham (see VALENTIA, V)

    1c Honora; bapt 17 May 1649; m 1st Sir William Egerton, KB (see GREY EGERTON, Bt), and had issue; m 2nd c 5 Oct 1692 3rd Baron Willoughby of Parham (see WILLOUGHBY DE ERESBY, B) and d 11 Sept 1730

    2c Jane; m 4th Baron and Viscount Tracy of Rathcoole (see SUDELEY, B)

1b Elizabeth; m 3rd Baron and Viscount Tracy of Rathcoole and had issue (see SUDELEY, B)

2b Vere; m Sir Justinian Isham, 2nd Bt (qv), and had issue

(1) ALICE Leigh, DUCHESS DUDLEY [sic] (E), so cr 23 May 1644 for life; b c 1579; m by 25 Sept 1597, as his 2nd w of three (the last, however, he married bigamously), Sir Robert Dudley (went through a form of marriage by 27 Jan 1606/7 with his cousin Elizabeth, dau of Sir Robert Southwell, of Woodrising, Norfolk, and d 6 Sept 1649, leaving by her issue), s (almost certainly illegitimate) of Robert Dudley, 1st and last Earl of Leicester of the 1564 cr (see LEICESTER, E, preliminary remarks); a doctor, engineer, gun-dog trainer, mathematician, naval architect and navigator; Sir Robert failed to establish his legitimacy in England and settled in Tuscany, the EMPEROR FERDINAND II purporting to recognise his claim to the title 'Duke of Northumberland' 9 March 1620 (see NORTHUMBERLAND, D, preliminary remarks); she dspm 22 Jan 1668/9, when her title expired

3 William (Sir), of Newnham Regis, Warwicks, ancestor of the Leigh Earls of Chichester (see GREY EGERTON, Bt)

1 Mary; m 1st Robert Andrews, of London; m 2nd — Cobb

2 Alice; m Thomas Connye, of Lincs

3 Katherine; m Edward Barber, of Somerset, Serjeant-at-law

4 Winifred; m Sir George Bond, Ld Mayor London

JAMES HENRY LEIGH d 27 Oct 1823; his only son,

CHANDOS LEIGH, 1st Baron Leigh of Stoneleigh, Co Warwick (UK), so cr 11 May 1839; b 27 June 1791; educ Ch Ch Oxford; High Sheriff Warwicks 1825–26; m 8 June 1819 Margarette (d 5 Feb 1860), est dau of Rev William Shippen Willes, of Astrop Ho, Northants, and had:

1 WILLIAM HENRY, 2nd Baron

2 Edward Chandos (Sir), KCB, KC,JP Warwicks; educ Oriel Coll Oxford; Fell All Souls, Bencher Inner Temple, Recorder Nottingham 1881–1909, Counsel to Speaker H of C 1883–1907; b 22 Dec 1832; m 1 June 1871 Katherine Fanny (d 3 Aug 1920), est dau of James Rigby, DL, of Moss Ho, Lancs, and d 18 May 1915, having had:

    (1) Chandos, DSO; Maj KOSB, attd Egyptian Army, Boer War 1899–1900, WW I, 3rd Cl Medjidie, 4th Cl Osmanieh; b 29 Aug 1873; m 6 June 1912 Winifred Madeline (m 2nd 7 Oct 1925 Sir Christopher Boyd William Magnay, 3rd and last Bt, MC (d 4 Sept 1960), and d 28 Sept 1966), est dau of Arthur Frederick Jeffreys (see JEFFREYS, B), and was ka 25 Aug 1914

    (2) Edward Henry; Lt Rifle Bde; b 14 July 1888; ka 9 May 1915

    (1) Violet Agnes Evelyn; b 7 Feb 1875; m 26 Oct 1899 Sir Bertram Hardy, 3rd Bt (qv), and had issue

    (2) Katherine Margaret; b 8 June 1877; d 30 Oct 1887

    (3) Audrey Cecilia; b 20 Oct 1880; d 18 Sept 1923

3 James Wentworth (Very Rev); DD Cantab, FSA, Dean Hereford 1894–1919, Rector St Mary's Bryanston Sq; b 21 Jan 1838; m 29 June 1871 Frances (d 18 Dec 1910), dau of Pierce Butler (see BUTLER, Bt, of Cloughgregnan), and d 5 Jan 1923, having had:

    (1) Pierce Butler; b 2 Nov 1879; d 25 Sept 1880

    (1) Alice Dudley; b 2 July 1874; m 2 June 1906 Sir Richard Pierce Butler, 11th B, of Cloughgrenan (qv), and d 13 July 1965, leaving issue

    (2) Frances; d an infant, 14 May 1878

1 Julia Anna Eliza; m 28 July 1842 1st Baron Norton (qv) and d 8 May 1887, leaving issue

2 Emma Margarette; d 20 Feb 1892

3 Caroline; m 18 Aug 1857 10th Baron Saye and Sele (qv) and d 21 July 1909, having had issue

4 Augusta (twin with Caroline); d 11 July 1898

5 Mary; m 4 May 1848 Rev and Hon Henry Pitt Cholmondeley, bro of 2nd Baron Delamere (qv), and d 24 Aug 1906, leaving issue

6 Louisa Georgina; m 1 March 1870 Lt-Col Francis William Newdigate, Coldstream Gds (d 9 March 1893), of Allesley Pk, Warwicks, and dsp 7 Aug 1907

7 Sophia (twin with James Wentworth); LGStJ; m 21 May 1861 Granville William Gresham Leveson Gower (see SUTHERLAND, D) and d 12 July 1926, having had issue

The 1st BARON d 27 Sept 1850; his est son,

WILLIAM HENRY LEIGH, 2nd Baron Leigh of Stoneleigh, PC (1895), JP Glos; b 17 Jan 1824; educ Harrow and Trin Coll Cambridge; fought N Warwicks as Free Trader 1895; High Steward Sutton Coldfield 1859–92 and 1902–05; Govr and Tstee Rugby Sch; Col 3rd Bn Warwicks Regt, Ld Lt Warwicks 1856–1905, Hon LLD Cantab; m 22 Aug 1848 Caroline Amelia (d 24 March 1906), dau of 2nd Marquess of Westminster (see WESTMINSTER, D), and d 21 Oct 1905, having had:

    1 Gilbert Henry Chandos, JP, DL; b 1 Sept 1851; educ Harrow and Magdalene Coll Cambridge; MP S Warwicks; d unm 15 Sept 1884

2 FRANCIS DUDLEY LEIGH, 3rd Baron Leigh of Stoneleigh, TD, JP (Warwicks); b 30 July 1855; educ Harrow and Trin Coll Cambridge; Assist Sec to Sec State India 1886–91, memb LCC for St George's Hanover Sq 1904–07, Hon Col 7th Bn Roy Warwicks Regt, Col Warwicks Vol Regt, Maj and Hon Col Warwicks Yeo, WW I, Ld Lt Warwicks, Tstee and Govr Rugby Sch; m 1st 29 Nov 1890 Frances Helen Forbes (dsp 28 April 1909), dau of Hon N M Beckwith, of New York; m 2nd 2 Oct 1923 Marie (d 13 March 1949), dau of Alexander Campbell, of New York, and dsp 16 May 1938

3 Rupert; b 10 Dec 1856; Maj 4th Dragoon Gds (formerly 15th Hus), staff employment under War Office 1915–16, Afghan War 1878–79 (medal), Egypt 1882 (medal with clasp, bronze star), Bechuanaland FF 1884–85, ADC to Govr NSW 1890–94, NWF India 1897 (medal with two clasps), Mil Sec to Govr Bombay 1900; m 14 July 1906 Beatrice Mary (d 12 Dec 1922), dau of Dudley Robert Smith, of 47 Belgrave Sq, SW, and d 14 Aug 1919, leaving:

    (1) RUPERT WILLIAM DUDLEY, 4th Baron

4 Rowland Charles Frederick; barrister, MA Cantab; b 23 May 1859; m 31 Oct 1898 Mabel (d 5 Nov 1951), dau of Gen William Washington Gordon, US Army, of Savannah, Ga., and d 26 Jan 1943, leaving:

    (1) Rowland Henry Gordon; b 16 May 1902; m 17 Nov 1937 (divorce 1943) Catherine, dau of Count Pierre de Bernard de la Fosse, of Château de Beaumont, Loir et Cher, France, and dsp 8 Oct 1963

    (1) Margaret Ethel (Jane Gordon, authoress); b 24 Jan 1901; m 17 Dec 1929 Charles Patrick Ranke Graves (d 21 Feb 1971), author, 5th s of Alfred Perceval Graves, and d 29 Aug 1962

1 Margaret Elizabeth, DBE, JP London; Govr Charterhouse; b 29 Oct 1849; m 19 Sept 1873 7th Earl of Jersey (qv) and d 22 May 1945, leaving issue

2 Agnes Eleanor; b 24 May 1853; d unm 29 March 1942

3 Mary Cordelia Emily; b 3 July 1866; d unm 27 Feb 1956

The 3rd BARON's nephew,

RUPERT WILLIAM DUDLEY LEIGH, 4th Baron Leigh of Stoneleigh, TD, JP (Warwicks 1962), DL (1946); b 14 March 1908; educ Eton and RMC Sandhurst; Lt-Col Roy Glos Hus, Lt 11th Hus, High Steward Sutton Coldfield, owner and trainer of racehorses, memb Nat Hunt Ctee; m 27 April 1931 Anne (d 1977), 2nd dau of Ellis Hicks Beach (see SAINT ALDWYN, E), and d 24 June 1979, having had:

1 JOHN PIERS LEIGH, 5th and present Baron Leigh of Stoneleigh

2 +William Rupert [The Hon William Leigh, Ranaghan, Collooney, Co Sligo, Ireland], late Lt 11th Hus (PAO); b 13 Sept 1938; educ Eton and RMA Sandhurst; m 20 May 1965 *Priscilla Elizabeth, yr dau of Lt-Cdr Edward Francis Patrick Cooper, RN, of Markree Castle, Co Sligo, and has had:

    (1) +James Rupert; b 15 Feb 1967

    (2) +Edward William; b 1968

    (3) Richard Thomas; b 1974; d 1978

    (4) +Francis Dudley; b 1982

3 +Benjamin Chandos [The Hon Benjamin Leigh, Little Rissington House, Little Rissington, Glos GL54 2NB]; late 11th Hus (PAO), amateur jockey; b 24 Oct 1942; educ Eton; m 1 Aug 1979 *Jennifer Vivian, dau of Capt Peter Winser and formerly w of Hon Richard Henry Strutt (see BELPER, B), and has:

    (1) *Samantha Jane Hazel; b 1980

4 +Michael James; b 27 March 1945; educ Eton and Keble Coll Oxford; m 12 May 1972 (divorce 1980) Cherry Rosalind (m 2nd 23 Jan 1987 Christopher Stewart Moorsom, see also LINDSEY and ABINGDON, E), dau of David Long-Price

LEIGH, Bt

Arms: Argent on a cross engrailed quadrant gules a garb or between in chief two roses of the second, barbed and seeded proper.
Crest: A cubit arm, vested gules, cuffed argent, grasping a staff in bend sinister proper, pendant therefrom a banner of the second, charged with a cross couped of the first. **Motto:** Fides servand est ('Faith must be kept'). **Creation:** Bt. (UK) 9 Feb 1918.

SIR RICHARD HENRY LEIGH, 3RD BT, of Altrincham, Co Chester [Sir Richard Leigh Bt, Trythall Vean, Maldron, Penzance, Cornwall TR20 8SY]; b 11 Nov 1936; s unc 1992; educ Aiglon Coll Switzerland; m 1st 4 Dec 1962 (divorce 1977)

Barbro Anna Elizabeth, er dau of Stig Carl Sebastian Tham and Baroness Ebba Tham, of Rydboholm, Rydbo, Sweden; *m* 2nd 1977 *Cherie Rosalind, er dau of Douglas Donald Dale, of La Blanchie, Cherval, France, and widow of Alan Reece, RMS

Lineage: JOHN LEIGH, JP, of Woodbourne, Brooklands, Cheshire; had:

Sir John Leigh, 1st Bt (UK), so *cr* 9 Feb 1918, JP (Lancs); *b* 3 Aug 1884; *educ* Manchester GS; MP (C) Clapham 1922–45, Tstee Manchester Acad Fine Arts, proprietor *The Pall Mall Gazette* (before amalgamation with *Evening Standard*), funded offrs' hosp in WW I, fndr/chm Canadian Offrs' Club; *m* 23 Jan 1908 Norah Marjorie, CBE (1920) (*d* 13 Jan 1954), dau of John Henry New, of Melbourne, Australia, and *d* 29 July 1959, leaving:

1 **Sir John Leigh, 2nd Bt**; *b* 24 March 1909; *educ* Eton and Balliol Coll Oxford (MA 1935); RAF WW II India 1943–46; *m* 29 Sept 1959 Ariane, yst dau of Joseph William Allen, of Beverley Hills, California, and widow of Harold Wallace Ross, of New York, and *dsp* 1992

2 Eric; *b* 13 April 1913; *educ* Radley; Lt-Cdr RNVR WW II; *m* 1st 21 Nov 1934 (*divorce* 1939) Joan Fitzgerald Lane, er dau of Maurice Charles Lane Freer, of Kenya, and had:

  (1) **Sir RICHARD HENRY LEIGH, 3rd and present Bt**

2 (cont.) Lt-Cdr Eric Leigh *m* 2nd 14 Dec 1939 Mary Babette (*d* 18 Jan 1993), formerly w of Basil Butcher and est dau of Joseph Hodgson Jacques and Mrs John Clervaux Chaytor, of The West House, Thirsk, Yorks, and by her had:

  (2) +CHRISTOPHER JOHN [Christopher Leigh Esq, The Spinney, Wendens Ambo, Essex CB11 4UL]; *b* 6 April 1941; heir presumptive; *educ* Radley; *m* 5 Oct 1963 *Gillian Ismay, only dau of William King Lowe, of The Bell House, Guiting Power, Glos, and has:

    1a *Edward John; *b* 1 April 1970; *educ* Bishops Stortford Coll

    1a *Caroline Nicola [Mrs James Lewis, Cucumber Hall, Burnt House Rd, Great Tey, Colchester, Essex]; *b* 12 Sept 1967; *m* July 1991 *James Robert Lewis, s of Ian Lewis, and has:

      1b *Oliver James; *b* 19 April 1995

      2b *Thomas Patrick; *b* 11 Dec 1997

      1b *Georgia Louise; *b* 19 Nov 1993

  (1) *Victoria Anne; *b* 19 Sept 1945; *educ* St James's Malvern; *m* 10 Feb 1967 *Capt Jasper Rodney Archer, 4th/7th Roy Dragoon Gds, er s of Lt-Col Rodney Archer, MC, of Millfield, Haslemere, Surrey, and has:

    1a *Nicholas Jasper; *b* 30 Jan 1971

    1a *Sophie Louise; *b* 1973

3 +David [David Leigh Esq, High Coombe, Coombe Hill, Bruton, Somerset BA10 0QA]; *b* 6 Feb 1921; *educ* Eton and New Coll Oxford (MA 1946); BM, BCh; *m* 23 Aug 1945 *Rosemary Eleanor, only dau of William Henry Wyburn-Mason, of Clytha Park, Newport, Mon, and has:

  (1) +Peregrine William Roger Wyburn; *b* 1 June 1955; *educ* Eton, Exeter U (BA) and RAC Cirencester (Dip Surv); *m* 1992 *Laura Dawn, dau of Col Vincent Warwick Calmady-Hamlyn, of Leawood, Bridestowe, Devon, and has:

    1a +Ranald Geoffrey Merlin; *b* 1992

    1a *India Frances Larissa; *b* 8 Dec 1994

  (1) *Eleanor Elizabeth Corinna Wyburn; *b* 19 May 1951; *educ* Westonbirt; *m* 1992 *Col Keith George Turner, MBE, s of Maj Herbert George Turner

1 *Marjorie Joan; *m* 21 July 1939 Maj William Frederick Bovill, OBE, JP, 5th Roy Inniskilling Dragoon Gds, only s of Frederick William Bovill, of Sondes House, Bekesbourne, Canterbury, and has:

  (1) *Bristow Charles; *b* 24 Sept 1940; *educ* Harrow; Capt 5th Roy Inniskillin Dragoon Gds; *m* 11 June 1968 *Kerry Anne, est dau of Sydney Beresford Reynolds, of Morrlands, Rosalie Plains, Toowoomba, Qld, and has:

    1a *Skye Laurette; *b* 5 Sept 1969; *m* 1993 *Earl of Hopetoun (*see* LINLITHGOW, M) and has issue

  (2) *Miles William; *b* 6 Nov 1945; *educ* Harrow

  (3) *Rex Anthony; *b* 12 Feb 1948; *educ* Nautical Coll Pangbourne

LEIGHTON

Arms: Quarterly per fess indented or and gu. **Crest:** A wyvern, wings expanded sa. **Motto:** Dread shame.
Creation: Bt. (E) 2 March 1692/3.

SIR MICHAEL JOHN BRYAN LEIGHTON, 11TH BT, of Wattlesborough, Shropshire [Sir Michael Leighton Bt, Loton Park, Salop SY5 9AJ]; *b* 8 March 1935; *s* f 1957; *educ* Stowe, Tabley Ho Ag Sch and RAC Cirencester; *m* 1st July 1974 (*divorce* 1980) Mrs Amber Mary Ritchie; *m* 2nd 1991 *Mrs Diana Mary Gamble and by her has:

  1 *Eleanor Angharad Diana; *b* 1992

Lineage: TIHEL de LATHUNE; living 1155–66; had:

RICHARD Fitz TIHEL; held the Manor of Leighton, Salop, as a kt's fee in the feudal Barony (territorial) of FitzAlan; had:

Sir RICHARD, to whom William Fitz Alan confirmed Leighton and the advowson of the church there *c* 1200; living 1203; had:

RICHARD; Verderer Salop, a Justice at Shrewsbury 1241; had:

WILLIAM; Constable Oswestry 1256; had:

RICHARD de LEIGHTON; Constable Oswestry; of age by 1284; asserted his right to make a park at Leighton 1300; had:

Sir RICHARD de LEIGHTON; MP Salop 1312–19, Commr of Array Salop; summoned 1324 to attend a council at Westminster; f or gf of:

RICHARD de LEIGHTON; MP Salop 1339; had:

JOHN de LEIGHTON; of age by 1346; living 1359; had:

JOHN LEIGHTON; *m* Margaret, dau of Sir John Drake, and had:

JOHN LEIGHTON; *m* 1383 Ellen, dau and heiress of Watkyn Cambray, of Stretton-in-le-Dale, Salop, who brought the LEIGHTONs an estate and manor-house at Church Stretton which was the family residence for some generations, and *d* 1428, leaving:

EDWARD LEIGHTON, of Stretton-in-le-Dale; *m* Elizabeth, dau and coheir of Sir John Stapleton, of Stapleton, Salop, and *d* 1455, leaving, with other issue (including a 2nd s Edward, ancestor of the LEIGHTONs of Cotes), an est s:

JOHN LEIGHTON, of Stretton-in-le-Dale; MP Salop 1460, thrice Sheriff Salop, Constable Oswestry Castle; Steward Montgomery Castle for Richard, Duke of York, but switched to HENRY VII before Bosworth; acquired Manors of Cardeston, Loton and Wattlesborough, Salop; *m* Ankaret, dau and coheir of Sir John Burgh, of Wattlesborough, feudal Ld of Dinas Mawddwy, Merioneths, by Jane, dau and heiress of Sir William Clopton, of Radbroke, Glos, thus acquiring also the feudal Ldship of Bausley, Montgomeryshire, and *d* 1493, leaving, with two yr sons (Cuthbert, Kt of Rhodes and St John, *dsp*; William, *m* Margery, dau and coheir of Sir Fulk Sprencheaux, of Plash, Salop, and was ancestor of the extinct LEIGHTONs of Plash) and a dau (Elizabeth, *m* William Lyster, of Rowton):

Sir THOMAS LEIGHTON; *b* 1454; Salop: Sheriff 1495 and MP; memb Ct of Marches of Wales, Kt of the Body to HENRY VII; served in the hostilities between Brittany (supported by HENRY VII) and France; ktd following Battle of Tournai 1513; *m* Elizabeth, dau of 1st Lord (Baron) Ferrers (of Chartley) (*see* HEREFORD, V) and widow of Sir Richard Corbet, of Moreton Corbet (*see* 1970 edn CORBET, Bt), and had:

JOHN LEIGHTON; Esq of the Body to HENRY VIII, MP Salop; *m* 1st Matilda (*dsp*), dau and coheir of John Harewell; *m* 2nd Joyce, dau of 2nd Lord (Baron) Dudley (*qv*), and *d* 1532, leaving with other issue, including a yr s (Thomas (Sir), Govr Jersey, MP Worcs, granted by ELIZABETH I the Manor of Feckenham, Worcs (confiscated from the Throgmortons), member Court Marches of Wales, *m* Elizabeth, dau of Sir Francis Knollys (*see* KNOLLYS, V), *dsp*):

Sir EDWARD LEIGHTON; Salop: MP 1563, twice Sheriff, custos rotulorum; twice Sheriff Montgomeryshire, memb Ct Marches of Wales; *m* Anne, dau of Paul Darrell, of Lillingstone Darrell, Bucks, and *d* 1593, leaving:

THOMAS LEIGHTON; MP Salop 1597, Capt Salop trained bands; *m* Elizabeth, dau of Sir William Gerrard, Ld Chllr Ireland, and *d* 1600, leaving:

ROBERT LEIGHTON; *m* Anne, dau of Sir Edward Devereux, 1st Bt (*see* HEREFORD, V), and *d* 1625, leaving:

EDWARD LEIGHTON; *m* 1st Abigail, dau and heiress of William Stephens, of Shrewsbury; *m* 2nd Martha, dau of Thomas Owen, and *d* 1632, leaving by his 1st w:

ROBERT LEIGHTON; MP Shrewsbury 1660–78, Sheriff Salop, one of the proposed Knights of the Oak (a chivalric order mooted by CHARLES II but never instituted); *m* Gertrude, dau of Edward Baldwyn, of Diddlebury, Salop, and *d* 1689, leaving, with a yr s (Capt Baldwyn Leighton, Whig agent on a secret mission to the then Prince of Orange in JAMES II's reign):

Sir Edward Leighton, 1st Bt (E), so *cr* 2 March 1692/3; MP Salop 1695 and Shrewbury, Sheriff Salop; *m* 1st 1679 Dorothy (*d* 1688), dau of Sir Job Charlton, Bt, Speaker H of C, and had, with other issue:

  1 EDWARD (Sir), **2nd Bt**

Sir Edward *m* 2nd 1693 Jane, dau of Daniel Nicholl, of London, and by her had, with other issue:

2 Daniel, of Bausley; MP Herefs 1747, Lt-Col Gen Evans's Regt of Horse, served Battle of Fontenoy (British defeat by French) 1745; *b* 1694; *m* Jane, widow of Capt Michael Barkham and dau of Nathaniel Thorold, of Lincoln, and *d* 1765, leaving, with other issue:

  (1) Herbert; Army Capt, Gentleman Usher to FREDERICK PRINCE OF WALES; *m* Harriet, dau of Henry Wilson, of Aswelthorpe, Norfolk, and had:

    1a Francis (Rev), of Bausley; *m* 1st Clare, sis and coheir of John Boynton Adams, of Cambleforth, Yorks; *m* 2nd Victoria, dau of Baldwin Leighton, and by his 1st w had:

      1b Francis Knyvett; Lt-Col Militia; *m* Louisa Anne, dau of 1st Viscount Doneraile (*qv*), and *d* 1834, leaving, with two daus:

      1c Francis Knyvett (Rev), of Ballasley, Montgomeryshire; DD, Fell and Warden All Souls, Canon Westminster; *b* 2 July 1806; *m* 23 Feb 1843 Catherine (*d* March 1911), dau of Hon and Ven James St Leger, 3rd s of 1st Viscount Doneraile (*qv*), and *d* 13 Oct 1881, having had:

        1d Francis St Leger Knyvett; *b* 27 Aug 1850; *d* 28 Aug 1855

        2d Charles Arthur Baldwin Knyvett; Maj 1st Bn RWF; *b* 9 Nov 1854; *m* 17 April 1879 Agatha Georgina (*d* 10 May 1940), dau of Lt-Gen

Edward Arthur Somerset, CB (*see* BEAUFORT, D), and *dsp* 18 May 1889

1d Louisa Catherine Clare; *m* 1879 Maj Maurice Charles O'Connell, Roy Dublin Fus, and *d* 29 May 1928

2d Caroline Alice Jane; *m* 1st 5 Jan 1875 (*divorce* 1892) Lt-Col Montague Cecil Broun, Maj 15th Hus; *m* 2nd 20 Dec 1893 Horace Charles George West (*d* 2 Dec 1926), MVO, est s of Sir Algernon West, KCB, and *d* 19 Nov 1919, leaving issue

3 Francis; Lt-Gen, Col 32nd Foot, MP Herefs; *b* 1696; *m* Renea, dau of Col Charles Pinfold, Govr Barbados, and *d* 1773, having had:

(1) Renea; *m* 1st Capt Hon Schaw Cathcart (*see* CATHCART, E); *m* 2nd 26 Jan 1758 Jonathan Cope (*dvp* 2 Nov 1763) and by him had issue

(2) Frances; *m* 16 May 1783 Sir Hew Whiteford Dalrymple, 1st Bt (*see* HAMILTON-DALRYMPLE, Bt)

1 Jane; *m* 1st Thomas Jones, MP Shrewsbury; *m* 2nd Sir Charles Lloyd, Bt, of Garth

The 1st Bt *d* 1711; his only surv son by his 1st w,

Sir Edward Leighton, 2nd Bt; *b* 1681; *m* 1st Rachel, dau of Sir William Forester, of Watling Street, Salop (*see* SALISBURY, M); *m* 2nd Judith (*dsp* 1764), widow of Capt Thwaite and dau of John Elwick, of Mile End, Dir HEIC 1713–1720, and *d* 6 March 1756, having by his 1st w had, with other issue:

1 **Sir Charlton Leighton, 3rd Bt**; Maj RM, Col Salop Militia, High Sheriff Salop 1749–50; *b* 1715; *m* 1st Anna Maria (*d* Aug 1750), dau of Richard Mytton, of Halston, Salop, by Letitia, sis and sole heiress of Thomas Owen, of Condover Hall, Condover, Salop, and had, with two daus:

(1) **Sir Charlton Leighton, 4th Bt**; MP Shrewsbury 1780–84; *d* unm 9 Sept 1784

(1) Anna Maria; *s* to the Condover estate; *m* Nicholas Smythe, of Nibley, and was great-grandmother of Reginald Cholmondeley, of Condover

1 (cont.) **Sir Charlton** *m* 2nd 22 Oct 1751 Emma, dau of Sir Robert Maude, 1st Bt (*see* HAWARDEN, V), and *d* 5 May 1780, having by her had:

(2) **Sir Robert Leighton, 5th Bt**; High Sheriff Salop 1786; *b* 1752; *d* unm Feb 1819

(2) Emma; *m* John Corbet, of Sundorne, Salop

2 Baldwin; Capt 9th Regt; *b* 1717; *m* Anne, dau of Capt Smyth, and had, with six daus:

(1) Edward (Rev); Rector Pontesbury and Cardiston, Salop; *b* 1745; *dsp* 21 May 1804

(2) BALDWIN (Sir), **6th Bt**

(3) Thomas; Maj-Gen HEICS; *b* 1751; *m* Mary Louisa, dau of Capt Everett, HEICS, and *d* 22 May 1808, leaving:

1a Francis (Rev); Rector Cardiston; *b* 5 Dec 1801; *m* 12 Feb 1829 Catherine (*d* 22 April 1884), 3rd dau of Samuel Amy Severne, of Thenford, Northants, and *d* 15 Dec 1870, having had, with other issue:

1b Edward William Forester; Capt 9th Regt; *b* 20 Dec 1839; *m* 28 Aug 1886 Beatrice Jane (*d* 6 Aug 1940), dau of John Eyre, of Eyrecourt Castle, Co Galway, and *d* 14 Oct 1932, leaving:

1c Charlton Dudley Forester; Capt 1st Bn Cameronians (Scottish Rifles) WW I, ADC to Govr-Gen Bermuda; *b* 17 June 1887; *m* 1st 29 Aug 1921 (*divorce* 1927) Doris Hastings, only dau of William Hastings Barber, of S Kensington; *m* 2nd 2 July 1940 *Eleanor Gertrude, formerly w of Sir Ernest Gordon Graig and dau of William Cook, of Clifton, Bristol

1c Olga Beatrice; *m* 1st 14 Dec 1920 Frank Jay Mackey, of USA (*d* 24 Feb 1927); *m* 2nd 19 Nov 1927 Antonio, Marqués de Portago, Grandee of Spain (*d* May 1942), and had:

1d Alfonso, Marqués de Portago, Grandee of Spain; *b* 11 Oct 1928; *m* — (*m* 2nd 22 May 1969 Richard Pistell) and was *k* racing in the Mil Millas 12 May 1957, leaving issue

1d *Soledad; *m* Marqués de Moratalla

1c (cont.) The Marquesa de Portago *m* 3rd 17 April 1943 Don Isidro Martin-Montis, s of the Marqués de Linares, of Madrid

(4) Francis (Rev); Vicar Condover; *b* 1757; *d* 1809

(5) Burgh; Lt-Col 4th Light Dragoons Battle of Albuera; *b* 1760; *m* Jane, dau of Rev Thomas Holme, and *dsp* 1836

(6) Forester (Rev); *b* 1763; *m* Honoria, dau of Gen Barclay, and *d* 12 May 1807, leaving:

1a Forester Owen, Maj 56th Regt; *b* 1797; *m* 9 June 1827 Mary (*d* 16 Nov 1859), est dau of William Whateley, of Wandsworth, Staffs, and *d* 29 Feb 1876, leaving a dau (*d* unm)

2a Baldwin Francis (Rev); *b* 31 March 1804; *m* 8 March 1849 Sarah Catherine (*d* 21 June 1864), dau of Rev Sir Richard Hughes, 4th Bt (*qv*)

1 Rachel; *m* Thomas Jenkins, of Charlton Hall

The 5th Bt's cousin,

Sir Baldwin Leighton, 6th Bt; *b* 15 Jan 1747; Govr Carrickfergus, Col 9th Garrison Bn, served War American Independence (wounded), Brig Peninsular War, Govr Jersey, Gen; *m* 1st May 1780 Anna (*dsp*), dau of Rev William Pigott, Rector Edmond, Salop; *m* 2nd 25 Nov 1802 Margaretta Louisa Anne (*d* 8 Jan 1842), 2nd dau of Sir John Thomas Stanley, 6th Bt (*see* STANLEY OF ALDERLEY, SHEFFIELD and, B), and *d* 13 Nov 1828, leaving:

Sir Baldwin Leighton, 7th Bt; *b* 14 May 1805; Salop: MP S Div 1859, Sheriff 1835, Chm QS 1855–71 and Montgomeryshire QS 1846–51; *m* 9 Feb 1832 Mary (*d* 5 March 1864), dau of Thomas Netherton Parker, of Sweeney Hall, Oswestry, Salop, and sis and eventual heiress of Rev John Parker, of Sweeney Hall and had:

1 BALDWIN (Sir), **8th Bt**

2 Stanley, JP, DL, of Sweeney Hall; *b* 13 Oct 1837; MA, MP N Salop 1876–85 and W Salop 1885–1901; *m* 28 Aug 1873 Jessie Marie (*d* 16 Dec 1939), dau and coheir of Henry Bertie Watkin Williams Wynn (*see* WILLIAMS-WYNN, Bt), and *d* 4 May 1901, leaving:

(1) Bertie Edward Parker, JP, DL Salop, of Sweeney Hall; *b* 26 Nov 1875; *educ* Eton; Maj 1st (Roy) Dragoons, Boer War 1899–1902 (two medals and six clasps), WW I (wounded); MP Oswestry 1929–45; *m* 24 Sept 1936 Margaret

Evelyn, CBE (1957), er dau of Rev Hugh Hanmer (*see* HANMER, Bt), and *dsp* 15 Feb 1952

(1) Rachel Frances Marion; *d* unm 23 Oct 1956

1 Frances Christina, JP; *m* 23 April 1862 Rev Edward George Baldwin Childe (*d* 22 Feb 1898), of Kyre Pk, Worcs, Preb Hereford, s of William Lacon Childe, of Kinlet Hall, Salop, and *d* 21 Feb 1930

2 Isabella; *m* 1st 28 Oct 1857 Beriah Botfield, MP, of Norton Hall, Northants, and Hopton Ct, Salop. He *d* 7 Aug 1863. She *m* 2nd 18 Aug 1866 Alfred Seymour and *d* 7 April 1911, having had issue (*see* SOMERSET, D)

3 Charlotte; *m* 7 April 1893 Gen Hon William Henry Adelbert Feilding (*see* DENBIGH and DESMOND, E) and *dsp* 28 June 1928

4 Margaret; *d* unm 11 Sept 1883

The 7th Bt *d* 26 Feb 1871; his er son,

Sir Baldwin Leighton, 8th Bt, DL; *b* 27 Oct 1836; *educ* Oxford; MP (C) S Salop 1877–85; *m* 30 Jan 1864 Hon Eleanor Leicester LEIGHTON-WARREN (1900), sis and eventual heiress of 3rd and last Baron de Tabley (*see* 1895 edn), and *d* 10 Aug 1914, having had:

1 BRYAN BALDWIN MAWDDWY (Sir), **9th Bt**

2 Cuthbert LEIGHTON later LEICESTER-WARREN (roy licence 9 Feb 1899 on succeeding his mother in the de Tabley properties), JP and DL Cheshire; *b* 6 Nov 1877; *educ* Radley and Merton Coll Oxford; Hon Maj RASC, MT (V), Capt and Adj 16th Bn London Regt WW I; High Sheriff Cheshire 1921–22; WW II as Army Welfare Offr; *m* 21 July 1904 Hilda Marguerite (*d* 2 Nov 1954), only dau and heir of Edmund Henry Davenport, of Davenport, and *d* 2 Jan 1954, having had:

(1) John LEICESTER-WARREN later LEIGHTON BYRNE, TD, JP (Cheshire 1948), High Sheriff 1965, V-Lt 1968 (DL 1955–68), barrister Inner Temple 1933, Lt-Col Cheshire Yeo (TA) WW II 1939–41 (POW), Lt-Col Staff JAG (War Crimes) 1946, cmded Cheshire Yeo 1949–52; *b* 25 Sept 1907; *educ* Eton and Magdalen Coll Oxford (BA 1928, MA 1933); *d* unm 10 Aug 1975

(2) Edmund Cuthbert; *b* 26 Sept 1915; *d* 27 Jan 1917

(1) Margaret Alice; *m* 18 Jan 1933 Lt-Gen Sir Oliver William Hargreaves Leese, 3rd Bt (*qv*), and *dsp* 30 April 1964

1 Catherina Barbara; *m* 28 Sept 1909 Alfred Frederick Sotheby (*d* 9 Oct 1949), yst s of Adml Sir Edward Southwell Sotheby, KCB, and *d* 2 Oct 1952

2 Meriel Gundrede; *m* 9 April 1890 Algernon Edward Perkins (*d* 1 Oct 1926), s of George Perkins, and *d* 20 Feb 1947, leaving issue

Sir Baldwyn *d* 22 Jan 1897; his son,

Sir Bryan Baldwin Mawddwy Leighton, 9th Bt, TD, JP Salop; *b* 26 Nov 1868; Bechuanaland Landberg Campaign 1897, Spanish-American War 1898, Boer War 1899–1900, war correspondent Russo-Japanese War 1904, with Turkish Forces Balkan War 1913, Maj TFR and F/O RFC WW I, also cmdg Westmorland and Cumberland Yeo; *m* 3 Dec 1890 Margaret Frances (*d* 26 June 1944), dau of Maj John Fletcher, of Saltoun Hall, Haddington, and *d* 19 Jan 1919, having had:

1 John Burgh Talbot, MC, Capt (T/Maj) Scots Gds and S/Cdr RFC WW I (despatches twice); *b* 9 Feb 1892; *dsp* 7 May 1917 of wounds recd in action

2 **Sir Richard Tihel Leighton, 10th Bt**, TD, JP and DL Salop, High Sheriff 1956, patron of one living, Lt-Col and Brevet-Col TAR, Salop Yeo, Westmorland and Cumberland Yeo, F/O RFC, WW I (wounded, POW), WW II as S/Ldr RAFVR; *b* 13 Feb 1893; *educ* Eton; *m* 5 Jan 1932 Kathleen Irene Linda (*d* 1993), only dau of Maj Albert Ernest Lees, of Rowton Castle, Salop, and *d* 26 Sept 1957, leaving:

(1) Sir MICHAEL JOHN BRYAN LEIGHTON, **11th and present Bt**

(1) *Lavinia Ann [Mrs Edward Bonnor-Maurice, Bodynfoel Hall, Llanfechain, Montgomeryshire]; *b* 17 Nov 1932; *m* 12 April 1958 *Maj Edward Arthur Trevor Bonnor-Maurice, Coldstream Gds, only s of Trevor Bonnor-Maurice, of Llanfechain, and has:

1a *Emma Mary; *b* 12 Nov 1959; *m* 1986 *Mark William Fane and has:

1b *Harry Lachlan; *b* 1992

1b *Alice Daisy (twin); *b* 1992

2a *Frances Flavia; *b* 11 Feb 1962

(2) *Judy Johanna Kathleen [Miss Judy Leighton, Loton Park, Salop SY5 9AJ]; *b* 7 Jan 1937

(3) *Elizabeth Mary Linda; *b* 25 Nov 1938; *m* 1st 1977 (*divorce* 1984) David James Treasure, Mon Regt; *m* 2nd *Vyvian Clover, Parachute Regt

Seat: Loton Park, nr Shrewsbury. The oldest part of this house would seem to date from the early 17th century but it is known that certain of the very features which are most Jacobean in appearance date from the end of the 18th century at the earliest, notably the gables, and may well be as late as Queen Victoria's accession. More additions were made in the last quarter of the 19th century, possibly ones in the Jacobean style but so adroitly fashioned that they are hard to tell from the real thing.

The Georgian section is of less cryptic provenance. It was the **2nd Bt** who moved from Wattlesborough Castle, the ancient family seat, to Loton, and certainly a good deal of the house dates from his time. But it seems to have been **Sir Charlton**, the **3rd Bt**, who made major alterations, calling in Robert Mylne (who was later to work on Inveraray Castle; *see* ARGYLL, D). The project was not effected till the mid–1770s, shortly before another **Sir Charlton**, the **4th Bt**, succeeded. Further modifications were carried out in the year **Sir Robert**, the **5th Bt**, died, and were presumably his commission. The result is a Jacobean(?) core, added to in QUEEN ANNE's time and fronted on the north side with a red brick High-Georgian-period skin.

LEIGHTON OF St MELLONS

Arms: Az. a cross moline between in bend dexter two lymphads and in bend sinister as many mullets, all arg. **Crest:** Between two wings az., each charged with a mullet, a cross moline arg. **Motto:** *Animo et fide* ('By courage and faith'). **Creation:** Bt. (UK) 1 July 1952, B. (UK) 25 Jan 1962.

THE 2ND BARON LEIGHTON OF SAINT MELLONS, of Saint Mellons, Co Monmouth, and a **Baronet** (Sir John Leighton Seager, Bt) [The Rt Hon The Lord Leighton of St Mellons, 24 Clwyd, Northcliffe, Penarth CF64 1DZ]; *b* 11 Jan 1922; *s* f 1963; *educ* Leys Sch Cambridge; dir W H Seager and Co, late ptnr Probity Industrial Maint Servs and chm Bristol Channel Shipowners Assoc; *m* 1st 31 Oct 1953 Elizabeth Rosita (*d* 1979), only dau of Henry Hopgood, of Cardiff, and has had:

1 +ROBERT WILLIAM HENRY LEIGHTON; *b* 28 Sept 1955
2 +Simon John Leighton; *b* 25 Jan 1957
1 Christine Mary; *b* 24 Aug 1954; *d* 19 March 1955
2 *Carole Mary Leighton; *b* 7 Dec 1958

The 2nd BARON *m* 2nd 1982 *Ruth Elizabeth, widow of John Hopwood

Lineage: WILLIAM SEAGER, of Cardiff; *b* 1827; *m* 1858 Mary Jane, dau of William Berry, of Ilfracombe, and *d* 1895, leaving:

Sir WILLIAM HENRY SEAGER, JP Cardiff , DL Glamorgan, of Cardiff; *b* 13 March 1862; md WH Seager and Co Cardiff, Tempus Shipping Co, Victory Shipping Co, Sir William Seager and Sons Ltd, dir Br Steamship Owners' Assoc, N of England Protecting and Indemnity Assoc, chm Cardiff Pilotage Authority, Tstee Cardiff Roy Infirmary, Govr Hamadryad Seamen's Hosp, Rep Cardiff Inc Chamber of Commerce on Ctee Lloyd's Register of Shipping, memb Exec Cncl Shipping Fedn, Pres Chamber Shipping UK, Cardiff and Bristol Channel Shipowners Assoc, Cardiff Chamber Commerce, chm Cardiff Inst for the Blind, MP E Cardiff 1918–22, ktd 1918, High Sheriff Mon 1932–33; *m* 8 Nov 1890 Margaret Annie (*d* 6 July 1955 aged 93), 2nd dau of John Elliot, of Cardiff, and *d* 10 March 1941, leaving:

1 John Elliot, MC, JP, DL; *b* 30 July 1891; *educ* Cardiff High Sch and Queen's Coll Taunton; Hon Advsr Ships' Stores to Min of Food, dir W H Seager & Co, Seager's Shipping Supplies, Fell Inst Chartered Shipbrokers, chm Cardiff Pilotage Authority, S Wales and Mon Discharged Prisoner's Aid Soc, Govt Business Trg Scheme Wales, chm Cardiff and Bristol Channel Shipowners' Assoc, Pres Cardiff Inst for the Blind, Publicity Club Cardiff, Cardiff Inc Chamber Commerce, V-Pres Cardiff Business Club, V-Chm Min Labour and Nat Service, Cardiff and Dist Employment Ctee, Govr Queen's Coll Taunton, memb Cardiff Local Marine Bd, Bd Management Cardiff Roy Infirmary, Cardiff Appeals Tbnl, Min Nat Insur, Welsh Nat Cncl, YMCA, Tstee S Wales Fedn Boys' Clubs, Treas Charity of Sir David R Llewellyn for Clergymen and Ministers, memb Priory for Wales HQ Ctee, KStJ, High Sheriff Glam 1937–38, WW I with S Wales Borderers; *m* 26 May 1922 Dorothy Irene, MBE, JP, dau of D R Jones, of Pontypridd, and *d* 8 Jan 1955, leaving:
   (1) *Gerald Elliot; *b* 29 June 1923
   (1) *Pamela Elliot; *b* 2 Nov 1925; *m* 12 Sept 1951 *William Stephen Gilbart, yr s of John Gilbart, of Penarth, Glam, and has issue
   (2) *Malveen Elliot; *b* 15 Nov 1926; *m* 15 Feb 1956 *Michael Gibbon, 2nd s of Frank O Gibbon, of Tydraw Rd, Cardiff, and has issue
   (3) *Valerie Elliot; *b* 21 June 1929; *m* 4 Jan 1951 *Maj Ronald Robert Sands, RA, s of R B Sands, of Nottingham, and has issue
2 William Henry; Lt 10th Bn S Wales Borderers WW I; *b* 28 Jan 1893; *ka* 7 Feb 1916
3 (GEORGE) LEIGHTON (Sir), **1st Baron**
1 Margaret Annie; *m* 26 June 1929 Maj Charles Ellis Feneley, s of Rev Charles Feneley, of Bristol, and had two daus

Sir WILLIAM's yst son,
   Sir (George) Leighton Seager, 1st Bt, and **1st Baron Leighton of Saint Mellons**, of Saint Mellons, Co Monmouth (both UK), so *cr* 1 July 1952 and 25 Jan 1962,

respectively, CBE (1932), JP (Mon); *b* 11 Jan 1896; *educ* Queen's Coll Taunton; WW I with Artists Rifles (invalided); High Sheriff Mon 1938, V-Lt 1957, underwriting memb Lloyd's, Chm and Treas Nat Lib Party, ptnr W H Seager & Co and Seager's Shipping Supplies, dep chm Mountstuart Dry Docks Ltd, Victory Insur, dir Tempus Shipping, Victory Shipping, Cardiff Channel Dry Dock, Barry Graving Dock, New Egypt and Levant Shipping Co, Atlantic Shipping and Trading Co, chm Cardiff Post Office Advsy Ctee, Port of Cardiff Employment Ctee, S Wales Advsy Ctee to Unemployment Assistance Bd, Hamadryad Seamen's Hosp Ctee of Visiting Justices, Cardiff Prison, dir Br Sailor's Soc, dir and treas Roy Merchant Navy Sch, memb Gen Ctee Lloyd's Register, Monmouthshire Ag Wages Ctee, Pres Chamber Shipping UK, Cardiff Chamber Commerce, chm Cardiff and Bristol Channel Shipowners' Assoc, Govr Cardiff Roy Infirmary, Tstee Kingswood Sch, Govr U Coll Cardiff, memb Tramp Shipping Advsy Ctee, Warden Shipwrights' Co, Freeman City London; ktd 1938; *m* 19 Jan 1921 Marjorie, JP (Mon 1954) (*d* 1992), dau of William Henry Gimson, of Brecon, and *d* 17 Oct 1963, having had:

1 JOHN LEIGHTON SEAGER, **2nd and present Baron Leighton of St Mellons**
2 +Douglas Leighton [The Hon Douglas Seager, Leighton House, 5929 Hudson, Vancouver 13, BC, Canada]; *b* 24 Nov 1925; *educ* Leys Sch Cambridge; Capt S Wales Borderers WW II, ptnr Georgia Shipping Ltd, md Sir William Seager and Sons Ltd and Leighton Investments Ltd; dir Heaton Developments Ltd; *m* 3 Dec 1960 *Gillian Claire, only dau of Leonard Warwick Greenwood, of Astley, Worcs, and has:
   (1) *Nicola Claire Leighton; *b* 25 Nov 1961
   (2) *Wendy Elizabeth Leighton; *b* 31 Oct 1963
   (3) *Michelle Leighton; *b* 24 April 1967
1 *Thelma Margaret [The Hon Mrs Lloyd, Darenth Lodge, Shoreham, Kent]; *b* 6 Nov 1923; *m* 1st (*divorce* 1981) 12 Jan 1951 Michael Leighton Edmonds, ARIBA, only s of James Edmonds, of Bristol, and has:
   (1) *Christopher Leighton; *b* 24 Nov 1958; *m* 1992 *Diane, dau of William Burnell
   (1) *Susan Leighton; *b* 1 July 1952; *m* 1971 *Timothy Vicary
   (2) *Jane Leighton; *b* 23 April 1954; *m* 1984 *John Nelson
1 (cont.) The Hon Mrs Thelma Edmonds *m* 2nd 1983 *Joseph Evan Lloyd
2 *Zoë Leighton [The Hon Mrs Stewart, Westwood House, Hardgate, Castle Douglas, Kirkcudbrightshire DG7 3LD]; *b* 28 April 1928; *m* 1st 31 March 1955 Malcolm James Peniston, MA (*d* 1981), yr s of John Ernest Peniston, of Amersham, Bucks, and has:
   (1) *Douglas James; *b* 22 March 1959; *m* 1990 *Lyana, dau of Peter Hodgson, of Tiverton, Cheshire, and has:
      1a *Charlotte Eloise; *b* 1991
      2a *Arabella Leighton; *b* 1993
   (1) *Angela Clare; *b* 28 May 1956; *m* 1982 *Jeremy J Adams
   (2) *Rosemary Leighton; *b* 8 Aug 1964; *m* 21 Dec 1996 *Simon O'Hea, er s of Jerome O'Hea, of Chichester
2 (cont.) The Hon Mrs Peniston *m* 2nd 1984 *Alan Carnegie Stewart

LEINSTER

Arms: Arg. a saltire gu. **Crest:** A monkey statant ppr. environed about the middle with a plain collar and chained or. **Supporters:** Two monkeys, environed and chained as in the crest. **Motto:** *Crom a boo* ('Croom to victory'). **Creations:** E. (Kildare) (I) 14 May 1316, B. (I) 26 June 1620 (Offaly), V. (GB) 21 Feb 1746/7, E. (Offaly) and M. (I) 3 March 1761, D. (I) 26 Nov 1766, B. (UK) 3 May 1870 (Kildare).

THE 8TH DUKE OF LEINSTER, **Marquess of Kildare** and **Earl of Kildare**, Co Kildare, **Earl of Offaly**, **Viscount Leinster of Taplow**, Co Buckingham, **Baron Offaly** and **Baron Kildare** (Gerald FitzGerald) [His Grace The Duke of Leinster, Kilkea House, Wilcote Lane, Ramsden, Oxon OX7 3BA]; *b* 27 May 1914; *s* f 1976, also as premier (indeed sole) Duke, premier Marquess and premier Earl in the peerage of Ireland; *educ* Eton and RMC Sandhurst; Maj 5th Roy Inniskilling Dragoon Gds WW II (wounded, invalided), joint MFH N Kilkenny 1937–40, MFH W Percy 1945–46 and Portman 1946–47; *m* 1st 17 Oct 1936 (*divorce* 1946) Joane, est dau of Maj Arthur McMorrough Kavanagh, MC (*see* BUXTON, Bt) and has had:

1 Pamela Hermione; *b* 6 Nov 1937; *d* 3 April 1938

2 *Rosemary Anne [The Lady Rosemary FitzGerald, Beggars Roost, Lilstock, Somerset TA5 1SU]; *b* 4 Aug 1939; *educ* LMH Oxford; *m* 9 Feb 1963 (*divorce* 1967, resumed maiden name) Mark Killigrew Wait, only s of Peter Lothian Killigrew Wait, of Kensington

3 *Nesta [The Lady Nesta Tirard, Coolnabrune, Borris, Co Carlow, Ireland]; *b* 8 Jan 1942; *m* 1977 Philip Charles Seppings Tirard (*d* 1993) and has:

  (1) *Siobhan Eleanor; *b* 1978

  (2) *Eithne; *b* 1982

The 8th DUKE *m* 2nd 12 June 1946 *Anne, yr dau of Lt-Col Philip Eustace Smith, MC, TD, of Rothley Crag, Cambo, Morpeth, Northumberland, and by her has:

1 +MAURICE, *Marquess of Kildare* [Marquess of Kildare, Courtyard House, Oakley Park, Frilford Heath, Oxon OX13 6QW]; *b* 7 April 1948; *educ* Millfield; *m* 19 Sept 1972 *Fiona Mary Francesca, dau of Harry Hollick, of Thames Cottage, Wargrave, Berks, and has had:

  (1) Thomas, *Earl of Offaly*; *b* 12 Jan 1974; *d* 9 May 1997

  (1) *Francesca Emily Purcell; *b* 6 July 1976

  (2) *Pollyanna Louisa Clementine; *b* 1982

2 +John [The Lord John FitzGerald, Graham Lodge, Newmarket, Suffolk]; *b* 3 March 1952; *educ* Millfield and RMA Sandhurst; late Capt 5th Roy Inniskilling Dragoon Gds; *m* 11 Dec 1982 *Barbara, er dau of Andreas and Daniele Zindel, of Lausanne, Switzerland, and has:

  (1) +Edward; *b* 1988

  (1) *Hermione; *b* 1985

Leinster, previous creations: For the Earldom of Leinster of the March 1645/6 *cr* see CHOLMONDELEY, M. Another Earldom of Leinster was conferred for life on Sophia, Baroness Kielmansegge, mistress of GEORGE I, in 1721. (The peerage might be for life but the post of royal mistress was closer to being hereditary since her mother had stood in the same relationship to GEORGE's father the Elector of Hanover.) For a previous Dukedom of Leinster *cr* March 1691 *see* BANGOR, V, preliminary remarks.

Lecale, previous creation: The Earl of Ardglass (*see* CROMWELL, B, preliminary remarks) was granted as a subsidiary title the Viscountcy of Lecale.

Lineage: WALTER Fitz OTHER; tenant-in-chief (*i.e.*, holding direct of the Crown) of lands in Berks, Bucks, Hants, Middx and Surrey at the time of the Domesday Survey 1086; Castellan Windsor and Keeper Gt Forest there; *m* Beatrice — and *d* in or after 1100, leaving, with an est s (William, *see* PLYMOUTH, E) and a yst one (Robert de Windsor, feudal Baron of Eston, Essex):

GERALD Fitz WALTER; Constable Pembroke Castle by 1092, when he held off a Welsh attack; cmded troops against native Welsh in SW Wales 1095; travelled to Ireland 1100 to seek the hand in marriage of King Murrogh's dau for his overlord Arnulf de Montgomery; on Arnulf's disgrace 1102 was made full Keeper of Pembroke Castle by HENRY I; *m* Nest (who also had by Stephen, Constable of Cardigan, a s (Robert fitz Stephen) and by HENRY I another s (Henry, *k* 1158, f of Meiler fitz Henry), dau of Rhys ap Tudor Mawr, Prince of S Wales, and *d* apparently by 1136, having had:

1 William; *see* CAREW, Bt

2 MAURICE

3 David; Bp St David's 1147; *d* 1176; had:

  (1) Milo fitz David/fitz Bishop; feudal Baron of Iverk, Co Kilkenny; ancestor of the BARRONs of Brownsford, Co Kilkenny

1 Angharad/Ankeret; *m* William de Barri and had:

  (1) Gerald de Barri *alias* Giraldus Cambrensis, the historian

The 2nd s,

MAURICE Fitz GERALD; *b* probably *c* 1100; feudal Ld of Llanstephan, Wales, by inheritance; in 1167 Dermot MacMurrogh, King of Leinster, who had been deprived of his kingdom by Roderick O'Connor, King of Connaught and High King of Ireland, pledged Wexford to MAURICE and his half-bro Robet Fitz Stephen (*see* above) if they would help restore him; MAURICE accordingly went to Ireland in 1169 and not only secured Wexford but, in concert with Dermot, took Dublin, from which Roderick failed to dislodge him in 1171, by which time Dermot had died; HENRY II subsequently went to Ireland and made MAURICE Jt Keeper of Dublin, granting him also the middle cantred (akin to a hundred, or subdivision of a county) of Ophelan in Co Kildare (approximately that part of the county centred on Naas) and that of Co Wicklow between Bray and Arklow; *d* 1 Sept 1176, leaving by a 1st w:

1 William Fitz MAURICE; feudal Baron of Naas; made over to his (half-?) bro GERALD half the cantred of Ophelan; his legitimate male issue appears to be extinct

MAURICE Fitz GERALD had by a 2nd w:

2 Alexander; had large grants of land in Munster; *dsp*

3 GERALD

4 Thomas

5 Maurice, of Kiltrany (subsequently Burnchurch); ancestor of the FitzGERALD feudal Barons of Burnchurch, Co Kilkenny

6 Robert (*see* LANSDOWNE, M)

The 2nd son,

GERALD FitzMAURICE FitzGERALD, 1st Baron of Offaly (not a peerage of Parliament but a designation of the ancestors of the Earls of Kildare); *b c* 1150; took part in the conquest of Limerick *c* 1197 and acquired Croom in that Co (hence the wording of the family motto); *m c* 1193 Eve (*m* 2nd Geoffrey FitzRobert (*d* 1211) and 3rd by Feb 1217/8 Geoffrey de Marisco/Mareis, Justiciar of Ireland, and *d* by Dec 1226), thought to have been dau of Robert de Bermingham, by which marriage he acquired the territorial Barony of Offaly (an entity wholly distinct from Ophelan aforementioned), though Offaly was in his w's 3rd husb Geoffrey de Marisco's hands following her death (it was forfeited by Geoffrey in 1234, however, and passed to GERALD's heir); GERALD *d* 1245, having had:

MAURICE FitzGERALD, 2nd Baron of Offaly, called '*an Bráthair*' (the friar); *b c* 1190; ktd 1217; Justiciar Ireland 1232–45; took part in the subjugation of Connaught 1235, where he acquired manors and built castles in Sligo, Banada and Ardcree, Co Sligo, at Lough Mask, Co Mayo, and Ardrahan and Kilcolgan, Co

Galway; Commr Treasury and Cncl Ireland 1250; fnded the Franciscan Friary at Youghal and Dominican Friary at Sligo and took vows as a friar before his death; *m* allegedly Juliane — and *d* 1257, having had:

1 Gerald; *b c* 1220; *dvp* 1243, leaving:

  (1) Maurice, 3rd Baron of Offaly, called *Ruadh* ('The Red'); *m* 1st — and had a s; *m* 2nd 1266 Agnes (*dsp* 2 Jan 1310), dau of William de Valence, Earl of Pembroke, and was lost at sea returning to Ireland from England 28 July 1268; his s by his 1st w:

    1a Gerald, 4th Baron of Offaly, called *Rothfalyaght* ('The Red Man of Offaly'); *m* Joan, dau of Sir Geoffrey de Geneville/Joinville, Justiciar Ireland, and *d* 20 July 1286

  (1) Juliane; *m* 1st John de Cogan (*d* by 1276); *m* 2nd John de Peneys; *dsp*

2 Maurice, called *Mael* ('The Bald'); Justiciar Ireland 1272; s to his f's lands in Co Cork, Tyrconnell, Fermanagh and Connaught; *m* 1st Maud, dau and coheir of Gerald de Prendergast (*see* GORT, V) and widow of Maurice de Rocheford and had a dau (Amabel, *m* Andrew Avenel, *dsp*); *m* 2nd Emeline, dau of Stephen de Longespée and gdau of Walter de Ridelisford, who brought him the Manors of Kilkea and Castledermot, and *d* Ross, Co Wexford, by 10 Nov 1286, leaving a dau (Juliane, *m* 1st Thomas de Clare and had issue, *m* 2nd Nicholas Avenel)

3 David; *dsp*

4 Thomas, of Banada, Co Sligo; alleged fndr Trinitarian Abbey at Adare, Co Limerick; *d* Ballyloughmask, Co Mayo, 1271, leaving:

  (1) JOHN FitzTHOMAS FitzGERALD, **1st Earl of Kildare** (I), so *cr* 14 May 1316; a legend is told of him similar to that about the ancestor of the FitzGERALD Bts of Valencia (*qv*), viz., that when he was a baby in the Castle of Woodstock, nr Athy, Co Kildare, a fire broke out, he was overlooked in the panic and rescued by a monkey, who climbed a tower holding him in its arms; subsequently the FitzGERALDs adopted a monkey as crest and occasionally the additional motto *Non immemor beneficii* ('Not forgetful of a helping hand'); *m* Blanche de la Roche (living 1327), and *d* 12 Sept 1316, having had, with other issue:

    1a THOMAS, **2nd Earl**

    1a Joan; *m* 1302 Edmund Butler/le Botiller and had issue (*see* MOUNTGARRET, V)

The 1st EARL's son,

THOMAS FitzJOHN FitzGERALD, **2nd Earl of Kildare**; Dep Justiciar Ireland 1320, Ld Justice Ireland 1326–28, Justiciar Ireland 1327 and 1328; *m* 16 Aug 1312 Lady Joan de Burgh (*m* 2nd 3 July 1329 Sir John D'Arcy, Ld Justice of Ireland, and *d* 22 April 1359), 3rd dau of Richard 'The Red', Earl of Ulster, and *d* 9 April 1328, having had, with a yst s (John, *dsp* 1383):

1 John; *b* 1314; *dvp* 1323

2 RICHARD FitzTHOMAS FitzGERALD, **3rd Earl of Kildare**; *b c* 1319; *dsp* 7 July 1331

3 MAURICE FitzTHOMAS FitzGERALD, **4th Earl of Kildare**; ktd 1347; Justiciar Ireland 1356–61 and 1376; *b* 1318; *m* 1347 Elizabeth, dau of 1st Lord (Baron) Burghersh, KG, of the Jan 1329/30 *cr*, and *d* 15 Aug 1390, leaving:

  (1) GERALD FitzMAURICE FitzGERALD, **5th Earl of Kildare**; Justiciar Ireland 1405; *m* 1st *c* 1381 Margaret, dau and heiress of Sir John Rocheford of Tobernea, Co Limerick, a marriage which may have been annulled as she was possibly mother of Richard FitzGerald, described as the **4th Earl's** illegitimate s but who was 1st in remainder to Margaret's lands 1388, *m* (dispensation 10 April 1405) Joan, dau and heiress of Sir Nicholas Castlemain, of Dunsany, and *d* by 1409, leaving a dau and heiress (Anne, *m* 1st Baron of Dunsany, *qv*), and had:

    1a Thomas; *dsp*

    1a Joan; *m* 4th Earl of Ormonde (*qv*, 1970 edn)

  (1) (cont.) The **5th Earl** *m* 2nd by 18 Nov 1397 Agnes (*d* 29 Sept 1439), dau of 4th Lord (Baron) Darcy de Knayth (*qv*) and widow of Sir Brian/Urien Cokeshay, and *d* 16 Oct 1432, leaving by her:

    1a Elizabeth; *b* 1398; *m* 1st 2nd Lord (Baron) Grey (*qv*) (of Codnor); *m* 2nd 1432 4th Earl of Ormonde (*qv*, 1970 edn) and *dsp* 6 Aug 1452, and *dspml* 11 Dec 1432

  (2) JOHN, **6th Earl**

  (3) Richard; living 1397

  (4) Maurice; *dsp* by 1397

  (5) Thomas; *dspl* by 1388

  (1) Joanna; *m* Donald MacCarthy, Prince of Desmond, and had issue

The 5th EARL's bro,

JOHN Fitz MAURICE *Cam* ('Crouchback') FitzGERALD, of Castletown-Kildrought, Co Kildare, *de jure* 6th EARL OF KILDARE, as which according to modern doctrine almost certainly s his bro since he was undoubtedly living Aug 1425, though never so referred to in contemporary records, the 4th Earl of Ormond having seized his lands on the pretext that he had a right to them through his w (*see* above); allegedly *m* 1st Margaret Delaherne; probably *m* (2nd?) Rose Basset, on whom his trustees settled lands (after his death?) 10 July 1435, and had, presumably by her:

THOMAS FitzMAURICE FitzGERALD, **7th Earl of Kildare**; *b c* 1421; Justiciar Ireland 1454 and 1461–70, Chllr Ireland 1462; *m* Lady Joan *Cam* FitzGerald (*d* 13 June 1486), dau of 7th Earl of Desmond, and had:

1 GERALD, **8th Earl**

2 Thomas (Sir), of Lackagh; Ld Chllr Ireland 1484; *k* Battle of Stoke 1487 fighting for Lambert Simnel; ancestor of the FitzGERALDs of Lackagh (*see* WELLINGTON, D), Kilrush and Narraghbeg, Co Kildare

3 James (Sir); *m* Eleanor FitzGibbon, dau of the White Kt, and *d* 1513, leaving issue

1 Eleanor; *m* CONN MORE O'NEILL, KING OF ULSTER (*see* O'NEILL, B), and *d* 14 Nov 1497

2 Anne; *m*? Gerald Kavanagh

The 7th EARL *d* 25 March 1477; his est son,

GERALD FitzGERALD, **8th Earl of Kildare**, KG (1505), called *Geroit More* ('Gerald the Great'); *b* seemingly after Jan 1455/6; Dep King's Lt Ireland; supported imposture of Lambert Simnel 1487 but after its failure submitted to HENRY VII; under suspicion also of conspiring with Perkin Warbeck 1493, hence attainted 1494, forfeiting his estates and titles and being imprisoned in the Tower of London; attainder reversed 1495; Ld Dep Ireland 1496 (as which in 1504 he defeated a rising by Clanricarde and a confederacy of Irish chiefs at the Battle of Knock Tuagh or Knockdoe ('Hill of Slaughter'), Co Galway), Treasurer Ireland 1505, Ld Justice Ireland 1509, Ld Dep Ireland 1510 (as which, during an expedition against Lemyvannon, or O'Carroll's Castle, now called Leap Castle, in Co Offaly, he was shot by one of the O'Mores of Leix (modern Co Laois), at Kilkea and *d* a few days later 3 Sept 1513); *m* 1st *c* 1478 Alison (*d* 22 Nov 1495), dau of 1st Baron Portlester (*see* DUNSANY, B), and had:

1 GERALD, **9th Earl**

1 Ellis; *m* as his 1st w 8th Lord (Baron) Slane

2 Elizabeth; *m* 1st Baron Delvin (*see* WESTMEATH, E)

3 Margaret; *m* 8th Earl of Ormonde (*see* MOUNTGARRET, V)

4 Eleanor; *m* 1st (contract 1497) Donal MacCarthy Reagh, Lord or Prince of Carbery; *m* 2nd Manus O'Donnell, Lord or Prince of Tirconnell

The **8th Earl** *m* 2nd 1496 Elizabeth (*m* 2nd Sir John Wallop, KG, collateral ancestor of the Earls of Portsmouth (*qv*), and *d* 28 June 1516), dau of Sir Oliver St John, of Lydiard Tregoze, Wilts (*see* BOLINGBROKE and SAINT JOHN, V), and by her had:

2 Henry; *dsp*

3 Thomas called *Bacach* ('The Lame') (Sir), of Leixlip, Co Kildare; *m* an illegitimate dau of 3rd and last Duke of Buckingham of the 1444 *cr* (*see* STAFFORD, B) and *dsp* 1532

4 James (Sir), of Leixlip, Co Kildare; Kt of St John; *m* Margaret, dau of Sir William Darcy, of Platten, Co Meath and *dspl*:

5 Oliver; *m* Maeve (*m* 2nd Donough O'Kelly, of Hy Many, Connaught), dau of Cahir O'Conor Failghe, and was ancestor of the FitzGERALDs of Newcastle and Portanure, Co Longford

6 Richard, of Fassaral, Co Wicklow; *m* Maud (*m* 3rd Sir Thomas Cusack, Ld Chllr Ireland), dau of George Darcy, of Platten, and widow of James Marword, feudal Baron of Skreen, and *dsp*

7 John (Sir); Kt of St John

8 Walter; *m* Elizabeth Plunkett, dau of 5th Baron of Dunsany (*qv*), and *dsp*

The 8th Earl also had an illegitimate dau:

1 Catherine; *m* Sir Peter Talbot (*see* TALBOT OF MALAHIDE, B)

The 8th EARL's only s by his 1st w,

GERALD FitzGERALD, **9th Earl of Kildare**, called *Geroit Oge* ('Gerald the Younger') and *Garrett McAlison* ('Gerald Alison's son); *b* 1487; High Treasurer Ireland 1503–13; Ld Justice Ireland and Ld Deputy 1513, 1524/5 and 1532–34, Dep to King's Lt Ireland 1533; *m* 1st 1503 Elizabeth (*d* 6 Oct 1517), dau of Sir John Zouche, of Codnor, Derbys (*see* ZOUCHE, B), and had:

1 THOMAS FitzGERALD, **10th Earl of Kildare**, called 'Silken Thomas' from the silken fringes adorning the helmets of his 140 mounted retainers the day (11 June 1534) he came out in rebellion against the Crown, having been misinformed that his father had been beheaded; *b* 1513; before he was forced to surrender he killed John Allen, Archbp of Dublin; he submitted 5 Aug 1535 to the Ld Deputy of Ireland and was sent to the Tower of London for 16 months, being beheaded 3 Feb 1536/7 (contrary to a pledge that he would be pardoned), while five of his uncles (Sir James, Oliver, Richard, Sir John and Walter FitzGerald, two of whom seem to have had no part in his insurrection, HENRY VIII's aim probably being to wipe out the family altogether) were hanged, drawn and quartered; *m* seemingly by Dec 1529 Frances, dau of Sir Adrian Fortescue, but *dsp*, the Earldom having been forfeited by attainder 1 May 1536 in the Irish Parl and *c* 1537 in the E Parl

1 Mary; *m* Briann O'Connor, of Offaly

2 Catherine; *m* 3rd Viscount Gormanston (*qv*)

3 Cicely; nun

4 Ellis; *m* apparently by 8 July 1528 9th Lord (Baron) Slane and *dsp*

The **9th Earl** *m* 2nd 1519 Lady Elizabeth Grey, dau of 1st Marquess of Dorset (*see* 1970 edn STAMFORD, E), and *d* in the Tower of London 13 Dec 1534 under suspicion of plotting a rebellion, having by her had, with other further issue:

2 GERALD FitzGERALD, **11th Earl of Kildare**, as which restored by Act of I Parl 23 Feb 1568/9, also 1st EARL OF KILDARE and BARON OF OFFALY (both I), so *cr* 13 May 1554 (before the reversal of the attainder), with precedence of the earlier forfeited Earldom, called 'The Wizard Earl', PC (I March 1557/8), JP (Cos Dublin and Kildare 1556); *b* 25 Feb 1525; aged ten at the time of his half-brother's giving himself up, he was spirited away by well-wishers anxious to keep him out of HENRY VIII's clutches to his sister Mary (*see* below), to whom he was conveyed in a covered basket while in the throes of smallpox; from Mary he was bundled off to his aunt Eleanor and from her he was shipped to the Low Countries, arriving in Liège aged 15; from there he subsequently went to Rome, reportedly doubled back to Nantes, in western France, where the French were alleged to be getting ready a fleet to invade Ireland; also, however, helped the Knights 'of Rhodes' repel what contemporaries refer to as the Moors, though since the Kts of St John had lost Rhodes to the Ottoman Turks in 1522 this may refer to the Knights of St John at Malta; entered service of Cosmo de' Medici, Duke of Florence, who appointed him Master of his Horse; went to England following EDWARD VI's accession 1547, his estates being restored him 1552; ktd *c* 1552; supported Lady JANE GREY's candidature for the Crown 1553 but after MARY's coming to the throne took a leading part in suppressing Sir Thomas Wyatt's Revolt 1554, hence the revival of the Earldom in his favour some months later; apparently sympathetic to rising led by the Earl of Desmond 1574, hence arrested 1575 and sent over to London, where imprisoned by Jan 1575/6; nevertheless allegedly helped suppress a further rising stirred up by the Earl of Desmond in Munster with Spanish aid 1579–82; again imprisoned on suspicion of subversion first in Dublin then in the Tower of London 1580; allowed to go back to Ireland 1583; *m* 29 May 1554 Mabel (*d* 25 Aug 1610), sis of Anthony Browne, 1st Viscount Montagu, and *d* 16 Nov 1585, having had:

1 Gerald, styled (incorrectly according to modern notions) *Lord Garratt/Gerald*; *b* 28 Dec 1559; *m* Oct 1578 Catherine (*m* 2nd Sir Philip Boteler, of Watton Woodhall, Herts), dau of Sir Francis Knollys, KG (*see* KNOLLYS, V), and *dvp* June 1850, having by her had an only dau:

1a LETTICE FitzGerald, **Baroness Offaly** (I) in her own right, so *cr* (effectively so, being in fact recognised as such, she having styled herself Baroness Offaly from 1599, when her unc WILLIAM, **13th Earl of Kildare** of the 1316 *cr* and 3rd and last EARL OF KILDARE and BARON OFFALY of the 1554 *cr* died, and claiming both the title and associated lands) by 26 June 1620, when the Crown ruled that the Barony should after her death pass to her FitzGerald cousin holding the Earldom of Kildare rather than to her children; *b c* 1580; *m c* 19 April 1598 Sir Robert Digby (*see* DIGBY, B) and *d* 1 Dec 1658, leaving issue

(2) HENRY FitzGERALD, **12th Earl of Kildare**, called *na Tuagh* ('Of the Battleaxes'); *b* 1562; though suspected of disaffection by the English and taken to England, he fought against the Spaniards in Ireland 1588 and lost his life helping suppress the Earl of Tyrone's rising in Ulster; *m* by 22 Feb 1589/90 Lady Frances Howard (*m* 2nd 22 May 1601 11th Lord (Baron) Cobham (attainted 1603; *see* COBHAM, V, preliminary remarks) and *d* 1628), dau of 1st Earl of Nottingham (*see* NORFOLK, D), and *dspm* 1 Aug 1597 of wounds recd earlier that year, having had, with other issue:

1a Bridget; *b c* 1590; *m* 1st by 1606 Roderick or Rory O'Donnell, 1st and last Earl of Tyrconnell (attainted by 23 Feb 1607/8, when his titles were forfeited; *d* 28 July 1608) and had an only s:

1b Hugh, *Baron Donegall*; *b c* 1 Oct 1606; left Ireland with his f Sept 1607 (the episode known as the 'Flight of the Earls'); Col of a regt of Irishmen in Spanish service in Low Countries and Spain; Kt Order of Alcantara Spain; *m* Anna Margaret, dau of Maximilian de Hennin, Count of Boussu, and *dsp* at sea *c* 1 July 1642 in a naval battle against the French off Barcelona

1a (cont.) The Countess of Tyrconnell *m* 2nd by 7 July 1617 1st Viscount Barnewall of Kingsland (*see* BARNEWALL, Bt) and *d* by 25 Dec 1682, having by him had issue

2a Elizabeth; *m* well before 1611, as 1st of his three ws, 1st Earl of Fingall (*see* 1970 edn) and *dsp*

(3) WILLIAM FitzGERALD, **13th Earl of Kildare**; *d* unm early April 1599, shipwrecked or drowned while crossing from England to Ireland to help suppress the Earl of Tyrone's rising, when the titles *cr* 1554 expired

(1) Mary; *m* 1582 3rd Baron Delvin and *d* 1 Oct 1610, leaving with other issue (*see* WESTMEATH, E):

1a Elizabeth; *m* her cousin **14th Earl of Kildare** (*see* below)

(2) Elizabeth; *m* as his 2nd w 3rd Earl of Thomond (*see* INCHIQUIN, B) and *d* 12 Jan 1617, leaving issue

3 Edward; *b* 17 Jan 1528; Lt Gentlemen Pensioners; *m* Agnes, widow of Sir John Paston and dau and heiress of Sir John Leghe, of Stockwell, Surrey, and had, with three daus:

(1) GERALD FitzGERALD, **14th Earl of Kildare**; ktd 1599, Govr Offaly 1600, Commr Connaught 1604; *m* after 1600 his cousin Elizabeth, dau of 3rd Baron Delvin (*see* WESTMEATH, E), and *d* 11 Feb 1611/2, leaving:

1a GERALD FitzGERALD, **15th Earl of Kildare**; *b* 26 Dec 1611; *d* 11 Nov 1620

(2) Thomas, of Walton-on-Thames, Surrey; *m* Frances, est dau of Thomas Randolph, PMG and Chamberlain Exchequer under ELIZABETH I, and *d* 1619, having had, with two er sons (*d* young) and four daus:

1a GEORGE, **16th Earl**

1 Elizabeth, 'The Fair Geraldine'; *m* 1st Sir Anthony Browne, KG; *m* 2nd 1st Earl of Lincoln (*qv*)

2 Mary; *m* by 1582 3rd Baron Delvin (*see* WESTMEATH, E)

The 15th Earl's cousin,

GEORGE FitzGERALD, **16th Earl of Kildare**, also 2nd BARON OFFALY, as which *s* cousin 1658, called from his small stature 'The Fairy Earl'; *bapt* 23 Jan 1611/2; *educ* (as a Protestant) Ch Ch Oxford; *m* 15 Aug 1630 Lady Joan Boyle (*d* 11 March 1656/7), 4th dau of 1st Earl of Corke (*see* CORK and ORRERY, E) and *d* 1660, having had, with other issue:

1 WENTWORTH FitzGERALD, **17th Earl of Kildare**, PC (I 1661); *b* 1634; MP E Retford 1660–61, Govrs Co Kildare and King's and Queen's Cos; *m c* 1655 Lady Elizabeth Holles, 2nd dau of 2nd Earl of Clare (*see* CHICHESTER, E), and *d* 5 March 1663/4, leaving, with a dau:

(1) JOHN FitzGERALD, **18th Earl of Kildare**; *b* 1661; MP (Whig) Tregony 1694–95; *m* 1st Mary, dau of Henry, Lord O'Brien (s of 6th Earl of Thomond; *see* INCHIQUIN, B); *m* 2nd 12 June 1684 Lady Elizabeth Jones, dau of 1st Earl of Ranelagh, and *dsps* 9 Nov 1707, having by his 1st w had:

1a Henry, *Lord Offaly*; *dvp* 18 Feb 1683/4 aged less than eight months

2 Robert, PC (I 1678), of Grangemellon, Co Kildare; *b c* 1637; Cornet 1659, Lt Horse Gds 1664, Capt of Horse 1684; Commr forfeited estates; Govr Co Kildare; *m* 4 Aug 1663 Mary, dau and heiress of James Clotworthy, of Monnimore, Co Londonderry, bro of 1st Viscount Massereene (*see* MASSEREENE and FERRARD, V), and *d* 31 Jan 1697/8, having had, with other issue:

(1) ROBERT, **19th Earl**

(1) Margaret; *m* 1712 Toby Hall (*d* 4 May 1734), of Mount Hall, and *d* 8 Dec 1758, leaving issue

1 Elizabeth; *m* 1st 3rd Earl of Clancarty (*d* 21 Nov 1676) of the 1658 *cr* (*see* CLANCARTY, E, preliminary remarks) and had issue; *m* 2nd 17 June 1682 Sir William Davis, Ch Justice King's Bench Ireland, and was *bur* 15 Feb 1697/8

The 18th EARL's cousin,

ROBERT FitzGERALD, **19th Earl of Kildare**, PC (I 1710); *b* 4 May 1675; a Ld Justice Ireland 1714; *m* 7 March 1708/9 Lady Mary O'Brien, est dau of 3rd Earl of Inchiquin (*see* INCHIQUIN, B), and had, with three other sons and six other daus:

1 JAMES, **1st Duke**

1 Margaretta; *m* 1747, as his 1st w, 1st Marquess of Downshire (*qv*) and had issue

2 Frances; *m* 1691/2 William Tisdale (*d* 1725) and *d* 26 Aug 1917, leaving issue

The 19th EARL *d* 20 Feb 1744; his only surv son,

JAMES Fitz GERALD, **1st Duke of Leinster**, so *cr* 26 Nov 1766, as also earlier 3 March 1761 EARL OF OFFALY and MARQUESS OF KILDARE (all I) and earlier still 21 Feb 1746/7 VISCOUNT LEINSTER OF TAPLOW, Co Buckingham (GB), PC (I March 1744/5); *b* 29 May 1722; MP Athy 1741–44, a Ld Justice V-Regent Ireland 1756–57, Master-Gen Ordnance 1758–66, Col Roy Irish Artillery 1760–66, Maj-Gen 1761, Lt Gen 1770, Govr Co Kildare 1761; *m* 7 Feb 1746/7 Emilia Mary (*m* 2nd 1774 William Ogilvie, former tutor to her children and alleged f of the last child born to her while she was still Duchess of Leinster; as her husb he fathered three more children on her), dau of 2nd Duke of Richmond (*see* RICHMOND and GORDON, D), and had, with two other sons and four other daus:

1 George, *Earl of Offaly*; *b* 15 Jan 1748; *d* 26 Sept 1765

2 WILLIAM ROBERT, **2nd Duke**

3 CHARLES JAMES FitzGERALD, 1st and last BARON LECALE OF ARDGLASS, Co Down (I), so *cr* 27 Dec 1800; *b* 30 June 1756; *b* 30 June 1756; R-Adml 1790, MP (I Parl) Co Kildare 1776–90, Cavan 1790–97 and Ardfert 1798–1800 and (UK Parl) Arundel Jan-April 1807, Sheriff Co Down 1798, Commr Customs 1789–92, Muster Master-Gen Ireland 1792–1806; *m* 1st(?) —; *m* (?)2nd(?) 18 July 1808 Julia (*d* 6 May 1844), widow of Thomas Carton, of Monkstown, Co Dublin, and *d* 18 Feb 1810, when the title expired, having allegedly had (by his putative 1st w?):

(1) Henry; *ka* at sea off Civita Vecchia 14 Sept 1803

(1) Anna Maria

4 Henry; *b* 30 July 1761; *m* 1791 Charlotte Boyle, Baroness de Ros (*qv*) in her own right, and had issue

5 Edward; *b* 15 Oct 1763; served British forces War American Independence; *m* 27 Dec 1792 Stephanie Caroline Anne Syms, known as 'Pamela' (*m* 2nd — Pitcairn, US Consul Hamburg, and *d* 1831), allegedly illegitimate dau of Philippe ('Egalité'), Duke of Orleans, and *d* 4 June 1798 in prison in Dublin of blood poisoning from wounds recd in resisting arrest for participation in the 1798 Uprising, leaving:

(1) Edward Fox; Capt 10th Hus, 3rd Dragoons and 52nd Foot; *b* 10 Oct 1794; *m* 6 Nov 1827 Jane (*d* 2 Nov 1891), dau of Sir John Dean Paul, Bt (*see* 1970 edn), and *d* 25 Jan 1863, leaving:

1a Pamela Frances Lucy Augusta Charlotte; *b* 29 Sept 1830; *m* 7 Dec 1850 James Turner, of Llwynderid, Montgomeryshire, and had issue

(1) Pamela; *m* 21 Nov 1820, as his 2nd w, Sir Guy Campbell, 1st Bt (*qv*), and *d* 25 Nov 1869, leaving issue

(2) Lucy Louisa; *m* 1825 Capt G F Lyons, RN (*d* 1832), and *d* 1826

6 Robert Stephen; *b* 1765; *m* 1792 Sophia Charlotte, dau of Capt Fielding, RN, and *d* 2 Jan 1833, leaving, with three daus:

(1) George; *b* 24 Dec 1809; *m* 8 Sept 1834 Mary (*d* 25 Jan 1866), dau of Thomas Barton, of Grove, Co Tipperary, and *dsp* 29 Jan 1853

7 Gerald; RN; lost at sea 1788 aged 22

1 Emily Mary Margaretta; *m* 1774 1st and last Earl of Bellamont (*see* COOTE, Bt)

2 CHARLOTTE MARY GERTRUDE FitzGerald, *cr* BARONESS RAYLEIGH (*qv*) OF TERLING PLACE

3 Sophia Mary Sarah; *d unm* 21 March 1845

4 Lucy Anne; *m* 31 July 1802 Adml Sir Thomas Foley, GCB (*d* 1833), and *d* 1851

The 1st DUKE *d* 19 Nov 1773; his est son,

WILLIAM ROBERT FitzGERALD, **2nd Duke of Leinster**, KP (1783), PC (I 1777); *b* 12 March 1748/9; *educ* Eton and (possibly) Cambridge; Cornet of Horse 1765, MP (Whig) Dublin City 1767–73, Sheriff Co Kildare 1772, Govr Co Kildare 1773, Master Rolls Ireland 1788–89 and Clerk of the Crown and Hanaper Ireland 1795–97; *m* 7 Nov 1775 Emilia Olivia, only dau and heiress of St George SAINT-GEORGE formerly USHER, 1st and last Baron Saint George of Hatley Saint George of the 1763 *cr* (*see* ST GEORGE, Bt), and had, with other issue:

1 George, *Marquess of Kildare*; *b* 20 June 1783; *d* Feb 1784

2 AUGUSTUS FREDERICK, **3rd Duke**

1 Emily Elizabeth; *m* 1801 John Joseph Henry, of Straffan, Co Kildare and had:

(1) Charles John; *m* 25 June 1838 Lady Selina Constance Rawdon-Hatsings, dau of 1st Marquess of Hastings (*see* LOUDOUN, E)

(1) Olivia; *m* 1850, as his 2nd w, Sir Thomas Sebright, 8th Bt (*qv*)

2 Cecilia Olivia Geraldine; *m* 18 Aug 1806 3rd Baron Foley (*qv*) and *d* his widow 27 July 1863

3 Olivia Letitia Catherine; *m* 8 May 1806 8th Lord Kinnaird (*see* 1970 edn) and *d* his widow 28 Feb 1858

The 2nd DUKE *d* 20 Oct 1804; his er surv son,

AUGUSTUS FREDERICK FITZGERALD, **3rd Duke of Leinster**, PC (I May 1831, GB June 1831); *b* 21 Aug 1791; *educ* Eton and Ch Ch Oxford; Ld Lt and custos rotulorum Co Kildare 1831–74, Commr Nat Educn Ireland 1836–41, Gd Master Freemasons Ireland; *m* 16 June 1818 Charlotte Augusta (*d* 15 Feb 1859), yst dau of 3rd Earl of Harrington (*qv*), and had:

1 CHARLES WILLIAM, **4th Duke**

2 Gerald; Capt Scots Fus Gds; *b* 6 Jan 1821; *m* 9 June 1862 Anne Agnes (*d* 6 June 1913), dau of James Barker, and *d* 23 Sept 1886, leaving:

(1) Edward Gerald; *b* 2 Sept 1863; *m* 20 Feb 1913 Anne Josephine, 3rd dau of C L Throckmorton, and *d* 5 Aug 1919

3 Otho Augustus, PC; *b* 10 Oct 1827; served RHG, Gentleman Bedchamber to Ld Lt Ireland, MP Co Kildare 1865–74, Treasurer Household 1866, Comptroller Household 1868–74; *m* 14 Dec 1861 Ursula Lucy Grace (*d* 12 Nov 1883), widow of 1st Baron Londesborough (*qv*) and dau of V-Adml Hon Charles Orlando Bridgeman (*see* BRADFORD, E), and *d* 19 Nov 1882, leaving:

(1) Gerald Otho; Capt and Hon Maj 5th Bn KRRC; *b* 25 Sept 1862; *d* 20 March 1919

(1) Ina Blanche Georgie; *b* 12 Jan 1864; *m* 29 Jan 1885 Lt-Col Arthur Leopold Paget and *d* 6 July 1910, leaving issue (*see* ANGLESEY, M)

1 Jane Seymour; *m* 5 Sept 1848 George William John Repton, MP (*d* 30 Aug 1906), only s of George Stanley Repton, and *d* 3 Nov 1898, leaving issue

The 3rd DUKE *d* 10 Oct 1874; his son,

CHARLES WILLIAM FitzGERALD, **4th Duke of Leinster**, PC (I 1879); *b* 30 March 1819; *educ* Ch Ch Oxford; Commr Nat Educn Ireland 1841–87, MP (Lib) Co Kildare 1847–52, Chllr Queen's U Ireland 1870–81, Hon Col 3rd Bn Roy Dublin Fus; *cr* 3 May 1870 *vp* BARON KILDARE OF KILDARE, Co Kildare (UK),

author *The Earls of Kildare*; *m* 13 Oct 1847 Lady Caroline Sutherland-Leveson-Gower (*d* 13 May 1887), 3rd dau of 2nd Duke of Sutherland (*qv*), and had:

1 GERALD, **5th Duke**

2 Maurice; RN, Ld Lt and custos rotulorum Co Wexford; *b* 16 Dec 1852; *m* 13 April 1880 Lady Adelaide Jane Frances Forbes (*d* 18 Nov 1942), est dau of 7th Earl of Granard (*qv*), and *d* 24 April 1901, leaving:

(1) Gerald Hugh, Capt 4th Dragoon Gds; *b* 11 April 1886; *m* 5 Aug 1914 Dorothy Violet (*m* 2nd Sept 1928 Thomas William Jefferies (*d* 4 May 1951), s of Thomas Jefferies, JP, of Wexford, and *d* 5 April 1974), dau of Spencer Calmeyer Charrington, of Winchfield, Hants, and was *ka* 13 Sept 1914

(1) Geraldine Mary; *b* 26 March 1881; *m* 23 Oct 1907 Gerald More O'Ferrall, DL, JP (*d* 30 Dec 1951), of Lisard, Edgeworthstown, Co Longford, and *d* 5 July 1954, leaving issue

(2) Kathleen; *b* 25 March 1892; *m* 18 July 1914 Maj Michael Lawrence Lakin, DSO, MC, 11th Hus, of Horetown Ho, Foulke's Mill, Co Wexford, 4th s of Sir Michael Henry Lakin, 1st Bt (*qv*), and *d* 23 Feb 1930, leaving issue

(3) Marjorie; *b* 31 Aug 1896; *d* 2 Jan 1899

3 Frederick; Commr Nat Educn Ireland, Maj 60th Rifles; *b* 18 Jan 1857; *d* 8 March 1924

4 Walter, Capt 60th Rifles; *b* 22 Jan 1858; *d* 31 July 1923

5 Charles; *b* 20 Aug 1859; *m* Nov 1887 Alice Sidonia (*d* July 1909), dau of Pericles Claudius, and *d* 28 June 1928, leaving:

(1) George Frederick, MC; Capt AIF WW I; *b* 25 April 1890; *m* 1939 Kathleen Mary, dau of C E Stedman, of Sandringham, Victoria, Australia, and *dsp* 28 June 1970

(2) Charles Otho; WW I with Australian Light Horse; *b* 1895; *m* 16 May 1931 Mary Pearl, dau of John McIntosh, of Western District, Victoria

(3) Rupert Augustus; *b* 2 June 1900; *m* 1st 18 Sept 1923 (*divorce* 1932) Irene, dau of J Jennings, of Melbourne, and had:

1a +Peter Charles; WW II with AMF; *b* 22 March 1925; *m* 1950 *June, dau of W Murray, of E St Kilda, Victoria, and has:

1b +Stephen Peter; *b* 1953

1b *Lynette Pamela; *b* 1951

(3) (cont.) Rupert FitzGerald *m* 2nd 1936 Ivy (*d* 1945), dau of J Simmons, of Melbourne, and *d* 8 June 1969, having by her had:

1a *Elizabeth Mary [Mrs Ronald Smith, 24 Ireland Ave, Doncaster East, Victoria, Australia]; *b* 1937; *m* 1958 Ronald Smith and has:

1b *Gary Ronald; *b* 1960

1b *Amanda Elizabeth; *b* 1962

(1) Nesta Sidonia; *b* 22 Sept 1888; *m* Sept 1926 (*divorce* 1936) Frank Moloney, BEng, BSc, and had issue

(2) Mabel Geraldine; *b* 30 Sept 1891; *m* 1914 Robert Alan McCracken (*d* 28 June 1967), Lt Australian Res of Offrs, and had issue

6 George; BA Oxon, Priv Sec to Govr Jamaica; *b* 16 Feb 1862; *d* 23 Feb 1924

7 Henry, JP Suffolk; Assist to Col i/c Records 1916–19, Capt and Hon Maj 4th Bn Bedford Regt; *b* 9 Aug 1863; *educ* Eton; *m* 21 Jan 1891 Inez Charlotte Grace (*d* 30 Jan 1967), 2nd dau and coheir of Cdr William John Casberd Boteler, RN, of Eastry, Kent, and *d* 31 May 1955, having had:

(1) Dermot; Capt Army Remount Serv WW I; *b* 8 Nov 1891; *educ* Eton; *d* 23 Jan 1939

(2) Brian Boteler; *b* 21 Jan 1908; *educ* Eton; *m* 28 July 1936 Elizabeth Dorothea Maud (*d* 1991), yst dau of Maj Charles Hesketh Fleetwood-Hesketh (*see* BIBBY, Bt), and *d* 1977

(3) +Denis Henry, DSO (1945), OBE (1951) [Brig Denis FitzGerald DSO OBE, Glenshelane House, Cappoquin, Co Waterford, Ireland]; *b* 25 Sept 1911; *educ* Eton and RMC Sandhurst; ADC to GOC NI Dist 1938–39, WW II in Norway and NW Europe, Instr Staff Coll Camberley 1942–43, Palestine 1947, cmded Irish Gds 1950–52, Brig cmdg 4th Gds Bde 1952–55, IDC 1956, Dir Plans War Office 1957–58, memb Stock Exchange

8 Robert; *b* and *d* 23 Dec 1868

1 Geraldine; *d* 15 Nov 1867

2 Mabel; *d* 13 Sept 1850

3 Alice; *m* 2 May 1882 Col Sir Charles John Oswald FitzGerald, KCB, IA (*d* 28 Feb 1912), s of Gen James FitzGerald, and *d* 16 Dec 1941, leaving issue

4 Eva; *d unm* 13 Feb 1931

5 Mabel; *d unm* 8 Dec 1939

6 Nesta; *d unm* 7 Dec 1944

7 Margaret; *d young* 26 Oct 1867

The 4th DUKE *d* 10 Feb 1887; his est son,

GERALD FitzGERALD, **5th Duke of Leinster** PC (I 1888); *b* 16 Aug 1851; *educ* Eton; Ld Lt Co Kildare 1892–93; *m* 17 Jan 1884 Lady Hermione Wilhelmina Duncombe (*d* 19 March 1895), dau of 1st Earl of Feversham (*see* FEVERSHAM, B), and *d* 1 Dec 1893, having had, with a dau (*d* an infant 5 Feb 1886):

1 MAURICE FitzGERALD, **6th Duke of Leinster**; *b* 1 March 1887; *educ* Eton; *d unm* 2 Feb 1922

2 Desmond, MC; Maj Irish Gds WW I (wounded twice, despatches); *b* 21 Sept 1888; *ka* 3 March 1916

3 EDWARD FitzGERALD, **7th Duke of Leinster**; *b* 6 May 1892; *educ* Eton; Lt 8th Service Bn W R Regt, Lt Irish Gds, WW I (wounded), WW II 1939–42 (ret as Capt); *m* 1st 12 June 1913 (*divorce* Scottish Courts 1930) May (*d* 11 Feb 1935), dau of Jesse Etheridge, and had:

(1) GERALD FitzGERALD, **8th and present Duke of Leinster**

3 (cont.) The **7th Duke** *m* 2nd 1 Dec 1932 (*divorce* 1946) (Agnes) Raffaelle (*d* 1993), formerly w of Clare Van Neck and dau of Robert Davidson Kennedy; *m* 3rd 11 March 1946 Jessie (Denise Orme) (*d* 20 Oct 1960), formerly w of (a) 3rd Baron Churston (*qv*) and (b) Theodore William Wessel and only dau of Alfred Smither; *m* 4th 12 May 1965 Vivien Irene (*d* 1992), formerly w of George William Conner and 3rd dau of Thomas Albert Felton, of London, and *d* by his own hand 8 March 1976, leaving by Yvonne Denison Percy PROBYN later fitzGERALD by deed poll 1952 (*d* 17 Aug 1973), er dau of Col Percy J Probyn, DSO, RAMC:

(2) +Adrian Dighton Desmond FITZGERALD [Adrian FitzGerald Esq, 2 Trevarrian Mews, Trevarrian, Mawgan Porth, Cornwall TR8 4AU]; *b* 17 Oct 1952; *educ* Bluecoat Sch, Wavertree, Liverpool; sales and marketing dir; *m* 1st 29 April 1972 (*divorce* 1975) Colleen Teresa, dau of Gordon James Cross, of Foxhole, St Austell, Cornwall; *m* 2nd 31 July 1982 (*divorce* 1992) Linda Jane Harris, dau of Charles James Clark, of London, and by his 1st w has:

  1a *Kirsty; *b* 30 March 1973; *m* 17 Sept 1993 *Andrew Keetch, s of David John Keetch

LEITH-BUCHANAN

Arms: 1st and 4th grandquarters, or a cross crosslet fitchée sa. between three crescents in chief and as many fusils in base gu. (for LEITH); 2nd grandquarter, or a lion rampant sa. holding in its dexter paw a man's heart ppr. within a double tressure flory counterflory of the second, a bordure compony arg. and az. (for BUCHANAN); 3rd grandquarter counter-quartered, 1st, arg. a lion rampant gu. armed or, 2nd, or a dexter hand couped in fess holding a cross crosslet fitchée in pale gu., 3rd, or a lymphad oars in saltire sa. and in base undy vert a salmon naiant arg., 4th, arg. an oak tree vert surmounted of an eagle displayed or, the third grandquarter with a bordure invected gu. (for MACDONALD). **Crests:** 1 A cross crosslet fitchée sa. (for LEITH), 2 A dexter hand holding a dagger ppr. (for BUCHANAN). **Mottoes:** 1 Trusty to the end, 2 God with my right. **Creation:** Bt. (GB) 21 Nov 1775.

SIR CHARLES ALEXANDER JAMES LEITH-BUCHANAN, 7TH BT, of Burgh St Peter, Norfolk [Sir Charles Leith-Buchanan Bt, 7510 Clifton Rd, Clifton, VA 22024, USA]; *b* 1 Sept 1939; *s* kinsman 1973; pres Utd Business Machines Inc Alexandria, Va., 1978–; *m* 1962 (*divorce* 1987) Marianne, dau of Col Earle Wellington Kelly, and has:

  1 +GORDON KELLY McNICOL; *b* 18 Oct 1974

  1 *Mary Elizabeth; *b* 1964

Lineage: WILLIAM LEITH; Provost Aberdeen 1350; ancestor through sr line of:

JOHN LEITH, of Leith Hall; had, with other issue (including James, of Leith Hall, ancestor of the LEITHs of Leith Hall and LEITHs of Glenkindie and Freefield):

ALEXANDER LEITH; gf of:

ALEXANDER LEITH; *m* Margaret, dau of Walter Halket of Cairnstoun; his est s:

ALEXANDER LEITH; Provost Aberdeen; *ka* cmdg artillery Battle Havana 1763; *m* Anne, widow of John Milet and had, with a dau (Anne, *m* Lucius Ferdinando Cary, est s of 7th Viscount Falkland; *qv*):

Sir Alexander Charles George Leith, 1st Bt (GB), so *cr* 21 Nov 1775; Lt-Col 88th Foot, MP Tregony 1774–78; *m* 1st Margaret, est dau of Thomas Hay, of Huntingdon, Ld of Session, and widow of — Wren, and had issue:

  1 GEORGE ALEXANDER WILLIAM (Sir), **2nd Bt**

  2 Thomas; *d* young

Sir Alexander *m* 2nd 1 March 1775 —, dau of Gen Sir John Cope, KB, and *d* Jamaica 3 Oct 1780

His est son,

  Sir George Alexander William Leith, 2nd Bt, KCB; Maj-Gen; *m* 10 Dec 1798 Albinia (*d* 2 Feb 1842), yst dau of Thomas Wright Vaughan, of Molesey, Surrey, and had, with two daus (*d* unm):

  1 ALEXANDER WELLESLEY WILLIAM (Sir), **3rd Bt**

  2 George Gordon Browne, of the Hermitage, Ancaster, Canada; *b* 26 Jan 1812; *m* 1843 Eleanor, dau of John Ferrier, WS, of York Place, Edinburgh, and *d* 2 Jan 1887, leaving a s and four daus (the yst, Eleanor Alma, *m* 3 Dec 1878 Stair Dick-Lauder; *see* DICK-LAUDER, Bt)

Sir GEORGE *d* 25 July 1842; his est son,

  Sir Alexander Wellesley William Leith, 3rd Bt; *b* 30 Oct 1806; *m* Oct 1832 Jemima (*d* 6 Aug 1877), 2nd dau of Hector Macdonald Buchanan, of Ross, Dunbartonshire, and *d* 3 April 1842, leaving an est s:

Sir GEORGE HECTOR LEITH later LEITH-BUCHANAN (added on mother's death), **4th Bt**, DL and JP Dunbartonshire, Capt 17th Light Dragoons; *b* 10 Aug 1833; *m* 1st 1 March 1856 Ella Maria (*d* 10 Feb 1857), est dau of David Barclay Chapman, of Roehampton, Surrey, and had a dau (*d* an infant 11 Feb 1857); *m* 2nd 24 April 1861 Eliza Caroline (*d* 1 May 1899), only child of Thomas Tod, of Drygrange, and *d* 29 Sept 1903, having by her had, with other issue:

1 **Sir Alexander Wellesley George Thomas Leith-Buchanan, 5th Bt**, JP, DL Dunbartonshire; V-Chm TAA Dunbartonshire, Lt-Col cmdg 9th Bn Argyll and Sutherland Highrs (later Hon Col); *b* 5 Dec 1866; *m* 19 Jan 1888 Agnes Maude Mary (*d* 22 Feb 1956), dau of Alexander Grant, and *d* 29 April 1925, leaving:

  (1) **Sir George Hector Macdonald Leith-Buchanan, 6th Bt**, JP (Dunbartonshire 1929); *b* 30 Jan 1889; *m* 16 Sept 1933 *Barbara, dau of Willard Phelps Leshure, of Springfield, Mass., and *dspm* 1 Aug 1973, having had:

    1a *Helen Elizabeth [Mrs Peter Selfe, Abermill Cottage, Gartocharn, Dunbartonshire]; *m* 14 Oct 1967 *Peter Michael Selfe, s of Cecil John Hunt Selfe, MBE, of High Burnside, Lanarks

  (2) Alexander Wellesley Grant; Lt 9th Bn Argyll and Sutherland Highrs; *b* 29 April 1890; *d* unm 29 Jan 1943

2 George Hector, MC; Lt MGC WW I (despatches); *b* 25 Jan 1871; *m* 22 Sept 1904 Mathilda Mary Charlotte (*dsp* 8 Feb 1908), dau of Isadore McWilliam Bourke, of Rahasane, Co Galway, and Curragh Leigh, Co Mayo, and *d* 30 Jan 1948

3 James Macdonald Buchanan; Capt TFR Boer War 1901–02 (medal with five clasps), recruiting staff 1916–19; *b* 11 Nov 1872; *m* 23 Aug 1905 Katie Isabel (*d* 16 Dec 1943), 2nd dau of George E Porter, of Australia, and *d* 2 June 1946, leaving:

  (1) John Wellesley Macdonald; Able Seaman RNVR WW II; *b* 22 May 1908; *m* 1st 26 June 1939 (*divorce* 1947) Jane Elizabeth Macdonald (*d* 1955), dau of Ronald McNicol, of Wick, Scotland, and had:

    1a Sir CHARLES ALEXANDER JAMES LEITH-BUCHANAN, **7th and present Bt**

  (1) (cont.) John Leith-Buchanan *m* 2nd 12 Jan 1947 *Isabel Sim Cumming, dau of A W Fraser, of Birchwood, Inverness, and *d* 1956

  (2) David Gustavus James; MA Edin, Lt RA WW II; *b* 25 Sept 1916; *ka* Feb 1941

  (1) *Jean Isobel Barbara [Miss Jean Leith-Buchanan, 645 Chelsea Cloisters, Sloane Ave, SW3]; *b* 18 April 1911

4 Charles John; *b* 21 June 1875; Pte 125th Canadian Regt WW I (wounded); *m* 25 Feb 1905 Mary Eleanor (*d* 24 May 1946), dau of William Farmer, of Ancaster, Ontario, and *d* 22 April 1948, leaving:

  (1) George William Hector; *b* 1 Nov 1905; *d* unm 17 Feb 1968

  (2) Thomas Wellesley Macdonald, CD; Lt RCN (ret); *b* 11 May 1907; *m* 1932 Mary C, dau of Allan J Cameron, barrister, of Halifax, NS, and *d* 11 Jan 1967, leaving:

    1a *Eleanor Clare [Mrs William Shaw, 99 Carrington Court, Ancaster, Ontario, Canada]; *b* 1935; *m* 17 Sept 1955 *William Hugh Shaw and has issue

  (1) *Mary Elizabeth Warburton; *b* 1911

5 Thomas Tod; Pte 173rd Canadian Highrs WW I; *b* 6 Dec 1877; *m* 1 Feb 1928 Frances Meredith, dau of William Farmer, and *dsp* 12 May 1947

1 Caroline Elizabeth; *b* 10 Oct 1865; *m* 16 April 1885 John Galbraith Horn, Advocate, of Edinburgh (*d* 10 Sept 1925), and *d* 2 July 1949, leaving issue

2 Margaret Georgina Jemima; *b* 23 Jan 1868; *m* 27 April 1897 William MacNish Porter (*d* 28 May 1931) and *d* 29 June 1942, leaving issue

3 Kathleen Nora; *b* 19 Sept 1876; *m* 1st 5 July 1904 Capt James Marshall McLaren, Gordon Highrs (*d* 24 Dec 1910), s of William St Clair McLaren, of the Transvaal; *m* 2nd 8 June 1912 Maj Gustavus Henry Spencer Fowke, Gordon Highrs, 2nd s of Maj Frederick Gustavus Fowke (*see* FOWKE, Bt), and *d* 12 Aug 1958

LE MARCHANT

Arms: Az. a chevron or between three owls arg., legged of the second. **Crest:** Out of a ducal coronet an owl's leg erect or. **Motto:** *Me Minerva lucet* ('Minerva is my light'). **Creation:** Bt. (UK) 14 Oct 1841.

SIR FRANCIS ARTHUR LE MARCHANT, 6TH BT, of Chobham Place, Surrey [Sir Francis Le Marchant Bt, Hungerton Hall, nr Grantham, Lincs]; *b* 6 Oct 1939; *s* f 1987; *educ* Gordonstoun and RA Schools; artist

Lineage: The LE MARCHANTs of Guernsey are probably a branch of the LE MARCHANTs of Bouville, La Manche, France. In a French charter *c* 1200 occurs the name WILLIAM MERCATOR of the Isles, alleged fndr of the Guernsey branch. Other persons of this name are James Le Marchant, Jurat Royal Court 1204, and Robert Le Marchant, who acquired land at Bursenhall, Hants, *temp* HENRY III.

PETER LE MARCHANT; Bailiff (ch civil offr) and Lt-Govr Guernsey *temp* EDWARD I; *m* Matilda — and had:

DENIS LE MARCHANT; Prévôt (Ch Magistrate) 1331; *m* 1st Bonita de Garis; *m* 2nd Perronelle Le Moigne and by his 1st w had:

JOHN LE MARCHANT; Bailiff 1359–83; had:

DENIS LE MARCHANT; Lt Bailiff; *m* Jeanne, dau of Sir William de Chesney, and *d c* 1303, leaving, with a yr s (Janequin, *dsp*) and a dau (Michelle, *m* Janequin de Plessis):

PETER LE MARCHANT; Jurat (Magistrate) Roy Court; *m* Janette Lemprière and *d* 1436, having had, with two er sons (Denis, Lt Bailiff and Seneschal fief of Le Comte 1438, *dsp*; John, Jurat, *m* Collette de la Cour and was ancestor of the LE MARCHANTs of the IoW):

DROUET LE MARCHANT; living 1460; Capt Castle of Beauregard, St Peter Port, Guernsey, *temp* EDWARD IV; had, with a dau (Janette, *m* Thomas Effart):

WILLIAM LE MARCHANT; Lt Bailiff; *m* Laurence Perrin and had, with two daus (Michelle; Laurence, *m* Michael le Petit):

NICHOLAS LE MARCHANT; living 1546; *m* Philippine de la Roque and had, with two yr sons (Nicholas, *dsp*; William, *dsp*):

THOMAS LE MARCHANT; Jurat; *m* Thomasse de la Marche and *d* by 1586, having had, with two yr sons (Thomas, *dsp*; Eleazer, *dsp*) and a dau (Rachael, *m* Giles German):

WILLIAM LE MARCHANT; Lt Bailiff; *m* Margaret du Port and had, with other issue, including a yr s (Josias, ancestor of the LE MARCHANTs of Melrose, St Peter Port):

THOMAS LE MARCHANT; Jurat; *m* Anne de Beauvoir and *d* 1619, having had, with other issue, including two er sons (James, Jurat, *b* 1613, *m* Rachel le Moyne de Vitré and had issue; William, *m* 1st Elizabeth Knapton and 2nd Marie de Saumarez and left issue):

THOMAS LE MARCHANT; *m* Martha de Lisle and had, with two daus:

THOMAS LE MARCHANT, of Le Marchant Manor, Guernsey; Lt Bailiff; *m* Catharine Mauger and had, with an er s (Thomas, Militia Col, *m* Esther Fiott and *dsp* 1816) and four daus:

JOHN LE MARCHANT, of Le Marchant Manor; Col 7th Dragoons Seven Years' War; *m* Mary Catherine Hirzel and *d* 1794, leaving, with a yr s (James, *m* Susannah Falla and had issue):

JOHN GASPARD LE MARCHANT; *b* Amiens 9 Feb 1766; invented the sword exercise, Maj-Gen, Lt-Govr RMC Sandhurst; *m* Mary (*d* 21 Aug 1811), dau of John Carey, Jurat, and was *ka* leading the Heavy Bde on the British side at Salamanca 22 July 1812, having had, with other issue:

  1 Carey; Capt 1st Foot Gds; *b* 5 Dec 1791; *dsp* 12 March 1814 of wounds recd Battle of the Nive

  2 DENIS (Sir), **1st Bt**

  3 John Gaspard (Sir), GCMG , KCB; Gen, Lt-Govr Newfoundland, Halifax and Malta, C-in-C Madras, Col 11th Regt, Kt St Ferdinand 1st and 3rd Cl, Kt Cdr San Carlos Spain; *b* 1803; *m* 28 May 1839 Margaret Anne (*d* 23 Aug 1903), 3rd dau of Rev Robert Taylor and coheir of Rev John Watkins, of Clifton Hall, Staffs, and *d* 6 Feb 1874, having had issue

  4 Thomas, JP, of New Lodge, Herts; Col; *b* 21 Aug 1811; *m* 2 July 1846 Frances Mary Isabella (*d* 15 Oct 1902), only dau of James Smith, of Ashlyus Hall, Herts, and *dsp* 8 Aug 1873

  1 Catherine Stephens; *m* 11 Oct 1821 Rev Thomas Lewis Fanshawe (*d* 5 March 1858), of Parsloes, Essex, and *d* 1 July 1881, leaving issue

  2 Helen; *m* 20 March 1827 Henry Shaw-Lefevre (*d* 3 Dec 1880), bro of Viscount Eversley, GCB (*see* 1928 edn), and *d* Feb 1883, leaving issue

The 2nd son,

Sir Denis Le Marchant, 1st Bt (UK), so *cr* 14 Oct 1841; *b* 3 July 1795; *educ* Eton; MP Worcester, Sec BOT and Treasury, U-Sec Home Dept, Ch Clerk H of C; *m* 9 Jan 1835 Sarah Eliza (*d* 6 March 1894), sis of Sir Charles Smith, 1st Bt (*see* SPENCER-SMITH, Bt), and had:

  1 HENRY DENIS (Sir), **2nd Bt**

  2 Francis Charles; memb Cncl India 1896–1906; *b* 1843; *educ* Eton and Balliol Coll Oxford (BA 1866); *d* 9 Dec 1930

  1 Helen Augusta; *d* 11 Feb 1924

  2 Emma Mary; *d* 3 Feb 1851

The 1st Bt *d* 30 Oct 1874; his er son,

Sir Henry Denis Le Marchant, 2nd Bt, JP (Surrey); *b* 15 Feb 1839; *educ* Eton and Ch Ch Oxford; barrister; *m* 7 Sept 1869 Hon Sophia Strutt (*d* 2 Dec 1928), est dau of 1st Baron Belper (*qv*), and *d* 21 Jan 1915, having had:

  1 **Sir Denis Le Marchant, 3rd Bt**; *b* 8 June 1870; *educ* Trin Hall Cambridge; *m* 1915 Katherine Chisholm (*d* 2 Dec 1965), dau of William Mackey, of Bonar Bridge, and *dsp* 29 April 1922

  2 EDWARD THOMAS (Sir), **4th Bt**

  3 William Gaspard; Lt 6th Bn KRRC; *b* 10 Nov 1873; *educ* Eton and Exeter Coll Oxford (BA); *m* 3 Oct 1903 Ada Constance, yst dau of Albert Mott, and *dsp* 5 May 1944

  4 Herbert Carey; *b* 16 Feb 1875; *educ* Marlborough and King's Coll Cambridge (BA 1896); *d* unm 25 July 1950

  5 Spencer Henry; *b* 4 Aug 1881; barrister, 2nd Lt 6th Bn Roy Fus WW I; *d* 25 May 1915 of wounds recd in action

  1 Amy Frances; *b* 31 Oct 1878; *d* unm 23 Nov 1947

The 3rd Bt's bro,

Sir Edward Thomas Le Marchant, 4th Bt, KCB (1943), CBE (1919), JP (Notts), DL; *b* 23 Oct 1871; *educ* Eton; Notts: CC 1928–37, High Sheriff 1930, dep chm QS 1933–45, chm TAA 1931–45, Army Welfare Offr 1940–44; Col Res of Offrs, Hon Brig-Gen occupation of Crete 1897–98, Boer War 1899–1900, WW I; *m* 11 May 1899 Evelyn Brooks, JP (Notts) (*d* 25 Sept 1957), er dau and coheir of Robert Millington Knowles, JP, DL, of Colston Bassett Hall, Notts, and had:

  1 DENIS, **5th Bt**

  2 Alfred Gaspard; *b* 28 Feb 1906 (twin); *educ* Radley; *m* 12 Sept 1929 Turdis (*d* 11 March 1986), yr dau of Einar Mortensen, of Holte, Denmark, and *d* 3 March 1986, having had:

    (1) Spencer (Sir); commissioned Sherwood Foresters 1949–54, memb Westminster CC 1956–71, MP (C) High Peak Derbys 1970–83, PPS to: Ch Sec Treasury 1972–74, Dept Energy 1974, Leader H of C 1981–82 and For Sec 1982–83, Oppn Whip 1974–79, Jt Sec C Energy Ctee 1979–81, ktd 1984; memb London Stock Exchange 1954–86, ptnr L Messel & Co 1961–86; *b* 15 Jan 1931; *educ* Eton; *m* 5 May 1955 *Lucinda Gaye [Lady Le Marchant, The Saltings, Yarmouth, IoW PO41 0RH], only child of Brig Hugh Nugent Leveson-Gower (*see* SUTHERLAND, D), and *d* 7 Sept 1986, leaving:

      1a *Perronelle Jane; *b* 22 March 1956; *m* 30 May 1979 *James Hudleston, yr s of W A Hudleston, of Bulawayo, and has:

        1b *Hugh Edward; *b* 23 Aug 1983

        1b *Tamara Avril; *b* 16 May 1980

      2a *Geva Ann; *b* 30 Oct 1958; *m* 1991 *Dr Michael McCaldin, er s of Dr John McCaldin, of Natal, and has:

        1b *Elvira Joy; *b* 21 Nov 1994

        2b *Leonora Xa; *b* 25 Nov 1997

    (2) +MICHAEL; *b* 28 July 1937; heir presumptive; *educ* Eton; *m* 1st 2 March 1963 (*divorce* 1980) Philippa Nancy, er dau of Ralph Batchelor Denby, of Sussex; *m* 2nd 1981 (*divorce* 1997) Sandra Elisabeth Champion (*née* Kirby) and by his 1st w has:

      1a +Piers Alfred [Piers Le Marchant Esq, 16 Elms Rd, London SW4 9EX]; *b* 11 April 1964; *m* 1995 *Hon Silvia Pearson, er dau of Baron Pearson of Rannoch (*qv*), and has:

        1b *Edward Charles Carey; *b* 16 Jan 1998

        1b *Olivia Francesca Mary; *b* 9 Feb 1996

      2a +Dickon John; *b* 14 Jan 1968

      1a *Melissa Winifred [Mrs Guy Linley-Adams, The Knapp, Aston, Kingsland, Herefs]; *b* 25 Nov 1965; *m* 1995 *Guy Edward Linley-Adams and has:

        1b *Serena Mary; *b* 31 Aug 1996

      2a *Antonia Ruth; *b* 4 July 1970; *m* 1996 *John Chapple

    (1) *Pamela [Mrs Patrick Mitchell, The Deanery, Windsor Castle, Berks SSL4 1NJ]; *b* 12 July 1933; *m* 1st 26 Oct 1957 Henry Douglas-Pennant (*see* PENRHYN, B); *m* 2nd 1988 Very Rev Patrick Reynolds Mitchell, Dean Windsor, and by her 1st husb has issue

  1 Ruth Alice; *b* 12 Feb 1900; *m* 1st 24 April 1924 (*divorce* 1939) Col John Bury, OBE, 17th/21st Lancers, s of John Bury, of Cheshire; *m* 2nd 15 Nov 1939 Brig Sir Gerald Thomas Fisher, KBE, CSI, CIE (*d* 6 Sept 1965), and *d* 10 Jan 1982, leaving by her 1st husb:

    (1) *John Edward, DL (Devon 1989) [John Bury Esq DL, Buckland Manor, Braunton, N Devon EX33 1HN]; *b* 26 Sept 1927; *educ* Oxford (MA); *m* 28 June 1961 *Diana Mary, er dau of Lt-Col G S Incledon-Webber, TD, DL, MA, OStJ, and Angela Frances, dau of Sir Pierce Lacy, 1st Bt (*qv*), and has had:

      1a *Henry Incledon; *b* 5 May 1962

      2a Edward John; *b* 11 March, *d* 18 April 1970

      1a *Mary Helen; *b* 7 March 1964; *m* 27 June 1987 *Marc Arthur Richard Cumberlege, s of Lt-Col Jeremy Richard Parbury Cumberlege, and has:

1b *Edward Jeremy Parbury; *b* 3 Aug 1991

2b *Nicholas Antony; *b* 4 Oct 1993

2a *Anne Ruth; *b* 21 May 1965

3a *Eleanor Frances; *b* 30 May 1967; *m* 1 Aug 1998 *James Grant Mac-Donald-Smith, s of William Ian MacDonald-Smith

4a *Jane Angela; *b* 10 May 1971

5a *Clare Elizabeth; *b* 6 Oct 1972; MA

(1) *Rosemary; *b* 23 Oct 1930; *m* 9 July 1960 *Maj John Angus McKay Forbes, RE, s of Brig L W McKay Forbes, and has:

1a *Robert Angus; *b* 2 March 1964

1a *Joanna Elizabeth; *b* 27 Jan 1962

(2) *Margaret; *b* 15 Nov 1931; *m* 6 Sept 1958 *Christopher Eldred Hindson, est s of Lt-Col Richard Eldred Hindson and Margaret Eacy, dau of Sir Henry Hayes Lawrence, 2nd Bt, of Lucknow (*qv*), and has:

1a *Richard Charles; *b* 11 June 1959; *m* 3 Dec 1994 *Catherine, dau of C G Headlam, and has:

1b *John Francis; *b* 13 Oct 1996

1b *Camilla Sarah; *b* 2 May 1998

1a *Catherine Margaret; *b* 7 June 1961; *m* 18 March 1994 *Peter Thomas Martin and has:

1b *Tighe Patrick Martin Hindson; *b* 29 Oct 1997

2 Joan Margaret, JP (Oxon 1953); *b* 11 April 1901; *m* 29 Sept 1921 Maj Noel Brand Brooks and had issue (*see* CRAWSHAW, B)

3 Geva; *b* 19 Aug 1914; *d* 28 Feb 1932 following a hunting accident

4 Barbara; *b* 26 March 1916; *d* 30 July 1938

Sir EDWARD *d* 17 Nov 1953; his er son,

Sir Denis Le Marchant, 5th Bt, of Huntington Hall, Lincs; *b* 28 Feb; *educ* Radley; Capt Cheshire Yeo (Res), Lt Nottingham (Sherwood Rangers) Yeo 1906, High Sheriff Lincs 1958; *m* 30 June 1933 *Elizabeth Rowena [Lady Le Marchant, Hungerton Hall, Grantham, Lincs], yst dau of Arthur Hovenden Worth, of Hovenden Ho, Fleet, Lincs, and *d* 1987, having had:

1 Peter Edward; *b* 11 June 1934; *educ* Eton and Lincoln Coll Oxford; *d* unm 11 July 1972

2 Sir FRANCIS ARTHUR LE MARCHANT, **6th and present Bt**

1 *(Penelope) Clare [Mrs Frederick Connell, Colston Bassett House, Colston Bassett, Notts]; *b* 18 March 1944; *m* 1st 3 Oct 1964 (*divorce* 1989) Capt John Henry Warrand Hanmer (*see* HANMER, Bt) and has issue; *m* 2nd *Frederick Connell

LEON

Arms: Gules two sunflowers erect, slipped, leaved and eradicated or, seeded sable. **Crest:** Issuant from a mural crown or a demi-lion gules, grasping between the paws a sunflower erect, leaved and slipped or, seeded sable. **Motto:** Seek the truth. **Creation:** Bt. (UK) 5 July 1911.

SIR JOHN RONALD LEON, 4TH BT, of Bletchley Park, Bletchley, Co Buckingham [Sir John Leon Bt, c/o ICM Ltd, Oxford House, 76 Oxford St, London W1N 0AX]; *b* 16 Aug 1934; *s* f 1964; *educ* Eton, Millfield and Byam Shaw Sch of Art; late 2nd Lt KRRC; actor (as John Standing); *m* 1961 (*divorce* 1972) Jill, actress, dau of Jack Melford, and has:

1 +ALEXANDER JOHN; *b* 3 May 1965; *educ* Bryanston; *m* 30 Nov 1996 *Susan Brooks

Sir JOHN *m* 2nd 1984 *Sarah Kate, dau of Bryan John Forbes, film dir, and by her has:

2 +Archie; *b* 1986

1 *India; *b* 1985

2 *Octavia; *b* 1989

Lineage: GEORGE ISAAC LEON, of Gloucester Place, Portman Sq, London W, and First Ave, Brighton; *m* Julia Ann (*d* 15 June 1901), dau of John Samuel, of London, and *d* 6 Feb 1885, having had, with other issue:

Sir Herbert Samuel Leon, 1st Bt (UK), so *cr* 5 July 1911, JP (Bucks); *b* 11 Feb 1850; MP (Lib) N Bucks 1891–95, CA Bucks, High Sheriff Bucks 1909; *m* 1st 4

June 1873 Esther Julia (*d* 15 May 1875), dau of Edward Henry Beddington, of 98 Lancaster Gate, London W, and had:

1 GEORGE EDWARD (Sir), **2nd Bt**

1 Mabel Julia; *b* April 1874; *m* 2 Dec 1897 Henry Hyman Haldin, KC (*d* 30 Nov 1931), s of Philip Haldinstein, of Norwich, and *d* 6 April 1970, leaving issue

Sir Herbert *m* 2nd 4 Aug 1880 Fanny (*d* 20 Jan 1937), dau of David Hyman, of Bloomsbury, and by her had:

2 Reginald Herbert; *b* 13 May 1882; memb London Stock Exchange; *m* 1st 8 Nov 1906 (*divorce* 1916) Rita Ethel, dau of Abram de Mattos Mocatta, and had:

(1) Herbert Geoffrey; *b* 2 Oct 1907; *d* 3 Nov 1911

(2) Richard Neville; *b* 29 Aug 1909; *educ* privately and Edinburgh U (MA); *m* 11 Jan 1941 Marjory Frances (*d* 1991), only dau of Sir William Henry Robinson, KCMG, CBE, and *d* 1981, having had:

1a +David Richard [David Leon Esq, Benton Cottage, Peters Green, Bodiam, E Sussex TN32 5UN]; *b* 12 Oct 1946; *educ* Epsom; *m* 1970 *Maria Amelia da Conceicao, only dau of Domingos Jacinto, of Lisbon, and has:

1b +Daniel James; *b* 1976

1b *Jennifer Rachel; *b* 1972

(3) Derek Noel; *b* 15 Dec 1912; *m* 24 June 1936 Nancy Juliet (*m* 2nd 3 Feb 1940 Walter Duncan Spicer), yr dau of Percy Shirley, of London, and *d* 6 March 1938

2 (cont.) Reginald Leon *m* 2nd 2 Dec 1920 Mary Millicent (*d* 12 March 1950), dau of James Blagbrough, and *d* 3 Sept 1960

2 Margaret Alice; *b* 1 June 1881; *m* 7 Dec 1899 Cecil Frank Raphael (*d* 15 Dec 1936), yst s of Henry Lewis Raphael, of 31 Portland Place, London W, bro of Sir Herbert Raphael, 1st and last Bt (*see* 1924 edn), and had issue

Sir HERBERT *d* 23 July 1926; his er son,

Sir George Edward Leon, 2nd Bt; *b* 7 May 1875; *educ* Eton; barrister Lincoln's Inn 1898; memb London Stock Exchange; *m* 1st 19 Jan 1899 (*divorce* 1923) Mildred Ethel (*d* 7 March 1951), dau of Louis J Jennings, MP Stockport, and had:

1 RONALD GEORGE (Sir), **3rd Bt**

1 Esther Mildred; *b* 16 Dec 1899; *m* 20 March 1920 Maj Hon Philip Plantagenet Cary, 2nd surv s of 12th Viscount Falkland (*qv*), and *d* 1972, leaving issue

Sir George *m* 2nd 23 July 1928 Anne Dorothy (*m* 3rd 5 July 1952 Thomas Parrington; *d* 16 March 1963), est dau of Edward Cazalet Browne and formerly w of Capt Victor Charles Hugh Gordon-Lennox (*see* RICHMOND and GORDON, D), and *d* 14 May 1947

His only s,

Sir Ronald George Leon, 3rd Bt; *b* 22 Oct 1902; *educ* Eton and Magdalen Coll Oxford; Capt KRRC WW II, memb London Stock Exchange; *m* 1st 28 Oct 1924 Rosemary, dau of George Armstrong, and had:

1 Anne Elizabeth; *b* 8 Dec 1925; *m* 19 Dec 1950 (*divorce* 1964) Michael Gough, actor, s of Francis Berkeley Gough, of Manyuki, Kenya, and had:

(1) *Emma Frances; *b* 13 Aug 1953

Sir Ronald *m* 2nd 9 Nov 1932 (*divorce* 1945) Dorothy Katherine (Kay Hammond, the actress, who *m* 2nd 1946 Sir John Selby Clements, CBE, actor and dir (*d* 1988), and *d* 1980), dau of Sir Guy Standing, KBE, and by her had:

1 Sir JOHN RONALD LEON, **4th and present Bt**

2 +Timothy Michael George [Timothy Leon Esq, 26 Benbow Rd, London W6; Fermor House, Somerton, Oxon]; *b* 31 May 1938; *educ* Stowe; late Sub-Lt RNVR; *m* 1969 *Suzanne, dau of Col H Kinnear, JP, late KOYLI

Sir Ronald *m* 3rd 23 June 1947 Alice Mary, only dau of Dr Thomas Holt, of Whalley, Lancs, and *d* 29 Aug 1964

LESLIE

Arms: Quarterly, 1st and 4th, arg. on a bend az., between two holly leaves vert three buckles or; 2nd and 3rd, or a lion rampant gu., debruised by a ribbon sa. **Crest:** A griffin's head erased gu. **Motto:** Grip fast. **Creation:** Bt. (UK) 21 Feb 1876.

SIR JOHN NORMAN IDE LESLIE, 4TH BT, of Glaslough, Co Monaghan [Sir John Leslie Bt, Glaslough, Co Monaghan, Ireland; Badia di St Sebastiano di Alatri,

Alatri, Frosinone, Italy]; *b* 6 Dec 1916; *s f* 1971; *educ* Downside and Magdalene Coll Cambridge (BA 1938); Capt Irish Gds WW II (POW), Kt Hon and Devotion SMO Malta, Kt Cdr St Gregory the Great

Lineage: Sir ANDREW de LESLIE of Leslie (*see* ROTHES, E); *d* by 28 Nov 1324, leaving a 5th s:

Sir GEORGE LESLIE of Balquhain, Aberdeenshire, allegedly erected into a (territorial) Barony by charter from DAVID II 1340; *d* 1351, leaving:

Sir HAMELIN LESLIE, 2nd of Balquhain; *d* 1378, leaving:

Sir ANDREW LESLIE, 3rd of Balquhain; *k* in a feud with the FORBESes 22 Jan 1420, leaving:

Sir WILLIAM LESLIE, 4th of Balquhain; Baillie (Magistrate) Regality of Garioch; *m* 1st Elizabeth, dau of Hugh Fraser, 6th of Lovat (*see* LOVAT, L), and had:

1 Alexander, 5th of Balquhain; ancestor of the (territorial) Barons Balquhain, Counts Leslie of the Holy Roman Empire

2 William, 1st of Kincraigie

Sir WILLIAM *m* 2nd Agnes, dau of Alexander Irvine, 5th of Drum, and by her had:

3 ALEXANDER

4 George, 1st of New Leslie

5 Thomas, Minister of Kingussie

Sir WILLIAM *m* 3rd Euphemia, only child of William Lindsay of Cairney and by her had:

6 David, 1st of Pitcople

7 James, 2nd of Pitcople

The est son by the 2nd w,

ALEXANDER LESLIE, 1st of Wardis; Comptroller Household to JAMES III; *m* Isabel Lauder, who brought him Balcomie, Fife, and *d* 1500, having had, with at least one dau (Elizabeth, *m* 1st William Seton of Meldrum (*see* SETON, Bt, of Pitmedden) and 2nd John Collison, of Aberdeen):

JOHN LESLIE, 2nd of Wardis; Baillie Regality of Garioch; had free charters of Kintore and extensive lands in Garioch; *b* 1460, *m* 1st —, dau of Alexander, Bp Moray (*see* MORAY, E); *m* 2nd Margaret, dau of 1st Lord Crichton, of Frendraught; *m* 3rd Margaret, widow of Walter Stewart of Dryland and dau of Forbes of Ech; *m* 4th Agnes, dau of Patrick Gordon of Haddo; *m* 5th Annabella, dau of Chalmers of Balbithan, and *d* 1546, having had:

ALEXANDER LESLIE, 3rd of Wardis; *m* 1st Margaret, dau of Alexander Forbes of Towie, and *m* 2nd Elizabeth, dau of Sir William Seton of Meldrum; *m* 3rd Isabel Menzies and *d* 1574, having had by his 1st w (and by one or other of his ws at least one dau, Marjorie, *m* 1545 John Innes of Edingight; *see* INNES, Bt, of Balvenie):

WILLIAM LESLIE, 4th of Wardis; Falconer to JAMES VI; *m* Janet, dau of Robert Innes of Innermarkie, and had, with other issue:

1 John, 5th of Wardis; *m* Jane, dau of Sir James Crichton of Frendraught, and had:

(1) Sir JOHN LESLIE, 1st Bt (NS), so *cr* 1 Sept 1625, with remainder to heirs male whatsoever; *m* Elspeth (*m* 2nd 24 June 1641 Sir Alexander Gordon, 1st Bt, of Cluny, and *d* 2 Dec 1642), dau of John Gordon of Newton, and *d* 1640, having had, with two other sons:

1a Sir JOHN LESLIE, 2nd Bt; *d unm* 1645

1a Janet; *m* 1st John Gordon of Avochie; *m* 2nd George Gordon of Newton

2a Elizabeth; *m* Sir John Gordon of Cluny

3a Marjory; *m* 1st Sir Alexander Bannerman of Elsick (*see* BANNERMAN, Bt); *m* 2nd Sir John Fletcher, King's Advocate

(2) William, *de jure* 3rd Bt, though he neither assumed the title (which on his death became dormant till 1800) nor inherited the estates; *m* Helen, dau of George Gordon of Newton, and had four sons (*dsp*) and three daus

(3) Norman; *m* Marjory, dau of John Leith of Harthill, and had:

1a John, of New Rayne; *m* Janet Gordon, of Newton, and had:

1b Patrick, of New Rayne, which he sold 1700; *m* Margaret, dau of Gordon of Braco, and had:

1c William, of Aberdeen; had a s (William, *dsp*)

2c John; had:

1d Sir JOHN LESLIE, 4th Bt; WS; assumed the title 1800; *m* 15 July 1794 Caroline Jemima (*d* 1810), only dau and heiress of Abraham Leslie of Dindrassie, and *d* 30 Sept 1825, having had:

1e Sir CHARLES ABRAHAM LESLIE, 5th Bt; *b* 4 July 1796; *m* 1822 Anne (*d* 7 Oct 1868), dau of Adam Walker, and *d* 1 March 1847, having had:

1f Sir NORMAN ROBERT LESLIE, 6th Bt, Lt 19th Bengal Native Inf; *b* 10 Dec 1822; *m* 17 Dec 1846 Jessie Elizabeth (*d* at Lucknow 1 July 1876), 3rd dau of Major Robert Wood Smith, 6th Bengal Lt Cav, and was *k* Indian Mutiny 12 June 1857, having had:

1g Sir CHARLES HENRY (Sir), 7th Bt, CB; *b* 27 Nov 1848; Col IA, Cmdt 2nd Bn 4th Gurkhas, CO Cawnpore 1900–04; *m* 7 Jan 1879 Emma May (*d* 12 Aug 1937), dau of R M Edwards, Bengal CS, and *d* 12 Oct 1905, leaving:

1h Sir NORMAN RODERICK ALEXANDER DAVID LESLIE, 8th Bt, CMG, CBE; *b* 10 Jan 1889; W/Cdr RAF, Maj KGO Centl India Horse IA, RFC 1916, RAF 1919, Air Attaché Paris 1919, Sec CID 1924, Imp Wireless and Cables Conf 1928, Imp Communications Advsy Ctee 1929; jt md Cable and Wireless 1933; *m* 4 Oct 1919 Betty Elise , dau of John Thomas Beadsworth Sewell, CBE, and *d* 16 June 1937, leaving:

1i Sir (HENRY JOHN) LINDORES LESLIE, 9th Bt; *b* 26 Aug 1920; *educ* Stowe; Capt 12th Lancers SRO WW II 1939–40 with E R Yorks Yeo (POW), ACIS; *m* 12 July 1950 *Colette Kathleen [Lady Leslie, 10 Sloane Gate Mansions, London SW1], formerly w of Lt-Cdr Trevor Russell-Walling, RN, and only dau of George Theodore Cregan, MC, MB, of Commonside House, Rogate, Hants, and *d* 21 June 1967, when the btcy once more became dormant, leaving:

1j *(Elizabeth) Jean; *b* 21 April 1952; *m* 10 Nov 1972 *Sir Richard William Hyde Parker, 12th Bt, of Melford Hall, Suffolk (*qv*), and has issue

1i *Nancy Jean [Mrs William Gerard Leigh, 15 Eaton Mansions, Cliveden Place, London SW1; Hayes, East Woodhay, Berks RG15 0AN]; *b* 20 Nov 1923; *m* 29 Oct 1946 *Col William Henry Gerard Leigh, CVO, CBE, Life Gds, Gentleman Usher to HM THE QUEEN, s of Lt-Col John Cecil Gerard Leigh, of Thorpe Satchville Hall, Melton Mowbray, Leics, and has:

1j *John Norman [John Gerard Leigh Esq, The Old Rectory, Doynton, Bristol]; *b* 24 July 1949; *educ* Eton; *m* 1977 *Lavinia Sheila, dau of Leopold Richard Seymour (*see* HERTFORD, M), and has:

1k *Louisa Helen; *b* 1980

2k *Emily Rose; *b* 1982

3k *Laura Katherine; *b* 1984

2j *David William Philip [David Gerard Leigh, 16 Ormeley Rd, London SW12 9QE]; *b* 28 Aug 1958 (HRH THE DUKE OF EDINBURGH stood sponsor); *m* 1990 *Julie S, est dau of H A Rall, of Johannesburg, and has:

1k *James Henry; *b* 1991

1k *Jessica Rose; *b* 1993

1j *Carolyn Jane; *b* 12 Nov 1947; *m* 1977, as his 2nd w, *Charles Edward Riou Benson, and has:

1k *Honor May; *b* 1980

2j *Camilla Madeleine; *b* 4 July 1952; *m* 1979, as his 2nd w, her bro's bro-in-law Hugh Leopold Seymour (*see* above)

1h Marjory Scott; *m* 31 Jan 1901 Col A E Sealy, 4th Bn Gurkha Rifles, yst s of Rev A F Sealy, of Cochin, and *d* 1903, leaving issue. He *d* Feb 1920

2h Margaret Jean, MBE (1919); *m* 5 March 1903 Lt-Col Albert Elijah Walter, OBE, IMS, s of E Walter, JP, of Putford, Devon, and *d* April 1966, leaving issue. He *d* 11 Jan 1933

3h Jessie Helen May; *m* 14 Sept 1905 Maj Gilbert Lewis, Centl India Horse, s of Hon J Lewis, MLC, Australia, and *d* 16 Nov 1961, leaving issue

4h Rothes Beatrix; *m* 29 Feb 1908 Adml Sir Charles James Colebrooke Little, GCB, s of Louis S Little, of Mayfair, and *d* 9 May 1939, having had issue. He *d* 20 June 1973

1g Annie Josephine; *m* 27 July 1871 Bradford Smith, Bengal SC, and had issue

2g Ada Mary Susan; *m* 30 March 1872 Col John Arthur Barlow, Manchester Regt, and *d* 27 June 1889

3g Georgina Julie; *m* 1870 Col Henry Metcalfe Rose, DSO, IA, and *d* 18 July 1908. He *d* 22 Dec 1909

4g Catherine Louisa; *m* 26 Dec 1872 Maj Frederick Whitworth Russell Jones, Highland LI, and *d* 1926, leaving issue. He *d* 1894

5g Emily Helen; *m* 1874 Lt-Col William Henry Gregg, MD, IMS, and *d* 28 May

2f John Lloyd; *dvp* 18 June 1845

1f Georgina Elizabeth Gordon; *m* 9 July 1847 Rev George Turnbull

2f Ada Walker; *b* 1830; *m* 1 Sept 1857 James Robertson Turnbull, of Paignton, S Devon, 2nd s of Mark Turnbull, and *d* 13 March 1918. He *d* 9 Nov 1907

2e John; Capt 42nd Highrs; had an only child (Caroline, *m* Capt Thomas Jenkins, Madras Army, s of Sir R Jenkins, GCB)

3e Thomas; *b* 1800; *m* 1839 Pennel, est dau of John Grant, Capt 78th Regt, and had, with another s:

1f John; *b* 1840; *m* 1868 Elizabeth (*d* 1902), dau of Henry Myhill, of Mercury House, Brentford, and *d* 1913, leaving:

1g Frank Harvey; *b* 2 Sept 1874; *educ* Christ's Hosp; *m* 1st 1915 Amelia Caroline (*d* 1918), dau of Alexander Russon, rlwy engr, and had:

1h +(Percy) Theodore; *b* Nov 1915; probable heir to the btcy *cr* 1625 and dormant since 1967

1g (cont.) Frank Leslie *m* 2nd 1918 Agnes Maude (*d* 1948), dau of Frank Spooner, artist, and *d* 9 April 1965

1g Eliza Myhill; *b* 1872; *m* 1897 John Leslie Brown and *d* April 1946, leaving issue. He *d* 1928

2g Josephine Ann; *b* 1878; *d unm* 23 Sept 1945

1e Caroline Jemima; *m* John Murray

2e Rothes Beatrix; *m* 16 July 1831 Hugh Inglis and *d* 14 Feb 1884 aged 79, having had issue

3e Cecilia Margaret; *m* 1st James Grant; *m* 2nd Claud Russell and *d* 6 Nov 1889, leaving issue

2 George; had:

(1) John; *b* Scotland; *educ* Aberdeen and Oxford (DD); Bp of the Isles 1628, Raphoe 1633 and Clogher 1661; acquired the Castle Lesley estate, otherwise called Glaslough, Co Monaghan; *m* Katherine, dau of Alexander Conyngham (*see* CONYNGHAM, M), and *d* 4 Sept 1671, leaving a 2nd s:

1a Charles (Rev), of Glaslough; *b* 17 July 1650; Chllr Diocese of Connor 1686; *m* Jane, dau of Very Rev Richard Griffith, Dean Ross, and *d* 13 April 1722, leaving:

1b Robert, of Glaslough; *m* 1730 Frances, 4th dau of Stephen Ludlow, and *d* 17 Dec 1743, having had, with a dau (Annabella, *m* Robert Leigh, of Rosegarland, Co Wexford):

1c Charles Powell, of Glaslough; MP Co Monaghan; *m* 1st 22 May 1765 Prudence Penelope, dau of 1st Viscount of Dungannon (*see* DOWNSHIRE, M), and had:

1d Charles Powell, of Glaslough, JP, High Sheriff 1788, MP Co Monaghan 1802–26, Col Co Monaghan Militia; m 1st Anne (d Jan 1819), dau of Rev Dudley Charles Ryder, of Merrion Sq, Dublin, and had three daus; m 2nd 24 May 1819 Christiana (d 24 April 1869), yst dau of George Fosbery, of Clorane, Co Limerick, and d 15 Nov 1831, having by her had:

1e Charles Powell, of Glaslough; b 13 Sept 1821; Co Monaghan: HM Lt, Hon Col Militia, MP 1842–71; d unm 26 June 1871

2e JOHN (Sir) 1st Bt

3e Thomas LESLIE later SLINGSBY (roy licence 9 April 1869), JP and DL Yorks; b 12 Oct 1826; Capt RHG Crimean War, original bearer of the message to the Light Bde which was snatched from him by the overzealous Capt Nolan and relayed by the latter in garbled form, with the well-known disastrous consequences; m 19 July 1860 Emma Louisa Catherine (dsp 1 July 1899), only sis and heiress of Sir Charles Slingsby, Bt (see 1869 edn), and d 6 Sept 1903

1e Christiana; m 20 Feb 1843 4th Marquess of Waterford (qv) and d 19 May 1905, leaving issue

2e Prudentia Penelope; m 14 Aug 1850 Rt Hon George Augustus Cavendish-Bentinck, MP, and d 22 June 1896, leaving issue (see PORTLAND, E)

3e Julia; d unm

4e Emily; d unm 16 April 1909

2d John (Rt Rev); DD; b 12 Oct 1772; Bp Dromore 1812, Elphin 1820; m 8 Aug 1808 Isabella (d 10 Nov 1830), 2nd dau of Rt Rev Hon Thomas St Lawrence, Bp Cork and Ross (see 1909 edn HOWTH, E), and d 22 July 1854, leaving issue

1c (cont.) Charles Leslie m 2nd 9 May 1785 Mary Anne (d March 1830), dau and heiress of Rev Joshua Tench, of Bryanstown, Co Wexford, and d Aug 1800, having by her had:

3d Edward (Rev); Treasurer Dromore Cathedral 1817–47, Rector Annahilt, Co Down, 1847; b 8 Nov 1792; educ Ch Ch Oxford (BA); m 1820 Margaret (d 13 Nov 1872), dau of Rev Thomas Edward Higginson, of Lisburn, Co Antrim, and d 2 Jan 1865, leaving issue

1d Emily Jane; m Rev J Hallward, Vicar Assington, Suffolk

2d Harriet; m Rev William Hallward, Rector Minden, Suffolk

3d Mary Anne; d unm

4d Isabella Frances; m 23 June 1821 Anthony Cliffe, of Bellvue, Co Wexford

The 2nd s,

Sir John Leslie, 1st Bt (UK), so cr 21 Feb 1876 , of Glaslough, JP and DL Cos Donegal and Monaghan; b 16 Dec 1822; educ Ch Ch Oxford (MA); MP Co Monaghan 1871–80, Capt 1st Life Gds; m 26 Aug 1856 Lady Constance Wilhelmina Frances (d 25 June 1925), sis of 4th Earl of Portarlington (qv), and had:

1 JOHN (Sir), **2nd Bt**

1 Mary; Médaille de la Reine Elisabeth Belgium; b 30 Sept 1858; m 20 July 1893 Robert Thompson Crawshay, 2nd s of Robert Thompson Crawshay, of Cyfarthfa Castle, Glam, and d 18 April 1936, leaving issue

2 Constance Christina; b 23 Sept 1861; m 2 June 1881 Sir Edward Stanley Hope, KCB, and d 30 May 1945, leaving issue (see LINLITHGOW, M)

3 Theodosia, DGStJ, RRC; b 5 Jan 1865; m 1st 11 June 1885 Josceline Fitzroy Bagot (see BAGOT, B) and had issue; m 2nd 3 June 1920 Rev Sidney Bellingham Swann, Vicar Lindfield, and d 21 Feb 1940

4 Olive Louisa Blanche; b 14 Sept 1872; m 1st 30 Aug 1894 Walter Murray Guthrie (d 24 April 1911), of Torosay Castle, Isle of Mull, MP Tower Hamlets, yst s of James Alexander Guthrie of Craigie, and had issue; m 2nd 30 Dec 1914 (divorce 1920) Lt-Col John Alexander Stirling, DSO, MC (d 28 Nov 1957), of Kippenross and Kippendavie, of Perthshire, and d 3 July 1945

The 1st Bt d 23 Jan 1916; his only son,

Sir John Leslie, 2nd Bt, CBE (1919); HM Lt Co Monaghan 1921–22, High Sheriff 1905, Hon Col 5th Bn Roy Irish Fus, Lt Gren Gds, Egypt 1882 (medal with clasp, bronze star), Boer War 1900, T/Lt-Col cmdg 12th Res Bn Roy Inniskilling Fus 1915; b 7 Aug 1857; m 2 Oct 1884 Leonie Blanche, DGStJ, Médaille de la Reine Elisabeth (d 21 Aug 1943), dau of Leonard Jerome, of NY, and sis of Lady Randolph Churchill (see MARLBOROUGH, D), and had:

1 (JOHN RANDOLPH) SHANE (Sir), **3rd Bt**

2 Norman Jerome Beauchamp; Capt Rifle Bde; b 20 Nov 1886; ka 18 Oct 1914

3 Seymour William; Sec Queen Charlotte's Hosp, author: Glaslough in Oriel, The Silent Queen and The Jerome Connexion; b 30 Sept 1889; m 9 Oct 1929 Gwyneth Rawdon, dau of Rawdon Roden, of Knaresborough, Yorks, and d 21 July 1979, leaving:

(1) *Jennifer Constance [Miss Jennifer Leslie, Castle Leslie (West), Glaslough, Co Monaghan, Ireland]; b 16 June 1930

4 Lionel Alistair David; Capt Cameron Highrs WW II (despatches), sculptor, explorer, author: Wilderness Trails in Three Continents, One Man's World and Ladies from Hell; b 27 June 1900; educ Eton; m 12 Jan 1942 Barbara Yvonne, dau of Edwin Alexander Enever, and d 1987, having had:

(1) *Leonie Deirdre Elise [Mrs Luiz Monteiro de Barros, 38 Bloemfontein Ave, London W12 4BL]; b 28 April 1944; educ Trin Coll Dublin (BA 1967); m 1975 *Luiz Monteiro de Barros, of Rio de Janeiro, and has:

1a *Leo Alexander; b 1976

2a *Jaime Norman Jerome; b 1977

Sir JOHN d 25 Jan 1944; his est son,

Sir (John Randolph) Shane Leslie, 3rd Bt; b 24 Sept 1885; educ Eton and King's Coll Cambridge (BA 1907, MA 1909); author of nearly 40 books (including poetry, biography, anthology and ghost stories), memb Irish Academy of Letters, Kt Cdr St Gregory the Great; m 1st 11 June 1912 Marjorie (d 8 Feb 1951), dau of Hon Henry C Ide, of Vermont, Govr-Gen Philippine Islands and US Min Spain, and had:

1 Sir JOHN NORMAN IDE LESLIE, **4th and present Bt**

2 +DESMOND ARTHUR PETER [Desmond Leslie Esq, Castle Leslie, Glaslough, Co Monaghan]; b 29 June 1921 (HRH THE DUKE OF CONNAUGHT stood sponsor); heir presumptive; educ Ampleforth and Trin Coll Dublin; WW II as F/Sgt (Pilot) RAF, author: Careless Lives, Pardon my Return, Angels Weep, Flying Saucers Have Landed, Hold Back the Night, The Amazing Mr Lutterworth; m 18 Aug 1945 (divorce Mexico) Agnes Elizabeth, only dau of Rudolf Bernauer, producer and playwright, of Budapest, and has:

(1) +Shaun Rudolph Christopher; b 4 June 1947; educ Ampleforth; m 1987 (divorce 1989) Charlotte Bing

(2) +(Christopher) Mark; b 7 Dec 1952; m 1982 *Cliona Manahan and has:
1a +Luke Daniel; b 1987
1a *Leah; b 1992

(1) *Antonia Kelvey Oriel; b 1 Nov 1963; m 7 July 1995 *Colm Nolan, s of Padraig and Anne Nolan, of Dublin

2 (cont.) Desmond Leslie has by *Jennifer Helen, est dau of Lt-Col Ian Strong, of Wiveliscombe, Somerset:

(2) *Samantha Helen; b 1966

(3) *Camilla Patricia; b 1968

1 Anne (Anita) Theodosia Moira; b 21 Nov 1914; S African Army 1940–42, ambulance driver 1st Armoured Div French Army 1944–45 (Croix de Guerre Feb 1945), author: Train to Nowhere, Love in a Nutshell, The Remarkable Leonard Jerome, Mrs Fitzherbert, Jennie, A Life of Lady Randolph Churchill, The Tempestuous Career of Cousin Clare and Cousin Randolph; m 1st 29 April 1937 (annulled 1948, resumed maiden name by deed poll May 1947) Col Paul Rodzianko, CMG (d 16 April 1965), s of Gen Paul Rodzianko and Princess Marie Galitzine; m 2nd 1 Jan 1949 *Cdr William (Bill) Donald Ælian King, DSO and bar, DSC, RN, only s of Lt-Col William Albert de Courcy King, DSO, and d 5 Nov 1984, having had:

(1) *(Richard) Tarka Bourke [Tarka Leslie-King Esq, Pentridge House, Pentridge, Wilts]; b 27 Aug 1949; educ Milton Abbey; m 3 July 1976 *June Henrietta Mary, dau of Sir Hamish Stewart Forbes, 7th Bt, of Neme (qv) and has:
1a *William Peter Wilfred; b 22 Nov 1981
1a *Olivia Maude; b 1 Feb 1985

(1) *Leonie Rose [Mrs Alec Finn, Oranmore Castle, Oranmore, Co Galway, Ireland]; b 10 Oct 1951; m *Alec Finn and has:
1a *Cian
1a *Heather

Sir Shane m 2nd 30 May 1958 Iris Carola (d 1994), widow of Capt Donald Alexander Frazer and yst dau of Charles Miskin Laing, barrister, of Bury Knowle, Headington, Oxford, and d 13 Aug 1971

Seat: Glaslough, Co Monaghan, Ireland. Formerly known as Castle Leslie, but re-Gaelicised to accommodate modern (i.e., backward-looking) Irish susceptibilities (see also LONGFORD, E, sub Tullynally), Glaslough is not at all Celtic in style. But neither is it Georgian. It was erected around 1870, the heyday of the style that has become known as Victorian Institutional. It had two architects. One was Sir Charles Lanyon, who was first and foremost a civil engineer and whose major works include the Belfast Court House, County Gaol and Custom House and homes for deaf mutes and the blind. At Glaslough he was supposedly responsible for the softer touches, such as the Cloister in neo-Renaissance style, allegedly modelled on one by Michelangelo in Rome. The somewhat grim exterior is by W H Lynn, whose angular lines on gables and polygonal bow windows with their heavy sash glazing interspersed by vertically crenellated polychrome brick adornments contrast with the more feminine archs to the ambulatory but are inevitably what first arrest the eye of the newcomer.

Outside, geopolitical considerations predominate. A corner of the estate edges over into Northern Ireland so that a wise resident will turn a blind eye to nocturnal toings and froings in the woods. The lake to the front of the building is entirely charming, however, and the shrub-dotted lawns that sweep down to it add to the sense of tranquillity. Internally the walls are enlivened with Italianate wall paintings by the **1st Bt**. Many of the ceilings are also highly decorated, particularly those in the hall, drawing room and dining room. The house is much in demand both sides of the border for functions.

LESTER OF HERNE HILL

Creation: B. (LP, UK) 1993.

THE BARON LESTER OF HERNE HILL, of Herne Hill, in the London Borough of Southwark (Anthony Paul Lester) [The Rt Hon The Lord Lester of Herne Hill, 2 Hare Court, Temple, London EC4Y 7BH]; b 3 July 1936; educ City of London Sch, Trin Coll Cambridge (BA) and Harvard Law Sch (LLM); 2nd Lt RA 1955–57; barrister Lincoln's Inn 1963, QC 1975, Bencher 1985, NI Bar 1984, Irish Bar 1983, Recorder SE Circuit 1987–93; Special Advsr: Home Sec 1974–76, Standing Advsy Commn Human Rights NI 1975–77, Lib Dem working peer; Pres Lib Dem Lawyers' Assoc; Chm: Govrs James Allen's Girls' Sch 1987–91 (memb 1984–94) and Interights (Internat Centre for Legal Protection of Human Rights) (Pres 1991–), co fndr, former chm and tstee Runnymede Tst 1991–97; Memb: Bd Overseers Pennsylvania Law Sch 1978–89, Ct Govrs LSE, Internat Law Assoc Ctee on Human Rights, American Law Inst 1985–; Govr Br Inst Human Rights, Bd Dirs Salzburg Seminar Austria; Winner Human Rights Lawyer award 1997; Hon Visiting Prof Law UCL; Ed-in-Ch Butterworth's Human Rights Cases; consultant ed Constitutional Law and Human Rights (1997); author: Justice in the American South (1964), Shawcross and Beaumont on Air Law (co-author, 3rd edn, 1964), Race and Law (1972); m 1971 *Catherine Elizabeth Debora, dau of Michael Morris Wassey, of London, and has:

1 *Gideon; b 1972

1 *Maya; b 1974

Lineage: HARRY LESTER, of London; m Kate — and had an only s:

ANTHONY PAUL, cr a **Baron**

LETHBRIDGE

Arms: Arg. over water ppr. a bridge of five arches embattled, on the centre arch a turret gu., in chief an eagle displayed sa., charged on the breast with a bezant. **Crest:** Out of a mural crown or a demi-eagle displayed ppr., charged on the breast with a leopard's face or. **Motto:** *Spes mea in Deo* ('My hope is in God').
Creation: Bt. (UK) 15 June 1804.

SIR THOMAS PERIAM HECTOR NOEL LETHBRIDGE, 7TH BT, of Westaway House, Pilton, and Winkley Court, Co Devon [Sir Thomas Lethbridge Bt, Lloyds House, Honeymead, Somerset TA24 7JX]; *b* 17 July 1950; *s f* 1978; *educ* Milton Abbey and RAC Cirencester; *m* 9 Aug 1976 *Susan Elizabeth, est dau of Lyle Rocke, of Md., and has:

1 +JOHN FRANCIS BUCKLER NOEL; *b* 10 March 1977
2 +Edward Christopher Wroth; *b* 10 Aug 1978
3 +Alexander Ralph Periam; *b* 24 June 1982
4 +Henry Charles Hesketh; *b* 1984
1 *Georgina Rose Alianore; *b* 1980
2 *Rachel Elizabeth Mary; *b* 1986

Lineage: JOHN LETHBRIDGE, of Hatherleigh and Exbourne, Devon; *m* 10 Dec 1543 Alienor, dau of Symon Westlake, of Exbourne, and had an er s:

THOMAS LETHBRIDGE, of Dunsland Court, Jacobstowe; *m* Elizabeth — and *d* 28 June 1621, having had, with other issue, including a yr s (George, of Dunsland Court, *m* 25 Oct 1602 Katherine, dau and ultimate coheir of Nicholas Poyntingdon, of Pennycott in Shobrooke and Cheriton Fitzpaine, and was ancestor of the LETHBRIDGEs of Exbourne Manor, Devon, and other branches in Devon and Cornwall) and a dau (Joan, *m* 1st Edward Cholwich, of Newton Ferrers, Devon, *m* 2nd Andrew Hart, of Yarsacombe Manor, Modbury, Devon):

JOHN LETHBRIDGE, of Walston in Clannaborough, Devon; *m* Zenobia Stafford (*d* 1655), of Stafford in Dolton, and *d* 1626, having had, with other issue:

1 JOHN
2 Christopher, of Exeter; merchant; *b* 1610; *m* 1st Mary Jourdain, of Exeter; *m* 2nd Eleanor Taylor, of Bradninch, and *d* 1669, leaving an only dau
3 Alexander; *b* 1616; *m* Priscilla, dau of Rev R Reynolds, Rector Stoke Fleming, and had an only son
1 Charitie; *m* 1st her cousin John Lethbridge, of Ingleigh Green, Devon; *m* 2nd William Trevithick, Vicar Hatherleigh, ejected as a non-juror 1662
2 Margery; *m* 1617 John Fisher, of Bow, and left issue

The est surv son,

Rev JOHN LETHBRIDGE; *b* 1608; *educ* Exeter Coll Oxford (MA); Rector Ashprington 1639, ejected as a royalist 1647; *m* his bro's sis-in-law Mary, dau of Rev R Reynolds, Rector Stoke Fleming, and *d* 1655, having had, with other issue, including a dau (Frances, *m* Rev Lewis Burnett, Sub-Dean Exeter):

CHRISTOPHER LETHBRIDGE, of Walston and Westaway; *m* 1681 Margaret, dau of Philip Bowchier, of Pilton and Tavistock, Devon, and *d* 30 June 1713, having had, with other issue:

1 Christopher, of Pilton; *b* 1685; *m* Mary Cannon, of Bishop's Lydeard, Somerset, and *d* 7 Aug 1746, leaving:
 (1) Elizabeth Cannon; *m* as his 1st w Lt-Col Hon Hugh Somerville, of Fitzhead, Somerset (*d* 7 May 1795 aged 66), 2nd s of 12th Lord Somerville (*see* 1868 edn) by his 1st w, and had:
  1a JOHN SOUTHEY SOMERVILLE, 14TH LORD SOMERVILLE; *b* 21 Sept 1765; *educ* Harrow and St John's Coll Cambridge; Col W Somerset Yeo, rep S peer 1796–1807, Pres Bd Ag 1798–1800, a Ld Bedchamber 1799–1810; *d* unm 5 Oct 1819
2 THOMAS
3 Philip, of Santon Court, Barnstaple; *b* 1700; *m* Elizabeth, only dau and heiress of Rev Francis Tucker, and had:
 (1) Christopher Lethbridge (Rev); *d* unm 1779

The 3rd (but 2nd here noticed) son,
THOMAS LETHBRIDGE, of Clement's Inn; *b* 1698; *m* 1719 Sarah, dau of John Periam, of Milverton, Somerset, and had:

JOHN LETHBRIDGE, of Westaway Ho, Pilton; *m* 1744 Grace, dau of Amos Cardor, of Westdown, and *d* 10 Dec 1761, leaving:

Sir John Lethbridge, 1st Bt (UK), so *cr* 15 June 1804; *b* 12 March 1746; *m* June 1776 Dorothea (*d* Nov 1831), est dau and coheir (with her sis, Mary, w of Sir Francis Dugdale Astley, Bt, of Everley; *see* 1970 edn) of William Buckler, of Boreham, Wilts, and *d* 15 Dec 1815, having had, with two daus (Dorothea, *m* Henry Powell Collins, of Hatch Court, Somerset; Frances Maria, *m* Sir Charles Rich, 2nd Bt (*see* 1970 edn), and *d* 20 Feb 1852):

Sir Thomas Buckler Lethbridge, 2nd Bt, of Sandhill Park; *b* 21 Feb 1778; Col 2nd Somerset Militia, MP Somerset; *m* 1st 14 May 1796 Jessy Catherine (*d* 31 Aug 1801 aged 25), sis of Sir Thomas Dalrymple Hesketh, 3rd Bt (*see* HESKETH, B), and had:

1 JOHN HESKETH (Sir), **3rd Bt**
1 Jessy Catherine; *m* 1 Aug 1818 Ambrose Goddard, of Swindon, MP Wilts, and *d* 6 March 1843, leaving issue

Sir Thomas *m* 2nd 14 May 1803 his dau's sis-in-law Anne (*d* 25 Jan 1857), 2nd dau of Ambrose Goddard, and by her had:

2 Ambrose Goddard, of Eastbrooke Ho, nr Taunton, JP, DL; Fell All Souls; *m* 10 May 1856 Fanny (*d* 25 Nov 1912), dau of Rev R Follett and n of Sir William Follett, MP, and *dsp* 21 Nov 1875
3 Thomas Prowse (Rev); Rector Combe Florey, Somerset; *m* 10 April 1834 Isabella (*d* 1860), yst dau of Rev Thomas Sweet Escott, of Hartrow Manor, Somerset, and *d* 27 June 1851, having had:
 (1) Charles, JP Somerset and Hants; High Sheriff Hants 1895; *b* 16 May 1836; *m* 25 Jan 1865 Susan Anne (*d* 21 May 1908), yst dau of George John Yarburgh, of Heslington Hall, Yorks, and *d* 8 Dec 1922, having had:
  1a Ambrose Yarburgh; Lt Gren Gds; *b* 2 Nov 1874; *m* Feb 1898 Violet (*m* 2nd 6 Jan 1926 Brig-Gen Laurence George Frank Gordon, CB, DSO; *see* HUNTLY, M), dau of Charles Townsend Murdoch, MP, and *d* 11 Sept 1909, leaving:
   1b Thomas Charles; *b* 23 March 1901; *educ* Wellington and Trin Coll Cambridge (BA 1923, MA 1937); explorer, archaeologist and occultist; author: *Gogmagog: The Buried Gods, Ghost and Goul*; Maj HG WW II; *m* 1st 6 Feb 1924 (*divorce* 1943) Sylvia Frances (*d* 5 May 1973), only child of Rev Canon Arthur Gordon Robertson, of The Close, Salisbury, and had:
    1c Christopher John; *b* 18 March 1925; *educ* Wellington and St John's Coll Cambridge; *d* 1996
    2c Hugh Periam, Lt Gordon Highrs; *b* 21 July 1926; *d* 7 Jan 1948 of illness contracted on active service,
    1c *Belinda Mary; *b* 12 April 1930
   1b (cont.) Maj Thomas Lethbridge *m* 2nd 18 July 1944 *Mina Elizabeth, only dau of Rev Matthew Graham Leadbitter, of The Rectory, Moretonhampstead, Devon
   2b Ambrose William Speke; *b* 6 April 1907; *d* 15 March 1919
   1b Jacintha; *b* 7 June 1904; *m* 29 March 1928 Thomas Rogers, s of William Henry Rogers, FSA, of Orleigh Ct, Devon, and *d* 1940, leaving issue
  2a Bertram Escott; 2nd Lt Rifle Bde; *b* 5 June 1878; *d* of wounds Boer War 11 Nov 1899
  1a Mary; *b* 18 Oct 1865; *m* 19 April 1888 Rev Herbert Barnett (*d* 23 Nov 1937), Hon Canon Ch Ch Oxford, Vicar Bracknell Berks 1886–1919, and *d* 14 Oct 1953, leaving issue
  2a Dorothea; *b* 10 Sept 1866; *m* 17 Nov 1892 Arthur Finch Charrington (*d* 1 May 1922), of East Hill Ho, Oxted, Surrey, and *d* 28 June 1930, leaving issue
  3a Ellinor; *b* 22 July 1868; *d* unm 17 May 1948
  4a Ruth; *b* 2 June 1870; *m* 14 Jan 1904 Willoughby Arthur Pemberton (*d* 19 June 1923) and *d* 11 June 1943, leaving issue
  5a Susan; *b* 7 Oct 1881; *m* 16 Jan 1907 Geoffrey Charlton Wolryche-Whitmore (*d* 5 March 1969), est s of Francis Alexander Wolryche-Whitmore, JP, of Salop, and *dsp* 3 April 1907
  6a Rachel; *b* 3 June 1885; *m* 26 Sept 1914 Lt-Col Alan David Greenhill Gardyne, JP, Gordon Highrs (*d* 14 March 1953), of Finavon Castle, Forfar, and had:
   1b David; *b* 5 May 1918; *educ* Charterhouse; T/Maj Gordon Highrs WW II; *ka* El Alamein 3 Nov 1942
   1b *Susan Patience; *b* 1 March 1917; *m* 21 July 1949 *Stanislaw Mazur, Lt Polish Forces, and has:
    1c *Ian David; *b* 13 June 1954
    2c *Andrew Stanislaw; *b* 3 March 1962
    1c *Carolyne Sarah Jane; *b* 23 Sept 1958
   2b *Maryel Alice; *b* 25 July 1919
 (2) Edward; Capt 1st Bn S Wales Borderers, 90th Regt Kaffir and Zulu wars 1878–79 (medal with clasp); *b* 25 Nov 1846; *m* 4 April 1877 Constance (resumed maiden name 1922, *d* 25 Feb 1930), dau of Francis Capper Brooke, of Ufford Place, Suffolk, and *d* 1894, having had:
  1a Sybil; *m* 29 June 1909 Maj Charles Francis Sewell, KRRC (*d* 1937), s of Charles Sewell, and *d* 1927, leaving issue
  2a Miriam; *m* 4 Feb 1908 (*divorce* 1928) Maj Robert Cotesworth and *d* 25 Jan 1961, having issue
  3a Hester; *k* in an accident 30 Dec 1947
  4a Joan; *m* 2 June 1921 Sir Richard Roy Maconachie, KBE, CIE, ICS (*d* 18 Jan 1962), s of James Robert Maconachie, ICS, and had issue
 (1) Mary; *m* 29 April 1865 Vincent Stuckey, DL (*d* 20 Jan 1902), of Hill Ho, Langport, and *d* 18 Sept 1906, leaving issue
 (2) Jessie; *m* 27 Sept 1859 Vincent John Reynolds (*d* 1883), of Canon Grove, Somerset, and *d* 21 Jan 1901, having had issue
2 Anna Maria; *m* 7 June 1848 Lt-Gen Sir Richard Goddard Hare-Clarges, KCB (*d* 1857), and *d* 20 March 1886 aged 80
3 Lucy Sarah; *m* 9 Aug 1831 Lt-Col Hugh FitzRoy (*see* GRAFTON, D) and *d* 1855
4 Emma Dorothea; *m* 18 Nov 1826 Sir Francis Dugdale Astley, 2nd Bt (*see* 1970 edn), and *d* 9 Dec 1872

5 Frances Margaret; *m* 3 March 1836 Rev Charles Augustus Thurlow and *d* 12 April 1861, leaving issue (*see* THURLOW, B)

Sir THOMAS *d* 17 Oct 1849; his est son,

Sir John Hesketh Lethbridge, 3rd Bt, DL Somerset; *b* 1798; *m* 1st 27 March 1817 Harriett Rebecca (*d* 13 March 1826), only dau of John Mytton, of Halston, Salop, and Dinas Mowddy, Merioneths, and had:

1 Thomas Christopher Mytton, Lt 85th Regt; *d* 31 March 1844 at St Kitts of yellow fever

2 John Periam; *b* 9 Nov 1824; *d* 13 March 1867

1 Harriet Agatha Mytton; *m* 25 May 1840 Henry Pratt, MD, and *d* 24 April 1898, leaving issue

2 Jessy Catherine Hesketh; *m* 25 Oct 1854 Capt Frederick Dampier Rich, RN (*d* 17 Jan 1876), s of Sir Charles Rich, 2nd Bt (*see* 1970 edn), and *d* 6 Oct 1907, having had issue

3 Annette; *m* 22 Feb 1840 Christopher G Rigbye Collins (*d* 1891), of Helena Ho, Sidmouth, Capt 16th Lancers, and *d* 14 May 1893

4 Caroline Giffard; *m* 28 Sept 1849 John Tharp Burton Phillipson (*d* 10 Dec 188), est s of Rev Burton Phillipson Phillipson, of Herringswell Ho, Suffolk

Sir John *m* 2nd 15 March 1827 Julia (*d* 29 May 1855), 2nd dau of Sir Henry Hugh Hoare, 3rd Bt, of Barn Elms (*qv*); *m* 3rd 11 Sept 1855 Anna (*d* 14 July 1880), est dau of Robert Wright, MD, and by his 2nd w had:

3 WROTH ACLAND (Sir), **4th Bt**

4 Ernest Acland; served RN aboard HMS *Trafalgar*; *d* Malta 1 May 1848

5 Albert Arthur Erin; 13th Light Dragoons; *b* 24 May 1840; *m* 11 Oct 1862 Jane (*d* July 1922), only child of Robert A Hill, of Hamilton, Ontario, and *d* 7 Nov 1872, leaving

(1) Julia Mary; *m* 27 June 1888 3rd Baron Carew (*qv*) and *d* 28 Sept 1922

(2) Jane Anne Gordon; *m* 25 Jan 1893 Sir Clifford John Cory, 1st Bt (*d* 3 Feb 1941; *see* 1970 edn), of Llantarnam Abbey, Mon, and *d* 8 Feb 1947

6 Walter Buckler; Kt Charles III of Spain and Medjidie; *b* 10 March 1845; *m* 1st 19 Dec 1864 Eleonore Marie (*d* 1896), dau of Peter Alexander Boyer, of Paris, and had:

(1) Walter Alexander Charles; Capt Northants Yeo, Lt Roy Bucks Hus, WW I; *b* 4 Oct 1865; *m* 1st 1885 (*divorce* USA) Rosa Maria, dau of Miguel del Monte, of Havana, and had:

1a Walter Miguel, MC; served USN, WW I as Lt Gds MGR; *b* 13 Sept 1886; *m* 1st 29 Jan 1907 (*divorce* 19–) Anna Agnes, dau of J V Ganter, and had:

1b *Frances Rose; *b* 19 Nov 1907

1a (cont.) Walter Lethbridge *m* 2nd 17 June 1913 (*annulled* 19–) Catherine Matilda, dau of F M Marsh; *m* 3rd 1919 Carmela (*d* 1980), dau of Miguel I Aguilera, of Havana, and *d* 13 July 1964, having by her had:

1b +Walter Miguel; *b* 18 Nov 1923; *m* 1st 1949 (*divorce* 1955) Nora, dau of Eduardo Barrios, and has:

1c +Walter Alexander [Walter Lethbridge Esq, 100 rue St Honoré, 75001 Paris, France]; *b* 27 Oct 1950; *m* 1st 1971 (*divorce* 1988) Elsie, dau of Guy Derozières-Le Comte, of Lille; *m* 2nd 1988 *Patricia Douglas, and by his 1st w has:

1d +Alexis Guillaume; *b* 1971

1d *Chloé; *b* 1980

1b (cont.) Walter Lethbridge *m* 2nd 1957 (*divorce* 1982) Jill Margaret, dau of Robert Gibson Nethery, MRCS, LRCP, and by her has:

1c *Arabella Margaret [Mrs Charles Budgett, 18 Mythern Meadow, Bradford-on-Avon, Wilts]; *b* 8 May 1962; *m* 1986 *Charles Edward Budgett, s of Rev Preb Anthony Thomas Budgett, of Wellington, Som, and has:

1d *Holly Catharine; *b* 1989

2d *Vanessa Margaret; *b* 1992

1b (cont.) Walter Lethbridge *m* 3rd 1982 *Silvely, dau of Viktor Kalve Grandin, of Riga, Latvia

2b Rodney Thomas; *b* 21 Dec 1925; *m* 1st 1942 (*annulled* 1944) Sara, dau of R Miranda; *m* 2nd 1949 (*divorce* 1955) Fedora, dau of Ernesto Moya, and had:

1c *Doris Elizabeth; *b* Oct 1950

2b (cont.) Rodney Lethbridge *m* 3rd 1956 Marcelle Goulet and *d* 1978, leaving by her:

1c +Rodney Thomas; *b* Oct 1957

2c +Michael Walter; *b* 1964

2c *Suzanne Carmen; *b* 1962

3b +Douglas Nelson [Douglas Lethbridge Esq, 84th St, No 240–Apt Z, Surfside 33141, Miami Beach, FL, USA]; *b* 1933; *m* 1st 1954 (*divorce* 196–) Margaret, dau of George Isher, and has:

1c +Michael; *b* 1955

1c *Maureen; *b* 1956

3b (cont.) Douglas Lethbridge *m* 2nd —, 3rd —, 4th —, 5th —, 6th 19– (*divorce* 19–) Maria Cecilia Urrutia, of Columbia; *m* 7th —, 8th — and had two further children

2b *Carmen Rosa; *b* April 1927; *m* 1st 1950 (*divorce* 19–) Luis F Pinêiro; *m* 2nd 19– — Menendes and has by her 1st husb:

1c *Luis Felipe; *b* 1952

1c *Rose Marie; *b* 1959

2c *Katherine; *b* 1968

2a John George Jules; F/Lt RAF and USN WW I; *b* 1888; *m* 1917 Dorothy Josephine, dau of Le Roy M Taylor, of Washington, and had:

1b +John George; *b* 15 Oct 1917

2b +Robert Mortimer; *b* 20 June 1921

(1) (cont.) Walter Lethbridge *m* 2nd 1902 (*divorce* France 1922) Blanche, er dau of John Bingham, Judge High Ct New York; *m* 3rd 18 April 1922 Marie José Léona, yst dau of Josef Léon Mondron, of Belgium, and *d* 3 Jan 1931

6 (cont.) Walter Lethbridge *m* 2nd 1896 Julia (*d* 31 July 1930), widow of Henry Hamblen and dau of Matthew Hawkins, and *d* 11 July 1907

5 Ada Cicely Georgina; *m* 1st 3 May 1845 George Stone, of Blisworth, Northants; *m* 2nd 12 Feb 1863 Sir Henry Moore Brownrigg, 3rd Bt (*qv*), and *d* 17 Feb 1911, having had issue

6 Adora Julia; *m* 10 Jan 1848 Peter Wells (*d* 22 March 1908), of Forest Farm, Windsor Forest, and *d* 21 April 1850, leaving issue

7 Anna Maria; *m* 23 Sept 1854 Edmund Peel (*d* 17 March 1903), of Bryn-y-pys, Flints, and Downham Hall, Norfolk, and *d* 28 Nov 1860

8 Grace Catherine; *d* unm 31 July 1871

9 Alda Gertrude; *m* 8 Dec 1857 William Henry Purcell Weston, of Kilcorney, Co Cork, and Weymouth, Dorset, and *d* 17 July 1906, leaving issue

10 Agnes Maria; *m* 1st 29 Sept 1855 Peter Valentine Purcell (*d* 2 July 1964), Capt 13th Light Dragoons, of Halberstown Ho, Co Kildare, and had issue; *m* 2nd 20 Nov 1866 Col Henry St John Vaughan Thomas Le Marchant, RHA, est s of Le Marchant Thomas Le Marchant, of Haye-du-Puits, Guernsey, and Seaview, IoW, and *d* 24 Feb 1915

11 Julia Decima; *m* 15 March 1860 Col Hercules Walker-Myln (*d* 1895) and *d* 24 Nov 1900, leaving issue

12 Susanna Octavia; *m* 1 July 1861 Capt Edward Raleigh King (*d* 14 March 1900), 13th Light Dragoons, of Chadshunt, Warwicks, and *d* 14 June 1920, having had issue

Sir JOHN *d* 1 March 1873; his est surv son,

Sir Wroth Acland Lethbridge, 4th Bt, JP and DL Somerset, JP Cambs; Rifle Bde; *b* 2 Jan 1831; *m* 1st 29 Oct 1861 Ann Williams (*d* 11 Feb 1882), 2nd dau of Thomas Benyon, of Thorp Arch, Yorks; *m* 2nd 4 May 1889 Gertrude Elizabeth (*dsp* 14 April 1890), dau of Rev Charles Theodore Mayo, Vicar St Andrews, Hillingdon, and by his 1st w had:

1 WROTH PERIAM CHRISTOPHER (Sir), **5th Bt**

2 Ernest Astley Edmund, CMG, DSO; Col Oxon and Bucks LI, Boer War 1899–1902 (Queen's medal with three clasps, King's medal with two clasps, despatches twice), cmded 1st Bn Mesopotamia WW I (POW, despatches twice, Brevet-Col, Croix de Guerre); *b* 26 Dec 1864; *m* 9 July 1919 Ruth Mary (*d* 29 Aug 1960), widow of Maj Charles Evelyn Forrest, DSO, and dau of Lt-Col Hon Edward Alexander Holmes à Court (*see* HEYTESBURY, B), and *d* 29 April 1943, having had:

(1) Elinor Anne Mary; *b* 6 July 1920; *d* 21 Feb 1921

(2) *Diana Ruth; *b* 10 Jan 1922; *m* 15 Sept 1950 *Alexander Haig Anderson, of Sussex, s of Alexander Cunningham Anderson, of Ayrshire, and has:

1a *Charles Ernest Haig; *b* 13 July 1951; *educ* Eton

1a *Fiona Diana; *b* 3 Aug 1953; *educ* N Foreland Lodge

3 Thomas Buckler Valentine; Lt 3rd Bn Somerset LI; *b* 14 Feb 1866; *m* 1901 Eva Henrietta Wyndham (*d* 1 July 1936), dau of Reginald William Templer, of Powderham Ho, Teignmouth, and *d* 7 Feb 1914, leaving:

(1) Montagu Benyon Templer; *b* 8 Sept 1902; accidentally drowned Oct 1931

(2) Wroth Thomas Coull; Capt P&O Service; *b* 24 March 1904; *m* 18 Feb 1954 *Edith Marian, widow of Hugh Wansey Bayly, MC, and dau of W H N Edwards, and *dsp* 9 April 1976

(1) Linda Cecely Geraldine; *b* 12 Feb 1906; *m* 1946 Michael Harold Selby (*d* 1965)

4 Hugh Francis Hesketh; Lt 3rd Bn Somerset LI, Matabele Campaign 1896 (medal), Boer War (Queen's medal with four clasps), Natal Rebellion 1906 (medal and clasp); *b* 25 Oct 1867; *m* 1912 Edith Maude, er dau of Thomas Mellor Robinson, of Natal, and *d* 3 July 1935, leaving:

(1) +Hugh Mytton Fitzwarine; *b* 1913; *m* 1945 *Elsie Murray, dau of Very Rev George Bartlet, of Aberdeen, and has:

1a +Hugh George; *b* 1948

1a *Jennifer Murray; *b* 1946

(2) +Wroth Thomas Hesketh Bourchier; *b* 28 Dec 1914

(1) *Delphine Edith Conyers Bourchier; *b* 20 May 1922

5 John Acland Musgrave; Capt Imp Yeo Boer War; *b* 28 Feb 1869; *m* 1894 Florence Martin (*d* 26 Oct 1931), dau of Sidney Wood Cooper, of New York, and *d* 18 April 1934, leaving:

(1) Duncan John Leghe; Oxon and Bucks LI WW I, WW II as Capt RASC and on Gen Staff; *b* 15 Dec 1898; *educ* Kilkenny Coll and RMC Sandhurst; *m* 17 June 1922 Phyllis Muriel (*d* 3 May 1971), formerly w of Col Rowland James Percy Anderson, CMG, DSO, 11th Hus, and dau of Thomas Stanley Chappell, of Chadshunt, Warwicks, and *d* 26 March 1962, leaving:

1a *Jacqueline Auriol Phyllis Leghe; *b* 19 April 1923

2a *June Florence [Mrs Mario Fog, 217A Lucy Creek Dve, Beaufort, SC 29902, USA]; *b* 10 June 1926; *m* 1944 *Mario Fog and has:

1b *Duncan Lethbridge; *b* 1948; *m* 1989 *Sarah McLane

2b *Stephen Chase; *b* 1952; *m* 1979 *Wendy Merritt Dixon and has:

1c *Merritt Lawrence; *b* 1981

2c *Courtnay Andrews; *b* 1984

3a *Ann [Mrs Graham Platt, 40 Walnut Tree Lane, Cold Spring Harbor, Long Island, NY 11724, USA]; *b* Feb 1930; *m* 11 Aug 1951 *Graham Lusk Platt, and has:

1b *Graham Leghe; *b* 1959; has:

1c *Jeremy Redding Knox; *b* 1983

2b *Gordon Lethbridge; *b* 1962; *m* 1993 *Mary M Walsh

1b *Christina May *b* 1956; *m* 19– *Michael J Nelson and has:

1c *Adrien Leghe; *b* 1979

2c *Lindsay Ann; *b* 1981

3c *Louisa May *b* 1985

4c *Sandi Grey; *b* 1989

(2) Harold Reginald; *b* 19 May 1901; *educ* St Paul's; *m* 1942 Mrs Shirley Ivy Grace Lidstone, dau of William Mascall, of Cambs, and *d* 19 March 1972, leaving:

1a +Duncan Stuart; *b* 22 March 1943; *m* 1969 *Catherine Jean Beveridge, dau of John Sneddon, of Kinross, and has:

1b +Duncan Reginald John; *b* 1973

1b *Claire Cecilia; *b* 1975

2a +Reginald Martin Peter; *b* 7 Nov 1946

3a Richard Christopher Noel; *b* 1 July 1949; *d* 1968

(1) Violet Martin; *b* 1895; *m* 6 March 1913 Samuel Francis Beeke Lane (*d* Aug 1950), yr s of William Lane, of Mount Vernon, Co Cork, and has issue

(2) Annie Gwendoline; *m* 1st 11 Jan 1916 Capt Guy Clavering Weatherall, RASC; *m* 2nd 12 Feb 1945 Capt Thorold Murray-Smith, MC, and *d* 13 Dec 1978 aged 84, having by her 1st husb had:

1a *Peter Martin; *b* 1919

(3) Phyllis Henrietta; *m* 25 March 1933 George Francis Ackroyd (*d* 1938)

(4) Mabel Florence, OBE (1917); sole survivor of Hayes, Middx, munitions explosion 1917; Ambulance Driver WW II; author: *Fortune Grass* and *Against the Tide*; *m* 5 Sept 1922 (*divorce* 1932, resumed maiden name) Noel Eric Kalenberg, s of Dr Allan Kalenberg, and *d* 14 July 1968, having had issue

6 Alan Bourchier; Resident N Nigeria 1903–06, FO and Min Info WW I, author: *The New Russia*, *The Soul of the Russian*; *b* 21 Jan 1878; *m* 14 Dec 1912 Marjorie Colt (*m* 2nd 23 Sept 1925 Thomas Alfred Bell, of Sherborne, Dorset, s of Thomas Bell, of Durham), only child of Brig-Gen Byrne, US Army, and *d* 25 Feb 1923

1 Dorothea Anne; *b* 4 July 1874

The 4th Bt *d* 26 Nov 1902; his est son,

Sir Wroth Periam Christopher Lethbridge, 5th Bt, JP Somerset; Capt Gren Gds, Signalling Offr Home Dist 1892–97, WW I: Dep Assist Censor BEF 1914, Egyptian Expdny Force 1917, Mil Mission USA 1918, Special Constable Gen Strike 1926, HG WW II 1940–44, Pres Ormskirk and Dist ATC from 1941; *b* 19 Dec 1863; *m* 1st 22 Oct 1892 (*divorce* 1911) Alianore (*d* 24 Feb 1952), yst dau of Edward Sacheverell Chandos-Pole, of Radbourne Hall, Derbys; *m* 2nd 9 Dec 1911 (*divorce* 1928) Kathleen (*d* 10 July 1962), formerly w of Richard Cecil Leigh, of Lyburn Pk, Lyndhurst, Hants, and only child of Robert O'Hara, barrister; *m* 3rd 29 Sept Hilda (*d* 1 March 1951), yst dau of Rev Canon Thomas Hollinshead-Blundell, Rector Halsall, Ormskirk, and by his 1st w had:

1 HECTOR WROTH (Sir), **6th Bt**

1 Torfrida Alianore; SStJ; *m* 14 April 1920 Col Hubert Francis Grant-Suttie, CBE, DSO, MC, RA (*see* GRANT-SUTTIE, Bt), and *d* 30 Aug 1971, leaving issue

2 Dulcibel Margaret (twin with bro); BRCS WW II; *m* 3 Sept 1921 Maj Robert James Wordsworth, DSO, TD, Notts and Derbys Regt (*d* 23 Jan 1969), s of Robert Walter Wordsworth, of Whitemoor, Ollerton, Notts, and *d* 12 Feb 1962, leaving issue

The 5th Bt *d* 20 Feb 1950; his only son,

Sir Hector Wroth Lethbridge, 6th Bt; *b* 26 Aug 1898; *educ* Radley; Capt Rifle Bde WW I 1917–18, India 1919–20, WW II in W Africa (invalided home); *m* 13 April 1946 Evelyn Diana (*d* 8 July 1996, having *m* 3rd 1979 as his 3rd w, David James Douglas Nugent, Baron Nugent; *see* WESTMEATH, E), widow of Maj John Vivian Bailey, Roy Scots Fus, and er dau of Lt-Col Francis Arthur Gerard Noel (*see* GAINSBOROUGH, E), and *d* 29 June 1978, leaving:

1 Sir THOMAS PERIAM HECTOR NOEL LETHBRIDGE, **7th and present Bt**

1 *Mary Jacintha [Mrs Richard Heywood, Pond Farm, Holme Hale, Thetford, Norfolk IP25 7EE]; *b* 5 Sept 1948; *m* 27 March 1974 *Brig Richard John Heywood, OBE, Coldstream Gds, only s of Peter Heywood, and has:

(1) *Richard Anthony; *b* 2 Sept 1977

(1) *Anna Rose; *b* 17 Nov 1975

LEVEN and MELVILLE

Arms: Quarterly, 1st, azure a thistle slipped proper, ensigned with an Imperial Crown or (a coat of augmentation to the arms of LESLIE); 2nd, gules three crescents within a bordure argent, charged with eight roses of the first (for MELVILLE); 3rd, argent a fess gules (for MELVILLE of Raith); 4th, argent on a bend azure three buckles or (for LESLIE). **Crests:** 1 A demi-chevalier in complete armour, holding in his right hand a dagger, point down proper, the pommel and hilt or (for LESLIE), 2 A ratchet hound's head, erased proper, collared gules (for MELVILLE). **Supporters:** Dexter, a knight in complete armour, holding in his dexter hand the banner of Scotland, all proper (for LESLIE); sinister, a ratchet hound proper, collared gules (for MELVILLE). **Mottoes:** 1 *Pro rege et patria* ('For King and country'), 2 *Denique coelum* ('Heaven at last'). **Creations:** L. (S) 30 April 1616 (Melville of Monymaill); E. (Leven) and L. (Balgonie) (S) 11 Oct 1641, E. (Melville), V. and L. (S) 8 April 1690.

THE 16TH EARL OF LEVEN and **13th EARL OF MELVILLE, Viscount of Kirkcaldy, Lord Melville of Monymaill, Lord Balgonie,** and **Lord Raith, Monymaill and Balwearie** (Alexander Robert Leslie Melville) [The Rt Hon The Earl of Leven and Melville, Glenferness House, Nairn IV12 5VP]; *b* 13 May 1924; *s f* 1947; *educ* Eton; Capt Coldstream Gds WW II (wounded), ADC to Govr-Gen NZ 1951–52; Ld Lt Nairn 1969– (DL 1961–69), Chm Nairn CC 1970–74, Chm Govrs Gordonstoun 1971–89, Pres Br Ski Fedn 1981–85, Hon Pres Scot Nat Ski Cncl; *m* 30 April 1953 *Susan, er dau of Lt-Col Ronald Steuart-Menzies of Culdares, JP, DL, of Arndilly House, Craigellachie, Banffshire, and has:

1 +DAVID ALEXANDER, *Lord Balgonie* [Lord Balgonie, The Old Farmhouse, West St, Burghclere, Berks RG20 9LB]; *b* 26 Jan 1954; *educ* Eton; Lt (A/Capt) QO Highrs (1975) RARO 1979–89, dir Wood Conservation Ltd 1984– and Treske Ltd 1996–; *m* 1981 *Julia Clare, dau of Col Ian Ranald Critchley, OBE, Black Watch, of Greenden, by Brechin, Angus, and has:

(1) +Alexander Ian; *b* 29 Nov 1984

(1) *Louisa Clare; *b* 18 Sept 1987

2 +Archibald Ronald [The Hon Archibald Leslie Melville, Orwell House, Manse Rd, Milnathort, Kinross-shire KY13 7YQ]; *b* 15 Sept 1957; *educ* Gordonstoun; Lt QO Highrs; *m* 1987 *Julia Mary Greville, yr dau of Basil Fox, of Kensington, and has:

(1) *Alice Catherine; *b* 12 Nov 1990

(2) *Camilla Jane; *b* 29 Aug 1992

(3) *Joanna Julia; *b* 6 July 1994

1 *Jane Catherine [The Lady Jane Hudson, Southcott Lodge, Pewsey, Wilts SN9 5JF]; *b* 5 May 1956; *m* 1977 *Philip Mark Gurney Hudson and has:

(1) *Katherine Laura; *b* 24 Dec 1983

(2) *Susanna Jane; *b* 26 Feb 1986

Lineage (of Leslie): WILLIAM LESLEY, of a branch of the LESLIEs Earls of Rothes (*qv*); *fl temp* JAMES II (1437–60) and III (1460–88); had charters under the Great Seal of the lands and (territorial) Barony of Balquhain; had, with other issue:

WILLIAM; ancestor of:

WILLIAM LESLIE, 4th territorial Baron of Balquhain; had:

GEORGE LESLIE of New Leslie; *m* Comney Ramsay of Dalhousie (*see* DALHOUSIE, E) and had a 2nd s:

ALEXANDER LESLIE, 1st of Kininvie (which he was granted by charter from John Stewart, 1st Earl of Atholl, 1520; *see* MORAY, E); *m* Margaret Calder of Napherson and *d* 1549, having had:

WALTER LESLIE, 2nd of Kininvie; Capt Scottish Gd of FRANCIS I OF FRANCE; *m* Katherine Grant, of Ballindalloch, and *d* 1562, leaving, with other issue, including an er s (Robert, 3rd of Kininvie):

GEORGE LESLIE; had the lands of Drummuir from his f; *m* Mary, dau of Stewart of Kilcowie, and had:

GEORGE LESLIE of Balgonie, Fife; Capt garrison Blair Castle *temp* JAMES VI; *m* 1st Anne, dau of Stewart of Ballechin; *m* 2nd a local girl of Rannoch, Perthshire, and by her had:

ALEXANDER LESLIE, **1st Earl of Leven**, so *cr* 11 Oct 1641, as also LORD BALGONIE (both S), PC (S 1641); *b c* 1580 before his parents' marriage but by that marriage was legitimated; soldier of fortune on the Continent: served in Lord Vere's Regt in Holland against the Spaniards, quickly becoming Capt, also under GUSTAVUS ADOLPHUS OF SWEDEN 1627–30 in Thirty Years War (ktd 1627, FM 1636), C-in-C Tsar of Russia's armies Jan 1631/2; returned to Scotland 1639 and cmded Covenanters' army; defeated English royalists Newburn 1640 and captured Newcastle; Keeper Edinburgh Castle 1641; Gen Scottish armies in Ireland 1642 but went over to England with 21,000 men and contributed to the Parly victory of Marston Moor 1644; Ld-Gen of Scotland 1647; royalist following CHARLES I's execution, fighting at Battle of Dunbar 1650; captured by Cromwellians 1651 and imprisoned Tower of London 1651–53 (released by QUEEN CHRISTINA OF SWEDEN's putting in a good word for him in gratitude for his past servs to her f and gf); *m c* 1610 Agnes (*d* 26 June 1651), dau of David Renton, of Billie, Berwicks, and *d* 4 April 1661, having had:

1 Gustavus; *dsp* & *vp*

2 Alexander, *Lord Balgonie*; Col; *m* 1636 his distant cousin Lady Margaret Leslie (*m* 2nd *c* 25 July 1646 2nd Earl of Buccleuch (see BUCCLEUCH and QUEENSBERRY, D); *m* 3rd 13 Jan 1652/3 2nd Earl of Wemyss, *qv*), dau of 6th Earl of Rothes (*qv*), and *dvp* shortly after 12 Jan 1644, having by her had:

(1) ALEXANDER LESLIE, **2nd Earl of Leven**; *b c* 1637; since he had no sons he procured a regrant of the Earldom 12 Feb 1663 with remainder to heirs male, failing whom heirs female of his body, with further remainder to John Earl of Rothes's 2nd s and the heirs male of the latter's body, failing whom to his (the **2nd Earl of Leven**'s) sister (see below) Catherine Countess of Melville's 2nd s and the latter's heirs male of the body, failing whom to the second son of his (the **2nd Earl of Leven**'s) mother Margaret, Countess of Wemyss, with further remainder to his (the **2nd Earl of Leven**'s) heirs male whomsoever and with remainder beyond that to his heirs and assignees whomsoever; *m* 30 Dec 1656 Margaret (*d* 30 Sept 1664), sis of 1st Earl of Carlisle (*qv*), and *dspm* 15 July 1664, leaving:

1a MARGARET Leslie, **Countess of Leven** in her own right; *m c* 10 Oct 1673 Francis MONTGOMERIE, 2nd s of 7th Earl of Eglinto(u)n (see EGLINTON and WINTON, E), but *dsp* 6 Nov 1674

2a CATHERINE LESLIE, **Countess of Leven** in her own right; *b* 1663 or 1664; *d* unm 21 Jan 1676

(1) Catherine; *m* 18 Jan 1655 **1st Earl of Melville** (see below) and had, with other issue:

1a DAVID, **5th/2nd Earl**

1 Barbara; *m* Gen Sir John Ruthven

2 Christian; *m* Walter Dundas of that Ilk

3 Janet; *m* after 1 Oct 1639, as his 1st w, James Crichton, 1st Viscount of Frendraught, and *dspm* 24 Nov 1640

4 Anes/Anne; *m* 1st Hugh Fraser, Master of Lovat, s of 7th Lord Lovat (*qv*); *m* 2nd Ralph de la Val and had issue

5 Mary; *m c* 10 July 1643 William, 3rd Lord Cranstoun

Lineage (of Melville): GALFRID de MALEVILLE; *fl temp* DAVID I (1124–53), MALCOLM IV (1153–65) and WILLIAM I (1165–1214); first known Justiciar of Scotland; had:

1 Gregory, whose line ended in an heir female:

(1) Agnes; *m* Sir John Ross of Halkhead and brought him the Melville lands

2 Philip; ancestor of:

(1) Alexander, of Glenbervie; *d* 1468, leaving:

1a Elizabeth; *m* Sir John Auchinleck of Auchinleck and was grandparent with him of:

1b Elizabeth; took the territorial Barony of Glenbervie to her husb Sir William Douglas, 2nd s of 5th Earl of Angus

3 Walter; gf of:

(1) John (Sir); one of the leading Scots whose agreement was sought to the marriage of QUEEN MARGARET with PRINCE EDWARD of England 1290; swore fealty to EDWARD I 1296; ancestor of:

1a John (Sir), of Raith; had charters jointly with his (2nd) w 23 May 1536 and 23 Oct 1542 of Crown lands of Murdoc(hc)airnie, Fife; Master-Gen Ordnance and Capt-Gen Dunbar Castle *temp* JAMES V; *m* 1st —; *m* 2nd Helen, est dau of Sir Alexander Napier of Merchiston (see NAPIER, Bt, of Merchiston), and was executed for treason 13 Dec 1548, having had, with an er or est s (*d* young):

1b John, of Raith; had his f's forfeited estates restored him *c* 1553; *d* 13 Jan 1605, leaving:

1c John, of Raith; *m* Margaret, dau of Sir John Scott of Balwearie, and *d* 17 Jan 1626, leaving:

1d JOHN MELVILLE, **3rd Lord Melville of Monymaill**; *m c* 27 Oct 1627 Anne, est dau and coheir of Sir George Erskine of Innerteil/Inverteill, a Ld of Session, and *d* 22 May 1643, leaving:

1e GEORGE MELVILLE, **1st Earl of Melville**, so *cr* 8 April 1690, as also VISCOUNT OF KIRKCALDY and LORD RAITH, MONYMAILL AND BALWEARIE (all S); *b* 1636; involved in the rebellion of the Duke of Monmouth but escaped to Holland; his estates were consequently forfeited by act of attainder 1685, but he returned to England 1688 with WILLIAM III and was reinstated; Sec State Scotland 1689–90, High Commr to S Parl 1690, Privy Seal Scotland 1691–96, Pres Cncl Scotland 1696–1702, Commr for executing office of Ld High Adml Scotland 1697; *m* 18 Jan 1655 Catherine Leslie (*d* 2 April 1713), gdau of **1st Earl of Leven** (see above), and *d* 20 May 1707, having had:

1f Alexander, *Lord Raith*; *b* 23 Dec 1655; Treasurer-Depute Scotland; *m* 17 Aug 1689 Barbara (*d* 23 Feb 1719), dau of Walter Dundas, and *dsp* & *vp* 27 March 1698

2f DAVID MELVILLE later LESLIE, **2nd Earl of Melville** and **5th Earl of Leven** (as which he styled himself from 21 Jan 1676, when

his cousin CATHERINE, **Countess of Leven** in her own right, died, although until the 1st and last Duke of Rothes *dspm* 27 July 1681 (see ROTHES, E), he was not recognised as such since in the event of the Duke having male issue certain of that male issue would have had a prior claim to the Earldom), PC (S 1689); *b* 5 May 1660; took part with his f in Momouth's rising, fled also to Holland then went to Germany where in service of Duke of Brandenburg; Col 25th Foot 1689–94, which he raised from Scotsmen in the Low Countries and Germany on behalf of WILLIAM III, fought Battle of Killiecrankie 1689 and in Flanders 1692, Brig Gen 1702, Maj Gen 1704, Lt Gen 1707, Master Ordnance Scotland 1705, Constable Edinburgh Castle 1689–1702 and 1704–12, Commr to pacify Highlands 1689, Commr Exchequer Scotland 1689, Govr Bank Scotland 1697–1728, C-in-C Forces Scotland 1706, a Commr for the Union of E and S Parls 1707, rep S peer 1707–10; *m c* 3 Sept 1691 Anne (*d* 9 Jan 1702), dau of James Wemyss, Lord Burntisland, by Margaret, Countess of Wemyss in her own right (see WEMYSS, E), and *d* 6 June 1728, having had:

1g George, *Lord Balgonie*; *b* Jan 1695; *m* Aug 1716 Margaret (*d* 7 July 1722), dau of 4th Earl of Northesk (*qv*), and *dvp* 20 Aug 1721, having had:

1h DAVID LESLIE, **6th Earl of Leven** and **3rd Earl of Melville**; *b* 17 Dec 1717; *d* unm June 1729

1h Anna; *d* unm

2g ALEXANDER, **7th/4th Earl**

3f James, of Balgarvie; had with other issue:

1g George, of Balgarvie

2g David

1g Margaret; *m* March 1719 John Erskine of Carnock and Cardross, author *Institutes of the Law of Scotland*, and *d* 1 March 1768, leaving issue

1f Margaret; *m* 4th Lord Balfour of Burleigh (*qv*) and had, with other issue:

1g Mary; *m* Maj Alexander Bruce of Kennet

2b Sir ROBERT MELVILLE, **1st Lord Melville of Monymaill** (S), so *cr* 30 April 1616, with remainder, failing heirs male of his body, to his er bro John and the latter's heirs male of the body, PC (S 1562 and 1583), of Murdoc(hc)airnie; *b c* 1527; as a youth at court of HENRY II of France; Amb England 1562; Hereditary Keeper Linlithgow Palace Feb 1566/7; captured fighting for MARY QUEEN OF SCOTS Battle of Langside 1568 and again at taking of Edinburgh Castle by the Regent Morton (see MORTON, E) 1573; ktd 1581; Treasurer Depute Scotland 1582–96; Jt Amb England 1586 to beg that MARY QUEEN OF SCOTS' life be spared; V-Chllr Scotland 1589, Extra Ld of Session 1594–1601 as Lord Murdochairnie; *m* 1st by 14 Feb 1563/4 Catherine, dau of William Adamson of Craigcrook, Co Edinburgh; *m* 2nd by 1593 Lady Mary Leslie, dau of 5th Earl of Rothes (*qv*), and *d* 1621, leaving by his 1st w:

1c Sir ROBERT MELVILLE, **2nd Lord Melville of Monymaill**, PC (S 1600); ktd *vp*, Extra Ld of Session as Lord Burntisland 1601–26; granted 10 Aug 1627 a novodamus changing his title's remainder to the heirs of his body whomsoever, failing whom 'to his heirs male, general or of conquest or either of them, bearing the name and arms of Melville, as it should please him to designate at any time during his life and his assignees whatsoever'; *m* 1st *c* late Oct 1584 Margaret (*dsp* 24 May 1594), sis of Andrew Ker, 1st Lord Jedburgh (see LOTHIAN, M); *m* 2nd by 24 Feb 1601 Jean (*d* May 1631), est dau of Gavin Hamilton of Raploch and widow of 5th Lord Ross, and *dsp* 19 March 1635

3b James (Sir), of Hall Hill, Fife, PC (S); Envoy to England; *d* 1617, leaving issue

4b William; Ld of Session 1587–1614

5b Andrew (Sir), of Garvock; Master of the Household to MARY QUEEN OF SCOTS and JAMES VI

6b David, of Newmill

1b Janet; *m* Sir James Kirkaldy, of Grange, High Treasurer of Scotland, and had:

1c William (Sir)

2c James (Sir); executed 1573 with his bro for conspiring on behalf of MARY QUEEN OF SCOTS

2b Margaret; *m* Sir James Johnstone of Elphinstone

The 6th/3rd EARL's uncle,

ALEXANDER LESLIE, **7th Earl of Leven** and **4th Earl of Melville**; *b* 5 May 1660; a Ld of Session and High Commr to Gen Assembly Ch of Scotland 1741–53, rep s peer 1747–54; *m* 1st 23 Feb 1721 Mary (*d* 12 July 1723), dau of Hon Col John Erskine of Carnock, see BUCHAN, E), and *d* 2 Sept 1754, having had:

1 DAVID, **8th/5th Earl**

The 7th/4th Earl *m* 2nd 10 March 1726 Elizabeth (*d* 15 March 1783), dau of David Monypenny of Pitmilly, and by her had:

2 Alexander; *b* 1731; Gen; *m* 1760 the dau of Walter Tullideph of Tullideph, Forfarshire, and had:

(1) Mary Anne; *m* 1787 John Rutherford, of Edgerstown; *dsp*

1 Anne; *m* 1748 6th Earl of Northesk (*qv*) and *d* 1779

2 Elizabeth; *m* 10 June 1767 2nd Earl of Hopetoun (see LINLITHGOW, M) and *d* 10 April 1788, leaving issue

3 Mary; *m* 1762 James Walker of Innerdovat

The 7th/5th EARL's er son,

DAVID LESLIE, **8th Earl of Leven** and **5th Earl of Melville**; *b* 4 May 1722; High Commr to Gen Assembly Ch Scotland 1783–1801; *m* 29 July 1747 Wilhelmina (*d* 10 May 1798), dau of William Nisbet of Dirleton, and *d* 9 June 1802, having had:

1 ALEXANDER, **9th/6th Earl**

2 William; Offr Army; *k* War American Independence 1777

3 David; Gen; *m* 16 Jan 1787 Rebecca, dau of Rev John Gillies, DD, and *dsp* 21 Oct 1838

4 John; *b* 20 Nov 1759; Lt-Gen; *m* 13 Sept 1816 Jane, est dau and heiress of T Cuming, took the name CUMING and *dsp* 1824

5 George; *b* 21 April 1766; *m* 27 Nov 1802 Jacomina Gertrude, only dau of William Jacob van der Graaff, and *d* 8 March 1812, leaving an only dau:

(1) Mary Christiana; *d* 6 Nov 1892

1 Jane; *m* 9 Nov 1775 Sir John Wishart Stuart, Bt, and *d* 28 Oct 1829

2 Mary Elizabeth; *m* 5th Lord Ruthven (*see* CARLISLE, E) and *d* 1820

3 Charlotte; *d* unm 1830

The 8th/5th EARL's est son,

ALEXANDER LESLIE later LESLIE-MELVILLE (1805), **9th Earl of Leven** and **6th Earl of Melville**; *b* 7 Nov 1749; rep S peer 1806–07; *m* 12 Aug 1784 Jane (*d* 13 Feb 1818), dau of John Thornton, of London, and *d* 22 Feb 1820, having had:

1 DAVID LESLIE-MELVILLE, **10th Earl of Leven** and **7th Earl of Melville**; *b* 22 June 1785; V-Adml 1858, rep S peer 1831–60; *m* 21 June 1824 Elizabeth Anne (*d* 6 Nov 1863), dau of Sir Archibald Campbell, 2nd Bt, of Succoth (*qv*), and *d* 8 Oct 1860, having had:

(1) Alexander; *Lord Balgonie*; *b* 19 Nov 1831; Maj, Chev Legn Hon; *dvp* 29 Aug 1857

(2) David Archibald; *b* 14 Oct 1833; *dvp* 20 Oct 1854

(1) Elizabeth Jane; *m* 2 Nov 1858 Thomas Robert Brook Leslie Melville Cartwright (*d* 23 Jan 1921), s of Sir Thomas Cartwright, GCH, and *d* 25 Jan 1892, having had issue

(2) Anna Maria; *m* 26 April 1865 Sir William Stirling Maxwell, 9th Bt (*qv*), and *d* 8 Dec 1874

(3) Susan Lucy; Ldy of the Bedchamber to HRH THE PRINCESS CHRISTIAN 1868–83; *d* unm 8 June 1910

(4) Emily Eleanor; *m* 28 March 1864 1st Baron Hamilton of Dalzell (*qv*) and *d* 11 Nov 1882, having had issue

2 JOHN THORNTON, **11th/8th Earl**

3 William Henry; *b* 1788; dir HEIC; *d* 1856

4 Robert Samuel; in holy orders; *d* 24 Oct 1826

5 Alexander, of Branston Hall; *b* 18 June 1800; *m* 19 Oct 1825 Charlotte (*d* 26 April 1879), yst dau of Samuel Smith, of Herts, and *d* 19 Nov 1881, having had, with other issue:

(1) Alexander Samuel, of Branston Hall, JP and DL (Lincs); *b* 28 July 1829; High Sheriff 1888; *m* 30 Sept 1858 Albinia Frances (*d* 18 March 1918), dau of 6th Viscount Midleton (*qv*), and *d* 27 Jan 1919, leaving:

1a Alexander Brodrick; *b* 19 Dec 1872; Capt and Adj 2nd/8th Bn Sherwood Foresters, Notts and Derbys Regt, WW I (despatches); *m* 25 March 1905 Aileen (*d* 25 July 1941), only dau of Col Harvey Hamilton Harvey-Kelly and widow of Allan Daly, and *d* 8 Oct 1941, leaving:

1b Alexander Ronald; *b* 13 Dec 1905; F/O RAF, ATA WW II; *m* 29 April 1937 *Méry Henriette, dau of Emile Dallinges, of Lausanne, and *das* 12 June 1942

2a Charles le Despencer; *b* 23 Jan 1877; Capt Gren Gds; *m* 1911 Rose (*d* 13 Dec 1968), dau of Joseph Chesney, and *d* 31 Jan 1929

1a Emma Charlotte; *m* 16 June 1887 Rev John Otter Stephens (*d* 14 Aug 1925), Vicar All Saints, Tooting Graveney, Hon Canon Southwark, and *d* 29 Aug 1946, leaving issue

2a Albina Harriet; *m* 25 May 1896 Maj Edward Henry Evans Lombe, DL (*d* 5 April 1952), and *d* 22 Jan 1956, leaving issue

3a Lucy Victoria; *m* 13 Nov 1890 Claude George Melville Pym (*see* PYM, B) and *d* 10 May 1957, leaving issue

4a Edith Mary; *m* 30 May 1901 Thomas Walter Bacon (*d* 2 Dec 1950), 4th s of Sir Henry Hickman Bacon, 10th and 11th Bt (*qv*), and *d* 18 April 1950, leaving issue

5a Constance Alice, CBE (1919); *m* 22 June 1893 Sir Nicholas Henry Bacon, 12th and 13th Bt (*d* 1 Jan 1947), and *d* 11 Feb 1962, leaving issue

(2) Frederick Abel (Rev); *b* 17 Sept 1833; *educ* Cambridge (MA); Rector Welbourn, Preb Lincoln; *m* 9 June 1869 Susan Georgina (*d* 19 July 1922), dau of Robert Balfour Wardlaw-Ramsay, of Whitehill, Midlothian, and *d* 14 April 1908, having had:

1a Ruthven Wardlaw; *b* 27 July 1879; *d* 5 Dec 1928

2a Henry William; *b* 9 June 1881; *d* 26 Aug 1915

3a Malcolm Alexander; *b* 11 Dec 1882; *m* 6 Sept 1924 Ruth Ellen (*m* 2nd 31 March 1951 Arthur Ernest Mallett (*d* 29 Oct 1960) and *d* 1982), yr dau of James Dowker, of Mount Tolmie, Victoria, BC, and *d* 12 Dec 1946, leaving:

1b *Eleanor Constance [Mrs David Metcalfe, 640 Fernhil Rd, Victoria, BC, Canada]; *b* 5 July 1926; *m* 9 May 1953 *David William Metcalfe, s of George Metcalfe, and has:

1c *Margaret Rose; *b* 4 July 1955; *m* 1979 *Albert Lawson Munday

2c *Sandra Gail; *b* 16 May 1957; *m* 1976 *Bruce Douglas Crowe and has:

1d *Andrew Jackson; *b* 1989

3c *Heather May; *b* 1 May 1965

1b *Margaret Wardlaw [Miss Margaret Leslie Melville, 1833 West 37th Ave, Vancouver V6M 1N3, BC, Canada]; *b* 29 Nov 1928

4a Douglas Montague; *b* 12 Feb *d* 26 Aug 1886

1a Annie Louisa; *b* 2 Aug 1871; *d* 26 April 1938

2a Lucy Mabel; *b* 4 Oct 1873; *d* unm 10 Aug 1961

3a Eleanor; *b* 19 Sept 1875; *d* unm 11 March 1958

(3) Arthur Henry, OBE (1918), JP Lincs; *b* 12 March 1842; KGStJ; *d* 21 April 1922

(1) Charlotte Elizabeth; *m* 2 May 1866 William Elphinstone Malcolm, DL (*d* 30 Dec 1907), and *dsp* 27 Nov 1892

(2) Marianne; *m* 27 Jan 1852 Francis Brown Douglas (*d* 1885), advocate, and *d* 1899, having had issue

(3) Caroline; *m* 9 Oct 1879 Very Rev William Robert Fremantle (*d* 8 March 1895), bro of 1st Baron Cottesloe (*qv*), and *d* 10 Feb 1926

(4) Lucy Sophia; *m* 28 Oct 1857 Rev Henry Wright (*d* 13 Aug 1880) and *d* 7 Feb 1902, having had issue

1 Lucy; *m* 14 July 1824 Henry Smith (*d* 7 Feb 1874) and *d* 23 Dec 1865, having had issue

2 Jane Elizabeth; *m* 13 Oct 1816 Francis Pym (*see* PYM, B) and *d* 25 April 1848, leaving issue

3 Marianne; *m* 28 Aug 1822 Abel Smith, JP (*d* 23 Feb 1859), and *d* 22 March 1823

The 10th/7th EARL's bro,

JOHN THORNTON LESLIE-MELVILLE, **11th Earl of Leven** and **8th Earl of Melville**, JP, DL; *b* 18 Dec 1786; rep S peer 1865–76; *m* 1st 15 Sept 1812 Harriet (*d* 26 July 1832), yst dau of Samuel Thornton, of Clapham, MP Surrey, and had, with other issue:

1 ALEXANDER LESLIE-MELVILLE, **12th Earl of Leven** and **9th Earl of Melville**; *b* 11 Jan 1817; rep S peer 1880–89; *d* unm 22 Oct 1889

2 Alfred John; *b* 5 June 1826; HEICS; *d* Penang 25 May 1851

1 Emily Maria; *m* 18 Nov 1858 Robert Williams (*see* WILLIAMS, Bt, of Bridehead) and *dsp* 10 March 1896

2 Julia Louisa; *m* 29 March 1869 Lt-Gen Richardson-Robertson (*see* STEWART-RICHARDSON, Bt), of Tulliebelton, Perthshire, and *d* 24 Oct 1870

The **11th/8th Earl** *m* 2nd 23 April 1834 his cousin Sophia (*d* 28 June 1887), 4th dau of Henry Thornton, MP, and *d* 8 Sept 1876, having by her had, with other issue:

3 RONALD RUTHVEN, **13th/10th Earl**

4 Norman; *b* 5 Feb 1839; Capt Gren Gds; *m* 4 Dec 1861 Georgina (*d* 30 Dec 1922), dau of Capt William Shirley Ball, 8th Hus, of Abbeylara, Co Longford, and *d* 13 Nov 1923 having had:

(1) Galfrid John; *b* 11 Nov 1863; *m* 2 Sept 1895 Nora French (*m* 2nd 29 March 1913 Arnold Ceresole and *d* 17 June 1924), dau of George Ambler Stead, of Pool, nr Leeds, and *d* 25 Oct 1910, leaving:

1a (Norman) Victor; *b* 30 May 1896; *educ* Wellington; Lt Roy Scots SR, WWs I and II; *m* 15 Aug 1918 Dorothea (*d* 1982), er dau of Walter Stead, and *d* 7 Jan 1974, leaving:

1b Xenia Winifred; *b* 18 May 1919; *m* 28 Sept 1939 John Michael Richmond Paton, s of Edward Richmond Paton, of Hareshawmuir by Kilmarnock, and *d* 12 Aug 1984, leaving:

1c *Alasdair Donald; *b* 14 Sept 1952; *educ* Gordonstoun

1c *Frances Dorothea; *b* 30 March 1948; *m* 25 May 1968 *Harold Abbott and has:

1d *John; *b* 1971

1d *Clare; *b* 8 March 1969

2c *Fiona Jacqueline Richmond [Mrs Colin Graham, Mackeanston House, Doune, Perthshire FK18 6AX]; *b* 1 Aug 1951; *m* 4 April 1986 *Colin Hugh Campbell Graham (see GRAHAM, Bt, of Larbert), and has issue

2b *Joan Frances Ruth [Mrs Richard Amphlett, The Close, Fairford, Glos GL7 4BB]; *b* 1 March 1922; *m* 1st 18 Jan 1941 (*divorce* 1954) Norman Henry Gibbs (*d* 1990), DPhil, Prof Mil Hist, of All Souls, yr s of W B Gibbs, of Ilford, and has:

1c *(Kathleen) Vanessa [Mrs Peter Quarrell, Vyners Cottage, Long Compton, Shipston-on-Stour, Warwicks CV36 5JJ]; *b* 15 April 1942; *m* 14 Aug 1965 *Peter John Quarrell, yr s of Prof Arthur George Quarrell, DSc, PhD, of Sheffield U, and has:

1d *Rachel Emma Louise; *b* 31 March 1968; *educ* Bryanston; PhD

2d *Philippa Kathryn; *b* 22 May 1970; *educ* Bryanston

2c *Judith Rowena; *b* 25 Aug 1946; *m* 21 Oct 1967 *William Rupert Brent Pelly (*see* PELLY, Bt) and has issue

2b (cont) Mrs Joan Gibbs *m* 2nd 6 Oct 1955 Richard John Marshall Amphlett (*d* 1978), only s of Richard Ferrand Amphlett

3b *Anne [Mrs Anne McDermott, Kitebrook House, nr Moreton-in-Marsh, Glos]; *b* 13 Dec 1929; *m* 1953 (*divorce* 1977) Matthew Joseph McDermott

2a Kenneth; *b* 30 Nov 1901; *d* unm 13 Oct 1943

(1) Sylvia Beryl; *b* 1899; *m* 6 Sept 1924 René Lara (*d* 194–), ed *The Gaulois*, s of André Lara, and *d* 1989, having had issue

1 Florence Evelyn; *d* Malta 31 May 1864

2 Kathleen Mabel; *m* 16 Jan 1894 Charles Henry Farrer (*d* 10 June 1927), of Green Hammerton Hall, Yorks, and *d* 8 Jan 1958, leaving issue

The 12th/9th EARL's half-bro,

RONALD RUTHVEN LESLIE MELVILLE, **13th Earl of Leven** and **10th Earl of Melville**, KT (1905), PC (1902), DL (Nairn); *b* 19 Dec 1835; *educ* Eton and Ch Ch Oxford; Lt City London, rep S peer 1891–1906, Keeper Privy Seal Scotland, Ld High Commr Gen Assembly Ch Scotland 1898–1905; *m* 7 May 1885 Hon Emma Selina (*d* 1 March 1941), dau of 2nd Viscount Portman (*qv*), and *d* 21 Aug 1906, having had:

1 JOHN DAVID LESLIE MELVILLE, **14th Earl of Leven** and **11th Earl of Melville**; *b* 5 April 1886; Lt Lovat Scouts Yeo, rep S peer 1910–13; *d* unm 11 June 1913

2 ARCHIBALD ALEXANDER, **15th/12th Earl**

3 David William, MBE (1919); *b* 23 May 1892; Capt 2nd Lovat Scouts, formerly 10th Hus, Order Redeemer Greece 5th Cl; *m* 1st 6 March 1914 (*divorce* 1928) Susanna Elizabeth Johanna, dau of Francis Sleigh, of Cape Town; *m* 2nd 1929 Eleanor Mary Barrell (*m* 2nd 24 Aug 1939 Capt Arthur Miller (*das* 1942) and *d* 1974), dau of Arthur John Abrahall, of Shustoke, Warwicks, and *d* 10 Dec 1938, having by her had:

(1) John David; *b* 28 Feb 1933; *m* 14 July 1961 (*divorce* 1964) Lady Zinnia Denison, only child of 4th Earl of Londesborough (*see* LONDESBOROUGH, B), and formerly w of Peter Comins, and *d* 1984

(1) *Gillian Mary; *b* 24 Sept 1930; *m* 1st 9 Sept 1950 (*divorce*) Peter Riley, only s of Maj J H Riley, of Waterloo, Gt Crosby, Liverpool; *m* 2nd *Martin Dowling and by him has:

1a *David; *b* 19–

1a *Eleanor; b 19–
4 Ian, TD; b 14 Aug 1894; educ Eton and Balliol Coll Oxford (BA 1917, MA 1932); Lt-Col Lovat Scouts, WWs I and II; dep chm Dalgety and Co 1949–55, md Glyn Mills and Co, memb Scottish Bd Legal and Gen Ass Soc, memb Roy Co Archers; m 26 Aug 1915 Charlotte Isobel (d 7 Nov 1968), dau of Maj William Stirling, DL, of Fairburn, Muir of Ord, Ross-shire, and d 10 Feb 1967 having had:
  (1) Michael Ian, TD, DL (Selkirks 1974); b 12 Aug 1918; educ Eton and Balliol Coll Oxford (BA 1946, MA 1949); FRICS; Maj Lovat Scouts WW II; memb Roy Co Archers; m 31 July 1943 Cynthia (d 1986), sis of Baron Hambro (qv), and d 22 Jan 1997, leaving:
    1a +(Ian) Hamish [Hamish Leslie Melville Esq, Lochluichart, by Grave, Ross-shire]; b 22 Aug 1944; educ Eton and Ch Ch Oxford (MA, Dip Econ), memb Roy Co Archers; dir Hambros Bank 1975–, chm Dunedin to 1996; m 30 March 1968 *Lady Elizabeth Compton, yr dau of 6th Marquess of Northampton (qv), and has:
      1b +James ('Jake') Ian; b 4 Sept 1969; m 25 Oct 1997 *Emma, yr dau of Geoffrey Thorpe, of Guildford
      2b +Henry Bingham; b 30 Jan 1975
    1a *Pamela; b 6 Sept 1947
    2a *Fiona Evelyn; ARCM; b 10 Feb 1950; m 2 June 1973 *James Campbell David Brodie, yr s of Maj David James Brodie, of Lethen, OBE, DL, and has:
      1b *Alexander John; b 1974
      1b *Charlotte Sophia; b 1976
      2b *Anna Louise; b 1979
  (1) Judith Betty; b 26 Oct 1916; m 2 Sept 1939 (divorce 1961) 2nd Baron Dulverton (qv) and d 1983, leaving issue
  (2) Helen Selina; b 6 March 1921; m 14 June 1941 Maj John Hugh Gilbert Wyld, Lovat Scouts, er s of Maj Hugh James Wyld, of Beverston Old Rectory, Tetbury, Glos, and d 15 June 1946, leaving issue
  (3) *Elisabeth Marion; b 9 April 1928; m 27 March 1952 4th Baron Joicey (qv) and has issue
1 Constance Betty; b 7 Aug 1888; d 13 Aug 1922

The 14th/11th EARL's bro,
ARCHIBALD ALEXANDER LESLIE MELVILLE, **15th Earl of Leven** and **12th Earl of Melville**, KT; b 6 Aug 1890; educ Eton and RMC Sandhurst; rep S peer 1922–47, Ld-Lt Nairn 1935–47, Lt-Col and Brevet Col Lovat Scouts and Capt RSG WW I (wounded); m 3 Sept 1918 Lady Rosamond Sylvia Diana Foljambe (d 12 April 1974), 6th dau of 1st Earl of Liverpool (qv), and d 15 Jan 1947, leaving:
1 ALEXANDER ROBERT LESLIE MELVILLE, **16th and present Earl of Leven and 13th and present Earl of Melville**
2 George David; b 13 May 1924; educ Eton and Trin Coll Cambridge (BA); Maj Black Watch (TAR), WW II as Capt Rifle Bde (wounded); FLAS, FRICS, FAI; m 30 April 1955 *Diana Mary [The Hon Mrs George Leslie Melville, Inneshewen, Aboyne, Aberdeenshire AB34 5BH], yr dau of Brig Sir Henry Walter Houldsworth, KBE, DSO, MC, TD, of Dallas Lodge, Forres, Morayshire, and d 23 June 1997, leaving:
  (1) +James Hugh; b 5 Nov 1960; m 1987 *Clare Jean, 2nd dau of Robert Henry Heywood-Lonsdale (see ROLLO, L), and has:
    1a +John (Jack); b 1991
    2a +George; b 1993
    1a *Rosanna Clare; b 1995
  (1) *Annabel Clare [Mrs Nigel Savory, Thorpland Hall, Fakenham, Norfolk NR21 0HD]; b 18 July 1956; m 1979 *Nigel R Savory, s of John Savory, of Bridge Cottage, Thorpland
3 Ronald Jocelyn; b 22 Nov 1926; educ Eton and Worcester Coll Oxford (BA 1950); m 17 May 1962 *Ruth [The Hon Mrs Ronald Leslie Melville, Little Deuchar, Fern, Angus DD8 3QZ], only dau of Dr John Duckworth, and d 1987, leaving:
  (1) Andrew John; b 16 April, d 18 Dec 1964
  (2) +Roderick Justice; b 12 Aug 1965
  (3) +Robert Jeffrey; b 13 May 1967
  (4) +Angus Jack; b 4 Aug 1968
  (1) *Rosamond Joscelyn; b 31 Dec 1962
4 +Alan Duncan [The Hon Alan Leslie Melville, Fingask, Kirkhill, Inverness]; b 11 Oct 1928; educ Eton; Capt (ret) Rifle Bde; m 1 Nov 1997 *Mrs Sally Haywood, of Fettes Farmhouse, Muir of Ord, Ross-shire
1 *Jean Elizabeth [The Lady Jean Leslie Melville, Flat 24, Homesmith House, Evesham, Worcs WR11 4EH]; b 25 June 1921

LEVENE OF PORTSOKEN

Arms: Per pale gules and azure between three swords palewise in fesse the outer two with their points downwards all three argent their hilts pommels and quillons or two towers also argent masoned proper in front of the portal of each tower a cartwheel gules and on a chief per pale azure and gules a boar's head couped or langued gules tusked argent between two loving cups of silver. **Crest:** A mail gauntlet clenched argent in front of two vine branches in saltire leaved and fructed. **Supporters:** Dexter, a scorpion or the stinger azure; sinister, a scorpion or the stinger gules.
Motto: Industria atque fortuna ('By industry and fortune').
Creation: B. (LP, UK) June 1997.

THE BARON LEVENE OF PORTSOKEN, of Portsoken, City of London (Sir Peter Keith Levene, KBE (1989), JP (City London 1984)) [The Rt Hon The Lord Levene of Portsoken KBE JP, House of Lords, London SW1A 0PW]; b 8 Dec 1941; educ City of London Sch (Govr 1986–) and Manchester U; United Scientific Hldgs: joined 1963, md 1968–85, chm 1982–85; Ch Def Procurement MOD 1985–91; UK Nat Armaments Dir 1988–91, Chm European Nat Armaments Dirs 1989–90; Personal Advsr: Def Sec 1984 and Pres BOT 1992–95, Special Advsr: Environment Sec 1991–92 and Chllr Exchequer on competition and purchasing 1992; chm: Docklands Light Rlway 1991–94 and Canary Wharf Ltd 1993–96 (also ch exec), dep chm Wasserstein Perella 1991–94; advsr to PM on efficiency 1992–97; memb Court HAC 1984–, City London: Alderman Portsoken Ward 1984–, Sheriff 1995–96, Ld Mayor 1998–99; Liveryman Carmens' Co 1984–; CIMgt, FRSA, FCIT, FCIPS, OStJ 1996, Cdr OM France; m 1966 *Wendy Ann Fraiman and has two sons and a dau

Lineage: MAURICE LEVENE; m Rose — and had:

PETER KEITH (Sir), cr a **Baron**

LEVER

ANIMO ET FIDE

LEVERHULME

MUTARE VEL TIMERE SPERNO

Arms: Quarterly, 1st and 4th, tierce in pale sable, gules and azure, three bear's heads, one and two erased, muzzled or; 2nd and 3rd, argent a chevron invected ermines between two keys erect, the wards to the dexter in chief sable, and an Esquire's helmet in base proper. **Crests:** 1 In front of a rising moon proper a cormorant sable, 2 A dexter arm embowed in armour, the hand proper holding a key in bend sinister, the wards upwards sable, and encircled above the elbow with a chaplet of roses argent, leaved vert. **Motto:** *Animo et fide* ('By spirit and faith'). **Creation:** Bt. (UK) 8 Feb 1911.

Arms: Quarterly, 1st and 4th, per pale argent and barry of eight or and azure two bendlets sable, the upper one engrailed (for LEVER); 2nd and 3rd, per chevron or and gules, in chief two chaplets of roses and in base a lion's head all counterchanged (for HULME). **Crest:** A trumpet fesswise, thereon a cock proper, charged on the breast with a rose as in the arms. **Supporters:** On either side an elephant or, the dexter charged on the shoulder with a rose gules, barbed and seeded proper, the sinister with a chaplet of roses also gules. **Motto:** *Mutare vel timere sperno* ('I scorn to change or fear'). **Creations:** Bt. (UK) 6 July 1911, B. (UK) 21 June 1917, V. (UK) 27 Nov 1922.

SIR (TRESHAM) CHRISTOPHER ARTHUR LINDSAY LEVER, 3RD BT, of Hans Crescent, Chelsea [Sir Christopher Lever Bt, Newell House, Winkfield, Berks SL4 4SE]; *b* 9 Jan 1932; *s* f 1975; *educ* Eton and Trin Coll Cambridge (BA 1954, MA 1957); late 2nd Lt 17th/21st Lancers, former accountant, stockbroker, naturalist, consultant Born Free Fndn 1991–, memb IUCN Species Survival Commn 1988–, patron: Rhino Rescue Tst 1985–, Lynx Educnl Tst for Animal Welfare 1991– and Respect for Animals 1995–, chm and patron Tusk Tst 1990–, hon life memb Brontë Soc 1988–, memb exec ctee Earth 2000 1996–, author: *Goldsmiths and Silversmiths of England* (1975), *The Naturalized Animals of the British Isles* (1977), *Naturalized Mammals of the World* (1985), *Naturalized Birds of the World* (1987), *The Mandarin Duck* (1990), *They Dined on Eland: the story of the acclimatisation societies* (1992), *Naturalized Animals: the ecology of successfully introduced species* (1994), *Naturalized Fishes of the World* (1996); *m* 1st 11 Aug 1970 (*divorce* 1974) Susan Mary, only dau of Prof John Armytage Nicholson, of Enniscoe, Crossmolina, Co Mayo; *m* 2nd 6 Nov 1975 *Linda Weightman McDowell, dau of James Jepson Goulden, of Tennessee

Lineage: JOSEPH LEVY, of Knighton, Leics; *b* 13 Feb 1829; *m* 8 Aug 1855 Cordelia (*d* 4 Dec 1906), dau of Michael Hart, of Manchester, and *d* 22 Nov 1899, having had:

  1 David, of 38 Porchester Square, London W; *b* 9 Oct 1856; *m* 14 Feb 1888 Kate, dau of David Benjamin, of Westbourne Terrace, London W, and had issue
  2 MAURICE LEVY (Sir), *cr* 1913 a Baronet (UK) (*see* 1970 edn)
  3 ARTHUR (Sir), **1st Bt**
  1 Lulie; *m* 9 Jan 1889 Sir John Henry, JP, DL (*d* 23 Dec 1930), and *d* 12 Aug 1955, leaving issue

JOSEPH LEVY's 3rd son,
  Sir ARTHUR LEVY later LEVY LEVER (deed poll 1896, roy licence 7 Feb 1911), **1st Bt** (UK), so *cr* 8 Feb 1911, JP (Essex); *b* 17 Nov 1860; Maj London Regt, Roy Fus WW I, MP (Lib) Harwich 1906–10 and Centl Hackney (Nat Lib)1922–23, memb Commn on Coast Erosion; *m* 12 Feb 1896 Beatrice Hilda (*d* 28 May 1917), 3rd dau of Philip Falk, of Kensington, and *d* 23 Aug 1924, leaving:

Sir Tresham Joseph Philip Lever, 2nd Bt; *b* 3 Sept 1900; *educ* Harrow and Univ Coll Oxford (BA 1921, MA 1928); barrister Inner Temple 1925, High Sheriff Leics 1962, author: *Profit and Loss* (1933), *The Life and Times of Sir Robert Peel* (1942), *The House of Pitt; a family chronicle* (1947), *Godolphin, his life and times* (1952), *The Letters of Lady Palmerston* (ed, 1957), *The Herberts of Wilton* (1967), *Lessudden House, Sir Walter Scott and the Scots of Raeburn* (1971), and *Clayton of Toc H* (1972); *m* 1st 23 April 1930 Frances Yowart (*d* 3 Oct 1959), yr dau of Lindsay Hamilton Goodwin, of Neston, Cheshire, and widow of Cecil Parker, of Walton Hall, Lancs, and had:

  1 Sir (TRESHAM) CHRISTOPHER ARTHUR LINDSAY LEVER, **3rd and present Bt**

Sir Tresham *m* 2nd 5 March 1962 *(Clodagh) Pamela [Pamela Lady Lever, Lessudden Cottage, St Boswells, Roxburghshire TD6 0BH], only child of Lt-Col Hon Malcolm Bowes-Lyon, CBE (*see* STRATHMORE AND KINGHORNE, E), and formerly w of Lord Malcolm Avondale Douglas-Hamilton, OBE, DFC (*see* HAMILTON and BRANDON, D), and *d* 30 April 1975

THE 3RD VISCOUNT LEVERHULME, of the Western Isles, Cos Inverness and Ross and Cromarty, **Baron Leverhulme**, of Bolton-le-Moors, Co Lancaster, and a **Baronet** (Sir Philip William Bryce Lever, Bt, KG (1988),TD, JP) [The Rt Hon The Viscount Leverhulme KG TD JP, Thornton Manor, Thornton Hough, Wirral, Cheshire L63 1JB; Badanloch, Kinbrace, Sutherland; Flat 6, Kingston House East, Prince's Gate, London SW7 1IJ]; *b* 1 July 1915; *s* f 1949; *educ* Eton and Trin Coll Cambridge (BA); Hon Col Cheshire Yeo (TA), Hon A/Cdre No 610 (Co Chester) Sqdn RAuxAF, Hon A/Cdre 663 Air OP Sqdn RAuxAF, TAVR 1972–; Ld Lt Cheshire 1949–90, Advsy Dir Unilever Ltd, Pres Cncl Liverpool U 1957– (Chllr 1980–93, Hon LLD 1967); memb Nat Hunt Ctee, Sr Steward Jockey Club and Co-Chm Jt Racing Bd 1973–76, KStJ, Hon FRCS 1970; *m* 1 July 1937 Margaret (Ann) (*d* 1973), only child of John Moon, of Tiverton, Devon, and has:

  1 *Susan Elizabeth Moon [The Hon Mrs Pakenham, Dibbinsdale Lodge, Bromborough, Wirral, Cheshire]; *b* 5 May 1938; *m* 1 June 1957 (*divorce*) (Hercules) Michael Roland Pakenham (*see* LONGFORD, E) and adopted a s and dau
  2 *Victoria Marion Ann [The Hon Mrs Tower, 8 Mulberry Walk, London SW3]; *b* 23 Sept 1945; Extra Ldy-in-Waiting to HRH (THE) PRINCESS ANNE (ROYAL) 1974–; *m* 1st 27 Sept 1966 (*divorce* 1973) Sir Richard Carew Pole, 13th Bt (*qv*); *m* 2nd 3 Oct 1975 (Robert) Gordon Lennox O'Reilly Apsion; *m* 3rd 1990 *Brig Peter Tower and by her 2nd husb has:
    (1) *Philip Gordon William; *b* 1976
    (2) *Robert George Neville; *b* 1978
    (1) *Victoria Alexander; *b* Sept 1983
  3 *(Margaret) Jane [The Hon Mrs Heber-Percy, Hodnet Hall, Market Drayton, Salop TF9 3NN]; *b* 22 June 1947; *m* 6 July 1966 *Algernon Eustace Hugh Heber-Percy (*see* NORTHUMBERLAND, D) and has issue

Lineage: ALEXANDER LEVER, of Darcy Lever; *bapt* 18 March 1666 (s of John Lever); *m* 24 Oct 1689 Elizabeth Ramsbottom and was *bur* March 1739, having had (with six daus):

  1 James, of Darcy Lever; *b c* 1695; *m* 21 Jan 1718 Hannah (*bur* 26 April 1779), dau of Thomas Wolfenden, and was bur *sp* 16 Dec 1778
  2 JOHN
  3 Robert; *bapt* 25 July 1708; *d* by 1778, leaving issue

The 2nd son,
  JOHN LEVER, of Darvy Lever; *b* 7 May 1701; *m* 1 Jan 1722 Alice (*bur* 20 Oct 1790), dau of John Norris, of Little Bolton, and *d* 12 Aug 1794, having had, with five other sons and two daus:

ALEXANDER LEVER, of Great Bolton, Lancs; *bapt* 11 Oct 1730; *m* 23 April 1749 Mary (*bur* 24 Nov 1797), dau of John Smith, of Haulgh, and *d* 1 June 1800, having had, with two yr sons and five daus:

ROBERT LEVER, of Gt Bolton; *bapt* 10 July 1757; *m* 5 Sept 1777 Mary, dau of William Rothwell, of Haulgh, and was *bur* 2 Sept 1783, having had, with a yr son and two daus:

JAMES LEVER, of Gt Bolton; *bapt* 16 Aug 1778; *m* 19 Jan 1802 Elizabeth, dau of John Parkinson, of Gt Bolton, and was *bur* 22 Aug 1825, having had:

  1 Robert; *bapt* 19 Jan 1803
  2 Ralph; *bapt* 1 Feb 1804
  3 William, of Gt Bolton; *bapt* 25 Dec 1805; *m* Jane — (*bur* 15 Feb 1843), and *d* 2 Feb 1830, having had issue

4 JAMES

5 Darcy; *b* 1813; *bur* 25 Dec 1814

1 Elizabeth; *bapt* 19 June 1811; *d* an infant

The 4th son,

JAMES LEVER, of Gt Bolton; *b* 26 Aug 1809; *m* 10 April 1839 Eliza (*d* 28 Nov 1893), dau of William Hesketh, of Manchester, and *d* 26 May 1897, having had:

1 WILLIAM HESKETH, **1st Viscount**

2 James Darcy, of Thornton House, Thornton Hough, Cheshire; *b* 10 Feb 1854; *m* 26 April 1882 Anne (*d* 25 Nov 1935), dau of Joshua Kershaw, of Bolton, and *d* 29 March 1910, having had issue

1 Elizabeth; *b* 31 March 1840; *d* 21 June 1849

2 Eliza Emma; *b* 9 Nov 1841; *m* 1st 28 Nov 1867 John Spencer Howarth; *m* 2nd 28 Aug 1878 Arthur Bromley and *d* 21 May 1920

3 Mary; *b* 14 Aug 1843; *m* 20 April 1870 William Frederick Tillotson and *d* 23 Feb 1918

4 Jane; *b* 30 Sept 1845; *m* 6 Sept 1871 John Smith Ferguson and *d* 20 Aug 1936

5 Emily; *b* 11 Oct 1847; *d* unm 18 Sept 1939

6 Alice; *b* 31 Aug 1849; *d* unm 20 May 1944

7 Harriette; *b* 1 Dec 1855; *d* unm 16 June 1946

8 Lucy Anne; *b* 25 Feb 1859; *m* 20 July 1893 Alexander Paul and *d* 1 Nov 1944

The est son,

Sir William Hesketh Lever, 1st Bt, so *cr* 6 July 1911, as also 27 Nov 1922 **1st Viscount Leverhulme**, of the Western Isles, Cos Inverness and Ross and Cromarty, and earlier 21 June 1917 BARON LEVERHULME, of Bolton-le-Moors, Co Lancaster (all UK), JP (Cheshire); *b* 19 Sept 1851; *educ* Bolton Church Institute; grocer 1867–86, soap mfr 1886 on, fndr Port Sunlight, Chm Lever Bros, Port Sunlight; MP (Lib) Wirral 1906–10, High Sheriff Lancs 1917, Mayor Bolton 1918–19, Hon FRIBA, FRGS, and LLD Edin, Hon Col 2nd Vol Bn Cheshire Regt, Grand Offr Order Leopold II Belgium, Jr Warden Grand Lodge England 1918, Messel Medal Soc Chemical Industry 1924; *m* 15 April 1874 Elizabeth Ellen, FRGS (*d* 24 July 1913), dau of Crompton Hulme, of Bolton, and *d* 7 May 1925, leaving:

WILLIAM HULME LEVER, **2nd Viscount Leverhulme**, JP and DL (Cheshire); *b* 25 March 1888; *educ* Eton and Trin Coll Cambridge (BA 1909, MA 1913); Capt 4th/5th Cheshire Regt (TA), Hon Air Cdre No. 919/923 (W Lancs) Balloon Sqdn AAF 1940, Hon Col 4th AA Div RASC 1941; High Sheriff Cheshire 1923, Govr Lever Bros and Unilever Ltd, Pres London Chamber Commerce 1931–34, Inst Chemical Engrs 1932–34, Roy Inst Public Health 1933–39, Chm Liverpool Sch Tropical Med, Hon FRIBA, a Pro-Chllr Liverpool U 1932–36, KJStJ, Pres: Soc Chemical Industry 1936 and 1937, Roy Inst Pub Health 1933–39, Epsom Coll and Caterham Sch, Charter Mayor Bebington 1937, Osborne Reynolds Medal 1937, Hon LLD Liverpool U 1937; *m* 1st 13 April 1912 (*divorce* 1936) Marion Beatrice, yst dau of Bryce Smith, of Whalley and Manchester, and had:

1 PHILIP WILLIAM BRYCE LEVER, **3rd and present Viscount Leverhulme**

1 (Elizabeth) Ruth, JP (1950) Liverpool; *b* 9 April 1913; *d* unm 16 April 1972

2 *Rosemary Gertrude Alexandra; *b* 23 April 1919; *m* 19 Oct 1938 Lt-Col William Erskine Stobart Whetherley, 1st King's Dragoon Gds, er s of Lt-Col William Stobart Whetherly, DSO, late 19th Hus, and had:

  (1) *Dennis William Stobart; *b* 27 Jan 1940; *educ* privately

  (2) *Robin Christopher Philip; *b* 19 Oct 1947; *educ* Harrow; late Lt RHG (Blues and Royals); *m* 30 June 1971 *Sally Ann, dau of Major R C S Price, of Birdhurst, Alderbury, Wilts, and has:

    1a *A dau; *b* 30 Jan 1976

  (1) *Dawn Elizabeth Evelyn [Mrs Dawn Little, College Farm, Wyck Rissington, Glos GL54 2PN]; *b* 12 Feb 1946; *m* 1st 2 May 1967 (*divorce* 1981) Andrew James Little, only s of John Douglas Little, DSC, of Llanferres, nr Mold, Flintshire; *m* 2nd 1987 (*divorce*) Kevin S Perrett and by her 1st husb has:

    1a *Mark William Douglas; *b* 17 Oct 1969

    1a *Emma Louise; *b* 1973

    2a *Alexandra Rose; *b* 1977

The **2nd Viscount** *m* 2nd 20 Jan 1937 Winifred Agnes (Freda), JP (Cheshire1950), OStJ (*d* 19 Feb 1966), yr dau of Lt-Col J E Lloyd, of Brentwood, Bidston, Cheshire, and formerly w of Capt George Lee Morris, VD, RNVR, and *d* 27 May 1949

LEVINGE

Arms: Vert a chevron or, in chief three escallops arg.
Crest: An escallop arg. within a garland ppr. **Motto:** *Vestigia nulla retrorsum* ('No footsteps backwards'). **Creation:** Bt. (I) 26 Oct 1704.

SIR RICHARD GEORGE ROBIN LEVINGE, 12TH BT, of High Park, Co Westmeath [Sir Richard Levinge Bt, Clohamon House, Bunclody, Co Wexford, Ireland]; *b* 18 Dec 1946; *s f* 1984; *educ* Hawkhurst Sch W Sussex, Mahwah High Sch NY and Craibstone Ag Coll; *m* 1st 27 June 1969 (*divorce* 1978) Hilary Jane, dau of Dr Derek Mark, of Wingfield, Bray, Co Wicklow, and has:

1 +RICHARD MARK; *b* 15 May 1970

Sir RICHARD *m* 2nd 1978 *Maria Isabella d'Ardia Caracciolo, yr dau of Prince Ferdinando d'Ardia Caracciolo dei Principi di Cursi, of Haddington Rd, Dublin, and by her has:

2 +Robin Edward; *b* 1978

1 *Melissa Louise; *b* 1980

Lineage: THOMAS LEVINGE, allegedly of Derbyshire but said by W Woolley, *History of Derbyshire* (MS 1712), and S Lysons, *Magna Britannia*, Vol V, *Derbyshire* (1816), to have been of Norfolk; living 1413; had:

VALENTINE LEVINGE; had a yr s:

WALTER LEVINGE, of Coleshill, Warwicks; *m* Margery Longshaw, of Lancs, and had, with a dau (Mrs Pecke):

1 THOMAS

2 Francis; *m* Persis, dau of Thomas Diccons, of Napton, Warwicks, and had:

  (1) Thomas; *b* 1601

  (1) Catherine

3 William; living 1611; *m* Dorothy, dau of William Hitson, of Baddesley, Warwicks, and had:

  (1) Timothy; living 1611

  (1) Sarah; living 1611

4 Timothy; Serjeant-at-law; MP Derby 1621–27

The est s,

THOMAS LEVINGE, of Derby; barrister; bought Parwich Hall, Derbys, 1561; Recorder Derby 1621–36; *m* Dorothy, dau of John Beresford, of Newton Grange, Derbys, and had, with two yr sons (Daniel; Timothy) and three daus (Persis; Frances; Sarah):

THOMAS LEVINGE, of Parwich Hall; Recorder Chester; had:

RICHARD LEVINGE, of Parwich Hall; *m* 1653 Anne, dau of George Parker (*see* PARKER, Bt, of Shenstone), and had:

Sir Richard Levinge, 1st Bt (I), so *cr* 26 Oct 1704, of Parwich; MP Chester 1690–95 and Derby 1710–11, Recorder Chester 1686–87 and Derby; Speaker Irish H of C 1692, Slr-Gen Ireland 1692 and 1704–09, Attorney-Gen 1711–14, Ch Justice Common Pleas 1720–24; *b* 2 May 1656; *m* 1st 1680 Mary, dau and coheir of Sir Gawen Corbyn, of London, and had:

1 **Sir Richard Levinge, 2nd Bt**, of Parwich and High Park, Co Westmeath; MP; *m* 1718 Isabella (*d* 2 Nov 1731), dau of Sir Arthur Rawdon, 2nd Bt (*see* LOUDOUN, E), and *dsp* 1748

2 CHARLES (Sir), **3rd Bt**

1 Mary; *m* 2nd Earl Ferrers (*qv*)

2 Dorothea; *m* 1st Sir John Rawdon, 3rd Bt (*see* LOUDOUN, E); *m* 2nd Charles Cobbe, DD (*d* 14 April 1765), Archbp Dublin, and had issue

3 Grace; *m* Edward Kennedy, of Mullow, Co Longford

Sir Richard *m* 2nd Mary (*m* 2nd 9 Nov 1732 Capt Charles Annesley, Battleaxe Gds, and *d* 2 Dec 1756), dau of Hon Robert Johnson, Baron Exchequer Ireland, and *d* 13 July 1724, having by her had:

3 Richard, of Calverstown, Co Kildare; *m* Alice, dau of Thomas Marlay, Ld Ch Justice King's Bench Ireland, and had:

  (1) Mary; *m* 28 April 1770 James Cuffe, 1st and last Baron Tyrawley of Ballinrobe (*dspl* 15 June 1821), and *dsp* 11 May 1808

The 2nd Bt's bro,

Sir Charles Levinge, 3rd Bt; *b* 1693; *m* 1722 Anne, dau and coheir of Maj Samuel Greene, of Killaghy Castle, Co Tipperary, MP Cashel, and *d* 29 May 1762, leaving:

Sir Richard Levinge, 4th Bt; *b* 1724; *m* 1st 17 April 1744 Dorothea, dau and coheir of William Kennedy, MP, of Mullow, Co Longford, and had, with three daus:

1 CHARLES (Sir), **5th Bt**

2 Richard, of Lurgo, Co Tipperary, and Belview, Co Kilkenny; *b* 1760; *m* 1st 1788 Anne, 3rd dau of Godfrey Taylor, of Noan, Co Tipperary, and had, with other issue:

  (1) Charles; Lt 27th Regt; *ka* Badajoz

  (2) Godfrey, of Lurgo and Cullean, Co Westmeath, JP; *d* unm

2 (cont.) Richard Levinge *m* 2nd Eleanor O'Keefe and *d* 25 May 1828, having by her had:

  (3) Richard Hastings; *s* to Belview; *b* 1812; *m* 20 March 1839 Ellen (*d* 19 Oct 1864), yst dau of Thomas Chippen Faulconer, of Newhaven and Henfield, Sussex, and *d* Jan 1847, leaving:

    1a Richard Reginald Augustus; *b* 3 Jan 1843

    2a Charles

  (1) Ellen Augusta Helena; *m* 1 Feb 1839 Joseph Ledwith, MD (*d* 16 April 1882), and had issue

  (2) Fanny Maria Louisa

Sir Richard *m* 2nd Mary, dau of Sir Henry Tuite, and by her had:

3 Henry

4 Richard Hugh, JP, of Levington, Co Westmeath; *m* 1 May 1797 Jane (*d* 17 Oct 1840), dau of Thomas Child, and *d* 2 Sept 1864, leaving:

  (1) Charles William, JP; *b* 30 May 1817; *m* 6 Jan 1842 Annie (*d* 23 June 1880), dau of Robert Barlow, MD, and *d* 15 May 1868, leaving:

    1a Richard William Chaworth, of Levington and Corteen, Co Longford, JP; Sec Co Longford Grand Jury 1895–99 and CC 1899–1905; *b* 29 Dec 1843; *m* 21 March 1873 Fanny Ellen (*d* 1941), dau of George David Donkin, Lt 7th Roy Fus, of Wylford Court, Oxon, and gdau of Sir Rufane S Donkin, KCB, and *d* 13 Dec 1905, leaving:

      1b Charles Edward Robert, of Levington Park and Violetstown, Co Westmeath, and Corteen, Co Longford, JP Co Westmeath; *b* 16 Jan 1874; *m* 18 Jan 1900 Norah Violet (*d* 8 March 1950), only child of Capt Henry Loftus Lewis, RE, of Violetstown, and *d* 7 Nov 1951, leaving:

        1c Avice Jocelyn; *b* 1902; *d* unm 7 March 1962

      2b Richard Hugh; Capt RASC, Boer War 1899–1902, 2nd Bn Scots Gds (two medals, five clasps), WW I; *b* 15 July 1879; *m* 1914 Jennie Moncrieth Howitt (*d* March 1977), only dau of George Bell McCreedy, of Belfast and S Africa, and *d* 24 Oct 1926, leaving:

        1c Evelyn Hugh (Rev); Chaplain RN 1952; *b* 1915; *educ* King's Coll London; *m* 9 April 1955 Sheila Joy (*d* 1992), dau of S L R Etherton, MA, LLB, BSc, of Detroit, and *d* 1981, having had:

          1d +Richard St John [Richard Levinge Esq, Broadway, 8 Hall Rd, Leckhampton, Glos GL53 0HE]; late Sub-Lt RN; *b* 4 June 1956; *m* 1979 *Mary Juliet, dau of Radnor Outhwaite, of Cheshire, and has:

            1e +Daniel Richard; *b* 1983

            1e *Victoria Louise; *b* 1984

        1c *May Frances Jenoyr [Miss Mary Levinge, 21 Ridgeway Rd, Headington, Oxford]; *b* 1918; SRN, Nursing Offr Churchill Hosp Oxford

      3b Reginald Markham; Supt Trades and Customs; *b* 4 March 1885; *m* 21 May 1929 Vera Alexandra (*d* 1 Jan 1954), formerly w of Granville Altman-Wild and yst dau of Theodore Bogosoff, of Clifton, Bristol, and *dsp* 22 June 1960

      4b Arthur Tenison; Capt RASC and Roy Irish Rifles WW I, bank manager; *b* 5 June 1887; *d* unm 19 April 1958

      5b Frederick Rufane; WW I with Assam Valley Light Horse Vol Cav Corps and Indian Defence Force, tea-planter Assam; *b* 12 July 1890; *m* 13 Jan 1929 Rona Elizabeth (*d* 29 June 1971), er dau of Richard M Hawker, of S Australia, and *d* 1981, leaving:

        1c +Frederick Charles Richard [Frederick Levinge Esq, Messamurray, Box 20, Narracoorte, S Australia 5271]; *b* 20 Feb 1939; *educ* Scotch Coll, Adelaide; *m* 25 Oct 1969 *Tessa Mary, only dau of R W Barton, of Gisborne, NZ, and has:

          1d +Charles Richard Wynn; *b* 1 May 1973; *educ* Geelong GS

        1d *Georgina Rona [Mrs Richard Oates, Elovera, Purlewaugh, via Coonabarabran, NSW 2357, Australia]; *b* 27 Aug 1971; *m* 19 Oct 1996 *Richard Allan Oates

      1b Eva; *b* 7 Feb 1875

      2b Violet Frances; *b* 28 March 1876; *m* 20 Aug 1914 Charles (*d* 26 Jan 1945), est s of George Scott, of Co Wicklow, and had:

        1c *Richard Levinge Colthurst; Maj RASC WW II (despatches); *b* 28 June 1915; *educ* Downing Coll Cambridge (BA 1937); *m* 1946 *Peggy Amelia, dau of Percy Albert Parfitt, of Cambridge, and has:

          1d *Susan Margaret; *b* 9 Jan 1950

        1c Dorothy Mabel; *b* 4 April 1917; *d* unm 6 Aug 1959

      3b Annie Caroline; *m* 16 Aug 1911 Col William Theodore Redmond Browne, DSO, RASC (*d* 27 Oct 1962), 2nd s of Maj J Browne, Devonshire Regt, and had:

        1c *Patrick Theodore Levinge; Maj RA WW II; *b* 19 Oct 1915; *m* 30 April 1955 *Patricia, yst dau of James Lewis Tyler, LDS, and has:

          1d *Vanessa Madeleine; *b* 9 April 1957

      4b Frances Ellen; *b* 12 July 1883; *m* Dec 1917 Maj Thomas Marshall Llewellyn Fuge, IA (*d* 20 Nov 1965), s of Maj Thomas William Marshall Fuge, and *d* 17 Aug 1955, leaving issue

    2a Edward; Surgn-Maj IMS; *b* 4 March 1850; *m* 1 May 1888 Mary Ellen Davies, dau of Bryce McMaster, MICE, and *d* 7 May 1892, leaving:

      1b Edward Vere Bryce; *b* 25 March 1889; *m* 20 Jan 1916 Ethel Violet (*d* 1924), dau of George Cardwell Porter, MRCS, of Castleacre, Norfolk, and *d* 1922, leaving:

        1c Reginald Vere Noel; Lt RNR WW II 1939–40 (posted missing); *b* 21 Dec 1918

        2c +Bryce Leonard; *b* 6 June 1922; farmer

        1c *Avice Ethel Mary; *m* 1st 24 June 1944 Ward Shepard, Jr (*d* 3 Jan 1953), s of Ward Shepard, of Vienna, Va., and has:

          1d *Carol Jean; *b* 11 March 1946

         1c (cont.) Mrs Ward Shepard, Jr, *m* 2nd 11 June 1953 *George Alfred Robinson, Lt US Army, s of William Orrin Robinson, and by him has:

          1d *Bryce Levinge; *b* 17 Sept 1954

          2d *Guy Herrick; *b* 1957

          2d Joan Hilda; *d* unm 27 Feb 1950

      3a Robert Childe; *b* 21 May 1853; *d* 1912

      4a Reginald Thomas Alexander; BA Dublin LRCSI, Dep Inspr-Gen Hosps and Fleets RN; *b* 9 Sept 1860

      1a Francis Lavinia; *m* 1 June 1874 Dr Whittaker and *d* 21 June 1908

      2a Edith Jane; *m* 20 Oct 1877 George Richard Armstrong, MD, of Dublin, and had issue

      3a Rosa Violet Avice; *m* 1883 George Porter, MD (*d* 1918), of Norfolk, and had issue

  (1) Avice; *d* 5 July 1878

  (2) Elizabeth; *m* 25 June 1828 Rev James Brabazon

  (3) Mary Jane; *m* 10 Sept 1841 Rev Alexander Orme and *dsp* 26 Oct 1861

  (4) Charlotte; *m* 18 Nov 1854 Sir Mark Anthony Henry Tuite, 10th Bt (*qv*), and *dsp* 9 April 1878

5 Mark Anthony; *m* 1812 Caroline (*d* 11 March 1856), dau of John Lyons, of Ledeston, Co Westmeath, and *d* 1847, leaving:

  (1) Marcus Anthony, of New Park, Co Roscommon; *b* 1 Jan 1818; *m* 1st 5 Dec 1842 Elinor Anne (*d* 23 Dec 1878), dau of William Armstrong Hodson, of Middleton, Co Westmeath, and had:

    1a William, of Carnagh, Co Roscommon; *b* Dec 1845; *m* 19 April 1876 Annie Georgina (*d* 1908), dau of Daniel Bailey, of Moorock, King's Co, and *d* 1880, leaving:

      1b Evelyn Violet, of Carnagh, Athlone and Menton, France; *m* 15 July 1901 Walter Cecil Michell, Straits Settlements CS, and had issue

    2a Henry Mark; MD, LRCS Edinburgh, Surgn RN; *b* 2 June 1847; *educ* Trin Coll Dublin (BA); *m* 1886 Jessie (*d* 1951), dau of Philip Ness, Govt Surveyor-Gen and Architect, of Bermuda, formerly Capt RE, and *d* 1919, leaving:

      1b Henry Marcus Tenison Tuite; *b* 1891; *ka* 1917

      1b Jessie Ness (Nessie)

    3a Tenison Francis, JP Co Westmeath; *b* 24 June 1848; *m* 18 Aug 1882 Elizabeth Joanna Naomi (*d* 13 June 1933), dau of Hon George Charles Hawker, of S Australia, and *d* 27 May 1920, leaving:

      1b George Marcus Tenison; Australian Light Horse WW I (wounded); *b* 14 Feb 1888; *educ* Trin Coll Dublin (BA); *d* 1938

      1b Alleen Eleanor; *m* 5 Sept 1914 George Fitzgerald Mortimer and *d* 22 Sept 1969, leaving two daus

      2b Ierne Althea; *m* 29 Oct 1908 Iver Edmund de Breon MacLaverty (*d* 1956), Lt Hants Regt, 2nd s of Graeme A MacLaverty, and had issue

    4a Robert Degennes; *b* 1850; *m* 1889 Hester M Shine (*d* 20 May 1907) and *d* 1940, leaving:

      1b Walter Hodson; *b* 1894; *m* 1945 Marion Blanche, dau of Rev Francis Cockle, Rector Aasleagh, Leenane, Co Galway, and *d* 1982, leaving:

        1c *Hester Sylvia [Mrs Trevor Scott, Mount Venus House, Woodtown Rd, Rathfarnham, Co Dublin, Ireland]; *b* 1947; *m* 1970 *Trevor David Scott

        2c *Daphne Elaine Sybil; *b* 19 Jan 1950; PhD; *m* 1979 *Jonathan Joseph Shackleton and has:

          1d *David Levinge; *b* 1981

          1d *Jane Hester; *b* 1981

          2d *Hannah Lydia; *b* 1987

        3c *Marion Alison Patricia [Mrs Charles Couper, Creughduff, Athlone, Co Meath, Ireland]; *b* 1951; *m* 1981 *Charles Gillard Couper and has:

          1d *Alister Milne; *b* 1984

          1d *Sally Marion; *b* 1981

      1b Florence Ida; *m* 5 Dec 1922 Col Keble Theodore ANDREWS later ANDREWS-LEVINGE, OBE, est s of Rev P T Andrews, of Southbourne, Hants, and had:

        1c *Patricia Ierne

        2c *Betty Maureen

      2b Vera Hester; *m* 1948 Dr Charles Sutton Hillis, LRCS, LRCP

    5a Edward George, MBE (1918), MB Dublin; *b* 1852; *d* 22 Nov 1929

    6a Frederick; *b* 1862; *d* 22 April 1933

    1a Caroline Euphemia; *m* 19 Oct 1871 Charles Seymour (*d* 1901), of Gisborne, NZ, and *d* May 1908, leaving issue

    2a Emma Isabella

    3a Louisa Henrietta; *m* 24 Dec 1884 Oliver James Carthew, 2nd s of John Carthew, of Crediton, Devon, and *d* 1933, leaving issue

  (1) (cont.) Marcus Levinge *m* 2nd 6 March 1884 Clara Alice, dau of John Cardwell, of Tullyelmer, Co Armagh, and *d* 21 July 1908

1 Charlotte; *d* 9 Nov 1856 aged 95

Sir RICHARD *d* 30 Oct 1786; his est son,

Sir Charles Levinge, 5th Bt; *b* 17 April 1751; *m* 26 June 1779 Elizabeth Frances (*d* 19 May 1828), only dau of Nicholas Reynell, of Reynella, Co Westmeath, and had, with other issue:

1 RICHARD (Sir), **6th Bt**

2 Charles; Lt-Col; b 20 March 1796; m 2 June 1825 Barbara (d 14 June 1838), dau of Hugh Johnston, of St John's, New Brunswick, and d 1843, having had two sons and three daus

1 Anne; m 18 Aug 1817 Rev William Gregory (d 22 Dec 1874), 2nd s of Rt Hon William Gregory, U-Sec Dublin Castle, by Anne, dau of 1st Earl of Clancarty (qv), and had issue

Sir CHARLES d 10 Jan 1796; his er son,

Sir Richard Levinge, 6th Bt; b 29 Oct 1765; m 3 Dec 1810 Elizabeth Anne (d 28 Oct 1853), est dau and ultimate coheir of 1st Baron Rancliffe (see 1970 edn PARKYNS, Bt), and d 12 Sept 1848, having had, with other issue:

1 **Sir Richard George Augustus Levinge, 7th Bt**; b 1 Nov 1811; Army Capt, Lt-Col Westmeath Rifles, MP Co Westmeath 1857–1865, author: *Historical Records of the Forty-third Regiment* (1868); m 1st 20 March 1849 Caroline Jane (d 1858), est dau of Col Rolleston, MP, of Watnall Hall, Notts; m 2nd 10 Feb 1870 Margaret Charlotte (d 5 Nov 1871), widow of D Jones, of Pantglâs, MP Carmarths, dau of Sir George Campbell and n of 1st Baron Campbell of St Andrews (see STRATHEDEN and CAMPBELL, B), and dsp 28 Sept 1884

2 **Sir Vere Henry Levinge, 8th Bt**; Madras CS; b 28 Nov 1819; d unm 22 March 1885

3 William James; b 22 Jan 1821; m 15 Aug 1848 Anna Maria (d 2 July 1868), only dau of John Michael Henry, Baron de Robeck (see 1956 edn Foreign Titles Section), and d 22 Oct 1867, having had:

   (1) WILLIAM HENRY (Sir), **9th Bt**

   (2) Richard; b 23 Jan 1852

   (3) Reginald, Lt 13th LI; b 24 Sept 1854; d unm 1882

   (4) Godfrey Charles Rawdon; b Feb 1858; d unm 1898

   (5) George Edward; Maj Remount Dept WW I; b 1862; m 1895 Elizabeth Louisa, dau of John Wiley, of Brisbane, and d 22 Aug 1926, leaving:

     1a George Onslow; b 1896

     2a William John; b 19 June 1903

   (1) Emily Caroline; m 3 Aug 1874 Ernest C F James, est s of Maj-Gen Sir Henry James, and d 21 July 1937

   (2) Gertrude; d unm 1886

   (3) Mary Georgina; m 29 April 1880 Rev Arthur Prestwood-Clayton (d 9 June 1933), Vicar Holy Trinity Ventnor IW 1889–1918, and had issue

4 Edward Parkyns; Judge Supreme Ct Calcutta; b 30 Nov 1825; d 2 March 1865

5 Harry Corbyn, DL; High Sheriff Co Westmeath 1886, Sec to Bengal PWD; s to the Knockdrin estate, Co Westmeath, on death of **8th Bt**; b 1 Dec 1828; m 6 April 1857 Ellen Hawes (d 1918), dau of R Barnes, and d 11 March 1896, having had:

   (1) Harry George; Capt and Brevet Maj 1st Bn Norfolk Regt, Capt and Hon Maj 3rd Bn Norfolk Regt, Lt-Col cmdg 6th Bn Roy N Lancs Regt; b 9 Sept 1864; m 31 Aug 1905 Maureen Elizabeth (d 7 May 1963 aged 88), only dau of Capt William Addis Fagan, 12th Lancers, and was ka 10 Aug 1915

   (2) Edward Vere (Sir), KCIE (1916), CSI (1911); ICS, Ch Sec Govt Bengal 1910, MEC Bihar and Orissa 1912–17, Actg Lt-Govr 1918; b 24 May 1867; educ Cheltenham and Balliol Coll Oxford (BA 1888); m 1 Dec 1900 Alys Adèle (d 1 May 1952), dau of Maj-Gen Charles Frederic Thomas, and d 24 Jan 1954, leaving:

     1a *Vera Alys [Countess Althann, A3435, Zwentendorf am der Donau, Lower Austria]; b 20 June 1911; m 28 April 1938 Count (Michael) Karl Althann (d 1978), of Zwentendorf and Rhodesia, and has:

       1b *(Michael) Robert [Father Robert Althann SJ, Pontifical Biblical Inst, via della Pilotta 25, 1–00187 Rome, Italy]; b 1939

       2b *(Michael) Alexander [Alexander Althann Esq, A–3435 Zwentendorf am Donau, Lower Austria]; b 1940; m 1978 *Maria Kammerlander and has:

         1c *Wenzel; b 1979

         2c *Quintin; b 1982

         3c *Severin; b 1984

         1c *Clementine; b 1980

       3b *(Michael) Victor [Victor Althann Esq, 1105 Park Ave, Apt 2c, New York, NY 10128, USA]; b 1944; m 1972 *Maria de la Natividad del Valle, of Haverford, Pa., and has:

         1c *Charles; b 1982

         2c *Robert; b 1987

         1c *Caroline; b 1980

       1b *Maria Olga [Olga Althann, rue de Sous-Ville 1, CH–1908 Riddes, Switzerland]; b 1941; m 1975 (divorce 1988, annulled 1989) Count Ferdinand von Coreth zu Coredo and has:

         1c *Julie; b 1976

         2c *Isabelle; b 1978

       2b *Maria Christina [Dña Christina Althann Vda de Ruiz, Calle Maria Cabnera 9, E–29400 Ronda, Málaga, Spain]; b 1942; m 1966 José Manuel de Ruiz Gonzalez (d 1980) and has:

         1c *José Carlos; b 1967

         2c *Alejandro Miguel; b 1970

         1c *Veronica; b 1974

       3b *Marie-Thérèse Margarethe [Mme François-Charles Pictet, 6 rue Robert-de-Traz, 1206 Geneva, Switzerland]; b 1949; m 1983 *François-Charles Pictet, Swiss Amb to: Canada 1975–79, UN Office and Internat Organisations Geneva 1980–84, UK 1984–89, Netherlands 1989–90, Austria 1990–94 and Holy See 1993–97

   (1) Florence; b 24 May 1861; m 22 Oct 1885 Col Irton Eardley-Wilmot and d 25 Sept 1946, leaving issue (see EARDLEY-WILMOT, Bt)

   (2) Constance; b 21 Dec 1872; m 22 Aug 1895 Maj Thomas Gibbons Hawkesworth Smyth (d 15 Nov 1953), DL, E Yorks Regt, and d 27 Oct 1960, leaving issue

The 8th Bt's nephew,

Sir William Henry Levinge, 9th Bt; b 21 May 1849; MA Oxon, Capt 9th Bn Rifle Bde, Maj 5th Vol Bn Hants Regt; m 2 Nov 1886 Emily Judith (d 12 Jan 1921), 2nd dau of Sir Richard Sutton, 4th Bt (qv), and had:

1 RICHARD WILLIAM (Sir), **10th Bt**

2 Thomas Vere; Maj Northumberland Fus; b 4 June 1880; m 22 Feb 1928 Dorothy, est dau of John Thomas Ingman, of Northampton, and d 1949, leaving:

   (1) William James; b 17 Dec 1929; m 31 July 1954 *Heather Mary [Mrs William Levinge, 41 Bridge Rd, Welwyn Garden City, Herts], dau of Harold Alfred Johnson, Brackley, Northants, and d 1987, leaving:

     1a +Nicholas Vere; b 27 April 1955; m 1983 *Kathryn Bampton and has:

       1b +Thomas John; b 1986

     2a +Edward James; b 6 May 1957; m 1984 *Sandra Ann Dunne and has:

       1b +Andrew William; b 1992

       1b *Joanna Louise; b 1990

     1a *Sarah Jennifer Louise; b 19 April 1961

   (2) +Thomas Gerald [Thomas Levinge Esq, Broadley Farm, Llantony, Abergavenny, Mon]; b 22 Dec 1934; m *Stella Field and has:

     1a +A son; b 4 Nov 1964

     1a *A dau

3 Reginald Augustus; Capt RA, Lt Wicklow Artillery, WW I (despatches), WW II in Roy Observer Corps; b 7 Oct 1883; m 5 Nov 1925 Evelyn Mary, dau of Rev H E Robeson, Rector Broad Blunsdon, Wilts, and d 24 May 1953

4 Charles Horace; 17th Bn 1st AIF WW I; b 17 Nov 1884; m 25 Oct 1918 May Victoria, 4th dau of William Henry Thomas, of Canterbury, NSW, and d 23 Feb 1952, leaving:

   (1) Gerald Cecil Charles; b 26 Oct 1919; m 19 March 1946 Enid Lorraine, dau of Edward Rowling, of Sydney, and had:

     1a +Colin Gerald; b 21 Sept 1954

     1a *Lorraine Gay; b 1 May 1948

     2a *Margaret Kay; b 22 July 1951

   (1) *Dorothy Mabel Judith; b 6 April 1923; m 19– *Albert Douglas Pope, BEcon Sydney, and has two daus

   (2) *Joan Beatrice Annie; b 4 June 1927; m 19– *Albert Joseph Hall, of Benalia, Victoria, Australia, and has a s and two daus

5 Bernard George; b 4 July 1887; m 7 July 1912 Stella Parsons and d 1953, leaving:

   (1) +Percy Douglas; b 18 Feb 1919; m 21 Aug 1953 *Mary, dau of Thomas E G Munday, of Penrith, NSW

   (2) +Reginald Noel [Reginald Levinge Esq, 9 Dent St, Penrith, NSW, Australia]; b 12 March 1927; m 18 Oct 1950 *Pearl Kathleen, dau of Walter Wright Armstrong, of NSW, formerly of Co Fermanagh, and has:

     1a +Geoffrey Paul; b 8 Feb 1952; m 1970 *Sandra, dau of A Kiggins, and has:

       1b +Mark Andrew; b 1974

       1b *Kerry Ann; b 1971

       2b *Tracy Maree; b 1980

     1a *Maureen Ann; b 5 Feb 1956; m 1978 *Christopher Fehon and has:

       1b *Luke; b 1985

       1b *Rebecca; b 1982

       2b *Emma (twin); b 1985

     2a *Sharon Maree; b 21 May 1963; m 1983 *Christopher Carl and has:

       1b *Michael James; b 1985

       2b *Adrian Noel; b 1986

       1b *Amanda Lee; b 1984

6 Gerald Henry; b 6 Oct 1889; ka 5 April 1918

1 Dorothy Mary Gertrude; b 13 June 1882; m 22 Dec 1904 George Travers Heigham (d Oct 1934), s of Maj Clement Heigham, of Hunston, Suffolk, and d 7 Dec 1954, leaving issue

2 Beatrice Maud Cecil; b 9 March 1886; m 5 July 1923 Brig Henry Chambré Ponsonby and d 4 Feb 1961, leaving issue (see BESSBOROUGH, E)

The 9th Bt d 17 April 1900; his est son,

Sir Richard William Levinge, 10th Bt, DL Co Westmeath; b 12 July 1878; Lt 8th Hus, S Irish Horse and 1st Life Gds; m 15 Feb 1910 Irene Marguerite (d 29 March 1975) (m 2nd 31 Aug 1916 Lt-Col Robert Vere Buxton, see BUXTON, Bt), er dau of J H C Pix, of Bradford, Yorks, and was ka between 24 and 26 Oct 1914, leaving:

Sir Richard Vere Henry Levinge, 11th Bt, MBE (1941), of Knockdrin Castle, Co Westmeath; b 30 April 1911; educ Eton and Balliol Coll Oxford (BA 1933); Maj Lovat Scouts (TA) WW II (despatches), chm William Nuttall and GPG Holidays, dir Arthur Guinness Son & Co, Purdy Machinery, Jobenoil 1973–84 and GEI Internat 1975; m 1st 30 July 1935 (divorce 1976) Barbara Mary (d 8 Nov 1997), 2nd dau of George Jardine Kidston, CMG, of Hazelbury Manor, Box, Wilts, and had:

1 Sir RICHARD GEORGE ROBIN LEVINGE, **12th and present Bt**

2 *Michael James [Michael Levinge Esq, 2 Vicarage Crescent, Hatfield Peverel, Essex]; b 28 Jan 1948

1 *Elizabeth Anne; b 20 Feb 1937; m 17 June 1957 *Walter Wright Lee, Jr, only s of Walter Wright Lee, of New York

2 Patricia Mary; b 24 July 1939; d 16 Jan 1940

3 *Susan Maureen; b 3 June 1944; m 2 Oct 1965 *Douglas P W Wright, yr s of Rev E H Wright

4 *Mary Irene [Mrs Charles Cooper, Markree Castle, Co Sligo, Ireland]; b 23 June 1952; m 12 Nov 1976 *Charles Philip Cooper, yst s of Lt-Cdr Edward Francis Patrick Cooper, RN, of Markree Castle

Sir Richard m 2nd 1976, as her 2nd husb, *Jane Rosemary [Jane Lady Levinge, Abbey Lodge, Rectory Lane, Itchen Abbas, Hants SO21 1BN], dau of John Thomas Stacey, of East Dereham, Norfolk and d 1984

LEVY

Creation: B. (LP, UK) 2 Aug 1997.

THE BARON LEVY, of Mill Hill, London Borough of Barnet (Michael Abraham Levy) [The Rt Hon The Lord Levy, House of Lords, London SW1A 0PW]; *b* 11 July 1944; *educ* Hackney Downs GS; FLA 1966, with Lubbock, Fine (CA) 1961–66, Pncpl M Levy & Co 1966–69, Ptnr Wagner Prager Levy & Ptnrs 1969–73, chm: Magnet Gp 1973–88, D&J Securities 1988–92, M & G Records 1992 and M & G Music Ltd 1992–, Jewish Community Care Fndn 1995–, v-chm Phonographic Performance Ltd 1979–84, Patron Br Music Industry Awards 1995–, Tstee Lab Pty For Policy Centre; *m* 1967 *Gilda Altbach and has a s and dau

LEWIN

FLEXIBLE · BUT · FIRM · OF · PURPOSE

Arms: Quarterly gules and azure, three boar's heads, two and one, couped or, tusked argent, on a chief barry wavy of four bleu celeste and argent, a naval gun *c* 1800 proper mounted on its carriage gold. **Crest:** Out of a naval crown azure a lion rampant in trian aspect or, on its head a baron's coronet and cap of estate proper, brandishing in the dexter paw a sword proper, hilt, knuckle guard and pommel in the form of an eagle's head gold. **Supporters:** Dexter, an Able Seaman of HMS *Victory*; sinister, a Royal Marine, both wearing the South Atlantic Medal, the compartment comprising a grassy mount with outcrops of rock proper and having on each side a sea inlet barry wavy argent and azure. **Motto:** Flexible but firm of purpose.
Creation: B. (LP, UK) 1982.

THE BARON LEWIN, of Greenwich in Greater London (Sir Terence Thornton Lewin, KG (1983), GCB (1976, KCB 1973), MVO (1958), DSC (1942)) [The Rt Hon The Lord Lewin KG GCB MVO DSC, House of Lords, London SW1A 0PW]; *b* 19 Nov 1920; *educ* The Judd Sch Tonbridge; WWII: RN, Home and Mediterranean Fleets (despatches); cmded HMS *Corunna* 1955–56, HM Yacht *Britannia* 1957–58; Capt (F) Dartmouth Trg Sqdn and HMS *Urchin* and *Tenby* 1961–63; Dir Naval Tactical and Weapons Policy Div MOD 1964–65; cmded HMS *Hermes* 1966–67; Assist Ch Naval Staff (Policy) 1968–69; Flag Offr 2ic Far East Fleet 1969–70; V-Ch Naval Staff 1971–73; C-in-C Fleet 1973–75; C-in-C Naval Home Cmd 1975–77; Flag ADC to HM 1975–77; First and Pncpl ADC to HM 1977–79; Ch Naval Staff and First Sea Lord 1977–79; CDS 1979–82; memb: Cncl White Ensign Assoc 1982– (Chm Cncl and Assoc 1983–87), Tstee Nat Maritime Museum 1981– (Dep Chm 1986–87, Chm 1987–95), Museums and Galleries Commn 1983–87; Er Bro Trin Ho 1975; Pres: Shipwrecked Fishermen and Mariners' Roy Benevolent Soc 1984–, British Schs Exploring Soc 1985–, George Cross Island Assoc 1988–, Soc for Nautical Research 1989–; Hon Freeman: Skinners' Co 1976, Shipwrights' Co 1978; Life Col Comdt RM 1995; Hon FNI; Hon DSc City U; Hon DLitt Greenwich U 1993; *m* 1944 *Jane, dau of Rev Charles James Branch-Evans, and has:

1 *Timothy Charles Thornton; *b* 1947; *m* 1973 *Carolyn Thain
2 *Jonathan James; *b* 1959; *m* 1990 *Madeline Marsh
1 *Susan; *b* 1949; *m* 1969 *Peter Roe and has:
  (1) *Cosmo; *b* 1972
  (1) *Emily; *b* 1975
  (2) *Jessica; *b* 1982

Lineage: E H LEWIN; had:

TERENCE THORNTON, *cr* a **Baron**

LEWIS OF NEWNHAM

Creation: B. (LP,UK) 1989.

THE BARON LEWIS OF NEWNHAM, of Newnham, Co Cambridge (Sir Jack Lewis) [The Rt Hon The Lord Lewis of Newnham, Robinson College, Grange Rd, Cambridge CB3 9AN]; *b* 13 Feb 1928; *educ* Barrow GS, London U (BSc 1949, DSc 1961), Nottingham U (PhD 1952), Manchester U (MSc 1964) and Cambridge (MA 1970, ScD 1977); lecturer: Sheffield U 1954–56, Imp Coll London 1956–57, UCL 1957–61 (Reader 1957–61); Visiting Prof Sheffield U 1967; Prof Chemistry: Manchester U 1962–67, UCL 1967–70 and visiting Prof 1996, Cambridge U 1970–95; Warden Robinson Coll Cambridge 1975–; memb: CNAA Ctee 1964–70, Exec Standing Ctee on U Entry 1966–71, Schs Cncl 1966–70; SERC Polytechnic Ctee 1973–79 (Chemistry Ctee Chm 1975–82, Sci Bd 1975–82, Cncl 1980–), SERC/SSRC Jt Ctee 1979–84, UGC 1975–81, Cncl Roy Soc 1982–84, DES Visiting Ctee Cranfield Inst 1983 (Chm 1985–93), Roy Commn Environmental Pollution 1985–92 (Chm 1986–92), Ho Lds Select Ctee Environmental Pollution 1993–95 (Chm Sub Ctee C 1993–95); Pres Roy Soc Chemistry 1986–88; Tstee Croucher Fndn 1989–; Dir BOC Fndn 1990, ktd 1982; Patron Student Community Action Devpt Unit 1985–; For Memb American Acad Arts and Sci 1983; For Assoc Nat Acad Sciences USA 1987; Chevalier l'Ordre des Palmes Academiques 1993; Fell American Philosophy Soc 1994; Hon DU: Rennes 1980, OU 1982, Kingston 1993: Hon DSc UEA, Nottingham 1983, Keele 1984, Waterloo (Canada) 1988, Birmingham 1988, Leicester 1988, Manchester 1990, Wales 1990, Sheffield 1992, Cranfield 1993, Edinburgh 1994, Bath 1995 and Durham 1996; Hon Fell: UCL 1990, UMIST 1990, Centl Lancs U 1993; FRS 1973; FRIC; FRSA; FRSC; FNA 1980; *m* 1951 *Elfreida Mabel, dau of Frank Alfred Lamb, of Manchester, and has:

1 *Ian Peter; *b* 1958; *educ* Leys Sch Cambridge
1 *Penelope Jane; *b* 1956; *m* 1982 *Howard Allaker Chase and has:
  (1) *George Howard; *b* 1984
  (1) *Charlotte Elizabeth; *b* 1986

Lineage: ROBERT LEWIS, of Askham; had:

JACK LEWIS (Sir), *cr* a **Baron**

LEWTHWAITE

Virtus · ad · æthera · tendens

Arms: Erm. a cross flory az. fretty or. **Crest:** A garb or, bound by a serpent nowed ppr., holding in the mouth a cross-crosslet fitchée gu. **Motto:** *Virtus ad æthera tendens* ('Virtue reaching towards heaven'). **Creation:** Bt. (UK) 26 Jan 1927.

SIR RAINALD GILFRID LEWTHWAITE, 4TH BT, of Broadgate, Parish of Thwaites, Co Cumberland, CVO (1975), OBE (1974), MC (1943) [Brig Sir Rainald Lewthwaite Bt CVO OBE MC, Broadgate, Millom, Cumbria LA18 5JY]; *b* 21 July 1913; *s* bro 1993; *educ* Rugby and Trin Coll Cambridge (BA 1934); WW II: Brig Scots Gds, cmded 1st Bn 1945 (wounded, despatches twice, Croix de Guerre with palm), Jt Servs Mission Washington 1950–52, Actg Sec (Mil) Cabinet Office 1953–65, SHAPE Paris 1955–58, GSO(1) DCIGS Co-Ord War Office 1958, Col NATO HQ Paris 1960, Def and Mil Attaché Paris 1964–68, Dir Protocol Hong Kong 1969–76; *m* 3 Jan 1936 Margaret Elizabeth, MBE (1941) (*d* 1990), yr dau of Harry Edmonds, of New York, and has had:

1 +DAVID RAINALD [David Lewthwaite Esq, 49 Ranelagh Grove, London SW1W 8PB]; *b* 26 March 1940; *educ* Rugby and Trin Coll Cambridge (BA 1960); *m* 11 Oct 1969 *Diana Helena, twin dau of William Robert Tomkinson, TD, of Kingswood, Surrey, by his w Helen Mary, only dau of Cdr Sir Charles Rodney Blane, 4th Bt, RN (*see* 1916 edn), and has:
  (1) *Emma Victoria; *b* 26 Nov 1971
  (2) *Mary-Claire; *b* 11 Dec 1972

2 (John) Valentine; *b* 9 Sept 1944; *educ* Eton; *m* 16 Sept 1967 *Elizabeth Georgiana, only dau of Lt-Cdr Richard John Bramble Mildmay-White by Hon

Helen Winifred, only dau of 1st Baron Mildmay of Flete, PC (*see* ST JOHN-MILDMAY, Bt), and *d* 4 Dec 1990, leaving:
(1) *Alice Georgiana; *b* 11 March 1969
(2) *Martha Grace; *b* 1 June 1970
1 Margaret Sylvia; *b* 23 Aug 1937; *d* 22 Oct 1994
2 Mary Rose; *b* 19 July 1946; *d* 11 Feb 1949

Lineage: JAMES LEWTHWAITE, of Whicham, Cumberland; *m* Elizabeth — and *d* on or after 26 March 1619, leaving:

THOMAS LEWTHWAITE, of The Groopes, Whicham, Millom, Cumberland; *m* — Newby, of Haverigg, Cumberland, and had:

THOMAS LEWTHWAITE; yeoman; bought Broadgate 1642; *b* 8 Dec 1588; *m* Nov 1619 Frances (*bur* 25 March 1670), widow of Christopher Toto and dau of Hugh Askew, of Graymains, Muncaster, Cumberland, and was *bur* 15 Feb 1667, leaving:
1 John; Capt royalist foot regt; *ka* Battle of Edgehill 1642
2 JAMES
1 Margaret; *m* 2 Nov 1658 William Benson, of Waberthwaite, and had issue
2 A dau; *m* Thomas Muncaster, of Selcroft, Wicham, and had issue
3 Agnes; *m* Richard Bulfell

The yr son,
JAMES LEWTHWAITE, of Broadgate, Cumberland; *m* Agnes, dau of William Dickson, of Beck Bank, Thwaites, Cumberland, and was *bur* 29 March 1677, having had:
1 JOHN
2 Thomas; *b* 1656; *d* an infant
3 Ralph; *bapt* 5 June 1664; *dsp* Oct 1697
4 William; mercer at Gateshead, Co Durham; *b* 7 Dec 1667; *m* 1700 Catherine, dau of Wilfrid Lawson, of Brayton, and gdau of Sir Wilfrid Lawson, Bt, of Isell, Cumberland, and had:
(1) William, of Ryhope, Co Durham; mercer; *m* Sarah, dau of George Sparrow, of Washington, Co Durham, and *d* by 19 May 1739
(2) Alfred; *d* young
(3) John; merchant of Whitehaven, Cumberland; *b* 1701; *m* 1733 Grace, dau of Francis Jackson, of Bransty Ho, Whitehaven, and *d* 22 Oct 1790 aged 89, having had:
1a Gilfrid; merchant Whitehaven; *bapt* 2 Sept 1737; drowned while bathing behind the North Pier, Whitehaven, 3 Aug 1779
5 Anthony; *d* 18 May 1696
6 James, of Lady Hall, near Millom, Cumberland; yeoman; *m* —, dau of Myles Wennington, of Greystone Ho, Thwaites, and had:
(1) James, of Whitehaven and Chester; *b* 1713; anchorsmith and blacksmith; *m* 1st 1736 Joyce, dau of Thomas Cragg, of Cragghall, Thwaites, *m* 2nd Elizabeth (*bur* 1795 aged 80), and by her had issue
(2) John; *m* Elizabeth, dau of James Lancaster, and had:
1a John, sadler, of London 1792; had issue
2a George, of Ulverston; *dsp*
1 Elizabeth; *d* unm 1686
2 Agnes; *bapt* 15 Dec 1670; *d* unm
3 Margaret; *b* 1661; *m* Christopher Mitchell, of Strickland, Kendal, Westmorland, and *d* 1697
4 Eleanor; *m* 1703 William Robinson, of Waberthwaite, and *d* 1755, leaving a dau

The est son,
JOHN LEWTHWAITE, of Broadgate; yeoman; *m* Eleanor (*bur* 24 Aug 1723), dau of William Whinfield, of Woodland, Kirkby Ireleth, Lancs, and was *bur* 1 May 1737, having had:
1 James; *bapt* 3 Nov 1692; *d* 2 July 1699
2 WILLIAM
1 Eleanor; *bapt* 2 May 1697; *m* John Lewes, hosier, of St James's St, London, and had, with a dau:
(1) Charles Lee; *b* 1740; celebrated actor and gf of George Henry Lewes, philosopher and companion of George Eliot; *d* 1803
2 Elizabeth; *bapt* 6 June 1703; *m* Henry Addison, custom offr, of Ravenglass, Cumberland, and had two sons and two daus

The only surv son,
WILLIAM LEWTHWAITE, of Broadgate and Kirkby Hall, Kirkby Irebeth, N Lancs; *bapt* 17 May 1700; *m* 1727 Agnes, dau of Thomas Towers, of Houkler Hall, Blawith, N Lancs, and *d* 1767, leaving:
1 John, of Broadgate; merchant Antigua and Dominica; *b* 1730; *m* Elizabeth (*d* 1804), widow of — Grice, of Antigua, and *dsp* Dominica 21 June 1781
2 WILLIAM
3 George; *bapt* 26 Jan 1744; merchant in Antigua; *dsp* 1777
1 Elizabeth; *b* 1751; *m* 1766 William Hunter, yeoman, of Cross Ho, Millom, Cumberland, and *d* 1815
2 Agnes; *bapt* 1737; *m* 1787 Thomas Bailiff, yeoman, of Wreaks End, Broughton-in-Furness, Lancs, and *dsp*
3 Margaret; *bapt* 1747; *m* Matthew Taylor, slr Liverpool, and *dsp*
4 Eleanor; *m* Capt William Postlethwaite, mariner, of Elenfoot, now Maryport, Cumberland, and had two sons and two daus

The 2nd s,
WILLIAM LEWTHWAITE, of Broadgate and Whitehaven, JP Cumberland; *bapt* 1 March 1740; *educ* Hawkshead GS; *m* Feb 1765 Mary (*d* 29 Aug 1807), dau and coheir of Joseph Nicholson, of Milholme, Bootle, Cumberland, yeoman, and *d* 30 Oct 1809, having had:
1 WILLIAM
2 John, of Stott Park, Finsthwaite, N Lancs; attorney, Town Clerk Lancaster 1802–21, Clerk of the Peace, Under Sheriff Lancs; *b* 1771; *educ* Hawkshead GS; *m* 1797 Margaret, 2nd dau of Roger Taylor, of Stott Pk, Finsthwaite, Lancs, and *d* 1849, leaving:

(1) William, of Richmond Ho, Lancaster, later of Parramatta, NSW; *b* 1798; slr, Coroner Parramatta; *m* 9 Feb 1832 Sarah, er dau of Michael Clapson, of NSW, and *d* 21 Nov 1851, leaving:
1a John; *b* 11 Sept 1840; *educ* Westhall Sch Suffolk and Caius Coll Cambridge; *d* 1861
1a Frances Jane, of Stott Park; *b* 16 Oct 1836; *d* unm 17 Jan 1914
2a Maria Margaret; *m* — Jackson, of NSW
(2) Gilfrid, of Stott Park; *b* 1801; *dsp* 4 Jan 1890
(1) Marianne, of Stott Park; *b* 1801; *d* unm 10 March 1875
(2) Frances Jane, of Stott Park; *b* 1804; *d* unm 29 Dec 1876
3 George (Rev), JP; Rector Adel Yorks 1809–54; *b* 28 July 1772; *educ* Hawkshead GS and Queen's Coll Oxford (BD, MA); *m* 21 May 1816 Martha (*d* Oct 1861 aged 84), dau of Thomas Birley, of Low Mill, Cumberland, and Kirkham, Lancs, and *d* 2 July 1854, leaving:
(1) William Henry (Rev); Incumbent Clifford, Curate Adel 1840–42, RC priest London (ordained 1854), Order of Charity; *b* 6 April 1817; *educ* Oakham Sch and Trin Coll Cambridge (MA); *d* 17 April 1892
(2) George (Rev); *b* 1818; Curate Adel 1842–60; *educ* Rugby and Univ Coll Oxford (MA); *d* unm 22 May 1893
(1) Margaret; *b* 1820; *m* 1865 Rev George Brewin, Vicar Wortley, Yorks, and *dsp* 11 June 1908
4 Joseph; merchant W Indies; *b* 1782; *d* unm Dominica 28 Nov 1815, leaving issue
5 Myles; *b* 1780; *d* an infant
6 Thomas; *b* 1787; *d* 1805
1 Elizabeth; *b* 1768; *d* an infant
2 Agnes; *b* 1769; *m* 14 Sept 1796 Rev Richard Armitstead, JP, DL (*d* 18 May 1821), Rector Moresby, Min St James's Whitehaven, and *d* 15 April 1853, having had four sons and three daus
3 Mary; *b* 1776; *m* 31 Oct 1799 Milham Hartley, JP (*d* 30 May 1839), banker, of Rose Hill, Moresby, Cumberland, High Sheriff Cumberland 1818, and *d* 19 Dec 1833, having had four sons and three daus
4 Ann; *b* 1777; *m* 1802 Peter Dixon (*d* 1835), surgn and apothecary, of Newington, Surrey, s of Thomas Dixon, of Rheda, Cumberland and *dsp* 1803
5 Margaret; *b* 1783; *m* 1816 Peter Taylor (*d* 1827), of Belfield, Bowness-on-Windermere, Westmorland, and Prospect Hill, Whitehaven, Maj Roy Westmorland Militia, and *dsp* 1835
6 Fanny, of Monkfoss Manor, Whitbeck, Cumberland; *b* 1786; *d* unm 27 Aug 1812
7 Betsy (twin with Fanny), of Hazel Mount, nr Millom, Cumberland; *d* unm 1 Dec 1862

The est son,
WILLIAM LEWTHWAITE, of Broadgate, JP, Cumberland; *b* 1766 (*bapt* 18 Feb 1766); *educ* Hawkshead GS; *m* 7 March 1791 Eleanor (*d* 18 Nov 1830), dau of Thomas Cragg, of Lowscales, Millom, Cumberland, and *d* 31 March 1845, having had:
1 JOHN
1 Mary; *b* 1793; *m* 1825 William Postlethwaite (*m* 2nd 1858 Agnes Armitstead and *d* 1876), merchant and banker in Ulverston, s of John Postlethwaite, of Broughton Ho, Broughton-in-Furness, and *dsp* 1853
2 Agnes; *b* 1795; *m* 23 Sept 1823 Robert Postlethwaite, JP, DL (*d* 25 Feb 1859), of Broughton Ho and The Oaks, Millom, s of John Postlethwaite, and *d* 1853, having had three sons and a dau
3 Eleanor; *b* 1798; *d* unm 10 Nov 1827
4 Elizabeth; *b* 26 Aug 1801; *d* unm 21 July 1827

The only son,
JOHN LEWTHWAITE, of Broadgate, JP, DL Cumberland; *b* 24 March 1792; *educ* Macclesfield GS; *m* 18 May 1820 Anne (Nancy) (*d* 10 Aug 1857), dau of William Kirkbank, JP, DL, of Beckside, Whicham, Cumberland, and *d* 11 April 1863, having had:
1 WILLIAM
2 Joseph (Rev); Vicar Kelstern Lincs 1857–86; *b* 26 Sept 1834; *educ* privately and Christ's Coll Cambridge (MA); *d* unm 7 Feb 1886
3 George, of Littlebank, Settle, W R Yorks, JP Cumberland; *b* 29 Aug 1839; *educ* Rugby and Trin Coll Cambridge (BA); *m* 27 Oct 1864 Margaret (*d* 11 May 1924), dau of Christopher Atkinson, of Ivytree, Blawith, Lancs, and *d* 13 June 1912, having had:
(1) John Gilfrid, of Broadgate Farm, Sintaluta, Saskatchewan, Canada; *b* 5 July 1866; *educ* Giggleswick; *m* 2 Dec 1902 Annie Caroline Munro Murray (*d* 25 Feb 1948), dau of Dr W Berkeley Murray, of Tenbury Wells, Worcs and *d* 5 May 1940, having had:
1a Gilfrid Murray; *b* 10 Aug 1907; *m* 1st 21 Oct 1936 Clara Roberta Railton (*d* 31 Oct 1962) and had:
1b *Robert Gilfrid [Robert Lewthwaite Esq, Box 272, Indian Head, Saskatchewan, Canada]; *b* 8 Feb 1939; *m* 21 Oct 1963 *Royal Beverley King and has:
1c *Bradley Robert; *b* 1970; *m* 1992 *Teresa Rea Meheden
1c *Leslie Anne; *b* 4 Feb 1966; *m* 1989 *Larry Ross Bailey
1b *Peggy Elizabeth; *b* 24 Dec 1945; *m* 15 July 1967 *Robert Leslie Paterson, of Edmonton, Alberta, and has:
1c *Aaron Robert; *b* 1979
1c *Jennifer Lee; *b* 1976
1a (cont.) Gilfrid Lewthwaite *m* 2nd 1 July 1964 *Helen Mahala Fraser and *d* 1 Dec 1984
2a George Edward Bruce; *b* 6 Aug 1909; *m* 5 Oct 1938 *Mae Coyman and *d* 1983, leaving:
1b *Sharon Ann [Mrs Terry Russell, 174 Bench Drive, Victoria, BC, Canada]; *b* 24 May 1940; *m* 27 July 1963 *Terry Allen Russell, PhD (Psychology) and adopted:
*Paul Edward; *b* 8 Jan 1969
*Sarah Jean; *b* 1970

*Kathleen Mae; b 1973; educ Saskatchewan U

2b *Judy Lynne; b 17 May 1944; m 9 Dec 1967 *Vernon Richard Threinen, BA, and has issue:

  1c *Timothy Mark; b 1971

  2c *Samuel Matthew; b 1976

  1c *Jennifer Leah; b 1973

3b *Terri Lee; b 24 April 1952; m 19– *Harold Wesley Sexsmith and has:

  1c *Christopher Todd; b 1973

  1c *Tina Marie; b 1972; m 1994 *Keith Atrill

3a William Harold; b 7 Feb, d 24 Aug 1911

1a Margaret Berkeley; b 3 Oct 1903

2a Phyllis Elizabeth; b 22 Sept 1905; m 8 Aug 1964 Edwin Preston Mackay (d 1990)

(2) William Atkinson, of Vancouver; b 2 Sept 1867; educ Giggleswick; m 29 Jan 1896 Margaret Evelyn Armstrong and d 13 Aug 1944, leaving:

1a Violet Evelyn; b 28 Nov 1896; m March 1952 Maj Ernest Ingle (d 1977)

2a Margaret Inez; b 25 June 1899; m 12 Sept 1922 Douglas Barrington Taylor (d 1969) and had:

  1b *William Barrington; b 11 Sept 1923

  2b *Allan Douglas; b 27 Jan 1929; m 17 Sept 1954 *Wooneytha Oliver, dau of Dr W Archibald Hunter, and has:

    1c *Douglas Hunter; b 31 Jan 1959

    1c *Margaret Susan; b 14 Nov 1955

3a Noelle Victoria; b 25 Dec 1900; m Edmund Steward Withers and d 1975, leaving:

  1b *Edmund William Bennett; b 5 Oct 1929; m 30 July 1960 *Joan McLowan and has:

    1c *Kathleen Anne; b 13 May 1961

    2c *Beverley Jean; b 24 Oct 1962

  1b *Margaret Anne; b 24 Feb 1932; m 25 Aug 1951 *Jack Alan Sheldon and has:

    1c *Michael Alan; b 12 Aug 1952

    2c *Ted William; b 1 Oct 1954

  2b *Judith Lambert; b 29 June 1939; m 29 Sept 1955 *Wilfred John Hogg and has:

    1c *Mark John; b 12 April 1957

    1c *Sandra Lea; b 20 Dec 1958

4a Helen Armstrong; b 23 Nov 1906; m 23 July 1947 Maj Ernest Ingle (d 1977), and d 15 Feb 1951

(3) George (Rev); Vicar Old Milverton Warwicks 1925–38; b 13 Dec 1868; educ Giggleswick and Keble Coll Oxford (BA); m 25 Oct 1898 Robena Mary (d 10 Feb 1948), widow of Henry Marshall, of Gainsborough, and only dau of Samuel Kelsey, JP, CC, of Holly Ho, Morton, Lincs, and d 10 July 1941, leaving:

1a George Kelsey, of Coppice Corner Farm, Henley-in-Arden, Warwicks; b 23 July 1899; educ Sedbergh; m 1 May 1940 Hilda Frost (d Sept 1960) and d 1969, leaving:

  1b *George Thomas; b 15 March 1946

  1b *Janette Barbara; b 22 May 1941; m 19– *— and has issue

2a John Gilfrid, of Warwicks; b 16 Feb 1901; educ Sedbergh; m 6 March 1940 Maud, dau of Courteney Bigger, of Falmore Hall, Dundalk, and d 2 Sept 1971, leaving:

  1b *John David [John Lewthwaite Esq, Home Farm, Pillerton, Warwicks]; b 19 March 1941; m 1971 *Jennifer Jane, dau of Kenneth William Pow, and has:

    1c *Katherine Jane; b 1974; educ King's High Sch Warwick and Durham U (BSc)

3a Charles Aubrey Elsham; b 5 June 1903; educ Dover Coll; m 30 Oct 1944 Edna (d 1989), dau of Thomas Page, of Bushwood Common Farm, Henley-in-Arden, and d 1985, leaving:

  1b *Richard Charles Osborn [Richard Lewthwaite Esq, High Chimneys Farm, Bushwood, Warwicks]; b 12 Sept 1945

  2b James Michael; b 25 Oct 1947; d 19–

1a *Ethel Mary Robena; b 20 Aug 1909; m 23 Dec 1935 Col William John Cockerill (d 1982), est s of Charles William Cockerill, of Hampton-in-Arden, Warwicks, and has:

  1b *Timothy James, JP Suffolk [Timothy Cockerill Esq JP, Old Mill House, Weston Colville, Cambridge CB1 5NY]; b 6 June 1940; educ St Edward's Oxford; Sen Slr and Dep Area Dir Legal Aid Bd (E Reg) to 1994; m 2 July 1971 *Chloë A, dau of Michael William Gibson, of Park Ho, Berechurch, Essex

  1b *Jane [Mrs Malcolm Van Biervliet d'Overbroek, 75 Kingston Rd, Oxford]; b 11 May 1948; educ Bedford High Sch; m 1980 *Malcolm Van Biervliet d'Overbroek, LLM, s of Paul Van Biervliet d'Overbroek by April Penelope, only dau of Sir Malcolm Lyall Darling, KCIE, ICS, and has:

    1c *Oliver Robin; b 1985

    1c *Emmie April Jessica; b 1983

(4) Joseph Harold, of Canada; b 2 Oct 1871; educ Giggleswick; d unm 13 Aug 1910

(5) Charles, of Stott Pk, Finsthwaite, Lancs; slr 1900; b 8 Nov 1872; educ Giggleswick; d unm 13 Dec 1902

(6) Henry, of Canada; b 29 June 1874; educ Giggleswick; m Kathleen Josephine Webb (d 1944) and d 4 Aug 1954, leaving:

1a Earl Henry John; b 1903; m 1937 Dorothy Evelyn Thomson (d 1988); d 6 May 1988

(7) Arthur Edwyn; b 25 May 1876; educ Giggleswick; m 1910 Louise Swain and d 26 April 1951

(8) Alfred; MRCS, LRCP, Resident MO Winsley Sanatorium, Ho Physician Brompton Hosp; b 22 Oct 1877; educ Giggleswick and UCL (MB); m 31 Oct 1911 Dorothy Bertha (d 18 Oct 1942), widow of Col C J O'Neill Ferguson, RE, and dau of Rev W H West, of Bath, and d 22 May 1918, leaving:

1a *Christopher; MRCS, LRCP, Lt-Cdr RNVR; b 29 June 1915; educ Epsom and U Coll Hosp London (DObst, RCOG); m 9 Oct 1940 *Joan Diana, dau of Stanley Holliday, and has:

  1b *Elisabeth Anne; b 13 Sept 1946; m *Mark Jenkins and has two daus

1a *Jeanette Margaret; b 27 Feb 1913; m 1934 *Eric Norman De Voy and has issue

(1) Elizabeth; b 5 Aug 1865; m 4 Dec 1902 Percy Drake Brockman, of Saskatchewan, and d 21 June 1929, having had two sons

(2) Margaret Ethel; b 12 Feb 1870; m 29 Sept 1900 Richard Jebb, JP, MA (d 25 June 1953), of The Lyth, Ellesmere, Salop, s of Arthur Trevor Jebb, of The Lyth, and d 16 May 1949, leaving issue

(3) Edith Maud; b 22 April 1881; m 6 Nov 1911 George Cockburn, est s of Jamison Cockburn, MB, of Ulverston, Lancs, and d March 1944, leaving a s

1 Mary; b 11 March 1821; m 22 Aug 1854 Walter Buchanan, of Lower Bebington, Cheshire, and d 3 Sept 1890, having had a s and three daus

2 Elizabeth; b 1822; d unm 1 Dec 1859

3 Eleanor; b 4 Feb 1824; m 25 Aug 1853 Robert Francis Calrow (d 4 July 1897), of Kirkby Lonsdale, Westmorland, 3rd s of William Calrow, JP, DL, of Walton Lodge, Walton-le-Dale, Lancs, and d 2 Dec 1901, having had four sons and four daus

4 Anne; b 1829; d unm 7 Aug 1868

5 Agnes; b 13 May 1829; m 6 Sept 1860 William Adam Allen (d 22 July 1873), of Woodplumpton, Lancs, and d 17 Feb 1885, leaving a dau

The est son,

WILLIAM LEWTHWAITE, of Broadgate, JP, DL; b 5 March 1826; educ Macclesfield and Trin Coll Cambridge (MA); m 11 Dec 1851 Mary (d 6 Oct 1904), dau of William Challinor, of Leek, Staffs, and d 23 April 1867, having had:

1 WILLIAM, 1st Bt

1 Anne; m 25 April 1878 Hamlet Riley, JP, DL (d 14 Oct 1922), of Ennim, nr Penrith, Cumberland, and d 21 April 1933, leaving issue

2 Mary; m 19 Aug 1880 Hon William Henry Cross, MP, and d 8 Nov 1946, leaving issue (see CROSS, V)

WILLIAM LEWTHWAITE's only son,

Sir William Lewthwaite, 1st Bt (UK), so cr 26 Jan 1927, JP, DL; CC Cumberland; b 29 Oct 1853; educ Rossall, Rugby and Trin Coll Cambridge (BA 1876); dep chm Cumberland QS, chm C Assoc Whitehaven 1904–24; m 16 Aug 1881 Helena Jane (d 8 Feb 1934), dau of Charles Challinor, of Basford Hall, Stoke-on-Trent, Staffs, and had:

1 WILLIAM (Sir), 2nd Bt

2 Charles Gilfrid, MC; WW I as Lt 2nd N Midland Bde RFA (wounded, despatches); b 15 April 1884; educ Rugby and Trin Coll Cambridge (BA); ka 29 July 1917

1 Violet Mary, JP (Salop 1943); m 16 June 1920 Robert Edward Morris-Eyton, JP (d 24 Jan 1936), of Calvington, Salop, 2nd s of Charles Edward Morris-Eyton, of Wood Eaton Manor, Staffs, and had issue

The 1st Bt d 13 Dec 1927; his son,

Sir William Lewthwaite, 2nd Bt, JP and CC; educ Trin Coll Cambridge (BA); WW I with RFA; b 20 June 1882; m 26 Oct 1910 Beryl Mary Stopford (d 10 July 1970), only child of Maj Stopford Cosby Hickman, JP, DL, of Fenloe, Co Clare, and d 13 June 1933, leaving:

1 **Sir William Anthony Lewthwaite, 3rd Bt**; b 26 Feb 1912; educ Rugby and Trin Coll Cambridge (BA 1933); slr 1937, ptnr Tatham and Burgis 1959–66 and Southall and Co, Roy Signals and Gren Gds (Lt) WW II, memb: Cncl CLA 1948–64 and Ctee City of Westminster Law Soc 1964–73; m 9 July 1936 *Lois Mairi [Lois Lady Lewthwaite, 73 Dovehouse St, London SW3 6JZ], only child of Capt Struan Robertson Kerr-Clark (see 1949 edn INVERCHAPEL, B) by Lady Beatrice Minnie Ponsonby (see DROGHEDA, E, and RANKEILLOUR, B), and d 25 Dec 1993, having had:

  (1) Elizabeth Mary; b 30 Aug 1950; educ Francis Holland Sch (scholarship to LMH Oxford); d in a walking accident in Wasdale 6 July 1969

  (2) *Catherine Jane; b 16 March 1954; m 1986 *William Tobias Hall, 2nd s of S J Hall, and has:

    1a *Francesca; b 22 July 1990

    2a *Sophie (twin); b 22 July 1990

2 Sir RAINALD GILFRID LEWTHWAITE, **4th and present Bt**

3 Gilfrid MacIver; S/Ldr RAFVR WW II; b 15 April 1922; educ Rugby; kas 22 July 1943

LEY

POST·MORTEM·SPERO·VITAM

Arms: Arg. a bend lozengy gu. between two broken tilting spears erect of the last. **Crest:** In front of a cubit arm in armour, holding in the hand a broken tilting spear in bend sinister ppr., four lozenges conjoined fessways gu. **Motto:** *Post mortem spero vitam* ('I hope for life after death'). **Creation:** Bt. (UK) 27 Dec 1905.

SIR IAN FRANCIS LEY, **5TH BT**, of Epperstone Manor, Epperstone, Co Nottingham [Sir Ian Ley Bt, Fauld Hall, Tutbury, Staffs DE13 9HR]; *b* 12 June 1934; *s f* 1995; *educ* Eton; late 2nd Lt 10th Roy Hus, dep chm 1972–80 (chm 1981–82) Ley's Foundries and Engrg plc, High Sheriff Derbys 1985; *m* 29 July 1957 *Caroline Margaret, er dau of Maj George Henry Errington, MC, of Monkton Ranch, Figtree, Zimbabwe, and has:

(1) +Christopher Ian; *b* 2 Dec 1962
(1) *Virginia Mary; *b* 1 May 1960; *m* 1988 *Samuel C Thomasson, est s of Christopher Thomasson, of Boothby, Graffoe, Lincs, and has:
  1a *Jack James; *b* 1990
  2a *Laurie Francis; *b* 1992
  1a *Cicely Rose; *b* 1996

Lineage: WILLIAM LEYE, of Middle Matherfield, Staffs; *m* Constance — (*d* on or after 17 Sept 1557) and *d* by 19 Sept 1550, leaving, with four daus:

GEORGE LEY, of Mayfield; *m* Katherine, dau of Sampson Beresford, of Beresford and Enton, Staffs, gs of John Beresford, of Beresford and Euston (*see* WATERFORD, M), and *d* 1598, having had, with three yr sons (William; Sampson; Thomas) and a dau (Anne, *m* John Warner):

ADEN LEY, of Mayfield Hall, which he rebuilt 1608; *m* Izobell — and had, with an er s (Francis, of Northfield, *dsp* by 6 Oct 1675):

GEORGE LEY, of Catton, Derbys; *b* 1608; *m* Jane — and had, with an er s (Christopher, Ld Manor of Mayfield, *m* 7 July 1676 Dorothy, dau of George Gaunt, of Bradley, and was *bur* 31 Oct 1701; ancestor of the LEYs of Mayfield, extinct in the male line when Thomas Ley *dsp*; he, however, left his estate to his cousin Robert C GREAVES later LEY (roy warrant 1820)) five yr sons and a dau, a 2nd s:

GEORGE LEY; *m* 26 May 1674 Hannah, dau of John Wakefield, of Burton-on-Trent, where he settled; *bur* 22 Jan 1693, having had, with three yr sons:

GEORGE LEY, of Burton-on-Trent; *bapt* 7 Feb 1675; *m* 22 Jan 1694 Elizabeth Smith (*d* between 13 Jan 1719 and 9 June 1720) and was *bur* 15 July 1712, having had, with other issue:
  1 Lucas/Luke, of Burton-on-Trent; *bapt* 25 April 1696; *m* Sarah — and was *bur* 22 July 1729, having had a s (*d* young) and a dau (Ann, *bapt* 14 Nov 1721)
  2 GEORGE
  3 Christopher, of Burton; surgn; *bapt* 13 Dec 1699; *bur* 17 Feb 1779, having had issue

The 2nd son,
  GEORGE LEY, of Burton-on-Trent; *bapt* 11 Jan 1697; *m* Elizabeth — and was *bur* 28 May 1733, having had, with other issue:

GEORGE LEY, of Burton-on-Trent; *bapt* 16 Oct 1725; *m* 30 May 1749 Elizabeth Morris (*bur* 23 Sept 1792), of Burton, and was *bur* 20 May 1804, having had an est s:

JOSEPH LEY, of Burton-on-Trent; *bapt* 7 Sept 1751; *m* Margaret — and was *bur* 28 Sept 1825, having had, with three daus and four other sons (two of whom were *k* Peninsular War):

GEORGE LEY, of Burton-on-Trent; *bapt* 31 Oct 1784; *m* 12 Sept 1820 Anne Phillips (*bur* 9 Feb 1832) and was *bur* 16 Oct 1843, having had, with another s (Charles):

GEORGE PHILLIPS LEY, of Winshill, Burton-on-Trent; High Bailiff Staffs Co Ct; *bapt* 25 Oct 1821; *m c* 11 Oct 1841 Sarah (*d* 7 June 1883), dau of John Potts, of White Meer Farm, Yoxall, Staffs, and *d* 28 Jan 1886, having had an only surv child:

Sir Francis Ley, 1st Bt (UK), so *cr* 27 Dec 1905, JP Derbys and Notts, of Epperstone Manor, Notts; High Sheriff Notts 1905, Ld Manors of Epperstone and Lazonby, Staffield, Glassonby and Kirkoswald, Cumberland, fndr and dir Ley's

Works, Derby; KGStJ; *b* 3 Jan 1846; *m* 1st 24 Aug 1870 Georgina Townsend (*d* 23 Dec 1886), 3rd dau of George Willis, of Aislaby Hall, Whitby, Yorks, and had:
1 HENRY GORDON (Sir), **2nd Bt**
1 Agnes Willis; *b* 4 June 1871; *d* unm 7 March 1958
2 Ethel, MBE; *b* 2 Jan 1873; *m* 16 Dec 1902 Henry John Boyd-Carpenter (*d* 1 June 1923), barrister (*see* BOYD-CARPENTER, B), and *d* 29 Sept 1953, leaving issue

Sir **Francis** *m* 2nd 24 April 1888 Alison Catherine (*d* 13 Aug 1940), 3rd dau of John Jobson, JP, of Spondon, Derbys, and by her had:
2 Christopher Francis Aden; Capt S Notts Hus Yeo, attd RFC, served Gallipoli 1915; *b* 7 June 1893; accidentally *kas* 16 March 1918
3 Maurice Aden; 2nd Lt E Kent Regt; *b* 5 Aug 1895; *ka* Nov 1914

Sir FRANCIS *d* 17 Jan 1916; his er surv son,
  Sir Henry Gordon Ley, 2nd Bt, JP Derbys and Cumberland; *b* 12 March 1874; Maj TFR WW I, Ld Manors Lazonby, Staffield, Glassonby and Kirkoswald, Cumberland; *m* 1st 6 Sept 1899 (*divorce* 1927) Rhoda (*d* 2 Sept 1935), yr dau of Herbert Prodgers, JP, of Kingston St Michael, Wilts, and had:
1 **Sir Gerald Gordon Ley, 3rd Bt**, TD; *b* 5 Nov 1902; *educ* Eton and New Coll Oxford (BA); Capt 1st Derbys Yeo, RAC (TA), High Sheriff Cumberland 1937, Ld Manors Lazonby, Staffield, Glassonby and Kirkoswald, Cumberland; *m* 1st 19 Feb 1936 (*divorce* 1956) Rosemary Catherine (*d* 26 Sept 1977), formerly w of Harwood Lawrence Maurice Cotter and yr dau of Capt Duncan Macpherson, RN, of Somerset; *m* 2nd 21 Aug 1958 (*divorce* 1968) Grace, dau of Harold Foster, of Pershore, Worcs, and *d* 24 March 1980, having by his 1st w had:
  (1) *Elizabeth Bridget Rhoda [Mrs Roger Boissier, Easton House, The Pastures, Repton, Derbys, DE65 6GG]; *b* 1 March 1937; *m* 30 Oct 1965 *Roger Humphrey Boissier, CBE, yr s of Ernest Gabriel Boissier, DSC, of Derby, and has:
    1a *Rupert John; *b* 25 May 1967; *m* 1996 *Isabel Mary, dau of Spencer Barratt, of Hampstead
    1a *Clare Louise; *b* 16 Nov 1968
  (2) *Annabel Alison [Mrs David Stapleton, Armathwaite Place, Armathwaite, Carlisle]; *b* 30 April 1939; *m* 1 March 1960 *David Eric Cramer Stapleton, er s of Edward Eric Stapleton, of Knockrobin, Co Wicklow, and has:
    1a *Serena Jane Clare; *b* 17 July 1961; *m* 1990 *David Hugo Martyn Williams-Ellis, s of John Williams-Ellis, of Carregfelen, Porthmadog, and has had:
      1b *Hugo John George; *b* 1992
      1b Emily Rose; *b* and *d* 1991
      2b *Phoebe Constance Mary; *b* 1994
    2a *Charlotte Jessica Louise [Mme Bertrand Van Houtte de la Chaise, 30 rue Montmartre, 75001 Paris, France]; *b* 20 Feb 1963; *m* 1987 *Bertrand Maurice Van Houtte de la Chaise, s of Jacques Van Houtte de la Chaise, of Deauville, and has:
      1b *Edward Henri Cramer; *b* 1991
      1b *Alexandra Constance Marie; *b* 1989
    3a *Victoria Lucy Annabel; *b* 5 April 1967
    4a *Lara Alexandra Mary-Rose; *b* 1974
  (3) *Caroline Sheila; *b* 10 May 1943; *m* 3 Dec 1975 *7th Earl of Lonsdale (*qv*) and has issue
2 FRANCIS DOUGLAS LEY (Sir), **4th Bt**
1 *Mary Rhoda [Mrs Geoffrey Bishop, Nesley Down, Westonbirt, Glos]; *b* 8 April 1906; *m* 25 March 1944 Maj Geoffrey Charles Bishop, 9th Lancers (*d* 17 April 1970), only s of Maj Charles Bishop

Sir **Henry** *m* 2nd 29 Sept 1927 (*divorce* 1938) Mabel Annie, dau of Sir Philip Brocklehurst, 1st Bt (*see* 1970 edn); *m* 3rd 23 Jan 1939 Dorothea Gertrude (*d* 1986), formerly w of 2nd Baron Borwick (*qv*) and dau of Charles Grey, of Anerley, and *d* 27 Sept 1944

The 3rd Bt's bro,
  Sir Francis Douglas Ley, 4th Bt, MBE (1961), TD, JP (Derbys 1939), DL (Derbys 1957); *b* 5 April 1907; *educ* Eton and Magdalene Coll Cambridge (MA); Maj Derbys Yeo (TA), chm Ley's Malleable Castings Co Ltd, High Sheriff Derbys 1956; *m* 25 June 1931 Violet Geraldine (*d* 1991), est dau of Maj James Gerald Thewlis Johnson, DSO, of Foston, Derbys, and *d* May 1995, leaving:
1 Sir IAN FRANCIS LEY, **5th and present Bt**
1 *Susan Alison [Mrs Charles Weatherby, Mixbury Lodge Farm, Brackley, Northants NN13 5RW]; *b* 14 May 1937; *m* 2 April 1960 *Charles Edward Weatherby, only s of Edward William Weatherby, of Croughton Lodge, Brackley, Northants, and has:
  (1) *Camilla Jane [Mrs William Hiley, Ashley Hill House, Clarendon, Wilts SP5 3HA]; *b* 23 March 1963; *m* 1993 *William J H Hiley, s of Peter Hiley (*see* LINLITHGOW, M), and has issue
  (2) *Fiona Mary [Mrs Paul Webber, Cropnedy Lawn, Mollington, Oxon OX17 1DR]; *b* 13 March 1965; *m* 1990 *Paul R Webber, s of John Webber of Cropredy, Oxon

LICHFIELD

NIL + DESPERANDUM

Arms: Quarterly, 1st, arg. three bends engrailed gu., in the sinister chief a crescent of the last (for ANSON); 2nd, erm. three cats-a-mountain passant guardant in pale sa. (for ADAMS); 3rd, az. three salmon naiant in pale per pale or and arg. (for SAMBROOKE); 4th, sa. a bend or between three spear heads arg. (for CARRIER).

Crests: Dexter, out of a ducal coronet or a spear head ppr. (for ANSON); sinister, a greyhound's head erased ermines, gorged with a collar double gemel or. **Supporters:** Dexter, a sea-horse; sinister, a lion guardant, both ppr. and each gorged with a collar double gemel or. **Motto:** *Nil desperandum* ('Despair of nothing'). **Creations:** V. and B. (UK) 17 Feb 1806, E. (UK) 15 Sept 1831.

THE 5TH EARL OF LICHFIELD, Viscount Anson, of Shugborough and Orgrave, Co Stafford, and **Baron Soberton**, of Soberton, Co Southampton ([Thomas] Patrick John Anson, DL (Staffs (1996)) [The Rt Hon The Earl of Lichfield DL, Shugborough Hall, Stafford ST17 0XB; Lichfield Studios, 133 Oxford Gdns, London W10 6NE]; *b* 25 April 1939 (HM QUEEN ELIZABETH THE QUEEN MOTHER stood sponsor); *s gf* 1960; *educ* Harrow and RMA Sandhurst; Lt Gren Gds 1959–62; photographer as Patrick Lichfield, Freeman City London 1981, FBIPP, FRPS, former dir Burke's Peerage Ltd and proprietor Burke's Club; author: *The Most Beautiful Women* (1981), *Lichfield on Photography* (1981), *A Royal Album* (1982), *Patrick Lichfield's Unipart Calendar Book* (1982), *Patrick Lichfield Creating the Unipart Calendar* (1983), *Hot Foot to Zabriskie Point* (1985), *Lichfield on Travel Photography* (1986), *Not the Whole Truth* (autobiography, 1986), *Courvoisier's Book of the Best* (ed, 1986, 5th edn 1994), *Lichfield in Retrospect* (with Charles Mosley (see CUNINGHAME, Bt), 1988), *Queen Mother: the Lichfield selection* (ed, 1990), *Elizabeth R: a photographic celebration of 40 years* (ed, 1991); *m* 8 March 1975 (*divorce* 1986) Lady Leonora Mary Grosvenor, LVO, er dau of 5th Duke of Westminster (*qv*), and has:

1 +THOMAS WILLIAM ROBERT HUGH, *Viscount Anson*; *b* 19 July 1978

1 *Rose Meriel Margaret; *b* 27 July 1976

2 *Eloise Anne Elizabeth; *b* 1981 (HRH THE PRINCESS ROYAL stood sponsor)

Lichfield, previous creations: For the Earldom of Lichfield created 1645 *see* MORAY, E. In 1674 Sir Edward Lee, 5th Bt, of Quarendon, Bucks, was created Earl of Lichfield. His faithfulness to the Stuarts was such that he withdrew from public life at the Glorious Revolution, having been one of only four peers to join JAMES II in his flight from Whitehall to Rochester in December 1688. But then he had married into the family, albeit the wrong side of the blanket, having taken to wife Lady Charlotte FitzRoy some two and a half years after his ennoblement. She was CHARLES II's daughter by Barbara Villiers, Duchess of Cleveland (*see* JERSEY, E), and like her mother a beauty, though less wanton. The marriage appears to have been a happy, or at any rate a busy, one as they had 18 children. The sixth of their 13 sons succeeded as 2nd Earl in 1716. Like his maternal grandfather CHARLES II he turned papist. One of their five daughters, Charlotte, was ancestress by her husband the 5th Baron Baltimore of the wife of Robert E Lee, the Confederate commander in the American Civil War (*see* Introduction to AMERICAN PRESIDENTIAL FAMILIES, 1994, Morris Genealogical Books SA). The title expired with the death of the 4th Earl in 1776, the estates, chief of which was the Ditchley Park property in Oxfordshire, going to the Dillons (*see* DILLON, V) via his niece, another Charlotte, whose husband was 11th Viscount Dillon.

Lineage: WILLIAM ANSON (of a family that had lived in Staffs for several generations); lawyer *temp* ELIZABETH I; bought Manors of Shugborough, Staffs, and Bolehall and Glascott, Warwicks, *temp* JAMES I; *m* Joan, dau of Richard Mitchel *alias* Whitehall, of Oldbury, Warwicks, and *d* by 7 Oct 1644, leaving:

WILLIAM ANSON, of Shugborough; *b* 1628; unsuccessful in establishing to the heralds' satisfaction at the visitation of Staffs 1663 that his family bore arms licitly; *m* Elizabeth, dau of Thomas Stafford, of Botham Hall, Derbys, and had:

WILLIAM ANSON, of Shugborough; *m* Isabella, dau and coheir (with her sis, Countess of Macclesfield, *qv*) of Charles Carrier, of Wirkworth, Derbys, and *d* Aug 1720, having had, with several yr daus:

1 Thomas, of Shugborough; MP Lichfield; *dsp*

2 GEORGE ANSON, 1st and last LORD ANSON, BARON OF SOBERTON, Co Southampton (GB), so *cr* 13 June 1747, PC (1750); *b* 23 April 1697; RN: joined

Feb 1711/2, Midshipman 1716, 2nd Lt 1718, Cdr 1722, Post Capt 1724 (served off Carolina coast to 1730, being so fondly remembered by the inhabitants ashore that they named Anson County after him); circumnavigated the world 1740, R-Adml: the Blue 1740, the White 1745, V-Adml: the Blue 1746, the Red 1747, Adml: the Blue 1748, the White 1757, a Ld Admlty 1744–51, C-in-C Channel Fleet 1746 and 1758, won engagement off Cape Finisterre over French May 1747 (capturing six men of war), V-Adml GB 1749–62, First Ld Admlty 1751–56 and 1757–62, Adml and C-in-C Fleet 1761–62; MP (Whig) Hedon 1744–47, Trin House: Er Bro 1749–62, Master 1752–56; a Ld Justice GB 1752 and 1755; *m* 25 April 1748 Lady Elizabeth Yorke (*d* 1 June 1760), dau of 1st Earl of Hardwicke (*qv*), and *dsp* 6 June 1762, when the Barony expired

1 Janette; *m* Sambrooke Adams, of Sambrooke, Salop, and had a 4th s:

(1) George ADAMS later ANSON (roy licence 30 April 1773 after inheriting the Shugborough estate from his uncle), of Orgrave, Staffs; *bapt* 25 July 1731; MP (Whig) Lichfield 1770–83; *m* 5 Jan 1763 Mary, dau of 1st Baron Vernon (*qv*), and had, with other issue:

1a THOMAS, **1st Viscount**

2a George (Sir), GCB; *b* 1769; MP, Gen, Col 4th Dragoon Gds, served Peninsular War; Equerry to HRH THE DUCHESS OF KENT (mother of HM QUEEN VICTORIA), Groom Bedchamber to HRH THE PRINCE CONSORT, Govr Chelsea Hosp; *m* 1800 Frances (*d* 1834), sis of Sir Frederic Hamilton, 5th Bt, of Silverton Hill (*qv*), and *d* 4 Nov 1849, leaving with other issue:

1b Octavius Henry St George; 9th Lancers; had:

1c George Wemyss; Lt-Col; *m* 1912 Gertrude Ann, 5th dau of William Nicholson (*see* NICHOLSON OF WINTERBOURNE, B)

3a Sir WILLIAM ANSON, 1st Bt (*qv*)

4a Edward; *b* 1775; *m* 1808 Harriott, dau of J Ramsbottom, and *d* 1837, having had issue

5a Sambrooke; Lt-Col 1st Foot Gds; *b* 18 Feb 1778; *m* Elizabeth Hawkins (*d* 22 March 1866), of Staffs, and *d* 10 Oct 1846, leaving:

1b Elizabeth Grace; *m* 1st 29 March 1831 Thomas King (*d* 23 Dec 1863), of Alvediston Ho, Wilts; *m* 2nd 22 Nov 1867 Thomas Jarvis Bennett, MD, of Wilton, Wilts, and *d* 24 Jan 1882

6a Frederick (Very Rev); DD, Dean Chester; *b* 23 March 1779; *m* 1807 Mary Anne, only dau of Rev Richard Levett, of Milford, Staffs, and *d* 8 May 1867, having had issue

1a Mary; *m* 1785 Sir Francis Ford, 1st Bt (*see* ST CLAIR-FORD, Bt), and *d* 1837

2a Catherine Juliana; *m* 1807 Henry Stuart and *d* 5 July 1843, leaving issue (*see* ST CLAIR-FORD, Bt)

GEORGE ANSON *d* 27 Oct 1789; his est son,

THOMAS ANSON, **1st Viscount Anson**, of Shugborough and Orgrave, Co Stafford, so *cr* 17 Feb 1806, as also BARON SOBERTON, of Soberton, Co Southampton (both UK); *b* 14 Feb 1767; MP (Whig) Lichfield 1789–1806; *m* 15 Sept 1794 Anne Margaret (*d* 23 May 1843), 2nd dau of 1st Earl of Leicester (*qv*) of Holkham, and had, with other issue:

1 THOMAS WILLIAM, **1st Earl**

2 George; Maj-Gen, C-in-C India; *b* 13 Oct 1797; *m* 30 Nov 1830 Isabella Elizabeth Annabella (*d* 29 Dec 1858), 3rd dau of 1st Baron Forester (*qv*), and *d* 27 May 1857, leaving:

(1) Isabella Maria Katherine; *m* 8 Feb 1858 3rd Earl Howe (*qv*) and *d* 29 March 1922, leaving issue

(2) Alice Louisa; *m* 18 March 1865 Hon George Wentworth Fitzwilliam (*d* 4 March 1874) and *d* 14 Jan 1879, leaving issue (*see* 1970 edn FITZWILLIAM, E)

(3) Geraldine Georgiana Mary, LGStJ; *m* 4 March 1862 3rd Marquess of Bristol (*qv*) and *d* 25 Jan 1927, leaving issue

3 Charles Littleton; Midshipman RN; *k* 1812 by a gun accidentally exploding aboard HMS *Bacchante*

1 Anna Margaret; *m* 1819, as his 2nd w, 4th Earl of Rosebery (*qv*) and *d* 19 Aug 1882, leaving issue

2 Frances Elizabeth; *m* 1st Sept 1835 Hon Charles John Murray, s of 4th Earl of Mansfield and Mansgfield (*qv*); *m* 2nd 10 Sept 1853 Ambrose Isted (*d* 13 May 1881), of Ecton, Northants, and *d* 25 Dec 1899

3 Frederica Sophia; *m* 21 April 1838 her sister's stepson Hon Bouverie Francis Primrose, 2nd s of 4th Earl of Rosebery (*qv*) by his 1st w, and *d* 11 Oct 1867

4 Elizabeth Jane, VA; Extra Lady of the Bedchamber to HM QUEEN VICTORIA; *m* 18 July 1837 3rd Baron Waterpark (*qv*) and *d* 15 Sept 1894

The 1st VISCOUNT *d* 31 July 1818; his est son,

THOMAS WILLIAM ANSON, **1st Earl of Lichfield**, Co Stafford (UK), so *cr* 15 Sept 1831, PC (1830); *b* 20 Oct 1795; *educ* Eton and Ch Ch Oxford; MP (Whig) Yarmouth June-July 1818, Master Buckhounds 1830–34, PMG 1835–41 (during his term of office the penny post was inaugurated), High Steward Yarmouth 1836–54; *m* 11 Feb 1819 Louisa Barbara Catherine (*d* 20 Aug 1879), dau of Nathaniel Phillips, of Slebech Hall, Pembs, and had:

1 THOMAS GEORGE, **2nd Earl**

2 William Victor Leopold Horatio; RN; *b* 1 Aug 1833; *d* 1856

3 Augustus Henry Archibald, VC; Lt-Col 8th Hus, MP Lichfield 1859–68; *b* 5 March 1835; *m* 1 Dec 1863 Amelia Maria (*m* 2nd 13 Aug 1881 8th Duke of Argyll (*qv*) and *d* 4 Jan 1894), est dau of Rt Rev Thomas Legh Claughton, DD, Bp St Albans, and sis of Sir Gilbert Henry Claughton, 1st and last Bt (*see* 1821 edn), and *dsp* 17 Nov 1877

4 Adelbert John Robert (Rt Rev); DD Oxon; Assist Bp Lichfield, 2nd Canon Residentiary and Chllr, Bp Qu'Appelle Canada 1884–92; *b* 20 Dec 1840; *d* unm 27 May 1909

1 Louisa Mary Anne; *m* 26 Nov 1838 Lt-Col Edward King-Tenison (*d* 19 June 1878), of Kilronan Castle, Co Roscommon, and *d* 27 Aug 1882, leaving, with another dau:

(1) France Margaret Christina; *b* 9 July 1845; *m* 8th Earl of Kingston (*qv*) and had issue

2 Anne Frederica; *m* 29 Aug 1843 10th Earl of Wemyss (*qv*) and *d* 22 July 1896, leaving issue

3 Harriet Frances Maria; m 7 June 1851 6th Baron Vernon (qv) and d 15 Feb 1898, leaving issue

4 Gwendoline Isabella Anna Maria; m 19 April 1865 Nicholas Power O'Shee (d 30 March 1902), of Gardenmorris, Co Waterford, and d 14 March 1912, leaving issue

The 1st EARL d 18 March 1854; his est son,

THOMAS GEORGE ANSON, **2nd Earl of Lichfield**; b 15 Aug 1825; educ Eton; FO 1846–47, MP (Lib) Lichfield 1847–54, Ld Lt Staffs 1863–71; m 10 April 1855 Lady Harriet Georgiana Louisa Hamilton (d 23 April 1913), est dau of 1st Duke of Abercorn (qv), and had:

1 THOMAS FRANCIS, **3rd Earl**

2 George Augustus (Sir), KCB (1937), CBE (1925), MVO (1907), KPM (1918), DL Staffs; b 22 Dec 1857; educ Harrow; Lt-Col RFA, TFR, 3rd N Midland Bde RFA, Capt RA, Ch Constable Staffs 1888–1929; m 27 Sept 1884 Blanche Mary (d as result of enemy action 16 April 1941), dau of George Miller, of Brentry, Glos, and d 25 May 1947, having had:

(1) John George, MC; Maj 62nd, N Midland Bde, RFA, TAR; b 14 July 1886; d 19 Sept 1931

(2) Claud Ronald, JP Hants; Lt 3rd N Midland Bde RFA WW I (wounded); b 3 May 1895; educ Harrow; m 1st 9 Nov 1915 Frederica Heath (d 25 Feb 1941), yst dau of Frederic James Harrison, of Maer Hall, Staffs, and had:

1a Yvonne; b 15 Nov 1916; m 5 April 1941 Brig Francis Edward Buckland, RAMC (d 2 May 1965), only s of Francis Mathew Buckland, of Laleham, and had issue

2a *Mary [Mrs Mary Dene, Lyons Hill, Minterne Magna, Dorchester, Dorset]; b 2 July 1918; m 22 Feb 1940 (divorce 1960) Lt-Col John Anthony Dene, cmdg Staffs Yeo (Queen's Own Royal Regt), late DCLI, s of Col Arthur Pollard Dene, of The Priory, Badingham, Suffolk, and has:

1b *John Michael; b 15 April 1946; educ Harrow

2b *David Frederick; b 3 March 1948; educ Harrow

1b *Margaret Katherine [Mrs Patrick Lucas, Chalknewton House, Maiden Newton, Dorset]; b 10 Jan 1942; m 1st 6 Oct 1962 (divorce 1976) Michael Charles Power, only s of Maj Charles Alfred Power, RM, of Kent; m 2nd 1977 *Patrick Bernard Lucas and by her 1st husb has:

1c *Anthony George Bertram; b 23 April 1968

1c *Katharine Mary; b 27 May 1965

2c *Erica Margaret; b 5 April 1967

3a *Joan; b 7 Nov 1919; m 14 Nov 1945 Maj J C Lee, Roy Netherlands Army (d 1963)

(2) (cont.) Claud Anson m 2nd 24 Dec 1944 (divorce 1949) Mrs Lilian Gallia Meiklejohn, dau of David George Davies, of New York; m 3rd 11 Nov 1949 Noreen Stella, formerly w of W V Cross, of Home Farm, Spralton, Northants, and Boundary Ford, Sway, dau of H G Barlow, and d 10 Feb 1965

(1) Barbara Grace; b 4 March 1889; d as a result of enemy action 16 April 1941

3 Henry James; Maj 2nd Bn HLI, ADC to Govr-Gen Canada; b 29 Dec 1858; m 27 Oct 1902 Lady Adelaide Audrey Ryder (d 23 Dec 1956), dau of 4th Earl of Harrowby (qv), and dsp 26 Feb 1904

4 Frederic William, JP Herts; b 4 Feb 1862; m 1st 3 Aug 1886 Florence Louisa Jane (d 11 Feb 1908), dau of Lt-Col John Henry Bagot Lane, of King's Bromley, Staffs, and had:

(1) Ernald Henry; Maj 3rd Co London Yeo WW I; b 28 June 1893; educ Harrow; m 21 May 1924 (divorce) Mabel Elizabeth Flake Manning, dau of Albert Flake, of New York, and d 29 Sept 1953

(2) Frederic, MC; Lt-Col Gren Gds WW I (wounded), WW II; b 3 March 1896; educ Eton; d unm 2 Feb 1963

(3) Arthur; Lt Gren Gds; b 3 March 1896; ka France 8 Oct 1915

(1) Helen Frances; b 7 June 1892; m 28 June 1917 Maj Frederick Horace Gale, Beds Regt, only s of Frederick Gale, of Notting Hill, and d 9 Jan 1957, leaving issue

(2) Sibyl Florence; b 24 Sept 1894; d unm April 1914

(3) Beryl Susan; b 12 Nov 1904; m 1st 29 Feb 1928 (divorce) Claude A Cutbill (d 27 Sept 1962), 2nd s of Edward Cutbill; m 2nd 24 Feb 1938 (divorce 1948) Capt Harold Winchester Sanderson, Gren Gds, est s of Harold Arthur Sanderson (see SANDERSON OF AYOT, B); m 3rd 1952 Arthur Temple Thorne (d Oct 1970) and d 10 July 1976

4 (cont.)The Hon Frederic Anson m 2nd 16 June 1915 Edith (d 3 Feb 1961), dau of S E Rowland, of Slinfold, Sussex, and d 2 April 1917

5 Claud, JP; V-Lt Co Waterford, High Sheriff 1909; b 11 Jan 1864; educ Harrow; m 27 Feb 1901 Lady Clodagh Beresford (d 17 April 1957), yst dau of 5th Marquess of Waterford (qv), and d 25 Dec 1947, leaving:

(1) Anthony John; Roy Corps of Signals WW II; b 1 Jan 1904; m 17 Aug 1926 Rosalind Désirée (d 1985), only dau of R-Adml Sir Robert Keith Arbuthnot, 4th Bt, of Edinburgh (qv), and d 1981 leaving:

1a +John Anthony Robert [Dr John Anson, 30 Tibbets Close, London SW19 6EF]; MRCS, LRCP; b 26 March 1927; m 1st 27 Oct 1962 (Fiona) Brook, MB, BS (d 1987), dau of Colin Frederick George Wills; m 2nd *(Angela) Jane Millican and by his 1st w has had:

1b +Martin Anthony Wills; b 7 Oct 1963

1b Annabel Frances Rosalind; b 12 June 1967; d 1988

2a +Colin Shane [Colin Anson Esq, 18 Ripplevale Grove, London N1 1HU]; b 29 July 1931; educ Stowe

1a *Sarah Rose [Mrs Robin Kerr, 3 Lansdown Place East, Bath]; b 12 July 1944; m 5 July 1969 *Capt Robin Gifford Kerr, RN, yr s of William Mark Kerr, WS, of Edinburgh, and has:

1b *Bryony Charlotte; b 1972

2b *Julia Emily; b 28 March 1974

(2) Hugo Edward; Maj Rifle Bde; b 1 June 1908; m 1st 24 Jan 1935 (divorce 1946) Elizabeth (d 22 Feb 1997), er dau of Capt Sir Harold George Campbell, KCVO, DSO, RN, of Rockhill Ho, Egerton, Kent, and had:

1a +Michael [Michael Anson Esq, Windrush Hill, Hawling, Glos GL54 5SZ]; Page of Hon to TM GEORGE VI 1950–52 and THE QUEEN 1952–53; b 5 May 1937; educ Stowe and Edinburgh U; m 10 Aug 1963

*Claire-Elizabeth Seymour, dau of Lt-Col Frederick Arthur Morris, of Malvern, Worcs, and has:

1b *Alexandra Albinia [Mrs Marcus Hodge, Whitehouse Lodge, 31 Whitehouse Rd, Oxford OX1 4PA]; b 7 Dec 1965; m 1992 *Marcus A Hodge, er s of Spencer Hodge, of Roquebrune, France, and has:

1c *Clara Albinia; b 29 Jan 1987

2b *Josephine Emma [Mrs Alastair Graham-Campbell, 22 Cleaver Sq, London SE11 4OW]; b 1968; m 1996 *Alastair John Graham-Campbell, yr s of Niall Graham-Campbell, of Pitlochry

3b *Catherine Elizabeth; b 1971

(2) (cont.) Maj Hugo Anson m 2nd 8 June 1946 Annina (d 14 Dec 1991), widow of Duke Paolo Badoglio and dau of Marchese Silj, of Rome, and d 24 Oct 1991, leaving by her:

2a +Bernard Anthony [Bernard Anson Esq, Villa Silj, via di Santa Cornelia, 008891 Prima Porta, Rome, Italy]; b 26 Sept 1948; educ Harrow and Trin Coll Dublin; m 1st 1975 (divorce 1984) Anna, dau of John Cooper; m 2nd 1984 *Eleonora, dau of Carlo Monini and has:

1b +Edoardo; b 1 Feb 1991

2b +Daniel; b 16 March 1995

3a +Andrea Victor [Andrea Anson Esq, 203 Prince St, New York, NY 10012, USA]; b 5 June 1951; educ Harrow

(1) Clodagh Blanche; b 28 Feb 1902; d unm 23 Feb 1992

6 Francis; T/Capt Brecknockshire Bn S Wales Borderers 1915–16; b 7 March 1867; m 15 June 1892 Caroline (d 10 Jan 1951), 2nd dau of George Cleveland, of Coleman, Tex., and d 13 April 1928, leaving:

(1) Thomas George; Maj 4/7th Dragoon Gds WWs I (wounded twice) and II; b 27 July 1894; educ Harrow and RMC Sandhurst; m 6 Oct 1930 Mrs Enid Moore, dau of Rev Arthur Durrant, and dsp 18 Sept 1954

(2) Henry Adelbert; W/Cdr (T) RAF, Lt Brecknockshire Bn S Wales Borderers, WWs I (despatches) and II; b 21 Dec 1895; educ Harrow; m 1st 2 June 1927 (divorce 1930) Hilda Suzanne, only dau of S Carson Allen, of St John's Wood, and had:

1a +David Richard; b 29 Jan 1929; educ Harrow

(2) (cont.) W/Cdr Henry Anson m 2nd 25 Jan 1930 Muriel Irene, only dau of Edgar Cecil Smith, of Putney, and d 16 Nov 1955, having by her had:

2a Charles Henry; b 6 June 1944; educ Rosenberg Coll St Gallen; d unm 31 Jan 1967

1a Deirdre Henrietta; b 3 Sept 1933; d 25 April 1948

2a *Vanessa Irene [Lady Hannam, 27 Fentiman Rd, London SW8 1LD]; b 10 March 1940; m 1st 6 July 1962 John Edward Robert Wauchope, er s of Lt-Col Charles Edward Wauchope, MC, RA, of Sussex, by Elaine Margaret, er dau of Sir Robert Armstrong-Jones (see SNOWDON, E); m 2nd 1983 *Sir John Gordon Hannam, MP, and by her 1st husb has:

1b *Andrew Charles Anson; b 1974

1b *Arabella Jane [Mrs Harry Huddart, 101 Camberwell Grove, London SE5]; b 30 April 1963; m 1986 *G H C P (Harry) Huddart, only s of Edward William Huddart, of Littlecourt, Derriford, Devon, and has:

1c *Joseph Edward Anson; b 1989

1c *Georgiana Rose; b 1986

2c *Augusta Louisa (twin); b 1989

3c *Flora Vanessa Elizabeth; b 1990

2b *Lucy Anne Margaret; b 24 April 1965; m 1987 *James F D Rolls, only s of John Rolls, of Spain

3b *Alexandra Gladys; b 9 Dec 1968

(3) William Alfred; Maj 13th/18th Hus WW I (wounded); b 19 March 1897; educ Harrow; m 7 Oct 1919 Dorothy Helme (d 1988), only dau of Richard Mashiter, of S Kensington and Glam, and d 29 Oct 1952, leaving:

1a Francis Richard; Lt 13th/18th Hus; b 12 March 1926; educ Harrow; m 1st 16 Dec 1948 (divorce 1960) Ann, only dau of Capt Sir John Lionel Armytage, 8th Bt (qv), and has:

1b +Anthony Francis [Anthony Anson Esq, Pigeon House, Pigeon Lane, Hanmer, Salop]; b 4 Nov 1951; educ Harrow; m 1985 *Sally C, dau of Col Geoffrey Vardon Churton, MBE, MC, TD, and has:

1c +Patrick Francis; b 5 Aug 1996

1c *Caroline Myra; b 1990

1b *Amanda Jane [Mrs Jeremy Pratt, 63 Colehill Lane, London SW6 5EF]; b 16 May 1950; m 1982 Jeremy D P Pratt, s of David Pratt, of Suffolk

1a (cont.) Francis Anson m 2nd 30 April 1960 (divorce 1983) Bridgett Ann, only dau of Dudley Gerald David Greenhough, of Mayfair; m 3rd *Elisabeth Gilroy [Mrs Francis Anson, 11 Anley Rd, London W14], dau of Edward Philip Shaw, of Englefield Green, and formerly w of Oliver Simon Willis Fleming, and d 1989, leaving by his 2nd w:

2b *Juliet May [Mrs Graeme Pentolpe, 39 Court Rd, Greendale, Harare, Zimbabwe]; b 31 May 1961; m April 1983 *Graeme Pentolpe and has:

1c *Michael John; b 23 Dec 1985

2c *Nicholas Anson; b 17 July 1992

1c *Alexandra May; b 13 April 1988

3b *Emma Louise [Mrs Alan Hargreaves, c/o Gleneagles Dve, Durban 4051, S Africa]; b 10 Dec 1963; m 1988 *Dr Alan Hargreaves, s of Eric Hargreaves, of Durban, and has:

1c *Christopher John; b 14 Sept 1990

2c *Matthew James; b 9 Dec 1992

3c *Timothy Adam; b 11 Oct 1996

3c *Nicole Louise; b 19 Jan 1995

2a +Edward William; b 11 March 1929; educ Harrow

1a *Harriet Louise; b 24 Sept 1924

(4) Francis Edward; b 16 Feb 1901; d 8 June 1918

(1) Frances; b 10 May 1893; m 24 July 1929 Claude St John Garle Miller, ARIBA (d 26 June 1951), only s of Edward Miller, of Bickenhall Mansions, and d 18 April 1967, leaving issue

7 William; *b* 19 April 1872; *m* 17 July 1917 Louisa Goddard (*d* 10 Feb 1952), dau of Frederick de Voe Van Wagenen, of Fulton, NY, and *d* 22 June 1926, leaving:

(1) *Edith [Mrs Ford Boulware, 1104 Montecito Dve, San Angelo, TX 76901–4560, USA]; *b* 2 Dec 1921; *m* 1st 14 Aug 1943 Capt Alfred Ryland Howard, 90th Div Field Regt, Liaison Pilot (*ka* Normandy 4 July 1944), s of Dr Alfred Philo Howard, of Houston, and has:

1a *Alfred Ryland III [Alfred Howard III, 114 Park Hill, San Antonio, TX 78212, USA]; *b* 16 Nov 1944; *m* 1985 *Pamela, only dau of Hugh A Fitzsimmons, of San Pedro Ranch, Carrizo Springs, Texas, by Mrs William Negley, of San Antonio, and has:

1b *Anson Boulware; *b* 1987

1b *Laura Isabel; *b* 1989

2b *Louisa Carrigan; *b* 1992

(1) (cont.) Mrs Alfred Howard *m* 2nd 15 April 1947 *Lt-Col Ford Millspaugh Boulware, US Army Engrs Amphibians, s of Lemuel Ford Boulware, of Lexington, Ky.

8 Alfred; Capt Sussex Yeo WW I, Offr Crown Italy; *b* 15 April 1876; *educ* Harrow; *m* 1 July 1912 Leila (*d* 14 July 1953), widow of John Josiah Emery, of New York, and dau of Gen Charles T Alexander, of Washington, DC, and *dsp* 25 March 1944

1 Florence Beatrice; *m* 15 Aug 1885 Col Sir Henry Streatfeild, GCVO, CB, CMG, TD, Gren Gds (*d* 26 July 1938), of Chiddingstone, Kent, Priv Sec and Equerry to HM QUEEN ALEXANDRA 1910–25, and *d* 25 Sept 1946, leaving issue

2 Beatrice; *m* 30 July 1890 Lt-Col Richard Hamilton Rawson, DL (*d* 12 Oct 1918), of Gravenhurst, Sussex, MP Reigate, and *d* 15 Dec 1919, having had issue

3 (Mary) Maud, OBE (1920); *m* 19 July 1893 Hon Edward Alan Dudley Ryder, s of 4th Earl of Harrowby (*qv*), and *d* 22 Sept 1961, leaving issue

4 Edith; *m* 29 April 1895 3rd Earl of Lovelace (*qv*) and *d* 8 Oct 1932, leaving issue

5 Evelyn; *d unm* 2 July 1895

The 2nd EARL *d* 7 Jan 1892; his est son,

THOMAS FRANCIS ANSON, **3rd Earl of Lichfield**, JP, DL, CA Staffs; *b* 31 Jan 1856; *educ* Harrow and Trin Coll Cambridge (BA); dir Nat Provincial Bank and Bank of Australia, Pres MCC, fndr Social Welfare Assoc London; *m* 5 Nov 1878 Lady Mildred Coke (*d* 12 May 1941), dau of 2nd Earl of Leicester (*qv*) of Holkham, and *d* 29 July 1918 following a shooting accident, having had:

1 THOMAS EDWARD, **4th Earl**

2 Arthur Augustus; *b* 29 July 1887; *educ* Harrow; *m* 31 July 1929 Mrs Beatrice Dora Sassoon, dau of Walter James, and *d* 30 Aug 1960

3 Rupert; Capt 7th Bn Royal Fus, Maj KRRC; *b* 7 Nov 1889; *educ* Harrow; *m* 26 Nov 1919 Marion Emma Ruthven (Mollie) (*d* 11 Sept 1965), yst dau of James Halliday, and *d* 20 Dec 1966, leaving:

(1) Geoffrey Rupert; Lt 4th Hus; *b* 28 Jan 1929; *educ* RNC Dartmouth and RMA Sandhurst; *m* 28 Dec 1957 *Verna Grace [Mrs Geoffrey Anson, 2000 Jonathan Dve, Martinsburg, WV 25401, USA], dau of Edward Leonard Hall, of N Ontario, and *d* 5 June 1997, having had:

1a +George Rupert [George Anson Esq, Nash End Farmhouse, Nash Rd, Thornborough, Bucks MK18 2DN]; *b* 7 June 1960; *m* 1987 *Kirsty Jane, dau of A S D Day, of Billesdon, Leics, and has:

1b +Douglas Rupert; *b* 1992

2b +Peter Francis; *b* 1997

1b *Josceline Elizabeth; *b* 1989

2a +Christopher Leonard; *b* 11 Sept 1963

3a Edward Peter; *b* 24 March 1965; *d* 1982

1a *Jennifer Marion; *b* 10 Nov 1961

(2) +(Thomas) Peter [Maj Peter Anson, Coneygre Farmhouse, Hardwick, Oxon OX6 9SU]; Maj Queen's Roy Irish Hus; *b* 5 March 1933; *educ* Harrow and RMA Sandhurst; *m* 19 Dec 1964 *Judith Hilary, 2nd dau of Capt John Nicholl Kennard, RN (*see* KENNARD, Bt), and has:

1a +Henry James; *b* 2 Jan 1967; *m* 1992 *Joanna C, dau of D R Lamb, of W Littleton, Bath, and has:

1b +Archie Augustus; *b* 26 Feb 1996

2a +Patrick John; *b* 27 Feb 1969

(1) *Ann Rosemary [Mrs Ann Coombe, c/o Coutts & Co, 440 Strand, London WC2R 0GS]; *b* 1924; *m* 4 Dec 1946 (*divorce* 1974) Capt Paul Norrish Coombe, only s of William Frederick Coombe, and has:

1a *Geoffrey Paul [Geoffrey Coombe Esq, Dianalaan 7, Amstelveen, Holland]; *b* 28 July 1951; *educ* Queen Elizabeth's Sch Crediton

2a *Michael Anthony [Michael Coombe Esq, PO Box 171, Milsons Point, NSW 2061, Australia]; *b* 1955; *m* 1st 1975 Karen Elizabeth O'Hara (*d* 1990) and has:

1b *Benjamin Michael; *b* 1982

2a (cont.) Michael Coombe *m* 2nd 1992 *Karin Penny South and by her has:

1b *Lucy Romy; *b* 1992

1a *Diana Mary; *b* 25 Sept 1947; *m* 1st 17 June 1967 (*divorce* 1986) Timothy Dennis Gaines, s of Orgel Fay Gaines, of Pomana, Calif., and has:

1b *David Allan; *b* 1970

2b *Daniel Anson; *b* 1972

3b *Devon Ashley; *b* 1974

1a (cont.) Mrs Diana Gaines *m* 2nd 1987 (*divorce* 1989) Jess Mount; *m* 3rd 1990 *Richard Stewart

(2) *Felicity Marian [Mrs John Woodhouse, Shepherds, Ansty, Dorset DT2 7PX]; *m* 2 Jan 1952 John Arbon Woodhouse (*d* 1986), 2nd s of Col Harold Sealy, Woodhouse, TD, of West Lodge, Blandford, and has:

1a *Mark John Michael [Mark Woodhouse Esq, Cherrington Farm Cottage, N Cheriton, Somerset BA8 0AP]; *b* 29 Sept 1955; *m* 16 June 1979 *Teresa Anne, only dau of Michael Kennedy Merriam (*see* AILSA, M)

2a *Andrew Harold Rupert; *b* 1957

1a *Clare Marian; *b* 7 July 1965

1 Bertha; *b* 22 Aug 1879; *m* 23 Oct 1902 Hon Thomas Henry Frederick Egerton and *d* 30 Aug 1959, leaving issue (*see* SUTHERLAND, D)

2 Mabel; *b* 18 July 1882; *m* 12 Oct 1914 22nd Lord Forbes (*qv*) and *d* 21 March 1972, leaving issue

3 Violet; *b* 21 April 1886; *m* 29 July 1912 Col Lancelot Mare Gregson, OBE (*d* 7 Nov 1935), Gren Gds, 2nd s of Rev Charles Gregson, of Burdon and Murton, Co Durham, and *d* 17 Sept 1974, leaving issue

The 3rd EARL's est son,

THOMAS EDWARD ANSON, **4th Earl of Lichfield**, JP, DL; CA Staffs; *b* 9 Dec 1883; *educ* Harrow and Trin Coll Cambridge; Ld High Steward Stafford 1933–60, Capt 5th City of London Rifles WW I, ADC Actg Master Horse to Ld Lt Ireland 1906–10; *m* 1st 11 July 1911 Evelyn Maud (*d* 16 April 1945), only dau of Col Edward George Keppel, MVO (*see* ALBEMARLE, E), and had:

1 Thomas William Arnold, *Viscount Anson*; *b* 4 May 1913; *educ* Harrow, psc, Lt-Col Gren Gds WW II; *m* 1st 28 April 1938 (*divorce* 1948) Anne Ferelith Fenella (*d* 1980), dau of Hon John Herbert Bowes-Lyon (*see* STRATHMORE AND KINGHORNE, E), and had:

(1) (THOMAS) PATRICK JOHN ANSON, **5th and present Earl of Lichfield**

(1) *Elizabeth Georgiana [The Lady Elizabeth Shakerley, 56 Ladbroke Grove, London W11 2PB]; *b* 7 June 1941 (HM GEORGE VI stood sponsor); granted rank of earl's dau 12 July 1961; fndr Party Planners 1960, dir Debrett's Peerage Ltd 1979–83, Pres Action for ME 1995–; *m* 27 July 1972, as his 2nd w, Sir Geoffrey Adam Shakerley, 6th Bt (*qv*), and has issue

1 (cont.) *Viscount Anson m* 2nd 12 May 1955 Monica (*m* 4th 29 July 1959 (*divorce*) Lt-Col Eric Astley Cooper-Key, MBE, MC, Roy Norfolk Regt, only s of Capt Astley Dunas Cooper Cooper-Key, DSO, RN, and *d* 8 Nov 1969), formerly w of (a) Maj Peter Holdsworth Hunt, MC, Coldstream Gds, and (b) Robert Maxtone Inglis and only dau of Cdr Ralph Neville, RN (*see* BRAYBROOKE, B), and *d* 18 March 1958

2 Edward John; Lt RN WW II; *b* 19 Feb 1919; *das* following an accident 6 Oct 1943

1 *Betty Marjorie [The Lady Betty Winnington, 182 Rivermead Ct, Ranelagh Gdns, London SW6 3SG]; *b* 12 March 1917; *m* 20 May 1944 *Col Thomas Foley Churchill Winnington (*see* WINNINGTON, Bt) and has issue

2 Cecilia Evelyn; WRNS WW II; *m* 30 Sept 1947 (*divorce* 1961) Maj John Henry Wiggin (*see* WIGGIN, Bt) and *d* 16 Jan 1963, leaving issue

The **4th Earl** *m* 2nd 23 Feb 1949 Violet Margaret (*d* 1988), formerly w of Lt-Col Humphrey Burgoyne Philips, of Heybridge, Tean, Staffs, and yr dau of Henry Dawson Dawson-Greene, of Slyne and Whittington Hall, Lancs, and *d* 14 Sept 1960

Seat: Shugborough Hall, Staffs. Although the house has now been made over to the National Trust and is administered by Staffordshire County Council, Lord Lichfield is allowed to keep a suite of rooms for his own use and indeed some of his best landscape photographs have been taken at Shugborough. The house dates from the late 17th century, when the substantial main section was put up with its three floors. It was not till the 1740s that the wings were built. Although it was Thomas, elder brother of George Anson, the naval hero, who commissioned the work, his younger brother made a large fortune in prize money, particularly from his capture of the Acapulco treasure ship in 1743, and some of this funded the building programme, notably the various Greek Revival temples and summer houses scattered throughout the park by James 'Athenian' Stuart. Doubtless it was in gratitude as well as genuine admiration that Thomas put up a commemorative arch to his brother.

Samuel Wyatt later worked on the house too, his embellishments consisting chiefly of the bow-fronted addition to the main facade, the elliptical hall surrounded by scagliola pillars and the Red Room. The interior has important plasterwork by Joseph Rose.

LIFFORD

Arms: Gu. a chevron engrailed between three owls arg. **Crest:** On a stump of a tree, with one branch growing thereon, an owl, all ppr. **Supporters:** Dexter, a vulture or, wings inverted arg., gorged with a plain collar az., thereon three bezants; sinister, a griffin or, wings elevated arg., gorged as the dexter. **Motto:** Be just and fear not. **Creations:** B. (I) 9 Jan 1768, V. (I) 8 Jan 1781.

THE 9TH VISCOUNT LIFFORD, Co Donegal, and **Baron Lifford of Lifford**, Co Donegal ((Edward) James Wingfield Hewitt) [The Rt Hon The Viscount Lifford, Field House, Hursley, Hants SO21 2LE]; *b* 27 Jan 1949; *s f* 1987; *educ* Aiglon Coll Switzerland; memb London Stock Exchange, dir: Cobbold Neilson Ltd 1991–, City of Winchester Investments plc, Rathbone Bros plc and WCIMS plc; *m* 7 Feb 1976 *Alison Mary, dau of Robert Law, of Turnpike Ho, Withersfield, Suffolk, and has:

1 +JAMES THOMAS WINGFIELD; *b* 29 Sept 1979

1 *Annabel Louise; *b* 16 Jan 1978

2 *Alice Mary; *b* 14 Sept 1990

Lineage: JAMES HEWITT, of Churchtown, Rockcliffe, Cumberland; *m* Nov 1679 Mary Urwin and had:

WILLIAM HEWITT; mercer, draper, Mayor Coventry 1744; *b* 14 Sept 1683; *m* 1710 Hannah Lewis (*d* 4 April 1760) and *d* 22 Nov 1747, leaving. With two yr sons (William, Commr for sale of ceded lands W Indies 1766, *b* 3 Oct 1719, *d* unm 16 May 1781; Joseph, *b* 14 May 1725, *d* unm 1813):

JAMES HEWITT, **1st Viscount Lifford**, Co Donegal, so *cr* 8 Jan 1781, as also earlier 9 Jan 1768 BARON LIFFORD OF LIFFORD, Co Donegal (both I); *b* probably 1709; barrister Middle Temple 1742, Serjeant-at-law 1754, King's Serjeant 1759, MP (Whig) Coventry 1761–66, a Justice King's Bench 1766–68, Ld Chllr Ireland 1767–89, Ld Justice Ireland 1787; *m* 1st by 1750 Mary (*d* 1765), only dau of Ven Rice Williams, DD, Archdeacon Carmarthen and Preb Worcester, and had:

1 JAMES, **2nd Viscount**

2 William Williams; *m* 16 Dec 1773 Anne, only dau of Thomas Strettell, of Cork, and *d* April 1798, leaving two sons and three daus

3 Joseph; a Judge King's Bench Ireland 1791; *d* 1 April 1794

4 John (Very Rev); Dean Cloyne; *m* Aug 1779 Jane (*d* 22 May 1848), dau of Dr Moore, of Dorset St, Dublin, and *d* 14 May 1804, having had:

   (1) Mary; *m* 1802 Lt-Gen Hon Sir Henry King, KCB, and *d* 26 May 1821, leaving issue (see KINGSTON, E)

   (2) Jane; *m* 1 Dec 1824 Acheson St George (*d* 3 Dec 1855), of Woodpark, Co Armagh, and had issue

The **1st Viscount** *m* 2nd 15 Dec 1766 Ambrosia (*d* 26 March 1807), dau of Rev Charles Bayley, of Navestock, Essex, and by her had:

5 George; Offr 31st Foot; *d* 22 Feb 1792 unm

1 Ambrosia; *d* unm

2 Elizabeth; *d* unm

The 1st VISCOUNT *d* 28 April 1789; his est son,

Very Rev JAMES HEWITT, **2nd Viscount Lifford**; *b* 27 Oct 1750; *educ* Trin Coll Dublin and Ch Ch Oxford; Dean Armagh 1796–1830; *m* 1st 25 July 1776 Henrietta Judith (*dsp* 22 April 1778), est dau of 1st Viscount Harberton (*qv*); *m* 2nd 23 Dec 1781 Alicia (*d* 15 March 1845), est dau of Ven Rev John Oliver, DD, Archdeacon Ardagh, s of R Oliver, of Castle Oliver, Co Limerick, and by her had:

1 JAMES, **3rd Viscount**

2 James John Pratt (Rev); Rector Desterlyn; *b* 26 May 1796; *m* 1st 19 Oct 1819 Juliana (*d* 29 Aug 1827), dau of Alexander Hamilton, and had, with other issue:

   (1) James; *b* 19 Sept 1822; *m* 24 Sept 1846 Frances Dorothy (*m* 2nd 1 Aug 1853 Maj David Philip Brown, 7th Hus, and *d* 21 Jan 1900), only dau of Francis Synge Hutchinson (see SYNGE, Bt), and *d* 21 May 1851, having had:

      1a Louisa Frances; *m* 10 Sept 1870 Hon Arthur Cecil Crampton Plunket and *d* 3 Dec 1929, leaving issue (see PLUNKET, B)

2 (cont.) The Rev James Hewitt *m* 2nd 7 July 1829 Elizabeth (*d* 12 March 1886), dau of Rev Francis Gervais, of Cecil, Co Tyrone, and *d* 5 Jan 1880, having by her had, with other issue:

(2) James John (Rev); Vicar Pagham Sussex 1877–92, Rector Teffont Ewyas Wilts 1892–1912; *b* 22 April 1830; *educ* Trin Coll Dublin (BA); *d* 17 Feb 1913

(3) James Francis Katharinus; Bengal CS 1859–85; *b* 21 June 1835; *m* 10 March 1870 Constance (*d* 10 June 1908), yst dau of Edward Stanley, of Ponsonby Hall, Cumberland, and *d* 14 March 1908, having had:

   1a John Stanley; *b* 17 July 1875; *m* 15 Feb 1909 Avice Alureda (*d* 6 Feb 1939), est dau of Rev Arthur Langdale Langdale-Smith, Rector Holton, and *d* 6 Feb 1937, having had:

      1b Edward James Stanley; WW II with RE; *b* 6 Dec 1909; *d* unm 4 Dec 1959

      2b +Terence John Lifford [Terence Hewitt Esq, Holton Cottage, Holton, Wheatley, Oxon]; Lt 2nd/9th Gurkha Rifles WW II (POW); *b* 30 Aug 1911; *m* 26 April 1946 *Rowena Edith Mabel, 2nd dau of Ernest Daniel Taylor England, and has:

         1c *Anthea Avice Yvonne [Mrs Richard Kemp, Slaymaker, Holton, Oxon]; *b* 14 June 1947; *m* 12 Sept 1970 *Richard Geoffrey Horsford Kemp, est s of Athole Stephen Horsford Kemp, OBE, of Lockey Ho, Langford, Glos

      3b +Theodore Denis; Actg Capt 1st and 4th/9th Gurkha Rifles WW II; *b* 21 April 1918

   1b Constance Avice Irene; *b* 24 Jan, *d* 17 May 1916

2a Brian Lifford, OBE (1919); Cdr RN Boxer Rising China 1899–1900, WWs I and II, Sec Navy League, Order Crown Italy; *b* 17 Nov 1881; *m* 9 July 1914 Roie, dau of Alfred Nathan, of NZ, and *d* 5 Jan 1962, leaving:

   1b Michael James Alfred Lifford; *b* 6 June 1916; *m* 9 Jan 1947 Sybil Grace (*d* Sept 1995), yst dau of William Arthur Izard (see EGLINTON and WINTON, E), and *d* 1993, leaving:

      1c +Peter Lifford [Peter Hewitt Esq, 3 Kawau Rd, One Tree Hill, Auckland, New Zealand]; *b* 21 Jan 1948; *m* 1983 *Mary, dau of J A Parkinson, and has:

         1d +Christopher; *b* 1984

         1d *Ellen; *b* 1986

      2c +Anthony James [Anthony Hewitt Esq, 26 Martin Way, Woking, Surrey]; *b* 1951; *m* 1978 *Susan Elizabeth, dau of Lt-Col M J J Rolt, of Byfleet, and has:

         1d +Oliver Michael James; *b* 1985

         1d *Victoria Louise; *b* 1980

         2d *Emily Kate; *b* 1982

      1c *Rosemary Ruth [Mrs Geoffrey Brodie, 31 Carlton Mill Rd, Merivale, New Zealand]; *b* 1949; *m* 1975 *Geoffrey Martin Brodie and has:

         1d *Thomas Nathan; *b* 1982

         2d *Timothy Paul; *b* 1984

         1d *Caroline; *b* 1977

         2d *Amy; *b* 1979

      2c *Elizabeth Grace [Mrs Kevin Bradley, 36 Fancourt St, Meadowbank, Auckland, New Zealand]; *b* 1956; *m* 1990 *Kevin Francis Bradley and has:

         1d *Hamish Michael Patrick; *b* 1993

         2d *Samuel James Joseph; *b* 1994

         1d *Olivia Roie; *b* 1992

2b +Patrick Francis [Patrick Hewitt Esq, 31 Dell Ave, Remuera, Auckland, New Zealand]; *b* 5 Feb 1921; *m* 1st 10 July 1944 (*divorce*) Mary, dau of Trevor N Holmden, of Remuera; *m* 2nd 1954 *Judith, dau of John Hellaby, of Remuera, and by his 1st w has:

   1c +Brian James Lifford [Lt-Col Brian Hewitt, RMB 825, Birchmans Grove, via Bungendore, NSW 2621, Australia]; *b* 26 July 1945; Roy NZ Army 1965–87, active serv Vietnam 1969–70, Cwlth Monitoring Force Zimbabwe-Rhodesia 1979–80; Lt-Col Australian Army 1989–95; *m* 1st 1972 (*divorce* 1984) Erin Margaret, est dau of Keith Charles Walshe, of NZ, and has:

      1d +Richard James Lifford; *b* 1975

      1d *Rebecca Roie Cecilia; *b* 1978

   1c (cont.) Lt-Col Brian Hewitt *m* 2nd 1984 *Julie Margaret-Anne, est dau of Maurice James Beuth, of Ashburton, NZ, and by her has:

      2d *Danielle Margaret; *b* 1985

      3d *Antonia Julie; *b* 1987

1a Averil Mary; Anglican nun Malvern Link, Worcs; *d* 11 May 1963

2a Beatrix Constance Henrietta; *m* 6 July 1910 Charles Alexander Mackenzie, s of Gen Colin Mackenzie, and *d* Nov 1934

(4) James Charles Archibald, JP and DL Herefs; 24th Foot; *b* 17 March 1837; *m* 18 May 1870 Jane Harvey (*d* 17 Nov 1919), dau of Zaccheus Andrew, RN, and *d* 23 Oct 1910, leaving:

   1a HAROLD later HARALD (deed poll 2 July 1929) Charles Harvey; *b* 15 May 1873; *educ* Trin Coll Cambridge (BA); *d* unm 31 May 1936

   2a John Wilfred, JP Herefs; barrister Inner Temple 1901; *b* 29 May 1876; *m* 12 Aug 1903 Florence Mabel (*d* by 1946), dau of W Laurence, of Meldon Ho, Weston-super-Mare, and *d* 12 Aug 1946, having had:

      1b James Andrew; *b* 12 March 1914; *d* 29 April 1924

   3a Cecil James; Lt Gren Gds (SR) WW I (wounded twice); *b* 31 Jan 1882; *m* 30 Dec 1916 Katherine Sybil Learmonth, dau of R-Adml Norman Craig Palmer, CVO, and *d* 23 May 1951, having had:

      1b Anthony; *b* 1919; *kas* 19–

   1a Ella Charlotte; *b* 9 Feb 1872; *d* 8 Aug 1884

   2a Kathleen Susanna Jane; *b* 16 Nov 1878; *d* unm 29 Oct 1936

(5) James Dudley Ryder; Capt RN; *b* 17 Nov 1840; *m* 6 Sept 1873 Thomasine (*d* 1942), dau of Daniel Riddeford, and *d* May 1913, leaving:

   1a John Edward; *b* 29 June 1874; *m* 30 Jan 1901 Ellen Edith (*d* 28 Jan 1958), dau of V T Hitchings, of Woodstock, Levin, NZ, and *d* 21 June 1949, leaving:

1b William Robert Riddiford; *b* 17 July 1903; *m* 8 April 1930 Nancy Charlotte Ellen (*d* 1988), dau of Sydney Arthur Robert Mair, of NZ, and *d* 1976, leaving:

  1c Ian Robert; *b* 28 July 1931; *m* 1955 *Jean Hamilton, dau of Henry Nicholas Johnson, MD, and *d* 1992, leaving:

    1d +Robert Johnson [Robert Hewitt Esq, Nokomai, Hanmer Springs, New Zealand]; *b* 1962; *m* 1992 *Margot Joan, dau of Ian Hanmer Atkinson, of Hanmer Springs, and has:

      1e +William Ian Atkinson; *b* 1994

    1d *Louise Johnson; *b* 1958; *m* 1983 *Malcolm Lawrence Sincock and has:

      1e *James Robert; *b* 1986

      2e *Matthew Thomas; *b* 1990

      1e *Tara Jane; *b* 1985

    2d *Mary-Anne Johnson; *b* 1959; *m* 1984 *Christopher William and has:

      1e *Rebecca Mary; *b* 1989

      2e *Stephanie Louise; *b* 1991

  2c +Peter David [Peter Hewitt Esq, Balfour Farm, RD4, Pahiatua, New Zealand]; *b* 28 Aug 1937; *m* 8 June 1963 *Heather Jean, dau of Robert Allen Donald, and has:

    1d +James Donald; *b* 15 Dec 1965; *m* 1991 *Susan Jean, dau of David Petersen, of Waipukurau, NZ, and has:

      1e +Hamish William; *b* 21 Aug 1996

      1e *Anna Charlotte; *b* 6 May 1994

    2d +Peter John; *b* 9 Jan 1967; *m* 1998 *Jody Lee, dau of Perry Jones, of Bull, NZ

    3d +Timothy David; *b* 19 Nov 1968; *m* 1995 *Nicola Jane, dau of Geoffrey Dunn, of Waipukurau, NZ, and has:

      1e +George Geoffrey; *b* 17 March 1996

      2e +Edward Alexander; *b* 17 March 1996

    1d *Teena Anne; *b* 5 May 1964; *m* 1994 *Stephen Scoular Richards, of Windwhistle, Canterbury, NZ, and has:

      1e *James Francis; *b* 7 March 1996

  1c *Judith Anne [Mrs John Armstrong, 121a Waiwhetu Rd, Lower Hutt, New Zealand]; *b* 19 Aug 1936; *m* 24 April 1965 *John Henry Armstrong, s of Lt-Col John Dickenson Armstrong, and has:

    1d *Jane Margaret; *b* 30 July 1966; *m* 1994 *Paul Andrew Hanson

    2d *Kate Amanda; *b* 1969

    3d *Nicola Anne; *b* 1972

1b *Helen Mary Gervais; *b* 24 Jan 1902; *m* 16 Dec 1926 Thomas Westbury Abraham (*d* 29 Jan 1968), s of Lionel Abraham, and has:

  1c *David Thomas; *b* 22 Dec 1937; *m* 19 Oct 1963 *Susan Winifred Nelson and has:

    1d *Thomas Nelson; *b* 29 Aug 1968

    1d *Nicola Jane; *b* 4 March 1967

  2c *Brian Lionel John; *b* 13 Jan 1940; *m* 17 Dec 1968 *Diana Margaret Cranstone

  1c *Mary Helen [Mrs John Collier, 17 Higgins St, Marewa, Napier, New Zealand]; *b* 22 Aug 1932; *m* 18 Oct 1957 *John Ernest Collier, s of C A Collier, and has:

    1d *David John; *b* 30 Aug 1961

    1d *Susan Mary; *b* 11 Sept 1959

2a Dudley Riddiford, CIE (1919); Lt-Col IA, Boer War, WW I, WW II CD; *b* 30 March 1877; *m* 1905 Marjorie Middlemas (*d* 1954), yr dau of William Fleming Inglis, of Shanghai, and *d* 1971, leaving:

  1b *Dorothy Mary Riddiford [Mrs William Lysley, Flint House, Gt Barton, Suffolk IP31 2SW]; *b* 1914; *m* 19 May 1948 Capt William James Lysley, 11th Hus (*d* 19–), est s of Maj William Lowther Lysley, JP, of Pewsham Ho, Chippenham, Wilts, and has:

    1c *Rachel Marjorie Sarah Anne; *b* 19 Oct 1949; *m* 1979 *Michael Norman Scott Ruddock and has:

      1d *Alexander James Scott; *b* 1984

      1d *Camilla Dorothy Scott; *b* 1982

  2b *Patricia Frances Thomasine; *b* 1916; *m* 1st 5 Oct 1940 Capt Herbert Eldon Hope, RA (*d* 2 Feb 1946), er s of Herbert Ashworth Hope, and has:

    1c *Michael Lifford Ashworth; Capt 14th/20th King's Hus; *b* 16 June 1942; *m* 21 Jan 1966 *Alison, dau of Brig Ernest Shaw Lough, MBE, S Staffs Regt, and has:

      1d *Simon Ashworth; *b* 7 June 1967

      2d *Justin William Ashworth; *b* 19 June 1969

    2c *Jeremy Fleming Ashworth [Capt Jeremy Hope, c/o Lloyds Bank Ltd, Wincanton, Somerset]; Capt 14th/20th King's Hus; *b* 24 May 1944; *m* 22 Oct 1966 *Rosemary Ann, dau of Cdr Alfred Coxon, RN

    1c *Sally Patricia Ashworth; *b* 24 May 1944; *m* 13 Aug 1965 *Christopher John Russell, s of Herbert Francis Russell, of Major's Green, Solihull, Warwicks, and has:

      1d *Kimberley Hope; *b* 23 April 1967

  2b (cont.) Mrs Herbert Hope *m* 2nd 1 May 1948 (*divorce* 1958) Lt-Col Gilbert Hannington, REME, 2nd s of R A G Hannington; *m* 3rd 1959 Lt-Col Brian Charles Lascelles Tayleur, OBE, 14th/20th King's Hus, s of Brig Charles Lancelot Oliver Tayleur, DSO

3a James Francis Daniel; *b* 7 April 1881; *m* 1st 18 Feb 1908 Ellen Westbury (*d* 19 July 1938), dau of R S Abraham, of Palmerston North, NZ; *m* 2nd 1942 May Evelyn (*m* 2nd Maunchell Hobbs), dau of E J Wright, and *d* 22 June 1963, having by his 1st w had:

  1b Richard Walter; *b* 1909; *m* 1951 *Joan Millicent [Mrs Richard Hewitt, 35 Kitchener St, Masterton, New Zealand], dau of Thomas Edward Holdgate, and *d* 1974, leaving:

  1c +Timothy James [Timothy Hewitt Esq, Taratanui, Ponatahi, Carterton, Wellington, New Zealand]; *b* 1954; *m* 1978 *Judith Clair, dau of Trevor Simson, and has:

    1d +Richard James; *b* 1979

    2d +Thomas Cameron; *b* 1987

    1d *Catherine Jane; *b* 1981

  1c *Mary Ellen [Mrs David Hadfield, Kelmarsh, Valley Rd, Paraparaumu, Wellington, New Zealand]; *b* 1952; *m* 1975 *David Carleton Hadfield, est s of Barry Hadfield, and has:

    1d *Richard Henry; *b* 1979

    2d *Samuel Mark; *b* 1984

    1d *Melissa Maisie; *b* 1976

2b James; *b* 1911; *m* 1945 *Frances Meta, dau of F Unlacke, of Stratford, NZ

1b *June Lifford [Mrs Robert Young, 14 Matenga St, Walkanae, New Zealand]; *b* 1910; *m* 1934 *Robert Oswald Young, est s of Maj-Gen Robert Young, CB, CMG, DSO, and has:

  1c *Robin Slingsby; *b* 1935

  2c *Simon Vivian Riddiford; *b* 1936

  3c *James Francis; *b* 1940

  4c *Thomas Lifford; *b* 1951

  1c *Ellen Jennifer; *b* 1938

4a Charles Horace Gervais; *b* 1885; *m* 1911 Elsie Mary (*d* 1974), er dau of Herbert Pryce, and *d* 7 Aug 1970, having had:

  1b Beryl Elizabeth; *b* 1912; *d* unm 23 Oct 1963

  2b *Cushla Mary; *b* 1916

  3b *Ruth Lifford; *b* 1918

5a Arthur Lifford Oliver; Lt Wellington NZ Mtd Inf; *b* 1888; *d* of wounds recd in action Gallipoli 1916

1a Hallette Thomasine Elizabeth; *b* 13 April 1879; *m* 27 Jan 1904 Daniel Jarvis Willis, 2nd s of Maj Willis, and had issue

2a Alice Margaret; *b* 1883

(6) James Robert Silver Oliver; Col RA; *b* 10 Oct 1844; *m* 20 July 1880 Celina, dau of John Metayer, of Quebec, and *dsp* 6 April 1899

The 2nd VISCOUNT *d* 15 April 1830; his er son,

JAMES HEWITT, **3rd Viscount Lifford**; *b* 29 Aug 1783; *educ* Ch Ch Oxford; Sheriff Co Donegal 1815, Resident Commr Excise Scotland 1823–32; *m* 15 April 1809 Mary Anne (*d* 3 Jan 1877), 8th dau of 1st Viscount Hawarden (*qv*), and *d* 22 April 1855, having had, with other issue, including a dau (Alicia Anne, *m* 15 April 1841 Sir Edwin Pearson, FRS, and *d* 8 March 1895, leaving issue):

JAMES HEWITT, **4th Viscount Lifford**, DL (Co Donegal); *b* 31 March 1811; *educ* Ch Ch Oxford; Sheriff Co Donegal 1841, rep I peer 1856–87; author: *Ireland and the Irish Church* (1842), *Thoughts on the Present State of Ireland* (1849) and *A Plea for Irish Landlords* (1867); *m* 1st 9 July 1835 Lady Mary Acheson (*d* 13 March 1850), dau of 2nd Earl of Gosford (*qv*), and *d* 20 Nov 1887, having had:

  1 JAMES WILFRID HEWITT, **5th Viscount Lifford**, JP Co Donegal; *b* 12 Oct 1837; *educ* Rugby; Ensign 4th Foot 1856, Lt 3rd Foot 1857, Hon Col Donegal Roy Field Res Artillery; *m* 4 July 1867 Annie Frances (*d* 12 April 1927), est dau of Sir Arthur Hodgson, KCMG, of Clopton, Warwicks, and Qld, and *dsp* 20 March 1913

  2 Evelyn John, Lt RA; *b* 19 July 1842; *d* 4 July 1867

  3 ARCHIBALD ROBERT HEWITT, **6th Viscount Lifford**; *b* 14 Jan 1844; RNB: joined 1858, ret as Capt 1890; *m* 5 Dec 1878 Helen Blanche (*d* 4 June 1942), only dau of Charles S Geach, and *d* 22 May 1925, having had:

    (1) EVELYN JAMES HEWITT, **7th Viscount Lifford**, DSO (1916) and bar (1918); *b* 18 Dec 1880; *educ* Haileybury; Lt-Col Dorset Regt, Boer War 1902, WW I (despatches); *m* 8 July 1919 Charlotte Rankine (*d* 2 April 1954), widow of Capt Edgar Walker (*see* WALKER, Bt, of Sand Hutton) and yr dau of Sir Robert Maule, of Edinburgh, and *dsp* 5 April 1954

    (2) Archibald Rodney, DSO; Capt E Surrey Regt WW I (despatches); *b* 25 May 1883; *ka* 25 April 1915

    (1) Norah; *b* 5 Nov 1879

    (2) Anne Rachel Millicent; *b* 26 Nov 1885; *m* 11 April 1917 Maj Melvil Farrant, RFA (*d* 29 June 1961), yr s of Col Henry Cecil Binstead Farrant, Roy N Lancs Regt, and *d* 25 May 1967, leaving:

      1a *Michael Rodney; *b* 1918; *educ* Blundell's; served WW II

      2a *Anthony; *b* 6 Dec 1919; Maj Border Regt WW II; *m* 21 May 1960 *Kathleen Joan, widow of Peter Kirkland Rylands, of Moore, Warrington, and 2nd dau of Surgn-Cdr Richard Connell, RN

  4 Cornwallis Charles (Rev); Preb Tuam; *b* 3 March 1847; *m* 7 Dec 1881 Maria (*d* 19 Aug 1882), dau of Sir Edmund Samuel Hayes, 3rd Bt, of Drumboe (*see* 1896 edn), and *dsp* 4 Sept 1889

  5 Edward, JP Denbighs and Wilts; *b* 31 March 1848; *m* 10 Dec 1890 Evelyn Frances Charlotte (*d* 17 June 1956), dau of Edmond Robert Stronge (*see* STRONGE, Bt), and *d* 4 Sept 1931

  1 Mary Anne; *m* 4 Sept 1866 John Gathorne Wood (*d* 3 Aug 1929), of Thedden Grange, Hants, and *d* 27 May 1913, leaving issue

  2 Isabella; *m* 7 Jan 1879 Richard Southby and *d* 19 March 1924, leaving issue

The **4th Viscount** *m* 2nd 9 Dec 1851 Lydia Lucy (*d* 28 April 1919), widow of Charles Purdon Coote, JP, DL (*see* COOTE, Bt), and est dau of Rev John Digby Wingfield Digby, Vicar Coleshill, and by her had:

6 William James, JP Fife; *b* 6 April 1836; *educ* Bromsgrove and Trin Coll Dublin; *m* 26 April 1887 Evelyn Frances (*d* 21 Oct 1946), yst dau of Lt-Gen Francis Carey, and *d* 28 Oct 1948, having had:

(1) James Francis; Lt 1st Bn Scottish Rifles; *b* 23 Jan 1888; *ka* 26 Oct 1914

(2) William George; Lt 3rd Bn Royal Scots; *b* 7 June 1892; *ka* 13–14 Oct 1914

7 George Wyldbore, JP Hants; *b* 16 Nov 1858; *m* 24 Jan 1891 Elizabeth Mary (*d* 24 May 1959), est dau of Charles Rampini, DL, LLD, and *d* 23 April 1924, leaving:

(1) Denis George Wyldbore, VC; 2nd Lt Hants Regt; *b* 18 Dec 1897; *ka* 31 July 1917

(2) ALAN WILLIAM WINGFIELD, 8th Viscount

3 Lettice Lucy; *m* 4 Feb 1875 Capt Alexander William Maxwell Clark Kennedy, DL, Coldstream Gds (*d* 21 Dec 1894), of Knockgray, Scotland, and *d* 13 Aug 1930, leaving issue

4 Alice Anne; *m* 25 July 1878 Sir Samuel Hercules Hayes, 4th Bt (*d* 7 Nov 1901), of Drumboe Castle, Co Donegal, and *d* 11 Feb 1943, leaving issue

5 Georgiana Rosamund; *m* 13 Dec 1883 John Kenelm Digby Wingfield Digby (*d* 25 Dec 1904), of Sherborne Castle, Dorset, and *d* 9 May 1887 aged 29, leaving issue

6 Anne Eliza; *d unm* 5 Sept 1957 in her 98th year

The 7th VISCOUNT's cousin,

ALAN WILLIAM WINGFIELD HEWITT, **8th Viscount Lifford**; *b* 11 Dec 1900; *educ* Winchester and RMC Sandhurst; Lt Hants Regt; *m* 16 Jan 1935 *Alison Mary Patricia [The Rt Hon Mary Viscountess Lifford, The Barn, Hursley, Hants], 2nd dau of Thomas Wingrave Ashton, of The Cottage, Hursley, and *d* 1987, leaving:

1 (EDWARD) JAMES WINGFIELD HEWITT, **9th and present Viscount Lifford**

1 *Lydia Mary (does not use courtesy title) [Mrs Lydia Swann, Quedley Farm, Flimwell, Wadhurst, E Sussex]; *b* 10 May 1938; *m* 24 April 1965 (*divorce* 1983) Michael Christopher Swann, only s of Sir Antony Charles Christopher Swann, 3rd Bt (*qv*), and has issue

2 *Belinda Anne [The Hon Mrs Warburton, The Rectory, Hartley Wintney, Hants]; *b* 21 Dec 1939; *m* 27 July 1963 *Rev Piers Eliot de Dutton Warburton, er s of Piers Grove Eliot Warburton, of Kingsworthy Court, Winchester, Hants, and has:

(1) *(Piers) Richard Grove; *b* 24 Sept 1964

(1) *Elizabeth Jane; *b* 22 Aug 1967

3 *Flora Elizabeth; *b* 19 Feb 1947; *m* 11 Aug 1965 (*divorce* 1975) Edward Bell Henderson, only s of Dr Edward Henderson, of New York, and has:

(1) *Samantha Elizabeth; *b* 20 April 1967

(2) *Victoria Amanda; *b* 2 April 1971

LIGHTON

Fortitudine et prudentia

Arms: Barry of eight argent and vert, over all a lion rampant crowned with an Eastern crown or, armed and langued azure, a canton of Ireland. **Crest:** A lion's head erased, crowned with an Eastern crown or, langued azure. **Motto:** *Fortitudine et prudentia* ('By fortitude and prudence'). **Creation:** Bt. (I) 1 March 1791.

SIR THOMAS HAMILTON LIGHTON, 9TH BT, of Merville, Co Dublin [Sir Thomas Lighton Bt, c/o Waddington Galleries, 11 Cork St, London W1X 2LT]; *b* 4 Nov 1954; *s f* 1993; *educ* Eton; Chm Soc London Art Dealers 1993–95; *m* 1990 *Belinda Jean, er dau of John Fergusson, of Barnhillies, Castle Douglas, Kirkcudbrightshire, and has:

1 +JAMES CHRISTOPHER HAMILTON; *b* 20 Oct 1992

2 +Harry John Hamilton (twin); *b* 1992

3 +A son; *b* 1994

1 *Celina Hamilton; *b* 1991

Lineage: JOHN LIGHTON, of Glasgow; *m* Catherine, dau of Thomas Bond, of Bond's Glen, Co Derry, and had:

JOHN LIGHTON, of Raspberry Hill, Co Derry; *m* Elizabeth, dau of John Walker, of Tisdern, Co Tyrone, and had:

Sir Thomas Lighton, 1st Bt (I), so *cr* 1 March 1791, of Merville, Co Dublin, MP, High Sheriff Co Dublin 1790; *m* 11 Dec 1777 Anne (*d* 1804), dau of William Pollock, of Strabane, Co Tyrone, and *d* 27 April 1805, having had, with other issue:

1 **Sir Thomas Lighton, 2nd Bt**; *b* 19 May 1787; *m* 14 Dec 1811 Sylvia, dau of John Brandon, and *d* 11 May 1816, leaving:

(1) **Sir Thomas Lighton, 3rd Bt**; *d* in infancy 1817

2 JOHN (Sir), **4th Bt**

1 Elizabeth; *m* Sir Samuel Hayes, Bt

The 3rd Bt's uncle,

Rev Sir John Lighton, 4th Bt; *b* 1 Jan 1792; Rector Donoughmore, Co Donegal; *m* 23 Jan 1817 Mary Hamilton, 2nd dau of Christopher Robert Pemberton, MD (descended from 1st Lord Paisley; *see* ABERCORN, D), of Newton, Cambs, by Eleanora, dau of James Hamilton, of Woodbrooke, Strabane, by Eleanor, sis of 1st Earl Castle Stewart (*qv*), and *d* 5 April 1827, having had, with other issue:

1 **Sir John Hamilton Lighton, 5th Bt**; *b* 26 May 1818; *d unm* 29 April 1844

2 CHRISTOPHER ROBERT (Sir), **6th Bt**

3 Andrew; *b* 26 Dec 1822; MA Cantab; Capt 4th Bn Gloucester Regt; *m* 25 May 1860 Eliza Amelia (*d* 11 Jan 1899), yst dau of Henry Sumner Joyce, of Freshford, Somerset, and *dsp* 13 Nov 1904

The 5th Bt's bro,

Rev Sir Christopher Robert Lighton, 6th Bt; *b* 28 May 1819; *educ* St John's Coll Cambridge (MA); Vicar Ellastone, Staffs; *m* 2 June 1843 Mary Anne Elizabeth (*d* 22 March 1902), only dau of Rev Digby Joseph Stopford Ram, of Brookville, Co Cork, and had, with other issue:

1 CHRISTOPHER ROBERT (Sir), **7th Bt**

2 Andrew Hamilton Digby; *b* 28 April 1850; RN; *m* 11 Feb 1897 Anna Elizabeth (*d* 1 April 1931), dau of Count van Zuylen van Nyevelt, of The Hague, Netherlands, memb Cncl of State, and *d* 4 March 1929

3 John Hamilton Plumptre; *b* 26 June 1855; *k* when hit by a cricket ball 6 July 1872

4 Claud Hamilton Dallas (Rev); *b* 19 Oct 1860; *educ* Clare Coll Cambridge (MA); Rector Credenhill Herefs 1910–23; *m* 30 April 1895 Georgina Caroline, dau of Rev Patrick Leslie Miller and widow of H H Taylor, of Thurnscoe, Yorks, and *d* 23 April 1938

1 Eleanor Anne Pemberton; *m* 24 April 1877 Rev Robert Hereford (*d* April 1894), Rector Mordiford, 2nd s of Richard Hereford, of Sufton Court, Herefs, and *d* 27 June 1929, leaving issue

2 Emily Stuart Hamilton; *d unm* 25 March 1943

3 Isabel Penelope Hamilton; *d unm* 15 April 1950

The 6th Bt *d* 12 April 1875; his est son,

Sir Christopher Robert Lighton, 7th Bt, JP and DL (Herefs); *b* 4 July 1848; *educ* Repton and Trin Coll Cambridge (BA 1870); barrister 1874; High Sheriff Herefs 1885; *m* 6 April 1880 Helen Frances (*d* 12 Jan 1927), est dau of James Houldsworth, JP, DL, of Coltness, Lanarks, and had issue:

1 CHRISTOPHER ROBERT (Sir), **8th Bt**

1 Mabel Katharine Mary; *b* 24 Aug 1888; *d* 19 Nov 1972

2 Winifred Helen; *b* 12 Jan 1891; *m* 11 May 1922 Horatio John Ross (*d* 19 Aug 1965), est s of Edward C R Ross, of Rossie Castle, Forfar, and had issue

3 Florence Hamilton; *b* 26 Jan 1894; *m* 25 Oct 1923 Maj Alexander Caldwell Stewart, MC, The Cameronians (*d* 8 Feb 1927), 2nd s of Sir Robert King Stewart, KBE, of Murdostoun, and had issue

The 7th Bt *d* 15 Aug 1929; his only son,

Sir Christopher Robert Lighton, 8th Bt, MBE (1945), JP (Somerset); *b* 30 June 1897; *educ* Eton and RMC Sandhurst; WW I KRRC (wounded), WW II Lt-Col War Office; *m* 1st 4 Nov 1926 (*divorce* Scottish Courts 1953) Rachel Gwendoline, yr dau of R-Adml Walter Somerville Goodridge, CIE, of Rudgwick Grange, Rudgwick, Sussex, and had:

1 *Bridget Mary [Mrs Anthony Lithgow, c/o Barclays Bank Ltd, Oakham, Rutland]; *b* 29 Oct 1927; *m* 6 Nov 1949 Brig Anthony Onslow Lawrence Lithgow, MC, The Black Watch (*d* 1988), yr s of Capt Douglas Plenderleath Lithgow, Roy Dragoons, of South Newington, Banbury, Oxon, by Dorothy Kathleen, only dau of Maj Arthur Hughes-Onslow (*see* ONSLOW, E), and has:

(1) *Nigel Christopher Douglas; *b* 4 Sept 1950; *educ* Harrow and RMA Sandhurst; commnd Black Watch

(1) *Sara Vivienne Hamilton; *b* 15 April 1952

(2) *Clare Grania Bridget; *b* 25 May 1953

2 *Virginia Hamilton; *b* 4 July 1929

Sir Christopher *m* 2nd 26 June 1953 Horatia Edith, dau of Armand Temple Powlett, of Godminster Manor, Bruton, Somerset, and by her had:

1 Sir THOMAS HAMILTON LIGHTON, **9th and present Bt**

Sir Christopher *m* 3rd 1985 *Eve, only dau of R-Adml Alexander Livingston Penrose Mark-Wardlaw, of Loseberry, Claygate, Surrey, and widow of Maj Henry Stopford Chetwode Ram, RE, and *d* 1993

LILFORD

Arms: Or a lion's gamb bendwise erased between two cross crosslets fitcheé gu. **Crest:** A bear's gamb erased and erect gu., holding a sceptre, also erect, headed with a fleur-de-lys or.
Supporters: Dexter, a reaper with ears of corn round his hat, a reap-hook in his exterior hand and a garb erect at his feet, all ppr.; sinister, a soldier of the Northamptonshire Yeomanry Cavalry, habited vert, doubled buff, booted, his exterior hand resting upon his sword, the point on the ground, all ppr. **Motto:** *Parta tueri* ('Acquisitions are to be guarded'). **Creation:** B. (GB) 26 Oct 1797.

THE 7TH BARON LILFORD OF LILFORD, Co Northampton (George Vernon Powys) [The Rt Hon The Lord Lilford, Le Grand Câtelet, St John, Jersey JE3 4FL]; *b* 8 Jan 1931; *s* kinsman 1949; *educ* Stonyhurst; *m* 1st July 1954 (*divorce*) Mrs Eveline Bird; *m* 2nd 29 June 1957 (*divorce* 1958) Anuta, only dau of L F Merritt, of Johannesburg, and Mrs H F Crossland, of Zambia; *m* 3rd 12 Sept 1958 (*divorce* 1961) Norma Yvonne, only dau of V Shell, of Johannesburg; *m* 4th 23 Dec 1961 (*divorce* 1969) Muriel Norma, formerly w of Nigel Spottiswoode and dau of — Cooke, and by her has:

1 *Clare Lynette; *b* 2 April 1962
2 *Emma-Jane; *b* 20 April 1964

The 7th BARON *m* 5th 7 Aug 1969 (*divorce* 1991) Margaret Penman and by her has:

1 +MARK VERNON; *b* 16 Nov 1975
3 *Sarah Margaret; *b* 1971
4 *Hannah Victoria; *b* 1974

Lineage: WILLIAM POWYS; *m* Emma — (living 1313) and had:

THOMAS POWYS; had:

RICHARD POWYS; had:

JOHN POWYS, of Myfod/Myvott, Montgomeryshire; had, with two est sons (Edward; Morris) and a 4th s (Lewis, ancestor of the POWYSes of Cockshoulton, Salop):

JAMES POWYS; had, with an er s (Humphrey):

WILLIAM POWYS, of Ludlow, Salop; *b* 1465; *m* 1st Anne — and had three sons; *m* 2nd Margaret, dau of Richard Rowbury, and by her had, with four yr sons (including Edward, of Ludlow; John, of Brindrinock, ancestor of the POWYSes of Berwick Ho and of Westwood) and two daus:

THOMAS POWYS, of Snitton, Salop; *b* 1558; *m* Elizabeth, dau of Richard Smith, of Credenhill, Herefs, and *d* 19 Nov 1639, having had, with other issue (including Christopher; Peter, *m* 1st Elizabeth, dau of William Cupper, and 2nd Jane, dau and heiress of John Morris, of Rochford) an est s:

THOMAS POWYS, of Henley Hall, Bitterley, Salop; Serjeant-at-law, Bencher Lincoln's Inn; *b* 1620; *m* 1st Anne, dau of Sir Adam Littleton, 1st Bt, of Stoke Milburgh, Ch Justice of N Wales, a descendant of Sir Thomas Littleton, author of the *Treatise on Tenures* (see HATHERTON, B), and had, with other issue:

1 Littleton (Sir), of Henley Hall; Bencher Lincoln's Inn, Ch Justice N Wales 1692, Baron Exchequer 1695–1720, Judge King's Bench 1720–26; *b* 1647; *m* Agnes Carter (*dsp*) and *d* 13 March 1731
2 THOMAS (Sir)
1 Anne; *m* 1697 Andrew Hill, of Court of Hill, of the sr branch of the HILLs of Hawkestone

THOMAS POWYS *m* 2nd Mary, dau of John Cotes, of Woodcote, Salop, and by her had five sons and a dau

The 2nd son of the first marriage,
Sir THOMAS POWYS, of Lilford, Northants, which Manor he bought 1711; Slr-Gen 1686, ktd 1686, Attorney Gen 1687, Judge Queen's Bench 1713; *m* 1st Sarah, dau of Ambrose Holbech, of Mollington, Warwicks, and had, with other issue:

1 THOMAS
Sir THOMAS *m* 2nd Elizabeth, dau of Sir Philip Medows, and by her had:

2 Philip; *m* Isabella, only child and heiress of Richard Lybbe, of Hardwick, and was ancestor of the POWYS-LYBBEs of Hardwick

Sir THOMAS *d* 4 April 1719; his er son,
THOMAS POWYS, of Lilford; *m* Catherine, dau and coheir of Thomas Ravenscroft, of Broadlane, Flints, and *d* 1720, leaving:

THOMAS POWYS, of Lilford; *b* 24 Sept 1719; inherited the Salop estate from his great-uncle Sir Littleton Powys 1731; *m* 1740 Henrietta, dau of Thomas Spence, of Palgrave, Northants, Serjeant H of C, and *d* 2 April 1767, having had, with a yr s (Littleton (Rev), Rector Tichmarsh and Thorpe, Northants, *m* 21 Nov 1778 Maria Priscilla (*d* 21 Dec 1833), dau of Rev George Shaw and aunt of Viscount Eversley, GCB (see 1928 edn), and had issue) and two daus:

THOMAS POWYS, **1st Baron Lilford of Lilford**, Co Northampton (UK), so *cr* 26 Oct 1797; *b* 4 March 1743; *educ* Eton and King's Coll Cambridge; High Sheriff Northants 1768–69, MP Northants 1774–97 (Whig to 1793, Pittite thereafter); *m* 31 March 1772 Mary (*d* Jan 1823), dau of Galfridus Mann (see CORNWALLIS, B) and sis of Sir Horace Mann, 2nd Bt, and had, with other issue:

1 THOMAS, **2nd Baron**
2 Littleton (Rev); *b* 23 Jan 1781; Rector Tichmarsh, Northants; *m* 24 July 1809 Penelope (*d* 22 Nov 1864), dau of James Hatsell, of Morden Park, and *d* 22 Jan 1842, having had, with five daus:
1 Littleton POWYS later HATSELL-POWYS (roy licence 18 March 1853); *d* 10 Aug 1878
2 Frederick (Rev); *b* 13 March 1782; *m* 15 Oct 1807 Mary (*d* 19 Jan 1837), sis of 19th Lord (Baron) Grey (of Ruthin) (see GREY, B), and *d* 21 Dec 1850, leaving, with other issue:
(1) Spencer Merceval (Rev); Rector Achurch, Northants; *b* 27 March 1814; *m* 1st 21 June 1852 Harriet (*d* 7 Jan 1856), est dau of William Hole, of London; *m* 2nd 8 Oct 1857 Caroline (*d* 24 Feb 1867), yst dau of T G R Bishop, and *dsp* 17 Aug 1868
(1) Barbara Yelverton; *m* 17 Sept 1844 Roger Dawson, of Tyddynroe, nr St Asaph, and *d* 9 Nov 1887 aged 78, leaving issue
3 Henry; Capt 83rd Regt; *d* of wounds Peninsular War April 1812
1 Eleanor; *m* 1800 Rev Hon Richard Bruce Stopford, 4th s of 2nd Earl of Courtown (*qv*), and *d* his widow 10 Dec 1854

The 1st BARON *d* 26 Jan 1800; his est son,
THOMAS POWYS, **2nd Baron Lilford of Lilford**; *b* 8 April 1775; *educ* Eton and St John's Coll Cambridge; *m* 5 Dec 1797 Henrietta Maria (*d* 11 Aug 1820), est dau and coheir of Robert Vernon ATHERTON formerly GUILLYM, of Atherton Hall, Lancs, by Henrietta Maria, est dau and coheir of Peter Legh (see LEIGH, B) and first cousin of George Anthony Legh-Keck, of Stoughton Grange, Leics, and Bank Hall (*d* 4 Sept 1860), whose latter estate passed to the Barons Lilford, and *d* 4 July 1825, having had:

1 THOMAS ATHERTON POWYS, **3rd Baron Lilford**; *b* 2 Dec 1801; *educ* Eton and Ch Ch Oxford; a Ld Bedchamber 1831–35 and 1835–37, a Ld in waiting 1837–41; *m* 20 May 1830 Hon Mary Elizabeth Fox (*d* 7 Dec 1891), dau of 3rd Baron Holland of Foxley (see ILCHESTER, E), and *d* 15 March 1861, having had:

(1) THOMAS LITTLETON POWYS, **4th Baron Lilford**; *b* 18 March 1833; *educ* Harrow and Ch Ch Oxford; author: *Birds of the British Isles*; *m* 1st 14 June 1859 Emma Elizabeth (*d* 9 July 1884), yst dau of Robert William Brandling, of Low Gosforth, Northumberland, and had:
1a Thomas Atherton; *b* 5 April 1861; *educ* Eton; Lt 4th Bn Northants Regt; *d* unm 22 Nov 1882
2a JOHN POWYS, **5th Baron Lilford**, DL; *b* 12 Jan 1863; *educ* BNC Oxford; Capt and Hon Maj 3rd Bn Northants Regt; *m* 9 Aug 1894 Milly Louisa Isabella (*d* 8 April 1940), est dau of George William Culme Soltau-Symons, of Chaddlewood, Devon, and *d* 17 Dec 1945, having had:
1b Thomas Atherton; *b* 8 May 1896; *d* 3 Aug 1909
3a STEPHEN POWYS, **6th Baron Lilford**; *b* 8 March 1869; *educ* Harrow and Trin Coll Cambridge (BA 1890); Kt SMO Malta; *d* unm 19 Sept 1949
(1) (cont.) The **4th Baron** *m* 2nd 21 July 1885 Clementina, OStJ (*d* 7 April 1929), 2nd dau of Kerr Baillie Hamilton, CB (see HADDINGTON, E), and *d* 17 June 1896
(2) Leopold William Henry POWYS later FOX-POWYS (roy licence 1890), of Bewsey Hall, Warrington, DL; 30th Regt; *b* 17 Sept 1837; *m* 27 Feb 1862 Lady Mary (*d* 30 Jan 1892), 2nd dau of 3rd Earl of Gosford (*qv*), and *d* 18 July 1893, having had:
1a Edith Galfrida; *m* 1st 9 Aug 1888 Capt Charles Blood Mulville (*dsp* 28 March 1901), 3rd Dragoon Gds; *m* 2nd 12 July 1904 Edward Chenevix Austen Leigh (*d* 18 Sept 1949), est s of Cholmeley Austen Leigh, and *d* 18 Feb 1932
2a Emily Marion Emma; *m* 1 Dec 1892 Maj Ellis Houlton Ward, 60th Rifles (*d* 5 Dec 1919), and *d* 1 Nov 1923
3a Maud Blanche; *d* 29 Oct 1920
4a Mary Theresa Gwendoline; *m* 15 April 1896 her cousin Mervyn Owen Wayne Powys (see below)
5a Hilda Geraldine; *d* unm 25 Feb 1936
6a Louise Christina; *b* 9 Sept 1879; *m* 9 June 1906 Hubert Graves Archer, er s of Graves T Archer (*d* 23 Sept 1940), of Mount John, Co Wicklow, and *d* 19 March 1937, leaving issue
(3) Edward Victor Robert (Rev); LLB Cantab; Vicar Kemsing, Kent; *b* 11 Feb 1839; *m* 8 June 1865 Elizabeth Gwenllian (*d* 21 Nov 1870) only child of William Watkyn-Wayne, of Plas Newydd, Aberdare, and *d* 16 Feb 1930, having had:
1a Mervyn Owen Wayne; Hon Lt 18th Bn Co of London Vol Regt, Lt 4th Bn Northants Regt, MA Cantab; *b* 5 March 1866; *m* 15 April 1896 Mary Theresa Gwendoline, dau of Hon Leopold Fox-Powys (see above), and *d* July 1942
2a George Percy Wayne; *b* 10 Nov, *d* 31 Dec 1868
3a Edward William Wayne; *b* 6 Nov 1870; *m* 1919 Sarah Rebecca (*d* 9 Nov 1942), dau of Samuel Phenix Franks, of Wisbech
1a Helen Constance; *d* an infant 26 Sept 1867

(4) Charles James Fox; Col 2nd Bn Welsh Regt; *b* 25 April 1840; *m* 9 Nov 1871 Amy Charlotte (*d* 30 Sept 1911), dau of William George Rose, of Wolston Heath, and *dsp* 14 April 1893

(1) Adelaide Mary; *d* 14 Feb 1873

(2) Edith Galfrida; *m* 20 April 1858 Thomas Henry Burroughes (*d* 17 Jan 1924) and *d* 10 Feb 1864

(3) Georgiana Caroline; *m* 28 April 1859 John Nicholas Fazakerley (*d* 21 April 1909), s of J N Fazakerley, MP, and *d* 7 April 1897

(4) Mary Elizabeth Frances; *d* unm 10 Oct 1908

(5) Constance Emma Augusta; *m* 7 May 1867 Arthur William Crichton (*d* 4 Feb 1882), of Broadward Hall, Salop, and *d* 3 Sept 1931, having had issue

(6) Caroline Mary; *m* 19 Oct 1897 Frederic George Dawtrey Drewitt, MA, MD, FRCP (*d* 29 July 1942), of Kensington, and *d* 6 April 1940

2 Robert Vernon; HEIMS; *b* 3 Dec 1802; *m* 14 April 1825 Jane (*d* 10 Nov 1842), 3rd dau of William Beckett, of Enfield, Middx, and *d* 26 May 1854, having had, with other issue:

(1) Robert Horace; *b* 21 June 1826; *m* 4 Dec 1856 Ellen Elizabeth (*d* 10 July 1916), est dau of Lt-Col William Henry Budd, IA, and *d* 17 Sept 1913, having had:

1a John Edward; *b* 21 Sept 1857; *d* 13 Sept 1923

2a Robert Vernon; *b* 14 Sept 1860; *m* 1889 Wilhelmina Hart (*d* 16 April 1940) and *d* 6 Oct 1933, leaving:

1b Robert Horace; *b* 4 Dec 1889; *m* 6 April 1926 Vera Grace Bryant and *d* 28 Jan 1940, leaving:

1c GEORGE VERNON POWYS, **7th and present Baron Lilford of Lilford**

1c *Hilary Betty [Mrs Philip Millar, 4 Braeside Rd, Kenilworth, CP 7700, S Africa]; *b* 19 Jan 1929; *m* 1950 Philip Donald Millar (*d* 31 May 1967) and has:

1d *Christopher; *b* 1961; *m* 1989 *Tracey Lynn Boddington and has:

1e *Guy Philip; *b* 1992

1d *Philippa Ann [Mrs Paul Sater, 4 Westcroft Mews, London W6 0TL]; *b* 1958; *m* 1989 *Paul Edward Roisen Sater

2c *Beryl Irene; *b* 11 June 1932

1b Magdalen; *b* 24 Dec 1890

2b Agnes; *b* 17 May 1892

3b Ellen Mona; *d* young

4b Nesta; *b* 1896

3a Charles Horace Lilford; *b* 12 Oct 1862; *d* unm 28 Sept 1928

4a Henry Littleton; *b* 10 Sept 1866; *m* 5 July 1900 Alice Maud Hammond (*d* 7 March 1927) and *d* 16 March 1929, having had:

1b Frank Lilford; *b* 23 April 1902; *m* 6 July 1929 *Gertrude Frances Elizabeth [Mrs Frank Powys, Erensrust, 3 Hilltop Rd, Hillcrest, Natal, S Africa], dau of G G F Meyer, and *d* 15 Sept 1972, leaving:

1c +Robert Charles Lilford [Robert Powys Esq, PO Box 2138, Port Alfred 6170, CP, S Africa]; *b* 15 Aug 1930; *m* 14 Dec 1957 (*divorce* 1972) Charlotte Webb, *m* 2nd 1973 *Janet Wightwick and by her has:

1d +Matthew Robert Lilford; *b* 25 June 1974

2b Harold Littleton; *b* 1908; *d* 29 Nov 1919

5a Wilfred Owen; *b* 25 Feb 1873; *m* 8 June 1905 Constance Mary (*d* 20 Jan 1948), dau of Robert Michael Bradford, of Germiston, and *d* of injuries 10 Dec 1944, leaving:

1b Horace Victor; *b* 18 May 1907; *m* 1928 Olive Maude Peetz, of Durban, and *d* 1956, leaving:

1c *Michael John [Michael Powys Esq, PO Box 661, Link Hills 3652, Natal, S Africa]; *b* 1934; *m* 1957 *Lynette Bernice Hodges, of Durban, and has:

1d +Victor Michael [Victor Powys Esq, PO Box 710, Link Hills 3652, Natal, S Africa]; *b* 1961; *m* 1986 *Yvonne Joan McCort and has:

1e *Victoria Amy; *b* 1993

2d Andrew John; *b* 1970; *k* car crash 1985

3d Paul Michael; *b* 1974; *k* car crash 1985

1d *Susan Lynn; *b* 1958; *m* 1978 *Peter Gary Bahrs and has:

1e *Justin Peter; *b* 1983

1e *Jacqueline Susan; *b* 1979

2e *Nicola Susan; *b* 1981

3e *Megan Lynn; *b* 1986

1c *Pamela Ann [Mrs Harry Rowntree, 24 Meyer Gdns, Umbilo, Durban 4001, Natal, S Africa]; *b* 1929 *m* 1st 1949 (*divorce* 1959) Ian Falconer and has:

1d *Malcolm; *b* 1950

2d *Donald; *b* 1952

3d *Colin; *b* 1955

4d *Neil; *b* 1956

1c (cont.) Mrs Pamela Falconer *m* 2nd 1959 *Harry Rowntree and by him has:

5d *Mark; *b* 1960

1d *Anne; *b* 1961

1b *Marjory Gladys [Mrs Cecil Collier, 124 Northway, Durban N 4051, Natal, S Africa]; *b* 29 April 1911; *m* 15 July 1933 Cecil Wilme Collier (*d* 1986) and has:

1c *Frank Wilme [Frank Collier Esq, 2 Lister Court, Lister Ave, Durban, Natal, SA]; *b* 11 April 1942; *m* 11 Jan 1969 *Christine Alice Dewar, of Vryheid, Natal, and has:

1d *Andrew Blaine; *b* 16 June 1972

1d *Claire; *b* 1974

2c *David Owen; *b* 17 April 1947; *m* 28 March 1970 *Fay McKenzie, of Richmond, Natal, and has:

1d *Vicky; *b* 1974

2d *Paula; *b* 1976

3d *Kate; *b* 1978

1a Mary Augusta, OBE (1919); *m* 6 Aug 1885 Edward Peter Mathers (*d* 13 Oct 1924) and *d* 20 June 1934, leaving issue

2a Ellen Jane Beatrice; *m* 22 Dec 1896 Lionel Herbert Herbert and *d* 1921, leaving issue

(2) John; Lt 61st Bengal NI; *b* 30 March 1828; *m* 1855 Caroline Louisa, dau of Rev W A Holmes, DD, and was murdered with his w and infant child Caroline Jane in the Indian Mutiny 8 June 1857

3 Horatio (Rt Rev); DD; Bp Sodor and Man; *b* 28 Nov 1805; *m* 21 Feb 1833 Percy Gore (*d* 7 April 1886), sr dau of William Currie, of E Horsley Pk, Surrey, and *d* 31 May 1877, having had, with other issue:

(1) William Percy (Rev); Rector Thorpe Achurch 1877–94; *b* 25 April 1838; *m* 7 Oct 1890 Mary Kathleen (*d* 5 July 1941), est dau of Rev Frederick Manners Stopford (*see* COURTOWN, E), and *d* 19 Jan 1918

(2) Henry Lyttelton; Col Oxon LI; *b* 14 May 1839; *m* 7 Aug 1869 Helena Cecilia (*d* 27 June 1886), est dau of Rt Rev Charles Graves, DD, Bp Limerick, and *d* 9 Oct 1919, having had:

1a John; Lt 2nd Bn Oxon LI; *b* 17 June 1870; *d* unm Dec 1897

1a Norah

(1) Sophia Vernon; *m* 14 Nov 1878 Rev Boscawen Thomas George Henry Somerset (*see* BEAUFORT, D) and *d* 5 April 1935

4 Atherton Legh (Rev); Rector Tichmarsh; *b* 23 Sept 1809; *educ* Trin Coll Cambridge; *m* 23 Sept 1841 Charlotte Elizabeth (*d* 2 Nov 1869), dau of Richard Norman, and *d* 28 Aug 1886, having had:

(1) Arthur Lyttelton; *b* 17 Oct 1842; *d* 8 Oct 1875

(2) Richard Atherton Norman; Sec Roy Veterinary Coll Camden Town 1876–1913; *b* 19 Sept 1844; *m* 23 Dec 1882 Florence Martha (*d* 29 April 1905), dau of H Hussey, and *d* 10 July 1913, leaving:

1a Atherton Richard Norman; slr 1912; *b* 15 Aug 1888; *educ* London U (LLB 1912); *m* 1st 16 Feb 1915 Elsie Dyus (*d* 1957), dau of Frederick R Mattingly, and had:

1b +John Frederick Atherton; *b* 5 July 1916

2b +Richard Atherton Legh; *b* 20 March 1923; *m* Sept 1962 *Ann Patricia Blanchard and has:

1c +Anthony Richard Atherton; *b* 4 Nov 1963

2c +David John Atherton; *b* 6 March 1965

3c +Christopher James Atherton; *b* 22 May 1966

4c +Michael Paul Atherton; *b* 1970

5c +Nicholas; *b* 1971

1b *Mary Elizabeth Anne; *b* 12 Nov 1921

1a (cont.) Atherton Powys *m* 2nd 1957 Edith (*d* 1977), dau of John Smart, of Edinburgh, and *d* 1976 leaving by her:

3b *Ian Atherton [Ian Powys Esq, 97 Robin Hood Lane, London SW15 3QR]; *b* 1930; *educ* Haileybury and RMA Sandhurst; *m* 1955 *Beryl Mary, dau of Percy Hirst Lomax, of Bolton, and has:

1c *Richard Ian Lomax; *b* 1955

2c *Andrew John; *b* 1961

(3) Walter Norman; *b* 28 July 1849; *m* 10 March 1880 Ada Marion (*d* 1939), dau of G T Vaughan, and *d* 7 Jan 1892, leaving:

1a Evelyn Marian; *b* 14 Oct 1882; *m* 1st 23 March 1915 Alexander William Harvey Grant, W African Medical Staff (lost in SS *Falaba* 28 March 1915); *m* 2nd F E Quipp, of NJ, USA, and *d* 22 March 1965

2a Averil Frances; *b* 7 March 1890; *d* unm 2 April 1971

(1) Evelyn Mary; *m* 19 Oct 1869 Edward Pennefather Wade Browne (*d* 20 April 1904) and *d* 4 March 1934

(2) Alice Elizabeth Juliana; *m* 7 Sept 1880 Rev Frederick Armine Wodehouse (*see* KIMBERLEY, E) and *d* 7 March 1934

5 Henry Littleton POWYS later POWYS-KECK (roy licence 16 Feb 1861), of Stoughton Grange, Leics; Maj 60th Roy Rifles; *b* 28 March 1812; *m* 1st 20 Nov 1840 Margarette Matilda (*d* 21 June 1845), 3rd dau of J J Bancho, of Parsonstown, Ireland, and had:

(1) Harry Leycester, of Stoughton Grange and The Knoll, Kingston Hill, Surrey, JP and DL Leics, High Sheriff 1871, BA Oxon; Lt Leics Yeo Cav; *b* 16 Oct 1841; *m* 6 Aug 1891 Agnes Cecil (*d* 20 April 1926), widow of James Milward and 4th dau of Lord Cecil James Gordon-Moore (*see* HUNTLY, M), and *dsp* 20 April 1912

(2) Charles Horatio Gardiner; Lt 60th Roy Rifles; *b* 7 May 1843; *d* 9 March 1870

(3) Thomas Bancho; Lt 60th Roy Rifles; *b* 28 May 1845; *m* 24 Oct 1870 Sarah Matilda (*m* 2nd 3 Feb 1886 Capt William Freeman and *d* 26 Jan 1925), 2nd dau of James Johnston, of Kincardine, Perthshire, and *d* 27 Nov 1877, having had:

1a Thomas Charles Leycester, of Stoughton Grange; Lt 5th Bn KRRC WW I; *b* 12 Aug 1871; *educ* Charterhouse and BNC Oxford (BA); *m* 27 Sept 1917 Clare Hephzibah (*d* 13 June 1958), dau of Richard Dowson, and *d* 4 April 1931, leaving:

1b Thomas Leycester, of Stoughton Grange; RAF; *b* 14 Dec 1919; *educ* Malvern; *m* 5 Nov 1949 Joyce [Mrs Thomas Powys-Keck, Clarence Dve, Littlehampton, Sussex], dau of Albert Hills, of Worthing, and *d* 19 March 1959, leaving:

1c +Thomas Charles Leycester; *b* 17 Oct 1951; *m* 1st 1979 (*divorce* 1983) Judith Harris and has:

1d +Leycester Charles; *b* 1981

1c (cont.) Thomas Powys-Keck *m* 2nd 1985 *Evelyn K Dobner and has by her:

2d +Christian Rhys; *b* 1992

1d *Jacqueline Lauren; *b* 1989

2c +(Piers) Anthony Leycester [Anthony Powys-Keck Esq, 12 Meadow Way, Ferring, W Sussex BN12 5LD]; *b* 7 Oct 1954; *m* 19– (*divorce* 1995) Pauline Ann Short and has:

1d +Thomas Anthony Leycester; *b* 1988

1d *Emma Leigh; *b* 1983

2d *Danielle Kelly; *b* 1985

2a Horatio James POWYS-KECK later POWYS (1930); *b* 7 March 1873; *educ* Malvern and Monkton Combe; Capt 5th Bn KRRC and RDC, ADC to Govr Newfoundland 1900–01, served Boer War and WW I; *m* 18 Oct 1902 Edith Mary Cockburn (*d* 8 June 1971 aged 89), only dau of Alexander J Harvey, of St John's, Newfoundland, and *d* 31 Jan 1952, leaving:

1b Clodagh Betty; *b* 14 March 1907; *m* 1st 21 Feb 1933 (*divorce*) Colin Alfred Lampson, est s of Alfred Curtis Lampson, and had issue; *m* 2nd José Jorge Brugada (*d* 7 July 1954), Spanish Press Attaché UK, er s of Mariano Brugada, of Barcelona, and *d* 10 Aug 1964

2b *(Gwladys) Maïta Joan [Mrs Maïta Fenwick, Oratory Lodge, Bromp-ton Rd, London SW7 2RW]; *b* 5 July 1911; *m* 2 June 1933 (*divorce* 1959) David Fenwick (*d* 1982), er s of Herbert George Fenwick, JP, of Harbrook, Ramsbury, Wilts, and has had:

1c *(Anthony) Benedict Xavier [Benedict Fenwick Esq, Sholebroke, Towcester, Northants]; dir Investment Intelligence Ltd, Morgan Grenfell Funds Management; *b* 3 Aug 1934; *educ* Ampleforth; *m* 28 Nov 1958 *Susan Deirdre, 2nd dau of Lt-Col Peter Heber-Percy (*see* NORTHUMBERLAND, D), and has:

1d *Alexius John Benedict [Alexius Fenwick Esq, 15 Glazbury Rd, London W14]; *b* 1959; *m* 1st 1984 (*divorce* 1988) Briony Gretel, er dau of Bruce Gyngell, of Sydney; *m* 2nd 3 March 1990 *Lady Sophia Anne Crichton-Stuart, only surv dau of 6th Marquess of Bute (*qv*), and by her has:

1e *Georgia Jessie; *b* 1990

1d *Celestria Chantal Arabella [Mrs James Alexander-Sinclair, Blackpitts House, Whittlebury, Northants NN12 8TD]; *b* 1963; *m* 1987 *James B Alexander-Sinclair, er s of Maj-Gen David Boyd Alex-ander-Sinclair, CB, and has:

1e *Archie Benedict Boyd; *b* 1988

2e *Maxim Boyd; *b* 1994

1e *Stroma Georgina; *b* 1990

2c Jerome Dunstan; *b* 9 March 1936; *educ* Ampleforth and New Coll Oxford; *d* following an accident 4 March 1956

3c *Charles Christopher Sebastian, LVO (1977) [Maj Charles Fenwick LVO, Barhams Manor, Higham, Essex]; *b* 7 April 1946; *educ* Ampleforth; Maj Gren Gds; Adj 1973–75, Equerry to HRH THE DUKE OF EDINBURGH 1975–77

4c *Timothy Dominic Ignatius [Timothy Fenwick Esq, rue du Mont 1, 5650 Biesmes-la-Colonoise, Belgium]; *b* 24 Sept 1947; *educ* Ampleforth; *m* 1971*Jeanne Marie, only dau of Joseph Marechal, of Bastogne, Belgium

5c *Justin Francis Quintus, QC (1983) [Maj Justin Fenwick QC, Geldeston Hall, Geldeston, Norfolk]; *b* 11 Sept 1949; *educ* Ampleforth and Clare Coll Cambridge; Maj Gren Gds, Adj 1977–79, Equerry to HRH THE DUKE OF EDINBURGH 1979–81; barrister Inner Temple 1980; *m* 1975 *Marcia Mary, er dau of Archibald Dunn, of Overbury Hall, Hadleigh, Suffolk (*see* 1970 edn ASTLEY, Bt), and has:

1d *Hubert George Francis; *b* 1990

1d *Corisande Mary; *b* 1983

2d *Rosamond Xanthe; *b* 1985

3d *Madeleine Isobel; *b* 1988

6c *Sebastian Edmund Stephen [Sebastian Fenwick Esq, Puslinch, Yealmpton, Devon PL8 2NN]; *b* 15 Jan 1953; *educ* Ampleforth

1c *Serena Mary [Miss Serena Fenwick, Hope Cottage, Marsham Lane, Gerrards Cross, Bucks]; *b* 30 March 1944; *educ* New Hall Essex

1a Haidee Alma Alice; *b* 8 June 1876; *m* Jan 1901 George R A Wilson and *d* 28 Jan 1934, leaving issue

5 (cont.) Maj The Hon Henry Powys-Keck *m* 2nd 16 July 1862 Maria (*d* 8 March 1902), yst surv dau of Adml Sir John Gore, KCB, GCH, and *d* 10 July 1863

6 Charles; Lt-Col 9th Lancers, formerly RN, served Sikh War and Indian Mutiny, cmdg 9th Lancers Relief Lucknow; *b* 4 March 1813; *m* 1st 29 March 1836 Mary (*dsp* 12 Feb 1854), only surv child of William Scott Kennedy; *m* 2nd 15 Aug 1854 Agnes Anne (*d* 26 April 1906), only dau of John Richards, of Penzance, and *d* 16 Oct 1897, having by her had:

(1) Charles Warwick; *b* 14 May 1855

(2) Vernon Henry; *b* 28 June 1863; *d* unm 29 Sept 1913

(3) Warwick Gurney; *b* 7 Jan 1872

(1) Agnes Mary Edith; *b* 29 Sept 1856; *d* unm 21 Feb 1877

1 Henrietta Maria; *m* 10 Sept 1827 John Campbell Colquhoun (*d* 17 April 1870), of Killermont and Garscadden, Scotland, and Chartwell, Kent, and *d* 21 Jan 1870

2 Eleanor; *m* 8 July 1839, as his 2nd w, Sir John Murray Naesmyth, of Posso, 4th Bt (*d* 19 July 1876; *see* 1928 edn), and *d* 13 March 1880, having had issue

3 Mary; *m* 11 May 1830 Rev James Drummond (*d* 18 Nov 1882), Rector Galby, Leics, and *d* 5 Nov 1883

4 Elizabeth Atherton; *m* 15 Feb 1828 Rev R Leonard Adams (*d* 22 Aug 1875), Rector Shere, Surrey, and *d* 8 Jan 1891

5 Frances Hester; *m* 5 April 1831 Rev Thomas Henry Causton (*d* 15 May 1854), and *d* 17 June 1840

6 Jane Lucy; *m* 18 May 1836 Rev John Pierce Maurice (*d* 17 July 1874), Rector Michael Marsh, Hants, and *d* 4 Dec 1905, leaving issue

LIMERICK

Arms: Quarterly, 1st and 4th quarterly, gu. and or, on a bend arg. three lions passant sa. (for PERY); 2nd and 3rd, per chevron engrailed or and sa. three pellets in chief and in base a stag passant of the first (for HARTSTONGE). **Crests:** 1 A hind's head erased ppr. (for PERY), 2 A demi-Saracen, supporting on the dexter shoulder a sword, the point resting on the palm of the hand, the sinister arm extended, holding a battle-axe (for HARTSTONGE).
Supporters: Dexter, a lion erm.; sinister, a fawn ppr., ducally collared and chained or. **Motto:** *Virtute, non astutia* ('By courage, not by craft'). **Creations:** B. (I) 2 June 1790 (Glentworth of Mallow), V. (I) 29 Dec 1800, E. (I) 1 Jan 1803, B. (UK) 11 Aug 1815 (Foxford of Stackpole Court).

THE 6TH EARL OF LIMERICK, **Viscount Limerick of the City of Limerick**, **Baron Glentworth of Mallow** and **Baron Foxford of Stackpole Court**, Co Clare (Sir Patrick Edmund Pery, KBE (1983), DL (W Sussex)) [The Rt Hon The Earl of Limerick KBE DL, Chiddinglye, West Hoathly, W Sussex RH19 4QT; 30 Victoria Rd, London W8 5RG]; *b* 12 April 1930; *s f* 1967; *educ* Eton and New Coll Oxford (BA 1953, MA 1963); late Maj City of London Yeo, Rifle Bde (TA); dir: Kleinwort Benson 1967–87 (v-chm 1983–85, dep-chm 1985–87), Kleinwort Benson Gp 1982–90, Kleinwort Benson Australian Income Fund Inc 1986– and Robert Benson, Lonsdale and Co Ltd; Cncl memb London Chamber Commerce, chm: Ctee Middle East Trade (COMET) 1975–79, Br Nat Export Cncl Ctee Middle East Trade 1979–83; Parly U-Sec DTI 1972–74, memb Overseas Trade Bd 1975–91, pres Inst Export 1983–95; chm: Br Invisibles 1984–91 (Bd memb 1983–91), Pirelli UK plc 1989–, AMP Asset Management plc 1992–, Tstees City Parochial Fndn 1992– (tstee 1971–), De La Rue plc 1993–97 (dir 1983–) and Ct Govrs London Guildhall U 1984–; pres: Hispanic and Luso-Brazilian Cncl 1994– and S of England Ag Soc 1993–; CA Scotland; *m* 22 April 1961 *Sylvia Rosalind, CBE (1991), MA Oxon, pres: Nat Assoc Maternal and Child Welfare 1973–, Health Visitors' Assoc 1984–,; dir Tanganyika Concessions 1976–, chm Cncl BRCS 1985–; *m* 1961 *Sylvia Rosalind, er dau of Brig Maurice Stanley Lush, CB, CBE, MC, of Brantridge Forest, Balcombe, Sussex, and has:

1 +EDMUND CHRISTOPHER, *Viscount Glentworth* [Viscount Glentworth, c/o Deutsche Morgan Grenfell (Moscow Office), 23 Great Winchester St, London EC2P 2AX]; *b* 10 Feb 1963; *educ* Eton, New Coll Oxford (MA), Pushkin Inst Moscow and City U (Dip Law); barrister Middle Temple 1987, FCO 1987–92, slr: Clifford Chance 1992–93, Freshfields 1993–94, Milbank Tweed 1994–96; dir Deutsche Morgan Grenfell Moscow 1996–; *m*1990 *Emily Kate, only dau of Michael Gavin Lynam Thomas, of Worcester, and has:

(1) +Felix Edmund; *b* 16 Nov 1991

(2) +Ivo Patrick; *b* 1993

2 +Adrian Patrick; *b* 14 June 1967; *educ* Eton, Reading U and RMA Sandhurst; Army Capt; *m* 5 July 1997 *Suzanne, dau of Peter Wartnaby, of Leek Wootton

1 *Alison Dora; *b* 27 Oct 1964

Limerick, previous creations: The Roger Palmer created Earl of Castlemaine (*see* CASTLEMAINE, B, preliminary remarks) in 1661 was also granted as a subsidiary title the Barony of Limerick. Although this Barony did not expire until Roger's death in 1705 an Earldom of the same title was created in January 1685/6 for Sir William Dongan or Dungan, 4th Bt. The new Earl of Limerick was a supporter of JAMES II and after the latter's defeat at the Battle of the Boyne in July 1690 accompanied his master to France. He was accordingly attainted and normally his titles would have been forfeited as a concomitant punishment. Nevertheless the title was assumed after his death by his younger brother Thomas, who under the special remainder in the creation of the Earldom would have been the next heir had no forfeiture been operative. Moreover he seems to have been recognised as such. Whatever the precise legal position, it would seem that the Earldom expired on Thomas's death without issue in 1715.

Four years later the James Hamilton who was later promoted Earl of Clanbrassill was made Viscount of the City of Limerick. Both these titles expired in 1798. The town of Limerick has featured as a part of the subsidiary wording in two other peerage titles: Grandison of Limerick (*see* JERSEY, E) and a Barony of Esmond of Limerick, which was created in 1622 and expired 23 years later.

Lineage: EDMUND PERY; *m* Susannah (*d* 1671), only dau of Edmond Sexten and heiress of her nephew, Edmond Sexten, of St Mary's Abbey, and *d* 1655, leaving:

EDMUND PERY; Col; *m* Dymphna, dau and heiress of Bartholomew Stackpole, of Stackpole Court, Co Clare, and *d* 1721, leaving, with an est s (Sexten, *d* 1730):

Rev STACKPOLE PERY; MA; *m* 1716 Jane, dau of Ven William Twigg, Archdeacon Limerick, by Diana, widow of Rev Peter Rilands, of Limerick, and dau and heiress of Sir Drury Wray, 8th Bt, of Glentworth (commemorated in his gs's choice of peerage title; see below), Lincs (whose mother Albinia was dau of 1st and last Viscount Wimbledon; *see* EXETER, M), and had, with other issue:

1 EDMOND SEXTEN PERY, 1st and last VISCOUNT PERY OF NEW-TOWN-PERY, near the City of Limerick (I), so *cr* 30 Dec 1785, PC (I 1771); *b* April 1719; *educ* Trin Coll Dublin and Middle Temple; barrister Ireland 1745, MP (I Parl) Wicklow 1751–60 and Limerick 1761–85, Speaker Irish H of C 1771–85; *m* 1st 11 June 1756 Patty (*dsp* 1757), yr dau of John Martin, of Dublin; *m* 2nd 27 Oct 1762 Hon Elizabeth Vesey, sis of 1st Viscount de Vesci (*qv*) and widow of Robert Handcock (*see* CASTLEMAINE, B), and *dspm* 24 Feb 1806, when the Viscountcy expired, having by her had:

(1) Diana Jane; *m* 1786 1st Earl of Ranfurly (*qv*) and *d* 24 Nov 1839

(2) Frances; *m* 9 Jan 1789 Nicolson Calvert (*d* 1841), of Hunsdon House, Herts, MP and had issue (*see* STRONGE, Bt)

2 Rt Rev WILLIAM CECIL PERY, **1st Baron Glentworth of Mallow** (I), so *cr* 2 June 1790; *b* 26 July 1721; *educ* Trin Coll Dublin (DD 1781); Bp Killaloe 1781–84 and Limerick 1784–94; *m* 1st 2 April 1755 Jane (*d* 20 June 1792), est dau of John Minchin Walcott, of Croagh, Co Limerick, and had:

(1) EDMOND HENRY, **1st Earl**

(1) Eleanor; *m* 1784 Sir Vere Hunt, 1st Bt, of Curragh Chase (*see* 1904 edn), and *d* 21 Jan 1821

2 (cont.) The **1st Baron** *m* 2nd 14 Oct 1792 Dorothea (*dsp*), dau of Ven William Lewis, Archdeacon Kilfenora, and widow of General Crump, and *d* 4 July 1794

1 Diana; *m* 8 Oct 1733 Rev Henry Smyth, s of Thomas Smyth, DD, Bp Limerick

2 Dymphna; *m* 1751 William Monsell, of Tervoe, Co Limerick

3 Lucy; *m* 23 Dec 1751 Sir Henry Hartstonge, Bt

4 Jane; *m* 1774 Launcelot Hill and *dsp*

The 1st BARON's son,

EDMOND HENRY PERY, **1st Earl of Limerick**, so *cr* 1 Jan 1803, as also earlier 29 Dec 1800 VISCOUNT LIMERICK OF THE CITY OF LIMERICK (both I) and 11 Aug 1815 BARON FOXFORD OF STACKPOLE COURT, Co Clare (UK), PC (I 1797); *b* 8 Jan 1758; *educ* Trin Coll Dublin; MP Limerick 1786–94, Keeper Signet and Privy Seal Ireland 1795–97, Clerk Crown and Hanaper Ireland 1797–1806; rep I peer 1801–44; *m* 29 Jan 1783 Mary Alice (*d* 13 June 1850), only dau and heiress of Henry Ormsby, of Cloghan, Co Mayo, by Mary, sis and heir of Sir Henry Hartsonge, Bt, of Bruff, Co Limerick, and had, with other issue:

1 Edmond Cecil; *d* 10 May 1793 aged 7

2 Henry Hartstonge, *Lord Glentworth*; *b* 26 May 1789; *educ* Winchester; *m* 11 May 1808 Annabella (*d* 18 Sept 1868), 2nd dau of Tenison Edwards, of Old Court, Co Wicklow, and *dvp* 7 Aug 1834, leaving:

(1) Edmund Henry, styled (improperly, as have been all subsequent est sons and heirs so styled, since the family does not possess a Viscountcy of Glentworth, only a Barony thereof) *Viscount Glentworth*; *b* 3 March 1809; *m* 8 Oct 1836 Eve Maria (*m* 2nd 29 Dec 1847 Col Hugh S Baillie, RHG, and *d* 28 Aug 1903 in her 101st year), 2nd dau of Henry Villebois, of Marham Ho, Norfolk, and *dsp* 16 Feb 1844

(2) WILLIAM HENRY TENNISON, **2nd Earl**

(3) John Hartstonge; Army Capt; *b* 1813; *d* 8 Oct 1842 in Canada

(4) Henry Frederick; HEICS; *b* 1820; *m* 12 June 1841 Amelia Mary (*m* 2nd Robert William King, 9th Lancers, only surv s of R-Adml Hon James William King (*see* KINGSTON E), and *d* 1873), 2nd dau of Capt Rowland Money, CB, RN, and *d* in the E Indies 16 Aug 1843

(1) Annabella Erina; *m* 11 Sept 1832 Robert Gun Cuninghame, of Mount Kennedy, Co Wicklow, and *d* 25 April 1841

(2) Mary Georgiana; *d* unm

(3) Emile Caroline; *m* 21 May 1835 Rev Henry Gray (*d* 1864), Vicar Almondsbury, Glos, s of Rt Rev Dr Robert Gray, Bp Bristol, and *d* 4 Sept 1888, having had issue

(4) Cecilia Annabella; *m* 10 Jan 1843 Rev George Herbert Repton (*d* 8 April 1852), Canon of Westminster, and *d* 5 March 1902, leaving issue

(5) Augusta Maria; *m* 19 Oct 1854 Sir Edward Kennedy, 2nd Bt (*qv*), and *d* 10 Nov 1865

3 Edmund Sexton, of Bury Ho, Cottingham, Northants; *b* 7 Feb 1797; *m* 14 Feb 1825 Elizabeth Charlotte (*d* 21 April 1833 aged 84), 5th dau of Hon William Cokayne (*see* CULLEN OF ASHBOURNE, B), and *d* 31 Dec 1860, having had, with other issue:

(1) Edmond Henry Cockayne PERY later PERY-KNOX-GORE (roy licence 1891), of Bury Ho, Cottingham, and Coolcronan Ho, Ballina, Co Mayo, JP and DL Co Mayo; *b* 9 April 1827; *m* 19 Dec 1860 Sarah Jane (*d* 19 May 1919), 3rd dau of Sir Francis Arthur Knox-Gore, 1st Bt (*see* 1899 edn), and *d* 3 March 1900, leaving:

1a Edmond Arthur Gore, of Coolcronan; Lt 6th Bn Connaught Rangers; *b* 3 July 1861; *m* 9 Nov 1898 Amy (*d* 6 Nov 1958), yst dau of Rev Francis Gordon Sandys-Lumsdaine, and *d* 25 Dec 1935, leaving:

1b Edmond Myles; Maj Gren Gds; *b* 30 July 1904; *educ* Eton; *m* 1st 30 April 1929 (*divorce* 1948) Gundrede Mary, formerly w of Col Courtenay Fergus Ochoncar Grey Forbes (*see* FORBES, L) and yr dau of Capt Graham Owen Robert Wynne, and had:

1c +Simon [Simon Pery-Knox-Gore Esq, 12 East Brook Rd, London SE3]; *b* 4 Nov 1937; *educ* Eton; *m* 20 May 1961 *Moira, dau of Thomas Jaraith Egan, of Sevenoaks, and has:

1d +Myles; *b* 14 July 1970

1d *Caroline; *b* 10 March 1962

2d *Katherine Lucy; *b* 10 June 1964

3d *Siobhan; *b* 11 Aug 1966; *m* 19– *Steven Way and has:

1e *Edward Sean; *b* 1993

1b (cont.) Maj Edmond Pery-Knox-Gore *m* 2nd 4 Aug 1948 *Ingrid Margaret Mary [Mrs Edmond Pery-Knox-Gore, Coolcronan Cottage, Ballina, Co Mayo, Ireland], widow of Capt Francis Holdsworth ffrench Davis, RASC (*see* MOWBRAY, SEGRAVE and STOURTON, B), and est dau of Henry MacDermot, KC, of Fitzwilliam Sq, Dublin, and *d* 15 July 1965, having by her had:

2c +Mark [Mark Pery-Knox-Gore Esq, 173 Orwell Rd, Rathgar, Dublin 14, Ireland]; *b* 28 May 1955; *educ* Ampleforth; *m* 1986 *Ann, dau of Patrick Mallon, of Ambrosetown Ho, Duncormick, Co Wexford and has:

1d *Flora; *b* 30 June 1997

1c *Sarah [Mrs James McLoughlin, Saurora, Glencree, Co Wicklow, Ireland]; *b* 5 Dec 1950; *m* *James McLoughlin

1b Sarah Frances; *b* 21 Aug 1900; *d* 20 May 1923

2a Cecil Charles James PERY; Col RE, Dir Works 1915–16, Ch Engr Northern Cmd 1916; *b* 12 Sept 1864; *m* 2 Sept 1916 Flora Isabella (*d* 7 May 1946), est dau of Capt H B Kelley, Roy Lancs Artillery, of Ireton Ho, Cheltenham, and *d* 29 Nov 1931

3a Wilfred Henry Cullen; Lt-Col RCT, Maj RWF, WW I (despatches); *b* 1 Sept 1880; *educ* Cheltenham; *d* unm 3 Aug 1947

4a Arthur Francis Gore, CB (1937), DSO (1917); Col RASC (Hon Brig 1937) WW I, AQMG Br Salonika Force and Army of Black Sea 1917–20 (despatches), Orders Redeemer Greece and White Eagle Serbia, Offr Legn Hon, Medal Mil Merit Greece, Silver Jubilee Medal 1935, Coronation Medal 1937; *b* 1 Sept 1880; *educ* Cheltenham; *m* 11 Oct 1909 Evangeline (*d* 18 Feb 1967 aged 87), yst dau of Capt John William St John Hughes (*see* HUGHES, Bt), and *d* 18 Feb 1954, having had:

1b Edmond Arthur; F/O RAFVR WW II; *b* 4 Aug 1922; *educ* Sherborne; missing presumed k on air operations 6 Sept 1943

1b Diana Frances; *b* 5 March 1914; *m* 1st 14 Sept 1936 Nigel Horatio Trevor FitzRoy (*see* GRAFTON, D) and had issue; *m* 2nd 27 Nov 1958 William Edward Yates (*d* 10 Nov 1964), s of Maj S P Yates, of Broughton Grange, Banbury, Oxon, assumed by deed poll Aug 1965 the name Fitz-ROY-YATES, and *d* 21 Oct 1995

2b *Mary Agnes [Lady Barrowclough, The Old Vicarage, Winsford, Somerset TA24 7JF]; WW II in WAAF; *b* 21 Nov 1923; *m* 17 Dec 1949 *Sir Anthony Richard Barrowclough, QC, s of Sidney Barrowclough, and has:

1c *Richard Edmond [Richard Barrowclough Esq, Pyncombe Farm, Wiveliscombe, Somerset]; *b* 27 July 1953; *educ* Eton; *m* 1978 *Laura Selina Madeline, only dau of Prof Sir (Albert) Raymond Maillard Carr (*see* STRICKLAND-CONSTABLE, Bt), and has:

1d *Milo Edmond; *b* 1984

2d *Conrad Oliver; *b* 1986

3d *Theodore Charles; *b* 17 Dec 1990

1d *Sibell Augusta; *b* 1982

1c *Claire Cecilia; *b* 27 Oct 1956; *m* 1982 *Nicholas Welham Paul and has:

1d *Flora Valentine; *b* 1985

2d *Phoebe Henrietta; *b* 1986

2d *Dominica Rose; *b* 1989

5a Aubrey Edmond OBE (1916); Maj KOYLI, Bde Maj 1916, WW I (wounded, despatches); *b* 27 Oct 1883; *m* 17 May 1916 Monica (*d* 3 Dec 1973), dau of Capt John Strachan Bridges, RA, of Woodcote, Fleet, Hants, by Lady Grace Harriet, 4th dau of 5th Earl of Courtown (*qv*), and *d* 25 Sept 1960, leaving:

1b +Cullen; *b* 5 Nov 1917; *m* 1st 28 Dec 1941 Barbara (*k* at sea by enemy action Dec 1942), only dau of G L Stuart; *m* 2nd 25 Sept 1948 *Priscilla Wendy, dau of J S Corr, of Johannesburg, and by her has:

1c *Janet Barbara; *b* 27 Jan 1950

2c *Diana Wendy; *b* 7 July 1951

2b +David Edmond Strachan; Lt RNVR WW II (despatches); *b* 28 Feb 1920; *m* 1 June 1948 *Molly, widow of Maj Frank Robertson, SAAF, and dau of A Daly, of Pretoria

6a Ivan Cokayne, DSO (1918), MC; Maj RFA WW I (despatches), WW II as Lt-Col HG; *b* 15 Sept 1886; *educ* RMA Woolwich; *d* unm 23 June 1971

1a Isabel Sarah; *d* unm 5 Dec 1945

2a Alice Gertrude Nina; *m* 27 Nov 1893 Sir Robert Lynch Blosse, 12th Bt (*qv*), and *d* 25 May 1959, leaving issue

3a Ethel Frances Theodora Pery; *d* unm 18 May 1951

4a Augusta Helen; *m* 9 Nov 1909 Frederick Hellewell Mills, barrister, and *d* 3 Sept 1954, leaving issue

5a Edith Maud Gore; *m* 5 Oct 1904 Sir Elliot Philipson Philipson-Stow, 2nd Bt (*qv*), and *d* 19 Nov 1943, leaving issue

(1) Louisa; *m* 28 July 1925 Sir Peter Van Notten Pole, 3rd Bt, of Wolverton (*qv*), and *d* 6 Aug 1852, leaving issue

(2) Caroline Alicia; *m* 16 Feb 1832 George Russell (*d* 1878), s of Rt Hon Sir Henry Russell, Bt, and *d* 11 Dec 1890 aged 87

The 1st EARL *d* 7 Dec 1844; his est surv gs,

WILLIAM HENRY TENNISON PERY, **2nd Earl of Limerick**; *b* 19 Oct 1812; Magistrate and Supt Ag NSW; *m* 1st April 1838 Susanna (*d* 21 Aug 1841), dau of William Sheaffe and niece of Sir Roger Sheaffe, Bt (*see* 1851 edn), and had:

1 WILLIAM HALE JOHN CHARLES, **3rd Earl**

The **2nd Earl** *m* 2nd 6 April 1842 Margaret Jane (*d* 25 Nov 1875), only dau of Capt Nicholas Horsley, 96th Regt, of Durham, and by her had:

2 Henry Harstonge; *b* 2 Sept 1843; *m* 19 March 1873 Sarah Annie (*d* 5 April 1934), dau of John James Hooper, and *d* 28 Sept 1919, leaving:

(1) Henry Vernon Horsley; AIF WW I (wounded, medals); *b* 19 Dec 1880; *m* 11 March 1925 Dorothy Maud, est dau of Capt D H T M Knight-Eaton, of Qld, and *d* 1942

(1) Violet Mabel Horsley; *b* 1884; *m* 19– —

3 Edmund Aubrey Templar; Sub-Lt RN, present bombardment Simonoseki, Japan, 1864, JP NSW, Police Magistrate Macleay River, Capt cmdg Res Forces

NSW; *b* 6 Jan 1845; *m* 21 Jan 1875 Clara Julia (*d* 15 Oct 1901), dau of Lt James O'Brien Croker, RN, and *d* 1924, having had:

(1) Edmond Aubrey Horsley de Vere; served Boer War (medal and clasp); *b* 9 Dec 1875; *m* 2 Nov 1902 Margrieta Allitza, dau of Jacobus Hendrik Coetzee, of S Africa, and had:

1a Clara Violet; *b* 8 June 1903

2a Lily Aileen; *b* 3 Aug 1904

3a *Jacoba Hendrika; *b* 2 May 1908

4a *Myrtle Croker; *b* 20 Aug 1913

(2) Harry Reddall de Vere; AIF WW I (medal and clasp); *b* 19 April 1877; *m* 23 April 1907 Bertha, dau of John Edward Fouscha, of NSW, and *d* 1937, leaving:

1a +Lyndon de Vere [Lyndon Pery Esq, 20 Wyandra Cres, Port Macquarie, NSW 2444, Australia]; *b* 23 Feb 1914; *m* 1934 *Eileen May, dau of Henry Ernest Reid, and has:

1b +Barry Lyndon de Vere [Barry Pery Esq, 9/120 Ramsgate Rd, NSW 2217, Australia]; *b* 1935

1b *Carol Ann [Mrs James Fletcher, 45 Bibaby St, Carlton, NSW 2218, Australia]; *b* 1940; *m* 19– *James Fletcher

1a Claudia Thelma de Vere; *b* 15 Nov 1909

2a *Gretta de Vere; *b* 2 Sept 1911; *m* 1944 *Daniel John Foster

(3) Percy de Vere; *b* 17 Aug 1878

(4) George Terence Croker de Vere; *b* 1 Oct 1879; *d* 23 July 1884

(5) William Vere de Vere; *b* 12 June 1882; *m* 5 Nov 1912 Annie Tombs, of London, and *d* 23 July 1956

(1) Mary Margaret Aileen de Vere; *d* unm 14 Feb 1902

(2)Violet Isabella de Vere; *m* 2 Nov 1918 Hugh Harold Heathcote, AIF, yst s of Frederick Heathcote, of Hendon

4 Cecil Standish Stackpole; *b* 23 Nov 1847; *m* 20 Aug 1875 Katherine Mary (*d* 24 Dec 1946), dau of John Gavin, of Qld, and *d* 6 June 1935, having had:

(1) Neville John Tenison, JP King's Co, Nova Scotia; *b* 17 Jan 1877; *m* 5 Feb 1905 Dolores Harriet, 2nd dau of Harvey Davis, of Upton Hall, Worcs, and *d* 11 March 1958, leaving:

1a Kathleen Dolores de Vere; *b* 27 April 1906; *m* 9 Oct 1937 Kenneth Campbell-Watson, s of Dr D T C Campbell-Watson, of Halifax, Nova Scotia, and Kingston, Jamaica, and had:

1b *Kenneth David Campbell; *b* 19 Jan 1944

1b *Kayleen Elizabeth Hinshaw; *b* 27 April 1939

2b *Katherine Louise; *b* 26 May 1940

(2) Cecil de Vere; Lt 1st Middx Regt WW I (medals and star); *b* 21 Feb 1881; *ka* 25 Sept 1915

(1) Margaret Alice; *m* 12 Dec 1899 Harry Hamilton Hinshaw (*d* 26 Oct 1918), 3rd s of John Hinshaw, of Balgreen Ho, Hamilton, Lanarks, and *dsp* 31 May 1956

5 John Sexton; *b* 15 June 1849; *d* 19 Sept 1921

6 Harry de Vere; Sub-Lt, RN, Capt and Instr Musketry 5th Bn Roy Munster Fus, Ashanti War 1873–74 (medal), RM Ireland 1885–1916; *b* 2 June 1951; *m* 10 Dec 1874 Harriette (*d* 31 Dec 1933), dau of Robert Knox, Dip Serv, and *d* 1 Sept 1935

7 Neville Calder; *b* 12 Dec 1852; *d* unm May 1896

1 Alice Louisa; *m* 1st 5 Aug 1868 Capt Percy Hughes Hewitt, 6th Dragoon Gds; *m* 2nd 7 March 1874 Edward Martin Langworthy, barrister, and *d* 15 Sept 1876

The 2nd EARL *d* 5 Jan 1866; his est son,

WILLIAM HALE JOHN CHARLES PERY, **3rd Earl of Limerick**, KP (1892), PC (1889), JP, DL; *b* 17 Jan 1840; ADC to HM QUEEN VICTORIA, Hon Col 5th Bn Roy Munster Fus, Ld-in-Waiting 1886–89, Capt Yeomen Gd 1889–92 and 1895–96; *m* 1st 28 Aug 1862 his cousin Caroline Maria (*d* 24 Jan 1877), dau of Rev Henry Gray, and had:

1 WILLIAM HENRY EDMOND DE VERE SHEAFFE PERY, **4th Earl of Limerick**, DL Co Limerick; *b* 16 Sept 1863; *educ* Eton; Lt 4th Bn Rifle Bde 1884–90, Capt and Hon Maj 5th Bn Roy Munster Fus; *m* 23 July 1890 May Imelda Josephine, CBE (1920) (*d* 11 March 1943), dau of Joseph Burke Irwin, RM, of The Priory, Co Limerick, and *d* 18 March 1929, having had:

(1) Edmond William Claude Gerard de Vere, *Lord Glentworth*; Capt RAF and Lt Warwicks Yeo; *b* 14 Oct 1894; *ka* 18 May 1918

(1) Imelda Sybil; *b* 10 and *d* 12 Nov 1891

(2) Victoria May; *b* 4 May 1893; *m* 14 Oct 1914 James Cox Brady (*d* 1927), of New York, s of Anthony Brady, and *d* 27 Dec 1918, leaving issue

The **3rd Earl** *m* 2nd 20 Oct 1877 Isabella (*m* 2nd 22 Feb 1898 Maj Sir Edmund Halbert Elliot, MVO (*see* MINTO, E), and *d* 10 Nov 1927), dau of James Charles Henry Colquhoun, and *d* 8 Aug 1896, having by her had:

2 EDMUND COLQUHOUN, **5th Earl**

1 Florence Louise Beatrice Esterelle Isabelle; *d* unm 7 March 1955

2 May Katherine Leila; *m* 22 Oct 1908 Capt Frederick Lewis Maitland Boothby, CBE, RN (*d* 3 Jan 1940), er s of Alexander Cunningham Boothby, CE (*see* 1970 edn BOOTHBY, B), and *d* 29 June 1959, leaving issue

The 4th EARL's half-bro,

EDMOND COLQUHOUN PERY, **5th Earl of Limerick**, GBE (1953), CH (1960), KCB (1945), DSO (1918), TD; *b* 16 Oct 1888; *educ* Eton and New Coll Oxford; Lt City London; Brevet Col RA (TA), cmdg City London Yeo Battery, RHA (TA) and 11th Bde RHA (TA), Hon Col City London Yeo RAC (TA) 1932–52, WW I in Egypt, Gallipoli and France (despatches), chm City London TAAFA 1941–50 (v-chm 1937–41), pres Cncl TAFAs 1954–56 (v-chm 1942–49 and chm 1949–54), chm Medical Research Cncl 1952–60, dir London Life Assoc Ltd, Industrial and Commercial Finance Corp; *m* 1 June 1926 Angela Olivia, GBE (1954, DBE 1946), CH (1974), DL (W Sussex 1977) (*d* 1981), Govr Stowe and Charterhouse to 1976, memb LCC 1936–46, v-chm BRCS 1942–63, chm Standing Commn Internat Red Cross, pres Multiple Sclerosis Soc, Austrian Order Merit 1959, DStJ, Henry Dunant Medal 1975, dau of Lt-Col Sir Henry Trotter, KCMG, CB, and *d* 4 Aug 1967, having had:

1 PATRICK EDMUND PERY, **6th and present Earl of Limerick**

2 +Michael Henry Colquhoun [The Hon Michael Pery, Ardtur, Appin, Argyll PA38 4DD]; late 2nd Lt 12th Roy Lancers, Lt Inns of Court and City Yeo, chm

ECOSCI, OPTOSCI, formerly md Sifam Ltd, dir London Life Assoc; *b* 8 May 1937; *educ* Eton and New Coll Oxford (BA 1960); *m* 13 July 1963 *Jennifer Mary, BA Oxon, er dau of John Anthony Stuart-Williams, of Causeway Ho, Braughing, Herts, and has:

(1) +Marcus Alexander Kemal; *b* 2 Oct 1965; *educ* Eton

(2) +Fergus Anthony Colquhoun; *b* 4 March 1967; *educ* Eton; *m* 10 May 1997 *Emma, dau of Dr Rhind Tutt, of Wargrave, Berks

(1) *Pervaneh Frances; *b* 20 Feb 1969

(2) *Azelle Fiona; *b* 7 April 1971

1 *Anne Patricia [The Lady Anne Thorne, Chiddinglye Farmhouse, W Hoathly, Sussex RH 19 4QS]; Sr Research Fell Imperial Coll London, chm Ardingly Coll Cncl; *b* 3 Oct 1928; *educ* North Foreland Lodge and St Hugh's Coll Oxford (MA, DPhil 1954); author *Spectrophysics* (1988) and many papers in physics journals; *m* 16 May 1959 *Lt-Col Sir Peter Francis Thorne, KCVO, CBE, ERD, late Gren Gds, Serjeant at Arms H of C 1976–82, yst s of Gen Sir (Augustus Francis) Andrew (Nicol) Thorne, KCB, CMG, DSO, DL, of Knowl Hill Ho, Reading, and has:

(1) *Andrew Henry; *b* 15 Sept 1965; *m* 25 June 1994 *Sarah, er dau of H T Fanconi, of Sticklepath, Devon

(1) *Bridget Iolanthe; *b* 5 July 1961; *m* 3 June 1995 *Peter Sychta, s of Dr Stanislaw Sychta, of Horsham, Sussex

(2) *Meriel Patricia; *b* 18 May 1963; *m* 10 Jan 1998 *Philip Stinson, er s of Robert Stinson, of Englefield Green, Surrey

(3) *Janet Melinda; *b* 26 March 1968

LINCOLN

Arms: Argent six cross-crosslets fitchée sable, three, two and one, on a chief azure two mullets or pierced gules. **Crest:** Out of a ducal coronet gules a plume of five ostrich feathers argent banded with a line laid chevronwise azure. **Supporters:** Two greyhounds argent, plain collared and lined gules. **Motto:** *Loyaulté n'a honte* ('There is no shame in loyalty'). **Creation:** E. (E) 4 May 1572.

THE 18TH EARL OF LINCOLN (Edward Horace Fiennes-Clinton) [The Rt Hon The Earl of Lincoln, Flat 45, Elanora Villas, 37 Hastie St, Bunbury, WA 6230, Australia]; *b* 23 Feb 1913; *s* kinsman 1988; *m* 1st 1940 Leila Ruth Millen (*d* 19 July 1947), dau of John James Millen, of Kalgoorlie, W Australia; *m* 2nd 3 Dec 1953 Linda Alice (*d* 19–), dau of Charles Creed and widow of James O'Brien, of Kalgoorlie, and by his 1st w has:

1 +EDWARD GORDON [The Hon Edward Fiennes-Clinton, 6 Jasminum Place, Carcoola Estate, Pinjarra, W Australia 6208]; *b* 7 Feb 1943; *m* 12 Dec 1970 *Julia Eleanor, 1st dau of William Thomas Howson, of 10 Waltham Rd, Armadale, Perth, and has:

(1) +Robert Edward; *b* 19 June 1972

(2) +William Roy; *b* 1980

(1) *Marian Dawn; *b* 3 July 1973

1 *Patricia Ruth [The Lady Patricia Elrick, 2 Tucker St, PC 6271, Capel, W Australia 6084]; *b* 1 Feb 1941; *m* 27 Jan 1959 (*divorce* 1970) Alexander George Stuart Elrick (*d* 1979), s of Francis Elrick, and has:

(1) *Nicholas James; *b* 24 Aug 1959; *m* 1st 1979 (*divorce* 1992) Rosa Audino; *m* 2nd 19– *Monique Veronica Gardner (*née* Truman) and by his 1st w has:

1a *Steven John; *b* 1980

2a *Peter James; *b* 1981

(2) *David Wayne; *b* 29 June 1961

(3) *Warren Stuart; *b* 4 Dec 1962

(1) *Leilani Yvonne; *b* 1974

Lincoln, previous creations: HENRY I's widow ADELIZ married in 1138 William d'Aubigny, who the next year, probably as a result, was created Earl of Lincoln. William's father was a Norman immigrant to England in HENRY I's reign. His son, who by this advantageous marriage came into the former Queen's dowry of Arundel Castle, together with its Honour (feudal administrative unit embodying several knight's fees), has been held thereby to have become Earl of Arundel (*see also* NORFOLK, D). By 1142 he had been deprived of his Earldom of Lincoln and thereafter, indeed even before, was spoken of sometimes as Earl of Arundel and sometimes as Earl of Chichester or Earl of Sussex (*see* CHICHESTER, E, for elaboration on this point).

Meanwhile one William de Roumare, also a Norman, who seems to have had a close though ill-defined connection with Lincolnshire in terms of land-holdings via his mother Lucy, apparently resented the grant of the Earldom of that county to d'Aubigny. He and his half-brother the Earl of Chester therefore appropriated Lincoln Castle in 1140 and fortified it against KING STEPHEN, who swiftly laid siege to it but was made prisoner by Chester and another ally of his, the Earl of Gloucester. STEPHEN was eventually set free and having patched up the quarrel with de Roumares created him Earl of Lincoln in or about 1141. That the patching was somewhat threadbare may be inferred from the fact that only six or so years later STEPHEN made Gilbert de Ga(u)nt Earl of Lincoln, although de Roumares had not apparently been deprived of the dignity. Like de Roumares, de Ga(u)nt had ancestral links with the county, his grandfather having held one of its most substantial agglomerations of manors at the time of the Domesday Survey in 1086.

De Roumare's grandson and successor, another William, seems never to have been styled Earl of Lincoln and died without issue in any case. The Earldom of Lincoln was revived nearly twenty years after the putative 2nd Earl's death in favour of his cousin Ranulph Earl of Chester, who of course also had a long-standing connection with the county through their common ancestress Countess Lucy. Ranulph's prominent role in defeating the French invaders at the Battle of Lincoln earlier in 1217, the year he was made Earl of Lincoln, played a part in his elevation. Soon after Michaelmas 1230 he made over the Earldom to his sister Hawise, from whom it was conveyed to her son-in-law John de Lacy, the traffic in the dignity being approved by HENRY III in both cases in the autumn of 1232.

The Earldom of Lincoln continued to be held by the de Lacys for another two generations, the 3rd Earl dying without surviving male issue. His daughter Alice is discussed in the preliminary remarks to the article SALISBURY (*qv*). Here it will be sufficient to say that she was deemed to have become Countess of Lincoln on her father's death and to have transmitted the lands that went with the Earldom of Lincoln to her son by Thomas, Earl of Lancaster (the same Earl of Lancaster who rebelled against his cousin EDWARD II and was defeated at Boroughbridge in March 1321/2). This son, Henry, was created in 1349 Earl of Lincoln, which suggests that by now the dignity of an earldom and the territorial possessions that went with it were coming to be looked on as two separate entities. Henry died leaving only daughters, the younger of whom married John of Gaunt, who among other titles arrogated the Earldom of Lincoln to himself. With the accession of Gaunt's son to the throne as HENRY IV the Earldom must be regarded as having merged in the Crown.

The title was once again revived, and once again in favour of a close connection of the King, in March 1466/7, when John de la Pole, nephew of EDWARD IV through his mother, was made a peer. He strengthened his ties with EDWARD by marrying the latter's niece through the Queen Consort Elizabeth Woodville. He was even declared in May 1485 by RICHARD III to be his heir, should the new King fail to beget male issue, but the events of that summer put an end to such glittering possibilities when RICHARD was defeated and killed at Bosworth, his nephew and heir apparent the 1st and last Earl of Lincoln of the 1466/7 creation fighting at his side. Unlike his uncle, Lincoln survived. He swiftly made his peace with HENRY VII but the next year went abroad and started agitating on behalf of Lambert Simnel. He was killed at the ensuing Battle of Stoke in 1487, when the Earldom expired. He was in any case posthumously attainted.

The last pre-Clinton creation occurred in 1525, when HENRY VIII's nephew Henry Brandon, eldest son of Charles Brandon, Duke of Suffolk, by HENRY's sister MARY, QUEEN DOWAGER OF FRANCE, was so ennobled. The boy was only nine at the time. He died just under nine years later and the title expired with him.

The choice of Lincoln as Edward Clinton/Fiennes's title when promoted in the peerage in 1572 is partly explicable by his having been granted substantial monastic lands in the county back in HENRY VIII's reign and appointed its Lord Lieutenant shortly before the end of EDWARD VI's. He had also married as his first wife one of HENRY VIII's mistresses, and the close association of the Lincoln title with hangers-on of the Sovereign over the past four hundred years, starting with William d'Aubigny, the man who married a former king's widow, may well have helped commend it.

Lineage: EDWARD CLINTON alias FIENNES, 9th LORD (Baron) CLINTON (*qv*) and **1st Earl of Lincoln** (E), so *cr* 4 May 1572; had by his 2nd w, with other issue (*see* BURGH, B, and WILLOUGHBY DE ERESBY, B):

HENRY CLINTON alias FIENNES, **2nd Earl of Lincoln** and 10th LORD (Baron) CLINTON; had by his 1st w:

1 THOMAS CLINTON alias FIENNES, **3rd Earl of Lincoln** and 11th LORD (Baron) CLINTON; had, with other issue:

(1) THEOPHILUS CLINTON alias FIENNES, **4th Earl of Lincoln** and 12th LORD (Baron) CLINTON; had by his 1st w:

1a Edward, *Lord Clinton*; *dvp* 1657, leaving issue:

1b EDWARD CLINTON alias FIENNES, **5th Earl of Lincoln** and 13th LORD (Baron) CLINTON; *dsps* 25 Nov 1692, when the Barony of Clinton fell into abeyance between his aunts or their issue

(1) Margaret; *m* Hugh Boscawen, of Tregothnan, Cornwall, and had issue (*see* FORTESCUE, E)

2 Edward (Sir); *m* Mary, dau of Thomas Dighton, of Stourton Parva, Lincs, and had, with two er sons (*dsp*):

(1) Francis, of Stourton Parva; *m* Priscilla, dau of John Hill, and had an only s:

1a FRANCIS CLINTON, **6th Earl of Lincoln**; *b c* 1635; ktd 1661, Gent Privy Chamber 1669; *m* 1st Elizabeth (*dsps* and was *bur* 1677), dau of Sir William Killigrew, and had a son (*d* in infancy); *m* 2nd *c* 1683 Susannah, dau of Rev Anthony Penyston, and was *bur* 3 Sept 1693, having by her had, with an er s (*d* young):

1b HENRY CLINTON, **7th Earl of Lincoln**, KG (1721), PC (1715); *b* 1684; a Ld Bedchamber to QUEEN ANNE's husb PRINCE GEORGE OF DENMARK 1708 and GEORGE I 1714–27, Master Horse to PRINCE OF WALES 1714, Jt Paymaster-Gen Forces (Whig) 1715–20, Constable Tower London 1723–25, Cofferer Household 1725–28, Ld Lt Cambs March-Sept 1728; allegedly bequeathed by Lord Torrington (presumably the then Earl of Torrington, *qv*) property worth £6,000 (some £83,500 in late–1990s terms) p.a. on no better grounds than that Lord Torrigton loathed his heir and Lord Lincoln was an impoverished nobleman, since the testator had never seen the beneficiary when he made his will; *m* 16 May 1717 Lucy (*d* 20 July 1736), dau of 1st Baron Pelham of Laughton (*see* CHICHESTER, E) and sis of 1st Duke of Newcastle-under-Line, so *cr* 17 Nov 1756 with special remainder to his nephew, Henry, **9th Earl of Lincoln**, and *d* 7 Sept 1728, leaving:

1c GEORGE CLINTON, **8th Earl of Lincoln**; *b* 15 Jan 1718; *d* unm 30 April 1780,

2c HENRY CLINTON later PELHAM-CLINTON (roy licence 1 Dec 1768), **9th Earl of Lincoln** and 2nd DUKE OF NEWCASTLE-UNDER-LINE, KG (1752), PC (1768); *b* 16 April 1720; *educ* Eton and Clare Hall Cambridge; Ld Lt Cambs 1742–57 and Notts 1768–94, Ld Bedchamber to GEORGE II and GEORGE III 1743–62, Master Jewel Office 1744, Cofferer Household 1746–54, Auditor Exchequer 1751–94; *m* 16 Oct 1744 his cousin Catherine (*d* 27 July 1760), est dau of Rt Hon Henry Pelham (*see* CHICHESTER, E), and *d* 22 Feb 1794, having had:

1d George, *Lord Clinton*; *b* 26 Nov 1745; *dvp* 19 Aug 1752

2d Henry Fiennes, *Earl of Lincoln*; *b* 5 Nov 1750; *educ* Eton; MP (Tory) Aldborough 1777–74 and Notts 1774–78; *m* 21 May 1775 Lady Frances Seymour-Conway, dau of 1st Marquess of Hertford (*qv*), and *dvp* 18 Oct 1778, having had:

1e Henry, *Earl of Lincoln*; *b* 23 Dec 1777; *d* 23 Sept 1779

1e Catherine; *b* 6 April 1776; *m* 2 Oct 1800 3rd Earl of Radnor (*qv*) and *dspm* 18 May 1804

3d THOMAS PELHAM-CLINTON, **10th Earl of Lincoln** and 3rd DUKE OF NEWCASTLE-UNDER-LINE; *b* 1 July 1752; *educ* Eton; joined Army 1769 (Capt 1st Foot Gds and ADC to his cousin Gen Sir Henry Clinton in America 1779–80, ADC to GEORGE III 1780–87, Maj-Gen 1787, Col 75th Foot 1782–83, Col 17th Light Dragoons 1785–95), MP (Tory) Westminster 1774–80 and E Retford 1781–94, Ld Lt Notts 1794–95; *m* 2 May 1782 Anna Maria (*m* 2nd 7 Feb 1800 Lt-Gen Sir Charles Gregan Craufurd, GCB (*see* CRAUFURD, Bt), and *d* 18 Oct 1834), yst dau of 2nd Earl of Harrington (*qv*), and *d* 18 May 1795, leaving:

1e HENRY PELHAM PELHAM-CLINTON, **11th Earl of Lincoln** and 4th DUKE OF NEWCASTLE-UNDER-LINE, KG (1812); *b* 30 Jan 1785; *educ* Eton (where the Newcastle scholarship was founded by him); Ld Lt Notts 1809–39, DCL 1834, Steward and Keeper Sherwood Forest, High Steward Retford; *m* 18 July 1807 Georgiana Elizabeth (*d* 20 Sept 1822), dau of Edward Miller Mundy, of Shipley, Derbys, and *d* 12 Jan 1851, having had, with other issue:

1f HENRY PELHAM PELHAM-CLINTON, **12th Earl of Lincoln** and 5th DUKE OF NEWCASTLE-UNDER-LINE, KG (1860), (PC GB 1841, I 1846); *b* 22 May 1811; *educ* Eton and Ch Ch Oxford; MP (C) S Notts 1832–46 and (Peelite) Falkirk Burghs 1846–51, a Ld Treasury 1834–35, First Commr Woods and Forests 1841–46, Ch Sec Ireland with Cabinet seat Jan-July 1846, Colonial Sec 1852–54 and 1859–64, Sec State War 1854–55, Ld Lt Notts 1857–64, Ld Warden Stannaries 1862–64; *m* 27 Nov 1832 (*divorce* 1850) Lady Susan Harriet Catherine Hamilton (*m* 2nd 2 Jan 1860 — Opdebeck, of Brussels, and *d* 28 Nov 1889), only dau of 10th Duke of Hamilton (*see* HAMILTON and BRANDON, D), and *d* 18 Oct 1864, having had:

1g HENRY PELHAM ALEXANDER PELHAM-CLINTON, **13th Earl of Lincoln** and 6th DUKE OF NEWCASTLE-UNDER-LINE; *b* 25 Jan 1834; *educ* Eton and Ch Ch Oxford; MP (Lib) Newark 1857–59; *m* 11 Feb 1861 Henrietta Adela (*m* 2nd 7 April 1880 Thomas Theobald Hohler (*d* 2 May 1892), yst s of Rev Frederick William Hohler, Rector Winstone and Colesborne, Glos, and *d* 8 May 1913), illegitimate dau but heiress of Henry Thomas Hope, of the banking family who at one time owned the Hope Diamond, of Deepdene, Surrey, and Castle Blayney, Co Monahan, by Anne Adèle Bichet (whom he afterwards married), dau of Joseph Bichet, and *d* 22 Feb 1879, leaving:

1h HENRY PELHAM ARCHIBALD DOUGLAS PELHAM-CLINTON, **14th Earl of Lincoln** and 7th DUKE OF NEWCASTLE-UNDER-LINE, DL Notts; *b* 28 Sept 1864; *educ* Eton and Magdalen Coll Oxford; KGStJ, Master Forester Dartmoor, Keeper St Briavel's Castle; *m* 20 Feb 1889 Kathleen Florence May, OBE (1920) (*d* 1 June 1955), dau of Maj Henry Augustus Candy, 9th Lancers, by Hon Frances Kathleen, dau of 3rd Baron Rossmore (*qv*), and *dsp* 30 May 1928

2h HENRY FRANCIS HOPE PELHAM-CLINTON later PELHAM-CLINTON-HOPE (roy licence 7 April 1887), **15th Earl of Lincoln** and 8TH DUKE OF NEWCASTLE-UNDER-LINE; *b* 3 Feb 1866; Lt Notts Yeo Cav, High Sheriff Co Monaghan 1891 and 1917; *m* 1st 27 Nov 1894 (*divorce* 1902) Mary Augusta (*d* 27 Aug 1938), dau of William Yohé; *m* 2nd 27 Feb 1904 Olive Muriel (*d* 30 Aug 1912), formerly w of Richard Owen and yr dau of George Horatio Thompson, of Melbourne, and *d* 20 April 1941, having by her had:

1i HENRY EDWARD HUGH PELHAM-CLINTON-HOPE, **16th Earl of Lincoln** and 9th DUKE OF NEWCASTLE-UNDER-LINE, OBE (1945), DL (1937–48), JP (Notts 1933–48); *b* 8 April 1907; *educ* Eton and Magdalene Coll Cambridge (BA); cmded 616 RAF Sqdn 1938–39, A/W/Cdr RAuxAF WW II; *m* 1st 23 March 1931 (*divorce* 1940) Mrs Jean Banks Gimbernat (*d* 2 Sept 1968), yst dau of David Banks, of Park Ave, NY, USA; *m* 2nd 30 Nov 1946 (*divorce* 1959) Lady (Mary) Diana Montagu-Stuart-Wortley (*d* 19

Sept 1997), 2nd dau of 3rd Earl of Wharncliffe (qv), and had:

1j *Patricia [The Lady Patricia Pelham-Clinton-Hope, 6901 Washington Rd, W Palm Beach, FL 33450, USA]; b 20 July 1949; film actress; m 1st 1971 (divorce 1974, resumed maiden name) Alan Pariser; m 2nd 1981 (divorce 1983, resumed maiden name again) Nick Mancuso, actor, of Toronto, and has:

1k *Dorian Henry Navarr PELHAM-CLINTON-KOLE; b 1990

2j *Kathleen Marie Gabrielle [The Lady Kathleen Pelham-Clinton, The Cottage, Ballinakil, Kilfinny, nr Croom, Co Limerick, Ireland]; b 1 Jan 1951; m 1st 27 Feb 1970 (divorce, resumed maiden name) Edward Vernon Reynolds, s of Henry Reynolds, of The Mall, Kenton, Middx; m 2nd 19– (divorce) —, of Thailand and has had by *Alan Dawson:

1k Sean; b July 1971; d in infancy

1k *Roxanna; b 23 Nov 1973

1i (cont.) The **16th Earl** m 3rd 23 Oct 1959 *Mrs Sally Ann Wemyss Hope, formerly w of Fikret Jemal and er dau of Brig John Henry Anstice, DSO and bar, of Kyrenia, Cyprus, and d 4 Nov 1988

1i Doria Lois; b 17 June 1908; m 1st 22 Feb 1930 (divorce) Maj Frederick Baldwin Childe, only surv s of Lt-Col Frederick Childe, of Roundhay, Oxford. He d 20 June 1967. She m 2nd 26 Feb 1936 Stefan Newmann, s of Alfred Neumann, of Vienna, and d 26 Sept 1942, leaving issue

2i Mary; b 4 July 1910; m 1st 20 Sept 1930 (annulled 1933) (Charles) Kenneth Horne (d 14 Feb 1969), s of Rev Sylvester Horne; m 2nd 1939 (divorce 1946) Romain Alphonse Stemmer; m 3rd 1947 William Serge Belaieff and d 27 June 1982. He d 15 Oct 1964

1h Beatrice Adeline; b 12 Feb 1862; m 16 Sept 1880 Sir Cecil Edmund Lister-Kaye, 4th Bt (qv), and d 16 June 1935, leaving issue

2h Emily Augusta Mary; b 28 March 1863; m 24 June 1882 Prince Alfonso Doria Pamphilj, Duke d'Avigliano, s of Prince Philip Doria Pamphilj Landj, and d 23 Dec 1919, leaving issue. He d 6 Dec 1914

3h Florence Josephine; b 18 Sept 1868; d 15 April 1935

2g Edward William (Sir), GCVO, KCB, DL Notts, Groom-in-Waiting to TM QUEEN VICTORIA 1881–94 and EDWARD VII 1901–07, Master Household 1894–1901, Col London Rifle Bde, MP N Notts 1865–68; b 11 Aug 1836; m 22 Aug 1865 Matilda Jane (dsp 23 Oct 1892), 3rd dau of Sir William Edmund Cradock-Hartopp, 3rd Bt (qv), and d 9 July 1907

3g Arthur, Lt RN, MP Newark; b 23 June 1840; d 18 June 1870

4g Albert Sidney; b 22 Dec 1845; m 17 Nov 1870 (divorce 23 Nov 1877) Frances Evelyn, widow of Capt Edward Stotherd, 60th Rifles, and dsp 1 March 1884

1g Susan Charlotte Catherine; m 23 April 1860 Lt-Col Lord Adolphus Vane-Tempest, 3rd s of 3rd Marquess of Londonderry (qv), and d 6 Sept 1875, leaving issue

2f Charles Pelham; Capt 1st Life Gds, MP Sandwich; b 3 Dec 1813; m 10 Aug 1848 Elizabeth (d 7 Nov 1899), only surv child of William Grant, of Congalton, and d 15 Dec 1894, leaving issue:

1g Charles Stapleton, of Woodrow High Ho, Amersham, Bucks, and Waterfall, Berehaven, Co Cork, JP Co Cork and S Bucks; Lt Leinster Regt; b 23 July 1857; m 6 Oct 1886 Elizabeth (d 29 Sept 1946), only dau of Louis H Zerega di Zerega, of New York, and dsp 22 Oct 1911

2g Henry William; b 21 Oct 1860; m 21 July 1886 Mary (d 31 Oct 1936), dau of Lt-Gen Frederick Green Wilkinson, CB, and d 18 Dec 1927, leaving:

1h (Henry Charles) Frederick; F/Lt RAFVR, Capt Notts Yeo WW I Dardanelles, Macedonia and Palestine (wounded twice); b 6 Sept 1892; educ Eton; m 24 Nov 1920 Dorothy Charlotte Middleton (d 14 Oct 1969), only child of Capt J Carlon, of Toronto, and d 8 June 1968, leaving:

1i *Ethne Mary [Mrs Jasper Hubbard, Hammonds, Lewes Heath, Kent TN12 8EE]; b 22 Sept 1923; m 6 Feb 1951 *Jasper Picton Hubbard, yr s of Eric Wyndham Hubbard, JP (see ADDINGTON, B), and has issue

2h Guy Edward, MC; BA Cambridge, Capt RE WW I (despatches); b 11 April 1894; m 30 July 1918 Hermione Edith Agnes, yst dau of Arthur Frederick Churchill Tollemache (see TOLLEMACHE, Bt), and d 18 Dec 1934, leaving:

1i EDWARD CHARLES PELHAM-CLINTON, **17th Earl of Lincoln** and 10th and last DUKE OF NEWCASTLE-UNDER-LINE; b 18 Aug 1920; educ Eton and Trin Coll Cambridge; Capt RA WW II (despatches), lepidopterist, Assist Keeper Roy Scottish Museum Edinburgh 1960–80; d unm 25 Dec 1988, when the Dukedom expired

2i Alastair Henry; F/O RAF WW II; b 29 March 1923; ka over Bay of Biscay 24 May 1943

1h Kathleen Lettice Mary; b 15 Aug 1887; d unm 19 April 1946

3g Hubert Edward; b 30 March 1862; m 1st 23 Sept 1893 Louisa Brooks (d 27 Aug 1911), widow of Henry Fitzwilliam Browne and dau of E Macaulay Arnaud, of Bath; m 2nd 28 Oct 1911 Helen (d 1963), yst dau of James William Halcrow, of Burton-on-Trent, and d 29 Aug 1913, leaving:

1h *Marjorie; b 1910; m 1940 Edward Date Long (d 1982) and has:

1i *Richard Pelham [Richard Long Esq, 58 Northcroft Lane, Newbury, Berks, RG13 1BN]; b 1941; educ Harrow, Queens' Coll Cambridge (MA) and Stanford U, Calif (MBA); m 1973 (divorce 1985) Roslyn Vera, only dau of Capt Gordon Britton, RN, and has:

1j *Camilla Elizabeth; b 1978

2j *Zoë Rebecca; b 1980

1i *Alison Jean [Mrs Gerry Rowe, 1887 Stonepath Crescent, Mississauga, Ont LAX 1Y1, Canada]; b 1945; m 1969 *Gerry Rowe and has:

1j *Jonathan Oliver; b 1974

1j *Deborah Elizabeth; b 1971

2h *Georgiana Elizabeth May [Mrs John Bordewich, Highgrove House, 32 Winchester Rd, Worthing, Sussex]; b 7 May 1913, adopted 1916 by her aunt Mrs Charles Stapleton Pelham-Clinton (see above); m 3 March 1951 John Stuart Bordewich, MVO (d 1986), yst s of Peter Magnus Roness Bordewich, of Kensington, and has:

1i *John Peter Pelham; b 10 Jan 1955

4g A son; b and d Dec 1862

1g Emily Dora; m 9 Feb 1881 Sir George William Hervey, KCB (see BRISTOL, M), and d 30 Sept 1921, leaving issue

2g Adela Harriett; m 1st 2 Aug 1871 John Campbell, 2nd Queen's Regt, est s of Colin Campbell, of Stonefield, Argyllshire, and had issue. He d 1885. She m 2nd 24 Feb 1903 Col George Hastings Brooke (see BROOKEBOROUGH, V) and d 21 May 1915

3g Edith Elizabeth; d 11 May 1859

3f Thomas Charles; b 3 Dec 1813; m 31 July 1843 Marianne (got judicial separation 1865 and d 3 May 1887), dau of Francis Gritton, and d 28 Feb 1882

4f Robert Renebald; MP N Notts; b 15 Oct 1820; d 25 July 1867

1f Caroline Augusta; m 29 Jan 1852 Sir Cornwallis Ricketts, 2nd Bt (qv), and d 3 June 1898, leaving issue

2f Henrietta; m 1 March 1859 Adml Edwin Clayton Tennyson-d'Eyncourt, CB, of Bayons Manor, Lincs, and d 19 Aug 1890, leaving issue. He d 4 Jan 1903

2e Thomas; d 8 Oct 1804

1e Anna Maria; m 1 Jan 1801 1st Viscount Combermere (qv) and dsp 31 May 1807

2e Charlotte; d 23 May 1811

4d John; MP; b 1781

2b George; Sr Adml the White, Govr Newfoundland 1732 and New York 1741; m Anne (d 5 Aug 1761), dau and coheir of Gen Peter Carle, and d 10 July 1761, leaving:

1c Henry (Sir), KB; C-in-C Land Forces America War American Independence; m Feb 1767 Harriet (d 29 Aug 1772), dau and coheir of Thomas Carter, and d 13 Dec 1795, leaving:

1d William Henry (Sir), GCB; Gen, Col 55th Foot, Lt-Govr Chelsea Hosp; b 23 Dec 1769; m 14 March 1797 Louisa Dorothea (d 14 May 1854), dau of 1st Earl of Sheffield (see STANLEY OF ALDERLEY, SHEFFIELD and, B), and d 15 Feb 1846, leaving, with other issue:

1e Henry, of Earlsbury Park, Royston, Herts; Col; b 24 Feb 1802; m 17 Aug 1863 Priscilla, dau of James Loder, and d 13 March 1881, leaving:

1f Henry; b 28 May 1865; d 28 June 1888

2f Frederick; b 11 Dec 1868; m Isabella, er dau of Robert Lambert

2e Frederick; Col Gren Gds; b 28 Aug 1804; m 9 July 1840 Hon Mary Margaret Montagu (d 30 July 1885), 2nd dau of 2nd and last Baron Montagu of Boughton (see BUCCLEUCH and QUEENSBERRY, D), and d 9 Nov 1870, leaving:

1f Henry Renebald, of Ashley Clinton, Lymington, Hants, JP Hants; Lt-Col Gren Gds; b 23 March 1841; d 1916

2f Walter Francis; RN; b 6 April 1845; d 30 Dec 1859

3f William Osbert (Rev); Rector Padworth, Berks; b 11 Sept 1850; educ Trin Coll Cambridge (MA); m 12 May 1880 Margaret (d 24 April 1905), yst dau of Rev William L Eliot, Rector Creeting, Suffolk, and d 12 Nov 1921, leaving:

1g Walter Laurence, of Ashley Clinton; Capt KRRC WW I; b 18 May 1883; d unm 22 Nov 1918

1g Frances Elinor; b 2 April 1881

1f Lucy Dorothea; m 9 July 1872 George Selwyn Marryat and had issue. He d 1896

1e Anna Maria; m 28 April 1855 Robert Pigot and d 6 Nov 1880. He d 9 Jan 1873

2d Henry (Sir), GCB, GCH; Lt-Gen; m 23 Dec 1799 Susan (d 17 Aug 1816), 2nd dau of Francis, Lord Elcho (see WEMYSS, E), and dsp 11 Dec 1829

1d Augusta; m 1778 Henry Dawkins, MP, and had issue. He d 1852

2d Harriet; m 3 Sept 1799 Maj-Gen Harry Chester

1c Mary; m Sir Francis Willes, of Hampstead

2c Lucy Mary; m Adml Robert Roddam and d 1750

1b Susannah; m her cousin Capt Robert Booth, bro of Very Rev Penyston Booth (see BERNERS, B), and had issue

The **2nd Earl** m 2nd Elizabeth (d 1611), widow of William Norreys (see LINDSEY and ABINGDON, E) and dau of Sir Richard Morrison, of Cashiobury, Herts, and by her had:

3 Henry (Sir), of Kirkstead, Lincs; b 1587; m 1st Eleanor, dau of Sir James Harrington, and had issue; m 2nd 1624 Elizabeth, dau of Dr Henry Hickman, and d 1641, having by her had had issue; by his 1st w he left, with other issue:

(1) Henry; dspm, leaving a yst dau and coheir (Catherine, m 1674 Daniel Disney, of Swinderby)

(2) Harrington; *d* unm

(3) Norreys; gggf of:

1a Charles CLINTON later FYNES-CLINTON (roy licence 26 April 1821) (Rev); LLD; Rector Cromwell, Notts, Preb St Peter's, Westminster; *m* 15 July 1779 Emma (*d* 15 Aug 1881), dau of Job Brough, of Newark, Notts, and *d* 13 Nov 1827, leaving:

1b Henry, of Welwyn, Herts; MP Aldborough, Yorks; *b* 14 Jan 1781; *m* 1st 22 June 1809 Harriet (*dsp* 2 Feb 1810), dau of Rev Charles Wyld, DD; *m* 2nd 6 Jan 1812 Katherine (*d* 25 April 1871), dau of Rt Rev H W Majendie, Bp Bangor, and *d* 24 Oct 1852, leaving, with other issue (*d* unm):

1c Anne Emma Katherine; *m* 4 Oct 1838 William Robert Baker, of Bayfordbury, and *d* 2 May 1894, leaving issue. He *d* 29 Nov 1896

2c Anna Maria Isabella; *m* 13 Aug 1839 Thomas Gambier Parry, JP, DL, of Highnam Ct, Glos, and *d* 11 March 1848, leaving issue. He *d* 28 Sept 1888

3c Louisa Emma Mary; *m* 23 Aug 1853 Rev T W Weare, of Hampton Ho, and *d* 11 Jan 1865, leaving issue. He *d* 24 Feb 1871

4c Margaretta; *m* 14 April 1852 Rev J R P Hoste, Rector Meonstoke, Hants, Canon Winchester, and *d* 2 May 1893, leaving issue

5c Agnes; *m* 26 Nov 1846 Rev Hon Richard Godolphin Henry Hastings and *d* 6 March 1872, having had issue (*see* HUNTINGDON, E)

6c Ida; *m* 1st 21 June 1855 Henry Negus Burroughes, RN (*dsp* 9 Jan 1856); *m* 2nd 8 July 1858 James Hollway and had issue

2b Clinton James FYNES-CLINTON later FYIENNES-CLINTON; MP Aldborough, Yorks, barrister; *b* 13 Dec 1792; *m* 8 May 1825 Penelope (*d* 5 June 1834), dau of Sir William Earle Welby, 2nd Bt (*qv*), and *d* 11 April 1833, leaving, with a dau (*d* unm):

1c Henry (Rev); MA Durham; Rector Cromwell, Notts; *b* 5 Feb 1826; *m* 9 July 1850 Sarah Katherine (*d* 23 March 1898), dau of Rev John B Smith, DD, and *d* 17 Oct 1911, having had:

1d Henry Glynne (Rev); BA Oxon; Rector St James, Vancouver, BC; *b* 31 Jan 1854; *d* unm 29 Jan 1912

2d Charles Edward; *b* 24 July 1855; *m* 5 April 1885 Alice Gertrude (*d* 1917), dau of William Waring, MD, and *d* 11 Jan 1888, having had:

1e Edward Henry; *b* 4 April 1886; *m* 1912 Edith Annie (*m* 2nd 1923 Robert Johnston Lynn), dau of Capt Horace Guest, and was *kas* WW I with ANZAC, leaving:

1f EDWARD HORACE FIENNES-CLINTON, **18th and present Earl of Lincoln**

2f +Gilbert Henry; *b* 21 May 1914

3d Clement Walter; slr; *b* 3 Dec 1856; *m* 1885 Lucy Eleanor (*d* 2 Nov 1944), dau of Henry J Hassell, and *d* 5 Jan 1919, leaving:

1e Henry; *b* 1885; *m* 26 Sept 1924 Catherine, dau of Rev Edmund Thomason, and had:

1f Henry Bernard; *b* 9 Oct 1929; *m* 14 Oct 1961 (*divorce* 1980) Carol Priscilla, dau of James Greig, of Toronto, and *d* 1990, leaving:

1g +Gregory Edward [Gregory Fiennes-Clinton Esq, 2 Lissom Crescent, N York, Ontario M2R 2P1, Canada]; *b* 6 Jan 1970; *m* 1994 *Sharon Quammie, of Toronto

2g +Richard James [Richard Fiennes-Clinton Esq, 27 Pintail Crescent, N York, Ontario M3A 2Y6, Canada]; *b* 4 March 1972

1e Lucy Eleanor Clement; *b* 1886

4d Henderson; *b* 27 Feb 1860; *dsp* 2nd May 1898

1d Eleanor Katherine; *m* 15 Oct 1872 Rev Seymour Bently, of Bute, Whitby, N R Yorks, Vicar Markham Clinton 1872–1902, and had issue. He *d* 1918

2d Ida Mary; *m* 31 Dec 1878 Anthony Swainson Allen, of Lower Wick Ho, Worcester, and *d* Dec 1932. He *d* 13 Feb 1923

3d Susan Charlotte Catherine; *m* 7 Aug 1884 Alfred Temple Roberts and *d* 26 Feb 1936, leaving issue. He *d* 1911

4d Madeline Isabella; *m* 20 Aug 1889 Rev Cecil Warburton Knox, BA Cantab, Curate St Margaret's Westminster 1906–11, and *d* 10 May 1952 aged 89, leaving issue

5d Adela Rachel; *m* 23 July 1891 Henry Mitchell Hull, CMG, of 42 The Strand, Walmer, Kent, s of Rev John Winstanley Hull, and *dsp* 1942. He *d* 3 Oct 1946

1c Mary Katherine; *m* 12 Dec 1855 Maj-Gen Thomas Knox, RA, and *d* 15 Dec 1873, leaving issue. He *d* 29 Oct 1878

3b Charles John (Rev); Rector Cromwell; *b* 16 April 1799; *m* 1st 10 March 1826 Caroline (*d* 11 Jan 1827), dau of Joseph Clay; *m* 2nd 20 May 1820 Rosabella (*d* 8 Dec 1871), dau of John Mathews, and *d* 10 Jan 1872, leaving:

1c Dormer (Rev); BA Oxon; *b* 21 Feb 1830; *m* 16 Dec 1862 Mary, dau of Maj J N Hewson, and *dsp* 8 May 1880

2c Charles Henry (Rev); Rector Blandford 1877–1913; *b* 5 June 1835; *educ* St John's Coll Cambridge (MA); *m* 1st 24 Feb 1863 Ellen Graeme (*d* 29 May 1871), dau of P R Falkner, and had:

1d Idonea; *d* unm 3 Dec 1881

2c (cont.) The Rev Charles Fynes-Clinton *m* 2nd 14 Jan 1873 Thomasina Gordon (*d* 1 April 1929), dau of James Shaw, and *d* 6 July 1915, having by her had:

1d Henry Joy (Rev); Rector St Magnus-the-Martyr's City of London 1921, Hon Chaplain to and Past-Master Plumbers' Co, Hon Chaplain Roy Soc St George (City branch), Fell Roy Empire Soc, Fell Coll Gdns Walsingham and Sion Coll, Chm Govrs St Michael's Sch, Otford, Govr Quainton Hall Sch, Harrow, Dir Catholic League, Fndr and Gen Sec Anglican and Eastern Churches Assoc 1906–20, Sec Archbishop's E Churches Ctee 1920–23, 1st Cl Order St Sava Serbia, 4th Cl Order St George Greece, 1st Cl Insignia Archpriest Church Serbia 1919 and Church of Russia 1930; *b* 6 May 1875; *educ* Trin Coll Oxford (BA 1808, MA 1901) and Ely Theol Coll; *d* unm 4 Dec 1959

2d Charles Pelham (Rev), MA; *b* 6 Oct 1878; *m* 19 Jan 1907 Grace Elizabeth MacDougall (*d* 28 June 1959 aged 91), only dau of Col James Graham, of Killiney, Co Dublin, and *dsp* 25 June 1933

1d Mary Gordon, RRC; WW II in CD; *d* unm 4 Feb 1953

2d Ida Norah Katherine; *m* 1st 23 April 1903 William Arthur Bedford Brennand, of Blandford, and had issue. He *d* 1908. She *m* 2nd 1916 Rev William Kilbride Gallagher. He *d* 1967

3c Osbert (Rev); BA Cantab; Rector Barlow Moor; *b* 18 July 1839; *m* 24 Jan 1867 Louisa (*d* 13 Feb 1915), dau of Edward Lloyd, and *d* 7 Nov 1900, leaving:

1d Charles Edward (Rev); Rector Lawford Essex 1934–43; *b* 14 Aug 1868; *educ* St John's Coll Cambridge (BA 1891, MA 1896); *m* 9 Sept 1902 Quenilda Mary (*d* 5 Aug 1917), dau of James Begg Shaw, of Didsbury, and *d* 1 Oct 1955, having had:

1e +Charles John; BSc Lond, ARSM; *b* 13 Oct 1909; *m* March 1943 Martha, dau of Samuel Mannes, of Aue, Saxony

2e Hugh Arthur; Inspr Schs Dept African Educn 1956–61, Pncpl Khaiso Sch Pietersburg Transvaal 1945–50, Headmaster St Chad's Coll Ladysmith 1950–54 ; *b* 8 Jan 1913; *educ* St John's Coll Cambridge (BA 1935, MA 1939); *m* 9 July 1945 *Pauline Ruth Ashton Dold [Mrs Hugh Fynes-Clinton, 2 Downash Ct, Rosemary Lane, Flimwell, E Sussex], of Cape Town, S Africa, and *d* 1991, leaving:

1f +Oliver John [Oliver Fynes-Clinton Esq, Trees, Priory Rd, Forest Row, Sussex]; *b* 2 Aug 1948; *educ* Cape Town U (BA); *m* 1978 *Christine Elisabeth Brittaine and has:

1g +Francis Bernard Peter; *b* 1979

1g *Laura Emily; *b* 1984

1f *Rozanne Jean; *b* 5 Oct 1946

1e Mary; *b* 3 Sept 1903; *m* 2 Sept 1939 *Alfred Denis Jenkins and *d* 19 Aug 1952, leaving issue

2e *Quenilda Margaret; late Matron Evelyn Nursing Home Cambridge; *b* 12 Oct 1905

3e *Eleanor Lloyd [Miss Eleanor Fynes-Clinton, 12 Pakenham Close, Cambridge]; *b* 4 Aug 1907

2d Osbert Hendry; Prof French and Romance Philology U Coll N Wales; *b* 9 Nov 1869; *educ* St John's Coll Oxford (MA, DLitt); *m* 10 July 1907 Gwladys Mabel, yr dau of Rev William Hughes, Vicar Llanuwchllyn, Merioneth, and *d* 9 Aug 1941, leaving:

1e David Osbert; Consul-Gen Zagreb; *b* 25 Jan 1909; *educ* Clifton and St John's Coll Oxford; *m* 1st 3 July 1933 (*divorce* 1947) Laure Léoncie Mathilde Reyne, only dau of Pierre Félix Suquet; *m* 2nd 22 Feb 1947 (*divorce* 1958) Betty Annie (*d* 1989), dau of Arthur C Lawrence, of Iquique, Chile, and by her had:

1f +Michael Peter; *b* 25 May 1949; *m* 1973 (*divorce* 1978) Paula Valerie Neuss (*d* 1988)

3d Arthur (Rev); Vicar St Michael's Walthamstow 1929–36; *b* 25 Feb 1878; *educ* Lincoln Coll Oxford (BA 1912, MA 1916); *m* 14 Jan 1913 Louisa Caroline (*d* 1961), dau of Rev William Hughes, Vicar Llanuwchllyn, and *dsp* 21 May 1961

4d Robert; *b* 7 Oct 1879; *m* 27 June 1907 Margaret Emma (*d* 1949), yr dau of Rev Stephen Phillips, DD, Hon Canon Peterborough, and *d* 28 March 1962, leaving:

1e +Pelham; *b* 10 July 1910; *educ* Radley; *m* 16 June 1937 Joan Elizabeth (*d* 1984), only dau of Alfred Chaplin, of W Kirby, and has:

1f *Margaret Julia; *b* 25 May 1949

1d Edith; *m* 7 Nov 1899 Charles Frederick Brenan, of Rhosneigr, Anglesey, and *d c* 1940, leaving issue. He *d* 8 March 1927

2d Ethel Rosa; *m* 14 Sept 1899 Frederick Alsop Eyre, and *d* 29 Jan 1951, leaving issue. He *d* 30 Jan 1939

3d Mabel; *m* 3 June 1897 John Frederick Binyon, of Grange-over-Sands, and *d* 22 June 1918, leaving issue. He *d* 4 Feb 1936

4d Hilda Mary; *m* 23 Sept 1908 Rev Arthur David Phillips, Vicar Hambleton, Oakham, and *d* 1 Sept 1932, leaving issue. He *d* 18 Aug 1932

5d *Muriel Agnes; *m* 26 July 1938 Herbert Septimus Phillips, s of Rev Stephen Phillips, DD, Hon Canon Peterborough. He *d* 23 March 1961

4c John; *b* 11 Aug 1841; *m* 1880 Eleanor (*d* 1896), dau of John Holden, and *d* 22 July 1898, leaving:

1d Rose Eleanor; *m* Rev Frank Swan and *d* 1921

5c Eustane; Headmaster Wimborne Sch; *b* 4 July 1845; *educ* St John's Coll Cambridge (MA); *m* 1 Jan 1879 Louisa Richenda (*d* 9 July 1933), dau of Rev Francis Macaulay Cunningham, and *d* 11 Jan 1928, leaving:

1d Margaret Alice; *m* 9 Nov 1907 Ernest Norman Travers Cummins, 3rd s of Maj-Gen James Turner Cummins, CB, DSO, and *d* 4 Jan 1970, leaving issue. He *d* 1953

2d Eleanor Mabel

3d Katharine

4d Rosalind Mary, MBE (1946); *b* 28 July 1890; *educ* LMH Oxford (MA 1928); *d* 23 Aug 1989

6c Geoffrey (Rev); Vicar All Saints Gladstone Invercargill NZ 1914–30, Canon Dunedin; *b* 17 March 1847; *m* 1873 Frances (*d* 24 Sept 1888), dau of Henry Searle, and *d* 3 July 1934, having had:

1d Geoffrey de Berdt Granger; *b* 5 Jan 1878; *m* 1902 Maybelle (*d* 1971), dau of John Finamore Edwards, and *d* 28 Sept 1922, leaving:

1e Geoffrey Noel; *b* 24 Dec 1902; *d* 19–

2e Philip Neville; *b* 22 June 1908; *m* 24 Dec 1931 Isobel Maud (*d* 19–), dau of William Wilks, and *d* 25 Jan 1996, leaving:

1f Geoffrey William Norreys; *b* 9 Sept 1932; *educ* Queensland U (BA, LLB); *m* 1957 *Joyce Kathleen Lynch [Mrs Geoffrey Fynes-Clinton, 9 Ormond St, Ascot, Qld, Australia], and *d* 1987, leaving:

1g +Stephen Philip; *b* 1960; *educ* Queensland U (B Econ LLB); *m* 1994 *Sarah Burgess

2g +Matthew James; *b* 1963; *m* 1988 *Jane Williams and has:

1h +Alexander Geoffrey; *b* 4 Feb 1991

1h *Kate Margaret; *b* 7 Sept 1992

2h *Amelia Jane; *b* 12 May 1994

3g +Timothy Pelham; *b* 1965; *educ* Queensland U (LLB)

1g *Emma Mary; *b* 1968; *educ* Queensland U (B Econ)

2f +Arthur Nevill [Arthur Fynes-Clinton Esq, 13 Pantheon St, Jindalee, Qld 4074, Australia]; *b* 21 July 1934; *educ* Queensland U (BA); *m* 1956 *Jacqueline Baker and has:

1g +Jamie; *b* 1957; *m* 1987 *Elizabeth Jean Morgan and has:

1h +Ben Thomas; *b* 1988

1h *Tegan Jane; *b* 14 Dec 1990

2g +Alan; *b* 1958

3g +Neil; *b* 1962; *educ* U of S Queensland (BEd); *m* 1992 *Janeece Wilson and has:

1h *Sophie Frances; *b* 13 April 1994

2h *Marissa Jane; *b* 4 Oct 1997

3e Pelham Osbert Grainger; *b* 10 March 1912; *d* unm 31 March 1982

1d Bertha; *d* unm 1966

2d Rosalind Margaret; *m* 1906 Most Rev Samuel Tarratt Nevill, DD, Primate NZ (*d* 29 Oct 1921)

3d Maud Marion; *b* 1880; *d* unm 1947

4d Mabel Fanny *b* 1881; *m* 1905 Alfred Hillier Newton, of Timaru, NZ

5d Irene; *m* 19 July 1911 Herbert Charles Stevens (*d* 1957), of Myross Bush, Invercargill, NZ, and had:

1e *Charles Clinton; Capt RNZN WW II, Cdr RNAS HMS *Curlew* Cornwall 1953–54, Capt Australian Navigation, Torpedo and Anti-Submarine Estab HMAS *Watson* Sydney 1961, Cdre and 2nd Naval Memb and Dir Personnel NZ Naval Bd 1961–64, Hon ADC to HM THE QUEEN; *b* 21 June 1912; *m* 1st 14 Oct 1939 (*divorce* 1965) Kathleen Mary McQuilken; *m* 2nd 15 April 1966 *Eileen Marguerite, widow of — Gaffikin and dau of Jock Bruce Tailyour Renny, and by his 1st w has:

1f *Geoffrey Fynes-Clinton [Geoffrey Stevens Esq, 49, Paddington St, Paddington, NSW 2021, Australia]; *b* 7 Nov 1940; *educ* RNC Dartmouth; with Price, Waterhouse, Sydney, NSW, 1967, Sub-Lt RNZN 1962, ret 1965 as Lt, served Far East Station 1963–64; *m* 21 Dec 1966 *Elizabeth Georgina, er dau of Maj Herbert Johnes Lloyd-Johnes, TD, of Fosse Hill, Coates, Cirencester, Glos, and has:

1g *Alexander Clinton Johnes; *b* 20 Jan 1970

1g *Georgina Anne; *b* 14 Aug 1967; *m* 22 July 1995 *Timothy Ruthven, s of Michael St Clair Ruthven

1e *Nora Pelham; *b* 1915; *m* 1939 Rupert Garland and has issue. He *d* 1 March 1969

7c Arthur Norreys; *b* 18 June 1850; *m* 30 July 1881 Georgina Anne (*d* 6 July 1940), dau of G E Gill, and *d* 25 July 1916

1c Caroline; *m* 15 Sept 1859 James Wilson Holme and *d* 27 Sept 1919, leaving issue. He *d* 1892

2c Anna Rosa; *d* unm 1855

3c Emma; *m* 31 Jan 1871 Rev Herbert Alfred Holme, MA, Rector Whiston, Rotherham, and *d* 9 March 1926, leaving issue. He *d* 1920

4c Bertha; *m* 14 June 1865 Rev Trueman Tully Falkner, MA, and *d* 20 April 1927, having had issue. He *d* 1876

5c Rosabella Paulina; *d* unm 16 Sept 1918

1b Caroline Frances; *m* 13 Sept 1814 Very Rev James Webber, DD, Dean Ripon, Rector St Margaret's Westminster, and had issue. He *d* 3 Sept 1847

(1) Elizabeth; *m* Sir Michael Livesey, Bt, and *dspm c* 1666

4 Kendal

LINDSAY, Earl

Arms: Quarterly, 1st and 4th, gules a fess chequy argent and azure, in chief three mullets of the second; 2nd and 3rd counter-quartered, 1st and 4th, argent a fess between three lozenges or; 2nd and 3rd, argent on a chevron sable an otter's head erased of the first, all within a bordure embattled gold. **Crest:** A swan with wings expanded proper. **Supporters:** Two griffins gules, armed and beaked or. **Mottoes:** 1 (over crest) *Je ayme* ('I love'), 2 (under shield) Live but dreid. **Creations:** L. (S) by Oct 1444 (Lindsay of the Byres), E. and L. (Parbroath) (S) 8 May 1633 , V. and L. (Kilbirny and Drumry) (S) 26 Nov 1703.

THE 16TH EARL OF LINDSAY, Viscount of Garnock, Lord Lindsay of the Byres, Lord Parbroath and Lord Kilbirny and Drumry (James Randolph Lindesay-Bethune) [The Rt Hon The Earl of Lindsay, Lahill, Upper Largo, Fife KY8 6JE]; *b* 19 Nov 1955; *s f* 1989; *educ* Eton, Edinburgh U (MA Hons) and U of Calif (Davis); md J W T G P 1975–95, a Ld-in-Waiting (Govt Whip) 1995, Parly U-Sec Scottish Office 1995–97, landscape architect and environmental consultant, Tstee Gardens for Disabled Tst 1984–, chm Landscape Fndn 1992–95 (Tstee 1992–), V-Pres Internat Tree Fndn 1993–95 (Pres 1995–), memb Advsy Cncl World Resource Fndn 1994–; memb: Select Ctee EC Affrs, Environment, Public Health and Consumer Protection Sub-Ctee 1993–95 and 1997–, Inter-Parly Ctee Environment and Sustainable Devpt 1993–95 (V-Chm 1994–95 and Select Ctee 1994–95); V-Chm Scottish Salmon Growers Assoc 1997–; Chm Assured Br Meat 1997–, author: *Garden Ornament* (jt, 1989), *Trellis* (1991); *m* 2 March 1982 *Diana, er dau of Maj Nigel Chamberlayne-Macdonald (*see* BOSVILLE-MACDONALD, Bt), and has:

1 +WILLIAM JAMES, *Viscount Garnock*; *b* 30 Dec 1990

2 +David Nigel; *b* 1993

1 *Frances Mary; *b* 1986

2 *Alexandra Penelope; *b* 1988

3 *Charlotte Diana (twin with David); *b* 1993

Lineage: Sir DAVID de LINDESAY (*see* CRAWFORD and BALCARRES, E); *d* 1355, leaving a 3rd s:

Sir WILLIAM LINDSAY of the Byres, Haddingtonshire, which granted by charter 17 Jan 1365/6 on its resignation by his bro, Sir Alexander Crawford of Glenesk; *m* Christina, dau of Sir William Mure of Abercorn, who brought him that (territorial) Barony, and *d c* 1 July 1393, leaving an er s:

Sir WILLIAM LINDSAY of the Byres, *m* Christiana, dau of Sir William Keith, Marischal of Scotland (*see* KINTORE, E), who brought him the (territorial) Barony and Castle of Dunnottar, Kincardineshire, which he afterwards exchanged with the Keiths for Struthers, Fife, allegedly stipulating that the infant est s and heir of the LINDSAYs should in time of feuding within the family be sheltered in the Castle, which was thought impregnable; *d* 1414, leaving:

JOHN LINDSAY, **1st Lord Lindsay of the Byres** (S), so *cr* just prior to Oct 1444, PC (S); a hostage for JAMES I's ransom by the English 1424; Justiciar Scotland N of the Forth 1457, a Ld of Session March 1457/8; *m* allegedly a dau of Robert Stewart, 1st Lord Lorn (*see* MORAY, E), and *d* 6 Feb 1482, having had, with at least three daus (Christian, *m* 1st John, Master of Seton (*see* EGLINTON and WINTON, E), *m* 2nd Robert, s of 1st Earl of Glencairn (*see* CUNINGHAME, Bt); Margaret, *m* 3rd Lord Lorn (*see* MORAY, E); Mariot, *m* as his 1st w 1st Lord Itay of Yester; *see* TWEEDDALE, M):

1 DAVID LINDSAY, **2nd Lord Lindsay of the Byres**; fought for JAMES III Battle of Sauchieburn 1488 at head of 1,000 horse and 3,000 foot against the King's rebellious s, later JAMES IV; *m* probably between 16 April 1458 and 14 Jan 1458/9 Janet, dau and heiress of Walter Ramsay of Carnock and Pitcruvie, and *dsp* 1490

2 JOHN LINDSAY, **3rd Lord Lindsay of the Byres**, called 'John out-with-the-sword'; *m* Marion/Mariott (*m* between 1500 and 1503, as his 3rd w, Robert Douglas of Lochleven *see* MORTON, E), dau of Sir William Baillie of Lamington, and *dspm* after 26 Oct 1498, leaving:

(1) Margaret; *m* 3rd Lord Innermeath (*see* MORAY, E)

3 PATRICK LINDSAY, **4th Lord Lindsay of the Byres**; advocate who successfully defended his er bro from the new King JAMES IV's attempt to try him for disaffection after Sauchieburn; fought at Flodden Sept 1513, following which disaster (in which JAMES IV was killed) was one of the four peers apptd Dec 1513 to advise the widowed QUEEN MARGARET; recognised as Sheriff of Fife, with reversion to his s and gs,1525; *m* Isabella, dau of Henry Pitcairn of Pitcairn and Forthar, and *d* after 8 March 1526, leaving:

(1) John (Sir), of Pitcruvie, *Master of Lindsay*; *m* by 8 Sept 1521 Elizabeth (*m* 2nd David Lundie), dau of Sir Robert Lundie of Balgonie, and *dvp* shortly after 28 Aug 1525, having had, with a dau (Janet *m* Sir David Murray of Arngask etc; *see* MANSFIELD and MANSFIELD, E):

1a Sir JOHN LINDSAY, **5th Lord Lindsay of the Byres**, PC (1545); Sheriff Fife 1526; Extrdy Ld of Session 1532; one of four peers charged with caring for the infant MARY QUEEN OF SCOTS 1542, cmded Scots forces victory over English of Ancrum Muir 6 March 1544/5; hereditary Justiciar St Andrews; *m* Helen (*m* 2nd 1563 Thomas Moncur and *d* 1577), dau of John Stewart, 2nd Earl of Atholl (*see* MORAY, E), and *d c* 17 Dec 1563, having had, with other issue:

1b PATRICK LINDSAY, **6th Lord Lindsay of the Byres** (PC (S 1565); *b* 1521; one of the first proponents of a reformed church in Scotland; a Ld of Congregation; leader in murder of Rizzio, the secretary and favourite of MARY QUEEN OF SCOTS, as also the deposition of the QUEEN herself; Jt Ld Lt and Justice Fife 1572, Ld Provost Edinburgh 1573, Sheriff Fife 1574, granted bailliership (magistracy) of regality of Archbishopric of St Andrews (held by his descendants till abolition of heritable jurisdictions 1747); involved in 'Raid of Ruthven' 1582 (an attempt to kidnap JAMES VI), following the failure of which he escaped to England; *m c* May 1545 Euphemia, dau of Sir Robert Douglas of Lochleven, and *d* 11 Dec 1589, leaving, with a dau (Margaret, *m* 1575 James, Master of Rothes, *see* ROTHES, E):

1c JAMES LINDSAY, **7th Lord Lindsay of the Byres**, PC (S Jan 1593/4); *b* 1554; Gentleman King's Chamber 1580; *m c* 9 May 1573 Euphemia, dau of 4th Earl of Rothes (*qv*), and *d* 5 Nov 1601, leaving, with other issue:

1d JOHN LINDSAY, **8th Lord Lindsay of the Byres**, PC (S 1605); *m c* 4 July 1599 Anne, sis of 5th Lord Oliphant, and *d* 5 Nov 1609, leaving:

1e Anne; *m* 1619 Alexander, Lord Falconer of Halkerton (*see* 1963 edn)

2d ROBERT LINDSAY, **9th Lord Lindsay of the Byres**, PC (S 1610 and 1616); Ecclesiastical High Commr Scotland; *m* between Jan and April 1610 Christian (*m* 2nd 1617 7th Lord Boyd; *see* KILMARNOCK, B), dau of 1st Earl of Haddington (*qv*), and *d* 9 July 1616, leaving:

1e JOHN LINDSAY, **1st Earl of Lindsay**, so *cr* 8 May 1633, as also LORD PARBROATH (both S), with remainder to him and his heirs male bearing the name and arms of Lindsay; in addition 17th EARL OF CRAWFORD, as which *s* distant cousin (16th Earl of Crawford, *see* CRAWFORD and BALCARRES, E) under terms of regrant of latter's title, probably 1652 but undoubtedly by 1663, accordingly calling himself 'Earl of Crawford-Lindsay', PC (S 1641 and Feb 1660/1); *b* 1596; Jt Treasurer Scotland 1641, Extrdy Ld of Session 1641–49 and 1661–64, High Treasurer Scotland 1644 and 1661, Pres Scottish Parl Jan 1644/5 and 1661; after advising CHARLES I to accept Parliament's terms 1646 he supported the latter's son and was imprisoned by the Commonwelath/Protectorate authorities 1651–60; *m c* 1630 Margaret, dau of 2nd Marquess of Hamilton (*see* HAMILTON and BRANDON, D), and *d* 1678, leaving, with other daus (one of whom *m* Sir Robert Sinclair of Stevenson):

1f WILLIAM LINDSAY, **2nd Earl of Lindsay** and 18th EARL OF CRAWFORD, PC (S 1690); *b* April 1644; obliged by his f's extravagance to put his estates in trust so as to meet his debts, the trust lasting over 70 years; leading Presbyterian, Pres S Cncl 1689–93, Pres S Parl, Commr Treasury Scotland 1689–92; *m* 1st 8 March 1670 Mary, dau of 1st Earl of Annandale and Hartfell (*qv*), and had:

1g JOHN LINDSAY, **3rd Earl of Lindsay** and 19th EARL OF CRAWFORD, PC (S 1702); *b* by 1672; Brig Gen 1703, Maj-Gen 1707, Lt Gen 1710, Col 2nd Horse Gren Gds 1704–Jan 1713/4; rep S peer 1707–10; *m* by 1702 Amelia (*d* 18 Feb 1711), dau of James, Lord Doune (*see* MORAY, E), and widow of Alexander Fraser, 5th of Strichen (*see* LOVAT, L), and *d* 4 Jan 1713/4, having had:

1h JOHN LINDSAY, **4th Earl of Lindsay** and 20th EARL OF CRAWFORD, called 'The Gallant Earl of Crawford', Kt Banneret (1743); *b* 4 Oct 1702; *educ* Glasgow U and Mil Acad Vaudeuil, Paris; joined army 1726, Capt Scots Gds 1734; rep S peer 1732–49, Gentleman Bedchamber to PRINCE OF WALES 1733; served Imperial forces against Turks Battle of Claussen 1735 and with Russian army, also against Turks, 1738, present Battle of Krotzha, nr Belgrade, 22 July 1739; Adj-Gen in GB 1739–43, fought at Dettingen 1743, Col 43rd Foot (later called 'The Black Watch') 1739–40, Col 2nd Horse Gren Gds 1740–43, Col 4th Horse Gren Gds 1743–46, fought at Fontenoy 1745, Brig-Gen 1744, Maj-Gen 1745, holding the Lowlands during the Jacobite Uprising while the DUKE OF CUMBERLAND campaigned in the Highlands; Col 25th Foot 1746–47, present at French victory over British and allies at Roucoux 1746; Col 2nd Dragoons (Scots Greys) 1747–49; Lt Gen 1747; *m* 3 March 1747 Jean (*d* 10 Oct 1747), dau of 2nd Duke of Atholl (*qv*), and *dsp* 24 Dec 1749

2h William; Capt RN; *dsp*

1h Catherine; *m* John Wemyss

2h Mary; *m* Dougal Campbell of Glensaddell, whose gs Col Claud Campbell of Newfield claimed 1809 the Crawford-Lindsay estates against Lady Mary Lindsay-Crawford (*see below*); the eventual rep of this family

was Albert Johnstone Campbell, heir of line of the CRAWFORD-LINDSAYs

2g James; Col; *ka* Battle of Almanza 1707

3g Patrick; *dsp*

1f (cont.) The **2nd Earl** *m* 2nd Henrietta (*d* April 1681), dau of 2nd Earl of Dunfermline (*see* EGLINTON and WINTON, E) and widow of 5th Earl of Wigton, and *d* 6 March 1698, having by her had further issue

2f Patrick LINDSAY later CRAWFORD; *m* 1664 Margaret, yr dau and coheir of Sir John Crawford of Kilbirnie, Ayrshire, and *d* Oct 1681, leaving, with other issue (*dsp*):

1g JOHN CRAWFORD alias LINDSAY-CRAWFORD, **1st Viscount of Garnock, Lord Kilbirny** and **Drumry** (S), so *cr* 26 Nov 1703, with remainder to him and his nearest heirs male, having been previously *cr* 10 April 1703 VISCOUNT OF MOUNT CRAWFORD, LORD KILBIRNY, KINGSBURN and DRUMRY (S), but having had it changed to the November (and current) designation, PC; *b* 12 May 1669; MP Ayrshire 1693–1703; *m* Jan 1697 Margaret, dau of 1st Earl of Bute (*see* BUTE, M), and *d* 24 Dec 1708, leaving, with yr sons (*dsp*) and a dau (Margaret, *m* MacNeal of Ugadale):

1h PATRICK LINDSAY-CRAWFORD, **2nd Viscount of Garnock**; *bapt* 30 Nov 1697; *m c* 19 April 1720 Margaret, dau of George Home of Kello, Berwicks, and *d* 24 May 1735, leaving:

1i JOHN LINDSAY-CRAWFORD, **3rd Viscount of Garnock**; *b* 5 July 1722; *d* unm 22 Sept 1739

2i GEORGE LINDSAY-CRAWFORD, **4th Viscount of Garnock**, also **5th Earl of Lindsay** and 21st EARL OF CRAWFORD, as both of which *s* cousin 1749; *b* 14 March 1728/9; Kilbirnie Castle having burnt down April 1757, he erected a house at Struthers, Fife (the ancient seat of the LINDSAYs of the Byres; *see* above), called Crawford Lodge or Crawford Priory; *m* 26 Dec 1755 Jean, dau and heiress of Robert Hamilton of Bourtreehill, Ayrshire, and *d* 11 Aug 1781, leaving, with other issue:

1j GEORGE LINDSAY-CRAWFORD, **6th Earl of Lindsay** and 22nd EARL OF CRAWFORD; *b* 31 Jan 1758; *educ* Eton; joined Army 1776, Col 2nd Bn 71st Regt 1782–83, Col 63rd Foot 1789–1808, Maj-Gen 1805, Ld Lt Fifeshire 1794–March 1807 and May 1807–08; *d* unm 30 Jan 1808, when the Earldom of Crawford passed to 6th Earl of Balcarres (*see* CRAWFORD and BALCARRES, E)

1j Joan; *m* 1772 11th Earl of Eglinto(u)n (*see* EGLINTON and WINTON, E) and *d* 1778

1i Christian Graham; *m* Patrick Bogle and *dsp* 1748

1g Margaret; *m* 19 April 1687 1st Earl of Glasgow (*qv*)

2g Anne; *m* Henry Maule of Kelly, bro of the Earl of Panmure (*see* DALHOUSIE, E)

3g Magdalen; *m* George Dundas of Duddingston

1f Anne; *m* between Jan and Feb 1647/8 7th Earl of Rothes (*qv*) and *d* on or after 1 July 1689, leaving issue

2f Christian; *m* 4th Earl of Haddington (*qv*) and had issue

3f Elizabeth; *m* 3rd Earl of Northesk (*qv*) and *d* Jan 1688

1d Helen; *m* by 23 April 1623, as his 2nd w, 2nd Lord Cranstoun (*see* 1869 edn) and *dsp* 1658

2b Norman, of Kilquhiss; his male-line descendants died out in the 17th century

1b Isabel; *m* 1st Norman Leslie, Master of Rothes (*see* ROTHES, E); *m* 2nd 1554 William Christisson; *m* 3rd John Innes of Leuchars

2b Janet; *m c* June 1547, as his 1st w, 5th Lord Sinclair (*qv*)

2a Patrick, of Kirkforther; *dsp*

3a David, of Kirkforther; *m* Helen Crichton and *d* 1592; his only s:

1b John, of Kirkforther; *m* 1st Marjory Pitcairn and *d* by 4 Dec 1599, leaving an est s:

1c Patrick, of Kirkforther; *m* Sept 1584 Helen, dau of David Orme of Priorlethame and *d* 24 March 1638, leaving an est s:

1d David, of Kirkforther; *m* 1609 Elizabeth, dau of Robert Bethune of Balfour, and *dvp* by April 1631, leaving an est s:

1e David, of Kirkforther; *m* 1621 Jean, dau of Henry Pitcairn of that Ilk, and *d* in or after 1672, leaving an est s:

1f David, of Kirkforther; *m* 1st 7 June 1660 Elizabeth, dau of Alexander Pearson of Southall, Ld of Session, and *d* by 1714, leaving an est s:

1g John, of Kirkforther; *m* Catherine, est dau of Christopher Seton of Careston, and *d* by 1740, leaving a 4th s:

1h John; allegedly a 'common soldier'; *d* in or after 1760, leaving an only s:

1i DAVID LINDSAY, *de jure* 7th EARL OF LINDSAY etc according to the Ho Lds decision of 5 April 1878; served heir male of the LINDSAYs of Kirkforther 23 Aug 1808; Army Sgt; *dsp* and was *bur* 5 May 1809

2d James; had:

1e Patrick, of St Andrews; *m* Beatrice, dau of William Daes, and *d* in or after 1646, having had a 2nd but est surv s:

1f Patrick (Rev); Rector St Andrews GS; *m* Janet, dau of John Lindsay of Newton, and *d c* 1722, having had an est surv s:

1g Patrick; MP, Provost Edinburgh; *m* 1st Margaret, dau of David Monteir, Edinburgh merchant, and *d* 20 Feb 1753, leaving:

1h Patrick, of Eaglescairnie, E Lothian; *b c* 1718; *dspm* 18 Oct 1801

2h John; Lt-Col 53rd Foot; *m* 1776 Margaret Maria, dau of Charles Hackett Craigie Halkett, of Hawhill and Dunbarnie, and *d* 8 April 1780, leaving:

1i Sir PATRICK LINDSAY, *de jure* 8th EARL OF LINDSAY etc, KCB (1838), KCH (1834); *b* 24 Feb 1778; served Army 44 years, notably at taking of Coorg, India; Maj Gen 1837; *dsp* 14 March 1839

(2) William, of Pyotston; *m* Isabel Logan and *d* by March 1546/7, having had a 4th s:

1a John, of Cupar, Fife; *m* Janet Williamson and *d* by 12 July 1580, leaving an only s:

1b Patrick, of Wormiston, Fife; *b c* 1571; Commissary Archbishopric of St Andrews; *m* 1st Margaret Lundie; *m* 2nd Elizabeth, dau of Peter Arnot of Balcarno and *d* June 1621, leaving by one or other of his ws an est s:

1c John, of Wormiston; living 1647; *m* Elizabeth, dau of David Lentron of Newgrange, and *d* Feb 1666, leaving:

1d Patrick, of Wormiston; captured by CROMWELL's troops Battle of Worcester 1651; *m* Catherine, dau of Robert Bethune of Bandon, and had, with a yr s (William, ancestor of the LINDSAYs of Feddinch):

1e John, of Wormiston; served heir to Pyotston 1699; advocate; *m* Margaret, est dau of George Haliburton of Denhead, Bp Aberdeen, and *d* 23 Sept 1715, having had, with an er s (Patrick, executed Carlisle 1745, presumably for Jacobitism, ancestor of the LINDSAYs of Leith) and a dau (Agnes, *m de jure* 5th Viscount of Oxfuird, *qv*):

1f George, of Wormiston; advocate; *m* Margaret, est dau of Thomas Bethune of Kilconquhar, Fife, and *d* 10 Feb 1764, leaving, with five er sons:

1g Henry LINDSAY later BETHUNE (roy licence 2 Oct 1779 on inheriting Kilconquhar from his mother's bro); *b c* 1736; *m* 1st Elizabeth, dau of Thomas Kyd, and had an only dau (Rachel, *m* Lt-Gen James Dickson); *m* 2nd Margaret, dau of Martin Eccles, MD, of Edinburgh, and *d* 11 March 1819, having by her had an est s:

1h Martin Eccles Lindsay; Maj; *m* Margaret Augusta, dau of Gen James Tovey, and *dvp* 22 July 1813, leaving:

1i Sir HENRY BETHUNE, 1st Bt (UK), so *cr* 7 March 1836, of Kilconquhar, *de jure* 9th EARL OF LINDSAY etc; *b* 12 April 1787; joined HEICS, attd as Maj to Court of Shah of Persia, where helped the Crown Prince form an artillery force, later granted rank of full Agent; ktd 1832, Cdr Persian forces against Russia 1804–19 and the rebel Zulli Sultan 1834–36; *m* 9 July 1822 Coutts (*d* 31 Dec 1877), dau of John Trotter, of Dyrham Park, Herts (bro of Sir Coutts Trotter, 1st Bt), and *d* 19 Feb 1851, leaving:

1j Sir JOHN TROTTER BETHUNE, 2nd and last Bt, and **10th Earl of Lindsay** etc, as which recognised by Ho Lds 5 April 1878; *b* 3 Jan 1827; Lt 91st Highrs, rep S peer 1885–94; *m* 18 July 1858 Jeanne Eudoxie Marie (*d* 24 June 1897), dau of Jacques Victor Duval, of Bordeaux, and *dsp* 12 May 1894, when the btcy expired

2j Henry James Hamilton; *b* 8 June 1834; *dsp* Marseilles 5 July 1862

3j Martin William; *b* 17 June 1843; *dsp* 15 Sept 1859

1j Anne Katherine; *m* 29 April 1856 John Thomas Campbell, only s of Maj John Campbell, 74th Foot, and *d* 23 March 1903, leaving issue

2j Stewart; *m* 7 Nov 1848 3rd Earl of Norbury (*qv*) and *d* 5 March 1904, leaving issue

3j Caroline Felicie; *d unm* 30 Jan 1891

4j COUTTS later JANE COUTTS (deed poll 1899); *m* 25 July 1878 James Stuart Trotter, 3rd s of Archibald Trotter, of Dreghorn, and *dsp* 17 July 1909

5j Charlotte Jane; *d unm* 28 Sept 1855

2g Patrick, of Coats; *b* 1745; bought Wormiston from his er bro Henry; *d* 1823, leaving, with a dau:

1h David LINDSAY later AYTON-LINDSAY, of Wormiston, JP Fife; *b* 31 Dec 1798; *m* 1824 Jane Emilia (*d* 22 Nov 1872), dau of John Ayton of Kippo, Fife, and *d* 5 May 1872, leaving an est s:

1i DAVID CLARK, **11th Earl**

2i Alexander Monypenny; *b* 7 April 1836; advocate; *m* 13 Nov 1872 Mary (*d* 1902), dau of Alexander Sproat, of Brig House, Kirkcudbrightshire, and *dsp* 22 March 1905

1i Emilia; *m* 29 April 1862 Eric Rudd, barrister (*d* 3 Jan 1868), and *d* 2 Dec 1901, leaving issue

2i Elizabeth; *m* Edward Cliff (*d* 13 Dec 1874) and *d* 2 March 1865, leaving issue

3i Margaret; *m* 1875 Archibald Rodan Hogg, WS (*d* 1892), of Edinburgh, and *d* 25 April 1924, leaving issue

2h Henry Bethune; *b* 11 Oct 1811; Maj 3rd Bengal Cav; *m* 9 March 1837 Elizabeth (*d* 1903), dau of Colin Campbell, MD, and *d* 22 June 1856, leaving:

1i Henry George; *b* 3 Dec 1843; *m* 1886 Jane Edith (*d* 15 Jan 1932), dau of Edward Fisher, of Spring Dale, Huddersfield, and *d* 15 Sept 1915, leaving:

1j Jane Kathleen Mary; *b* 14 March 1888

2j Constance Norah Edith; *b* 17 Nov 1889; *m* 21 July 1926 Arthur John Grinfield Cresswell and had issue

2i Edward Campbell; *b* 7 March 1855; *d unm* 1892

1i Jessie Frances; *d unm* 28 May 1928

2i Emily Florence

3i Constance Madeline; *m* 12 Sept 1877 Sharples Fisher, JP (*d* Sept 1921), of Helme Hall, Metham, Huddersfield, and *d* 1 March 1925, leaving issue

(3) DAVID, of Kirkforthar; *k* Flodden 1513

The 10th EARL's 2nd cousin once-removed,

DAVID CLARK LINDSAY later BETHUNE (assumed with arms but without official authority 1894), **11th Earl of Lindsay**, JP (Fife); *b* 18 April 1832; *educ* St Andrews and Edinburgh Us; *m* 15 Aug 1866 Emily Marian (*d* 17 Oct 1920), dau of Robert Crosse, of Doctors' Commons, and widow of Capt Edmund Charles Barnes, of St Helena Regt, and *d* 20 March 1917, leaving:

1 REGINALD BETHUNE later LINDESAY-BETHUNE [*sic*] (1981), **12th Earl of Lindsay**, JP and DL (Fife); *b* 18 May 1867; Maj 8th Hus Boer War and E R Yeo Reserve Regt WW I, rep S peer 1917–39; *m* 16 Oct 1892 Beatrice Mary, OStJ (*d* 9 Nov 1944), er dau of John Shaw, of Welburn Hall, Kirbymoorside, Yorks, and *dsp* 14 Jan 1939

2 ARCHIBALD LIONEL, **13th Earl**

1 Muriel Maud Stuart; *m* 1st 30 Sept 1893 Watkin James Yuille S Watkins (*d* 25 Nov 1921), of Shotton Hall, Salop, and had issue; *m* 2nd 31 Dec 1929 Joseph Alexander Drummond Kirkpatrick, Devonshire Regt, s of Lt-Col TD Kirkpatrick, Green Howards, of Locksley Hall, Torquay, and *d* 30 March 1936

The 12th EARL's bro,

ARCHIBALD LIONEL BETHUNE, **13th Earl of Lindsay**; *b* 14 Aug 1872; *m* 31 Jan 1900 Ethel (*d* 31 May 1942), dau of William Austin Tucker, of Boston, USA, and *d* 15 Oct 1943, leaving:

WILLIAM TUCKER BETHUNE later LINDSAY-BETHUNE (1939), **14th Earl of Lindsay**, DL (Fife 1956); *b* 28 April 1901; *educ* Groton and BNC Oxford (MA); Maj Scots Gds WW II (wounded), rep S peer 1947–59, Hon Col Fife and Forfar Yeo, Scottish Horse 1957–62; memb Roy Co Archers, memb Fife CC 1956–63, Pres Shipwrecked Fishermen and Mariners' Roy Benevolent Soc 1965–, KStJ, Prior OStJ Scotland 1947–50; *m* 6 Jan 1925 Marjory (*d* 1988), DStJ, dau of Arthur John Graham Cross and Lady Hawke, and *d* 1985, leaving:

1 DAVID BETHUNE, **15th Earl**

2 +John Martin [The Hon John Lindesay-Bethune, Muircambus, Elie, Fife KY9 1HD]; *b* 27 Nov 1929; *educ* Eton and Trin Hall Coll Cambridge; late Lt Scots Gds; *m* 1st 1 Jan 1953 (*divorce* 1976) Enriqueta Mary Jeanne, only dau of Peter Maurice Jacques Koch de Gooreynd, of Gooreynd, Belgium (*see* QUEENSBERRY, M); *m* 2nd 1977 *Jean Maxwell, dau of Brig Eric Brickman and formerly w of Stephen John Younger, and by his 1st w has had:

(1) +Nicholas John [Nicholas Lindesay-Bethune Esq, 89 East Sheen Ave, London SW14 8AX]; *b* 20 Jan 1956; *educ* Eton; *m* 1977 *Maria Teresa, dau of Luis Prats, of Manila, and has:

1a +Andrew Nicholas; *b* 1979

2a +Henry William; *b* 1983

3a +Dominic Luis; *b* 1985

(2) +Jonathan Patrick; *b* 14 Oct 1959; *m* 1st 1988 Heike, dau of M Christ, of Sencle, Germany; *m* 2nd 1996 *Wilma Anderson and by his 1st w has:

1a +Kevin Patrick; *b* 1989

(3) +Simon Charles; *b* 29 Sept 1962; *m* 1990 *Melissa Jane, only dau of Roderick Webb, of Ditchling, Sussex

(4) Crispin; *b* and *d* 2 Aug 1966

(1) *Sally Alexandra Jane [Mrs Peter Breeden, Woodside House, Freshford, Bath BA3 6EJ]; *b* 26 April 1954; *m* 24 Nov 1977 *Peter Breeden, only s of David Breeden, and has:

1a *Alexander Peter; *b* 1979

2a *Jamie George; *b* 1981

3a *Benjamin Jonathan; *b* 1985

1a *Rosie Alexandra Charlotte; *b* 1987

1 Elizabeth Marjory Beatrice; *b* 31 May 1932; *m* 26 May 1960 (*divorce* 1971) Maj David Laurence Greenacre, Welsh Gds, est s of Brig (Walter) Douglas Campbell Greenacre, CB, DSO, MVO, Welsh Gds, and *d* 20 Feb 1996, leaving:

(1) *Philip Laurence; *b* 6 Aug 1961; *m* 1993 *Anna Katharine, dau of Robin Muschamp Garry Simpson, QC, of Chelsea, and Lady Webster, of Bratton, Wilts, and has:

1a *Georgia; *b* 199–

(2) *Andrew Lindsay; *b* 15 Feb 1969

(1) *Louise Caroline; *b* 1 Feb 1967

2 *Mary Bethune [The Lady Mary Varney, Hill House, Dedham, Essex]; *b* 11 Dec 1935; *m* 14 Dec 1956 *Capt Owen Buckingham Varney, Scots Gds, only s of Edwin Thomas Varney, and has:

(1) *Mark Lindesay Buckingham; *b* 30 May 1958; late Scots Gds; *m* 1987 *Katie J, yr dau of Eric Bean, of Berks, and has:

1a *Alexander Edward Lindesay; *b* 1991

2a *Jocelyn James Buckingham; *b* 1993

(2) *Guy Nicholas Buckingham; *b* 15 Nov 1962; Capt late Scots Gds; *m* 1992 *Louise, er dau of Peter Owen, of Whitelands Farm, Ashington, Sussex

(1) *Georgina Mary Bethune; *b* 29 Sept 1960; *m* 1984 *Christopher Neil Hunter Gordon, yr s of Maj Patrick Hunter Gordon, CBE, MC, JP, DL, of Ballindoun House, Beauly, Inverness-shire, and has:

1a *Sam William; *b* 1988

2a *Ivan Patrick; *b* 1989

1a *Ione Mary; *b* 1992

The 14th EARL's er son,

DAVID BETHUNE LINDSAY-BETHUNE, **15th Earl of Lindsay**; *b* 9 Feb 1926; *educ* Eton and Magdalene Coll Cambridge; Scots Gds 1943–44; memb: Roy Co Archers 1960, Assoc American Railroads 1948–49, dir: John Crossley Carpet Trades Hldgs 1956, Festiniog Railway Co 1962, Severn Railways, Bank of Montreal 1976–89, John Junior Ltd 1963–89, Crossley Karastan Carpet Mills Ltd (Canadian) 1963, Abbey Life Insur Co of Canada 1967, memb Lloyd's 1967, OStJ; *m* 1st 31 Oct 1953 (*divorce* 1968) Hon Mary-Clare Douglas-Scott-Montagu (*m* 2nd 1979 Timothy Charles Austin Horn), yst dau of 2nd Baron Montagu of Beaulieu (*qv*), and had:

1 JAMES RANDOLPH LINDESAY-BETHUNE, **16th and present Earl of Lindsay**
1 *Caroline Janet [The Lady Caroline Wrey, Hollamoor Farm, Tawstock, Devon; 60 The Chase, London SW4]; *b* 7 July 1957; *m* 1981 *Sir George Richard Bourchier Wrey, 15th Bt (*qv*), and has issue

The **15th Earl** *m* 2nd 9 June 1969 *Penelope Georgina [The Rt Hon Penelope Countess of Lindsay, Steward's Cottage, Combermere, Salop SY13 4AJ], er dau of Anthony Crommelin Crossley, MP (*see* CROSSLEY, Bt), and formerly w of Maj Henry Ronald Burn Callendar, MC, Coldstream Gds, and *d* 1989

LINDSAY, Bt

Arms: Gu. a fess chequy arg. and az. between a mullet of the second in chief and the base barry undy and of the third, in a dexter canton arg. a sinister hand couped apaumé erect of the first. **Crest:** On a chapeau az., furred erm., a castle triple-towered ppr., port gu., tower-caps arg. **Supporters:** Two doves ppr. gorged of collars chequy arg. and az. **Motto:** *Firmus maneo* ('I remain firm'). **Creation:** Bt. (UK) 27 Feb 1962.

SIR RONALD ALEXANDER LINDSAY OF DOWHILL, 2ND BT, of Dowhill, Co Kinross [Sir Ronald Lindsay of Dowhill Bt, 104 Edith Rd, London W14 9AP]; *b* 6 Dec 1933; *s f* 1981, and as 23rd of Dowhill; *educ* Eton and Worcester Coll Oxford (MA); Lt Gren Gds 1952–54, memb Roy Co Archers, insur broker with Hogg Robinson and Minet 1958–80, gen manager UK branch Ocaso SA, of Madrid, 1980–84; Lloyd's membs' agent 1984–93, dir: AHJ Membs' Agency 1984–88, Sturge Hldgs Membs' Agencies 1989–93; memb Standing Cncl Baronetage (Chm 1987–89), Tstee Baronets' Tst 1986–95 (Chm 1990–92): V-Pres Anglo-Spanish Soc 1994– (V-Chm 1985–93); FCII; Encomienda Orden de Isabel la Católica (Spain) 1988; *m* 11 Jan 1968 *Nicoletta, yr dau of Capt Edgar Storich, Roy Italian Navy, of Madrid, and has:

1 +JAMES MARTIN EVELYN; *b* 11 Oct 1968
2 +Hugo Edgar; *b* 1970
3 +Robin Ronald Edward; *b* 1972
1 *Lucia Linda; *b* 28 Aug 1974

Lineage: Sir WILLIAM LINDSAY of Rossie (yr s of Alexander Lindsay of Glenesk and half-bro of 1st Earl of Crawford, *qv*); 1st of Crambeth or Dowhill, of which granted charter by ROBERT III 1398; *b c* 1350; *m c* 1376 Agnes, heiress of Crambeth, and had:

JOHN LINDSAY, 2nd of Dowhill, *d* 1447, leaving:

DAVID LINDSAY, 3rd of Dowhill; *d* 1472, leaving:

JOHN LINDSAY, 4th of Dowhill; had:

ADAM LINDSAY, 5th of Dowhill; *d* 1544, leaving:

JOHN LINDSAY, 6th of Dowhill; *d* 1566, leaving, with at least two daus (Margaret, *m* Robert Colville of Cleish and had issue; Janet, *m* 1st Andrew Lundie, 2nd Sir William Scott, 3rd, as his 1st w, Sir George Douglas; *see* MORTON, E):

JAMES LINDSAY, 7th of Dowhill; helped MARY QUEEN OF SCOTS escape from Lochleven 1567; *m* Janet, only dau of James Ross of Craigie, and *d* 1591, leaving, with 10 other children, including an er s (James, 8th of Dowhill, also held the town and lands of Logie and the territorial Barony of Kinloch, Perthshire, all of which he lost to his yr bro John, *m* Elizabeth Colville of Cleish and had a s Adam, who failed to recover them from his uncle):

JOHN LINDSAY, 9th of Dowhill; had, with a yr s, William, on whom he settled the (territorial) Barony of Kinloch:

JAMES LINDSAY, 10th of Dowhill; *b* 1601; *d* 1638, leaving, with five daus:

1 John, 11th of Dowhill; matriculated arms *c* 1673; *b* 1623; *m* 1644 Janet, est dau of Robert Ayton of Inerdorney, and *d* by 1692, leaving, with three other sons (*dsp*) and five daus:

(1) James, 12th of Dowhill; inherited the territorial Barony of Kinloch from his great-uncle William and sold it 1696; *dsp* 1705

2 William (Rt Rev); Bp Dunkeld 1677–79; *m* Katharine, dau of Sir Andrew Skene of Halyards, and *d* 1679, leaving:

(1) James, 13th of Dowhill; last actual holder of the Barony and Castle of Dowhill, his estates being sold or passing to creditors; *m* Mary Watson and had:

1a Martin, 14th of Dowhill; sold the last of the estate 1740, took part in the '45 Uprising; acquitted of treason; writer (legal practitioner) Record Office, Edinburgh; *b* 1710; *m* 1749 Jean, dau of Dr James Smythe, and *d* 1790, leaving, with other issue:

1b James, 15th of Dowhill; *b* 1753; *m* Ann Pillance and *d* 1837, leaving, with four daus:

1c Martin, CB, 16th of Dowhill; Col 78th (Seaforth) Highrs 1819–37; *b* 1782; *m* 1817 Elspeth, dau of James Hadden of Persley, Provost Aberdeen, and *d* 1847, having had:

1d James Martin; *b* 1818; *d* 1824

2d David Baird, 17th of Dowhill; merchant Calcutta; *b* 1822; *m* 1st 1843 Sophia, dau of Rev Norman Garstin, DD, and had:

1e Sophia Garstin; *m* 1st William Bury; *m* 2nd Thomas Hodges

2d (cont.) David Lindsay *m* 2nd 1856 Eleanor, dau of Rev Anthony Garstin, Chaplain Darjeeling, and *d* 1887, having by her had:

1e David Hugh, 18th of Dowhill; dir S Maharatta Railway; *b* 1859; *m* 1896 Caroline Offley (*d* 1902), dau of Hartington Offley Shaw, of Hartington Hall, Derbys, and *d* 1919, leaving:

1f Alison; *m* 7 Jan 1935 Lt-Col Horace Anthony Garstin, MC, PAVO Cavalry (*d* 4 April 1960), s of Col George Lindsay Garstin, Hodson's Horse IA, and *dsp* 1 Oct 1988

2e Norman Garstin, 19th of Dowhill; *b* 1862; *dsp* 1940

3e D'Arcy (Sir), CBE (1919), 20th of Dowhill; MLA India 1921–30, Kaisar-i-Hind Gold Medal 1911, ktd 1925; *b* 14 Nov 1865; *d* unm 17 April 1941

4e Bertram Alexander, 21st of Dowhill; *b* 1873; *dsp* 17 April 1948

2e Eleanor Charlotte; *m* George Penn Gaskell, barrister, and *dsp* 1938

3e Marion Ethel; *b* 1870; *m* 11 June 1902 Hugh Alexander Barclay McCulloch (*d* 27 June 1944), s of Hugh McCulloch, of Stranraer, Wigtownshire, and *d* 20 Nov 1962, leaving issue

4e Edith; *m* 21 July 1897 Hugh Charles Loudon Bloxam, FIC (*d* 14 July 1940), s of William Bloxam, MD, of Mount St, W1, and *d* 7 Nov 1964, leaving a dau, Rosalie (*dsp* 199–)

3d Edward James; *b* 1828; *m* 1862 and *dspm* 1886

4d Alexander Hadden, CB; Maj-Gen RA and RHA; *b* 10 Aug 1830; *m* 1870 Isabella Mary Frances (*d* 1874), dau of Maj-Gen Philip Harris, and *d* 1887, leaving:

1e Alexander Bertram; Lt-Col 2nd KEO Gurkhas, IA; *b* 11 Dec 1872; *m* 1904 Gladys (*d* 11 Jan 1961), widow of Lt Maurice Cay, RN, and dau of William Hutton, of Beetham Ho, Milnthorpe, Westmorland, and 33 Sloane Gdns, SW1, and *d* 16 Sept 1914, leaving:

1f MARTIN ALEXANDER (Sir), **1st Bt**

1f Elsy; *m* 6 Feb 1895 Brig-Gen Richard Boileau Gaisford, CB, CMG (*d* 25 Sept 1924), of Conynger Hurst, Ulverston, Lancs, s of Rev S H Gaisford, Rector Cowthorpe, Yorks, and *d* 21 March 1951, leaving a s and dau

Lt-Col ALEXANDER LINDSAY's s,

Sir Martin Alexander Lindsay of Dowhill, 1st Bt (UK), so *cr* 27 Feb 1962, 22nd of Dowhill, CBE (1952), DSO (1945), DL (Lincs 1938–45); *b* 22 Aug 1905; *educ* Wellington and RMC Sandhurst; 2nd Lt Roy Scots Fus 1925, seconded 4th Bn Nigeria Regt 1927, Surveyor Air-Route Expdn Greenland 1930–31 (King's Polar Medal), Leader Br Trans-Greenland Expdn 1934, WW II on staff (Norway 1940 (despatches)) and 1st Bn Gordon Highrs 51st Highland Div 1944–45 (despatches, wounded), Lt-Col 1945, MP Solihull 1945–64, chm W Midlands C and U Assocs 1949–52, memb Roy Co Archers, Gold Staff Offr Coronation 1953, author: *Sledge* (1934), *So Few Got Through* (1945) and *The Baronetage* (1977); *m* 1st 15 Dec 1932 (*divorce* 1967) Joyce Emily [Joyce Lady Lindsay, 40 Ladbroke Rd, London W11 3PH], er dau of Maj Hon Robert Hamilton Lindsay, RSG (*see* CRAWFORD and BALCARRES, E); *m* 2nd 1 Aug 1969 Hon Loelia (*d* 1993), formerly w of 2nd Duke of Westminster (*qv*) and only dau of 1st Baron Sysonby (*qv*), and *d* 1981, having by his 1st w had:

1 Sir RONALD ALEXANDER LINDSAY OF DOWHILL, **2nd and present Bt**
2 +Oliver John Martin; CBE (Mil 1993) [Col Oliver Lindsay CBE, Brookwood House, Brookwood, Surrey GU24 0NX]; *b* 30 Aug 1938; *educ* Eton and RMA Sandhurst; FRHistS, MICFM, Col Gren Gds, dir Treloar Tst, memb Roy Co Archers; author: *The Lasting Honour, The Fall of Hong Kong 1941* (1978), *At The Going Down of the Sun — Hong Kong and South East Asia 1941-45* (1981) and *Once a Grenadier . . . The History of the Grenadier Guards 1945–1995* (1996), ed: *A Guards General: The Memoirs of Sir Allan Adair* (1986) and *The Guards Magazine* 1992–; *m* 27 Oct 1964 *Lady Claire Rohais Antonia Elizabeth Giffard, yr dau of 3rd Earl of Halsbury (*qv*), and has:

(1) +Mark Oliver GIFFARD-LINDSAY; *b* 27 Dec 1968
(1) *Victoria Louise Elizabeth Clare; *b* 26 May 1967; *m* 1988 *Gregory F M T Wheatley, 2nd s of Anthony Wheatley
(2) *Fiona Emily Margaret; *b* 1 May 1972; Lt RAMC TA
1 *Jacynth Rosemary [The Lady Mark Fitzalan Howard, 13 Campden Hill Sq, London W8 7LB]; *b* 1 Dec 1934; *m* 17 Nov 1961 *Lord Mark Fitzalan Howard, OBE, bro of 17th Duke of Norfolk (*qv*), and has issue

LINDSAY OF BIRKER

Creation: B. (UK) 13 Nov 1945.

THE 3RD BARON LINDSAY OF BIRKER (James Francis Lindsay) [The Rt Hon The Lord Lindsay of Birker, c/o Australian Foreign Service, Department of Foreign Affairs, Barton, Canberra, ACT, Australia]; *b* 29 Jan 1945; *s f* 1994; *educ* Canberra High Sch, Geelong GS, Bethseda-Chevy Chase High Sch and Keele U; lecturer Dept Physics Tunghal U Taichung, Taiwan, Republic of China, Dep Australian High Commr: Islamabad 1993–96, Nairobi 1996–; *m* 1969 (*divorce* 1985) Mary Rose Thomas, dau of W G Thomas, of Cwmbran, Mon

Lineage: The Rev THOMAS M LINDSAY, of Glasgow; *b* 1843 (s of Rev A Lindsay); DD, LLD, Pncpl Utd Free Coll Glasgow 1902–14, Examiner Edin U, Assist to Prof Logic and Metaphysics, sometime Convener Foreign Mission Ctee Free Church Scotland, ecclesiastical historian; *m* 1872 Anna (*d* 1903), est dau of Alexander Colquhoun-Stirling-Murray-Dunlop, JP, of Corsock, Kirkcudbrightshire, and Edinbarnet, Duntocher, Dunbartonshire, sometime MP Greenock, and *d* 6 Dec 1914, leaving:

  1 ALEXANDER DUNLOP, **1st Baron**
  2 James H; ICS; *d* 30 March 1955
  3 Thomas; with Min Health; *d* 27 Dec 1967
  1 Esther; *m* W Alcock and *d* 25 Feb 1958
  2 Susan Irvine Martin; *m* 8 Sept 1909 Sir (Frederick) Maurice Powicke (*d* 19 May 1963), the historian, s of Rev Frederick James Powicke, DD, and *d* 25 Aug 1965 aged 89, having had issue

The Rev THOMAS's son,
  ALEXANDER DUNLOP LINDSAY, **1st Baron Lindsay of Birker**, of Low Ground, Co Cumberland (UK), so *cr* 13 Nov 1945, CBE (1919, MBE 1918); *b* 14 May 1879; *educ* Glasgow Acad, Glasgow U (MA 1899) and Univ Coll Oxford (BA 1902, MA 1908); Maj Gen List WW I (despatches), Hon LLD Glasgow 1925, St Andrews 1938, Princeton 1946 and Leeds 1950, Pncpl U Coll N Staffs 1949–52, Fell and Tutor Philosophy Balliol Coll Oxford 1906–22, Jowett Lecturer Philosophy 1910, Prof Moral Philosophy Glasgow U 1922, Master Balliol Coll Oxford, V-Chllr Oxford U 1935–38, Pro-V-Chllr 1941–45, Shaw Fell Edinburgh U and Lecturer Philosophy Victoria U Manchester, author: *Karl Marx's Capital* (1925), *The Nature of Religious Truth* (1927), *The Essentials of Democracy* (1929), *Christianity and Economics* (1933), *Kant* (1934), *The Churches and Democracy* (1934), *The Moral Teachings of Jesus* (1937), *The Two Moralities* (1940), *The Modern Democratic State* (1943); *m* 1907 Erica (*d* 28 May 1962), yst dau of F Storr, and had:

  1 MICHAEL FRANCIS MORRIS, **2nd Baron**
  2 Thomas Martin, MBE (1946); *b* 5 March 1915; *educ* Sidcot Sch and Edinburgh U (BMus 1935); Maj Sherwood Rangers WW II (despatches), lecturer FO German Section; *m* 1st 7 Sept 1939 (*divorce* 1950) Denise Theresa, dau of Gerald Albert Vaughan, and had:
    (1) +ALEXANDER SEBASTIAN [Alexander Lindsay Esq, 5 Cambridge Rd, Carshalton, Surrey]; *b* 27 May 1940; heir presumptive
    (2) +Thomas Martin; *b* 1 Sept 1942
    (1) *Teresa; *b* 3 Oct 1944
  2 (cont.) The Hon Thomas Lindsay *m* 2nd 1950 (*divorce* 1960) Felicitas, dau of Dr Martin Lange, and by her had:
    (3) +Stuart Martin; *b* 3 July 1951
    (4) +Alexander Gordon; *b* 16 Nov 1952
  2 (cont.) The Hon Thomas Lindsay *m* 3rd 2 Dec 1961 *Erica, dau of Maj Eric Thirkell-Cooper, and *d* 1995, leaving by her:
    (5) +Benjamin Martin; *b* 3 July 1962
    (6) +Robert William; *b* 11 June 1967
  1 *(Anna) Drusilla [The Hon Lady Scott, Ash House, Alde Lane, Aldeburgh, Suffolk IP15 5DZ]; *b* 15 April 1911; *m* 1937 *Sir Ian Dixon Scott, KCMG, KCVO, CIE, 2nd s of Thomas Henderson Scott, OBE, MInstCE, of Selkirk, and has:
    (1) *Peter John Lindsay; *b* 13 July 1948; *m* 1976 *Susan Dobson
    (1) *(Mary) Pauline; *b* 10 Jan 1939; *m* 1971 *Samih Sadek
    (2) *Rachel Erica; *b* 25 June 1940; *m* 1960 *David Britton
    (3) *Ann Catharine; *b* 9 Feb 1942; *m* 1975 *Jack Shepherd
    (4) *Monica Margaret; *b* 16 Feb 1947; *m* 1975 *Ian Lanman

The 1st BARON *d* 18 March 1952; his er son,
  MICHAEL FRANCIS MORRIS LINDSAY, **2nd Baron Lindsay of Birker**; *b* 24 Feb 1909; *educ* Gresham's and Balliol Coll Oxford; Lecturer Yenching U Peking 1937, served with 8 Route Army N China 1942–45, Visiting Lecturer Harvard U 1946–47, Lecturer U Coll Hull 1948–51, Sr Fell Australian Nat U 1951–59, Visiting Prof Yale U 1958, Prof Far Eastern Studies American U Washington, DC, 1959–; *m* 25 June 1941 *Hsiao Li, dau of Col Li Wen-Chi, Chinese Army, of Lishih Shansi, and *d* 1994, having had issue:

  1 JAMES FRANCIS LINDSAY, **3rd and present Baron Lindsay of Birker**
  1 Erica Susan; *b* 16 Oct 1942; *d* 1993
  2 *Mary Muriel; *b* 12 March 1951; *m* 1976 *Kenneth Kyle Abbot Jr and has:
    (1) *Thomas Lindsay; *b* 1978
    (2) *Michael William; *b* 1985

LINDSAY-HOGG

Arms: Per pale indented vert and azure, on a bend or three boar's heads couped sable. **Crest:** Issuant out of a mural crown argent a boar's head erect sable, holding in the mouth a sprig of oak fructed proper. **Motto:** *Mores ante nomen* ('Good conduct before a good name'). **Creation:** Bt. (UK) 22 Dec 1905.

SIR EDWARD WILLIAM LINDSAY-HOGG, 4TH BT, of Rotherfield Hall, Rotherfield, Co Sussex; *b* 23 May 1910; *s n* 1987; *educ* Eton; jockey, playwright and author; *m* 1st 18 Nov 1936 (*divorce* 1946) Geraldine Mary (the actress and producer Geraldine Fitzgerald), dau of Edward Martin Fitzgerald, of Greystones, Co Wicklow; *m* 2nd 30 Oct 1957 *Kathleen Mary, dau of James Cooney, of Carrick-on-Suir, Co Tipperary, and widow of Capt Maurice Cadell, MC, and by his 1st w has:

  1 +MICHAEL EDWARD; *b* 5 May 1940; theatre and film dir: *The Abbess of Crewe* (1976); *m* 1967 (*divorce* 1971) Lucy Mary (*m* 2nd 13 Dec 1978, as his 2nd w, 1st Earl of Snowdon (*qv*), only dau of Donald Davies, of Enniskerry, Co Wicklow, prodn assist Thames TV

Lineage: Rev PETER HOGG; Rector Pitchcombe and Hanscombe, Glos, *temp* ELIZABETH I; had:

Rev PETER HOGG; Rector Pitchombe and Hanscombe; had:
  1 Edward, of Pitchcombe; *m* Abigail — and *dsp* between 30 April 1687 and 13 April 1688
  2 Thomas
  3 Daniel, of Pitchcombe; *b* by 1687; *m* Alice (*d* between 18 May 1716 and 8 May 1724) and *d* between 29 May 1705 and 22 Oct 1712, leaving:
    (1) DANIEL
    (2) William; living 1716
    (3) Robert; living 1716
    (4) John; *m* 23 June 1711 Deborah White, of Pitchcombe, and was *bur* 17 Feb 1718/9
    (1) Alice; *m* 1st by 1705 William Lawrence; *m* 2nd by 1716 — Burford
    (2) Elizabeth; *m* by 1705 Henry Clayfield
    (3) Mary; living 1724
    (4) Sarah

DANIEL HOGG's est s,
  DANIEL HOGG, of Pitchcombe; *b* 1677; *m* Mary Gardener (*d* 1 Sept 1727), of Pitchcombe, and *d* 6 Sept 1737, leaving:
  1 Samuel; *m* Mary Burrows, of Tuffley Court, Glos; *m* 2nd Mary Stevens, of Painswick, Glos, and had two sons (Samuel, *d* W Indies; Capel) and a dau (Mary, *m* her 1st cousin William Hogg, *see below*)
  2 WILLIAM
  1 Edith; *m* William Hopson, of Randwick, Glos, and had issue

DANIEL HOGG's yr s,
  WILLIAM HOGG, of Painswick; *m* Sept 1734 Betty, dau of James Mitchell, of Harescombe Park, Glos, by Mary Hillier, and had, with eight other children:
  1 William; *b* 1735; *m* his 1st cousin Mary, dau of Samuel Hogg (*see* above), and had a s (William)
  2 THOMAS
  1 Elizabeth; *m* her cousin Miles Mitchell, of Randwick
  2 Mary; *m* Richard Glover, of Bowbridge, Glos

WILLIAM HOGG's 2nd s,
  THOMAS HOGG, of Painswick; *bapt* 15 Oct 1749; *m c* 1772 Sarah, dau of Henry Jordan by Elizabeth, dau of Josia Jenner and aunt of Dr Edward Jenner, the promoter of vaccination, and *d* 27 Jan 1795, having had, with other issue:
  1 Thomas Jenner (Rev); Perpetual Curate Clunbury, Salop; *b* 1773; *m* Rebecca Haines, of Haynes, and *d c* 1848, leaving two sons and three daus
  2 Samuel; *m* Elizabeth Cooke and had two sons (Thomas; Samuel) and two daus (Elizabeth; Sarah)
  3 HENRY
  4 Edward; *b* 1789 or 1790; MD; *m* Elizabeth Dunkheim and *dsp*

5 James; *b* 18 May 1791; *m* 24 June 1816 Mary Ann Hogg (*d* 30 April 1826) and had:

(1) Martha Sophia; *b* 25 April 1817; *m* Sept 1849 Lt Barrett, RN

1 Elizabeth; *m* Thomas Beard and had issue

2 Mary; *b* 1794; *m* Nehemiah Longshaw, of Pendlebury, Lancs, and *dsp* 6 May 1862

The 3rd s,

HENRY HOGG, of Davenshaw House, Congleton, Cheshire, JP; *b* 7 Aug 1787; *m* 1 June 1822 Charlotte (*d* 26 Aug 1878), dau of — Coppinger, of Congleton, and *d* 12 March 1864, having had, with other issue:

1 WILLIAM

2 James; *b* 23 June 1830; *m* Clara Louise, dau of George S Daintry, of The Grange, North Rode, Cheshire, and had:

(1) George Daintry; *m* Agnes, dau of Edward Fayer, MRCS, LRCP, of Southsea

(2) Reginald Ormsby; *m* Wilhelmina, dau of Pelham Richardson, Irrigation Dept India

3 Edward Jenner; *b* 15 Feb 1838; *m* Betty, widow of J Bell, of Shanghai, and *dsp*

4 Henry Jenner Holder; *b* 9 Nov 1839; *m* 6 Sept 1865 Georgina, widow of — Jacob, and *dsp*

5 Capel Wilson, JP; *b* 29 April 1841; *m* 1st Harriette, dau of Rev J T Robinson, Incumbent Mow Cop, Staffs, and had 12 children; *m* 2nd Hope, dau of — Chaddock, of Congleton

6 Herbert Octavius; *b* 25 Jan 1843; *m* 9 Nov 1873 Katherine Dowling (*m* 2nd 16 Oct 1879 Charles Elliott; *d* 12 June 1882) and *dsp* 5 April 1878

1 Mary Sophia; *b* 16 May 1836; *m* William Scott, MD (*d* 1865), and had issue

The est s,

WILLIAM HOGG, of Oakleigh, Pembury, Kent, and Bayswater; *b* 9 July 1825; Hanseatic Consul Shanghai, Chev Crown Italy; *m* 1 Oct 1850 Eliza Susannah (*b* 27 Aug 1832; *d* 28 May 1894), dau of George Hickson, of Chigwell, Essex, and *d* 12 April 1895, leaving:

1 William Henry Jenner, of Oakleigh, JP; *b* 12 July 1851; *m* 4 July 1877 Mary Elizabeth, dau of Jeremiah Dummett, of London, and *dsp* 1 May 1900

2 LINDSAY (Sir), **1st Bt**

1 Mary Edith; *b* 10 Oct 1855; *m* 5 April 1877 Francis Luscombe, of Crawley, Sussex, and *dsp* 17 Dec 1901

2 Alice Charlotte; *b* 7 Feb 1858; *m* 24 Oct 1882 Edward Adolph Horne, of London, and had two sons

WILLIAM HOGG's yr s,

Sir LINDSAY HOGG later LINDSAY-HOGG (roy licence 6 Jan 1906), **1st Bt** (UK), so *cr* 22 Dec 1905, of Rotherfield Hall, Rotherfield, Sussex, JP; *b* 10 March 1853; *educ* Harrow; CC E Sussex, MP Eastbourne or S Sussex 1900–06; *m* 12 Oct 1880 Alice Margaret Emma (*d* 23 Aug 1952 in her 97th year), dau of John Christian Cowley, of Heathfield, Addington, Surrey, by Julia, dau of Sir William Baynes, 2nd Bt (*see* BAYNES, Bt, of Harefield Place), and *d* 2 Nov 1923, having had:

WILLIAM LINDSAY-HOGG, JP (Sussex); *b* 27 Jan 1882; *m* 23 May 1907 Nora Cicely (*d* 16 Nov 1929), dau of John James Barrow, of Holmwood, nr Tunbridge Wells, Dornoch, Scotland, and Hyde Park Gdns, London, and *dvp* 1 May 1918, leaving:

1 **Sir Anthony Henry Lindsay-Hogg, 2nd Bt**; *b* 1 May 1908; S/Ldr RAF WW II, ADC to Govr Trinidad 1942–43; *m* 16 Dec 1929 (*divorce* 1934) Frances Mary Hyde (*d* 12 Dec 1969), er dau of Arthur Richard Dobie, of Montreal, and *d* 31 Oct 1968, leaving:

(1) **Sir William Lindsay Lindsay-Hogg, 3rd Bt**; *b* 12 Aug 1930; *educ* Stowe; Lt 17th/21st Lancers; *m* 31 Jan 1961 (*divorce* 1967) Victoria, twin dau of John Pares, of Priory House, Kingsclere, Berks; *m* 2nd 1987 *Marie Teresa, dau of John Foster, of St Helens, Lancs, and *d* 1987, leaving by his 1st w:

1a *Sarah Frances; *b* 15 July 1961; *m* 1982 *Simon John Gatliff and has had:

1b George Auben; *b* 1990; *d* 1991

2b *John William; *b* 1994

1b *Rosie Frances; *b* 1988

2 **Sir EDWARD WILLIAM LINDSAY-HOGG, 4th and present Bt**

1 Alice Violet; *b* 27 Jan 1882; *m* 19 May 1903 Capt Hugh Brodie Cardwell (*ka* 1918), of North Lea, Eastbourne, s of Col William Alexander Cardwell, of The Moat Croft, Eastbourne, and *d* 1 Aug 1965, leaving issue

2 Edith Vera; *b* 15 July 1889; *m* 20 Oct 1908 Capt Lancelot Mellish Fane Gladwin, er s of Hamilton Fane Gladwin, of Seven Springs, Glos, and *d* 5 May 1912, leaving issue

3 Cecily; *b* 18 Jan 1898; *m* 25 July 1918 Lt-Col Eden George Wallace (*d* 1 Feb 1968), of Hamford House, Claines, Worcester, and had issue

LINDSEY and ABINGDON

Arms: Arg. three battering-rams fesswise in pale ppr., headed and garnished az. charged on the breast with a fret azure. **Crest:** A Saracen's head, couped at the breast ppr., ducally crowned or. **Supporters:** Dexter, a pilgrim or friar vested in russet, his crutch and rosary or; sinister, a savage man wreathed about the temples and waist with ivy; each charged on the breast with a fret azure. **Mottoes:** *Loyauté m'oblige* ('Loyalty is my duty'); *Virtus ariete fortior* ('Valour is stronger than a battering ram'). **Creation:** B. (E) 6 May 1572, E. (E) 22 Nov 1626 (Lindsey) and 30 Nov 1682 (Abingdon).

THE 14TH EARL OF LINDSEY AND 9TH EARL OF ABINGDON and **Lord (Baron) Norreys of Rycote** (Richard Henry Rupert Bertie) [The Rt Hon The Earl of Lindsey and Abingdon, Gilmilnscroft, Sorn, Mauchline, Ayrshire KA5 6ND; 3 Westgate Terrace, London SW10 9BT]; *b* 28 June 1931; *s* cousin 1963; *educ* Ampleforth; late Lt Roy Norfolk Regt (SRO), insur broker and underwriting memb Lloyd's 1958–96, High Steward Abingdon 1963–, chm Anglo-Ivory Coast Soc 1974–77; *m* 5 Jan 1957 *Norah Elizabeth Farquhar-Oliver, yr dau of Mark Oliver (*see* FARQUHAR, Bt), and has:

1 +HENRY MARK WILLOUGHBY, *Lord Norreys* [Lord Norreys, Alameda de la Alcaldesa 1, Urb La Virginia, 29600 Marbella (Málaga), Spain]; *b* 6 June 1958; Kt Honour and Devotion SMO Malta 1995; Kt Justice Sacred Mil Constantinian Order St George 1998; Kt Order SS Maurice and Lazarus 1998; *educ* Eton and Edinburgh U; *m* 1989 *Lucinda Sol, 2nd dau of Christopher Stewart Moorsom, by his 1st w Maria del Pilar Sánchez y Betancourt has:

(1) +Willoughby Henry Constantine St Maur; *b* 15 Jan 1996

(2) +James Frederick Christopher St Ninian; *b* 26 Aug 1997

2 +Alexander Michael Richard; *b* 8 April 1970; *educ* Eton and The Queen's Coll Oxford (BA 1992); *m* 17 April 1998 *Catherine Davina, dau of Prof Gordon Cameron

1 +Annabel Frances Rose [The Lady Annabel Bertie, 3 Westgate Terrace, London SW10]; *b* 11 March 1969; *educ* St Mary's Ascot and Edinburgh U (MA 1991)

Lineage (of Bertie): ROBERT BARTUE, of Bearsted, Kent; stonemason; *d* between 4 Oct 1501 and 17 Feb 1501/2, leaving, with a yr s (William):

THOMAS BARTUE, of Bearsted; worked as master mason on Winchester Cathedral 1532, also built Calshot Castle 1539 and Hurst Castle, Hants, 1541, of which made Capt; granted arms 1550; *m* Alice — and *d* by 5 June 1555, leaving, with a yr s:

RICHARD BERTIE; *b c* Christmas 1516 or 1517; *educ* Corpus Christi Coll Oxford; allegedly served in the household of Sir Thomas Wriothesley, for whom his f had worked on the construction of Place House, Titchfield, Hants, 1538; Gentleman Usher to his future w, for whom he was working by Aug 1549; MP Lincs 1562/3–66/7; *m c* early 1553, as her 2nd husb, Katherine (*d* 19 Sept 1580), *de jure* Baroness Willoughby de Eresby (*qv*) in her own right according to later doctrine, dau and ultimately sole heir of 11th Lord (Baron) Willoughby de Eresby and widow of Charles Brandon, 1st Duke of Suffolk (whose 3rd w had been MARY, sis of HENRY VIII and widow of LOUIS XII OF FRANCE), unsuccessfully claimed the Barony of Willoughby de Eresby 1570 in right of his w and *d* 9 April 1582, leaving an only s:

PEREGRINE BERTIE, 13th LORD (Baron) WILLOUGHBY DE ERESBY (*qv*), whose claim to the Barony was accepted 11 Nov 1580; *b* 12 Oct 1555 at Wesel, Duchy of Cleves, in which Protestant German state his similarly inclined parents were staying; they later moved on to Strasbourg and Weinheim (such peregrinations being reflected in the name they gave their son), prudently staying away from England while the Marian persecution flared up there; naturalised as an Englishman 1559; *educ* Gray's Inn; Envoy Denmark 1582 and 1585, served with English forces Low Countries 1585–86 (saw action at Zutphen 22 Sept 1586), Govr Bergen-op-Zoom 1586–87; allegedly ktd for gallantry (KB) 7 Oct 1586, Col-Gen Inf June–Dec 1587, Capt Gen (cdr all English forces) Dec 1587, Lt-Gen English forces France assisting HENRY IV (when still Henry of Navarre, the Protestant leader in that country) Sept 1589–Jan 1589/90, Govr Berwick-on-Tweed and Warden E March March 1597/8, memb Cncl North 1599; *m* between Christmas 1577 and 12 March 1577/8 Lady Mary de Vere (*m* 2nd Sir

Eustace Hart and *d c* 24 June 1624), only dau of 16th Earl of Oxford (*see* SAINT ALBANS, D), and *d* 25 June 1601, having had, with four other sons:

ROBERT BERTIE, 14th LORD (Baron) WILLOUGHBY DE ERESBY and **1st Earl of Lindsey**, Co Lincoln (E), so *cr* 22 Nov 1626, KG (1630), KB (Jan 1604/5), PC (1628); *b* probably 16 Dec 1582; *educ* Corpus Christi Coll Cambridge and Gray's Inn; claimed the Earldom of Oxford and its associated dignities in right of his mother but successfully only as far as the post of Ld Gt Chamberlain, as which he was granted precedence at the head of the Barons in 13 April 1627, and which had presumably helped his promotion to Earl since it was proclaimed in his patent of creation that nobody below that rank had held the Ld Gt Chamberlainship in the earliest days of its existence; V-Adml Isle of Rhé Expdn 1627, cmded fleet to relieve La Rochelle 1628; Ld Lt Lincs 1628–42, Govr Berwick 1639, Col Foot Gds 1642 and Gen royalist forces on outbreak of Civil War; *m c* 1605 Elizabeth (*d* 30 Nov 1634), dau of 1st Baron Montagu of Boughton (*see* MANCHESTER, D), and *d* from wounds received at the drawn Battle of Edgehill 23 Oct 1642, leaving, with seven yr sons (including Roger, 2nd s, *m* Ursula —; Peregrine, 3rd s; Edward, 8th s, Collector Customs London 1676) and at least one dau (Mary, *m* Dr John Hewitt (beheaded Tower Hill May 1658)):

MONTAGU BERTIE, **2nd Earl of Lindsey** and 15th LORD (Baron) WILLOUGHBY DE ERESBY, KG (1661), PC (1643 and 1660); *b* just before 1608; *educ* Sidney Sussex Coll Cambridge; MP Lincs 1624–25 and Stamford 1625–26; called up to Ho Lds 3 Nov 1640 *vp* in f's Barony, Capt King's Gds Civil War, as which chose to be captured by Parly forces Battle of Edgehill 1642 rather than abandon his mortally wounded f; set free 1643, fought Battle of Naseby 1645 (wounded); Ld Lt Lincs 1660–66, Ld Gt Chamberlain CHARLES II's Coronation, Jt Commr for office of Earl Marshal 1662, Col of Horse 1662 and 1666; *m* 1st 18 April 1627 Martha (*d* 1641), widow of 1st Earl of Holderness and dau of Sir William Cokayne, of Rushden, Northants (*see* CULLEN OF ASHBOURNE, B), and had, with other issue (including Peregrine; Richard; Vere):

1 ROBERT BERTIE, **3rd Earl of Lindsey** and 16th LORD (Baron) WILLOUGHBY DE ERESBY, PC (1666–79 and 1682); *b c* 1630; MP (Tory) Boston 1661–66, Gent Bedchamber 1674–85, Ld Lt Lincs 1666–1700; *m* 1st *c* Nov-Dec 1654 Mary, yr dau and coheir of John Massingberd, of London, Treasurer HEIC, and had an only dau (Arabella, *m* 3rd Earl Rivers); *m* 2nd Elizabeth, dau of 4th Lord (Baron) Wharton (*qv*), by whom he had five sons; *m* 3rd Elizabeth, widow of Sir Francis Henry Lee, Bt, of Ditchley (by whom she was mother of 1st Earl of Lichfield of the 1674 *cr*; *see* LICHFIELD, E, preliminary remarks), and dau and heir of Thomas Pope, 2nd Earl of Downe, and *d* 8 May 1701, having by her had a s and dau (both *dsp*); his est s by his 2nd w:

(1) ROBERT BERTIE, **4th Earl of Lindsey**, 17th LORD (Baron) WILLOUGHBY DE ERESBY and 1st DUKE OF ANCASTER AND KESTEVEN (GB), so *cr* 26 July 1715, as also earlier 21 Dec 1706 MARQUESS OF LINDSEY (E), with in both cases special remainder, failing heirs male of his body, to the heirs male of the body of his parents, PC (1701); *b* 30 Oct 1660; MP Boston 1685–87 and 1689–90, Chllr Duchy Lancaster 1689–97; called up to Ho Lds 19 April 1690 *vp* in f's Barony; Ld Lt Lincs 1701–23; *m* 1st 30 July 1678 Mary (*d* 20 Sept 1689), dau of Sir Richard Wynn, 4th Bt, of Gwydir (*see* WILLIAMS-WYNN, Bt), and had one surv son; *m* 2nd 6 July 1705 Albinia (*m* 2nd James Douglas and *d* 29 July 1745), dau of Maj-Gen William Farrington, of Chislehurst, Kent, and *d* 26 July 1723, having by her had four other sons (including Montague, for whose dau *see* WESTMORLAND, E) and a dau; his s by his 1st w:

1a PEREGRINE BERTIE, **5th Earl of Lindsey**, 18th LORD (Baron) WILLOUGHBY DE ERESBY and 2nd DUKE OF ANCASTER AND KESTEVEN, PC (1708 and Jan 1723/3–42); *b* 29 April 1686; V-Chamberlain 1702, MP Lincs 1708–15; called up to Ho Lds 16 March 1714/5 *vp* in f's Barony; a Ld Bedchamber 1719–27, Ld Lt Lincs Feb 1723/4–Jan 1741/2, Ld Gt Chamberlain GEORGE II's Coronation; *m* June 1711 Jane (*d* 25 Aug 1736), dau and coheir of Sir John Brownlow, Bt (*see* BROWNLOW, B), and *d* 1 Jan 1741/2, having had, with other issue:

1b PEREGRINE BERTIE, **6th Earl of Lindsey**, 19th LORD (Baron) WILLOUGHBY DE ERESBY and 3rd DUKE OF ANCASTER AND KESTEVEN, PC (Feb 1741/2); *b* 1714; Ld Bedchamber 1755–65, Maj-Gen 1755, Lt Gen 1759, Gen 1772, Ld Gt Chamberlain GEORGE III's Coronation, Master Horse 1766–78; *m* 1st 22 May 1735 Elizabeth (*dsp* 17 Dec 1743), widow of Sir Charles Gunter Nicoll, KB, and dau and sole heir of William Blundell, of Basingstoke; *m* 2nd 27 Nov 1750 Mary (*d* 19 Oct 1793), dau of Thomas Panton, of Newmarket, Master of the King's running horses or what would now be called GEORGE II's racehorse trainer (and according to Horace Walpole, an unreliable source in this case, a jockey), and *d* 12 Aug 1778, having by her had (with another dau, *d* young):

1c ROBERT BERTIE, **7th Earl of Lindsey**, 20th LORD (Baron) WILLOUGHBY DE ERESBY and 4th DUKE OF ANCASTER AND KESTEVEN, PC (1779); *b* 17 Oct 1756; Ld Lt Lincs 1779; *d* unm 8 July 1779, when the Barony and Ld Gt Chamberlainship fell into abeyance between his sisters

1c PRISCILLA BARBARA ELIZABETH, BARONESS WILLOUGHBY DE ERESBY (*qv*) in her own right on termination of abeyance in her favour 1780; *m* and had issue

2c Georgiana Charlotte; *m* 25 April 1791 1st Marquess of Cholmondeley (*qv*) and *d* 23 June 1838, leaving issue

2b BROWNLOW BERTIE, **8th Earl of Lindsey** and 5th and last DUKE OF ANCASTER AND KESTEVEN, PC (1779); *b* 1 May 1729; MP Lincs 1761–79, Ld Lt Lincs 1779; *m* 1st 11 Nov 1762 Harriet (*dsp* 23 April 1763), dau and heir of George Morton Pitt, Govr Fort St George, India, of Twickenham; *m* 2nd 2 Jan 1769 Mary Anne (*d* 13 Jan 1804), dau of Maj Peter Layard, and *dspm* 8 Feb 1809, when the Dukedom and Marquessate expired, having by her had an only dau:

1c Mary Elizabeth; *m* 26 May 1793 Viscount Milsington, est s of William Charles, Earl of Portmore, and *d* 10 Feb 1797

(1) Jane; *m* Maj-Gen Edward Mathew, Govr Grenada, Equerry to GEORGE III, and had issue

(2) Caroline; *m* 31 Oct 1753 as his 2nd w, Capt George Dewar (*d* 12 July 1786), of Hants and St Kitt's, and *d* 8 June 1774

2 Peregrine; *m* Susan, dau and coheir of Sir Edward Monins, Bt, and *d* 4 Jan 1700, leaving two daus

3 Richard; Army Capt; *d* unm 1685

4 Vere; Judge of Common pleas; *d* unm 13 Feb 1680

5 Charles, of Uffington, Lincs; *b c* 1635; Envoy Denmark 1671, Sec Treasury 1673; *m* Mary, widow of Sir Samuel Jones and dau of Peter Tryon, of Harringworth, Northants, and *d* 22 March 1711, leaving, with a dau (Elizabeth, *m* 18th Lord (Baron) FitzWalter), an only s:

(1) Charles, of Uffington; *b c* 1678; *m* 1704 Mary, dau and heir of John Narbonne, of Gt Stewkeley, and *d* 1730, leaving, with other issue:

1a Peregrine, barrister Lincoln's Inn; *b* 1709; *m* 1736 Elizabeth, dau of Edward Payne, of Tottenham Wick, Wilts, and *d* 1779, leaving, with two daus, an only surv s:

1b ALBEMARLE BERTIE, **9th Earl of Lindsey**; *b* 17 Sept 1744; Col 9th Foot 1794, 77th Foot 1804 and 89th Foot 1808, Gen 1803, MP (Tory) Stamford 1801–09; *m* 1st 7 May 1794 Eliza Maria (*dsp* July 1806), widow of Thomas Scrope, of Coleby, Lincs, and dau of William Clay, of Burridge Hill, Notts; *m* 2nd 18 Nov 1809 Charlotte Susanna Elizabeth (*m* 2nd 14 April 1821 Rev Peter William Pegus (*d* 21 April 1860), and *d* 28 Nov 1858), est dau of Very Rev Charles Peter Layard, DD, FRS, Dean Bristol, and *d* 18 Sept 1818, having by her had:

1c GEORGE AUGUSTUS FREDERICK ALBEMARLE BERTIE, **10th Earl of Lindsey**, DL (Lincs); *b* 4 Nov 1814; *d* unm 21 March 1877

2c MONTAGU PEREGRINE BERTIE, **11th Earl of Lindsey**, JP, DL; *b* 25 Dec 1815; *educ* Eton; Capt Gren Gds; *m* 30 May 1854 Felicia Elizabeth (*d* 16 March 1927), dau of Rev John Earle Welby, of Harston (*see* WELBY, Bt), and *d* 29 Jan 1899, having had, with other issue, an only s:

1d MONTAGU PEREGRINE ALBEMARLE BERTIE, **12th Earl of Lindsey**, JP, DL Lincs; *b* 3 Sept 1861; *educ* Eton and Magdalene Coll Cambridge; Capt 4th Bn Northants Regt, ADC to Govr NSW 1885–88; *m* 12 Feb 1890 Millicent (*d* 17 Aug 1931), est dau of James Charles Cox, FRS, of Craig Cruich, Sydney, NSW, and *dspm* 2 Jan 1938, having had:

1e Muriel Felicia Vere, DJStJ; *m* 1st 20 Jan 1922 Capt Henry Herbert Liddell-Grainger, DL, Scots Gds (*d* 3 Nov 1935), of Ayton Castle, Berwicks, s of Henry Liddell-Grainger, and had:

1f *David Ian, DL (1963), CC (1958) Berwicks, FSA (Scot), Scots Gds, memb Roy Co Archers and Scottish Gas Consultative Cncl 1962–, CStJ; *b* 26 Jan 1930; *educ* St Peter's Coll Adelaide and Eton; *m* 14 Dec 1957 *Anne Mary Sibylla, er dau of Col Sir Henry Abel Smith, KCMG, KCVO, DSO, DL, Govr Queensland, and has:

1g *Ian Richard Peregrine; *b* 23 Feb 1959 (HRH THE LATE PRINCESS ROYAL stood sponsor)

2g *Charles Montague [Charles Liddell-Grainger Esq, 6 Trigon Rd, London SW8 1NH]; *b* 23 July 1960

3g *Simon Rupert; *b* 28 Dec 1962

4g *Malcolm Henry; *b* 14 Dec 1967

1g *Alice Mary; *b* 3 March 1965

1e (cont.) Lady Muriel Liddell-Grainger *m* 2nd 23 March 1938 Sir (Charles) Malcolm Barclay-Harvey, KCMG, JP, DL (*d* 17 Nov 1969), of Dinnet, Aberdeenshire

1c Charlotte Elizabeth; *m* 1st 29 July 1833 Sir Josiah John Guest, Bt, MP (*see* WIMBORNE, V); *m* 2nd 10 April 1855 Charles Schreiber (*d* 31 March 1884), MP Poole, est surv s of Lt-Col James Alfred Schreiber, JP, of Melton, Suffolk, and *d* 15 Jan 1895

The **2nd Earl** *m* 2nd between 1646 and 1653 BRIDGET, *de jure* BARONESS NORRIS in her own right (*d* March 1656/7), widow of Edward Sackville (yr s of 4th Earl of Dorset; *see* SACKVILLE, B) and dau and heir of Edward Wray by ELIZABETH, *de jure* BARONESS NORRIS in her own right, only dau and heir of **2nd Lord** (Baron) **Norris** (*see* below), and *d* 25 July 1666, having by her had, with a dau and another s (Edward):

6 JAMES BERTIE, **5th Lord** (Baron) **Norris** (as which *s* mother), summoned to Parliament as **Baron Norreys of Rycote** 13 April 1675, and **1st Earl of Abingdon**, Co Berkshire (E), so *cr* 30 Nov 1682; *bapt* 16 June 1653; Ld Lt and custos rotulorum Oxon 1674–87 and 1689–97; contributed £30,000 (something under £1.5m in late-1990s terms) to the expdn of the Prince of Orange to England, supposing the latter's purpose was merely to patch things up between JAMES II and his people, but withdrew support on discovering that the Prince intended to mount the throne; *m* 1st 1 Feb 1671/2 Eleanora (*d* 31 May 1691), dau and heir of Sir Henry Lee, 3rd Bt, of Quarendon (bro of the 1st husb of his half-bro the **3rd Earl of Lindsey**'s 3rd w), and had issue (including Bridget, *b c* 1682, *m c* 12 Feb 1702/3 4th Viscount Bulkeley of Cashel (see WILLIAMS-BULKELEY, Bt) and *d* 13 June 1753); *m* 2nd by licence 15 April 1698 Catherine (*m* 3rd Francis Wroughton, of Estcourt, Wilts, and *d* 9 Feb 1741/2), widow of 4th Viscount Wenman and est dau and coheir of Sir Thomas Chamberlayne, 2nd Bt, of Northbrook, and *d* 22 May 1699, having by her had no issue; his s by his 1st w:

(1) MONTAGU BERTIE later VENABLES-BERTIE (roy licence 10 Nov 1687), **2nd Earl of Abingdon**, (PC 1702 and 1714); MP Berks 1689–90 and Oxon 1690–96, Constable and Ld Lt Tower London 1702–05, Ld Lt Oxon 1702–05 and 1712–15; *m* 1st 22 Sept 1687 Anne (*dsp* 28 April 1715), Ldy Bedchamber to QUEEN ANNE, dau and sole heir of Peter Venables (*see* also VERNON, B); *m* 2nd 13 Feb 1716/7 Mary (*d* 10 Jan 1757), widow of Gen Charles Churchill (bro of 1st Duke of Marlborough, *qv*) and dau of James Gould, of Dorchester, and *dsps* 16 June 1743, having by her had an only child, a s (*d* an infant)

(2) James, of Stanwell, Middx, MP; *b* 13 March 1673; *m* 5 Jan 1691/2 Elizabeth (*d* 26 Sept 1716), only surv dau and eventual sole heir of 7th Baron Willoughby of Parham (*see* WILLOUGHBY DE ERESBY, B), and *d* 18 Oct 1735, leaving an est s:

1a WILLOUGHBY BERTIE, **3rd Earl of Abingdon**; *b* 28 Nov 1692; High Steward Abingdon and Wallingford 1743; *m* Aug 1727 Anna Maria (*d* 21 Dec 1763), dau of Sir John Collins, and *d* 10 June 1760, having had, with other issue:

1b WILLOUGHBY BERTIE, **4th Earl of Abingdon**; *b* 16 Jan 1739/40; *educ* Westminster, Magdalen Coll Oxford and Geneva; High Steward Abingdon and Wallingford 1761; *m* 7 July 1768 Charlotte (*d* 28 Jan 1794), dau and coheir of Adml Sir Peter Warren, KB, MP Westminster, of Warrenstown, Ireland, and *d* 26 Sept 1799, having had, with other issue:

1c MONTAGU BERTIE, **5th Earl of Abingdon**; *b* 30 April 1784; High Steward Abingdon 1826, Ld Lt Berks, DCL; *m* 1st 27 Aug 1807 Emily (*d* 28 Aug 1838), sis of 3rd Viscount Gage (*qv*); *m* 2nd 11 March 1841 Lady Augusta Kerr (*d* 26 Nov 1864), 5th dau of Charlotte, Countess of Antrim (*qv*) in her own right, by V-Adml Lord Mark Robert Kerr (*see* LOTHIAN, M), and *d* 16 Oct 1854, having by his 1st w had an est s:

1d MONTAGU BERTIE, **6th Earl of Abingdon**; *b* 19 June 1808; *educ* Eton and Trin Coll Cambridge; MP Oxon 1830–31 and 1832–52 and Abingdon 1852–54, DCL Oxon 1834, High Steward Oxford and Abingdon, Ld Lt and custos rotulorum Berks 1855–81; *m* 7 Jan 1835 Elizabeth Lavinia (*d* 16 Oct 1858), only dau and heir of George Granville Harcourt, MP (*see* VERNON, B), and *d* 8 Feb 1884, leaving:

1e MONTAGU ARTHUR BERTIE, **7th Earl of Abingdon**, JP, DL Berks, JP Oxon; *b* 13 May 1836; *educ* Eton; High Steward Abingdon, Hon Col 3rd Res Bn Princess Charlotte of Wales Regt Berks; *m* 1st 10 July 1858 Caroline Theresa (*d* 4 Sept 1873), est dau and in her issue coheiress of Charles Towneley, FRS, FSA, JP, DL, of Towneley, Lancs, and had:

1f Montagu Charles Francis BERTIE later TOWNELEY-BERTIE (assumed 1896), *Lord Norreys*, JP, DL Berks, JP Oxon; *b* 3 Oct 1860; Capt TFR, Capt 3rd Bn Princess Charlotte of Wales Berks Regt, KGStJ, served Imp Yeo Boer War 1899–1900; *m* 25 July 1885 Hon Rose Riversdale Glyn (*d* 21 Dec 1933), sis of 4th Baron Wolverton (*qv*), and *d* 24 Sept 1919, leaving:

1g MONTAGU HENRY EDMUND CECIL BERTIE, **8th Earl of Abingdon** (as which *s gf* 1928) **and 13th Earl of Lindsey** (as which *s* distant cousin 1938); *b* 2 Nov 1887; *educ* Eton; High Steward Abingdon, Tstee (family) Br Museum, Capt Gren Gds (SR) WW I (wounded); *m* 11 Aug 1928 Elizabeth Valetta (Bettine), Chev Legn Hon (*d* 24 Oct 1978 aged 82), formerly w of Capt Alastair Edward George Grant, 9th Lancers, and dau of Maj-Gen Hon Edward James Montagu-Stuart-Wortley, CB, CMG, DSO, MVO (*see* WHARNCLIFFE, E), and *dsp* 11 Sept 1963

1g Alexandra Rose Alice; granted rank of earl's dau 1928; *b* 17 Oct 1886; *d* unm 21 April 1952

1f Mary Caroline; *b* 11 Aug 1859; *m* 5 Aug 1879 1st Viscount Fitzalan of Derwent and *d* 21 April 1938, leaving issue (*see* NOR-FOLK, D)

2f Alice Josephine, JP Lancs; *b* 2 March 1865; *m* 1st 1 Feb 1890 Sir Gerald Herbert Portal, KCMG, CB (*see* PORTAL, Bt); *m* 2nd 5 Oct 1897 Maj Robert Reyntiens, Belgian Artillery (*d* 13 Oct 1913), son of Maj Robert Reyntiens, of Brussels, ADC to LEOPOLD II OF THE BELGIANS, and *d* 7 May 1950, leaving:

1g Priscilla Cecilia Maria, CBE (1963), JP (Co of London 1944), memb SE Regnl Hosp Bd and Bd Govrs Bethlem, Roy and Maudsley Hosps, v-pres Nat Assoc Mental Health and RCN; *s* mother in the Worsthorne section of the Towneley estates, ceding them to her er son 1952; *b* 20 March 1899; *m* 1st 1921 (*divorce* 1929) Col Alexander Louis Wynand KOCH De GOOREYND later WORSTHORNE (deed poll 1923) later still KOCH De GOOREYND again (deed poll 1937), OBE, Irish Gds (*d* 1985), est s of William Julien Maurice Koch de Gooreynd, of Gooreynd, Belgium, and Belgrave Square, SW (*see* also QUEENSBERRY, M), and had:

1h +Simon Peter Edmund Cosmo William KOCH De GOOREYND later WORSTHORNE later still TOWNELEY WORSTHORNE later still TOWNELEY (roy licence 18 Jan 1955) (Sir), KCVO (1994), JP (Lancs 1956) [Sir Simon Towneley KCVO JP, Dyneley Hall, Burnley, Lancs], Lancs: CC 1961–64, High Sheriff 1971–72, memb Cncl Duchy Lancaster 1986–97, KStJ, KCSG, Tstee Br Museum 1988–93, Hon Col Duke of Lancaster's Own Yeo 1979–88, WW II 1941–46 with KRRC in Italy; *b* 14 Dec 1921; *educ* Stowe and Worcester Coll Oxford (BA 1942, MA 1947, DPhil 1949); *m* 30 June 1955 *Mary, 2nd dau of Cuthbert Fitzherbert, of Street Ho, Mortimer, Berks, and has:

1i +Peregrine Henry; *b* 16 May 1962; *m* 1 Aug 1998 *Sarah, dau of Nicholas Marriner

1i +Alice Mary; *b* 14 April 1956; *m* 1984 *Michael O'Neill

2i +Charlotte Mary; *b* 19 April 1957; *m* 1986 *Arthur Edmund French and has issue (*see* DE FREYNE, B)

3i +Katharine Mary; *b* 6 Oct 1958; *m* 1985 *William Marr Couper Grant, WS, yr s of Douglas Marr Kelso Grant, of Drumellan Ho, Maybole, Ayrshire, and has:

1j +Cosmo Douglas; *b* 1991

1j +Clementine Priscilla; *b* 1986

2j +Eliza Mary; *b* 1989

4i +Victoria Mary; *b* 29 Feb 1964; *m* 1992 *Edward Bowen-Jones

5i +Cosima Cecilia; *b* 22 Nov 1967

6i +Frances Teresa; *b* 11 April 1969; *m* 29 Dec 1997 *Daniel Scoular, only s of Mrs Leslie Phillips

2h +Peregrine Gerard [Sir Peregrine Worsthorne, The Old Rectory, Hedgerley, Bucks SL2 3UY]; *b* 22 Dec 1923; *educ* Stowe, Peterhouse Cambridge and Magdalen Coll Oxford; Lt Oxford and Bucks LI and GHQ Liaison Regt (Phantom) WW II, jnlst, ed *Sunday Telegraph* 1986–89 (assoc ed 1976–86, dep ed 1961–76), ktd 1991; author *The Socialist Myth* (1971), *Tricks of Memory* (autobiog, 1993); *m* 1st 7 June 1950 Claudia

(Claudie) (*d* 1990), formerly w of Geoffrey Baynham and dau of Victor Bertrand de Colasse, of Paris, and has:

1i +Dominique Elizabeth Priscilla; *b* 18 Feb 1952; *m* 1978 *Jonathan Busil Maynard Keeling, s of Robert Keeling, of Hembury Knoll, Hook Heath Rd, Woking, Surrey

2h (cont.) Sir Peregrine *m* 2nd 1991 *Lady Lucinda Lambton (*see* DURHAM, E)

1g (cont.) Mrs Priscilla Worsthorne *m* 2nd 21 Jan 1933 1st and last Baron Norman, DSO, PC (*d* 4 Feb 1950; *see* 1949 edn), and *d* 1991

3f Cecil Josephine; *b* 22 July 1873; *m* 18 July 1895 Brig-Gen Paul Aloysius Kenna, VC, DSO (*d* 30 Aug 1915 of wounds received in action), s of James Kenna, and *dsp* 3 Oct 1895

1e (cont.) The **7th Earl of Abingdon** *m* 2nd 16 Oct 1883 Gwendoline Mary (*d* 16 Sept 1942), est dau of Lt-Gen Hon Sir James Charlemagne Dormer, KCB (*see* DORMER, B), and *d* 10 March 1928, having by her had:

2f Arthur Michael Cosmo, DSO (1917), MC (1918); Hon Attaché Petrograd, Maj Rifle Bde WW I (wounded twice, despatches twice); WW II in S African Def Force, CCG 1945–48; *b* 29 Sept 1886; *educ* in Austria and Balliol Coll Oxford; *m* 1st 15 May 1929 Aline Rose (*d* 5 July 1948), widow of Hon Charles Fox Maule Ramsay, MC (*see* DALHOUSIE, E), and er dau of George Arbuthnot-Leslie, of Warthill, Aberdeenshire, and had:

1g RICHARD HENRY BERTIE, **9th and present Earl of Abingdon and 14th and present Earl of Lindsey**

2f (cont.) Maj The Hon Arthur Bertie *m* 2nd 7 May 1949 *Lilian Isabel, widow of Lt-Cdr Frank Dayrell Montague Crackanthorpe, RN, and est dau of Charles Edward Cary-Elwes, of Staithe House, Beccles, Suffolk, and *d* 2 Feb 1957

3f James Willoughby; Lt-Cdr RN emergency list, served WWs I 1917–19 and II, Kt Honour and Devotion SMO Malta; *b* 22 Sept 1901; *m* 12 June 1928 Lady Jean Crichton Stuart (*d* 23 Oct 1995), Dame Grand Cross Honour and Devotion SMO Malta, yr dau of 4th Marquess of Bute (*qv*), and *d* 11 May 1966, leaving:

1g +Andrew Willoughby Ninian [His Most Eminent Highness Fra' Andrew Bertie, Palazzo Malta, via Condotti 68, 00187 Rome, Italy]; Lt Scots Gds SR, 78th Prince and Grand Master SMO Malta 1988– (Arms: Quarterly, 1st and 4th, gules a latin cross argent (Order of Malta); 2nd and 3rd, argent three battering rams fesswise in pale proper, armed and garnished azure (for BERTIE)); *b* 15 May 1929; *educ* Ampleforth, Ch Ch Oxford (MA) and London U

2g +(Charles) Peregrine Albemarle [Peregrine Bertie Esq, Frilsham Manor, Hermitage, Newbury, Berks RG18 9UZ]; Capt Scots Gds SR, Kt of Obedience SMO Malta, High Sheriff Berks 1986–87, Pres Br Assoc SMO Malta 1995, memb Roy Co Archers, Liveryman Armourers' and Braziers' Co, KStJ 1996, Kt Cdr Order St Gregory the Great 1983, Cdr Merit with Swords Order Pro Merito Malta; *b* 2 Jan 1932; *educ* Ampleforth; *m* 20 April 1960 *Susan Griselda Anne Lyon, er dau of Maj John Lycett Wills (*see* WILLS, Bt, of Hazelwood), and has:

1h +David Montagu Albemarle [David Bertie Esq, Seven Acres, Church Hill, Binfield, Berks RG42 5PY]; *b* 12 Feb 1963; *m* 12 Feb 1994 *Catherine Cecily, only dau of Anthony Feilden Mason-Hornby (*see* WIGAN, Bt), and has:

1i +Charlotte Iona Rose; *b* 27 March 1995

2i +Lucy Victoria Isabella; *b* 5 Feb 1998

1h +Caroline Georgina Rose; *b* 16 March 1965; *m* 3 Aug 1991 *Andrew L Carrington, s of Capt Norman Carrington, of Saxonmead, Haywards Heath, Sussex, and has:

1i +Charles Alexander Francis; *b* 27 July 1996

1i +Georgia Elizabeth Jean; *b* 9 July 1994

4f Gwendoline Theresa Mary; *b* 20 Nov 1885; *m* 8 Aug 1908 Maj John Strange Spencer Churchill, DSO, and *d* 7 July 1941, leaving issue (*see* MARLBOROUGH, D)

5f Elizabeth Constance Mary (Betty), OBE (1938); Sr Cdr ATS 1938–42; *b* 12 March 1895; *m* 1st 21 April 1914 Maj Sigismund William Joseph Trafford, Rifle Bde, of Wroxham Hall, Norfolk (*d* 8 Sept 1953), est s of Edward Southwell Trafford, and has:

1g +Edward Willoughby [Edward Trafford Esq, Broad House, Wroxham, Norfolk]; Lt Scots Gds WW II, Kt Honour and Devotion SMO Malta; *b* 2 July 1924; *educ* Harrow and Downside; *m* 3 April 1952 *June Imelda, only dau of Richard Joseph Anthony Harding, of Echo Valley, Springbrook, Qld, and has:

1h +Michael Francis; *b* 23 Aug 1953; *educ* Downside

2h +Bernard Edward [Bernard Trafford Esq, Kingstone Villa, Kingstone, Herefs HR2 9ET]; *b* 18 Sept 1955; *educ* Downside; *m* 1980 *Corinne Jean, dau of Alan Furnell, and has:

1i +Edward Alexander; *b* 1981

2i +Charles Henry; *b* 1983

3h +Andrew Martin David; *b* 30 Nov 1960

1h +Amanda Gabrielle Mary; *b* 8 Sept 1959; *m* 1984 *Mark Edmond Garthwaite and has:

1i +Alice Sophie Elizabeth; *b* 1987

1g +Helen Mary [Mrs Peter Fanshawe, 12 Lincoln Ave, London SW19 5JT]; *b* 27 Feb 1915; *m* 10 Dec 1936 Capt Peter Evelyn Fanshawe, CBE, DSC, RN (*d* 1994), est s of Capt Guy Dalrymple Fanshawe, RN, of Dalveagh, Aberfoyle, Perthshire, and has:

1h +Richard Henry William [Richard Fanshawe Esq, Rafters, Waldron, Heathfield, E Sussex TN21 0QY]; *b* 24 Aug 1939; *educ* Ampleforth and RNC Dartmouth; *m* 10 Sept 1966 *Hon Maura Clare, er dau of 11th Baron Carbery (*qv*), and has:

1i +Louisa Mary Constance; *b* 1987

1h +Veronica Evelyn; *b* 19 Oct 1947; *m* 1977 *Maj Charles Napier St Pierre Bunbury, MBE (*see* BUNBURY, Bt)

2g +Sophie Mary [The Rt Hon The Lady Lyell, Kinnordy House, Kirriemuir, Angus DD8 5ER]; *b* 10 Feb 1916; *m* 4 July 1938 2nd Baron Lyell, VC, (*qv*) and has issue

3g +Diana Rosemary [Mrs L Collins, 15 St Petersburgh Mews, London W2]; *b* 10 July 1920; *m* 1st 3 March 1951 John Reford, s of Andrew Drummond Reford, of The Guard Ho, Knowlton, PQ, Canada, and Countess de Nonancourt, of Ornans, France; *m* 2nd 1977 Col L M Collins (*d* 1984)

5f (cont.) Lady Elizabeth Trafford *m* 2nd 5 Sept 1956 Col Henry Antrobus Cartwright, CMG, MC (*d* 30 July 1957), s of Rev Arthur Rogers Cartwright, of Clevedon, Somerset

2e FRANCIS LEVESON BERTIE, 1st VISCOUNT BERTIE OF THAME (*see* 1953 edn)

3e Alberic Edward (Rev); Rector Gedling Notts 1887–1923; *b* 14 Nov 1846; *educ* Merton Coll Oxford (MA); *m* 26 April 1881 Lady Caroline Elizabeth McDonnell (*d* 23 Feb 1930), est dau of 5th Earl of Antrim (*qv*), and *d* 20 March 1928, having had:

1f Aubrey Charles; Lt-Cdr RN; *b* 22 Jan 1882; *m* 23 May 1916 Jeanne Georgina, dau of Arnold Vissers, and *d* 14 Jan 1944, leaving:

1g +Arnaud Albert [Arnaud Bertie Esq, Maison du Coin, Route du Coin, St Brelade, Jersey, CI]; *b* 10 June 1910; *m* 10 June 1950 *Joan Nelly, dau of Albert Edward Sidery, and has:

1h +John Peregrine; *b* 1952; *m* 1st 1972 (*divorce* 1977) Mary, dau of Cedric Rosenvinge, and had:

1i +Caroline Emma; *b* 1973

1h (cont.) John Bertie *m* 2nd 1986 *Belinda, dau of Timothy Orpe Adkin, and by her has:

2i +Georgina Anne; *b* 1990

3i +Harriet Olivia; *b* 1992

4i +Sabrina Dawn; *b* 1993

2h +Peter Mark; *b* 1959; *educ* Pembroke Coll Cambridge (MA); *m* 1993 *Karen, dau of Raymond Anthony Hewitts

1g +Christine Caroline; *b* 25 Dec 1917

2f Schomberg Montagu, Lt Notts Yeo; *b* 12 Aug 1888; *m* 5 Sept 1922 Edith Mary (*d* 1982), novelist as E M England (*m* 2nd 15 March 1941 Harry August Anders, s of August Anders, of Mount Alford, via Boonah, Qld), dau of John England, and *d* 17 Aug 1937, leaving:

1g +Caroline Edith [Mrs Gordon Ross, 6 Burley Griffin Place, Heidelberg, Melbourne, Australia]; *b* 2 Nov 1923; *m* 29 Jan 1952 Gordon Ernest Ross (*d* 1971), s of Alan Ross, of Perth, W Australia, and has:

1h +Alan Gordon Schomberg; *b* 11 Aug 1955

1h +Dagmar Caroline Edith; *b* 22 April 1953

2h +Hilary; *b* 1960

2g +Rose Patricia [Mrs Harold Kleinschmidt, 45 Kersley Rd, Kenmore, Brisbane, Qld, Australia]; *b* 8 May 1926; *educ* Queensland U (MSc Ag); *m* 3 Feb 1951 *Harold Edwin Kleinschmidt, BAgSc, s of Ernest Traugott Kleinschmidt, of Buranda, Qld, and has:

1h +Christopher Montagu; *b* 8 Jan 1963; *m* 1991 *Tammy Joan, est dau of Henry Vincent Neller

1h +Felicity Rose; *b* 28 April 1965; *m* 1989 *Raymond Andrew Hembrow, and has issue:

1i +Elise Robin; *b* 1994

2h +Elise Caroline; *b* 1970

3f Alberic Willoughby, MC; T/Capt RFA; *b* 10 Jan 1891; *educ* Eton and Balliol Coll Oxford; *m* 1st 1 Oct 1910 (*divorce*) Florence Winifred, dau of William Edward Kitts, CE; *m* 2nd 21 Dec 1922 Flore Maria (*d* 2 March 1925), dau of Jean Joseph Reinhart, and *d* 15 Feb 1969, having had:

1g John Edward; Lt 13th/18th Royal Hussars, QMO, attd 17th/21st Lancers WW II; *ka* N Africa 9 May 1943

1g +Marie Lucette [Mrs Ronald Kershaw, Firs House, Ramsdell, Hants; 4 Cheyne Court, London SW3]; *m* 4 Sept 1943 *Ronald Frank Kershaw, JP, late Capt 60th Rifles, yr s of Frank Kershaw, MA, barrister and slr, of Onston Hall, Crowton, Cheshire, and has:

1h +Martin John [Martin Kershaw Esq, Brights Farm, Christian Malford, Chippenham, Wilts SN15 4DA]; *b* 26 July 1954; *educ* Eton; *m* 1982 *Joanna Lucy, er dau of Lord Edward Anthony Charles FitzRoy (*see* GRAFTON, D), and has:

1i +Simon Edward; *b* 1985

2i +William Ronald; *b* 1987

3i +David Robert; *b* 1990

1i +Louisa; *b* 1992

1h +Clarissa Mary [Mrs Peter Roe, Clench Farm House, nr Marlborough, Wilts]; *b* 23 Dec 1944; *m* 1970 *Capt Peter Malcolm Roe, Roy Hussars (PWO), and has:

1i +Jeremy Malcolm Ninian; *b* 1973

2i +Christopher John Edward; *b* 1975

3i +Nicholas James Buxton; *b* 1982

2h +Serena Jane [Lady Graham, Kirkandrews Tower, Longtown, Cumbria CA6 5NF]; *b* 8 July 1948; *m* 1975 *Sir James Fergus Surtees Graham, 7th Bt, of Netherby (*qv*) and has issue

3h +Gabrielle Lavinia [Mrs Christopher Hodgson, Souldern Court, nr Bicester, Oxon]; *b* 26 June 1951; *m* 1975 *Christopher James Hodgson and has:

1i +Henry James; *b* 1977

1i +Clare Lucy; *b* 1979

2i +Sarah Rebecca; *b* 1982

3i +Camilla Rose; *b* 1984

4f Ninian Mark Kerr; 2nd Lt KRRC; *b* 19 Nov 1896; *ka* 8 May 1915

1f Irene Elsie; *b* 25 Dec 1883; *d* unm 30 Dec 1970

2f Lavinia May; *b* 10 March 1887; *m* 29 Sept 1921 Theodore Stephen Hubbard (*d* 8 Oct 1934), s of Thomas Hubbard (only bro of 1st Baron Addington, *qv*), and *d* 1978, having had:

1g +Theodore Bernard Peregrine [Lt-Cdr Theodore Hubbard RN, The Flat, Horsecroft Hall, Horsecroft Rd, Bury St Edmunds, Suffolk IP29 5NY]; *b* 19 Aug 1923; Lt-Cdr RN WW II; *m* 19 April 1952 Lady Miriam Fitzalan Howard, DL (*d* 1 Feb 1996), sis of 17th Duke of Norfolk (*qv*), and has:

1h +Martin Peregrine Thomas [Martin Hubbard Esq, Flat 6, Weston House, Weston Lane, Bridgetown, Totnes, Devon]; *b* 25 Feb 1954; *educ* Ampleforth

2h +Theodore Bernard Peter; *b* 28 Dec 1959; *educ* Cambridge (MA); *m* 1985 *Penelope D, est dau of Alan Thomas Street, of Ollerton Hall, Knutsford, Cheshire, and has:

1i +Francesca; *b* 1989

2i +Kinvara; *b* 1992

1h +Mary-Miranda Josephine [Mrs Roger Pratt, 32 High St, Haddenham, Ely, Cambs]; *b* 11 Jan 1956; *m* 1974 *Roger John Pratt and has:

1i +Alexander Roger Martin; *b* 1978

2i +James Malcolm; *b* 1980

3i +Matthew Charles; *b* 1982

2h +Lucinda Mary Lavinia, DL [Mrs Richard Blakiston Houston DL, Beltrim Castle, Gortin, Co Tyrone BT79 8PL]; *b* 22 Dec 1956; *educ* Leeds U (BSc), Liverpool U (Msc) and Queen's U, Belfast (PhD); *m* 1988 *Richard Patrick Blakiston Houston, JP, DL (*see* BLAKISTON, Bt), and has issue

3h +Vanessa Mary Teresa; *b* 21 Feb 1958; *m* 1st 1980 (*divorce* 1987) David St Vincent Llewellyn (*see* LLEWELLYN, Bt); *m* 2nd 1987, as his 2nd w, *John Austen Anstruther-Gough-Calthorpe (*see* ANSTRUTHER-GOUGH-CALTHORPE, Bt)

2g Thomas Francis ; Sub-Lt RN 1943–47, CA 1951; *b* 25 Nov 1925; *educ* Wadham Coll Oxford (BA 1949); *m* 27 Nov 1954 *Melise Marie [Mrs Thomas Hubbard Esq, 15 rue Cler, Paris VII, France], est dau of Marquis de Merindol, of 34 Gordon Place, W8, and *d* Jan 1998 leaving:

1h +John Francis; *b* 4 Nov 1955

2h +Mark Fernand; *b* 31 Jan 1957

3h +Richard Peter; *b* 2 Nov 1959

3f Olivia Bridget; *b* 5 Nov 1900; *d* 2 July 1987

4e George Aubrey Vere; Lt-Col Coldstream Gds Zulu War 1879; *b* 2 May 1850; *m* 13 Oct 1885 Harriet Blanche Elizabeth (*d* 30 Jan 1923), dau of Sir Walter Farquhar, 3rd Bt (*qv*), and *d* 8 Nov 1926, having had:

1f Claude Peregrine; Capt 6th Ammunition Column, 6th London Bde, RFA, and F/O RFC; *b* 13 July 1890; *ka* 19 March 1917

1f Vere Mary, BEM; *b* 30 Sept 1886; *d* unm 14 Jan 1964

2f Margaret Adine; *b* 29 April 1888; *d* 13 Dec 1978 aged 90

5e Charles Claude; Lt 47th Foot; *b* 31 Aug 1851; *m* 29 April 1890 Adelaide (*d* 28 Aug 1903), yst dau of Rev Jeremiah Burroughes, of Lingwood Lodge, Norfolk, and *d* 4 Sept 1920

6e Reginald Henry, CB (1900); Brevet-Col cmdg RWF Crete 1897–98, China 1900–01 (relief Peking (despatches)); *b* 26 May 1856; *educ* Eton; *m* 1st 1892 Lady Amy Evelyn (*d* 21 Dec 1948), sis of 14th Earl of Devon (*qv*), and *dsp* 15 June 1950

1e Elizabeth Emily; *d* 4 May 1923

2e Lavinia Louisa; *m* 16 Jan 1883 Robert Bickersteth (*d* 10 July 1916), of Downgate Ho, Wadhurst, Sussex, est s of Rt Rev Robert Bickersteth, DD, Bp Ripon, and *dsp* 5 July 1928

3e Frances Evelyn; nun Convent Visitation Harrow-on-the-Hill; *d* 29 Aug 1929

2c Frederic (Rev); Rector Albury, Oxon, and Wytham, Berks; *b* 12 Feb 1793; *m* 17 Oct 1825 Lady Georgina Anne Emily (*d* 20 May 1881), 2nd dau of Adml Lord Mark Kerr (*see* LOTHIAN, M), and *d* 4 Feb 1868, leaving, with other issue:

1d Charles McDonnell; *b* 17 Sept 1829; *d* 8 Sept 1884

2d Montagu Mark, RN; *b* 5 March 1831; *d* at sea 27 March 1850 aboard the *Cormorant*

3d Willoughby; *b* 29 Jan 1834; *d* 8 May 1860

4d Vere Clinton; Lt 1st Madras Fus Indian Mutiny 1857; *b* 19 Dec 1835; *d* unm 1907

5d Frederic Arthur; Capt Bengal Staff Corps; *b* 24 Sept 1837; *m* 15 July 1873 Rose Emily (*d* 19 March 1935), yr dau of John Pratt de Montmorency, of Castle Morres, and *d* 20 Sept 1885, having had:

1e Richard Frederic Norreys; Lt Berks Yeo; *b* 16 July 1876; *ka* 20 Nov 1917

1e Kathleen Adela Helen; *m* 9 Sept 1899 Charles Frederick McKee (*d* 17 Sept 1954), of Oundle, Northants, and *d* 1 May 1959

2e Mary Georgina Rose; *m* 27 April 1908 Cecil Edward Bateman Dashwood (*d* 1936), of Kenya, only child of Edward Pelham Dashwood, and *d* 5 March 1928

3e Henrietta Emily Cecil; *m* 11 Feb 1905 Hon Alec Puleston Henderson, 2nd s of 1st Baron Faringdon (*qv*), and *dsp* 7 June 1913

4e Margaret Grace; *m* 6 July 1914 Lt-Col Hugh Jagger, OBE, RAVC (TA) (*d* 6 Nov 1931), s of Francis Jagger, of Cadogan Ho, Shrewsbury, and had:

1f Richard Hugh; PO RAFVR WW II; *b* 18 April 1915; *kas* 14 April 1941

1f +Margaret Rosemary Helen; *m* 12 Aug 1950 *Drayton Alfred Wiltshire, s of Alfred Wiltshire, of Aberfoyle, Croydon, and has:

2g +Richard Drayton; *b* 5 Nov 1951

2g +Robin Cleivion; *b* 30 Nov 1956; *m* 1986 *Catherine Eva FitzSimon and has:

1h +Robert Charles; *b* 1993

3g +A son

6d Peregrine Francis, RN; *b* 18 Dec 1841; *m* 22 Feb 1888 Elizabeth Anne (*d* 12 Nov 1899), only dau of Richard Satchwell, of Beaumont St Peter, Jersey, and *dsp* 26 Nov 1905

7d Albemarle Henry, late 17th Foot; *b* 26 Feb 1847; *m* 1888 Rose (*d* 1913), dau of Henry Weston, of Montreal, and *d* 24 Feb 1906, leaving:

1e Adela Harriet Blossom; *b* 1889

7 Edward; *d* young

8 Henry; *m* Philadelphia, dau of Sir Edward Norris, of Weston and *dsp* 1734

1 Mary; *m* 2nd and last Earl of Carnarvon of the 1628 *cr* (*see* DORMER, B)

Lineage (of Norris): ALANE NORREYS, of Sutton, Lancs, before the reign of HENRY III; had:

ALANE NORREYS, of Sutton; had:

Sir HENRY NORREYS, of Sutton; had:

ALANE NORREYS, of Sutton; had:

HENRY NORREYS, of Sutton; had:

THOMAS NORREYS, of Sutton; had:

WILLIAM NORREYS, of Sutton, Lancs; *m* Joan, dau of Sir John Molyneux, of Sefton (*see* 1970 edn SEFTON, E), through whom he acquired half the feudal lordship of Speke, Lancs, and had:

Sir HENRY NORREYS, of Speke and Sutton; had:

Sir JOHN NORREYS, of Speke; *m* Katherine, dau of Robert Balderstone, and had:

Sir HENRY NORREYS, of Speke; living 1421; juror 1429; *m* Alice, dau and heir of Roger de Ernys, of Chester, by Joane, dau and heir of Sir William Molyneux, of Crosby, thus acquiring the other half of the lordship of Speke, and had, with an er s (William, ancestor of the NORREYSes of Speke):

JOHN NORREYS, of Bray, Berks; living 1456; *m* Millicent Ravenscroft, of Coton End, Northants, and had a yr s:

ROGER NORREYS, of Bray; had:

WILLIAM NORREYS, of Bray; *m* 1st Christian, dau and heir of William Sereth, of Ruscombe, Berks, and had issue; *m* 2nd Anne de la Rivers and by her had issue; his s by his 1st w:

Sir JOHN NORREYS, KB, of Bray and Pattenden, Berks; Usher of the Chamber, Esquire of the Body (also to EDWARD IV) and Master Wardrobe to HENRY VI; Sheriff Devon and Berks; *m* 1st Alice, dau and heir of Richard Merbrooke, feudal Ld Yattendon, Berks, and had issue; *m* 2nd Eleanor, dau and heir of Roger Clitherow, of Goodnestone, Kent, and by her had issue; *m* 3rd by 20 Sept 1459 Margaret (*m* 3rd 1st Duke of Norfolk; *qv*), widow of Nicholas Wyfold, Ld Mayor London 1450, and dau of Sir John Chedworth, and *d* 1466, having by her had issue (a dau by one of his ws *m* Sir John Harcourt; *see* VERNON, B); his s by his 1st w:

Sir WILLIAM NORREYS, of Yattendon; Kt of the Body to EDWARD IV; cmded troops for HENRY VII Battle of Stoke 1487 against Lambert Simnel and his followers; granted 1504 the Manor of Langley, also stewardship of several other manors in Oxon; *m* 1st 25 April 1472, as her 2nd husb, Elizabeth/Isabel (*d* 20 May 1476), widow of Sir John Nevill(e), 1st Marquess of Montagu (*see* ABERGAVENNY, M), and dau and heir of Sir Edmund Ingaldesthorpe; *m* 2nd Lady J(o)ane de Vere, dau of 12th Earl of Oxford (*see* SAINT ALBANS, D), and by her had a s and three daus; *m* 3rd Anne, widow of Sir John Harcourt and dau of Sir John Horne, of Sarsden, and by her had further issue; his s by his 2nd w:

Sir EDWARD NORREYS, of Yattendon; *m* Frideswide Lovel, dau of 8th Lord (Baron) Lovel by Joan Beaumont (*see* NORFOLK, D) and had, with an er s:

Sir HENRY NORREYS/NORRIS (the former version now being preferred where an Earl of Lindsey and Abingdon's est son and heir is concerned); Usher Black Rod 1527, Esquire of the Body and Gentleman Privy Chamber; *m* Mary, dau of 8th Lord (Baron) Dacre (*qv*), and was beheaded 17 May 1536 after being accused of adultery with ANNE BOLEYN (being also posthumously attainted), leaving, with a dau:

HENRY NORRIS, **1st Lord** (Baron) **Norris** (E), so *cr* by writ of summons 6 May 1572 (and restored in blood by Act of Parl 1575/6, following an earlier Act of Parl of 1539 restoring him in blood and to him such of his f's property as had not been forfeited to the Crown or had belonged to his attainted great-uncle Viscount Lovel), of Rycote, Oxon; *b c* 1525; MP Berks 1547–52 and Oxon 1571–72, ktd 1566; Amb France 1566–71; Porter Outer Gate and Keeper Armoury Windsor Castle *c* 1580; Ld Lt Berks and Oxon 1587–99; *m* Margaret, dau and coheir of John, Lord (Baron) Williams, of Thame, thus acquiring the Manor of Rycote, and *d* 27 June 1601, having had, with other issue:

1 William; *b c* 1545–50; Marshal of Berwick, campaigned in Ireland 1573–76 and 1579; *m c* 1576 Elizabeth, dau of Sir Richard Morrison, of Cashiobury, and *dvp* 25 Dec 1579, leaving an only child:

(1) FRANCIS, **2nd Lord**

2 Thomas; Pres Munster, Justice Ireland; had an only dau and heiress:

(1) Elizabeth; *m* Sir John Jephson, of Froyle, Hants, and was ancestor of Sir Charles Denham Orlando Jephson Norreys, Bt (*see* 1902 edn)

The 1st BARON's gs,

FRANCIS NORRIS, **2nd Lord (Baron) Norris** and 1st and last EARL OF BERKSHIRE, so *cr* 28 Jan 1620/1, as also VISCOUNT THAME (both E), KB (Jan 1604/5); *b* 6 July 1579; *m* just after 28 April 1599 Lady Bridget de Vere, dau and coheir of 17th Earl of Oxford (*see* SAINT ALBANS, D), and *dspl* 29 Jan 1621/2, when the

Earldom and Viscounty expired, leaving by a mistress Sarah Rose, who *m* Samuel Hayward, a s Francis Rose *alias* Norris, and by his w an only dau:

ELIZABETH Norris, *de jure* BARONESS NORRIS in her own right; *m* 27 March 1622 Edward Wray, Groom Bedchamber to CHARLES I, 3rd s of Sir William Wray, 1st Bt, of Glentworth, Lincs, and was *bur* 28 Nov 1645, having had an only dau and heir:

BRIDGET WRAY, *de jure* BARONESS NORRIS in her own right; *m* 1st Hon Edward Sackville (*dsp* 1646), 2nd son of 4th Earl of Dorset (*see* SACKVILLE, B); *m* 2nd, as his 2nd w, **2nd Earl of Lindsey** (*see* above) and was *bur* 24 March 1656/7, having had:

1 JAMES, **5th Lord** (Baron) **Norris** (subsequently **Lord** (Baron) **Norreys of Rycote** and **1st Earl of Abingdon**

2 Henry, Capt in the Army

1 Mary; *m* Charles Dormer, 2nd Earl of Carnarvon (*see* DORMER, B), and *dsp* 30 June 1709

LINKLATER OF BUTTERSTONE

Creation: B. (LP, UK) 2 Aug 1997.

THE BARONESS LINKLATER OF BUTTERSTONE, of Riemore, Perth and Kinross (Veronica Lyle) [The Rt Hon The Baroness Linklater of Butterstone, House of Lords, London SW1A 0PW]; *b* 15 April 1943; *educ* Cranborne Chase and Sussex and London (DipSoc) Us; Child Care Offr Tower Hamlets 1967–68, Co-Fndr Visitors' Centre Pentonville Prison 1971–77, with Winchester prison project Prison Reform Tst 1981–82, Fndr/Chm The New School Butterstone 1991–; Tstee: Butler Tst 1987– (Fndr/Administrator 1983–87, Consultant), Cancer Care Western General Hosp, Esmee Fairbairn Charitable Tst 1991–, Young Musicians' Tst 1993–, Dir Maggie's Cancer Caring Centre 1997–; Lib Dem Parly candidate Perth and Kinross May 1995; JP Inner London 1985–88; *m* 21 Jan 1967 *Magnus Duncan Linklater, jnlst, er s of Eric Robert Linklater, CBE, TD, LLD, author, of Pitcalzean House, Nigg, Ross-shire, and has:

1 *Alexander Ragnar; *b* 19 Dec 1968

2 *Saul Archibald Robert; *b* 20 Sept 1970

1 *Freya Elizabeth Erica; *b* 1975

Lineage: *See* LYLE

LINLITHGOW

Arms: Azure on a chevron or between three bezants a bay leaf, slipped vert. **Crest:** A globe, fracted at the top, under a rainbow with clouds at each end, all proper. **Supporters:** Two female figures in loose garments, hair dishevelled, each holding in the exterior hand an anchor, all proper (the emblem of Hope). **Motto:** *At spes non fracta* ('But my hope is not broken'). **Creations:** E. V and L. (S) 15 April 1703, B. (UK) 3 Feb 1809 (Hopetoun of Hopetoun) and 17 May 1814 (Niddry of Niddry), M. (UK) 27 Oct 1902.

THE 4TH MARQUESS OF LINLITHGOW, Co Linlithgow or W Lothian, **Earl of Hopetoun**, **Viscount of Aithrie**, **Lord Hope**, **Baron Hopetoun of Hopetoun**, and **Baron Niddry of Niddry**, Co Linlithgow (Adrian John Charles Hope) [The Most Hon The Marquess of Linlithgow, Hopetoun House, South Queensferry, West Lothian EH30 9SL; 123 Beaufort St, London SW3]; *b* 1 July 1946; *s* f 1987; *educ* Eton; *m* 9 Jan 1968 (*divorce* 1978) Anne Pamela, est dau of Arthur Edmund Leveson, of Hall Place, Ropley, Hants, by Margaret Ruth, dau of G/Capt Christopher Edward Maude, of The Red House, Crookham, Hants, and has:

1 +ANDREW VICTOR ARTHUR CHARLES, *Earl of Hopetoun*; *b* 22 May 1969; *educ* Eton and Exeter Coll Oxford; Page of Honour to HM QUEEN ELIZABETH THE QUEEN MOTHER 1984–86; *m* 1993 *Skye Laurette, er dau of Maj Bristow Charles Bovill (*see* LEIGH, Bt), and has:

(1) *Olivia Rose; b 11 March 1997

2 +Alexander John Adrian; b 3 Feb 1971

The 4th MARQUESS m 2nd 1980 Peta Carol, dau of Charles Victor Ormond Binding, of Congresbury, Somerset; m 3rd 1 Nov 1997 *Auriol Veronica, dau of Graham Mackeson-Sandbach (see MACKESON, Bt), and formerly w of Sir John Ropner, 2nd Bt of Thorp Perrow (qv), and by his 2nd w has:

3 +Robert Charles Robin Adrian; b 1984

1 *Louisa Vivienne; b 1981

Linlithgow, earlier creation: Alexander Livingston, 7th Lord Livingston, was broadly speaking a supporter of JAMES VI in the turbulent years in Scotland of that King's youth. For instance, he collected troops and captured Stirling in the King's name in 1584. He was promoted Earl of Linlithgow around Christmas 1600 — it is hard to pinpoint the date because no enrollment of the patent is extant. Lord Linlithgow had been appointed Baillie of the Crown estates in Linlithgowshire three years before his investiture with the Earldom and his son the 2nd Earl was Hereditary Constable of Linlithgow Palace.

The 3rd Earl initially supported the Parliamentarians in the English Civil War, leading a Scottish army to attack Newcastle in 1644, but later switched his support both to CHARLES I and the latter's successor CHARLES II. He somehow sat as a member of the Scottish House of Commons, despite being a peer. After the Restoration he was briefly Commander-in-Chief in Scotland, taking a leading part in Monmouth's victory over the Covenanters of Bothwell Bridge in 1679, but his involvement in at least one Jacobite conspiracy following the Glorious Revolution suggests he would not have prospered in the new reign. He died shortly afterwards in any case, expiring on the first of February 1690.

The 4th Earl fought alongside his father at Bothwell Bridge, giving a good account of himself. Like his father, however, he was not a wholehearted supporter of WILLIAM OF ORANGE and was locked up in Edinburgh Castle for five days on suspicion of plotting with the Jacobites following their shortlived victory of Killiecrankie in 1689. His nephew and successor the 5th Earl openly fought for the Jacobites at Sheriffmuir in 1715, being accordingly attainted the following year, when he was stripped of his titles. Shortly afterwards he fled to Italy, where the titular James III was then residing. He died without surviving male issue in 1723.

Lineage: Sir THOMAS HOPE, 1st Bt (qv); had a 6th s:

Sir JAMES HOPE of Hopetoun; advocate; mining engr; Govr Mint 1641, Ld of Session 1649; m 1st Anne, only dau and heiress of Robert Foulis of Leadhills, Lanarks (see FOULIS, Bt), who brought him valuable lead mines there, and had, with other issue:

1 JOHN

2 Sir WILLIAM HOPE, 1st Bt (NS), so cr 1 March 1698, with remainder to his heirs male whatsoever, of Kirkliston, formerly Balcomie; b 15 April 1660; Dep Govr Edinburgh Castle, ktd; m c 1682 Elizabeth, dau of — Clerk, and d 1 Feb 1724, leaving an only s:

(1) Sir GEORGE HOPE, 2nd Bt; b c 1685; Capt of Foot; m 29 Nov 1724 Anne, dau of Sir John Mackenzie, 3rd Bt, of Coul (qv), by his 2nd w Helen, dau of 3rd Lord Elibank (qv), and d Ireland 30 Nov 1729, leaving an only s:

1a Sir WILLIAM HOPE, 3rd Bt; b c 1726; Lt RN 1749, later Lt 31st Foot and Capt HEICS; m —, of Holland, and was k sp Bengal 1763, when the btcy became dormant

Sir JAMES m 2nd Lady Mary Keith, est dau and coheir of 6th Earl Marischal (see KINTORE, E), and d 1661

His er surv son,

JOHN HOPE of Hopetoun; b c 1650; bought the (territorial) Barony of Niddry from 4th Earl of Winto(u)n (see EGLINTON and WINTON, E) and took up residence at Niddry Castle 1678, also the (territorial) Barony of Abercorn and the heritable Shrievalty of Linlithgowshire from Sir Walter Seton; MP Linlithgowshire; m Margaret, est dau of 4th Earl of Haddington (qv), and d 5 May 1682, lost in the wreck of the frigate Gloucester, leaving, with a dau (Eleanor, m 6th Earl of Haddington, qv):

CHARLES HOPE, **1st Earl of Hopetoun**, so cr 15 April 1703, as also VISCOUNT OF AITHRIE and LORD HOPE (all S), KT (1738), PC (S 1703); b 1681; MP Linlithgowshire 1702–03, Ld Lt Linlithgowshire 1715–42, rep S peer 1722–42, Ld High Commr Gen Assembly Ch Scotland 1723, a Ld of Police Scotland 1734–42, Govr Bank Scotland 1740–42; m 31 Aug 1699 Lady Henrietta Johnstone (d 25 Nov 1750), only dau of 2nd Earl of Annandale and Hartfell (qv), and d 26 Feb 1742, having had, with other issue:

1 JOHN, **2nd Earl**

2 Charles HOPE later HOPE-VERE of Craigiehall, Linlithgowshire; b 8 May 1710; m 1st 26 July 1733 Catherine (d 5 Dec 1743), dau and heiress of Sir William Weir, Bt, of Blackwood, Lanarks, and had:

(1) William, of Blackwood and Craigiehall; b 17 May 1736; 1st Dragoon Gds; Muster-Master-Gen forces Scotland; m 5 Jan 1775 Sophia, dau of Joseph Corrie, of Dumfries, and d Sept 1811, having had:

1a James Joseph, of Blackwood and Craigiehall, DL; b 3 June 1785; m 7 Sept 1813 Lady Elizabeth Hay (d 19 Dec 1868), 4th dau of 7th Marquess of Tweeddale (qv), and d 19 May 1843, leaving:

1b William Edward, of Blackwood and Craigiehall, JP, DL; b 5 March 1824; Brig-Gen Roy Co Archers, Offr Gren Gds; m 24 July 1857 Lady Mary Emily Boyle (m 2nd 24 Feb 1873 Lord David Kennedy (see AILSA, M) and d 25 Nov 1916, leaving issue, sis of 9th Earl of Cork and Orrery (qv), and d 3 Oct 1872, leaving:

1c James Charles, of Blackwood, TD, JP and DL (Lanarks); b 13 July 1858; Maj and Hon Lt-Col Lanarks Imp Yeo WW I (despatches); m 1st 17 July 1879 Hon Louisa Maud (dsp 20 April 1882), sis of 2nd Baron Churston (qv) and widow of Hon Reginald James Greville-Nugent (see WESTMEATH, E); m 2nd 4 June 1884 (divorce 1905) Marie Elizabeth Françoise (d 15 Aug 1937), dau of Auguste Guillemin and gdau of the Duc de Montebello, and had:

1d Edward James, JP (Lanarks); b 10 Feb 1885; 1st Sec Dip Serv, memb Roy Co Archers, Kt SMO Malta 1921; d 4 Nov 1924

2d Ralph Jean James, of Blackwood, OBE (1944), AFC; b 13 Dec 1887; Midshipman RN, Lt-Col RFC, WW I (despatches twice), WW II cmdg 1st Dumfries Bn HG, V-Chm TAFA Dumfriesshire, Silver Medal Italy for valour, CC Dumfriesshire; m 18 Oct 1928 Esmée, er dau of Lt-Col H Crabbe, Scots Greys, of Duncow, Dumfries, and widow of Lt-Col T G J Torrie, Life Gds, and d 12 Oct 1959, leaving:

1e Adrian Ralph; b 31 Aug 1929

1d Rachel Madeleine Mary; b 24 May 1886; m 20 July 1908 Maj Hon Philip Henderson (see FARINGDON, B) and d 28 Oct 1953, leaving issue

1c (cont.) Lt-Col James Hope-Vere m 3rd 20 Jan 1906 Mabel Ellis Vandervort (d 26 Jan 1954), est dau of Alkman Henryson Foster Barham, UK V-Consul Pau, and d 6 Sept 1933, having by her had:

2d Rosemary Marguerite; b 9 Feb 1907; m 1st 22 Oct 1930 (divorce 1933) Maj John Drury Boteler Drury-Lowe, Scots Gds (d 1 June 1960), and had issue; m 2nd 11 Feb 1933 (divorce 1942) Quintin Holland Gilbey (see GILBEY, Bt) and by him had issue; m 3rd 15 July 1943 Col Sir Roderic Napoleon Brinckman, 5th Bt (qv), and by him had issue

1c Mary St Lawrence, JP (Kent); m 10 April 1886 Sir Everett Millais, 2nd Bt (qv), and d 10 Nov 1948, leaving issue

2b Charles Edward; b 3 Oct 1828; m 22 March 1866 Julia (d 13 Jan 1910), yst surv dau of Maj-Gen John Craigie-Halkett, CB, of Ravelrigg, and dsp 16 Jan 1900

1b Hannah Charlotte; m 17 May 1844 Keith William Stewart-Mackenzie of Seaforth (d 18 June 1881), and d 4 June 1868, leaving issue (see GALLOWAY, E)

2b Sophia Jane; d 15 April 1878

3b Harriet; m 1st 17 Oct 1839 Sir Edward Sherlock Gooch, 6th Bt (qv); m 2nd 30 June 1858 Maj John St Leger (d 20 April 1868) and d 17 Oct 1883

4b Jane, VA; Ldy Bedchamber to HM QUEEN VICTORIA; m 29 Oct 1844 3rd Marquess of Ely (qv) and d 11 June 1890, leaving issue

5b Georgina, VA; m 13 June 1855 Lt-Col Charles Townshend Wilson, Coldstream Gds, and d 26 Dec 1894

6b Henrietta Vane; d Oct 1863

2a Edward Hamilton; b Jan 1792; d 1835

1a Jane Sophia; m 3 July 1813 Adml Hon Edmund Sexton Pery Knox (see RANFURLY E) and d 11 Jan 1875, leaving issue

(2) John Hope; b 7 April 1739; London merchant; m 1762 Mary (d 25 June 1767), only dau of Elia Breton, of Enfield, and d 1785, leaving:

1a Charles, of Granton; b 29 June 1763; Ld Pres Court Session; m 8 Aug 1793 Charlotte, 6th dau of **2nd Earl of Hopetoun** (see below), and d 31 Oct 1851, having had, with other issue:

1b John; b 26 May 1794; Ld Justice Clerk Scotland; m Aug 1824 Jessie Scott (d 26 Jan 1872), dau of Thomas Irvine, and d 14 June 1857, having had:

1c William, VC; b 12 April 1834; Col cmdg City London Artillery and 1st Bn Roy Fus; m 29 April 1857 Margaret Jane (d 11 Dec 1909), 3rd dau of Robert Cunninghame Cunninghame-Graham, of Gartmore, Perthshire, and d 17 Dec 1909, having had:

1d Adrian Charles Francis; b 8 March 1858; m 2 Aug 1888 Laura (d 15 March 1929), 2nd dau of Sir Thomas Hope Cochrane Troubridge, 3rd Bt, CB (qv), and d 11 May 1904, leaving:

1e Jaqueline Louise Rachel; m 1 June 1916 (William) Hedley Kenelm NICHOLSON later HOPE-NICHOLSON (d 18 July 1964) and d 17 Dec 1972, leaving:

1f (Charles) Felix Otho Victor Gabriel John Adrian; b 1921; educ Eton and Ch Ch Oxford (BA 1946, MA 1948); d 198–

1f *(Mary) Lauretta Jaqueline Carola Desirée Valentine Esmée; b 1919; m 1948 *Jean Hugo, descendant of the author Victor Hugo, and has:

1g *Charles Louis Victor Marie; b 1949

2g *Jean Baptiste Victor Marie Leopold; b 1953

1g *Marie Pauline Victorine Leopoldine; b 1951

2g *Adèle Marie Julie Laure Victorine; b 1954

3g *Jeanne Marie Laure Victorine; b 1955

4g *Sophie Marguerite Marie Victorine; b 1957

5g *Leopoldine Charlotte Marie Victorine; b 1958

2f *Marie-Jaqueline; b 1922; jnlst, author: Brian Howard: portrait of a failure (1965); m 1945 *Herbert Maurice Lancaster and has:

1g *Carolyn Sarah Louise; b 1945; m 1965 *Gareth Wickens Wright, 2nd s of W Matvyn Wright, and has:

1h *Merlin Wyndham; b 1965

1h *Zephyra Melisande; b 18 Oct 1968

2g *Maria Shirley Harriet; b 1948

2e Esmée Laura Diamond; d young 17 Feb 1905

2d John Archibald Graham; b 29 Oct 1864; d 28 May 1897

3d Charles Douglas; b 15 April 1867; educ Trin Coll Oxford (BA 1890, MA 1900); Pncpl Potchefstroom Coll Transvaal; m 1896 Alice (d May 1947), dau of Hon A Wilmot, MLC, of Cape Town, and d Jan 1947, having had:

1e Adrian Alexander; b 19 Nov 1897; educ Trin Coll Oxford (BCL); Maj Transvaal Scottish, IA, WW II; barrister; m 24 July 1926 *Eleanor, dau of Lt-Col George Ritchie-Thomson, CMG, MB, of Johannesburg, and was ka Italy 17 April 1945, leaving:

1f +William Adrian [William Hope Esq, 9 Montagu St, Knysna 6570, S Africa]; b 13 June 1927; educ Michaelhouse Natal, Witwatersrand U (BA 1948) and Trin Coll Oxford (BA 1951, MA 1955); SA Artillery WW II; advocate Johannesburg and Salisbury, Rhodesia; author: A Digest of Rhodesian Mining Law (1965); m 27 Feb 1960 *Hazel, dau of Adelbert Johnstone, of Gwelo, S Rhodesia, and has:

1g +Adrian Charles; b 10 Oct 1962

2g +James Graham; *b* 1970

1g *Patricia Anne; *b* 29 May 1961

2g *Sarah Jane; *b* 25 July 1964

1f *Anne Eleanor; *b* 12 Feb 1930; *educ* Rhodes U S Africa (BA), Dip Ed Oxford

2f Joan Alice; *b* 17 Dec 1931; *educ* Witwatersrand U (BSc 1951); *m* 9 June 1954 *James Ecclestone Stewart of Cape Town, and had issue

2e James; *b* 26 May 1899; Lt Br Bechuanaland Police, Lt Scottish Borderers, WWs I and II; *m* 1937 *Doreen, dau of Prof Armstrong, and *d* 1970, leaving:

1f +Christopher James [Christopher Hope Esq, 273 Burton Rd, Oakville, Ontario L6K 2K7, Canada]; *b* 1938; *m* *Erica — and has:

1g +Thomas

2f +Alastair Frederick [Alastair Hope Esq, 5 Malleson Rd, Mowbray, CP, S Africa,]; *b* 5 Feb 1941; *m* 12 Oct 1963 *Mary Elizabeth, dau of Arthur Cecil Bilbrough, of Somerset West, S Africa, and has:

1g +Charles Andrew; *b* 1 July 1966

2g +Paul James; *b* 1968

1g *Bridget Moira; *b* 20 June 1964

1f *Angela Ruth Alice; *b* 1939; *m* (*divorce*) Warwick Manning **and** has:

1g *Joanne; *b* 19–

3e Henry Francis; *b* 11 July 1900; co dir; *m* 18 Sept 1930 Aileen Elinor (*d* 1993), yr dau of William Falkiner Harnett, CBE, ICS, and *d* 19 April 1971, leaving:

1f *Gillian Margaret; *b* 13 Aug 1933; *m* 1955 *Neville Price Boyce and has:

1g *Richard Henry Price; *b* 27 Sept 1957

1g *Diana Mary; *b* 9 Dec 1959

2g *Margaret Louise; *b* 31 Dec 1961

2f *Rosemary Patricia; *b* 15 Sept 1936; *m* 23 Feb 1963 *Guy Everingham Hitchings, of Kent, s of Douglas Brigstocke Hitchings, and has:

1g *Charles Robin; *b* 22 May 1967

2g *Mark Alexander; *b* 28 April 1969

3g *Andrew Hope; *b* 1971

1g *Alice Elizabeth [Mrs Michael Bennett, 2 The Ridgeway, London SW19]; *b* 22 Oct 1965; *m* 1994 *Michael Andrew Bennett

4e Charles Christopher; *b* 15 Sept 1902; Capt Ceylon Planters' Rifle Corps and F/Lt RAFVR WW II, Colonial Aux Forces Efficiency Medal; tea planter; *m* 5 Jan 1937 Una Mainguy (*d* 1989), dau of P Le Feuvre, MD, of Kenilworth, CP, S Africa, and *d* 18 Feb 1963, leaving:

1f +Charles Richard Christopher; *b* 3 April 1938; *educ* Downside, MAA, Dip LPA, Toronto U (BA); *m* *Mary Lou, dau of John Francis Fitzpatrick, of New Brunswick, and has:

1g *Mary Mainguy; *b* 1971

2g *Tiffany Anne Granton; *b* 1972

1e Alice Margaret Mary; *b* 6 Oct 1906

2e Patricia Anne; *b* 17 March 1908; *m* 17 March 1937 Capt Sebastian Francis Newdigate, DSC, RD, RNR (*d* 20 Jan 1954), yst s of Alfred Newdigate, and had:

1f *Anne Charlotte; *b* 3 Feb 1938; *m* 1960 *Humphrey Edward Waldock, barrister, s of Sir Humphrey Waldock, and has:

1g *Harold Sebastian; *b* 28 May 1961

2g *Henry Bernard; *b* 9 Nov 1962

3g *Thomas Edward; *b* 26 May 1965; *m* 1988 *Jane Little

1g *Mary Beatrice; *b* 7 May 1969; *m* 1991 *Michael Markwick

2g *Alice Patricia; *b* 1973

3g *Susan Katherine Margaret; *b* 1973

2f *Lilah Mary Amphelis [Sister Mary Lucy, Carmelite Monastery, PO Box 6, Kew, Vict 3101, Australia]; *b* 15 Oct 1940

3e Mary Monica (Sister M Emmanuel, OP); *b* 3 June 1912

1d Laura Charlotte; *b* 12 Dec 1859; *m* 22 Aug 1894 Thomas William Allen, Fell Queen's Coll Oxford; *d* 25 March 1936

2d Jesse Margaret; *b* 15 Jan 1870; *d* 20 April 1920

3d Margaret Elizabeth Horatia; *b* 24 Nov 1873; *m* 26 April 1893 (*divorce* 1923) Francis Horatio Napier, MB, FRCS, and *d* March 1947, leaving issue (*see* NAPIER and ETTRICK, L)

2b Charles; *b* 12 April 1798; R-Adml; *m* 1st 12 Sept 1826 Anne (*d* 24 Nov 1836), est dau of R-Adml Webley-Parry, and had:

1c Charles Webley; *b* 21 April 1829; R-Adml, ADC to HM QUEEN VICTORIA; *m* 23 April 1861 Ellen Evelyn Elizabeth (*d* 5 Dec 1897), est dau of G B J Jordan, of Pembs, and gdau of Sir John Owen, Bt, and *d* 13 Feb 1880, having had:

1d Charles William Webley; *b* 9 Aug 1864; ICS, High Sheriff Cards 1919; *m* 18 July 1916 Florence Mary (*d* 27 Dec 1954), 4th dau of Col John Lewes, of Llanlear, Cards, and *d* 28 June 1926

2d George Webley (Sir), KCB (1923, CB 1918), KCMG (1919); *b* 11 Oct 1869; Adml, ADC to HM GEORGE V 1915–17, Flag Capt to V-Adml, C-in-C E Mediterranean Sqdn 1915, Dir Ops Div Admlty War Staff 1916–17, Dep First Sea Lord 1918 (despatches), cmded 3rd Light Cruiser Sqdn 1919–21, Pres and Flag Offr cmdg RNC Greenwich 1923–26, Legn Honour 2nd Cl, Order Rising Sun Japan, Order St Maurice and St Lazarus Italy, US DSM; *m* 24 Aug 1899 Arabella Phillippa (*d* 5 May 1945), yr dau of John Sutton Sams, and *d* 11 July 1959, leaving:

1e Maurice Webley, DSO (1944); *b* 26 Sept 1901; *educ* Winchester and RMA Woolwich; Brig RA WW II, FZS; *m* 22 May 1943 *Pamela

[Mrs Maurice Hope, Ivy Bank, Vinegar Hill, Milford-on-Sea, Hants], er dau of J K Osborne, of NSW, and *d* 1986, leaving:

1f +David George Osborne; *b* 17 July 1944; *educ* Winchester and Balliol Coll Oxford; *m* 1970 *Jane Lesley, dau of Edward Ellis, of Durham, and has:

1g +Joseph Cornelius Ellis; *b* 1971

2f Michael John; *b* 24 Feb 1947; *educ* Winchester; *d* May 1966

1e Philippa; *b* 7 June 1900; *m* 1 May 1922 Brig Alfred Geoffrey Neville, CBE, MC, RA and had issue (*see* BRAYBROOKE, B)

1d William Henry Webley, CMG (1918); *b* 4 June 1871; Lt-Col RA; *m* 19 Sept 1900 Florence (*d* 19 Feb 1918), dau of Charles Walter Hill, of Clapham, and *d* 13 May 1919, leaving:

1e Charles Webley; *b* 22 March 1902; Lt-Cdr RN WW II; *m* 13 Nov 1933 Harriott Barbara (*d* 1970), dau of Lt-Col Richard Goord Edwal Locke, JP, DL, of Hartlip House, Kent, and was *ka* aboard HMS *Bonaventure* 31 March 1941, leaving:

1f *Mary; *b* 15 Aug 1934

2f *Janet; *b* 12 Oct 1937; *m* 8 Oct 1960 *Richard Wilson Froggatt, s of Surgn-Cdr Thomas Wilson Froggatt, OBE, RN, and has:

1g *Ian Wilson; *b* 11 May 1962

2g *Peter Webley; *b* 21 Nov 1964; *m* 1990 *Michele Hobday and has:

1h *Hayley Louise; *b* 1990

3g *Nigel Thomas; *b* 4 April 1966

4g *Eric Charles; *b* 4 April 1966

1g *Jenny Patricia; *b* 11 May 1962; *m* 1987 *Simon John Pickhaver and has:

1h *Joanna Ruth; *b* 1990

2h *Sarah Elizabeth; *b* 1992

2g *Alison Clare; *b* 21 Nov 1964

2e +James Webley, OBE (1945) [Lt-Col James Hope OBE, 60 Kenilworth Gdns, Bowral, NSW 2576, Australia]; *b* 9 Oct 1903; Lt-Col S Wales Bdrs, Waziristan 1937 (despatches), Burma 1945 (despatches), ret 1950; *m* 1st 17 April 1928 Harriett Mary (*d* 27 Jan 1931), er dau of Henry Louis King, JP, DL, of Ballylin, Ferbane, King's Co; *m* 2nd 22 Feb 1934 Veda Annie (*d* 1986), er dau of Dr Alfred Walter Campbell, of Sydney, and by her has:

1f *Gillian Florence; *b* 28 April 1935; *m* 18 March 1961 *Maj George Mark Chirnside, 13th/18th Roy Hus (QMO)

4d Adrian Victor Webley, CIE (1919); *b* 16 Feb 1873; Col IA, cmdg Bn 32nd Sikh Pioneers 1917; *m* 14 April 1920 Ethel Mary (*d* 22 March 1938), dau of J S Middleton, of Cadamaney, Mysore, and *d* 19 Aug 1960, leaving:

1e *Margaret Isobel [Mrs James Hepburn, 68 Parliament Hill, London NW3 2TJ]; *b* 17 May 1921; *educ* Reading U (BA); *m* 1st 6 Oct 1943 (*divorce* 1949) James Veitch Telfer and has:

1f *Alison; *b* 1944; *educ* Oxford (BA 1966) and King's Coll, London U (PhD 1971); *m* 1970 *Terence Parry Jones and has:

1g *William George Parry; *b* 1976

1g *Sally Louise Parry; *b* 1974; BA

2f *Kate TELFER later HEPBURN (deed poll 1963); *b* 11 June 1947; DipAd, MA (RCA); has:

1g *Usha Junge; *b* 1978

1e (cont.) Mrs Margaret Telfer *m* 2nd 30 March 1950 S/Ldr James Geoffrey Cutcliffe Hepburn, DFC (*d* 1995), est s of Patrick Henry Hepburn, and by him had:

3f *Harriet Rose; *b* 31 March 1965; *educ* Oxford (BA); ACA 1992

5d John Owen Webley, CMG; *b* 22 Aug 1875; Provisional Commr Kenya Colony; *d* 15 Sept 1927

6d Herbert Willes Webley, CB (1917), CVO (1925), DSO (1919), JP, DL Cards; *b* 26 May 1878; Adml, naval ADC to HM GEORGE V 1926–36, served WW I, Russian Order St Anne, Italian Order Mil Valour, Ch of Staff to C-in-C The Nore 1923–24, cmded HMS *Repulse* 1924–26, Pres Ordnance Ctee Roy Arsenal Woolwich 1928–32; *m* 16 Sept 1905 Katherine Maria Antoinette (*d* 17 June 1966), yr dau of Rev Francis Kewley, and *d* 26 April 1968, leaving:

1e Adrian Price Webley, CB (1961), CBE (1952), OBE (1943); *b* 21 Jan 1911; *educ* Winchester and RMC Sandhurst; Maj-Gen KOSB WW II and i/c Admin Far East Land Forces 1959–61, Dir Equipment Policy War Office 1961–64, Dep Master-Gen Ordnance MOD 1964, ret 1966; *m* 9 Sept 1958 Mary Elizabeth (*d* 28 May 1990), er dau of Graham Partridge, and *d* 12 Dec 1992

1e *Ellen Katherine Webley [Mrs Charles King, Sutton Manor Nursing Home, Sutton Scotney, Winchester, Hants SO21 3JX]; *b* 10 Aug 1907; *m* 1st 10 Aug 1929 (*divorce* 1937) David William Heneker, 17th/21st Lancers, est s of Gen Sir William Charles Giffard Heneker, KCB, KCMG, DSO, and has:

1f *Peter David Grenfell [Peter Heneker Esq, Parc Helyg, Llechryd, Dyfed SA43 2NJ]; *b* 6 May 1931; *educ* Wellington and BNC Oxford; with ITN; *m* 5 Nov 1954 *Josephine Anne, est dau of Lt-Col James William Lewis-Bowen, and has:

1g *David Marius; *b* 11 Oct 1958

2g *Sam Gerald William; *b* 20 July 1961

3g *Nicholas Charles Adrian; *b* 3 Feb 1963

4g *Piers Herbert; *b* 24 July 1964

5g *Simon Thomas; *b* 18 July 1965

1e (cont.) Mrs Ellen Heneker *m* 2nd 22 Nov 1941 Lt-Col Charles Vaughan King, OBE, Devonshire Regt (*d* 27 March 1994), s of Adml Richard Matthew King, DSO, and by him has:

2f *Adrian Charles Richard; *b* 25 May 1944

2e Jaqueline Elizabeth Webley; *b* 13 June 1914; *m* 11 Nov 1938 Maj John Malcolm Douglas, RA (*d* Jan 1997), yr s of J P Douglas, and *d* 9 July 1952, leaving issue

1d Evelyn Ellen; *d* unm 25 July 1939

2d Alice Anne Elizabeth; *m* 11 Jan 1888 Reginald Austin Bewes (*d* 1892) and had issue

1c Anna Maria; *m* 15 Nov 1855 Rev William Gill (*d* 6 May 1872) and *d* 23 April 1875, leaving issue

2c Charlotte Maria; *m* 25 March 1856 Cdr Adam Alexander Dundas of Dundas, RN (*d* 6 March 1904), and *d* 24 Jan 1905, leaving issue

2b (cont.) R-Adml Charles Hope *m* 2nd 19 Jan 1854 Mary Elizabeth (*d* 1882), dau of Joseph Sykes, of Raywell, and *d* 6 Aug 1854

3b James; *b* 28 May 1803; Dep Keeper Signet; *m* 2 Dec 1828 Elizabeth (*d* 20 July 1880), est dau of David Boyle, Lord Justice Gen Scotland, and *d* 14 Feb 1882, having had, with other issue:

1c Charles William; *b* 23 Jan 1832; civ engr PWD India; *m* 15 Jan 1874 Lucy Harriet (*d* 27 Jan 1882), dau of Robert King, and *d* 16 Feb 1904, leaving:

1d Adrian James Robert, CIE (1922); *b* 3 Nov 1874; India Serv of Engrs Burma; *m* 19 Aug 1914 Jessie Newall (*d* 21 March 1950), dau of David McLellan, of Kirkcudbright, and widow of Maj David James Welsh, 2nd Bn Border Regt, and *d* 8 March 1963, leaving:

1e Charles Adrian, ARIBA; *b* 9 June 1918; *educ* Edinburgh Acad and RMC Sandhurst; Capt 4th/5th Roy Scots RA (TA) WW II; *m* 30 May 1951 *Susan Elizabeth Rona [Mrs Charles Hope, 23 Ann St, Edinburgh EH4 1PL], dau of Eric Cuthbert Kruse, of Winsham, Somerset, and *d* 1986, leaving:

1f +Adrian Kruse Anthony [Adrian Hope Esq, The Old Smithy, Stobo, Peeblesshire EH45 8NS]; *b* 7 Aug 1953; *educ* Edinburgh Acad, Sheffield and Edinburgh Colls of Art Design; designer and silversmith; *m* 1977 *Linda Caroline Lewin and has:

1g +Adam Poyntz; *b* 1981

2g +Thomas Joseph; *b* 30 Dec 1994

1g *Claire Evelyn; *b* 1984

2f +James William Drever [James Hope Esq, 10 Brondesbury Pk Mansions, 132 Salusbury Rd, London NW6 6PD]; *b* 9 March 1957; *educ* Edinburgh Acad and Bristol Old Vic Theatre Sch; actor

1d Elizabeth Emily Vere; *d* unm 9 Nov 1949

2d Lucy Helen Montgomerie; *m* 9 Oct 1917 Richard D Wilson (*d* 6 June 1953), s of Ralph Wilson, of Holy Island, Northumberland, and *d* 6 May 1951, leaving issue

2c David Boyle; *b* 21 Aug 1833; advocate, Sheriff Roxburgh, Berwick and Selkirk; *m* 19 April 1863 Letitia Augusta (*d* 14 Sept 1896), yst dau of Arthur Burgh Crofton, of Roebuck Castle, Co Dublin, and *d* 9 Sept 1896, leaving:

1d James Arthur, VD, WS; *b* 21 Jan 1865; *educ* Edinburgh U (MA, LLB); Lt-Col RASC (TA Res); FZS (Scotland); *m* 17 April 1895 Geraldine Lucy (*d* 20 April 1949), dau of Rev Charles Hope Robertson, and *d* 2 March 1925, having had:

1e Arthur Henry Cecil, OBE (1939), TD, WS; *b* 18 July 1896; *educ* Edinburgh Acad, Rugby and Edinburgh U (BL); Lt-Col Roy Scots TA and RA (TA), WWs I and II (despatches twice, medals); *m* 2 April 1937 *Muriel Ann Neilson [Mrs Arthur Hope, 8A Randolph Cliff, Edinburgh EH3 7TZ], yr dau of James Anderson Collie, of Edinburgh, and *d* 1986, leaving:

1f +JAMES ARTHUR DAVID HOPE, *cr* BARON HOPE OF CRAIGHEAD (*qv*)

2f +John William Lewis; *b* 14 Jan 1940; *educ* Edinburgh Acad and St Andrews (MA 1962); *m* 1974 *Hazel Goh Mei Ling, dau of Goh Siew Hiong, of Sarawak, and has:

1g +Charles Arthur Robertson; *b* 1976

2g +Thomas John Alexander; *b* 1978

1g *Geraldine Katherine Anne; *b* 1982

3f +Alexander Robertson Boyle [Alexander Hope Esq, Croftinloan Sch, Pitlochry, Perthshire]; *b* 22 June 1947; *educ* Edinburgh Acad, Rugby and St John's Coll Durham (BA 1969)

1f Charlotte Ann Margaret Lucy; *b* 14 March 1945; *educ* St Andrews; *d* unm air crash Uganda 17 April 1971

2f *Elspeth Mary Neilson [Mrs Elspeth Mogendorff, 77 Irvine Place, Aberdeen AB10 6HE]; *b* 22 June 1947; *educ* Strathclyde U; *m* 11 July 1969 (*divorce* 1994) Dolf Andries Mogendorff, of Arnhem, Holland, and has:

1g *Andrew Michael Alexander; *b* 1972

2g *Richard Arthur John; *b* 1974

3g *David Martin James; *b* 1978

4g *Robin Paul Neilson; *b* 1980

3f *Angela Muriel Evelyn [Mrs Angela Anscombe, 812 Linkleas Ave, Victoria, BC V8S 5C3, Canada]; *b* 22 Dec 1948; SRN; *m* 1976 (*divorce* 1995) Brian Richard Anscombe and has:

1g *Philip Hayward; *b* 1979

1g *Jacqueline Hope; *b* 1981

2e John Charles David; *b* 30 Sept 1897; *educ* Edinburgh Acad; F/Lt RAFVR, French Red Cross, WW I, WW II with RAF, Croix de Guerre; *d* unm 10 Oct 1956

3e James Louis, TD, WS; *b* 31 Jan 1906; *educ* Edinburgh Acad, Rugby and Edinburgh U (MA 1927, LLB 1929); Hon Lt-Col Roy Scots (TA) WW II; *m* 5 June 1939 Kathleen Colquhoun (*d* 16 Oct 1968), dau of Henry Archibald Kerr Sconce, MICE, and *d* 25 Oct 1995, leaving:

1f +Charles Louis [Charles Hope Esq, Woodside, Ockham Rd North, W Horsley, Surrey KT24 6PF]; *b* 9 May 1940; *educ* Edinburgh Acad, Rugby and Magdalene Coll Cambridge (BA 1962);

CEng MIEE; *m* 30 March 1963 *Susan Jane Elizabeth, dau of Robert William McDowall, of Guildford, and has:

1g *Joanna Mary; *b* 23 July 1968

2g *Fiona Jane; *b* 7 Sept 1972

2f +Michael Edmund [Michael Hope Esq, The Hermitage, Evershot, Dorset DT2 0PQ]; *b* 31 Jan 1943; *educ* Edinburgh Acad, Rugby, Trin Coll Dublin (BA 1965) and St Andrews (MA 1970)

1e Kathleen Isabel; *d* 20 Sept 1909

1d Kathleen Elizabeth; *d* unm 26 Aug 1898

2d Matilda; *m* 5 April 1897 Maj T R Morse, OBE, of Hungerford, and *d* 19 Nov 1910, having had issue

1c Lucy Anne; *m* 9 Aug 1870 Maj-Gen George Skene Hallowes (*d* 4 May 1911), 25th Regt, and *d* 14 April 1931, leaving issue

4b William; *b* 11 Sept 1807; Maj; *m* 14 Sept 1835 Stratyra Livedostro (*d* 10 Nov 1881) and *d* 2 Oct 1858, having had:

1c Charles Erroll; *b* 8 April 1837; Col 2nd Bn KOSB; *m* 19 April 1865 Helen Rae (*d* 25 Oct 1933), dau of John Hamilton Colt, of Gartsherrie, Lanarks, and *d* 9 Jan 1920

2c Hamilton; *b* 31 Oct 1840; *m* Emmie, dau of William Rolland, and *dsp* 1880

3c James, JP; *b* 6 March 1857; Maj KOSB; *m* 1894 Constance Marion (*d* 18 Oct 1934), dau of Sir David Brewster, KH, and *d* 26 March 1936, leaving:

1d Vere Constance Brewster; *b* April, *d* July 1895

1c Zoe; *d* unm 15 March 1936

2c Kalitza; *d* unm 26 May 1941

2a John (Sir), GCH; *b* 15 July 1765; Lt-Gen, Col 72nd Foot; *m* 1st 20 Sept 1806 Margaret, only dau and heiress of Robert Scott, of Logie, and had three daus; *m* 2nd 21 April 1814 Jane Hester (*m* 2nd Rev William Knight, Rector Steventon, Hants, and *d* 10 Nov 1880), dau of John Macdougall, of Ardintriva, and *d* 1836, having by her had three sons

3a William HOPE later JOHNSTONE-HOPE (Sir), GCB; *b* 16 Aug 1766; V-Adml; *m* 1st 8 July 1792 Lady Anne Hope-Johnstone (*d* 28 Aug 1818), est dau of **3rd Earl of Hopetoun**, and had issue (*see* ANNANDALE AND HARTFELL, E); *m* 2nd 30 Oct 1821 Maria, Dowager Countess of Athlone (*d* 4 March 1851), but had no further issue

2 (cont.) The Hon Charles Hope-Vere *m* 2nd 20 March 1745/6 (*divorce* 1757) Anne Vane (*d* Sept 1776), dau of 3rd Baron Barnard (*qv*) of Barnard's Castle, and by her had:

(3) Henry; Lt-Govr Canada; *m* Sarah, dau of Rev John Jones, LLD, Preb Mullaghbrack, and *dsp* 13 April 1789

(4) Charles; Commr Chatham Docks; *m* Susan Anne (*d* 10 July 1802), dau of Adml Sawyer, and *d* 10 Sept 180, leaving, with other issue:

1a Henry (Sir), KCB; *b* 1787; Adml the White; *m* 21 July 1828 Jane Sophia (*d* 6 Aug 1829), yst dau of Adml Sir Herbert Sawyer, KCB, and *dsp* 2 Sept 1863

2a Frederick Hope; *b* 1 March 1799; Maj-Gen; *m* 15 Jan 1829 Eliza (*d* 25 June 1877), est dau of Maj Gen James Cockburn, RA, and *d* 2 Aug 1869, having had:

1b Frederick Henry; *b* 24 June 1832; Capt 1st Royals, ADC to Govr of Madras; *m* 4 Jan 1860 Anna Maria Elizabeth (*d* 6 March 1864), est dau of Maj Gen Henry Charles Gosling, IA, and was accidentally drowned Madras 23 Dec 1866, having had:

1c Frederick Henry Vansittart; *b* 28 Sept 1860; *d* 5 March 1864

1c Beatrice Helen Katherine; *d* 6 March 1864

2b Charles, JP (Northumberland); *b* 18 July 1845; *m* 13 April 1871 Leonora Louisa Isabella (*d* 22 Nov 1901), yst dau of Rev Leonard Shafto Orde, of Weetwood, Northumberland, and *d* 2 Dec 1912, leaving:

1c Frederick Jocelyn; *b* 12 April 1872; *educ* Loretto and Merton Coll Oxford; *m* 4 May 1901 Hilda Mary (*d* 1968), yr dau of Rev Hugh Bellamy, Chaplain RN Hosp Gt Yarmouth, and *dsp* 1 Nov 1952

2c Charles Henry Sawyer; *b* 1 May 1880; Paris rep RAC; *m* 5 Nov 1913 Olive Lois (*d* 4 March 1954), dau of Arthur Francis Godwin, and *d* 12 Oct 1964, leaving:

1d *Jaqueline; State Registered Physiotherapist Norfolk and Norwich Hosp, Supt Physiotherapist U Coll Hosp W Indies Jamaica 1953–55, WW II with Naval VAD

2d *Anne Vere [Miss Anne Hope, 42 Telegraph Lane East, Norwich]; WW II in ATS, architectural draughtswoman

3c George Leonard Nelson; *b* 21 Oct 1884; *educ* Pembroke Coll Cambridge (BA 1905); Lt RNVR, assist master RNC Dartmouth 1908–14; joined FO 1919, ret 1946; *m* 29 Dec 1908 Honoria Mary Victoria (*d* 29 Jan 1968), yst dau of John Giffard Riddell, of Felton Park, Northumberland, and had:

1d +(Charles) Peter (Sir), KCMG (1972, CMG 1956), TD (1945) [Sir Peter Hope KCMG TD, Guillard's Oak House, Midhurst, W Sussex GU29 9JZ]; *b* 29 May 1912; *educ* Oratory Sch and London U [BSc Engrg 1933]; WW II as Maj RA; Dip Serv 1946 as 1st Sec Paris, Assist Head UN Dept FO 1950, Cnsllr Bonn 1953, Head News Dept FO 1956–59, Min Madrid 1959–63, Consul-Gen Houston 1963–65, Alternate Br Delegate to UN New York 1965–68, Amb Mexico 1968–72, Grand Cross Order Aztec Eagle Mexico; KStJ 1984; *m* 15 Feb 1936 *Hazel Mary, yr dau of G L Turner, and had:

1e +(Charles) Jeremy [Jeremy Hope Esq, Netherhill, Awbridge, Hants SO51 0HG]; *b* 20 July 1937; *educ* Downside and RMA Sandhurst; Capt (ret) Gren Gds; Kt Honour & Devotion SMO Malta; manager London Office Hamburger Lloyd Ltd; *m* 18 Feb 1961 *Judith Ann, only dau of Harold T Pearce, of Cornwall, and has:

1f +Dominic Mark; *b* 17 Oct 1963

2f +Jonathan Paul; *b* 24 Feb 1965

2e +Adrian Philip; *b* 11 July 1942; *educ* Downside and Trin Coll Cambridge; researcher *Time-Life* New York

3e Richard Andrew; *b* 8 April 1947; *educ* Downside and St Thomas U, Houston, Texas; *d* 10 Dec 1985

1c Nora; *m* 26 July 1892 Rev Henry James Lawes Arnold (*d* 13 June 1928), Rector N Creake Norfolk 1911–27, Hon Canon Norwich, and *d* 23 April 1953

2c Louisa; *m* 23 April 1896 Rev Lionel Peere Williams-Freeman (*d* 22 April 1918), Rector Narborough, Leics, and had issue

3c Charlotte Gwendoline Frances; *m* 1st 31 Dec 1913 Capt Francis Hugh Beaufort (*ka* Festubert 15 May 1915), Oxon and Bucks LI, er s of Maj Francis Beaufort, RA; *m* 2nd Nov 1917 Capt William Harvey Cobbett, RASC

4c Gwendoline Katherine Leonora; *b* 30 March 1878; *m* 26 Oct 1907 Capt Donald Charles Hugh MacLean, DSO (*d* 12 April 1909), Roy Scots (Lothian Regt), and *d* 28 March 1970, leaving issue (*see* VYVYAN, Bt)

1b Eliza Louisa; *m* 28 July 1862 Andrew Inglis, WS (*d* 1892), and *d* 6 Aug 1914, leaving issue

2b Katherine; *m* 7 Jan 1886 Rev George Francis Edward Shaw (*dsp* 21 March 1904), Rector Edgeworth, Cirencester, and *d* 5 Dec 1919

3b Louisa Margaret; *m* 29 April 1869 Lionel A A Tollemache (*see* DYSART, E) and *d* 22 Nov 1909

3a George; *b* 30 May 1801; Capt RN; *m* 1st 2 Jan 1833 Charlotte (*d* 14 April 1837), dau of Adml John Tollemache (*see* TOLLEMACHE, B), and had:

1b Selina Elizabeth; *m* 22 Aug 1854 Rev Thomas Edmund Franklyn (*d* 6 Aug 1901) and *d* 8 Feb 1919, leaving issue

2b Charlotte; *m* 9 Aug 1864 Rev Samuel B Browne, Rector Plumtree, Notts, yst s of Ven J H Browne, Archdeacon Ely, and *d* 3 Sept 1870

3a (cont.) George Hope *m* 2nd 23 April 1845 Katherine Frances (*d* 26 Feb 1880), dau of William Leveson-Gower (*see* SUTHERLAND, D), and *d* 1 April 1893, having by her had:

3b Frances Katherine; *d* unm 21 Dec 1914

2 (cont.) The Hon Charles Hope-Vere *m* 3rd 2 April 1766 Helen (*d* 18 Sept 1794), dau of George Dunbar, and *d* 30 Dec 1791, having by her had, with other issue:

(5) George (Sir), KCB; *b* 6 July 1767; Adml; *m* 1st 1803 Jemima (*d* 5 Sept 1808), 5th dau of **3rd Earl of Hopetoun** (*see* below), and had, with a dau (Helen):

1a James (Sir), GCB; *b* 3 March 1808; V-Adml, pncpl naval ADC to HM QUEEN VICTORIA, C-in-C W Indies and N America Stations, Chev Legn Hon; *m* 1st 16 Aug 1838 Frederica Eliza (*d* 27 May 1856), 2nd dau of 8th Lord Kinnaird (*see* 1970 edn); *m* 2nd 6 Dec 1877 Elizabeth, dau of Gen Sir Arthur Thomas Cotton, KCSI, and *dsp* 9 June 1881

(5) (cont.) Adml Sir George Hope-Vere *m* 2nd 1814 Georgiana Mary Anne (*d* 16 Dec 1848), dau of 7th Lord Kinnaird (*see* 1970 edn), and *d* 2 May 1818, having by her had:

1a Eliza; *m* 1835 Sir Harry Verney, 2nd Bt, of Claydon (*qv*), and *d* 2 Jan 1857, leaving issue

(1) Henrietta; *m* 14 March 1729 5th Lord Napier (*see* NAPIER and ETTRICK, L) and *d* 17 Feb 1745, leaving issue

1 Sophia; *m* 1723, as his 2nd w, 2nd Earl of Seafield (*qv*)

The 1st EARL's er son,

JOHN HOPE, **2nd Earl of Hopetoun**; *b* 7 Sept 1704; a Ld Police Scotland 1744–60, Ld High Commr to Gen assembly Ch Scotland 1754; *m* 1st 14 Sept 1733 Anne (*d* 8 Sept 1759), 2nd dau of 2nd Earl of Seafield (*qv*), and had, with other issue:

1 JAMES HOPE later HOPE-JOHNSTONE (on inheriting estates and right to another Earldom from his great-uncle; *see* ANNANDALE AND HARTFELL, E), **3rd Earl of Hopetoun**; *b* 23 Aug 1741; served 3rd Foot Gds 1758–64 (fought Battle of Mindedn 1759), Ld Lt Linlithgowshire 1794–1816; *cr* 3 Feb 1809 BARON HOPETOUN OF HOPETOUN, Co Linlithgow (UK), with remainder, in default of male issue, to the heirs male of his f; *m* 16 Aug 1766 Elizabeth (*d* 19 Aug 1793), est dau of 6th Earl of Northesk (*qv*), and *d* 29 May 1817, having had, with other issue:

(1) Anne; inherited the Annandale estates; *m* 8 July 1792, as his 1st w, her cousin V-Adml Sir William Johnstone-Hope, GCB (*see* above), and *d* 28 Aug 1818, leaving issue (*see* ANNANDALE AND HARTFELL, E)

(2) Georgiana; *m* 20 Nov 1793 Hon Andrew James Johnstone-Cochrane and *d* 17 Sept 1797, leaving issue (*see* DUNDONALD, E)

(3) Jemima; *m* 1803, as his 1st w, her cousin Adml Sir George Hope-Vere, KCB, and *d* 5 Sept 1808, leaving issue (*see* above)

1 Elizabeth; *m* 24 July 1754 Henry, Earl of Drumlanrig (*see* QUEENSBERRY, M), and *dsp* 7 April 1756

2 Sophia; *m* 30 April 1779 8th Earl of Haddington (*qv*) and *d* 8 March 1813, leaving issue

The **2nd Earl** *m* 2nd 30 Oct 1762 Jane (*d* 16 March 1767), dau of Robert Oliphant, of Rossie, Perthshire, and by her had:

2 JOHN, **4th Earl**

3 Jane; *m* 1st 2 April 1793 1st Viscount Melville (*d* 29 May 1811); *m* 2nd 16 Feb 1814 1st Baron Wallace (*d* 23 Feb 1844)and *dsp* 9 June 1829

The **2nd Earl** *m* 3rd 10 June 1767 Lady Elizabeth Leslie (*d* 10 April 1788), 2nd dau of 5th Earl of Leven and (2nd Earl of) Melville (*qv*), and *d* 12 Feb 1781, having by her had, with other issue:

3 Charles; *b* 16 Oct 1768; Gen; *m* 30 April 1807 Louisa Anne (*d* 1 March 1875), est dau of George Finch Hatton (*see* WINCHILSEA and NOTTINGHAM, E), and *d* 1 July 1828, leaving:

(1) Elizabeth; *b* 23 Jan 1810; *m* 18—Louis Billard and *d* 30 May 1868

4 Alexander (Sir), GCB; *b* 2 Dec 1769; Gen; MP, Lt-Govr Chelsea Hosp; *m* 23 Oct 1805 Georgina (*d* 2 Dec 1855), dau of George Brown, and *d* 19 May 1837, leaving:

(1) John Thomas; *b* 10 Jan 1807; *m* 2 March 1835 Lady Frances Anne Lascelles (*d* 6 Dec 1855), dau of 2nd Earl of Harewood (*qv*), and *dsp* 17 March 1835

(2) George William, of Luffness; *b* 4 July 1808; MP Windsor; *m* 5 March 1836 Caroline Georgiana (*d* 5 Dec 1891), dau of 2nd Baron Montagu of Boughton

(*see* BUCCLEUCH and QUEENSBERRY, D), and *d* 18 Oct 1863, leaving, with other issue:

1a Henry Walter, of Luffness, JP, DL (E Lothian and Fifeshire); *b* 17 Aug 1839; Capt Gren Gds; *m* 8 Oct 1885 Lady Mary Catherine Constance Primrose (*d* 3 Sept 1935), sis of 5th Earl of Rosebery (*qv*), and *d* 25 Oct 1913, having had:

1b George Everard, of Luffness and Over Rankeillour, MC, JP (Fife); *b* 4 Nov 1886; Capt Gren Gds, Actg Lt-Col Lancs Fus; *m* 8 April 1911 Margaret (*m* 2nd 3 Oct 1919 Lionel Clement Erskine Clark and *d* 5 Jan 1923), only dau of John Cockton, JP, of Kirkborough, Cumberland, and was *ka* 10 Oct 1917, leaving:

1c Archibald John George, of Luffness, MBE (1946); *b* 9 Oct 1912; *educ* Eton and RMA Woolwich; Col RA WW II (despatches); *m* 6 April 1937 Mary Pilar Elizabeth (*d* 1989), yr dau of Brig-Gen Alister Fraser Gordon, CMG, DSO, and *d* 18 Jan 1987, leaving:

1d +George Archibald [George Hope of Luffness, Luffness, Aberlady, E Lothian EH32 0QB]; *b* 15 June 1938; *educ* Eton and Edinburgh U; late Gren Gds and Roy Scots (TA), Kt Honour & Devotion SMO Malta; CA, Fell Hong Kong Soc Accountants; *m* 15 June 1996 *Anna Maria Willemina Jacoba, widow of Jean Gaspard Haitsma Mulier and dau of Frederick Wilhelm Fabius and Mrs Anna Maria Wilhelmina Jacoba Labouchere Crommelin, of Zeist, Utrecht, Netherlands

1d *(Mary) Margaret Lucy [Mrs Richard Baillie, Allanbank, Lauder, Berwicks TD2 6RW]; *b* 27 Dec 1940; *m* 1978 *Richard Simon Baillie, er s of Capt Alexander Maciej Gucewicz-Baillie, of Kelso, and has:

1e *Alexander Simon; *b* 1982

2e *Edward George; *b* 1985

2d *(Mary) Catherine Elizabeth [Mrs Yalçin Hope-Adar, 9 Ames Place, Morristown, NJ 07960, USA]; *b* 12 May 1943; *m* 1989 *Bey Yalçin Adar, of Istanbul

3d *(Elizabeth) Caroline [Mrs Patrick Scott, 6 Rede Place, London W2 4TU]; *b* 11 Dec 1948; *m* 1984 *(James) Patrick Scott, s of Munro Mackenzie Scott, of Cakemuir, Pathhead, Midlothian, and has:

1e *James William Hope; *b* 4 June 1988

1e *Catriona Mary; *b* 22 Sept 1984

4d *Cecilia Mary [Mrs Christopher Latilla-Campbell, Lochton, Abernyte, Perthshire PH14 9TA]; *b* 2 Feb 1952; *educ* St Andrews (MA); *m* 1987 *Christopher Peter Latilla-Campbell, er s of Peter Latilla-Campbell, of Bulawayo

1c Wilhelmine Mary Margaret; Sister Marina memb Soc of St Margaret, St Margaret's Convent, Sussex; *d* 2 July 1988

2a Montagu; *b* 4 March 1844; Col 2nd Bn Gordon Highrs; *m* 2 Nov 1876 (*divorce* 1882) Constance Maud (*d* 1914), only dau of James Fletcher, of Rosehaugh, Scotland, and *d* 1 March 1890, leaving:

1b Caroline Violet Mary, OBE (1920); *b* 11 Sept 1878; *m* 28 April 1904 Maj Ian Ashley Moreton Brodie of Brodie, DSO (*d* 15 Feb 1943), and *d* 10 Oct 1958, leaving issue

3a Edward Stanley (Sir), KCB; *b* 1 Feb 1846; Lunacy Commr 1908–14, barrister, Charity Commr 1879–99, Registrar Privy Cncl 1899–1909; *m* 2 June 1881 Constance Christina (*d* 30 May 1945), dau of Sir John Leslie, 1st Bt (*qv*), and *d* 15 Feb 1921, leaving:

1b John Alexander Henry; *b* 1 March 1882; Maj Canadian Scottish Regt WW I (despatches); *m* 15 April 1907 (*divorce* 1923) Elizabeth Maud (*d* 27 Dec 1962), dau of Hon James Dunsmuir, Lt-Govr BC, Canada, and *d* 18 Oct 1938, leaving:

1c Edward James, MC; *b* 19 July 1911; *educ* Eton; T/Maj Scots Gds WW II; *m* 1st 16 Dec 1937 (*divorce* 1950) Enid (*d* 1988), yr dau of Robert Louis George Gunther, of Surrey, and had:

1d David Edward Geoffrey; *b* 28 Dec 1939; *educ* Eton; *d* in bathing accident 3 Sept 1961

1d *Sarah Elizabeth [Mrs Sarah Wordsworth, Avendale, 6 Nags Head Lane, Avening, Glos GL8 8NZ]; *b* 27 May 1942; *m* 11 July 1964 (*divorce* 1987) Benjamin Laurie Copinger Wordsworth, yst s of John Theodore Wordsworth, of Badminton, Glos, and has:

1e *Marcia; *b* 30 May 1965; *m* 1993 *Mark Walton, of Christchurch, NZ, and has:

1f *George Wordsworth; *b* 27 July 1997

1f *Sophie Wordsworth; *b* 9 Dec 1994

2e *Lucy; *b* 30 May 1965; *m* 1992 *Kostka Garcia Minaur de la Rica and has:

1f *Lucas Dylan; *b* 1992

2f *Theo Gregory; *b* 27 Jan 1995

3f *Joe Patrick; *b* 23 May 1996

3e *Rebecca; *b* 29 Oct 1967; *m* 1st 1989 (*divorce* 19–) Julian A Lloyd, of Stroud, and has:

1f *Oscar Benjamin; *b* 1989

3e (cont.) Mrs Rebecca Lloyd *m* 2nd 1996 *Jason Peter Moore and has by him:

1f *Flora Wordsworth; *b* 12 Sept 1997

2f *Imogen Wordsworth; *b* 12 Sept 1997

1c (cont.) Edward Hope *m* 2nd 2 Dec 1952 *Winifred Gwendolyn Marie [Mrs Edward Hope, Ibstock Close, Little Tew, Oxon OX7 4JF], er dau of Maj John Byng Paget, of Co Wicklow, and former w of Maj Guy Montgomerie Carleton Paget, and *d* 1989

2c Alexander Douglas Byng; *b* 20 Aug 1918; *educ* Eton and Balliol Coll Oxford; T/Maj 10th Roy Hus WW II (despatches); BBC 1955; *m* 3 Nov 1951 *Florence Leslie, JP Essex (1961), dau of Graham St Clair-Keith, of Cap Martin, France

1b Elizabeth Caroline; *b* 4 March 1885; JP and CC Wilts; *m* 1st 16 Feb 1904 6th Marquess of Lansdowne (*qv*) and had issue; *m* 2nd 14 Feb 1941 Lord Colum Edmund Crichton-Stuart (*d* 18 Aug 1957), 3rd s of 3rd Marquess of Bute (*qv*), and *d* 25 March 1964

4a Herbert James (Sir); *b* 3 Jan 1851; *educ* Ch Ch Oxford (BA); barrister, Bankruptcy Registrar 1891–1926, ktd 1925; *d* unm 23 May 1930

1a Lucy Georgiana; *d* unm 14 March 1946

(3) James Robert HOPE later HOPE-SCOTT, QC, of Abbotsford; *b* 15 July 1812; *m* 1st 19 Aug 1847 Charlotte Harriet Jane (*d* 20 Oct 1858), dau of John Gibson Lockhart and gdau of the author Sir Walter Scott, Bt (*see* 1850 edn), and had:

1a Walter Michael; *b* 2 June 1857; *d* 11 Dec 1858

1a Mary Monica, of Abbotsford; *b* 2 Oct 1852; *m* 21 July 1874 Hon Joseph MAXWELL later MAXWELL-SCOTT (*see* HERRIES OF TERREGLES, L) and *d* 15 March 1920

(3) (cont.) James Robert HOPE-SCOTT *m* 2nd 7 Jan 1861 Lady Victoria Alexandrina Fitzalan-Howard (*d* 20 Dec 1870), est dau of 14th Duke of Norfolk (*qv*), and *d* 29 April 1873, having by her had:

2a Philip James; *b* 8 April, *d* 9 April 1868

3a JAMES FITZALAN HOPE HOPE-SCOTT; *cr* BARON RANKEILLOUR (*qv*)

2a Minna Margaret; *m* 13 April 1887 Sir Nicholas R O'Conor, GCB, GCMG, PC, of Dundermott, Co Roscommon (*d* 19 March 1908), Amb Constantinople, and *d* 29 Jan 1934, leaving issue

3a Catherine Mary (twin sis); *d* at birth

4a Josephine Mary; *m* 24 Nov 1887 Wilfrid Ward (*d* 1916) and *d* 20 Nov 1932, leaving issue

5a Theresa Anne; nun; *d* 1 Nov 1891

(4) Alexander; *b* 1814; *d* 1835

(1) Louisa Dorothea; *m* 10 Sept 1832 Lord Henry Kerr and *d* 18 Jan 1884, leaving issue (*see* LOTHIAN, M)

The 3rd EARL's half-bro,

JOHN HOPE, **4th Earl of Hopetoun**, GCB (1815, KB 1809), PC (I 1812); *b* 17 Aug 1765; Cornet 10th Dragoons 1784, Maj-Gen 1802, Lt-Gen 1808, Gen 1819, served W Indies 1796–97 and Egypt 1801, 2ic to Gen Sir John Moore Peninsular War, succeeding him after his death following Corunna 1809, also saw action Bayonne 1814; MP (Tory) Linlithgowshire 1790–1800; Cdr Forces Ireland 1812–13; Col 6th Bn 60th Rifles 1805–06, 92nd Regt 1806–20 and 42nd Regt 1820–23; Capt Gen Roy Co Archers 1819–23, Ld Lt Linlithgowshire 1816–23; *cr* 17 May 1814 BARON NIDDRY OF NIDDRY, Co Linlithgow (UK); *m* 1st 7 Aug 1798 his cousin Elizabeth (*dsp* 20 March 1801), yst dau of Hon Charles Hope-Vere (*see* above); *m* 2nd 9 Feb 1803 Louisa Dorothea (*d* 16 July 1836), 3rd dau of John Wedderburn by his 2nd w (*see* OGILVY-WEDDERBURN, Bt), and *d* 27 Aug 1823, having by her had, with other issue:

1 JOHN, **5th Earl**

2 James HOPE later HOPE-WALLACE (on inheriting Lord Wallace's estates), of Featherstone Castle, DL (Linlithgowshire); *b* 7 June 1807; Lt-Col Coldstream Gds; *m* 4 March 1837 Lady Mary Frances Nugent (*d* 23 May 1904), yst dau of 7th Earl of Westmeath (*qv*), and *d* 7 Jan 1854, leaving, with other issue:

(1) John George Frederick, of Featherstone Castle, JP (Northumberland); *b* 15 April 1839; High Sheriff Northumberland 1871; *m* 19 June 1867 Mary Frances (*d* 17 Feb 1929), est dau of Adml Charles Ramsay Drinkwater Bethune, CB, of Balfour, Fife, and *d* 14 July 1900, leaving:

1a James, of Featherstone Castle, JP; *b* 20 Feb 1872; Lt Northumberland Fus; *m* 3 Nov 1909 Hon Ursula Mary Addington (*d* 24 Aug 1962), er dau of 4th Viscount Sidmouth (*qv*), and was *ka* 15 Sept 1917, leaving:

1b *Ruth [Mrs Eric Cairns, Hallbank Head, Featherstone, Haltwhistle, Northumberland]; *b* 25 Sept 1911; *m* 3 Sept 1937 Capt Eric Cairns, Roy Northumberland Fus, est s of Russell Cairns, of Duke's House, Hexham, and has:

1c *Jane [Mrs Peter Butcher, Crooks Farm, Gilsland, Cumbria]; *b* 1939; *m* 1965 *Peter Butcher and has:

1d *David James Peter; *b* 1967

2c *Clare [Mrs Michael Steinberg, 1216 Cornell Ave, Berkeley, CA 94706, USA]; *b* 1947; *m* 1985 *Michael Jefferey Steinberg

2b Ann; *b* 2 April 1914; *m* 2 Jan 1944 Capt Robert Byrt Jordan, RAC, only s of Frederick Hudson Jordan, of Thika, Kenya, and had:

1c *Richard; *b* 11 March 1945

1c *Elizabeth Mary; *b* 27 June 1947

2c *Dorothy Margaret; *b* 21 Nov 1949

2a Charles Nugent, MBE (1918); *b* 3 Feb 1877; *educ* Eton and Balliol Coll Oxford (BA 1899, MA 1902); barrister Lincoln's Inn 1904, Pncpl Clerk Charity Commn; *m* 12 Jan 1905 Mabel Florence (*d* 20 June 1970), dau of Col Alan Chaplin, Madras Army, of Bencomb, Dorking, and *d* 15 Oct 1953, leaving:

1b Philip Adrian, CBE (1975); *b* 6 Nov 1911; *educ* Charterhouse and Balliol Coll Oxford (BA 1933); Press Offr Air Min WW II, music and drama critic *The Times*, *Time and Tide* and *Manchester Guardian* 1946 on; *d* unm 3 Sept 1979

1b Nina Mary; *b* 14 Dec 1905; *m* 1 Oct 1932 Sir Edward O'Bryen Hoare, 7th Bt, of Annabella (*qv*), and *d* 15 Oct 1995, leaving issue

2b *(Dorothy) Jaqueline, CBE (1958) [Miss Jacqueline Hope-Wallace CBE, 17 Ashley Court, Morpeth Terrace, London SW1P 1EN]; *b* 29 May 1909; *educ* LMH Oxford (BA 1931); Min Labour 1932, Nat Assistance Bd 1934 (Assist Sec 1946–58, U-Sec 1958–65), U-Sec Min Housing and Local Govt 1965–69, ret, Cwlth Fell 1952–53, Commr Public Works Loan Bd 1974–78

3a Ernest; *b* 29 Oct 1880; *d* 1959

1a Emily Mary; *d* unm 15 Jan 1956

2a Evelyn Frances; *d* unm 25 Oct 1926

3a Alice Maud; *d* unm 4 July 1947

4a Anna Louisa; *d* unm 19 Dec 1965

(2) James Louis Alexander HOPE; *b* 24 Dec 1843; High Sheriff Herefs 1901; *m* 1st 11 Feb 1873 Anna Louisa (*dsp* 15 April 1873), 2nd dau of Robert Oliphant, of Rossie; *m* 2nd 24 April 1884 Eliza (*d* 7 May 1906), dau of Sir Peter Coats (*see* COATS, Bt), and *d* 15 Oct 1904, having had:

1a Peter Oliver Louis; *b* 19 March, *d* 12 July 1885

2a Laurence Nugent, JP (1920), DL (1953); *b* 14 Oct 1890; *educ* Clifton and Trin Hall Cambridge (BA 1912); Capt Res Offrs Welsh Gds, Capt Roy N Devon Yeo (TA), WW I, WW II 1940–41 as Staff Offr Middle East; High Sheriff Herefs 1923; *m* 1st 23 Sept 1919 Hilda Mary (*d* 21 March 1938), only dau of Michael Joseph Hunter, JP, of Derbys, and had:

1b +John Nugent [John Hope Esq, The Power House, Whitney-on-Wye, Herefs]; *b* 7 Oct 1924; *educ* Eton and Magdalene Coll Cambridge (BA 1946); *m* 1st 15 Aug 1953 Polly, er dau of Lt-Gen Sir Hugh Charles Stockwell, KBE, CB, DSO, and has:

1c +Augustine Jason Nugent; *b* 11 July 1961; *m* 1991 *Maureen Patricia, dau of Douglas Hymers, of Seattle, and has:

1d +John Gabriel; *b* 1992

1b (cont.) John Hope *m* 2nd *Penelope Berengaria Walker, dau of Lawrence George Durrell, FRSL, the writer

1b *Jocelyn Mary; *b* 15 July 1922; *m* 2 Dec 1948 *Michael Fortune Cleghorn, of Cape Town, yr s of W R Cleghorn, of Tunbridge Wells

2a (cont.) Laurence Hope *m* 2nd Feb 1941 Constance Elizabeth (*d* 19–), dau of E A Shell

1a Violet Mary; *b* 21 April 1887; *m* 1st 30 July 1912 Capt Edward Archibald Hume (*ka* 1915), barrister, Ch Magistrate Gambia; *m* 2nd 21 April 1925 Maj Sir Duncan McCallum, MC, MP, FRGS, FZS (*d* 10 May 1958), 3rd s of Colin Whitton McCallum, and *d* 30 Oct 1964

(3) Adrian Henry; *b* 5 May 1849; Maj KOSB; *m* 16 Dec 1875 Mary, est dau of Hugh Lee Pattinson, of Scots House, Durham, and *d* 9 April 1932, leaving:

1a Edith Frances Mary; *d* unm 17 Nov 1935

3 Charles, JP, DL (Linlithgow); *b* 11 Sept 1808; MP Linlithgow 1838–45; Lt-Govr IoM 1845–60; *m* 26 Oct 1841 Lady Isabella Helen Douglas (*d* 4 July 1893), dau of 5th Earl of Selkirk (*qv*), and *d* 31 Oct 1893, leaving:

(1) John, JP, DL, of St Mary's Isle, Kirkcudbright; *b* 30 Jan 1843; Capt RN; *m* 13 Aug 1872 Rebecca Marion (*d* 20 June 1914), 2nd dau of Peter Blackburn, MP, of Killearn, Stirling, and *d* 27 Feb 1915, having had issue (*see* HOPE-DUNBAR, Bt)

(2) Thomas, of Summerhill, Dumfriesshire, JP, DL (Linlithgowshire); *b* 3 Feb 1848; Capt Bombay SC; MP Linlithgow 1893–95; *m* 14 July 1909 Mary Louisa (*d* 9 June 1943), er dau of Gen Horace A Browne and widow of Col W G Cumming, RE, and *d* 28 March 1925

(3) Charles, VD; *b* 28 Jan 1850; Col cmdg 2nd Vol Bn KOSB, Capt KRRC; Ld Lt Berwicks 1922; *m* 4 Oct 1881 Julie Isabella (*d* 1 Nov 1930), dau of David Carnegie (*see* FIFE, D), and *d* 25 Aug 1930

(1) Jean; *d* unm 20 Feb 1924

(2) Louisa Dorothea; *d* 5 March 1870

(3) Isabella Helen; *d* 25 Aug 1920

4 George; *b* 12 April 1811; Capt RN; *m* 29 April 1847 Hon Anne Carmichael Napier (*see* NAPIER and ETTRICK, L) and *d* 14 Nov 1854, leaving a dau

5 Louis; *b* 29 Oct 1817; Capt Coldstream Gds; *m* 12 Oct 1859 Susan Frances Sophia (*d* 4 Dec 1901), er dau of William John Dumaresq, Capt RSC, and *d* 15 Aug 1894, leaving:

(1) Reginald William; *b* 2 June 1864; *d* unm 11 Nov 1915

(2) Edmund Louis, MIME; *b* 9 June 1866; *d* unm 12 Oct 1913

(3) Herbert George, MBE (1918); *b* 23 May 1875; *m* 1920 May Winifred (*d* 3 Oct 1960), dau of Lt-Col F F Sheppee, RA, and widow of John Harley, and *d* 19 Dec 1956, having had:

1a John Francis; *b* 20 March 1921; *d* unm 21 April 1944

1a*(Isabel) Susan [Mrs Peter Hiley, 7 St John's St, Chichester PO19 1VR]; *b* 9 Dec 1922; *m* 21 May 1955 *Peter Haviland Hiley, only s of Col Sir (Ernest) Haviland Hiley, KBE, s of Rev Walter Hiley by Henrietta Jemima Forbes (*see* STUART-FORBES, Bt), and has:

1b *William John Haviland [William Hiley Esq, Ashley Hill House, Clarendon, Wilts SP5 3HA]; *b* 1 Feb 1960; *m* 1993 *Camilla Jane, er dau of Charles Edward Weatherby (*see* LEY, Bt), and has:

1c *Tara Elizabeth; *b* 28 Oct 1995

(1) Florence Mary Susan; *d* unm 26 April 1943

(2) Henrietta Isabella; *d* unm 7 Feb 1918

(3) Elinor Alice; *d* 1869

(4) Edith Aimée; *d* unm 31 May 1942

(5) Laura Caroline; *m* 22 Nov 1905 Sir Donald James Boyd, KCIE, ICS (*d* 12 Dec 1953), and *d* 25 July 1931, leaving issue

6 Adrian, CB; *b* 8 March 1821; Brig-Gen, Lt-Col 93rd Highrs; *k* Rowdennal, Oudh, 15 April 1858

The 4th EARL's est son,

JOHN HOPE, **5th Earl of Hopetoun**; *b* 15 Nov 1803; *m* 4 June 1826 Louisa (*d* 1 Sept 1854), dau of Sir Godfrey Bosville-Macdonald, 11th Bt (*qv*) who was also 3rd Baron Macdonald (*qv*) of Sleat, and *d* 8 April 1843, leaving:

JOHN ALEXANDER HOPE, **6th Earl of Hopetoun**; *b* 22 March 1831; *educ* Harrow; Offr 1st Life Gds 1851–52; Ld Lt Linlithgowshire 1863–73; *m* 3 Jan 1860 Etheldred Ann (*d* 15 Oct 1884), est dau of Charles Thomas Samuel Birch-Reynardson, of Holywell Hall, Lincs, and *d* 1 April 1873, having had, with a yr s (Charles Archibald, *b* 12 May 1863, *d* 2 April 1888) and two daus (Estella, *d* unm 6 Nov 1958; Dorothea Louisa, *d* unm 20 June 1943):

JOHN ADRIAN LOUIS HOPE, **1st Marquess of Linlithgow** (UK), so *cr* 27 Oct 1902, KT (1900), GCVO (1900), GCMG (1889), PC (1895), DL (Haddingtonshire, Linlithgowshire, Dumfriesshire and Lanarks); *b* 25 Sept 1860; *educ* Eton; Hon Col Forth Div Submarine Miners, Maj Lanarks Yeo Cav, KStJ, Sub-Prior OStJ; Ld-in-Waiting 1885–86 and 1886–89, Ld High Commr Gen Assembly Ch Scotland 1887–89, Govr and C-in-C Victoria 1889–95, Paymaster-Gen 1895–98, Ld Chamberlain 1898–1900, Govr-Gen and C-in-C Australian Cwlth 1900–02, Sec State Scotland Feb-Dec 1905, Dep Govr Bank Scotland 1904–08, Pres Inst Naval Architects 1895–1900; *m* 18 Oct 1886 Hon Hersey Alice Eveleigh de Moleyns, DGStJ (*d* 3 April 1937), dau of 4th Baron Ventry (*qv*), and *d* 29 Feb 1908, having had:

1 VICTOR ALEXANDER JOHN, **2nd Marquess**

2 Charles Melbourne, DL (W Lothian); *b* 20 Feb 1892; *educ* Eton; Capt Lothians and Border Horse Yeo WW I, Lt 1st Life Gds, WW II as Maj 3rd Bn London Scottish and cmdg W Lothian Bn HG; *d* unm 11 June 1962

1 Jaqueline Alice; *b* 16 June, *d* 21 June 1896

2 Mary Dorothea, CVO (1947); *b* 1903; Ldy-in-Waiting to HRH PRINCESS MARINA, DUCHESS OF KENT 1934–49, Extra Ldy-in-Waiting 1949–68, Hon 1st Offr WRNS; *m* 27 July 1936 16th Earl of Pembroke and (13th Earl of) Montgomery (*qv*) and *d* 1995, leaving issue

The 1st MARQUESS's er son,

VICTOR ALEXANDER JOHN HOPE, **2nd Marquess of Linlithgow**, KG (1943), KT (1928), GCSI (1936), GCIE (1929), OBE (1919), TD, PC (1935), DL (W Lothian); *b* 24 Sept 1887; *educ* Eton; WW I as Capt Lothians and Border Horse Yeo (despatches), cmded a Bn Roy Scots 1916–20, Maj cmdg 1st Lothians and Border Armoured Car Co 1920–26, Hon Col 1926–46, Hon Col Edin U OTC; Capt Roy Co Archers 1920–34, Ensign 1934–41, Lt 1941–46; V-Lt W Lothian 1927 (Ld Lt 1929–52), FRS Edinburgh; Hon LLD Edinburgh, Dep Chm U Party Orgn 1924–26, chm Midland Bank Ltd, Pres Br Bankers' Assoc, dir Scottish Widows' Fund and Life Assur Soc, Edinburgh Chm Ctee Distbn and Prices Ag Produce 1923, Pres Edinburgh and E Scotland Coll Ag 1924–33, memb Roy Fine Art Commn Scotland 1933–36, Chm MRC and Govrs Imp Coll Sci and Tech 1934–36, Viceroy India 1936–43, Ld High Commr Gen Assembly Ch Scotland 1944 and 1945, Chm Tstees Natl Galleries Scotland 1944–52, Chllr Edinburgh U 1944–52, Pres Empire Cotton Growing Corp 1945–50, Pres Navy League 1924–31, Chm Roy Commn Ag India 1926–28, Chm Jt Select Ctee Indian Constitutional Reform 1933–34, Civ Ld Admlty 1922–24, KGStJ; *m* 19 April 1911 Doreen Maud, CI (1936), DGStJ, Kaiser-i-Hind gold medal (*d* 2 Aug 1965), yr dau of Rt Hon Sir Frederick George Milner, 7th Bt (*qv*), and *d* 5 Jan 1952, having had:

1 CHARLES WILLIAM FREDERICK, **3rd Marquess**

2 +JOHN ADRIAN HOPE; *cr* BARON GLENDEVON (*qv*)

1 *Anne Adeline [The Lady Anne Southby, Robins Mill, Overbury, Tewkesbury, Glos]; *b* 27 Jan 1914 (twin); *m* 6 Nov 1939 *Lt-Cdr Patrick Henry James Southby, RN, yr s of Cdr Sir Archibald Richard James Southby, 1st Bt (*qv*), and has issue

2 Joan Isabella; *b* 21 Sept 1915; *m* 22 April 1952 *Col Ian William Gore-Langton, MBE, Coldstream Gds, only son of Maj Francis Wilfred Gore-Langton, of Little Tingewick House, Buckingham, and *d* 20 April 1982, leaving:

   (1) *Mary Jane; *b* 4 May 1955

   (2) *Margaret; *b* 26 Sept 1956

3 Doreen Hersey Winifred; *b* 17 June 1920; Govr Enham Alamein Tst 1958–92, Pres Rehabilitation Assoc and Lhas Apso Soc; *m* 9 Jan 1948, as his 2nd w, Maj-Gen George Erroll Prior-Palmer, CB, DSO, 9th Lancers (*d* 18 Aug 1977), s of Prior Spunner Prior-Palmer, of Dublin, and *d* 22 Jan 1998, leaving:

   (1) *Simon Erroll; *b* 5 Feb 1951; *educ* Eton; *m* 1984 *Lady Julia Margaret Violet Lloyd George, dau of 3rd Earl Lloyd George of Dwyfor (*qv*), and has:

      1a *George Errol Owen; *b* 1988

      2a *Arthur Frederick Victor; *b* 1991

      3a *Harold; *b* 3 April 1998

      1a *Laura Ruth Hope; *b* 1994

   (1) *Lucinda Jane, MBE (1978); *b* 7 Nov 1953; show-jumper; *m* 1981 *David Green, s of Barry Green, of Brisbane, and has:

      1a *Frederick; *b* 1985

      1a *Lissa; *b* 1989

The 2nd MARQUESS's er son,

CHARLES WILLIAM FREDERICK HOPE, **3rd Marquess of Linlithgow**, MC; *b* 7 April 1912; *educ* Eton and Ch Ch Oxford (BA 1936); Lt Scots Gds WW II 1939–40 (POW), Capt Lothian and Border Horse RAC (TA); Ld Lt W Lothian 1964–87; *m* 1st 24 July 1939 Vivien (*d* 23 Sept 1963), er dau of Maj Robert Orlando Rodolph Kenyon-Slaney (*see* KENYON, B), and had:

1 ADRIAN JOHN CHARLES HOPE, **4th and present Marquess Linlithgow**

1 *(Mary) Sarah-Jane [The Lady Sarah-Jane Learoyd, East Lodge, Hopetoun, S Queensferry, W Lothian EH30 9SL]; *b* 25 May 1940 (HRH THE PRINCESS ROYAL stood sponsor); *m* 3 Oct 1967 (*divorce* 1978) Michael Gordon Learoyd, yr s of Philip Halkett Brook Learoyd, of Britwell Salome, Oxon, and has:

   (1) *Jeremy Anthony Gordon; *b* 23 March 1971; *educ* Milton Abbey

The **3rd Marquess** *m* 2nd 18 Feb 1965 *Judith, dau of Stanley Matthew Lawson, of Cincinnati, Ohio, and widow of Lt-Col Esmond Charles Baring, OBE (*see* ASHBURTON, B), and *d* 1987

Seat: Hopetoun House, South Queensferry, Lothian. The site of Hopetoun is on the Abercorn estate acquired by the father of the 1st Earl and the house itself was started before the latter even came of age. Sir William Bruce, 1st Bt, of the 1668 creation (*see* ELGIN and KINCARDINE, also ROYAL FAMILY sub Holyroodhouse), drew up the initial plans and the first phase of building was finished the year the Earldom was created, 1703. This consisted of the main block, in particular the side facing onto the parkland and lake with the D-shaped pediment above the main door punctured by two oculi to break up the otherwise over-rectilinear facade.

From the early 1720s to the late 1740s William Adam worked to extend Hopetoun, adding on the colonnaded bays that reach out to embrace the onlooker either side of the main block on the eastern side of the house, which he refaced, and rounding them off at each end with bulky but squat wings. These rise higher than the main block by reason of their belvederes. The effect is nevertheless a little stark, particularly as there is no very elaborate entrance door and the fact that the house sits on the southern shore of the Firth of Forth, one of Britain's bleaker spots, does not help. Presumably Adam strove for this effect deliberately.

The interior was taken care of by Robert and John Adam, William's sons, though they had enough restraint to leave Bruce's best work relatively untouched, notably the splendid staircase, the Garden Room and the Library. The brothers Adam made their own distinctive contribution in the form of the Yellow and Red Drawing Rooms. The latter has a Rysbrack chimney piece, a magnificent object but more than a shade chunky for such a delicate apartment. It is particularly discordant when compared with the ceiling, whose exquisite gilt tracery is one of the best things Robert Adam ever did. Later work includes the State Banqueting Room, put together a few years after the end of the Napoleonic Wars in which its sponsor the 4th Earl had played such a distinctive role. The murals above Bruce's staircase are the work of William McLaren in the 1960s.

LISBURNE

Arms: Sa. a chevron between three fleurs-de-lys arg.
Crest: An armed arm embowed, holding in the hand a sword ppr.
Supporters: Dexter, a dragon regardant, wings elevated vert, gorged with a collar sa., edged arg., and charged with three fleurs-de-lys of the last, thereto a chain or; sinister, a unicorn regardant arg., armed, maned, tufted and unguled or, collared and chained as the dexter.
Motto: *Non revertar inultus* ('I will not return unavenged').
Creations: V. and B. (I) 5 June 1695, E. (I) 18 July 1776.

THE 8TH EARL OF LISBURNE, *Viscount Lisburne* and **Lord Vaughan, Baron of Fethard** (John David Malet Vaughan, DL (Dyfed 1992)) [The Rt Hon The Earl of Lisburne DL, Cruglas, Ystrad Meurig, Dyfed SY25 6AN]; *b* 1 Sept 1918; *s* 1965; *educ* Eton and Magdalen Coll Oxford (MA); Capt Welsh Gds WW II, barrister Inner Temple 1948, dep chm Westward TV, dir: BHS 1964–87, Lloyds Bank SW Regnl Bd 1978–; chm Wales Cncl for Vol Action 1976–; *m* 4 Dec 1943 *Shelagh, er dau of Timothy Alfred Macauley, of 1266 Redpath Crescent, Montreal, Canada, and has:

1 +DAVID JOHN FRANCIS MALET, *Viscount Vaughan* [Viscount Vaughan, 4 Porthmeor Studios, Porthmeor Sq, St Ives, Cornwall]; *b* 15 June 1945; *educ* Ampleforth; *m* 1973 *Jennifer Jane, only dau of James Desire John William Fraser Campbell, of Glengarry, Inverness-shire, and has:

   (1) +Digby Dylan; *b* 1973

   (1) *Lucy Bronwyn; *b* 1971

2 +Michael John Wilmot Malet [The Hon Michael Vaughan, 44 Tite St, London SW3 4JA]; *b* 26 June 1948; *educ* Ampleforth and New Coll Oxford (MA); chm Vaughan Ltd 1983–, Pres Vaughan Designs Inc 1996–; *m* 16 Sept 1978 *Lucinda, er dau of 7th Baron Ashburton (*qv*), and has:

   (1) *Emma Rose Nightingale; *b* 19 Jan 1993

   (2) *Sophie Louise Malet; *b* 14 July 1994

3 +John Edward Malet [The Hon John Vaughan, 19 Bowerdean St, London SW6 3TN]; *b* 3 Oct 1952; *educ* Ampleforth; *m* 1st 17 Sept 1977 (*divorce* 1983) Catharine Euphan, only dau of J P Waterer, of Coombe Bissett, Salisbury; *m* 2nd 1989 *Sandra Caroline Janet, dau of Brian Harold Thomson, of Kemback Ho, by Cupar, Fife, and formerly w of Michael Charles Craufurd Cooper, and by her has:

   (1) +Henry John Augustus; *b* 1990

Lisburne, previous creation: *See* ELY, M.

Lineage: The VAUGHANs Earls of Lisburne have in their time alleged an ancestry stretching back to EINION ap GOLLWYN, whose issue were settled predominantly in Glamorgan. The descent as regards the first couple of generations (*see* below) is not absolutely certain, however.

GOLLWYN (probably s of Cadrod of Senghenydd ab Einion ap Gollwyn; *see* above); had:

GRUFFUDD Ap GOLLWYN; had:

LLYWELYN Ap GRUFFUDD; had:

LLYWELYN FYCHAN Ap LLYWELYN; a juror in the district known as 'Ultra' (Upper reaches of the River) Aeron 1292; had:

ADDA Ap LLYWELYN FYCHAN; probably the person of the same name who was Beadle (parish offr with punitive powers over minor offenders) at Creuddyn 1331, Escheator (royal official implementing escheats, or reversions of property to the Crown in cases where a person had died without direct heirs) of S Wales 1344–46 and Dep Steward Cards to 1348 (when deprived of office as a Welshman, though performing the duties of the office again 1349–50 and 1352–57); *m* Tudo, dau of Ieuan Goch, of Trawsgoed, Llanafan, and had:

MAREDUDD Ab ADDA, of Trawsgoed; probably the person of the same name who was Constable of Genau'r-glyn, Cards, 1357–59 and Mefenydd 1360–61; *m* Efa, dau of Llywelyn, and had:

ADDA Ab MAREDUDD Ab ADDA, of Trawsgoed; probably the person of the same name who was Constable Mefenydd 1389–90, Beadle Creuddyn 1391–94, Escheator Cards 1395 and Reeve (official in a manorial society representing the overlord) of Creuddyn 1391–94 and 1397–98; *m* Gwerful, dau of Llywelyn Goch ap Llwelyn Gaplan, of Glyn Aeron, and had:

LLYWELYN Ab ADDA Ap MAREDUDD; living 1434–64; Beadle Creuddyn 1434–45, Reeve Creuddyn 1457–58; *m* Margaret, dau of Thomas Fychan ap Thomas Fychan, of Llangathen, Carmarths, and had:

IEUAN Ap LLYWELYN; possibly the person of the same name who was Beadle Creuddyn 1518–20; *m* Gwenllian Fechan, dau of Gruffudd ab Ieuan, of Ceulan, Genau'r-glyn, and had:

MORUS FYCHAN Ab IEUAN, of Trawsgoed; *m* 1st Tangwystl, dau of Dafydd ap Llywelyn, and had a s; *m* 2nd —, dau and coheir of Llywelyn Goch, of Glynaeron, and had another s (Thomas); his s by his 1st w:

RICHARD Ap MORUS FYCHAN; living 1547; *m* Mawd, dau of Rhys ap Dafydd ap Llywelyn ap Gwilym Llwyd, of Ffoshelyg, Lladysul, Cards, and had, with three other sons and three daus:

MORUS FYCHAN, of Trawsgoed; living 1586; *m* after 10 June 1547 Elliw, dau and heir of Hywel ap Jenkin, of Creuddyn, and had, with four yr sons and seven daus:

IEUAN LLWYD FYCHAN; *m* 1st Margaret, dau of Dafydd Lloyd ap Jenkin, of Berthlwyd, Steward Arwystli, Montgomeryshire, and had four sons and two daus; *m* 2nd Gwenllian, dau of Dafydd ab Ieuan Llwyd Fychan; his est s by his 1st w:

EDWARD VAUGHAN, of Trawscoed; *m* 1st after 10 Dec 1601 Lettice, dau of John Stedman, of Strata Florida, Cards, and had six sons and four or five daus; *m* 2nd after 28 Oct 1624 Agnes/Anne, dau of Thomas Jones, of Abermarlais, Carmarths, and widow of John Stedman, of Cilcennin, Cards, and by her had one or two daus; *d* 1635, leaving by his 1st w an est s:

Sir JOHN VAUGHAN; *b* 14 Sept 1603; barrister 1630, MP Cardigan 1640 and Cards 1661, Ch Justice Common Pleas 1668–74; *m* after 28 Oct 1624 Jane (*d* by 1680), est dau and coheir of John Stedman, of Strata Florida and Cilcennin, by Anne, dau of Sir Thomas Jones, of Abermarlais, and *d* 10 July 1674, having had:

EDWARD VAUGHAN, of Trawscoed; MP Cardigan 1678/9–81, a Ld Admlty; *m* after 23 March 1664/5 Letitia (*d* 1716), dau of Sir William Hooker, Ld Mayor London, and *d* 1683, leaving an est s:

JOHN VAUGHAN, **1st Viscount Lisburne**, Co Antrim, so cr 5 June 1695, as also BARON OF FETHARD, Co Tipperary (both I); *b c* 1670; MP (Whig) Cards 1694–98, Ld Lt Cards 1714; *m* 18 Aug 1692 Lady Malet Wilmot (*d* 13 Jan 1708/9), 3rd dau of 2nd Earl of Rochester by Elizabeth, dau of John Malet, of Enmore, Somerset, and *d* 20 March 1720/1, having had, with other issue:

1 JOHN VAUGHAN, **2nd Viscount Lisburne**; *b c* 1695; Ld Lt Cards 1721–Jan 1740/1, MP (Whig) Cards 1727–34; *m* 1st Anne (*dsp* 31 July 1723), dau of Sir John Bennet, Serjeant-at-Law; *m* 2nd Feb 1725/6 Dorothy (*d* 26 Nov 1790), dau of Capt Richard Hill, of Henblâs, Montgomeryshire, and widow of — Waller, of Cards, and *dspm* 15 Jan 1740/1, having had:

   (1) Malet; *m* Capt George Langley, RM, of Frampton Cottrell, Glos, and had issue

2 WILMOT, **3rd Viscount**

1 Anne; *m* 12 April 1719 Sir John Prideaux, Bt, of Netherton

The 2nd s,

WILMOT VAUGHAN, **3rd Viscount Lisburne**; Ld-Lt Cards 1744–69; *m* Dec 1727 Elizabeth (*d* 19 Jan 1764), est dau of Thomas Watson, of Berwick-on-Tweed, and had:

1 WILMOT, **1st Earl**

2 John (Sir), KB, Lt Gen, Col 46th Regt, Govr Berwick; *d* unm 30 June 1795

1 Elizabeth; *m* 11 July 1765 Morgan Thomas Lloyd, of Abertrinant, and had issue

The 3rd VISCOUNT *d* 4 Feb 1766; his er son,

WILMOT VAUGHAN, **1st Earl of Lisburne**, Co Antrim (I), so cr 18 July 1776; *b c* 1730; *educ* Eton; MP (Tory 1783, thereafter pro Fox-North Coalition then Whig) Cards 1755–61 and 1768–96 and Berwick-upon-Tweed 1765–68, Sec to Chllr Exchequer 1761–62, Ld Lt Cards 1762–1800, Commr Trade and Plantations 1768–70, a Ld Admlty 1770–82; *m* 1st 3 July 1754 Elizabeth Gascoigne (*d* 19 May 1755), only dau of Joseph Gascoigne Nightingale, of Mamhead, Devon, and Enfield, Middx, and had an only s:

1 WILMOT VAUGHAN, **2nd Earl of Lisburne**; *b* 3 May 1755; *educ* Eton and Magdalen Coll Oxford; *d* unm 6 May 1820

The **1st Earl** *m* 2nd 19 April 1763 Dorothy (*d* 12 Sept 1805), est dau of John Shafto, of Whitworth, Co Durham, and *d* 6 Jan 1800, leaving by her:

2 JOHN, **3rd Earl**

1 Dorothy Elizabeth; *m* 15 May 1792, as his 2nd w, Sir Laurence Palk, Bt (*d* 20 June 1813; *see* 1940 edn), and *d* 15 Feb 1849

2 Malet; *d* unm Jan 1858

3 Theodosia Charlotte; *b* 27 Feb 1773

The 2nd EARL's half-bro,

JOHN VAUGHAN, **3rd Earl of Lisburne**; *b* 3 March 1769; Col 1800, MP Cards 1796–1818; *m* 2 Aug 1798 Lucy (*d* 27 Jan 1822), 5th dau of 2nd Viscount Courtenay (*see* DEVON, E), and had:

1 John Wilmot Courtenay; *b* 4 May 1799; *d* unm 8 Feb 1818

2 ERNEST AUGUSTUS, **4th Earl**

3 George Lawrence; Capt Army; *b* 8 Feb 1802; *m* 4 Oct 1830 Mary Josephine Roche (*d* 10 June 1895), dau of Henry O'Shea, of Madrid, and niece and coheir of Gen Sir Philip K Roche, and *d* 19 Aug 1879, having had:

   (1) Ernest Courtenay; Maj RA; *b* 7 March 1832; *d* unm 27 Oct 1875

   (2) George Augustus; Capt 33rd Regt; *b* 7 Sept 1833; *m* 12 Aug 1862 Laura Mary (*d* 9 Jan 1898), 3rd dau of Charles Moore, MP, of Mooresfort, Co Tipperary, and *d* 26 Sept 1914, leaving:

1a Wilmot Charles; T/Lt-Col cmdg 22nd Bn Lancs Fus, Maj 20th Hus; *b* 21 Dec 1863; *m* Nora (*d* 1957), dau of Frederick Fane, and *d* 23 Jan 1944, leaving:

   1b Bertha Yvonne; *b* 23 June 1894

   2b Muriel Alice Katherine Evelyn; *b* 10 Aug 1897; *m* July 1921 John Abbott Bosvile Boshell (*d* 13 June 1969)

1a Christine Mary; *m* June 1890 John Charles Ogilvie Forbes (*d* 8 May 1941), of Boyndlie, Aberdeenshire, and *d* 5 Nov 1897, leaving issue

(1) Christine Harriet; *m* 22 Sept 1859 Domingo Arcos (*d* 28 July 1872)

(2) Mary Celeste; *m* 26 April 1877 her cousin Edmund Malet Vaughan, DL, and *d* 2 Aug 1916, leaving issue (*see* below)

4 John Shafto; *b* 31 Oct 1803; *m* and had issue

5 William Malet; Lt 4th Dragoon Gds; *b* 18 May 1807; *m* 24 June 1838 Louisa Emily (*d* 11 Jan 1842), only dau of Edmund Wigan, of Lapley, Staffs, and *d* 13 Dec 1867, leaving:

   (1) Edmund Malet, of Lapley, DL Cards; *b* 12 Feb 1840; *m* 26 April 1877 his cousin Mary Celeste (*d* 2 Aug 1916), dau of Hon George Lawrence Vaughan (*see* above), and *d* 10 May 1882, having had:

     1a Eugène Napoléon Ernest Malet, DSO, JP, Maj Gren Gds Boer War 1899 and WW I (despatches); *b* 19 Nov 1878 (THE EMPRESS EUGENIE and THE PRINCE IMPERIAL stood sponsor); *m* 25 June 1914 Hilda Winifred (*d* 1972), er dau of Neville Hanbury Mander, of Penn, Wolverhampton (*see* MANDER, Bt), and *d* 11 March 1934, leaving:

       1b +Edmund Bernard Malet [Maj Edmund Vaughan, The Bath Farm, Codsall Wood, Wolverhampton, Staffs], Maj Gren Gds WW II; *b* 6 June 1920; *m* 27 Sept 1950 *Jean Elizabeth, dau of Lt-Col J W Nelson, MC, of Sevenoaks, Kent, and has:

         1c +David John; *b* 10 May 1953

         2c +Michael Edmund; *b* 2 March 1957

         1c *Diana Mary (twin); *b* 10 May 1953

       1b *Mary Christine; *b* 18 May 1916

     2a George Edmund, MC; Maj Coldstream Gds WW I 1914–16 (despatches); *b* 1 March 1881; *ka* 15 Sept 1916

     1a Louise Mary; *b* 15 Nov 1879; *d* 10 Oct 1918

1 Lucy Harriet; *d* unm 29 March 1867

The 3rd EARL *d* 18 May 1831; his est son,

ERNEST AUGUSTUS VAUGHAN, **4th Earl of Lisburne**; *b* 30 Oct 1800; MP (C) Cards 1854–59, High Sheriff 1851; *m* 1st 27 Aug 1835 his cousin Mary (*d* 23 July 1851), 2nd dau of Sir Lawrence Palk, 2nd Bt (*see* 1940 edn), and had:

1 ERNEST AUGUSTUS MALET, **5th Earl**

2 Wilmot Shafto; *b* 1839; *d* 27 Jan 1853

3 Edward Courtenay; Capt Rifle Bde; *b* 23 Oct 1841; *d* 3 Oct 1876

1 Elizabeth Malet; *m* 6 Aug 1860 John Inglis Jones, RHG (*d* 15 Dec 1879), of Derry Ormond, Cards, and *d* 12 Nov 1921, having had issue

The **4th Earl** *m* 2nd 5 April 1853 Hon Elizabeth Augusta Harriet (*d* 13 Dec 1883), Maid of Honour to QUEEN ADELAIDE, dau of Col Henry Hugh Mitchell by Lady Harriet Isabella Elizabeth Somerset, dau of 5th Duke of Beaufort (*qv*), and by her had:

2 Gertrude Dorothy Harriet Adelaide; *d* 8 Sept 1869

The **4th EARL** *d* 8 Nov 1873; his est son,

ERNEST AUGUSTUS MALET VAUGHAN, **5th Earl of Lisburne**; *b* 26 June 1836; *educ* Eton and Ch Ch Oxford; High Sheriff Cards 1878; *m* 1st 24 June 1858 Laura Gertrude (*d* 29 March 1865), 3rd dau of Edwyn Burnaby, of Baggrave Hall, Leics, and had:

1 GEORGE HENRY ARTHUR, **6th Earl**

1 Ida Constance; *m* 4 Dec 1886 Brig-Gen Seymour Charles Hale Monro, CB (*d* 30 Sept 1906), est s of Charles Hale Monro, of Ingsdon, Devon, and *d* 16 Jan 1941, having had issue

2 Enid Maud Rose; *d* unm 12 Dec 1877

3 Lucy; *m* 17 Oct 1883 Capt Martin Albirt-Silber, 3rd Bn Middx Regt, and *d* 6 Aug 1916, leaving issue

The **5th Earl** *m* 2nd 15 May 1878 Alice D'Alton (*m* 2nd 25 Sept 1880 3rd Earl Amherst (*dsp* 14 Aug 1910; *see* AMHERST OF HACKNEY, B); *m* 3rd 16 Dec 1914 HSH Prince Jean Sapieha-Kodenski and *d* 27 April 1933), est dau of Edmund Probyn, of Huntley Manor, Glos, and *d* 31 March 1888

His only son,

GEORGE HENRY ARTHUR VAUGHAN, **6th Earl of Lisburne**; DL Cards; *b* 30 July 1862; *m* 24 Oct 1888 his stepmother's sister Evelyn (*d* 30 Aug 1931), dau of Edmund Probyn, and *d* 4 Sept 1899, leaving, with a dau (Enid Evelyn Malet; *m* 18 Nov 1914 Sir James Hamlyn Williams Williams-Drummond, 5th Bt (*see* 1970 edn), and *dsp* 14 April 1958):

ERNEST EDMUND HENRY MALET VAUGHAN, **7th Earl of Lisburne**, JP Cards; *b* 8 Feb 1892; *educ* Eton; WW I in Scots Gds to 1915, thereafter Maj Welsh Gds (wounded, despatches), High Sheriff Cards 1923, Ld Lt 1923–56, V-Pres U Coll Wales 1929, re-employed WW II, KStJ; *m* 1st 16 July 1914 Maria Isabel Regina Aspasia, OStJ (*d* 22 Jan 1944), dau and coheir of Julio Fermin Albert de Bittencourt, Chilean Legation London, and had:

1 JOHN DAVID MALET VAUGHAN, **8th and present Earl Lisburne**

1 Gloria Regina Malet; *m* 1st 7 June 1935 (*divorce* 1952) Maj Sir Nigel Thomas Loveridge Fisher, MC, MP, only s of Cdr Sir Thomas Fisher, KBE, RN, and had:

   (1) *Mark Nigel Thomas Vaughan [Mark Fisher Esq MP, 110 Victoria St, Hartshill, Stoke-on-Trent ST4 6DU]; *b* 1944; MP (Lab) Stoke-on-Trent Central 1983–, Oppn Whip 1985–86, Parly U-Sec Heritage Dept 1997–98; *m* 1971 (*divorce*) Mrs Ingrid Hunt, dau of James Hoyle Geach, and has two sons and two daus

   (1) *Amanda Gloria Morvyth Vaughan; *b* 1939; *m* 1967 *John Klampfer, and has:

     1a *Matthew; *b* 1972

1 (cont.) Lady Gloria Fisher *m* 2nd 10 June 1952 Lt-Col Ronald Philip Flower, OBE (*d* 1993), only s of Philip Arthur Flower and Mrs William Sturges (*see* BANBURY OF SOUTHAM, B), and *d* 27 Feb 1998, leaving by him:

(2) *Philip Ronald [Philip Flower Esq, 9 Dewhurst Rd, London W14 0ET]; b 8 April 1953; educ Eton; barrister; m 1991 *Kate, only dau of Michael Percival, of London SW1, and has:

1a *Joshua Ronald; b 1992

1a *Saskia Martha Nina; b 1995

2 *Honor Morvyth Malet, JP (Cards 1968) [The Lady Honor Llewellyn JP, 4 St Omer Rd, Guildford, Surrey GU1 2DB]; Sub-Visitor St David's Coll Lampeter 1963; m 2 Jan 1943 *Maj William Herbert Rhydian Llewellyn, MC, yst s of Sir David Richard Llewellyn, 1st Bt (qv), and has issue

3 *Auriel Rosemary Malet [The Lady Auriel Vaughan, Haute Folie de Breux, par Tillière sur Avre, 27570 Eure, France]; writer as Oriel Malet; b 1923

The 7th Earl m 2nd 14 Nov 1961 Audrey Maureen Leslie, DStJ (d 18 Feb 1978), widow of Hon Robert Godfrey de Bohun Devereux, JP (see HEREFORD, V), and yr dau of James Meakin, of Westwood Manor, Staffs, and Countess Sondes (see MONSON, B), and d 30 June 1965

LISLE

Arms: Arg. three spears erect gu., on a chief az. a lion of England passant guardant or. **Crest:** A dexter arm embowed in armour, the hand holding a sword, all ppr. **Supporters:** Two lions or. **Motto:** *Bella! horrida bella!* ('Wars! Horrid wars!'). **Creation:** B. (I) 18 Sept 1758.

THE 8TH BARON LISLE OF MOUNTNORTH, Co Cork (John Nicholas Horace Lysaght) [The Rt Hon The Lord Lisle, 30 Springhurst House, Newbury, Berks]; b 1 May 1931; s unc 1997; educ Shrewsbury; late 2nd Lt Gren Gds; m 12 Nov 1957 (divorce) Mary Louise, formerly w of Sir Euan Guy Shaw-Stewart, 10th Bt (qv), and 2nd dau of Lt-Col Geoffrey Reginald Devereux Shaw, of Scottow Hall, Norwich, and has:

1 +JOHN NICHOLAS GEOFFREY [The Hon John Lysaght, 50 The Fairstead, Scotton, Norwich]; b 20 May 1960

2 +David James [The Hon David Lysaght, Wayside Cottage, Sydney St, Ingham, Norfolk NR12 9TQ]; b 10 Aug 1963

1 *Mary Jane [The Hon Mrs Roberts, Carpenters Town, Castle Pollard, Co Westmeath, Ireland]; b 4 June 1959; m 1986 *Paul Stephen Roberts, s of Mrs D McCarthy, of Bingham, Notts, and has:

(1) *Lucy; b 1988

Previous creations: See DE L'ISLE, V, preliminary remarks.

Lineage: JOHN LYSAGHT; Cornet in the Army under Lord Inchiquin (qv) engaged in suppressing the 1641 Rising in Ireland; subsequently settled at Mountnorth, Co Cork; had an est s:

NICHOLAS LYSAGHT; Col of Horse in WILLIAM III's Regt Battle of the Boyne; m Grace, dau of Col Thomas Holmes, of Kilmallock, Co Cork; had an est s:

JOHN LYSAGHT, **1st Baron Lisle of Mountnorth**, Co Cork (I), so cr 18 Sept 1758; b c 1702; educ Trin Coll Dublin; MP Charleville 1727–58; m 1st 17 Dec 1725 Catharine, 3rd dau and coheir of Joseph Deane, of Crumlin, Co Dublin, Ch Baron Exchequer Ireland, by Margaret, sis of 1st Earl of Shannon (qv), and had:

1 JOHN, **2nd Baron**

2 Joseph; m 1795 Henrietta, widow of John Godsell and est dau of 1st Viscount Doneraile (qv), and dsp 1799

3 James; d unm

1 Margaret; m William Hodder, of Hoddersfield

2 Mary; m Kingsmill Pennefather, MP Cashel, est s and heir of R Pennefather, of New Park, Co Tipperary

The **1st Baron** m 2nd 1746 Elizabeth, only dau of Edward Moore, of Mooresfort, Co Tipperary, by whom he had further issue

The 1st BARON d 15 June 1781; his est son,

JOHN LYSAGHT, **2nd Baron Lisle of Mountnorth**; b c 1729; educ Trin Coll Dublin; MP Castlemartyr 1753–60 and Co Cork 1765–68, Sheriff Co Cork 1757; m 1778 Mary Anne (d 19 Oct 1815), dau of George Connor, of Ballybracken, Co Cork, and d 8 Jan 1798, having had:

1 JOHN LYSAGHT, **3rd Baron Lisle of Mountnorth**; b 6 Aug 1781; educ Eton; m 14 Sept 1809 Sarah (d 20 Sept 1857), est dau of William Gibb, of Inverness, and dsp in a hunting accident 26 Nov 1834

2 GEORGE, **4th Baron**

1 Elizabeth; m James Hall and d 1813

2 Catharine; m 1803 Thomas Delany Hall

The 3rd BARON's bro,

GEORGE LYSAGHT, **4th Baron Lisle of Mountnorth**; b 6 June 1783; m 1st 11 Oct 1810 Elizabeth (d 12 April 1815), est dau of Samuel Knight, and had:

1 JOHN ARTHUR, **5th Baron**

1 Elizabeth Mary Anne; d 3 March 1872

The **4th Baron** m 2nd 14 Oct 1816 Elizabeth Anne (d 1 Nov 1825), 2nd dau of John Davy Foulkes, and by her had, with six sons:

2 Catherine Charlotte; m 19 Dec 1844 Rev John Eyre Yonge, MA (d 11 June 1890), Rector Hempstead, Norfolk, and d 22 Dec 1905, leaving issue

The **4th Baron** m 3rd 16 Aug 1836 Elizabeth (d 9 April 1855), 2nd dau of John Church, of Bedford Place, London, and by her had:

2 George Octavius; b 25 Feb, d 20 Oct 1839

The 4th BARON d 7 July 1868; his son by his 1st w,

JOHN ARTHUR LYSAGHT, **5th Baron Lisle of Mountnorth**; b 12 Oct 1811; m 6 March 1837 Henrietta (d 1860), dau of John Church, and had:

1 John Arthur; b 19 Nov 1831; d Jan 1872

2 GEORGE WILLIAM JAMES, **6th Baron**

3 Frederick; b 27 May 1841; m 1st 31 Dec 1867 Annie Elizabeth (d 24 May 1868), est dau of Aycliffe Langford, of Jersey; m 2nd 10 Nov 1868 Elizabeth Lavinia, yst dau of D Le Couteur, of Jersey, and d 1914, having by his 1st w had:

(1) Frederick Edward John; b 1868; m Elizabeth, of Cross Ave, Dublin, and d 26 Feb 1951

4 Henry (Rev); Vicar St Mary's Middleton 1892–1908; b 10 March 1847; m 14 Jan 1875 Susan Isabelle (d 10 March 1926), 3rd dau of Philip Scott, of Hill Ho, Queenstown, Co Cork, and d 7 Dec 1915, leaving:

(1) John Arthur Constantine (Rev); Vicar Carham Northumberland 1904–08; b 13 Sept 1876; educ Pembroke Coll Oxford (BA); m 8 April 1902 Mary Nicholl (d 14 April 1967 aged 86), dau of Adam Fettiplace Blandy, and d 22 Sept 1950, leaving:

1a John Charles Fettiplace; b 1 Jan 1909; educ Clifton; m 1939 *Phyllis Jean, dau of T H Massey, of Newcastle, NSW, and d 1976, leaving:

1b +John Daniel Blandy [John Lysaght Esq, Bank of NSW, Port Kembla, NSW, Australia]; b 1943

2b +Nicholas Richard Fettiplace; b 1946

1b *Primrose Mary; b 1940; m *Jorgen Hendlos Andersen and has two sons

2b *Sarah Louise; b 1953

2a Nicholas Henry Lyster; WW II as Maj Australian Inf; b 5 Nov 1911; educ Clifton; m 1950 *Gillian Mary [Mrs Nicholas Lysaght, 6 Hafod Gdns, Ponthir, Newport, Gwent], dau of R F Huggett, of Risca, Mon, and d 1977, having had:

1b *Mary Susan; b 1952; m 1988 *John Wallace Lanning, s of Maj E C Lanning, MBE, FSA, of S Godstone, Surrey, and has:

1c *Sophie Alexandra Rose; b 1991

2b *Philippa Jane; b 25 April 1954; m 1985 *Nicholas M S Dale-Harris, est s of T I Dale-Harris, of W Kensington, and has:

1c *Lucy Annabel; b 1986

2c *Polly Louise; b 1988

3c *Chloë Alexandra; b 1989

3b Alison; b 15 Aug, d 29 Aug 1959

4b *Elizabeth Anne [Mrs Wayne Lysaght-Mason, Walnut Tree Cottage, 112 Chester Rd, Hazel Grove, Cheshire SK7 6HE]; b 2 June 1961; m 1986 *Wayne Vernon MASON later LYSAGHT-MASON, 2nd s of B A Mason, of Coventry, and has:

1c *Charlotte Jennifer; b 1991

2c *Abigail Frances; b 1992

3a Philip Michael Vaughan; W/Cdr AAF WW II; b 26 Sept 1914; m 1941 Christine (m 2nd 1948 Cdr C G Procter, RN, and d 8 April 1968), dau of J Edwards, of Inverness, and was ka Feb 1943, leaving:

1b *Diana Mary Philippa [Mrs Graham Snell, 2B Moore Park Rd, London SW6 2JT]; b 27 Jan 1943; m 20 Oct 1962 *Graham Edward Frank Snell and has:

1c *Matthew Michael Charles; b 9 June 1965

1c *Louise Jane; b 18 July 1969

4a +Christopher David Blandy; b 20 July 1919

1a *Winifed Joyce; b 4 May 1903

2a Kathleen Mary Lalage; b 28 Jan 1905; m 16 July 1938 John St Barbe Collins (d 1954); s of Lt-Col C B Collins, CMG, DSO, RE, and had issue

3a *Renée Primrose; b 7 April 1907; m 4 July 1936 Edward Montgomery Miles (d 18 Aug 1949), s of Lt-Col Archibald Edward Miles

1 Henrietta Elizabeth; d unm 1891

2 Elizabeth Octavia; d 7 May 1870

3 Philippa Charlotte; m 1884 Arthur Octavius Marwood (d 1912), of Folkestone, and d 5 May 1937, leaving issue

4 Mary Anne Clara; d unm 1858

The 5th BARON d 18 April 1898; his est surv son,

GEORGE WILLIAM JAMES LYSAGHT, **6th Baron Lisle of Mountnorth**; b 20 Jan 1840; educ Plymouth GS; served Maori War 1864–65; m 31 Oct 1868 Amy Emily (d 1918), dau of Ayliffe Langford, of Ventnor, IoW, and St Heliers, Jersey, and d 25 Feb 1919, having had:

1 Horace George, JP Co Cork; b 16 Feb 1873; m 28 June 1899 Alice Elizabeth, 6th dau of Sir John Wrixon-Becher, 3rd Bt (qv), and dvp 30 Sept 1918, leaving:

(1) JOHN NICHOLAS HORACE LYSAGHT, **7th Baron Lisle of Mountnorth**; *b* 10 Aug 1903; *m* 1st 21 April 1928 (*divorce* 1939) Vivienne (*d* 1948), dau of Rev M Brew; *m* 2nd 14 Jan 1939 *Marie Helen [The Rt Hon The Lady Lisle, The Chestnuts, Barge Farm, Taplow, Bucks SL6 0AE], dau of Adolph D Purgold, of Ebnal Lodge, Gobowen, Salop, and *dsp* 29 Dec 1997

(2) (Horace) James William; works manager John Lysaght Ltd, Newport, Mon; *b* 22 Sept 1908; *educ* Wesley Coll Dublin; *m* 1st 1930 (*divorce* 1951) Joanna Mary (José) (*d* 1985), er dau of Dr Jeremiah Stock Nolan, of Bedwas, Mon, and had:

  1a PATRICK JAMES LYSAGHT, **8th and present Baron Lisle of Mountnorth**

  2a Philip Henry; *b* 9 Oct 1933; *educ* Dauntseys; *d* May 1984

  3a +Dermot Edward [Dermot Lysaght Esq, Crews Court, Upton Bishop, Ross-on-Wye HR9 7UF]; late 2nd Lt 8th Kings Roy Irish Hus; *b* 19 Jan 1935; *educ* Dauntseys; *m* 25 Nov 1961 *Tessa Susan, only dau of Capt Terence Hugh Back, CBE, RN, of Blaisdon Ho, nr Longhope, Glos, and has:

    1b +Cornelius James Terence [Cornelius Lysaght Esq, 16A Dunraven Rd, London W12]; *b* 27 Jan 1965; *educ* Eton

    1b *Georgina Mary; *b* 26 Aug 1966; *educ* Exeter U (BA 1988)

  4a Roderic Desmond John; *b* 9 March 1940; *educ* King's Canterbury; *m* July 1970 *Josephine Harrison, and *dsp* 21 Nov 1975

(2) (cont.) James Lysaght *m* 2nd 1953 *Vyrna, dau of J Jones, of Pontypool, and *d* 1977, having by her had:

  1a *Deirdre Elizabeth Jane; *b* 1954

  2a *Philippa Jane; *b* 1956; *m* 1982 *Capt Paul McMahon, RCT, s of J J McMahon, of Gosport, Hants

(3) George Henry; *b* 5 July 1911; *m* 22 Oct 1935 *Pauline Ann, er dau of Patrick J Dillon, of The Grove, Girley, Kells, Co Meath, and *d* 1985, leaving:

  1a +Horace George [Horace Lysaght Esq, Abbeycourt, Kinsale, Co Cork, Ireland]; *b* 3 Aug 1936; *m* 1961 *Anne Phyllis, dau of David Daly, of Cork, and has:

    1b +Stephen Henry; *b* 1963

    2b +John Gareth; *b* 1965

    1b *Susan Anne; *b* 1962

    2b *Jennifer Mary; *b* 1967

  2a +Lawrence George [Lawrence Lysaght Esq, Killestry, Killaloe, Co Clare, Ireland]; *b* 26 Aug 1937; LRCPI, LRCSI

  3a +John Patrick George; *b* 17 May 1939

  1a *Pauline Anne; *b* 4 June 1942

  2a Maire; *b* 11 May 1943

(1) Alice Amy; *m* 14 March 1930 Henry Lysaght (*d* 11 June 1963), 5th s of William Lysaght, JP, of Hazlewood, Co Cork, and had issue

(2) Elizabeth Maude; *b* 9 Aug, *d* 10 Aug 1901

(3) Emily Catherine; *d* 19–

1 Kathleen Emily; *b* 31 Oct 1876

LISTER-KAYE

Arms: Quarterly, 1st and 4th, argent two bendlets sable (for KAYE); 2nd and 3rd, ermine on a fess sable three mullets or (for LISTER); the whole within a bordure wavy azure. **Crests:** 1 A goldfinch proper, charged on the breast with a rose gules (for KAYE), 2 A buck's head proper, erased wavy or attired sable, in the mouth a bird-bolt bendways of the third, flighted argent (for LISTER). **Motto:** *Kynd kynn knawne kepe* ('Keep your own kin kind'). **Creation:** Bt (UK) 28 Dec 1812.

SIR JOHN PHILLIP LISTER LISTER-KAYE, 8TH BT, of Grange, Co York [Sir John Lister-Kaye Bt, House of Aigas, Beauly, Inverness-shire IV4 7AD]; *b* 8 May 1946; *s* f 1982; *educ* Allhallows Sch; lecturer, writer and broadcaster on Conservation of Nature and the Environment, fndr/dir Aigas Tst 1979–, exec dir Aigas Field Centre 1980–, memb Internat Ctee World Wilderness Fndn 1983–, chm Scottish Advsy Ctee RSPB 1986–92, Nature Conservancy Cncl Scotland Ctee 1989–91, NW regnl chm Nature Conservancy Cncl and Scottish Natural Heritage 1992–96, Pres Scottish Wildlife Tst 1996–, hon degree Stirling U 1995, author:

The White Island (1972), *Sea Cull* (1979), *The Seeing Eye* (1980), *One For Sorrow* (1994), *Ill Fares the Land* (1995); *m* 1st 24 June 1972 (*divorce* 1988) Lady Sorrel Deirdre Bentinck, dau of 11th Earl of Portland (*qv*), and has:

  1 +JOHN WARWICK NOEL; *b* 10 Dec 1974; *educ* Trin Coll Glenalmond and RMC Sandhurst; commissioned HLDRS 1996

  1 *Amelia Helen; *b* 12 Oct 1976

  2 *Melanie Jenifer; *b* 12 Oct 1976

Sir JOHN *m* 2nd 1989 *Lucinda Anne, JP (Ross-shire), est dau of Robin Law, of Withersfield, Suffolk, and formerly w of Hon Evan Michael Ronald Baillie (*see* BURTON, B), and by her has:

  3 *Hermione Anne Lucinda Lorne; *b* 1990

Lineage: Sir JOHN KAYE, of Woodsome, Almondbury, Yorks; MP Eye 1610–11; *m* Anne, dau of Sir John Ferne, Sec Cncl of North, and *d* 9 March 1640/1, leaving:

Sir JOHN KAYE, 1st Bt (E), so *cr* 4 Feb 1641/2, of Woodsome; *bapt* 15 Aug 1616; ktd 1641, Col royalist regt horse Civil War, as which raised 700 men in time for Battle of Naseby, being promised an earldom by CHARLES I in the event of victory; *m* 1st 27 April 1637 Margaret, dau and coheir of Thomas Moseley, of Northcroft, sometime Mayor York; *m* 2nd by 1649 Elizabeth, dau of Sir Ferdinand Leigh, of Middleton, nr Leeds, and widow of Thomas Burdett, of Birthwaite, Yorks, and by her had nine children (all *dsp*); *m* 3rd 12 Feb 1660 Catharine, dau of Sir William St Quentin, 1st Bt, and widow of Michael Wentworth, of Woolley, Yorks, but by her had no issue and *d* 23 July 1662; his s by his 1st w:

Sir JOHN KAYE, 2nd Bt; *b* 1641; MP Yorks 1685–98 and 1701–06; *m* by 1663 Ann, dau of William Lister, of Thornton in Craven, and *d* 8 Aug 1706, leaving:

  1 Sir ARTHUR KAYE, 3rd Bt; *b* 1660; *educ* Ch Ch Oxford; MP Yorks 1710–26; *m* c 22 July 1690 Anne, est dau and coheir of Sir Samuel Marow, Bt, of Berkswell, Warwicks, and *dspm* 10 July 1726, leaving:

    (1) Elizabeth; inherited Woodsome; *m* 1st Viscount Lewisham (*see* DARTMOUTH, E) and had issue; *m* 2nd 1st Earl of Guilford (*qv*) and *d* 21 April 1745, having had further issue

  2 Thomas KAYE later LISTER (on inheriting his cousin Christopher Lister's estates Nov 1701); *d* unm 1745, when the estates passed to his n the **4th Bt**

  3 George; *m* Dorothy, dau of Robert Savile, of Bryan Royd, nr Eland, Yorks, and was *bur* 4 April 1710, leaving:

    (1) Sir JOHN KAYE later LISTER-KAYE, 4th Bt, of Denby Grange, Yorks; *bapt* 4 Sept 1697; *educ* Ch Ch Oxford; York: MP 1734–40, Alderman 1735, Ld Mayor 1737; *m* 1st Ellen (*d* 1729), dau of John Wilkinson, and had:

      1a Sir JOHN LISTER-KAYE, 5th Bt, of Denby Grange; *b* 26 June 1725; *educ* Lincoln Coll Oxford; Sheriff Yorks 1761–62; *dspl* 27 Dec 1789, leaving his estates to his illegitimate s:

        1b JOHN (Sir), **1st Bt**

    (1) (cont.) Sir JOHN *m* 2nd 29 July 1730 Dorothy, dau of Richard Richardson, MD, of N Bierley, W R Yorks, and *d* 5 April 1752, leaving by her:

      2a Sir RICHARD KAYE, 6th and last Bt; *b* 11 Aug 1736; *educ* BNC Oxford; Dean Lincoln, 1st Vinerian Scholar Laws Oxford, BCL 1761, DCL 1770, Chaplain to GEORGE III 1766, Rector Kirkby Clayworth, Notts, Preb: York 1768–83, Southwell 1774–80 and 1783–1809, Durham 1777–84, Archdeacon Notts 1780–1809, FRS, FSA; *m* 29 Aug 1791 Helen, dau of William Fenton, of Glasshouse, Yorks, and widow of Thomas Mainwaring, of Goltho', Lincs, and *dspm* 25 Dec 1809, when the btcy expired

The 5th Bt's illegitimate s,

Sir John Lister-Kaye, 1st Bt (UK), so *cr* 28 Dec 1812; *m* 18 Oct 1800 Lady Amelia Grey (*d* 29 Oct 1849), 5th dau of 5th Earl of Stamford (*see* 1970 edn), and *d* 28 Feb 1827, having had, with other issue:

  1 JOHN LISTER (Sir), **2nd Bt**

  2 George Lister; *b* 14 Nov 1803; Lt Col 5th W Yorks Militia, formerly 10th Hus; *m* 24 Aug 1847 Louisa Jessie (*d* Oct 1862), 2nd dau of Capt Dowker, of W Huntington Hall, Yorks, and *d* 18 Sept 1871, having had, with other issue:

    (1) Charles Wilkinson; *b* 28 March 1849; *m* 5 May 1881 Lucy Adela (*d* 16 July 1948), dau of John Champion, of Ranby House, Notts, and *d* 8 Jan 1935, having had:

      1a George Lister; *b* 19 March 1885; Lt Sherwood Rangers and Lincs Yeo (TA); *m* 16 Sept 1919 Susan Katherine (*d* 4 Sept 1951), dau of Frederick Tooth and widow of Lt Col Percival Naylor Kent, and *d* 4 Sept 1951

      2a Russell, OBE (1919), JP (Derbys); *b* 1887; Cdr RN, Gentleman Usher to HM GEORGE VI 1937–39; *m* 1st 16 Oct 1913 Anna (*d* 5 Oct 1947), dau of Capt Edward Bridges, 7th Fus, and widow of Hugh Alleyne Sacheverell Bateman; *m* 2nd 2 March 1948 Katharine Sylvia, dau of Maj Algernon Pilkington, of Florence, and *dsp* 17 Feb 1960

      3a Charles; *b* 1890; Capt Notts Yeo; *m* 1st 6 June 1917 (*divorce* 1928) Mabel (Mavis) Violet, er dau of C M Bramald; *m* 2nd 19 Nov 1935 Vera May (*d* 18 Oct 1983), er dau of Rev (Walter) Hindley, and *d* 14 Aug 1965

      1a Marie; *d* young 23 Jan 1894

      2a Kathleen; *m* 19 June 1907 Alexander Frederic Cecil Talbot Baines, T/Maj RASC (*d* 26 April 1917 of wounds recd in action), yst s of Lazarus Threlfall Baines, JP, of Bawtry Hall, Yorks, and *d* 28 May 1968, leaving issue

    (2) Alan; *b* 21 Aug 1854; *m* 1st 12 June 1879 Mary Jane (*d* 22 June 1915), est dau of Rev Edward Stansfield, Vicar Rustington, Sussex, and had, with two other daus (*d* young):

      1a Dorothea; *b* 1885; *m* 12 Nov 1910 Arthur d'Anyers Willis (*d* 23 Aug 1953), yst s of Rev Canon Frederick William Willis, Rector Warrington, and *d* 14 Dec 1926, leaving issue

      2a Rhoda; *b* 1889; *m* 1st 22 Oct 1914 Maj Guy Spencer Mitchell (*ka* 15 May 1917), King's Liverpool Regt, er s of Capt Spencer Mitchell, Border Regt; *m* 2nd 23 Nov 1918 Reginald Arnold Ball, est s of E J O Ball, of Melbourne, and *d* 5 May 1967, leaving issue

    (2) (cont.) Alan Lister-Kaye *m* 2nd 22 Nov 1916 Mary Clare (*d* 28 Jan 1940), er surv dau of Thomas Fletcher, and *d* 25 Aug 1925

    (1) Jessie Maria; *m* 6 Feb 1872 Joseph Charlton Parr (*d* 1920) and *d* 28 Aug 1929, leaving issue

(2) Louisa; *d* unm 9 Oct 1946

1 Sophia Charlotte; *m* Oct 1831 Rev Henry Spencer Markham (*d* 1844), Canon Residentiary York, Rector Clifton, Notts, and *d* 17 Feb 1877, leaving issue

2 Henrietta; *m* 1st 4 Feb 1836 John Ward (*d* 13 Oct 1840) and had issue; *m* 2nd 24 Feb 1852 V-Adml Russell Eliott, s of Sir William Eliott of Stobs, 6th Bt (*qv*), and *d* 15 Oct 1878

3 Georgiana; *m* 15 Oct 1839 William Ford Hulton, of Hulton Park, Lancs, and *d* 29 July 1877, leaving issue (*see* 1970 edn HULTON, Bt)

The er s of the 1st Bt of the 1812 cr,

Sir John Lister Lister-Kaye, 2nd Bt; *b* 18 Aug 1801; *m* 21 Oct 1824 Matilda (*d* 4 April 1867, only dau and heiress of George Arbuthnot; *m* 2nd 10 Aug 1869 Elizabeth Margaret, 2nd dau of Rev John William Bower, and *d* 13 April 1871, having had by his 1st w, with other issue:

1 Lister; *b* 3 Sept 1827; *m* 25 May 1852 Lady Caroline Pepys (*d* 21 Jan 1902), 3rd dau of 1st Earl of Cottenham (*qv*), and *dvp* 12 April 1855, leaving:

(1) **Sir John Pepys Lister-Kaye, 3rd Bt**, OBE, DL (W R Yorks); *b* 18 Feb 1853; Lt RHG and Yorks Hus, Groom-in-Waiting to HM EDWARD VII 1908–10; *m* 5 Dec 1881 Natica (*d* 13 Feb 1943), 2nd dau of Antonio Yxnaga del Valle, of New York, and *dsps* 27 May 1924, having had:

1a John Digby; *b* 15 Sept 1882, *d* same year

(2) **Sir Cecil Edmund Lister-Kaye, 4th Bt**, JP, DL (W R Yorks); *b* 16 Jan 1854; *m* 16 Sept 1880 Lady Beatrice Adeline (*d* 16 June 1935), dau of 6th Duke of Newcastle (*see* LINCOLN, E), and *d* 27 Jan 1931, having had:

1a Pelham Henry Alexander; *b* 4 Aug 1890; *d* 26 Feb 1891

2a **Sir Kenelm Arthur Lister-Kaye, 5th Bt**; *b* 27 March 1892; *educ* Eton and Trin Coll Oxford; Capt 3rd Bn W Yorks Regt, S/Ldr RAF WWs I (wounded) and II; *m* 19 Jan 1949 Jean Agnes (*d* 22 Sept 1975), dau of John Labett, of London, Ontario, and widow of Maj Ralph E Balders, MC, Roy Canadian Regt, and *dsp* 28 Feb 1955

1a Adeline Cecilia; *b* 24 Sept 1881; *m* 22 Sept 1920 Guglielmo Count de la Feld (*d* 28 Sept 1927)

2a Frances Lois; *b* 28 Oct 1882; *m* 1st 19 Oct 1905 5th Earl of Rosse (*qv*) and had issue; *m* 2nd 15 May 1920 5th Viscount de Vesci (*qv*)

3a Florence; *b* 2 May 1885; *m* 3 March 1908 Col Charles Jerome Vaughan, OBE, JP, DL, RE (*d* 30 Jan 1948), and *d* 19 Oct 1961, leaving issue

2 Alick; RN; *b* 2 Jan 1833; *m* 1856 Sarah, gdau of William Grange, of Meeway, Pa., and *d* 28 Jan 1874

3 Arthur; Capt RA; *b* 12 May 1834; co-fndr Rugby Portland Cement Co; *m* 8 Oct 1867 Eugenia (*d* 12 July 1909), yst dau of Rev John William Bower, Rector Barmston, Yorks, and *d* 5 Dec 1893, leaving:

(1) LISTER (Sir), 6th Bt

(2) Arthur; *b* 15 March 1876; *m* 1st 1895 Lottie Emmeline, dau of John Woodward, and had:

1a John Arthur, of Leslieville, Alberta; *b* 1895; *m* 1923 Emily Alice, dau of James Henry Cooper, of Hayling Island, and *d* 1974 leaving:

1b +Warwick Arthur; *b* 1929

1b *Stella Maude; *b* 1924; *m* 1943 *William John Stewart Boyd, of Victoria, BC

1a Helen; *b* 1896

(2) (cont.) Arthur Lister-Kaye *m* 2nd 1900 Gertrude (*d* 16 June 1945), dau of J Hall, and *d* 26 June 1943, having by her had:

2a Reginald Aubrey; *b* 19 Jan 1902; *d* 2 April 1905

3a Arthur Lister; *b* 22 Sept 1903

(1) Hermione; *m* 12 Dec 1893 William Howard Murphy Grimshaw (*d* 27 Jan 1926), of Stranmills, Co Antrim, and *d* 27 July 1935, leaving issue

(2) Amelia; *m* 10 Oct 1905 Capt Gerald Elliot Kenworthy Browne (*d* 1910), Lancs Fus, and *d* 8 April 1951

(3) Violet Eugenia; *m* 25 April 1899 Arthur Hyde Hulton (*d* 23 June 1966), 3rd s of Sir William Wilbraham Blethyn Hulton, 1st Bt (*see* 1970 edn), and *d* 14 Aug 1962, leaving issue

1 Marcia; *m* 25 Aug 1859 Robert Hartley Bower, JP, DL (*d* 25 May 1886), and *d* 7 April 1906, leaving issue

2 Rosa; *m* 7 Feb 1860 Col James Crosbie (*d* 5 Sept 1897), of Ballyheigue Castle, Co Kerry, and *d* 19 Jan 1925, leaving issue

The 5th Bt's cousin,

Sir Lister Lister-Kaye, 6th Bt, JP (Warwicks); *b* 19 Dec 1873; *educ* privately; Co-fndr and dir Rugby Portland Cement Co; *m* 8 Nov 1910 Emily Mary (*d* 10 May 1944), 2nd dau of John Frederick Starkey, DL (*see* STARKEY, Bt), and *d* 12 Feb 1962, leaving:

1 **Sir John Christopher Lister Lister-Kaye, 7th Bt**; *b* 13 July 1913; *educ* Oundle and Loughborough Coll Technology; dir Bath and Portland Gp; *m* 7 March 1942 Audrey Helen (*d* 20 July 1979), est dau of Edwin James Carter, and *d* 1982, leaving:

(1) Sir JOHN PHILLIP LISTER LISTER-KAYE, **8th and present Bt**

(1) *Mary Eugenia Helen; *b* 5 April 1944; *m* 1970 (*divorce* 1994) Nigel Carrel and has:

1a *Christopher James; *b* 1971

2a *Gareth Nigel Andrew; *b* 1974

3a *Huw Stephen; *b* 1981

1a *Lucinda Helen Jane; *b* 1977

2 Aubrey Robert Lister; *b* 22 Nov 1917; *educ* Oundle; POW WW II; *m* 28 Aug 1965 Nora May, dau of Edward Gratton, of Okehampton, Devon, and *d* 9 Oct 1985

1 *Rosamond Eugenia Mary [Mrs Edward Simpson, 7275 Balaclava St, Vancouver V6N 1M7, BC, Canada]; *b* 5 June 1912; *m* 10 Nov 1945 Maj Edward Osmond Thornhill Simpson (*d* 1992), only s of Edward Thornhill Beckett Simpson, of Walton Hall, Wakefield, and has:

(1) *Mark Thornhill; *b* 28 Dec 1951

(1) *Sarah Thornhill; *b* 27 Oct 1946

(2) *Julia Thornhill; *b* 24 Nov 1947

LISTOWEL

Arms: Gu. two bars or, a chief indented of the last. **Crest:** A demi-lion, couped arg., ducally gorged or. **Supporters:** Two dragons erm., armed and langued gu., wings elevated. **Motto:** *Odi profanum* ('I hate whatever is profane'). **Creations:** B. (I) 31 July 1800 (Ennismore), V. (I) 15 Jan 1816, E. (I) 5 Feb 1822, B. (UK) 8 Dec 1869 (Hare).

THE 6TH EARL OF LISTOWEL, Viscount Ennismore and Listowel, Baron Ennismore, Co Kerry, and **Baron Hare of Convamore**, Co Cork (Francis Michael Hare) [The Rt Hon The Earl of Listowel, House of Lords, London SW1A 0PW]; *b* 28 June 1964; *s f* 1997

Lineage: RICHARD HARE, of Ennismore, Co Kerry; *m* Catherine/Margaret, dau of Samuel Maylor, and had, with an er s (John, *d* unm 1774) and two daus (Mary, *m* 1774 John Bagwell, of Marlfield, Co Tipperary, MP Co Tipperary; Margaret Anne, *m* Edward Croker, of Ballinagarde, Co Limerick):

WILLIAM HARE, **1st Earl of Listowel**, so *cr* 5 Feb 1822, as also earlier 31 July 1800 BARON ENNISMORE, Co Kerry, and 15 Jan 1816 VISCOUNT ENNISMORE AND LISTOWEL (all I); *b* Sept 1751; MP (I Parl) Cork 1796–97 and Athy 1797–1800; *m* 1st 30 May 1772 Mary (*d* 1810), dau of Henry Wrixon, of Ballygiblin, Co Cork; *m* 2nd 5 March 1812 Anne (*d* 2 Oct 1859), 2nd dau of John Latham, of Meldrum, Co Tipperary, and by his 1st w had:

1 Richard, *Viscount Ennismore*; *b* 20 March 1773; MP Athy 1797–1800 and (Whig) Co Cork 1812–27; *m* 10 June 1797 Hon Catherine Bridget Dillon (*d* 13 Oct 1828), est dau of 1st Baron Clonbrock (*see* 1926 edn), and *dvp* 24 Sept 1827, leaving:

(1) WILLIAM, **2nd Earl**

(2) Richard; Lt-Col; *b* July 1803; *m* 20 Oct 1835 Mary Christina (*d* 22 Jan 1888), 4th dau of Adml William Windham, of Felbrigg, Norfolk, and *d* 5 Aug 1881, having had:

1a Richard Charles, CB; Col Cheshire Regt, cmdg 63rd and 24th Regtl Dists, Ashanti Expdn 1873–74, Egyptian Campaign 1882; *b* 8 Aug 1844; *m* 4 Nov 1875 Mary (*d* 22 Feb 1932), only dau of Lt-Gen Sir Charles Ashe Windham, KCB, and *d* 31 Oct 1917, leaving:

1b Richard; Capt Roy Fus WW I; *b* 20 March 1877; *educ* Wellington and RMC Sandhurst; *m* 19 April 1933 Beatrice Lilian Mary, 2nd dau of Rev Henry Teasdale Hutchinson, Rector Reymerston, Norwich, and *d* 7 Jan 1959, having had:

1c Richard Charles; *b* 18 Aug 1934; *d* 4 March 1935

2b Joseph Doughty; *b* 7 Jan 1882; *d* 22 March 1892

3b Francis; *b* 15 March 1884; *educ* Repton and Cooper's Hill Engrg Coll; *d* unm 2 Oct 1906

4b Charles Beresford; *b* 5 Aug 1889; *educ* Haileybury and Keble Coll Oxford; *d* unm 31 Aug 1956

1b Mary Windham; *b* 28 Dec 1878; *d* 13 Jan 1879

2b Mary Windham; *b* 20 March 1880; *d* unm 30 Oct 1954

3b Dorothy; *b* 21 Dec 1885; *d* unm 23 March 1965

2a William Aldworth Home; Col RE; *b* 30 Nov 1846; *d* unm 29 April 1900

3a Francis Augustus; Lt 74th Highrs; *b* 21 Feb 1849; *d* unm 2 Feb 1876

4a Sydney Henry Robert; *b* 22 May 1853; *d* 7 April 1854

1a Catherine Anne; *m* 27 March 1860 Hamilton Sabine Pasley and *d* 21 July 1872, leaving issue (*see* PASLEY, Bt)

2a Mary Letitia; *d* unm 22 May 1916

3a Cecilia Maria; *m* Francesco Figurelli and *d* his widow 28 Dec 1918

4a Beatrice Christine; *m* 5 Dec 1871 Capt Edward Sealy Vidal, 57th Regt (*d* 13 March 1878), and *d* 16 May 1903, having had issue

5a Alice Caroline; *m* 15 Aug 1899 John Windham, 3rd s of Lt-Gen Sir Charles Ashe Windham, KCB, and *d* his widow 15 Nov 1923

6a Evelyn Sohpia; *m* 29 April 1875 Adml Hon William John Ward (*see* BANGOR, V) and *dsp* 24 Sept 1925

(3) Robert; *b* 5 Aug 1808; *m* 9 Jan 1840 Louisa Augusta (*d* 9 Oct 1852), dau of Thomas G French, of Marino, Co Cork, and *d* 8 July 1865, having had:

1a Robert Dillon, of Ballymore, Queenstown, Co Cork, JP; 9th Foot; *b* 25 Jan 1842; *m* 25 Nov 1871 Flora (*d* 17 Oct 1921), est dau of Col William Henry Longfield, of Ashgrove, Co Cork, and *d* 22 April 1936, having had:

1b Robert William, CMG (1919), DSO (1900), DL (Norfolk); *b* 14 Nov 1872; *educ* Harrow and RMC Sandhurst; Brig-Gen Norfolk Regt, Sec Norfolk TAA 1923–38, Actg Sec April 1940–Jan 1941, V-Pres Norfolk SSAFA, Army Welfare Offr Norfolk 1941–53, S Africa 1896, Boer War 1899–1902 (despatches, Queen's medal, five clasps, King's medal, two clasps), WW I on Gen Staff (despatches, Offr Legn Hon); *m* 5 Sept 1908 Helen Mary (*d* 1972), dau of Lt-Col Guy Newcomen Atkinson, of Cangort, King's Co, and *d* 26 Dec 1953, leaving:

1c Robert Gerald Dillon; Lt-Col Roy Norfolk Regt WW II, ADC to Govr and C-in-C Gibraltar 1937–39; *b* 11 Dec 1910; *educ* Gresham's and RMC Sandhurst; *m* 27 March 1951 Eve(lyn) Nora, dau of Thomas Pratt, of Teddington, and *d* 14 Oct 1997, leaving:

1d +Anthony Gerald; *b* 16 Aug 1956

1d *Carol(yn) Elizabeth; *b* 10 April 1952

1c *Elizabeth [Elizabeth Lady Shakespeare, Clare Park, Crondall, Farnham, Surrey]; Section Offr WAAF WW II (despatches, US Bronze Star), Freeman City London 1974; *b* 4 May 1914; *m* 29 Feb 1952, as his 2nd w, Sir Geoffrey Hithersay Shakespeare, 1st Bt (*qv*)

2c *Nancy Violet [Lady Temple, Picton Gorse, Chester]; *b* 9 Nov 1915; *m* 17 Nov 1942 Sir John Meredith Temple, JP, MP (*d* 10 Dec 1994), and has:

1d *Guy; *b* 30 April 1946; *educ* Rugby; *m* 1972 *Philomena Henrietta Baynes, of Seal, Kent, and has:

1e *Christina Philomena Nancy; *b* 1973

1d *Diana Mary, CBE, DL [Mrs Robert McConnell CBE DL, The Priests House, Puddington, Wirral L64 5SS]; *b* 15 Oct 1943; *m* 11 Dec 1955 *Robert Frederick McConnell, er s of Arthur Frederick Vavasour McConnell, of Hampton Hall, Worthen, Salop, and has:

1e *Frederick Bruce; *b* 22 June 1970

1e *Anne Helen; *b* 22 March 1968; *m* 12 June 1993 *Alexander Adam Smith

1b Edith Letitia; *b* 23 April 1874; *d* unm 8 March 1950

2b Winifred Anna Georgina; *d* young 14 Aug 1881

2a Charles Pascoe, Lt Roy Scots Regt; *b* 23 Jan 1849; *d* 1874

3a Thomas George; *b* 1 Sept 1850; *m* 24 July 1895 Catharine (*d* 15 Feb 1947), dau of John Francis, Count de Salis (see 1956 edn Foreign Titles Section), and *d* 26 May 1915, leaving:

1b Adelaide Mary

2b Frances Letitia; *d* 26 Nov 1919

1a Letitia Louisa; *m* 8 Sept 1868 Maj-Gen H W H D Dumaresq, RE (*d* 19 Dec 1898), and *d* 23 Feb 1927, leaving issue

2a Louisa Augusta Anne; *m* 1 Jan 1874 Capt Charles Vernon Anson, RN, and *d* 1898

(4) Henry; Army Offr; *b* 1812; *m* 13 June 1841 Marie Louise (*m* 2nd Alfred Collingwood, of Upper Norwood, and *d* 9 Oct 1878), yr dau of Dominico Santiero, of Turin, and *d* 9 April 1848, leaving:

1a Richard Henry, Capt 13th Regt; *b* 2 Oct 1845; *d* 22 June 1878

1a Henrietta; *m* 15 Aug 1866 Capt John Thomson Bowers, 6th Roy Warwicks Regt (*d* 1889), and *d* 1915, leaving issue

2a Kathleen; *m* 5 Aug 1890 Rev John Campbell Strickland, DD, Vicar Ch Ch Tunbridge Wells, and *d* 3 March 1893

(5) Charles Luke; Capt 7th Roy Fus; *d* unm 22 Sept 1854 of wounds recd the Alma

(1) Letitia; *m* 1824 Richard Oliver Aldworth (*d* Feb 1887) and *d* 19 Sept 1874

(2) Katherine Anne; *m* 1837 Lt-Gen Charles William Morley Balders (*d* 1875), CB, of W Barsham, Norfolk, and *d* 30 Sept 1895, having had issue

2 William Henry; *b* July 1782; *m* 17 July 1806 Charlotte, only dau of Isaac Baugh, and *d* 1848, leaving:

(1) William; *b* 18 June 1808; *d* 1873

1 Margaret Anne; *m* 1799 1st Earl of Bantry (see 1891 edn) and *d* 1835

2 Mary; *m* 1st 1803 Charles Morley Balders, of Barsham, Norfolk; *m* 2nd 1824 Thomas Royse Morgell, Capt of Hus, and *d* 1841

3 Louisa; *m* 1817 John Bushe (*d* 1870), est s of Ch Justice Bushe, and *dsp* 18 April 1855

4 Catharine; *m* 1808 Richard Maunsell (*d* 17 March 1819) and *d* 30 June 1864

The 1st EARL *d* 13 July 1837; his gs,

WILLIAM HARE, **2nd Earl of Listowel**, KP (1839); *b* 22 Sept 1801; *educ* Eton; MP (Whig) Co Kerry 1826–30 and St Albans 1841–46, Sheriff Co Cork 1834, V-Adml Munster 1838, Ld-in-Waiting 1840–41, 1846–52 and 1853–56; *m* 23 July 1831 Maria Augusta (*d* 31 Oct 1871), widow of George Thomas Wyndham, of Cromer Hall, Norfolk, and 2nd dau of V-Adml William WINDHAM [*sic*] formerly LUKYN, of Felbrigge Hall, and had:

1 WILLIAM, **3rd Earl**

2 Richard; R-Adml; *b* 25 Aug 1836; *m* 16 July 1874 Caroline Acland (*d* 8 Jan 1942), dau of Capt George Rideout Pinder, Madras Army, and *d* 16 July 1903, leaving:

(1) William Victor; *b* 17 June 1875; *d* 18 May 1879

(2) Arthur Hugh; *b* 1 June 1877; *d* 12 Dec 1920

(3) Harry Vivian; Capt Durham LI; *b* 10 June 1881; *m* 30 Sept 1909 Ellen Louisa Marie (*d* 8 Feb 1969), 6th dau of Sir Edward Hudson Hudson-Kinaham, 1st Bt (see 1949 edn), and was *ka* France Sept 1914, leaving:

1a Richard George Wyndham, OBE (1942); Capt RN WW II (despatches); *b* 1910; *m* 10 April 1937 Doreen (*d* 1993), 3rd dau of Rev Nixon Chetwode Ram, of Wentworth House, Newbury, and *d* 21 Feb 1995, leaving:

1b *(Rosemary) Vivien [Mrs Roger Clarke, 26 Gowan Ave, London SW6 6RF]; *b* 11 Jan 1939; SRN; *m* 18 Aug 1961 *Roger Philip Lawrence Chetwode Clarke, 3rd s of Reuben Clarke, OBE, of Aylmerton, Norfolk, and has:

1c *Dominic Wyndham; *b* 2 Jan 1963

1c *Cleone Rachen Vivien; *b* 13 April 1964

2b *Caroline Veronica [Mrs Richard Bradley, 14 Moore St, London SW3 2QN]; *b* 21 March 1941; *m* 30 March 1968 *Capt Richard Baden Bradley, Roy Fus, yr s of Baden Redvers Bradley, of Christchurch, NZ, and has:

1c *Robert Edward Baden; *b* 17 Feb 1969

1c *Virginia Clare Baden; *b* 21 June 1970

2c *Victoria Elizabeth Baden; *b* 1973

3b *(Shelah) Virginia; *b* 21 March 1941; *m* 13 June 1964 (*divorce* 1983) James Alan Edward Morshead, er s of A/Cdre Alan Vernon Dillon Edward Morshead, of North Cheriton Manor, Templecombe, Somerset, and has:

1c *Charmian Juliet; *b* 1966

2c *Veronica Anne; *b* 1969

3c *Caroline Violet; *b* 1971

1a *Emily Lavender; *b* 20 April 1912; *m* 1st 1 March 1935 Thomas Edward Montgomery (*d* of wounds recd Arnhem Sept 1944), of Careysville, Fermoy, and has issue; *m* 2nd 1948 Ronald Paul Lancaster Rose (see ROSE, Bt, of Rayners), and by her 1st husb has:

1b *Thomas Carey; *b* 1937

1b *Dawn Vivian [Mrs David Connington, Warden's Lodge, Kingston, Ilminster, Somerset]; *b* 1936; *m* 1963 *David Connington and has:

1c *Sarah Rose; *b* 1964

2c *Lucy Clare; *b* 1966

(1) Eleanor Mary; *b* 3 Dec 1890; *m* 11 July 1914 Harold Godfrey Twist (*d* 6 Feb 1978) and had issue

3 Ralph; Maj RHA; *b* 19 Feb 1838; *d* 19 July 1879

4 Hugh Henry; Lt Bengal SC, Queen's Messenger 1865–95; *b* 1 April 1839; *m* 18 June 1860 Georgiana Caroline (*d* 12 Jan 1920), 3rd dau of Col Birnie Browne, Bengal Artillery, and *d* 25 Jan 1927, having had:

(1) Hugh Henry; *b* 6 Nov 1862; *d* 8 April 1863

(2) Granville Worsley; *b* 12 June 1868; *d* 26 March 1869

(3) Percy Richard, TD; Capt TF 3rd Co London Yeo Matabele War 1897 (medal with clasp), Boer War (Queen's medal with three clasps), WW I Egypt, Gallipoli and Salonika (1915 star, two medals); *b* 2 April 1870; *m* 21 April 1903 Matilda Gertrude (*d* 1972), dau of Henry Frederic Tiarks, of Foxbury, Chislehurst, and *d* 8 Feb 1937, leaving:

1a Hugh Percy; Capt WW II; *b* 1906; *educ* Eton; *m* 1948 (*divorce* 1959) Madeleine Marie Louise Tritter, of Asnières, France

1a Joan Agnes; *b* 25 Oct 1904; *m* 10 April 1934 (*divorce* 1961) G/Capt Peter Warren Johnson and *d* 2 Dec 1975, leaving issue (see JOHNSON, Bt, of New York)

2a Sybil Rika; *b* 7 Oct 1907; *m* 27 July 1934 Maj Hon Robert Edward Udny Hermon Hodge (see WYFOLD, B)

3a Victoria Katherine; *b* 7 Feb 1914; *m* 23 June 1961, as his 2nd w, Maj George Seton Wills, TD (*d* 1979), yst s of Sir Ernest Salter Wills, 3rd Bt, of Hazlewood (*qv*)

4a *Lilah Mary; *b* 26 Aug 1915; *m* 1st 30 Oct 1935 (*divorce* 1946) George Seton Wills (*d* 1979), yst s of Sir Ernest Salter Wills, 3rd Bt, of Hazlewood (*qv*), and has issue; *m* 2nd 14 Nov 1946, as his 2nd w, Col Nigel Victor Stopford Sackville (see COURTOWN, E)

(1) Eleanor Georgiana; *b* 8 April 1861; *m* 10 April 1888 Sir Robert Wilmot, 6th Bt, of Osmaston (*d* 16 Aug 1931; see 1931 edn WILMOT-HOTON, Bt), and *d* 31 Oct 1921, leaving issue

(2) Lina Augusta; *d* an infant 30 July 1867

(3) Katherine Mary; *b* 1 Oct 1872; *m* 1st 22 June 1893 (*divorce* 1902) 6th Marquess of Downshire (*qv*) and had issue; *m* 2nd 19 Nov 1902 Brig-Gen Sir Joseph Frederick Laycock, KCMG, DSO (*d* 10 Jan 1952), of Wiseton Hall, Doncaster, Yorks, and *d* 2 Feb 1959, leaving issue

(4) Florence Adela; *b* 11 May 1876; *m* 2 Aug 1898 Claude Garrard, of Hawkhurst Court, Sussex, and *d* 3 Jan 1923, leaving issue

5 Edward Charles; *b* 8 Jan 1842; *d* 1844

1 Augusta Maria; *m* 19 July 1853 4th Earl of Carysfort (see PROBY, Bt) and *d* 24 March 1881

2 Emily Catherine; *m* 6 May 1857 Sir John Wrixon-Becher, 3rd Bt (*qv*), and *d* 31 Dec 1916, having had issue

3 Sophia Eliza; Hon Lady Bedchamber to HRH THE PRINCESS LOUISE, DUCHESS OF ARGYLL (*qv*); *m* 28 Sept 1854 Arthur Macnamara, DL (*d* 11 Feb 1906), of Caddington Hall, Herts, and *dsp* 8 Dec 1912

4 Victoria Alexandrina (HM QUEEN VICTORIA stood sponsor); *m* 1st 3 Aug 1858 3rd Earl of Yarborough (*qv*) and had issue; *m* 2nd 16 July 1881 John Maunsell Richardson (*d* 22 Jan 1912), of Edmundthorpe Hall, Oakham, and *d* 7 March 1927, having had further issue

5 Adela Maria, Hon Ldy-in-Waiting to HRH THE DUCHESS OF CONNAUGHT; *m* 2 June 1864 Col Cuthbert Larking (*d* 31 Oct 1910), 15th Hus, est s of John Wingfield Larking, of The Firs, Lee, Kent, and *d* 9 Nov 1912, having had issue

6 Eleanor Cecilia (twin with Adela); *m* 9 June 1864 1st Baron Heneage, PC (*d* 10 Aug 1922), and *d* 29 Sept 1924, leaving issue (see 1967 edn)

The 2nd EARL *d* 4 Feb 1856; his son,

WILLIAM HARE, **3rd Earl of Listowel**, KP (1873), JP (Co Cork); *b* 29 May 1833; *educ* Eton; Lt Scots Fus Gds 1852–56 (wounded Battle of the Alma 20 Sept 1854), fought Co Cork (Lib) 1855 gen election; *cr* 8 Dec 1869 BARON HARE OF CONVAMORE, Co Cork (UK), Ld-in-Waiting May-Sept 1880, V-Adml Munster; *m* 31 Aug 1865 Lady Ernestine Mary (*d* 27 Dec 1936), yr dau of 3rd Marquess of Ailesbury (*qv*), and had:

1 RICHARD GRANVILLE, **4th Earl**

2 Charles Ambrose; *b* 5 Sept 1875; *d* 4 May 1885

1 Margaret Ernestine Augusta; *m* 25 July 1895 Reginald Bernhard Loder (see LODER, Bt) and *d* 15 July 1951, leaving issue

2 Beatrice Mary; *m* 4 April 1899 Hon Edward Donough O'Brien (*d* 27 Dec 1943), yst s of 14th Baron Inchiquin (*qv*), and *d* 1960, leaving issue

The 3rd EARL *d* 5 June 1924; his son,

RICHARD GRANVILLE HARE, **4th Earl of Listowel**; *b* 12 Sept 1866; *educ* Eton and Ch Ch Oxford; Maj Co London Vol Regt and Roy Munster Fus, Lt 1st Life Gds 1890–92, Imp Yeo Boer War 1900–01, WW I; *m* 1 Dec 1904 Freda (*d* 10 March 1968), dau of 2nd Baron Derwent (*qv*), and *d* 16 Nov 1931, leaving:

1 WILLIAM (BILLY) FRANCIS HARE, **5th Earl of Listowel**, GCMG (1957), PC (1946); *b* 28 Sept 1906; *educ* Eton, Balliol Coll Oxford, Magdalene Coll Cambridge, Sorbonne and London U (PhD); worked Toynbee Hall, fndg Neighbours Ltd (assoc aiming to redistribute wealth), V-Chm Nat Jt Cttee for Spanish Relief, Chm Friends of Chinese People, Pres China campaign Cttee, memb LCC for E Lewisham 1937–46, 2nd Lt Intell Corps WW II, Assist Lab Whip Ho Lds 1941–42, Ch Lab Whip 1942–44, Parly U-Sec India and Burma 1944–45, PMG 1945–47, Dep Ldr Lds 1947–51, Sec State India and Burma 1947, Sec State Burma 1947–48, Min State Colonial Affrs 1948–50, Jt Parly Sec Min Ag and Fisheries 1950–51, Chm Ctees Ho Lds 1965–76, Govr Gen and C-in-C Ghana 1957–60, Jt Pres Anti-Slavery Soc, author *A Critical History of Modern Aesthetics* (1933); *m* 1st 24 July 1933 (*divorce* 1945) Judith, only dau of Raoul de Marffy-Mantuano, formerly Min Plen Budapest, and had:

(1) *Deirdre Mary Freda [The Rt Hon Deirdre Lady Grantley, Markenfield Hall, Ripon; Flat 2, 2 Warwick Sq, London SW1V 2AA]; *b* 13 Feb 1935; *educ* LMH Oxford; *m* 18 Jan 1955 7th Baron Grantley (*qv*) and has issue

1 (cont.) The **5th Earl** *m* 2nd 1 July 1958 (*divorce* 1963) Stephanie (Stevie) Sandra Yvonne, jazz singer, dau of Sam Wise, of Toronto, and formerly w of Hugh Currie, and by her had:

(2) *Fiona Eve Akua [The Lady Fiona Mackintosh, 133 Sunnyside Ave, Ottawa, ON K15 0R2, Canada]; *b* 24 Feb 1960; *m* 1987 *Christopher G D Mackintosh, s of Charlach Mackintosh, of Calgary, and has:

1a *Billy Douglas; *b* 1990
1a *Emma Frances; *b* 1988
2a *Zoë Beatrice; *b* 1992

1 (cont.) The **5th Earl** *m* 3rd 4 Nov 1963 *Pamela Mollie [The Rt Hon The Countess of Listowel, 10 Downshire Hill, London NW3], hairdresser, dau of Francis Day, of Croydon, and formerly w of John Alexander Reid, middleweight boxer, and *d* 12 March 1997, leaving by her:

(1) FRANCIS MICHAEL HARE, **6th and present Earl of Listowel**
(2) +TIMOTHY PATRICK; *b* 23 Feb 1966; heir presumptive
(3) *Diana France; *b* 7 Dec 1965; *m* 1990 *Timothy J Voss, yst s of Douglas J Voss, of Adelaide, Australia

2 Richard Gilbert; *b* 5 Sept 1907; MA Balliol and Queen's Coll Oxford; Sec Dip Serv, FO and Min Info 1939–46, Fell Stanford U, California, 1947, and Sch Slavonic Studies London U 1949, Visiting Prof Russian Studies U of Indiana 1958, Prof Slavonic Studies London, author: *Russian Literature from Puskhin to the Present Day, Pioneers of Russian Social Thought, Portraits of Russian Personalities between Reform and Revolution, Maxim Gorky, Romantic Realist and Conservative Revolutionary*, and *The Art and Artists of Russia*; *m* 21 Nov 1936 Dora, FRBS, dau of Mark Goudine, of St Petersburg, and *dsp* 14 Sept 1966

3 JOHN HUGH HARE, *cr* VISCOUNT BLAKENHAM (*qv*)

4 Alan Victor, MC (1944); *b* 14 March 1919; *educ* Eton and New Coll Oxford ; Maj Life Gds WW II, served MI6, shot down *Financial Times*; *m* 5 Nov 1945 *Jill Peggotty [The Hon Mrs Alan Hare, 53 Rutland Gate, London SW7], yr dau of Frank William Gordon North, of Pinner, and *d* 10 April 1995, leaving:

(1) +(Alan Simon) Mercury [Mercury Hare Esq, 11 Denbigh St, London SW1V 2HF]; *b* 22 June 1948; *educ* Eton; *m* 1988 *Hon (Alexandra) Elizabeth Charmian Amery, yst dau of Baron Amery of Lustleigh (*see* STOCKTON, E), and has:

1a *Alice Alexandra; *b* 1989
2a *Florence; *b* 25 Jan 1993

(1) *Marcia Persephone; *b* 13 Sept 1946; *m* 12 Jan 1965 her cousin 2nd Viscount Blakenham (*qv*) and has issue

1 *(Ethel) Patricia [The Lady Patricia Milnes-Coates, Moor House Farm, Helperby, York YO6 2RG]; *b* 29 Oct 1912; *m* 1st 12 Nov 1936 Lt-Col Charles Thomas Milnes Gaskell (*k* air crash 5 Nov 1943), Coldstream Gds, only s of Evelyn Milnes Gaskell (*see* RANFURLY, E), and had:

(1) *James; *b* 1937; *educ* Eton and Queens' Coll Cambridge; *m* 1982 *Celia Elizabeth Voelcker, of Montpelier, Nevis, WI, and has:

1a *Charles Paul; *b* 1983
1a *Anna Elizabeth; *b* 1985

(2) *Andrew; *b* 1939; *educ* Eton and Trin Coll Dublin
(3) *Thomas; *b* 1942; *educ* Eton and McGill U

1 (cont.) Lady Patricia *m* 2nd 4 Sept 1945 Sir Robert Milnes-Coates, 3rd Bt (*qv*), and by him has issue

2 Elizabeth Cecilia; *b* 8 May 1914; *m* 1st 22 July 1936 Viscount Elveden (*ka* Feb 1945), only s of 2nd Earl of Iveagh (*qv*), and had issue; *m* 2nd 30 Sept 1947 Edward Rory More O'Ferrall (*d* 1991), yst s of Dominic More O'Ferrall, of Kildangan, Co Kildare, and *d* 1990

LITHGOW

Arms: Per chevron sable and argent three estoiles in chief of the second, and in base in a sea undy azure and of the second a galley, sails furled of the first, flagged gules. **Crest:** An otter on a rock proper. **Motto:** (over crest) *Per mare, per terras* ('By sea and land'). **Creation:** Bt. (UK) 1 July 1925.

SIR WILLIAM JAMES LITHGOW, 2ND BT, of Ormsary, Co Argyll [Sir William Lithgow Bt DL, Ormsary House, by Lochgilphead, Argyll PA31 8PE]; *b* 10 May 1934; *s f* 1952; *educ* Winchester; industrialist and farmer; CEng, FRINA, CIMgt; dir: Lithgows Ltd 1956– (chm 1959–), Bank of Scotland 1962–86, Hunterston Devpt Co 1971– (chm 1987), Lithgows Pty Ltd 1972–, Scott Lithgow 1968–78); memb: Roy Co Archers 1964–, Hon Pres Strathclyde U Students' Assoc 1963–69, Hon LLD Strathclyde 1979, FRSA 1990; *m* 1st 31 Jan 1964 Valerie Helen (*d* 6 Aug 1964), 2nd dau of Denis Herbert Scott, CBE, of Farley Grange, Westerham, Kent; *m* 2nd 29 Sept 1967 *Mary Claire DL (Argyll & Bute 1998), 2nd dau of Col Frank Moutray Hill, CBE, of E Knoyle, Wilts, and by her has:

1 +JAMES FRANK [James Lithgow Esq, Drums, Langbank, Port Glasgow, Renfrewshire PA14 6YH]; *b* 13 June 1970; *m* 6 Sept 1997 *Claire Felicity, yr dau of Lt-Cdr Nicholas John du Cane Wilkinson, RN, of Croy, Inverness-shire
2 +John Alexander; *b* 8 Dec 1974
1 *Katrina Margaret; *b* 5 Oct 1968; MA, BA

Lineage: DANIEL LITHGOW, of Boathaugh, Lanarks, living 1668; *m* Isobel Prentice and had:

DANIEL LITHGOW; *b* 1701; *m* Marion Hamilton and *d* 1776, leaving:

WILLIAM LITHGOW; smith in Biggar, Lanarks; *b* 1730; had:

JOHN LITHGOW; *bapt* 28 March 1754; *m* Anne Paterson and had:

JAMES LITHGOW; *bapt* 26 Nov 1775; *m* Elizabeth Wilson and had:

JAMES LITHGOW, of Huntly Bank, Port Glasgow; *b* 26 Oct 1799; *m* Margaret McNicol (*d* 13 Aug 1861) and had:

WILLIAM TODD LITHGOW, of Drums, Langbank, Renfrewshire, and Ormsary, Argyll; *b* 24 Sept 1854; shipbuilder; *m* 12 Feb 1879 Agnes (*d* 12 June 1929), dau of Henry Birkmyre, of Springbank, Port Glasgow, and *d* 7 June 1908, leaving:

Sir James Lithgow, 1st Bt (UK), so *cr* 1 July 1925, GBE (1945), CB (1947), MC, TD, JP; *b* 27 Jan 1883; Hon Col 416 Coast Regt RA (Clyde) (TA) WW I (despatches), Dir Merchant Shipbuilding Admlty 1916–19, chm: Renfrewshire TA&AFA and Lithgow Ltd, memb: Bd of Admlty 1940–46, Centl Electricity Bd 1927–30, Pres Fedn Br Industs 1930–32, Br Employers' Delegate Internat Labour Conf Geneva 1922–25 and 1933–35, extrdy dir Roy Bank of Scotland, V-Lt Renfrewshire, Hon LLD Glasgow 1946, first Freeman Burgh of Port Glasgow 1951, Order Orange Nassau Netherlands; *m* 11 Sept 1924 Gwendolyn Amy (*d* 14 Sept 1975 aged 78), only dau of John Robinson Harrison, of Scalesceugh, Cumberland, and *d* 23 Feb 1952, leaving:

1 Sir WILLIAM JAMES LITHGOW, **2nd and present Bt**

1 *Margaret Helen [Mrs Geoffrey Rickman, Sullington Old Rectory, Storrington, W Sussex]; *b* 4 Feb 1928; *m* 14 April 1951 *Geoffrey Robert Rickman, yr s of Maj Eric Rickman, of Regents Park, and has:

(1) *Stephen Lithgow; *b* 18 June 1952
(2) *Robert James; *b* 29 Sept 1957
(3) *Andrew George; *b* 2 March 1960
(1) *Catherine Margaret; *b* 23 Oct 1953

2 *Ann Barlow [Mrs William Wilson, Ballochmorrie House, Barrhill, by Girvan, Ayrshire]; *b* 6 July 1931; *m* 29 March 1952 *William Simon Wilson, yr s of W A Wilson, of Renfrewshire, and has issue

(1) *Mark Lithgow; *b* 27 Nov 1960
(1) *Sarah Rosalind; *b* 4 Oct 1953
(2) *Judith Clare; *b* 22 Feb 1957

LIVERPOOL

Arms: Sable a bend between six escallops or and (as an honourable augmentation) on the bend in chief an escutcheon vert thereon a key surmounted by a baton in saltire, or.
Crests: 1 (honourable augmentation) On a chapeau gules doubled ermine a lion rampant of the first, charged on the shoulder with a bezant, thereon an eagle displayed sable, and resting the dexter hind paw on a plate charged with a bend azure, thereon three garbs or, and surmounted by an escutcheon argent charged with an eagle, also sable, charged on the breast with a fleur-de-lys, also or, the lion crowned gold and supporting with the forepaws a man-of-war's church pennant proper, 2 (dexter) A seaweed rock proper, thereon a heraldic sea-lion sejant azure, resting the dexter paw on an escutcheon per fess wavy argent and of the second; in chief a cormorant sable, legged and beaked gules, holding in the beak a branch of seaweed (called laver) inverted vert, and in base a hawk, wings elevated and addorsed of the third, 3 (sinister) A man's leg, unarmed excepting the spur, couped at the thigh quarterly or and sable, spurred gold. **Supporters:** On either side a griffin, wings elevated or, beaked, membered, ducally gorged and on the wing three fleurs-de-lys one and two all azure, the dexter charged on the breast with a torteau thereon a cross-crosslet fitchée argent, the sinister with a pellet, thereon a stag's head cabossed also argent. **Mottoes:** 1 (under the arms) *Soyes ferme* ('Be steadfast'), 2 (over the 1st crest) *Bydd ddiys gog* ('Be steadfast'), 3 (over the 2nd crest) *Demovres ferme* ('Be fast'); 4 (over the 3rd crest) Bee fast. **Creations:** B. (UK) 24 June 1893, E. and V. (UK) 22 Dec 1905.

THE 5TH EARL OF LIVERPOOL, *Viscount Hawkesbury of Kirkham*, Co York, **and of Mansfield**, Co Nottingham, and **Baron Hawkesbury of Haselbech**, Co Northampton, **and of Ollerton**, Sherwood Forest, Co Nottingham (Edward Peter Bertram Savile Foljambe) [The Rt Hon The Earl of Liverpool, 56 Bolingbroke Rd, London W14 0AH; Scotton Farm House, Osberton, Notts S81 00EJ]; *b* posthumously 14 Nov 1944; *s* great-uncle 1969; *educ* Shrewsbury and Perugia U; Jt chm Melbourns Brewery 1975– (md 1970–87), chm and md Rutland Properties Ltd 1987– (dir 1986–), dir Hart Hambleton plc 1986–92, J W Cameron and Co 1987–90, Hilstone Developments Ltd 1987–91, Rutland Management Ltd 1989–, Naylor Automatics Ltd 1988–92; *m* 29 Jan 1970 (*divorce* 1994) Lady Juliana Mary Alice Noel, est dau of 5th Earl of Gainsborough (*qv*); *m* 2nd 1995 *Marie-Ange, er dau of Comte Géraud Michel de Pierredon, and by his 1st w has:

1 +LUKE MARMADUKE PETER SAVILE, *Viscount Hawkesbury*; *b* 25 March 1972

2 +Ralph Edward Anthony Savile; *b* 24 Sept 1974

Lineage: Lady SELINA CHARLOTTE Jenkinson, 2nd dau of 3rd and last Earl of Liverpool of the 1796 *cr* (*see* JENKINSON, Bt); *b* 3 July 1812; *m* 1st 15 Aug 1833 William Charles, Viscount Milton (*d* 8 Nov 1835), est s of 5th Earl Fitzwilliam (*see* 1970 edn), and had:

1 Mary Selina Charlotte; *m* 21 June 1855 2nd Viscount Portman (*qv*) and *d* 4 Jan 1899, leaving issue

VISCOUNTESS MILTON *m* 2nd 28 Aug 1845 George Savile FOLJAMBE (*d* 18 Dec 1869), of Osberton, Notts, and Aldwarke, Yorks, and *d* 24 Sept 1883, having by him had, with two other sons and another dau:

1 CECIL GEORGE SAVILE, **1st Earl**

2 Elizabeth Anne; *m* 31 Jan 1888 Rev William Bury, Rector Ickenham, Middx, Canon Peterborough, and *d* 2 Jan 1930, having had an only dau

3 Frances Mary; *m* 10 Oct 1876 Rev Savile Richard William L'Estrange Malone (*d* 16 Sept 1908), of Pallas Park, King's Co, Rector Dalton Holme, Yorks, and *d* 25 Jan 1921, leaving issue

4 Caroline Frederica; *m* 4 Aug 1881 Arthur Francis Gresham Leveson-Gower and *d* 20 Oct 1895, leaving issue (*see* SUTHERLAND, D)

The est son,
CECIL GEORGE SAVILE FOLJAMBE, **1st Earl of Liverpool**, so *cr* 22 Dec 1905, as also VISCOUNT HAWKESBURY OF KIRKHAM, Co York, AND OF MANSFIELD, Co Nottingham, also earlier 24 June 1893 BARON HAWKESBURY OF HASELBECH, Co Northampton, AND OF OLLERTON, Sherwood Forest, Co Nottingham (all UK); PC (1906), JP and DL (Notts and E R Yorks), JP (W and N R Yorks, Northants and Leics); *b* 7 Nov 1846; *educ* Eton; Lt RN, with Naval Bde NZ War 1863–64 (despatches, medal); MP (Lib) N Notts 1880–85 and Mansfield 1885–92, Ld-in-Waiting 1894–95, Ld Steward Household 1905–07; CA Notts 1891–98; *m* 1st 22 July 1869 Louisa Blanche (*d* 7 Oct 1871), est dau of Frederick John Howard (*see* CARLISLE, E), and had:

1 ARTHUR WILLIAM DE BRITO SAVILE FOLJAMBE, **2nd Earl of Liverpool**, PC (1917), GCB (1920), GCMG (1914), GBE (1918), MVO (1900), JP (Kesteven and Lindsey, Lincs), DL (Lincs); *b* 27 May 1870; *educ* Eton and RMC Sandhurst; Lt-Col cmdg 8th Bn London Regt, formerly Maj Rifle Bde, ADC to Ld Lt Ireland 1898–1900, Boer War 1901–02 (Queen's medal with three clasps), State Steward and Chamberlain to Ld Lt Ireland 1906–09, Comptroller Household 1909–12, NZ: Govr and C-in-C 1912–17, Govr-Gen 1917–20, Hon Col 11th Regt (Taranaki Rifles) and NZ Rifle Bde, KGStJ; *m* 27 July 1897 Hon Annette Louise Monck, GBE, DGStJ (*d* 25 May 1948), only dau of 5th Viscount Monck (*qv*) of Ballytrammon, and *dsp* 15 May 1941

2 Frederick Compton Savile; *b* 20; *d* 21 Aug 1871

The **1st Earl** *m* 2nd 21 July 1877 Susan Louisa (*d* 19 Dec 1917), est dau of Lt-Col William Henry Frederick Cavendish (*see* DEVONSHIRE, D), and *d* 23 March 1907, having by her had with other issue:

3 GERALD WILLIAM FREDERICK SAVILE FOLJAMBE, **3rd Earl of Liverpool**, DSO (1918), JP (Leics); *b* 12 May 1878; *educ* Eton; Lt-Col, Capt Oxford and Bucks LI, Boer War 1899–1902 (two medals, four clasps), ADC to Govr Bombay 1904–05, WW I: cmded 21st Bn KRRC (despatches); *m* 29 July 1909 Constance Isabelle (*d* 29 March 1976), only surv dau of John Holden, JP, DL, of Nuthall Temple and Hawton, Notts, and *dsp* 27 July 1962

4 Josceline Charles William Savile; *b* 16 Oct 1882; *educ* Eton; Capt and Brevet Maj Oxford and Bucks LI; *ka* 6 April 1916

5 ROBERT ANTHONY EDWARD ST ANDREW SAVILE FOLJAMBE, **4th Earl of Liverpool**; *b* 3 April 1887; *educ* Malvern; memb Norton (E R Yorks) RDC 1927–47 and Norton Centl Gp Hull and E R Inf Ctees 1940–45, Inspr (Driffield Div) E R Special Constabulary 1926–45 (Long Service Medal and two bars); *d* unm 13 March 1969

6 Bertram Marmaduke Osbert Savile, MC (1915); *b* 6 Jan 1891; *educ* Eastbourne Coll and RMC Sandhurst; Capt and Brevet Maj W Yorks Regt WW I (despatches), Adj 5th Bn 1923–26, Co Cdr RMC Sandhurst 1926–30; Bursar Haileybury 1931–39; served WW II 1939–42; Sec W R Yorks TA&AFA 1942–47; *m* 15 Jan 1916 Joyce Norton (*d* 21 May 1963), er dau of W B Edmondson, and *d* 13 Oct 1955, having had:

(1) Peter George William Savile; *b* 23 April 1919; *educ* Eton and Trin Coll Cambridge; Capt Herts Regt (TA) WW II; *m* 15 Aug 1942 *Elizabeth Joan (*m* 2nd 9 May 1947 Maj Andrew Antony Gibbs, *see* ALDENHAM and HUNSDON OF HUNSDON, B), yr dau of Maj Eric Charles Montagu Flint, DSO, of Hembury Castle, nr Torrington, N Devon, and was *ka* 2 Sept 1944, leaving:

1a EDWARD PETER BERTRAM SAVILE FOLJAMBE, **5th and present Earl of Liverpool**

1a *Jane Rosamond Mary [The Lady Jane Foljambe, Kilvington Hall, Thirsk, Yorks]; *b* 8 July 1943; *educ* Durham U (BA), SRN 1982; granted rank of earl's dau 28 June 1971

(1) *Ursula Susan Annette Mary [Mrs Stephen Smith, Dawnedge Lodge, Aspley Guise, Bucks]; *b* 8 Nov 1916; *m* 12 Oct 1939 Maj Stephen Carrington Smith (*d* 3 Oct 1998), only s of George Carrington Smith, of Stafford House, Broxbourne, Herts, and has:

1a *Nigel Antony Carrington [Maj Nigel Smith, Redwings, Orchard Close, Brancaster Staithe, King's Lynn, Norfolk PE31 8AX]; *b* 19 March 1943; *educ* Stowe; Maj Light Infantry; *m* 1980 *Jane Elizabeth Lee and has:

1b *Guy Savile; *b* 1983

2b *Miles Stephen; *b* 1985

1b *Sarah Jane; *b* 1982

2b *Diana Mary; *b* 1989

1a *Angela Selina Carrington; *b* 28 Feb 1948; *m* 1971 *John Bunker and has:

1b *Nicholas James; *b* 1977

1b *Alice Louise; *b* 1974

7 Victor Alexander Cecil Savile; *b* 19 Jan 1895 (HM QUEEN VICTORIA stood sponsor); *d* unm 4 June 1975

1 Edith Margaret Emily Mary; *m* 19 Nov 1908 Brig Gen d'Arcy Legard and *d* 3 Nov 1962, leaving issue (*see* LEGARD, Bt)

2 Alice Etheldreda Georgiana Mary; *d* 3 June 1922

3 Mabel Evelyn Selina Mary; *m* 15 April 1909 William Young Woodburn, MD (*d* 1945), of Southsea, s of John Woodburn, of Dennkeld, Victoria, Australia, and *d* 12 Nov 1915, leaving:

(1) Barbara Constance; *b* 1910; *m* 1937 Brig Geoffrey Reginald Grove, 6th Gurkha Rifles (*d* 1993), leaving:

1a *Josceline Philip [Josceline Grove Esq, 34 Stevenage Rd, London SW6 6ET]; *b* 1938; late Capt Cheshire Regt and RGJ; *m* 1970 *Jennifer Clifton Calvert (*see* BROWN, Bt) and has:

1b *Miranda Clifton; *b* 6 July 1974

2b *Venetia Mary; *b* 17 Dec 1976

2a Giles Reginald William; *b* 1945; *m* 1971 *Annette Wakely and *d* 1984 in an accident at sea, leaving:

1b *Thomas Reginald; *b* 1980

1b *Sarah Charlotte; *b* 1972

1a *Alison Rosamond; *b* 1939; *m* 1969 (*divorce* 19–) Graham Finch and has:

1b *Jason Patrick; *b* 1970

2b *Duncan Alexander; *b* 1971

(2) Rosamond Helen, MBE, TD; *b* 1912; *dsp* 1974

(3) *Mabel Evelyn Selina Mary; *b* 1915; *m* 1943 Maj Michael Lewes Dix Hamilton, Lovat Scouts (*d* 1981), and has had:

  1a *Stephen Alexander Michael; *b* 1947

  1a *Selina Mary; *b* 1944; *m* 1968 *John Cedric Eger and has:

    1b *Elizabeth Selina; *b* 1971

    2b *Helen Esther; *b* 1973

  2a Elizabeth Medley (twin); *b* 1947; *d* 1997

4 Margaret Susan Louisa Mary; *b* 14; *d* 16 Jan 1884

5 Constance Blanche Alethea Mary; *m* 13 Dec 1911 Rev Hezekiah Astley Kemp Hawkins, Vicar St Mary, Kilburn, Yorks (*d* 1927), 2nd s of Hezekiah Hawkins, of Margate, and *d* 16 Aug 1977, leaving issue

6 Rosamond Sylvia Diana Mary; *m* 3 Sept 1918 13th Earl of Leven and Melville (*qv*) and *d* 12 April 1974, leaving issue

LLEWELLYN

Arms: Per chevron or and gules, in chief a lion passant and in base three chevronels all counterchanged. **Crest:** A demi-dragon holding in the mouth a dexter hand couped proper. **Motto:** *Moribus fortuna vincitur* ('Character is destiny'). **Creation:** Bt. (UK) 31 Jan 1922.

SIR HENRY (HARRY) MORTON LLEWELLYN, 3RD BT, CBE (1953, OBE 1945), DL (Mon 1952) [Sir Harry Llewellyn Bt CBE DL, Ty'r Nant, Llanarth, Raglan, Gwent NP5 2AR]; *b* 18 July 1911; *s* bro 1978; *educ* Oundle and Trin Coll Cambridge (BA 1933, MA 1937); Lt-Col Warwicks Yeo WW II Middle East, N Africa, Italy and NW Europe (despatches twice, US Legn Merit); High Sheriff Mon 1966, JP 1954–68; chm C L Clay & Co Ltd 1936–47, Davenco (Engineers) Ltd, Whitbread Wales Ltd 1958–74 (Pres 1974–), Wales Bd Eagle Star Insur 1962–82 and Wales Branch Nationwide Bldg Soc 1974–86; dir: TWW Ltd 1958–68, Lloyds Bank (S Wales Region) 1963–82, Chepstow Racecourse 1952–; memb: Nat Hunt Ctee 1946–, Jockey Club 1969–, Pres IOD (Wales) 1963–65, Chm Civic Tst (Wales), memb Welsh Tourist Bd 1969–75, Chm Sports Cncl for Wales 1971–80, memb cncl WWF 1985–, Pres Br Show Jumping Assoc 1967–69, Br Equestrian Fedn 1975–79, Roy Welsh Ag Soc 1985 and Roy Internat Show 1990–92; Bronze Medal Show Jumping Olympic Games 1948, Gold Medal 1952, MFH Monmouthshire 1952–57 and 1963–65, Roy Humane Soc Medal 1956, ktd 1977; *m* 14 April 1944 Hon Christine Saumarez (*d* 20 April 1998), yr dau of 5th Baron de Saumarez (*qv*), and has:

1 +DAVID (DAI) ST VINCENT; *b* 2 April 1946; *educ* Eton; dir Dorchester Club 1994–95, International Sportsmen's Club Aug–Oct 1997; *m* 1980 (*divorce* 1987) Vanessa Mary Theresa, yr dau of Lt-Cdr Theodore Bernard Peregrine Hubbard, RN (*see* NORFOLK, D), and has:

  (1) *Olivia Anna Christina; *b* 1980

  (2) *Arabella Dominica; *b* 1983

2 +Roderic (Roddy) Victor [Roderic Llewellyn Esq, Old George House, Leafield, Oxon OX8 5NP]; *b* 9 Oct 1947; *educ* Shrewsbury; landscape gardener, jnlst, broadcaster and author; *m* 1981 *Tatiana Manora Caroline, dau of Paul Soskin, film producer, and has:

  (1) *Alexandra Manora Tatiana; *b* 1982

  (2) *Natasha Anna Christina; *b* 1984

  (3) *Rose-Anna Alice; *b* 1987

1 *Anna Christina [Mrs Christopher Elletson, 5a Egerton Terrace, London SW3 2BX]; *b* 29 May 1956; *m* 1987 *Christopher Charles Elletson, s of C E Elletson, of Douglas, IOM

Lineage: DAVID LLEWELLYN; *b* 1775; *m* Margaret — and had:

DAVID LLEWELLYN, of Parc Isaf and Parc Usha Farms, Cwmparc, Glam; *b* 1810; *m* Elizabeth Jones, of Ogmore Valley, Glam, and *d* 1890, leaving, with two er sons (Griffith, *b* 1846, *m* Elizabeth Jones and *d* 1917, leaving issue; David, *b* 1847, *d* unm 1865) and a dau (Elizabeth, *b* 1849, *d* 1866):

REES LLEWELLYN, JP, of Bwllfa House, Glam; *b* 23 June 1851; chm Welsh Associated Collieries, Lysaght Iron and Steel; High Constable Muskin Higher 1899, High Sheriff Glam 1916, Provincial Grand Master (Freemasons) Glam; *m* 15 May 1877 Elizabeth Llewellyn (*d* 1929) and *d* 21 Aug 1919, leaving:

1 DAVID RICHARD (Sir), **1st Bt**

2 Walter Powell; *b* 7 Nov 1882; *dsp* 28 May 1922

3 Rees Thomas; *b* 16 June 1885; *d* 8 May 1886

4 William Morgan; *b* 11 June 1887; MFH Bwllfa 1920–43, High Sheriff Breconshire 1928; *d* unm 19 Sept 1943

5 Griffith; *b* 8 Aug 1888; sr ptnr Llewellyn & Hann, dir Powell Duffryn; *m* 1916 Lilian Sandbrook and *dsp* 26 June 1967

6 Morton Howell; *b* 7 April 1890; Capt RE, High Sheriff Breconshire 1938; *m* 14 April 1916 Hannah White (*d* 1951) and *d* following a shooting accident 15 Sept 1958, leaving issue

1 Anne Matilda; *b* 3 Nov 1880; *m* 12 Sept 1906 Charles Edwards and had issue

The est s,

Sir David Richard Llewellyn, 1st Bt (UK), so *cr* 31 Jan 1922, of Bwllfa, Aberdare, Co Glamorgan, JP (Glam); *b* 9 March 1879; LLD; chm Welsh Assoc Collieries Ltd, Graigola Merthyr Co, North's Navigation Collieries (1889) Ltd and John Lysaght Ltd, v-chm Amalgamated Anthracite Collieries Ltd, dir GKN, Powell Duffryn Assoc Collieries Ltd, Powell Duffryn Steam Coal Co Ltd, Past-Pres U Coll Cardiff, MFH Bwllfa, CStJ; *m* 19 April 1905 Magdalene Anne (*d* 1 Feb 1966), dau of Rev Dr Henry Harries, DD, of Porthcawl, Glam, and *d* 15 Dec 1940, leaving:

1 **Sir Rhys Llewellyn, 2nd Bt**; *b* 9 March 1910; *educ* Oundle and Trin Coll Cambridge (BA 1931, MA 1935); Lt-Col Welsh Gds Supp Res of Offrs June 1939, WW II (despatches), RARO 1945–61; High Sheriff Glamorgan 1950–51, MFH Talybont 1936–40, CStJ; *d* unm 25 April 1978

2 Sir HENRY (HARRY) MORTON LLEWELLYN, **3rd and present Bt**

3 David Treharne (Sir); *b* 17 Jan 1916; *educ* Eton and Trin Coll Cambridge (BA 1938); Capt Welsh Gds WW II; MP (C) Cardiff N 1950–59, Parly U-Sec Home Office 1951–52, memb Bdcstg Cncl Wales 1960–61, Welsh Advsy Cncl Civ Aviation 1961, dir Br Telemeter Home Viewing Ltd and James Howell and Co Ltd, jnlst (J Bliss *Sporting Life*), broadcaster, author: *Nye The Beloved Patrician*, ktd 1960; *m* 18 Feb 1950 *Joan Anne, OBE [Lady Llewellyn OBE, The Well House, Yattendon, nr Newbury, Berks], dau of Robert Henry Williams, of Bonvilston House, Bonvilston, nr Cardiff, and *d* 1992, having had:

  (1) +Robert Crofts Williams [Robert Llewellyn Esq, 5 Drakefield Rd, London SW17 8RT]; *b* 19 Nov 1952; *educ* Eton; *m* 1st 10 Oct 1975 Susan Constance (*d* 1980), est dau of Hubert Millet-Stirling, of Cape Town, S Africa; *m* 2nd 1981 (*divorce* 1989) Lucinda Roberte, only dau of Alexander Clement Gilmour (*see* GILMOUR OF CRAIGMILLAR, B); *m* 3rd 1989 *Sarah Dominica, dau of Maj Gavin Anderson, of Swallow Cottage, Little Cressingham, Norfolk, and Mrs Michael Giles (*see* KILMAINE, B), and by his 2nd w has:

    1a +Dominic Robin Crofts; *b* 1984

    1a *Zara Marie-Louise; *b* 1986

  (2) +David Rhidian; *b* 21 Aug 1957; *m* 1984 *Mrs Susan Edwards, er dau of Edward Edmiston, Headmaster Papplewick Sch, Ascot

  (1) *Emma Victoria [Mrs Bruce Dinwiddy, c/o FCO, King Charles St, London SW1A 2AH]; *b* 28 Feb 1951; *m* 29 June 1974 *Bruce H Dinwiddy, HC Tanzania, yst s of T L Dinwiddy, of Aldeburgh, Suffolk, and has:

    1a *Thomas Rhidian; *b* 1979

    1a *Celia Rose; *b* 22 Sept 1976

4 +(William Herbert) Rhidian, MC, DL (Cards 1963) [Maj Rhidian Llewellyn MC DL, 4 St Omer Rd, Guildford, Surrey GU1 2DB]; *b* 8 July 1919; *educ* Eton and RMC Sandhurst; Maj Welsh Gds WW II (despatches); CC Cards 1961–70, High Sheriff Cards 1967, memb Hosp Bd Wales 1964–70; *m* 2 Jan 1943 *Lady Honor Morvyth Vaughan, JP (1968), 2nd dau of 7th Earl of Lisburne (*qv*), and has:

  (1) +Trefor Wilmot [Trefor Llewellyn Esq, Hill Farm House, Ipsden, Oxon]; *b* 2 July 1947; *educ* Eton and U Coll Wales Cardiff; *m* 1 Dec 1973 *Heather Mary, dau of Richard Lucas, of The Lydiate, Heswall, Cheshire, and has:

    1a *Catrin Sarah Malet; *b* 1981

    2a *Elinor Victoria Sian; *b* 1985

  (1) *Cordelia [Mrs Angus Lamont, Beech House, Chiddingfold, Surrey GU8 4XJ]; *b* 14 April 1949; *m* 12 July 1969 *Angus Ross Lamont, yr s of Charles Lamont, of Virginia Water, and has:

    1a *Douglas Ross; *b* 1973

    1a *Camilla Rose; *b* 1971

  (2) *Gaynor Malet [Mrs Edward Garrett, 146 New Kings Rd, London SW6]; *b* 28 March 1952; *m* 1977 *Edward James Sutcliffe Garrett and has:

    1a *Nicholas Edward Sutcliffe; *b* 1982

    1a *Lucinda Felicity; *b* 1979

    2a *Melissa Kinvara; *b* 1987

1 *Margaret Elaine [Lady Anderson, 9 Hamilton House, Vicarage Gate, London W8 4HL]; *b* 7 March 1913; *m* 1st 28 Feb 1935 Sir Donald Forsyth Anderson (*d* 1973), yr s of Sir Alan Garratt Anderson, GBE, and had:

  (1) *Gillian Elizabeth [Mrs Gillian Davies, 27 Earl St, Randwick, NSW 2031, Australia]; *b* 15 Jan 1936; MB, MS 1962, MRCS, LRCP 1961; *m* 24 May 1966 (*divorce* 19–) William Peter Grant Davies, only s of Grant Davies, of NSW, and has issue

  (2) *Jennifer Forsyth [Mrs Anthony Loehnis, Haughton House, Churchill, Oxon]; *b* 10 Nov 1937; *m* 7 Aug 1965 *Anthony David Loehnis CMG, only s of Sir Clive Loehnis, KCMG, and has issue (*see* HARROWBY, E)

  (3) *Lindsay Garrett [Mrs Robert Fox, Cheriton House, Alresford, nr Winchester, Hants SO24 0QA]; *b* 4 Dec 1942; *m* 6 Sept 1962 *Robert Trench Fox (*see* ASHTOWN, B) and has issue

  (4) *Susan Elaine [The Rt Hon The Countess of Darnley, Netherwood Manor, Tenbury Wells, Worcs]; *b* 4 Sept 1945; *m* 14 Oct 1965 *11th Earl of Darnley (*qv*) and has issue

2 *Elizabeth Aileen Maud [Mrs David Prichard, Gobion Manor, Abergavenny, Gwent NP7 9AY]; *b* 9 Oct 1914; WW II as W/O WAAF; MFH; *m* 25 June 1946 Lt-Col David Mathew Caradoc Prichard (*d* 1986), Roy Welsh Fus, yr s of Col Hubert Cecil Prichard, CBE, of Pwllywrach, Cowbridge, and has had:

  (1) Robert David Caradoc; *b* 17 Nov 1947; *educ* Wellington and Corpus Christi Coll Cambridge; with Kleinwort Benson; *d* unm 1995

(2) *Colin Hubert Llewellyn [Colin Prichard Esq, Lodge Farm, Barcombe, E Sussex BN8 4TH]; *b* 19 Aug 1949; *educ* Wellington; *m* 1977 *Jane Helen, dau of Paul Chamberlain, of Groombridge, E Sussex, and has:

  1a *Claire Helen; *b* 1982

  2a *Eleanor Jane; *b* 1984

  3a *Lydia Diana; *b* 1988

(3) *William De Burgh [William Prichard Esq, Gobion Manor, Abergavenny, Gwent NP7 9AY]; *b* 31 March 1953; *educ* Wellington; Capt Welsh Gds; *m* 1983 *Judith Elizabeth Thorneycroft, dau of Richard Thorneycroft Salt, of The Old Farm, Over Whitacre, Warwicks, and has:

  1a *Thomas David Caradoc; *b* 1990

  1a *Georgina Lydia; *b* 1986

  2a *Olivia Charlotte; *b* 1988

3 Marjorie Joyce; *b* 22 March 1917; WW II as W/O WAAF (despatches); *m* 24 June 1947 Frank May Reid Byers (*d* 13 April 1973), yst s of Sir John William Byers, MD, of Waterfoot House, Newcastle, Co Down, and *d* 24 Oct 1971, having had issue

4 *Magdalene Clare [Mrs Alexander Stewart-Moore, Moyarget Farm, 98 Moyarget Rd, Ballycastle, Co Antrim]; *b* 3 Feb 1922; *m* 1 June 1948 *Alexander Wyndham Hume Stewart-Moore, 2nd s of James Stewart-Moore, of Ballydivity, Dervock, and has:

(1) *Christopher Wyndham Hume [Christopher Stewart-Moore Esq, 71 Milson Rd, London W14 0LH]; *b* 10 Aug 1949; *educ* Shrewsbury; *m* 1981 *Penelope Sarah, yr dau of Edward Foster James, CMG, OBE, and has:

  1a *Henry Wyndham Hume; *b* 1983

  1a *Eliza Caroline Clare; *b* 1987

(2) *Michael David; *b* 10 Oct 1950; *educ* Shrewsbury and Trin Coll Dublin; *m* 1981 *Susan Jane, est dau of John Alan Lionel Kinnaird, of Capeldale, Killinchy, Co Down, and has:

  1a *Thomas John; *b* 1983

  2a *Edward Alexander; *b* 1986

  1a *Sally Frances; *b* 1990

(3) *(James) Anthony; *b* 7 July 1953; *educ* Shrewsbury; *m* 1982 *Guion, yr dau of Edward Fifield, of Greensboro, NC, USA, and has:

  1a *James Alexander; *b* 1987

  1a *Gillian; *b* 1989

(1) *Gillian Clare [Mrs Donald Keith, The Manor House, Carleton Green, Yorks]; *b* 30 March 1956; *m* 1987 *Donald Murray Keith, s of Donald Keith, FRACOG, and has:

  1a *Frederick Donald David; *b* 1993

  1a *Emily Margaret; *b* 1989

LLOYD

Arms: Per bend sable and gules a lion rampant regardant argent, goutté gules, surmounted of a fess or charged with a barrulet dancettée azure, a bordure invected or. **Crest:** A demi-lion argent goutté and langued gules, holding in bend forward two spears sable, points upwards or. **Motto:** (over the shield) *Honorabile et fortiter* ('Honourably and bravely'). **Creation:** Bt. (UK) 23 July 1960.

SIR RICHARD ERNEST BUTLER LLOYD, 2ND BT, of Rhu, Co Dunbarton [Sir Richard Lloyd Bt, Sundridge Place, Sundridge, Kent TN14 6DD]; *b* 6 Dec 1928; *s f* 1987; *educ* Wellington and Hertford Coll Oxford (BA 1952, MA 1957); commissioned Black Watch 1948, Capt and ADC to GOC Malaya 1948–49, dir Glyn Mills and Co 1964–70, ch exec Williams and Glyn's Bank 1970–78, dep chm Hill Samuel and Co 1978–80 (ch exec 1980–87, chm 1987–91) chm: Vickers plc 1992–97 and Argos plc 1995–, V Chm Advsy Ctee OECD 1996–, non exec dir SIEBE plc 1988–; Govr Ditchley Fndn, Pres Br Heart Fndn, memb: Ind Devpt Advisy Bd 1972–76, NEDC 1973–77, Cncl CBI 1978–96, Overseas Projects Bd 1981–85, Advsy Bd Roy Coll Def Studies 1987–95; *m* 6 June 1955 *Jennifer Susan Margaret, er dau of Brig Ereld Boteler Wingfield Cardiff, CB, CBE, of Easton Court, Ludlow, Salop, and has:

1 +(RICHARD) TIMOTHY BUTLER [Timothy Lloyd Esq, Howe Combe Farmhouse, Howe Rd, Watlington, Oxon OX9 5EY]; *b* 12 April 1956; *educ* Wellington and RAC Cirencester; FRICS; *m* 1989 *Wilhelmina S M, yr dau of G H A Schut, of Amstelveen, The Netherlands, and has:

  (1) +Sebastian George Butler; *b* 1996

  (1) *Daphne Florence Wilhelmina; *b* 1993

2 +Simon Wingfield Butler; *b* 26 July 1958; *educ* Eton and Hertford Coll Oxford (BA); *m* 1984 *Catherine Rosemary Chanter and has:

  (1) +Christopher Timothy Butler; *b* 1986

  (2) +Jeremy Richard Butler; *b* 1988

  (1) *Jessica; *b* 1991

3 +Henry Butler; *b* 22 Feb 1965; *educ* Eton and Bristol U (BSc); *m* 1992 *Joanna M, er dau of James Gourlay Freeland, of Grenna House, Chilson, Oxon, and has:

  (1)+Edward James Butler; *b* 1994

  (2) +Thomas Butler; *b* 1996

  (1) *Alice Elizabeth; *b* 1997

Lineage: LEWIS LLOYD, of Alberbury, Salop; living 1582; had:

JOHN LEWIS LLOYD, of Shrewsbury; burgess 1582; had, with two other sons (Lewis, *d* 1670; Thomas, of Shrewsbury, *d* 1676, leaving William, *d* 1686):

WILLIAM LLOYD, of Shrewsbury; *d* 1646, leaving:

JOHN LLOYD, of Shrewsbury; burgess 1677; had:

JOHN LLOYD, of Abbey Foregate, Shrewsbury; burgess 1677 but declared too young to vote; had:

THOMAS LLOYD, of Rowton, Salop; had property at Wattlesborough, Salop, 1708; burgess Shrewsbury 1721; *m* Sarah — (*bur* 1781 aged 78) and was *bur* 15 Aug 1736, leaving, with other issue:

JOHN LLOYD, of Shrewsbury; burgess 1774; *m* 22 June 1758 Mary, dau of William Bucknall, of Shrewsbury, and was *bur* 20 May 1794, leaving, with other issue:

THOMAS LLOYD, of Shrewsbury; burgess 1783, Mayor 1810; *m* 18 Aug 1789 Eliza Bella (*d* 30 June 1831), dau of Thomas Wright, of Poultry, London, and *d* 17 Jan 1829, having had, with three daus (Mary, *m* 9 May 1823 Rowland Hunt (*bur* 27 Feb 1835), of Boreatton, and *d* 1861, having had issue; Frances, *m* Rev James Williams, DD, Rector Llanfairnghornwy; Charlotte, *d* 28 May 1827):

JOHN THOMAS LLOYD, of The Stone House, Shrewsbury; burgess 1812; *m* 5 Oct 1819 Harriet (*d* 12 March 1880), yr dau of Rt Rev Samuel Butler, DD, Bp Lichfield, and *d* 4 May 1826, leaving:

1 Thomas Bucknall (Ven), of The Whitehall, Shrewsbury; *b* 23 May 1824; *educ* St John's Coll Cambridge (MA); Vicar St Mary's Shrewsbury, Rector Edgmond, Archdeacon Salop; *m* 21 Aug 1849 Sophia Elizabeth (*d* 27 Nov 1858), est dau of

Rev Percival Spearman Wilkinson, of Mount Oswald, Durham, and *d* 25 Feb 1896, leaving:

(1) John Bucknall, of The Whitehall and later Dorrington Grove, Salop, JP; *b* 30 Dec 1852; *educ* Winchester and St John's Coll Cambridge; *m* 23 July 1884 Adela Maud (*d* 17 May 1907), 2nd dau of Percival Spearman Wilkinson, of Mount Oswald, and *d* 15 Dec 1932, having had:

1a Lewis John Bucknall; *b* 19 Sept 1887; Lt King's Salop LI WW I; *ka* France 25 April 1915

1a Violet Maud; *b* 6 April 1889; *m* 1 March 1927 Maj Walter Norman Withers and had issue

2a Gwyneth Mary Sophia; *b* 5 Aug 1892; *m* 11 Sept 1928 Capt Arthur John William Allan, RA, s of Maj L F Allan, of Johannesburg, and had issue

(1) Sophia Harriet; *m* 12 April 1877 Rev Robert Mowbray Tillard (*d* 8 June 1915), Rector Rodington, Salop, 4th s of Philip Tillard, of Stukeley Hall, Hunts, and *d* 12 Nov 1937, leaving issue

(2) Alice Mary; *d* 11 Nov 1949

(3) Ellen Isabella; *m* 1883 Charles Mercer Adam and *d* 7 July 1936

(4) Mary Beatrice; *d* 8 Oct 1941

2 WILLIAM BUTLER

1 Eliza Harriet; *d* 19 Oct 1907

2 Mary Lucy; *m* Rev John Adams Cree, Vicar Marlow

3 Mary Jane; *m* 27 Sept 1849 Rev William Joseph Whately, Rector Rise, Preb York

JOHN LLOYD's yr son,

WILLIAM BUTLER LLOYD, of Monkmoor and Preston Montford, Salop, JP, DL; *m* 21 May 1851 Jane Emilia (*d* 1913), 5th dau of Rev George Hunt, of Wadenhoe, Northants, and had:

1 George Butler, of Shelton Hall, Salop, JP (Shrewsbury); *b* 8 Jan 1854; *educ* Marlborough and St John's Coll Cambridge; CC Salop; MP Shrewsbury 1913–22; *m* 22 Jan 1880 Constance Mary, 2nd dau of Col Richard Jenkins, 1st Bengal Cav, of Bicton Hall, Salop, and *d* 28 March 1930, leaving:

(1) William Butler; *b* 6 Nov 1880; *educ* Ch Ch Oxford (BA 1904, MA 1907); Judge Supreme Ct Nigeria; barrister Inner Temple; *m* 14 April 1909 Kathleen, only dau of Andrew George O'Farrell, of Middleton Lodge, Co Cork, and *d* 25 Feb 1944, leaving:

1a *Helen Mary; *m* 16 April 1936 William Ewart Matthews and has:

1b *David William, FGC, AMIMM; *b* 23 Feb 1939; *educ* Peterhouse Cambridge (MA, PhD)

2b *Patrick Kenneth, MSc; *educ* U Coll N Wales and New Brunswick, Canada

2a *Barbara Kathleen; *b* 9 May 1924; *m* 15 Sept 1946 William Robert McIlroy

(2) Thomas Butler; *b* 17 Nov 1880; *m* 1st 14 Jan 1914 (*divorce* 1942) Sibyl Mary Grace (*d* 16 Nov 1969), er dau of Maj-Gen Arthur Domville Corbet, CB (*see* 1970 edn CORBET, Bt); *m* 2nd Brenda Lort Lloyd and *dsp* 16 Feb 1916

(1) Mary Constance; *b* 1 Feb 1882; *m* 26 April 1916 Maj Alfred Wynne Corrie (*d* 4 April 1919), of Park Hall, Oswestry, and *d* 10 Feb 1966, leaving issue

(2) Margaret Helen; *b* 27 Sept 1885; *m* 14 June 1911 Leonard Cookson (*d* 1928), of Foxleigh, Wem, Salop, and *d* 8 Feb 1936, having had issue

2 Edward William CB (1911); *b* 1855; *educ* HMS *Britannia*; Cdr RN; *m* 1883 Charlotte McCrea, dau of Rev Hayden Aldersey Taylor, and *d* 1946, leaving:

(1) Montagu Aubrey; *b* 1888; *educ* Cambridge (BA); *m* 24 Aug 1915 Dorothea Marie, dau of Col Ryley, Loyal N Lancs Regt, and *d* 11 Sept 1946, leaving:

1a Robert Harold; *b* 19 July 1916; *educ* Shrewsbury and RMC Sandhurst; *m* 3 Aug 1940 *Lois Ann Vaughan, dau of Maj C Vaughan Phillips, of Carmarthen, and had:

1b *Christopher Edward; *b* 6 Sept 1942

2a Edward Herbert; *b* 13 Oct 1918; *educ* Eastbourne Coll; *m* 1st (*divorce* 1966) Jessie Doreen —; *m* 2nd 8 July 1967 *Winifred Florence, widow of — Muddiman

3a *Geoffrey McCrea; *b* 15 Jan 1923; *m* *Dorothy Evelyn, dau of Henry James McGregor, and has issue:

1b *Graham McCrea McGregor; *b* 13 June 1955

2b *Robert Allen; *b* 19 July 1959

1b *Ada Jean; *b* 23 Nov 1952

2b *Valerie Ann; *b* 8 March 1954

1a *Krithia Mary Drake [Mrs David Westmacott, White Swan Inn, Mainsbridge Rd, West End, Hants]; *b* 14 Aug 1929; *m* 8 Dec 1950 *David Westmacott, s of James Westmacott, of Lyons Gate, Dorset, and has:

1b *Jonathan Grant; *b* 22 Aug 1951

2b *David William; *b* 17 April 1953

3b *James Arthur; *b* 3 March 1959

1b *Dorothea Diana; *b* 2 March 1963

(2) Lionel Vavasseur; *b* 15 Dec 1893; *educ* RNCs Osborne and Dartmouth; Cdr RN, Croix de Guerre; *m* 27 April 1921 Margery Cecil, dau of John William Holdron, of Regent's Park, London

(1) Lilian Aldersey; *b* 1886; *m* 22 April 1909 Henry Delacombe Roome (*d* car crash 8 June 1930), barrister, est s of Dr Henry A Roome, of Twickenham

3 ERNEST THOMAS

1 Harriet Mary, MBE; *d* unm 22 April 1948

2 Edith Lucy; *d* unm 30 July 1942

WILLIAM LLOYD *d* 9 April 1874; his yst son,

ERNEST THOMAS LLOYD; *b* 7 July 1860; *educ* Charterhouse, Shrewsbury and Ch Ch Oxford (MA); barrister; ICS Bengal 1887–93, Ch Constable York 1893–97, RM Ireland 1897–1910, WW I as Maj King's Salop LI (Res Bn), Cmdt POW Camp 1914–18; *m* 29 Aug 1889 Ethel Mary (*d* 12 July 1961), 2nd dau of Sir Richard Dansey Green-Price, 2nd Bt (*qv*), and had:

1 (ERNEST) GUY RICHARD (Sir), **1st Bt**

2 Owen Robert, MC (1917); *b* 10 Jan 1893; *educ* Rossall; Capt 6th King's Salop LI WW I; *ka* France 1917

3 Reginald John; *b* 26 March 1894; *educ* Shrewsbury; *m* 1926 Frances (*d* 1965), dau of Francesco Fernandez, of Telen, Argentina, and had:

(1) John Robert; *b* 15 July 1928; *m* 1957 *Margaret Chappell, of Pico, Argentina, and has:

1a *Robert Daniel; *b* 1958

(1) *Frances Mary; *b* 1928; *m* J Lawrie (*d* 1965) and has issue

4 Wilfrid Lewis, CBE (1942), DSO (1940) and bar (1941), MC (1917); *b* 1 March 1897; *educ* Shrewsbury and Trin Coll Dublin; WW I as Capt 7th Bn King's Salop LI, IA 1918, Brig 4th Indian Bde WW II, Maj-Gen 1943; *m* 5 Jan 1922 Phyllis Janet (*m* 2nd Francis Arnold Benedict Jones), yr dau of John M B Turner, slr, of Bournemouth, and *das* Jan 1944, leaving:

(1) *Peter John Ernest [Lt-Cdr Peter Lloyd RN, Home Farm, The Green, Foxton, Cambs CB2 6ST]; *b* 25 June 1923; *educ* RNC Dartmouth, MIPM, served WW II; with Metals Research Ltd; *m* 1st 9 March 1946 Heloise (*d* 9 Feb 1979), dau of Col L F Goodwin, of Ontario; *m* 2nd 6 June 1980 *Angela Mary Gillham and by his 1st w has:

1a *Nigel David Wilfrid; *b* 28 June 1948

2a *Matthew Sinclair; *b* 18 Jan 1958

1a *Philippa Helen; *b* 1 May 1951

2a *Deborah Claire; *b* 15 Oct 1952

(2) David Owen Reginald; *b* 16 Dec 1931; *d* 1934

(1) Maureen Joan; *b* 1927; *d* 25 Jan 1943

(2) *Patricia Jane; *b* 16 Oct 1938; SRN; *m* 2 April 1960 *Jon Bredal, s of Erling Michael Holtsmark Bredal, of Asker, and has:

1a *Erling Michael; *b* 25 Nov 1964

1a *Kristin Jane; *b* 22 Feb 1961

2a *Caroline; *b* 25 April 1962

1 Ethel Winifred; *b* 15 Nov 1891; *d* 1891

2 Kathleen Mary; *b* 20 Sept 1899; *d* unm 23 Aug 1969

3 Evelyn Nesta Violet; *b* 22 March 1903

4 Frances Gwenda; *b* 3 May 1908; *educ* Cheltenham Ladies' Coll and St Anne's Coll Oxford (MA, DipEd); Headmistress St Martin's Sch, Brentwood

Maj ERNEST LLOYD *d* 4 Jan 1935; his est son,

Sir (Ernest) Guy Richard Lloyd, 1st Bt (UK), so *cr* 23 July 1960, DSO (1917), of Rhu, Dunbartonshire, DL (Dunbartonshire 1953); *b* 7 Aug 1890; *educ* Rossall and Keble Coll Oxford (BA 1913, MA 1919); Maj King's Salop LI WW I (despatches), 2ic 5th Loyal Regt (TA) 1930, Roy Warwicks Regt WW II 1939–40; MP (U) E Renfrewshire 1940–1959; dir Jas Chadwick and Bros Bolton 1921, memb Bolton Town Cncl 1923–31, administrator J & P Coats, Glasgow and Paisley, 1931, ktd 1953; *m* 5 March 1918 Helen Kynaston, yr dau of Col Ernest William Greg, CB, VD, JP, of Norcliffe Hall, Styal, Cheshire, and *d* 1987, having had:

1 Sir RICHARD ERNEST BUTLER LLOYD, **2nd and present Bt**

1 Irene Marion; *b* 13 March 1919; *m* 19 Jan 1937 Sir John Green-Price, 4th Bt (*qv*), and *d* 27 Sept 1955, leaving issue

2 *Margaret Kynaston [Mrs Bruce Fowler, Shirley Holms, South Park Dve, Gerrards Cross, Bucks SL9 8JH]; *b* 23 Sept 1920; *m* 10 March 1948 *(Percy) Bruce Southmayd Fowler, DM, FRCP, and has:

(1) *Michael Bruce; *b* 6 May 1951; *educ* Harrow; MB, FRCP, FACC; *m* 1st 1978 Dr Linda Jane Fenney and has:

1a *Jack; *b* 1981

1a *Katherine Jane; *b* 1980

2a *Emily Louise (twin); *b* 1981

(1) (cont.) Michael Fowler *m* 2nd 1992 *Sherry Farr and has by her:

3a *Jenna Morgan; *b* 1994

(2) *Guy Richard John; *b* 1 April 1961; *educ* Harrow; MB, BS; *m* 1994 *Vanessa Stuttaford and has:

1a *Holly Victoria; *b* 1997

(1) *Susanne Jane; *b* 23 Dec 1949; FRCGP; *m* 1970 *Richard Anthony Savage, FRCGP, and has:

1a *Thomas Michael; *b* 1978

2a *Samuel Richard; *b* 1984

1a *Emma Louise; *b* 1981

(2) *Amanda Jill; *b* Dec 1952; MRCP, MRCGP; *m* 1979 *Andrew Duncan Platts, FRCS Edin and London, FRCP, and has:

1a *Nicholas James; *b* 1982

1a *Helen Jane; *b* 1981

2a *Catherine Frances; *b* 1987

3 Pamela Rathbone; *m* 3 July 1954 *Alfred Robert Petrie Hall, AMIMechE, only s of Alfred Petrie Hall, MB, ChB, of Perthshire, and has:

(1) *James Stewart; *b* 30 May 1955; *educ* Bishops Stortford Coll and Cambridge

(1) *Irene Anne; *b* 8 March 1958

4 *Elizabeth Hunt [Lady Denny, Crombie Cottage, Abercrombie, Anstruther, Fife KY10 2DE]; *b* 8 Jan 1925; *m* 18 April 1949 Sir Alistair Maurice Archibald Denny, 3rd Bt, of Dumbarton (*qv*), and has issue

LLOYD OF BERWICK

Arms: Per fess gules and or, a pale per fess and a fess per fess, in chief an escallop between two hedgehogs and in base a hedgehog between two escallops, all counterchanged. **Crest:** A hedgehog gules, spined or, holding in its dexter claw an ostrich plume erect proper. **Motto:** *Nisi Dominus* ('Only the Lord').
Creation: B. (LP, UK) 1993.

THE BARON LLOYD OF BERWICK, of Ludlay, Co E Sussex (Sir Anthony John Leslie Lloyd, PC (1984), DL (E Sussex 1983)) [The Rt Hon The Lord Lloyd of Berwick PC DL, Ludlay, Berwick, E Sussex BN26 6TE; 68 Strand-on-the-Green, London W4 3PF]; *b* 9 May 1929; *educ* Eton and Trin Coll Cambridge; 1st Bn Coldstream Gds 1948; barrister Inner Temple 1955, QC 1967, Bencher 1976, Reader 1998–99, Treasurer 1999; Attorney-Gen to HRH THE PRINCE OF WALES 1969–77; High Court Judge Queen's Bench 1978–84 , ktd 1978, Ld Justice Appeal 1984–93, Ld Appeal in Ordinary 1993–; memb: Top Salaries Review Body 1971–77, Bishop's Cncl Chichester 1972–76, Criminal Law Revision Ctee 1981–, Parole Bd 1983–84 (v-chm 1984–85); Chm: Chichester Diocesan Bd Finance 1972–76, Glyndebourne Arts Tst 1975–, Civ Serv Security Appeals Panel 1982–, Sussex Assoc Rehabilitation Offenders 1985–91, Security Commn 1992– (v-chm 1985–92); Tstee Smith's Charity 1971– (Chm 1975–94); Dir RAM 1979–; V-Pres: Br Maritime Law Assoc 1983– and Corp Sons of Clergy 1996–; Fell Eton 1974–86; Hon Fell Peterhouse Cambridge 1981; Hon FRAM 1985; Hon Memb Salters' Co 1988; *m* 1960 *Jane Helen Violet, High Sheriff E Sussex 1994, dau of Cornelius William Shelford, of Chailey Place, nr Lewes

Lineage: EDWARD JOHN BOYDELL LLOYD, of Little Bucksteep, Dallington, Sussex; *m* Leslie Johnston Fleming and had an only *s*:

ANTHONY JOHN LESLIE, *cr* a **Baron**

LLOYD OF HIGHBURY

Creation: B. (LP, UK) 15 June 1996.

THE BARONESS LLOYD OF HIGHBURY, of Highbury, London Borough of Islington (Dame June Kathleen Lloyd, DBE (1990)) [The Rt Hon The Baroness Lloyd of Highbury DBE, 37 Allingham St, London N1 8NX]; *b* 1 Jan 1928; *educ* Roy Sch Bath, Bristol U and Durham U (DPH); Research Fell and Lecturer Child Health Birmingham U 1958–65, Sr Lecturer, Reader Paediatrics Inst Child Health 1965–73, Prof Paediatrics London U 1973–75, Prof Child Health St George's Hosp Med Sch London U 1975–85, Sci Advsr Assoc Med Research Charities 1992–, Chm Dept Health Advsy Ctee Gene Therapy 1993–, Nuffield Prof Child Health Br Postgrad Med Fedn London U 1985–92, Emeritus 1992–, Pres Br Paediatric Assoc 1988–91, FRCP 1969, FRCPE 1989, FRCGP 1990, Hon DSc Bristol 1991, Birmingham 1993

Lineage: ARTHUR CRESSWELL LLOYD; *m* Lucy Bevan and had:
JUNE KATHLEEN, *cr* a **Baroness**

LLOYD GEORGE OF DWYFOR

Arms: Az. over water barry wavy, in base a bridge of one arch ppr., on a chief arg. a portcullis sa. between two daffodils stalked and leaved, also ppr. **Crest:** A demi-dragon gu., holding between the claws a portcullis sa. **Supporters:** Dexter, a dragon or; sinister, an eagle, wings addorsed or, each gorged with a collar vert.
Motto: *Y gwir yn erbyn y byd* ('The truth against the world').
Creation: E. and V. (UK) 12 Feb 1945.

THE 3RD EARL LLOYD GEORGE OF DWYFOR and **Viscount Gwynedd**, of Dwyfor, Co Carvarvon (Owen Lloyd George, DL (Dyfed 1993)) [The Rt Hon The Earl Lloyd George DL, Ffynone, Boncath, Dyfed SA37 0HQ; 47 Bruton Court, London SW3 4SZ]; *b* 28 April 1924, *s f* 1968; *educ* Oundle; Capt Welsh Gds WW II Italy 1944–45, Underwriting memb Lloyd's; *m* 1st 8 Sept 1949 (*divorce* 1982) Ruth Margaret, only dau of Richard Coit, of S Kensington; *m* 2nd 16 June 1982 *(Cecily) Josephine, widow of 2nd Earl of Woolton (*qv*), formerly *w* of 3rd Baron Forres (*qv*) and er dau of Maj Sir Alexander Penrose Gordon Cumming 5th Bt (*qv*), and by his 1st *w* has:

1 +DAVID RICHARD OWEN, *Viscount Gwynedd*; *b* 22 Jan 1951; *educ* Eton; *m* 1985 *Pamela Alexandra, only dau of Alexander Kleyff, and has:

  (1) +William Alexander; *b* 16 May 1986

  (2) +Frederick Owen; *b* 1987

2 +Robert John Daniel [The Hon Robert Lloyd George, 23 Shek O, Big Wave Rd, Hong Kong]; *b* 13 Aug 1952; *educ* Eton and Univ Coll Oxford; author: *A Guide to Asian Stock Markets* (1989) and *The East West Pendulum*; chm Lloyd George Mangement (Hong Kong); *m* 1st 8 Sept 1977 (*divorce* 1991) Kim, only dau of Earl Fischer, of New York, and has:

  (1) +Richard Joseph; *b* 4 March 1983

  (1) *Alice Margaret; *b* 1987

2 (cont.) The Hon Robert Lloyd George *m* 2nd 1992 *Donna Jean, only dau of John Archbold Hufty, of Palm Beach, Fla., and by her has:

  (2) +Alexander Gwilym; *b* 1994

  (2) *Julia Frances; *b* 1993

1 *Julia Margaret Violet; *b* 19 May 1958; *m* 1984 *Simon Erroll Prior-Palmer and has issue (see LINLITHGOW, M)

Lineage: WILLIAM GEORGE, of Bulford, Pembs, and Liverpool; Master Hope Street Unitarian Schools, Liverpool; *m* Elizabeth, dau of Rev David Lloyd, of Caernarvon, and had:

1 DAVID LLOYD, **1st Earl**

2 William, MBE, Hon LLD U of Wales 1947, slr, author, chm Centl Welsh Bd; *b* 23 Feb 1865; *m* — (*d* 1943) and *d* 25 Jan 1967, leaving:

  (1) *William; won Crown Nat Eisteddfod Wales 1974; *b* 1912

The er son,

DAVID LLOYD GEORGE, **1st Earl Lloyd George of Dwyfor**, so *cr* 12 Feb 1945, as also VISCOUNT GWYNEDD, of Dwyfor, Co Caernarvon (both UK), OM (1919), PC (1905), JP, DL (Caernarvs); *b* 17 Jan 1863; *educ* Llanystymdwy Ch Sch and privately; slr 1884 with Lloyd George and George, of Criccieth and Portmadoc, MP (Lib) Caernarvon April 1890–December 1944, Pres BOT 1905–08, Chllr Exchequer 1908–15, Min Munitions and memb Cabinet War Cncl 1915–16, Sec State War and memb Army Cncl 1916, PM and 1st Ld Treasury 1916–22, Ch Br Rep Paris Peace Conference 1919, Sessional Chm Lib Party 1924–31, Constable Caernarvon Castle 1908–45, Ld Rector Edin U 1920, CA Caernarvs, chm Caernarvs QS 1929–38; Freeman London, Birmingham, Manchester, Cardiff, Bristol, York, Glasgow and Barnsley 1921, Aberystwyth and Leeds 1922, Montreal, Brecon, Llandovery, Carmarthen, Llanelly and Swansea 1923, Hon LLD U of Wales 1908, Glasgow 1917, Edinburgh 1918, Cambridge 1920, Birmingham 1921 and Leeds 1922, Hon DCL Oxford 1908 and Durham 1919, Hon DLitt Sheffield 1919, Hon Fell Jesus Coll Oxford 1910, Grand Cordon Legion of Honour, Order of St Maurice and St Lazarus of Italy, KGStJ, Prior and Chllr Wales Welsh Priory Order St John Jerusalem; *b* 17 Jan 1863; *m* 1st Jan 1888

Margaret, GBE (1920), LLD, LGStJ, JP (*d* 20 Jan 1941), dau of Richard Owen, of Mynydd Ednyfed, Criccieth, Caernarvs, and had issue; *m* 2nd 23 Oct 1943 Frances Louise, CBE (1918), BA Lond, author: *Makers of New World* (1922) (*d* 5 Dec 1972), dau of John Stevenson, of Wallington, Surrey, and by his 1st w had:

1 RICHARD, **2nd Earl**

2 GWILYM LLOYD GEORGE, *cr* VISCOUNT TENBY (*qv*)

1 Olwen Elizabeth, DBE (1969); *b* 3 April 1892; *m* 19 June 1917 Maj Sir Thomas John Carey Evans, MC, FRCS, IMS (*d* 25 Aug 1947), est s of Dr R D Evans, JP, of Blaenau Festiniog, and had:

(1) *Robert Rufus, DFC [Robert Carey Evans Esq DFC, 2a Fisher Avenue, Vaucluse, Sydney, NSW 2030, Australia], F/Lt RAFVR WW II, barrister Middle Temple 1949; *b* 21 Sept 1923; *m* May 1968 *Elizabeth Margaret, yr dau of Walter R J Laing, of Sydney

(2) *David Lloyd [David Carey Evans Esq, Eisteddfa Farm, Criccieth, Gwynedd]; Lt RNVR WW II; *b* 14 Aug 1925; *m* 1959 *Annwen, est dau of W Williams, of Cae Mawr, Llanerchymedd, and has:

1a *Thomas Robert; *b* 1961

2a *William Lloyd; *b* 1962

3a *Richard Huw; *b* 8 Nov 1968

1a *Davina; *b* 1964

(1) *Margaret Lloyd [Mrs Michael Barrett, 22 Rowan Court, Ely Rd, Llandaff, Cardiff CF5 2JB]; *b* 25 April 1918; *m* Nov 1948 Capt (Robert) Michael Stewart Barrett, USAF (*d* 31 Oct 1995), of Edinburgh, s of J C W Barrett

(2) *Eluned Jane [Mrs Robert MacMillan, Box 728, 9605 Dufferin St, Maple, Ontario L6A 1S7, Canada]; *b* 3 March 1921; *educ* Roedean and U of Toronto (BSc Med); *m* 1942 *Robert Laidlaw MacMillan, MD, BA Toronto, MRCP Lond FRCP Canada, FACP, Assoc Prof of Med, U of Toronto, late Surgn-Lt RCNVR, and has:

1a *Thomas Carey; *b* 1948

2a *Robert David Hugh; *b* 1951

3a *David John; *b* 1953

1a *Margaret Olwen; *b* Nov 1943; *educ* Sherborne Sch for Girls, Trin Coll U of Toronto (BA) and St Hilda's Coll Oxford (B Phil)

2a *Ann Elizabeth; *b* 1946; *educ* N Toronto Collegiate and Victoria Coll, U of Toronto (BA)

2 Megan, CH (1966), MP (Lib) Anglesey 1929–51 and Carmarthenshire 1957–66, JP Caernarvs; Hon LLD U of Wales 1949, Dep Leader Lib Party 1949–51, Welsh Church Commr 1942–66, Chm Welsh Parity Party 1944–45, Pres Women's Lib Fedn 1936 and 1945; *b* 22 April 1902; *d* unm 14 May 1966

The 1st EARL *d* 26 March 1945; his er son,

RICHARD LLOYD GEORGE, **2nd Earl Lloyd George of Dwyfor**; *b* 15 Feb 1889; *educ* Portmadoc and Christ's Coll Cambridge (BA 1910); AMICE, Maj RE, served WW I and WW II, author: *Dame Margaret*; *m* 1st 7 April 1917 (*divorce* 1933) Roberta Ida Freeman (*d* 10 March 1966), 5th dau of Sir Robert McAlpine, 1st Bt (*qv*), and had:

1 OWEN LLOYD GEORGE, **3rd and present Earl Lloyd George of Dwyfor**

1 *Valerie Davidia [The Lady Valerie Daniel, 67 Cae Ffynnon, St Michael's Rd, Llandaff, Cardiff CF5 2AN]; *b* 14 Feb 1918; *educ* St Hilda's Coll Oxford (BA 1939); *m* 28 March 1940 *Sir Goronwy Hopkin Daniel, KCVO, CB, DPh, and has:

(1) *David Llewelyn [David Daniel Esq, 31 Westway, Petts Wood, Kent BR5 1LN]; *b* 23 Aug 1950; *m* 1977 *Mary Helen, dau of A Kent Maytham, of Cabinteely, Co Dublin, and has:

1a *Owen Maytham; *b* 11 April 1982

2a *Katherine Megan; *b* 14 Sept 1984

(1) *Anne Margaret [Mrs Bernard Harrison, 29 St Stephen's Rd, London W13 8HJ]; *b* 4 March 1944; *m* 1977 *Bernard Thomas Harrison and has:

1a *Florence Ceridwen Dorothy; *b* 7 Sept 1977

2a *Eleanor Mary Gwyneth; *b* 11 March 1979

(2) *Gwyneth Roberta [Mrs Avi Shlaim, 8 Chalfont Rd, Oxford]; *b* 10 Sept 1946; *m* 1971 *Avi Shlaim and has:

1a *Tamar Megan; *b* 24 June 1980

The **2nd Earl** *m* 2nd 1935 *Winifred Emily, formerly w of — Calve and dau of Thomas William Peedle, and *d* 1 May 1968

LLOYD-WEBBER

Creation: B. (LP, UK) 31 Dec 1996.

THE BARON LLOYD-WEBBER, of Sydmonton, Co Southampton (Sir Andrew Lloyd Webber) [The Rt Hon The Lord Lloyd-Webber, 22 Tower St, London WC2H 9NS]; *b* 22 March 1948; *educ* Westminster, Magdalen Coll Oxford and RCM (FRCM 1988); composer (*Variations* [on Paganini's A minor caprice No 24] (1977), *Requiem Mass* (1985), also film scores and musicals (*Joseph and the Amazing Technicolor Dreamcoat* (1968), *Jesus Christ Superstar* (1970), *Evita* (1976), *Jeeves* (1975), *Tell Me on a Sunday* (1980), *Cats* (1981), *Song and Dance* (1982), *Starlight Express* (1984), *The Phantom of the Opera* (1986), *Aspects of Love* (1989), *Sunset Boulevard* (1993), *Whistle Down the Wind* (1996)); theatrical producer, author of books of his musicals, ktd 1992; *m* 1st 1971 (*divorce* 1983) Sarah Jane Tudor, *née* Hugill, and has, with a dau:

1 *Nick; *b c* 1980

BARON LLOYD-WEBBER *m* 2nd 1984 (*divorce* 1990) Sarah Brightman; *m* 3rd 1991 *Madeleine Astrid Gurdon and by her has two sons and a dau

Lineage: WILLIAM SOUTHCOMBE LLOYD WEBBER, CBE; DMus, FRCM, FRCO; *m* Jean Hermione Johnstone and had:

1 ANDREW, *cr* a **Baron**

2 * Julian [Julian Lloyd Webber Esq, c/o IMG Artists Europe, Media House, 3 Burlington Lane, London W4 2TH]; *b* 14 April 1951; *educ* U Coll Sch London and RCM (ARCM 1967, FRCM 1994); 'cellist; *m* 1st 1974 (*divorce* 1989) Celia Mary Ballantyne; *m* 2nd 1989 *Princess Zohra Mahmud Ghazi and by her has a s

LOCKWOOD

Creation: B. (LP, UK) 1977

THE BARONESS LOCKWOOD, of Dewsbury, Co of W Yorkshire (Betty Lockwood, DL (W Yorks 1987)) [The Rt Hon The Baroness Lockwood DL, 6 Sycamore Dve, Addingham, W Yorks LS29 0NY]; *b* 22 Jan 1924; *educ* Eastborough Girls' Sch Dewsbury and Ruskin Coll Oxford; Ch Woman Offr and Assist Nat Agent Lab Party 1967–75, Chm Equal Opportunities Commn 1975–83, Pres Mary MacArthur Holiday Tst 1990– (Chm 1971–90), chm Nat Coal Mining Museum for England 1995–; Memb Cncl: Bradford U 1983– (Pro-Chllr 1983–97 and Chllr 1997–), Leeds U 1985–91; ed *Labour Woman* 1967–71; Pres Birkbeck Coll London 1983–89, Dep Speaker Ho Lds 1989–; *m* 1978 Lt-Col Cedric Hall (*d* 1988)

Lineage: ARTHUR LOCKWOOF; *m* Edith Alice — and had:

BETTY, *cr* a **Baroness**

LODER

Arms: Az. on a fess between two escallops or three buck's heads cabossed ppr. **Crest:** Between two escallops or a buck's head cabossed, transfixed with an arrow bendwise, point to the sinister, all ppr. **Motto:** *Murus aeneus conscientia sana* ('A sound conscience is a wall of brass'). **Creation:** Bt. (UK) 27 July 1887.

SIR GILES ROLLS LODER, 3RD BT, of Whittlebury, Co Northampton, and the High Beeches, Sussex, JP (1949), DL (W Sussex 1977) [Sir Giles Loder Bt JP DL, Ockenden House, Cuckfield, Sussex RH17 5LD; Leonardslee Gardens, Horsham, Sussex RH13 6PP]; *b* 10 Nov 1914; *s* gf 1920; *educ* Eton and Trin Coll Cambridge (BA 1936, MA 1944); late Lt 98th (Surrey and Sussex Yeo) Field Bde RA (TA); High Sheriff Sussex 1948, FLS; *m* 11 July 1939 *Marie Violet Pamela, only dau of

Capt Bertram Hanmer Bunbury Symons-Jeune, of Runnymede House, Old Windsor, and has:

1 +EDMUND JEUNE [Edmund Loder Esq, Eyrefield Lodge, The Curragh, Co Kildare, Ireland]; *b* 26 June 1941; *educ* Eton; ACA (1964); *m* 1st 23 June 1966 (*divorce* 1971) Penelope Jane, only child of Ivo Matthew Leopold Dieskan Forde, OBE, of Norther Farm, Cranleigh, Surrey; *m* 2nd 1992 *Susan Warren, dau of V W Warren Pearl, of Lindfield, Sussex, and by his 1st w has:

(1) *Gillian Marie; *b* 12 March 1968; *m* 1992 *James D P Morgan, s of David Morgan, of Northchapel, Sussex, and has:

1a *Matthew; *b* 199–

1a *Olivia; *b* 11 May 1996

2 +Robert Reginald [Robert Loder Esq, Leonardslee Gardens, Horsham, Sussex]; *b* 12 Nov 1943; *educ* Eton and Trin Coll Cambridge (BA 1965); *m* 1 April 1967 *(Quenelda) Jane, yr dau of Sir John Ledward Royden, 4th Bt (*qv*), and has:

(1) +Christopher Giles; *b* 25 July 1968

(2) +Peter Thomas; *b* 2 April 1972

(1) *Catherine Marie Violet; *b* 7 March 1970

(2) *Mary Charlotte; *b* 2 April 1972

Lineage: JOHN LODER, of Hazelbury Bryan, Dorset; living 1563; *d* 1597, leaving a 3rd s:

WILLIAM LODER; *b* 1580; *m* 1619 Gratia Gilbert (*d* 1670) and *d* 1665; his 4th s:

JAMES LODER; *b* 1625; *m* 1st Edith — (*d* 1681); *m* 2nd Frances — (*d* 1688) and *d* 1684, leaving:

JAMES LODER; *b* 1673; *m* Elizabeth — (*d* 1743) and *d* 1745, leaving:

GILES LODER; *b* 3 Jan 1705; *m* Anna — (*d* 1792) and *d* 1774, leaving:

GILES LODER; *b* 28 Aug 1754; *m* Susannah Pinkney (*d* 1824 aged 65) and *d* 15 Oct 1834, leaving:

GILES LODER, of Wilsford, Wilts; *b* 9 Oct 1876; *m* 1st 1816 Elizabeth (*d* 7 June 1848), dau of John Higginbotham, of St Petersburg; *m* 2nd 12 July 1849 Elizabeth (*d* Dec 1877), dau of Richard Murcott Satchwell and widow of Capt John Bott, 5th Bengal Light Cav, and *d* 19 Aug 1871, leaving by his 1st w:

Sir Robert Loder, 1st Bt (UK), so *cr* 27 July 1887, JP, DL Sussex; *b* 7 Aug 1823; High Sheriff 1877, MP Shoreham; *m* 25 March 1847 Maria Georgiana (*d* 15 Nov 1907), 4th dau and coheir of Hans Busk, JP, DL, of Glenalder, Radnorshire, and Culverden Grove, Kent, and had surv issue:

1 EDMUND GILES (Sir), **2nd Bt**

2 Wilfrid Hans, JP and DL (Sussex); *b* 4 Oct 1851; *educ* Trin Coll Cambridge (BA); High Sheriff 1891; *m* 6 June 1878 Sarah Winifred (*d* 16 April 1943), dau of Charles Rowe, and *d* 19 Aug 1902, leaving:

(1) Giles Harold, MC, DL (Sussex); *b* 2 Jan 1884; *educ* Eton and RMC Sandhurst; Lt-Col Scots Gds WW I; High Sheriff 1942, Order Rising Sun Japan; *d* unm 1 Feb 1966

(2) Norman Wilfrid; *b* 2 Oct 1885; Lt RASC, 7th Bn The Buffs (E Kent Regt); *m* 24 Oct 1914 Phyllis Sydney (*m* 2nd 2 April 1943 Capt Lindesay Harry Compton Shedden (*d* 1971)), yst dau of Sydney Fisher, of Amington Hall, Tamworth, and *d* 2 Aug 1940, having had:

1a John Wilfrid; *b* 31 Dec 1915; *d* 16 April 1937

(3) Hubert Sydney; *b* 13 March 1888; *educ* Eton and Magdalen Coll Oxford; Lt 1st Roy E Kent Yeo; *m* 8 Nov 1918 (*divorce* 1944) Brenda Mary Adela (*d* 1981), er dau of Charles Fitzroy Ponsonby McNeill, of Paris, and *d* 1982, having had:

1a David Eustance; *b* 10 Oct 1920; Lt Scots Gds WW II; *ka* Italy 23 Oct 1943

2a +Simon John; *b* 4 April 1932; *educ* Eton and RMA Sandhurst; late Capt Gren Gds; stockbroker; dir Jersey External Tst 1974–; *m* 1st 23 June 1962 (*divorce* 1978) Kathleen Alexandra, est dau of Maj Richard Evelyn Fleming (*see* WYFOLD, B), and has:

1b +David Richard; *b* 26 Jan 1964; *m* 1990 *Cressida, dau of Ian Landless, of Duns Tew, Oxon, and has:

1c *Katherine Rose; *b* 14 Jan 1996

2c *Flora; *b* 19 Nov 1997

2b +Alexander Hugh; *b* 10 Nov 1965

3b +John Alistair; *b* 22 Jan 1968

2a (cont.) Simon Loder *m* 2nd 1979 *Penelope Anne Mary, dau of Sir Charles Marcus Mander, 3rd Bt (*qv*), and formerly w of Michael Rollo Hoare, and by her has:

4b +James Robert; *b* 1981

1a *Jean Mary [Mrs Stephen Player, Dam Farm House, Brailsford, Derbys]; *b* 17 Sept 1919; *m* 31 Jan 1939 Stephen Dane Player (*d* 1979), 4th s of William Goodacre Player, JP, of Whatton Manor, Notts, and has had:

1b *Peter Dane [Peter Player Esq, Whatton Manor, Whatton in the Vale, Notts]; *b* 4 Oct 1941; *educ* Harrow; late Capt RSG; *m* 1970 *Catherine Esther, est dau of Col Gerald Vigors de Courcy O'Grady (The O'Grady), MC, of Kilballyowen, Bruff, Co Limerick, and formerly w of Rupert Hugh Stobart, and has:

1c *Edward Dane; *b* 1973

1c *Alice Mary; *b* 1971

2b *James Stephen [James Player Esq, Bradley Park South, Brailsford, Derbys]; *b* 19 March 1945; *educ* Harrow; *m* 7 Dec 1968 *Philippa Hedley, est dau of Andrew Hedley Richardson, of Broadstone End, Ticknall, Derbys, and has:

1c *Andrew Headley; *b* 1970

2c *Duncan James; *b* 1972

3b Nicholas Charles William; *b* 4 Sept 1948; *educ* Harrow; *d* car crash 30 June 1969

1b *Karen Jean [Mrs Dermot Kelly, The Coach House, Dowdeswell, Glos GL5 J44]; *b* 27 March 1940; *m* 16 Jan 1963 *Dermot Lindsay Patrick Kelly, yr s of Col Lindsay Patrick Grellan Kelly, MC, of Leesthorpe Hall, Leics, and has:

1c *Patrick Dermot Stephen; *b* 12 Aug 1968

1c *Doone; *b* 30 Dec 1963

2c *Anna; *b* 8 Feb 1966

2a *Gillian [Mrs John Kirkpatrick, Horn Park, Beaminster, Dorset]; *b* 11 Dec 1925; *m* 21 April 1952 *John Johnston Kirkpatrick, FLAS, FRICS, MBH, only s of Cdr Kenneth Clarke Kirkpatrick, DSC, JP, DL, RN, of Church Hill, Newcastle, Co Down, and has:

1b *Christopher James [Christopher Kirkpatrick Esq, Compton Graze, Little Compton, Glos GL56 0RT]; *b* 1 Feb 1953; *m* 1978 *Annabel Susan, dau of Frederick McLean Hayward, of Gosebury Hall Farm, Nonnington, Kent, and has:

1c *Lucy Diana; *b* 1984

2c *Sophie Clare; *b* 1986

3c *Chloe Laura; *b* 1991

2b *Nicholas Yvone John; *b* 21 Aug 1959; *m* 1990 *Hon Joanna Norrie FitzRoy Newdegate, only dau of 3rd Viscount Daventry (*qv*), and has:

1c *A son; *b* 1992

1c *A dau; *b* 1994

3b *Francis Hugh [Francis Kirkpatrick Esq, 52 Walham Grove, London SW6 1QR]; *b* 20 Dec 1962; *m* 1990 *Miranda J, est dau of David Fitzwilliam-Lay, of Bloxham, Savernake Forest, Wilts, and has:

1c *George Hugh; *b* 1992

2c *Henry James; *b* 1993

4b *Robin Kenneth Anthony; *b* 21 Feb 1969

1b *Rose Cecilia [Mrs James Wigan, Biddlesgate Farm, Cranborne, Dorset BH21 5RS]; *b* 13 May 1955; *m* 1979 *James Adair Wigan and has issue (*see* WIGAN, Bt)

2b *Sara Gillian [Mrs Preston Rabl, Winterbourne Manor, Newbury, Berks RG16 8AU]; *b* 26 Dec 1956; *m* 1983 *Preston Martin Charles Rabl and has:

1c *Francesca Sara; *b* 1984

2c *Sophia Rose; *b* 1986

3c *Georgina Moira; *b* 1988

(1) Winifred Mary; *m* 20 June 1918 William Young Woodburn, MD, Capt RAMC (T) (*d* 1945), s of John Woodburn, of Australia, and *d* 28 July 1958

(2) Brenda Cicely; *m* 15 Jan 1916 Maj Arthur Compton Lethbridge Dumville Lees, KSLI (Res) (*d* 11 Sept 1961), 2nd s of George John Dumville Lees, JP, of Woodhill, Oswestry, Salop, and *d* Feb 1936, leaving issue

(3) Edith Margaret; *m* 8 Aug 1918 Maj John Wyndham Aylmer, MC, 4th Dragoon Gds (Res) (*d* 22 March 1953), of Courtown, Co Kildare, and *d* 29 Oct 1964, leaving issue

3 Alfred Basil, of Aldwickbury, Herts, JP (Herts and Bucks); *b* 25 March 1855; Lt-Col Roy Bucks Hus Imp Yeo; *m* 1st 9 Aug 1882 Annie Katherine (*d* 9 Dec 1891), er dau of Rev Charles Henry Crosse, Rector Fincham, Norfolk, and had:

(1) Basil Charles Robert; *b* 14 July 1885; Maj 4th Bn Beds and Herts Regt, formerly Scots Gds; *m* 8 Jan 1908 Katie Blanche (*d* 16 April 1957), est dau of W G Davies, of Pembroke, and *d* 6 July 1934, leaving:

1a Robert Eric, CBE (1965), DL (Sussex 1972); *b* 23 March 1911; *educ* Lancing and RMC Sandhurst; Brig late Roy Sussex Regt, Cmdt Roy Mil Sch of Music 1958–61, Head Cwlth Liaison Mission UN Cmd Korea 1961, Dep Col 3rd Bn Queen's Regt (Roy Sussex) 1968 (Dep Col (Sussex) Queen's Regt 1969), ADC to Govr NSW 1938, WW II 1939–40 (POW), Cdr Order House of Orange 1968; won London-Brighton Vintage Car Race 1975

1a Barbara Ellaline Joy; *b* 5 Nov 1908; *m* 17 July 1934 George Maitland Christian, only s of Frederick Henry Christian, of Midlington, Hants, and had:

1b *Ewan Loder; *b* 11 June 1936; *educ* Eton; Maj Queen's Regt; *m* 25 Aug 1962 *Elizabeth Iola, dau of Cdr William Scott Thomas, DSC, of Findon, Sussex, and has:

1c *Andrew Fletcher; *b* 19 Sept 1964

2c *James Ewan; *b* 19 Jan 1967

1c *Sarah Elizabeth; *b* 5 July 1963

(2) Eric Raymond; *b* 15 March 1888; *educ* Eton; Maj 4th Bn Beds Regt WW I (despatches three times); *m* 1st 1 March 1912 (*divorce* 1915) Gabrielle Elizabeth Clifford Ray, former 'Gaiety Girl' (*d* 21 May 1973 aged 90), dau of William Austin Cook; *m* 2nd May 1920 (*divorce* 1928) Iris Mary (*d* May 1940), er dau of Hon Eustace Robert Southwell FitzGerald (*see* 1889 edn FitzGERALD, B) and formerly w of Sir Digby Lawson, 2nd Bt (*qv*), and by her had:

1a Pamela Katherine; *b* 28 July 1921; *d* unm 23 May 1941

(2) (cont.) Maj Eric Loder *m* 3rd Dec 1932 Eleanor (*d* Monte Carlo 5 March 1977), dau of John Curran, of Louisiana, and widow of Sir Mortimer Barnett Davis, and *d* 27 July 1966

(1) Audrey Kathleen; *b* 17 May 1883; *m* 9 July 1907 11th Earl of Cavan (*qv*) and *d* 8 April 1942, leaving issue

3 (cont.) Lt-Col Alfred Loder *m* 2nd 17 Oct 1894 Henrietta Mabel, MBE (1920), Order Crown Belgium with Palms (*d* 27 Feb 1953), only dau of Lt-Col James Poynter, 14th Hus, of Belgravia, and *d* 17 April 1905

4 Clare Robert; *b* 25 Feb; *d* 18 April 1857

5 GERALD WALTER ERSKINE LODER, *cr* BARON WAKEHURST (*qv*)

6 Reginald Bernhard, of Maidwell Hall, Northampton, JP (Northants); *b* 8 June 1864; MA Trin Coll Cambridge; Hon Maj Roy Bucks Hus; High Sheriff 1899; *m* 25 July 1895 Lady Margaret Ernestine Augusta Hare (*d* 15 July 1951), er dau of 3rd Earl of Listowel (*qv*), and *d* 28 Oct 1931, leaving:

(1) Marjorie Kathleen; *b* 1897; *m* 10 Nov 1921 Lt-Col Cuthbert Henry Dawnay and *d* 1986, leaving issue (*see* DOWNE, V)

7 Sydney; *b* 16 May 1867; Capt Royal Bucks Hus; *m* 25 July 1907 Nelly (*d* 9 Jan 1972 aged 91), yst dau of Binyoun Francis Drage, of Grange, Chapel Brampton, Northants, and *dsp* 29 April 1944

8 Eustace; *b* 16 May 1867 (twin), JP (Co Kildare); Maj 12th Lancers; High Sheriff 1912; *d* unm 27 July 1914

1 Etheldreda Mary; *b* 1 May 1853; *m* 23 July 1872 Sir Charles Raymond Burrell, 6th Bt (*qv*), and *d* 25 Sept 1921, leaving issue

2 Adela Maria; *m* 1st 12 June 1833 Gen Hon Alexander Stewart, 3rd s of 9th Earl of Galloway (*qv*), and had issue; *m* 2nd 25 April 1899 Col Basil Lloyd-Anstruther (*see* ANSTRUTHER, Bt) and *d* 22 March 1915

Sir ROBERT *d* 27 May 1888; his est son,

Sir Edmund Giles Loder, 2nd Bt, JP (Sussex and Northants); *b* 7 Aug 1849; *educ* Eton and Trin Coll Cambridge (MA); High Sheriff 1888; *m* 21 Nov 1876 Marion (*d* 12 June 1920, yst dau of William Egerton Hubbard, of Leonardslee, Horsham, and *d* 14 April 1920, having had:

1 Robert Egerton; *b* 10 March 1887; *educ* Trin Coll Cambridge (BA); Capt 1st/4th Bn Roy Sussex Regt, Bde Machine Gun Offr and Staff Capt 1916, WW I Gallipoli and Egypt 1915 (despatches); *m* 9 Aug 1913 Muriel Rolls, Alderman W Sussex CC 1938–52 (granted by roy warrant 14 June 1921 rank of bt's w; *d* 10 Feb 1955), dau of James Rolls Hoare, of Mayfair, and *d* 29 March 1917 of wounds recd in action, leaving:

  (1) Sir GILES ROLLS LODER, **3rd and present Bt**

1 Patience Marion; *b* 4 Feb 1882; *m* 21 June 1904 Walter William Otter (*d* 6 Aug 1940), s of Francis William Otter, of Horsham, and *d* 27 Jan 1963, leaving issue

LOFTHOUSE OF PONTEFRACT

Arms: Azure, on a pale between and conjoined to two grills throughout or, the whole surmounted by three chevronels argent overall on a pale sable three ellipses palewise or. **Crest:** A canary or holding in the dexter foot a miner's lamp sable glazed proper. **Supporters:** On either side a mole sejant erect sable holding in the mouth a rose argent barbed slipped and leaved or. **Motto:** Stick and lift. **Creation:** B. (LP, UK) 19 April 1997.

THE BARON LOFTHOUSE OF PONTEFRACT, of Pontefract, Co W Yorks (Sir Geoffrey Lofthouse, JP (Pontefract, 1970)) [The Rt Hon The Lord Lofthouse of Pontefract JP, 67 Carleton Crest, Pontefract, W Yorks WF8 2QR]; *b* 18 Dec 1925; *educ* Featherstone Sch and Leeds U; memb: Pontefract Borough Cncl 1962–74 (Mayor 1967–68), Wakefield Met DC 1974– (Chm Housing Ctee), NUM 1939–64, APEX 1970–; personnel manager NCB Fryston 1970–78; MP (Lab) Pontefract and Castleford 1978–97, Dep Chm Ways and Means 1992–97, Dep Speaker H of C 1992–97, ktd 1995; author: *A Very Miner MP* (1986); *m* 1946 Sarah — (*d* 1985) and has a dau

Lineage: ERNEST LOFTHOUSE; *m* Emma — and had:

GEOFFREY (Sir), *cr* a **Baron**

LONDESBOROUGH

Arms: Quarterly, 1st and 4th, erm. a bend az. cotised sa. between a unicorn's head erased in chief and a cross crosslet fitchée in base gu. (for DENISON); 2nd and 3rd, arg. a shakefork between three mullets, one and two, sa. (for CONYNGHAM). **Crests:** 1 Issuant from clouds an arm in bend ppr., vested gu., cuffed erm., and charged with a covered cup or, the forefinger pointing to an estoile radiated gold (for DENISON), 2 A unicorn's head erased arg., maned and armed or (for CONYNGHAM). **Supporters:** Dexter, a horse arg., maned, unguled, and charged on the shoulder with an eagle displayed or; sinister, a stag arg., attired, unguled and charged on the shoulder with a griffin's head erased or, both charged on the body with a crescent sa. **Motto:** *Adversa virtute repello* ('I repel adversity with courage'). **Creation:** B. (UK) 4 March 1850.

THE 9TH BARON LONDESBOROUGH, in the East Riding, Co York (Richard John Denison TD) [The Rt Hon The Lord Londesborough TD, Edw Cottage, Aberedw, Powys LD2 3UR]; *b* 2 July 1959; *s f* 1968; *educ* Wellington and Exeter U; AMICE; *m* 1987 *Rikki, dau of J E Morris, of Bayswater, and has:

1 +JAMES (JACK) FREDERICK; *b* 4 June 1990

1 *Laura Rose; *b* 1992

Lineage: The 1st MARQUESS CONYNGHAM (*qv*) had by Elizabeth, dau of Joseph Denison, of Denbies, nr Dorking, Surrey, a 2nd surv s:

ALBERT DENISON CONYNGHAM later DENISON (roy licence 4 Sept 1849 under terms of will of his unc, William Joseph Denison, of Denbies, Seamer (Yorks) and Pall Mall, MP Surrey), **1st Baron Londesborough**, in the East Riding, Co York (UK), so *cr* 4 March 1850, KCH (1829); *b* 21 Oct 1805; *educ* Eton; Offr Horse Gds (Blues), Attaché Berlin 1824 and Vienna 1825, Sec Legation Florence 1828 and Berlin 1829–31; MP (Lib) Canterbury 1835–41 and 1847–50, First Pres Br Archaeological Assoc 1844–45, V-Adml Yorks Coast, FSA 1840, FRS 1850, author: *Wanderings in Search of Health* (1849), trans *Der Bastard* (Carl Spindler, 1835); *m* 1st 6 July 1833 Henrietta Maria (*d* 22 April 1841), 4th dau of 1st Baron Forester (*qv*), and had:

1 WILLIAM HENRY FORESTER DENISON, **2nd Baron Londesborough** and 1st EARL OF LONDESBOROUGH, in the North Riding of Co York, so *cr* 1 July 1887, as also VISCOUNT RAINCLIFFE OF RAINCLIFFE, in the North Riding of Co York (both UK), JP (E R and N R Yorks); *b* 19 June 1834; *educ* Eton; MP (Lib) Beverley 1857–59 and Scarborough 1859–60, V-Adml Yorks Coast, CA E R Yorks, Hon Col 4th E Yorks Artillery Vols and 2nd Vol Bn E Yorks Regt (Vol Offrs' decoration); *m* 10 Sept 1863 Lady Edith Frances Wilhelmina Somerset (*d* 15 May 1915), yst dau of 7th Duke of Beaufort (*qv*), and *d* 19 April 1900, having had:

(1) WILLIAM FRANCIS HENRY DENISON, **3rd Baron Londesborough** and 2nd EARL OF LONDESBOROUGH, KCVO (1907), DL (E R Yorks); *b* 30 Dec 1864; served RN, V-Adml Yorks Coast, Hon Col 5th Bn E Yorks Regt, Lt Yorks Yeo Cav; *m* 11 Aug 1887 Lady Grace Adelaide Fane (*d* 13 June 1933), er dau of 12th Earl of Westmorland (*qv*), and *d* 30 Oct 1917, leaving:

1a GEORGE FRANCIS WILLIAM HENRY DENISON, **4th Baron Londesborough** and 3rd EARL OF LONDESBOROUGH; *b* 17 July 1892; V-Adml Yorks Coast; *d unm* 12 Sept 1920

2a HUGO WILLIAM CECIL DENISON, **5th Baron Londesborough** and 4th and last EARL OF LONDESBOROUGH; *b* 13 Nov 1894; Capt Gen Res Offrs Household Cav WW I (wounded three times); *m* 4 Sept 1935 Marigold Rosemary Joyce (*m* 2nd 19 July 1948 (*divorce* 1954) Zygmunt Stanislaw de Lubiez-Bakanowski, s of Waclaw de Lubiez-Bakanowski, of Poland and *d* 15 May 1976), Sr Cdr ATS WW II 1939–43, 3rd dau of Edgar Lubbock (*see* AVEBURY, B), and *d* 17 April 1937, when the Earldom and Viscountcy expired, leaving:

1b Zinnia Rosemary; *b* posthumously 25 Nov 1937; *m* 1st 8 May 1957 (*divorce* 1961) Peter Crawford Melhuish Comins, s of Capt Dennis Comins, MC, of Coddington Moor, Newark-on-Trent, and had:

1c *Timothy Hugo COMINS later POLLOCK (1968); *b* 19 Dec 1958; *m* 1993 *Jeanie Anne, er dau of Capt Simon Hugh Walford (*see* BELLEW, B)

1b (cont.) Lady Zinnia *m* 2nd 14 July 1961 (*divorce* 1964) John David Leslie Melville (*see* LEVEN and MELVILLE, E); *m* 3rd 26 June 1964 (*divorce* 1967) Maj Hugh Cantlie, Scots Gds, est s of Col Kenneth Cantlie, and by him had:

2c *Charles Edgar; *b* 27 Feb 1965

1b (cont.) Lady Zinnia *m* 4th 1 Feb 1968 (Ralph) John Hamilton Pollock (*see* POLLOCK, Bt); *m* 5th 1982 *James Hubert Judd, s of Leslie Ashurst Judd by Enid Irene Crichton (*see* ERNE, E), and *d* 13 July 1997

1a Irene Frances Adza, GBE (1938); DJStJ, Spanish Order Maria Luisa; *b* 4 July 1890; *m* 19 July 1917 1st Marquess of Carisbrooke (*see* MILFORD HAVEN, M) and *d* 16 July 1956, leaving issue

(1) Edith Henrietta Sibyl; *m* 3 Feb 1887 Sir Gerald William Henry Codrington, 1st Bt, of the 1876 *cr* (*qv*), and *d* 6 May 1945, leaving issue

(2) Lilian Katharine Selina; *m* 26 Nov 1895 Newton Charles Ogle (*d* 23 July 1912), of Kirkley, and *d* 31 July 1899, leaving issue

(3) Ida Emily Augusta; *m* 23 Nov 1886 Sir George Reresby Sitwell, 4th Bt (*qv*), and *d* 12 July 1937, leaving issue

(4) Mildred Adelaide Cecilia; *m* 15 July 1902 (*divorce* 1925) Sir William Henry Charles Wemyss Cooke, 10th Bt (*qv*), and *d* 25 Jan 1953, leaving issue

2 Albert Denison Somerville, of Woodside, Wootton, IoW; R-Adml; *b* 4 Oct 1835; *m* 14 Oct 1873 Louisa Crichlow (*d* 6 July 1933), yst dau of Antonio Fabris, of Springcroft, Beckenham, and *d* 2 Sept 1903, having had:

(1) ERNEST WILLIAM DENISON, **6th Baron Londesborough**, MBE (1946); *b* 9 Aug 1876; Capt RN WW I, WW II CD, Russian Order St Stanislas 2nd Cl with swords; *m* 1 June 1905 Sybil May (*d* 5 July 1963), dau of Capt Henry Thomas Anley, The Buffs, of IoW, and *dsp* 31 Dec 1963

(1) Daisy; *b* 18 May 1875; granted with sisters rank of baron's daus 10 May 1938; *m* 6 June 1900 Robert Lockhart Hobson, CB (*d* 5 June 1941), 2nd s of Rev Canon W T Hobson, and *d* 11 Aug 1967, leaving issue

(2) Ivy; *b* 19 Aug 1878; *m* 25 April 1905 Herbert Guy Sturges Mitchison (*d* 10 Oct 1946) and *d* 10 March 1950, leaving issue

(3) Lily; *b* 31 Jan 1882; *m* 23 Aug 1916 F/Lt Reginald Marsh Everett, RAF (*d* 1953), s of T M Everett, of Ruislip, and *dsp* 23 May 1954

1 Henrietta Elizabeth Sophia; *m* 18 July 1861 Sir Phillip Grey Egerton, 11th Bt (*qv*), and *d* 15 July 1924, leaving issue

2 Selina Camerina Charlotte; *d* 11 Sept 1852

3 Isabella Maria; *d* 5 April 1856

4 Augusta Elizabeth; *m* 18 July 1861 3rd Baron Wrottesley (*qv*) and *d* 20 Jan 1887, leaving issue

The **1st Baron** *m* 2nd 21 Dec 1847 Ursula Lucy Grace (*m* 2nd 14 Dec 1861 Lord Otho Augustus FitzGerald (*see* LEINSTER, D) and *d* 12 Nov 1883), est dau of R-Adml Hon Charles Bridgeman (*see* BRADFORD, E), and *d* 15 Jan 1860, having by her had:

3 Henry Charles; Capt RHA; Hon Lt RN Arty Vols; *b* 28 Oct 1849; *m* 1 June 1887 Beatrice (*d* 8 Dec 1926), dau of James Alexander Guthrie, of Craigie, and widow of Maj Wilfred Arbuthnot Gough, 52nd Regt, and *d* 23 July 1936, leaving:

(1) Edward Conyngham, MVO (1931); Capt RN, WWs I and II (despatches), Cdr HM Yacht *Victoria and Albert* 1930–32, Capt-in-Ch Naval Establishment Bermuda 1936–38, Cdre Convoys 1941–44; *b* 6 Sept 1888; *m* 2 Jan 1919 Maria Amy Brabazon (Betty), yst dau of Lt-Col Sir Charles Henry Brabazon Heaton-Ellis, CBE, DL, of Wyddiall Hall, Herts, and *d* 13 Nov 1960, having had:

1a Philip Henry Charles; Lt KRRC WW II; *b* 4 Dec 1919; *k* by air attack while POW Germany 14 April 1945

1a *Sonia Myrtle [Mrs Roderick Heathcoat-Amory, Allington Grange, Chippenham, Wilts SN14 6LW]; *b* 12 Feb 1921; *m* 1st 7 Sept 1940 Maj Gerald Heathcoat-Amory (*see* HEATHCOAT-AMORY, Bt) and has issue; *m* 2nd 28 April 1947 his cousin *Brig Roderick Heathcoat Amory and by him has issue

4 Conyngham Albert; Cdr RN; *b* 5 March 1851; *m* 5 Dec 1878 Evelyn Maude (*d* 7 June 1951), dau of Charles Fox Webster (*see* 1923 edn WEBSTER, Bt), and *d* 25 May 1938, having had:

(1) CONYNGHAM CHARLES DENISON, **7th Baron Londesborough**, DSO; *b* 6 April 1885; Cdr RN, WWs I (despatches) and II 1939–44 as Capt-in-Charge Trinidad; *m* 1st 8 Feb 1912 (*divorce* 1925) Vera, only dau of Francis Hugh Baxendale, of Framfield Place, Sussex; *m* 2nd 18 June 1926 Mabel Violet (*d* 30 July 1951), dau of Mathew George Megaw; *m* 3rd 23 Jan 1952 *Jocelyn Helen [The Rt Hon Jocelyn Lady Londesborough, Anchor Cottage, Bembridge, IoW], dau of Lt-Cdr Hugh Duppa Collins, RN, of Bembridge, and *dsp* 31 Oct 1967

(2) Gerald Evelyn Henry; 2nd Lt 12th Bn Rifle Bde; *b* 22 Dec 1892; *ka* 25 Sept 1915

(1) Beatrice Mildred; *b* 31 Dec 1887; *m* 1st 20 Feb 1912 Lt-Col Algernon Corbet Turnor (*d* 25 June 1930), MC, RHG, only s of Lt-Col Wyatt William Turnor, of Pinkney Park, Malmesbury, and had issue (*see* STUART-FORBES, Bt); *m* 2nd 3 July 1943 Maj Sir Ralph St George Claude Gore, 10th Bt (*qv*)

5 Harold Albert; Lt RN; *b* 26 March 1856; *m* 3 Aug 1899 Katherine (*d* 15 Jan 1961), dau of Sir Thomas Villiers Lister, KCMG, and *d* 2 Jan 1948, leaving:

(1) JOHN ALBERT LISTER, **8th Baron**

6 Evelyn Albert; *b* 4 Sept 1859; *d* 20 Jan 1833

5 Ursula Elizabeth; *m* 12 May 1870 Rev George Cockburn Dickinson and *d* 23 April 1880, leaving issue

6 Albertina Agnes Mary; *m* 31 July 1873 1st and last Baron Treowen, CB, CMG (*d* 18 Oct 1933), and *d* 20 Oct 1929, leaving issue

The 7th BARON's cousin,

JOHN ALBERT LISTER DENISON, **8th Baron Londesborough**, TD; *b* 30 May 1901; *educ* Wellington and Trin Coll Cambridge, AMICE, WW II in RA and REME; *m* 1st 8 Jan 1949 (*divorce* 1953) Lesley Maxwell Gordon, MBE, dau of Lt-Col Herbert Forbes Churchill, OBE, and widow of Lt-Col J H Wooldridge, IA; *m* 2nd 15 June 1957 Elizabeth Ann (*d* 1994), dau of Edward Little Sale, ICS, and formerly w of Thomas Chambers Windsor Roe, CBE, and *d* 5 April 1968, leaving:

RICHARD JOHN DENISON, **9th and present Baron Londesborough**

LONDONDERRY

Metuenda · Corolla · Draconis

Arms: Quarterly, 1st and 4th, or a bend counter compony arg. and az. between two lions rampant gu. (for STEWART); 2nd, arg. a bend engrailed between six martlets sa. (for TEMPEST); 3rd, az. three sinister gauntlets or (for VANE). **Crests:** 1 A griffin's head erased, per pale arg and sa, beaked gu. (for TEMPEST), 2 A dragon statant or (for STEWART), 3 A dexter cubit arm in armour, the hand in a gauntlet ppr., grasping a sword also ppr., pommel and hilt or (for VANE). **Supporters:** Dexter, a Moor wreathed about the temples arg. and az., holding in his exterior hand a shield of the last, garnished or, charged with the sun in splendour gold; sinister, a lion or, gorged with a collar arg., charged with three mullets sa. **Motto:** *Metuenda corolla draconis* ('The dragon's crest is to be feared'). **Creations:** B. (I) 20 Sept 1789 (Londonderry), V. (I) 1 Oct 1795 (Castlereagh), E. (I) 8 Aug 1796 (Londonderry), M. (I) 13 Jan 1816 (Londonderry), B. (UK) 1 July 1814 (Stewart of Stewart's Court and Ballylawn), E. (Vane) and V. (Seaham) (UK) 8 July 1823.

THE 9TH MARQUESS OF LONDONDERRY, Earl of Londonderry, Earl Vane, Viscount Castlereagh, Viscount Seaham of Seaham, Co Durham, **Baron Londonderry** and **Baron Stewart of Stewart's Court and Ballylawn** (Alexander (Alistair) Charles Robert Vane-Tempest-Stewart) [The Most Hon The Marquess of Londonderry, PO Box 8, Shaftesbury, Dorset SP7 OLR]; *b* 7 Sept 1937; *educ* Eton; *s f* 1955; *m* 1st 16 May 1958 (*divorce* 1970) Nicolette Elaine Katherine (*d* by her own hand 1993, having *m* 2nd Georgie Fame, the pop singer), only dau of Michael Harrison, of Nether Hampton, nr Salisbury, Wilts, by Maria Madeleine Benita, dau of Baron Alexander Karl Wilhelm von Koskull, and has:

1 *Sophia Frances Anne; *b* 23 Feb 1959; *m* 1987 *Jonathan Mark Pilkington, yst s of Ronald Charles Leslie Pilkington, of Hill House, Stanstead Abbots, Herts, and has:

(1) *Hermione Alice; *b* 1989

(2) *Allegra Rose; *b* 1991

2 *Cosima Maria-Gabriella; *b* 25 Dec 1961; *educ* St Paul's Girls' Sch; claims that Robin Douglas-Home (*d* 1968, *see* HOME, E) was her true f; *m* 1st 1 Oct 1982 (*divorce* 1986) Cosmo Fry, s of Jeremy Fry, of Bath; *m* 2nd 1990 (*divorce* 1996) Lord John Robert Somerset and by him has issue (*see* BEAUFORT, D)

The 9th MARQUESS *m* 2nd 1972 (*divorce* 1989) Doreen Wells, ballerina Roy Ballet 1955–74, and by her has:

1 +FREDERICK AUBREY, *Viscount Castlereagh*; *b* 6 Sept 1972

2 +Reginald Alexander; *b* 1977

Londonderry, previous creations: In 1622 Thomas Ridgeway was created Earl of Londonderry in the Irish peerage. His father had bought from the Seymours in 1599 the remains of Tor Abbey in Devon but the Ridgeways seem to have been established in the county already. Like many Devonians at that time, Ridgeway was a naval adventurer, and contributed a ship to the Earl of Essex's plundering enterprise which in 1597 descended on the Azores. He also took part in one of ELIZABETH I's more or less continuous attempts to assert her rule in Ireland, rising to Vice-Treasurer and Treasurer of that kingdom in the early years of JAMES I's reign. He was a Privy Counsellor in Ireland and MP for Ballinakill, Queen's Co, also Co Tyrone, being involved in JAMES I's plantation of Ulster, much of which he surveyed and where he acquired at least 4,000 acres. He outbid all comers for a blank patent of earldom in the possession of Sir James Erskine, who as a favourite of JAMES I had been given this desirable document by the King, and thus secured his promotion in the peerage, having been made Lord Ridgeway, Baron of Gallen-Ridgeway six years earlier.

With the death in March 1713/4 of his great-grandson, whose father the 3rd Earl had married one of the Temples of Stowe (*see* TEMPLE OF STOWE, E), the title expired.

It was revived some five years later for Thomas Pitt, uncle of Pitt the Elder, Earl of Chatham (*see* JERSEY, E), who had married in March 1716/7 Lady Frances Ridgeway, the only offspring of the last Earl of the old creation to have children. The new Earldom descended first to Thomas's elder son then to his younger, expiring with the latter's death in 1765.

Lineage (of Stewart): ALEXANDER STEWART; had:

JOHN STEWART; had an est s:

JOHN STEWART; ggf of:

ALEXANDER STEWART, of Mount Stewart, Co Down, and Ballylawn Castle, Co Donegal; MP Londonderry; *b* 1699; *m* 30 June 1737 his cousin Mary, only surv dau of Alderman John Cowan, of Londonderry, and sis and heiress of Sir Robert Cowan, Govr Bombay, and had, with other issue:

1 ROBERT, **1st Marquess**

2 Alexander, of Ards; ancestor of the STEWARTs of Ards and STEWARTs of Rockhill; *b* 26 March 1746; *m* 2 Oct 1791 Mary Moore (*d* 22 Feb 1842), 3rd dau of 1st Marquess of Drogheda (*see* DROGHEDA, E), and *d* Aug 1831, having had issue

ALEXANDER STEWART *d* 2 April 1781; his est son,

ROBERT STEWART, **1st Marquess of Londonderry**, so *cr* 13 Jan 1816, as also earlier 20 Sept 1789 BARON LONDONDERRY, 1 Oct 1795 VISCOUNT CASTLE-REAGH and 8 Aug 1796 EARL OF LONDONDERRY (all I), PC (I 1782); *b* 27 Sept 1739; MP Co Down 1771–83, rep I peer 1801–21; *m* 1st 3 June 1766 Sarah Frances (*d* 18 July 1770), 2nd dau of 1st Marquess of Hertford (*qv*), and had:

1 ROBERT STEWART, **2nd Marquess of Londonderry** (better known as the statesman Lord Castlereagh), KG (1814), GCH (1821), PC (I 1797, GB 1798); *b* 18 June 1769; *educ* St John's Coll Cambridge; MP (I Parl) Co Down 1790–1800, (GB Parl) (Tory) Tregony 1794–96, Orford 1796–97and (UK Parl) 1821–22, Co Down (UK Parl) 1800–05 and 1812–20, Boroughbridge 1806, Plympton 1806–12, Ireland: Sec State 1798–1801 and Ch Sec to Ld Lt 1798–1800, a Ld Treasury 1797–1804, Keeper Privy Seal 1797–1801; UK: Pres India Bd 1802–06, Sec War and Colonies 1805–06 and 1807–09, For Sec 1812–22 (also Plen Congress of Vienna); *m* 9 June 1794 Amelia Anne (*d* 12 Feb 1829), yst dau and coheir of 2nd Earl of Buckinghamshire (*qv*), and committed suicide by cutting his throat 12 Aug 1822

The **1st Marquess** *m* 2nd 7 June 1775 Frances (*d* 18 Jan 1833), est dau of 1st Earl Camden (*see* CAMDEN, M), and *d* 6 April 1821, having by her had:

2 CHARLES WILLIAM, **3rd Marquess**

1 Frances Anne; *m* 10 March 1799 Lord Charles FitzRoy and *d* 9 Feb 1810, leaving issue (*see* GRAFTON, D)

2 Caroline; *m* 23 Dec 1801 Thomas Wood (*d* 26 Jan 1860), MP, of Littleton, Middx, and of Gwernevet, Breconshire, Col E Middx Militia, and *d* 10 Aug 1865, leaving issue

3 Georgina; *m* 13 July 1803 1st Baron Garvagh (*qv*) and *d* 17 Nov 1804

4 Selina; *m* 22 Feb 1814 David Kerr (*d* 30 Dec 1844), of Portavo, Down, and *d* 5 Feb 1871, leaving issue

5 Matilda; *m* 14 Sept 1815 Michael Edward Ward and *d* 3 Oct 1842, leaving issue (*see* BANGOR, V)

6 Emily Jane; *m* 1st 29 June 1814 John James (*d* 4 June 1818); *m* 2nd 10 Dec 1821 1st Viscount Hardinge (*qv*) of Lahore and Kings Newton and *d* 18 Oct 1865, leaving issue

7 Octavia; *m* 11 Dec 1813 1st Earl of Ellenborough (*see* ELLENBOROUGH, B) and *dsp* 5 March 1819

The 2nd MARQUESS's half-bro,

CHARLES WILLIAM STEWART later VANE (roy licence 5 May 1821), **3rd Marquess of Londonderry**, KG (1853), GCB (1815, KB 1813), PC (1814); *b* 18 May 1778; *educ* Eton; Lt Macnamara's Foot 1794, Lt-Col 5th Dragoons 1797–99 and 18th Dragoons 1799, MP (I Parl) Thomastown March-May 1800 and Co Derry May-Dec 1800 and (UK Parl) 1810–14, ADC to GEORGE III 1803, U-Sec War and Colonies 1807–09, non-resident Govr Ft Charles Jamaica 1809–22, Adj Gen 1809–12 Peninsular War, Maj-Gen 1810, Envoy Extrdy and Min Plen Berlin also Mil Commr Allied Armies 1813–14, Col 25th Light Dragoons 1813–18, Lt Gen 1814, Amb Vienna 1814–23 during which period acted as Plen at Congress of Vienna, Col 10th Hus 1820–43, Gen 1837, Col 2nd Life Gds 1843–54, Ld Lt Co Durham 1842–54, Govr Co Londonderry 1823, Custos Rotulorum Cos Londonderry 1821 and Down 1822; *cr* 1 July 1814 BARON STEWART OF STEW-ART'S COURT AND BALLYLAWN, Co Donegal (UK), and 28 March 1823 EARL VANE and VISCOUNT SEAHAM OF SEAHAM, Co Durham (UK), with remainder to heirs male by his 2nd and current wife; Groom Bedchamber 1812–14, Ld Bedchamber 1814–27, Kt Cdr Tower and Sword Portugal, Kt St George Russia 4th Cl, Kt Black Eagle Prussia, Kt Grand Cross of Sword Sweden, all 1813; Kt Red Eagle Prussia 1814; *m* 1st 8 Aug 1804 Catherine (*d* 11 Feb 1812), yst dau of 3rd Earl of Darnley (*qv*), and had:

1 FREDERICK WILLIAM ROBERT STEWART, **4th Marquess of Londonderry**, KP (1856), PC (1835); *b* 7 July 1805; *educ* Eton; MP (Tory) Co Down 1826–52, a Ld Admlty 1828–30, V-Chamberlain Household 1834–35, Ld Lt Co Down 1845–64, Col Down Militia; *m* 2 May 1846 Elizabeth Frances Charlotte (*d* 2 Sept 1884), dau of 3rd Earl of Roden (*qv*) and widow of 6th Viscount Powerscourt (*qv*), and *dsp* 25 Nov 1872

The **3rd Marquess** *m* 2nd 3 April 1819 Frances Anne Emily (*d* 20 Jan 1865), only dau and heiress of Sir Henry Vane-Tempest, 2nd Bt (*see* below), and by her had:

2 GEORGE HENRY ROBERT CHARLES WILLIAM, **5th Marquess**

3 Adolphus Frederick Charles William VANE later VANE-TEMPEST; Lt-Col Scots Gds, MP; *b* 2 July 1825; *m* 23 April 1860 Susan (*d* 6 Sept 1875), only dau of 5th Duke of Newcastle (*see* LINCOLN, E), and *d* 11 June 1864, leaving:

(1) Francis Adolphus; Maj Durham LI; *b* 4 Jan 1863; *m* 30 Nov 1901 Gertrude Magdalen (*d* 1925), dau of F A Elliott by Charlotte Bell (later Lady Jones-Parry), and *d* 10 Dec 1932, leaving:

1a Francis Charles Joseph; F/Lt RAFVR WW II; *b* 25 Jan 1911; *educ* Downside; *m* 1st 2 June 1931 (*annulled* 1935) Pamela Mary (*d* 17 Dec 1953), 2nd dau of Maj Edwin Philip Abel Smith, of Great Kimble House, Princes Risborough, Bucks; *m* 2nd 1935 (*divorce* 1952) Penelope Joan, dau of Edmund Henry Bevan, JP, of Hilston Park, Mon (*see* GRANTLEY, B), and *d* 5 Oct 1994, having had:

1b Peregrine Francis Edmund; *b* 27 May 1947

1a (cont.) Francis Vane-Tempest also adopted:

*Richard Conyers (*né* Lowndes-Stone Norton); *b* 9 July 1941

4 Ernest McDonnell VANE later VANE-TEMPEST; *b* 29 Feb 1836; *m* 12 Jan 1869 Mary Townshend (*d* 8 Oct 1891), dau of Thomas Hutchinson, of Howden Hall, Co Durham, and *d* 14 Aug 1885, leaving:

(1) Charles Henry; *b* 22 Feb 1871; *m* 13 April 1893 Florence Mary (*d* 1942, having *m* 2nd 3 June 1903 Nigel Sydney Augustine Harrison), est dau of William Kirk, JP, of Norton, Stockton-on-Tees, and *d* 20 Feb 1899, leaving:

1a Ernest Charles William, DSC; Lt RNVR WW I (despatches); *b* 24 July 1894; *educ* Eton and Trin Coll Cambridge; *m* 1st 19 Dec 1918 (*divorce* 1933) Aline Mary Loftus (*m* 2nd 7 Nov 1933 (*divorce* 1948) Michael Seely Sandford Pakenham (*see* LONGFORD, E) and *d* 1967, est dau of Loftus St George (*see* ST GEORGE, Bt); *m* 2nd 23 Dec 1933 Anne Elizabeth (*d* 1968), dau of Capt Evan Humphreys, of Carnarvon, and *d* 24 Aug 1957, having by his 1st w had:

1b +Charles Stewart McDonnell; F/O RAF 1940–48; *b* 2 Dec 1921; *educ* Haileybury; *m* 1st 2 Sept 1948 (*divorce* 1956) Diana Constance, only dau of Maj Kenneth Arthur Seth-Smith, of Chesterwood Grange, Haydon Bridge, Northumberland, and has:

1c +(Charles) Stewart Martin St George [Stewart Vane-Tempest Esq, Lower House Farm, The Endway, Steeple Bumpstead, Suffolk CB9 7DW]; *b* 18 April 1950; *educ* Stowe; *m* 1st 1 July 1972 (*divorce* 1976) Pamela Elizabeth, dau of M Jenkins, of Myrtle Grove House, Patching, Sussex; *m* 2nd 1977 *Jillian Barbara, dau of Dr John Evelyn Bulow, of Cheam, Surry, and by her has:

1d +Christopher James Stewart; *b* 1978

2d +James Alexander Stewart; *b* 1981

1c *Aline Mary Anne; *b* 10 Dec 1952; *m* 1984 *Philip John Lester Nash and has:

1d *Jonathan Guy Randell; *b* 1988

1d *Camilla Judith; *b* 1986

1b (cont.) Charles Vane-Tempest *m* 2nd 1957 *Maija-Lilsa, dau of Col Erkki Elias Puomi, and by her has:

2c +Charles Erkki William; *b* 28 April 1958; *m* 1981 *Stina Maria Veronica, dau of Per-Erik Tornblom, of Virkby, Finland

3c +Donald John Ernest; *b* 29 Jan 1961; *m* 1985 *Pirkko Maritta, dau of Vaino Salminen, of Alastaro, Finland, and has:

1d +Thomas Christopher; *b* 1986

4c +Harold Michael St George; *b* 28 Dec 1962; *m* 1987 *Merja Anneli, dau of Teuvo Karinkanta, of Vantaa, Finland

2c *Mary-Anne Elizabeth; *b* 28 Dec 1962

1b Theresa Anne Mary Stewart; *b* 1 Feb 1920

2a Charles Stewart; Lt 5th Bn Durham LI and RFC; *b* 5 May 1896; *d* 25 March 1917 of wounds recd in action

1 Frances Anne Emily, VA; *m* 12 July 1843 7th Duke of Marlborough (*qv*) and *d* 16 April 1899, leaving issue

2 Alexandrina Octavia Maria; *b* 29 July 1823; *m* 2 Sept 1847 3rd Earl of Portarlington (*qv*) and *dsp* 15 Jan 1874

3 Adelaide Emelina Caroline; *m* 11 Feb 1852 Rev Frederick Henry Law, Rector Lee, Kent, and *d* 3 Feb 1882

The 4th MARQUESS's half-bro,

GEORGE HENRY ROBERT CHARLES WILLIAM VANE later VANE-TEMPEST (roy licence 28 June 1851), **5th Marquess of Londonderry**, KP (1874); *b* 26 April 1821; *educ* Eton and Balliol Coll Oxford; Lt 1st Life Gds 1845–48, MP (C) N Durham 1847–54; special mission 1867 to invest Tsar of Russia with KG, hence given Grand Cross Order of St Alexander Nevski; Ld Lt Co Durham 1880–84, Col 4th Bn Durham LI, Lt-Col Cmdt Seaham Artillery Vol Bde; *m* 3 Aug 1846 Mary Cornelia (*d* 19 Sept 1906), only dau and heiress of Sir John Edwards, 1st and last Bt, of Garth, Montgomeryshire (*see* 1850 edn), and had:

1 CHARLES STEWART, **6th Marquess**

2 Henry John, of Machynlleth, Montgomeryshire, VD, JP, DL Merioneths and Montgomeryshire; Lt 2nd Life Gds, Lt-Col 2nd Durham Seaham Vol; *b* 1 July 1854; *d* unm 28 Jan 1905

3 Herbert Lionel Henry (Sir), KCVO, VD, of Machynlleth, JP Montgomeryshire and Merioneths; High Sheriff Montgomeryshire 1910, Maj and Hon Lt-Col Durham Artillery Vols; *b* 6 July 1862; *k* Welsh Railway accident 26 Jan 1921

1 Frances Cornelia Harriet Emily; *d* 2 March 1872

2 Avarina Mary; *d* 26 June 1873

3 Alexandrina Louisa Maud; *b* 8 Nov 1863; *m* 12 Nov 1889 1st Viscount Allendale (*qv*) and *d* 31 July 1945, leaving issue

The 5th MARQUESS *d* 6 Nov 1884; his est son,

CHARLES STEWART VANE-TEMPEST later VANE-TEMPEST-STEWART (roy licence 3 Aug 1885), **6th Marquess of Londonderry**, KG (1888), GCVO (1903), PC (GB 1886, I 1892), JP, DL Co Durham, DL Montgomeryshire; *b* 16 July 1852; *educ* Eton and Ch Ch Oxford; MP (C) Co Down 1878–84, Ld Lt Ireland 1886–89, chm London Sch Bd 1895–98, PMG 1900–02, Pres Bd Educn 1902–05, Ld Pres Cncl 1903–05, CA Co Durham, Lt Co Down 1902–15 and Co Belfast 1900–03, Hon Col 3rd Northumbrian Bde RFA, 3rd Bn Durham LI and 4th Bn Roy Irish Rifles, ADC to HM, Hon LLD Trin Coll Dublin and Durham, Mayor of Durham 1910; *m* 2 Oct 1875 Theresa Susey Helen, LGStJ (*d* 16 March 1919), est dau of 19th Earl of Shrewsbury and Waterford (*qv*), and had:

1 CHARLES STEWART HENRY, **7th Marquess**

2 Charles Stewart Reginald; *b* 4 Dec 1879; *d* unm 9 Oct 1899

1 Helen Mary Theresa; *b* 8 Sept 1876 (HRH PRINCE LEOPOLD stood sponsor); *m* 25 Jan 1902 6th Earl of Ilchester (*qv*) and *d* 14 Jan 1956, leaving issue

The 6th MARQUESS *d* 8 Feb 1915; his only surv son,

CHARLES STEWART HENRY VANE-TEMPEST-STEWART, **7th Marquess of Londonderry**, KG (1919), MVO, ED, PC (I 1918, NI 1922, GB 1925), JP Co Durham and Down; *b* 13 May 1878; *educ* Eton and RMC Sandhurst; HM Lt Co Down; Ld Lt Co Durham, MP (C) Maidstone 1906–15; Hon LLD Belfast, Chllr Queen's U Belfast 1923 and Durham U 1931, Hon DCL Durham 1929, Mayor Durham 1936 and Hon Freeman 1938, KGStJ, U-Sec State Air 1920–21, Min Educn NI and Ldr Senate 1921–26, 1st Commr Works and Public Buildings 1928–29 and 1931, Sec State Air Nov 1931–35, Ld Privy Seal and Ldr Ho Lds to Nov 1935, Maj and Brevet

Lt-Col Maj RHG, Hon Col 3rd Northumbrian (Co of Durham) Bde RA (TA), 3rd Bn Durham LI and 4th Bn Roy Ulster Rifles, Hon A/Cdr No 502 (Ulster) Bomber Sqdn AAF 1938– and No 607 (Co of Durham) Fighter Sqdn AAF 1934–39, Master Guild of Air Pilots and Air Navigatiors 1937–49, Ch Commr Civil Air Gd 1938–49, Cmdt ATC (NI) 1942–46, WW I: despatches, ADC to Lt-Gen Pulteney 1914, 2ic RHG 1916–17; Hon Col 28th London Regt (Artists' Rifles) 1934–38, memb Lloyd's, Pres NI Red Cross Ctee 1941–49, memb NI Advsy Cncl Civil Aviation 1947–49, author: *Ourselves and Germany* and *Wings of Destiny*; m 28 Nov 1899 Hon Edith Chaplin, DBE (1917), JP Cos Durham and Down (d 23 April 1959), er dau of 1st Viscount Chaplin (see 1970 edn), and had:

1 EDWARD CHARLES STEWART ROBERT, **8th Marquess**

1 Maureen Helen; CC Westmorland; b 6 Dec 1900; m 4 Nov 1920 Rt Hon Oliver Frederick Stanley, MC, PC, MP (see DERBY, E), and d 20 June 1942, leaving issue

2 Margaret Frances Anne; b 9 March 1910; m 1st 21 Nov 1934 (*divorce* 1939, resumed maiden name 1941) Frederick Alan Irving Muntz; m 2nd 18 July 1952 (*divorce* 1958, resumed maiden name by deed poll 15 Sept 1958) Hugh Falkus, actor and writer, s of James Everest Falkus, of Devon, and dsp 19 Oct 1966

3 Helen Maglona; b 8 July 1911; m 1st 14 Feb 1935 (*divorce* 1960) 2nd Baron Jessel (see JESSEL, Bt) and had issue; m 2nd 23 March 1960 Dennis Cecil Whittington Walsh, est s of Sir Cecil Henry Walsh, KC

4 *Mairi Elizabeth, JP Co Down [The Lady Mairi Bury JP, Mount Stewart, Newtownards, Co Down BT22 2AD]; b 25 March 1921; Patron Br Red Cross Soc NI, Fell Roy Philatelic Soc; m 10 Dec 1940 (*divorce* 1958) Derek William Charles Keppel, Viscount Bury (dvp 8 Nov 1968), est s of 9th Earl of Albemarle (qv), and has issue

The 7th MARQUESS d 11 Feb 1949; his only son,

EDWARD CHARLES STEWART ROBERT VANE-TEMPEST-STEWART, **8th Marquess of Londonderry**, JP, DL (Co Down 1931, Co Durham 1950); b 18 Nov 1902 (HM EDWARD VII stood sponsor); educ Eton and Ch Ch Oxford (BA 1923); MP Co Down Oct 1931–June 1945, Hon Capt RA (TA), Hon Col 12th Bn (Cadet) Durham LI WW II, memb House Laity Ch Assembly 1950–55, Hon Attaché Rome 1924–25; m 31 Oct 1931 Romaine (d 19 Dec 1951), er dau of Maj Boyce Combe, JP, of Great Holt, Dockenfield, Surrey, and d 17 Oct 1955, leaving:

1 ALEXANDER CHARLES ROBERT VANE-TEMPEST-STEWART, **9th and present Marquess of Londonderry**

1 *Jane Antonia Frances [The Rt Hon The Lady Rayne, 33 Robert Adam St, London W1M 5AH]; b 11 Aug 1932; m 2 June 1965, as his 2nd w, *Baron Rayne (LP) and has:

 (1) *Nicholas Alexander; b 15 Jan 1969

 (1) *Nata; b 8 March 1966

2 *Annabel [The Lady Annabel Goldsmith, Ormeley Lodge, Ham Common, Surrey]; b 13 June 1934; m 1st 10 March 1954 (*divorce* 1975) Marcus Lecky Oswald Hornby Birley, only s of Sir Oswald Joseph Hornby Birley, MC, and has had:

 (1) Rupert Oswald Robin; b 20 Aug 1955; educ Eton; missing presumed drowned at sea Lomé W Africa 1986

 (2) *Robin Marcus; b 19 Feb 1958; Referendum Party parly candidate Kensington and Chelsea 1997 gen election

 (1) *(India) Jane; b 14 Jan 1961; m 1st 1988 (*divorce* 1988) Jonathan Halsey Luke Colchester, s of Rev Halsey Sparrowe Colchester, CMG, OBE; m 2nd 1993 *Francis Bruce Pike, s of Esmund Francis Victor Wallace Pike

2 (cont.) Lady Annabel m 2nd 1978, as his 3rd w, Sir James Michael Goldsmith (d 19 July 1997) and by him has:

 (3) *Zach(arias) Frank; b 1975

 (4) *Ben(jamin) James; b 1980; educ Eton

 (2) *Jemima Marcelle (took names Jamila Haiqa following marriage); b 1974; m Paris May 1995 and London 20 June 1995 *Imran Ahmed Khan Niazi, cricketer, s of Ikramullah Niazi, of Lahore, and has:

  1a *Sulaiman Isa; b 17 Nov 1996

Lineage (of Tempest): — TEMPEST; had, with a (yr?) s (Richard, living c 1150):

ROGER TEMPEST; of age by 1120; held land in Craven, Yorks; d in or after 1151, leaving, with another s:

RICHARD TEMPEST; living 1153; had an est s:

ROGER TEMPEST, newly enfeoffed with land at Bracewell, Yorks, by 1166; m c 1188 Alice, dau of Elias de Rilleston, and d in or after 1209, leaving:

RICHARD TEMPEST; presented the advowson of Bracewell to Kirkstall Abbey in or after 1222; m Elena, sis of Richard de Tong, and had, with a yr s:

Sir RICHARD TEMPEST, of Bracewell; ktd by April 1246; d c 1268, leaving, with a yr s:

Sir ROGER TEMPEST, of Bracewell; fedual Ld of Waddington by 1268; held land in Bracewell, Keighley, Laycock, Rilleston, Skipton and Stock by 1272; ktd by 1277; m Alice (d 8 March 1301/2), dau and coheir of Walter de Waddington, and had:

RICHARD TEMPEST, of Bracewell; of age by 1267; m by 1283 — and d 29 Sept 1297, leaving:

Sir JOHN TEMPEST, of Bracewell; b 24 Aug 1283; sided with Thomas Earl of Lancaster (gs of HENRY III) in his attempt to overthrow EDWARD II's favourite Piers Gaveston, pardoned for this 1313, and again 1322 (this time after joing Lancaster against other favourites, the Despensers; see FALMOUTH, V); joint holder of the feudal Ldships of Bracewell, Stock and Waddington by 1316; m Margaret, dau of 1st Lord (Baron) Holand (see HOLLAND, Bt), and d 1359, leaving:

1 John (Sir), of Bracewell; ktd by 1349; m Katherine, dau of Sir Robert Sherburne, and had, with a yr s:

 (1) Richard (Sir), of Bracewell; b c 1334; m Maria, dau of Sir Thomas Talbot, and d c 1386, having had, with two yr sons and two daus:

  1a Richard (Sir); b 1356; ktd by 1380; held a command in Aquitaine during Hundred Years War, a Warden Roxburgh Castle 1385, Warden Berwick 1386, Lt Carlisle Castle 1396; MP Lancs 1401 and Yorks 1403; served Agincourt campaign 1415; m allegedly (1st?) Isabel (she or her successor wife was apparently abducted by the Scots 1385), dau of John Grassus (i.e.,

'the Fat'), of Gemelyn; m 2nd(?) Margaret, dau of Robert de Stainforth, and had, with other issue:

  1b Piers (Sir); of Bracewell; ktd 24 Oct 1415, just prior to battle of Agincourt, hence presumably served in that campaign; cmded troops in France 1417; m c 1400 Grace (m 2nd 1422 Sir William Frank; m 3rd by 1434 Thomas Darcy), dau of Sir Nicholas de Hebden, and d c 1417, leaving:

  1c John (Sir), of Bracewell; Sheriff Yorks 1440 and 1459 and Lincs 1456; m Alice, dau of Sir Robert Sherburne, of Stonyhurst, Lancs, and had, with other issue:

  1d Nicholas, of Bracewell; m Margaret, dau of John Pilkington, and had:

  1e Richard (Sir), of Bracewell; cmded troops Battle of Flodden 1513; m Rosamiond, dau of Tristram Bolling, of Bollling Hall, Yorks, and had a yst s:

  1f Henry, of Bradford; m Ellinor, dau of Christopher Mirfield, of Tong Hall, thus coming into possession of that property, and d 1591, leaving:

  1g Richard, of Tong Hall; m Elizabeth, dau of Thomas Savile, of Overthorpe, Yorks, and d 1607, leaving:

  1h Richard, of Tong Hall; m Alice, dau of William Mauleverer, of Arncliffe, Yorks, and d 1613, leaving:

  1i John, of Tong Hall; m Katherine (m 2nd Henry Fairfax, of Bolton Percy, Yorks), dau of Robert Duckenfield, of Duckenfield, Cheshire, and d 1623, leaving:

  1j Henry, of Tong Hall; bapt Sept 1621; MP Yorks 1654 and 1656; m Mary, dau of Nicholas Bushall, of Bagdall Hall, Yorks, and d 1657, leaving:

  1k Sir JOHN TEMPEST, 1st Bt (E), so cr 25 May 1664; b 1645; m by Jan 1664/5 Henrietta, dau of Sir Henry Cholmeley, of West Newton Grange, Yorks, and d 23 June 1693, leaving, with three er sons (d young):

  1l Sir GEORGE TEMPEST, 2nd Bt; carried out alterations to Tong Hall 1702; bapt 22 May 1672; m 19 Oct 1694 Anne (d 1746), dau of Edward FRANK alias ASHTON, of Campsall, Yorks, and was bur 11 Oct 1745 (having willed the Tong estate to his 2nd s Nicholas, on whose death sp it passed to the bro of ELIZABETH (see below), and from him to John PLUMBE later PLUMBE TEMPEST), leaving, with three yr sons and a dau:

  1m Sir HENRY TEMPEST, 3rd Bt, of Campsall; bapt 1 Sept 1696; educ Univ Coll Oxford; m 31 Aug 1749 Maria, est dau of Francis Holmes, of Wigston, Leics, and d 9 Nov 1753, leaving:

  1n Sir HENRY TEMPEST, 4th and last Bt, of Thorpe Lee, Surrey; b 13 Jan 1753; Sheriff Herefs 1779; m 24 Jan 1791 Susanna Pritchard, only child of Henry Lambert, of Hope End, Herefs, and dsp 29 Jan 1819, when the btcy expired

  2m John, of Nottingham; Capt Churchill's Dragoons; m Elizabeth, dau of William Scrimshire, of Colgrave, Notts, and had, with other issue:

  1n Elizabeth, of Tong Hall; m Thomas Plumbe, s and heir of William Plumbe, of Wavertree Hall and Augton, Lancs, and d Sept 1823, leaving, with another s and five daus:

  1o John PLUMBE later PLUMBE TEMPEST (roy licence 1824), JP, DL Lancs, of Tong Hall and Aughton; sold Wavertree to Sir Joshua Walmsley, JP, MP; Col 1st Roy Lancs Militia; m Sarah, dau of Rev William Plumbe, and d 6 April 1859, having had, with a s and four er sisters:

  1p Frances Penelope; m 26 July 1824 Thomas Rawson, of Nidd Hall, Yorks, s of Benjamin Rawson, of Darley Hall, Lancs, and d 4 May 1825, leaving:

  1q Frances Penelope; m 11 Feb 1844 13th Viscount Mountgarret (qv)

  2p Henrietta; m 31 May 1834 Adml Sir Cornwallis Ricketts, 2nd Bt (qv), and had issue

2b Robert (Sir); was serving in Hundred Years War in France (where ktd) 1420; m c 1407 Alice, dau of John Lacy, and d between 26 Aug 1427 and 30 Sept 1428, leaving:

 1c Richard (Sir), of Giggleswick and Stainforth, Yorks; of age by 1437; m Mabel, dau of Walter Strickland, of Sizergh, and d Feb 1488/9, leaving:

  1d Dowsabel; m as his 1st w 1st Lord (Baron) Darcy of the cr made some time between Jan 1503/4 and autumn 1509 (see DARCY DE KNAYTH, B)

3b Roger, of Broughton-in-Craven, Yorks; m c 1407 Catherine, dau and heiress of Piers Gilliot, of Broughton, thus uniting the two halves of the Broughton property, and d 1467, having had, with three yr sons and two daus:

 1c William, of Broughton; m 1st c 7 July 1437 Johanna, dau of James Metcalfe, of Nappa, Yorks, and had two sons (including a yr one, Thomas, ancestor of the TEMPESTs of Marton); m 2nd Elizabeth (m 2nd Nicholas Towneley (see O'HAGAN, B) and had issue), dau of Richard Catterall, of Catterall, Lancs, and d by July 1480; his er s by his 1st w:

  1d John; m c 20 June 1455 Agnes, dau of Richard Banastre, and dvp by 1490, leaving, with four yr sons:

  1e Roger, of Broughton; m 1st c 1499 Anne, dau of Robert Carre, and had four sons and four daus; m 2nd Elizabeth, dau of William

Huddleston and widow of Edward Redman, and *d* by Nov 1537; his 2nd s by his 1st w:

1f Stephen, of Broughton; *b* 1500; *m* 1st *c* 1525 Agnes, dau of William Lister, of Midhope, and had two sons; *m* 2nd Anne, sis of Anthony Preston, and *d* 14 Aug 1549, having by her had issue (*d* young); his er s by his 1st w:

1g Henry, of Broughton, where he built a new house 1598; *b* 1527; *m c* 7 July 1543 Isabel, illegitimate dau of Sir Ing(el)ram Percy (*see* NORTHUMBERLAND, D), and *d* 17 Feb 1604/5, having had, with four yr sons and four daus:

1h Stephen (Sir), of Broughton; *b* 1553; ktd 1603; *m* 1st Anne, dau of Edmund Eltofts, of Farnhill, Yorks, and had a s and five daus; *m* 2nd Oct 1591 Catherine, dau of Henry Lawson, of Nesome, Co Durham, and *d* 30 Sept 1625, having by her had, with an est s (*d* young) and six yr sons:

1i Stephen; *b* 1593; royalist Civil War; *m* 1st 1612 Susan, dau and coheiress of William Oglethorpe, of Roundhay Grange, Yorks, and had issue; *m* 2nd 1629 Frances (*dsp*), dau of Sir Cotton Gargarve, of Nostel, Yorks, and *d* 1651; his 3rd s by his 1st w:

1j Thomas, of Roundhay Grange (confiscated during the Interregnum); *m* 1653 Anne, only dau and heiress of Henry Scrope, of Danby, Yorks, and *d* 24 June 1697, having had, with three yr sons and four daus:

1k Stephen, of Broughton, which with other family estates he inherited from his f's est bro (who *dsp*); *b* 9 April 1654; Col of Horse 1688; *m* 1687 Elizabeth, 3rd dau of Richard Fermor, of Tusmore, Oxon, and *d* 10 April 1742, having had, with four yr sons and three daus:

1l Stephen, of Broughton; *b* 14 Oct 1689; author *Religio Laici; m* April 1714 Elizabeth, yst dau of Sir Henry Lawson, 2nd Bt, of Brough, Yorks (*see* HOWARD-LAWSON, Bt), and *d* 12 Aug 1771, having had, with a yr s and four daus:

1m Stephen Walter, of Broughton; *b* 23 May 1719; *m* 21 Dec 1748 Frances Olive, 3rd dau and coheir of George Meynell, of Aldborough and W Dalton, Yorks, and *d* 9 Sept 1784, having had, with seven other sons and four daus, an est surv s:

1n Stephen of Broughton Hall; *b* 1 May 1756; *m* 1 May 1789 Elizabeth, 2nd dau and ultimate coheir of Henry Blundell, of Ince Blundell, Lancs, and *d* 28 Nov 1824, having had, with six other sons and five daus:

1o Sir CHARLES ROBERT TEMPEST, 1st and last Bt (UK), so *cr* 1841, of Broughton Hall and Coleby, Lincs; *b* 21 April 1794; High Sheriff Yorks 1839; *d* unm 8 Dec 1865, when the btcy expired

2o Henry, of Heaton, Lancs; *b* 18 Oct 1795; *m* 6 July 1829 Jemima, dau of Sir Thomas de Trafford, 1st Bt (*qv*), and *d* 25 March 1860, having had, with four other sons and four daus:

1p Sir CHARLES HENRY TEMPEST, 1st and last Bt (UK), so *cr* 30 July 1866, of Heaton, Lancs, JP, DL; *b* 5 Jan 1834; *m* 1st 21 May 1862 Cecilia Elizabeth Tichborne, 4th dau of John Hubert Washington Hibbert, of Bilton Grange, Warwicks, and had:

1q Henry Arthur Joseph; *b* 31 March 1863; *m* 16 Nov 1885, as her 1st husb, Mary Boleyn, est dau of Adml Sir Charles Frederick Knowles, 4th Bt (*qv*), and *dsp & vp* 16 April 1891

1q Mary Ethel; inherited the Heaton estate; *m* 7 Nov 1893 10th Lord (Baron) Beaumont and *d* 19 Jan 1937, leaving issue (*see* NORFOLK, D)

1p (cont.) Sir CHARLES *m* 2nd 1 June 1874 (*divorce* 1878) Harriette, only dau of Capt Rowland Hill Gordon, 42nd Highrs, and *dspms* 1 Aug 1894, when the btcy expired

2p Arthur Cecil, of Broughton Hall, Yorks, and Coleby Hall, Lincs, which he inherited from his unc the 1st and last Bt of the 1841 *cr*, JP (Lincs and W R Yorks), DL (W R Yorks); *b* 2 June 1837; Maj 11th Hus; *m* 28 April 1873 Eleanor Blanche, 2nd dau of Edward Horner Reynard, of Sunderlandwick and Hobgreen, Yorks, and *d* 21 June 1920, leaving, with a dau:

1q Roger Stephen, CMG (1918), DSO (1917), JP (Parts of Kesteven and Yorks 1899), DL (W R Yorks 1934), of Broughton; *b* 26 May 1876; *educ* Oratory and Stonyhurst; sold the Coleby estate; Ld manors Burnsall and Thorpe; Lt-Col and Brevet Col Scots Gds, Boer War 1900–02 (despatches), WW I (despatches, Brevet, Croix de Guerre with palm); *m* 31 Oct 1912 Valerie Arthur, er dau of Arthur Leone Glover, of Ryarsh Place, W Malling, Kent, and *d* 12 Feb 1948, leaving, with an er s (Stephen, *d* unm 1970):

1r *Henry Roger, DL (N Yorks 1982) [Henry Tempest Esq DL, Broughton Hall, Skipton, N Yorks BD23 3AE]; *b* 2 April 1924; *educ* Oratory and Ch Ch Oxford; Scots Gds WW II, Staff Capt 1946, with Britannia Rubber 1947–51, accountant N Rhodesia and S Africa 1952–61, fin offr Oxford U Dept Nuclear Physics 1962–72; memb N Yorks CC 1973–85 and exec ctee Yorks CLA 1973–87; pres Skipton branch Roy Br Legion 1974–91; ACIS, FCIS 1971; Kt of Malta; *m* 1957 *Janet Evelyn Mary, dau of Harold Longton, of Johannesburg, and has:

1s *Roger Henry; *b* 1963

2s *Piers; *b* 1973

1s *Bridget Mary; *b* 1957

2s *Anne Valerie; *b* 1959; *m* 1991 *James McConnel

3s *Mary Hazel; *b* 1961; *m* 1985 (*divorce* 1996) Geoffrey Stocker

1r *Iris Mary; *b* 6 Nov 1921; ATS WW II; *m* 3 Sept 1949 Richard Whiteside Leeming, s of James Whiteside Leeming, of Skirsgill Park, and has:

1s *Antony [Antony Leeming Esq, Skirsgill Park, nr Penrith, Cumbria]; *b* 22 June 1950; *educ* Ampleforth and Keble Coll Oxford; *m* 1 Sept 1990 *Lady Elizabeth Mary Cecilia Bowes Lyon (*see* STRATHMORE AND KINGHORNE, E)

2s *James; *b* 27 April 1952; *educ* Ampleforth

3s *Nicholas; *b* 14 Nov 1954; *educ* Ampleforth

2 Richard (Sir); ktd by 1349; Sheriff Berwick-on-Tweed 1350, Sheriff Roxburghs and Berwicks and Govr Berwick, Roxburgh and Scarborough Castles 1351–75; *m* 1st 1342 Joan (*dsp*), dau of Sir Thomas de Hertford, of Hertford, Yorks; *m* 2nd *c* 1355 Isabel, dau of Sir Thomas de Bourne, of Studley, Yorks, and *d* by Oct 1379, leaving, with an er s:

(1) William (Sir); of Hertford and Studley, both Yorks, also Treffham, Co Durham; *m* by 1401; *m* Alianore, dau and heiress of Sir William de Washington, and had a s (whose own s *d* in infancy) and two daus; he also had an illegitimate s:

1a Rowland; left land in Thornton le Strete by his f 1440; *m* Isabel, dau of William de Elemeden, and had:

1b Robert; *m* Anne, dau of — Lambton, of Lambton, Co Durham, and had:

1c Nicholas; *m* Agnes, dau of John Marley, of Gibside, and *d* 1539, leaving:

1d Thomas; *m* Elizabeth, dau of Rowland Place, of Halnaby, Yorks, and had, with at least one other s:

1e Sir NICHOLAS TEMPEST, 1st Bt (E), so *cr* 23 Dec 1622, of Stella, Co Durham; *b c* 1553; ktd March 1603/4; *m* Isabel, dau of Robert Lambton, of Lambton, Co Durham, and *d* 26 March 1626, having had, with two yr sons (*dsp*) and four daus:

1f Sir THOMAS TEMPEST, 2nd Bt, of Stella; *m* his distant cousin Troth, dau of Sir Richard Tempest, of Bracewell and Bolling, by Elizabeth, dau of Sir Francis Rodes, Judge Common Pleas, and *d* Aug 1641, having had, with four daus:

1g Sir RICHARD TEMPEST, 3rd Bt, of Stella; *b c* 1620; *educ* Queen's Coll Oxford and Lincoln's Inn; royalist Col of Horse Civil War; *m* 9 Oct 1641 Sarah, dau of Thomas Cambell (3rd s of Sir Thomas Cambell, Ld Mayor London 1609–10) by his 1st w Sarah (sis of Obadiah Sparkes), and was *bur* 5 Feb 1662, leaving:

1h Sir THOMAS TEMPEST, 4th Bt, of Stella; *b c* 1642; *m* Alice, 2nd dau and coheir of William Hodgson, of Hepburn, Co Durham, by Margaret, dau of Sir Thomas Haggerston, 1st Bt (*see* 1970 edn), and *d* Aug 1692, leaving:

1i Sir FRANCIS TEMPEST, 5th Bt, of Stella; *d* unm 1698

1i Jane; inherited Stella; *m c* 13 April 1700, as his 1st w, 4th and last Baron Widdrington of Blankney (*m* 2nd Catherine, dau of Sir Richard Graham, 3rd Bt, of Esk (*qv*), and *d* 1743) and *d* 9 Sept 1714

2g Nicholas; *m* Halliwell; *m* Margaret, dau of William Swinburne, of Capheaton, Northumberland, and had a dau

3g Thomas; *m* Jane, dau of Sir Jordan Metham, of Metham, Yorks, and had, with two er sons (*dsp*):

1h Sir NICHOLAS TEMPEST, 6th and last Bt; *b c* 1664; *m* Anne, dau of — Price, and *dsp* 31 May 1742, when the btcy expired

2e Rowland; *m* Barbara, sis of Sir John Calverley, of Littlebourne, Co Durham, and had, with a yr s (Francis, barrister Gray's Inn, Recorder Durham 1642, *bur* 22 Dec 1644):

1f Thomas (Sir), of the Isle, Co Durham; barrister, Attorney-Gen Ireland 1640; *m* his distant cousin Eleanor, dau of William Tempest (4th s of Thomas Tempest, of Holmside, Yorks), and had:

1g John, of the Isle; one of the projected Kts of the Roy Oak (a chivalric order mooted by CHARLES II), MP Co Durham 1675–77; *m* 27 Oct 1642 Elizabeth (*d* Oct 1684), only dau and heiress of John Heath, of Old Durham, and had, with other issue:

1h WILLIAM

1h Margaret; *b* 1645; *m* Sir Richard Shuttleworth, of Forcet, Yorks, and Gawthorpe, Lincs (*see* SHUTTLEWORTH, B)

2h Dorothy; living 15 Oct 1686; *m* William Sanderson, of Armathwaite Castle, Cumberland, and *dsp*

JOHN TEMPEST was *bur* 26 July 1697; his est son,

WILLIAM TEMPEST, of Old Durham; MP Durham 1678–89; *bapt* 31 Jan 1653; *m* 23 Dec 1677 Elizabeth (*bur* 25 June 1728), sis of Sir John Sudbury, 1st and last Bt, of Eldon, Co Durham, and had, with other issue:

1 JOHN

2 FitzHerbert; Capt Army; *bapt* 26 July 1687; *bur* 16 April 1724

3 Francis; Army Offr; *bapt* 18 Sept 1688; *bur* 3 Nov 1724

1 Margaret; *m* 9 July 1723 Rev Robert Blakiston, Vicar Berwick-on-Tweed

2 Elizabeth; *m* 26 Feb 1714 Anthony Salvin, of Sunderland-on-Bridge

WILLIAM TEMPEST was *bur* 15 March 1699/1700; his est son,

JOHN TEMPEST, of Old Durham; MP Durham 1705; *bapt* 17 April 1679; *m* 24 June 1706 Jane (*bur* 21 May 1736), dau and sole heiress of Richard Wharton, of Durham, and was *bur* 3 Jan 1737, having had, with other issue, including a dau (Anne, *m* 28 Oct 1732 Basil Foster, of Hartler House, and *dsp* 1771):

JOHN TEMPEST, of Sherborne, Co Durham; MP Durham 1741–54 and 1761; *bapt* 28 April 1710; *m* 9 May 1738 Frances (*bur* St Giles 18 June 1771), dau of Richard Shuttleworth, of Forcet and Gawthorpe (*see* SHUTTLEWORTH, B), and *d* 12 May 1776, leaving:

1 John, of Wynyard and Brancepeth Castle; MP Durham 1768–84 and 1790; *m* Anne, dau of Joseph Townsend, of Honington Hall, Warwicks, and *dsps* 12 Aug 1794, having had:

(1) John Wharton; *dvp* unm Brighton 13 May 1793

1 FRANCES Tempest; *m* 3 March 1708 Rev Sir Henry VANE, 1st Bt (*d* 7 June 1794), of Long Newton, Co Durham, Preb Durham, LLD Cantab, yr s of George Vane (*d* 25 July 1750), of Long Newton, and bro of Lionel Vane (*d* unm 20 Feb 1793), of Long Newton, and *d* 19 Jan 1796, leaving, with a dau (Frances Anne, *m* Michael Angelo Taylor, MP Durham):

(1) Sir HENRY VANE later VANE-TEMPEST (added under terms of unc's will, under which he inherited The Brancepeth Castle, Old Durham and Wynyard properties), 2nd Bt, of Long Newton; *b* 25 Jan 1771; MP Durham 1794–1800; *m* 25 April 1799 Lady Anne Katharine Mac Donnell (*m* 2nd 24 May 1817 Edmund PHELPS later McDONNELL [*sic*] and *d* 30 June 1834), Countess of Antrim in her own right (*see* ANTRIM, E) and est dau of 1st and last Marquess of Antrim, and *d* 1 Aug 1813, having by her had an only dau and heiress:

1a FRANCES ANNE EMILY VANE-TEMPEST; *m* 3 April 1812 as his 2nd w, CHARLES WILLIAM STEWART, **3rd Marquess of Londonderry** (*see* above)

LONG

Arms: Sa. within two flaunches and semée of cross-crosslets or a lion rampant arg. **Crest:** A lion's head arg., erased or, holding in the mouth a dexter hand erased gu. **Supporters:** On either side a lion arg., holding a flagstaff erect ppr., flowing therefrom a pennon sa., that on the dexter charged with a portcullis chained, that on the sinister with a fetterlock or. **Badge:** Issuant out of a coronet or, charged with three cross-crosslets sa., a demi-lion rampant arg. **Motto:** *Pieux quoique preux* ('Pious, though valiant'). **Creation:** V. (UK) 4 June 1921.

THE 4TH VISCOUNT LONG, of Wraxall, Co Wilts (Richard Gerard Long, CBE 1993) [The Rt Hon The Viscount Long, Owles Hall, Buntingford, Herts SG9 9PL]; *b* 30 Jan 1929; *s f* 1967; *educ* Harrow; Wilts Regt 1947–49, Oppn Whip 1974–79, Ld in Waiting 1979–97, Freeman City London 1991; *m* 1st 2 March 1957 (*divorce* 1984) Margaret Frances, only dau of Ninian Bannatyne Frazer, of 59 Hyde Park Gate, London, and has had:

1 +JAMES RICHARD; *b* 31 Dec 1960

1 *Sarah Victoria; *b* 14 Aug 1958; *m* 1990 *George G C Littler

2 Charlotte Helen; *b* 9 Oct 1965; actress; *d* 1984 in a motor accident

The 4th VISCOUNT *m* 2nd 1984 (*divorce* 1990) Mrs Catherine Patricia Elizabeth Mier Woolf, dau of Charles Terrence Miles-Ede, of S Africa; *m* 3rd 1990 *Helen Millar Wright Fleming-Gibbons

Lineage: JOHN LONG, of Marston, Potterne, Wilts; *m* Anne (*d* 1626), dau of John Merewether, of Great Cheverell, and *d* 1597, leaving, with other issue:

THOMAS LONG, of Little Cheverell and Melksham, Wilts; High Sheriff 1652; *bapt* 1597; *m* — Floyer, of Devon (*see also* ACLAND, Bt, of Columb-John), and was *bur* 8 May 1654, leaving, with an est s (John, High Sheriff Wilts 1668, *dsp*) and two yst sons (Thomas, ancestor of the LONGs of Preshaw; William, ancestor of the LONGs of Baynton):

RICHARD LONG, of Collingbourne Kingston, Wilts; *m* 9 April 1657 Elizabeth, dau of Edward Long and sis and heiress of Henry Long, of Rood Ashton, Wilts, and had:

1 Henry; *bapt* 20 May 1658; *m* Anne, dau of John Long and sis of Hope Long, of S Wraxall, and *d* 31 March 1686, leaving:

(1) Henry; *m* Ellen, dau of William Trenchard, of Cutteridge, Wilts, and *d* 1727, having had three sons (all *dsp*), and four daus

2 RICHARD

1 Dorothy; *m* 17 Oct 1685 Richard Kenn, MD, of Chippenham, and had issue

2 Dionysia; *bapt* 23 Jan 1661; *m* Edward Thresher, of Bradford-on-Avon, and had issue

RICHARD LONG *d* 1676; his 2nd son

RICHARD LONG, of Rood Ashton; *bapt* 7 April 1668; *m* 1st Elizabeth, dau of Thomas Long, of Monkton and Rowden, Wilts; *m* 2nd Grace (*dsp* April 1746), dau of John Stileman, of Steeple Ashton, and widow of John Martyn, of Hinton, Steeple Ashton, and *d* 19 Jan 1729/30, having had by his 1st w, with a yr s (Thomas, *d* unm 1711):

RICHARD LONG, of Rood Ashton; *m* Anne (*d* aged 71), sole dau and heiress of John Martyn, and had:

1 RICHARD

2 John; DD; Fell All Souls, Rector Chelsfield, Kent; *d* unm 17 Oct 1797 aged 65

1 Anne; *m* as his 2nd w Gifford Warriner, of Conock, Wilts, and *dsp* 1815

2 Elizabeth; *m* 1764 Rev Richard Pocock, Rector Mildenhall, Wilts, ggs of Dr Edward Pocock, the Orientalist, and *d* 18 Sept 1805 aged 83

3 Ellen; *m* Daniel Jones (*d* 1772), of Bradford-on-Avon, and *d* 17 May 1794, leaving issue

RICHARD LONG *d* 6 May 1760 aged 68; his er son,

RICHARD LONG, of Rood Ashton; *m* Meliora, dau of Sir John Lambe and widow of Joseph Poulden, of Imber, Wilts, and had:

1 RICHARD GODOLPHIN

2 John, of Monkton Farleigh; *b* 1768; *m* Mrs Lucy Anne Kinnear (*d* 11 Feb 1812 aged 48), dau of Rev John Warneford, of Corpus Christi Coll Oxford, Camden Prof Ancient History, and *d* 20 Oct 1833, having had, with three daus:

(1) John, of Monkton Farleigh and Baynton, Wilts, JP and DL; *b* 14 Aug 1793; *m* Mary, dau of Edward Daniel, barrister, and had issue

(2) Walter (Rev); *b* 1795; *m* Anne, dau of Rev R Gunning

1 Ellen Anne

2 Dionysia; *b* 29 Oct 1766; *m* 31 March 1792 John Bodmin Vince, 2nd s of Henry Chivers Vince, of Clyffe Hall, Wilts, and *d* 23 April 1814

RICHARD LONG *d* 3 Sept 1787 aged 69; his er son,

RICHARD GODOLPHIN LONG, of Rood Ashton; fndr Wilts Yeo, MP Wilts 1806–18; *bapt* 12 Nov 1761; *m* Florentina (*d* 1835), dau of Sir Bourchier Wrey, 5th Bt (*qv*), and *d* 1835 aged 74, having had, with other issue, including two daus (Ellen, *m* 1812 John Walmesley, of Wigan and Bath; Dionysia Mellora, *m* 6 Dec 1838 Rev Joseph Medicott, Vicar Potterne, Wilts):

WALTER LONG, of Rood Ashton, Wraxall, and Whaddon, JP, DL Wilts, Somerset and Montgomeryshire; Maj Roy Wilts Yeo Cav, MP N Wilts 1835; *b* 10 Oct 1793; *educ* Ch Ch Oxford (MA 1812); *m* 1st 3 Aug 1819 Mary Anne (*d* 15 March 1856), 2nd dau of Rt Hon Archibald Colquhoun, of Killermont, Dunbartonshire, Ld Register Scotland; *m* 2nd 15 April 1857 Mary Bickerton, est dau of R-Adml Sir James Hillyar, KCB, KCH, and widow of Rev Sir Cecil Augustus Bisshopp, Bt (*see* 1870 edn), and by his 1st w had:

1 Walter; *b* 27 Sept 1823; *m* Avarina Brunetta Herbert (*d* 26 Jan 1847), of Dolforgan, Montgomeryshire, and *dsp* Rome 17 April 1847

2 RICHARD PENRUDDOCKE

3 Henry William; Rector Hilperton, Trowbridge, Wilts; *b* 12 June 1829; *educ* Trin Coll Oxford (BA); *m* 1868 Jane, dau of Edwyn Statham, of S Lambeth, Surrey, and *dsp* 30 Jan 1876

1 Mary Anne Catherine; *m* 1st Bryan Edward Duppa; *m* 2nd John Philip Green, of the Temple-trees, Ceylon

2 Flora Henrietta; *m* 26 April 1853 Charles Penruddocke (*d* 1899), of Compton Park, Wilts, and *d* 1902

3 Jane Agnes; *m* 26 Aug 1860 Charles Forbes (*see* STUART-FORBES, Bt)

WALTER LONG *d* 31 Jan 1867; his 2nd son,

RICHARD PENRUDDOCKE LONG, of Rood Ashton, and Dolforgan Hall, Montgomeryshire, JP and DL; High Sheriff Montgomery 1858, MP Chippenham 1859, N Wilts 1865–68; *b* 19 Dec 1825; *educ* Trin Coll Cambridge (MA 1852); *m* 4 Oct 1853 Charlotte Anna (*d* 18 Dec 1899), only surv child of Rt Hon W W DICK formerly HUME, of Humewood, MP, and had:

1 WALTER HUME, **1st Viscount**

2 RICHARD GODOLPHIN WALMESLEY LONG later CHALONER, *cr* BARON GISBOROUGH (*qv*)

3 Robert Chaloner Critchley, JP and DL Wilts; 7th Dragoon Gds, Warwicks RHA (TA), Berks Yeo; *b* 4 Sept 1858; *m* 6 Feb 1884 Maud Felicia Frances Ann (*d* 1916), jt heiress with her two sisters of Llanerchydol Hall, Welshpool, 3rd and yst dau of Capt Willes Johnson, RN, by his 3rd w Margaret Ann, est dau of D Pugh, of Llanerchydol Hall, Welshpool, and *d* 5 Oct 1938, having had:

(1) Muriel Millesaintes Lilian; *b* 11 Nov 1884; *m* 28 June 1904 Lt-Col D H Campbell, 7th Dragoon Gds, and *d* 1944

(2) Margaret Bruce; *b* 1 Jan 1889; *m* 14 Jan 1914 Lt-Col Jack Giffard (*d* Feb 1956), OBE, RHA, Chev Legn Hon, twin s of Henry Rycroft Giffard, of Lockeridge House, Marlborough, and had issue

(3) Millesaintes Laura Joan; *b* 14 Aug 1897; *m* 1st 1916 (*divorce* 1921) Thomas Maitland Lovett, of Henlle Hall, Oswestry; *m* 2nd 12 May 1934 Donald Graham Bennett and *d* 1942

4 Henry Hope Giffard; *d* June 1866

5 William Hoare Bourchier; Capt 2nd Bn QO Roy W Kent Regt; *b* 22 March 1868; *d* 17 July 1943

1 Florence Frideswyde; *m* 5 July 1882 Sir Arthur Henderson Fairbairn, 3rd Bt (*qv*), and *dsp* 22 March 1941

2 Margaret Henrietta Georgina; *m* 6 Aug 1887 Hugh Frank Clutterbuck and *d* 1 Feb 1914, leaving issue

3 Charlotte Ethel; *m* 31 Jan 1889 John Evan Martin (*d* 1918) and *d* 5 Feb 1936, leaving issue

4 Frances Laura Arabella; *m* 1st 18 July 1882 (*divorce* 1888) Harry Willis Darell de Windt (*d* 30 Nov 1933); *m* 2nd 1892 Anthony George Lyster (*d* 1921) and *d* 29 April 1932

5 Maud Avarina Millesaintes; *d* 14 May 1880

RICHARD LONG *d* 16 Feb 1875; his est son,

WALTER HUME LONG, **1st Viscount Long**, of Wraxall, Co Wilts, so *cr* 4 June 1921, PC (4 July 1895), JP (Wilts); *b* 13 July 1854; MP N Wilts 1880–85, Devizes 1885–92, Liverpool (W Derby) 1893–1900, S Bristol 1900–06, S Dublin 1906–10, Middx Strand 1910–18 and St George's Westminster 1918–21, Sec Local Govt Bd 1886–92, Pres Bd Ag 1895–1900, Pres Local Govt Bd 1900–05 and 1915–16, Ch Sec to Ld Lt Ireland 1905–06, Sec State Colonies 1916–19, 1st Ld Admlty 1919–21, Lt-Col and Hon Col Roy Wilts Imp Yeo, Ld Lt Somerset, Hon LLD Birmingham 1909, FRS; *m* 1 Aug 1878 Lady Dorothy Blanche Boyle (*d* 7 June 1938), 4th dau of 9th Earl of Cork and Orrery (*qv*), and *d* 26 Sept 1924, having had:

1 Walter, CMG, DSO; Brig-Gen 2nd Dragoons, Boer War (wounded Kimberley Feb 1900), WW I, Order St Stanislas Russia 2nd Cl with swords; *b* 26 July 1879; *m* 17 Dec 1910 Sibell, OBE (*m* 2nd 25 April 1921 Maj 1st and last Baron Glyn, MC, DL (*d* 1 May 1960), and *d* 23 March 1958), er dau of 2nd Baron Derwent (*qv*), and was *ka* 27 Jan 1917, leaving:

(1) WALTER FRANCIS DAVID LONG, **2nd Viscount Long**; *b* 14 Sept 1911; *educ* Eton; Maj Coldstream Gds WW II; *m* 14 Nov 1933 (*divorce* 1942) Frances Laura, 2nd dau of Hon Guy Lawrence Charteris (*see* WEMYSS, E), and was *ka* Uden, Holland, 23 Sept 1944, leaving:

1a *(Antoinette) Sara Frances Sibell [The Hon Mrs Sara Morrison, 16 Groom Place, London SW1X 7BA]; CC then CA Wilts 1961–71, v-chm C Party 1971–75; dir: GEC 1980–, Abbey Nat 1979–95, Carlton TV 1992–; Govr Imp Coll London 1986– (Hon Fell 1993), FRSA; *b* 9 Aug 1934; *m* 28 Oct 1954 (*divorce* 1984) Hon Sir Charles Andrew Morrison, MP, 2nd s of 1st Baron Margadale (*qv*), and has issue

2 RICHARD ERIC ONSLOW, **3rd Viscount**

1 Victoria Florence de Burgh, CBE; *m* 26 Nov 1901 1st Baron Wraxall (*qv*) and *d* 29 March 1920

2 Doreen Ethel Nora; *b* 17 Feb 1884; *d* 8 May 1885

3 Lettice Margaret; *m* 18 April 1904 Sir (William George) Daniel Cooper, 4th Bt, of Woollahra (*qv*), and *d* 1 Sept 1950, leaving issue

The 2nd VISCOUNT's unc,

RICHARD ERIC ONSLOW LONG, **3rd Viscount Long**, TD, JP, DL; *b* 22 Aug 1892; *educ* Harrow; Maj Roy Wilts Yeo TA, MP (C) Westbury 1927–31, served WWs I (despatches) and II 1939–42, Freeman City of Athens, Kt Cdr Order George I of Greece; *m* 21 Oct 1916 Gwendolyn Hague (*d* 19 Jan 1959), dau of Thomas Reginald Hague Cook, and *d* 12 Jan 1967, having had:

1 Walter Reginald Basil; Lt RA WW II; *b* 13 Dec 1918; *das* (drowned) Greece 28 April 1941

2 RICHARD GERARD LONG, **4th and present Viscount Long**

3 +John Hume [The Hon John Long, Mount Cottage, Kleine Constantia, CP, S Africa]; *b* 4 July 1930; *educ* Harrow; late Black Watch, BSA Police Rhodesia 1951; *m* 29 Nov 1957 (*divorce* 1969) Averil Juliet, only dau of Henry Stobart, of Arcturus, Rhodesia; *m* 2nd 30 July 1994 *Anne, dau of Capt and Mrs H L Taunton, of Jersey, and by his 1st w has:

(1) *Bridget Gwendolyn; *b* 26 Aug 1963

1 *Noreen [The Hon Mrs Bartholomew, Poulshot Court, Devizes, Wilts]; *b* 21 Jan 1921; *m* 14 June 1947 *Maj John Cairns Bartholomew, Roy Wilts Yeo, only s of John Bartholomew, of Rowde Court, Devizes, and has:

(1) *Charles J E; *b* 1951; *m* 1979 *Rosemary Anne, dau of Rev Canon V H Julien, of The Rectory, Hamilton, Vict, Australia, and has:

1a *Toby; *b* 1986

1a *Camilla; *b* 1984

(2) *William W; *b* 1956; *m* 3 Sept 1982 *Carolyn, er dau of Barry Pride, of Knock House, Stone-in-Oxney, Kent, and has:

1a *Jack William; *b* 1989

1a *Sophie Virginia; *b* 1990

(1) *Susan; *b* 1949; *m* 19– *— Bruce and has:

1a *Rupert; *b* 19–

1a *Natasha; *b* 19–

LONGFORD

Arms: Quarterly, 1st, quarterly or and gu., in the first quarter an eagle displayed vert (for PAKENHAM); 2nd, arg. on a bend indented sa., cotised az., three fleurs-de-lys of the field, each cotise charged with three bezants (for CUFF); 3rd, erm. a griffin segreant az. (for AUNGIER); 4th, per bend crenelle arg. and gu. (for BOYLE).
Crest: Out of a mural crown or an eagle displayed gu.
Supporters: Dexter, a lion az., charged on the shoulder with an escarbuncle or; sinister, a griffin segreant az., wings erm., beaked and clawed or. **Motto:** *Gloria virtutis umbra* ('Glory is the shadow of virtue'). **Creations:** B. (I) 7 May 1756 (Longford), E. (I) 20 June 1785 (Longford), B. (UK) 17 July 1821 (Silchester) and 12 Oct 1945 (Pakenham of Cowley).

THE 7TH EARL OF LONGFORD, **Baron Longford**, Co Longford, **Baron Silchester**, Co Southampton, and **Baron Pakenham**, of Cowley, City of Oxford (Sir Francis Aungier Pakenham, KG (1971), PC (1948)) [The Rt Hon The Earl of Longford KG PC, Bernhurst, Hurst Green, Sussex TN19 7QN; 18 Chesil Court, Chelsea Manor St, London SW3 5QP]; *b* 5 Dec 1905; *s* bro 1961; *educ* Eton and New Coll Oxford (BA 1928, MA 1934); tutor U Tutorial Courses Stoke-on-Trent 1929–31, CRD 1930–32, lecturer politics Ch Ch Oxford 1932, 2nd Lt Oxon and Bucks LI (TA) 1939 (resigned due ill-health 1940), Sub-Cdr 'S' Co Oxford City Bn HG, PA to Lord Beveridge 1941–44, Ld-in-Waiting 1945–46, Parly U-Sec War 1946–47, Chllr Duchy Lancaster 1947–48, Min Civil Aviation 1948–51, 1st Ld Admlty May–Oct 1951, Ld Privy Seal 1964–65 and 1966–68, Ldr Ho Lds 1964–68, Sec State Colonies 1965–66, chm Nat Bank 1955–63 and Sidgwick and Jackson 1970–80 (dir 1980–85), Nat Youth Employment Cncl 1968–71; fndr New Bridge for Ex-Prisoners 1956, Dir The Help Charitable Tst 1986; Gd Cross Order St Gregory 1975, author: *Peace by Ordeal* (1935), *Born to Believe* (autobiography, 1953), *Causes of Crime* (with Roger Opie, 1958), *The Idea of Punishment* (1961), *Five Lives* (autobiography, 1964), *Humility* (1969), *Eamon de Valera* (with Thomas P O'Neill, 1970), *The Grain of Wheat* (autobiography, 1974), *Abraham Lincoln* (1974), *Jesus Christ* (1974), *Kennedy* (1976), *St Francis of Assisi* (1978), *Nixon* (1980), *Ulster* (with Anne McHardy, 1981), *Pope John Paul II* (1982), *Diary of a Year* (1982), *Eleven at No. 10: a personal view of Prime Ministers* (1984), *One Man's Faith* (1984), *The Search for Peace* (1985), *The Bishops* (1986), *Saints* (1987), *A History of the House of Lords* (1989), *Suffering and Hope* (1990), *Punishment and the Punished* (1991), *Prisoner or Patient* (1992), *Young Offenders* (1993), *Avowed Intent* (autobiography, 1994); *m* 3 Nov 1931 *Elizabeth, CBE (1974), author: *Points for Parents* (1956), *Catholic Approaches* (ed, 1959), *Jameson's Raid* (1960), *Victoria RI* (1964, James Tait Black memorial Prize 1964), *Wellington: Years of the Sword* (1969, Yorkshire Post Prize), *Wellington: Pillar of State* (1972), *The Royal House of Windsor* (1974), *Churchill* (1974), *Byron's Greece* (1975), *Life of Byron* (1976), *A Pilgrimage of Passion: the life of Wilfrid Scawen Blunt* (1979), *Louisa: Lady in Waiting* (ed, 1979), *Images of Chelsea* (1980), *The Queen Mother, a biography* (1981), *Eminent Victorian Women* (1981), *Elizabeth R* (1983), *The Pebbled Shore* (autobiography, 1986), *The Oxford Book of Royal Anecdotes* (1989), *Darling Loosy: Letters to Princess Louise 1856–1939* (1991), *Poet's Corner* (anthology, 1992), *Royal Throne: the future of the Monarchy* (1993), er dau of Nathaniel Bishop Harman, FRCS, of 108 Harley St, London W1, and has had:

1 +THOMAS FRANK DERMOT (does not use courtesy title) [Thomas Pakenham Esq, 111 Elgin Crescent, London W11 2JF; Tullynally, Castlepollard, Co Westmeath, Ireland]; *b* 14 Aug 1933; *educ* Ampleforth and Magdalen Coll Oxford (BA 1955); jnlst with *TES* 1958–60, *Sunday Telegraph* 1961, *Observer* 1961–64, Treas British-Irish Assoc 1972–, Sec and Co-Fndr Christopher Ewart-Biggs Memorial Tst 1976–, Fndr and Chm Irish Tree Soc 1990–; author: *The Mountains of Rasselas: an Ethiopian adventure* (1959), *The Year of Liberty: the story of the Great Irish Rebellion of 1798* (1969), *The Boer War* (1979, Cheltenham Prize 1980), *Dublin: a travellers' companion* (with Valerie Pakenham, 1988), *The Scramble for Africa* (1992), *Meetings with Remarkable Trees* (1996); *m* 23 July 1964 *Valerie Susan, yst dau of Maj Ronald McNair Scott, of Huish House, Old Basing, Hants, and has:

(1) +Edward Melchior; *b* 6 Jan 1970

(2) +Frederick Augustus; *b* 27 Nov 1971

(1) *Anna Maria; *b* 26 July 1965

(2) *Eliza; *b* 3 Nov 1966; *m* 1983 *Alexander James Chisholm (*see* WINDLESHAM, B) and has:

    1a *Aidan Carus; *b* 29 July 1996

2 +Patrick Maurice [The Hon Patrick Pakenham, 24 Chesil Court, Chelsea Manor St, London SW3]; *b* 17 April 1937; *educ* Ampleforth and Magdalen Coll Oxford; barrister Inner Temple 1966; *m* 27 July 1968 *Mary Elizabeth, er dau of Maj Henry Aldren James Plummer, of Winchester, and has:

(1) +Richard; *b* 22 April 1969

(2) +Guy; *b* 19 July 1970

(3) +Harry Michael; *b* 8 Jan 1972

3 +Michael Aidan CMG (1993) [The Hon Michael Pakenham CMG, 23 Sutherland Pl, London W2; 3062 P St, Washington, DC, USA]; *b* 3 Nov 1943; *educ* Ampleforth, Trin Coll Cambridge (MA) and Rice U Texas, USA; FO 1965–, UK Perm Rep EC Brussels 1987–91, Amb and Consul Gen Luxembourg 1991–94, Min Paris 1994–; *m* 1980 *Meta (Mimi) Landreth, er dau of William Conway Doak, of Philadelphia, and formerly w of — Lavine, and has:

(1) *Alexandra Clio; *b* 1981

(2) *Clio Isabelle Blaise; *b* 1985

4 +Kevin John Toussaint; *b* 1 Nov 1947; *educ* Ampleforth and New and St Antony's Colls Oxford; sr economist Rothschild Intercontinental Bank, md John Govett (fund manager), Pres Irish Club London 1997–, Treas Ireland Fund of GB, author *A Gathering Bunker* (golf stories, 1996); *m* 1st 1972 (*divorce* 1984) Ruth Lesley, dau of Leslie Douglas Colbeck Jackson, and has:

(1) +Thomas John Chamberlain; *b* 23 May 1977

(1) *Catherine Ruth; *b* 4 May 1975

4 (cont.) The Hon Kevin Pakenham *m* 2nd, as her 2nd husb, *Mrs Claire Chatel (novelist as Clare Harkness), er dau of John Edward Melvill Hoare, of Montague House, Holton St Peter, Suffolk, and by her has:

(2) +Benjamin John; *b* 1983

(3) +Dominic Balthazar; *b* 1989

(2) *Hermione Clare; *b* 1984

1 *Antonia [The Lady Antonia Fraser, c/o Curtis Brown, Haymarket House, 28/29 Haymarket, London SW1Y 4SP]; *b* 27 Aug 1932; *educ* LMH Oxford (MA); author: *King Arthur and the Knights of the Round Table* (1954), *Robin Hood* (1955), *Dolls* (1963), *A History of Toys* (1966), *Mary Queen of Scots* (1969, James Tait Black Memorial Prize), *Cromwell Our Chief of Men* (1973); *King James: VI of Scotland, I of England* (1974), *Quiet as a Nun* (1977), *The Wild Island* (1978), *King Charles II* (1979), *A Splash of Red* (1981), *Cool Repentance* (1982), *The Weaker Vessel: woman's lot in seventeenth century England* (1984, Wolfson History Award, Prix Caumont-La-Force 1985), *Oxford Blood* (1985), *Jemima Shore's First Case* (1986), *Your Royal Hostage* (1987), *Boadicea's Chariot: the Warrior Queens* (1988), *The Cavalier Case* (1990), *Jemima Shore at the Sunny Grave* (1991), *The Six Wives of Henry VIII* (1992, Schlossbauverein Prize 1997), *Political Death* (1994), *The Gunpowder Plot: terror and faith in 1605* (1996, CWA Non-fiction Gold Dagger 1996 and St Louis Literary Award 1996); chm Soc Authors 1974–75; chm CWA 1979–80, V Pres English PEN 1989–90, Pres 1990–; *m* 1st 25 Sept 1956 (*divorce* 1977) Hon Sir Hugh Charles Patrick Joseph Fraser, MBE, MP (*see* LOVAT, L), and has issue; *m* 2nd 1980 *Harold Pinter, CBE, playwright

2 *Judith Elizabeth (does not use courtesy title) [Mrs Judith Kazantzis, 32 Ladbroke Grove, London W11 3BQ]; *b* 14 Aug 1940; *educ* Somerville Coll Oxford (BA); *m* 26 Feb 1963 (*divorce* 1982) Alexander John Kazantzis, yr s of Constantine Kazantzis, of Ealing, and has:

(1) *Arthur Constantine; *b* 27 Nov 1967

(1) *Miranda Elizabeth; *b* 13 Nov 1964

3 *Rachel Mary [The Lady Rachel Billington, 33 Courtnell St, London W2 5BU; The Court House, Poyntington, Dorset DT9 4LF]; *b* 11 May 1942; author: *All Things Nice* (1969), *The Big Dipper* (1970), *Lilacs out of the Dead Land* (1971), *Cock Robin* (1973), *Beautiful* (1974), *A Painted Devil* (1975), *A Woman's Age* (1979), *Rosanna and the Wizard-Robot* (for children, 1981), *Occasion of Sin* (1982), *The First Christmas* (for children 1983), *Star-Time* (for children, 1984), *The Garish Day* (1985), *The First Easter* (for children, 1987), *Loving Attitudes* (1988), *The First Miracles* (for children, 1990), *Theo and Matilda* (1990), *Bodily Harm* (1992), *The Family Year* (1992), *The Great Umbilical: mother, daughter, mother* (1994), *Magic and Fate* (1996), *Life of Jesus* (for children, 1996), *Perfect Happiness: the sequel to Emma* (1996), *Tiger Sky* (1998); Pres English centre PEN 1998–; *m* 1967 *Kevin Billington, film, theatre and TV dir, and has:

(1) *Nathaniel Kevin; *b* 6 Dec 1970

(2) *Caspar Leo; *b* 1979

(1) *Catherine Rose; *b* 6 Feb 1973

(2) *Chloe Margaret; *b* 28 March 1976

4 Catherine Rose; *b* 25 Feb 1946; jnlst *Daily Telegraph Magazine*; *k* car crash 11 Aug 1969

Longford, previous creations: Francis Aungier, son of a leading lawyer in ELIZABETH I's reign, was created Baron Aungier of Longford in 1621, the Earldom and Viscountcy of Longford being conferred on his grandson, another Francis, half a century later. The elder Francis was Master of the Rolls, a Privy Counsellor and briefly joint Lord Keeper, all in the Kingdom of Ireland, where he won a reputation as a hanging judge. His younger brother John was known by the anglicised form of his surname as Hanger and another brother, Richard, was hanged for murdering their father, a blot on the family record which may account for the severity of Judge Francis as a form of overcompensation. What was apparently a criminal streak in the family would keep breaking out, however. The younger Francis, the 1st Earl, embezzled £1,500 (some £72,000 in late-1990s terms) that was in his care for weapons procurement when Captain of Horse late in CHARLES II's reign. The view of him by a contemporary as a 'skilled financier' rings a little hollow in the circumstances. A few years later he was sacked from his post of Commissioner of Irish Revenue, though this may have been for religious reasons as the new Lord Lieutenant was a Catholic, whereas the Aungiers, at any rate in the 16th century, had been noted Protestants. With the death in 1704 of his brother and successor, the childless 2nd Earl, the titles expired. Alice, their sister, married Sir James Cuffe and was great-grandmother of the Countess of Longford of the 1785 creation (*see* below).

Lineage: WALTER; held the Manor of Netherhall, Pakenham, Suffolk, by the end of the 11th century as vassal of the Abbey of Bury St Edmunds; founded the church at Pakenham *c* 1100; had an est s:

PETER; had an illegitimate s:

ANSELM; seized the manor to the exclusion of his f's sisters; *m* Ingrethe — and had:

ROBERT de PAKYNHAM; inherited f's manor; granted 1252 lands in Kertling, Cambs, to his sons; had:

JOHN de PAKENHAM, called 'le Clerk' (probably from his having been literate); *m* Muriel — and had, with an er s (Sir John, *d* by 1305, his male line dying out in the 14th century):

Sir WILLIAM de PAKENHAM; King's Justice on circuit; *m* Joan — and *d* 1304, leaving, with three er sons and coheirs (Sir Edmund, feudal Ld of Netherhall, *m* Rose, dau and coheir of Robert de Valoignes, his line dying out 1361; Thomas, feudal Ld of Ixworth thorpe, Suffolk, whose last male-line descendant *d* 1396; William, feudal Ld of Fakenham Aspes, Suffolk, whose branch died out by 1381):

JOHN de PAKENHAM, of Garboldisham, Norfolk; *m* Margery, dau and heir of Robert de Northwold, and *d* 1315, leaving, with two er sons (Aubrey, *d* unm; Richard, *m* Joan, widow of (a) Sir William de Cricketot and (b) Sir John Fitz-Rauf, and *d* 1383 (last of the family to live at Netherhall), leaving a dau Anne):

THOMAS de PAKENHAM, of Garboldisham; *m* Agnes, sis and heiress of Henry le Bretton, feudal Ld of Shropham, Norfolk, and *d* by 1386, leaving, with an er s (Henry, ancestor of the PAKENHAMs of Garboldisham and Shropham, extinct 1495):

EDMUND de PAKENHAM; executor of his uncle Richard's will 1383; tstee for lands in Ampton and Thorpe 1404; had:

JOHN de PAKENHAM; Collector Customs Southampton 1380; *m* Joan (*m* 2nd John Wespall, of Hartley Wespall, Hants, and *d* 1451), widow of Henry Machon, and *d* 1420, having had, with a yr s (John, priest, Treasurer York Minster, executor Cardinal Kemp's will, *d* 1477):

HUGH PAKENHAM; Sheriff Wilts 1459, Ld Manor Eastcourt, Finchampstead, Berks; *s* to his step-f's Manor of Hartley Wespall 1451; Constable Odiham Castle 1457; *m* Constance, dau and coheir of Richard de la Hay, and *d c* 1478, leaving, with a yr s (Nicholas, Town Clerk City London 1489–1516, *d* unm) and a dau (Agnes, Dominican nun Dartford Priory):

JOHN PAKENHAM, of Eastcourt; *m* Margaret, dau and coheir of John Bramshott, of Bramshott and Titden (and sis of Elizabeth, w of John Dudley, mother of HENRY VII's notorious Minister John Dudley and grandmother of John, Duke of Northumberland; *see* NORTHUMBERLAND, D, preliminary remarks, also DUDLEY, B, and DE L'ISLE, V), and with his w *d* of plague 1 Oct 1485, having had, with an er s (Sir Edmund, Gentleman-Usher to CATHERINE OF ARAGON, Ld of Manor of Eastcourt and Lordington, Sussex, *d* 1528; his er dau Constance *m* Sir Geoffrey Pole; *see* ABERGAVENNY, M):

HUGH PAKENHAM; *m* Anne, eventual coheiress to her bro Sir Richard Clement, of Ightam Moat, Kent, so becoming Ld Manors Ightam Moat and Stretton-on-Fosse, Warwicks, and had, with two daus (Anne, *m* 1st Sir William FitzWilliam (*k* Flodden 1513), *m* 2nd Sir William Sydney (*see* DE L'ISLE, V); Elizabeth, *m* Sir Francis Lovell, of E Harling, Norfolk):

ROBERT PAKENHAM; Clerk Green Cloth; bought 1548 Manor of Tooting Bec, Surrey; *m* Elizabeth, dau and heiress of Maurice Berkeley, of Wymondham, Leics, who brought him large estates in Leics, Lincs, Rutland and Yorks, and *d* 1552, leaving, with other issue:

1 Robert; Sheriff Hunts; *m* Ursula, dau of Clement Chicheley, of Wimpole, Cambs, and had, with other issue:

(1) Henry (Sir), of Belton and N Witham, Lincs; his male line expired 1651

2 John, of Wimbledon; lawyer; *d* unm 1602

3 Edmund; *b c* 1547; Sec to his first cousin Sir Henry Sydney, Ld Dep Ireland; Clerk-Comptroller of the Revels to ELIZABETH I 1595; *m* Frances, dau of Francis Seckford, of Seckford Hall, Suffolk, and *d* 1605, having had, with other issue (*dsp* or unm):

(1) Philip (Sir); ktd 1617, Col English Bde in service of Dutch Republic; *dsp* abroad 1638

(2) Edmund; Ensign under er bro; *dsp*

(3) Robert; *b* 1592; *m* Jane, dau of Jasper Horsey, of Willen, Herts, and *d* of plague with his w July 1638, leaving, with two other sons (*dsp*):

    1a HENRY

    2a Philip; Offr Royalist Army 1644; *d* unm Ireland 1683

    3a Robert; *m* Anne Stearne and *d* 1703, leaving issue in Ireland

The est son,

HENRY PAKENHAM; *b c* 1618; Parly Capt Dragoons Ireland 1642–65; granted 17 Oct 1665 lands that included acreage in the Barony of Bantry, Co Wexford, and Tullynally, Co Westmeath, in lieu of £4,363 arrears of pay; MP Navan 1667; *m* 1st Mary (*d* 12 June 1665), dau of Robert Lill, of Trim, Co Meath, and had, with two other sons (Philip, *b* 1653; Henry) and three other daus (Eleanor, *m* Archdeacon Smith, of Clogherissue; Mary; *m* — Robinson; Martha, *m* — Rider):

1 THOMAS (Sir)

2 William, of Carne; *m* Rebekah, 2nd dau of Nicholas Ogle, of Dysart, Co Westmeath, and *d* 1740, leaving three sons (William; Robert; Thomas) and two daus (including Martha, *m* — Troke; —, *m* —Eaton)

HENRY PAKENHAM *m* 2nd 1670 Anne, widow of Capt James Pierce and sis of Sir Thomas Pigot, Master Court of Wards, and by her had:

3 Robert; Rector Kilbeggan, Co Westmeath; *m* Lucretia (*d* 1755), dau of Sir Elias Best, Ld Mayor Dublin and *d* by 1760, having had, with three other sons (*dsp*):

(1) Edward; *m* Elizabeth, dau of Adml John Weller, of Rolvenden, Kent, and *d* by 1765, leaving:

    1a John; *b* 1743; V-Adml the Red; *m* Frances Thomas and *dsp* 1807

    2a Edward; Capt RN; *d* unm 1798

    1a Helen; *m* Fleming French, of Ripple Vale (*see* 1970 edn YPRES, E)

2a Elizabeth Lucretia, of Bernhurst House, Hurst Green, Sussex; *d unm*

4 Anne; *m* Robert Beatty, of Springtown, Co Longford

HENRY PAKENHAM *d* 1690; his est son,

Sir THOMAS PAKENHAM; ktd 1693, Prime Serjeant-at-law Ireland 1695, MP Augher, Co Tyrone, 1695–99; *b* 1649; *m* 1st 1673 Mary, dau of Richard Nelmes, Alderman London; *m* 2nd 18 Feb 1696 Mary (*dsp*), dau of Sir Daniel Bellingham, 1st Bt (*qv*), and by his 1st w had, with two other sons (*d unm*):

1 EDWARD

2 Thomas, of Craddenstown, Co Westmeath; *m* Anne, dau of Thomas Smyth, of Kiltomb, Co Westmeath, and *d* 1722, leaving:

  (1) Eleanor; *m* Abraham Fuller, of Violet Hill, Co Dublin

1 Frances; *m* George Nugent, of Castlerichard, Co Westmeath, and *d* 1756

Sir THOMAS *d* 1706; his est son,

EDWARD PAKENHAM, of Pakenham Hall, Co Westmeath; MP Co Westmeath 1714–21; *m* 1708 Margaret (*m* 2nd Rev Ossory Medlicott), dau and heiress of John Bradestan, and had:

1 THOMAS, **1st Baron**

2 George Edward; Hamburg merchant; *b* 1717; *m* Frances, dau of Frederick Voquel, and *d* 1768, leaving, with four other sons (*dsp*):

  (1) John Henry; Capt 1st Dragoon Gds; *m* 1st 27 Sept 1780 Henrietta Maria Edgar; *m* 2nd Anne Sherrard and *dsp*

  (2) Richard; Capt 27th Foot; *d* St Lucia 1779

  (3) Robert; *d* 1721

  (1) Elizabeth; *d* 1722

EDWARD PAKENHAM *d* 1721; his est son,

THOMAS PAKENHAM, **1st Baron Longford**, Co Longford (I), so *cr* 7 May 1756 following his marriage; *b* May 1713; *educ* Queen's Coll Oxford; MP Longford 1745–56; *m* 5 March 1739/40 ELIZABETH (*bapt* 26 July 1719; *d* 27 Jan 1794), **Countess of Longford** in her own right (I), so *cr* 20 June 1785, dau and sole heiress of Michael Cuffe, MP Ballinrobe, Co Mayo (*d* 24 July 1744, s of Francis Cuffe, MP Co Mayo (*d* 26 Dec 1694), himself est s of Sir James Cuffe by Alice, sis of Ambrose Aungier, 2nd and last Earl of Longford of the 1677 *cr*), and *d* 27 Jan 1794, leaving:

1 EDWARD MICHAEL, **2nd Baron**

2 Robert; MP Co Longford 1768–75, Capt 33rd Foot; *d unm* 1775

3 William; *b* 1756; *d* 1769

4 Thomas (Sir), GCB; Adml the Red, MP Longford 1783–90 and 1797–1800 and Kells 1790–97, Master-Gen Ordnance Ireland; *b* 1757; *m* 24 June 1785 Louisa (*d* 1833), dau of John Staples, PC, MP (*see* STAPLES, Bt), and *d* 2 Feb 1836, leaving, with other issue:

  (1) Edward Michael PAKENHAM later CONOLLY, of Castletown, Co Kildare; Col Donegal Militia, MP Co Donegal; *b* 23 Aug 1786; *m* 25 May 1819 Catherine Jane (*d* July 1861), dau of Chambré Brabazon Ponsonby Barker, and *d* 4 Jan 1848, leaving, with other issue:

    1a Thomas, of Castletown and Cliff, Co Donegal; MP Donegal; *b* 23 Feb 1823; *m* 1 Sept 1868 Sarah, dau of Joseph Shaw, of Celbridge, Co Kildare, and *d* 10 Aug 1876, leaving, with other issue:

      1b Thomas; Lt Scots Greys; *b* 1 Sept 1870; *ka* Boer War 11 July 1900

      2b Edward Michael, CMG (1919); Maj RA, Capt W R RA (TA) Boer War 1899–1901 (despatches) and WW I (despatches); *b* 20 Feb 1874; *d unm* 22 Oct 1956

      1b Catherine; *b* 20 Oct 1871; *m* 21 April 1904 5th Baron Carew (*qv*) and *d* 20 March 1947, leaving issue

    2a Arthur Wellesley; Capt 30th Foot; *b* April 1828; *ka* Inkerman 5 Nov 1855

    3a John Augustus, VC; Lt-Col Coldstream Gds; *b* 30 Nov 1829; *m* 4 Aug 1864 Ida Charlotte (*d* 1886), dau of Edwyn Burnaby, of Baggrave Hall, Leics, and *d* 28 Jan 1889, leaving:

      1b John Richard Arthur; *b* 22 July 1870

      1b Aileen Geta Katherine; *m* 10 Nov 1891 Eustace Abel Smith (*d* 10 July 1938), of Longhills, Lincs, and *d* 12 July 1912, leaving issue

      2b Oonah Edwina; *m* 22 Jan 1891 Lt-Col John McNeile (*ka* Dardanelles 12 July 1915), 4th Bn KOSB, Maj Coldstream Gds, and *d* 15 Oct 1960 aged 93, leaving issue

      3b Louisa Augusta

      4b Irene Beatrice; *d unm* 28 Dec 1928

    4a Richard; 3rd Sec Legation Peking; *d unm* 28 Aug 1870

    1a Louisa Augusta; *m* 28 July 1846 3rd Baron Langford (*qv*) and was accidentally drowned 4 Nov 1854, leaving issue

    2a Henrietta; *m* 29 May 1880 Rev Edward Montgomery Moore

    3a Mary Margaret; *m* 6 June 1854 Rt Hon Henry Bruen (*d* 8 March 1912), of Oak Park, Co Carlow, and *d* 13 May 1894, leaving issue

  (2) Thomas; HEIC CS; *b* 12 Oct 1787; *m* 1st 1813 Isabella Mary (*d* 10 Nov 1827), dau of Lt-Gen Sir Frederic Augustus Wetherall, GCH; *m* 2nd 1 May 1838 Sarah Jane, dau of William Mills, of Cradoxton, and widow of W Johnstone, and *d* 17 Oct 1846, leaving by his 1st w:

    1a George Dent; Capt 4th Bengal Lancers; *b* 12 June 1824; *m* 1st 13 June 1850 Rosa (*dsp* 7 June 1852), dau of Justin McCarthy; *m* 2nd 1853 Elizabeth (*d* 1909), dau of Rev Robert Hume, and *d* 19 June 1888, having by her had:

      1b Thomas Robert; Colonial Sec Sierra Leone; *b* 27 Nov 1854; *d unm* 5 Sept 1885

      2b Gustavus Conolly; *b* 27 Oct 1856; *m* 14 Nov 1889 Ella Compton (*d* 14 Aug 1913), only dau of William George Bayne, of Japan, and *d* 1 Nov 1924, having had, with a s (*d* in infancy):

        1c Compton Thomas, MC; Lt Coldstream Gds WW I (despatches); *b* 11 May 1893; *m* 1st 1915 (*divorce* 1920) Phyllis Mona, dau of Col William Price, RE, and had:

          1d *Simona Vere [Mrs Kenneth Middleton, Cobbler's Cottage, Ledwell, Oxon OX7 7AN]; *b* 1916; *m* 1939 Noel Paterson Durnford Iliff (*d* 1984) and *m* 2nd 1984 *Kenneth William Bruce Middleton and by her 1st husb has:

            1e *David Anthony [David Iliff Esq, Green Willows, Station Rd, Woodmancote, Glos GL52 4HN]; *b* 1939; *m* 1966 *Celia Winifred Foot and has:

              1f *Stephanie Brigid Laura; *b* 1968

              2f *Alison Deborah Caroline; *b* 1970

        1c (cont.) Compton Pakenham *m* 2nd 1921 Alma Clark and by her had:

          1d Compton Christopher; *b* 8 July 1921; *m* 11 March 1947 Dorothy Rebecca (*d* 1984), dau of Walter Thomas Cullingford, and *d* 1996, leaving:

            1e *Diane; *b* 17 June 1949; *m* 1980 *— Pennington

            2e *Monica; *b* 5 April 1954

            3e *Jennifer [Mrs Gary Sawhill, Mattix Run Equestrian Center and Polo Club, Moss Mill Rd, Towne of Smithville, NJ 08201, USA]; *b* 5 April 1954; *m* 1983 *Gary Sandy Sawhill

        1c (cont.) Compton Pakenham *m* 3rd 1925 Sara (*d* 1976), dau of Charles Manning Furman, of Clemson, SC, and *d* 17 Aug 1957, having by her had:

          2d +Edward Michael; *b* 1932; *ed New York Daily News*

          2d *Joan Compton; *b* 1932; *m* 19– *— Breiter

        2c Hercules Ivo; *b* 22 June 1897; *d unm* 4 March 1954

        3c A son; *b* and *d* 3 Sept 1898

        1c Cynthia Hume Barnard; *b* 16 Aug 1890; *m* 6 June 1912 Gilbert Lyall (*d* 8 Oct 1949), 5th s of George Lyall, of Hong Kong, and had issue

        2c Hermione Bayne; *b* 25 July 1896; *m* 8 June 1921 Norman Hubert Rutherford (*d* 3 Jan 1962) and *dsp* 5 Jan 1940

        3c Daphne Eliot Araminta; *b* 29 April 1901; *m* 24 Nov 1926 Geoffrey Charles Kingham and had:

          1d *Michael Francis Pakenham [Michael Kingham Esq, Ridgway House, Runwick, Farnham, Surrey]; Lt (Res) Roy Welch Fus; *b* 19 Sept 1928; *educ* Marlborough; *m* 15 March 1958 *Ann Augusta Cardamine, only dau of Edgar Percival Chance, of Sandhurst, and has:

            1e *Charles Edgar Justin; *b* 8 Sept 1962

            1e *Camilla Lucinda Jane; *b* 4 July 1960

    3b John Arthur; *b* 19 July 1859; *m* 1888 Agnes Noble Stuart (*d* 30 July 1948), dau of David Millons, of Edinburgh, and *d* 1907

    4b Richard James; T/Capt 9th Bn S Wales Borderers; *b* 1 Aug 1861; *m* 1887 Sarah Llewellyn (*d* 1893), dau of L L Dillwyn, MP, and *d* 29 Nov 1923

    5b Frederick Edward; bandsman 131st Bn Canadian Expdny Force; *b* 26 Oct 1869; *m* 30 April 1906 Nancy Jane, dau of Charles Youmans, of Hazleton, BC, and *d* 1923, having had:

      1c Thomas Hume; *b* 7 March 1907; *m* 1st 1928 (*divorce* 1945) Margaret Olwen, dau of Capt Thomas Corrance, of Ervin, Wigtownshire; *m* 2nd 1946 Isabella Nimmo, dau of Archie Cowie, of Airdrie, Scotland, and had:

        1d +Thomas David Corrance [Thomas Pakenham Esq, 1100 Normandy Crescent, Ottawa, ON K2C 0L8, Canada]; *b* 1929; *m* 1951 *Edith McDerby and has:

          1e +Thomas McDerby [Thomas Pakenham Esq, 1024 Arrowhead Pl, Ottawa, ON K1C 2S4, Canada]; *b* 1961; *m* 1987 *Maura Ann, dau of William Tubridy, of Toronto, and has:

            1f *Kathryn Tubridy; *b* 1993

          2e +James Arthur; *b* 1962

          1e *Teresa Christine [Miss Teresa Pakenham, 156F Woodbridge Crescent, Ottawa, ON K2B 7S9, Canada]; *b* 1952; *m* 1977 (*divorce* 1984, resumed maiden name) Michael Sabourin and adopted:

            *Angela Sarah Christine PAKENHAM; *b* 1976

            *Candace Debra Elaine PAKENHAM; *b* 1984

          2e *Jocelyn Patricia [Mrs Warren Reade, SS3 Site 9, Comp 87, Prince George, BC V2N 2S7, Canada]; *b* 1955; *m* 1975 *Warren Reade and has:

            1f *Jennifer Alison Ella; *b* 1979

            2f *Kathryn Ann Dorothy; *b* 1981

          3e *Edith Lorraine [Mrs Donald Bond, 1388 Chatelaine Ave, Ottawa, ON K1Z 8A8, Canada]; *b* 1958; *m* 19– *Donald Bond and has:

            1f *Shaun Donald Pakenham; *b* 1980

            2f *Daniel Scott; *b* 1983

          4e *Maria Aline; *b* 1964

         2d +John Edwin; Col Seaforth Highrs of Canada; *b* 11 May 1930; *m* 1st 1954 (*divorce* 1959) Wendy Eileen, dau of Charles Larson Cox, of Ontario, and has:

          1e *Cheryl Owen; *b* 1955

        2d (cont.) Col John Pakenham *m* 2nd 12 Oct 1962 *Gaylynn Evon, dau of Weir Powellson Armstrong, of California, and by her has:

          1e +Sean Thomas; *b* 17 Aug 1963

          2e +Edwin Austin Westmoreland; *b* 1967

          2e *Naja Christiana; *b* 1968

      2c +Arthur Godfrey [Arthur Pakenham, 1210 NE 124th St, Seattle, WA 98125, USA]; *b* 23 Jan 1910; *m* 1st 1939 (*divorce* 1950) Wanda Hatcher; *m* 2nd 1951 *Rose Marie, dau of Anton Eberly, and by her has:

        1d *Patricia Eve; *b* 1956

      3c Frederick Edward; *b* 23 Oct; *d* 1 Nov 1911

      4c +William Christopher; *b* 1922; *m* 1st 1943 (*divorce* 1954) Mona May Morris and has:

        1d +Frederick Edward; *b* 1944

      4c (cont.) William Pakenham *m* 2nd 1955 *Marjorie Jane, dau of Duncan Reid Wilson, of Montrose, Scotland, and by her has:

        2d +Ronald Arthur; *b* 1957

      1c Viola Gwendoline Elizabeth; *b* 1908

2c Norma Muriel Doreen; *b* 6 Nov 1913; *m* 1938 Donald Holmes and had issue

3c Fiona Evelyn Pauline; *b* 16 June 1916; *m* 1939 Gordon Gatenby

(3) John; Adml; *b* 18 Oct 1790; *m* 1st Aug 1817 Caroline Emily (*d* 2 Aug 1844), dau of R-Adml Sir Home Popham; *m* 2nd 8 May 1845 Frances Julia (*d* 26 July 1894), dau of Henry Peters, of Betchworth Castle, Surrey, and widow of Hon Felix Tomas Tollemache (*see* TOLLEMACHE, Bt), and *d* 1 June 1876, having by his 1st w had, with two daus (*d* unm):

1a Thomas Conolly; *b* 21 March 1825; Offr 15th Hus, UK Consul Madagascar 1862; *d* 22 June 1883

2a Wellington Montagu; *b* 28 Aug 1840; *m* 4 June 1863 Emma Sophia Julia (*d* 21 Nov 1927), yst dau of George Rust, of Cromwell House, Hunts, and *d* 10 Oct 1916, leaving:

1b William Law; *b* 4 May 1869; *m* 1 Feb 1894 Ada Mary (*d* 3 Oct 1940), dau of J B Phillips, of Llanelly, and *d* 18 April 1927, leaving:

1c George Robin Montagu; Lt Rifle Bde WW I (wounded); *b* 18 Jan 1895; *m* 30 July 1932 *Rosemary Fiona Buchanan, only dau of Brig-Gen Sir Godfrey Davenport Goodman, KCB, CMG, DSO, VD, TD, of Eccles House, Chapel-en-Frith, and *dsp* 2 April 1957

2c John Walter Deaven; 2nd Lt London Regt; *b* 24 Nov 1898; *ka* 21 Sept 1918

3c Thomas Arthur Charles (Rev); ordained 1963, Chaplain Menton, Capt RN WWs I and II; *b* 4 Sept 1900; *m* 19 Dec 1925 Clara Talbot (*d* 1985), only child of William Middleton, of Monks Pond, Lymington, and *d* 1981, leaving:

1d +William Thomas Talbot [Capt William Pakenham RN, Croft Mews, Botley, Hants SO32 2BX]; Capt Dockyard and Queen's Harbour Master Gibraltar 1974, Dir Naval Signals and Ch Naval Signal Offr 1976, Dir RN Staff Coll, Greenwich 1979, served WW II; *b* 28 Nov 1926; *m* 4 May 1957 *Antonia Mary, only dau of Capt Anthony Coleby, RN, of Hapton House, Hambledon, and has:

1e +Robin Thomas Cliff; *b* 23 May 1963; *m* 1974 *Susan Mary, dau of Frederick Henry Timson, of Keyworth, Notts, and has:

1f +Benjamin Thomas William; *b* 6 Jan 1997

2e +John Neville; *b* 24 July 1964

1e *Katherine Clara; *b* 16 Sept 1960

2d +Stephen Walter [Rev Stephen Pakenham, 9 Chattis Hill Stables, Spitfire Lane, Stockbridge, Hants SO20 6JS]; Lt RN (ret), 1968 record singlehanded-sailing Atlantic (21 days 15 hours 7 minutes), Vicar Donnington and Apuldram 1964–75, Durrington 1975–81 and St Mary Bourne and Woodcott 1981–88; *b* 10 Dec 1929; *educ* Queens' Coll Cambridge (MA); *m* 29 June 1957 *Elizabeth Ann, only dau of Rt Rev Kenneth Edward Norman Lamplugh, Bp Southampton, and has:

1e +Jonathan Hugh Rust; *b* 19 April 1958; *m* 1985 *Nina Diana, dau of Lawrence Woodhouse Mason, of Winchester, and has:

1f +George Lawrence; *b* 1987

2f +Timothy James; *b* 1990

3f +Henry Francis Benjamin; *b* 1997

2e +Marcus Charles; *b* 24 Feb 1960; *m* 1st 1991 Lisa A M, dau of Bengt Delaryd, of Repulse Bay, Hong Kong; *m* 2nd 1996 *Stephanie, dau of Byung Gap Ahn, of S Korea

1e *Olivia Judith Clare; *b* 17 Aug 1963; *m* 1992 *Mark Elton, est s of Ronald George Johnson, and has:

1f *Samuel Luke Pakenham; *b* 1996

1f *Bethany Charlotte Pakenham; *b* 1993

1c Emma Joyce; *b* 9 Dec 1896; *d* unm 18 April 1962

2b Walter Maurice; *b* 18 June 1872

3b Arthur McClellan, RD; Cdr RNR WW I; *b* 18 May 1876; *m* 1st 1 Nov 1910 Ethel Louise (*d* 23 Aug 1934), dau of R A W Holwell; *m* 2nd 2 July 1938 Katharine Joan (*m* 2nd 29 Aug 1951 Brian Merry), dau of Sidney A Horstmann, of Fair Lawn, Bath, and *d* 27 Feb 1948, having by his 1st w had:

1c Peter Hugh Percy Holwell; Capt RA; *b* 8 June 1913; *m* 1st 3 June 1939 Nancy (*d* 2 Dec 1966), dau of Herbert George Alexander, of Westonbirt, Glos; *m* 2nd 1973 *Ailsa Jean [Mrs Peter Pakenham, The Red Cottage, Roode Ashton, Trowbridge, Wilts], widow of Kenneth George Marsh, and *d* 1982, leaving by his 1st w:

1d +Jeremy Edwin Montagu [Jeremy Pakenham Esq, The Old Manor, Rudge, Frome, Somerset]; *b* 21 March 1948; *m* 1974 *Caroline, yst dau of A M Redman, of Wonham House, Bampton, Devon, and has:

1e +James Edwin Helwell; *b* 30 Aug 1977

2e +Edward Charles Montague; *b* 1980

1e *Victoria Louise; *b* 1984

1d *Susan Daphne [Mrs Gerald Blakey, Farrington House, Farrington, Dorset]; *b* 11 April 1942; *m* 1965 *Capt Gerald G Blakey, RE, only s of A Blakey, of Haslemere, Surrey, and has:

1e *Lucinda Jane; *b* 6 Dec 1967

2c +Patrick Christopher Montagu Holwell [Patrick Pakenham Esq, 2 Ave de Bude, Geneva 1202, Switzerland]; Capt Roy Signals WW II (despatches twice); *b* 8 Feb 1922

1c Daphne Margaret Holwell; *m* 20 April 1932 *Capt Sir (Francis Richard) Jonathan Peel, CBE, MC, DL, Ch Constable Essex 1933–62, and *d* 9 Sept 1983, leaving issue

1b Emma Mary; *b* 25 Nov 1866; *d* 15 June 1918

2b Mary Josephine; *b* 25 Sept 1881; *m* 27 April 1904 Rev Hugh Banastre Langton (*d* 1960) and *d* Feb 1959, leaving issue

1a Louise Barbara; *m* 20 Oct 1848 Gerard Lake Brooks, s of Maj-Gen and Hon Amabel Brooks and maternal gs of 1st Viscount Lake, and *d c* 1886, leaving issue

(4) Richard (Sir), KCB (1848), PC (1843); *b* 19 May 1797; Min Mexico, Washington and Lisbon; *d* 30 Oct 1868

(5) Robert (Rev), DD; Vicar Straffan; *b* 4 June 1799; *m* 1st 30 June 1829 Harriet Maria (*d* 23 May 1865), dau of Rt Hon Denis Browne, and had, with other issue:

1a Thomas Samuel, of Glen Oak, JP Co Antrim; *b* 3 May 1830; *m* 4 Jan 1859 Josephine Maria (*m* 2nd 9 May 1866 Robert Conway Dobbs Ellis, Capt 22nd Regt, and *d* 1889), est dau of Peter Bancroft, of Lancs, and *d* 11 Aug 1863, having had, with a s (*d* young):

1b Evelyn Georgina Harriet; *m* 13 April 1882 David Browne McCorkell (*d* 27 June 1897), JP, DL, barrister, and *d* 26 April 1952, leaving issue

2b Elizabeth Josephine; *d* young 26 Feb 1866

2a Robert Edward; *b* 29 March 1830; *m* April 1856 Mary Elizabeth (*m* 2nd L Smith), 2nd dau of Isaac Goodall, and *d* April 1869, having by her had:

1b Arthur Edward, of Childers, Australia; *b* 22 Aug 1859

2b Hugh Charles; *d* young

3b Edward Roberts; *b* Aug 1863

1b Helen Anna Louisa

2b Mary Elizabeth

3b Gertrude; *m* 9 May 1888 Daniel Gunn and had issue

3a Hugh Arthur; Capt 11th Bengal Cav; *b* 6 Oct 1828; *m* Jan 1863 Clara Marianne (*d* 31 March 1896), dau of Rev Frank Hutton, Sr Presidency Chaplain, Calcutta, and *d* 31 May 1869, having had:

1b Robert Dent; *b* 8 Jan 1864

2b Hugh Horsburgh; *b* 13 March 1865; *m* 1st 23 Dec 1889 Nellie (*d* 1 June 1913), dau of James Standen, and had:

1c Hugh Richard Hercules; *b* 7 Aug 1893; *d* 9 May 1910

2c Robert Charles Aungier; *b* 7 Aug 1893; *d* 7 Jan 1895

3c James William Lygon; *b* 15 July 1896

2b (cont.) Hugh Pakenham *m* 2nd 15 Aug 1921 Louisa, dau of William Jennings, of Stubblefield, Otterden, Kent, and by her had:

1c Clara Primrose; *b* 19 April 1922

3b Lygon Graham; *b* 23 Aug 1866; *m* 1889 Katharine, dau of Rev G H Heslop, and had:

1c Violet Marianne; *b* 1890; *d* unm 12 Dec 1969

4b Aleck James; *b* 4 Oct 1867; *d* 1891

4a Charles George, of Headon Hall, Alum Bay, IoW; 101st Roy Bengal Fus, Maj and Adj 3rd Bn Roy Irish Fus; *b* 1844; *m* 21 Feb 1872 Emily Blanche (*d* 1899), only dau of Charles Hercules Harrison, of Singapore, and *d* 5 July 1918, having had:

1b Charles William Lygon; *b* 20 Jan 1873; *d* 14 Feb 1877

2b Robert Edward Michael; Capt Roy Munster Fus, Boer War 1899–1902 and WW I; *b* 28 July 1874; *m* 12 Sept 1900 Nancy (*d* 19 March 1934), 2nd dau of William Fowler, of Broadlands, Liverpool, and *d* 17 Jan 1915 of wounds recd in action, having had:

1c Ivo Robert Raymond Lygon; Capt Roy Berks Regt WW II; *b* 4 Dec 1903; *educ* Wellington

2c Osmund Edward Michael; *b* 26 April 1905; *d* 13 April 1906

1c Emile Estelle Rosemary; *b* 4 Feb 1907; *m* 9 Nov 1932 Kenneth Evelyn Parker (*d* 2 March 1969), W/Cdr RAF, yst s of Evelyn Stuart Parker, and *d* 22 Sept 1952

3b George de la Poer Beresford, CMG (1918), CBE (1922), DSO (1915); Col Border Regt, IA, WW I on staff (despatches six times, Brevet); *b* 4 Dec 1875; *m* 1st 23 Feb 1905 Emilie Elsie (*d* 15 July 1921), 4th dau of William Fowler, of Liverpool; *m* 2nd 1923 Marie Marthe Amalie (*d* 1968), widow of Capt Jacques Henri Joucia, French Army, and *d* 29 Dec 1960, having by his 1st w had:

1c +Raymond Beresford; Lt-Col Border Regt and G/Capt RAF WW II; *b* 31 Dec 1907; *educ* Haileybury; *m* 1st 30 Sept 1930 (*divorce* 1934) Sheila Barbara Kathleen, only dau of Joseph Mason, of Thorleby House, Skipton-on-Craven; *m* 2nd 24 Jan 1934 (*divorce* 1937) Sophia Patricia, dau of Capt R D Pollock, of Bangor, Co Down; *m* 3rd Oct 1948 Catherine Lillian Elizabeth, est dau of H Smith, of Salisbury, S Rhodesia

2c William Antony Beresford; Maj Border Regt WW II; *b* 24 Nov 1910; *educ* Haileybury and Queens' Coll Cambridge (BA 1932); *d* 9 June 1968

4b Hewitt John Havelock; *b* 26 Aug 1880; Capt E Lancs Regt, Lt Coldstream Gds, Boer War 1902, Lancs Fus WW I; *m* 1st Feb 1906 Claire May (*d* 7 Oct 1944), only dau of Edmond Berdoe-Wilkinson, of Godalming, and formerly w of Sir William Hollingworth Quayle Jones; *m* 2nd 16 May 1946 Molly (*d* 1976), dau of William Henry Cook, of The Old Cross House, Herts, and widow of Capt Oswell Jones, MBE, Roy W Kent Regt, and *d* 1978, having by his 1st w had:

1c (Arthur) John Edmond, TD; Maj 5th Bn Queen's Roy Regt (TA) WW II; *b* 10 June 1907; *m* 1st 15 Oct 1932 (*divorce*1949) Sarah, er dau of Capt Rowland Alston, Coldstream Gds, formerly of Odell Castle, Beds; *m* 2nd 2 April 1952 *Heidi [Mrs John Pakenham, Eastlands Close, Oxted, Surrey RH8 0EX], dau of Emil Wegmann, of Switzerland, and *d* 15 April 1996, having by her had:

1d Michael Dermot; *b* 27 Sept 1955; *d* 16 Feb 1960

2d +Timothy James Robert; *b* 13 Oct 1961; *m* 1989 *Kim, dau of John Gibson, of Bayston Hill, Salop, and has:

1e *Sophie; *b* 1991

2e *Hannah; *b* 199–

1d *Christine Catherine; *b* 17 April 1953; *m* 1980 (*divorce* 1989) Nigel Buckler Cooper and has:

1e *Robert John; *b* 1987

1c *Cynthia Marion Blanche [Mrs Guy Batho, The Hollies, 3A Compton Way, Olivers Battery, Winchester, Hants]; *b* 12 Nov 1909; *m* 1st 27 April 1935 (*divorce* 1942) Alexander Grazebrook Acton Pierce; *m* 2nd 8 Feb 1947 Guy Fothergill Batho, MBE (*d* 1992), and by him has:

1d *William Nicholas Pakenham; *b* 1948; *educ* Canford and RNC Dartmouth; Cdr RN; *m* 1973 *Jennifer, dau of W R Best, of Embleton, Northumberland, and has:

1e *William Guy Pakenham; b 1980

1e *Julia Elizabeth; b 1978

1a Charlotte Emily; b 16 April 1837; m 10 May 1866 Rev Thomas Tomlinson (d 1889), Rector St James's Dublin, and d 29 March 1903

2a Elizabeth Sophia; b 14 June 1942; m 26 Feb 1869 James J Mills (d 1895), of Castle Odder, Co Meath, and d 1904, leaving issue

(5) (cont.) The Rev Robert Pakenham m 2nd 28 Sept 1865 Elizabeth, widow of — Hayes; m 3rd 6 July 1876 Elizabeth (m 2nd 19 Aug 1885 Rev William Lawder, of Munsarabad, Mysore), 2nd dau of Robert Whitelaw, of Ardross, Co Kildare, and d 30 Dec 1883, having by her had:

3a Eveleen Frances; b 27 May 1880; d 25 Oct 1895

(1) Louisa Anne; b 12 March 1792; m 1 Sept 1814 William Dutton Pollard (d 25 Sept 1839), of Castle Pollard, Co Westmeath

(2) Henrietta; b 20 Sept 1795; m 10 April 1826 Rev John Hare (d Nov 1886) and d 8 March 1869

(3) Sarah; b 17 April 1802; m 1 March 1831 Samuel Law

1 Frances; b 1744; m John Ormsby Vandeleur, of Maddenstoun, Co Kildare, and d 1776, leaving issue

2 Helena; b 1745; m William Sherlock, of Sherlockstoun, Co Kildare, and d 1777, leaving issue

3 Mary; b 1749; m 1768 Thomas Fortescue, MP Dromlaken, Co Louth, and d 1775, leaving issue

The 1st BARON d 30 March 1766; his est son,

EDWARD MICHAEL PAKENHAM, 2nd Baron Longford, PC (I 1777); b 1 April 1743; RN 1761–66, ret as Post-Capt RN, MP Co Longford 1765–66; m 25 June 1768 Catherine (d 12 March 1816), 2nd dau of Rt Hon Hercules Langford Rowley by Elizabeth, Viscountess Langford (qv) in her own right, and had:

1 THOMAS, **2nd Earl**

2 Edward Michael (Sir), GCB; b 19 March 1778; Maj-Gen; ka 8 Jan 1815 Battle of New Orleans

3 Hercules Robert (Sir), KCB; Lt-Gen; b 29 Sept 1781; m 25 Dec 1817 Hon Emily Stapleton (d 26 Jan 1875), dau of 12th Lord (Baron) le Despenser (see FAL-MOUTH, V), and d 7 March 1850, having had:

(1) Edward William, of Langford Lodge, Co Antrim; Lt-Col Gren Gds, MP; b 1819; ka Inkerman

(2) Arthur Hercules (Rev), of Langford Lodge; b 25 Nov 1824; d unm 29 March 1895

(3) Thomas Henry, CB, JP, DL Co Antrim; b 28 June 1826; Lt-Gen, Col E Lancs Regt, MP Co Antrim, served Crimea 1854, Fenian Raid 1866; m 25 Feb 1862 Elizabeth Staples (d 6 Feb 1919), est dau of William Clarke, of New York, and d 20 Feb 1913, having had:

1a Hercules Arthur, CMG (1917), JP, DL Co Antrim; Senator NI Parl 1928, High Sheriff Co Antrim 1906; b 17 Feb 1863; Capt Gren Gds, Maj 4th Bn Roy Irish Rifles, Lt-Col cmdg 18th Bn London Regt (London Irish Rifles), GSO(2) 1918, Hon Col 1919, served Sudan Expdn 1885 (medal with clasp, bronze star), WW I, Offr Legn Hon, ADC to Govr-Gen Canada 1886 and Viceroy India 1888; m 16 Nov 1895 Lilian Blanche Georgiana (d 14 Sept 1939), dau of Rt Hon Evelyn Ashley (see SHAFTESBURY, E), and d 28 March 1937, leaving:

1b Hercules Dermot Wilfrid; Maj Gren Gds WW II; b 29 July 1901; m 9 Nov 1927 *Hetty Margaret (m 2nd 3 Aug 1950 (divorce 1959) Lt-Col Richard Walter Byng Pembroke, OBE (see TORRINGTON, V), dau of Capt Roland Stuart Hebeler, Queen's Roy Regt, and d of wounds recd in action 2 June 1940, leaving:

1c +(Hercules) Michael Roland [Michael Pakenham Esq, Old Hall, Penaley, Wrexham, Clwyd]; late 2nd Lt Gren Gds; b 4 Feb 1935; educ Eton; m 1 June 1957 (divorce 1973) Hon Susan Elizabeth Moon Lever, est dau of 3rd Viscount Leverhulme (qv), and adopted:

*Dermot Philip Michael; b 1 Sept 1961; m 1988 *Johanna, er dau of Dr Ian Perry, of The Old Farm House, Grateley, Hants, and has:

1e *Arthur; b 1992

1e *Emma; b 1989

2e *Alice (twin); b 1989

3e *Claire Alexandra (Anna); b 1990

*Caroline Susan Margaret; b 9 June 1963; m 1990 *A Henry M Wilson, yst s of John Wilson, of Chelsea, and has:

1e *Alexander James Kirkland; b 1991

1e *Madeline Rose Kirkland; b 1993

1c (cont.) Michael Pakenham m 2nd 15 Nov 1973 (divorce 1982) Margaret Fisher (m 2nd 198– Johnny Munn), dau of Charles William Fisher, of Hants; m 3rd 1984 (divorce 19–) Fiona Jane, dau of Gordon Barrie Peters, of Dorking, and by his 2nd w had:

1d *Rebecca Kate; b 1977

1c Ann Penelope; b 8 Aug 1928

2c Katharine Susan; b 1 Dec 1930

1b *Joan Esther Sybella, JP (Nantwich 1949); b 2 Feb 1904; m 30 June 1926 Hon Angus Dudley Campbell, CBE (d 5 Dec 1967), JP, yr s of 1st Baron Colgrain (qv), and has issue

2b Beatrix Helen Constance; b 3 Jan 1910; m 17 July 1929 (divorce 1943) Lt-Col Nigel Victor Stopford Sackville and has issue (see COURTOWN, E)

2a Harry Francis; Maj KRRC Boer War 1900; b 6 Nov 1864; m 7 Feb 1905 Gwendolen Beatrice Sanchia May (m 2nd 20 April 1910 Brian Baskerville Molloy, Capt Oxon Hus (ka 1 Nov 1914), and d 4 June 1948), dau of Lt-Col William Thomas Markham, of Becca Hall, and dsp 11 Feb 1905

(4) Robert Maxwell; Capt 84th Regt; b 14 April 1834; k relief of Lucknow 25 Sept 1857

(5) Edmund Powerscourt; b 24 Dec 1837; d Gwalior Fort, India 28 Sept 1861

(6) Charles Wellesley; Lt-Col Gren Gds; b 23 June 1840; d 16 Oct 1873

(1) Emily; m 3 July 1837 Sir Edmund S Hayes, Bt (d 30 June 1860), and d 21 April 1883, leaving issue

(2) Elizabeth Catherine; m 6 Aug 1850 Thomas Thistlethwayte (d 2 Jan 1900), of Southwick Park, Hants, and d 22 Jan 1885, having had issue

(3) Mary Frances Hester; m 6 Aug 1850 Sir William Verner, 2nd Bt (see 1970 edn), and had issue

4 William; Capt RN; drowned 4 Dec 1811

5 Henry (Very Rev); Dean St Patrick's; b 24 Aug 1787; m 15 Jan 1822 Eliza Catherine Sandford (d 1867), sis and coheir of 2nd Baron Mount Sandford of Castlerea (see 1845 edn), and d 26 Dec 1863, having had, with other issue:

(1) Henry Sandford PAKENHAM later PAKENHAM-MAHON, of Strokestown, Co Roscommon, JP and DL, 8th Hus; b 6 Feb 1823; m 11 March 1847 Grace Catherine (d 4 Jan 1914), dau of Maj Denis Mahon, of Strokestown, and cousin and heiress of the 3rd and last Baron Hartland (see 1845 edn), and d 18 March 1893, having had:

1a Henry, of Strokestown, DL Co Roscommon; Capt Scots Gds; b 13 July 1851; m 13 Jan 1890 Mary (d 18 March 1944), only dau of Lt-Col Sidney Burrard, Gren Gds (see 1963 edn BURRARD, Bt), and d 12 Jan 1922, leaving:

1b Olive; m 1st 4 July 1914 Capt Edward Charles Stafford-King-Harman (dvp 6 Nov 1914, ka), Irish Gds, of Rockingham, Co Roscommon, er s of Sir Thomas Stafford, 1st Bt, CB (see 1970 edn STAFFORD-KING-HARMAN, Bt), and had issue; m 2nd 19 Dec 1921 Maj Wilfrid Stuart Atherstone HALES later HALES PAKENHAM MAHON (deed poll 18 April 1923), E Yorks Regt, and RE (TA), only s of Col Atherstone Hales, Govr Parkhurst Prison, and by him had issue

1a Henrietta Grace; m 7 March 1874 William Henry Foster (d 9 March 1934), DL, of Apley Park, Salop, and d 17 Nov 1939, leaving issue

2a Florence; d unm 7 Dec 1900

3a Maud; d unm 14 Feb 1903

(2) William Sandford; b 10 Jan 1826; m 15 Jan 1857 Constantia Henrietta Frances (d 7 Dec 1923), yst dau of Sir William Verner, 1st Bt (see 1970 edn), and d 26 Nov 1886, leaving:

1a William Wingfield Verner; Lt-Col 79th Carnatic Inf IA; b 14 Nov 1857; m 1 Jan 1883 Frances Josephine (d 1924), dau of Surgn-Gen Marcus Joseph, MD, and d 1942, leaving:

1b William Henry Verner; served WW I (wounded); b 2 June 1885; m 1905 Alice (d 2 May 1966), dau of Charles Smith, of Fulwood Park, Liverpool, and d 1956, leaving:

1c William Wingfield Verner; b 1906; d unm 27 June 1991

1c Ida Dorothy; b 1912; m 1931 William J Wright and d 16 Sept 1969, leaving:

1d *Daphne; b 19–

2c *Frances Josephine [Mrs Eric Rowlands, 2 Acorn Grove, Scholes, Holmfirth, Huddersfield HD7 1SE]; b 1919; m June 1946 *Eric Douglas Rowlands and has:

1d *William Verner Pakenham [William Rowlands Esq, 5 Highfield Rd, Highburton, W Yorks HD8 0RQ]; b 1947; BSc, LIM; m 1974 *Ann, only dau of John Tyas, of Skelmanthorpe, Yorks, and has:

1e *Richard William; b 1976

1e *Victoria Nicola; b 1977

1d *Cynthia Jane Olive [Mrs Cynthia Fisher, 299 Shenley Fields Rd, Selly Oak, Birmingham 29]; b 1951; m 1974 (divorce 19–) Andrew Fisher and has:

1e *Daniel Andrew; b 1976

1e *Emily Jane (twin); b 1980

2e *Sarah Elizabeth; b 1980

1b Ida Constance; b 3 April 1893; d unm 3 April 1968

2a Frederick Edward Sandford; b 15 April 1859; m 1898 Marguerite Louisa (d 1961), dau of Maurice Ceely Maude (see HAWARDEN, V), and d 24 March 1950, leaving issue:

1b Michael Ceely Sandford; b 26 April 1903; m 1st 7 Nov 1933 (divorce 1948) Aline Mary Loftus (d 1967), dau of Loftus St George (see ST GEORGE, Bt) and formerly w of Ernest Charles William Vane-Tempest, DSO (see LONDONDERRY, M); m 2nd 1948 Patricia (d 1986), dau of Capt William Harvey Murray, of Mill House, Boyton, Essex, and formerly w of — McHugh, and d 8 Nov 1978, having by his 1st w had:

1c *Aline Marguerite Constance Sandford; b 19 Aug 1934; m 9 May 1959 *Keith William Boyd, only s of W J Boyd, of Melbourne, and has:

1d *William Michael Sandford; b 8 March 1964

1d *Jane Maria Loftus; b 18 July 1960

2d *Christina Theresa; b 22 Sept 1961

3a Henry Wingfield Hamilton; b 15 July 1861; d 14 May 1862

4a Francis Henry Godfrey, LDS; b 21 Jan 1865; m 1st 1890 Mary Josephine (d 1 April 1933), only dau of John Russell, of Newry, Co Down; m 2nd 6 Feb 1937 Violet Mary, yst dau of Mrs C A Iles, of Redlands, Bristol, and dsp 23 Jan 1957

5a Robert Sandford; b 1 May 1866; m 1st 1910 Edith Carter (d 1912); m 2nd 1920 Mildred Alice Armstrong (d 1940) and d 1959, having by his 1st w had:

1b Robert Wingfield; b 1912; educ Malvern and Trin Coll Cambridge (BA 1934, MA 1938); ARICS; m 14 Sept 1941 (Alice) Gwendoline (d 1982), 2nd dau of T H James, of Haverfordwest, Pembs, and d 15 March 1998, leaving:

1c +Clive Sykes [Clive Pakenham Esq, 31 Barton Gdns, Sherborne, Dorset]; b 8 Oct 1947; m 1973 *Jane, yst dau of H J Antell, of Sherborne, and has:

1d +Daniel Nicholas; b 1973

2d +Adam Geoffrey; b 1978

6a Hamilton Richard, MB, BCh; b 25 Nov 1867; m 1901 Emilie Willis, dau of Thomas Stringer, and d 6 Feb 1957, having had:

1b Arthur Hamilton; b 24 Sept 1903; d 28 July 1904

2b (Richard) Hercules Wingfield, CBE (1955, OBE 1949, MBE 1943); Sr Commr Zanzibar 1948–56, Gen Sec Lebanon Evangelical Mission 1956–69, Order Brilliant Star Zanzibar 2nd Cl 1956; b 15 May 1906; educ

Monkton Combe and Trin Coll Cambridge (MA); *m* 10 June 1947 *Eileen Isolde [Mrs Hercules Pakenham, Apt 20, Flete, Ivybridge, Devon PL21 9NZ], er dau of Oscar Faber, CBE, DCL, DSc, MInstCE, of Chateley Dene, Harpenden, Herts, and *d* 1993, leaving:

  1c +John Hubert [John Pakenham Esq, Tor Down House, Belstone, Okehampton, Devon EX20 1QY]; *b* 8 May 1951; *educ* Monkton Combe; *m* 1991 *Maureen Denise, dau of W/Cdr Patrick Woolley, RAF, of Rayleigh, Essex

2b (cont.) Mr and Mrs Hercules Pakenham also adopted:

  *Richard Arthur [Richard Pakenham Esq, Stoney Lane Cottage, Little Haseley, Oxford OX9 7LU]; *b* 14 Aug 1949; *educ* Grenville Coll; *m* 9 Jan 1971 *Hilary Julia, dau of John Priestman Doncastor, CBE, of Harpenden

3b +(Henry) Desmond Verner, CBE (1964) [Desmond Pakenham Esq CBE, The Mill House, 46 Prentice St, Lavenham, Suffolk CO10 9RD]; Dep HC Sydney, Counsellor Buenos Aires, Counsellor and Consul-Gen Tel Aviv; *b* 5 Nov 1911; *educ* Monkton Combe and St John's Coll Oxford; *m* 1st 14 Sept 1946 (*divorce* 1960) Crystal Elizabeth, yst dau of Lt-Col Edward York Brooksbank (*see* BROOKSBANK, Bt), and has had:

  1c Edward Desmond; *b* 13 Aug 1950; *d* 10 Feb 1951

  2c +Anthony Edward; *b* 23 Aug 1952; *educ* Eton and Ch Ch Oxford

  1c *Pandora Clare; *b* 1 Oct 1948; *m* 1969 *Matthieu Millet, 2nd son of Claude Millet, of Paris, and has:

    1d *Alexandre François; *b* 1974

    2d *Thomas; *b* 1990

    1d *Sophie Emilie; *b* 1976

    2d *Catherine; *b* 1981

3b (cont.) Desmond Pakenham *m* 2nd 1963 *Venetia, only dau of William Paterson Doyle and formerly *w* of Maurice Christopher Maude, and by her has:

  3c +Mark Edmund; *b* 10 Feb 1965

  2c *Sarah Catherine; *b* 27 Oct 1966

  1a Constance Selina; *b* 24 July 1863; *d* unm 11 Jan 1946

  (3) Hamilton Sandford; Capt 2nd Life Gds; *b* 14 Feb 1840; *m* 15 Sept 1864 Gwenwydd Frances (*m* 2nd 2 Jan 1866 Hugh Hebry Erskine (*d* 4 Jan 1907), yst s of Sir David Erskine, 1st Bt, of Cambo (*qv*), and *d* 8 June 1932, having had issue), est dau of Hon R T Rowley (*see* LANGFORD, B), and *dsp* 20 Oct 1864

  (1) Emily; *m* 6 June 1867 Capt Charles J Coote (*d* 11 March 1925), 18th Regt, and *d* 23 May 1896

1 Elizabeth; *m* Jan 1793 Henry Stewart (*d* Sept 1840), of Trycallen, Co Donegal, and *d* 10 Aug 1851, leaving issue

2 Catherine; *m* 10 April 1806 1st Duke of Wellington (*qv*) and *d* 24 April 1831

3 Helen; *m* 1799 James Hamilton (*d* 1805), est s of John Hamilton, of Brown Hall, Co Donegal, and *d* 1807

4 Caroline Penelope; *m* 1808 Henry Hamilton (*d* 1850), est s of Rt Hon Sackville Hamilton, and *d* Aug 1854

The 2nd BARON *dvm* 3 June 1792; his est son,

  THOMAS PAKENHAM, **3rd Baron Longford**, also **2nd Earl of Longford**, as which *s* grandmother 1794, also 1st BARON SILCHESTER, Co Southampton (UK), so *cr* 17 July 1821, KP (1813); *b* 14 May 1774; *m* 23 Jan 1817 Lady Georgiana Emma Charlotte Lygon (*d* 12 Feb 1880), dau of 1st Earl Beauchamp (*see* 1970 edn), and *d* 24 May 1835, having had, with other issue:

1 EDWARD MICHAEL PAKENHAM, **3rd Earl of Longford**; *b* 30 Oct 1817; *educ* Winchester; Maj 2nd Life Gds; *d* unm 27 March 1860

2 WILLIAM LYGON, **4th Earl**

3 Thomas Alexander; R-Adml; *b* 3 March 1820; *m* 21 Sept 1853 Sophia Frances (*d* 15 Nov 1898), dau of Sir Tatton Sykes, 4th Bt, of Sledmere (*qv*), and *d* Jan 1889, leaving:

  (1) Edward Tatton; Capt KRRC, Capt and Hon Maj 3rd Bn Roy Irish Rifles; *b* 12 Sept 1859; *d* unm 19 April 1931

  (2) William Christopher (Sir), GCB, KCMG, KCVO; Adml, Naval Attaché Tokyo 1904–05, a Ld Admlty 1911–13, ADC to HM GEORGE V 1912–13, cmdg 3rd Cruiser Sqdn 1913–16, Battle-Cruiser Fleet 1916–19, Pres RNC Greenwich 1919–20, C-in-C N America and WI Station 1920–23, Bath King of Arms 1930–33, Grand Cordon Rising Sun Japan, Excellent Crop China, Order St Stanislas Russia 1st Cl with swords, Legn Hon, Croix de Guerre, US DSM; *b* 10 July 1861; *d* 28 July 1933

  (3) Thomas Cecil; *b* 18 Sept 1864; *d* unm 26 May 1894

  (1) Georgiana Mary; *m* 16 Oct 1893 Rev Thomas Geoffrey Wyatt, Vicar St Wilfrid's, Haywards Heath, and *d* 2 June 1922

  (2) Selina Frances; *d* unm 20 March 1951

  (3) Katherine Louisa; *d* unm 20 May 1912

  (4) Margaret Elizabeth; *m* 4 Aug 1898 Lt-Col Frederick Charles Strickland-Constable and *d* 17 June 1961, leaving issue (*see* STRICKLAND-CONSTABLE, Bt)

4 Charles Reginald; *b* 21 Sept 1821; *d* 1 March 1857

5 Henry Robert (Rev); *b* 26 Sept 1822; *d* April 1856

6 Frederick Beauchamp; Maj 10th Hus and 27th Regt; *b* 25 Sept 1823; *d* unm 15 Feb 1901

7 Francis John (Sir), KCMG; Envoy Extrdy and Min Plen Sweden and Norway 1895–1901; *b* 29 Feb 1832; *m* 29 July 1879 Caroline Matilda (*d* 25 June 1938), 7th dau of Rev Hon Henry Ward (*see* BANGOR, V), and *dsp* 29 Jan 1905

1 Katherine Felicia; *m* 14 Oct 1851 Col Hon Fenton John Evans-Freke and *d* 26 Dec 1911, leaving issue (*see* CARBERY, B)

2 Georgina Sophia; *m* 17 Oct 1848 3rd Marquess of Exeter (*qv*) and *d* 26 March 1909, leaving issue

The 3rd EARL's bro,

  WILLIAM LYGON PAKENHAM, **4th Earl of Longford**, GCB (1881, KCB 1861, CB 1855); *b* 31 Jan 1819; *educ* Winchester and Oriel Coll Oxford; Ld Lt and custos rotulorum Co Longford, Gen, Col 5th Fus, Offr Leg Hon, Cdr St Maurice and St Lazarus Italy, Kt Medjidie, Adj-Gen forces Crimea and Indian Mutiny, U-Sec

War 1866–68; *m* 12 Nov 1862 Hon Selina Rice-Trevor (*d* 22 Jan 1918), 4th dau of 4th Baron Dinevor (*qv*), and had:

1 William, **Lord Silchester**; *b* 19 Oct 1864; *d* 16 Feb 1876

2 THOMAS, **5th Earl**

3 Edward Michael; Maj Coldstream Gds Boer War 1899–1902 (despatches, Queen's medal with five clasps, King's medal with two clasps), WW I (1914–15 star, two medals); *b* 20 Feb 1866; *d* 27 Dec 1937

1 Georgiana Frances Henrietta; *m* 35 Oct 1889 3rd Viscount Gough (*qv*) and *d* 30 July 1943, leaving issue

2 Katherine Louisa; *m* 27 Jan 1904 Col Hon William Lyonel Vane (*d* 23 Jan 1920) and *d* 9 March 1954, having had issue (*see* BARNARD, B)

The 4th EARL *d* 19 April 1887; his er surv son,

  THOMAS PAKENHAM, **5th Earl of Longford**, KP (1901), MVO (1909), JP Co Westmeath and Oxon; *b* 19 Oct 1864; *educ* Winchester and Ch Ch Oxford; 2nd Lt 2nd Life Gds 1887, Lt 1888, Capt 1895, Maj 1903, Brevet Lt-Col 1906, Capt 45th Imp Yeo and 2nd Life Gds Boer War 1899–1900 and 1902 (wounded, Queen's medal with four clasps), Ld Lt and Custos Rotulorum Co Longford 1887, Brig Gen 2nd S Midland Mounted Bde 1912–15, served WW I (despatches); *m* 8 Nov 1899 Lady Mary Julia Child-Villiers (*d* 21 Nov 1933), dau of 7th Earl of Jersey (*qv*), and was *ka* Gallipoli 21 Aug 1915, leaving:

1 EDWARD ARTHUR HENRY PAKENHAM, **6th Earl of Longford**; *b* 29 Dec 1902; *educ* Eton and Ch Ch Oxford (BA 1925, MA 1928); Hon LittD Dublin 1954, memb Roy Irish Acad 1952; memb Irish Senate 1946–48; *m* 18 July 1925 Christine Patti, dau of Richard Trew, of Cheddar, Somerset, and *dsp* 4 Feb 1961

2 FRANCIS AUNGIER PAKENHAM, 1st BARON PAKENHAM, of Cowley, City of Oxford (UK), so *cr* 12 Oct 1945, also **7th and present Earl of Longford**

1 *(Margaret) Pansy Felicia [The Lady Pansy Lamb, via di Santo Stefano del Cacco 22, Rome, Italy]; *b* 18 May 1904; *m* 15 Aug 1928 Henry Taylor Lamb, MC, RA (*d* 8 Oct 1960), s of Prof Sir Horace Lamb, and has:

  (1) *Valentine Edward Martin [Valentine Lamb Esq, Stable Block, Castletown House, Celbridge, Co Kildare, Ireland]; *b* 26 Jan 1939; *educ* King's Sch Bruton; *m* 1970 *Ann Graecen and has:

    1a *Celia Margaret; *b* 1971

    2a *Stephanie Christine; *b* 1972

    3a *Fiona; *b* 1977

  (1) *Henrietta Frances [Mrs William Phipps, 31 Chepstow Villas, London W11 3DR]; *b* 9 Dec 1931; *educ* Somerville Coll Oxford (BA 1953); *m* 23 June 1960 *William Anthony Dominic Phipps and has issue (*see* NORMANBY, M)

  (2) *(Horatia Mary) Felicia [Mrs William Palmer, Low Winsley Farm, Burnt Yates, Yorks]; *b* 21 Oct 1933; *m* 26 July 1958 *William Henry Tugwell Palmer, only s of Col Henry Wellington Tuthill Palmer, DSO, OBE, and has had:

    1a *Rufus Henry; *b* 28 July 1967; *d* 1986

    1a *Primrose Felicia; *b* 18 Feb 1960; *m* 1993 *Lt-Col Hon Alastair James Calthrop Campbell, yr s of Baron Campbell of Croy (*qv*)

    2a *Harriet Eve; *b* 6 July 1961

2 Mary Katharine [The Lady Mary Clive, Whitfield, Allensmore, Herefs HR2 9BA]; *b* 23 Aug 1907; author: *Christmas with the Savages* (1955), *The Day of Reckoning* (1964), *This Sun of York* (1973); *m* 30 Dec 1939 Maj Meysey George Dallas Clive, Gren Gds (*ka* N Africa 1 May 1943), er s of Lt-Col Percy Archer Clive, MP, JP, DL, of Whitfield, Herefs, and has:

  (1) *George Meysey; *b* 29 Dec 1940; *educ* Eton and Ch Ch Oxford

  (1) *Alice Mary [The Rt Hon The Viscountess Boyd of Merton, Ince Castle, Saltash, Cornwall PL12 4QZ]; *b* 24 March 1942; *m* 24 July 1962 *2nd Viscount Boyd of Merton (*qv*) and has issue

3 *Violet Georgiana [The Lady Violet Powell, The Chantry, nr Frome, Somerset]; author: *Irish Cousins* (1970), *Flora Annie Steele — Novelist of India* (1981), *The Life of a Provincial Lady — A Study of E M Delafield and her Works* (1988), *A Substantial Ghost, A Compton-Burnett Compendium, Five Out of Six, The Family Circle, The Constant Novelist*; *b* 13 March 1912; *m* 1 Dec 1934 *Anthony Dymoke Powell, CH, CBE, writer, only s of Lt-Col Philip Lionel William Powell, CBE, DSO, Welch Regt, and has:

  (1) *Tristram Roger Dymoke [Tristram Powell Esq, 3 Stockwell Park Crescent, London SW9 0DQ]; TV dir; *b* 25 April 1940; *educ* Eton and Trin Coll Oxford; *m* 25 April 1968 *Virginia Beatrice, twin dau of Archibald Julian Lucas, and has:

    1a *Archibald John Llewelyn; *b* 1970

    1a *Georgia; *b* 18 Feb 1969

  (2) *John Marmion Anthony [John Powell Esq, 137 Kennington Park Rd, London SE11 4JJ]; *b* 11 Jan 1946; *educ* Eton and Cornell

4 Julia Agnes Cynthia; *b* 5 Nov 1913; *educ* Somerville Coll Oxford (BA 1934); *m* 5 March 1938 Robert Francis Mount, 2nd s of Sir William Arthur Mount, 1st Bt (*qv*), and *d* 10 Sept 1956, leaving issue

Seat: Tullynally Castle, Castlepollard, Co Westmeath, Ireland. Long known as Pakenham Hall (though references to Pakenham Hall Castle survive in records dating from the beginning of the 19th century), this generously proportioned neo-Gothic dwelling reverted to the Irish name of Tullynally in 1961 (the year of the **6th Earl's** death), in keeping with post-independence Irish nomenclature trends generally.

The core of the place was apparently a two-storey classical mansion, allegedly 17th-century in origin. The first phase of growth occurred in the late 18th century, apparently in the decade just prior to the creation of the Earldom, when Graham Myers, who also worked on Trinity College Dublin, is thought to have superimposed the top floor. The high-Georgian remains of what is probably his work can best be seen on the south front, where the sash windows (one of which is a dummy, inserted for harmony's sake) are untouched. From 1803, just as the second half of the epic struggle between Napoleon and the rest of the world was beginning in which the Pakenhams were to play such a distinguished part, Francis Johnston was recruited to impose an aura of romanticised medievalism. It is piquant that battlements, machicolations and turrets should have been erected so profusely on what was home to two of the leading generals and the wife (Kitty,

Duchess of Wellington) of the supreme exponent of warfare in the early Industrial Age.

The next addition, five years after Waterloo, was the three-sided bay on the eastern front by James Shiel. It forms the facade to one end of the dining-room, which internally is decorated with a wood dado, a splendid groined plaster ceiling and wallpaper originally designed by Pugin for the Houses of Parliament. The west front was built at the end of the 1830s, at right-angles to the old 18th-century block, by Richard Morrison, being a private suite of apartments for the family. The most noticeable internal decorative feature here is the elaborate grill-work covering the vents for central heating, the installation of which in UK dwellings the Pakenhams pioneered. Externally a focus for the eye is provided by Morrison's octagonal tower, which marries his new wing to the original structure. The gabled kitchen wing on the garden side by the swimming pool is also his work. Another tower was put up in 1860 by J Rawson Carroll.

Despite its new name, 'Hall' is perhaps a more appropriate one for Tullynally in that the entrance chamber is the chief glory of the internal apartments. This soars up two floors in height to deeply sloping groins. The walls are embellished with ogival niches. There is even an organ. In recent years a conservatory has been added to the garden front by the fashionable Dublin architect Jeremy Williams.

LONSDALE

Arms: Or six annulets, three, two and one, sa. **Crest:** A dragon passant arg. **Supporters:** Two horses arg., each gorged with a wreath of laurel vert. **Motto:** *Magistratus indicat virum* ('The office displays the man'). **Creations:** Bt. (GB) 22 Aug 1764, B. and V. (GB) 26 Oct 1797, E. (UK) 7 April 1807.

THE 7TH EARL OF LONSDALE, Co Westmorland, **Baron and Viscount Lowther of Whitehaven** and a Baronet (Sir James Hugh William Lowther, Bt) [The Rt Hon The Earl of Lonsdale, Askham Hall, Penrith, Cumbria CA10 2PF]; *b* 3 Nov 1922; *s* gf 1953; *educ* Eton; Capt E R Yeo RAC WW II (despatches); dir: Border TV, NE Housing Assoc and Internat Life Insur (UK); memb: Minister's Hill Farming Advsy Ctee, Westmorland Ag Ctee, N Regn Ec Planning Cncl, Ct Newcastle U and English Tourist Bd; chm Northern Advsy Cncl Sport and Recreation, Pres NW Area Br Legion and NW Div YMCA, Warden Farmers' Co 1972 (Master 1973); *m* 1st 18 June 1945 (*divorce* 1954) Tuppina Cecily (*d* 1984), dau of Capt Geoffrey Henry Bennet by Cecily Clayton (*m* 2nd A/Cdre Victor Bruce Bennett, DFC), dau of Col Robert Clayton Swan, of Barrowby, Lincs, and has:

1 +HUGH CLAYTON, *Viscount Lowther* [Viscount Lowther, Towcett House, Newby, Cumbria]; *b* 27 May 1949; *m* 1st 2 Oct 1971 Pamela Colleen, dau of John Middleton, of Stannington, Northumberland; *m* 2nd 1986 *Angela Mary, dau of Capt Peter Wyatt, of Dartmouth

1 *Jane Helen Harbord [The Lady Jane Benson, Glebe House, Lowther, Cumbria]; *b* 13 Nov 1947; *m* 1st 19 Dec 1968 Gary Hunter Wooten, s of Thomas M Ray, of California; *m* 2nd 1978 *Robert Charles Benson (*see* RUTLAND, D) and by him has:

(1) *Laura Jane; *b* 1980

(2) *Sophie Camilla; *b* 1984

The 7th EARL *m* 2nd 9 Sept 1954 (*divorce* 1962) his cousin Hon Jennifer Lowther (*see* ULLSWATER, V) and by her has:

2 +William James; *b* 9 July 1957

2 *Miranda *b* 1 July 1955; *m* 1st 1978 Martin Dunne; *m* 2nd 1986 Ian Cronshaw and by him has:

(1) *Samantha; *b* 1986

2 (cont.) Lady Miranda *m* 3rd 19– *Michael Glen and by him has:

(2) *Sarah; *b* 1992

3 *Caroline [The Lady Caroline Lawson, Heckwood, Sampford Spiney, Devon PL20 6L9]; *b* 11 March 1959; *m* 1st 1978 (*divorce* 19–) Guy P T Forrester; *m* 2nd 1982 Stephen Christopher Ernest Hunt and by him has:

(1) *George Stephen; *b* 1982

3 (cont.) Lady Caroline *m* 3rd 1987 *Charles John Patrick Lawson and by him has issue (*see* LAWSON, Bt, of Weetwood Grange)

The 7th EARL *m* 3rd 6 March 1963 (*divorce* 1975) Nancy Ruth, dau of Thomas F Cobbs, of Pacific Palisades, California, and formerly *w* of — Stephenson, and by her has:

3 +James Nicholas; *b* 4 Dec 1964

The 7th EARL *m* 4th 3 Dec 1975 *Caroline Sheila, yst dau of Sir Gordon Ley, 3rd Bt, TD (*qv*), and by her has:

4 +Charles Alexander James, *b* 27 Feb 1978

4 *Maria Louisa Kate; *b* 1976

Lineage: THOMAS de LOWTHER, Sir GERVASE de LOWTHER and GERVASE de LOWTHER, Archdeacon Carlisle, all lived *temp* HENRY III; presumably kin to:

Sir HUGH de LOWTHER; Attorney Gen 1292, MP Westmorland 1300 and 1305, Justice Itinerant and Escheator (official implementing reversion of property to Crown where no heirs exisitng) North of the Trent, Judge King's Bench 1312; *m* —, dau of Sir Peter de Tilliol, and had, with a 2nd s (Thomas, living 1293):

Sir HUGH LOWTHER; sided with Thomas Earl of Lancaster (gs of HENRY III) in his attempt to overthrow EDWARD II's favourite Piers Gaveston, pardoned for this 1313; MP Cumberland 1328, Commr of Array Cumberland and Westmorland 1329, MP Westmorland 1341 and 1373 and Cumberland 1322, 1344 and 1345, Sheriff Cumberland 1353, 1354 and 1355; *m* (1st?) —, dau of 1st or 2nd (Baron) Lucy, of Cockermouth (*see* also NORTHUMBERLAND, D); *m*(?) 2nd Margaret, dau and heiress of William de Qualc, and had by one or other of these ws, with two yr sons (John, MP Westmorland 1377, 1379 and 1380; William, Sheriff Cumberland 1401 and 1407):

Sir ROBERT LOWTHER; MP Cumberland 1394, 1401, 1404, 1407 and 1415; *m* Margaret, dau and heiress of William Strickland, Bp Carlisle, and *d* 1431, having had, with three daus (Anne, *m* Sir Thomas Curwen, of Workington; Mary, *m* Sir James Pickering, of Killington; Elizabeth, *m* William Lancaster):

Sir HUGH LOWTHER; fought Agincourt 1415, Sheriff Cumberland 1440; *m* Anne/Margaret, dau of John de Derwentwater, and had:

Sir HUGH LOWTHER; Cumberland: MP 1449, Sheriff 1456; *m* Mabel, dau and heiress of Sir William Lancaster, of Stockbridge, and *d c* 1476, leaving:

Sir HUGH LOWTHER, KB (1502), of Lowther; *m* Anne, dau of Sir Lancelot Threlkeld, and *d c* 1511, leaving, with other issue, including a dau (Joan, *m* John Fleming, of Rydal):

Sir JOHN LOWTHER; Sheriff Cumberland 1516, 1543 and 1551; *m* Lucy, dau of Sir Christopher/Thomas Curwen, of Workington, and had, with a dau (Mabel, *m* Christopher Dalton, of Uldale):

Sir HUGH LOWTHER, of Lowther, *m* Dorothy, dau of 10th Lord (Baron De) Clifford (*qv*), and had issue:

1 RICHARD (Sir)

2 Gerard, of Penrith; Bencher Lincoln's Inn; *m* — Dudley

1 Margaret; *m* John Richmond, of Highhead Castle, Cumberland

2 Barbara; *m* Thomas Carleton, of Carleton, Cumberland

3 Frances; *m* Sir Henry/John Goodyere, of Polesworth, Warwicks

4 Anne; *m* Thomas Wybergh, of Clifton

The er son,

Sir RICHARD LOWTHER; *b* 14 Feb 1532; High Sheriff Cumberland 1568 and 1588, as which recd MARY QUEEN OF SCOTS when she fled to England after the defeat of Langside; Ld Warden W Marches; *m* Frances, dau of John Midleton, of Middleton Hall, Westmorland, and *d* 27 Jan 1607, leaving, with an est s (John, *dsp*), two yr sons (George; Richard; both *dsp*) and five other daus (*d* unm):

1 CHRISTOPHER (Sir)

2 Gerard (Sir); Judge Court Common Pleas Ireland 1610, ktd 1618; granted large tracts of land in Cos Tyrone and Fermanagh, where he built the castle later called Lowtherstown; *m* 1st Grace (*d* 1594 aged 36), dau of Alan Bellingham (*see* BELLINGHAM, Bt) and widow of Edmund Cilburn, of Cilburn, Westmorland; *m* 2nd Anne Welbury, widow, of Castle Eden, dau and coheir of Sir Ralph Bulmer, of Wetton, Co Durham, and *dsp* 16 Oct 1624

3 Hugh, of Lowtherstown, agent for his bro; Army Capt; *m* —, widow of — Borough, and *dsp*

4 Lancelot (Sir); Baron Exchequer 1617, ktd 1631; *m* 1st Elizabeth (*dsp*), dau of Anthony Welbury, of Castle Eden, Co Durham; *m* 2nd Anne, dau of Thomas Coote, and *d* 10 Jan 1637, heaving had a s (*dvp*)

5 William, of Ingleton, Yorks; *m* Elinor Welbury and had an est s, Richard

1 Ann; *m* Alexander Fetherston, of Fetherston, and had issue

2 Frances; *m* Thomas Cilburn, of Cilburn, and had issue

Sir RICHARD's est surv son,

Sir CHRISTOPHER LOWTHER; memb Cncl of the North; *b* 8 Sept 1557; *m* 1st Eleanor Middleton (*dsp*); *m* 2nd Eleanor, dau of William Musgrave, of Hayton Castle, Cumberland (*see* MUSGRAVE, Bt, of Hartley Castle), and *d* 1617, having had:

1 JOHN (Sir)

2 Gerard; soldier of fortune; *k* in wars against the Turks

3 Richard, JP Middx, of St Giles, Cripplegate; barrister; *m* —, dau of John Williams, and had an only dau, Eleanor

4 Christopher (Rev); Rector Lowther

5 William; Clerk Warrants Ct Common Pleas Ireland; *dsp*

6 Lancelot (Rev); Rector Long Marton, Westmorland

7 Robert; Alderman London; *m* 1st Margaret, dau of Thomas Cutler, of Stainborough, Yorks; *m* 2nd Elizabeth, dau of William Holcroft, of Lancs, and was *bur* 9 Jan 1655, having had:

(1) Anthony, of Marske, Yorks; MP Appleby 1678–79; *m* Feb 1666/7 Margaret, dau of Adml Sir William Penn, and *d* 27 Jan 1692, having had:

1a Sir WILLIAM LOWTHER, 1st Bt (E), so *cr* 15 June 1697, of Marske; MP Lancaster 1702–5; *b* 1670; *m* Catherine, dau and heiress of Thomas Preston, of Holker, Lancs, and *d* April 1705, leaving, with other issue:

1b Sir THOMAS LOWTHER, 2nd Bt, of Marske and Holker; MP Lancaster 1722–45; *m* 2 July 1723 Elizabeth (*d* 7 Nov 1747), dau of 2nd Duke of Devonshire (*qv*), and *d* 23 March 1745, having had:

1c Sir WILLIAM LOWTHER, 3rd Bt; *b* 1727; *d* unm 3 Feb 1753, when the btcy expired, leaving Holker and the other Preston estates to his maternal cousin Lord George Augustus Cavendish, from whom they passed to the Dukes of Devonshire

(2) John, of Danzig; *m* Mary, dau of Col John Lowther, and had issue (*see* below)

1 Eleanor; *m* Richard Fallowfield, of Gt Strickland, Westmorland

Sir CHRISTOPHER's est son,

Sir JOHN LOWTHER, of Lowther; MP Westmorland *temp* JAMES I and CHARLES I; *m* Eleanor, dau of William Fleming, of Rydal, Westmorland, and *d* 15 Sept 1637, having had, with two daus:

1 Sir JOHN LOWTHER, 1st Bt (NS), so *cr c* 1638, of Lowther; *b* 20 Feb 1605; MP Westmorland 1628–29 and 1660, Sheriff Cumberland 1661–62; *m* 1st by 1655 Mary, dau of Sir Richard Fletcher (*see* AUBREY-FLETCHER, Bt), and had, with other issue:

(1) John, of Hackthorpe and Mauds Meaburn; Col, MP Appleby 1661–67; *b* 1628; *m* 1st 1665 Elizabeth, dau and coheir of Sir Henry Bellingham, 1st Bt, of Hilsington, and had:

1a Sir JOHN LOWTHER, 2nd Bt, and 1st VISCOUNT LONSDALE, Co Westmorland, so *cr* 28 May 1696, as also BARON LOWTHER OF LOWTHER, Co Westmorland (both E), PC (Feb 1688/9); *b* 25 April 1655; *educ* Sedbergh and Queen's Coll Oxford; barrister Inner Temple 1677, MP (Whig) Westmorland 1677–79, 1681, 1685–87 and 1689–96, V-Chamberlain Household 1689–94, Ld Lt Cumberland and Westmorland 1689–94, First Ld Treasury March-Nov 1690, a Ld Treasury 1690–92, Ld Privy Seal 1699–1700; *m* 3 Dec 1674 Katherine (*d* by 25 June 1713), sis of 1st Viscount Weymouth (*see* BATH, M), and *d* 10 July 1700, leaving:

1b RICHARD LOWTHER, 2nd VISCOUNT LONSDALE; *d* unm of smallpox 1 Dec 1713

2b HENRY LOWTHER, 3rd and last VISCOUNT LONSDALE, PC (1726); *b* 1694; mustered 10,000 men to counter the Jacobites 1715, a Ld Bechamber 1717–27, Constable Tower London 1726–31, Ld Privy Seal 1733–35, Ld Lt Cumberland and Westmorland 1738–March 1750/1; *d* unm 12 March 1750/1, when the Viscounty and Barony expired

3b Anthony; *d* unm 24 Nov 1741

1b Mary; *m* 1692 Sir John Wentworth, 1st Bt, of N Elmsal, and *dspm* 16 April 1706

2b Elizabeth; *m* 6 Aug 1695 Sir William Ramsden, 2nd Bt (*qv*), and *d* 1764, leaving issue

3b Jane; *d* unm 1752

4b Margaret; *m* 20 March 1706 Sir Joseph Pennington, 2nd Bt, and had, with other issue (*see* 1917 edn MUNCASTER, B):

1c Katherione; *m* her cousin Robert Lowther (*see* below)

5b Barbara; *m* Thomas Howard, of Corby (*see* NORFOLK, D)

1a Mary; *m* John Lowther, of Dantzig (*see* above)

(1) (cont.) Col John Lowther *m* 2nd Mary dau of William Withins, of Eltham, and *dvp* by March 1667/8, having by her had:

2a William, MP Carlisle; *d* unm

(2) Richard, of Maulds Meaburn, MP Appleby 1688; *m* Barbara, dau of Robert Prickett, and had, with four daus:

1a Richard; Capt in Ireland; *dsp*

2a Robert, of Mauds Meaburn; Govr Barbados; *b* 13 Dec 1681; *m* 22 June 1731 his cousin Katherine (*d* 7 Dec 1764), dau of Sir Joseph Pennington, 2nd Bt, and *d* Sept 1745, having had:

1b Sir JAMES ('Wicked Jimmy') LOWTHER, 5th and last Bt, and 1st and last EARL OF LONSDALE, Co Westmorland and Co Palatine of Lancaster, so *cr* 24 May 1784, as also BARON LOWTHER of Lowther, Co Westmorland, BARON OF THE BARONY OF KENDAL, Co Westmorland, BARON OF THE BARONY OF BURGH, Co Cumberland, VISCOUNT OF LONSDALE, Co Westmorland and Co Palatine of Lancs, and VISCOUNT OF LOWTHER, Co Westmorland (all GB), with remainder to heirs male of his body, but being childless he got himself *cr* 26 Oct 1797 **Baron and Viscount Lowther of Whitehaven**, with remainder to the heirs male of his cousin, **Rev Sir William Lowther, 1st Bt** (*see* below); *b* 5 Aug 1736; *educ* Cambridge; patron of Pitt the Younger (*see* JERSEY, E), whose first seat as MP was for Appleby, a pocket borough of Sir JAMES's, hence his profusion of titles following Pitt's appointment as PM; MP (Whig) Cumberland 1757–61, 1762–68 and 1774–84, Westmorland 1761–62 and Cockermouth 1769–74; Ld Lt Westmorland 1758–1802 and Cumberland 1759–1802; Col: Army 1794, Westmorland Militia 1759 and Cumberland Militia 1792; *m* 7 Sept 1761 Mary, dau of 3rd Earl of Bute (*see* BUTE, M), and *dsp* 24 May 1802, when all his titles bar the 1797 *cr* expired

2b Robert; *d* unm

1b Margaret; *m* 19 March 1757 2nd Earl of Darlington and *d* 10 Sept 1800, leaving issue (*see* BARNARD, B)

2b Katherine; *m* 8 April 1765 6th Duke of Bolton and *d* 21 March 1809, leaving issue (*see* WINCHESTER, M)

3b Barbara; *d* unm

(1) Margaret; *m* as his 1st w Sir John Aubrey, 2nd Bt (*see* AUBREY-FLETCHER, Bt)

1 (cont.) Sir JOHN *m* 2nd Elizabeth (*d* by 21 Oct 1699), sis of Sir Ralph Hare, 1st Bt, and widow of Woolley Leigh, of Addington, Surrey, and *d* 30 Nov 1675, having by her had, with other issue:

(3) Ralph; *b* 3 July 1655; *m* Mary, dau of Godfrey Lawson, and had a s and three daus

(4) William; barrister; *b* 27 April 16–; *m* Elizabeth, dau of William Rawlinson

2 Sir CHRISTOPHER LOWTHER, 1st Bt (E), so *cr* 11 June 1642, of Whitehaven; Sheriff Cumberland 1640; *m* Frances (*m* 2nd John Lamplugh, of Lamplugh), dau and heiress of Christopher Lancaster, of Stockbridge, Westmorland, and *d* Sept 1644, having had:

(1) Sir JOHN LOWTHER, 2nd Bt; *bapt* 20 Nov 1642; *educ* Balliol Coll Oxford; MP Cumberland 1665–81, 1685–87 and 1689–1700, a Commr Admlty 1689–96; *m* his uncle's stepdau Jane, dau of Woolley Leigh, and was *bur* 17 Jan 1705/6, leaving:

1a Sir CHRISTOPHER LOWTHER, 3rd Bt; *b c* 1666; *educ* Queen's Coll Oxford; barrister Middle Temple 1690; his f disinherited him (because of his (2nd?) marriage?), other than paying over a small weekly sum; *m* 1st Jane, dau of Rev Philip Nanson, Rector Newnham, Hants; *m* 2nd Hannah (Taylor?) and *dsp* 2 Oct 1731

2a Sir JAMES LOWTHER, 4th and last Bt; *b c* 1673; *educ* Queen's Coll Oxford; barrister and Bencher Middle Temple, MP Carlisle 1694–1702, Appleby 1723–27 and Cumberland 1708–22 and 1727–55, V-Adml Cumberland; *d* unm 2 Jan 1755, when the btcy expired, leaving property allegedly worth £2,000,000 (some £160,000,000 in late–1990s terms) to his cousin the **1st Earl** (*see* below)

1a Jane; *d* unm 27 Feb 1730/1

(1) Frances; *m* Richard Lamplugh, of Ribton

3 William (Sir), of Swillington, Gt Preston and Garforth, Yorks; MP Pontefract 1661–78; *m* Jane, 2nd dau of William Busfield, of Leeds, and *d* Feb 1687, leaving, with six daus:

(1) William (Rev); Rector Swillington; *m* Margaret, dau of John Adams, of Rowcliff, and had:

1a William (Sir), of Swillington; MP Pontefract 1695–6; *b* Aug 1639; *m* Catherine, dau of Thomas Harrison, of Dancers Hill, Herts, and *d* 7 Dec 1705, having had, with other issue:

1b Sir WILLIAM LOWTHER, 1st Bt (GB), so *cr* 6 Jan 1714/5; MP Pontefract 1701–10 and 1715–29; *m* 1691 Annabella (*d* 8 Aug 1734), dau of 3rd Baron Maynard (*see* 1865 edn), and *d* 6 March 1728/9, having had, with two daus (*d* unm):

1c Sir WILLIAM LOWTHER, 2nd and last Bt; MP Pontefract 1729–41; *m* 1st 1719 Diana (*d* 1 Jan 1736), dau of Thomas Condon; *m* 2nd 17 Aug 1736 Catherine (*d* 5 Jan 1778), dau of Sir William Ramsden, 2nd Bt (*qv*), but *dsp* 22 Dec 1763, when the btcy expired

2c Henry, of Newcastle, MD; *dsp* 1743

3c John; Govr Surat; *dsp*

2b Christopher, of Little Preston, Yorks; *m* Elizabeth, dau of Daniel Maude, of Alverthorpe, and *d* 1718, leaving a dau (Martha; *m* 1750 George Thompson), and a s:

1c **Rev Sir William Lowther, 1st Bt** (GB), so *cr* 22 Aug 1764, of Little Preston; *b* 10 July 1707; *educ* Trin Coll Cambridge (MA); Preb York, Rector Swillington; *m* 31 Aug 1753 Anne (*d* 3 April 1759), dau of Rev Charles Zouch, Vicar Sandal, and had:

1d WILLIAM, **1st Earl**

2d Sir JOHN LOWTHER, 1st Bt (*qv*)

The Rev Sir WILLIAM *d* 15 June 1788; his er son,

Sir William Lowther, 2nd Bt, and **1st Earl of Lonsdale**, Co Westmorland, so *cr* 7 April 1807, also **2nd Baron and Viscount Lowther of Whitehaven**, as which *s* cousin 1802, KG (1807); *b* 29 Dec 1757; MP (Tory) Carlisle 1780–84, Cumberland 1784–90 and Rutland 1796–1802, Ensign 80th Foot 1794, Lt 1794, Lt-Col 1800, Ld Lt Cumberland and Westmorland 1802–44; *m* 12 July 1781 Augusta (*d* 6 March 1838), est dau of 9th Earl of Westmorland (*qv*), and *d* 19 March 1844, having had:

1 WILLIAM LOWTHER, **2nd Earl of Lonsdale**; *b* 30 July 1787; *educ* Harrow and Trin Coll Cambridge; MP (Tory) Cockermouth 1808–13, Westmorland 1813–31 and 1832–41 and Dunwich Feb-Dec 1832, a Ld Admlty 1809, Commr Indian Affrs 1810–18, a Ld Treasury 1813–27, Ch Commr Woods and Forests 1828–30, V-Pres BOT and Treasurer Navy 1834–35, PMG 1841–45, and Ld Pres Cncl Feb-Dec 1852, Ld Lt of Cumberland and Westmorland 1844–68, called up to Ho Lds in f's Barony/Viscountcy *vp* 8 Sept 1841, FRS, FSA; *d* unm 4 March 1872

2 Henry Cecil, of Barley Thorpe, Rutland, DL Cumberland; MP Westmorland, Col Cumberland Militia; *b* 27 July 1790; *m* 19 May 1817 Lady Lucy Eleanor Sherard (*d* 8 June 1848), est dau of 5th Earl of Harborough (*see* 1859 edn), and *d* 6 Dec 1867, having had:

(1) HENRY, **3rd Earl**

(2) Arthur; Capt Rifle Bde and 6th Inniskilling Dragoons; *b* 12 July 1820; *d* unm 15 Feb 1855

(3) William, of Capsea Ashe, Wickham Market, Suffolk, and Lowther Lodge, London SW, JP (Beds, Cumberland, Suffolk, Westmorland), DL (Cumberland, Westmorland); *b* 14 Dec 1821; granted with sisters rank of earl's dau/yr s; Sec Legation Naples, St Petersburg and Berlin, Min Plen Argentina; MP Westmorland 1867–85 and Appleby 1885–92; *m* 17 Dec 1853 Charlotte Alice (*d* 5 Jan 1908), dau of 1st and last Baron Wensleydale of Walton (*see* 1868 edn), and *d* 23 Jan 1912, leaving:

1a JAMES WILLIAM LOWTHER, *cr* VISCOUNT ULLSWATER (*qv*)

2a Sir GERARD AUGUSTUS LOWTHER, 1st and last Bt (UK), so *cr* 19 Jan 1914, GCMG, CB, PC (1908); *b* 16 Feb 1858; Dip Serv 1879–1913, Amb Constantinople 1908–13; *m* 28 Feb 1905 Alice, Order Queen Elisabeth Belgium, Coronation Medal 1911, Star Order Shefakat (*d* 20 Nov 1939), dau of Atherton Blight, of Philadelphia, and *dspm* 5 April 1916, when the btcy expired, having had:

1b Edith Alice Cecilia; *b* 2 Aug 1906; *m* 1st 30 Oct 1933 Baron Jacques Thenard (*ka* May 1940), s of Baron Thenard, of Château de la Ferté, Saone-et-Loire, France, and had:

1c *Arnould [Baron Arnould Thenard, La Ferté-sur-Grosne, Sennecey Le Grand, S et L, France]; *b* 3 March 1940; *m* 1963 *Anne de MacMahon and has issue

1c *Anne; *b* 14 Aug 1934; *m* 1958 *Jean Lemut and has issue

2c *Irène; *b* 3 Aug 1936; *m* 1956 *Nicolas de Vilmorin, and has issue

1b (cont.) Baroness Jacques Thenard *m* 2nd 1945 Roger de Vilmorin and by him had:

2c *Philippe Victoire; *b* 11 Nov 1948

3c *Elenore [Countess Guy de Dampierre, 38 rue St Sulpice, 75006 Paris, France]; *b* 28 Feb 1947; *m* *Count Guy de Dampierre

2b Gladys Mabel; *b* 22 Oct 1908; *m* 1st 20 Dec 1933 Capt Charles Nevile Fane (*see* CLINTON, B) and had issue; *m* 2nd 14 Feb 1942 Lt-Col James Hayton Greenhill Black (*d* 23 Dec 1966), Argyll and Sutherland Highrs, and by him had issue

3b Violet Eleanor; *b* 20 Sept 1910; *d* 17 Jan 1911

3a Harold Arthur; Lt 3rd Bn Beds Regt; *b* 23 July 1864; *d* 20 Dec 1929

4a (Henry) Cecil (Sir), KCMG, CB, CVO, DSO; *b* 27 Jan 1869; Col Scots Gds, Mil Attaché Paris 1905–09, Mil Sec to HRH THE DUKE OF CONNAUGHT 1911–13, Bde Cdr 1914–15, Mil Sec to C-in-C 1915, Maj-Gen Staff HQ Forces 1917–18, Boer War 1899–1902 (despatches, Queen's medal with six clasps, King's medal with two clasps), WW I (wounded, despatches, Brevet), Cdr Legn Hon, MP Appleby 1915–18 and Penrith and Cockermouth 1921–22; *m* 28 June 1920 Dorothy Maude Isabel (*d* 3 Oct 1967), yst dau of John Selwyn Harvey and formerly w of Gordon Bois, and *d* 1 Nov 1940

1a Mary Eleanor Rose; *m* 29 April 1897 Paul Vicugue, French Dip Serv, and *d* 14 Aug 1929

2a Mildred Alice; *d* 8 Sept 1876

3a Mabel Cecily; *m* 3 May 1912 James Bey (*d* 26 Jan 1941), est s of HE Elias Pasha

(1) Eleanor Cecily; *m* 22 April 1844 John Talbot Clifton, DL (*d* 16 April 1882), of Lytham Hall, Lancs, and *d* 24 Nov 1894, leaving issue

(2) Augusta Mary; *m* 30 June 1863 Rt Hon Gerard Noel, 2nd s of 1st Earl of Gainsborough (*qv*), and *d* 1916, leaving issue

(3) Constantia; *m* 24 July 1850 Maj-Gen Robert Blucher Wood, CB, and *d* 10 May 1864, leaving issue

1 Elizabeth; *d* unm Orleans 12 Feb 1869

2 Mary; *m* 16 Sept 1820 Maj-Gen Lord William Frederick Cavendish-Bentinck, CB (*d* 11 Feb 1828), yst s of 3rd Duke of Portland, and *d* 21 Oct 1863, leaving issue (*see* PORTLAND, E)

3 Anne; *m* 20 Jan 1817 Sir John Beckett, 2nd Bt (*see* GRIMTHORPE, B), and *d* 8 Nov 1871

4 Caroline; *m* 3 July 1815 3rd Duke of Cleveland (*see* BARNARD, B) and *dsp* 1 Nov 1883

The 2nd EARL's nephew,

HENRY LOWTHER, **3rd Earl of Lonsdale**; *b* 27 March 1818; *educ* Westminster and Trin Coll Cambridge; served 1st Life Gds 1841–52 (ret as Capt), MP W Cumberland 1847–52, Ld Lt and custos rotulorum Westmorland and Cumberland 1868; *m* 31 July 1852 Emily Susan (*d* 15 July 1917), est dau of St George Francis Caulfeild (*see* CHARLEMONT, V), and *d* 15 Aug 1876, leaving:

1 ST GEORGE HENRY LOWTHER, **4th Earl of Lonsdale**, DL Cumberland; *b* 4 Oct 1855; *educ* Eton; Col Roy Cumberland Militia; *m* 6 July 1878 Lady Constance Gwladys Herbert (*m* 2nd 7 May 1885 2nd Marquess of Ripon (*see* 1923 edn) *d* 27 Oct 1917), sis of 13th Earl of Pembroke and (12th Earl of) Montgomery (*qv*), and *d* 8 Feb 1882, leaving:

(1) (Gladys Mary) Juliet; *b* 9 April 1881; *m* 1st 9 June 1903 Sir Robert (Robin) George Vivian Duff, 2nd Bt (*ka* 16 Oct 1914), only s of Sir Charles Garden Assheton-Smith, 1st Bt, of Vaynol (*see* 1970 edn DUFF, Bt), and had issue; *m* 2nd 12 June 1919 (*divorce* 1926) Maj Keith Trevor, MC, resumed name of Duff and *d* 23 Sept 1965

2 HUGH CECIL LOWTHER, **5th Earl of Lonsdale**, called 'The Yellow Earl', KG (1928), GCVO (1925), TD, JP, DL Westmorland and Rutland; *b* 25 Jan 1857; *educ* Eton; V-Adml Cumberland and Westmorland and Ld Warden Marches; Ld Lt and custos rotulorum Cumberland 1917–44, Chm Westmorland QS 1908–36, chm Jt Ctee Cumberland and Westmorland TAA, Mayor Whitehaven 1894–96, Col Cumberland Vol Regt, Hon Col: Westmorland and Cumberland Yeo, 4th E Lancs Bde RFA, 3rd Bn Border Regt and 2nd King Edward's Horse, raised 11th (Serv) Bn (Lonsdale) Border Regt, Chev Legn Hon; *m* 25 June 1878 Lady Grace Cecilie Gordon, CBE (1920) (*d* 20 May 1941), 3rd dau of 10th Marquess of Huntly (*qv*), and *dsp* 13 April 1944

3 Charles Edwin; *b* 11 July 1859; *m* 12 June 1878 Mrs Kate Benjamin, dau of Charles Fink, and *dsp* 2 April 1888

4 LANCELOT EDWARD, **6th Earl**

1 Sibyl Emily; *m* 30 April 1886 Maj-Gen John George Williams Knox, CB, Scots Gds (*d* 6 March 1894), and *d* 11 June 1932, leaving issue

2 Verena Maud, VA; *m* 1 Jan 1887 (*divorce* Scottish Court 1927) 1st Viscount Churchill (*qv*) and *d* 25 Dec 1938, having had issue

The 5th EARL's bro,

LANCELOT EDWARD LOWTHER, **6th Earl of Lonsdale**, OBE (1919), JP and DL Cumberland, JP Rutland and Westmorland; *b* 25 June 1867; *educ* Cheltenham and Magdalene Coll Cambridge; Capt 3rd Bn Border Regt, Gen Staff WW I (despatches twice, Mons 1914 Star, two medals, Order Nile); *m* 1st 24 April 1889 Sophia Gwendoline Alice (*d* 4 Nov 1921) est dau of Sir Robert Sheffield, 5th Bt (*qv*), and had:

1 Anthony Edward, *Viscount Lowther*, JP and DL Westmorland, DL Cumberland; *b* 24 Sept 1896 (HM EDWARD VII stood sponsor); *educ* Wellington and RMC Sandhurst; Lt 10th Hus WW I, WW II 1940–43, Hon Col 4th Bn Border Regt (TA), Page Honour to TM EDWARD VII 1908–10 and GEORGE V 1910–13; ADC Personal Staff 1920, Westmorland: High Sheriff 1930, Ld Lt 1939–45; *m* 1 Feb 1922 Muriel Frances, CC Westmorland (*d* 25 Feb 1968), 2nd dau of Sir George Farrar, 1st Bt, DSO (*see* 1915 edn), and *d* 16 Oct 1949, leaving:

(1) JAMES HUGH WILLIAM LOWTHER, **7th and present Earl of Lonsdale**

(2) Anthony George, MBE (1954), DL (1964); *b* 23 Sept 1925; *educ* Eton and RMC Sandhurst; granted 1 July 1954 with sis rank of earl's dau/yr s; Westmorland: CC 1960, High Sheriff 1964, Capt 12th Roy Lancers WW II, Palestine 1946–47 and Malaya 1951–54, Dep MFH Ullswater 1956, Jt MFH 1957; *m* 22 July 1958 *Lavinia [The Hon Mrs Anthony Lowther, Whitbysteads, Askham, Penrith, Cumbria], only dau of Thoma H Joyce, of San Francisco, and *d* 1981, leaving:

1a +Thomas Scott Anthony; *b* 2 April 1966; *m* 13 Sept 1997 *Victoria, dau of David Wheteley, of Shaftesbury, Dorset, and has:

1b +Anson; *b* 10 Jan 1998

1a *Camilla Ann; *b* 24 July 1959

2a *Arabella Mary; *b* 6 Dec 1962

3a *Sarah Lavinia; *b* 27 June 1964; *m* 1990 *Steven G Husband

(1) Ann Mary; *b* 30 Aug 1927; *m* 27 April 1949 Col Julian Patrick Fane, MC, 12th Roy Lancers and The Life Gds, only s of Col Cecil Fane, CMG, DSO, and *d* following a car crash Germany 23 Aug 1956, leaving issue

1 Barbara; *b* 8 April 1890; *m* 8 April 1914 (*divorce* 1921, resumed maiden name) Lt-Col James Archibald Innes, DSO (*d* 16 Aug 1948), s of James Innes, of Roffey Park, Horsham, and had issue

2 Marjorie; *b* 6 Feb 1895; *m* 15 Sept 1917 8th Baron Rodney (*qv*) and *d* 29 July 1968, leaving issue

The **6th Earl** *m* 2nd 8 Oct 1923 Sybil Beatrix (*d* 10 March 1966), only child of Maj-Gen Edward Feetham, CB, CMG, of Farmwood, Ascot, by Isabel Beatrix, only dau of Col Ewen Grant, Bombay SC, and *d* 11 March 1953, having by her had:

2 Timothy Lancelot Edward; Lt RN; *b* 27 April 1925; *m* 1st 11 May 1966 (*divorce* 1976) Margaret Elizabeth, er dau of John Herring, MC, of 50 Harley St, W1, and Mrs J J Kino, of Cannes, and formerly w of Baron Giovanni Testaferrata-Abela; *m* 2nd *Susan Ann [The Hon Mrs Timothy Lowther, Ivy-Stone House, La Rue de la Croix, St Clements, Jersey, CI JE2 6LQ], dau of Capt Leonard Stephen Smallwood, of Jersey, and *d* 1984, leaving:

(1) *Melinda Clare, *b* 16 June 1978

Seat: Askham Hall, Penrith, Cumbria. The old and sumptuous seat of the Earls of Lonsdale, Lowther Castle, had its roof taken off by the current **Lord Lonsdale** in the mid-1950s, having proved too expensive even for the enormously rich **5th Earl** before the War. The Lowthers therefore moved to Askham, which in its oldest section (the pele tower) dates back to the 14th century. It was added to in ELIZABETH I's reign and later in the 17th century, when the southerly aspect of the tower was given cross-mullion windows and a D-shaped overhang to the main door. The crenellation of this tower, however, only dates from the 19th century. Internally the best features are the 17th-century wood staircase and panelling in the dining-room. The place belonged between the Middle Ages and the 1680s to the Sandfords, a younger branch of whom held a baronetcy between 1641 and 1723. It was sold by the executors of the last Sandford in the male line to a family called King, by whom it was disposed of to another family called Bolton. The **1st Earl of Lonsdale** of the present creation only acquired it in 1815. Even then it was used for a time as a dwelling house for the local parson before becoming the family seat.

LOTHIAN

Arms: Quarterly, 1st and 4th, azure a sun in splendour proper, a coat of augmentation (for LOTHIAN); 2nd and 3rd, gules on a chevron argent three mullets of the field (for JEDBURGH).
Crests: 1 A sun in splendour or, 2 A stag's head erased proper.
Supporters: Dexter, an angel proper, vested azure, surcoat vert, winged and crined or; sinister, a unicorn argent, armed, unguled, maned and tufted or. **Motto:** *Sero sed serio* ('Late, but in earnest').
Creations: L. (S) 2 Feb 1622 (Jedburgh); E. (Lothian) and L. (Ker of Newbattle) 31 Oct 1631; E. (Ancram) and L. (Kerr of Nisbet, Langnewtoun, and Dolphinstoun) (S) 24 June 1633; M., E. (Ancram), V. (Briene) and L. (Ker of Newbottle, Oxnam, Jedburgh, Dolphinstoun and Nisbet) (S) 23 June 1701; B. (UK) 17 July 1821.

THE 12TH MARQUESS OF LOTHIAN, Earl of Lothian, Earl of Ancram (twice), **Viscount of Briene, Lord Jedburgh, Lord Ker of Newbattle, Lord Ker of Nisbet, Langnewtoun, and Dolphinstoun, Lord Ker of Newbottle, Oxnam, Jedburgh, Dolphinstoun and Nisbet** and **Baron Ker of Kersheugh,** Co Roxburgh (Sir Peter Francis Walter Kerr, KCVO (1983), DL (Roxburghshire 1962)) [The Most Hon The Marquess of Lothian KCVO DL, Ferniehirst Castle, Jedburgh, Roxburghshire TD8 6NX]; *b* 8 Sept 1922; s kinsman 1940; *educ* Ampleforth and Ch Ch Oxford; Lt Scots Gds WW II; memb Deptl Ctee Homosexual Offences and Prostitution 1954, memb Br Delegation UN Gen Assembly 1956–57, European Parl 1973, UK Del Cncl Europe and WEU 1959, PPS to For Sec 1960–63, Ld-in-Waiting (Govt Whip Ho Lds) 1962–63 and 1972–73, Jt Parly Sec Min Health April–Oct 1964, Parly U-Sec FCO 1970–72, Cmdt Special Constabulary Roxburgh, Berwick and Selkirk, memb Roy Co Archers, Ld Warden Stannaries and Keeper Privy Seal Duchy Cornwall 1977–83, memb Prince's Cncl 1976–83, Chm Standing Conf Br Vol Refugee Orgs 1966, FRSA, Hon Pres Maltese Nobility, Kt SMO Malta; *m* 30

April 1943 *Antonella OBE (1977), dau of Maj-Gen Sir Foster Reuss Newland, KCMG, CB, by Agnes Carr, of Ditchingham Hall, Norfolk, and has:

1 +MICHAEL ANDREW FOSTER JUDE KERR, *Earl of Ancram*, PC (1996) QC, DL (Roxburgh, Ettrick and Lauderdale 1990) [The Rt Hon The Earl of Ancram PC QC DL MP, House of Commons, London SW1A 0AA]; *b* 7 July 1945; *educ* Ampleforth, Ch Ch Oxford and Edinburgh U (BA, LLB); advocate Edinburgh 1970; MP (C) Berwick and E Lothian Feb–Sept 1974, Edinburgh S 1979–87, Devizes 1992–, memb Ctee Energy 1979–83, Chm C Party Scotland 1980–83, Parly U-Sec .Scottish Off 1983–87, NI Off 1993–94, Min State NI 1994–97, Oppn Constitutional Affrs Spokesman 1997–98, C Pty Chm Oct 1998– (Dep Chm June–Oct 1998), memb Roy Co Archers; *m* 7 June 1975 *Lady (Theresa) Jane Fitzalan-Howard, yst dau of 16th Duke of Norfolk (*qv*), and has had:

  (1) Sarah Margaret; *b* and *d* 13 June 1976
  (2) *Clare Therese; *b* 25 Jan 1979
  (3) *Mary Cecil; *b* 1981

2 +Ralph William Francis Joseph [The Lord Ralph Kerr, Melbourne Hall, nr Derby DE7 1EN]; *b* 7 Nov 1957; *educ* Ampleforth; *m* 1st 1980 (*divorce* 1987) Lady Virginia Mary Elizabeth FitzRoy, 2nd dau of 11th Duke of Grafton (*qv*); *m* 2nd 1988 *Marie-Clare, yr dau of (Michael) Donald Gordon Black, MC, of Cupar, Fife, and by her has:

  (1) +John Walter Donald Peter; *b* 8 Aug 1988
  (2) +Frederick James Michael Ralph; *b* 1989
  (3) +Francis Andrew William George; *b* 1991
  (1) *Amabel Amy Antonella; *b* 31 March 1998

1 *Mary Marianella Anne; *b* 20 March 1944; *m* 1970 *Charles Von Westenholtz, of Little Blakeswar, Widford, Herts, and has:

  (1) *Alexander Peter Frederick; *b* 1971
  (2) *Mark Henry Cosimo; *b* 1973
  (3) *Nicholas Anthony Philip; *b* 1975

2 *Cecil Nennella Therese [The Lady Cecil Cameron, Achnacarry, Spean Bridge, Inverness-shire; 26 The Little Boltons, London SW10 9LP]; *b* 22 April 1948; *educ* London U (BA); *m* 1 June 1974 *Donald Angus Cameron, Yr. of Lochiel, est s of Col Sir Douglas Hamish Cameron of Lochiel, KT, TD, JP, DL, and has:

  (1) *Donald Andrew John; *b* 1976
  (1) *Catherine Mary; *b* 1975
  (2) *Lucy Margot Therese; *b* 1980
  (3) *Emily Frances; *b* 1986

3 *Clare Amabel Margaret [Countess of Euston, The Racing Stables, Euston, Thetford, Norfolk; 6 Vicarage Gdns, London W8]; *b* 15 April 1951; *m* 16 Sept 1972 *Earl of Euston and has issue (see GRAFTON, D)

4 *Elizabeth Marian Frances [Countess of Dalkeith, Dabton, Thornhill, Dumfriesshire]; *b* 8 June 1954; *m* 31 Oct 1981 *Earl of Dalkeith and has issue (see BUCCLEUCH and QUEENSBERRY, D)

Lothian, previous ascription of title: The 4th and 7th Earls of Dunbar (*see* DUNBAR, Bt, of Mochrum) are very occasionally referred to in contemporary sources as Earl of Lothian. No formal creation under this title is known of, however.

Lineage: The name KER(R) first occurs in Scotland in the late 12th century. But a detailed pedigree only begins with:

JOHN KERR, of the Forest of Selkirk; had a charter of part of Auldtounburn 5 Feb 1357/8 and another 4 Oct 1358 to himself and his w Mariot of a further part, together with the lands of Molle; his er gs:

ROBERT KERR of Auldtounburn; had a charter of Smailholm 20 June 1404 from 4th Earl of Douglas; had, with an er s (Richard, of Auldtounburn; *dsp* Jan 1437/8):

ANDREW KERR of Auldtounburn; had various charters of lands in Roxburghshire, including one of Cessford from the Earls of Douglas 1430–48; *d* 1444, having had:

  1 ANDREW
  2 James; ancestor of the KERRs of Linton
  3 Thomas; ancestor of the KERs of Gateshaw
  1 Margaret; *m* George Roule

The est son,

ANDREW KERR of Auldtounburn and Cessford; with the eclipse of the DOUGLASes and his consequent tenure directly of the Crown his power increased; had a charter of Crown lands of the (territorial) Barony of Old Roxburgh 1451; Warden Middle March 1457; *m* 1st a dau of William Douglas of Cavers; *m* 2nd Margaret, dau of James Tweedie of Drummelzier, and *d c* 8 May 1481, having had:

  1 Andrew; pardoned for helping abduct JAMES III from Linlithgow 1466; *m* Margaret, dau of 1st Lord Hailes (*see* BUCHAN-HEPBURN, Bt) and widow of 2nd Lord (Halyburton) of Dirletoun, and *d c* 27 April 1467, leaving:
    (1) Margaret; *m* Sir John Home and had issue (see HOME, E)
  2 Walter, of Caverton and later Cessford, of which had a Crown charter 13 March 1493–99; *m* 1st allegedly Isabel, dau of 1st Lord Hay of Yester (*see* TWEEDDALE, M); *m* 2nd after 1487 Agnes, dau of 1st Lord Crichton (*see* ERNE, E) and widow of 2nd Lord Glamis (*see* STRATHMORE AND KINGHORNE, E), and *d* 25 Nov 1501, having had:
    (1) Robert (Sir), Yr. of Cessford; Master King's Artillery; *m* (contract 12 Feb 1484) Christian, dau of James Rutherfurd of that Ilk, and *dvp* by 6 Nov 1500, leaving:
      1a Andrew (Sir), of Cessford; had sasine of his estates 30 Sept 1511, fought at Flodden 9 Sept 1513, Warden Middle March 1515; *m* Agnes, dau of Sir Patrick Crichton of Cranstoun Riddell and widow of George Sinclair, Yr. of Rustin, and was *k* nr Melrose while escorting JAMES V to Edinburgh 18 July 1526, leaving:
        1b Walter (Sir), of Cessford, whose male issue died out; ancestor in the female line of the Dukes of Roxburghe (*qv*)
        2b Mark; Abbot 1547 then as the Reformation developed Commendator (titular or lay Abbot, without duties but with revenues) Newbottle, MP 1560 and 1563, a Ld of Session 1569, Auditor Exchequer 1580; *m* Helen

(*d* 26 Oct 1594), dau of 4th Earl of Rothes (*qv*) and widow of Gilbert Seton, Yr. of Parbroath, and *d* 29 Aug 1584, having had, with other issue:

          1c MARK KERR, 1st LORD NEWBOTTLE, so *cr* 15 Oct 1591, with remainder to his heirs male and assigns, as also 10 July 1606 EARL OF LOTHIAN (both S), with remainder to heirs male; *b c* 1553; Vicar Linton, Peeblesshire, 1567, Master of Requests 1577–1606, Commendator Newbottle 1581; Gentleman Bedchamber 1580, Extra Ld Session 1584–1609, had Crown charters of (territorial) Baronies of Newbottle and Preston Grange 1587, had his lands erected into the (feudal) Barony of Newbottle prior to his creation as a Ld of Parl; *m* by 1592 Margaret (*d* 8 Jan 1617), dau of Sir John Maxwell by Lady Herries (*qv*) of Terregles, and *d* (by witchcraft according to his siblings, the seriousness of the charge leading the Privy Council to appoint commissioners to investigate two women suspected of the act of sorcery) 8 April 1609, having had, with other issue:

            1d ROBERT KERR, 2nd and presumably last LORD NEWBOTTLE and 2nd and presumably last EARL OF LOTHIAN, KB (1603); *educ* Padua U; Master of Requests 1606; having no male issue, he obtained a regrant of the Ldship of Parl 29 March 1621, with remainer to himself and the heirs male of his body, whom failing to his eldest unmarried heir female, she to then marry a husb called Kerr, legitimately born and of honourable descent, he to take the name and arms of the Earldom of Lothian and House of Newbottle, which failing (for instance if the est female heir married before his death) to his next unmarried female with the same conditions attached, which failing to his brother James, whom failing to his cousins Robert Earl of Roxburghe and Sir Walter Kerr of Fawdonside; no such regrant appears to have been made with regard to the Earldom, which on his death expired accordingly (unless the revival of the Earldom in 1631 be viewed as a regrant following a surrender, the lack of any record of the patent making it hard to decide); *m c* May 1611 Annabella (*d* 1652), dau of 7th Earl of Argyll (*see* ARGYLL, D), and *dspms*, having cut his throat during the night of 5/6 March 1624, it is thought from having run up huge debts, having had:

              1e Charles; *dvp*
              1e ANNE KERR; would have appeared to have met the requirements of the regrant of 1621 whereby she could inherit her f's Ldship of Parl, and certainly did so as regards the estates, but the conferring of a similarly worded title on her husb, together with the decreet of 1 July 1695 ranking the Earl of Roxburghe above the 2nd Earl of Lothian of the 1631 *cr*, which in effect rejected the latter's claim both to the Earldom of Lothian of 1601 and the Ldship of Parl of Newbottle of 1591 would seem to militate against such an interpretation; *m* 9 Dec 1630 her cousin **1st Earl of Lothian** of the 31 Oct 1631 *cr* (see below)
              2e Joanna
            2d William (Sir), of Blackhope; *dsp* by 1650
            3d Mark (Sir), of Mauldslie; ktd 1633; *dspm* Nov 1652
            1d Jean; *m* 1st Robert Boyd, Master of Boyd (*see* KILMARNOCK, B); *m* 2nd 12th Earl of Crawford (*see* CRAWFORD and BALCARRES, E); *m* 3rd Thomas Hamilton of Roberton and *d* 17 Aug 1632, leaving issue by her first two husbs
            2d Janet; *m* 8th Earl of Glencairn (*see* CUNINGHAME, Bt)
            3d Margaret; *m* 1st 7th Lord Hay of Yester (*see* TWEEDDALE, M); *m* 2nd Andrew Kerr, *Master of Jedburgh* (see below), and *dsp* 15 March 1645
            4d Isabel; *m* 1st Earl of Queensberry (*see* QUEENSBERRY, M) and *d* 1628
            5d Elizabeth; *m* 9th Lord Borthwick (*qv*) and *d* 10 July 1659, leaving issue
           2c Andrew, of Fentoun and Romanno Grange; *m* Isabella Whitlaw and *dspms*
           3c William, of Ewinstoun; *m* by 1589 Jean, dau of James Johnstone, Yr. of that Ilk (*see* ANNANDALE AND HARTFELL, E), and widow of (a) William, Master of Carlyle and (b) 6th Lord Saltoun (*qv*) of Abernethy, and *dspm*
           1c Catherine; *m* 5th Lord Herries of Terregles (*qv*) and *d* March 1600, leaving issue
         3b Andrew; *dsp* by 1573
         1b Catherine; *m* her cousin Sir John Kerr of Ferniehirst
      2a George, of Fawdonside; *m* Margaret, dau of 5th Lord (Halyburton) of Dirleton by his 1st w, and *d* by 12 March 1553/4; his descendant, Sir Walter Ker of Fawdonside, who became heir male of Ker of Cessford, resigned any rights to that estate 1664 and his branch died out in the male line
    (2) Mark, of Maxton, Roxburghshire; guardian of Cessford; *m* Marjorie, dau and heiress of John Ainslie of Dolphington; ancestor in the female line of the KERs of Littledean, of whom the heir male Maj-Gen Walter Ker unsuccessfully claimed the Roxburgh titles and estates; *d* 1433, leaving an only s (*d* unm 1481)
    (3) Ralph; living 1494
    (1) Elizabeth; *m* 1st (contract 12 Feb 1484/5) Philip Rutherford, Yr. of that Ilk; *m* 2nd Sir Walter Scott of Buccleuch (*see* BUCCLEUCH and QUEENSBERRY, D) and *d* 19 Oct 1548
    (2) Margaret

3 Thomas, initially of Smailholm, later of Ferniehirst; in 1483 exchanged Smailholm for Crailing and Hownam with John Home of Whitrig; *m* Margaret, dau and heiress of Sir Thomas Ker of Ferniehirst, which he thus acquired, holding it from the Earl of Angus; *d* 24 June 1484, having had:

  (1) Andrew (Sir), of Ferniehirst; Warden Middle March, Baillie (Magistrate) Jedburgh; had Crown charters of (territorial) Barony of Oxnam 17 Jan 1523/4 and of Ferniehirst 21 May 1540; *m* by 6 Nov 1501 Janet, dau of Sir Patrick Home of Polwarth, and *d c* 4 Oct 1545, having had, with other issue:

    1a Thomas; *dvp* 1524

2a John (Sir), of Ferniehirst; Warden Middle March, Heritable Baillie Jedburgh; *m* Catherine, dau of Sir Andrew Kerr of Cessford (*see above*), and *d* 1562, having had, with other issue:

　1b Thomas (Sir), of Ferniehirst; supported MARY QUEEN OF SCOTS; *m* 1st (contract 10 Feb 1561/2) Janet, dau and heiress of Sir William Kirkaldy of Grange, Fife, and had:

　　1c ANDREW KERR, **1st Lord Jedburgh**, so *cr* 2 Feb 1621/2, with remainder to his heirs male and successors in the family of Ferniehirst bearing the name and arms of Kerr; Gentleman Bedchamber Feb 1584/5; *ktd* by 1604; hereditary Baillie Jedburgh Forset; *m* 1st (contract 20 Oct 1584) Anne, dau of Andrew Stewart, Master of Ochiltree, s of 2nd Lord Ochiltree (*see* MORAY, E); *m* 2nd *c* 2 July 1621 Katherine, dau of — McCulloch and widow of William Houston of Cottreoch, and *dspms* after 20 April 1633, having by his 1st w had, with other issue (including a dau, Mary, who *m* — Keie and had issue; *see* HOUSTOUN-BOSWALL, Bt):

　　　1d Andrew, *Master of Jedburgh*, PC; Capt King's Gds 1618, Extrdy Ld of Session 1628; *m c* 15 Dec 1609 Margaret, 3rd dau of 1st EARL OF LOTHIAN (*see above*) and widow of James, Lord Hay of Yester (*see* TWEEDDALE, M), and *dsp* & *vp* 20 Dec 1628

　　2c William KERR later KIRKALDY (on inheriting that family's estates) of Grange; *m* (contract 14 Feb 1586/7) Elizabeth Lyon, dau of 8th Lord Glamis (*see* STRATHMORE AND KINGHORNE, E), and *d c* 13 Jan 1598/9, having had, with other issue:

　　　1d ALEXANDER KIRKALDY later KERR, *de jure* 2nd LORD JEDBURGH; *b c* 1590; made over the Grange estate to the heir male of the name of Kirkaldy; had:

　　　　1e JOHN KERR, *de jure* 3rd LORD JEDBURGH; served heir male of the Ferniehirst family 24 June 1654, but like his f did not assume the title; *dsp* by 1670

　　1c Mary; *m* James Douglas, Commendator of Melrose, 2nd son of 8th Earl of Morton (*qv*), and had issue

　　2c Julian; *m* 1st Sir Patrick Home of Polwarth (*see* POLWARTH, L); *m* 2nd 1613 1st Earl of Haddington (*qv*) and was *bur* 30 March 1637, leaving issue

　　3c Margaret; *m* (contract 28 Oct 1584) 2nd Lord Melville (*qv*) and *dsp* 24 May 1594

　1b (cont.) Sir Thomas *m* 2nd 1569 Janet, sis of William Scott of Branxholme, and *d* 30 March 1585/6, having by her had:

　　3c Thomas, of Oxnam and Over Crailing; *dsp*, *k* Jedburgh Fair 14 Sept 1601

　　4c James (Sir), of Oxnam and Crailing; MP Co Roxburgh 1630; *m* Mary, dau and heiress of James Rutherford of Hunderlie, Jedburgh, and *d* 1645, having had, with other issue:

　　　1d ROBERT KERR, **4th Lord Jedburgh**, of which title got a regrant 11 July 1670, with remainder, in default of heirs male of his body, to William Kerr, Master of Newbottle, later **2nd Marquess of Lothian** (*see below*), and the heirs male of the latter's body; *m* by 1656 Christian, dau of Sir Alexander Hamilton of Innerwick and widow of Sir Patrick Hume, 1st Bt, of Polwarth (*see* POLWARTH, L), and *dsps* 4 Aug 1692

　　5c ROBERT CARR/KER(R), 1st and last EARL OF SOMERSET, so *cr* 3 Nov 1613, as also BARON BRANCEPETH, Co Durham, and earlier 25 March 1611 VISCOUNT ROCHESTER (all E), KG (1611), PC (E 1612, S 1613); *b c* 1587; Page of Honour to JAMES VI (and I), whose particular favourite he was before the rise of the Duke of Buckingham (*see* JERSEY, E); *ktd* 1607, Gentleman Bedchamber 1607, granted Jan 1608/9 the disgraced Sir Walter Ralegh's Sherborne estate in Dorset and Jan 1609/10 much of the disgraced Lord Maxwell's estates (*see* MAXWELL, Bt, of Monreith) in Scotland; Keeper Westminster Palace 1611, granted Rochester Castle July 1611, High Steward Westminster 1612, Actg Sec State 1612–14, Actg Ld Keeper Privy Seal 1614–15, provisional Ld Warden Cinque Ports 1614–15, Ld Chamberlain 1614–15, imprisoned Tower of London 1615 with his w for murder of Sir Thomas Overbury, found guilty (on a plea of innocence, whereas his w had pleaded guilty) 1616, but set free (with her) Jan 1621/2 (though rusticated with her first to Oxon then to Herts and later still to Surrey) and pardoned 26 Dec 1613 Lady Frances Howard (*d* 23 Aug 1632), dau of 1st Earl of Suffolk (*see* SUFFOLK and BERKSHIRE, E) and divorced w of 3rd Earl of Esssex (*see* HEREFORD, V), *dspm* and was *bur* 17 July 1645, leaving an only dau:

　　　1d Anne; *b* 9 Dec 1615; *m* 11 July 1637 1st Duke of Bedford (*qv*) and had issue

　　4c Anne; *m* (contract 30 Aug 1613) 2nd Lord Balmerinoch (*see* ELPHINSTONE, L) and *d* 27 Feb 1649/50, leaving issue

　2b Andrew, of Nethergogar; *d* by 24 Aug 1581, leaving issue, whose male line died out

　1b Margaret; *m* 5th Lord Hay of Yester (*see* TWEEDDALE, M)

3a Robert, of Ancram and Woodheid; *m* Isabel, dau of David Home of Wedderburn (*see* POLWARTH, L) and *d* Feb 1588, having had, with other issue:

　1b William, of Ancram and Woodheid, of which had sasine 27 Nov 1598; *m* Margaret (*m* 3rd Sir George Douglas Mordington), dau of Archibald Douglas of Fingask and widow of David Home of Fishwick, and was murdered Edinburgh 20 Dec 1590 by Sir Robert Ker, Yr. of Cessford (later Earl of Roxburghe; *see* ROXBURGHE, D), leaving:

　　1c Sir ROBERT KERR, **1st Earl of Ancrame** [*sic*], so *cr* 24 June 1633, as also LORD KERR OF NISBET, LANGNEWTOUN, AND DOLPHINSTOUN (all S), with special remainder to his heirs male by his 2nd w Lady Anne Stanley, in default of whom to heirs male general, KB (probably by 1603, certainly by 1625); *b* 1578; signed the 'Letters of Slains' with his bros 1607 in forgiveness of Lord Roxburghe for the murder of his f; had charters 1611 of lands at Whitchester, 1631 of the Ldship of Newbottle and 1632 of the (territorial) Barony of Langnewton; Capt King's Bodygd to 1613; banished (from Court after

killing Charles Maxwell of Terregles *c* 1 Feb 1620 in a duel, which in extenuation seems not to have been of his own seeking; MP Aylesbury Jan-Aug 1625 and Preston 1628–29; Gentleman Bedchamber 1625; Keeper Privy Purse Scottish Coronation 1633; *m* 1st *c* 24 Jan 1607 Elizabeth (*d* by 1620), sis of Sir Archibald Murray, 1st Bt, of Blackbarony (*qv*), and had:

　　　1d Sir WILLIAM KERR, **1st Earl of Lothian**, so *cr* 31 Oct 1631, as also LORD KER OF NEWBATTLE [*sic*] (both S), PC (1641); *b c* 1605; *educ* Cambridge and Paris; served expdn to Isle of Rhé 1627 (*see* JERSEY, E, sub Duke of Buckingham) and in Dutch serv 1629, Commr Highways 1633, supported Covenanters 1638 and served Scottish army in invading England 1640, Lt-Gen Scottish forces Ireland 1642 and 1645, imprisoned *c* 1643–44 by CHARLES I, to whom he was pretty implacably opposed throughout the Civil War years, Sec State Scotland 1649–52; *m* 9 Dec 1630 his cousin Lady Anne Kerr (*d* 26 March 1667), est dau and heiress of line of 2nd EARL OF LOTHIAN of the 1606 *cr* (*see above*), and *d* Oct 1675, having had, with other issue:

　　　　1e ROBERT KERR, **1st Marquess of Lothian**, so *cr* 23 June 1701, as also EARL OF ANCRAM, VISCOUNT OF BRIENE, LORD KER OF NEWBOTTLE, OXNAM, JEDBURGH, DOLPHINSTOUN AND NISBET (all S), with remainder to heirs male of his body, in default of which to the other heirs of entail succeeding him in his estate for ever, also **3rd Earl of Ancram**, as which *s* half-unc 1690; *s* cousin (**4th Lord Jedburgh**) as heirs male of Kerr, Cessford and Kerr, Ferniehirst and Chief of The Name of Kerr 1692 (but not in the actual Ldship of Parl (which passed instead to his *s*) due to the terms of its regrant 1670, for which *see above*), PC (Jan-Sept 1686 and 1689); *b* 8 March 1636; *educ* Scotland, Leyden and Saumur; unsuccessfully claimed Earldom of Roxburghe 1658; serve Third Dutch War 1673, Capt Roxburghshire Militia Horse to 1675, a Commr Supply 1678–96, Justice-Gen Scotland 1689–Feb 1702/3, Sheriff Pncpl Midlothian, Commr Exchequer and Treasury 1690, Justice Gen and Commr to negotiate Parly Union 1702, Ld High Commr Gen Assembly Ch Scotland; *m* (contract Jan 1660/1) Lady Jean Campbell (*see* ARGYLL, D) and *d* 15 Feb 1702/3, having had, with other issue:

　　　　　1f WILLIAM KERR, **2nd Marquess of Lothian**, also **5th Lord Jedburgh**, as which *s* cousin 1692 under terms of regrant of 1670, KT (1705); *b* 1661; Col 7th Dragoons 1696–1707, 3rd Foot Gds 1707–13, Brig-Gen 1702, Maj-Gen 1704, Lt Gen 1707; rep S peer 1707–08/9 (unseated on petition due irregularity in his election) and 1715–22; *m* (contract 30 June 1685) his cousin Jane (*d* 31 July 1712), sis of 1st Duke of Argyll (*qv*), and *d* 28 Feb 1721/2, leaving:

　　　　　　1g WILLIAM, **3rd Marquess**

　　　　　　1g Anne; *m* 1st 7th Earl of Home (*qv*) and had issue; *m* 2nd Henry Ogle and *d* 1727

　　　　　　2g Jean; *m* 5th Lord Cranstoun (*see* 1869 edn) and *d* 1768, leaving issue

　　　　　　3g Elizabeth; *m* George, 13th Lord Ross (extinct 1754) and *d* 22 May 1758, leaving issue

　　　　　　4g Mary; *m* her cousin Alexander Hamilton and *d* 17 Nov 1768, leaving issue (*see* HADDINGTON, E, also STRATHMORE AND KINGHORNE, E)

　　　　　2f Charles, of Cramond; Dir Chancery; *m* Janet (*d* 1 Dec 1755), est dau of Sir David Murray of Stanhope, and *d* 1735, leaving issue

　　　　　3f Mark; *bapt* 1 April 1676; Gen, Govr Edinburgh Castle; *d* unm 2 Feb 1752

　　　　　1f Mary; *m* 13 Dec 1692 as his 2nd w, 2nd Marquess of Douglas and *d* 22 Jan 1736, leaving issue (*see* HAMILTON and BRANDON, D)

　　　　2e William (Sir), of Halden; *b* 22 Dec 1638; Dir Chancery Scotland; *m* (contract 30 June 1664) Agnes, dau of John Cockburn of Ormiston, and had:

　　　　　1f William; *d* 1721

　　　　3e Charles, of Abbotrule; *b* 17 July 1642; *m* Cecily, dau of Patrick Scott of Langshaw, and was ancestor of the KERs of Abbotrule

　　　　1e Elizabeth; *m* Sir Alexander Hamilton, 11th of Ballincrieff and 2nd of Fenton, and had issue (*see* HADDINGTON, E)

　　　　2e Anne; *b* 26 Nov 1631; *m c* 11 Jan 1651/2 Alexander, Master of Saltoun (*see* SALTOUN, L), and *d* 30 Aug 1658, leaving issue

　　　　3e Vere; *b* 24 April 1649; *m* 28 Jan 1668 Lord Neil Campbell (*see* ARGYLL, D) and *d* 17 April 1674, leaving issue

　　　　4e Henrietta; *b* 2 Feb 1653; *m* (contract 27 Nov 1673) Sir Francis Scott of Thirlestane (*d* March 1712) and *d* 30 June 1741, leaving issue (*see* NAPIER and ETTRICK, L)

　　　　5e Margaret; *m* 1666 Sir James Richardson, 4th Bt (*see* STEWART-RICHARDSON, Bt), and had issue

　　1c (cont.) The **1st Earl** *m* 2nd 1621 Anne (*bur* 15 Feb 1656/7), only dau of 6th Earl of Derby (*qv*) and widow of Sir Henry Portman, 2nd Bt (*see* PORTMAN, V), and *d* Amsterdam just after 9 Dec 1654, having by her had:

　　　2d CHARLES KERR, **2nd Earl of Ancram**; MP St Michael's 1647–48 (when unseated for royalism), Thirsk July-Dec 1660 and Wigan 1661–81 and 1685–87; *m* just prior to 1 May 1662 — and *dsps* Sept 1690, having had a *s* (*dsp* & *vp* on or after 5 Feb 1675/6)

　　　3d Stanley; living 1666

　　　　1d Vere; *m* Dr Wilkinson, of Oxford

　　　　2d Elizabeth; *m* Col Nathaniel Rich

　　2c William, of Overtoun, Oxnam, Roxburghshire, of which had a charter 30 Aug 1625 but resigned them by 28 Feb 1629, when they were granted to William Ker of Linton

　　3c Thomas (Sir), of Redden; *ktd* 1633; *m* 1st Jean, dau of James Ker of Chatto and was ancestor of the KERRs of Bughtrig and KERRs of the Hale; *m* 2nd Mary Douglas

4c Andrew; allegedly *d* unm

5c George

1c Isabel; *m* John Ker of Corbet

2b Robert, of Newton; *m* (contract 14 Oct 1586) Helen, dau of John Grahamshaw of Newton, and had:

1c Robert, of Newton, of which had a charter 7 Feb 1622; served heir to his f 3 Nov 1618; *m* Euphemia Douglas and had issue

1a Janet; *m c* 1530, as his 2nd w, Sir Walter Scott of Buccleuch (*see* BUCCLEUCH and QUEENSBERRY, D)

2a Isabel; *m* her cousin Sir Walter Ker of Cessford (*see* ROXBURGHE, D)

(2) Ralph, of Primside; *m* 1st Margaret, dau of Murray of Falahill; *m* 2nd Margaret Rutherfurd and *d* by 29 Nov 1525, having had:

1a Andrew, of Primside and Greenhead; ancestor of Kerr, Bt, of Greenland, and the KERs of Helton

2a George; ancestor of the KERs of Cavers

3a William; Commendator Kelso; *k* by the KERRs of Cessford Aug 1566

4a John; living 1540

(3) Thomas; Rector Yetholme 1506, Abbot Kelso 1517; *d* by 14 Aug 1539

(4) George; living 1539

(5) William, of Langlie and Gillistongues; living 1568

4 Robert; Abbot Kelso; *d* by June 1505

5 William, of Yair; ancestor of the KERs of Yair

6 Ralph; ancestor of Ker, Bt, of Greenland (extinct 1779) and the KERRs of Chatto

1 Margaret; *m* 1st Sir James Sandilands of Calder (*see* TORPHICHEN, L); *m* 2nd, as his 2nd w, 4th Earl of Erroll (*qv*)

The 2nd MARQUESS's only son,
WILLIAM KERR, **3rd Marquess of Lothian**, KT (Feb 1733/4); *b c* 1690; rep S peer 1731–61, Ld High Commr Gen Assembly Ch Scotland 1732–38, Ld Clerk Register 1739–56; *m* 1st Dec 1711 Margaret (*d* 30 Sept 1759), dau of Sir Thomas Nicolson, 1st Bt, of Kemney, Aberdeenshire, and had two sons (the yr, Robert, Capt Gren Gds, *ka* Culloden 16 April 1746) and a dau; *m* 2nd 1 Oct 1760 his cousin Jean Janet (*dsp* 26 Dec 1787), est dau of Lord Charles Kerr, of Cramond (*see* above), and *d* 28 July 1767; his er s by his 1st w:

WILLIAM HENRY KERR, **4th Marquess of Lothian**, KT (1768); *b* 1710; Cornet 1735, Capt 11th Foot 1739 and 1st Foot Gds 1741, ADC to DUKE OF CUMBERLAND 1745–46, wounded Battle of Fontenoy 1745, cmded Cavalry Culloden 1746, Maj-Gen 1755, Lt Gen 1758, Gen 1770, Col 24th Foot 1747–52 and 11th Dragoons 1752–75, MP (Whig) Richmond, Yorks, 1747–63, rep S peer 1768–74; *m* 6 Nov 1735 Lady Caroline D'Arcy (*d* 15 Nov 1778), only dau of 3rd Earl of Holderness (*see* DARCY DE KNAYTH, B), and *d* 12 April 1775, having had:

1 WILLIAM JOHN, **5th Marquess**

1 Louisa; *m* 25 Dec 1759 Lord George Lennox, 2nd s of 2nd Duke of Richmond, and had issue (*see* RICHMOND and GORDON, D)

2 Wilhelmina Frances; *m* 2 Jan 1783 Maj-Gen John MacLeod, RA, and had issue

The 4th MARQUESS's only son,
WILLIAM JOHN KERR, **5th Marquess of Lothian**, KT (1776); *b* 13 March 1737; *educ* Eton; joined Army 1754, Maj Gen 1777, Lt Gen 1782, Gen 1796, Col 1st Horse Gds 1777–89, 11th Dragoons 1798–1813 and 2nd Dragoons 1813–15; rep S peer 1778–90; *m* 29 June 1762 Elizabeth (*d* 30 Sept 1780), only dau of Chichester Fortescue, of Dromisken, Co Louth, and gdau of 1st Baron Mornington (*see* WELLINGTON, D), and *d* 4 Jan 1815, having had, with other issue:

1 WILLIAM, **6th Marquess**

2 Charles Beauchamp; *b* 19 July 1775; *m* Elizabeth (*d* 10 Nov 1830), dau of William Crump, of Farnham, and *d* 2 March 1816, having had, with other issue:

(1) Charles William John (Rev); *b* 3 Sept 1801; *d* unm 23 Jan 1869

(2) Mark Henry James (Rev); *b* 9 Nov 1802; *d* 3 Sept 1855

(3) Beauchamp; *b* 29 May 1806; Capt 55th Foot; *m* 15 Aug 1832 Caroline Elizabeth (*d* 1889), yst dau of James Irwin, HEICS, and *d* 13 July 1872, leaving issue

(4) William Henry; *b* 8 July 1811; *m* 17 Nov 1841 Maria, yst dau of Richard Power, of Cork, and *d* 28 Sept 1865, leaving:

1a Frances Caroline; *b* 11 March 1843; *d* unm

3 Mark Robert; *b* 12 Nov 1776; V-Adml; *m* 18 July 1799 Charlotte, Countess of Antrim in her own right, and *d* 9 Sept 1840, leaving issue (*see* ANTRIM, E)

4 Robert, KH; *b* 14 Sept 1780; Maj-Gen; *m* 14 June 1806 Mary (*d* 27 Nov 1861), dau of Rev Edmund Gilbert, and *d* 23 June 1843, leaving, with other issue:

(1) William Walter Raleigh; *b* 26 Nov 1809; Treasurer Mauritius; *m* 12 Feb 1850 Mary Rouet (*d* 4 Aug 1911), dau of James Wilson, Ch Justice Mauritius, and *d* 26 May 1881, leaving:

1a Henry Teviot; *b* 25 May 1857; Lt 80th Regt; *m* 1st 1885 Eva Mary Orde (*dsp* 20 June 1895), dau of Arthur Bigge Wither; *m* 2nd 1896 Harriett (*d* 13 Feb 1913), dau of J Andrews, RN, and widow of A Linberry, and *d* 1910

2a Mark Ancram, CB (1904); *b* 2 May 1859; Brevet Col IA, Tibet Expdn, cmdg 13th Bn Liverpool Regt 1914; *d* unm 19 Nov 1941

3a William Walter Raleigh; *b* 8 Feb 1863; Capt RAF, Lt 3rd Bn Gordon Highrs, Hon Attaché St Petersburg 1888, Priv Chamberlain to TH POPES PIUS X and BENEDICT XV, WW I BEF (Médaille de la Reconnaissance Française); *m* 22 Sept 1888 Annabel (*d* 1 April 1954), dau of Hon James Jackson Jarves, of Boston, USA, and *d* 22 Aug 1942, having had:

1b Walter Raleigh Mark Edward Joseph; *b* 4 Feb 1891; *d* 1901

2b (Louis William) Howard (Sir), KCVO (1948, CVO 1924, MVO 1929), CMG (1935), OBE (1922); *b* 25 Nov 1894; *educ* Lower Canada Coll Montreal and Trin Coll Cambridge; Maj 11th Hus WW I, ADC to Ld Lt Ireland 1921–22 and C-in-C Scottish Cmd 1923, Equerry to HRH THE DUKE OF GLOUCESTER 1924–47, Comptroller 1947–49 (PA to HRH with BEF France 1939–40, Ch Staff tour MEF, India and Ceylon 1942), served WW II; Roy Humane Soc's Medal (Canada) Saving Life, Chev Order Leopold Belgium, Order Sacred Treasure Japan, Priv Chamberlain to HH THE POPE 1928, Life Govr Queen Mary's Hosp 1929, Garter Mission Japan

1929, dir West End branch Commercial Union Assur, Govr Roy Nat Orthopaedic Hosp; *m* 12 June 1928 Christina Stephanie Mary (*d* 1986), dau of Arthur Archibald Ram, of Wexford, and *d* 11 July 1977, leaving:

1c +Henry Howard Philip Sackville Casamayor Ram [Henry Kerr Esq, 13 Westbourne Gdns, Hove, Sussex BN3 5PL]; *b* 13 Jan 1932; *educ* The Oratory; *m* 13 Nov 1973 *Christina Annie, dau of Herbert Charles Button, RN, of Lowestoft

2c +Andrew Robert Stephen Casamayor [Andrew Kerr Esq, Ninian House, Glasserton, Wigtownshire]; *b* 21 March 1936; *educ* Nautical Coll Pangbourne; *m* 1988 *Jacqueline Helen Andrée, dau of Frederick John Bryan, CA, of Vancouver

3c +Julian James Casamayor [Julian Kerr Esq, 53 Belper Rd, Derby DE1 3EP]; *b* 12 March 1941; *educ* Gordonstoun; *m* 14 May 1966 *Glenys Ann, dau of Rev Thomas Hugh Roberts, of Grantham, Lincs, and has:

1d +Andrew James; *b* 11 Nov 1967; *educ* St Hugh's Coll Tollerton Hall Nottingham and Manchester U (LLB); *m* 17 May 1997 *Jane Kathryn, dau of David Thomas Wilkinson, of Barrow-in-Furness, Cumbria

2d +Philip Hugh; *b* 18 Oct 1971; *educ* St Hugh's Coll Tollerton Hall, St Benedict RC Sch Derby and Manchester U (MA)

3d +Robert Michael; *b* 1974

1b Marie Constance Annabel; *b* 17 Aug 1889; *m* 29 July 1915 her cousin Capt Andrew William Kerr, RN (*see* below), and had issue

4a Charles Arthur Humphrey; *b* 22 Dec 1864; *dsp*

1a Mary Louisa Cranstoun; *m* 3 Aug 1869 Sir Edward Newton, KCMG, and *d* 3 May 1870

2a Sophie Mary Frances; *m* 15 Jan 1877 Maj-Gen Sir George Joseph Hamilton Evatt, KCB, MD, Army Med Staff (*d* 5 Nov 1921), and *d* 7 Oct 1934, leaving issue

3a Ethel Georgiana; *d* unm 13 Aug 1950

4a Mary Caroline Alice; *m* 10 Aug 1897 V-Adml John Douglas Edwards, CB (*d* 30 March 1952), s of Dr C F Edwards, and *dsp* 16 Jan 1955

(2) Robert Dundas; *b* Jan 1824; Col RE; *m* 17 June 1852 Harriett Marianne (*d* 21 Sept 1910), 4th dau of John Arnold, of Halstead, Kent, and Toronto, and *d* 20 Oct 1877, leaving:

1a Schomberg; *b* 11 Jan 1861; Capt Rifle Bde; *m* 1st 1884 Ada Jessie (*d* 1896), dau of J Wilson, and had:

1b Charles Lester, DSO; *b* 1886; Cdr RN, WW I (despatches twice), WW II (severely wounded Sept 1940), 4th Cl Order Kara-George Serbia with swords, 4th Cl Order White Eagle Serbia, Orders Crown Italy, George I Greece and Croix de Guerre; *m* 1st 21 Nov 1908 Innes Margaret Annie (*d* 6 March 1953), dau of Col P Archer Chapman, RFA, and had:

1c Mark Barrington; *b* 22 Aug 1910; *educ* Downside; WW II as Capt RA (despatches); Pncpl Overseas Dept Bank of England

1b (cont.) Cdr Charles Kerr *m* 2nd 16 April 1953 Dorothea Blanchard, dau of Capt Reeves and widow of Capt Martin Martin-Smith, Worcs Regt, and *d* 29 Oct 1965

1a (cont.) Capt Schomberg Kerr *m* 2nd 11 Oct 1904 Rosa Williamina (*d* 19 July 1926), dau of Archibald Dymock, JP, MD, of Louth, Lincs, and *d* 23 Sept 1930

1a Rosamond Eliza; *d* unm 1 Jan 1911

2a Louisa Grace Charlotte Mary; *m* 20 May 1880 Col Thomas Ryder Main, CB, CMG, RE (*d* 1 May 1934), and *d* 5 July 1939, leaving issue

3a Constance Lucy; *m* 30 Sept 1884 Lester Ramsay de Fonblanque (*d* 16 March 1925) and *d* 29 June 1944, leaving issue

(1) Elizabeth Anne; *m* 13 Jan 1830 FM Sir William Maynard Gomm, GCB, Col Coldstream Gds (*d* 15 March 1875), and *d* 30 Nov 1877

(2) Louisa Grace; *m* 4 May 1841 Maj-Gen William Henry Cornwall (*d* 21 July 1855) and *d* 5 Sept 1856

(3) Mary Frances; *m* 3 Jan 1846 1st and last Baron Hammond of Kirkella (*d* 29 April 1890) and *d* 14 June 1888, leaving issue

(4) Emily Caroline Fortescue; *m* 17 July 1841 Andrew Morton Carr (*d* 17 Sept 1852), barrister, and *d* 19 April 1893, leaving issue

(5) Lucy Mary; Maid-of-Honour to HM QUEEN VICTORIA; *d* unm 27 June 1874

1 Mary; *m* 8 Dec 1788 Gen Hon Frederick St John and *d* 6 Feb 1791, leaving issue (*see* BOLINGBROKE and SAINT JOHN, V)

The 5th MARQUESS's est son,
WILLIAM KERR, **6th Marquess of Lothian**, KT (1820); *b* 4 Oct 1763; *cr* 17 July 1821 BARON KER OF KERSHEUGH, Co Roxburgh (UK); Col Edinburgh Militia, Ld Lt Midlothian and Roxburghshire, rep S peer 1817–21; *m* 1st 14 April 1793 Lady Harriet Hobart (*d* 14 July 1805), est dau of 2nd Earl of Buckinghamshire (*qv*) and formerly w of 1st Earl Belmore (*qv*), and had:

1 JOHN WILLIAM ROBERT, **7th Marquess**

2 Schomberg Robert; *b* 15 Aug 1795; Capt 3rd Regt; *d* 12 Aug 1825

3 Henry Francis Charles (Rev); *b* 17 Aug 1800; Rector Dittisham, Devon; *m* 10 Sept 1832 Louisa Dorothea (*d* 18 Jan 1884), only dau of Gen Hon Sir Alexander Hope, GCB (*see* LINLITHGOW, M), and *d* 7 March 1882, leaving:

(1) William Hobart (Rev); *b* 25 July 1836; Dep Sec Govr Madras and Superintendent Coorg, later RC priest; *d* 24 March 1913

(2) Henry Schomberg (Rev); *b* 15 Aug 1838; Cdr RN, later RC priest; *d* 18 Aug 1895

(3) Francis Ernest; *b* 10 Aug 1840; Lt Rifle Bde, Govr Mil Prison Malta; *m* 4 Oct 1870 Mary Frances (*d* 6 Sept 1916), est dau of Robert Monteith, of Carstairs, Lanarks, and *d* 30 May 1884, having had:

1a Henry Francis Hobart; *b* 1 Sept 1878; Capt 3rd Bn Cameronians Boer War; *m* 18 Nov 1915 Gertrude Mary (*d* 2 Sept 1969), dau of James Anthony, and had:

1b Francis Robert Newsam, OBE (1961), MC; *b* 12 Sept 1916; *educ* Ampleforth; Lt-Col (TA), Maj Roy Scots, Palestine 1939, WW II (wounded), V-Lt Berwicks 1971; *m* 7 Oct 1941 *Anne Frederica, yr dau of William Edmundstoun Kitson, of Blanerne House, and *d* 19 Oct 1995, leaving:

1c +Henry Mark William [Henry Kerr Esq, Sea Moss, Keveral Gdns, Seaton, Cornwall PL11 3JH]; b 7 Aug 1946; educ Ampleforth; m 1982 *Pamela Christine, dau of Alfred Edward Noel Delafield, of Plymouth

2c +David Anthony Francis [David Kerr Esq, Howden, Jedburgh, Roxburghs]; b 26 May 1953; m 1975 *Julia Veronica, dau of William Bertram, and has:

1d *Sarah Anne; b 1978

2d *Jane Elizabeth; b 1980

1c *Susan Mary Kerr [Mrs Susan Kerr, 7 Chelmsford Rd, Mount Lawley, Perth 6050, W Australia]; b 2 April 1952; kept maiden name; m 1981 *Andrew Robert King and has:

1d *Rory Francis KING; b 1985

1b *Monica Mary Cecil [Mrs William Devas, 3 Cavendish St, Chichester, W Sussex]; b 26 Oct 1917; m 14 Nov 1939 *G/Capt William George Devas, CBE, DFC, AFC, RAF, and has:

1c *Christopher William Kerr, JP 1992 [Christopher Devas Esq JP, Wadmill Farm, Stour Row, Dorset SP7 0QB]; b 26 July 1944; educ Ampleforth and RMA Sandhurst; m 1st 9 May 1970 (divorce 1983) Hon Penelope Anne, only dau of Baron O'Neill of the Maine (see O'NEILL, B); m 2nd 1 June 1994 *Veronica Susan, widow of Michael Conway-Phayne-Mudge and dau of — Scott, and by his 1st w has:

1d *William Thomas; b 1975

2c *John Robin Ambrose [John Devas Esq, 4 St Martin's Sq, Chichester, W Sussex]; b 26 May 1947; educ Ampleforth; AA Dip, ARIBA; m 5 Sept 1970 *Rachel Geraldine, yr dau of Capt Gerald Tuck, DSO, RN, of Chichester, and has:

1d *Frederic Seymour; b 1978

1d *Claire Noelle; b 1976

2b *Anne Margaret D'Arcy [Mrs Christopher Scott, Hollybush, Galashiels, Selkirkshire; Flat 27, 50 Sloane St, London SW1]; b 30 April 1923; m 16 Sept 1948 *Christopher Bartle Hugh FRERE later SCOTT of Gala (1940) only s of Philip Beaumont Frere, of London, and has had:

1c *John Philip Henry Schomberg; b 20 June 1952; m 1977 *Jacqueline Dawn, er dau of Colin Rae, of Little Weston, Somerset, and has:

1d *Alexander Hugh Frere; b 1982

2d *James Julian Frere; b 1985

2c *Dominic Christopher Hugh [Dominic Scott Esq, Netherbarns Farm House, Netherbarns Farm, by Galashiels]; b 24 Aug 1955; m 1984 *Melanie Lydia, er dau of Craven Nicholas Charrington, of Reigate, and has:

1d *Samara Olga Frere; b 1985

2d *Isabella Zinaida Frere; b 1986

3d *Anastasia Amelia Frere; b 1989

4d *Sasha Scarlett Frere; b 1991

3c Julian Sebastian Frere; b 8 Dec 1956; m 1982 *Alexandra Hough and d 1984

4c *Rupert Benjamin Bartle Frere [Rupert Scott Esq, 2 Whitehorse St, London W1]; b 12 Oct 1958

5c *Sebastian Simon Frere; b 1 Aug 1961

2a Francis Robert; b 3 March 1880; d 12 March 1881

3a Robert Joseph; b 12 March 1882; d 20 Nov 1883

1a Wilhelmina Mary Henrietta, OBE (1920); b 16 April 1872; m 23 Oct 1895 Charles John Philip Cave, JP, Capt RE (d 8 Dec 1950), of Stoner Hill, Petersfield, and d 8 Jan 1944, leaving issue

2a Dorothy Margaret Mary; b 11 Dec 1873; nun; d 26 May 1964

3a Henrietta Mary Monica; b 28 Nov 1874; nun; d 28 Nov 1943

4a Cecil Mary; b 11 March 1876; d unm 16 Sept 1962

5a Mary Christina; b 1 May 1877; m 22 Feb 1906 Capt Adrian Laurence Cave, 10th Roy Hus (d 21 June 1931), s of Laurence Trent Cave, of Ditcham Pk, Buriton, Hants, and had:

1b Dan Adrian Francis; b 29 Nov 1906; educ Eton; Lt Somerset LI WW II; m 28 Aug 1934 Marion Margaret Josephine, dau of Col Oswald Turville-Petre (see PETRE, B), and had:

1c *Adrian Oswald Wynn; b 18 Oct 1935; educ Ampleforth; AA Dip, ARIBA, AA Dip TP; m 1 Feb 1964 *Felicity Mary, est dau of Martin du Pré Cooper, of London, and has:

1d *Benedict Blaise; b 2 Nov 1967

2c *Peter Dan Gabriel (Rev); b 24 April 1938; educ Ampleforth; RC priest 1968

2b *John Laurence Mark, TD; b 9 June 1910; Maj RA WW II N Africa and Italy; m 5 Aug 1936 *Georgiana Helen, yr dau of Edward Somerset Charrington, of Bures Manor, Surrey, and has:

1c *Jennifer Anne; b 8 Oct 1947; m 2 March 1968 *Capt Patrick Michael Corbett, Irish Gds, s of John Corbett, of Tyrella House, Downpatrick, Co Down

6a Anne Maude Mary; b 10 Feb 1881; d 9 March 1882

7a Mary Alice; b 21 May 1883; d unm 16 Feb 1959

(1) Henrietta Mary Emma; d unm 1 Dec 1884

(2) Mary D'Arcy; m 4 Oct 1871 John George Kenyon and d 2 Feb 1937, leaving issue (see KENYON, B)

(3) Alice Dorothea; d unm

1 Isabella Emily Caroline; d 19 Dec 1858

The **6th Marquess** m 2nd 1 Dec 1806 Harriet (d 18 April 1833), dau of 3rd Duke of Buccleuch and (5th Duke of) Queensberry (qv), and d 27 April 1824, leaving by her:

4 Charles Lennox; b 1 July 1814; Lt-Col 3rd Bn Black Watch, ADC to Ld Lt Ireland; m 22 Oct 1839 Charlotte Emma (d 10 April 1887), est dau of Sir Thomas Hanmer, 2nd Bt (qv), and d 15 March 1898, having had:

(1) Charles Wyndham Rodolph; b 9 Nov 1849; m 17 June 1873 Anna Maria Olivia (d 20 Jan 1937), yst dau of Adml Sir George Elliott, KCB (see MINTO, E), and dvp 7 Feb 1894, leaving:

1a CHARLES IAN KERR, cr BARON TEVIOT (qv)

2a Walter William, MC; b 2 Oct 1875; Capt 2nd E African Rifles, Lt 3rd London Yeo; m 22 June 1898 Evelyn Mary (d 10 Dec 1934), dau of Maj-Gen Sir Arthur Ellis, KCVO, CSI (see HOWARD DE WALDEN, B), and d 1 May 1947, leaving:

1b Alister Walter Mark; b 17 Oct 1900; educ Wellington; d March 1915

3a Basil, DSC; b 22 Sept 1879; Maj Scottish Horse Yeo WW I; m 6 Feb 1912 Winifred Katherine (d 19 Feb 1974), est dau of George Blezard by Hon Katherine Chetwynd (see CHETWYND, V), and d 19 Sept 1957, having had:

1b Mark George; b 27 Oct 1912; ADC to Viceroy India 1937, Lt-Col Rifle Bde WW II; m 14 Oct 1942 *Anne, dau of T Haydn, of USA; das Italy 13 Jan 1945

1b *Diana Katherine, MBE (1977) [Lady Clowes MBE, 235 Cranmer Ct, Whiteheads Grove, London SW3 3HD]; m 1 March 1941 Col Sir Henry Nelson Clowes, KCVO, DSO, OBE, Scots Gds (d 1993), yr s of Maj Ernest Clowes DSO, 1st Life Gds by Blanche, dau of R-Adml Hon Algernon Littleton (see HATHERTON, B), and has:

1c *Andrew Henry [Andrew Clowes Esq, 52 Bowerdean St, London SW6 3TW]; b 27 Oct 1942; educ Eton; Capt Scots Gds, Equerry to HRH THE DUKE OF GLOUCESTER 1966–67; m 8 July 1968 *Georgiana Elizabeth, est dau of Richard Edward Osborne Cavendish, JP, DL (see DEVONSHIRE, D), and has:

1d *Richard (Dickon) William Andrew; b 1971

1d *Emma Georgiana; b 1975

2b *Elizabeth [Mrs George Demetriadi, 9 Wilton St, London SW1]; m 26 June 1946 Lt-Col George Demetriadi, MBE, TD, Roy Welch Fus (d 1991), er s of George Constantine Demetriadi, of Cheshire

1a Violet; m 30 April 1902 Rev Hon Nigel Campbell (see CAWDOR, E) and d 15 March 1940, leaving issue

2a Olive; m 28 April 1903 Maj Hon George Henry Edwardes (see KENSINGTON, B) and d 27 June 1968, leaving issue

3a Helen Cicely; m 1st 6 July 1910 Capt Archibald Edward Butter, CMG (d 6 Jan 1928), er s of Col Archibald Butter, DL, and had:

1b Archibald Charles (Rev); b 15 June 1911; educ Stowe; ordained Bloemfontein 1943, Diocesan Relieving Staff Diocese of Johannesburg; m 25 May 1968 *Margaret Janet, dau of Rees William Haddock and widow of Douglas Christison

2b Ian Edward; b 4 May 1912; d 14 Sept 1923

3b *John Henry, CMG (1963), MBE (1946); b 20 April 1916; educ Charterhouse and Ch Ch Oxford; Fin Advsr Treasury Kenya Govt; m 25 Nov 1950 *Joyce, dau of Wilfred Platt, of Bradford, and has:

1c *Ian Peter; b 28 March 1952

2c *Andrew Edward; b 5 June 1953

3c *David Charles; b 3 Dec 1956

4b Peter Herbert; b April 1921; educ Charterhouse and Balliol Coll Oxford; Regius Prof English Glasgow U; m 30 Aug 1958 *Bridget, dau of Maj H J Younger, of Baro, Haddington, E Lothian, and had:

1c *Archibald Simon; b 21 Sept 1962

1c *Rachel Mary Cecilia; b 23 Nov 1965

3a (cont.) Mrs Archibald Butter m 2nd 28 April 1939 Brig-Gen Edward William David Baird, CBE, JP, DL (d 8 Aug 1956), of Whitehill, Gordon, Berwick, and d 14 June 1976

(2) John Hanmer; b 7 May 1851; Capt Black Watch; d unm 14 Oct 1890

(3) Walter Montagu; b June 1852; CE; d unm 23 April 1888

(1) Harriet Georgiana Edith; m 10 Nov 1864 William Warcop Peter Consett, DL (d 6 May 1910), of Brawith Hall, Yorks, and d 15 Jan 1924, leaving issue

(2) Florence Elizabeth; m 29 April 1869 4th Earl of Dunraven and Mount-Earl (qv) and d 16 Sept 1916, leaving issue

(3) Amy Frances; m 15 April 1871 Henley Eden and d 7 Aug 1939, having had issue (see EDEN OF WINTON, B)

5 Mark Ralph George (Sir), GCB; b 15 Dec 1817; Gen, Col Prince Albert's Somerset LI; d unm 17 May 1900

6 Frederick Herbert; b 30 Sept 1818; Adml; Groom-in-Waiting to HM QUEEN VICTORIA 1868–91, Extra Groom-in-Waiting and Bath King of Arms 1891–96; m 13 Jan 1846 Emily Sophia (d 16 Dec 1891), dau of Gen Sir Peregrine Maitland, GCB, and d 15 Jan 1896, leaving:

(1) Arthur Herbert; b 10 Feb 1862; Pres Land Agents' Soc 1912–13; m 23 July 1889 Mildred Caroline (d 8 Oct 1950), dau of Sir James Walker, 2nd Bt, of Sand Hutton (qv), and d 8 Jan 1930, leaving:

1a Mark Peregrine Charles; b 20 Oct 1891; Cdr RN, WW I (despatches), N Russia 1919, WW II, Russian Order St Anne 3rd Cl; m 9 Oct 1918 Mary Catherine (d 1982), only child of Henry Offley Wakeman (see WAKEMAN, Bt), and d 22 Feb 1951, leaving:

1b +Frederic Mark, DFM; b 6 July 1919; educ Canford; WW II as W/O RAFVR (POW); m 1st 24 Jan 1947 (divorce 1952) Iris Margaret Urquhart, dau of William Palk Tully; m 2nd 1 April 1952 *June, dau of Capt Lancelot Gerrard Laurence, and by her has had:

1c +Peregrine Gerrard Mark [Peregrine Kerr Esq, Charlton Cottage, Flax Bourton, Bristol]; b 27 Sept 1955; m 1988 *Susan Jane, dau of Dennis Tucker, of Cumnor, Oxford

2c +Christian Anthony Mark; b 11 Aug 1960

1c Angela Caterina; b 27 Aug 1952; d 13 Oct 1957

2b +(Mark) David [David Kerr Esq, 4/5 Russell Garth Cottage, High St, Eynsford, Kent DA4 0AB]; b 3 Feb 1921; educ Canford; F/O RAFVR WW II (despatches); m 17 Nov 1959 *Diana Law, dau of Arthur Fawcett, of Newmarket

3b +John Anthony [John Kerr Esq, East Membury Farm, Membury, E Devon EX13 7JR]; b 13 Nov 1926; educ Radley

4b +Andrew Philip [Andrew Kerr Esq, Rectory Cottage, Church End, Standlake, Oxon OX8 7BG]; b 29 Nov 1933; educ Radley

1b *Elizabeth Mary; b 29 Nov 1928 [Mrs Walter Woodin, Oak Tree Cottage, Appleton, Oxon OX13 5LA]; m 5 Sept 1957 *Walter Michael Woodin, s of Walter Benjamin Woodin, and has:

1c *Mark Chandler [Mark Woodin Esq, 2 Gatehouse Cottages, Chilton, Aylesbury, Bucks HP18 9LR]; b 16 Feb 1966; m 13 Oct 1990 *Joanna Franklin

1c *Elizabeth Mary Anne [Mrs Robert Florey, Rectory Farm, Northmoor, Oxon OX8 1SX]; b 27 Dec 1960; m 1982 *Robert Patrick Frank Florey and has:

1d *James Edward Robert; b 1985

2d *Samuel Michael Thomas; b 1987

1a Margaret Vere; b 26 Sept 1890; m 12 Dec 1917 Maj-Gen Cecil Percival Heywood (see HEYWOOD, Bt) and d 25 Oct 1958, leaving issue

2a Irene Mildred; b 28 Aug 1896; m 17 July 1928 Hugh Watson Pearson, Maj E R Yeo (d 13 April 1946), s of Hugh Watson Pearson, and had:

1b Hugh Gerard Kerr; b 23 March, d 31 Aug 1933

1b *Sarah Evelyn; b 24 Aug 1934; m 24 Aug 1968 *Lt-Cdr George Stephen Rae-Fraser, RN, s of Douglas Rae-Fraser, of Waltham St Lawrence, Berks

(2) Mark Edward Frederic, CB (1913), MVO (1903); b 26 Sept 1864; Adml; Egypt 1882 and 1891 (medal and star), WW I (wounded and gassed), Naval Attaché Rome, Vienna, Constantinople and Athens 1903–04, Naval ADC to HM GEORGE V 1912–13, C-in-C Roy Hellenic Navy and Naval Advsr to KING CONSTANTINE 1913–15, cmdg Br Sqdn Adriatic 1916–17; instrumental in founding RAF 1917; T/Maj-Gen RAF 1918, Dep CAS and memb Air Cncl 1918, Area Cdr RAF 1918; author, Roy Humane Soc's medal for saving life at sea, Grand Cross King George I of Greece, Kt Cdr Stefan and St Stanislas Russia, Iron Crown Lombardy, Crown Italy and Mil Cross Savoy Italy, Redeemer Greece, Spanish Naval Order Merit 3rd Cl, Grand Offr Order St Maurice and St Lazarus Italy; m 10 July 1906 Rose Margaret, OBE (d 12 Dec 1944), only child of Maj Wilfred A Gough, and d 20 Jan 1944, leaving:

1a Alix; b 10 May 1907; m 28 July 1937 Maurice Arthur Liddell (see RAVENSWORTH, B) and had issue

2a *Luise Rosemary [Miss Luise Kerr, 19 Draycott Ave, London SW3; 26 Upper Strand St, Sandwich, Kent]; b 22 Nov 1908

(3) Frederic Walter, DSO; b 20 May 1867; Page of Honour to HM QUEEN VICTORIA 1879–83; Col Gordon Highrs, Chitral, Tirah, Bde-Maj Boer War, DAQMG 1st Army Corps 1904–06, GSO(2) Aldershot 1905–08, Dep Assist Dir Movements WO 1908–12, GSO(1) Scottish Cmd 1913–14, WW I in BEF (despatches); m 5 April 1902 his cousin Helen Victoria Lillian (d 4 June 1968), dau of 9th Marquess of Lothian, and was ka 31 Oct 1914, leaving:

1a Schomberg David Frederic; b 8 June 1903; d unm Sept 1947

2a Ronald William, WS; b 24 May 1906; educ Wellington, Keble Coll Oxford (BA 1927) and Edinburgh U (LLB 1931); WW II as Lt RNVR; m 15 Nov 1939 *Barbara Helen [Mrs Ronald Kerr, Barnacarry, Kilninver, Oban, Argyllshire PA34 4QU], dau of Charles John Crawford, of St Andrews, and d 29 May 1972, leaving:

1b *Patricia Margaret [Mrs Robert Wakeford, The Hatch, Staverton, Northants NN11 6JH]; b 28 Oct 1940; m 28 Aug 1965 *Robert James Wakeford, er s of Robert Lionel Wakeford, and has:

1c *Mark Robert [Mark Wakeford Esq, Home Farm, School Lane, Badby, Northants NN11]; b 3 March 1966; m 1993 *(Julie) Belinda Stannage and has:

1d *Lucy Georgina; b 15 Jan 1996

2c *James Richard; b 10 July 1968

3c *Ian Frederick; b 1974

2b *Angela Helen [Mrs John Goddard, 20 Hackthorne Rd, Cashmere, Christchurch, New Zealand]; b 2 Jan 1942; m 11 March 1971 *John Goddard and has had:

1c *Nicholas James; b 27 Sept, d 16 Nov 1995

1c *Penelope Helen; b 1978

3b Elizabeth Daphne; b 9 June 1949; m 1975 Charles Colclough Butterworth (d 1988) and d 24 June 1997, leaving:

1c *Thomas William [Thomas Butterworth Esq, Camus Darach, Ganavan Rd, Oban, Argyll PA34 5TU]; b 17 Oct 1978

1c *Janet Helen; b 1980

(1) Emily Georgina; m 4 Aug 1866 5th Earl of Strafford (qv) and d 27 Oct 1929, leaving issue

(2) Sidney Katherine; m 7 June 1887 Rev Gordon Bolles Wickham (d 19 Dec 1920), Vicar Bradford Abbas, Dorset, and d 21 May 1928

(3) Edith Harriet; d unm 6 March 1942

(4) Mary Frances; m 3 April 1880 George Henry Longman (d 19 Aug 1938), 2nd s of Thomas Longman, of Farnborough Hill, Hants, and d 17 April 1941

(5) Constance Honoria; Extra Maid of Honour to HM QUEEN VICTORIA 1886–1901; d unm 9 Oct 1940

(6) Cecil Nona; Ldy-in-Waiting to Marchioness of Milford Haven (qv); m 24 Jan 1915 Lt-Col Richard Edward Crichton (see ERNE, E) and d 28 Dec 1960

2 Elizabeth Georgiana; m 25 Oct 1831 19th Lord (Baron) Clinton (qv) and d 19 March 1871, leaving issue

3 Harriet Louisa Anne; m 13 June 1834 Sir John Stuart FORBES later HEPBURN-FORBES, 8th Bt (see STUART-FORBES, Bt), and d 24 April 1884, leaving issue

4 Frances; m 11 June 1848 George Wade and d 25 March 1863

5 Anne Katherine; d 6 Dec 1829

6 Georgiana Augusta (GEORGE IV stood sponsor); m 25 July 1849 Rev Granville Hamilton Forbes, Rector Broughton, Northants, and d 12 Feb 1859, leaving issue

The 6th MARQUESS's est son,

JOHN WILLIAM ROBERT KERR, 7th Marquess of Lothian; b 1 Feb 1794; MP (Tory) Huntingdon 1820–24, Col Edinburgh Militia, Ld Lt Roxburghshire 1824–41; m 19 July 1831 Lady Cecil Chetwynd Talbot (d 13 May 1877), yr dau of 2nd Earl Talbot (see SHREWSBURY and WATERFORD, E), and d 14 Nov 1841, having had:

1 WILLIAM SCHOMBERG ROBERT KERR, 8th Marquess of Lothian; b 12 Aug 1832; educ Eton and Ch Ch Oxford; m 12 Aug 1857 Lady Constance Harriet Mahonese Talbot (d 10 Oct 1901), dau of 18th Earl of Shrewsbury and Waterford (qv), and dsp 6 July 1870

2 SCHOMBERG HENRY KERR, 9th Marquess of Lothian, KT (1878), PC (1886); b 2 Dec 1833; educ Glenalmond, Eton and Ch Ch Oxford; Dip Serv 1858–65, Attaché Frankfurt and Teheran, Ld Keeper Privy Seal 1874–1900, Sec State Scotland 1887–92, Ld Rector Edinburgh U 1887–90, Hon Col 3rd Bn Roy Scots Lothian Regt, Capt-Gen Roy Co Archers 1884–1900, Gold Stick Scotland, PRSA Scotland, KGStJ; m 23 Feb 1865 Lady Victoria Alexandrina Montagu-Douglas-Scott (m 2nd 21 Feb 1903 Bertram Talbot and d 19 June 1938), est dau of 5th Duke of Buccleuch and (7th Duke) of Queensberry (qv), and d 17 Jan 1900, having had:

(1) Walter William Schomberg, Earl of Ancram; b 29 March 1867; Capt 3rd Bn Roy Scots Lothian Regt, ADC Govr NSW; accidentally shot dead NSW 15 June 1892

(2) Schomberg Henry Mark; b 4 Aug 1869; d 25 Aug 1870

(3) ROBERT SCHOMBERG KERR, 10th Marquess of Lothian, DL (Roxburghshire); b 22 March 1874; educ Eton and Ch Ch Oxford; d unm 16 March 1930

(1) Cecil Victoria Constance; b 14 Feb 1866; m 4 June 1889 her cousin 2nd Baron Montagu of Beaulieu (qv) and d 13 Sept 1919, leaving issue

(2) Margaret Isobel; b 12 June 1868; d unm 2 Sept 1964

(3) Mary; b 25 Dec 1870; m 7 Dec 1897 Henry Kidd (d 23 June 1923), of Lowood, Melrose, 2nd s of Robert Charles Kidd, of Lowood and Bridgend, Roxburghshire, and d 31 Dec 1958, leaving issue

(4) Helen Victoria Lilian; b 9 Dec 1872; m 5 April 1902 her cousin Col Frederic Walter Kerr, DSO, and d 4 June 1968, leaving issue (see above)

(5) Victoria Alexandrina Alberta; b 7 Nov 1876 (HM QUEEN VICTORIA stood sponsor); m 12 Nov 1903 Maj William Sullivan Gosling, DL, Scots Gds (d 2 Oct 1952), 2nd s of Robert Gosling, of Hassobury, Essex, and d 23 May 1956, leaving issue

(6) Isobel Alice Adelaide; b 25 Sept 1881; m 28 Oct 1907 James Cospatrick Hepburn-Scott and d 26 Dec 1975, leaving issue (see POLWARTH, L)

3 Ralph Drury, KCB; b 11 Aug 1837; Maj-Gen, Col 10th Hus, GOC troops Curragh 1891–96; m 24 July 1878 Lady Anne Fitzalan-Howard, OBE (d 7 Jan 1931), dau of 14th Duke of Norfolk (qv), and d 18 Sept 1916, having had:

(1) PHILIP HENRY KERR, 11th Marquess of Lothian, KT (1940), CH , PC (1939), DL (Midlothian); b 18 April 1882; educ New Coll Oxford (MA); LLD (Edinburgh) 1936; Assist Sec Inter-Colonial Cncl Transvaal and Orange River Colony 1905–08, ed Round Table 1910–16, Sec to PM 1916–21, Sec Rhodes Tst 1925–39, Chllr Duchy Lancaster Aug–Nov 1931, Parly U-Sec State India 1931–32, Amb Washington 1939–40, Hon DCL Oxon 1939; d unm Washington 12 Dec 1940

(2) David Anselm; b 21 April 1893; 2nd Lt Roy Scots; ka 13 Oct 1914

(1) Mary Cecil; b 14 April, d 27 April 1880

(2) Anne Cecil; b 30 June 1883; granted with sisters rank of marquess's dau 23 July 1930; d unm 9 Aug 1941

(3) Margaret Mary, MBE (1955); b 22 Aug 1884; d unm 24 Jan 1962

(4) (Gertrude) Minna; b 5 Oct 1887; m 9 March 1918 Capt Francis Wendell Butler-Thwing, Coldstream Gds (d 14 April 1964), only s of Charles Thwing, Pres W Reserve U, Cleveland, USA, and dsp 27 Dec 1963

4 Walter Talbot, GCB, JP and DL (Derbys); b 28 Sept 1839; Adml of the Fleet Baltic Crimean War 1854–55, Indian Mutiny 1857–58, Naval ADC to HM QUEEN VICTORIA 1887–88, 1st Sea Ld Admlty 1892–95, cmded Channel Sqdn 1895–97, 1st Sea Ld 1899–1904, Grand Cross Charles III Spain, Constantinian Order St George, Silver Medal Roy Humane Soc; m 18 Nov 1873 Lady Amabel Cowper (d 15 Oct 1906), yst dau of 6th Earl Cowper (see LUCAS OF CRUDWELL, B), and d 12 May 1927, having had:

(1) Ralph Francis (Rev); b 1 Oct 1874; educ Ch Ch Oxford (BA); Superior Brompton Oratory 1925; d 16 Oct 1932

(2) Andrew William; b 23 March 1877; Capt RN, Chev Constantinian Order St George; m 29 July 1915 Marie Constance Annabel, dau of Capt William Walter Raleigh Kerr (see above), and d 28 March 1929, leaving:

1a PETER FRANCIS WALTER KERR, 12th and present Marquess of Lothian

2a +John Andrew Christopher [The Lord John Kerr, Holly Bank, Wootton, Oxon OX20 1AE]; b 4 July 1927; granted rank of marquess's yr s 1941; educ Ampleforth and Ch Ch Oxford; late Capt Scots Gds; m 12 July 1949 *Isabel Marion, 2nd dau of Sir Hugh Gurney, KCMG, MVO (see FIFE, D), and has:

1b +William Walter Raleigh [William Kerr Esq, The Dower House, Melbourne, Derbys; 11 Micklethwaite Rd, London SW6 1QD]; b 17 Aug 1950; educ Ampleforth and Ch Ch Oxford; m 3 Aug 1983 *Griselda Mary, er dau of Brig John Robert Edward Hamilton-Baillie (see HADDINGTON, E), and has:

1c +Robert John Edward; b 1987

2c +Walter William Raleigh; b 1992

1c *Cordelia Isabel Marie; b 1988

2b +David John; b 25 Sept 1952; educ Ampleforth; m 1980 *Carol Prior and has:

1c +John Andrew David; b 1981

2c +Andrew Christopher; b 1984

3b +Andrew Peter Hugh [Andrew Kerr Esq, 29 The Green, Steventon, Oxon OX13 6SN]; b 5 May 1955; educ Ampleforth and Exeter U

1b *Marion Isabel [Mrs Simon May, 17 Campion Way, Witham, Chelmsford, Essex]; b 5 March 1960; m 1987 *Simon David May, er s of C J May, of Marlow, Bucks, and has:

1c *Susannah Isabel Catherine; b 1990

2c *Rebecca Isabel Laura; b 1994

2b *Catherine Richenda Margaret [Mrs Darren Williams, 19/9 Nilson Ave, Hillsdale, NSW, Australia]; b 9 Jan 1965; m 1st 1991 (divorce) Alan McCallie and has:

1c *Beau James (twin); b 1991

2c *Matthew Ross; *b* 1991

2b (cont.) Mrs Catherine McCallie *m* 2nd 19– *Darren Williams, of Sydney, and by him has:

1c *Isabel Richenda Eileen; *b* 1996

(3) John David, MC, TD, JP, DL; *b* 28 Feb 1883; Lt-Col, Brevet Col (Hon Col 1939), 5th Bn Sherwood Foresters WW I (despatches), WW II; CC Derbys; *m* 1 March 1924 Annabel Mary (*d* 22 March 1974), yst dau of Richard Ward, of London, and *dsp* 7 March 1954

(4) Philip Walter, MVO (1937); *b* 19 Oct 1886; *educ* Pembroke Coll Cambridge (BA); Capt RFA (SR) WW I, WW II as P/O RAFVR; FSA, Rouge Croix Pursuivant of Arms 1921–41, Kt SMO Malta; *m* 12 May 1936 *Dorothy Lucy Ethelreda, dau of John Philip Cave, JP, of Stoner Hill, Hants, and *das* 10 Feb 1941

(1) Mary Catherine Cecil; *b* 15 Nov 1878; nun; *d* 19 July 1957

(2) Margaret Mary; *b* 15 Feb 1880; *d* unm 12 March 1943

5 John Montagu Hobart; *b* 24 April 1841; *d* 2 Jan 1855

1 Cecil Elizabeth; nun; *d* 13 Feb 1866

2 Alice Mary; *m* 20 June 1870 Thomas Galsford, JP, DL (*d* 26 Feb 1898), of Offington, Sussex, and *d* 25 Jan 1892, leaving issue

Seats: Melbourne Hall, Melbourne, Derbyshire; Ferniehirst Castle, Jedburgh, Roxburghshire.

Melbourne was acquired by the Kerrs quite late, through the marriage in 1873 of Lady Amabel, the Cowper heiress of her day, with the present **Marquess**'s grandfather. The Cowpers had in turn acquired it by the marriage of Lady Amabel's grandfather the 5th Earl Cowper with Emily, sister of Queen Victoria's first Prime Minster Lord Melbourne and long-time mistress (she eventually took him as her second husband) of the Queen's most assertive one, Lord Palmerston. Lord Melbourne's father the first Viscount was granted three peerages, each designated by the name Melbourne, his grandfather Matthew having been land agent to the Cokes who leased Melbourne Hall from the Bishops of Carlisle.

The house, for all its changes of ownership, has not been the subject of a commercial transaction since GEORGE I's time: it has simply passed from family to family by inheritance. It is not strictly speaking a country mansion: the approach is from Melbourne High Street, by no means a pretty one until the last few hundred yards, and it was long a rectory. Although the celebrated east-facing elevation which invariably features in illustrations is a fine example of Palladian architecure (by the father-and-son master builder team of Francis and William Smith), the rest of the house is a mélange of Elizabethan remnants and early Georgian improvisatory work. Money may be the root of it all. The Coke lessees were evidently too honest to salt away cash for themselves as public servants. (Sir John, who took up residence in 1620, was CHARLES I's Secretary of State; his great-great grandson Sir Thomas, who bought the freehold from his episcopal landlord, was Vice-Chamberlain from 1711 to 1727.) The limited building programme of the early 18th century may reflect some difficulty in scraping funds together even after it became their very own.

Sir Thomas appears to have been more under Voltaire's influence than most members of the Whig Ascendancy: that is, he cultivated his garden rather than spend money on bricks-and-mortar. It is Melbourne's gardens, whose early 18th-century designer, Henry Wise, looked up to the master, Le Nôtre, that justify its fame, though their centrepiece is a wholly man-made object. This is an elaborately baroque, urn-shaped contrivance in lead, adorned with sphinx heads, fruit and foliage towards its crown and dancing characters at it waist — the work of Jan van Nost, the gift to Coke of QUEEN ANNE. It perches atop a plinth in the middle of the principal circus. From it radiate six avenues, one dog-legged, one the top of a cruciform extension of lesser avenues, one debouching into another circus a relatively short way away. Twin lines of over-arching yew and the natural focus of the entire grounds, the pond, best viewed from the house so as to take in the distant hills across it, combine, it has been said, to suggest a miniature Powerscourt.

Other delights include the gilt and paint wrought-iron arbour, usually called the bird cage, by Robert Bakewell of Derby; a grotto with some bad poetry by Lady Caroline Lamb inscribed on a slab inside it; statues of squabbling urchins or putti kissing and making up. Inside the house an inevitably more prosaic note is struck, though it is all very comfortable and in good taste, and indeed the furniture incudes some masterpieces. The stair-case rises from inside an arch leading to its base from the main hall. The dining-room panels and timber chimney piece hark back to the early Stuart period. For all its French and Italian influences, the mixture is extraordinarily English, urbane yet *terre-à-terre*, like Prime Minister Melbourne himself. In 1990 Melbourne was made over to Lord Ralph Kerr.

Ferniehirst dates back to the second half of the 15th century, built by that Sir Thomas Ker who was father-in-law of Thomas, originally of Smailholm and third son of the Andrew Kerr who died in 1481 (*see* above). Being on the Borders the Castle came in for a number of attacks by the English, particularly in the almost continuous strife between the two nations of the early 16th century. It was besieged in 1523, 1544 and 1549, when the English captured and briefly held it. Yet another English attack occurred in 1570, when the Sir Thomas Kerr who supported MARY QUEEN OF SCOTS mounted a raid across the Borders, less with a view to plunder, as one account insisted, than to stir up the English. He succeeded only too well. The English streamed north to counterattack, hitting Ferniehirst once again and this time totally destroying it. Nearly thirty years passed before Sir Thomas's son the **1st Lord Jedburgh** could get permission to rebuild. When he did so he first put up a new tower, but with the obsolescence of fortified dwellings more apparent as the 17th century wore on he began to turn the place into a country house, extending the building to encompass a chapel and great hall on the north side of the keep.

In later centuries the Castle was let, until Walter Earl of Ancram, the son of the house accidentally shot dead in Australia, took a fancy to it and had it fitted up to suit a late Victorian gentleman's idea of comfort. In the 20th century it underwent some 50 years of alien occupation as a Youth Hostel, but since 1985 has again been used as a home, under a family trust, by the present **Marquess** and his wife, who commissioned the Scottish architect James Simpson to carry out further restoration.

LOUDOUN

Arms: Quarterly, 1st and 4th, argent a maunch sable (for HASTINGS); 2nd and 3rd, or on a chief gules a demi-lion issuant argent (for ABNEY). **Supporters:** Dexter, a man in armour, plumed on the head with three feathers gules and holding with the right hand a spear in bend proper; sinister, a lady richly apparelled, plumed on the head with three feathers argent and holding in the left hand a letter of challenge. **Creations:** L. (S) 30 June 1601 ((Campbell of) Loudoun) and 12 May 1633 (Tarrinzean and Mauchline), E. (S) 12 May 1633.

THE COUNTESS OF LOUDOUN, Lady (Campbell of) Loudoun, of Loudoun, **Lady Tarrinzean and Mauchline** (Barbara Huddleston Abney-Hastings) [The Rt Hon The Countess of Loudoun, Mount Walk, Ashby-De-La-Zouche, Leics LE65 1BG]; *b* 3 July 1919; *s* mother 1960 as 13th holder of the Earldom; *m* 1st 5 Sept 1939 (*divorce* 1945) Capt Walter Strickland Lord, s of Capt Arthur Francis Lord, of Kerswell Rock, Chudleigh, Devon, and has:

1 +MICHAEL EDWARD LORD later ABNEY-HASTINGS (deed poll 1946), *Lord Mauchline* [Lord Mauchline, 74 Coreen St, Jerilderie, NSW 2716, Australia]; *b* 22 July 1942; *educ* Ampleforth; *m* 1969 *Noelene Margaret, dau of W J McCormick, of Barham, NSW, and has:

(1) +Simon Michael; *b* 1974

(2) +Marcus William; *b* 1981

(1) +Amanda Louise; *b* 1969

(2) +Lisa Maree; *b* 1971

(3) +Rebecca Lee (twin with Simon); *b* 1974

The COUNTESS *m* 2nd 21 Nov 1945 Capt Gilbert Frederick Greenwood (*d* 24 May 1951), s of Frederick Greenwood, of Sheffield, and by him has:

2 +Frederick James ABNEY-HASTINGS; *b* 29 Jan 1949

1 +Selina Mary [The Lady Selina Newman, Old Place, Ansty, West Sussex]; *b* 19 Dec 1946; *m* 1967 *William Newman and has:

(1) +Christopher James Loudoun; *b* 1972; *m* 1997 *Jocelyn Rachel Brown

(1) +Selina Anne; *b* 1968; *m* 1995 *Jonathan Robert Lamb and has:

1a +William Anthony Louden; *b* 1996

1a +Harriet Selina; *b* 1993

The COUNTESS *m* 3rd 15 Sept 1954 *Peter GRIFFITHS later ABNEY-HASTINGS (deed poll with his w 1955), s of William Griffiths, of Hastings, and by him has:

2 +Margaret Maude; *b* 10 Feb 1956; *m* 1977 *Brian Peter Ludlow and has:

(1) +Thomas William; *b* 1983

(2) +Peter Arthur; *b* 1987

(1) +Kathleen Rose; *b* 1981

(2) +Iona Clare (twin); *b* 1981

(3) +Alice Selina; *b* 1985

(4) +Joy Elizabeth; *b* 1990

3 Mary Joy; *b* 18 March 1957; *m* 1982 *David John Flowers and *d* 17 June 1997, leaving:

(1) +Robert Eric (twin); *b* 1989

(1) +Clare Hannah; *b* 1987

(2) +Catherine Barbara; *b* 1989

4 +Clare Louise; *b* 8 Dec 1958; *m* 1988 *Peter William Lacey and has:

(1) +Laurie; *b* 1991

(1) +Lily Edith; *b* 1993

Lineage: LAMBINUS; held *temp* DAVID I (1124–53) the (territorial) Barony of Loudoun, Ayrshire; had:

JAMES LOUDOUN of Loudoun, of which he obtained a charter, with other lands, from Richard de Morville, Constable of Scotland; had an only dau:

MARGARET de Loudoun; *m c* 1200 Sir Reynald de CRAWFORD, Heritable Sheriff Ayrshire, and had:

HUGH CRAWFORD, of Loudoun; ggf of:

Sir REGINALD CRAWFORD, of Loudoun; Sheriff Ayrshire, d 1303, leaving:

SUSANNA Crawford, of Loudoun; m c 1318 Sir Duncan CAMPBELL, s of Donald Campbell (2nd s of Sir Colin Campbell of Lochow; see ARGYLL, D), and had:

Sir ANDREW CAMPBELL of Loudoun; Heritable Sheriff Ayrshire; allegedly gggggggf of:

Sir MATTHEW CAMPBELL of Loudoun; m Isabel, dau of Sir John Drummond of Innerpeffray (see PERTH, E), and had, with a dau (Jean, m 1598, as his 2nd w, 2nd Duke of Lennox; see MORAY, E):

Sir HUGH CAMPBELL, 1st Lord (Campbell of) Loudoun, of Loudoun (S), so cr 30 June 1601 (having sat in Parl as a minor Baron 1597 and 1599), but resigned by him by 1619 in favour of his gs-in-law, to whom it was confirmed after 25 Jan 1622/3, PC (S 1601); Sheriff Ayr and ktd 1572, MP Irvine 1579; m 1st 1572 Margaret, dau of Sir John Gordon of Lochinvar (see HUNTLY, M) by his 1st w Julian (dau of David Home of Wedderburn; see POLWARTH, L), and had:

1 George, Master of Loudoun; m Lady Jean Fleming, dau of 1st Earl of Wigtoun by his 1st w Lilias, only dau of 3rd Earl of Montrose (see MONTROSE, D), and dspm & vp March 1611/2, leaving:

(1) MARGARET Campbell, Lady Loudoun in her own right (but see above); b c 1605; m by 8 March 1620 Sir John CAMPBELL of Lawers (see CAMPBELL, Bt, of Aberuchill), 2nd Lord (Campbell of) Loudoun by resignation of his gf-in-law (see above), also cr 12 May 1633 Earl of Loudoun, as also LORD TARRINZEAN AND MAUCHLINE (all S), but the patent suspended till 1641 due his opposition to the King (he being a Covenanter and even shut up in the Tower of London on suspicion of treason after signing a letter from the Covenanters seeking help from France; apptd Ld Chllr Scotland 1641, however; First Commr Treasury Scotland 1641–44, Pres Scottish PC, fought for CHARLES II Battle of Dunbar 1650, after which he fled to the Highlands and enrolled with the royalists there; d 15 March 1661/2), and outlived her husb, leaving:

1a JAMES CAMPBELL, 2nd Earl of Loudoun; m after 25 Nov 1666 Margaret, dau of 7th Earl of Eglinto(u)n (see EGLINTON and WINTON, E), and d Holland 1684, being disaffected to the post-Restoration regime in Britain, having had, with other issue:

1b HUGH CAMPBELL, 3rd Earl of Loudoun, KT (1706), PC (S, 1697 and 1703, and E, 1707); Extrdy Ld of Session 1699–1731, a Commr S Treasury 1703–05, Jt Sec State Scotland 1705–07, rep S peer 1707–31, Ld Keeper Scotland 1708–13, fought against Jacobites Battle of Sheriffmuir 1715; resigned and got his titles regranted 7 Feb 1707 with remainder to the heirs male of his body, in default of which to the heirs gen of the body of the 1st Earl but of his nomination, in default of which to the heirs male whatsoever of the 1st Earl; m 6 April 1700 Lady Margaret Dalrymple (d 3 April 1777), dau of 1st Earl of Stair (qv), and d 20 Nov 1731, leaving:

1c JOHN CAMPBELL, 4th Earl of Loudoun; b 5 May 1705; rep S peer 1734–82; Govr Stirling Castle 1741–63 and Edinburgh Castle 1763–82, ADC to GEORGE II 1743–45, Col of a Highr regt 12 companies strong, all taken prisoner by Jacobites Battle of Prestonpans June 1745, though soon after he in his turn took prisoner the Jacobite Lord Lovat (qv); beaten also by Jacobites Dornoch Firth 20 March 1746 when cmdg 3,500 men, being forced to take refuge in the Highlands; Govr Gen Virginia and C-in-C forces N America 1756–57, his slowness off the mark against the French there causing his recall; C-in-C forces in Portugal ranged against Spain 1762, Maj-Gen 1755, Lt Gen 1758, Gen 1770, Col 30th Foot 1749–70, Col in Ch 60th Rifles (Royal Americans) 1755–57, Col 3rd Foot Gds 1770–82; d unm 27 April 1782

2b John, of Shanktoun; Col; dsp

3b James (Sir), of Lawers, KB (1743); Col Scots Greys; fought Battle of Dettingen 1743; m Lady Jane Boyle, est dau of 1st Earl of Glasgow (qv) by his 2nd w Jean, dau and heiress of William Mure of Rowallan, Ayrshire, and was fatally wounded cmdg British Horse detachment Battle of Fontenoy 29 April 1745, leaving:

1c JAMES, 5th Earl

2c Elizabeth; m Sir Hugh Campbell of Cessnock

1b Eleanor; m 1st Viscount Primrose (see ROSEBERY, E); m 2nd 1714 2nd Earl of Stair (qv)

The 1st Lord m 2nd Isabel, 5th dau of 1st Earl of Gowrie (see CARLISLE, E) and divorced w of his bro-in-law Sir Robert Gordon of Lochinvar, by whom he had two daus (Jean; Margaret); m 3rd c 11 Oct 1617 Margaret (m 3rd, as his 3rd w, Sir Archibald Stewart of Ardgowan and Blackhall), dau of Sir George Home of Wedderburn and widow of Thomas MacDougall of Makerston, and d 15 Dec 1622, having had no issue by her

The 4th EARL's cousin,

JAMES CAMPBELL later MURE-CAMPBELL (on inheriting by the death 13 Dec 1729 of his mother his grandmother's estate), 5th Earl of Loudoun; b 11 Feb 1726; Capt Scots Greys 1745, MP (Whig) Ayrshire 1754–61, Lt-Col 2nd Dragoon Gds then 21st Dragoons 1757–63, Maj-Gen 1781; m 30 April 1777 Flora (d 2 Sept 1780), est dau of John Macleod of Raasay, Inverness-shire, and dspm 28 April 1786, leaving:

FLORA Campbell, Countess of Loudoun in her own right; b Aug 1780; m 12 July 1804 Francis RAWDON-HASTINGS formerly RAWDON, 1st Marquess of Hastings etc, 14th Lord (Baron) Hastings (of Hastings) and de jure 17th Lord (Baron) Botreaux, 13th Lord (Baron) Hastings (of Hungerford), 16th Lord (Baron) Hungerford and 14th Lord (Baron) Moleyns, also Baron Rawdon of Rawdon, KG (1812), GCB (1818), GCH (1818), PC (1806), and d 8 Jan 1840, having had:

1 GEORGE AUGUSTUS FRANCIS, 7th Earl

1 Flora Elizabeth; b 11 Feb 1806; Ldy Bedchamber to HRH THE DUCHESS OF KENT (mother of HM QUEEN VICTORIA); d unm 5 July 1839, her mortal illness of a tumour on the liver and the swollen stomach it caused making the young QUEEN VICTORIA suspect she was pregnant; when the truth became known the QUEEN was mortified, but damage to her prestige, particularly among the Hastings family, had already been sustained by then

2 Sophia Frederica Christina; m 10 April 1845 2nd Marquess of Bute (qv) and d 28 Dec 1859

3 Selina Constance; m 25 June 1838 Charles John Henry, s of John Joseph Henry, of Straffan, Co Kildare, by Lady Emily Elizabeth FitzGerald, dau of 2nd Duke of Leinster (qv), and d 8 Nov 1867

4 Adelaide Augusta Lavinia; m 8 July 1854 Sir William Keith Murray, 7th Bt, of Ochtertyre (qv), and d 6 Dec 1860

The COUNTESS's only son,

GEORGE AUGUSTUS FRANCIS RAWDON-HASTINGS, 7th Earl of Loudoun, 2nd MARQUESS OF HASTINGS and 15th LORD (Baron) HASTINGS (of Hastings), also de jure 18th LORD (Baron) BOTREAUX, 14th LORD HASTINGS (of Hungerford), 17th LORD (Baron) HUNGERFORD and 15th LORD (Baron) MOLEYNS; b 4 Feb 1808 (GEORGE IV when PRINCE OF WALES stood sponsor); a Ld Bedchamber 1830–31, Bearer Golden Spurs (in right of his w) Coronation 1831; m 1 Aug 1831, as her 1st husb, Barbara, Baroness Grey (of Ruthin) (see GREY, B) in her own right (m 2nd 9 April 1845 Adml Sir Hastings Reginald HENRY later YELVERTON, GCB, and d 19 Nov 1858, having by him had issue; see CHURSTON, B), and d 13 Jan 1844, leaving:

1 PAULYN REGINALD SERLO RAWDON-HASTINGS, 8th Earl of Loudoun, 3rd MARQUESS OF HASTINGS and 16th LORD (Baron) HASTINGS (of Hastings), also de jure 19th LORD (Baron) BOTREAUX, 15th LORD (Baron) HASTINGS (of Hungerford), 18th LORD (Baron) HUNGERFORD and 16th LORD (Baron) MOLEYNS; b 2 June 1832; educ Eton; Ensign 52nd Foot 1850; d unm 17 Jan 1851

2 HENRY WEYSFORD CHARLES PLANTAGENET RAWDON-HASTINGS, 9th Earl of Loudoun, also 4th and last MARQUESS OF HASTINGS and 17th LORD (Baron) HASTINGS (of Hastings) and (as which s mother 1858) 21st LORD (Baron) GREY (of Ruthin), also de jure 20th LORD (Baron) BOTREAUX, 16th LORD (Baron) HASTINGS (of Hungerford), 19th LORD (Baron) HUNGERFORD and 17th LORD (Baron) MOLEYNS; b 22 July 1842; educ Eton and Ch Ch Oxford; MFH Quorn 1866–68; m 16 July 1864 Florence Cecilia (m 2nd 9 June 1870 Sir George Chetwynd, 4th Bt (qv), and d 3 Feb 1907), yst dau of 2nd Marquess of Anglesey (qv), and dsp 10 Nov 1868, when the Marquessate, Earldom of Moira, Earldom of Rawdon, Viscountcy of Loudoun, Barony of Rawdon of Moira and Barony of Rawdon of Rawdon expired, while the Barony of Grey fell into abeyance between his full sisters and half-sister on his mother's side (see CHURSTON, B) and that of Hastings, plus right to those of Botreaux, Hungerford and Moleyns fell into abeyance between his full sisters only

1 EDITH MAUD Rawdon-Hastings, Countess of Loudoun (10th holder of the title) in her own right, also LADY LOUDOUN (11th holder) and LADY TARRINZEAN AND MAUCHLINE (10th holder), also (on termination of abeyance in those Baronies 6 Nov 1871) BARONESS BOTREAUX (21st holder of the title), BARONESS HASTINGS (of Hastings) (18th holder), BARONESS HUNGERFORD (20th holder) and BARONESS MOLEYNS (18th holder) in her own right; b 10 Dec 1833; m 30 April 1853 Charles Frederick CLIFTON later ABNEY-HASTINGS (Act of Parliament 1859 following his inheritance by an instrument of 1844 of the estates of his w's kinsman Sir Charles Abney-Hastings, 2nd Bt, gs through an illegitimate descent of 10th Earl of Huntingdon, qv; Charles ABNEY-HASTINGS was b 17 June 1822; educ Eton and Ch Ch Oxford; cr 4 May 1880 BARON DONINGTON, of Donington Park, Co Leicester (UK); d 24 July 1895), 3rd s of Thomas Clifton, of Lytham and Clifton, Lancs, and d 23 Jan 1874, leaving:

(1) CHARLES EDWARD HASTINGS ABNEY-HASTINGS later RAWDON-HASTINGS (roy licence 8 April 1887), 11th Earl of Loudoun, 2nd BARON DONINGTON (as which s f), also (as which s mother) 22nd LORD (Baron) BOTREAUX, 19th LORD (Baron) HASTINGS (of Hastings), 21st LORD (Baron) HUNGERFORD and 19th LORD (Baron) MOLEYNS, DL (Ayrshire); b 5 Jan 1855; Lt Leics Yeo Cav; bore one of the Gold Spurs at 1902 and 1911 Coronations, though as a favour not by right; m 4 Feb 1880 Hon Alice Elizabeth Fitzalan-Howard (d 10 May 1915), 3rd dau of 1st Baron Howard of Glossop (see NORFOLK, D), and dsp 17 May 1920, when all his Baronies bar that of Donington fell once more into abeyance

(2) Paulyn Francis Cuthbert ABNEY-HASTINGS later RAWDON-HASTINGS (roy licence 1887); b 21 Oct 1856; Maj 3rd Bn Leics Regt; m 20 Dec 1881 Lady Maud Grimston (d 3 Sept 1929), dau of 2nd Earl of Verulam (qv), and d 19 Oct 1907, leaving:

1a Paulyn Charles James Reginald; b 27 Nov 1889; Capt 5th Bn Leics Regt; ka 13 Oct 1915

2a Edward Hugh Hastings; b 31 Aug 1895; 2nd Lt 2nd Black Watch; das 15 Sept 1915

1a EDITH MAUD Rawdon-Hastings, Countess of Loudoun (12th holder of title) and on termination of abeyance of those Baronies 23 Feb 1921 BARONESS BOTREAUX, BARONESS HASTINGS and BARONESS STANLEY; b 13 May 1883; m 12 Dec 1916 (divorce 1947) Maj Reginald Mowbray Chichester HUDDLESTON later ABNEY-HASTINGS and d 24 Feb 1960, when the Baronies again fell into abeyance (between her daus), having had:

1b Ian Huddleston, Lord Mauchline; b 23 March 1918; Capt RA WW II; ka 11 July 1944

1b BARBARA HUDDLESTON ABNEY-HASTINGS, present Countess of Loudoun

2b Jean Huddleston Abney-Hastings later Campbell of Loudoun (on having the Loudoun estate made over to her by her mother); b 3 Oct 1920; m 1st 23 March 1940 (divorce 1949) Edgar Wright Wakefield, est s of Raymond Edgar Wakefield, of Toronto, and had:

1c +Sheena [Mrs Donald Williams, Loudoun, 7840 North Desert Pass Rd, Tuscon, AZ 85743, USA]; b 9 May 1941; m 1968 *Donald Russell Williams, of New York, and has:

1d +Amanda Sarah Edith; b 1970

2b (cont.) Lady Jean Wakefield m 2nd 1 Sept 1954 (divorce 1964) Capt Arthur Alexander Hubble, Queen's Bays (d 13 June 1979), s of Arthur Whibley Hubble, of Hunton, Kent, and d 1981, leaving by him:

2c +Flora Ann Madeleine [Mrs John Kerr, Peelhill Farm, Drumclog, Strathaven, Lanarks ML10 6RQ]; b 12 June 1957; m 1975 (divorce 1992) John Robert Kerr and has:

1d +John Campbell; b 1980

1d +Britt Jean; b 1975

2d +Emma Jennifer; *b* 1977

3b Fiona Mary Huddleston; *b* 17 March 1922; WW II in WAAF; *m* 26 April 1951 Robert Alexander French, TD (*d* 2 Sept 1970), yr s of James Andrew French, of Glasgow

4b Fiona Huddleston; *b* 26 Feb 1923; *m* 27 Sept 1940 Robert CONROY-ROBERTSON later DE FRESNES (deed poll 1944 when s maternal gf as 12th Baron de Fresnes (*cr* France 1642)), Capt RA, and *d* 1990, having had:

  1c +(Christopher) Ian [Baron de Fresnes, Elm Tree House, High Halden, Kent TN26 3BP]; *b* 8 May 1942; *educ* Ampleforth and Glasgow Sch of Art; *m* 1st 1969 (*divorce* 1971) Elvira Maria, dau of W/Cdr Marcel Pustelniak, and has:

    1d +Robert Marcel; *b* 1970

  1c (cont.) Baron de Fresnes *m* 2nd 1973 *Angela Margaret, dau of Lt-Col Denys Ainsworth Yates, and by her has:

    2d +Rawdon Alexander Denys; *b* 1974

    1d +Nicola Margaret; *b* 1975

  2c +Nigel Diarmid [Baron Nigel de Fresnes, 8839 Broadway St, Chilliwack, BC, Canada; *b* 28 April 1944; *educ* Ampleforth; *m* 1965 *Dolores Emelyn, dau of Isidore Douglas Grinder, of Clinton, BC, and has:

    1d +Robert Aaron Bryan; *b* 1969

    1d +Christel Rose Helen; *b* 1966; *m* 1993 *Michael John Fisher and has:

      1e +Adrian Isidore Robert; *b* 1991

      2d +Iona Elizabeth Louise; *b* 1968

  3c Adrian Michael; *b* 30 July, *d* 31 July 1947

  4c +Paulyn Armand; *b* 9 June 1949; *educ* Ampleforth; *m* 1973 (*divorce*) Kaija, dau of Dr Franf, of Finland, and has:

    1d +Ida Piri Pulikukka Fiona; *b* 1974

  5c +Vivian Robert James George; *b* 1 July 1960; *educ* Merchiston; *m* 1988 *Jill, dau of Peter Hendrie, of Edinburgh, and has:

    1d +Peter James; *b* 1989

    2d +Joseph Robert; *b* 1990

  1c +(Iona Mary) Nicole [Mrs Timothy Kirkwood, Culfoichmore, Advie, Grantown on Spey, Morayshire]; *b* 30 June 1957; *m* 1982 *Timothy John Kerr Kirkwood and has:

    1d +Toby John; *b* 1989

    2d +Arthur George; *b* 1992

    1d +Harriet Mary; *b* 1984

    2d +Matilda Alice; *b* 1986

    3d +Jemima Jane; *b* 1987

    4d +Phoebe Maud; *b* 1990

    5d +Augusta Fiona; *b* 1994

5b +Edith Huddleston [The Lady Edith Maclaren, Ard Daraich, Ardgour, by Fort William, Inverness-shire]; *b* 19 Jan 1925; *m* 23 May 1947 *Maj David Kenneth Maclaren, yst s of Dr Norman Maclaren, of Curieshaw, West Kilbride, Ayrshire, and has had:

  1c +Norman Angus; *b* 6 May 1948; *educ* The Abbey Sch Fort Augustus

  2c +Roderic John [Roderic Maclaren Esq, Ardvullin, Ardgour, by Fort William, Inverness-shire]; *b* 9 March 1950; *m* 1st 1981 (*divorce* 1993) Victoria Helen Elizabeth Glaysher and has:

    1d +Christopher Rory James; *b* 1988

  2c (cont.) Roderic Maclaren *m* 2nd 1993 *Kirsty Rowena Amabel, yr dau of Sir Charles Edward McGrigor, 5th Bt (*qv*), and formerly w of David Norman G Barraclough, and by her has:

    1d +Catriona Mary Edith; *b* 1993

  1c Sarah Margaret; *b* 19 Feb 1959; *d* 1 March 1960

2a ELIZABETH FRANCES Abney-Hastings; *s* 1921 her unc Charles (**11th Earl of Loudoun**) on termination of abeyance in her favour as BARONESS HUNGERFORD and BARONESS MOLEYNS and her remote ancestor the 5th Earl of Derby (*qv*) as BARONESS STRANGE (of Knokyn) all in her own right (*see* SAINT DAVIDS, V); *b* 19 June 1884; granted with yr sisters 9 Oct 1920 rank of earl's dau; *m* 27 April 1916, as his 2nd w, 1st Viscount St Davids (*qv*) and had issue

3a Flora Anne; *b* 12 Sept 1885; *d* unm 14 Feb 1950

4a Isabel Jacqueline; *b* 8 Aug 1887; *m* 20 Sept 1916 Capt Hubert James Cecil Rostron, of South Warnborough Manor, Winchfield, Hants, and *d* 14 July 1917

(3) GILBERT THEOPHILUS CLIFTON ABNEY-HASTINGS later CLIFTON-HASTINGS-CAMPBELL (roy licence 2 Jan 1896), 3rd and last BARON DONINGTON; *b* 29 May 1859; Maj 3rd Bn Sherwood Foresters; *m* 12 July 1894 Maud Kemble (*d* 18 Nov 1947), only surv dau of Sir Charles Edward Hamilton, 1st and last Bt (*see* 1876 edn), and *dspm* 31 May 1927, when his Barony expired, having had:

1a Margaret Selina Flora Maud; *b* 7 July 1895; *m* 15 July 1917 Sir Edward Orde MacTaggart-Stewart, 2nd Bt (*see* 1949 edn), Capt Gren Gds (*d* 19 Oct 1948), and *d* 27 Feb 1975, leaving issue (*see* SAINT DAVIDS, V)

2a Edith Winifred Lelgarde; *b* 21 Jan 1897; *d* 11 Sept 1908

3a Irene Mary Egidia; *b* 9 Feb 1898; *m* 17 Oct 1927 Lt-Col Richard St Barbe Emmott, MFH, 6th Gurkha Rifles (*d* in a hunting accident 14 Aug 1949), s of S St Barbe Emmott, and *d* 8 April 1961, leaving:

  1b +Patricia Egidia Hastings [Mrs Stafford Floyer-Acland, The Dairy House, W Stafford, Dorset]; *b* 1929; *m* 1950 Lt-Col Stafford Nugent Floyer-Acland, CBE, KO Yorks LI (*d* 1994), and has issue (*see* ACLAND, Bt, of Columb-John)

  2b +Moira Anne St Barbe [Mrs Alec Dow, 1 Parkway, Ruiston, Taunton, Somerset TA3 5JX]; *b* 1931; *m* 1st 1953 (*divorce* 1965) Capt David Anderson Vetch, Queen's Roy Irish Hus; *m* 2nd 1980 Lt-Col Alec Dow (*d* 1987) and by her 1st husb has:

  1c +James William Anderson [James Vetch Esq, 47 New North Rd, S Pk, Reigate, Surrey RH2 8LZ]; *b* 1958; *m* 1978 *Patricia Eileen, dau of Daniel Haste, of Tadworth, Surrey, and has:

    1d +Rachel Anne; *b* 1980

    2d +Amanda Jane; *b* 1982

  1c +Belinda Louise [Ms Belinda Annakin, 41 Charlotte St, Lilyfield, NSW 2040, Australia]; *b* 1956; has by Ian James McKee:

    1d *Aniella Caitlin Emmott McKEE

3b +Bridget Griselda Kemble [Mrs Anthony Copley, Winterfield Farm, Melbury Abbas, Dorset]; *b* 1934; *m* 1955 *Anthony Copley, JP, DL, and has:

  1c +Robert Anthony; *b* 1960; *m* 1986 *Diana Mary, yst dau of Charles Talbot Rhys Wingfield (*see* POWERSCOURT, V), and has:

    1d +Jack Anthony Talbot; *b* 1989

    1d +Alice Florence Hastings; *b* 1992

  1c +Jane Belinda [Mrs John Beaton, Wester, Balchrystie by Colinsburgh, Fife]; *b* 1957; *m* 1985 *John David Beaton and has:

    1d +Camilla Jane Moira; *b* 1987

    2d +Emily Rose Margaret; *b* 1989

  4a Alicia Moira Stuarta; *b* 2 Jan 1909; *d* 22 June 1916

(4) Henry Cecil Plantagenet; *b* 19 June 1860; *d* unm 22 Nov 1886

(1) Flora Paulyna Hetty Barbara; *b* 13 Feb 1854; *m* 21 Nov 1877 15th Duke of Norfolk (*qv*) and *d* 11 April 1887, leaving issue

(2) Egidia Sophia Frederica Christina; *b* 9 May 1870; *d* unm 6 March 1892

2 BERTHA LELGARDE, BARONESS GREY (of Ruthin) on termination of abeyance in that Barony (*see* GREY, B)

3 Victoria Maria Louisa; *m* 31 Oct 1859 John Forbes Stratford Kirwan (*d* 1892), of Moyne, Co Galway, and *d* 30 March 1888, leaving issue (*see* SAINT DAVIDS, V, and GREY, B)

4 Frances Augusta Constance; *m* 30 July 1863 4th Earl of Romney (*qv*) and *d* 1 Sept 1910, having had issue

Lineage (of Botreaux): REYNOLD de BOTREAUX, of Botreaux Castle (Boscastle), Cornwall; *d* 1273, leaving:

WILLIAM de BOTREAUX; *d* 1302, leaving:

WILLIAM de BOTREAUX; *d c* 1342, leaving:

REYNOLD de BOTREAUX; *d* 1346, leaving:

WILLIAM de BOTREAUX; Sheriff Cornwall; *m* Isabel, yr dau and coheir of Sir John Moels, 4th Lord (Baron) Moels (*dspm* 21 Aug 1337, since when by later doctrine the Barony is deemed to have fallen into abeyance between his daus and their reps), of N Cadbury, Somerset, and E Berkhamsted, Herts, and *d* 22 July 1349, leaving:

WILLIAM de BOTREAUX, 1st LORD (Baron) BOTREAUX (E), so *cr* (according to later doctrine) by writ of summons 24 Feb 1367/8; *m c* Feb 1369/70 Elizabeth (*d* May 1433), dau of Sir Ralph Daubeny, and *d* 10 Aug 1391, leaving:

WILLIAM de BOTREAUX, 2nd LORD (Baron) BOTREAUX; *b c* 1367; *m* Elizabeth, dau of Sir John St Lo, of Newton St Lo, Wilts, by his 2nd w Margaret, dau of John Clyveden, and *d* 25 May 1395, leaving:

WILLIAM de BOTREAUX, 3rd LORD (Baron) BOTREAUX; *b* 20 Feb 1388/9; *m* 1st by 1411 Elizabeth, dau of 4th Lord (Baron) Beaumont (*see* BEAUMONT, Bt) and had a s (William, *d* an infant) and two daus (of whom the er, Anne, *m* 1426 Sir John Stafford and *dvp* without issue surv her f); *m* 2nd by 1458 Margaret, dau of 8th Lord (Baron) Ros of Helmsley (*see* DE ROS, B) and *dspms* 16 May 1462, leaving a yr dau by his 1st w:

MARGARET de Botreaux, BARONESS BOTREAUX in her own right according to later doctrine (and indeed self-styled 'Lady Botreaux' in her lifetime); *b c* 1412; *m* Robert HUNGERFORD, 2nd Lord (Baron) Hungerford (*see* ST DAVIDS, V), and *d* 7 Feb 1477/8, having had

ROBERT HUNGERFORD, 3rd LORD (Baron) HUNGERFORD and 1st LORD (Baron) MOLEYNS (*see* SAINT DAVIDS, V); attainted after the Lancastrian defeat at Towton 1461, when both Baronies were forfeited, and beheaded after the further Lancastrian defeat at Hexham 1464, leaving:

Sir THOMAS HUNGERFORD; *m* by 16 Oct 1460 Ann, dau of 2nd Earl of Northumberland of the 1415/6 *cr* (*see* NORTHUMBERLAND, D), and was attainted and executed Jan 1468/9, leaving an only dau and heiress:

MARY Hungerford, BARONESS BOTREAUX (as which s great-grandmother Feb 1477/8) and BARONESS HUNGERFORD and MOLEYNS following reversal of their forfeiture 1485; *b c* 1468; *m* 1st after 8 June 1478 Edward HASTINGS, 2nd Lord (Baron) Hastings and 1st Lord (Baron) Hastings (of Hungerford) (*see* HUNTINGDON, E); *m* 2nd 1511 Sir Richard Sacheverell and *d* between 1528 and 1531/2, leaving by her 1st husb:

GEORGE HASTINGS, 6th LORD (Baron) BOTREAUX (as which s mother, also in the Baronies of Hungerford and Moleyns), also 1st EARL OF HUNTINGDON (E), so *cr* 8 Dec 1529; in addition s f in Baronies of Hastings (of Hastings) and Hastings (of Hungerford); all these Baronies passed down with the Earldom till the 10th Earl of Huntingdon *d* unm 2 Oct 1789, when the Earldom became dormant (*see* HUNTINGDON, E) while the Baronies passed to his only surv sis:

ELIZABETH Hastings, BARONESS BOTREAUX, HASTINGS (of Hastings), HASTINGS (of Hungerford), HUNGERFORD and MOLEYNS in her own right; *b* 23 March 1731; *m* 26 Feb 1752, as his 3rd w, John RAWDON, 1st Earl of Moira (*d* 20 June 1793), and *d* 11 April 1808, having had:

1 FRANCIS RAWDON later RAWDON-HASTINGS (roy licence 1790 under terms of will of his maternal uncle Francis Hastings, 10th Earl of Huntingdon), 1st MARQUESS OF HASTINGS, so *cr* 13 Feb 1817, as also VISCOUNT LOUDOUN and EARL OF RAWDON (all UK); in addition s mother as 14th LORD (Baron) HASTINGS (of Hastings) and *de jure* 17th LORD (Baron) BOTREAUX, 13th LORD (Baron) HASTINGS (of Hungerford), 16th LORD (Baron) HUNGERFORD and 14th LORD (Baron) MOLEYNS; *b* 7 Dec 1754; *educ* Harrow and Univ Coll Oxford; joined Army 1771, Maj-Gen 1793, Lt-Gen 1798, Gen 1803, Col 105th Foot 1781–83 and 27th Foot 1804–26, ADC to GEORGE III 1782–93, War American Independence: wounded Bunker Hill

1775, cmded a div Battle of Camden, SC, 16 Aug 1780, defeated a numerically greater enemy at Hobkirk's Hill 25 April 1781; MP (I Parl) Randalstown, Co Antrim, 1780–83, Cdr Forces Scotland 1802–06, *cr* vp 5 March 1783 BARON RAWDON OF RAWDON, Co York (GB); Cdr Forces Scotland 1802–06, Master-Gen Ordnance 1806–07, Constable Tower London 1806–26, Govr-Gen and C-in-C India 1813–22 and Malta 1824–26; Govr Charterhouse, FRS 1787, FSA 1793, MRIA; *m* 12 July 1804 Flora Mure-Campbell, **Countess of Loudoun** in her own right and had issue (*see above*)

2 John Theophilus; *b* 19 Nov 1756; *m* 30 Oct 1792 Frances, dau of Joseph William Hall Stevenson and gdau of John HALL later STEVENSON), of Skelton Castle, Yorks, and *d* 5 May 1808, leaving:

   (1) Elizabeth Anne; *m* 21 June 1817 Lord George William Russell and *d* 10 Aug 1874, leaving issue (*see* BEDFORD, D)

3 George; Maj 16th Foot; *dvm* 25 May 1800

1 Anne Elizabeth; *m* 14 Feb 1788 1st Earl of Ailesbury (*see* AILESBURY, M) and *dsp* 8 Jan 1813

2 Selina Frances; *m* 10 May 1779 6th Earl of Granard (*qv*) and *d* May 1827, leaving issue

3 Charlotte Adelaide Constantia; *m* 10 April 1814 Hamilton Fitzgerald and *d* 1834

LOUTH

Arms: Sa. a bend arg., in the sinister chief point a castle of the second. **Crest:** A horse passant arg. **Supporters:** Dexter, a pegasus per fess or and arg.; sinister, a heraldic antelope arg., horned, tufted, unguled and collared or. **Motto:** *Festina lente* ('Make haste with care'). **Creation:** B. (I) 15 June 1541.

THE 16TH BARON LOUTH, Co Louth (Otway Michael James Oliver Plunkett) [The Rt Hon The Lord Louth, Les Sercles, 8 La Grande Pièce, St Peter, Jersey, CI JE3 7AE]; *b* 19 Aug 1929; *s* f 1950; *educ* Downside; *m* 9 Aug 1951 *Angela Patricia, dau of William Cullinane, of St Helier, Jersey, and has:

1 +JONATHAN OLIVER [The Hon Jonathan Plunkett, Les Sercles, La Grande Pièce, St Peter, Jersey, CI JE3 7AE]; *b* 4 Nov 1952; *educ* De La Salle Coll, Jersey, Hautlieu Sch Jersey and Hull U (BSc); AMIEE; *m* 1981 *Jennifer, dau of Norman Oliver Hodgetts, of Weston-super-Mare, and has:

   (1) +Matthew Oliver; *b* 22 Dec 1982

   (1) *Agatha Elizabeth; *b* 1985

2 +Otway Jeremy Oliver [The Hon Otway Plunkett, 1 Holttums Yard, Linton, Cambridge CB1 6JN]; *b* 18 Oct 1954; *m* 1st 1971 (*divorce* 1982) Ruth Levine; *m* 2nd 1983 *Alice Veronica Tierney and by his 1st w has:

   (1) +Oliver; *b* 1972

   (2) +Benjamin Otway; *b* 1974

3 +Timothy James Oliver [The Hon Timothy Plunkett, 17 South Riding, Bricket Wood, St Albans, Herts AL2 3NG]; *b* 25 April 1956; *educ* De La Salle Coll Jersey; *m* 1984 *Julie Anne Cook and has:

   (1) +Joseph Timothy Oliver; *b* 1989

   (1) *Sophie Louise; *b* 1987

   (2) *Emma Jane; *b* 1991

   (3) *Stephanie Anne; *b* 1993

1 *Olivia Jane [The Hon Mrs Olivia Billingsley, Sylverwind, Portelet, St Brelade, Jersey, CI JE3 8AL]; *b* 4 Oct 1953; *m* 1974 (*divorce* 1982) Trevor Billingsley and has:

   (1) *James Michael; *b* 1975

   (1) *Nicola Jane; *b* 1977

2 *Stephanie Patricia [The Hon Stephanie Plunkett, Forest Farm, Forest Lane, Hanbury, Worcs B60 4HP]; *b* 1963

Louth, previous creation: In 1319 John de Bermingham, commander of the English forces in Ireland, was created Earl of Louth. He died without surviving male issue in a skirmish with the local sheriff and a posse comitatus at Ballybraggan, when the title expired..

Lineage: JOHN PLUNKETT, of Bewley, Co Louth; ancestor of:

JOHN PLUNKETT, of Bewley, *temp* HENRY III; *m* Alice — and was living 1322; had, with a 2nd s (Richard, ancestor of the Earls of Fingall (*see* 1970 edn) and the Barons of Dunsany, *qv*):

JOHN PLUNKETT, of Bewley; living 1337; had:

RICHARD PLUNKETT, of Bewley; King's Serjeant-at-law 1361; *m* Alice (*d* 8 Oct 1362), dau of — D'Arcy, of Trim, Co Meath and *d* 17 Sept 1360, leaving:

WALTER PLUNKETT, of Bewley; Sheriff Co Louth 1401; *m* Joan, dau of Thomas Netterville, and *d* 1 Feb 1436, leaving:

WALTER PLUNKETT, of Bewley; living 1418; *m* Genet, dau of John Luttrell, and had:

WALTER PLUNKETT, of Bewley; living 1455; *m* — Bellew, of Bellewstown, and had:

Sir JOHN/PHILIP PLUNKETT, of Bewley, Kilsaran, and Talanstown; Sheriff Co Louth 1497; *m* Catherine, dau of Thomas Nangle, of Navan, by Ismay, dau of Sir William Wells, Ld Chllr Ireland, and had, with other issue:

1 Thomas, of Kilsaran; *m* Alice, dau of James Fitzgerald, 3rd s of 7th Earl of Kildare (*see* LEINSTER, D), and had:

   (1) Eleanor; *m* 1st Thomas More, of Barmeath; *m* 2nd Thomas Barnewall, of Robertstown

   (2) Anne; *m* Sir James Gernon, of Kilnecoole

2 OLIVER (Sir), **1st Baron**

3 John (Sir), of Bewley; living 1560; ancestor of the PLUNKETTs of Bewley, the representative of whom, William Plunkett, was Capt in the 1641 Uprising, and *d* 21 July 1644, leaving a s (Thomas)

Sir JOHN/PHILIP *d* 14 Feb 1508; his 2nd son,

OLIVER PLUNKETT, **1st Baron Louth**, Co Louth (I), so *cr* 15 June 1541; *m* 1st Catherine, dau and heiress of John Rochfort, of Carrick, Co Kildare, and had, with other issue:

1 THOMAS, **2nd Baron**

2 Christopher; *m* Margaret, dau of Walter Cusack, of Kilcarne

3 John; *m* Alison, dau of Edward Bate, of Donnancarney, and had issue

4 Alexander, of Carstown, Co Louth; *m* Anne, dau of Francis Hope, of Mullingar, and was ancestor of the PLUNKETTs of Castle Plunkett, Co Roscommon

1 Margaret; *m* Sir John Bellew (*see* BELLEW, B)

The **1st Baron** *m* 2nd Maud (*m* 3rd Richard Bellew), dau and coheir of Walter Bath, of Rathfreigh, and widow of Walter Golding, by whom he had:

5 Edward; *m* —, illegitimate dau of Richard Bellew

6 Alexander; *m* — Dowdall, of Artreston

2 Catherine; *m* Robert Bath, of Mullagh

3 Eleanor; *m* Roger Garland, barrister

The 1st BARON *d* between Dec 1549 and 1 May 1553; his est s,

THOMAS PLUNKETT, **2nd Baron Louth**; ktd 1566; *m* Margaret, dau and heiress of Nicholas Barnewall, of Dromnah, and *d* 1 May 1571, having had, with three daus:

1 PATRICK PLUNKETT, **3rd Baron Louth**; *b c* 1548; *m* by 1571 Maud, dau of 7th Lord (Baron) Killeen (*see* 1970 edn FINGALL, E), and *dspm c* 1 May 1578, *k* by Evyr Boy McMahon in recovering stolen cattle at Essexford, Co Monaghan

2 OLIVER, **4th Baron**

3 John; *m* Margaret, dau of Robert Cusack, of Cussington, and had issue

The 3rd BARON's bro,

OLIVER PLUNKETT, **4th Baron Louth**; *m* 1st Frances, dau of Sir Nicholas Bagnall, Kt Marshal Ireland; *m* 2nd Genet (*dsp*), dau of Patrick Dowdall, of Termonfeighan, and by his 1st w had, with six other children:

1 MATTHEW, **5th Baron**

1 Margaret; *m* 1st Viscount Fitzwilliam of Merrion

The 4th BARON *d* 5 March 1607; his est son,

MATTHEW PLUNKETT, **5th Baron Louth**; *m* Mary, sis of 1st Viscount FitzWilliam of Merrion, and had, with other issue:

1 OLIVER, **6th Baron**

2 Thomas; Col Spanish serv; *m* Mary, dau of Henry Whitfleet, of Brussels, and had issue

3 Patrick, Col; *m* Mary, dau of Sir Oliver Tuite, 1st Bt, of Sonagh (*qv*), and had issue

4 Ignatius; *m* Catherine, dau of Christopher Barnewall, of Crackanstown, and had issue

1 Frances; *m* Sir Christopher Bellew, of Castletown (*see* BELLEW, B)

2 Jane; *m* Ignatius Nugent, Col in France, s of 1st Earl of Westmeath (*qv*), and had issue

3 Catherine; *m* 1st Nicholas Dowdall, of Brownestown; *m* 2nd Lawrence Taaffe, of Dowanstown

The 5th BARON *d* 19 July 1629; his est son,

OLIVER PLUNKETT, **6th Baron Louth**; *b* March 1588; participated in rising of 1639; *m* after 1629 Mary, widow of 2nd Viscount Dillon and dau of 1st Earl of Antrim (*qv*), and *d c* 1679, leaving:

MATTHEW PLUNKETT, **7th Baron Louth**, (PC temp JAMES II); Col Foot 1687, Ld Lt Co Louth; outlawed as a Jacobite 1689; *m* 1st *c* 4 Feb 1664 Jane dau of Sir Luke Fitzgerald, of Tecroghan, Co Meath, and had, with two other daus:

1 OLIVER, **8th Baron**

2 Thomas, of Portland, Co Tipperary; *m* 1st Sarah Blunt (*dsp*); *m* 2nd Anne, dau of John Cheevers, of Carneton, and had, with two daus:

   (1) Matthew; Capt Imp Inf

1 Eleanor; *m* Sir James Cotter, of Cotter's Lodge

2 Alice; *m* as his 1st w Stephen Taaffe and *d* 1707 aged 36

The **7th Baron** *m* 2nd *c* 7 March 1684/5 Anne (*m* 3rd John Eyre, of Eyrecourt, Co Galway), dau of William Hamilton, of Lisclony, King's Co, and widow of Claud Francis Hamilton, of King's Co, and *d* Sept 1689

His er son by his 1st w,

OLIVER PLUNKETT, **8th Baron Louth**; *b* 1668; was prevented from taking his seat in the Irish Ho Lds on the grounds that he had not proved the reversal of his gf's outlawry for rebellion 1642, even though the gf had not been formally attainted; *m* Mabel, dau of 2nd Viscount Barnewall of Kingsland, and *d* 1707, leaving, with two daus (Jane, *m* Darcott Talbot, of Mornington, Co Meath; Mabel):

MATTHEW PLUNKETT, *de jure* 9th BARON LOUTH; *b* 1698; *m* 20 April 1716 Susanna (*d* 21 Feb 1767), sis of Christopher Mason, of Blackheath, and had, with three other daus:

1 OLIVER

2 Matthew; *b* 22 Sept 1728

1 Elizabeth; *m* Plunkett Henry Talbot, of Mornington

The 9th BARON *d* 20 June 1754; his er son,

OLIVER PLUNKETT, *de jure* 10th BARON LOUTH; *bapt* 2 April 1727; *m c* 1750 Margaret (*d* 1787), dau of Hon Luke Netterville (3rd s of 3rd Viscount Netterville of Douth), and had:

1 THOMAS, **11th Baron**

2 Matthew; *b* 1765; *m* 1800 Sydney, dau of Col — Shaw, of Killough Castle, Co Tipperary, and *d* July 1825, leaving, with other issue:

(1) Oliver, of Killough Castle; *m* April 1838 Bessie Jane, dau of William Drought, of Parsonstown, and *dsp* 23 Oct 1860

(2) Merrick Shaw, of Gwersylit Hill, Denbighs; *b* 1814; *m* 21 April 1860 Caroline Mary (*d* 5 Nov 1897), yst dau of Thomas Penson, of Gwersyllt, DL, and had:

1a Thomas Oliver; *b* 26 Aug 1863; *d* 24 Oct 1926

2a Merrick Richad; *b* 2 Nov 1865; *d* 18 Aug 1916

3a Anthony Percy; *b* 3 Oct 1869; *m* 1899 Maud (*m* 2nd Dr Selby and *d* Jan 1956), dau of George Fuller Sandys, of Royston, and *d* 23 July 1902, leaving:

1b Kathleen Penson; *b* 28 Oct 1900; *m* 19 June 1923 Sir Harold George Sanders, PhD, and *d* 27 Oct 1973, leaving:

1c *Peter Plunkett; *b* 10 July 1938; *educ* Marlborough and St John's Coll Cambridge; *m* 28 July 1962 *Rosemary Anne Gravely, dau of Frederick James Rose, of Sonning-on-Thames, Berks, and has:

1d *Francesca Rose Gravely; *b* 14 Dec 1964

2d *Fiona Rosemary Anne; *b* 18 Jan 1967

1c *June Penson; *b* 23 June 1926; *m* 21 Dec 1949 *Lt-Col Stanley Thomas Baldry, MBE, RE

4a Matthew Penson; *b* 7 May 1872; *m* 9 Jan 1899 Matilda Myfanwy (*d* 15 Dec 1952), dau of Rev Samuel Evans, Rector Llysfaen, N Wales, and *d* 6 Feb 1940, leaving:

1b Sydney Penson; *b* 31 Dec 1903; *m* 4 Dec 1928 (*divorce* 1955) Helen Margaret, only dau of H A Pattullo, MB, of Kelsall, Cheshire, and *d* 1976, having had:

1c +Anthony Penson; *b* 21 Feb 1931; *m* 30 June 1956 *Anne Malkin, dau of Joseph Malkin White, of Harpenden, Herts, and has:

1d +Timothy Penson; *b* 16 Jan 1959; *m* 1982 *Carol Anne Parr, of Fetcham, Surrey

2d +Andrew Christopher; *b* 31 March 1961; *m* 1985 *Christine Anne Meysner, of Leicester

1c *Jean Margaret; *b* 5 Sept 1929; *m* 2 April 1955 *John Charles Travers Clark and has:

1d *Charles James Travers; *b* 10 March 1961; *m* 1988 *Maura Teresa Lynch

1d *Caroline Travers; *b* 27 March 1957; *m* 1985 *S/Ldr Clive Wood and has:

1e *Benjamin Richard; *b* 1987

2d *Bridget Travers; *b* 14 April 1959; *m* 1981 *Richard Pilling and has:

1e *Katherine Anne; *b* 1987

1b Caroline Frances; *b* 16 Oct 1899

5a Algernon Venables; *b* 10 Nov 1876; *ka* 19 April 1915

1a Sydney Frances Anna; *m* 1st 6 Aug 1890 Andrew Oliphant Kelso (*dsp* 14 Jan 1899), yr s of Archibald Kelso, of Rhyl; *m* 2nd 6 Nov 1908 George Knott, Surveyor Customs, and *d* 20 Aug 1913

(1) Anna Shaw; *m* 21 Jan 1822 Thomas Leeke (*d* 25 Dec 1836), of Longford Hall, Salop, and *dsp* 13 Dec 1884

1 Susannah; *d unm*

2 Anne; *m* Anthony Tisdall, of Charleville, Co Louth, and *d* 5 March 1837

The 10th BARON *d* 4 March 1763; his 3rd and est surv son,

THOMAS OLIVER PLUNKETT, **11th Baron Louth**; *b* 28 Aug 1757; claimed and was allowed the peerage 1798; *m* 7 July 1808 Margaret (*m* 2nd Lt-Col — Tisdall, of Charleville, Co Louth, and *d* 28 July 1831), est dau of 13th Baron of Dunsany (*qv*), and had surv issue:

1 THOMAS OLIVER, **12th Baron**

2 Randal Matthew; *b* 31 Oct 1810; *d* 5 Nov 1833

3 Charles Dawson; Maj-Gen, Lt-Col 1st Foot, Kt Medjidie; *m* 22 Aug 1874 Harriet Amelia (*d* 1893), dau of Biddulph Warner and widow of Joseph Kirkwood, and *d* 19 May 1886, leaving:

(1) Anna Georgina Constance; *m* 19 April 1898 Lionel E A Bennett (*d* 7 June 1921), Oxon LI, of Castle Roe, Coleraine, and *d* 27 May 1900

4 Henry Luke; *b* 6 Aug 1815

5 Edward Sidney; Maj; *b* 1817; *m* 1st 1 April 1845 Caroline Mary (*d* 23 Dec 1861), dau of George Templer; *m* 2nd 23 Feb 1865 Sophia Augusta (*dsp* 15 April 1877), est dau of Edward Litton, MP Coleraine, Master Chancery Ireland, of Altmore, Co Tyrone, and *d* 19 Oct 1875, having by his 1st w had:

(1) Harry Edward; *b* Feb 1848; *m* 28 Sept 1877 Marianne, 2nd dau of George Smith, of Dalkey, Co Dublin, and *d* 1906

(2) Charles Seale; Lt 95th Regt; *b* 13 Feb 1850; *m* 15 Aug 1776 Fanny Elizabeth (*d* 8 May 1879), dau of William Wilmott and *d* 17 March 1879, leaving:

1a Sydney Wilmott; served WW I; *b* 4 Nov 1877; *educ* Blue Coat Sch Dublin; *m* 24 Aug 1904 Elizabeth Josephine (*d* 10 Aug 1960), dau of John Patrick Higgins, of Rathmines, Co Dublin, and *d* 1 Jan 1955, leaving:

1b +Charles Seale [Charles Plunkett Esq, 180 Perth St W, Hull]; served WW II (despatches); *b* 16 March 1908; *m* 24 Jan 1934 Julia Elizabeth, dau of Walter Brown, of Hull, and has:

1c +Merrick Shawe [Merrick Plunkett Esq, 51 Woodlands Rd, Willerby, Hull]; served BAOR 1952–55; *b* 13 Sept 1934; *m* 6 Oct 1956 *Eileen, dau of Thomas Armstrong, of Leeds, and has:

1d +Patrick Allan; *b* 27 May 1958; *educ* Hull GS and Bretton Hall Coll (BEd)

2d +Glenn Charles; *b* 2 March 1966

1d *Angela; *b* 5 July 1963

2b +Norman Dawson [Norman Plunkett Esq, 14 Ashdown Crescent, London NW5]; *b* 6 Aug 1910; *educ* Bp Wordsworth Sch Salisbury, Muresk Ag Coll W Australia and Sch of Mines and Metallurgy W Australia

3b +Randal Otway [Randal Plunkett Esq, 5 Brompton Cl, Bricknell Ave, Hull, Yorks]; served WW II; *b* 4 Feb 1914; *m* 26 Jan 1935 *Sylvia May, dau of E Rutherford, of Hull, and has:

1c +Anthony Patrick [Anthony Plunkett Esq, 29 Davenport Ave, Hessle, E Yorks HU13 0RL]; *b* 20 April 1939; *educ* Hull GS; *m* 1969 *Ann Elisabeth Bennett and has:

1d +Matthew Patrick; *b* 30 Nov 1972

2d +Simon James; *b* 27 Feb 1975

1c *Eve; *b* 29 Sept 1935; *m* 4 March 1958 *Philip John Turner and has:

1d *Mark Stephen; *b* 11 Feb 1959; *m* 1994 *Francesca, dau of K E Dodd, of Welwyn, Herts

2d *Nicholas Matthew; *b* 14 Dec 1960

4b +Oliver Penson [Oliver Plunkett Esq, 4 Hartoft Rd, Hull, Yorks]; *b* 27 Sept 1917; *m* 31 May 1947 *Jean Elizabeth, dau of H Hewson, of Hull, and has:

1c +Sean Patrick [Sean Plunkett Esq, 14 Burghley Rd, St Andrews, Bristol BS6 5BN]; *b* 1948; *educ* Hull GS and Ealing Tech Coll; *m* 1985 *Antonia Susan, dau of Florian Brann, of London, and has:

1d +Leo Joseph; *b* 4 Oct 1988

1d *Caitlin Martha; *b* 28 July 1986

1b Frances Louisa; *b* 4 Sept 1905; *m* 20 Nov 1925 Walter Grundy and *d* 1989, leaving issue

The 11th BARON *d* 25 June 1823; his son,

THOMAS OLIVER PLUNKETT, **12th Baron Louth**; *b* 5 Aug 1809; *m* 29 Nov 1830 Anna Maria (*d* 18 Jan 1878), yst dau of Philip Roche, of Donore, Co Kildare, by Anna Maria, yst dau of 13th Baron of Dunsany (*qv*), and had:

1 RANDAL PERCY OTWAY, **13th Baron**

2 Thomas Oliver Westenra; RM Belfast, Capt 1st Foot; *b* 8 April 1838; *m* 1st 24 July 1862 Clara Anne (*d* 27 July 1867), only dau of John Kirkby, of Sheffield; *m* 2nd 20 June 1874 Caroline Alicia Victoria (*m* 2nd 4 July 1892 Annesley Horace Packe (*d* 7 Nov 1950), s of Capt Horatio Packe, RN, and *d* 30 July 1898), only dau of Col Henry Musters, JP, DL, of Brianstown, Co Longford, and *d* 6 Dec 1889, having by his 1st w had:

(1) Thomas Oliver Clarence; Lt 4th Bn Royal Munster Fus; *b* 15 July 1867

3 Algernon Richard Hartland; Offr 73rd Foot; *b* 1843; *d* 1873

1 Augusta Anna Margaret; *m* 20 Jan 1869 Col John Douglas Johnstone, DL, Roy Sussex Regt, of Snow Hill, Kisbellaw, Co Fermanagh, and *d* 27 Aug 1907, leaving issue

2 Adelaide Constance; *d* 19 July 1866

3 Randalina Anna Maria Louisa; *m* 1st 20 Aug 1884 Thomas A Farrell (*dsp* 29 Dec 1898); *m* 2nd 21 Feb 1900 Francis Arthur Farrell (*d* 1914), of 37 Merrion Sq, Dublin, 2nd s of John Farrell, DL, of Moynalty, Co Meath, and Thornhill, Bray, Co Wicklow, and *d* 6 Feb 1932

The 12th BARON *d* 26 June 1849; his est son,

RANDAL PERCY OTWAY PLUNKETT, **13th Baron Louth**; *b* 28 Aug 1832; *educ* Eton; Offr 79th Highrs 1851–54 and 1855–60; *m* 1st 4 Oct 1867 Anne Maria MacGeough (*d* Dieppe 27 Oct 1868), 2nd dau of Walter MacGeough Bond, of Drumsill and The Argory, Co Armagh; *m* 2nd 14 July 1877 Elizabeth Lily (*m* 2nd 12 Aug 1886 Richard Muldowney), est dau of John Black, of Ceylon, and *d* 19 July 1883, leaving by his 1st w:

RANDAL PILGRIM RALPH PLUNKETT, **14th Baron Louth**, JP and DL Co Louth; *b* 24 Sept 1868; Maj 2nd Co of London Yeo (Westminster Dragoons), Lt 3rd Bn Wilts Regt, WW I, WW II; *m* 1st 17 March 1890 (*divorce* 1912) Eugénie de Miaritze (*d* 13 Oct 1947), dau of Edmund Hooke Wilson Bellairs, UK V-Consul Biarritz, and had:

1 OTWAY RANDAL PERCY OLIVER, **15th Baron**

1 Eugénie Anne Westenra; *b* 16 April 1891; *m* 1st 11 Sept 1915 Walter Digby Buddicom, MC, Lt 4th Hus (*d* of wounds recd in action 6 June 1918), only s of Harry William Buddicom, DL, of Penbedw, Flints; *m* 2nd 1919 (*divorce* 1940) Maj William Campbell, 2nd s of J D Campbell, of Howden Ct, Tiverton, and had issue; *m* 3rd 3 July 1940 Maj Arthur Macdonald Harbord (*d* 3 Feb 1963), RA, yst s of Rev Harry Harboard, of E Hoathly, Sussex

The **14th Baron** *m* 2nd 2 Aug 1913 Dorothy Lettice (*d* 16 Aug 1923), 2nd dau of Col Thomas Lewis Hampton-Lewis, of Henllys and Bodior, Anglesey; *m* 3rd 12 March 1926 Marie Ethel (*d* 21 April 1941), dau of Charles Read, of Hampstead, and widow of Sir John Prichard-Jones, 1st Bt (*qv*), and by his 2nd w had:

2 Randall Patrick Ralph Oliver; 2nd Lt 5th Inniskilling Dragoons Gds; *b* 9 Dec 1914; *m* 13 Feb 1936 *Gwendoline Mary, dau of E A Cowling, and *d* in an accident 14 July 1936

The 14th BARON *d* 28 Oct 1941; his only surv son,

OTWAY RANDAL PERCY OLIVER PLUNKETT, **15th Baron Louth**; *b* 26 April 1892; *educ* Downside; WW I with Canadian Forces; *m* 4 July 1927 Ethel Molly (*d* 1992), dau of Walter John Gallichan, of Jersey, and *d* 3 Feb 1950, leaving:

OTWAY MICHAEL JAMES OLIVER PLUNKETT, **16th and present Baron Louth**

LOVAT

Arms: Quarterly, 1st and 4th, azure three cinquefoils argent; 2nd and 3rd, argent three antique crowns gules. **Crest:** A buck's head erased or, attired argent. **Supporters:** Two bucks proper. **Motto:** *Je suis prest* ('I am ready'). **Creations:** L. (S) 1457–64, B. (UK) 28 Jan 1837.

THE 16TH LORD (FRASER OF) LOVAT and **Baron Lovat of Lovat**, Co Inverness (Simon Christopher Joseph Fraser) [The Rt Hon The Lord Lovat, Beaufort Lodge, Beauly, Inverness-shire; Balblair House, Beauly, Inverness-shire]; *b* 13 Feb 1977; *s* gf 1995, also as Chief of Clan Fraser; *educ* Harrow and Edinburgh U; Col-in-Ch 78th Fraser Highrs 1997–

Lineage: Sir ANDREW FRASER, Yr. of Touchfraser (*see* SALTOUN, L); Sheriff Stirling; *m* Beatrix —, an heiress, probably of the Le CHENs of Duffus, and *d* by 1306, leaving, with other issue:

Sir SIMON FRASER, of Brotherton and 1st of Lovat; probably the Simon commemorated in the Gaelic name for the Chief of the House *MacShimi*, *MacShimidh* or *Mac Simi* ('son of Simon'); Sheriff Kincardine 1317; *m* Margaret, dau of John, Jarl of Orkney and Earl of Caithness (*qv*), by his w, who was possibly dau but evidently ultimate heiress of Sir David Grahame, feudal Ld of Lovat, and was *k* Battle of Halidon Hill, having had, with another s and a dau:

1 Simon (Sir), 2nd of Lovat; *d* unm 1346 of wounds recd Battle of Durham

2 Alexander (Sir), 3rd of Lovat; *m* —, dau of Sir Andrew Moray of Bothwell, and had:

(1) Hugh, 4th of Lovat; territorial Baron of Kynnell and Linton, which latter he surrendered with the remant of his lands in Tweeddale; *m* Isobel, dau of Sir John Wemyss of Leuchars by his 2nd w Isabel, dau of Sir Alan Erskine of Inchmartin, and *d c* 1409, having had:

1a Alexander, 5th of Lovat; *m* 1st Elizabeth Keith (*d* by April 1414); *m* 2nd Marion, dau of Sir Robert Keith (*see* KINTORE, E), and having no son made over his lands to his yr bro *c* 1410 and became a monk, leaving by his 1st w (as well as an illegitimate s by an unknown woman):

1b Marjorie; just conceivably the Mariota (although the latter is an alternative version for 'Mary' rather than 'Marjorie') who *m c* 1414, as his 1st w, Sir William Keith, Marischal of Scotland (*see* KINTORE, E)

2a Hugh, 6th of Lovat; *b c* 1376; High Sheriff Inverness-shire 1431; *m* 1st 1425 Janet (*d* by Dec 1429), sis of William de Fenton of Beaufort; *m* 2nd by Dec 1429 Isabel, dau of Sir John Wemyss of Wemyss (*see* WEMYSS, E) and *d* by July 1440, having had by his 1st w:

1b Thomas, 7th of Lovat

2b Hugh, 8th of Lovat; *b c* 1417; *m* Janet, dau of Thomas de Dunbar, 2nd Earl of Dunbar (*see* DUNBAR, Bt, of Mochrum), and *d c* 1450, leaving:

1c HUGH, **1st Lord**

1b Elizabeth; *m* as his 1st w Sir William Leslie of Balquhain (*see* LESLIE, Bt)

3a William; *m* —, heiress of the SCRYMGEOURs

1a Agnes/Euphemia; *m* 1st Lachlan Mackintosh, Capt of Clan Chattan; *m* 2nd Sir Walter Innes of that Ilk (*see* ROXBURGHE, D)

HUGH FRASER, 8th of Lovat's s,

HUGH FRASER, **1st Lord (Fraser of) Lovat** (S), so *cr* 1457–64; came to an arragement 1464 with his distant cousin Alexander Fraser of Philorth that each was to be heir male to the other in the event of either failing to beget heirs male of his body; *m* by 1464 Violet, est dau of 3rd Lord Glamis (*see* STRATHMORE AND KINGHORNE, E), and had:

1 THOMAS, **2nd Lord**

2 Hugh; *k* Flodden

3 John, Rector Dingwall, memb King's Cncl

1 Margaret; *m* Hector de Kilmalew

2 Agnes; *m* Kenneth MacKenzie of Kintail (*see* CROMARTIE, E)

3 Egidia/Marjory; *m* Ferquherd Mackintosh of Mackintosh

The 1st LORD *d* between 1 Nov 1499 and 30 April 1501; his est son,

THOMAS FRASER, **2nd Lord (Fraser of) Lovat**; *b c* 1461; Justiciar N of Scotland; *m* 1st (contract Jan 1493) Janet (*d* 1503), dau of Sir Alexander Gordon of Abergeldie, and had, with two er daus (Margaret; Isobel):

1 HUGH, **3rd Lord**

2 William, of Teachers; had at least one dau (Agnes, *m c* 1544, as his 2nd w, John Grant of Glenmoriston; *see* STRATHSPEY, B)

3 James; *k* Battle of Loch Lochy (feud between Frasers and Macdonalds) 15 July 1544; ancestor of the FRASERs of Culbokie

1 Janet; *m c* 1527 John Crichton of Ruthven

The **2nd Lord** *m* 2nd 1506 Janet (*m* 3rd 9th Earl of Crawford, *see* CRAWFORD and BALCARRES, E), dau of 2nd Lord Gray (*qv*) and widow of Sir Alexander Blair of Balthayock, and *d* allegedly 21 Oct 1524, having by her had:

4 Robert; *m* Janet Gelly; ancestor of the FRASERs of Kinnell

5 Andrew; allegedly *m* —, dau of the Laird of Grant

6 Thomas; allegedly *m* Anna, dau of Macleod of Harris

The est s,

HUGH FRASER, **3rd Lord (Fraser of) Lovat**; *b* 1494; got a new charter 1539 incorporating the territorial Baronies of Abertarf, Lovat, Stratherrick and others into a free Barony of Lovat, to be held of him and heirs male of his body, in default of which to his next heirs male whosoever bearing the arms, insignia and name of Fraser, in default of which to heirs whomsover; Justiciar N of Sotland for MARY QUEEN OF SCOTS; *m* 1st *c* 1512 Anne, dau of John Grant 2nd of Freuchie (*see* STRATHSPEY, B) and widow of John Hallyburton of Pitcur, and had:

1 Hugh, *Master of Lovat*; *k* with his f Battle of Loch Lochy

The **3rd Lord** *m* 2nd by 19 July 1536 Janet (*d* 1565), dau of Walter Ross of Balnagowan, and by her had, with a yr dau (Margaret):

2 ALEXANDER, **4th Lord**

3 William, of Struy; *b c* 1537; *m* 1561 Janet, dau of the Laird of Grant

4 Hugh; *b c* 1539

1 Agnes; *m* 1st by 3 March 1540/1 William Macleod of Macleod, 9th Ch of Macleod (*d* 1551); *m* 2nd Alexander Bayne of Tulloch and *d* 29 Jan 1594/5

The 3rd LORD was also *k* at Loch Lochy 15 July 1544; his 2nd son,

ALEXANDER FRASER, **4th Lord (Fraser of) Lovat**; *m* Janet (*m* 2nd Donald McDonald of Sleat), dau of Sir John Campbell of Cawdor (*see* CAWDOR, E), and *d* Dec 1557, having had, with other issue:

1 HUGH UISDEAN RUADH FRASER, **5th Lord (Fraser of) Lovat**; *m* 24 Dec 1567 Elizabeth (*m* 2nd 1578 (*divorce* due his impotence) 2nd Earl of Lennox of the 1572 *cr* and later 1st Earl of March (*see* MORAY, E); *m* 3rd 1581 James Stewart, Earl of Arran; *see* MORAY, E), dau of John Stewart, 4th Earl of Atholl (*see* MORAY, E), and *d* 1 Jan 1576, leaving, with an est and yst s (both *d* in infancy) and three other daus:

(1) SIMON FRASER, **6th Lord (Fraser of) Lovat**; *b c* 1569; Sheriff Inverness; *m* 1st 1589 Katherine (*d* 1593), dau of Sir Colin Mackenzie of Kintail (*see* CROMARTIE, E), and had, with an er s (*dsp* & *vp*):

1a HUGH FRASER, **7th Lord (Fraser of) Lovat**; *b* 1592; *m* 1614 Isabel, dau of Sir John Wemyss of Wemyss (*see* WEMYSS, E), and *d* 16 Feb 1646, having had, with other issue:

1b Simon, *Master of Lovat*; *b* 1621; *educ* Aberdeen and St Andrews Us; *dvp* unm by June 1640

2b Hugh, *Master of Lovat*; *m* by 30 June 1642 Anne, 3rd dau of 1st Earl of Leven (*see* LEVEN and MELVILLE, E), and *dvp* 1643, leaving:

1c HUGH FRASER, **8th Lord (Fraser of) Lovat**; *b* 2 May 1643; *m* July 1659 Anne, 2nd dau of Sir John Mackenzie, 1st Bt, of Tarbat (*see* CROMARTIE, E), and *d* 27 April 1672, leaving, with three daus:

1d HUGH FRASER, **9th Lord (Fraser of) Lovat**; *b* 28 Sept 1666; *m* Amelia (*d* 6 May 1743), dau of 1st Marquess of Atholl (*see* ATHOLL, D), and *d* 14 Sept 1696 after settling his estates 20 March 1696 on his cousin and heir male (4th s of **7th Lord**), having had, with two sons (*d* young):

1e Amelia; as heir general of her f assumed on his death the title 'Lady Lovat' and the Court of Session 2 Dec 1702 decided that she was entitled both to the title and the Lovat estates, rejecting a counter-claim by her cousin Simon, **11th Lord**, the heir male; she held the estates till 1715, when her husb's participation in the Jacobite Rising led to his attainder and forfeiture of his life-rent interest in the estate; on 3 July 1730, by a decree of reduction in the Court of Session at the instigation of the **11th Lord**, she was deprived of the title and though her right to the estates was not subject to court action she parted with them to the **11th Lord** for £12,000 ready money (some £700,000 in late-1990s terms); *m* 1702 Alexander MACKENZIE of Prestonhall later FRASER OF FRASERDALE (*d* 3 June 1755 aged 72) and *d* 22 Aug 1763, having had:

1f Hugh; self-styled 'Lord Lovat'; *b c* 1703; sold 1733 the reversion of any claim he might have on the family estates to the **11th Lord**; *d* 9 Nov 1770

1f Amelia; *d* 22 Aug 1763

2e Anne; *b* 1689; *m* 1st Sept 1703 Norman Macleod of Macleod, 20th Chief; *m* 2nd Peter Fothringham of Powrie; *m* 3rd 2nd Earl of Cromarty (*see* CROMARTIE, E) and *d* 10 Aug 1734

3e Katherine; *m* 23 July 1706 Sir William Murray, Bt, of Ochtertyre (*qv*), and *d* 4 March 1771

3b Alexander; *b* 1626; *m* Sybilla, dau of 1st Lord Mackenzie of Kintail (*see* CROMARTIE, E) and widow of Ian *Mor* ('The Great' or 'The Elder') Macleod, 16th Ch of Macleod, and *d* 27 June 1671, leaving a dau

4b THOMAS FRASER, of Beaufort, Inverness-shire, *de jure* 10th LORD (FRASER OF) LOVAT; *m* Sibylla (*d* June 1682), 4th dau of Ian *Mor* Macleod of Macleod, 16th Chief, and *d* May 1699, having had, with three other sons (*d* young and/or unm):

1c SIMON FRASER, **11th Lord (Fraser of) Lovat**; *b c* 1667; *educ* King's Coll Aberdeen; after the **9th Lord**'s death induced his cousin Amelia to elope with him but she soon returned to her mother; he then abducted Amelia's mother and forced her to go through a form of marriage with him, for which he was tried *in absentia* 1698 for high treason, outlawed and sentenced to death (his f, who was an accessory, was also found guilty of high treason); sentence quashed 1700; having initially conspired with the Jacobites he switched sides in the 1715 Rising to the Govt, to whom he presented Inverness Castle (of which he was apptd Govr 1716) and as a reward was granted his cousin Amelia's husb's forfeited life-rent of the Lovat estates; unsuccessfully asserted his right to the Ldship of Lovat at elections of Scottish rep peers 1721, 1722 and 1727; finally acquired the title through the Court of Session judgement of 1730; despite his treachery towards them 22 years earlier was accepted into the the Jacobite circle that from *c* 1737 planned Prince Charles Edward's landing in Scotland and this time stayed relatively true ('relatively' since as late as the last week before his apprehension he was writing letters proclaiming his loyalty to the Hanoverians); *cr* 14 March 1739/40 titular Lord Lovat of Beaulieu, Viscount of the Aird and Strathglass, Earl of Stratherrick and Abertarf, Marquess of Beaufort and Duke of Fraser by the titular James III; gathered his clansmen from late Sept 1745 (following the Jacobite victory at Prestonpans) on; arrested 11 Dec 1745, escaped 2 Jan 1745/6, rearrested on Lake Morar, having fruitlessly urged Prince Charles Edward to continue the struggle even after the rout of Culloden; *m* 1st Margaret, dau of Ludovic Grant of Grant (*see* STRATHSPEY, B), and had, with other issue (*d* unm):

1d Simon, *Master of Lovat*; *b* 19 Oct 1726; joined f in 1745 Rising, pardoned 1750; MP Inverness 1761–82; served Portugal and War American Independence; got back f's forfeited lands 1774; *dsp* 8 Feb 1782

1d Janet; *m* Ewan Macpherson of Cluny and *d* 1765

1c (cont.) The **11th Lord** *m* 2nd 1733 Primrose (*d* 1796), dau of Hon John Campbell, bro of 4th Duke of Argyll (*qv*), was impeached (prosecution by House of Commons before House of Lords as jury) 11 Dec 1746, found unanimously guilty of high treason 19 March 1746/7, when his title and estates were forfeited, and was beheaded 9 April 1747 on Tower Hill when not far short of 80, having by her had:

2d Archibald Campbell; *b* 16 Aug 1736; Br Consul Algiers 1766; MP Inverness 1782; recruited a regt ('Fraser Fencibles') which was stationed in Ireland throughout the Napoleonic Wars; willed his estates to his distant cousin Thomas Alexander (later **12th Lord**) 1808; *m* 1763 Jane, dau of William Fraser of Leadclune, and *dsps* 8 Dec 1815, having had five sons (all *dvp* unm)

5b James; *b* 1633; *k* 1657 in service of King of Poland

1b Mary; *b* 1617; *m* 1635 David Ross of Balnagowan and *d* 1659

2b Anne; *b* 1619; *m* 24 Jan 1638/9, as his 2nd w, 14th Earl of Sutherland (*qv*) and *dsp* 23 July 1658

3b Catherine; *b* 1622; *m* 1st Sir John Sinclair of Dunbeath; *m* 2nd, as his 2nd w, 1st Viscount of Arbuthnott (*qv*); *m* 3rd *c* 1660 3rd Lord Fraser (*see* SALTOUN, L) and *d* 18 Oct 1663

1a Elizabeth; *b* 1591; *m* John Dunbar, Sheriff Morayshire

(1) (cont.) The **6th Lord** *m* 2nd 1596 Jean (*d* 1622), dau of 1st Lord Doune (*see* MORAY, E), and *d* 1633, having by her had:

2a Simon (Sir), 1st of Inverallochy; *b c* 1598; *m* Jean (*m* 2nd 1621 Sir Thomas Burnett, 1st Bt, of Leys; *see* 1970 edn), dau of Sir John Moncreiffe of that Ilk (*see* ERROLL, E), and *dvp* 1620, having had:

1b Simon, 2nd of Inverallochy; *m* Lady Marjory Mary Erskine (*m* 2nd 4th Lord Fraser; *see* SALTOUN, L), dau of 7th Earl of Buchan (*qv*), and had:

1c Simon, 3rd of Inverallochy; had:

1d Alexander, 4th of Inverallochy; *m* Elizabeth (*d* 1744), dau of 3rd Earl of Kellie (*see* MAR and KELLIE, E), and *dsp* 1698

2d William, 5th of Inverallochy; *dsp*

3d Charles, 6th of Inverallochy, titular Lord Fraser of Muchall, so *cr* 1723 by titular James III; *m* Anne, dau of John Udny of that Ilk by Martha, dau of 1st Earl of Aberdeen (*see* ABERDEEN AND TEMAIR, M), and had:

1e Charles, Yr. of Inverallochy; *ka* Culloden 1746

2e William, 7th of Inverallochy; *dsp* 1789

1e Martha, 8th of Inverallochy; *m* Colin Mackenzie of Kilcoy and *d* 1803, having had, with two er sons:

1f Alexander MACKENZIE later MACKENZIE-FRASER, 9th of Inverallochy; also *s* 1814 his aunt Elizabeth (*see* below) at Castle Fraser; *m* 1st 1786 Helen (*d* 25 April 1808), dau of Maj William Mackenzie (gs of 4th Earl of Seaforth, *see* CROMARTIE, E); *m* 2nd 21 Sept 1843 Georgiana Augusta (*d* 23 June 1851), dau of Sir Charles Bagot, GCB (*see* BAGOT, B), and by his 1st w had:

1g Charles, 10th of Inverallochy and 6th of Castle Fraser; *b* 9 June 1792; *m* 25 April 1817 Jane, dau of Sir John Hay, Bt, of Smithfield and Hayston (*see* 1949 edn), by Mary Elizabeth, dau of 17th Lord Forbes (*qv*), and *d* 7 March 1871, having had:

1h Frederick, 11th of Inverallochy

1h Eleanor Jane

2e Elizabeth, of Castle Fraser, formerly the territorial Barony of Muchall; *d* unm 1814

3a Thomas; *dsp* 1613

4a James (Sir), of Brae; had:

1b James; min Culross, later of Inverness; his dau and heiress *m* 1692 as his 2nd w, Hugh Rose, 15th of Kilravock

2b David; left an only s:

1c Simon; *dsp*

(1) Anne; *m* Hector Munro of Foulis (*see* MUNRO, Bt, of Foulis-Obsdale, also Section Monroe AMERICAN PRESIDENTIAL FAMILIES, 1994, Morris Genealogical Books SA)

2 Thomas, of Knockie and (1st of) Strichen; *b c* 1550; *m* Isobel, allegedly dau of John (more probably James) Forbes of Corsindae and widow of his cousin Thomas Fraser of Strichen (*see* SALTOUN, L), and *d* 2 Oct 1612, leaving:

(1) Thomas, 2nd of Strichen; Sheriff Inverness; *m* 1st Christian, dau of William Forbes of Tolquhon; *m* 2nd Margaret Macleod and *d* March 1647/8, leaving (by his 1st w?):

1a Thomas, 3rd of Strichen; *m* 1628 Christian, dau of Sir John Forbes of Pitsligo, and *d* 1656, leaving:

1b Thomas, 4th of Strichen; *m* 1656 Marion, yr dau of Robert Irvine of Fedderet by Elizabeth, dau of Sir Duncan Campbell, 1st Bt, of Glenorchy (*see* 1970 edn BREADALBANE AND HOLLAND, E), and had:

1c Alexander, 5th of Strichen; *m* 1st —, dau of Cockburn of Ormiston; *m* 2nd 1697 Amelia (*see* LINDSAY, E), dau of James, Lord Doune (*see* MORAY, E), and *d* 1702, having by her had:

1d James, 6th of Strichen; *dsp*

2d Alexander, 7th of Strichen; a Ld of Session, as Lord Strichen, 1730–75; *m* 19 Sept 1731 Anne, dau of 1st Duke of Argyll (*qv*) and widow of 2nd Earl of Bute (*see* BUTE, M), and *d* 1775, leaving an only s:

1e Alexander, 8th of Strichen; *m* 1764 Jean Menzies and had, with other issue:

1f Alexander, 9th of Strichen; Capt 1st Dragoon Gds; *m* 1801 Amelia Mary (*d* Aug 1860), dau of John Leslie of Balquhain (*see* LESLIE, Bt), and *d* 1803, leaving:

1g THOMAS ALEXANDER FRASER, **12th Lord (Fraser of) Lovat** on reversal of attainder 13 Aug 1857 (following his petition 32 years earlier), also 1st BARON LOVAT OF LOVAT, Co Inverness (UK), so *cr* 28 Jan 1837, KG (1865); *b* 17 June 1802; Ld Lt Inverness-shire 1853–73; *m* 6 Aug 1823 Charlotte Georgina (*d* 28 May 1876), est dau of 2nd Baron Stafford (*qv*), and *d* 28 June 1875, having had:

1h SIMON, **13th Lord**

2h Alexander Edward; *b* 13 Jan 1831; Lt-Col Scots Gds Crimea; *m* 13 Jan 1858 Georgina Mary (*d* 28 March 1928), only dau of George Fieschi Heneage, of Hainton Hall, Lincs (*see* 1967 edn HENEAGE, B), and *dsp* 20 Sept 1885

3h George Edward Stafford; *b* 17 Feb 1834; *d* 4 May 1854

4h Henry Thomas; *b* 2 Dec 1838; Col 1st Bn Scots Gds; *d* unm 3 Aug 1904

1h Amelia Charlotte; *m* 17 Sept 1846 Charles Robert Scott-Murray (*d* 27 Aug 1882), of Danesfield, Bucks, and *d* 17 Aug 1912, leaving issue

2h Frances Georgiana; *m* 9 May 1844 Sir Piers Mostyn, 8th Bt (*qv*), and *d* 25 Dec 1899

3h Charlotte Henrietta; *m* 27 Nov 1866 Sir Matthew Sausse, QC (*dsp* 4 Nov 1867), Ch Justice Bombay, and *d* 21 July 1904

1d Marian; *m* James Craig of Riccarton

2b Hugh

(1) Jean; *m* 1st Sir James Stewart of Kilcoy; *m* 2nd Alexander Mackenzie of Kilcoy

(2) Magdalene; *m* June 1603 Hugh Rose, 12th of Kilravock (*d* 10 June 1643), and *d* 26 Dec 1644, leaving issue

3 James, of Ardachy; *m* and had issue

1 Anne; *m* Fraser, of Dalcross Alexander

The 12th LORD's est son,

SIMON FRASER, **13th Lord (Fraser of) Lovat**; *b* 21 Dec 1828; Lt-Col 2nd Bn QO Cameron Highrs Militia, Ld Lt Inverness-shire 1873–87, ADC to HM QUEEN VICTORIA 1883–87; *m* 14 Nov 1866 Alice Mary (*d* 3 June 1938), dau of Thomas Weld-Blundell, of Ince Blundell, and *d* 6 Sept 1887, having had:

1 Simon Thomas Joseph; *b* 17 Aug 1867; *d* 28 Sept 1868

2 SIMON JOSEPH, **14th Lord**

3 Hugh Joseph, MVO; *b* 6 July 1874; Maj Scots Gds, Boer War, WW I; *ka* Oct 1914

4 Alastair Thomas Joseph, DSO (1918); JP, DL (Invernessshire); *b* 1 Aug 1877; *educ* Magdalen Coll Oxford (BA 1899); Hon Lt Army, Maj 1st Lovat Scouts, Boer War, WW I (despatches); chm Cornbrook Brewery and Champion Reef and Ooregum Gold Mines India; *m* 16 March 1915 Lady Sibyl Grimston (*d* 1 Aug 1968), 5th dau of 3rd Earl of Verulam (*qv*), and *d* 14 Oct 1949, leaving:

(1) Alastair Hugh Joseph, MC; *b* 26 Sept 1919; *educ* Ampleforth and Magdalen Coll Oxford; Maj Lovat Scouts WW II; *m* 1 July 1950 *Philippa Margaret [Mrs Alastair Fraser, Moniack Castle, Kirkhill, Inverness-shire IV5 7PQ], only dau of Sir Anselm William Edward Guise, 6th Bt (*qv*), and *d* 1986, leaving:

1a +Alastair James [Alastair Fraser Esq, Petit Moniack, CH-1873 Val d'Illiez, VS, Switzerland]; *b* 10 June 1951; *educ* Ampleforth; *m* 1981 *Elizabeth von Wartburg and has:

1b *Victoria Alexandre; *b* 1982

1a (cont.) Mr and Mrs Alastair Fraser also adopted:

*Philip; *b* 1985

*Anne-Sophie; *b* 1983

2a +Roderick Joseph [Roderick Fraser Esq, Moniack Castle, Inverness IV5 7PQ]; *b* 25 Jan 1953; *educ* Ampleforth; *m* 1981 *Mary Jean, yr dau of Hon Charles Richard Strutt (*see* RAYLEIGH, B), and has:

1b +Charles Alastair; *b* 1982

2b +Harry Edward; *b* 1984

1b *Caroline Mary; *b* 1988

2b *Georgina; *b* 1990

3a +Christopher (Kit) James [Christopher Fraser Esq, Moniack Castle, Kirkhill, Invernesshire]; *b* 25 July 1954; *educ* Ampleforth; *m* 1983 *Sarah Louise, only dau of J H Gladwin, of Bishops Stortford, and has:

1b +Sandy John; *b* 1988

1b *Angelica Ishbel; *b* 1987

4a +(Peter) Anselm [Anselm Fraser Esq, Myreside Grange, Gifford, E Lothian]; *b* 18 Jan 1957; *educ* Ampleforth; *m* 1981 *Antonia Hope, dau of

Lt-Col Thomas Holroyd Gibbon, OBE, of The Field House, Sutton, W Sussex, and has:

  1b +James Anselm; *b* 1986

  2b +Thomas Alastair; *b* 1987

1a *Arabella Mary [The Rt Hon The Lady Huntingfield, 1 Clanricarde Mansions, Clanricarde Gdns, London W2]; *b* 21 Nov 1959; *m* 1982 *7th Baron Huntingfield (*qv*) and has issue

2a *Sophia Margaret; *b* 21 Nov 1964; *m* 1992 *Robin Yates

(2) +Ian James (Sir), CBE (1972), MC [Sir Ian Fraser CBE MC, South Haddon, Skilgate, Somerset TA4 2DR]; *b* 7 Aug 1923; *educ* Ampleforth and Magdalen Coll Oxford; Capt Scots Gds WW II; foreign corresp Reuters 1946–56, merchant banker 1956–69, dir S G Warburg 1962–69, Dir-Gen Panel on Takeovers and Mergers 1969–72, chm: Rolls-Royce Motors 1971–80, Lazard Bros 1980–85, Lloyd's Syndicate 90 (1982) Names Assoc 1990–95; ktd 1986, dep chm Vickers 1980–89 and TSB Gp 1985–91, FRSA 1970, Kt Honour and Devotion SMO Malta 1971; *m* 1st 25 Oct 1958 (Elizabeth) Anne (*d* 1984), yr dau of Capt Allaster Edward George Grant, DSO, 9th Lancers, and has:

1a +Alexander Charles Evelyn; *b* 18 July 1962

2a +James Hector Ian; *b* 10 July 1963

1a *Consuelo Catherine Sibyl; *b* 27 July 1959; *m* 23 Sept 1989 *Guy William Antony Barker, only s of Kenneth W Barker, and has:

  1b *Inigo Julian Clare; *b* 1993

  1b *Theodora; *b* 1990

2a *Domenica Margaret Anne; *b* 31 July 1960; *m* 1989 *Philip Martin Dunne, er s of Thomas Raymond Dunne, of Gatley Park, Leominster, Herefs, and has:

  1b *Thomas Hugo Rendel; *b* 9 June 1995

  1b *Evelyn Anne; *b* 1 June 1990

  2b *Matilda Rose; *b* 29 June 1992

(2) (cont.) Sir Ian *m* 2nd 1993 *Fiona Margaret, dau of Maj Hon Henry Montagu Douglas-Home, MBE (*see* HOME, E), and formerly w of Gregory Martin

(3) Roderick Andrew; *b* 20 Feb 1927; *educ* Ampleforth; Lt Scots Gds; *m* 8 April 1958 *Ethel Mary (*m* 2nd 7 July 1969 Edward Eyre; *see* ACTON, B), er dau of Cdr Charles Hardinge Drage, RN, and *d* 3 Aug 1964, leaving:

1a +Anthony Henry Joseph [Anthony Fraser Esq, Keeper's Cottage, Spanhoe Wood, Deene Rd, nr Corby, Northants NN17 3AB; 4, Wilmington House, Highbury Cres, London N5]; *b* 4 Jan 1959; *educ* Ampleforth and Downing Coll Cambridge; Capt Scots Gds, co dir; *m* 1994 *Hon Fiona Mary Maitland-Biddulph, only dau of 4th Baron Biddulph (*qv*), and has:

  1b *Rory Ivor Charles; *b* 17 May 1996

2a +Archibald Ian Charles (Archie) [Archibald Fraser Esq, 70 St Dionis Rd, London SW6 4TU]; *b* 5 Feb 1960; *educ* Ampleforth and Magdalen Coll Oxford; slr 1986; *m* 26 July 1997 *Rosalind Henrietta, dau of Robert Martin Mays-Smith, of Chaddleworth, Berks

3a +Thomas William Gerard; *b* 17 Feb 1964; *educ* Ampleforth; *m* 1989 (*divorce* 1994) Emma Louise, dau of Ronald Russell Hobbs, of Harrogate, N Yorks

1a *Eleanor Clare [Countess Olivier de Rosmorduc, Château de Pencran, F-2 800, Pencran, France]; *b* 13 May 1961; *m* 1993 *Count Olivier Tanguy Antoine Marie-Ghislain de Rosmorduc, s of Count Tanguy de Rosmorduc, and has:

  1b *Marguerite Marie-Gabrielle Alexandra; *b* 21 July 1994

  2b *Sophie Amelia Sybille; *b* 21 July 1994

(4) +Simon Joseph [Simon Fraser Esq, 33 Clarendon Rd, London, W11]; *b* 13 March 1929; *educ* Ampleforth and Magdalen Coll Oxford; *m* 6 Oct 1956 *(Elspeth) Jane, yr dau of Hugh Stewart Mackintosh, and has:

1a +Rupert James [Rupert Fraser Esq, 98 Clarendon Drive, London SW15]; *educ* Ampleforth and Magdalen Coll Oxford; *b* 13 Jan 1958; *m* 1987 *Anne Elizabeth, dau of J H Kingston, and has:

  1b +Simon Peter James; *b* 1993

  1b *Lucy Miranda Jean; *b* 1989

  2b *Alice Felicity Jane; *b* 1991

1a *Cordelia Jane; *b* 9 Nov 1959; *m* 1986 *Arthur I Trueger, of San Francisco, and has:

  1b *Alastair William James; *b* 1987

  2b *Hugh Robin Charles; *b* 1988

  3b *Ruari Simon Paul; *b* 1990

  4b *Ian Julian Joseph; *b* 1992

  5b *Archibald Rupert Leo; *b* 1996

2a *Katharine Julia [Mrs Mark Rowan, Kerswell Priory, Broadhembury, Devon EX15 2EA]; *b* 19 Feb 1961; *m* 1990 *Mark D R Rowan, yr s of Sir Thomas Leslie Rowan, KCB, CVO, and has:

  1b *Thomas Simon Leacroft; *b* 1992

  2b *Alexander Charles Hugh; *b* 1994

3a *Olivia Mary Juliet; *b* 7 June 1965; *m* 1991 *William Benedict Hamilton-Dalrymple, yst s of Sir Hew Fleetwood Hamilton-Dalrymple, 10th Bt (*qv*), and has issue

4a *Perdita Rachel Josephine; *b* 22 July 1967; *m* 19– *Davide Taliente

5a *Helen Jane; *b* 1972

(1) *Frances Mary [Mrs Humphrey Weld, Chideock Manor, Dorset]; *b* 26 Jan 1916; *m* 12 June 1948 *Lt-Col Humphrey Joseph Giles Weld, MC, Queen's Bays, only s of Humphrey Weld, and has:

1a *Charles Humphrey Joseph; *b* 1949; *m* 1991 *Georgina Helen, 2nd dau of Sir Francis John Vernon Hereward Dashwood, 11th Bt, of West Wycombe (*qv*)

1a *Gabrielle Mary Frances; *b* 1950; *m* 1980 *Amyas Michael George Martelli, of Wooth Manor, Bridport, Dorset, and has:

  1b *Frederick Amyas; *b* 1984

  2b *Bartholomew Michael Augustus; *b* 1989

  1b *Anna Rose; *b* 1983

2a *Lucinda Mary Rose; *b* 1952; *m* 1977 *Thomas Alastair Christie, of Kellas House, by Elgin, Moray, and has:

  1b *Alexander Thomas; *b* 1980

  2b *Robert Sylvester; *b* 1981

  3b *Ewen Humphrey; *b* 1988

  1b *Isabella Frances Mary; *b* 1984

  2b *Georgina Mary Rose; *b* 1986

3a *Candida Mary Sibyl; *b* 1956; *m* 1980 *Sebastian Anthony Arbuthnot-Leslie, of Warthill, Aberdeenshire, and has:

  1b *William Anthony; *b* 1982

  2b *John Alexander; *b* 1989

  1b *Sophia Louisa; *b* 1984

  2b *Rose Eleanor; *b* 1987

  3b *Portia Elizabeth; *b* 1990

(2) Elizabeth Alice Mary; *b* 20 June 1921; *m* 24 June 1942 Maj Hon Peter James Mowbray Rous, 27th Lancers, 4th s of 3rd Earl of Stradbroke (*qv*), and *d* 8 Feb 1968, leaving issue

1 Mary Laura; *b* 2 April 1869; *m* 25 May 1898 Viscount Encombe and *d* 3 Dec 1946, leaving issue (*see* ELDON, E)

2 Alice Mary Charlotte; *b* 3 March 1870; *m* 30 April 1890 Hon Bernard Constable Maxwell (*d* 27 Oct 1938), 4th son of 10th Lord Herries of Terregles (*qv*), and *d* 7 Aug 1958, leaving issue

3 Etheldreda Mary; *b* 22 Nov 1872; *m* 12 Jan 1903 Sir Francis Lindley, GCMG, CB, CBE (*d* 17 Aug 1950; *see* 1939 edn LINDLEY, B), and *d* 9 Oct 1949, leaving issue

4 Margaret Mary, OBE (1920), JP; *b* 25 June 1881; *m* 14 April 1910 Brig-Gen Archibald Stirling of Keir (*see* HERON-MAXWELL, Bt) and *d* 4 Aug 1972, leaving issue

5 Muriel Mary Rose; *b* 12 July 1884; a Sister of St Vincent de Paul

The 13th LORD's est surv son,

SIMON JOSEPH FRASER, **14th Lord (Fraser of) Lovat**, KT (1915), GCVO (1932), KCVO 1908, CVO 1903), KCMG (1919), CB (1902), DSO (1900), TD; *b* 25 Nov 1871; MA Oxford; ADC to HM GEORGE V, Col TA, Hon Maj-Gen 1931, Boer War with Lovat Scouts, which he raised (despatches twice) and cmded, Lt 1st Life Gds, V-Lt Inverness-shire, Mily memb TAA, WW I (despatches), Legn Hon, Order Crown Belgium; Rhodes Tstee, Parly U-Sec Dominion Affrs 1926–28, dir Forestry, Chm Forestry Commn 1919–27; *m* 15 Oct 1910 Hon Laura Lister (*d* 24 March 1965), 2nd dau of 4th and last Baron Ribblesdale (*see* 1925 edn), and *d* 18 Feb 1933, leaving:

1 SIMON CHRISTOPHER JOSEPH, **15th Lord**

2 Hugh Charles Patrick Joseph (Sir), MBE (1945), PC (1962); *b* 23 Jan 1918; *educ* Ampleforth and Balliol Coll Oxford; Maj Lovat Scouts (TA) WW II; MP (C) Stone 1945–50 and Stafford and Stone 1950–84, Parly U-Sec War, Fin Sec War Office 1958–60, Parly U-Sec Colonies 1960–62, Sec State Air July 1962–64, Min Def RAF April-Oct 1964, Chev Order Leopold II with Palm, Croix de Guerre Belgium with Palm; *m* 25 Sept 1956 (*divorce* 1977) Lady Antonia Pakenham (*see* LONGFORD, E), and *d* 1984, leaving:

(1) +Benjamin Hugh; *b* 28 March 1961; *m* 1991 *Hon Lucy Elspeth Roper-Curzon, 3rd dau of 20th Baron Teynham (*qv*), and has:

  1a +Thomas Roper; *b* 1992

  2a +William Melville; *b* 28 March 1995

  3a +Hugh Douglas; *b* 16 Aug 1996

  1a *Eliza Wedderburn; *b* 1993

(2) +Damian Stafford [Damian Fraser Esq, Esopo 55, Polanco, Mexico DF 11560]; *b* 26 Oct 1964; Mexican corresp *Financial Times*; *m* 14 Nov 1992 *Paloma Porraz del Amo, Curator Museum del Chop Mexico City, dau of Don Alfredo Porraz Ortiz de la Huerta, owner Gen Motors franchise Mexico, of Mexico City, and has:

  1a *Ana Sofia; *b* 20 Dec 1996

  2a *Oriana Paloma; *b* 14 May 1998

(3) +Orlando Gregory; *b* 9 May 1967

(1) *Rebecca Rose; *b* 4 May 1957; writer; *m* 1988 *Edward Hamilton Fitzgerald, yr s of Carroll Fitzgerald, and has:

  1a *Blanche Catherine; *b* 1990

  2a *Atlanta Rose; *b* 1992

  3a *Honor Antonia; *b* 3 Aug 1995

(2) *Flora Elizabeth; *b* 30 Oct 1958; *educ* St Paul's Girls' Sch and Wadham Coll Oxford; author: *Double Portrait, Beloved Emma, The Life of Emma Lady Hamilton* (1986), *The English Gentlewoman, The Diaries of Maud Berkeley* (ed), *Tamgar* (novel, 1990), *Queen Caroline* (1996); *m* 1st 1980 (*divorce* 1992) Robert J Powell-Jones, barrister, s of John Ernest Powell-Jones, CMG, and has:

  1a *Stella Elizabeth; *b* 1987

(2) (cont.) Mrs Flora Powell-Jones *m* 2nd 29 Jan 1997 *Peter, er s of Paul Soros, of New York, and n of the financier George Soros and by him has:

  1a *Simon Tivadar; *b* 10 March 1998

(3) *Natasha Antonia; *b* 10 March 1963; *m* 12 July 1997 *Jean-Pierre Cavassori, s of Giovanni Cavassori

1 Magdalen Mary Charlotte, OBE (1953); *b* 1 Aug 1913; Dep Pres Devon BRCS; *m* 10 April 1934 4th Earl of Eldon (*qv*) and *d* 27 Sept 1969, leaving issue

2 *Veronica Nell [The Hon Lady Maclean of Dunconnel, Strachur House, Strachur, Argyll PA27 8BX]; *b* 1920; *m* 1st 6 Aug 1940 Lt Alan Phipps, RN (*ka* Leros 16 Nov 1943, *see* NORMANBY, M); *m* 2nd 12 Jan 1946 Sir Fitzroy Maclean of Dunconnel, 1st Bt, KT CBE, MP (*qv*), of Strachur, and has further issue

3 Mary Diana Rose; *b* 15 April 1926; *d* unm 31 Aug 1940

The 14th LORD's est son,

SIMON (SHIMI) CHRISTOPHER JOSEPH FRASER, **15th Lord (Fraser of) Lovat**, DSO (1942), MC (1942), TD (1953), JP (Inverness-shire 1944), DL (1942); *b* 9 July 1911; *educ* Ampleforth and Magdalen Coll Oxford (MA); Lt Scots Gds 1932–37, Lt-Col 1942, Brig 1943, cmdg Lovat Scouts (TA), cmded also No 1 Special Serv Bde, WW II (wounded); Jt U-Sec For Affrs May–July 1945, memb Inverness CC, Chm: Shikar Club and Anglo-Scottish Cattle Co, Kt SMO Malta, Kt Cdr St Gregory with star 1982, CStJ, Hon LLD Nova Scotia 1952 and Simon Fraser U of BC, Legn Hon, Croix de Guerre, Liberation Cross Norway, Russian Order Suvorov, author *March Past* (memoirs 1978); *m* 10 Oct 1938 *Rosamund, only dau of Maj Sir Henry John Delves Broughton, 11th Bt (*qv*), and *d* 16 March 1995, having had:

　1 Simon Augustine, *Master of Lovat*; *b* 28 Aug 1939; *educ* Ampleforth; Lt Scots Gds; *m* 21 Feb 1972 *Virginia [The Hon Mrs Simon Fraser, Beaufort Lodge, Beauly, Inverness-shire], dau of David Grose, of Chelsea, and *d* 26 March 1994 while out hunting, leaving:

　　(1) SIMON FRASER, **16th and present Lord (Fraser of) Lovat**

　　(2) *Jack; *b* 1984

　　(1) *Violet; *b* 25 Oct 1972

　　(2) *Honor; *b* 1973; model

　2 +Kim Maurice; *b* 4 Jan 1946; *educ* Ampleforth; 2nd Lt Scots Gds; *m* 18 Oct 1975 *Joanna, 2nd dau of Maj Geoffrey Edward Ford North, MC (*see* WALSINGHAM, B), and has:

　　(1) +Thomas Oswald Mungo; *b* 25 Aug 1976

　　(2) +Joseph Oscar Edward; *b* 1981

　　(3) *Maximillian Alexander Kim; *b* 1981

　3 +Hugh Alastair Joseph; *b* 14 Nov 1947; *educ* Ampleforth and Ch Ch Oxford; *m* 1 May 1976 *Drusilla Jane Montgomerie, dau of Alastair Montgomerie, of Gilmilnscroft Mains, Sorn, Ayrshire, and has had:

　　(1) Cosmo Alexander Raoul; *b* and *d* 9 March 1977

　　(2) +Raoul Alastair Joseph; *b* 1980

　　(1) *Poppy Augusta; *b* 1979

　　(2) *Eloise Hermione; *b* 1986

　4 Andrew Roy Mathew; *b* 24 Feb 1952; *educ* Ampleforth and Ch Ch Oxford; *m* 1979 *Lady Charlotte Anne Greville [The Lady Charlotte Fraser, 1 Petyt Place, London SW3 5DJ], only dau of 8th Earl of (Brooke and) Warwick (*qv*), and was fatally gored by a buffalo in Tanzania 15 March 1994, leaving:

　　(1) *Daisy Rosamond; *b* 1985

　　(2) *Laura Alfreda; *b* 1987

　1 *Fiona Mary [The Hon Mrs Allen, PO Box 6655, Dubai, UAE]; *b* 6 July 1941; *m* 1982 *Robin Richard Allen

　2 *(Annabel) Térèse (Tessa) [The Hon Mrs Keswick, 6 Smith Square, London SW1P 3HT]; *b* 15 Oct 1942; political advsr to Chllr Exchequer 1988–95, Dir Centre Policy Studies 1995–; *m* 1st 14 Sept 1964 (*divorce* 1978) 14th Lord Reay (*qv*) and has issue; *m* 2nd 1985 *Henry Neville Lindley Keswick, est s of Sir William Keswick, of Glenkiln, Shawhead, Dumfries (*see* 1949 edn LINDLEY, B)

LOVELACE

LABOR · IPSE · VOLUPTAS ·

Arms: Sa. three spear heads arg., imbrued ppr., on a chief or as many battle-axes az. **Crest:** A cubit arm, vested az., charged with three erm. spots in fess or, cuffed arg., grasping in the hand ppr. the broken shaft of a spear in bend sinister sa., the butt arg. **Supporters:** On either side a mastiff dog regardant ppr., collared gu. **Motto:** *Labor ipse voluptas* ('Labour itself is a pleasure'). **Creations:** B. (GB) 29 May 1725, E. and V. (UK) 30 June 1838.

THE 5TH EARL OF LOVELACE, Viscount Ockham of Ockham, Co Surrey, and **Lord King, Baron of Ockham,** of Ockham, Co Surrey (Peter Axel William Locke King) [The Rt Hon The Earl of Lovelace, Torridon House, Torridon, Ross-shire IV22 2HA]; *b* 26 Nov 1951; *s* f 1964; *educ* privately; *m* 1st 1980 (*divorce* 1989) Kirsteen Olhrig, dau of Calum Kennedy, of Leethland Ho, Leethland, Renfrewshire; *m* 2nd 1994 *Kathleen Anne Smolders, of Melbourne, Australia

Lovelace, previous creation: Richard Lovelace, of Hurley, Berkshire, who was MP for Berkshire, Abingdon and Windsor, was created Baron Lovelace of Hurley in 1627. His son the 2nd Baron was a royalist in the Civil War and accordingly subjected to a huge fine, which was however reduced by degrees, and in 1655 imprisoned in the Tower of London. He married Lady Anne Wentworth, daughter of the Earl of Cleveland, who after his death became Baroness Wentworth in

her own right (*see* LYTTON, E). The 2nd Baron died owing £20,000 (over £900,000 in late-1990s terms), but his son the 3rd Baron managed to find enough money to lead a life of great luxury and profusion, though before his death he had to sell most of his property. The title passed on his death in 1693 to a cousin, son of a Governor of New York, whose own two sons inherited it thereafter. It expired with the death of the younger of these in 1736. The 3rd Baron's daughter meanwhile inherited her grandmother's Barony of Wentworth, which unlike that of Lovelace of Hurley could pass to female heirs, and was ancestress of Lady Byron, the poet's wife, and through her of the **1st Earl of Lovelace**'s wife, hence his choice of title when promoted to an earldom.

Lineage: JEROME KING, of Exeter; grocer; *m* Anne, dau of Peter Locke and cousin of the philosopher John Locke, and had:

PETER KING, **1st Lord King, Baron of Ockham**, Co Surrey (GB), so *cr* 29 May 1725, PC (1715); *b* 1669; *educ* Exeter GS; apprentice to his f, barrister Middle Temple 1698, MP (Whig) Beeralston 1701–14, Recorder: Glastonbury 1705, London 1708–15; ktd 1708, Ld Ch Justice 1714–25, Speaker Ho Lds 1725, Ld Chllr 1725–33; *m* Sept 1704 Anne (*d* 1 July 1767), dau of Richard Seys, of Boverton Court, Glam, and *d* 22 July 1734, having had, with two daus (Elizabeth; Anne; *d* unm):

　1 JOHN KING, **2nd Lord King, Baron of Ockham**; *bapt* 13 Jan 1705/6; Outranger Windsor Forest 1726–40, MP (Whig) Launceston 1727–34; *m* May 1726 Elizabeth (*d* 28 Jan 1732/3), dau of John Fry, of Yarty, Devon, and *dsp* 10 Feb 1740

　2 PETER KING, **3rd Lord King, Baron of Ockham**; *bapt* 13 March 1708/9; *d* unm 22 March 1754

　3 WILLIAM KING, **4th Lord King, Baron of Ockham**; *b* 15 April 1711; *d* unm 16 April 1767

　4 THOMAS KING, **5th Lord King, Baron of Ockham**; *b* 19 March 1712; *m* 17 Aug 1734 Catherina (*d* 3 June 1784), dau of John Troye, Judge Sovereign Cncl Brabant, and *d* 4 April 1779, leaving, with a yr s and two daus:

　　(1) PETER KING, **6th Lord King, Baron of Ockham**; *b* 6 Oct 1736; *educ* Eton and Trin Coll Cambridge; *m* 24 Nov 1774 Charlotte (*d* 25 Oct 1829), dau of Edward Tredcroft, of Horsham, and had:

　　　1a PETER, **7th Baron**

　　　2a William; *b* 24 Feb 1780; *d* 3 Dec 1798

　　　3a George; *b* 28 Jan 1783; *m* 30 Oct 1808 his cousin Charlotte (*d* 25 July 1853), dau of Nathaniel Tredcroft, of Horsham, and *d* 21 Dec 1885, having had, with two daus (*d* unm):

　　　　1b Frederick, of Fryern, Sussex, Capt 27th Foot; *b* 13 June 1815; *m* 25 April 1854 Charlotte Mary (*d* 14 Aug 1927), dau of James Maitland-Heriot (*see* LAUDERDALE, E), and *d* 3 Dec 1893, leaving:

　　　　　1c William Frederick, Capt RA; *b* 31 March 1855; *dsp* 1893

　　　　　2c Robert Maitland, of Fryern, Storrington, Sussex; *b* 15 Oct 1856; Lt RN; *d* 29 May 1926

　　　　　3c Henry Somerset; Brevet Col RE; *b* 21 Feb 1860; *m* 19 April 1893 Alice Mary Louisa (*d* 27 Oct 1935), dau of Augustus Pechell (*see* 1970 edn PECHELL, Bt), and *d* 30 Jan 1935, leaving:

　　　　　　1d William Augustus Henry; *b* 23 Feb 1894; *educ* Eton and Balliol Coll Oxford (MA 1921); Dep Keeper Br and Medieval Antiquities Br Museum; Lt 3rd Bn Roy Sussex Regt WW I, Lt RA WW II 1940–42, FO 1942–45; *m* 4 Aug 1926 Dorothy Elizabeth, only dau of Henry Campbell Booth, and *dsp* 23 Feb 1958

　　　　　　1d Ida Winifred; *d* 28 Nov 1907

　　　　　4c Edward George; BA Cambridge; *b* 19 Sept 1863; *d* unm 15 June 1940

　　　　　1c Charlotte Isabella; *b* 29 May 1858; *m* 20 May 1886 Cdr William Heriot Maitland-Dougall, DL, RN, and *d* 10 Oct 1953, leaving issue (*see* LAUDERDALE, E)

　　　　　2c Ethel Louisa; *b* 19 Sept 1863; *m* 18 Oct 1892 John Henry Baxter (*d* 30 March 1908), of Gilston, Fife, and *d* 11 Dec 1945, leaving issue

　　　　2b Henry, of Chithurst, Petersfield, Sussex, Capt RN; *b* 30 June 1819; *m* 1st 29 Nov 1850 Isabella Louisa (*d* 15 April 1853), dau of James Maitland-Heriot (*see* LAUDERDALE, E), and had:

　　　　　1c George Henry Maitland KING later MAITLAND KING, of Aubletts, Petersfield, Hants, JP Surrey; *b* 9 April 1853; *m* 17 Feb 1883 Maud Giffard (*d* 1957), dau of Rev F Tate, and *d* 4 May 1937, leaving:

　　　　　　1d Frank Jerome Maitland; Col RE; *b* 30 March 1884; *m* 1914 Elizabeth Agnes (*d* June 1944), dau of Charles Elliott, and *d* 24 June 1941

　　　　　　1d Mysie Caroline Maitland, OBE (1941), JP (Norfolk 1928); *b* 21 Jan 1892; *m* 12 June 1923 Cyril Grosvenor Sargent, only s of C G M Sargent, and had:

　　　　　　　1e *Hugh Peter [Hugh Sargent Esq, Friars Farm, Norning Throupe, Norfolk]; *b* 7 Sept 1925; *m* 1952 *Bridget Katherine Tucker and has:

　　　　　　　　1f *Michael Peter; *b* 10 May 1953

　　　　　　　1e *Caryl Maitland [Mrs Caryl Hinde, End Farm, Fritton Common, Long Stratton, Norfolk]; *b* 29 Dec 1927; *m* 1952 (*divorce* 19–) Capt John D'Oyley Hinde, Roy Ulster Rifles, and has:

　　　　　　　　1f *Margaret; *b* July 1954

　　　　2b (cont.) Capt Henry King *m* 2nd 11 Sept 1856 Charlotte (*d* 1890), dau of Rev George Palmer, and *d* 1891, having by her had:

　　　　　2c Arthur Montague; Maj Rifle Bde; *b* 21 Oct 1869; *m* 26 Feb 1897 Dorothy Lee (*d* 10 March 1953), dau of William Congreve, of Congreve and Burton (*see* 1940 edn CONGREVE, Bt), and was *ka* March 1915, leaving:

　　　　　　1d *Diana Charlotte; *m* 6 Sept 1934 Geoffrey Desmond Roper, s of Freeman Roper, and has:

　　　　　　　1e *Mark; *b* 27 June 1935; *educ* Bradfield and Magdalene Coll Cambridge; *m* 30 Sept 1967 *Elizabeth Dorothy, 2nd dau of Oliver Robin Bagot (*see* BAGOT, B), and has:

　　　　　　　　1f *Alice Katherine; *b* 1 Aug 1968

　　　　　　　　2f *A dau; *b* 9 Feb 1970

　　　　　　　2e *John Fitzgerald; *b* 27 Dec 1936; *educ* Bradfield and Magdalene Coll Cambridge

3e *Christopher; b 8 Dec 1939; educ Bradfield and Magdalene Coll Cambridge; m 29 Oct 1965 (divorce 1975), as her 1st husb, Hon Penelope Christina Plowden, yr dau of Baron Plowden (LP; qv)

1e *Charlotte Belinda; b 26 Aug 1941

The 6th LORD d 23 Nov 1793; his est son,

PETER KING, **7th Lord King, Baron of Ockham**; b 31 Aug 1775; educ Eton and Trin Coll Cambridge; m 26 May 1804 Lady Hester Fortescue (d 17 Dec 1873), dau of 1st Earl Fortescue (qv), and had:

1 WILLIAM, **1st Earl**

2 Peter John Locke, JP and DL, MP E Surrey 1847–74; b 25 Jan 1811; m 22 March 1836 Louisa Elizabeth (d 21 July 1884), dau of William Henry Hoare, of Mitcham Grove, Surrey, and d 12 Nov 1885, having had, with two other sons and five daus (all d unm):

(1) Hugh Fortescue Locke, JP (Surrey and Sussex), of Brooklands, Weybridge; barrister; b 7 Oct 1848; m 3 Jan 1884 Ethel (Dame Ethel King, DBE; d 5 Aug 1956 aged 92), dau of Sir Thomas Gore-Browne, KCMG, CB, and dsp 28 Jan 1926

(1) Hester; m 15 Feb 1843 Rev Sir George Cregan Craufurd, 3rd Bt (qv), and d 18 March 1848, leaving issue

(2) Anne Emily; d unm 1872

(3) Charlotte Louisa; m 7 Sept 1841 Rev Demetrius Calliphronas, Rector Walpole St Andrew, Norfolk, and d 13 Aug 1863, leaving issue

The 7th LORD d 4 June 1833; his est son,

WILLIAM KING later KING-NOEL (roy licence 29 Sept 1860), **1st Earl of Lovelace**, so cr 30 June 1838, as also VISCOUNT OCKHAM OF OCKHAM, Co Surrey (both UK); b 21 Feb 1805; educ Eton and Trin Coll Cambridge; Hon Col 3rd Bn Roy W Surrey Regt, Ld Lt and custos rotulorum Surrey 1840–93; m 1st 8 July 1835 Hon Augusta Byron (d 29 Nov 1852), mathematician and pioneer of computing, though her application of these talents to inventing a system for betting on horses proved disastrous, only child of 6th Baron Byron (qv), and had:

1 BYRON NOEL KING later KING-NOEL, 12th LORD (Baron) WENTWORTH (as which s maternal grandmother 16 May 1860), and (by courtesy) Viscount Ockham, RN; b 12 May 1836; placed in Royal Navy by his f but deserted, working his passage back to Britain, where he found employment in a shipyard, dropped his title and became an out-and-out radical; dvp unm 1 Sept 1862

2 RALPH GORDON NOEL KING later KING-NOEL (roy licence 29 Sept 1860) later still KING-MILBANKE (roy licence 6 Nov 1861), **2nd Earl of Lovelace** and 13th LORD (Baron) WENTWORTH (as which s bro 1862), DL Surrey; b 2 July 1839; m 1st 25 Aug 1869 Fanny (d 13 July 1878), 3rd dau of Rev George Heriot, of Fellow Hills, Berwicks, Vicar St Anne's Newcastle; m 2nd 30 Dec 1880 Mary Caroline (d 18 April 1941), est dau of Rt Hon James Stuart Wortley (see WHARNCLIFFE, E), and d 28 Aug 1906, having by his 1st w had surv issue:

(1) ADA MARY MILBANKE, BARONESS WENTWORTH (as which s f 1906) in her own right; b 26 Feb 1871; d unm 18 June 1917

1 ANNE ISABELLA NOEL, BARONESS WENTWORTH in her own right (as which s niece 18 June 1917); b 22 Sept 1837; m 8 June 1869 Wilfrid Scawen Blunt (d 10 Sept 1922), of Crabbett Park, Sussex, and d 15 Dec 1917, leaving issue (see LYTTON, E)

The **1st Earl** m 2nd 29 March 1865 Jane Crawford (d 27 Jan 1908), widow of Edward Jenkins, Bengal Civ Serv, and dau of John Jenkins, auctioneer, of Calcutta, and d 29 Dec 1893, having by her had:

3 LIONEL FORTESCUE NOEL-KING later KING (roy licence 5 May 1908), **3rd Earl of Lovelace**, DSO, JP and DL Surrey; b 16 Nov 1865; educ Eton and RMC Sandhurst; Maj Gen List and Northumberland Fus, Capt 9th Lancers; m 29 April 1895 Lady Edith Anson (d 8 Oct 1932), 4th dau of 2nd Earl of Lichfield (qv), and had:

(1) PETER MALCOLM, **4th Earl**

(1) Evelyn Catherine; b 3 March 1896; m 1st 17 June 1918 (divorce 1930) Maj-Gen Sir Miles William Arthur Peel Graham, KBE, CB, MC (d 8 Feb 1976), of Wiverton Hall, Bingham, Notts, yst s of Maj Henry Graham, 20th Hus, by Ellen, later Lady Askwith, 3rd dau of Archibald Peel, DL (see PEEL, E), and had:

1a Clyde Euan Miles; F/O RAF WW II; b 30 Oct 1920; m 25 May 1944 Daphne Marion (m 2nd 1 June 1948 Alexander David Stewart, est s of Lt-Col Walter Robert Stewart, DSO, MC; see GALLOWAY, E), only dau of Sir Reginald Bonsor, 2nd Bt (qv), and das Sept 1944

1a *Sheila Valerie; b 31 July 1919; m 14 July 1945 *Maj David Victor Bonsor, MC, yr s of Sir Reginald Bonsor, 2nd Bt (qv), and has issue

(1) (cont.) Mrs Evelyn Graham m 2nd 18 Dec 1930 Mark Patrick, MP (d 8 Jan 1942), Dip Serv, s of Colin Grant Patrick, and d 19 Oct 1974, leaving by him:

2a *John Evelyn Mark; b 30 Aug 1932; educ Eton

(2) Phyllis Edith; b 19 March 1897; m 6 Dec 1922 (divorce 1933) William Edward David Allen, OBE (d 18 Sept 1973), s of William Edward Allen, of Commonwood Ho, Chipperfield, Herts, and d 3 Dec 1947, leaving issue

(3) Rosemary Diana; b 6 Feb 1902; m 1st 28 April 1927 (divorce 1940) Alistair Monteith Gibb (k in a polo accident 29 July 1955), est s of Sir Alexander Gibb, CBE, CB; m 2nd 9 Oct 1941 Martin de Hosszu (d 24 Nov 1953), s of Alexander Hosszu, of Kolozsvar, Hungary, and dsp 15 Nov 1955

The 3rd EARL d 5 Oct 1929; his only son,

PETER MALCOLM KING, **4th Earl of Lovelace**; b 30 March 1905; educ Eton; m 1st 30 March 1939 Doris Evison (d 30 Sept 1940); m 2nd 18 June 1951 Manon Lis (d 1990), widow of Carl Fredrik Gustaf, Baron von Blixen-Finecke, and dau of Axel Sigurd Transö, of Copenhagen, and d 4 Dec 1964, leaving:

PETER AXEL WILLIAM LOCKE KING, **5th and present Earl of Lovelace**

LOVELL-DAVIS

Creation: B. (LP, UK) 1974.

THE BARON LOVELL-DAVIS, of Highgate, Greater London (Peter Lovell Lovell-Davis) [The Rt Hon The Lord Lovell-Davis, 80 North Rd, London N6 4AA.]; b 8 July 1924; educ Christ's Coll Finchley, King Edward VI Sch Stratford-on-Avon and Jesus Coll Oxford (MA); F/Lt RAF 1943–47; memb Press Gallery H of C 1951–71; Chm: Centl Press Features Ltd 1952–71, The Features Syndicate Ltd 1971–74, Colour Features Ltd, Lee Cooper Licensing Servs 1983–90, Perrifor Morrow & Assocs 1986–; md Davis & Harrison 1971–73; Ld-in-Waiting 1974–75; Parly U-Sec Energy 1975–76; Memb: Bd Cwlth Devpt Corp 1977–84, London Consortium 1978–88, Islington Health Authority 1982–85; V-Pres YHA 1977–; Tstee Academic Centre Whittington Hosp 1980–; m 1950 *Jean, dau of Peter Foster Graham, and has:

1 *Stephen Lovell; b 1955

1 *Catherine Ruth; b 1958

Lineage: WILLIAM LOVELL DAVIS; m Winifred Mary — and had:

PETER LOVELL, cr a **Baron**

LOWE

Arms: Erminois, on a bend engrailed cotised plain azure between two Stafford knots sable, three wolf heads erased or.
Crest: A demi-gryphon erminois, resting the sinister paw on a Stafford knot sable. **Motto:** Spero meliora ('I hope for better things').
Creation: Bt. (UK) 30 Jan 1918.

SIR THOMAS WILLIAM GORDON LOWE, 4TH BT, of Edgbaston, City of Birmingham [Sir Thomas Lowe Bt, 45 Limerston St, London SW10 0BL; 2 Gray's Inn Sq, London WC1R 5JH]; b 14 Aug 1963; s f 1986; educ Stowe, LSE (LLB) and Jesus Coll Cambridge (LLM); barrister; m 1996 *Mozhgan, dau of Hassan Asilzadeh

Lineage: WILLIAM LOWE, of Edgbaston; slr; m Emma (d 1892), dau of William Griffiths, of Moseley, Birmingham, and d Jan 1892, leaving an est s:

Sir Francis William Lowe, 1st Bt (UK), so cr 30 Jan 1918, PC (1929), JP (Birmingham and Warwicks), DL (Warwicks); b 8 Jan 1852; slr 1875, MP (C) Edgbaston 1898–1929, Jt Pres Birmingham U Assoc, Pres C Assoc, ktd 1905; m 12 Sept 1883 Mary (d 11 Sept 1945), only child of William Holden, of Scarborough, and had:

1 (FRANCIS) GORDON (Sir), **2nd Bt**

2 Arthur Holden; b 29 Jan 1886; m 28 March 1924 Evelyn (d 22 July 1949), dau of Alfred Philpot, of Bexhill-on-Sea, and d 22 Oct 1958, having had:

(1) Arthur Brian; b 28 Jan 1925; d 16 Aug 1939

(2) +John Evelyn [John Lowe Esq, Paillole-Basse, Cours, 47360 Praysass, France]; b 23 April 1928; educ Wellington and New Coll Oxford (MA); FSA, FRSA; Sgt Instr RAEC 1947–49; V&A Museum (Woodwork Dept) 1953–56, Dep Story Ed Pinewood Studios 1956–57, V&A Ceramics Dept 1957–61 (Assist to Dir 1961–64), Dir City Museum and Art Gallery Birmingham 1964–69, Dir Weald and Downland Open Air Museum 1969–74, Pncpl W Dean Coll Chichester 1972–78, lit ed Kansai Time Out 1983–88, Visitg Prof Br Cultural Studies Doshisha U Japan 1979–81, fndr ed Faber Furniture Series 1954–56, author: Thomas Chippendale (1955), Cream Coloured Earthenware (1958), Japanese Crafts (1983), Into Japan (1985), Into China (1986), Corsica (1988), A Surrealist Life — Edward James — Poet, Patron & Eccentric (1991), Glimpses of Kyoto Life (1996) and The Warden, A Portrait of John Sparrow (1998); m 1st 22 Sept 1956 (divorce 1981) Susan Helen Sanderson and has:

1a +Mark John; b 1957

2a +Dominic Simon; b 1961

1a *Judith Anne; b 1962

(2) (cont.) John Lowe m 2nd 1989 *Yukiko Nomura and by her has:

2a *Miki; b 19–

(1) *Jill Rosemary [Mrs Lal Singh Yadav, 170 Cambridge St, London SW1]; *b* 31 July 1937; *m* 1st 2 Dec 1957 Peter Gibbons; *m* 2nd 3 Dec 1997 Lal Singh Yadav, s of Ghanshyam Singh, of Zainabad, India, and by her 1st husb has:

  1a *Nicholas Arthur; *b* 1960

  1a *Caroline Evelyn; *b* 1958

  2a *Lucinda Mary; *b* 1961

  3a *Julia Anne; *b* 1963

  4a *Mary Jane; *b* 1967

3 John Claude Malcolm; *b* 21 Feb 1888; *educ* Uppingham and Oriel Coll Oxford (BA 1910); W/Cdr RAF (ret 1939), WW I in RNAS, R and E Dept Min Home Security 1939–45, Planning Div Home Off 1945; *m* 21 March 1912 Winifred Olsson (*d* 1968) and *d* 1970, having had:

  (1) +Anthony John [Anthony Lowe Esq, Unicorn Cottage, Wallcrouch, Wadhurst, Sussex]; *b* 12 Dec 1913; *m* 1 May 1948 *Mrs Rosemary Beatrice Richards, er dau of Capt A H Hollins, and has:

    1a +Charles; *b* 5 March 1949

    2a +Nicholas; *b* 5 March 1949; *m* 1974 *Rosemary Jane, dau of Maurice Henry Frank Charman, and has:

      1b *Elizabeth Jane; *b* 1980

      2b *Katherine Louise; *b* 1981

    3a +Timothy; *b* 20 Jan 1953

    1a *Joanna; *b* 1958

  (1) Pauline Muriel; *b* 18 Feb 1916; *m* 11 Oct 1943 Desmond Kirkness and had issue

  (2) *Elizabeth Sidney [Mrs Edward Richardson, 540 Banbury Rd, Oxford]; *b* 19 Oct 1929; *m* 20 July 1957 *Edward C Richardson and has:

    1a *Henry Edward Carleton; *b* 1961

    2a *Conan Sacheverell Carleton; *b* 1963

    1a *Emma; *b* 1958

    2a *Sophie; *b* 1959

1 Dorothy Mary; *b* 15 June 1893; *m* 24 July 1916 (*divorce* 1934) Maj Robert Harley Egerton Bennett, MC, Somerset LI (*d* 29 Sept 1970), and *d* 14 May 1969, having had:

  (1) Peter Egerton; *b* 1917; *educ* Malvern and RADA; actor and dir; *m* 1971 *Sheila [Mrs Peter Bennett, 39 Bedford Gdns, London W8 7EF], dau of Rev William Bramwell-Jones, and *d* 1989

Sir FRANCIS *d* 12 Nov 1929; his est son,

  Sir (Francis) Gordon Lowe, 2nd Bt; *b* 21 June 1884; *educ* Charterhouse and Clare Coll Cambridge (BA 1905); IARO WW I 1916–19 Mesopotamia (despatches); Proprietor Gordon Lowe Sports, internat lawn tennis–player and jnlst; *m* 1st 4 May 1914 (*divorce* 1926) Margaret Alice Manley (*d* 1961), dau of George Manley Sims; *m* 2nd 17 Nov 1926 Dorothy Honor, dau of Col Humphrey Stephen Woolrych, of Croxley, and *d* 1972, leaving:

Sir Francis Reginald Gordon Lowe, 3rd Bt; *b* 8 Feb 1931; *educ* Stowe and Clare Coll Cambridge (BA, LLB); barrister Middle Temple 1959; *m* 1st 18 Feb 1961 (*divorce* 1971) Francesca Cornelia, dau of Siegfried Steinkopf, of Berlin, and had:

  1 Sir THOMAS WILLIAM GORDON LOWE, **4th and present Bt**

  2 +CHRISTOPHER FRANCIS; *b* 25 Dec 1964; heir presumptive

Sir Francis *m* 2nd 22 Jan 1971 *Helen Suzanne [Helen Lady Lowe, Pelham House, 9 Bath Rd, Cowes, IoW PO31 7QN], yr dau of Sandys Macaskie and Mrs R Beresford-Peirse, and *d* 1986, having adopted:

  *William John; *b* Dec 1972

LOWRY

Creation: B. (LP, UK) 1979.

THE BARON LOWRY, of Crossgar, Co Down (Sir Robert Lynd Erskine Lowry, PC (NI 1971, GB 1974)) [The Rt Hon The Lord Lowry PC, White Hill, Crossgar, Co Down BT30 9HJ]; *b* 30 Jan 1919; *educ* Roy Belfast Academical Inst (Govr 1956–71) and Jesus Coll Cambridge (MA 1944, Hon Fell 1977); WW II: Roy Iniskillen Fus 1940, commissioned Roy Irish Fus 1941 (Hon Col 5th Bn 1967–71, 7th Bn 1969–71), 38th Irish Infantry Bde Tunisia 1942–43, Maj 1945; barrister NI 1947, Bencher 1955, QC NI 1956; Counsel to Attorney-Gen 1948–56; dep chm: Boundaries Commn NI 1964–71, Ld Chllr's Ctee on NI Supreme Court; High Court Judge NI 1964–71, ktd 1971, Ld Ch Justice NI 1971–88, Ld Appeal in Ordinary 1988–94; memb: Nat Equestrian Fedn 1969–78, Deptl Ctees on Charities Legal Aid and Registration of Title, Jt Law Enforcement Commn 1974, Judicial Ctee FEI 1991– (Chm 1995–); Chm: Richmond Lodge Sch 1956–77, Governing Bodies Assoc NI 1965, Interim Boundary Commn NI Constituencies 1967, Perm Boundary Commn 1969–71, SJAI Exec 1969–72, NI Constnl Convention 1975, Cncl Legal Educn NI 1976–79; Internat Showjumping Judge 1973, Official Internat Judge 1987–93; Hon Col 5th (Vol) Bn Roy Irish Rangers 1971–76; Hon Bencher Middle Temple 1973 and King's Inns Dublin 1973; Hon LLD Qeen's U Belfast 1980, Hon DLitt New U Ulster 1981; Visitor Ulster U 1989–; *m* 1st 1945 Mary Audrey (*d* 1987), dau of John Martin, of Belfast, and has:

  1 *Sheila Mary [The Hon Mrs Corrall, 5 Beaconsfield Rd, St Albans, Herts]; *b* 1950; *m* 1974 *Jonathan Austyn Corrall

  2 *Anne Lynd; *b* 1952; *m* 1980 *Neville McCoubrey, QGM, and has a s and two daus

  3 *Margaret Ina; *b* 1956

THE BARON LOWRY *m* 2nd 1994 *Mrs Barbara Adarnson Calvert, QC, dau of Albert Parker, CBE

Lineage: The Rt Hon Mr Justice WILLIAM LOWRY had:

ROBERT LYND ERSKINE, *cr* a **Baron**

LOWSON

Arms: Quarterly, 1st and 4th, per saltire arg. and az. a sea-lion sejant in chief and a fleur-de-lys sa. in base, in each flank a garb or (for LOWSON); 2nd, per chevron arg. and pean a chevronel invected on the upper side between two sealions sejant sa. in chief and another in base of the first (for FLOWERDEW); 3rd, erminois three catherine wheels, two and one, sa. within a bordure engrailed az., over all a chief gu., thereon a hill with lines of defence all ppr., in dexter chief a mullet arg. (for SCOTT). **Crests:** 1 A garb or, 2 A demi-man habited az., garnished gu., wreathed about the temples arg. and sa., holding in the right hand a sprig of two roses, one of the second, the other of the third, stalked and leaved ppr. **Mottoes:** 1 *Deus dat incrementum* ('God giveth increase'), 2 Flower dew.
Creation: Bt. (UK) 27 June 1951.

SIR IAN PATRICK LOWSON, 2ND BT, of Westlaws, Co Perth [Sir Ian Lowson Bt, 23 Flood St, London SW3 5ST]; *b* 4 Sept 1944; *s f* 1975; *educ* Eton and Duke U, NC, USA; OStJ; *m* 1979 *Mrs Tanya Theresa H Du Boulay, only dau of Raymond F A Judge, and has:

  1 +HENRY WILLIAM; *b* 10 Nov 1980

  1 *Katherine Louisa Patricia; *b* 16 July 1983

Lineage: ALEXANDER LOWSON, of Arbroath, Forfarshire; writer (legal practitioner); *m* Margaret, dau of Capt Andrew Small, of Dunernain, Perthshire, and *d* 8 March 1818, leaving:

WILLIAM LOWSON, DL Perthshire, of Balthayock; *b* 1814; *m* 1851 Helen (*d* 1896), dau of William Allan Flowerdew, of Gray Bank, Dundee, and had:

  1 William, JP Edinburgh; *b* 1852; *m* 1880 Elizabeth Steele, dau of James Cunningham, of Blackford Brae, Edinburgh, and *d* 4 May 1924

  2 Patrick Alexander; *b* 1857; drowned 1872

  3 JAMES GRAY FLOWERDEW

  1 Eliza; *m* 5 July 1876 Sir Mitchell Mitchell-Thomson, 1st Bt (*d* 16 Nov 1918), and *d* 17 May 1877, leaving issue (*see* SELSDON, B)

  2 Margaret; *m* 21 Sept 1876 Wilberforce Bryant, JP (*d* 3 Feb 1906), of Stoke Park, Bucks, and *d* 4 June 1923, leaving issue

  3 Helen; *m* 1888 Rev William Veitch, TD, MA (*d* 31 Dec 1937), of Edinburgh, and *d* 8 July 1951, leaving issue

  4 Anne Inches; *d* 1 March 1926

  5 Louise; *m* 1891 Arthur Anthony Macdonell (*d* 28 Dec 1930), of Lochgarry, Prof Sanskrit Oxford, of Lochgarry, and *d* 11 June 1932, having had issue

WILLIAM LOWSON *d* 1893; his 3rd son,

JAMES GRAY FLOWERDEW LOWSON, of Quarwood, Stow-on-the-Wold, Glos, formerly of Snitterfield Park, Warwicks, JP Warwicks; *b* 7 July 1860; *educ* Edinburgh and Heidelberg Us (PhD); CC Midlothian, Capt 9th Bn Roy Scots (the Roy Regt), memb Roy Co Archers, Life Govr U Coll Dundee, Govr Shakespeare Meml Theatre Stratford-on-Avon, 1st Dist Commr Boy Scouts Stratford-on-Avon; *m* 19 April 1890 Adelaide Louisa (*d* 21 May 1948), yr dau of Col Courtenay Harvey Saltren Scott, of Shankhill, Co Dublin, Bengal Staff Corps, and had:

  1 Courtenay Patrick Flowerdew; *b* 1897; Lt Rifle Bde attd RFC WW I; *ka* 3 Nov 1917

  2 DENYS COLQUHOUN FLOWERDEW (Sir), **1st Bt**

  1 Eleanor Margaret (Norma); *b* 1892; Offr First Aid Nursing Yeo WW I (despatches), Croix de Guerre with Bronze Star, Medaille de la Reine Elizabeth with Croix Rouge, WW II Cmdg 200 FANY/ATS Drivers attd Southern Cmd and Recruiting Offr Midlands (despatches); *m* 1920 Maj-Gen William Revell Revell Smith, CB, CBE, DSO, MC, AM, GOC Malta 1947–49, RHA (*d* 4 June 1956), and had:

    (1) *Peter Anning; *b* 1924; *m* 5 June 1961 *Jacine Marie-Therese Ravel, of Isère

    (1) *Lurleen Margaret; *b* 1922; *m* 19– *Capt J R Groves, RN

JAMES LOWSON *d* 16 Sept 1942; his 2nd son,

Sir Denys Colquhoun Flowerdew Lowson, 1st Bt (UK), so cr 27 June 1951, JP; b 22 Jan 1906; educ Winchester and Ch Ch Oxford (MA); barrister Inner Temple 1930, Sheriff City London 1939–40, memb Ct Common Cncl 1940, HM Lt City London 1942, Alderman 1942–73, FCIS, memb Roy Co Archers 1948, Hon Col 290 Field Regt RA City London (TA) 1950, High Steward Stratford-on-Avon 1952, Ld Mayor London 1950–51, memb LCC for Cities London and Westminster 1949–52, Master: Glaziers' 1947–48, Loriners' 1950–51, Gold and Silver Wyre Drawers' Cos 1951–52, Hon Memb Ct Assistants Haberdasher's Co 1951, Prime Warden Shipwrights' Co 1955–56, Pres CIS 1962–63, Fell Roy Philatelic Soc, Life Govr Roy Shakespeare Theatre Stratford-on-Avon, Ch Commr England 1948–62, Life Govr and Almoner St Bartholomew's Hosp 1948–67, Govr Bridewell, Bethlehem and Roy Hosps, V-Pres League Mercy, Hon Treas Princess Louise Hosp for Children 1938–48, V-Pres St Mary's Hosp Paddington to 1948, Life Govr U Coll Dundee, V-Pres 1940 and Dep Commr St John's Ambulance Bde Prince of Wales's No 1 Dist London 1945–66, Hon Freeman London Ontario, Nanaimo Vancouver, Granby Quebec, Halifax Nova Scotia and Lewes Sussex, KJStJ, Order Mercy, Defence and Coronation Medals, Grand Offr Orange Nassau Netherlands, Kt Cdr Order Dannebrog Denmark, Kt Cdr with Star Order St Olaf Norway and Order Lion Finland; m 17 July 1936 *Hon Ann Patricia Macpherson, OStJ [The Hon Lady Lowson, Oratory Cottage, 33 Ennismore Gdns Mews, London SW7 1HZ], yr dau of 1st Baron Strathcarron (qv), and d 10 Sept 1975, leaving:

1 Sir IAN PATRICK LOWSON, **2nd and present Bt**

1 *Gay Ann [The Rt Hon the Countess of Kinnoull, 15 Carlyle Sq, London SW3 6EX]; b 10 Jan 1938; m 1 June 1961 *15th Earl of Kinnoull (qv) and has issue

2 *Melanie Fiona Louisa [Mrs Charles Black, 1 Astell St, London SW3 3RT]; b 12 June 1940; m 17 Sept 1964 *Charles Archibald Adam Black, only s of Archibald Alan Gordon Black, of Crocks, Bentley, Hants, by Violet Rosamund Hyde-Villiers (see CLARENDON, E), and has:

  (1) *Adam Sebastian; b 25 Aug 1965

  (1) *Holly Patricia Louisa; b 27 Jan 1968

LOWTHER

Arms: Or six annulets, three, two and one sa., a crescent for difference. **Crest:** A dragon passant arg. **Motto:** *Magistratus indicat virum* ('The office displays the man'). **Creation:** Bt. (UK) 3 Nov 1824.

SIR CHARLES DOUGLAS LOWTHER, 6TH BT, of Swillington, Co York [Col Sir Charles Lowther Bt, Erbistock Hall, Wrexham, Clwyd LL13 0DE]; b 22 Jan 1946; s f 1982; educ Winchester; Lt QRIH 1966, served BAOR, ADC to CDS 1974–76, psc 1978–79, Staff Offr 1981, Col QRIH 1986–89, High Sheriff Clwyd 1997–98; memb Gentlemen at Arms 1997; m 1st 14 Feb 1969 (divorce 1975) Melanie Pensée FitzHerbert, dau of Roderick Christopher Musgrave by Mrs John Sholto Henry Douglas (see MORTON, E); m 2nd 1975 *(Florence) Rose, yst dau of Col Alexander James Henry Cramsie, OBE, of O'Harabrook, Ballymoney, Co Antrim, and by her has:

1 +PATRICK WILLIAM; b 15 July 1977

1 *Alice Rose; b 20 Sept 1979

Lineage: Sir John Lowther, 1st Bt (UK), so cr 3 Nov 1824; b April 1759 (bro of 1st Earl of Lonsdale, qv); MP; m 4 Sept 1790 Elizabeth, 2nd dau of 9th Earl of Westmorland (qv), and d 11 May 1844, having had:

1 **Sir John Henry Lowther, 2nd Bt**; MP Wigton and York; b 23 March 1793; d unm 23 June 1868

2 George William; b 17 Oct 1795; d 1805

3 CHARLES HUGH (Sir) **3rd Bt**

1 Elizabeth d unm 2 Oct 1863

Sir JOHN's yr bro,

Sir Charles Hugh Lowther, 3rd Bt; b 26 Sept 1803; m 10 May 1834 Isabella (d 2 July 1887), est dau of Rev Robert Morehead, DD, Rector Easington, and had:

1 George William; b 28 March 1837; m 29 Aug 1872 Mary Frances Alice (d 2 Dec 1921), est dau of Col Charles Bingham, DAG RA, and dvp 6 Feb 1890, leaving:

  (1) CHARLES BINGHAM (Sir), **4th Bt**

  (2) John George, CBE (1953) DSO (1919), MC, TD, JP, DL Northants; b 9 Aug 1885; educ Winchester; Col cmdg 4th Bn Northants Regt 1924–28 and 1939–40, cmded Northants Yeo 1920–24, Hon Col 1928–50, Capt 11th Hus,

Chm Little Bowden Bench 1943–60, served WW I (wounded, despatches twice) and WW II, chm Northants TA 1946–50 and Northants and Hunts 1950–52, Pres Kettering C Assoc, Jt MFH Pytchley 1923–40 and 1949–60, CA Northants; m 1 June 1911 Hon Lilah Charlotte Sarah White (d 1976), er dau of 3rd Baron Annaly (qv), and d 1977, having had:

1a George Hugh; b 17 Feb 1912; educ Eton; Capt Life Gds WW II, CC Northants 1948, Jt MFH Pytchley 1949–60 and 1963–66; m 10 Nov 1938 Sheila Rachel Isabel (Mit) (d 1980), dau of Maj Phipps Foster, and d 1976, leaving:

1b +James [James Lowther Esq, Holdenby House, Northampton]; b 27 Jan 1947; educ Eton; m 1987 *Karen H, dau of James Wallace, of Boston, USA, and has:

1c +James William Dolfin; b 1991

1c *Natasha Jane; b 1988

2c *A dau; b 1994

1b *Sheila Anne [Mrs John Paget, 40 Gloucester Walk, London W8]; b 5 Feb 1943; m 8 April 1964 *John Byng Oswald Carleton Paget and has:

1c *James Nicholas; b 1966

2c *William Byng; b 1968

3c *Rory Edward; b 1971

2b Georgina Jane; b 19 Jan 1944; d unm 18 Dec 1970

2a +John Luke (Sir), KCVO (1997), CBE 1983), JP (1984) [Sir John Lowther KCVO CBE JP, Nortoft Grange, Guilsborough, Northants NN6 8QB]; b 17 Nov 1923; educ Eton and Trin Coll Oxford (MA 1949); Ld Lt Northants 1984– (DL 1977–84), CC Northants 1970–84, High Sheriff 1971, Hon Col Roy Anglian Regt TA 1986–89; Capt KRRC 1942–47 (wounded); m 21 Feb 1952 *Jennifer Jane, er dau of Col John Henry Bevan CB, MC, TD, and has:

1b +Hugh William [Hugh Lowther Esq, Guilsborough Court, Guilsborough, Northants NN6 8QW]; b 12 Jan 1956; m 1985 *Hon Amanda Ursula Georgina Vivian, er dau of 4th Baron Swansea (qv), and has had:

1c Bertie; b and d 1989

1c *Flora Miriam; b 1988

2c *Georgia; b 1991

3c *Lucia; b 1994

1b *Sarah Charlotte Margaret; b 4 Jan 1954 (HRH PRINCESS MARGARET, COUNTESS OF SNOWDON stood sponsor); m 4 Feb 1977 *Harry M Henderson, yr s of John Henderson, of W Woodhay House, Newbury, Berks, and has:

1c *Harry Oliver; b 1979

1c *Katie Sarah; b 1981

2b *Lavinia Mary [Mrs Julian Tomkins, South Lodge Farm, Holdenby, Northampton NN6 8DL]; b 11 Nov 1958; m 1 Oct 1983 *Julian Tomkins, s of Sir Edward Tomkins, GCMG, CVO, of Winslow Hall, Winslow, Bucks, and has:

1c *Benjamin Henry; b 1988

2c *Geordie Edward; b 1991

1a *Bridget Elizabeth; b 23 May 1921; m 14 June 1947 *Robert Alistair Henderson, s of Robert Evelyn Henderson, of Sedgwick Park, Horsham, and has had:

1b *Robert David Charles [Robert Henderson Esq, Battle House, Goring-on-Thames, Oxon]; b 6 Nov 1948; educ Eton; m 1975 *Odette Anne, dau of Lloyd Llewellyn Andersson, of Johannesburg, and has:

1c *Camilla Elizabeth; b 1977

2c *Laura Catherine; b 1979

3c *Celia Anne; b 1982

2b James; b 3 Feb 1955; educ Eton; m 1978 *Susan Clare Evelyn (m 2nd 19— Charles Dingwall), dau of David Cuthbert Tudway Quilter (see QUILTER, Bt), and d 1991, leaving:

1c *Sophie Elizabeth; b 1979

2c *Emily Anne; b 1981

3c *Alice Beatrice; b 1985

1b *Emma Mary [Mrs Paul Irby, Garth House, Highclere, Berks RG20 9RE]; b 5 Nov 1950; m 1st 1971 (divorce 1978) Hugh Leopold Seymour (see HERTFORD, M); m 2nd 1979 (divorce 19–) J L David Aschan and has by him:

1c *Clare Louise; b 1979

2c *Eliza Beatrice; b 1981

1b (cont.) Mrs Emma Aschan m 3rd 29 Jan 1982 *Paul Anthony Irby and has issue by him (see BOSTON, B)

(1) Henrietta Isabella, MBE (1920), JP Salop; b 12 June 1873; m 21 May 1898 Maj Robert Lambert, DSO, and d 31 Jan 1950, leaving issue (see LAMBERT, Bt)

(2) Elizabeth Ida, MBE (1918); b 1 July 1875; m 28 Jan 1904 Col Sir Robert William Herbert Watkin Williams-Wynn, 9th Bt, KCB, DSO (qv), and had issue

(3) Helen Katharine; b 29 Dec 1876; m 5 Feb 1903 Sir Hugh Douglas Blackett, 8th Bt (qv), and d following an accident 10 Jan 1943, leaving issue

(4) Emma Alice, OBE (1918), JP; DGStJ, Hon Sec Lincs SSAFA 1939–47; b 1 May 1878; m 27 June 1903 Henry John Hope Barton (d 20 Sept 1951), of Saxby Hall, Lincs, s of John Hope Barton, of Saxby Hall and Stapleton Park, Yorks, and d 5 March 1964, leaving issue

2 James, PC, JP, DL, of Wilton Castle, Redcar, Yorks; b 1 Dec 1840; MA Cantab, barrister, CA N R Yorks, MP York 1865–80, N Lincs 1881–85 and Isle of Thanet 1888–1904, Parly Sec Poor Law Bd 1868, U-Sec Colonies 1874–78, Ch Sec Ireland 1878–80; d unm 12 Sept 1904

1 Frances Elizabeth; m 27 Jan 1869 William Gerard Lysley, JP (d 6 Oct 1887), of Pewsham, Wilts, er s of William John Lysley, JP, DL, MP, of Mimwood, Herts, and Pewsham, Wilts, and d 14 April 1918, leaving issue

Sir CHARLES d 6 Nov 1894; his gs,

Sir Charles Bingham Lowther, 4th Bt, CB (1948), DSO (1917), JP and DL Denbighs; High Sheriff Northants 1926; b 22 July 1880; educ Winchester and

RMC Sandhurst; Lt-Col Northants Yeo 1917–20, formerly 8th Hus, Boer War 1900–01 (Queen's medal, five clasps), WW I (despatches, Brevet); chm Denbighs TA&AFA, Croix de Guerre, Order Crown Italy, CStJ; *m* 1st 14 April 1909 Marjorie Noel (*d* 3 Dec 1925), dau of Thomas Fielden, MP, of Grimston, Yorks; *m* 2nd 3 Nov 1936 Ruth Kynaston (*d* 28 Feb 1995), dau of Charles Francis Kynaston Mainwaring, of Seven Sisters, Ellesmere, Salop, and by his 1st w had:

1 (WILLIAM) GUY (Sir), **5th Bt**

1 Doreen Margaret, JP (Flints); *b* 23 March 1910; *d* Oct 1996

Sir CHARLES *d* 22 Jan 1949; his only son,

Sir (William) Guy Lowther, 5th Bt, OBE (1952) DL (Denbighs 1969), High Sheriff 1959; *b* 9 Oct 1912; *educ* Winchester and RMC Sandhurst; Lt Col 8th Hus, cmdg 1951–54, Palestine 1936 (despatches), WW II (POW), Korea 1950–51 (despatches), memb Gentlemen-at-Arms 1962–82, OSt J; *m* 18 July 1939 *Grania Emerald Suzanne [Grania Lady Lowther, Cefyndd Farm, Erbistock, Clwyd], yst dau of Maj Archibald James Hamilton Douglas Campbell, of Blythswood, OBE, and *d* 7 May 1982 leaving:

1 Sir CHARLES DOUGLAS LOWTHER, **6th and present Bt**

1 *Grizelda Leonora; *b* 14 Nov 1948; *m* 19 April 1968 *Capt Timothy Michael Bell, Scots Gds, est s of Col Michael Allgood Bell, of Staward Manor, Langley-on-Tyne, Northumberland, and has:

(1) *Matthew Guy; *b* 1974

(1) *Katherine Leonora; *b* 18 Jan 1971

LUCAN

Arms: Az. a bend cotised between six crosses patée or. **Crest:** On a mount vert a falcon rising, wings expanded ppr., armed, membered and belled or. **Supporters:** Two wolves az., plain collared and chained or. **Motto:** *Spes mea Christus* ('Christ is my hope'). **Creations:** Bt. (NS) 7 June 1634, B. (I) 24 July 1776 (Lucan of Castlebar), E. (I) 1 Oct 1795 (Lucan), B. (UK) 26 June 1934 (Bingham).

THE 7TH EARL OF LUCAN, Baron Lucan of Castlebar, Baron Bingham, of Melcombe Bingham, Co Dorset, and a **Baronet** (Sir Richard John Bingham, Bt); *b* 18 Dec 1934; *s* f 1964; *educ* Eton; Lt Coldstream Gds (Res); disappeared 7 Nov 1974; wanted for questioning by the police in connection with the murder of his children's nanny Sandra Rivett but has not been legally declared dead, though his w was reported in spring 1998 to be about to try and get him declared dead; *m* 28 Nov 1963 *Veronica, dau of Maj Charles Moorehouse Duncan, MC, and has:

1 +GEORGE CHARLES, *Lord Bingham*; *b* 21 Sept 1967; *educ* Eton and Trin Hall Cambridge; assist manager capital mkts Kleinwort Benson

1 *Frances; *b* 24 Oct 1964; *educ* St Swithun's Winchester and Bristol U; slr

2 *Camilla; *b* 30 June 1970; *educ* St Swithun's Winchester and Balliol Coll Oxford; barrister

Lucan, titular creation: Patrick Sarsfield, younger brother of the William Sarsfield whose granddaughter married **Sir John Bingham, 5th Bt** (*see* below), was son of another Patrick Sarsfield, of Lucan, Co Dublin, by Anne, dau of Rory O'More, the brains behind the 1641 Irish Uprising. A professional soldier under CHARLES II, Sarsfield recruited cavalry to fight for JAMES II in Ireland as that King's rule was crumbling in England. He played a leading part in the first Siege of Limerick in 1690 and in covering the withdrawal of JAMES's men at their defeat by the Williamites of Aughrim 12 July 1691. JAMES accordingly created him in January 1690/1 Earl of Lucan in the Irish peerage. By now the King had been deposed not just in England but in Ireland too, so that in effect the creation was a titular one. Nevertheless, Sarsfield in his capacity as Commander-in-Chief of the Jacobite forces in Ireland so skilfully handled the surrender of Limerick in October 1691, following its second Siege, that he extracted remarkably generous terms for the defeated party. In the articles of capitulation he is referred to as Lord Lucan, an implicit recognition by both sides of his creation. He then moved to France, where he commanded the second troop of Irish Life Guards in LOUIS XIV's service. He was killed in action leading a division of the French army at the Battle of Landen 29 July 1693. His son, who served in the Spanish forces, died unmarried in 1719, when the Earldom expired.

Lineage: RALPH de BINGHAM, of Sutton Bingham, Somerset (descended from Sir John de Bingham, living *temp* HENRY I); had, with a yr s (Robert, Bp Salisbury; *d* 3 Nov 1246):

RALPH de BINGHAM, of Sutton Bingham; had, with other issue:

ROBERT BINGHAM; held lands in Manor of W Stafford 1246; *m* Lucy, dau and heiress of Robert Turberville, and had:

ROBERT BINGHAM, of Melcombe Bingham, Dorset; *m* Eleanor, dau of Sir Andrew Wake, and *d* 1307, having had:

RICHARD BINGHAM, of Melcombe; *m* Pernell, dau of Sir Galfrid Warnhill, and *d* 1317, having had:

ROBERT BINGHAM, of Melcombe; *b c* 1295; *m* Catherine, dau of Sir Thomas Aston, and had:

RICHARD BINGHAM, of Melcombe; *m* Catherine, dau of Thomas Silvester, and *d* by 1404, having had:

ROBERT BINGHAM, of Melcombe; *m* Margaret, dau of John Frampton, of Moreton, Dorset, and *d* 1431, having had, with an er s (Sir John, *dsp*):

RICHARD BINGHAM, of Melcombe; *d* 1480, having by his 1st w Margaret, dau of John Basket, of Dawlish, had:

ROBERT BINGHAM, of Melcombe; *m* Joan, dau of John de la Lynde, of Winterborne, Clenston, Dorset, and *d* 1524, having had, with other issue:

ROBERT BINGHAM, of Melcombe; *m* Alice, dau of Thomas Coker, of Mapowder, and *d* 1561, having had, with other issue:

1 Robert, of Melcombe; *m* Joan, dau of Robert Williams (*see* WILLIAMS, Bt, of Bridehead), and *d* 1593, leaving issue

2 Richard (Sir), of Connaught; Marshal of Ireland, Govr Leinster; *b c* 1528; *m* 11 Jan 1558 Sarah, dau of John Heigham, of Sifford's Hall, Suffolk, and *d* 19 Jan 1598/9, leaving an only dau:

(1) Martha; *m* 15 July 1612 Nicholas Bacon, s of Edward Bacon, of Shrubland (*see* BACON, Bt)

3 GEORGE (Sir)

4 John (Sir); served Ireland with his bro; *m* Alice Mills and *dsp*

ROBERT BINGHAM's 3rd son,

Sir GEORGE BINGHAM, of Ballymot, Co Sligo; ktd by 23 Dec 1588, Mil Govr Co Sligo 1596; *m* 1569 Cicely, dau of Robert Martin, of Atherhampton, Dorset, and was *bur* 27 Sept 1599, having had, with a yr s (John, had issue; see CLANMORRIS, B):

Sir Henry Bingham, 1st Bt (NS), so *cr* 7 June 1634, of Castlebar, Co Mayo; *b* 1573; MP Co Mayo 1634–35 and 1639–48, Sheriff Co Galway 1607 and Co Mayo 1639; *m* Catherine (*d* between 31 Oct 1673 and 21 July 1674), dau of John Byrne, of Ballinclough, and *d* by 27 Jan 1658/9, having had:

1 **Sir George Bingham, 2nd Bt**; MP Castlebar 1661–66, Sheriff Co Mayo 1662–63 and 1678–79, custos rotulorum Co Mayo 1663; *m* 1st — and had:

(1) **Sir Henry Bingham, 3rd Bt**; MP Co Mayo 1692–99 and 1703–14, High Sheriff 1684–85 and 1694, custos rotulorum 1682; *m* 1st (licence 3 Feb 1677/8) Jane, dau of Sir James Cuffe, ancestor of 1st and last Baron Tyrawley of Ballinrobe; *m* 2nd Lettice (*d* by 1728), dau of Charles Bingham, of Newbrook, Co Mayo, and *dspm* 1714

1 (cont.) **Sir George** *m* 2nd 1 June 1661 Anne Pargiter (*dsp*); *m* 3rd (by licence 5 Dec 1661) Rebecca, dau of Sir William Middleton, Bt, and *d* by 1 June 1682, leaving by her:

(2) **Sir George Bingham, 4th Bt**; *m* 1st 1688 Mary Scott and had three sons (including two yr ones, Henry; George); *m* 2nd Phoebe Hawkins and had another s (George); his est s by his 1st w:

1a **Sir John Bingham, 5th Bt**; Govr and MP Co Mayo, High Sheriff 1721; *b* 1696; *m* 1730 Anne (*b* 8 Feb 1697/8; *d* Feb 1761), dau of Agmondesham Vesey, of Lucan, Co Dublin (*d* 23 March 1738), by Charlotte (*b c* 1673; *m* 26 Feb 1696/7; *d* 7 Oct 1699), dau and heiress of William Sarsfield, of Lucan (*d* 13 April 1675) by his w Mary (*b* 1655/6, illegitimate dau of CHARLES II by Lucy Walters (*see* also BUCCLEUCH and QUEENSBERRY, D); *m* 1670; *d* April 1693), and *d* 21 Sept 1749, leaving, with other issue:

1b **Sir John Bingham, 6th Bt**, MP Mayo 1740–50; *b* 1730; *d* unm 10 Oct 1752

2b **Sir Charles Bingham, 7th Bt**, and **1st Earl of Lucan**, so *cr* 1 Oct 1795, as also earlier 24 July 1776 BARON LUCAN OF CASTLEBAR, Co Mayo (both I); *b* 22 Sept 1735; Sheriff Co Mayo 1756, MP (I Parl) Co Mayo 1761–76 and (GB Parl) (Whig) Northampton 1782–84; *m* 25 Aug 1760 Margaret (*d* 27 Feb 1814), dau and coheir of James Smith, MP, of Canons Leigh, Devon, and St Audries, Somerset, and had, with two other daus:

1c RICHARD, **2nd Earl**

1c Lavinia; *m* 6 March 1781 2nd Earl Spencer (*qv*) and *d* 8 June 1831, leaving issue

2c Margaret; *m* Thomas Lindsey, of Hollymount, and had an est dau:

1d Margaret Lavinia; *m* 1816 Rev John Grey Porter (*see* DUNLEATH, B, section **Seat**) and had issue

The 1st EARL *d* 29 March 1799; his son,

RICHARD BINGHAM, **2nd Earl of Lucan**; *b* 4 Dec 1764; *educ* Westminster and Ch Ch Oxford; MP (Whig) St Albans 1790–1800, rep I peer 1801–39; *m* 26 May 1794 (separated 1804) Elizabeth (*d* 24 March 1819), 3rd dau and coheir of Henry Belasyse, 3rd and last Earl of Fauconberg of Newborough and divorced w of 12th Duke of Norfolk (*qv*), and had:

1 GEORGE CHARLES, **3rd Earl**

2 Richard Camden; Sec Legation Munich, Turin, Lisbon and Naples, Chargé d'Affaires Venezuela 1852–58; *b* 2 May 1801; *m* 11 Dec 1848 Maria, dau of Charles Thomas, and *dsp* 23 Jan 1872

1 Elizabeth; *m* 27 May 1815 George Granville Harcourt (*see* VERNON, B) and *d* 9 Sept 1838, leaving issue

2 Anne; *m* 18 July 1816 Alexander Murray, MP (*d* 15 July 1845), of Broughton, and *d* 28 Oct 1850

3 Louisa; *m* 22 Aug 1817 9th Earl of Wemyss (*qv*) and *d* 16 April 1882, leaving issue

4 Georgiana; *m* 15 June 1821 Charles Nevill, of Nevill Holt (*d* 18 Oct 1848), and *d* 1 July 1849, leaving issue

The 2nd EARL *d* 30 June 1839; his er son,

GEORGE CHARLES BINGHAM, **3rd Earl of Lucan**, GCB (1869, KCB 1855); *b* 16 April 1800; *educ* Westminster; Ensign 6th Foot 1816, Lt 8th Foot Gds 1818, Capt 1st Life Gds 1822, Maj 1825, Lt-Col 1826, Maj-Gen 1851, cmdg a division Crimean War 1854 (wounded Balaclava, Crimean Medal and four clasps), Lt Gen 1858, Gen 1865, FM 1887; MP (Tory) Co Mayo 1826–30, rep peer 1840–88, Col: 8th Hus 1855–65, 1st Life Gds 1865–88, Chev Legn Hon, Kt 1st Cl Medjidie, Kt St Anne of Russia 2nd Cl (having had a staff appointment with the Russian Army in Bulgaria back in 1826), Lt Co Mayo 1845–88, Gold Stick in Waiting 1886; *m* 21 Feb 1829 Anne (*d* 2 April 1877), dau of 6th Earl of Cardigan (*see* AILESBURY, M), and had, with two other daus:

1 GEORGE, **4th Earl**

2 Richard; R-Adml; *b* 6 Jan 1847; *m* 1st 26 Sept 1877 Mary Elizabeth (*d* 23 Feb 1908), yst dau of Edward Henry Cole, of Stoke Lyne, Oxon; *m* 2nd 30 April 1914 Ida (*d* 22 Nov 1925), dau of Charles Galton, ICS, and *d* 12 Nov 1924, having by his 1st w had:

(1) Violet Mary; *b* 26 March 1880; *m* 29 Nov 1911 Maj Edward John Lake Baylay, DSO, RHA, s of Col C E Baylay, and *d* 29 Aug 1931, leaving issue

(2) Edith Lavinia; *b* 27 July 1881; *m* 30 April 1913 Brig-Gen Duncan Alwyn Macfarlane, CB, DSO, DL (*d* April 1941), of Dunain Park, Inverness, s of Rev James Duncan Macfarlane, and *d* 2 Dec 1960, leaving issue

1 Augusta; *m* 10 Sept 1853 1st Baron Alington (*see* 1940 edn) and *d* 3 July 1888, leaving issue

2 Lavinia; *m* 10 April 1856 2nd Viscount Hardinge (*qv*) and *d* 15 Sept 1864, leaving issue

The 3rd EARL *d* 10 Nov 1888; his er son,

GEORGE BINGHAM, **4th Earl of Lucan**, KP (1898), JP (Middx); *b* 8 May 1830; *educ* Rugby; Lt-Col Coldstream Gds 1851–59, ADC to his f Crimean War, Kt Legn Hon and Medjidie 5th Cl 1857, MP (C) Co Mayo 1865–74, rep I peer 1889–1914, V-Adml Coastguard 1889, Lt and custos rotulorum Co Mayo 1901, CA Middx; *m* 17 Nov 1859 Lady Cecilia Catherine (*d* 5 Oct 1910), yst dau of 5th Duke of Richmond and Gordon (*qv*), and had:

1 GEORGE CHARLES, **5th Earl**

2 Cecil Edward (Sir), GCVO, KCMG, CB; *b* 7 Dec 1861; Maj-Gen, Col 1st Life Gds, Col 2nd Life Gds 1919, cmdg 4th Cavalry Bde 1914, 1st Cav Div 1915, cmdg Cavalry Corps 1915, Sr ADC to HRH THE DUKE OF CONNAUGHT Indian Tour 1903; Boer War 1899–1901 and WW I (despatches, promotion, Cdr Legn Hon); *m* 1st 28 June 1884 Rose Ellinor (*d* 18 Sept 1908), dau of James Alexander Guthrie, of Craigie, Forfar; *m* 2nd 3 Feb 1911 Alys Elizabeth (*d* 1 Nov 1953), dau of Col Henry Montgomery Carr, of Kentucky, and widow of Samuel Sloane Chauncey, of New York, and *d* 31 May 1934, having by his 1st w had:

(1) Ralph Charles, CVO (1953), DSO (1917); *b* 15 April 1885; *educ* Eton; Lt-Col Res Offrs Coldstream Gds, Lt-Col 4th City London Regt (TA), Lt 1st Life Gds Instruction MGC 1916 WW I (despatches, three times, Italian silver medal Mil Valour), Exon Yeomen Gd, Adj and Clerk Cheque 1950, Sec OStJ 1926–37; *m* 16 June 1913 Dorothy Louisa (*d* 12 Feb 1967), er dau of Edward Roger Murray Pratt (*see* DUNLEATH, B), and *d* 4 Nov 1977, leaving:

1a +(John) Nigel [Nigel Bingham Esq, Stone House, Brimpton, Berks RG7 4TD]; *b* 26 Aug 1915; *educ* Eton and Trin Coll Cambridge (BA 1936); Capt Coldstream Gds SR Offrs WW II (wounded); *m* 26 June 1943 *Elizabeth Rosamund, yr dau of Maj Sir Algernon Thomas Peyton, 7th Bt (*qv*), and has:

1b *Lavinia Frances [Mrs Robert Barbour, Baglake Farm, Litton Cheney, Dorset DT2 9AD]; *b* 14 Jan 1949; *m* 1975 *Robert David Barbour, only s of Brig David Charles Barbour, OBE, of Shortheath House, Sulhamstead, Berks, and has:

1c *Henry George; *b* 1979

1c *Alexandra Frances; *b* 1981

2b *Veronica Annabel [Mrs Raymond Williams, Stone House, Brimpton Berks RG7 4TD]; *b* 26 July 1952; *m* 1988 *Raymond John Williams and has:

1c *Anna Grace Joan; *b* 1994

1a *Rachel Cecilia; WW II as 3rd Offr WRNS; *b* 9 April 1917; *m* 26 Oct 1945 *Baron Alport (*qv*) and has issue

(2) David Cecil; Lt Coldstream Gds; *b* 18 March 1887; *m* 12 Feb 1912 Lady Rosabelle Millicent St Clair-Erskine (*m* 2nd 20 May 1919 Lt-Col John Charles Brand; *see* HAMPDEN, V), only dau of 5th Earl of Rosslyn (*qv*), and was *ka* 14 Sept 1914, leaving:

1a Rose; *b* 14 March 1913; *m* 1st 11 July 1933 (*divorce* 1938) 7th Earl of (Brooke and) Warwick (*qv*) and had issue; *m* 2nd 8 Sept 1938 P/O William M L Fiske III, RAF (*d* from injuries recd in action 17 Aug 1940), s of W M L Fiske, of New York; *m* 3rd 17 March 1945 (*divorce* 1950) Sir John Charles Arthur Digby Lawson 3rd Bt (*qv*); *m* 4th 1951 (*divorce*) Theodore Sheldon Bassett and *d* 29 Dec 1972

(1) Cecilia Mary Lavinia; *b* 19 April 1893; *m* 24 April 1915 Col Frederick George Beaumont-Nesbitt, CVO, MC, Gren Gds (*d* 14 Dec 1971), er s of Edward John Beaumont-Nesbitt, DL, of Penton Lodge, Andover, and *d* 26 Aug 1920, leaving issue

3 Francis Richard (Sir), KCB, KCMG, JP (Bucks 1932); *b* 5 July 1863; Maj-Gen RA, ADC to C-in-C Madras 1893–95 and 1896–98, Ch Instr Sch of Gunnery 1911–13, Assist Dir War Office 1913–15, Dep Dir War Office 1915–16, memb Cncl Min Munitions 1916–19, Ch Br Section Mil Inter-Allied Control Commn Germany 1919–24, Lt-Govr Jersey 1924–29, Col Cmdt RA 1931–33, Hon Col Roy Militia Jersey 1925, Cdr Order Crown Belgium and Italy and Legn Hon and St Stanislas Russia 1st Cl; *m* 10 June 1896 Kathleen (*d* 18 Sept 1963), dau of Gen Sir Charles Mansfield Clarke, 3rd Bt, of Dunham Lodge (*qv*), and *d* 5 Nov 1935, leaving:

(1) Francis Humphrey, OBE (1953); *b* 3 July 1899; Colonial CS, Lt RA WW I, WW II in Somaliland and Abyssinia with Gold Coast Regt and as Maj E Afri-

can Artillery; *m* 15 Nov 1927 Evangeline Marguerite Gladys, yst dau of Col William Henry Wilson Elliot, DSO, IMS

4 Alexander Frederic; *b* 3 Aug 1864; *d* unm 26 May 1909

5 Albert Edward; *b* 30 June 1866 (HM EDWARD VII stood sponsor); *m* 3 Sept 1892 Christine Graham (*d* 14 April 1966 aged 101), dau of Archibald Smith, and *dsp* 6 Nov 1941

6 Lionel Ernest; *b* 4 Nov 1876; Capt RFA WWI (wounded twice); *d* 26 July 1927

1 Rosalind Cecilia Caroline, DBE (1936); *b* 26 Feb 1869; Hon LLD Queen's U Belfast (1944), Hon Associate OStJ, freedom of Belfast 1935; *m* 1 Nov 1894 3rd Duke of Abercorn (*qv*) and *d* 18 Jan 1958, leaving issue

The 4th EARL *d* 5 June 1914; his est son,

GEORGE CHARLES BINGHAM, **5th Earl of Lucan**, GCVO (1939), KBE (1920), CB (1919), TD (1920), PC (1938), JP and DL Middlesex, DL Co Mayo; *b* 13 Dec 1860; *educ* Harrow and RMC Sandhurst; MP Chertsey 1904–06, Chm City London TA&AFA 1914–41, Capt Rifle Bde, Col TAR, Hon Col 5th Bn Lond Regt, Hon Lond Rifle Bde 1923–46, ADC to HM GEORGE V 1920–28, Hon Brig-Gen 1917, Brig-Gen cmdg 1st Lond Inf Bde, Ld-in-Waiting 1920–Jan 1924 and Dec 1924–29, Capt Gentlemen-at-Arms Jan-Jun 1929 and 1931–40, served Bechuanaland Expdn 1884–85 and WW I (despatches), Order St Stanislas Russia 2nd Cl, Order Nile 3rd Cl, rep I peer, *cr* 26 June 1934 BARON BINGHAM, of Melcombe Bingham, Co Dorset (UK); *m* 30 Nov 1896 Violet Sylvia Blanche, OBE (1920) (*d* 31 Jan 1972 aged 94), only dau of Joseph Spender Clay, of Ford Manor, Surrey, and had:

1 GEORGE CHARLES PATRICK, **6th Earl**

2 John Edward, TD; Maj AAC TAR, WW II in Derbys Yeo, N Africa and SAS; *b* 29 Feb 1904; *educ* Eton and Trin Coll Cambridge (BA 1925); *m* 7 Nov 1942 *Dorothea [The Hon Mrs John Bingham, Nicholls, Udimore, Rye, E Sussex], yr dau of Rev John Kyrle Chatfield, and *d* 1992, leaving:

(1) +Nicholas Charles [Nicholas Bingham Esq, Court Lodge Oast, Udimore, E Sussex TN31 6BB]; *b* 9 Aug 1943; *educ* Eton and INSEAD (MBA); *m* 30 March 1976 *Catherine Violet, er dau of Maj Nigel Stuart Hunter, of S Kensington, and has:

1a +Charles Nigel; *b* 1979

1a *Alexandra Romina; *b* 31 March 1977

(2) +Peter John [Peter Bingham Esq, Lambsland Farm, Rolvenden, Kent TN17 4PX]; *b* 10 June 1945; *educ* Eton and RNC Dartmouth; Lt RN; *m* 5 Nov 1971 *Penelope Ann, only dau of Dr E C Herten-Greaven, of Buenos Aires, and has:

1a +Philip Charles; *b* 1974

2a +Richard Patrick; *b* 1978

(3) +David Julian [David Bingham Esq, 31 Crescent Grove, London SW4 7AF]; *b* 9 May 1951; *educ* Eton and Trinity Coll Cambridge (MA); FRICS

1 Barbara Violet; *b* 17 Aug 1902; *m* 18 Jan 1927 Col John Henry Bevan, CB, MC, TD, yst s of David Augustus Bevan, of Rowney Priory, Ware Herts, and *d* 17 Dec 1963, leaving issue

2 Margaret Diana, GBE (1954), JP (Berks 1956); *b* 16 Sept 1905; *m* 14 Oct 1931 1st Earl Alexander of Tunis (*qv*) and *d* 17 Aug 1977, leaving issue

The 5th EARL *d* 20 April 1949; his er son,

GEORGE CHARLES PATRICK BINGHAM, **6th Earl of Lucan**, MC (1918); *b* 24 Nov 1898 (HRH THE DUKE OF CONNAUGHT stood sponsor); *educ* Eton and RMC Sandhurst; Col Coldstream Gds WW I (wounded), ADC to Govr-Gen S Africa 1924–26, Bde Maj Br Troops Sudan 1932–34 and 11th Inf Bde 1934–36, DAA&QMG London Dist 1937–40, cmded 1st Bn 1940–42, Dep Dir Ground Defence Air Min 1942–45, Capt Yeomen Gd 1950–51, Parly U-Sec CRO June–Oct 1951, Opposition Ch Whip Ho Lds 1954–64; *m* 23 Dec 1929 Kaitlin Elizabeth Anne, only child of Capt Hon Edward Stanley Dawson, RN, 2nd s of 1st Earl of Dartrey (*see* 1933 edn), and *d* 21 Jan 1964, leaving:

1 RICHARD JOHN BINGHAM, **7th and present Earl of Lucan**

2 +Hugh [The Hon Hugh Bingham, 6 Gledhow Gdns, London SW5]; *b* 24 April 1939; *educ* Charterhouse and Hertford Coll Oxford

1 *Jane [The Lady Jane Griffin, 444 East 66th St, New York, NY 10021, USA]; *b* 13 Oct 1932; *educ* Badminton Sch Bristol and Roy Free Hosp Medical Sch (MB, BS); *m* 18 June 1960 *James Driscoll Griffin, est s of Edwin G Griffin, of Evanston, Ill., and has:

(1) *Nicholas Driscoll; *b* 17 Oct 1962

(2) *John Christopher; *b* 15 Dec 1963

(3) *Benjamin Alexander Dawson; *b* 2 Nov 1966

(1) *Kaitilin Bingham; *b* 22 June 1961

2 *Sarah Kaitilin [The Lady Sarah Gibbs, The Vicarage, Guilsborough, Northampton NN6 8PU]; *b* 5 Sept 1936; *educ* Badminton Sch, Bristol; *m* 17 June 1958 *Rev William Gilbert Gibbs (*see* ALDENHAM and HUNSDON OF HUNSDON, B) and has:

(1) *Oliver John; *b* 30 Sept 1961; *m* 1993 *Isabelle, dau of Lt-Col John Halford, of Paris

(1) *Marcia Kaitilin; *b* 17 Dec 1959; *m* 1986 *Capt Charles H C Lynch-Staunton, LI, yr s of Maj A C Lynch-Staunton, of The Coach House, Nunney, Somerset, and has:

1a *George Henry; *b* 1988

2a *Nicholas John; *b* 1989

3a *Patrick Charles; *b* 1993

(2) *Selina Helen; *b* 3 April 1964; *m* 1989 *Abdullah Akinci, s of A O Akinci, of Umraniye, Istanbul, and has:

1a *Mustafa Noah; *b* 1990

1a *Lütfye; *b* 1992

(3) *Madeleine Susannah; *b* 3 Nov 1965

LUCAS

SPES · ET · FIDES

Arms: Per bend argent and gules a bend dovetailed between six annulets counterchanged. **Crest:** Issuing from a wreath of oak or a dragon's head, wings addorsed gules, semée of annulets argent.
Motto: *Spes et fides* ('Hope and faith').
Creation: Bt. (UK) 25 July 1887.

SIR THOMAS EDWARD GUBBINS LUCAS, 5TH BT, of Ashtead Park, Surrey [Sir Thomas Lucas Bt, Shermans Hall, Dedham, Essex CO7 6DE]; *b* 16 Sept 1930; *s* cousin 1980; *educ* Wellington and Trin Hall Cambridge (MA); CEng, FBIM, MIMC, engr and research analyst, tech dir Vacuum Research (Cambridge) 1959–62, Bourdon Tools 1973–82, St George Fields Ltd 1982–, Vacuum Metallising Processes, fndr Engrg Capacity Exchange London 1963, dir: Columbia Industrial Gp 1969–72, Utopian Housing Soc (Group One) 1973, SGF Properties plc, external consultant to DG XIII, EC and other orgs, FRSA; *m* 1st 1958 Charmian Margaret (*d* 6 Oct 1970), only dau of Lt-Col J C Powell, of Drayton Court, London SW10; *m* 2nd 1980 *Mrs Anne Graham Moore and by his 1st w has:

1 +STEPHEN RALPH JAMES; *b* 11 Dec 1963; *educ* Wellington and Edinburgh U (BCom)

Lineage: JAMES JONATHAN HUGHES DELIGHT LUCAS, of Lowestoft, Suffolk; *b* 13 March 1792; *m* 21 Feb 1812 Elizabeth (*d* 26 Jan 1865), dau of Thomas Pearman, of Chipping Norton, Oxon, and had, with three other sons and three daus:

1 Charles Thomas, JP, DL, of Warnham Court, Sussex; *b* 26 Oct 1820; High Sheriff 1879; *m* 27 April 1842 Charlotte Emma, dau of Charles Tiffin, and *d* 4 Dec 1895, leaving issue

2 **Sir Thomas Lucas, 1st Bt** (UK), so *cr* 25 July 1887, VD, JP (Suffolk, Surrey and Middx), DL, of Ashtead Park, Surrey; *b* 18 July 1822; Col Engrg and Rlwy Vol Staff Corps; *m* 1st 2 Sept 1845 Jane Rolfe (*d* 13 June 1849), dau of Charles Golder, of Folkestone, and had:

(1) Kate Golder Lucas; *b* 10 June 1846; *m* 14 July 1869 (*divorce* 1876) Athol Edward Maudslay (*d* 15 Nov 1923), 4th s of Joseph Maudslay, and *d* 1913, leaving issue

2 (cont.) **Sir Thomas** *m* 2nd 2 June 1852 Mary Amelia (*d* 7 Nov 1905), 3rd dau of Robert Chamberlain, DL, of Catton House, Norfolk, and *d* 6 March 1902, having by her had:

(1) **Sir Arthur Charles Lucas, 2nd Bt**, JP (Middx and Suffolk), of Ashtead Park; *b* 22 May 1853; Maj Engrg and Rlwy Staff Corps RE; *m* 8 Nov 1876 Agnes (*d* 17 Aug 1914), dau of George Jamieson, of S Kensington, and *dsp* 14 June 1915

(2) **Sir Edward Lingard Lucas, 3rd Bt**; *b* 15 Feb 1860; *m* 1st 16 Jan 1886 Mary Helen (*d* 24 April 1915), dau of Henry Chance, DL, of Thornbridge, Leamington, Warwicks, and had:

1a Thomas Farquhar; *b* 25 Nov 1886; Lt 10th Bn Roy Warwicks Regt and RFC; *ka* 16 June 1917

2a **Sir Jocelyn Morton Lucas, 4th Bt**, KBE (1959), MC; *b* 27 Aug 1889; *educ* Eton and RMC Sandhurst; Maj 4th Bn Roy Warwicks Regt WWI (wounded, prisoner), ADC to Lt-Gen Sir S Lawford, KCB, served NFS 1938–42 (twice wounded in air raids), MP Portsmouth S 1936–66, v-chm (chm Hospitality Ctee 1938) Roy Overseas League, fndr and chm Allies Welcome Ctee and Returned Prisoners of War Advice Ctee, Cdr Order Orange Nassau, Czechoslovak Mil Medal Merit 1st Cl; *m* 1st 20 Dec 1933 Edith (*d* 21 Jan 1956), dau of Very Rev David Barrie Cameron, DD, JP, of Dundee, and widow of Sir Trehawk Herbert Kekewich, 1st Bt (*see* 1932 edn); *m* 2nd 20 Oct 1960 Thelma Grace (*d* 23 Jan 1974), only dau of Harold Denison Arbuthnot (*see* ARBUTHNOT, Bt, of Kittybrewster) and formerly w of Somerset Struben De Chair, and *d* 2 May 1980

(2) (cont.) **Sir Edward** *m* 2nd 1915 Anna Maria del Carmen (*d* 23 Dec 1921), 2nd dau of Capt William Henry O'Shea, 18th Hus; *m* 3rd Delia Dorothy (*m* 1st Hon Robert de la Poer Horsley Beresford (*see* DECIES, B); *m* 2nd Sir Charles Philip Huntington, 3rd Bt, *see* 1928 edn), dau of Daniel John O'Sullivan, of The Green, Killarney, Co Kerry, and *d* 3 Aug 1936

(3) Ernest Murray, JP (Co Wicklow); *b* 24 April 1861; Hon Maj, T/Maj Army Remount Serv, formerly Duke of York's Own Loyal Suffolk Hus, WW I; *m* 24 Jan 1900 Ada Catherine (*d* 29 Oct 1962), dau of Joseph Fletcher Moore, JP, DL, of Manor Kilbride, Co Wicklow, and *d* 3 April 1936, leaving:

1a Geoffrey Arthur; *b* 6 Nov 1900; *d* unm 14 June 1969

2a Ralph John Scott; *b* 26 Jan 1904; Lt Coldstream Gds WW II (despatches posthumously); *m* 20 Nov 1929 Dorothy (*d* 1985), yr dau of Maj Henry Thomas Timson, of Tatchbury Mount, Totton, and Stydd House, Lyndhurst, by Edith Theodosia, 3rd dau of St Leger Richard Glyn (*see* WOLVERTON, B), and was *ka* Sollum 20 June 1941, leaving:

1b Sir THOMAS EDWARD GUBBINS LUCAS, **5th and present Bt**

2b +Patrick Timson, VRD and bar; *b* 14 Sept 1933; *educ* Wellington; Maj RMR; *m* 1 March 1958 *Anne, dau of J Westcott, of Yeovil, and has:

1c +Simon James Timson; *b* 26 May 1960; *educ* Wellington and City U London (BSc)

2c +Julian Patrick; *b* 23 March 1962; *educ* Wellington and U Coll Cardiff (BSc)

3a +George Charlton; *b* 14 June 1907; *m* 14 July 1950 *Daphne Gertrude, dau of George William Bryant, MCS (ret)

1a Mary Gladys; *b* 16 Feb 1902; *m* 1st 1943 Arthur Cyril Jennings, OBE, MICE (*d* 20 April 1954), s of J A Jennings, of Canterbury; *m* 2nd 1 May 1966 Wilfred Brinton, JP, yst s of Alfred John Brinton, formerly of Chilworth Tower, Chilworth, Hants, and *d* 19–

2a *Marjorie Dorothy Bertha; *b* 26 Oct 1913; *m* 22 May 1947 Baron Upjohn, CBE, PC, DL, Ld Appeal in Ordinary (*see* 1970 edn)

(4) Francis Granville Lewis (Rev); *b* 16 May 1862; *educ* Trin Coll Cambridge (MA); Rector Campsea Ashe Suffolk 1905–15; *m* 8 Nov 1892 Mary Frances (*d* 18 April 1958), dau of John E Bovill, of Sondes Place, Dorking, and *d* 15 Aug 1939, having had:

1a Alan Reginald Farrar, MC; *b* 23 Aug 1893; *educ* Eton and Trin Coll Cambridge (BA 1914); Maj RHA and RFA WW I (despatches); *m* 30 March 1930 Vera Eleanor Myre, widow of Rev Guy Seymour Black, of Dymchurch, Kent, and *dsp* 12 Nov 1967

2a Hubert Francis, CBE (1946); *b* 21 Jan 1897; *educ* Harrow, RMA Woolwich and Trin Coll Cambridge; Brig RE WW I (despatches), i/c Admin Malaya 1940–42 (POW), Sec Dorset T&AFA 1947–57; *m* 24 Aug 1921 Evelyn Irene Sophie Phipps, er dau of Brig-Gen Edmund John Phipps Hornby, VC, CB, CMG, and had:

1b Diana Joan; *b* 29 April 1931; *m* 2 Jan 1954 Capt John Brian St Vincent Hawkins, Dorset Regt, only s of Brig Victor Francis Staples Hawkins, DSO, MC, of Athelleaze, Athelhampton, Dorchester, and *d* 1994, leaving:

1c *Rowena Fay [Mrs David Ward-Barrow, Brownston House, School Lane, Harby, Leics LE14 4BZ]; *b* 2 March 1955; *m* 1st 1986 Lt Cdr David Lawrence Barrow (*d* 1989); *m* 2nd 1996 *Michael Richard Ward

2c *Wendy Susan [Mrs Robert Hawkins-Creed, 166 Hatton Rd, Bedfont, Middx]; *b* 7 Nov 1957; *m* 1988 *Robert Leonard Creed and has:

1d *Martin Geoffrey Hubert; *b* 1989

2d *Richard David; *b* 1991

2b Rosemary Anne; *b* 10 Sept 1932; *m* 14 June 1962 *Lt-Cdr William Beauchamp Tower, RN [Lt-Cdr William Tower RN, The Home House, Stoke St Michael, Bath, Somerset BA3 5JH]; only s of Robert Beauchamp Tower, MC, of 31 Wyke Road, Weymouth, and *d* 29 May 1981, leaving:

1c *Alan Francis Beauchamp; *b* 3 Sept 1964; *m* 2 July 1988 *Margaret Pate and has:

1d *Anna Clare; *b* 18 March 1991

2d *Helen Rebecca; *b* 13 Dec 1993

2c *Christopher John ; *b* 31 March 1972; *m* 14 Oct 1995 *Clare Louise Webb

1c *Annabel Jane; *b* 8 Oct 1965; *m* 11 April 1992 *Kyle Alexander McFarlane and has:

1d *Benjamin Alexander; *b* 19 Feb 1994

2d *Oliver Philip; *b* 21 Oct 1996

2c *Sophie Elisabeth; *b* 6 Oct 1967

3a Arthur John; *b* 31 July 1903; *educ* Harrow; Maj RE WW II; *m* 7 Aug 1930 Margaret Ruth (*d* 1989), dau of Col Joseph Francis Noel Baxendale, CB, JP, DL, of Froxfield Green, Petersfield, Hants, and *d* 1986, leaving:

1b *James Granville [Lt-Cdr James Lucas RN, Yew Tree Cottage, Port Navas, Falmouth, Cornwall TR11 5RJ]; *b* 8 March 1932; *educ* Harrow and HMS *Hawke*; joined RN 1950, Lt-Cdr (ret), insur broker; *m* 1st 5 Oct 1957 (*divorce* 1973) Suzanne Molly, only dau of Edward Fitzroy Talbot-Ponsonby (*see* SHREWSBURY and WATERFORD, E), and has:

1c +Jonathan Delight; *b* 14 April 1964; FRCS; *m* 19– *—

2c +Charles Granville; *b* 14 April 1964; BSc; *m* 19– *—

1b (cont.) Lt-Cdr James Lucas *m* 2nd 1973 *Ann Marie Mason and by her has:

1c *Serena Kate; *b* 1977

1b *Jennifer [Mrs Hugh Toomer, 5 Eccleston Sq, London SW1]; *b* 3 Jan 1936; *m* 1972 *Hugh Cecil Toomer

(5) Reginald Jaffray; *b* 28 Dec 1865; *educ* Eton and Trin Coll Cambridge; MP Portsmouth 1905–06, Capt 3rd Bn Hants Regt; *d* unm 9 May 1914

(6) Evelyn Penn, MC; *b* 26 June 1875; *educ* Eton; Maj 4th Roy Berks Regt WW I (wounded, despatches); *m* 29 April 1902 Mary Georgetta (*d* 9 June 1948), only dau of Rev Canon Richard Stovin Mitchinson, Rector Barby, Rugby, and *d* 30 May 1950, having had:

1a Timothy Stovin, MC, TD; *b* 20 April 1916; Capt KRRC WW II; *m* 15 Aug 1942 *Joanna Repington [Mrs Timothy Lucas, The Lodge, Boroughbridge, York YO5 9AM], only child of Charles Bernard Mathews, of Lob's Wood, Ilkley, Yorks, and *d* 1981, leaving:

1b +Charles [Charles Lucas Esq, The Lodge, Boroughbridge, York YO5 9AM]; *b* 27 June 1943; *educ* Eton; *m* 9 Nov 1967 (*divorce* 1989) Antoinette Maria, only dau of Baron Henri von Westenholz, of Little Blakesware, Much Hadham, Herts, and has:

1c +Piers Timothy Everard; *b* 23 Oct 1970
2c +Harry Rudolph Penn; *b* 11 Dec 1976
1c *Nina Antoinette; *b* 1971
1b *Charlotte Theresa Stovin [Mrs Charlotte Irwin, Weavers, Fewcott, nr Bicester, Oxon]; *b* 4 Feb 1945; *m* 11 Oct 1966 (*divorce* 1971) Christopher Frank Stuart Irwin, only s of Angus Charles Stuart Irwin, of Crouch Green, Codicote, Herts, and has:

    1c *Alexander Christian Stovin; *b* 17 June 1970
    1c *Sophie Georgetta Kate; *b* 2 May 1968
1a Mary Evelyn; *b* 4 March 1903; *d* 21 March 1937
(2) Constance Mary; *b* 7 May 1855; *m* 20 June 1877 William Penn (*d* 1921) and *d* 6 March 1942, leaving issue
(3) Amy Florence; *b* 25 Jan 1857; *m* 23 July 1885 Lt-Col Aubrey Maude and *d* 18 Dec 1931, leaving issue (*see* HAWARDEN, V)
(4) Evelyn Emma; *b* 20 June 1858; *d* 28 Sept 1870
(5) Mary Alice; *b* 16 Feb 1864; *m* 14 Feb 1885 Frederick Eustace Reade Fryer, JP (*d* 1 Oct 1917), of Bury Hill, Woodbridge, Suffolk, est s of Frederick Daniel Fryer, JP, DL, of Moulton Paddocks, Cambs, and *d* 21 Nov 1930, having had issue

LUCAS OF CHILWORTH

Arms: Per fess wavy or and azure, in chief between two annulets a rose gules barbed and seeded proper, in base two bars wavy argent surmounted by a bull's head cabossed sable. **Crest:** A representation of Apollo affronté or. **Supporters:** Dexter, a lion or; sinister, a Russian bear sable, each resting the interior paw upon an annulet, therein a rose gules barbed and seeded proper. **Motto:** *Labor omnia vincit* ('Labour conquers all'). **Creation:** B. (UK) 27 June 1946.

THE 2ND BARON LUCAS OF CHILWORTH, of Chilworth, Co Southampton (Michael William George Lucas) [The Rt Hon The Lord Lucas of Chilworth, House of Lords, London SW1A 0PW]; *b* 26 April 1926; *s* f 1967; *educ* Peter Symonds Sch, Winchester; AMBIM; late Roy Tank Regt; memb Ho Lds Select Ctee Science and Technology 1980–83, T Eng (CEI); FIMI (memb council 1972–76), FInstTA, Pres: Inst HGV Instrs 1972–76, League of Safe Drivers 1976–80, Inst of Tport Admin 1980–83, V-Pres: RoSPA 1980–, Inst Motor Industry 1992–, memb Public Policy Ctee RAC 1981–83, Ld-in-Waiting 1983, Parly U-Sec DTI 1984–87; *m* 9 June 1955 (*divorce* 1990) Ann-Marie, only dau of Ronald William Buck, of Southampton, Hants, and has:

1 +SIMON WILLIAM; *b* 6 Feb 1957; *educ* Churchers Coll Petersfield and U of Leicester (BSc); *m* 1993 *Fiona, yr dau of Thomas Mackintosh, of Vancouver, and has:

    (1) +John Ronald Muir; *b* 21 May 1995
2 +Timothy Michael [The Hon Timothy Lucas, 23 Common Lane, Weybridge, Surrey]; *b* 23 Sept 1959; *educ* Lancing and U of Surrey (BSc)
1 *Rachel Ann; *b* 13 Feb 1963; *educ* Atherley Sch and Peter Symonds Coll; *m* 1991 *Howard J Wilder, er s of John R Wilder, of Eastleigh, Hants, and has:

    (1) *A dau; *b* 1993
    (2) *A dau; *b* 1997

Lineage: GEORGE WILLIAM LUCAS, **1st Baron Lucas of Chilworth**, of Chilworth, Co Southampton (UK), so cr 27 June 1946; *b* 29 March 1896 (s of Percy William Lucas, of Oxford); WW I with RNAS; Pres MAA 1927–29 and 1941–46, memb Motor Vehicle Maintenance Advsy Ctee 1941, Chm Nat Jt Industl Cncl Motor Trade 1943–46, memb New Forest Deptl Ctee 1946–47, memb English Nat Ctee Forestry Commn 1945–48, Chm Ag Mktg Acts Ctee 1947, a Ld-in-Waiting 1948–49, Capt Yeomen Gd 1949–50, Parly Sec Min Tpt 1950–51; *m* 24 Feb 1917 Sonia (*d* 1979), dau of Marcus Finkelstein, of Libau, Latvia, and *d* 11 Oct 1967, leaving:

1 MICHAEL WILLIAM GEORGE LUCAS, **2nd and present Baron Lucas of Chilworth**
2 +Ivor Thomas Mark, CMG (1980) [The Hon Ivor Lucas CMG, 65 Newstead Way, London SW19 5HR]; *b* 25 July 1927; *educ* St Edward's Oxford and Trin Coll Oxford (BA 1951, MA 1956); Capt late RA; Dip Serv 1951–87: Persian Gulf 1952–56, FO 1956–59 and 1966, Karachi 1959–62, Tripoli Libya 1962–66,

Cnsllr Aden 1968–69, Dep HC Kaduna Nigeria 1969–71, Amb Oman 1979–81 and Syria 1982–84, Assist Sec-Gen Arab-Br Chamber Commerce 1985–87, chm edtl bd *Asian Affairs* 1995–, tstee Cwlth Linking Trust 1996–, memb Central Cncl Roy Overseas League 1996–, V pres Anglo-Omani Soc, author: a chapter on Syria in *The Middle East: a handbook* (1988) and *A Road to Damascus; Mainly Diplomatic Memoirs from the Middle East* (1997); *m* 27 April 1954 *Christine Mallorie, er twin dau of Cdr Arthur Mallorie Coleman, OBE, DSC, RN, of Greenwich, and has:

(1) +Mark Haselden; *b* 12 April 1955; *m* 1983 *Melinda Jane, yr dau of Sir Alastair Frederick Down, OBE, MC, of Brieryhill, by Hawick, Roxburghshire, and has:

    1a +Nicholas Alastair James; *b* 1988
    1a *Georgina Sophie; *b* 1986
    2a *Laura Evelyn; *b* 1990
    3a *Eleanor Grace; *b* 1994
(2) +Crispin Mallorie; *b* 1 Oct 1958; *m* 1993 *Heather Patricia, er dau of William Boyd, of Aldeburgh, Suffolk, and has:

    1a +William Mallorie; *b* 1996
(3) +Adrian George; *b* 6 Dec 1963; *m* 26 July 1997 *Elisabeth, est dau of Charles Schmitz, of Bethesda, Md., and Mrs Barbara Putnam, of New York
1 *Nadia [The Hon Mrs Nadia Selkirk, 49 Ancastle Green, Henley-on-Thames, RG9 1TS]; *b* 19 Jan 1923; *m* 4 March 1944 (*divorce* 1980) F/Lt Hamish Rattray Selkirk, DFC, RAF, s of James Logie Selkirk, of Moffat, Dumfriesshire, and has had:

(1) *Christopher Rattray Lucas; *b* 27 Jan 1949; *educ* Henley GS and Queen's U Belfast
(2) Alastair Hamish Lawson; *b* 27 Jan 1949; *educ* Henley GS; *d* 1982
(1) *Lindsay Alexandra; *b* 31 July 1945; *m* 1st 4 Sept 1965 (*divorce* 1970) Alan Stuart-Hutcheson and has:

    1a *Guy James; *b* 29 Sept 1966
(1) (cont.) Mrs Lindsay Stuart-Hutcheson *m* 2nd 1 Aug 1979, as his 3rd w, *David Lewis Jacobs, s of David Jacobs
2 *Tatiana Sonia [The Hon Mrs Bradford, Nashdom, 13 Woodlands Rd, Surbiton, Surrey KT6 6PR]; *b* 10 Jan 1933; *educ* Convent High Sch Southampton and Eastbourne Sch of Domestic Economy; *m* 17 Sept 1964 *Kenneth Bradford, s of Arthur Bradford, of Charmouth, Dorset, and has:

(1) *Adam George; *b* 17 Jan 1966; *m* 1992 *Caroline Louise, est dau of R John Dorrell, of Surbiton, Surrey
(2) *Justin Nicholas; *b* 26 July 1967; *m* 1993 *Anne Caroline, yr dau of Mrs S Horwood, of Claygate, Surrey

LUCAS OF CRUDWELL

Arms: Argent, two bars sable, charged with three trefoils slipped of the field; in chief a greyhound courant of the second, collared or. **Crest:** A mount vert, thereon a greyhound sejant sable, collared or, charged on the shoulder with a trefoil slipped argent. **Supporters:** On either side a wyvern with wings erect or. **Motto:** *Palma virtuti* ('To virtue the palm'). **Creations:** B. (E) 1663 and L. (S) 8 June 1609.

THE 12TH BARON LUCAS OF CRUDWELL and 8th Lord Dingwall (Ralph Matthew Palmer) [The Rt Hon The Lord Lucas of Crudwell and Dingwall, House of Lords, London Sw1A 0PW]; *b* 7 June 1951; *s* mother 1991; *educ* Eton and Balliol Coll Oxford (BA); BDO Binder Hamlyn 1972–76, S G Warburg 1976–88, a Ld-in-Waiting (Govt Whip) 1994–97; *m* 1st 22 July 1978 (*divorce* 1995) Clarissa Marie, only dau of Maj George Vivian Lockett, TD, of Stratford Hills, Stratford St Mary's, Essex; *m* 2nd 1995 *Amanda Atha and by his 1st w has:

1 +LEWIS EDWARD; *b* 7 Dec 1987
1 *Hannah Rachel Elise; *b* 1984

Lineage (of Barony of Lucas of Crudwell): Sir THOMAS LUCAS, of Colchester; High Sheriff Essex 1617; *m* Elizabeth, dau and coheir of John Leighton, and *d* 25 Sept 1625, leaving, with other issue:

1 Thomas (Sir); *b* before his parents' marriage but included in his yr bro's ennoblement (*see* below); had:

(1) CHARLES LUCAS, 2nd BARON LUCAS OF SHENFIELD; *m* Penelope, dau of Francis Leke, 1st Earl of Scarsdale, and *d* 1688, having had:

  1a Anne; *m* Edward Cary and had issue (*see* FALKLAND, V)

  2a Penelope; *m* Isaac Selfe, of Benacre, and had, with other issue:

    1b Anne; *m* Thomas Methuen and had issue (*see* METHUEN, B)

(2) THOMAS LUCAS, 3rd and last BARON LUCAS OF SHENFIELD; Constable Tower of London 1688–1702, Er Bro Trinity House 1692–1705 (Master 1697–99), Col 34th Foot 1702–05; *d unm* 1705, when the Barony expired

2 Sir JOHN LUCAS, 1st BARON LUCAS OF SHENFIELD, Co Essex (E), so *cr* 13 Jan 1644/5, with remainder to his bros Sir Charles and Sir Thomas in default of his own male issue, and to the heirs male of their bodies; *b* 1606; royalist Civil War; *m* 17 Dec 1628 Anne (*d* 22 Aug 1660), dau of Sir Christopher Nevill(e) (*see* ABERGAVENNY, M), and *d* 2 July 1671, having had, with a s (*d* young):

  (1) MARY LUCAS, *cr* **Baroness Lucas of Crudwell**, for whom *see* further below

3 Charles (Sir); shot on CROMWELL's orders 1648 after Colchester's surrender to the Parliamentarians

The 1st BARON LUCAS OF SHENFIELD's dau,

  MARY Lucas, **Baroness Lucas of Crudwell**, Wilts (E), so *cr* 7 May 1663, with remainder in default of male heirs by her husb to the heirs of her body by him (which could include females), but without the usual division (and abeyance) between coheiresses in the event of the failure of heirs male; *m* 2 March 1662/3 Anthony GREY, 11th EARL OF KENT (*see* GREY, B), and *d* 1 Nov 1702, leaving:

HENRY GREY, **2nd Baron Lucas of Crudwell**, 12th and last EARL OF KENT and 1st and last DUKE OF KENT (GB), so *cr* 28 April 1710, as also earlier 14 Nov 1706 MARQUESS OF KENT (E) and 19 May 1740 MARQUESS GREY (GB), with special remainder in the case of the last title to his gdau Jemima Campbell (*see* below) and her heirs male, KG; *bapt* 28 Sept 1671; *m* 1st 16 April 1695 Jemima (*d* 27 July 1728), dau and coheir of 2nd Baron Crewe, and had, with other issue (*d* young):

1 ANTHONY GREY, **3rd Baron Lucas of Crudwell**, as which called up to Ho Lds *vp* 8 Nov 1718, previously known as *Earl of Harold* by courtesy; *b* 21 Feb 1695/6; *m* 17 April 1718 Mary (*m* 2nd 16 May 1736 1st Earl Gower (*see* SUTHERLAND, D) and *d* 12 Feb 1785), dau and coheir of 6th Earl of Thanet, and *dsp* & *vp* 21 July 1723

2 Henry; *d unm* 1717 aged 21

1 Amabel; *m* 20 Feb 1717/8 3rd Earl of Breadalbane and Holland (*qv*, 1970 edn) and *d* 2 March 1726, having had, with a s (*d* in infancy):

  (1) JEMIMA CAMPBELL; *s gf* as MARCHIONESS GREY and **Baroness Lucas of Crudwell** (*see* below)

2 Jemima; *m* 4 Feb 1723/4 1st Earl of Ashburnham (*d* 10 March 1736/7; *see* 1924 edn) and *d* 7 July 1731, leaving issue

3 Anne; *m* 9 Jan 1727 Lord Charles Cavendish, MP, s of 2nd Duke of Devonshire (*qv*), and *d* 20 Sept 1733, leaving issue

4 Mary; *m* 1743 Dr Gregory, Dean Ch Ch, Oxford, and *d* 1 Jan 1761, leaving issue

The **2nd Baron Lucas of Crudwell** (and 1st DUKE OF KENT) *m* 2nd 24 March 1728/9 Lady Sophia Bentinck (*d* 5 June 1741), dau of 1st Earl of Portland (*qv*), and *d* 5 June 1740, when the Viscountcy of Goderich, the Earldom of Harold and the Earldom, Marquessate and Dukedom of Kent expired, having by her had:

3 George, *Earl of Harold*; *b* 22 Aug 1732; *dvp* 3 Feb 1732/3

5 Anne Sophia; *m* 24 March 1780, John Egerton, DD, Bp Durham, and had issue (*see* GREY EGERTON, Bt)

The 2nd BARON's gdau,

  JEMIMA Campbell, **Baroness Lucas of Crudwell** and MARCHIONESS GREY; *b* 9 Oct 1722; *m* 22 May 1740 Philip YORKE, 2nd Earl of Hardwicke (*qv*) and *d* 11 Jan 1797, when the Marquessate of Grey expired, having had:

1 AMABEL Yorke, *s* mother as **Baroness Lucas of Crudwell**; *b* 22 Jan 1750; *cr* 25 Oct 1816 COUNTESS DE GREY OF WREST, Co Bedford (UK), with remainder to her only sis and the heirs male of her body; *m* 16 July 1772 Alexander Hume-Campbell, Viscount Polwarth (*see* POLWARTH, L), and *dsp* 4 May 1833

2 MARY JEMIMA Yorke; *m* 17 Aug 1780 Thomas ROBINSON, 2nd Baron Grantham (*d* 20 July 1786), and *d* 7 Jan 1830, having had:

  (1) THOMAS PHILIP ROBINSON later WEDDELL (roy licence 7 May 1803) later still DE GREY (roy licence 23 June 1833), **6th Baron Lucas of Crudwell** and 3rd BARON GRANTHAM, KG; *s* aunt 1833 as 2nd EARL DE GREY OF WREST; *b* 8 Dec 1781; *educ* St John's Coll Cambridge; *m* 20 July 1805 Lady Henrietta Frances Cole (*d* 2 July 1845), dau of 1st Earl of Enniskillen (*qv*), and *d* 14 Nov 1859, having had, with other issue (*d* young):

    1a Frederick William Weddell; *b* 11 April 1810; *dvp unm* 6 Feb 1831

    1a ANNE FLORENCE Weddell; *s f* as **Baroness Lucas of Crudwell**; *b* 8 June 1806; *m* 7 Oct 1833 GEORGE COWPER, 6th EARL COWPER (*see* below)

    2a Mary Gertrude; *m* 5 July 1832 Henry Vyner (*d* 22 Jan 1861), s of Robert Vyner, of Gautby, Lincs, and *d* 11 July 1892, having had:

      1b Henry Frederick Clare, of Gautby; *b* 1836; *d unm* 11 Nov 1882

      2b Reginald Arthur, DL (Yorks); *b* 1839; MP Ripon 1860–65; *dsp* 28 Sept 1870

      3b Robert Charles de Grey, of Gautby, Lincs, and Newby Hall and Fairfield House, Yorks, DL (Yorks); *b* 13 Feb 1842; Capt Gren Gds; High Sheriff Cheshire 1893; *m* 10 July 1865 Eleanor Margaret Duncombe (*d* 7 Dec 1913), dau of Rev Slingsby Duncombe Shafto, and *d* 19 March 1915, leaving:

        1c Mary Evelyn VYNER later COMPTON later still COMPTON-VYNER (roy licence 30 Sept 1915); *m* 31 July 1886 Lord Alwyne Frederick Compton, DSO, and *d* 10 Aug 1939, leaving issue (*see* NORTHAMPTON, M)

        2c Violet Aline; *m* 1st 19 July 1890 (*divorce* 1902) 5th Earl of Rosslyn (*qv*) and had issue; *m* 2nd 12 Aug 1903 Charles Jarott and *d* 17 Feb 1945

      4b Frederick Grantham; *b* 1847; murdered by brigands in Greece 21 April 1870

    1b Henrietta Anne Theodosia, CI; *m* 8 April 1851 her cousin 1st MARQUESS OF RIPON and *d* 28 Feb 1907, leaving issue (*see* below)

2b Theodosia; *m* 5 July 1859 3rd Marquess of Northampton (*qv*) and *d* 18 Nov 1864

(2) FREDERICK JOHN ROBINSON, 1st EARL OF RIPON, so *cr* 13 April 1833, as also earlier 28 April 1827 VISCOUNT GODERICH (both UK); *b* 1 Nov 1782; Sec of State Colonies, Ld Privy Seal, PM 1827–28; *m* 1 Sept 1814 Lady Sarah Albinia Louisa Hobart (*d* 9 April 1867), only dau and eventual coheir of 4th Earl of Buckinghamshire (*qv*), and *d* 28 Jan 1859, having had:

  1a GEORGE FREDERICK SAMUEL ROBINSON, 2nd EARL OF RIPON, 3rd EARL DE GREY (as which *s unc* 1859) and 1st MARQUESS OF RIPON (UK), so *cr* 23 June 1871; *b* 24 Oct 1827; MP Hull 1852–53, Huddersfield 1853–57 and W R Yorks 1857–59, Ld Pres Cncl 1868–73, Viceroy India 1880–84, 1st Ld Admlty 1886, Ld Privy Seal 1905–08, Ld Lt N R Yorks 1873–1906, Mayor Ripon 1895; *m* 8 April 1851 his cousin Henrietta Theodosia, CI (*d* 28 Feb 1907), dau of Capt Henry Vyner, of Gautby Hall, Lincs, and *d* 9 July 1900, having had, with a dau (*an infant*):

    1b FREDERICK OLIVER ROBINSON, 2nd MARQUESS OF RIPON, GCVO; *b* 29 Jan 1852; MP (Lib) Ripon 1874–80, Treas to HM QUEEN ALEXANDRA 1901, Tstee Wallace Collection 1912; *m* 7 May 1885, as her 2nd husb, Hon Constance Gladys Herbert (*d* 27 Oct 1917), 3rd dau of 1st Baron Herbert of Lea (*see* PEMBROKE and MONTGOMERY, E), and *dsp* 22 Sept 1923, when all his titles expired

(3) Philip; *b* 18 Oct 1783; *d* June 1794

Lineage (of Lordship of Dingwall): Sir RICHARD PRESTON, of Halltree, Edinburgh, **1st Lord Dingwall**, of Co Ross (S), so *cr* 8 June 1609, and 1st and last EARL OF DESMOND and BARON DUNMORE, Co Kilkenny (both I), so *cr* 11 July 1619, as also again 7 Nov 1622 EARL OF DESMOND (I), with remainder in reversion to his prospective (but not in the event actual) s-in-law George Feilding (*see* DENBIGH and DESMOND, E), KB; Gent of the Bedchamber to JAMES I; *m* 1614 Elizabeth (*d* 10 Oct 1628), only surv child of 10th Earl of Ormonde (and 3rd Earl of) Ossory (*see* 1970 edn, ORMONDE, M) and widow of Theobald Butler, Viscount Butler of Tulleophelim, and *dspm* 28 Oct 1628, when the Earldom of Desmond of the 1622 *cr* and Barony of Dunmore expired, leaving:

ELIZABETH Preston, **Lady Dingwall**; *b* 25 July 1615; *m* Sept 1629 her cousin James BUTLER, 1st DUKE OF ORMONDE (*see* MOUNTGARRET, V) and *d* 21 July 1684, having had, with other issue:

1 THOMAS BUTLER, 6th EARL OF OSSORY, as which called up to Irish Ho Lds *vp* 8 Aug 1662 and to E Ho of Lds by writ 14 Sept 1666 as LORD (Baron) BUTLER OF MOORE PARK (the effect of the summons by writ making the Barony heritable by heirs general, which could include females), KG; *b* 8 July 1634; *m* 17 Nov 1659 Amilia (*bur* 27 Jan 1684), est dau of Lodewyk van Nassau, Lord of Beverweerd *alias* Louis de Nassau, Lord of Auverquerque (illegitimate s of PRINCE MAURICE OF NASSAU by Margaretha van Mechelen) and *dvp* 30 July 1680, having had, with other issue:

  (1) JAMES BUTLER, **3rd Lord Dingwall** and 2nd DUKE OF ORMONDE, KG (1688), PC (I, 1690 and 1702; E, 1696–1714); *b* 29 April 1665; attainted under an Act of the GB Parl 1715 when all his titles save the Irish ones were forfeited (and they only escaped by a legal oversight); *m* 1st 15 July 1682 Lady Anne Hyde (*d* 25 Jan 1684/5), dau of 1st Earl of Rochester (*see* CLARENDON, E), and had:

    1a Mary; *d* young 1688

  (1) (cont.) The **3rd Lord Dingwall** *m* 2nd 3 Aug 1685 Lady Mary Somerset (*d* 19 Nov 1733), dau of 1st Duke of Beaufort (*qv*), and *d* in exile 16 Nov 1745, having by her had two daus

  (1) Henrietta; *m* 12 Jan 1697 her cousin Henry de/van Nassau, *alias* d'Auverquerque, Earl of Grantham (*d* 5 Dec 1754 when his titles expired) and *d* 11 Oct 1724, having had, with two sons (*d unm*) and two er daus (*dsp*):

    1a Henrietta; *m* 27 June 1732 William COWPER later CLAVERING-COWPER, 2nd EARL COWPER (*d* 18 Sept 1764), and *d* 23 Sept 1747, having had:

    1b GEORGE NASSAU CLAVERING-COWPER, 3rd EARL COWPER; *b* 26 Aug 1738; *cr* by JOSEPH II 31 Jan 1778 a Prince of the HRE; *m* 2 June 1775 Anne (*d* 5 Sept 1826), dau and coheir of Charles Gore, of Horkstowe, Lincs, and *d* 22 Dec 1789, having had:

      1c GEORGE AUGUSTUS CLAVERING-COWPER, 4th EARL COWPER, Prince of the HRE; *b* 9 Aug 1776; *educ* St John's Coll Cambridge (MA 1795); *d unm* 12 Feb 1799

      2c PETER LEOPOLD LOUIS FRANCIS NASSAU CLAVERING-COWPER or COWPER, 5th EARL COWPER; *b* 6 May 1778; *m* 20 July 1805 Hon Emily Mary Lamb (*b* 21 April 1787; *m* 2nd 16 Dec 1839 3rd and last Viscount Palmerston (*see* TEMPLE OF STOWE, E) and *d* 11 Sept 1869), dau of 1st Viscount Melbourne, and *d* 21 July 1837, leaving:

        1d GEORGE AUGUSTUS FREDERICK, 6th EARL COWPER, for whom *see* further below

        2d WILLIAM FRANCIS COWPER, 1st and last BARON MOUNT TEMPLE (UK), so *cr* 25 May 1880; *b* 13 Dec 1811; *m* 1st 27 June 1843 Harriet Alicia (*d* 28 Aug 1843), dau of Daniel Gurney, of N Runcton, Norfolk; *m* 2nd 21 Nov 1848 Georgiana (*d* 17 Oct 1901), sis of 1st Baron Tollemache (*qv*), and *dsp* 17 Oct 1888, when the Barony expired

        3d Charles Spencer; *b* 7 June 1816; *m* 1st 1 Jan 1852 Lady Harriet Anne Frances (*d* 17 Dec 1869), dau of 1st Earl of Blesington of the 1816 *cr* (*see* STEWART, Bt, of Ramelton), and widow of Alfred Count d'Orsay, and had:

          1e Mary Henrietta, *b* 1853; *d* 1854

        3d (cont.) The Hon Charles Cowper *m* 2nd 11 April 1871 Jessie Mary (*d* 7 Oct 1901), only surv child of Col Clinton McLean, and *dsps* 30 March 1879

        1d Emily Caroline Frances; *m* 10 June 1830 7th Earl of Shaftesbury (*qv*) and *d* 15 Oct 1872, leaving issue

        2d Frances Elizabeth; *m* 29 April 1841 Robert, Viscount Jocelyn, s of 3rd Earl of Roden (*qv*), and *d* 26 March 1880, leaving issue

        3c Edward Spencer, of Digswell, Herts, MP, *b* 16 July 1779; *m* 23 May 1808 Catherine (*m* 2nd 29 Jan 1827 Rev G A Hamilton and *d* 1830), yst dau of Thomas March Phillipps, of Garendon Park, Leics, and *dsp* 1 Feb 1823

1b Caroline; *m* 26 July 1753 Henry Seymour and *d* 2 June 1773, having had issue (*see* SOMERSET, D)

The 5th EARL COWPER's est s,

GEORGE AUGUSTUS FREDERICK COWPER, 6th EARL COWPER; *b* 26 June 1806; Offr RHG, Lt 31st Foot 1835, MP (Whig) Canterbury 1830–34, U-Sec For Affrs Nov-Dec 1834, Prince HRE, Ld Lt Kent 1846–56; *m* 7 Oct 1833 Anne Florence, **Baroness Lucas of Crudwell** in her own right (*see* above; she *d* 1880), er dau and coheir of 2nd Earl de Grey, KG, and *d* 15 April 1856, having had:

1 FRANCIS THOMAS DE GREY COWPER, 7th EARL COWPER, **8th Baron Lucas of Crudwell**, also **4th Lord Dingwall** and 3rd LORD (Baron) BUTLER OF MOORE PARK (both of which titles he was declared 15 Aug 1871 to have inherited as heir general of 6th Earl of Ossory, the attainder affecting them having been reversed that year), in addition a Prince of the HRE, KG, PC, DL (Kent and Notts); *b* 11 June 1834; Ld Lt Beds, Hon Col 1st Vol Bn Beds Regt, Capt Gentlemen-at-Arms 1871–74, Ld Lt Ireland 1880–82; *m* 25 Oct 1870 Lady Katrine Cecilia Compton (*d* 23 March 1913), est dau of 4th Marquess of Northampton (*qv*), and *dsp* 18 July 1905, when the Earldom of Cowper, Viscountcy of Fordwich, Barony of Cowper and the Imperial title all expired, the Barony of Butler of Moore Park fell into abeyance among his sisters and their heirs and the Barony of Lucas and Lordship of Dingwall passed to his nephew

2 Henry Frederick, JP, DL; MP Herts 1865–85, *b* 18 April 1836; *d* unm 10 Nov 1887

1 Henrietta Emily Mary, *d* unm 28 June 1853

2 Florence Amabel, *m* 9 Aug 1871 Hon Auberon Edward William Molyneux Herbert (*d* 5 Nov 1906), DCL Oxford, of Old House, Berry Wood, Ringwood, Hants, MP Notts 1870–74, 3rd s of 3rd Earl of Carnarvon (*qv*), and *d* 26 April 1886, having had:

(1) Rolf; *b* 23 July 1872; *d* 13 April 1882

(2) AUBERON THOMAS HERBERT, **9th Baron Lucas of Crudwell** and **5th Lord Dingwall**, PC (1912); *b* 25 May 1876; Capt Hampshire Carabiniers, F/Cdr RFC, Priv Sec to Sec of State War 1907–08, Parly U-Sec: War and Memb Army Cncl 1908–11 and Colonies 1911, Parly Sec Bd Ag and Fisheries 1911–14 and Pres 1914–15, war correspondent Boer War (wounded), attached RFC WW I, Serbian Order Karageorge 4th Cl with swords; missing presumed killed during a flight over German lines 3 Nov 1916

(1) Clair Mimram; *b* 28 Sept 1874; *d* 8 Jan 1893

(2) NAN INO Herbert, **Baroness Lucas of Crudwell** and **Lady Dingwall**; *b* 13 June 1880; granted rank of baron's dau 7 Sept 1907; *m* 30 April 1917 Lt-Col Howard Lister COOPER, AFC, RAF, and *d* 23 Nov 1958, leaving:

1a ANNE ROSEMARY Cooper, **Baroness Lucas of Crudwell** and **Lady Dingwall**; *b* 28 April 1919; *m* 11 May 1950 Maj Hon Robert Jocelyn PALMER, MC, late Coldstream Gds, 3rd s of 3rd Earl of Selborne (*qv*), and *d* 31 Dec 1991, leaving:

1b RALPH MATTHEW PALMER, **12th and present Baron Lucas** and **8th Lord Dingwall**

2b +Timothy John [The Hon Timothy Palmer, West Woodyates Manor, Salisbury, Wilts SP5 5QS]; *b* 10 April 1953; *educ* Eton and Balliol Coll Oxford; *m* 1984 *Adèle Cristina Sophia, 4th dau of Lt-Col Hon Henry Anthony Camillo Howard, CMG (*see* HOWARD OF PENRITH, B), and has:

1c +Henry Jocelyn; *b* 1987

2c +Robert Dominic; *b* 1993

1c +Nan Cristina; *b* 1985

2c +Isabella Spring; *b* 1989

1b +Anthea Amabel; *b* 28 June 1956; added christian name Amabel by deed poll 1963; *educ* Westfield Coll London

2a Rachel; *b* 25 Feb 1921; *m* 1 April 1948 4th and last Baron Loch, MC (*d* 1991; *see* 1970 edn), and *d* 6 Nov 1976, leaving, with two sons (*dsp*):

1b +Sarah Nan [The Hon Sarah Loch, The Old House, The Close, Blandford, Dorset DT11 7HA]; *b* 1949

3 Adine Eliza Anne, *m* 29 Sept 1866 Hon Julian Henry Charles Fane (*d* 19 April 1870), 4th s of 11th Earl of Westmorland (*qv*), and *d* 20 Oct 1868, having had:

(1) John Francis Henry, *b* 18 July 1868; *d* 9 March 1876

(1) Ethel Anne Priscilla; *b* 27 June 1867; *m* 17 Feb 1887 1st and last Baron Desborough, KG, GCVO (*see* GRENFELL, B), and *d* 28 May 1952, leaving:

1a Monica Margaret; *b* 1893; *m* 2 June 1924, as his 2nd w, Marshal of the RAF Sir John Maitland Salmond, GCB, CMG, CVO, DSO (*d* 1968), and *d* 1978, leaving:

1b +Julian John William [Julian Salmond Esq, Old Manor House, Didmarton, Badminton, Avon]; *b* 1926; *m* 1950 *Brigid Louise, dau of FitzHerbert Wright (*see* POWERSCOURT, V), and has:

1c +David John Julian; *b* 11 Nov 1969

1c +Alicia Brigid [The Rt Hon The Viscountess Head, Throope Manor, Bishopstone, Wilts SP5 4BA]; *b* 14 June 1951; *m* 11 May 1974 *2nd Viscount Head (*qv*) and has issue

2c +Georgiana Monica; *b* 1952; *m* Dec 1971 (*divorce*) Stephen Roberts and has:

1d +Miran (son); *b* May 1972

3c +Venetia Anne [Mrs David Morrison, 21 Albert Bridge Rd, London SW11]; *b* 6 Aug 1957; *m* 1984 *David John Morrison and has issue (*see* MARGADALE, B)

1b Rosemary Laura; *b* 1928; *m* 1947 (*divorce* 1974) 3rd Baron Ravensdale (*qv*) and *d* 1991

2a Alexandra Imogen Clare; *b* 1905; *m* 1931 6th Viscount Gage (*qv*) and *d* 1969

4 Amabel Frederica Henrietta, *m* 18 Nov 1873 Adml-of-the-Fleet Lord Walter Talbot Kerr, GCB (*d* 12 May 1927), 4th s of 7th Marquess of Lothian (*qv*), and *d* 15 Oct 1906, having had issue

LUCAS-TOOTH

Arms: Quarterly, 1st and 4th, gu. a demi-griffin segreant between three feathers arg. (for TOOTH); 2nd and 3rd, az. on a bend between in chief two crescents and in base an estoile arg. three vine-leaves ppr. (for LUCAS). **Crests:** 1 A griffin segreant gu., semée of mullets and holding in the sinister claw a feather arg. (for TOOTH), 2 A demi-dragon az., holding in the paws a vine branch, fructed and leaved ppr. (for LUCAS). **Motto:** *Perseverantia palmam obtinebit* ('Perseverance will win'). **Creation:** Bt. (UK) 1 Dec 1920.

SIR (HUGH) JOHN LUCAS-TOOTH, 2ND BT, of Bught, Co Inverness [Sir John Lucas-Tooth Bt, Parsonage Farm, E Hagbourne, Oxon OX11 9LN]; *b* 20 Aug 1932; *s* f 1985; *educ* Eton and Balliol Coll Oxford; late Lt Scots Gds; *m* 29 June 1955 *Hon Caroline Poole, est dau of 1st Baron Poole (*qv*), and has:

1 *(Caroline) Maria [Mrs William Hibbert, 41 Lancaster Rd, London W11]; *b* 12 May 1956; *m* 1980 *William John Hibbert, yr s of Sir Reginald Alfred Hibbert, GCMG, and has:

(1) *Cosima Mary; *b* 1984

(2) *Clover Frances; *b* 1988

2 *(Lucinda) Kate; *b* 20 March 1958; *m* 1980 *David Mark Ackroyd, s of L M Ackroyd, and has:

(1) *Frederick William; *b* 1981

(1) *Nancy Caroline; *b* 1983

(2) *Beatrice Alice Violet; *b* 1988

3 *(Belinda) Alice; *b* 22 Dec 1966; *m* 1990 *Aubrey Duarte Simpson-Orlebar, er s of Sir Michael Keith Orlebar Simpson-Orlebar, KCMG

Lineage (of Lucas-Tooth of Kensington): WILLIAM TOOTH, of Cranbrook, Kent; *bapt* 28 May 1773; *m* 9 April 1792 Catherine Butler, of Cranbrook (*d* 30 March 1820), and *d* 2 Oct 1832, having had, with two er sons, three yr sons and five daus):

ROBERT TOOTH, of Swifts Park, Cranbrook, Kent, and of London; merchant; *b* 15 Feb 1799; *m* 1st 13 July 1820 Mary Ann Reader, of Tenterden (*d* 26 Feb 1845 aged 44), and had:

1 Robert, of Sydney, NSW; *b* 28 May 1821; *m* 1st 1 May 1849 Marcia Lisle (*dsps*), dau of Capt Forster, RN, of Brighton, Tasmania; *m* 2nd 24 June 1871 Elizabeth, dau of Joseph Mansfield, of Hatcham, and *d* 19 Sept 1893, having by her had issue

2 EDWIN

3 Alfred, of Bayswater; *b* 10 Dec 1824; *m* 12 Aug 1852 Adelaide, dau of John Lainson, London Alderman and Sheriff 1835–36

4 Frederick, of Sydney; *b* 14 Feb 1827; *m* 1st 22 Aug 1848 Jane Jackson, of Southsea, and had issue; *m* 2nd Susan Frances Gosling and by her had two daus; *m* 3rd Fanny Peach

5 Charles (Rev); *b* 14 Feb 1831; *m* 1st 1 Feb 1855 Eliza Tabberer, of Tutbury (*d* 1892); *m* 2nd 1894 Louisa Janette Anne (*d* 18 Sept 1899), widow of Richard Meredyth Richards, DL, of Caerynwch, Merioneths, and only child and heiress of Edward Lloyd Edwards, of Cerrig Llwydion, Denbighs, and *d* 2 Aug 1894

6 Henry; *b* 27 March 1833; *m* 23 Nov 1854 Ann, dau of William Edwards, of Hastings, Sussex

7 William Augustus (Rev); Chaplain Warren Farm Schools Brighton 1873–92; *b* 9 Nov 1834; *educ* Trin Coll Cambridge (MA); *m* 31 Aug 1865 Eliza Petar, of Midhurst, Sussex (*d* 26 Feb 1875)

8 Arthur (Rev); Warden St Raphael's Coll Croydon; *b* 17 June 1839; *educ* Trin Coll Cambridge (MA)

1 Mary Ann; *b* 27 Feb 1837; *m* Rev Christopher Nevile, of Thorney Hall, Notts, and *d* 24 Sept 1919, having had issue. He *d* 8 Aug 1877

2 Eliza Jane; *b* 30 June 1841; *m* 1st Marmaduke Coghill Cramer Roberts, RN (*dsp* 13 April 1877); *m* 2nd — Smith

ROBERT TOOTH *m* 2nd 16 Nov 1847 his cousin Fanny, dau of Edward Tooth, of Petworth, Sussex, and by her had:

3 Fanny Blanche; *b* 8 Dec 1848; *m* John Edward Fincham

4 Annie Maud; *b* 1 June 1850; *m* Col Compton Norman, RWF, and had issue

5 Roberta Catherine Anne; *b* 19 Nov 1852; *m* Ernest W Cotterill and *d* 1900, leaving issue

6 Gertrude Gower; *b* 26 March 1856; *m* George Robins

The 2nd son,

EDWIN TOOTH, of Sydney, NSW; *b* 28 Aug 1822; *m* Feb 1844 Sarah (*d* 28 Aug 1854), dau of Francis Lucas, of Blackheath, and had, with another *s* (*d* an infant):

1 ROBERT LUCAS (Sir), 1st Bt

2 Edwin Forster; *b* 8 May 1848; *d* unm 28 Dec 1865

1 Mary Anne; *b* 9 June 1846; *m* 19 Dec 1867 Ernest de Satgé, Vicomte de Satgé de St Jean, and *d* 16 Feb 1871, leaving issue. He *d* 29 June 1901

2 Julia Lucas; *b* 7 April 1852; *m* 21 April 1874 John Taylor Lingen, barrister, of Hereford, and *d* 16 Sept 1912, leaving issue

3 Sarah Lucas; *b* 18 June 1854; *m* 15 Jan 1874 Henry de Satgé, 3rd *s* of Vicomte de Satgé, and *d* 20 July 1876, having had issue

EDWIN TOOTH *d* 29 Aug 1858; his est son,

Sir ROBERT LUCAS TOOTH later LUCAS-TOOTH (roy licence 15 Aug 1904), 1st Bt (UK), so *cr* 26 July 1906, of Queen's Gate, Kensington, and Kamaruka, NSW, JP (Herefs); *b* 7 Dec 1844; Ld Manor of Holme Lacy; Memb for Monaro NSW Parl 1879–84; *m* 2 Jan 1873 Helen (*d* 17 Aug 1942), dau of Frederick Tooth, of Goderich, Sydney, and *d* 19 Feb 1915, having had:

1 Selwyn Lucas, Capt 3rd Bn Lancs Fus; *b* 19 March 1879; *m* 16 June 1908 Everild Blanche Marion (*d* 18 Oct 1928), 2nd dau of Sir Edward Law Durand, 1st Bt, CB (*qv*), and *dvp* *ka* 20 Oct 1914, leaving:

(1) Everild Vera Undine, FRGS; *b* 27 March 1909; *m* 1st 24 Sept 1932 (*divorce* 1940) Cdr Reginald Seymour Young, RN (*d* 1996), only *s* of Dr C W F Young, of Kensington; *m* 2nd 27 Jan 1949 Kjeld Helweg-Larsen (*d* 8 June 1971), *s* of Dean Poul Helweg-Larsen, of Copenhagen, and *d* 2 Sept 1992, leaving by him:

  1a *Robin [Robin Helweg-Larsen, 327 Burlage Circle, Chapel Hill, NC 27514–2703, USA]; *b* 28 Sept 1950; *educ* Stowe; *m* 1st 31 Dec 1975 (*divorce* 1992) Pamela Boyes; *m* 2nd 23 Aug 1992 *Elizabeth Sharon Drake, dau of — Heaton, and by his 1st w has:

    1b *Simon Garth; *b* 14 April 1978

    1b *Kelda Jane; *b* 31 Jan 1977

    2b *Tessa Molly Danica; *b* 14 April 1983

  2a *Brian [Brian Helweg-Larsen Esq, 3 Weedon Lane, Amersham, Bucks HP6 5QS]; *b* 28 May 1952; *educ* Stowe and Pembroke Coll Oxford (BA); *m* 12 July 1975 *Elizabeth Sarah Fitch and has:

    1b *Timothy; *b* 6 July 1978

    2b *Nicholas; *b* 29 Sept 1981

    1b *Gillian; *b* 8 Aug 1986

2 Douglas Keith Lucas, DSO (posthumous); Capt 9th Lancers, Boer War (despatches) and WW I (despatches); *b* 10 Oct 1880; *d* unm *vp* 14 Sept 1914 of wounds recd in action Battle of the Aisne

3 Sir ARCHIBALD LEONARD LUCAS, 2nd and last Bt, Maj HAC WW I; *b* 3 June 1884; *m* 4 Jan 1916 Rosa Mary (*m* 2nd 17 April 1923 Maj John Greville Smyth-Osbourne, RWF, *s* of John Smyth Smyth-Osbourne, JP, DL, of Ash, Devon, and had issue), dau of Charles Arthur Bovill, of Smeeth Paddocks, Ashford, Kent, by Penelope Magdalen, dau of 1st Baron Basing (*qv*), and *das* & *spm* 12 July 1918, when the btcy expired, leaving:

(1) *Rosemarie Helen, JP; *b* 24 Oct 1916; *m* 1st 14 July 1936 Capt Algernon Robert Augustus Dorrien-Smith, 15th/19th King's Roy Hus (*ka* 20 May 1940), est *s* of Maj Arthur Algernon Dorrien-Smith, DSO, of Tresco Abbey, Scilly Isles; *m* 2nd 8 Feb 1945 Maj Bertram William Jepson Turner, MC, Rifle Bde, er *s* of Maj William Jepson Turner, of Garlogs, Nether Wallop, Hants

(2) *Christine Leonard; *b* 11 Dec 1918; *m* 28 Nov 1945 Maj Herbert Frederick Brudenell Foster, JP, The Scottish Horse, er *s* of Col Herbert Anderton Foster, of Littlemore, Queensbury, Yorks, and has:

  1a *John Leonard William; *b* 20 July 1948

  2a *Francis Derick; *b* 25 Feb 1953

  1a *Madeline Rosa Edith; *b* 1 Nov 1946; *m* 29 March 1967 Clive Lyon, only *s* of Lt-Col Ivan Lyon, DSO, MBE, Gordon Highrs

1 Beatrice Maude Lucas; *m* 24 April 1901 Maj Hugh Munro Warrand, 3rd Bn QO Cameron Highrs (*b* 8 July 1870; *d* 11 June 1935), 2nd *s* of Alexander John Cruickshank Warrand, of Bught, Inverness-shire, and Pitlochie, Aberdeenshire, and *d* 25 June 1944, leaving:

(1) HUGH VERE HUNTLY DUFF (Sir), **1st Bt**

(2) Selwyn John Power; Cdr RN WW II; *b* 6 Feb 1904; *m* 25 March 1933 *Frena Lingen (*m* 2nd 1947 Henry Richard Charles Humphries), 2nd dau of Everard Crace, of Canberra, Australia, and was *ka* in HMS *Hood* 24 May 1941, leaving:

  1a +JAMES LINGEN [James Warrand Esq, Ryefields, Cobbity, NSW 2570, Australia]; *b* 6 Oct 1936; heir presumptive; *m* 16 Oct 1960 *Juliet Rose, yr dau of T A Pearn, of Ford Park Rd, Plymouth, and has:

    1b *Patrick Duncan; *b* 18 March 1962; *m* 1989 *Elizabeth Margaret, yst dau of Bernard Bowen, of Perth, W Australia

    2b +Edward Jonathan; *b* 9 June 1968; *m* 1993 *Lisa Ann, est dau of Graham Wagg, of Kentlyn, NSW

    1b *Anna-Claire; *b* 11 Oct 1964; *m* 1991 *Christopher George Coore, yst *s* of George Coore, of Canberra, ACT, and has:

      1c *George Thomas; *b* 1993

  1a *Joanna Christine; *b* 3 July 1938

(1) *Beatrice Helen Fitzhardinge [Mrs Lyndall Urwick, Poyntington, 83 Kenneth St, Longueville, NSW, Australia]; *b* 1908; *m* 27 Sept 1941 *Lt-Col Lyndall Fownes Urwick, OBE, MC, only *s* of Sir Henry Urwick, JP, of Malvern, Worcs

2 Murielle Dorothea Lucas; *m* 23 April 1912 Maj Richard George Tyndall Bright, CMG, Rifle Bde, yst *s* of Charles Edward Bright, CMG, and *d* 27 Oct 1969, leaving *d* 10 July 1944

3 Vera Helen Lucas; *m* 29 July 1913 Maj Sir Edward Percy Marion Durand, 2nd Bt (*qv*), and *dsp* 23 Dec 1968

---

4 Yvonne Marjorie Lucas; *m* 14 Jan 1932 W/Cdr Reginald George Spencer-Booth, RAuxAF, er *s* of Capt Frank Booth, of Frizinghall, Yorks, and *d* 9 May 1967, leaving a dau

Maj and Mrs HUGH WARRAND's er *s*,

Sir HUGH VERE HUNTLY DUFF WARRAND later LUCAS-TOOTH (roy licence 1920) later still MUNRO-LUCAS-TOOTH (deed poll 3 Feb 1965, with territorial suffix 'of Teananich'), 1st Bt (UK), so *cr* 1 Dec 1920, with remainder to the heirs male of the body of his mother; *b* 13 Jan 1903; *educ* Eton and Balliol Coll Oxford (BA 1924); MP (C) Isle of Ely Oct 1924–May 1929 and Hendon S July 1945–70, Parly U-Sec Home Office Feb 1952–Dec 1955, barrister Lincoln's Inn 1933, Lt-Col QO Cameron Highrs; *m* 10 Sept 1925 Laetitia Florence, OBE (1958), JP (Hants 1951) (*d* 5 July 1978), er dau of Sir John Findlay, 1st Bt, KBE, of Aberlour (*see* 1970 edn), and had:

1 Sir (HUGH) JOHN LUCAS-TOOTH, **2nd and present Bt**

1 *Laetitia Helen [Lady Oppenheimer, L'Aiguillon, Rue des Cotils, Grouville, Jersey, CI JE3 9AP]; *b* 30 Dec 1926; *m* 12 July 1947 *Sir Michael Bernard Grenville Oppenheimer, 3rd Bt (*qv*), and has issue

2 *Jennifer Mary [Mrs John Henderson, Brimpton Lodge, Brimpton, Reading, Berks]; *b* 17 May 1929; *m* 1 Oct 1949 *Maj John Desmond Henderson, Scots Gds, only *s* of John Kenneth Henderson, of The Moot, Downton, Wilts, and has:

  (1) *John Richard; *b* 18 Oct 1951; *educ* Radley

  (2) *Alexander; *b* 15 Aug 1971

  (1) *Patricia Catherine; *b* 27 July 1950

LUKE

Arms: Arg. on a saltire sa., between four daggers, the points downwards gu., a sun in splendour or, on a chief of the third three cushions of the fourth. **Crest:** A spur between two wings or. **Supporters:** Dexter, a heron; sinister, a flamingo, both ppr. **Motto:** *Nunquam non paratus* ('Never unprepared'). **Creation:** B. (UK) 9 July 1929.

THE 3RD BARON LUKE, of Pavenham, Co Bedford (Arthur Charles St John Lawson Johnston) [The Rt Hon The Lord Luke, Odell Manor, Beds MK43 7BB]; *b* 13 Jan 1933; *s f* 1996; *educ* Eton and Trin Coll Cambridge (BA 1954); CC Beds 1965–70, High Sheriff 1969–70, FRSA, KStJ, Warden Drapers' Co 1993, Opposition (C) Whip Ho of Lds 1997–; *m* 1st 6 Aug 1959 (*divorce* 1971) Silvia Maria, yr dau of Honorio Roigt, Argentine Amb Netherlands, and has:

1 +IAN JAMES ST JOHN; *b* 3 Oct 1963; *educ* Eton

1 *Rachel Honoria; *b* 9 June 1960; *m* 1984 *Anthony William Parrack and has:

  (1) *Archie Beach; *b* 1989

  (2) *Felix Honorio Beach; *b* 1991

  (1) *Betsy Dorothy Mary; *b* 11 April 1998

2 *Sophia Charlotte; *b* 5 March 1966; *m* 23 Sept 1995 *Charles Reggie Kirk, only *s* of Maj J O Kirk, of Kirklington, N Yorks, and has:

  (1) *Mamie Honoria; *b* 30 Sept 1997

The 3rd BARON *m* 2nd 7 June 1971 *Sarah Louise, dau of Richard Hearne, OBE, and by her has:

2 +Rupert Arthur; *b* 12 May 1972

Lineage: JOHN LAWSON JOHNSTON; a Scot; migrated to Canada; following Franco-Prussian War won contract to supply French Army with tinned beef, mfg 'Johnston's Fluid Beef' in Canada till 1884 and then founded Bovril; later of Kingswood, Kent; *m* Elizabeth — and *d* 1900, having had, with other issue:

GEORGE LAWSON JOHNSTON, **1st Baron Luke**, of Pavenham, Co Bedford; (UK), so *cr* 9 July 1929, KBE (1920), JP and Ld Lt Beds, High Sheriff 1924, Chm Revenue Ctee, Hon Sec King Edward's Hosp and Fund London, Chm Br Charities Assoc, memb Cncl Br Empire League and PO Advsy Cncl, memb Cncl London Chamber Commerce, Chm: Br Nat Ctee Internat Chambers Commerce and Nutrition Advsy Ctee Min Health, V-Pres Roy Northern Hosp, Hon Sec League Mercy, dir Lloyds Bank and Nat Bank Australia, dir *Daily Express* to 1917; *b* 9 Sept 1873; *m* 4 Dec 1902 Hon Edith Laura St John, Order Mercy with bar (*d* 2 Aug 1941), 5th dau of 16th Baron St John of Bletso (*qv*), and *d* 23 Feb 1943, leaving:

1 IAN ST JOHN LAWSON JOHNSTON, **2nd Baron Luke**, KCVO (1976), TD (1949), JP (Beds 1939), DL (1938); *b* 7 June 1905; *educ* Eton and Trin Coll Cam-

bridge (BA 1927, MA 1933); Lt-Col Beds and Herts Regt WW II 1940–43 (Hon Col 5th Bn TA); Beds: CC 1943–52 (chm Standing Jt Ctee), High Sheriff; Lt City London 1976; memb: Ch Assembly (Ho Laity) 1935 and Ch House Cncl, Gen Advsy Cncl BBC 1947–52; MFH Oakley 1947–49, Master Drapers' Co 1962–63, chm: Beds TAA 1943, Duke of Gloucester's Red Cross and St John Fund 1943–46, Moorfields, Westminster and Centl Eye Hosp 1947–56, Outdoor Advertising Industry Advsy Ctee, Nat Playing Fields Assoc 1950–76, Bovril Ltd 1943–70 and Argentine Estates of Bovril Ltd, Virol Ltd and Electrolux Ltd, dir: Ashanti Goldfields Corp, Electrolux, IBM, Lloyds Bank, Australian Mercantile Land and Finance, pres London Chamber Commerce 1952–55, Advertising Assoc 1955–58, Inst Packaging 1957–60, Operation Britain Organisation 1957 on; CStJ; m Feb 1932 *Barbara [The Rt Hon Barbara Lady Luke, Odell Cottage, High St, Odell, Beds], yr dau of Sir FitzRoy Hamilton Anstruther-Gough-Calthorpe, 1st Bt (qv), and d 25 May 1996, leaving:

(1) ARTHUR CHARLES ST JOHN LAWSON JOHNSTON, **3rd and present Baron Luke**

(2) +(Ian) Harry Calthorpe [The Hon Harry Lawson Johnston, Coldstone House, Logie Coldstone, Aberdeenshire AB34 5NP]; 2nd Lt 5th Beds Regt (TA), late RN; b 29 May 1938; educ Harrow; m 4 Apr 1970 *Lady (Pamela) Lemina Gordon, only dau of 12th Marquess of Huntly (qv), and has:

1a +Percy FitzRoy; b 6 July 1971

1a *Henrietta Lemina; b 2 May 1973

(3) +(George) Andrew [The Hon Andrew Lawson Johnston, Inverenan House, Strathdon, Aberdeenshire]; composer; b 15 Nov 1944; educ Eton; m 22 Jun 1968 *Sylvia Josephine Ruth, est dau of Richard Michael Lloyd Hayes, DL (see SHELLEY, Bt), and has:

1a *Justin; b 5 April 1971

2a +Giles Spencer; b 5 April 1974

3a +Daniel George [Daniel Lawson Johnston Esq, 101 Brackenbury Road, London W6]; b 29 Nov 1978; glass engraver

1a *Tania Georgiana; b 29 March 1977

(4) +Philip Richard [The Hon Philip Lawson Johnston, 307 Woodstock Rd, Oxford OX2 7NY]; b 20 Nov 1950; educ Eton; m 17 Dec 1977 *(Saskia) Moyne, est dau of Terence George Andrews, MBE, of Carneshire House, Longstock, Hants, and has:

1a +Harry Alexander; b 9 Sept 1979

2a +Edward Philip; b 9 Sept 1979 (twin)

3a +Samuel; b 1982

1a *Saskia Rose; b 1985

(1) *Caroline Jean [The Hon Mrs Bristow, Penmorfa, Seaview, IoW PO34 5HE]; b 25 Dec 1935; m 19 April 1958 *James Bristow, s of James Percy Bristow, of Glebe House, Biddenham, Beds, and has:

1a *Timothy Dominic Ian James [Timothy Bristow Esq, Manor Farm House, Hulcote, Northants NN12 7HT]; b 1 July 1959; educ Bedford Sch and Exeter U; m 3 March 1984 (divorce 1992) Annabel J D, yr dau of David Palmer, of The Old Vicarage, Biddenham, Beds, and has:

1b *Arthur Timothy James; b 1986

1b *Lily Annabel Mary; b 1989

2a *George Edward FitzRoy; b 18 Sept 1961; educ Bedford Sch; m 1987 *Juliet J, only dau of Paul Knocker, of Windsor, and has:

1b *Edward George; b 1990

2b *Lucinda Joy; b 1989

3a *Barnaby James St John; b 9 Aug 1966

1a *Melissa Caroline; b 7 Nov 1963; m 1994 *Mathew Thurlow Laws and has:

1b *James; b 1997

1b *Isabella; b 1995

1b *Lara; b 1996

2 +Hugh de Beauchamp, TD (1951), DL (Beds 1964) [The Hon Hugh Lawson Johnston TD DL, Flat 1, 28 Lennox Gardens, London SW1 0DJ]; Woodleys Farm House, Melchbourne, Beds]; High Sheriff Beds 1961–62, Capt 5th Bn Beds and Herts Regt (TA), dir Bovril Ltd, Tribune Investment Tst; b 7 April 1914; educ Eton and Corpus Christi Coll Cambridge (BA 1934, MA 1938); m 18 July 1946 *Audrey, er dau of Col Frederic Warren Pearl, of Knightsbridge, and has:

(1) *Primrose Pearl [Mrs Martin Hudson, 7 Grove Park Gardens, London W4 3RY]; b 2 April 1948; m 1975 *Martin Arthur Hudson and has:

1a *Hugh James; b 1977

2a *Mark Oliver; b 1978

3a *Ian Alexander; b 1979

4a *Christopher Martin; b 1981

(2) *Juliet Amy; b 23 June 1950 [Mrs Simon Crocker, 62 Battledean Rd, London N5]; m 21 Nov 1975 *Simon Crocker and has:

1a *Barnaby William de Beauchamp; b 1976

1a *Amy; b 1979

(3) *Marguerite Laura [Mrs Timothy Clark, Wappenham Manor, nr Towcester, Northants]; b 5 July 1952; m 1977 *Timothy John Clark and has:

1a *Jamie Duncan; b 1979

2a *Thomas Edward; b 1986

1a *Anna Camilla; b 1981

2a *Jessica Roddie; b 1984

1 Olive Elizabeth Helen; Sr Cmdt ATS, 2nd Offr WRNS, WW II; b 22 Jan 1904; m 18 Dec 1934 (annulled 1936) Frederick Lothair Lawson Johnston (d 15 July 1963)

2 Margaret Beaufort; Order Mercy; m 28 Apr 1927 Sir Isaac James Pitman, KBE, Hon DLitt, chm Initial Teaching Alphabet Fndn, and had issue

3 Charlotte Enid; m 3 Oct 1933 George McCorquodale, yst s of Norman McCorquodale, OBE, JP, of Winslow Hall, Bucks (see 1970 edn McCORQUODALE OF NEWTON, B), and had issue

4 *(Laura) Pearl, OBE (1946), JP (Beds 1941), DL (Beds 1976) [The Hon Pearl Lawson Johnston OBE JP DL, Woodleys Stud House, Melchbourne, Beds MK44 1AG]; V-Pres Cadets St John Ambulance Bde Beds, DStJ, High Sheriff Beds 1985–86

LUSHINGTON

Arms: Or on a fess wavy between three lion's heads erased vert, langued gu., as many erm. spots of the field. **Crest:** A lion's head erased vert, charged on the erasure with three erm. spots or, ducally gorged arg. **Motto:** Fides nudaque veritas ('Faith and naked truth').
Creation: Bt. (GB) 26 April 1791.

SIR JOHN RICHARD CASTLEMAN LUSHINGTON, 8TH BT, of South Hill Park, Berkshire [Sir John Lushington Bt, The Glebe House, Henham, Herts CM22 6AH]; b 28 Aug 1938; s f 1988; educ Oundle; m 21 May 1966 *Bridget Gillian Margaret, only dau of Col John Foster Longfield, of Knockbeg, Saunton, N Devon, and has:

1 +RICHARD DOUGLAS LONGFIELD; b 29 March 1968; BA; F/Lt RAF

2 +Greville Edmund Longfield; b 9 May 1969; BA

3 +Thomas Robert Longfield; b 28 Nov 1975

Lineage: Sir Stephen Lushington, 1st Bt (GB), so cr 26 April 1791, of S Hill Park, Berks (3rd s of Rev Dr Lushington by Mary, dau of Rev Dr Altham, Archdeacon Middx, and gs of Stephen Lushington, of Sittingbourne); m 6 June 1771 Hester (d 6 Dec 1830), dau of John Boldero, of Aspenden Hall, Herts, and had, with three other daus:

1 HENRY, (Sir), **2nd Bt**

2 Stephen; MP, DCL, Judge Admlty, Chllr Dioceses Rochester and London; b 14 Jan 1782; m 8 Aug 1821 Sarah Grace (d 20 Sept 1837), dau of Thomas William Carr, and d 19 Jan 1873, leaving, with three other daus (d unm):

(1) Edward Harbord, JP, of Brackenhurst, Cobham, Surrey; Bengal CS 1842–71; b 29 July 1822; m 26 Nov 1848 Mary (d 25 Feb 1895), dau of Col Michael Ramsay, and d 29 Oct 1904, having had:

1a Edward Eardley, Lt-Col 8th Hus; b 11 Feb 1850; m 1st 1882 Caroline Anna (d 1884), dau of Sir Bradford Leslie, KCSI; m 2nd 1897 Maria Thomasine (d 23 June 1918), dau of Maj T B Sharpe, 20th Regt; m 3rd 18 Jan 1921 Adeline Charlotte (d 28 April 1939), yst dau of Alexander Gordon, KC, and d 17 Feb 1930

2a Sidney George; BCL Oxford, barrister; b 6 April 1859; m 6 Aug 1890 Georgina Caroline Elizabeth Chippindall (d 30 Sept 1900), est dau of Capt John Chippindall Healey, Manchester Regt, and d 18 Aug 1909, leaving:

1b Franklin; b 23 March 1892; educ Eton; Lt-Col RA WW I (wounded), WW II 1939–43 (despatches); novelist; m 1st 14 Oct 1916 (divorce 1948) Mary Marjorie Bridget (d 1977), dau of Ernest Howard, of Heath End, Farnham; m 2nd 31 March 1949 Eleanora (d 9 Dec 1964), dau of Niels Illeris, of Denmark, and formerly w of M E H Coggin, of Totnes, Devon, and d following a car crash 2 Sept 1964, leaving by his 1st w:

1c +Stephen [Stephen Lushington Esq, 9 High Wickham, Hastings, Sussex]; b 29 July 1917; educ Eton and New Coll Oxford; Nuffield Fell Linguistics and English Teaching, late RA; m 1st 1 Oct 1941 (divorce 1951) Maureen, dau of Maj John Pook, and has:

1d +Mark; b 14 Dec 1942; educ Westminster and King's Coll Cambridge; m 1966 *Cora, dau of Sidney Kaplan, of Northampton, Mass., and has:

1e +Jacob; b 1968

1c (cont.) Stephen Lushington m 2nd 10 Feb 1951 (divorce 1972) Sonia, dau of Harry Ratoff; m 3rd June 1972 *Beatrice, dau of Irvan O'Connell, of Winchester, Va., and widow of Theodore Roethke, and by his 2nd w has:

1d *Catherine Rachel; b 16 Dec 1953; m 14 Feb 1975 *Richard Marc Greenblatt

2b Sydney Edward James Chippindall; b 20 May 1895; T/Lt 11th (Service) Bn Hants Regt; ka 1916

1b Mary Frances; b 23 Sept 1897; m 14 Nov 1923 John Dudley Lucie-Smith, OBE, Assist Colonial Sec Jamaica (d 10 March 1943), s of John Barkley Lucie-Smith, PMG Jamaica, and had:

1c *(John) Edward McKenzie, [Edward Lucie-Smith Esq, c/o Coleridge & White, 20 Powis Mews, London W11 1JN]; art critic and poet, FRSL; b 27 Feb 1933; educ King's Sch Canterbury and Merton Coll Oxford (MA)

3a Guy; barrister; b 10 Sept 1861; d 11 Sept 1916

4a Stephen, CB, CMG, JP Hants; Hon Brig-Gen RFA, Inspr-Gen Police Br Guiana 1902–07, WW I (despatches), Offr Mil Order Savoy; *b* 18 Jan 1864; *m* 1891 Mabel Louise (*d* 14 Jan 1950), dau of Col Frederick Wood Macmullen, Duke of Connaught's Own 13th Bengal Lancers, and *dsp* 21 Dec 1940

1a Helen; *m* 18 Aug 1881 His Hon Judge Francis Reynolds Yonge Radcliffe, KC (*d* 23 April 1924), and *d* 26 Feb 1938, leaving issue

(2) William Bryan; barrister; *b* 23 July 1824; *m* 22 Oct 1873 Augusta Victoria (*d* 6 April 1942), 3rd dau of Robert Alfred Cloyne Godwin-Austen, of Shalford House, Surrey, and *d* 21 Dec 1888, leaving:

1a Philip Austen (Rev); Preb Hereford; *b* 10 Oct 1874; *educ* Winchester and Balliol Coll Oxford (BA 1897, MA 1902); *m* 17 April 1907 Frances Anne Katherine (*d* 3 Jan 1964), only dau of G C Harrison, and *dsp* 4 Sept 1966

(3) Stephen; *d* 1860

(4) Vernon, KC, of Pyports, Cobham, Surrey; DJAG 1864–69, Sec Admlty 1869–77, Judge Co Courts Surrey and Berks 1877–1900; *b* 8 March 1832; *m* 28 Feb 1865 Jane (*d* 1884), 3rd dau of Francis Mowatt, MP, and *d* 24 Jan 1912, having had:

1a Katherine; *m* 23 Dec 1890 Leopold James Maxse (*see* BERKELEY, B) and *d* 4 Oct 1922

2a Margaret; *m* 18 July 1895 Maj Stephen Langton Massingberd, JP, DL (*d* 21 May 1925), of Gunby Hall, Lincs, and *dsp* 11 Sept 1906

3a Susan, MBE (1943); *d* unm 16 Feb 1953 aged 82

(5) Godfrey (Sir), GCMG, KCB; barrister, Fell All Souls, Counsel Home Office 1869–76, Assist U-Sec 1876–1885, U-Sec 1885–95; *b* 8 March 1832; *m* 3 June 1865 Beatrice Anne Shore (*d* 7 Sept 1914), dau of Samuel Smith, of Combe Hurst, Surrey, and *dsp* 5 Feb 1907

(1) Hester; *m* 26 June 1844 Capt Robert Russell, RN (*d* 27 Nov 1848), of Newton House, Bedale, and *d* 12 March 1900, leaving issue

(2) Edith Grace; *m* 28 April 1858 Ven John Pilkington Norris (*d* 1891), Archdeacon and Canon Bristol, and *d* 11 Jan 1928, having had issue

3 Charles; *b* 14 April 1785; MP Westminster 1847–52; *m* 1st 1805 Sarah (*d* 24 Dec 1839), dau of Gen — Gascoigne; *m* 2nd Oct 1844 Julia (*d* 17 Feb 1866), widow of Thomas Teed, of Stanmore, and *dsp* 23 Sept 1866

1 Hester; *m* 28 Aug 1797 Thomas Butler, of Berry Lodge, Hants, and had issue

2 Sophia; *m* 20 Sept 1800 Gen Denzil Onslow (*d* 21 Aug 1838) and *d* 17 March 1860, having had issue

Sir STEPHEN *d* 12 Jan 1807; his est son,

Sir Henry Lushington, 2nd Bt; *b* 27 Oct 1775; Consul-Gen Naples 1815–1832; *m* 8 April 1799 Fanny Maria (*d* 20 May 1862), est dau of Matthew Lewis, U-Sec War, and sis and coheir with her sis Sophia (w of Col — Shedden) of Matthew Gregory Lewis, MP, author *The Monk*, and *d* 25 Jan 1863, having had, with other issue:

1 **Sir Henry Lushington, 3rd Bt;** HEICS; *b* 10 Oct 1802; *m* 1st 26 March 1825 Eliza Louisa (*d* 1862), dau of William Trower, and had:

(1) **Sir Henry Lushington, 4th Bt;** *b* 24 Jan 1826; Judge Allahabad; *m* 29 Dec 1849 Elizabeth (*d* 6 June 1902), dau of Anstruther Cheape, of Rossie, Fife, and *d* 15 March 1898, having had:

1a Henry Cornwallis Cartwright; *d* 11 Feb 1866

2a **Sir Arthur Patrick Douglas Lushington, 5th Bt;** *b* 19 Jan 1861; Maj 3rd Dragoon Gds, Boer War 1899–1902, WW I; *m* 1st 21 Jan 1892 Florence (*d* 7 May 1926), est dau of James A Burness, of The Lodge, Melton, Suffolk; *m* 2nd 21 Nov 1929 Mabel Marie (*d* 29 Oct 1955), yr dau of George Hatfield D Gossip, of Hatfield, Yorks, and formerly w of Gerald Purcell FitzGerald, and *d* 13 April 1937, having by his 1st w had:

1b Florence Lisette; *m* 19 March 1929 (*divorce* 1938) Cecil Frank Drury-Lowe Bruce Durham, of Bull's Farm House, Herriard, Basingstoke, and *d* following an accident 5 Dec 1942, leaving issue

1a Caroline Alison; *m* 29 Dec 1874 Sir Charles Hawkes Todd Crosthwaite, KCSI (*d* 28 May 1915), and *d* 10 Oct 1893, leaving issue

2a Annette Louisa; *m* 5 Sept 1873 Donald Mackenzie Smeaton, CSI, MP (*d* 19 April 1910), s of David James Smeaton, of St Andrews, Fife, and *d* 1880, leaving issue

3a Edith Emily; *d* unm 15 Jan 1942

(1) Louisa Fanny Maria; *m* 10 Oct 1849 Reginald Thornton, Bengal CS (*d* 29 Aug 1895), of Birkin House, Dorset, and *d* 18 Sept 1918, having had issue

(2) Laura; *m* 11 Nov 1850 Gen Hon Sir Henry Ramsay, KCSI, CB (*d* 16 Dec 1893), bro of 12th Earl of Dalhousie (*qv*), and *d* 29 July 1914, leaving issue

1 (cont.) **Sir Henry** *m* 2nd 17 June 1863 Eliza Hannah (*d* 26 March 1889), dau of John Shelley, and *d* Sept 1897, having by her had:

(3) Geraldine; *d* unm 15 Jan 1937

2 Stephen (Sir), GCB; *b* 12 Dec 1803; Adml, Supt Indian Navy, C-in-C S American station, Lt-Govr Greenwich Hosp, cmded naval bde on shore capture Sebastopol, Kt St Louis, the Redeemer, Kt Cdr Legn Hon; *m* 1841 Henrietta (*d* 22 Sept 1875), dau of Adml Sir Henry Prescott, KCB, and *d* 28 May 1877, having had:

(1) Henrietta; *d* unm 15 Dec 1902

(2) Agnes; *m* 19 May 1864 Henry Kirke, JP (*d* 9 July 1925), and *d* 28 July 1916, leaving issue

3 Charles (Rev); Vicar Walton-on-Thames; *b* 29 Nov 1805; *m* 29 July 1835 Rose (*d* 5 Sept 1877), dau of Capt J Tweedale, HEIS

4 Matthew; *b* 5 Oct 1808; *d* Jamaica 16 May 1839

5 Franklin, CB; Col Scots Fus Gds; *b* 20 April 1811; *m* June 1853 Anne Dobrée (*d* 17 Dec 1887), dau of Gen Sir Philip Bainbridge, KCB, and *d* 18 Jan 1890, leaving:

(1) Eleanor Fanny; *m* 9 Oct 1877 2nd Earl Kitchener of Khartoum and of Broome (*qv*) and *d* 1 June 1898, leaving issue

6 Frederick Astell, of Rosiere, Hants, JP; Bengal CS; *b* 1 Nov 1815; *m* 24 Sept 1846 Lady Margaret Julia Hay, dau of 15th Earl of Erroll (*qv*), and *d* 18 Sept 1892, leaving:

(1) Algernon Hay, of Lansdowne, Shanklin, IoW; *b* 29 Sept 1847; *m* 1st 2 April 1872 Emma Jane (*d* 4 Oct 1879), only child of Charles Castleman, and had:

1a HERBERT CASTLEMAN (Sir), **6th Bt**

1a Muriel Evelyn; *d* unm 7 Feb 1969 aged 90

(1) (cont.) Algernon Lushington *m* 2nd 6 Jan 1881 Effie Lilian (*d* 26 July 1946), 2nd dau of Capt W E Newall, 92nd Gordon Highrs, and *d* 13 Sept 1930, having by her had:

2a Montague Hay; T/Capt RFA (despatches twice); *b* 24 Nov 1881; *m* 1st 2 June 1909 Annette Caroline (*d* Nov 1953), dau of Rev George Richard Dupuis, of Sessay Hall, Yorks; *m* 2nd 1 Jan 1954 Rosemary Phyllis, er dau of Stanley Edwards, of Reydon Covert, Southwold, Suffolk, and *dsp* 10 May 1961

(2) Herbert Gurney; Lt 31st Regt; *b* 11 Jan 1848; *d* unm 19 Feb 1871

(3) Frederick Seton Karr; Lt 64th Regt; *b* 29 Jan 1849; *d* unm 23 Dec 1874

(4) Somerville Henry (Rev); Vicar Thorpe, Surrey; *b* 24 May 1856; *d* unm Dec 1916

(1) Beatrice Harriet; *d* unm 18 Oct 1913

(2) Constance Fanny; *m* 1889 R-Adml Henry Compton Aitchison (*d* 1901), of Shrubbs Hill, Lyndhurst, and *d* 6 Dec 1924, leaving issue

(3) Violet Margaret; *m* 1st 3 May 1899 Henry A Court Pigott (*see* PIGOTT, Bt); *m* 2nd 12 Sept 1917 Max Georges de Crelier (*d* 15 June 1923) and *d* 9 Nov 1951

1 Louisa; *m* 8 April 1826 Adml Sir Charles Burrard, 2nd Bt (*see* 1956 edn), and *d* 17 Feb 1885 aged 83

The 5th Bt's cousin,

Sir Herbert Castleman Lushington, 6th Bt; *b* 15 Sept 1879; WW I in Yeo, WW II 1940–43 in RASC; *m* 1st 22 Feb 1908 Barbara Henrietta (*d* 13 Feb 1927), 2nd dau of Rev William Greville Hazlerigg (*see* HAZLERIGG, B), and had:

1 HENRY EDMUND CASTLEMAN (Sir), **7th Bt**

2 Algernon Herbert Greville; *b* 22 Oct 1910; *educ* Dauntsey's Sch; Capt AIF (despatches) WW II; *m* 1st 1948 Mary Elizabeth Gwenyth (*d* 15 Sept 1959), dau of J C Dunbar, of Dunbarton, Bairnsdale, Vict; *m* 2nd 18 Aug 1961 Mrs Marjory Lorrainé Breheny (*d* 1994), dau of Cecil Wood Le Plastrier, of Woodend, Vict, and *d* 11 Jan 1995

3 Stephen Arthur Hay; *b* 17 June 1914; *m* 1st 1941 Joyce, dau of J Crump, of Melbourne; *m* 2nd 19– Joy — (*d* 26 April 1991) and *d* 15 May 1990

Sir Herbert *m* 2nd 18 Aug 1928 Roselia May, only dau of Ernest Edward Elliot, MRCS, LRCP, of Maison Dieu Lodge, Dover, and by her had:

4 +Patrick Hay Castleman [Patrick Lushington Esq, 56 Suzanne Ave, Morphett Vale, S Aust 5162]; *b* 6 Aug 1931; late RAF; *m* 13 July 1957 *Anne Marie, er dau of Ferdinand Mohr, of Mainz, and has:

(1) +Kurt; *b* 30 March 1958; *m* 6 April 1985 *Susane Annette, dau of Lionel Burton, of Adelaide, and has:

1a +Joshua Hay Castleman; *b* 31 March 1991

2a +Caleb James; *b* 16 Oct 1997

1a *Grace Alexandra; *b* 12 Nov 1992

2a *Hanna Victoria; *b* 6 Dec 1995

(2) +Werner; *b* 28 July 1960; *m* 25 May 1985 *Sylvia Angelika, dau of Sigismund Krause, and has:

1a +Sean Matthew; *b* 1 April 1987

2a +Alexander James; *b* 8 Jan 1992

1a *Tarryn Rebecca; *b* 23 Sept 1985

(3) +Horst; *b* 19 Sept 1966; *m* 2 Dec 1995 *Farlie, est dau of Colin Gordon, of Kangarilla, SA, and has:

1a +Finneas Colin Ross; *b* 27 Aug 1997

(1) *Elke Christine; *b* 4 Dec 1964; *m* 10 Oct 1992 *Robert Melten, of Melbourne

1 *Pamela Anne [Mrs Peter Jones, 19 Aberdare Ave, Drayton, Cosham, Hants PO6 2AT]; *b* 21 July 1929; *m* 5 April 1952 *Peter Lindsay Jones, 2nd s of Lt-Cdr H Jones, and has:

(1) *Alistair; *b* 1953; *m* 1st 1975 (*divorce* 1986) Heather McKennes; *m* 2nd 1993 *Shaari Horowitz

(2) *Laurence; *b* 1959

(3) *Martin Edward; *b* 1964

(1) *Margaret Amanda; *b* 1955; *m* 1976 *Michael Joseph Reilly, of Denver, USA, and has:

1a *Patrick Joseph; *b* 1977

2a *Dennis John; *b* 1979

(2) *Rosemary Anne; *b* 1957; *m* 1989 *Nicholas John Pullen and has:

1a *Adam James; *b* 1990

1a *Rebecca Louise; *b* 1992

(3) *Sarah Louise; *b* 1966

Sir HERBERT *d* 5 Oct 1968; his est son,

Sir Henry Edmund Castleman Lushington, 7th Bt; *b* 12 May 1909; *educ* Dauntsey's Sch; F/Lt RAFVR WW II 1941–46, Supt Met Police 1935–58, legal exec with Amery Parkes & Co 1958–88; *m* 2 Oct 1937 *Pamela Elizabeth Daphne [Pamela Lady Lushington, Gramerci, Eversley Centre, Hants RG27 0NB], er dau of Maj Archer Richard Hunter, of Hare Hatch Grange, Twyford, Berks, and *d* 1988, leaving:

1 Sir JOHN RICHARD CASTLEMAN LUSHINGTON, **8th and present Bt**

1 *Caroline Elizabeth [Mrs Patrick Bloss, Dene House, The Green, Shamley Green, Surrey GU5 0UA]; *b* 4 April 1942; *m* 19 Sept 1964 *Patrick Donald Bloss, FCA, and has:

(1) *James Patrick; *b* 1972

(1) *Diana Elizabeth; *b* 2 March 1967

(2) *Victoria Caroline; *b* 31 March 1970

2 *Penelope Daphne [Mrs Ronald Gulliver, The Old Chapel, New Mill, Eversley, Hants]; *b* 21 April 1945; *m* 16 Sept 1967 *Ronald Gulliver, LLB, FCA, s of Ronald Charles Gulliver, and has:

(1) *Christopher Ronald; *b* 5 April 1974

(1) *Patricia Jean; *b* 1976

LYELL

FORTI NON IGNAVO

Arms: Or a cross parted and fretty azure between four crosses patée gules, all within a bordure of the last. **Crest:** Upon a rock a dexter cubit arm erect in armour proper, charged with a cross parted and fretty gules, the hand grasping a sword in bend sinister also proper. **Motto:** *Forti non ignavo* ('To the brave, not to the dastardly'). **Creations:** Bt. (UK) 24 Jan 1894, B. (UK) 4 July 1914.

THE 3RD BARON LYELL, of Kinnordy, Co Forfar, and a **Baronet** (Sir Charles Lyell, Bt, DL (Angus 1988)) [The Rt Hon The Lord Lyell DL, Kinnordy, Kirriemuir, Angus DD8 5ER; 20 Petersham Mews, London SW7 5NR]; *b* 27 March 1939; *s* f 1943; *educ* Eton and Ch Ch Oxford; 2nd Lt Scots Gds 1957–59; chartered accountant; memb Roy Co Archers, Oppn Whip Ho Lds 1975–79, Ld-in-Waiting (Govt Whip) 1979–84, Parly Under-Sec NI 1984–89

Lineage: CHARLES LYELL, of Kinnordy, Forfarshire; *b* 1734; *m* Mary Beale (*d* 16 May 1813), of Westloe, Cornwall, and *d* 19 Jan 1796, having had:

1 CHARLES

1 Mary; *d* unm 30 April 1843

2 Anne; *m* Feb 1809 Capt Gilbert Heathcote, RN (*see* HEATHCOTE, Bt, of Hursley), and *d* 30 April 1854, leaving issue

The only son,

CHARLES LYELL, of Kinnordy, JP; *b* March 1769; *m* 11 Oct 1796 Frances (*d* 4 Dec 1850), only dau of Thomas Smith, of Maker Hall, Swaledale, Yorks, and *d* 8 Nov 1849, leaving, with six other daus:

1 Sir CHARLES LYELL, 1st and last Bt (UK), so *cr* 22 Aug 1864, of Kinnordy, DL; *b* 14 Nov 1797; DCL, FRS, author: *Principles of Geology*, fndr memb The Sunday League, ktd 1848; *m* 12 July 1832 Mary Elizabeth (*d* 24 April 1873), est dau of Leonard Horner, FRS, of Montagu Sq, London W, and *d* 11 Feb 1875, when the btcy expired

2 Thomas; *b* 24 Feb 1799; Lt RN; *d* 1871

3 Henry; *b* 1 Dec 1804; Lt-Col 43rd Bengal LI; *m* 25 Jan 1848 Katherine Murray (*d* 18 Feb 1915), 4th dau of Leonard Horner, FRS, of Montagu Sq, London W, and *d* Feb 1875, leaving:

  (1) LEONARD (Sir), **1st Baron**

  (2) Francis Horner; *b* 11 Feb 1852; *m* 1st 12 Aug 1879 Emily (*d* 1887), only dau of Francis Guise, of Dean Hall, and had issue; *m* 2nd 13 March 1889 Mary (*d* 29 July 1934), dau of Capt Nicholson, and *d* 24 June 1934

  (3) Arthur Henry; *b* 26 Nov 1853; *m* 11 July 1883 Florence (*d* 22 July 1938), dau of David Chambers, and *d* 1 Jan 1925, leaving issue

  (1) Rosamond Frances Anne; *d* unm 21 Dec 1901

1 Maria; *m* 15 Jan 1840 Rev Gilbert Heathcote and *dsp* 24 Dec 1843, leaving issue (*see* HEATHCOTE, Bt, of Hursley)

The Bt's n,

Sir Leonard Lyell, 1st Bt, and **1st Baron Lyell**, of Kinnordy, Co Forfar, so *cr* 24 Jan 1894 and 4 July 1914 respectively (both UK), JP and DL; *b* 21 Oct 1850; BSc (London); MP (Lib) Orkney and Shetland 1885–1900; *m* 4 July 1874 Mary (*d* 24 Feb 1929), dau and coheir of Rev John Mayne Stirling by Rosetta, dau of Capt George Cheyne, RN, and had:

1 Charles Henry, JP (Forfarshire); *b* 18 May 1875; Maj Fife RGA; MP (Lib) E Dorset 1904–10 and S Edinburgh 1910–17, PPS to For Sec 1906 and PM 1911, Assist Mil Attaché Washington 1918 (despatches); *m* 18 May 1911 Rosalind Margaret, MBE (1918), JP (Co London) (*d* 22 May 1957), er dau of Vernon James Watney, of Cornbury Park, Charlbury, Oxon, by Lady Margaret Wallop, dau of 5th Earl of Portsmouth (*qv*), and *d* 18 Oct 1918, leaving:

  (1) CHARLES ANTONY, **2nd Baron**

  (1) Margaret Laetitia (Letty); *b* 22 April 1912; BSc Econ (London); Assist Commercial Sec Moscow 1944–45; *m* 1st 23 Jan 1937 Maj Hon Francis Alan Stewart Mackenzie of Seaforth, Surrey and Sussex Yeo (*ka* Sept 1943), 2nd son of 1st Earl of Midleton (*see* MIDLETON, V); *m* 2nd 6 June 1944 Charles Henry Pearson Gifford, OBE (*d c* 1993), er s of Thomas Johnstone Carlyle Gifford, of Edinburgh, and *d* Nov 1995, leaving:

1a *Patrick Antony Francis; *b* 24 May 1945; *educ* Winchester and Magdalene Coll Cambridge (BA 1966); *m* 22 March 1969 *Mary, MSc, dau of John Kilgour, of Farnham, Surrey, and has:

  1b *Antony Patrick Carlyle; *b* 25 May 1971

2a *John Vernon; *b* 24 Dec 1946; *educ* Bradfield and New Coll Oxford (BA)

3a *William Lyell; *b* 22 Aug 1950; *educ* Bedales and Birmingham U; *m* 5 Aug 1972 *Carolyn Mortimore

4a *Andrew Graham; *b* 3 Feb 1953; *educ* Bedales

1a *Mary Charlotte; *b* 11 June 1948; *educ* North London Collegiate Sch and Barnard Coll Columbia U (BA); *m* 17 May 1971 *R Michael Neumann, yr s of Leopold Newman and Mrs Herbert Marcuse, of La Jolla, Calif

1 Mary Leonora; *m* 9 Oct 1912 Arthur Pierson, of Calgary, Canada, and *d* 18 Feb 1916

2 Eleanor Katherine; *m* 5 Jan 1904 Sir Archibald Lawrence Langman, 2nd Bt, CMG (*see* 1970 edn), and *d* 18 Nov 1963, leaving issue

The 1st BARON *d* 18 Sept 1926; his grandson,

  CHARLES ANTONY LYELL, **2nd Baron Lyell**, VC (posthumous 1943); *b* 14 June 1913; Capt Scots Gds WW II; *m* 4 July 1938 *Sophie Mary, CC Angus [The Rt Hon The Lady Lyell, Kinnordy, Kirriemuir, Angus DD8 5ER], 2nd dau of Maj Sigismund William Joseph Trafford (*see* LINDSEY and ABINGDON, E), and was *ka* 27 April 1943, leaving:

CHARLES LYELL, **3rd and present Baron Lyell**

LYLE

AN·I·MAY

Arms: Gules fretty or, surmounted of a galley, oars in saltire, sails furled sable, flagged gules, the sails charged with a crescent of the second for difference. **Crest:** A cock or, crested gules. **Motto:** (over crest) *An I may*. **Creation:** Bt. (UK) 26 March 1929.

SIR GAVIN ARCHIBALD LYLE, 3RD BT, of Glendelvine, Co Perth [Sir Gavin Lyle Bt, Glendelvine, Caputh, Perthshire PH1 4JN]; *b* 14 Oct 1941; *s* gf 1946; *educ* Eton; estate manager, farmer, co dir; *m* 26 Sept 1967 (*divorce* 1985) Suzanna, only dau of John Royston Vaughan Cooper, of Cheslsea, by Mrs John Claud Armitage, and has:

  1 +IAN ABRAM; *b* 25 Sept 1968

  2 +Jake Archibald; *b* 4 Nov 1969

  3 +Matthew Alexander; *b* 1974

  4 +Joshua; *b* 1979

  5 +Samuel; *b* 1981

  1 *Rachel; *b* 31 March 1971

Lineage: JOHN LYLE; *b* 1669; merchant in Greenock, Renfrewshire; *m* Margaret — and *d* 25 March 1728, having had, with three yr sons:

JOHN LYLE, of Greenock; *b* 12 Aug 1700; *m* 10 Aug 1728 Isabel, dau of John Forrest, and had, with other issue:

ABRAM LYLE; *b* 14 Sept 1741; fndr Abram Lyle & Sons 1796; *m* 10 Dec 1774 Rachael McAulay and had:

ABRAM LYLE, of Greenock; *b* 18 Jan 1783; *m* 8 Dec 1806 Mary Campbell (*bur* 16 March 1855) and was *bur* 19 Sept 1849, leaving:

ABRAM LYLE, of Oakley, Greenock, JP; *b* 14 Dec 1820; Provost Greenock; *m* 14 Dec 1846 Mary (*d* 24 June 1881), dau of William Park, Greenock merchant, and had, with other issue:

1 ALEXANDER PARK (Sir), **1st Bt**

2 Charles, of Brooke Hall, Norwich, and Knightsbridge; *b* 1851; *m* Margaret (*d* 1915), yst dau of James Brown, of Dunedin, and *d* 13 June 1929, leaving:

  (1) Sir CHARLES ERNEST LEONARD LYLE, 1st Bt, and 1st BARON LYLE OF WESTBOURNE, of Canford Cliffs, Poole, Co Dorset (both UK), so *cr* 22 June 1932 and 13 Sept 1945 respectively, JP (Bournemouth); *b* 22 July 1882; *educ* Harrow and Trin Hall Cambridge; WW I as Capt RASC (MV) and BRCS; Pres (formerly Chm) Tate and Lyle Ltd, Treasurer Roy Wanstead Sch, Dep-Pres and Chm Queen Mary's Hosp for the E End, MP (C) Stratford 1918–22, Epping 1923–24 and Bournemouth 1940–45, PPS to Food Controller 1919, V-Pres (formerly Chm) Br Empire League and Empire Industries Assoc, Life V-Pres (Chm 1932) Lawn Tennis Assoc, ktd 1923; *m* 14 Jan 1904 Edith Louise

(*d* 22 Dec 1942), 2nd dau of John Levy, of Rochester, and *d* 6 March 1954, leaving:

　1a CHARLES JOHN LEONARD LYLE, 2nd and last BARON LYLE OF WESTBOURNE, JP (Surrey 1951); *b* 8 March 1905; *educ* Harrow and Pembroke Coll Cambridge; dir Tate and Lyle Ltd, Zambia Sugar Co Ltd, Lusaka (Rhodesia) Sugar Refineries Ltd, Dep-Dir Sugar Div Min of Food 1939–50; *m* 24 Nov 1927 Joyce Jean, er dau of Sir John Jarvis, 1st Bt, and *dsp* 1976, when his titles expired

　1a Nancy Margaret; *m* 1st 20 April 1938 Capt Philip Foster Glover, RN (*d* 26 April 1957), yr s of John Weatherald Glover, of Mereleigh, Chelford, Cheshire, and had:

　　1b *John Philip Leonard; *b* 22 April 1940; *educ* Harrow; dir Moira Investments Ltd, Trent Gravels Ltd, A W Webb Ltd, C Spalding Ltd; *m* 20 Sept 1963 *Rosemary Beryl, dau of William Peter Manners, of The Cottage, Rolleston, Burton-on-Trent, and has:

　　　1c *James Philip John; *b* 20 July 1965

　　　2c *Peter Lyle; *b* 29 Sept 1966

　　　3c *Simon Foster; *b* 20 May 1968

　　1b *Margaret Ann; *b* 28 April 1942

　1a (cont.) Mrs Philip Glover *m* 2nd 20 Dec 1969 Ryder Gardyne Maltwood

　2a *(Barbara) Suzanne; *b* 1915; *m* 30 June 1938 (*divorce* 1953) (William) Thomas Charles Skyrme (later Sir Thomas, KCVO (1974)), CB (1966), CBE, JP, barrister, s of Charles George Skyrme, of S Kensington, and has:

　　1b *Anthony Lyle; *b* 20 Aug 1946; *educ* Harrow and U of Neuchâtel; *m* 1972 *Carole-June, dau of W J Glover, of Sandown House, Belfast, and has:

　　　1c *Sebastian; *b* 1976

　　　1c *Samantha; *b* 1973

　　1b *Carolyn Anne [Mrs Philip Holbrook, The Pond House, Well, Long Sutton, Hants]; *b* 20 July 1940; *educ* Heathfield and Paris; *m* 19 Jan 1966 *Maj Philip Norman Elston Holbrook, s of Sir Claude Vivian Holbrook, CBE, JP, DL, of Upper Durford, Hants, and has:

　　　1c *Charles Philip Elston; *b* 9 Oct 1968

　　　1c *Miranda Carolyn; *b* 20 July 1967

　2b *Diana Suzanne, JP [Lady Waterlow JP, Rushall Lodge, Pewsey, Wilts SN9 6EN]; *b* 21 March 1943; *educ* Heathfield and Theatre Workshop Acting Sch; a dir Securities and Futures Authority 1987–; *m* 19 July 1965 *Sir (James) Gerard Waterlow, Bt, of Harrow Weald (*qv*) and has issue

3 Sir ROBERT PARK LYLE, 1st and last Bt (UK), so *cr* 16 June 1915; *b* 17 Oct 1859; Maj 1st Vol Bn Argyll and Sutherland Highrs, chm Tate and Lyle, Pres Br Sugar Refiners' Assoc; *m* 16 Aug 1882 Agnes (*d* 14 Oct 1943), 4th dau of William Jamieson, shipowner in Greenock, and *dspm* 11 July 1923, when the btcy expired, having had:

　(1) Gertrude Agnes; *m* 1st 10 Dec 1902 Maj John Hendley Morrison Kirkwood, DSO (*d* 7 Feb 1924), of Yeo Vale, Bideford, N Devon, only s of James Morrison Kirkwood, of Yeo Vale, and had issue; *m* 2nd 4 Sept 1924 Lt-Col John Hill Pattisson, DSO, Essex Regt, s of William Henry Luard Pattisson, of Writtle, Essex, and *d* 28 July 1961

　(2) Mary Elizabeth; *m* 7 June 1905 Charles John Baker, of Upper Chedglow, Malmesbury, and *d* 25 May 1917, leaving issue

ABRAM LYLE *d* 30 April 1891; his est son,

Sir Alexander Park Lyle, 1st Bt (UK), so *cr* 26 March 1929, JP (Perthshire); *b* 2 Aug 1849; shipowner, chm Lyle Shipping Co Ltd, Pres Greenock Philosophical Soc and Chamber of Commerce, dir Clyde Lighthouse Tst; *m* 30 April 1880 Grace Eleanora (*d* 1918), dau of Archibald Moir, JP, of Alloa, Clackmannanshire, and had:

　1 ARCHIBALD MOIR PARK (Sir), **2nd Bt**

　1 Eleanora; *m* 17 July 1912 Count Paolo Manassei di Collestatte (*d* 10 Sept 1938), Min of San Marino to the Holy See, and *d* 10 Feb 1967, leaving issue

Sir ALEXANDER *d* 10 Dec 1933; his est son,

Sir Archibald Moir Park Lyle, 2nd Bt, MC, TD, JP, DL; *b* 5 Feb 1884; *educ* Oxford (MA); Col Scottish Horse WW I (despatches), memb Roy Co Archers, V-Lt Perthshire; chm Lyle Shipping Co Ltd; *m* 24 Nov 1908 Dorothy (*d* 27 May 1967), est dau of Sir James de Hoghton, 11th Bt (*qv*), and *d* 3 Dec 1946, having had:

　1 Ian Archibald de Hoghton; *b* 1 Sept 1909; *educ* Eton and Trin Coll Oxford; Lt Scottish Horse Scouts (TA), Capt Black Watch WW II; *m* 26 Jan 1938 Hon Lydia Yarde-Buller [Lydia Duchess of Bedford, Little Ribsden, Windlesham, Bagshot, Surrey] (*m* 2nd 12 Feb 1947 (*divorce* 1960) 13th Duke of Bedford, *qv*), 3rd dau of 3rd Baron Churston (*qv*), and was *ka* El Alamein 23 Oct 1942, leaving:

　　(1) Sir GAVIN ARCHIBALD LYLE, **3rd and present Bt**

　　(1) *Lorna; *b* 28 June 1939; *m* 1st 2 Oct 1959 (*divorce* 1969) Timothy Cyprian George Thomas Elwes and has issue (see RENNELL, B); *m* 2nd 1979 *Walter Ronald Alexander

　2 Robin Alexander; *b* 17 Sept 1910; *educ* Eton and Trin Coll Oxford; Maj Scottish Horse Scouts (TA) WW II; *m* 30 Jan 1939 Emilia (*m* 2nd Feb 1948 Capt Michael Aubrey Bankier, late Welsh Gds (*d* following a car crash 21 Aug 1966), yr twin s of W A Bankier, of Court Hill, House, Letcombe Regis, Berks; resumed name LYLE by deed poll 18 March 1952; *m* 3rd 30 April 1953 Count Sigmund Berchtold, s of Count Leopold Berchtold, Austro-Hungarian For Min; *m* 4th 28 March 1956 (*divorce* 1961) HH Prince Vsevolode Joannovitch of Russia), dau of Col Eugene von Gosztonyi, of Budapest, and was *ka* Normandy 9 June 1944

　3 +(Archibald) Michael, JP (Perthshire 1950), DL (1961) [Lt-Col Michael Lyle JP DL, Riemore Lodge, Dunkeld, Perthshire]; *b* 1 May 1919; *educ* Eton and Trin Coll Oxford (MA); Lt-Col Scottish Horse, Maj Black Watch (RHR) WW II (discharged with wounds 1944), cmded Scottish Horse RAC (TA) 1955–57, memb Roy Co Archers, Hon Attaché Rome 1938–39, CC 1945, chm TA&AFA Perthshire 1959–; *m* 18 July 1942 Hon Elizabeth Sinclair (*d* 1994), yr dau of 1st Viscount Thurso (*qv*), and had:

　　(1) *VERONICA, *cr* BARONESS LINKLATER OF BUTTERSTONE (*qv*)

　　(2) *Janet Lyle; *b* 27 Sept 1944; *m* 19 July 1975 *Richard D B Cooper, squash player, s of A B Cooper, of Bristol, and has:

　　　1a *Daisy; *b* 1983

　　　2a *Hester; *b* 1985

3a *Matilda; *b* 1988

　(3) Diana; *b* 27 Oct 1946; *d* 1972

　*Sarah Caroline; *b* 29 Jan 1963 (adopted); *m* Sept 1996 *Owen Day and has:

　　*Alistair; *b* June 1997

1 *Dorothea; *b* 25 April 1914; *m* 4 March 1937 (*divorce* 1962) Viscount Kelburn, later 9th Earl of Glasgow (*qv*), and has issue

LYNCH-BLOSSE

Arms: Az. a chevron between three trefoils, slipped or. **Crest:** A lynx passant coward arg. **Motto:** *Nec temere, nec timide* ('Neither rashly nor timidly'). **Creation:** Bt. (I) 8 June 1622.

SIR RICHARD HELY LYNCH-BLOSSE, 17TH BT [Sir Richard Lynch-Blosse Bt, The Surgery, Watery Lane, Clifton Hampden, Oxon OX14 3EL]; *b* 26 Aug 1953; *s* f 1971; *educ* Welwyn Gdn City and Roy Free Hosp (U of London); MRCS, LRCP 1978, MB, BS 1979, DRCOG 1983, MRCGP 1984, Capt RAMC 1975–85, GP 1985–; *m* 1976 *Cara Lynne, only dau of George Longmore Sutherland, of St Ives, Cambs, and has:

　1 *Katherine Helen; *b* 1983

　2 *Hannah Victoria; *b* 1985

Lineage: Sir Henry Lynch, 1st Bt (I), so *cr* 8 June 1622; MP Galway (4th s of Nicholas FitzStephen Lynch, Mayor Galway 1584, and gs of Stephen FitzArthur Lynch, Mayor Galway 1546 and 1560, who *d* 15 Aug 1579); *m* Elizabeth, widow of James D'Arcy and dau of Richard Martin, and had:

　1 ROBUCK (Sir), **2nd Bt**

　2 Nicholas; student Middle Temple 1634

　3 Maurice; *m* Gennet, yst dau of Sir Peter French, of Galway

　1 Elizabeth; *m* Thomas Lynch, of Galway, ancestor of the LYNCHes of Drimcong

　2 Mary; *m* Geoffrey Browne, of Carrowbourne (see ORANMORE AND BROWNE, B)

　3 Ellinor; *m* c 27 June 1632 Sir Valentine Blake, 3rd Bt, of Menlough (*qv*), and *d* 1692, having had issue

Sir HENRY *d* 21 Feb 1634; his est son,

Sir Robuck Lynch, 2nd Bt; Mayor Galway 1638, MP 1639 and 1641; Resident Counsel Connaught during 1641 Uprising; *m* Ellis, 3rd dau of Sir Peter French, and had, with other issue:

　1 HENRY (Sir), **3rd Bt**

　2 Peter; *m* Bibyan O'Flaherty and had:

　　(1) Mary; *m* Thomas Blake, of Brendrim (see BLAKE, Bt, of Menlough)

　3 Arthur, ancestor of the LYNCHes of Partry, Co Mayo

Sir ROBERT *d c* 1667; his est son,

Sir Henry Lynch, 3rd Bt, of Castlecarra, Co Mayo; lawyer; Baron Exchequer 1686; granted 23 July 1678 6,400 acres Co Mayo (including Castlecarra); *m* 1st Margaret, dau of 3rd Viscount Mayo (see MAYO, E); *m* 2nd Mary (*d* 1712), dau of Nicholas Blake, of Crumlin, Co Galway (see 1917 edn WALLSCOURT, B), and *d* Brest 1691, after accompanying JAMES II to France, having had, with two yr sons (Dominick; James):

Sir Robuck Lynch, 4th Bt, of Castlecarra; *m* 29 Nov 1683 Katharine, only dau of Henry Blake, of Lehinch and Renvyle, and had:

　1 HENRY (Sir), **5th Bt**

　2 John, of Clogher, Co Mayo; *m* Mary, dau of Valentine Browne, of Mount Browne, Co Mayo (see SLIGO, M)

　1 Catherine; *m* Theobald Bourke, of Moneycrower

　2 Jane; *m* John Darcy, of Kiltullagh, Co Galway

Sir ROBERT *d* in or after 1736; his est son,

Sir Henry Lynch, 5th Bt, of Corrandulla; *m* before 1723 Mary, widow of Marcus French, of Rahassaney, and dau and coheir of John Moore, of Moat, Co Mayo, and had, with two other sons:

　1 ROBERT (Sir), **6th Bt**

　1 Harriet; *m* 1754 Col Dominick Browne, of Castlemacgarrett

　2 Anna; *m* Hon Henry Browne, 5th s of 1st Earl of Altamont (see SLIGO, M)

Sir HENRY *d* 1762; his est son,

Sir ROBERT LYNCH later LYNCH-BLOSSE, **6th Bt**, of Moat, Co Mayo; *m* 14 Jan 1749 Elizabeth (*d* 1756), dau and heiress of Francis Barker, of Sibton, Suffolk, and heiress of Tobias Blosse, of Little Belstead, Suffolk, and *d* 1775, having had:

1 **Sir Henry Lynch-Blosse, 7th Bt**, of Moat, Co Mayo; *b* 14 Oct 1749; *dspl* 1788.

2 Francis; 14th Light Dragoons; *m* Hatton, dau of John Smith, of Rathcooney, Co Cork, and had:

(1) **Sir Robert Lynch-Blosse, 8th Bt**, of Moat, Co Mayo, later Gabalga, nr Cardiff; *b* 25 Feb 1784; *m* 1st Elizabeth, dau of William Gorman, of Carlow, and had:

1a **Rev Sir Francis Lynch-Blosse, 9th Bt**; *b* Aug 1801; *m* April 1824 Hon Elizabeth Plunket (*d* 3 April 1885 aged 84), est dau of 1st Baron Plunket (*qv*), and *d* 1840, leaving:

1b **Sir Robert Lynch-Blosse, 10th Bt**; High Sheriff Co Mayo 1847; *b* 15 Feb 1825; *m* 31 March 1853 Lady Harriet Browne (*d* 29 June 1904), dau of 2nd Marquess of Sligo (*qv*), and *d* 3 Dec 1893, having had:

1c **Sir Henry Lynch-Blosse, 11th Bt**; JP and DL Co Mayo; High Sheriff 1897; *b* 21 April 1857; *m* April 1881 Annie Stokes (*d* 20 Oct 1925) and *dsp* 17 Aug 1918

2c **Sir Robert Lynch-Blosse, 12th Bt**, JP Co Kilkenny, JP and DL Co Mayo; High Sheriff 1921, Maj 3rd Res Garrison Bn Roy Irish Fus, formerly Capt King's Own Borderers; Staff Offr Burmese Expdn 1899–1900, served WW I; *b* 14 Feb 1861; *m* 27 Nov 1893 Alice Gertrude Nina (*d* 25 May 1959), dau of Edmund Cockayne Pery-Knox-Gore (*see* LIMERICK, E), and *dspm* 23 June 1942, leaving:

1d Alice Cecil Emily; *m* 27 Sept 1934 Lt-Col Robert Arthur Milne, RE, s of Arthur Pledge Milne, of Aberdeen, and had:

1e *Robert Cecil; *b* 5 Nov 1935; *educ* Wellington

1e *Mary Elizabeth; *b* 6 Dec 1936; *m* 24 Aug 1963 Rev Peter John van de Kasteele, only s of Lt William John van de Kasteele, RN, of Munster Ho, Plymouth

3c William Conyngham; *b* 15 Feb 1864; *d* 19 Nov 1870

4c Francis; Capt 2nd West India Regt; *b* 27 Nov 1868; *d* 17 Feb 1915

1c Harriet; *b* 25 May 1862; *m* 6 Nov 1883 Rt Hon Sir Henry Augustus Robinson, 1st Bt (*see* LYNCH-ROBINSON, Bt), and *d* 14 Jan 1942, leaving issue

2c Mary; *b* 3 July 1865; *m* 8 March 1892 Hon Robert Nicholas Hardinge, s of 2nd Viscount Hardinge (*qv*), and *d* 25 Aug 1955, having had issue

2b William Conyngham; Capt RA; *b* March 1826; *d* 21 Dec 1863

3b Francis; Lt 85th Regt, Capt N Mayo Militia; *b* Dec 1831; *d* Anstruther, Canada West, 26 July 1864

1b Katherine; *d* unm 24 Nov 1915

1a Mary; *m* 27 March 1830 Very Rev Hon Robert Plunket, Dean Tuam and Rector Headfort (*see* PLUNKET, B)

(1) (cont.) **Sir Robert** *m* 2nd 13 March 1807 Charlotte (*d* 5 Oct 1834), dau of John Richards, of Cardiff, and *d* Jan 1818, having by her had:

2a Henry; MA, Dean Llandaff; *b* 11 Feb 1813; *m* 16 July 1844 Charlotte Frances (*d* 1 May 1892), dau of Sir Robert Knight, of Tythegston, and *d* 28 Jan 1879, leaving, with other issue:

1b Robert Charles (Rev); Vicar Tidenham, Chepstow; *b* 5 Aug 1848; *m* 6 Dec 1881 Mary Carwardine (*d* 10 Sept 1936), dau of Rev George Alfred Walker, Vicar Chidham, Sussex, and *d* 13 July 1933, leaving:

1c **Sir Robert Cyril Lynch-Blosse, 13th Bt**; Capt and Hon Maj 3rd Bn Roy Welch Fus, WWs I and II; *b* 17 Jan 1887; *m* 1st 25 April 1911 Dorothy Mary (*d* 9 March 1926), er dau of Edward Cunliffe Owen, CMG, and had:

1d **Sir Robert Geoffrey Lynch-Blosse, 14th Bt**; Lt-Cdr RN WW II; *b* 1 April 1915; *educ* Nautical Coll Pangbourne; *d* unm 21 April 1963

1d Evelyn Mary; *b* 16 Jan 1912

1c (cont.) **Sir Robert** *m* 2nd 16 April 1932 Frances Dorothy (*d* 4 Nov 1975), dau of Charles Edward Banks, Civ Serv, and *d* 4 July 1951, having by her:

2d *(Frances) Clodagh [Mrs Paul Nevell, 7 Sea Lane, Goring-by-Sea, Worthing, Sussex]; *b* 1 Sept 1936; *m* 30 April 1960 *Paul Richard Nevell, er s of James Richard William Nevell, of Worthing, and has:

1e *Christopher Paul; *b* 21 Sept 1965

2e *James Robert; *b* 1 May 1968

1c Ethel Margaret; *b* 9 July 1885; *d* 6 March 1939

2b Henry Francis; *b* 20 Jan 1852; *d* 18 Jan 1896

3b Edward Falconer JP; CC Glam; *b* 25 Dec 1853; *m* 11 Dec 1883 Edith Caroline (*d* 20 Jan 1953), dau of Rev George Alfred Walker, Vicar Chidham, and *d* 25 Oct 1926, leaving:

1c **Sir Henry Lynch-Blosse, 15th Bt**; *b* 29 Oct 1884; *educ* Repton; Capt RE, Lt 7th Bn Welsh Regt, WW I, mining engr; *m* 17 Feb 1914 Cicely Edith (*d* 11 April 1970), yr dau of Francis Thomas Bircham, of Chepstow, and had:

1d Elizabeth Cicely; *b* 10 Jan 1916; Subaltern ATS WW II; *m* 1 March 1951 Francis Cade Gordon Harris, only s of Boris Gordon Harris, of Swansea, and had:

1e *Alan Gordon; *b* 11 Jan 1952; *educ* Worksop Coll

1e *Margaret Jane; *b* 2 Sept 1954

2d *Susan Frances [Mrs Brian Noble, Old Inn Cottage, Inwardleigh, Okehampton, Devon]; *b* 29 Nov 1917; Section Offr WAAF WW II; *m* 7 March 1942 *W/Cdr Brian Noble, RAF, er s of Herbert James Noble, of Esher, and has:

1e *Nigel Brian; *b* 12 July 1947; *educ* Lindisfarne Coll; Lt-Col RAPC; *m* 1974 *Diana Mary Fogg and has:

1f *James Colin; *b* 1975

2f *Charles Christopher; *b* 1977

1e *Elizabeth Hilary; *b* 18 Oct 1945; *m* 1974 *Richard Charles Perry and has:

1f *Charles Edward Bruce; *b* 1978

1f *Katherine Jane Susannah; *b* 1979

2c Edward Knight; *b* 20 April 1886; *d* 23 Jan 1935

3c Hely Richard; ICS; *b* 6 Sept 1887; *educ* BNC Oxford (BA); *m* 25 April 1922 Evangeline Margaret Victoria, dau of Charles William Maitland Hudson, of W Kensington, and *d* 21 April 1928, leaving:

1d DAVID EDWARD (Sir), **16th Bt**

1d *Sylvia Diana [Mrs Robert Sullivan-Tailyour, The Curate's Egg, Dymocks Lane, Sutton Veny, Wilts]; *b* posthumously 5 Dec 1928; *m* 22 March 1958 *Maj Robert Basil Sullivan-Tailyour, Worcs and Sherwood Foresters Regt, only s of Lt-Col Eric Eyre Sullivan-Tailyour, OBE, MC, of Grange Cottage, North Curry, Somerset, and has:

1e *James Robert; *b* 5 Nov 1960

1e *Sarah Jane; *b* 28 April 1963

4c Cecil Eagles; *b* 4 Dec 1890; Indian Police, Ch Constable Montgomeryshire 1925, Assist Ch Constable Lancs 1927, Ch Constable Leics 1928–49, WW I with Poona Horse, WW II 1943–44 as Lt-Col, KPM 1946; *m* 1st 31 Oct 1915 (*divorce* 1940) Dorothy Delahaize (*d* 26 Oct 1962), dau of Rev John Delahaize Ouvray, Vicar Haydon, Dorset, and had:

1d +(ERIC) HUGH, OBE (1952) [G/Capt Hugh Lynch-Blosse OBE, 17 Queen's Acre, Newnham, Glos GL14 1DJ]; *b* 30 July 1917; heir presumptive; *educ* Blundells and RAF Coll; G/Capt RAF WW II 1939–41 (despatches, POW); *m* 27 March 1946 *Jean Evelyn, dau of Cdr Andrew Robertson Hair, RD, RNR, of Edinburgh, and has:

1e +David Ian; *b* 14 Jan 1950; *educ* Blundells; *m* 1st 1984 Mrs Barbara Susan McLaughlin (*d* 1985); *m* 2nd 1989 *Nadine, dau of J Baddeley, and by her has:

1f +Oliver Daniel; *b* 12 Nov 1989

1f *Jessica Hannah; *b* 1992

1e *Valerie Jean [Mrs Irvine Cormack, Fieldridge, Broombarn Lane, Gt Missenden, Bucks]; *b* 7 Sept 1947; *m* 1974 *Irvine Cormack

2e *Fiona Carol; *b* 8 Aug 1955

2d Anthony Cecil; *b* 7 Sept 1919; F/Lt RAF WW II; *m* 1st 13 Oct 1942 (*divorce* 1946) Margaret, dau of Maj-Gen David Graeme Ridgeway, CB, DSO, of Kenya; *m* 2nd 4 Dec 1948 *Marjorie Elizabeth [Mrs Anthony Lynch-Blosse, Malegash Terrace, PO Box 1602, Lunenburg, Nova Scotia B0J 2C0, Canada], dau of James Joseph William Morris, of Portland, Maine, and by her has:

1e +Michael Anthony [Michael Lynch-Blosse Esq, 18 Clear Spring Court, Sugarland, TX 77479, USA]; *b* 28 Jan 1950; *m* 1977 *Barbara Lorraine, dau of Jack Haberthur, of St Augustine, Florida, and has:

1f *Danielle Bryann; *b* 1981

2f *Shannon Elizabeth; *b* 1983

3f *Heather Michelle; *b* 1985

4f *Brittany Noel; *b* 1989

2e +Sean James [Sean Lynch-Blosse Esq, Lunenburg, NS B0J 2C0, Canada]; *b* 11 Nov 1960; has:

1f *Sean James SANTIAGO; *b* 1984

1e *Sharon Delahaize [Mrs Robert Reuter, 8 Green Tree Lane, Dover, NJ 07801, USA]; *b* 11 Nov 1960; *m* 11 Oct 1997 *Robert James Reuter

4c (cont.) Lt-Col Cecil Lynch-Blosse *m* 2nd 14 Feb 1943 his cousin Violet Emily (*d* 2 Dec 1976), dau of Francis Traherne Lynch-Blosse (*see* below), and *d* 17 Nov 1966

5c (George) Robert; *b* 25 Jan 1895; tea planter Ceylon; *m* 22 June 1929 Lucy Myra (*d* 1988), dau of Bertram Edward Adams, of Auckland, NZ, and had:

1d +Robert Edward [Robert Lynch-Blosse Esq, 8 Cassandra Grove, Sunnynook, Auckland, New Zealand]; *b* 7 July 1932; *m* 20 Oct 1954 *Alannah Marie, 2nd dau of John Donald Graham Drought, and has:

1e +Robert Mark; *b* 11 Oct 1955

2e +Brendon Scott; *b* 27 March 1960

1e *Jennifer Sue; *b* 5 July 1957

2d +Gerald Bertram; *b* 21 July 1936; *m* 15 Oct 1966 *Moira Jean, dau of R B Johns, of Takapuna, Auckland, NZ, and has:

1e +Craig Allan; *b* 4 Aug 1967

2e +Blair Robert; *b* 1974

1e *Catherine Mary; *b* 1970

2e *Joanne Maree; *b* 1972

3d +Timothy Richard [Timothy Lynch-Blosse Esq, 31A Coldham Crescent, St Johns Park, Auckland 5, New Zealand]; *b* 15 Nov 1939; Sr Police Sgt (ret); *m* 24 Feb 1962 *Joan, dau of William George Whittington, of Auckland, and has:

1e +Stephen John; *b* 31 July 1964

2e +David Paul; *b* 1 Aug 1966

4d +Andrew John [Andrew Lynch-Blosse Esq, 7 Catherine St, Onehunga, Auckland, New Zealand]; *b* 4 Feb 1946; *m* 9 March 1968 *Janice Marie, dau of E Swinburne, and has:

1e +Christopher Andrew; *b* 1972

2e +Timothy Nigel; *b* 1974

6c Patrick Windsor, DFC; Actg W/Cdr RAF WW II; *b* 11 April 1900; *m* 1st 25 April 1920 (*divorce* 1925) Beatrice Marjorie, dau of Thomas Roland Lamb Polden Laughrane, of Green Ore, Wells, Somerset; *m* 2nd — (*m* 2nd 19– —) and was *ka* April 1942, leaving:

1d *A dau; *m* 19– —

1c Constance Diana; *b* 6 July 1889; *m* 17 June 1918 Capt (Ernest) Norman Bock, S Lancs Regt, s of Richard Bock, of Larkhill, Bowden, Cheshire, and had:

1d Richard Norman Walker; F/Lt RAF WW II; *b* 22 May 1920; *ka* 14 Jan 1944 unm

1d *Margaret Diana Mary; b 28 Feb 1922; m 17 Feb 1951 George Bernard Richardson, s of George Richardson, of Mechin, Cornwall, and has:

    1e *Gerald Norman; b 23 May 1955
    2e *Peter George; b 12 Oct 1960
    1e *Pauline Diana; b 22 Nov 1951
    2e *Carol Jane; b 12 May 1953

2d *Pauline Ann; b 31 Aug 1926; m 7 Oct 1950 John Hunter Dolan, s of John Dolan, of Pawtucket, RI, and has:

    1e *Roderick Norman; b 26 Nov 1952
    1e *Heather Ann; b 6 Jan 1954
    2e *Robin Elizabeth; b 23 Aug 1961

2c Theodora Mary; b 20 Feb 1893; m 23 Dec 1923 Glenton de Glenton Hunt, s of Henry Gardiner Hunt, of Suva, Fiji, and had:

1d *Moira Evelyn; b 16 Jan 1925; m 1951 Archie Couper, of Ontario, and has issue

2d *Gillian Frances; b 18 Oct 1927; m 1953 *John Burton Camping and has issue

4b Francis Traherne; b 28 April 1859; m 15 Dec 1885 Emily Vivian (d 21 Aug 1936), dau of Richard Cory, JP, of Cardiff, and d 1 June 1926, leaving:

1c Francis Courtenay; Lt Irish Gds (SR) WW I (wounded); b 31 Oct 1898; m 17 Sept 1932 Dorothy Guthrie (d 23 July 1965), widow of Charles Ivan Lynn-Thomas and dau of Duncan MacRae, of Ruthven, Kingussie, and d 1 March 1943, leaving:

1d +Richard Courtenay [Richard Lynch-Blosse Esq, Hugletts Farm, Old Heathfield, Sussex]; b 16 Dec 1937; educ Wellington; m 12 March 1965 Deirdre Geraldine Mary (d 28 June 1965), formerly w of Sheridan Young and dau of Commandant Patrick Butler, of Dublin

1c Violet Emily; m 1st 9 April 1913 (divorce 1925, resumed maiden name by deed poll 11 Aug 1925) Hew James Brown (d 6 Dec 1934), est s of James William Brown, of Eastrop Grange, Highworth, Wilts; m 2nd 14 Feb 1943 her cousin Lt-Col Cecil Eagles Lynch-Blosse (see above) and d 2 Dec 1976

2c Constance Mabel Frances; m 7 Dec 1918 Leonard Robert Arthur Bate, Capt KRRC (d 22 March 1959), est s of Arthur Bate, of Hagley, Worcs, and had:

1d *Rosemary Suzanne; b 10 Oct 1920; m 6 Dec 1948 *Maj Michael Thomas Jerome Bate Williams, only s of Lt-Col Walter Williams, OBE, of Weald, Kent, and has:

    1e *Christopher Michael Leonard; b 23 Sept 1949
    2e *John Robert Alexander; b 25 Sept 1951

1b Katherine Marion; m 1903 Lewis Price and d 27 Oct 1943. He d 31 July 1934

3a Edward Lynch; Lt-Col; b 23 Feb 1814; m 1st 19 Aug 1858 Eliza Grace (d 19 Feb 1861), widow of Rev Edward Illingworth and dau of Henry Percy, and had:

1b Edward Falconer Lynch; Lt York and Lancaster Regt, Staff Maj Japanese Intell Branch; b 21 July 1859; m 1st 21 June 1884 Eva Lilian (d 1893), dau of Rev T R Brownrigg, Vicar St Jude's, Southsea; m 2nd 30 May 1893 Anna Maria (dsp June 1904), dau of Edward Wright, and d 25 Oct 1927

3a (cont.) Col Lynch-Blosse m 2nd 15 Jan 1863 Eularia Bruce (d 22 May 1913), yst dau of Capt Harry Gough Ord, RA, of Bexley, Kent, and d 9 Jan 1890

1a Charlotte Diana; m James Lewis, MD, and dsp 6 May 1876

2a Catherine Diana; m Nov 1844 Rev Hely Rickards and d 4 Dec 1889

Sir HENRY d 17 May 1969; his nephew,

Sir David Edward Lynch-Blosse, 16th Bt; b 24 Nov 1925; educ Marlborough and Jesus Coll Oxford; RN 1944–48; m 8 March 1950 *Elizabeth, er dau of Thomas Harold Payne, of Welwyn Gdn City, and d 15 Oct 1971, leaving:

1 Sir RICHARD HELY LYNCH-BLOSSE, **17th and present Bt**

1 *Caroline Susan [Mrs Caroline Rollnick, 67 Conway Rd, Cardiff CF1 9NW]; b 22 Aug 1951; m 1st 1978 (divorce 1984) Christopher Elliot Stuart, only s of Anthony Stuart, of Birstall, Leics, and has:

  (1) *Josephine Rachel Blosse; b 1979

1 (cont.) Mrs Caroline Stuart m 2nd 1987 (divorce 1994) Steven Rollnick and by him has:

  (1) *Jacob Julian Blosse; b 1987

1 (cont.) Mrs Caroline Rollnick also has:

  (2) *Efa Grug Blosse MASON; b 29 Feb 1996

2 *Bridget Ruth; b 10 Feb 1958; has:

  (1) *Charlie James Brosse BARRY; b 1994

LYNCH-ROBINSON

Arms: Quarterly, 1st and 4th, vert a chevron engrailed between three stags at gaze or, each charged with a fleur-de-lys azure (for ROBINSON); 2nd and 3rd, azure a chevron between three trefoils slipped or, all between two voiders of the second (for LYNCH).
Crests: 1 Out of a crown vallery or a mount vert, thereon a stag as in the arms, 2 A lynx passant cowed argent collared gules, a chain flexed over the back or. **Motto:** Legi regi fidus ('Faithful to the law and the king'). **Creation:** Bt. (UK) 30 Jan 1920.

SIR DOMINICK CHRISTOPHER LYNCH-ROBINSON, 4TH BT, of Lisnacarrig, Foxrock, Co Dublin [Sir Dominick Lynch-Robinson Bt, Flat 3, 25 Manchester Sq, London W1M 5AP]; b 30 July 1948; s f 1996; m 1973 *Victoria, dau of Kenneth Weir, of Sale, Cheshire, and has:

1 +CHRISTOPHER HENRY JAKE; b 1 Oct 1977
1 *Anna Elizabeth Seaton; b 1973

Lineage: BRYAN ROBINSON; allegedly of the ROBINSONs of Newby Hall, Yorks; had:

CHRISTOPHER ROBINSON; b 1647; MD; m Mary — and was bur 17 Jan 1688/9, leaving:

BRYAN ROBINSON; b 1682; educ Dublin (MB 1709, MD 1711); lecturer anatomy, Regius Prof Physic 1745–54; d Jan 1754, leaving:

1 CHRISTOPHER
2 Robert; MD, State Physician 1742–70; m Elizabeth, dau and heiress of Thomas Lyster, of Lysterfield, Co Roscommon, and had:
  (1) Elizabeth; m 25 May 1785 1st Baron Ashtown (qv) and d 1844
3 Bryan; educ Dublin (BA 1737)

The est s,

CHRISTOPHER ROBINSON; b 1716; MP Co Kilkenny, Judge King's Bench Ireland; m May 1758 Elizabeth, dau of Rev Hartstonge Martin, of Kilkenny, by Sarah, dau of Sir Henry Wemys, of Danesfort, and d Jan 1787, leaving, with other issue (d unm):

CHRISTOPHER ROBINSON; b 1761; Rector Granard; m Elizabeth, 2nd dau of Sir Hercules Langrishe, 1st Bt (qv), and d 1837, having had, with eight other sons (the yst, Sir Bryan, being Judge Supreme Ct Newfoundland 1858–77):

HERCULES ROBINSON, JP (Co Westmeath), DL; b 16 March 1789; Midshipman Trafalgar, Adml, High Sheriff Co Westmeath 1842; m 22 June 1822 Frances Elizabeth, only child of Henry Wildman-Wood, by Anne, dau of Joseph Henry, of Straffan, Co Kildare, and d 15 May 1864, leaving, with other issue:

1 HENRY (Sir), for whom see further below
2 HERCULES ROBINSON, cr 1896 BARON ROSMEAD, KCMG, PC (see 1933 edn)
3 William Cleaver Francis (Sir), KCMG; b 14 Jan 1834; Colonial Govr; m 7 April 1862 Olivia, dau of Most Rev Thomas Townsend, Bp Meath, and d 2 May 1897
4 Frederick Charles Brian; b 1836; V-Adml; m 1st 1864 Williamina, dau of William Bradley; m 2nd 1889 Alice, dau of Col Cyril Blackburne Tew, and d 1896, leaving issue

The est s,

Sir HENRY ROBINSON, KCB, of Rosmead, Co Westmeath; b 1823; V-Pres Local Govt Bd Ireland 1879–91; m 12 Jan 1853 Hon Eva Arthur Henry Medora Annesley, 4th dau of 10th Viscount Valentia (qv), and d March 1893, leaving, with other issue:

Sir Henry Augustus Robinson, 1st Bt (UK), so cr 30 Jan 1920, KCB, PC (I); b 8 Nov 1857; Sec: Local Govt and Taxation of Town Commn and Poor Law and Lunacy Inquiry Commn Ireland, Commr Municipal Boundaries Ireland 1878–79, Inspr Local Govt Bd 1879–91, Commr 1891–98 and V-Pres 1898–1920; m 6 Nov 1883 Harriet (d 14 Jan 1942), er dau of Sir Robert Lynch-Blosse, 10th Bt (qv) and d 16 Oct 1927, having had:

1 CHRISTOPHER HENRY (Sir), **2nd Bt**
2 Bryan Arthur; b 26 Oct 1889; m 26 Oct 1919 Gertrude Susannah (Pamela) (d 20 Jan 1970), 3rd dau of Ambrose Pickard, of Leeds, and dsp

3 Adrian, CBE (1951), of Seymour Ho, Dunmurry, Co Antrim; *b* 14 April 1892; *educ* Charterhouse and Trin Coll Dublin (BA); Perm Sec Min Home Affairs NI; *m* 17 June 1919 Agnes Patricia, dau of Hugh Dorrien, of Donegal, and had:

  (1) Henry Adrian; *b* 29 March 1920; FRIBA, MRIAI

The 1st Bt's est s,

  Sir CHRISTOPHER HENRY ROBINSON later LYNCH-ROBINSON (letters patent 13 Feb 1947), **2nd Bt**; *b* 18 Oct 1884; *educ* Wellington and RMC Sandhurst; Roy Fus 1903–12, Priv Sec to Govr Jamaica 1910–12, memb Old Age Pensions Ctee Local Govt Bd Ireland 1912, barrister King's Inn Dublin 1920, RM 1912–22; *m* 1st 9 March 1912 (*divorce* 1957) Dorothy Mary Augusta (*d* 24 June 1970 aged 88), er dau of Henry Charles Jackson Warren, of Carrickmines, Co Dublin (*see* WARREN, Bt); *m* 2nd 23 March 1957 Olive Louise (*d* 23 March 1976), dau of George Bartholomew, of Tonbridge, Kent, and formerly w of Walter Bartaby-Smith, and *d* 22 Nov 1958, leaving by his 1st w:

1 **Sir Niall Bryan Lynch-Robinson, 3rd Bt**, DSC (1941); *b* 24 Feb 1918; *educ* Stowe; Lt RNVR WW II, chm Leo Burnett Ltd 1970–78, Croix de Guerre; *m* 30 March 1940 *Rosemary Seaton [Rosemary Lady Lynch-Robinson, Flat 25 Headbourne Worthy House, Headbourne Worthy, Hants SO23 7JG], er dau of Harold John Eller, and *d* 3 June 1996, having had:

  (1) Sir DOMINICK CHRISTOPHER LYNCH-ROBINSON, **4th and present Bt**

Sir Niall and Lady Lynch-Robinson also adopted:

  Anthea ('Penny') Lucy; *b* 1956; *m* 19– *Steve — and *d* 1993

LYTTON

Arms: Quarterly; 1st and 4th, erm. on a chief dancettée az. three ducal crowns or, a canton arg., charged with a rose gu., barbed and seeded ppr. (for LYTTON); 2nd and 3rd, gu. on a chevron arg., between three eagles regardant or, as many cinquefoils sa. (for BULWER); 3rd, or a dove regardant, holding in the beak an olive branch ppr. (for WIGGETT). **Crests:** 1 A heraldic tiger's head, erased erm., crined and armed or (for BULWER), 2 A bittern in flags ppr., charged with a rose gu., as in the arms (for LYTTON), 3 A dove regardant arg., holding in the beak an olive branch ppr., fructed gold (for WIGGETT). **Supporters:** On either side an angel ppr., vested arg., holding in the exterior hand an eastern crown or. **Motto:** *Hoc virtutis opus* ('This is the work of valour'). **Creations:** B. (E) by 2 Dec 1529 (Wentworth), Bt. (UK) 18 July 1838, B. (UK) 14 July 1866 (Lytton of Knebworth), E. and V. (UK) 28 April 1880.

THE 5TH EARL OF LYTTON, Co Derby, **Viscount Knebworth of Knebworth**, Co Hertford, **Lord** (Baron) **Wentworth**, **Baron Lytton of Knebworth**, Co Hertford, and a **Baronet** (Sir John Peter Michael Scawen Lytton, Bt) [The Rt Hon The Earl of Lytton, Estate Office, Newbuildings Place, Shipley, W Sussex RH13 7JQ]; *b* 7 June 1950; *s* f 1985; *educ* Worth, Downside and Reading U (BSc); FRICS 1987 (ARICS 1976), IRRV 1990, sole proprietor John Lytton & Co chartered surveyors 1988–, chm Leasehold Enfranchisement Advsy Serv (now Leasehold Advsy Serv) 1994–, Pres Newstead Abbey Byron Society, Chm Horsham Chamber of Commerce 1993–95 (Pres 1995–), Pres Sussex Assoc Local Cncls 1997–, Hon FABE 1997; *m* 7 June 1980 *Ursula Alexandra, yr dau of Anton Komoly, of Vienna, and has:

1 +PHILIP ANTHONY SCAWEN, *Viscount Knebworth*; *b* 7 March 1989

1 +Wilfrid Thomas Scawen; *b* 1992

1 *Katrina Mary Noel; *b* 1985

Lineage (of Lytton): HENRY de LITTON, of Litton/Lytton in Tideswell, Derbys; living between 1214 and 1222; putative f of:

GILBERT de LITTON, of Litton; had:

ROBERT fitz GILBERT de LITTON; enacted a fine 3 Nov 1290; had:

THOMAS de LITTON, of Litton; had, with a yr s (Richard, living 1383):

JOHN fitz THOMAS de LITTON, also of Grimston, Yorks; living 1375; *m* Christiana — and was ancestor of:

ROBERT LYTTON, of Litton; gentleman; living 1448; had:

Sir ROBERT de LYTTON, of Litton; Comptroller Household to HENRY VI, Receiver-Gen Queen's rents in Honour (chief feudal administrative unit) of High Peak and agister (officer responsible for cattle taken in to graze for payment) of the forest there; *m* Agnes, dau of John Hotoft, Sheriff London, and had:

1 William, of Lytton; *d* 1488, leaving:

  (1) William, of Lytton and Monyash; living between 1534 and 1546; gentleman; had:

    1a Thomas

    1a Lucy; *m* Thomas Moseley

2 ROBERT (Sir)

The yr s,

Sir ROBERT de LYTTON, KB, PC, of Lytton; Under-Treasurer Exchequer *temp* HENRY VII, Keeper Gt Wardrobe; bought 1492 the Knebworth estate, Herts, from Sir Thomas Bourchier; *m* Elizabeth, dau and coheir of John Andrews, of Weston, Norfolk, and widow of Thomas Windsor, of Hanwell, and had, with a dau (Fides, *m* Richard Deveneish, of Hellengleigh):

WILLIAM de LYTTON, of Knebworth; Govr Castle of Boulogne, Sheriff Herts and Essex; *m* Audrey, dau and heiress of Sir Philip Booth, of Shrubland Hall, Suffolk, by Margaret, dau of Sir Wittin Hopton, of Swillington, and had, with an er s (Sir Robert, KB, of Knebworth and Shrubland Hall, Sheriff Herts and Essex, *m* 1st Frances, dau of Anthony Cavalery, *m* 2nd Elizabeth, dau of Thomas Munden, and widow of Robert Burgoyne, and *d c* 1551, leaving by his 1st w three daus):

ROWLAND LYTTON, of Knebworth; Govr Boulogne; *m* 1st Margaret, dau of John Tate, of Calais, s of Sir John Tate; *m* 2nd Anne, dau of George Carleton, of Brightwell, Oxon, and *d* 1582, leaving, with a dau (Frances, *m* Sir Anthony Cope, 1st Bt; *see* 1970 edn):

Sir ROWLAND LYTTON, of Knebworth; Lt Herts, MP Herts *temp* ELIZABETH I and JAMES I, one of the 'Voluntary Gentlemen' in the Earl of Essex's Cavalry in the Low Countries 1585–86, ktd 1603; *m* Anne, dau of 3rd Lord (Baron) Saint John of Bletso (*qv*) and widow of Sir Robert Corbet (*see* 1970 edn CORBET, Bt) and had:

1 WILLIAM (Sir)

1 Anne; *m* Sir William Webbe and *d* 1612

2 Judith; *m* 1st Sir George Smyth, of Annables, Herts; *m* 2nd Sir Thomas Barrington, of Barrington Hall, Essex

3 Elizabeth; *m* Thomas Windham, of Felbrigg Hall, Norfolk

4 Jane; *m* Sir Charles Crofts

Sir ROWLAND *d* 1615; his son,

Sir WILLIAM LYTTON, of Knebworth Park; MP Herts; *m* 1st Anne, dau and heiress of Stephen Slaney, of Norton, Salop; *m* 2nd Ruth, dau of Francis Barrington (*see* BARRINGTON, Bt), and had:

1 ROWLAND (Sir), his heir

1 Margaret; *m* 1st Thomas Hillersdon, of Elstow, Beds; *m* 2nd Sir Thomas Hewett, 1st Bt, of Pishiobury, and *d* 1689, leaving by him:

  (1) Sir GEORGE HEWETT, 2nd and last Bt, and 1st and last VISCOUNT HEWYTT OF GORAN, Co Kilkenny, so *cr* 9 April 1689, as also BARON of JAMES-TOWNE, Co Longford (both I); *b* 1625; *d* unm 2 Dec 1689, when his titles expired

  (1) Arabella; *m* 16 May 1664, as his 2nd w, Sir William Wiseman, 2nd Bt (*qv*)

2 Dorothy; *m* Sir John Barrington, 3rd Bt (*see* below), and *d* 1703

3 Mary; *m* Sir Edward Gostwick, 3rd Bt, of Willington, Beds, and had issue

4 Jane; *m* Sir Thomas Bosville

Sir WILLIAM *d* 1660; his only son,

Sir ROWLAND LYTTON, of Knebworth Park; MP Herts *temp* CHARLES II; *m* 1st Judith, dau of Sir Humphrey Edwards, and had, with other issue:

1 William (Sir), of Knebworth Park; High Sheriff and MP Herts; *m* 1st Mary, dau of Sir John Harrison; *m* 2nd Philippa, dau of Sir John Kelyng, of Southill, and *dsp* 14 Jan 1704/5

1 Anne; *m* Sir Francis Russell, of Strensham, Worcs, and *d* 1705, leaving:

  (1) Anne; *m* 1st Richard Lygon, of Madresfield, Worcs (*see* 1970 edn BEAUCHAMP, E); *m* 2nd Sir Henry Every, 3rd Bt (*qv*); *m* 3rd Sir John Guise, 3rd Bt (*qv*), and *d* 1734/5

  (2) Mary; *m* Thomas Jones, of Shrewsbury

  (3) Elizabeth; *m* 1st William Dansey, of Brinsop; *m* 2nd — Lloyd

2 Judith; *m* 1st Maurice Abbot, of Fulmere, Cambs; *m* 2nd Sir Nicholas Strode, of St John's Close, Middx, and Etchingham, Sussex, and had:

  (1) George (Sir); *m* 1687 Margaret, dau of John Robinson, of Gwersyllt, and sis of William Robinson, and had:

    1a Lytton STRODE later LYTTON, of Knebworth Park; *m* Bridget, dau of Richard Mostyn (*see* MOSTYN, B), and *dsp* 1710, willing the estates to his 1st cousin through his mother

Sir ROWLAND *m* 2nd by 1662 Rebecca, dau and coheir of Thomas Chapman, of Wormley, and widow of Sir Richard Lucy, 1st Bt, of Broxbourne (*see* RAMSAY-FAIRFAX-LUCY, Bt), and *d* 1674, having by her had:

3 Rebecca; *m* 5th Viscount Falkland (*qv*)

LYTTON STRODE later LYTTON's cousin,

WILLIAM ROBINSON later ROBINSON-LYTTON, of Knebworth Park (s of William Robinson and gs of John Robinson, of Gwersyllt; *see* above); *m* Elizabeth (*d* 1737), dau and coheir of Giles Heysham, of London, and *d* 18 Nov 1732, having had, with other issue:

1 John, of Knebworth Park; DCL Oxon; *b* 1725; MP Bishop's Castle; *m* 12 April 1744 Leonora (*d* 13 March 1790), dau and heir of Humphrey Brereton, of Borras, Denbighs, and *dsp* 1762, when he was *s* by his sis

1 Barbara; *bapt* 3 April 1710; *m* William Warburton, of Yarrow, Queen's Co, and had:

  (1) Richard WARBURTON later WARBURTON-LYTTON, of Knebworth; *b* 1745; *m* 1768 Elizabeth, dau of Paul Jodrell, of Lewknor, Oxon, and *d* 1810, leaving:

1a Elizabeth Barbara; *b* 1773; *m* 1798 Gen William Earle Bulwer (s of William WIGGETT later BULWER (Act of Parl 1756), of Guestwich, Norfolk, s of Rice Wiggett by Sarah, sis of William Bulwer, of West Dalling), of Wood Dalling and Heydon, Norfolk, and *d* 19 Dec 1843, leaving:

1b William Earle Lytton, of Wood Dalling and Heydon; *b c* 1799; *d* 21 July 1877, leaving issue

2b WILLIAM HENRY LYTTON EARLE BULWER, 1st and last BARON DALLING AND BULWER OF DALLING, Norfolk (UK), so *cr* 23 March 1871, GCB (1851, KCB 1848), PC (1845); *b* 13 Feb 1801; *educ* Harrow and Trin and Downing Colls Cambridge; Offr 1st Life Gds 1824 and 58th Foot 1826; joined Dip Serv 1827, Sec Legn Brussels 1835–37, Sec Embassy Constantinople 1837–38, St Petersburg 1838–39 and Paris 1839–43, Envoy Extrdy and Min: Madrid 1843–48 (recalled at the host govt's insistence for meddling with political appointments there), Washington 1849–52 and Florence 1852–54, Amb Constantinople 1858–65, MP (Lib) Wilton 1830–31, Coventry 1831–35, Marylebone 1835–37 and Tamworth 1868–71; *m* 9 Dec 1848 Hon Georgiana Charlotte Mary Wellesley (*d* 2 Aug 1878), yst dau of 1st Baron Cowley (*see* COWLEY, E), and *dsp* 23 May 1872, when the title expired

3b Sir EDWARD GEORGE EARLE LYTTON BULWER later BULWER-LYTTON (roy licence 20 Feb 1844 on inheriting the Knebworth estate from his mother), **1st Bt**, of Knebworth, Herts, and **1st Baron Lytton of Knebworth**, Co Hertford (both UK), so *cr* 18 July 1838 and 14 July 1866 respectively, GCMG (1869), PC (1858); *b* 25 May 1803; *educ* Trin Hall Cambridge; author: *Rienzi*, *The Last Days of Pompeii*, *Ernest Maltravers*, *The Caxtons*, *My Novel* and other works of fiction, not least the account he used to give of his own ancestry, claiming that BULWER was a corruption of 'Bolver', the name the Norse God Odin assumed in battle; MP (extreme Lib) St Ives 1831–32 and Lincoln 1832–41 and (C) Herts 1852–66, Sec State Colonies 1858–59, Hon DCL Oxon, Hon LLD Cantab, Ld Rector Glasgow U 1856 and 1858; *m* 29 Aug 1827 (separated 1836) Rosina Doyle (author: *Chevely, or the Man of Honour* (1839), consisting of abuse of her husband; also delivered an oral attack on him to the electors of Hertford from the hustings when in June 1858 he was up for re-election; was certified insane but set at liberty July 1859; *d* 12 March 1882), only surv dau of Francis Massy Wheeler, of Lizzard Connell, Co Limerick; and had:

1c EDWARD ROBERT, **1st Earl**

1c Emily Elizabeth; *d* 29 April 1848

The 1st BARON *d* 18 Jan 1873; his only son,

EDWARD ROBERT LYTTON BULWER-LYTTON, **1st Earl of Lytton**, in the County of Derby, so *cr* 28 April 1880, as also VISCOUNT KNEBWORTH OF KNEBWORTH, Co Hertford (both UK), GCB (1878), GCSI (1880), CIE (1880), PC (1888); *b* 8 Nov 1831; *educ* Harrow and U of Bonn; Dip Serv: Attaché Washington 1849, Florence 1852, Paris 1854, The Hague 1856, St Petersburg 1858, Constantinople 1858, Vienna 1859, Consul Belgrade 1860, Sec Legn Copenhagen 1863, Athens 1864, Lisbon 1865 and Madrid 1868, Sec Embassy Vienna 1868 and Paris 1872–74, Min Lisbon 1874–76, Viceroy India 1876–80, Amb Paris 1887–91, Ld Rector Glasgow U; *m* 4 Oct 1864 Edith, CI, VA (*d* 17 Sept 1936), Ldy Bedchamber to TM QUEENs VICTORIA and ALEXANDRA, 2nd dau of Hon Edward Villiers (*see* CLARENDON, E), and *d* 24 Nov 1891, having had:

1 Edward Rowland John; *b* 19 Sept 1865; *d* 24 July 1871

2 Henry Meredith Edward; *b* 22 March 1872; *d* 1 March 1874

3 VICTOR ALEXANDER GEORGE ROBERT BULWER-LYTTON, **2nd Earl of Lytton**, KG (1933), GCSI (1925), GCIE (1922), PC (1919), JP, DL (Herts); *b* 9 Aug 1876; *educ* Eton and Trin Coll Cambridge (BA 1898); Civil Ld Admlty 1916–17 and 1919–20, addnl Parly Sec Admlty 1917–18, Br Commr Propaganda France 1918, Parly U-Sec India 1920, Govr Bengal 1922–27, T/Viceroy India 1925, Ldr Indian Delegn League Nations 1927–28 and Br Delegate 1931; chm Jt Ctee Houses Parl London Traffic Bill 1931, chm: League Nations Manchurian Commn 1932, permanent Commn of Conciliation and Arbitration Turkey-Holland, Centl London Electricity Ltd and Palestine Potash Ltd, KJStJ, Hon LLD Manchester, Grand Cross Belgian Order Crown 1926; *m* 3 April 1902 Pamela, CI, DGStJ (*d* 6 July 1971 aged 97), dau of Sir Trevor John Chichele Chichele-Plowden, KCSI, and *d* 25 Oct 1947, having had:

(1) (Edward) Antony James, *Viscount Knebworth*; *b* 13 May 1903 (HM EDWARD VII stood sponsor); *educ* Eton and Magdalen Coll Oxford (BA); P/O AAF, MP Hitchin 1931–33; *dvp* unm 1 May 1933 following an air accident

(2) Alexander Edward John, *Viscount Knebworth*; *b* 11 March 1910 (HM QUEEN ALEXANDRA stood sponsor); *educ* Trin Coll Cambridge (BA); Maj The Bays WW II, OStJ; *ka* El Alamein 4 July 1942

(1) *(Margaret) Hermione (Millicent) [The Lady Hermione Cobbold, Lake House, Knebworth, Herts]; *b* 31 Aug 1905 (the late CROWN PRINCESS OF SWEDEN stood sponsor); *m* 3 April 1930 1st Baron Cobbold (*qv*) and has issue

(2) *Davidema Katharine Cynthia Mary Millicent (Davina); *b* 23 April 1909; *m* 1st 15 July 1931 5th Earl Erne (*qv*) and has issue; *m* 2nd 28 Aug 1945 5th Baron Terrington (*qv*) and has further issue

4 NEVILLE STEPHEN, **3rd Earl of Lytton**

1 Elizabeth Edith; *b* 12 June 1867; *m* 21 Dec 1887 2nd Earl of Balfour (*qv*) and *d* 28 March 1942, leaving issue

2 Constance Georgina; *b* 12 Feb 1869; author: *Prisons and Prisoners* (1914), memb WSPU; *d* 22 May 1923

3 Emily; *b* 26 Dec 1874; *m* 4 Aug 1897 Sir Edwin Landseer Lutyens, OM, KCIE, PRA, LL.D, architect (*d* 1 Jan 1944), and *d* 3 Jan 1964, leaving issue

The 2nd EARL's bro,

NEVILLE STEPHEN BULWER-LYTTON later LYTTON, **3rd Earl of Lytton**, OBE (1918); *b* 6 Feb 1879; portrait and landscape painter, Maj 11th Bn Roy Sussex Regt WW I (wounded, despatches, Legn Hon), memb Société Nationale des Beaux Arts Paris 1936; *m* 1st 2 Feb 1899 (*divorce* 1923) Judith Anne Dorothea, **Baroness Wentworth** (*d* 8 Aug 1937, *see* below) and had:

1 NOEL ANTHONY SCAWEN, **4th Earl of Lytton**

1 Anne LYTTON later LYTTON-MILBANKE (deed poll 23 Feb 1925) later still LYTTON again (deed poll 1947); *b* 24 Aug 1901; *d* unm 26 June 1979

2 Winifred; *b* 19 March 1904; *educ* Priory of Our Lady of Good Counsel Haywards Heath; *m* 9 Nov 1921 Claude Tryon (*d* 19 Sept 1949), MIMechE, est surv s of John Tryon, of Grove Mill House, Watford, Herts

The **3rd Earl** *m* 2nd 1 May 1924 Alexandra Fortel and by her had:

1 *Madeleine Elizabeth [The Lady Madeleine Lytton, 4 rue des Hauts-Tillets, 92310 Sèvres, France]; *b* 1921; dancer, choreographer and teacher; has:

(1) *Eleanore LYTTON; *b* 1957; lyricist

The 3rd EARL *d* 9 Feb 1951; his only son,

NOEL ANTHONY SCAWEN LYTTON later LYTTON-MILBANKE (deed poll 23 Feb 1925) later still LYTTON again (deed poll 1951), **4th Earl of Lytton** and **17th Lord** (Baron) **Wentworth**, as which *s* mother 1957, OBE (1945); *b* 7 April 1900; *educ* Downside and RMC Sandhurst; Lt-Col Rifle Bde, attd KAR 1922–26, Instr Economics RMC 1931–35, Staff Capt and DAQMG War Office 1936–39, served WW II, Ch Staff Offr Br Mil Govt Vienna; *m* 30 Nov 1946 *Clarissa Mary [The Rt Hon Dowager Countess of Lytton, Garden Wing, Newbuildings Place, Shipley, W Sussex RH13 7JQ], est dau of Brig-Gen Cyril Eustace Palmer, CB, CMG, DSO, RA, of Verno, Christchurch, Hants, by Nina Kathleen, only dau of Henry Scarlett, JP, of Preston, Firle, Sussex, and *d* 1985, leaving issue (the females among whom are in remainder to the Barony of Wentworth only):

1 JOHN PETER MICHAEL SCAWEN LYTTON, **5th and present Earl of Lytton**

2 +(Thomas) Roland Cyril Lawrence [The Hon Roland Lytton, Bratton Court Farm, Minehead, Somerset TA24 8SL]; *b* 10 Aug 1954; *educ* Worth, Downside and RAC Cirencester

1 +Caroline Mary Noel; *b* 29 Dec 1947; *educ* Shaftesbury, Birmingham U and Sir John Cass Sch of Art; silversmith

2 +Lucy Mary Frances; *b* 29 Jan 1957; *educ* Woldingham and Vienna State Conservatory of Music

3 +Sarah Teresa Mary; *b* 15 Oct 1959; *educ* Woldingham; *m* 1984 *P David Nash Solly, yst s of Lt-Col R J N Solly, and has:

(1) +A dau; *b* 1992

Lineage (of Wentworth): WILLIAM WENTWORTH, of Wentworth Woodhouse, Yorks; *d* 1308, leaving a yr s:

JOHN WENTWORTH; living 1314; gf of:

JOHN WENTWORTH, of N Elmsall, Yorks; living 1413; had a yr s:

ROGER WENTWORTH, of Nettlestead, Suffolk, which he acquired through marriage (by 25 June 1423, originally secretly because of their difference in rank) with Margery (*d* 20 April 1478), *de jure* Baroness le Despenser (of the 1387 *cr*) in her own right (according to later doctrine), widow of 7th Lord (Baron) De Ros (*qv*) of Helmsley and dau and heir of 2nd Lord (Baron) le Despenser of the 17 Dec 1387 *cr* (*see* FALMOUTH, V, preliminary remarks; the 2nd Lord le Despenser was *b c* 1365; *m* Elizabeth, dau and coheir of Sir Robert Tybotot, 3rd Lord (Baron) Tybotot, of Nettlestead, Suffolk, and *dspm* 20 June 1424); *d* 21 or 24 Oct 1452, leaving, with a yr s (Henry, had issue, *see* below):

Sir PHILIP WENTWORTH; *dvm*, beheaded 18 May 1464 after the Lancastrian defeat of Hexham 14 May 1464, leaving:

Sir HENRY WENTWORTH, *de jure* 4th LORD (Baron) LE DESPENSER, KB, of Nettlestead; *d* between 17 Aug 1499 and 27 Feb 1499/1500, leaving, with other issue (including at least one dau, Margery, *m* Sir John Seymour, KB; *see* SOMERSET, D):

Sir RICHARD WENTWORTH, *de jure* 5th LORD (Baron) LE DESPENSER, of Nettlestead; *m* Anne, dau of Sir James Tyrrell, of Gipping, Suffolk, and had:

Sir THOMAS WENTWORTH, **1st Lord** (Baron) **Wentworth** (E), so *cr* (but whether by patent, proclamation ('*par parole*') or writ is unknown) soon after 3 Nov 1529, also *de jure* 6th LORD (Baron) LE DESPENSER, PC (by 9 Oct 1549); *b* 1501; served French Campaigns of 1523 and 1544, ktd 1523, MP Suffolk 1529, Ld Chamberlain Feb 1549/50–March 1550/1; *m c* 1520 Margaret, est dau of Sir Adrian Fortescue (*see* CAMOYS, B), and *d* 3 March 1550/1, leaving an est s:

THOMAS WENTWORTH, **2nd Lord** (Baron) **Wentworth** and *de jure* 7th LORD (Baron) LE DESPENSER, PC (1553); *b* 1525; *educ* St John's Coll Cambridge; ktd 1547 following victory over Scots of Pinkie; MP Suffolk 1547–51; Jt Ld Lt Suffolk 1552 and 1553; last Govr of English-held Calais 1553–7 Jan 1557/8; Ld Lt Norfolk and Suffolk 1569; *m* 1st 9 Feb 1545/6 his cousin Mary (*dsp c* 1554), dau of Sir John Wentworth, of Gosfield (gs of Henry Wentworth, yr s of Roger; *see* above); *m* 2nd 1555/6 his 1st w's cousin and his own more distant cousin Anne (*d* 2 Sept 1571), dau of Henry Wentworth, of Mountnessing, Essex, and *d* 13 Jan 1583/4, leaving by her, with other issue, including an er s (William, *m* Elizabeth, dau of 1st Baron Burghley (*see* SALISBURY, M), *dsp* & *vp* 7 Nov 1582) and at least one dau (Cecily, *m* Sir Robert Wingfield, of Letheringham; *see* POWERSCOURT, V):

HENRY WENTWORTH, **3rd Lord** (Baron) **Wentworth** and *de jure* 8th LORD (Baron) LE DESPENSER; *b* by 20 Aug 1558; *m c* 1585 Anne (*m* 2nd 1595 Sir William Pope, Bt, *cr* Earl of Downe after her death, and was *bur* 10 May 1625), dau of Sir Owen Hopton, and *d* of plague 16 Aug 1593, leaving:

THOMAS WENTWORTH, **4th Lord** (Baron) **Wentworth** and *de jure* 9th LORD (Baron) LE DESPENSER, also EARL OF CLEVELAND, Co York (E), so *cr* 5 Feb 1625/6, KB (1610); *b* 1591; *educ* Trin Coll Oxford and Gray's Inn; Jt Ld Lt Beds 1625–39 and 1660–67, solely 1639–42; Capt Gentlemen Pensioners 1642–43/4 and 1660–67, cmdg a royalist cav bde 1644, helping win the Battle of Cropredy Bridge 29 June 1644, taken prisoner 2nd Battle of Newbury 27 Oct 1644 and held in Tower of London till late 1648, when he fled abroad; went with CHARLES II to Scotland 1650 and fought Battle of Worcester 1651, when again taken prisoner and imprisoned once more in the Tower of London (till 1658); *m* 1st just prior to 1612 Anne (*d* 16 Jan 1637/8), dau of Sir John Crofts, of Little Saxham, Suffolk, and had issue; *m* 2nd by 25 Oct 1638 Lucy (*d* 23 Nov 1651, leaving an only child, ANNE, **Baroness Wentworth** in her own right etc; *see* below), dau and coheir of Sir John Wentworth, 1st Bt, of Gosfield, and *dspms* 25 March 1667, when the Earldom of Cleveland expired, leaving, with other issue by his 1st w (*dsp* & *vp*):

1 THOMAS WENTWORTH, **5th Lord** (Baron) **Wentworth**, KB (Feb 1625/6), PC (1654); *bapt* 2 Feb 1612/3; served against Scots in both Bishops' Wars 1639–40, MP Beds 1640, called up to Ho Lds *vp* 3 Nov 1640 in f's Barony of Wentworth; Col (royalist) Prince of Wales's Regt Horse and Sgt-Maj-Gen of Horse Civil War, serving at Tipton Green 11 June 1644, Cropredy Bridge 29 June 1644 and it is

thought at 2nd Newbury 27 Oct 1644, Marshal of the Field West Country 1645, when fought at Parly victory of Langport 10 July; Gentleman Bedchamber to CHARLES II 1649–March 1664/5, fought Battle of Worcester 1651, Col Gren Gds 1656 and 1660–March 1664/5; *m* by 11 March 1657/8 Philadelphia (*d* 4 May 1696), dau of Sir Ferdinando Carey, and *dvp* 1st March 1664/5, leaving:

(1) HENRIETTA MARIA WENTWORTH; presumably **Baroness Wentworth** in her own right and certainly *de jure* BARONESS LE DESPENSER in her own right; *b* 11 Aug 1660; mistress of Duke of Monmouth (*see* BUCCLEUCH and QUEENSBERRY, D); *d* unm 23 April 1686

1 ANNE Wentworth, **Baroness Wentworth** in her own right and *de jure* BAR-ONESS LE DESPENSER in her own right; *bapt* 29 July 1623; *m* 11 July 1638 John LOVELACE, 2nd Baron Lovelace of Hurley (*d* 14 Nov 1670; *see also* LOVELACE, E), and *dspms* 7 May 1697, having had:

(1) JOHN LOVELACE, 3rd BARON LOVELACE OF HURLEY; *b c* 1640; *m* 28 Aug 1662 Martha, dau and coheir of Sir Edmund Pye, 1st and last Bt, and *dspms* & *vm* 27 Sept 1693, leaving:

1a MARTHA Lovelace, **Baroness Wentworth** in her own right and *de jure* BARONESS LE DESPENSER in her own right; *b c* 1667; *m* 11 March 1692/3, as his 2nd w, Sir Henry JOHNSON (*d* 29 Sept 1719), of Friston Hall, Suffolk, and *dsp* 18 July 1745

(1) MARGARET Lovelace; *b c* 1644; *m* 30 Oct 1660, as his 1st w, Sir William NOEL, 2nd Bt (*m* 2nd 9 July 1672 Frances, dau of 1st Baron Ward of Birmingham (*see* DUDLEY, E), and *d* 13 April 1675), only s of Sir Varney Noel, 1st Bt (*cr* 6 July 1660; and *d* 1670), of Kirkby Malory, Leics, by Elizabeth, sis of Sir Wolstan Dixie, 1st Bt (*see* 1970 edn), and *d* 14 April 1671, leaving:

1a Sir THOMAS NOEL, 3rd Bt; *b* 1662; *m* Anne (*d* 8 Jan 1737), dau of Sir William Whitlock, and *dsp* 1688

2a Sir JOHN NOEL, 4th Bt; *b* 1668, *m* Mary, dau and heir of Sir John Clobery, and *d* 1 July 1697, having had an est s:

1b Sir CLOBERY NOEL, 5th Bt; MP Leics; *b* 1695; *m* 24 Aug 1714 Elizabeth (*d* 25 June 1743), dau of Thomas Rowney, MP Oxford, and *d* 30 July 1733, leaving, with other issue:

1c EDWARD NOEL, **9th Lord** (Baron) **Wentworth** and *de jure* 13th LORD (Baron) LE DESPENSER, also 1st VISCOUNT WENTWORTH OF WELLESBOROUGH, Co Leicester (GB), so *cr* 5 May 1762; *b* 30 Aug 1715; *educ* Eton and New Coll Oxford; *m* 20 July 1744 Judith (*d* 3 Dec 1761), dau and coheir of William Lamb, of Wilby, Northants, and Farndish, Beds, and *d* 31 Oct 1774, leaving:

1d THOMAS NOEL, **10th Lord** (Baron) **Wentworth** and *de jure* 14th LORD (Baron) LE DESPENSER, also 2nd VISCOUNT WENTWORTH OF WELLESBOROUGH; *b* 18 Nov 1745; *educ* Eton and BNC Oxford; MP (Tory) Leics 1774, a Ld Bedchamber 1790–1815; *m* 2 Feb 1788 Mary (*d* 29 June 1814), dau of Robert Henley, 1st Earl of Northington and widow of Edward, Earl Ligonier of Clonmell, and *dspl* 17 April 1815, when the Viscounty and bty expired but the Barony of Wentworth and right to that of Le Despenser (of the 1387 *cr*) fell into abeyance between his sisters or their heirs, leaving, by an unknown mother:

1e Thomas NOEL (Rev); *b* 1774; *educ* Rugby and Ch Ch Oxford; Rector Kirkby Mallory till 1853; performed the marriage ceremony between his cousin **Baroness Wentworth** and 6th Baron Byron (*qv*); *d* unm 22 Aug 1853

1d Judith; *m* 9 Jan 1777 Adml Sir Ralph MILBANKE later NOEL (roy licence1815), 6th Bt, MP (*d* 19 March 1825), and *d* 22 Jan 1822, leaving an only child:

1e ANNE ISABELLA Milbanke later Noel, **Baroness Wentworth** in her own right, as which s on natural termination of abeyance 1856, also *de jure* BARONESS LE DESPENSER; *b* 17 May 1792; *m* 2 Jan 1815 George Gordon BYRON later NOEL, 6th Baron Byron (*qv*) of Rochdale, the poet (*d* 19 April 1824), and *d* 26 May 1860, having had:

1f Ada Augusta; *m* 8 July 1835 1st Earl of Lovelace (*qv*) and *dvm* 29 Nov 1852, leaving:

1g BYRON NOEL KING later KING-NOEL (roy licence 29 Sept 1860), **12th Lord** (Baron) **Wentworth** and *de jure* 16th LORD (Baron) LE DESPENSER, as which s grandmother 1860, also by courtesy *Viscount Ockham*; *b* 12 May 1836; served RN; *dvp* unm 1 Sept 1862

2g RALPH GORDON KING later KING-NOEL (roy licence 29 Sept 1860) later still KING-MILBANKE (roy licence 6 Nov 1861), **13th Baron Wentworth**, *de jure* 17th LORD (Baron) LE DESPENSER, also 2nd EARL OF LOVELACE; *b* 2 July 1839; *educ* privately and Univ Coll Oxford; *m* 1st 25 Aug 1869 (legal separation 1871) Fannie (*d* 13 July 1878), 3rd dau of Rev George Heriot, of Fellow Hills, Co Berwick, Vicar St Anne's, Newcastle; *m* 2nd 30 Dec 1880 Mary Caroline (*d* 18 April 1941), est dau of Rt Hon James Stuart-Wortley (*see* WHARNCLIFFE, E), and *dspm* 28 Aug 1906, when the Earldom of Lovelace, Viscountcy of Ockham and Barony of King passed to his half bro (*see* LOVELACE, E), leaving by his 1st w:

1h ADA MARY KING-MILBANKE, **Baroness Wentworth** in her own right and *de jure* BARONESS LE DESPENSER in her own right, *b* 26 Feb 1871; *d* unm 18 June 1917

1g ANNE ISABELLA King, **Baroness Wentworth** in her own right and *de jure* BARONESS LE DESPENSER in her own right; *b* 22 Sept 1837; *m* 8 June 1869 Wilfrid Scawen BLUNT (*d* 10 Sept 1922), of Crabbet Park, Poundhill, Crawley, Sussex, and Newbuildings Place, Southwater, Sussex, and *d* 15 Dec 1917 aged 80, having had, with other issue:

1h JUDITH ANNE DOROTHEA Blunt, **Baroness Wentworth** in her own right and *de jure* BARONESS LE DESPENSER in her own right; owned Crabbet Arabian Stud and Burton Park Thoroughbred Stud, author: *Thoroughbred Racing Stock and its Ancestry, The World's Best Horse, The Authentic Arabian Horse and his Descendants, Horses in the Making, The Swift*

Runner, The Arabian Horse, Drift of the Storm, Passing Hours, Arab Horse Nonsense Cartoons, Horses of Britain, Love in a Mist, Toy Dogs and their Ancestors and other works; *m* 2 Feb 1899 (*divorce* 1923, took name BLUNT-LYTTON by deed poll 24 Oct 1904) **3rd Earl of Lytton** (*see* above) and *d* 8 Aug 1957, having had issue

2d Elizabeth, *m* 19 June 1777 Sir James Bland Burges, Bt, and *dsp* 25 Jan 1779

3d Sophia Susanna; *m* 18 Aug 1777 2nd Baron Scarsdale and *d* 28 June 1782, having had:

1e NATHANIEL CURZON, 3rd BARON SCARSDALE; *d* unm 12 Nov 1856, when the abeyance of the Barony of Wentworth terminated in favour of his cousin Anne Isabella, Lady Byron, the only surv descendant of their gf Viscount Wentworth (*see* above)

1e Juliana; *m* Sir Ralph MILBANKE later NOEL, Bt (*see* 1949 edn MILBANKE, Bt)

2e Sophia Caroline; *m* 5 Aug 1800 Robert, Viscount Tamworth, s of 7th Earl Ferrers (*qv*), and *dsp* 3 Feb 1849

LYVEDEN

Arms: Quarterly; 1st and 4th, arg. a fret sa. (for VERNON); 2nd and 3rd, gu. three bars gemelles arg., a chevron erm., on a chief of the second three blackamoor's heads ppr., a canton of the field charged with a battle-axe or, all within a bordure counter-compony of the second and az. (for SMITH). **Crests:** 1 A boar's head erased sa., ducally gorged or (for VERNON); 2 A cubit arm erect in armour ppr., charged with a battle axe sa., the hand grasping two wreaths of laurel pendant on either side, also ppr. (for SMITH).
Supporters: Dexter, a boar sa. ducally gorged, suspended therefrom by a chain an escutcheon or, charged with a rose gu., slipped ppr.; sinister, a wyvern vert, plain collared, suspended therefrom by a chain an escutcheon or, charged with a rose gu., slipped ppr.
Motto: *Vernon semper viret* ('Vernon always flourishes').
Creation: B. (UK) 28 June 1859.

THE 6TH BARON LYVEDEN OF LYVEDEN, Co Northampton (Ronald Cecil Vernon) [The Rt Hon The Lord Lyveden, 20 Farmer St, Te Aroha, New Zealand]; *b* 10 April 1915; *s f* 1973; *m* 21 May 1938 *Queenie Constance, dau of Howard Ardern, and has:

1 +JACK LESLIE [The Hon Jack Vernon, 17 Carlton St, Te Aroha, New Zealand]; *b* 10 Nov 1938; *educ* Te Aroha Coll; *m* 11 Nov 1961 *Lynette June, dau of William Herbert Lilley, of Taupaki RD, Auckland, and has:

(1) +Colin Ronald; *b* 3 Feb 1967; *educ* Te Aroha Coll

(1) *Wendy Caroline; *b* 5 Oct 1962

(2) *Karen Marie; *b* 11 May 1964

2 +Robert Howard [The Hon Robert Vernon, 2175 Avenue Rd, Apt 6, Toronto, Ontario M5M 4B6, Canada]; *b* 2 Oct 1942; *educ* Te Aroha Coll; *m* 1968 *Louise Smith and has:

(1) +Russell Sydney [Russell Vernon Esq, 213 Atlas St, Toronto M6C 3P6, Canada]; *b* 1969; *m* 1995 *Kathryn Johnston and has:

1a +Mitchell Robert Allan; *b* 1998

3 +Grant [The Hon Grant Vernon, 40 Emma St, Te Aroha, New Zealand]; *b* 29 April 1952; *educ* Te Aroha Coll; *m* 1992 *Karen Teresa Margaret Green and has:

(1) +Daniel Grant James; *b* 1993

Lineage: ROBERT PERCY SMITH, of Cheam, Surrey; JAG India, MP Lincoln; *b* 7 May 1770 (bro of Rev Sydney Smith, the celebrated wit); *m* 1798 Caroline Maria, 2nd dau and coheir of Richard Vernon, MP (of the VERNONs of Hilton, Staffs), MP Newcastle-under-Lyme, Okehampton and Bedford, by Lady Evelyn, sis of 1st Marquess of Stafford (*see* SUTHERLAND, D), and *d* 10 March 1845, leaving:

ROBERT SMITH later VERNON (roy licence 14 July 1859), **1st Baron Lyveden of Lyveden**, Co Northampton (UK), so *cr* 28 June 1859, GCB (1872); *b* 23 Feb 1800; *educ* Eton and Ch Ch Oxford; MP (Whig) Tralee 1829–31, Northampton 1831–59; Mety Commr Lunacy 1830–45, Commr Lunacy 1845–60, a Ld Treasury 1830–34,

Sec Bd Control 1835–39, Parly U-Sec Colonies 1839–41, Sec at War Feb–March 1852, Pres Bd Control 1855–58; *m* 15 July 1823 Emma Mary Fitzpatrick (*d* 22 Sept 1882), sis of 1st Baron Castletown of Upper Ossory (*see* 1937 edn), and *d* 10 Nov 1873, having had:

1 FITZPATRICK HENRY VERNON, **2nd Baron Lyveden of Lyveden**, JP, DL (Northants); *b* 27 April 1824; *educ* Eton and Durham U; Attaché Madrid 1846–48, Hanover 1848–49, Berlin 1849, Priv Sec to Head Woods and Forests Dept 1840 and to f at War Office 1852 and at Bd Control 1855–58; *m* 1st 21 June 1853 Albreda Elizabeth (*dsp* 11 Nov 1891), dau of 5th Earl Fitzwilliam (*see* 1970 edn); *m* 2nd 15 Oct 1896 Julia Kate, Sister Columba at the Convent of the Poor Clares York (*d* 19 March 1949), dau of Albert Emary, of Hastings, and *dsp* 25 Feb 1900

2 Gowran Charles; *b* 9 Nov 1825; barrister, Recorder Lincoln; *m* 4 Aug 1857 Caroline (*d* 16 Oct 1884), est dau of John Nicholas Fazakerly, MP Peterborough, and *d* 15 Jan 1872, having had, with a s (*d* young) and a dau (*d* unm):

(1) Eleanor Emma Albreda; *m* 29 Nov 1884 Lt-Col George Lancelot McLean Farmer, KRRC (*d* 7 Jan 1920), 3rd s of William Francis Garmul Farmer, JP, DL, of Nonsuch Park, Surrey, and *dsp* 24 Sept 1949

(2) Gertrude; *m* 15 Oct 1889 Sir Andrew Noel Agnew of Lochnaw, 9th Bt (*qv*), and *d* 3 April 1932

3 Courtenay John (Rev); *b* 27 July 1828; Rector Grafton Underwood, Northants; *m* 25 March 1856 Alice Gertrude (*d* May 1913), 2nd dau of Rev Maurice Fitzgerald Stephens Townshend, of Castle Townshend, Co Cork, and *d* 2 July 1892, leaving:

(1) COURTENAY ROBERT PERCY VERNON, **3rd Baron Lyveden of Lyveden**; *b* 29 Dec 1857; *educ* Eton; Capt 3rd Bn HLI, Pres Br Ctee Study For Municipal Instns; actor from 1881, also sailor, purser, waiter, cab driver and nurseryman; co dir 1910–14, Lt-Cdr RNVR WW I; *m* 1st 12 Feb 1890 Fanny Zelle (*d* 10 Sept 1924), dau of Maj Charles Hill, of Wollaston Hall, Northants; *m* 2nd 1925 Ada (the actress Lynda Martell), dau of Arthur Hodgkinson, of Accrington, and formerly w of Richard Springate, and *d* 25 Dec 1926, having by his 1st w had:

1a ROBERT FITZPATRICK COURTENAY VERNON, **4th Baron Lyveden of Lyveden**; *b* 1 Feb 1892; *educ* Harrow; Paymaster Lt RNR; *m* 28 Oct 1949 Doris Violet (*d* 1985), dau of Henry Francis Coghlan White, of Courtlands W Hoathly, Sussex, and widow of Capt Eric Paterson, and *dsp* 9 Jan 1969

1a Victoria Wyndham Dorothy; *b* 14 June 1898; *m* 24 Sept 1919 Rev Walter Frift (*d* Nov 1938), Rector Irthlingborough, Northants, s of John Frift

(2) Sydney Charles Fitzpatrick; *b* 14 July 1862; *m* Emilie Louise, dau of C Lorkin, and *d* 1924

(1) Evelyn Mary Geraldine; *m* 7 Aug 1877 Rev Canon Hugh Hodgson Gillett (*d* 1915), Rector Compton, Surrey, and *d* 28 Jan 1930, leaving issue

4 Greville Richard, of Auchans House, Kilmarnock, JP and DL Ayrshire; MP Ayrshire 1886–92; *b* 6 March 1835; *m* 13 April 1858 Susan Caroline (*d* 3 Oct 1901), 2nd dau of Cdr Richard Howe Cockerell, RN, by Theresa, later Countess of Eglinton (*see* EGLINTON and WINTON, E) and sis of Countess of Shrewsbury (*see* SHREWSBURY and WATERFORD, E), and *d* 19 Feb 1909, having had, with other issue:

(1) Howe William Leveson; *b* 21 Dec 1859; *d* Jan 1882

(2) Cecil Sydney Archibald; *b* 18 Feb 1862; *m* 16 Feb 1887 Jessie Jane Munroe and *d* 22 Oct 1944, leaving:

1a SIDNEY MUNROE ARCHIBALD, **5th Baron**

2a Ronald Greville; *b* 1890; *m* 1932 Ethel Mary Ely, of Wimbledon, and *d* 13 Aug 1956

3a John Lyveden; *b* 1895; *m* 1922 Catherine Mary Draffin (*d* 3 July 1970) and *d* Jan 1970, leaving:

1b *Bettina Mary [Mrs Bettina Nair, 81 Charles St, Westshore, Napier, New Zealand]; *b* 1926; *m* 1950 (*divorce* 1977, took name NAIR) Archie Reid McLeay, of Westshore, and has:

1c *Eain Dougald John; *b* 1953; *m* 1977 *Jennifer Raye Thomsen and has:

1d *Devin Eain; *b* 1983

1d *Holley Jennifer; *b* 1981

2d *Casey Leah; *b* 1986

1c *Jane Imelda; *b* 1951; has:

1d *Amber Lea; *b* 1977

2c *Leah Paule (twin); *b* 1951; *m* 1974 *Ralph John Johansson, of Bucklands Beach, Auckland, NZ

3c *Victoria Catherine Ethel (twin); *b* 1953; *m* 1974 (*divorce* 1977) Lee Nicholas Fatouros and has:

1d *Marley Reid; *b* 1980

2b *Jillyan Imelda [Mrs Charles Locke, 55 Pacific Parade, Whangaparaoa Peninsula, Auckland, New Zealand]; *b* 1935; *m* 1955 *Charles Woolnough Locke and has:

1c *Gregory Charles Woolnough; *b* 1957

1c *Antoinette Marie [Mrs William Stuart, 12 Cameron St, Sydney, Australia]; *b* 1956; *m* 1977 *William Sylvester Stuart and has:

1d *William Gregory Charles; *b* 1978

1d *Kellie Ann Imelda; *b* 1979

2c *Katherine Hélène; *b* 1961; *m* 1987 *Olivier Michele Jean Wardecki, of Ferme de Vaufron, Vézelay, France, and has:

1d *Ava Alice; *b* 29 Nov 1996

1a Dorothy Ann; *b* 1902; *m* 1924 Leonard Ross and had issue

(3) Ronald James; Capt 4th Bn KRRC; *b* 25 Jan 1866; *ka* Boer War 26 Dec 1899

(4) Eustace; Capt W Australian MI Boer War 1900; *b* 8 Feb 1871; *m* 1898 Jane, dau of William Baillie Rankin, MD, and widow of William Henry Cutts, MD, and *d* 24 Oct 1914, leaving:

1a Greville Rupert Eustace; *b* 13 May 1899; *m* 28 Oct 1925 *Francesca [Mrs Greville Vernon, 88 Elphin Rd, Launceston, Tasmania 7250, Australia], dau of John Henry Little, of Hobart, and *d* 11 Sept 1967, leaving:

1b +Greville Richard Eustace [Greville Vernon Esq, 2/16 Diana Court, Riverside, Tasmania 7250, Australia]; BSc (Tas) TTC; *b* 17 Sept 1926; *m*

24 Jan 1953 *Nancy Grace, dau of Geoffrey Haslam, of Lamona, Beauty Point, Tasmania, and has:

1c *Jane Suzanne [Mrs Laurence Rogers, 17 Tanner Dve, Legana, Tasmania]; *b* 27 March 1957; *m* 1978 *Laurence James Rogers and has:

1d *Jonathan; *b* 1986

1d *Kate Frances; *b* 1984

2b Robert Harcourt; *b* 27 Aug 1929; *m* 25 Nov 1953 *Isobel Jennifer [Mrs Robert Vernon, 2 Kenyon St, Launceston, Tasmania 7250, Australia], dau of John Schoular Miller, of Hobart, and *d* 25 May 1987, having had:

1c +Robert Courtenay John [Robert Vernon Esq, 59 Grandview Ave, Burnie, Tasmania 7320, Australia]; *b* 5 March 1955; *educ* Launceston Church GS; *m* 1982 *Vicki Maree Davis and has:

1d +Robert Andrew; *b* 4 Oct 1983

2d +Christopher Richard; *b* 15 Jan 1986

2c +Hugh Gowran [Hugh Vernon Esq, 2 Kenyon St, Launceston, Tasmania 7250, Australia]; *b* 2 May 1957; *educ* Launceston Church GS

3c +David Stewart Lyveden [David Vernon Esq, 117 Poplar Parade, Launceston, Tasmania 7250, Australia]; *b* 49 Sept 1958; *educ* Launceston Church GS; BEd, TCAE; *m* 1982 *Meredith Caroline Reeve and has:

1d *Stephanie Caroline; *b* 1985

2d *Rebecca Isobel; *b* 1988

3d *Georgina Amy; *b* 1991

2a William Baillie; *m* 1925 Dorothy O'Grady

(5) Rupert Robert Charles, DSO, JP Somerset; Lt W Australian MI Boer War 1900, CA and CC Somerset; *b* 31 Dec 1872; *m* 18 Oct 1906 Dorothy Inez Elinor (*k* car crash 19 Feb 1965 aged 84), dau of George Benjamin Thorneycroft, of Dunston, Staffs, and *d* 4 May 1940, having had:

1a Greville Archibald Fitzpatrick; 2nd Lt Gren Gds; *b* 2 July 1908; *educ* Eton; *d* 27 Dec 1929 in a car crash

2a Mervyn Sydney Bobus, MVO (1936); Maj Gren Gds Res Offrs WW II (despatches); *b* 8 April 1912; *educ* Eton and RMC Sandhurst; *m* 28 Jan l937 Lady Violet Mary Baring (*d* 2 July 1978), yr dau of 2nd Earl of Cromer (*qv*), and *d* 1991, having had:

1b +Greville Edward Mervyn [Greville Vernon Esq, Newington Farm, Kingscote, Glos]; *b* 19 July 1944; *educ* Eton; *m* 17 July 1969 *(Fiona) Dawn Cory, only dau of Lt-Col William Handley Ferguson (*see* CORY, Bt) and has:

1c +James Fitzpatrick Greville; *b* 1971

1c *Zara Caroline; *b* 28 Sept 1973

2c *Sasha Elizabeth; *b* 1979

2b +(Hugh) Richard Mervyn [Richard Vernon Esq, Stairaird, Mauchline, Ayrshire]; *b* 19 Jan 1947; *educ* Eton; *m* 1976 *Hon Victoria Arthur, yr dau of 3rd Baron Glenarthur (*qv*), and has:

1c +Andrew Robert Richard; *b* 1979

1c *Catherine Victoria; *b* 1977

2c *Emma Mary; *b* 1983

1b *Veronica Elizabeth [Mrs Jonathan Hargreaves, Glen Cottage, Luckington, Chippenham, Wilts]; *b* 2 Nov 1938; *m* 19 Nov 1968, as his 3rd w, (George) Jonathan Hargreaves (*d* 1991), s of Lt-Col J C Hargreaves, of Twyford Hall, Dereham, Norfolk

1a *Susan Diana Mary [Mrs Francis Reitman, The West Wing, Triscombe House, Bishop's Lydeard, Somerset TA4 3HG]; *b* 1 Aug 1915; *m* 14 Dec 1946 Francis Reitman, MD, DPM (*d* 25 Aug 1955), s of — Reitman, of Budapest, and has:

1b *Robert Vernon Michael [Robert Reitman Esq, Thiat, Bussière, Poitevin 87320, France]; *b* 7 Sept 1947; *educ* Radley

1b *Susan Theresa Maria [Miss Susan Reitman, The West Wing, Triscombe House, Bishop's Lydeard, Somerset TA4 3HG]; *b* 6 July 1950

2b *Roseanna Mary Blanche [The Rt Hon the Countess of Stradbroke, Mt Fyans, RSD Darlington, VIC 3271, Australia]; *b* 31 July 1953; *m* 1977, as his 2nd w, *6th Earl of Stradbroke (*qv*) and has issue

(6) Guy Fitzpatrick Roger; *b* 8 Oct 1878; *m* 30 April 1914 Marjorie (*m* 2nd 16 Aug 1922 16th Earl of Eglinton and Winton (*qv*) and *d* 7 Dec 1963), dau of Thomas Walker McIntyre, of Sorn, and *d* 11 June 1914 from injuries recd in a car crash

(1) Florence Albreda; *b* 2 Dec 1867; *m* 28 Nov 1894 Lt-Col Ranald Macdonald Laurie (*d* 21 Oct 1927), DSO, RA, of Ford Place, Grays, Essex, and *d* 10 March 1940, leaving issue

(2) Hermione Helen; *b* 27 June 1875; *m* 1 June 1912 Maj John Brown Black, Cameron Highrs, of Bayford Lodge, Wincanton, Somerset, yr s of Gavin Black, of Wester Moffat, Airdrie, Lanarks, and *d* 27 Nov 1947, leaving issue

1 Evelyn Elizabeth; *b* 5 Sept 1829; *m* 19 Sept 1850 George Wodehouse Currie (*dsp* 8 Jan 1887) and *d* 22 Jan 1873

The 4th BARON's cousin,

SIDNEY MUNROE VERNON, **5th Baron Lyveden of Lyveden**; *b* 21 Nov 1888; *m* 1st 2 July 1912 Ruby (*d* 26 Jan 1932), dau of Robert John Shandley, of Hobart; *m* 2nd 1957 Gladys (*d* 1986), widow of John Cassidy, and *d* 19 Sept 1973, having by his 1st w had:

1 RONALD CECIL VERNON, **6th and present Baron Lyveden of Lyveden**

1 Eileen Dorothy; *b* 3 Jan 1914; *m* 11 July 1932 John Robert Grindrod and had:

(1) *John Vernon; *b* 19 Jan 1938

2 Valda Jean; *b* 11 July 1918; *m* 10 July 1937 Basil George Garrett and had issue

3 *Audrey Joan [The Hon Mrs Parker, Kennington St, Waihi, New Zealand]; *b* 8 Jan 1922; *m* 14 Nov 1940 *Russell Parker and has:

(1) *Robert Barry; *b* 1944; *m* 1965 *Helen Wilkinson and has:

1a *Michelle; *b* 1965

(2) *Allan Sydney Russell [Allan Parker Esq, 12 Argus St, Rotorua, New Zealand]; *b* 1946; *m* 1967 *Judi Patterson and has:

1a *Kerry James; *b* 1968

2a *Grant Allen; *b* 1970

(3) *Raymond John; *b* 1953

(1) *Barbara Joan; *b* 1942; *m* 1961 *John Sydney Barnett and has:

1a *Craig John; *b* 1963

2a *Gregory Mark; *b* 1965

1a *Tracy Megan; *b* 1969

4 *Maureen Dawn [The Hon Mrs Surrell, 10 Koha Rd, Taupo, New Zealand]; *b* 19 Oct 1926; *m* 16 Nov 1945 *Noel Surrell and has had:

(1) Carey Wayne; *b* 22 Aug 1947; *d* 9 Nov 1965

(2) *Andrew Gray [Andrew Surrell Esq, 49A Huka Falls Rd, Taupo, New Zealand]; *b* 13 Feb 1952; *m* 1970 *Rowena Anne Doel and has:

1a *Jason Carey; *b* 1971

1a *Carlene; *b* 1974

MacAndrew

Creation: B. (UK) 8 Dec 1959.

THE 3RD BARON MacANDREW, of the Firth of Clyde (Christopher Anthony Colin MacAndrew) [The Rt Hon The Lord MacAndrew, Hall Farm, Archdean Newton, Darlington DL2 2YB]; *b* 16 Feb 1945; *s* f 1989; *educ* Malvern; Commr Income Tax 1996–; *m* 13 Dec 1975 *Sarah Helen, only dau of Lt-Col Peter Hendry Brazier, of Nash Court Farmhouse, Marnhull, Dorset, and has:

1 +OLIVER CHARLES JULIAN; *b* 3 Sept 1983

1 *Diana Sarah; *b* 24 June 1978

2 *Tessa Deborah; *b* 2 Aug 1980

Lineage: JOHN MacANDREW, of Park Circus Place, Glasgow; *b* 1803; *m* 1840 Janet Orr, of Glasgow and *d* 1891, leaving:

FRANCIS GLEN MacANDREW, of Knock Castle, Largs, Ayrshire; *b* 30 Nov 1854; *educ* Glasgow HS and Abbey Park St Andrews; *m* 17 Nov 1886 Elizabeth Muir (*d* 8 Dec 1938), dau of John Graham, and had, with four other children:

1 CHARLES GLEN (Sir), **1st Baron**

2 James Orr, TD (1950) DL (Ayrshire 1966); *b* 22 June 1899; *educ* Trin Coll Glenalmond and Trin Hall Cambridge; Lt-Col TARO, MP Ayrshire 1931–35, MFH Eglinton 1939–40, WW I with RAF (wounded), Capt Ayrshire Yeo (TA) 1928, Maj 1938, Lt Col 1939, WW II as OC Ayrshire Yeo 1939–40 and 151st (Ayrshire Yeo) Field Regt RA 1940–41, Hon Col Ayrshire Yeo 1955–60; *m* 9 Sept 1944 *Eileen May, dau of Robin Butterfield, of Oxford, and *d* 11 July 1979, leaving:

(1) *Amanda Rose [Mrs John Nicholson, Adstockfields, Adstock, Bucks MK18 2JD]; *b* 7 June 1947; *m* 31 Oct 1969 *John Hartshorne Courtney Nicholson, s of Claude Nicholson, and has:

1a *John Hempe; *b* 5 Oct 1970

FRANCIS MacANDREW *d* 10 Sept 1908; his est son,

CHARLES GLEN MacANDREW, **1st Baron MacAndrew**, of The Firth of Clyde (UK), so *cr* 8 Dec 1959, TD (1923), PC (1952), JP (1929), DL (Ayrshire 1955); *b* 15 Jan 1888; *educ* Uppingham and Trin Coll Cambridge; joined Ayrshire Yeo 1907, WW I in France, Lt-Col Ayrshire Yeo (TA) 1932–36, Brevet-Col 1936, MP (C) Kilmarnock Oct 1924–May 1929, Partick Oct 1931–Oct 1935 and Bute and N Ayrshire Nov 1935–Sept 1959, T/Chm Ctees H of C 1934–50, Dep Chm Ways and Means May–July 1945 and March 1950–Oct 1951, Chm Oct 1951–Sept 1959, memb Racecourse Betting Control Bd 1938–61, OStJ, Hon LLD St Andrews, ktd 1935; *m* 1st 7 Feb 1918 (*divorce* 1938) Lilian Cathleen (*d* 1978), dau of James Prendergast Curran, of St Andrews, and had:

1 COLIN NEVILL GLEN, **2nd Baron**

2 Ronald; *b* 19 Feb 1922; *educ* Eton; *m* 18 Dec 1943 Jean (*m* 2nd 17 Nov 1949 George Maurice Barber), dau of Geoffrey John Lee-Barber, of Torquay, and *dsp* 18 April 1946

1 *Elizabeth Lilian Graham [The Hon Lady Coats, The Cottage, Symington, Ayrshire KA1 5QG]; *b* 23 Aug 1929; *m* 8 Feb 1950 *Sir William David Coats, DL, er s of Thomas Heywood Coats, of Nitshill, Glasgow (*see* 1970 edn GLENTANAR, B), and has:

(1) *Brian Glen Heywood; *b* 1951; *educ* Eton; *m* 1979 *Consuelo, dau of Luis Eduardo Marquez, of Colombia, and has:

1a *Andrew William Heywood; *b* 1983

1a *Julia Caroline; *b* 1981

(2) *Adrian James MacAndrew; *b* 1955; *educ* Eton; *m* 1979 *Mary Elizabeth, dau of George Robin Clover, and has:

1a *Alistair Thomas Edward; *b* 1984

1a *Rachel Olivia Askernish; *b* 1982

(1) *Frances Alice; *b* 1958; *m* 1982 *Michael John Adam Fowle and has:

1a *Jonathan Richard Adam; *b* 1986

1a *Alexandra Jane Adam; *b* 1985

The **1st Baron** *m* 2nd 2 Feb 1941 Mona (*d* 1994), dau of James Alexander Ralston Mitchell, of Perceton House, Irvine, Ayrshire, and *d* 11 Jan 1979, leaving by her:

2 *Mary Margaret Hastings [The Hon Mrs Ramsay, Bughtrig, Coldstream, Berwicks TD12 4JP]; *b* 23 March 1942; *m* 1 Aug 1967 *Maj-Gen Charles Alexander Ramsay, CB, OBE (*see* RAMSAY, Bt), and has issue

His only surv son,

COLIN NEVILL GLEN MacANDREW, **2nd Baron MacAndrew**; *b* 1 Aug 1919; *educ* Eton and Trin Coll Cambridge; WW II with Ayrshire Yeo, MFH Zetland; *m* 15 Sept 1943 Ursula Beatrice (*d* 1986), yr dau of Capt Joseph Steel, of Kirkwood, Lockerbie, Dumfriesshire, and *d* 1989, leaving:

1 CHRISTOPHER ANTHONY COLIN MacANDREW, **3rd and present Baron MacAndrew**

2 +Nicholas Rupert [The Hon Nicholas MacAndrew, The Old Chapel, Greywell, Hook RG29 1BS]; *b* 12 Feb 1947; *educ* Eton; *m* 1st 17 May 1975 (*divorce*

1995) Victoria Rose, dau of George Patrick Renton, of Paddock Lodge, Isington, Alton GU34 4PR, and has:

(1) +Robin Glen; *b* 2 June 1978

(1) *Rose Clare; *b* 12 April 1980

(2) *Rachel Emma; *b* 27 Jan 1984

2 (cont.) The Hon Nicholas MacAndrew *m* 2nd 14 March 1998 *Joy Meadows

1 *Deborah Jane [The Hon Mrs Faulkner, Hollintree House, Newsham, N Yorks YO7 4DH]; *b* 13 Nov 1956; *m* 8 Dec 1979 *Lt-Col Mark William Bingham Faulkner (*see* DE TRAFFORD, Bt) and has issue

Macara

Arms: Erm. an oak tree eradicated in bend dexter, surmounted by a sword in bend sinister ppr., hilt and pommel or, supporting on its point an Imperial crown of the second, on a chief of the third a spider sa. between two thistles, also ppr. **Crest:** A stag lodged regardant in front of an oak tree ppr. **Motto:** *Consilio non vi* ('By argument not force'). **Creation:** Bt. (UK) 9 Feb 1911.

SIR HUGH KENNETH MACARA, 4TH BT, of Ardmore, St Anne-on-the-Sea, Co Lancaster; *b* 17 Jan 1913; *s* bro 1982

Lineage: Rev WILLIAM MACARA; Min Free Church Scotland at Strathmiglo, Fife; *b* 27 May 1812 (s of Charles Macara); *m* 5 April 1844 Charlotte Grace (*d* 12 March 1882), dau of Thomas Cowpar, of Memus, Kirriemuir, Forfar, and niece of Maj-Gen Sir Archibald Galloway, Chm HEIC, and *d* 11 March 1889, leaving:

Sir Charles Wright Macara, **1st Bt** (UK), so *cr* 9 Feb 1911, JP Lancs; *b* 11 Jan 1845; Chm Manchester Master Cotton Spinners' Assoc 1892–1926, Pres Fedn Master Cotton Spinners' Assocs 1894–1914, Chev Legn Hon and Leopold Belgium, Grand Cross Order Merito Agricola Spain, Red Eagle Germany 4th Cl and Cdr Crown Italy; *m* 14 Jan 1875 Marion (*d* 12 June 1938), dau of William Young, of Bournemouth, and had:

1 WILLIAM COWPER (Sir), **2nd Bt**

2 Charles Douglas; *b* 14 Aug 1885; *d* 29 Jan 1891

1 Marion Grace Macara; *b* 11 June 1877; *m* 14 Nov 1908 Charles Henry Ritchings and had issue

2 Beatrice Mary; *b* 14 Oct 1878; *m* 21 Dec 1906 Frederick Ballard (*d* 13 Sept 1940), of Herefs, and *d* 1 Feb 1955

3 Lillian Emily; *b* 8 Oct 1880; *d* unm 17 Jan 1949

4 Alice Maud; *b* 16 May 1882; *d* unm 4 July 1952

Sir CHARLES *d* 2 Jan 1929; his only surv s,

Sir William Cowper Macara, 2nd Bt; *b* 4 Nov 1875; Lt 2nd W Lancs Bde RFA; *m* 18 Feb 1903 Lillian Mary (*d* 17 Feb 1971 aged 96), dau of John Chapman, of Boyton Court, E Sutton, Kent, and *d* 18 March 1931, leaving:

1 Sir (Charles) Douglas Macara, **3rd Bt**; *b* 19 April 1904; *educ* Fettes; *m* 20 Nov 1925 (*divorce* 1945) Quenilda Mary, dau of Herbert Whitworth, of St Anne's-on-Sea, and had:

(1) William Barry; *b* 29 July 1930; *d* unm 10 Oct 1954

(1) *Pamela Alison [Mrs John Romer, Tan-y-Maes, Glan Conwy, Colwyn Bay, Clwyd LL28 2LQ]; *b* 10 March 1927; *m* 9 July 1954 *John Gordon Raymond Romer and has:

1a *Charles John; *b* 3 Dec 1958

2a *Gordon Clive; *b* 6 May 1960

1a *Gillian Avril; *b* 22 Sept 1955

2a *Susan Claire; *b* 1970

(2) *Quenilda Jennifer [Mrs Peter Dobson, 7 Clyst Valley Rd, Clyst St Mary, Exeter]; *b* 23 April 1929; *m* 6 March 1954 *Peter Graham Dobson and has had:

1a *Trevor William; *b* 27 July 1957

2a John Keith; *b* 9 Dec 1961; *d* 1982

1a *Susan Jane; *b* 25 Dec 1954

2a *Valerie Anne; *b* 25 March 1956

3a *Kay Elizabeth; *b* 19 Feb 1960

2 John Keith; *b* 29 Oct 1905; *m* 18 April 1948 Joan Florence Mary (*d* 19 June 1956), est dau of Oswald Frances Gerard Stonor, CMG (*see* CAMOYS, B) and formerly w of John Colburn Bennett

3 William Donald; *b* 17 July 1909; *m* 15 April 1939 *Rosalind Verena, yst dau of Frederick Harrild, of Sevenoaks

4 Sir HUGH KENNETH MACARA, **4th and present Bt**

1 *Aileen Lillan [Mrs Hart, The Old Manor, Fore St, Seaton, Devon EX12 2AN]; *b* 9 Jan 1908; *m* 19– — Hart

2 Margaret Alison; *b* 11 Jan 1912; *m* 1st 15 April 1933 Roger Edwards (*d* 25 Dec 1955); *m* 2nd 19 Feb 1958 Harry Winchurch, s of Enoch Winchurch, of Staffs, and by her 1st husb had issue

MACARTNEY

STIMULAT · SED · ORNAT

Arms: Or a stag trippant within a bordure gules. **Crest:** A hand holding a slip of a rose-tree with three roses thereon, all proper. **Motto:** *Stimulat sed ornat* ('It stimulates, but it adorns'). **Creation:** Bt. (I) 4 Jan 1799.

SIR JOHN BARRINGTON MACARTNEY, 6TH BT, of Lish, Co Armagh [Sir John Macartney Bt, 37 Meadow St, N Mackay, Queensland 4740, Australia]; *b* 21 Jan 1917; *s* unc 1960; retired dairy farmer; *m* 1944 Amy Isobel Reinke (*d* 1978) and has:

1 +JOHN RALPH [John Macartney Esq, 1 Kookaburra St, Slade Point, Qld 4740, Australia]; *b* 24 July 1945; Petty Offr RAN Malaya 1964–65 and Vietnam 1968–69, teacher Bruce Coll Technology and Further Educn 1979–82, Head Dept 1982–; *m* 1966 *Suzanne Marie Fowler, of Nowra, NSW, and has:

  (1) *Donna Maree; *b* 1968

  (2) *Karina Lee; *b* 1971

  (3) *Katharine Ann; *b* 1974

  (4) *Anita Louise; *b* 1979

Lineage: ISAAC MACARTNEY; High Sheriff Co Antrim 1690; *m* Anne/Grace, sis and coheir of John Haltridge, MP Killyleagh, and had, with an er s and a dau (Grace, *m* 1729, as his 2nd w, Sir Robert Blackwood, 2nd Bt, and had issue; *see* DUFFERIN AND CLANEBOYE, B):

WILLIAM MACARTNEY, of Lish, Co Armagh; *b* 1715; MP (I Parl) Belfast 1747–61; *m* 1743 Catherine, dau of Thomas Bankes, and *d* 1797, having had, with an er s (Arthur Chichester, KC, of Lish and Murlough, Co Down, *b* 1744, Ch Remembrancer Court Exchequer, *m* 1779 Anna (*d* 1841), dau of Samuel Lindsay, of Turin Castle, Co Mayo, and *d* 29 Sept 1827, leaving issue) and five daus:

Sir John Macartney, 1st Bt (I), so *cr* 4 Jan 1799, of Lish; *b* 9 March 1747; MP (I Parl) Fore 1793–97 and Naas 1798–1800, ktd 1796 for promoting Irish canals, Dep Ch Remembrancer Exchequer Ireland; *m* 1st *c* 26 Feb 1778 Anne, dau of Edward Scriven by Elizabeth, dau of John Barclay, of Dublin, and had, with five other children:

1 WILLIAM ISAAC (Sir), **2nd Bt**

1 Maria; *m* her cousin Joseph Macartney and *d* 3 June 1869, leaving issue

Sir John *m* 2nd 4 Nov 1794 Catherine (*b c* 1770; *d* 17 Sept 1840), dau of Walter Hussey-Burgh, PC, Ch Baron Exchequer Ireland 1782–83, and *d* 29 May 1812, leaving by her:

2 Hussey Burgh (Very Rev), DD; *b* 10 April 1799; first Dean Melbourne, Australia; *m* 7 March 1833 Jane (*d* 10 Jan 1885), dau of Edward Hardman by Rebecca, dau of John McClintock, MP (*see* RATHDONNELL, B), and *d* 8 Oct 1894, having had:

  (1) John Arthur, of Ormiston House, Ormiston, Qld; *b* 5 April 1834; *m* 15 Jan 1861 Annie Flora (*d* 14 Oct 1911), dau of Alexander Cuningham Fairlie Wallace Dunlop, and *d* 1917, having had:

    1a Hussey Burgh John Arthur; *b* 1 Aug 1873; *d* 1936

    2a Alexander Wallace Dunlop; *b* 8 Jan 1875; *d* unm 20 Dec 1907

    3a Arthur John Edward McClintock; *b* 13 March 1877; *d* young

    4a Henry Dundas Keith, CMG (1919), DSO (1918); *b* 1 Feb 1880; Lt-Col Roy Australian Artillery WW I (despatches); *m* 1911 Alexandrina Vans, dau of Stanislaus Zichy Woinarski, and *d* 24 Oct 1932

1a Constance Madeline Frances; *m* 1st 23 Sept 1884 Capt William Mountifort Longfield (*ka* Boer War 4 June 1901), Hants Imp Yeo, of Ashgrove, Co Cork, and had issue; *m* 2nd 1916 John Godolphin Rich (*d* 1951)

2a Jane Catherine Nina Henrietta; *m* 1890 James G K Snape (*d* 1922), of Woodlawn, Quirindi, NSW, and had:

  1b John Edward MACARTNEY-SNAPE, MC and bar; *b* 189–; early pioneer tobacco grower Tanganyika, 1st AIF; *m* 1st — and had issue; *m* 2nd — and had, with two other daus:

    1c *Tim; *b* 19–; first Australian to climb Mt Everest

    1c *Susan; *b* 19–; artist with *Sunday Telegraph*

3a Flora Charlotte Antonia

4a Jemina Vans Anna Mabel; *m* 1917 A Buxton Kenrick (*d* 1922)

(2) Edward Hardman; *b* 19 May 1835; *m* 6 May 1862 Georgiana Henrietta (*d* 8 Aug 1923), dau of James Moore, of Kew, Melbourne, and *d* 17 Oct 1903, leaving:

  1a Edward Hussey Burgh; *b* 25 Dec 1867; *educ* Melbourne U (BA, BCE); *m* 1st 1904 Jane Alexandra (*d* 1909), dau of Alexander Richardson McNab, and had:

    1b Jean Marion Isobel; *b* 1908; *m* 1954 William Balston (*d* 1960)

  1a (cont.) Edward Macartney *m* 2nd 1910 Constance May (*d* 1960), dau of Edward Griffith, and *d* 8 Sept 1930, leaving by her:

    1b James Edward; *b* 18 July 1911; md W Australian Newspapers; *m* 1946 *Margaret Casson, dau of Herbert Ernest Bennett, and *d* 1977, leaving:

      1c +John Alexander; *b* 1947; *m* 1977 *Lynette Kathleen, dau of Gordon Vaughan, and has:

        1d +Edward John; *b* 1978

      2c +William James; *b* 1948; *m* 1970 *Sherryl, dau of Wallace George Humfry, and has:

        1d +Benjamin Wallace; *b* 1972

        2d +Christopher John; *b* 1973

        3d +Jack Hussey Burgh; *b* 1981

    2b +John Hussey Burgh [John Macartney Esq, 7 Tutus St, Balgowlah, Sydney, NSW 2093, Australia]; *b* 14 June 1915; Lt Cdr RAN (ret); *m* 1945 *Geraldine, dau of Eli Leach, of Darwen, Lancs, and has:

      1c *Francesca May; *b* 25 Jan 1948; *educ* Sydney U (BA, LLB); *m* 1972 *Christopher William Beale, LLB (Sydney), MBA (Harvard), and has:

        1d *Julian Macartney; *b* 1986

        2d *Andrew Macartney; *b* 1988

    2b *Catherine Frances; *b* 1913; *m* 1st 1933 A N Magnus and has issue; *m* 2nd 19– *A H Telfer

    3b *Constance Eleanor; *b* 1922; *m* 1950 *David Howley and has issue

2a James Moore; *b* 20 Sept 1871; Australian Light Horse and 14th Inf Bn WW I; *m* 4 March 1935 Vera, dau of D G E Alsop, and *d* 8 June 1956

3a Charles Perry; *b* 3 Nov 1880; *m* 2 Dec 1912 Daphne Violet (*d* 1976), 2nd dau of Lt-Col Henry James King, and *d* 1947, leaving:

  1b *Violet Moore [Miss Violet Macartney, 33 Proctors Rd, Dynnyrne, Hobart, Tasmania 7005]; *b* 24 Feb 1914

  2b *Nancy Gower [Mrs Leonard Basterfield, 43 Tramway Pde, Beaumaris, Victoria 3193, Australia]; *b* 24 Jan 1920; *m* 30 Aug 1958 Leonard James Basterfield (*d* 1988) and has:

    1c *Josephine Nancy; *b* 29 Oct 1960

  3b Elizabeth Catherine; *b* 23 July 1923; *m* 1945 Frederick James Byrne and *d* 5 March 1993, leaving:

    1c *Frederick Michael [Frederick Byrne Esq, 1/42 Queen St, Bellerive, Hobart, Tasmania, Australia 7018; *b* 12 April 1946; *m* 1968 (*divorce* 19–) Helen Miller West

    2c *Damien Charles; *b* 15 Oct l947

    3c *Anthony Gerard; *b* 13 July 1962

    4c *Paul Leonard Dominic; *b* 14 Oct 1966

    1c *Catherine Anne [Mrs Geoffrey Taylor, 19 Currajong St, Mornington, Hobart, Tasmania 7018]; *b* 27 May 1949; *m* 1972 *Geoffrey Francis Taylor and has:

      1d *Gabriel Francis; *b* 1973

      2d *Adam Gerard; *b* 1975

      3d *Justin Marcus; *b* 1977

      4d *Joshua Frederick; *b* 1983

      5d *Tristan Luke (twin); *b* 1985

      6d *Liam Geoffrey; *b* 1987

      1d *Simone Elizabeth; *b* 1974

      2d *Jenna Therese (twin); *b* 1985

    2c *(Margaret) Louise [Miss Louise Byrne, 23 Erica Avenue, St Albans, Melbourne, VIC 3021, Australia]; *b* 7 Feb 1957; *m* 1977 (*divorce*) Jon Lewryk and has:

      1d *Anton Alexander James; *b* 1981

1a Harriet Maria; *m* 14 March 1894 Charles Rawdon Cuningham and *d* 1953, leaving issue (*see* FAIRLIE-CUNINGHAME, Bt)

2a Georgiana Maude; *m* 1 June 1887 Sir William Edward Fairlie-Cuningham, 13th Bt (*qv*), and *d* Feb 1951, leaving issue

3a Jane Catherine; *d* unm 3 Oct 1947

4a Agnes Henrietta; *m* 5 July 1899 Peter Corsar Anderson, CBE, MA, BD (St Andrews) (*d* 1955), Pncpl Scotch Coll Perth, W Australia, and *d* 8 Jan 1961, leaving issue

5a Anne Constance; *d* unm 31 May 1938

6a Charlotte Mary

(3) Hussey Burgh (Rev); *b* 30 Sept 1840; MA Dublin; incumbent Caulfield, Victoria; *m* 7 March 1872 Emily (*d* 15 May 1900), dau of Henry Addenbrooke and widow of Hon Robert Quayle Kermode, of Tasmania, and *d* 21 Oct 1908, leaving:

  1a Hussey Burgh George; *b* 10 Feb 1875; *educ* Trin Coll Cambridge (BA); Capt Roy Fus Boer War 1899–1900 (wounded) and WW I; *ka* 25 June 1915

1a Jane Elizabeth Catherine; *m* 10 April 1913 Lt-Col Robert Hall Hayes, CMG, Middx Regt (*d* 23 Aug 1946), s of G H Hayes, of Melbourne, and *d* 29 April 1965, leaving:

  1b *Katherine Hussey de Burgh [Miss Katherine Hayes, Radipole Manor, Weymouth, Dorset DT3 5HS]; *b* 1915

(1) Henrietta Rebecca; *d* unm 1917

(2) Anna Catharine; *d* unm 17 Sept 1852

(3) Jane Frances; *m* 11 Aug 1868 Sir William Watson and *d* 15 Oct 1876, leaving issue

(4) Charlotte Elizabeth Caroline

(5) Frances Marianne; *d* unm 29 May 1885

2 Catherine Anne Mona; *m* 16 May 1826 Rev Henry Brougham and *d* 5 Jan 1892, leaving issue (*see* BROUGHAM AND VAUX, B)

The 1st Bt's est s,

Rev Sir William Isaac Macartney, 2nd Bt; *b* 25 Oct 1780; *educ* Trin Coll Dublin (BA 1801, MA 1812); Rector Desertegny; *m* 28 May 1818 Ellen (*d* 7 Sept 1875), illegitimate dau of Sir John Barrington, 9th Bt, of Barrington Hall, and *d* 31 July 1867, having had, with six daus (Sophia; Anna Maria; Eliza; Georgiana; Frances Catherine; Maria Louisa):

1 JOHN (Sir), **3rd Bt**

2 William George; *b* 1835; *m* 1872 Bessie, dau of Robert Bayley Tyser, of Wellington, NZ, and *d* 188–, having had two sons (Henry Tyser, *b* 1872; Ernest George, *b* 1880) and two daus (Edith Isabel; Eileen Agnes)

The 2nd Bt's er s,

Sir John Macartney, 3rd Bt; *b* 10 Oct 1832; *m* 1 Sept 1865 Catherine (*d* 5 May 1904), 2nd dau of Alexander Miller, of Merindindi, Victoria, and *d* 7 Dec 1911, having had:

1 **Sir William Isaac Macartney, 4th Bt**; *b* 13 Oct 1867; *d* unm April 1942

2 **Sir Alexander Miller Macartney, 5th Bt**; *b* 24 July 1869; *d* unm 30 Sept 1960

3 John Barrington; *b* 26 Oct 1873; *m* May 1910 Selina, dau of J Koch, and *d* June 1951, leaving:

(1) Sir JOHN BARRINGTON MACARTNEY, **6th and present Bt**

(1) *Evelyn Catherine [Mrs Albert Ellwood, 23 Milne Lane, West Mackay, Queensland 4740, Australia]; *b* 1910; *m* 1931 *Albert Edward Ellwood and has:

  1a *Alan John [Alan Ellwood Esq, 4740 Gargett via Mackay, Queensland, Australia]; *b* 1935; *m* 1963 *Hester, dau of H Lewis, of Mackay, and has:

    1b *Derek John; *b* 1968

    1b *Charmaine Mary; *b* 1964

    2b *Dianne Lucy; *b* 1966

  2a *Edward Graham; *b* 1945; *m* 19– *Helen Mary, dau of Thomas Chadwick, of Dalby, Qld, and has:

    1b *Damian Ralf; *b* 1974

  1a *Audrey Philomene [Mrs Nathaniel Perry, Matcham, Gracemere, via Rockhampton, Queensland 4702, Australia]; *b* 1932; *m* 1952 *Noel Nathaniel Perry and has:

    1b *Gregory John; *b* 1957

    2b *Shane Nathaniel; *b* 1971

    1b *Christine Anne; *b* 1953

    2b *Janette Patricia; *b* 1955

    3b *Judith Marie; *b* 1956

    4b *Kathleen Ellen; *b* 1959

  2a *Marie Claire; *b* 1934; *m* 1956 *Franciscao Antonius Brieffres and has:

    1b *Frank John; *b* 1957

    2b *Peter Eugene; *b* 1961

    3b *Anthony John; *b* 1964

    1b *Lynette; *b* 1958

    2b *Trudy Bernadette; *b* 1959

    3b *Melita Maree; *b* 1963

    4b *Yvonne; *b* 1966

(2) *Constance [Mrs Stanley Desbois, Mail Serv 656, Mackay, Qld 4740, Australia]; *b* 1911; *m* 1939 Stanley Dan Desbois (*d* 1983) and has:

  1a *Kevin; *b* 1941; *m* 1966 *Janet Elizabeth Gordon, of Mackay, and has:

    1b *Sean Kevin; *b* 1975

    1b *Michelle Maree; *b* 1968

    2b *Andrea Jane; *b* 1969

  2a *Clive John; *b* 1948; *m* 1973 *Bernadette Mary Murphy and has:

    1b *Timothy John; *b* 1976

    2b *Graham Stanley; *b* 1983

    1b *Sharon Ann; *b* 1978

    2b *Jennifer Mary; *b* 1981

4 Herbert Charles; *b* 11 March 1876; *m* 1913 Frances, dau of J E Tooker, of Leura Castle Station, Rockhampton, and *d* 1953, leaving:

(1) *Patricia Catherine; *b* 1917; *m* 27 Jan 1941 *Leslie John Campbell, s of William Blair Campbell, of Inverness Station, and has:

  1a *Alan Leslie John Macartney; *b* 14 Jan 1952

  1a *Diana Ruby; *b* 10 Dec 1942

  2a *Rosemary Frances; *b* 3 Jan 1945

  3a *Ailsa Catherine; *b* 10 Dec 1947

(2) *Frances Evelyn; *b* 1924; *m* 12 Sept 1953 *John Smith, of Brisbane, Queensland

5 Robert Graham; *b* 7 Dec 1878; *d* 20 Aug 1879

6 David Edwin; *b* 5 July 1880; *m* 1st 1912 Flora (*d* Dec 1914), dau of E K Ogg, of Rockhampton; *m* 2nd July 1920 Ella Margaret McCulloch (*d* 1978), of Qld, dau of Daniel Craig, of Longreach, and *d* 6 July 1957, leaving by her:

(1) +Alexander Macdonald [Alexander Macartney Esq, 11 Chermside Dve, Warwick, Queensland 4370, Australia]; *b* 21 Oct 1921; F/Lt RAAF; *m* 1959 *Penelope Ann, dau of C B Freeman, of Brisbane, and has:

1a +John Alexander [John Macartney Esq, Crane Rd, Castle Hill, NSW 2154, Australia]; *b* 1961; F/Lt RAAF; *m* 1986 *Robyn Mary, dau of E M Norling, of Wellington, NZ

1a *Deborah Ann; *b* 1962; *m* 1985 (*divorce* 1994) — and has:

  1b *Arianna Ella; *b* 1990

(2) +David Edwin; *b* 1924; late RAN; *m* 1948 *Elizabeth Lillias, dau of L Ewert, of Rotorua, NZ, and has:

1a +David Edwin; *b* 1951

2a +Anthony Craig; *b* 1956

1a *Diane Ewert; *b* 1952; *m* 1977 *David John McBryde and has:

  1b *James David; *b* 1983

  1b *Fiona Diane; *b* 1981

(3) John Craig; *b* 9 July 1927; late AIF; *m* 1951 *Betty Katrine [Mrs John Macartney, L6/356 Blunder Rd, Durack, Qld, Australia], dau of Dr Leckie, of Ingham, Qld, and *d* 19 Feb 1992, having had:

1a Paul Alexander; *b* 1955; *d* 5 June 1979

1a *Belinda Lee; *b* 1952

(4) +Wallace Herbert [Wallace Macartney Esq, 49 Nevin St, Aspley, Brisbane, Qld 4034, Australia]; *b* 9 July 1929; *m* 1973 *Judith Anne, dau of A K Addison, of Brisbane, and has:

1a *Robyn Judith; *b* 1976

(1) *Margaret Miller [Mrs David Hopton, PO Box 242, Edge Hill, Cairns, N Qld 4870, Australia]; *b* 1932; *m* 1949 *Capt David Hopton, formerly with Ansett Airways, and has:

1a *John Craig Macartney; *b* 1950; *m* 1980 *Diane Rita Cavanagh

2a *Peter Coulter; *b* 1955; *m* 1980 *Christine Ann Cosgriffe and has:

  1b *James Duncan; *b* 1988

  1b *Stephanie Lee; *b* 1984

  2b *Angela Margaret; *b* 1986

3a *Jason Craig; *b* 1956; *m* 1983 *Julie Ann McLaren and has:

  1b *Toby John; *b* 1985

  2b *Fraser McLaren; *b* 1987

  3b *Joshua Craig; *b* 1989

(2) *Catherine Ella [Mrs Donald Grayling, 13 Cliff Ave, Winston Hills, Sydney, NSW 1253, Australia]; *b* 1926; *m* 1962 *Donald Grayling, RN, and has:

1a *Donald David; *b* 28 March 1968

1a *Fiona Ella; *b* 14 Jan 1964

7 Harold Eric Joseph; *b* 1882; served 5th Australian LI; *ka* 5 July 1915

8 Victor Alan, of The Gully, Ourimbah, NSW; *b* 1887; *m* Aug 1915 Elsie Maria, dau of Robert McKie, of Brisbane, and *d* 1969, leaving:

(1) +Harold Kenneth; *b* Feb 1919; AIF Singapore 1941 (POW); *m* 1951 *Beatrice, dau of Henry Apsley Carlyle Lowe, of NSW, and has:

1a +William John; *b* 1959

1a *Diana Eileen; *b* 1955

(1) *Elinor; *b* 1917; sis Australian Army Nursing Serv Middle East 1940–41; *m* 1942 *Maj Francis Stephen Small, AIF, and has:

1a *Roderick Cameron Macartney; *b* 1943

2a *Robert Francis (twin); *b* 1949

1a *Rosemary Elinor; *b* 1945

2a *Margaret Anne (twin); *b* 1949

MACAULAY OF BRAGAR

Creation: B. (LP, UK) 1989.

THE BARON MACAULAY OF BRAGAR, of Bragar, Co Ross and Cromarty (Donald Macaulay) [The Rt Hon The Lord Macaulay of Bragar, House of Lords, London SW1A 0PW]; *b* 14 Nov 1933; *educ* Clydebank HS and Glasgow U (MA, LLB); advocate 1963; QC (Scotland) 1975; *m* 1962 *Mary, dau of Murdo Morrison, of Bragar, and has two daus

Lineage: JOHN MACAULAY; shipyard labourer, of Clydebank; *m* Effie McLean and had:

DONALD, *cr* a **Baron**

MACCLESFIELD

Arms: Gu. a chevron between three leopard's faces or. **Crest:** A leopard's head affrontée, erased at the neck or, ducally gorged gu. **Supporters:** Two leopards, regardant ppr., each gorged with a ducal coronet gu. **Motto:** *Sapere aude* ('Dare to be wise'). **Creations:** B (GB) 10 March 1716, E. and V. (GB) 15 Nov 1721.

THE 9TH EARL OF MACCLESFIELD, Co Chester, **Viscount Parker of Ewelm**, Co Oxford, and **Baron Parker of Macclesfield** (Richard Timothy George Mansfield Parker) [The Rt Hon The Earl of Macclesfield, Shirburn Castle, Watlington, Oxon OX9 5DL]; *b* 31 May 1943; *s f* 1992; *educ* Stowe and Worcester Coll Oxford (BA 1965); *m* 1st 11 Aug 1967 (*divorce* 1985) (Tatiana) Cleone Anne, only dau of Maj Craig Wheaton-Smith (*see* 1933 edn CRAIG, Bt), of Wenham, Mass., by Tatiana, dau of Prince Serge Wiasemsky; *m* 2nd 1986 *Mrs Sandra Hope Mead, dau of Sylvio Fiore, of Florida, and by his 1st w has:

1 *Tanya Susan; *b* 27 Aug 1971
2 *Katherine Anne; *b* 19 June 1973
3 *Marion Jane; *b* 19 June 1973 (twin)

Macclesfield, previous creation: Charles Gerard, of a Lancashire family, also great-grandson of a Master of the Rolls in ELIZABETH I's reign, commanded an infantry brigade at Edgehill, the opening battle of the Civil War, and handled it so well that it played a very large role in bringing about a draw that day (23 Oct 1642) rather than a victory for Parliament. He went on to become royalist Commander-in-Chief in South Wales and was created Baron Gerard of Brandon in November 1645. After the Restoration he was made Lieutenant-General of all English forces, despite his past record of peculation, *viz.*, concealing news of some of his soldiers' deaths so as to divert their pay to himself, and promoted Earl of Macclesfield in 1679. (Dishonesty seems to have been a failing of the other 1st Earl of Macclesfield, the one so created in 1721: he was tried for having accepted bribes three weeks after leaving office as Lord Chancellor by the Commons before the Lords (the process known as impeachment), found guilty without a single dissentient voice and fined £30,000 (some £1,680,000 in late-1990s terms)).

The 1st Earl of Macclesfield of the 1679 creation was one of the conspirators with the Duke of Monmouth to bring about a Protestant succession in the final years of CHARLES II's reign and was forced to flee abroad for a time, being outlawed, but was rehabilitated under WILLIAM III. His London house was in what is now Gerrard Street, Soho, hence the name.

His son the 2nd Earl of Macclesfield was thought also to have been involved in treasonable activity during CHARLES II's reign and was briefly held in custody in the Tower of London during the late summer and early autumn of 1683. He was later attainted for his part in the Rye House Plot, a conspiracy actually to assassinate CHARLES II as well as his brother the future JAMES II, but was pardoned by the latter on his ascending the throne.

The 2nd Earl seems to have led a charmed life for the evidence against him on the count of treason was strong and in CHARLES's time, when he was only 19, he had been reprieved after being found guilty of actual rather than contemplated homicide, namely killing a pageboy while drunk. His marriage to Anne Mason, dau of a wealthy country squire from Shropshire, ended effectively after less than two years, when they were separated, although the divorce did not come through till 1698. This dissolution of marriage was a milestone in the history of English family law in that it was the first such under an Act of Parliament (the standard method until modern times) that had not been preceded by an Ecclesiastical Court judgement. By the Act of Parliament Anne's children were bastardised. They were indeed not by her husband but almost certainly by Richard Savage, 4th Earl Rivers (whose only surviving legitimate child was buried by an odd coincidence at Macclesfield). The poet Richard Savage, whose work *The Bastard* (1728) was so reproachful towards Lady Macclesfield (and which persuaded Dr Johnson to put Savage into his *Lives of the Poets*), claimed but is now reckoned not to have been one of these illegitimate children. Lady Macclesfield's daughter by her second marriage was a mistress of GEORGE I in his old age.

The 2nd Earl was clearly savage by nature as when only 14 he had beaten up a janitor at the Bedlam lunatic asylum. He made a will appointing as executor the

4th and last Lord Mohun (himself the murderer or accessory to murder of three men, for none of which crimes he was punished). The will left Mohun all Macclesfield's real property should he die without sons. This he did (at any rate without legitimate ones). The ensuing litigation between Mohun and the 4th Duke of Hamilton (*see* HAMILTON and BRANDON, D), another interested party through his wife, Macclesfield's niece, resulted in the death of both Mohun and Hamilton in a duel.

The Earldom expired a year after the 2nd Earl's death with the demise of his younger brother Fitton, who never married and did little harm, despite sitting as a Whig MP for all but two of the last 13 years of his life.

Lineage: THOMAS PARKER, of Leek, Staffs (*see* PARKER, Bt, of Shenstone Lodge); attorney; *m* Anne (*d* 27 June 1699), dau and coheir of Robert Venables, of Nuneham, Cheshire, and had:

THOMAS PARKER, **1st Earl of Macclesfield**, so *cr* 15 Nov 1721, as also VISCOUNT PARKER OF EWELM [*sic*], Co Oxford, and earlier 10 March 1716 BARON PARKER OF MACCLESFIELD, Co Chester (all GB), all with remainder, in default of heirs male of the grantee's body, to his only dau, PC (1710); *b* 23 July 1667; *educ* Trin Coll Cambridge and Inner Temple; barrister 1691, MP (Whig) Derby 1705–10, Serjeant-at-law and Queen's Serjeant 1705, ktd 1705, Ld Ch Justice Queen's Bench 1710–18, Ld Chllr 1718–Jan 1724/5, Ld Lt Warwicks 1719; *m* 23 April 1691 his cousin Janet (*d* 23 Aug 1733), dau and coheir of Charles Carrier, of Wirksworth, Derbys (s of Richard Carrier by Janet, dau of Thomas Parker, of Browsholme in Bolland, Yorks, the latter being ggf through his yr s George of the **1st Earl**), and *d* 28 April 1732, leaving, with other issue, including a dau (Elizabeth, *m* 7 April 1720 Sir William Heathcote, 1st Bt, of Hursley (*qv*), and *d* 21 Feb 1747, leaving issue):

GEORGE PARKER, **2nd Earl of Macclesfield**; *b c* 1697; *educ* Clare Coll Cambridge; Teller Exchequer 1719–64, MP (anti-Walpole Whig) Wallingford 1722–27, PRS 1752–64 (FRS 1722), FSA 1752, V-Pres Foundling Hosp, High Steward Henley-on-Thames, DCL Oxon; *m* 1st 18 Sept 1722 Mary (*d* 4 Sept 1753), er dau and coheir of Ralph Lane, Turkey merchant; *m* 2nd 20 Dec 1757 Dorothy Nesbitt (*dsp* 14 July 1779) and by his 1st w had:

1 THOMAS, **3rd Earl**
2 George Lane; Lt Gen, MP Tregony; *b* 4 Sept 1724; *m* 1782 Jane (*d* 29 July 1802), dau and coheir of Charles Adelmare Caesar and widow of Sir Charles Cottrell-Dormer, of Rousham, and *dsp* 6 Sept 1791

The 2nd EARL *d* 17 March 1764; his er son,

THOMAS PARKER, **3rd Earl of Macclesfield**; *b* 12 Oct 1723; *educ* Hertford Coll Oxford (MA, DCL 1773); MP (Whig) Newcastle-under-Lyme 1747–54, Oxon 1754–61 and Rochester 1761–64; *m* 12 Dec 1749 his cousin Mary (*d* 20 May 1812), est dau of Sir William Heathcote, 1st Bt, of Hursley (*qv*), and *d* 9 Feb 1795, leaving:

1 GEORGE PARKER, **4th Earl of Macclesfield**, PC (1791); *bapt* 21 March 1755; *educ* Eton and Exeter Coll Oxford; MP (Tory) Woodstock 1777–84 and Minehead 1790–95, Ld Bedchamber to PRINCE OF WALES 1780–89, Comptroller Household 1791–97, Ld Bedchamber 1797–1804, Capt Yeomen Gd 1804–30, Pres Bd Ag 1816–18, Ld Lt Oxon 1817–42; *m* 25 May 1780 Mary Frances (*d* 1 Jan 1823), dau and coheir of Rev Thomas Drake, DD, Rector Amersham, Bucks, and *d* 20 March 1842, having had an only surv dau:

  (1) Maria; *m* 13 Nov 1802 9th Earl of Haddington (*qv*) and *dsp* 11 Feb 1861
2 THOMAS, **5th Earl**
1 Elizabeth; *m* 16 Nov 1773 John Fane and *d* 10 June 1829, leaving issue (*see* WESTMORLAND, E)

The 4th EARL's bro,

THOMAS PARKER, **5th Earl of Macclesfield**; *b* 9 June 1763; Offr Coldstream Gds 1780–82, Sheriff Oxon 1808–09, DCL Oxon 1834, High Steward Henley 1842; *m* 1st 16 March 1796 the est dau (*d* 9 April 1803) of Lewis Edwards, of Talgarth, Merioneths, and had, with another dau (*d* unm):

1 Amelia; *m* March 1817 William Montgomery, DL, JP (*d* 3 May 1831), of Grey Abbey, Co Down, and *d* 5 Feb 1881, leaving issue
2 Matilda Anne; *m* 26 May 1825 Arthur Hill Montgomery, of Tyrella, Co Down, and *d* 25 May 1888, leaving issue
3 Ellen Katherine; *m* 3 Nov 1829 John William Fane and *d* 23 Sept 1844, leaving issue (*see* WESTMORLAND, E)

The **5th Earl** *m* 2nd 19 March 1807 Eliza (*d* 1 Jan 1862), yst dau of William Breton Wolstenholme, of Holly Hill, Sussex, and by her had:

1 THOMAS AUGUSTUS WOLSTENHOLME, **6th Earl**
4 Laura Cecilia; *m* 3 May 1836 4th Earl of Antrim (*qv*) and *d* 26 Jan 1883, leaving issue
5 Lavinia Agnes; *m* 19 July 1836 Hon John Thomas Dutton (*d* 22 June 1884), 2nd s of 2nd Baron Sherborne (*see* 1970 edn), and *d* 24 Nov 1893, leaving issue

The 5th EARL *d* 31 March 1850; his only s,

THOMAS AUGUSTUS WOLSTENHOLME PARKER, **6th Earl of Macclesfield**; *b* 17 March 1811; *educ* Eton and Ch Ch Oxford; MP (C) Oxon 1837–41, V-Lt Oxon (previously DL); *m* 1st 11 July 1839 Henrietta (*d* 19 Nov 1839), dau of Edmond Turnor, of Stoke Rochford, Lincs; *m* 2nd 25 Aug 1842 Mary Frances (*d* 2 Jan 1912), Extra Ldy Bedchamber to HM QUEEN ALEXANDRA, dau of 2nd Marquess of Westminster (*see* WESTMINSTER, D), and by her had:

1 George Augustus, *Viscount Parker*; *b* 19 Oct 1843; *educ* Eton and Ch Ch Oxford; Maj Oxon Yeo Cav, Lt 1st Life Gds; *m* 1st 14 March 1878 Edith (*d* 4 April 1895), dau of Frederick Paul Harford, of Down Place, Windsor, and widow of Thomas Rumbold Richardson, 1st Life Gds; *m* 2nd 26 Jan 1887 Carine Agnes (*m* 2nd 28 April 1897 Maj LW Matthews and *d* 7 Jan 1919), dau of Pryse Loveden, of Gogerddan, Cards (*see* 1959 edn PRYSE, Bt), and *dvp* 24 Sept 1895, having by her had:

  (1) GEORGE LOVEDEN WILLIAM HENRY, **7th Earl**
2 Cecil Thomas, JP Cheshire and Wilts; Lt Rifle Bde; *b* 27 March 1845; *m* 24 May 1870 Rosamond Esther Harriet (*d* 4 April 1936), dau of Most Rev Charles Thomas Longley, DD, Archbp Canterbury and *d* 12 Jan 1931, leaving:

  (1) Gerald Longley; Boer War 1900–01 and WW I as Capt RASC, Priv Sec to Govr W Australia 1901–02; *b* 24 Feb 1871; *m* 16 June 1936 Blanche (*d ca* May 1947), yst dau of Rupert Pennefather Fetherstonhaugh-Frampton, of More-

ton House, Dorset, and widow of Frederick Bathurst, OBE, of The Warren, Lydney, Glos, and *dsp* 17 May 1947

(2) Arthur Cecil; *b* 15 Aug 1873; *m* 27 Oct 1909 Millicent Taylor (*d* 10 May 1967), est dau of G Davenport, of Foxlowe, Leek, Staffs, and *dsp* 3 Dec 1948

(3) Geoffrey; Inspr-Gen Irrigation Sudan, Order Ismail, Grand Offr Order Nile; *b* 6 Feb 1880, *educ* Radley and Trin Coll Cambridge; *m* 15 Oct 1912 Isolda Mabel Cecil (*d* 11 June 1955), 3rd dau of Sir Charles William Frederick Craufurd, 4th Bt (*qv*), and *d* 11 March 1954, leaving:

1a *Cecily Mary Caroline; *b* 15 Sept 1913

2a *Isolda Rosamond; WW II as Sr Cdr ATS; *b* 26 June 1918; *m* 27 April 1940 2nd Viscount Hanworth (*qv*) and has issue

(4) Wilfred (Rt Rev); Hon CF, WW I (Italian Croix de Guerre), Vicar St George's, Parktown, Johannesburg, 1919–23, Priest-in-Charge St Cyprian's Native Mission Johannesburg 1923–31, Archdeacon Pretoria and Dir Native Missions 1931, Bp Pretoria 1933–50, Sub-Prelate OStJ; *b* 23 Jan 1883; *educ* Radley and Ch Ch Oxford (BA 1905, MA 1908); *m* 5 Sept 1933 Charlotte Frederika (*d* 28 Nov 1965), est dau of Sir George Albu, 1st Bt (*qv*), and *dsp* 23 June 1966

(1) Caroline Beatrix, DBE (1924), JP Salop; V-Chm House Laity Church Assembly 1942–47, Chm Women's Orgn Nat U Assoc, Govr BBC 1935–39; *m* 30 April 1895 1st Viscount Bridgeman (*qv*) and *d* 26 Dec 1961, leaving issue

(2) Cecily Mary, OBE (1918); OStJ; *m* 14 June 1906 Lt-Col William Scott Warley Radcliffe, KSLI (*d* 30 April 1954), yr s of Lt-Gen Robert Parker Radcliffe, RA, and *d* 8 April 1955, leaving issue

3 Algernon Robert (Rev); *b* 17 Nov 1849; *educ* Oxford; Rector Bix, Oxon, 1877–97 and St Oswald Malpas, Cheshire, 1897–1904, RD Malpas 1904–17; *m* 26 April 1877 Emma Jane (*d* 17 May 1933), only dau of Hon Edward Kenyon (*see* KENYON, B), and *d* 20 May 1940, leaving:

(1) Robert Edward; *b* 16 Feb 1878; *m* 6 Sept 1904 Emily (*d* 5 Dec 1951), yst dau of Joseph John Dawson Paul, JP, DL, of Eaton Grove, Norwich, and *d* 5 July 1942, leaving:

1a Robert Kenyon; Maj RA (TA); *b* 15 Feb 1907; *m* 1st 12 June 1935 Frances Mary (*d* July 1964), dau of Robert William Gawthropp, of Little Somerford, Wilts, and had:

1b +Nigel Kenyon [Nigel Parker Esq, 3 Hopetoun Terrace, Bucksburn, Aberdeen]; *b* 19 March 1942; *m* 1964 *Joey, dau of John Jack, and has:

1c *Karen Antonia; *b* 1965

2c *Lisa Anne; *b* 1969

1b *Jennifer Elizabeth [Miss Jennifer Parker, 63 Onslow Gdns, London SW7]; *b* 23 Nov 1938

1a (cont.) Robert Parker *m* 2nd 7 Oct 1965 *Ealga Hester Balgriffin [Mrs Robert Parker, Water Meadows, Station New Rd, Brundall, Norfolk], Order Merit Internat Union Child Welfare Geneva 1948, er dau of Cyril Joseph Kildare Burnell, CF, of Dublin and *d* 23 Sept 1968

2a Alexander Patrick; *b* 2 Sept 1910; *m* 1st 1948 (*divorce* 1962) Joan Olive, dau of Benjamin Sayer, of Saxlingham Thorpe, Norwich, and had:

1b +Patrick Edward Benjamin; *b* 1956

1b *Tania Lynn [Mrs Thomas Moore, 22 The Plantation, Aldeburgh, Suffolk]; *b* 1950; *m* 1st 1970 (*divorce* 1975) Stephen William Widdows and has:

1c *Matthew Adam; *b* 1973

1b (cont.) Mrs Tania Widdows *m* 2nd 1978 *Thomas Patrick Moore and by him has:

2c *Thomas Edward Alexander; *b* 1982

1c *Tiphanie Anne; *b* 1980

2b *Alexandra Vanessa [Mrs Alexandra Parker-Milne, Read Mead, Glastonbury, Somerset]; *b* 1952; *m* 1976 (*divorce* 1986) William Andrew Milne and has:

1c *Charlotte Francesca; *b* 1977

2c *Jessica Emily; *b* 1980

3b *Amanda Rose; *b* 25 Oct 1960; *m* 1988 *Rodney William Beckwith

2a (cont.) Alexander Parker *m* 2nd 21 Sept 1965 *Helen Mary [Mrs Alexander Parker, Algarsthorpe, Marlingford, Norfolk], dau of John Owen Bond, of Eaton Hill, Norwich

3a +Michael Edward [Michael Parker Esq, Paddock Farm, Mulbarton, Norwich]; WW II as Lt-Col Norfolk Yeo; *b* 9 Jan 1916; *educ* Eton; *m* 1st 1940 (*divorce* 1956) Florence Margaret Catto, dau of James Catto Duffus, OBE, MC; *m* 2nd 31 March 1958 *Estella Mary, er dau of H A Dalby, of Fairfield House, York, and widow of George Hall, of Stittenham, Yorks, and by his 1st w has:

1b +Timothy Robert Walter; *b* 1944

2b +Alexander Michael; *b* 4 April 1950

1b *Elizabeth Susan; *b* 1947

1a Isobel; *b* 28 Nov 1905; *m* 1946 Alfred George Douglas Greenshields (*d* 20 July 1947)

2a *Elizabeth Mary; *b* 25 July 1914; *m* 1940 Frederick Colin George Preston and has:

1b *Frederick Robert [Frederick Preston Esq, Toad Hall, Mulbarton, Norfolk NR14 8JT]; *b* 30 Nov 1947

1b *Anna Susan [Mrs Dirk Bouwens, Ivy Green House, Wymondham, Norfolk]; *b* 20 Sept 1943; *m* 1979 *Dirk Murray Bouwens and has:

1c *Theodore Frederick Thomas; *b* 1981

(2) Hugh Algernon; Capt Yeo WW I (despatches); *b* 15 April 1879; *educ* Eton; *m* 26 April 1911 Averil Francis (*d* 31 Aug 1969 aged 85), 2nd dau of Brownlow Richard Christopher Tower, of Ellesmere, Salop, and *d* 1 Jan 1954, leaving:

1a *Camilla Mary [Mrs John Pisani, 21 Chancellor House, 17 Hyde Park Gate, London SW7 5DQ]; *b* 13 Feb 1916; *m* 1st 2 Sept 1939 Capt Sir Lionel Francis Phillips, 2nd Bt (*qv*), and has issue; *m* 2nd 18 July 1950 John George Pisani (*d* 1982), s of George Constantine Pisani

2a *Juliet Leonora [Mrs Frederick McCreery, Swallowfield Park, Reading, Berks RG7 1TG]; *b* 28 Aug 1920; *m* 29 Sept 1945 (John) Frederick Cathers

McCreery (*d* 1993), RNVR and Overseas Civ Serv, s of Rev William John McCreery, BD Dublin, and has:

1b *Crispin Hugh; *b* 26 Aug 1953

2b *Sean Frederick; *b* 16 July 1964; *m* 19 July 1997 *Alexandra, dau of C B d'A Fearn, of Haywards Heath, Sussex

(3) Thomas Frederick; *b* 19 Sept 1882; *d* 22 Sept 1925

(4) Eustace PARKER later PARKER BOWLES (roy licence 14 Aug 1920), of Far Croft, Market Drayton, Salop, JP; Dep Chm QS 1947–52; *b* 5 July 1884; *educ* Marlborough; *m* 11 June 1913 Wilma Mary Garnault (*d* 10 Oct 1928), only child of Col Sir Henry Ferryman Bowles, 1st and last Bt, of Forty Hall, Enfield (*see* 1943 edn), and *d* 15 Nov 1952, having had:

1a A son; *b* 20, *d* 23 March 1914

2a Derek Henry, JP (Berks 1964); High Sheriff 1966, RHG; *b* 18 Dec 1915; *educ* Eton and Cambridge; *m* 14 Feb 1939 Ann (*d* 1987), DCVO (1977), Ch Commr Cwlth Girl Guides Assoc, est dau of Capt Sir Humphrey Edmund de Trafford, 4th Bt (*qv*), and *d* 4 Feb 1977, leaving:

1b +Andrew Henry; late Adj Blues and Royals, ADC to Govr Gen NZ 1965–66, Brig, late Silver Stick-in-Waiting; racehorse owner; *b* 27 Dec 1939; *educ* Ampleforth and RMA Sandhurst; *m* 1st 4 July 1973 (*divorce* 1995) Camilla Rosemary, er dau of Maj Bruce Middleton Hope Shand (*see* ASHCOMBE, B), and has:

1c +Thomas Henry Charles; *b* 18 Dec 1974; *educ* Eton; with Dennis Davidson Assocs, film publicists 1997–

1c *Laura Rose; *b* 1978

1b (cont.) Brig Andrew Parker Bowles *m* 2nd 7 Feb 1996 *Rosemary, formerly w of Hugh Pitman

2b +Simon Humphrey [Simon Parker Bowles Esq, 17 Scarsdale Villas, London W8]; late Coldstream Gds, proprietor Green's Restaurant, Duke St, St James's; *b* 6 Nov 1941; *educ* Eton; *m* 1974 *Carolyn, dau of Sir Ian Potter, of Melbourne, Australia, and has:

1c +Luke Derek Ian; *b* 31 March 1978

2c +Sam William Francis; *b* 1981

3b +Richard Eustace; *b* 7 Nov 1947; *educ* Ampleforth; *m* 1973 (*divorce* 1976) Camilla, dau of Charles Younger of Gledswood, Melrose, Roxburghs, and has:

1c *Emma Teresa; *b* 1974

1b *Mary Ann [Mrs Mary Paravicini, North Lodge Farm, Warfield, Berks]; *b* 9 June 1945; *m* 4 April 1967 (*divorce* 1987) Capt Nicolas Vincent Somerset Paravicini, s of Col Vincent Paravicini (*see* GLENDEVON, B), and has:

1c *Charles Vincent Somerset; *b* 21 June 1968

2c *Derek Nicolas Somerset; *b* 1979

1c *Elizabeth Ann; *b* 11 Feb 1970

1a Daphne Wilma Kenyon; *b* 4 Dec 1917; *m* 1st 27 April 1939 (*divorce* 1950) Brig Algernon George William Heber Percy (*see* NORTHUMBERLAND, D), and had issue; *m* 2nd 9 May 1952 (*divorce* 1965) 1st Baron Poole (*qv*) and *d* 12 Sept 1995

(5) Leonard; 2nd Lt 15th Hus, Maj and Sqdn Cdr RFC, WW I (wounded); *b* 25 Feb 1886; *ka* in the air 7 Jan 1917

(6) Eric; Lt RASC; *b* 28 Jan 1892; *m* July 1921 Florence May (*d c* 1949), dau of Thomas Cowman, of Richmond, Va., and *d* 28 Jan 1932

(1) Algitha; *b* 18 Nov 1880; *m* 14 Feb 1911 Maj Cloudesley Henry Marsham and *d* 14 April 1972, leaving issue (*see* ROMNEY, E)

(2) Constance Jessie; *b* 10 Aug 1889; *m* 31 Jan 1912 Lt-Col Hugh John Howell Evans, DSO (*d* 8 Feb 1961), s of Canon William Howell Evans, of Oswestry, Salop, and *d* 29 April 1969, leaving issue

4 Francis; MA Oxon, barrister, MP Henley 1886–95; *b* 15 Aug 1851; *m* 16 Feb 1882 Henrietta (*d* 5 Sept 1940), dau of Henry Lomax Gaskell, of Kiddington Hall, Oxon, and *d* 22 Oct 1931, leaving:

(1) Ronald Francis, MBE (1919); *b* 26 Jan 1883, *educ* Eton; Maj RE WW I, Gold Stick-in-Waiting 1937 Coronation, Assist Ch Constable War Dept Constabulary 1940–42, King's Messenger 1942–45; *d* unm 9 March 1959

(2) Oliver Ivan; Capt Roy Fus WW I; *b* 3 March 1891; *m* 14 Feb 1921 Margaret Noel, er dau of Frederick Kerr, of Twynceri, Barry, Wales, and *d* 15 Jan 1968, leaving:

1a Timothy Oliver; Capt Gren Guards; *b* 7 Nov 1924; *m* 30 April 1952 Rosemary (*d* 1984), yr dau of Maj John Henry Dent-Brocklehurst (*see* TREVOR, B), and *d* 12 April 1995, leaving:

1b +Oliver John [Oliver Parker Esq, 18 Elia St, London N1 8DE]; *b* 4 July 1953; *educ* Eton; *m* 1990 *Amanda Jane, yr dau of Lt-Col W D H McCardie

2b +Michael Henry; *b* 6 Oct 1955; *educ* Eton; *m* 1991 *Julia Jane Craven, er dau of Nigel Craven Humphreys, of Meadow House, Smannell, Hants, and has:

1c +Thomas Edward; *b* 1992

1b *Emma Mary [Mrs James Garvin, 30 Trygon Rd, London SW8 1NH]; *b* 19 Jan 1964; *m* 1991 *James M Garvin, s of Stephen Garvin, MBE, of Sussex, and has:

1c *Eliza Rose Clare; *b* 1994

1a Pamela Dione; *m* 1st 17 May 1944 (*divorce* 1947) Maj Timothy Tufnell, MC, Gren Gds (*d* Dec 1997), yr s of Col Neville Charsley Tufnell, of Fairfield, Sunninghill, Berks; *m* 2nd 4 Sept 1947 (*divorce* 1950) Hon Peter Robert Thellusson (*see* RENDLESHAM, B); *m* 3rd 25 Nov 1955 Peter Alexander Buchanan, yst s of John Neville Buchanan, DSO, MC, of The Old House, Bledlow Ridge, Bucks, and *d* 7 Dec 1968

(3) Ivo Murray; WW I with Coldstream Gds, WW II with RA; *b* 14 July 1899; *educ* Eton; *m* 24 Aug 1923 Ellen Dulcibella (*d* 1974), yst dau of Capt Charles William Daubeny, of Bath, and *d* 2 Jan 1957, leaving:

1a *Penelope Joan [Mrs Arthur Hughes, Vineyards, Welwyn, Herts AL6 9NE]; *b* 14 Aug 1924; *m* 15 June 1946 Arthur John Hughes, MC, TD, CA (*d* 1984), est s of Arthur Hubert Hughes, of Bexley, Kent, and has:

1b *Max Ivo Arthur [Max Hughes Esq, Chaffeymoor House, Bourton, Gillingham, Dorset]; b 16 April 1947, educ Lancing; m 1970 *Clara Christabel Harries and has:

1c *James Ivor Arthur; b 1976

1c *Emma Penelope; b 1975

1b *Jane Philippa [Mrs Richard Ware, The Elms, Little Wymondley, Hitchin, Herts]; b 14 Nov 1948; m 15 April 1972 *Richard Ivor Wakefield Ware and has:

1c *Christopher Arthur Corry; b 1973

1c *Samantha; b 1975

2c *Georgina; b 1977

3c *Henrietta Daubeny; b 1979

(1) Norah Henrietta; b 2 March 1885; m 7 March 1910 Sir Ivor Walter Heron-Maxwell, 8th Bt (qv), and d 9 Aug 1971, leaving issue

(2) Phyllis Blanche; b 6 May 1889; m 16 Jan 1919 Brig-Gen Robert Henry More, CMG, CBE, RAF (d 1 Nov 1951), s of Robert Jasper More, DL, MP, of Linley Hall, Salop, and d 17 March 1943

5 Sidney; b 3 Oct 1852; d 21 May 1897

6 Reginald; b 14 July 1854; m 17 Oct 1876 Katharine Mary (d 20 Nov 1939), dau of Henry Metcalfe Ames, of Linden, Northumberland, and d 23 March 1942, having had:

(1) Victor; Lt 1st Northumbrian Bde RFA; b 29 Aug 1877; das 5 March 1916

(1) Doreen Maud; b 30 Aug 1879; m 1st 29 Sept 1904 Capt James Randolph Innes Hopkins (ka 1915), yst s of W R Hopkins, of Grimstone Manor, Yorks, and had issue; m 2nd 6 Oct 1915 Thomas Sackville Manning, only s of Augustus Sackville Manning, and d 29 July 1943, leaving further issue

(2) Ethel Henrietta; b 6 Nov 1880; m 1 June 1899 Sir Wilfred Forbes Home Thomson, 1st Bt , of Old Nunthorpe (qv), and d 24 Jan 1968, leaving issue

(3L) Winifred Mary; b 19 Nov 1883; m 1st 1 Nov 1906 Lt-Col Cecil George Wellesley and had issue (see WELLINGTON, D); m 2nd 24 Oct 1933 Lt-Col Clifford Charles Horace Twiss, DSO (d 13 Feb 1947), s of Col Godfrey Twiss, and d 26 Feb 1959

7 Hugh Lupus; b 2 Oct 1855, d 11 March 1859

8 Edmund William; High Sheriff Warwicks 1919; b 2 March 1857; m 11 July 1883 Fanny Emma (d 18 April 1942), dau of Capt William Baldwin, of Dunedin, and d 27 March 1943, having had:

(1) Cyril Edmund; T/Lt KRRC; b 15 May 1884; ka 1 Jan 1915

(2) Wilfred Henry, MC; Lt Suffolk Regt WW I; b 29 Sept 1888; educ Trin Coll Cambridge (MA); m 8 Jan 1913 Audrey Elizabeth Peareth, MBE (d 24 Oct 1955), only dau of Thomas Rawson Vickers, JP, of Hollyberry Hall, Leics, and d 11 Jan 1938, leaving:

1a Michael Cyril Edmund; b 10 July 1920; educ Eton and Corpus Christi Coll Cambridge (BA 1947, MA 1951); Lt RNV(S)R WW II, Info Offr Allied HC Germany 1948–53, Scandinavian correspondent Economist 1954; d 19–

(1) Gwendoline Mary; b 8 Oct 1886; m 1 June 1921 Lt-Cdr John Edmund Power Bickford, RN, 3rd s of Adml Andrew Kennedy Bickford, CMG, and d 30 Dec 1928, leaving issue

9 Archibald (Rev); MA Oxon, Rector and RD Wem, Preb Lichfield; b 4 April 1859; m 8 Jan 1890 Hon Maud Frances Bateman-Hanbury (d 23 Feb 1932), est dau of 2nd Baron Bateman (see 1931 edn), and d 9 Jan 1931, leaving:

(1) Charles Edward, MC; Admin Offr Nyasaland 1922–44, Capt 1st Bn KSLI WW I; b 17 Nov 1890; educ Eton; m 28 Jan 1915 Hilda Margaret (d 1970), er dau of Sir John Ralph Starkey, 1st Bt (qv), and d 20 March 1962, leaving:

1a +Charles George Archibald, JP, DL (Oxon) [Charles Parker Esq JP DL, The White House, Nuffield, Oxon RG9 5SR; 19 Lennox Gdns, London SW1X 0DB]; Capt Rifle Bde WW II (POW), High Sheriff Oxon 1989, V-Ld Lt 1996; b 30 Jan 1924; educ Eton and New Coll Oxford; m 3 Nov 1958 *Shirley Follett, 2nd dau of Lt-Col Frank Follett Holt, TD, JP, of Riffhams, Danbury, Essex, and formerly w of David John Stanley Rutland, and adopted her dau by him:

*Davina Jane [Mrs John Walter, 5 Elms Rd, London SW4 9ER]; b 1954; m 1986 *John Walter, only s of John Walter, of Lugano, Switzerland, and Mrs Vladimir Daskaloff (see ENNISKILLEN, E), and has:

*John Charles; b 1987

*Edward William; b 1990

(2) Frederic Archibald (Deric); Lt 4th Bn KSLI WW I; b 16 July 1894; educ Eton and Trin Coll Cambridge (BA 1919, MA 1922); m 28 June 1927 Evereld Adela (d 1980), dau of Capt James Randolph Innes-Hopkins, of S Kensington, and d 13 May 1977, leaving:

1a Archibald Henry; b 7 June 1928; educ Wellington; m 6 Oct 1951 (divorce 1979) Una-Mary, novelist, only child of Hugh Power Nepean-Gubbins, of Rumbling Bridge Cottage, by Dunkeld, Perthshire, and d 7 Feb 1984, leaving:

1b +Philip ('Buffy') Archibald Reginald [Philip Parker Esq, Hazel Down House, Fullerton, Andover, Hants SP11 7LJ]; b 3 March 1955; m 1st 1981 Kathryn Jane Micaela, dau of Dr John Frederick Lewis Aldridge, OBE, of E House, Charlton, W Sussex, and has:

1c +Archie William Charles; b 1987

1c *Lucy Elizabeth Rebecca; b 1983

2c *Amelia Kathryn Louise; b 1984

3c *Charlotte Laura Mary; b 1990

1b (cont.) Philip Parker m 2nd 3 May 1997 *Gabrielle, dau of Tom Salter by his w Frances

1b *(Una-Mary) Diana [Mrs Robert Hobart, 12 Brunswick Gdns, London W8 4AJ]; b 15 Aug 1953; m 1976 *Robert Henry Hobart (see HOBART, Bt)

1a *Joan Sylvia [Mrs Theodore Landon, Great Bromley House, Gt Bromley, Essex CO7 7TP]; b 19 June 1931; m 29 Sept 1956 *Theodore Luke Giffard Landon, est s of Rev Sylvanus Luke Landon, of Furzebeam, Chagford, Devon, and has:

1b *Mark Eustace Palmer; b 19 Nov 1958; educ Downside; m 1st 1983 (divorce 1987) Julia Ruth, er dau of John Luddington, of Mill House,

Brancaster, Norfolk; m 2nd 1987 *Veronica Claire, only dau of Harvey Jones, of Llandaff, and by her has:

1c *Samuel; b 1994

1c *Bethan Emily; b 1990

2b *Philip James Aislabie; b 17 Feb 1962; educ Downside and Kent U (BA)

3b *Benjamin Edward Giffard; b 1 Nov 1967; educ Worth, Durham U (BA) and Keele U (MA)

1b *Felicity Juliana Mary; b 11 Oct 1960; educ New Hall; m 1990 *Christopher Gerald Payne and has:

1c *Edward Charles Aislabie; b 1992

2b *Rohais Elizabeth Jane [Mrs David Haughton, Forge View, Lower Rd, Somersham, Ipswich IP8 4PH]; b 22 March 1964; educ New Hall and Warwick U (MA); m 1992 *David Peter Haughton and has:

1c *William George Rosgill; b 28 June 1994

(1) Violet Maud, JP (Salop 1944); b 7 July 1892; m 10 Feb 1931 Brig-Gen Hugh Cecil Cholmondeley (see DELAMERE, B) and had issue

(2) Evelyn Sylvia; b 22 Aug 1897; m 14 April 1920 Col Thomas Marshall Brooks (see CRAWSHAW, B) and d 17 Dec 1967, leaving issue

10 Henry, JP and CC Oxon; Sub-Librarian Ho Lds; b 14 Dec 1860; educ Eton; m 11 Oct 1916 Henrietta Judith (d 8 Oct 1946), dau of Rev Robert Lowbridge Baker, of Ramsden House, Oxon, and d 26 June 1952, having had:

(1) +Peter Henry, JP (Oxon 1962), DL [Maj Peter Parker JP DL, The Hays, Ramsden, Oxon OX7 3BA]; b 9 March 1918; educ Eton and New Coll Oxford; Oxon: CC 1967, High Sheriff 1973, KRRC WW II (ret 1961); m 16 May 1953 Susan Rosemary, JP (Oxon 1969) (d 12 Feb 1997), est dau of Maj Mowbray Louis Buller (see PORTSMOUTH, E), and has:

1a +Henry Mowbray [Henry Parker Esq, Downes, Crediton, Devon EX17 3PL]; b 22 Feb 1957; educ Eton and Exeter Coll Oxford; m 1991 *Susan Jane, dau of John William Alvin and Mrs A Thomson, and has:

1b +Redvers Charles; b 28 June 1992

1b *Stroma Anne; b 8 March 1995

1a *Belinda Rosemary; b 2 April 1955; m 1990 *Hon (Anthony) Julian Aylmer, only s of 13th Baron Aylmer (qv), and has issue

(2) Richard Cecil; P/O RAF WWII; b 11 Sept 1919; das 17 Oct 1940

11 Alexander Edward, OBE (1949), JP, DL (Warwicks); b 1 July 1864; m 30 Dec 1896 Winifred Florence (d 30 Sept 1958), dau of Albert Octavius Worthington, of Maple Hayes, and d 2 Sept 1958, leaving:

(1) Sidney Alexander; Lt RA 1917–19; b 18 July 1899; educ Eton; m 1st 6 Oct 1937 Adelaide Mary (d following a hunting accident 27 Nov 1947), dau of Maj Sidney George Everitt, 23rd Roy Welch Fus, of Knowle Hall, Warwicks, and had:

1a +David Alexander [David Parker Esq, Greghams Farm, Fords Water, Axminster, Devon]; b 15 Dec 1943; educ Wellington; m 1971 *Frances Marie, dau of Francis W Meehan, and has:

1b +Christopher Alexander; b 1976

2b +Charles Edward; b 1977

1b *Sarah Adelaide; b 1973

1a *Anne Mary [Mme Paul Clément, Mas de Valetière, Le Fontanil, 38120 St Egrève, France]; b 14 Aug 1940; m 20 Dec 1961 *Paul G E Clément, est s of Jean Clément, of Nice, and has had:

1b *Germaine Anne Marie; b 1962

2b *Dominique Jeanne Alice; b 1964

3b Adelaide; b and d 1968

4b *Marie-Jeanne Paule Andrée; b 1969

5b *Alexandra Paule Emmanuelle; b 1970

2a *Rosemary Elizabeth [Mrs Walter Taylor, Cricket St Thomas, Chard, Somerset]; b 14 May 1945; m 1964 *Walter John Dawe Taylor and has:

1b *Jeremy John Alexander; b 1967

1b *Celia May Adelaide; b 1966

2b *Olivia Anne Nicola; b 1972

(1) Sidney Parker m 2nd 10 Jan 1951 June Rosemary (d 3 March 1954), only child of Rev Herbert Arthur Wadman, of Filleigh Rectory, N Devon; m 3rd 28 Sept 1955 *Rosemary Moon [Mrs Sidney Parker, Conygree Farm, Aldsworth, Glos], only dau of Capt Henry Errington Moon Ord, of Kirk Fenwick, Northumberland, and widow of Derek Welton, and d following a hunting accident 14 Nov 1969

1 Elizabeth Amelia; d unm 26 June 1916

2 Adelaide Helen; m 22 April 1875 Hon William Frederick Dawnay (see DOWNE, V) and d 14 July 1941, leaving issue

3 Mary Alice; m 21 July 1896 Rt Rev Charles Fane De Salis (d 24 Jan 1942), Assist Bp Bath and Wells, and d 11 Jan 1930, leaving issue

4 Evelyn Florence; d unm 16 March 1957

The 6th EARL d 24 July 1896; his gs,

GEORGE LOVEDEN WILLIAM HENRY PARKER, **7th Earl of Macclesfield**, JP (Oxon 1911); b 24 May 1888; educ Eton and Ch Ch Oxford; Lt Oxon Yeo, ADC Personal Staff, WW I; Oxon: Ld Lt 1954–63 and CC (Chm 1937–75); m 9 June 1909 Lilian Joanna Vere (d 9 April 1974), Order Mercy, only dau of Maj Charles John Boyle (see CORK and ORRERY, E), and had:

1 GEORGE ROGER ALEXANDER THOMAS, **8th Earl**

2 William Richard Christopher Boyle; P/O RAFVR WW II; b 25 Dec 1917; m 19 April 1941 Lavender Amy (m 2nd 12 Sept 1947 Michael Fulwar Horne and d 3 Nov 1964, leaving issue), yr dau of Col Arthur St Leger Glyn (see WOLVERTON, B), and was ka Dec 1941

3 +Jocelyn George Dudley [The Hon Jocelyn Parker, Pyrton Field Farm, Watlington, Oxon]; b 23 April 1920, educ Stowe; Lt RNVR WW II; m 20 Nov 1948 *Daphne Irene, 2nd dau of Maj George Cecil Whitaker, JP, of Britwell House, Watlington, Oxon, and has:

(1) +Robert George; b 16 March 1955

(1) *Mary Joanna Isabel [Mrs Peter Boone, Eastfield Farm, Shirburn, Watlington, Oxon]; *b* 18 July 1951; *m* 1973 Peter Robert Boone (*d* 1986), s of Maj RE Boone, of Rockliffe House, Upper Slaughter, Glos

The 7th EARL *d* 20 Sept 1975; his est s,

GEORGE ROGER ALEXANDER THOMAS PARKER, **8th Earl of Macclesfield**, JP (Oxon 1955), DL (1965); *b* 6 May 1914; *educ* Stowe; Lt RNVR WW II; *m* 18 June 1938 Hon Valerie Mansfield (*d* June 1995), 1st woman Chm Oxon CC, only dau of 4th Baron Sandhurst (*qv*), and *d* 1992, leaving:

1 RICHARD TIMOTHY GEORGE MANSFIELD PARKER, **9th and present Earl of Macclesfield**

2 +(JONATHAN) DAVID GEOFFREY [The Hon David Parker, Model Farm, Shirburn, Oxon OX9 5DX]; *b* 2 Jan 1945; heir presumptive; *educ* Stowe and RAC Cirencester; *m* 7 Dec 1968 *Lynne Valerie, yr dau of George William Butler, of Middle Barton, Oxon, and has:

(1) +Timothy George; *b* 23 Aug 1969; *educ* Stowe

(1) *Elizabeth Anne; *b* 1971

(2) *Jessica; *b* 1977

Seat: Shirburn Castle, Watlington, Oxon. This property, formerly known as Sherborne Castle, belonged at one time to John Chamberlain, whose eldest daughter Mary married Sir Thomas Gage, 2nd Bt (*see* GAGE, V). Mary's fourth son by Sir Thomas inherited but, becoming a Jesuit, sold it to the **1st Earl of Macclesfield** in 1716.

MACDONALD

Arms: Quarterly, 1st, argent a lion rampant gules, armed and langued azure; 2nd, or a hand in armour fessways, holding a cross-crosslet fitchée gules; 3rd, or a lymphad, sails furled and oars in action sable, flagged gules; 4th, vert a salmon naiant in fess proper; over all, on an inescutcheon en surtout or, an eagle displayed gules, surmounted of a lymphad, sails furled, oars in action sable (as Chief of the name and arms of MACDONALD). **Crest:** A hand in armour fessways, couped at the elbow proper, holding a cross-crosslet fitchée gules. **Supporters:** Two leopards proper. **Mottoes:** 1 (over the crest) *Per mare per terras* ('By sea and land'), 2 (on the compartment) *Fraoch eilean* ('The heathery isle'). **Creation:** B. (I) 25 July 1776.

THE 8TH BARON MACDONALD OF SLATE, Co Antrim (Godfrey James Macdonald of Macdonald) [The Rt Hon The Lord Macdonald, Kinloch Lodge, Isle of Skye IV43 8QY]; *b* 28 Nov 1947; *s* f 1970, also as Chief of the name and arms of Macdonald; *educ* Eton; *m* 14 June 1969 *Claire, est dau of Capt Thomas Noel Catlow, CBE, RN, of Gabriel Cottage, Tunstall, Lancs, and has:

1 +(GODFREY EVAN) HUGO THOMAS; *b* 24 Feb 1982

1 *Alexandra Louisa; *b* 19 Aug 1973

2 *Isabella Clare; *b* 2 Oct 1975

3 *Meriel Iona; *b* 1978

Lineage: Sir ALEXANDER MACDONALD, 7th Bt, of Slate (*see* BOSVILLE MACDONALD, Bt); had by his 2nd w a 2nd s:

Sir ALEXANDER MACDONALD, 9th Bt, as which *s* er bro 26 July 1766, and **1st Baron Macdonald of Slate**, Co Antrim (I), so *cr* 25 July 1776; *b c* 1745; *educ* Eton; Ensign Coldtream Gds 1761–68; *m* 3 May 1768 Elizabeth Diana (*d* 18 Oct 1789), est dau of Godfrey Bosville, of Gunthwaite, Yorks, and maternal gdau of Sir William Wentworth, 4th Bt, of Bretton, and *d* 12 Sept 1795, having had, with other issue:

1 ALEXANDER WENTWORTH MACDONALD, **2nd Baron Macdonald of Slate**; *b* 9 Dec 1773; Offr 10th Light Dragoons, MP Saltash 1796–1806; *d* unm 19 June 1824

2 GODFREY, **3rd Baron**

3 Archibald; *b* 21 May 1777; *m* 29 Oct 1802 Jane (*d* Oct 1860), dau and coheir of Duncan Campbell of Ardneave, Argyll, and *d* 5 Feb 1861, having had issue

1 Diana; *b* 28 Sept 1769; *m* 5 March 1788, as his 2nd w, Sir John Sinclair, 1st Bt (*see* THURSO, V), and *d* 22 April 1845, leaving issue

The 2nd BARON's yr bro,

GODFREY MACDONALD later BOSVILLE (roy licence 11 April 1814 on inheriting his unc William Bosville's Gunthwaite estate) later still BOSVILLE-MACDONALD (roy licence 20 July 1824 on inheritng the Barony), **3rd Baron Macdonald of Slate**; *b* 14 Oct 1775; *educ* Harrow and Oriel Coll Oxford; Ensign Loyal Kelso Regt 1794 and 60th 1795, Lt 70th, Capt 86th 1796 (served Low Countries Campaign 1798), Maj 55th, Lt-Col 24th (served WI 1801–02 and retaking Cape Good Hope 1805–06), Lt-Col 1st Gren Gds 1808, Brevet Col 1811 (served Peninsula War 1812), Maj-Gen 1814, Lt Gen 1830; *m* 29 Dec 1803 Louisa Maria La Coast/Laccoast (*d* 10 Feb 1835), probably illegitimate dau of THE DUKE OF GLOUCESTER (yr bro of GEORGE III) by Lady Almeria Carpenter (dau of 1st Earl of Tyrconnell of the 1761 *cr*), and ward of Farley Edsir, the DUKE's steward and tenant of a farm in the vicinity of Hampton Court, and had, with other issue (*see* BOSVILLE-MACDONALD, Bt):

1 GODFREY WILLIAM WENTWORTH, **4th Baron**

2 James William, CB; *b* 31 Oct 1810; Lt-Gen, Col 21st Hus, Chev Legn Hon and Medjidie, ADC, Equerry and Priv Sec to HRH THE 2nd DUKE OF CAMBRIDGE; *m* 26 Sept 1859 Hon Elizabeth Nina Blake (*d* 21 July 1890), 2nd dau of 3rd Baron Wallscourt (*see* 1917 edn WALLSCOURT, B), and *d* 4 Jan 1882, leaving:

(1) George Godfrey; *b* 17 May 1861; Capt Gren Gds, Page of Honour to HM QUEEN VICTORIA; *d* 18 July 1930

(1) Mary Selina Honoria; *b* 5 April 1865; *m* 14 Aug 1889 Hon Alexander Hugh Willoughby and *d* 12 Jan 1925, leaving issue (*see* MIDDLETON, B)

3 William; Col; *b* 27 Sept 1817; *d* 11 May 1847

1 Elizabeth Diana; *b* 27 Feb 1804; *m* 20 June 1825 Duncan Davidson of Tulloch and *d* 9 June 1839, leaving, with other issue:

(1) Adelaide Lucy; *m* George William Holmes Ross and had issue (*see* below)

2 Julia; *b* 30 Oct 1805; *m* 11 Oct 1838 Rev Charles Walter Hudson, Rector Trowell, Notts, maternal gs of 1st Marquess Townshend (*qv*), and *d* 11 July 1884

3 Susan Hussey; *b* 25 Aug 1807; *m* 9 Feb 1832 Capt Richard Beaumont, RN (*see* ALLENDALE, V) and *d* 5 Nov 1879, leaving issue

4 Diana; *b* 12 April 1812; *m* 25 April 1837 Col John George Smyth (*see* SMYTH, Bt) and *d* 8 Dec 1880

5 Jane; *b* 25 May 1815; *d* unm 13 Jan 1888

6 Marianne; *b* 27 July 1816; *m* 28 July 1840 Henry Martin Turnor, Capt King's Dragoon Gds (*d* 8 Jan 1902), and *d* 12 July 1876, leaving issue

7 Octavia Sophia; *m* 7 Dec 1841 William James Hope-Johnstone, Yr. of Annandale, and *d* 22 Jan 1897, leaving issue (*see* ANNANDALE AND HARTFELL, E)

The 3rd BARON *d* 13 Oct 1832; his 1st s *b* in wedlock (*see* also BOSVILLE MACDONALD, Bt):

GODFREY WILLIAM WENTWORTH BOSVILLE-MACDONALD, **4th Baron Macdonald of Slate**; *b* 16 March 1809; *educ* Eton; *m* 21 Aug 1845 Maria Anne (*d* 21 April 1892), dau of George Thomas Wyndham, of Cromer Hall, Norfolk, and *d* 25 July 1863, having had, with two other daus (*d* in infancy):

1 SOMERLED JAMES BRUDENELL BOSVILLE-MACDONALD, **5th Baron Macdonald of Slate**, DL (Inverness-shire); *b* 2 Oct 1849; *educ* Eton; *d* unm 25 Dec 1874

2 RONALD ARCHIBALD, **6th Baron**

3 Godfrey Alan; *d* in infancy 7 July 1858

1 Eva Maria Louisa; *m* 1st 7 June 1873 Capt Henry Algernon Langham, Gren Gds (*d* 20 Dec 1874); *m* 2nd 27 Jan 1885 2nd Baron Napier of Magdala (*qv*) and *d* 7 Feb 1930, leaving issue

2 Flora Matilda; *d* in infancy 12 March 1851

3 Lilian Janet; *m* 1st 2 Aug 1876 2nd Earl of Cromartie (*qv*) and had issue; *m* 2nd 7 Nov 1895 Reginald Frederick Cazenove, 6th Dragoon Gds (*dsp* 5 Sept 1905), est s of Frederick Cazenove, of Warfield Grove, Bracknell, and *d* 20 Nov 1926

4 Alexandrina Victoria (HM QUEEN VICTORIA stood sponsor); *m* 11 Nov 1886 Sir Anthony Charles Sykes Abdy, 3rd Bt (*qv*), and *d* 4 March 1953, leaving issue

The 5th BARON's bro,

RONALD ARCHIBALD (BOSVILLE-)MACDONALD, **6th Baron Macdonald of Slate**, JP, DL (Inverness-shire); *b* 9 June 1853; *educ* Eton; *m* 1 Oct 1875 his cousin Louisa Jane Hamilton (*d* 20 Aug 1922), 2nd dau of Col George William Holmes Ross, of Cromarty House, Cromarty, by Adelaide Lucy Davidson (*see* above), and had:

1 Somerled Godfrey James; *b* 21 July 1876; *educ* Eton; Sub-Lt RNVR; *dvp* unm 11 April 1913

2 Godfrey Evan Hugh, JP (Inverness-shire); *b* 5 March 1879; Lt Scots Gds WW I; *m* 28 April 1908 Helen (*d* 7 Nov 1928), dau of Maj Meyrick Bankes and gdau of William Meyrick Bankes, of Winstanley Hall, Lancs, and Letterewe, Ross-shire, and *d* of wounds recd in action 2 Nov 1914, having had:

(1) ALEXANDER GODFREY, **7th Baron**

(2) James Archibald; *b* 11 Dec 1911; BA, LLB; Capt 4th Bn Cameron Highrs (TA) WW II 1939–42; *ka* Middle East 22 Oct 1942

3 Archibald Ronald Armadale; *b* 20 May 1880; 2nd Lt 9th Lancers; *ka* Boer War 17 April 1901

4 Ronald Ian; *b* 1 Oct 1884; Capt 5th Bn Cameron Highrs WW I, Legn Hon; *m* 5 May 1915 Helen Elizabeth (*m* 2nd 20 Jan 1932 Maj-Gen Charles John Wallace, CB, DSO, OBE, MC, HLI (*das* 20 Dec 1943), and *d* 30 April 1966), yr dau of Sir Thomas Swinnerton Dyer, 11th Bt (*qv*), and *das* 17 Oct 1918

1 Iona Mary Adelaide Hope; *b* 1 Dec 1888; *m* 3 April 1929 Rt Rev Norman Maclean, DD (*d* 15 Jan 1952), Chaplain to HM GEORGE VI, s of Kenneth Maclean, of Portree, and *dsp* 1 Feb 1972

The 6th BARON *d* 20 Jan 1947; his gs,

ALEXANDER GODFREY (BOSVILLE-)MACDONALD, **7th Baron Macdonald of Slate**, MBE (1944), TD, JP (1936) and DL (1942); *b* 27 June 1909; *educ* Eton and Magdalene Coll Cambridge (MA); Maj 4th QO Cameron Highrs (TA) WW II; CC Inverness-shire 1932 (V-Convener 1952, Convener 1968–70), Ld Lt Inverness-shire 1952–70, Grand Master Mason Scotland 1953–57; Chm Skye DC 1945–64, Skye Hosp Bd Management 1948–70 and Consultative Cncl N Scotland Dist 1962–70, Pres Assoc County Cncls Scotland 1958–60, memb N Scotland Hydro-

Electric Bd; arms of Macdonald of Macdonald restored him as Chief of the Name and Arms of Macdonald and as Inheritor of the Feudal Barony of Macdonald by Lord Lyon 1 May 1947; *m* 14 June 1945 Anne (*d* 1988), only dau of Alfred Whitaker and Mrs Andrew McKenzie McLaghlan, of Itchenor, Sussex, and *d* 29 Nov 1970, leaving:

1 GODFREY JAMES (BOSVILLE-)MACDONALD, **8th and present Baron Macdonald of Slate**

2 +(Alexander Donald) Archibald; *b* 3 Sept 1953; *educ* Eton

1 *Janet Anne [The Hon Janet Macdonald, Ostaig House, Isle of Skye]; *b* 2 Nov 1946

MACDONALD OF GWAENYSGOR

Creation: B. (UK) 13 April 1949.

THE 2ND BARON MACDONALD OF GWAENYSGOR, of Gwaenysgor, Co Flint (Gordon Ramsay Macdonald) [The Rt Hon The Lord Macdonald of Gwaenysgor, Littleworth House, Littleworth Common, Bucks SL1 8PP]; *b* 16 Oct 1915; *s* f 1966; *educ* Upholland GS and Manchester U (BA 1938, MA 1939); WW II with RA, GSO(2) (Maj), Middle East, India, Burma and Malaya (despatches), Assist Sec Lancs Associated Collieries 1939, Admin Offr BOT 1946, Pncpl 1947, UK Trade Commr Australia 1947–53, md Tube Investment (Exports) Ltd, sr exec The Plessey Gp, ch exec Hayek Engrg Ltd]; *m* 6 May 1941 *Leslie Margaret, dau of John Edward Taylor, of Rainford, Lancs, and has:

1 *Susan [The Hon Mrs Susan Stride, 73 Swinburne Rd, London SW15]; *b* 21 Feb 1947; *m* 9 March 1968 (*divorce* 1991) David Hensley Adair Stride and has had:

  (1) *Toby David Macdonald; *b* 1972

  (1) Jessica Charlotte Macdonald; *b* 1970; *d* 1984

2 *Helen Margaret; *b* 21 April 1950; *m* 1974 (*divorce* 19–) James Edward Richard Prisinzano

3 *Marylyn Jane; *b* 10 Oct 1951; *m* 1977 *Peter Jost and has:

  (1) *Edward Peter; *b* 1980

  (2) *Thomas William; *b* 1983

Lineage: THOMAS MACDONALD, of Ashton-in-Makerfield, nr Wigan, had:

GORDON MACDONALD, **1st Baron Macdonald of Gwaenysgor**, of Gwaenysgor, Co Flint (UK), so *cr* 13 April 1949, KCMG (1946), PC (1951), JP Lancs; *b* 27 May 1888; *educ* St Luke's Elementary Sch Stubshaw Cross and Ruskin Coll Oxford; memb Wigan Bd of Guardians 1920, chm 1929–30, MP (Lab) Ince 1929–42 (resigned), Jr Lab Whip 1931–34, chm Ctees H of C 1934–41, Regnl Controller Min Fuel and Power Lancs, Cheshire and N Wales 1942–46, Govr Newfoundland and chm Commn of Govt of Newfoundland and Dependencies 1946–49, Paymaster Gen 1949–51, Leader UK Delegn Cwlth Conf Sydney 1950, memb Br Delegn to 5th Annual Conf of UN Gen Assembly 1950–51, dir Colonial Devpt Corp Jan 1952–59, Govr BBC and chm Nat Broadcasting Cncl for Wales Aug 1952–60, Hon LLD Mount Allison U Canada 1947 and U of Wales 1950; *m* 1913 Mary (*d* June 1967 aged 82), yst dau of William Lewis, of Blaenau Festiniog, and *d* 20 Jan 1966, leaving:

1 GORDON RAMSAY MACDONALD, **2nd and present Baron Macdonald of Gwaenysgor**

2 Kenneth Lewis; RAFVR WW II with RAF Coastal Cmd, Priv Sec and ADC to his f as Govr Newfoundland 1946–49; *b* 3 Feb 1921; *m* 1952 *Maureen Margaret [The Hon Mrs Kenneth Macdonald, Fir Trees, Frog Lane, Balsall Common, West Midlands CV7 7FP], only dau of David Watson Allan, of Churston Ferrers, Devon, and *d* 1990, leaving:

  (1) *Sarah Margaret; *b* 27 Jan 1954; *m* 1974 *David Henry Waldron and has:

    1a *William David Macdonald; *b* 1980

    1a *Charlotte Sarah; *b* 1978

  (2) *Laura Jane; *b* 13 May 1966; *m* 1994 *James Edward Reeve and has:

    1a *Frederick James; *b* 13 Nov 1996

1 Elsie, JP Mon, memb Broadcasting Cncl Wales (BBC); *b* 1917; *m* 1938 Rev Llywelyn Williams (*d* 4 Feb 1965) and had:

  (1) *Richard Gareth Macdonald; *b* 9 Feb 1946

  (1) *Margaret Eryl Macdonald; *b* 11 April 1942

2 *Glenys, JP Lancs; *b* 1923; Commr Girl Guides' Assoc; *m* 1949 *Robert Fullard, BSc, and has:

  (1) *Judith Mary; *b* 14 May 1952; *m* 1973 *Christopher John Norton Ellis and has:

    1a *Richard Gordon; *b* 1979

    1a *Laura Kate; *b* 1981

  (2) *Cathryn Elisabeth; *b* 9 March 1955; *m* 1978 *Michael John Morris and has:

    1a *Robert James; *b* 1982

    1a *Rachel Elisabeth; *b* 1984

MACFARLANE OF BEARSDEN

Creation: B. (LP, UK) 1991.

THE BARON MACFARLANE OF BEARSDEN, of Bearsden in the District of Bearsden and Milngavie (Sir Norman Somerville Macfarlane, KT (1996), DL (Dunbartonshire 1993)) [The Rt Hon The Lord Macfarlane of Bearsden KT DL, 50 Manse Rd, Bearsden, Glasgow G61 3PN]; *b* 5 March 1926; *educ* Glasgow HS; commissioned RA 1945, Palestine 1945–47; fndr N S Macfarlane & Co 1949–73, chm Macfarlane Gp (Clansman) plc 1973– (md 1973–90), Chm: Fine Art Soc plc 1976–, Govrs Glasgow HS 1979–92, American Tst 1984–97, Glasgow Action 1985–90, United Distillers 1987–96, United Distillers UK 1989–, Guinness plc 1987–89 (Jt Dep Chm 1989–92), Glasgow Devpt Agency 1990–92; Dir: Clydesdale Bank plc 1980–96 (Dep Chm 1993–96), Gen Accident Fire & Life Assur 1984–96, Edinburgh Fund Managers 1980–97, Glasgow Chamber Commerce 1976–79, Scottish Nat Orchestra 1977–82, Third Eye Centre 1978–81; Pres: Glasgow HS Club 1970–72, Stationers' Assoc GB and Ireland 1965, Stationers' Co Glasgow 1968–70, Roy Glasgow Inst Fine Arts 1976–87; Memb: Bd Scottish Devpt Agency 1979–87, Roy Fine Art Commn Scotland 1980–82, Court Glasgow U 1980–88; Govr Glasgow Sch Art 1976–87; V-Chm Scottish Ballet 1983–87 (dir 1975–83); Scottish Patron Nat Art Collection Fund 1978–; Ld High Commr Gen Assembly Ch Scotland 1992, 1993 and 1997; Tstee Nat Heritage Meml Fund 1984–97, Nat Galleries Scotland 1986–97; Hon V-Pres Glasgow Bn Boys' Bde; Underwriting Member Lloyd's 1978–, ktd 1983; Hon FRIAS 1984; Hon LLD Strathclyde 1986, Glasgow 1988; Hon DU: Stirling 1992, Glasgow Caledonian 1993, Aberdeen 1995; Hon RSA 1987; HRGI 1987; FRSE 1991; Hon FScotvec 1991; Hon FRCPS Glasgow 1992; Hon Dr Edinburgh 1992; Hon Fell Glasgow Sch Art 1993; *m* 1953 *Marguerite Mary, dau of John Johnstone Campbell, of Whitecraigs, and has:

1 *Hamish; *b* 1961; *m* 1990 *Laura Pitt

1 *Fiona; *b* 1955; *m* 1982 *J S M McNaught

2 *Gail; *b* 1957; *m* 1992 *Lt Simon Allbutt, RN

3 *Marjorie; *b* 1960; *m* 1991 *J B (Jack) s of J B Roberts, of Bearsden, Glasgow

4 *Marguerite; *b* 1966

Lineage: DANIEL ROBERTSON MACFARLANE; *m* Jessie Lindsay Somerville and had:

NORMAN SOMERVILLE, *cr* a **Baron**

MACGREGOR

Arms: Argent from a mount in base an oak-tree, surmounted by a sword in bend proper, in chief two Eastern crowns gules, all within a bordure engrailed of the last. **Crest:** A human hand, couped at the wrist, and holding a dagger erect proper, pommel and hilt gold. **Motto:** *E'en do and spair nocht* [spare not]. **Creation:** Bt. (UK) 17 March 1828.

SIR EDWIN ROBERT MACGREGOR, 7TH BT, of Savile Row, Co Middlesex [Sir Edwin Macgregor Bt, 3886 King's Rd, East Bay, NS B0A 1H0 Canada]; *b* 4 Dec 1931; *s* f 1963; *educ* U of BC (BA Sc 1955, MA Sc 1957); memb Assoc Prof Engrs Prov BC, with Union Carbide Canada 1965–74, Dep Min: Min of Crown Lands BC 1989–91, Min of Lands and Parks BC 1991–92 (ret); *m* 1st 1952 (*divorce* 1981) Margaret Alice Jean, dau of A Peake, of Haney, BC, and has had:

1 Robert Lionel Frederick; *b* 10 May 1953; *d* 19–

2 +IAN GRANT; *b* 22 Feb 1959

1 *Valerie Jean; *b* 1956

Sir EDWIN and Lady MACGREGOR also adopted:

*Jessie Marlene Elizabeth; *b* 6 Oct 1963

Sir EDWIN *m* 2nd 1982 *Helen Linda Herriott

Lineage: JAMES MACGREGOR, of Raigmore, Inverness-shire; *m* Margaret, dau of Alexander Grant, of Tullochgorum, Inverness-shire, and had:

Sir Patrick Macgregor, 1st Bt (UK), so *cr* 17 March 1828; Serjeant-Surgn to HM GEORGE IV and personal surgn to WILLIAM IV as DUKE of YORK; *m* 12 Nov 1806 Bridget (*d* 24 July 1863), dau and heiress of James Glenny, of Quebec, and *d* 17 July 1828, having had, with five other daus:

  1 **Sir William Macgregor, 2nd Bt**; *b* 14 March 1817; Capt 92nd Highrs; *d unm* 29 March 1846

  2 CHARLES (Sir), **3rd Bt**

  1 Bridget Margaret; *m* 1st 10 Sept 1833 Rev Joseph Sortain (*d* 16 July 1860); *m* 2nd 31 Aug 1869 Charles Reginald Buller (*d* 22 April 1879), of Erie Hall, Devon, and *d* 18 Aug 1885

The 2nd Bt's bro,

  Rev Sir Charles Macgregor, 3rd Bt; *b* 8 Nov 1819; Rector Swallow, Lincs; RD Lincoln; *m* 2 Oct 1845 Eliza Catherine (*d* 4 May 1887), dau of John Jeffreys, FRS, of Fynone, nr Swansea, and *d* 12 Oct 1879, leaving:

    1 **Sir William Gordon Macgregor, 4th Bt**; *b* 11 Sept 1846; *m* 5 April 1903 Alice, 4th dau of Capt Gulliver, RN, and *dsp* 14 June 1905

    2 Charles Reginald, CB, DSO; *b* 22 Oct 1847; Brig-Gen cmdg Assam Dist; *m* 15 March 1893 Maud (*m* 2nd 27 July 1903 Addison Yalden Thomson, s of Rev Yalden Thomson), 3rd dau of Augustus des Moustiers Campbell, of Oakley House, Abingdon, Berks, and *d* 29 June 1902, leaving:

      (1) Helen Maud

    3 Patrick Eugene; *b* 28 Jan 1856; *m* 1879 Gertrude (*d* 1926), dau of J F M'Connell, and *d* 10 Sept 1895, leaving:

      (1) **Sir Cyril Patrick M'Connell Macgregor, 5th Bt**; *b* 1887; *d unm* 30 Jan 1958

      (2) **Sir Robert James M'Connell Macgregor, 6th Bt**, MM; *b* 1890; 10th Canadian Inf Bn WW I; *m* 1930 Annie Mary, dau of Joseph Lane, of Nanaimo, BC, and *d* 21 Jan 1963, leaving:

        1a **Sir EDWIN ROBERT MACGREGOR, 7th and present Bt**

        2a +Arthur Joseph [Dr Arthur Macgregor, 2597 Vista Bay Rd, Victoria, BC, Canada]; *b* 7 Sept 1933; *educ* U of BC (MD 1958); *m* 1st 23 Dec 1957 Carole Isabel (*d* 1984), BSc (Nursing) 1958, dau of Dr W L Valens, and has:

          1b *Ann Lorraine; *b* 15 Sept 1960

          2b *Jean Louise; *b* 13 Sept 1962

        2a (cont.) Dr Arthur Macgregor *m* 2nd 1985 *Brenda Margaret Hanson

        1a *Margaret Gertrude [Mrs Cyril White, 6172 Pepperell St, Nova Scotia, Canada]; *b* 1937; *m* 1963 *Cyril George White

        2a *Patricia Elizabeth; *b* 1939; *educ* U of BC (BA 1961); *m* 1966 *John Peramaki

        3a *Nancy Lane; SRN Vancouver Gen Hosp 1964; *b* 1942; *m* 1972 Hubert Foulds (*d* 1991)

      (1) Gladys May; *m* 1925 Aylmer McNeil Wickwire and *d* 1963

  1 Annie Francis; *m* 31 Dec 1885 Thomas John Perry (*d* 1901) and *d* 1925, leaving issue

  2 Helen Grant; *m* 1 Feb 1876 Edward Williams Byron Nicholson (*d* 17 March 1912), librarian Bodleian, Oxford, and *d* 19 Dec 1938, having had issue

  3 Alma Anna Margaret Gwyn; *m* 13 April 1875 (*divorce* 1895) Rev George William Henry Hanford, Vicar Forest Gate, Essex, and had issue

MAC GREGOR OF MAC GREGOR

SRIOGHAL · MO · DHREAM

E'EN · DO · AND · SPAIR · NOCHT

Arms: Arg. an oak-tree eradicated in bend sinister ppr., surmounted of a sword in bend az., supporting on its point in dexter canton an antique crown gu. **Crest:** A lion's head ppr., crowned with an antique crown or. **Supporters:** Dexter, a unicorn arg., crowned, horned or; sinister, a deer ppr., tyned az. **Mottoes:** 1 E'en do, and spair nocht, 2 S'rioghal mo dhream ('Royal is my race'). **Creation:** Bt. (GB) 3 July 1795.

SIR GREGOR Mac GREGOR OF Mac GREGOR, 6TH BT, of Lanrick and Balquhidder [Brig Sir Gregor Mac Gregor of Mac Gregor Bt, Bannatyne, Newtyle, Perthshire PH12 8TR]; *b* 22 Dec 1925; *s* f 1958, also as Chief of Clan Gregor; *educ* Eton; Brig Scots Gds (ret 1980), WW II, Palestine 1947–48, Malaya 1950–51 and Borneo 1965, Bde Maj 16th Parachute Bde Gp 1961–63, Jt Servs Staff Coll 1965, cmded Scots Gds 1966–69, Br Liaison Offr US Army Inf Center 1969, Col 'A' Recruiting HQ Scotland 1971, Lt-Col cmdg Scots Gds 1971–73, Defand Mil Attaché Athens 1975–78, OC Lowlands 1978–80, ADC 1979, Grand Master Mason Scotland 1988–93, memb Roy Co Archers; *m* 8 Feb 1958 *Fanny, only dau of Charles Hubert Archibald Butler, of Le Pavillon, Newport, Essex, and has:

  1 +MALCOLM GREGOR CHARLES [Malcolm Mac Gregor of Mac Gregor Yr, Bannatyne, Newtyle, Angus PH12 8TR]; *b* 23 March 1959; *educ* Eton; Maj Scots Gds (ret 1997), memb Roy Co Archers, QBGS; *m* 1988 *Cecilia Margaret Lucy, er dau of Sir Ilay Mark Campbell, 7th Bt, of Succoth (*qv*)

  2 +Ninian Hubert Alexander; *b* 30 June 1961

Lineage: The Chiefs of Clan Gregor have for many centuries claimed to be of royal race, like the other dynastic Highland chiefs. They are thought to descend from the hereditary Abbots of Glendochart, who according to Celtic monastic custom had to be royal, whether chosen from the local dynasty who gave the abbey lands or from the kin of their royal founder saint, St Fillan. By the 16th century the Gregarach or Mac Gregors held that their royal ancestor was ALPIN (King of Kintyre March-Aug 834) and the Clan Gregor is often known as the Clan Alpin. Owing to their long period of persecution, when the very names of Gregor and Mac Gregor were banned on pain of death (1603–61; *see* below against the 11th Chief for details) and following the Glorious Revolution and much of the reigns of the first three Hanoverians (1693–1774), they are perhaps the only clan who can be reasonably certain that all who bear the surname are genuine scions of the ancient chiefly blood, although some branches have never yet resumed it. There are now no reliable records of the clan before 1390, but a number of ancient Gaelic heroic poems and the Dean of Lismore's MS. genealogy, known by the title *From the Books of the Royal Sennachie*, agree in deriving the Chiefs of Clan Gregor from:

AIDH of Glenorchy; living *c* 1150; had:

GIOLLA FAOLAIN ('the Devotee of St Fillan'); had:

DUNCAN A STRAILEACH; had:

DUNCAN *Beg* ('Little', or in this context probably 'The Younger'; called also 'The first who was lord of this land' by Mac Giolla Fhionntog, the Man of Songs); had:

MALCOLM ('The Lame Lord'); had:

DUNCAN; had:

GREGOR ('Of Golden Bridles', the true name-father of the clan and thus 1st Ch of the Gregarach); had:

IAIN Mac GREGOR; held the three glens of the rivers Orchy, Strae and Lochy on the opposite watershed to Strathfillan and Glendochart; *d* 1390, leaving:

IAIN Mac GREGOR OF GLENORCHY, 2nd Chief of Clan Gregor; called *Cam* ('The One-eyed'); *d* 19 April 1390, leaving:

  1 Iain, 3rd Chief of Clan Gregor; called *Dubh* ('The Dark'); *m* Dervogill (*d* 1424), dau of Ewen Maclachlan, probably Ch of Clan Lachlan, and *d* 1415, leaving:

    (1) Malcolm, 4th Chief of Clan Gregor; *m* Mary — and *d* 20 April 1440, leaving:

      1a Patrick, of Glenstrae, 5th Chief of Clan Gregor; *d* 28 April 1461, leaving:

        1b Iain, of Glenstrae, 6th Chief of Clan Gregor; called *Dubh*; it was in his time that the Book of the Dean of Lismore was compiled; *m* Marion Stewart (living 1522) and *d* 24 May 1519, leaving:

          1c Malcolm, Yr. of Glenstrae; *dvp* 22 June 1498

  2 Gregor; called *Aluin* or 'The Handsome'; *d* 1415, allegedly leaving, with other issue:

    (1) Iain, almost certainly the est s, fndr of the line of *Breachd-sliabh* or Brackly; had:

      1a Malcolm; sold Auchinrevach in Glendochart 1463 to Campbell of Glenorchy (*see* 1970 edn BREADALBANE AND HOLLAND, E)

      2a Gregor *Mor* ('The Great' or 'The Elder'); fndr of the line of Gregor Maclain; had:

        1b Patrick; *d* 9 July 1518, leaving:

          1c Gregor Patrickson; probably became rightful Ch of Clan Gregor 1519 but the Campbells promoted instead the Gregarach chieftain of the Clan Dugall Ciar (*see* below); nevertheless acted as leader of the clan 1528–45 during the next Ch's long minority and his descendants recovered the chiefship after 1774; *d* 6 March 1547, leaving:

            1d DUNCAN, of Ardchoille (*see* below)

            2d Iain; ancestor of the later Mac GREGORs of Brackly, who were Keepers of Kilchurn Castle for the Campbells of Glenorchy

  (2) Duncan; had:

    1a Duncan *Beg*; *d* 17 Feb 1477/8; ancestor of the MacGREGORs of Roro in Glenlyon, of whom the Jacobite agent Alasdir Mac Gregor of Balhaldie *alias* Drummond (chosen as 17th Ch 1714, assumed the style of Ch of Clan Gregor but was not recognised by the Government, nor did he matriculate arms as Ch in Lyon Register; Jacobite agent from 1689 on, took part in the 1715 Rising, was *cr* 14 March 1740 a Bt by the titular James III; *m* 26 March 1686 Margaret, dau of Sir Ewen Cameron of Lochiel, 17th Ch, and *d* by 23 Dec 1743, leaving issue) was a cadet; from this branch allegedly descend the McGRIGOR Bts (*qv*)

  (3) Dugall; called *Ciar* ('The Dusky'); ancestor of the Clan Dugall Ciar, which included the MacGREGORs of Glengyle, of whom the celebrated Rob Roy MacGregor was a cadet; had:

    1a Alasdair; had:

      1b Evan; had:

        1c Iain, of Glenstrae, also Chieftain of the Clan Dugall Ciar; recognised perforce as 7th Ch although according to the Campbells' own Black Book of Taymouth he 'was not righteous heir to The MacGregor', which implies that Dugall Ciar was not the est s of Gregor Aluin; the Gaelic MS. *c* 1467 implies that Iain *Dubh* had another bro Patrick, f of

Malcolm, and it has been suggested that they were 3rd and 4th Chiefs of Clan Gregor and held Glenorchy, that Malcolm *d c* 1432 and so Glenorchy fell vacant to the Campbells; but if so it is strange that their deaths and burials in Dysart were not recorded in the Chronicle of Fortingall; in 1523 the Menzies Ch complained that Mac Gregor was of 'far greater power' than the Menzieses and was withholding Rannoch from them by force; the 7th Ch ravished and afterwards *m* Helen, widow of two other Highland chiefs, MacIain of Ardnamurchan and MacIain of Lochbuie and dau of Sir Colin Campbell of Glenorchy (*see* 1970 edn BREADALBANE AND HOLLAND, E), which relationship was no doubt the reason why the Campbells advanced him to the chiefship, and *d* 12 April 1528, leaving an est surv s:

1d Alasdair, of Glenstrae, 8th Ch of Clan Gregor; was 'blooded' at his effective accession by leading a raid (with Duncan *Ladasach* ('The Lordly') as his mentor) to burn the House of Trochrie in Strathbran 1545, killing four Robertsons and capturing their Ch, Struan; with Maclean of Duart he fought on the left wing against the English at the Battle of Pinkie 1547; *m* —, dau of Campbell of Ardkinglas and widow of — Macnaghten of Dundarave, Ch of Clan Naghten (*see* MACNAGHTEN, Bt), and *d c* 1550, having had, with other issue:

1e Iain, of Glenstrae, 9th Chief of Clan Gregor; *k* before Aug 1561 by an arrow while going from Glenlyon into Rannoch

2e Gregor, of Glenstrae, 10th Chief of Clan Gregor, also called 'Mac Gregor of that Ilk' as holding his clan direct from the Crown, also *Ruadh* ('The Red'); fought with Campbell of Glenorchy, who had bought the superiority of Glenstrae from Argyll and refused to recognise Gregor *Ruadh*'s succession to that glen; the latter was outlawed for murder and other crimes 1561 together with several of his clan; formed an alliance with young Stewart of Appin 1563; took part with Argyll in Chatelherault's rebellion in 1565 but was pardoned; *m* Marion, dau of Duncan Campbell of Glenlyon, and was beheaded at Balloch 7 April 1570 on the orders of Sir Colin Campbell of Glenorchy ('Grey Colin'), who asked Atholl and other guests to be present for the spectacle, leaving:

1f Alasdair, of Glenstrae, 11th Chief of Clan Gregor, called 'the Arrow of Glenlyon' for his prowess as hunter and archer; denounced by the PC 1589 with 138 of his clansmen because when some Gregarach (of the branch called the 'Children of the Mist') brought him the head of their victim John Drummond of Drummond-Ernoch (a Royal Forester of Glenartney who had punished Mac Gregor poachers) he summoned the whole clan together at the Church of Balquhidder, where they each laid their hand upon the severed head in turn, took upon themselves the blood-guilt and swore to defend the slayers; nevertheless pardoned 1591/2; in 1591 the Macauley Chief recognised Alasdair as his own Chief, both asserting a common descent from Clan Alpin; in 1596 gave a bond of good behaviour in the presence of JAMES VI and the PC and remained in the Royal Household as a pledge for his clan, later sending hostages in his place; his territory was raided by Maclean of Duart and the Clan Cameron, while some of his wilder Gregarach raided the Colquhouns of Luss 1602 when JAMES VI's sympathy was aroused by the Colquhoun women bringing him the bloody shirts of their dead and wounded (some say a few extra shirts dyed in sheep's blood); two months later Alasdair himself raided Luss with 400 clansmen, defeating the Colquhouns (now invested with the royal authority) at the Battle of Glenfruin 1603, for which the whole clan Gregor were outlawed and the Name of MacGregor proscribed on pain of death; Alasdair was captured by Campbell of Ardkinglas, escaped by swimming a loch, but was retaken by Argyll, who had promised to send him safe to England but sent him only to Berwick under guard then brought him back at once for trial; he was executed at the Mercat Cross of Edinburgh 20 Jan 1604 with 11 of his principal clansmen, being hanged his own height above the rest

2f Iain *Dubh nan Luiraig* ('Black John of the Coat of Mail'); outlawed 1589; one of the Laird of Mac Gregor's 'own gang' 1599; *m* —, dau of John Murray of Strowan, and was *k* by an arrow while leading that half of the Gregarach force which took the Colquhouns of Luss in rear at the Battle of Glenfruin 7 Feb 1603, having had:

1g Gregor, of that Ilk, 12th Chief of Clan Gregor; took the alias 'John Murray' and was obliged to sell Glenstrae with the tower of Stronmelochan to Campbell of Glenorchy 1624, settling in Stirlingshire; during his boyhood the Clan Gregor were driven homeless into the hills, being hunted with bloodhounds and when caught the men butchered while the women were branded on their faces with a key-mark; those who survived were forced to take another name and in one case may well have been ancestors of that line of STEWARTs who were eventually ennobled as Marquesses of Londonderry (*qv*); eventually the persecution abated and in 1626 as 'Laird of MacGregor' Gregor prosecuted Buchanan of Leny for the slaughter of some of the Clan Gregor; nevertheless he and his bro were imprisoned in Edinburgh for being MacGregors 1635–36; *m* Margaret Sinclair, widow of John Grant of Carron (murdered 1628), but *dsp*

2g Patrick, of that Ilk, 13th Chief of Clan Gregor; called *Ruadh*; seized lands in Rannoch in 1641 from the Menzies chief; a royalist, in 1644 he raised his clan for Montrose (*see* MONTROSE, D), who promised to restore the MacGregors if he were victorius, and fought at the Battles of Inverlochy and Kilsyth 1645; *m* Jean (*m* 3rd by 10 July 1656 Duncan Stewart of Appin), widow of Archibald Campbell of Glenlyon and dau of Sir Robert Campbell of Glenorchy, and *d* by Aug 1649, leaving:

1h James, of that Ilk, 14th Chief of Clan MacGregor; lived in 'MacGregor's Hall' on the isle in Loch Rannoch, which he held by the sword; in 1661 an Act of Parl was passed rescind-

ing the penal laws against those bearing the names of Gregor and MacGregor; in 1671 entered into a bond of friendship with the Mackinnon chief (whose family had formerly held the abbacy of Iona), asserting the common origin of their clans (as did the Macnab chief also with Mackinnon); in 1671 he and his clansmen joined with the Macdonalds of Glencoe and Keppoch in raiding the Menzies chief's lands, where they settled, driving out his tenants, sending out scouts and posting sentinels; accordingly a commission was given to Menzies and the Campbells of Glenorchy and Glenlyon to apprehend him, but they failed; *dsp* by April 1678

1h Jean; *m* Aug 1666 Allan Cameron, yr bro of Sir Ewen Cameron of Lochiel ('The Great Lochiel'), 17th Ch

3g Evan (given as a child into his maternal gf's custody), served as an officer under KING GUSTAVUS ADOLPHUS OF SWEDEN in the Thirty Years War in Germany 1631

3e Evan, Tutor (Guardian) of Glenstrae during the 11th Ch's minority 1584, when he was summoned to appear personally before JAMES VI and the PC to answer for the suppression of 'broken men', although he had himself been outlawed for murder and other crimes 1561; *d* by 1601, leaving:

1f Gregor; executed with his Ch 20 Jan 1604

2f Iain *Dubh*; hostage for his Ch 1599; hanged with eight other Gregarach at the Mercat Cross of Edinburgh 17 Feb 1604, leaving:

1g Alasdair; was required to provide securities for keeping the peace 1637

3f Duncan; Tutor of Glenstrae after the execution of the 11th Ch 1604; fortified the isle of Eilean Mharnoch in Loch Katrine, whence he broke through his besiegers with 7 score Gregarach and 'headed the Clan in every adventure', harrying the land from Loch Awe to Fortingall 1610–11; his name appeared first with £1,000 (over £45,000 in late-1990s terms) on his head on the official list of those MacGregor chieftains for whose slaughter the pardon of all past faults was promised; he himself pardoned 1611 through Argyll's influence and took the alias Douglas (probably out of compliment to Argyll's countess); *m* 1603 Margaret, dau of Malcolm Macfarlane of Gartartan, and had:

1g Malcolm, Tutor of MacGregor during the minority of the 14th Ch 1649; royalist, held the passes at the Heads of Forth for CHARLES II 1651; during Glencairn's royalist rising of 1653 (*see* CUNINGHAME, Bt) the clans involved assembled at 'MacGregor's Hall' in the isle of Loch Rannoch and he led 200 Gregarach at the Battle of Aberfoyle, made peace between some Gregarach and the Laird of Buchanan 1655 and was the pncpl MacGregor chieftain cited by the PC 1661; lived at Stuckinroy on the eastern shore of Loch Lomond and western shoulder of Ben Lomond; *m* Mary, dau of Campbell of Glenlyon and widow of John Macnab of Bovain, Ch of Macnab, and had:

1h Gregor, of that Ilk, 15th Chief of Clan Gregor; settled at Gregoriestoun in Luss's country; Col in JAMES II's army 1689 but seems to have entrusted the command of the clan in the field to his Lt-Col, Donald MacGregor of Glengyle; *d* unm 9 Feb 1693

2g Evan, of Kilmanan, of which he had a charter from Montrose 1659; Col, Capt of an armed Highland Watch for protecting the cattle of the Lennox; *m* Mary, dau of William Napier of Ardinmoir, bro of 1st Lord Napier (*see* NAPIER and ETTRICK, L), and had:

1h John, of Kilmanan, living 1673; *dspl*

2h Archibald, of that Ilk, 16th Chief of Clan Gregor; authorised to maintain an armed Highland Watch for the security of Loch Lomond side against 'broken men' 1691; took the name of Graham of Kilmanan when the penal laws against Clan Gregor were revived by WILLIAM III June 1693; one of the Highland chiefs summoned before the PC 1704; while drunk in 1694 he shot and killed his ghillie Malcolm MacCurich; had acquired Craigrostan from Luss 1693 but made that territory in 1706 over to the famous Rob Roy MacGregor; afterwards went to Ireland and is said to have been last heard of at a horse-fair in Antrim; with him the male line of the usurping 7th Ch came to an end (although other Clan Dugall Ciar cadets continued), and so in July 1714 (in the hope of collecting the Govt pension paid to the Chiefs of Clans to keep quiet) 14 MacGregors descended of the old chiefly house (including the chieftains of Brackly, Roro and Glengyle) met and chose as their chief Balhaldie, a prominent cadet of Roro (*see* above under the 2nd Chief); *m* (contract 31 May 1679) Anna, dau of John Cochrane, Minister of Strathblane, and had:

1i Hugh, Yr. of MacGregor; *dvp c* 1705

After the 17th Chief's death in 1743 the Mac GREGORs continued officially chiefless and nameless until 1774, when, largely through the efforts of Gregor *Boidheach* MacGregor, a cadet of Glengyle, an Act of Parl was passed repealing the statutes against Clan Gregor and allowing the names Gregor and MacGregor to be used again; soon afterwards 856 clansmen of the name MacGregor subscribed a deed admitting John MacGregor or Murray of Lanrick (ancestor of the present Ch) to be 'proper and true Chief of Clan Alpin' and in 1795 he was formally reinvested in the chiefship by the Crown through the Lord Lyon King of Arms, by recording in his name the heraldic insignia of the ancient chiefs

Lineage (of the 18th Chief): DUNCAN Mac GREGOR OF ARDCHOILLE, called *Ladasach* (s of Gregor Patrickson; *see* above); leader of all the most recalcitrant Gregarach of his time, doubtless as 'righteous heir to The MacGregor'; a feud with the MacLarens perhaps arose from MacGregor claims through a MacLaren heiress as their crests are similar and in 1532 the Gregarach slew the MacLaren Minister of Balquhidder, claiming the right to share with the MacLarens (descendants of a local Abbot) the privilege of being first to enter Balquhidder Church on Sundays; the MacGregors were desperate for land and in Easter Week 1543 DUN-

CAN led a surprise night attack on peaceful homesteads which, followed by another MacGregor onslaught in 1558, nearly exterminated the Clan Laren and overran their lands in Balquhidder; he was mentor of the young 8th Chief in the raid that captured Struan Robertson 1545, and in 1548 the Menzies chief inserted a special clause in leases forbidding lands to be sub-let to 'Duncan MacGregor MacPhadrig' (*Ladasach*'s patronymics); he became Tutor of Glenstrae during the 9th Chief's minority *c* 1550 and killed Alasdair Odhar MacGregor of Morenish for acknowledging Campbell of Glenorchy as his chief; outlawed for murder 1551 and became a noted freebooter, 'Ardchoille' becoming the MacGregor slogan; was captured and beheaded at Finlairg by Sir Colin Campbell of Glenorchy ('Grey Colin') 16 June 1552; *m* Mary Campbell of Ardkinglas and had, with other issue:

1 GREGOR

2 Malcolm *Ruadh*; beheaded with his father and er bro 1552

3 Patrick *Dubh*; murdered in Balquhidder by rival Gregarach of the Clan Dugal Ciar, the usurping ch branch, 4 Oct 1574; after DUNCAN *Ladasach*'s execution his branch of the Gregarach led such wild and hunted lives in the misty mountains that they became known as *MacEagh* ('Sons of the Mist')

DUNCAN Mac GREGOR's est son,

GREGOR Mac GREGOR, Yr. of Ardchoille; *m* Isabel Cameron of Stronhead and was beheaded with his f by the Campbells 1552, leaving, with other issue:

1 DUNCAN

2 Patrick, called *Adholach* because brought up in Atholl; hanged at Edinburgh with the 11th Ch 20 Jan 1604; three of his sons took the name of Livingstone and two that of Balfour

GREGOR Mac GREGOR's est son,

DUNCAN Mac GREGOR in Ardchoille, Chieftain of the Children of the Mist; called *Aberach* as he was brought up in Lochaber; outlawed with his brothers and ten other MacGregors for murder 1568; taken into favour by Argyll 1573; appears in an official list as one of the chieftains of 'the House and Gang of Gregor MacIain' *c* 1587; *k* in a skirmish with the Campbells at Bintoig April 1604; *m* —, dau of Macfarlane of that Ilk, and had, with other issue:

1 PATRICK

2 Robert *Aberach*; allegedly planned the fatal attack on the Colquhouns 1603; later took the alias Ramsay; bought his pardon with six rival MacGregor heads and surrendered with a rope round his neck, giving up his sword to the Chllr of Scotland and being imprisoned 1624, but released and banished to fight in 'the wars abroad' 1626

3 Gregor; fatally shot in the back with an arrow by a rival MacGregor Aug 1604

DUNCAN Mac GREGOR's est son,

PATRICK Mac GREGOR, Chieftain of the Children of Mist, called *Aberach* after his f; among the Gregarach reconciled to the Buchanans 1629; allegedly fought under Montrose at Kilsyth; *m* Marion Macdonald of Auchatrichatan in Glencoe and had, with other issue:

1 IAIN

2 James; Maj; settled America, where *k* by Indians

PATRICK Mac GREGOR's er son,

IAIN Mac GREGOR in Glenlochy, Chieftain of the Children of the Mist, against whom with their Ch a 'commission of fire and sword' was issued 1679; fought for JAMES II Battle of Killiecrankie 1689; *m* Ann, dau of Gregor MacGregor of Roro, his fellow chieftain, and had an est s:

JOHN Mac GREGOR of Glencarnoch in Balquhidder, Chieftain of the Children of the Mist; took the alias Murray; *b* 1668; quarrelled with Rob Roy MacGregor (of the Clan Dugal Ciar branch of the Gregarach), who ambushed him and 30 of his men 1722; it is said that at a meeting at Blair Atholl with the Grants in 1726 the MacGregors offered to take the name of Grant of Glencarnoch if JOHN was recognised as Chief of the united Clan Alpin, to include all the Grants; *m* Catherine (*d* 14 May 1774), dau of Hugh Campbell of Lix, and *d* 18 Sept 1744, leaving:

1 Robert, of Glencarnoch, Chieftain of the Children of the Mist, (territorial) Baron Bailie of Balquhidder; Jacobite cdr of a regt of MacGregors in the 1745 Uprising; was in hiding in the hills for a while before surrendering to Gen John Campbell (afterwards Argyll) Sept 1746; several former prisoners of his certifying his kindness to them, he was not executed but imprisoned for three years in Edinburgh Castle; *m* 1st Christian, dau of John MacGregor of Roro; *m* 2nd Robina, dau of Maj Donald Cameron, yr s of Sir Ewen Cameron of Lochiel, 17th Ch; *m* 3rd Barbara Mary, dau and heiress of William Drummond of Hawthornden, and *d* Oct 1758; by his 2nd w he had:

(1) John, Yr. of Glencarnoch; Lt Fraser's Highlanders; *k* Siege of Louisburg, America, 1758

2 Peter; *d* before his er bro

3 Duncan; Jacobite 1745, his heel being shot away at the Battle of Prestonpans; became Chieftain of the Children of the Mist 1758; *m* Beatrix, dau of David MacNiven, and *d* Feb 1787, having had:

(1) John; Cdre Bombay Marine HEICS; *dvp* Batavia 23 March 1784

4 EVAN

5 John; Capt-Lt Perry's Regt; *k* Ticonderoga in America 1759

The 4th son,

EVAN Mac GREGOR *alias* MURRAY; Jacobite Maj, ADC to Prince Charles Edward Stuart 1745; fired the first shot against Sir John Cope's army and distinguished himself at Prestonpans, the Prince presenting him with a dirk (worn by subsequent Chiefs); Lt 88th Highrs Seven Years War; *m* Janet, dau of John Macdonald of Balcomie, s of Sir James Macdonald of Sleat, 2nd Bt (*see* BOSVILLE MACDONALD, Bt), and had:

1 JOHN (Sir), **1st Bt**

2 Alexander; Col Royal Clan Alpin Fencibles; *b* 25 Aug 1746; *m* 1st Frances (*d* 1788), dau of Maj — Pascal; *m* 2nd 25 March 1790 Grace, dau of James Hay, and by his 1st w had, with another s (*d* young):

(1) Alexander Murray; Maj-Gen; *b* 27 Nov 1778; *m* 21 May 1810 Lady Charlotte Sinclair (*d* 7 April 1854), dau 12th Earl of Caithness (*qv*), and *d* 20 Aug 1827, leaving issue

3 Peter; Col HEICS, Adj-Gen Bengal Army; *m* Eliza Turing and was *ksp* on board the *Lord Nelson* East Indiaman

4 Robert; Lt-Col Roy Clan Alpin Fencibles; *m* Barbara, widow of Kenneth Murchison of Tarradall and sis of Sir Alexander Mackenzie, Bt, of Fairburn, and had:

(1) Jeannetta Catherine; *m* 1st Robert Sutherland; *m* 2nd William Darley Hull and *d* 1883

(2) Barbara; *m* 1826 Lt-Col Hort, Dep Adj-Gen Windward and Leeward Cmd, and *d* 1841

EVAN Mac GREGOR *d* 29 Oct 1778 aged 63; his est son,

Sir John Murray Mac Gregor of Mac Gregor, 1st Bt (GB), so *cr* 3 July 1795; resumed the original surname of the family after the Act repealing the statues against the Mac Gregors and was officially recognised as 18th Ch of Clan Gregor; Lt-Col HEICS, Auditor-Gen Bengal; *b* 10 April 1745; *m* 1774 Anne (*d* 5 Feb 1830), dau of Roderick Macleod of Bernera, and *d* 28 June 1822, leaving:

Sir EVAN JOHN MURRAY Mac GREGOR later Mac GREGOR OF Mac GREGOR (roy licence 22 Dec 1822), **2nd Bt**, KCB, GCH; 19th Chief of Clan Gregor; *b* Jan 1785; Maj-Gen, Govr Windward Islands; *m* 28 May 1808 Lady Elizabeth Murray (*d* 12 April 1846), dau of 4th Duke of Atholl (*qv*), and had, with three other daus:

1 JOHN ATHOLL BANNATYNE (Sir), **3rd Bt**

2 Evan William John; Offr Austrian Army; *b* 1819; *d* 28 June 1850

3 James Strathallan; *b* 1821; *d* Dominica W Indies 12 Jan 1843

4 Francis Alexander Robert; HEICS; *b* 1823; *k* Indian Mutiny 25 Sept 1857

5 Ernest Augustus; Lt-Col 4th Regt European Light Cav; *b* 1825; *d* Calcutta 17 Jan 1869

1 Jane Anna Maria; *m* 1st John James Hamilton Burgoyne, 93rd Highrs, 2nd s of Sir J J Burgoyne; *m* 2nd — Le Maout and *d* 19 July 1880

Sir EVAN *d* 14 June 1841; his son,

Sir John Atholl Bannatyne Mac Gregor of Mac Gregor, 3rd Bt, 20th Chief of Clan Gregor; *b* 20 Jan 1810; Lt-Govr Virgin Islands; *m* 14 Nov 1833 Mary Charlotte (*d* 29 April 1896), yst dau and coheir of R-Adml Sir Thomas Masterman Hardy, Bt, GCB (*see* 1834 edn), Nelson's Flag-Capt aboard the *Victory*, and had:

1 MALCOLM (Sir), **4th Bt**

2 Atholl; Madras CS, Br Resident Travancore; *b* 22 July 1836; *m* 23 April 1878 Caroline Mary Stuart (*d* 10 Dec 1906), er dau of Sir Robert Menzies, 7th Bt, of that Ilk (*see* 1902 edn), and *d* 2 March 1902, leaving:

(1) John Atholl; Lt Coldstream Gds; *b* 27 Nov 1880; *ka* 1916

(2) Robert Menzies, CMG (1929); Ind Serv Engrs (ret 1929), Irrigation Advsr Sudan Govt (ret 1937), 2nd Cl Order Nile, Hungarian Order Merit 2nd Cl; *b* 24 July 1882; *d* unm 8 Jan 1946

(3) Evan Malcolm, JP Perthshire; *b* 16 Oct 1883; *d* unm 22 Nov 1960

(1) Morna; BRC WW I, Scottish Branch BRCS POW Food Parcels Depot WW II; *d* unm

3 Evan (Sir), GCB, ISO, JP; *b* 31 March 1842; Admlty 1860–1907, Pncpl Clerk 1880, Perm Sec 1884–1907; *m* 28 Oct 1884 Annie Louise (*d* 21 May 1922), dau of Col William A Middleton, CB, RA, and *d* 21 March 1926, leaving:

(1) Eva Mary, SRN; *d* unm 8 April 1964

4 Alpin; *b* 20 June 1846; Gentleman Usher to HM QUEEN VICTORIA; *d* unm 13 Nov 1899

1 Emily Louisa; *m* 6 Aug 1857 William David, Viscount Stormont, and *d* 9 April 1919, having had issue (*see* MANSFIELD and MANSFIELD, E)

2 Mary Elizabeth; *m* 25 April 1871 John Charles Thynne and *d* 30 July 1934, having had issue (*see* BATH, M)

Sir JOHN *d* 11 May 1851; his est son,

Sir Malcolm Mac Gregor of Mac Gregor, 4th Bt, 21st Chief of Clan Gregor; *b* 29 Aug 1834; R-Adml, Crimean Medal and clasp for Sebastopol, Turkish War Medal, Roy Humane Soc Medal; *m* 26 Oct 1864 Lady Helen Laura McDonnell (*d* 17 March 1922), only dau of 4th Earl of Antrim (*qv*), and had:

1 MALCOLM (Sir), **5th Bt**

2 Alexander Ronald (Alasdair), JP Perthshire; WW II in Roy Observer Corps; *b* 20 June 1878; *m* 12 June 1907 Gertrude Blanche (*d* 4 Aug 1959), 3rd dau of Charles Archibald Murray (*see* MANSFIELD and MANSFIELD, E), and *d* 21 May 1960, leaving:

(1) (Malcolm) Findanus; Lt-Cdr RNVR WW II; *b* 2 March 1908; *educ* RNC Dartmouth; *m* 1st 14 June 1930 (*divorce* 1940) Rachel Katherine, only child of Hon Eustace Hamilton-Russell, OBE, JP (*see* BOYNE, V); *m* 2nd 1940 *Mariquita Gwen Alison [Mrs Findanus Mac Gregor, Cardney, Dunkeld, Perthshire PH8 0EY], 3rd dau of A J Webbe, of Fulvens, Abinger Hammer, and *d* 5 May 1990, leaving:

1a +Alpin Findanus [Alpin Mac Gregor Esq, 79 Stockwell Park Rd, London SW9 0DB]; *b* 25 Jan 1941; *educ* Wellington and Trin Coll Cambridge (MA); chartered accountant, ptnr KPMG; *m* 9 Oct 1965 *Maria Christina Elisabeth, yr dau of Dage Collin Brunow, of Kotka, Finland, and Baroness Dana von Uexkull, of Helsinki, and has:

1b +Euan Alexander; *b* 8 Oct 1972; *educ* Shiplake and Warwick

2b +Callum Randal; *b* 23 Aug 1977; *educ* Wellington Coll

3b +Alasdair Duncan; *b* 1979; *educ* Wellington Coll

(2) Donnchadh Tearlach, ERD; *b* 18 April 1914; *educ* Malvern; psc, Maj RSG (2nd Dragoons), ret 1960, Capt Reserve of Offrs Coldstream Gds, WW II (wounded) and Malaya 1945–48, memb Roy Co Archers; *m* 1st 29 Jan 1944 (*divorce* 1949) Nighean, WAAF, only child of Col Alastair Norman Fraser, DSO, MB, ChB, RAMC, of Bridgford, Notts, and *d* 1974, leaving:

1a +Randal Alasdair [Randal Mac Gregor Esq, Came House, Dorchester, Dorset DT2 8NU]; *b* 17 Nov 1945; *educ* Gordonstoun; Lt RSG (2nd Dragoons); *m* 1st 1973 (*divorce* 1977) Lynn Vanessa, dau of Maj Tommy Vale, MBE, of Kingston Broadway, W Sussex; *m* 2nd 1978 *Sarah, dau of Maj Nigel Martin, of Came House, and has:

1b *Morag Nicotina; *b* 1978

2b *Malvina Iona; *b* 1982

(2) (cont.) Donnchadh Mac Gregor *m* 2nd 14 Oct 1954 Roxana Mary Jocelyn (*d* 1989), dau of Jocelyn Walker, of Isfield, Sussex, and by her has:

1a *Isabel Maryel; *b* 27 April 1956

2a *Catriona Gabrielle; *b* 14 May 1968

(1) Dorviegelda Malvina; *b* 5 April 1910; *m* 1st 30 March 1939 S/Ldr Hon Greville Baird, RAF (*see* KINTORE, E), and had issue; *m* 2nd 15 Nov 1947 S/Ldr Algernon Ivan (Toby) Sladen, DSO (*d* 2 July 1976), only s of Maj Algernon Ryder Lambart Sladen, of Norfolk Cottage, Virginia Water, and *d* 1997, leaving:

    3a *Angus Murray [Angus Sladen Esq, Glen Carron, Achnashellach, Rossshire]; *b* 1950

1 Malvina Charlotte; *b* 26 Oct 1865; *m* 11 June 1892 Hon Granville William Richard Somerset (*see* RAGLAN, B) and *d* 4 Dec 1924, leaving issue

2 Margaret Helen Mary; *b* 15 Jan 1867; *m* 20 April 1899 6th Earl of Mansfield and Mansfield (*qv*) and *d* 13 Feb 1933, leaving issue

3 Maryel Alpina, MBE (1919); *b* 1 April 1875; *m* 23 Oct 1911 Ernest Penleton Magruder, AM, MD (*d* 8 April 1915), Prof Clinical Surgery Georgetown U, s of Hon C C Magruder, Clerk Court Appeals Md., and *d* 27 Nov 1967, having had issue

Sir MALCOLM *d* 31 Aug 1879; his er son,

Sir Malcolm Mac Gregor of Mac Gregor, 5th Bt, CB (1919), CMG (1917), JP and DL Perths; 22nd Chief of Clan Gregor; *b* 3 Aug 1873; Capt RN, WW I as Cdre 1st Cl (despatches four times, Legion of Honour and Croix de Guerre with palm), chm Ag Exec Ctee 1939–47; *m* 22 Jan 1925 Hon Gylla Constance Susan Rollo, OBE (1948), Swedish Order of Vasa 1st Cl (*see* ROLLO, L), and *d* 5 Dec 1958, leaving:

1 Sir GREGOR Mac GREGOR of Mac GREGOR, **6th and present Bt**

1 Anna Gylla; *b* 26 May 1929; *m* 15 July 1950 *James Christopher Ellis [James Ellis Esq, Localitá Coi 11, Torri del Benaco, 37010 Verona, Italy], AADip, ARIBA, FBIM, late Capt RE (despatches 1946), yst s of Francis Henry Ellis, of Elmton House, Creswell, Notts, and *d* 1996, leaving:

    (1) *Giles Christopher; *b* 30 June 1951; *educ* Downside

    (2) *Conrad James; *b* 23 May 1965

    (1) *Anna Gabrielle; *b* 25 March 1953

    (2) *Katherine Gylla; *b* 23 Feb 1957

MACKAY OF ARDBRECKNISH

Creation: B. (LP, UK) 1991.

THE BARON MACKAY OF ARDBRECKNISH, of Tayvallich, District of Argyll and Bute PC (1996), JP, DL (Glasgow) (John Jackson Mackay) [The Rt Hon The Lord Mackay of Ardbrecknish PC JP DL, Innishail, 51 Springkell Drive, Pollokshields, Glasgow G41 4EZ]; *b* 15 Nov 1938; *educ* Glasgow U (BSc, Dip Ed); Head Maths Dept Oban HS; MP (C) Argyll 1979–83, Argyll and Bute 1983–87; PPS to Sec State Scotland 1982, Parly U-Sec Scottish Office 1982–87; Ch Exec Scottish C Centl Office 1987–90, Chm Sea Fish Industry Authority 1990–93; memb Ho Lds: Select Ctee EC 1991–93, Sub Ctee Energy, Industry and Tport 1991–93, Delegated Powers Scrutiny Ctee 1992–93; Ld-in-Waiting 1993–1994; Parly U-Sec Tport 1994, Min State Social Security 1994–97, Oppn Spokesman Treasury Affrs, Constitution and Scotland 1997; Pres Glasgow Bn Boys' Bde 1993–; *m* 1961 *Sheena, dau of James Wagner, of Bishopton, Renfrewshire, and has:

1 *David Ferguson; *b* 1967; *educ* Glasgow U (BSc Civil Engrg); *m* 19– *Jacqui, dau of Brian MacNulty, of Ardrossan, and has:

    (1) *Lisa Jane; *b* 1993

    (2) *Gemma May; *b* 1997

2 *Colin James; *b* 1969; *educ* Glasgow U (LLB)

1 *Fiona Jackson; *b* 1964; *educ* Glasgow U (MA); *m* 1992 *Richard Sales, of Noulten-Le-Clay, Lincs, and has:

    (1) *Ross Laurence; *b* 1996

    (1) *Amy Helen; *b* 1993

Lineage: JACKSON MACKAY, of Tayvallich, Argyll; *m* Jean — and had:

JOHN JACKSON, *cr* a **Baron**

MACKAY OF CLASHFERN

Arms: Azure on a chevron argent, between two bear's heads couped argent, muzzled gules, in chief and a fleece argent in base, a roebuck's head erased between two hands grasping daggers, the points turned towards the buck's head, all proper. **Crest:** A dexter arm, couped at the elbow proper, the hand grasping a pair of balances or. **Supporters:** Dexter, a male figure attired in the Robes of the Lord High Chancellor; sinister, a male figure attired in the Robes of one of Her Majesty's Counsel learned in the Law in Scotland proper, **Motto:** *Manu justi* ('With a just hand'). **Creation:** B. (LP, UK) 1979.

THE BARON MACKAY OF CLASHFERN, of Eddracchillis in the District of Sutherland (Sir James Peter Hymers Mackay, KT (1997), PC (1979)) [The Rt Hon The Lord Mackay of Clashfern KT PC, Lord Chancellor's Residence, House of Lords, London SW1A 0PW]; *b* 2 July 1927; *educ* George Heriot's Sch Edinburgh and Edinburgh U (MA 1948); BA Camb 1952; LLB Edinburgh 1955; Lecturer St Andrews 1948–50; advocate 1955, QC Scotland 1965, Standing Jr Counsel to: Queen's and Ld Treasurer's Rembrancer, Scottish Home and Health Dept, Commrs Inland Revenue Scotland; Sheriff Pncpl Renfrew and Argyll 1972–74; dir Stenhouse Hldgs 1976–77; memb Insurance Brokers' Registration Cncl 1977–79; V-Dean Faculty Advocates 1973–76, Dean 1976–79, Ld Advocate Scotland 1979–84, Ld of Session 1984–85; Ld Justice Appeal Ordinary 1985–87; Ld Chllr 1987–97; Chllr Heriot-Watt U 1991–, ed-in-chief *Halsbury's Laws of England* 1998–, memb part-time Scottish Law commn 1976–79; Commr Northern Lighthouses 1975–84; Hon Bencher Inner Temple 1979; Fell: Internat Academy Trial Lawyers 1979, Inst Taxation 1981, American Coll Trial Lawyers 1990; Er Bro Trin Ho 1990; FRSE 1984; Hon memb SPTL 1986; Hon FICE 1988; Hon Fell: Trin Coll Cambridge 1989, Girton Coll Cambridge 1990; Hon FRCSE 1989; Hon FRCP 1990; Hon LLD: Edinburgh 1983, Dundee 1983, Strathclyde 1985, Aberdeen 1987, St Andrews 1989, Cambridge 1989, William and Mary Coll Va. 1989, Birmingham 1990; Hon DCL Newcastle 1990; author: *Armour on Valuation for Rating* (consultant ed, 5th edn, 1985); *m* 1958 *Elizabeth Gunn Hymers and has:

1 *James; *b* 1958; *educ* Cambridge (MA) and Edinburgh Us (MB, ChB); Hon Registrar and Research Fell Dept Clinical Surgery Edinburgh U; *m* 1991 *Marion E., dau of J E McArthur, of Edinburgh, and has:

    (1) *Heather Mairi; *b* 1992

1 *Elizabeth Janet; *b* 1961; *m* 1982 *James Campbell, of Milton of Ness Side, Inverness, and has two sons and a dau

2 *Shona Ruth; *b* 1968

Lineage: JAMES MACKAY; *m* Janet Hymers and had:

JAMES PETER HYMERS, *cr* a **Baron**

MACKAY OF DRUMADOON

Creation: B. (LP, UK) 1997.

THE BARON MACKAY OF DRUMADOON, of Blackwaterfoot, in the District of Cuninghame (Donald Sage Mackay, PC (1996)) [The Rt Hon The Lord Mackay of Drumadoon PC, 39 Hermitage Gdns, Edinburgh EH10 6AZ; Kinneil Cottage, Lamlash, Isle of Arran KA27 8JT]; *b* 30 Jan 1946; *educ* George Watson's Boys' Coll Edinburgh, Edinburgh U (LLB1966, LLM 1968) and U of Virginia (LLM 1969); law apprentice 1969–71; slr Allan McDougall & Co 1971–76; barrister (Scotland) 1976, Advocate Depute 1982–85, QC (Scotland) 1987; memb Criminal Injuries Compensation Bd 1989; Slr Gen Scotland 1995–96, Ld Advocate 1996–97; *m* 1979 *Lesley Ann Waugh and has a s and two daus

Lineage: Rev DONALD GEORGE MACKINTOSH MACKAY; *m* Jean Margaret — and had:

DONALD SAGE, *cr* a **Baron**

MACKENZIE of Coul

Arms: Quarterly, 1st and 4th, az. a deer's head cabossed or (for MACKENZIE); 2nd and 3rd, gu. a boar's head couped arg. (for CHISHOLM). **Crest:** A boar's head erect or, between the attires of a stag fixed to the scalp sa. **Supporters:** Dexter, an armed Highlander in full costume ppr.; sinister, a roebuck ppr.
Motto: *Pulchrior ex arduis* ('The more graceful for pressure').
Creation: Bt. (S) 16 Oct 1673.

SIR PETER DOUGLAS MACKENZIE, 13TH BT, of Coul, Ross-shire; *b* 23 April 1949; *s* kinsman 1990; *m* 1982 *Jennifer, dau of Ridley Boyce, and has:

  1 *Alison Douglas; *b* 1985
  2 *Sarah Douglas; *b* 1988

Lineage: ALEXANDER MACKENZIE, of Coul (illegitimate s of Colin *Cam* ('One--eyed') Mackenzie, 11th of Kintail (*d* 1594, having made over Coul to him; *see* CROMARTIE, E), by Mary, dau of Roderick Mackenzie of Davochmaluach); had sasine of Applecross 10 March 1582; *m* 1st Annabella, dau of Murdoch Mackenzie of Fairburn and widow of Thomas Mackenzie of Ord, and *d* March 1650, having had:

  1 Roderick, of Applecross; *m* Finguala, dau of Murdoch Mackenzie of Redcastle, and had issue
  1 Isabel; *m* Alexander Mackenzie, 5th of Gairloch
  2 Marjory; *m* Rev William MacCulloch, of Park

ALEXANDER MACKENZIE *m* 2nd 1617 Christian, dau of Hector Munro of Assynt (*see* MUNRO, Bt, of Foulis-Obsdale), and by her had:

  2 KENNETH (Sir), **1st Bt**
  3 Alexander; *d* unm 1639
  4 Hector, of Assynt; *m* — dau of Hugh Fraser of Belladrum
  3 A dau; *m* John Chisholm of that Ilk and had issue
  4 Mary; *m* 1649, as his 2nd w, Sir Alexander Innes, 3rd of Coxton (*see* INNES, Bt, of Coxton)

The 2nd son,

  Sir Kenneth Mackenzie, 1st Bt (NS), so *cr* 16 Oct 1673, of Coul; *m* 1st Jean, er dau of Alexander Chisholm of that Ilk; *m* 2nd —, dau of Thomas Mackenzie of Invertail and by both ws had issue; his sons by his 1st w:

  1 **Sir Alexander Mackenzie, 2nd Bt**; had his lands erected into a (territorial) Barony 1681; MP (S Parl) Ross-shire 1692–1702; *m* 1st Jean, dau of Sir Robert Gordon, 1st Bt, of Gordonstoun later of Lettefourie, Banff (*see* 1902 edn), and had two daus (the er *m* Mackintosh of Cullachy; the yr, Janet, *m* 1695 her

cousin Alexander Mackenzie of Davochmaluach; *see* also CROMARTIE, E); *m* 2nd Janet Johnston, of Warriston, and *d* 1702, leaving by her, with another s and a dau:

  (1) **Sir John Mackenzie, 3rd Bt**; attainted as a Jacobite 1716; *m* 1st Margaret, dau of Hugh Rose of Kilravock, and had a dau (*m* Bayne of Delny); *m* 2nd 1703 Helen, dau of 3rd Lord Elibank (*qv*), and *dspm*, leaving two daus
  (2) **Sir Colin Mackenzie, 4th Bt**; Clerk to the Pipe in Exchequer; *m* Henrietta, dau of Sir Patrick Houston of Houston and widow of Andrew Brown of Braid, and *d* 1740, having had:

    1a **Sir Alexander Mackenzie, 5th Bt**; had a crown charter of Coul as heir male of his gf 1742; *m* Janet, dau of Sir James Macdonald, 6th Bt, of Sleat (*see* BOSVILLE MACDONALD, Bt), and *d* 1792, having had, with other issue:

      1b **Sir Alexander Mackenzie, 6th Bt**; Maj-Gen Bengal Army, Provisional C-in-C Bengal 1790–92; *m* 1778 Katherine, dau of Robert Ramsay of Camno, and *d* 1796, leaving:

        1c **Sir George Steuart Mackenzie, 7th Bt**, DL Ross-shire; *b* 22 June 1780; V-Pres Roy Soc Edinburgh, Gen Offr Roy Co Archers, FRS; *m* 1st 8 June 1802 Mary (*d* 13 Jan 1835), 5th dau of Donald MacLeod of Geanies, Sheriff Ross-shire, and had, with three daus:

          1d **Sir Alexander Mackenzie, 8th Bt**; *b* 10 Jan 1805; served Bengal Army 1825–51, present Siege Bhurtpore 1825–26 and Sutlej Campaign 1845–46, also Battle of Maharajpore 29 Dec 1843, DJAG army Gwalior; *d* 3 Jan 1856
          2d **Sir William Mackenzie, 9th Bt**; *b* 20 May 1806; *m* 16 Aug 1858 Agnes (*m* 2nd Sept 1881 Baron di San Felici, of Florence), 2nd dau of Ross Thompson Smyth, of Ardmore, Co Londonderry, and *d* 21 Dec 1868
          3d George; *b* 21 July 1807; *d* Madeira June 1839
          4d **Sir Robert Ramsay Mackenzie, 10th Bt**; *b* 21 July 1811; *m* Sept 1846 Louisa Alexandrina (*d* 13 May 1906), dau of Richard Jones, MLA Sydney, NSW, and *d* 19 Sept 1873, having had:

            1e **Sir Arthur George Ramsay Mackenzie, 11th Bt**, JP and DL Ross-shire; *b* 2 May 1865; *m* 11 May 1901 Evelyn Mary Montgomery (*d* 10 May 1908), yst dau of Maj-Gen Sir Edward Wolstenholme Ward, KCMG (*see* BANGOR, V), and *d* 28 April 1935, leaving:

              1f **Sir Robert Evelyn Mackenzie, 12th Bt**; *b* 15 Feb 1906; *educ* Eton and Trin Coll Cambridge; Maj Intell Corps WW II, 1st Sec For Serv 1945–52; memb Lloyd's 1932–90; *m* 1st 28 June 1940 Jane Adams-Beck (*d* 1 Nov 1953), dau of Maurice Beck, of Saltwood, Hythe, Kent; *m* 2nd 5 April 1963 Elizabeth (*d* 16 June 1996), dau of Renard Pearth, of Pittsburg, Pa., and formerly w of Col Archie Campbell, and *d* 1990
            1e Mary Louisa; *m* 19 May 1871 Alexander Archer, of Brisbane, Qld and *d* with him in the wreck of the *Quetta* Feb 1890
            2e Katherine Elizabeth; *d* unm 4 July 1899
            3e Louisa Stewart; *m* 26 Feb 1885 James G L Archer (*d* 1919), of Grace Mere, Qld, and Laurvig, Norway, and *d* 13 May 1933, leaving issue
            4e Frances Philadelphia; *d* unm 13 Dec 1933
          5d John (Rev); *b* 13 Feb 1813; *m* 13 Aug 1839 Eliza, dau of Rev Dr Thomas Chalmers, and *dsp* 25 May 1878
          6d Donald Macleod; *b* 18 Sept 1815; V-Adml; *m* 20 April 1865 Dorothea (*d* 26 May 1901), est dau of Adml Sir Michael Seymour, GCB (*see* CULME-SEYMOUR, Bt), and *dsp* 25 Jan 1894
          7d James (Rev); *b* 23 Dec 1819; *m* 11 May 1847 Philadelphia (*m* 2nd 19 Oct 1858 W T Knapp (*d* 1887) and *d* 27 Dec 1904), yst dau of Sir Percival Hart Dyke, 5th Bt (*qv*), and *dsp* 20 Aug 1857

        1c (cont.) **Sir George** *m* 2nd 27 Oct 1836 Catherine (*d* 2 Aug 1857), 2nd dau of Sir Henry Jardine of Harwood and widow of Capt John Street, RA, and *d* Oct 1848, having by her had:

          8d Henry Augustin Ornano, CE; *b* 24 April 1839; *m* 1st 20 Oct 1859 Mary Anne (*d* 1881), dau of Louis Francis Botte, and had:

            1e George Henry Louis; *b* 27 May 1872; *m* 23 Jan 1907 Lilian Mary (*d* 19 March 1969), est dau of Richard Rodney Pope, late ICS, and *d* 10 May 1960, leaving:

              1f *Mary Zeta Bingham; *b* 6 March 1909; *m* 18 April 1931 Lt Philip Henry Burch, DCLI (*d* 24 Aug 1932), yst s of Maj F Burch, Roy Dragoons, and has:

                1g *Deirdre Raine Mary; *b* 12 Feb 1932
                2g *Phillida Mary; *b* (posthumously) 27 April 1933; *m* 30 Oct 1965 *Aloysius John Zadnik, of Alberta, and had:

                  1h *Philip John; *b* 10 April 1967
                  2h *Michael Peter; *b* 26 June 1968
                  1h *Elizabeth Anne [Miss Elizabeth Zadnik, c/o National & Grindlays Bank, 13 St James's Sq, London SW1]; *b* 1970

              2f *Eira Margaret Antonia; *b* 25 Feb 1913; *m* 19 Feb 1938 Owen James Esmonde (*d* 1993) and has issue (*see* ESMONDE, Bt)
            2e Robert Alfred Steuart; *b* 5 July 1873; *d* 16 May 1894
            3e Alexander Augustin Donald (Very Rev); *b* 19 Feb 1876; *educ* Bp Hatfield Hall, Durham (BA 1904, MA 1907); Rev Canon, Provost Inverness Cathedral 1918–49; *m* 6 Aug 1913 Louisa Barbara (*d* 9 April 1958), dau of Capt Norman Macleod, of Orbost, Skye, and *dsp* 1 July 1969
            4e Cameron James Jardine; *b* Jan 1878; *d* 14 Nov 1879
            1e Catherine Mary Aimée; *d* unm 6 March 1941

         8d (cont.) Henry Mackenzie *m* 2nd 10 Oct 1892 Josephine Emily (*d* 24 Jan 1951), dau of Charles Bolton, of Clapham, London, and *d* 29 May 1909, having by her had:

            5e Ramsay Malcolm Bolton (Rev); *b* Aug 1893; *educ* Trin Coll Oxford (BA 1904, MA 1907); Capt RAF WW I (despatches); Rector Edgmond Salop 1955–60, Vicar St Mary's Shrewsbury 1938–55, RD Shrewsbury 1952, Sec Additional Curates Soc 1932–34, Sec

Centl Bd Finance C of E, Fin Sec to Ch Assembly 1934–37; *m* 18 Aug 1920 Margaret Cecilia (*d* 19 Feb 1965), only dau of Rev George Augustus Seymour Metford, of Sutton Bonington, Notts

1b Henrietta; *m* Thomas Wharton

2b Margaret; *m* William Mackenzie of Suddie

3b Stewart; *m* William Dallas of Cautray

2a William, of Achilty and Kinnahaird, whose male issue died out 1850

1a Anne; *m* John Mackenzie of Applecross and *dsp*

2 Simon, of Torridon and Lentran; *m* 1673 Catherine, dau of John Mackenzie of Invertail, and had:

(1) Alexander, of Lentran and Tarradale; had, with other issue:

1a Kenneth, of Torridon; entertained Prince Charles Edward 1745; *m* 1703 Anne, dau of Alexander Mackenzie, 7th of Gairloch (*see* INGLIS, Bt), and had, with a dau (*m* Colin Mackenzie, Baillie (Magistrate) of Dingwall):

1b John, of Torridon; fought on Jacobite side Culloden 1746 but escaped attainder; *m* Isabel, dau of Kenneth Mackenzie of Dundonnell, and had, with a dau (Janet, *m* Alexander Mackenzie, 2nd s of Sir Roderick Mackenzie, Bt, of Scatwell, *qv*):

1c Kenneth; sold Torridon to his bro John; *m* — Cockerell and had issue

2c John, of Torridon; *b* 1754; *m* Anne Isabella van Dam (*d* 3 May 1831) and *d* 20 Jan 1820, having had:

1d John; sold Torridon to J A Stewart Mackenzie of Seaforth; *m* Katherine Yallop (*d* 1844) and *dsp* 1852

2d Anthony van Dam; *d* unm 1824

3d Charles (Rev); *b* 28 Feb 1807; Rector Allhallows, London, Preb St Paul's; *m* 9 July 1832 Henrietta (*d* 1895), dau of Henry Simonds, of Reading, and *d* April 1888, having had

1e Henry Douglas; *b* 26 Sept 1849; Col cmdg Tasmanian Cwlth Mil Forces, Lt RN; *m* 7 Jan 1873 Julia Nina Sofala (*d* Oct 1917), dau of Hon John Bligh Suttor, of Bathurst, NSW, and *d* 24 Oct 1910, having had:

1f Dudley Bligh Douglas; *b* 26 Dec 1875; *d* unm

2f Keith Douglas; *b* 19 Sept 1879; Boer War (medals with four clasps); *m* 10 Nov 1904 Anna Hildagonda (*d* 1937), dau of George Reitz, of Riversdale, CP, and *d* 1948, leaving:

1g Henry Douglas; *b* 14 Sept 1905; *m* 1941 Irene Carter Freeman, of S Africa, and *d* 4 Nov 1965, leaving:

1h Sir PETER DOUGLAS MACKENZIE, **13th and present Bt**

1h *Ann Douglas [Mrs Ann Mayne, PO Box 10036, Rivonia 2128, S Africa]; *b* 1943; *m* 1975 *Michael Wallace Mayne and has:

1i *Douglas Wallace; *b* 1976

2i *Rory Douglas; *b* 1979

2g Keith Douglas; *b* 16 Aug 1912; *m* 1937 *Thelma Reeders and *d* 1984, having had:

1h *Judy Douglas; *b* 1940; *m* 1962 *Lt Graham Douglas Ferguson, SAAF, and has:

1i *Ian Douglas; *b* 1964

1i *Kim Douglas; *b* 1962; *m* 1984 *David James Sharp

2i *Lynn Douglas; *b* 1968

3i *Lee-Ann Douglas; *b* 1971

2h *Jenifer Mary Douglas [Mrs Jeremy Garrett, 7 Dromedaris Rd, Land en Zeezicht, Somerset West 7130, CP, S Africa]; *b* 1944; *m* 1965 *Jeremy David Garrett, of CP, and has:

1i *Craig Douglas; *b* 1968

2i *Geoffrey Keith; *b* 1972

1i *Nikki Jane; *b* 1970

1g Helen Douglas; *b* 18 Jan 1908; *m* 1933 John Shaw and had issue

2g Joan Douglas; *b* 16 Aug 1909; *m* 1943 Maj Kenneth David Harris, King's Dragoon Gds (*d* 1967), and had:

1h *Peter David; *b* 1949; *m* 1981 *Anne Elizabeth, dau of Anwyl Davies

1h *Gillian Diana; *b* 1947; *m* 1981 *Raymond Wright and has:

1i *David William Benedict; *b* 1988

1i *Eleanor Faith Rosina; *b* 1986

1f Maude Nina Douglas; *m* 8 Feb 1900 Lt-Col Stanley Stewart Ryrie (*d* 4 Dec 1945), RAFA Res, s of Alexander Ryrie, of Micalago, NS, and *d* 10 Feb 1943, leaving issue

2f Helen Douglas; *m* 16 Nov 1898 J Laurence Brown and had issue

3f Florence Douglas; *m* 23 Sept 1908 William Lionel Russell Clarke (*d* 14 May 1954), 3rd s of Sir William John Clarke, 1st Bt, of Rupertswood (*qv*), and *d* 23 Jan 1961, leaving issue

4f Ethel Douglas; *m* 31 Dec 1902 Colin Smith and had issue

1e Mary Louisa; *m* 25 March 1856 Rev Alexander St David Francis Pringle (*d* 1908), Vicar Blakeney, and *d* 9 Jan 1916, having had issue

2e Anna Isabella; *m* 23 Aug 1860 Edward Picton Warlow Baumgarten (*d* 1914), Capt 10th Hus, and *d* 1927, leaving issue

3e Henrietta Helen; *m* Edwin A B Crockett (*d* 1916) and *d* 21 Oct 1862, having had issue

4e Florence Emma; *m* 21 April 1863 Duncan Stewart (*d* 1887), barrister, and had issue

4d Henry (Rt Rev), DD; *b* 16 May 1808; Bp Suffragan Nottingham 1870–77; *m* 1st 1834 Elizabeth (*d* 1840), dau of Robert Ridley, of Demerara, and had:

1e Edith; *m* 18 Feb 1862 Rev Henry John Fellowes (*d* 1902), Rector Over Wallop, Hants, and *d* 22 Feb 1904, leaving issue

4d (cont.) The Rt Rev Henry Mackenzie *m* 2nd 10 Aug 1842 Antoinette Margaret Campbell (*d* 20 Dec 1907), est dau of Sir James Henry Turing, 7th Bt (*qv*), and *d* 15 Oct 1878, having by her had:

1e Henry Turing; *b* 7 Dec 1843; *m* 1887 Mary Adelaide (*d* 31 Dec 1947), dau of Rev Walter Clarke, and *d* 23 Feb 1896, leaving:

1f Roderick Henry Turing, MICE; *b* 4 July 1891; *educ* St Paul's and London U; Lt-Col AAF India, Capt Middx Regt, Ch Eng State of Bikaner India, Kaisar-i-Hind Gold Medal Public Services India 1942; *m* 1st 20 Jan 1920 (*divorce* 1933) Helen Margaret, dau of I Pagan Dalzell, of Musselburgh, Edinburgh, and had:

1g Keith Roderick Turing, OBE (1983), MC (1945); *b* 19 Jan 1921; *educ* Uppingham and RMC Sandhurst; Maj 6th Gurkhas IA WW II; *m* 2 Aug 1949 *Barbara Kershaw [Mrs Keith Mackenzie, Garden Cottage, 3 Thistle Lane, South St, St Andrews, Fife KY16 9EL], dau of W H Miles, of Deal, Kent, and *d* 7 Oct 1990, having had:

1h +MILES RODERICK TURING [Miles Mackenzie Esq, 55 Lansdowne Parade, Oatley, NSW 2223, Australia]; *b* 18 April 1952; heir presumptive; *educ* Essex U (MA); *m* 1983 *Hiroko Sato, of Tokyo

2h +Angus Keith Turing; *b* 31 Aug 1965; *m* 30 Sept 1995 *Funda Perseiner, of Istanbul

1h *Sarah Jane Kershaw [Mrs Alan Franchi, 9 Osborne Place, Aberdeen AB2 4BX]; *b* 15 Oct 1950; *m* 1975 *Alan Forrest Franchi

2h *Susannah Mary [Mrs Seumas Lorimer, Spott Mill, Spott, E Lothian]; *b* 19 Feb 1957; *m* 1979 *Seumas McKinnon Lorimer

1f (cont.) Lt-Col Roderick Mackenzie *m* 2nd 23 Oct 1934 *Helen Monica Bradley [Mrs Roderick Mackenzie, 14 Gybbons Rd, Rolvenden, Kent], dau of Lt-Col William Bradley Roberts, DSO, IA, of Fleet, Hants, and *d* 7 Jan 1963, having by her had:

2g +Bruce Sydenham [Maj Bruce Mackenzie, Chestnut Cottage, Flimwell, Wadhurst, E Sussex TN5 7NR]; *b* 24 Oct 1935; *educ* Berkhamsted Sch and RMA Sandhurst; Maj Queen's Lancs Regt; *m* 14 Sept 1963 *Sheila Hope Evan, est dau of Rev Aubrey Lionel Evan Hopkins, of Folkestone, and has:

1h +Kevin Roderick; *b* 17 Aug 1964; *educ* Lancaster U (BA) and Hong Kong U (MA); *m* 22 Aug 1992 *Alexandra Mary Morton and has:

1i +Joseph Michael; *b* 10 May 1994

1i *Esme Elizabeth; *b* 22 Nov 1996

2h +Neil Kenneth; *b* 2 Sept 1966; *educ* Nene Coll Northampton (BA) and Lancaster U (MA); *m* 6 July 1996 *Teresa Mary Brayshaw

1h *Tessa Claire; *b* 28 Jan 1970; *educ* Leeds U (BA)

2h *Kirsty Celia; *b* 27 Aug 1971; *educ* Leeds U (BA)

3g Colin Sydenham; *b* 9 March 1938; *d* 23 Feb 1939

4g +Michael-Sydenham; *b* 9 Dec 1940; *educ* Berkhamsted and Trin Coll Dublin (BA 1965)

1f Mary Lilias, MVO (1945); *educ* Newnham Coll Cambridge (MA); Registrar Roy Archives Windsor Castle 1929–53; *d* unm 17 Sept 1953

2e Stanley John MACKENZIE later WYNN-MACKENZIE; *b* 2 Oct 1847; *m* 1st 17 Nov 1869 Charlotte Arthur (*d* 1888), dau of Thomas Wynn, and had:

1f Stanley Charles William; *b* 11 Dec 1870; *m* 1900 G Whitehouse and had:

1g +Douglas Stanley; *b* 1903

2f Alexander Evan Lindsay; *b* 31 May 1872; *d* unm 6 May 1908

3f Esmé Hugh Henry; *b* 16 Aug 1875

4f Ronald Gerald; *b* 21 Feb 1878; *d* young

5f Archibald Thomas; *b* 1 July 1879; *d* young

6f Kenneth Maurice; *b* 11 Oct 1880; *m* 1917 and had issue

7f Robert Fraser; *d* an infant 11 Oct 1882

1f Charlotte Gladys Sissa; *m* Newbury Thomas and had issue

2f Antoinette Gwyneth Wynn; *m* 1908 George Cochran and had issue

2e (cont.) Stanley Mackenzie *m* 2nd 1892 Lizzie Adeline, dau of George Gordon Bennet, and *d* 1904, having by her had:

8f Noel Donald George; *b* 1899; *m* 23 July 1931 *Elsie Kate, dau of William Henry Mitchell, and *d* 1981, having had:

1g +Donald William John [Donald Mackenzie Esq, c/o Hong Kong and Shanghai Banking Corp, Ocean Centre, Hong Kong]; *b* 1 Dec 1935; *m* 20 Sept 1969 *Cheryl Patricia Elizabeth, dau of Cyril Leslie Charles Allen, of Llyswen, Breconshire, and has:

1h +Nicholas Richard John; *b* 1974

2h +Christopher Stuart; *b* 1977

1g *Marian Audrey; *b* 1944; *m* 1966 (*divorce* 1975) Kaddour Amari and has:

1h *Nadia; *b* 1966

2h *Samira; *b* 1970

3f Lillie Marguerite

3e Walter Turing; *b* 19 April 1856; *m* 1st 15 Jan 1880 Sophie (*d* 17 Oct 1894), dau of W A Howie; *m* 2nd 23 Sept 1905 Mabel Grace (*d* 9 Feb 1919), dau of John Scott Bankes, of Soughton Hall, Flints, and widow of Arthur Wiggin, of Ceylon, and *d* 13 June 1919, leaving by his 1st w:

1f Walter Robert Turing; *b* 12 Nov 1881; *m* 1911 Bertha Mary, dau of Herman Alexander Krohn, CBE, JP, DL, of Maldon Court, Essex, and *d* 26 Nov 1932

4e James Henry Turing; *b* 4 July 1858; *d* 13 June 1923

5e Evan Charles (Rev); MA Oxon; *b* 8 Sept 1860; Vicar Old Brampton, Derbys; *m* 21 Sept 1899 Mary Georgiana (*d* 12 May 1924), dau of William Waring, of Chelsfield, Kent, and *d* 17 March 1929

6e Kenneth Edward; *b* 12 Sept 1862; *m* 15 June 1909 Katherine Avenel, 2nd dau of Col G J van Someren, IA, and *d* 23 Oct 1928

2e Antoinette Mary; *d* unm 16 Feb 1928

3e Alice Margaret; *d* 9 Jan 1926

4e Gertrude Eliza; *m* 30 April 1872 John Wigram, of Collingham, Notts, and *d* 18 June 1929, leaving issue (*see* WIGRAM, Bt)

5e Lilias Dalton; *d* unm 30 March 1888

6e Ethel Fitzgerald; *d* unm 14 Jan 1919

3 John, of Delvine; *m* twice and by each w had two sons (*dsp & vp*); *m* 3rd Margaret, dau of Sir John Hay, 1st Bt, of Alderston (*qv*), and *d* 1731, having by her had:

(1) Alexander, of Delvine; Advocate 1681, Pncpl Clerk of Session; *m* Anne, dau of Fothringham of Powrie, and *d* 1731, leaving:

1a Margaret; *m* George Muir of Cassencarrie, s of William Muir of Cassencarrie, Kirkcudbrightshire, by Agnes, dau of John Sharp, of Hoddam, and *d* 1767, leaving issue (*see* MUIR MACKENZIE, Bt)

(2) Kenneth; advocate, Prof Law Edinburgh U, served heir male in Delvine to his bro Alexander 1738; *m* Grizel Hume, dau of Andrew Broune of Dolphinton, Lanarks, and *d* 1756, having had:

1a John, of Dolphinton; *m* Alice, dau of Robert Ord, Ch Baron Exchequer, and *d* 1788, leaving:

1b Richard, of Dolphinton; *b* 1780; *m* 1810 Jane, dau of Capt Hamilton, and *d* 1850, leaving:

1c John Ord, of Dolphinton, WS, JP, DL; *b* 18 March 1811; *m* 1st 23 April 1833 Margaret Hope (*d* 3 May 1873), dau of Sir Thomas Kirkpatrick, 5th Bt (*qv*), and had:

1d Alice Ord; *m* 15 Sept 1864 Francis Borthwick (*see* BORTHWICK, L) and *d* 28 Aug 1935, leaving issue

2d Margaret Mary; *m* 5 Oct 1869 John Wharton DUFF formerly TOD, WS, and *d* 10 Feb 1932

3d Eleanor Susan; *m* 2 Aug 1876 John C R Marshall and *d* 18 Dec 1925

1c (cont.) John Mackenzie *m* 2nd 20 Jan 1881 Joanna (*d* 15 Feb 1928), dau of William Spens, and *d* 14 March 1902, having by her had:

1d Kenneth, WS Edinburgh, JP Lanarks; *b* 10 March 1882; Capt Roy Scots; *m* 4 Oct 1910 May Eudora, CBE (1952, OBE 1947) (*m* 2nd 1920 John Douglas Boswell Campbell (*d* 1943)), dau of Henry Moncrieff Horsbrugh, of Edinburgh (*see* 1970 edn HORSBRUGH, B), and was *ka* 27 Aug 1918, leaving:

1e John Moncrieff Ord, WS Edinburgh (1936), JP (1947), DL (1953); *b* 13 Aug 1911; *educ* Rugby and Corpus Christi Coll Cambridge; Capt Lanarks Yeo (TA) and GHQ Liaison Regt WW II (despatches), US Bronze Star Medal; CC Peeblesshire, V-Lt 1965, memb Border Ag Exec Ctee, *m* 15 Oct 1936 *Delia Alice [Mrs John Mackenzie, Dolphinton House, Dolphinton, Lanarks], 2nd dau of Lt-Col Wyndham Damer Clark, JP, DL, of Tal-y-Garn (*see* MAYO, E), and *d* 1986, having had:

1f +Richard Wyndham John; *b* 14 Nov 1939; *m* 1969 *Diane Gracie Petters and has:

1g +Douglas John; *b* 1972

1g *Delia Joan; *b* 1970

1f *Elizabeth Anne; *b* 23 Dec 1937

2f *Diana Ord; *b* 9 June 1944

3f *Cynthia Rose; *b* 5 Aug 1946; *m* 1969 *Capt Colin Grant Ogilvie Hogg, KOSB, and has had:

1g *Vanessa Charlotte Ogilvie; *b* 1972

2g Nicola Joanna Ogilvie; *b* and *d* 1974

3g *Sarah Jane Ogilvie; *b* 1976

4f *Angela Viviane; *b* 1949

2e Kenneth Ord; *b* 28 Nov 1912; *m* 20 Jan 1955 *Penelope June [Mrs Kenneth Mackenzie, Springfield Cottage, Sherborne St John, Hants RG24 9HP], dau of Neville Brace Colt, of Ringmer, Sussex, and *d* 30 March 1994, leaving:

1f *Virginia Anne [Mrs Hans von Celsing, Pyt House, Ashampstead, Berks RG8 8RA]; *b* 8 March 1958; *m* 1988 *Hans H von Celsing, yr s of Capt Folke von Celsing, of Stockholm, and has:

1g *Henrik Alexander Folke; *b* 1990

2g *Christian Frederick; *b* 1992

1g *Isabel Alexandra; *b* 1995

2f *Caroline Jane [Mrs Hector Sants, Court Farm, Worminghall, Aylesbury, Bucks]; *b* 18 Oct 1960; *m* 1987 *Hector W H Sants, s of John Sants, of Killin, Perthshire, and has:

1g *Hector Alexander; *b* 1989

2g *Edward Kenneth Richard; *b* 1990

3g *Arthur Frederick Joseph; *b* 1994

3e Alastair Douglas; *b* 10 April 1917; Col Roy Scots; *m* 31 Jan 1945 *Diane, yr dau of Lt-Col Arthur John Henry Sloggett, CBE, DSO, DL, Rifle Bde, of Tremabyn, Paignton, Devon, and *d* 1989, leaving:

1f +Mark Tresloggett; *b* 12 April 1950

1e Margaret Hermione, MBE (1945); *b* 29 March 1915; Maj WRAC WW II

(3) John, of Delvine (made over to him by his bro Kenneth), WS; Pncpl Clerk of Session; *m* — Renton, of Lamberton, and *dsp* 1778

(1) Anne; *m* Alexander Robertson of Faskally and *d* 1772

(2) Helen; *m* Crawford Balfour of Bingrey

(3) Rebecca; *m* John Mackenzie of Belmaduthy

4 Roderick; *m* —, dau of Kenneth Mackenzie of Davochmaluach

1 A dau; *m* Colin Mackenzie of Redcastle and had issue

2 Agnes; *m* Sir John Munro of Foulis, 4th Bt (*qv*), and had issue

3 Jean; *m* Alexander Baillie of Dunain

4 Christian; *m* John Dunbar, Yr., of Bennetsfield

5 Lilias; *m* John Munro of Inverawe and had issue

6 Mary; *m* Kenneth Mackenzie of Davochmaluach and had issue

7 A dau; *m* — Gordon of Cluny

MACKENZIE
of Glen Muick

Arms: Per pale indented azure and or, a stag's head cabossed counterchanged. **Crest:** A dexter hand grasping a sword bendways proper. **Motto:** *Sic itur ad astra* ('This is the way to the stars'). **Creation:** Bt. (UK) 21 March 1890.

SIR (JAMES WILLIAM) GUY MACKENZIE, 5TH BT, of Glen Muick, Co Aberdeen [Sir Guy Mackenzie Bt, Tresowes Hill Farm, Ashton, Cornwall TR13 9SY]; *b* 1946; *s* cousin 1993; *educ* Stowe; v-pres Crown Royale Internat USA 1979–81, v-chm Kerrier Direct Serv Bd 1994–95 (chm 1995–), memb (Ind) Kerrier DC 1993–; *m* 1st 1972 (*divorce* 1980) Paulene Patricia Simpson and has:

1 *Amanda Louise; *b* 1972

2 *Iona Elizabeth Rose; *b* 1978

Sir GUY *m* 2nd 1996 *Sally Ann Mackenzie *neé* Howard

Lineage: The MACKENZIEs of Glen Muick allegedly descend from the MACKENZIEs of Suddie, Ross-shire.

WILLIAM MACKENZIE, of Aberdeen; *m* Feb 1737 Barbara, est dau of William Moir, of the Bridgend of Cruden, nr Aberdeen, and *d* on or after 6 March 1765, leaving:

KENNETH MACKENZIE, of Aberdeen; *m* 16 Aug 1766 Margaret (*d* 1802), dau of Alexander Garioch, of Kinstairs, Aberdeen, and Mergie, Kincardine, and *d* April 1804, leaving:

GEORGE MACKENZIE, of Aberdeen; *b* 17 April 1773; *m* 16 Oct 1806 Margaret (*d* 26 Oct 1851), only child of William Allan, of Aberdeen, and *d* 21 Jan 1852, leaving an only surv s:

Sir James Thompson Mackenzie, 1st Bt (UK), so *cr* 21 March 1890, DL (Ross-shire and Middx); *b* 27 Dec 1818; *m* 27 March 1849 Mary (*d* 18 Aug 1912), 2nd dau of Charles Du Pré Russell, Bengal CS, and had:

1 ALLAN RUSSELL (Sir), **2nd Bt**

2 Randolph Douglas; *b* 15 Dec 1853; *d* unm 26 Feb 1887

3 Claud Longueville; *b* 15 June 1857; *m* 22 April 1884 Ilona (*m* 2nd 1 March 1890 (*divorce* 1899) Count Ladislas Telcki; *m* 3rd 22 Sept 1901 Baron Nickolaus Wessalenyl (*d* 4 Dec 1921); *d* 20 March 1932), only child of Oliver Paget, of Gyeres, and *d* 21 Aug 1890, leaving:

(1) Olive Leonora; *m* 2 Oct 1915 Lt-Col William Percival Cosnahan Tenison, DSO, FLS, RA, er s of Col William Tenison, DL, of Lough Bawn, Co Monaghan, and had issue

1 Mary Leonora; *m* 20 May 1875 Col Lennox Logan and *d* 13 Aug 1881, leaving issue

2 Alice Louisa Raynsford; *m* 19 Aug 1879 Sir George Pigot, 5th Bt (*qv*), and *d* 25 June 1934, leaving issue

3 Margaret Allan Stuart; *m* 11 Jan 1881 Col Thomas Davison, 16th (Queen's) Lancers, and *d* 7 May 1905, leaving issue

Sir JAMES *d* Aug 1890; his est s,

Sir Allan Russell Mackenzie, 2nd Bt, JP and DL Ross-shire and Aberdeenshire; *b* 29 March 1850; memb Roy Co Archers, Lt RHG; *m* 2 July 1874 Lucy Eleanora (*d* 20 April 1926), dau of Duncan Davidson, of Tulloch, and *d* 19 Aug 1906, having had:

1 Allan James Reginald; *b* 26 May 1880; Lt RHG Boer War 1902; *d* unm 28 Sept 1903

2 **Sir Victor Audley Falconer Mackenzie, 3rd Bt**, DSO (1916), MVO 5th Cl (1906), DL; *b* 15 Dec 1882; Col Scots Gds WW I (wounded twice, despatches), Cdr 153rd Black Watch and Gordon TA 1930–32, Groom-in-Waiting to HM

GEORGE V 1932–36, Extra Groom-in-Waiting to TM EDWARD VIII 1936 and GEORGE VI 1937–44, medal of Republic of Panama; *d* unm 18 April 1944

3 Allan Keith; *b* 26 April 1887; Capt Gren Gds WW I (wounded); *m* 19 Dec 1911 Hon Alexandra Louvima Elizabeth Knollys (*m* 2nd 10 Nov 1922 Richard Henry Spencer Checkley; *d* 30 May 1958), only dau of 1st Viscount Knollys (*qv*) and *d* 16 Sept 1916 of wounds recd in action, leaving:

> (1) **Sir (Alexander George Anthony) Allan Mackenzie, 4th Bt**, CD; *b* 4 Jan 1913 (TM GEORGE V and QUEEN ALEXANDRA stood sponsors); *educ* Stowe; Page Honour to HM GEORGE V 1924–31, Capt Black Watch (RHR) Canada WW II, RCMP 1932–37; *m* 24 Aug 1937 *Marjorie [Lady Mackenzie, RR2, Oliver, BC V0H 1T0, Canada], dau of A F McGuire, of Vancouver, and *d* 5 Jan 1993, having had:
>
>> 1a Margaret Ann; *b* 7 June 1939; *m* 1974 *Richard L Mullin and *dsp* 1989
>>
>> 2a *Kathryn Heather; *b* 8 May 1946
>>
>> 3a *Linda Alexandra; *b* 19 Nov 1949; *m* 1970 *Brock J Eayrs, BA, LLB, and has:
>>
>>> 1b *Jennifer Alexandra; *b* 1973
>>>
>>> 2b *Alison Marjorie Ellen; *b* 1977
>>>
>>> 3b *Elizabeth Brooke Jane; *b* 1989
>>
>> 4a *Allain Fenton; *b* 23 June 1953; *m* 1974 *J F M Beltgens and has:
>>
>>> 1b *Christopher John Mackenzie; *b* 1978
>>>
>>> 1b *Jessica Kathryn Ann; *b* 1982

4 Eric Dighton, CMG (1935), CVO (1939), DSO (1917), JP (Argyll 1953); *b* 22 Aug 1891; *educ* Eton; Comptroller Govr-Gen Canada 1931–39, Col Scots Gds, served WWs I (despatches twice, wounded three times) and II, DStJ; *m* 15 Nov 1948 *Elizabeth Kathrine Mary, formerly w of Lt-Col James Robertson-McIsaac, Gordon Highrs, and dau of Capt James William Guy Innes, CBE, DL, RN (*see* INNES, Bt, of Balvenie), and *d* 8 Aug 1972, leaving:

> (1) Sir (JAMES WILLIAM) GUY MACKENZIE, **5th and present Bt**
>
> (2) +ALLAN WALTER; *b* 6 Nov 1952; heir presumptive; *educ* Eton
>
> (1) *Lucy Elizabeth Victoria; *b* 12 Aug 1949

1 (Mary) Lucy Victoria; *m* 22 May 1900 21st Earl of Erroll (*qv*) and *d* 18 Jan 1957, leaving issue

MACKENZIE of Scatwell

Arms: Quarterly, 1st, az. a deer's head cabossed or (for MACKENZIE of Scatwell); 2nd, or a mountain az. inflamed gu.; 3rd, gu. three legs of a man in armour ppr. flexed in triangle, garnished and spurred or (for MACLEOD of Lewis); 4th, az. a deer's head cabossed or within a bordure of the last, charged with eight crescents of the first (for MACKENZIE of Findon). **Crest:** The sun in his splendour or. **Supporters:** Dexter, a savage wreathed about the head and middle with laurel and carrying with his dexter hand a club over his shoulder, all ppr.; sinister, a deer ppr. **Mottoes:** (above) *Luceo non uro* ('I shine but do not burn'), (below) *Sine macula* ('Spotless'). **Creation:** Bt. (NS) 22 Feb 1702/3.

SIR RODERICK McQUHAE MACKENZIE, 12TH BT, of Scatwell, Ross-shire [Sir Roderick Mackenzie Bt, 2431 Udell Rd NW, Calgary, AB T2N 4H9, Canada]; *b* 17 April 1942; *s* f 1986; *educ* Sedbergh, King's Coll London and St George's Hosp (MB, BS); MRCP, FRCP (Canada), DCH; *m* 1970 *Nadezhda (Nadine), Baroness von Rorbas, dau of Georges Frederic Leon Schlatter, Baron von Rorbas, of Buchs-K-Zurich, Switzerland, and has:

1 +GREGORY RODERICK McQUHAE; *b* 8 May 1971

1 *Nina Adelaïda; *b* 1973

Lineage: Sir RODERICK MACKENZIE of Castle Leod, Cogeach and Tarbat (*see* CROMARTIE, E); *d* Sept 1626; his 2nd s:

KENNETH MACKENZIE of Scatwell, Ross; *m* 1st 1634 Margaret, er dau and coheir of Sir Robert Munro of Foulis, 3rd Bt (*qv*), and had, with three daus:

> 1 John; *m* Anne, dau of Roderick Mackenzie of Redcastle, and *d* 13 May 1677, having had:
>
>> (1) Lilias *m* Colin Mackenzie of Kincraig

KENNETH MACKENZIE of Scatwell *m* 2nd Janet, dau of Walter Ross of Inver-charron and widow of Thomas Ross of Priesthill, and *d* 3 March 1662, having by her had, with two daus:

> 2 Alexander; *s* his f in Scatwell; *m* Janet Ross (*d* March 1699), of Ulladale, and *dsp* 18 March 1680
>
> 3 **Sir Kenneth Mackenzie, 1st Bt** (NS), so *cr* 22 Feb 1702/3, of Scatwell; *s* his bro Alexander in Scatwell 1699; MP; *m* 1st his cousin Lilias (*d* 21 Oct 1703), dau and heiress of Sir Roderick Mackenzie of Findon, 3rd s of Kenneth Mackenzie of Kilcoy (*see* CROMARTIE, E), and *d* 1729, having had:
>
>> (1) George; *d* unm 1705
>>
>> (2) RODERICK (Sir), **2nd Bt**
>>
>> (3) Simon, of Scotsburn; *m* 1st Jean, dau of William Mackenzie of Bal-maduthy; *m* 2nd Vere, dau of Patrick Campbell of Edinchip, and had further issue; *d* 23 July 1761, leaving by his 1st w, with two daus:
>>
>>> 1a Roderick, of Scotsburn; *m* 1st — (*dsp*), dau of Mackenzie of Muirton; *m* 2nd Anne (*d* 1816), dau of Alexander Chisholm of Chisholm, and had, with a dau (Lilias, *m* 28 Oct 1825 James Walker of Dalry):
>>>
>>>> 1b Alexander, of Scotsburn; *m* 1812 Jane Henderson and *d* 1843, leaving:
>>>>
>>>>> 1c Charles Roderick; *m* 28 March 1846 Madeline, dau of Rev Sir Wil-liam Murray, 9th Bt of Dunerne (*qv*), and *dsp* 1893
>>
>> (1) Margaret; *m* 1st Eneas Macleod of Cadboll; *m* 2nd Roderick Mackenzie of Applecross
>>
>> (2) Isabel; *m* 1st Kenneth Bayne of Tulloch; *m* 2nd Roderick Chisholm of Chisholm
>>
>> (3) Elizabeth; *m* William Mackenzie of Belmaduthy
>>
>> (4) Margaret; *m* James Cuthbert, of Inverness, merchant
>
> 3 (cont.) **Sir Kenneth** *m* 2nd 1707 Christian (*dsp*), dau of Rev Roderick Macken-zie, of Avoch; *m* 3rd 1718 Abigail, dau of John Urquhart of Newhall, and by her had:
>
>> (4) Kenneth; HEICS
>>
>> (5) Jean; *m* Kenneth Mackenzie of Dundonnell
>>
>> (6) Anne; *m* 1750 Thomas Mackenzie of Ord

Sir KENNETH's 2nd son,

Sir Roderick Mackenzie, 2nd Bt; *m* 1710 Janet (*d* 10 Feb 1761), dau of Ludo-vick Grant, 1st of Grant and 8th of Feuchie (*see* STRATHSPEY, B), and 24 April 1750, having had:

> 1 LEWIS (Sir), **3rd Bt**
>
> 2 Alexander (Capt); *m* 1st Lilias, dau of Simon Mackenzie of Scotsburn, and had issue
>
> 1 Janet; *m* Sir Alexander Mackenzie, 2nd Bt, of Gairloch (*see* INGLIS, Bt), and had issue
>
> 2 Elizabeth; *m* Colin Mackenzie of Mountgerald
>
> 3 Margaret; *m* James Cuthbert of Milncraig

Sir RODERICK's er son,

Sir Lewis Mackenzie, 3rd Bt; *b* 1715; *m* 1739 Isabel (*d* 4 May 1786), dau of Colin Mackenzie of Mountgerald, and *d* 13 Sept 1756, having had, with other issue:

> 1 **Sir Roderick Mackenzie, 4th Bt**; *m* 7 April 1764 Catherine (*d* 11 March 1804), dau of Sir James Colquhoun, of Luss, 1st Bt (*qv*), and *d* 11 June 1811, leaving, with two daus:
>
>> (1) Lewis; Col Ross and Cromarty Rangers; *m* 22 Feb 1794 Grace, dau of Tho-mas Lockhart, and *dsvp* 1810
>>
>> (2) **Sir James Wemyss Mackenzie, 5th Bt**; Ld Lt and MP Ross-shire; *b* 19 Aug 1770; *m* 26 March 1810 Henrietta Wharton (*d* 14 Nov 1840), only surv dau of William Mackenzie of Suddy and sis and sole heiress of Maj-Gen John Ran-doll Mackenzie of Suddy (*ka* Battle of Talavera Aug 1809), and *d* 8 March 1843, leaving:
>>
>>> 1a **Sir James John Randoll Mackenzie, 6th Bt**, JP, DL Ross and Cromarty; *b* 20 June 1814; *m* 1st 10 Oct 1838 Lady Anne Wentworth Fitzwilliam (*d* 29 April 1879), dau of 5th Earl Fitzwilliam (*see* 1970 edn); *m* 2nd 5 Aug 1879 Mary Anne, dau of James McNeill, of Toxteth Park, Lancs, and *dsp* 28 Feb 1884
>
> 2 Colin; London merchant; *b* 13 April 1749; *m* Janet, dau of John Sprot, of Edin-burgh, and *d* 3 Feb 1814, leaving, with two other sons:
>
>> (1) Lewis; *b* 20 Aug 1788; Maj Scots Greys; *m* 16 Oct 1820 Nancy (*d* 22 Jan 1870), dau and heiress of Samuel Forester Bancroft, and *d* 30 May 1853, leav-ing, with other issue:
>>
>>> 1a **Sir James Dixon Mackenzie, 7th Bt**, JP, DL Ross-shire; *b* 22 April 1830; Maj 79th Highrs and 14th Foot; *m* 5 Oct 1858 Julia Stanley (*d* 18 Feb 1898), dau of Dr Samuel Clutsam, TCD, and *d* 24 June 1900, having had:
>>>
>>>> 1b **Sir (James) Kenneth Douglas Mackenzie, 8th Bt**; *b* 31 Aug 1859; Capt RAF; *m* 24 Nov 1888 Stephanie Corinne (*d* 6 Dec 1921), yst dau of Dr Jules Espinet, MD, of Trinidad, and *d* 5 Dec 1930, having had:
>>>>
>>>>> 1c **Sir Lewis Roderick Kenneth Mackenzie, 9th Bt**; *b* 8 Aug 1902; *educ* Oakham Sch; WW II in RAF; with Empire Cotton Growing Corp Rhode-sia; *d* unm 10 Dec 1972
>>>>>
>>>>> 1c Corinne Maud; *d* unm 20 Oct 1940
>>>>
>>>> 1b Alice Nancy; *d* unm 6 July 1917
>>>>
>>>> 2b Julia Marion; *d* unm 5 Jan 1881
>>>>
>>>> 3b Louise Augusta; *m* 12 Dec 1901 her cousin Baron Arild Rosenkrantz, yst s of Baron Iver Holger Rosenkrantz, of Denmark (*see* below), and *d* 9 May 1944
>>>>
>>>> 4b Lillian Geraldine; *d* unm 25 Dec 1935
>>>>
>>>> 5b Evelyn; *d* unm 9 Oct 1957
>>>
>>> 1a Nancy Copley; *m* 17 June 1854 Thomas Anthony Lister, of Gargrave (*d* 1873), and *d* 11 Jan 1905, leaving issue
>>>
>>> 2a Julia Louisa; *m* 22 Dec 1864 Baron Iver Holger Rosenkrantz (*d* 1873) and *d* 10 April 1911, leaving issue (*see* above)
>
> 3 George; *b* 6 April 1748; Col 72nd Regt; *m* 20 Feb 1775 Joan (*d* 20 Oct 1825), dau of John Campbell of Wellwood, Ayrshire, and *d* 9 April 1840, having had, with other issue:

(1) Lewis; b 1778; Offr 72nd Regt; m 6 April 1801 Jane (d 1843), dau of William Logan, and d 26 May 1807, leaving:

  1a Margaret; m 1836 Rev Stair McQuhae, DD (d 8 March 1872), and d 1840

(2) John; b 3 Sept 1779; Dep Commissary Gen 5th Regt; m 11 April 1814 Marie Barbier Deshayeux (d 24 May 1852) and d 14 Nov 1824, leaving:

  1a George Salvador; HEICS; drowned 1844

  2a John Francis Campbell; b 3 Aug 1820; Adml; m 6 Aug 1850 Annabella Fullerton (d 9 May 1906), dau of Rev Dr John Stirling, and d 1892, leaving:

    1b John Campbell; b 12 Jan 1852; Lt RN; d unm 26 Nov 1875

    2b Edmund Lyons; b 25 Jan 1858; m 18 July 1888 Julia (d 25 Jan 1937), only dau of Peyton Skipwith Coles, of Estouteville, Va., and d 19 Sept 1945, leaving:

      1c Kenneth Roderick; b 2 Aug 1891; m 18 Feb 1954 *Elizabeth Carrington, dau of William Barbee Settle, lawyer, of Boston, USA, and d 27 Nov 1960, leaving:

        1d **Sir Roderick Campbell Mackenzie, 10th Bt**; b 15 Nov 1954; d unm 1981

      1c Julia Mary Louise; b 24 Oct 1889; m 4 Dec 1919 Frederick Brewer de Hamel Krom, s of Louis J Krom, and had issue

      2c Grace Stuart; b 14 April 1897; d 29 Jan 1903

    3b Frank; b 11 Dec 1859; dsp 4 Feb 1911

    4b Kenneth Lester; b 7 Oct 1862; m 1892 Grace Stuart (d 13 March 1902), dau of Peter Hall, and dsp 27 May 1899

    1b Annie; m 4 Sept 1878 Rev Edward Moore, DD, Pncpl St Edmund Hall, Oxford, Canon Residentiary Canterbury, and d 1906, leaving issue

    2b Louise; m 10 Aug 1899 Rev Charles Dennis Mason-Cox (d 1935), of Château Pont Pillet, Lehon, France, Vicar St Peter's, Stockport, and d 1944, leaving issue

    3b Laura Maynard; m 1896 William Reginald Karslake (d 1911), of Herefs, and d 1950, leaving issue

  3a François; b 16 Sept 1823; Maj Bengal LI; m 4 April 1854 Julia (d Dec 1884), dau of John Mercer, of Maidstone, and d 18 March 1893, leaving:

    1b George Frederic Campbell, CB; b 22 Oct 1855; Col Suffolk Regt; m 31 Dec 1885 Emily Mary (d 12 Jan 1953), dau of Capt Joseph Boulton, 14th Hus, and d 6 Feb 1909, leaving:

      1c Geraldine; m 15 May 1918 Marcel Pierre Léonce Potez (d 1 Nov 1921), s of Auguste Joseph Jérome Potez, of Saint-Ouen, France, and d 9 Aug 1923, leaving issue

      2c Olive; m 1st 28 April 1908 (divorce 1925) Rev Henry Tregarthen Percy Smith, Govt Chaplain Lucknow, est s of Maj-Gen Percy Smith, RE, and had issue; m 2nd 25 Oct 1925 Leslie Frederick Jackson (d 17 April 1944), Indian State Rlwys, s of Isaac Jackson, of Delhi, and d 6 July 1964

      3c Norah, MBE (1945); WVS

    2b François Donald, KGStJ; b 16 Sept 1860; m 12 May 1904 Edith (d 25 Oct 1957), dau of Rev Duncan Campbell Mackenzie of Glack, Aberdeenshire, and dsp 26 Jan 1910

    3b John Roderick Kenneth; b 29 April 1869; educ Wellington; civ serv BC, Canada, Assist Commr Min Food, Hon Sec Surrey Assoc Empire Settlement; m 27 May 1893 Kathleen Elizabeth, dau of Capt Thomas Howard Blennerhasset Coulson, RIM, and d 26 May 1958, leaving:

      1c RODERICK EDWARD FRANÇOIS McQUHAE (Sir), **11th Bt**

      1c Iris Louisa Ida; b 17 Jan 1897

      2c Phyllis Marion; b 7 Aug 1899; m 29 June 1922 Capt James Millar Begg, RN (d 22 Feb 1954), and had:

        1d Kathleen Mary Iris; b 19 April 1923; m 26 July 1947 Brig Henry Lionel Broome Salmon, s of Capt Lionel Mordaunt Broome Salmon, Welch Regt, of Apperley, Glos, and had:

          1e *Marion Jane Broome [Mrs Thomas Sowler, Unthank Hall, Haltwhistle, Northumberland NE49 0HX]; b 11 Jan 1949; m 1974 *Thomas Richard Holland Sowler, TD, FTII, slr, and has:

            1f *Thomas Henry James Holland; b 1982

            2f *Richard Mordaunt George Holland; b 1989

            1f *Phyllis Elisabeth May Holland; b 1977

          2e *Anthea Maud Broome [Mrs John Streeter, The Dower House, Sizewell, nr Leiston, Suffolk]; b 18 Oct 1953; m 1991 *John Alexander Streeter

    1b Julie Louise Clara; d unm March 1946

    2b Lilias Fynuola; d unm Aug 1946

  1a Lilias; d unm

  2a Louisa Georgina; m 1843, as his 2nd w, Rev Stair McQuhae, DD (d 8 March 1872), and had issue

The 10th Bt's cousin,

Sir Roderick Edward François McQuhae Mackenzie, 11th Bt, CBE (1945), DSC (1916); b 11 Dec 1894; educ RNCs Osborne and Dartmouth; Capt RN, WW I (despatches), WW II (despatches, US Medal Freedom with silver clasp); m 3 Dec 1938 Marie Evelyn Campbell (d 1993), only child of William Ernest Parkinson, of Farnham, Surrey, and d 1986, having had:

1 Sir RODERICK McQUHAE MACKENZIE, **12th and present Bt**

1 *Marie Isobel Campbell [Mrs Richard Allerton, Bicton Mill, Bicton, Liskeard, Cornwall]; b 17 Oct 1939; m 14 March 1964 *AVM Richard C A Allerton, CB, RAF, and has:

  (1) *James Roderick Orde; b 1967

  (2) *Christopher Edward Orde; b 5 May 1970

2 *Fiona Louise [Mrs Timothy Havers, Corner House, 153 Dalling Rd, London W6 0ER]; b 24 Nov 1943; m 22 Nov 1969 *Lt-Cdr Timothy Patrick Havers, RN, and has:

  (1) *(James) Angus; b 1978

  (1) *Louisanna Marie; b 7 June 1973

  (2) *Laetitia Anastasia Sophie; b 1982

MACKENZIE-STUART

Creation: B. (LP, UK) 1988.

THE BARON MACKENZIE-STUART, of Dean in the District of the City of Edinburgh (Alexander John Mackenzie Stuart) [The Rt Hon The Lord Mackenzie-Stuart, 7 Randolph Cliff, Edinburgh EH3 7TZ; Le Garidel, Gravieres, 07140 Les Vans, Ardèche, France]; b 18 Nov 1924; educ Fettes (Govr 1962–72), Sidney Sussex Coll Cambridge (BA 1949, Hon Fell 1977) and Edinburgh U (LLB 1951); served RE 1942–47, T/Capt 1946; advocate 1951, QC (S) 1963; Keeper Advocates Library 1970–72; Standing Jr Counsel: Scottish Home Dept 1956–57, Inland Revenue Scotland 1957–63; Sheriff Pncpl Aberdeen, Kincardine and Banff 1971–72; Ld of Session 1972; Pres: Court Justice ECs 1984–88 (Judge 1972–84), Br Acad Experts 1989–92, European Movement Scotland 1991; Hon Prof Coll d'Europe Bruges 1974–77; Hon Bencher Middle Temple 1978 and King's Inn Dublin 1983; Prix Bech 1989; Hon DU Stirling 1973; Hon LLD: Exeter 1978, Edinburgh 1978, Glasgow 1981, Aberdeen 1983, Cambridge 1987, Birmingham 1988; Hon memb SPTL 1982; Grand Cross Crown of Oak Luxembourg 1988; author: Hamlyn Lectures: The European Communities and the Rule of Law (1977), A French King at Holyrood (1995); m 1952 *Anne Burtholme, dau of John Sidney Lawrence Millar, WS, of Edinburgh, and has:

1 *Amanda Jane [The Hon Mrs Hay, 8 Swan St, Osney, Oxon]; b 1954; m 1977 *Michael George Hay, s of George Ronald Hay, and has:

  (1) *Daisy Elizabeth; b 1981

  (2) *Marianna Clare; b 1985

2 *Katherine Anne [The Hon Katherine Mackenzie-Stuart; 99a Grosvenor Ave, London N1]; b 1956

3 *Laura Margaret [The Hon Mrs Borkowy, 85 Riverview Gdns, London W6]; b 1961; m 15 Feb 1997 *Tomek Borkowy, s of Dr Borkowy, of Warsaw

4 *Judith Mary; b 1964; m 1989 *Nicholas David Aspinall, er s of Dr Dennis L Aspinall

Lineage: ALEXANDER MACKENZIE STUART, KC, of Aberdeen; Prof; m Amy Margaret Dean and had:

ALEXANDER JOHN, cr a **Baron**

MACKESON

Arms: Vair, four roses, three and one, or. **Crest:** A lion's gamb erased or, supporting an escutcheon gules charged with a rose or.
Motto: Inest sua gratia parvis ('His grace is inherent in little things').
Creation: Bt. (UK) 29 Jan 1954.

SIR RUPERT HENRY MACKESON 2ND BT, of Hythe, Co Kent; b 16 Nov 1941; s f 1964; educ Harrow and Trin Coll Dublin (BA 1964, MA 1967); 2nd Lt The Buffs (TA) 1961, Lt 1963, 2nd Lt Roy Horse Gds 1964, Lt 1965, Capt 1967, ret 1968, author as Rupert Collens: 'Snaffles' on Racing and Point-to-Pointing (1988), 'Snaffles' on Hunting (co-author, 1989), Look at Cecil Aldin's Dogs and Hounds (1990), 25 Legal Luminaries from Vanity Fair (1990) and Cecil Aldin's Dog Models (1994); m 22 July 1968 (divorce 1972) Hon Camilla Margaret Keith, dau of Baron Keith of Castleacre (LP, qv)

Lineage: HENRY BEAN MACKESON, JP, of Hythe, Kent; had, with a dau (Mildred Adair, m Col H W Murray and d 17 Oct 1964, leaving issue):

HENRY MACKESON, JP, of Littlebourne House, Littlebourne, Kent; b 4 March 1865; educ Uppingham; m 25 Jan 1895 Ella Cecil (d 8 April 1933), dau of John Anthony Ripley, and d 15 May 1935, leaving:

1 HARRY RIPLEY (Sir), **1st Bt**

2 Graham Lawrie MACKESON later MACKESON-SANDBACH; b 24 Jan 1907; educ Rugby; Capt Irish Gds, Capt Gen Staff WW II 1939–43, QALAS; m 5 Oct 1932 *Geraldine Pamela Violet, JP (1942), only child of Maj-Gen Arthur Edmund Sandbach, CB, DSO, JP, of Hafodunos, Denbighs, and Bryn Gwyn,

Bwlch-y-Cibau, by Hon Ina Douglas-Pennant, OBE, 5th dau of 2nd Baron Pen-ryhn (*qv*), and *d* 1984, leaving:

(1) +Ian Lawrie [Ian Mackeson-Sandbach Esq, 20 Hanover Terrace, London NW1 4RJ]; *b* 14 June 1933; *educ* Eton and New Brunswick U Canada; Lt Welsh Gds 1951–53, md France Fenwick Ltd 1969–75, ch exec Ernest Not-cutt Gp 1976–82, Crown Estate Paving Cmmn 1972 (chm 1983–); *m* 6 May 1967 *Annie Marie Antoinette Eugenie, dau of Jan van Lanschot, of The Netherlands, and has:

  1a *Antoinette Geraldine; *b* 15 Feb 1969

  2a *Sara Emilie; *b* 29 Aug 1970; *m* 6 June 1997 *Fabio Fabrizio

  3a *Louise Catherina; *b* 15 Nov 1973

  4a *Megan Annie; *b* 26 July 1976

(1) *Rosemary Daphne (twin); *b* 14 June 1933

(2) *Auriol Veronica; *b* 27 May 1943; *m* 9 Nov 1970 (*divorce* 1994), as his 2nd w, Sir John Ropner, 2nd Bt (*see* ROPNER, Bt, of Thorp Perrow), and has issue; *m* 2nd 1 Nov 1997 *4th Marquess of Linlithgow (*qv*)

HENRY MACKESON's er s,

Sir Harry Ripley Mackeson, 1st Bt (UK), so *cr* 25 Jan 1964; *b* 5 May 1905; *educ* Rugby and RMC Sandhurst; RS: 2nd Lt 1925, Adj 1932–35, psc 1937, Bde Maj Egypt 1938–40, GSO 1940–42, BGS HQ RAC 1942, Bde Cdr NW Europe 1943–44, ret as Brig 1946; MP (C) Hythe 1945–50 and Folkestone 1950–59, Whip 1947, Dep Ch Whip 1950–52, Sr Ld Commr Treasury 1951–52, Sec Overseas Tde BOT 1952–53; *m* 22 Feb 1940 Alethea Cecil, only dau of Lt-Cdr Reginald George Chetwynd-Talbot, CBE (*see* SHREWSBURY and WATERFORD, E), and *d* 25 Jan 1964, leaving:

1 Sir RUPERT HENRY MACKESON, **2nd and present Bt**

1 *Fiona Mariella [Mrs Hamish Gray-Cheape, Hill House, Walcot, Warwicks BB49 6LZ]; *b* 5 May 1946; *m* 6 Oct 1965 *Capt Hamish Leslie Gray-Cheape, JP, DL (Warwicks 1990), Gren Gds, High Sheriff Warwicks 1984, est s of Lt-Col Leslie George Gray-Cheape, JP, of Carse Gray, Forfar, Angus, and has:

  (1) *Hugo James; *b* 21 Nov 1968; *educ* Eton

  (2) *George Hamish; *b* 16 Aug 1971

MACKIE OF BENSHIE

Creation: B. (LP, UK) 1974.

THE BARON MACKIE OF BENSHIE, of Kirriemuir, Co Angus (George Yull Mackie, CBE (1971), DSO (1944), DFC (1944)) [The Rt Hon The Lord Mackie of Benshie CBE DSO DFC, Benshie Cottage, Oathlaw, by Forfar, Angus DD8 3PQ]; *b* 10 July 1919; *educ* Aberdeen GS and Aberdeen U; WW II: RAF Bomber Command, Air Staff 1944; farmer Kirriemuir 1945–89; MP (Lib) Caithness and Sutherland 1964–66, Pres Scottish Lib Party 1983–88 (V-Chm 1960–65, Chm 1965–70); Memb: Ho Lds EEC Scrutiny Ctee (D), Inter-Parly Union Exec, Govrs GB-East Europe Centre, Scottish Advsy Ctee Br Cncl, Cncl of Europe 1986–97, WEU 1986–; Ho Lds Lib Spokesman: Devolution, Ag, Scotland, Industry; chm: Caithness Glass Ltd, Cotswold Wine Co 1983–85; Rector Dundee U 1981–83; Dir Scottish Ballet 1986–88; author: *Policy for Scottish Agriculture* (1963), Hon LLD Dundee; *m* 1st 1944 Lindsay Lyall (*d* 1985), dau of Alexander Sharp, advocate, by Isobelle Sharp, OBE, of Aberdeen, and has had, with a s (*d* young):

1 *Lindsay Mary; *b* 1945; *m* 1982 *Alan Rusbridger, ed *The Guardian*, and has two daus

2 *Diana Lyall [The Hon Mrs Hope, 3 St Bernard Cres, Edinburgh]; *b* 1946; *m* 1968 *John Carlyle Hope and has issue

3 *Jeannie Felicia; *b* 1953; *m* 1982 *David Leigh and has issue

BARON MACKIE OF BENSHIE *m* 2nd 1988 *Jacqueline, dau of Col Marcel Rauch, French Air Force, and widow of Andrew Lane

Lineage: MAITLAND MACKIE, OBE; Dr; *m* Mary Yull and had, with an er dau:

1 JOHN MACKIE later JOHN-MACKIE, BARON JOHN-MACKIE, of Nazeing in the County of Essex (LP, UK), so *cr* 1981; *b* 24 Nov 1909; *educ* Aberdeen GS and N of Scotland Coll of Ag (Govr 1942–64, V-Chm 1956–64); md Mackie family agricultural co Waltham Abbey, Essex, 1953–94; MP (Lab) Enfield E 1959–Feb 1974, Jt Parly Sec MAFF 1964–70, Oppn Spokesman Ho Lds on ag, fisheries, food and forestry 1983–88; chm Glentworth Scottish Farms Ltd 1947–68 and Forestry Commn 1976–79; *m* 1934 *Jeannie Inglis Milne and *d* 25 May 1994, leaving three sons and two daus

2 Maitland (Sir), CBE (1965), JP (Aberdeen 1956); *b* 16 Feb 1912; *educ* Aberdeen GS and Aberdeen U; farmer; CC Aberdeenshire 1951–75 (Convener 1967–75), Chm: NE Devpt Authority 1969–75, Jt Advsy Ctee Scottish Farm Bldgs Investigation Unit 1963–96, Aberdeen Milk Mktg Bd 1965–82, Peterhead Bay Management Co 1975–86, Oil Policy Ctee of Scottish Cncl Devpt and Industry 1975–96; dir: Scottish Telecom 1969–85, Aberdeen Petroleum 1980–96; Burgess Guild Aberdeen 1978, Ld Lt Aberdeenshire 1975–87, KstJ 1977, Hon LLD Aberdeen 1977; author: *A Lucky Chap* (1993); *m* 1st 1935 Isobel Ross (*d* 1960), *m* 2nd 1963 Martha Pauline Turner (*d* 1993) and *d* 18 June 1996, leaving by his 1st w two sons and four daus

3 GEORGE YULL, *cr* a **Baron**

1 *Catherine Hay [Mrs Ian Aitken, 52a North Hill, London N6 4RH]; Dr; *m* 1956 *Ian Levack Aitken, political ed *The Guardian* 1975–90, s of George Aitken, and has two daus

MACKINTOSH OF HALIFAX

Arms: Or on a chevron between two lions rampant in chief and a lymphad in base sable a bezant charged with a representation of the head of St John the Baptist proper between two hearts of the field. **Crest:** Upon a rock proper charged with two roses argent, barbed and seeded, a cat sejant also proper. **Supporters:** On either side a squirrel proper, about the neck a cord and pendant therefrom a purse, both or. **Motto:** By faith and work. **Creations:** Bt. (UK) 28 Jan 1935, B. (UK) 6 Feb 1948, V. (UK) 10 July 1957.

THE 3RD VISCOUNT MACKINTOSH OF HALIFAX, of Hethersett, Co Norfolk, **Baron Mackintosh of Halifax**, of Hethersett, Co Norfolk, and a **Baronet** (Sir John Clive Mackintosh, Bt) [The Rt Hon The Viscount Mackintosh of Halifax, House of Lords, London SW1A 0PW]; *b* 9 Sept 1958; *s f* 1980; *educ* The Leys Sch (Cambridge) and Oriel Coll Oxford; FCA, ptnr Price Waterhouse; *m* 1st 1982 (*divorce* 1993) Elizabeth, only dau of D G Lakin and Mrs F E G Melener, of Esher, and has:

1 +THOMAS HAROLD GEORGE; *b* 8 Feb 1985

2 +George John Frank; *b* 24 Oct 1988

The 3rd VISCOUNT *m* 2nd 12 June 1995 *Claire Jane, yst dau of Stanislaw Nowak and formerly w of Charles Wishart

Lineage: WILLIAM McINTOSH, at Spittal and later at Bridge of Don, Old Machar, Aberdeenshire; *m* Jean Gibson and had, with other issue:

WILLIAM MacKINTOSH, of Hyde, Cheshire, and later Ashton-under-Lyne, Lancs; *b* April 1809; *m* Isabella Trinkle and had, with other issue:

JOSEPH MacKINTOSH, of Hyde; *b* 19 July 1840; *m* July 1865 Mary Jane (*d* 23 Dec 1912), dau of Henry Burgess, and *d* 30 April 1891, leaving:

JOHN MACKINTOSH, JP, of Greystones, Halifax, Yorks; *b* 7 July 1868; *m* 29 Sept 1890 Violet, dau of James Taylor, of Clover Hill, Halifax, and *d* 27 Jan 1920, leaving:

Sir Harold Vincent Mackintosh, 1st Bt, so *cr* 28 Jan 1935, and **1st Viscount Mackintosh of Halifax**, of Hethersett, Co Norfolk, so *cr* 10 July 1957, as also earlier 6 Feb 1948 BARON MACKINTOSH OF HALIFAX, of Hethersett, Co Norfolk (all UK), JP, DL (WR Yorks); *b* 8 June 1891; *educ* New Sch Halifax and abroad; Lt RNVR WW I, ktd 1922, pres: World Cncl Christian Educn and Sunday Sch Assoc 1928–58 (chm 1558–64, hon treasurer Br Ctee), Nat Sunday Sch Union, Advertising Assoc 1942–46, Nat Advertising Benevolent Soc 1946 and 1947, Internat Advertising Convention 1951, Yorks Ag Soc, Roy Norfolk Ag Assoc 1960, v-pres TSB Assoc and Nat Cncl YMCA, chm: Nat Savings Ctee 1943–64 (also pres 1958–64), John Mackintosh & Sons, Promotion Ctee UEA, Central Bd Finance Methodist Church and Yorks Cncl Br Empire Cancer Campaign (memb Grand Cncl), dir Martins Bank and RHM, tstee E Anglia Savings Bank and York Co Savings Bank, Chllr UEA, Hon LLD Leeds U, memb Arts Cncl, Hon Freeman Halifax CC 1954, jt hon treasurer: Home Missionary Ctee Methodist Church and Ashville Coll Harrogate, author: *Early English Figure Pottery*; *m* 8 June 1916 Constance Emily (*d* 11 Dec 1975), 2nd dau of Edgar Cooper Stoneham, OBE, and *d* 27 Dec 1964, leaving:

1 JOHN, **2nd Viscount**

1 *Mary, JP (Norfolk) [The Hon Mrs Watt JP, Wychwood House, Hethersett, Norfolk NR9 3AT]; *b* 18 April 1927; chm Norwich Juvenile Court 1978–82; *m* 17 June 1949 *(Charles) Michael Watt, only s of Charles Skinner Watt, of Norwich, and has:

  (1) *Charles Jonathan [Charles Watt Esq, Narborough House, Stoke Holy Cross, Norfolk NR14 8RF]; *b* 20 Aug 1950; *educ* Millfield and Boston U; *m* 1974 *Catherine Anna Lilley and has:

    1a *Henry Charles William; *b* 1980

    2a *Edward Alastair Donald; *b* 1984

    1a *Elizabeth Anna; *b* 1977

  (2) *Henry Donald; *b* 17 April 1962; *m* 1992 *Tania Elizabeth, only dau of Charles Ian Strafford, of Chelmsford, Essex, and has:

    1a *Natasha Constance Frances; *b* 1994

(1) *Susan Mary [Mrs Alexander Shenkman, 41 Kensington Place, London W8]; b 26 Sept 1952; m 1980 *Ivan Alexander Shenkman and has:

1a *Maximilian Ivan Michael; b 1982

2a *Alexander Ivan Marcus; b 1988

1a *Melissa Alexandra Mary; b 1984

The 1st VISCOUNT's s,

JOHN MACKINTOSH, **2nd Viscount Mackintosh of Halifax**, OBE (1976), BEM (1946); b 8 Oct 1921; educ Bedales and Trin Coll Hertford (Conn, USA); served RAOC WW II 1942–47, chm: Norwich Savings Ctee 1965–75, The 54 Gp Norwich and Norwich Ctee IOD 1968–78, v-chm E Regn Industrial Savings Ctee, dir: John Mackintosh and Sons, A J Caley, Thickthorn Farm Ltd 1955–80, Tom Smith & Co 1956–76, Mead and Field Ltd and Tudor Auto Servs 1961–72, hon treasurer Methodist Youth Guest Ho Mundesley 1947–64, pres: Confectioners' Benevolent Fund 1959–60, Norwich Wanderers Cricket Club 1964–65, Leeds Branch Inst Mktg 1966–68; m 1st 6 Dec 1946 (divorce 1956) Bronda, only dau of Louis John Fibiger, of South Shields, Co Durham, and had:

1 *Diana Mary [The Hon Diana Mackintosh, Homewood, Water Lane, Storrington, W Sussex RH20 3LY]; b 14 Sept 1947

2 *Elizabeth Constance [The Rt Hon The Lady Astor of Hever, Frenchstreet House, Westerham, Kent TN16 1PW]; b 4 May 1950; m 1st 29 April 1972 Timothy Cutting; m 2nd 1980 (divorce 19–) Nicolas Chagrin, actor, and has:

(1) *Natalya Isabel; b 1981; educ Benenden

2 (cont.) The Hon Mrs Elizabeth Chagrin m 3rd 5 May 1990, as his 2nd w, *3rd Baron Astor of Hever (qv) and has issue by him

The **2nd Viscount** m 2nd 30 Aug 1956 *Gwynneth Charlesworth [The Rt Hon Gwynneth Viscountess Mackintosh of Halifax, The Old Hall, Barford, Norwich NR9 4AY], dau of Charles Henry Gledhill, of Halifax, and d 2 Nov 1980, leaving by her:

1 JOHN CLIVE MACKINTOSH, **3rd and present Viscount Mackintosh of Halifax**

2 +Graham Charles; b 12 March 1964; educ The Leys Sch, Newcastle U (BSc) and Coll of Estate Management Reading; surveyor; m March 1994 *Anjella Fisher

MACKWORTH

Arms: Per pale indented sable and ermine on a chevron gules five crosses-patée or. **Crest:** A cock proper. **Motto:** Gwell angau na cywlydd ('Death before dishonour'). **Creation:** Bt. (GB) 16 Sept 1776.

SIR DIGBY JOHN MACKWORTH, 10TH BT, of the Gnoll, Glamorgan [Sir Digby Mackworth Bt, Blagrove Cottage, Fox Lane, Boars Hill, Oxford OX1 5DS]; b 2 Nov 1945; s f 1998; educ Wellington; Lt AAAC (helicopter pilot) 28 Cwlth Inf Bde Malaysia and Singapore 1968–70, 161 Flight Vietnam 1970–71; with Iranian Helicopters (Bristow) 1972–76, BA Helicopters N Sea 1977–89, pilot with BA Heathrow 1989–; m 26 Aug 1971 *Antoinette Francesca, dau of Henry James McKenna, and has:

1 *Octavia; b 1977

Lineage: This family's origins are connected with Mackworth, Derbys. The manor of Ash or Eisse, Derbys, seems to have been held by a family called Mackworth in 1385.

JOHN MACKWORTH; Preb Empingham, Rutland, 1404, Dean Lincoln 1422; d 1451; his yr bro:

THOMAS MACKWORTH; living c 1434; settled at Normanton Hall, Mackworth; m Alice, dau of Sir John de Basings or Basynges, feudal Ld of Empingham, and d c 1446, leaving:

HENRY MACKWORTH, of Mackworth and Empingham; living c 1482; had:

1 John, of Mackworth and Empingham; d by c 1489; had:

(1) George; Sheriff Rutland c 1497, 1523, 1531 and 1535; m Anne, dau of Geoffrey Sherard, of Stapleford, and d 1536, leaving:

1a Francis, of Normanton; Sheriff Rutland c 1539, 1544 and 1556; m Ellen, dau of Humphrey Hercy, of Grove, Notts, by Elizabeth, dau of Sir John Digby, of Ketterley, and d 1557, leaving:

1b George; thrice Sheriff Rutland temp ELIZABETH I; m 1st Grace, dau of Ralph Rokeby; m 2nd Anne, dau of Edmund Hall, of Gretford, and by his 1st w had:

1c Sir THOMAS MACKWORTH, 1st Bt (E), so cr 4 June 1619; Serjeant at Law, Sheriff Rutland 1598/9, 1599–1600 and 1609–10; m Margaret, dau of Henry Hall, of Gretford, Lincs, and d March 1625/6, leaving:

1d Sir HENRY MACKWORTH, 2nd Bt; Sheriff Rutland 1627–28; m Mary, dau of Robert Hopton, of Witham, Somerset, sis and coheir of 1st and last Baron Hopton of Stratton (the Cavalier General Sir Ralph Hopton) and widow of Sir Thomas Hartopp, and d Aug 1640, leaving:

1e Sir THOMAS MACKWORTH, 3rd Bt; fined as a royalist March 1647/8, Sheriff Rutland 1666–67, MP Rutland 1679–94; m 1st Dorothy (dspm), dau of Capt George Darell, of Calehill, Kent, and had:

1f Dorothy; had issue

1e (cont.) Sir THOMAS m 2nd his distant cousin Anne, dau of Humphrey Mackworth, of Betton, Salop (see below), and d Nov 1694, leaving by her an only surv s:

1f Sir THOMAS MACKWORTH, 4th Bt; MP: Rutland 1694–95, 1701–08 and 1721–27 and Portsmouth 1713–15, Sheriff Rutland 1696–97; d unm Feb 1744/5

2e Robert; b c 1623; d 1 Feb 1717/8, leaving, with an er s:

1f Robert, of Huntingdon; m Mary, dau of William Dowse, merchant, of Huntingdon, and had an only s:

1g Sir THOMAS MACKWORTH, 5th Bt; apothecary in Huntingdon, Alderman Huntingdon; m 1st c 1737 Elizabeth (dspm), dau of John Maule, of Ecton, Northants; m 2nd Mary, dau of Rev Leonard Reresby, of Thribergh, Yorks, and widow of Rev — Waller, and dspm 17 Oct 1769

3e Henry; m Dorothy Hall, of Gretford, and had:

1f Henry; m Katharine Roberts, of Empingham, and had:

1g Sir HENRY MACKWORTH, 6th Bt; m Elizabeth, dau of Rev Edward Lamb, Rector Acle, Norfolk, and d 14 Jan 1774, leaving:

1h Sir HENRY MACKWORTH, 7th and last Bt; b c 1728; almsman Charter House, London, 1786–1803; dsp 1 Aug 1803, when the btcy expired

2 Thomas; Groom Privy Chamber to HENRY VII; held Meole Brace, Salop, c 1507; m Agnes — and had:

(1) Arthur, of Meole Brace; m — Barker and had, with three daus:

1a Thomas; disinherited by his f; ancestor of John Mackworth, of Shrewsbury

2a William; mortgaged his f's property of Meole Brace and left issue

3a Richard; had issue

(2) JOHN

3 William; London clothworker; m Agnes, sis of Robert Meredith, and d between 5 June and 25 July 1534, leaving a dau

4 Robert

THOMAS MACKWORTH's 2nd s,

JOHN MACKWORTH; m Elizabeth, dau of Thomas Hosier, of Shrewsbury, and had, with two daus:

THOMAS MACKWORTH, of Betton Grange, Meole Brace; m c 25 July 1566 Dorothy, dau of Richard Lee, of Langley, Salop, and d on or after 10 Jan 1585/6, leaving, with another s and four daus:

RICHARD MACKWORTH, of Betton Grange; m Dorothy (m 2nd Adam Ottley; m 3rd John Gorton), dau of Lawrence Cranage, gentleman, of Keele, Staffs, and had:

HUMPHREY MACKWORTH, of Betton Grange; Col Parly army at taking of Ludlow Castle May 1646, Govr Shrewsbury June 1646, memb CROMWELL's Cncl, MP Salop CROMWELL's 2nd Parl; m 1st c 28 May 1624 Anne, dau of Thomas Waller, of Beaconsfield, Bucks, and a relation of the poet Edmund Waller, and had:

1 THOMAS

2 Humphrey; Town Clerk and MP Shrewsbury, Col Parly army, Govr Shrewsbury after his f's death

1 Dorothy; m Thomas Baldwin, s and heir of Edward Baldwin, of Diddlebury, Salop

2 Anne; m as his 2nd w her distant cousin Sir THOMAS MACKWORTH, 3rd Bt, of Normanton (see above)

HUMPHREY MACKWORTH m 2nd c 12 July 1638 Mary, dau of Thomas Venables, so-called Baron (territorial rather than parly but by long usage) of Kinderton, Co Palatine of Chester, and was bur 26 Dec 1654, having had:

3 Peter; d an infant

3 Mary; d 22 Oct 1663

HUMPHREY MACKWORTH's est s,

THOMAS MACKWORTH, of Betton Grange; aged 35 on 24 Aug 1663, MP Salop; m 1652 Anne, dau and heiress of Richard Bulkeley, of Buntingsdale, Salop, and had, with a dau:

1 Bulkeley, of Buntingsdale; b 1653; d unm 18 Feb 1730/1

2 Humphrey (Sir); b Jan 1657; educ Magdalen Coll Oxford; barrister Middle Temple 1682, ktd 15 Jan 1682/3, MP Cards 1700–01, 1702–05 and 1710–13 and Totnes 1705–07, Constable Neath Castle 1703, pamphleteer and religious polemicist; m 1686 Mary (d by 1705), dau and ultimately by the death of her four sisters sole heir of Sir Herbert Evans, of Gnoll, Glamorgan, by his w Anne, dau and heir of William Morgan, of Pencrûg House, Llanhenog, Mon; by this marriage Sir Humphrey acquired large estates in Glamorgan and Monmouthshire, which in addition he developed assiduously as to mineral deposits, though not without opposition locally and in Parl; d 25 Aug 1727, having had:

(1) HERBERT

(2) Kingsmill Evans; b 2 Oct 1688; had issue

(3) William MACKWORTH later MACKWORTH-PRAED (added on his friend John Praed's deeding him his (John's) estates 19 Jan 1715 in gratitude

for given by the MACKWORTHs); *b* 3 Nov 1694; MP St Ives,; *m* 1715 Anne, only dau of Robert Slaney, of Rudge, Salop, and *d* 1752, having had issue

Sir HUMPHREY MACKWORTH's est s,

HERBERT MACKWORTH, of Neath; *b* 7 Sept 1687; MP Neath 1739–65; *m* 29 April 1730 Hon Juliana Digby (*d* 9 Aug 1785), dau of 5th Baron Digby (*qv*), and *d* 20 Aug 1765, leaving, with three other daus (*d* unm):

1 HERBERT (Sir), **1st Bt**

1 Frances; *b* 28 Aug 1731; *m* 1st 25 June 1757 5th Lord Falconer of Halkertoun (*see* KINTORE, E); *m* 2nd 22 July 1765 7th Viscount Montagu (*d* 9 April 1787) and *d* 3 March 1814, having had issue

2 Catherine; *b* 24 Oct 1735; *m* 1769 Rev James Stillingfleet, Preb Worcester, and had issue

3 Susanna; *b* 25 July 1738; *m* Sir John Hotham, 9th Bt (*qv*), Bp Clogher, and had issue

HERBERT MACKWORTH's s,

Sir Herbert Mackworth, 1st Bt (GB), so *cr* 16 Sept 1776, of Gnoll Castle, Glamorgan; *b* 1 Jan 1736/7; *educ* Magdalen Coll Oxford (BA 1757, MA 1760); barrister Lincoln's Inn 1759, MP Cardiff 1766–90, Col Glamorgan Militia, v-pres Marine Soc, FRS; *m* 1759 Eliza (*b* 24 Jan 1738; *d* 19 Dec 1799), dau of Robert Cotton Trefusis (*see* CLINTON, B), and *d* 25 Oct 1791 of blood poisoning following failure to pull out a thorn, leaving:

1 **Sir Robert Humphrey Mackworth, 2nd Bt**, of Gnoll Castle; *b* 16 Nov 1764; *m* 6 Dec 1792 Mary or Molly Anne (*d* 27 June 1846), dau of Nathaniel Miers or Myers, of Neath, Glamorgan, and Richmond, Surrey, and *dsp* 13 Sept 1795, leaving Gnoll Castle and other estates to his widow, who *m* 2nd 14 Sept 1797, as his 1st w, Capel Hanbury-Leigh, of Pontypool Park, Ld Lt Mon, er bro of 1st Baron Sudeley (*qv*)

2 DIGBY (Sir), **3rd Bt**

1 Elizabeth Anne; *m* 1795 Francis Drake

The 2nd Bt's bro,

Sir Digby Mackworth, 3rd Bt, of Glen Usk, Mon; *b* 14 May 1766; *educ* Magdalen Coll Oxford (DCL 1799); Lt-Col Oxford City Loyal Vols 1798 and 1803–04; *m* 1st 1788 Jane (*d* 11 Jan 1808), only dau and heir of Rev Matthew Deere by his w Margaret, dau and coheir of Anthony Maddocks, of Cefn-yd-fa, Glam; *m* 2nd 10 July 1821 Philippa (*dsp* 18 July 1851), sis of Sir Robert Affleck, 4th Bt (*see* 1939 edn AFFLECK, Bt), and *d* 2 May 1838, having by his 1st w had, with other issue:

1 DIGBY (Sir), **4th Bt**

2 Herbert; *b* 1 Oct 1791; Lt RN, High Sheriff Trinidad, WI; *m* 2 June 1821 Jessie (*d* 5 Aug 1869), dau of James Anderson, and *d* 17 March 1848, having had:

(1) Herbert Francis; *b* 27 Sept 1823; *m* 6 Oct 1853 his cousin Julia Henrietta (*d* 3 Feb 1883), dau of **Sir Digby Mackworth, 4th Bt** (*see* below), and *d* 13 July 1858, having had:

1a Herbert Digby; *b* 4 Oct 1854; *dsp*

2a Audley; *b* 13 May 1857; *m* 1896 Mary (*d* 24 Feb 1955 aged 87), dau of Henry Mason, of Caterham, and *d* 12 April 1914, leaving:

1b Philip Herbert, CB (1949), CBE (1942), DFC (1918); *b* 22 Oct 1897; *educ* Uppingham; served RNAS WW I 1916–19, RAF 1919, WW II (despatches), Comdt Empire Central Navigation Sch 1944–45, SASO HQ Coastal Cmd 1945–47, AOA HQ Tport Cmd 1947–50, Air V-Marshal (ret 1950); *m* 4 Oct 1921 Winifred Kathleen June (*d* 28 July 1967), dau of William Moss, of London, and *d* 30 Aug 1958, leaving:

1c +Richard Charles Audley [Richard Mackworth Esq, 27 Wellington Sq, London SW3]; *b* 29 Oct 1924; *educ* Upper Canada Sch and Pembroke Coll Cambridge (MA 1951); F/Lt RAF WW II, MSc (Eng) London 1952, MIMechE, MIWE, DIC 1952; *m* 2 July 1960 *Rosalind Jean, only child of Rev Albert Walters, FRMetS, Vicar Wychbold, Worcs, and has:

1d *Julia Kathleen; *b* 27 June 1968

2d *Victoria Alma Louise; *b* 17 Feb 1971

2c +James Digby [Maj James Mackworth, The Old School House, Littleworth, Oxon SN7 8ED]; *b* 2 Sept 1927; *educ* Cambridge (MA 1956); Maj REME; *m* 1st 1952 Marjorie Wilding and has:

1d +Charles Digby; *b* 5 Nov 1958

2d *Amanda Jane; *b* 22 June 1956

2c (cont.) Maj James Mackworth *m* 2nd 1968 Anna Marjorie Wilson Melling (*d* 1983); *m* 3rd 1984 *Susan Elizabeth Parsons

1c Sheila Margaret; *b* 5 June 1922; *m* 7 June 1952 (*divorce* 1962) Osmond Francis and had:

1d *David FRANCIS later FRANCIS-MACKWORTH; *b* 27 April 1953

1b Christabel Mary; *b* 25 June 1899

2b Joan Evelyn; *b* 24 May 1903; MB and ChB Bristol 1938, MRCS Eng, LRCP London 1939, DPM 1943

3b Margaret Julia; *b* 2 Nov 1906; *m* 15 Sept 1938 Maj Eldred O'Flaherty Wilson, DSO, TD, er s of R E Wilson, of Harpley Dams House, and had:

1a Constance; *d* 4 Nov 1924

2a Theodora; *d* 4 June 1919

(2) William Augustus; *b* 3 March 1825; *m* 22 Sept 1852 Juliet Anne, dau of Francis Valpy, of Dunedin, and *d* 4 Dec 1855, leaving:

1a Wilhelmina Jessie

(1) Jessie Philippa; *m* 15 July 1851 Rev George Woodfield Paul (*d* 7 April 1911), Vicar Finedon, Northants, Hon Canon Peterborough, and *d* 14 Oct 1924, having had issue

(2) Jane Deere; *m* 24 Feb 1862 George Sinclair Brodie (*d* 1880), of Bayswater, and *dsp*

(3) Martha Amelia; *d* unm 27 Dec 1904

(4) Frances; *m* 5 May 1859 Thomas Bagnell, DL, 3rd s of Thomas Bagnell, of Great Barr, Staffs, and had issue

(5) Mary; *m* 8 Sept 1864 Maj-Gen Edmund Lewin Taverner (*d* 1891) and had issue

(6) Augusta Octavia

(7) Sophia Matilda; *m* 29 Sept 1868 Rev Penyman Worsley and *d* 30 April 1875

3 Arthur Francis John; *b* 7 Sept 1804; Army Capt; *m* 14 July 1831 Augusta Mary (*d* 1884), dau of Joseph Gilbert, and *d* 12 Sept 1835, leaving:

(1) Fanny Augusta Matilda; *d* unm 2 Jan 1926

4 William Harcourt Isham MACKWORTH later MACKWORTH-DOLBEN (roy licence 14 July 1835); *b* 3 Sept 1806; *m* 1 July 1835 Frances (*d* 1892), yst dau and coheir of William Somerset Dolben, est s and heir for Sir John English Dolben, 4th and last Bt of the 1704 *cr* (*see* 1834 edn), of Finedon, and *d* 2 Nov 1872, leaving:

(1) Ellen; *d* unm 2 Feb 1912

1 Mary; *m* 1819 Rev William Cleaver, est s of Dr Cleaver, Archbp Dublin

The 3rd Bt's est s,

Sir Digby Mackworth, 4th Bt, KH (1832), of Glen Usk; *b* 13 June 1789; served Peninsular War and Waterloo Campaign, ret as Col, ADC to 1st Viscount Hill of Hawkestone and of Hardwicke (*qv*), v-pres London Soc for promoting Christianity among Jews; *m* 1st 16 Sept 1816 Marie Alexandrine Ignatie Julie de Richepance (*d* 1818), only dau of Gen and the Baroness de Richepance, niece of the Duke de Damas-Crux, and had:

1 DIGBY FRANCIS (Sir), **5th Bt**

Sir Digby *m* 2nd 3 April 1823 Sophia Noel (*d* 5 Jan 1882), dau of James Mann, of Linton, by Lucy, dau of Sir Horace Mann, 2nd and last Bt of the 1755 *cr*, by Lady Lucy *née* Noel (dau of 4th Earl of Gainsborough, *qv*), and *d* 23 Dec 1852, having by her had, with two other daus:

2 Horace Eugene; *b* 8 May 1829; *m* 1874 Jane (*d* 23 Dec 1907), dau of William Sangster, and *d* 7 April 1892, leaving:

(1) Norman Walter; *b* 1878; Lt-Col IMS, MB, ChB, FRCS; *m* 1908 Isabel Largie, MA (*d* 1967), dau of William Anderson, and *d* 3 May 1950, leaving:

1a Eliot Digby; *b* 1910; MB, ChB Aberdeen U 1932, MRCP London 1939; *m* 1941 — and *d* 23 Aug 1955

2a +NORMAN HUMPHREY [Dr Norman Mackworth, 16232 Camellia Terr, Los Gatos, CA 95030, USA]; *b* 1917; heir presumptive; *educ* Aberdeen (MB, ChB 1939) and Cambridge Us (PhD 1947); Lecturer Stanford U; *m* 12 June 1941 *Jane Felicity, MB, BChir, PhD, yr dau of Capt Walter Hugh Charles Samuel Thring, CBE, RN, and has:

1b +Alan Keith [Alan Mackworth Esq, 4433 West 9th Ave, Vancouver, BC, Canada V6R 2C9]; *b* 1945; *m* 30 April 1969 *Marian Elizabeth, dau of J V Fry, of Markham, Ontario, and has:

1c *Bryn Sarah; *b* 1972

2b +Hugh Francis; *b* 1948

1b *Jean Clare [Mrs David Surry, 44 Lois Dve, Shepperton, Middx]; *b* 1942; *m* June 1964 *David Surry and has:

1c *Patrick David; *b* 1969

1c *Susan Alicia Mackworth; *b* 1971

2c *Kathleen Jane Mackworth; *b* 1973

(1) Caroline Jane; *b* 1881; *m* 4 Oct 1912 Lt-Col Richard Edward Flowerdew, CIE, MB, ChB, IMS, 9th s of Arthur John Blomfield Flowerdew, of Billingford Hall, Scole, Norfolk, and *d* 12 Oct 1957, leaving issue

1 Julia Henrietta; *m* 6 Oct 1853 her cousin Herbert Francis Mackworth and *d* 2 Feb 1883, leaving issue (*see* above)

The 4th Bt's er s,

Sir Digby Francis Mackworth, 5th Bt, of Glen Usk; *b* 7 July 1817; Ensign 90th Foot 1834–44; *m* 1840 Mathilde Eleanor Eliza, 2nd dau of Lt-Col Peddie, KH, 90th LI, and *d* 8 Sept 1857, leaving:

1 ARTHUR WILLIAM (Sir), **6th Bt**

2 William; *b* 10 Jan 1846; *d* 13 Nov 1923

3 Rowland; *b* 20 March 1848; *d* unm 3 April 1908

1 Louisa Juliana; *b* 1845; *m* 23 May 1874 William Cubitt, of New Ho, Cardiff, only s of Joseph Cubitt, CE, and *d* March 1885

2 Sophia Julia; *b* 1852; *m* 13 Sept 1883 Charles Edward Whitting, MA Trin Coll Cambridge, of Sandcroft, Uphill, Weston-super-Mare, and *d* 2 Dec 1891

The 5th Bt's est s,

Sir Arthur William Mackworth, 6th Bt, CB (1897), JP, DL (both Mon), of Glen Usk; *b* 5 Oct 1842; RE: Lt 1861, Capt 1873, Maj 1881, Lt-Col 1882, Col 1886, Egyptian Campaign 1882 (3rd Cl Medjidie), cmded RE S Wales 1883–88, WI 1888–89 and Aldershot 1894–99, Hon Col 1st Bn Mon Regt (chm TF); *m* Br Embassy Paris 18 Oct 1865 Alice Kate (*d* 25 March 1915), yr dau of Joseph Cubitt, CE, of Park St, Westminster, and *d* 8 March 1914, having had:

1 Digby; *b* 20 May 1868; Capt and Brevet Maj 2nd Bn Queen's Roy W Surrey Regt; *ka* Boer War 6 Jan 1900

2 **Sir Humphrey Mackworth, 7th Bt**, JP (Mon); *b* 11 July 1871; *educ* Marlborough and Oxford Mil Coll; Lt 3rd Bn Roy W Surrey Regt and Capt Roy Mon RE S Africa 1902 and Remount Serv WW I 1915–19, MFH Llangibby 1908–20; *m* 1st 9 July 1908 (*divorce* 1923) Margaret Haig Thomas, later Viscountess Rhondda in her own right (*d* 20 July 1958), only child and heir of 1st Viscount Rhondda (*see* 1956 edn); *m* 2nd 15 Sept 1923 Dorothy Cecil Cleeves (*d* 16 April 1971), 2nd dau of John Charles Llewellin, of Caerleon House, Caerleon, Mon, and *d* 2 May 1948

3 Francis Julian Audley; *b* 15 Sept 1876; Capt RFA WW I (despatches); *m* 4 Aug 1910 Dorothy Conran (*m* 2nd 22 Nov 1922 Charles Edward Gatehouse; *d* 1976), only dau of Arthur Hastings Lascelles, of Narbeth, Pembs, and was *ka* 1 Nov 1914, leaving:

(1) *Cecily Joan; *b* 15 Aug 1911; *m* 1st 1935 Leon Donckier de Donkeel (*d* 1938); *m* 2nd 11 July 1956 Marquis de Chabannes la Palice (*d* 1980) and has by her 1st husb:

1a *Pascale; *b* 1936

(2) Helen Margaret; *b* 18 Feb 1914; *d* 24 Sept 1938

4 **Sir Harry Llewellyn Mackworth, 8th Bt**, CMG (1918), DSO (1900); *b* 17 March 1878; Boer War 1899–1902 (despatches twice, Queen's medal with six clasps, King's medal with two clasps), E Africa 1903–04 (medal with two clasps) and WW I (despatches, brevet), 4th Class Osmanieh, Serbian Order White Eagle 4th Cl with swords, Col RE and Roy Signals, Ch Signal Offr Egypt 1924–27; *m* 8 Oct 1913 Leonie Georgette, only dau of Professor Franklin Sievewright Peterson, MusB, of Edinburgh, and *dsp* 18 Nov 1952

5 Geoffrey, CMG (1920), DSO (1918); *b* 20 June 1879; ADC to HM GEORGE V 1929–30, served WW I (despatches) and as Cdre Convoys WW II 1939–42, V-Adml; *m* 26 April 1910 Noel Mabel, only dau of William T Langford, of Charford Manor, S Devon, and *d* 4 March 1952, leaving:

(1) **Sir David Arthur Geoffrey Mackworth, 9th Bt;** *b* 13 July 1912; *educ* Farnborough Sch and RNC Dartmouth; Cdr RN (ret 1956), naval advsr to Dir Guided Weapon R & D Min Supply 1946–49, md South Coast Rod Rigging Co, memb Roy Inst Navigation; *m* 1st 20 Nov 1941 (*divorce* 1971) Mary Alice Robinson-Smith (*d* 1993), dau of Thomas Henry Grylls, of Bloomsbury, and had:

1a **Sir DIGBY JOHN MACKWORTH, 10th and present Bt**

(1) (cont.) **Sir David** *m* 2nd 11 Dec 1973 *Beryl Joan [Beryl Lady Mackworth, 36 Wittering Rd, Hayling Island, Hants PO11 9SP], 3rd dau of Pembroke Henry Cockayn Cross and formerly w of Ernest Henry Sparkes, and *d* 8 Feb 1998

(1) *Betty Mabel; *b* 29 April 1911

(2) *Lorna Alice; *b* 16 July 1918

6 Arthur Christopher Paul; *b* 24 Jan 1886; *educ* Magdalen Coll Oxford (MA, Fell 1913); T/Lt Rifle Bde; *d* 25 Nov 1917

7 John Dolben, CBE (1918); *b* 26 June 1887; *educ* Corpus Christi Coll Oxford (MA); Col RAF and Queen's Roy Regt, Legn Hon; *m* 8 April 1913 Marianne Annette (*d* 19 Aug 1968 aged 81), only dau of H W Sillem, of The Pines, Horsell, Surrey, and *d* 5 Sept 1939, having had:

(1) Christopher Charles Dolben; *b* 21 Jan 1919; P/O RAF WW II; *m* 21 March 1940 Janet (*m* 2nd 26 Oct 1946 Capt E P G Barrett), only dau of Maj Norman Mackinnon, of Bucklebury, Berks, and was *ka* 15 May 1940

(1) *Josephine Ann [Mrs Noel James, Tower Ho, 4 Bath Rd, Cowes, IoW]; *b* 30 Jan 1914; *m* 1st 24 Nov 1937 Maj Patrick Owen Lyons, RA (*ka* SE Asia 1941), s of E Lyons, of Co Wicklow, and has:

1a *Mary Annette; *b* 1939

2a *Bridget Carol Dolben; *b* 1940

(1) (cont.) Mrs Patrick Lyons *m* 2nd 1 Jan 1942 *Lt-Col Noel James, MBE, RAOC, and by him has:

1a *Christopher Noel; *b* 1946

2a *John Gwyn Mackworth; *b* 1951

1 Gwyneth; *b* 2 Aug 1866; *m* 26 June 1894 Col Gwynnedd Conway Gordon, CBE, RASC (*d* 22 Oct 1936), 2nd s of Col Lewis Conway Gordon, CIE, RE, and *d* 25 Aug 1938, leaving issue

2 Helen; *b* 15 Feb 1870; *d* unm 19 Aug 1951

3 Mary Josephine; *b* 25 Oct 1872; *d* unm 24 Dec 1960

4 Beryl Katherine; *b* 2 Feb 1875; *d* unm 1 Jan 1954

5 Dorothy; *b* 20 Sept 1880; *d* unm 23 April 1943

MacLAURIN OF KNEBWORTH

Arms: Arms granted, but official blazon not available at the time of going to print. **Motto:** *Alta peto* ('I seek the heights'). **Creation:** B. (LP, UK) Aug 1996.

THE BARON MacLAURIN OF KNEBWORTH, of Knebworth in the County of Hertfordshire (Sir Ian Charter MacLaurin, DL (Herts 1992)) [The Rt Hon The Lord MacLaurin of Knebworth DL, c/o Tesco plc, Tesco House, Delamare Rd, Cheshunt, Herts EN8 9SL]; *b* 30 March 1937; *educ* Malvern (later Govr); RAF 1956–58; Tesco: joined 1959, dir 1970, md 1973–85, dep chm 1983–85, chm 1985–97; dir: Guinness plc 1986–95, Nat West Bank 1990–, Gleneagles Hotels 1992–, Enterprise Oil 1984–90; Pres Retail Consortium 1997–, Tstee ROH Tst 1992, Chllr U of Herts 1996–, memb ctee MCC 1986–, chm England and Wales Cricket Bd 1997–; FRSA 1986, FIM 1987, Hon FCGI 1992, Liveryman Carmens' Co 1982–; DUniv Stirling 1987, Hon LLD Herts 1995; *m* 1961 *Ann Margaret Collar and has a s and two daus

Lineage: ARTHUR GEORGE MacLAURIN; *m* Evelina Florence — and had:

IAN CHARTER, *cr* a **Baron**

MACLAY

Arms: Or a lion rampant azure, armed and langued gules, resting its sinister paw on an anchor sable, all within an orle of the second. **Crest:** A lymphad, sails furled sable, flagged gules. **Supporters:** Two wolves proper, each gorged with a chain, pendant therefrom an escutcheon argent, charged with a salmon on its back holding a ring in its mouth proper. **Motto:** *In Deo fides* ('Faith in God'). **Creations:** B. (UK) 21 Nov 1922, Bt. (UK) 20 July 1914.

THE 3RD BARON MACLAY, of Glasgow, Co Lanark, and a **Baronet** (Sir Joseph Paton Maclay, Bt, DL (Renfrewshire 1986)) [The Rt Hon The Lord Maclay DL, Duchal, Kilmacolm, Renfrewshire PA13 4RS]; *b* 11 April 1942; *s f* 1969; *educ* Winchester, Sorbonne U; md: Denholm Maclay 1970–83, Denholm Maclay (Offshore) 1975–83, Triport Ferries (Management) 1975–83, Milton Timber Services 1984–90, dep md Denholm Ship Management 1982–83, dir: Milton Shipping Co 1970–83, Marine Shipping Mutual Insur Co 1982–83, Br Steamship Short Trades Assoc 1978–83, N of England Protection and Indemnity Assoc 1976–83, Denholm Ship Management (Holding) 1991–93, Altnamara Shipping plc, pres Hanover Shipping Inc 1982–83, gp mktg exec Acomarit Gp Geneva, chm Scottish branch Br Sailors Soc 1979–81, v-chm Glasgow Shipowners and Shipbrokers Benevolent Assoc 1982–83 and 1997–98, Commr Northern Lighthouse Bd 1996–; *m* 1976 *Elizabeth Anne, only dau of G M Buchanan, of Delamere, Pokataroo, NSW, Australia, and has:

1 +JOSEPH PATON; *b* 6 March 1977; *educ* Loretto

2 +Thomas Maxwell; *b* 25 Jan 1981; *educ* Loretto

1 *Rebecca Delamere; *b* 14 March 1979; *educ* Queen Margaret's Sch

Lineage: EBENEZER MACLAY, of Glasgow; *m* Janet Paton (*d* 1895) and *d* 30 Oct 1894, leaving:

Sir Joseph Paton Maclay, 1st Bt, and 1st Baron Maclay, of Glasgow, Co Lanark (both UK), so *cr* 20 July 1914 and 21 Nov 1922 respectively, PC (1916), JP (Glasgow), DL (Glasgow and Renfrews); *b* 6 Sept 1857; ptnr Maclay and MacIntyre (Glasgow shipowners), Min Shipping and Memb War Cabinet 1916–21 (the historian John Grigg (*see* ALTRINCHAM, B) has recently argued that this appointment was perhaps the most vital of all those Lloyd-George made on becoming PM), memb: Ctee on Nat Expenditure 1921, Glasgow Town Cncl, Clyde Tst; Freeman Glasgow 1922, Hon LLD Glasgow U; *m* 18 April 1889 Martha (*d* 28 Sept 1929), dau of William Strang, of Glasgow, and *d* 24 April 1951, having had:

1 Ebenezer; *b* 27 Dec 1891; *educ* Cambridge (BA); Lt Scots Gds; *ka* 1918

2 William Strang; *b* 8 July 1895; Lt 8th Bn Cameronians (Scottish Rifles); *ka* 25 June 1915

3 JOSEPH PATON, **2nd Baron**

4 Walter Symington, CB (1955), OBE (1944); *b* 29 Oct 1901; *educ* Fettes and St John's Coll Cambridge (BA 1925, MB 1928, MD 1934); Medical Sr Commr Bd Control 1945–60, FRCP (London) 1954, Hon Physician to HM THE QUEEN 1959–64, Regnl Psychiatrist Wessex Regnl Hosp Bd 1960–64, Hon DSc McGill U 1961; *m* 26 April 1928 Dorothy Russell (CC Berks 1964; *d* 1993), dau of William Lennox, WS, of Abbotsford Park, Edinburgh, and *d* 27 April 1964, leaving:

(1) Walter Strang Symington; *b* 9 Aug 1931; *educ* Winchester and St John's Coll Cambridge (MA, MB, BCh); *m* 23 June 1956 Elizabeth Ann (*m* 2nd 1991 Thomas Roderick Loxley Waring), est dau of Willis Charles Cooper, of Esher, and *d* 1987, leaving:

1a +Andrew Strang; *b* 17 Sept 1958; *m* 1987 *Felicity Neal

2a +Christopher Willis; *b* 17 Feb 1964; *m* 1988 *Louise Nelson

1a *Janet Susan; *b* 23 Sept 1960

(2) +John Lennox Sim [John Maclay Esq, 12 Stafford Ct, London W8 7DJ; 3 Fairfield Close, Lymington SO41 3NP]; *b* 11 April 1937; *educ* Winchester and St John's Coll Cambridge (MA); *m* 19– *—

(3) +Mark Paton [Mark Maclay Esq, Sladen Green, Binley, Andover, Hants]; *b* 30 April 1943; *educ* Winchester and RAC Cirencester; ARICS; *m* 24 June 1967 *Elizabeth Ruth, er dau of Worsfold McClenaghan, and has:

1a +James Paton; *b* 14 April 1971

2a +Alasdair Worsfold; *b* 1973

1a *Caroline Elizabeth; *b* 1976

(1) *(Shirley) Georgina, OBE (1991) [Mrs Michael King OBE, Cedar House, Hellidon, Northants NN11 6LG]; *b* 4 July 1933; *m* 1st 25 June 1955 (*divorce* 1973) (Robert) David Ogden, JP (*d* 1992), s of Dr Robert James Ogden, of Almondbury, Yorks, and has:

　1a *Robert Nicholas; *b* 16 May 1958

　2a *Joseph Jeremy; *b* 16 May 1958

　3a *Benjamin Patrick; *b* 15 Nov 1966

　1a *Emma Maclay; *b* 25 March 1961

(1) (cont.) Mrs Georgina Ogden *m* 2nd 1989 *Prof Michael Stuart King

(2) Janet Russell; *b* 4 Jan 1936; *d* following a riding accident 28 April 1954

5 JOHN SCOTT MACLAY, 1st and last VISCOUNT MUIRSHIEL, of Kilmacolm, Co Renfrew (UK), so *cr* 16 July 1964, KT (1973), CH (1962), CMG (1944), PC (1952); *b* 26 Oct 1905; *educ* Winchester and Trin Coll Cambridge; 57th Searchlight Regt RA WW II, MP (Nat Lib) Montrose 1940–50 and (Nat Lib then C) Renfrew W 1950–64, memb Br Shipping Mission to Washington (Head 1944), Min Tport and Civ Aviation 1951–52, Min State Colonial Office 1956–57, Sec State Scotland 1957–62; *m* 1930 Betty L'Estrange (*d* 1974), dau of Maj Delaval Graham L'Estrange Astley, CB (*see* HASTINGS, B), and *dsp* 17 Aug 1992, when the Viscountcy expired

1 Lilias; *b* 25 July 1897; *educ* Glasgow U (MB, ChB 1917); *m* 22 Sept 1926 Rev John Edmund Hamilton, MC, s of Rev John Sinclair Hamilton, of Dublin, and *d* 26 Oct 1965, leaving issue

2 Janet, JP (Bristol); *b* 3 March 1897; *m* 18 April 1923 Sir John Hampden Inskip, KBE, and *d* 4 April 1974, leaving issue (*see* CALDECOTE, V)

The 1st BARON's 3rd s,

　JOSEPH PATON MACLAY, **2nd Baron Maclay**, KBE (1946); *b* 31 May 1899; *educ* Fettes and Trin Coll Cambridge (MA); MP (Lib) Paisley 1931–45, Min War Transport's Rep USSR 1941–42, Pres UK Chamber Shipping 1946–47, chm: Internat Chamber Shipping 1947, Clydesdale and N of Scotland Bank, Maclay and MacIntyre Ltd; pres Boys Bde, Ld Dean of Guild Glasgow 1952–54, Cdr Order Orange Nassau, Netherlands; *m* 24 Sept 1936 *Nancy Margaret [The Rt Hon The Dowager Lady Maclay, Milton, Kilmacolm, Renfrewshire]; 3rd dau of Robert Coventry Greig, of Hall of Caldwell, Uplawmoor, Renfrews, and *d* 7 Nov 1969, leaving:

　1 JOSEPH PATON MACLAY, **3rd and present Baron Maclay**

　2 +David Milton [The Hon David Maclay, Hilcott Farm House, Hilcott, Pewsey, Wilts]; *b* 21 March 1944; *educ* Winchester; *m* 29 Nov 1968 *Valerie, dau of Lt-Cdr J P Fyfe, of Kinkell, St Andrews, Fife, and has:

　　(1) +Duncan; *b* 1974

　3 +Angus Grenfell [The Hon Angus Maclay, Whitelee, St Boswells, Roxburghshire]; *b* 11 Aug 1945; *educ* Winchester and RAC Cirencester; *m* 1st 8 Aug 1970 Hon (Elizabeth) Victoria Baillie (*d* 1986), er dau of 3rd Baron Burton (*qv*), and has:

　　(1) +Robert Michael; *b* 1972

　　(2) +Fergus; *b* 1981

　　(1) *Sarah Elizabeth; *b* 1977

　3 (cont.) The Hon Angus Maclay *m* 2nd 1990 *Jane Elizabeth Angela, dau of Lt-Col Alistair Monteith Gibb, Roy Wilts Yeo (*see* COWDRAY, V), and formerly w of 13th Marquess of Huntly (*qv*)

　1 *Sarah [The Hon Mrs Hayes, Muir of Knock, Pityoulish, Inverness-shire PH22 1RD]; *b* 4 July 1937; *m* 17 Dec 1968 *David Richard Hayes, s of Capt E G Hayes, RFC, by Margaret, sis of Sir John Muir, 3rd Bt (*qv*), and has:

　　(1) *James Richard; *b* 15 Oct 1969

　　(2) *(Calum) Joseph; *b* 25 Nov 1970

　　(3) *Benjamin David; *b* 6 Sept 1973

　2 Lucy; *b* 24 July 1938; *m* 9 Sept 1966 *James Ian Alexander Robertson, est s of Capt Ian Greig Robertson, DSO, DSC and bar, JP, RN, of Forneth, Blairgowrie, Perths, and *d* 1987, leaving:

　　(1) *Hugh Sebastian; *b* 4 Sept 1967

　　(2) *David Ian; *b* 31 Dec 1969

　　(3) *Dominic James; *b* 1973

　　(1) *Anna Marcelle; *b* 1977

MACLEAN of Dowart

Arms: Quarterly, 1st, arg. a rock gu; 2nd, arg. a dexter hand fesswise, couped gu., holding a cross-crosslet fitchée in pale az.; 3rd, or a lymphad, oars in saltire, sails furled, sa., flagged gu.; 4th, arg. a salmon naiant ppr., in chief two eagle's heads respectant gu. **Crest:** A tower embattled arg. **Supporters:** Dexter, a seal ppr.; sinister, an ostrich with a horseshoe in its beak ppr. **Motto:** Virtue mine honour. **Creation:** Bt. (NS) 3 Sept 1631.

SIR LACHLAN HECTOR CHARLES MACLEAN, 12TH BT, of Dowart and Morvern, Argyllshire, DL (Argyll and Bute 1993) [The Hon Sir Lachlan Maclean Bt DL, Arngask House, Glenfarg, Perthshire PH2 9QA]; *b* 25 Aug 1942; *s f* 1990, also as Chief of Clan Maclean; *educ* Eton; Maj Scots Guards (ret); *m* 2 Nov 1966 *Mary Helen, est dau of William Gordon Gordon of Lude, Blair Atholl, Perths, and has had:

1 +MALCOLM LACHLAN CHARLES; *b* 20 Oct 1972

2 +Andrew Lachlan William; *b* 1979

1 *Emma Mary; *b* 15 Sept 1967; *m* 29 June 1996 *Giovanni Amati, s of Dr Luigi Amati and Carla Amati Ponziania, of Lecco, Italy

2 Sarah Elizabeth Helen; *b* 26 Sept 1969; *d* 1971

3 *Alexandra Caroline; *b* 1975

Lineage: GILLEAN, called *Gillean nan Tuaighe* ('Gillean of the Battle-Axe'); fndr Clan Gillean; had:

MAOLIOSA or MALISE; *d c* 1300, leaving:

GILLIECALLUM or MALCOLM; fought Battle of Bannockburn 1314; *m* —, dau of the (feudal) Lord of Carrick, and had:

JOHN *Dubh* ('The Dark'); held Dowart and other lands on the Isle of Mull; *m* —, dau of Comyn, feudal Lord of Lochaber, and had, with a 2nd s (Hector Reganach, ancestor of the MACLEANs of Urquhart and the MACLAINEs of Lochbuie):

LACHLAN *Lubanach*, of Dowart, of which with Brolas, on Mull, and other lands had charters 1390; House Steward to the Lord of the Isles; *m* Elizabeth, dau of John, Lord of the Isles (*see* BOSVILLE MACDONALD, Bt), and *d c* 1405, leaving:

EACHAN *Ruadh nan Cath* ('Red [with blood] from Battles'), of Dowart; *k* Battle of Harlaw 1411, leaving:

LACHLAN *Bronnach* ('Big-bellied'), of Dowart; *m* Janet, dau of Alexander Stewart, 11th Earl of Mar (*qv*) in right of his w, and *d c* 1472 (having had by —, dau of — Macearchan of Kingerloch, a s (Donald, 1st of Ardgour), and by Finovola, dau of — Macleod of Harris, two other sons (Neil, ancestor of the MACLEANs of Lehire, Ross and Shuna; John Garbh, 1st of Coll), leaving by his w:

LACHLAN *Og* ('The Younger'), of Dowart; *b c* 1432; *m* Catherine, dau of 1st Earl of Argyll (*see* ARGYLL, E), and had:

HECTOR *Odhar*, of Dowart; *m* —, dau of Mackintosh, Ch of Clan Chattan, and was *k* at Flodden 1513, having had:

LACHLAN *Cattanach*, of Dowart; *m* 1st Marion, dau of — Maclean of Treshnish; *m* 2nd Catherine/Elizabeth (*m* 2nd Archibald Campbell of Auchinbreck (*see* CAMPBELL, Bt, of Auchinbreck), and *dsp*), dau of 2nd Earl of Argyll (*see* ARGYLL, D), and was murdered in Edinburgh 1523 by her bro, Sir John Campbell of Calder, having by his 1st w had, with a 2nd s (Allan *nan Sop*) and at least one dau (Catherine, *m* 1st, as his 3rd w, 4th Earl of Argyll (*see* ARGYLL, D), *m* 2nd Calvagh, The O'Donell of Tir Conaill, *m* 3rd, as his 2nd w, Shane *an Diomair* O'Neill; *see* O'NEILL, B):

HECTOR *Mor* ('The Great'), of Dowart and Morvaren; *m* Mary, dau of Alexander Macdonald of Islay, and *d* 1568, having had, with seven daus (one of whom, Mary, *m* Donald *Gormeson*, 6th of Sleat (*see* BOSVILLE MACDONALD, Bt), and another, Janet, *m* Aeneas Macdonnell, 5th of Glengarry; *see* BOSVILLE MACDONALD, Bt) and a 2nd s (John *Dubh* ('Dark') of Morvern, ancestor of the MACLEANs of Drimnin, Calgary and Pennycross):

HECTOR *Og*; *m* 1557 Lady Janet Campbell, dau of 4th Earl of Argyll (*see* ARGYLL, D), and *d* 1573, leaving:

Sir LACHLAN *Mor* MACLEAN of Dowart; fought Battle of Glenlivet 1594; *m* Lady Margaret Cunningham, dau of 6th Earl of Glencairn (*see* CUNINGHAME, Bt), and was *k* at the Battle of Traigh-Ghruinneirt on Isla 5 Aug 1598, having had, with three other sons (including Lachlan *Og*, ancestor of the MACLEANs of Torloisk):

HECTOR *Og* MACLEAN of Dowart; *m* 1st Jennette, 2nd dau of Colin Mackenzie of Kintail (*see* CROMARTIE, E), and had:

1 Hector *Mor*; *m* Margaret, dau of Sir Rory Macleod of Dunvegan, and *dsp c* 1631

2 **Sir Lachlan Maclean, 1st Bt** (NS), so *cr* 3 Sept 1631, with remainder to his heirs male whatsoever, of Morvaren; MP (S Parl) Tarbert Sheriffdom 1628–33; royalist Civil War, assisting at Battles of Inverlochy and Kilsyth 1645 (*see* MONTROSE, D); *m* Mary, dau of Roderick Macleod of Macleod, and *d* 18 April 1649, leaving:

(1) **Sir Hector Maclean, 2nd Bt**; *b c* 1625; royalist; *k* leading 700 of his clansmen Battle of Innerkeithing 1651

(2) **Sir Allan Maclean, 3rd Bt**; *b c* 1637; *m* Giles, 3rd dau of John Macleod of Macleod, and *d* 1674, leaving, with other issue:

1a **Sir John Maclean, 4th Bt**; Jacobite, led his clansmen Battles of Killiecrankie 1689 and Sheriffmuir 1715; *m* by 1704 Mary, dau of Sir Æneas Macpherson of Invereshie, and *d* by 1719, having had, with other issue:

1b **Sir Hector Maclean, 5th Bt**; *b c* 1704; imprisoned 1745–47 Tower of London on suspicion of Jacobitisim; *d unm* Jan/Feb 1751

1 Finovola

HECTOR *Og* MACLEAN *m* 2nd Isabelle, dau of Sir Archibald Acheson, 1st Bt, of Gosford (*see* GOSFORD, E), and *d* 1623, having by her had:

3 Donald, of Brolas; *m* Finovola, dau of John Garbh, 7th of Coll, and had:

(1) Lachlan, of Brolas; *b* 1650; MP Argyllshire 1685–86; *m* Isabelle, dau of Hector Maclean of Torloish, and *d* 1687, leaving:

1a Donald, of Brolas; *b* 1671; *m* Isabella, dau of Allan Maclean of Ardgour, and *d* 1750, leaving:

1b **Sir Allan Maclean, 6th Bt**; Capt in Dutch serv; fought War American Independence, Maj 119th Regt; *m* Una, dau of Hector Maclean of Coll, and *dspm* 10 Dec 1783, having had:

1c Maria; *m* Charles Maclean of Kinlochaline

2c Sibella; *m* John Maclean of Inverscadell

3c Ann; *m* Dr Mackenzie Grieve, of Edinburgh, and *dspms* 10 Dec 1783

2a Allan; *d unm* 1722

(2) Hector *Og*; *m* Jennette, dau of Macneil of Barra, and had:

1a Donald; *d unm* 1738

2a John; *m* Finovola/Florence, dau of Allan Maclean of Garmony, and had, with a 2nd s (*d unm*):

1b Donald; Collector Customs Montego Bay Jamaica; *m* 1st Mary, dau of John Dickson, of Glasgow, and had:

1c **Sir Hector Maclean, 7th Bt**; *d unm* 2 Nov 1818

1b (cont.) Donald Maclean *m* 2nd Margaret, dau of James Wall, of Clonea Castle, Co Waterford, and *d c* 1770, leaving by her:

2c FITZROY JEFFREYS GRAFTON (Sir), **8th Bt**

4 John; ancestor of the extinct Counts Maclean of Sweden

The 7th Bt's half-bro,

Sir Fitzroy Jeffreys Grafton Maclean, 8th Bt; joined Army 1787, served WI, assisting at taking of Tobago, attack on Martinique and Guadaloupe (medals and clasps) and taking of St Thomas and St John, of which islands apptd Govr 1808, Gen 1837, Col 54th Foot 1841; *m* 1st 17 May 1794 Elizabeth (*d* 1832), only child of Charles Kidd and widow of John Bishop, of Barbados; *m* 2nd 17 Sept 1838 Frances (*d* 12 June 1843), dau of Rev Henry Watkins and widow of Henry Campion, of Malling Deanery, Sussex, and *d* 5 July 1847, leaving by his 1st w:

1 CHARLES FITZROY (Sir), **9th Bt**

2 Donald, MP; *b* 1800; Chancery barrister; *m* 7 Sept 1827 Harriet (*d* 20 Sept 1850), dau of Gen Frederick Maitland (*see* MAITLAND, Bt), and *dsp* 21 March 1874

Sir FITZROY's est son,

Sir Charles Fitzroy Maclean, 9th Bt; *b* 14 Oct 1798; *educ* Eton and RMA Woolwich; joined Scots Fus Gds 1818, Lt-Col 81st Foot 1832–39, Mil Sec Gibraltar, Col 1846; *m* 10 May 1831 Emily Eleanor (*d* 12 April 1838), 4th dau of Rev Hon Jacob Marsham, DD (*see* ROMNEY, E), and *d* 27 Jan 1883, having had:

1 FITZROY DONALD (Sir), **10th Bt**

1 Emily Frances Harriet; *d unm* 10 Sept 1908

2 Louisa Marianne; *m* 12 July 1860 Hon Ralph Pelham Nevill (*see* ABERGAVENNY, M), and *d* 6 July 1919, leaving issue

3 Fanny Henrietta; *m* 2 Oct 1855 1st Baron Hood of Avalon, GCB (*dspm* 15 Nov 1901; *see* 1970 edn ST AUDRIES, B), and *d* 29 Aug 1919

4 Georgina Marcia; *m* 20 Oct 1868 1st Baron Llangattock (*d* 24 Sept 1912; *see* 1916 edn) and *d* 1 April 1923, leaving issue

Sir CHARLES's son,

Sir Fitzroy Donald Maclean, 10th Bt, KCB, JP, DL; Ch of Clan Gillean; *b* 18 May 1835; Col W Kent Yeo Cav, Lt-Col cmdg 13th Hus, Bulgaria, Crimea (present Alma and Sebastopol, medal and two clasps, Turkish war medal), Canada 1866–69; Order of Mercy; *m* 17 Jan 1872 Constance Marianne (*d* 8 March 1920), dau and coheir of George Holland Ackers, of Moreton Hall, Cheshire, and *d* 22 Nov 1936, having had:

1 Hector Fitzroy; *b* 17 Feb 1873; Maj Scots Gds, Boer War (medal, four clasps), WW I (two medals); *m* 3 Sept 1907 Winifred Joan (*d* 20 June 1941), yr dau of John Hodgkiss Wilding, and *d* 25 July 1932, having had:

(1) Donald Iain Andrew; *b* 29 Nov 1913; *d* 27 May 1923

(2) CHARLES HECTOR FITZROY (Sir), **11th Bt**

(1) Joan Sybil; *b* 26 April 1909; *m* 3 Feb 1940 Lt Col David John Graham-Campbell, KRRC, Warden Trin Coll Glenalmond, yst s of Sir Rollo Frederick Graham-Campbell, and had:

1a *John Malcolm, ACA [John Graham-Campbell Esq, Porchway Cottage, Taplow, Maidenhead, Berks]; *b* 28 April 1941; *educ* Eton and Trin Coll

Cambridge (MA); *m* 29 Nov 1969 *Margaret, yr dau of Percival Harold Fry Britton, of Kilkhampton, Cornwall, and has:

1b *Katherine Louise; *b* Aug 1971

2a *James Alastair [James Graham-Campbell Esq, Fernbank, Crathes, Banchory, Kincardineshire]; *b* 7 Feb 1947; *educ* Eton and Trin Coll Cambridge (BA 1968)

3a *Angus Charles David [Angus Graham-Campbell Esq, Fernbank, Crathes, Banchory, Kincardineshire]; *b* 30 June 1949; *educ* Eton and Trin Coll Cambridge

2 Charles Lachlan, JP Perthshire; *b* 20 Sept 1874; Capt RN, Benin Expdn 1897 (medal with clasp), China 1900–01 (medal), WW I (1915 star, two medals); *m* 1st 15 June 1904 Hon Philadelphia Sybil Robertson (*d* 12 Feb 1945), only dau of Baron Robertson of Forteviot, a Lord of Appeal in Ordinary; *m* 2nd 31 March 1952 Christian Mary (*d* 1983) dau of Rev M Taggart, of Lyne, Peeblesshire, and widow of Hedley Briggs-Constable, and *d* 27 Aug 1958, leaving by his 1st w:

(1) Philadelphia Constance; *b* 23 Oct 1905; *m* 8 June 1926 Richard Kennedy Lingard Guthrie, yr s of Roger Lingard Guthrie, of Carnoustie House, Angus, and had issue

(2) *Finovola Sybil; *b* 31 Dec 1907; *m* 24 April 1929 *Henry Norman Wilson, Black Watch, yst s of Very Rev John Skinner Wilson, Dean Edinburgh, and has:

1a *Charles Jeremy; *b* 1930

2a *Robert Malcolm; *b* 1935

3 Fitzroy Holland; *b* 10 May 1876; *d* 13 April 1881

4 John Marsham; *b* 24 Oct 1879; Lt RA; *ka* Boer War 4 Nov 1901

1 Finovola Marianne Eleanor; *b* 14 Feb 1887; *m* 1st 7 April 1908 Capt Roger Cordy Simpson (*d* 1919) and had issue; *m* 2nd 19 April 1922 Col Francis William Bullock-Marsham, DSO, MC (*see* ROMNEY, E)

Sir FITZROY's gs,

Sir Charles Hector Fitzroy Maclean, 11th Bt, and BARON MACLEAN, of Duart and Morven Co Argyll (LP, UK), so *cr* Feb 1971, KT (1969), GCVO (1971), KBE (1967), PC, JP (Argyllshire 1955); *b* 5 May 1916; *educ* Canford; Ld Lt Argyllshire 1954–90, Maj Scots Gds WW II (despatches), ret 1949; Pres T&AFA Argyllshire, Brig Roy Co Archers, Ld Chamberlain 1971–90, Grand Cross Dannebrog 1974; *m* 7 June 1941 *(Joan) Elizabeth [The Rt Hon Elizabeth Lady Maclean, Wilderness House, Hampton Court Palace, Surrey KT8 9AR; Duart Castle, Isle of Mull], er dau of Francis Thomas Mann (*see* MANN, Bt), and *d* 1990, leaving:

1 Sir LACHLAN HECTOR CHARLES MACLEAN, **12th and present Bt**

1 *Janet Elizabeth [The Hon Mrs Barne, Blofield House, Blofield, Norfolk]; *b* 27 Dec 1944; *m* 9 May 1974 *Capt Nicholas Michael Lancelot Barne, Scots Gds, yr s of Lt-Col Michael Ernest St John Barne, JP, of Sotterley Hall, Beccles, Suffolk, and has:

(1) *Alasdair Michael Fitzroy; *b* 23 Jan 1979

(2) *Hamish Nicholas Charles; *b* 1981

MACLEAN of Dunconnel

Arms: Quarterly, 1st, arg. a lion rampant gu., armed and langued az; 2nd, az. a castle triple-towered arg., masoned sa., windows, portcullis and flags gu.; 3rd, or a dexter hand couped fessways gu., holding a cross crosslet fitchée az.; 4th, or a galley, sails furled, oars in saltire sa., flagged gu., in a sea in base vert a salmon arg.; at the centre point a portcullis sa. for difference. Behind the shield in saltire a key, wards outwards or, and a rod gu., garnished or (insignia of Hereditary Keeper and Capt Dunconnel Castle); above the shield a chapeau gu. doubled erm. **Crest:** A lochaber axe in pale between a branch of laurel and a branch of cypress in open chaplet, all ppr. **Motto:** *Altera merces* ('Another reward').
Creation: Bt. (UK) 22 July 1957.

SIR CHARLES EDWARD MACLEAN OF DUNCONNEL, 2ND BT, of Dunconnel, Co Argyll [Sir Charles Maclean of Dunconnel Bt, Inverglen, Stachur, Cairndow, Argyll PA27 8DG]; *b* 31 Oct 1946; *s f* 1996; *educ* Eton and New Coll Oxford (BA 1969); *m* 1986 *Deborah, dau of Lawrence Young, of Chicago, and has:

  1 *Margaret Augusta; *b* 1986
  2 *Katharine Alexandra; *b* 1988
  3 *Charlotte Olivia; *b* 1991

Lineage: DOMNHALL or DONALD (s of Lachainn *Bronnach* ('Big-bellied') Lachlan of Dowart; *see* MACLEAN, Bt, of Dowart), seized the MacMasters' lands of Ardgour, which 1432 he was formally granted by his cousin Alexander, 3rd Lord of the Isles (roy confirmation 1494); *m* Evere, dau of Ewen Cameron of Lochiel and gdau of Donald *Dubh* ('The Dark'); his est s:

EWEN, 2nd of Ardgour (from whom the Chieftains of Ardgour derive the patronymic Mac-Mhic-Eoghain); *m* a dau of Chisholm of Strathglass and fought Battle of Bloody Bay 1482; had:

TERLACH or CHARLES, 3rd of Ardgour; claim to Chiefship disputed by his bro Lachlan; had:

IAIN Mac TERLACH, 4th of Ardgour; lands erected into Crown (territorial) Barony of Ardgour in the Lordship of the Isles 18 October 1542; *dsp c* 1549; *s* by his first cousin:

ALLAN MACLEAN, 5th of Ardgour; *m* a dau of Ewen Cameron of Lochiel and had:

EWEN MACLEAN, 6th of Ardgour, known from his agility as Eoghan *na h-Iteige* ('Ewen of the feather'); *m* a dau of Stewart of Appin and had:

ALLAN MACLEAN, 7th of Ardgour; granted by JAMES II/VII 12 Sept 1688 a fresh charter of the Barony of Ardgour, *m* Catherine, dau of Allan Cameron of Lochiel, and had:

IAIN *Crubach* ('Lame John') MACLEAN, 8th of Ardgour; *m* 1630 Anne, dau of Archibald Campbell, 8th Captain of Dunstaffnage, and had:

EWEN MACLEAN, 9th of Ardgour; *m* Mary, dau of Lachlan Maclaine of Lochbuie, and had:

ALLAN MACLEAN, 10th of Ardgour; *b* 1668; *m* Ann, 2nd dau of Sir Ewen Cameron of Lochiel, and gdau of Sir Lachlan Maclean of Duart, and *d* 1756, leaving:

JOHN MACLEAN, 11th of Ardgour; *b c* 1720; *m* 1735 Marjorie, dau of Lachlan MacLachlan of Corrie, and *dvp* March 1739, leaving:

HUGH MACLEAN, 12th of Ardgour; *b* 1736; *m* 1763 Elizabeth, dau of Alexander Houstoun, and *d* 1768, leaving:

ALEXANDER MACLEAN, 13th of Ardgour; *b* 1764, Ensign 1780, Lt-Col; *m* 1793 Margaret, dau of 2nd Earl of Hopetoun (*see* LINLITHGOW, M), and *d* 1855, leaving a yst s:

PETER MACLEAN; Maj-Gen RA; *b* 1813; *m* 21 Sept 1841 Elizabeth Harriet Frances (*d* 9 Nov 1869), dau of Lt-Gen Sir Henry Somerset, KCB, KH (*see* BEAUFORT, D), and *d* 15 Jan 1901, leaving an est s:

ALLAN HENRY MACLEAN; Lt-Col RHA; *m* Lucy Henrietta (*d* 13 May 1912), dau of John Norton Kyshe, Colonial Service, and *d* 20 Aug 1898, leaving a 4th s:

CHARLES WILBERFORCE MACLEAN, DSO (1918), OBE (1932); Maj QO Cameron Highrs; *b* 1875; *m* 1905 Frances Elaine (*d* 1954), dau of Lt-Cdr Royle, RN, and had an only s:

Sir FitzRoy Hew Maclean, 1st Bt (UK), so *cr* 22 July 1957, KT (1993), CBE (1944), 15th Hereditary Keeper and Captain of Dunconnel in the Isles of the Sea; *b* 11 March 1911; *educ* Eton and King's Coll Cambridge (BA 1932, MA 1968); Dip Serv: 3rd Sec 1933, 2nd Sec 1938 Paris and Moscow, Queen's Own Cameron Highrs and 1st SAS Regt WW II, 2nd Lt 1941, Capt 1942, Lt-Col 1943, Brig cmdg British Mission Yugoslav Partisans 1943–45, Croix de Guerre 1943, Order Kutuzov USSR 1944, Partisan Star 1st Cl Yugoslavia 1945, Order Merit Yugoslavia 1969, Order Yugoslav Star with ribbon 1981, MP (C) Lancaster 1941–1959 and Bute and N Ayrshire 1959–74, Parly U-Sec and Fin Sec War Office 1954–57, Glasgow 1969, author: *Eastern Approaches* (1949), *Disputed Barricade* (1957), *A Person From England* (1958), *Back to Bokhara* (1959), *Jugoslavia* (1969), *A Concise History of Scotland* (1970), *The Battle of Neretva* (1970), *To the Back of Beyond* (1974), *To Caucasus* (1976), *Take Nine Spies* (1978), *Holy Russia* (1979), *Tito* (1980), *The Isles of the Sea* (1985), *Portrait of the Soviet Union* (1988), *Bonnie Prince Charlie* (1988), *All the Russias* (1992), *Highlanders* (1995); *m* 12 Jan 1946 *Hon Veronica Nell, 2nd dau of 16th Lord Lovat (*qv*) and widow of Lt Alan Phipps, RN (*see* NORMANBY, M), and *d* 15 June 1996, leaving:

  1 Sir CHARLES EDWARD MACLEAN, **2nd and present Bt**
  2 +(ALEXANDER) JAMIE SIMON AENEAS [Jamie Maclean Esq, Flat 4, 49 Drayton Gdns, London SW10]; *b* 9 June 1949; heir presumptive; *educ* Eton; *m* 1st 1983 (*divorce* 1989) Sarah, est dau of Hugh Janson, of Barn House, Aldbourne, Wilts; *m* 2nd 1993 *Sarah C, dau of Nicolas Thompson, of Ennismore Gdns, London SW7

MACLEHOSE OF BEOCH

Arms: Argent on a chevron ensigned at the top with a cross patée sable between two escutcheons azure, each charged of a mullet of the first in chief and a demi-double-headed eagle displayed azure, beaked sable; in base, a book expanded argent. **Crest:** A dragon's head erased affrontée or, armed and langued gules. **Supporters:** Dexter, a Chinese dragon or, armed and langued gules, gorged of a collar indented sable; sinister, a black-faced ram proper. **Motto:** *Spe vitae melioris* ('In hope of a better life').
Creation: B. (LP, UK) 1981.

THE BARON MACLEHOSE OF BEOCH, of Maybole, in the district of Kyle and Carrick, and of Victoria in Hong Kong (Sir (Crawford) Murray MacLehose, GBE (1976, MBE 1946), KCMG (1971, CMG 1964), KCVO (1975), DL (Ayr and Arran 1983)) [The Rt Hon The Lord MacLehose of Beoch GBE KCMG KCVO DL, Beoch House, Maybole, Ayrshire KA19 8EN]; *b* 16 Oct 1917; *educ* Rugby and Balliol Coll Oxford; WW II: Lt RNVR; Malayan Colonial Serv 1939–46, For Serv 1947–82; Actg Consul Hankow 1947–48 and Actg Consul-Gen 1948–49, 1st Sec 1949, FO 1950, 1st Sec and Consul Prague 1951–54, seconded Wellington NZ 1954–56, 1st Sec Paris 1958–59, Counsellor and Political Advsr Hong Kong 1959–62, Head Far Eastern Dept FO 1963–65, Pncpl Priv Sec to For Sec 1965–67, Amb: Vietnam 1967–69, Denmark 1969–71, Govr and C-in-C Hong Kong 1971–82; dir Nat West Bank 1982–88, ktd 1983; Pres GB China Centre 1982–93; Chm: Scottish Tst for Physically Disabled 1982–90, Margaret Blackwood Housing Assoc 1982–90, Victoria League Cwlth Friendship 1983–87, Govrs SOAS 1985–90, Hon Fell SOAS 1983; Hon LLD: York 1983, Strathclyde 1984; KtStJ 1972; *m* 1947 *Margaret Noël, yst dau of Sir (Thomas) Charles Dunlop, TD, of Doonside, Ayrshire, and has:

  1 *Elfrida Sandra [The Hon Mrs Wedgwood, Collalis, Gartocharn, Dunbartonshire]; *b* 1949; *m* 1971 *Martin Amery Wedgwood and has issue
  2 *Sylvia Margaret [The Hon Mrs Sandeman, Rosgaradh, West Dhuhill Dve, Helensburgh, Dunbartonshire G84 9AW]; *b* (twin) 1949; *m* 1970 *Ronald Leighton Sandeman and has issue

Lineage: HAMISH A MACLEHOSE, of Grange, Culroy, Ayrshire; *m* Margaret Bruce Black and had:

(CRAWFORD) MURRAY, *cr* a **Baron**

MACLEOD OF BORVE

Creation: B. (LP, UK) 1971.

THE BARONESS MACLEOD OF BORVE, of Borve, Isle of Lewis (Evelyn Hester Blois, JP (Middx 1955), DL (Gtr London 1977)) [The Rt Hon The Baroness Macleod of Borve JP DL, Luckings Farm, Coleshill, Bucks HP7 0LS]; *b* 19 Feb 1915; Chm: Nat Gas Consumers' Cncl 1972–77, Nat Assoc Leagues Hosp Friends 1973–85 (Pres 1985–89); Pres Nat Assoc Widows 1976–; memb IBA 1972–75; Govr Queenswood Sch 1978–85; co-fndr Crisis at Christmas 1967; *m* 1st 1937 Mervyn Charles Mason (*k* by enemy action 1940); *m* 2nd 1941 Iain Norman Macleod, PC, MP (*d* 1970), and by him has:

1 *Torquil Anthony Ross; *b* 1942; *educ* Harrow; *m* 1967 (*divorce* 1973) (Elizabeth) Meriol, dau of Brig Arthur Pelham Trevor, DSO, and has:

  (1) *Iain Ross; *b* 1970

1 *Diana Hester [The Hon Mrs Heimann, Hertfordshire House, Coleshill, Bucks]; *b* 1944; *m* 1968 *David Heimann and has:

  (1) *Hugo Iain Philip; *b* 1972
  (2) *James Iain Philip; *b* 1974
  (3) *Charles Gervase Andrew; *b* 1977

Lineage: *See* BLOIS, Bt

MACLEOD

Arms: Azure a castle triple-towered argent, masoned sable, windows and portcullis gules, on a chief of the second an open book proper, leaved of the fourth. **Crest:** A bull's head cabossed sable, horned or, between two keys wards uppermost of the last. **Motto:** Hold fast. **Creation:** Bt. (UK) 3 March 1924.

SIR (JOHN) MAXWELL NORMAN MACLEOD, 5TH BT, of Fuinary, Morven, Co Argyll [The Hon Sir Maxwell MacLeod Bt, Dowie's Mill House, Dowie's Mill Lane, Cramond, Edinburgh PA34 5XU]; *b* 23 Feb 1952; *s* f 1991; *educ* Gordonstoun

Lineage: NORMAN MacLEOD had:

Very Rev NORMAN MacLEOD, DD, of St Columba Church, Glasgow, Dean and Chaplain Chapel Royal, Moderator Gen Assembly Ch Scotland; *b* Dec 1783; *m* Agnes, dau of Maxwell of Aros, Chamberlain to Duke of Argyll, and *d* 25 Nov 1862, having had, with four yr sons and six daus:

Very Rev NORMAN MacLEOD, DD, of the Barony Church, Glasgow; one of HM's Chaplains Scotland, Moderator Gen Assembly Ch Scotland, Dean of the Thistle; *b* 3 June 1812; *m* 11 Aug 1851 Catherine Ann (*d* 30 March 1903), dau of William Mackintosh, of Geddes, Nairn, by Jane, dau of James Jollie, WS, and *d* 16 June 1872, leaving:

1 Norman; *b* 3 Oct 1853; *m* Dec 1877 Jessie Caldwell Gifford and *d* Chicago 1897, leaving:

  (1) Norman, Maj 15th Sikhs; *d* 13 March 1924
  (2) Eric Olaf, 11th Bengal Lancers; *d* India 1906
  (1) Norma Agnes Maxwell; *m* 1910 Charles Maitland and had issue

2 JOHN MACKINTOSH (Sir), **1st Bt**

3 William Mackintosh; *b* 15 June 1861; *m* 8 Jan 1902 Constance Helen (*d* 16 May 1928), dau of Professor W J Sellar, of Edinburgh U, and widow of Cecil Scott Arkcoll, and *d* 30 June 1931

1 Jane; *d* 8 Feb 1939

2 Anne; *m* 16 Sept 1888 Sir James Wilson, KCSI (*d* 22 Dec 1926), and *d* 13 April 1921

3 Agnes Maxwell; *m* Nov 1895 Anstruther Frank Simson, of Brunton, Fife, and *d* 3 March 1913

4 Catherine Ann; *m* Sept 1879 Hardinge Hay Cameron, Ceylon CS, and *d* 1880

---

5 Mary; *d* unm 28 Feb 1947

6 Elizabeth; *m* 10 Jan 1898 Ralph Buller Hughes-Buller (*d* 13 Dec 1949), CIE, CBE, ICS, s of Gen Sir William Templer Hughes, KCB, of Bovey Tracey, Devon, and *d* 5 Feb 1960, leaving issue

The Very Rev NORMAN MacLEOD's 2nd s,

Sir John Mackintosh MacLeod, 1st Bt (UK), so *cr* 3 March 1924, JP, DL Glasgow; *b* 5 May 1857; MP (C U) Glasgow Centl 1915–18 and Kelvingrove 1918–22, ptnr Kerr, MacLeod and Macfarlan, CA, Glasgow, dir Clydesdale Bank and Scottish Union of Nat Insur, Memb Gen Assembly Ch Scotland and Roy Co Archers, LLD; *m* 4 Jan 1888 Edith (*d* 25 Sept 1942), 3rd dau of Joshua Fielden, of Todmorden and Nutfield Priory, Redhill, Surrey, and *d* 6 March 1934, leaving:

1 **Sir John Mackintosh Norman MacLeod, 2nd Bt**; *b* 10 Aug 1891; ptnr Kerr, Macleod and Macfarlan, Unicorn Pursuivant of Arms 1925–29, Rothesay Herald 1929–39, Lt RNVR WW I; *m* 29 Aug 1918 Isa (*d* 1968), dau of Francesco Brutsati, of Milan, and *d* 23 Sept 1939, leaving:

  (1) **Sir Ian Francis Norman MacLeod, 3rd Bt**; *b* 25 Sept 1921; Capt Intell Corps WW II; *das* April 1944

2 **Very Rev Sir George MacLeod, 4th Bt**, and BARON MACLEOD OF FUINARY, of Fuinary in Morven, Co Argyll (LP, UK), so *cr* 6 Feb 1967, MC (1917); *b* 17 June 1895; *educ* Winchester and Oriel Coll Oxford (BA 1919, Hon Fell 1969); served 1914–19 as T/Capt Argyll and Sutherland Highlanders WW I (Croix de Guerre avec palmes 1918), Hon DD Glasgow 1937, Min Govan Parish Church 1930–38, Leader Iona Community 1938–67, Moderator Gen Assembly Ch Scotland 1957–58, Chaplain to HM Scotland 1956; *m* 28 Aug 1948 Lorna Helen Janet (*d* 1984), er dau of Rev Donald MacLeod, of Balvonie of Inshes, Inverness, and *d* 1991, leaving:

  (1) Sir JOHN MAXWELL NORMAN MacLEOD, **5th and present Bt**
  (2) +NEIL DAVID; *b* 25 Dec 1959; heir presumptive; *educ* Edinburgh Acad
  (1) *Eva Mary Ellen; *b* 5 April 1950

1 Ellen; *m* 17 Dec 1918 Rev James Alan Cameron Murray (*d* 1966), MA, BD, and had issue

MACLURE

Arms: Arg., on a chevron engrailed az., between two roses in chief and a quatrefoil in base gu., a martlet between two escallops of the field **Crest:** An eagle's head erased arg. between four roses gu., stalked and leaved, two on either side, ppr. **Motto:** *Paratus sum* ('I am prepared'). **Creation:** Bt. (UK) 12 March 1898.

SIR JOHN ROBERT SPENCER MACLURE, 4TH BT, of The Home, Whalley Range, nr Manchester, Co Palatine of Lancaster [Sir John Maclure Bt, Croftmhor, Pitlochry, Perthshire PH16 5JR; Wild Goose Cottage, Gooseham, Cornwall EX23 9PG]; *b* 25 March 1934; *s* f 1980; *educ* Winchester; Headmaster Croftinloan Sch Pitlochry, Perthshire 1978–92, 1996–98; *m* 26 Aug 1964 *Jane Monica, dau of Rt Rev Thomas Joseph Savage, Bp Zululand and Swaziland, and has:

1 +(JOHN) MARK [Mark Maclure Esq, Stable Cottage, Rectory Lane, Fringford, Oxon OX6 9DX]; *b* 27 Aug 1965; *educ* Winchester; *m* 17 Aug 1996 *Emily, yr dau of Peter Frean, of Aberdeen, and Mrs Elisabeth Austing, of Salisbury, and has:

  (1) +John James; *b* 4 Sept 1997

2 +Thomas Stephen; *b* 11 Dec 1967

3 +Graham Spencer; *b* 1970

4 +Stephen Patrick Ian; *b* 1974

Lineage: JOHN McCLURE; *m* 13 June 1723 Margaret Martin and had:

MARTYN McCLURE; *b* 1724; *m* 1st — and had an est s:

WILLIAM McCLURE, of Middle Hulton, Lancs; *m* Alice Iriam (*d* 1796) and *d* Feb 1793, leaving:

WILLIAM McCLURE, of Tyldesley, Lancs, and Manchester; *b* 16 Oct 1773; *m* 1796 Hannah (*d* 31 Jan 1856), dau of George Grundy, of Wigan, and *d* 1847, leaving:

JOHN McCLURE, of Manchester; *b* 10 Nov 1800; *m* 20 Dec 1827 Elizabeth (*d* 27 Nov 1881), dau of William Kearsley, Manchester merchant, and had:

1 Edward Crig McCLURE later MACLURE (Very Rev); DD Oxon, LLD Owen's Coll Manchester, Dean Manchester, Curate St John's Ladywood, Birmingham, 1857–61, St Pancras 1861–63, Vicar Harbergham-Eaves 1863–77, Rochdale 1877–90, Hon Canon Manchester 1878–90, RD Rochdale 1881–90, Archdeacon designate Manchester 1890; b 10 June 1833; m May 1863 Mary Ann, dau of Johnson Gedge, of Bury St Edmunds, Suffolk, and d 8 May 1906, leaving surv issue two sons and three daus

2 JOHN WILLIAM (Sir), **1st Bt**

3 Henry Martyn, of Maida Hill, London; b 26 Feb 1837; m Sept 1863 Fanny Maria, dau of Robert Smith of Manchester, and d 8 April 1902, leaving a s and dau

1 Mary; d unm 12 Sept 1907

2 Elizabeth; m 9 May 1867 Rev Henry Isaac Sharp (d 17 March 1892), Rector Downham, Hon Canon Ely, Cambs, and d 12 June 1902, leaving issue

JOHN McCLURE d 4 Dec 1858; his 2nd s,

Sir JOHN WILLIAM McCLURE later MACLURE, **1st Bt** (UK), so cr 12 March 1898, of The Home, Whalley Range, Manchester, JP Manchester, JP and DL Lancs; b 22 April 1835; MP Stretford 1886–1901, KGStJ, Maj 40th Lancs Rifle Vols, Hon Sec Cotton Famine Relief Fund 1862–65; m 13 Dec 1859 Eleanor (d 1 April 1910), 2nd dau of Thomas Nettleship, of E Sheen, Surrey, and had:

1 JOHN EDWARD STANLEY (Sir), **2nd Bt**

2 William George Percy, OBE (1925); b 19 March 1871; educ Rossall; MIMech E, MILocoE; d unm 13 Dec 1953

3 Alan Francis, CB (1921), TD, DL Lancs; b 24 Sept 1873; Col TA, cmdg 1st/7th Bn Lancs Fus, Hon Col 1927; d unm 23 May 1929

1 Ethel Annie; m 19 Sept 1885 Edward Sholto Douglas, of Bexhill, Sussex, and d 9 Aug 1944, having had:

2 Mildred Campbell; m 11 Aug 1885 Maj John Sington, DL (d 11 Aug 1922), of Dunham House, Dunham Massey, Cheshire, and d 1950, leaving issue

3 Margaret Eleanor, MBE (1918), JP Lancs; d unm 25 May 1929

4 Constance Mary; m 6 Sept 1899 Col William Hancock Tucker, IMS (d 7 Dec 1934), and d 14 June 1955, leaving issue

Sir JOHN d 28 Jan 1901; his est s,

Sir John Edward Stanley Maclure, **2nd Bt**; b 25 Feb 1869; Col, Ch Paymaster, Staff GOC Scottish Cmd, formerly Manchester Regt; m 14 April 1898 Ruth Ina Muriel (d 3 Dec 1951), er dau of Cdr Wallace Bruce McHardy, RN, Ch Constable Lanarks, and had:

1 JOHN WILLIAM SPENCER (Sir), **3rd Bt**

2 +Edward Stanley Winton [Lt-Cdr Edward Maclure RN, Flat No 1, Hinton House, Jubilee Rd, Waterlooville, Hants PO7 7QX]; b 11 April 1909; m 22 Dec 1938 Jeanette Kathleen (d 15 Jan 1969), er dau of Anton Bakker, of Sydney, NSW, and has:

(1) *Caroline Eleanor Kathleen [Mrs Caroline van Tienen, Abeelstraat 154, 3329 A H Dordrecht, Netherlands]; b 27 Oct 1939; educ London U (BA); m 22 Sept 1964 (divorce 1989) Gerard Jozef van Tienen, s of A J van Tienen, of Leiden, and has:

1a *Robbert Rudolf; b 25 Feb 1967; m 19– *Emma — and has:

1b *Elizabet; b 18 Sept 1996

2a *Richard Mark; b 21 Feb 1970

(2) *Margaret Elizabeth Anne [Mrs Raymond Hibberd, 1A Spur Rd, Waterlooville, Hants]; b 2 Feb 1941; m 26 April 1969 *Raymond Hibberd, s of H Hibberd, of Portsmouth, and has:

1a *Simon Philip; b 2 June 1972

2a *Nicholas Adam; b 21 Nov 1975

(3) *Yvonne Irene Valerie [Mrs Brian Thompson, 35 George V Ave, Westbrook, Margate, Kent]; b 27 Feb 1943; m 1st 23 May 1964 (divorce 1972) Albert Brian Challinor and has:

1a *Ian Grant; b 10 July 1965

1a *Susan Jane; b 13 Sept 1967

(3) (cont.) Mrs Yvonne Challinor m 2nd 1972 *Brian Henry Thompson, RN, and by him has:

2a *Fiona Kate; b 3 June 1973

3a *Alexandra Louise; b 27 June 1975

4a *Caroline Elizabeth; b 21 Feb 1978

1 Ruth Ina Margaret; b 24 June 1900; d 5 March 1977

2 *Edith Mary Ursula [Mrs Louis Hutchison, Ramon, Salles 47150, Monflanquin, France]; b 9 Jan 1916; m 2 Sept 1939 F/O Louis Gordon Oliphant Hutchison, RAF (d 4 Jan 1959), 2nd s of Alexander Hutchison, of Strathairly, Upper Largo, Fife, and has:

(1) *Alexander Gordon Oliphant [Alexander Hutchison Esq, Batworthy Mill, Batworthy, Devon]; b 27 May 1943; m 1967 *Jennifer Marilyn, yr dau of Alun Blackwell, and has:

1a *Alexander Valentine Oliphant; b 1968

2a *William Lawrence Oliphant; b 1969

3a *James Hardy Oliphant; b 1973

(1) *Susan Ruth Oliphant [Mrs Colin Costello-Jones, Les Bourges, Salles 47150, Monflanquin, France]; b 29 June 1941; m 1st 19 Sept 1959 John Chislett (d 5 Jan 1962) and has:

1a *Miles Gordon; b 8 May 1960; m 1986 *Elizabeth Robinson and has:

1b *Hannah Georgina; b 1986

(1) (cont.) Mrs John Chislett m 2nd 25 June 1962 (divorce 1975) Jonathan Frederick Macnaught Ruddick and by him has:

2a *Francis Louis; b 17 Oct 1962

3a *Simon William; b 3 Oct 1964

1a *Charlotte Nina; b 3 Aug 1966

2a *Romany Lara; b 1974

(1) (cont.) Mrs Susan Ruddick m 3rd 1976 *Colin Costello-Jones and by him has:

4a *Benjamin Llewelyn; b 1981

3a *Harriet; b 1984

(2) *Philippa Anne Oliphant; b 30 May 1946; m 1st 4 May 1963 (divorce 1970) Donald Stuart Oldham, est s of Stanley Allan Oldham, of Cippenham, Bucks, and has:

1a *Tamsin; b 29 Sept 1963; m 1985 *Jonathan Seymour and has:

1b *Alice; b 1986

2a *Jessica; b 25 March 1966; m 1988 *James Eager and has:

1b *Amy; b 1989

(2) (cont.) Mrs Philippa Oldham m 2nd 1972 *Patrick John Bugg and by him has:

*Fletcher Charlie; b 1973

Sir JOHN d 16 Nov 1938; his er s,

Sir John William Spencer Maclure, **3rd Bt**, OBE (1945); b 4 Feb 1899; educ Wellington and RMC Sandhurst; Lt-Col KRRC WW I, Russia 1919, WW II in BAOR 1944–47, cmded 41 Garrison Hook of Holland 1947–49; m 27 April 1929 Elspeth King, er dau of Alexander King Clark (see CLARK, Bt, of Dunlambert), and d 1 March 1980, leaving:

1 Sir JOHN ROBERT SPENCER MACLURE, **4th and present Bt**

2 +Patrick Stanley Winton King [Patrick Maclure Esq, Flat 2, 25 Christchurch Rd, Winchester, Hants SO23 9SU]; b 12 March 1939; educ Winchester; consultant, Ch Exec Friends of Winchester Coll

1 *Elspeth Rosemary [Mrs Michael Matthews, Selhurst, Barton's Lane, Old Basing, Hants RG24 8AN]; b 31 Aug 1930; SRN 1954; m 16 July 1955 Maj-Gen Michael Matthews, CB, DL, AMBIM, RE (d 1993), s of William Matthews, of Chagford, Devon, and has:

(1) *Graeme Michael Ian [Graeme Matthews Esq, 110 Newland, Witney, Oxon]; b 19 Aug 1959; m 1987 *Sophie L K, yr dau of Ralph Denne, of Henley-on-Thames, and Lady Hodson, of Romsey, and has:

1a *Benjamin Michael David; b 1989

2a *Oscar William; b 1991

3a *Mungo George; b 1993

4a *Hamish Max; b 1995

(2) *James Binding; b 17 May 1966; m 1990 Jennifer J Harper-Hill and has:

1a *Katherine Olivia Elspeth; b 1993

2a *Annabel Jane Elspeth; b 1995

(1) *Nichola Jane; b 15 May 1957

(2) *Elspeth Julie; b 11 Oct 1963

MACNAGHTEN

Arms: Quarterly, 1st and 4th, argent a dexter arm fessways proper, holding a cross-crosslet fitchée azure; 2nd and 3rd, argent a tower embattled gules. **Crest:** A tower embattled gules. **Supporters:** Two roebucks proper. **Motto:** I hope in God. **Creation:** Bt. (UK) 16 July 1836.

SIR PATRICK ALEXANDER MACNAGHTEN, 11TH BT, of Macnaghten and Dundarave, Co Antrim [Sir Patrick Macnaghten Bt, Dundarave, Bushmills, Co Antrim BT57 8ST]; b 24 Jan 1927; educ Eton and Trin Coll Cambridge; s f 1972; m 10 Sept 1955 *Marianne, yr dau of Dr Erich Schaefer, of Clement Place, Cambridge, and has:

1 +MALCOLM FRANCIS; b 21 Sept 1956

2 +Edward Alexander; b 24 July 1958

3 +David Charles; b 22 Sept 1962

Lineage: The MACNAGHTENS are one of three clans descended from the old Mormaers (see BUCHAN, E, preliminary remarks) of Moray. In the 12th century MALCOLM IV granted lands to the MACNACHTANs (as they were then known) as part of a policy of breaking the power of the former Mormaers of Moray. The MACNACHTANs in question were for a time styled Thanes of Loch Tay but by the 13th century their Chiefs had settled in Argyllshire. In 1267 ALEXANDER III granted custody of the island castle of Frechelan in Lochawe to Gillechrist MacNachdan. By the 16th century the Chiefs' principal residence was Dunderave Castle on Loch Fyne, which remained in their possession till the 18th century. In 1627 Alexander Macnachtan raised a force of bowmen to help relieve the Huguenot stronghold in France of La Rochelle. In 1653 his nephew Alexander participated in a rising against the Commonwealth led by the Earl of Glencairn (see

CUNINGHAME, Bt). On 10 July 1689 Alexander's son John fought on the Jacobite side in the victory over the Williamites of Killiecrankie. Although the forfeiture of the clan lands which followed was soon rescinded, the MACNACHTENs had accumulated such debts in support of the STUARTs that their Chiefs had to sell most of their property. Alexander, John's elder son, was a Captain in the Guards in QUEEN ANNE's reign and was killed in Spain at the start of the War of the Spanish Succession in 1702. His brother John, Inspector-General of Customs in Scotland, succeeded to the Chiefship but died without issue after 1753, by which time all the clan property had been lost.

A yr s of the MACNACHTANs of Dunderave,

JOHN *Shane Dhu* ('Black John') MACNACHTEN; went to Ireland *c* 1580 as secretary to his bro-in-law Sorley *Buie* Macdonnell (*see* ANTRIM, E); had an est s:

JOHN MACNAGHTEN, of Ballymagarry; *d* 1630, leaving an est s:

DANIEL MACNACHTEN, of Benvarden, Co Antrim; had:

DANIEL MACNACHTEN; *m* Catherine, dau of George Dowdale, Archbp Armagh, and had:

JOHN MACNACHTEN, of Benvarden, Co Antrim; *m* Helen, dau of Francis Stafford, of Portglenone, and had a 4th s:

EDMUND MACNACHTEN, of Beardiville, Co Antrim; *b* 10 Aug 1679; present as a child at Siege of Londonderry; refused the chiefship of the MACNAGHTANs despite a clan deputation having travelled from Scotland to offer it to him following the extinction of the Scottish line; *m* 1st Leonora Vesey, by whom he had no issue; *m* 2nd 1761 Hannah, dau of John Johnstone, and *d* 1781 having by her had, with an er s (Edmund Alexander, of Beardiville, *b* 2 Aug 1762, barrister, MP Co Antrim (I Parl) 1788–1800, (UK Parl) 1800–12 and 1826–30 and Oxford 1812–26, a Ld Treasury 1819–30, recognised 1818 as Chief of the MACNAGHTENs by warrant of Ld Lyon, *d* unm March 1832):

Sir FRANCIS MACNAGHTEN later WORKMAN-MACNAGHTEN (roy licence 18 Nov 1809), **1st Bt** (UK), so *cr* 16 July 1836, of Dundarave, Co Antrim; *b* 2 Aug 1763; barrister 1788, Judge Supreme Court Madras 1809–15, Calcutta 1815–25, ktd 1809; *m* 6 Dec 1787 Letitia, est dau of Sir William Dunkin of Clogher, sometime a Judge of the Supreme Court of Judicature at Calcutta, and *d* 22 Nov 1843, having had:

1 EDMUND CHARLES (Sir), **2nd Bt**

2 Sir WILLIAM HAY MACNAGHTEN, 1st and last Bt (UK), so *cr* 18 Jan 1840; *b* 24 Aug 1793; BCS; *m* 2 Aug 1823 Frances (*m* 2nd 5 Feb 1853 2nd Marquess of Headfort (*qv*) and *d* 2 March 1878), dau of John Livingstone Martyn, and *dsp* (*k* Kabul during Afghan War) 25 Dec 1841, when the btcy expired

3 Francis; *b* 21 Feb 1789; BCS; *m* 6 Jan 1831 Ellen (*d* 17 March 1893), dau of Valentine Conolly, and *d* 6 Nov 1869, having had:

(1) Francis; BCS; *m* 8 Oct 1861 Bessie (*d* 7 Feb 1901), dau of G Westoby, and *dsp* 1 May 1879

(2) Arthur William; *b* 19 May 1835; Col Bombay Cav; *m* 12 Oct 1861 Louisa (*d* 30 Oct 1929), dau of Nelson Howard, HEICS, and *d* 24 Oct 1919, leaving:

1a Francis William; *b* 10 Dec 1865; *d* 18 Sept 1938

1a Blanche Alice; *m* 2 Oct 1889 Maj-Gen Edward Hughes Hemming, CMG (*ka* 20 April 1943), RE, and *d* 8 Nov 1942, leaving issue

2a Minnie Louisa; *m* 25 April 1900 Peter William Barker, est s of Rev Canon J T Barker, of Rushden, Northants, and *dsp* 9 Oct 1902

3a Mabel Margaret; *m* 1 Dec 1898 Edward Perceval Parsons (*d* 8 March 1934) and *d* 28 Nov 1951, leaving issue

4a Ellen Mary; *m* 9 April 1902 Maurice Walter Brodie Brockwell, s of Rev J C Brockwell, and *d* 4 Feb 1951, leaving issue

5a Kathleen Florence; *m* 24 Oct 1908 Maj George Maconchy Lee, DSO, MC (*d* 18 March 1960), Roy Fus, and *d* 13 April 1965, having had a s

6a Olive; *d* unm 1 June 1933

(3) Elliot Henry; *b* 1839; Capt 20th Hus; *m* 20 Jan 1864 Maria (*d* 5 Nov 1920), dau of William Mills Edye, and was *ka* 8 May 1878, leaving:

1a Steuart Edye; *b* 1873; *d* unm 9 Dec 1952

1a Ellen Emily; *d* unm 29 Nov 1949

2a Isabella; *d* unm 22 May 1952

3a Mary; *d* unm Feb 1942

(4) Steuart Lambert; *b* 1841; *m* 1878 Caroline Matilda (*d* 4 April 1929), dau of Rev Christopher J Garstin, and *d* 29 Sept 1900, having had:

1a Edmund Loftus (Rev); *b* 1879; *educ* Trin Coll Dublin (BA 1902); Capt RE, Rector Stanhoe with Barwick Norfolk 1938; *m* 1912 Ethel May, dau of Francis Scaife, and *d c* 1942

2a Steuart Cecil; *b* 4 Oct 1881; Capt RASC; *m* 6 Feb 1915 Hilda Marion (*d* 28 Dec 1957), dau of Henry Jenks, of Dunairds, Birnam, Perthshire, and Barrow Hedges, Carshalton, and *d* 9 Nov 1918, leaving:

1b (Steuart) Patrick; *b* 5 April 1917; *educ* Sherborne; Maj Derbys Yeo; *m* 2 Dec 1961 Beatrix, widow of Stanley Wyatt-Smith and dau of Lt-Col Sir Francis Metford, KCB, OBE, DL, of Burleigh, Glos

(5) Edmond Ross; *b* 1845; *m* 20 Sept 1876 Harriet (*d* 21 Feb 1923), dau of Rev Christopher J Garstin, and *d* 28 Jan 1905, having had:

1a Ellen Maria; *b* 1877; *d* unm 26 Feb 1969

2a Norah Elizabeth; *m* 15 Nov 1911 Thomas Joseph Collins (*d* 3 May 1937), s of Patrick Collins, of Dublin, and *d* 1943, leaving issue

(6) Alfred Hill; *b* 12 Nov 1848; *m* 27 Nov 1873 Arabella Marie (*d* 4 June 1931), dau of William Betts, of Frenze Hall, Norfolk, and *d* 13 Nov 1915, having had:

1a Balfour, DSO (1917); *b* 23 Dec 1875; Lt-Col 12th Roy Lancers, Boer War 1902 (medals and clasps), W Africa 1905–07 (medal with clasps), WW I (wounded, despatches); *m* 8 Feb 1902 Hilda (*d* 26 Nov 1958), est dau of William George Lardner, of Hove, and *d* 23 July 1945, having had:

1b Steuart Balfour; *b* 18 April 1903; *d* 2 March 1920

1b Daphne; *b* 7 Nov 1914; *m* 1 March 1940 Lt-Col Richard Percival Hawksley Burbury, DCLI (*ka* 8 June 1944), of Yorks

2a Steuart Maxwell; *b* 25 May 1880; 2nd Lt KRRC; *ka* S Africa 26 June 1901

1a Ella Margaret; *m* 19 March 1910 Capt John Colloyran Michell (*ka* 28 Aug 1914), 12th Roy Lancers, est s of John Michell, ISO, and *dsp* 31 Aug 1965

2a Violet Eileen; *d* unm 20 May 1958

4 Elliot; *b* 1 April 1807; memb Supreme Court Calcutta and India Cncl; *m* 1st 4 Feb 1833 Isabella (*d* 1 May 1871), dau of John Law; *m* 2nd 5 Sept 1872 Anne (*dsp* 4 May 1903), dau of George Chester (*see* BAGOT, B), and *d* 24 Dec 1888, having had, with three other daus (*d* unm):

(1) Elliot; *b* 13 Jan 1837; ICS, barrister; *m* 10 Sept 1859 Jane Maria (*d* 27 Jan 1891), dau of Thomas Gowan Vibart, BCS, and *d* 18 March 1875, leaving:

1a Russell Elliot; *b* 19 Nov 1860; BA Cantab; barrister, Prof Greek U Coll BC, Assist Prof Classics McGill, Montreal; *m* 1891 Mary (*d* 1950), dau of Frederick Berry, and *d* 6 July 1918 leaving:

1b Ronald Frederick, DSO (1918); *b* 1893; *educ* Vancouver and New Coll Oxford; barrister, slr, memb BC Law Soc and Vancouver Bar Assoc, WW I as Capt Canadian Inf (despatches); *d* unm 11 Feb 1958

1b Eva Fraoch; *b* 1895; *m* 1922 Frederick Ivor Jackson and had issue

2b *Kathleen Edith; *b* 1903; *m* 1934 Edward C R Cardinall of Skaha Lake, Penticton, BC, and has:

1c *Edward Russell; *b* 1936

1c *Sandra Margaret; *b* 1934

2c *Chloe Joan; *b* 1936 (twin)

2a Hugh Vibart; *b* 30 Jan 1862; MA Cantab, V-Provost Eton, Fell Trin Coll Cambridge; *d* unm 11 Aug 1929

3a Terence Charles, CMG (1923), CBE (1918); *b* 3 Dec 1872; *educ* Hertford Coll Oxford (BA); Colonial Office, Adminr St Christopher and Nevis 1929–31, ret 1931; *d* unm 30 June 1944

1a Kathleen Maria; *d* unm 22 Sept 1926

2a Eva Mary; *d* unm 18 April 1936

(2) Francis Hill; *b* 1840; Capt 5th Bombay Cav; *m* Emma Casement (*m* 2nd Rev A L Barnes Lawrence and *d* 1 Dec 1927), dau of T R Davidson, and *dsp* 14 Jan 1868

(3) William Hay, CB; *b* 1842; Col 13th Bengal Cav; *m* 15 April 1869 Alice Ellen (*d* 1926), dau of Lt-Gen Mangles James Brander, ISC, and *d* 1 July 1889, leaving:

1a Frank Chester; *b* 4 Aug 1871; Lt Roy Irish Regt; *d* unm 3 Aug 1897

2a Ernest Brander, CMG (1917), DSO (1915); *b* 11 Sept 1872; *educ* Wellington and RMA Woolwich; Col RA, Hon Brig-Gen 1920, ADC to HM GEORGE V 1920, served W Africa 1898–99 and 1906, Boer War 1899–1902, Somaliland 1902–04 (despatches twice), WW I (despatches eight times), Croix de Guerre, Chm Municipal Cncl Shanghai Internat Settlement; *m* 4 Oct 1906 Yvonne Marie (*d* 24 April 1950), only dau of Surgn-Col James Samuel Forrester, RHG, and *d* 21 Nov 1948, leaving:

1b James Steuart; *b* 19 June 1914; *educ* Eton and Ch Ch Oxford (MA 1937); Maj RA, with ICI 1949 on; *d* unm 15 March 1997

1b Susan May; *b* 26 July 1909; *m* 3 Oct 1936 Sir Duncan Morris Oppenheim, ARCA, 2nd s of Watkin Oppenheim, TD, and *d* 14 Sept 1964 leaving a s and dau

2b *Joan Yvonne Marie; *b* 29 March 1911

3b *Awdry Clarisse Macnaghten; *b* 19 June 1914; *m* 23 July 1936 Brig Anthony Donald Macdonald Teacher, CBE, DL (*d* 18 Sept 1969), RA, est s of Donald Macdonald Teacher, of Spittal-on-Rule, and has:

1c *(Anthony) James Moreton [James Teacher Esq, Hadlow Place, nr Tonbridge, Kent TN11 0BW]; *b* 8 Aug 1937; *educ* Wellington and Ch Ch Oxford (MA 1964); *m* 26 April 1969 *(Rosemary) Chloe, DL (Kent 1997), High Sheriff 1994, yr dau of Sir Henry Joseph d'Avigdor-Goldsmid, 2nd Bt, DSO, MC, MP (*see* 1970 edn), and has:

1d *Harry Donald Macdonald; *b* 14 Oct 1970; *educ* Eton and Ch Ch, Oxford (BA)

1d *(Laura) Poppy; *b* 30 May 1973; *educ* Wycombe Abbey and LMH Oxford (BA)

2d *Petra Rose; *b* 8 June 1980; *educ* Wycombe Abbey

3d *Sarah Cordelia; *b* 23 March 1983; *educ* Wycombe Abbey

2c *Hugh Macdonald; *b* 7 Dec 1943; *educ* Wellington, Goethe Institute Munich, Trin Coll Dublin and Oatridge Ag Coll; *m* 14 July 1977 *Rosemary, only dau of Sir David John Hatherley Page Wood, 7th Bt (*qv*), and has:

1d *James Henry Macdonald; *b* 5 July 1979

4b *Renée Gavrelle; *b* 18 July 1918; *m* 1st 9 April 1938 Lt-Cdr Alexander Arthur Wyndham Baker, RN (*d* 12 July 1969), only s of Frank Wyndham Baker; *m* 2nd 1971 William Henry Guilland Stenson, CBE and has by her 1st husb:

1c *Mark Alexander Wyndham, CBE [Mark Baker Esq CBE, The Old School, Fyfield, Oxon OX13 5LR]; *b* 19 June 1940; *educ* Prince Edward Sch Salisbury Rhodesia, U Coll of Rhodesia and Nyasaland (BA 1961) and Ch Ch Oxford (BA 1964); *m* 30 July 1964 *Meriel, yr dau of Capt Edward Hugh Frederick Chetwynd Talbot, MBE (*see* SHREWSBURY and WATERFORD, E), and has:

1d *Alexander Duncan; *b* 28 Sept 1968

1d *Miranda Gavrelle; *b* 1970

2c *Gavin Jeremy Wyndham; *b* 2 Aug 1944; *educ* St Stephen's Coll Balla Balla; *m* 1971 *Joanna Gwendoline, dau of G/Capt G B Bell, RAF, and has:

1d *Rebecca Beatrice; *b* 27 Sept 1973

2d *Lisa Renée; *b* 5 Feb 1975

3a Leslie Hay; *b* 12 Sept 1875; *educ* Wellington; Dir Public Works Somaliland, Somaliland Field Force 1920 (despatches); *m* 27 March 1906 Hilda Mary Ethelind (*d* 11 Dec 1973), dau of Rev Jocelyn Barnes, Vicar St Breage and St Germoe, Cornwall, and *d* 11 Aug 1950, having had:

1b Cyril Jocelyn Gillichrist; *b* 31 Oct 1907; *educ* Wellington; Lt RNVR WW II; *m* 18 Feb 1932 Mary Evelyne (*d* 1 Jan 1954), yr dau of G E Mullens, of Teddington, Australia, and was *ka* 9 June 1943, leaving:

1c +Alexander Michael Gillichrist [Alexander Macnaghten Esq, Jabiru Jetty, 12 Kiap Rd, Yunderup Canals, W Australia 6208]; *b* 27 April 1940; *educ* Wellington and RAC Cirencester; Memb Cwlth Inst Valuers; *m* 1st 1971 (*divorce* 1975) Vanessa, dau of Duncan Charles

Beresford-Ord, of Beverley Lodge, Mill Point Rd, S Perth, Australia; m 2nd 1983 *Vanessa Keran, 2nd dau of David Pay, of Guernsey

1c *Angela Kay [Mrs John Woodward, High House, Scopwick, Lincs LN4 3PA]; b 24 June 1935; m 3 Sept 1960 *John Woodward, s of Edward Gerard Woodward, of Estoril, Portugal, and has:

  1d *Andrew St John; b 29 Nov 1965

  1d *Sarah Mary; b 14 July 1963

2b +Geoffrey Leslie [Geoffrey Macnaghten Esq, 123 Old Church St, London SW3 6EA]; b 22 June 1909; educ Malvern; F/Lt RAFVR WW II, Appeals Sec Imperial Cancer Research Fund, MIPR; m 9 Sept 1937 Hilary Marriott (d 1989), yr dau of Thomas Amelius Marriott Castle, of Tangier, and has:

  1d *Jennifer Rosemary [Mrs David Mattinson, 14 Rectory Gdns, Broadwater, W Sussex BN14 7TE]; b 30 Sept 1939; m 1968 *David Guthrie Mattinson and has:

    1e *John; b 1974

    1e *Michelle; b 1966

  2d *Sarah Lynne; b 25 July 1954

3b +Douglas Melville [Douglas Macnaghten Esq, Hill Brow, Beacon Hill Rd, Ewshot, Surrey GU10 5DB]; b 14 March 1911; educ Wellington; Maj RASC WW II (Africa star, Italy star, 1939–45 star), late with Spicers Internat; m 23 April 1946 Thecla Isabel (d 1987), twin dau of John Mundell Reid, of Greenock, and has:

  1c *Lorraine Thecla Ethelind; b 8 June 1947; m 1982 *Alastair Ford-Young and has:

    1e *Jeremy David; b 1984

    2e *Nicholas James; b 1985

  2c *Camilla Dawn [Mrs Camilla Whittle, The Cottage, Holmwood Place, Ide Hill Rd, Four Elms, Kent TN8 6NT]; b 22 May 1950; m 1971 (divorce 1979) Timothy William Whittle; has:

    1e *Anastasia Isabella b 1993

1b Phyllis Eileen; b and d 5 Jan 1907

2b Millicent; b and d 5 Jan 1907

4a Arthur Edward Hay; b 1887; 2nd Lt 20th Bn Roy Sussex Regt; ka 31 July 1916

1a Violet Isabella; m 1st 1898 F Harold Carlyon, MD, of Johannesburg, and had issue; m 2nd 8 Nov 1912 Edmund Hugh Farrer, CMG (d 19 Feb 1955), and d 1918

2a Maud; m 1904 Ivor Miller and d Jan 1929

(4) Chester; b 4 May 1843; educ Trin Coll Cambridge (MA); Pncpl Rajkumar Coll India; m 1st Isabella Julia (d 1880), dau of Rev G Hodgkinson; m 2nd 1882 Susan Ferrier (d 25 July 1906), dau of James John Kinloch, of Kair, Kincardineshire, and dsp 10 Feb 1896

(5) Henry Alexander (Rev); Rector Tankersley, Yorks; Canon Sheffield; b 1850; educ King's Coll Cambridge (MA); m 1st 28 Aug 1873 Louisa (d 28 Dec 1921), dau of Ross Donnelly Mangles; m 2nd 3 Feb 1925 Evelyn Vere (d 7 Nov 1939), only dau of William L Boyle, MP Mid Norfolk (see CORK and ORRERY, E), and d 17 July 1928, having had by his 1st w:

  1a Henry Pelham Wentworth (Sir); b 4 Sept 1880; educ Eton and King's Coll Cambridge (BA 1902, MA); E Indian merchant, ktd 1924; m 16 July 1919 Frances Alice (d 12 Oct 1969), yr dau of Very Rev James Cropper, Rector Penshurst, Kent, and d 29 May 1949, having had:

    1b Edward Cropper; b 10 June, d 5 Nov 1920

    2b Angus David Henry; b 17 June 1923; educ Eton; Capt Rifle Bde WW II (wounded); m 30 Jan 1952 Sally (d 1991), only child of Edmund Hannay Watts, of Kensington, and d 1988, leaving:

      1c +David Edmund; b 12 May 1954; educ Stowe

      2c +Stuart Ben; b 2 May 1957; m 1st 1988 Joanna Crittall; m 2nd 1993 *Mrs Emma Monaghan, née Majdalany, and has by his 1st w:

        1e +Ben Henry; b 1989

      3c +Patrick Henry Donnelly; b 8 Jan 1959; m 19– *Pamela J, yr dau of S/Ldr K J White of Skellingthorpe, Lincs

    3b +Robin Donnelly [Robin Macnaghten Esq, Prospect House, Tisbury, Wilts SP3 6QQ]; b 3 Aug 1927; educ Eton and King's Coll Cambridge; Eton Coll housemaster, headmaster Sherborne 1974–88; m 12 Aug 1961 *Petronella Anne, er dau of Lt-Col Arthur Trevor Thompson Card, of The Old Vicarage, Holt, Wimborne, Dorset, and adopted:

      *Alexander Hugh [Alexander Macnaghten Esq, 3 Ballard Rd, Willingham, Cambridge]; b 24 July 1965; m 1994 *Gillian, dau of Ronald Law, of Dundee; and has:

        1d *James George; b 17 Oct 1997

      *James Donnelly; b 17 Nov 1969

      *Frances Bridget [Mrs Trevor Jolley, 3 Emmington, N Thame, Oxon]; b 1 Feb 1967; m 1990 *Trevor William Jolley, yr s of Rev Arthur Jolley, of Boston, Lincs, and has:

        1d *Hannah; b 1992

        2d *Laura; b 1994

    1b Pauline Frances; b 26 May 1925, d Dec 1925

    2b Caroline Priscilla; b 21 May 1931; m 21 May 1966 *Don Collis, s of Ernest Collis, of Birmingham, and had:

      1c *Chayley Zillah; b 20 Feb 1969

  2a Norman Donnelly, OBE (1918); b 26 Sept 1881; educ Eton and King's Coll Cambridge (BA 1903); Min Interior Egypt, Order Nile; m 9 May 1916 Ida Shackell (d 1 Jan 1978), dau of Edmund Gunning, of Twerton-on-Avon, and dsp 26 Nov 1964

    1a Ethelred Theodora; b 19 Oct 1883; m 24 Jan 1918 Very Rev Richard Henry Malden, BD (d 19 Aug 1951), Dean Wells, s of Charles Edward Malden, Recorder Thetford, and d 21 Aug 1960

(6) Melville Leslie (Sir), CB, JP Middx; b 16 June 1853; Assist Commr Met Police 1903–13, ktd 1907, Kt Cdr White Mil Order Spain, Cdr Order Dannebrog 2nd Cl; m 3 Oct 1878 Dora Emily (d 8 Jan 1929), est dau of Rev Canon Robert Edward Sanderson, DD, and d 12 May 1921, leaving:

1a Charles Melville, CMG; b 18 Nov 1879; BA Cantab, Lt-Col cmdg 4th Bn Australian Inf 1915–16 (wounded, despatches); m 30 Dec 1904 Nina, dau of Dr Hopcroft, and d Feb 1931

2a Gillichrist Edward Melville; b 25 Nov 1894; Capt 21st Bn London Regt; m 1918 Eleanor, dau of His Hon Judge John William McCarthy, and d 10 July 1939

1a Julia Mary Melville; b 10 Sept 1881; m 3 Oct 1903 Edward Oscar Donner (d 23 June 1926), s of Julius Donner, of Priesthill, Englefield Green, and d 2 Oct 1938, having had issue (see SANDERSON, Bt)

2a Christabel Mary Melville; b 12 Dec 1890; m 19 July 1910 2nd Baron Aberconway (qv) and d 7 Aug 1974, leaving issue

(1) Helena; m 20 Oct 1863 Rev Canon John Thomas Barker (d 1890), Rector Rushden, and d 10 Jan 1907, leaving issue

(2) Mary Charlotte; m 3 Dec 1867 F S Chapman (d 1887) and d 19 July 1905

(3) Alice Catherine; m 14 June 1870 Rev Canon Charles James Hamilton, of Walton Warren, Burton-on-Trent, Vicar St John, Derby, and d 10 May 1919, leaving:

(4) Fanny; m 3 Dec 1867 A A Dick and d 29 Dec 1882

(5) Eliza; d 26 Aug 1923

5 John Dunkin; b 12 May 1810; Capt Bengal Cav; d 1862

6 Steuart (Sir), of Bitterne Manor, Hants, JP, DL Hants; b 20 June 1815; Chm Southampton Dock Co, barrister; m 1st 5 Oct 1848 Agnes (d 28 April 1863), only child of James Eastmont and widow of Captain Lewis Shedden; m 2nd 7 July 1864 Emily Frances (d 5 June 1874), dau of Charlotte, Countess of Antrim (qv) in her own right, and widow of Henry Richardson, of Somerset, Co Derry; m 3rd 10 April 1877 Amy Katharine (d 2 Nov 1906), only dau of Rev Arthur Thomas, of Rottingdean (see 1970 edn WILLINGDON, M), and d 28 June 1895, having by her had:

(1) Angus Charles Rowley Steuart; b 1 June 1883; Lt 3rd Bn Black Watch; m 3 Jan 1911 Hazel Enid (d 23 Dec 1956), dau of Col Lyndon Irwin, IA, and was ka Oct 1914, leaving:

  1a Angus Derek Iain Jacques; b 29 May 1914; educ Eton and Trin Coll Cambridge (BA 1935); Br Cncl 1946, WW II as Maj Intell Corps (despatches); m 1 May 1957 Daphne (d 1984), only dau of Horace Nettleship Soper, and d 1992, having adopted:

    *Fiona Macnaghten; b June 1962; m 1990 *Martin K Asquith, only s of E Asquith, of Blewbury, Oxon, and has:

      1c *Eleanor Daphne; b 1993

(1) Letitia Julia Hannah; b 23 April 1879; d unm 10 June 1949

(2) Laura Maud Amy; b 5 Sept 1880; m 29 May 1908 Cdr Evelyn Culme-Seymour, RN, and d 23 Sept 1958, leaving issue (see CULME-SEYMOUR, Bt)

1 Anne; m 20 July 1809 Rev Richard Olphert (d 1849) and d 10 June 1828

2 Eliza Emeline; m 15 May 1813 Maj-Gen Sewell and d his widow 3 May 1862

3 Letitia; m 12 May 1814 David Hill, HEICCS, and d his widow 8 Feb 1880

4 Matilda; m 6 Dec 1817 John Trotter (d 13 Nov 1852) and dsp March 1852

5 Jane Russell; m 17 Nov 1821 Thomas Gowan Vibart, Bengal CS, and d 13 Oct 1886

6 Maria; m 17 Aug 1822 Thomas Robarts Thellusson (d 29 March 1869) and d 23 Jan 1881, having had issue

7 Caroline; m 20 July 1824 Capt Alfred Chapman (d 9 Nov 1876) and d 2 April 1875, leaving issue

8 Alicia; m 1 June 1826 Capt George Probyn (d 1855), Er Bro Trin Ho, and d 9 Sept 1864

9 Ellen; d unm

10 Hannah; d unm May 1852

The 1st Bt's s,

Sir Edmund Charles Workman-Macnaghten, 2nd Bt; b 1 April 1790; MP Co Antrim; m 17 May 1827 Mary Anne (d 25 April 1885), only child of Edward Gwatkin, and d 6 Jan 1876 having had:

1 **Sir Francis Edmund Workman-Macnaghten, 3rd Bt**, PC; b 9 July 1828; HM Lt Co Antrim, Hon Col 3rd Bn Roy Irish Rifles, Lt-Col 8th Hus; m 6 June 1866 (divorce 1883) Alice Mary, est dau of William Howard Russell, LLD, and dspms 21 July 1911, having had:

(1) Edmund Francis; b 14 Nov 1870; Lt 16th Lancers; d unm 12 Oct 1899

(2) Kenneth William; b 20 March 1875; Capt Roy Fus; d unm 15 April 1903

(1) Mary Alice; b 6 Oct 1867; m 28 Aug 1893 William Robert Young, PC (d 12 Sept 1933), of Galgorm Castle, Co Antrim (see SAINT HELENS, B), and d 9 May 1946, having had issue

(2) Hilda Margaret; b 23 Dec 1868; m 1st 14 Nov 1892 Henry Cecil Phillips, of Clifford, Co Cork; m 2nd 7 March 1907 Richard Arthur Grove Annesley (see ANNESLEY, E) and d 4 March 1961, leaving issue

2 EDWARD (Sir), **4th Bt**

3 William Henry; b 1835; Capt 1st Bengal Light Cav; m 11 Feb 1879 Mary Louisa (d 1 July 1926), yst dau of George Gough, of Rathronan, Clonmel, Co Tipperary, and d 5 May 1915

4 Fergus; b 1836; Bombay CS; d 27 April 1867

5 Edmund Charles; RA; ka 17 March 1861 at Waitara, NZ

1 Mary; d unm 18 May 1857

2 Octavia Helen; m 9 Sept 1869 Colin Glencairn Campbell (d 1889), s of Adml Colin Campbell, of Ardpatrick, Scotland, and nephew of Col Campbell of Islay and Shawfield, and d 20 March 1914, having had issue

The 3rd Bt's bro,

Sir Edward Macnaghten, 4th Bt, and BARON MACNAGHTEN OF RUNKERRY, Co Antrim (LP, UK), so cr 25 Jan 1887, GCB (1911), GCMG (1902), PC (1887); b 3 Feb 1830; educ Queen's Coll Belfast and Trin Coll Cambridge (MA, Fell, Hon Fellow 1902); barrister Lincoln's Inn 1857 (Bencher 1883, Treasurer 1907), QC 1880, MP (C) Co Antrim 1880–85 and N Antrim 1885–87, Hon LLD Dublin, Ld Appeal in Ordinary 1887; m 18 Dec 1858 Frances Arabella (d 22 Oct 1903), dau of Sir Samuel Martin, PC, of Crindle, Co Londonderry, and d 17 Feb 1913, when his Barony expired, having had:

1 **Sir Edward Charles Macnaghten, 5th Bt**, KC (1897), DL Co Antrim; b 9 Oct 1859; BA Cantab; barrister Lincoln's Inn 1885, Bencher 1904; m 1st 20 March

1888 Hon Gwen Elca Violet Abbott (*d* 5 Dec 1891), yst dau of 3rd Baron Tenterden (*see* 1939 edn), and had:

(1) Hugh Aubrey; *b* 1889; *d* 13 March 1894

1 **Sir Edward** *m* 2nd Jan 1894 Edith Minnie (*d* 20 Aug 1948), only dau of Thomas Powell, of Coldra, Mon, and *d* 31 Dec 1914, having by her had:

(2) **Sir Edward Harry Macnaghten, 6th Bt**; *b* 12 Feb 1896; 2nd Lt Black Watch, Roy Highrs, attd 12th Bn Roy Irish Rifles; officially reported missing believed *k* 1 July 1916

(3) **Sir Arthur Douglas Macnaghten, 7th Bt**; *b* 25 Jan 1897; 2nd Lt 8th Bn Rifle Bde, WW I; *ka* 15 Sept 1916

(1) Minnie Frances Edith; *b* 6 May, *d* 28 May 1903

2 **Sir Francis Alexander Macnaghten, 8th Bt**, JP, DL; *b* 18 May 1863; *educ* Eton; *m* 6 July 1905 Beatrice (*d* 12 July 1963), dau of Sir William Ritchie, Ch Justice Supreme Court Canada, and *dsp* 1 Nov 1951

3 **Sir Frederic Fergus Macnaghten, 9th Bt**; *b* 16 May 1867; *educ* Eton and Trin Coll Cambridge (BA); slr 1891; *m* 22 Dec 1914 Ada (*d* 1 Sept 1969), dau of John Webster, and *dsp* 18 Nov 1955

4 Malcolm Martin (Sir), KBE (1920), PC (1948), KC (1919); *b* 12 Jan 1869, *educ* Eton and Trin Coll Cambridge (BA 1891, MA 1895); MP Londonderry N June 1922, Londonderry Co and City 1922, 1923 and 1924–28, barrister Lincoln's Inn 1894, Bencher 1915, Treasurer 1938, memb Bar Cncl 1922, Recorder Colchester 1924–28, Commissary Cambridge U 1936–55, High Court Judge King's Bench 1928–47; *m* 4 Feb 1899 Antonia Mary (*d* 18 Jan 1952), est dau of Charles Booth, PC, FRS (*see* BOOTH, Bt), and *d* 24 Jan 1955, leaving:

(1) ANTONY (Sir), **10th Bt**

(1) *Mary Frances [Mrs Mary Perí, 8 Redwoods, Alton Rd, London SW15]; *b* 2 Feb 1903; *m* 1931 Laszlo Peri (*d* 1965) and has:

1a *William; *b* 1936

2a *Matthew; *b* 1942; *d c* 1960

3a *Anne; *b* 1931

(2) Brigid Alison; *b* 18 Dec 1904; *m* 1933 W JUNGMITTAG later YOUNGDAY (deed poll) and had issue

(3) *Anne Catherine [Mrs Anne Ashby, 23 Wymondley Rd, Hitchin, Herts]; *b* 9 Aug 1908; *m* 1st James Ernest Skilbeck (*d* 22 Jan 1947) and has:

1a *John SKILBECK later ASHBY (changed 1954) [John Ashby Esq, 7 Leazes Place, Durham City]; *b* 3 Oct 1942; *m* *Esther Newman and has:

1b *Rebecca; *b* 14 Feb 1966

2b *Emma Louise; *b* 5 April 1967

(3) (cont.) Mrs James Skilbeck *m* 2nd 1947 Arnold Richardson Ashby (*d* 1994) and by him has:

1a *Catherine; 26 Dec 1947

5 Maurice Patrick; *b* 2 March 1874; Capt Roy Scots Fus, attd Egyptian Army, served Boer War 1899–1900, 3rd Cl Medjidie; *m* 14 Oct 1912 Sybil Torbock (*m* 2nd 31 Dec 1925 Maj Gerald Aylmer, MC (*d* 14 July 1939), and *d* 28 Feb 1969), only dau of Col Henry Graham, 16th Lancers, of Castle House, Hampton, and *dsp* 5 May 1914

1 Frances Helen; *d* unm 12 March 1950 in her 90th year

2 Beatrice Mary; *d* unm 26 July 1950

3 Florence Mary; in charge Canadian Mission, Kangra, Punjab, Kaisar-i-Hind Medal 1st Cl; *d* unm 26 Jan 1941

4 Edith Arabella Mary; *b* 12 Dec 1865; *d* 16 Jan 1866

5 Octavia Mary; *d* unm 8 Aug 1946

6 Anne Julia Mary; Dir Dr Barnardo's Homes; *d* unm 7 March 1949

7 Ethel Mary; *d* unm 18 May 1951

The 9th Bt's nephew,

Sir Antony Macnaghten, 10th Bt; *b* 15 Nov 1899; *educ* Eton and Trin Coll Cambridge (BA 1922); *m* 27 Feb 1926 *Magdalene [Magda Lady Macnaghten, Dundarave, Bushmills, Co Antrim], est dau of Edmund Fisher, and *d* 12 Dec 1972, leaving:

1 Sir PATRICK ALEXANDER MACNAGHTEN, **11th and present Bt**

2 +(Antony) Martin [Martin Macnaghten Esq, Ballyvester House, Donaghadee, Co Down BT21 0LL]; *b* 23 Sept 1930; *educ* Eton and Trin Coll Cambridge (BA 1954); *m* 30 May 1959 *Catherine Frances, only dau of Rev Charles ffolliot Young, of The Vicarage, Castlerock, Co Londonderry, and has:

(1) +Philip Martin; *b* 6 Aug 1965

(2) +Antony Charles; *b* 15 Nov 1971

(1) *Ruth Helen; *b* 19 April 1964; *m* 1992 *Dr Jonathan Holbrook and has:

1a *Hannah Claire; *b* 23 Sept 1995

2a *Rachel; *b* 1 July 1997

(2) *Imogen Alice; *b* 8 June 1970

3 +Charles Edmund [Charles Macnaghten Esq, The Croft, Church St, Seal, Kent]; *b* 4 April 1937; *educ* Eton and Trin Coll Cambridge; *m* 25 Sept 1976 *Mary Jane, dau of John W Saunders, of W Hartford, Conn., and has:

(1) +Alexander; *b* 1977

(1) *Mary Joanna; *b* 1979

1 *Diana Mary [Mrs Myles Eckersley, Elm View, East Dean Rd, Lockerley, Hants SO51 0HQ]; *b* 9 Jan 1929; *m* 31 July 1951 *Myles Richard Eckersley, only s of Capt Peter P Eckersley, and has:

(1) *Alison; *b* 22 April 1954; *m* 1979 (*divorce* 1984) Mark Baines and has:

1a *Thomas Oliver ECKERSLEY; *b* 24 Oct 1988

(2) *Fiona Jane; *b* 30 Sept 1955; *m* April 1988 *Alan Kent, s of John Kent, and has:

1a *John Myles; *b* 2 June 1991

1a *Alice Vanessa; *b* 16 Oct 1990

MACPHERSON OF DRUMOCHTER

Arms: Per fess or and az. a lymphad, sails furled, flags and pennon flying, counterchanged, between in chief a dexter hand fesswise, couped at the wrist, grasping a dagger, point upwards, and a cross crosslet fitchée gu., and in base an oak free eradicated ppr., fructed or **Crest:** A wildcat sejant guardant ppr., holding a cross crosslet fitchée gu. **Supporters:** Dexter, a lion gu., gorged with a collar, pendant therefrom an escutcheon or, charged with a garb az.; sinister, a bull, also gu., armed and unguled az., gorged with a collar, pendant therefrom an escutcheon, also or, charged with a boar's head couped, also az. **Motto:** Touch not this cat but with a glove. **Creation:** B. (UK) 30 Jan 1951.

THE 2ND BARON MACPHERSON OF DRUMOCHTER, of Great Warley, Essex ((James) Gordon Macpherson), JP (Essex 1961) [The Rt Hon The Lord Macpherson of Drumochter JP, Kyllachy, Tomatin, Inverness-shire IV13 7YA]; *b* 22 Jan 1924; *s f* 1965; *educ* Loretto and Wells House Malvern; chm and md Macpherson, Train and Co and subsidiary and assoc cos 1964–, Dep Chm Brentwood Bench 1972–76, memb Essex Magistrates Court Ctee 1974–76, Hon Game Warden Sudan 1974, Fndr Pres Br Importers Confedn and Hartswood Golf Club, Govr Brentwood Sch, Crest of memb Council Lond Chamb Commerce 1958–73, memb Exec Ctee West India Ctee, Chm Clan Macpherson Assoc 1960–63, memb Cncl E European Trade Cncl 1969–71, Chm A J Macpherson and Co (Bankers) 1973–, memb Lloyd's 1980, Freeman City London 1969, PLA 1971, memb Butchers' Co 1969–, Life Managing Govr Roy Scottish Corp, Chm W India Ctee 1973–, RAF WW II, FRES 1940, FZA 1966, FRSA 1984; *m* 1st 15 April 1947 (Dorothy) Ruth (*d* 8 Oct 1974), dau of Rev Henry Coulter, BD, of Bellahouston, Glasgow, and has had:

1 Thomas Ian; *b* 25 July 1948; *educ* Wells House Malvern; *d* unm 28 Aug 1978

1 *Wendy Shona Coulter; *b* 30 Sept 1950; *m* 1st 15 Sept 1972 (*divorce* 1980) Brian Anthony Fountain, twin s of Herbert L Fountain, of Essex, and has:

(1) *Stewart James Coulter; *b* 4 April 1978

(1) *Shona Fountain; *b* 1981

1 (cont.) The Hon Mrs Wendy Fountain *m* 2nd 1987 *Derek Everest and by him has:

(2) *Douglas; *b* 1988

2 *(Shirley) Elizabeth [The Hon Mrs Shaw, 3 Olympic Rd, Blairgowrie, Randburg, S Africa]; *b* 31 March 1953; *m* 1st 30 Sept 1978 (*divorce* 1989) Mark William Ransone, s of Harold Augustus Ransome, of Johannesburg; *m* 2nd 1990 *Robert Frederick Shaw and by her 1st husb has:

(1) *James Gordon; *b* 1981

(1) *Sarah Emma Ashley; *b* 1984

The 2nd BARON *m* 2nd 3 March 1975 *Catherine Bridget, only dau of Dr Desmond MacCarthy, of Brentwood, Essex, and by her has:

2 +JAMES ANTHONY; *b* 27 Feb 1979

3 *Jennifer Margaret; *b* 1976

4 *Anne Alexandra; *b* 18 May 1977

Lineage: JAMES MACPHERSON, of Muirhead, Chryston, Lanarks; had, with two daus:

THOMAS MACPHERSON, **1st Baron Macpherson of Drumochter**, of Great Warley, Co Essex, so *cr* 30 Jan 1951; *b* 9 July 1888; Chm Thames Passenger Services Ctee 1948–65, memb PLA 1949–65, chm and jt md Macpherson, Train & Co, Foreign and Colonial Food & Produce Importers and Exporters, London, Fndr Pres Hides Shippers' and Agents' Assoc, Chm Domestic Poultry Keepers' Cncl England and Wales 1951–52, memb Inst Tport, WW I with Highland LI, MP Romford 1945–50, London Provision Exchange 1941, Regnl Port Dir Scotland Min of War Tport 1942–45, memb Re-Organisation Ctee for Hops 1947 and Brown Ctee Organisation Domestic Food Producers 1949, Fndr Chm Clan Macpherson Assoc 1946–51, Chm Cncl Scottish Clan Societies 1952–57, Freeman City London, Offr Order Orange-Nassau Netherlands, US Medal Freedom with Silver

Palms; *m* 29 Jan 1920 Lucy, dau of Arthur Butcher, of Heybridge Basin, Maldon, Essex, and *d* 11 June 1965, leaving:

1 JAMES GORDON MACPHERSON, **2nd and present Baron Macpherson of Drumochter**

1 Annie Butcher; *b* 21 Sept 1920; *m* 15 April 1944 *Sir Richard Harries Davies, KCVO (1984), CBE, BSc, AMIEE, Equerry to HRH THE DUKE OF EDINBURGH, s of Thomas Harries Davies, of Glamorgan, and *d* 24 Sept 1976 leaving:

(1) *Gregory Thomas Harries; *b* 23 Oct 1946; *educ* Phillips Exeter Acad, NH, USA, and Sussex U

(2) *Richard Harries; *b* 2 June 1949; *educ* Cheltenham

(1) *Lucy Anne; *b* 14 July 1956

(2) *Nancy Caroline; *b* 5 Oct 1958

2 *Shona Catherine Greig [The Hon Mrs Campbell, The Old Rectory, Wingfield, Wilts BA14 9LW]; *b* 31 July 1929; *m* 6 Sept 1952 *Donald le Strange Campbell, MC, est s of Donald Fraser Campbell, of Summer Hill, Heacham, Norfolk, and has:

(1) *(Donald) Bruce le Strange [Bruce Campbell Esq, Thurles, Ham Green, Holt, Wilts BA14 6PZ]; *b* 10 July 1956; *m* 18 Sept 1982 *Kristine, er dau of Maj L H Nash, of Haslemere, Surrey

(1) *Victoria Louise [Mrs Russell Crockford, Broadlands Farm Cottage, Bagshot Rd, Sunninghill, Berks SL5 9JN]; *b* 3 April 1959; *m* 1985 *Russell Charles Crockford, s of Charles Crockford, of Camberley, Surrey, and has:

1a *Alexander Charles; *b* 1990

MACREADY

Arms: Argent on a chevron azure between three leopard's faces gules two swords, the points in saltire proper, pommels and hilts or.
Crest: In front of two swords, points upwards in saltire proper, pommels and hilts or, a cubit arm also proper grasping a snake vert.
Motto: *Ad extremum tenax* ('Tenacious to the end').
Creation: Bt. (UK) 1 March 1923.

SIR NEVIL JOHN WILFRID MACREADY, 3RD BT, of Cheltenham, Co Gloucester, CBE (1983) [Sir Nevil Macready Bt CBE, The White House, Odiham, Hants RG29 1LG]; *b* 7 Sept 1921; *s* f 17 Oct 1956; *educ* Cheltenham and St John's Coll Oxford (MA 1947); served RA WW II 1942–47 (field despatches), Staff Capt 1945, with BBC European Serv 1947–50, md Mobil Oil 1975–85, chm: Crafts Cncl 1984–91, Horseracing Advsy Cncl 1986–93, dep chm Br Horseracing Bd 1993–95, Tstee V&A 1985–95, chm Mental Health Fndn 1993–97, pres: Roy Warrant Holders' Assoc 1979–80 and Inst of Petroleum; *m* 16 Sept 1949 *Mary, only dau of Sir (John) Donald Balfour Fergusson, GCB, of Manor Farm, Ebbesbourne Wake, Wilts, and has:

1 +CHARLES NEVIL; *b* 19 May 1955; *m* 1981 (*divorce* 1994) Lorraine, dau of Brian McAdam, of Connah's Quay, Deeside, Clwyd, and has:

(1) +James Nevil; *b* 26 Nov 1982

(1) *Laura Mary; *b* 1984

1 *Caroline Elisabeth [Mrs Clive Tucker, Whitewold Ho, Woldingham, Surrey CR3 7DX]; *b* 20 Dec 1950; *m* 1978 *Clive F Tucker and has two daus

2 *Sarah Diana Mary; *b* 22 July 1953; *m* 1st 1976 (*divorce* 19–) Bruce Geddes; *m* 2nd 1987 *Rodney Clough and by him has issue

3 *Anna Louise; *b* 26 Sept 1963

Lineage: WILLIAM MACREADY, of Dublin (s of a Dublin upholsterer); actor and manager, playwright: *The Irishman in London, or the Happy African* (first performed 1793) and *The Bank-note, or a Lesson for Ladies* (first performed 1795); *m* 18 June 1786 Christina Ann Birch (*d* 31 Dec 1803 aged 38), a surgeon's dau of Lincs, and *d* 11 April 1829 aged 74, leaving, with other issue:

WILLIAM CHARLES MACREADY; *b* 3 March 1793; *educ* Rugby; actor (arguably the leading rival of Kean from *c* 1819), notably as Othello, King John, Richard III, Romeo and William Tell, also manager (especially Covent Garden 1837), in which capacity he was the first person since the Restoration to mount Shakespeare's plays using the lines as they had actually been written; *m* 1st 24 June 1823 Catherine Frances Atkins, actress (*d* 18 Sept 1852), and had, with many other children, a dau Joan (*d* 1840) and a further s and dau who survived him; *m*

2nd 3 April 1860 Cecile Louise Frederica (*d* 19 Sept 1908), 5th dau of Henry Spencer, and *d* 27 April 1873, leaving by her an only child:

Sir (Cecil Frederick) Nevil Macready, 1st Bt (UK), so *cr* 1 March 1923, GCMG (1918, KCMG 1915), KCB (Mil 1912, CB Mil 1906, CB Civ 1911), PC (I 1920), JP (Co London); *b* 7 May 1862; served Gordon Highrs Egyptian Expdn 1882 (medal with clasp, bronze star), Boer War 1899–1902 (despatches twice, two medals, eight clasps, Brevet Lt-Col), AAG Cape Colony 1902–04, AQMG 1904–06, AAG HQ 1907–09, Brig-Gen cmdg 2nd Inf Bde Aldershot 1909–10, Dir Personal Servs War Office 1910–14, Adj-Gen BEF WW I (despatches) 1914–16, Adj-Gen to Forces and Memb Army Cncl 1916–18, Commr Metropolitan Police 1918–20, GOC-in-C Forces Ireland 1920–22, Grand Offr: Legn Hon, Crown Belgium and Crown Italy, Croix de Guerre Belgium, Grand Cordon Sacred Treasure Japan, Hon LLD Aberdeen; *m* 7 May 1886 Sophia Geraldine (*d* 13 April 1931), yst dau of Maurice Uniacke Atkin, and *d* 9 Jan1946, leaving:

1 GORDON NEVIL (Sir), **2nd Bt**

1 Louise Geraldine; *m* 24 Jan 1916 (*divorce* 1923) Lt-Col Frederick Kaye Puckle, CMG, RASC (*d* 23 June 1959), only surv s of Col H G Puckle, MSC, and had issue

2 Joan Isabel; *d* unm 28 Feb 1957

The only s,

Sir Gordon Nevil Macready, 2nd Bt, KBE (1945, OBE 1919), CB (1942), CMG (1932), DSO (1918), MC; *b* 5 April 1891; *educ* Cheltenham and RMA Woolwich; served WW I (despatches 5 times), AA and QMG 66th Div BEF 1917–18, AAG Supreme War Cncl Versailles 1918, AA and QMG Br Mil Mission Berlin 1919, Ch of Mission to Organise Polish Nat Police 1919–20, Assist Sec Ctee Imp Def 1926–32, T/Brig and Dep Dir Staff Duties War Office 1936–38, Maj-Gen and Ch Br Mil Mission to Egyptian Army 1938–40, Assist CIGS War Office 1940–42, Ch Br Army Staff Washington, DC, 1942–46, Regnl Commr Hanover 1946–47, Br Chm Bipartite Ec Control Office Germany 1947–49, Regnl Commr N Rhine-Westphalia 1948, Ec Advsr to UK HC 1949–51, Rep UK, US and French Zones W Germany on Internat Authority for Ruhr 1950, Lt-Gen late RE, Cdr US Legn Merit 1946, Legn Hon 1947, Grand Offr Order Orange Nassau 1947, Hon Memb Fedl Bar Assoc USA; *m* 24 Nov 1920 Elisabeth (*d* 7 Dec 1969), yr dau of 8th Duke de Noailles, of Maintenon and Paris, and *d* 17 Oct 1956, leaving:

Sir NEVIL JOHN WILFRED MACREADY, **3rd and present Bt**

MACTAGGART

Arms: Arg. on a bend sa. between two owls ppr. three escallop shells or. **Crest:** A tower ppr., masoned sa., windows and port gu.
Motto: For commonweal and liberty.
Creation: Bt. (UK) 2 Feb 1938.

SIR JOHN AULD MACTAGGART, 4TH BT, of King's Park, City of Glasgow [Sir John Mactaggart Bt, 63a South Audley St, London W1Y 5FB]; *b* 21 Jan 1951; *s* f 1987; *educ* Shrewsbury and Trin Coll Cambridge (MA); chm Central and City Hldgs 1981– and Western Heritable Investment Co 1987–; dir Scottish Ballet 1988–; *m* 1st 20 May 1977 (*divorce* 1990) Patricia, yst dau of Harry Alastair Gordon, MC (*see* 1953 edn WAVELL, E); *m* 2nd 17 May 1991 *Caroline, yst dau of Eric Charles Williams, of Esher, and by her has:

1 +JACK AULD; *b* 11 Sept 1993

2 +Sholto Auld; *b* 16 Dec 1996

1 *Kinvara May; *b* 1992

Lineage: JOHN MACTAGGART, in Campeltown; *b* 10 Sept 1802; *m* 25 April 1834 Jean Mactaggart and *d* 1867, leaving:

NEIL MACTAGGART; settled Glasgow; *b* 3 Feb 1835; *m* 25 June 1862 Anne (*d* 17 Jan 1906), dau of John Auld, of Glasgow, and had:

1 JOHN AULD (Sir), **1st Bt**

2 Neil; *b* 28 July 1874; *d* 7 April 1879

1 Annie Macbride; *b* 31 Dec 1865; *d* unm 9 May1944

2 Jeanie; *b* 16 Oct 1869; *m* 1906 James Campbell Anderson and *d* 18 Feb 1943

NEIL MACTAGGART *d* 25 Oct 1904; his only surv s,

Sir John Auld Mactaggart, 1st Bt (UK), so *cr* 2 Feb 1938, of King's Park, in the City of Glasgow (which he presented to that city), JP; *b* 30 Sept 1867; housing expert, Chm Western Heritable Investment Co, of Glasgow and London; treasurer 1st Labour branch under Keir Hardie; memb Nat Govt 1931; m 1st 10 Sept 1897 Margaret Lockhart (d 15 May 1927), dau of Robert Curtis, of Ramelton, Co Donegal; m 2nd 27 Jan 1928 Elizabeth Anna (Lena) (d 20 Nov 1958), dau of Rev David Orr, BD, of Glasgow, and by his 1st w had:

1 JOHN (JACK) AULD (Sir), **2nd Bt**

1 Isa Anna Auld; b 22 April 1901; m 1st 1927 (divorce 1934) Archibald Thomson Clow Campbell; m 2nd 27 Aug 1934 Stanley Eustace Woods and d 27 Aug 1936, leaving issue

Sir JOHN d 24 Nov 1956; his only s,

Sir John (Jack) Auld Mactaggart, 2nd Bt; b 22 June 1898; RGA (TF) WW I (wounded); m 27 June 1922 Betty (d 14 Sept 1951), dau of Robert Thomson, of Kilmarnock, and had:

1 JOHN (IAN) AULD (Sir), **3rd Bt**

2 +Neil Auld [Neil Mactaggart Esq, PO Box EE 16979, Nassau, Bahamas]; b 17 Aug 1925; educ Eton, Queen's Coll Ontario and MIT (BS 1952); late Capt RE; m 1st 15 May 1953 Sheila (d 1990), yst dau of Hon Herbert A McKinney, of Nassau, Bahamas; m 2nd 199– *Betty Jane, only dau of Lucius E Petersen, of New Jersey, and by his 1st w has:

(1) +Neil Auld; b 4 Aug 1959

(2) +Andrew Auld; b 6 Jan 1962

(1) *Ann Elizabeth; b 12 Dec 1955

(2) *Robin; b 7 July 1957

(3) *Tara; b 13 Oct 1960

3 +Alastair (Sandy) Auld [Alastair Mactaggart Esq, PO Box 3160, Edmonton, Alberta, Canada]; b 11 March 1928; educ Harvard U (AB 1950, MBA 1952); late Lt (P) RCNR; m 18 July 1959 *Cecile Macy, est dau of Josiah Macy Erickson, of Inagua, Bahamas, and Meads Point, Greenwich, Conn., and has:

(1) +Alastair Auld; b 2 Aug 1966

(1) *Mara Macy; b 25 Feb 1963

(2) *Fiona Osborn; b 3 Sept 1964

Sir JOHN d 8 April 1960; his est s,

Sir Ian John Auld Mactaggart, 3rd Bt; b 19 April 1923; educ Oundle and Clare Coll Cambridge; Lt RE India and Burma WW II 1942–45, md Western Heritable Investment Co, memb LCC 1949–52, Chm Exec Ctee Soc for Individual Freedom, C parly candidate 1945 and 1970 gen eletions, memb Monday Club; m 18 June 1946 (divorce 1969) Rosemary, only dau of Sir Herbert Geraint Williams, 1st Bt, of Cilgeraint (qv), and had:

1 Sir JOHN AULD MACTAGGART, **4th and present Bt**

2 +Philip Auld; b 26 Feb 1956; m 7 July 1978 (divorce 1997) Frances, only dau of Christy George Peters, of New York

1 *Jane Lindsay [Mrs Jane Mactaggart, Ardilistry, Southdown, Wanborough, Wilts SN4 0DB]; b 6 Feb 1949; m 1974 (divorce 1978, resumed maiden name) Keith Douglas Henry Baines

2 *Fiona Margaret [Ms. Fiona Mactaggart MP, House of Commons, London SW1A 0AP]; b 12 Sept 1953; educ Cheltenham Ladies' Coll and King's Coll London; lecturer, late Leader Lab Gp Wandsworth Cncl, MP (Lab) Slough 1997–, PPS to Culture Sec 1997–

MADDEN

Arms: Sable a falcon, wings expanded, preying on a mallard, all argent, on a chief ermine out of a naval crown, between two cross-crosslets gules, from a staff in bend sinister a flag of St George all proper. **Crest:** On a ducal coronet or a falcon rising argent, holding in his beak a cross-crosslet fitchée gules.
Motto: Fortior qui se vincit ('He is stronger who conquers himself').
Creation: Bt. (UK) 7 Oct 1919.

SIR CHARLES EDWARD MADDEN, 2ND BT, of Kells, Co Kilkenny, GCB (1965, KCB 1961), CB (1955), DL [Adml Sir Charles Madden Bt GCB CB DL, 21 Eldon Rd, London W8 5PT]; b 15 June 1906; s f 1935; served WW II (despatches twice), Naval Assist to 1st Sea Ld 1946–47, Cdr and Ch NZ Naval Staff 1953–55, R-Adml 1955, Dep Ch Naval Personnel 1955–57, Flag Offr Malta 1957–59, V-Adml 1958, Flag Offr Flotillas Home Fleet 1957–60, C-in-C Plymouth 1960–63, Adml 1961, C-in-C Home Fleet 1963–65, C-in-C Atlantic Command NATO 1963–65, ret

1965; chm Roy Nat Mission to Deep Sea Fishermen 1971–81, Tstee Nat Maritime Museum 1968 (Chm 1972–77), V-Chm Sail Trg Assoc 1968–70, V-Lt Gtr London 1969–; m 8 Oct 1942 Olive (d 1989), dau of George Winchester Robins, of Caldy, Cheshire, and has:

1 *Roseann [Mrs John Beddington, The Old School House, Hook End, Berks RG8 0UL]; b 25 Jan 1945; m 11 July 1972 *John Richard Beddington, er s of C Richard Beddington, of Cuckfield, Sussex, and has:

(1) *James Edward; b 20 Oct 1973

(2) *David Paul Madden; b 16 Oct 1975

Lineage: Rev SAMUEL MADDEN, DD, of Kilkenny; Vicar-Gen Diocese of Ossory; b 1728; m 21 Sept 1756 Cassandra, dau and heiress of Michael Travers, of Skehenore, Co Cork, and d 22 Sept 1800, leaving, with other issue:

SAMUEL MADDEN, JP, of Kells Grange; b 15 March 1769; Maj 15th Regt; m 8 Oct 1798 Margaret Grace, er dau of Sir Alexander Penrose Gordon-Cumming, 1st Bt (qv), and d 20 June 1822, leaving:

Rev SAMUEL MADDEN, of Kilkenny; b 25 Aug 1801; m 11 Nov 1822 Hannah Thomasine (m 2nd Edward Macdonnell, of New Hall, Co Clare, and d 17 Aug 1868), only child of Thomas Duckett, of Friarstown, Co Carlow, and d 15 Jan 1834, leaving a 3rd s:

JOHN WILLIAM MADDEN; b 12 Oct 1828; Ensign 70th Regt 1850, Lt 1854, Capt 4th Regt 1858; m 1858 Emily (d 30 June 1920), dau of John Busby, of Kingstown, Co Dublin, and d 23 Sept 1875, leaving, with other issue:

Sir Charles Edward Madden, 1st Bt (UK), so cr 7 Oct 1919 (with thanks of Parliament and grant of £10,000 (over £180,000 in late-1990s terms)), GCB (1919, KCB 1916), OM (1931), GCVO (1920, CVO 1907), KCMG (1916); b 5 Sept 1862; Lt RN 1884, Cdr 1896, Capt 1901, R-Adml 1911, V-Adml 1916, Adml 1919, Adml of the Fleet 1924 (ret 1930), served Egypt 1882 (medal, bronze star), 4th Sea Ld 1910–11, cmded: 1st Div Home Fleet 1912, 2nd and 3rd Cruiser Sqdns 1913–14, Ch of Staff to C-in-C Atlantic Fleet 1919–22, 1st Pncpl ADC to HM GEORGE V 1922–24, 1st Sea Ld 1927–30; Hon LLD Cantab, Hon DCL Oxford; m 28 June 1905 Constance Winifred (d 18 Nov 1964), yst dau of Sir Charles Cayzer, 1st Bt (qv), and d 5 June 1935, leaving:

1 Sir CHARLES EDWARD MADDEN, **2nd and present Bt**

2 John Wilmot, MC (1944); b 20 Dec 1916; educ Winchester and RMA Woolwich; Offr RA; d 20 Dec 1916; m 18 Sept 1941 Beatrice Catherine (d 1989), only dau of William Arthur Sievwright, WS, of Benmore, St Andrews, Fife, and d 25 Aug 1990, leaving:

(1) +PETER JOHN [Peter Madden Esq, Kaymito Cottage, San Carlos Heights, Quiot Pardo, Cebu, Philippines]; b 10 Sept 1942; heir presumptive; educ Blundell's and RMA Sandhurst; Lt RA; m 1993 *Mrs Vellie Laput Co, dau of Cirilo Laput and widow of Roberto Co

(2) +Charles Jonathan [Charles Madden Esq, Katherine Bank, Earlsferry, Fife KY9 1AD]; b 11 Aug 1949; BSc, MTech, MBA; m 1980 *Kirsteen Victoria, dau of John Ronald Noble, of St Andrews, and has:

1a *Samuel Charles John; b 1984

1a *Sophie Emma; b 1981

(1) *Susan Kate [Mrs Richard Jenkins, Delbridge House, Wendy, Herts SG8 0HJ]; b 7 March 1946; m 26 Sept 1970 *Richard Leoline Jenkins, LVO, TD, 1st Queen's Dragoons, s of Cdr H L Jenkins, of Little Somerford, Wilts, and has:

1a *Sarah Alexandra; b 1972

2a *Caroline Louise Gore; b 1973

1 Conn; b 28 June 1908; m 25 June 1929 Neil Brodie Henderson, 2nd s of Brig-Gen Sir Brodie Haldane Henderson, KCMG, CB (see (FARINGDON, B), and had issue

2 *Joan [Mrs Henry Vere Nicoll, North Field, Manton, Rutland]; b 21 June 1912; m 30 Dec 1939 her sister's 1st husb's bro *Lt-Col Henry Morison Vere Nicoll, DSO, OBE, RA, est s of Dr Charles Vere Nicoll, MRCS, LRCP, of Dockenfield, Surrey, and has:

(1) *Graham Morison; b 9 Nov 1940; educ Eastbourne Coll and RMC Sandhurst; Capt Welsh Gds, Extra Equerry to HRH THE DUKE OF EDINBURGH 1968–; m 1st 24 July 1963 (divorce 1972) Lucinda Marjorie, yr dau of Timothy John Gurney, of Buntingford, Herts, and has:

1a *Simon Morison; b 29 April 1968

(1) (cont.) Graham Vere Nicoll m 2nd 1972 Jane Kidd (see BEAVERBROOK, B); m 3rd 1980 *Mrs Jacquelyn Alexander, née Bray, and by her has:

2a *Harry Michael; b 1983

(2) *Kenneth Charles [Kenneth Vere Nicoll Esq, 52 Bassett Rd, London W10]; b 18 Sept 1942; educ Marlborough and U of Aix; m 12 June 1968 *Veronica Gillian, dau of Colin P Payne, of Cape Town, and has:

1a *Alastair Charles; b 1973

1a *Sara Jane; b 1971

2a *Georgina Clare; b 1981

(3) *Adrian Michael [Adrian Vere Nicholl Esq, Freynestown Stud, Dunlavin, Co Wicklow, Ireland]; b 1949; educ Marlborough; m 1976 *Meriel Jane, dau of Capt James McCarthy, of Navan, Co Meath, and has:

1a *James Henry; b 1981

1a *Annabel Jane; b 1979

(4) *Neville Henry [Neville Vere Nicoll Esq, 6119 Andrus Rd, Boulder, CO 80301, USA]; b 11 July 1954; educ Marlborough; m 1984 *Carrie Virginia, only dau of Dr W Robert Wentz, of Durham, NC, and has:

1a *Alexander Robert; b 1986

2a *John Morison; b 1988

1a *Sabrina Fiennes; b 1993

3 *Hope [Mrs John Batten, 120 Northumberland Court, Northumberland Rd, Leamington Spa, Warwicks CV2 6HN]; b 5 Oct 1914; m 27 July 1939 (divorce 1947) Maj John Henry Beardmore Batten, Roy Fus, only s of Lt-Col John Beardmore Batten, DSO, of Pennington, Hants, and has:

(1) *Patrick John Beardmore [Patrick Batten Esq, 2 Manor Cottages, Leamington Hastings, Warwicks]; b 24 Aug 1941; educ Ampleforth; m 1 June 1965 (divorce 1978) Diana Lyn, er dau of H L Brooke, GM, of Edgbaston, Birmingham, and has:

1a *Annabell Jane Beardmore; b 19 Oct 1965

2a *Katherine Nicola Beardmore; *b* 17 Jan 1968
3a *Sally Elizabeth Beardmore; *b* 1970
4 *Mary Elizabeth [Mrs Charles Barrett, 25 Eldon Rd, London W8]; *b* 4 Aug 1920 (HM QUEEN MARY stood sponsor); *m* 1st 16 Sept 1939 (*divorce* 1952) Raymond Guy Vere Nicoll, MC (*d* 1981); *m* 2nd 23 July 1952 (*divorce* 1956) Maj Desmond Richard FitzGerald, Irish Gds, s of Capt Derek FitzGerald, of Heathfield Park, Sussex; *m* 3rd 8 Oct 1968 Cdr Charles Raymond Barrett, RN (*d* 3 July 1970), and had by her 1st husb:

(1) *Mark Raymond [Mark Vere Nicoll Esq, 24 Eldon Rd, London W8]; *b* 18 April 1942; *educ* Eton; *m* 26 April 1968 *Virginia Anne, only dau of Maj James Christopher Vernon Miller, of Blackwell Grange, Shipston-on-Stour, Warwicks, by Eila Christian, yr dau of Capt Nigel James Christian Livingstone-Learmouth, and has:

1a *James; *b* 1971
2a *Edward; *b* 1971 (twin)
1a *Claire; *b* 1 July 1970
2a *Tamara Ann; *b* 1978
(2) *Nigel Edward; *b* 3 April 1947; *educ* Eton; *m* 1st 11 April 1969 *Corinna Jane, dau of John Goring (*see* GORING, Bt), and has:

1a *Adam Nigel; *b* 1972
2a *Rory Raymond; *b* 1978
1a *Zoe Gabrielle; *b* 16 April 1971
2a *Corinna Mary; *b* 1980
(2) (cont.) Nigel Vere Nicoll *m* 2nd 1991 *Catharine Euphan, only dau of J P Waterer, of Coombe Bissett, Wilts, and formerly w of John Vaughan, and by her has:

3a *Frederick John; *b* 1993

MADDOCK

Creation: B. (LP, UK) 1997.

THE BARONESS MADDOCK, of Christchurch, Co Dorset (Diana Derbyshire) [The Rt Hon The Baroness Maddock, House of Lords, London SW1A 0PW]; *b* 19 May 1945; *educ* Brockenhurst GS, Shenstone Training Coll and Portsmouth Poly; teacher: Weston Park Girls' Sch Southampton 1966–69, Extra Mural Dept Stockholm U 1969–72, Sholling Girls' Sch Southampton 1972–73, Anglo-Continental Sch of English Bournemouth 1973–76, Greylands Sch of English Southampton 1990–91; memb Southampton CC 1984–93; MP (Lib Dem) Christchurch 1993–97, V-Chm All Party Parly Gp Homelessness and Housing Need; *m* 1966 *Robert Frank Maddock and has two daus

Lineage: REGINALD DERBYSHIRE; *m* Margaret Evans and has:

DIANA, *cr* a **Baroness**

MAGNUS

Arms: Bendy of six gules and vert, on a fess or an open book proper between two martlets sable. **Crest:** A magnolia tree flowered proper. **Motto:** *Fide et labore* ('By faith and work'). **Creation:** Bt. (UK) 22 June 1917.

SIR LAURENCE HENRY PHILIP MAGNUS, 3RD BT, of Tangley Hill, Wonersh, Co Surrey [Sir Laurence Magnus Bt, Flat 8, 44 Lower Sloane St, London SW1W 8BP]; *b* 24 Sept 1955; *s* uncle 1988; *educ* Eton and Ch Ch Oxford (MA); exec dir Samuel Montagu & Co 1988–95; dir DLJ Phoenix Securities 1995–; *m* 1983 *Jocelyn Mary, est dau of Robert Henry Foster Stanton, and has:

1 +THOMAS HENRY PHILIP; *b* 30 Sept 1985
2 +Edmund Robert Hilary; *b* 26 Jan 1991
1 *Iona Alexandra; *b* 6 April 1988

Lineage: L MAGNUS, of Chatham, Kent; *d* 13 May 1837, leaving:

JACOB MAGNUS, of Chatham; *b* 9 Dec 1805; *m* Caroline (*d* 20 Feb 1894), dau of Joel Barnett, and *d* 11 Jan 1888, having had, with an est s (Laurie, *b* 4 June 1840, *d* 9 Nov 1862), a yst s (Edward, *b* 1 Dec 1848, *d* 5 Aug 1922) and two daus (Sarah, *d* 3 March 1927; Josephine, *d* 23 Feb 1927):

Sir Philip Magnus, 1st Bt (UK), so *cr* 22 June 1917, JP (Surrey); *b* 7 Oct 1842; *educ* U Coll Sch, UCL and Berlin U; MP (U) London U 1906–23, Memb Senate and Fell London U, Pres Coll Preceptors, Govr LSE, RSA (chm 1927), Hon Fell BMA, Organising Dir and Sec City and Guilds London Inst 1880–88 (Supt and Sec Dept Tech 1888–1915), memb Roy Commn Tech Educn 1881–84, ktd 1886; *m* 29 March 1870 Katie (*d* 2 March 1924), only dau of Emanuel Emanuel, JP, of Southsea, and *d* 29 Aug 1933, having had:

1 Laurie; *b* 5 Aug 1872; *educ* Magdalen Coll Oxford (MA); Maj Roy Defence Corps, dir George Routledge & Sons, chm Cncl Girls' Public Day Sch Tst, memb Cncl Roy Soc Lit; *m* 22 July 1903 Dora Marian (*d* 24 Dec 1972 aged 90), est dau of Sir Isidore Spielman, CMG, and gdau of Sir Joseph Sebag Montefiore, and *d* 28 April 1933, leaving:

(1) Sir PHILIP MAGNUS later MAGNUS-ALLCROFT (deed poll 1951), **2nd Bt**, CBE (1971), JP (Salop 1953); *b* 8 Feb 1906; *educ* Westminster and Wadham Coll Oxford (BA 1929, MA); Civ Serv 1928–32 and 1945–51, Maj RA and Intell Corps WW II, Salop: CC 1952, CA 1968, chm County Planning Ctee, Chm Govrs Attingham Coll, Tstee Nat Portrait Gallery, FRSL, FRHistS, author (as Philip Magnus): *Life of Edmund Burke* (1939), *Sir Walter Raleigh* (1951), *Gladstone — A Biography* (1954), *Kitchener — Portrait of An Imperialist* (1958), *King Edward the Seventh* (1964); *m* 14 July 1943 Jewell, only dau of Herbert John Allcroft, of Stokesay Court, Onibury, Salop, and *dsp* 1988

(2) Hilary Barrow, TD, QC (1957), JP (1949); *b* 3 March 1909; *educ* Westminster and Ch Ch Oxford (MA); barrister Lincoln's Inn 1933, Bencher 1963, Lt-Col Rifle Bde WW II, Nat Insur Commr 1964; *m* 9 Aug 1950 *Rosemary Vera Anne [Mrs Hilary Magnus, Cragmore House, Wye, Kent TN25 5BJ], est dau of George Henry Masefield, of Chelsea, and widow of Quentin Berkeley Hurst, and *d* 15 Jan 1987, leaving:

1a Sir LAURENCE HENRY PHILIP MAGNUS, **3rd and present Bt**

1a *Caroline Anne [Miss Caroline Magnus, Stokesay Court, Onibury, Shropshire SY7 9BD]; *b* 9 Dec 1951; *educ* Benenden

(1) *Jessie Dora [Mrs David Sandell, 44 Burton Court, London SW3]; *m* 9 April 1935 *David Hugh Sandell, MD, FRCS, and has:

1a *Robert Laurie [Robert Sandell Esq, 56 Dale St, London W4 2BZ]; *b* 8 March 1938; *educ* Eton and Ch Ch Oxford; *m* 7 Nov 1969 (*divorce* 1991) Stephanie Day, est dau of William Ainsworth Getz, of Moline, Ill., and has:

1b *Adam Jonathan William; *b* 1972
1b *Alexandra Jessica Laurie; *b* 1975
1a *Jenifer Celia Emily [Mrs Nicholas Bridges-Adams, Fornham Cottage, Fornham St Martin, Suffolk]; *b* 23 Jan 1936; *educ* LSE; barrister Lincoln's Inn 1958; *m* 9 Aug 1962 *(John) Nicholas William Bridges-Adams, barrister, s of William Bridges-Adams, CBE, of Hermitage, Waterfall, Bantry, Co Cork

(2) Pamela Lucy; *m* 10 Dec 1936, as his 1st w, Denzil Charles Sebag-Montefiore, est s of Charles Edward Sebag-Montefiore, OBE, of Ferney, Whitbourne, Worcs, and *d* 28 April 1944, leaving:

1a *Susan Penelope Dora; *b* 1938; *m* 1960 *William van Laun and has:

1b *Timothy Denzil; *b* 1965; *m* 1994 *Emma Thompson and has:

1c *Samuel James; *b* 1996
1b *Sarah Ruth; *b* 1962; *m* 1990 *Charles Lionel Cohen, s of Hon Hugh Lionel Cohen (*see* 1970 edn COHEN, B), and has:

1c *Emily; *b* 1992
2c *Henrietta; *b* 1993
3c *Charlotte; *b* 1997
(3) *Ruth Emily [Mrs Denzil Sebag-Montefiore, 129 Rivermead Court, Ranelagh Gdns, London SW6 3SD]; *m* 1 July 1946, as his 2nd w, her deceased er sis's widower Denzil Charles Sebag-Montefiore (*d* 15 Jan 1996) and has:

1a *Charles Adam Laurie [Charles Sebag-Montefiore Esq, 21 Hazlewell Rd, London SW15 6LT]; *b* 25 Oct 1949; *educ* Eton and St Andrews U; *m* 1979 *Pamela Mary Diana, yr dau of Archibald Tennant (*see* GLENCONNER, B), and has:

1b *Archibald Edward Charles; *b* 1987
1b *Elizabeth Anne; *b* 1982
2b *Laura Rose; *b* 1984
1a *Mary Pamela; *b* 1951; barrister Middle Temple 1974; *m* 1973 *David Murray Davidson, s of Col Robert St Clair Davidson, of The Manor House, Upham, Hants, and has:

1b *Denzil Jonathan Robert; *b* 1975
1b *Susanna Mary; *b* 1978
2b *Felicity Dora; *b* 1982
2 Leonard Arthur; LLB; *b* 12 Dec 1879; *d* 11 Sept 1924

1 Lucy Amy; *m* 17 June 1891 Frederic Samuel Franklin (*d* 17 April 1918), of Elcot, Sheringham, Norfolk, s of Ellis Abraham Franklin, of Bayswater, and *d* 25 May 1964, leaving issue

MAHON

Moniti · meliora · sequamur ·

Arms: Per fess sable and argent an ostrich counterchanged, holding in the beak a horseshoe or. **Crest:** A dexter arm in armour embowed proper, garnished or, grasping a sword wavy argent, pommel and hilt gold. **Motto:** *Moniti meliora sequamur* ('Having been warned, let us follow better things'). **Creation:** Bt. (UK) 14 April 1819.

SIR WILLIAM WALTER MAHON, 7TH BT, of Castlegar, Co Galway [Sir William Mahon, c/o Guinness Mahon, 9 Idol Lane, London EC3 5AW]; *b* 4 Dec 1940; *s f* 1987; *educ* Eton; Irish Gds 1959–92, Col, memb Gentlemen at Arms 1993; *m* 20 April 1968 *Rosemary Jane, yr dau of Lt-Col Michael Ernest Melvill, OBE, of The Old Manse, Symmington, Lanarks, and has:

1 +JAMES WILLIAM; *b* 29 Oct 1976

1 *Annabel Jane; *b* 12 May 1970; *m* 19 July 1995 *Richard Amphlett, s of Philip Amphlett, of Ombersley, Worcs

2 *Lucy Caroline; *b* 15 April 1972; *m* 30 Aug 1997 *Alexander Stroud, s of Geoffrey Stroud, of Kensington

Lineage: BRYAN MAHON; owned land at Loughrea, Co Galway, *c* 1656, and leased other property in the area from *c* 1663 on; *m* Magdalen Power (*d* Feb 1703) of Rathroddy, Co Galway, and *d* March 1695, having had:

1 James; *m c* 21 Sept 1672 Alice, dau and heiress of Thomas Cullen, of Oughter-cloony, Co Galway, and *d* April 1716, leaving, with other issue:

(1) Bryan, of Oughtercloony or Beech Hill; *dsp* 1731/2

(2) Thomas; *m* Bridget, dau of Ross Gaynor, of Black Castle, Co Westmeath, and sis of his unc's w (*see* below), and was ancestor of the MAHONs of Beech Hill, extinct in the male line when James Cullen Mahon *d* unm 17 Jan 1858

2 Bryan, of Castlegar, Co Galway; estate manager to 8th and 9th Earls of Clanricarde (*see* SLIGO, M); Lt Clanricarde's Regt of Inf in JAMES II's Army 1689, Capt Grenadiers Clanricarde's Regt 1690 Battle of the Boyne 1 July 1690; *m* 1693 Ellinor, dau of Ross Gaynor (*see* above) and widow of Daniel McNaghten (*d* 1689), and *d* 30 Oct 1719, having had, with two other daus (Alice; Ellinor; *d* young):

(1) ROSS

(2) James, of Ballyglass, Co Galway; *d* unm Aug 1752

(3) Peter, of Dublin; *d* unm by 21 March 1734

(1) Mary; *m* Feb 1719 William Kelly (*d* 14 July 1746), of Mucklon, Co Galway, and had issue

(2) Elizabeth; *m* Thomas Tully (*d* 1741), of Rafarn, Co Galway, and had issue

(3) Hester; *m* 1st 1729 — Molyneux (*d* by Nov 1733); *m* 2nd 1736/7 Edward Forster, 4th s of Capt Francis Forster, of Clooneene or Ashfield, Co Galway

The es *s*,

ROSS MAHON, of Castlegar; inherited bulk of bros' fortune 1751; *m* (licence 27 Dec 1721) Jane (*bapt* 17 Feb 1693/4; *d* 1768), dau of John Ussher, LLD, of Mount Ussher, Co Wicklow, and *d* April 1767, having had, with other issue:

1 ROSS

2 John; *b* 1728; *educ* Trin Coll Dublin (BA 1749); *d* unm by 18 Aug 1785

1 Alice; *m* 6 Nov 1748 John King (*see* KING, Bt, of Charlestown) and *d* Sept 1769, leaving, with other issue:

(1) Rebecca; *m* Rev Henry King; their dau *m* **Sir William Mahon, 4th Bt** (*see* below)

The er *s*,

ROSS MAHON, of Castlegar; *b* 1725; *educ* Trin Coll Dublin (BA 1746); *m* 12 Oct 1762 Lady Anne Browne (*d* 21 Feb 1815), only dau of 1st Earl of Altamont (*see* SLIGO, M), and *d* 17 March 1788, having had, with other issue:

1 ROSS (Sir), **1st Bt**

2 John of Besborough, Co Tipperary; *b* 24 Nov 1764; Lt 68th (Durham) Regt and 67th (S Hants) Regt; *m* 9 Jan 1794 Lady Charlotte Browne (*d* 23 Jan 1849), 4th dau of 2nd Earl of Altamont (*see* SLIGO, M), and *d* 23 Oct 1834, leaving:

(1) Elizabeth; *m* 28 Dec 1814 Gen Hon Arthur Grove-Annesley and *d* 26 Feb 1863, leaving issue (*see* ANNESLEY, E)

3 Henry (Rev), of Killegally, King's Co; *b* 25 Feb 1771; BA 1796, Rector Tessau-ran, King's Co; *m* 23 July 1802 Anne (*d* 12 May 1818), dau of Rev Abraham

Symes, DD, of Hillbrook, Rector Carnew, Co Wicklow, and *d* 29 July 1838, leaving:

(1) Louisa; *b* 1809; *m* her cousin Rev William Filgate, est s of Thomas William Filgate, of Arthenstown, Co Louth, and *d* 1843, leaving issue

4 James (Very Rev); *b* 20 April 1774; barrister Lincoln's Inn 1793, called Irish Bar 1795, Dean Tuam 1807–09 and Dromore 1809–37; *m* 1 Oct 1812 Frances Catherine (*d* 21 Oct 1868), dau of David Ker, of Portavo and Montalto, Co Down, and *d* 20 March 1837, having had issue

5 George, of Mount Pleasant, Co Mayo; *b* July 1778; High Sheriff Co Mayo 1812; *m* 9 Aug 1813 his er bro's sis-in-law Sophia (*d* 6 Dec 1844), dau of David Ker, and *d* 1 May 1843, having had issue

1 Anne; *m c* 7 Dec 1790 Denis Browne, PC, MP, and *d* 30 Dec 1833, leaving issue (*see* SLIGO, M)

2 Harriette; *m* 28 July 1793 Annesley Gore Knox (*d* 4 July 1839), of Rappa Castle, Co Mayo, and *d* 3 Nov 1840, having had issue

3 Amelia (Emily); *m* 30 Sept 1796, as his 1st w, Thomas William Filgate (*d* 17 Nov 1846), of Arthurstown, Co Louth, and had issue

ROSS MAHON's est *s*,

Sir Ross Mahon, 1st Bt (UK), so *cr* 14 April 1819, JP; *b* 2 Sept 1763; MP (I Parl) Granard 1798–1800 and (UK Parl) Ennis 1820; *m* 1st *c* 25 July–6 Aug 1786 Lady Elizabeth Browne (*see* SLIGO, M) and had, with two other daus:

1 Elizabeth Louisa; *b* 8 Sept 1787; *m* 25 Sept 1806 John Cator, JP (*d* 20 Aug1858), of Beckenham Place, Kent, and Woodbastwick Hall, Norfolk, and *d* 11 Feb1847, leaving issue

2 Anne Charlotte; *b* 13 Sept 1788; *m* 23 April 1822 Rev Rawdon Griffith Greene (*d* 28 Dec 1862), Vicar Stillorgan, Co Dublin, Precentor Kildare, and *dsp* 1833

3 Charlotte; *m* 1 July 1813 John Henry Blakeney, JP, DL (*d* 17 Nov 1858), of Abbert, Co Galway, and *d* 9 Aug 1865, having had issue

Sir Ross *m* 2nd 19 Sept 1805 Diana (*dsps* 2 Dec 1807), dau of Edward Baber, of Mayfair; *m* 3rd 1 Oct 1809 Hon Mary Geraldine (*d* 20 March 1859), dau of James FitzGerald, PC, KC, MP (I Parl) Fore 1776–1783, Tulske 1783–97, Kildare 1797–1800 and (UK Parl, Tory) Ennis 1802–08 and 1812–13, of Inchicronan, Co Clare, Prime Serjeant-at-law Ireland, by Catherine, Baroness FitzGerald and Vesey of Clare and of Inchicronan in her own right (*see* 1860 edn), and *d* 10 Aug 1835, having had by her, with other issue (*unm*):

1 **Sir Ross Mahon, 2nd Bt**; *b* 18 July 1811; Lt KRRC (60th Rifles), ADC to Ld Lt Ireland; *d* unm 5 April 1842

2 **Sir James FitzGerald Ross Mahon, 3rd Bt**, JP, DL (Co Galway); *b* 3 June 1812; *educ* Trin Coll Dublin (BA); barrister King's Inns 1831; *d* unm 11 March 1852

3 WILLIAM VESEY ROSS (Sir), **4th Bt**

1 Catherine Geraldine; *b* 1810; *m* 8 June 1842, as his 2nd w, Rev William John Purdon (*m* 1st Charlotte Emily (*dspm* 29 April 1838), dau of Rt Hon Denis Browne and Anne Mahon (*see* above); *dspm* 25 Aug 1880), Rector Carlow, and *dsp* 5 March 1890

2 Letitia Anne; *b* 1815; *m* 1 Sept 1843 John Adair (*d* 14 Sept 1883), barrister, of Dublin, and *d* 30 July 1892, having had issue

3 Henrietta Louisa; *m* 4 Dec 1845 James Thomas Foster-Vesey-FitzGerald, JP, DL (*d* 10 Dec 1893), of Moyriesk, Co Clare, and *d* 10 Dec 1893, having had issue

4 Georgina; *m* 1st 12 Nov 1851 Rev Samuel Hill (*d* 29 May 1858); *m* 2nd 8 Feb 1866 Robert Hudson (*d* 30 April 1872) and *dsp* 28 July 1897

5 Jane Alicia; *b* 1824; *m* 17 July 1855 Rev Peter William Browne (*d* 28 May 1861), Incumbent Blackrod, Lancs, only s of John Browne, of Mountjoy Sq, Dublin, and *d* 13 June 1907, having had issue

6 Caroline; *b* 1826; *m* 6 May 1857 Thomas Adair Hunt (*d* 3 Aug 1906), s of Rev Henry Hunt, Vicar-Gen Elphin, and *dsp* 9 Aug 1913

The 3rd Bt's yr bro,

Rev Sir William Vesey Ross Mahon, 4th Bt; *b* 14 July 1813; *educ* Trin Coll Dublin (MA); Rector Rawmarsh, Yorks, 1844–93; *m* 12 Oct 1853 Jane (*d* 7 June 1895), 2nd dau of Rev Henry King by Rebecca (*see* above), and *d* 14 Aug 1893, having had:

1 Ross; *b* and *d* Nov 1854

2 Ross; *b* 10 Jan 1856; *d* unm 24 June 1876

3 WILLIAM HENRY (Sir), **5th Bt**

4 John FitzGerald; *b* 20 Jan 1858; *m* 19 Oct 1898 Lady Alice Evelyn Browne (*see* SLIGO, M) and *d* 5 Nov 1942, leaving:

(1) (John) Denis (Sir), CBE (1967) [Sir Denis Mahon CBE, 33 Cadogan Sq, London SW1X 0HU]; *b* 8 Nov 1910; *educ* Eton and Ch Ch Oxford (BA 1932; MA 1936); art historian specialising in Caravaggio, Guercino and Poussin, Tstee Nat Gallery 1957–64 and 1966–; medal for Benemeriti della Cultura Italy 1957, Accademico d'Onore of Clementine Acad Bologna 1964, Serena Medal Italian Studies Br Acad 1972, ktd 1986, FBA 1964, Hon DLitt Newcastle 1969

5 James Vesey (Rev); *b* 23 Feb 1860; MA Oxon 1885; Curate Rawmarsh 1883–87; *d* unm 27 June 1887

6 Edward; *b* 1 June 1862; BA Oxon 1884; *m* 26 April 1911 Lilette Caroline Julia (*d* May 1956), dau of James K Rebbeck, of Victoria, BC, and *d* 18 June 1937, leaving:

(1) +Bryan Edward [Bryan Mahon Esq, 2003 82nd Ave SE, Mercer Island, WA 98040, USA]; *b* 29 June 1913; *m* 1960 *Marolyn Miriam, dau of C Laverne Smith, MD, of Seattle, and has:

1a +Ross Mackenzie; *b* 1961

1a *Lilette Elizabeth; *b* 1963

7 Gilbert; *b* 7 Oct 1865; *m* 19 March 1895 Frances (*dsp* 17 March 1931), 3rd dau of John Blakeney, DL, JP, of Abbert, Co Galway, and *d* 2 Jan 1947

1 Mary Geraldine; *b* 1859; *m* 14 Jan 1896 23rd Lord (Baron) De Ros (*qv*) of Helmsley and *dsp* 28 Dec 1921

2 Alice Jane; *b* 1861; *m* 8 Jan 1889 Harry Polhill Chambers (*d* 13 Oct 1919), s of George Wilton Chambers, JP, DL, of Clough House, Rotherham, Yorks, and *dsp* 25 Sept 1937

The 4th Bt's est surv *s*,

Sir William Henry Mahon, 5th Bt, DSO, JP (Co Galway and W R Yorks), DL (Co Galway); High Sheriff 1898, Maj 4th (Militia) Bn W Yorks Regt Boer War

1900–02; *b* 31 Dec 1856; *m* 25 Jan 1905 Hon Edith Augusta Dillon (*d* 24 April 1964), 2nd dau of 4th Baron Clonbrock (*see* 1926 edn), and *d* 13 Aug 1926, having had:

1 William Gerald Ross; *b* 2 Sept 1909; *d* 31 Aug 1910

2 GEORGE EDWARD JOHN (Sir), **6th Bt**

3 Luke Bryan Arthur DILLON later DILLON-MAHON (deed poll 1966); *b* 12 April 1917; *educ* Eton and Trin Coll Cambridge; *m* 28 May 1949 *Audrey Doreen [Mrs Luke Dillon-Mahon, Cooleen, Moycullen, Co Galway, Ireland], only dau of Ernest John Vipond, MBE, MC, of Hove, Sussex, and *d* 23 July 1997, leaving:

(1) +Robert John George; *b* 10 April 1954; *educ* Stowe; *m* 1983 *Caroline Mary, yst sis of 10th Earl of Granard (*qv*) and formerly w of Dominick Charles Hamilton (*see also* WILIAMS-WYNN, Bt), and has:

1a +Luke John; *b* 1984

(1) *Susan [Mrs George Gossip, Tullanisk, Birr, Co Offaly, Ireland]; *b* 3 July 1950; *m* 1978 *George Wilmer Hatfeild Gossip and has:

1a *William Luke George Hatfeild; *b* 1983

1 Ursula Augusta Jane; *b* 17 Jan 1906; *m* 17 July 1929 (*divorce* 1946) Hon Arthur Marcus Lowther Crofton (*see* CROFTON, B) and *d* 25 July 1987, having had issue

2 Mary Edith Georgiana; *b* 22 June 1911; *d* 17 Nov 1918

The 5th Bt's est s.

Sir George Edward John Mahon, 6th Bt; *b* 22 June 1911; *educ* Eton and Trin Coll Cambridge (BA 1933); *m* 1st 20 Sept 1938 Audrey Evelyn (*d* 4 April 1957), only child of Walter Jagger, MB, CM, and had:

1 Sir WILLIAM WALTER MAHON, **7th and present Bt**

2 +Timothy Gilbert [Timothy Mahon Esq, 7 Sunbury Gdns, Dartry, Dublin 6, Ireland]; *b* 24 April 1947; *educ* Crookham Court Sch; *m* 7 Aug 1971 *Penelope Telfer, er dau of Maj T B McDowell, of St Thomas, Rathfarnham, Co Dublin, and has:

(1) +Rupert Thomas George; *b* 1974

(2) +Myles Francis; *b* 1980

(1) *Antonia Margaret; *b* 1976

1 *Jane Evelyn (Jinnie) [Mrs Jinnie Moore, 12 Althorp Rd, London SW17 7ED]; *b* 23 Aug 1944; *m* 5 Aug 1967 (*divorce* 1978) Peter Alexander Charles Moore, est s of Lt-Col Alec Cecil Sutherland Moore, of Little Quantock, Crowcombe, Somerset, and has:

(1) *Alannah Katherine; *b* 26 Aug 1969

Sir George *m* 2nd 14 Sept 1958 *Suzanne [Suzanne Lady Mahon, 16 St James's Terrace, Winchester, Hants SO22 4PP], only dau of Thomas Donnellan, of Pirbright, Surrey, and *d* 1987, leaving by her:

2 *Sarah Caroline [Mrs Charles Loane, 133 Westbridge Rd, London SW11 3PF]; *b* 22 Oct 1959; *m* 8 March 1997 *Charles David Montgomery Loane, s of Warren Loane, of Crocknacrieve, Enniskillen, Co Fermanagh

MAITLAND

Arms: Or a lion rampant gu., couped in all his joints of the field, within a double tressure flory counter-flory az., a bordure erm.
Crest: A lion sejant erect and affrontée gu., holding in his dexter paw a sword ppr., hilted and pommelled or, and in his sinister a fleur-de-lys arg. **Motto:** *Consilio et animis* ('By counsel and courage'). **Creation:** Bt. (UK) 30 Nov 1818.

SIR CHARLES ALEXANDER MAITLAND, 10TH BT, of Clifton, Midlothian; *b* 3 June 1986; *s f* 1994

Lineage: Sir Alexander Maitland, 1st Bt (UK), so *cr* 30 Nov 1818; *b* 21 March 1728 (5th s of 6th Earl of Lauderdale; *qv*); *m* 6 July 1754 Penelope (*d* 22 Dec 1805), dau of Col Martin Madan, Foot Gds, MP, Groom Bedchamber to FREDERICK PRINCE OF WALES, by Judith, dau of Mr Justice Spencer Cowper, bro of Earl Cowper (*see* LUCAS OF CRUDWELL, B), and had:

1 ALEXANDER CHARLES (Sir), **2nd Bt**

2 William; *b* 1757; drowned Bay of Bengal 1781

3 Augustus; Lt-Col Gds; *d* 31 Oct 1797 of wounds recd in Low Countries during French Revolutionary Wars

4 Frederick; Gen, Col 58th Regt; *b* 3 Sept 1763; *m* 1790 Catherine, dau of John Prettyjohn, of Barbados, and *d* 27 Jan 1848, having had:

(1) John Madan; *b* 12 Aug 1793; *m* 1st 24 Oct 1822 Ellinor (*d* 15 Oct 1823), only dau of Gilbert Annesley, and had an only child (Ellinor Jane Susan, *d* 4 June 1870); *m* 2nd 21 July 1829 Harriet, est dau of Rev Joseph Pratt, and *d* 14 Oct 1842

(2) Frederick Thomas; Lt-Col; *b* 18 Sept 1807; *m* 18 July 1842 Emily Augusta Mary (*d* 12 April 1855), dau of Maj Richard Bingham Newlands, of Drayton, Hants, and *d* 1883, leaving:

1a Frederick; Cdr RN; *b* 23 March 1848; *m* 1887 Elizabeth Ann, dau of William Bennett, and *dsp* 9 April 1892

2a Reginald Paynter; Maj RA; *b* 6 March 1851; *m* 4 Feb 1875 Ann Eliza (*d* 12 Jan 1927), dau of Capt G F Oldfield, and *d* 10 April 1926, leaving:

1b Reginald Charles Frederick, DSO; Lt-Col RA WW I (despatches), Croix de Guerre; *b* 10 Oct 1882; *m* 2 Dec 1913 Marjorie Agnes Jane (*d* 26 Jan 1958), dau of Very Rev Ernald Lane, Dean Rochester, and *d* 24 April 1939, leaving:

1c Alastair Reginald; *b* 22 Sept 1915; *educ* Down House Sch; *m* 24 May 1947 *Mary [Mrs Alastair Maitland, Gables, Linden Chase, Uckfield, Sussex TN22 1EE], dau of Campbell Mansbridge, and *d* 1990, leaving:

1d +Iain David Paynter [Iain Maitland Esq, 67 The Avenue, Lewes, E Sussex BN7 1QU]; *b* 20 Jan 1954; *educ* Northease Manor, Lewes; *m* 10 Jan 1981 *Robyn Jane Nicholl and has:

1e +James Alastair Patrick; *b* 28 March 1985

1e *Fiona Jane; *b* 4 Sept 1982

2d +Andrew Reginald Campbell; *b* 7 March 1963; *m* 1995 *Vivienne Pemberton

1d *Penelope Mary; *b* 16 March 1948; *m* 1975 Peter Bayed (*d* 1987) and has:

1e *Clare; *b* 1976

2d *Carolyn Judith; *b* 25 June 1951; *m* 1978 (*divorce* 1996) John McArthur and has:

1e *Steven; *b* 1979

2e *Christopher; *b* 1980

3e *David; *b* 1983

2c Geoffrey Ernald; aerial photographer, Maj RA; *b* 1 June 1918; *educ* Winchester; *m* 1st 3 Feb 1945 (*divorce* 1967) Diana Joy, dau of Maj James Pridham, RA, and *d* 11 July 1992, leaving:

1d +Alastair Charles Frederick; *b* 8 June 1958

1d *Diana Jane [Mrs Michael Brooke, Woods Farm, Burrow Hill, Surrey GU24 8BY]; *b* 26 Nov 1945; *m* 11 March 1967 *Michael John Brooke and has:

1e *Mark Alexander; *b* 15 July 1969

2e *James; *b* 1971

3e *Christopher; *b* 1983

1e *Katie; *b* 1976

2d *Patricia Anne; *b* 22 Aug 1947; *m* 1st 1977 (*divorce* 1981) Robert Campbell and has:

1e *Julian; *b* 1980

2d (cont.) Mrs Patricia Campbell *m* 2nd 1991 *Richard Law and by him has:

2e *David; *b* 1992

3d *Susan Mary [Mrs Patrick Blackwell, PO Box 438, Woollahra, NSW 2025, Australia]; *b* 5 Sept 1952; *m* 1991 (*divorce* 1997) Patrick Blackwell

4d *Gabrielle Gillian Sarah [Mrs David Briggs, 27 Ellerby St, London SW6 EX]; *b* 16 Sept 1954; *m* 1987 *David Hylton Briggs, est s of W/Cdr G H Briggs, of The Farmhouse, Settrington, Sussex, and has:

1e *Thomas; *b* 1990

1e *Lucy; *b* 1992

2c (cont.) Geoffrey Maitland *m* 2nd 3 May 1971 (*divorce* 1980) Mrs Eleanor Williamson, dau of James Salter, and *d* 1992, leaving by her:

2d +James Alexander; *b* 24 Sept 1971

1b Muriel Penelope; *b* 10 March 1885; *m* 30 April 1913 Col Edward Forbes Cooke-Hurle, DSO, Somersetshire LI (*d* 21 Dec 1923 following a hunting accident), and *d* 23 Jan 1961, leaving issue

1a Catherine Penelope; *m* 13 Dec 1871 Adml William Henry Maxwell, of Holywych, Cowden, Kent, and *d* 9 June 1910, leaving issue

2a Frederica Charlotte Mary; *m* 21 April 1868 Sir Thomas George Freake, 2nd Bt (*d* 22 Dec 1920; *see* 1949 edn), and *d* 26 Nov 1932, leaving issue

(1) Charlotte; *m* 18 April 1820 Capt Garth, RN, of Haines Hill, Berks, and *d* his widow 2 Aug 1868

(2) Harriet; *m* 8 Sept 1827 Donald Maclean, 2nd s of Sir Fitzroy Maclean, 8th Bt, of Dowart (*qv*), and *d* 20 Sept 1850

1 Penelope; *m* Rev Thomas Marsham and *d* 1846

2 Charlotte; *d* 28 May 1853

Sir ALEXANDER *d* 14 Feb 1820; his s,

Sir Alexander Charles Maitland, 2nd Bt; *b* 21 Aug 1755; *m* 30 April 1786 Helen, dau and heiress of Alexander Gibson-Wright (*see* GIBSON-CRAIG-CARMICHAEL, Bt), and *d* 7 Feb 1848, having had, with other issue:

1 Alexander; advocate; *b* 14 Sept 1787; *m* 25 March 1819 Susan (*d* Sept 1831), est dau of George Ramsay, of Barnton, and *dvp* Sept 1828, having had:

(1) Sir ALEXANDER CHARLES MAITLAND later RAMSAY-GIBSON-MAITLAND (added 1856 on inheriting the Barnton, Co Edinburgh, and Sauchie, Stirling, estates from his Ramsay kinsman), **3rd Bt**; MP Edinburgh, Col Stirlingshire Militia; *b* 7 Jan 1820; *m* 3 Feb 1841 Thomasina Agnes, er dau of James Hunt, JP, of Pittencrieff and Logie, Fife, and *d* 16 May 1876, having had, with three daus (*d* unm):

1a **Sir James Ramsay-Gibson-Maitland, 4th Bt**, JP, DL; Convener Stirling-shire, FGS, FLS; *b* 29 March 1848; *m* 12 May 1869 Fanny Lucy Fowke (*d* 17 March 1896), yst dau of Sir Thomas Wollaston White, 2nd Bt, of Walling-wells (*qv*), and *d* 9 Nov 1897, having had:

  1b Mary; *b* 6 Oct 1871; *m* 10 July 1901 Sir Arthur Herbert Drummond Ramsay-Steel-Maitland, 1st Bt, PC, MP (*d* 30 March 1935; *see* 1963 edn), and *d* 25 May 1944, leaving issue

  2b Sybile; *b* 6 May; *d* 23 Sept 1873

2a William Forbes; *b* 16 April 1852; *d* 30 Dec 1863

3a Keith; MA, LLB, barrister, Capt 3rd Bn Argyll and Sutherland Highrs; *b* 5 July 1855; *m* 27 Nov 1886 Ina Blanche (*d* 25 Jan 1892), dau of G Ralston Caldwell, of Ayre, and *d* 25 June 1897, having had:

  1b Esmay Frances; *m* 1915 Rev Geoffrey Charles Edward Ryley (*d* 19 June 1947), Hon Canon Rochester, and *d* 28 May 1921

(2) George Ramsay, WS, of Edinburgh; *b* 19 Jan 1821; *m* 19 Sept 1848 Alice Anne (*d* 27 Oct 1869), est dau of Josiah Nisbet, HEICCS, and *d* 24 June 1866, leaving:

  1a JOHN NISBET (Sir), **5th Bt**

  2a George Keith; *b* 11 Jan 1854; *m* 1877 Christina Mary Theresa (*d* 29 Dec 1932), dau of Angus McDonell of Keppoch, and *d* 17 March 1896, leaving:

    1b Alexander McDonell; *b* 17 July 1878; *d* 7 May 1920

    2b Keith Andrew Ramsay, MC and bar; Capt RFA (SR) WW I (despatches); *b* 1882; *ka* 4 Oct 1917

    3b Angus Charles Marjoribanks; Capt RASC WW I (despatches), memb War Material Commn 1919–20 and Control Commn Germany and Austria 1946–47; *b* 29 Jan 1887; *m* 13 Dec 1923 Mary Brigid (*d* 1 July 1946), dau of Thomas O'Callaghan, of Claremorris, Co Mayo, and *d* 1986, leaving:

      1c +Keith Marjoribanks (Rev); RC priest; *b* 1 Sept 1925

      1c *Natalie Mary [Mrs Joseph Bibbing-Maitland, 15 Bellevue, Clifton, Bristol BS8 1DB]; *b* 1924; RNMS; *m* 1980 Joseph Bibbing (*d* 1989)

      2c *Joan Mary [Mrs Noel Fisher, 37A Lyncombe Hill, Bath BA2 4PQ]; *b* 1928; *m* 5 July 1952 *Noel Martin Fisher, DSC, s of Rev Maxwell Fisher, and has:

        1d *Dominic Mayne Maitland [Dominic Fisher Esq, 16 Boston Rd, Bristol BS7 0HB]; *b* 4 May 1953; *educ* St Brendan's Coll Bristol; *m* 1982 *Christine Robin Lindop, of Auckland, NZ, and has:

          1e *Robin Jordi Lindop; *b* 7 July 1988

        2d *Andrew Martin; *b* 9 Nov 1954; *educ* St Brendan's Coll Bristol

        3d *Aidan Hugh; *b* 24 Jan 1959

        4d *Paul Gregory; *b* 28 April 1960

        1d *Mary Brigid; *b* 28 Feb 1956

        2d *Catharine Mary; *b* 16 July 1957

        3d *Lucy Elizabeth; *b* 22 March 1963

        4d *Anna Clare; *b* 9 Feb 1964

        5d *Jane Frances; *b* 17 Aug 1965

      3c *Angela Helena Mary [Mrs Raymond Daniel, Willow House, Willow Vale, Frome, Somerset]; *b* 30 April 1933; *m* 1959 *Raymond Geoffrey Daniel, s of Alfred Martin Daniel, of Marston Gate House, Frome, Somerset, and has:

        1d *Charles Martin; *b* 19 Oct 1961

        2d *Francis Keith; *b* 1965

        1d *Brigid Mary; *b* 22 Nov 1959

        2d *Helen Margaret; *b* 1963

  1b Alice Marie; *m* 1900 George Kirby and had issue

  2b Christina Claire; *m* 12 April 1909 Percy Alan Cleaver (*d* 1945), s of H P Cleaver, of Clavis, Cheshire, and had issue

  1a Alice Rachel; *d* unm 18 Oct 1909

  2a Susan Rachel; *d* unm 15 June 1950

(3) William Ramsay; *b* 1825; *d* 1831

(4) Keith Ramsay; Col 79th Foot (Crimean medal with three clasps, India medal with clasps); *b* 20 Oct 1827; *m* 27 July 1861 Georgina Harriet (*d* 15 Dec 1916), dau of Alexander Grant Glass, and *d* 30 Oct 1893, having had:

  1a Keith Ramsay, WS, JP Midlothian and Stirling; *b* 13 Oct 1865; *d* unm 27 July 1929

  1a Agnes Mary; *d* unm 30 Sept 1934

  2a Caroline; *m* 17 Sept 1902 Lt-Col John Stirling Napier (*see* NAPIER, Bt, of Merchistoun) and *dsp* 1908

(1) Jean Hamilton; *m* 16 July 1856 Archibald Redfoord Bulwer, of Tomard, Co Kildare, and *d* 1877, leaving issue

(2) Helen; *m* 8 April 1851 James Alexander Hunt, JP (*d* 10 Oct1890), of Pitten-crieff and Logie, Fife, and *d* 9 Dec 1889, having had issue

2 Augustus; *b* 27 March 1800; *m* 1 June 1843 Elizabeth Jane, dau of Rev William Page Richards, DCL, and gdau of Sir J Strachan, Bt, and *d* 26 Jan 1855, leaving:

(1) Augustus Alexander William John Strachan; *b* 28 April 1844; *dsp* 1899

(2) Alexander Charles Richards; barrister; *b* 30 Nov 1845; *educ* Corpus Christi Coll Oxford (MA); *d* 4 Oct 1929

(3) William James, CIE; Dep Govt Dir Indian Rlwys 1892–1912; *b* 22 July 1847; *m* 7 Aug 1878 Agnes Magdalene (*d* 30 Oct1908), est dau of Ralph Neville-Grenville (*see* BRAYBROOKE, B), and *d* 8 May 1919, having had, with a s (*d* unm):

  1a Marjorie; *b* 29 June 1884; *m* 24 April 1913 ACM Sir Arthur Murray Long-more, GCB, DSO, RAF (*d* 10 Dec 1970), only s of Murray Longmore of Upa-von, Wilts, and *d* 8 May 1959, leaving issue

(4) Frederick Henry; *b* 13 May 1849; *m* 20 May 1875 Georgina Douglas (*d* 14 March 1932), est dau of J Henry Mackenzie, and *d* 1928, having had:

  1a Arthur Frederick; *b* 22 May 1876; *d* 2 Feb1897

  1a Maud; *b* 10 Jan 1878; *d* unm 1954

3 John; Accountant-Gen Court of Session; *b* 27 Jan 1803; *m* 9 Nov 1852 Mary Isabella (*d* 8 Feb 1886), dau of John Philip Wood, and *d* 23 Jan 1865

4 Frederick Charles; *b* 7 April 1812; *m* 8 Feb 1872 Emily Jeannette (*d* 6 Jan 1890), er dau of Col John Craigie and widow of J W Maxwell Lyte, of Berry Head, Devon, and *d* 31 Aug 1890

1 Margaret; *m* 9 Aug 1819 William Logan White, of Kellerstain, Midlothian, and *d* 19 Jan 1840

2 Anne Charlotte; *m* 1822 Capt William Stirling, 1st Dragoon Gds (*d* Dec 1826), only s of James Stirling of Keir by his 2nd w and heir through her of the Milton and Castlemilk estates, Lanarks, and *d* 17 Sept 1875, having had issue

3 Helen; *m* 7 Aug 1827 James Maitland Hog (*d* 1 Aug 1858), of Newliston, Lin-lithgow, and *d* 26 Jan 1893 aged 87

The 4th Bt's cousin,

  Sir John Nisbet Maitland, 5th Bt; *b* 26 Nov 1850; *educ* Haileybury and Edin-burgh U; *m* 9 Feb 1877 Annie Florence (*d* 21 Jan 1899), dau of Philip Rickman, and *d* 14 Dec 1936, leaving:

1 **Sir John Maitland, 6th Bt**, TD (1932); *b* 25 Nov 1879; *educ* Haileybury and Trin Coll Cambridge (BA and LLB 1901, MA 1925); barrister, Inner Temple 1903, Capt OTC and Lt RGA (SR), WW I (despatches), assist master Dulwich 1920–49; *m* 7 Sept 1915 Kathleen Offley (*d* 31 July 1959), dau of Henry Thomas Keates, of Petersfield, and *d* 27 Nov 1949, leaving:

  (1) *Petronilla Kathleen Florence [Mrs Malcolm Park, Stourhill, Sturminster Newton, Dorset DT10 1ED]; *b* 9 July 1916; *m* 15 Sept 1951 Malcolm Park, OBE, Colonial Ag Serv Antigua (*d* 16 March 1963), s of Horace William Park, and has:

    1a *Malcolm John Maitland; *b* 17 Oct 1955; *m* 1982 *Nicola Anne Jackson and has:

      1b *David Malcolm (twin); *b* 29 Sept 1986

      1b *Emma Caroline; *b* 4 March 1984

      2b *Marianne Beatrice; *b* 29 Sept 1986

2 GEORGE RAMSAY (Sir), **7th Bt**

1 Claire Marjoribanks, MBE (1920); DGStJ; *m* 3 June 1905 1st Baron Milne (*qv*) and *d* 15 Dec 1970, leaving issue

The 6th Bt's bro,

  Sir George Ramsay Maitland, 7th Bt, DSO (1918), JP (Angus 1932), DL (1942); *b* 20 Dec 1882; *educ* Cheltenham and RMA Woolwich; Lt-Col, 14th Murray's Jat Lancers IA, Boer War 1901–02, WW I (despatches), Belgian Croix de Guerre, memb Roy Co Archers; *m* 19 Feb 1919 Jean Hamilton, MBE (1920), only surv dau of Robert Findlay, of Easterhill, Lanarks, and had:

1 ALEXANDER KEITH (Sir), **8th Bt**

2 +John Ramsay; S/Ldr RAF Korea with USAF; *b* 11 Oct 1924; *m* 1st 29 Oct 1952 (*divorce* 19–) Nan Margaret, 3rd dau of Brig Charles Bannatyne Findlay, CBE, MC, RA, and has:

  (1) +David Ramsay; *b* 12 Nov 1954

  (2) +James; *b* 11 Aug 1957; *m* 1987 *Sarah Elizabeth, only dau of Malcolm Selwyn Shaw

  (1) *Jean Findlay; *b* 25 Oct 1959

2 (cont.) John Maitland *m* 2nd 1968 *Kathleen Mary, dau of Vivian Charles Desmond, and by her has:

  (3) +Keith John; *b* 1969

3 +James [James Maitland Esq, Clathic Crieff, Perthshire PH7 4JY]; late Lt QO Cameron Highrs; *b* 3 Sept 1927; *educ* Rugby; *m* 19 Sept 1959 *Mavis Ann, er dau of H J Kennaway, of Keithock, Brechin, Angus, and has:

  (1) +Alexander Henry; *b* 1964; *m* 1991 *Fiona Margaret, yst dau of W C Drummond, of Broomhill, Forteviot, Perthshire, and has:

    1a *Emma Jean; *b* 1993

    2a *Georgina Harriot; *b* 1995

  (1) *Amanda Helen; *b* 25 Oct 1960; *m* 1994 *Maj David Limb, MBE, yst s of Roy Limb, of Hadley Wood, Herts, and has:

    1a *Alice Helen; *b* 1995

  (2) *Fiona Ann (twin); *b* 25 Oct 1960

1 *Helen Florence [Mrs Thomas Lloyd-Jones, Reswallie, Forfar, Angus]; *b* 1923; *m* 9 Aug 1952 *Lt-Col Thomas David Lloyd-Jones, 20th Lancs Fus, only s of Rev Iowarth Lloyd-Jones, Rector St Kessogs, Auchterarder, Perthshire, and has:

  (1) *John Ramsay; *b* 23 March 1954; *m* 1982 *Henrietta Cicely, only dau of Henry Gabriel Richards Pickthorn (*see* PICKTHORN, Bt), and has:

    1a *Alexander; *b* 1986

    1a *Lucy; *b* 1989

    2a *Celia; *b* 1992

  (2) *Peter Neil; *b* 31 Oct 1956; *m* 1989 *Victoria Rees and has:

    1a *Frederick; *b* 1990

    2a *George; *b* 1991

  (1) *Caroline Margaret; *b* 28 Feb 1961; *m* 1987 *Marc Villiers Townsend, s of Reginald Townsend, of Rugby

Sir GEORGE *d* 1 Nov 1960; his est son,

  Sir Alexander Keith Maitland, 8th Bt; *b* 26 Oct 1920; *educ* Rugby and Peter-house Cambridge; Maj QO Cameron Highrs WW II, Malaya 1948; *m* 17 March 1951 *Lavender Mary Jex [Lavender Lady Maitland, Burnside, Forfar, Angus], yst dau of Francis William Jex Jackson, of Kirkbuddo, Forfar, and had:

1 RICHARD JOHN (Sir), **9th Bt**

2 +ROBERT RAMSAY [Robert Maitland Esq, Dowalty, Crathes, Banchory, Kincardineshire]; *b* 14 July 1956; heir presumptive; *educ* Rugby; *m* 1984 *(Georgina) Claire, yst dau of John Drysdale, of Kilrie, Kirkcaldy, Fife, and has:

  (1) +Harry Robert; *b* 1986

  (2) +John Richard; *b* 1992

  (1) *Cara Claire; *b* 1989

  (2) *Anna Victoria; *b* 1991

1 Lucy Diana; *b* 22 Aug 1961; *d* 12 Feb 1962

2 *Janey Fiona; *b* 25 April 1963; *m* 23 July 1988 *Hugo Peter Haig (*see* BESS-BOROUGH, E) and has:

  (1) *Christopher Edward (Kit); *b* 18 Sept 1993

(1) *Archie-Anne Rose; *b* 4 March 1992

Sir ALEXANDER *d* 18 July 1963; his er son

Sir Richard John Maitland, 9th Bt; *b* 24 Nov 1952; *educ* Rugby; *m* 1981 *Carine C A, er dau of J St G Coldwell, of Somerton, Oxford, and *d* 1994, leaving:

1 Sir CHARLES ALEXANDER MAITLAND, **10th and present Bt**

1 *Alice Emma; *b* 1983

MAKINS

IN · LUMINE · LUCE

Arms: Argent, on a fess embattled counter-embattled gules, between in chief two falcons proper belled or and in base a lion's face of the second, an annulet or between two bezants. **Crest:** A dexter arm embowed in armour proper, encircled by an annulet or and holding a flagstaff, therefrom flowing a banner argent charged with a lion's face gules. **Motto:** *In lumine luce* ('Shine thou in the light').
Creation: Bt. (UK) 9 Jan 1903.

SIR PAUL VIVIAN MAKINS, 4TH BT, JP (City and Garrison of Gibraltar 1964–70) [Sir Paul Makins Bt, Casas Cortijo 135, 11310 Sotogrande, Provincia de Cadiz, Spain]; *b* 12 Nov 1913; *s* bro 1969; *educ* Eton and Trin Coll Cambridge (MA); Maj Welsh Gds WW II; Kt of Magistral Grace SMO Malta 1955; *m* 30 Aug 1945 Maisie (*d* 2 July 1986), dau of Maj Oswald Henry Pedley, of Gibraltar, widow of Maj Cecil Leander John Bowen, Irish Gds, and mother of Most Rev Michael Bowen, RC Archbp Southwark

Lineage: WILLIAM MAKINS, of Epworth, Lincs; had:

WILLIAM MAKINS, of Thorne, Yorks; *b* 1756; *m* 1780 Mary (*d* 4 June 1837), dau of Robert Ambler, of Thorne, by Mary, dau of William Thompson, of Low Hall, Farnham, Yorks, and sis and coheir of William Thompson, banker, of Bridlington, Yorks, and *d* 5 Nov 1847, leaving, with other issue:

1 William Thompson MAKINS later THOMPSON (roy licence 1806); *b* 25 March 1785; *d* unm 10 Dec 1860

2 Charles; *b* 7 April 1797; *m* 7 Sept 1837 Frances (*d* 31 Jan 1876), dau of Thomas Kirkby, of Leeds, banker, and *d* 8 Aug 1878, having had:

(1) WILLIAM THOMAS (Sir), **1st Bt**

(2) Henry Francis; *b* 30 July 1841; barrister Middle Temple; *m* 6 June 1866 Keziah Elizabeth (*d* 15 Oct 1918), 2nd dau of John Hunt, of Holmwood, Dorking, Surrey, and *d* 11 Jan 1914, leaving:

1a Ernest (Sir), KBE (1938), CB (1917), DSO (1902); *b* 14 Oct 1869; *educ* Winchester and Ch Ch Oxford; Boer War 1899–1902 (despatches) and WW I (despatches), T/Brig-Gen cmdg Cav Bde 1914, Hon Brig-Gen 1919, Col 1st Roy Dragoons 1931–46, raised and cmded Palace of Westminster Home Gd 1940, ret 1941; MP (C) Knutsford 1922–45; Order St Maurice and St Lazarus Italy; *m* 31 Jan 1903 Maria Florence (*d* 11 Aug 1972 aged 95), 3rd dau of Sir James Robert Mellor, of Bayswater (see 1970 edn MELLOR, Bt), and *d* 18 May 1959, having had:

1b Sir ROGER MELLOR MAKINS; *cr* BARON SHERFIELD (*qv*)

2b Guy Henry; *b* 5 July 1906; *educ* Winchester; *d* following an accident 17 Sept 1923

3b Geoffrey Ernest, MC; *b* 19 Oct 1915; *educ* Winchester and Ch Ch Oxford; Maj 1st Roy Dragoons WW II; *d* unm from wounds recd in action Normandy 4 Sept 1944

2a Geoffrey, MVO; *b* 30 Dec 1877; Capt KRRC Boer War 1899–1900 (medal with clasps) and WW I; *ka* 23 Aug 1915

3a Hugh; *b* 18 Nov 1881; *educ* Oxford (BA); barrister; Capt Queen's Westminster Rifles; *ka* 4 Nov 1915

1a Beatrice; *m* 17 Aug 1892 Col Charles Cameron Leveson-Gower and *d* 2 Nov 1952, leaving issue (see SUTHERLAND, D)

2a Josephine; *m* 31 Oct 1899 James Granville Legge (*d* 17 Jan 1940), est s of Rev J Legge, of Oxford, and *d* 15 Sept 1956, leaving issue

3a Constance; *m* 22 July Very Rev Hastings Rashdall, DD, DCL, DLitt, Fell and Tutor New Coll Oxford, Dean Carlisle (*d* 9 Feb 1924), and *dsp* 9 Feb 1958

4a Isabel; *m* 25 Feb 1911 her bro-in-law Brig-Gen Sir James Gilbert Shaw Mellor, KBE, CB, CMG, KC, JP (*d* 16 April 1947; see 1970 edn MELLOR, Bt)

5a Pauline; *m* 5 Oct 1904 Hon Nigel Christopher Walsh (*d* 10 Sept 1931), 3rd s of 2nd Baron Ormathwaite (see 1970 edn), and *d* 5 Oct 1956, leaving issue

CHARLES MAKINS's er s,

Sir William Thomas Makins, 1st Bt (UK), so *cr* 9 Jan 1903, VD, JP (Oxon and Essex), DL (Essex), of Rotherfield Court, Oxon; *b* 16 March 1840; *educ* Trin Coll Cambridge (MA); barrister, Lt City London, MP (C) S Essex 1874–92, Hon Col 1st Essex Art, E Div RA Voly Bde; dep chm GER, govr Gas Light and Coke Co; *m* 3 June 1861 Elizabeth (*d* 3 Nov 1911), 2nd dau of Lightly Simpson, chm GER, and *d* 2 Feb 1906, having had:

1 William Henry; *b* 6 Dec 1863; Lt 13th Hus; *m* 19 Aug 1886 Mary Agnes (*m* 2nd 18 March 1891 Warine Martindale, of Haistwell Ho, Sunningdale, and *d* 18 July 1915), only dau of Sir Charles Lawrence Young, 7th Bt, of North Dean (*qv*), and *dvp* 1 Dec 1889, leaving:

(1) Marjorie Florence; *b* 13 Sept 1887; *m* 8 Sept 1909 Maj Alexander Vaughan Leipzic Wood, DSO, 5th Lancers (*d* 27 Jan 1933), 2nd s of Capt Charles Watkins Arthur Harcourt Wood, of Pontefract, and *d* 198–, having had issue

2 Francis Kirkby; *b* 28 July, *d* 28 Aug 1865

3 Basil Thomas, JP; *b* 6 Sept 1872; Lt Roy Bucks Hus; *dvp* unm 3 March 1905

4 PAUL AUGUSTINE (Sir), **2nd Bt**

5 Oscar Matthew; *b* 21 Sept 1872; Capt RN, served China 1900 (medal); *m* 7 June 1909 Marianne, only dau of W C Hoylake, late of Constantinople, and *dsp* 5 July 1942

1 Mary Elizabeth; *m* 23 July 1890 Maj Sir Eugene Clauson, KCMG, CVO, RE (*d* 31 Dec 1918), HC Cyprus, s of C Clauson, and *d* 1 July 1949, having had issue

2 Agatha Caroline, MBE; Cmdt Aux Mily Hosp Henley-on-Thames 1914–18; *d* unm 8 Jan 1933

3 Veronica Luce; *m* 14 April 1896 Allan Edward Batchelor, JP, BA (*d* 15 Nov 1916), of Greystoke, Warwicks, and *d* 29 April 1957, leaving issue

4 Audrey Katherine; *m* 28 April 1906 Walter Woodbine Parish (*d* 18 March 1952), est s of Charles Woodbine Parish, and *d* 29 April 1957, leaving issue

Sir WILLIAM's 4th s,

Sir Paul Augustine Makins, 2nd Bt, JP (Oxon); *b* 8 June 1871; *educ* Trin Coll Cambridge (BA); Maj Remount Serv 1915, High Sheriff Oxon 1911; *m* 1st 14 Feb 1900 Gladys Marie (*d* 23 April 1919), dau of William Vivian, of S Kensington, and had:

1 **Sir William Vivian Makins, 3rd Bt,** JP (Hants 1948), DL (Hants 1960); *b* 19 Jan 1903; *educ* Eton; Lt-Col Welsh Gds, seconded Sudan Def Force 1928–30 (despatches), Assist Mil Sec Gibraltar 1937–39, served WW II (despatches), Cmdt RMC (OCTU) 1944–46, Assist Mil Sec N Cmd 1947–48, memb Gentlemen-at-Arms 1951, High Sheriff Hants 1953; chm: Hants Co Probation Ctee 1954, Winchester Diocesan Bd Fin 1954; *m* 4 April 1932 Jean (*d* 1993), dau of Lord Arthur Hay (see TWEEDDALE, M), and *d* 22 April 1969, having had:

(1) *Carolyn Diana Mary [Mrs LeRoy Morgan, 25214 Peach Tree Rd, Clarksburg, MD 20871-9101, USA]; *b* 12 March 1933; *m* 1 June 1956 *LeRoy Tuttle Morgan, yr s of Charles Carroll Morgan, of Chevy Chase, MD, and has:

1a *Diana Vivian; *b* 3 May 1958

2a *Teresa Adelaide; *b* 15 Sept 1959

3a *Eleanora Carroll; *b* 22 Jan 1961

4a *Cecilia Hay; *b* 23 April 1964

5a *Maria Abell; *b* 23 April 1964

6a *Olivia Dudley; *b* 24 July 1972

(2) Penelope Anne Makins; *b* 30 Sept 1935; *m* 25 April 1957 2nd Baron Harvey of Tasburgh (*qv*) and *d* 8 June 1995, having had issue

2 Sir PAUL VIVIAN MAKINS, **4th and present Bt**

1 Diana Vivian, JP; *b* 22 Dec 1900; *m* 2 March 1926 Lt-Col Hugh Granville Leveson Dudley Ryder and *d* 12 Dec 1951, leaving issue (see HARROWBY, E)

2 Elisabeth Mary Savile; *b* 28 July 1904; Dir WAGS Club Sloane St, London SW1, WW II, memb Grail Community Pinner 1934–97; *d* unm 8 Jan 1997

3 Marcia Evelyn; *b* 2 March 1907; *d* unm 5 Jan 1977

4 Monica Vivian; *b* 8 Sept 1910; *m* 1st 16 Sept 1930 Maj Francis Savile Hoole Lowsley-William (see MEXBOROUGH, E) and had issue (see SKELMERSDALE, B); *m* 2nd 7 Oct 1948 Sir Edward Allan Greene, 3rd Bt, MC, TD (*d* 26 Dec 1966; see 1967 edn), and *d* 29 Sept 1967

Sir Paul *m* 2nd 27 June 1921 Dorothy (*d* 6 May 1956), yst dau of William Samuel Wakefield, of Calcutta, and *d* 10 Sept 1939

MALCOLM

Arms: Or a saltire az. between four stag's heads couped gu., within a bordure indented of the third. **Crest:** A pyramid encircled by a laurel wreath ppr. **Mottoes:** 1 (over crest) *Ardua tendo* ('I attempt difficult things'), 2 (below arms) *Dei dono sum quod sum* ('By the grace of God I am what I am'). **Creation:** Bt. (NS) 25 July 1665.

SIR JAMES WILLIAM THOMAS ALEXANDER MALCOLM, 12TH BT, of Balbedie and Innertiel, Co Fife [Col Sir James Malcolm Bt, Thatchers Barn, Worplesdon, Surrey GU3 3RD]; *b* 15 May 1930; *s* cousin 1995; *educ* Eton and RMA Sandhurst; Col cmdg Welsh Gds 1972–76, High Sheriff Surrey 1991–92; *m* 10 June 1955 *Gillian Heather, dau of Elton Humpherus, of The Coach House, Tunbridge Wells, Kent, and has:

1 +ALEXANDER JAMES ELTON; *b* 30 Aug 1956; Lt-Col Welsh Gds; *m* 1982 *Virginia Elizabeth, dau of Capt Alfred Coxon, RN, and has:
  (1) +Edward Alexander Humpherus; *b* 1984
  (2) +Thomas William; *b* 1990
  (1) *Camilla Petronell; *b* 1987
2 +Robin William; *b* 29 Nov 1958
1 *Julia Mary; *b* 31 Oct 1960; *m* 1984 *Julian Neville Guy Spurling and has:
  (1) *Jonathan Henry William; *b* 1987
  (2) *Frederic James Lovett; *b* 1989
  (3) *Harry Alexander; *b* 1992
2 *Annabel Heather; *b* 25 June 1967; *m* 1993 *Capt Patrick C D Toyne Sewell, s of Maj-Gen Timothy Toyne Sewell and has:
  (1) *Charles; *b* 1997

Lineage: JOHN MALCOLM of Balbedie, Lochore and Innertiel; Chamberlain Fife 1641; had a Crown charter of the land and (territorial) Barony of Balbedie 15 July 1646, which was erected with the Barony of Lochore into one Barony 16 Aug 1662; *m* Margaret (*d* 8 May 1698), dau of Sir Michael Arnot of that Ilk, and *d* 8 Feb 1692, having had, with other issue:

1 JOHN (Sir), **1st Bt**
2 Michael, of Balbedie and Nuthill; *b* 1648; *m* Jean, dau of Sir William Blair, and *d* 19 June 1733, having had a dau (Margaret, *m* George Mackenzie)
3 Alexander, of Lochore; *b* 13 Dec 1650; Ld of Session 1687 as Lord Lochore, a Ld of the PC, Ld Justice Clerk 1688; *dsp* 17 Sept 1692
4 James, of Grange, Fife; *b* 1664; fought as a Jacobite Battle of Killiecrankie 1689, Commissary-Gen Army; attainted as a Jacobite 1708, when his estate was forfeited; *d* unm
1 Margaret; bought back Grange

The est son,

Sir John Malcolm, 1st Bt (NS), so *cr* 25 July 1665, of Innertiel and Lochore; MP Kinross-shire 1711; *m* Emilia (*d* 12 Jan 1732), dau of 3rd Lord Balfour of Burleigh (*qv*), and *d* 30 March 1729, having had:

1 **Sir John Malcolm, 2nd Bt**, of Lochore; *b* 4 May 1681; *m* 1709 Isabel (*d* 14 Dec 1763), dau of Lt-Col Hon John Balfour, of Fernie, Fife, s of 3rd Lord Balfour of Burleigh (*qv*), and *d* 12 Aug 1753, having had, with other issue:
  (1) Robert; had:
    1a Anne; *m* Alexander Graham
  (2) **Sir Michael Malcolm, 3rd Bt**; *m* 1 Feb 1752 Katherine (*d* 30 Oct 1794), dau of Peter Bathurst, of Clarendon Park, Wilts, MP, by Lady Selina Shirley, dau of 1st Earl Ferrers (*qv*), and *dsps* 5 May 1793, having had issue (*d* young)
2 Robert, of Grange; *b* 25 Oct 1682; *m* Isabella (*d* 7 Aug 1793), yst dau of Robert Herries of Halldykes, gs of Robert Herries of Hartwood and Halldykes, Minister Dryfesdale, and *d* 3 June 1769, having had:
  (1) Robert; *d* 1770
  (2) **Sir James Malcolm, 4th Bt**, of Grange; Lt-Govr Sheerness; *dsp* 25 Oct 1805
    (1) Emilia; *m* her cousin James Malcolm (*see below*)
3 Michael, of Balbedie; *b* 1683; *m* 1st Herries (*d* Feb 1733), dau of Col William Grahame of Balwhapell by Janet, dau of William Herries of Hartwood, est s of Robert Herries, Minister Dryfesdale (*see above*), and had:
  (1) Michael; *d* 1737

(2) James, of Balbedie; served heir of entail of his f 6 March 1760; *m* his cousin Emilia (*d* Sept 1798), dau of Robert Malcolm of Grange (*see above*), and *dsp* 11 Aug 1798
(1) Emilia; *m* 1742 Christopher Lindsay of Kirkforthar
3 (cont.) Michael Malcolm *m* 2nd Anne Blackwood and *d* 10 April 1754, having by her had, with other issue:

(3) **Sir John Malcolm, 5th Bt**, of Balbedie and Grange; *b* 1749; *m* Jean Hutton (*d* Dec 1826) and *d* 23 May 1816, having had, with other issue:
1a **Sir Michael Malcolm, 6th Bt**, of Balbedie and Grange; *m* 1st 18 Dec 1809 Isabella (*dsp*), dau of Thomas Davie of Kirkaldie; *m* 2nd June 1824 Mary (*d* 13 Feb 1897), yst dau of John Forbes of Bridgend, Perthshire, and *d* Oct 1828, having by her had, with two other daus (*d* unm):
  1b **Sir John Malcolm, 7th Bt**, of Balbedie and Grange; *b* 1 April 1828; *m* 1861 Jane (*d* Nov 1875), dau of John McDougal, and *dsp* 24 Dec 1865
  1b Jean, of Balbedie and Grange, Fife; *m* 1850 Thomas LYDE later MALCOLM-LYDE, of Sidhouse, Devon, and *d* his widow 29 Sept 1907, having had issue
2a James; *m* 22 May 1818 Helen, est dau of James Duncan of Abernethy, and *d* 30 June 1826, having had, with two daus (*d* unm):
  1b John; *d* unm 1848
  2b **Sir James Malcolm, 8th Bt**, of Balbedie and Grange, JP Fife; *b* 11 April 1823; *d* unm 8 June 1901
4 Charles; *bapt* 19 Aug 1687; *m* Margaret Lindsay and had:
(1) Alexander; *b* 1720; *m* 18 July 1760 Elizabeth Malcolm and *d* 11 Sept 1809, having had, with other issue:
1a William; *bapt* 5 Oct 1767; *m* Margaret (*d* 12 July 1845), dau of Rev D Cormack, and *d* 3 Aug 1838, having had, with other issue:
  1b James; *b* 10 Oct 1804; *m* 1st Caroline Nesbit (*d* 15 Nov 1853), dau of Rev Daniel Wilkie, of Rathobyres, Midlothian, and had a s and dau (both *d* young); *m* 2nd 1 Feb 1860 Adeline (*m* 2nd 19 Nov 1885 John Ramsay-L'Amy, of Dunkenny, Forfar, and *d* 28 Feb 1915), est dau of James Attye, DL, 52nd Regt, of Pinchbeck, Lincs, by Catherine Adeline, dau of Adlard Welby, DL, of S Rauceby, Lincs, and *d* 16 July 1878, having by her had:
    1c **Sir James William Malcolm, 9th Bt**, JP Norfolk and Suffolk; *b* 29 March 1862; Admin Assist Min Munitions WW I, Capt Roy Pembs Artillery Militia; *m* 14 Nov 1885 Evelyn Alberta (*d* 6 Jan 1947), 3rd dau of Albert George Sandeman, of Presdales, Herts, and gdau of Viscount de Moncorvo, and *d* 30 April 1927, having had:
      1d **Sir Michael Albert James Malcolm, 10th Bt**; *b* 9 May 1898; *educ* Eton; Maj Scots Gds (Res), ADC to GOC Scottish Cmd 1919–23 and HC Ch Scotland Edinburgh 1924 and 1925, memb Roy Co Archers, WW I (severely wounded), WW II (AG's Branch, MS Branch FO), memb Exec Ctee Standing Cncl Btage 1954–76; *m* 1st 10 Jan 1918 (*divorce* 1946) Hon Geraldine Margot Digby (*d* 1 June 1965), 2nd dau of 10th Baron Digby (*qv*), and had:
        1e **Sir David Peter Michael Malcolm, 11th Bt**; *b* 7 July 1919; *educ* Eton and Magdalene Coll Cambridge (BA); Maj Scots Gds WW II (Staff Capt 1944, GSO(2) 1945), memb: Roy Co Archers, ICA Scotland 1949, Stock Exchange 1956–80 and Stock Exch Cncl 1971–80; *m* 6 June 1959 *Hermione [Hermione Lady Malcolm, Whiteholm, Whim Rd, Gullane, E Lothian EH31 2BD], er dau of Maj Sir David George Home, 13th Bt (*qv*), and *d* 30 Nov 1995, leaving:
          1f *Fiona Alice Jane; *b* 4 Aug 1962; *m* 1992 *Oliver George Stephenson (*see* STEPHENSON, Bt)
        1e *Margaret Jane Venetia [Mrs Christopher Vesey Holt, Westbury Manor, W Meon, Petersfield, Hants GU32 1ND]; *b* 11 Jan 1923; WW II (3rd Offr WRNS); *m* 1 June 1945 Lt-Cdr Christopher Robert Vesey Holt, CVO, VRD, RNVR (*d* 11 Nov 1997), er s of V-Adml Reginald Vesey Holt, CB, DSO, MVO, of Shirley Holms, nr Lymington, Hants, and has:
          1f *Nicholas James Vesey; *b* 21 Feb 1947; *educ* Eton
          1f *Ianthe Evelyn Vesey; *b* 15 Oct 1950; *m* 1975 *Rodney Charles Hudson and has:
            1g *Julian Charles; *b* 23 June 1979
            1g *Felicity Jane; *b* 28 May 1983
        2e *Morar Catherine Beryl [Mrs Oswald Ainscough, Abbots Brow, Kirkby Lonsdale, Lancs]; *b* 28 April 1929; *m* 8 Aug 1959, as his 2nd w, *Maj Oswald Whitwell Ainscough, s of John Ainscough, of Briars Hall, Latham, Lancs
      1d (cont.) **Sir Michael** *m* 2nd 22 April 1947 *Kathleen [Kathleen Lady Malcolm, Flat 1, 11 Onslow Sq, London SW7], dau of Cdr George Jonathan Gawthorne, RN, and formerly w of James Melvin, and *d* 10 Jan 1976
      2d Alexander Ernest William, TD; *b* 4 Oct 1900; *educ* Wellington; Maj RA (TA); *m* 1st 16 March 1925 Olive Leah, yst dau of Walter Scott, of Sydney, NSW; *m* 2nd 25 June 1941 *Sybil Mary (*m* 3rd 5 March 1963 Aubrey Vernon, of La Bergerie, Valbonne, France), yr dau of Hugh Peacock, of Greatford Hall, Stamford, and formerly w of Lt-Cdr Geoffrey Seymour Grenfell, RN (*see* GRENFELL, B), and *d* 30 Oct 1958, leaving:
        1e *Alexandra Mary [Mrs Simon Ward, 22 Antrim Mansions, London NW3]; *b* 22 Jan 1943; *m* 31 Jan 1964 *Simon Ward, actor, s of Leonard Ward, of Petts Wood, Kent, and has:
          1f *Sophie; *b* 29 Dec 1964, actress; *m* 1988 *Paul Hobson, s of George Hobson
          2f *Claudia Thomasine; *b* 14 Feb 1969
      1d Elspeth Mary Isabel; *m* 8 Jan 1936 *Thomas Cottrell-Dormer, JP, only surv s of Capt Charles Walter Cottrell-Dormer, of Rousham Park, Oxford, and *d* 7 April 1977, leaving:
        1e *Charles; *b* 13 Nov 1936; *educ* Eton; *m* 16 Sept 1961 (*divorce* 1966) Caroline Catherine, dau of Col Clayton Davis, DSO, of NSW, and has:
          1f *Julia Hilary Marigold; *b* 2 Sept 1963
         1e *Frances Mary; *b* 21 Feb 1938

2d *Griselda Helen Adeline; *m* 1st 8 Jan 1936 Capt Frederick William Gray (*d* 11 March 1938); *m* 2nd 21 July 1944 Cmdt Willem Galdermans, Chasseurs Ardennais, Chevalier Ordre de Leopold, Ordre de la Couronne, Dist Commr Belgian Congo (*d* 3 May 1953)

2c Charles Edward; *b* 2 Dec 1865; Maj Bucks Yeo, Lt Scots Gds; *m* 28 Dec 1894 (*divorce* 1914), as her 2nd husb, Hon Beatrix Mary Leslie Hore-Ruthven (*d* 24 March 1930), only dau of 9th Lord Ruthven of Freeland (*see* CARLISLE, E), and *d* 16 April 1935, having had:

1d James Alexander; *b* 5 Nov 1898; *d* 8 June 1904

2d Arthur William Alexander, CVO (1954, MVO 1949); *b* 31 May 1903; *educ* Repton; ADC to Govr Victoria 1926–28, Lt-Col Welsh Gds WW II (POW), Assist Mil Attaché Paris 1950–53, Priv Sec to Govr S Australia 1953–55, Queen's Messenger 1955–89; *m* 11 Sept 1928 Hester Mary (*d* 1992), dau of Samuel Furneaux Mann, of Victoria, Australia, and *d* 1989, leaving:

1e Sir JAMES WILLIAM THOMAS ALEXANDER MALCOLM, **12th and present Bt**

2e +Ian (John) William Ruthven [John Malcolm Esq, 76 Adelaide St, Woollahra, NSW 2025, Australia]; *b* 20 Aug 1933; *educ* Eton and Magdalene Coll Cambridge (BA 1957, MA 1960); *m* 10 Aug 1963 *Christie, only dau of John Bramley, of Bloemfontein, S Africa, and formerly w of John Moss, and has:

1f +Robert van Riet; *b* 19 Sept 1965; *m* 1993 *Susan, dau of T H Cass, of Ruislip, Middx, and has:

1g *Kim Kanga; *b* 24 Feb 1996

2g *Josephine Ivy; *b* 30 Sept 1997

2f +William David; *b* 1 March 1967

3f +John Alexander; *b* 25 July 1968

1d Honoria Adeline; *m* 1st 15 July 1914 Reginald Fitzroy Lewis Johnstone (*ka* 9 Sept 1914), Lt QO Cameron Highrs, 2nd s of Col Montague George Johnstone, DSO (*see* JOHNSTONE, Bt); *m* 2nd Dec 1916 2nd Lt James Gordon Lumsden, Scots Gds; *m* 3rd Capt Charles Gordon, s of Alexander Gordon of Pitlurg, Aberdeenshire, and *d* 8 April 1929, leaving issue

2d Bettine Violet; *m* 2 Dec 1922 Capt Henry Robert Somers FitzRoy de Vere Somerset, DSO, and had issue (*see* BEAUFORT, D)

5 James, of Nuthill and Lathrisk; *b* 19 Oct 1693; *m* Elizabeth Durward, of Kirkaldie, and *d* 22 June 1742, having had issue

1 Isabella; *b* 9 Aug 1684; *m* 1725 David Balfour

2 Margaret; *b* 5 Sept 1685; *d* 2 April 1771

3 Emilia; *b* 8 Oct 1688; *m* James Moutray of Roscobie

MALET

Arms: Az. three escallops or. **Crest:** Out of a ducal coronet or a heraldic tiger's head issuant erm. **Motto:** *Ma force de en hault* ('My strength comes from on high'). **Creation:** Bt. (GB) 24 Feb 1791.

SIR HARRY DOUGLAS ST LO MALET, 9TH BT [Sir Harry Malet Bt, Wrestwood, RMB 184, Boyup Brook, WA 6244, Australia]; *b* 26 Oct 1936; *s* f 1990; *educ* Downside and Trin Coll Oxford; late Lt QRI Hus; *m* 28 Aug 1967 *Julia Gresley, dau of Charles Harper, of 54 Irvine St, Pepermint Grove, Perth, W Australia, and has:

1 +CHARLES EDWARD ST LO; *b* 30 Aug 1970; *educ* Blundell's; lte Lt QRI Hus; *m* 20 Sept 1997 *Rachel, dau of Timothy P S Cane, of Kirby Bedon, Norfolk

Lineage: WILLIAM MALET, of Granville, Normandy; also held lands in Lincs before 1066 (possibly by virtue of his mother's putative status of Englishwoman); granted the feudal Barony of Eye, Suffolk, following the Conquest, in which he was one of WILLIAM I's chief lieutenants, being allegedly given the task by WILLIAM of burying HAROLD's body after Hastings; Sheriff Yorks 1068; *m* Hesilia Crispin (living 1086), gggdau of ROLLO THE DANE, DUKE OF NORMANDY, and *d* c 1071, leaving:

1 Robert, of Eye, which he was holding as a tenant-in-chief of the Crown 1086, along with 220 other Manors in Suffolk, 32 in Yorks, eight in Lincs, three in Essex, two in Notts and one in Hants; Sheriff Suffolk, Gt Chamberlain by the start of HENRY I's reign, but banished after 1105 for supporting HENRY's bro

ROBERT OF NORMANDY; *m* Elisée/Helise, gggdau of RICHARD I DUKE OF NORMANDY and was allegedly *k* Battle of Tinchebrai 1106, leaving:

(1) William; banished from England 1109 but inherited his f's lands in Normandy and was ancestor of the MAL(L)ETs de Graville in Caux, Normandy, and the MAL(L)ETs of Jersey

2 GILBERT;

1 Beatrice; *m* William de Arches

The 2nd s,

GILBERT MALET; had:

ROBERT MALET, of Curry Malet, Somerset; living 1137; had:

1 William, of Curry Malet; Steward to HENRY II, had:

(1) Gilbert, of Curry Malet; Steward to HENRY II 1170–83; *m* Alice, dau and coheir of Ralph Picot, of Milton, Kent, and had:

1a William, of Curry Malet and Shepton Mallet, Somerset; *fl* 1195–1217; Sheriff Dorset and Somerset 1211; one of the 25 magnates charged with seeing that Magna Charta was complied with; *m* Alice, dau and coheir of Thomas Basset, of Headington, Oxon, and *d c* 1219, leaving:

1b Mabel; *m* Hugh de Vivonia, of Chewton, Somerset, and was ancestor of the BEAUCHAMPs

2b Helewise; *m* 1st Sir Hugh Poyntz, of Tokington, Glos, and had issue; *m* 2nd Sir Robert de Muscegros, of Brewham, Somerset

3b Bertha; *dsp*

2a Ralph (Sir), of Bedgrave, Bucks, and Sheppey, Kent; *m* Lucy — and *d c* 1230, leaving:

1b William (Sir), of Bedgrave; *m* Lucy, dau and coheir of Sir Ralph, s of William of Brompton Ralph, Somerset, and had two daus

2 Baldwin, of Enmore, Somerset; mentioned 1166 by William Malet of Curry Malet as the third largest tenant of Curry Malet; *m* Emma — and *d* between 1191 and 1197, leaving:

(1) William (Sir), of Enmore and Sutton Malet 1199; Sheriff Somerset 1209–12; *m* 1st —; *m* 2nd Maud, dau of Adam de Kitemore, and *d c* 1223, having had:

1a WILLIAM

2a Richard

The er s,

Sir WILLIAM MALET, of Enmore; *m* Sara, dau of Raymund de Sully, of Llanmaes, Glam, and *d* 1251, leaving:

Sir WILLIAM MALET, of Enmore; *m* Maria — and had, with a yr s (Raymund):

Sir BALDWIN MALET, of Enmore; *m* Mabel, dau and heiress of Hamelyn de Deardon, whose arms were assumed by her s and remained those of this branch of the MALETs, and *d* 1279, leaving:

Sir JOHN MALET, of Enmore; allegedly *m* Sibylla, dau of Sir Robert de St Cleere, of Stapleton, and *d* 1287, having had:

Sir BALDWIN MALET, of Enmore and Deardon; *b* 1284; called to a Gt Cncl 1324; *m* Avicia, dau of Sir Simon Ralegh, and *d* 1343, leaving:

Sir JOHN MALET, of Enmore and Deardon; *m* Elizabeth, dau of Sir John Kingston, and *d c* 1349, having had:

Sir BALDWIN MALET, of Enmore, Deardon and St Audries; Kt of the Body to HENRY IV; called to a Gt Cncl 1401; *m* 1st Elizabeth, dau of Sir Thomas Trivett; *m* 2nd Amicia, dau and coheir of Richard Lyffe, of Corypole, and *d* 1416, leaving by her:

HUGH MALET, of Enmore, Deardon and St Audries; *m* Joan, dau of John Roynon, of Bickfold, and had:

THOMAS MALET, of Enmore, Deardon and St Audries; *m* 1st Joan, dau of Sir William Wadham, of Meryfield, fndr Wadham Coll Oxford; *m* 2nd Elizabeth — ; *m* 3rd Isabella, dau of Sir William Courtenay, and *d* 1502, having had:

1 William, of Enmore and Deardon; *b* 1471; *m* Alice, only dau and heiress of Thomas Young, of Easton in Gordano, and *d* 1511, having had, with other issue:

(1) Hugh, of Enmore and Deardon; *m* Isable Michell, of Cannington, and *d* 1541, leaving:

1a Richard, of Enmore and Deardon; *b* 1523; *m* Elizabeth, dau of Sir Andrew Luttrell, and *d* 1552, leaving:

1b Thomas, of Enmore and Deardon; High Sheriff Somerset 1576; *m* Elizabeth, dau of Humphrey Colles, of Barton, and *d* 1580, leaving, with other issue:

1c John (Sir), of Enmore and Deardon; High Sheriff Somerset 1601, ktd 1603; *m* Mary, dau of Sir John Popham, Ld Ch Justice, and *d c* 1614, having had, with other issue:

1d John, of Enmore and Deardon; MP Bath 1623, High Sheriff Somerset 1638; *m* Anne, dau of Sir John Tracy, and had:

1e John, of Enmore; *m* Unton, dau of 1st Baron Hawley of Duncannon, and *d* 1656, leaving:

1f Elizabeth; *m* 29 Jan 1666/7 John Wilmot, 2nd Earl of Rochester of the 1652 *cr*, the celebrated Restoration wit, poet and rake, and was *bur* 20 Aug 1681

(2) Richard, of Ash, Devon; ancestor of the MALLETs of Ash

(3) William, of Sutton Mallet

2 Baldwin (Sir), of St Audries; Slr-Gen to HENRY VIII; *m* 1st Joan, dau and heiress of John Tacle, of Honiton, and had:

(1) Michael, of St Audries; *b* 1511; *m* Joan Stawell, of Cothelstone, and *d* 1547, leaving:

1a Richard, of St Audries; *b* 1541; *m* Joan, dau of Richard Warre, of Hestercombe, and *d* 1614, having had, with two yr sons (Michael and Gawen):

1b Arthur, of St Audries; *b* 1564; *m* 1583 Mary Coffin and *dsp* 1644

2 (cont.) Sir Baldwin *m* 2nd Anne, dau and heiress of Thomas Hache, of Ullegh, and by her had, with two yr sons (Thomas and Adam):

(2) John, of Ullegh; *m* Margaret, dau of Humphrey Moncke, of Potheridge, and *d c* 1570, leaving, with other issue:

1a Malachi, of Poyntington; b 1582; m Elizabeth, dau of Richard Trevanion, of Cornwall, and d by 1636, leaving:

1b Thomas (Sir), of Poyntington; Slr-Gen to QUEEN HENRIETTA MARIA, Judge King's Bench 1641, imprisoned Tower of London by Parliamentarians 1642–44; granted 1663 a patent of btcy which he omitted to have passed the Gt Seal; m Jane, dau of Francis Mills, and d 1666, leaving, with other issue:

1c JOHN (Sir)

2c Baldwin; k in a skirmish with the Parliamentarians aged 20

The er s,

Sir JOHN MALET, of Poynington and St Audries, which latter he inherited from his cousin Arthur 1644; b c 1625; MP Bridgewater, ktd 1666; m Florentia, dau of John Wyndham, of Orchard Wyndham, and d 1686, leaving, with other issue:

BALDWIN MALET, of St Audries; Receiver Gen Somerset; b c 1650; m 1st Anne, dau of Sir John Horner; m 2nd Anne, dau of George Harbin, and by her had, with other issue:

Rev ALEXANDER MALET, of St Audries; Rector Combe Flory, Somerset, and Maiden Newton, Dorset; Preb Gloucester and Wells; b1704; m Anne, dau of Rev Laurence St Lo, Rector Pulham, and had:

1 Baldwin; d young

2 CHARLES (Sir), **1st Bt**

3 Alexander; b 1756; m 1788 Alice, dau of Nathaniel Lucas, of Bridgetown, and dsp

1 Margaret; d unm

2 Catherine; m Col William Dansey, CB, of Brinsop Court, Herefs

3 Elizabeth; m Thomas Charter, of Bishop Lydeard

4 Anne; d unm 7 May 1836

The Rev ALEXANDER MALET's er son,

Sir Charles Warre Malet 1st Bt (GB), so cr 24 Feb 1791, of Wilbury; bapt 30 Dec 1752; FRS, FSA; m 23 Sept 1799 Susanna (d 21 Dec 1868), dau and coheir of James Wales, of Bombay, and d 15 Dec 1815, leaving:

1 **Sir Alexander Malet, 2nd Bt**, KCB (1866), JP, DL Wilts; b 23 July 1800; Envoy Extrdy and Min Plen Germanic Conf Frankfurt, Min Plen Hesse-Cassel, Hesse-Darmstadt and Nassau to 1886; m 22 Dec 1834 Mary Anne Dora (d 2 Jan 1891), dau of John Spalding, of The Holme, by Marianne, dau of Thomas Eden (see EDEN OF WINTON, B), and d 28 Nov 1886, leaving:

(1) **Sir Henry Charles Eden Malet, 3rd Bt**, JP Wilts; Lt-Col Gren Gds; b 25 Sept 1835; m 19 Feb 1873 Laura Jane Campbell (d 9 May 1922), yr dau of John Hamilton, of Hilston Park, Mon, and dspm 12 Jan 1904, having had:

1a Dora; d young

2a Vera Jean Hamilton; b 5 July 1881; m 21 Jan 1903 Dorotheos Antoniadi, s of Michael Antoniadi, of Constantinople, and d 9 Dec 1951, leaving issue

(2) **Sir Edward Baldwin Malet, 4th Bt**, GCB, GCMG, PC; b 10 Oct 1837; Amb Germany 1884–95, memb Court Arbitration The Hague 1900–06, Tstee Wallace Collection; m 19 March 1885 Lady Ermyntrude Sackville Russell, LGStJ (d 22 March 1927), dau of 9th Duke of Bedford (qv), and d 29 June 1908

2 Charles St Lo; b 10 Jan 1802; Lt-Col cmdg 8th Regt; m 1st 27 Feb 1837 his cousin Jane St Lo (d 28 Dec 1868), only child of James Clarke, of Burbage, Leics, and heiress of the ST LOs; m 2nd 12 Aug 1871Caroline Emilia (dsp 9 March 1879), dau of John Thomas Ansley, Madras CS, and d 20 Sept 1889, having by his 1st w had:

(1) William St Lo; Capt 8th Hus.; b 20 Nov 1843; m 1st 12 Sept 1871 Helen (d 26 May 1878), est surv dau of Sir William Eden, 6th Bt (see EDEN OF WINTON, B), and had:

1a **Sir Edward St Lo Malet, 5th Bt**; b 14 Sept 1872; BA Cantab; m 12 Nov 1901 Louise Michelle (d 23 April 1949), dau of Philibert Dubois, and d 24 Dec 1909, leaving:

1b **Sir Charles St Lo Malet, 6th Bt**; b 1 Nov 1906; d at school 21 Nov 1918

2a HARRY CHARLES ST LO MALET (Sir), **7th Bt**

1a Elfrida St Lo; b 9 Feb 1875; m 14 July 1898 Capt Richard John Carey Oakes (d 27 May 1929), of Brookside, Bens, Oxford, and d 17 Nov 1947, leaving issue

2a Helen Avice Harriet St Lo; b 12 Sept 1878; d unm 31 March 1966

3a Hilda Mary Jeanne St Lo; b 25 April 1879; m 3 April 1900 Farquhar Celynin Lloyd, only s of Lt-Col Albert Lloyd, KOYLI, and d 1955, leaving issue

(1) (cont.) Capt William Malet m 2nd 4 Dec 1879 Nora Mary (d 19 Jan 1942), dau of Gilbert James Blane, of Foliejon Park, Windsor, and d 26 Aug 1885, leaving by her:

3a William Gilbert St Lo; b 27 Jan 1881; d 2 Sept 1928

4a Audley Forbes St Lo; b 3 Oct 1882; d 23 April 1929

5a Alexander Derwin St Lo; b 23 Nov 1883; dsp 1959

4a Mary St Lo; b 20 June 1885; m 20 Aug 1907 George Herbert Griffith, CBE (d 11 April 1947), s of Rev J W Griffith, of Pentreath, Angelesey, and d 22 Feb 1934

(2) Alexander George William St Lo; Maj 39th Regt.; b 25 Oct 1845; d unm 11 Jan 1922

(3) Thomas St Lo; Capt Dorset Militia; b 26 June 1855; d unm 5 Feb 1887

(1) Florence Dora St Lo; m 6 Aug 1861 Rev Edmond Warre, CB, CVO, DD (d 22 Jan 1920), Preb Wells, Provost Eton, and d 2 Nov 1922, leaving issue

(2) Amelia Ella St Lo; d unm

(3) Jane Blanche St Lo; m Feb 1870 Walter Rosebrook Dutts and d 3 June 1913, leaving issue

3 William Wyndham (Rev); Vicar Ardeley, Herts; b 29 Sept 1804; m 9 March 1837 Eliza Drake (d 24 Jan 1862), yr dau of Edward Jeffries Esdaile, JP, of Cothelstone House, Somerset, and d 12 June 1885, having had:

(1) Guilbert Edward Wyndham; Maj RHA, KStJ; b 12 July 1839; m 1st 29 July 1869 Florence (d 14 Sept 1877), dau of Charles Willes Wilshere, of The Fruthe, Welwyn, and had:

1a Sydney Francis Wyndham; b 10 Sept 1877; d 21 Jan 1879

(1) (cont.) Guilbert Malet m 2nd 20 Aug 1880 Gertrude Agnes Cunliffe (d 13 Nov1923), dau of Sir Philip Cunliffe-Owen, KCB, KCMG, CIE, and d 15 Oct 1918, having by her had:

2a Godfrey Charles Wyndham; Capt 6th Bn Somerset LI; b 5 Sept 1884; educ Keble Coll Oxford; m 1st 22 July 1918 (divorce 1934) Marian Clinton, 2nd dau of F Clinton-Baddeley, of Dibden Lodge, Hythe, Hants; m 2nd 1940 Isabelle Fergusson, dau of C W F Middleton, of NSW, and d 12 Jan 1969, having by his 1st w had:

1b Susanna Wyndham; b 27 Jan 1922; m 10 May 1947 Gerald Stewart Parker, s of Capt Basil Steward Parker, Hants Regt, and dsp 10 March 1948

3a Alexander Wyndham, MVO (1932); b 28 Feb 1886; Lt-Col IA, RAF Levies, WW I, NWF India 1922–23 (despatches), Burma 1930–32 (despatches), WW II (despatches); m 17 May 1921 Kathleen Betty (d 1993), only dau of Brig Ben Alexander Cadell, IA, and d 20 July 1956, leaving:

1b +Richard Wyndham; b 7 Jan 1923; educ St Edward's Sch Oxford; manager tea estates India and Africa 1947–60, management advsy offr Cncl for Small Industries in Rural Areas, Capt IA WW II Burma and Java, AMBIM, AIWSP; m 25 Feb 1956 *Judith Winifred Ferguson, yst dau of David McEwen, of Kirkby Lonsdale, Westmorland, and has had:

1c *Claire Alexandra; b 25 April 1965; m 1993 *Simon Hale

2c Sarah Agnes; b 23 Jan 1969; d 1985

1b *Sylvia Mary Fanshwaw [Mrs John Tapp, Southborough House, Ashcombe Avenue, Surbiton, Surrey]; b 7 Sept 1925; ARCM, LRAM; m 13 Nov 1948 *John Theodore William Theodore Tapp, AMICE, er s of Maj William Henry Tapp, MC, FRGS, Queen's Bays, and has:

1c *Nicholas Charles Theodore; b 5 Nov 1952

1c *Caroline Linda; b 2 March 1956

2b *Kathleen Mary Wyndham; b 4 Feb 1934; ARCM, LRAM

4a Owen Wyndham (Rev), of Wyndham Lodge, 2 Bennetts Way, Clevedon, Somerset; b 2 Aug 1887; Lt RNVR, Rector St Mary's Cayon, St Kitts, 1949–51, Chaplain St Raphael's Home Torquay 1951; m 1st 8 Aug 1914 Florence Elsie (d 5 Jan 1956), dau of W Hickie; m 2nd 27 Dec 1956 Christine Mary, dau of Sidney Bond

5a Edward Barnabas Wyndham; Lt RM; b 26 Oct 1894; m 1st 30 April 1921 (divorce 1950) Esther Grace MacDonald (d 6 Sept 1969), er dau of Rev Gilbert Lyon, Vicar Cloford, Somerset; m 2nd 1950 Aileen Nina Mary (d 1981), dau of F W Cuming, and d 12 May 1961, leaving by his 1st w:

1b +Michael Edward Guilbert [Maj Michael Malet, Adastra, Pound Rd, Over Wallop, Hants SO20 8JX]; b 12 Sept 1922; educ Marlborough; Maj RA; m 24 April 1953 Judith Ann Rowley (d Dec 1996), er dau of Ernest Rowley Lewis, of Battledown, Cheltenham, and has:

1c +Mark Wyndham [Mark Malet Esq, 3258 Route de Vaudaghes, 74310 Les Houches, France]; b 29 Oct 1956; m 1984 *Lilyan, dau of Capt M N Herrera, of Caracas, and has:

1d +Barnabas Wyndham; b 1986

1d *Alexandra Sophie; b 1988

2c +James Edward Barnabas Wyndham [James Malet Esq, 31 Atalanta St, London SW6 6TU]; b 30 March 1964

1c *(Mary) Pepita Wyndham; b 2 Feb 1954; m 9 July 1977 *Michael O' Kelly Webber, er s of Julien Linden O'Kelly Webber, of Rome, and has:

1d *Thomas Edward O' Kelly; b 1984

1d *Jessica Grace; b 1982

1b *Wendy [Miss Wendy Malet, 4 Church View, Bourton, Gillingham, Dorset SP8 5BT]; b 21 March 1926

1a Heloise Mary Wyndham; b 22 April 1883; m 5 April 1910 William St John Fenton Miles (d Oct 1936) and d 8 July 1960, leaving issue

2a Eva Mary Wyndham; b 19 Oct 1890; d unm 25 April 1918

3a Monica Mary Wyndham; LRAM; b 12 Aug 1893; m 27 Jan 1921 Rev William Wheldale Tunnicliffe, Vicar Middleton, Warwicks, and d 13 Sept 1951, leaving issue

(2) Harold Esdaile Wyndham, JP Kent; T/2nd Lt 4th Bn Hants Vol Regt, Col cmdg 18th Hus; b 17 Feb 1841; m 1 Sept 1868 Emily Constance (d 2 Nov 1920), dau of John Banks Friend, and d 26 June 1918, leaving:

1a Harold Wyndham; Maj 18th Hus, Bde-Maj 1916–18; b 7 July 1882; m 18 Jan 1908 Bertha Emily (d 6 Dec 1937), er dau of William Philip Pearson, and d 15 April 1937, leaving:

1b John Wyndham; b 12 Oct 1910; educ Wellington; Capt 10th Hus WW II; m 8 July 1937 June Rosalind (m 2nd 1943 Capt Wladyslaw Galica (d 7 June 1951), est s of Gen Andre Galica, of Poland, and d 1991), er dau of Capt John Broadley Harrison-Broadley, of Welton House, Brough, E Yorks, and was ka 27 May 1940, leaving:

1c +Greville John Wyndham, OBE [Lt-Col Greville Malet OBE, The Weald House, Hatherop, Cirencester, Glos]; Lt-Col 10th Roy Hus; b 6 Dec 1939; educ Harrow; m 22 Jan 1972 (divorce 1993) Hon (Margaret) Cherry Wigram (see WIGRAM, B), and has:

1d +Charles Neville Wyndham; b 24 Sept 1976; educ Eton

1d *Henrietta Margaret June; b 8 Sept 1978; educ St Mary's Wantage

1c *(Leola) Dawn Wyndham [Mrs David Nicholson, c/o Lloyds Bank, 6 Pall Mall, London SW1]; m 23 March 1961 Capt (John) David (Graham) Nicholson, RHA, only s of Gen Sir Cameron Gordon Graham Nicholson, GCB, KBE, DSO, MC, and has:

1d *John Andrew Graham; b 2 Feb 1964

2d *Edward Wyndham Graham; b 1966

1d *Davina June; b 30 March 1962

1a Sibyl Harold Wyndham; b 6 July 1877; d unm 5 May 1952

(3) Sydney Law Wyndham; b 19 April 1843; educ St Mary's Coll Winchester; d 29 Dec 1860

(4) Clement Drake Elton Wyndham (Rev); Vicar Stoke Courcy, RD of E Quantockshead; b 19 March 1845; educ Pembroke Coll Oxford (BA); m 3 Oct 1872 Agnes Bessie (d 11 April 1909), dau of Charles Knighton Webb, MD, of Exeter, and d 7 Jan 1930, leaving:

1a Clement Hugh Weston Wyndham; *b* 10 May 1877; *educ* Winchester; served Roy 1st Devon Yeo WW I (despatches), Order Nile 4th Cl; *m* 20 Feb 1930 Violet Frances, est dau of Jefferys Philip Thomas Allen, of Lyngford

1a Beatrice Elizabeth Wyndham; *b* 21 Aug 1873; *d* unm 5 March 1965

2a Agnes Cecilia Wyndham; *b* 27 Sept 1874; *m* 3 Oct 1905 Thomas Wood Shaw (*d* 24 March 1934), of Culmington Manor, Salop, and *d* 28 Sept 1947, leaving issue

3a Florence Wyndham; *b* 9 Sept 1879; *d* unm 6 Dec 1955

4a Winefride Joan Wyndham; *b* 9 Nov 1884; *d* unm 9 March 1971

4 George Grenville; Lt-Col cmdg 3rd Bombay Light Cav; *b* 7 March 1806; *m* 31 March 1851 Mary Maria Fleming (*d* 26 Jan 1905), dau of Col John Taylor, HEICS, and was *ka* Persian War 9 Dec 1856, leaving:

(1) Allan Arthur Grenville; *b* 22 Feb 1856; MICE, Public Works Dept India, Dept Ch Engr; *m* 1890 Elizabeth Anne (*d* 29 Jan 1953), dau of William Lysaght, of Beechmount, Co Cork, and *d* 12 Sept 1937, having had:

1a Hugh Arthur Grenville; Lt KOS Bdrs; *b* 22 Sept 1891; *educ* Harrow; *ka* 18 April 1915

2a George Edward Grenville, OBE (1943); *b* 15 Feb 1898; *educ* Harrow; Col RAOC, WW I, WW II; *m* 1st 15 July 1922 (*divorce* 1938) Gwendoline Iliffe (*m* 2nd 1938 R-Adml Ernest William Leir, DSO, and *d* 1980), only dau of Brig-Gen James Aubrey Gibbon, CMG, and had:

1b +(Baldwin) Hugh Grenville [Dr Hugh Malet, The Vyne, Blue Anchor, Somerset TA24 6JX]; *b* 18 Feb 1928; *educ* Wellington and King's Coll Cambridge (MA); PhD Salford; late Sudan Political serv, author, Dir Studies Brasted Theological Training Coll, Lecturer Local History Salford U 1973; *m* 25 July 1959 Kathleen Patricia (*d* 16 April 1983 aged 49), only dau of Arthur Morris, and has:

1c +Durand David Grenville; *b* 22 Jan 1965; *educ* St Chad's Coll Durham; barrister

1c *Phoebe Jane Grenville; *b* 2 Oct 1962

1b *Barbara Madeleine Anne [Mrs Edward Counsell, The Monks House, Montacute, Somerset]; *b* 4 Aug 1924; *m* 17 July 1947 *Edward Hugh Michael Counsell, CBE, and has:

1c *John Aubrey Malet; *b* 27 Sept 1949; *educ* Downside

2c *Christopher Anthony Hugh Malet; *b* 4 Dec 1952; *educ* Downside

3c *Hugh Michael Malet; *b* 15 Oct 1962

2a (cont.) Col George Malet *m* 2nd 1939 *Margaret Bell Wright (*m* 2nd 24 June 1967 Patrick Walsh, JP (*d* 1980), s of Luke Walsh, of Co Kerry), and *d* 1 Aug 1952, having by her had:

2b +Michael Ian Grenville; *b* 2 Nov 1939; *educ* Berkhamsted and St Andrews (MA), PhD LSE; *m* 1st 1964 (*divorce* 1980) Alison Little; *m* 2nd 1980 *Jennifer Jones and by his 1st w has:

1c +Ian Martin; *b* 1964

1c *Saffron Margaret; *b* 15 Aug 1968

2b *Zenobia Margaret Grenville [Mrs Michael Venner, Libra, Loders, nr Bridport, Dorset DT6 3SA]; *b* 7 Jan 1942; *educ* St Anne's Coll Oxford (BA); *m* 26 Aug 1967 *Michael Venner and has:

1c *Miriam Anna; *b* 1 Feb 1969

2c *Catriona Jeanne; *b* 6 April 1979

1a Elizabeth Enid; *m* 19 July 1916, Lt-Col Clive Vincent Moberly Bell, OBE, Loyal N Lancs Regt, and *d* 15 March 1951, leaving issue

2a Margaret Mary; *d* 16 Nov 1904 aged 9

(1) Agnes Susanna; *d* unm 27 April 1936

(2) Margaret Julia Mary; *d* unm 1949

(3) Elizabeth Jessie; *m* 9 July 1878 Sydney Eggers Bates (*d* 3 March 1924), of Manydown Park, Hants, and *d* 13 Oct 1940, leaving issue (*see* BATES, Bt, of Bellefield)

5 Arthur; memb Cncl Bombay; *b* 7 Nov 1806; *m* 1st 3 Sept 1846 Mary Sophia (*d* 6 Oct 1853), 3rd dau of Sir J P Willoughby, Bt, and had:

(1) Edith Eliza Rose; *m* 1 Aug 1872 Lt-Col Francis William Nixon, RE (*d* 15 Jan 1924), s of 1st Bp Tasmania, and *d* 19 March 1924

5 (cont.) Arthur Malet *m* 2nd Dec 1854 Annie Louisa (*d* 3 Sept 1900), dau of George Powney Thomps, HEICS, and *d* 13 Sept 1888, having by her had:

(1) Arthur Elphinstone; *b* 11 Feb 1858; *m* 1891 Janet, dau of I Henders, and *dsp* 16 May 1900

(2) Herbert Rivers; Cdr RNVR; *b* 12 May 1864; *m* 1st 1888 Violet (*d* 8 May 1946), dau of Maj J H King, 2nd Dragoons; *m* 2nd 19– Gertrude Fox and *d* 13 Jan 1951, having by his 1st w had:

1a Francis Arthur Rivers; *b* 23 Nov 1892; Flight Sub-Lt RNAS; accidentally *kas* Nov 1916

2a Henry Guy Rivers; *b* 30 Sept 1894; S/Ldr RAF; *m* 1st 23 June 1917 (*divorce*) Olga Muriel, 3rd dau of James Balfour, of Paignton, Devon; *m* 2nd Tessa West and had by his 1st w:

1b Guy Anthony Rivers; *b* 21 June 1920; Lt RNR WW II; *m* 1943 Elizabeth Barbara (3rd Offr WRNS) (*m* 2nd 3 Jan 1947 Lt (L) John Henry Guy Ellingham, RN, er s of J Ellingham, DFC, of Hoveton, Norfolk), dau of Maj A C Pitts, of Wroxham, and was *ka* March 1944

2b Francis Ivo Rivers; *b* 1 June 1922; *d* 8 Oct 1928

3b +Vivian Arthur Rivers; *b* 14 Feb 1925

1b *Olga Diana Valentine Rivers [Mrs F Hellingbrunner, 310 McFarlane St, Peterborough, Ontario, Canada]; *b* 1925; *m* 1951 *F A Hellingbrunner

2b *Patience Violet Rivers; *b* 26 April 1930; *m* 1954 (*divorce*) Leslie G Walton

1a Violet Rivers; *b* 5 Aug 1889; *d* 2 Aug 1891

(2) Alice Louisa; *m* 23 Aug 1883 John P Ramsden (*d* 27 Jan 1911),and *d* 13 July 1924, leaving issue (*see* RAMSDEN, Bt)

(3) Mary Harriett; *d* unm Nov 1944

(4) Fertrude Evelyn; *d* unm Jan 1940

(5) Ethel Maud; *m* 31 Dec 1894 Herbert George Brand (*d* 1942) and *dsp* May 1947

(6) Hilda Margaret; *d* unm 31 July 1894

(7) Esther Janet; *d* unm 9 Aug 1959

6 Hugh Poyntz; HEICS; *b* 13 Aug 1808; *m* 1839 Rosa (*dsp* 1884), dau of Charles Lucas, and *d* 10 March 1904

7 Octavius Warre; HEICS; *b* 7 May 1811; *m* 24 June 1852 Alice Anna Catherine (*d* 9 Aug 1905), dau of Thomas Hawkes, of Himley House, Staffs, MP Dudley, and *d* 11 Dec 1891, having had:

(1) Francis Blundell Warre; *b* 26 March 1855

(2) John Warre; Maj 1st Bn Northumberland Fus; *b* 6 May 1856; *m* 7 June 1893 Frances Anne Mary (*d* 3 Oct 1934), dau of William Scarborough Jacks, of Moor House, Headingley, Leeds, and *d* 20 Jan 1913, leaving surv issue:

1a Guy Seymour Warre, of Fairmead, N End, Ditchling, Sussex; RBA 1936; *b* 6 Aug 1900; *educ* Downside; painter and engraver, Camouflage Offr Air Min and Min Home Security WW II; *m* 3 July 1943 Dorothy Mary, dau of Atwell John Coxon

(3) Thomas Herbert Warre; *b* 8 April 1859; *m* 14 July 1909 Cicely Florence (*d* 28 Dec 1948), est dau of William Thomas Hartcup, of Sprowston Court, Norfolk, and Upland Hall, Suffolk, and *d* 21 Nov 1942, having had:

1a Sylvia Mary Warre; *b* 4 March 1920; *d* unm 20 Nov 1940

(1) Mabel Warre; *d* unm 27 April 1932

(2) Ethel Warre; *d* unm 19 April 1938

8 Alfred Augustus; Capt 8th Foot; *b* 29 Aug 1814; *m* 20 June 1840 Ellen von Passow, of Brandenburg, and *d* 21 March 1898, having had:

(1) Charles Frederick; Capt 8th Regt; *b* 11 May 1843; *d* 1879

The 6th Bt's uncle,

Sir Harry Charles Malet, 7th Bt, DSO, OBE, JP Wilts and Somerset; Lt-Col 8th Hus and AQMG Boer War 1899–1902 (two medals, six clasps), WW I (despatches three times), Ordre du Mérite Agricole; *b* 21 Sept 1873; *m* 1 Feb 1906 Mildred Laura Lambert-Swiney (*d* 7 March 1951), dau of Capt Henry Stephen Swiney, 69th Regt, of The Limes, Hawkhurst, Kent, and Stanmore, Canterbury, and *d* 14 Oct 1931, leaving:

1 EDWARD WILLIAM ST LO (Sir), **8th Bt**

1 Ermyntrude Virginia St Lo; *b* 16 Aug 1907; *m* 14 May 1937 Geoffrey Wynne Severn Conan-Davies, Dist Offr Colonial Admin Serv, of Tasmania, s of Rev J J Conan-Davies, of Worcester, and had:

2 *Helen Agnes St Lo [Mrs Alan Stoddart, Middle Halsway, Crowcombe, Somerset TA4 4BA]; *b* 5 Jan 1911; *m* 6 Sept 1934 *Alan Douglas Stoddart and has issue

Sir HARRY's only son,

Sir Edward William St Lo Malet, 8th Bt, OBE (1953); *b* 27 Nov 1908; *educ* Dover Coll and Ch Ch Oxford (BA 1932); served Palestine (GS Medal) 1935–36, N Africa (despatches) 1937–42, attd Br Embassy Ankara 1942–43, Col 8th Hus (ret 1955) NW Europe 1944–45, High Sheriff Somerset 1966; *m* 24 July 1935 Baroness Benedicta von Maasburg, est dau of Baron Wilhelm von Maasburg, and *d* 1990, leaving:

1 Sir HARRY DOUGLAS ST LO MALET, **9th and present Bt**

1 *Mary Jane St Lo [Mrs Robert Pickering, 101 North Rd, Bassendean, Perth, W Australia]; *b* 16 Sept 1938; *educ* Ruskin Sch of Art Oxford; *m* 1970 *Robert Pickering and has:

(1) *Samuel Thomas Carrington St Lo; *b*1970

(2) *William Benedict St Lo; *b* 1972

2 *Micaela Elizabeth Benedicta St Lo; *b* 26 Sept 1939; *educ* Ruskin Sch of Art Oxford; *m* 1963 *Maj-Gen Edwin H A Beckett, CB, MBE, POW Own Yorks Regt, and has:

(1) *Simon Turlo; *b* 25 Jan 1965

(2) *Alexander Crispin; *b* 1979

(3) *Thomas James; *b* 1980

(1) *Diana Viola; *b* 1964

MALLALIEU

MAL·A·LUI   QUI·MAL   EN·DIT

Arms: Azure on a chevron ermine between three fleurs-de-lys argent four bezants, on a chief ermines a rose of the third barbed and seeded proper. **Supporters:** Dexter, a horse argent; sinister, a fox-hound proper, both gorged with a torse argent and azure and each statant erect on a field of stubble with a hedgerow, that on the dexter having a stile and palings and that on the sinister a gate with palings, all in perspective proper. **Motto:** *Mal à lui qui mal en dit* ('Evil be to him who evil speaks'). **Creation:** B. (LP, UK) 1991.

THE BARONESS MALLALIEU, of Studdridge, Co Bucks (Ann Mallalieu, QC (1988)) [The Rt Hon The Baroness Mallalieu QC, House of Lords, London SW1A 0PW]; *b* 27 Nov 1945; *educ* Holton Park Girls' GS Wheatley, Oxon, and Newnham Coll Cambridge (MA, LLM, Pres Union 1967, Hon Fell 1992); barrister Inner Temple 1970, Bencher 1992, Recorder 1985–93, Memb Gen Cncl Bar 1973–75; chm Leave Country Sports Alone, Oppn Spokesman Home and Legal Affrs 1992–97; *m* 1979, as his 2nd w, *Timothy Felix Harold Cassel, est s of His Honour Sir Harold Felix Cassel, 3rd Bt (*qv*), and has two daus

Lineage: Sir (JOSEPH PERCIVAL) WILLIAM MALLALIEU; *m* 1945 *Harriet Rita Riddle Tinn and *d* 1980, leaving:

ANN, *cr* a **Baroness**

MALLINSON

· INDE · QUERCUS ·

Arms: Ermine three pallets gules, in chief two crescents or and in base an acorn, leaved and slipped proper. **Crest:** A cubit arm, the hand grasping a stock of a tree snagged and eradicated proper. **Motto:** *Inde quercus* ('Thence the oak'). **Creation:** Bt. (UK) 6 July 1935.

SIR (WILLIAM) JAMES MALLINSON, 5TH BT, of Walthamstow, Co Essex [Sir James Mallinson Bt, The Watch House, Bembridge, IoW PO35 5NQ]; *b* 22 April 1970; *s* f 1995; *educ* Eton and Balliol (BA) and St Peter's Coll Oxford (MA)

Lineage: Sir William Mallinson, 1st Bt (UK), so *cr* 6 July 1935, JP; *b* 6 July 1854 (4th s of John Mallinson, of Forest Gate, Essex); chm Justices Becontree Bench,

Essex; *m* 5 June 1878 Amelia Louisa (*d* 3 Dec 1913), dau of Henry Tucker, of Plumstead, Kent, and *d* 5 May 1936, having had:

1 WILLIAM JAMES (Sir), **2nd Bt**

2 Stanley Tucker, JP (Bury St Edmunds); *b* 9 Jan 1884; *m* 29 April 1919 Dora Selina (*d* 14 Aug 1960), dau of William Millman Burridge, of Boscombe, Hants, and *d* 21 Feb 1955, leaving:

(1) +ANTHONY WILLIAM [Anthony Mallinson Esq, 15 Douro Place, London W8 5PH]; *b* 1 Dec 1923; heir presumptive; *educ* Marlborough and Gonville and Caius Coll Cambridge (BA 1948, LLB 1949, Exhibitioner 1948–49, Tapp Post-Graduate Scholar 1949–51); Maj RA, slr 1952; *m* 30 April 1955 *Heather Mary, only dau of Thomas Arthur Mansfield Gardiner, of Gerrards Cross, Bucks

3 Stuart Sidney (Sir), CBE (1938), DSO (1918), MC (1915), JP (Essex 1938), DL (Essex 1937–66, Co London 1966); *b* 14 April 1888; *educ* Ashville Coll Harrogate and Leys Sch Cambridge; Lt-Col RE, Hon Col 563 (Essex) Regt RA (TA) 1938, High Sheriff Essex 1939, served WWs I (despatches thrice) and II as Sector Cdr HG, Co Welfare Offr Essex, v-pres ESU, chm Anglo-American Liaison Ctee, OStJ 1952, ktd 1954, Pres Essex Co FA, Hon Pres Wm Mallinson & Sons 1962, Pres Timber Research and Devpt Assoc of UK; *m* 13 Jan 1916 Marjorie Gray, CBE (1959) (*d* 2 Nov 1969), dau of Rev Alfred Soothill, of Ashville Coll, Harrogate, and *d* 1981, having had:

(1) Michael Stuart, MC; *b* 8 Dec 1919; *educ* Marlborough; Maj Essex Regt WW II; *ka* 22 April 1944

(2) +Justin Stuart [Justin Mallinson Esq, Bredy Farm, Burton Bradstock, Dorset DT6 4ND]; *b* 28 Sept 1923, *educ* Marlborough and Jesus Coll Cambridge; Capt Gren Gds WWII, chm Dorset NFU 1970; *m* 2 June 1944 *Juliana Beatrice, only dau of Samuel Martin, of St Helens, IoW, and has:

1a +John Michael Stuart [John Mallinson Esq, Black Down Cottage, Hemyock, Cullompton, Devon EX15 3RJ]; *b* 23 Sept 1945; *educ* Marlborough and Reading U (BSc Ag 1977); *m* 28 Dec 1968 *Elizabeth Margaret, BSc Reading 1967, est dau of John Cloke, of Walsall, Staffs, and has:

1b +Jonathan Justin Stuart; *b* 1971

1b *Elspeth May Stuart; *b* 1974

2b *Jane Majorie; *b* 1979

1a *Jennifer Jane Stuart; *b* 6 Sept 1949; *m* 1971 *Lt-Cdr Nicholas Graham Talbot Harris, RN, and has issue (see SHREWSBURY and WATERFORD, E)

(3) +Terence Stuart, CBE, DL (Gtr London) [Terence Mallinson Esq CBE DL, 28 Albion St, London W2 2AX]; *b* 9 Sept 1929; *educ* Marlborough and Jesus Coll Cambridge (BA 1952, MA 1959); Forestry Commr 1989–96; *m* 4 June 1955 *Anne Mary, JP (Westminster), Ld Mayor Westminster 1986–87, twin dau of D Butler Wilson, MC, of Burlington Lodge, Alderley Edge, Cheshire, and has:

1a +Lawrence Stuart [Lawrence Mallinson Esq, 8 Crieff Rd, London SW18 2EA]; *b* 4 Sept 1957; *educ* Marlborough and Jesus Coll Cambridge (MA); ACA; *m* 1990 *Angela Marie Christine, dau of Henry Sulivan, of Weybridge, Surrey, and has:

1b +Barnaby Henry Stuart; *b* 17 June 1993

1b *Mathilda Anne Kate; *b* 7 March 1995

2b *Phoebe Agnes Henrietta; *b* 24 June 1997

2a +Michael David Stuart [Michael Mallinson Esq, 16 Elvaston Place, London SW7 5QF]; *b* 22 April 1959; *educ* Marlborough, and Fitzwilliam and Darwin Coll Cambridge (MA, DipArch); RIBA; *m* 1987 *Helen P M, Head Coll of Arch & Design N London U, est dau of Alan Powell, of Cheltenham, Glos, and has:

1b +Saul Antony Terence; *b* 20 June 1996

1b *Rosanna Marjorie Bernice; *b* 17 March 1989

3a +Roland Arthur Stuart; *b* 13 July 1966; *educ* Marlborough and Edinburgh U (BSc); *m* 1995 *Fiona, dau of Ian Hunter Craig, of Reigate, Surrey

1a *Sheila Mary Anne [Mrs Nicholas Charrington, Layer Marney Tower, Colchester, Essex CO5 9US]; *b* 24 May 1961; *educ* Marlborough and Manchester U (BA); *m* 1988 *Nicholas Spencer Charrington, est s of Maj Gerald Anthony Charrington, and has:

1b *John Spencer; *b* 24 June 1995

1b *Alice Calmeyer; *b* 8 April 1990

2b *Hannah Mary; *b* 31 Oct 1991

3b *Grace Elizabeth; *b* 15 Nov 1993

(1) Sheila Stuart; *b* 21 March 1917; *d* 10 July 1934

4 Lancelot Victor; *b* 23 Nov 1892; Maj Tank Corps WWI; *m* 1st 1918 Elizabeth McLellan and had:

(1) *Pamela; *b* 1920

(2) *Marie Louise; *b* 1923

4 (cont.) Maj Lancelot Mallinson *m* 2nd 1932 *Madelon Edson Holmes [Mrs Lancelot Mallinson, 14 rue des Sablons, Paris XVI, France] and *d* 23 Oct 1953, leaving by her:

(1) Alastair; *b* 23 Sept 1932; *educ* Eton; 2nd Lt Roy Fus; *m* 1 Oct 1955 *Rosemary [Mrs Alastair Mallinson, rue Des Saulniers, 44420 Mesquer, France], dau of Charles Cecil Harvey, of Minehead, Somerset, and *d* 1986, having had:

1a +Guy; *b* 12 Dec 1957

2a +Alexander; *b* 4 June 1964

1a Louise; *b* 10 Nov 1960; *d* 26 April 1962

2a *Florence; *b* 8 March 1962

1 Amelia Agnes; *b* 2 May 1890

2 Gertrude Mabel; *m* 1st Norman Healey Swallow (*d* 7 Oct 1916) and had issue; *m* 2nd 1921 Frederick Henry Harkness (*d* 27 Dec 1935) and *d* 22 May 1969, leaving further issue

3 Daisy Florence; *d* unm 27 Jan 1971

4 Ethel Maudie; *m* 23 July 1912 Herbert Frederick Green and *d* 14 Feb 1935

5 Evangeline Dorothea; *m* 11 April 1916 Philip Smith, MC, MD, BS, DPH, MRCS, LRCP, Capt RAMC (*d* Dec 1965), of Kettering, Northants

6 Gwyneth Elaine; *m* 11 Oct 1917 Arthur Herbert Harkness, FRCS, of Wimpole St, London W1, and *d* 1968

The 1st Bt's, est s,

Sir William James Mallinson, 2nd Bt, JP (Co London and Surrey), DL (Co London); *b* 25 July 1879; High Sheriff Surrey 1933; *m* 16 Nov 1905 Mabel (*d* 22 Dec 1948), dau of John William Rush, of Tunbridge Wells, Kent, and *d* 26 Feb 1944, leaving:

1 **Sir (William) Paul Mallinson, 3rd Bt**; *b* 6 July 1909; *educ* Westminster and Ch Ch Oxford (MA, BM, BCh 1935); MRCP London 1938, FRCP 1953, consultant psychiatrist St George's Hosp London, consultant psychological medicine RN, Surg Lt-Cdr RNVR WWII, chm Wm Mallinson & Sons; *m* 1st 22 Jan 1940 (*divorce* 1967) Eila Mary, dau of Roland Graeme Guy, of Hastings, NZ; *m* 2nd 15 Feb 1968 *Mrs Margaret Cooper Gorrill, BA, MB, BS [Lady Mallinson, 25 Wimpole St, London W1M 7AD], and *d* 1989, leaving by his 1st w:

(1) **Sir William (Willie) John Mallinson, 4th Bt**; *b* 8 Oct 1942; *educ* Charterhouse; *m* 6 April 1968 (*divorce* 1978) Rosalind Angela, only dau of Rollo Hoare, TD, of The Dower Ho, Dogmersfield, Hants, and *d* 1995, leaving:

1a Sir (WILLIAM) JAMES MALLINSON, **5th and present Bt**

1a *Kate Sophia; *b* 12 March 1972; *educ* Edinburgh U

(1) *Angela Mary [Mrs Arthur Scrase, Prospect Farm, Llanidloes, Powys]; *b* 9 Aug 1941; MRCS (UK), LRCP (London 1965), DPM; *m* 7 March 1964 *Edward Tuppin Scrase, BA, MB, BCh, s of Lt-Col Arthur B Scrase, of Bartons, Stoughton, Chichester, Sussex, and has:

1a *James Ivan; *b* 21 Oct 1968

2a *Aeron Michael; *b* 1980

1a *Hannah; *b* 4 Jan 1967

(2) Hilary Eila; *b* 9 Sept 1947; *m* 1st 3 July 1965 (*divorce* 19–) Robin St Clair Barrow, 2nd s of Hugh Barrow, MC, of Springfield Lodge, Marlow, Bucks, and has:

1a *Paul Achilles St Clair; *b* 9 Feb 1966

(2) (cont.) Mrs Hilary Barrow *m* 2nd 19– *Michael Gooley and had by him:

2a *Tristan [Tristan Gooley Esq, 7 Richards Place, Chelsea, London SW3 2LA]; *b* 4 Oct 1973

1a *Siobhan; *b* 19 Dec 1975

MALMESBURY

Arms: Azure a chevron erminois between three hedgehogs or, on a chief argent the eagle of Prussia displayed sable, beaked, legged and langued gules, on the breast the cipher F R, and over it the electoral cap, in the dexter claw a sceptre and in the sinister a mound, all or, and on each wing a trefoil slipped of the last. **Crest:** A hedgehog or charged on the side with three arrows, one in pale and two in saltire, argent, and across them barways a key azure. **Supporters:** Dexter, the Prussian eagle, wings elevated sable, crowned and charged on the breast and wings as that on the chief of the arms; sinister, a reindeer proper, attired and unguled or. **Mottoes:** 1 (over the crest on an orange-coloured label) *Je maintiendrai* ('I will maintain' [motto of the House of Nassau]) 2 (under the shield) *Ubique patriam reminisci* ('Everywhere to remember one's country'). **Creations:** B. (GB) 19 Sept 1788, E and V. (GB) 29 Dec 1800.

THE 6TH EARL OF MALMESBURY, **Viscount FitzHarris**, of Hurn Court, Co Southampton, and **6th Baron Malmesbury**, of Malmesbury, Co Wilts (William James Harris, TD two clasps (1944), JP (Hants 1950)) [The Right Hon The Earl of Malmesbury TD JP, The Ford, Deptford Lane, Greywell, Hants RG29 1BS]; *b* 18 Nov 1907; *s* f 1950; *educ* Eton and Trin Coll Cambridge (BA 1930, MA 1938); CC Hants 1952, Ld Lt Hants and IoW 1973–74 (V-Lt 1960, DL 1957), Ld Lt Hants 1974–, Maj Hants Regt TA (ret), Gold Staff Offr Coronation 1937, ARICS 1937, Official Verderer New Forest 1966–74, Min Ag's personal liaison offr Western Counties SE Regn 1959–64, chm: Hants Ag Exec Ctee 1960–67 (Dep Chm 1952–60), CLA (Hants Branch) 1954–55, Hants and IoW T&AFA 1960–68, Eastern Wessex TAVRA 1968–70, Master Skinners' Co 1951–52; *m* 1st 7 July 1932 Hon Diana Claudia Patricia Carleton (*d* 1990), er dau of 2nd Baron Dorchester (see 1897 edn); *m* 2nd 1991 Margaret Fleetwood, OBE (*d* 25 Dec 1994), yst dau of Col Robert William Pigott Clarke Campbell-Preston, of Ardchattan Priory,

Argyllshire (*see also* COWDRAY, V), and widow of Capt Raymond Alexander Baring (*see* BARING, Bt); *m* 3rd 4 July 1996 *Bridget Graham Hawkings and has by his 1st w:

1 +JAMES CARLETON HARRIS, *Viscount FitzHarris*, DL (Hants 1997) [Viscount FitzHarris DL, Greywell Hill, Greywell, Hants RG29 1DG]; *b* 19 June 1946; *educ* Eton and Queen's Coll St Andrews; *m* 14 June 1969 *Sally Ann, yr dau of Sir Richard Newton Rycroft, 7th Bt (*qv*), and has:

(1) +James Hugh Carleton; *b* 29 April 1970; *m* 12 July 1997 *Jemima, est dau of Capt Michael Fulford-Dobson, RN, of Cerne Abbey, Dorset

(2) +Charles Edward; *b* 26 April 1972

(3) +Guy Richard; *b* 28 April 1975

(1) *Frances Maria; *b* 1979

(2) *Daisy Catherine; *b* 1981

1 *Sylvia Veronica Anthea [The Lady Sylvia Maltby, The Coach House, Greywell Hill, Hants RG29 1DG]; *b* 17 May 1934; *m* 28 July 1956 *John Newcombe Maltby, CBE, only surv s of AVM Sir Paul Copeland Maltby, KCVO, KBE, CB, DSO, AFC, DL, of Rotherwick, Hants, and has:

(1) *William John; *b* 5 Sept 1959; *m* 1985 *Sarah Catherine, dau of Cdr James Ekins, of Old Lime House, Easton, Hants, and has:

1a *George de Blaquiere; *b* 1989

1a *Alice Diana; *b* 1992

2a *Poppy Elizabeth; *b* 1994

(1) *Caroline Jane; *b* 14 May 1957; *m* 1990 *Alexander F J Roe, er s of Frederic Roe, of The Bacchus House, Elsdon, Northumberland, and has:

1a *Edward Frederick John; *b* 1994

2a *James; *b* 1996

1a *Charlotte Louise; *b* 1992

(2) *Sophia Louise; *b* 11 Nov 1963; *m* 23 Sept 1995 *Alexander Ross, est s of David Ross, and has:

1a *Jasper David; *b* 1996

1a *Natasha Sylvia (twin); *b* 1996

2 *Nell Carleton [The Lady Nell Boyle, The Dower House, Greywell, Hants]; *b* 3 July 1937; *m* 28 July 1962 *Capt Michael Patrick Radcliffe Boyle, Irish Gds (*see* SHANNON, E) and has issue

Malmesbury, previous creations: A Marquessate of Malmesbury was one of two peerages of that rank conferred on the 5th Baron Wharton (*qv*) in February 1714/5. A titular creation of Earl of Malmesbury was one of the subsidiary peerages conferred on Wharton's son by the titular James III in 1716.

Lineage: WILLIAM HARRIS, of Orcheston St George, Wilts; *m* 7 July 1561 Cicely, widow of — Sherne, and *d* between 13 July and 25 Nov 1570, having had:

THOMAS HARRIS, of Orcheston St George; *bapt* 15 March 1565; *m* Praxid, only dau of Robert Perry, of Orcheston, and had, with three er sons (Thomas; John; Robert) and three daus (Praxis; Sicell; Lucy):

JAMES HARRIS, of New Sarum, Wilts; *bapt* 6 Oct 1605; *m* Gertrude (*d* 1678), dau of Robert Tounson, Bp Salisbury, and *d* 24 Aug 1679, leaving, with a dau (Margaret, *m* 8 July 1669 Capt Gabriel Ashley, of Sarum, and *d* 23 June 1679) and other issue (*d* young):

THOMAS HARRIS, of the Close, Sarum, Wilts; *b* 22 Feb 1643; *m* 1st Dorothy (*dsp* 25 March 1672), dau of George Cary, DD, Dean Exeter; *m* 2nd 21 July 1673 Joan (*d* 20 Jan 1734 aged 84), dau of Sir Wadham Wyndham, of Norrington, Wilts, and *d* 13 Jan 1678-9, having had, with a yr s (Wadham, *d* aged 6):

JAMES HARRIS, of the Close, Sarum; *b* 17 April 1674; *m* 1st 3 Aug 1704 Catherine (*d* 13 June 1705), dau of Charles Cocks, MP, of Worcester, by Maria, sis and coheir of 1st and last Baron Somers (*qv*) of the 1697 *cr*, and had a dau (Catherine, *m* 23 June 1730 Sir Wyndham Knatchbull Wyndham, 5th Bt; *see* BRABOURNE, B); *m* 2nd 20 April 1707 Elizabeth (*d* 20 Jan 1743/4), 3rd dau of 2nd Earl of Shaftesbury (*qv*), and *d* 26 Aug 1731, having by her had:

1 JAMES

2 Thomas, Master in Chancery; *b* 1 Jan 1711–12; *m* 11 June 1754 Catharine (*d* 8 June 1796), sis of Sir Wyndham Knatchbull-Wyndham, 5th Bt (*see* BRABOURNE, B), and *dsp* 21 Feb 1785

3 George William (Rev); Preb Sarum, Rector Excliffe, Co Durham; *b* 19 Sept 1714; *d* unm 23 Aug 1777

2 Gertrude; *b* 22 Feb, *d* 20 Sept 1708

The est s,

JAMES HARRIS, of the Close, Sarum, and Manor Ho, Gt Durnford, Wilts; *b* 25 July 1709; FRS; Tstee Br Museum; author: *Hermes* and other works on philosophy and philology, MP Christchurch 1761–80, Ld Commr Admlty 1762 and Treasury 1763–65, Sec and Comptroller to QUEEN CHARLOTTE 1774–80; *m* 8 July 1745 Elizabeth (*d* 16 Oct 1781), dau of John Clarke, MP, of Sandford, Somerset, and *d* 22 Dec 1780, having had, with other issue, including a dau (Catherine Gertrude, *m* 11 June 1785 Hon Frederick Robinson (*d* 28 Dec 1792), 2nd s of 1st Baron Grantham, *see* LUCAS OF CRUDWELL, B), and *dsp* 8 June 1834):

JAMES HARRIS, **1st Earl of Malmesbury**, so *cr* 29 Dec 1800, as also VISCOUNT FitzHARRIS, of Hurn Court, Co Southampton, and earlier 19 Sept 1788 BARON MALMESBURY, of Malmesbury, Co Wilts (all GB), KB (1779), PC (1784); *b* 21 April 1746; *educ* Salisbury GS, Winchester, Merton Coll Oxford and Leyden U; MP (Whig) Christchurch 1770–74 and (Pittite from 1784) 1780–88; Madrid: Sec Embassy 1768, Chargé D'Affaires 1769, Min 1771–72, Envoy Berlin 1772–76 and 1793, Amb St Petersburg 1776–83, Envoy 1784–88 and Amb 1788–89 The Hague, Envoy Brunswick 1794, Amb Paris 1796 and 1797, Ld Lt Hants 1807–20; *m* 28 July 1777 Harriot Mary (*d* 20 Aug 1830), yr dau of Sir George Amyand, 1st Bt (*see* MINTO, E, also 1959 edn CORNEWALL, Bt), and *d* 21 Nov 1820, leaving, with other issue:

1 JAMES EDWARD, **2nd Earl**

2 Thomas Alfred (Rev); Preb York, Rector Hartley, Hants; *b* 24 March 1782; *m* 28 Sept 1812 Maria (*d* 12 Nov 1851), 4th dau of Very Rev George Markham, DD, Dean York, and *d* 15 Dec 1823, leaving:

(1) Alfred; *b* 31 Oct 1813; *d* unm 12 Nov 1841

(2) George; Consul-Gen Lombardo-Venetian States; *b* 1 April 1816; *m* 4 June 1857 Ellen (*d* 27 May 1897), dau of Daniel Magniac, and *dsp* 13 Nov 1857

(1) Louisa Cecilia; *m* 5 Aug 1844 Alfred Urbain Jameron, of Chateney, nr Tours, France, and *d* 1 April 1852, leaving issue

1 Catherine (CATHERINE II OF RUSSIA stood sponsor); *m* 14 June 1821 Gen Sir John Bell GCB, Col 4th Foot (*d* 20 Nov 1876), and *dsp* Dec 1855

2 Frances; *m* 15 June 1815 Lt-Gen Hon Sir Galbraith Lowry Cole (*d* 4 Oct 1842), GCB, 2nd s of 1st Earl of Enniskillen (*qv*), and *d* 1 Nov 1847, leaving issue

The 1st EARL's est s,

JAMES EDWARD HARRIS, **2nd Earl of Malmesbury**; *b* 19 Aug 1778; *educ* Eton and Ch Ch Oxford; Sec BOT 1801, MP (Tory) Helston 1802–04, Horsham 1804–07, Heytesbury 1807–12 and Wilton 1816–20, a Ld Treasury 1804–06, U-Sec For Affrs March-Aug 1807, last V-Adml IoW 1807–41; *m* 17 June 1806 Harriet Susan (*d* 4 Sept 1815), dau of Francis Bateman Dashwood, of Well Vale, Lincs, and *d* 10 Sept 1841, leaving:

1 JAMES HOWARD HARRIS, **3rd Earl of Malmesbury**, GCB (1859), PC (1852); *b* 25 March 1807; *educ* Eton and Oriel Coll Oxford; MP (C) Wilton June–Sept 1841, For Sec Dec 1852 and 1858–59, Ld Privy Seal 1866–68 and 1874–76, Hon Col 2nd Bde Southern Div RA, DCL; *m* 1st 13 April 1830 Lady Corisande Emma Bennet (*dsp* 17 May 1876), only dau of 5th Earl of Tankerville (*qv*); *m* 2nd 1 Nov 1880 Susan, DGStJ (*m* 2nd 18 Feb 1896 Maj-Gen Sir John Charles Ardagh, KCMG, KCIE, CB, LLD (*d* 30 Sept 1907), and *d* 21 Nov 1935, dau of John Hamilton, of Fyne Court, Somerset, and *dsp* 17 May 1889

2 Edward Alfred John (Sir), KCB; *b* 20 May 1808; Adml RN, Min The Hague 1867–Nov 1877, MP Christchurch 1844–52, Chargé d'Affaires and Consul-Gen Denmark 1852, Chile 1853, Min Berne; *m* 4 Aug 1841 Emma Wylly (*d* 30 July 1896), yst dau of Capt Samuel Chambers, RN, and *d* 17 July 1888, having had, with other issue:

(1) EDWARD JAMES, **4th Earl**

(2) Alfred Charles; *b* 16 Nov 1843; Lt RN; *d* unm 25 July 1877

(3) John Williams, JP (Hants); *b* 21 Feb 1849; barrister, Bengal CS 1869–78, Consul Denmark 1880–87, Tuscany 1887–88; *m* 31 July 1880 Amelia Frances Wardlaw (*d* 9 May 1926), only child of Lt-Col H W Cumming, Coldstream Gds, and *dsp* 17 Feb 1932

(1) Blanche Harriet Emma; *m* 1 Sept 1877 Capt Francis Baillie, KRRC, last surv s of Henry Baillie, PC (*d* 7 Nov 1879), of Redcastle, Ross-shire, and *d* 13 April 1911, leaving issue

(2) Rose Matilda; *m* 19 June 1878 Francis H Carew and *d* 2 Nov 1881, leaving issue (*see* CAREW, Bt)

(3) Florence Lucia; *m* 15 Oct 1890, as his 2nd w, Sir Charles Grant, KCSI (*d* 10 April 1903), and *d* 27 Jan 1909, leaving issue

(4) Alice Mary; *m* 7 April 1900 Lt-Col Henry Robert Eyre (*d* 12 March 1904), Coldstream Gds, of Middleton Tyas, Yorks, and *dsp* 6 April 1940

3 Charles Amyand (Rt Rev); DD, Bp Gibraltar 1868–73, Archdeacon Wilts, Rector Bremhill-cum-Highway, Wilts; *b* 4 Aug 1813; *m* 20 April 1837 Hon Katharine Lucia (*d* 31 Jan 1865), sis of 13th Baron Inchiquin (*qv*), and *d* 16 March 1874, having had:

(1) James Edward; *b* 14 March 1838; *d* 23 July 1845

The 3rd EARL's nephew,

EDWARD JAMES HARRIS, **4th Earl of Malmesbury**, DL (Hants); *b* 12 April 1842; *educ* RMC Sandhurst; Lt-Col Roy Irish Rifles; *m* 16 Nov 1870 Sylvia Georgina (*d* 3 April 1934), yst dau of Alexander Stewart, of Ballyedmond Castle, Co Down, and *d* 19 May 1899, having had:

1 JAMES EDWARD, **5th Earl**

2 Alexander Charles; *b* 18 Dec 1872; BA Oxon, Capt Roy Defence Corps, Lt Westminster Dragoons, 2nd Co Lond ImpYeo, Assist Priv Sec to Govr NSW 1900; *d* unm 12 May 1927

3 Arthur William; *b* 20 Jan 1876; *d* unm 15 Oct 1897

4 Edward Frederick William; *b* 24 June 1877; *educ* Ch Ch Oxford; Brevet Lt-Col KRRC, Boer War 1899–1900 and 1902 (severely wounded), WW I (despatches, severely wounded); *m* 21 June 1921 Margaret Elizabeth Hamilton (*d* 21 May 1965), sis of 11th Lord Belhaven and Stenton (*qv*), and *dsp* 10 Jan 1943

1 Catherine Sylvia; *b* 24 Dec 1871; *d* 24 June 1872

The 4th EARL's est s,

JAMES EDWARD HARRIS, **5th Earl of Malmesbury**, JP (Hants), DL; *b* 18 Dec 1872; *educ* Ch Ch Oxford (BA 1895, MA 1913), Assist Priv Sec to U-Sec Colonies 1901, Maj Special Res Offrs, 3rd Bn Hants Regt, Capt Hants Militia, WW I, Ld-in-Waiting to HM GEORGE V 1922–24, CA Hants, chm Hants CC 1927–38, Prov Grand Master Hants and IoW Freemasons, memb LCC for Stepney 1904–05, chm Lond Hosp Saturday Fund 1921–38, Pres Library Assoc 1923, Hon Treasurer Anti-Socialist Union 1917, V-Pres Soc Genealogists 1923; *m* 27 April 1905 Hon Dorothy Gough-Calthorpe, CBE (1920), DGStJ, Order Mercy with bar (*d* 23 Jan 1972 aged 86), yst dau and coheir of 6th Baron Calthorpe (*see* 1970 edn), and *d* 12 June 1950, leaving:

1 WILLIAM JAMES HARRIS, **6th and present Earl of Malmesbury**

2 Elizabeth; *b* 8 Jan 1906; *m* 1st 16 Feb 1926 (*divorce* 1944) 4th Baron Cottesloe (*qv*) and had issue; *m* 2nd 6 Feb 1944 Lt-Col Edward Walter Hall Berwick, Roy Canadian Dragoons, of Hove, s of Walter Mark Berwick, of Toronto, and *d* 11 Dec 1983, leaving further issue

MALVERN

Arms: Argent on a fess sable between three human hearts gules a lion passant guardant or. **Crest:** A lion sejant guardant erect or, the sinister paw resting on a fountain. **Supporters:** Dexter, a lion guardant gules, grasping in the exterior forepaw a rod of Aesculapius proper; sinister, a sable antelope guardant proper. **Motto:** *Cuncti perseveramus* ('Let us persevere together'). **Creation:** V. (UK) 18 March 1955.

THE 3RD VISCOUNT MALVERN, of Rhodesia and Bexley, Co Kent (Ashley Kevin Godfrey Huggins) [The Right Hon The Viscount Malvern, Standard Bank, Cecil Sq, Harare, Zimbabwe]; *b* 26 Oct 1949; *s* f 1978

Lineage: JOHN HUGGILL/HUGGINS, of St Lawrence, Reading, Berks; fisherman; *m* 1st 10 June 1548 Joan (*d* by May 1558), sis of Thomas and William Keblewhyte, of Blewburym and widow of — Palmer; *m* 2nd 14 May 1558 Alice Thicke (*bur*1560/1) and *d* by 19 April 1561, having by his 1st w had, with two er sons (John, of St Lawrence, *d* by 13 April 1583; Henry/Harry, *b* after 1540):

NICHOLAS HUGGILL, of Blewbury; *m* c 1588 Margaret — (*bur* 12 Sept 1621) and was *bur* 18 March 1618/9, having had, with three yr sons (Francis, *bapt* 18 Aug 1597, *d* by 5 Oct 1671, having had two sons; Nicholas, *bapt* 12 Aug 1600; John, of Blewbury, husbandman, *bapt* 4 April 1607, *bur* 10 Oct 1671) and three daus (Elizabeth, *bapt* 2 April 1592; Sybil, *bapt* 22 May 1594; Ann, *bapt* 17 May 1604):

THOMAS HUGGILL/HUGGINS, of Blewbury; *bapt* 4 Feb 1588/9; *m* 18 Sept 1615 Ann Lewenden (*bur* 3 Jan 1676/7) and was *bur* 3 Jan 1646/7, having had, with three er sons (William, *bapt* 19 Nov 1615, *bur* 11 Jan 1644/5; John, *bapt* 12 July 1621, *bur* 14 Feb 1634/5; Thomas, of Blewbury, *bapt* 16 April 1629, *m* Dorothy — and *d* on or after 5 Oct 1671, leaving a s Thomas, butcher, *bapt* 31 Oct 1659, *m* Martha, dau of Henry Butler, of Blewbury, and had issue) and two daus (Anne, *bapt* 27 Sept 1618; Joane, *bapt* 20 July 1626):

FRANCIS HUGILL, of Blewbury; butcher; *bapt* 7 July 1633; *m* Sarah — and was *bur* 4 Oct 1671, leaving, with a yr s (Francis, cobbler, *bapt* 31 Oct 1670, *m* 9 Oct 1699 Ann Blisset (*bur* 11/2 May 1730) and was *bur* 1 April 1735, having had issue:

WILLIAM HUGGINS, of Blewbury; *b* c 1660; *m* Mary — and *d* on or after 5 Oct 1671, leaving:

WILLIAM HUGGINS, of Blewbury; *bapt* 6 Oct 1688; *m* Mary — and *d* 24 Feb 1734/5, having had, with four yr sons (John, blacksmith, *bapt* 14 April 1717; *m* 23 July 1758 Mary King and *d* 1781 (leaving a s William, who *m* 24 Aug 1789 Elizabeth Pink and *d* between 6 July 1830 and 3 March 1831, having had two sons, Samuel and Elisha); Richard, *bapt* 25 June 1721; James, *bapt* 15 Sept 1723; Francis, *bapt* 30 April 1732) and a dau (Elizabeth, *bapt* 24 July 1726):

WILLIAM HUGGILL/HUGGINS, of Blewbury; blacksmith; *bapt* 10 July 1715; *m* 2 May 1740 Ann Messenger and was *bur* 18 June 1758, leaving, with an est s (William, *bapt* 16 March 1740/1) and two yst sons (James, *bapt* 2 Feb 1745/6; Richard, *bapt* 11 June 1749) a 2nd s:

JOHN HUGGILL/HUGGINS, of Blewbury; blacksmith; *bapt* 22 June 1743; *m* c 17 June 1771 Mary (*bapt* 22 May 1748), dau of Ambrose Boham, cordwainer, of Ilsley, Berks, and was *bur* 27 Jan 1801, leaving, with an est s (Robert, *bapt* 28 Oct 1772) and two yst sons (Ambrose, *bapt* 26 Sept 1779; Job, *bapt* 24 Feb 1781) a 2nd s:

JOHN HUGGINS, of Blewbury, later Somers Town, St Pancras; blacksmith; *b* 15 March 1777; *m* c 1804 Hannah, dau of William Pickton, and had:

1 William; *b* 26 Sept 1804; *m* c 1831 Mary Ann, dau of Henry Gibson, and had:

(1) John; *b* 16 May 1834

(2) William Henry; *b* 21 March 1836; *m* — Rawlins and *d* 26 Feb 1921, leaving:

1a William Armstrong; *m* Dare Copping and had:

1b Sidney

2b Herbert

3b Frederick; *m* Harriet Cats

2a Leonard Rawlins

(1) Jane; *b* 11 Aug 1832

2 Edward, DL (Middx); brewer, granted arms 12 June 1852; *b* 14 Oct 1808; *m* 1st *c* 1832 Mary Eales and had:

(1) Amy

(2) Lillie; *b* by 1 July 1837; *d* unm

2 (cont) Edward Huggins *m* 2nd (licence) 22 July 1847 Ellen, dau of John Meacock, farmer, of Ealing, and by her had:

(1) Charles Edward; *b* 26 Aug 1853; *d* unm

(2) Albert Edward; *b* 6 April 1855; *m* Mary Ann Jakes and had five daus

(3) Florence Marion; *b* 1 Sept 1849

(4) Stella Constance; *b* 18 April 1852

3 John; brewer; *b* 15 Jan 1811; *m* Sarah Holloway and *d* on or after 17 June 1861, having had issue

4 George, of Camden Town; brewer; *b* 22 Feb 1813; *m* 28 July 1838 Margaret Saul (*d* 13 June 1891), dau of William Saul Else, jeweller, of Burlington Arcade, Piccadilly, and *d* 16 May 1861, having had:

(1) George; migrated to NZ; *b* 3 March 1839; *m* 12 Oct 1869 Eliza (*d* 30 April 1928), dau of James Heather, slr, of Camden Town, and had:

1a George Heather; *b* 24 Jan 1872; *d* unm 19 Oct 1942

2a Harry Ralph; *b* 12 Nov 1874; *m* 26 Sept 1906 Ethel Albina Grace (*d* 31 May 1947), dau of Walter Schofield, and *d* 30 April 1950, leaving two daus

3a Gerald Francis; *b* 21 Jan 1882; *d* unm 10 Oct 1960

1a Ethel; *b* 13 Aug 1870; *d* unm 27 March 1958

2a Margaret Ann; *b* 5 April 1877; *d* unm 11 June 1927

(1) Harriet; *b* 21 May 1840; *m* Charles Thomas Browne, barrister, and *d* 30 July 1926, leaving issue

(2) Kate; *b* 10 May 1847; *m* 1st 8 April 1876 William Collis; *m* 2nd 27 Sept 1890 Samuel Owen and *d* 21 Oct 1933

(3) Ellen; *b* 30 April 1851; *d* unm 15 July 1938

5 HENRY

6 James; *b* 14 Dec 1820; *m* Eliza Franks

1 Mary; *b* 3 Oct 1806; *m* — Moore

The 5th s,

HENRY HUGGINS, DL (City London), of Gordon House, Highgate; *b* 20 Feb 1817; *m* 14 March 1844 Catherine Letitia (*d* 21 March 1895), dau of Thomas Bird, borough architect and surveyor St Pancras, and *d* 30 Jan 1874, having had:

1 Henry Thomas; *b* 3 Feb 1845; *m* 29 July 1883 Eleanor Frances (*d* 4 Aug 1919), est dau of John Driscol, of London, and *d* 25 May 1927, leaving issue

2 Arthur Erat; *b* 11 July 1846; *m* his cousin Alice Susan Bird and *d* 23 April 1932, leaving issue

3 GODFREY

4 Neville, of Staines, Middx; *b* 17 April 1860; memb London Stock Exchange 1882–1902, ptnr H E Huggins and Co, stock jobbers; *m* Ada Llewellyn and *d* 10 May 1907, leaving a s and two daus

5 Frank; *b* 3 Nov 1862; migrated to Australia; *d* 30 April 1911, leaving issue

1 Alice; *b* 3 Sept 1847; *m* 30 April 1868 Alfred Watson (*d* 15 March 1899), slr, s of Robert Watson, and *d* 4 May 1930, leaving issue

2 Edith; *b* 3 July 1851; *m* 30 July 1870 Edward Charles Robson Roose (*d* 12 Feb 1905), MD, FRCP, s of Francis Finley Roose, and *d* 1 Oct 1901, leaving issue

3 Catherine; *b* 8 July 1853; *d* 9 Feb 1855

4 Mabel; *b* 28 Nov 1856; *m* 23 Feb 1885 George Guy Vertue (*d* 1 Nov 1917), slr, and *d* 3 Dec 1947, leaving issue

5 Marion; *b* 25 Oct 1858; *m* Joseph James Smith (*d* 21 Dec 1906) and *d* 23 Aug 1929, leaving issue

6 Blanche Mary; *b* 13 Aug 1865; *d* unm 22 June 1935

HENRY HUGGINS's 3rd s,

GODFREY HUGGINS, of Gordon House, Highgate; *b* 19 May 1855; memb London Stock Exchange; *m* 27 Jan 1881 Emily (*d* 21 April 1937), yst dau of Alexander Melville Blest, of St Peter's, Belsize Park, and *d* 6 Feb 1937, leaving:

1 GODFREY MARTIN, **1st Viscount**

2 Philip Michael, of Normandy, Surrey; *b* 28 May 1893; Civ Serv Tanganyika, WW I E Africa with 2nd Rhodesian Regt, Dorsetshire Regt and KAR, Capt; *m* 2 July 1928 Helen (*d* 5 Feb 1963), 2nd dau of Rev Edward Taswell Richardson, of Widemouth Bay, Cornwall, and had:

(1) Paul Philip; *b* 28 March 1929; *educ* Sherborne and Trin Coll Oxford (BA 1952); *d* 6 Oct 1952 while on the Oxford U Exploration Club Scientific Expdn to Tehri Gahrwal in course of descending Mount Gangotri

(1) Penelope Helen; *b* 11 June 1941; *educ* Tormead Sch Guildford and St Thomas's Hosp; SRN

3 Reuben Hugh; *b* 6 Jan 1895; *d* unm 28 June 1919

1 Mary Faith; *b* 18 Jan 1882; *m* 2 July 1908 Harold Robert Unwin, MB, BCh Cantab, FRCS Eng, of Yeovil, and had issue

2 Catherine Naomi; *b* 26 Jan 1885; *d* unm 15 Dec 1968

3 Gabriel Ruth; *b* 12 Aug 1886; *m* 3 July 1923 William Ramsay and *dsp* Sept 1963

4 Madeline Joan; *b* 28 Sept 1888; *m* 19 Oct 1918 Andrew Malcolm Drummond (*d* 17 April 1943) and *d* Jan 1965, having had issue

GODFREY HUGGINS's est s,

GODFREY MARTIN HUGGINS, **1st Viscount Malvern**, of Rhodesia and Bexley, Co Kent (UK), so *cr* 18 March 1955, CH (1944), KCMG (1941), PC (1947); *b* 6 July 1883; *educ* Malvern and St Thomas's Hosp; MRCS and LRCP 1906, FRCS Eng 1908, Capt RAMC WW I, Surgn Maj Br S African Police, Consultant Surgn S Rhodesia 1921, MLA Salisbury N 1923–33, Salisbury Dist 1934–39 and Salisbury N 1939–53, MLA Fedl Parl Salisbury Suburbs 1953–58, Min Native Affrs 1933–49, PM S Rhodesia 1933–53, Min Educn 1941–42, Min Def 1948–53, PM Fedn Rhodesia and Nyasaland, Min External Affrs and Def 1953–56, KGStJ, Freeman Salisbury 1955, Hon DCL Oxon 1951, Hon LLD Witwatersrand 1953, London 1955, Hon DL Rhodes U Grahamstown, Hon FRCP Edin 1960, Hon Fell British Orthopaedic Assoc, Assoc of Surgns of GB and I, Internat Coll Surgns and Roy Coll Physicians Edinburgh 1960; *m* 21 Nov 1921 Blanche Elizabeth (*d* 30 July 1976 aged 89), dau of James Slatter, of Pietermaritzburg, and *d* 8 May 1971, leaving:

1 JOHN GODFREY HUGGINS, **2nd Viscount Malvern**; *b* 26 Oct 1922; *educ* Winchester; F/Lt RAF, BAOR, WW II; *m* 1 Jan 1949 *Patricia Marjorie, dau of Frank Renwick Bower, of Durban, Natal, *d* 28 Aug 1978, having had:

1 Michael Paul John; *b* 13 Oct 1946; *d* 19–

2 +ASHLEY KEVIN GODFREY HUGGINS, **3rd and present Viscount Malvern**

1 *Haoli Elizabeth Jane; *b* 20 March 1953

2 +(Martin) James; *b* 13 Jan 1928; *educ* Hilton Coll, Natal

MANCHESTER

DISPONENDO ME NON MUTANDO ME.

Arms: Quarterly, 1st and 4th, arg. three lozenges conjoined in fess gu. within a bordure sa. (for MONTAGU); 2nd and 3rd, or an eagle displayed vert, beaked and membered gu. (for MONTHERMER).
Crest: A griffin's head couped, wings expanded or, gorged with a collar arg., charged with three lozenges gu. **Supporters:** Dexter, a heraldic antelope or, armed, tufted and hoofed arg.; sinister, a griffin or, gorged with a collar, as in the crest. **Motto:** *Disponendo me, non mutando me* ('By disposing of me, not by changing me').
Creations: B. and V. (E) 19 Dec 1620; E. (E) 5 Feb 1626; D. (E) 28 April 1719.

THE 12TH DUKE OF MANCHESTER, Earl of Manchester, Co Lancaster, **Viscount Mandeville** and **Baron Kimbolton of Kimbolton**, Co Huntingdon (Angus Charles Drogo Montagu) [His Grace The Duke of Manchester, House of Lords, London SW1A 0PW]; *b* 9 Oct 1938; *s* bro 1985; *educ* Gordonstoun; *m* 1st 22 Nov 1961 (*divorce* 1970) Mary Eveleen, dau of Walter Gillespie McClure, of Geelong, Australia, and has:

1 +ALEXANDER CHARLES DAVID DROGO, *Viscount Mandeville*; *b* 11 Dec 1962

2 +Kimble; *b* Oct 1964

1 *Emma; *b* Sept 1965

The 12th DUKE *m* 2nd 1971 (*divorce* 1985) Diane Pauline, dau of Arthur Plimsaul, of 50 Highmoor Rd, Corfe Mullen, Wimborne, Dorset; *m* 3rd 1989 *Mrs Ann-Louise Bird, dau of Dr Alfred Butler Taylor, of Cawthorne, S Yorks

Lineage: WILLIAM LADDE (*see also* MONTAGU OF BERLIEU, B, preliminary remarks), of Hanging Houghton, Lamport, Northants, where he bought up land from 1425, settling at least some of it on his son April 1447; had:

RICHARD LADDE later MONTAGU (from *c* 1453), of Hanging Houghton; yeoman; *m* by April 1447 Agnes — and *d* by Sept 1484, leaving:

THOMAS MONTAGU, of Hemington, Northants; *educ* Oxford; attorney; *m* 1st by Sept 1485 Agnes, dau of William Dudley, of Clopton, Northants; *m* 2nd by 1512 Mary (*d* 1524), dau of William Lane, of Finedon, Northants, and *d* 5 Sept 1516, leaving by his 1st w:

Sir EDWARD MONTAGU, PC; *b c* 1487; *educ* Cambridge and Middle Temple; ktd 1537, Ch Justice King's Bench 1539–45 and Common Pleas 1545–54 ('a descent,' says Fuller in his *Worthies*, 'in honour, but an ascent in profit'); executor HENRY VIII's will, Govr to EDWARD VI, the passages in whose will settling the crown on Lady Jane Grey he drafted, possibly under duress, though this, if the case, did not save him from imprisonment in the Tower of London on MARY's accession July 1553; he bought his way out, however, by a substantial payment of cash and landed property two months later; *m* 1st Sept 1512 Cicely, dau of William Lane, of Orlingbury, Northants, and had issue (the sons all *d* in infancy); *m* 2nd 1527 Cicely, dau of George Kirkham, of Warmington, Northants; *m* 3rd by May 1533, as her 3rd husb, Ellen, est dau of John Roper, Attorney-Gen, by Jane, er dau of Sir John Fyneux, Ch Justice King's Bench, and *d* 10 Feb 1556/7, leaving by her, with four yr sons (Roger; Thomas; William; Simon):

Sir EDWARD MONTAGU, of Boughton, Northants; *m* Elizabeth, dau of Sir James Harington, of Exton, Rutland (*see* HARINGTON, Bt), and had:

1 EDWARD MONTAGU, 1st BARON MONTAGU OF BOUGHTON (E), so *cr* 29 June 1621, KB (1603); *b c* 1562; *educ* Ch Ch Oxford and Middle Temple; MP Beeralston 1584–86, Brackley 1601 and Northants 1604–11, 1614 and 1620–21, during which he proposed in the H of C the motion to commemorate annually the Gunpowder Plot of 1605; High Sheriff Northants 1595–96 and

1600–01, Ld Lt Northants 1642, royalist Civil War; *m* 1st by 21 Sept 1585 Elizabeth, dau of Sir John Jeffrey, of Chiddingly, Sussex; *m* 2nd 24 Feb 1611/2 Frances, dau of Thomas Cotton; *m* 3rd 16 Feb 1624/5 Anne, dau of John Crouch and widow of (a) Robert Wyncoll, (b) Richard Chamberlain and (c) Sir Ralph Hare, and *d* 15 June 1644, leaving by his 2nd w:

(1) EDWARD MONTAGU, 2nd BARON MONTAGU OF BOUGHTON; *b* 11 July 1616; *educ* Sidney Sussex Coll Cambridge; MP Huntingdon 1640–44, Parliamentarian Civil War but opposed trying CHARLES I and later took public office under Restoration (Recorder Northampton 1681); *m c* 1633 Anne, dau of Sir Ralph Winwood, and *d* 10 Jan 1683/4, having had:

  1a Edward; *educ* Westminster, Oxford and Sidney Sussex Coll Cambridge; Master of the Horse to CATHERINE OF BRAGANZA, CHARLES II's w, till 1664, when he was sacked for squeezing her hand while attending her to her carriage; *ka vp* Aug 1665 Second Dutch War

  2a RALPH MONTAGU, 1st DUKE OF MONTAGU, so *cr* 14 April 1705, as also MARQUESS OF MONTHERMER and earlier 9 April 1689 VISCOUNT MONTHERMER, of Monthermer, Co Essex, and EARL OF MONTAGU (all E), PC (Jan 1671/2–79 and Feb 1688/9); *bapt* 24 Dec 1638; *educ* Westminster; Amb Paris 1666, 1669, 1676 and 1677–78, MP (Whig) Northampton 1678–79 and 1679–81 and Hunts Feb–July 1679, Ld Lt Northants 1697–1702; *m* 1st 24 Aug 1673 Elizabeth, yst dau of 4th Earl of Southampton (*see* SOUTHAMPTON, B) and widow of Joceline Percy, Earl of Northumberland (*see* NORTHUMBERLAND, D); *m* 2nd 8 Sept 1692 Elizabeth ('the mad Duchess'), est dau of Henry Cavendish, Duke of Newcastle-upon-Tyne (*see* DEVONSHIRE, D) and widow of 2nd Duke of Albemarle (*see* MONCK, V), and *d* 9 March 1708/9, having had by his 1st w, with two er sons (*d* young):

    1b JOHN MONTAGU, 2nd and last DUKE OF MONTAGU, KG (1718), KB (1725), PC (Jan 1735/6); *b* 29 March 1690; Ld High Constable for GEORGE I's Coronation 1714, Gen 1746, Col 1st Horse Gds 1715–21 and June-Aug 1737 and 3rd Horse 1740–49, Ld Lt Northants and Warwicks 1715–49, Govr IoW 1733–34, Capt Gentlemen Pensioners 1734–40; *m* 20 March 1704/5 Lady Mary Churchill, yst dau of 1st Duke of Marlborough (*qv*) and *dspms* 6 July 1749, having had:

      1c John, *Marquess of Monthermer*; *b* 9 Nov 1706; *dvp* 26 Aug 1711

      2c George; *d* aged 3 or 4 months

      3c Edward Montagu Churchill, *Marquess of Monthermer*; *bapt* 27 Dec 1725; *dvp* May 1727

      1c Isabella; *m* 1st her cousin **2nd Duke of Manchester** (*see* below); *m* 2nd Edward Hussey later Hussey-Montagu, 1st and last Earl of Beaulieu, and *dsp*

      2c Mary Montagu; *m* 7 July 1730 George BRUDENELL later MONTAGU (*dspms* 23 May 1790), 4th Earl of Cardigan, also 1st and last Duke of Montagu, so *cr* 5 Nov 1766, as also 1st and last Marquess of Monthermer, and later 21 Aug 1786 Baron Montagu of Boughton, Co Northampton (all GB), with in the last case remainder to the 2nd and every other yr s of his dau Elizabeth, Duchess of Buccleuch (*see* BUCCLEUCH and QUEENSBERRY, D), and *d* 1 May 1775, having had a s (*see* AILESBURY, M) and three daus (the est of which is mentioned in the details of the remainder above; the two yr *d* unm)

    1b Anne; *m* Alexander Popham, MP, of Littlecote, Berks, and had issue (*see* SANDWICH, E)

2 Walter (Sir)

3 HENRY (Sir), **1st Earl**

4 Charles (Sir); *m* Mary, dau of William Whitmore (*see* WHITMORE, Bt)

5 James, Bp Winchester

6 Sydney (Sir); had issue (*see* SANDWICH, E)

1 Theodosia; *m* Sir Henry Capell (*see* ESSEX, E)

Sir EDWARD's 3rd son,

HENRY MONTAGU, **1st Earl of Manchester**, Co Lancaster, so *cr* 5 Feb 1626, as also earlier 19 Dec 1620 BARON KIMBOLTON OF KIMBOLTON, Co Huntingdon, and VISCOUNT MANDEVILLE (all E), PC (1620), KC (1607); *b c* 1563; *educ* Christ's Coll Cambridge; barrister Middle Temple, Reader 1606, MP Higham Ferrers 1593, 1597–98 and 1601 and City London 1604–11 and 1614, Recorder London 1603–16, ktd 1603, Serjeant-at-law and King's Serjeant 1611, Ch Justice King's Bench 1616–21, Ld High Treasurer 1620–21, First Commr Gt Seal May-July 1621, Ld Pres Cncl 1621–28, Ld Privy Seal 1628–42, Ld Lt Hunts 1627; *m* 1st 1 June 1601 Catherine (*d* 7 Dec 1612), 2nd dau of Sir William Spencer, of Yarnton, Oxon, 3rd s of Sir John Spencer, of Althorp (*see* SPENCER, E), and had:

1 EDWARD, **2nd Earl**

2 Walter; Abbot St Martin's Abbey, nr Pontoise, diocese of Rouen; *d* 1670, and was *bur* in the church belonging to the Hospital of Incurables, Paris

3 James, of Lackham, Wilts; *m* 11 Nov 1635 Mary, dau and heiress of Sir Robert Baynard, of Lackham, Wilts, through whom he acquired that estate, and *d* Feb 1665, leaving an est s:

  (1) James, of Lackham; *m* Diana, dau of Anthony Hungerford, and had:

    1a Edward, of Lackham, *dsp* 1701

    2a James, of Lackham; *m* 1716 Elizabeth, dau of Sir John Eyles, and *d* 4 Aug 1747, leaving:

      1b James, of Lackham; *m* 1744 Elizabeth, dau and heiress of William Hedges, and *d* 25 April 1790, leaving:

        1c James, of Lackham; *b* 1749; *d* unm 12 July 1797

        2c George, of Knowle, Devon; Lt-Col, ornithologist; *b* 1755; *m* 1773 Anne (*d* 10 Feb 1816), dau of William Courtenay, and *d* 19 June 1815, leaving, with other issue:

          1d George Conway Courtenay, of Lackham; *b* 24 June 1776; *m* 1st 29 Dec 1803 Margaret Green (*d* 7 May 1834), dau of Richard Green Wilkson, of Lancaster, and had:

            1e Frederick Conway; *b* 3 Oct 1805; *d* unm 20 Oct 1891

            2e James Augustus (Rev), of Sutton Hall, Rochford, Essex; BA Cantab, Curate and Rector Hawkwell Essex 1843–91; *b* 5 July 1810; *d* unm 10 Aug 1905

            1e Eleanor Louisa, author: *Edith of Greystock, The Feast of Camelot, Our Legends and Lives* and other poems and *Snooded Jessaline*, a

novel; *b* 16 Nov 1811; *m* 17 Oct 1843 Thomas Kebble Hervey (*d* 12 Feb 1849) and *d* 27 Oct 1903, leaving issue

          1d (cont.) George Montagu *m* 2nd 23 Jan 1840 Jessy (*m* 2nd 16 June 1853 Cyrus Mason, JP (*d* 8 Aug 1915), of Melbourne, and *d* 21 Nov 1909 aged 84), dau of John Elphinstone Campbell, and *d* 30 May 1847, having had:

            2e Jane Stuart Courtenay; *b* 1844; *d* 13 Aug 1938

            3e Edith Mary Wortley; *d* unm 27 May 1911

          1d Louisa Matilda; *m* Matthew Crawford (*d* Sept 1862) and *d* 29 Dec 1857

2b Edward; a Master in Chancery; *m* 1st 16 April 1745 Ann, dau of James Wroughton, and had issue; *m* 2nd 15 April 1754 Joanna Magdalena (*d* 21 Feb 1799), widow of Edward van Harthals and dau of Gerard Bolwark, and *d* 1798, having by her had:

  1c Gerard, of Burlingham Hall, Burlingham St Peter's, Norfolk; *b* 13 May 1756; *m* 5 June 1785 Mary Anne (*m* 2nd 16 Feb 1809 Rev George Lucas and *d* 19 July 1835), dau of George Doughty, of Theberton Hall, Suffolk, and *d* 7 Oct 1807, having had:

    1d Edward Proudfoot, Cdr RN; *b* 23 April 1791; *m* 4 Sept 1817 Mary Anne (*d* 19 June 1859), dau of Capt James Everard, and *d* 8 Jan 1862, leaving, with three daus (*d* unm):

      1e Edward; Offr 6th Foot; *b* 15 June 1818; *d* 21 June 1839

      2e Gerard, RM; *b* 2 Dec 1821; *d* 23 Feb 1890

      3e John; *b* 20 Sept 1823; *d* 4 Sept 1868

      4e Frederick (Rev); *b* 1 Nov 1825; *d* 2 June 1868

      5e Herbert, RN; *b* 2 May 1827; *d* 11 April 1868

      6e Arthur; *b* 22 Nov 1828; *d* unm 13 March 1909

      7e Octavius; *b* 21 July 1832; *m* Sophia Martha Morris and *d* 8 Oct 1892, leaving:

        1f Frances Wales

        2f Alice Teresa; *m* Sydney William Humphrey

      8e Everard; *b* 1836; *d* 28 June 1911

      9e Decimus; Offr 30th Foot; *b* 1837; *d* 30 July 1874

      10e Henry; *b* 1839; *d* 10 Sept 1873

  2d George (Rev); Rector S Pickenham, Norfolk; *b* 10 March 1793; *m* 18 Nov 1817 Emily (*d* 1 Feb 1880), 4th dau of Rev W Yonge, Chllr Diocese of Norwich, and *d* 6 July 1865, having had:

    1e Edgar William (Rev); Rector Kettlestone Nortolk, MA Cantab; *b* 20 July 1819; *m* 1st 20 June 1872 Arabella (*dsp* 3 July 1874), yr dau of Rev Cremer Cremer, of Beeston Regis, Norfolk; *m* 2nd 12 June 1880 Charlotte Adele (*dsp* 24 April 1895), dau of Rev Richard Aldous Arnold, and *d* 12 April 1902

    2e George (Rev); Rector Thenford; *b* 1 June 1820; *d* unm 22 Feb 1904

    3e Horace William (Sir), KCB; Gen, Col Cmdt RE 1887, Kt Legion of Honour Sardinian Order of Merit, 5th Cl Medjidie, served Crimean War; *b* 16 May 1823; *m* 4 Aug 1859 Catherine Frances (*d* 9 June 1925), est dau of Gen Poole V England, RA, and *d* 14 Nov 1916, having had:

      1f Charles; *b* 29 April 1860; *d* 27 June 1862

      2f Edward, CBE (1919); Col cmdg 1st Bn Suffolk Regt, served Hazara Expdn, NWF India 1888, Chin-Lushai Expdn Burma 1889–90 and WW I; *b* 23 Nov 1861; *m* 21 Aug 1894 Charlotte Eva (*d* 29 Sept 1952), only surv dau of Edward Kemble, Judge Supreme Court, Jamaica, and *d* 14 Jan 1941, leaving:

        1g Charles Edward; *b* 28 Nov 1900; Capt (ret) RE; *educ* Wellington and RMA Woolwich; *m* 8 May 1928 Rachel Alice (*d* 1996), est dau of W H Martin, of Swaffham, Norfolk, and *d* 11 March 1995, leaving:

          1h +Michael Drogo [Maj Michael Montagu, Pound Farm, Ringsfield, Beccles, Suffolk NR34 8LN]; *b* 2 Nov 1929; Maj RA; *m* 31 Dec 1955 *Verity Jane, yr dau of William James Coode, OBE, The Old Manor, Polgooth, Cornwall, and has:

            1i +Richard Lionel James [Richard Montagu Esq, Jocks Lodge, Geldeston, Norfolk]; *b* 1 Oct 1956; *m* 1984 *Aileen Amanda, dau of Charles Gordon Birchall, of the Close, Norwich, and has:

              1j +George Charles Drogo; *b* 1993

              1j *Lucy Elizabeth: *b* 1990

            2i +Alan Edward; *b* 5 June 1958; *m* 1990 *Louise Helen, twin dau of A G H Gaden, of Trull, Taunton, Som, and has:

              1j +Miles; *b* 1994

              1j *Madeleine; *b* 1993

            3i +James Robert; *b* 8 June 1962

          2h +Ralph Edward [Ralph Montagu Esq, Old Hall Farm, Ringsfield, Beccles, Suffolk]; *b* 5 March 1932; *m* 1st 23 Feb 1963 June Margaret (Lisa) (*d* 1979), dau of James William Finlayson, of Vaucluse, NSW, and has:

            1i +David Charles; *b* 1 Dec 1965

            1i *Caroline Elizabeth; *b* 7 April 1964

            2i *Victoria Jane; *b* 21 Sept 1967

            3i *Katharine Fiona (twin); *b* 21 Sept 1967

          2h (cont.) Ralph Montagu *m* 2nd 1989 *Stephanie Roberta, dau of Patrick Arthur Cattell, of Pallastown, Belgooly, Co Cork

      3f William; *b* 15 April 1867; *m* 30 March 1937 Lydia Dennis and *d* 3 Aug 1955

      4f Drogo, Supt Telegraphs Ceylon; *b* 16 Aug 1870; *m* 1 Jan 1901 Marion Kate Evelyn (*d* 16 Jan 1950), dau of R-Adml F Proby Doughty, and *dsp* 9 June 1944

      1f Mary; *b* 27 Sept 1863; *d* unm 11 Nov 1946

2f Alice; *b* 1865; *m* 11 Aug 1892 Rev Archibald Downes Downes-Shaw, Rector Scotton Lincs 1915–24, and *d* 3 April 1946, leaving issue

3f Madeline; *b* 26 Aug 1868; *d* unm 25 March 1958

4f Lena; *b* 27 April 1872; *m* 25 Aug 1909 Charles Scott Watson (*d* 14 July 1931), of Ealing, and *d* 24 March 1960

4e Charles E H; RN; *b* April 1832; *ka* Finland 7 June 1854

1e Mary Anne Fanny; *m* 3 March 1843 Cdr Benjamin Sharpe, RN (*d* 23 April 1883), of Hanwell Park, Middx, and *d* 20 April 1898, leaving issue

2e Louisa; *d* unm 23 March 1902

3e Agnes; *d* unm 21 March 1902

4e Charlotte; *d* unm 3 Aug 1912

5e Emily Augusta Reynolds; *m* 27 April 1852 Rev John William Dolignon (*d* 15 June 1896), Rector Cockley Cley, Norfolk, and *d* 19 March 1918, having had issue

6e Grace; *d* 26 June 1919

7e Elizabeth Georgiana Jane; *d* unm 3 July 1871

3d Edgar; barrister; *b* 1796; *m* 8 April 1847 Marianne Henrietta (*d* 1873), dau of Maj George Mackenzie, and *d* 21 May 1851, leaving:

1e Ernest Edgar; *b* 17 Aug 1849; *d* unm 11 Aug 1875

2e Cecil Edgar; Capt 21st Hus; *b* 2 July 1851; *m* 11 Sept 1883 Alice Ethel (*d* 1 Dec 1919), only dau of John Asheton Critchley, of Stapleton Tower, Dumfriesshire, and *d* 4 Aug 1923, leaving:

1f James Gerard Edgar Drogo; Maj Res of Offrs RA WW I; *b* 5 Jan 1893; *educ* Eton and Trin Coll Cambridge; *m* 1st 30 July 1919 (*divorce* 1928) Anne Gladys, only dau of Sir Harry Ross-Skinner, of Sunningdale and S Africa, and had:

1g William Gerard Drogo; Lt-Cdr RN; *b* 22 Feb 1921; *educ* Stowe and Chillon Coll Switzerland; *m* 29 July 1950 *Charlotte Delma [Mrs William Montagu, 7 Shernfold Park, Frant, E Sussex TN3 9DL], only dau of Frank Reitmeyer Calburn, of Cowden Cross House, Edenbridge, Kent, and *d* 1991, leaving:

1h +Charles Edward Drogo; *b* 15 Dec 1952; *educ* Tonbridge and Corpus Christi Coll Oxford; *m* 1986 *Marie-Jocelyne, dau of Gabriel Dardenne, of Tottenham, and has:

1i +Edward Harry; *b* 1990

2i +Robert William; *b* 29 Sept 1997

1i *Emily Frances; *b* 1993

2h +Francis Gerard Drogo [Francis Montagu Esq, White Lodge, Ropers Lane, Wrington, Somerset BS40 5NF]; *b* 15 Dec 1952; *educ* Tonbridge and Pembroke Coll Cambridge; slr; *m* 1991 *Olivia Mary, dau of Dr Patrick John Hardie, MBE, of Elm Cottage, Shipton Moyne, Tetbury, Glos

3h +James William Drogo [James Montagu Esq, Culvers, Hartfield, E Sussex]; *b* 12 Feb 1954; *educ* Tonbridge; *m* 1979 *Charlotte Elizabeth, dau of Richard John Goad Crosfield, of May Hill House, Droxford, Hants, and has:

1i *Elizabeth Charlotte Ann; *b* 1983

2i *Sarah Caroline; *b* 1985

1f (cont.) James Montagu *m* 2nd 19 Aug 1948 *Mary Rose, widow of Dietrich von Weber, previously w of Heinz von Kusserow and yr dau of Baron Robert Parry-Grainger, of Munich, and *d* 26 April 1978

1f Sydney Eleanor; *b* 29 Dec 1884; *m* 15 July 1913 Francis Bridger Dutton, BM, barrister, only s of Sir Frederick Dutton, and *d* 6 Jan 1942, leaving issue

1d Magdalena; *m* 1821 Capt R Hockings (*d* 1849), RN, and *d* 5 Dec 1948

2d Louisa Henrietta; *m* 16 April 1838 V-Adml Sir David Dunn, KCH (*d* 16 June 1859), and *d* 31 Jan 1849

3d Mary Anne; *m* 19 Aug 1834 Rev Frederick Ensor (*d* 1887), Rector Lustleigh, Devon, and *d* 2 July 1895, leaving issue

3b John; Adml; *b* 1719; *m* 11 Dec 1748 Sophia (*d* 14 April 1802), dau of James Wroughton, of Wilcot, and *d* Sept 1795, leaving:

1c John (Rev), DD; *b* 11 Nov 1749; *d* unm 25 July 1818

2c George (Sir), KCB; Adml the Red; *b* 12 Dec 1750; *m* 9 Oct 1783 Charlotte, dau and coheir of George Wroughton, and *d* 24 Dec 1829, leaving:

1d George Wroughton MONTAGU later WROUGHTON, of Wilcot, Wilts; Lt-Col; *b* 24 Sept 1788; *d* 8 June 1871

2d John William; Adml; *b* 18 Jan 1790; *m* 12 March 1840 Isabella Elizabeth (*d* 21 July 1864), dau of Charles George Beauclerk (*see* SAINT ALBANS, D), and *d* 12 Dec 1882, leaving:

1e George Edward, JP Wilts; *b* 19 Feb 1841; Capt 84th Foot; *m* Sept 1876 Annie Mary Augusta (*m* 2nd 19 Aug 1881 — Curry and *d* 1933), dau of Edward Delvin, of Enniskillen, Co Fermanagh, and *dvp* 23 Nov 1878, having had:

1f John William; *b* 1876; *m* 16 Sept 1913 Violet Irene (*d* 1970), dau of James Shuter, of Wilcot Manor, Pewsey, Wilts, and *d* 22 Sept 1954, leaving:

1g +John Drogo [Lt-Col John Montagu, The Officer's House, Coastguard Lane, Freshwater, IoW PO40 9QX]; Lt-Col IA (ret), served 2nd Punjab Regt 1936–50, WW II in Burma (despatches); *b* 30 May 1916; *educ* Exeter Sch and RMC Sandhurst; *m* 24 Nov 1952 Dorothy Boreham (*d* 1990), yr dau of Charles Edward Chuter, of Brisbane, and has:

1h +Michael Charles Drogo; *b* 28 June 1956; Lt-Col LI; *m* 1984 *Caroline Louise Marie, only dau of John George Griffiths, of the Algarve, Portugal, and has:

1i +James Robert Drogo; *b* 1985

2i +Frederic Charles; *b* 1988

3i +Arthur John; *b* 1992

2h +Nigel Edward; *b* 28 Jan 1958; Maj RE

3h +Richard John; *b* 25 April 1959; Capt LI 1981–90; *m* 1986 *Jane Emma, dau of Bruce Pearson, of Twynholm, Galloway, and has:

1i +Edward Drogo; *b* 27 April 1989

2i +George Ferdinand; *b* 29 Dec 1990

1h *Sally Ann; *b* 30 Dec 1954; *m* 1988 *Lt Col Harold Crispin Hardy Ellison, MBE, RTR, s of His Honour Judge (John Harold) Ellison, of Egham, Surrey, and has:

1i *Henry John Montagu; *b* 24 Aug 1995

2i *Robert Hamilton Montagu; *b* 17 July 1997

1i *Harriet Dorothy Montagu; *b* 1992

2h *Felicity Jane; *b* 12 Sept 1960; *m* 1985 *Alan Sutherland Nixon, s of Prof George Sutherland Nixon, of St Andrews, and has:

1i *Luke Sutherland; *b* 10 Aug 1996

1i *Olivia Chuter; *b* 1990

2g +James Edward [James Montagu Esq, 64 Hill Rd, Barrow-in-Furness, Lancs LA14 4EV]; *b* 18 Feb 1920; WW II as Capt RA; *m* 17 May 1946 *Joan, dau of James McPherson, of Fieldway, Barrow-in-Furness, and has:

1h +Philip James [Philip Montagu Esq, 7 Goldstone Lane, Hove, E Sussex BN3 7BB]; *b* 14 March 1949; *m* 1971 *Jennifer, dau of Leonard Edmund Lower, of Brighton, and has:

1i +Darren James; *b* 11 Sept 1971; *m* 1997 *Helen Kay, dau of Wolf Roller, of Edinburgh

2i +Paul Andrew; *b* 9 Sept 1974

1i *Rachel Mary; *b* 18 March 1980

2h +Robin William [Robin Montagu Esq, 26 Hornedale Ave, Barrow-in-Furness, Lancs LA13 9AS]; *b* 17 May 1953; *m* 1986 *Janice, dau of John Threlkeld Taylor, of Oldham

1g Mary Hamilton; *b* 1914; *d* 29 June 1997

2f James Drogo, CBE (1937); Commr Nicosia and Kyrenia, Cyprus, 1934–39, MEC and MLC Cyprus 1935–39, Lt 5th Bn Roy Irish Rifles, Boer War and WW II in 5th Bn Wilts HG as Capt, Silver Jubilee Medal 1935 and Coronation Medal 1937; *b* 10 July 1878; *d* unm 1 Aug 1958

2e John; *b* March 1843; *d* 29 May 1848

1e Anne Diana; *m* 19 May 1881 Rev William Francis Dashwood Lang (*d* 1912), of Lisburne, Torquay, Rector Deane, Hants

2e Emily Stuart; *m* 15 Jan 1884 Col Arthur Corbet Maurice, Royal Munster Fus, and had issue

3d James, Adml; *b* 10 April 1791; *d* 1872

1d Georgiana; Woman of Bedchamber to QUEEN ADELAIDE; *m* 15 Aug 1808 V-Adml Sir John Gore, KCB (*d* 21 Aug 1836), and *d* 14 Nov 1854

2d Sophia; *d* unm 21 May 1845

3c James; Capt RN; *b* 12 Aug 1752; *ka* June 1794

4c Edward; Lt-Col of Artillery, EICS; *b* 20 Feb 1755; *m* 17 May 1792 Barbara (*d* 3 June 1848), dau of John Fleetwood, and *d* 8 May 1799, leaving:

1d Edward; barrister; *b* 7 July 1796; *d* 1830

2d John; served 52nd Regt Waterloo, Colonial Sec Cape Good Hope; *b* 21 Aug 1797; *m* 7 Aug 1823 Jessy (*d* 3 Nov 1876), dau of Lt-Gen Edward Vaughan Worsley, RA, and *d* 4 Nov 1853, having had:

1e John Edward; Registrar-Gen Cape Good Hope; *b* 27 June 1824; *m* 1st 6 Jan 1848 Anna Maria (*d* 11 Nov 1867), dau of Maj H Piers, and had:

1f John Charles Worsley; *b* 31 May 1849; *m* 7 March 1871 Mary (*d* 1880), dau of John S Distin, and *d* 3 May 1877, having had:

1g Annie Selina; *d* 17 Dec 1923

2g Mabel Ruby; *m* 22 April 1891 Charles Roland Chambers, RMS (*d* 12 Sept 1923), African Civ Serv, and had issue

3g Violet Ida; *b* 15 May 1876; *m* 13 Jan 1897 Percy Gilbert Nevile (*d* 21 Jan 1938), est s of Percy Sandford Nevile, of Skelbrooke Park, Yorks, and *d* 25 June 1945, leaving issue

2f Edward Vaughan; *b* 23 Jan 1851; *m* 3 Aug 1876 Annie Dorothy, dau of Francis R Thompson, and *d* 13 Feb 1878, leaving:

1g John Francis Vaughan; *b* 19 Oct 1877; *m* 17 July 1909 Ada Mary (*d* 3 March 1957), dau of James Dougal Coley, of Claremont, Cape Town, and *d* 21 Nov 1960, leaving:

1h John Edward Coley; WW II as Lt 6th S African Armoured Div (wounded); *b* 2 Aug 1910; *m* 1st 19 Dec 1936 (*divorce* 1955) Flora Elizabeth (*d* 1981), dau of Capt James Robertson-Cumming, of Langrigg, Strathearn, Scotland; *m* 2nd 12 July 1958 *Anne Alice Henriet, est dau of Col Donald Rolfe Hunt, of Blackridge, Natal, and *d* 6 June 1983, leaving by his 1st w:

1i +John Anthony Francis [John Montagu Esq, 3 Kelvin Grove, Beacon Bay, East London, S Africa]; *b* 19 April 1938; *m* 14 May 1966 *Denise Catherine, er dau of James Peters Dallas, of East London, S Africa, and has:

1j +James Anthony John; *b* 1976

1j *Joanne Catherine; *b* 14 April 1969

2j *Leigh Frances; *b* 9 Jan 1971

2i +David Vaughan [David Montagu Esq, 16 Abelia Rd, Kloof, Natal, 3600, S Africa]; *b* 3 April 1948; *m* 1976 *Victoria Alice, yr dau of Allan Cunningham, of Newquay, Cornwall, and has:

1j +Christopher John Allan; *b* 1977

1j *Laura Ann; *b* 1979

1i *Gillian Denise [Mrs Michael Glover, 35 Esmerelda Crescent, Robindale Extn No 1, Randburg, Transvaal, S Africa]; *b* 13 April 1940; *m* 26 Jan 1966 *Michael Keyworth

Glover, s of Sydney Keyworth Glover, of Kimberley, and has:

1j *Mark Keyworth; b 13 March 1968

1j *Marguerite Tracey; b 7 Jan 1967

2j *Jenny Lynne; b 26 July 1972

2h +Dennis Vaughan [Denis Montagu Esq, 65 Gold Reef Village, Brakpan, Transvaal, S Africa]; b 30 March 1913; m 1st 21 Jan 1939 Margarieta (d 1981), dau of Henry Usher Gradwell, of Bloemfontein; m 2nd 1983 *Joan Patricia Chambers

3f Henry Southey Maclear; Capt Cape Mounted Rifles; b 7 June 1854; m 18 Oct 1916 Lily Rose (d 1954), dau of E Pearce, of East London, and d 4 Jan 1932

4f Frederick George; b 30 Jan 1856; m 26 Dec 1894 Bertha (d 22 June 1936), dau of Colin Turing Campbell, of Kimberley, and d 24 Dec 1923, having had:

1g Arthur Drogo Turing; DPSA, AICTA, Col Ag Service (ret 1948); b 17 Sept 1900; m 5 Sept 1934 *Dorothy Rittener, dau of Harry Taylor Pitt, of Sussex, and d 9 Jan 1969, leaving:

1h +John Drogo; b 27 May 1935; m 1980 *Margaret, 2nd dau of Lt-Cdr John Richard Windle, RNR, of Broadway House, Broadway, Northumberland

2h +William Pitt [William Montagu Esq, 13 Windsor Rd, Oosterzee, 7500 S Africa]; b 29 July 1939; educ St George's GS Cape Town; m 5 Feb 1966 *Elsa, dau of Jacobus Andries Fourie, of Morelig, Penhill Estate, CP, and has:

1i *Michelle; b 16 Oct 1969

2i *Colleen [Mrs Craig Blanckenberg, 61 Bremerhof, Oosterzee 7500, S Africa]; b 1971; m 21 Sept 1996 *Craig Reinier Blanckenberg

3i *Wendy [Mrs Werner van Wyk, 83 4th Ave, Boston, Bellville, S Africa] (twin); b 1971; m 28 Dec 1996 *Werner Nicholas van Wyk

1h Margaret Helen; b 10 Sept 1937; m 6 Dec 1961 *Hendrik de la Rey Winter and d 12 March 1979, leaving issue

1g Helen Bertha Piers Ashburnham; b 24 Feb 1896; m 7 April 1918 Capt Francis Henry Snow (d May 1958), and had issue

2g Isobel Flora Worsley; b 15 Oct 1898; d 30 Nov 1899 in Siege of Mafeking

5f Arthur Boyle; b 8 Oct 1859; d 26 Aug 1882

6f Ernest William Sanders (Sir); ktd 1923, Sec Mines and Works, MLA S Rhodesia, Cape Colony Civ Serv; b 6 Dec 1862; d unm 20 Nov 1952

1f Jessy Worsley; b 15 Aug 1852; m 4 Aug 1874 S J Brodribb and dsp 25 June 1878

2f Anna Elizabeth; b 16 Nov 1860; d unm March 1939

3f Louisa Georgiana; b 12 Jan 1865; d unm 21 Dec 1903

1e (cont.) John Montagu m 2nd 23 June 1869 Elizabeth Adams (d 31 Dec 1904), est dau of Capt S Bush Brodribb, 14th Dragoons, and d 3 March 1879, having by her had:

4f Louisa Worsley; b 11 Jan 1872; m 2 Oct 1901 Vyvyan Howard Owen Christian (d 27 Oct 1953), of Port Elizabeth, and d 8 March 1957, leaving issue

2e George; Dep Surveyor-Gen Cape Good Hope; b 1 Nov 1825; d 3 Aug 1863

3e Alfred Worsley; Lt-Gen ISC; b 25 Sept 1829; m 19 Aug 1854 Emily (d 26 Nov 1903), dau of G A Ward, and d 7 March 1898, having had:

1f John Augustus Worsley; b 29 July 1855; d 27 Aug 1857

2f Charles Gore Worsley; b 26 Jan; d 28 Aug 1857

3f Alfred Worsley; b 27 Sept 1860; m 5 Sept 1887 Ruth Lily Wallace, of Stawell, Victoria, Australia, and had:

1g Herbert Clive; b 2 June 1897

1g Ruth Mabel Josephine; b 1888

2g Jeffie Ina; b 1891

3g Vere Faerle; b 1894

4f Arthur Henry, Maj IA; b 4 June 1862; m 26 April 1905 Elsie Augusta Edith, 2nd dau of Wallace Crothers, of Edgcumbe, Guildford, and dsp 18 Dec 1907

5f Francis Ward; b 6 March 1864; d 16 Sept 1885

1f Florence; b 6 Aug; d 30 Oct 1858

4e Frederick Gore; b 6 June 1832; d 30 Sept 1836

5e Arthur Thomas; b 2 June 1841; d 12 July 1872

1e Jessy; d 26 Aug 1829

2e Mary Babara; d 2 Feb 1838

3e Eliza Raynor; d 2 Jan 1870

4e Emily Mary; b 16 Aug 1845; m 1 May 1896 Samuel William Percy Gordon Shute Barrington (see BARRINGTON, V) and d 1933

3d George, Maj; b 11 Dec 1798; had issue

1c Sophia; m 20 Dec 1782 Sir George Thomas, 3rd Bt, of Yapton (see 1970 edn), and d 21 Oct 1854

(1) Mary; m Thomas Ewes and had issue (see SHAFTESBURY, E)

4 Henry; Master St Katherine's Hosp, nr Tower of London, 1638; dsp

1 Elizabeth; m 1st Sir Lewis Ma(u)nsel(l), 2nd Bt (see MANSEL, Bt); m 2nd Sir Edward Sebright, 1st Bt (qv)

The **1st Earl** m 2nd Anne (dsp), dau and heiress of William Wincoll, of Langham, Staffs, and widow of Sir Leonard Halliday, Ld Mayor London; m 3rd 26 April 1620 Margaret (d Dec 1673), dau of John Crouch, of Cornbury, Herts, and widow of John Hare, and by her had:

5 George; m Elizabeth, dau of Sir Anthony Irby, and had, with another s (Christopher, m as her 2nd husb his cousin Anne, 3rd dau of 1st Earl of Sandwich, qv):

(1) Edward; m Elizabeth, dau of Sir John Pelham, Bt (see CHICHESTER, E), and had:

1a GEORGE MONTAGUE [sic], 2nd BARON HALIFAX (as which s unc; see below), and 1st EARL OF HALIFAX, so cr 14 June 1715, as also VISCOUNT SUNBURY, Co Middx (both GB), KB (1725), PC (1717); b by 1685; MP (Whig) Northampton 1705–15, Auditor Exchequer 1714–39; m 1st 8 April 1706 Ricarda Posthuma, only dau of Richard Saltonstall, and had:

1b Lucy; m 1st Earl of Guilford (qv)

1a (cont.) The 1st EARL OF HALIFAX of the 1715 cr m 2nd Lady Mary Lumley, est dau of 1st Earl of Scarbrough (qv), and d 9 May 1739, leaving by her an only s:

1b GEORGE MONTAGUE later MONTAGUE-DUNK, 2nd and last EARL OF HALIFAX of the 1715 cr, PC (Jan 1748/9); b 6 Oct 1716; educ Eton and Trin Coll Cambridge; Col 1745, Lt Gen 1759, First Ld Trade 1748–61, gave his name to Halifax Nova Scotia, Ld Lt Northants 1749–71, Ld Lt Ireland 1761–63, First Ld Admlty June–Oct 1762, Sec State North 1762–63 and Jan–une 1771 and South 1763–65, Ld Privy Seal 1770–71; m 2 July 1741 Anne, dau of William Richards (later Dunk?), ironmonger, citizen of London and possibly illegitimate s of Sir Thomas Dunk, Sheriff London 1709–10, since Anne is referred to in contemporary sources as Miss Anne Dunk before her marriage and credited with a fortune of £100,000 (just under £4,900,000 in late-1990s terms), and dspm 8 June 1771, when all his titles expired, leaving (with an illegitimate dau):

1c Mary; m 1 March 1766, as his 1st w, her cousin 5th Earl of Sandwich (qv) and d 1 July 1768

(2) CHARLES MONTAGU, 1st and last EARL OF HALIFAX, so cr 19 Oct 1714, as also VISCOUNT SUNBURY, Co Middx, and earlier 13 Dec 1700 BARON HALIFAX, Co York (all E), with in the last case remainder to his n George, KG (1714), PC (1694–March 1701/2 and 1714); b 16 April 1661; educ Westminster and Trin Coll Cambridge; Clerk PC 1689–92, MP (Whig) Maldon 1689–95 and Westminster 1695–1700, a Ld Treasury 1692–94, Chllr Exchequer 1694–99, First Ld Treasury 1697–99 and 1714–15, Ld Lt Surrey 1714–15; m just prior to 12 May 1688 Anne, dau of Sir Christopher Yelverton, 1st Bt, and widow of his cousin 3rd Earl of Manchester, and dsp 19 May 1715, when his two higher titles expired

(2) Edward

2 Susan; m 14 Dec 1637, as his 1st w, 6th Baron Chandos of Sudeley (see KINLOSS, L)

The 1st EARL d 7 Nov 1642; his est son,

EDWARD MONTAGU, **2nd Earl of Manchester**, KG (1661), KB (1626), PC (Jan 1639/40, S Feb 1660/1); b 1602; MP Hunts 1624–26, called up to Ho Lds vp 22 May 1626 in f's Barony; Parly Gen Civil War (cdr Marston Moor 1644, but later objected to trying CHARLES I and in 1660 promoted the Restoration), Ld Lt Hunts 1642 and Northants 1643, Ld Chamberlain 1660–61; m 1st 6 Feb 1622/3 Susanna (dsp), dau of John Hill, of Honiley, Devon, by Dorothy Beaumont, aunt of 1st Duke of Buckingham (see JERSEY, E); m 2nd 1 July 1626 Lady Anne Rich, dau of 2nd Earl of Warwick (see WARWICK, BROOKE and, E), and by her had:

1 ROBERT, **3rd Earl**

1 Frances; m Henry Saunderson

2 Anne; m Robert Rich, Earl of Holland

The **2nd Earl** m 3rd 20 Dec 1642 Essex (d 28 Sept 1658), widow of Sir Robert Bevill, KB, and dau of Sir Thomas Cheke, of Pirgo, Essex, and by her had other issue; m 4th July 1659 Eleanor (dsp), widow of (a) Robert Lee, of Quarendon, (b) 6th Earl of Sussex (see FITZWALTER, B) and (c) Robert Rich, Earl of Warwick (see WARWICK, BROOKE and, E), 4th dau of Sir Richard Wortley; m 5th 31 July 1667 Margaret (dsp Nov 1676), widow of James Hay, Earl of Carlisle (see KINNOULL, E), and dau of 4th Earl of Bedford (see BEDFORD, D), and d 5 May 1671; his est s by his 2nd w:

ROBERT MONTAGU, **3rd Earl of Manchester**; bapt 25 April 1634; MP (Whig) Hunts 1660–71, Ld Lt Hunts 1671–81; m 27 June 1655 Anne (m 2nd her husband's cousin 1st EARL OF HALIFAX (see above) and d 21 July 1698), dau of Sir Christopher Yelverton, 1st Bt, of Eastern Mauduit, and d 14 March 1682/3, having had, with other issue, including two daus (Anne, m 3rd Earl of Suffolk (see SUFFOLK and BERKSHIRE, E); Elizabeth, m Sir James Montagu, Ch Baron Exchequer):

CHARLES MONTAGU, **1st Duke of Manchester**, so cr 28 April 1719, PC (1698, 1702, 1714); b c 1662; educ St Paul's and Trin Coll Cambridge; one of the first and strongest supporters of the Glorious Revolution, served Battle of the Boyne 1690 and Siege of Limerick, Capt Yeomen Gd March 1688/9–1702, Ld Lt Hunts 1689–Jan 1721/2, Ld Gt Chamberlain 1694, Amb Venice 1697–98 and 1706–08 and Paris 1699–1701, Sec State South Jan–May 1702, a Ld Bedchamber 1714–Jan 1721/2; m c 19 Feb 1690/1 Dodington (d 16 Feb 1720), 2nd dau and coheir of 4th Baron Brooke of Beauchamps Court (see WARWICK, BROOKE and, E), and d 20 Jan 1721/2, having had, with two other daus:

1 WILLIAM MONTAGU, **2nd Duke of Manchester**, KB (1725); b France April 1700; Ld Lt Hunts 1722–39, Capt Yeomen Gd 1737–39; m 16 April 1723 his cousin Isabella (m 2nd 1st and last Earl of Beaulieu (dsp 1802) and d 20 Dec 1786), dau of John, Duke of Montagu (see above), and dsp 21 Oct 1739

2 ROBERT, **3rd Duke**

1 Charlotte; m 2nd Viscount Torrington (qv)

2 Dodington; b c 1694; d in a fire at her house in Lower Grosvenor Street 8 Jan 1774

The 2nd DUKE's bro,

ROBERT MONTAGU, **3rd Duke of Manchester**; b c 1710; MP (Whig) Hunts 1734–39, Ld Lt Hunts 1739–62; m 3 April 1735 Harriet (d 25 Feb 1755), dau and coheir of Edmund Dunch, of Little Wittenham, Berks, by Elizabeth, dau of Col Charles Godfrey and niece of 1st Duke of Marlborough (qv), and had:

1 GEORGE, **4th Duke**

2 Charles Greville; b 1741; m 20 Sept 1765 Elizabeth, dau of James Bulmer, and had issue

1 Caroline; m 1775 Charles Herbert, bro of 1st Earl of Carnarvon (qv), and d 1818

2 Louisa; d unm

The 3rd DUKE *d* 10 May 1762; his er son,

GEORGE MONTAGU, **4th Duke of Manchester**, PC (1782); *b* 6 April 1737; MP (Whig) Hunts 1761–62, Ld Lt Hunts 1762–88, Master of the Horse 1780, Ld Chamberlain 1782–83, Amb Paris April-Dec 1783; *m* 23 Oct 1762 Elizabeth (*d* 26 June 1832), est dau of Sir James Dashwood, 2nd Bt, of Kirtlington (*qv*), and had:

1 WILLIAM, **5th Duke**

2 Frederick; *b* 8 Nov 1774; *d* unm 4 Oct 1827

1 Caroline Maria; *m* 24 July 1790 3rd Duke of Montrose (*qv*)

2 Anna Marie; *d* 12 April 1796

3 Emily; housekeeper at Hampton Court Palace; *d* 21 April 1838

The 4th DUKE *d* 2 Sept 1788; his er son,

WILLIAM MONTAGU, **5th Duke of Manchester**; *b* 21 March 1771; *educ* Harrow and Winchester; Ld Lt Hunts 1793–1841, Govr Jamaica 1808–27, PMG 1827–30; *m* 7 Oct 1793 Lady Susan Gordon (*d* 26 Aug 1828), 3rd dau of 7th Marquess of Huntly (*qv*), and had:

1 GEORGE, **6th Duke**

2 William Francis; *b* 5 Aug 1800; *m* April 1830 Emily (*m* 2nd 7 Dec 1844 Richard Tonson Evanson, MD, and *d* 5 Dec 1848), dau of James Dupré, of Wilton Park, Bucks, and *d* 30 March 1842, leaving:

(1) Francis Dupré; Lt 38th Foot; *b* 7 Feb 1834; *k* Battle of the Alma 20 Sept 1854

(1) Emily; *m* 23 Nov 1865 John Cromie (*d* 17 Jan 1879), of Cromore, Co Londonderry, and *d* 25 May 1905

(2) Louisa Katherine; *m* 19 July 1859 Rev Owen Luttrel Mansel and *d* 30 Oct 1901, leaving issue (*see* MANSEL, Bt)

1 Jane; *d* unm 27 Sept 1815

2 Elizabeth; *m* 10 Aug 1819 Maj Gen Thomas Steele (*d* 8 May 1845) and *d* 9 Jan 1857

3 Susan; *m* 28 March 1816 8th Marquess of Tweeddale (*qv*) and *d* 5 March 1870, leaving issue

4 Georgiana Frederica; *m* 11 Oct 1823 Evan Baillie, of Dochfour, nr Inverness (*d* April 1883), and *d* 30 July 1892, leaving issue (*see* BURTON, B and WYNFORD, B)

5 Caroline Catherine; *m* 13 Feb 1828 John Hales Calcraft (*d* 13 March 1880), MP, of Rempston Hall, Dorset, and *d* 10 Sept 1892, aged 88, leaving issue (*see* WALDEGRAVE, E)

6 Emily; *d* unm 2 Feb 1827

The 5th DUKE *d* at Rome 18 March 1843; his er son,

GEORGE MONTAGU, **6th Duke of Manchester**, DL (Co Armagh); *b* 9 July 1799; *educ* Eton; Cdr RN 1822, MP (Tory) Hunts 1826–37; *m* 1st 8 Oct 1822 Millicent (*d* 21 Nov 1848), only dau and heiress of Brig-Gen Robert Bernard Sparrow, of Brampton Park, Hunts, by Lady Olivia Acheson, est dau of 1st Earl of Gosford (*qv*), and had:

1 WILLIAM DROGO, **7th Duke**

2 Robert, PC, JP and DL Co Antrim; MA Cantab, High Sheriff Co Antrim 1855, MP Hunts 1859–74 and Co Westmeath 1874–80, v-pres Educn Ctee 1867–68; *b* 24 Jan 1825; *m* 1st 12 Feb 1850 Ellen Mary (*d* 11 July 1857), only child and heiress of John Cromie, of Cromore, Co Antrim, and had:

(1) John Cromie; *b* 1 July 1852; *d* 30 March 1854

(2) Robert Acheson Cromie, JP and DL Co Derry, JP Co Antrim; Lt-Cdr RN; *b* 29 Aug 1854; *m* 1st 24 Nov 1880 Annie Margaret (*d* 6 Oct 1916), dau of Gilbert McMicking, of Miltonise, Wigtownshire; *m* 2nd 17 April 1917 Edith (*d* 1948), dau of Col Eldred Pottinger, CMG, of Portrush, Co Antrim, and *d* 12 Oct 1931, leaving by his 1st w:

1a John Michael Cromie, DL Co Londonderry; *b* 22 Aug 1881; *m* 6 April 1907 Libia (*d* 1979), dau of Martin Montes, of Quilmes, Buenos Aires, and *d* 11 Oct 1966, leaving:

1b +Robert Alexander [Robert Montagu Esq, 88 Chestnut Rise, London SE18 1RL]; *b* 16 March 1917; *m* 1946 *Eileen Teresa, dau of John Lamont, and has:

1c +Michael Anthony; *b* 1955

1c *Eileen Patricia [Mrs Hugh McGarry, 3 Antrim Gdns, Portrush, Co Antrim]; *b* 1947; *m* 1968 *Hugh McGarry and has:

1d *Stephen Hugh; *b* 1968

2d *Michael Edward Drogo

1d *Shirley Ellen; *b* 1969

2d *Alicia Patricia Teresa; *b* 1971

3d *Susan Mary Doreen; *b* 1975

2c *Sylvia Valerie Heather [Mrs Colin Brooks, 12 Leckwith Avenue, Bexleyheath, Kent]; *b* 1949; *m* 1969 *Colin Sidney Brooks and has:

1d *Stuart Robert; *b* 1971

2d *Steven Alexander; *b* 1982

1d *Cheryl Ann; *b* 1973

3c *Cynthia Christine Jeanette (twin); *b* 1949; *m* 1st 1967 (*divorce* 1979) David Nicholls and has:

1d *Michael David NICHOLLS later PAWLEY (deed poll 1979); *b* 1967

2d *Robert Alexander NICHOLLS later PAWLEY (deed poll 1979); *b* 1972

3c (cont.) Mrs Cynthia Nicholls *m* 2nd 1979 *Victor Pawley, of Portsmouth, and by him has:

1d *Rebecca Jane; *b* 1974

2d *Dawn Michele (twin); *b* 1974

4c *Helena May [Mrs Peter Suckling, 21st First Ave, Bexleyheath, Kent DA7 5SS]; *b* 1951; *m* 1973 *Peter George Suckling and has:

1d *Jayne Ellen; *b* 1981

2d *Louise Ann; *b* 1984

5c *Deirdre Veronica [Mrs Brian Richards, 132 Sutherland Ave, Welling, Kent]; *b* 1959; *m* 1982 *Brian Richards and has:

1d *Barry Charles Montagu; *b* 1984

2d *Alan James Montagu; *b* 1986

3d *Michael Anthony Montagu; *b* 1988

1b *Alicia May [Mrs Alicia Johnson Montagu, 30 Canterbury Court, Station Rd, Dorking, Surrey RH4 1HH]; *b* 1 Nov 1919; *m* 1st 1941 F/Lt Stuart James Lovell, RAF (*ka* over France 1944); *m* 2nd 1946 (*divorce* 1963, took name JOHNSON MONTAGU by deed poll 1963) John Dobney Johnson, PhD, and by him has:

1c *Adrian Michael Montagu; *b* 7 Aug 1947; *m* 1982 *Elizabeth Ann, dau of T J O'Shea, of Maesteg, S Wales

2c *Warwick Martin Montagu; *b* 21 June 1950; *m* 1970 *Gaye Marina Harding and has:

1d *Robert James; *b* 1978

2d *Simon David; *b* 1981

1d *Melissa Gaye; *b* 1973

2d *Sarah Louise; *b* 1975

3c *Philip Leicester Montagu [Philip Johnson Esq, Brook Cottage, Yeovil Marsh, Somerset]; *b* 21 July 1951; *m* 1973 *Fiona Madeleine Williams and has:

1d *Rebecca Claire Montagu; *b* 1981

1c *Michele Veronica Montagu; *b* 16 Feb 1953; *m* 1st 1973 (*divorce* 1982) Alan Craig Worrell; *m* 2nd 1984 *David John Robinson

2a George Frederick MONTAGU later WELD-BLUNDELL (roy licence Nov 1923); Capt RN, served WW I and WW II, Russian Order St Anne; *b* 12 March 1883; *m* 15 Oct 1912 Mary Teresa (*d* 6 June 1957), er dau of Charles Joseph Weld-Blundell (*see* YARBOROUGH, E), and *d* 21 Feb 1958, leaving:

1b Frederica Mary Montagu; *b* 16 Dec 1918; *m* 26 Aug 1966 *Jocelyn Philip Pereira, ARCS, yst s of Maj-Gen Sir Cecil Edward Pereira, KCB, CMG

3a Cuthbert Francis; WW I as Capt RE (despatches twice); *b* 29 May 1884; *m* 24 June 1917 Rosa Benedicta (*d* 1965), yst dau of Rev John Sanderson, Rector Winchfield, Hants, and *dsp* 7 Sept 1966

4a Austin Robert; *b* 26 May 1885; *m* 15 Feb 1934 Violet Vera (*d* 1982), dau of Charles William Sandles, of Wilmslow, Cheshire, and *d* 1958, leaving:

1b +Henry Robert Sanderson [Henry Montagu Esq, 22 Sandpiper St, Florida Lake, Florida 1710, S Africa]; *b* 2 Jan 1935; *m* 1963 *Margaret Elizabeth, dau of Norman Sinclair Pyper, of Sandpiper St, Florida Lake, and has:

1c *Gail; *b* 1968; *m* 1986 *John Dugmore and has:

1d *Lloyd John; *b* 1986

2d *Robyn Jail; *b* 1991

2c *Janet Frances; *b* 1972; *m* 1993 *Craig John Fraser

2b +Cyril John Sanderson [Cyril Montagu Esq, 101 Melville Ave, Discovers Park, Florida 1709, S Africa]; *b* 7 June 1937; *m* 1966 *Annette Mary, dau of Castlyn Barnard, and has:

1c +Graeme Peter; *b* 1967

2c +Christopher John; *b* 1968

3b +Gerard Phillip Sanderson [Gerard Montagu Esq, 35 Boeing Dve, Helderkruin ext 1, Roodeport 1725, S Africa]; *b* 9 Aug 1940; *m* 1963 *Elizabeth Sinden, dau of John Sinden Jarvis, and has:

1c +Matthew Gerard; *b* 1976

1c *Alison Elizabeth; *b* 1971

5a Walter Philip (Rev), SJ; T/Capt Army; *b* 7 May 1886; *d* 31 Oct 1918 of wounds recd in action

6a Gilbert Paul; *b* 30 June 1887; *m* 1st 3 July 1918 Frances Lazarre (*dsp* 14 May 1929), dau of — Aicher, of Mount Stirling, Kentucky; *m* 2nd 2 Jan 1932 Beatrice (*d* 24 June 1973), dau of William McNeill, of Australia, and widow of Lawrence Mendels, of Baltimore, Md.

7a Alexander Cyril; Lt RN; *b* 17 Sept 1890; lost in HMS *Bulwark* 26 Nov 1914

1a Mary Emily Winifred; *b* 26 June 1892

(1) Olivia Millicent; *b* 14 Nov 1850; *m* 14 May 1873 Henry Lyons (*d* 26 Sept 1885), of Croome House, Co Limerick, and *d* 3 Jan 1928, leaving issue

(2) Ellen Mary Elizabeth; *b* 23 Aug 1853; *d* unm 31 Aug 1951

2 (cont.) Lord Robert Montagu *m* 2nd 18 Oct 1862 Elizabeth Catherine (*d* 29 Dec 1908), dau of William Wade, and *d* 6 May 1902, having by her had:

(3) Monthermer Stanley Hume, MC; Capt Namaqualand Border Scouts Boer War 1899–1902 (wounded, two medals, six clasps), E Africa WW I (star, two medals, despatches); *b* 5 April 1868; *educ* Wellington; *m* 2 Oct 1913 Harriet Jessie (*d* 1959), dau of James Keith Forbes, of Valparaiso, and *d* 31 Dec 1954, having had:

1a Walter Bernard St John, TD; Capt RA (TA) (attd RAF as AOP) WW II (wounded); *b* 5 Dec 1915; *educ* Canford; *m* 29 June 1948 Doris Jean (*d* Jan 1992), WRNS 1942–45, dau of J Albany Morton, of Culzean, Busby, Lanarks, and *d* April 1992, leaving:

1b +John Charles Monthermer Albany [John Montagu Esq, c/o Child's Bank, 1 Fleet St, London EC4Y 1BZ]; *b* 4 Jan 1951; *educ* Gordonstoun and Hull U (LLB); Gren Gds and HAC

1b *Elizabeth Anne Kennedy [Mrs Elizabeth Hippisley, 15 Priory Rd, Cambridge CB5 8HT]; *b* 5 May 1949; *m* 1971 (*divorce* 1983) Victor Bayntun Hippisley and has:

1c *Antonia Frances Serena Olivia; *b* 1975

2a Charles Sydney Beattie, DFC; F/Lt RAFVR WW II; *b* 8 June 1918; *ka* W Desert 24 July 1942

1a Olivia Millicent Jane; WW II with Women's Tport Serv (E Africa); *b* 24 Oct 1914; *m* 29 May 1943 Edward Rodwell, FRGS, and *d* 1997

(4) Henry Bernard; Capt RN; *b* 19 Aug 1872; *m* 12 July 1922 Rosamond (*d* 1972), dau of Dudley Bowditch Fay, of Boston, Mass., and *d* 10 July 1941, leaving:

1a +John Drogo [John Montagu Esq, High Acre, Hunger Hill, East Stour, Dorset SP8 5JR]; *b* 18 Dec 1923; MRCS Eng and LRCP Lond 1946, late Surgn-Lt RNVR; *m* 16 Nov 1946 *Katharine Mary, dau of Brig-Gen Noble Fleming Jenkins, CMG, CBE, of Berkhamsted, Herts, and has:

1b +Robert Drogo [Robert Montagu Esq, 7 St Margaret's Close, Barming, Maidstone, Kent]; *b* 18 May 1947; *m* 1st 1970 (*divorce* 1985) Glenis Diane Littaur; *m* 2nd 12 Oct 1985 *Lancy Lim and by his 1st w has:

   1c +James Drogo; *b* 25 April 1975

   1c *Rachel Bernard; *b* 15 Jan 1974

2b +Christopher Bernard [W/Cdr Christopher Montagu, c/o National Westminster Bank, Covent Garden, London WC2]; *b* 18 May 1950; W/Cdr RAF; *m* 1975 *Christine Elizabeth Peatfield and has:

   1c +David William; *b* 8 Nov 1976

   2c +Thomas Edward; *b* 27 Nov 1979

1b *Rosamond Anne [Mrs Jonathan Chapple, 30 Barham Rd, London SW20]; *b* 23 March 1953; *m* 1984 *Jonathan Chapple and has:

   1c *Katharine Rose; *b* 19 Nov 1984

1a *Katharine Anne; *b* 21 Feb 1925

(5) St John Edward, OBE (1919); Maj Northumberland Fus, Boer War 1899–1902 (despatches, two medals, six clasps) and WW I (despatches, 1914 star, two medals, Legn Hon); *b* 26 Jan 1878; *d* unm 14 Jan 1946

(3) Elizabeth Catharine Mary; *b* 20 July 1863; *d* unm 13 May 1949

(4) Millicent; *b* 31 Dec 1864; *m* 27 Oct 1891 Walter Lionel Fenwick (*d* 15 July 1914), JP, of Witham Hall, Bourne, Lincs, and *d* 31 May 1942, leaving, with an intermediate s (*ka* unm 1916):

1a Keld Robert George; *b* 1892; Capt RHG; *m* 1st Oct 1916 (*divorce* 1924) Gladys Mary, dau of Sir William Nelson, 1st Bt (*qv*); *m* 2nd 1925 (*divorce* 1928) Anabel Bertha Greenough; *m* 3rd 1929 Dorothy Kimberley, dau of Walter Duncan, of New York, and *d* 1934, leaving by her:

1b *(John David) Keld [Keld Fenwick Esq, Pentlow Tower, Sudbury, Suffolk CO10 7JN]; *b* 17 Jan 1930; *educ* Eton; late Lt Roy Inniskilling Dragoon Gds; *m* 8 May 1954 *Eugenie Pamela, dau of James Edward Shaw, of Melbourne, Australia, and has:

   1c *Paul Anthony Ian Keld; *b* 30 July 1955

   2c Robin James Montagu; *b* 11 March 1957; *d* 21 April 1978

   3c *Nicholas Michael Walter; *b* 7 May 1960

   1c *Antonia Helen Eugenie; *b* 10 Aug 1965

2a Montagu John, JP (Hunts), of Great Stukeley Hall, Hunts; *b* 8 June 1896; *educ* Harrow; Lt RFC and RAF WW I, S/Ldr RAFVR WW II; *m* 17 Oct 1923 Marguerite Cecily, dau of Hugh Peacock, of Greatford Hall, Stamford, Lincs, and had:

1b *Anthony Walter; *b* 1928; *educ* Ampleforth; *m* July 1953 *Caroline Susan, sis of Baron Kimball (LP, *qv*), and has:

   1c *Mark John; *b* 1962

   1c *Claire Sonia; *b* 1954

   2c *Tania Jane; *b* 1955

   3c *Susan Antonia; *b* 1960

1b *June Mary; *b* 1925; *m* Baron Kimball (LP, *qv*) and has issue

(5) May Miriam; *b* 2 Dec 1866; *m* 5 Aug 1896 Cuthbert David Giffard Riddell (*d* 16 Oct 1937), est s of Giffard Riddell, of Felton Park and Swinburn Castle, Northumberland, and *d* 14 June 1897, having issue

3 Frederick, 12th Foot; *b* 5 Oct 1828; *d* 29 Oct 1854

1 Olivia; *m* 29 Jan 1850 6th Earl of Tankerville (*qv*) and *d* 15 Feb 1922, leaving issue

The **6th Duke** *m* 2nd 29 Aug 1850 (Harriet) Sydney (*m* 2nd 16 Dec 1858 Sir Stevenson Arthur Blackwood, KCB (*see* DUFFERIN AND CLANEBOYE, B), and *d* 30 May 1907), dau of Conway Richard Dobbs, of Castle Dobbs, Co Antrim, and *d* 18 Aug 1855, having by her had:

4 George Francis, Lt RA, Sec Dip Serv; *b* 18 Jan 1855; *d* 12 March 1882

2 Sydney Charlotte; *m* 14 Aug 1873 9th Earl of Kintore (*qv*) and *d* 21 Sept 1932, leaving issue

His est son,

WILLIAM DROGO MONTAGU, **7th Duke of Manchester**, KP (1877), DL; *b* 15 Oct 1823; Capt Gren Gds, Hon Col Huntingdon Militia, MP (C) Bewdley 1847–52 and Hunts 1852–55; *m* 22 July 1852 Countess Louise Fredericke Auguste (*m* 2nd 16 Aug 1892 8th Duke of Devonshire (*qv*) and *d* 15 July 1911), dau of Count von Alten, of Hanover, and had:

1 GEORGE VICTOR DROGO, **8th Duke**

2 Charles William Augustus, CVO, DL Hunts; Hon Lt-Col, T/Col and Co Cmdt 1st Bn Hunts Vol Regt, Lt N Somerset Yeo Cav, KGStJ, Legn Hon; *b* 23 Nov 1860; *m* 4 Dec 1930 Hon Mildred Cecilia Harriet (*d* 17 Dec 1942), widow of Sir Hedworth Meux (*see* DURHAM, E) and dau of 1st Baron Alington (*see* 1940 edn), and *dsp* 10 Nov 1939

1 Mary Louisa Elizabeth, OBE (1918); *m* 1st 10 Dec 1873 12th Duke of Hamilton and Brandon (*qv*) and had issue; *m* 2nd 20 July 1897 Robert Carnaby Forester (*d* 23 June 1925), of Easton Park, Wickham Market, Suffolk, and *d* 10 Feb 1934

2 Louisa Augusta Beatrice, DBE (1920); DGStJ, Ldy Bedchamber to HM QUEEN ALEXANDRA; *m* 10 Aug 1876 4th Earl of Gosford (*qv*) and *d* 3 March 1944, leaving issue

3 Alice Maude Olivia; DGStJ, Extra Ldy Bedchamber to HM QUEEN ALEXANDRA; *b* 1862; *m* 5 Jan 1889 17th Earl of Derby (*qv*) and *d* 23 July 1957, having had issue

The 7th DUKE *d* 22 March 1890; his er son,

GEORGE VICTOR DROGO MONTAGU, **8th Duke of Manchester**; *b* 17 June 1853; *educ* Eton; MP (C) Hunts 1877–80, Capt 3rd Bn Royal Irish Fus; *m* 22 May 1876 Consuelo (*d* 20 Nov 1909), dau of Don Antonio Yznaga del Valle, of Ravenswood, La., New York and Cuba, and *d* 18 Aug 1892, leaving, with two daus (Jaqueline Mary Alva, *d* unm 15 March 1895; Alice Aleanor Louise (twin with her sis), *d* unm 10 Jan 1900):

WILLIAM ANGUS DROGO MONTAGU, **9th Duke of Manchester**, PC, JP and DL Co Armagh; *b* 3 March 1877; *educ* Eton; Capt Yeomen Gd 1906–07, Capt 6th Bn Lancs Fus and 5th Bn KRRC; *m* 1st 14 Nov 1900 (*divorce* 1931) Helena (*d* 15 Dec 1971), dau of Eugene Zimmerman, of Cincinatti, USA; *m* 2nd 17 Dec 1931 Kathleen (*d* 28 March 1966), dau of W H Dawes, and by his 1st w had:

1 ALEXANDER GEORGE FRANCIS DROGO, **10th Duke**

2 Edward Eugene Fernando; *b* 26 July 1906 (HM EDWARD VII stood sponsor); *educ* Harrow; served US Forces; *m* 1st 10 Aug 1929 (*divorce* 1937) Norah Macfarlane, dau of Albert Edward Potter, of Ontario, Canada; *m* 2nd 28 Aug 1937 (*divorce* 1947) Dorothy Vera Peters; *m* 3rd 1947 Martha Matthews Hatton Bowen (*d* 5 Feb 1951); *m* 4th Aug 1952 Baroness Cora Kellie, portrait painter; *m* 5th 28 Sept 1953 Roberta Herold (*d c* 1964), dau of — Joughlin, of Los Angeles, and *d* 4 May 1954, leaving by his 1st w:

(1) +Roderick Edward Alexander [Roderick Montagu Esq, 71 St George's Crescent, Edmonton, Alberta, Canada]; *b* 1 June 1930; *m* 1968 *Mary Deas

1 Mary Alice; *b* 26 Oct 1901; *m* 1949 *Fendall Littlepage Gregory [Fendall Gregory Esq, Calle Miguel Salinas 20, Guernavaca, nr Mexico City, Mexico] and *d* 9 Oct 1962

2 Ellen Millicent Louise; *b* 5 Jan 1908; *m* 1st 1936 (*divorce* 1944) Herman Marten Hofer, 2nd s of John Jacob Hofer, of Zurich; *m* 2nd 30 Aug 1945 Maj John Norman Shairp, s of Col Alexander Shairp, CMG, IA, and *d* 2 Aug 1948

The 9th DUKE *d* 9 Feb 1947; his er son,

ALEXANDER GEORGE FRANCIS DROGO MONTAGU, **10th Duke of Manchester**, OBE (1940); *b* 2 Oct 1902; *educ* RNCs Osborne and Dartmouth; Cdr RN WW II; *m* 1st 5 May 1927 Nell Vere (*d* 2 Sept 1966), dau of Sydney Vere Stead, of Melbourne, Australia, and had:

1 SIDNEY ARTHUR ROBIN GEORGE DROGO MONTAGU, **11th Duke of Manchester**; *b* 5 Feb 1929; *m* 1st 5 Feb 1955 (*divorce* 1977) Adrienne Valerie, er dau of John Kenneth Christie, of Sedgefield, CP, S Africa; *m* 2nd 25 Aug 1978 Andrea (*d* 21 Jan 1996), dau of Lt-Col Cecil Alexander Joss, MC, TD, and formerly wife of (a) Maj Stuart Whitehead, AFC, (b) G J W Kent, and *d* 1985

2 ANGUS CHARLES DROGO MONTAGU, **12th and present Duke of Manchester**

The **10th Duke** *m* 2nd 7 Feb 1969 *Elizabeth [Her Grace Elizabeth Duchess of Manchester, PO Box 303, Pebble Beach, CA 93953, USA], dau of Samuel Clyde Fullerton, of Miami, and formerly w of W W Crocker, and *d* 23 Nov 1977

MANCROFT

Arms: Gules a chevron chequy argent and sable, between in chief two portcullises chained and in base a castle triple-towered or, on a chief of the last a lion passant guardant of the third. **Crest:** In front of a castle with three cupolas, issuant from each a staff proper flying therefrom a banner argent, charged with a cross gules, a sword sheathed also gules, garnished or, pommel and hilt of the last, and a mace gold in saltire. **Supporters:** On either side a Whiffler of the Corporation of the City of Norwich. **Motto:** Courage, patience. **Creations:** Bt. (UK) 15 Jan 1932, B. (UK) 23 Feb 1937.

THE 3RD BARON MANCROFT, of Mancroft, in the City of Norwich, and a **Baronet** (Sir Benjamin Lloyd Stormont Mancroft, Bt) [The Rt Hon The Lord Mancroft, House of Lords, London SW1A 0PW]; *b* 16 May 1957; *s* f 1987; *educ* Eton; MFH, chm: Drug and Alcohol Fndn 1994–, European Union Bank to Sept 1996, Inter Lotto (UK) 1995–; *m* 1990 *Emma, est dau of Thomas Peart, of Kensington, and has:

1 +ARTHUR LOUIS STORMONT; *b* 3 May 1995

1 *Georgia Esmé; *b* 1993

Lineage: AARON SAMUEL, of Norwich; *b* 1775; had:

MICHAEL SAMUEL, of Norwich; *b* 1799; *d* 1857, leaving:

BENJAMIN SAMUEL, of Norwich; *b* 19 April 1840; *m* 14 Feb 1872 Rosetta (*d* 29 April 1907), est dau of Philip Haldinstein, of Norwich, by Rachel, dau of David Soman, of Norwich, and *d* 16 April 1890, leaving:

1 ARTHUR MICHAEL, **1st Baron**

2 Frank Victor; *b* 28 March 1874; *educ* Oxford (MA); barrister; *m* 30 July 1913 Lily Valentine Mendel (*m* 2nd 1924 H Haldin-Davis, MD, FRCP, FRCS (*d* 1949), and *d* Nov 1953), and *d* 27 Dec 1922, leaving:

(1) *Jane Rosetta [Mrs Jane Page, 2 St Leonard's Terrace, London SW3]; *b* 19 July 1914; *educ* London U (BSc Econ); *m* 19 June 1939 (*divorce* 1960) Alan Thomas Page, MBE, and has:

1a *Andrew Frank Philip [Andrew Page Esq, 2 St Leonard's Terrace, London SW3]; *b* 18 July 1945

1a *Georgina Mancroft [Mrs Richard Ivor, 7 Rectory Rd, London SW15]; *b* 2 March 1944; *m* 20 Sept 1969 *Richard Alexander Burkhand Ivor, s of Dr Alexander Emil Albert Ivor, of Findon, Sussex

BENJAMIN SAMUEL's er s,

Sir Arthur Samuel, 1st Bt, and **1st Baron Mancroft**, of Mancroft in the City of Norwich (both UK), so *cr* 15 Jan 1932 and 23 Feb 1937 respectively; *b* 6 Dec 1872; *educ* King Edward VI GS Norwich; Ld Mayor Norwich 1912–13, Assist Dir Army Contracts (Munitions) WO 1914–15, memb Cncl Assoc Br Chambers Commerce 1915–24, MP (C) Farnham 1918–37, Parly U-Sec For Affrs, Parly Sec BOT, Min Dept Overseas Trade 1924–27, Fin Sec Treasury 1927–29, Chm H of C Select Ctee Public Accounts 1930 and 1931, Hon Freeman Norwich 1928, author: *Life of Giovanni Battista Piranesi*, *The Mancroft Essays* and other works; *m* 19 Dec 1912 Phoebe (*d* 18 Dec 1969), 2nd dau of George Alfred Chune Fletcher, MRCS, MO Charterhouse, London, and *d* 17 Aug 1942, leaving:

1 STORMONT MANCROFT, **2nd Baron**

1 Waveney Mancroft; *b* 25 Feb 1916; *m* 1 Dec 1950 Anthony William Garthwaite, 2nd s of Sir William Garthwaite, 1st Bt (*qv*), and had issue

2 *Rosetta Mancroft [The Hon Mrs Holm, Flat 2, 12 Eaton Place, London SW1X 8AD]; *b* 5 Oct 1918; *m* 1st 2 July 1947 Alfred John Bostock Hill (*d* 20 Aug 1959), Puisne Judge Supreme Court Penang, er s of Dr A Bostock Hill, of Weybridge; *m* 2nd 20 July 1966 Dr Cai Christian Holm (*d* 1983), 3rd s of Hans Christian Holm, of Aarhus, Denmark

The 1st BARON MANCROFT's only s,

Sir STORMONT MANCROFT SAMUEL later MANCROFT (deed poll 1925), **2nd Bt**, and **2nd Baron Mancroft**, KBE (1959, MBE 1945), TD; *b* 27 July 1914; *educ* Winchester and Ch Ch Oxford (MA); barrister Inner Temple 1938, memb Bar Cncl 1947–51, Lt-Col RA (TA) WW II (despatches twice), Ld in Waiting 1952–54, Parly U-Sec Home Dept 1954–57, Parly Sec MoD Jan-June 1957, Min without Portfolio June 1957–Oct 1958, memb St Marylebone Borough Cncl 1947–52, Chllr Primrose League 1952–54, dep chm Cunard Line 1966–87, dir GUS 1958–66 and Norwich Union Insur, pres: Inst Mktg and Sales Management 1959–62, St Marylebone C Assoc 1961–67, St Marylebone Soc 1964–69, London Tourist Bd, chm: USA Ctee of BNEC 1967–70, Restaurateurs Assoc GB, Wallis & Co (Costumiers) 1974–87, Br Greyhound Racing Fedn 1977–87, memb C working party reform Ho Lds 1977–87, author: *Booking the Cooks* and *A Chinaman in My Bath*; *m* 8 May 1951 *Diana Elizabeth, only dau of Lt-Col Horace Lloyd, DSO (see NUTTALL, Bt, and STOCKTON, E), and formerly w of Richard Bridges St John Quarry, and *d* 1987, leaving:

1 BENJAMIN LLOYD STORMONT MANCROFT, **3rd and present Baron Mancroft**

1 *Victoria [HRH Princess Nicholas von Preussen, Maperton House, Wincanton, Somerset BA9 8EJ]; *b* 7 March 1952; *m* 1980 *HRH PRINCE (FREDERICK) NICHOLAS VON PREUSSEN and has:

(1) *Frederick Nicholas Stormont; *b* 11 June 1990

(1) *Beatrice Victoria; *b* 10 Feb 1981

(2) *Florence Jessica; *b* 28 July 1983

(3) *Augusta Lily; *b* 15 Dec 1986

2 *Jessica Rosetta [The Hon Mrs Dickinson, Wortley House, Wotton-under-Edge, Glos GL12 7PQ]; *b* 10 May 1954; *m* 15 Oct 1983, as his 2nd w, *Simon Dickinson, s of Peter Dickinson, of Newbrough, Northumberland, and has:

(1) *Milo Clervaux Mancroft; *b* 1989

(1) *Phoebe Victoria; *b* 1984

(2) *Octavia Jessica; *b* 1986

MANDER

Arms: Gu. on a pile invected erminois three annulets interlaced two and one of the field. **Crest:** A demi-lion couped erm., holding in the paws two annulets fessways gu., between two buffalo horns of the last. **Motto:** *Vive bene* ('Live well'). **Creation:** Bt. (UK) 8 Oct 1911.

SIR CHARLES MARCUS MANDER, 3RD BT, of The Mount, Tettenhall, Co Stafford [Sir Charles Mander Bt, Little Barrow, Moreton-in-Marsh, Glos GL56 0XU; Greville House, Kinnerton St, London SW1]; *b* 22 Sept 1921; *s* f 1951; *educ* Eton

and Trin Coll Cambridge; Capt Coldstream Gds WW II, dir Mander Bros (Wolverhampton) 1948–58, chm Arlington Securities, High Sheriff Staffs 1962; *m* 24 Nov 1945 *Maria Dolores Beatrice, yr dau of Alfred Brödermann, of Gross Fontenay, Hamburg, and has:

1 +(CHARLES) NICHOLAS [Nicholas Mander Esq, Owlpen Manor, Uley, Glos GL11 5BZ]; *b* 23 March 1950; *educ* Downside and Trin Coll Cambridge (MA); co-fndr Mander Portman Woodward (private tutors) Kensington 1973, dir publishers and land companies UK and Spain, memb Lloyd's; *m* 24 June 1972 *Karin (Kajsa) Margareta, yr dau of (Gustav) Arne Norin, of Stockholm, and has:

(1) +(Charles) Marcus Septimus Gustav; *b* 26 July 1975; *educ* Eton and Peterhouse Cambridge (BA)

(2) +Benedict Edward Arthur; *b* 6 Feb 1977; *educ* Eton and St John's Coll Cambridge

(3) +Hugo Richard Theodore; *b* 3 April 1981; *educ* Eton

(4) +Fabian Edmund Quintin; *b* 3 May 1987

(1) *Sarra Mary; *b* 10 March 1973; *educ* St Mary's Ascot and Edinburgh U (BA)

2 +Francis Peter Edward [Francis Mander Esq, Heath Barn, Donnington, Glos GL56 0XU; 11A Cambridge Rd, London SW11 4RT] *b* 4 Dec 1952; *educ* Downside and RAC Cirencester; commercial pilot, fndr Mandair Promotions 1983 and Francis Mander Photography 1990; memb Lloyd's; *m* 1990 *Georgina Jane, er dau of Cdr Edward Theodore Thring, RN, and has:

(1) +Luke Edward Charles; *b* 27 April 1994

(2) +Frederick George Arthur; *b* 13 May 1996

1 *Penelope Ann Mary [Mrs Simon Loder, Marsh Court, Caundle Marsh, Sherborne, Dorset]; *b* 22 Sept 1946; *m* 1st 4 May 1965 Michael Rollo Hoare, only s of Rollo Hoare, of The Dower House, Dragmersfield, Hants, and has:

(1) *Venetia Elizabeth; *b* 3 Sept 1965; *educ* Wycombe Abbey and Trin Coll Cambridge; ptnr C Hoare & Co; *m* 19– *Hamish Peter Leng, s of Gen Sir Peter Leng, KCB, MBE, MC, and has:

1a *Harry Archie Peter; *b* 13 Sept 1997

(2) *Fiona Mary; *b* 1969

1 (cont.) Mrs Hoare *m* 2nd 1979 *Capt Simon John Loder, Gren Gds (see LODER, Bt), and by him has:

(1) +James Robert; *b* 22 July 1981; *educ* Wellington

Lineage: The MA(U)NDERs were originally yeomen of Tredington, Warwicks, where John Maundwer held land 1291.

HENRY MANDER; *b* June 1601; *m* 13 Feb 1636 Anne (*d* Sept 1662), dau of Robert Wegham, of Aston Cantlow, Warwicks, and was *bur* 18 May 1672, leaving, with other issue:

SAMUEL MANDER; of Lapwood Park, Henley-in-Arden, Warwicks; *b* Jan 1648; *m* Feb 1670 Mary (*d* May 1694), dau of Thomas Shakespeare, and *d* Nov 1716, leaving, with other issue:

ROBERT MANDER, of Ireland's Farm, Lapworth, nr Henley-in-Arden, Warwicks; *m* 1st 2 March 1708 Catherine (*d* 1724), dau of John Cotterell, of Bushwood Hall, Warwicks, and *d* 1749, having had, with four er sons, a sixth s and two daus:

THOMAS MANDER, of Wolverhampton, where settled by *c* 1745; *b* 1720; *m* 9 Sept 1742 Elizabeth (*m* 2nd 1775 Charles Hunter (*d* 1788), of Wolverhampton, and *d* Aug 1804), dau and coheir of Samuel Clemson, of Wolverhampton, and *d* Dec 1764, having had, with other issue:

1 BENJAMIN

2 John, of Wolverhampton; nonconformist, pioneer industrialist and chemist, establishing one of Britain's largest laboratories; *b* 13 July 1754; *m* 1st 20 Jan 1778 Esther (*d* 1802), dau of John Lea, of Kidderminster, and had issue; *m* 2nd — and *d* 22 Aug 1827

3 Thomas, of Birmingham; *b* 7 June 1757; *m* 1 July 1784 Elizabeth, dau of Edward Urwick, of Felhampton Court, Wistanstow, Salop, and *d* 26 April 1813, leaving issue

THOMAS MANDER's est surv s,

BENJAMIN MANDER, of Wolverhampton; *b* 10 May 1752; Town Commr 1777, fndr Mander Bros (varnish-mfrs, later also mfrs of paint and printing ink) 1773; *m* 5 Dec 1776 Elizabeth Hanbury (*d* 20 May 1828), dau and coheir of Samuel Read, of Kidderminster, and *d* 30 Oct 1819, having had:

CHARLES MANDER, of Wolverhampton; *b* 21 March 1780; *m* 1st 17 Dec 1812 Jemima (*d* 1 Nov 1834), dau of Thomas Small, of Boston, Lincs; *m* 2nd his deceased w's sis Elizabeth, and *d* 22 Dec 1853, having by his first w had, with two other sons and four daus:

1 CHARLES BENJAMIN

2 Samuel Small, of Wolverhampton; *b* 8 Feb 1822; *m* 26 Sept 1850 Mary, dau of Paul Wilkes, of Wolverhampton, and *d* 5 Nov 1881, leaving:

(1) Samuel Theodore, JP Staffs, of Wightwick Manor, Wolverhampton; *b* 25 Feb 1853; *educ* London U and Clare Coll Cambridge (BA); *m* 29 May 1879 Flora St Clair (*d* 15 April 1905), dau of Henry Nicholas Paint, of Halifax, Nova Scotia, and *d* 14 Sept 1900, leaving:

1a Geoffrey Le Mesurier (Sir), JP Staffs; *b* 6 March 1882; *educ* Harrow and Trin Coll Cambridge (BA 1903, MA 1906); barrister Inner Temple 1921, High Sheriff Staffs 1921, MP Wolverhampton East 1929–45, PPS to Sec State Air 1942–45, chm Mander Bros, WW I in RFC and RFA, ktd 1945; *m* 1st 10 Oct 1906 (*divorce* 1930) Rosalind Florence, dau of Col Frank Caverhill, of Montreal, and had, with other issue:

1b Mervyn Caverhill; *b* 14 Jan 1910; *educ* Harrow, Chillon Coll, Trin Coll Cambridge and Pennsylvania U; *m* 1st 29 Oct 1935 Elizabeth Maria Dorothea Mettlich, of Cologne, and had:

1c *(Mervyn) Nicholas [Nicholas Mander Esq, 6 Melbourne Terrace, London SW6]; *b* 22 Jan 1943; *educ* Shrewsbury and Trin Coll Cambridge; *m* 14 March 1986 *Marcia Prudencia, yst dau of Ulpiané Garcia, of Salamanca, Spain, and has:

1d *Sophia Vivien; *b* 1990

1b (cont.) Mervyn Mander m 2nd 27 Nov 1952 *Janet Prangley, er dau of Leslie Philip, and d 28 March 1978

1b Mavis Flora Rosalind; b 19 May 1909; m 1st Fitzroy Roger Partridge and had issue; m 2nd Fitzroy Philips and d 23 Jan 1953, leaving further issue

2b *Elizabeth Brehaut; b 19 July 1916

1a (cont.) Sir Geoffrey m 2nd 18 Nov 1930 Mary Rosalie Glynn (d 2 April 1988), only child of Archibald Campbell Glynn Grylls, and d 9 Sept 1962, having by her had:

2b John Geoffrey Grylls; b 28 May 1932; educ Eton and Trin Coll Cambridge (MA); author; m 1st 17 Dec 1956 (divorce 1968) Gertrude Bracher, of Stuttgart; m 2nd 19 April 1969 Penelope Loveday, est dau of Lt-Cdr James Dennis Williams, RN, by Pamela Winifred Mary Green, and dsp 2 Sept 1978

3b *Anthea Loveday Veronica [Mrs Anthea Mander-Lahr, Wightwick Manor, Wolverhampton, Staffs]; jnlst; b 16 Jan 1945; m 12 Aug 1965 *John Henry Christopher Lahr, s of Bert Lahr, actor, and has:

1c *Christopher David; b 1976

2a Lionel Henry; film actor and playwright (as Miles Mander); b 14 May 1888; educ Harrow, Loretto and McGill; m 1st (divorce) Princess Pretiva, dau of Maharajah of Cooch Behar; m 2nd (divorce) Bunty French and d 7 Feb 1946, having by her had:

1b Theodore, CBE; b 31 May 1926; educ Sherborne, Milton Acad, Pace Coll and Columbia U USA; US Merchant Marine 1942–44, with Standard Oil of New Jersey 1945–49, with Penn Mutual Life Insur 1949–62, Pres Balanced Pension and Profit Sharing Plans Inc 1962–90; m 1st May 1946 (divorce 1952) Diantha F, dau of Connor Lawrence, of New York, and had:

1c *Richard C; b Nov 1950; m and has:

1d *Theodore

1c *Melanie R; b June 1949

1b (cont.) Theodore Mander m 2nd May 1953 (divorce) Elizabeth Stuart, dau of Richmond Brown, of Greenwich, Conn., and had:

2c *Fabienne H B; b 6 Aug 1956

1b (cont.) Theodore Mander m 3rd 19– Lois Doherty and d 24 June 1990

3a Alan Jocelyn; b 28 Jan 1891; educ Trin Coll Glenalmond; m Princess Sudhira Devi (d 7 Jan 1968), dau of Maharajah of Cooch Behar, and d 21 Dec 1967, having had a s and two daus

1a Marjorie Mima; m 6 Jan 1910 Gervas Clifton Nevile (d 20 June 1943), er s of Edward Horatio Nevile, JP, of Skellingthorpe Manor, Lincs, and d 4 Aug 1968, leaving a s

(2) Benjamin Howard, of Trysull Manor, Staffs; b 1861; ptnr Mander Bros; m 1892 Lilian, dau of G H Nelson, of Warwick, and d 1912, leaving:

1a Howard Vivian, MC; b 1894; educ Wellington and Oxford; dir Mander Bros; Lt-Col; m 1st 19– (divorce 19–) — and had, with other issue:

1b Howard Anthony; b 1920; ka 1944, leaving a dau

1b *Pauline; m 1953 James Guinness (see GUINNESS, Bt) and has issue

1a (cont.) Lt-Col Howard Mander m 2nd Margaret, dau of R Graham, of Wolverhampton, and d 1950, leaving:

2b *Martin Ian; b 1929; educ Winchester; m 19– (divorce 19–) Mary Jane Fuller and has:

1c *Simon Vivian; b 1954

3b *Michael

1a Lilian Brenda; m 16 Jan 1919 Sir Alfred Edward Howard Hickman, 2nd Bt (qv), and had issue

CHARLES MANDER's est s,

CHARLES BENJAMIN MANDER, JP, of The Mount, Compton, Wolverhampton; b 9 July 1819; m 1st 14 April 1850 Sophia (d 29 Oct 1869 aged 42), dau of John Weaver, MRCS, of Chester; m 2nd 1874 Harriet Spooner (d 27 Aug 1915 aged 80) and d 18 Aug 1878, leaving by his 1st w:

1 CHARLES TERTIUS (Sir), **1st Bt**

2 Neville Hanbury, JP (Staffs); b 30 June 1862; m 19 June 1890 Emily Louise (d 9 March 1957), yst dau of Maj-Gen Archibald Edwardes Campbell, ISC, and d 7 July 1919, having had issue

3 John Harold, OBE; Capt DCLI Boer War, Ch Constable Norfolk; b 3 Aug 1869; m 27 Sept 1894 Maria Elinor Lloyd (d 31 Aug 1957), dau of John Philipps Allen Lloyd Philipps, DL, of Dale Castle, Pembs, and d 9 Dec 1927, leaving:

(1) Eileen Cicely, OBE (1950); b 1897; m 4 Feb 1920 Capt Francis Rudolph Phillips, MC (d 24 June 1942), yr s of Sir Lionel Phillips, 1st Bt (qv), and d 15 Nov 1962

(2) Rosemary Dorothy Esther; b 1902; m 1932 Robert L D Barnett

1 Amy Matilda; d 27 July 1919

2 Janetta; m 23 June 1885 Col Henry Sparke Stabb (d 22 Oct 1888), 32nd LI, and d Sept 1913, leaving issue

3 Sophie Emmeline; m 23 Jan 1894 Rev Canon Henry Paine Stokes, LLD, LittD, FSA (d 16 June 1931), Hon Fell Corpus Christi Coll Cambridge, Rector Little Wilbraham, Cambs, and d 2 July 1937, leaving issue

4 Annie Julia; m 17 July 1879 Robert Edward Turnbull and d 7 July 1902, leaving issue

5 Laura Louisa; m 9 June 1881 George Reginald Leeper, MD (d 26 June 1904), of Dublin, and had issue

CHARLES MANDER's est s,

Sir Charles Tertius Mander, 1st Bt (UK), so cr 8 July 1911, TD, JP (Wolverhampton and Staffs), DL (Staffs); b 16 July 1852; educ Rugby and Corpus Christi Coll Cambridge (MA); High Sheriff Staffs 1903, Mayor Wolverhampton 1892–96, Maj and Hon Lt-Col Staffs Yeo, first chm Mander Bros; m 25 May 1882 Mary Le Mesurier (d 10 Sept 1951), 2nd dau of Henry Nicholas Paint, of Halifax, Nova Scotia, MP (Dominion Parl) 1882–87, and d 8 April 1929, leaving:

1 CHARLES ARTHUR (Sir), **2nd Bt**

2 Gerald Poynton; b 13 Nov 1885; educ Eton and Trin Coll Cambridge (BA 1907, MA 1930); dir Mander Bros; FSA; m 5 June 1913 Nancy Steward (d 20

Nov 1960), 2nd dau of Lt-Col Robert Halstead Hargreaves, JP, DL, of Knightley Grange, Staffs, and d 10 Dec 1951, leaving:

(1) Philip FitzGerald, JP (Wolverhampton 1956); b 29 Sept 1915; educ Eton and Trin Coll Cambridge (BA 1937); WW II in RAOC, chm Manders Hldgs; m 20 July 1942 *Priscilla Patricia [Mrs Philip Mander, The Folley, Stableford, Bridgnorth, Salop], er dau of Lt-Col Edmund de Warrenne Waller, MC, IA, and d 2 June 1972, leaving:

1a (Patrick) Oliver; b 24 March 1951; educ Eton; m *Gabrielle [Mrs Oliver Mander, St Andrew's East, Bedchester, Dorset SP7 0JU], only dau of Geoffrey Weaver, of Hayling Island, Hants, and d 1982, leaving:

1b *Hannah Rachel; b 1982

1a *Philippa Hazel Jeanetta (Rev) [The Rev Mrs John Thorneycroft, The Vicarage, 11 Brookhouse Lane, Featherstone, Wolverhampton WV10 7AW; Poole's Yard, Kemberton, Shropshire TF11 9LL]; b 18 Feb 1944; educ Cheltenham Ladies' Coll, Exeter U (BA) and Queen's Theological Coll; deacon 1988, priest 1994; m 16 Oct 1965 *John Patrick Thorneycroft, slr, er s of Gerald Thorneycroft, of Park House, Codsall Wood, Staffs, and has:

1b *Hugh Martin Sumner; b 26 June 1967; educ Wellington and Durham U (BA); m 3 June 1995 *Caroline Anne, BA (Durham U), dau of George Riddington, of Crowland, Lincs, and has:

1c *Olivia Sophie; b 13 Dec 1996

2b *Martin Philip; b 1977; educ Winchester and St Edmund Hall Oxford

1b *Veryan Ruth; b 29 Jan 1971; educ Cheltenham Ladies' Coll and Exeter U (BA); m 3 May 1997 *Paul David Evans, s of John Evans, of Caversham, Reading

2b *Naomi Priscilla; b 1975; educ Oakham Sch and Brookes U Oxford

(1) *Catherine Daphne; b 12 March 1914; ATS, FANY WW II

(2) *Hilary Nancy [Mrs Anthony Jarrey, Oldbeams, Sarsden, Oxford OX7 6PT]; b 14 April 1924; RN VAD 1942–46, SEN; m 1st 5 Oct 1946 (divorce 1981) William Reginald Purslow (d 1991), s of Charles Purslow, of Cheshire, and has had:

1a *Ian Gerald Steward [Ian Purslow Esq, Château Saint Maur, par Mirande 32300, France]; b 28 Jan 1949; educ Cheltenham; 2nd Lt 16th/5th Queen's Roy Lancers; m 1st 1971 (divorce 1982) Sally Anne, only dau of Gordon Matthews, of Milton House, Shipton-under-Wychwood, Oxon; m 2nd 1988 *Susan Kathryn, dau of Capt Colin McKeand Little, RN, and has:

1b *Margaux Rose; b 2 Jan 1991

2b *Flora Louise; b 7 Sept 1994

2a Hugh Charles; b 28 Oct 1950; educ Cheltenham and Keele U; d 1975

1a Valerie Christine; b 29 Aug 1947; d 23 April 1966

(2) (cont.) Mrs Hilary Purslow m 2nd 31 Aug 1985 *Anthony Michael Jarrey

1 Daisy St Clair, JP Staffs; b 27 Dec 1887; d unm 24 June 1968

The 1st Bt's er s,

Sir Charles Arthur Mander, 2nd Bt, TD, JP and DL (Staffs); b 25 June 1884; educ Eton and Trin Coll Cambridge (BA 1907); High Sheriff Staffs 1926, Mayor Wolverhampton 1932 and 1936 (Hon Freeman 1945), V-Chm National Savings Ctee, Maj Staffs Yeo, md Mander Bros; m 29 April 1913 Monica Claire Cotterill (d 28 Feb 1964), yst dau of George Harding Neame, and d 25 Jan 1951, leaving:

1 Sir CHARLES MARCUS MANDER, **3rd and present Bt**

1 *Ann Marietta Patience, JP (Co London) [Mrs Patrick Stirling JP, Witney House, Leafield, Oxon]; b 16 Oct 1914; Fell King's Coll London; m 7 Jan 1939 (Hugh) Patrick Stirling, barrister, twice Mayor Westminster, only s of Kenneth Stirling, of Paris, and adopted:

*(Nicholas) Charles [Charles Stirling Esq, Dipton Cottage, Corbridge, Northumberland]; b 3 Oct 1947; educ Eton; 16th/5th Queen's Roy Lancers; FCA, AIIT; MFH; m 1975 *Elizabeth Emma, dau of Brig V W Barlow, DSO, OBE, KSLI, and has:

1a *William Nelson; b 20 Feb 1979; educ Eton and Edinburgh U

1a *Frances; b 1980

2a *Patience; b 1983

3a *Alexandra Emma; b 30 June 1988

*Charlotte Amelia [Mrs Paul Sandilands, Falcutt House, Helmdon, Northants]; b 27 Jan 1950; educ Cranborne Chase and Bristol U (BA); m 1973 *Paul Francis Sandilands, yr s of Sir Francis Sandilands, CBE, and has:

1a *Frederick James; b 1982

1a *Marietta Minette; b 1980

2 *Carinthia Jill, JP (1958) [Mrs James Wallis JP, Le Friquet, Bailiff's Cross Rd, St Andrews, Guernsey, CI GY6 8RZ]; b 16 Jan 1920; WRNS WW II; m 1st 2 Dec 1944 James Ramsden (d 22 Oct 1956), yst s of Henry Ramsden, of Edinburgh, and has:

(1) *(James) Tobit (Toby); b 26 Oct 1948; educ Radley and Sheffield U (BA); FCA; m 1st 1973 (divorce 1983) Linda, dau of Walter Critchlow, of Quebec, and has:

1a *Sarah Jill; b 1977

(1) (cont.) Toby Ramsden m 2nd 1985 *Ann Miller-Williams and by her has:

1a *Edward Henry James; b 17 Oct 1988

2a *Sian Amelia; b 24 May 1986

3a *Daisy Katherine; b 9 May 1990

(2) *(Charles) Riordan (Rory) [Rory Ramsden Esq, 1 King's Close, Lymington, Hants]; b 20 Dec 1949; educ Radley; m 1974 *Elizabeth Mary, only dau of Stewart Kilpatrick, of Fogdens Barn, Bury, Sussex

2 (cont.) Mrs James Ramsden m 2nd 22 Feb 1964 *Lt-Cdr James de Votier Grosvenor Wallis, RN (ret), s of William Frederick Wallis, of Norwich

MANN

Arms: Argent a chevron sable between in chief two crosses moline and in base an annulet gules. **Crest:** A demi-man in profile in armour proper, the helmet adorned with four feathers argent, holding in the dexter hand a cross as in the arms. **Motto:** *Homme d'Etat* ('Statesman'). **Creation:** Bt. (UK) 29 Dec 1905.

SIR RUPERT EDWARD MANN, 3RD BT, of Thelveton Hall, Thelveton, Norfolk [Sir Rupert Mann Bt, Billingford Hall, Diss, Norfolk IP21 4HN]; *b* 11 Nov 1946; *s* great-unc 1971; *educ* Malvern; *m* 6 July 1974 *Mary Rose, dau of Geoffrey Butler, of Cheveley Cottage, Stetchworth, Suffolk, and has:

1 +ALEXANDER RUPERT; *b* 6 April 1978
2 +William Edward; *b* 31 Oct 1980

Lineage: THOMAS MANN, of Thelveton Hall, Norfolk, and Roseneath House, Winchmore Hill, Middx; *b* 27 July 1822; *m* 4 Nov 1846 Fanny (*d* 19 Jan 1897), dau of Robert Spence, of Elvington, Yorks, and *d* 9 Oct 1886, leaving:

1 Thomas James, JP, of Hyde Hall, Sawbridgeworth, Herts; *b* 1848; *m* 1871 Rose, dau of Paul Bell, of Vale House, Stiffkey, Norfolk, and *d* 25 Aug 1897, leaving issue

2 EDWARD (Sir), **1st Bt**

1 Fanny; *m* 5 June 1877 Sir William Thomas Paulin, JP (*d* 26 Feb 1931), of Broadfields, Winchmore Hill, and *d* 5 Feb 1901, leaving issue

2 Julia; *b* 7 Oct 1857; *d* unm 3 Sept 1948

THOMAS MANN's 2nd s,

Sir Edward Mann, 1st Bt (UK), so *cr* 29 Dec 1905, JP (Norfolk); *b* 2 March 1854; High Sheriff Norfolk 1909, 1st Mayor Stepney 1900–01; *m* 20 April 1882 his sis-in-law Anna Jane (*d* 1 March 1928), dau of Paul Bell, and *d* 29 Sept 1943, leaving:

1 **Sir Edward John Mann, 2nd Bt**; *b* 26 Jan 1883; *educ* Marlborough and Pembroke Coll Cambridge (BA 1904), High Sheriff Norfolk 1939, Capt 4th Bn Norfolk Regt WWI (wounded), Master Brewers' Co 1921–22; *m* 25 April 1951 Clare Helen, CBE (1962, OBE 1950), 2nd dau of Robert Graham Dryden Alexander, and *dsp* 1971

2 William Edgar, DSO (1917); *b* 19 Jan 1885; *educ* Marlborough; Maj RA WW I (wounded twice, despatches); *m* 9 July 1913 Sarah Douglas, 4th dau of Sir Alexander Sprot, 1st Bt (*see* 1929 edn), and *d* 14 Feb 1969, leaving:

(1) Edward Charles, DSO (1940), MC (1945); *b* 4 Oct 1918; *educ* Malvern; Maj 12th Lancers WW II (wounded, despatches twice); *m* 20 Oct 1945 *Pamela Margaret, Subaltern ATS, only dau of Maj Frank Haultain Hornsby, RFA (*see* BELPER, B), and *d* 9 Aug 1959, leaving:

1a Sir RUPERT EDWARD MANN, **3rd and present Bt**

2a Malcolm Alexander; *b* 22 Oct 1947; *educ* Malvern; *d* 16 Dec 1976

3a +Andrew William [Andrew Mann Esq, 27 Limerick Rd, Redland, Bristol BS6 7DY]; *b* 23 Oct 1947; *educ* Malvern; *m* 3 May 1985 *Ann Christina, dau of Michael Lesley, of St Peter Port, Guernsey, and has:

1b +Jack Malcolm; *b* 3 Feb 1993
1b *Lucy Clare; *b* 15 Nov 1987
2b *Daisy Sarah; *b* 14 Nov 1989
3b *Camilla Mary; *b* 3 Feb 1993

(1) *Ann Sara Mann [Mrs Charles Cunningham, Westcott Barton Lodge, Middle Barton, Chipping Norton, Oxon OX7 7AA]; ATS WW II (despatches); *m* 12 May 1950 Charles John Cunningham, MA, FRIBA (*d* 1994), only s of Capt Kenneth Edward Cunningham, Duke of Wellington's Regt, and has:

1a *Alexander Kenneth; *b* 15 Nov 1956; *m* 1980 *Frances, dau of Judge John da Cunha, and has:

1b *Maximilian Edward; *b* 1986
2b *Ivo Alexander James; *b* 1991
1b *Camilla Lucy; *b* 1988

2a *Edward James; *b* 16 May 1962; *m* 1990 *Melissa Ann, dau of Daryl H Foster, of Perth, W Australia, and has:

1b *James Alexander; *b* 1992

2b *Thomas Henry; *b* 20 Jan 1995
1a *Sara Mary; *b* 29 March 1952
2a *Clare Margaret; *b* 4 Oct 1953; *m* 1983 *Edward Gold, s of Dr S C Gold, MD, FRCP, and has:

1b *Christopher Charles; *b* 1984
2b *Simon Piers; *b* 1988

(2) *Penelope Jane, JP (Norfolk) [Mrs Michael Keith JP, Keepers Cottage, Hoe, Dereham, Norfolk NR20 4BD]; ATS WW II; *m* 21 June 1950 Michael Telfair Keith, TD, MA (*d* 24 Dec 1966), yr s of Edward Charles Keith (*see* KEITH OF CASTLEACRE, B), and has:

1a *James Edward; *b* 5 March 1960; *m* 1987 *Victoria Rosemary, dau of Roy E Cook, and has:

1b *Edward Michael; *b* 1991
1b *Rosanna Victoria; *b* 1989
2b *Alicia Rose Juliet; *b* 1993

1a *Rosemary Ann [Mrs Michael Fetherston-Dilke, Maxstoke Castle, Warwicks B46 2RD]; *b* 18 April 1951; *m* 1983 *Michael Charles Fetherston-Dilke, s of Capt Charles Beaumont Fetherston-Dilke, RN, and has:

1b *George Michael; *b* 1985
2b *Edward Charles; *b* 1986
1b *Sarah; *b* 1989

2a *Priscilla Mary [Mrs Fergus Laing, Craggan, Grantown-on-Spey, Moray PH26 3NT]; *b* 12 Aug 1953; *m* 1979 *Fergus Hew Grant Laing and has issue (*see* STAIR, E)

3 Francis Thomas; *b* 3 March 1888; *educ* Malvern and Pembroke Coll Cambridge; Capt 1st Bn Scots Gds WW I (wounded three times, despatches twice), played cricket for Cambridge 1909–11, Middx 1909–31 (Capt 1921–28, Pres 1947–49) and England *v* S Africa 1922–23 (Capt), Test Selector 1930; *m* 8 Nov 1916 Enid Agnes (*d* 1976), only dau of George Adams Tilney, and *d* 6 Oct 1964, leaving:

(1) +(Francis) George, DSO (1945), MC [Maj George Mann DSO MC, Great Farmhouse, West Woodhay, Berks RG15 0BL]; *b* 6 Sept 1917; *educ* Eton and Pembroke Coll Cambridge; Maj Scots Gds WW II (wounded), played cricket for Cambridge 1938–39, Middx 1937–54 (Capt 1948–49), England *v* S Africa 1948–49 (Capt), *v* NZ 1949 (Capt); *m* 1 Dec 1949 *Margaret Hildegarde, er dau of William Marshall Clark, OBE, BSc, MICE, of Johannesburg, and has:

1a +Simon Francis; *b* 26 June 1952; *educ* Eton and RMA Sandhurst; Capt Scots Gds 1971–81 and 1991–92; *m* 1977 (*divorce* 1986) Jennifer, dau of David Barham, of Hole Park, Rolvenden, Kent, and has:

1b +Peter George; *b* 1980
2b +Jack; *b* 1982
1b *Sophie; *b* 1985

2a +Richard William [Richard Mann Esq, Goosedown Farm, Dolton, Winkleigh, Devon]; *b* 12 Nov 1953; *m* 1983 *Selina Rose Thoroton, only dau of Maj Robert Christopher Thoroton Hildyard, MC, RA, and has:

1b +Edgar; *b* 1985
1b *Perdita; *b* 1986

3a +Edward John [Edward Mann Esq, 101 Studdridge St, London SW6 3TD]; *b* 6 April 1961; *m* 1986 *D Clare de C, dau of Archie A de C Hunter, and has:

1b +A son; *b* 1989
1b *Georgia; *b* 1991

1a *Sarah Marguerite; *b* 12 Jan 1960; *m* 1989 *Hugh Grootenhuis, s of Peter Grootenhuis

(2) +John Pelham, MC [Maj John Mann MC, 290 Weed St, New Canaan, CT 06840, USA]; *b* 13 June 1919; *educ* Eton and Pembroke Coll Cambridge; Maj Scots Gds WW II; *m* 3 Oct 1942 (*divorce* 1975) Ann Marguerite, only dau of Col John Graham Brockbank, CBE, DSO, RTR, of The Manor House, Steeple Langford, Wilts; *m* 2nd 1978 *Isabel, dau of Dr Alton Ochsner, of New Orleans, and has by his 1st w:

1a +James John Francis [James Mann Esq, Bricklayers Farm, West Woodhay, Berks RG15 0BP]; *b* 4 April 1946; *educ* Eton; *m* 1976 (*divorce*1994) Effie Sarah Anne, dau of Norman Hepple, RA, and has:

1b +Thomas James; *b* 1979
2b +Frederick John; *b* 1986
1b *Rachel Poppy Jillian; *b* 1977

2a +Charles Edward Lionel; *b* 24 Jan 1948; *educ* Eton; *m* 1980 *Jane, dau of Thomas Elliott, and has:

1b *Charlotte Joanna; *b* 1981

1a *Celia Marguerite [Celia Lady Norrie, 17 Fairview Rd, Hungerford, Berks RG17 0BP]; *b* 21 Sept 1943; *m* 10 April 1964 (*divorce* 1997) 2nd Baron Norrie (*qv*) and has issue

(1) *Joan Elizabeth [The Rt Hon The Lady Maclean, Wilderness House, Hampton Court Palace, Surrey KT8 9AR]; *b* 30 May 1923; *m* 7 June 1941 Baron Maclean (LP) and has issue (*see* MACLEAN, Bt, of Dowart)

(2) *Margaret Enid [Mrs Patrick Simonds, Manor Farm, Syde, Cheltenham, Glos GL53 6PN]; *b* 13 Dec 1924, WRNS WW II; *m* 7 Nov 1951 *Maj (Seaton) Patrick Hayes Simonds, MC, RA, est surv s of Maj Maurice Hayes Simonds, and has:

1a *Peter Hayes; *b* 18 May 1966; *educ* Cheltenham, Bristol U and Hughes Hall Cambridge; *m* 1990 *Karen Louise, dau of Daniel Smith, of Wellesly, Landkey, Barnstaple, and has:

1b *George Hayes; *b* 5 Oct 1995
1b *Alexandra Margaret; *b* 18 March 1997
2b *Hannah Louise; *b* 18 March 1997

1a *Susan Enid; *b* 28 Jan 1954; *m* 1978 (*divorce* 1983) Timothy Rees

2a *Anne Margaret [Mrs John Treadwell, 66 Howards Lane, London SW15 6QD]; *b* 18 Feb 1958; *m* 1989 *John Treadwell, s of Lt-Col G W Treadwell, OBE, and has:

1b *Edward James Christopher; *b* 1 July 1991
2b *William Patrick John; *b* 30 Nov 1994
1b *Louisa Frances; *b* 19 Feb 1993

3a *Nicola Mary; b 1 March 1968
4a *Catherine Elizabeth; b 14 July 1970
4 Charles Julian; b 14 April 1892; Lt 14th Hus WWI; ka 3 Oct 1918
1 Fanny Julia; b 20 Dec 1896; m July 1947 Reginald Stanley Henry Warn

MANNERS

POUR·Y·PARVENIR

Arms: Or two bars az, a chief quarterly az. and gu., the 1st and 4th quarters charged with two fleurs-de-lys or, the 2nd and 3rd with a lion of England. **Crest:** On a chapeau gu. doubled erm. a peacock in his pride ppr. **Supporters:** Dexter, a unicorn arg, armed, maned, tufted and unguled or, charged on the shoulder with a cross flory az.; sinister, a like unicorn, charged on the shoulder with a portcullis sa. **Motto:** *Pour y parvenir* ('So as to accomplish it').
Creation: B. (UK) 20 April 1807.

THE 5TH BARON MANNERS OF FOSTON, Co Lincoln (John Robert Cecil Manners, DL (Hants 1987)) [The Rt Hon The Lord Manners DL, Sabines, Avon, Dorset BH23 7BQ]; b 13 Feb 1923; s f 1972; educ Eton and Trin Coll Oxford; F/Lt RAFVR WW II, slr Supreme Court 1949, consultant Osborne, Clarke & Co, slrs (ptnr 1952–84), Official Verderer New Forest 1983–93; m 6 Oct 1949 Jennifer Selena (d 4 May 1996), only dau of (Stephen) Ian Fairbairn, and has:

1 +JOHN HUGH ROBERT [The Hon John Manners, 14 North Ripley, Avon, Dorset BH23 8EP]; b 5 May 1956; educ Eton; m 1983 *Lanya Mary Patricia, dau of Dr H E Heitz and Mrs Ian Jackson, and has:

(1) *Harriet Frances Mary; b 1988
(1) *Catherine Mary Patricia; b 1992

1 *Venetia Jane [The Hon Mrs Colborne-Malpas, Keeper's Cottage, Ramsdell, Hants RG26 5SH]; b 30 July 1950; m 1972 *Alasdair John Colborne-Malpas, est s of Lt-Col John Frederick Colborne-Malpas, RN

2 *Selena Mary [The Hon Mrs Langlands, Hartgrove House, Shaftesbury, Dorset SP7 0JY]; b 4 Oct 1952; m 1974 *Maj Christopher Jeremy George Langlands, 1st Queen's Dragoon Gds, and has:

(1) *Andrew Charles; b 1981
(2) *George William; b 1987
(1) *Lucinda Mary; b 1977

Barony of Manners: A title under this name was created by writ of summons to the Parliament of 1309 in favour of Baldwin de Manners, whose father Walter had supported Simon de Montfort against HENRY III and been killed at the Battle of Evesham 1265. Baldwin died without issue in 1320. No connection has been established between him and the Mannerses subsequently created Dukes of Rutland (qv), the first of which was called in 1679 to Parliament during his father's lifetime as Lord Manners (of Haddon).

Lineage: Lord GEORGE MANNERS-SUTTON (see RUTLAND, D) had a 5th s:

THOMAS MANNERS-SUTTON, **1st Baron Manners of Foston**, Co Lincoln (UK), so cr 20 April 1807, PC (GB April I May 1807), KC (1800); b 24 Feb 1756; educ Charterhouse and Emmanuel Coll Cambridge; barrister Lincoln's Inn 1775, Commr Bankrupts 1783, MP (Tory) Newark 1796–1805, Ch Justice N Wales 1797–1802, Slr-Gen to PRINCE OF WALES 1800 and GB 1802–05, ktd 1802, a Baron Exchequer 1805–07, Ld Chllr Ireland 1807–27, V-Chllr Dublin U 1826; m 1st 4 Nov 1803 Anne (dsp 5 Aug 1814), dau of Sir Joseph Copley, Bt, of Sprotsborough; m 2nd 28 Oct 1815 Jane (d 2 Nov 1846), dau of 9th Baron Caher and sis of 1st Earl of Glengall, and d 31 May 1842, having by her had:

JOHN THOMAS MANNERS-SUTTON, **2nd Baron Manners of Foston**; b 17 Aug 1818; m 28 Sept 1848 Lydia Sophia (d 1 Feb 1916), 3rd dau of V-Adml William Bateman Dashwood, and d 14 Nov 1864, leaving:

1 JOHN THOMAS, **3rd Baron**
2 Arthur; b 19 July 1855; Capt 15th Hus; d unm 24 Aug 1888
3 Claud Henry; b 15 Sept 1856; d unm 6 July 1913
4 Charles William; b 26 Feb 1859; d unm 14 July 1879
1 Mildred Jane; d unm 16 Feb 1935
2 Mary Theresa; m 6 Dec 1881 Col Ralph Leeke, Gren Gds (d 30 Oct 1943), of Longford Hall, Newport, Salop, and d 21 Aug 1947, leaving issue

3 Etheldreda Mary; m 29 Oct 1891 Maj-Gen Bertram Reveley Mitford, CB, CMG, DSO (d 23 Feb 1936), and d 17 Nov 1950, leaving issue

The 2nd BARON's est s,

JOHN THOMAS MANNERS-SUTTON later MANNERS, **3rd Baron Manners of Foston**; b 15 May 1852; educ Eton and Trin Coll Cambridge (MA); 20th MFH Quorn, rode in only two races throughout his entire life (Grand National on Seaman 1882 and Grand Military Gold Cup on Lord Chancellor 1882) and won both; Lt Gren Gds 1857–83, Capt 3rd Bn Hants Regt; m 1st 12 Aug 1885 Constance Edwina Adeline (d 4 March 1920), dau of Col Henry Edward Hamlyn Fane, MP, of Clovelly, Devon, and Avon Tyrrell, Hants (see WESTMORLAND, E); m 2nd 5 Sept 1922 Zoë Virginie (d 28 Nov 1953), dau of Albert Llewellyn Nugent, 3rd Baron Nugent (Austria; see WESTMEATH, E), and widow of Claud Hume Campbell Guinness (see GUINNESS, Bt), and d 19 Aug 1927, having by his 1st w had:

1 John Neville; b 6 Jan 1892; educ Balliol Coll Oxford; Lt Gren Gds (despatches); ka France 2 Sept 1914
2 FRANCIS HENRY, **4th Baron**
1 Mary Christine; b 4 Dec1886; d unm 15 Feb 1904
2 Betty Constance; b 15 June 1889; inherited 1936 Clovelly Court, Devon, from her aunt Mrs Hamlyn; m 30 April 1918 Brig-Gen Hon Arthur Melland Asquith, DSO, 3rd s of 1st Earl of Oxford and Asquith (qv), and d 12 Sept 1962, leaving issue
3 Angela Margaret, ARRC; b 15 June 1889; m 26 May 1925 Col Hon Christian Malise Hore-Ruthven, CMG, DSO (d 3 May 1969; see CARLISLE, E), and d 1 Feb 1970, leaving issue

The 3rd BARON's est surv s,

FRANCIS HENRY MANNERS, **4th Baron Manners of Foston**, JP (1933), DL (1939), MC; b 21 July 1897; educ Eton and Trin Coll Cambridge; Lt-Col and Brevet Col 5th/7th Bn Hants Regt, Capt Res Offrs Gren Gds WWs I (despatches) and II, CA Hants 1952; m 29 Jan 1921 Mary Edith (d 1994), twin dau of Rt Rev Lord William Rupert Gascoyne-Cecil, DD, Bp Exeter (see SALISBURY, M), and d 1972, leaving:

1 JOHN ROBERT CECIL MANNERS, **5th and present Baron Manners of Foston**
2 +Richard Neville [The Hon Richard Manners, South Wing, Cromer Hall, Norfolk]; b 4 April 1924; educ Eton; m 14 July 1945 *Juliet Mary, est dau of Sir Edward Preston, 5th Bt (qv), and has:

(1) +Edward Preston [Edward Manners Esq, Askania, Askania Park, Ourimbah, NSW 2258, Australia]; b 8 April 1948; educ Gresham's; m 1973 *Catherine, dau of Mr Justice (William) Ash, of NSW, and has:

1a *Sarah; b 1981

(2) +Rupert Francis Henry [Rupert Manners Esq, Box 788, Armidale, NSW 2350, Australia]; b 13 April 1950; educ Gresham's; m 1975 *Wyn, dau of W Miller, of Sydney, and has:

1a +Stephen Francis; b 1978
1a +Philip; b 1979

(3) +(Thomas) Benjamin MANNERS later CABBELL MANNERS [Benjamin Cabbell-Manners, West Wing, Cromer Hall, Cromer, Norfolk]; b 12 Aug 1954; educ Gresham's; m 1981 *Diana (Dido) Dorothy Elizabeth, yr dau of Maj Anthony Richard Gurney, and has:

1a +Rupert; b 1990
2a +Hugh; b 1993
1a *Jessica; b 1990 (twin)

(1) *Christine Margaret Lavender [Mrs Timothy Pallister, The Old Vicarage, Tunstead, Norfolk NR12 8HT]; b 19 Aug 1946; m 1970 *Timothy John Barry Pallister and has:

1a *James Francis Timothy; b 1971
2a *Richard John; b 1976
1a *Charlotte Henrietta; b 1972

3 +Thomas Jasper [The Hon Thomas Manners, Old Malt House, Ashford Hill, Thatcham, Berks RG19 8BN]; b 12 Dec 1929; educ Eton; m 29 March 1955 *Sarah, er dau of Brig Roger Peake, DSO, OBE, of The Manor House, Little Missenden, Bucks, and has:

(1) +Charles Henry [Charles Manners Esq, Christacorn House, Woodend, Towcester, Northants NN12 8RX]; b 21 Oct 1957; m 1986 *Nichola E, dau of Peter Thompson, and has:

1a +Joseph Peter; b 1991
1a *Zoe; b 1989
2a *Mary; b 1994

(2) +Arthur Roger [Arthur Manners Esq, Wardens Lodge, Knowl Hill, Kingsclere, Hants RG20 8PA]; b 29 July 1959; m 1984 *Anna, dau of Roger Ryland, and has:

1a +Hugo; b 1989
1a *Olivia
2a *Laura; b 1996

(3) +Robert Hugh [Robert Manners Esq, The Barn House, Kimpton, Andover SP11 8NU]; b 14 Dec 1962; m 1989 *Samantha S, dau of Richard Jukes, and has:

1a +Archie Thomas; b 1993
2a +Orlando Douglas; b 9 Nov 1995

1 *Patricia Anne Manners; b 13 May 1927; m 6 April 1946 John Bonham Kidston (d 26 Sept 1968), only s of George Jardine Kidston (see BONHAM, Bt), and has:

(1) *Francis George; b 1947
(2) *Jonathan James; b 1951; m 1981 *Joanna R, dau of Col Michael Panton
(1) *Virginia Lilian; b 1953

MANSEL

Arms: Argent a chevron between three maunches sable. **Crest:** A cap of maintenance gules doubled ermine, enflamed on the top proper. **Motto:** *Quod vult valde vult* ('What he wishes, he wishes fervently'). **Creation:** Bt. (E) 14 Jan 1621/2.

SIR PHILIP MANSEL, 15TH BT, of Muddlescombe, Co Carmarthen [Sir Philip Mansel Bt, 2 Deyncourt Close, Darras Hall, Ponteland, Northumberland NE20 9RP]; *b* 3 March 1943; *s* 6 April 1947; *educ* Carlisle GS and Grosvenor Coll Carlisle; md Eden-Vale Engrg, Fell Inst Sales Management; *m* 24 Aug 1968 *Margaret, only dau of Arthur Docker, of Hainings Gate, Moorhouse, Carlisle, and has:

  1 +JOHN PHILIP; *b* 19 April 1982

  2 +Richard James; *b* 1990

  1 *Nicol; *b* 1978

Lineage: The origins of this family, whose name is spelled variously MANSEL, MANSELL, MAUNSELL and even MANSFEELD well into the 17th century, are not easily pinpointed.

One WALTER MANSEL; *b c* 1166; held serjeanty (type of tenure based on service to a superior lord) of Little Missenden, Bucks, and other lands in Bucks, Berks and Staffs; *m* Hawisia, dau of John de Somerie, and may have been f of:

JOHN MANSEL or MAUNSELL; appointed 1234 to a position in the roy exchequer, possibly as Chllr; served in expdn sent by HENRY III 1238 to assist the Holy Roman Emperor against various towns in N Italy; designated Prebendary of Thame, Oxon, 1241 but declined to take up post in deference to feelings of Bp Grosseteste; went with HENRY III to France 1242 and was present at Battle of Saintes (skirmish between French and English attempting to recover the Angevin domains), ch adviser to HENRY III from 1244, envoy to arrange royal marriage alliances with Brabant 1247, Scotland 1251 and Castile 1253–54, also with French 1256 and electors of Holy Roman Empire in Germany 1256, roy delegate to arrange implementation of Provisions of Oxford (concessions for governing England won from HENRY III by barons) 1258, held bishopric of Durham in temporal capacity while actual see vacant 1260; said to have held up to 300 benefices and was principally: Chllr St Paul's 1243, Dean Wimborne Minster 1246, Provost Beverley 1247 and Treasurer York 1256; Keeper Gt Seal 1246–47, 1248–49 and 1262; *d* 20 Jan 1265.

But the JOHN MANSEL mentioned above was a clerk (cleric), albeit a worldly pluralist, who is therefore unlikely to have married. Again, his f is said to have been a rural priest rather than the considerable landed proprietor implied by a list of WALTER MANSEL's holdings. Then again, another JOHN MANSEL held land contemporaneously at Rossington, Yorks.

Nevertheless a JOHN MA(U)NSEL(L) apparently *m* Joan, dau of Simon Beauchamp, of Bedford, and had:

  1 THOMAS (Sir)

  2 Walter; was granted Munster 20 Jan 1251 as tenant-in-chief, Govr Occonath Castle 1 March 1251

  3 Richard; living 20 April 1284

  4 Robert; Sheriff Tipperary 1304

  5 Philip; living 1307

The est s,

  Sir THOMAS MA(U)NSEL(L); Kt Banneret, Escheator (roy official implementing escheats, or reversions of land to its lord on a tenant's death) Bucks 1251, and Jurat (memb of a borough cncl) Essex 1255, wounded and captured at Siege of Northampton (during civil war between HENRY III and Simon De Montfort's party) 1264; held lands in Oxon, Bucks and Berks; *m* 1st Hana, dau of Sir Henry Grey; *m* 2nd Johanna — and by his 1st w had, with other issue:

HENRY MA(U)NSEL(L); apparently the first of the family to settle in Glamorgan; *m* Elina/Ellinor, dau of Hugh Haels, and had, with other issue, an est s:

Sir WALTER MA(U)NSEL(L); Kt of the Sepulchre, held manor of Missenden, Bucks, as a tenant-in-chief of EDWARD I; *m* Emma, dau of Sir William Langton, and *d c* 1327, leaving:

Sir ROBERT MA(U)NSEL(L), of Missenden; Kt of the Sepulchre; *m* Dorothy, dau of Sir Richard Fry, and had:

RICHARD MA(U)NSEL(L); *m* Lucy, dau and heiress of Philip Scurlage, of Scurlage Castle, Glamorgan, and had:

Sir HUGH MA(U)NSEL(L); living 1367; *m* Elizabeth, dau and heiress of Sir John Penrys, of Penrice, nr Oxwich in the Gower Peninsula, and left issue:

Sir RICHARD MA(U)NSEL(L), of Oxwich; *m* Elizabeth, dau of Hamon Turberville, and *d* 1435, having had:

JOHN MA(U)NSEL(L); *m* Cecily, dau and heiress of Sir William Cantelupe or Cauntelo, and *dvp*, leaving:

PHILIP MA(U)NSEL(L); Lancastrian in Wars of Roses (attainted in Parl 1464 during Yorkist ascendancy), captured at Battle of Tewkesbury (decisive Yorkist victory) 1471 and beheaded; *m* 1st *c* 1444 Mabel, dau of Griffiths or Griffith ap Nicolas, of Newton, Carmarthenshire; *m* 2nd *c* 1460 Elizabeth, dau and heiress of Sir Philip Long; his est surv s by his 1st w:

JENKIN MA(U)NSEL(L); got his f's attainder reversed 1486; *m* Edith, dau and coheir of Sir George Kyme, of Kent, and had, with four daus:

  1 RICE (Sir)

  2 Hugh; *m* Jane, dau and coheir of Richard Owgan, of Kent

  3 Philip; *m* Anne, dau of W Danbridgecourt

JENKIN MA(U)NSEL(L)'s est s,

  Sir RICE MA(U)NSEL(L); ktd *c* 1536, led troops to help Ld Deputy of Ireland suppress the rebellion of 10th Earl of Kildare (*see* LEINSTER, D) *c* 1536; Chamberlain Co Palatine of Chester 1537, granted former monastic lands at Margam, Glamorgan; *m* 1st Eleanor, dau of James Basset, but had no surv issue; *m* 2nd Anne, dau of Sir Giles Bruges, and had three sons (all *dvp*) and two surv daus; *m* 3rd Cecily, dau of John Danbridgecourt, of Stratfield Saye, Hants, and *d c* 1559, leaving by her (with a yr s and dau):

Sir EDWARD MA(U)NSEL(L); ktd 1572, Chamberlain Co Palatine of Chester; *m* Lady Jane Somerset (*d* 16 Oct 1597), yst dau of 2nd Earl of Worcester (*see* BEAUFORT, D), and *d* 5 Aug 1595, having had, with other issue:

  1 Sir THOMAS MA(U)NSEL(L), 1st Bt (E), so *cr* 22 May 1611; ktd by 1593, Sheriff Glamorgan 1593–94, 1603–04 and 1622–23; *m* 1st 30 May 1582 Mary Mordaunt, dau of 3rd Lord (Baron) Mordaunt; *m* 2nd Jane, dau of Thomas Pole/Powell and widow of (a) John Fuller and (b) John Bussey, and *d* 20 Dec 1631, leaving by his 1st w:

  (1) Sir LEWIS MA(U)NSEL(L), 2nd Bt; *b c* 1594; *educ* BNC Oxford and Lincoln's Inn; ktd 1603, Sheriff Glamorgan 1636–37; *m* 1st after 1603 Lady Katharine Sydney (*dsp*), dau of 1st Earl of Leicester (*see* DE L'ISLE, V); *m* 2nd Katharine (*dspm*), dau of Sir Edward Lewis, of Vann, Glamorgan; *m* 3rd 25 Aug 1627 Lady Elizabeth Montagu, dau of 1st Earl of Manchester (*see* MANCHESTER, D), and *d* 4 April 1638, leaving:

  1a Sir HENRY MA(U)NSEL(L), 3rd Bt; *b c* 1630; *d c* 1640

  2a Sir EDWARD MA(U)NSEL(L), 4th Bt; *b c* 1637; MP Glamorgan 1660, 1670–79, 1681 and 1685–87, appointed Sheriff Glam 1688 but refused to undertake duties of office; *m c* 1665 Martha, dau and coheir of Edward Carne, of Ewenny, Glam, and *d* 17 Nov 1706, having had issue, with an er s (*d* young):

  1b Sir THOMAS MA(U)NSEL(L), 5th Bt, 1st BARON MANSELL OF MARGAM (GB), so *cr* 1 Jan 1711/2 (one of eight peers *cr* that day to give the Tory administration a majority in the Ho of Lds), PC (1704–08 and 1711–14), of Penrice and Margam; *b c* 1668; *educ* Jesus Coll Oxford (BA 1686, MA 1699); MP (Tory) Cardiff 1689–98 and Glamorgan 1699–1712, a Commr Treasury 1710–11, a Teller Exchequer 1712–14, Sheriff Glam 1700–01, V-Adml S Wales 1704, Comptroller Household to QUEEN ANNE 1704–08 and 1711–12, Govr Milford Haven 1713–14; *m* 18 May 1686 Martha (*d* 10 June 1718), only dau and heir of Francis Millington, a London merchant, and *d* 10 Dec 1723, having had, with three other daus:

  1c Robert; *b* 2 Nov 1695; *m c* April 1718 Anne (she *m* 2nd John Blackwood; *d* 20 Oct 1741), dau and coheir of Adml Sir Cloudesley Shovel, of May Place, Crayford, Kent and *dvp* 29 April 1723, leaving:

  1d Sir THOMAS MA(U)NSEL(L), 6th Bt, 2nd BARON MANSELL OF MARGAM; *b* 26 Dec 1719; *educ* Ch Ch Oxford; sat as Tory in Ho of Lds; *d* unm 29 Jan 1743/4

  2c Sir CHRISTOPHER MA(U)NSEL(L), 7th Bt, 3rd BARON MANSELL OF MARGAM; Tory in Ho of Lds; *d* unm 26 Nov 1744

  3c Sir BUSSY MA(U)NSEL(L), 8th and last Bt of the 1611 *cr* and 4th and last BARON MANSELL OF MARGAM; MP (Tory) Cardiff 1723–34 and Glamorgan 1737–44; *m* 1st 17 May 1724 Lady Elizabeth Hervey (*b* 9 Dec 1697; *dsp* Sept 1727), dau of 1st Earl of Bristol of the 1714 *cr* (*see* BRISTOL, M); *m* 2nd 13 March 1728/9 Lady Barbara *née* Villiers, only dau of 2nd Earl of Jersey (*qv*) and widow of Sir William Blackett, 2nd Bt of the Jan 1684/5 *cr* (*see* BLACKETT, Bt, of Newcastle), and *dspm* 29 Nov 1750, when his titles expired

  1c Martha

  2c Elizabeth

  3c Mary; *m* John Ivory Talbot, of Lacock Abbey, Wilts, and had issue

  2 FRANCIS (Sir), **1st Bt**

  3 Robert (Sir); *b* 1573; served in naval expedn against Cadiz 1596, commanded small squadron off Ireland 1600, naval cdr in English Channel with title of 'V-Adml of the Narrow Seas' 1603, Treasurer of the Navy 1604–18, V-Adml of England 1618; MP: King's Lynn 1601, Carmarthen 1603, Carmarthenshire 1614, Glamorgan 1623, 1625 and 1627–28 and Lostwithiel 1626; granted by JAMES I *c* 1617 exclusive right to manufacture glass; *m* 1st by 1600 Elizabeth, dau of Sir Nicholas Bacon, 1st Bt (*qv*); *m* 2nd 1617 Anne (Maid of Honour to QUEEN ANNE (OF DENMARK), w of JAMES I; *d* 1663), dau of Sir John Roper, and *dsp* by 20 June 1656

Sir EDWARD MA(U)NSEL(L)'s 2nd s,

Sir Francis Mansel(l), 1st Bt (E), so *cr* 14 Jan 1621/2, of Mud(d)lescombe, Carmarths; Sheriff Carmarths 1594–95 and 1610–11; *m* 1st Catharine, dau and coheir of Henry Morgan, of Muddlescombe, and had, with three other daus:

1 **Sir Walter Mansel, 2nd Bt**; *bapt* 25 July 1586; *educ* Oriel Coll Oxford (BA 1603) and Lincoln's Inn 1605; *m* 11 Dec 1623 Elizabeth (*d* 11 Sept 1643), dau of Charles Fotherby, Dean Canterbury, and was *bur* Kidwelly 12 April 1640, having had, with three other daus (*d* young):

  (1) **Sir Francis Mansel, 3rd Bt**; *bapt* 9 May 1633; *d* unm 27 Oct 1654

  (1) Elizabeth; *bapt* 21 Oct 1631; *m* 1672 Thomas Bro(o)me (*d* 1673), Serjeant-at-Law, of Tuppendence, Kent

2 Anthony (Sir); ktd 19 July 1629, Sheriff Glam 1630–31; *m* Jane, dau and heiress of William Price, of Briton Ferry, and widow of Arthur Mansel, and was *k* fighting on the Royalist side at Second Battle of Newbury 27 Oct 1644 (in which Parly forces blocked CHARLES I's advance on London but failed to prevent him withdrawing to Oxford), leaving, with other issue:

  (1) **Sir Edward Mansel, 4th Bt**, of Mud(d)lescombe; Sheriff Carmarths 1661; *m* Jane (*d* by 1692), dau of Humphrey Wyndham, of Dunraven, Glam, and widow of Sir Roger Lort, 1st Bt, of Stacpoole, Pembs, and *dspms* by 10 March 1690/1

3 Francis; *bapt* 23 March 1578/9; *educ* free sch Hereford and Jesus Coll Oxford (BA Feb 1608/9, MA 1611, BD and DD 1624); Fell All Souls 1614, Pncpl Jesus Coll Oxford June–Nov or Dec 1620 and 1630–61 (ejected for royalist proclivities 1648 but restored 1660), Rector: Easington, Oxon, 1630 and Elmley Chapel, Kent, 1631, Preb St Davids 1631, Treasurer Llandaff 1631; *d* 1 May 1665

4 Richard; *m* 14 Feb 1612/3 Catherine (*d* 27 Jan 1631/2), dau and heiress of Rees Morgan, of Iscoed, and *d* between 1634 and 17 March 1635/6, leaving, with other issue:

  (1) Anthony; *bapt* 6 March 1613/4; BA Oxford 1635; *m* Mary (*d* Aug 1667), dau of Sir Edward Carne, of Nash, by Ann Mansel, of Margam, and *d* Dec 1670, leaving:

    1a Anthony; *dsp* and was *bur* 4 April 1679

    2a **Sir Richard Mansel, 5th Bt**, of Iscoed; *bapt* 6 Jan 1641; *m* Alice (*bur* 11 Dec 1689), dau and heiress of Rees Davies, of Pentre-yr-istill, Swansea, Glam, and was *bur* 24 Aug 1691, leaving:

      1b **Sir Richard Mansel, 6th Bt**, of Iscoed; *d* unm 1696

      2b **Sir William Mansel, 7th Bt**, of Iscoed and Clonakilty, Co Cork; *bapt* 15 March 1670; *m* 18 Oct 1700 Amy (*b* 29 June 1684), 4th dau of Sir Richard Cox, 1st Bt, Ld Chllr Ireland, and *d c* 1732, having had, with a yr s and three daus:

        1c RICHARD (Sir), **8th Bt**

Sir Francis *m* 2nd his s-in-law's sis Dorothy, sis of Sir John Stepney, 1st Bt, of Prendergast, Pembs, and dau of Alban Stepney by Mary Philips (*see* SAINT DAVIDS, V), and *d c* 1628, having by her had:

5 John; *bapt* 8 Dec 1611; *m* Mary, dau of Sir Henry Vaughan, of Derwydd, and widow of Charles Philips, and had:

  (1) Henry, of Stradey, Carmarths; *m* as her 1st husb Frances, only dau of Sir John Stepney, 2nd Bt, of Prendergast, and *d* by 1683, leaving:

    1a Sir EDWARD MANSEL(L), 1st Bt (E), so *cr* 22 Feb 1696/7, of Trimsaran, Carmarths; admitted Lincoln's Inn 1683, Sheriff Carmarths 1689; *m* Dorothy (*d* Sept 1721), sis and heir of Edward Vaughan, of Trimsaran, and widow of — Lloyd, and *d* 19 Feb 1719/20, having had, with ten other children:

      1b Sir EDWARD MANSEL, 2nd Bt, of Trimsaran and Stradey; Sheriff Carmarths 1728–29; *m* 1st Anne (*dsp* 1 Nov 1731), dau of Thomas Price, of Garth Llwyn, Caernarvs; *m* 2nd Nov 1740 Mary, widow of — Bayley, and *d* 10 May or 4 Nov 1754, leaving:

        1c Sir EDWARD VAUGHAN MANSEL, 3rd Bt, of Trimsaran and Stradey; Sheriff Carmarths 1778; *m* Mary, dau of Joseph Shewen, of Swansea, and *d* Jan 1788, leaving:

          1d Sir EDWARD JOSEPH SHEWEN MANSEL, 4th and last Bt of the Feb 1696/7 *cr*; *d* unm 6 April 1798, when the btcy expired

6 Edward, of Beauley, Carmarths; Army Capt; *m* Honor (*d* Dec 1660), dau of Thomas William Lloyd, of Alltycadno, and *d* May 1671, leaving:

  (1) Rawleigh; *m* as her 2nd husb his 1st cousin's widow Frances, dau of Sir John Stepney, 2nd Bt, and widow of Henry Mansel

7 Rawleigh; *b* 1622; *m* Ann, dau of Sir Richards Philips, of Picton, and *dsp* 1674

1 Jane; *m* Sir John Stepney, 1st Bt, and *d* in or after Jan 1628/9

2 Cicely; *m* George Jones, of Abercothy, Carmarths

The 7th Bt's er s,

Sir Richard Mansel, 8th Bt, of Iscoed, Pembrey, Carmarths, and Woodstone, Co Cork; *m* 1st 1732 Susanna Warner; *m* 2nd 1737 Rebecca (*bur* 8 Dec 1791), est dau of William Ware, of Farrana Lough, Co Cork, and was *bur* 20 Feb 1749, leaving by his 2nd w an only s:

Sir William Mansel, 9th Bt, of Iscoed and Woodstone; *b* 1 March 1738/9; Sheriff Carmarths 1781–82, MP Carmarths 1784; *m* 26 Aug 1765 Mary (*d* 27 Dec 1811), only dau of John Philipps, of Coedgaing, Carmarths, and was *bur* 14 Jan 1804, having had, with other issue:

1 **Sir William Mansel, 10th Bt**; *b* 29 April 1766; *m* Dec 1790 Elizabeth (*d* 12 Aug 1843), dau and heiress of John Bell, of Harefield, Middx, and *d* 1829, having had:

  (1) William John (Rev); *b* 1792; Rector Ellesborough, Bucks; *m* 27 July 1814 Harriet Charlotte (*d* 19 Jan 1877), 3rd dau of Laver Oliver, of Brill House, Bucks, and *dvp* 5 April 1823, leaving:

    1a Elizabeth Harriet Anne; *m* 1st 2 June 1842 Sir Thomas Phillipps, 1st and last Bt (*d* 1872), of Middle Hill; *m* 2nd 3 Aug 1875 Rev George Digby and *d* 5 Nov 1879

    2a Caroline Mary; *m* 28 July 1847 Rev Frederick Leigh Colvile (*d* 28 March 1886), of Kempsey House, Worcs, Vicar Leek Wootton, Warwicks, and *d* 5 June 1907, having had issue

    3a Frances Henrietta; *m* 3 Feb 1853 Rev Cuthbert John Carr (*d* 30 Oct 1888), Rector Witton Gilnert and Kimblesworth, Co Durham, and *d* 5 March 1877, leaving issue

    4a Augusta; *m* 21 Oct 1845 Rev Heller Touzel, MA (*dsp* 1888), Rector Martyr Worthy, Hants, and *d* Dec 1905

  (2) **Sir John Bell William Mansel, 11th Bt**, JP, DL; *b* 5 Oct 1806; barrister Lincoln's Inn 1831, High Sheriff Carmarths 1846; *m* 31 July 1832 Mary Georgiana (*b* 7 Feb 1801; *d* 18 Oct 1888 aged 81), sis of Sir Henry Dymoke, 1st Bt (*see* 1866 edn), and *dspm* 14 April 1883, leaving:

    1a Maria Emma; *m* 2 Sept 1869 Sir Edward Bradford Medlycott, 4th Bt (*qv*), and *d* 1 May 1912, leaving issue

    2a Elizabeth; *d* unm 5 April 1928

    3a Emma Jane (twin); *d* unm 26 June 1923

2 Richard MANSEL later PHILIPPS (roy licence 24 Jan 1793), of Coedgaing; *b c* 1777; Cdr RN; *m* 17 Aug 1797 Caroline (*d* 20 Sept 1850), only dau and heiress of B Bond Hopkins, MP, and *d* 20 Aug 1844, leaving:

  (1) Courtenay PHILIPPS later MANSEL (roy licence 12 May 1866); *b* 13 Jan 1801; Maj 15th; *m* in Scotland *c* 1838 for the first time Eliza, dau of Rev John Sidney (a decree in the Court of Session, Edinburgh, validating this marriage in Scotland was obtained 9 Nov 1906; up till then, or at any rate up till 1903 (*see* below), lack of general recognition of the validity of the 1838 marriage had led to Edward Berkeley Mansel being regarded as illegitimate, hence unable to assume the title), and had:

    1a Sir EDWARD BERKELEY PHILIPPS later MANSEL, **12th**(b) **Bt**, JP (Suffolk and Norfolk), of Old Catton House, Norwich; *b* 2 Feb 1839; Hon Col and Lt-Col 1st Vol Bn Norfolk Regt, previously 15th Hus and 6th Dragoons; from 1903 assumed the title with the consent of his n COURTENAY (*see* below), whose f RICHARD had been the titular (for such he must *ex post facto* be supposed) **12th Bt** (a) from 14 April 1883 (when Sir JOHN BELL WILLIAM MANSEL, **11th Bt**, *d*) to his (RICHARD's) death on 2 June 1892; nevertheless the assumption by Sir EDWARD of the title was not recognised by Col Edmund Morton Mansel-Pleydell (*see* below), who until the birth 1910 of Sir JOHN PHILIP FERDINAND MANSEL, **14th Bt**, was the heir presumptive; *m* 7 May 1870 Julia Vertue (*m* 2nd 6 Oct 1912 Rev Canon Stanley Swinburne, Rector Radcliffe, Lancs, and *d* 13 June 1944), er dau of Rev Henry Evans Lombe, of Bylaugh Park, and Melton Hall, Norfolk, and *dsp* 8 Jan 1908

    1a Eliza; *b* 16 May 1843; *m* 1 Sept 1881 Richard R Cole and had issue

    2a Florence; *b* 12 Jan 1845; *m* 1 Oct 1867 Charles Rhodes (*d* 1882) and had issue

    3a Caroline; *b* 3 June 1846; *m* 1st George Mervyn (*d* 7 May 1900); *m* 2nd 12 Dec 1881 Richard George Ford and *dsp* 26 April 1890

  (1) (cont.) Maj Courtenay PHILIPPS later MANSEL *m* for the second time (at St Paul's, Liverpool) 7 June 1847 Eliza etc (*d* 23 May 1879) and *d* 9 Sept 1875, having had further issue:

    2a Courtenay; *b* 4 May 1848; *d* unm 5 Jan 1874

    3a Sir RICHARD PHILIPPS later MANSEL, **12th** (a) **Bt**, of Coedgaing, Carmarths; *b* 2 Dec 1850; *educ* Eton; declared bankrupt Aug 1883; *m* 1st 4 Sept 1878 Maud Margaretta Bowen (*d* 12 Sept 1885), dau of John Jones, of Maes-y-crugiau Hall, Carmarths; *m* 2nd 1891 Ada Alice (*d* 1916), music hall entertainer and dau of James Lea, and *d* 2 June 1892, having had by his 1st w an only s:

      1b COURTENAY CECIL (Sir), **13th Bt**

    4a Arthur; *b c* 1852; *d* an infant

    4a Harriot; *b* 13 Aug 1849; *m* 6 Nov 1880 Henry Davies (*d* 29 Dec 1895) and *d* 12 Dec 1883, leaving:

  (2) Edward Berkeley; *b* 6 Aug 1803; Capt 53rd Regt; *m* 20 Aug 1831 Mary (*d* 22 Jan 1870), dau of Rev John Secker, and *dsp* 29 May 1879

  (1) Harriette; *m* 29 Aug 1823 Capt G C Carpenter, 15th Hus (*d* 8 April 1861), and *d* leaving issue

3 John, CB, of Smedmore, Dorset; *b* 16 Aug 1776; Col; *m* 1st Mary (*d* 25 July 1806); *m* 2nd July 1815 Louisa (*d* 6 May 1863), dau and heiress of Edmund Morton Pleydell, of Whatcombe House, and *d* 29 Jan 1863, leaving by her:

  (1) John Clavell MANSEL later MANSEL-PLEYDELL (1872), JP, DL (both Dorset), of Whatcombe, Dorset; *b* 4 Dec 1817; *educ* Cambridge (BA); Dorset: memb CC, High Sheriff 1876, FGS, FLS; *m* 1st 1844 Emily (*dsp* 1845), dau of Capt A B Bingham, RN; *m* 2nd 21 June 1849 Isabel (*d* 13 July 1912), dau of Capt Frederick Charles Acton Colvile, Scots Gds, by his w Mary, sis of 1st Baron Leigh (*qv*), and *d* 3 May 1902, having by her had:

    1a Edmund Morton, JP and DL (Dorset), of Whatcombe; *b* 30 June 1850; Col 12th Royal Lancers and Dorset Yeo Cav; *m* 6 June 1885 Emily Kathleen (*d* 30 March 1945), dau of Sir Thomas Fraser Grove, 1st Bt (*qv*), of Ferne, Wilts, and *d* 13 Oct 1914, leaving:

      1b Edmund Morton, of Whatcombe; *b* 23 Dec 1886; Lt 3rd Bn Dorsetshire Regt; *ka* 12 March 1915

      2b Henry Grove Morton, MC, of Whatcombe; *b* 20 March 1894; Lt 1st Bn Dorset Regt WW I (despatches, wounded); *ka* 15 May 1916

      1b Vivien, of Whatcombe; *b* 12 Sept 1889; *m* 22 April 1919 Lt-Col Henry George Moreton RAILSTON later PLEYDELL-RAILSTON (deed poll 1920), DSO, DL, Rifle Bde (*d* 23 Feb 1936), and had:

        1c *June [Mrs Richard Carlyle-Clarke, Clenston Manor, Blandford, Dorset]; *b* 23 July 1920; *m* 12 Aug 1950 *Richard John Saint-Clair Carlyle-Clarke, late 60th Rifles, s of William Carlyle-Clarke, of Salisbury, S Rhodesia, and has:

          1d *Giles Richard Morton [Giles Carlyle-Clarke Esq, Cottage in the Woods, Clenston, Dorset DT11 0NX]; *b* 23 July 1957; antique dealer; *m* 1st Jan 1992 (*divorce* 1994) Marcella Gazzolo and has:

            1e *Jessica; *b* 11 July 1992

          1d (cont.) Giles Carlyle-Clarke *m* 2nd June 1994 (*divorce* 1996) Sumiati, of Central Java, and has by her:

            1e *Maximilian Kusuma; *b* 4 Jan 1996

          1d *Caroline June; *b* 27 Jan 1952

        2c Patricia; *b* 8 Nov 1921; *m* 11 Aug 1951 Desmond Shane Chichester, yr s of Shane Randolph Chichester, OBE (*see* DONEGALL,M), and *d* 1987, leaving issue

      2b Daphne; *b* 20 July 1893; *m* 25 June 1919 Capt John Anthony Arnold-Forster, OBE, RFA (*d* 19 June 1958), s of Hugh Oakely Arnold-Forster, PC, MP (Lib U) W Belfast 1892–1906 and (U) Croydon 1906–09, Sec State War 1903–06, and had issue

2a John Colvile Morton (Rev Canon); *b* 21 Oct 1851; *educ* Trin Coll Cambridge (MA); Vicar Sturminster Newton, Dorset, 1899–1915, Canon and Preb Salisbury 1911–38; *m* 23 Oct 1879 Beatrice Maud (*d* 9 June 1940), est dau of Robert Smith, of Goldings, Herts, and *d* 12 July 1938, having had:

  1b John Morton; *b* 16 March 1884; *educ* Trin Coll Camb (BA); Lt RFA; *ka* 22 Sept 1916

  2b Evan Morton; *b* 16 March 1884; Lt RHA; *d* unm 22 May 1910

  3b Harry Percy Morton, OBE (1921); *b* 12 May 1891; Maj RFA WW I (despatches, Gallipoli 1915–16 and Mesopotamia 1916–21); *m* 6 Feb 1931 *Jessica Gertrude, dau of Richard Gerrard, of Bromley, Kent, and *dsp* 16 Jan 1960

  4b Ralph Morton; *b* 17 May 1895; Capt RFA WW I (despatches twice); *m* 11 Feb 1920 Countess Marguerite Marie Louise Barbe Ghislaine d'Ursel (*d* 4 Oct 1968), 4th dau of Count Aymard d'Ursel, of Brussels, and *d* 10 April 1932, leaving:

    1c John Aymard Morton; *b* 22 Nov 1920; *educ* Ampleforth; 2nd Lt Leics Regt; *ka* 17 Nov 1940

    2c +Philip Morton [Lt-Cdr Philip Mansel-Pleydell RN, 2 Lower Clenston, Winterborne Clenston, Dorset DT11 0NY]; *b* 16 Feb 1922; *educ* Ampleforth; Lt-Cdr (E) RN WW II and Korea 1951; *m* 21 Aug 1961 *Dagmar Rosalie, only dau of Theodore Louis Bowring, CMG, OBE, of Knsington, and has:

      1d +John Bowring Morton [John Mansel-Pleydell Esq, 06534 Flickinger Rd, Nev, OH 43549, USA]; *b* 2 Nov 1963; *m* 1995 *Rebecca, 4th dau of Robert Shininger, of Defiance, Ohio, and has:

        1e *Rose Magdalen; *b* 5 May 1996

      1d *Rosanna Vivien [Mme Rosanna Mansel-Pleydell, 10 Rue Aime Smekens, 1040 Schaerbeek, Belgium]; *b* 19 Feb 1965; *m* 1990 Werner van Zuylen, est s of Baron Edouard van Zuylen, of Argenteau, and has:

        1e *Edmond Marc Dominic; *b* 20 April 1992

        2e *Charles Tobias Edward; *b* 5 June 1994

    3c David Gabriel Morton, DFC; *b* 26 March 1923; *educ* Ampleforth; F/Lt RAFVR WW II 1942–45 (POW Jan–May 1945); *m* 5 Dec 1963 *Elizabeth Susan [Mrs David Mansel-Pleydell, 42 Bloomfield Terr, London SW1; Barneston Manor, Steeple, Dorset], only dau of John McVean Luard, of Woodlands, Little Baddow, Essex, and *d* 1973, leaving:

      1d +Toby Edmund Luard Morton; *b* 30 Sept 1964

      2d +Harry Rupert Delalynde Morton; *b* 27 May 1966

      3d +Thomas Oliver Clavell Morton; *b* 26 March 1969

      4d +Charles David Luttrell Morton; *b* 5 Sept 1973

  1b Dorothy Isabel Morton; *b* 2 Sept 1881; *m* 27 April 1910 Maj Edward Pelham Smith, RA (*d* 17 March 1937), yr s of Abel Smith, DL, of Woodland Park, Herts, and *d* 20 Dec 1927, leaving issue

  2b Cicely Morton; *b* 12 Dec 1882; *m* 16 Jan 1906 Col Nevile Hugh Cairns Sherbrooke, DSO, RA (*d* 6 March 1944), 2nd s of Rev Henry Nevil Sherbrooke, and *d* 27 Dec 1938, leaving issue

  3a Henry Bingham Morton; *b* 6 Dec 1852; Capt 1st Bn Roy Fus Sudan 1884 (medal with clasp, bronze star); *d* unm 21 Feb 1886

(2) George Pleydell, JP, DL, of Smedmore, Dorset; *b* 4 Dec 1817; Capt 60th Rifles, Hon Col Dorset Rifle Vols; *m* 7 March 1848 Jemima Henrietta (*d* 2 June 1896), dau of William Gambier by his w Henrietta (whose 1st husb had been 7th Earl of Athlone of the March 1691/2 *cr*), and *d* 26 March 1896, having had:

  1a John Delalynde, JP, of Smedmore; *b* 3 Oct 1850; Col Rifle Bde, Assist Mil Sec and ADC to Lt-Gen Sir John Ross, KCB, in Canada, served Jowaki campaign 1877–78 (medal with clasp), Afghan campaign 1878–80 (medal with two clasps and bronze star) and S Africa 1900 (medal with five clasps); *m* 24 April 1888 Mildred Ella (*d* 11 March 1942), dau of Arthur Edward Guest, 5th s of Sir Josiah John Guest, 1st Bt (*see* WIMBORNE, V), and *d* 11 Dec 1915, leaving:

    1b Rhys Clavell, JP (1930–52), DL (Dorset 1933–52), of Smedmore and Ropley Manor, Alresford, Hants; *b* 3 Feb 1891; *educ* Eton; Maj Rifle Bde WWs I (despatches, wounded) and II, High Sheriff Dorset 1938; *m* 1st 12 Jan 1916 Sylvia Nina (*d* 11 May 1944), only dau of Lt-Col Sir Guy Theophilus Campbell, 3rd Bt (*cr* 1815, *qv*), and had:

      1c +John Clavell, DL (Dorset 1974) [Maj John Mansel DL, The Old Parsonage, Kimmeridge, Dorset BH20 5PE]; *b* 9 Jan 1917; *educ* Eton and Ch Ch Oxford (BA 1938, MA 1968); served Rifle Bde WW II (Capt 1942, Maj 1946) and MELF and BAOR thereafter, ret 1958, High Sheriff Dorset 1968, pres Corfe Castle branch S Dorset C Assoc 1974–95, JP Wareham 1961–82; *m* 11 Aug 1945 *Damaris Joan, only dau of Hyde Hyde-Thomson, of Kensington, and has had:

        1d Richard John Clavell; *b* 22 May 1949; *educ* Eton; *d* 1993

        2d +Philip Robert Rhys; *b* 19 Oct 1951; *educ* Eton; writer

        1d *Lavinia Sylvia; *b* 8 Oct 1946; *educ* St Anne's Coll Oxford (BA 1967, BPhil 1969); *m* 21 July 1968 (*divorce* 1991) (Alexander) Quentin Jones, of Oxford, est s of Gwilym I Jones, of Shaftesbury Rd, Cambridge, resumed 1991 her maiden name and has:

          1e *Alexander Daniel Mansel; *b* 1978

          2e *Benjamin Robin Clavell; *b* 1980

          3e *Owen Toby Rhys; *b* 1984

      1c *Elizabeth Madeline Nina [Elizabeth Lady Crofton, Flat 11, St Martin's House, 30 North St, Wareham, Dorset BH20 4AQ]; *b* 3 Oct 1919; *m* 14 Jan 1961 (*divorce* 1966) Capt Sir Malby Sturges Crofton, 5th Bt of Longford House (*qv*)

      2c *Felicité Mary Adeline [Mrs Felicité Warner, 29 Ruttan Bay, Winnipeg, Manitoba, Canada R3T 0H5]; *b* 20 Dec 1924; *m* 5 Sept 1952 (*divorce* 1978) Peter Thomas John Christopher Plumbly Warner, MD PhD, FCPath, s of William Francis Warner, of NZ, and has:

        1d *William Francis; *b* 25 Feb 1957

        1d *Susanna Elizabeth Juliet; *b* 10 June 1953; *m* 19– *Harold Polsky and has:

          1e *Elizabeth; *b* 19–; has:

            1f *Alura Rachelle Poschner BOLDUC POLSKY; *b* 19–

          2d *Ianthe Sylvia; *b* 28 Sept 1954

          3d *Sarah Adeline [Ms Sarah Warner, 274 1st St East (Box 4194), The Pas, Manitoba R9A 1R2, Canada]; *b* 17 Feb 1959; *m* 1993 *Thomas Peter Kobar and has:

            1e *Kimberley Dana Warner; *b* 28 March 1995

            2e *Samantha Kelsey Warner; *b* 24 Feb 1997

          4d *Charlotte Anne; *b* 10 Jan 1965

          5d *Oenone Jane; *b* 2 July 1966

      3c *Pamela Sylvia [Mrs Nicholas McClintock, Lower Westport, Wareham, Dorset BH20 4PR]; *b* 22 May 1926; *m* 2 Sept 1953 *Nicholas Cole McClintock, CBE, KStJ, late Overseas CS Nigeria, yr s of Col Robert Singleton McClintock, DSO, RE, of Brakey Hill, Godstone, Surrey, and has:

        1d *Alexander Edward Franklin (Frank) [Alexander McClintock Esq, Baranco da Estrada, 7665 Santa Clara a Velha, Baixo Alentejo, Portugal]; *b* 12 Feb 1959; *educ* Eton; *m* 1986 *Julia (Lulu) Adeline, yr dau of Thomas Henry Luckock, of Flint Ho, Barkway Royston, Herts, and has:

          1e *Archie; *b* 29 Jan 1988

          1e *Araby Tessa; *b* 1989

          2e *Alexandra Adeline; *b* 1992

        2d *Michael Leopold Elphinstone [Michael McClintock Esq, 6 Westport Rd, Wareham, Dorset BH20 5PR]; *b* 19 Oct 1960; *educ* Milton Abbey; *m* 1991 (*divorce* 1997) Mrs Anne K Lee, dau of R T Greenwood, of Shipley, W Yorks, and has:

          1e *Jonathan Michael; *b* 29 May 1994

        1d *Sylvia Araby Jane [Mrs Malcolm Wright, Cricket Green Cottage, Ewhurst Green, Surrey GU6 7RR]; *b* 18 July 1954; *m* 1979 *Malcolm Wright and has:

          1e *Pamela Melesina Marion; *b* 12 Dec 1981

          2e *Katherine Elizabeth Jane; *b* 9 Nov 1984

        2d *Elizabeth Melesina [Mrs Anthony Loring, 2 Wingate Rd, London W6 0UR]; *b* 12 Jan 1961; *m* 1992 *Anthony F Loring, s of Brig Walter Loring, CBE, of Slingsby, Yorks, and has:

          1e *Joshua; *b* 21 Aug 1995

          2e *Thomas; *b* 3 March 1997

        1e *Frances Claudia; *b* 22 Nov 1993

    1b (cont.) Rhys Mansel *m* 2nd 12 Oct 1944 (*annulled* 1946) Mrs Margaret Georgina Walker, dau of Dr H F G Noyes; *m* 3rd 8 Oct 1947 Archie Anne (*d* 1986), er dau of Hugh Montgomery Cairnes, of Fox Hall, Raheny, Co Dublin, and *d* 9 Sept 1969, having by her had:

      2c +Hugh Clavell [Hugh Mansel Esq, Thornmoor House, nr Wareham, Dorset BH20 5DY]; *b* 19 Oct 1948; *educ* Eton; *m* 1st 2 June 1973 Jennifer Ann, dau of Brian Ashford-Russell, of Chelsea, and The Lindens, Alresford, Hants; *m* 2nd 2 Feb 1984 *Diana Theresa Violet, yst dau of Lt-Col Conyers Stephen Scrope, MC (*see* SUTHERLAND, D), and by her has:

        1d +Rhys Clavell; *b* 1987

        1d *Isabella Maria; *b* 1985

  1b Marcia Eugenia; *b* 12 March 1890; Croix de Guerre; *m* 1st 14 Dec 1910 Capt Oswald Bethell Walker (*ka* 1914, *see* WALKER, Bt, of Sand Hutton) and had issue; *m* 2nd 17 Feb 1920 François de Juge Montespieu (*d* 30 Dec 1940) and had further issue

  2b Juliet Ella Meimei; *b* 9 March 1893; Croix de Guerre; *d* unm 10 Sept 1982

  2a Eustace Gambier; *b* 31 Oct 1853; Capt Oxfordshire LI Sudan 1884 (medal with clasp and bronze star); *m* 19 May 1883 Mary Eleanor (*d* 2 Nov 1950), dau of Cdr Thomas Belgrave, RN, and *d* 31 Dec 1915, leaving:

    1b Eustace Philip Belgrave; *b* 20 July 1884; *educ* Radley and Pembroke Coll Oxford; Lt RNVR WW I, HG WW II; *m* 7 Oct 1925 Contessina Giorgina Mannini, 2nd dau of Count Ottavio Mannini, and *dsp* 25 Nov 1955

    1b Lily Dorothy; *m* 10 June 1926 Victor Napoleon Douetil (*d* 1936) and *dsp* 12 July 1949

  3a Ernest Digby; *b* 10 Oct 1855; Maj Highland LI; *m* 1 Nov 1882 Henrietta Cecilia (*d* 17 Feb 1939), dau of Sir John Don-Wauchope, 8th Bt (*qv*), and *dsp* 8 May 1911

  4a George Clavell, DSO; *b* 9 Feb 1861; Lt-Col and Brevet Col Durham LI S Boer War 1899–1902 (medal with four clasps); *d* unm 12 July 1910

  1a Elizabeth Henrietta; *d* unm 12 Dec 1934

  2a Louisa Mary; *d* unm 24 Aug 1934

(3) Morton Grove, of Puncknoll, Dorset; *b* 9 July 1823; Lt 10th Foot; *m* 30 May 1848 Elizabetha Arundell (*d* 1893), dau and co-heir of Rev George Clutterbuck Frome, of Puncknoll, and *d* 26 Feb 1859, having had:

  1b George Morton, JP, of Puncknoll Manor, Dorset; *b* 11 April 1849; Lt RN; *d* unm 4 July 1907

  2b Walter Luttrell, JP, of Puncknoll Manor; *b* 19 June 1851; Lt-Col S Lancs Regt; *m* 1886 Helen (*d* 27 Oct 1934), dau of George Ogilvy, of Cove, Dumfriesshire, and widow of Maj Charles Stepney Perceval Egmont Mansergh, of Clifford, Co Cork, and *d* 20 Feb 1913

  3b Charles Pleydell; *d* 1854

  1b Emma Louisa Arundell; *m* 12 May 1897 Col Henry Archibald Mallock (*d* 7 Feb 1923), IA, of Friar Mayne House, Dorset, and *d* 31 May 1924

(4) Owen Luttrell (Rev); *b* 24 Jan 1827; *educ* Trin Coll Camb (MA); Rector Church Knowle, Dorset; *m* 19 July 1859 Louisa Catherine (*d* 30 Oct 1901), yst dau and coheir of Lord William Montagu (*see* MANCHESTER, D), and *d* 12 July 1900, leaving:

  1b Francis Montagu; *b* 30 Nov 1861; *d* 1891

  2b Owen Llewellyn; *b* 25 July 1864; *d* 23 Nov 1931

  3b Edward Luttrell; *b* 14 May 1866; Lt 1st Bn E Surrey Regt; *d* unm

4b William Du Pré; *b* 12 Sept 1869; Assist Commr Basutoland, Capt 12th Bn Lancs Fus, Lt 4th Bn King's Own Regt; *ka* 1916

5b Charles Pleydell; *b* 7 Feb 1873; Lt-Cdr RN WW I 1914–15; *d* at sea 26 March 1915

6b James Morton; *b* 8 Feb 1876; *d* 4 March 1937

1b Katharine Louisa; *d* unm 11 March 1951

2b Emily Magdalene; *d* unm 21 March 1951

3b Winifred Emma; Sister of Charity of the Order of St Vincent de Paul

4b Theresa Mary; *m* 17 April 1894 Algar Labourchere Thorold (*d* 30 May 1936), est s of Rt Rev Anthony Wilson Thorold, Bp Winchester, and *d* 15 March 1944, leaving issue (*see* THOROLD, Bt)

5b Gwendoline Henrietta; Carmelite nun

(5) Arthur Edmund, JP (Dorset), of Grove House, Dorchester; *b* 10 April 1828; Capt 3rd Hus; *m* 6 Dec 1860 Clare Henrietta (*d* 10 Nov 1917), est dau of Hon Arthur Lascelles, s of 2nd Earl of Harewood (*qv*), and *d* 20 July 1905, leaving:

1a Algernon Lascelles; *b* 6 Sept 1868; *educ* Winchester; *m* 12 June 1906 Isita Rodger (*d* 16 Sept 1948), est dau of William Wilson, of S Kensington, and *d* 10 Aug 1942, leaving:

1b John William Morton, TD; *b* 2 Aug 1909; *educ* Winchester; Maj 5th Bn The Queen's Roy Regt (TA) WW II (POW, despatches), FRIBA; *m* 3 May 1952 *Gillian Valerie [Mrs John Barnard, Kingsmoor Cottage, Salford, Oxon OX7 5YN] (*m* 2nd 1977 John M S Barnard, who *d* 1979), er dau of Douglas Harold Whinney, of South Moreton Manor, Didcot, Berks, and *d* 29 July 1974, leaving:

1c *Isita Susan; *b* 24 Jan 1954; *m* 1st 16 Aug 1978 (*divorce*198–) J Peter Raffe, est s of Joseph Raffe; *m* 2nd 1988 *Roy Thomas Pickering, of Hook Norton, Oxon, and has by her 1st husb:

1d *Jonathan Luke; *b* 1980

1d *Sally Jane Isita; *b* 1979

2c *Philippa Clare; *b* 26 April 1955

2b (Edmund) Clavell, OBE (1960), MC; *b* 14 Jan 1915; *educ* Winchester and RMA Woolwich; Lt-Col RA (ret 1962) WW II (despatches); *m* 15 May 1954 *Ann [Mrs Clavell Mansel, Chestnuts, Bishop Wilton, York YO4 1RU], only dau of Capt Claud Anthony Merriman, RN (*see* 1956 edn MERRIMAN, B), and *d* 27 March 1997, having had:

1c +Timothy Mervyn Charles; *b* 16 May 1961; *educ* Winchester and Bristol U (BSc)

1c *Catherine Gillian [Mrs Rupert Dilnott-Cooper, 23 Glenmore Rd, London NW3 4BY]; *b* 11 Oct 1956; *m* 20 Jan 1979 *Rupert Michael Walter James Dilnott-Cooper and has:

1d *Edward Kenneth Timothy; *b* 9 Feb 1989

2d *William Rupert Mansel; *b* 4 Jan 1993

2c Elizabeth Jane; *b* 31 July 1963; *d* 10 June 1972

3b Mervyn Lascelles; *b* 2 Nov 1917; *educ* Winchester; Maj 1st Bn The Queen's Roy Regt WW II (despatches); *ka* Jail Hill, Burma, 13 May 1944

1b Isita Clare, OBE (1964); *b* 8 April 1907; G/Offr WAAF (despatches) WW II, memb: St Pancras Borough Cncl 1949–56, 1958–62 and 1963–65, LCC 1955–58, Alderman 1961–65, memb GLC 1967 and Peterborough Devpt Corp 1968, and *d* 27 July 1986

2a Hugh Arthur; *b* 7 Nov 1869; Capt late Dorset Regt, served Tirah Expdn 1897–98 (medal) and S Africa 1900 (wounded, two medals seven clasps); *d* 11 Jan 1931

1a Evelyn Louisa; *d* unm 4 Sept 1929

2a Margaret Blanche; *d* unm 23 March 1928

3a Susan Emma; *d* unm 15 Sept 1951

4a Clare Frances; *m* 16 Aug 1905 Capt Francis de Sausmarez Shortt (*d* 20 March 1956), Royal Scots Fus, s of V-Adml F H Shortt, of Martinstown, Dorset, and *d* 25 Jan 1958, leaving issue

5a Eleanor Maud; *m* 30 Sept 1909 Robert Lionel Foster, JP (*d* May 1952), 2nd s of John Foster, JP, DL, of Coombe Park, Whitchurch, Oxon, and Egton Manor, Egton Bridge, Yorks, and *d* 1944, leaving issue

6a Rhoda Caroline; *d* unm Feb 1902

(1) Louisa Mary; *d* Aug 1829

(2) Eliza Sophia; *d* 1834

(3) Emma Georgina; *m* 14 April 1852 Charles Richard Hoare (*d* Jan 1871), barrister, est s of Ven C Hoare, Archdeacon Surrey, and *dsp* 9 April 1905

4 Thomas; *b* 14 Oct 1783; Adml; *m* Selina Fleming, dau of Capt Benjamin Leigh, RN, and *d* 1 April 1869, having had:

(1) Selina Elizabeth Courtenay; *m* 16 July 1850 Cdr Alfred Young, RN (*d* 18 Nov 1861), and had issue

(2) Alexina Louisa

5 Robert Christopher, KH; *b* 12 Feb 1789; Lt-Gen, Col 68th Regt; *m* 2 Sept 1824 Amelia (*d* 10 Nov 1881), dau of Adml Sir Charles Tyler, GCB, and *d* 8 April 1864, having had:

(1) Emily; *d* unm 7 Aug 1914 aged 89

(2) Georgiana; *m* 23 Dec 1848 Maj John Davy Brett, 17th Lancers (*d* 2 April 1866), and *d* 28 June 1901

Sir RICHARD MANSEL, 12th (a) Bt's s and Sir EDWARD BERKELEY MANSEL, 12th (b) Bt's n,

Sir Courtenay Cecil Mansel, 13th Bt, JP (Cards and Carmarths); *b* 25 Feb 1880; assumed the title 1892 on his f's death, but relinquished it 1903 to his unc **Sir Edward Berkeley Mansel, 12th (b) Bt** (*see* above), only to resume it on the latter's death *sp* 8 Jan 1908; barrister Middle Temple 1918, Capt RAF, MP (Lib) Penryn and Falmouth 1923–24 (fought Coventry 1918), Conservative from 1926, author: *Masque of King Charles VI* and *The South Wind*; *m* 2 Oct 1906 Mary Philippa Agnes Germaine (*d* 6 March 1958), dau of Frederick Littlewood, and *d* 4 Jan 1933, leaving:

1 JOHN PHILIP FERDINAND (Sir), **14th Bt**

2 Rauf; *b* 30 Aug 1915; served RM 1942–45; *d* unm 2 July 1967

3 Regnier Ranulf Dabridgecourt; *b* 6 July 1919; RA WW II; *m* 14 June 1941 *Mary Germaine [Mrs Regnier Mansel, Taliaris, Maes-y-crugiau, Dyfed], dau of

W/Cdr W St J Littlewood, OBE, of Braemar, Stanmore, Middx, and *d* 1984, leaving:

(1) +Anthony Ranulf; *b* 22 Oct 1946; Capt RCT (V), AInstBM; *m* 19– *Joan Evans, of Neath, and has:

1a +Richard Mark; *b* 1973

2a +Robert Courtney; *b* 1976

(2) +Robert Edward; *b* 1 Feb 1948; MB, BS London, FRCS Eng, LRCP London, Capt RAMC (V); *m* 1st 19– Ingrid Powell and has:

1a *Joanna Margaret; *b* 1971

2a *Juliet Claire; *b* 1977

(2) (cont.) Robert Mansel *m* 2nd 1987 *Elizabeth C Skone, n of Bp of Tonbridge, and by her has:

1a +Rhys Edward Regnier; *b* 1989

2a +Courtenay Robert John; *b* 1994

3a *Charlotte Elizabeth; *b* 1988

(3) +Roderick Rhys; *b* 20 Dec 1959

(1) *Isabel Theresa; *b* 13 Jan 1949

(2) *Frances; *b* 28 July 1952

1 *Margaretta Cecil [Mrs Ralph West, Ty-Mawr, Trefilan, Talsarn, nr Lampeter, Dyfed]; *b* 7 Dec 1913; *m* 30 March 1940 *Lt-Cdr Ralph Leonard West, RN, s of R W West, of White Ho, Gosmore, Hitchin, and has:

(1) *Richard Mansel; *b* 6 July 1946

(2) *Christopher Leonard; *b* 23 Sept 1951

(1) *Aileen Margaretta [Mrs Robert Barrett, 6 Stony Croft, Stevenage, Herts]; *b* 18 March 1941; *m* 25 July 1964 *Robert John Barrett

2 *Juliet [Mrs Richard Burns, Corner Cottage, Ashby Lane, Bitteswell, Lutterworth, Leics]; *b* 1917; *m* 1939 G/Capt Richard Eric Burns, CBE, DFC, RAF, s of Owen Harcourt Burns, and has:

(1) *Richard Harcourt; *b* 1943

(1) *Christine Georgina; *b* 1941

(2) *Gillian; *b* 1948

Sir COURTENAY's est s,

Sir John Philip Ferdinand Mansel, 14th Bt; *b* 22 Aug 1910; *m* 16 July 1940 *Hannah [Mrs Harrison, Hall Flatt, Scalbey, Carlisle, Cumbria] (*m* 2nd 1947 — Harrison), dau of Ben Rees, of Cwmhuplyn, Pencader, and *d* 6 April 1947, leaving:

Sir PHILIP MANSEL, **15th and present Bt**

MANSFIELD and MANSFIELD

Arms: Quarterly, 1st and 4th, azure three mullets argent within a double tressure flory counterflory or (for MURRAY); 2nd and 3rd, gules three crosses patée argent (for BARCLAY). **Crest:** A buck's head couped or, a cross-patée between the attires argent. **Supporters:** Two lions gules, armed or. **Mottoes:** 1 (below the shield) *Uni æquius virtuti* ('More inclined to pure virtue'), 2 (over the crest) *Spero meliora* ('I hope for better things'). **Creations:** L. (S) 7 July 1604 (Scone) and 17 Nov 1641 (Balvaird), V. (S) 16 Aug 1621, E. (GB) 31 Oct 1776 (Mansfield, Co Notts) and 1 Aug 1792 (Mansfield, Co Middx).

THE 8TH EARL OF MANSFIELD, Co Nottingham, and **9TH EARL OF MANSFIELD**, Co Middx, also **Viscount (of) Stormont, Lord Scone** and **Lord Balvaird** (William David Mungo James Murray, JP (1975), DL (Perth and Kinross 1980)) [The Rt Hon The Earl of Mansfield and Manfield JP DL, Scone Palace, Perthshire, PH2 6BE; 16 Thorburn House, Kinnerton St, London SW1X 8EX]; *b* 7 July 1930; *s* f 1971; *educ* Eton and Ch Ch Oxford; Lt Scots Gds (RARO) Malaya 1949–50; barrister Inner Temple 1958–71; memb Tay Salmon Fisheries Bd 1971–79, Br Rep European Parl Strasbourg 1973–75, Min State Scottish Office 1979–83, NI Office 1983–84, First Crown Estate Commr 1985–95, dir Gen Accident Fire and Life Assur 1972–79 and 1985–, American Tst 1985–, Pinneys of Scotland 1985–89,

Ross Breeders Ltd 1989–90, dir Roy Highland and Ag Soc 1976–79, Pres Fédération des Assocs de Chasse de l'Europe 1977–79, Scottish Assoc for Care and Resettlement of Offenders 1974–79, Scottish Assoc Boys Clubs 1976–79, Roy Scottish Country Dance Soc 1977–, Chm Scottish branch HHA 1976–79, memb Perth CC 1971–75, Hon Sheriff Perthshire 1974, Hon memb RICS 1994; *m* 19 Dec 1955 *Pamela Joan, only dau of Wilfred Neill Foster, CBE (*see* COCHRANE OF CULTS, B), and has:

1 +ALEXANDER DAVID MUNGO, *Viscount Stormont; b* 17 Oct 1956; *educ* Eton; *m* 1985 *Sophia Mary Veronica, only dau of Philip Biden Derwent Ashbrooke (*see* MOWBRAY, SEGRAVE and STOURTON, B), of St John, Jersey, and has:

  (1) +William Philip David Mungo, *Master of Stormont; b* 1 Nov 1988

  (1) *Isabella Mary Alexandra; b* 19 June 1987

  (2) *Iona Margaret Sophie; b* 13 March 1992

  (3) *Louisa Frederica Olivia; b* 18 Dec 1996

2 +James William; *b* 7 June 1969

1 *(Georg)ina Dorothea Mary; b* 10 March 1967; *educ* Wycombe Abbey; *m* 24 Oct 1998 *John Bullough, only s of Michael Bullough, of Westmains of Huntingtower, Perth

Lineage: Sir WILLIAM MURRAY of Tullibardine (*see* also ATHOLL, D, for further details); *d c* 1459, leaving:

1 William (Sir), of Tullibardine; *d* 10 Feb 1524/5, having had:

  (1) William (Sir), of Tullibardine; *ka vp* Flodden 1513, leaving:

    1a William (Sir), of Tullibardine; *d* 1562, leaving:

      1b William (Sir), of Tullibardine; *d* 1583, leaving, with other issue:

        1c JOHN MURRAY, 1st EARL OF TULLIBARDINE, so *cr* 1606; *d* 1613, leaving, with other issue, including two er sons (*see* ATHOLL, D):

          1d Sir MUNGO MURRAY of Drumcairn, **2nd Viscount (of) Stormont**, as which *s* 3rd cousin twice-removed 1631 (*see* below); ktd 1607, Cornet King's Gds 1607–11, Sheriff Perthshire 1627, Gentleman Privy Chamber 1628; *m* 1st probably by 30 May 1606 his cousin Anne, n of **1st Viscount** (*see* below); *m* 2nd *c* 18 Oct 1639 Anne, dau of 1st Earl of Wemyss (*see* WEMYSS and MARCH, E) and widow of David Lindsay of Edzell, and *dspl* just prior to 11 March 1641/2

2 Andrew (Sir); *m* Margaret, dau and sole heiress of James Barclay of Balvaird, who brought him the Arngask, Balvaird, Kippo estates among others; his er s:

  (1) David (Sir), of Arngask, Balvaird, Kippo etc; *m* Janet, sis of 5th Lord Lindsay of the Byres (*see* LINDSAY, E), and *d* 1550, having had:

    1a Andrew (Sir), of Arngask and Balvaird; *m* 1st —; *m* 2nd Lady Janet Graham, 4th dau of 2nd Earl of Montrose (*see* MONTROSE, D), and *d* between 30 April 1572 and 23 July 1573, having had:

      1b Andrew (Sir); *m* as her 1st husb Margaret (*m* 2nd Sir Mungo Murray of Claremont and had by him William Murray), dau of John Crichton of Strathurd, and *d* 13 Nov 1590, leaving:

        1c Andrew (Sir), of Balvaird; *dsp* 1624

        1c Anne; *m* as his 1st w her cousin **2nd Viscount (of) Stormont** (*see* above) and *dsp* 13 May 1639

        2c Margaret; *m* Myrton of Cambo

    2b Sir DAVID MURRAY, **1st Lord Scone** (S), so *cr* 7 July 1604 and by charter 18 Aug 1608 granted the dissolved Scone Abbey lands, which were now converted to the temporal Ldship and Barony of Scone with the associated dignity of Baron and Lord of Parl by the title Lord Scone, with remainder to him and the heirs male of his body, in default of which with similar limitation to his nephew Sir Andrew Murray of Balvaird (who, however, predeceased him, whereupon the **1st Lord/Viscount** *s* to Balvaird); by a later charter of 29 April 1612 the remainder was expanded to include (a) the grantee's nephew Sir Andrew's bro-in-law and distant cousin Sir MUNGO MURRAY of Drumcairn (*see* above), (b) John Murray of Reidkirk (later 1st Earl of Annandale, who was apparently no relation despite having the same surname, but whose s JAMES MURRAY, 2nd EARL OF ANNANDALE, *s* as **3rd Viscount (of) Stormont**; *dsp* 28 Dec 1658, when the Earldom of Annandale expired), (c) Gilbert Murray (the grantee's late cousin once-removed on his f's side), (d) the latter's yr bro Andrew (later **1st Lord Balvaird**) and (e) William Murray (Sir Andrew Murray of Balvaird's half-bro by their mother, William Murray's f being Sir Mungo Murray of Claremont, a cousin of the grantee's), with identical limitation to the initial remainder, with ultimate remainder to his heirs male whatsoever bearing the name and arms of Murray of Balvaird; the **1st Lord Scone** was also *cr* 16 Aug 1621 (**1st**) **Viscount of Stormont**, with identical extended limitation to that of the earlier peerage creation, PC (S 1599); Cupbearer to JAMES VI by 1580, Master of the Stable 1583/4, Keeper Falkland Palace by 1596, ktd 1599, Provost Perth 1601–09 and 1612–Feb 1627/8, Comptonitor Scottish Treasury 1601–08, Capt King's Gd Scotland 1603–11, Commr Scottish Exchequer 1610; *m c* Feb 1603/4 Elizabeth, dau of James Beaton of Creich, Fife, and *dsp* 27 Aug 1631

    3b Robert; Archdeacon Dunkeld

    4b Patrick (Sir), of Byn and Drumcairn; Gds Offr; employed by JAMES VI in settling the church; *dsp*

  2a William, of Letter Bannathy; *d* 1589, having had an est s:

    1b David, of Balgony and Kippo; *m* Agnes, dau of (probably William, 11th) Moncreiffe of that Ilk (*see* ERROLL, E), and *d* 1627, having had:

      1c Gilbert; living 1645; *dsp* by 1658

      2c Sir ANDREW MURRAY, **1st Lord Balvaird** (S), so *cr* 17 Nov 1641, with remainder to his heirs male; ktd 1633, granted a charter of Pitlochrie 1636, memb Gen Assembly Ch Scotland 1638, his pliable behaviour there winning him his peerage; *m* Elizabeth, 5th dau of 1st Earl of Southesk (*see* FIFE, D), and *d* 24 Sept 1644, leaving an est s:

        1d DAVID MURRAY, **2nd Lord Balvaird**, as which *s* f, and **4th Viscount (of) Stormont**, as which *s* bro-in-law 1659; *m* 9 Aug 1659 Jean, est dau of 2nd Earl of Southesk (*see* FIFE, D) and widow of the **3rd Viscount (of) Stormont**/2nd Earl of Annandale, and *d* 14 July 1668, leaving:

          1e DAVID MURRAY, **5th Viscount (of) Stormont**; held in custody on suspicion of involvement in the pro-Jacobite French invasion of

---

Scotland March 1707/8 but set free on bail three months later, imprisoned and fined for Jacobite activity 1715–16; *m c* 31 Jan 1688 Marjory, only dau of David Scott of Scotstarvet, Fife, by Nicola, dau of Sir John Grierson of Lag (*see* GRIERSON, Bt), and *d* 9 Nov 1731, having had, with three other daus (*dsp*) and six other daus:

  1f DAVID MURRAY, **6th Viscount (of) Stormont**; *b c* 1689; *m* 1726 Anne, only dau and heiress of John Stewart of Innernytie, and *d* 1748, having had:

    1g DAVID MURRAY, **7th Viscount (of) Stormont**, as which *s* f 1748, and **2nd Earl of Mansfield**, Co Middx, of the 1 Aug 1792 *cr*, as which *s* unc (*see* below) 20 March 1793, KT (1768), PC (1763); *b* 9 Oct 1727; *educ* Westminster and Ch Ch Oxford; Attaché Paris, Envoy Dresden and Warsaw 1756–61, Amb Vienna 1763–72 and Paris 1772–78, Ld Justice Gen Scotland 1778–94, Sec State North Dept 1779–82, Ld Pres Cncl April-Dec 1783 and 1794–96, rep S peer 1754–93; *m* 1st 16 Aug 1759 Henrietta Frederica (*d* 10 March 1766), dau of Henry, Count von Bünau, of Saxony, and widow of — de Beragaard, and had:

      1h Elizabeth Mary; *m* 1785 George Finch Hatton and *d* 17 Feb 1823, leaving issue (*see* WINCHILSEA and NOTTINGHAM, E)

    1g (cont.) The **7th Viscount/2nd Earl** *m* 2nd 5 May 1776 Louisa, **Countess of Mansfield**, Co Nottingham, of the 31 Oct 1776 *cr*, in her own right, as which she *s* her 1st husb's unc (*see* below) 20 March 1793 (she *m* 2nd 19 Oct 1797 Hon Robert Fulke Greville, *see* WARWICK, BROOKE and, E), 3rd dau of 9th Lord Cathcart (*see* CATHCART, E), and *d* 1 Sept 1796, having by her had:

      1h DAVID WILLIAM, **3rd Earl**

      2h George; *b* 1780; Lt-Gen; *d* 1848

      3h Charles; *b* 22 Aug 1781; Maj; *m* 21 Sept 1802 Elizabeth, dau of Rev Robert Law, DD, and *d* 17 Sept 1859, leaving:

        1i Charles Robert; Army Offr; *d* 1872

        2i William; Maj 10th Hus; *m* 12 Oct 1854 Josephine, dau of M J Drapié, of Brussels, and *dsp* 1891

        1i Louisa; *d* 13 May 1872

      4h Henry (Sir), KCB; *b* Aug 1784; Gen, Col 14th Dragoons, served Peninsular War and Waterloo Campaign; *m* 28 June 1810 Emily (*d* 23 Nov 1873), dau of Gerard de Vismé, and *d* 29 July 1860, having had:

        1i Henry Stormont; *b* 1812; *d* 12 Aug 1863

        2i Frederick Stormont; *b* 23 March 1813; RN; *d unm* 23 March 1903

        3i Arthur Stormont; *b* 1820; Army Capt; *m* Mary (*m* 2nd 1851 (*divorce*) J C Hawker), dau of Capt Polkinghorne, RN, and *d* 1848

        1i Susan Emily; *d* 9 Feb 1874

        2i Gertrude Louisa; *d unm* 26 March 1904

      2h Caroline; *d* 21 Jan 1867

    2g James; *d unm*

    1g Anne; granted with sis rank of earl's dau 30 April 1793; *d unm* 9 July 1818

    2g Marjory; *d* 19 April 1799

  2f James; *b c* 1690; advocate 1710, MP Dumfriesshire 1711–13 and Elgin 1713–15 (unseated); joined Jacobite Uprising 1715; *cr* by titular James III 2 Feb 1720/1 Earl of Dunbar in the Shire of East Lothian, Viscount of Drumcairn in the Shire of Fife and Lord of Hadykes in the Shire of Dumfries (all S), with special remainder to his er bro, also titular KT 1725; *dsp* Avignon Aug 1770

  3f WILLIAM MURRAY, **1st Earl of Mansfield**, Co Nottingham (GB), so *cr* 31 Oct 1776, with special remainder in default of heirs male of his body to his nephew-and-heir-presumptive's w Louisa (*see* above); (the curious nature of this destination is thought to have arisen from the belief then current — and underpinned by a resolution of the House of Lords of 1711 which was only revoked in 1782 — that no title in the peerage of GB descending to a person holding a title in the peerage of Scotland would enable the latter to sit in the House of Lords even though it were by inheritance rather than direct grant), also **1st Earl of Mansfield**, Co Middlesex (GB), so *cr* 1 Aug 1792, with special remainder in default of heirs male of the grantee's body to his nephew (the above-mentioned Ho Lds resolution having by then been revoked), as also earlier 8 Nov 1756 LORD MANSFIELD, BARON OF MANSFIELD, Co Nottingham (GB), PC (1756); *b* 2 March 1704/5; *educ* Perth GS, Westminster and Ch Ch Oxford; barrister Lincoln's Inn 1730, KC 1742, MP (Whig) Boroughbridge 1742–56, Slr Gen 1742–54, Attorney Gen 1754–56, Ld Ch Justice 1756–88, Chllr Exchequer April-June 1757 and Sept–Oct 1767, Speaker Ho Lds Oct 1760 and 1770–71; *m* 20 Sept 1738 Elizabeth, dau of 7th Earl of Winchilsea and (2nd Earl of) Nottingham (*qv*), and *dsp* 20 March 1793, when the Barony expired

  1f Marjory; *m* Col John Hay of Cromlix, Perthshire

  2f Amelia; *m* Sir Alexander Lindsay of Evelick

The **2nd EARL's** surv son,

DAVID WILLIAM MURRAY, **3rd Earl of Mansfield**, of Co Middlesex, KT (1835); *b* 7 March 1777; *educ* Westminster, Leipzig and Ch Ch Oxford; Lt 7th Foot, Ld Lt Clackmannanshire 1803–40; *m* 16 Sept 1797 Frederica (*d* 29 April 1860), dau of Dr William Markham, Archbp York, and *d* 11 Feb 1840, having had, with four other daus:

1 WILLIAM DAVID, **4th/3rd Earl**

2 Charles John; *b* 25 Jan 1810; *m* 12 Sept 1835 Hon Frances Elizabeth Anson (*m* 2nd 10 Sept 1853 Ambrose Isted, of Ecton, and *d* 25 Dec 1899), 2nd surv dau of 1st Viscount Anson (*see* LICHFIELD, E), and *d* 1 Aug 1851, having had:

(1) Charles Archibald; *b* 10 Oct 1836; *m* 1st 27 April 1865 Adelaide Emily (*d* 24 May 1870), 3rd dau of 7th Earl of Denbigh and (6th Earl of) Desmond (*qv*), and had:

1a Ronald William; *b* 10 May 1866; *m* 16 Feb 1904 Constance Mary Jane (*d* 1 Dec 1950), est dau of Gen Sir Richard Chambré Hayes Taylor, GCB (*see* HEADFORT, M), and *d* 2 Jan 1917

2a Archibald John Percy; *b* 16 July 1867; *m* 9 April 1907 Dulcibella Maria Lindsay (*d* 28 Aug 1949), er dau and coheir of Collingwood Lindsay Wood, of Freeland, Perthshire, bro of Sir Lindsay Wood, 1st Bt, and *d* 8 April 1943, leaving:

1b Joan Noël; *b* 28 Dec 1911; *m* 1st 10 Jan 1933 William Neil Graham Menzies (*d* 27 July 1945), yst s of William Dudgeon Graham Menzies, of Perthshire, and had:

1c *Cynthia Lindsay; *b* 22 Jan 1936; *m* 28 June 1962 *Col Charles Timothy Llewellen Palmer, MC, 7th Hus, of Chippenham, Wilts, yst s of Col William Llewellen Palmer, MC, JP, DL, and has issue

1b (cont.) Mrs William Menzies *m* 2nd 19 Jan 1950 Lt-Col Michael John Lindsay, DSO, King's Dragoon Gds, s of Lt-Col Michael Egan Lindsay, DSO, DL, of Dairsie, Fife, and by him had:

1c *William Murray; *b* 15 March 1952; *educ* Strathallan Sch

1a Margaret Frances; *m* 10 July 1902 Arthur Holford, 19th Hus, and *d* 17 May 1916, leaving issue

2a Alice Grace; *d* 17 Feb 1895

(1) (cont.) Charles Murray *m* 2nd 11 June 1878 Blanche (*d* 4 July 1926), 5th dau of Sir Thomas Moncrieffe of that Ilk, 7th Bt (*see* ERROLL, E), and *d* 23 Aug 1924, having by her had:

3a Charles John; *b* 1 Dec 1881; Lt Coldstream Gds, ADC to Govrs N Nigeria 1907–09 and Br E Africa 1909–11; *ka* 27 Oct 1914

3a Gertrude Blanche; *m* 12 June 1907 Alexander Ronald (Alasdair) MacGregor (*see* MAC GREGOR, Bt) and *d* 4 Aug 1959, leaving issue

4a Lillian Edith; *m* 10 July 1919 Brig Harold Senhouse Pinder, CBE, MC, Roy Leics Regt, s of Rev J G Pindar, and had:

1b *John Humphrey Murray; *b* 20 June 1924; *educ* King's Coll Cambridge (MA); *m* 2 April 1964 *Pauline Hawtayne, dau of Herbert William Lewin

1b *Margaret Lilian; *b* 4 May 1920; V-Pres Br Rheumatism and Arthritis Assoc, fndr Margaret Pinder House, first recuperative hospital for Arthritics, V-Pres Maremma Sheepdog Club

(2) Frederick John George; *b* 18 May 1839; Col 3rd Dragoon Gds; *d* unm 27 May 1918

(3) David Henry; *b* 9 Feb 1811; Maj; *m* 5 Nov 1840 Margaret, Lady Gray in her own right (*see* GRAY, L), and *dsp* 5 Sept 1862

(1) Frederica Louisa; *m* July 1820 Lt-Col Hon James Hamilton Stanhope (*see* 1967 edn CHESTERFIELD and STANHOPE, E) and *d* 1823

(2) Emily; *m* 9 May 1839 5th Marquess of Hertford (*qv*) and *d* 24 June 1902, having had issue

The 3rd EARL's er son,

WILLIAM DAVID MURRAY, **4th Earl of Mansfield**, of Co Middlesex, as which *s f* 1840, and **3rd Earl of Mansfield**, of Co Nottingham, as which *s* grandmother 1843, KT (1843); *b* 21 Feb 1806, *educ* Westminster and Ch Ch Oxford 1843; MP (Tory) Aldborough 1830–31, Woodstock 1831–32, Norwich 1832–37 and Perths 1837–40, a Ld Treasury 1834–35, Ld Lt Clackmannanshire 1852–98; *m* 8 April 1829 Louisa (*d* 24 Nov 1837), 3rd dau of Cuthbert Ellison, JP, DL, of Hebburn Hall, Co Durham, and *d* 2 Aug 1898 (by then being 'Father of the House of Lords'), having had:

1 William David, *Viscount Stormont*, DL (Dumfriesshire); *b* 22 July 1835; Lt Gren Gds, Col cmdg 3rd Black Watch, V-Lt Perthshire, ADC to HM QUEEN VICTORIA 1892; *m* 6 Aug 1857 Emily Louisa (*d* 9 April 1919), est dau of Sir John Atholl Mac Gregor of Mac Gregor, 3rd Bt (*qv*), and *dvp* 12 Oct 1893, leaving:

(1) WILLIAM DAVID MURRAY, **5th Earl of Mansfield**, of Co Middlesex, and **4th Earl of Mansfield**, of Co Nottingham, PC (1905), JP and DL (both Perthshire), JP (Clackmannanshire and Dumfriesshire); *b* 20 July 1860; Capt Gren Gds and Roy Gds Res Regt; CC Perthshire, Order of Mercy 1902; *d* unm 29 April 1906

(2) Andrew David; *b* 28 Sept 1863; granted with surv siblings rank of earl's dau/yr s 13 March 1899; Capt and Brevet Lt-Col QO Cameron Highrs, Nile Expdn 1885, Sudan Frontier Field Force 1885–86, Sudan 1898 (despatches three times, Brevet of Maj), Boer War cmdg Lovat's Scouts 1899–1901 (despatches, Brevet of Lt-Col); *ka* 20 Sept 1901

(3) ALAN DAVID, **6th/5th Earl**

(4) Angus David; *b* 4 June 1869; Lt RN; *d* 4 Oct 1898

(5) Alexander David; *b* 3 May 1871; Maj 3rd Bn Black Watch; *m* 24 Nov 1908 Christian Maule (*d* 24 Sept 1964), dau of Sir James Thomas Stewart-Richardson, 14th Bt (*qv*), and *d* 28 July 1924, leaving:

1a +David John, TD (1951) [Maj David Murray TD, Moy House, Forres, Morayshire]; *b* 6 June 1919; *educ* Wellington and Magdalene Coll Cambridge; Maj Seaforth Highrs WW II; *m* 2 Aug 1961 *Joanna, dau of Lt John Godfrey Lincoln, RN, and has:

1b +Alexander David; *b* 8 Nov 1962; *m* 1987 *Susan Jayne, dau of Brian Savage, and has:

1c *Emma Kate; *b* 1988

2b +William John David; *b* 1976

1a *Maryot Louisa [Miss Maryot Murray, Windyridge, Dunphail, Morayshire]; *b* 19 Jan 1910

2a *Elizabeth Helen; *b* 16 Feb 1912; *m* 21 Aug 1937 (*divorce* 1945) T/Lt-Col Charles Richard Wynn Brewis, MC, The Welch Regt (*d* 23 May 1967), s of Capt Charles Richard Wynn Brewis, CBE, RN, and has had:

1b *Simon David Richard Wynn, MBE; *b* 31 Dec 1941; *educ* Canford; Lt-Col Parachute Regt

1b Jennifer Helen; *b* 12 March 1940; *d* 18 Dec 1956

3a *Christian Anne [Miss Christian Murray, Easter Dunfallandy, Pitlochry, Perthshire]; *b* 16 Aug 1913; WW II in WRNS

---

(1) Marjory Louisa, CBE (1920); *m* 8 April 1891 Sir Kenneth John Mackenzie, 7th Bt, of Gairloch (*see* INGLIS, Bt), and *d* 18 Feb 1943, leaving issue

(2) Mabel Emily; *b* 24 Oct 1866; *m* 30 March 1905 Adml Sir Herbert Goodenough King-Hall, KCB, CVO, DSO (*d* 20 Oct 1936), s of Adml Sir William King-Hall, KCB, and *dsp* 18 July 1969

1 Louisa Nina; *m* 21 July 1851 Hon George Edwin Lascelles (*see* HAREWOOD, E) and *d* 30 Dec 1909, leaving issue

The 5th/4th EARL's bro,

ALAN DAVID MURRAY, **6th Earl of Mansfield**, of Co Middlesex, and **5th Earl of Mansfield**, of Co Nottingham, DL (Perthshire); *b* 25 Oct 1864; Gentleman Usher Green Rod 1895–1917, T/Lt-Col Cmdt Perthshire Vol Regt 1917–19, Lt Black Watch; *m* 20 April 1899 Margaret Helen Mary (*d* 13 Feb 1933), dau of R-Adml Sir Malcolm Mac Gregor of Mac Gregor, 4th Bt (*qv*), and *d* 14 March 1935, leaving:

MUNGO DAVID MALCOLM MURRAY, **7th Earl of Mansfield**, of Co Middlesex, and **6th Earl of Mansfield**, of Co Nottingham, JP (Dumfriesshire), DL (1947), JP (Perthshire); *b* 9 Aug 1900; *educ* Ch Ch Oxford (BA 1922); Lt 6th/7th Bn Black Watch; FSA Scot, FZS, FZS (Scot), FLS, FRHS, MBOU; Ld Lt Perths 1960–71 (V-Lt 1959), CC Perthshire, Ld High Commr Gen Assembly Ch Scotland 1961 and 1962, memb Cncl Zoological Soc London 1934–35 (V-Pres 1956–71), Pres Perthshire Ag Soc and Scottish Chamber of Ag 1936–38, memb Perthshire Educn Authority, Govr Edinburgh and E of Scotland Coll of Ag 1925–30, MP Perth and Kinross 1931–35, Hon Pres Perth C and U Assoc 1935 (Chm 1945–60), Brig Roy Co Archers, memb Deptl Ctee Scottish Farm Bldg 1943–45, memb advsy ctee Scottish Water Supplies 1946–71, Statutory Advsy Ctee to Sec State Scotland on Bird Protection 1954–71, Pres Wildfowlers' Assoc GB and Ireland, Tstee Wildfowl Tst Slimbridge, memb Scottish Wildfowl Refuge Ctee Nature Conservancy, V-Pres Scottish Landowners' Fedn, memb Exec W India Ctee; *m* 19 July 1928 Dorothea Helena (*d* 1985), yr dau of Sir Lancelot Douglas Carnegie, GCVO, KCMG, PC (*see* FIFE, D), and *d* 2 Sept 1971, having had:

1 WILLIAM DAVID MUNGO JAMES, **8th/7th and present Earl of Mansfield**

1 *Malvina Dorothea [The Rt Hon The Countess of Moray, Doune Park, Doune, Perthshire FK16 6HA]; *b* 27 Jan 1936; *m* 27 Jan 1964 *20th Earl of Moray (*qv*) and has issue

2 *Mariota Cecilia [The Lady Mariota Napier, Bardmony House, Alyth, Perthshire]; *b* 26 Jan 1945; barrister Inner Temple 1969; *m* 25 Jan 1969 *Hon (Charles) Malcolm Napier, 2nd s of 13th Lord Napier and (4th Baron) Ettrick (*qv*), and has issue

Seat: Scone Palace, Scone, Perths. The name 'palace' is misleading to southern Britons as far as the actual building is concerned. Not uncommon in Scotland, the term means no more than that the site in question was once the location of a court , *e.g.*, of justice (*c.f. Palais de Justice* in France). Yet in some ways Scone *is* a palace: its internal decor and ancien regime furnishings are of the highest quality and sumptuosity. Moreover, long before the present structure was built the first Parliaments were convened on the spot, with the famous Stone of Destiny being kept there and coronations of some 40 Kings of Scots taking place in its precincts.

First the building: following the dissolution of the religious houses in Scotland the Abbey lands of Scone were granted to the Ruthvens, Earls of Gowrie between 1581 and 1600 (*see* CARLISLE, E), who put up a house *c* 1580. After their disgrace the property was conferred on the first Lord Scone. His collateral descendant the 3rd Earl of Mansfield of the Middlesex creation commissioned William Atkinson to remodel the place in the Gothick taste in the early years of the 19th century. Atkinson, who invented and promoted his own formula for cement and as a young man had, appropriately for Scone, won an Academy gold medal for designs for a court of justice, was a pupil of James Wyatt. Here his simple, even somewhat stark work evokes his master's more restrained manner. The pink sandstone material alone gives a hint of the riot of colour and luxury within: ivory bibelots and looking-glasses in the dining-room, Chinese Chippendale chairs in the silver-and-white anteroom, a fine collection of boulle in the drawing-room, as well as a Riesener escritoire constructed for MARIE-ANTOINETTE and chairs of the time of her father-in-law LOUIS QUINZE upholstered in glowing tapestry. Just to remind the visitor of Scone's past as a place of national importance, there is a set of embroidery worked by MARY QUEEN OF SCOTS and her attendants. The gardens contain a collection of pine trees that is notable even for central Scotland, where such vegetation flourishes to the point of tedium, including what is claimed as the original Douglas Fir.

MANTON

Arms: Argent on a chevron azure between four martlets, three in chief and one in base sable, a crescent between two roses of the field. **Crest:** A gryphon passant sable in front of an oak-tree proper. **Supporters:** On either side a gryphon per fess azure and argent, charged on the shoulder with a rose also argent. **Motto:** *Mea gloria fides* ('Fidelity is my glory'). **Creation:** B. (UK) 25 Jan 1922.

THE 3RD BARON MANTON, of Compton Verney, Co Warwick ((Joseph) Rupert Eric Robert Watson, DL (Humberside 1980)) [The Rt Hon The Lord Manton DL, Houghton Hall, Sancton, York YO4 3RE]; *b* 23 Jan 1924; *s f* 1968; *educ* Eton; late Capt 7th Hus and Life Gds, Sr Steward Jockey Club 1982–85, Jockey Club Rep Horserace Betting Levy Bd 1970–75; *m* 9 Jan 1951 *Mary Elizabeth (Mimi)*, twin dau of Maj Thomas Dennehy Hallinan, of Ashbourne, Glounthaune, Co Cork, and has:

1 +MILES RONALD MARCUS; *b* 7 May 1958; *educ* Eton; Maj Life Gds; *m* 1984 *Elizabeth Adams, est dau of Julian Russell Story, of Westcott, Surrey, and has:

  (1) +Thomas Nigel Charles David; *b* 19 April 1985

  (2) +Ludovic Waldo Rupert; *b* 1989

2 +Thomas Philip; *b* 7 May 1958; *educ* Eton and RAC Cirencester; late Lt QOH, Lt Yorks Yeo; *m* 1988 *Venetia Margaret Cadogan, dau of Paul Spicer, and has:

  (1) +Alexander Paul Rupert; *b* 1989

  (1) *Tara Cadogan; *b* 1993

1 *Claire Georgina [The Rt Hon The Lady Hesketh, Easton Neston, Towcester, Northants]; *b* 7 Jan 1952; *m* 21 May 1977 *3rd Baron Hesketh (*qv*) and has issue

2 *Fiona Caroline Mary; *b* 26 Sept 1953; *m* 1978 *Mark Swinfen Cottrell, s of D V S Cottrell, of Tewkesbury, Glos, and has:

  (1) *George; *b* 1993

  (1) *Laura Marina; *b* 1988

3 *Victoria Monica [The Hon Mrs Westropp, Wootton Downs Farmhouse, Woodstock, Oxon OX20 1AF]; *b* 7 May 1958; *m* 6 May 1993, as his 2nd w, *Anthony Henry (Harry) Westropp, yr s of Col Lionel Henry Mountifort Westropp, of Wye, Kent, and has:

  (1) *Marina Monica; *b* 22 Dec 1993

Lineage: JONAS WATSON, of Tyre House, Woodside, Horsforth, Yorks; *b* 1786; *m* 1st 1 June 1809 Rebecca (*d* 11 March 1842), 2nd dau of James Wright, of Guiseley, Yorks; *m* 2nd 4 Sept 1844 Mary (*d* 4 Nov 1873), er dau of Joseph Lupton, of Armley, Leeds, and widow of Benjamin Atkinson, of Leeds, and *d* 23 March 1868, leaving by his 1st w, with an est s, two yr sons and six daus:

JOSEPH WATSON; *b* 19 March 1814; *m* 1837 Hannah (*d* 17 Oct 1890), only dau of George Pratt, of Kirkstall, Yorks, and *d* 24 Feb 1873, leaving, with two daus (*d* young) and an er s (Charles, *b* 3 March 1838, *m* 17 May 1871 Ann Elizabeth (*d* 7 Nov 1896), est dau of Richard Waite, of Leeds, and *dsp* 31 March 1916):

GEORGE WATSON, of Donisthorpe House, Moor Allerton, Yorks, JP; *b* 15 Jan 1840; *m* 17 June 1867 Mary Ann (*d* 21 Feb 1906), yr dau of Thomas Walker Hornsby, of Flockton-cum-Denby Grange, Yorks, and *d* 18 May 1905, leaving:

  1 JOSEPH, **1st Baron**

  1 Clara; *b* 4 April 1863; *m* 19 Nov 1890 James Ashwin, JP, DL (*d* 8 July 1941), of Bretforton Manor, Worcs, and *d* 17 May 1946, leaving issue

  2 Florence; *b* 10 June 1869; *m* 8 Dec 1892 John Till (*d* 17 Dec 1921), of Kemerton Court, Glos, 2nd s of William Till, and *d* 23 May 1946, leaving issue

  3 Gertrude Watson; *b* 9 May 1871; *m* 6 April 1899 Rev Colin Ashwin (*d* 12 Nov 1938), Rector Dumbleton, Glos, 5th s of William Henry Ashwin, of Bretforton Manor, and *d* 8 Feb 1901, leaving issue

GEORGE WATSON's only s,

  JOSEPH WATSON, **1st Baron Manton**, of Compton Verney, Co Warwick (UK), so *cr* 25 Jan 1922, JP; *b* 10 Feb 1873; *educ* Repton and Clare Coll Cambridge; chm Joseph Watson & Sons and Olympia Ag Co, dir LNWR; *m* 5 July 1898 Frances Claire (*d* 19 Jan 1944), 3rd dau of Harold Nickols, and *d* 13 March 1922, leaving:

1 GEORGE MILES WATSON, **2nd Baron Manton**, JP; *b* 21 June 1899; *educ* Harrow; Capt Life Gds, dir Newmarket Bloodstock Ltd; *m* 1st 18 April 1923 (*divorce* 1936) Alethea Alice Mary Pauline (*d* 1979), 2nd dau of Col Philip Joseph Langdale, OBE, JP, DL, of Houghton Hall, Sancton, Yorks (*see* MOW-BRAY, SEGRAVE and STOURTON, B); *m* 2nd 1 June 1938 Leila Joan (*m* 3rd 14 May 1969 6th Baron Brownlow (*qv*), only dau of Maj Philip Guy Reynolds, DSO, and widow of John Dane Player, and *d* 10 June 1968, leaving by his 1st w:

  (1) (JOSEPH) RUPERT ERIC ROBERT WATSON, **3rd and present Baron Manton**

2 Robert Fraser, of Thankerton Ho, Windlesham, Surrey; *b* 30 Aug 1900; *educ* Wellington, RMC Sandhurst and Trin Coll Cambridge; md Newmarket Bloodstock Ltd 1946–75; *m* 1st 26 April 1928 Angela Blanche Gladwin (*d* 18 Nov 1959), 2nd dau of Lt-Col George Talbot Lake Denniss, Wilts Regt; *m* 2nd 1961 Mrs Ewen Cameron (*d* 1993), dau of Arthur Levita, and *d* 1975, leaving by his 1st w:

  (1) *Shirley Angela Josephine [Mrs John Kennedy, The Old Court, Nethergate St, Clare, Suffolk CO10 8NP; 48 Egerton Gdns, London SW3]; *b* 7 March 1932; *m* 1st 18 Oct 1958 (*divorce* 1974) David Thomas Chantler, only s of David Everett Chantler, of Pittsburgh; *m* 2nd 11 Sept 1977 *John Hines Kennedy, MD, of Ohio, and has by 1st husb:

    1a *Peter David Robert; *b* 2 July 1963

    2a *Angela Margaret Jennifer; *b* 8 April 1961

3 Alastair Joseph; *b* 20 Aug 1901; *educ* Eton and Magdalene Coll Cambridge (MA); Capt Suffolk Regt WW II, Quartering Cmdt Herts 1940–46; *m* 13 July 1925 Joan (*d* 1988), er dau of Philip Wyndham Cobbold by Cicely Augusta, *née* Nevill (*see* ABERGAVENNY M), and *d* 13 Dec 1955, leaving:

  (1) +Michael Oliver, JP [Michael Watson Esq JP, Chillesford Lodge, Sudbourne, Woodbridge, Suffolk IP12 2AN]; *b* 20 Dec 1926; *educ* Stowe; Capt Life Gds 1945–48; *m* 7 Dec 1950 *Virginia, only dau of Eustace Benyon Hoare, of Pirton Court, Worcs, and has:

    1a +Alastair James; *b* 7 Nov 1958; *educ* Stowe; late Capt Life Gds; *m* 1991 *Camilla Jane, dau of Maj Christopher Wordsworth, Life Gds, and has:

      1b *Katherine Rachel; *b* 1996

    2a +George William; *b* 16 Feb 1962; *educ* Stowe and Wye Coll London (MSc); Lt RN; *m* 1997 *Alison Beryl, dau of James Crane, of Ware

    1a *Amanda Virginia Watson; *b* 19 Dec 1956; *m* 1985 *Antony Richardson Finley and has:

      1b *Harry George; *b* 1987

      2b *Thomas Geoffrey; *b* 1989

      3b *Toby Michael; *b* 1995

  (2) +Andrew Philip [Andrew Watson Esq, Faldonside, Melrose, Roxburghshire]; *b* 7 Feb 1930; *educ* Eton and Magdalene Coll Cambridge (BA 1952, MA 1957); QALAS; *m* 6 July 1957 *Annette Mary Helena, yr dau of Gerald Wellington Williams, JP (*see* NORTHUMBERLAND, D), and has:

    1a +Simon Mark; *b* 4 March 1959

    2a +Nicholas Andrew; *b* 21 Feb 1961

    3a +Jonathan Philip; *b* 19 June 1965

    4a +Hugh Gerald; *b* 29 Sept 1968

4 Richard Mark; *b* 18 July 1906; *educ* Eton; Attaché Washington 1930–32, Paris 1932–34, F/Lt RAFVR WW II, Order Icelandic Falcon 1965

MAR

Arms: Azure a bend between six cross-crosslets fitchée or. **Crest:** Upon a chapeau gules furred ermine two wings each of ten pen feathers, erected and addorsed, both blazoned as the shield. **Supporters:** Two griffins argent, armed, beaked and winged or. **Motto:** *Pans plus* ('Think more'). **Creation:** By prescription (S) from *c* 1114/5, but given precedence of 1404 (the oldest evidence the **18th Earl** could produce) at the Decreet of Ranking of 1606; his successors from time to time protested at such a relatively lowly place (for the weakness of mere antiquity, however, as a criterion in assigning precedence in Scotland before 1707 see CRAWFORD and BALCARRES, E, preliminary section **Creation**). The 1885 Act of Parliament (*see* below) placed the Earldom in its existing position among Scottish Peerages.

THE COUNTESS OF MAR, 30th holder of the title (Margaret of Mar) [The Rt Hon The Countess of Mar, St Michael's Farm, Great Witley, Worcs WR6 6JB]; *b* 19 Sept 1940; *s f* 1975, having been recognised in surname of 'of Mar' by warrant of Lord Lyon 5 July 1967; *educ* Kenya HS for Girls Nairobi and Lewes County GS for Girls; Dep Speaker Ho Lds 1997–; lay memb Immigration Appeal Tbnl 1985–, chm Environmental Medicine Fndn 1997–; Patron: Dispensing Dr's Assoc 1985–, Gulf Veterans Assoc 1995–, Worcs Mobile Disabled Gp 1991–; Pres Elderly Accommodation Cncl 1994–, Govr King's Sch Glos 1984–87; maintains a private offr of arms called Garioch Pursuivant; *m* 1st 30 May 1959 (*divorce* 1976) Edwin Noel ARTISS later Of MAR (so recognised by warrant of Lord Lyon 1969), s of Edwin E Artiss, FREconS, of Northfield, Birmingham, and has:

1 +SUSAN HELEN, *Mistress of Mar* [The Mistress of Mar, Firethorn Farm Cottage, Plough Lane, Ewhurst Green, Surrey GU6 7SG]; *b* 31 May 1963; *educ* King Charles I Sch Kidderminster and Christie Coll Cheltenham; interior designer; *m* 1989 *Bruce Alexander Wyllie and has:

(1) +Isabel Alice; *b* 10 Sept 1991

(2) +Frances Alexandra; *b* 1 Nov 1994

The COUNTESS *m* 2nd 30 April 1976 (*divorce* 1981) her cousin John Leslie SALTON later OF MAR (so recognised by warrant of Lord Lyon 26 May 1976), s of Norman Leslie Salton, of Walkington, N Humberside; *m* 3rd March 1982 *John H Jenkin, MA, FRCO, LRAM, ARCM

Mar, Earldom of, other holders of: Between 1435, when the **11th Earl** in right of his wife died, and 23 June 1565, the Earldom of Mar was appropriated by the Crown of Scotland. Judicial cloak to this purloining was lent by an instrument called 'an assize of error' of 15 May 1457 reinforced by a retour (here a ratification by Parliament) of 5 Nov 1457 which rested on four points. Each of these was subsequently shown to be invalid and one (the assertion, backed up by an error-strewn genealogy, that JAMES II was ISABEL **Countess of Mar**'s heir) to be a downright falsehood.

Be that as it may, John, fourth son of JAMES II, was ennobled by the title 'Earl of Mar and Garioch' at some point after 21 June 1458 but before 25 June 1459. He died unmarried twenty years later, when the creation expired. His elder brother Alexander, better known as Duke of Albany, enjoyed the additional title of 'Earl of Mar and Garioch' for a few months from January 1482/3 on but was stripped of it by the autumn of that year for trafficking with the English. The two brothers' nephew, John, youngest son of JAMES III, had an identically worded title conferred on him in March 1485/6 but died unmarried almost exactly seven years later, when this Earldom too expired.

Some sources writing in the early 16th century refer to one Thomas Cochrane, a master builder who was a favourite of JAMES III, as Earl of Mar, crediting him with having been so created *c* 1479/80. The latter's lynching in 1482 by certain nobles who found his swift advancement more than they could stomach put an end to whatever peerage dignity he may have enjoyed. Finally, the 1st Earl of Moray (*qv*), who was an illegitimate son of JAMES V by Margaret, daughter of JOHN ERSKINE, *de jure* 16th EARL OF MAR (*see* below), chose that title when given a second earldom a week after his first one of Moray. He seems to have been happy to surrender it for regrant to his kinsman a few months later, however. Even so it was three years before the Earldom was restored to its rightful owner (*see* below against **17th Earl of Mar**).

Lineage: (For a discussion of Mormaers, the predecessors of holders of such ancient earldoms as Mar, *see* BUCHAN, E, preliminary remarks, also for a short account of the period in which Buchan and Mar formed a single Mormaership.)

RODERICK/ROTHRI/RUADRI, *Comes* (*i.e.*, 'Mormaer' or (**1st**) **Earl**) **of Mar** (S), so mentioned in the foundation charter of Scone Abbey 1114/5; witnessed a charter of DAVID I KING OF SCOTS (1124–53) to Dunfermline Abbey 1124–29; living 1131/2; his successor (and kinsman?):

MORG(R)UND Mac GYLOCHER, **2nd Earl of Mar**; witness by 1152 to a charter of DAVID I and his son Henry to Dunfermline, also a confirmatory charter to the same foundation by DAVID's successor MALCOLM IV in the mid-1150s; *m* Agnes — and *d* by 30 March 1183, leaving possibly five or six sons (Malcolm; James; Duncan; David/Donald (possibly the same person); John); one of his sons may have been the man who was his undoubted successor as Earl:

GILCHRIST, **3rd Earl of Mar**; witness to foundation charter of St Peter's Hospital, Aberdeen, between 1182 and 1199; possibly *m* Orabilis, dau of Nes (s of William of Leuchars); she was definitely w of Robert de Quincy, by whom he had Saer de Quincy, Earl of Winchester (*see* WINCHESTER, M, preliminary remarks); GILCHRIST, **3rd Earl of Mar**'s successor was a yr s (but perhaps the est legitimate one) of MORG(R)UND, **2nd Earl of Mar**, by Agnes:

DUNCAN, **4th Earl of Mar**, which dignity he held by 29 Aug 1228, though his right to it was challenged at some point prior to 1231; witness to the Anglo-Scottish agreement sealed autumn 1237; *d* by 7 Feb 1243/4, leaving a son:

WILLIAM, **5th Earl of Mar**; Chamberlain to ALEXANDER III KING OF SCOTS *c* 1252; intermittently memb of the Cncl of Regency of Scotland in the 1250s and 1260s, also Chamberlain 1262–64 and Sheriff Dunbartonshire 1264–66; *m* 1st Elizabeth (*d* 1267), dau of William Comyn, Earl of Buchan (*see* BUCHAN, E, preliminary remarks); *m* 2nd Muriel (*dsp* 1291), dau of Malise, 1st Earl of Strathearn, and *d* 1281, leaving by his 1st w:

DONALD (Sir), **6th Earl of Mar**; ktd 1270; one of the leading Scottish nobles who recognised ALEXANDER III's daughter MARGARET as heir to the throne after her f's death Feb 1283/4; following MARGARET's death 1290 supported ROBERT (THE) BRUCE but was one of the seven Earls of Scotland who referred a decision in the matter to EDWARD I OF ENGLAND, to whom he swore fealty as overlord 13 June 1291; nevertheless was a leading participant in the Scottish Uprising against the English shortly afterwards, being captured by them following the Battle of Dunbar 27 April 1296 and renewing his allegiance to EDWARD I thereafter; *m* Helen (living Feb 1294/5), dau of LLEWELYN, PRINCE OF NORTH WALES, and widow of Malcolm, Earl of Fife, and *d* shortly after 25 July 1297, leaving:

1 GARTNEY/GRATNEY, **7th Earl**

2 Duncan

3 Alexander

1 Isabel; *m c* 1295, as his 1st w, ROBERT I (THE BRUCE) and was ancestor by him of the Royal House of STUART

2 Marjory/Mary; *m* 1st 8th Earl of Atholl (*see* STRABOLGI, B); *m* 2nd 4th Earl of Sutherland (*qv*)

The 6th EARL's est son,

GARTNEY/GRATNEY, **7th Earl of Mar**; Jt Sheriff Aberdeenshire 1297; *m c* 1292, as her 1st husb, Lady Christian Bruce (*m* 2nd Sir Christopher Seton, *m* 3rd *c* Oct 1325 Sir Andrew Moray of Bothwell, *d c* 1356/7), sis of ROBERT I, who granted her the lands of Garioch for her life, but whereby the Earls of Mar acquired the (feudal) Ldship of Garioch (not a peerage dignity) and were even latterly styled 'Earls of Garioch', and *d* by Sept 1305, leaving:

1 DONALD, **8th Earl of Mar**; reared at EDWARD I's court in England, choosing to remain there rather than return to Scotland in an exchange of prisoners between Scots and English after Bannockburn; was subsequently often in the retinue of EDWARD II OF ENGLAND, notably as Keeper Newark Castle Jan 1321/2; raised a force in Scotland 1327 and invaded England seeking to restore EDWARD II; apptd Regent of Scotland 1332 despite his Anglophilia; *m* Isabel, just conceivably dau of Sir Alexander Stewart of Bonkyl (*see* MORAY, E), and was *ka* Battle of Dupplin 12 Aug 1332, when disaffected Scottish nobles under Edward Balliol and with English support invaded Scotland to assert Edward's claim to the throne, leaving:

(1) THOMAS, **9th Earl of Mar**; *b c* 1330; following his paternal grandmother's death (*see* above) he called himself Lord of Garioch, the lands of which he was granted by roy charter 27 Jan 1356/7; Great Chamberlain Scotland 1358 and 1359; nevertheless pledged allegiance to EDWARD III OF ENGLAND; his Castle of Kildrummy accordingly seized by DAVID I KING OF SCOTS and held by the latter till at least 1364 (*see* below against **12th Earl**); *m* 1st *c* 1353 (*divorce* by Feb 1358/9) Margaret Graham, Countess of Menteith in her own right, widow of John Moray of Bothwell; *m* 2nd after 1361 Margaret Stewart, Countess of Angus in her own right (*see* MORAY, E), and *dsp* between 22 Oct 1373 and 21 June 1374

(1) MARGARET, **Countess of Mar** in her own right (10th holder of the title); *m* 1st by 13 Nov 1357 1st Earl of Douglas (*see* QUEENSBERRY, M) but self-styled (apparently without official authority for so doing) Earl of Douglas and Mar (*d* 1384) and had with other issue (*see* QUEENSBERRY, M):

1a ISABEL Douglas, **Countess of Mar** in her own right (11th Holder of the title); *b c* 1360; *m* 1st by July 1388 Sir Malcolm Drummond of Drummond (murdered while confined in prison prior to 8 Nov 1402; *see* PERTH, E); *m* 2nd between 5 and 9 Dec 1404, as his 1st w, Sir Alexander STEWART, 'The Wolf of Badenoch', thereafter **11th Earl of Mar** in right of his w (*dspl* 25/6 July 1435, having had by an unknown mother Sir Thomas Stewart, *Master of Mar*, granted Ldship of Badenoch by his f by 1424, *m c* 1425 Elizabeth (*m* 3rd 1st Earl of Caithness, *qv*) widow of John Stewart, Earl of Buchan (*see* BUCHAN, E, preliminary remarks, and MORAY, E), and *dsp* & *vp*), illegitimate s of Alexander, Earl of Buchan; the **11th Earl** (as he was to become) had the preceding 12 Aug forced his future w to sign a charter making over to him, in supposed view of their forthcoming marriage, the Earldom of Mar 'and Garioch', with remainder to heirs of their bodies, failing whom to his heirs and assigns (*i.e.*, to the exclusion of heirs on her side of the family who had the better right); this charter was never confirmed by roy charter, however, and next month the future **11th Earl** (who *m* 2nd 1409/10 Marie (dau of William van Hoorn, of Duffel, Brabant, and widow of Thierry de Linden), defeated the Lord of the Isles at Harlaw 1411, was Adml of the Scottish Kingdom 1419/20 and 1423 and illegally got the Earldom of Mar regranted to himself and his bastard Thomas 1426), restored to her Kildrummy Castle, which he had previously seized; she granted the Earldom to him and their heirs by charter 9 Dec 1404 (roy confirmation 21 Jan 1404/5), reserving its descent to her own lawful heirs, and *dsp* Aug-Sept 1408

(1) (cont.) MARGARET, **Countess of Mar** in her own right, *m* 2nd by 27 July 1388, as his 1st w, Sir John Swinton of Swinton (*ka* at Scottish defeat by the English of Homildon Hill 14 Sept 1402) and *dspms* by 19 Oct 1393

1 Ellen; *m* Sir John Menteith of Arran and had:

(1) John (Sir), of Strathgartney; *dsp c* 6 Aug 1363

(1) Christian; *m* 1st Sir Edward Keith of Synton (*d c* 1350; *see* KINTORE, E) and had:

1a Janet; *m* 1st Sir David Barclay of Brechin (*d* by 8 Sept 1368); *m* 2nd by 13 April 1370 Sir Thomas Erskine of that Ilk (*d* 1403/4), s of Sir Robert Erskine (*see* below) and *d* 1412/3, leaving:

1b ROBERT, *de jure* 12th EARL

2b John, of Dun; ancestor of the ERSKINEs of Dun

(1) (cont.) Lady Keith *m* 2nd 1352 Sir Robert Erskine (f by his 1st w Beatrix Lindsay (*see* CRAWFORD and BALCARRES, E) of Sir Thomas Erskine (*see* above); *d c* 1385) and *d c* 1387

(2) A dau; transmitted right to half the Mar estates to Sir Robert Lyle (*see* below) by some form of kinship the details of which remain unkown

ISABEL COUNTESS OF MAR's 2nd cousin once-removed,

ROBERT ERSKINE, *de jure* 12th EARL OF MAR (retoured heir to ISABEL, **Countess of Mar**, 22 April and 16 Oct 1438 as regards half the estates, enfeoffed thereto 21 Nov 1438; the rest of the estates were claimed by the jr coheir Sir Robert Lyle and by his successor(s) up to 1452; the *de jure* 12th EARL as sr coheir had a right to Kildrummy Castle and its immediate lands, which carried with it according to the doctrine of the day the full dignity of the Earldom, but the Crown continued to hold Kildrummy and its immediate lands, meanwhile drawing their rents (*see* above against **9th Earl**), and withheld recognition of ROBERT as **12th Earl**), also 1st LORD ERSKINE (S), so *cr* by 1438; *m* shortly after 20 Dec 1400 Elizabeth, dau of 1st Earl of Crawford (*see* CRAWFORD and BALCARRES, E), and *d* between 7 Sept 1451 and 6 Nov 1452, leaving:

THOMAS ERSKINE, *de jure* 13th EARL OF MAR and 2nd LORD ERSKINE; ktd by late Jan 1440/1, Sheriff Stirling 1483; *m* by 1445 Janet Douglas and *d* by 1493, leaving, with at least two daus (Elizabeth, *m* Alexander Seton of Touch (*see* SETON, Bt, of Abercorn); Helen, *m* Humphrey Colquhoun, 12th of Luss; *see* COLQUHOUN, Bt):

ALEXANDER ERSKINE, *de jure* 14th EARL OF MAR and 3rd LORD ERSKINE, (PC); Govr Dumbarton Castle; *m* 1st by 9 Oct 1466 Christian, dau of Sir Robert Crichton of Sanquhar (*see* BUTE, M) and widow of Sir Robert Colville of Oxnam; *m* 2nd just prior to 15 July 1480 Helen, sis of 1st Lord Home (*see* HOME, E) and widow of Sir Adam Hepburn, Master of Hailes, and *d* between 10 March 1507/8 and 10 May 1509, leaving by his 1st w, with other issue (including a dau, Agnes, *m* Sir William Menteth of W Kerse; *see* STUART-MENTETH, Bt):

ROBERT ERSKINE, *de jure* 15th EARL OF MAR and 4th LORD ERSKINE; *m c* 1485 Isabel, dau of Sir George Campbell of Loudoun, and was *ka* Flodden 9 Sept 1513, having had, with an er s (Robert *dvp* and unm) and at least three daus (Margaret, *m* (contract 11 July 1527) Sir Robert Douglas of Lochleven (*see* MORTON, E) and *d* 5 May 1572; Elizabeth, *m* Sir Walter Seton of Touch (*see* SETON, Bt, of Abercorn); Christian, *m* as his 1st w Sir John Colquhoun of Luss (*see* COLQUHOUN, Bt) and *d* 1564):

JOHN ERSKINE, *de jure* 16th EARL OF MAR and 5th LORD ERSKINE; ktd by June 1510, Envoy France 1515, Govr to young JAMES V, Constable Stirling Castle by 1525, Keeper Edinburgh Castle; *m* Margaret, dau of 2nd Earl of Argyll (*see* ARGYLL, D), and *d* July–Nov 1555, having had, with other issue (*see* MAR and KELLIE, E), a 3rd s:

JOHN ERSKINE, **17th/1st Earl of Mar**, as which restored by charter 23 June 1565 (ratified by Parl 9 April 1567), together with some of the Mar lands (the Manor of Migvie was substituted for Kildrummy since the latter castle had been alienated by the Crown, while Dunnydeer Castle was substituted for Garioch Castle, which also had been alienated; the feudal Ldship of Garioch and the lands were restored him, however), and 6th LORD ERSKINE, PC (S 1561); (by a decision of the Ho Lds Privileges Ctee 1875 this restoration was deemed a new creation, only with remainder to heirs male (*see* MAR and KELLIE, E) instead of heirs general as before, hence the dual numbering from here on); Abbot Dryburgh, Commendator (lay Abbot, on dissolution of religious houses, taking the revenues but not undertaking spiritual duties) Inchmaholme 1548; Keeper Edinburgh (to March 1566/7) and Stirling Castles, as which *s* f; a moderate memb of the Reforming party in ecclesiastical matters; Regent of Scotland 1571, having helped incarcerate MARY QUEEN OF SCOTS in Lochleven castle 1567; *m* by 29 Jan 1556/7 Annabel, dau of Sir William Murray of Tullibardine (*see* ATHOLL, D), and *d* 28 Oct 1572, leaving an only s:

JOHN ERSKINE, **18th/2nd Earl of Mar** and 7th LORD ERSKINE, also 1st LORD CARDROSS (S), as which *cr* 10 June 1610 with right to nominate his successor (as which he chose his 3rd s Henry; *see* BUCHAN, E), KG (1603), PC (S 1577, E 1603); *b* 1562; brough up with JAMES VI and I, with whom he was on close terms; joined in the Raid of Ruthven (an attempt to get JAMES away from his Catholic pro-French advisers) 1582, hence banished Jan 1583/4; returned to Scotland March 1583/4 and briefly held Stirling Castle till obliged to escape south to England; accordingly stripped with his w of honours by Parl Aug 1584 till he won back JAMES's favour Nov 1585 and his titles and lands restored him Dec 1585; Amb England 1601, Constable and Justiciar Brechin 1613, High Treasurer Scotland 1616–30, Collector Gen Taxation 1619; recovered much of the old Mar lands alienated by the Crown during its usurpation of the title, in particular the Kildrummy estate; *m* 1st 29 Oct–1 Nov 1580 Agnes/Anne, dau of 2nd Lord Drummond (*see* PERTH, E), and had issue; *m* 2nd 7 Dec 1592 Mary, dau of Esmé Stuart, Duke of Lennox (*see* MORAY, E), and *d* 14 Dec 1634, having by her had seven sons (*see* ROSSLYN, E) and five daus (*see* BUCHAN, E, ROTHES, E and STRATHMORE AND KINGHORNE, E); his only child by his 1st w:

JOHN ERSKINE, **19th/3rd Earl of Mar** and 8th LORD ERSKINE, KB (1610), PC (S 1617); *b c* 1585; Govr Edinburgh Castle 1615–38, Extrdy Ld Session 1620–26 and 1628–30; royalist Civil War; *m* 6 Feb 1609/10 Jean, dau of 9th Earl of Erroll (*qv*), and *d* 1653, leaving, with at least one dau (Elizabeth, *m* Sir Archibald Napier, 2nd Bt, of Merdistoun, *qv*):

JOHN ERSKINE, **20th/4th Earl of Mar** and 9th LORD ERSKINE, PC (S Feb 1660/1); royalist Civil War, present defeat of Philiphaugh 1645, hence his estates sequestrated, throwing the family into relatively straitened circumstances for generations to come; Capt and Govr Stirling Castle 1661, Capt Scots Gds 1662; *m* 1st 1641 Elizabeth (*dsp*), dau of 1st Earl of Buccleuch (*see* BUCCLEUCH and QUEENSBERRY, D); *m* 2nd *c* 8 Oct 1647 Jean (*m* 2nd, as his 2nd w, 3rd Lord Fraser (*see* SALTOUN, L), dau of 2nd Earl of Seaforth (*see* CROMARTIE, E), and *d* Sept 1668, leaving, with at least one dau (Barbara, *m* as his 1st w, 2nd Marquess of Douglas; *see* HAMILTON and BRANDON, D):

CHARLES ERSKINE, **21st/5th Earl of Mar** and 10th LORD ERSKINE, PC (E 1682–86 and 1688 on); *b* 19 Oct 1650; fndr-Col Roy Scots Fus 1678–86; *m c* 2 April 1674 Lady Mary Maule (*m* 2nd 29 April 1697 Col John Erskine), dau of 2nd Earl of Panmure, and *d* 23 May 1689, having had:

1 JOHN, **23nd/6th Earl**

2 James; Ld of Session as Lord Grange; *m* Rachel, dau of John Chiesly, of Dalry, and *d* 24 Jan 1754, having had, with two other daus (*d* unm):

(1) Charles; *dsp* 1 Dec 1776

(2) James; *m* 1740 his cousin Lady Frances Erskine, dau of **22nd/6th Earl of Mar**, and had issue (*see* below)

(3) John; Dean Cork

(1) Mary; *m* (contract 21 Aug 1729) 3rd Earl of Kintore (*qv*) and *dsp* 19 Feb 1772

3 Henry; Col; *ka* Almanza 14 April 1707

1 Jean; *m* 21 Feb 1712 Sir Hugh Paterson, Bt, of Bannockburn (*d* 23 March 1777), and *d* 16 Nov 1763, leaving issue

The 21st/5th EARL's est son,

JOHN ERSKINE, **22nd/6th Earl of Mar** and 11th LORD ERSKINE, KT (1706), PC (S 1697, GB 1707–14); *b* Feb 1675; Col of Foot 1702–06, rep S peer 1707–13, Sec State Scotland 1705–09 and 1713–14, when relieved of office by GEORGE I despite having got the Highland Clans to present him a loyal address; accordingly joined the Jacobites 1715 and was their C-in-C, as which was beaten (seemingly from inattention) at Sheriffmuir 13 Nov 1715 by 4,000 Govt supporters while leading 12,000 on his own side; attainted 17 Feb 1715/6 when his titles and lands forfeited, though the latter were bought by his bro Lord Grange and kinsman David Erskine of Dun; the remaining Mar estates were entailed 6 Jan 1739 on his son Thomas, *Lord Erskine*, and his heirs, with remainder to Lady Frances Erskine and heirs whomsoever; *cr* by the titular James III 22 Oct 1715 Duke of Mar, Marquess Erskine, Earl of Kildrummie, Viscount Garioch, Lord of Alloa, Ferriton and Forest (all S), with remainder to his heirs general, also 10 Nov 1717 Earl of Mar, Co York (E), with remainder to heirs male of his body, and 13 Dec 1722 Duke of Mar (I), also titular KG 1716; ch advsr to James III till 1724, when he ended his support for the Jacobites; *m* 1st 6 April 1703 Margaret (*d* 25 April 1707), dau of 7th Earl of Kinnoull (*qv*), and had:

1 Thomas, *Lord Erskine*; *b c* 1705; *educ* Westminster; MP (Whig) Stirling 1728–34 and Clackmannan 1747–54; *m* 1 Oct 1741 Charlotte (*d* 24 Nov 1788), dau of 1st Earl of Hopetoun (*see* LINLITHGOW, M), and *dsp* 16 March 1766

The **22nd/6th Earl** *m* 2nd 20 July 1714 Lady Frances Pierrepont (*d* insane 4 March 1761), 3rd dau of 1st Duke of Kingston-upon-Hull, and *d* Aix-la-Chapelle May 1732, leaving:

1 FRANCES Erskine; *m* 1740 her cousin James ERSKINE (*d* Feb 1785), yr s of Lord Grange (*see* above) and from 1 Dec 1776 heir male of the ERSKINEs, and *d* 20 June 1776, leaving:

(1) JOHN FRANCIS ERSKINE, **23rd/7th Earl of Mar**, as which restored by Act of Parl 17 June 1824; *b* 1741; *s vp* to the Alloa estates on his mother's death; Capt 1st Horse, as which ret from Army 1770; *m* 17 March 1770 Frances (*d* 20 Dec 1798), dau of Charles Floyer, Govr Madras, and *d* 20 Aug 1825, leaving, with other issue (*see* MAR and KELLIE, E):

1a JOHN THOMAS, **24th/8th Earl**

2a Henry David; had issue (*see* MAR and KELLIE, E)

The 23rd/7th EARL's est son,

JOHN THOMAS ERSKINE, **24th/8th Earl of Mar**; *b* 18 June 1772; *m* 17 March 1795 Janet (*d* 25 Aug 1825), dau of Patrick Miller, of Dalswinton, Dumfriesshire, and *d* 20 Sept 1828, leaving:

1 JOHN FRANCIS MILLER ERSKINE **25th/9th Earl of Mar** and 11th EARL OF KELLIE, as which *s* distant cousin (*see* MAR and KELLIE, E) 3 Dec 1829 but did not establish right thereto till 3 Sept 1835; *b* 28 Dec 1795; *educ* Westminster; served Waterloo Campaign; *m* 24 April 1827 Philadelphia Stuart (*d* 15 Feb 1853), dau of Sir Charles Stuart-Menteth, 1st Bt (*qv*), and *dsp* 19 June 1866, when the Earldom of Kellie and right to the 1565 Earldom of Mar passed to his cousin and heir male (*see* MAR and KELLIE, E)

1 Frances Jemima; *m* 12 Oct 1830 William James Goodeve (*d* 22 Dec 1861), MD, of Clifton, Somerset, and *d* 20 June 1842, having had:

(1) Rev JOHN FRANCIS ERSKINE GOODEVE later GOODEVE-ERSKINE (19 June 1866), **26th Earl of Mar**, though implicitly not recognised as such by the Ho Lds Privileges Ctee of Decision 1875; an 1885 Act of Parl, however, did so, albeit in half-hearted wording; *b* 29 March 1836; *educ* Bristol GS and Queens' Coll Cambridge (MA); Hon MA Oxford, Curate Tedstome Wafer, Herefs; rep S peer 1886–1922; *m* 12 Sept 1866 Alice Mary Sinclair (*d* 6 June 1924), dau of John Hamilton, of Hilston Park, Mon, and *d* 17 June 1930, leaving:

1a JOHN FRANCIS HAMILTON SINCLAIR CUNLIFFE BROOKS FORBES GOODEVE-ERSKINE, **27th Earl of Mar**; *b* 27 Feb 1868; *educ* Eton and Magdalene Coll Cambridge; *m* 15 Sept 1903 Sibyl May Dominica (*d* 20 July 1958), only dau of Robert Heathcote (*see* HEATHCOTE, Bt, of London), and *dsp* 29 Sept 1932

(1) Frances Jemima; *b* 1831; granted with sisters by roy warrant 15 Oct 1885 rank of dau of countess in her own right; *m* 29 March 1854 Lt-Gen James Nowell Young (*d* 13 Jan 1917), JAG Bengal, and *d* 11 Aug 1887, leaving:

1a Charles Walter; *b* 25 Nov 1862; Maj W India Regt; *m* 1885 Constance Barnes (*d* 28 June 1936), dau of Rev John Lovick Johnson, of Saxlingham Lodge, Long Stratton, Norfolk, and *d* 1898, leaving:

1b LIONEL WALTER YOUNG later YOUNG-ERSKINE (registered Court of Lord Lyon 1932), **29th Earl of Mar**; *b* 13 June 1891; V-Pres Roy Martyr Church Union; *d* unm 27 Nov 1965

1a Alice; *b* 26 March 1858; *m* 2 March 1878 James Horsburgh Lane (*d* 11 Dec 1915), est s of James Lane, slr, and *d* 25 April 1951, having had:

1b Charles Macdonald, CSI (1935); ISE; *b* 26 Jan 1882; *m* 14 Jan 1914 Jessie Helen (*d* 15 Dec 1968), est dau of John Brown Grant, of Lower Beeding, Sussex, and *d* 30 April 1956, having had:

1c JAMES CLIFTON, **29th Earl**

2c Frank Horsburgh; *b* 3 Jan 1923; *educ* Wellington; Lt RE WW II; *ka* Burma 18 Oct 1944

1c Margaret Isabel; *b* 28 March 1921; granted rank of earl's dau 20 Nov 1967; *m* 1943 Maj John Bulley Bray Ayre, RA (*d* 18 July 1994), and *d* 1989, leaving:

1d +Michael Desmonde Erskine [Michael Ayre Esq, 419 Wilverside Way, Calgary SE, Alberta, Canada T2J 1Z6]; *b* 1944; *educ* Sir George Williams U Montreal (BEng 1968); *m* 8 May 1971 *Jane Erica, er dau of Cdr E G Lock, RN, and has:

1e +Nicholas Robert Erskine; *b* 1973

2e +Robin Michael; *b* 1975

1d +Rosemary Bray [Ms Rosemary Ayre, Apt 507, 95 La Rose Ave, Etobicoke, ONT M9P 3T2, Canada]; *b* 13 Nov 1950; *educ* McGill U (BA)

2b Frank Nowell; *b* 4 Jan 1888; Capt 2nd/7th Gurkha Rifles, IA; *das* Palestine 11 Aug 1918

1b Mildred; *b* 8 Jan 1879; *d* unm 3 Oct 1969

2a Isabel; *b* 31 Aug 1860; *d* unm 14 May 1943

(2) Charlotte Erskine; *b* 1833; *m* 30 Nov 1857 Charles Bell (*d* 2 Sept 1859), of Siam, and *d* 9 Sept 1859, leaving:

1a Amy Elizabeth; *b* 13 Feb 1859; *d* unm 11 March 1920

(3) Eliza Philadelphia Erskine; *b* 1834; *m* 14 Aug 1862 Rev Edward Maule Cole (*d* 30 March 1911), Vicar Wetwang, Yorks, and *d* 15 March 1917, leaving:

1a Seymour Hamilton Maule, VD; *b* 1866; Maj ISR Rifles WW I (despatches); *m* 1892 Lillian May (*d* 9 Oct 1952), dau of Michael Sullivan, and *d* 10 Dec 1938, leaving:

1b Douglas Seymour Francis Erskine Maule; *b* 1898; Lt Dorsetshire Regt, Capt MGC and RFC, WW II as S/Ldr RAFO and Maj IA; *m* 1st 1924 (*divorce* 1935) Iris (*d* 1972), dau of Col G S Broome, IA, and had:

1c +Louis Malcolm Erskine [Louis Maule-Cole Esq, 20 St Catherine's Road, Pound Hill, W Sussex RH10 3TA]; *b* 1931; *m* 1955 *Kathleen Ida May Jarvis and has:

  1d +Julia Erskine [Mrs Timothy Barber, 3 Kenmara Close, Three Bridges, W Sussex]; *b* 1961; *m* 1989 *Timothy John Barber and has:

    1e +Matthew James; *b* 1989

    2e +Philip John; *b* 1993

    1e +Rachael Eleanor Alice; *b* 1991

  2d +Louise Erskine [Ms Louise Maule Cole, 25 Coltash Rd, Crawley, W Sussex]; *b* 1963; has issue by Russell Short:

    1e *Eve Erskine MAULE-COLE; *b* 1989

1c +Iris Erskine [Mrs Roger Harrison, Hipica Internacional, Camino de la Sierra, Churriana, Malaga, Spain]; *b* 1929; *m* 1950 *Roger Harrison, MPS, and has:

  1d +Sally Erskine; *b* 1951; *m* 1st 1970 Andrew Aitkenhead (*d* 1971); *m* 2nd 1973 (*divorce* 1976) Grenville Stacey; *m* 3rd 1978 (*divorce* 1987) Anthony Curtis *m* 4th 1988 *Duncan McLaren and has by her 3rd husb:

    1e +Candice Samantha; *b* 1978

  2d +Victoria Erskine [Mrs Garry Doherty, 1 Lilac Grove, Chadderton, Manchester]; *b* 1956; *m* 1975 *Garry Stephen Doherty and has:

    1e +Lorraine Ann; *b* 1982

1b (cont.) S/Ldr Douglas Maule Cole *m* 2nd 1942 Rosa Florence (*d* 1983), only dau of Lt Stanley George Bartley, RN, and *d* 1985

2b EDWARD ROBERT ERSKINE MAULE COLE later COLE-ERSKINE (warrant of Lord Lyon 1946) later still WILMOT OF MAR (officially recognised 1961, matriculating the plain arms of Mar with a crescent gules in chief of the bend for difference); *b* 1903; Lt (Sp) RINVR; feudal superior of Meikle Migvie, Mar Province, Aberdeenshire

1b Florence Violet Erskine; *b* 1893; *m* 1st 1911 (*divorce* 1924) Col John Alexander Barclay Penn Bowen, RE, and had:

  1c John Ivor Erskine Penn; *b* 1916; *m* 7 May 1939 Kate Molly Faith (*d* 1990), dau of Capt Bernard Arthur Mildmay, IA, and *d* 1967, leaving:

    1d +Hugh Erskine [Hugh Penn Bowen Esq, 36 Porter Way, Clacton-on-Sea, Essex]; *b* 8 June 1945; *m* 1st 1963 (*divorce* 1983) Marion May Wells; *m* 2nd 1989 *Mrs Bernadette Evelyn Grace Widlake (*née* Carlsson) and has by his 1st w:

      1e +Mark James; *b* 1964; *m* 1st 1987 (*divorce* 1992) Susan Aspridge; *m* 2nd 1993 *Catherine Anne, dau of Brian Paul Taylor

      2e +Jason Ivor; *b* 1970; *m* 1st 1989 (*divorce* 1992) Shirley M Szafinski; *m* 2nd 1994 *Mrs Sarah Jane Parker, dau of Dieter Heinz McDonald, and by her has:

        1f +Holly May; *b* 1994

    1d +Elizabeth Angelo [Mrs Elizabeth Penn Bowen, PO Box 129, Urangan, Qld 4655, Australia]; *b* 27 May 1947; *m* 1966 (*divorced*, resumed maiden name) (David) Peter D Gregory and has:

      1e +David; *b* 19–

      1e +Samantha Georgette; *b* 1967

      2e +Phaedra Simone; *b* 1968

    1d (cont.) Mrs Elizabeth Penn Bowen also has:

      2e *Liam; *b* 19–

      3e *Jesse; *b* 19–

  2d +Halcyon [Mrs Halcyon Simpson, 6 Juno Mews, Colchester, Essex CO2 9PQ]; *b* 12 Aug 1949; assumed surname of Simpson by deed poll 1982; *m* 1st 1968 (*divorce* 1973) Brian Sidney Mole; *m* 2nd 1974 (*divorce* 1981) Andrew David Lee and has by her 1st husb:

    1e +Wendy Lynn; *b* 1965; *m* 1986 *Carl Gary Baker and has:

      1f +James Carl; *b* 1988

      1f +Holly Sarah; *b* 1991

1c +Barbara Lilian [Mrs Raleigh Amesbury, 503 President Ave, Sutherland, NSW 2232, Australia]; *b* 1918; *m* 12 May 1941 Raleigh Cornwallis Amesbury (*d* 1986), s of George Amesbury, and has:

  1d +Christopher Raleigh Cornwallis [Christopher Amesbury Esq, 31 Annesley Ave, Stanwell Tops, NSW 2508, Australia]; *b* 4 June 1943; *m* 1966 *Wendy Lloyd and has:

    1e +Richard Anthony; *b* 1971

    1e +Michelle Ann; *b* 1967

    2e +Heather Marie; *b* 1969

  2d +Bruce Hamilton; *b* 4 Nov 1944; *m* 1st 1964 (*divorce* 1971) Maureen Patricia Presswell and has:

    1e +Joanne Patricia; *b* 1966

  2d (cont.) Bruce Amesbury *m* 2nd 1981 *Maria Luz Pritchett and by her has:

    1e +Grant Raleigh Ross; *b* 1983

    2e +Crystal Luzette; *b* 1982

  3d +Gary John [Gary Amesbury Esq, 92 Beaconsfield Rd, Revesby, NSW 2212, Autralia]; *b* 5 May 1949; *m* 1980 *Marilyn Watts and has:

    1e +Jason Raleigh; *b* 1982

    1e +Melanie Rae; *b* 1985

  4d +Stephen Antony [Stephen Amesbury Esq, 8 Eames Ave, Baulkham Hills, NSW 2153, Australia]; *b* 25 July 1953; *m* 1982 *Jacquelene, dau of D Hunt, of Blaxland, NSW, and has:

    1e +Caitlin Maree; *b* 1987

  1d +Valentina Maria [Mrs Harry Ivison, Lot 33 Hume Dve, Helensburgh, NSW 2508, Australia]; *b* 1959; *m* 1985 *Harry Ernest Ivison and has:

    1e +Danielle Barbara; *b* 1987

1b (cont.) Mrs Florence Bowen *m* 2nd 1925 Maj Henry William Fitzroy Clive, IA (*d* 1932), and by him had:

2c +Henry Robert Somerset [Henry Clive Esq, 1-21 Burke St, Concorde West, NSW 2137, Australia]; *b* 1926; *educ* Wellington; *m* 1949 *—, dau of Mohintri Passi, of Raniganj, W Bengal, and has had:

  1d Saluchna; *b* 1950; *d* 1952

1b (cont.) Mrs Henry Clive *m* 3rd 1933 (*divorce* 1944, resumed name Clive 1948) Frederick James St John Croley, of Bexhill, Sussex, and *d* 26 Feb 1967

2b Crystal Mary Vera Erskine; *b* 1895; *m* 1915 (*divorce* 1925) Leonard Charles Simpson (*d* 1958) and *d* 1972, leaving:

  1c Robert Seymour; *b* 15 June 1917; *educ* Dulwich; WW II as F/Lt RAF; *m* *Ivy May Jackson [Mrs Robert Simpson, 33 Woodley Cres, Melville Heights, WA 6165, Australia] and *d* 1994, leaving:

    1d +Robert Neil [Robert Simpson Esq, 48 Riverview Terrace, Mount Pleasant, WA 6153, Australia]; *b* 1952; *educ* Dulwich; Air Traffic Controller Perth; *m* 1978 *Catherine Faull and has:

      1e +Alicia Catherine Faull; *b* 1986

      2e +Hannah Jackson; *b* 1987

    1d +Jean Elizabeth [Mrs Johan Ravn, 49 Barbican St, Shelly, W Australia 6155]; *b* 1947; *m* 1968 *Johan Daniel Stub Ravn and has:

      1e +Johan Daniel Stub; *b* 1970

      2e +Kristian Robert; *b* 1973

      1e +Ingrid Kirsten; *b* 1974

1c +Yvonne Lilian [Mrs Frank Dator, 7927 Plantation Lakes Dve, Port St Lucie, FL 34986, USA]; *b* 4 Sept 1919; *m* 4 Sept 1941 Frank Dator (*d* 1985) and has:

  1d +(Frank) William [William Dator, 597 Wyckof Ave, Mahwah, NJ 07430, USA]; *b* 5 March 1943; *m* 1964 *Linda O'Lear, of Mahwah, and has:

    1e +William Frank; *b* 1971

    1e +Lisa Lynn; *b* 1965

    2e +Rebecca Ann; *b* 1969

  2d +(Raymond) James [Jamie Dator, 12 S Railroad Ave, Mahwah, NJ 07430, USA]; *b* 21 May 1946; *m* 1967 (*divorce* 1978) Barbara Ann Roosa, of Mahwah, and has:

    1e +Michele Lynn; *b* 1966

    2e +Erin Ashley; *b* 1969

  1d +Darryl [Mrs Darryl Dator, 14 Snow Dve, Mahwah, NJ 07430, USA]; *b* 1947; *m* 1976 (*divorce* 1993, resumed maiden name) Thomas John Kopplin, of Denver, Colo., and has:

    1e +Michael Thomas; *b* 1985

    1e +Katherine Elizabeth; *b* 1981

2c +Pamela Bernadene [Mrs Reginald Isaac, 10 Albert St, King's Lynn, Norfolk PE30 1ED]; *b* 30 Oct 1921; *m* 1st 1940 (*divorce* 1948) Thomas Wallace Greenwood and has:

  1d +Patricia Frances, JP (W Norfolk 1991) [Mrs Peter Knights JP, The Old Music House, 5 London Rd, King's Lynn, Norfolk PE30 5PY]; *b* 26 March 1941; Dip Serv 1962–74; *m* 1981 *Peter Knights

  2d +Marilyn Evelyn; *b* 4 Feb 1946

2c (cont.) Mrs Pamela Greenwood *m* 2nd 4 Dec 1948 Lt-Col Reginald John Isaac, OBE, MC, Intell Corps (*d* 1984), and by him has:

  1d +James Robert [James Isaac-Cole Esq, 106 Manns Rd, Narara, NSW 2250, Australia]; *b* 20 July 1950; *educ* Millfield; *m* 1973 *Suzanne Gaye Musgrove, of Sydney, and has:

    1e +Russell Jason; *b* 1984

  2d +Lionel Seymour John [Lionel Isaac Esq, 1 Cristella Close, Capalaba, Qld 4157, Australia]; *b* 8 Nov 1954; *educ* Wells Cathedral Sch Somerset and Loughborough U (BSc); *m* 1984 *Beth Slater and has:

    1e +Alexander; *b* 1993

    1e +Philadelphia Jane; *b* 1987

    2e +Natasha; *b* 1989

3b Edna Beryl Mavis Erskine; *b* 29 July 1896; *m* 23 Oct 1919 Constantine Demetriadi, MBE (*d* 1 Aug 1951), and *d* 3 Sept 1984, leaving:

  1c +Michael Anthony, OBE (1992), TD (1960) [Col Michael Demetriadi OBE TD, Office Farm House, Mutton Lane, Brandeston, Suffolk IP13 7AR]; *b* 20 Oct 1920; *educ* Radley; WW II as Maj Roy Welch Fus (wounded, despatches twice, Burma Star), TA 1948–75, Lt-Col 1959, Brevet Col 1967, Col T&AVR 1968–75, JP Dumbartonshire 1973–76, ADC to HM 1974–75, MInst PS; MInst AM, memb Sec State Scotland's Advsy Ctee to Ld Lt on appointment JPs, memb TAA Lowlands Scotland 1968–75, E Anglia 1976–85; cotton expert with J & P Coats Ltd Glasgow, Commr St John's Ambulance Bde Suffolk 1978–86 (Comdt 1984–93), Dir St John Assoc Suffolk 1986–90, Dep Sec Diocese St Edmundsbury & Ipswich 1979–86, KJStJ 1988; *m* 18 Sept 1948 his cousin *Nancy Anna, est dau of Ambrose John Rodocanachi, and has:

    1d +Peter Michael [Peter Demetriadi Esq, Lower Lodge Farm House, Oversley Green, Warwicks B49 6LJ]; *b* 4 Jan 1953; *educ* Radley and UCL; *m* 6 Sept 1980 *France Marie Anne Nicole, est dau of Judge Paul Bodson, of Brussels, and has:

      1e +Guy Peter Michael Erskine; *b* 17 April 1983; *educ* Radley

      2e +James Paul Christian Erskine; *b* 5 Dec 1985

      1e +Jennifer Anna Nancy; *b* 10 Jan 1982; *educ* St Mary's Wantage

    1d +Philippa Nancy [Mrs Jan Demetriadi-Doman, Dostjevského Rad 1, Bratislava 811-09, Slovakia]; *b* 2 Sept 1949; *educ* Priors Field; *m* 1st 31 May 1975 (*divorce* 14 Sept 1983) Nikos Stamatopoulos, of Athens; *m* 2nd 1986 *Jan Doman and has by her 1st husb:

      1e +Lucinda Polixeni; *b* 21 June 1976; *educ* Felixstowe Coll

    2d +Antonia Claire [Miss Antonia Demetriadi, 12A Porchester Sq, London W2 6AD]; *b* 29 Oct 1959; *educ* Wycombe Abbey; editor

4b Lilian Maude Erskine; *b* 2 Dec 1900; *m* 1st 1926 (*divorce* 1933) Cyril Ernest Musgrave Ridsdale (*d* 1957) and had:

  1c +Suzanne June Toye [Mrs Claude Biard, Silver Wood, 10 Sulley Rd, Thame, Oxon OX9 2EE]; *b* 23 July 1928; *m* 1st 1951 (*divorce* 1955)

David Jonathan Lush, 2nd Lt King's Own Dragoon Gds; *m* 2nd 1957 *Claude Guy de la Faye d'Entrains Biard (*d* 1991) and by her 1st husb has:

  1d +Sarah Jane Judith [Mrs Andrew Steggall, Ormond House, Temple St, Brill, Bucks]; *b* 4 May 1952; *m* 1974 (*divorce* 1981) Christopher John Dean and has:

    1e +Matthew Christopher; *b* 1975

    2e +Adam James; *b* 1977

  1d (cont.) Mrs Sarah Dean *m* 2nd 1982 *Andrew Quinton Steggall and by him has:

    3e +Edward Dicken; *b* 1984

4b (cont.) Mrs Lilian Ridsdale *m* 2nd 1933 William Louis Charles Gerard Cook, OBE, Indian Imp Police, and *d* 13 Sept 1965, leaving by him:

  1c +David William Erskine Gerard; *b* 1936; *educ* Bedford Sch; Sub-Lt RNVR; *m* 4 June 1960 *Joanne Elizabeth, dau of J Fisher, of Sydney, NSW, and has:

    1d +Jonathan David; *b* 14 June 1961

    2d +Jeremy Nicholas; *b* 15 Oct 1963

    1d +Caroline Louise; *b* 28 March 1965

5b Cecile Erskine; *b* 1906; *d* unm 29 May 1954

2a Edward Wilmot Maule; *b* 1868; *m* 1st 8 June 1898 Helen (*d* 1930), only dau of George Anderson; *m* 2nd 18 Feb 1936 Jean Campbell (*d* 10 Jan 1967), yst dau of Capt Owen E Wheeler, Leics Regt, of Weybridge, Surrey, and *d* 2 Oct 1948

3a Maurice St Michael Maule; *b* 1872; *d* unm 14 April 1956

4a John Francis Erskine Maule; *b* 1877; *d* unm 11 Feb 1948

1a Beatrice Madeline Erskine; *b* 1863; *m* 1884 Henry Tanner Ferguson, MICE (*d* 1909), of Wolleigh, Bovey Tracey, and *d* 20 Dec 1936, leaving:

  1b Donald Harry, MC, VRD; *b* 1890; WW I with IA Cav and MGC (Order Nile, Medal Militare al Valore), ISR, with CCG 1945–46; *m* 1st 1920 (*divorce* 1927) Helen Emily Woods (*d* 1967); *m* 2nd 1 Dec 1930 Margaret, widow of Algernon G H Richards, and had by his 1st w:

    1c Bryan Gratney; *b* 31 May 1922; Black Watch; *das* 22 Feb 1944

  2b Gerald William, MC, AFC; *b* 1891; WW I with RFC; Assam-Bengal Rlwy, ret as DLS 1929, started Sch of Navigation, Heston Airport, Ch Naval Instr Straight Corp; *m* 1925 Jean Clapham and *d* Aug 1940

  3b George Hamilton, KPM; *b* 1896; WW II as Lt-Col Intell Corps; Dep Inspr-Gen Ceylon Police, ret 1939, Assist Inspr-Gen Overseas Special Police Corps CCG 1945–50, Dep Ch Br Police Mission Greece 1950–51; *m* 8 Oct 1931 (*divorce* 1948) Dorothy Mary Kate Susie Emily Vaughan, dau of Sir Robert Vaughan Gower, KCVO, OBE, DCL, MP, of Sandown Court, Tunbridge Wells, and *d* 1970, leaving:

    1c +Robert Maule Gower; *b* 9 Aug 1932; *educ* Harrow

    1c +Beatrice Margaret (Kiki) [Mrs Carey Creek, 9433 Ardmore Drive, RR2 Sidney, BC, Canada]; *b* 4 Nov 1933; *m* 1963 *(Norman) Carey Booth Creek and has:

      1d +Carey Hamish Ferguson; *b* 22 March 1964

      2d +Benjamin Robert; *b* 9 Dec 1965

      1d +Nicola Robin; *b* 13 Aug 1967

      2d +Karina Susanna Erskine; *b* 1970

    2c +Sally Pauline June [Mrs Ian Cochrane, c/o Royal Bank of Scotland, Oban, Argyll]; *b* 29 June 1941; has:

      1d *Frances Sarah Nicola; *b* 1960; adopted by her step-f 1968

    2c (cont.) Sally Ferguson *m* 8 May 1968 Lt-Cdr Ian Cochrane, RN (*d* 1988), and has:

      2d +Harriet Elizabeth Alexandra; *b* 1970

      3d +Emma Catherine Anne; *b* 1972

4b Roland Edward Stuart; *b* 1899; WW I with RNAS and RAF, later IA, WW II in RASC (invalided); Indian Imp Police; *m* 6 Sept 1941 *Veronica Catherine, yr dau of Henry Gore Hawker, of Devon, and *d* 1976, leaving:

  1c +Andrew Stuart [Andrew Ferguson Esq, Penllyn, Cathedine, Bwlch, Powys]; *b* 20 Nov 1948; ionosphericist and Base Cdr Br Antarctic Survey 1971–74, Nature Conservancy Cncl/Countryside Cncl for Wales 1979–; *m* 1975 *Helen Alice, only dau of Col P N Lodge, RA, of Compton Abdale, Glos, and has:

    1d +Geoffrey Roland; *b* 1976

    2d +Ian Anthony; *b* 1980

  1c +Janet Erskine [Mrs Adrian Bomback, Cracklewood, Didworthy, S Brent, S Devon]; *b* 9 June 1946; WRNS 1964–68; *m* 1st 26 Aug 1971 (*divorce* 1977) John Goodwin Fisk, 8th Hus; *m* 2nd 1978 Lt-Cdr Adrian John Bomback, MC, RN (*k* by falling tree in storm 25 Jan 1990), and has by her 1st husb:

    1d +Adrian John Stewart; *b* 10 Nov 1970

    2d +Peter Maule Erskine; *b* 1973

1b Helen Evelyn; *b* 23 Feb 1886; *m* 14 Nov 1914 Harold Henry Wyndham Newman (*d* 15 July 1963), yr s of Rev W F Newman, of Hockworthy, Devon, and S Town House, Dartmouth, and *d* 31 Oct 1962, leaving:

  1c +Durnford Frederick Wyndham [S/Ldr Durnford Newman, Roleystone Cottage, Golf Club Rd, Hook Heath, Surrey GU22 0LS]; *b* 4 Aug 1917; Dip Faraday House Engrg Coll; WW II as Capt RE, S/Ldr RAF 1951–54; CEng, FIEE; Ch Engr and Dep Dir BAA Heathrow 1972–77; *m* 11 Sept 1948 *Joan (Jane) Merriel, dau of Richard G Hollway, and has:

    1d +(James) Richard Wyndham [Richard Newman Esq, Studlands, 8 The Knoll, Fairmile Park Rd, Cobham, Surrey KT11 2PN]; *b* 7 Aug 1950; BSc; *m* 1st 5 July 1975 Ann Caroline Lawrence (*d* 16 Dec 1984); *m* 2nd 2 Aug 1985 *Carole Ann Dove and by her has:

      1e +Thomas Philip Wyndham; *b* 23 April 1987

      2e +James Frederick Wyndham; *b* 10 July 1991

    1d +Clare Marian Wyndham [Mrs Robert Alter, 11145 NW 1st Place, Coral Springs, FL 33071, USA]; *b* 28 March 1953; *m* 15 Oct 1982 *Robert Tony Alter and has:

      1e +Edward Donald; *b* 14 Aug 1989

    1e +Katharine Dora; *b* 23 Sept 1994

2b Kathleen Erskine; *b* 1887

3b Mary Beatrice Erskine; *b* 1888; *m* 1st 11 June 1912 Capt Hubert Symons, RFA (*ka* 22 March 1918); *m* 2nd 7 Sept 1937 Graham Parsons Earwaker (*d* 14 April 1971) and *d* 13 June 1970, leaving by her 1st husb:

  1c Peter Nicholas; *b* 7 July 1917; WW II with S Wales Borderers and Capt Roy W African Frontier Force India and Burma; *m* 26 Oct 1940 *Suzanne Penzer [Lady Marshall, Hatt House, nr Saltash, Cornwall] (*m* 2nd 19 Dec 1953 Cdr Sir Douglas Marshall, FZS, RNVR (*d* 24 Aug 1976)), dau of H Penzer Haynes, of Edgbaston, Birmingham, and *d* 29 Sept 1951, leaving:

    1d +Heugh Sherwood [Heugh Symons Esq, Bicton Farm House, Hatt, nr Saltash, Cornwall]; *b* 9 Oct 1949; *m* 4 Sept 1976 *Fiona Ann, dau of Dr A S Mitchell, of St Austell, and has:

      1e +Genevieve Penn; *b* 1979

      2e +Emily Penn; *b* 1980

      3e +Suzanna Penn; *b* 1984

    1d +Nicola Penn [Mrs John Coverdale, Bevere Manor, Bevere, Worcs WR3 7RG]; *b* 4 April 1942; *m* 14 Sept 1963 *John Philip Coverdale, only s of Philip Frederick Coverdale, and has:

      1e +Peter John; *b* 1970

      2e +Philip Anthony; *b* 1978

      1e +Anna Frances Mary; *b* 19 April 1966; *m* 1990 *Andrew Christopher Kennedy Davis and has:

        1f +Oliver John Kennedy; *b* 1991

      2e +Sarah Elizabeth; *b* 28 May 1968

    2d +Celia Mary [Mrs Celia Rinagl, Swiftaford Farm House, Hatt, Cornwall PL12 6PP]; *b* 20 Jan 1947; *m* 1973 (*divorce* 1988) Erich Gerhard Rinagl, of Austria, and has:

      1e +Marc Gerard Penn; *b* 1979

      1e +Nina Penn; *b* 1983

    2d +Melanie Anne [Mrs Jeremy Shales, 70 Princes Rd, Teddington, Middx]; *b* 20 Jan 1947 *m* 2 May 1970 *Jeremy John Shales, 2nd s of J H Shales, of E Sheen, and has:

      1e +Joanna Penn; *b* 1979

      2e +Louise Alexandra Penn; *b* 1980

  1c +Jean Erskine [Mrs Richard Joscelyn, Withycombe, Winsford, Somerset TA24 7AB]; *b* 3 Feb 1916; *m* 31 Aug 1940 Richard Andrew Joscelyn, MC (*d* 1992), and has:

    1d +Andrew Michael Hubert; *b* 11 Aug 1946; Col Gren Gds

    1d +Sarah Anne [Mrs A Blishen, 8 York Square, London E14 7LU]; *b* 10 June 1941; *m* 6 July 1963 *Anthony Owen Blishen, OBE, Capt Roy Hants Regt, later with FCO s of Henry Charles Adolphus Blishen, of Newport, IoW, and has:

      1e +James Peter Anthony; *b* 1 April 1966

      2e +Robert Edward Henry; *b* 1970

      3e +David Francis Andrews; *b* 1972

      1e +Catherine Annabelle; *b* 18 May 1964

4b +Violet Madeline; *b* 1893; *m* 1919 (*divorce* 1926) Philip Eric Bernard (*d* 25 Nov 1953) and has:

  1c +Barbara Nancy [Mrs Barbara Hyde, 11 Unsworth Rd, N Ringwood VIC 3134, Australia]; *b* 1920; *m* 1945 Ronald Hyde, JP, MRCS, LRCP (*d* 24 Jan 1965), and has:

    1d +Timothy David Erskine [Timothy Hyde Esq, c/o PO Box 879, Bowral, NSW 2576, Australia]; *b* 18 Oct 1946; late memb Sydney Stock Exch 1983; *m* 1987 *Caroline Noell Scheidat and has:

      1e +Philippa Annabelle Jane; *b* 1987

    2d +Robin Paul Christopher; *b* 22 April 1948; memb Australian Inst Export; *m* 1st 1975 (*divorce* 1979) Margaret Anne Weichelt; *m* 2nd 1979 *Aoura Sangsingkeo and by her has:

      1e +Andrew Chatvalin; *b* 1985

      1e +Samantha Darupat; *b* 1983

    3d +Max Anthony John; *b* 27 June 1951; *educ* Monash U (BA); *m* 1983 (*divorce* 1989) Carla Lavinia Holding and has:

      1e +Rebecca Louise Austen; *b* 1984

    4d +James Rupert; *b* 7 Aug 1955; *m* 1988 *Stella Moutos and has:

      1e +Jeremy; *b* 1989

      1e +Stephanie Anne; *b* 1987

      2e +Bianca Natalie; *b* 1991

    1d +Lucy Susan Elizabeth (twin); *b* 7 Aug 1955; *m* 1976 *Anthony John Lemprière Sheaffe and has:

      1e +Jonathan Lemprière; *b* 1979

      1e +Susan Elizabeth; *b* 1980

      2e +Alexandra Jane; *b* 1984

2a Edith Marguerite Erskine; *b* 1865; *d* unm 19 May 1951

3a Mary Christian Janet Erskine; *b* 1869; nun Community Resurrection; *d* 23 Dec 1956

(4) Madeline Erskine; *d* unm 31 Jan 1919

2 Jane Janetta; *m* 29 April 1830 Edward Wilmot Chetwode, JP (*d* 9 May 1874), of Woodbridge, Queen's Co, and *d* 16 May 1861, leaving issue

The 28th EARL's 1st cousin once-removed,

JAMES CLIFTON LANE later OF MAR (recognised by Lord Lyon 1959), **29th Earl of Mar**; *b* 22 Nov 1914; *educ* Marlborough; *m* 1st 1939 (*divorce* 1958) Millicent Mary, dau of William Salton, and had:

1 David Charles, *Lord Garioch*; *b* 10 Aug 1944; *educ* Gosfield Sch Essex; *d* unm 8 Jan 1967

1 MARGARET OF MAR, **present Countess of Mar**

2 +Janet Helen [The Lady Janet of Mar, 2 Lyndhurst Rd, Maidstone, Kent ME15 7EQ]; *b* 31 Jan 1946; *educ* St Andrews (MA 1968); *m* 22 March 1969 Lt-Cdr *Laurence Duncan McDiarmid ANDERSON later OF MAR (recognised by Lord Lyon 19 Oct 1969), RN, s of Archibald Anderson, of Aberdeenshire, and has:

(1) +Elizabeth; *b* 17 Jan 1970

(2) +Catherine Jane; *b* 13 May 1971; *m* 1 June 1995 *Stuart Kelly and has:

1a +Jack Alexander; *b* 13 Aug 1996

1a +Eleanor Louise; *b* 15 Oct 1997

The **29th Earl** *m* 2nd 1960 Marjorie Aileen (*d* 25 Nov 1975), dau of John Reginald Miller and widow of Maj C W S Grice, Centl Indian Horse, IA, and *d* 21 April 1975

MAR and KELLIE

Arms: Quarterly, 1st and 4th, argent a pale sable (for ERSKINE); 2nd and 3rd, azure a bend between six cross-crosslets fitchée or (for MAR); over all on an escutcheon gules the Royal Crown of Scotland proper within a double tressure flory counter-flory or, ensigned with an Earl's coronet (for KELLIE); behind the shield in saltire a key, wards outwards or, and a baton gules, garnished or, and ensigned with a castle of the last (for the Hereditary Keepership of Stirling Castle). **Crests:** 1 On a cap of maintenance gules, doubled ermine, a dexter hand holding a skene dhu in pale argent, hilted and pommelled or (for ERSKINE), 2 On a like cap a demi-lion rampant guardant gules, armed argent (for KELLIE). **Supporters:** Two griffins gules, armed, beaked and winged or. **Mottoes:** 1 *Je pense plus* ('I think more') (for ERSKINE), 2 *Decori decus addit avito* ('He augments ancestral honour with his own') (for KELLIE), 3 (under shield) *Unione fortior* ('The stronger for unity'). **Creations:** L. (S) 12 March 1619 (Dirletoun), B. (S) 8 July 1604 (Erskine of Dirletowne), V. (S) 18 March 1606 and 12 March 1619, E. (S) 29/30 July 1565 (Mar) and 12 March 1619 (Kellie).

THE 14TH EARL OF MAR AND 16TH EARL OF KELLIE, Viscount (of) Fentoun (twice), **Baron Erskine of Dirletowne** and **Lord Dirletoun** (James Thorne Erskine, DL (Clackmannan 1991)) [The Rt Hon The Earl of Mar and Kellie DL, Erskine House, Kirk Wynd, Clackmannan FK10 4JF]; *b* 10 March 1949; *s* 1993, also as Premier Viscount of Scotland and Hereditary Keeper Stirling Castle; *educ* Eton, Moray Coll of Educn and Inverness Coll; Page of Honour to HM THE QUEEN 1962 and 1963; P/Offr RAuxAF 1979, attd 2622 Highland Sqdn, RAuxAF Regt, F/Offr RAuxAF 1982–86, Memb RNAuxS 1985–89; community serv vol York 1967–68, community worker Richmond Craigmillar Parish Church Edinburgh 1971–73, sr social worker Family and Community Serv Sheffield DC 1973–76, social worker Grampian Regn Cncl Elgin 1976–77, Forres 1977–78, Highland Regn Cncl Aviemore 1979, Inverness Prison 1979–81, community worker Merkinch Centre Inverness Jan–July 1982, community serv supervisor Inverness 1983–87, building technician 1989–91, project worker SACRO Intensive Probation Project Falkirk 1991–93, boatbuilder 1993; *m* 23 March 1974 *Mary, yr dau of Dougal McDougal Kirk, of Edinburgh, and formerly w of Roderick James Mooney

Lineage: HENRY de ERSKINE, whose name probably derives from lands held by the family on the banks of the Clyde in Renfrewshire, witnessed a charter *temp* ALEXANDER II (1214–49); had:

Sir JOHN ERSKINE; witnessed charters 1260, 1263 and 1271; had:

Sir JOHN ERSKINE of that Ilk; swore fealty to EDWARD I OF ENGLAND 1296; had:

Sir WILLIAM ERSKINE of that Ilk; living 1331; had:

Sir ROBERT ERSKINE of that Ilk; supported DAVID II against the Balliol faction (*see* MAR, E, sub **8th Earl**); High Chamberlain Scotland 1350–57 and 1363–64, Constable Stirling Castle, Amb England; had a roy charter 1368 granting Alloa to himself and his 2nd w in exchange for Strathgartney, subsequently a Menteith possession; *m* 1st Beatrix, dau of Sir Alexander de Lindsay (*see* CRAWFORD and BALCARRES, E) and widow of Sir Archibald Douglas, and had two sons (the yr of whom, Nichol, was ancestor of the ERSKINEs of Kinnall); *m* 2nd 1352, as her 2nd husb, Christian (*dsp* by him), dau of Sir John Menteith of Arran by Ellen, dau of 7th Earl of Mar (*qv*), and *d* 1385; his er s by his 1st w:

Sir THOMAS ERSKINE of that Ilk; *m* 1st *c* 1365 — (*dsps*), only dau and heiress of Sir William Douglas of Liddesdale; *m* 2nd *c* 13 April 1370 Janet, dau and heiress

of Christian (dau of Ellen (dau of 7th Earl of Mar) by Sir John Menteith of Arran) by Sir Edward Keith of Synton (*see* KINTORE, E) and widow of Sir David Barclay of Brechin, and *d* 1403/4, having had, with a yr s (John, ancestor of the ERSKINEs of Dun; *see* AILSA, M, against 1st Marquess)

Sir ROBERT ERSKINE, 1st LORD ERSKINE (S), so *cr* by 1438, and *de jure* 12th EARL OF MAR (*qv*); had, with two daus (Janet, *m* (dispensation 1421) Walter Stewart, est s of Murdoch, Duke of Albany (*see* MORAY, E); Christian):

THOMAS ERSKINE, 2nd LORD ERSKINE and *de jure* 13th EARL OF MAR; had, with three daus:

ALEXANDER ERSKINE, 3rd LORD ERSKINE and *de jure* 14th EARL OF MAR; had by his 1st w:

ROBERT ERSKINE, 4th LORD ERSKINE and *de jure* 15th EARL OF MAR; had, with other issue (including James, ancestor of the ERSKINEs of Balgony):

JOHN ERSKINE, 5th LORD ERSKINE and *de jure* 16th EARL OF MAR; had:

1 Robert, *Master of Erskine*; *m c* 17 Feb 1534/5 Margaret, dau of 2nd Earl of Montrose (*see* MONTROSE, D), and was *ka spl* Battle of Pinkie 10 Sept 1547

2 Thomas, *Master of Erskine*; Commendator (lay Abbot, in wake of dissolution of religious houses, drawing revenues but undertaking no spiritual duties) Dryburgh 1541–47, Amb England 1551; *m* (contract 30 Jan 1548/9) Margaret, dau of 3rd Lord Fleming and widow of Robert, Lord Graham (*see* MONTROSE, D), and *dspl* 1551

3 JOHN ERSKINE, **1st Earl of Mar** (S), so *cr* 29/30 July 1565 (according to a Ho Lds Privileges Ctee decision of 26 Feb 1875, but also 17th EARL OF MAR (*qv*) of the older *cr*), and 6th LORD ERSKINE; had, with a dau (Mary, *m* 13 June 1573 8th Earl of Angus, *see* HAMILTON and BRANDON, D):

(1) JOHN ERSKINE, **2nd Earl of Mar** (also 18th EARL OF MAR) and 7th LORD ERSKINE; *m* 1st 29 Oct–1 Nov 1580 Agnes/Anne, dau of 2nd Lord Drummond (*see* PERTH, E), and had:

1a JOHN ERSKINE, **3rd Earl of Mar** (also 19th EARL OF MAR) and 8th LORD ERSKINE; had, with other issue:

1b JOHN ERSKINE, **4th Earl of Mar** (also 20th EARL OF MAR) and 9th LORD ERSKINE; had by his 2nd w, with other issue:

1c CHARLES ERSKINE, **5th Earl of Mar** (also 21st EARL OF MAR) and 10th LORD ERSKINE; had:

1d JOHN ERSKINE, **6th Earl of Mar** (also 22nd EARL OF MAR) and 11th and last LORD ERSKINE, attainted for Jacobitism when his titles were forfeited; *m* 1st and had a s (Thomas, *dsp*); *m* 2nd and by her had:

1e Frances; *m* 1740 her 1st cousin James Erskine (*see* below) and *d* 20 June 1776, leaving:

1f JOHN FRANCIS ERSKINE, **7th Earl of Mar** (also 23rd EARL OF MAR), as which restored 1824; had, with five daus (*d* unm):

1g JOHN THOMAS ERSKINE, **8th Earl of Mar** (also 24th EARL OF MAR); had, with other issue (*see* MAR, E):

1h JOHN FRANCIS MILLER ERSKINE, **9th Earl of Mar** (also 25th EARL OF MAR) and **11th Earl of Kellie**, as last of which *s* distant cousin 1829 but did not establish right thereto till 3 Sept 1835; *dsp* 19 June 1866, when the Earldom of Mar (*qv*) of the medieval *cr* passed to his sister's son

2g James Floyer; Capt 26th Cameron Regt; *m* 12 Nov 1796, as her 1st w, Susan (*m* 2nd 8 Aug 1800 William Walker; *m* 3rd 16 June 1806 Shirley F S Perkins; *d* 8 Feb 1827), dau of Charles Kirkpatrick Sharpe, of Hoddam, and *dsp* 15 May 1798

3g Henry David; *b* 10 May 1776; *m* 22 Oct 1805 Mary Anne (*d* 4 March 1860), dau of John Cooksey, and *d* 31 Dec 1846, having had, with two er sons (*d* young):

1h WALTER CONINGSBY ERSKINE, *de jure* 10th EARL OF MAR, which title he claimed 1867 but *d* before the Ho of Lds reached a decision, and **12th Earl of Kellie**, CB (1860); *b* 12 July 1810; joined Bengal Army 1826; Lt-Col, Commr Jubbulpore at time of Indian Mutiny (recd thanks of Parl for servs); rep S peer 1869–72; *m* 11 Sept 1834 Elise (*d* 14 July 1895), dau of Col Youngson, of Bowscar, Cumberland, and *d* 15 Jan 1872, having had:

1i WALTER HENRY, **11th Earl of Mar** and **13th Earl of Kellie**

2i Augustus William, JP (Cumberland); *b* 18 June 1841; Offr 17th Lancers; *m* 18 April 1871 Harriet Susannah (*d* 24 Feb 1884), dau of William Forbes of Medwyn (*see* STUART-FORBES, Bt), and *d* 17 July 1914, having had:

1j Henry Walter Coningsby; *b* 11 May 1872; *d* 7 Nov 1933

2j Walter Augustus; *b* 22 July 1880; Capt RGA WW I (despatches); *ka* 24 May 1915

3j William Forbes; *b* 21, *d* 22 Feb 1884

1j Eveline Mary Elise; *b* 25 Nov 1874; *m* 20 May 1896 Col Henry Lowther, IA (*d* 25 Jan 1925), and had issue

2j Agnes Helen; *b* 16 April 1876; nun Community St Mary the Virgin Wantage; *d* unm 1 April 1943

3j Dorothy Christian; *b* 31 March 1878; *m* 27 June 1906 James Chapman, s of Rev Edward William Chapman, Hon Canon Carlisle, by Hon Theodosia, sis of 2nd Baron Monteagle of Brandon (*qv*), and *d* 1 Oct 1940, leaving issue

3i Charles Herbert Stewart; *b* 11 Sept 1853; Maj 3rd Bn Princess Louise's Argyll & Sutherland Highrs; *d* 6 April 1896

2h James Augustus; *b* 27 March 1812; granted with sis rank of earl's dau/yr s 1866, Kt St Ferdinand Spain, Assist Commissary Gen HM Forces; *m* 1st 15 June 1837 Fanny (*d* 17 Sept 1851), dau of Gen Henry Ivatt Dalacombe, CB, and had:

1i Augustus; *b* 15 May 1843; 108th Regt, Melbourne CS; *m* 6 Aug 1888 Kathleen (*d* 22 Nov 1924), dau of Edmund Lyons, of N Melbourne, and *d* 28 Jan 1918, leaving:

  1j Busby Lyons; *b* 21 Aug 1890; Capt and Hon Maj 4th Bn Manchester Regt; *m* 31 Dec 1919 Lilian, dau of Francis William Blenkey, of Beckenham, and *d* 1962, leaving:

    1k *Sheelah Katherine; *b* 1921; *m* *— Tortonese, resumed maiden name

  2j Fenton Augustus; *b* 29 June 1895; 2nd Lt RM WW I (despatches); *ka* 8 May 1915

1i Fanny Eliza; *m* 1873 Thomas Bushby Jamieson and *d* 10 June 1897

2i Caroline; *m* 1 Nov 1864 Col George Pearson, MSC, and *d* 21 Nov 1865, leaving issue

3i Marianne Craig; *m* 10 Nov 1868 John Henry Gordon of Aikenhead and *d* 24 Feb 1870

2h (cont.) The Hon James Erskine *m* 2nd 4 Nov 1852 Elizabeth Bogue (*d* 9 Feb 1882), dau of George Brodie, Historiographer Roy Scotland, and *d* 24 July 1885, having had:

2i William Alexander Ernest; *b* 24 March 1857; *m* 1st 27 Dec 1878 Edith Elizabeth (*d* 1879), est dau of William Frank Elliot, of Wilton, Taunton, and widow of C A Turner, of Staplegrove, and had:

  1j Eva Edith Mar ERSKINE later ERSKINE MACONOCHIE (deed poll 1918); *d unm* 1958

2i (cont.) William Erskine *m* 2nd 4 Jan 1881 Amelia Esther, dau of Capt John Ovens, 57th Regt, and *d* 24 March 1934, having by her had:

  2j Marguerite Ernestine Louise; *m* 1st 20 Oct 1902 (*divorce* 1908) Richard Murray McGusty, of Dublin, and had issue; *m* 2nd 1921 Arthur Bendir (*d* 30 Oct 1957) and *d* 23 Feb 1954, having had further issue

3i Charles Henry Stuart; *b* 19 Sept 1858; *m* 7 Sept 1880 Constance Claire (*d* 9 Sept 1934), dau of William Frank Elliot, of Taunton, and *d* 11 April 1910, leaving:

  1j Constance Gwendoline Erskine; *m* 7 June 1915 Maj Eric Charles Robert Hudson, Worcs Regt, er s of Rev Thomas William Hudson, Rector Gt Shefford, Berks, and *d* 22 Dec 1963, leaving issue

  2j Marion Esmé Erskine; *d unm* Feb 1963

  4j Kathleen Nadine Erskine; *d unm* 6 Feb 1919

4i Edmond Waterton Coningsby; *b* 9 Nov 1860; *m* 1st 6 Dec 1882 (*divorce* 1894) Evelina Florence (*d* 15 May 1949), dau of George Jones, of Cupar, Grange, Trinidad, and had:

  1j Lowiny Leta Arabella; *b* 1883; *d* 4 Nov 1971

4i (cont.) Edmond Erskine *m* 2nd 1894 Edith (*d* 25 Sept 1957), dau of Maj Alexander Crombie, 72nd Regt, and *d* 2 July 1926, having by her had:

  2j Monica Violet; *b* 1897; *m* 1st 1923 Lt-Col G D Maynard (*d* 1923); *m* 2nd 1926 Lt-Col Hugh Alan Heber-Percy, OBE (*see* NORTHUMBERLAND, D), and by him had issue

5i Walter Kellie; *b* 16 July 1868; *d unm* 2 Jan 1901

6i Evelyn Pierrepont; *b* 7 Sept 1870; CS W Australia; *m* 1897 Amy Maria (*d* 1959), dau of Joseph Hough, of Collie River, WA, and *d* 1953, leaving:

  1j Augustus Evelyn; *b* 7 Dec 1901; WW II with AIF (POW); *d unm* 7 Sept 1963

  2j +Charles Seymour [Charles Erskine Esq, 21 Bellevue Terrace, Swanbourne, WA 6010, Australia]; *b* 1903; *m* 1923 Mona Roselyn, dau of George Murphy, of Co Cork

  3j +Gratney Pierrepont [Gratney Erskine Esq, 12 Devon Rd, Swanbourne, PC 6010, W Australia]; *b* 1911; WW II with AIF; *m* 1st 1931 (*divorce* 1935) Elsie Evelyn, dau of I Nutall, and has:

    1k *Yvonne Constance [Miss Yvonne Erskine, 23 Catesby St, City Beach, PC 6015, W Australia]; *b* 1932

  3j (cont.) Gratney Erskine *m* 2nd 21 Sept 1940 *Beth Rosemary, dau of William Henry Kenworthy, of Mosman Park, W Australia, and by her has:

    1k +Gratney Evelyn [Gratney Erskine Esq, 20 Knight St, Wembley Down, W Australia]; *b* 24 July 1941; *m* 28 Jan 1967 *Elaine Joy, dau of F D Marchant, of Claremont, W Australia, and has:

      1l +Gregory Bryce; *b* 1972

      1l *Janine Gaye; *b* 9 Sept 1969

  4j Robert Fallowfield; *b* 1913; WW II with RAAF

  1j Maimie Rhoda Wilhelmina; *b* 1898; *m* 1926 Lawrence Ridley Field (*d* 1971) and had:

    1k *Spencer Erskine; *b* 1927; *m* 1956 *Coral, dau of F White of Albany, W Australia, and has:

      1l *Murray; *b* 1958

      1l *Susan; *b* 1957

      2l *Kay; *b* 1961

    2k *Barry Ridley [Barry Field Esq, 5 Crocker Way, Innaloo 6018, W Australia]; *b* 1930; *m* 1956 *Gwen Murphy, of Victoria Park, WA, and has:

      1l *Stephen; *b* 1955

      2l *Clinton; *b* 1958

      3l *Bradley; *b* 1959

      1l *Marilyn; *b* 1954

3k *Robin Erskine [Robin Field Esq, 155 Hare St, Albany, W Australia]; *b* 1938; *m* 1960 *Lorraine Whitfield and has:

  1l *Alan; *b* 1966

  1l *Yvonne; *b* 1963

  2l *Beverley; *b* 1965

1k *Naomi Laurel Erskine; *b* 1928; *m* 1949 *John O'Keefe, of W Australia, and has:

  1l *Neil; *b* 1959

  1l *Carol; *b* 1950; *m* *Gary Thomas Adams, of Albany, W Australia, and has:

    1m *Tracy Lana; *b* 1966; *m* 1983 *Trevor White and has:

      1n *Ryan Trevor; *b* 1983

      1n *Jade; *b* 1986

    2m *Michelle Lisa; *b* 1968; *m* 1989 *Larry Hill, of Osborne Park, W Australia, and has:

      1n *Jacinta Bree; *b* 1985

  2l *Linda; *b* 1952; *m* 1st 1970 Kevin Albert Wallinger, of Albany, W Australia, and has:

    1m *Brent; *b* 1976

    1m *Hayley; *b* 1972

  2l (cont.) Mrs Wallinger *m* 2nd 1984 *Wayne Alexander Halliday and by him has:

    2m *Cher Odette; *b* 1986

  3l *Diane; *b* 1954; *m* 1971 *Lindsay Horton, of Albany, W Australia, and has:

    1m *Wade; *b* 1972

    2m *Chad; *b* 1976

2k *Derrice; *b* 1933; *m* 1953 *John Joseph Jones, of Parkerville, W Australia, and has:

  1l *Laurence John; *b* 1955; *m* 1988 *Nadine Alger

  2l *Mark; *b* 1957

  3l *Matthew; *b* 1961

  1l *Rachel; *b* 1963; *m* 1988 *Clement Foley

2j Azelma Aileen; *b* 1900

3j Edna May; *b* 25 Nov 1903; *d unm* 5 May 1952

4j Alice Amy Mar; *b* 1906; *m* 1927 Wallace Kendall Ross (*d* 1971) and had issue

5j Bessie Constance; *b* 1910; *d unm* 20 March 1936

7i Hugh Bushby Erskine later JOHNSON (deed poll for self only 4 June 1952); *b* 16 Sept 1872; *educ* Dulwich; Lt Australian Inf; *m* 5 Jan 1897 Mae (*d* 1950), dau of Dennis Valentine, of Bunbury, WA, and *d* 1956, leaving:

  1j John Patrick William; *b* 27 Jan 1899; *m* and had:

    1k +Hugh Walter Bushby; *m* Doris Gwen Crundwell and has:

      1l *Christine Maria; *b* 1946

  2j Kellie Edmund; *b* 25 Oct 1901; *m* 1924 Annie (*d* 1975), dau of Robert Knox, and had:

    1k +Kellie Knox [Kellie Erskine Esq, 4 Palermo Place, Allambie Heights, Sydney, NSW 2100, Australia]; *b* 1931; *m* 25 May 1959 *Pamela Ann, dau of Alfred Ernest Leer, AIF, and has:

      1l +Bryan Andrew; *b* 30 Sept 1966

      1l *Robyn Ann; *b* 10 April 1963

      2l *Keryn Maree; *b* 9 March 1971

  3j Hugh Pierrepont Clayhills; *b* April 1903; *m* 1935 Edith Wilhelmina, dau of James Ralphs, of Sydney, NSW

  4j James Keith Brodie; *b* 16 March 1907; AIF; *m* 1949 *Mary Douglas, dau of Arthur Ernest Savage, of Sydney, and *d* 1981, leaving:

    1k *Lynette Mary; *b* 1950; *m* 1978 *Patrick Philip Duncan, s of Patrick Duncan, of Wellington, NZ, and has:

      1l *Guy Philip; *b* 1980

      1l *Stacey Mary; *b* 1982

    2k *Catherine Evelyn; *b* 1953

    3k *Joanne Margaret; *b* 27 June 1960

  1j *Esmé Mai Lydia [Mrs Claud Jefferson, 1 Budgdree St, Norah Head, NSW 2263, Australia]; *b* 10 July 1910; *m* 1935 Claud Wentworth Jefferson, F/Lt RAAF (*d* 1974), and has:

    1k *Ian David; *b* 1945; *m* 1968 *Kay Leslie, dau of John Farren Price, of Sydney, and has:

      1l *Kalena Ann; *b* 1971

      2l *Fiona; *b* 1975

4i Rachel Georgina; *m* 1882 Rev Edward Field Norman, Vicar Watford, Rugby, and had issue

5i Elizabeth Mai; *m* 16 June 1897 Alexander Cockburn McBarnet, CBE (*d* 5 Feb 1934), barrister, Judge Mixed Court Appeal Egypt, and *d* 30 June 1951, leaving issue

6i Lowiny Ida; *m* 16 Aug 1892 Maj Charles James Addison, RAMC (*d* 1929), and *d* 1949, leaving issue

7i Augusta Helena; *b* 1875; *m* 15 March 1898 Thomas George Harkness (*d* 20 Dec 1906), s of Christopher Harkness, of Dumfries, and *d* 1958, leaving issue

3h Henry David; *b* 15 June 1814; Capt RM; *m* 27 June 1846 Eliza (*d* 1881), 3rd dau of John Ingle, and *d* 7 Dec 1852, having had:

1i Henry David; *b* 27 April 1847; *dsp* May 1881

2i Coningsby James; *b* 27 April 1849; *m* 3 July 1872 Louisa Jane (*d* 9 Dec 1928), est dau of Thomas Henry Baylis, KC, and *d* 29 Aug 1925, leaving:

1j Evelyn; *b* 1874; *d* unm 9 Aug 1959

1h Anne Caroline; *m* 18 June 18– Rev Joseph Haskoll (*d* 26 Feb 1871), and *d* 4 Dec 1891 aged 68, leaving issue

4g Thomas (Rev); *b* 10 July 1785; Vicar Beighton, Derbys; *m* 4 June 1817 Charlotte (*d* 1 Dec 1876), dau of Maj Watson, and *d* 1 Jan 1859, leaving, with other issue:

1h Thomas Floyer; *b* 10 July 1819; Admlty; *m* 28 Aug 1856 Emma (*d* 2 Dec 1918), dau of Boughey Hepworth, and *d* 30 Sept 1872, leaving:

1i Alice Mary; *b* 1858; *d* unm Jan 1946

2i Frances Anne Janet; *b* 1861; *d* unm 18 May 1956

3g Mary Margaret Anna; *m* 27 Dec 1864 Rodolph Zwilchenbart, of Dean Wood, Berks (*d* 2 April 1883; she added maiden name 30 Aug 1884) and *d* 31 Oct 1906, leaving:

1h Gratney Rodolph; *b* 1871; *m* 1896 Theodora (*d* 1958), dau of W H Laverton, of Leighton, Wilts, and *d* 1930, leaving:

1i Helen Mary; *b* 1901; *m* 1928 Brig Alec Palmer ffleetwood Churchill, OBE, IA (*d* 1947), and had:

1j *John ffleetwood [John Churchill Esq, Victoria Lodge, Charters Rd, Sunningdale, Berks SL5 9QB]; *b* 1934; *educ* Wellington and Trin Hall Cambridge; *m* 1970 (*divorce* 19–) Stephanie, dau of H van den Bergh, of The Hague, and has:

1k *John Edward ffleetwood; *b* 1973

1k *Gratia Mary Anne ffleetwood; *b* 1975

2k *Juliet Kathleen ffleetwood; *b* 1978

2j *Charles ffleetwood [Charles Churchill Esq, 31 Irsha St, Appledore, N Devon EX39 1RZ]; *b* 1937; *educ* Wellington and Jesus Coll Cambridge

2f James; Col; *m* Matty Baller, of Berne, Switzerland, and *d* 5 April 1806, having had issue (*dsp*)

2d James; Ld of Session as Lord Grange; *m* Rachel, dau of John Chiesly, and *d* 24 Jan 1754, having had, with other issue (see MAR, E):

1e James; *m* 1740 his 1st cousin Lady Frances Erskine, only dau of **6th Earl of Mar**, and had issue

1c Jean; *m* 5 Aug 1673, as his 1st w, 11th Earl of Glencairn (see CUNINGHAME, Bt), and had issue

2c Sophia; *m* 1676 3rd Lord Forbes of Pitsligo (see FORBES, Bt, of Newe) and had issue

1b Elizabeth; *m* 2nd Lord Napier (see NAPIER and ETTRICK, L) and had issue

(1) (cont.) The **2nd Earl** *m* 2nd 7 Dec 1592 Mary (*d* 11 May 1644), dau of 1st Duke of Lennox (see MORAY, E), and *d* 14 Dec 1634, having by her had, with other issue (see BUCHAN, E):

2a Charles (Sir), of Alva; had issue (see ROSSLYN, E)

1a Mary; *m* (contract 12 Oct 1609) 5th Earl Marischal (see KINTORE, E) and had issue

2a Anna; *m* (contract 28 Dec 1614) 6th Earl of Rothes (*qv*) and had issue

4 Alexander (Sir), of Gogar; Guardian of JAMES VI and Keeper of Stirling Castle, from which ejected 1578 by his nephew, **2nd Earl of Mar**; *m* *c* 20 March 1563/4 Margaret, dau of 4th Lord Home (*qv*), and *d* *c* 3 April 1592, having had, with an est s (*d* young), four yr sons and four daus:

(1) Sir THOMAS ERSKINE, **1st Earl of Kellie**, so *cr* 12 March 1619, as also VISCOUNT OF FENTOUN and LORD DIRLETOUN, with remainder to heirs male bearing the name and arms of Erskine, as also earlier 8 July 1604 BARON ERSKINE OF DIRLETOWNE and 18 March 1606 VISCOUNT OF FENTOUN, with remainder to heirs male whatsoever (all S), KG (1615), PC (S 1601, E Jan 1609/10); *b* 1566; Gentleman Bedchamber 1585, Groom Stole Feb 1604/5, Capt Yeomen Gd 1617; *m* 1st 30 Nov 1587 Anne, dau of Sir Gilbert Ogilvy of Powrie, and had:

1a Alexander, *Viscount Fentoun*, KB (1616); *m* 1610 Lady Anne Seton, est dau of 1st Earl of Dunfermline (see EGLINTON and WINTON, E), and *dvp* 11 Feb 1633, leaving:

1b THOMAS ERSKINE, **2nd Earl of Kellie**; *bapt* 4 May 1615; *d* unm 3 Feb 1642/3

2b ALEXANDER ERSKINE, **3rd Earl of Kellie**, PC (S 1661); royalist Civil War, captured by CROMWELL's forces Battle of Worcester 1651; *m* 1st 1661 Anna, dau of Col John Kirkpatrick, Govr Bois-de-Duc, and had:

1c Anne; *m* her cousin Sir ALEXANDER ERSKINE, 2nd Bt, of Cambo, and had issue (see below)

2b (cont.) The **3rd Earl** *m* 2nd (contract 8 July 1665) Mary, niece of 1st Earl of Carnwath (see 1940 edn), and *d* May 1677, having by her had:

1c ALEXANDER ERSKINE, **4th Earl of Kellie**; *bapt* 14 Sept 1677; *m* 11 June 1699 Anne (*m* 2nd (contract 16 April 1714) 3rd Viscount of Kingston (see EGLINTON and WINTON, E) and *d* 4 Feb 1742/3), dau of 3rd Earl of Balcarres (see CRAWFORD, E), and *d* 8 March 1710, leaving, with a dau (Jean, *m* 1719 John Scott of Harden and had issue; see POLWARTH, L):

1d ALEXANDER ERSKINE, **5th Earl of Kellie**; Col Jacobite Army 1745 Uprising, fought at Preston, Falkirk and Cullloden, accordingly imprisoned Edinburgh Castle 1746–49; *m* 1st 1726 Louisa (*dsp* 11 Nov 1729), dau of William Moray, 12th of Abercairny, Perths; *m* 2nd Oct 1731 Janet (*d* 7 June 1775), dau of Dr Archibald Pitcairn, a Jacobite physician and poet, and *d* 3 April 1756, having had, with other issue:

1e THOMAS ALEXANDER ERSKINE, **6th Earl of Kellie**; *b* 1 Sept 1732; *educ* Edinburgh HS; composer for and perfomer on the violin; sold his entire estates apart from the mansion at Kellie; *d* unm at Brussels 9 Oct 1781

2e ARCHIBALD ERSKINE, **7th Earl of Kellie**; *b* 22 April 1736; Lt-Col 104th Foot 1782, rep S peer 1790–96; *d* unm 8 May 1797

1e Elizabeth; *m* 1st 23 April 1760 Walter Macfarlan of that Ilk (*d* 5 June 1767); *m* 2nd 1 Oct 1768 6th Lord Colville of Culross (*qv*) and *d* 2 Nov 1794

2e Janet; *m* 18 Aug 1863 Sir Robert Anstruther, Bt, of Balcaskie (*qv*), and *d* 14 Oct 1770, leaving issue

2c Elizabeth; *bapt* 15 Sept 1673; *m* Alexander Fraser of Inverallochy (see LOVAT, L) and *d* 11 Dec 1744

3b Sir CHARLES ERSKINE, 1st Bt (NS), so *cr* 20 Aug 1666, of Cambo, Fifeshire; Lyon King of Arms 1663; *m* 1663 Penelope, dau of Arthur Barclay of Colhill, Gentleman of the King's Chamber, and *d* Feb 1677, leaving, with other issue:

1c Sir ALEXANDER ERSKINE, 2nd Bt, of Cambo; MP Fifeshire 1710–13; Lyon King of Arms 1681; *m* 1680 his cousin Lady Anne Erskine, dau of **3rd Earl of Kellie**, and *d* 1727, having had, with other issue:

1d Sir CHARLES ERSKINE, 3rd Bt; *bapt* 1 Oct 1687; Lyon Clerk 1715–24; *d* unm 8 Feb 1753

2d Sir JOHN ERSKINE, 4th Bt; *bapt* 18 May 1690; *d* unm 20 July 1754

3d Sir WILLIAM ERSKINE, 5th Bt; *bapt* 13 April 1695; *d* unm 15 Oct 1781

4d David; Lyon Depute and Lyon Clerk 1724–69; *m* 1st — Grant and had two daus; *m* 2nd — Young and *d* 7 Oct 1769, having by her had, with three other sons (*d* unm):

1e Sir CHARLES ERSKINE, 6th Bt, of Cambo; *b* 1730; *m* 1758 Margaret, dau of John Chiene of Crail, and *d* 6 March 1790, having had, with other issue:

1f Sir WILLIAM ERSKINE, 7th Bt; *b* 1759; Lt 26th Foot; *d* unm 2 Oct 1791

2f Sir CHARLES ERSKINE, 8th Bt, and **8th Earl of Kellie**; *b* *c* 1764; Capt Fifeshire Light Dragoons; *d* unm 28 Oct 1799

2e THOMAS ERSKINE, 9th Bt, and **9th Earl of Kellie**; *b* *c* 1745; Br Consul Gothenburg, Sweden; rep S peer 1804–06 and 1807–28; Kt Cdr Order Gustavus Vasa; *m* 1771 Anne (*d* 20 March 1829), dau of Adam Gordon of Ardoch, and *dspl* 6 Feb 1828; his illegitimate son's s was *cr* a Bt (see ERSKINE, Bt)

3e Sir METHVEN ERSKINE, 10th and last Bt, and **10th Earl of Kellie**; *b* *c* 1750; merchant in Bengal; *m* 10 July 1781 Joanna, dau of Adam Gordon of Ardroch and sister of his er bro's w, and *dsp* 3 Dec 1829, when the btcy expired

5d Thomas; *bapt* 17 Jan 1699; *m* Jean Rue and *d* 2 Feb 1783, leaving three sons (*dsp*)

6d Colin; painter; had:

1e Charles; Cardinal; *b* 9 March 1811

1c Margaret; *m* Sir William Sharp, 1st Bt, of Scotscraig (see 1970 edn SHARP BETHUNE, Bt), and *d* March 1726, leaving issue

2c Mary; *bapt* 21 May 1667; *m* 1687 *de jure* 5th Lord Colville of Culross (*qv*) and had issue

4b George; *d* unm 31 Dec 1656

1b Mary; *m* *c* 14 Dec 1663 2nd Earl of Carnwath (see 1940 edn) and *dsp*

2b Sophia; *m* 5 Aug 1663 Alexander, Master of Saltoun, s of 11th Lord Saltoun (*qv*) of Abernethy, and had issue

1a Anna; *m* Sir Robert Mowbray of Barnbougie

(1) (cont.) The **1st Earl** *m* 2nd 1604 Elizabeth (*dsp* 27 April 1621), dau of Sir Henry Pierrepont, of Holme Pierrepont, Notts, and widow of Sir Edward Norreys; *m* 3rd, as her 4th husb, Dorothy, dau of Ambrose/Humphrey Smith, of London, and widow of (a) Benedict Barnham, of London, (b) Sir John Pakington, KB (see HAMPTON, B), and (c) 1st Viscount Kilmorey (see KILMOREY, E), and *d* 12 June 1639

5 Arthur, of Blackgrange; *m* (contract 7 Jan 1561/2) Magdalen, dau of 5th Lord Livingston, and *dsps* *c* Jan 1570/1

1 Catherine; *m* (contract 20 Nov 1525) 2nd Lord Elphinstone (*qv*)

2 Margaret; illegitimately mother by JAMES V of 1st Earl of Moray (*qv*); *m* (contract 11 July 1527) Robert Douglas of Lochleven and *d* 5 May 1572

3 Janet; *m* (contract 1 Sept 1532) John Murray of Touchadam and had issue

The 12th EARL OF KELLIE's est son,

WALTER HENRY ERSKINE, **11th Earl of Mar**, as which confirmed in his claim by Ho Lds 25 Feb 1875, and **13th Earl of Kellie**; *b* 17 Dec 1839; *educ* Radley and BNC Oxford; rep S peer 1876–88; *m* 14 Oct 1863 Mary Anne (*d* 22 May 1927), est dau of William Forbes of Medwyn (see STUART-FORBES, Bt), and *d* 16 Sept 1888, having had:

1 WALTER JOHN FRANCIS, **12th and 14th Earl**

2 William Augustus Forbes (Sir), GCMG, MVO, PC; *b* 30 Oct 1871; *educ* Eton and Magdalen Coll Oxford; Br Del Internat Commn Athens 1913, Chargé d'Affaires Athens 1914, Rome 1917, Envoy Extrdy and Min Plen Cuba 1919–21, Bulgaria 1921–28, Poland 1928, Amb Poland 1928–34; *m* 18 Feb 1908 (Georgiana) Viola Eleanor (*d* 14 May 1972), 2nd dau of Capt William Humble Dudley Ward (see DUDLEY, E), and *d* 17 July 1952, leaving:

(1) Cynthia Romola; *b* 30 March 1910; *m* 20 May 1943 Pierre Bressy (*d* 1973), Amb in French Dip Serv, and *d* Aug 1997, leaving:

1a *François Pierre Erskine [M François Bressy, L'Englos, rue Gabrielle Bénier, Bouviers, 78280 Guyancourt, France]; *b* 1946; *m* 1975 *Monique Vanwelsenaere and has:

1b *Jean Sebastien Erskine; *b* 1979

2a *Catherine Marie Charlotte [Vicomtesse de Bourgoing, 54 Boulevard de la Tour-Maubourg, Paris VII]; *b* 1945; *m* 1972 *Vicomte Jean-Marie de Bourgoing and has:

1b *Guillaume Pierre Denis; *b* 1976

2b *Philippe Marie François; *b* 1978

1b *Marguerite Roseline Romola; *b* 1975

(2) *Margaret Elsie Viola [Mrs Denys Oglander, c/o West Lodge, Nunwell Park, Brading, IoW]; *b* 13 Dec 1913 (HRH CROWN PRINCESS OF SWEDEN stood sponsor); *m* 17 Jan 1950 Maj Denys Ernest Glynn Oglander (*d* 22 March 1977), of Brading, only surv s of Lt-Col Auberon Claud Hegan Kennard (*see* KENNARD, Bt), and has:

  1a *William Auberon Erskine; *b* 1953

  2a *John Peter Erskine [John Oglander Esq, West Lodge, Nunwell Park, Brading, IoW PO36 0JQ]; *b* 1957; *m* 1987 (*divorce* 1988) Fiona Stuart, dau of Ronald Stuart Brisbane, of Leicester, and has:

    1b *Susanna Anastasia; *b* 1987

  1a *Frances Mary; *b* 1951; *m* 1977 *Michael Solosy, of IoW, and has:

    1b *Robert John Solosy OGLANDER; *b* 1981

  2a Mary Theresa Catherine Joan; *b* 1955; *m* 1981 *Josef Hubbard and *d* 1982

3 Alexander Penrose Forbes (Rev); *b* 13 Aug 1881; *educ* Eton and New Coll Oxford (MA); *m* 11 July 1916 Irene Annette (*d* 17 Jan 1968, having *m* 2nd 15 July 1930 Rt Rev Frederic Llewellyn Deane, DD, Bp Aberdeen and Orkney 1917–43), est dau of Rt Rev Archibald Ean Campbell, DD, DCL, Bp Glasgow and Galloway, by Hon Helen Anna, dau of 8th Viscount Midleton (*qv*), and *d* 20 June 1925, having had:

(1) +Archibald Walter Forbes [Dr Archibald Erskine, 130 Walm Lane, London NW2 4RT]; *b* 22 July 1918; *educ* Eton and New Coll Oxford (BM, BCh 1942, MA 1946); *m* 8 Nov 1958 *(Joan Mary) Thérèse Frances, est dau of John Benedict Heppel, of Bromley, Kent, and has:

  1a +James Alexander [Dr James Erskine, Box 86, Banjul, The Gambia]; *b* 6 Oct 1959; MB, BS, DA, DTM & H, MRCGP; *m* 1993 *Debbie de Lacy-Leacy and has:

    1b *Abigail Mia Thérèse; *b* 1995

  2a +Robert John [Dr Robert Erskine, The Mount, Yeldersley, Ashbourne, Derbyshire DE6 1LS]; *b* 15 Nov 1960; MB, BS, FRCA; *m* 1990 *Dr Gillian Margaret Turner, dau of Charles Thomas Turner, and has:

    1b *Lucy Emmeline; *b* 1994

    2b *Eleanor Kathryn; *b* 1996

  3a +Benjamin David [Benjamin Erskine Esq, 29 rue Ste Eugénie, 33000 Bordeaux, France]; *b* 14 Jan 1971

(2) +David Alexander John, TD [David Erskine Esq TD, Les Loriers, Rue Beau Repaire, St Peter Port, Guernsey]; *b* 18 Feb 1921; *educ* Eton and New Coll Oxford (BA 1948); Capt 5th Bn QO Cameron Highrs (TA) WW II; *m* 1st 14 March 1947 (*divorce*) Margaret Eleanor, twin dau of R-Adml Steuart Arnold Pears, CBE, DL, of Warwick, and has:

  1a +Robin David [Robin Erskine Esq, East Deanraw, Langley-on-Tyne, Northumberland NE47 5LY]; *b* 18 Feb 1948; *educ* Eton; *m* 1985 *Belinda Ann, 2nd dau of Thomas Aydon Bates (*see* MUSGRAVE, Bt, of Tourin), and formerly w of David Pulford, and has:

    1b +Caspar James Pears; *b* 1986

    1b *Imogen Felicia Anne; *b* 1989

  2a +Peter Alexander [Peter Erskine Esq, Packwood Haugh, Ruyton-XI-Towns, Salop]; *b* 24 March 1950; *educ* Eton; *m* 1976 *Charlotte, twin dau of W/Cdr Sir (Eric) John Hodsoll, CB, and has:

    1b +Andrew John Hodsoll; *b* 1985

    1b *Emily Clare; *b* 1978

    2b *Harriet Alice; *b* 1981

  3a +Alistair John [Alistair Erskine Esq, 58 Ravenslea Rd, London SW12]; *b* 30 Jan 1959; *m* 1987 *Fiona Sue Awdry, est dau of Maurice Lovett-Turner, of Surrey, and has:

    1b *Oliver Stewart; *b* 1989

    2b +Edmund Alexander; *b* 1993

(2) (cont.) David Erskine *m* 2nd 1970 *Mrs Joan Mary Gilmour, dau of Brig James Brindley Bettington, DSO, MC

1 Elyne Mary; *d* unm 4 Oct 1891

2 Constance Elise; *b c* 1869; *d* unm 22 Feb 1959

3 Mary; *d* an infant, 1873

4 Louisa Frances; *b* 1875; nun Community St Mary the Virgin Wantage; *d* 15 Dec 1965

5 Frances Elisabeth; *m* 29 July 1899 Rev Frederick Tufnell (*d* 28 Feb 1920), Rector Sudbury, Derbys, and *d* 22 Jan 1967, leaving issue

6 (Alice) Maud Mary; *b* 1878; *d* unm 24 May 1967

The 11th and 13th EARL's est son,

WALTER JOHN FRANCIS ERSKINE, **12th Earl of Mar** and **14th Earl of Kellie**, KT (1911), TD; *b* 29 Aug 1865; *educ* Eton; Lt Scots Gds 1887–92, rep S peer 1892–1955; Hon Col 7th Bn Argyll and Sutherland Highrs, Clackmannshire: Ld Lt 1896–1955 and Pres TAA; confirmed as Hereditary Keeper Stirling Castle by roy warrant 17 Feb 1923; Capt Roy Co Archers to 1948, Chllr Order Thistle 1932–49, Ld Clerk Register and Keeper Signet Scotland 1936–48; *m* 14 July 1892 Lady Violet Ashley, JP Clackmannanshire (*d* 16 Dec 1938), dau of 8th Earl of Shaftesbury (*qv*), and *d* 3 June 1955, having had:

1 John Francis Ashley, *Lord Erskine*, GCSI (1940), GCIE (1934); *b* 26 April 1895; Maj Scots Gds WW I, Assist Priv Sec to 1st Ld Admlty 1920–21, MP Weston-Super-Mare 1922–23 and 1924–34, Brighton 1940–41, PPS to: PMG 1923, Home Sec 1924–29; Govt Whip 1931–34, KCStJ, Govr Madras 1934–40; *m* 2 Dec 1919 Lady Marjorie Hervey (*d* 22 Nov 1967), er dau of 4th Marquess of Bristol (*qv*), and *dvp* 3 May 1953, having had:

  (1) JOHN FRANCIS HERVEY, **13th and 15th Earl**

  (2) Alistair Robert Hervey, MC; *b* 21 March 1923; *educ* Eton; Lt Scots Gds WW II; *ka* 19 April 1945

  (3) +David Hervey, JP, DL (Suffolk) [The Hon David Erskine JP DL, Felsham House, Felsham, Suffolk; 17 Clareville Ct, Clareville Grove, London SW7]; *b* 5 Nov 1924; *educ* Eton and Trin Coll Cambridge (MA 1957); Capt Scots Gds WW II (Italy Star), Lt RARO; barrister Inner Temple 1950, Hon Sec Navy Records Soc 1963–, CC W Suffolk 1968; *m* 1st 5 Dec 1953 Jean Violet (*d* 1983), er dau of Lt-Col Archibald Vivian Campbell Douglas (*see* 1932 edn DE BUNSEN, Bt); *m* 2nd 1985 *Caroline Mary, yr dau of Sir Alan Frederick Las-

celles, GCVO, KCB, CMG, MC, PC (*see* HAREWOOD, E), and widow of 2nd Viscount Chandos (*qv*), and has by his 1st w:

  1a *Janet Cicely [Mrs Gordon Arthur, Highfields, Smeeton Westerby, Leics LE8 0LT]; *b* 28 Dec 1955; *m* 1980 *Gordon Drake Arthur, er s of Allan Arthur, MBE, DL, of Boreham, Essex, and has:

    1b *Allan Douglas Erskine; *b* 1987

    1b *Isobel Jean Douglas; *b* 1984

    2b *Margaret Frances Ramsay; *b* 1989

  2a *Catherine Marjorie; *b* 20 Feb 1958; *m* 1979 *Edward Georges Rossdale, s of John Rossdale, and has:

    1b *Venetia; *b* 1981

    2b *Sophie; *b* 1982

    3b *Caroline; *b* 1986

  3a *Mary (Molly) Viola [Mrs Seymour Adams, 33 Radipole Rd, London SW6 5DN]; *b* 26 Sept 1962; *m* 1987 *(Edward) Seymour Adams, s of Philip Adams, of Havant, Hants, and has:

    1b *Max Philip Erskine; *b* 1992

    2b *Ellen Catherine Jean; *b* 1990

    3b *Rosalind Elizabeth; *b* 1994

  (4) +Robert William Hervey [The Hon Robert Erskine, 100 Elgin Crescent, London W11 2JL]; *b* 13 Oct 1930; *educ* Eton and King's Coll Cambridge; 2nd Lt Scots Gds; *m* 1st 21 May 1955 (*divorce* 1964) Jennifer Shirley, yr dau of L J Cardew Wood, of Kintbury, Berks; *m* 2nd 2 Oct 1969 (*divorce* 1975) Anne-Marie, dau of Jean Lattès, of Paris, and by her has:

  1a +Alistair Robert; *b* 1970

  (4) (cont.) The Hon Robert Erskine *m* 3rd 1977 *Belinda Mary Rosalind, dau of Raymond Blackburn, of London, and by her has:

  2a +Thomas Gerald; *b* 1978

  3a +Felix Benjamin; *b* 1980

2 Francis Walter; *b* 9 Jan 1899; *educ* Eton; Capt Scots Gds, WWs I and II, ADC to Govr-Gen Canada 1921–25, memb London Stock Exchange 1928–47; *m* 24 Sept 1925 Phyllis (*d* 29 Sept 1974), dau of John Francis Burstall, of Quebec, and *d* 20 Sept 1972, having had:

  (1) Robin Francis; *b* 26 Aug, *d* 18 Oct 1929

  (1) *(Rosemary) Susan; *b* 16 Aug 1927; *m* 1st 27 Nov 1947 (*divorce* 1974) Lt Mark Alastair Coats, Gren Gds (*d* 1996) (*see* 1970 edn GLENTANAR, B), and has:

    1a *Nicholas James [Nicholas Coats Esq, 8 Kempson Rd, London SW6 4PU]; *b* 19 April 1952; *m* 1987 *Belinda, dau of Gordon McKechnie, and has:

      1b *James Michael; *b* 1987

      1b *Rosanna Sarah; *b* 1992

    2a *Virginia Jane [Mrs Andrew Hay, 10 Favart Rd, London SW6 4AZ]; *b* 1954; *m* 1977 *Andrew Nicholas John Hay (*see* HERTFORD, M) and has:

      1b *Timothy George Nicholas; *b* 1980

      2b *Christopher James Philip; *b* 1984

      1b *Olivia Margaret Rose; *b* 1990

  (2) (Jean) Felicity; *b* 26 Feb 1931; *m* 1st 10 July 1951 (*divorce* 1961) Hon (Desmond) Rupert Strutt (*see* BELPER, B) and had issue; *m* 2nd 10 Jan 1963, as his 2nd w, *Hon Victor Patrick Hamilton Wills (*see* DULVERTON, B) and *d* 1984

1 Elyne Violet; *b* and *d* 2 Aug 1893

The 12th and 14th EARL's gs,

JOHN FRANCIS HERVEY ERSKINE, **13th Earl of Mar** and **15th Earl of Kellie**, JP (1962); *b* 15 Feb 1921; *educ* Eton and Trin Coll Cambridge; Maj Scots Gds WW II (despatches), ret 1954, Maj Argyll & Sutherland Highrs (TA) 1955–58; memb Roy Co Archers, CC Clackmannanshire 1955, Er Ch of Scotland, Chm Forth Conservancy Bd 1957–67, Keeper Stirling Castle, Ld Lt Clackmannanshire 1966, KStJ 1965; *m* 24 April 1948 Pansy Constance (*d* 9 Aug 1996), memb Admin Cncl King George's Jubilee Tst (for Youth) 1975, UK Pres Unicef 1979–84, Chm Youth at Risk Advsy Gp 1986–91, CStJ, yst dau of Gen Sir Andrew Nicol Thorne, KCB, CMG, DSO, DL (*see* PENRHYN, B), and *d* 1993, leaving:

  1 JAMES THORNE ERSKINE, **14th and present Earl of Mar and 16th and present Earl of Kellie**

  2 +ALEXANDER DAVID [The Hon Alexander Erskine, 34 Awaba St, Mosman, NSW 2088, Australia]; *b* 26 Oct 1952; heir presumptive; *educ* Eton and Pembroke Coll Cambridge (BA); *m* 1977 *Katherine Shawford, er dau of Thomas Clark Capel, of NSW (*see* BUTE, M), and has:

    (1) +Alexander Capel; *b* 1979

    (1) *Isabel Katherine; *b* 1982

  3 +Michael John (Rev) [The Rev and Hon Michael Erskine, The Manse, Kilmelfort, Argyllshire]; *b* 5 April 1956; *educ* Eton and Edinburgh U; *m* 1987 *Jill, er dau of Campbell S Westwood, and has:

    (1) +Euan Stewart; *b* 1992

    (1) *Laura Anne; *b* 1990

  1 *Fiona [The Lady Fiona Campbell, The Glebe House, Stobo, Peeblesshire EH14 8NU]; *b* 5 April 1956; *m* 1980 *Lt-Col Andrew P W Campbell, Argyll & Sutherland Highrs, yr s of Wilson Campbell, of Northumberland, and has:

    (1) *Barnabas William Erskine; *b* 1983

    (1) *(Elizabeth) Poppy; *b* 1985

    (2) *Rosanna Katherine; *b* 1986

MARCHAMLEY

MARCHWOOD

Arms: Per fess dancettée sable and gules, in chief a pale or, thereon three bars of the second, in base a fleur-de-lys argent. **Crest:** A stag's head couped argent attired or, holding in the mouth a bell gold. **Supporters:** Dexter a griffin sejant; sinister a hawk, both per fess gules and sable, armed and membered or, each charged on the fess line with a fleur-de-lys argent. **Motto:** Live to live. **Creation:** B. (UK) 3 July 1908.

Arms: Gules six fleurs-de-lys, three, two and one or, on a chief engrailed of the second three roses of the first, barbed and seeded proper. **Crest:** Issuant from a circlet or a demi-lion gules collared sable, charged on the shoulder with a rose and holding in the dexter paw a fleur-de-lys gold. **Supporters:** Dexter, a Malayan tiger; sinister, a sea-lion; both proper. **Motto:** *Semper paratus* ('Always prepared'). **Creations:** V. (UK) 13 Sept 1945, B. (UK) 8 June 1937, Bt (UK) 19 June 1933.

THE 4TH BARON MARCHAMLEY, of Hawkstone, Salop (William Francis Whiteley) [The Rt Hon The Lord Marchamley, Whetcombe, North Huish, Devon TQ10 9NG]; *b* 27 July 1968; *s* f 26 May 1994.

Lineage: GEORGE WHITELEY, of May Field House, Halifax, Yorks; had:

GEORGE WHITELEY, of Blackburn and Halifax; *b* 31 July 1825; *m* 13 July 1853 Margaret (*d* 19 Jan 1913), dau of James Pickop, MD, of Blackburn, and *d* 10 March 1873, having had:

1 GEORGE WHITELEY, **1st Baron**

2 Sir HERBERT JAMES WHITELEY, 1st Bt (*see* HUNTINGTON-WHITELEY, Bt)

GEORGE WHITELEY's er s,

GEORGE WHITELEY, **1st Baron Marchamley**, of Hawkstone, Co Salop (UK), so *cr* 3 July 1908, PC (1907), JP (Hants and Salop); *b* 30 Aug 1855; cotton-spinner and brewer, Mayor Blackburn, MP (C) Stockport 1893–1900 and (Lib) Pudsey 1900–08, patronage sec Treasury and Ch Lib Whip 1905–08; *m* 25 June 1881 Alice (*d* 10 March 1913), only child of William Tattersall, JP, of Quarry Hall, Blackburn, and St Anthony's Milnthorpe, and *d* 21 Oct 1925, leaving:

1 WILLIAM TATTERSALL, **2nd Baron**

2 Ronald George, OBE (1919); *b* 11 Aug 1890; *educ* Eton and Magdalen Coll Oxford (BA 1912); Maj RGA (SR) WW I; *m* 27 July 1939 Marjorie Gordon (*m* 2nd 2 Dec 1959 Adml Sir Desmond Parry Dreyer, GCB, CBE, DSC, JP and *d* 8 Sept 1997), dau of Ernest Jukes, of Rickmansworth, Herts, and *dsp* 22 April 1957

1 Muriel Cartmel; *m* 30 April 1908 (*divorce* 1949) Stanley Wyndham Jamieson, CBE, LLD (*d* 27 April 1970), er s of John Donaldson Jamieson, of Greenock, and *d* 16 Oct 1952, leaving issue

2 Dorothy; *m* 26 May 1911 Sir Alfred Bakewell Howitt, CVO, MA, MD, BCh (*d* 8 Dec 1954), yst s of Francis Howitt, MD, of Heanor, Derbys, and *d* 17 July 1942, leaving issue

The 1st BARON's er s,

WILLIAM TATTERSALL WHITELEY, **2nd Baron Marchamley**; *b* 22 Nov 1886; *educ* Eton and Hertford Coll Oxford; Lt-Cdr RNVR WW I 1915–18, Maj RAF and F/Lt RAFVR WW II 1939–44, High Sheriff Hants 1921, fought Leeds SE 1923 and 1924 gen elections; *m* 24 May 1911 (Margaret) Clara, yr dau of Thomas Scott Johnstone, of Glenmark, Waipara, NZ, and *d* 17 Nov 1949, leaving:

1 JOHN WILLIAM TATTERSALL WHITELEY, **3rd Baron Marchamley**; *b* 24 April 1922; Lt RAC and Capt 19th King George V Own Lancers WW II 1940–45 and attd IA; *m* 25 July 1967 *Sonia Kathleen Pedrick and *d* 26 May 1994, leaving:

(1) WILLIAM FRANCIS WHITELEY, **4th and present Baron Marchamley**

1 *Alice Tattersall [The Hon Mrs Bradford, Membland, Haddington, E Lothian EH41 4JH]; *b* 11 April 1917; Cmdt ATS WW II 1940–45; *m* 9 May 1946 Lt-Col Robert Danby Bradford, Coldstream Gds (*d* 1986), er s of Arthur Danby Bradford, of Ashwell Court, Gt Missenden, Bucks, and has:

(1) *Robert William Danby [Robert Bradford Esq, 8a Maunsel St, London SW1P 2QL]; *b* 20 May 1947; *educ* Fettes; *m* 1972 (*divorce* 1983) Dinah Jane, dau of Thomas Gerald Porter, and has:

1a *Lydia Jane; *b* 1973

2a *Antonia Sarah; *b* 1975

3a *Jessica Jennifer; *b* 1978

(2) *Andrew Mark Danby [Andrew Bradford Esq, 20 Gurney St, Stonehaven, Kincardineshire AB39 2EB]; *b* 7 June 1949; *educ* Fettes; *m* 1980 *Janice, er dau of A G Diverty, of Buckie, Banffshire, and has:

1a *Claire Alison; *b* 20 Oct 1981

2a *Sarah Gillian; *b* 16 Oct 1983

THE 3RD VISCOUNT MARCHWOOD, of Penang, and of Marchwood, Co Southampton, **Baron Marchwood**, of Penang, and of Marchwood, Co Southampton, and a **Baronet** (Sir David George Staveley Penny, Bt) [The Rt Hon The Viscount Marchwood, The Filberts, Aston Tirrold, Oxon OX11 9DG]; *b* 22 May 1936; *s* f 1979; *educ* Winchester; late 2nd Lt RHG, md Moët & Chandon (London) (chm 1997–); *m* 26 Sept 1964 Tessa Jane (*d* 17 Aug 1997), 2nd dau of Wilfred Francis Norris, of Timbers Chase, Chiddingfold, Surrey, and has:

1 +PETER GEORGE WORSLEY [The Hon Peter Penny, 44 Elsynge Rd, London SW18]; *b* 8 Oct 1965; dir Staveley plc 1996–; *m* 7 Oct 1995 *Annabel, dau of Rex Cooper, of E Bergholt, Suffolk, and has:

(1) *India Rose; *b* 21 March 1997

2 *Nicholas Mark Staveley; *b* 17 Dec 1967

3 +Edward James Frederick; *b* 26 June 1970; *m* 7 Sept 1996 *Selina Margaret, dau of Frederick Sasse (*see* HANMER, Bt), and has:

(1) +Alexander George Robert; *b* 23 June 1997

Lineage: THOMAS PENNY, of Chatham, Kent; *m* 30 Aug 1762 Susanna Simmons, and had:

RICHARD PENNY, of Marchwood, Hants; *b c* 1775; *m* 1st —; *m* 2nd 8 Feb 1817 Ann, dau of James Ch(e)ater, of Eling, Hants, and *d* 8 June 1845, leaving:

JAMES CHATER PENNY, of Marchwood, Hants; *b* 24 Aug 1827; *m* 12 June 1848 Ann (*d* 2 July 1899), dau of James Bowyer, seaman, and *d* 8 Feb 1874, leaving, with other issue:

1 FREDERICK JAMES, of whom presently

2 Herbert, of Cape Town; fndr RNVR Cape Good Hope; *b* 11 Jan 1867; *m* 20 Dec 1892 Carlotta Elvira de Concecia0 (*d* 27 Sept 1927), 5th dau of Chev Oscar W A Forssman, and *d* 14 Aug 1938, leaving an est s:

(1) Magnus Herbert Forssman; Lt-Cdr RNVR WW I; *b* 28 Dec 1893; *m* 1st 10 April 1930 Elizabeth (*d* 20 Aug 1973), dau of Johannes Swellengrebel le Sueur, and *d* 4 July 1984, leaving an est s:

1a *Errol (Erral) Forssman; DEOR WW II; *b* 20 March 1921; *m* 12 Jan 1946 Nina Vilna (*d* 14 Feb 1984), dau of John Charles August Hartdegen, and has, with three daus:

1b *Magnus John Forssmann; *b* 10 May 1947; *m* 2 June 1976 *Karen Denise, dau of Gordon Frank Vorster, and has:

1c *Wolf; *b* 21 Sept 1977

2c *Michael; *b* 29 Nov 1987

1c *Sarah Jane (Tia); *b* 25 March 1979

2b *Conrad Hugo, of The Tower, Chanwell, nr Johannesburg; *b* 31 May 1951; *m* 7 Aug 1978 *Maria-Theresia, Baroness Kotz von Döbrz, dau of Karl Christian, Baron Kotz von Döbrz, and has:

1c *Gustaf; *b* 23 July 1979

2c *Ludwig; *b* 9 Sept 1980

1c *Tamara; *b* 7 Sept 1984

2c *Jenna; *b* 23 Sept 1988

FREDERICK JAMES PENNY, of Bitterne, Hants; *b* 13 May 1849; *m* 17 July 1873 Elizabeth (*d* 7 March 1930), est dau of George Emerson Glover, of Liverpool, and *d* 4 March 1934, leaving:

1 Reginald James; *b* 4 June 1874; *m* 3 April 1929 Frances Constance, 3rd dau of Rev Alfred Legge, of St Germans, King's Lynn, and *d* 27 March 1952

2 (FREDERICK) GEORGE, **1st Viscount**

3 Gerald Evelyn, JP (Hants); *b* 28 Sept 1878; *m* 21 March 1912 Jane Maud Pierce, of Birkenhead, and *d* 2 Nov 1955, leaving issue

4 Thomas Algernon Edgar, JP (Hants); *educ* Cranleigh; Capt Hants Regt WW I, Liaison Offr to 14th Fareham Bn Hants HG WW II; *m* 21 March 1912 Eveline Mary, dau of Col Arthur Frederick Eden-Perkins, VD, JP, DL, Ceylon Rifles

1 Freda Margaret; *m* George Ernest Suter and had issue

2 Helena Mary, twin with her sis; *m* 15 March 1913 Henry Ashton Hornby Swayne and had issue

FREDERICK PENNY's 2nd s,

  Sir Frederick George Penny, 1st Bt, and **1st Viscount Marchwood**, of Penang and of Marchwood, Co Southampton, so *cr* 19 June 1933 and 13 Sept 1945 respectively, as also 8 June 1937 BARON MARCHWOOD, of Penang and of Marchwood, Co Southampton (all UK), KCVO (1937), JP; *b* 10 March 1876; *educ* King Edward VI GS Southampton; served Mercantile Marine (Master Mariner 1899), sr ptnr Fraser & Co, govt exchange brokers, of Singapore; md Eastern Smelting Co, dir: Phoenix Oil and Trading and Caroni's Sugar Estates (Trinidad), Federated Malay States rep in negotiations with Netherlands Indies, memb ctee Penang Chamber Commerce, MP (C) Kingston-upon-Thames 1922–37, PPS to Fin Sec War Office 1923, Govt Whip 1926–28, Jr Ld Treasury 1928–29 and 1931, V-Chamberlain Household 1931–32, Comptroller Household 1932–35, Treasurer Household 1935–37, Hon Treasurer C Party 1938–46, ktd 1929, Freeman City London, Order Crown Johore 1st Cl, Master Hon Co Master Mariners 1941–45; *m* 20 July 1905 Anne Boyle (*d* 20 April 1957), est dau of Sir John Gunn, JP, of St Mellons, Glam, and *d* 1 Jan 1955, leaving:

PETER GEORGE PENNY, **2nd Viscount Marchwood**, MBE (1944); *b* 7 Nov 1912; *educ* Winchester; Maj RA WW II, dir Geo Wimpey, chm and md Vine Products; *m* 30 July 1935 Pamela (*d* 1979), only child of John Staveley Colton-Fox, JP, of Todwick Grange, Yorks, and *d* 6 April 1979, leaving:

1 DAVID GEORGE STAVELEY PENNY, **3rd and present Viscount Marchwood**

2 +Patrick Glyn Staveley [The Hon Patrick Penny, 33 Wellington Sq, London SW3 4NR]; *b* 3 July 1939; *educ* Nautical Coll Pangbourne; Lt Roy Wilts Yeo 1962–65, late 2nd Lt RHG; *m* 1st 10 April 1968 (*divorce* 1974) Sue Eleanor Jane, dau of Charles Phipps Brutton, CBE, and Mrs Daniel Swinden, of S Kensington; *m* 2nd 1979 *Lynn Vanessa, dau of John Leslie Wyles, of Wimbledon, and formerly w of (a) Colin Hart and (b) John Birkett Knox, and has by his 1st w:

  (1) *Sasha Jane; *b* 5 Sept 1969

1 *Carol Ann [The Hon Mrs Quirk, 9 Lambourn Rd, London SW4 0LX]; *b* 30 Aug 1948; *m* 8 June 1978 *Patrick John Quirk, s of P J Quirk, and has:

  (1) *Tom Michael; *b* 1979

  (2) *Toby James; *b* 1983

MARGADALE

Arms: Tierced in pairle sable, azure and gules, in chief a Saracen's head couped affrontée and in base two Saracen's heads addorsed in profile, all argent, and at the fess point an inescutcheon parted per pale, dexter per bend sinister embattled gules and or, in dexter chief a battleaxe paleways argent, and in sinister base, issuant from a base undy azure and argent, a tower sable, masoned argent port gules (for MORRISON, of Islay); sinister, vert powdered with bezants, a horse rearing on its hind legs argent, langued and hoofed gules (for the Lordship of MARGADALE). **Crest:** Three Saracen's heads conjoined in one neck, one looking to the dexter, one affrontée and one to the sinister, all proper. **Supporters:** On a compartment below the shield of the sea undy, with dexter a cresting wave and sinister a rock issuant from the water, two woodcock close proper, which supporters are limited to him and his successors in the Peerage, but the inescutcheon is limited to his heirs male in the Peerage of Margadale, whom failing his feudal heirs in the Barony of Islay, whom failing the heir of the last heir-male in the name and designation of Morrison of Islay inalienably. **Motto** (over shield) *Praetio prudentia praestat* ('Prudence before any thought of a reward'). **Creation:** B. (UK) 1 Jan 1965.

THE 2ND BARON MARGADALE, of Islay, Co Argyll (James Ian Morrison, TD (1963), DL (Wilts 1977)) [Col The Rt Hon The Lord Margadale TD DL, Fonthill House, Tisbury, Salisbury, Wilts SP3 5SA; Islay Estate Office, Bridgend, Islay,

Argyll PA44 7PA]; *b* 17 July 1930; *s f* 1996; *educ* Eton and RAC Cirencester; 2nd Lt Life Gds 1949–50, Maj Roy Wilts Yeo 1960–68, Hon Col: A (RWY) Sqdn Roy Yeo RAC TA and B (RWY) Sqdn Roy Wessex Yeo 1982–89, Roy Wessex Yeo RAC TA 1984–89; memb Roy Co Archers 1960–; Wilts: CC 1955 and 1973–77, CA 1969–74, High Sheriff 1971, Chm W Wilts C Assoc 1967–71 (pres 1972–84); Chm: CLA 1978–81, Tattersalls Ctee 1969–80, co dir, farmer; *m* 14 Oct 1952 *Clare, est dau of Anthony Lister Barclay, of Broad Oak End, Herts, and has:

1 +ALASTAIR JOHN [The Hon Alastair Morrison, The Quadrangle, Tisbury, Wilts]; *b* 4 April 1958; *m* 1988 *Lady Sophia Sydney Louise Cavendish, yr dau of 11th Duke of Devonshire (*qv*), and formerly w of Anthony Murphy, and has:

  (1) +Declan James; *b* 11 July 1993

  (1) *Nancy Lorna; *b* 22 Jan 1995

2 +Hugh; *b* 7 Nov 1960; *m* 1986 *Jane, dau of Brian Jenks, of Monte Carlo, and has:

  (1) +Geordie Anthony; *b* 1989

  (1) *Amber Belinda; *b* 1993

1 *Fiona Elizabeth; *b* 11 Nov 1954; *m* 9 April 1975 *3rd Viscount Trenchard (*qv*) and has issue

Lineage: CHARLES JOHN JOSEPH MORRISON; *b* 1731; *m* Sarah (*d* 1803), dau of Marmaduke Grimston, of Hertford, and *d* 1804 aged 73, leaving, with other issue:

JAMES MORRISON, of Hants; head of Morrison, Dillon and Co, of Fore St, London; MP St Ives 1830, Ipswich 1832 and Inverness Burghs 1840–47, bought estates in Berks, Bucks, Kent, Wilts, Yorks and Islay; the story of a Morrison making a fortune by stockpiling black crepe just before a Sovereign's death, usually ascribed to HUGH MORRISON before QUEEN VICTORIA's, is more likely to refer, if at all, to this JAMES MORRISON just before WILLIAM IV's; *m* 1814 Mary Anne (*d* 20 Feb 1887), dau of Joseph Todd, of London, and *d* 30 Oct 1857, having had:

1 Charles, JP, DL, of Basildon Park, Berks, Hole Park, Kent, and Islay House, Argyllshire; *b* 20 Sept 1817; *d* unm 25 May 1909

2 ALFRED

3 Frank, of Hole Park; *b* 1824; *m* 26 Sept 1854 Henrietta (*d* 17 Dec 1909), 4th dau of James Murray Grant, 12th of Glenmoriston, and *dsp* 14 Jan 1904

4 Henry; *b* 1832; *educ* Eton; *d* 1850

5 Walter, JP (1895), of Basildon Park (which he inherited from his er bro and settled on his nephew James Archibald 1910) and Malham Tarn House, W R Yorks; *b* 21 May 1836; *educ* Eton and Balliol Coll Oxford (MA); MP Plymouth 1861–74 and Skipton Yorks 1886–92, High Sheriff W R Yorks 1883; *d* unm 18 Dec 1921

6 George, JP, of Hampworth Lodge, Salisbury; *b* 1829; *educ* Eton and Balliol Coll Oxford; *m* Barbara Jane Poore (*d* 24 June 1907) and *d* 4 April 1884

7 Allan; *b* 1842; *educ* Eton and Balliol Coll Oxford; *d* 1880

1 Lucy; *b* 1825; *m* 6 Aug 1856 George Moffatt (*d* 20 Feb 1878), of Goodrich Court, Herefs, and *d* 1 July 1876, leaving issue

2 Emily; *b* 31 Dec 1827; *m* 7 Aug 1850, as his 1st w, Capt John Grant, 42nd Highrs (*dvp* 17 Aug 1867), est s of James Murray Grant, 12th of Glenmoriston, and *dsp* 1854

3 Mary; *b* 15 June 1830; *m* Rev George Goodwin Pownall Glossop (*d* 23 April 1874), Vicar Twickenham, and had a dau

4 Ellen; *b* 12 March 1834; *d* unm 23 Dec 1909

JAMES MORRISON's 2nd son,

  ALFRED MORRISON, JP and DL (Wilts), of Fonthill House, Hindon, Wilts; *b* 28 April 1821; *educ* Edinburgh and Trin Coll Cambridge; High Sheriff Wilts 1857; *m* 12 April 1866 Mabel (*d* 1 March 1933), dau of Rev R S C Chermside, Rrector Wilton, Wilts, and *d* 22 Dec 1897, leaving:

1 HUGH

2 (James) Archibald, DSO (1916), of Basildon Park (sold 1929); *b* 1873; *educ* Eton and New Coll Oxford; 2nd Lt Gren Gds 1896, Lt 1898, Sudan (including Khartoum) 1898 (Br medal and Khedive's medal with clasps), Boer War 1899–1900; MP (U) Wilton 1900–06 and E Nottingham 1910–12; Capt (T/Maj 1915), Maj Lovat's Scouts Yeo, T/Lt-Col Territorial Bn Middx Regt 1916–17 WW I (wounded); *m* 1st 2 Jan 1901 (*divorce* 1913) Hon Mary Hill-Trevor (*d* 3 Sept 1962), 6th dau of 1st Baron Trevor (*qv*), and had:

  (1) Simon Archibald; *b* 19 Sept 1903; *d* unm 18 Aug 1969

  (1) Mary; *b* 6 Feb 1902; *m* 24 Jan 1924 Maj John Henry Dent Brocklehurst, OBE (*d* 20 July 1949), of Sudeley Castle, and had a s and three daus

  (2) Elizabeth, OBE, DL; *b* 5 July 1909; *m* 1st 28 April 1930 (*divorce* 1940) Nigel Eric Murray Gunnis, yst s of Francis Gunnis, of Hamsell Manor, Eridge, Sussex, and had:

    1a *Diana Marion, CVO (1998); *b* 24 May 1931; Ldy Bedchamber to HM THE QUEEN 1987–; *m* 19 Jan 1959 *12th Baron Farnham (*qv*) and has two adopted daus

    2a Gillian Elizabeth; *b* 30 April 1933; *d* 15 May 1997

  (2) (cont.) Mrs Elizabeth Gunnis *m* 2nd 4 May 1940 Eric Martin-Smith, MP (*d* 13 Aug 1951), of Codicote Lodge, Hitchin, Herts, and by him had two daus; *m* 3rd 2 July 1954 Michael Cory-Wright (*see* CORY-WRIGHT, Bt) and *d* 16 Dec 1995

2 (cont.) Lt-Col Archibald Morrison *m* 2nd 1920 Dorothy Halton; *m* 3rd 1931 Gwendoline Phyllis Talmage and *d* 27 Oct 1934

1 Katharine; *m* 21 Feb 1905 Sir Stephen Herbert Gatty, KC (*d* 29 March 1922), of Ossemsley Manor, Christchurch, Hants, Ch Justice Gibraltar, 3rd s of Rev Alfred Gatty, DD, and *d* 9 June 1949, leaving two sons and a dau

2 Dorothy; DGStJ; *m* 9 June 1912 Viscount St Cyres (*see* IDDESLEIGH, E) and *dsp* 20 Sept 1936

ALFRED MORRISON's er son,

  HUGH MORRISON, JP and DL (Argyllshire), of Fonthill House and Islay House; *b* 8 June 1868; *educ* Eton and Trin Coll Cambridge (BA 1889); MP Salisbury 1918–23 and 1924–31, High Sheriff Wilts 1904; *m* 16 Aug 1892 Lady Sophia Castalia Mary Leveson-Gower (*d* 22 March 1934), 2nd dau of 2nd Earl Granville (*qv*), and *d* 14 March 1931, leaving:

1 JOHN GRANVILLE, **1st Baron**

1 Marjorie; *b* 15 Dec 1910; *m* 16 Jan 1933 Lt-Col Scrope Arthur Francis Sutherland Egerton and *d* 1992, having had issue (*see* SUTHERLAND, D)

HUGH MORRISON's only son,

JOHN GRANVILLE MORRISON, **1st Baron Margadale**, of Islay, Co Argyll (UK), so *cr* 1 Jan 1965, TD (1944), JP (Wilts 1936, Argyllshire 1933), DL (Wilts 1950–69); *b* 16 Dec 1906; *educ* Eton and Magdalene Coll Cambridge; Maj Roy Wilts Yeo WW II, Hon Col Roy Wilts Yeo Sqdn 1965–71, Hon Col Roy Yeo 1965–71, Hon Col Wessex Yeo 1971–96, Yeo Cmdt and Chm Yeo Assoc 1965–71, memb Roy Co Archers; MP (C) Salisbury 1942–64, Chm 1922 Ctee 1955–64, Wilts: High Sheriff 1938, Ld Lt 1969–1981; Charity Commr 1951–56, MFH S and W Wilts 1932–65, KStJ 1972; *m* 16 Oct 1928 Hon Margaret Esther Lucie Smith, JP (Wilts 1943) (*d* 1980), yr dau of 2nd Viscount Hambleden (*qv*), and *d* 25 May 1996, having had:

1 +JAMES IAN MORRISON, **2nd and present Baron Margadale**

2 +Charles Andrew (Sir), DL (Hereford and Worcester 1995) [The Hon Sir Charles Morrison DL, Madresfield Court, Malvern, Worcs WR13 5AU]; *b* 25 June 1932; *educ* Eton; Capt Roy Wilts Yeo (TA) (ret), late 2nd Lt Life Gds; CC Wilts 1957–63, MP (C) Devizes 1964–92, Chm Nat Ctee for Electoral Reform 1985–91 and Game Conservancy 1987–94, ktd 1988; *m* 1st 28 Oct 1954 (*divorce* 1984) Hon (Antoinette) Sara Frances Sibell Long, only child of 2nd Viscount Long (*qv*), and has:

(1) +David John [David Morrison Esq, 21 Albert Bridge Rd, London SW11]; *b* 12 Jan 1959 (HRH PRINCESS ALEXANDRA stood sponsor); *m* 1984 *Venetia Anne, 2nd dau of Julian John William Salmond (*see* LUCAS OF CRUD-WELL, B), and has:

1a +Ivo Charles D; *b* 1990

1a *Tara Caolila; *b* 1988

(1) *Anabel Laura Dorothy [Mrs David Loyd, 17 Larkhall Rise, London SW4 6JB]; *b* 31 Dec 1955; *m* 1st 1979 (*divorce*) Michael Harry Stapleton and has:

1a *Harry Edward John; *b* 1982

1a *Scarlett Margaret Laura; *b* 1980

(1) (cont.) Mrs Anabel Stapleton *m* 2nd 1985 *David Arnold William Loyd and has issue (*see* ALBEMARLE, E)

2 (cont.) The Hon Sir Charles Morrison *m* 2nd 1984 Rosalind Elizabeth, dau of Hon Richard Edward Lygon (*see* 1970 edn BEAUCHAMP, E) and formerly w of Gerald John Ward (*see* DUDLEY, E)

3 Peter Hugh (Sir), PC (1988); *b* 3 June 1944; *educ* Eton and Keble Coll Oxford; MP (C) Chester 1974–92, Oppn Whip 1976–79, Govt Whip 1979–81, Parly U-Sec Employment 1981–83, Min State: Employment 1983–85, DTI 1985–86 and Energy 1987–90, Dep-Chm C Party 1986–89, PPS to PM 1990, ktd 1992; *d* unm 13 July 1995

1*Mary Anne, DCVO (1982) [The Hon Dame Mary Morrison DCVO, The Old Rectory, Fonthill Bishop, Wilts SP3 5ST; Knockdon, Bridgend, Isle of Islay, Argyllshire]; *b* 17 May 1937; *educ* Heathfield; Woman of the Bedchamber to HM THE QUEEN 1960–

MARGESSON

Arms: Sable a lion passant guardant argent, a chief engrailed or, thereon between two pallets azure a pale of the last charged with an ostrich feather erect of the second. **Crest:** Upon a coronet composed of four roses set upon a rim or, a lion passant guardant sable, collared gold and charged with a rose argent, barbed and seeded proper. **Supporters:** On either side a falcon, wings elevated argent, armed and belled or, and charged with a portcullis chained sable. **Motto:** *Loyauté me lie* ('Loyalty binds me'). **Creation:** V. (UK) 27 April 1942.

THE 2ND VISCOUNT MARGESSON, of Rugby, Co Warwick (Francis Vere Hampden Margesson) [The Rt Hon The Viscount Margesson, Ridgely Manor, Box 245, Stone Ridge, New York, NY 12484, USA]; *b* 17 April 1922; *s* 1965; *educ* Eton and Trin Coll Oxford; Sub-Lt RNVR WW II, dir Thames & Hudson Inc New York 1949–53, ADC to Govr Bahamas 1956, info offr Br Consulate-Gen New York 1964–70; *m* 18 Sept 1958 *Helena, dau of Heikki Backstrom, of Oulu, Finland, and has:

1 +RICHARD FRANCIS DAVID [Maj The Hon Richard Margesson, Cheney Cottage, 7 Glovers Lane, Middleton Cheney, Oxon OX17 2NU]; *b* 25 Dec 1960; *educ* St Paul's, NH, USA, Eton and Exeter U; Maj Coldstream Gds (commnd 1983); *m* 15 Dec 1990 *Wendy Maree, dau of James Hazelton, of Kempsey, NSW

1 *Rhoda ('Rhodie') Frances; *b* 31 May 1962

2 *Sarah Helena; *b* 18 Oct 1963

3 *Jane Henrietta; *b* 20 Oct 1965

Lineage: WILLIAM MARGESSON; *m* —, dau and coheir of William Newdigate, of Wootton, Surrey, Ld Manors Ockley and Wootton, and had:

WILLIAM MARGESSON or MARGETSON; *bapt* 26 July 1686; *m* 1712 Mary, sis and heiress of William Whitebread, of Offington, Sussex, and *d* 1763, leaving:

JOHN MARGESSON, of Offington and Ockley; *b* 31 March 1716; High Sheriff Sussex 1759; *m* Mary Penfold, of Steyning, Sussex, and *d* 19 May 1785, leaving, with two daus:

WILLIAM MARGESSON, of Offington and Ockley; *b* 11 Nov 1757; High Sheriff Sussex 1805; *m* 7 May 1790 Mary (*d* 21 July 1826), dau of John Hughes, of Cowfold, Sussex, and *d* 21 May 1843, leaving, with a yr s and a dau:

Rev WILLIAM MARGESSON, of Van, Ockley, Surrey, and Woodingfold, Sussex; *b* 7 Feb 1792; *educ* Harrow and Ch Ch Oxford; Rector Whatlington 1821–36, Vicar Mountfield 1836–71; *m* 8 June 1818 Mary Frances (*d* 3 April 1865), only dau of Bryan Cooke (*see* COOKE, Bt), and *d* 20 May 1871, having had:

1 William George; bought Findon Place, Sussex, 1872

2 Henry Davies; *b* 1 Sept 1822; lost at sea 17 June 1869

3 John James; *b* 31 Aug 1825; *d* unm 23 Jan 1840

4 Philip Davies; *b* 20 Sept 1826; Capt RA; *d* 14 June 1860

5 REGINALD WHITEHALL

1 Frances; *b* 9 July 1819; *m* 28 Oct 1853, as his 2nd w, Sir Charles Montolieu Lamb, 2nd Bt (*d* 21 March 1860; *see* 1949 edn LAMB, Bt) and *dsp* 1 July 1884

2 Marianne Harriet; *b* 29 June 1820; *d* 1 June 1835

3 Emily Charlotte; *b* 8 Nov 1823; *d* unm 17 March 1909

4 Julia Helena; *b* 12 April 1829; *m* 29 July 1890 Frederick Webster, s of Sir Godfrey Vassal Webster, 5th Bt (*see* 1923 edn), and *d* 13 Oct 1873, leaving:

(1) Godfrey Frederick; *b* 7 May 1873; *d* 1 July 1880

5 Helena Adelaide; *b* 25 July 1831; *d* unm 5 Dec 1905

The Rev WILLIAM MARGESSON's 5th s,

Rev REGINALD WHITEHALL MARGESSON; *b* 5 Dec 1827; Rector Blendworth, Hordean, Hants; *m* 3 May 1860 Louisa Sophia (*d* 2 Jan 1893), dau of Rev David Rodney Murray (*see* ELIBANK, L), and *d* 3 Oct 1901, leaving:

1 MORTIMER REGINALD (Sir)

2 Henry Philip Montolieu (Rev); *b* 26 Aug 1862; *educ* Salisbury Theological Coll; Vicar and Curate Windsor; *m* 20 Nov 1901 Mary Myfanwy (*d* 21 July 1953), dau of Rev R E Price, Vicar Morton, Salop, and *d* 5 March 1932, leaving:

(1) *Richard William [Richard Margesson Esq, West House, Ogbourne St Andrew, Wilts SN8 1SE]; *b* 7 Sept 1910; *m* 18 Sept 1935 *Margaret Whatley and has, with other issue:

1a *(Richard) David [David Margesson Esq, Burdcrop Farm House, Burdcrop, Wilts]; *b* 3 Jan 1937; *m* 20 May 1961 *Ruth Margaret Prince and has three children

2a *(Charles) Philip; *b* 3 March 1939; *m* 21 May 1966 *Franziska Anna Maria Ward and has three adopted children

3a *(William) Robert Stanley; *b* 2 Aug 1941; *m* 28 Jan 1969 *Lois Molland and has two children

1a *Mary Myfanwy [Mrs Simon Brown, Yew Tree Cottage, Hong Hill, Tring, Herts]; *b* 8 May 1943; *m* 20 May 1967 *Simon Fallowfield Brown and has three children

(1) Mary Paulina; *b* 25 Jan 1903; late MMCA; *d* unm 10 Jan 1965

(2) *Agatha Hope [Miss Agatha Margesson, 36 Dommetts Lane, Frome, Somerset]; *b* 5 Feb 1907

3 Reginald Elibank Murray; *b* 22 Sept 1863; *m* in USA

4 Philip Alexander; *b* 20 May 1865; *d* unm Oct 1923

5 William Anthony (Rev); *b* 6 Oct 1866; *d* Central Africa 5 April 1898

1 Mary Louisa; *b* 29 July 1869; *d* unm 5 March 1926

2 Amy Helena; *b* 29 Nov 1872

The Rev REGINALD MARGESSON's est s,

Sir MORTIMER REGINALD MARGESSON, JP (Worcs); *b* 16 March 1861; *educ* Harrow; ktd 1928; *m* 10 Nov 1886 Lady Isabel Augusta Hobart-Hampden, JP (Worcs) (*d* 1 July 1946), sis of 7th Earl of Buckinghamshire (*qv*), and *d* 6 April 1947, having had:

1 HENRY DAVID REGINALD, **1st Viscount**

2 *Thomas Vere Hobart, MM; *b* 15 July 1902; RA WW II 1940–45; *m* 21 Nov 1924 *Agneta Hoffman, of Copenhagen, and has:

(1) *Peter Reginald Hampden; *b* 18 Jan 1926

(2) *Michael Vere Hobart; *b* 27 Feb 1933

1 Catherine Sydney Louisa; *b* 29 Sept 1887; *m* 29 Dec 1930, as his 2nd w, 1st and last Baron Cushendun, PC (*see* 1928 edn), and *d* 11 Dec 1939

2 Albinia Helena; *b* 1889; *d* unm 12 Aug 1907

3 Isabel Joan Hampden; *b* 10 Feb 1898; *d* 13 April 1905

Sir MORTIMER MARGESSON's er s,

HENRY DAVID REGINALD MARGESSON, **1st Viscount Margesson**, of Rugby, Co Warwick (UK), *cr* 27 April 1942, MC, PC (1933); *b* 26 July 1890; *educ* Harrow and Magdalene Coll Cambridge; Capt 11th Hus WW I, MP (U) West Ham Upton 1922–23 and Rugby 1924–42, PPS (unpaid) to Min Lab 1922–23, Assist Govt Whip Nov 1924, Jr Ld Treasury 1926–29 and Aug–Oct 1931, Parly Sec Treasury and Govt Ch Whip 1931–40, Sec State War 1940–42, dir Martins Bank (London Bd) and Internat Nickel 1942–60; *m* 29 April 1916 (*divorce* 1940) Frances (*d* 1977), dau of Francis Howard Leggett, of New York, and *d* 24 Dec 1965, leaving:

1 HENRY DAVID REGINALD, **1st Viscount**

1 FRANCIS VERE HAMPDEN MARGESSON, 2nd and present Viscount Margesson

1 Janet Hampden; *b* March 1918; *educ* Newnham Coll Cambridge; *m* 22 Aug 1952 *George Henry Perrott Buchanan [George Buchanan Esq, 27 Ashley Gdns, London SW1], yr s of Rev Charles Henry Leslie Buchanan, of Kilwaughter, Co Antrim, and *d* 6 June 1968, leaving two daus

2 *(Mary) Gay Hobart [The Rt Hon The Lady Charteris of Amisfield, 11 Kylestrome Ho, Cundy St, London SW1W 9JT; Wood Stanway, Cheltenham, Glos GL54 5PG]; *b* 3 May 1919; *m* 16 Dec 1944 *Baron Charteris of Amisfield (LP, *qv*) and has issue

MARKHAM

Arms: Azure on a pale argent three lozenges sable, issuant from a chief engrailed or a demi-lion rampant gules. **Crest:** The winged lion of St Mark passant guardant or, resting its dexter fore-paw on a lozenge sable, the halo gules. **Motto:** *Tenax propositi* ('Firm of purpose'). **Creation:** Bt. (UK) 10 July 1911.

SIR CHARLES JOHN MARKHAM, 3RD BT, of Beachborough Park, Newington, Kent [Sir Charles Markham Bt, PO Box 42263, Nairobi, Kenya]; *b* 2 July 1924; *s* f 1952; *educ* Eton; Lt 11th Hus (despatches) 1943–47, v-chm Nairobi CC 1953–55, MLC Kenya 1955–60, Pres Roy Ag Soc Kenya 1958–59, Hon Tstee Kenya Nat Parks, KStJ 1973; *m* 27 Aug 1949 *Valerie, only dau of Lt-Col Evelyn Barry Johnston, of Makuyu, Kenya, and has:

1 +ARTHUR DAVID [Arthur Markham Esq, PO Box 42263, Nairobi, Kenya]; *b* 6 Dec 1950; *educ* Milton Abbey; *m* 1977 *Carolyn L, yr dau of Capt Mungo Park, and has:

  (1) *Tanya Valerie Helen; *b* 6 June 1979

  (2) *Joanna Mary Hilda; *b* 1981

2 +Richard Barry; *b* 18 April 1954; *m* 1985 *Anne C, yst dau of Ian Malcolm-Smith, of Mombasa, and Mrs Yvonne Malcolm-Smith, of Canterbury, Kent, and has issue:

  (1) +Nicholas Charles; *b* 1987

  (2) +Matthew James; *b* 1990

1 *Elizabeth Ann; *b* 23 Nov 1958; *m* 1983 *Peter J Bateman, er s of Col A J Bateman, and has:

  (1) *Jessica Elisabeth; *b* 1987

Lineage: WILLIAM MARKHAM, of Great Creaton, Northants, possibly descended from the MARKHAMs of Orton, themselves descended from the MARKHAMs of Markham, Notts, and Cotha; *d* 1605, having had:

1 GREGORY
2 John; *m* Dorothy Pearson
3 Thomas
1 Anne; *m* Edward Boone

WILLIAM MARKHAM's est s,

  GREGORY MARKHAM; merchant Cornhill, memb Skinner's Co; *m* Elizabeth (*bur* 29 Jan 1622/3) and was *bur* 28 June 1632, having had:

JOHN MARKHAM, of London; *b* 20 Aug 1609; *educ* Merchant Taylors'; merchant adventurer; *m* Elizabeth (*bur* 10 April 1703), dau of John Simpson, of St Albans, and sis of Sir John Simpson, lawyer, and *d* 1658, having had:

JOHN MARKHAM, of Staines, Middx; *m* Rose — (*bur* 1740) and was *bur* 1 Dec 1721, having had:

WILLIAM MARKHAM, of Northampton; a Clerk Chancery; *m* 1 Jan 1716/7 Elizabeth (*bur* 16 Oct 1745), dau of Henry Plowman, of Northampton, and *d* 28 Jan 1763, having had:

HENRY WILLIAM MARKHAM, of Northampton; attorney; *m* 1744 Frances (*bur* 27 Feb 1803), sis of Maj-Gen Mansel, of Cosgrove Hall, and was *bur* 5 Jan 1776, having had:

JOHN MARKHAM, of Northampton; *b* 6 May 1750; attorney, Clerk of Peace Northants; *m* 23 July 1778 Hannah Wagstaffe (*d* 7 May 1820) and was *bur* 9 Aug 1803, having had:

CHARLES MARKHAM; *b* 28 Dec 1778; Clerk of Ltcy and Clerk of Peace Northants 1823–46, Master Extrdy in Chancery; *m* 23 Sept 1811 Eliza Mary (*d* 17 Dec 1858), dau of John Packharness, of St Ann's, Jamaica, and *d* 20 Oct 1846, having had, with two other sons (*d* young):

1 Arthur Bayley; *b* 11 May 1815; *m* 28 Aug 1838 Ann (*d* 5 Sept 1872), dau of John William Smith, of Shrewsbury, and *d* 20 Dec 1873, having had issue

2 Henry Philip, DL, of Sedgebrooke, Pitsford, Northants; *b* 5 Aug 1816; Clerk of Peace Northants, Mayor Northampton 1862; *m* 6 Dec 1855 Edith (*d* 27 Dec 1915), dau of Robert Alexander, of Clifton, and *d* 24 Jan 1904, leaving issue

3 William Orlando; *b* 28 Jan 1818; MD Edin, FRCP; *m* 1st 29 April 1847 Eliza Emma (*d* 12 Aug 1848), dau of John William Smith, of Shrewsbury, and had issue; *m* 2nd 21 Sept 1854 Catharine (*d* 21 Jan 1902), dau of Professor James Hamilton, of Edinburgh, and widow of Thomas Seagrave, and *d* 23 Jan 1891, having by her had issue

4 CHARLES

5 Thomas Hugh; *b* 28 Nov 1825; *educ* BNC Oxford (MA); barrister; *d* unm 19 Sept 1868

1 Anna Maria Frances; *b* 22 March 1813; *m c* 1839 Rev John Cox (*d* 28 March 1867), and *d* 1 Jan 1878, leaving issue

2 Mary Helen; *b* 16 May 1827; *m* 7 June 1855 Isaac Edward Lovell, JP, of Guilsborough, Northants, and *d* 4 Aug 1907

CHARLES MARKHAM's 4th s,

  CHARLES MARKHAM, JP, of Brimington Hall and Tapton House, Derbys; *b* 1 March 1823; *m* 24 April 1862 Rosa (*d* 20 April 1912), 4th dau of Sir Joseph Paxton, MP, of Rock Hills, Kent, and *d* 30 Aug 1888, having had:

1 Charles Paxton, of Tapton House, JP and DL Derbys, High Sheriff 1914; *b* 14 April 1865; *m* 1st 6 June 1889 (*divorce* 1925) Margaret Hermine (*d* 9 Oct 1936), er dau of Thomas Hughes Jackson (see MATHER-JACKSON, Bt); *m* 2nd 14 Oct 1925 Frances Margery Nunneley and *d* 29 June 1926

2 ARTHUR BASIL (Sir), **1st Bt**

3 Ernest Whinfield; *b* 3 Oct 1867; *d* unm 21 April 1888

1 Geraldine; *b* 11 July 1873; *m* 25 April 1889 Samuel Hugh Franklin Hole (*d* 14 May 1948), barrister, only s of Very Rev Samuel Reynolds Hole, DD, Dean Rochester, and *d* 18 April 1955, leaving issue

2 Violet Rosa, CH (1917), JP (Derbys 1922, Chesterfield 1930); *b* 3 Oct 1872; Hon LLD Edin 1938, Mayor Chesterfield 1927, Freedom Chesterfield 1952, FRGS, FRHistS, chm Centl Ctee Women's Employment, memb Exec Nat Relief Fund and Unemployment Assistance Bd 1934–37 (dep chm 1937–46), assist dir Nat Serv Dept; *m* 11 Feb 1915 Lt-Col James Carruthers, MVO, DSO, RFA (*d* 27 June 1936), est s of Peter Carruthers, and *d* 2 Feb 1959

CHARLES MARKHAM's 2nd s,

Sir Arthur Basil Markham, 1st Bt (UK), so *cr* 10 July 1911, JP (Derbys, Leics); *b* 25 Aug 1866; MP (Lib) Mansfield 1900–16, Capt 3rd Bn Sherwood Foresters, Derbys Regt, dir Tredegar Iron & Coal, fndr Doncaster Amalgamated Collieries; *m* 1st 31 Jan 1889 (*divorce* 1895) Mary Louise Agnes Caroline, dau of Capt John Richard Welstead, 7th Dragoon Gds; *m* 2nd 17 Sept 1898 Lucy Bertram (CBE 1920; *m* 2nd 16 March 1922 Lt-Col James O'Hea, Lt 2nd Life Gds, Lt-Col cmdg 8th Bn King's Regt and S/Ldr AAF; *d* 5 Feb 1960), dau of Capt A B Cunningham, RHA, and *d* 5 Aug 1916, having by her had:

1 CHARLES (Sir), **2nd Bt**

2 Mansfield; *b* 30 Dec 1905; *educ* Radley; Hon Attaché Paris 1925, cmded RA 1939–42; *m* 1st 27 Aug 1927 (*divorce* 1942) Mrs Beryl Purves (*d* 1987), only dau of C B Clutterbuck, of Kenya; *m* 2nd 2 Feb 1944 Mary Ellen (*d* 1987), dau of Capt A Adley, of Calcutta, and *d* 1971, leaving by his 1st w:

  (1) Gervase; *b* 25 Feb 1929; *educ* Eton and Magdalen Coll Oxford; Lt Life Gds; *m* 28 July 1952 Viviane (*d* 1987), dau of Joseph Bruiltet, and *d* 1971, leaving:

    1a *Fleur; *b* 1953

    2a Valerie-Carol; *b* 1955; *m* 1982 *Daniel Rollet, of Lyons, s of Georges Rollet, and *d* 1988

3 Arthur; *b* 21 Oct 1911; *m* 1936 Althea (*m* 2nd 1946 William John Martin Begg (*d* 1986) and *d* 25 April 1996), dau of Warren David Heinly, of Los Angeles, and *d* 15 Dec 1943, leaving:

  (1) +Michael Arthur [Michael Markham Esq, Southerly, Smiths Parish, Bermuda]; *b* posthumously 20 June 1944; *educ* Trin Coll Sch Canada, Menlo Coll California (BS, BA) and Florida Atlantic U; *m* 1976 *Geke, dau of D de Jager, of Holland, and has:

    1a +Moshe Arthur; *b* 1977

    2a +John Lloyd; *b* 1979

    1a *Hanna Althea Marion; *b* 1981

    2a *Julia Grace; *b* 1990

    3a *Joy Elizabeth; *b* 1992

    4a *Christy Victoria; *b* 27 Feb 1996

1 Joyous; *b* 21 July 1902; *m* 24 July 1925 Count Edward Andre Raczynski, of Warsaw (Polish Amb London), and *d* 27 Feb 1931

Sir ARTHUR's est s,

Sir Charles Markham, 2nd Bt; *b* 28 Aug 1899; *educ* Harrow; Capt 24th (Derby Yeo) Armoured Car Co RTC, TAR, Lt 2nd Life Gds, Dip Serv 1919, Hon Attaché Cairo 1919, attd Br High Cmmd S Russia 1920, WW I 1918, FRGS, OStJ; *m* 1st 8 Dec 1920 (*divorce* 1928) Gladys Helen (*d* 22 Feb 1943), est dau of Hon Rupert Evelyn Beckett (see GRIMTHORPE, B), and had:

1 Sir CHARLES JOHN MARKHAM, **3rd and present Bt**

1 *Mary; *b* 1921; *m* 1st 18 Sept 1946 (*divorce* 19–) Senator Joseph Dana Roberts, of Seattle, est s of Arthur Roberts; *m* 2nd 1977 James Austin Hughes (*d* 19–)

2 Rose; *m* 29 July 1953 Hon Charles Christopher Philip Hodson, only surv s of Baron Hodson, PC, MC (LP; see 1970 edn), and had issue

Sir Charles *m* 2nd 2 March 1932 (*divorce* 1938) Anne, er dau of Arthur George Vanscolina, of Labuan, Br N Borneo, and by her had:

2 +John [Maj John Markham, c/o Williams & Glyn's Bank, 9 Pall Mall, London SW1]; *b* 12 June 1933; *educ* Gordonstoun; Maj RA; *m* 1st 18 Dec 1961 (*divorce* 1987) Yvonne Penelope, dau of Neil Buchanan, and has:

  (1) +Toby John; *b* 20 May 1966; *m* 1994 *Natasha, dau of Walter Brunn

(1) *Annalise Elizabeth; b 17 April 1963; m 1986 *Anthony Cowley

Sir Charles m 3rd 17 July 1942 *(Frederica) Betty Cornwallis [Betty Lady Markham, PO Box 583, Mbabane, Swaziland]; er dau of Lt-Col Hon Christian Edward Cornwallis Eliot, OBE (see SAINT GERMANS, E), and formerly w of Capt Robert Wigram Crawford, KRRC, and d 7 Sept 1952

MARKS OF BROUGHTON

Arms: Pily argent and azure a pair of scales or. **Crest:** A dove, wings addorsed argent, beaked and membered gules, gorged with an antique crown and in the beak a gimmel ring. **Supporters:** On either side a lion or supporting a cornucopia argent, fruit proper, that on the dexter holding aloft with the interior forepaw a red rose, slipped and leaved, also proper, and that on the sinister two interlaced triangles or. **Motto:** Strive, probe, apply.
Creation: B. (UK) 10 July 1961.

THE 2ND BARON MARKS OF BROUGHTON, of Sunningdale, Co Berks (Michael Marks) [The Rt Hon The Lord Marks of Broughton, Michael House, Baker St, London W1A 1DN]; b 27 Aug 1920; s f 1964; educ St Paul's and Corpus Christi Coll Cambridge; painter, author The Prince of the Golden Apple (1975); m 1st 10 Jan 1949 (divorce 1958) Ann Catherine, dau of Maj Richard James Pinto, MC; m 2nd 1960 (divorce 1965) Helene, dau of Gustave Fischer; m 3rd 1976 (divorce 1985) Toshiko Shimura, of Japan; m 4th 19– (divorce 19–) Liyang Zhang; m 5th Nov 1994 *Marina, dau of Demetrios Sakalis, slr, of Athens, and formerly w of Leslie Collins, and has by his 1st w:

1 +SIMON RICHARD; b 3 May 1950; educ Eton and Balliol Coll Oxford; m 9 Nov 1982 *Marion, only dau of Peter F Norton, of Bermuda, and has:

  (1) +Michael; b 13 May 1989

  (1) *Miriam Ann; b 1983

  (2) *Susannah Elizabeth; b 1986

  (3) *Rebecca; b 26 Jan 1997

1 *Naomi Anne; b 16 May 1952; m Jan 1980 *(Martin) Christian Wölffer, investment banker, of New York, and has:

  (1) *Joanna Claire; b 1982

  (2) *Georgina Chloe; b 1985

2 *Sarah Elizabeth; b 7 Aug 1953; m 1979 (divorce 1989) Nicholai Radomir and has:

  (1) *Michael Richard; b 1981

  (2) *Leo Mark; b 1985

Lineage: MICHAEL MARKS, of Manchester; b Russia 1863; migrated to UK 1880s; m 19 Nov 1886 Hannah (d 20 April 1917), dau of Reuben Cohen, of Manchester, and d 31 Dec 1907, leaving:

1 SIMON, **1st Baron**

1 Rebecca, OBE (1960); m 15 June 1910 Israel Moses Sieff, cr 13 Jan 1966 Baron Sieff (LP; d 1972), s of Ephraim Sieff and Sarah, née Saffer, and d 8 Jan 1966, leaving:

  (1) Michael David, CBE (1975); b 12 March 1911; educ Manchester GS; joined Marks & Spencer 1929 (dir 1950–78, assist md 1965–71, jt md 1971–76, jt v-chm 1972–76), served RAOC WW II (Col 1944), Hon Col TA 1956, memb: European Tde Ctee Br Overseas Tde Bd 1974–87 and Br Overseas Tde Advsy Cncl 1975–87, pres Br Overseas Tde Gp for Israel 1979–83 (chm 1972–78), v-chm Br-Israel Chamber Commerce 1969–87, Fndr Fell Roy Post-Grad Medical Sch 1972; m 1st 1932 (divorce 1975) Daphne Madge Kerin (m 2nd 1976 Sir Michael Hadow (d 1993); d 1988), dau of Cyril Aaron Michael, and had:

    1a *Jonathan; b 1933; educ Marlborough; m 1st 1959 (divorce 1966) Nicole, only dau of Francis Moschietto, of Monte Carlo, and has:

      1b *Mark; b 1959

      2b *Patrick; b 1963

    1a (cont.) Jonathan Sieff m 2nd 1966 (divorce 19–) Angela, dau of Brig Douglas Pringle, of Canterbury, and by her has:

      1b *Rebecca; b 1967

    1a (cont.) Jonathan Sieff m 3rd 1986 *Candy Seymour-Smith

---

(1) (cont.) The Hon Michael Sieff m 2nd 1975 *Elizabeth (m 2nd 20 July 1996 Baron Haslam (LP, qv)), dau of William Norman Pitt, of Hampton, Middx, and d 1987, leaving by her:

  2a *Daniel Marcus; b 1977

  1a *Elizabeth Anne; b 1980

(2) *MARCUS JOSEPH SIEFF, cr 1980 BARON SIEFF OF BRIMPTON (LP, qv)

(3) Daniel; d unm

(1) Judith Hannah; b 26 Sept 1921; m 1st June 1941 (divorce 1947) Konrad Steiner, s of Paul Steiner, of Zurich, and had a dau; m 2nd Aug 1947 (divorce 1962) Philip Giaquinto, s of Filiberto Giaquinto, of Boston, Mass., and had a s and dau; m 3rd 1962 *Abraham Shechterman [Abraham Shechterman, 20 Dubnow St, Tel Aviv, Israel] and d 199–

2 Miriam; b 1 Feb 1892; Hon Fell St Hilda's Coll Oxford; m 27 Dec 1915 Harry Sacher (d 10 May 1971 aged 89), s of Jacob Sacher, and d 14 Feb 1972, leaving:

  (1) *Michael [Michael Sacher Esq, 15 Upper Phillimore Gdns, London W8]; b 17 Oct 1917

  (2) *Gabriel; b 1 March 1920

3 Mathilda; b 16 Nov 1895; m 23 Aug 1951 Terence Frank Kennedy, s of Terence Frank Kennedy, of 5 Washington Sq, New York, and Elliswood, Orange County, NY, and dsp 1 Sept 1964

4 Elaine; m 1st (divorce) Norman Laski; m 2nd 5 Oct 1944, as his 2nd w, Neville Blond, CMG, OBE (d 4 Aug 1970; see also ROMNEY, E, SCARBROUGH, E and STRACHEY, Bt), s of Bernard Blond, of Manchester

MICHAEL MARKS's only s,

SIMON MARKS, **1st Baron Marks of Broughton**, of Sunningdale, Co Berks (UK), so cr 10 July 1961; b 9 July 1888; educ Manchester GS; chm and jt md Marks & Spencer, ktd 1944, Hon DSc (Econ) London 1939, Hon FRCS 1957, Hon Fell: Weizmann Inst Science, Rehovoth, Israel, and UCL 1960, Hon LLD Manchester U 1962, Hon PhD Hebrew U of Jerusalem 1962; m 27 July 1915 Miriam (d 26 Aug 1971), dau of Ephraim Sieff, of Manchester (see 1970 edn SIEFF, B), and d 8 Dec 1964, leaving:

1 MICHAEL MARKS, **2nd and present Baron Marks of Broughton**

1 *Hannah Olive [The Hon Mrs Marcow, Le Rocabella, 24 Ave Princesse Grace, Monte Carlo, 28000 Monaco]; b 17 Sept 1918; m 1st 21 April 1941 (divorce 1959) Dr Alec Lerner, s of Moses Lerner, of Winnipeg, Canada, and has:

  (1) *Joel David [Joel Lerner Esq, 25 Eaton Mews South, London SW1]; b 9 May 1942; educ Stowe and McGill U Montreal; m 1982 *Deborah, dau of C Travers, of Woking, and has:

  (1) *Diana Toby; b 2 April 1947; m 1969 *Michael John Glass, er s of Basil Glass, of 19 Blvd de Suisse, Monte Carlo, and has:

    1a *Samantha; b 19–

  (2) *Maureen Ann [Mrs Terence Willson, 78 Waterford Rd, London SW6 2DR]; b 3 Oct 1952; m 1983 *Terence A Willson, stepson of Edward Helliwell, and has:

    1a *Simon Zachary George; b 24 Aug 1985

    1a *Jessica Sophie Hannah; b 8 July 1989

1 (cont.) The Hon Mrs Hannah Lerner m 2nd 10 June 1960 Gerald William Harold Marcow (d 1992), s of Beno Marcow, dentist, of London

MARLBOROUGH

Arms: Quarterly, 1st and 4th, sa. a lion rampant arg., on a canton of the last a cross gu. (for CHURCHILL); 2nd and 3rd, quarterly, arg. and gu., in the 2nd and 3rd quarters, a fret or, over all, on a bend sa., three escallops of the first (for SPENCER); in chief an escutcheon arg., charged with the Cross of St George gu. (honourable augmentation granted by CHARLES II 1661 for Sir Winston Churchill's servs in the late Civil War), thereon an escutcheon of the arms of France (az. three fleurs-de-lys or), the whole arms borne upon an imperial eagle, as a Prince of the Holy Roman Empire; above the arms a princely coronet. **Crests:** 1 A lion couchant guardant arg., supporting with the dexter paw a banner gu. charged with a dexter hand appaumée of the first, staff or (for CHURCHILL), 2 Out of a ducal coronet or a griffin's head between two wings expanded arg., gorged with a collar gemelle and armed gu. (for SPENCER). **Supporters:** Two wyverns, wings expanded gu. **Motto:** *Fiel pero desdichado* ('Faithful, though unfortunate'). **Creations:** B. (E) 21 July 1603 (Spencer of Wormleighton) and 14 May 1685 (Churchill of Sandridge); E. (E) 6 June 1643 (Sunderland) and 9 April 1689 (Marlborough), D. and M. (E) 14 Dec 1702, Prince (HRE) 28 Aug 1704 (Mindelheim, later Mellenburg).

THE 11TH DUKE OF MARLBOROUGH, Marquess of Blandford, Co Dorset, **Earl of Sunderland, Earl of Marlborough**, Co Wilts, **Baron Spencer of Wormleighton**, Co Northampton, and **Baron Churchill of Sandridge**, Co Hertford, also **Prince of Mellenburg** (HRE) (John George Vanderbilt Henry Spencer-Churchill, JP and DL (Oxon) [His Grace The Duke of Marlborough JP DL, Blenheim Palace, Woodstock, Oxon OX20 1PX]; *b* 13 April 1926; *s f* 1972; *educ* Eton; late Capt Life Gds, CC (1961) Oxon; *m* 1st 19 Oct 1951 (*divorce* 1961) Susan Mary (*m* 2nd 1962 Alan Cyril Heber-Percy; *see* NORTHUMBERLAND, D), only dau of Michael Charles St John Hornby, of Pusey House, Faringdon, Berks, and has:

1 John David Ivor, *Earl of Sunderland*; *b* 17 Nov 1952 (HRH PRINCESS MARGARET stood sponsor); *d* 14 May 1955

2 +(CHARLES) JAMES, *Marquess of Blandford*; *b* 24 Nov 1955; *educ* Harrow; sometime mktg dir Brodie Brittain Racing, of Brackley, Northants; organiser VIP hospitality for Benetton Formula One Team 1996–; *m* 1990 (*divorce* 1998) Rebecca Mary, dau of Peter Few Brown, and has:

　(1) +George, *Earl of Sunderland*; *b* 28 July 1992

1 +Henrietta Mary [The Lady Henrietta Gelber, 60 Radnor Walk, London SW3]; *b* 7 Oct 1958; *m* 1980 (*divorce* 1989) Nathan Gelber and has:

　(1) +David Aba; *b* 1981

　(2) +Maximilian Henry; *b* 1985

The 11th DUKE *m* 2nd 23 Oct 1961 (*divorce* 1971) Athina (Tina) Mary (*d* 1974), dau of Stavros G Livanos, of 56 Avenue Foch, Paris XVI, and formerly wife of Aristotle Socrates Onassis; *m* 3rd 1972 *(Dagmar) Rosita Astri Libertas, dau of Count Carl Ludwig Douglas, and by her has:

3 +Edward Albert Charles; *b* 1974; *educ* Pembroke Coll Cambridge; management consultant with Bain & Co

2 +Alexandra Elizabeth Mary; *b* 1977

Previous creations: An Earldom of Marlborough was conferred on James Ley in February 1625/6. He was a Wiltshire man (though with a seemingly rather exotic streak in his background in that his mother was called Dionysia de St Mayne) who had clawed his way up the rungs of the legal profession till he had attained the Chief Justiceship of the King's Bench, the Commissionership of the Great Seal, both in Ireland, and the post of Lord High Treasurer in England. He may well have deserved his ennoblement — he was reckoned a competent judge, particularly by Milton, who put in a good word for him in bad verse. But the chief mover in the matter was almost certainly his third wife's uncle George Villiers, Duke of Buckingham (*see* JERSEY, E).

James's son the 2nd Earl was killed at the English victory of Sole Bay in 1665 during the Second Dutch War. The title expired on the death without issue of the 3rd Earl in 1679. When another nephew of the Duke of Buckingham, John Churchill,

was given a step up in the peerage in 1689 it was therefore natural for the Earldom of Marlborough to be revived.

For other titles embodying the names Churchill or Spencer *see* those articles. An Earldom of Sunderland was held between 1627 and 1630 by Emanuel Scrope but expired with him.

Lineage: WILLIAM CHURCHILL, of Rockbear, Devon; had:

GILES CHURCHILL; had:

CHARLES CHURCHILL; supported EDWARD IV in the Wars of the Roses as a retainer of Thomas Courtenay, Earl of Devon, but remained faithful when Devon deserted the King (possibly during EDWARD's temporary eclipse in 1470) and through EDWARD's influence *m* Margaret, dau and heiress of Sir William Woodvill, a member of the powerful family of the Earls Rivers and a relative of EDWARD IV's w Elizabeth; gggf of:

MATTHEW CHURCHILL, of Bradford-on-Avon, Wilts; *m* Alice, dau of James Gould, of Dorchester, and had:

JASPER CHURCHILL, of Bradford-on-Avon; *m* Elizabeth, dau of John Chaplet, of Herrington, Dorset, and had an e r s:

JOHN CHURCHILL, of Mintern, Dorset; *m* Sarah, dau and coheir of Sir Henry Winston, of Standish, Glos, and had:

Sir WINSTON CHURCHILL; Commr Court of Claims and Explanations Ireland 1662–68; *b* 1620; *m* May 1643 Elizabeth, dau of Sir John Drake, of Ash, Devon, by Elizabeth, niece of George Villiers, 1st Duke of Buckingham (*see* JERSEY, E), and had, with five other sons (Winston; Theobald, *d* unm 1684; Henry; Jasper; Mountjoy):

1 JOHN

2 George; Adml the Blue, MP St Albans, memb Cncl of PRINCE GEORGE OF DENMARK, QUEEN ANNE's husb; *b* 29 Feb 1653; *dsp* 8 May 1710

3 Charles; fought Battles of Steenkirk and Landen, where he captured his nephew the French cdr the Duke of Berwick; Lt-Gen, Govr Kingsale Ireland, Govr Tower of London, also fought at Blenheim, Govr Brussels, Col Coldstream Gds, Govr Guernsey; *b* 2 Feb 1656; *m* 1702 Mary (*m* 2nd 13 Feb 1716/7 2nd Earl of Abingdon (*see* LINDSEY and ABINGDON, E), dau and sole heiress of James Gould, of Dorchester, and *dspl* 29 Dec 1714

1 Arabella; *b* 23 Feb 1647; mistress of JAMES II, by whom she had issue:

　(1) JAMES FitzJAMES, 1st DUKE OF BERWICK-UPON-TWEED, so *cr* 19 March 1686/7, as also EARL OF TINMOUTH (*i.e.*, Tynemouth), Co Northumberland, and BARON OF BOSWORTH, Co Leicester (all E); served in the Imperial Army in Hungary against the Turks, rising to Maj-Gen 1687; Col 8th Foot 1687–88, Ld Lt Hants 1687–88, Govr Portsmouth 1687–89, Col RHG Feb–Nov 1688, Col 3rd Horse Gds 1688–89; fought on his f's side Battle of the Boyne 1690 and was accordingly attainted and his E titles forfeited 1695; Lt-Gen French Serv 1693, naturalised in France 17 Dec 1703; Marshal of France 1706; also *cr* 16 Oct 1707 DUKE OF LIRIA AND XERICA, Province of Valencia, Spain, and made a Kt of the Golden Fleece for his victory over an Anglo-Portuguese army at the Battle of Almanza 25 April 1707; also *cr* 23 May 1710 DUKE OF FitzJAMES, of Warty on the Oise, Beauvais, France (Warty being made into a Duke and Peer's territory), with special remainder to his issue by his 2nd w, Kt of the Holy Ghost 1724, Govr Strasbourg 1730; *b* 21 Aug 1670; *educ* Colleges of Juilly (nr Meaux), Plessis and La Flèche; *m* 1st 26 March 1695 Honora (*d* 16 Jan 1697/8), dau of 7th Earl of Clanricarde (*see* SLIGO, M) and widow of Patrick Sarsfield, titular 1st Earl of Lucan (*see* LUCAN, E, preliminary remarks); *m* 2nd 18 April 1700 Anne (*d* 12 June 1751), dau of Hon Henry Bulkeley (4th s of 1st Viscount Bulkeley), and was *k* at Siege of Philippsburg 12 June 1734, leaving issue by both wives, that of the senior branch (by 1st w) continuing as Dukes of Spain, that of the junior branch (by 2nd w) continuing as Dukes of France

　(2) Henry FitzJAMES, titular Duke of Albemarle, Earl of Rochford, and Baron of Romney, so *cr* by his f JAMES II while in exile 13 Jan 1696; *b* Aug 1673; Col of Infantry Battle of Boyne 1690, attainted 1695; Lt Gen and Adml of France 1702; *m* 20 July 1700 Marie Gabrielle (*m* 2nd 25 May 1707 2nd Earl of Melfort (*see* PERTH, E) and *d* 15 May 1741), dau of Jean d'Audibert, Count of Lussan, and *dspm* 16/27 Dec 1702, leaving issue

　　(1) Henrietta; *b* 1667; *m* 1st 29 Nov 1683 1st Baron Waldegrave of Chewton (*d* 14/24 Jan 1689/90; *see* WALDEGRAVE, E); *m* 2nd *c* 3 April 1695 3rd Viscount of Galmoye (*see* MOUNTGARRET, V), and *d* 3 April 1730, leaving issue by her 1st husb

　　(2) Arabella; Benedictine nun; *b c* 1674; *d* 7 Nov 1704 aged 31

1 (contd.) Arabella Churchill afterwards *m* Col Charles Godfrey, Master of the Jewel Office (*d* 23 Feb 1714), and *d* 4 May 1730, leaving further issue

Sir WINSTON's est surv son,

JOHN CHURCHILL, **1st Duke of Marlborough**, so *cr* 14 Dec 1702, as also MARQUESS OF BLANDFORD, Co Dorset, with a grant of £5,000 (just under £260,000 in late-1990s terms) p.a. during QUEEN ANNE's life, as also earlier 21 Dec 1682 LORD CHURCHILL OF EYEMOUTH, Co Berwick (S), 14 May 1685 BARON CHURCHILL OF SANDRIDGE, Co Hertford, and 9 April 1689 EARL OF MARLBOROUGH, Co Wilts (by Act of Parl 21 Dec 1706 he obtained a revised remainder, expanding the descent of his titles to heirs male of the body, whom failing, to his est dau Harriet and the heirs male of her body, whom failing to his 3rd dau Anne, and the heirs male of her body, whom failing to his yst dau Mary and the heirs male of her body, then to any other daus he might have by primogeniture, then Harriet's daus and their heirs male, and so on with his other daus, and lastly all and any other of his issue under the same terms), *cr* also 28 Aug 1704 PRINCE OF THE HRE by the EMPEROR LEOPOLD and granted 18 Nov 1705 the Principality of Mindelheim, Swabia, by the EMPEROR JOSEPH (exchanged 1713 for the County of Mellenburg, Upper Austria, which was then erected into a Principality), with all his descendants, of either sex, to be Princes of the HRE also, KG (March 1701/2), PC (Feb 1688/9–92 and 1698–1711 and 1714–22); *b* 24 June 1650; *educ* St Paul's; joined Foot Gds 1667, Page-of-Honour to JAMES II when DUKE OF YORK 1667; Gent Bedchamber 1673, throughout JAMES II's reign and 1689 on; MP Newtown (IoW) Feb–July 1679, Master Wardrobe 1679, Col: Roy Dragoons 1683–85, 3rd Horse Gds 1685–88 and 1689–92, Roy Fus 1689–92, 24th Foot 1702–04 and 1st Foot Gds 1704–12 and 1714–22, Amb Paris March–April 1685, Govr Hudson's Bay Co 1685–91, Lt Gen 1688, one of the first public figures to desert JAMES II for WILLIAM III in 1688, as certainly one of the most important (and in addition the most prone to dissemble his intended disloyalty); helped WILLIAM III conquer Ireland; Cdr English forces Netherlands 1690; relieved of all his appointments 1692 for suspected (indeed actual) plotting with JAMES II; Master Horse 1698–1700; C-in-C Br and Dutch forces Netherlands 1701, Amb to The Hague 1702; Capt Gen all English forces, Generalissimo Allied forces, Master Gen Ordnance 1702 on outbreak War of Spanish Succession; captured various Flemish fortresses autumn 1702, won victories of Donauwerth (over Bavaria) 2 July 1704 and over the French: Blenheim 2/13 Aug 1704, Tirlemont 18 July 1705, Ramillies 23 May 1706, Oudenarde 11 July 1708 and Malplaquet (something of a pyrrhic victory) 11 Sept 1709, taking also Mons and Bouchain 13 Sept 1711; Ld Lt Oxon 1706–12; relieved of all his posts 1711 but reappointed 1714 as Capt-Gen, Master Gen Ordnance, Col 1st Foot Gds, Govr Chelsea Hosp; m 1 Oct 1678 Sarah (d 18 Oct 1744), a favourite of QUEEN ANNE, dau and coheir of Richard Jenyns (usually nowadays spelled Jennings), of Sandridge, Herts, by Frances, dau of Sir Giffard Thornhurst, Bt, of Agnes Court, Kent, and yr sis of 1st and last Duke of Tyrconnel (see TALBOT OF MALAHIDE, B) and dspms 16 June 1722, having had:

1 John, *Marquess of Blandford*; b 13 Feb 1689/90; d of smallpox 20 Feb 1702/3

2 Charles; b 19 Aug 1690; d 22 May 1692

1 Harriet; b Oct 1679; d infant

2 HENRIETTA Churchill, **Duchess of Marlborough** in her own right; b 19 July 1681; m c 23 April 1698 Francis GODOLPHIN, 2nd Earl of Godolphin (d 17 Jan 1766), and d 24 Oct 1733, having had:

(1) William, *Marquess of Blandford*, MP Woodstock; m 25 April 1729 Maria Catherina (m 2nd 1 June 1734 Sir William Wyndham, 3rd Bt, and dsp 1 Sept 1779), dau of Peter de Jonge, of Utrecht, Holland, and sis of Isabella, Countess of Denbigh (qv), and dsp 24 Aug 1731

(1) Henrietta; m 2 April 1717 1st Duke of Newcastle (see CHICHESTER, E, and LINCOLN, E) and dsp 17 July 1776

(2) Mary; m 26 June 1740 4th Duke of Leeds (see 1963 edn) and d 3 Aug 1764, leaving issue

3 ANNE Churchill; b 27 Feb 1684; m 14 Sept 1699, as his 2nd w, Charles SPENCER, **3rd Earl of Sunderland** (see below), and d 15 April 1716, leaving, with two daus:

(1) ROBERT SPENCER, **4th Earl of Sunderland**; d unm 27 Nov 1729

(2) CHARLES, **3rd Duke**

(3) John; ancestor of EARL SPENCER (qv)

4 Elizabeth; b 15 March 1687; m 9 Feb 1703 1st Duke of Bridgwater and d 22 March 1713/4, leaving issue (see GREY EGERTON, Bt)

5 Mary; b 15 July 1689; m 17 March 1705 2nd Duke of Montagu and dspms 14 May 1751, leaving issue

The 1st DUKE's gs (through his 3rd dau)

CHARLES SPENCER, **3rd Duke of Marlborough** (as which s aunt 1733) and **5th Earl of Sunderland** (as which had previously s er bro 1729), KG (March 1740/1), KB (1743); b 22 Nov 1706; educ Eton; Lord Lt and custos rotulorum Oxon and Bucks 1738–58; Brig-Gen 1743, Maj-Gen 1745, Lt Gen 1758, cmded a Bde of Foot Gds at Battle of Dettingen 1743, C-in-C expdn against France and Br forces Germany summer 1758, Col: 38th Foot 1738–39, 1st Dragoons 1739–40, 2nd Horse Gds 1740–42, 2nd Foot Gds 1742–44, Ld Steward Household 1749–55, Ld Privy Seal Jan–Dec 1755, Master Gen Ordnance 1755–58; m 23 May 1732 Elizabeth (d 7 Oct 1761), dau of 2nd Baron Trevor of Bromham (see TREVOR, B, preliminary remarks), and had, with other issue:

1 GEORGE, **4th Duke**

2 Charles; b 31 March 1740; m 2 Oct 1762 Mary (d 13 Jan 1812), sis of 5th Duke of St Albans (qv), and d 16 June 1820, leaving:

(1) John; b 21 Dec 1767; m 5 Feb 1790 Elizabeth, dau of **4th Duke of Marlborough** (see below), and d 17 Dec 1831, leaving:

1a Frederick Charles (Rev); Rector Wheatfield, Oxon; b 18 March 1796; m 6 Oct 1823 Mary Anne (m 2nd 1835 Rev Edward Fanshawe Glanville and d 1882), dau of Sir Scrope Bernard Morland, Bt (see 1850 edn), and d 2 Oct 1831, leaving:

1b Charles Vere (Rev); Rector Wheatfield, Oxon; b 17 May 1827; m 22 June 1852 Emma Frederica (d 20 Jan 1907), only dau of John Robert à Court Gray, of Kingweston, Somerset, and d 27 May 1898, having had:

1c Aubrey John; barrister, JP; b 18 June 1853; educ Marlborough and Ch Ch Oxford (MA); m 9 April 1885 Florence Mary (d 23 Aug 1952), dau of Frederick Halsey Janson, and d 19 June 1935, leaving:

1d Aubrey Vere, DSO (1914), JP (Oxon 1938), DL (1944); b 4 April 1886; educ Marlborough and Wye Ag Coll; High Sheriff 1959, Lt-Col 3rd Bn Oxon and Bucks LI WW I (wounded, despatches), cmded a Bn Oxon HG 1940–44, Bursar Corpus Christi Coll Oxford, MA Oxon 1929, Land Agent to Oxford U 1946, FLAS, PASI; m 15 Sept 1926 Gwendoline Esther Hall (d 24 Sept 1968), dau of George Neame Murton, of Petleys, Downe, Kent, and widow of Capt Claude Holdsworth Hunt, RFA, and dsp 7 June 1973

1d Ethel Frances; b 16 Dec 1887

2d Frederica Elizabeth; b 31 March 1892; m 23 April 1919 Thomas Henry Bayley (d 3 Nov 1937) and had issue

3d Caroline Mildred; b 26 Nov 1898

2c George Trevor, RN; b 6 Feb 1855; d 8 Feb 1931

3c Edmund Vere; BA Oxon, Capt RE (T); b 13 Nov 1866; d unm 7 Feb 1944

4c Charles Gordon (Sir); ICS, Puisne Judge Madras; b 23 Feb 1869; m 13 Jan 1903 Edith Mary (d 18 Dec 1936), dau of Col Hugh Pearce Pearson, CB, and d 17 Nov 1934, leaving:

1d John Gray Churchill SPENCER later SPENCER BERNARD (deed poll 1955); MRCS Eng and LRCP Lond 1933, FRCS Eng 1940, Assist Surgn Roy Salop Infirmary, Pathologist Frenchay Hosp Bristol; b 26 May 1907; educ Marlborough and Magdalene Coll Cambridge (BA 1930, MA 1935, MD 1938); m 31 Aug 1933 *Elsie Phyllis [Mrs John Spencer Bernard, Nether Winchendon House, Aylesbury, Bucks], only dau of Ferrand Corley, of Christian College, Madras, and d 28 March 1977, leaving:

1e +Charles Francis Churchill [Charles Spencer Bernard Esq, 18 rue Barbette, 75003 Paris, France]; b 23 Jan 1942; educ Marlborough and Magdalene Coll Cambridge (BA 1964); 2nd Lt RA (TA) 1965; m 1974 *Rosalyn Anne, dau of Maj Patrick Plunkett, and has:

1f +Jane Beatrice; b 1979

2f +Sarah Penelope Katherine; b 1983

3f +Elizabeth Joanna; b 1986

2e +Robert Vere [Robert Spencer Bernard Esq, Nether Winchendon House, Aylesbury, Bucks HP18 0DY]; b 1 Dec 1944; educ Marlborough and Trin Coll Oxford; barrister Inner Temple 1969; m 1975 *Katharine Margaret, dau of Lt-Col Claud Everard Montagu Douglas Scott, MC (see BUCCLEUCH and QUEENSBERRY, D)

1e +Julia Diana [Mrs John Hopton, Village Farm House, Boarstall, Aylesbury, Bucks]; b 20 April 1936; educ LMH Oxford; m 12 Sept 1959 *John Simon Baskerville Cadwallader Hopton, s of Maj Otho Cadwallader Hopton, of Clyro, Herefs, and has:

1f +Richard Henry Cadwallader; b 20 April 1962

2f +Edward Charles Adams; b 28 June 1964

1f +Isobel Georgiana; b 16 March 1967

2e +Clare Rosemary [Mrs Rio Hohler, Chevreloup, 27 Route de Perdreauville, 78950 Gambais, France]; b 1 Nov 1938; educ Newnham Coll Cambridge (MA); m 10 Aug 1963 *Rio Tyrrell Arthur Hohler, er s of Henry Arthur Frederick Hohler, CMG, of Long Crendon, Bucks, and has:

1f +Rupert John Frederick; b 15 Nov 1972

1f +Harriet Valentine; b 1 Feb 1967

2f +Camilla Clare; b 9 Nov 1968

3f +Amanda Sophie; b 19 Nov 1970

2d Charles Bernard; b 9 Nov 1909; educ Marlborough and Corpus Christi Coll Oxford (BA 1932); m 1st 1 Aug 1936 Nora (d 13 June 1947), dau of Frederick Gibbs; m 2nd 29 Sept 1961 *Anne Margaret Helen (m 2nd 1969 Rock Noel Humphreys) [Mrs Rock Humphreys, Bark Barn Cottage, 12 West Dean, Salisbury, Wilts], dau of Alan George Marjoribanks, of Colinton, Edinburgh, and d 11 Sept 1963, leaving:

1e +Piers Bernard [Piers Spencer Esq, 36 Alma Sq, London NW8 9QD]; b 7 Feb 1963

1d Cynthia Mary; b 16 March 1904; m 5 Jan 1928 William H Peppercorn and d 1995, leaving:

1e John Julian; b 4 March 1935; m 1959 *Elizabeth, only dau of A S Grant, and d 1995, leaving issue

5c Frederick Augustus Morland (Rev); b 23 July 1878; educ Bradfield and BNC Oxford (BA 1901, John Locke Scholar 1902, MA 1904, DD 1929); Rector Gt Rollright 1935–48, Chaplain AIF WWI and BNC Oxford 1929–34, author: *Human Ideals*, *The Ethics of the Gospel*, *Civilisation Re-made by Christ*, *The Theory of Christ's Ethics* and *The Future Life*; m 3 June 1913 Gertrude Lucie (d 4 Oct 1970), dau of George John Burke, MICE, of St Kilda, Melbourne, and d 28 Sept 1962, leaving:

1d +Marion Gertrude [Mrs Marion Hoare, 9 Sympson Close, Abingdon, Oxon OX14 5RB]; b 15 Jan 1916; m 18 June 1940 (divorce 1971) Kenneth Ninian Hoare and has:

1e +Gillian Sheila [Mrs Richard Button, Gulf Stevedoring, Jeddah Islamic Port, PO Box 19860, Jeddah 21445, Saudi Arabia]; b 19 Sept 1947; m 22 May 1971 *Richard James Kenneth Button and has had:

1f Daniel Mark; b 13 March 1983; d 1 Aug 1987

1f +Sarah Nicola [Miss Sarah Button, 30 Farm Close Rd, Wheatley, Oxon OX33 1UQ]; b 6 Nov 1971

2f +Teresa Jane [Miss Teresa Button, 9 Sympson Close, Abingdon, Oxon OX14 5RB]; b 1 Feb 1974

2e +Celia Jennifer [Mrs Keith Reading, Hidcote, 10 Longdown Lane North, Ewell, Surrey KT17 3JQ]; b 1 May 1952; m 11 Oct 1975 *Capt Keith Reading, MN, and has:

1f +Kyle Gareth; b 21 Dec 1983

1f +Katrina Louise; b 4 April 1976

2d +Geraldine Mildred [Geraldine Spencer, 70c Currong Apartments, Braddon, Canberra 2601, Australia]; b 20 April 1920; educ Sydney U (BA)

1c Mildred Frances; d unm 16 May 1923

2c Frederica Marion; b 6 July 1858; d unm 3 Aug 1951

2b George Bernard; b 27 July 1829; d 2 Nov 1853

1b Harriet Frances; d unm 29 June 1899

1a Georgiana Elizabeth; d unm 13 April 1863

2a Caroline Susannah; m 14 Jan 1830 Vicomte Charles de Mentque and d 5 May 1840

3a Elizabeth; m 22 April 1823 Lacy Rumsey, Clerk of Bills Treasury, and had issue

(2) William Robert; b 9 Jan 1769; m 13 Dec 1791 Susan, widow of Count Spreti and dau of Ralph Jenison Count von Walworth, and d 23 Oct 1834, leaving, with other issue:

1a Aubrey George (Rt Rev); DD, Bp Jamaica; b 8 Feb 1795; m 14 July 1822 Eliza (d 1883), dau of John Musson, and d 24 Feb 1872, having had:

1b Ella Louisa; m 5 Sept 1842 Henry John Harvey (d 1878), Capt RN, 2nd s of Lt-Gen Sir John Harvey, KCB, and d 25 June 1906

2b Emily Jane Pembroke; m 23 Sept 1856 Rev Duncan Houston Campbell (d 1878)

3b Mary Shaftesbury; m 1 Feb 1849 Archdeacon Charles John Smith, of Jamaica, Vicar Erith, Kent, and d 20 May 1854

2a William; b 4 May 1796; m 20 July 1820 Frances, dau of John Garland, and had issue

3a George John Trevor (Rt Rev); DD, Bp Madras, Chllr St Paul's; b 11 Dec 1799; m 27 May 1823 Harriet, dau of Sir Benjamin Hobhouse, 1st Bt (qv), and d 16 July 1866, having had:

1b William Cavendish; BCS; *b* 19 Jan 1829; *m* 28 June 1858 Patience Caroline (*d* 20 Nov 1859), dau of Col J C Hannyngton, IA, and *d* 23 Jan 1860, leaving:

1c John Trevor; Lt-Col cmdg 4th Bn, Maj 1st Bn Essex Regt; *b* 13 Nov 1859; *m* 1889 Lilian (*m* 2nd 12 March 1910 Capt A H Rose (*ka* 23 Nov 1914), Essex Regt), dau of Robert Gordon, of New York, and *d* 16 Oct 1906, leaving:

1d Lillian Mary Latina; *b* 1 Dec 1890; *m* 1918 (*annulled* on her petition 1921) Maj Armistead L Feild, MC, Essex Regt and MGC, and *d* 17 July 1933

2b Almeric John Churchill (Rev); Incumbent Ear Sterndale, Derbys; *b* 23 Jan 1834; *m* 18 June 1857 Isabella Elizabeth (*d* 8 Dec 1924), dau of Rev Frederick Adrian Scrope Fane (*see* WESTMORLAND, E), and *d* 3 May 1864, leaving:

1c Harriette Isabella Barbara; *d* unm 8 Aug 1918

2c Adelaide Churchill; *m* 1st 11 Feb 1885 (*divorce* 1902) Col George M Davison, Durham LI, and had issue; *m* 2nd 16 Sept 1902 William Freeman O'Donoghue, Accountant-Gen IPWD, s of Col Charles O'Donoghue, 76th Regt, and *d* 22 April 1935

1b Theodora Amelia Mary; *m* 22 Sept 1840 Hatley Frere, Madras CS, and *d* 28 May 1848, leaving issue

2b Susan Ann Sophia Churchill, 1845; *m* Rev Robert Kerr Hamilton, Chaplain Madras, and *d* his widow 13 Nov 1866, having had a dau (*d* unm)

(3) Robert; *m* Henrietta, dau of Sir E Fawkener, KB, and widow of Hon E Bouverie (*see* RADNOR, E), and *dsp* 1831

1 Diana; *m* 1st 1757 (*divorce*) 2nd Viscount Bolingbrokeand (3rd Viscount) Saint John (*qv*) and had issue; *m* 2nd 1768 Topham Beauclerk (*see* ST ALBANS, D) and *d* 1808, leaving further issue

2 Elizabeth; *m* 1756 10th Earl of Pembroke (*see* PEMBROKE and MONTGOMERY, E), and *d* 1831

The 3rd DUKE *d* 28 Oct 1758; his est son,

GEORGE SPENCER, **4th Duke of Marlborough**, KG (1768), PC (1762); *b* 26 Jan 1738/9; *educ* Eton; Capt 20th Foot, Ld Lt Oxon 1760–1817, Ld Chamberlain 1762–63, Ld Privy Seal 1763–65; *m* 23 Aug 1762 Lady Caroline Russell (*d* 26 Nov 1811), only dau of 4th Duke of Bedford (*qv*), and had:

1 GEORGE, **5th Duke**

2 FRANCIS ALMERIC SPENCER, 1st BARON CHURCHILL (*see* CHURCHILL, V)

1 Caroline; *m* 19 March 1792 2nd Viscount Clifden (*see* 1970 edn) and *d* 23 Nov 1813, having had issue

2 Elizabeth; *m* John Spencer and *d* 1812

3 Charlotte; *m* 16 April 1797 Rev Edward Nares, DD, Regius Prof Modern History and Languages Oxford, and *d* 1802

4 Anne; *m* 1796 6th Earl of Shaftesbury (*qv*) and *d* 7 Aug 1865

5 Amelia Sophia; *m* 1812 Henry Pytches Boyce and *d* 30 Jan 1829

The 4th DUKE *d* 30 Jan 1817; his er son,

GEORGE SPENCER later SPENCER-CHURCHILL (roy licence 26 May 1817), **5th Duke of Marlborough**; *b* 6 March 1766; *educ* Eton and Ch Ch Oxford; MP (Whig) Oxon 1790–96 and (Tory) Tregony 1802–04; called up to Ho Lds *vp* 12 March 1806 in his f's Barony of Spencer of Wormleighton; *m* 15 Sept 1791 Lady Susan Stewart (*d* 2 April 1841), dau of 7th Earl of Galloway (*qv*), and had, with other issue:

1 GEORGE, **6th Duke**

2 Charles; Army Offr; *b* 3 Dec 1794; *m* 24 Aug 1827 Etheldred Catherine (*d* 6 Dec 1839), 2nd dau of John Benett, of Pyt House, MP Wilts, and *d* 28 April 1840, leaving, with two other daus:

(1) Charles Henry; Lt-Col 60th Rifles; *b* 27 May 1828; *m* 30 Oct 1862 Rosalie (*m* 2nd 9 Oct 1886 Baron von Fahnenberg Burckheim, of Burckheim, Rothwell, Grand Duchy of Baden), yst dau of Rev Gorges Paulin Lowther, Preb Salisbury, Rector Orcheston St George, Wilts, and *dsp* 3 April 1877

(2) John Kemys George Thomas, CMG; Govr Montserrat, Commr St Kitts and Nevis, Colonial Sec Bahamas 1895–96, Capt 8th Regt; *b* 27 Dec 1835; *m* 23 July 1884 Edith Maxwell Lockhart (*d* 28 June 1932), dau of Edward Lockhart, of Geneva, Dominica, W Indies, and *dsp* 9 Aug 1913

(1) Susan; *m* 27 Aug 1857 Rev Hon John Horatio Nelson and *d* 2 Feb 1898, leaving issue (*see* NELSON, E)

3 George Henry (Rev); *b* 18 May 1796; *m* 13 July 1824 his cousin Elizabeth Martha (*m* 2nd 18 Aug 1834 William Whately, QC, and *d* 14 Feb 1866), dau of Rev Edward Nares, DD, s of Mr Justice Nares, Court of Common Pleas, and *d* 1828

The 5th DUKE *d* 5 March 1840; his est son,

GEORGE SPENCER-CHURCHILL, **6th Duke of Marlborough**; *b* 27 Dec 1793; *educ* Eton and Ch Ch Oxford; MP (Ind) Chippenham 1818–20 and Woodstock 1826–31, 1832–35 and 1838–40, Ld Lt Oxon 1842–57, High Steward Oxford and Woodstock; *m* 1st 13 Jan 1819 his cousin Lady Jane Stewart (*d* 12 Oct 1844), est dau of 8th Earl of Galloway (*qv*), and had:

1 JOHN WINSTON, **7th Duke**

2 Alfred, JP and DL; 4th Light Dragoons, Lt-Col Oxon Yeo, MP Woodstock 1845–47 and 1857–65; *b* 24 April 1824; *m* 5 Feb 1857 Harriet Louisa Hester (*d* 20 July 1901), 3rd dau of 4th Baron Calthorpe (*see* 1970 edn), and *d* 21 Sept 1893, having had:

(1) Jane; *m* 5 Feb 1879 Sir Francis Salwey Winnington, 5th Bt (*qv*), and *d* 20 June 1940, leaving issue

(2) Olivia; *m* 6 Nov 1883 Brig-Gen Arthur Edward William Colville and *d* 28 May 1943, leaving issue (*see* COLVILLE OF CULROSS, V)

(3) Adeline; *m* 1 Aug 1895 Col William Hugh Williams, CMG, RA (*d* 20 Jan 1938), est s of Gen Sir J William Collman Williams, KCB, of Purbrook, Hants, and *d* 10 Jan 1937, leaving issue

(4) Violet; *m* 20 April 1908 Brig-Gen Charles FitzClarence and *d* 22 Dec 1941, leaving issue (*see* MUNSTER, E)

3 Alan; Offr 8th Hus; *b* 25 July 1825; *m* 2 July 1846 Rosamond (*m* 2nd 4 Aug 1874 Alfred Henry Caulfeild (*see* CHARLEMONT, V) and *d* 10 Dec 1888), dau of Thomas Dowker, of Huntingdon Hall, Yorks, and *d* 18 April 1873

1 Louisa; *m* 4 July 1845 Hon Robert C H Spencer (*d* 17 June 1881) and *d* 23 March 1882, leaving issue (*see* CHURCHILL, V)

The **6th Duke** *m* 2nd 10 June 1846 Charlotte Augusta (*d* 20 April 1850), dau of 4th Viscount Ashbrook (*qv*), and by her had:

4 Almeric Athelstan; *b* 1847; *d* 12 Dec 1856

2 Clementina Augusta; *m* 1st 12 July 1866 3rd Marquess Camden (*qv*) and had issue; *m* 2nd 28 Dec 1876 Capt Philip Green, 5th Lancers (*d* 18 Nov 1904), and *d* 27 March 1886, having had further issue

The **6th Duke** *m* 3rd 11 Oct 1851 Jane Frances Clinton (*d* 24 March 1897), dau of Hon Edward Richard Stewart (*see* GALLOWAY, E), and by her had:

5 Edward, DL Worcs; *b* 28 March 1853; *m* 15 Sept 1874 Augusta, CBE (1935, OBE 1920) (*d* following a car crash 1 Sept 1941), dau of Maj George Drought Warburton, RA, MP, by Hon Elizabeth Augusta, later Baroness Northwick (*see* 1887 edn), and *d* 5 May 1911, having had:

(1) Edward George, MC, of Northwick Park, Blockley, Glos; *b* 21 May 1876; *educ* Eton and Magdalen Coll Oxford (BA 1898); Capt Gren Gds, Boer War 1899–1901 (medals with seven clasps) and WW I (wounded twice, Croix de Guerre with palm), High Sheriff Worcs 1924, Tstee Nat Gallery 1943–50; *d* unm 24 June 1964

(1) Augusta Ruby; *b* 6 April 1877; *m* 22 April 1902 Lt-Col Hon (Allen) Benjamin Bathurst (*d* 8 Oct 1947), 3rd s of 6th Earl Bathurst (*qv*), and had issue

(2) Katharine Maude Mary; *b* 17 April; *d* 5 Aug 1878

(3) Agnes Beryl; *b* 20 Nov 1881; *m* 14 Nov 1905 2nd Viscount Cowdray (*qv*) and *d* 19 Feb 1948, leaving issue

The 6th DUKE *d* 1 July 1857; his est son,

JOHN WINSTON SPENCER-CHURCHILL, **7th Duke of Marlborough**, KG (1868), PC (1866); *b* 2 June 1822; *educ* Eton and Oriel Coll Oxford; MP (C) Woodstock 1844–45 and 1847–57, Ld Lt Oxon 1857–83, High Steward Woodstock, Ld Steward Household 1866–67, Ld Pres Cncl 1867–68, Ld Lt Ireland 1876–80; *m* 12 July 1843 Lady Frances Anne Emily Vane, VA (*d* 16 April 1899), dau of 3rd Marquess of Londonderry (*qv*), and had:

1 GEORGE CHARLES, **8th Duke**

2 Frederick John Winston; *b* 2 Feb 1846; *d* 5 Aug 1850

3 Randolph Henry, PC, JP, DL; *b* 13 Feb 1849; MA Oxon; MP (C) Woodstock 1874–85 and Paddington 1885–95, Sec State India 1885–86, Chllr Exchequer 1886, LLD Cantab; *m* Paris 15 April 1874 Jennie, CI, RRC, DGStJ (*m* 2nd 28 July 1900 (*divorce* 1913) Capt George Frederick Myddelton Cornwallis-West (*d* 1 April 1951) (*see* DE LA WARR, E); *m* 3rd 1 June 1918 Montague Phippen Porch, Resident Nigeria (*d* 9 Nov 1964), and *d* 29 June 1921), dau of Leonard Jerome, of New York, and *d* 24 Jan 1895, leaving:

(1) Winston Leonard (Sir), KG (1953), OM (1946), CH (1922), TD, PC (1907), DL (Kent 1949); *b* 30 Nov 1874; *educ* Harrow and RMC Sandhurst; Lt 4th Hus and S African Light Horse, served Cuba 1895, Malakand Field Force 1897 (despatches), Tirah Expdn 1898, Nile Expdn 1898, Boer War 1899–1900 (POW, escaped), WW I: Maj 100th (Worcs and Oxford Yeo) Bde (TA), attd Gren Gds 1915, T/Lt-Col cmdg a Bn Roy Scots Fus 1916, Col 4th QO Hus 1941–65, Col QRI Hus 1958, Hon Air Cdre No 615 (Co Surrey) Fighter Sqdn RAAF 1939–65, Hon Col 63rd Oxfordshire Yeo, Anti-Tank Regt RA (TA) 1939, Hon Col 489 (Cinque Ports), HAA Regt RA (TA 1942, Hon Col 6th Bn Royal Scots Fus 1940–65, Hon Col 4th/5th (Cinque Ports) Bn Royal Sussex Regt 1941, Hon Col 1st/4th Bn Essex Regt 1945, Hon Col 299 (Bucks and Oxon Yeo) Field Regt RA (TA); Hon Col 6th (Cinque Ports) Cadet Bn The Buffs; MP (C) Oldham Oct 1900–Jan 1906, (Lib) NW Manchester Jan 1906–April 1908, Dundee (Lib then Coalition Lib) May 1908–Oct 1922, Epping (Constitutional, C from 1931) Oct 1924–June 1945 and Woodford July 1945–Oct 1964, Parly U-Sec Colonies 1905–08, Pres BOT 1908–10, Home Sec 1910–11, 1st Ld Admlty 1911–15, Chllr Duchy of Lancaster May-Nov 1915, Min Munitions 1917–19, Sec State War and Air and Pres Army Cncl 1919–21, Sec State Colonies 1921–22, Chllr Exchequer 1924–29, 1st Ld Admlty and Memb War Cabinet Sept 1939–May 1940, PM, 1st Ld Treasury and Min Defence 10 May 1940–July 1945 and Oct 1951–April 1955, Ldr Oppn 1945–51, Min Def Oct 1951–Jan 1952, author: *The River War* (1899), *Savrola* (1900), *Lord Randolph Churchill* (1906), *The World Crisis* (4 vols, 1923–29), *My Early Life* (1930), *Marlborough, His Life and Times* (vol 1 1933, vol 2 1934, vol 3 1936, vol 4 1938), *Great Contemporaries* (1937), *The Second World War* (vol 1 1948, vol 2 1949, vol 3 1950, vol 4 1951, vol 5 1952, vol 6 1954), *History of The English Speaking Peoples* (vol 1 1956, vol 2 1956, vol 3 1957, vol 4 1958) and other works; Kt Gd Cross Order of Leopold of Belgium, Kt Gd Cross Order of the Netherlands Lion, Gd Cross with Chain Order of St Olav of Norway, Gd Cross Grand-Ducal Order Crown of Oak Luxemburg, Kt Order Elephant Denmark 1950, Danish Liberation Medal, Belgian Croix de Guerre avec palme 1915, French Croix de Guerre avec palme 1914, Medaille Militaire France, Mil Medal Luxemburg, Spanish Order Mil Merit 1st Cl, DSM USA, Cross of Liberation France 1958, Coronation Medals 1911 and 1937, Silver Jubilee Medal 1935; Albert Gold Medal Roy Soc of Arts 1945, Gold Medals of Cities of New York, Amsterdam and Rotterdam 1946, Golden Grotius Medal Netherlands 1949, Pilgrims Gold Medal 1958; 1st Hon Academician Extrdy RA 1948, Hon RBA 1948, memb Jockey Club 1950, Sunday Times Literary Award and Medal 1938 and 1949, Nobel Prize for Literature 1953, CLit 1971, Hon DCL Oxford 1925 (Romanes Lect 1930), DCL Rochester U USA 1941, Hon LLD Queen's U Belfast 1926, Bristol 1929, Harvard 1943, McGill 1944, Brussels and Louvain 1945, Miami, Westminster Coll Fulton Mo. and Columbia, Aberdeen and Leyden 1946, Liverpool 1949, Hon DPhil and Hist Oslo, Hon DLL Camb 1948, Hon DLitt London and DLL St Andrews 1948, DLL Liverpool 1949, DPhil Copenhagen 1950, Hon Fell Merton Coll Oxford 1942, Ld Rector Aberdeen U 1914–18 and Edin U 1929–32, Chllr Bristol U 1929–65, Hon LLD U of State of New York 1954, Hon Bencher Gray's Inn 1942, FRSL 1947, Hon FRCS 1943, FRS 1941, FRIBA 1941, FZS, FRAeS 1944, Fell Soc of Engrs 1946, FRGS 1948, Fell IOJ 1950, FRCP 1951, Hon Memb: Lloyd's, Inst of Municipal and Co Engrs and Inst of Naval Architects, Hon Pres UN Assoc, pres Constitutional Club, v-pres London Library 1948, Er Bro Trin House 1913–65, Liveryman Mercers' Co, Hon Freeman

Shipwrights' Co, Hon Life Memb Assoc of Men of Kent and Kentish Men, Constable Dover Castle and Ld Warden Cinque Ports 1941–65, Grand Master of Primrose League 1943–65, Hon Freeman Edinburgh 1942, City London 1943, Wanstead and Woodford, Brussels and Antwerp 1945, Aberdeen, City of Westminster, Luxemburg, Blackpool, Birmingham, Beckenham and Stafford 1946, Darlington, Ayr, Woodstock (Oxford), Brighton and Manchester 1947, Eastbourne, Perth and Aldershot 1948, Cardiff and Kensington 1949, Worcester, Bath, Wimbledon and Portsmouth 1950, Sheffield, Deal and Dover 1951, Leeds 1953, Poole 1954, Rochester, Harrow, Belfast and Londonderry 1955, Hastings 1957, Douglas, Malden and Combe and Margate 1958, Hon Citizen of Cuba 1941, Hon Citizen of Athens, Marathon, Thebes and Aeglion (Greece) 1945, Pinar Del Rio (Cuba) 1942, Paris 1945, Naupactos (Greece) 1946, Strasburg 1949, Nancy 1950, Roquebrune-Cap Martin and Cap d'Ail 1956; *m* 12 Sept 1908 Clementine Ogilvy (*d* 1977), GBE (1946), CStJ (*cr* LP as BARONESS SPENCER-CHURCHILL 1954), dau of Sir Henry Montague Hozier, KCB, and *d* 24 Jan 1965, leaving:

1a Randolph Frederick Edward, MBE (1944); *b* 28 May 1911; *educ* Eton and Ch Ch Oxford; Maj 4th Hus (SR Offrs) WW II, Br Mission to Yugoslav Army of Nat Liberation, MP (C) Preston Sept 1940–June 1945, author: *The Rise and Fall of Sir Anthony Eden*, *Lord Derby*, *King of Lancashire*, *The Fight for the Tory Leadership*, *Twenty-One Years*, *Winston S Churchill: Volume I, Youth 1874–1900*; *Volume II, Young Statesman 1901–14* and *The Six Days War* (with his son), etc, journalist; *m* 1st 4 Oct 1939 (*divorce* 1946) Hon Pamela Beryl Digby, 2nd dau of 11th Baron Digby (*qv*), and had:

1b +Winston; *b* Chequers 10 Oct 1940; *educ* Eton and Ch Ch Oxford; MP (C) Stretford 1970–83 and Manchester Davyhulme 1983–97, jnlst, special writer *The Times* 1969, co-author (with his father) *The Six Days War*, memb: Exec 1922 Ctee 1979–88 and Select Ctee Defence 1983–97, C Party Defence Spokesman 1976–78 and 1982–84, PPS to Min Housing and Construction 1970–72 and Min State FCO 1972–73; *m* 1st 15 July 1964 (*divorce* 21 Feb 1997) Mary Caroline (Minnie), yr dau of Sir Gerald John Regis Leo d'Erlanger, CBE, of Bayswater and Singleton Manor, Kent, and has:

1c +Randolph Leonard Spencer; *b* 22 Jan 1965; Lt RN (ret); *m* 1992 *Catherine Z, er dau of Antony Lancaster, of Kensington, and has:

1d +Serena Barbara Spencer; *b* 12 May 1996

2c +John (Jack) Gerard Averell; *b* 27 Aug 1975

1c +Jennie Spencer; *b* 25 Sept 1966; *m* 1993 *James P Repard

2b +Marina Spencer; *b* 11 Sept 1967

1b (cont.) Winston Churchill *m* 2nd 25 July 1997 *Luce Danielson

1a (cont.) Randolph Churchill *m* 2nd 2 Nov 1948 (*divorce* 1961) June (*d* 1980), only dau of Col Rex Hamilton Osborne, DSO, MC, of Little Ingleburn, Malmesbury, Wilts, and *d* 6 June 1968, having by her had:

1b +Arabella [Mrs Ian McLeod, 2 St Edmund's Cottages, Bove Town, Glastonbury, Somerset]; *b* 31 Oct 1949; Dir The Children's World Charity, Govr Avalon Special Sch; *m* 1st 10 Aug 1972 James J Barton and has:

1c +Jake Nicholas; *b* 1973

1b (cont.) Mrs Arabella Barton *m* 2nd 1988 *Ian McLeod (juggler, as Haggis McLeod), s of Harold Leonard Hodges, and has:

1c +Jessica Jules; *b* 1988

1a Diana, WW II in WRNS; *b* 11 July 1909; *m* 1st 12 Dec 1932 (*divorce* 1935) Sir John Milner Bailey, 2nd Bt (*qv*); *d* 13 Feb 1946); *m* 2nd 16 Sept 1935 (*divorce* 1960, resumed maiden surname by deed poll 11 April 1962), as his 1st w, (Edwin) Duncan Sandys, PC, MP (LP as BARON DUNCAN-SANDYS, so *cr* 1974; *m* 2nd 1962, as her 2nd husb, Marie-Claire, dau of Adrien Schmitt, of Paris, and formerly w of 2nd Viscount Hudson (*see* 1963 edn), and *d* 1987, leaving further issue), and *d* 19 Oct 1963, leaving by him:

1b Julian George Winston, QC (1983); *b* 19 Sept 1936; *educ* Eton, Salem and Melbourne U; served 4th Hus and TAR, barrister Inner Temple 1959, fought (C) Ashfield 1959 gen election; *m* 1970 *Elisabeth Jane [The Hon Mrs Julian Sandys, Charnwood, Shackleford, Surrey GU8 6AZ], only dau of John Besley Martin, CBE, and *d* 15 Aug 1997, leaving:

1c +Duncan John Winston; *b* 1973

2c +Jonathan Martin Edwin; *b* 1975

3c +Roderick Julian Frederick; *b* 1977

1c +Lucy Diana; *b* 1971

1b +Edwina, MBE; *b* 1938; sculptress; *m* 1st (*divorce* 1973) Piers(on) John Shirley Dixon (*m* 2nd Janet ('Tiger') Countess Cowley, *qv*), s of Sir Pierson Dixon, GCMG, CB, and has:

1c +Mark Pierson; *b* 1962; photographer

2c +Hugo Duncan; *b* 1963; jnlst

1b (cont.) The Hon Mrs Edwina Dixon *m* 2nd 1985 *Richard D Kaplan

2b +Celia Mary [The Hon Mrs Perkins, 4 Bedwyn Common, Gt Bedwyn, Wilts SN8 3HZ]; *b* 1943; author and lecturer, chm tstee Inernat Churchill Soc (UK), tstee Churchill Center Washington DC; *m* 1st 1965 (*divorce* 1970) Michael Kennedy and has:

1c +Justin; *b* 1967

2b (cont.) The Hon Mrs Celia Kennedy *m* 2nd 1970 (*divorce* 1979), as his 2nd of three ws, Sir Dennis Walters (ktd 1988), MBE, MP (C) Westbury 1964–92, and by him has:

2c +Dominic; *b* 1971

2b (cont.) The Hon Mrs Celia Walters *m* 3rd 1985 *Maj-Gen Kenneth Perkins, CB, MBE, DFC, and by him has:

3c +Alexander Winston Duncan; *b* 1986

1c +Sophie Rachel; *b* 1988

2a Sarah Millicent Hermione; actress and writer, WW II as Sectn Offr WAAF; *b* 7 Oct 1914; *m* 1st 25 Dec 1936 (*divorce* 1945) Vic(tor) Oliver (*d* 15 Aug 1964), actor, s of Baron Victor von Samek, of Vienna; *m* 2nd 18 Oct 1949 Antony Beauchamp (*d* 18 Aug 1957), s of Ernest George Entwistle; *m* 3rd 26 April 1962 23rd Baron Audley, MBE (*see* 1970 edn), and *dsp* 24 Sept 1982

3a Marigold Frances; *b* 15 Nov 1918; *d* 23 Aug 1921

4a +Mary, DBE (1980, MBE 1945), JP (E Sussex 1960); *b* 15 Sept 1922; WW II as Jr Cdr ATS; author; Hon Fell Churchill Coll Cambridge, Govr Harrow, chm: Roy Nat Theatre Bd 1989–95 and Winston Churchill Memorial Tst 1991–, Chev Legion Honour 1995, Hon DCL Kent 1997; *m* 11 Feb 1947 Baron Soames (LP, *d* 1987), GCMG, GCVO, CBE , PC, and has:

1b +(Arthur) Nicholas Winston [The Hon Nicholas Soames MP, House of Commons, London SW1A 0AA]; *b* 12 Feb 1949; *educ* Eton; 2nd Lt 11th Hus (PAO) 1967–70, Extra Equerry to HRH THE PRINCE OF WALES 1970–72; sometime dir Tollgate; MP Crawley 1983–97, Mid Sussex 1997–, PPS to Min State Employment and Chm C Party 1984–92, Parly U-Sec MAFF 1992–94, Min State Armed Forces MOD 1994–97, dir Network Technology 1997– and Wilton's 1998–; *m* 1st 1981 (*divorce* 1988) Catherine N, dau of Capt Anthony E Weatherall, of Cowhill Tower, Dumfries, and has:

1c +Arthur Harry David; *b* 1985

1b (cont.) The Hon Nicholas Soames *m* 2nd 1993 *Serena Mary, dau of Sir John Lindsay Eric Smith, CH, CBE (*see* NORTHESK, E), and by her has:

1c +Isabella; *b* 28 Nov 1996

2b +Jeremy Bernard; *b* 25 May 1952; *educ* Eton; *m* 1978 *Susanna, dau of (James) David (Agar) Keith, of W Barsham Hall, Fakenham, Norfolk, and has:

1c +Archie Christopher Winston; *b* 1988

1c +Gemma Mary; *b* 1979

2c +Flora Caroline; *b* 1982

3b +Rupert Christopher; *b* 18 May 1959; *educ* Eton; *m* 1988 *Camilla (Milly) Rose, dau of Thomas Raymond Dunne, of Gatley Park, Leominster, Herefs, and has:

1c +Arthur Christopher; *b* 1990

2c +Jack; *b* 22 Sept 1994

1c +Daisy; *b* 1992

1b +Emma Mary [The Hon Emma Soames, 26 Eland Road, London London SW11]; jnlst, ed *Tatler* 1988–90, sometime ed *Literary Review* and features ed *Vogue*, now ed *Daily Telegraph Magazine*; *b* 6 Sept 1949; *m* 1981 (*divorce* 1989, resumed maiden name) James N M MacManus, jnlst with *Guardian*, and has:

1c +Emily Fiona; *b* 16 April 1983

2b +Charlotte Clementine [The Rt Hon The Countess Peel, Kilgram Grange, Jervaulx, Ripon, N Yorks HG4 4PQ]; *b* 17 July 1954; *m* 1st 1973 (*divorce* 1982) (Alexander) Richard Hambro (*see* HAMBRO, B); *m* 2nd 1989 3rd Earl Peel (*qv*) and by her 1st husb has:

1c +Clementine Silvia; *b* 1976

(2) John Strange DSO (1918), TD; *b* Feb 1880; *educ* Harrow; Maj Oxon Yeo and TAR Boer War 1899–1900 (wounded, despatches, medals) and WW I (despatches), Legn Hon, Mil Order Avis Portugal, Croix de Guerre, memb London Stock Exchange, ptnr Vickers Da Costa; *m* 8 Aug 1908 Lady Gwendeline Theresa Mary Bertie (*d* 7 Jan 1941), dau of 7th Earl of Abingdon (*see* LINDSEY and ABINGDON, E), and *d* 23 Feb 1947, leaving:

1a John George; *b* 31 May 1909; *educ* Harrow; painter, sculptor and composer; WW II as Maj RE, author: *Crowded Canvas*; *m* 1st 13 May 1934 (*divorce* 1938) Angela Mary, dau of Capt George Culme-Seymour, KRRC (*see* CULME-SEYMOUR, Bt), and had:

1b +Sarah Cornelia [The Rt Hon The Lady Ashburton, Lake House, Northington, Hants SO24 9TG]; *b* 26 March 1935; *m* 1st 19 Nov 1957 James Colin Crewe and has:

1c +Peregrine John; *b* 12 July 1959

1c +Emma; *b* 9 March 1963; *m* 1993 *Nicholas G S Vester and has issue

2c +Annabel Sophia; *b* 21 Jan 1965 and has issue

1b (cont.) Mrs Sarah Crewe *m* 2nd 1987 *7th Baron Ashburton (*qv*)

1a (cont.) John Churchill *m* 2nd 20 May 1941 (*divorce* 1953) Mary, only dau of Kenneth Cookson, of Wynberg, CP, S Africa; *m* 3rd 5 March 1953 Mrs Kathlyn Maude Muriel Hall Tandy (*d* 25 June 1957), only dau of Maj-Gen Walter Samuel Hall Beddall, CB, OBE; *m* 4th 27 Aug 1958 (*divorce* 1972) Anna Gunvor Maria, dau of Johan Janson, of Kristianstad, Sweden, widow of Granger Boston, and *d* 1992

2a +Henry Winston (Peregrine) [Peregrine Spencer-Churchill Esq, Fairdown, Vernham Dean, Hants SP11 0EL]; *b* 25 May 1913; *educ* Harrow and Trin Coll Cambridge (BA); *m* 1st 15 Nov 1954 Patricia Ethel Louise (*d* 22 Oct 1956), dau of Thomas March, of Chesham, Bucks; *m* 2nd 21 Dec 1957 *Yvonne Henriette Marie, 2nd dau of Constant Jéhannin, of France

1a +(Anne) Clarissa [The Rt Hon The Countess of Avon, 32 Bryanston Square, London W1H 7LS]; *b* 28 June 1920; *m* 14 Aug 1952 1st Earl of Avon, KG, MC, PC (*see* EDEN OF WINTON, B)

4 Charles Ashley; *b* 1856; *d* 11 March 1858

5 Augustus Robert; *b* 4 July 1858; *d* 12 May 1859

1 Cornelia Henrietta Maria, OBE; *m* 25 May 1868 1st Baron Wimborne (*see* WIMBORNE, V) and *d* 22 Jan 1927, leaving issue

2 Rosamond Jane Frances; *m* 12 July 1877 2nd Baron de Ramsey (*qv*) and *d* 3 Dec 1920, leaving issue

3 Fanny Octavia Louisa; *m* 9 June 1873 2nd Baron Tweedmouth (*see* 1935 edn) and *d* 5 Aug 1904, leaving issue

4 Anne Emily, OBE, VA; *m* 11 June 1874 7th Duke of Roxburghe (*qv*) and *d* 20 June 1923, leaving issue

5 Georgiana Elizabeth; *m* 4 June 1883 4th Earl Howe (*qv*) and *d* 9 Feb 1906, leaving issue

6 Sarah Isabella Augusta, RRC, DGStJ; *m* 21 Nov 1891 Lt-Col Gordon Chesney Wilson (*ka* 6 Nov 1914), MVO, RHG, est s of Sir Samuel Wilson, MP, and *d* 22 Oct 1929, leaving issue

The 7th DUKE *d* 5 July 1883; his est son,

GEORGE CHARLES SPENCER-CHURCHILL, **8th Duke of Marlborough**, DL Oxford, Lt RHG; *b* 13 May 1844; *m* 1st 8 Nov 1869 (*divorce* on her petition 1883) Lady Albertha Frances Anne Hamilton (*d* 7 Jan 1932), 6th dau of 1st Duke of Abercorn (*qv*), and had:

1 CHARLES RICHARD JOHN, **9th Duke**

1 Frances Louisa; b 15 Sept 1870; m 6 June 1893 Sir Robert Gresley, 11th Bt (see 1970 edn), and d 13 Nov 1954, leaving issue

2 Lilian Maud; b 9 July 1873; m 8 Oct 1898 Col Cecil Alfred Grenfell and d 4 Jan 1951, leaving issue (see GRENFELL, B)

3 Norah Beatrice Henriette; b 1 Sept 1875; m 1 Dec 1920 Francis Bradley Bradley-Birt (d 11 June 1963), FRGS, of Birtsmoreton Court, Worcs, s of John Bradley-Birt, of Birtsmoreton and The Barrow, Worcs, resumed maiden name 1921 and dsp 28 April 1946

The **8th Duke** m 2nd 29 June 1888 Lillian Warren (m 3rd 30 April 1895 Lord William de la Poer Beresford, VC, KCIE (see WATERFORD, M), and d 11 Jan 1909), widow of Louis Hammersley, of New York, and dau of Cicero Price, Cdre USN, and d 9 Nov 1892

His son,

CHARLES RICHARD JOHN SPENCER-CHURCHILL, **9th Duke of Marlborough**, KG (1902), PC (1894); b 13 Nov 1871; educ Winchester and Trin Coll Cambridge; Paymaster-Gen 1899–1902, Parly U-Sec Colonies 1903–05, Jt Parly Sec Bd Ag and Fisheries 1917–18, CC Woodstock and Mayor Woodstock 1907–98, Lt Lt and custos rotulorum Oxon, Hon Col 3rd Bn Oxon and Bucks LI, Lt-Col Oxon Hus (TD), Staff Capt Imp Yeo Boer War 1900 (despatches, medal with clasp), Ld High Steward Coronation 1902; m 1st 6 Nov 1895 (divorce 1921, annulled by Vatican 19 Aug 1926) Consuelo (d 6 Dec 1964 aged 87), dau of William Kissam Vanderbilt, of New York, and had:

1 JOHN ALBERT EDWARD WILLIAM, **10th Duke**

2 Ivor Charles; b 14 Oct 1898; educ Eton and Magdalen Coll Oxford; WW I 1917–18 as Lt RASC, Legn Hon; m 15 Nov 1947 *Elizabeth [The Lady Ivor Spencer-Churchill, Fyning House, Rogate, Petersfield, Hants], er dau of James Cyril Cunningham, of Mayfair, and d 17 Sept 1956, leaving:

  (1) +Robert William Charles; b 7 Feb 1954; educ Eton; m 1979 *Jeanne M, er dau of Etienne Maze (s of Paul Maze, DCM, painter), and has:

    1a +John Robert I—; b 1984

    2a +Ivor Charles E—; b 1986

The **9th Duke** m 2nd 25 June 1921 *Gladys Marie, dau of Edward Parker Deacon, of Boston, USA, and d 30 June 1934

His er son,

JOHN ALBERT EDWARD WILLIAM SPENCER-CHURCHILL, **10th Duke of Marlborough**, DL (1936), JP (1936); b 18 Sept 1897; educ Eton; CC Oxon, High Steward City of Oxford 1937–72, Mayor Woodstock 1937–42, Lt-Col Life Gds WW I (two medals), WW II as Mil Liaison Offr to Regl Commr Southern Regn 1942, Lt-Col Liaison Offr US Forces 1942–45, Hon Treasurer Queen Mary's Hosp, USA Bronze Star Medal; m 1st 17 Feb 1920 Hon Alexandra Mary Cadogan, CBE (1953), JP Oxon, Ch Cmdt ATS 1938–40, CStJ (d 23 May 1961), gdau of 5th Earl Cadogan (qv), and had:

1 JOHN GEORGE VANDERBILT HENRY SPENCER-CHURCHILL, **11th and present Duke of Marlborough**

2 +Charles George William Colin [The Lord Charles Spencer-Churchill, 1 Shepherd's Place, Upper Brook St, London W1; Blenheim Palace, Woodstock, Oxon]; b 13 July 1940 (HRH THE late DUKE OF KENT stood sponsor); educ Eton; m 1st 23 July 1965 (divorce 1968) Gillian Spreckels, only child of Andrew D Fuller, of New York and Fort Worth, Texas; m 2nd 9 Dec 1970 *(Elizabeth) Jane, er dau of Hon Mark Hugh Wyndham (see EGREMONT, LECONFIELD and, B), and has:

  (1) +Rupert John Harold Mark; b 26 Nov 1971

  (2) +Dominic Albert Charles; b 1979

  (3) +Alexander David; b 9 June 1983

1 +Sarah Consuelo; b 17 Dec 1921; m 1st 15 May 1943 (divorce 1966) Lt Edwin F Russell, USN, est s of Lucius T Russell, of Beverly Hills, and has:

  (1) +Serena Mary Churchill [Mrs Neil Balfour, 55 Warwick Sq, London SW1V 2 AJ]; b 1944; m 1st 1966 (divorce Mexico 1967) R Stephen Salant; m 2nd 1968 Neil A McConnell and has issue:

    1a +Morgan Alexandra; b 1973

    2a +Lucinda Mary; b 1975

  (1) (cont.) Mrs Serena McConnell m 3rd 1978 *Neil Roxburgh Balfour and has:

    1a +Alastair Albert David; b 1981

    3a +Consuelo Lily; b 1979

  (2) +Consuelo Sarah; b 1946; m 1st 1968 (divorce Mexico 1969) James Toback; m 2nd 1970 Mark Schulman, of New York; m 3rd 19– *B William Judson and has:

    1a +Nicholas; b 1976

    2a +Ian; b 1978

  (3) +Alexandra Brenda; b 1949; m 1970 *Timothy Biech, of Camp Hill, Pa.

  (4) +Jacqueline; b 1958; m 19– *Eugene Williams

1 (cont.) Lady Sarah Russell m 2nd 11 Nov 1966 (divorce Mexico 1967) Guy Burgos, of Santiago, Chile; m 3rd Philadelphia 1967 *Theodorus Roubanis

2 Caroline; b 12 Nov 1923; m 5 Dec 1946 *Maj Charles Huguenot (Hugo) Waterhouse, Life Gds, est s of Capt Charles Waterhouse, MC, PC, JP, DL, Life Gds, of Middleton Hall, and has:

  (1) +Michael Thomas [Michael Waterhouse Esq, Middleton Hall, Bakewell, Derbys]; b 25 May 1949; educ Eton and Trin Coll Cambridge; m 1983 *Lucinda Ileene, dau of Lt-Col Robin Hood William Stewart Hastings, DSO, OBE, MC (see HUNTINGDON, E), and has:

    1a +Robin Hood E T; b 1987

    2a +Marcus Charles; b 1990

  (2) +David Charles; b 8 July 1956; educ Eton

  (1) +Elizabeth Ann; b 24 June 1951

3 +Rosemary Mildred [The Lady Rosemary Muir, Orange Hill House, Binfield, Bracknell, Berks]; b 24 July 1929; Train Bearer to HM THE QUEEN Coronation 1953; m 26 June 1953 Charles Robert (Robin) Muir (d 24 March 1972), only s of Rowland Huntly Muir, of Billingbear House, Bracknell, and has:

  (1) +Alexander Pepys; b 8 Nov 1954 (HRH THE PRINCESS MARGARET, COUNTESS OF SNOWDON stood sponsor); educ Gordonstoun

  (2) +Simon Huntly [Simon Muir Esq, Angel Farm, Monks Alley, Binfield, Berks RG42 5PA]; b 3 July 1959; m 1990 *Sarah-Jane E, only dau of Barry Jenkinson, of Chetton Grange, Bridgnorth, Salop, and has:

    1a +Robin Hugo; b 1993

    2a +Thomas Sebastian; b 1995

  (1) +Mary Arabella [Mrs Timothy Haynes, 29 Henning St, London SW11 3DR]; b 16 Jan 1962; m 1991 *J Timothy Haynes, s of J H Haynes, of Spain, and has:

    1a +Jack Cresswell; b 1993

    2a +Rowley James; b 1996

The **10th Duke** m 2nd 26 Jan 1972 (Frances) Laura (d 1990), widow previously w of (a) 2nd Viscount Long (qv) and (b) 3rd Earl of Dudley (qv) and yr surv dau of Capt Hon Guy Lawrence Charteris (see WEMYSS and MARCH, E), and d 11 March 1972

Lineage (of Spencer): Sir JOHN SPENCER; descended from a line of Midlands graziers and sheep-herders who had grown in prosperity throughout the 15th century; bought the Wormleighton, Warwicks, estate 3 Sept 1506 and the Althorp one in Northants; ktd by HENRY VII; m Isabel, dau and coheir of Walter Grant, of Snitterfield, Warwicks, which he acquired through her, and d 14 April 1522, leaving, with other issue:

Sir WILLIAM SPENCER, of Wormleighton and Althorp; High Sheriff Northants c 1532–33, ktd 1529; m Susan, dau of Sir Richard Knightley, of Fawsley, Northants, and d 22 June 1532, leaving, with six daus (one of whom, Jane, m 1st Sir Richard Bruges, of Shefford, Berks, and 2nd, as his 3rd w, Sir Simon Harcourt; see VERNON, B):

Sir JOHN SPENCER, of Wormleighton and Althorp; High Sheriff Northampton c 1552, MP Northants 1553 and 1571; m Katherine, dau of Sir Thomas Kitson, of Hengrave, Suffolk, and had, with other issue:

1 JOHN (Sir), his heir

2 William (Sir), ancestor of the Spencer Bts of Yarnton, Oxon

3 Richard (Sir), ancestor of the SPENCERs of Offley, Herts

1 Elizabeth; m 1st 2nd Baron Hunsdon (see ALDENHAM and HUNSDON OF HUNSDON, B, preliminary remarks); m 2nd 3rd Lord (Baron) Eure

2 Alice; m 1st 5th Earl of Derby (qv); m 2nd 2nd Viscount Brackley (see GREY EGERTON, Bt) and d 1637

3 Anne; m 1st 3rd Baron Monteagle (see DERBY, E); m 2nd 1st Baron Compton (see NORTHAMPTON, M); m 3rd 2nd Earl of Dorset (see SACKVILLE, B)

4 Katharine; m Sir Thomas Leigh, 1st Bt (see LEIGH, B), and had issue

Sir JOHN d 8 Nov 1586; his est son

Sir JOHN SPENCER, of Wormleighton and Althorp; ktd 1588; m Mary (m 2nd Edward Glascoke, of Castle Hedingham, Essex), only dau and heiress of Sir Robert Catlin, of Berne, Dorset, Ch Justice King's Bench, and d 9 Jan 1599/1600, leaving:

ROBERT SPENCER, **1st Baron Spencer of Wormleighton**, Co Warwick (E), so cr 21 July 1603; b 1570; MP 1597–98, ktd 1601; m 15 Feb 1587/8 Margaret (d 17 Aug 1597), dau and coheir of Sir Francis Willoughby, of Wollaton, Notts, and d 25 Oct 1627, having had, with other issue, including a dau (Elizabeth, m as his 1st w Sir George Fane (d 26 June 1640), MP, of Burton Woodfolde and Merewold Castle, Kent (see WESTMORLAND, E), and dsp):

WILLIAM SPENCER, **2nd Baron Spencer of Wormleighton**, KB (1616); bapt 4 Jan 1591/2; MP Brackley 1614 and Northants 1620–22, 1624–25 and 1626; m 1615 Lady Penelope Wriothesley (d 16 July 1667), est dau of 3rd Earl of Southampton (see SOUTHAMPTON, B, preliminary remarks), and had, with other issue:

1 HENRY, **1st Earl**

2 ROBERT SPENCER, 1st and last VISCOUNT TEVIOT, so cr 1685; dsp

3 William, of Ashton, Lancs; had at least one dau (Elizabeth, m Robert Hesketh; see HESKETH, B)

1 Elizabeth; b 1618; m 1st 1634 1st Baron Craven (see CRAVEN, E, preliminary remarks); m 2nd 1648 Henry Howard, 2nd s of 1st Earl of Berkshire (see SUFFOLK and BERKSHIRE, E); m 3rd 1st Baron Crofts and d 1672

2 Alice; b 1625; m 1st Earl of Drogheda (qv) and had issue

3 Margaret; b 1627; m 1st Earl of Shaftesbury (qv) and dsp 1693

The 2nd BARON d 19 Dec 1636; his est son,

HENRY SPENCER, **1st Earl of Sunderland** (E), so cr 6 June 1643; bapt 23 Nov 1620; royalist Civil War; m 20 July 1639 Lady Dorothy Sydney (m 2nd 8 July 1652 Robert Smythe, of Bounds, Kent, and d 5 Feb 1684), dau of Robert, Earl of Leicester (see DE L'ISLE, V), and was killed at the Battle of Newbury 20 Sept 1643, leaving an only s:

ROBERT SPENCER, **2nd Earl of Sunderland**, KG (1687), PC (1674–Jan 1680/1); b 1641; Amb Madrid 1671–72, Paris 1672–73 and July–Oct 1678, Jt Amb to negotiate peace with Dutch at Cologne 1673; Sec State for the North Feb 1678/9–April 1680 and Jan 1682/3–April 1684 and for the South 1680–Feb 1680/1 and 1684–88, Ld Pres Cncl 1685–88, turned RC July 1688, lived in exile 1688–91 but returned to England and was pardoned by WILLIAM III, to whom he became a confidential advsr; Ld Chamberlain April–Dec 1697; m 10 June 1665 Lady Anne Digby (d 26 April 1715), dau of 2nd Earl of Bristol (see DIGBY, B), and d 28 Sept 1702, leaving an only surv s:

CHARLES SPENCER, **3rd Earl of Sunderland**, KG (1719), PC (1706); b c 1674; MP (Whig) Tiverton 1695–1702, Envoy Extrdy Vienna 1705, a Commr for Union S and E Parls 1706, Sec State for South 1706–10, Ld Lt Ireland 1714 but never visited it, Ld Privy Seal 1715–16, Sec State North April 1717–March 1717/8, Ld Pres Cncl March 1717/8–Feb 1718/9, First Ld Treasury 21 March 1717/8–April 1721, when the South Sea Bubble, in which he was involved, brought his downfall; m 1st 12 Jan 1694/5 Lady Arabella Cavendish (d 4 June 1698), dau and coheir of 2nd Duke of Newcastle-upon-Tyne (see DEVONSHIRE, D), and had:

1 Frances; m 27 Nov 1717 4th Earl of Carlisle (qv), and d 27 July 1742, leaving issue

The **3rd Earl** *m* 2nd 14 Sept 1699 Anne (*d* 15 April 1716), 2nd dau of **1st Duke of Marlborough** (*see* above), and had:

> 1 ROBERT SPENCER, **4th Earl of Sunderland**; *b* 24 Oct 1701; *d* unm 15 Sept 1729
>
> 2 CHARLES, **5th Earl** and **3rd Duke of Marlborough**
>
> 3 John; had issue (*see* SPENCER, E)
>
> 2 Anne; *m* 1720 1st Viscount Bateman and *d* 19 Feb 1769, leaving issue
>
> 3 Diana; *m* 11 Oct 1731 4th Duke of Bedford (*qv*) and *dsps* 27 Sept 1735

The **3rd Earl** *m* 3rd 5 Dec 1717 Judith (*m* 2nd 10 Dec 1724 Sir Robert Sutton, KB, of Broughton, Lincs, and *d* 17 May 1749), dau and coheir of Benjamin Tichborne, and *d* 19 April 1722, having had:

> 4 William; *d* in infancy

Seat: Blenheim Palace, Woodstock, Oxon. Blenheim is perhaps more a gigantic war memorial than anything else. It is hard to think of a more striking one in all Europe, even bearing in mind the Arc de Triomphe, Les Invalides or Constantine's Arch. None of the last three offers much shelter to the human frame. In regard to Blenheim itself Consuelo, the Vanderbilt Duchess and as an American plutocrat preternaturally concerned with comfort, used to rail against the mausolean sleeping arrangements and remoteness of the kitchens from the dining room, which made hot meals a rarity. Laura, the **10th Duke**'s second wife and as a Charteris not readily overawed by magnificence, thought it very gloomy and called it 'the Dump'. There are some surprisingly close, cramped and ill-lit rooms hidden away among the servants' quarters. It is worth remembering that the architect, Vanbrugh, had once been confined in the Bastille.

Yet in visual terms he conceived a truly epic building. The dominant feature of the elevation is an array of square towers which to the onlooker with a classical education recall the topless ones of Ilium. (It is perhaps significant that the War of the Spanish Succession, in which Marlborough won his dukedom, lasted almost exactly the same length as the Trojan conflict.) They look pagan, un-European, plinth-like. Though not quite topless they are still very high, the finials alone soaring 30 feet before culminating in a ducal coronet. Each coronet rests on a bursting grenade in stone (a tour de force of sculpting), to remind us what the Dukedom was conferred for. Similar adornments to the top of the building include the Grinling Gibbons stone lions (Britain) clutching fluttering cocks (France). For Vanbrugh, like his patron, was a soldier. More, he was a man of the theatre, above all an opera impresario — Britain's first. The Blenheim forecourt is big enough to mount a regimental parade and the stable-block could accommodate a perfomance of Berlioz's *Les Troyens*, wooden horse, generous orchestra and all. The portico over the main entrance rests on Corinthian columns, enhanced by a pediment in which Athene, the Goddess of war and wisdom, presides over a chain-gang of defeated enemies.

Athene was a less formidable opponent than Sarah, Duchess of Marlborough, whose falling-out with Vanbrugh so bedevilled the Blenheim project. Despite her arrogance of character she was modest in her aims for a dwelling, settling for a relatively homely testament to public gratitude for her husband's skills as a general. The fact is, she was concerned about the expense, which did indeed in the end cause great vexation to almost everybody concerned: government, contractors, patron, architect. (It has been calculated that the final cost was some £300,000 [£14,500,000 in late-1990s terms], of which four-fifths came from the public purse.) Vanbrugh's notions could not have been more different, aiming at extremes of baroque magnificence all along, though he wished at first to incorporate because of its historical associations the old manor house at Woodstock. (The latter had been a royal manor for centuries and Blenheim is held from the Sovereign to this day by an annual payment of a banner depicting French fleurs-de-lys, thus commemorating the eponymous victory.) The Duchess's venomous persecution of Vanbrugh caused him to resign the commission in 1716 and the building was finished by her with the help of his assistants.

Internally Blenheim is little less vast. The hall rises to nearly seventy feet, adorned on the ceiling with a Thornhill painting of the **1st Duke** in Roman battle dress, as it were a Caesar in command of legions, gesturing towards a map of the field of Blenheim. The banqueting chamber, with murals and ceiling by Laguerre, has in the latter depiction the Duke airborne in a chariot. From the side of the room figures of onlookers gaze across *trompe l'oeil* balustrades onto the banquets involving real people at ground-level. One of the figures is Laguerre himself.

Less fanciful illustrations of the Duke's victories appear in tapestry form in the state apartments. The scale is still immense, however. The Long Library (by Hawksmoor, who greatly assisted Vanbrugh) is aptly named. The bedroom in which Sir Winston Churchill was born almost alone of the rooms on public display strikes a cosy note.

Vanbrugh prepared designs for the 22,000 acres of grounds initially granted by QUEEN ANNE which were largely executed during his time on the project, though they were greatly modified by Capability Brown some seventy years later. Formal gardens were landscaped in the **9th Duke**'s time. Apart from the house Vanbrugh's external masterpiece is generally recognised as being the bridge. Though lacking superstructure because of the Duchess's opposition (the bridge as a whole was the chief material cause of enmity between her and Vanbrugh), it is a formidable construction when seen from the lake level. The two chief piers' resemblance to pill boxes is yet another reminder of both the Duke's and Vanbrugh's military experiences.

MARLESFORD

Arms: Ermine on a roundel sable, between three griffin's heads erased vert, a cross engrailed or. **Crest:** A dexter arm in armour, the upper arrn charged with a roundel sable, thereon a cross engrailed or, the hand grasping a dagger, point downwards proper, hilt and pomel or. **Supporters:** Two griffins ermine, the aquiline parts vert, forelegs or, both collared with a ring of clouds radiated proper and each segreant on a grassy mount also proper. **Mottoes:** 1 *Deutlich und wahr* ('Faithful and true'), 2 *Post nubila Phoebus* ('After the clouds the sun'). **Creation:** B. (LP, UK) 1991.

THE BARON MARLESFORD, of Marlesford, Co Suffolk (Mark Shuldham Schreiber, DL (Suffolk 1991)) [The Rt Hon The Lord Marlesford DL, 5 Kersley St, London SW11 4PR; Marlesford Hall, Woodbridge, Suffolk IP13 0AU]; *b* 11 Sept 1931; *educ* Eton and Trin Coll Cambridge (MA); Lt Coldstream Guards 1950–51; Fisons Ltd 1957–63; CRD 1963–67, Dir C Public Sector Research Unit 1967–70; memb E Suffolk CC 1968–70; Special Advsr: Govt 1970–74, Leader Oppn 1974–75; memb Govt Computer Agency Cncl 1973–74; edtl consultant *Economist* 1974–91 (Parly Lobby correspondent 1976–91); dir: Roy Ordnance Factories 1972–74, BR Anglia 1988–92, Eastern Electricity 1989–95, Times Newspaper Hldgs 1991–; memb: Countryside Commn 1980–92, Rural Devpt Commn 1985–93; Chm CPRE 1993–; Ld Manor Marlesford and patron of the living; *m* 18 Oct 1969 *Gabriella Federica, dau of Conte Teodoro Veglio di Castelletto d'Uzonne, and has:

> 1 *Nicola Charlotte; *b* 8 Aug 1971
>
> 2 *Sophie Louisa; *b* 8 Sept 1973

Lineage: CARL SCHREIBER, of Durlach, Swabia; *b* 1680; migrated to England *c* 1721; *d* 1760, leaving:

JOHN CHARLES SCHREIBER, of Tewin House, Herts, and London; *b* 1723; *m* 1754 Elizabeth (*d* 1763), dau of William Mount (*see* MOUNT, Bt), and *d* 1800, leaving:

WILLIAM SCHREIBER, of Tewin House and Wickham Market, Suffolk; *b* 1759; *m* 1780 Mary, est dau and coheir of James Sewell, of Alton Hall, Suffolk, and *d* 1821, leaving, with other issue:

> 1 WILLIAM FREDERICK
>
> 2 James Alfred, JP (Suffolk), of Melton, Suffolk; *b* 21 Nov 1789; Lt-Col 11th Dragoons and 5th Dragoon Gds; *m* 23 July 1832 Mary, dau of Thomas Ware, of Woodford, Co Cork, and *d* 1840, leaving, with a yr s (*d* unm):
>
> > (1) Charles; *b* 10 May 1826; *educ* Trin Coll Cambridge (Fell 1852–53); MP Cheltenham 1865 and Poole 1880–84; *m* 10 April 1855 Lady Charlotte Elizabeth, only dau of 9th Earl of Lindsey (*see* LINDSEY and ABINGDON, E) and widow of Sir Josiah Guest, 1st Bt (*see* WIMBORNE, V), and *d* 31 March 1884

The er s,

WILLIAM FREDERICK SCHREIBER, of The Roundwood, Ipswich; *b* 1784; Capt 11th Light Dragoons and 18th Hus, served Penisular War (Silver Medal following Salamanca) and Waterloo Campaign; *m* 18 Jan 1814 Frances Mary (*d* 23 April 1832), est dau of William Shuldham, of Marlesford Hall, and *d* 28 April 1860, leaving, with other issue:

CHARLES ALFRED SCHREIBER, JP, DL (Suffolk), of The Roundwood; *b* 6 Jan 1816; Capt 34th Regt; *m* 1st 19 Aug 1845 Elizabeth Hester, dau of Owen Hogan, of Auburn, Co Westmeath, and had, with a yr dau (*d* unm):

> 1 William Frederick Duff; *b* 10 Dec 1847; Capt 34th Regt; *m* 1883 Alice Mary, yr dau of Henry Cazenove, JP, of Bucks, and *dsp*
>
> 1 Emma Augusta; *m* 1st 5 Oct 1866 Frederick Bernard Astley (*see* HASTINGS, B) and had issue; *m* 2nd 25 Jan 1879 Maj L M Carmichael and *d* 1883

CHARLES SCHREIBER *m* 2nd 11 Oct 1866 Rosa Alexandrina, dau of John Robert Thomson, of Blackstones, Surrey, and *d* 29 March 1879, leaving by her:

> 2 Charles Shuldham, JP (Suffolk 1904), of Marlesford Hall; *b* 17 May 1871; *educ* Rugby; Ld Manor and patron living Marlesford, Capt 1st Life Gds; *m* 10 Nov 1900 Hon Margaret Henderson, only dau of 1st Baron Faringdon (*qv*), and *d* 2 Jan 1943, leaving:

(1) John Shuldham, AE, DL (Suffolk 1964); *b* 30 Aug 1901; *educ* Eton and Trin Hall Cambridge; served AAF 1926, WW II RAF (W/Cdr 1941), Air Attaché Lisbon 1941–44, CC E Suffolk 1944, High Sheriff 1963, Ld Manor and patron living Marlesford; *m* 26 June 1930 Maureen (*d* 12 Dec 1980), dau of Charles Hastings Dent, of Maltravers House, Arundel, Sussex, and *d* 7 June 1968, leaving:

  1a MARK SHULDHAM, *cr* a **Baron**

  1a *(Theresa) Clare [Mrs Clare Evans-Schreiber, Weston Lodge, Kedleston, Derbys DE22 5JL]; *b* 31 March 1943; *m* 5 July 1978 (*divorce* 1982) Robert Evans and has:

    1b *Guy Shuldham; *b* 3 June 1979

    1b *Emily Rosina; *b* 21 June 1981

(2) Derek Shuldham, MVO (1935); *b* 7 May 1904; *educ* Harrow and RMC Sandhurst; joined 11th Hus 1923, Adj 1930–33, GSO(1) Gds Armoured Div and Brig cmdg 5th Indian Tank Bde WW II, Equerry and Ch Staff to HRH THE late DUKE OF GLOUCESTER 1934–35 and 1944–46 respectively; CStJ; *m* 24 Oct 1945 *Vida, only dau of Capt James Harold Cuthbert, DSO, Scots Gds, of Beaufront Castle, Northumberland, and widow of Viscount Clive (*see* POWIS, E), who was also 17th Lord (Baron) Darcy de Knayth (*qv*), and *d* 19 March 1972, leaving:

  1a *Susan Alice Margaret [Mrs Philip Gwyn, The Old Vicarage, Owslebury, Hants SO21 1LU]; *b* 13 Aug 1946; *m* 20 Aug 1970 *Philip Anthony Gwyn and has:

    1b *Richard Hwfa; *b* 11 March 1980

    1b *Katharine Henrietta; *b* 7 July 1972

    2b *Anna Elizabeth; *b* 1 Oct 1974

    3b *Christina Alice; *b* 6 March 1976

(3) Richard Shuldham; *b* 1 June 1907; *educ* Eton and RMC Sandhurst; ADC to Govr-Gen S Africa 1933–35, Maj Coldstream Gds WW II, OStJ, Commr St John's Ambulance Bde Suffolk; *m* 13 May 1954 *Rosemary Violet, dau of Sir William Cameron Gull, 2nd Bt (*qv*), and *dsp* 4 Dec 1978

(1) Pamela Shuldham; *b* 15 July 1910; FANY and ATS WW II; *d* 10 May 1985

Seat: Marlesford Hall, Woodbridge, Suffolk. The pediment, shutters either side of the windows and curvilinear classical portico screening the door to the main front elevation combine to give Marlesford the air of an antebellum mansion in the Deep South. It would seem to date from the mid-18th century, when it was still in the hands of a cadet branch of the Shuldhams, who were originally from Norfolk. It passed by marriage (*see* above) to the Schreibers in the early 19th century, although the father of the Shuldham heiress outlived his daughter by some eleven years, dying at the age of 101.

MARLING

Arms: Argent three bars gules, each charged with five bezants, in chief a lion passant of the second. **Crest:** In front of a tower embattled and domed, thereon a flagstaff proper with a pennon gules, three bezants. **Motto:** *Nulli præda sumus* ('We are nobody's prey'). **Creation:** Bt. (UK) 22 May 1882.

SIR CHARLES WILLIAM SOMERSET MARLING, 5TH BT, of Stanley Park and Sedbury Park, Co Gloucester [Sir Charles Marling Bt, The Barn, The Street, Eversley, Hants RG27 0PJ]; *b* 2 June 1951; *s* f 1977; *educ* Harrow; *m* 1979 *Judi P—, adopted dau of Thomas W Futrille, of Sunningdale, Berks, and has:

  1 *Georgina Katharine; *b* 1982

  2 *Aimy Frances; *b* 1984

  3 *Laura Beatrice; *b* 1990

Lineage: WILLIAM MARLING (s of Samuel Marling by Hester Webb); *b* 3 April 1776; *m* 28 March 1796 Sarah (*b* 9 Nov 1773; *d* 7 Aug 1856), dau of Nathaniel Hillman, of Woodchester, Glos, and *d* 16 Oct 1859, having had, with three other sons (*d* young or unm):

1 Nathaniel Samuel, JP, of Stonehouse Court, Glos; *b* 2 April 1797; *m* 1824 Lucina (*d* 12 Oct 1880), dau of William Summers, of Wickwar, Glos, and *d* 24 Jan 1861, leaving issue

2 John Figgins, of Ebley Court, Glos, later Toronto, Canada; *b* 6 Sept 1799; *d* 4 Nov 1869

3 Thomas JP, of Norton Court, Glos; *b* 1 Nov 1803; *m* 1st 16 April 1839 Maria Louisa (*dsp* 1858), dau of Joseph Overbury, of Cheltenham; *m* 2nd Catherine Anne (*d* 18 Nov 1863), dau of William Playne, of Longfords, Glos, and *d* 11 Nov 1879, having by her had:

  (1) William Playne (Sir), 1st Bt
  (1) William Playne; *b* 5 Nov 1863; Capt 4th Bn Glos Regt; *d* unm 25 Sept 1895

4 SAMUEL STEPHENS (Sir), **1st Bt**

1 Esther; *b* 28 July 1805; *m* 22 Sept 1835 Rev James Gallaway and *dsp* 30 Oct 1836

2 Sarah; *b* 1 July 1814; *m* 11 Oct 1842 James Apperly, of Dudbridge House, Glos, and *d* 25 Jan 1900

WILLIAM MARLING'S 6th s,

Sir Samuel Stephens Marling, 1st Bt (UK), so *cr* 22 May 1882, JP and DL (W Glos 1868–74, Stroud 1875–80), of Stanley Park and Sedbury Park; *b* 10 April 1810; *m* 23 Sept 1834 Margaret Williams (*d* 13 April 1885 aged 69), dau of William Bentley Cartwright, of Devizes, Wilts, and *d* 22 Oct 1883, having had, with a dau (*d* young):

1 WILLIAM HENRY (Sir), **2nd Bt**

2 Charles; *b* 25 April 1837; *d* unm 30 Nov 1862

3 Walter Bentley, JP (Mon), of Domus, Broadstairs, Kent; *b* 4 April, 1854; Col 4th Bn Glos Regt, formerly Capt and Adj 1st Bn Roy Ulster Rifles; *m* 3 Aug 1880 Mary Isabella Cunynghame (*d* 14 Sept 1933), dau of Col Robert Broome Baker, and *d* 28 Jan 1941, leaving:

  (1) Margaret Cicely; *m* 7 Aug 1902 Maj Arthur Henry Bathurst (*see* BLEDISLOE, V) and *d* 24 Aug 1968, leaving issue

  (2) Mary Helen; *m* 22 Oct 1913 her cousin Maj William John Paley Marling (*see* below)

  (3) Dorothy Barbara; MB, BS, MRCS, LRCP; *d* unm 3 Sept 1939

  (4) Elspeth Katharina; *m* 5 June 1915 Capt Norman Tyrer, Beds Regt, of Ramley, Hants, s of William Tyrer, of St Mary's Lodge, Bedford

1 Annie Louisa; *b* 16 May 1841; *m* 14 June 1866 George Robertson, Capt 25th Regt, and *d* 1 Feb 1896, leaving issue

Sir SAMUEL's s,

Sir William Henry Marling, 2nd Bt, JP, DL, CA Glos, High Sheriff 1888, JP Mon; *b* 1 July 1835; *m* 2 May 1860 Mary Emily (*d* 14 Feb 1918), dau and coheir of John Abraham, of Longridge, Lancs, and *d* 19 Oct 1919, leaving:

1 **Sir Percival Scrope Marling, 3rd Bt,** VC (1884), CB (1902), JP and DL (Glos and Bristol), JP (Mon); *b* 6 March 1861; *educ* Harrow; 2nd Lt KRRC, served Transvaal 1880–81, Egyptian War 1882, Suakin Campaign 1884 (despatches), Nile Expdn 1884–85 (despatches, Egyptian medal with five clasps and Khedive's Star, promoted Capt 18th Hus), Boer War 1899–1902 (despatches, two medals with seven clasps), Col cmdg 18th Hus, Brig-Gen cmdg Potchefstroom Dist Transvaal 1909–10, HQ Staff IA Corps France WW I (Mons Star with clasp, two medals), High Sheriff Glos 1923, Jubilee Medal 1935, Hon Col 5th Bn Glos Regt 1934–36; *m* 18 May 1899 Beatrice Caroline, OStJ (*d* 28 July 1941), est dau of Francis Henry Beaumont, JP, DL, of Buckland Court, Surrey (*see* BEAUMONT, Bt), and *dsp* 29 May 1936

2 Charles Murray (Sir), GCMG, CB; *b* 3 Dec 1862; *educ* Trin Coll Cambridge (MA); Envoy Extrdy and Min Plen Persia 1915–21 and The Hague 1921–26, Pres Int Plebiscite Commn Slesvig 1920; *m* 2 Sept 1909 Lucia, CBE (*d* 11 Sept 1927), only child of Maj-Gen Sir John Ramsay Slade, KCB (*see* SLADE, Bt), and *d* 16 Feb 1933, having had:

  (1) JOHN STANLEY VINCENT (Sir), **4th Bt**

  (1) Yvonne Mary; *b* 6 Dec 1912; *m* 6 Dec 1932 (*divorce* 1948), as his 1st w, Cdr Hon Gustaf Guthrie Rennell Rodd, OBE, RN (*d* 26 June 1974), yst s of 1st Baron Rennell (*qv*), and had issue

  (2) Marian Charlotte, MBE (1944); *b* 1 Aug 1915; CC Berks, Jr Cdr ATS WW II, OStJ 1957; *m* 9 May 1944 (*divorce* 1953) Lt Richard Oliver Bruce Long, RNVR (*see* LONG, V), and had issue

3 Samuel Stanley, JP (Glos); *b* 20 Sept 1864; *educ* Clifton; High Sheriff 1936, Lt-Col 5th Bn Glos Regt, *d* unm 18 April 1963

4 William John Paley, JP (Glos), High Sheriff 1932; *b* 23 Oct 1865; *educ* Trin Coll Cambridge (MA); Maj 3rd Bn Glos Reg; *m* 22 Oct 1913 his cousin Mary Helen, 2nd dau of Col Walter Bentley Marling (*see* above), and *dsp* 9 April 1939

Sir PERCIVAL's nephew,

Sir John Stanley Vincent Marling, 4th Bt, OBE (1945); *b* 26 July 1910; *educ* Winchester and RMC Sandhurst; Lt-Col 17th/21st Lancers WW II; *m* 1st 27 Oct 1939 (*divorce* 1957) Georgina Brenda (Betty) (*d* 29 June 1961), dau of Henry Edward FitzRoy Somerset (*see* BEAUFORT, D), and had:

1 Sir CHARLES WILLIAM SOMERSET MARLING, **5th and present Bt**

1 *Miranda Mary [Mrs Anthony Cordle, 23 Durand Gdns, London SW9]; *b* 1 Jan 1941; *m* 2 April 1966 *Capt Anthony John Cordle, Coldstream Gds (ret), est s of John Howard Cordle (*see* POWERSCOURT, V), and has:

  (1) *Lucia Georgina Diana; *b* 11 Nov 1968

  (2) *Jessica Grace Rosanne; *b* 1972

2 *Harriet Anne; *b* 7 March 1944

3 *Virginia Frances [Mrs Colin Bowie, Dragon's Lair, Moor Lane, Wincanton, Somerset BA9 9EJ]; *b* 7 Dec 1946; *m* 1978 *Colin Bowie and has:

  (1) *John Adrian Charles; *b* 1977

  (2) *Geoffrey David; *b* 1979

Sir John *m* 2nd 2 Nov 1957 Marjorie Francis Esclair-Monde, 2nd dau of Sir Francis Hugh Stewart, CIE, MA, of Little Hallands, Bishopstone, Sussex, and widow of Maj Gustavus Henry March-Phillips, DSO, MBE, RA, of Chelsea, and *d* 20 Sept 1977

MARR

Arms: Azure the mast and sail of a ship, pennon flying, within eight estoiles in orle or. **Crest:** A bell or, charged with a fouled anchor proper. **Motto:** *Labor omnia vincit* ('Work conquers all'). **Creation:** Bt. (UK) 12 May 1919.

(SIR) LESLIE LYNN MARR, 2ND BT, of Sunderland, Co Durham; *b* 14 Aug 1922; *s* gf 24 Nov 1932, but does not use title; *educ* Shrewsbury and Pembroke Coll Cambridge; late F/Lt RAF; *m* 1st 1948 (*divorce* 1956) Dinora Delores Mendelson and adopted:

> *Juliet; *b* 194–

LESLIE MARR *m* 2nd Sept 1962 *Lynn, er dau of Michael William Walker Heneage, and by her has:

> 1 *Joanne Lesley; *b* 1963
> 2 *Rebecca Lynn; *b* 1966

Lineage: CHRISTOPHER HALL MARR, of Newcastle-upon-Tyne; *m* Ellen (*d* 24 Feb 1906), dau of Archibald Bell, and *d* 17 Feb 1907, leaving:

Sir James Marr, 1st Bt (UK), so *cr* 12 May 1919, CBE (1918), JP; *b* 9 Sept 1854; chm: T W Greenwell & Co, ship repairers and dry dock owners, of Sunderland, Sir James Laing & Sons, Sunderland Forge & Engineering and Joseph L Thompson & Sons, memb Shipping Controller's Advsy Ctee and Admlty Shipbuilding Cncl WW I; Freeman City London; *m* 18 Oct 1876 Mary (*d* 21 Nov 1943), dau of John Lynn, of Hylton, Co Durham, and *d* 24 Nov 1932, having had:

1 John Lynn, OBE, TD; *b* 23 Sept 1877; Lt-Col and Brevet Col RGA (TAR), memb TAA Co Durham; *m* 14 April 1920 Amelia Rachel, dau of Robert Thompson, of Over Dinsdale Hall, Co Durham, and *d* 2 Sept 1931, leaving:

> (2) (Sir) LESLIE LYNN MARR, **2nd and present Bt**

2 William Bell; *b* 4 Oct 1881; *educ* Durham U (BSc); *m* 1 Aug 1906 Hilda, dau of George Carse, of Wilton, Salisbury, and had:

> (1) Allan James, CBE (1965); *b* 6 May 1907; *educ* Oundle and Durham U (BSc); chm and md Sir James Laing & Sons, dir Doxford and Sunderland Shipbuilding and Engrg; *m* 1 June 1935 Joan de Wolfe (*d* 19–), dau of John Ranken, of Sunderland, and *d* 1989, leaving:

>> 1a +JAMES ALLAN [James Marr Esq, 2 Peppermines, Brancepeth, Co Durham DH7 8ED]; *b* 17 May 1939; heir presumptive; *educ* Oundle and Newcastle U; *m* 28 July 1964 *Jennifer, yr dau of John William Edward Gill, of Ellerslie, Bishop Auckland, and has:

>>> 1b +Allan James William; *b* 8 Oct 1965; *educ* Strathallan; *m* 1988 *Dawn, dau of George Ridley, and has:

>>>> 1c +Liam James Allan; *b* 1991

>>> 2b +Roderick John; *b* 1971

>>> 1b *Lucy Joan; *b* 30 March 1968

>> 1a *Jennifer Wendy [Mrs Nicholas Willink, Greenhills, Crook, Kendal, Cumbria]; *b* 28 July 1936; *m* 30 April 1960 *Nicholas Warren Willink (*see* WILLINK, Bt) and has issue

>> 2a *Gillian Mary; *b* 23 Feb 1941; *m* 1974 *Richard Tatton Wedderburn Hewetson and has:

>>> 1b *Richard Allan Webster; *b* 1975

>>> 2b *Edward Anthony; *b* 1976

> (2) Norman Carse; *b* 20 Feb 1910; *educ* London U (BSc 1932); *m* 25 April 1935 Flora McDonald (*d* 1985), dau of Kenneth McDonald Cameron, of W Hartlepool, and *d* 1980, leaving:

>> 1a +Jeremy Norman [Jeremy Marr Esq, 4430 Piccadilly, W Vancouver, BC, Canada]; *b* 12 May 1940; *m* 14 Dec 1968 *Gillian Yvonne, only dau of P J Hugo, of Johannesburg, and has:

>>> 1b +Kyle Jeremy; *b* 1974

>>> 2b +Jordan Hugo; *b* 1977

>> 1a *Dair Norman; *b* 30 Sept 1941; *m* 1964 *Douglas Ian Henry Henderson and has:

>>> 1b *Stuart Philip; *b* 1968

>>> 1b *Karen Frances; *b* 1966

>>> 2b *Avril Louise; *b* 1971

2a *Alexandra Norman; *b* 17 May 1944; *m* 1975 *Ian Nicol

(3) Arthur Lynn; *b* 4 Aug 1914; *educ* Oundle; *m* 5 July 1941 *May Victoria [Mrs Arthur Marr, 12 King John's Court, Ponteland, Newcastle-upon-Tyne NE20 9AR], dau of Harry Bernard Bradshaw, of St Ouen, Jersey, and *d* 1991, leaving:

> 1a +Bernard Lynn [Bernard Marr Esq, Deneholme, Acomb Drive, Wylam, Northumberland]; *b* 9 Aug 1943; *educ* Oundle; *m* 9 Oct 1968 *Judith, dau of Ronald Henry Richards, and has:

>> 1b *Katherine Lynn; *b* 1972

>> 2b *Jane Victoria; *b* 1974

>> 3b *Helen Judith; *b* 1979

> 1a *Mary Singleton [Mrs Christopher Broom-Smith, Auchenskeoch Lodge, Dalbeattie, Kirkcudbrightshire DG5 4PG]; *b* 20 Nov 1946; *m* 1972 *Christopher Broom-Smith

> 2a *Victoria Lynn; *b* 30 June 1951; *m* 1976 (*divorce* 19–) Henry Jeremy Meadows and has:

>> 1b *Carl Jeremy; *b* 1980

>> 2b *James Arthur Henry; *b* 1983

>> 1b *Joanna Lynn; *b* 1977

1 Ellen Bell; *m* 23 April 1907 Harry Cecil Coatsworth (*d* 16 July 1943), of Sunderland, and *d* 5 May 1957, leaving issue

MARSDEN

Arms: Sable a fess dancettée ermine, in chief two fleurs-de-lys argent and in base a ship sailing to the sinister proper. **Crest:** In front of a unicorn's head erased sable, charged with two barrulets gules, as many roses argent, barbed and seeded proper. **Motto:** *Deo gratias* ('Thanks be to God'). **Creation:** Bt. (UK) 4 March 1924.

SIR SIMON NEVILLE LLEWELYN MARSDEN, 4TH BT, of Grimsby, Co Lincoln [Sir Simon Marsden Bt, The Presbytery, Hainton, Lincs LN3 6LR]; *b* 1 Dec 1948; *s* bro 1997; *educ* Ampleforth and Sorbonne; author *Tales of the Haunted Realm* (1990) and other coffee table books on the supernatural; *m* 1st 15 March 1971 (*divorce* 1978) Catherine, yr dau of Brig James Windsor-Lewis, DSO, MC; *m* 2nd 1984 *Caroline, yst dau of John Stanton, and by her has:

> 1 +TADGH ORLANDO DENTON; *b* 25 Dec 1990

> 1 *Skye Atalanta; *b* 1988

Lineage: JOHN DENTON MARSDEN, of Almondbury, Huddersfield; *d* 23 May 1858 aged 55, leaving:

WILLIAM DENT MARSDEN, of Almondbury; *d* 13 June 1922, having had:

Sir John Denton Marsden, 1st Bt (UK), so *cr* 4 March 1924, JP (Parts Lindsey), High Sheriff Lincs 1942; *b* 9 Nov 1873; *m* 6 May 1911 Agnes Mary (*d* 20 Sept 1951), dau of Thomas Robert Ronald, and *d* 25 April 1944, leaving:

1 JOHN DENTON (Sir), **2nd Bt**

1 *Agnes Isabelle [Mrs Frederick Storey, Baymead Cottage, 2 Baymead Lane, North Pemberton, Somerset]; *b* 1920; *m* 28 June 1941 *Capt Frederick William Tackaberry Storey, RASC, only s of Rev John William Storey, and has:

> (1) *Michael William Tackaberry; *b* 29 May 1942; *educ* Sherborne

> (2) *Jonathan William Tackaberry; *b* 8 Feb 1948; *educ* Sherborne

> (3) *Alastair William Tackaberry; *b* 3 Nov 1949

> (1) *Jane Patricia; *b* April 1951

> (2) *Penelope Caroline; *b* 8 July 1953

> (3) *Sally Anne; *b* 13 April 1957

Sir JOHN's s,

Sir John Denton Marsden, 2nd Bt, of Grimsby, Lincs, JP (Parts of Lindsey 1950); *b* 25 Aug 1913; *educ* Downside and St John's Coll Cambridge (BA 1935); Lt RA WW II (POW), chm and md Consolidated Fisheries , High Sheriff Lincs 1955; *m* 5 Sept 1939 *Hope [Hope Lady Marsden, Wold Cottage, Greetham, nr Horncastle, Lincs], yr dau of G E Llewelyn, and *d* 1985, leaving:

1 **Sir Nigel John Denton Marsden, 3rd Bt**; *b* 26 May 1940; *educ* Ampleforth; *m* 16 Sept 1961 *Diana-Jean [Diana-Jean Lady Marsden, 1 Grimsby Rd, Waltham, S Humberside DN37 0PS], er dau of Air Marshal Sir Patrick Hunter Dunn, KBE, CB, DFC, of Beaulieu, Hants, and *d* 16 Nov 1997, leaving:

(1) *Lucinda Ann; *b* 2 Sept 1962
(2) *Rose Amanda; *b* 11 Dec 1964
(3) *Annabel Juliet; *b* 24 Nov 1968
2 SIR SIMON NEVILLE LLEWELYN MARSDEN, **4th and present Bt**
1 *Vanessa Ann [Mrs Vanessa Whitehead, Wold Cottage, Greetham, Horncastle, Lincs LN9 6NT]; *b* 3 June 1941; *m* 15 Nov 1968 (*divorce* 19–) Francis John Whitehead, s of Maj Thomas B Whitehead, and has:
(1) *Mark John Bovil; *b* 1975
2 *Caroline Jane [Mrs Richard Noton, Bockingham Hall, Copford, Essex CO6 1DR]; *b* 22 March 1946; *m* 9 Sept 1970 *Richard Thomas Widdowson Noton, only s of L W Noton, of IoW

MARSH

NON·EST·VIVERE·SED·VALERE·VITA·

Arms: Argent four pallets wavy azure on a chevron over all gules a leopard's face between two keys, wards upwards and outwards or, on a chief gules a double-warded key, wards upwards, between two leopard's faces gold. **Crest:** Upon a mount vert a bear sejant upon its haunches and erect or, holding between its forepaws a mitra preciosa gold-panneled vert garnished and lined gules, the infulae vert and fringed at their ends gold. **Supporters:** On either side a Japanese crane (*grus japonensis*) proper, the interior wing and leg of each supporting the shield, the whole upon a compartment composed of water barry wavy of four azure and argent, between two banks of marshy ground proper, sprouting therefrom plants of marsh buckler fern, marsh mallow and bullrush, all slipped and leaved proper. **Motto:** *Non est vivere sed valere vita.* ('Life is not for living but for making the most of'). **Creation:** B. (LP, UK) 1981.

THE BARON MARSH, of Mannington, Co Wilts (Sir Richard William Marsh, PC (1966)) [The Rt Hon The Lord Marsh PC, House of Lords, London SW1A 0PW]; *b* 14 March 1928; *educ* Jennings Sch Swindon, Woolwich Poly and Ruskin Coll Oxford; Health Services Officer NUPE 1951–59; memb Whitney Cncl for Health Services 1953–59; MP (Lab) Greenwich 1959–71, memb Select Ctee Estimates 1961; chm Interdepartmental Ctee Industl Trng 1964, Parly Sec Min Labour 1964–5, Jt Parly Sec Mins: Technology 1965–66, Power 1966–68, Tport 1968–69; Pres Cncl ECSC 1968; memb NEDC 1971, Cncl CBI 1970–, Freight Integration Cncl 1971–; Chm: BR 1970–75, Newspaper Publishing Assoc 1975–90, Allied Medical Gp 1977–81, Allied Investments 1977–81, Br Iron and Steel Consumers Cncl 1977–83, Lee Cooper plc 1982–, TV AM 1983 (dep chm 1981), Mannington Management Servs 1989–, Gartmore Br Income and Growth Tst 1994–, Business for Sterling (anti-single currency lobby) 1998–; dep chm: United Medical Enterprises 1978–81, Lopex 1986–97 (dir 1985–97), Laurentian Finance Gp 1986–, China & Eastern Investment Tst 1990– (dir 1987–); Advsr: Nissan Motor Co 1981–, Fujitec 1982; dir: Imperial Life of Canada UK 1983–, Imperial Life Assur Co Canada 1983, Charles Church Devpts 1987–, Laurentian Gp Corp 1990–; Govr Br Transport Staff Coll; Chm London Business Sch, ktd 1976; FIMgt; FInstD; FInstM; FCIT; *m* 1st 1950 (*divorce* 1973) Evelyn Mary, dau of Frederick Andrews, of Southarnpton, and has:
1 *Andrew; *b* 1950
2 *Christopher; *b* 1960
The BARON MARSH *m* 2nd 1973 Caroline Dutton (*d* 1975); *m* 3rd 1979 *Hon Felicity Carmen Francesca McFadzean, dau of Baron McFadzean of Kelvinside (LP, *d* 1992)
Lineage: WILLIAM MARSH, of Belvedere, Kent; had:
RICHARD WILLIAM, *cr* a **Baron**

MARTONMERE

INTEGRITY AND UNDER STANDING

Arms: Arg. a three-masted merchant ship of the early 18th century, mainsails furled ppr., on a chief az. a portcullis chained between two roses or. **Crest:** A lion's head erased or, in the mouth a crescent gu. **Supporters:** Dexter, a lion or collared flory counterflory gu.; sinister, a stag gu., attired and unguled, collared flory counterflory or. **Motto:** Integrity and understanding. **Creation:** B. (UK) 13 May 1964.

THE 2ND BARON MARTONMERE, of Blackpool, Co Palatine of Lancaster (John Stephen Robinson) [The Rt Hon The Lord Martonmere, 390 Russell Hill Rd, Toronto, Ontario M4V 2V2, Canada]; *b* 10 July 1963; *s gf* 1989; *educ* Lakefield Coll Sch and Seneca U
Lineage: JOHN HARRISON ROBINSON, of Whitbarrow Hall, nr Penrith, Cumberland; *b* 30 June 1850; *educ* Penrith; *m* Jane (*d* 3 May 1920), dau of John Walkden, of Blackpool, and *d* 18 Feb 1935, leaving:
ROLAND WALKDEN, of Blackpool; *b* 25 Aug 1876; *educ* Blackpool; slr; *m* 21 Dec 1905 Mary Collier (*d* 5 Nov 1944), dau of Joseph Pritchard, of Blackpool, and *d* 9 Sept 1947, leaving:
1 (JOHN) ROLAND, **1st Baron**
2 (Leonard) Pritchard, MBE (1946); *b* 5 May 1908; *educ* Trin Hall Cambridge (BA 1929, LLB 1930, MA 1933); slr 1932, RAFVR WW II, Czechoslovak Medal of Merit 1st Cl 1946; *m* 1st 17 July 1932 (*divorce* 1948) Catherine, dau of William Gittus, of Barnsley, Yorks; *m* 2nd 1948 *Hilda (Faff) Glass, WAAF, dau of Walter Lawrence Butler, of Moss Hall, Handforth, and widow of — Naylor, and *d* 14 Sept 1976, leaving by his 1st w:
(1) *Martin Nigel, RN; *b* 17 April 1935; *educ* Malvern; *m* 19– *— and has:
1a *Alec
ROLAND ROBINSON *d* 9 Sept 1947; his er son,
JOHN ROLAND ROBINSON, **1st Baron Martonmere**, of Blackpool in the Co Palatine of Lancaster (UK), so *cr* 13 May 1964, GBE (1973), KCMG (1966), PC (1962); *b* 22 Feb 1907; *educ* Trin Hall Cambridge (BA 1928, LLB 1929, MA); barrister 1929, MP (C) Widnes 1931–35, Blackpool 1935–45 and S Blackpool 1945–64, WW II as W/Cdr RAFVR 1943; pres Assoc Health and Pleasure Resorts 1936–64 and Roy Lancs Ag Soc 1936, chm Gen Cwlth Parly Assoc 1960–61, dep chm UK Branch 1962–64, chm Cwlth Affairs Ctee H of C 1954–64, Govr and C-in-C Bermuda 1964–89, KStJ 1964, Offr US Legion Merit, ktd 1954; *m* 9 July 1930 Maysie, CStJ (*d* Oct 1989), dau of Clarence Warren Gasque, of Hampstead, and *d* May 1989, having had:
1 Richard Anthony Gasque; *b* 11 March 1935; *educ* Winchester, Selwyn Coll Cambridge (BA 1958) and Stanford U California (MBA 1960); *m* 8 Aug 1959 *Wendy Patricia [The Hon Mrs Richard Robinson, 390 Russell Hill Rd, Toronto, Ontario M4V 2V2, Canada], dau of James Cecil Blagden, of Bapchild Court, nr Sittingbourne, Kent, and *dvp* 1979, leaving:
(1) JOHN STEPHEN ROBINSON, **2nd and present Baron Martonmere**
(2) +David Alan; *b* 15 Sept 1965; *educ* Upper Canada Coll and Neuchâtel, Switzerland, and Queen's U, Weston U (BA, MBA)
(1) *Carolyn Elizabeth; *b* 29 Jan 1969
1 *Loretta Anne [The Hon Mrs Rogers, 3 Frybrook Rd, Toronto 7, Ontario M4V 1Y7, Canada]; *b* 13 April 1939; *m* 25 Sept 1963 *Edward Samuel Rogers, s of Edward Samuel Rogers, of Toronto, and has:
(1) *Edward Samuel; *b* 22 June 1969
(1) *Lisa Anne; *b* 9 Oct 1967
(2) *Melinda Mary; *b* 1971
(3) *Martha Loretta; *b* 1972

MASHAM OF ILTON

Creation: B. (LP, UK) 1970.

THE BARONESS MASHAM OF ILTON, of Masham, N Riding, Co York (Susan Lilian Primrose Sinclair, DL (N Yorks 1991)) [The Rt Hon The Countess of Swinton, Dykes Hill House, Masham, Ripon, Yorks HG4 4NS; 46 Westminster Gdns, Marsham St, London SW1P 4JG]; *b* 14 April, 1935; *educ* Heathfield Sch Ascot and London Poly; memb: Bd Visitors Wetherby Young Offenders Inst 1963–94, All-Party Disablement Ctee 1970–, Peterlee and Newton Aycliffe New Town Corp 1973–85, Parly All-Party Penal Affairs Gp 1975–, All-Party Children's Gp; V-Chm: Parly All-Party Drug Misuse Ctee 1984–, Parly All-Party Aids Ctee, Winston Churchill Meml Tst 1980–, Stonham Memorial Tst 1995–; Chm Phoenix House 1986–92 (Patron 1992–); Pres: N Yorks Red Cross 1963–88 (Patron 1989–), Yorks Assoc for the Disabled 1963–, Papworth and Enham Village Settlements 1973–85, Chartered Soc of Physiotherapy 1975–82, Spinal Injuries Assoc 1982–, Countrywide Workshops Charitable Trust 1993–; Hon Fell: Roy Coll General Practitioners 1981, Bradford and Ilkley Community Coll 1988; Hon MA OU 1981; DUniv York 1985; Hon Master of Law Leeds 1988; Hon DSc Ulster 1990; Hon LLD Leeds 1988, Teesside 1993; Hon Freeman Borough of Harrogate 1989; *m* 1959 *2nd Earl of Swinton (*qv*) and adopted two children

Lineage: *See* SINCLAIR, Bt

MASON OF BARNSLEY

Creation: B. (LP, UK) 1987.

THE BARON MASON OF BARNSLEY, of Barnsley, S Yorks (Roy Mason, PC (1968), DL (S Yorks 1992)) [The Rt Hon The Lord Mason of Barnsley PC DL, 12 Victoria Av, Barnsley, S Yorks S70 2BH]; *b* 18 April 1924; *educ* Carlton Jr and Royston Sr Schs and LSE; miner 1938–53, branch offr NUM 1947–53, memb Yorks Miners' Cncl 1949; MP (Lab) Barnsley 1953–83, Barnsley Centl 1983–87; Oppn Spokesman Def and PO 1960–64, Min State BOT 1964–67 and MOD (Equipment) 1967–68, PMG 1968, Min Power 1968–69, Pres BOT 1960–70, Oppn Spokesman Civ Aviation, Shipping, Tourism, Film and Trade Matters 1970–74; Chm: Yorks Gp Lab MPs 1972–74, Miners' Gp MPs 1974 (V-Chm 1980); Sec State: Def 1974–76, NI 1976–79; Oppn Spokesman Ag, Fisheries and Food 1979–81; memb Cncl Europe and WEU 1973; Hon Dr Sheffield Hallam 1993; *m* 1945 *Marjorie, dau of Ernest Snowden, of Royston, W R Yorks, and has:

1 *Susan Ann; *b* 1947; *m* 1969 *Allen Duke and has:
  (1) *Steven Allen; *b* 1975
  (1) *Caroline Ann; *b* 1978
2 *Jill Diane; *b* 1955; *m* 1979 *Kevin Charles Edward Martin and has:
  1 *Andrew Ian; *b* 1986

Lineage: JOSEPH MASON, of Carlton, nr Barnsley; *m* Mary — and had:

ROY, *cr* a **Baron**

MASSEREENE and FERRARD

Arms: Quarterly, 1st and 4th, argent three bull's heads erased sable, armed or (for SKEFFINGTON); 2nd and 3rd, azure a chevron between three chaplets or (for CLOTWORTHY). **Crest:** A mermaid with comb and mirror, all proper. **Supporters:** Two stags sable, attired and unguled or, each gorged with a chaplet of roses argent. **Motto:** *Per angusta ad augusta* ('Through difficulties to honours'). **Creations:** V. (Massereene) and B. (Loughneagh) (I) 21 Nov 1660, B. (I) 5 June 1790 (Oriel of Collon), V. (I) 22 Nov 1797 (Ferrard), B. (UK) 17 July 1821 (Oriel of Collon).

THE 14TH VISCOUNT MASSEREENE, Co Antrim, **AND (6TH VISCOUNT) FERRARD**, Co Louth, **Baron of Loughneagh**, Co Antrim, **Baron Oriel of Collon**, Co Louth, and **Baron Oriel of Ferrard**, Co Louth (John David Clotworthy Whyte-Melville Foster Skeffington) [The Right Hon The Viscount Massereene and Ferrard, House of Lords, London SW1A 0PW]; *b* 3 June 1940; *s* f 1992; *educ* Millfield and Inst Monte Rosa Switzerland; 2nd Bn Gren Gds 1959–61, stockbroker 1961–64 and 1970– with M D Barnard, in motor trade 1964–70; *m* 21 Nov 1970 *(Ann) Denise, er dau of Norman Rowlandson, of Kingston Hill, Surrey, and has:

1 +CHARLES CLOTWORTHY WHYTE-MELVILLE FOSTER; *b* 7 Feb 1973
2 +Henry William Norman Foster Clotworthy; *b* 1980
1 *Harriette Denise Margaretta Eileen; *b* 26 Jan 1975

Previous Barony of Ferrard: Henry Tichborne (*see* 1967 edn TICHBORNE, Bt) was created Baron Ferrard of Beaulieu in 1715 but died without surviving male issue in 1731, when the title expired.

Lineage (of Skeffington): THOMAS SKEFFINGTON, of Skeffington, Leics; had:

Sir WILLIAM ('The Gunner') SKEFFINGTON or SKEFFYNGTON; Ld Deputy Ireland *temp* HENRY VIII; Master Ordnance (hence his sobriquet); *m* 1st Margaret, dau of Sir Everard Digby, of Drystoke, and had issue; *m* 2nd Anne dau of Sir John Digby, of Eye Kettleby, Rutland, and *d* 1534, having had by her, with other issue:

Sir JOHN SKEFFINGTON, of Fisherwick(e), Staffs; Alderman London, Sheriff 1521; *m* Elizabeth Pecke (*m* 2nd Sir John Daunsey) and had:

WILLIAM SKEFFINGTON, of Fisherwick(e) and White Ladies; *m* Isa, dau of James Leveson, of Trentham, Staffs, and *d* 31 May 1550, having had:

JOHN SKEFFINGTON, of Fisherwick; *m* Alice, 7th dau of Sir Thomas Cave (*see* CAVE-BROWN-CAVE, Bt), of Stanford, Northants, and had:

Sir WILLIAM SKEFFINGTON, 1st Bt (E), so *cr* 8 May 1627, of Fisherwick(e); *m* by 1590 Elizabeth, dau of Richard Dering (*see* 1970 edn DERING, Bt), and was *bur* 16 Sept 1635, having had:

1 Sir JOHN SKEFFINGTON, 2nd Bt, of Fisherwick(e); *b c* 1590; MP Newcastle-under-Lyne 1626, Sheriff Staffs 1637–38, fined for royalism 1650; *m* his cousin Cicely, sis of Sir John Skeffington, of Skeffington, Leics, and *d* 19 Nov 1651, leaving an only s:
  (1) Sir WILLIAM SKEFFINGTON, 3rd Bt, of Fisherwick(e) and Skeffington; *m* Ursula —; *dsp* and was *bur* 7 April 1652
2 Richard (Sir), ktd 1624, MP Staffs 1646–47; *m* Anne, dau of Sir John Newdigate, of Arbury, Warwicks, and *d* 2 June 1647, having had an est s:
  (1) Sir JOHN SKEFFINGTON, 4th Bt and **2nd Viscount Massereene**, PC (I); *educ* Magdalene Coll Cambridge; MP (I Parl) Co Antrim 1661–65, Custos Rotulorum Co Londonderry 1666, Govr Co Antrim by 1683 and Derry and Coleraine 1685, attainted by JAMES II's I Parl 1689, restored by WILLIAM III 1692; *m* 20 July 1654 Mary Clotworthy (*d* 20 Sept 1686), only dau and heiress of **1st Viscount Massereene**, Co Antrim (I) (*dspm* 23 Sept 1665), so *cr* 21 Nov 1660 (as also BARON OF LOUGHNEAGH, Co Antrim), with remainder, in default of male issue of his own, to his s-in-law and the issue male of the latter's body, with further remainder in default of which to the heirs general of his own (the grantee's) body (the **1st Viscount** being s of Sir Hugh Clotworthy, of Massereene, Co Antrim, Sheriff Co Antrim), and *d* 21 June 1695, having had:

1a CLOTWORTHY SKEFFINGTON, **3rd Viscount Massereene**; *b c* 1660; attainted by JAMES II's I Parl 1689 but restored by WILLIAM III, MP (I Parl) Co Antrim 1692–93; *m c* 9 March 1679/80 Rachel (*d* Feb 1731), dau of Sir Edward Hungerford (*see* SAINT DAVIDS, V), and *d* 14 March 1713, leaving:

1b CLOTWORTHY, **4th Viscount**

1b Jane; *m* probably *c* 1705 Sir Hans Hamilton, 2nd and last Bt of the Feb 1682/3 *cr* (*dspm* 1729/30), s of Sir Robert Hamilton, 1st Bt, by Sarah, dau of Sir Hans Hamilton, 1st and last Bt of the 1662 *cr* (*see* HOLMPATRICK, B)

2b Rachel; *m* 1st 4th Earl of Antrim (*qv*) of the 1620 *cr*; *m* 2nd Robert Hawkins Magill (*d* 10 April 1745) and *d* 13 April 1739, leaving issue

3b Mary; *m* Rt Rev Edward Smyth, DD, Bp Down and Connor, and had issue (*see* ARRAN, E)

1a Margaret; *m* 1681 1st and last Baron Saint George of Hatley Saint George (*see* ST GEORGE, Bt)

The 3rd VISCOUNT's s,

CLOTWORTHY SKEFFINGTON, **4th Viscount Massereene**; MP Co Antrim 1703–14; *m* 8 Sept 1713 Lady Catherine Chicester (*d* 1 July 1749), est dau of 4th Earl of Donegall (*see* DONEGALL, M), and *d* 11 Feb 1738, having had, with other issue:

1 CLOTWORTHY, **5th Viscount**

2 Arthur, MP (Co Antrim); *dsp* 8 April 1747

3 John (Rev); *m* a dau of Henry Thornton, of Muffe, and *d* 25 Dec 1753

1 Catherine; *m* 3 Jan 1739 3rd Viscount Doneraile (*qv*) of the 1703 *cr* and *dsp* 3 April 1751

The 4th VISCOUNT MASSEREENE's est s,

CLOTWORTHY SKEFFINGTON, **5th Viscount Massereene** and 1st EARL OF MASSEREENE (I), so *cr* 28 July 1756, PC (I 1746); *educ* Trin Coll Dublin; *m* 1st 16 March 1738 Anne (*dsp* 24 March 1740), est dau of Richard Daniel, Dean of Down; *m* 2nd 25 Nov 1741 Anne (*d* 20 May 1805), only dau of Henry Eyre, of Row Tor, Derbys, and *d* 17 Sept 1757, having had, with other issue:

1 CLOTWORTHY SKEFFINGTON, **6th Viscount Masserenne** and 2nd EARL OF MASSEREENE; *b* 28 Jan 1742/3; *educ* Benet's Coll Cambridge; imprisoned Châtelet, Paris, for debt 1771–89 (escaped May 1789, two months before the Fall of the Bastille) after imprudent speculations in salt futures; *m* 1st 19 Aug 1789 Marie Anne (*d* Oct 1800), his prison govr M Barcier's dau; *m* 2nd Elizabeth Lane (*m* 2nd George Doran; *m* 3rd Hon George Massy (*see* MASSY, B); *d* 19 March 1838) and *dsp* 28 Feb 1805

2 HENRY CLOTWORTHY SKEFFINGTON, **7th Viscount Massereene** and 3rd EARL OF MASSEREENE; *b c* 1744; *educ* Harrow and Trin Coll Dublin; Lt-Col 2nd Regt Horse, MP Belfast 1768–97 and Antrim 1779–1800, Govr Cork 1792–1811; *d* unm 12 June 1811

3 CHICHESTER CLOTWORTHY SKEFFINGTON, **8th Viscount Massereene** and 4th and last EARL OF MASSEREENE; *b c* 1746; MP Antrim 1768–97, Sheriff Co Antrim 1797; *m* 1780 Lady Harriet Jocelyn (*d* 7 July 1831), est dau of 1st Earl of Roden (*qv*) and *dspm* 25 Feb 1816, when the Earldom and btcy expired, leaving:

(1) HARRIET Skeffington, **Viscountess Massereene** in her own right; *m* 20 Nov 1810 **2nd Viscount Ferrard** (*see* below)

1 Elizabeth; *m* 1st Earl of Leitrim (*see* 1953 edn)

2 Catherine; *m* 7 June 1784 1st Earl of Llandaff and *d* 9 Feb 1796

Lineage (of Foster): Col ANTHONY FOSTER, of Dunleer, Co Louth, but originally of a Cumberland family; had:

JOHN FOSTER, of Dunleer; MP Dunleer; *m* 10 Dec 1704 Elizabeth (*d* 29 Oct 1762), yst dau of William Fortescue, of Newrath, Co Louth, and *d* 16 May 1747, leaving:

1 ANTHONY

2 Thomas (Rev), DD; Rector Dunleer; *b* 16 Nov 1709; *m* 4 May 1740 Dorothy, dau of William Burgh, of Bert, Co Kildare, and *d* 1784, leaving:

(1) John Thomas, of Dunleer; MP Dunleer 1776–83 and Ennis, Co Clare, 1783–90; *m* 2 April 1776 Lady Elizabeth Hervey (*m* 2nd 19 Oct 1809 5th Duke of Devonshire (*qv*); *d* 30 March 1824), dau of 4th Earl of Bristol (*see* BRISTOL, M), and *d* 10 Oct 1796, having had:

1a Frederick Thomas; *b* 2 Oct 1777, MP Bury St Edmunds 1812–18

2a Sir AUGUSTUS JOHN FOSTER, 1st Bt (UK), so *cr* 30 Sept 1831, PC, GGH, of Glyde Court, Co Louth; *b* Dec 1780, Envoy-Extrdy and Min Plen: USA 1812, Sweden, Denmark and Sardinia; *m* 18 March 1815 Albinia (*d* 28 May 1867), dau of Hon George Vere Hobart (*see* BUCKINGHAMSHIRE, E), and *d* 1 Aug 1848, leaving:

1b Sir FREDERICK GEORGE FOSTER, 2nd Bt; *b* 3 Jan 1816; *d* unm 25 Dec 1857

2b Rev Sir CAVENDISH HERVEY FOSTER, 3rd Bt; *b* 7 May 1817; Rector Theydon Garnon 1843–87; *m* 15 Jan 1844 Isabella (*d* 3 June 1881), yst dau of Rev John Todd, and *d* 27 Nov 1890, having had:

1c John Frederick, JP and DL, High Sheriff 1875; *b* 18 Jan 1847, 13th Hus, Maj 6th Bn Roy Irish Rifles; *m* 20 April 1871 Caroline Emily (*d* 22 Sept 1892), dau of Thomas Coxhead Chisenhale Marsh, of Gaynes Park, Essex, and *dvp* 27 July 1890, leaving:

1d Sir AUGUSTUS VERE FOSTER, 4th and last Bt, JP and DL; *b* 31 March 1873; Capt Norfolk Yeo; *m* 25 Oct 1895 Charlotte Philippa Marion (*d* 29 Sept 1938), dau of Rev Henry Edward Ffolkes (*see* FFOLKES, Bt), and *d* 7 Nov 1947, when the btcy expired, having had:

1e Anthony Vere; *b* 21 Feb 1908; 2nd Lt Roy Berkshire Regt; *d* unm 4 Oct 1934

1e Philippa Eugenie Vere; *b* 23 April 1898; *d* unm 7 Jan 1962

2e Dorothy Elizabeth Charlotte Vere; *b* 24 March 1903; *m* 16 Aug 1940 Lt-Col Arthur Charles William May, MC, HLI, yst s of George Chichester May, KC, of 13 Fitzwilliam Sq, Dublin

1d Emily Albinia; *d* unm 29 Nov 1951

2d Mary Isabella; *m* 16 Oct 1902 Rev Edward M Hadow, Vicar Uffington Berks, 3rd s of Rev C E Hadow (*d* 16 March 1930), Rector E Barnet, and *d* 17 Dec 1948, having had issue

3d Alice Jane Blanche; *m* 6 Jan 1912 Maj-Gen Fitzgerald Wintour, CB, CBE (*d* 18 June 1949), Roy W Kent Regt, s of Rev Fitzgerald Wintour, and had issue

2c Hervey; *b* 20 June 1851; Lt Roy Irish Rifles; *d* unm 31 March 1887

1c Jane Vere; *m* 2 Oct 1872 Robert Boothby Heathcote (*see* HEATHCOTE, Bt, of London); *dsp* 1 Aug 1895

3b Vere Henry Lewis; educationist and philanthropist; *b* 26 April 1819; *d* unm 21 Dec 1900

3 John William of Rosy Park; MP Dunleer; ancestor of the FOSTERs of Ballynascanlon; had a dau (Patience, *m* John McClintock and had issue; *see* RATHDONNELL, B)

1 Margaret; *m* Stephen Sibthorpe, of Brownstown, Co Louth

2 Charlotte; *m* Nicholas Forster, of Tullaghan, and had issue (*see* 1904 edn FORSTER, Bt, of Coolderry)

3 Alice; *m* Thomas Bolton (*d* 17 March 1740)

The est s,

ANTHONY FOSTER, of Collon, Co Louth, PC; Ld Ch Baron Exchequer Ireland 1766–77, MP Dunleer 1737–60 and Co Louth 1761–67; *m* 1st 25 Feb 1736 Elizabeth (*d* 30 July 1744), dau of William Burgh, of Bert, Co Kildare, and had:

1 JOHN, **1st Baron**

2 William (Rt Rev), DD; Bp Cork 1789, Kilmore 1790 and Clogher 1796; *m* Catherine Letitia (*d* 1814), dau of Rev Henry Leslie, LLD, and *d* Nov 1797; ancestor of the FOSTER-VESEY-FitzGERALDs

1 Margaret; *bapt* 21 Feb 1737; *m* 1759 Rt Rev Hon Henry Maxwell and *d* 3 April 1778, having had issue (*see* FARNHAM, B)

The er s,

JOHN FOSTER, **1st Baron Oriel of Ferrard**, Co Louth (UK), so *cr* 17 July 1821, PC (GB 1821, I 1799); *bapt* 28 Sept 1740; *educ* Trin Coll Dublin; barrister Dublin 1766, MP (I Parl) Dunleer 1761–68, Co Louth 1761–1800 and (Tory, UK Parl) 1801–21, Chllr Exchequer Ireland 1784–85 and 1804–06 and a Commr Treasury 1807–11, last Speaker Irish H of C 1785–1800; *m* 14 Dec 1764 Margaret Amelia (*b c* 1737; *cr* 5 June 1790 Baroness Oriel of Collon, Co Louth, and 22 Nov 1797 **Viscountess Ferrard**, Co Louth (both I), both times with remainder to heirs male of her body; *d* 20 Jan 1824), dau of Thomas Burgh, of Bert, Co Kildare, and *d* 23 Aug 1828, having had, with other issue:

1 John, *b c* 1770; *educ* Eton and Trin Coll Cambridge; MP Dunleer 1790–92, *dvp* by 18 April 1792

2 THOMAS HENRY FOSTER later SKEFFINGTON (roy licence 8 Jan 1817), s mother 1824 as **2nd Viscount Ferrard** and **2nd Baron Oriel of Collon** and f 1828 as **2nd Baron Oriel of Ferrard**, PC (I 1809); *b c* 1772; *educ* Eton, Trin Coll Cambridge and Lincoln's Inn; MP Dunleer 1792–1800, Drogheda (Tory) 1807–12 and Co Louth 1821–24, Commr Customs (I) 1798–99, Sheriff Co Louth 1811 and Co Antrim 1818; *m* 20 Nov 1810 Harriet, **Viscountess Massereene** in her own right (*see* above; *d* 2 Jan 1831), and *d* 18 Jan 1843, having had, with other issue:

(1) JOHN, **10th/3rd Viscount**

(2) Chichester Thomas; *b* 29 Oct 1813; offr 27th Regt; *m* 29 Dec 1845 Amelia (*d* 23 Aug 1887), 2nd dau of Arthur Blennerhasset, of Ballyseedy, Co Kerry, and *d* 18 July 1880, leaving, with other issue:

1a Blennerhasset John; *b* 24 Feb 1846; Lt 3rd Bn S Lancs Regt Boer War 1900–01 and WW I; *m* 6 Feb 1900 Lily E Devoge (*d* 30 June 1932), dau of Thomas Wild, and *d* 13 Aug 1935

1a Anna Louisa; *m* 27 March 1869 Maj-Gen James Foord Hilton, of Archers Court, St Helens, Hastings, 2nd Bn Seaforth Highrs, and *d* 31 Jan 1915

2a Flora Georgina; *m* 23 Nov 1872 4th Baron Muskerry (*qv*) and *d* 20 Dec 1902, leaving issue

3a Ada Blennerhasset; *m* 22 Aug 1878 Bde Surg Lt-Col Rodolphe Harman, MB (*d* 1897). s of Ralph Harman, of Co Cavan, and *d* 20 Jan 1923

4a Henrietta; *m* 17 April 1895 Maj Arthur Dillon Denis Kelly, The O'Kelly (*d* 14 March 1936), Border Regt, est s of Gen Sir Richard Denis Kelly, KCB, of Mucklon, Ahascragh, Co Galway, and *dsp* 3 Jan 1939

(3) Thomas Clotworthy (Rev); *b* 1818; *m* 20 Feb 1841 Henrietta Catherine (*m* 2nd 18 March 1869 Edwin Arnold; *d* 16 Nov 1891), dau of 3rd Baron Dufferin and Clandeboye (*qv*), and *d* 20 Dec 1862, having had, with other issue:

1a Hungerford Clotworthy; *b* 8 April 1850; *m* 30 Dec 1878 Grace Marie Ruttinger and *d* 21 March 1881, leaving:

1b Hungerford Colwood Clotworthy; *b* 16 April 1879

1b Agnes Mary Grace Cecilia; *b* 7 Aug 1880

1a Alice Victoire; *m* 29 March 1865 Capt Samuel Henry Harford (*d* 14 March 1914 aged 99), Cape Mounted Rifles, 3rd s of Henry Charles Harford, of Frenchay Lodge, Glos, and *d* 7 Nov 1871

2a Agnes Elizabeth; *m* 14 Dec 1903 Lt-Gen William Henry Bradford, Col Roy Irish Rifles, and *d* 11 June 1910

(1) Harriet Margaretta; *m* 9 Dec 1843 David Ross (*d* 5 Nov 1866), of Rostrevor, Co Down, and *d* 31 Oct 1883 aged 67, having had issue

(2) Anne Elizabeth; *m* 15 March 1836 Robert Foster Dunlop, JP (*d* 11 Nov 1875), of Monasterboice, Co Louth, and *d* 1 June 1901, having had issue

(3) Elizabeth Mary; *m* 14 June 1854 William Thomas Poe, MA (*d* 14 Feb 1892), barrister, of Curraghmore, Co Tipperary, 2nd s of Rev James Hill Poe, Rector Nenagh, Co Tipperary, and *dsp* 19 June 1878, leaving issue

The 2nd VISCOUNT FERRARD's est s,

JOHN FOSTER later SKEFFINGTON (1843), **10th Viscount Massereene** and **3rd Viscount Ferrard**, KP (1851); *b* 30 Nov 1812; *educ* Eton and Ch Ch Oxford; *m* 1 Aug 1835 Olivia Deane (*d* 10 May 1874), 4th dau of Henry Deane Grady, of Lodge, Co Limerick, and Stillorgan Castle, Co Dublin, and *d* 28 April 1863, leaving:

1 CLOTWORTHY JOHN EYRE, **11th and 4th Viscount**

2 Hungerford Henry; *b* 25 July 1845; *m* 30 Nov 1868 his cousin Louisa Muskerry Deane (*m* 2nd Á Stepney; *d c* 1920), dau of Robert Deane Grady, and *dsp* 18 Dec 1870

3 Sydney William; *b* 30 May 1849; *m* 3 Oct 1872 Clementina Isabella Margaret (*m* 2nd 14 Feb 1885 Col James Craig (*dsp* 15 Oct 1910); *d* 2 Dec 1937), yr dau of Archibald Campbell Dennistoun of that Ilk, of Dunbartonshire and Park Hill, Torquay, and *d* 6 Feb 1876, having had:

(1) Florence Clementina, JP (Notts); *b* 23 July 1873; *m* 1st 21 Sept 1905 Lt-Col George Brenton Laurie, Roy Irish Rifles (*ka* Neuve Chapelle 14 March 1915; she added by deed poll 1 June 1915 name VERE), 2nd s of Lt-Gen John Winburn Laurie, CB, MP, and had:

1a George Halliburton Foster Peel, JP (1952), DL (Notts 1948), High Sheriff 1957; *b* 22 Aug 1906; *educ* Eton and RMC Sandhurst, Maj 9th Lancers, Lt-Col Roy Mil Police, WW II, Freeman City London, memb Court Assistants Saddlers' Co (Master 1965), Jt MFH S Notts 1956–68; *m* 1st 2 July 1932 (*divorce* 1968) Caroline Judith, yr dau of Edward Francklin JP, of Gonalston Hall, Notts; *m* 2nd 1968 (*divorce* 197–) Bridget Mary, dau of F Arthur Good; *m* 3rd 1979 *Joyce Mary Letts [Mrs George Vere-Laurie, The Dower House, Carlton-on-Trent, Newark, Notts] and *d* 1981, leaving by his 1st w:

1b *George Edward, DL (Notts 1993) [Lt-Col George Vere-Laurie DL, Carlton Hall, Carlton-on-Trent, Newark, Notts NG23 6NW]; *b* 3 Sept 1935; *educ* Eton and RMA Sandhurst, Lt-Col 9th/12th Lancers; *m* 1st 2 June 1962 (*divorce*1977) Georgina Nefert, dau of Maj Anthony Claud Riall; *m* 2nd 19– *Barbara Ann Tweed and by his 1st w has:

1c *George Anthony; *b* 8 May 1963

1c *Georgina Sylvia [Mrs Martin Hale, The Red House, Church Corner, Raydon, Suffolk IP7 5LW]; *b* 25 June 1965; *m* 1990 *C Martin Hale, only s of C Hale, and has:

1d *James George Hale; *b* 1991

2d *William Edward Hale; *b* 1992

3d *Frederick Clifford Hale; *b* 1994

1b *(Florence) Mary, JP [Mrs Christopher Fagan JP, Deane Hill House, Deane, Hants RG25 3AX]; *b* 11 Sept 1939; Ld Lt Hants 1994–; *m* 21 Oct 1960 *Capt Christopher Tarleton Feltrim Fagan, late Gren Gds, only s of Capt Christopher Frederick Feltrim Fagan, AMICE, and has:

1c Christopher Hugh Tarleton Feltrim; *b* 1964; Capt Grenadier Gds; *d* in a car crash 1987

2c *James Tarleton Feltrim; *b* 1965; Capt Greadier Gds

2a Sydney John Athelstane; *b* 10 July 1910; Hon Fell LCM, Freeman City London, Dir Imp Opera Co; *d* 1994

1a *Eleanor Blanche Helen Margaretta [Mrs Andrew Johnstone, Apt 312, 4646 Sherbrooke St West, Westmount, Quebec H32 22A, Canada]; *b* 21 Dec 1907; Freeman City London; *m* 15 Nov 1932 Andrew Wauchope Johnstone (*see* JOHNSTONE, Bt) and has issue

(1) (cont.) Mrs George Vere-Laurie *m* 2nd 17 Aug 1940 her cousin **12th Viscount Massereene** and **5th Viscount Ferrard** (*see* below) and *d* 14 Dec 1978

(2) Evelyn Isabella; *b* 7 July 1874; *d* 20 July 1887

(3) Mabel Anna Mary; *b* 8 Sept 1875; *m* 15 Jan 1919 Rev Francis Bartlett Proctor (*d* 16 March 1930), Fell King's Coll London, Rector Rishangles, Suffolk, and *d* 12 Feb 1938

4 Reginald George; *b* 5 Oct 1850; *d* 21 Feb 1873

1 Dorcas Louisa; *m* 8 July 1869 Percy FitzGerald (*d* 24 Nov 1925 aged 96), barrister, of Fane Valley, Co Louth, only surv s of Thomas FitzGerald, MP Co Louth, and *d* 27 Sept 1876

2 Olivia Margaretta Mary; *d* unm 13 Oct 1914

3 Florence Cecilia; *d* unm 4 Jan 1906

4 Blanche Amelia; *m* 6 Jan 1870 her cousin Lt-Col Sir John Foster George Ross, KCB, KCVO, Coldstream Gds (*d* 10 July 1926), of Rostrevor House, Rostrevor, Co Down, and *d* 8 Feb 1938

The 10th and 3rd VISCOUNT's est s,

CLOTWORTHY JOHN EYRE SKEFFINGTON, **11th Viscount Massereene** and **4th Viscount Ferrard**; *b* 9 Oct 1842; Lt Co Louth and Drogheda, Lt-Col Antrim Militia; *m* 4 Oct 1870 Florence Elizabeth (*d* 14 Oct 1929), only child of Maj George John Whyte-Melville, and *d* 26 June 1905, having had:

1 Oriel John Clotworthy Whyte-Melville; *b* 10 Oct 1871; barrister, Capt 4th Bn Roy Irish Rifles; *d* unm 30 April 1905

2 ALGERNON WILLIAM JOHN CLOTWORTHY, **12th and 5th Viscount**

1 Norah Florence Margaretta; *b* 15 Dec 1872; *m* 24 July 1897 Rev Charles Johnston (*d* 1942), Vicar Eaton Bray, Beds, and *d* 10 Feb 1944, leaving:

(1) Algernon George Henry; *b* 1899; *m* 1926 Eileen Magdalene, dau of — Kearney, of Creagh House, Doneraile, Co Cork, and *d* 1948, leaving:

1a *Anthony James Rex; *b* 1931

1a *Rosemary Margaretta Norah; *b* 1929

2a *Gabrielle; *b* 1943

(2) John Edward Arthur; *b* 1902; *m* 1933 *Grietje, yst dau of Jelle Zoethout, of Leeuwarden, Holland, and *d* 1958, leaving:

1a Michael John Anthony; *b* 1939; *m* 1965 *Myrtle Stevens, of Springs, S Africa, and *d* 1965, leaving:

1b *Craig Alastair; *b* 1964

2a *Peter Charles Anthony; *b* 1945; *m* 1967 *Deborah Jane, dau of John Wilding, and has:

1b *Christopher John; *b* 1970

1b *Katharine Ann; *b* 1973

2b *Susan Margaret; *b* 1974

2 Ethel Mary Catherine; *b* 12 Jan 1876; *m* 20 April 1904 Richard Altherton d'Anyers Willis (*d* 18 July 1823), of Halstead Park, Lancs, s of Henry Rodolph d'Anyers Willis, JP, DL, of Halstead Park, and *d* 27 May 1960, leaving:

(1) Charles Rodolph d'Anyers; *b* 1907; *m* 1936 Ursula (*m* 2nd 1963 Maj E J Fitz-Gerald, Coldstream Gds), only child of Brig-Gen Sir Robert Harvey Kearsley, KCVO, CMG, DSO (*see* PETO, Bt, of Somerleyton), and *d* 1961, leaving:

1a *Martin Atherton d'Anyers; *b* 1939; *educ* Eton

2a *Julian Charles d'Anyers [Julian Willis Esq, 53 Halford Rd, Durban, S Africa]; *b* 1945; *m* 1972 *Gillian Curtis, er dau of Earle Smith, of Pietermaritzburg, and has:

1b *Sean d'Anyers; *b* 1974

1a *Caroline Ann d'Anyers [Mrs Caroline Thorne, 2 Sandways Cottage, Bourton, Gillingham, Dorset]; *b* 1945; *m* 1st 1960 (*divorce* 1967) Col Dudley Lancelot Guy Carleton Smith (*d* 1984); *m* 2nd 1967 (*divorce* 1971) Richard Courtenay Thorne and by him has:

1b *David Courtenay; *b* 1968

(1) Winifred Alice d'Anyers; *b* 1910; *m* 1934 Lt-Col Count Peter Francis de Salis, Coldstream Gds (*d* 1982), and *d* 1977, leaving:

1a *Richard John [Maj Richard de Salis, Holly Hatch, Owslebury, Hants SO21 1LN]; *b* 1935; *educ* Downside and Trin Coll Cambridge (BA); Maj RA; *m* 1959 *Susan Elizabeth, dau of Cdr G H Thompson, RN, and has:

1b *Peter John Francis [Peter de Salis Esq, 52 Charlwood Rd, London SW15 1PZ]; *b* 1964; *educ* Downside; Capt RGBW (TA); *m* 1996 *Susan Mary, dau of John D Porter

1b *Elizabeth Mary [Mrs Charles Hezlet, Lingcroft House, Plealey, Shrewsbury, Salop SY5 0XT]; *b* 1961; *m* 1988 *Charles Tyson Richard Hezlet, s of Charles Maitland Richard Hezlet, and has:

1c *Charles Salis Richard; *b* 1990

2c *Edward Salis William; *b* 1992

2b *Jane Sarah [Mrs Rudolf Bihr, Altes Jagdhaus, Unterniesenberg, 5625 Kallern, Switzerland]; *b* 1962; *educ* St Mary's Shaftesbury and U of Bath (BSc Hort); landscape architect; BSLA; *m* 1986 *Rudolf Bihr, s of R Bihr, of Wädenswil, Switzerland, and has:

1c *Sophia Violanta; *b* 1992

3b *Anne Francis; *b* 1970

2a *Bernard Peter [Lt-Cdr Bernard de Salis RN, 12 Park Vista, London SE10 9LZ]; *b* 1936; *educ* Downside and RNC Dartmouth; Lt-Cdr RN; *m* 1967 *Monica Juanita, yst dau of Cdr Robert Tatton Bower, RN (*see* 1970 edn STRICKLAND, B), and has:

1b *Piers Robert; *b* 1969

2b *Hugo John; *b* 1971

3a *Nicholas George [Nicholas de Salis Esq, 20 Belmont Hill, London SE13]; *b* 1938; *educ* Downside; *m* 1964 *Norma Christine, dau of Maj C H Dennis, RAMC, and has:

1b *Alexander Edward; *b* 1969

2b *Christian Henry; *b* 1973

4a *James Anthony [James de Salis Esq, Fern Cottage, Milton-under-Wychwood, Oxon]; *b* 1949; *educ* Downside; *m* 1987 *Helen Margaret Guy

5a Thomas Peter [Thomas de Salis Esq, 26 Eastwell Close, Paddock Wood, Kent]; *b* 1950; *educ* Downside

3 Constance Harriet Georgina; *b* 15 May 1877; *m* 8 Nov 1905 Maj Herbert Rushton Sykes (*d* 15 March 1952), JP, only s of Arthur Henry Sykes, DL, of Lydham Manor, Salop (*see* 1940 edn SYKES, Bt, of Cheadle), and *d* 24 Feb 1965, leaving:

(1) *(Arthur) Patrick, MBE (1945), JP and DL Salop; *b* 1906; *educ* Eton and Magdalene Coll Cambridge (BA 1928); Lt Col KRRC WW II (wounded), High Sheriff 1961–62; *m* 1st 1936 (*divorce* 1967) Prudence Margaret, est dau of Maj-Gen Donald Elphinston Robertson, CB, DSO; *m* 2nd 1968 *Katharine Diana Bartlett and has by his 1st w:

1a *William; *b* 1939; *m* 1970 *Pamela Strickland Skailes and has:

1b *Camilla; *b* 1971

2b *Angela; *b* 1973

2a *(Gillian Diana) Juniper [Mrs John Greener, Langebride House, Long Bredy, Dorset DT2 9HU]; *b* 1937; *m* 1964 *Maj (William) John Martin Greener, OBE, DL, and has:

1b *James; *b* 1967

1b *Juliet; *b* 1970

(2) Humphrey Hugh; *b* 1907; *educ* Rugby; Maj 9th Lancers; *m* 1st 1936 (*divorce* 1948) Grizel Sophie, dau of AVM Sir Norman Duckworth Kerr MacEwen, CB, CMG, DSO; *m* 2nd 1958 *Muriel, dau of Col John Charles Hooper, DSO, and *d* 1991, leaving by his 1st w:

1a *Richard; *b* 1940

2a *Alexander; *b* 1942

1a *Jane; *b* 1938; *m* 1963 *John Deen and has:

1b *Emma Sophie Louise; *b* 1964

2a *Annabelle; *b* 1944

(2) *Robin George,TD [Col Robin Sykes TD, Greenwood, Shotley Bridge, Co Durham]; *b* 1917; *educ* Eton and Ch Ch Oxford (MA, BM BCh, DA, FFARCS); Col RAMC (TA), HM Hon Surg 1964; *m* 1947 *Jean, dau of H Cunningham, and has:

1a *Edward Colin Richard; *b* 1952

1a *Gillian; *b* 1950

4 Winifred Kathleen Rachel; *b* 3 Sept 1878; *d* unm 10 Oct 1909

5 Violet Florence; *b* 9 Nov 1879; *m* 20 June 1907 Corbet Radford (*d* 4 Aug 1934), yst s of Capt Frederick Radford, and *d* 19 May 1947, leaving issue

The 11th and 4th VISCOUNT's only surv s,

ALGERNON WILLIAM JOHN CLOTWORTHY WHYTE-MELVILLE SKEFFINGTON, **12th Viscount Massereene** and **5th Viscount Ferrard**, DSO (1900), JP and DL Co Antrim; *b* 28 Nov 1873; *educ* Winchester and RMC Sandhurs; Lt-Col NI Horse Yeo, Maj 17th Lancers, Boer War 1899–1902 (wounded, despatches, brevet) and WW I (despatches), Lt Co Antrim 1916–38, Pres TA&AFA, Parly Sec to PM NI, Memb Senate NI 1921–29, Hon Col 188th (Antrim) Heavy Bn RA (TA) 1937–56; *m* 1st 16 Feb 1905 Jean Barbara, JP (*d* 11 Dec 1937), er dau of Sir Stirling Ainsworth, 1st Bt (*qv*); *m* 2nd 17 Aug 1940 his cousin Florence Clementina, dau of Hon Sydney William Skeffington (*see* above), and *d* 20 July 1956, having by his 1st w had:

1 A son; *b* and *d* 24 April 1910

2 JOHN CLOTWORTHY TALBOT WHYTE-MELVILLE SKEFFINGTON, **13th Viscount Massereene** and **6th Viscount Ferrard**, DL (Co Antrim 1957); *b* 22

Oct 1914; *educ* Eton; Lt Black Watch (invalided 1940), Small Vessels Pool 1944, Freeman City London, memb Shipwrights' Co, Gold Staff Offr in Waiting Coronation 1953, memb Inter-Parly Union Delegn Spain 1960; *m* 15 March 1939 *Annabelle Kathleen, er dau of Henry David Lewis, of Combwell Priory, Kent, and *d* 1992, leaving:

(1) JOHN DAVID CLOTWORTHY WHYTE-MELVILLE FOSTER SKEFFINGTON, **14th and present Viscount Massereene and (7th Viscount) Ferrard**

(1) *Oriel Annabelle Diana Clotworthy Whyte-Melville [The Hon Mrs Stratford, Gt Paddock Farm, Challock, Kent]; *b* 6 Feb 1950; *m* 1st 4 Feb 1971 (*divorce* 1989) Dominik Luczyc-Wyhowski, er s of S J L Luczyc-Wyhowski, of Wooden, Kelso, Roxburghshire; *m* 2nd 1992 *Michael Francis Stratford and has by her 1st husb:

  1a *Sofia Oriel Laura; *b* 1973

  2a *Kassia Annabelle Susan; *b* 1980

1 Diana Elizabeth Margaret Clotworthy; *b* 12 Feb 1909; *d* unm 6 Nov 1930

MASSY

Arms: Argent on a chevron between three lozenges sable a lion passant or. **Crest:** Out of a ducal coronet or a bull's head gules, armed, sable. **Supporters:** Dexter, a lion; sinister, a leopard regardant, both proper and collared and chained or.
Motto: *Pro libertate patriæ* ('For my country's freedom').
Creation: B. (I) 4 Aug 1776.

THE 9TH BARON MASSY OF DUNTRILEAGUE, Co Limerick (Hugh Hamon John Somerset Massy); *b* 11 June 1921; *s f* 1958; *educ* Clongowes Wood Coll and Clayesmore Sch; Pte RAOC WW II; *m* 18 Sept 1943 *Margaret, dau of John Flower, of Barry, Co Meath, and has:

1 +DAVID HAMON SOMERSET; *b* 4 March 1947; *educ* St George's Coll Weybridge; Merchant Navy

2 +John Hugh Somerset; *b* 2 Jan 1950; *m* 1978 *Andrea, dau of Alan West, of Leicester

3 +Graham Ingoldsby Somerset; *b* 28 March 1952

4 +Paul Robert Somerset; *b* 18 Oct 1953; *m* 1976 *Anne Bridget, dau of James McGowan, of Leicester, and has:

  (1) +Kevin Hames Somerset; *b* 1978

  (2) +Colin Hugh Somerset; *b* 1979

1 *Sheelagh Louise Marie; *b* 10 Nov 1958

Lineage: HUGH MASSY, mil cdr putting down 1641 Uprising; *m* Margaret Percy and had:

HUGH MASSY, of Duntrileague, Co Limerick; *m* Amy, dau of John Benson, and had:

1 HUGH

2 John, of Knockaneevan, Co Limerick

3 William, of Stoneville, Co Limerick

4 Charles; Dean Limerick; had issue (*see* 1970 edn MASSY Bt)

1 Margaret; *m* William Baker

2 Amy; *m* George Benson

HUGH MASSY's est s,

  Col HUGH MASSY, of Duntrileague; *b* 1685; *m* Elizabeth, dau of George Evans, PC, and sis of 1st Baron Carbery (*qv*), and had, with four daus:

1 HUGH, **1st Baron**

2 George (Ven); Archdeacon Ardfert; *m* Jane, dau of Simon Purdon, and *dsp* March 1782

3 John; *k* in a duel

4 Godfrey (Rev); Preb Dysart; *m* his cousin Margaret, dau of William Baker, of Lismacue, and was ancestor of the MASSYs of Kingswell, Co Tipperary, and MASSYs of Granstown Hall

5 William; *m* Mary, dau of Eyre Evans, of Portrane, and *dsp* 1777

6 EYRE MASSY, 1st BARON CLARINA OF ELM PARK (*see* 1949 edn)

Col HUGH MASSY's est s,

  HUGH MASSY, **1st Baron Massy of Duntrileague** (I), so *cr* 4 Aug 1776; *b* 1700; Sheriff Co Limerick 1739, MP Co Limerick 1759–76 and Old Leighlin 1776; *m* 1st by 1733 Mary, dau and heiress of Col James Dawson, of Ballynacourte, Co Tipperary, and had:

1 HUGH, **2nd Baron**

2 James, of Ballynacourte; *b* Oct 1736; *m* Mary (*d* 26 May 1805), dau of John Leonard, of Carha, Co Galway, and Brownestown, Co Kildare, and *d* Dec 1790, leaving:

(1) James Hewitt MASSY later MASSY-DAWSON (roy licence 4 April 1827), of Ballynacourte, MP; *b* 13 Sept 1779; *m* 11 March 1800 Eliza Jane (*d* 14 March 1834), dau of Francis Dennis, of Jamaica, and *d* 2 Oct 1834, leaving, with other issue:

  1a Francis Dennis; *b* 23 Sept 1803; *m* 1st 6 Aug 1829 Susan (*d* 17 Sept 1856), dau of 4th/13th Lord Sinclair (*qv*), and had:

    1b Francis Staunton MASSY-DAWSON later STAUNTON-MASSY (deed poll 16 Aug 1924); *b* 27 Dec 1840; *m* 2 Aug 1870 Julia Eliza (*d* 4 Nov 1937), only dau of T C Gilmour, of New Orleans, and *d* 11 Dec 1908, leaving:

      1c Francis Evelyn, DSO; *b* 9 Sept 1872; Capt RN Boer War 1899–1902 (medal with three clasps), Gambia Expdn 1901 (despatches, medal, clasp) and WW I (despatches), Legn Honour, Cdr Orders Crown Romania and St Stanislas Russia; *m* 1st 1922 Emily Banner Clough (*d* 1 Feb 1928), dau of Lt-Cdr Somerset James Johnstone (*see* JOHNSTONE, Bt) and widow of Capt Herbert Algernon Adam, CBE, RN; *m* 2nd 14 April 1928 Mary Caroline (*d* 1950), dau of Herbert Taylor, and *d* 12 Feb 1939, leaving by her:

        1d +Francis Patrick; *b* 7 June 1934; *educ* Oundle; RN and RAF; *m* 10 June 1961 *Anne Marie, dau of Walter Henry Heritage, and has:

          1e *Suzanne; *b* 25 Oct 1963

          2e *Nicola Jane; *b* 21 Dec 1965

        1d *Rosemarie Julia; *b* 25 July 1933; *m* Nov 1961 *John William Halse, geologist

      2c Charles Godfrey; *b* 30 Sept 1873; T/2nd Lt Gen List, RFC; *m* 5 Sept 1903 Wilhelmina Geraldine, est dau of Samuel Haughton, Ceylon CS, and *d* 20 Aug 1936, leaving:

        1d Dennis Staunton; *b* 6 Dec 1909; Lt RN WW II; *m* 15 July 1939 Jean Mary (*m* 2nd 29 Sept 1941 Cdr (S) Alan Melville Ackery, OBE, RN), er dau of Lt-Col William Kentigern Hamilton-Campbell, DSO, DL, and was *ka* Jan 1940

        1d Nora St Clair; *b* 19 Sept 1904

        2d Morna Helena Casey; *b* 17 May 1915; *m* 9 Oct 1942 Lt-Col Derek Boileau Lang, DSO, MC, Cameron Highrs, and *d* 20 Aug 1953, leaving issue

      3c Robert Henry; *b* 13 Oct 1874 T/2nd Lt Gen List; *m* 1 June 1920 Elsie Mary Catherine (*d* 25 May 1933), only dau of John R Mackenzie and widow of Arthur Chambers Cordery, and *dsp* 27 May 1942

      1c Agnes Anne; *b* 24 June 1871; *m* 6 April 1910 Percy Charles Tweedie (*d* 1 Oct 1938), 3rd s of James Tweedie of Quarter, DL, and *d* 1 Oct 1957, leaving issue

    1b Mary Agnes; *d* 18 Oct 1859

    2b Jane Isabella; *m* 22 July 1856 the Chevalier D Pantaleone (*d* 1885) and had issue

    3b Susan St Clair; *m* 1 Jan 1857 Joseph Lewis Franklin and *dsp* 20 Oct 1857

  1a (cont.) Francis Massy-Dawson *m* 2nd 20 March 1861 Harriet (*d* 26 March 1867), only dau of Thomas Sparke Griffinhoof, of Arkesden, and *d* 16 Nov 1870, having by her had:

    4b Lilian Harriet; *m* 21 Jan 1891 Rev Edward Arthur Bagot

  2a George Staunton King, of Ballynacourte, JP, DL; High Sheriff Co Tipperary 1854; *b* 30 Nov 1816; Capt 14th Light Dragoons; *m* 1st 5 Sept 1854 Grace Elizabeth (*d* 9 Nov 1865), 2nd dau of Sir William Leeson (*see* 1970 edn MILLTOWN, E), and had:

    1b James; *b* 26 Jan 1857; Lt 3rd Dragoon Gds; *m* 4 March 1886 Alice, widow of J James Ingram, and *dsp* 1 Dec 1891

    2b George Henry Edward, of Ballynacourte, JP; *b* 8 Oct 1864; *m* 25 Sept 1894 Rosalie Margaretta, dau of Jean Hunziker, and *dsp* 13 Sept 1916

    1b Louisa Elizabeth; *b* 20 March 1867

    2b Grace Catherine Rose, CBE (1919); *m* 26 April 1881 Carew Davies Gilbert, JP, DL (*d* 1 Dec 1913), of Trelissick, Cornwall, and *d* 8 July 1951, leaving issue

    3b Maira Isabel; *m* 2 Oct 1894 Ven Thomas E Lindsay, Canon York, Archdeacon Cleveland, and *d* 31 March 1938

  2a (cont.) George Massy-Dawson *m* 2nd 20 May 1869 Harriett Sophia (*d* 5 Jan 1892), dau of Walter Steele, of Monalty, Co Monaghan; *m* 3rd 10 Jan 1893 Eliza (*d* 5 April 1920), dau of Rev James Rynd, Rector Galbally, and widow of George Eyre Massy, of Riversdale, Limerick (*see* below), and *d* 14 Nov 1897

  1a Mary Jane; *m* 12 July 1821 George Evelyn (*d* 15 Feb 1829), of Wotton, Surrey, and had issue

  2a Anna Maria; *m* 1st 16 May 1833 Robert Montague Poore (*see* POORE, Bt); 2nd 9 Dec 1839 Mark Anthony Saurin (*dsp* 3 July 1862) and *d* 15 May 1865

  3a Elizabeth Rosetta; *m* 1st 13 April 1828 Eyre Coote, of West Park, Hants (*d* 30 May 1834), and had issue (*see* COOTE, Bt); *m* 2nd 10 Sept 1842 R-Adml Armar Lowry Corry (*d* 1 May 1855), was granted precedence of a KCB's widow 1856 and *d* 7 Jan 1858, leaving issue

    4a Isabella Palmer; *m* 2 Aug 1838 Capt R D Dunn, 2nd Dragoon Gds, and *d* 19 Jan 1860

  5a Louisa Susan; *m* 15 Aug 1839 Edward O'Brien (*see* INCHIQUIN, B) and *d* 20 March 1908, leaving issue

(1) Elizabeth; *m* Robert Compton Bolton

(2) Maria; *m* Robert Bomford, of Rakinston, Co Meath, and had issue

3 John; *m* Elizabeth, sis of William Baker, of Lismacue, Co Limerick, and *dsp*

1 Elizabeth; *m* 1st John Arthure, of Seafield, Co Dublin; *m* 2nd Sir Michael Cox, Bt

The **1st Baron** *m* 2nd 16 April 1754 Rebecca, dau of Francis Delap, of Antigua, and *d* 30 Jan 1788, having by her had, with other issue:

4 Francis Hugh; *b* 13 Jan 1755; *m* 7 July 1777 Jane (*d* Aug 1813), only dau of William Cullum, of Dublin, and had:

(1) Francis Hugh, of Suir Castle, Co Tipperary; *m* Anne Bomford, dau of Daniel Molloy, and had:

1a Francis Hugh; *m* 14 Feb 1889 Gertrude Masterton (*d* 29 July 1919), only child of Capt Walter, 26th Cameronians, and *d* 3 March 1901, leaving issue

2a Daniel Molloy; Col Tipperary Art Militia; *m* 21 Oct 1876 Sophia (*d* 16 July 1919), dau of Alexander Grant and widow of William Massy, of Ballyglasheen, Co Tipperary (*see below*), and *dsp* 31 Oct 1908

1a Anne Bomford; *m* 21 Sept 1871 John Henry St George Whitty, of Ballintobber, Queen's Co

2a Jane Adelaide; *m* 29 April 1886 Austin Damer Cooper, of Drumnigh, JP, and *d* his widow 3 April 1906

3a Harriet; *m* Thomas Whitby and *d* 1869

5 Eyre; *b* 13 Feb 1757; *m* 1st Elizabeth, dau and heiress of John Leighton, and had:

(1) Anne; *m* Surgn — Doran

(2) Rebecca; *m* Harmon Gibborne, of Coolnagore, and had issue

(3) Elizabeth; *m* John Steele, of Kyle Park, and had issue

(4) Matilda Frances; *m* Richard Sadleir (*d* 1835), of Sadleir's Wells, Co Tipperary; *m* 2nd Rev Dawson-Massy and had issue (*see* 1949 edn CLARINA OF ELM PARK, B)

(5) Grace; *m* Oliver Mills, of Castlelake, Co Tipperary, and had issue

5 (cont.) Eyre Massy *m* 2nd Phoebe, dau of Gen John Head, and *d* Nov 1828, having by her had:

(6) Phoebe Letitia; *m* 20 Sept 1836 John Massy (*d* 23 Oct 1866), of Stagdale, Co Limerick, and had issue (*see* 1949 edn CLARINA OF ELM PARK, B)

6 George; *b* 19 Aug 1765; *m* 1st July 1787 Elizabeth (*d* 1819), est dau of Abel Onge, of Haystown, Co Dublin; *m* 2nd Constance (*dsp* 3 Dec 1819), dau of — Crone; *m* 3rd Elizabeth Lane (*d* 19 March 1838), widow of (a) 2nd Earl of Massereene (*see* MASSEREENE and FERRARD, V) and (b) George Doran, and *d* 13 Aug 1834, having had by his 1st w:

(1) Robert George, of Caervillahow, Golden, Cashel, Co Tipperary; *m* Helen (*d* 12 April 1859), dau of James Sutton, of Toxteth Park, Liverpool, and had:

1a William, of Caervillahow and Ballyglasheen, Co Tipperary; *b* 18 Feb 1815; *m* 30 Sept 1857 Sophia (*m* 2nd 21 Oct 1876 Col Daniel Molloy Massy (*d* 31 Oct 1908), dau of Alexander Grant, of New Brunswick, and *d* 22 July 1875, having had:

1b Godfrey Warburton, of Caervillahow; *b* 27 April 1863; Capt Roy Irish Rifles Boer War 1900–01; *m* 27 Dec 1904 Gertrude Annette Seton, only dau of Lt-Gen William Godfrey Dunham Massy, CB, DL, of Grantstown, Co Tipperary, and widow of Col James George Cockburn

2b George William Hughes; *b* 16 June 1864; *m* 1st 1889 Edith Margaret (*d* 1910), dau of John Birrell, and had:

1c Marjorie Geraldine; *b* 1890; *m* 1925 Hon Arthur Read Slipp (*d* 1958), County Court Judge

2c Muriel Frances; *b* 2 Oct 1891; *m* 1914 William Morrison McKie and had issue

2b (cont.) George Massey [*sic*] *m* 2nd 28 May 1912 Marion (*m* 2nd 1935 Brig Jesse (Jake) Pevensey Duke, DSO, MC, Roy Warwicks Regt; *d* 1973), dau of George Bryson Clarke, of Petton Grange, Salop, and *d* 19 June 1914, having by her had:

1c +Patrick Godfrey Goolden, MC (1945) [Lt-Col Patrick Massey MC, Arawai House, Liss, Hants GU33 7PB]; *b* 15 March 1913; *educ* Harrow and RMC Sandhurst; Hodson's Horse IA 1933, WW II India, Iraq, Iran and Burma (despatches), Lt-Col 5th/10th Baluch Regt, Cmdt Govr-Gen's Body Gd 1946, Lt-Col Roy Dragoons; *m* 1st 4 March 1941 Bessie Lee (*d* 1978), yst dau of W J Byrne, and has:

1d +Hamon Patrick Dunham [Col Hamon Massey, Pollachar, Isle of S Uist, Outer Hebrides]; *b* 18 Aug 1950; *educ* Harrow and RMC Sandhurst; Col Blues and Royals, cmdg Household Cavalry Mounted Regt 1992–95, Mil Attaché Buenos Aires 1997–; *m* 1st 1973 (*divorce* 1987) Caroline (*d* 1988), dau of Lt-Col George Baker, and has:

1e +Edward Hamon; *b* 1976

1e *Eleanore Joan Diana; *b* 1977

1d (cont.) Col Hamon Massey *m* 2nd 1988 *Mrs Cathleen Teresa Poole, dau of Neil Campbell, of Benbecula, and has:

2e *Lee; *b* 1989

3e *Garda; *b* 1990

2d +Peregrine Tatton Eyre [Peregrine Massey Esq, Boldshaves, Woodchurch, Ashford, Kent]; *b* 14 June 1952; *educ* Harrow and Magdalene Coll Cambridge (MA), barrister Middle Temple 1975; *m* 1977 *Deirdre Mary, est dau of Capt Spencer Heneage Drummond, DSC, RN (*see* PERTH, E), and has:

1e *Emma Rachel Lee; *b* 1981

2e *Alexandra Clare Louise; *b* 1983

3e +Laura Helena Ruth; *b* 1986

3d +William Greville Sale, QC (1996) [William Massey Esq QC, 30 Brodrick Rd, London SW17 7DY; The Barn, Beanacre, Melksham, Wilts]; *b* 31 Aug 1953; *educ* Harrow and Hertford Coll Oxford (MA); barrister Middle Temple 1977; *m* 1978 *Cecilia D'Oyly, 2nd dau of Daniel Edmund Awdry, TD, DL, of Old Manor, Beanacre, Wilts, and has:

1e +Patrick William Edmund; *b* 1983

2e +Richard Daniel Hugh; *b* 1985

3e +Edmund Greville Robert; *b* 1990

3b Hugh Francis; *b* 8 Nov 1866

1b Eva Sophia; *m* 1883 Edwin Richardson Goolden and had issue

2b Lillian; *m* 1890 Maj Anthony Hudson, Manchester Regt, and had issue

3b Helen Blanche; *m* 23 Aug 1898 Frederick Llewellyn Nash and had issue

4b Geraldine; *m* 7 July 1898 George Hugh Chetwood Townsend

5b Maud Constance

2a Joseph Thomas; *b* 26 April 1820; *dsp*

3a Richard; *b* 3 Feb 1824; *m* Anne Barrett and had issue

4a Hugh James; *b* 10 Aug 1826; *m* 21 April 1853 Mary Jane (*d* 14 March 1899), dau of Isaac Darby, and *d* 10 Aug 1899, having had, with other issue:

1b Hugh James; *b* 23 June 1854; *m* 1881 Isabella Rhymers (*d* 2 May 1925), dau of Horatio N Hope, and *d* 23 July 1934, having had:

1c Muriel Alexander; *d* unm 17 April 1909

2c Dolores Garay Hope; *b* 1888; ARRC, Canadian Army Medical Corps WW I

1b Rose Rebecca; *m* 1st 1888 Benjamin Lombard (*d* 16 Jan 1911), of Boston, USA; *m* 2nd 1914 de Putron Gleddon (*d* 1924) and *d* 2 June 1935

1a Helen Rose; *m* 1849 Rev A E Watson and had issue

2a Constance; *m* 6 July 1854 William Steele Studdert, JP (*d* 30 July 1892), and *d* 14 Jan 1911, leaving issue

3a Rebecca; *m* 15 June 1842 Alexander Wood, MD, and *d* 6 Feb 1894

(2) Hugh, of Tullow Lodge, Carlow; *b* 10 July 1800; *m* 11 July 1834 Mary Anne, dau of Maj Beresford Gahan, 5th Dragoons, and *d* 1886, having had, with other issue:

1a Beresford; *b* 15 May 1840; *m* 14 April 1869 Elizabeth Harriet (*d* 1926), dau of Rev G H Read, of Inniskeen Rectory, Dundalk, and *d* 13 March 1878, leaving:

1b Rev Cecil Hugh; *b* 18 April 1870; *educ* Trin Coll Dublin; Curate Staplestown, Co Carlow; *d* unm 1946

2b Sydney Beresford; *b* 18 Feb 1876; Capt Army; *m* 19– Eileen McMahon (*d* 1974), dau of Canon O'Grady, of Bantry, Co Cork, and *d* 1946

1b Frances Mary Georgina; *b* 18–; *d* unm 1955

2b Eva Constance; *b* 18–; *m* 3 Nov 1916 Frederick J Smissen, Lt Roy Irish Rifles, and *d* 1957

2a George Hugh; *b* 9 June 1844; *m* 15 April 1880 Georgina (*d* 1920), dau of George Fenwick, MD, and *d* 10 Jan 1912, leaving, with other issue:

1b Beresford Fenwick; *b* and *d* 1885 (twin)

2b Gordon Eyre; *b* 1886; *m* 1958 Irene Powell and *dsp* 1967

3b Hugh de Hertal; *b* 1893; *ka* 1915 Ypres

1b Mary Charlotte Robertson; *b* 1881; *m* 1914 Charles W Blackham (*d* 1961) and *d* 1950, having had a s (*ka* WW II) and dau

2b Constance Emily; *b* 1885 (twin); *m* 1913 Hugh Nehal Gahan (*d* 1975) and *d* 1970 leaving two sons and two daus

(1) Constance; *m* 5 March 1812 Charles Putland and *d* 26 Oct 1842

(2) Rebecca; *m* Robert Butler and *d* 17 Dec 1878

(3) Frances; *m* 13 Oct 1828 Richard Studdert (*d* 29 April 1870), of Mount Rivers, Co Clare, and had issue

2 Margaret; *m* 1st Godfrey Baker, est s of Godfrey Baker, of Cork, and had issue; *m* 2nd Capt Hugh Wheeler and *d* 1838

3 Rebecca; *m* Rev Godfrey Massy, of Rathkenny

4 Frances; *m* George Robbins, of Hymenstown

5 Caroline; *m* William Butler, of Drom, Co Tipperary, and *d* 1837, leaving issue

The 1st BARON's est s,

HUGH MASSY, **2nd Baron Massy of Duntrileague**; *b* 14 April 1733; *m* Sept 1760 Catherine (*d* 16 Aug 1791), est dau and coheir (with her sis Sarah, Countess of Carrick, *qv*) of Edward Taylor, of Ballynort, Co Limerick, and *d* 10 May 1790, having had:

1 HUGH, **3rd Baron**

2 Edward, of Ballynort; *b* 21 Dec 1766; *m* 29 Jan 1795 Catharine (*d* 29 Jan 1836), dau of John Villiers Tuthill, of St John's Island, Co Limerick, and *d* 2 Jan 1835, leaving:

(1) Edward Taylor, of Cottesmore, Pembs, JP, DL; *b* 4 July 1807; *m* 8 Oct 1835 Helen (*d* 25 July 1888), dau of Jonathan Haworth Peel, of Cottesmore, and *d* 27 July 1882, having had, with other issue:

1a Edward Hugh Hamon, JP Haverfordwest; *b* 6 Sept 1836; *m* June 1856 Ellena Antonia, dau of Giuseppe Buttigeig, of Malta, and *dsp* 31 July 1909

2a Haworth Peel; *b* 10 Oct 1842; Lt 22nd Foot; *m* 12 Aug 1873 Anne Justina, dau of Arthur Lloyd Davies-Lloyd, and *d* 28 Oct 1916, having had, with other issue:

1b John Hamon; *b* 3 March 1879; *ka* 11 Nov 1914

2b Hugh Dillon; *b* 23 Nov 1880

3b Haworth Peel; *b* 31 July 1882; Capt Leinster Regt WW I; *ka* 10 Dec 1914

4b Bertie Errol; *b* 1 Nov 1883; Maj Cheshire Regt WW I (wounded, POW); *m* 5 June 1918 Ine van Enst, widow of H Versteegh

3a Xavier Peel (Rev); *b* 28 Feb 1845; BA Dublin, Rector St Cuthbert's Colinton, Midlothian; *m* 1872 Harriet Emily (*d* June 1931), dau of Edward Hurlstone, and *d* 20 June 1906, having had:

1b Arthur Ernest; *b* 1873; T/Capt RAVC

2b Godfrey; *b* 1879; *m* 22 Aug 1908 Marianne (*d* 1950), er dau of Ezra Gooderidge, of Goole, Yorks, and *d* 1953, leaving:

1c Lawrence Xavier Peel [Lawrence Massy Esq, Box 165, Savona, nr Kamloops, BC, Canada]; *b* 1909; *m* 1934 *Hazel, dau of Edwin Hartt, of Alberta, and has:

1d *Winston; *b* 1936

1d *Marianne Belle; *b* 1938; *m* 19– Edward Heidinger

2c Godfrey Atcherley Peel; *b* 1914; *ka* WW II

3c Robert Alastair Peel; *b* 1918; *m* 1953 Shirley Grania, dau of Clarence James Wylde, MRCS, LRCP

3b Lawrence Peel, DSC (1917); *b* 1883; Lt RNR WW I (despatches); *m* 27 Oct 1914 Constance Jean Anne (*d* Sept 1949), er dau of John James Galletly, and *d* 22 Sept 1932, leaving:

1c Arthur Lawrence John Peel; *b* 12 Jan 1916; Maj W Yorks Regt WW II; *m* 1943 Margaret Alison (*d* 19–), dau of Rev Ernest Bell Sharpe, MA, of Purulia, India, and *d* 1992, having had:

1d +David Lawrence Peel; *b* 28 Nov 1949; Sub Lt (E) RNR; *m* 1976 *Linda, dau of Edgar Clarachan, of Malibu, Calif.

2d +John Eversdon Peel; *b* 15 July 1954

1c *Doreen Constance Peel [Mrs John Woolls, Maipenrai, Sea Dyke Way, Marshchapel, Lincs]; *b* 2 Sept 1919; LRAM, WRNS WW II; *m* 1st 1945 (*divorce* 1956) Conrad Laviolette and has:

1d *Derry Keith; *b* 8 Oct 1951; apprentice artificer RN

1d *Lorna Doreen; *b* 23 Sept 1946; WRNS 1964–68; *m* 23 Sept 1967 *Percival Northcott Skedgell and has:

1e *Elinor Peel; *b* 1971

2e *Lindsey Northcott; *b* 1976

1c (cont.) Mrs Doreen Laviolette *m* 2nd 1959 *John Woolls

2c Desirée Winifred Peel; *b* 9 Jan 1921; *m* 1939 W/Cdr Joseph Cargill Stevenson, RAF, and *d* 23 April 1962, leaving issue

1b Mary Augusta; *m* 1st 9 May 1899 Capt Charles Stanbrough Watson (*d* 16 Nov 1914), RMLI; *m* 2nd 5 June 1920 John Nevill English, only surv s of John Hampden English

2b Laura Gertrude; *m* 1st 5 Aug 1903 Harold MacFarlane (*d* 1919), LRCP, LRCSI, only surv s of William Alexander MacFarlane, MD; *m* 2nd 6 Oct 1920 Philip Peveril John Wodehouse, CIE (*see* KIMBERLEY, E), and *d* 2 Feb 1959

3b Helen Peel

4b Dorothy Peel

5b Marjory Joan; *m* 7 July 1909 Henry Curwen, CBE, MB, ChB, DPH (*d* 14 June 1946), s of Robert E Curwen, and *d* 10 Oct 1962, leaving two sons and two daus

4a Arthur Wellington, JP Pembs; *b* 21 Aug 1846; *m* 1881 Emma Elizabeth Rhys (*d* 22 July 1932), dau of John Stokes, DL, and *d* 6 May 1916, having had:

1b Edward Warren Stokes; *b* 1 Feb 1882; *d* young

2b Hugh Royds Stokes, CB (1940), DSO (1917), MC, JP (1916), DL (1944); *b* 5 Jan 1884; *educ* Bradfield and RMA Woolwich; WW I (despatches) and WW II, Brig S Cmd 1934–38, Dir Mil Trg War Office 1938–39, DCIGS 1939–40, County Commr Boy Scouts 1945–52, Hon Lt-Gen (ret 1943), Col Cmdt RA 1945, High Sheriff Pembs 1946; *m* 12 Nov 1912 Maud Ina Nest (*d* 9 Oct 1960), dau of Col Thomas James Roch, JP, DL, and *d* 21 May 1965, leaving:

1c +Hugh Peter Stokes [Lt-Col Hugh Massy, Long Acre, Owermoigne, Dorset DT2 8HY]; *b* 27 Feb 1914; *educ* Bradfield; Lt-Col RTR WW II (despatches) and Korean War; *m* 10 Oct 1945 Jean (*d* 1993), dau of S/Ldr M G Kidston, of Kenya, and has:

1d *Diana Rosamund; *b* 16 May 1947; *m* 1973 *Lt-Col Philip Eric Scott, 16th/5th Lancers, and has:

1e *James; *b* 1975

2d *Pauline Lorraine [Mrs Richard Scott, 34 Christchurch Rd, Longham, Wimborne, Dorset]; *b* 12 Nov 1951; *m* 1980 *Richard Malcolm Cyril Scott and has:

1e *Louise Sarah; *b* 1984

1c *Mary Nest [Mrs Mary Carter, Fulmar House, Twyford, Dorset]; *b* 1915; *m* 20 Sept 1940 (*divorce* 1947) Gerald Wilfred Charles Carter, RAF, and has:

1d *Miles Richard; *b* 11 Aug 1941

1d *Jandy; *b* 28 Nov 1943; *m* 1975 *Actg Cdr David Andrew Hobbs, MBE, s of A S Hobbs, and has:

1e *Andrew Arthur Duncan; *b* 1978

3b Herbert John; *b* 20 Feb 1885; *m* 18 Nov 1912 Amy, 2nd dau of Lt-Col Esmonde White, and *d* 24 June 1961

4b Charles Walter, CBE (1940), DSO (1918), MC, DL (Mon 1948–51); *b* 2 May 1887; *educ* Cheltenham and RMA Woolwich, Col (Hon Brig) RA WW I (wounded, despatches twice) and WW II, Roy Humane Society's Testimonial for saving life 1924; *m* 1st 1 Sept 1920 Muriel Lorna Bell (*d* 9 Sept 1958), er dau of Joseph Aloysius Hallinan, of Glandalane, Fermoy, Co Cork, and had:

1c +Hugh Charles [Hugh Massy, RR No 1, Box 30, South Woodstock, VT 05071, USA]; *b* 11 June 1921; *m* 12 Jan 1970 *Janice, dau of Maurice de Kay Thompson, of Boston, and widow of Grenville Goodwin

2c +John Royds [Dr John Massy, Hazel Lodge, Hensting Lane, Fishers Pond, Eastleigh, Hants SO50 7HH]; *b* 19 June 1925; *educ* Ampleforth, HMS *Worcester* and King's Coll London (MB, BS), MRCS, LRCP 1960, MCSP 1951, HT 1925, Merchant Navy 1943–48; *m* 2 April 1957 *Eileen Dulcie, dau of F Evans, and has:

1d +David Hugh; *b* 27 Aug 1962

2d +Peter John [Peter Massy Esq, 19 Netley Firs Rd, Hedge End, Hants SO30 4AY]; *b* 17 July 1964; *m* 1987 *Jennifer Freeman and has:

1e +Gregory Hugh; *b* 1995

1e *Helen Clare; *b* 1993

1d *Anne Sarah; *b* 4 Dec 1959; *m* 1991 *Kees de Koning, of Holland, and has:

1e *Robert John; *b* 1995

2e *Christopher Martin; *b* 1997

2d *Clare Muriel [Mrs Jonathan Evans, 34 Crichton Rd, Carshalton Beeches, Surrey SM5 3LS]; *b* 16 Nov 1960; *m* 1991 *Jonathan Brian Evans, s of T J Evans, and has:

1e *Harriet Frances; *b* 1994

2e *Philippa Lucy; *b* 1996

4b (cont.) Charles Massy *m* 2nd 25 Nov 1958 Irene Gillbee (*d* 1990), dau of Richard Gillbee Thorold (*see* THOROLD, Bt) and widow of Dr Clifford Hackney, and *d* 1 June 1973

5a George Eyre (Rev); *b* 25 May 1851; Rector Gumfreston, Pembs; *m* 1 Feb 1877 Katherine Frances (*d* 31 Dec 1912), only child of Surgn-Maj G Brown, and *d* 20 Sept 1905, leaving, with other issue:

1b Villiers Wilfrid Peel; *b* 4 March 1882; Capt 9th Bn Duke of Cornwall's LI; *m* 15 March 1915 Beatrice Emma (*d* 6 Dec 1952), dau of Carlos Vetter, and *d* 1932, leaving:

1c Patrick Wilfrid Villiers, DSO, DSC; *b* 24 Feb 1916; Lt (A) RN WW II; *m* Feb 1942 Ruth (*m* 2nd 25 June 1947 John Campbell Clarke (*d* 17 June 1966) and has issue), dau of Rev Dr Alan Hugh McNeile, and was *ka* 15 Nov 1942

1c *Bridget Ursula Elaine (Jane) [Mrs Leonard Riddett, Half Acre, Witheridge Hill, Highmoor, Oxon RG9 5PE]; *b* 16 Feb 1920; *m* 17 June 1948 *Leonard Arthur Hammond Riddett, MC, s of Arthur Elliott Riddett by Gwendolen Frances, yr dau of John Maude, and has:

1d *John Villiers [John Riddett Esq, 46 Back St, Ashwell, Herts]; *b* 17 Aug 1949; *m* 1985 *Linda Marie West and has:

1e *Paul James Massy; *b* 1990

2e *Guy Edward West; *b* 1992

3e *Leo Patrick; *b* 1995

2d *Patrick Hammond [Patrick Riddett Esq, Box 76, Takaka, NZ]; *b* 9 May 1951

3d *Philip Peel [Philip Riddett Esq, 4 Macquarie Terr, Balmain, NSW, Australia]; *b* 21 May 1957

1d *Sara Caroline [Mrs Dominic Scott, 34 St Andrew's Rd, Henley-on-Thames, Oxon RG9 1JB]; *b* 29 July 1953; *m* 1981 *Dominic Kingsley Eason Scott and has:

1e *Martha Jane; *b* 1983

2e *Jemima; *b* 1986

1b Gladys Mary; *b* 15 Feb 1880; *m* 25 April 1908 Geoffrey Lloyd Jones-Parry (*d* 21 July 1914), yr s of Thomas Parry Jones-Parry JP, DL, and *d* 4 Jan 1971, having had a s and two daus

1a Ellen Catherine; *m* 1st 11 Feb 1863 Rev Charles Henry Barham (*d* 15 Aug 1878), of Trecwn, Pembs; *m* 2nd 20 Nov 1879 Henry Hyde Nugent Bankes (*d* 26 March 1883); *m* 3rd 2 June 1885 Sir William Henry Marsham Style, 9th Bt (*qv*), and *d* 1 Sept 1922

2a Annette Jane; *m* 2 April 1867 William Grinfield Lely, JP (*d* 27 Sept 1886), of Framlingham Hall, Norfolk, and had issue

3a Gertrude; *m* 1st 30 Dec 1875 William CLIFFORD later PHELPS (roy licence Sept 1891 on inheriting property from his unc; *d* 31 May 1906), barrister; *m* 2nd 2 Dec 1909 Capt Maitland R Coleman, Roy London Militia, Lt 6th Dragoons, and *d c* 1912

4a Constance Grace; *m* 3 Dec 1880 Alan Peel (*d* 22 May 1908), s of William Peel, DL, of Taliaris, Carmarths, and *d* Jan 1931, leaving issue

(1) Elizabeth; *m* 1822 Lt-Gen Thomas Gerard Ball and *d* 17 Oct 1852

(2) Catherine; *m* 7 May 1838 John Green, of Cobh, Co Cork

(3) Anna; *m* 11 Sept 1828 Robert Chambre Vaughan (*d* 8 Aug 1876), of Burlton Hall, Salop, and *d* 6 April 1886

(4) Jane; *m* 16 Oct 1827 Thomas Dickin (*d* 1855), of Loppington House, Salop, and *d* 19 Nov 1890

3 George Eyre; *b* 29 July 1772; *m* Dec 1791 Elizabeth (*d* 4 Dec 1844), dau of Michael Scanlan, of Ballynahana, and *d* 29 Jan 1842, leaving:

(1) Hugh, of Riversdale, Co Limerick, JP and DL; High Sheriff 1853; *b* 1796; *m* 6 Nov 1821 Mary Anne (*d* 20 Aug 1869), only dau of Robert Harding, of Cherry Grove, Co Limerick, and *d* 28 Feb 1881, leaving:

1a George Eyre, of Riversdale; *b* 23 Nov 1822; High Sheriff 1885, Lt-Col Roy Limerick Co Militia; *m* 1st 24 Nov 1864 Rose Gertrude (*d* 1 Feb 1869), dau of Thomas de Moleyns, QC (*see* VENTRY, B), and had:

1b Hugh Hamon George, of Riversdale; *b* 17 March 1867; *educ* St Columba's; *m* 7 Nov 1894 Hortense Mary (*d* 30 May 1930), dau of Thomas John Pennefather, of Marlow, Goold's Cross, Co Tipperary, and *d* 9 April 1918, leaving:

1c Hugh Hamon de Moleyns; *b* 20 Aug 1895; *educ* Tipperary GS, King Edward VI Sch Stratford-on-Avon and Trin Coll Dublin; Lt Roy Inniskilling Fus WW I (wounded), Res Offrs 1919, emigrated S Africa 1923; *m* 3 Oct 1923 Helen Violet, dau of Allen Hamilton Morgan, slr, and *d* 1976, having had:

1d +Hugh Allen Oliver [Hugh Massy Esq, PO Box 361, Pietermaritzburg, Natal 3200, S Africa]; *b* 27 Dec 1926; *educ* Michaelhouse Natal; schoolmaster

2d +Evan Eyre Pennefather [Evan Massy Esq, 60 Maclean St, Umkomaas, Natal 4170, S Africa]; *b* 9 Sept 1930; *educ* Cordwalles Sch Pietermaritzburg and Estcourt High Sch; *m* 7 Aug 1965 *Lynette Marion, dau of Arthur Stuart Clark, and has:

1e *Jennifer Lynne; *b* 1 July 1966

2e *Helen Louise; *b* 3 April 1969

1c Noeline Hortense Pennefather; *b* 25 Dec 1906; *m* 1st 12 Dec 1933 Charles Lionel Day (*d* 30 July 1953) and had:

1d Maurice John; *b* 1934; Lt; *d* 1962

1d *Patricia Mary; *b* 1937

1c (cont.) Mrs Charles Day *m* 2nd 1964 Maj Gen Douglas Bluett, CB, OBE, MA, MB, RAMC, s of Rev R D Bluett, of The Rectory, Delgany, Co Wicklow, and *d* 22 July 1971

1b Geraldine; *b* 21 Dec 1865; *d* 8 Feb 1868

1a (cont.) George Massy *m* 2nd 6 July 1871 Eliza (*m* 2nd 10 Jan 1893 George Massy-Dawson, of Ballinacourte; *see* above), 3rd dau of Rev James W Rynd, Rector Galbally, and *d* 26 April 1885, having by her had:

2b James Eyre; *b* 16 Sept 1873; Capt Roy Dublin Fus WW I; *m* 21 May 1903 May Evelyn, dau of John Carmichael, JP, of Tracton Park, Co Cork, and *d* 7 Jan 1952, leaving:

1c George Eyre; *b* 31 July 1914; *m* 4 Nov 1950 *Marella Margaret Helen [Mrs George Massy, 19 Broome St, Nedlands, W Australia], dau of James McQueen, and *d* 1989, having had:

    1d +Timothy James Hamon; *b* 14 Jan 1953; *m* 1983 *Karen Maria, dau of Gerard McCrea, of W Australia, and has:

        1e *Lauren Elizabeth; *b* 1984

    1d *Jacqueline Cynthia; *b* 14 Jan 1952

    2d *Nicola Jane; *b* 17 Oct 1954

1c Beatrice Vera; *b* 2 May 1904; *m* H W Noyle

2c Theodora Patricia; *b* 5 Sept 1912; *m* 31 Jan 1948 Lt-Col Humphrey Rawstone Carmichael, MC, RAOC, 17th Dogra Regt, IA

3c *Cynthia Evelyn [Mrs Eric Reade, Conifers, The Close, Brighton Rd, Sway, Hants SO41 6ED]; *b* 19 July 1916; *m* 1938 *Eric Reade, s of Arthur Reade, DSO, MC, and has:

    1d *Michael Wildin [Michael Reade Esq, 93 Cow St, P Perth 6005, W Australia]; *b* 4 March 1949

    1d *Phyllida Anne [Miss Phyllida Reade, Conifers, The Close, Brighton Rd, Sway, Hants SO41 6ED]; *b* 26 Aug 1946

3b George Robert; *b* 20 March 1875; *d* 8 July 1954

4b Edmund Ingoldsby; *b* 26 April 1876; *m* 7 Dec 1910 Cicely Helen (*d* 23 Aug 1951), yst dau of Robert Ellis Cuncliffe

2b Vera

2a Robert Harding; *b* 12 Nov 1826; *m* 15 April 1874 Harriet Elizabeth, dau of Rev John Fetherstone, of Griffinstown, Co Westmeath, and *d* 20 Dec 1886, leaving:

    1b Everina Susanah Isabel

    2b Violet Augusta Mary; *m* 5 Feb 1902 Thomas A Howe, County Inspr RIC, and had issue

    3b Aileen Ismenia; *m* 17 April 1902 Brig-Gen Herbert Edward Trevor, CMG, DSO, KOYLI (*d* 23 March 1939), er s of Col G H Trevor, CSI

3a Hugh; *b* 20 June 1831; *d* 5 Aug 1887

1a Eliza Mary; *m* 19 April 1860 Lt-Col John Henry Lowndes, MVO (*d* 27 July 1909), 47th Regt, est s of Rev J Lowndes, and *d* 23 June 1907, leaving issue

2a Anne Catherine; *m* 13 March 1884 John Vanderkiste, JP (*d* 1892), and *dsp* 15 June 1918

3a Isabella Margaret; *m* 15 Jan 1880 George Massy Robins

4a Mary Anne; *m* 4 Dec 1872 Sir David Vandeleur Roche, 2nd Bt (*qv*), and *dsp* 29 Feb 1892

5a Emily; *m* 22 Nov 1871 Rev Edward Gabbett, Rector Croom, Co Limerick, and had issue

(2) George Michael (Rev); Rector Knockany; *m* 6 June 1837 Elizabeth, dau of Matthew O'Brien, and *dsp* 20 Nov 1863

(3) Edward; HEICS; *d* 17 Nov 1835

(4) John; Maj 5th Fus; *m* 17 Oct 1844 Henrietta Jane (*d* 25 March 1874), dau of Maj-Gen Thomas Bell, CB, 48th Regt, and *d* 22 Jan 1862, leaving:

    1a George Thomas Charles Eyre; *b* 15 Oct 1846; *d* 15 Jan 1919

    2a John Francis Hugh Bell; *b* 12 Nov 1848; *d* 10 May 1872

    1a Mary Selina Constance Evelyn; *b* 31 March 1851; *d* unm 3 March 1946

(1) Elizabeth; *m* 17 Nov 1812 Nathaniel Eyre Robins, of Hymenstown, and *d* 1826

(2) Catherine; *m* 1825 Rev William Hartford and *d* 10 Nov 1881

(3) Mary Anne; *m* 1829 Lt Charles Kearney, 2nd Dragoon Gds

4 John, of Barna, Co Limerick; *m* 16 June 1817 Maria (*d* 28 May 1880 aged 84), dau of Robert Maunsell, of Co Limerick, and *d* 6 July 1869, having had, with other issue:

(1) Hugh, Maj 85th LI; *m* 18 Sept 1860 Augusta (*m* 2nd 1 Nov 1866 5th Earl Castle Stewart (*qv*); *d* 4 Dec 1908, leaving issue), only child of Major Richardson Brady, 1st Life Gds, of Oaklands, Co Tyrone, and *dsp* 3 Jan 1862

(2) John Maunsell MASSY later MASSY-BERESFORD (roy licence 1871) (Very Rev), of St Hubert's, Co Fermanagh, and Macbie Hill, Peeblesshire; *b* 26 Sept 1823; Dean Kilmore; *m* 6 May 1851 Emily Sarah (*d* 29 July 1893), dau of Rev John Isaac Beresford and er sis and coheir of Capt George Robert Beresford, of Macbie Hill, and *d* 22 Oct 1886, having had, with other issue:

    1a John George Beresford, of St Hubert's, JP (Peeblesshire), DL (Co Fermanagh); *b* 7 Feb 1856; Capt Lanarks Yeo 1880–87, High Sheriff 1900, BRC WW I France; *m* 22 Nov 1892 Hon Alice Elizabeth Mulholland (*d* 23 Nov 1948), 3rd dau of 1st Baron Dunleath (*qv*), and *d* 25 July 1923, leaving:

        1b Tristram Hugh, DSO (1945), MC; *b* 10 April 1896; *educ* Eton and RMC Sandhurst; Brig Rifle Bde WW I (wounded severely twice) and WW II Far East (POW); *m* 25 Aug 1927 Helen Lindsay (*d* 1979), dau of Lindsay Crompton Lawford, of Montreal, and *d* 1987, having had:

            1c +Michael James [Maj Michael Massy-Beresford, 11 Charleville Mansions, Charleville Rd, London W14]; *b* 10 April 1935; *educ* Eton, RMA Sandhurst, Jesus Coll Cambridge (BA) and Roy Mil Coll Science; Maj Roy Green Jackets (43rd and 52nd)

            2c +Christopher Kerry [Christopher Massy-Beresford Esq, 4 Vaughan Ave, Stamford Brook, London W6]; *b* 22 April 1939; *educ* Eton and Ch Ch Oxford (MA); 2nd Lt Roy Wilts Yeo (TA) 1962–65; *m* 1979 *Marjory Snow and has:

                1d *Helen Emily; *b* 1980

            1c *Patricia Nell [Mrs James Paton, Park Corner Farm, Odiham, Hants RG29 1JB]; *b* 17 May 1931; *educ* St Hilda's Coll Oxford (MA, PhD); *m* 13 Dec 1958 *Maj James Otway George (Tim) Paton, 13th/18th Roy Hus (QMO) (ret), only s of Brig James Angus Paton, OBE, and has:

                1d *Timothy James; *b* 18 Nov 1964; *m* 13 May 1995 *Catherine Jane

                2d *Nicholas George; *b* 25 June 1968; *m* 8 July 1995 *Eliza Ann O'Driscoll and has:

                    1e *Emer Rose; *b* 22 July 1997

                1d *Penelope Loveday; *b* 17 July 1963; *m* 1992 *Matthew Alan Fleet and has

                    1e *Emily Charlotte Rose; b 14 June 1996

    2d *Elizabeth Gwendoline; *b* 4 Jan 1967

2b John Clarina; *b* 29 July 1897; Lt RFA; *ka* 23 Aug 1918

3b Desmond George; *b* 21 April 1905; *educ* Cheltenham, Trin Coll Glenalmond and McGill U; 2nd Lt Rifle Bde; *m* May 1940 *Alicia (*m* 2nd 1969 Dr John I Maran), dau of Prof Felix Markstein, of Vienna, and *dsp* 15 Feb 1966

1b Monica Emily; *b* 12 July 1894; Danish Resistance WW II; *m* 15 June 1916 Jorgen Adalbert Wichfeld (*d* Aug 1966), Sec Danish Legn London, s of Niels Henning Frederik Wichfeld, of Denmark, and *d* in a German prison 27 Feb 1945, having had issue

1a Emily Maria Louisa; *m* 31 Oct 1876 Cecil Edward St Lawrence Leslie, s of Bp of Kilmore, and *d* 3 Jan 1890

2a Selina Harriette Perotine; *m* 10 Nov 1892 Rev Charles Barrington Walters, Rector Stoke Climsland, Cornwall, and *d* 24 Jan 1902, leaving issue

(1) Catherine; *m* John Green (*d* 1847), of Greenstown, Co Limerick, and *d* 1826

(2) Mary Anne; *m* Dec 1784 Christopher Tuthill, of Faha

(3) Jane; *m* Oct 1789 Maj William Greene (*d* 3 June 1829), of Fota, Co Cork, and Jonesville, Co Waterford, and *d* 4 Jan 1848, leaving issue

(4) Sarah; *m* H C Gumbleton (*d* 1834), of Curraglass House, Co Cork, and *d* 1845

The 2nd BARON's est s,

HUGH MASSY, 3rd Baron Massy of Duntrileague; *b* 24 Oct 1761; *m* 2 March 1792 Margaret (*d* 1820), yst dau of William Barton, of Grove, and *d* 20 June 1812, having had:

1 **HUGH HAMSON, 4th Baron**

2 George William, of Bellmont, Co Limerick; *b* 12 Jan 1794; *m* 1st 28 April 1821 Narcissa (drowned 9 Jan 1831), 2nd dau of James Hugh Smith Barry, of Fota Island, and had, with other issue:

(1) Hugh Hamon John, of Hazelhurst, Hants; *b* 14 Aug 1822; Capt 44th Regt; *m* 25 May 1850 Annie Margaret (*d* 24 Sept 1882), 2nd dau of Morgan John Evans, and *d* 29 July 1867, having had:

    1a Hugh Hamon George William Carruthers; *b* 10 March 1851; Lt-Cdr RN, Commr Income and Land Taxes; *m* 1st 27 July 1882 Agnes Henrietta (*dsp* 5 Nov 1907), dau of John James Edward Hamilton (*see* HAMILTON, Bt); *m* 2nd 10 Nov 1908 his cousin Anne Emma Fetherstonhaugh (*d* 13 May 1926), dau of Col Robert Thomas Thompson, 56th Regt, by Grace Elizabeth Elinor, dau of Lt-Col Hon John Massy (*see* below), and *d* 6 Oct 1916, leaving:

        1b Hugh Carruthers; *b* 25 Oct 1914; *educ* Trin Coll Cambridge; Maj 4th/7th Roy Dragoon Gds WW II (despatches), Kenya Emergency 1953–55 and Kenya Game Dept 1955–59; *m* 27 May 1961 *Pamela, est dau of John Malcolm Drew, war artist, and widow of 4th Baron Rathdonnell (*qv*)

        1b Narcissa Catherine; *b* 12 Jan 1910

    2a Rollo Dillon Dunham, JP Hants; *b* 16 June 1856; *m* 22 Nov 1884 Emma (*d* 27 Oct 1926), dau of James Inman, and *d* 1 April 1934, leaving:

        1b Annie Narcissa; *b* 9 Dec 1885; nurse St Bartholomew's Hosp London; *d* 30 May 1948

        2b Louisa Bythia; *b* 23 April 1887

(2) George William; *b* 2 July 1823; *m* July 1845 Anne, yst dau of John Massy, of Glanville, Co Limerick, and *d* 29 May 1885, leaving:

    1a Caroline; *b* Jan 1849

    2a Narcissa; *b* Jan 1849

(3) Dunbar James; *b* 18 Jan 1829; *d* 1850

2 (cont.) The Hon George Massy *m* 2nd 1 Oct 1834 Mary Jane (*m* 2nd 13 Dec 1838 Rev Morris Yescombe), est dau of Lt-Col Crosbie, of Rusheen, Co Kerry, and *d* 5 Sept 1835

3 John; *b* 4 June 1795; Lt-Col; *m* 12 April 1828 Elizabeth (*d* 24 March 1857), yst dau of Edward Homewood, and *d* 7 March 1848, having had, with three sons:

(1) Grace Elizabeth Elinor; *m* 19 Sept 1866 Col Robert Thomas Thompson, 56th Regt, Cmdt Kneller Hall Roy Mil Sch Music

4 Dawson (Rev); *d* unm 1825

1 Grace Elizabeth; *m* 26 June 1823 Hon Waller O'Grady (*d* 1849), 2nd s of 1st Viscount Guillamore (*see* 1953 edn), and *d* 27 Sept 1841

2 Cathenne; *d* 28 Jan 1847

3 Susan Maria; *m* 27 March 1826 John Fetherstonhaugh, of Griffinstown

4 Margaret Evertina; *m* 17 July 1833 Francis Drew, of Drewsborough, Co Clare, and *d* 31 March 1885 aged 73

5 Elizabeth Jane Sarah Anne; *m* 1 July 1835 Thomas Lefroy (*d* 29 Jan 1891), 2nd s of Rt Hon Thomas Lefroy, and *d* 30 July 1874

The 3rd BARON's s,

HUGH HAMON MASSY, 4th Baron Massy of Duntrileague; *b* 13 Feb 1793; *m* 22 June 1826 Matilda (*d* 27 Feb 1883 aged 84), yst dau of Luke White, of Woodlands, Co Dublin, and sis of 1st Baron Annaly (*qv*), and *d* 27 Sept 1836, having had:

1 **HUGH HAMON INGOLDSBY MASSY, 5th Baron Massy of Duntrileague**; *b* 14 April 1827; *m* 4 Jan 1855 Isabella (*d* 19 July 1917), est dau of George More Nisbett, of Cirnhill, Lanarks, and *dsp* 27 Feb 1874

2 **JOHN THOMAS WILLIAM MASSY, 6th Baron Massy of Duntrileague**, JP and DL Co Leitrim and Limerick; *b* 30 Aug 1835; rep I peer, High Sheriff Co Leitrim 1863 and Limerick 1873; *m* 19 March 1863 Lady Lucy Maria Butler (*d* 25 July 1896), dau of 3rd Earl of Carrick (*qv*), and *d* 28 Nov 1915, having had:

(1) **HUGH SOMERSET JOHN MASSY, 7th Baron Massy of Duntrileague**; *b* 15 1864; *m* 16 Sept 1886 Ellen Ida Constance (*d* 1922), dau of Charles William Wise, of Rochestown, Co Tipperary, and *d* 20 Oct 1926, having had:

    1a **HUGH HAMON CHARLES GEORGE MASSY, 8th Baron Massy of Duntrileague**; *b* 13 July 1894; *educ* Harrow; *m* 1919 Margaret (*d* 6 March 1971), 2nd dau of Richard Leonard, of Meadsbrook, Ashbourne, Co Meath, and widow of Dr P G Moran, of Tara, Co Meath, and *d* 20 March 1958, having had:

1b HUGH HAMON JOHN SOMERSET MASSY, **9th and present Baron Massy of Duntrileague**

2a Francis John Ingoldsby Tristram; *b* 6 July 1895; Lt RFA; *m* 1920 Evelyn (*d* 1941), only dau of Capt Alexander Henry, of Richardstown Castle, Ardee, Co Louth, and *d* 24 Nov 1929 leaving:

1b Cyril John; *b* 20 May 1925; Lt 8th Hus; *d* unm 7 April 1947

1a Ida Lucy; *b* 16 Sept 1887; *d* unm 1957

2a Muriel Olive; *b* 21 June 1892

3a A dau; *b* and *d* 14 June 1893

4a Lilian Ierne Susan; *b* 29 Dec 1897; *m* 19 March 1929 Herbert Browne, s of George Browne, of Kenrick, Cumberland, and had issue

(1) Lucy Matilda Anne; *b* 21 May 1865; *m* 13 Nov 1889 Col Charles Davis Guinness and *d* 8 April 1941, leaving issue (*see* GUINNESS, Bt)

(2) Matilda Isabella; *b* 16 Aug 1867; *m* 13 Nov 1889 Spencer Charles Vansittart (*d* 9 Aug 1928), of Coolbawn, Co Limerick, and had issue (*see* 1956 edn VANSITTART, B)

MATHESON

Arms: Gyronny of eight sable and gules, a lion rampant or, armed and langued azure, overall on a canton argent a dexter hand apaumée gules. **Crest:** Issuant from an eastern crown or a dexter hand holding a scimitar in fess all proper. **Supporters:** Two brown bears proper, each gorged with an antique crown or.
Mottoes: 1 (over the crest) *Fac et spera* ('Do and hope'), 2 (under arms) *O'chian* ('Of old'). **Creation:** Bt. (UK) 15 May 1882.

SIR FERGUS JOHN MATHESON OF MATHESON, 7TH BT, of Lochalsh, Co Ross [Maj Sir Fergus Matheson of Matheson Bt, The Old Rectory, Hedenham, Norfolk NR35 2LD]; *b* 22 Feb 1927; *s* bro 1993; *educ* Eton; Maj Coldstream Gds 1945–64, memb Gentlemen at Arms 1979–97 (Standard Bearer 1993–97); *m* 17 May 1952 *Hon Jean Elizabeth Mary Willoughby, yr dau of 11th Baron Middleton (*qv*), and has:

1 +ALEXANDER FERGUS (Alexander Matheson Yr. of Matheson); *b* 26 Aug 1954; *educ* Eton and Durham U; Lt-Col Coldstream Gds, T/Equerry to HM THE QUEEN 1982–84, Ch of Staff Br Forces Belize 1992–94, Adj RMA Sandhurst 1995–96, Bde Maj Household Div 1996–98; *m* 8 Nov 1983 *Katharine Davina Mary, only dau of Michael and Lady Angela Oswald (*see* EXETER, M), and has:

(1) +Andrew William Fergus; *b* 12 March 1985

(2) +Archie James Torquhil; *b* 13 March 1987

(1) *Louisa Alexandra Matilda Matheson; *b* 3 Sept 1989

1 *Elizabeth Angela Matilda [Mrs Martin Thompson, The Old Rectory, Little Bytham, Lincs]; *b* 19 Feb 1953; *m* 15 April 1978 *Martin Thompson, er s of Maj E C O Thompson, and has:

(1) *Charles Guy Martin; *b* 1981

(1) *Mara Angela Matilda; *b* 1979

(2) *Siana Camilla Elizabeth; *b* 1989

2 *Fiona Jean Lucia [Mrs Andrew Kendall, 49 Lansdowne Gdns, London SW8]; *b* 4 April 1962; *m* 1986 *Andrew Thomas Kendall, er s of John Kendall, and has:

(1) *Edmund Andrew Fergus; *b* 1991

(1) *Lucia Amelia Fiona; *b* 1988

Lineage: FARQUHAR MATHESON, tacksman (lessee) of Fernaig, Lochalsh, 3rd s of Alexander Matheson; *m* 1st a dau of Efander Murchison, of Auchtertyre, without issue; *m* 1665, as his 2nd w, his cousin Mary, dau of Christopher Macrae, and *d* 1725, leaving, with three yr sons and five daus:

JOHN MATHESON of Attadale (which estate he bought 1730), tacksman Fernaig; *m* 1st a dau of Mackenzie of Achilty, and had two sons (*d* infants); *m* 2nd —, ggdau maternally of Kenneth Mackenzie of Gairloch by Ann, dau of Sir John Grant of Grant, and a descendant of Macdonnell of Glengarry by Margaret (gdau of Celestine of the Isles, to whom the Matheson lands in the neighbourhood of Lochalsh had passed 1427 on the arrest and execution of the chief of the Mathesons), and by her had five sons and three daus; *m* 3rd 1745 Elizabeth, dau of Simon Mackenzie of Allangrange, descended paternally from 1st Lord Mack-

enzie of Kintail (*see* CROMARTIE, E), and *d* 1760, having by his 3rd w had a s; his est surv s (by his 2nd w):

ALEXANDER MATHESON of Attadale; tacksman Fernaig, *m* 1765 his 1st cousin Catherine Matheson (*d* 1832 aged 88), and *d* 1804, leaving, with three daus:

JOHN MATHESON of Attadale, JP and DL (Ross-shire); tacksman Fernaig (gave it up 1810), Capt Lochalsh Vols; *m* 1804 Margaret (*d* 1850), dau of Capt Donald Matheson and sis of Sir James Matheson, Bt, of the Lews, Ross-shire (*see* 1878 edn), and *d* 1826, leaving, with four yr sons and two daus:

Sir Alexander Matheson, 1st Bt (UK), so cr 15 May 1882; *b* 16 Jan 1805; ptnr Jardine Matheson and Matheson & Co, bought 1839 and 1844 lands of Ardintoul and Inverinate, part of the ancient patrimony of the chiefs of the Mackenzies, from whom he descended several times over through females, also 1851 the territorial Barony of Lochalsh, the ancient patrimony of his family, MP (Lib) Inverness Burghs 1847–68 and Ross-shire 1868–84; *m* 1st 1840 Mary (*d* 1841), only dau of James Crawford Macleod of Geanies; *m* 2nd 19 July 1853 Lavinia Mary (*d* 30 Sept 1855), sis of 8th Baron Beaumont (*see* NORFOLK, D), and by her had:

1 **Sir Kenneth James Matheson, 2nd Bt**, JP and DL (Ross-shire); *b* 12 May 1854; *m* 1 Oct 1913 Ada Juliana (*d* 31 July 1922), dau of George E B Lousada and widow of Daniel C Stiebel, and *dsp* 25 Jan 1920

1 Mary Isabella; *m* 20 April 1881 Wallace Charles Houstoun (*d* 25 Oct 1923), of Wolverton House, Bucks, yst s of Col Alexander Houstoun, of Clerkington, and *d* 1 March 1933, leaving issue

Sir Alexander *m* 3rd 17 April 1860 Eleanor Irving (*d* 6 Dec 1879), dau of Spencer Perceval (*see* EGMONT, E), and *d* 27 July 1886, having by her had:

2 **Sir Alexander Perceval Matheson, 3rd Bt**; *b* 6 Feb 1861; Australian Senator; *m* 18 Oct 1884 (*divorce* 1925) Eleanor (*d* 10 July 1959), dau of Rev Kyrle Ernle Aubrey Money, of Much Marcle, Herefs, and *d* 6 Aug 1929, having had:

(1) Ian Kenneth; *b* 14 May 1893; Capt Seaforth Highrs; *d* unm 13 May 1917 of wounds recd in action

(2) Alexander Perceval; *b* 21 Jan 1895; Lt ASC and A/Flt/Cdr RFC; *ka* 13 July 1917

(3) Roderick Kyrle; *b* 14 Nov 1897; 2nd Lt Roy W Kent Regt; *d* unm 8 Sept 1916 of wounds recd in action

(1) Margaret Anna (Nancy); *d* unm 20 April 1948

(2) Norah; *m* 1 May 1915 Arthur Harry Gerald Dawson (*d* 1957), Surveyor-Gen Colombo, Ceylon, and had issue

(3) Muriel Helen; *m* 1st 18 Sept 1909 Patrick Wallace Gould, KRRC (*ka* 24 Aug 1916), only s of Alexander Gould, of Newquay, Cornwall, and had issue; *m* 2nd 1919 Herbert Bush, Lt Canadian MGC, and had further issue

(4) Eleanor; *m* 27 Feb 1922 John Lyne Harvey, MC, ARIBA, est s of Edward Lyne Harvey, of Plymouth, and had issue

3 **Sir Roderick Mackenzie Chisholm Matheson, 4th Bt**; *b* 26 Dec 1861; *m* 1st 15 March 1883 (*divorce* 1894) Jane Clark (*d* 1895), dau of John Grant; *m* 2nd 17 June 1899 Emma Frances (*d* 10 Oct 1929), only dau of James A Croft, of Putney and Swindon, Wilts; *m* 3rd 6 June 1931 Cecil (*d* 23 April 1975), dau of Sir Charles Lyall, KCSI, CIE, and widow of William Alexander Fleet, Gren Gds, of Culver, Indiana, and *d* 24 July 1944, having by his 1st w had:

(1) Ethel Ivy Flora, OBE (1919); *b* 17 Dec 1886; Divl Dir WRNS WW I; *d* March 1972

4 George Charles, *b* 9 June 1867, *d* 13 Dec 1870

5 **Sir Torquhil George Matheson, 5th Bt**, KCB (1921, CB 1918), CMG (1919); *b* 4 Feb 1871; *educ* Eton; 4th Bn Beds Regt (Herts Militia) 1890–94, Coldstream Gds: joined 1894, Adj 1st Bn 1897–1902 (Boer War; despatches, King's and Queen's medals), Regtl Adj 1903–05, attd Gen Staff London Dist, Bde Maj 1907–11, WW I: cmded 3rd Bn, 46th Scottish Inf Bde, 10th (Light) Div, 4th Div, Gds Div (despatches ten times, Brevet Lt-Col, Brevet Col Maj-Gen, Order St Stanislas Russia with Swords, Croix de Guerre with Palms), cmded Warziristan Field Force 1920–24 (despatches four times), Ch Political Offr Waziristan 1920–21, S Waziristan 1921–24, cmdg 54th E Anglian Div and E Anglian Area 1927–30, Lt-Gen 1930, GOC-in-C Western Cmd India 1931–35, Gen 1934, ret 1935, cmded D Co 2nd Ross-shire Bn HG 1940–42, memb: CC Ross and Cromarty 1938–45, Ag Wages Ctee No 11 Dist Scotland 1937–40; *m* 1st 2 July 1900 (*divorce* 1923) Ella Louisa, 2nd dau of Capt James Wingfield Linton, of Hemingford Abbotts, and the Countess of Aylesford (*qv*); *m* 2nd 23 July 1923 Lady Elizabeth Mary Gertrude Keppel, ARRC, VAD Nurse France 1915–18 (despatches), only dau of 8th Earl of Albemarle (*qv*), and *d* 13 Nov 1963, having by her had:

(1) **Sir Torquhil Alexander Matheson, 6th Bt**; *b* 15 Aug 1925; *educ* Eton; Maj Coldstream Gds, seconded KAR Kenya 1961–64, ret 1964, 4th Bn Wilts Regt (TA) 1965–67, Roy Wilts Territorials (TAVR 3) 1967–69; *m* 21 April 1954 *Serena Mary Francesca [Serena Lady Matheson of Matheson, Trees Farm, Standerwick, Frome, Somerset BA11 2PT], only child of Lt-Col Sir (James) Michael Peto, 2nd Bt of Barnstaple (*qv*), and *d* 1993, having had:

1a *Eleanor Mary Francesca; *b* 5 July 1955

2a *Isobel Sophia; *b* 20 Feb 1957; *m* 1986 *William George Craven, 2nd s of John Craven, MRCVS, and has:

1b *Frances Elizabeth; *b* 1987

2b *Emily Flora; *b* 1989

(2) Sir FERGUS JOHN MATHESON, **7th and present Bt**

2 Eleanor Margaret; *m* 25 Aug 1886 7th Baron Vaux of Harrowden (*qv*) and *d* 18 Sept 1896, leaving issue

3 Anna Elizabeth; *d* unm 31 Oct 1927

4 Flora; *m* 1st 4 Dec 1883 Sir Henry Philip Pauncefort-Duncombe, 2nd Bt (*qv*), and had issue; *m* 2nd 10 June 1908 Arthur Lucas (*d* 7 Feb 1926), of Moreton Manor House, Bucks, and *d* 7 Sept 1927

5 Hylda Nora Grace; *m* 13 May 1899 Walter Taylor and *dsp* 23 May 1902

MAXWELL

Arms: Arg. an eagle with two heads displayed sa., beaked and membered gu., on the breast an escutcheon of the first, charged with a saltire of the second, surcharged in the centre with a hurcheon (hedgehog) or, all within a bordure gu. **Crest:** An eagle rising ppr. **Motto:** *Reviresco* ('I renew my strength'). **Creation:** Bt. (NS) 8 Jan 1680/1.

SIR MICHAEL EUSTACE GEORGE MAXWELL, 9TH BT, of Monreith, Wigtownshire [Sir Michael Maxwell Bt, Laundry House, Farming Woods, Brigstock, Northants NN14 3JA; Monreith House, Port William, Newton Stewart DG8 9LB, Wigtownshire; 56 Queensmill Rd, London SW6 6JS]; *b* 28 Aug 1943; *s* unc 1987; *educ* Eton and London U; ARICS

Lineage: UNDWEYN, allegedly a Norseman; had:

MACCUS; witnessed charters of DAVID I KING OF SCOTS (1124–53); granted land (later called Springwood) on the Tweed where it meets the Teviot in what is now Roxburgh; from the fishing reach attached to it (still called Maxwheel) comes the name 'Maccus's well' or 'Maxwell'; had:

HERBERT de MACCUSWELL; Sheriff Teviotdale *c* 1200; *d c* 1206, leaving:

JOHN de MACCUSWELL; Envoy England, Chamberlain Scotland 1231–33; *d* by 1241; f or just possibly bro of:

Sir AYMER de MAXWELL; Chamberlain Scotland *c* 1257–60, Sheriff Dumfriesshire and Peeblesshire, Justiciar Galloway; *m* Mary, possibly dau of Robert de Mearns, by whom the MAXWELLs would thus have acquired the (territorial) Barony of Mearns, Clydesdale, which they undoubtedly did possess from about now, and had, with three yr sons (Edward, *dsp*; Sir John, Govr Dumbarton Castle, ancestor of the MAXWELLs of Pollok, Springkell and Calderwood, the Barons Farnham (*qv*) and the MAXWELLs of Cardoness, Newark, Stainlie and Dargavel; Sir Alexander, living *c* 1300):

Sir HERBERT de MAXWELL of Carlaverock, on the Solway Firth, which he held by 1300, when the celebrated Siege of it by the English took place; swore fealty to EDWARD I following the English victory over the Scots of Dunbar 27 April 1296; allegedly *ka* at the English victory over the Scots of Falkirk 22 July 1298, leaving:

Sir JOHN de MAXWELL; also swore fealty to EDWARD I 1296; living June 1307; had:

1 Eustace (Sir), of Carlaverock, which he occupied on behalf of EDWARD II OF ENGLAND till *c* 1312, shortly afterwards switching sides to ROBERT I (THE BRUCE) OF SCOTS, being in turn then besieged by the English; later supported claim of EDWARD BALLIOL (the English-backed candidate) to the Scottish throne and following BALLIOL's eclipse continued pro-English till he rose against them 1338, only to be pardoned by EDWARD III OF ENGLAND 1339; *d* apparently 3 March 1342

2 John (Sir); captured by English at their victory over the Scots of Neville's Cross 17 Oct 1346 and imprisoned Tower of London, where he allegedly died, leaving apparently two sons:

(1) Herbert; swore fealty to EDWARD III OF ENGLAND Sept 1347, for whom he held Carlaverock; accordingly outlawed by the Scots

(2) John (Sir); held Carlaverock on behalf of the Scots by April 1354; *m* Christian — and *d* in or after April 1373, leaving:

1a Robert (Sir); *d* by 8 Feb 1409/10, leaving:

1b Herbert (Sir); apptd Hereditary Steward of Annandale 8 Feb 1409/10; *m* by 10 Aug 1386 Katherine, dau of John Stewart of Dalswinton, and *d* by 16 Oct 1421, leaving:

1c HERBERT MAXWELL, 1ST LORD MAXWELL (S), so *cr* between 8 Jan 1440/1 and 3 July 1445; ktd 1424; *m* 1st —, dau of Sir Herbert Herries of Terregles (*see* HERRIES OF TERREGLES, L); *m* 2nd Catherine, dau of Sir William Seton of Seton (*see* EGLINTON and WINTON, E) and widow of Sir Alan Stewart of Darnley (*see* MORAY, E), and *d* by 14 Feb 1453/4, leaving by his 1st w:

1d ROBERT MAXWELL, 2ND LORD MAXWELL; Adml and Warden W March; *m* 13 Jan–4 Feb 1424/5 Janet, dau of Sir John Forrester of Corstorphine, and *d* between 22 April 1485 and 29 April 1486, having had:

1e John, Master of Maxwell; *m c* 1454 Janet, dau of George Crichton, Earl of Caithness (*qv*), by his 2nd w but *b* prior to their marriage, and was *k vp* in an affray against raiders from England led by exiled Scots at Kirtlemure 22 July 1484, leaving:

1f JOHN MAXWELL, 3RD LORD MAXWELL; *b* just after 1454; Warden W Marches; fought for JAMES III against the latter's rebellious son at Sauchieburn 1488; *m* between 15 Feb 1490/1 and 20 Feb 1491/2 Agnes, est dau of Sir Alexander Stewart of Garlies (*see* MORAY, E), and was *ka* Flodden 9 Sept 1513, leaving:

1g ROBERT MAXWELL, 4TH LORD MAXWELL, PC (S 1526); *b* probably 1493 or 1494; ktd by late 1510, Warden W Marches and Steward and Hereditary Sheriff Kirkcudbright by 1515, Capt Gd and Provost Edinburgh by 1524, Ch Carver to JAMES V 1528, First Gentleman of the Bedchamber, Extrdy Ld of Session 1533, Jt Warden W Marches and a Ld of Regency 1537; taken prisoner by English at their defeat of the Scots of Solway Moss 24 Nov 1542; promoted the Refomation in Scotland; *m* 1st after 4 July 1509 Janet, dau of Sir William Douglas 6th of Drumlanrig (*see* QUEENSBERRY, M); *m* 2nd 1520–15 Nov 1525 Agnes, illegitimate dau of James Stewart, Earl of Buchan (*see* MORAY, E), and widow of (a) 2nd Earl of Bothwell (*see* BUCHAN-HEPBURN, Bt) and (b) 3rd Lord Home (*see* HOME, E), and *d* 9 July 1546, leaving:

1h ROBERT MAXWELL, 5TH LORD MAXWELL, PC (S 1551); Warden W Marches 1542; *m* after 25 July 1530 Beatrice (*d* on or after 31 Oct 1583, having been a certified lunatic since 1562), 2nd dau and coheir of 3rd Earl of Morton (*qv*), and *d* 13 Sept 1552, leaving:

1i ROBERT MAXWELL, 6TH LORD MAXWELL; *b c* 1549; *d* a child between 31 Dec 1553 and 16 Jan 1554/5

2i JOHN MAXWELL, 7TH LORD MAXWELL, also 1st EARL OF MORTON (S), so *cr* 5 June 1581, though obliged to surrender this title on reversal of attainder on the Douglas Earls of Morton (*qv*) 29 Jan 1585/6; *b* 24 April 1553; Warden W March to 1577, as an RC found life in Scotland increasingly uncomfortable and went to Spain, where connected with the Armada enterprise against England; revisiting Scotland spring 1588, he was arrested as a traitor and imprisoned till 1589; *m* 17 Feb 1571/2 Elizabeth, 2nd and yr dau of 7th Earl of Angus (*see* HAMILTON and BRANDON, D), and was *k* in a skirmish with the JOHNSTONEs at Dryffe Sands 6 or 7 Dec 1593, leaving:

1j JOHN MAXWELL, 8TH LORD MAXWELL; *b* by May 1583; *k* Sir James Johnstone 1608 in revenge for his f's murder and was sentenced to death but fled abroad till 1612, when he returned to Scotland and was beheaded 21 May 1613; *m* by 19 April 1600 Margaret, dau of 1st Marquess of Hamilton (*see* HAMILTON and BRANDON, D), and *dsps*

2j ROBERT MAXWELL, 9TH LORD MAXWELL and 1st EARL OF NITHSDALE, so *cr* 29 Aug 1620, as also LORD MAXWELL, ESKDALE AND CARLEILL (all S), with remainder to heirs male whatsoever and with precedence from 29 Nov 1581 (the which f was *cr* EARL OF MORTON; *see* above), PC (S 1619); *b* after 1586; intermittently imprisoned Edinburgh Castle 1607–13, apparently for complicity with er bro; one of six membs of an inner circle of the PC advsg the King 1621; royalist Civil War; *m* 28 Oct 1619 Elizabeth, dau of Sir Francis Beaumont, and *d* May 16146, leaving an only s:

1k ROBERT MAXWELL, 2ND EARL OF NITHSDALE; *b* 1 Sept 1620; royalist Civil War; *d* unm 5 Oct 1667, when his titles passed to his cousin (*see* HERRIES OF TERREGLES, L)

1g Mary; *m* James Johnstone of Johnstone (*see* ANNANDALE AND HARTFELL, E)

2h John (Sir); *m* Agnes, Lady Herries of Terregles (*qv*) in her own right, and had issue

2d Edward (Sir), of Tinwald, Dumfriesshire; *m* Margaret, dau and coheir of Henry Munduell, of Tinwald, and had:

1e Edward, of Tinwald; had charter 15 Jan 1482 of quarter of the (territorial) Barony of Mureith (later called Monreith), with the chief messuage thereof called Ballingrene; *m* Egidia Douglas (*d c* 1509) and had:

1f Herbert; *m* Margaret Douglas (*m* 2nd 1st Lord Carlyle of Torthorwald) and *dvp*, leaving:

1g Edward, of Tinwald; *d c* 1518, having had:

1h Edward; *dvp c* 1514

2g William; had:

1h Edward; *m* his cousin Elizabeth (*m* 2nd Sir Robert Maxwell of Dinwiddie), heiress of Tinwald, and *d c* 1566, leaving three sons (Edward; James; Herbert, all of whose male issue apparently died out following the death *sp* of Francis Maxwell, gggs of Herbert, who sold Tinwald by 1712)

2h Herbert; *m* 1541 his cousin Margaret Maxwell, heiress of Monreith (*m* 2nd George Maxwell of Dumfries and had a s, Robert of Garrerie, for whose dau *see* below), and had:

1i John, of Monreith; *m* Agnes, dau of Sir Godfrey McCulloch of Myretown, and *d c* 1605, leaving, wih oher issue:

1j John, of Monreith; *m* his 2nd cousin Catherine, dau of Robert Maxwell of Garrerie (*see* above), and *d* 1670, leaving:

1k William, of Monreith; *m* 1632 Margaret, dau of John McCulloch of Myretown, and *d* 1670, having had:

1l John; *m* 1656 Margaret, dau of Sir Andrew Agnew, 2nd Bt, of Lochnaw (*qv*), and *d* Ireland 1668, leaving:

1m William; *d* 1671

1m Agnes; served heiress to her gf and bro 2 June 1681; *m* Robert Gordon of Shirmers

2l **Sir William Maxwell, 1st Bt** (NS), so *cr* 8 Jan 1680/1, of Monreith; *m* 1st Joanna, dau of Patrick McDouall of Logan; *m* 2nd Elizabeth, dau of Sir Thomas Hay, 1st Bt, of Park (*qv*), and *d* 1709, having by her had, with two daus (*d* unm):

1m William; *d* unm, drowned River Nith 1707

2m ALEXANDER (Sir), **2nd Bt**

3m John, of Ardwell and Killasar, Wigtownshire; *m* Mary McGhie and had:

1n William, of Ardwell; had:

1o Elizabeth; *m* her cousin Capt James Maxwell (*see below*) and had issue

1m Isabel; *m* William Stewart of Castle Stewart, gs of 2nd Earl of Galloway (*qv*)

2m Mary; *m* Andrew Heron (*d* 1730) of Bargaly and had issue

3m Mary; *m* 1708 Thomas, er s of Sir Charles Hay, 2nd Bt, of Park (*qv*), and *d* 24 Dec 1767, leaving issue

1d Catherine; *m* as his 1st w 1st Lord Kennedy *see* AILSA, M)

1c Jean; *m* Sir William Douglas, 2nd of Drumlanrig (*see* QUEENSBERRY, M), and had issue

The 1st Bt's 2nd son,

Sir Alexander Maxwell, 2nd Bt; MP Wigtown Burghs 1715; *m* 29 Dec 1711 Lady Jean (*d* 20 Feb 1745), dau of 9th Earl of Eglinto(u)n (*see* EGLINTON and WINTON, E), and *d* 23 May 1730, having had:

1 WILLIAM (Sir), **3rd Bt**

2 Alexander; *b* 7 March 1718; *dvp*

3 James; *b* 31 July 1724; Capt 42nd Highrs; *m* his cousin Elizabeth, dau of William Maxwell of Ardwell, and had, with other issue:

(1) Murray (Sir), CB (1815); Adml, ktd 1818; *m* 9 Sept 1798 Grace Callander (*d* 23 June 1857), dau of Col — Waugh, 57th Regt, and *d* 26 June 1831, having had:

1a John Balfour; Adml; *d* 31 Jan 1874, leaving, with other issue:

1b Rose Frances; *m* 11 Sept 1879 George E H Cates

1a Mary; *m* 1st 12 June 1828 Capt Charles Hallowell Carew, RN (*d* 2 Aug 1880), of Beddington, Surrey, s of Adml Sir Benjamin Hallowell Carew, and had issue; *m* 2nd 2 July 1850 Col Petrie Waugh, s of Gen Sir Andrew Scott Waugh

(2) Archibald Montgomerie, KH; Col 36th Regt; *m* 30 Oct 1823 Mary, 3rd dau of John Falconer Atlee, of Wandsworth, Surrey, and *d* 21 May 1845, leaving a dau (*d* unm)

1 Margaret; *m* — Carruthers of Dormont, Dumfriesshire

2 Elizabeth; *m* John Crawford Balfour of Powmill

3 Catharine; *m* William Booth

4 Susan; *m* Capt Alexander Hay, s of Sir Thomas Hay, 3rd Bt, of Park (*qv*), and *d* 22 Feb 1792

Sir ALEXANDER's est son,

Sir William Maxwell, 3rd Bt; *m* Magdalene, dau of William Blair of Blair, and *d* 22 Aug 1771, having had, with other issue:

1 WILLIAM (Sir), **4th Bt**

1 Catharine; *m* 28 Jan 1767 John Fordyce, of Ayton, Berwicks, Receiver-Gen land tax Scotland, and had issue

2 Jane; *m* 23 Oct 1767 7th Marquess of Huntly (*qv*) and had issue

3 Eglantine; *m* Sept 1772 Sir Thomas Wallace, Bt, of Craigie, Ayrshire (*see* 1850 edn DUNLOP-WALLACE, Bt)

Sir WILLIAM's est son,

Sir William Maxwell, 4th Bt; *m* 1776 his cousin Katharine (*d* 2 April 1798), dau and heiress of David Blair of Adamton, Ayrshire, and *d* 17 Feb 1812, having had, with other issue:

1 WILLIAM (Sir), **5th Bt**

2 Hamilton; Maj 43rd Bengal Inf, Capt 42nd Highrs; *m* Mary, dau of Sir Robert Grierson, 5th Bt (*qv*), and *d* 17 June 1829, having had, with other issue:

(1) William Robert Maxwell; Gen RM; *m* Caroline Delacombe and *d* March 1892

(2) Alexander Charles; *m* Amelia Helena, dau of Capt John Elliott Porch, Gren Gds, and had issue

1 Anne; *m* 11 June 1799 William Murray of Touchadam and Polmaise, Stirlingshire

2 Madeline; *m* 1801 James Du Pré, of Wilton Park, Bucks, and had issue

3 Jane; *m* 1802 John Maitland of Freugh and had issue (*see* LAUDERDALE, E)

Sir WILLIAM's est son,

Sir William Maxwell, 5th Bt; *b* 5 March 1779; Lt-Col 26th Foot, lost an arm Battle of Corunna 1809; *m* 23 April 1803 Catharine (*d* 19 July 1857), yst dau of John Fordyce of Ayton, Berwicks, and *d* 22 Aug 1838, having had, with three other daus:

1 WILLIAM (Sir), **6th Bt**

2 Eustace; RN; *d* Australia 1857

3 Edward Herbert, CB; *b* 30 July 1822; Gen, Chev Legn Hon and Medjidie; *m* 20 Nov 1865 Agnes Morgan (*d* 23 Feb 1926), 3rd dau of R-Adml James Hay (*see* TWEEDDALE, M), and *d* 24 Feb 1885

1 Catherine Helen; *m* 28 Feb 1824 H Hathorn, of Castlewigg, and *d* 28 Sept 1882

2 Louisa Cornwallis; *m* 25 July 1833 Caledon George Du Pré, of Wilton Park, MP Bucks, and *d* 24 April 1880, having had issue

3 Charlotte Queensberry; *m* Filippo Calandra di Roccolino and *d* 28 Aug 1889

Sir WILLIAM's est son,

Sir William Maxwell, 6th Bt; *b* 2 Oct 1805; Lt-Col Galloway Rifles Militia, Capt 14th Light Dragoons; *m* 10 June 1833 Helenora (*d* 27 Oct 1876), yst dau of Sir Michael Shaw-Stewart, 5th Bt (*qv*), and *d* 29 March 1877, having had, with three er sons:

1 HERBERT EUSTACE (Sir), **7th Bt**

2 Edward Adolphus Seymour; *b* 20 Oct 1849; *d* 25 Aug 1866

1 Catherine Shaw Stewart; *d* unm 27 July 1911

2 Anne Murray; *m* 24 April 1856 Robert Hathorn Johnston Stewart, of Physgill (*d* 10 July 1899), and *d* 27 April 1920, having had issue

3 Alan Eglantine; *d* Sept 1921

4 Eleanora Louisa; *m* 4 Feb 1885 Henry Macdowall (*d* 3 April 1927), of Garthland, Renfrewshire, and *dsp* 19 March 1908

Sir WILLIAM's er surv son,

Sir Herbert Eustace Maxwell, 7th Bt, KT (1933), PC (1897), JP; *b* 8 Jan 1845; Lt-Col 3rd Bn Roy Scots Fus; FRS, Hon LLD Glasgow, Hon DCL Durham; Wigtownshire: Pres TAA, MP 1880–1906 (a Ld Treasury 1886–92), Ld Lt 1903–35; chm Tstees Nat Library Scotland 1925–32, Pres Soc Scottish Antiquaries 1900–13, Chm Roy Commn Scottish Historical Monuments 1908–33; *m* 20 Jan 1869 Mary (*d* 3 Sept 1910), est dau of Henry Fletcher-Campbell of Boquhan, Stirlingshire, and *d* 30 Oct 1937, having had:

1 William; *b* 29 Sept 1869; *d c* 12–19 June 1897 nr Fort Gibbs, Mashonaland

2 Aymer Edward, JP, DL Wigtownshire; *b* 26 Oct 1877; Lt-Col cmdg Collingwood Bn 1st Naval Bde RND, Capt Gren Gds and Lovat Scouts Boer War, WW I; *m* 20 Oct 1909 Lady Mary Percy (*d* 18 March 1965), 5th dau of 7th Duke of Northumberland (*qv*), and *das* 9 Oct 1914, leaving:

(1) **Sir Aymer Maxwell, 8th Bt**, JP (Wigtownshire 1939); *b* 7 Dec 1911; *educ* Eton and Magdalene Coll Cambridge (BA 1933); Hon Capt Scots Gds; *d* unm 1987

(2) Eustace; *b* 24 Feb 1913; *educ* Winchester and RMC Sandhurst; Maj Argyll & Sutherland Highrs; *m* 18 May 1940 (*divorce* 1949) Dorothy Vivien, er dau of Capt George Bellville, of Fermyn Woods Hall, Brigstock, Northants, and *d* 12 April 1971, leaving:

1a Sir MICHAEL EUSTACE GEORGE MAXWELL, **9th and present Bt**

1a *Diana Mary; *b* 10 Jan 1942; has by Patrick Helmore:

1b *Katherine Diane; *b* 1984

2b *Charlotte Jessica (twin); *b* 1984

(3) Gavin; *b* 15 July 1914; *educ* Stowe and Hertford Coll Oxford (MA); Maj Scots Gds; FRSL, FZS (Scientific), FRGS, FIAI; author: *A Reed Shaken by the Wind, Ring of Bright Water, The House of Elrig, Raven Seek thy Brother* and other works; *m* 1 Feb 1962 (*divorce* 1964) Lavinia Joan, er dau of Sir Alan Frederick Lascelles, GCB, GCVO, CMG, MC, PC (*see* HAREWOOD, E), and formerly w of Maj Edward Westland Renton, and *dsp* 7 Sept 1969

(1) Christian; *b* 31 July 1910

1 Ann Christian; *b* 5 Sept 1871; *m* 12 Nov 1901 Sir John Maxwell Stirling-Maxwell of Pollok, 10th Bt, KT (*see* 1970 edn), and *d* 5 April 1937, leaving issue

2 Winifred Edith; *b* 19 July 1873; *m* 11 Nov 1897 Alastair Erskine Graham (*d* 5 Sept 1932) and *d* 30 Oct 1968, leaving issue

3 Beatrice Mary; *b* 24 Jan 1875; *m* 10 Oct 1901 Ernest Robert Walker (*d* 17 May 1942), yst s of Sir James Robert Walker, 2nd Bt, of Sand Hutton (*qv*), and *d* 11 April 1938, leaving issue

MAXWELL-SCOTT

Arms: Quarterly, grand-quarterly, 1st grand quarter, or two mullets in chief and a crescent in base az., within an orle of the second and charged at the middle chief point with a crescent sa. (for SCOTT); 2nd grand-quarter, az. on a bend cotised arg. three billets sa. (for HAGGERSTON of Haggerston); 3rd grand-quarter, quarterly, 1st and 4th quarters, arg. an eagle displayed with two heads sa., beaked and membered gu., surmounted on an escutcheon of the first charged with a saltire of the second and surcharged in the centre with a hurcheon (hedgehog) or (for MAXWELL, Earl of Nithsdale); 2nd quarter, counter quartered 1st and 4th, arg. a saltire sa., in chief a label of three points gu. (for MAXWELL); 2nd and 3rd, arg. three hurcheons sa. (for HERRIES of Terregles); 3rd quarter, quarterly, gu. vair a bend or (for CONSTABLE of Everingham); 4th grand-quarter, or on a bend az. three mascles of the first, in the sinister chief point a buckle of the second (for HALIBURTON); **Crests:** 1 A nymph richly attired holding in her dexter hand the sun and in her sinister the moon, all ppr. (for SCOTT), 2 A lion passant arg. (for HAGGERSTON). **Mottoes:** (both over crest) 1 *Reparabit cornua phoebe* ('The moon will replenish her horns'), 2 The Lord giveth. **Creation:** Bt. (E) 15 Oct 1642.

SIR DOMINIC JAMES MAXWELL-SCOTT, 14TH BT, of Haggerston, Northumberland [Sir Dominic Maxwell-Scott Bt,130 Ritherdon Rd, London SW17 8QQ]; *b* 2 July 1968; *s f* 1989; *educ* Eton and Sussex U

Lineage: JOHN de HAGARDESTON; had:

HUGH de HAGARDESTON; living *c* 1290; probably ancestor of:

ROBERT de HAGARSTON; fedual Lord of Hagerston; *d* by 1399; had:

HENRY de HAGARSTON; *b c* 1359; *m* probably Mary, dau of Alexander Selby, of Biddleston, Northumberland, and *d* by 1400, leaving:

THOMAS de HAGARSTON; *b c* 1390; *m* probably Catharine, dau of Miles Stapleton, of Wighill, Yorks, and *d* 1446, leaving, with other issue:

THOMAS de HAGARSTON; *b c* 1416; Receiver Norham and Island shires (subdivisions of Northumberland) 1465; *m* 1446 Agnes, dau of Sir Thomas Umframville and coheir of her bro Gilbert, and *d* 1 May 1470, leaving, with a dau (Margaret, *m* John Swinburne, of Nafferton):

THOMAS HAGGARSTON, of Haggarston; *b c* 1448; Justice of Gaol Delivery Northam and Island shires 1477; *m* Margaret Haslerigg, of Haslerigg, Northumberland and *d* 26 March 1502, leaving, with five other sons (Richard; George; Ralph, *m* Elizabeth (*d* 6 April 1537), dau and coheiress of John Manners, of Cheswick, and widow of Thomas Manners; Roger; Rowland):

THOMAS HAGGARSTON, of Haggerston; *b c* 1477; *m* Elizabeth (*m* 2nd — Carlisle), dau of George Collingwood, of Eslington, and *d* 26 Jan 1531, leaving, with three daus (Margaret; Ellinor; Esabel):

THOMAS HAGGARSTON, of Haggerston; *b c* 1517; *m* Dorothy, dau of Sir Cuthbert Ratcliffe, Warden E Marches, and was *ka* Battle of Pannyerhaugh, Scotland, 1545, leaving:

HENRY HAGGARSTON, of Haggerston; *m* Anne, dau and coheiress of Robert Beadnell, of Lemington, Northumberland, and had, with three other sons (John, Mayor Berwick-on-Tweed 1534, 1535, 1537 and 1539; Cuthbert; Henry, of Goswick) and two daus (Helen; Mary, *m* John Orde, of Berwick-on-Tweed):

WILLIAM HAGGERSTON, of Haggerston and Haslerigg; *m* Margaret (*bur* probably 18 Oct 1597), dau of Henry Butler, of Rowcliffe, Lancs, and was *bur* 24 June 1606, leaving, with a 2nd s (Luke) and two daus (Anne; Mary; both *d* unm):

Sir Thomas Haggerston, 1st Bt (E), so *cr* 15 Oct 1642, of Haggerston Castle; Col of a royalist regt Civil War; *m* Alice (*bur* 10 April 1673), dau and heir of Henry Banaster, of Bank, Lancs, and was *bur* 7 March 1673/4, having had:

1 John; *ka* Ormskirk Civil War

2 THOMAS (Sir), **2nd Bt**

3 Henry; *k* in a fall from his horse at Lambton Gates, Co Durham, and was *bur* 28 Oct 1682; *m* —, of Liège, and had a dau (*m* abroad)

1 Ellen; *m* Sir William Selby, of Biddleston

2 Anne; *m* William Blundell, of Crosby

3 Margaret; *m* 2nd William Hodson, of Hepburn

4 Alice; *bur* 22 Dec 1654

Sir THOMAS's 2nd son,

Sir Thomas Haggerston, 2nd Bt; Govr Berwick Castle; *m* 1st Margaret, dau of Sir Francis Howard, of Corby Castle (*see* NORFOLK, D); *m* 2nd Jane (*dsp*), dau and heir of Sir William Carnaby, and had by his 1st w, with other issue:

1 Thomas; *k* in the serv of JAMES II in Ireland

2 William; *m* Anne, dau of Sir Philip Mark Constable, 3rd Bt, of Everingham, Yorks, and *dvp*, leaving, with four daus (the 3rd, Anne, *m* Bryan Salvin, of Croxdale):

(1) CARNABY (Sir), **3rd Bt**

3 Henry (Rev); *b* 1658; *educ* St Omer and Douai; RC priest, ordained *c* 1688; *d* 12 March 1714

4 John (Rev); *b* 28 Jan 1661; *educ* St Omer; RC priest, ordained 1689; *d* 6 Feb 1726

5 Thomas; *educ* St Omer

Sir THOMAS's gs,

Sir Carnaby Haggerston, 3rd Bt; *b c* 1700; *m* 20 Nov 1721 Elizabeth (*d* Dec 1769), sis and coheir of William Midleton, of Kilvington and Stockeld, Yorks, and was *bur* 20 July 1756, having had:

1 **Sir Thomas Haggerston, 4th Bt**; *bapt* 11 Sept 1722; *educ* St Omer; *m* 1754 Mary (*d* 22 May 1778), dau of George Silvertop, of Minster Acres, Northumberland, and *d* 1 Nov 1777, having had, with other issue:

(1) **Sir Carnaby Haggerston, 5th Bt**; *b* May 1756, *m* Frances (*d* 1836), dau of Walter Smythe (s of Sir John Smythe, 3rd Bt, of Eshe, Co Durham) and sis of the Mrs Fitzherbert who went through a form of marriage with GEORGE IV, and *d* 3 Dec 1831, having had:

1a Mary; *m* Jan 1805 Sir Thomas Stanley, 9th Bt (*see* DERBY, E), and *d* 20 Aug 1857, leaving issue

(2) Thomas, of Sandoe, Northumberland; *educ* Bruges; *m* Winifred, dau of Edward Charlton, of Reedsmouth, and *d* 1829, leaving, with other issue:

1a **Sir Thomas Haggerston, 6th Bt**; *b* 13 July 1785; *m* 24 Jan 1815 Margaret (*d* 26 Oct 1823), only dau of William Robertson, of Ladykirk, Berwicks, and *dspm* 11 Dec 1842, having had:

1b Marianne Sarah; *m* 10 Sept 1834 David MARJORIBANKS later ROBERTSON, 1st and last Baron Marjoribanks of Ladykirk, Co Berwick (UK), so *cr* 12 June 1873 (*dspms* 19 June 1873 (a week after his ennoblement), when the title expired), 4th s of Sir John Marjoribanks, Bt (*see* 1888 edn), and *d* 19 Aug 1889, having had issue

2b Margaret Frances; *m* 2 July 1850 Lewis Joseph Eyre, yst s of Charles Eyre, of Derby, and *d* 25 Aug 1892, leaving, with other issue:

1c Marguerite Haggerston; *m* 11 Jan 1887 **Sir John Haggerston, 9th Bt** (*see* below)

3b Emma; nun St Mary's Priory Princethorpe

4b Winifred Mary; nun St André, Tournay, Belgium; *d* 31 Jan 1885

5b Charlotte Louisa; nun St Mary's Priory Princethorpe

2a **Sir Edward Haggerston, 7th Bt**; *b c* 1797; *dsp* 6 May 1857

3a **Sir John Haggerston, 8th Bt**; *b* 18 Aug 1798; Capt 80th Foot; *m* 5 Aug 1851 Sarah Anne (*d* 24 March 1883 aged 65), dau of Henry Knight, of Terrace Lodge, Axminster, Devon, and *d* 8 March 1858, having had:

1b **Sir John de Marie Haggerston, 9th Bt**; *b* 27 Nov 1852; *m* 11 Jan 1887 Marguerite Sarah Mary (*d* 18 Feb 1925), dau of Lewis Joseph Eyre, of S Kensington, and *dsp* 29 Nov 1918

2b **Sir Edward Charlton de Marie Haggerston, 10th Bt**, JP (Northumberland); *b* 8 Feb 1857; *m* 10 Oct 1904 Florence (*d* 6 Jan 1955), 3rd dau of William H Perrin, of Dublin, and *d* 1 April 1925, having had:

1c **Sir (Hugh) Carnaby de Marie Haggerston, 11th Bt**, JP (Northumberland 1939); *b* 7 March 1906; *educ* Oratory Sch; Capt Roy Northumberland Fus TA, Lt 1st Bn Roy Northumberland Fus 1926–37, TA RNF WW II; *m* 7 Jan 1933 Mary Ridgway, est dau of J Ridgway Macy, of 5th Avenue, New York, and *d* 11 Sept 1971, having had:

1d Charlton Peter de Marie; *b* 12 Dec 1935; *d* 11 March 1936

1d *Belinda Ann de Marie Haggerston [Lady Haggerston Gadsden, Harelaw House, Chathill, Northumberland NE67 5HE]; *b* 23 Sept 1933; *m* 16 April 1955 *Sir Peter Drury GADSDEN later HAGGERSTON GADSDEN (roy licence 1973), GBE, JP, Ld Mayor London 1979–80, er s of Rev Basil Claude Gadsden, of Whitney-on-Wye, Herefs, and has:

1e *Juliet Mary; *b* 4 March 1956; *m* 1978 *Nigel John Cartwright and has:

1f *Nicholas John Haggerston Gadsden; *b* 1980

2f *James Alexander Haggerston Gadsden; *b* 1982

3f *Charles Peter Haggerston Gadsden; *b* 1989

1f *Georgina Mary Haggerston Gadsden; *b* 1984

2e *Caroline Mabel [Mrs Graham Simpson, The Home Farm, Ellingham, Northumberland NE67 5HG]; *b* Aug 1957; *m* 1983 *Capt Graham C Simpson, RA, and has:

1f *Matthew Caveen Drury; *b*1985

2f *Oliver Peter Carnaby; *b* 1989

1f *Amelia Ann de Marie; *b* 1987

2f *Belinda Rose de Marie; *b* 1991

3e *Clare Louise; *b* 29 June 1960; *m* 1985 *Iain C H McWhirter, er s of Ross McWhirter, and has:

1f *(Alexander) Ross; *b* 1988

1f *Annabelle Louise; *b* 1986

2f *Lucy Belinda; *b* 1990

3f *Camilla Rosemary; *b* 1991

4f *Charlotte Elizabeth; *b* 1993

4e *Elizabeth Ann; *b* 28 Feb 1962

2d *Jennifer Veronica Louise de Marie [Mrs Anthony Forward, 43 Flood St, London SW3]; *b* 19 July 1938; *m* 28 March 1959 (*divorce* 19–) Anthony Lambert Forward, s of Frederick Bruce Forward, of Va., and has:

1e *Hugh Carnaby; *b* 18 Nov 1959; *m* 1988 (*divorce* 19–) Veronique Cavallier

2e *Andrew Lambert; *b* 4 March 1964

3d Helias Cecilia de Marie; *b* 13 April 1940; *d* 21 Oct 1957

4d *Phyllida Angela de Marie [Mrs Anthony Woosnam Mills, Mother Ivy Cottage, Trevose Head, Cornwall PL28 8SL]; *b* 18 June 1945; *m* 26 Aug 1967 *Antony Roland Woosnam Mills, s of Harry Roland Mills, and has:

1e *Alexander Ross Thomas; *b* 8 March 1984

1e *Victoria Ann Helen; *b* 30 Jan 1977

2c **Sir Ralph (Raphael) Stanley de Marie Haggerston, 12th Bt;** *b* 6 Aug 1912; *educ* Ampleforth; *m* 15 Dec 1956 *Joan Adeline [Lady Haggerston, 62 Lonston Park, Beadnell, Northumberland NE67 5BP], dau of William Blythe-Perrett, of Ludgershall, Wilts, and *dsp* 3 Jan 1972

1c Monica Winifred de Marie; *b* 28 June 1907; *m* 4 Dec 1940 Capt Geoffrey Russell Hudson, RA, s of Brig-Gen Thomas Roe Christopher Hudson, CB, of Pyle Hill, Newbury, and *d* 17 Nov 1967, leaving issue

2c *Ursula Edith de Marie [Mrs Richard Harrison, 2 Swan Lane Close, Burford, Oxon]; *b* 1 May 1910; *m* 22 July 1939 Richard Grenville Harrison, JP (*d* 16 Feb 1969), er s of Col Louis Kenneth Harrison, CBE, of Springfield House, Leicester, and has:

1d *Louis Bevill Grenville [Louis Harrison Esq, Weaver's Cottage, Clapton Rd, Bourton-on-the-Water, Glos GL54 2DN]; *b* 10 May 1940; *educ* Downside and RAC Cirencester; *m* 1975 *Katherine Sarah, yr dau of Charles Lindsay Lushington Picken, and has:

1e *Charles Richard Grenville; *b* 14 Dec 1980

1d *Elizabeth Rosemary [Mrs Guy Taylor, Kirkside House, Bonkyl, Duns, Berwickshire TD11 3RJ]; *b* 1943; *m* 1972 *Guy Martin Aldersey Taylor and has:

1e *James Edward Aldersey; *b* 1978

1e *Emma Mary Ursula; *b* 1981

1b Mary Julia; *m* 23 April 1879 Lt-Col Robert Lewis Arathoon, 58th Regt, of Court Lodge, Gillingham, Kent, and *d* 27 Sept 1920, leaving issue

2b Winifred Josephine de Marie; *b* posthumously 1858; *d* unm 3 Aug 1915.

1a Mary; *m* 23 Nov 1829 Henry S Stephens

2a Frances Emily; *m* 3 Jan 1825 Henry John William Collingwood, of Lilburn Tower

3a Winifred; *m* William Foster, of Alnwick

2 William HAGGERSTON later CONSTABLE (on inheriting 1746 the Everingham Park and other estates from his great-uncle Sir Marmaduke Constable, 4th Bt); *educ* St Omer; *m* 17 Oct 1758 Lady Winifred Maxwell, only surv dau and heir of William, s of 9th Lord Herries of Terregles (*qv*), and *d* 1797, leaving:

(1) Marmaduke William CONSTABLE later CONSTABLE-MAXWELL; had, with other issue (*see* HERRIES OF TERREGLES, L):

1a WILLIAM CONSTABLE-MAXWELL, 10th LORD HERRIES OF TERREGLES, as which recognised by Ho Lds 23 June 1858; *b* 25 Aug 1804; *m* 12 Nov 1835 Marcia Mary (*d* 13 Nov 188, aged 67), est dau of Hon Sir Edward Marmaduke Joseph Vavasour, 1st Bt (*qv*), and *d* 12 Nov 1876, leaving, with other issue:

1b Joseph CONSTABLE-MAXWELL later CONSTABLE-MAXWELL-SCOTT; *m* 21 July 1874 Mary Monica, dau of J Robert Hope-Scott (*see* LINLITHGOW, M), consequently adding SCOTT, and had, with other issue (*see* HERRIES OF TERREGLES, L):

1c Malcolm Joseph Raphael, DSO (1917); *b* 22 Oct 1883; *m* 6 Sept 1918 Fearga Victoria Mary, est dau of Sir Nicholas Roderick O'Conor (*see* LINLITHGOW, M), and *d* 23 Feb 1943, leaving:

1d MICHAEL FERGUS CONSTABLE-MAXWELL-SCOTT (Sir); **13th Bt**

2d Ian Malcolm; *b* 18 July 1927; *m* 14 Feb 1958 *Susan Mary [Mrs Ian Maxwell-Scott, 12 Kelmscott Rd, London SW11 6QY], yr dau of Sir Andrew Edmund James Clark, 3rd Bt, MBE, MC, QC, of Cavendish Square (*see* 1970 edn), and *d* 1993, leaving:

1e +Malcolm Fergus; *b* 24 Dec 1960; *m* 1990 (*divorce* 1993) Tanya, yr dau of William Church

2e +Simon Magnus; *b* 28 Dec 1962; *m* 1986 (*divorce* 1993) Gaynor, yst dau of Daniel Jones, and has:

1f +Hector George; *b* 1986

1f *Amelia Elizabeth; *b* 1989

3e +Andrew Nicholas Hugh; *b* 25 Nov 1966

1e *Lucy Ann; *b* 26 Sept 1958

2e *Sarah Secunda; *b* 15 Oct 1959

3e *Catherine Monica Jane; *b* 25 Nov 1966

1d Elizabeth Mary; *b* 28 May 1924; *d* 1991

(1) Mary; *d* unm 13 Jan 1829

(2) Anne; *m* Thomas Clifford, of Lytham, Lancs, and *dsp*

Sir RALPH's distant cousin,

Sir Michael Fergus Maxwell-Scott, 13th Bt; *b* 23 July 1921; *educ* Ampleforth and Trin Coll Cambridge; *m* 1963 *Deirdre Moira [Lady Maxwell-Scott, 10 Evelyn Mansions, Carlisle Place, London SW1; Dennett Cottage, Bembridge, Isle of Wight], dau of Alexander MacKechnie, and *d* 29 Nov 1989, leaving:

1 Sir DOMINIC JAMES MAXWELL-SCOTT, **14th and present Bt**

2 +Matthew Joseph; *b* 27 Aug 1976

1 *Annabel Jane; *b* 1973

MAY

Arms: Gu. on a chevron, between in chief three billets or and in base an eagle displayed arg., three roses of the field, barbed and seeded ppr. **Crest:** A demi-leopard ppr., holding in the dexter paw a bezant and resting the sinister paw on a terrestrial globe, also ppr. **Supporters:** Dexter, a griffin; sinister, a dragon or, each charged on the shoulder with a sprig of mayflower, slipped and leaved ppr. **Motto:** *Deo adjuvante labor proficit* ('With God's help work prospers'). **Creation:** Bt. (UK) 27 Jan 1931, B. (UK) 28 June 1935.

THE 3RD BARON MAY, of Weybridge, Co Surrey, and a **Baronet** (Sir Michael St John May, Bt) [The Rt Hon The Lord May, Gautherns Barn, Sibford Gower, Oxon OX15 5RY; 9 Palace Mews, London SW6 7TQ]; *b* 26 Sept 1931; *s* f 1950; *educ* Wycliff Coll and Magdalene Coll Cambridge; late Lt Roy Signals; *m* 1st 27 Dec 1958 (*divorce* 1963) Dorothea Catherine Ann, dau of Charles McCarthy, of Boston, USA; *m* 2nd 5 July 1963 *Jillian Mary, only dau of Albert Edward Shipton, of Wroxton Mill, Oxon, and has by her:

1 +JASPER BERTRAM ST JOHN; *b* 24 Oct 1965; *educ* Harrow

1 *Miranda Jane; *b* 17 Oct 1968

Lineage: Sir George Ernest May, 1st Bt, and 1st Baron May, of Weybridge, Co Surrey (both UK), so *cr* 27 Jan 1931 and 28 June 1935 respectively (s of William C May, of Cheshunt, Herts), KBE (1918); *b* 20 June 1871; MIA, chm Import Duties Advsy Ctee 1932–46 and Ec Ctee 1931, Manager American Dollar Securities Ctee 1916–18, Sec Prudential Assur Co, DQMG War Office in charge of canteens 1916–19; *m* 15 Oct 1903 Lily Julia, OBE (1920) (*d* 15 Jan 1955), yr dau G Strauss, of Earls Court, and had:

1 JOHN LAWRENCE, **2nd Baron**

2 Patrick William May; *b* 25 May 1911; *educ* Harrow; Maj RA WW II; *m* 1st 17 Feb 1934 (*divorce* 1948) Dorothy Patience, est dau of Francis du Croz, of Weybridge, and had:

(1) *Caroline May [Mrs Edwin Waldman, 45 Burleigh St, Waterville, ME 04901, USA]; *b* 1934; *m* 1954 *Edwin Waldman and has:

1a *Joshua Patrick; *b* 1957

2a *Noah William; *b* 1962

1a *Victoria Rose; *b* 1959

2a *Andrea Karen; *b* 1961

(2) *Valentine Virginia May [Mrs Malcolm MacLeod, 70 Belden Hill Rd, CT 06897, USA]; *b* 30 Nov 1938; *m* 1963 *Malcolm Walker MacLeod and has:

1a *Sarah Walker; *b* 1965

2a *Alexandra Louise; *b* 1968

2 (cont.) Maj The Hon Patrick May *m* 2nd 10 Feb 1951 Audrey Gillian (*d* 1989), dau of Edward Bagot, of Cross Farm, W Coker, Somerset, and formerly w of Frederick John Parland Jackson, and *d* 9 Sept 1956, having by her had:

(3) *Philippa Jane May [Mrs Anthony Crabtree, Cornwall House, Cross St, Tenbury Wells, Worcs WR15 8EG]; *b* 18 June 1952; *m* 1987 *Anthony Crabtree and has:

1a *Christopher; *b* 1987

1a *Melanie; *b* 1988

2a *Alice; *b* 1990

(4) *(Elisabeth) Patricia; *b* posthumously 17 Jan 1957; *m* 19– *— and has:

1a *Tanya; *b* 1980

2a *Samantha; *b* 1981

1 Elisabeth Frances; *b* 29 June 1907; F/Capt ATA WW II; *m* 10 Jan 1955 *George Leonard Brunton Henderson, BSc (Edin), MRCVS [George Henderson Esq, Oak Lodge, 4 Oak Hill Grove, Surbiton, Surrey KT6 6DS], s of Edward Joseph Henderson, of Portobello, Midlothian, and *d* 10 April 1995, leaving:

(1) *Christopher Iain; *b* 1959

(2) *Simon Neil; *b* 1960

The 1st BARON *d* 10 April 1946; his er son,

JOHN LAWRENCE MAY, **2nd Baron May;** *b* 15 Aug 1904; *m* 1st 1 July 1925 Cicely Beryl (*d* 1928), only dau of Ernest Fleming, of Watford; *m* 2nd 29 Oct 1928

*Elisabeth (m 2nd W H Hallam) [Mrs W Hallam, 46 Lyndon Rd, Bramham Mead, Yorks], dau of George Ricardo Thoms, and d 9 March 1950, having by her had:

1 MICHAEL ST JOHN MAY, **3rd and present Baron May**

1 *June Lisette May [The Hon Mrs Lisser, School House, Stanton, Broadway, Worcs]; b 1929; educ St Paul's and Sadler's Wells Sch of Dancing; m 8 Jan 1958 *Raymond Charles Lisser and has:

  (1) *Aidan Charles; b 13 Nov 1959; m 17 Dec 1994 *Caroline, yr dau of Allan Wordsworth, of Mayfield, E Sussex

Mayhew of Twysden

Creation: B. (LP, UK) 1997.

THE BARON MAYHEW OF TWYSDEN, of Kilndown in the County of Kent (Sir Patrick Barnabas Burke Mayhew), PC (1986), QC (1972) [The Rt Hon The Lord Mayhew of Twysden PC QC, House of Lords, London SW1A 0PW]; b 11 Sept 1929; educ Tonbridge and Balliol Coll Oxford; Capt 4th/7th Roy Dragoon Gds, barrister Middle Temple 1955, Bencher 1980, fought Camberwell and Dulwich 1970 gen election, ktd 1983, MP (C) Roy Tunbridge Wells Feb 1974–83 and Tunbridge Wells 1983–97, Parly U-Sec Employment 1979–81, Min State Home Office 1981–83, Slr-Gen 1983–87, Attorney-Gen 1987–92, NI Sec 1992–97, memb exec 1922 Ctee 1976–79, Pres Airey Neave Tst 1997–; m 15 April 1963 *Jean Elizabeth, OBE (1997), 2nd dau of John Gurney, JP (Norfolk), of Walsingham Abbey, Norfolk, by Ann, only child of Capt Frederick Charles Ashley Ogilvy, RN, 3rd s of Sir Reginald Ogilvy, 10th Bt (qv), and has:

1 *(James) Barnabas Burke; b 11 March 1964

2 *Henry Edmund Burke; b 10 Aug 1965

3 *Tristram Thomas Burke; b 12 April 1968; Capt Army; m 16 May 1998 *Rebecca K S, est dau of Richard Hobbs and Mrs John Morgan of Northchapel, W Sussex

4 *Jerome Patrick Burke; b 1970

Lineage: See FERMOY, B

Mayo

Arms: Per fess or and erm. a cross gu., in the 1st quarter a lion rampant, in the 2nd a dexter hand erect, couped at the wrist, both sa. **Crest:** A cat-a-mountain sejant guardant ppr., collared and chained or. **Supporters:** Two chevaliers in complete armour, each holding in the exterior hand a pole-axe ppr. **Motto:** A cruce salus ('Salvation from the Cross'). **Creation:** E. (I) 24 June 1785, V. (I) 13 Jan 1781, B. (I) 1 Aug 1776.

THE 10TH EARL OF THE COUNTY OF MAYO ,Viscount Mayo of Monycrower, Co Mayo, and **Baron Naas of Naas**, Co Kildare (Terence Patrick Bourke) [The Rt Hon The Earl of Mayo, Château d'Arlens, Couloumé, Mondebat, 32160 Plaisance-du-Gers, France]; b 26 Aug 1929; s unc 1962; educ St Aubyn's Rottingdean and RNC Dartmouth; Lt (P) RN (ret); m 1st 5 April 1952 (divorce 1987) Margaret Jane Robinson (d 1992), only dau of Gerald Joseph Cuthbert Harrison, DL, of Cumberland, and has:

1 +CHARLES DIARMUIDH JOHN BOURKE, Baron Naas [Lord Naas, Derryinver, Beach Rd, Clifden, Co Galway, Ireland]; b 11 June 1953; educ Portora Roy Sch and Queen's U Belfast; m 1st 1975 (divorce 1979) Marie Antoinette Cronnelly and has:

  (1) *Corinne Mary Jane Bourke; b 1975

1 (cont.) Lord Naas m 2nd 1985 *Marie Veronica, dau of Francis Mannion, of Clifden, and by her has:

  (1) +Richard Thomas Bourke; b 7 Dec 1985

  (2) +Eoin Patrick Bourke; b 1989

2 +Patrick Anthony Bourke; b 16 Dec 1955

3 +Harry Richard Bourke; b 23 Sept 1960

The 10th EARL m 2nd 1987 *Sally Anne, only dau of F G Matthews, of Bampton, Oxon, and by her has:

4 +James Edward Maurice Bourke; b 1986

Mayo, previous creation: Sir Richard Bourke, the MacWilliam Eighter (or 'Lower', i.e. of Sligo, or the Lower part of Connaught) had a son, Theobald, who is not to be confused with his contemporary, the man of the same name mentioned below. This first Theobald Bourke, although at first opposed to ELIZABETH I's attempt to bring Ireland under control, later sided with the English in opposing the Spaniards at Kinsale, was knighted, regranted his lands from the English authorities in Dublin and was in 1627 made Viscount Mayo or Bourke of Mayo. His son the second Viscount was as a Protestant made Joint Governor of the county from which his title took its name and married a granddaughter of the 3rd Earl of Clanricarde (see SLIGO, M). The 3rd Viscount, also a Protestant, was nevertheless executed by the Cromwellian authorities for rebellion, having previously been a royalist in the confused internecine war that had raged throughout Ireland during the 1640s and early 1650s. The 4th Viscount got his substantial estates in Co Mayo back after the Restoration (they amounted to 50,000 acres) but these were largely sold off by his successor the 5th Viscount. The 8th and last Viscount died without surviving male issue in 1767, when the title either expired or became dormant. It was assumed, though without official recognition, by three cousins in succession over the next thirty years. Both these lines of Bourkes were clearly themselves cousins of the Bourkes who were later created Earls of Mayo, but the precise relationship has not been determined.

Lineage: The MacWILLIAM BOURKEs (see also SLIGO, M, subsection **Lineage (of Clanricarde)**) derive from a common ancestor, WILLIAM Fitz ADELM de BURGO, who succeeded STRONGBOW as Ch Govr Ireland following the Anglo-Cambro-Norman incursion into Ireland in the 12th century.

Sir THEOBALD BOURKE, of Ardnaree, the last MacWilliam Bourke Eighter of his line in Ireland, migrated to Spain shortly after 1595 and was cr MARQUIS OF MAYO by PHILIP II

DAVID BOURKE, of Monycrower; living temp HENRY VIII, had:

1 Edmond, of Urey and Cornelaugh, Co Mayo, ancestor of the BOURKEs of Urey

2 JOHN, of Monycrower

3 Miles

The 2nd son,

JOHN BOURKE, of Monycrower; had:

THEOBALD BOURKE, of Monycrower; granted Carrowoutragh 1617; had a 3rd s:

JOHN BOURKE, of Kill, Co Kildare; Capt of Horse under the Marquess of Ormonde during the 1641 Uprising; m Catherine, dau of Mayler Fay and niece of Sir Paul Davys, and had, with three daus:

1 Miles; Cursitor Common Pleas Ireland, dsp

2 Walter, of Monycrower and Kill; m Anne, dau of Robert Annesley, of Ballysonan, Co Kildare, and had:

  (1) Theobald, of Monycrower and Kill; dsp 1751

  (1) Mary; m Rev T Murray

  (2) —; m 1749 Robert Stafford

3 Theobald, of Palmerston; MP Naas; dsp 1726

4 Rickard, of Dublin and Palmerston, Co Kildare; LLD; m Catherine, dau of Charles Minchin, of Ballinakill, Co Tipperary, and d 1727, leaving:

  (1) JOHN BOURKE, **1st Earl of the County of Mayo**, so cr 24 June 1785, as also earlier 1 Aug 1776 BARON NAAS OF NAAS, Co Kildare, and 13 Jan 1781 VISCOUNT MAYO OF MONYCROWER (all I), PC (I); b c 1700; Sheriff Co Kildare 1737 MP Naas 1727–60 and 1768–76 and Old Leighlin 1761–68; m 1726 Mary (d 21 July 1774), 3rd dau and coheir of Rt Hon Joseph Deane, Ld Ch Baron of Exchequer in Ireland, and d 2 Dec 1790, having had, with other issue:

1 JOHN BOURKE, **2nd Earl of the County of Mayo**; b c 1729; MP Naas 1763–90; m Feb 1764 Lady Mary Leeson, dau of 1st Earl of Milltown (see 1970 edn), and dsp 20 April 1792

2 JOSEPH DEANE, **3rd Earl**

1 Margaret; m Sir Thomas Newcomen, 8th Bt, of Kenagh

The 2nd EARL's bro,

JOSEPH DEANE BOURKE, **3rd Earl of the County of Mayo**, PC (I 1782); b 1736; Archbp Tuam 1782–94; m 1760 Elizabeth (d 13 March 1807), sis of 1st Earl of Clanwilliam (qv), and d 20 Aug 1794, having had, with five other daus:

1 JOHN BOURKE, **4th Earl of the County of Mayo**, GCH (1819), PC (I 1810); b 18 June 1766; MP Naas 1798 0–94, rep I peer 1816–49; m 24 May 1792 Arabella, Ldy-in-Waiting to QUEEN ADELAIDE (d 19 Nov 1943), 4th dau of William Mackworth-Praed, MP, of Bitton Court, Devon, and dsp 23 May 1849

2 Richard (Rt Rev); Bp Waterford and Lismore; b 23 April 1767; m 20 March 1795 Frances (d 1827), 2nd dau of Robert Fowler, Archbp Dublin, and d 15 Nov 1832, having had:

  (1) ROBERT, **5th Earl**

  (1) Mildred; granted with her surv sis 19 Oct 1849 rank of earl's dau; m Aug 1821 Robert Uniacke (d 1851), of Wodehouse, Co Waterford, and d 29 July 1869

  (2) Frances; m 10 June 1846, as his 2nd w, William Henry Carter (d 6 July 1859), of Castle Martin, Co Kildare, and d 21 Jan 1858

  (3) Catherine; m 1830 Rev Henry Prittie Perry, Rector Newcastle, Co Limerick, and d 12 Sept 1876, leaving issue

3 Joseph (Very Rev); Dean Ossory; b 24 Dec 1771; m 23 April 1799 Mary, est dau and coheir of Sackville Gardiner, and d 3 May 1843, having had, with two daus:

  (1) Sackville Gardiner (Rev); Rector Hatherop, Glos; b 1 May 1805; m 6 June 1839 Georgiana Sarah (d 25 June 1861), est dau of 4th Earl of Bessborough (qv), and d 30 Jan 1860, having had, with other issue:

    1a Cecil Frederick Joseph (Ven); b 1 Sept 1841; MA Oxon, Archdeacon Buckingham; d unm 15 April 1910

(2) John William (Rev); *b* Nov 1808; Rector Offerland, Queen's Co; *d* 15 Feb 1885

4 George Theobald (Rev); *b* 15 April 1770; *m* 1808 Augusta Georgiana (*d* 7 Oct 1863), 2nd dau of Thomas Webster, and *d* 22 Dec 1847, having had, with a dau (*d* unm):

(1) Richard; barrister; *b* 22 Feb 1811; *m* 26 June 1849 Gertrude (*m* 2nd 12 Aug 1858 Anthony North Peat (*d* 1870) and *d* 10 June 1910), dau of Robert Borrowes, of Gilltown, Co Kildare (*see* 1939 edn BORROWES, Bt), and had:

1a Southwell George Theobald; *b* 28 July 1851; Lt-Cdr RN, barrister Middle Temple, Stipendiary Magistrate Br Guiana 1897; *m* 27 July 1881 Catherine Jane (*d* 11 Sept 1951), only dau of William Cameron, and *d* 8 Nov 1919

2a Hubert Edward Madden BOURKE later BOURKE-BORROWES (roy licence 9 March 1925), of Gilltown and Feltimores, Harlow, Essex; *b* 7 Dec 1853; Lt RN, Roy Humane Soc Medal; *m* 4 Aug 1881 Rose (*d* 24 Dec 1948), dau of Henry Blackett, and *d* 11 Oct 1936, leaving:

1b Dermot Richard Southwell BOURKE later BOURKE-BORROWES (deed poll 27 Aug 1925); *b* 14 April 1884; Indian Forest Serv, Capt IA, served Mesopotamia 1916–18 (despatches); *educ* Winchester; *m* 9 April 1941 *Mrs Elizabeth Burton, dau of G F Burgess, of Hall Garth, Over Kellett, Lancs, and *d* 27 June 1968, leaving:

1c +Kildare Hubert, JP [Kildare Bourke-Borrowes Esq JP, The Lower House, North Aston, Oxon OX6 4JA]; *b* 21 Sept 1942; *educ* Wellington and Magdalene Coll Cambridge; *m* 1st 1971 (*divorce* 1983) Pippa Marguerite (*d* 1992), yr dau of Lt-Col O S Steel, of Chelsea, and has:

1d *Olivia Helene; *b* 10 July 1974

2d *Catherine; *b* 6 May 1977

1c (cont.) Kildare Bourke-Borrowes *m* 2nd 1984 *Sarah Louise, dau of John Robert McCready, of Kenya, and by her has:

1d +Hubert Alexander Robert; *b* 10 June 1985

3d *Thea Anne; *b* 7 Aug 1986

2b Cecil Hubert BOURKE later BOURKE-BORROWES (deed poll 27 Aug 1925), MBE (1953), TD, DL Essex; *b* 24 Jan 1892; *educ* Haileybury; Maj RE, TAR, WW I (despatches), WW II attd RAF North Weald and SHAEF HQ, Croix de Guerre 1946, Attaché Paris; *m* 11 June 1925 Hélène, only surv child of Maurice Casenave, Ministre Plénipotentaire, of Château des Rets, Chennevières-sur-Marne, and *dsp* 24 Dec 1967

1b Vivian Margaret Nellie; *m* 27 June 1912 Wyndham Damer Clark, JP, DL, Coldstream Gds (*d* 28 Nov 1961), and *d* 5 Aug 1957, leaving issue

1a Augusta Georgiana Clara; *m* 6 Dec 1867 Charles de Gannes, of Pierrefonds, and *d* 29 Feb 1870, leaving issue

(2) John (Rev); Vicar Kilmeaden, Co Waterford; *b* 15 Aug 1812; *m* 8 Feb 1842 Louisa Maria (*d* 14 Nov 1870), dau of James David Potts, and *d* 15 March 1891, leaving, with two daus (*d* unm):

1a John Frederick (Rev); *b* 16 Nov 1843; *educ* Jesus Coll Cambridge (BA); Curate Corfe Castle, Dorset; *dsp* 23 Jan 1873

2a William Theobald; *b* 21 June 1851; Cdr RN; *dsp* 1890

3a Arthur Edward Desborough; *b* 3 Dec 1852; BA Dublin, barrister, Inspr Local Govt Bd Ireland; *m* 2 April 1888 Maude Margaret (*d* 8 Nov 1923), dau of Henry Blake Mahon, of Belleville, Co Galway, and *d* 31 Jan 1903, leaving:

1b Arthur John Henry; *b* 9 May 1897; Brig IA; Lt Connaught Rangers WW I (wounded twice), Afghanistan 1919 and Waziristan 1919–21, Lt-Col cmdg 4th/8th Punjab Regt 1938–41, served NWF India and Waziristan 1936–38 (despatches) and WW II (despatches); *dsp* 12 Jan 1986

2b Eleanor Louise; *m* 29 April 1922, as his 2nd w, Maurice Collis, ICS (*d* 13 Jan 1973), author and critic, est s of William Stewart Collis, JP, of Killiney, Co Dublin, and *d* 8 March 1967, leaving issue

4a Henry Beresford, DSO; *b* 2 June 1855; Lt-Col 3rd WI Regt, W Africa 1892 and 1893–94, Sierra Leone 1898–99, WW I as DCO; *d* 1 Nov 1921

1a Alice Mildred; *d* unm 1 April 1950

(3) Thomas Joseph Deane; *b* 7 March 1815; Lt-Col 34th Regt; *m* Jan 1849 Mary (*d* 1895), 2nd dau of Ven Archdeacon Robert Willis, of Nova Scotia, and *d* 28 Feb 1875, leaving, with two daus (*d* unm):

1a George Deane Bourke (Sir), KCMG, CB; *b* 15 Oct 1852; Maj-Gen AMS, Nile Expdn 1884–85 and 1885–86, Burma 1887–89, Chin-Lushai Expdn 1889–90, Tirah 1897–98, Hon Physician to HM 1909–12; PM Offr Irish Cmd 1908–12, Col Cmdt RAMC 1921–22, DDMS Scottish Cmd 1915 and Aldersot Cmd 1916; *m* 24 Jan 1883 Mary Morrow (*d* 1939), est dau of John Stairs, JP, of Fairfield, Nova Scotia, and *d* 7 Dec 1936, leaving:

1b Ulick John Deane, CMG (1919); *b* 13 April 1884; G/C RAF, Capt and Brevet Maj Oxon and Bucks LI WW I (despatches, brevet); *m* 1917 (*divorce* 1932) Irene, dau of Lewis Ashurst, of Norwich, and *d* 4 March 1948, having had:

1c Dermot; *b* 13 July 1918; *d* 5 May 1919

2c *Bridget Deane [Mrs Leigh Parker, Sparrows, North Aston, Oxon]; *b* July 1920; barrister Lincoln's Inn 1956; *m* 1963 Leigh Edward Parker (*d* 1973)

2a Robert John, JP N R Yorks; *b* 18 April 1854; *d* 10 Oct 1933

3a Frederick Arthur Deane; *b* 6 July 1856; *m* 1887 Anne Caird, dau of Col Hutchison, 64th Regt, and *d* 1917

1 Mary Elizabeth; *m* 1789 21st Baron De Clifford (*qv*) and *d* 28 May 1845

2 Mary Anne; *m* 1806 Adml Thomas Scotheby and *d* 1830

3 Theodosia Eleanor; *m* 1807 Robert Hale, of Alderley, Glos, and *d* 23 Aug 1845

The 4th EARL's nephew,

ROBERT BOURKE, **5th Earl of the County of Mayo**; *b* 12 Jan 1797; rep I peer 1852–67; *m* 3 Aug 1820 Anne Charlotte (*d* 26 Jan 1867), only child of Hon Jocelyn (*see* RODEN, E), and *d* 12 Aug 1867, having had, with a dau (*d* unm):

1 RICHARD SOUTHWELL BOURKE, **6th Earl of the County of Mayo**, KP (1869), GCSI, PC (1852); *b* 21 Feb 1822; MP (C) Co Kildare 1847–52, Coleraine 1852–57 and Cockermouth 1857–68, Ch Sec Ireland 1852, 1858–59 and 1866–68, Viceroy India 1868–72; *m* 31 Oct 1848 Blanche Julia CI, VA (*d* 31 Jan 1918 aged 91), Extra Ldy Bedchamber to HM QUEEN VICTORIA, 4th dau of 1st Baron Leconfield (*see* EGREMONT, LECONFIELD and, B), and was assassi-

nated on a tour of inspection in the Andaman Islands 8 Feb 1872, having had, with a dau (*d* young):

(1) DERMOT ROBERT WYNDHAM BOURKE, **7th Earl of the County of Mayo**, KP (1904), PC (I 1900), JP and Lt Co Kildare; *b* 2 July 1851; *educ* Eton; rep I peer 1890, Senator IFS, Cornet 10th Hus and Lt Gren Gds; *m* 3 Nov 1885 Geraldine Sarah (*d* 29 Nov 1944), est dau of Hon Gerald Henry Brabazon Ponsonby (*see* BESSBOROUGH, E), and *dsp* 31 Dec 1927

(2) Maurice Archibald, CMG; *b* 22 Dec 1853; Capt RN, Extra Equerry to HRH THE DUKE OF SAXE-COBURG AND GOTHA, KG; served bombardment of Alexandria 1882; *d* unm 16 Sept 1900

(3) Algernon Henry; *b* 31 Dec 1854; *m* 15 Dec 1887 Guendoline Irene Emily (*d* 30 Dec 1967 aged 98), dau of Hans Sloane Stanley, of Paultons, Hants, and *d* 7 April 1922, leaving:

1a Daphne Marjorie; *b* 5 April 1895; *m* 7 June 1917 John Grenville Fortescue (*see* FORTESCUE, E) and *d* 22 May 1962, leaving issue

(4) Terence Theobald, OBE (1920); *b* 2 April 1865; Consul at Biserta; *m* 5 Aug 1896 Eveline Constance (*d* 16 July 1917), dau of Col Thomas William Haines, of Hasketon Manor, Suffolk, and *d* 13 May 1923, leaving:

1a Jasmine Eva; *b* 10 May 1898; *m* 22 April 1924 Harold Haydn-Morris (*d* 13 April 1950), 2nd s of Joseph Haydn Morris, and *d* 1964, leaving:

1b *Eva Myrtle [Miss Eva Haydn-Morris, 124 Elm Park Mansions, Park Walk, London SW10]; *b* 5 March 1931

2a Myrtle Mercy; *d* 24 Dec 1899

(1) Eva Constance Aline; *m* 7 July 1885 5th Earl of Dunraven and Mount-Earl (*qv*) and *d* 19 Jan 1940, leaving issue

(2) Florence Blanche Madeline; *b* 16 Aug 1861; *d* unm 1953

2 John Jocelyn, CB, JP and DL Co Meath; *b* 5 Oct 1823; Lt-Gen, Col Essex Regt, Kt Medjidie, 88th Connaught Rangers Crimea and Indian Mutiny; *d* unm 25 Sept 1904

3 ROBERT BOURKE, 1st and last BARON CONNEMARA, of Connemara, Co Galway (UK), so *cr* 12 May 1887, GCIE (1887), PC (1880), JP and DL E Lothian; *b* 11 June 1827; barrister Inner Temple 1852, MP (C) King's Lynn 1868–86, Parly U-Sec for Affrs 1874–80 and 1885–86, Govr Madras 1886–90; *m* 1st 21 June 1863 (*divorce* 1891) Lady Susan Georgina Broun-Ramsay, CI (*d* 22 Jan 1898), est dau of 1st Marquess of Dalhousie (*see* DALHOUSIE, E); *m* 2nd 22 Oct 1894 Gertrude (*d* 23 Nov 1898), widow of Edward Coleman, of Stoke Park, and *dsp* 3 Sept 1902, when the Barony expired

4 George Wingfield (Rev); *b* 16 Feb 1829; MA Durham; Rector Pulborough, Sussex, Hon Chaplain and Chaplain-in-Ordinary to HM QUEEN VICTORIA, RD Storrington and Treas Chichester Cathedral; *m* 9 Dec 1858 Mary Henrietta (*d* 22 Aug 1906), est dau of Most Rev Dr Longley, Archbp Canterbury, and *d* 9 Oct 1903, leaving, with a dau (*d* an infant):

(1) WALTER LONGLEY, **8th Earl**

5 Charles Fowley, CB; *b* 5 Sept 1832; chm General Prisons Bd Ireland, 1878–95; *m* 18 Dec 1895 Lady Albreda Mary Wentworth Fitzwilliam (*d* 9 Oct 1933), dau of 6th Earl Fitzwilliam (*see* 1970 edn), and *dsp* 4 April 1899

6 Edward Roden; *b* 13 Dec 1835; Maj 3rd Hus, Mil Sec to Govr-Gen India 1869–72; *m* 20 Nov 1872 Emma Mary Augusta (*m* 2nd 5 Aug 1908 5th Earl of Clarendon (*qv*) and *d* 9 March 1935), est dau of Lt-Gen George Cliffe Hatch, CSI, and *d* 7 June 1907, having had:

(1) Cecil Richard Donoughmore; *b* 29 Sept 1875; *d* 30 Nov 1884

(2) Nigel Edward Jocelyn; *b* 21 Aug 1886; Lt-Col 10th Manchester Regt; *m* 1927 Doris (*d* 1949), dau of Allan Wills, of Aberdeen, and *d* 27 Sept 1970, leaving:

1a +Josslyn Allen Roden; *b* 1930; *m* 17 Oct 1951 *Barbara Alison, dau of Wilson Braddock, of Errington, BC, and has:

1b *Alice Grania; *b* 1954

2b *Deborah Madeline; *b* 1958

3b *Susan Doris; *b* 29 Oct 1960

(1) Anne Kathleen Julia; *m* 1 Aug 1894 George Francis Burroughes, 2nd s of Rev Randall Burroughes, of Burlingham Hall, Norfolk, and *d* 16 March 1935, leaving issue

(2) Norah Mary Madeline; *m* 27 April 1895 Lt-Col Henry Edith Arthur Lindsay and *d* 20 June 1948, having had issue (*see* CRAWFORD and BALCARRES, E)

(3) Madeline Emmie Louisa; OStJ, pres Women's Land Army 1914–18 and Red Cross Beds; *m* 16 Jan 1904 Samuel Howard Whitbread, CB (*d* 29 July 1944), Ld Lt Beds, of Southill Park, Biggleswade, Beds, and *d* 5 Aug 1961, leaving issue

7 Henry Lorton, of Hayes, Beau Parc, Co Meath, and Wootton Hall, Ashbourne, Derbys, DL Middx; *b* 26 Sept 1840; BA Cantab; *m* 18 Dec 1876 Constance Una Elizabeth (*d* 2 July 1925), dau of Gustavus W Lambart, of Beau Parc, Meath (*see* 1970 edn LAMBART, Bt), and *dsp* 30 Jan 1911

The 7th EARL's cousin,

WALTER LONGLEY BOURKE, **8th Earl of the County of Mayo**, JP Lancs; *b* 28 Nov 1859; Maj Duke of Lancaster's Own Imp Yeo, MInst CE, FLAS, FRPS, engaged on Ch Engr's staff during construction of Forth Bridge, Resident Engr Manchester Ship Canal Construction, Tstee and Supt Bridgewater Estates 1891–1903, pres Land Agents Soc 1927–28 and College of Estate Management 1937–38; *m* 1st 8 June 1887 Ethel Kathleen Jane (*d* 12 Feb 1913), only dau of Capt John W Freeman, 16th Regt, of Rockfield, Herefs, and had:

1 Eustace George Walter; *b* 24 June 1888; Capt and Adj 9th Bn KRRC, ADC to Govr Gen S Africa, WW I (wounded); *ka* France 16 June 1915

2 ULICK HENRY BOURKE, **9th Earl of the County of Mayo**; *b* 13 March 1890; *educ* Wixenford and Uppingham; 2nd Lt (SR) KRRC, Lt KAR WW I; *m* 31 July 1937 Noel Jessie (*d* 1993), yst dau of William James Wilson, of High Park, nr Kendal, Westmorland, great-niece of 1st Baron Haliburton (*see* 1907 edn) and formerly w of her kinsman John Selwyn Haliburton, FRGS, and *dsp* 17 Dec 1962

3 Bryan Longley; *b* 18 July 1897; *educ* Rugby; WW I 1917–19 as Lt KRRC (wounded), WW II as Capt Roy Irish Fus; *m* 1st 4 April 1923 Violet Wilmot Heathcote (*d* 31 Dec 1950), dau of Col Charles Harcourt Stisted, JP, of King's Court, Chandler's Ford, Hants; *m* 2nd 11 Feb 1952 *Patricia May [The Hon Mrs Bryan Bourke, Dashells, Dog Village, Broadclyst, Devon EX5 3AB], BA Lon-

don, formerly JP Glos, er dau of Harold Bertie Dickinson, MD, FRCS, of Worcs, and *d* 11 June 1961, leaving by his 1st w:

(1) TERENCE PATRICK BOURKE, **10th and present Earl of the County of Mayo**

(1) *Sheelagh Wilmot [Mrs Frank Trier, Fairlawn, West Horsley, Surrey]; *b* 30 Aug 1925; *m* 4 Feb 1955 *Frank Merton Trier and has:

  1a *Terence Anthony Merton; *b* 6 Nov 1957

  1a *Ysolde Gwynedd; *b* 19 April 1956

4 Geoffrey John; *b* 2 July 1900; *educ* Repton; FRICS, FCLAS, pres Land Agents Soc 1947; *m* 3 Feb 1926 Nancy Lisette (*d* 19 June 1987), er dau of Douglas Theodore Thring, Bursar Merton Coll Oxford, and *d* June 1982, leaving:

(1) Mary Jennifer; *b* 8 Dec 1926; *m* 14 April 1953 *Digby Michael Auden [Digby Auden Esq, Dolphin House, 2 Back Lane, Hardingstone, Northampton NN4 0BX], yr s of Lt-Col Edward Humphry Auden, MBE, of Danesgate, Repton, Derbys, and *d* 27 Aug 1956, leaving:

  1a *Crispin Jeremy [Crispin Auden Esq, 21 Sturges Rd, Wokingham, Berks]; *b* 9 Aug 1954; *m* 19– *Lesley, er dau of Anthony Merrill and has:

    1b *Richard; *b* 16 Nov 1980

    1b *Alexandra Mary; *b* 18 March 1982

    2b *Lucinda Elizabeth; *b* 30 May 1987

  1a *Felicity Jennifer; *b* 12 Jan 1956; *m* 19– *Simon Andrew John White, er s of Geoffrey White, and has:

    1b *Robin Simon Auden; *b* 25 June 1985

    2b *Laurence Michael Geoffrey; *b* 29 Jan 1988

    1b *Helen Yvonne Kate; *b* 27 Dec 1991

(2) Elizabeth; *b* 27 Nov 1928; *m* 2 Oct 1954 John Anthony Lorimer Auden, only s of Maj John Lorimer Auden, MC, of The Laurels, Etwall, Derbys, and *d* 11 May 1991, leaving:

  1a *Christopher John Lorimer [Christopher Auden Esq, Weihermattstrasse 72, 4153 Reine Basel, Switzerland]; *b* 10 March 1958; *m* 19– *Astrid Bichsel and has:

    1b *Salonne; *b* 5 March 1991

    2b *Seraina; *b* 24 May 1993

  1a *Jennifer Mary [Mrs Ferhat Saadi, Gstadstrasse 30, 4153 Reinach, Basel, Switzerland]; *b* 28 Nov 1956; *m* 19– *Ferhat Saadi and has:

    1b *Malek Mokranes; *b* 11 Dec 1996

1 Margaret Ethel; *b* 3 Feb 1892; Cmdt BRCS 1946, WWs I and II VAD and nursing; *m* 6 Aug 1918 Lt-Cdr Edward James Trillo, RN (*d* 11 Jan 1958), s of James Trillo, of Trewalkin, Brecon, and *d* 4 April 1970, leaving:

(1) *Eustace Walter James [Eustace Trillo Esq, 100 Brent Court, Stevenage, Herts SG1 1JW]; *b* 4 Sept 1919; *educ* Hilsea Coll and SE Essex Tech Coll

(2) *Robert Longley; *b* 3 Feb 1927; CEng, FIMechE, FRAeS; *m* 12 Dec 1953 *Moira Darling, dau of Robert Thwaites, of Highcliffe, Hants, and has:

  1a *Richard James; *b* 2 Dec 1956

  2a *Duncan Patrick; *b* 1959

  3a *Robert Charles; *b* 17 Aug 1963

(1) *Kathleen Elizabeth Jane [Miss Kathleen Trillo, Erskine House, 7 Hinton Wood Ave, Highcliffe, Hants] *b* 26 April 1921

2 Mary Kathleen; *b* 19 Nov 1895; *m* 1st 19 June 1917 Capt Rev Percy Gordon Duff (*d* 27 Aug 1941), Rector St Mary Magdalen, St Leonards-on-Sea, and Chaplain RAFVR; *m* 2nd 23 Sept 1965 Lt-Col Richard Thomas Tarrant, VD, AMF, JP (NS Wales), s of James Tarrant, of Mudgee, NSW, and *d* 19 July 1971, leaving by her 1st husb:

(1) *Joyce Daphne [Mrs James Berry, The Woodlands, Newbarns Close, Arnside, Carnforth LA5 0BL]; *b* 8 April 1918; *m* 1943 James Percy Berry (*d* 7 Nov 1987)

(2) Pamela Kathleen; *b* 29 July 1919; *m* 1940 *Capt Cecil Lionel Bell, RASC [Cecil Bell Esq, 52 The Goffs, Eastbourne, E Sussex BN21 1HE] and *d* 18 Dec 1965, leaving:

  1a *Peter Gordon [Peter Bell Esq, 35 St Sampson Rd, Cottesmore Green, Crawley RH11 9RP]; *b* 25 April 1942; *m* 4 April 1970 (*divorce* 1 Oct 1990) Denise Estell Hawes and has:

    1b *James Gordon; *b* 25 April 1976

    1b *Sarah Louise; *b* 24 May 1972

    2b *Charlotte Marie; *b* 22 Jan 1980

    3b *Nannette Victoria; *b* 13 March 1982

  1a *Rosemary Wendy Pamela [Mrs George Risley, Garden House, 1 Church Rd, Egginton, Derby DE65 6HP]; *b* 27 March 1946; *m* 20 June 1975 *George Francis Risley and has:

    1b *Thomas Edward; *b* 8 Jan 1982

    1b *Jane Emma; *b* 9 Dec 1976

The **8th Earl** *m* 2nd 21 Dec 1916 Margaret Anah, Pres Girls Life Bde 1936–46, V-Pres Nat Assoc of Girls Clubs, Hon V-Pres Nat Assoc of Youth Clubs (*b* 29 May 1964), dau of Maj John Harvey Scott, IA, and *d* 6 May 1939, leaving by her:

3 *Betty Jocelyne [The Lady Betty Clarke, 361 Woodstock Rd, Oxford]; *b* 18 Aug 1917; *m* 1st 21 May 1943 Capt Ronald Banon (*d* 22 Aug 1943), late 60th Rifles, only child of Brig-Gen Lionel Banon, CB; *m* 2nd 27 April 1953 Samuel Clarke (*d* 1980) and by him has:

(1) *Elizabeth Charlotte; *b* 20 June 1955

(2) *Jocelyne Margaret; *b* 6 Jan 1957; *m* 1st 1981 (*divorce* 1988) Michael J Woodman; *m* 2nd 1992 *Carl Coert Grobler

McALPINE

Arms: Per chevron vert and or two chevronels, one in chief arg. and the other in base az. **Crest:** A cubit arm grasping a chaplet of pines fructed, all ppr. **Motto:** Build sure. **Creation:** Bt. (UK) 2 July 1918.

SIR WILLIAM HEPBURN McALPINE, 6TH BT, of Knott Park, Surrey [The Hon Sir William McAlpine Bt, Fawley Hill, Fawley Green, Henley-on-Thames, Oxon RG9 6JA]; *b* 12 Jan 1936; *s f* 1990; *educ* Charterhouse; dir Sir Robert McAlpine Ltd 1956–; *m* 1959 *Jill Benton, only dau of Lt-Col Sir Peter Fawcett Benton Jones, 3rd Bt (*qv*), and has:

1 +ANDREW WILLIAM; *b* 22 Nov 1960; *educ* Stowe; *m* 1991 *(Caroline) Claire, yr dau of Frederick A Hodgson, of Sheffield, Yorks, and has:

  (1) +Frederick William Edwin; *b* 25 Aug 1993

  (2) +Fergus Andrew Algernon; *b* 1994

1 *Lucinda Mary Jane; *b* 1964

Lineage: ROBERT McALPINE, of Newarthill, Lanarks; had:

Sir Robert McAlpine, 1st Bt (UK), so *cr* 2 July 1918, JP (Herts); head of Sir Robert McAlpine and Sons, civ engrg contractors; *b* 13 Feb 1847; *m* 1st 1867 Agnes (*d* 1888), dau of William Hepburn and *d* 3 Nov 1934, having had:

1 Sir Robert McAlpine, 2nd Bt; *b* 17 Oct 1868; *m* 1896 Lillias Cooper (*d* 1 Aug 1948), dau of Thomas George Bishop, of Helensburgh and Beattock, and *d* 16 Nov 1934, leaving:

(1) Sir Alfred Robert McAlpine, 3rd Bt, *b* 11 May 1907; *d* unm 25 Aug 1968

(1) Lillias Elizabeth McAlpine; *b* 21 Feb 1900; *m* 4 June 1925 S/Ldr Claude Alward Ridley, DSO, MC, RAF (*d* 27 June 1942), and *d* 9 April 1984, leaving:

  1a *Robert Louis McAlpine [Robert Ridley Esq, 12 Sheridan Court, Barkston Gardens, London SW5 0ET]; *b* 26 June 1926; *educ* Marlborough; *m* 15 Oct 1949 *Jacqueline, only dau of Louis Charles Bernard, of La Rochelle, France, and has:

    1b *Alain Patrick; *b* 20 Nov 1950; *m* 7 July 1979 *Valerie Susan Nettell and has:

      1c *Johnathan Claude; *b* 6 July 1984

      1c *Emma Louise; *b* 1 Feb 1981

    1b *Dominique Claudia; *b* 6 Aug 1952; *m* 10 Dec 1977 *Robert Leigh and has:

      1c *Alexandre Claude; *b* 19 March 1981

      1c *Vanessa Florence; *b* 17 Jan 1985

  1a *Elizabeth Lillias [Mrs William Kitto, Reef House, Douglas St, Castletown, IoM]; *b* 3 Nov 1927; *m* 22 June 1952 *William John Colin Kitto and has:

    1b *Nicholas John; *b* 9 Nov 1954

    1b *Joanna Elizabeth; *b* 10 Dec 1957

  2a *Eleanor Jean [Mrs Paul Longmire, 47 Egerton Crescent, London SW3]; *b* 26 Oct 1933; *m* 9 Nov 1957 *Paul Longmire and has:

    1b *Rupert; *b* 28 March 1964

    2b *Edward; *b* 26 Oct 1967

(2) *Zelie Agnes Elise Conde [Mrs Wilfred Chapman, Woodgates Cottage, Ford Manor, Dormansland, Lingfield, Surrey RH7 6NZ]; *b* 1910; *m* 7 March 1934 Wilfred Treize Rougier Chapman, VRD, LRCP, MRCS, Surgn-Cdr RNVR (*d* 1981), and has:

  1a *Zerelda Lillias; *b* 11 Nov 1939; *m* 1st 16 Feb 1962 (*divorce* 1970) Trevor Adrian Soutry, s of Capt Trevor Soutry, of Fletching; *m* 2nd 1977 *Alphonse Michaele Micallef, MD, of Lower Stonehurst Farm, E Grinstead, Sussex, and has by her 1st husb:

    1b *Giles Robert Adrian; *b* 5 May 1964; *m* 1994 *Mrs Anne Yolande Tranter Broadbent, dau of — Cartright

    1b *Lucinda Caroline; *b* 8 Jan 1969

  2a *Nonie Elizabeth; *b* 30 Sept 1942

  3a *Penelope Margaret [Mrs David Adam, Wayside Cottage, Dormansland, Surrey]; *b* 13 Aug 1944; *m* 24 Sept 1966 *David Ronald Adam, s of Ronald Adam, OBE, of Surbiton, Surrey, and has:

    1b *Angus Ronald; *b* 28 May 1969; *m* 1996 *Yasmin Osmond

1b *Annabelle Jane; *b* 30 Jan 1968; *m* 1993 *Maj Charles Andrew Stuart and has:

2c *William James; *b* 12 July 1996

2b *Katherine Lucy; *b* 1972; *m* 1997 *Michael Greville Tufnell and has:

1c *William James; *b* 1996

2 William Hepburn; *b* 31 Oct 1871; *m* 6 April 1898 Margaret Donnison (*d* 5 Jan 1970 aged 92), dau of Thomas George Bishop, and *d* 20 Feb 1951, leaving:

(1) **Sir Thomas George Bishop McAlpine, 4th Bt**; *b* 23 Oct 1901; *m* 1st 29 March 1934 Doris Frew (*d* 27 June 1964), dau of D C Campbell, of Gosforth, Newcastle-upon-Tyne, and widow of W E Woodeson; *m* 2nd 19 Aug 1965 *Kathleen Mary, dau of Frederick Best, of Hurworth-on-Tees, and Bickley, Kent, and widow of Charles Bantock Blackshaw, and *dsp* 5 April 1983

(2) (ROBERT) EDWIN (Sir), **5th Bt**

(3) Malcom Donnison; *b* 23 Dec 1909; *educ* Oundle; *m* 17 June 1939 *Diana Mary [Mrs Diana McAlpine, The White House, Burton Lazars, Leics], only dau of Sidney Bruce Askew of Patterson Court, Redhill, Surrey, and *d* 1982, leaving:

1a +Ian Malcolm OBE [Ian McAlpine Esq OBE, Peatling Hall, Peatling Parva, Leics LE17 5QA]; *b* 7 April 1942; *educ* Oundle and Clare Coll Cambridge (MA); High Sheriff Leics 1998–99; *m* 16 Sept 1967 *Caroline Mary, only dau of William Henry Ward, of The Warrens, Leverington, Cambs, and adopted:

*Julian Angus Ian; *b* 1970

*Susannah Melanie; *b* 1972

1a +Bruce Andrew [Bruce McAlpine Esq, 43 Elm Park Gdns, London SW10 9PA]; *b* 28 July 1947; *educ* Oundle and Clare Coll Cambridge; *m* 1st 1974 (*divorce* 1990) Ingrid Christliebe, dau of Alfred Reynolds Schlosshauer, of Neckarhausen, Germany; *m* 2nd 1993 Marina Ernestine Hirschberg, dau of Hubert, Baron von Breisky, of Salzburg

1a *Susan Mary [Mrs Leonard Harvey, Lyneham House, Yealmpton, Devon PL8 2LG]; *b* 2 June 1945; *m* 14 Sept 1968 *Leonard Maxwell Harvey and has:

1b *Damon; *b* 1971

(1) Agnes Hepburn; *b* 1903; *m* 18 Dec 1924 Maj James Henderson Mann, MBE, MA, FCA, late The Cameronians (*d* 13 Nov 1997), s of Sir John Mann, KBE, and had issue

(2) *Margaret Elizabeth Henderson; *b* 1905; has two adopted daus

3 (Thomas) Malcolm (Sir), KBE (1921); *b* 19 June 1877; *m* 2 Sept 1903 Maud (*d* 13 July 1969), 2nd dau of James Gibson Dees, of Whitehaven and *d* 12 April 1967, leaving:

(1) ROBERT later ROBIN (deed poll 1939) (Sir), CBE (1957); *b* 18 March 1906; *educ* Charterhouse; chm Sir Robert McAlpine and Sons Ltd (ret 1969), pres Fedn Civil Engrg Contractors, ktd 1969; *m* 1st 14 July 1939 Nora Constance (*d* 29 Sept 1966), yr dau of Horace Frank Perse, of Rochester, Kent; *m* 2nd 20 March 1970 Philippa Janet (*d* 1987), dau of Sir (Eustace) Gervais Tennyson d'Eyncourt, 2nd Bt (*qv*), and formerly w of Nigel Nicolson (*see* CARNOCK, B), and *d* 1993, leaving an adopted dau:

*Carolyn Peta [Mrs Nigel Elwes, Aylesfield, Alton, Hants GU34 4BY]; *b* 1944; *m* 22 June 1965 *Nigel Robert Elwes, er s of Col Robert Philip Henry Elwes, MBE, MC, of Ennistown, Co Meath, and has:

1b *Andrew Julian Robert; *b* 19 Nov 1969; *educ* Eton and Edinburgh U

1b *Serena Clare; *b* 13 Aug 1967; *m* 18 May 1996 *Jeremy John Chantler Bradbeer and has:

1c *Charles Julian Chantler; *b* 2 Aug 1997

2b *Melisa Jennifer; *b* 1973

(2) +Malcolm Hugh Dees [Lt-Col Malcolm McAlpine, Highfields, Withyham, Hartfield, Sussex]; *b* 24 July 1917; *educ* Charterhouse; late Lt-Col RE, dir Sir Robert McAlpine Ltd; *m* 14 Feb 1944 *Sheila Margaret, er dau of Maj F Raeburn Price, of Fordyce, N Foreland, Thanet, and has:

1a +Adrian Neil Raeburn; *b* 23 Dec 1944; *educ* Milton Abbey; dir Sir Robert McAlpine Ltd, govr Milton Abbey Sch 1987–; *m* 1983 *Angela Mary, yr dau of Dr George Hickie, of Mill House, Ashton Keynes, Wilts, and has:

1b +Angus Neil Adrian; *b* 1993

1b *Antonia Louise Philippa; *b* 1984

2b *Olivia Alice Gemma; *b* 1986

2a +MALCOLM ROBERT later CULLUM (deed poll 1963) [Cullum McAlpine Esq, Cold Ashton Manor, Chippenham, Wilts]; *b* 31 Jan 1947; *educ* Gordonstoun; dir Sir Robert McAlpine Ltd; *m* 1973 *Amanda Valerie, yst dau of R S Lamdin, of Klysford, Horsted Keynes, Sussex, and has:

1b +Robert Harry; *b* 1975

2b +Gavin Malcolm; *b* 1976

3b +Hector George; *b* 1980

4b +Douglas James; *b* 1983

3a +Hamish [Hamish McAlpine Esq, 79 Wardour St, London W1V 3TH]; *b* 12 Dec 1954; *educ* Harrow; film producer; *m* 1st (*divorce*) Bianca Juarez, dau of Bobo Sigrist, aviation heiress; has by Carina Bodle:

1b *Alex; *b c* 1986

1b *Sara; *b c* 1984

3a (cont.) Hamish McAlpine *m* 2nd 23 Aug 1997 *Karen Nicholls

(3) +Kenneth, OBE (1997), DL (Kent) [Kenneth McAlpine Esq OBE DL, The Priory, Lamberhurst, Kent TN3 8DS]; *b* 21 Sept 1920; *educ* Charterhouse; late F/O RAFVR, High Sheriff Kent 1973–74, Govr St Bartholomew's Hosp 1972–74, Govr and Dep Chm Eastbourne Coll 1968–84; FRAeS; *m* 24 Nov 1955 *Patricia Mary, dau of Capt Francis William Hugh Jeans, CVO, RN, of Summerfold, Rudgwick, Sussex and has:

1a +Richard Hugh; *b* 24 April 1958; *m* 1991 *Linda Elizabeth, only dau of William Leighton Wee, of San Francisco, and has:

1b +Thomas Leighton; *b* 1992

2a +James Thomas Hemery; *b* 29 Sept 1960; *m* 1995 *Heather Alison Baillie

4 Alfred David (Sir), JP (Denbighs); *b* 6 Nov 1881; High Sheriff 1923, memb Sir Robert McAlpine and Sons, civ engrg contractors, Hon Treas N Wales Div Nat

Union C and U Assocs, Life Govr Wrexham War Memorial Infirmary, OStJ; *m* 19 April 1907 Ethel May (*d* 24 Oct 1961), 2nd dau of James Williams, of Aboyne, Aberdeenshire, and *d* 25 May 1944, leaving:

(1) (Alfred) James; *b* 15 June 1908; *educ* Repton; chm Marchwiel Holdings Ltd, Sir Alfred McAlpine and Sons Ltd and assoc cos; *m* 1st 24 June 1931 (*divorce* 1940) Peggy Barbara, est dau of John Ernest Sanders, of Hurst Newton, Wrexham, and had:

1a +Robert James [Robert McAlpine Esq, Tilston Lodge, Tilston Fearnall, Tarporley, Cheshire]; *b* 6 May 1932; *educ* Harrow; dir Sir Alfred McAlpine & Son Ltd and Westminster Property; *m* 1st 8 Sept 1956 (*divorce* 19–) Jane Winifred Mary (*d* 1992), er dau of James Anton, of Tudor House, Rumsley, Salop, and has:

1b +Euan James; *b* 26 July 1958; *m* 1983 *Fiona Elizabeth, est dau of Charles Aylmer Eade, of Uppington House, Telford, Salop, and has:

1c +Thomas James; *b* 1991

1c *Flora Belinda; *b* 1989

2c *Roseanna Jane; *b* 1993

2b +Christopher William; *b* 1 Jan 1964; *m* 1991 *Sarah Louise, dau of Anthony Rundell, of Clapham

1b *Sara Jane; *b* 22 Oct 1961; *m* March 1982 *Hon (Herbert) Robin Cayzer, est s of 2nd Baron Rotherwick (*qv*), and has issue

1a (cont.) Robert McAlpine *m* 2nd 1981 *Mrs Angela J Bell, only dau of Maj E W Langford-Brooke, of Cheshire, and by her has:

2b *Emma Antonia; *b* 1982

2a Alfred William; *b* 9 Feb 1935; *educ* Harrow; *k* car crash 14 June 1962

(1) (cont.) James McAlpine *m* 2nd 1 April 1940 (*divorce* 1951) Mary Kinder, dau of Frank Musgrave Read, and by her had:

1a *Valerie Anne [Mrs Peter Shaw, Barley End, Aldbury, Herts]; *b* 19 Sept 1942; *m* 1st 29 Nov 1962 (*divorce* 1967) Julio Noyes, est s of Julius W Noyes, of New York, and has:

1b *William; *b* 15 Nov 1963

1a (cont.) Mrs Valerie Noyes *m* 2nd 1967 *Peter Shaw and by him has:

1b *Samantha Margaret; *b* 1969

2b *Joanna Mary; *b* 1972

(1) (cont.) James McAlpine *m* 3rd 17 Sept 1951 (*divorce* 1959) Mrs Rosemary Lavery (*d* 1983), dau of Maj Charles Hugh Gregory-Hood (*see* HOOD, V), and by her has:

2a *Sally Dorothy [Mrs Sally Argent, 49 Campden Hill Rd, London W8 7DY]; *b* 13 April 1952; *m* 1975 (*divorce* 1990), as his 3rd w, (Bernard) Godfrey Argent, and has:

1b *Jenna Charlotte; *b* 1980

(1) (cont.) James McAlpine *m* 4th 27 Oct 1959 (*divorce* 1979) Eleanor Margaret Rangel-Wallace, dau of John Nicholson Wallace, of Lisbon; *m* 5th 1979 *Cynthia Greenaway [Mrs James McAlpine, Gerwyn Hall, Marchwiel, nr Wrexham, Denbighshire; The Towers, Llanarmon, Dyffryn Ceiriog, Denbighshire], dau of Harry Whitney, and *d* 1991

(1) Gladys Gwendoline; *b* 7 Nov 1910; *m* 11 April 1935 (*divorce* 1943) Charles Phipps Brutton, OBE (*d* 11 May 1964), and *d* 1978

(2) *Ethel Mary [Mrs Peter Bell, Marchwiel Hall, Wrexham, Clwyd]; *b* 8 Oct 1915; *m* 19 April 1939 *Peter Henry Bell, s of Claude Bell, of Chester, and has:

1a *John Peter Blair; *b* 22 May 1950; *educ* Marlborough

1a *Susan Mary [Mrs William Gibbs, 10 Walton Place, London SW3]; *b* 14 March 1940; *m* 16 July 1960 (*divorce* 1968) William George Rendell Gibbs, s of Kenneth Henry Rendell Gibbs, of Rowden Abbey, Bromyard, Herefs

2a *Jane; *b* 2 April 1943; *m* 9 Aug 1969 *William Matthew Patterson

5 Granville Ramage; *b* 1883; *m* 1922 Beatrice Mary Donald (*d* 13 April 1936) and *d* 19 Oct 1928, leaving:

(1) *Maureen Agnes; *b* 17 March 1925; *m* 22 Oct 1949 Frederick Stanley Thornton, MBE (*d* 1994), and has:

1a *David Malcolm; *b* 14 Sept 1950; *educ* Gordonstoun and Exeter U; *m* 1973 *Stephanie Patricia Mills and has:

1b *Simon Edward; *b* 1983

2a *Andrew William [Andrew Thornton Esq, Willow Orchard, Frating Rd, Gt Bromley, Essex CO7 7JW]; *b* 24 July 1953; *educ* Gordonstoun; *m* 1981 *Jacqueline Mary Deane and has:

1b *James Ashley; *b* 1983

2b *Tobias William; *b* 1987

1 Mary Gibb; *m* 1897 Andrew Henderson Bishop (*d* 1957), s of Thomas George Bishop, of Beattock, Dumfriesshire, and *d* 16 Jan 1935, leaving issue

2 Agnes Hepburn; *m* 1905 (*divorce* 1915) Louis Fradin, Baron de Belabre (*d* 1945), and *d* 15 Dec 1952, leaving issue

3 Ethel Mary; *m* 1906 Walter Porteous Scott (*d* 1944) and *d* 1 Feb 1939

Sir Robert *m* 2nd 1889 Florence Margaret Palmer (*d* 1910) and *d* 3 Nov 1934, having by her had:

6 (Archibald) Douglas; *b* 19 Aug 1890; *educ* Cheltenham and Glasgow U (MB and ChB 1913, MD 1923); MRCP London 1921, FRCP 1932, T/Brig RAMC, WW I and WW II (despatches), Consultant Neurologist, MEF 1941–43 and India Cmd and SEAC 1943–45, Emeritus Consultant Middx Hosp; *m* 1st 1917 Elizabeth Meg Sidebottom (*d* 21 June 1941) and had:

(1) +(Robert Douglas) Christopher, CMG (1967) [Lt-Cdr Christopher McAlpine CMG RNVR, Longtree House, Cutwell, Glos GL8 8EB]; *b* 14 June 1919; *educ* Winchester and New Coll Oxford; Lt-Cdr RNVR (FAA) WW II, Dip Serv 1946–69 (Assist Private Sec to For Sec 1947–49, CCG as 2nd then 1st Sec 1949–52, Lima 1954–56 and Moscow 1956–59, Dep Consul-Gen NY 1962–65, Cnsllr Mexico City 1965–68), md Baring Bros 1969–79, dir Clarkson Hldgs 1980–87; *m* 4 Dec 1943 *Helen Margery Frances, dau of Capt Astley Cannan, and has:

1a +David Douglas Christopher [David McAlpine Esq, 64 Gloucester Rd, Kew, Surrey]; *b* 7 Oct 1949; *educ* Winchester and UEA; dir Edgar Investments 1973–; *m* 1973 *Susan Mary, dau of Richard John Boileau Walker, and has:

1b +Thomas David; *b* 1977

1b *Laura Esmé; *b* 1980

2b *Martha Rose; *b* 1983

3b *Jessica Mary Sucharita; *b* 1986

2a +Robert John [Robert McAlpine Esq, 12 Elizabeth Gdns, Meysey Hampton, Glos GL7 5LP]; *b* 1 Dec 1953; *m* 1987 *Sheila Maureen, dau of E J Arseneault, of Winnipeg, and has:

1b *Sophia Madeleine; *b* 1993

1a A dau; *b* 14 July 1944; *d* an infant

2a *Sarah Margaret [Mrs Timothy Holloway, Glebe House, Lamer Lane, Wheathampstead, Herts AL4 8RH]; *b* 1 Dec 1946; *m* 30 April 1971 *Timothy George Holloway and has:

1b *Benjamin Richard; *b* 31 March 1973

1b *Katharine Helen; *b* 14 May 1975

(1) *Florence Mary [Mrs Florence MacDonell, Windmill Hill, Woodhouse Eaves, Leics; Rosecourt, Fortrose, Scotland]; *b* 24 Aug 1922; late 3rd Offr WRNS; *m* 16 May 1952 Peter Alexander MacDonell (*d* 1986), yr s of Aeneas Ranald MacDonell, CBE, 21st Ch of Glengarry and Scotus, and has had:

1a A son; *b* 26 July 1953; *d* an inf

1a *Charlotte Anne; *b* 1954; *m* 1979 *Peter St Clair Aston Maltin and has:

1b *Charles Alexander; *b* 1992

1b *Zoe Alexandra; *b* 1987

2a *Maria Christian; *b* 15 Jan 1959; has:

1b *Molly Isolde; *b* 1992

2b *Calanach; *b* 1995

3b *Georgina Primrose; *b* 1996

6 (cont.) (Archibald) Douglas McAlpine *m* 2nd 3 July 1945 Diana Christina Dunscombe (*d* 1981), dau of Bertram Plummer, of Leicester, and *d* 1981, having by him had:

(2) +Alastair Bertram [Alastair McAlpine Esq, Flat 5, 65 Cadogan Gdns, London SW1]; *b* 23 April 1946; *m* 1st 6 May 1968 (*divorce* 1973) Ann Margaret, only dau of Maj Bernard N Winchester, of Long Hanborough, Oxon; *m* 2nd 1994 *Dena Brooking-Thomas (*see* CUNINGHAME, Bt)

4 Emma Margaret Florence; *m* 12 June 1920 (*divorce* 1933) Capt Hugo Chenevix Trench (*see* ASHTOWN, B) and *d* 12 July 1948, leaving issue

5 Roberta Ida Freeman; *b* 28 July 1898; *m* 1st 7 April 1917 (*divorce* 1933) 2nd Earl Lloyd George of Dwyfor (*qv*) and had issue; *m* 2nd 1933 His Hon David Eiflon Puleston Evans, QC, MA, LLB, late Maj RASC, s of John Owain Evans, CBE, and *d* 10 March 1966

The 4th Bt's bro,

Sir (Robert) Edwin McAlpine, 5th Bt, and BARON McALPINE OF MOFFAT, of Medmenham, Co Bucks (LP, UK), so *cr* 1979; *b* 23 April 1907; *educ* Oundle; ptnr Sir Robert McAlpine and Sons Ltd; *m* 8 Dec 1930 *Ella Mary Gardner, yr dau of James Gardner Garnett, of N Vancouver, BC, Canada and *d* 1990, having had:

1 Sir WILLIAM HEPBURN McALPINE, **6th and present Bt**

2 (ROBERT) ALISTAIR McALPINE, BARON McALPINE OF WEST GREEN (LP, *qv*)

3 +David Malcolm [David McAlpine Esq, Fawley House, Fawley Green, Henley-on-Thames, Oxon]; *b* 8 Oct 1946; *educ* Stowe; dir Sir Robert McAlpine & Sons Ltd; *m* 11 Sept 1971 (*divorce* 1993) Jennifer Anne, yr dau of Eric Hodges, of Brook Cottage, Streams Lane, Sidlescombe, E Sussex, and has:

(1) +Robert Edward Thomas William; *b* 1 Aug 1978

(1) *Katherine Alexandra Donnison; *b* 1972

(2) *Elizabeth Louise; *b* 1973

1 *Patricia Garnett [The Hon Mrs Robin Borwick, Neptune House, Newells Lane, Bosham, Sussex PO18 8PS]; *b* 5 Feb 1932; *m* 2 Dec 1950 *Hon Robin Sandbach Borwick, yr s of 3rd Baron Borwick (*qv*), and has issue

McALPINE OF WEST GREEN

Arms: Per chevron vert and or two chevronels, one in chief argent, the other in base azure. **Crest:** A cubit arm grasping a chaplet of pine fructed proper. **Supporters:** Dexter, an aborigine girt with a body belt, pendant therefrom a lonca-lonca, armed with a spear and in his sinister hand a boomerang, and extending the other to and behind the head of a kangaroo sejant beside him, all proper; sinister, a gardener in his working clothes wearing an apron of green baize, in his exterior hand a spade, and having perched upon the wrist and palm of his other hand a parrot proper. **Motto:** Give all, win all.
Creation: B. (LP, UK) 1983.

THE BARON McALPINE OF WEST GREEN, of West Green, Co Southampton ((Robert) Alistair McAlpine) [The Rt Hon The Lord McAlpine of West Green, 31 South Audley St, London W1]; *b* 14 May 1942; *educ* Stowe; joined Sir Robert McAlpine and Sons 1958, dir 1963–; Dir: ICA 1972–73, Geo Weidenfeld Hldgs 1975–83, Theatre Investment Fund 1981–90 (chm 1985–90); Hon Treas: European League Economic Co-operation 1974–75 (V-Pres 1975–), C and U Party 1975–90 (Jt Hon Treas 1981, Dep Chm 1979–83), European Democratic Union 1978–88; Memb: Friends of V & A Museam 1976–, Cncl English Stage Co 1973–75, Arts Cncl 1981–82; Chm Arts Cncl Touring Ctee and Referendum Party 1997; V-Pres: Friends Ashmolean Museum 1969–, Greater London Arts Assoc 1971–77, Contemporary Arts Soc 1973–80; Tstee ROH Tst 1974–80; Pres: Br Waterfowl Assoc 1978–81 (Patron 1981–), St Bart's Hosp Medical Coll 1993; Govr: South Bank Poly 1981–82, Stowe Sch 1981–84; author: *The Servant* (1992), *Journal of a Collector* (1994), *Letters to a Young Politician From His Uncle* (1995) and *Once a Jolly Swagman* (memoirs 1997); *m* 1st 1964 (*divorce* 1979) Sarah Alexandra, dau of Paul Hillman Baron, of Marylebone, and has:

1 *(Mary) Jane; *b* 1965; *m* 1987 *Simon J E du B Taylor, est s of Timothy Taylor, of Meadle, Bucks

2 *Victoria Alice; *b* 1967; *m* 1992 *Lionel Digby Sheffield Neave (*see* NEAVE, Bt) and has issue

The BARON McALPINE OF WEST GREEN *m* 2nd 1980 *Romilly Thompson, only dau of Alfred Thompson Hobbs, of Knights Farm House, W Green, Hants, and by her has:

3 *Skye; *b* 1984

Lineage: *See* McALPINE, Bt

McCARTHY

Creation: B. (LP, UK) 1975.

THE BARON McCARTHY, of Headington, City of Oxford (William Edward John McCarthy) [The Rt Hon The Lord McCarthy, 4 William Orchard Close, Old Headington, Oxford OX3 9DR]; *b* 30 July 1925; *educ* Holloway County Sch, Ruskin Coll, Merton Coll and Nuffield Coll Oxford (MA, DPhil); Research Fell Nuffield Coll 1959, Lecturer Industrial Relations Oxford, Research Dir Roy Commn Trade Unions and Employers' Assocs 1965–68; Sr Ec Advsr Dept Employment 1968–71; Special Advsr to Sec State Social Servs 1975–77; memb: Houghton Ctee Aid to Political Parties 1975–76, TUC Independent Review Ctee 1976; Pres Br Universities Industrial Relations Assoc 1975–78; Special Commr Equal Opportunities Commn 1977–80; Dep Chm Teachers' Nat Conciliation Ctee 1979–; Oppn Spokesman Employment 1980–97; memb: Ho Lds Select Ctee Unemployment 1980–82, All Party Motor Industry Gp 1989; Chm: Railway Staff Nat Tbnl 1973–86, TUC Newspaper Feasibility Advsy Study Gp 1981–83, Independent Inquiry into Rover Closure Proposals 1989–90; V-Chm All Party Friends of Music Gp 1992; Adjudicator Nursing and Midwifery Staffs Negotiating Cncl

1994–; author: *The Closed Shop in Britain* (1964), *The Role of Shop Stewards in British Industrial Relations* (1966), *Employers' Associations* (with V L Munns, 1967), *Disputes Procedures in Britain* (with A J Marsh, 1968), *The Reform of Collective Bargaining at Plant and Company Level* (1971), *Trade Unions* (ed, 2nd edn, 1972), *Coming to Terms with Trade Unions* (with A I Collier, 1973), *Management by Agreement* (with N D Ellis, 1973), *Wage Inflation and Wage Leadership* (with J F O'Brien and V E Dowd, 1975), *Making Whitley Work* (1977), *Change in Trade Unions* (jt author, 1981), *Strikes in Post-War Britain* (jt author, 1983), *Freedom at Work* (1985), *The Future of Industrial Democracy* (1988), *Employee Relations Audits* (with C Jennings and R Undy, 1989), *Legal Intervention in Industrial Relations* (ed, 1992), *New Labour at Work* (1996); *m* 14 Jan 1957 *Margaret, dau of Percival Godfrey

Lineage: EDWARD McCARTHY; *m* Louisa Kemp and had:

WILLIAM EDWARD JOHN, *cr* a **Baron**

McCLUSKEY

Creation: B. (LP, UK) 1976.

THE BARON McCLUSKEY, of Churchhill, District of City of Edinburgh (John Herbert McCluskey) [The Rt Hon The Lord McCluskey, 5 Lansdowne Cresc, Edinburgh EH12 5EQ]; *b* 12 June 1929; *educ* St Bede's GS Manchester, Holy Cross Acad Edinburgh and Edinburgh U (MA 1950, LLB 1952); F/O (Sword of Honour) RAF 1953; advocate 1955, QC Scotland 1967, Standing Jr Counsel Min Power Scotland 1963, Advocate Depute 1964–71; Chm: Medical Appeal Tbnls Scotland 1972–74, Scottish Assoc Mental Health 1985–94; Sheriff Pncpl Dumfries and Galloway 1973–74, Slr-Gen Scotland 1974–79; Ld of Session 1984–; Ind Chm: Scottish Football League's Compensation Tbnl 1988–, Scottish Football Assoc's Appeals Tbnl 1990–; author: *Law, Justice and Democracy* (1987), *Butterworth's Scottish Criminal Law and Practice* (ed, 1988–), *Criminal Appeals* (1992); *m* 1956 *Ruth, dau of Aaron Friedland, and has:

　1 *John Mark; *b* 1960; *m* 1986 (*divorce* 1996) Judith Fernie; *m* 2nd 1997 *Diane Sivas

　2 *David Francis; *b* 1963; *m* 1989 *—

　1 *Catherine Margaret; *b* 1962

Lineage: FRANCIS JOHN McCLUSKEY; slr; *m* Margaret Doonan and had:

JOHN HERBERT, *cr* a **Baron**

McCOLL OF DULWICH

Arms: Azure a cross or between in the first quarter a leg embowed in armour, in the second quarter a dove volant to the sinister, in the third quarter a flean and in the fourth quarter a fish haurient, all argent. **Crest:** A demi-lion rampant or, head and mane gules, gorged with three barrulets wavy argent, flanked by oak branches formed chevronwise as an 'M' leaved argent and fructed or, on an escroll proper. **Supporters:** Dexter, a dachshund rampant proper; sinister, an eagle close also proper, armed or and crowned with an ancient crown gold. **Mottoes:** 1 (over crest) *Veritas* ('Truth'), 2 (below shield) *Dare quam accipere* ('Giving rather than receiving').
Creation: B. (LP, UK) 1989.

THE BARON McCOLL OF DULWICH, of Bermondsey, London Borough of Southwark (Ian McColl, CBE (1997)) [The Rt Hon The Lord McColl of Dulwich CBE, House of Lords, London SW1A 0PW]; *b* 6 Jan 1933; *educ* Hutchesons' GS Glasgow, St Paul's London and London U (MB, BS 1957); Dr various London hosps 1957–67, Research Fell Harvard Medical Sch 1967, Moynihan Fellowship Assoc Surgns 1967, Reader Surgery St Bartholomew's Hosp Medical Coll 1967 (Sub Dean 1969); Hon Sec Br Soc Gastroenterology 1970–74, Examiner Pathology RCS 1970–76 (Advsr SE Regn 1975–80), Dir Surgical Unit Guy's Hosp 1971–; Prof Surgery London U 1971–; Visiting Prof: S Carolina U 1974, Johns Hopkins

Hosp 1976; Consultant Surgn: KCH 1971–, Guy's Hosp 1971–, Edenbridge Dist Memorial Hosp 1978–91, Lewisham Hosp 1983–; Medical Advsr BBC 1976–92; Hon Consultant Surgery to Army 1982–; Chm: King's Fund Centre Ctee 1976–86, Govt Working Party on Artificial Limbs, Wheelchairs and Appliance Centres in England 1984–86; Dir Surgery Guy's Hosp 1985–; V-Chm Special Health Authority Disablement Servs 1987–91; Dep Speaker Ho Lds 1994–; PPS to PM 1994–; Memb: Centl Health Servs Cncl 1972–74, Standing Medical Advsy Ctee 1972–82, Cncl Roy Coll Surgeons 1986–, Cncl Imperial Cancer Research Fund 1986–, Exec Ctee BLESMA 1991–; Govr-at-Large for England American Coll Surgns Bd Govrs 1982–88; Pres: Mildmay Mission Hosp 1985– (chm Bd Govrs 1994–), Soc Minimally Invasive Gen Surgery 1991–94, Limbless Assoc 1992– (Patron and Hon Consultant 1987–), Internat Wheelchair Fedn 1991–, Assoc Endoscopic Surgeons GB and Ireland 1994–, The Hosp Saving Assoc 1994–; V-Pres John Groom's Assoc Disabled People 1990–; Govr Dulwich Coll Prep Sch 1978–, James Allen's Girls' Sch 1994–; Barbers' Co: Renter Warden 1995–96, Middle Warden 1996–97 and 1997–98; FRCS 1962, FRCSE 1962, MS 1966, FACS 1975; author: *Intestinal Absorption in Man* (jt ed, 1975), *Talking to Patients* (1982), *NHS Data Book* (1984); *m* 1960 *Dr Jean Lennox, 2nd dau of Arthur James McNair (*see* McNAIR, B), and has:

　1 *Alastair James; *b* 25 July 1961

　1 *Caroline Lennox, MD; *b* 1963; *m* 1994 *Simon Brook Holmes

　2 *Mary Alison; *b* 1966; *m* 1989 *Rory Nicholas Knight

Lineage: FREDERICK GEORGE McCOLL, of Dulwich; *m* Winifred E — and had:

IAN, *cr* a **Baron**

McCONNELL, Baron

Creation: B. (LP, UK) 1995.

THE BARON McCONNELL, of Lisburn in the County of Antrim (Robert William Brian McConnell, PC (NI 1964) [The Rt Hon The Lord McConnell PC, 50a Glenavy Rd, Knocknadona, Lisburn, Co Antrim BT28 3UT]; *b* 25 Nov 1922; *educ* Sedbergh and Queen's U Belfast; barrister NI 1948, MP (NI Parl, U) S Antrim 1951–68, Dep Chm Ways and Means Ctee 1962, Parly Sec Min Health and Local Govt 1963, Min Home Affrs 1964–66, Min State, Min Devpt 1966–67, Leader H of C 1967–68, Pres Industl Court NI 1968–81, Soc Security Commr NI 1968–87; *m* 1951 *Sylvia Elizabeth Joyce Agnew and has two sons

Lineage: ALFRED E McCONNELL, of Belfast; had:

ROBERT WILLIAM BRIAN, *cr* a **Baron**

McCONNELL, Bt

Arms: Per pale azure and gules, in the dexter a ship in full sail proper, in the sinister an arm embowed and couped at the shoulder argent, the hand holding a trefoil slipped or, on a chief of the 4th three stag's heads cabossed sable. **Crest:** A stag's head erased azure, attired and charged on the neck with a bee volant or.
Motto: *Victor in arduis* ('Triumphant in spite of difficulties').
Creation: Bt. (UK) 25 Sept 1900.

Robert Shean; *b* 23 Nov 1930; *s f* 1987 but does not use title; *educ* Stowe, Queens' Coll Cambridge, Polytechnic Sch of Architecture and U of BC (MSc); ARICS, FRTPI; MIMgt; memb (Lib Dem) Lambeth Cncl 1996–

Lineage: ROBERT McCONNELL, of Clougher, Co Antrim; *b* 23 Jan 1797; *m* 26 March 1828 Margaret (*d* 9 Nov 1846), dau of James McKnight; *m* 2nd 18 March 1847 Margaret, dau of John Harvey, and *d* 3 Nov 1850, leaving by his 1st w:

JOSEPH McCONNELL, of Clougher; *b* 9 Jan 1829; *m* 24 Dec 1851 Elizabeth (*d* 23 July 1896), dau of James McBride, and *d* 17 May 1872, leaving:

Sir Robert John McConnell, 1st Bt (UK), so *cr* 25 Sept 1900, JP, DL, of the Moat, Strandtown, Belfast; *b* 6 Feb 1853; Ld Mayor Belfast 1900; *m* 1st 26 Jan 1874 Mary Elizabeth — (*d* 5 April 1896), dau of Thomas Smiley; *m* 2nd 27 April 1897

(*divorce* 1904) Elsie, dau of George Hewson, JP, DL, of Ennismore, Co Kerry, and *d* 22 April 1927, having had by his 1st w:

1 JOSEPH (Sir), **2nd Bt**

2 Alfred Edward; *b* 10 Nov 1880; *educ* Jesus Coll Cambridge; *m* 12 June 1919 Emma (Yvonne) Dougal (*d* July 1957) and *d* Jan 1963, leaving:

  (1) +Robert William Brian, PC (NI 1964) [The Rt Hon Robert McConnell, Aughnahough, Lisburn, Co Antrim]; *b* 25 Nov 1922; *educ* Sedbergh and Queen's U Belfast (BA, LLB); barrrister NI 1948, MP S Antrim NI Parl 1951–68, Dep Chm Ways and Means 1962–63, Parly Sec Min Health and Local Govt 1963–64, Min Home Affairs NI 1964–68; *m* 23 Aug 1951 *Sylvia Elizabeth Joyce, dau of Samuel Agnew, of Belfast, and has:

    1a +Richard Alfred; *b* 18 Feb 1955; *m* 1988 *Julie, dau of Eddie Ellis, and has:

      1b *Kira Elizabeth; *b* 4 Aug 1994

    1a +Samuel James; *b* 16 Sept 1958; *m* 1985 *Christine Molly Smyth and has:

      1b *Laura Elizabeth; *b* 9 July 1987

      2b *Ruth Mary; *b* 10 Oct 1990

      3b *Joanne Christine; *b* 16 Nov 1993

    1a *Helen Elizabeth; *b* 2 March 1964; *m* 4 April 1987 *Thomas Nelson and has:

      1b *Philip Thomas; *b* 26 Sept 1989

      1b *Rachel Elizabeth; *b* 11 Jan 1992

      2b *Sarah Jane; *b* 9 Jan 1994

3 Thomas Herbert; *b* 10 July 1883; *d* 21 Aug 1931

4 William Clarke; *b* 25 Feb 1885; Lt 3rd Bn Roy Irish Rifles; *ka* July 1916

5 Charles John; *b* Nov 1886; *d* 23 Dec 1887

1 Sarah Elizabeth; *d* young 1877

2 Mary Elizabeth; *b* 27 May 1879; *d* 18 Jan 1894

3 Margaret; *b* 27 May 1879; *m* 3 Jan 1899 Henry Herbert Martin and *d* 28 Jan 1924

4 Ethel Muriel; *b* 26 June 1890; *m* 3 Aug 1934 William Thomas Briggs, AMIEE (*d* 1958), Egyptian State Rlwys, and *d* 1965

The 1st Bt's est s,

Sir Joseph McConnell, 2nd Bt, DL (Belfast); *b* 17 Sept 1877; MP Co Antrim 1929–42; *m* 25 April 1900 Lisa (*d* 19 Aug 1956), dau of Jackson McGowan, JP, and *d* 27 Aug 1942, having had:

1 ROBERT MELVILLE TERENCE (Sir), **3rd Bt**

2 (Jackson) Desmond; *b* 12 June 1912; Lt RNVR; *m* 16 Jan 1948 *Honor Muriel [Mrs Desmond McConnell, Little Galleons, 52 Craigdarragh Rd, Helen's Bay, Bangor, Co Down BT19 1UB], dau of Robert Henry Cooke Ramsay, of Fairholme, Helens Bay, and widow of S/Ldr Richard Ashton Shuttleworth, RAF, and *d* 1986, having had:

  (1) +Rory Desmond Ramsay [Rory McConnell Esq, Ardville, Old Quay Rd, Holywood, Co Down]; *b* 3 May 1957; *educ* Marlborough; *m* 1982 *Karen, dau of James McClean, of Bangor, and has:

    1a +Jamie Desmond; *b* 1984

    1a *Hayley Elizabeth; *b* 1987

    2a *Alexandra Jane; *b* 1991

  (1) *Kathryn Fiona [Mrs Anthony Randel, Langdon, Langdon Cross, Launceston, Cornwall]; *b* 9 Dec 1948; *m* 1970 *Maj Anthony Randel and has:

    1a *Sophia Honor; *b* 1971; *m* 21 Sept 1996 *Matthew David Murr

1 Josephine Patricia; *b* 29 Feb 1908; *m* 12 Feb 1930 John Dermot Campbell, DL, MP (presumed *d* 23 Jan 1945), s of Robert Garrett Campbell, CBE, of Fort William Pk, Belfast, and *d* Dec 1989, leaving:

  (1) *(Godfrey) Garrett [Garry Campbell Esq, Walden House, Stonor, Oxon]; *b* 28 June 1934; *educ* Winchester; 1st King's Dragoon Gds 1953–54; *m* 3 July 1966 *Margaret Elizabeth, dau of Lt-Col L J D Reid, of Limpsfield, Surrey, and has:

    1a *Dermot John Hugh; *b* 13 March 1967

    1a *Fiona Annelisa; *b* 16 April 1973

  (2) *Colin Walter Joseph; *b* 18 May 1939; *educ* Stowe

  (1) *Lisa Alice Freda; *b* 5 Oct 1931; *m* 21 July 1956 *Peter Hartley Tom Lewis, s of Bruce Lewis, of Derbys

The 2nd Bt's er s,

Sir Robert Melville Terence McConnell, 3rd Bt, of Belfast; *b* 7 Feb 1902; *educ* Trin Coll Glenalmond and St John's Coll Cambridge; Cdr RNVR, VRD, ptnr R J McConnell & Co, surveyors, valuers and estate agents, Belfast; *m* 1st 4 Sept 1928 (*divorce* 1954) Rosamond Mary Elizabeth, dau of James Stewart Reade, JP, of Lisburn, Co Antrim; *m* 2nd 29 Sept 1967 *Alice Ann Mary [Lady McConnell, Pigeon Hill, Island Rd, Killyleagh, Co Down], dau of Robert Graham Glendinning, of Lennoxvale, Belfast, and formerly w of James Hillis, and *d* 1987, leaving by his 1st w:

1 Sir ROBERT SHEAN McCONNELL, **4th and present Bt**

2 +(JAMES) ANGUS [Angus McConnell Esq, Rory's Glen, 219 Old Holywood Rd, Holywood, Co Down]; *b* 18 Dec 1933; heir presumptive; *educ* Stowe; *m* 24 Sept 1957 *Elizabeth Jillian, dau of Derek Edmond Harris, of Sydenham, Belfast, and has:

  (1) +Terence Reade; *b* 16 Nov 1959; Maj Roy Irish Regt (ret); *m* 16 Nov 1987 *Lorel Natalie Willetts and has:

    1a +James Alexander; *b* 29 Aug 1989

    1a *Kitty Sarah; *b* 8 Aug 1991

  (2) +Edmund Fraser; *b* 9 Sept 1961

  (1) *Joanne Christina; *b* 30 June 1958; *m* 1979 *Richard Sholdis and has:

    1a *Robert James; *b* 1984

    2a *Christopher John; *b* 1989

    1a *Jennifer Elizabeth (twin); *b* 1984

    2a *Rachel Rosemary; *b* 1987

  (2) *Victoria Wylie; *b* 7 Jan 1965

  (3) *Emma-Jane Wylie; *b* 7 Jan 1965; *m* 23 Sept 1995 *David Michael Allen

  (4) *Alison Clare; *b* 6 Jan 1967

3 +William Donn [William McConnell Esq, Laurelbrae, Saintfield Rd, Lisburn, Co Antrim]; *b* 30 June 1938; *educ* Stowe; *m* 18 Sept 1963 *Daphne Elisabeth, only child of Robert Simms, of Bangor, and has:

  (1) +Robert Randal; *b* 1 Sept 1966; *m* 1993 *Sarah Annaliese Kirk and has:

    1a +Jacob Kirk; *b* 9 July 1997

  (2) +Stewart Neale; *b* 1972

  (1) Penelope Elisabeth; *b* 28 June 1964; *d* 25 Dec 1970

1 *Elisabeth Moyne [Mrs Robert Ramsay, Ardreagh, Marino, Holywood, Co Down]; *b* 27 April 1935; *m* 16 Sept 1954 *Robert Henry Cooke Ramsay, only s of Robert Henry Cooke Ramsay, of Belfast, and has:

  (1) *Richard Patrick James; *b* 24 April 1960; *m* 1994 *Carey, dau of Nicholas Duffin, and has:

    1a *Molly Rose; *b* 18 June 1997

  (2) *Magnus Robert Neal; *b* 5 Feb 1967

  (1) *Roslyn Moyne Elisabeth; *b* 7 April 1962

McCowan

Arms: Argent a saltire between four anchors sable, roped or.
Crest: An eagle rising proper. **Motto:** *Tendimus ad cœlum* ('We reach for the sky'). **Creation:** Bt. (UK) 26 June 1934.

SIR HEW CARGILL McCOWAN, 3RD BT, of Dalwhat, Co Dumfries [Sir Hew McCowan Bt, Vivenda Marbelo, Estrada da Lagoa Azul, Malveira da Serra, Cascais, Portugal]; *b* 26 July 1930; *s f* 1965

Lineage: HEW McCOWAN, of Ayr; *b* 7 Aug 1815; *m* 21 Aug 1855 Joanna (*d* 26 Jan 1908), dau of Rev William McCall, of Caitloch Moniave, Dumfriesshire, and *d* 9 Nov 1863, leaving, with other issue:

Sir David McCowan, 1st Bt (UK), so cr 26 June 1934, JP, DL (Glasgow); *b* 8 Dec 1860; Pres Glasgow U Assoc, memb Roy Co Archers, sr ptnr William Euing & Co, marine insur brokers, dir George Outram & Co and Burma Oils, Maj 8th Scottish Rifles, ktd 1928; *m* 1 Oct 1889 Gertrude Margaret, CBE (1932) (*d* 2 March 1935), est dau of David Sime Cargill, of Glasgow, and *d* 15 May 1937, having had:

1 Hew; *b* 13 Aug 1890; Lt 8th Bn Scottish Rifles; *ka* Gallipoli 28 June 1915

2 DAVID JAMES CARGILL (Sir), **2nd Bt**

1 Margaret Elizabeth; *b* 20 May 1894; *m* 24 Nov 1931 Alexander Osborne Bonnar, yst s of William Bonnar, of Edinburgh

The 1st Bt's est surv s,

Sir David James Cargill McCowan, 2nd Bt, DL (Dunbartonshire 1953–61); *b* 5 June 1897; *m* 24 Oct 1928 Muriel Emma Annie, dau of William Charles Willmott, of Grasmere, Deal, and *d* 29 Aug 1965, leaving:

1 Sir HEW CARGILL McCOWAN, **3rd and present Bt**

2 +DAVID WILLIAM CARGILL [David McCowan Esq, Auchendennan Farm, Nr Alexandria, Dunbartonshire G83 8RB]; *b* 28 Feb 1934; heir presumptive; *m* 19– *Jean McGhee and has:

  (1) +David; *b* 1975

  (2) *Caroline; *b* 19–

McEwen

Arms: Quarterly, 1st and 4th, or a lion rampant az., gorged with a ducal crown ppr., on a chief of the second three garbs of the field (for McEWEN); 2nd and 3rd, gu. three headless cranes arg. (as arms of affection for FINNIE). **Crest:** The trunk of an oak tree, sprouting ppr. **Mottoes:** 1 *Reviresco* ('I flourish again'), 2 *Dieu premier servi* ('God comes first'). **Creation:** Bt. (UK) 28 Jan 1953.

SIR JOHN RODERICK HUGH McEWEN, 5TH BT, of Marchmont, Co Berwick, and Bardrochat, Co Ayr [Sir John McEwen Bt, Polwarth Crofts, Greenlaw, Berwicks TD10 6YR]; *b* 4 Nov 1965; *s* bro 1983; *educ* Ampleforth and U Coll London.

Lineage: JAMES McEWEN, of Bardrochat, Ayrshire; *b* 1695; drowned in River Stinchar 1737, leaving:

JAMES McEWEN, of Bardrochat; *b* 1725; *m* Helen Pyper and *d* 1790, leaving:

ROBERT McEWEN; *b* 1759; Capt Ayrshire Militia; *m* 1799 Jean McIlwraith and *d* 1812, leaving:

1 James, of Bardrochat, WS; *b* 1801; *d* 1874
2 JOHN
3 Robert; *b* 1806; *d* 1887
4 Hugh; *b* 1808; *d* Calcutta 1857
5 David; *b* 1809; *d* 1842; ancestor of the McEWENs of Alloway Lodge, Ontario
1 Margaret; *b* 1800; *d* unm 1850

ROBERT McEWEN's 2nd son,

Rev JOHN McEWEN; Minister Kirkmichael in Carrick; *b* 9 July 1803; *educ* Ayr Acad and Glasgow U; *m* 12 Jan 1860 Isabella, dau of William Finnie, of Kilmarnock, and *d* 11 May 1866, leaving, with a dau (Janet, *b* 3 July 1862, *d* unm 27 Aug 1958):

ROBERT FINNIE McEWEN, of Marchmont, Berwicks, and Bardrochat, Ayrshire, JP and DL; *b* 1 Jan 1861; *educ* Edinburgh Acad and Trin Hall Cambridge (BA); memb Roy Co Archers 1910, memb Cncl RCM 1906–26, FSA Scot; *m* 20 July 1893 Mary Frances (*d* 8 Dec 1944), est dau of Henry Robert Duncan Dundas, and *d* 31 March 1926, having had:

1 JOHN HELIAS FINNIE (Sir), **1st Bt**
2 James Robert Dundas; *b* 29 July 1896; Lt Roy Scots Fus; *ka* France 12 Oct 1916
1 Katherine Isobel, DCVO (1962); *b* 26 Oct 1899; Extra Ldy of the Bedchamber to HM QUEEN ELIZABETH THE QUEEN MOTHER, DStJ, Kaisar-i-Hind Medal; *m* 12 July 1922 11th Earl of Scarbrough (*qv*) and *d* 1979, leaving issue
2 Elizabeth Jeannet Mary; *b* 22 July 1902; *d* 20 Aug 1913

ROBERT McEWEN's er son,

Sir John Helias Finnie McEwen, 1st Bt (UK), so *cr* 28 Jan 1953, JP (1931), DL (Berwicks 1933); *b* 21 June 1893; *educ* Eton and Trin Coll Cambridge (MA); Hon LLD Glasgow U; Capt QO Cameron Highrs and RFC WW I (POW), Dip Serv 1921–26 (2nd Sec 1925), memb Roy Co Archers 1927, MP (C) Berwick and Haddington 1931–45, Parly U-Sec Scotland 1939–40, Chev Legn Hon 1946, Pres Scottish U Assoc 1949–50, Tstee Nat Galleries Scotland 1952–62; *m* 16 June 1923 Bridget Mary (*d* 26 Sept 1971), est dau of Rt Hon Sir Francis Oswald Lindley, GCMG, CB, CBE (*see* 1921 edn LINDLEY, B) by Hon Etheldreda Mary Fraser, 3rd dau of 13th Lord Lovat (*qv*), and *d* 19 April 1962, leaving:

1 **Sir James Napier Finnie McEwen, 2nd Bt**; *b* 14 Dec 1924; *m* 6 Sept 1958 *Clare Rosemary [Mrs Kenneth Wagg, Flat 7, 80 Elm Park Gardens, London SW10 9PD] (*m* 2nd 19 Dec 1973 Kenneth Wagg), only child of Col John Eric William Graves Sandars, OBE, TD, JP, DL, of Gate Burton Hall, Gainsborough, Lincs, and *d* 2 July 1971, leaving:

(1) *Margaret; *b* 29 May 1959; *m* 1980 *Edward John Ivo Stourton (*see* MOWBRAY, SEGRAVE and STOURTON, B)
(2) *Mary Gabriel; *b* 5 Jan 1963; *m* 1989 *(Vincent) Patrick Byrne (*see* LAWRENCE, B)
(3) *Christina; *b* 19 Jan 1964; *m* 1992 *Anthony D L Norton

2 ROBERT LINDLEY (Sir), **3rd Bt**
3 Roderick; *b* 12 March 1932; *educ* Eton and Trin Coll Cambridge; QO Cameron Highrs; *m* 15 April 1958 *Romana [Mrs Roderick McEwen, 5 Netherton Grove,

London SW10 9TQ], dau of Raimund von Hofmannsthal and Mrs Pleydell-Bouverie (*see* RADNOR, E), and *d* 16 Oct 1982, leaving:

(1) +ADAM HUGO; *b* 9 Feb 1965; heir presumptive
(1) *Flora Mary Alice; *b* 21 Feb 1959; *m* 1988 *Anthony David Willard Mason and has:
  1a *Nathaniel; *b* 1993
  1a *Brooke Emily; *b* 1997
(2) *Samantha Mary; *b* 19 April 1960
(3) *Christabel Mary; *b* 2 June 1962; *m* 1983 (*divorce*) Lord Durham (*see* DURHAM, E) and has issue; has further issue by *Jools Miles Holland, actor and musician:
  1a *Mabel Ray Britannia; *b* 22 Nov 1990

4 +Alexander Dundas [Alexander McEwen Esq, Bardrochat, Colmonell, Ayrshire]; *b* 16 May 1935; *educ* Eton; late 2nd Lt QO Cameron Highrs; *m* 30 June 1960 *Cecilia, only child of Franz, 2nd Prince Weikersheim, and has:

(1) +Alexander Francis Charles; *b* 12 June 1962; *m* 1988 *Natasha Durac, er dau of Peter H D Marr, and has:
  1a +Thomas Peter Dundas; *b* 1989
  2a +Archie James; *b* 1992
  3a +Maximilian; *b* 1996
(2) +Hugo Gabriel; *b* 28 Feb 1965; *m* 6 July 1996 *Monica Blom, of Stockholm
(1) *Sophia Christina; *b* 8 April 1961 (HRH PRINCE MICHAEL OF GREECE stood sponsor)

5 David Fraser; *b* 25 Sept 1938; *educ* Eton and Trin Coll Cambridge; QO Cameron Highrs; *d* 23 June 1976
6 +John Sebastian [John McEwen Esq, 74 St Augustine's Rd, London NW1 9RP]; *b* 29 July 1942; *educ* Eton and Trin Coll Cambridge; *m* 1975 *Gillian, dau of D M Heeley, and has:
(1) +David; *b* 1977
(2) +Duncan Dundas; *b* 1979
1 *Christian Mary, OBE (1983), DL Northants [The Rt Hon Christian Lady Hesketh OBE DL, Pomfret Lodge, Hulcote, Northants; 20a Tregunter Rd, London SW10]; *b* 17 July 1929; High Sheriff Northants 1981, Hon LLD Leicester; *m* 22 Nov 1949 2nd Baron Hesketh (*qv*) and has issue

The 2nd Bt's bro,

Sir Robert Lindley McEwen, 3rd Bt; *b* 23 June 1926; *educ* Eton and Trin Coll Cambridge; Gren Gds, barrister Inner Temple 1951; *m* 18 Sept 1954 *Brigid Cecilia [Lady McEwen, Polwarth Crofts, Duns, Berwickshire TD10 6YR], only dau of James Laver, CBE, Hon RE, FRSA, FRSL, of Blackheath, and *d* 1980, leaving:

(1) **Sir James Francis Lindley McEwen, 4th Bt**; *b* 24 Aug 1960; *d* unm 18 June 1983
(2) Sir JOHN RODERICK HUGH McEWEN, **5th and present Bt**
(1) *Mary Christian; *b* 21 April 1956
(2) Catherine Veronica; *b* 25 April 1958; *d* unm 8 Sept 1983
(3) *Helena Mary Elizabeth; *b* 3 Nov 1961
(4) *Isabella Gabriel Anne; *b* 27 March 1968

McFarland

Arms: Argent a saltire engrailed gules between two roses in pale and a thistle and shamrock in fess, all proper. **Crest:** A demi-savage holding in the dexter hand an antique crown, all proper. **Motto:** This I'll defend. **Creation:** Bt. (UK) 23 Jan 1914.

SIR JOHN TALBOT McFARLAND, 3RD BT, of Aberfoyle, Co Londonderry, TD (1967) [Sir John McFarland Bt TD, Dunmore House, Carrigans, Co Donegal, Ireland]; *b* 3 Oct 1927; *s* f 1986; *educ* Marlborough and Trin Coll Oxford; memb Londonderry CBC 1955–69, High Sheriff Co Londonderry 1958 and City of Londonderry 1965 and 1966, Commr Londonderry Port and Harbour Bd 1969, memb Management Ctee NW Gp Hosps 1958–69, Capt RCT (TA) 1955–67, chm: Lanes (Business Equipment) 1977–97, T J McFarland Hldgs 1984–, McFarland Farms 1980–, dir or former dir: G Kinnaird & Son 1981–, Windy Hills Ltd 1994–,

Erinwind Ltd 1994–, Londonderry and Lough Swilly Rlwy (chm 1978–81), Londonderry Gaslight 1960, R C Malseed & Co (chm 1957–90), Alexander Thompson & Co (chm), Boscrane Investments, J W Corbett Ltd (chm), Mitchell Launderettes Ltd, Donegal Hldgs 1966 and Life Assur Adv, DL Londonderry 1962; *m* 5 March 1957 *Mary Scott, er dau of Dr William Scott Watson, of Londonderry, and has:

1 +ANTHONY BASIL SCOTT [Anthony McFarland Esq, 5 Smolenskaya NAB, Flat 20, Moscow, Russia]; *b* 29 Nov 1959; *educ* Marlborough and Trin Coll Dublin (BA); ACA; *m* 28 Oct 1988 *Anne Margaret, 3rd dau of Thomas Kennedy Laidlaw, of Gernonstown, Slane, Co Meath, and has:

   (1) +Max Anthony; *b* 13 July 1993

   (2) +Rory John; *b* 25 May 1996

   (1) *Amelia Elizabeth; *b* 13 Sept 1990

2 +Stephen Andrew John; *b* 23 Dec 1968; *educ* Trin Coll Glenalmond and RAC Cirencester

1 *Shauna Jane [Mrs Andrew Gailey, The Manor House, Eton, Berks]; *b* 11 Dec 1957; *educ* St Mary's Wantage and Trin Coll Dublin (BA); *m* 4 Sept 1982 *Andrew Louis Hamilton Gailey, PhD, and has:

   (1) *Emily; *b* 9 Dec 1988

2 *Fiona Kathleen [Mrs William Orme, The Orchard, 39 High St, Fen Ditton, Cambs CB5 8ST]; *b* 1 Feb 1963; *educ* St Mary's Wantage and Switzerland; *m* 25 Sept 1993 *William Orme and has:

   (1) *Shane; *b* 24 June 1994

   (2) *Patrick; *b* 14 Jan 1997

Lineage: Sir John McFarland, 1st Bt (UK), so *cr* 23 Jan 1914, JP (Cos Londonderry and Donegal); *b* 15 Sept 1848; Mayor Londonderry 1908, 1909, 1910 and 1912, High Sheriff 1904, memb Port and Harbour Commn, High Sheriff Co Londonderry 1905, chm Londonderry and Lough Swilly Rlwy; *m* 15 May 1893 Annie (*d* 13 Oct 1939), 2nd dau of John Talbot, JP, of Terryglass, Co Tipperary, and Londonderry, and *d* 28 May 1926, leaving:

Sir Basil Alexander Talbot McFarland, 2nd Bt, CBE (1954), ERD (1945), of Aberfoyle, Londonderry; *b* 18 Feb 1898; *educ* Bedford Sch, ADC (additional) to HM THE QUEEN 1952–60, High Sheriff City Londonderry 1930–38 and Co Londonderry 1952, HM Lt City Londonderry, Mayor Londonderry 1939 and 1945–50 (Hon Freeman), Senator NI 1945–50, Hon Col 9th Londonderry HAA Regt RA (SR), Hon Col 246(M) HAA Regt RA (TA) and 245(M) LAA Regt RA (TA), Chm Co Londonderry TA&AFA 1947–62, Pres TA&VR Assoc NI 1967–69, Cmdg Offr Londonderry HG, Artists Rifles WW I, WW II (despatches), chm: Sir Alfred McAlpine & Son (NI), Lanes (Derry) Ltd, Londonderry and Lough Swilly Rlwy, John W Corbett & Sons, Londonderry Port and Harbour Commrs, Londonderry Gaslight Co, Belfast Banking Co, Belfast Bank Executors and Tstee Co, Londonderry Branch St John Ambulance Assoc and Alexander Thompson & Co, dir Robert C Malseed & Co, local dir Commercial Union Assur, Cmmr Irish Lights, memb: Irish Rugby Int 1920–22, Co Donegal Rlwy, Jt Ctee Strabane and Letterkenny Railway Co, Cncl TA and AF Assoc, NI Air Advisory Cncl 1946–65 and London Midland Area Bd Br Tport Commn 1955–61, Tstee Magee U Coll 1962–65, CStJ; *m* 1st 10 Sept 1924 Annie Kathleen (*d* 28 Feb 1952), 2nd dau of Andrew Henderson, JP, of Parkville, Whiteabbey, Belfast; *m* 2nd 2 July 1955 Mary Eleanor, 2nd dau of William Dougan, of Londonderry, and *d* 5 March 1986, having by his 1st w had:

1 Sir JOHN TALBOT McFARLAND, **3rd and present Bt**

1 Annie Maureen; *b* 27 Sept 1926; *d unm* 6 Sept 1960

McFarlane of Llandaff

Creation: B. (LP, UK) 1979.

THE BARONESS McFARLANE OF LLANDAFF, of Llandaff in the County of South Glamorgan (Jean Kennedy McFarlane) [The Rt Hon The Baroness Mcfarlane of Llandaff, 5 Dovercourt Ave, Heaton Mersey, Stockport SK4 3QB]; *b* 1 April 1926; *educ* Howell's Sch Llandaff and Bedford and Birkbeck Colls London; SRN; SCN; Staff Nurse St Bartholomew's Hosp 1950–51; Health Visitor Cardiff CC 1953–59; Organising Tutor RCN 1960–62; Educn Offr Birmingham 1962–66; Research Project Leader London 1967–69; Dir Educn Inst Advanced Nursing Educ 1969–71; Sr Lecturer Nursing Manchester U 1971–73, Prof and Head Dept Nursing 1974–88, Prof Emeritus 1988–; Memb: Roy Commn NHS 1976–79, Cwlth War Graves Commn 1983–88, Gen Synod C of E 1990–; Chm English Bd for Nursing, Midwifery and Health Visiting 1980–83; FRCN 1976; FCNA 1984; Hon FRCP 1990; Hon MSc Manchester 1979; Hon DSc Ulster 1981; Hon DEd CNAA 1983; Hon MD Liverpool 1990; author: *The Problems of Developing Criteria of Quality for Nursing Care* (1969), *The Proper Study of the Nurse* (1970), *The Practice of Nursing using the Nursing Process* (with G Castledine, 1982)

Lineage: JAMES McFARLANE; *m* Elvina Alice — and had:

JEAN KENNEDY, *cr* a **Baroness**

McGowan

Arms: Per saltire arg. and az. two lions rampant in pale gu. and as many horse shoes in fess ppr. **Crest:** A tower or between two horseshoes ppr. **Supporters:** Dexter, a figure representing St Barbara ppr., holding in the exterior hand a tower or; sinister, a figure representing St Kentigern ppr., holding in the exterior hand his crozier or. **Motto:** *Juncta juvant* ('Union is strength').
Creation: B. (UK) 24 Feb 1937.

THE 3RD BARON McGOWAN, of Ardeer, Co Ayr ((Harry) Duncan Cory McGowan) [The Rt Hon The Lord McGowan, 12 Stanhope Mews East, London SW7 5QU; Highway House, Lower Froyle, Hants GU34 4NB]; *b* 20 July 1938, *s f* 1966; *educ* Eton; with Panmure Gordon 1968– (chm 1995–); *m* 16 May 1962 *Lady Gillian Angela Pepys, yst dau of 7th Earl of Cottenham (*qv*), and has:

1 +HARRY JOHN CHARLES; *b* 23 June 1971; stockbroker

1 *Emma Louisa Angela [The Hon Mrs Hill, 30 Westover Rd, London SW18]; *b* 13 June 1963; *m* 1987 *Guy H C Hill and has:

   (1) *Charles; *b* 1988

   (1) *Davina; *b* 1991

2 *Annabel Kate Cory; *b* 2 Nov 1965; interior designer; *m* 1991 *Ashley J Bealby

Lineage: HENRY McGOWAN, of Glasgow; *m* Agnes (*d* 1 Aug 1937), dau of Richard Wilson, and had:

HARRY DUNCAN McGOWAN, **1st Baron McGowan**, of Ardeer, Co Ayr (UK), so *cr* 24 Feb 1937, KBE (1918); *b* 3 June 1874; Hon LLD Glasgow and Birmingham 1934, St Andrews 1950, Hon DCL Oxford 1935, Durham 1949, Hon DSc McGill 1951; Hon Pres (chm 1930–50) ICI Ltd, Internat Nickel Co of Canada, pres Soc of Chemical Industry and Inst of Fuel; Hon Col 52nd (Lowland) Div Signals, Roy Signals 1934–39, pres Br Standards Inst 1947, Freeman Glasgow 1951; *m* 17 Dec 1903 Jean Boyle (*d* 8 April 1952), dau of William Young, of Paisley, and had:

1 HENRY WILSON, **2nd Baron**

2 William Johnston; *b* 10 July 1909; *educ* Uppingham and Clare Coll Cambridge; WW II 1939–43 with Scottish Horse and Notts (Sherwood Rangers) Yeo (severely wounded); *m* 26 Feb 1949 Helen Myrtle Dorothy (*d* 16 March 1976), MBE, JP (1954) Co London, chm Met Juvenile Courts 1959–76, yr dau of Arthur Atherley, JP, DL, of Landguard Manor, IoW, and widow of Col Edward Orlando Kellett, DSO, MP, and *d* 13 June 1977, leaving:

   (1) *Fiona Victoria Jean [The Rt Hon The Lady Hindlip, 18 Chester Square, London SW1W 9HS; The Cedar House, Inkpen, Berks RG15 ODT]; *b* 18 Nov 1947; *m* 18 April 1968 *6th Baron Hindlip (*qv*) and has issue

1 Isobel Young; *m* 12 June 1929 D'Arcy Melville Stephens (*ka* 10 Nov 1942) and *d* 25 Jan 1973, leaving issue

2 Agnes Wilson; *m* 1st 24 July 1936 (*divorce* 1949) Maj Dermot Ralph Daly (*d* 8 March 1974), Scots Gds, s of Maj Denis St George Daly, of Chipping Norton, and had issue; *m* 2nd 21 April 1949 George Berkeley Sheffield (*d* 2 July 1968), 3rd s of Sir Berkeley Sheffield, 6th Bt (*qv*), and *d* (murdered by robbers) 11 March 1976, leaving further issue

The 1st BARON *d* 13 July 1961; his er s,

HARRY WILSON McGOWAN, **2nd Baron McGowan**; *b* 18 May 1906; *educ* Uppingham and Clare Coll Cambridge (BA); Maj Middx Yeo WW II; *m* 22 April 1937 Carmen (*d* 6 Sept 1996), dau of Sir (James) Herbert Cory, 1st Bt (*qv*), and *d* 5 July 1966, leaving:

1 (HARRY) DUNCAN (CORY) McGOWAN, **3rd and present Baron McGowan**

2 +Dominic James Wilson [The Hon Dominic McGowan, Bragborough Hall, Daventry, Warwicks]; *b* 26 Nov 1951; *educ* Bradfield; *m* 19– *Brigitta, est dau of C Papadimitriou, of Athens

3 +Mungo Alexander Cansh [The Hon Mungo McGowan, Bragborough Farm, Daventry, Northants]; *b* 10 Dec 1956; *educ* Eton; *m* 12 Feb 1983 *(Arabella) Charlotte, yr dau of Baron Eden of Winton (*qv*), and has:

   (1) +James Alexander Cory; *b* 21 June 1985

   (1) *Laura Charlotte Iona; *b* 8 May 1987

   (2) *Rose Daisy Annabel; *b* 7 Feb 1991

1 *Moana Elizabeth Jean [The Hon Mrs Seth-Smith, The Old School House, Whilton, Daventry, Northants]; *b* 30 May 1948; *m* 1978, as his 2nd w, *John David Vaughan Seth-Smith, only s of Cdr David Keith Seth-Smith, and has:
  (1) *Edward David Harry; *b* 1979
  (2) *William Jonathan Cory; *b* 1985
2 *Catriona Carmen Harriet; *b* 8 Jan 1953

McGRIGOR

Arms: Argent a fir tree growing out of a mount in base vert, surmounted by a sword, point upwards in bend proper, pommel and hilt gold, in the dexter chief an eastern crown gules, on a chief azure a tower or, between the badge of the Order of the Tower and Sword on the dexter and that of the Crescent on the sinister.
Crest: A lion's head erased gules, crowned with an eastern coronet or. **Motto:** *S'rioghal mo dhream* ('Royal is my tribe').
Creation: Bt. (UK) 30 Sept 1831.

SIR CHARLES EDWARD McGRIGOR, 5TH BT, of Campden Hill, Middlesex, DL (Argyll and Bute 1987) [Sir Charles McGrigor Bt DL, Upper Sonachan, by Dalmally, Argyll PA33 1BJ]; *b* 5 Oct 1922; *s f* 1946; *educ* Eton; Capt Rifle Bde WW II (despatches), ADC to HRH THE DUKE OF GLOUCESTER 1945–47, memb Roy Co Archers, Exon Yeomen Gd 1970–85, memb ctee of Management and V-Pres RNLI and convenor Scottish Lifeboat Cncl; *m* 7 June 1948 *Mary Bettine, est dau of Sir Archibald Charles Edmonstone, 6th Bt (*qv*), and has:

1 +JAMES ANGUS RHODERICK NEIL [James McGrigor Esq, Ardchonnel House, by Dalmally, Argyll PA33 1BW]; *b* 19 Oct 1949; *educ* Eton; *m* 1988 (*divorce* 1993) Caroline F, dau of Jacques Roboh, of Paris; *m* 2nd 3 Oct 1997 *Emma, dau of David Lyon Fellowes, JP, of Inistrynich, Dalmally, Argyll, and by his 1st w has:
  (1) *Sibylla; *b* 1988
  (2) *Sarah; *b* 1989
2 +Charles Edward; *b* 7 Aug 1959; *m* 30 July 1996 *Melissa, dau of Thomas Merrywether, of Akron, Ohio
1 *Lorna Gwendolyn; *b* 18 Feb 1951
2 *Kirstie Rowena Amabel; *b* 3 Feb 1953; *m* 1st 1979 David Norman G Barraclough, est s of Geoffrey Barraclough, of Madrid, and has:
  (1) *Hector; *b* 1979
  (1) *Amabel; *b* 1983
2 (cont.) Mrs Barraclough *m* 2nd 1993, as his 2nd w, *Roderick John Maclaren and has issue (*see* LOUDOUN, E)

Lineage: GREGOR MacGREGOR, of Easter Drumnacharrie (Grigor MacGregor in Goularich), allegedly est s of John Dhu MacGregor, held Drumnacharrie and half Nether Urquhilare from John, Earl of Atholl; *m* Christian McWilliam and had:

JOHN MacGREGOR; fiar (owner of the fee simple) of Easter Drumnacharrie, known as Delavorar (or Dalrown) in Strathdown; *m c* 1658 a dau of Farquharson of Auchenheyle and gdau of John Couper of Blackchibrich and had:

GREGOR MacGREGOR; *m c* 1681 Marjory, dau of Robert Grant of Easter Elchies, and *d* 1731, leaving:

JAMES MacGREGOR; settled in Milton, by Duthill, Strathspey; *m* a dau of Grant of Abernethy and *d* 1761, leaving:

COLQUHOUN McGRIGOR; *b* Aberdeen 1740; merchant; *m* Ann, dau of Lewis Grant, of Lethendrie, and *d* 1798, leaving an est s:

Sir James McGrigor, 1st Bt (UK), so *cr* 30 Sept 1831, KCB (1851); *b* 9 April 1771; MA and MD Edin, Hon LLD, FRS, FRCP, joined Army medical dept 1793, Surgn 88th Connaught Rangers, served Holland, Flanders, W Indies and India, Superintending Surgn Egypt 1801, Inspr-Gen Hosps 1809, Ch Medical Staff Wellington's Army Peninsula 1811, Dir-Gen Army Medical Dept 1815–51, ktd 1814, Orders of Knight of the Tower and Sword; *m* 23 June 1810 Mary (*d* 1 April 1872), yst dau of Duncan Grant of Mullochard, Strathspey, and gdau of Grant of Arndilly, and *d* 2 April 1858, leaving:

1 CHARLES RHODERIC (Sir), **2nd Bt**

2 Walter James; *b* 18 March 1817; *educ* Trin Coll Camb (MA); Maj 2nd Bn QO Cameron Highrs; *m* 1st 29 Aug 1849 Marie Anne (*d* 24 Sept 1851), est dau of V-Adml Digby (*see* DIGBY, B); *m* 2nd 20 Sept 1870 Elizabeth Anna (*m* 2nd 20 Aug 1902 Capt Randolph Richards Luscombe, 4th Dragoon Gds, and *d* 14 Nov 1903), est dau of Rev John Hamilton, Vicar Linstead, Kent, and *d* 7 June 1891, leaving by his 1st w:
  (1) James Digby Walter (Rev); *b* 12 Sept 1851; *d* 17 Aug 1894
1 Jane Grant; *m* April 1845 Rev Frederick Parr Phillips (*d* 17 March 1903), Hon Canon Winchester, Rector Stoke d'Abernon, Surrey, and *d* 28 Jan 1902, leaving issue

The 1st Bt's er s,
  Sir Charles Rhoderic McGrigor, 2nd Bt; *b* 2 May 1811; *m* 17 Nov 1850 Elizabeth Anne (*d* 26 Nov 1874), 2nd dau of Maj-Gen Sir Robert Nickle, KH, and *d* 13 Jan 1890, leaving:

1 JAMES RHODERIC DUFF (Sir), **3rd Bt**
2 Charles Rhoderic Robert, CB, CMG; *b* 5 Sept 1860; *educ* Eton; Maj-Gen, cmded 3rd Bn KRRC, served E Griqualand, Transvaal, Eqypt, E Sudan, S Africa and WW I; *m* 18 Feb 1892 Ada Rosamond (*d* Jan 1945), dau of Robert Hartley Bower, JP, DL, of Welham, Yorks, and *d* 9 July 1927, leaving:
  (1) Rhoderick Robert (Sir), GCB (1951, KCB 1945), DSO (1943); *b* 12 April 1893; Adml of the Fleet, served WWs I and II (despatches), Capt (D) 4th Destroyer Flotilla 1936–38, Ch Staff to C-in-C China Station 1938–40, cmded HMS *Renown* in Force (H) 1941, Ld Commr Admlty and Assist Ch Naval Staff 1941–43, Naval Force Cdr capture Pantelleria and invasion Sicily 1943 (wounded), Flag Offr Sicily 1943, Taranto and Adriatic, Flag Offr liaison with Italy 1943–44, Flag Offr 1st Cruiser Sqdn 1944–45, V-Ch Naval Staff 1945–47, C-in-C Home Fleet 1948–50, C-in-C Plymouth 1950–51, 1st Sea Ld and Ch Naval Staff 1951–55, First and Pncpl Naval ADC to HM THE QUEEN 1952–53, Hon LLD St Andrews (1953), Aberdeen (1955), Ld Rector Aberdeen U 1954–57; *m* 28 Nov 1931 Louise Gwendoline (*d* 11 Nov 1961), only dau of Col Geoffrey Carr Glyn, CMG, DSO, MVO (*see* WOLVERTON, B), and widow of Maj Charles Henry Greville, DSO, Gren Gds (*see* WARWICK, BROOKE and, E), and *dsp* 3 Dec 1959, leaving adopted twin sons:
    *John [John McGrigor Esq, Downderry, Crescent Rd, Alverstoke, Hants]; *b* 4 July 1942; *educ* Marlborough and RNC Dartmouth; Lt RN; *m* 27 Oct 1962 *Anita Rence, yr dau of Elemer Nordberg, Chev Legn Honour, of St Germain-en-Laye, France, and has:
      1b *Alison Jean; *b* 27 April 1963
      2b *Helen Mary; *b* 10 Sept 1965
    *Andrew David; *b* 4 July 1942; *educ* Marlborough and St Andrews; Capt 2nd Bn Roy Green Jackets (KRRC); *m* 15 May 1971 *Susan, dau of Col George Brain, of Belfast
  (1) Mary Ada Bower; *b* 24 Sept 1894
3 William Colquhoun Grant; *b* 25 Nov 1861; *educ* Eton; Col Scots Gds, Hon Brig-Gen 1918, cmdg 2nd Bn Scots Gds, cmdg 174th Bde 1914–17, served Sudan 1885, S Africa 1899–1902 and WW I; *d* 4 Sept 1924
4 George Duncan, FRGS; *b* 26 Oct 1867; *educ* Eton; *m* 1 Aug 1903 Margaret Roberta (*d* 4 July 1956), dau of James Mackenzie, formerly of Shanghai, and *dsp* 12 Feb 1953
1 Mary Jane Dallas; *d* unm 29 Dec 1936
2 Elizabeth Anne, *d* unm 13 June 1938
3 Dona Edith; *m* 21 Jan 1886 Sir Thomas Swinnerton Dyer, 11th Bt (*qv*), and *d* 3 Feb 1909, leaving issue

The 2nd Bt's est s,
  Sir James Rhoderic Duff McGrigor, 3rd Bt; *b* 27 April 1857; *educ* Eton and Ch Ch Oxford; Capt Rifle Bde; *m* 30 Oct 1890 Helen Cornell (*d* 11 Nov 1942), 2nd dau of John Gilbert Meiggs, of New York, and *d* 4 Feb 1924, having had:

1 CHARLES COLQUHOUN (Sir), **4th Bt**
2 James Neil Grant; *b* 16 Nov 1894; Lt Gordon Highrs; *d* 7 Nov 1914 of wounds recd in action 24 Oct 1914
1 Jean Helen; *b* 28 July 1902; served WW II Middle East 1939–42 (despatches); *m* 2 Jan 1926 Maj-Gen Sir Michael O'Moore Creagh, KBE, MC, 15th/19th Hus, s of Gen Sir O'Moore Creagh, VC, GCB, GCSI, and had issue
2 Dona Mary; *b* 7 Feb 1908; *d* 25 June 1909

The 3rd Bt's only surv s,
  Sir Charles Colquhoun McGrigor, 4th Bt, OBE (1921); *b* 26 April 1893; Lt-Col Rifle Bde; *m* 7 Jan 1919 Amabel, only dau of Edward Lygon Somers Cocks, of Bake, St Germans, Cornwall, by his w Amabel Jemima, dau and coheir of Sir Charles Watson-Copley, 3rd Bt (*see* CROMWELL, B), and *d* 28 Oct 1946, having had:

1 James Neil; *b* 8 March 1920; Capt Rifle Bde WW II; *ka* Nov 1941
2 Sir CHARLES EDWARD McGRIGOR, **5th and present Bt**

McINTOSH OF HARINGEY

Creation: B. (LP, UK) 1982.

THE BARON McINTOSH OF HARINGEY, of Haringey in Greater London (Andrew Robert McIntosh) [The Rt Hon The Lord McIntosh of Haringey, 27 Hurst Ave, London N6 5TX]; *b* 30 April 1933; *educ* Haberdashers' Aske's Sch, Roy GS High Wycombe, Jesus Coll Oxford (MA) and Ohio State U; Fell Ec Ohio State U 1956–57; with Gallup Organisation 1957–61, Hoover Ltd 1961–63, mkt research manager Osram GEC 1963–65; memb: Hornsey Borough Cncl 1963–65, Haringey Borough Cncl 1964–68, GLC for Tottenham 1973–83 (Leader Oppn 1980–81); Ho Lds Oppn Spokesman: Industry 1983–87, Educn and Sci 1985–87, Home Affrs 1992–97, Dep Leader Oppn Ho Lds 1992–97, Dep Govt Ch Whip 1997–; Chm: Market Research Soc 1972–73, SVP UK 1983–, Fabian Soc 1985–86; dep chm IFF Research Ltd 1988– (md 1965–81, chm 1981–88); *m* 1962 *Naomi Ellen Sargant, Pro V-Chllr Student Affairs OU 1974–78, Prof Applied Social

Research 1978–81, sr commissioning ed Channel 4 TV 1981–88, chm Gt Ormond St Hosp for Children 1997–, dau of Thomas Sargant, OBE, JP, and formerly w of Peter Joseph Kelly, and has:

1 *Francis Robert; *b* 1962; *educ* Highgate Wood Sch and London Coll of Furniture

2 *Philip Henry Sargant; *b* 1964; *educ* Highgate Wood Sch and Kingston Poly

Lineage: Prof ALBERT WILLIAM McINTOSH, OBE; *m* Helena Agnes (Jenny) Britton and had:

ANDREW ROBERT, *cr* a **Baron**

McLeod

Arms: Ermine on a pile azure, between two lotus flowers in base or, a castle, triple-towered argent, masoned sable, windows and porch gules. **Crest:** In front of two flags in saltire gules, staves proper, a bull's head cabossed, also gules. **Mottoes:** 1 (beneath arms) *Murus aheneus esto* ('Be thou a brazen wall'), 2 (over crest) Hold fast. **Creation:** Bt. (UK) 22 Jan 1925.

SIR CHARLES HENRY McLEOD, 3RD BT, of The Fairfields, Cobham [Sir Charles McLeod Bt, Coombe Green Cottage, Lea, Wilts SN16 9PF]; *b* 7 Nov 1924; *s f* 1950; *educ* Winchester; memb London Stock Exchange 1955–, Dip Master Brewer 1950, rep India internat squash rackets 1956–58; *m* 5 Jan 1957 Ann Gillian (*d* 1978), 3rd dau of Henry Russell Bowlby, of Chelsea SW10, and has:

1 +JAMES RODERICK CHARLES; *b* 26 Sept 1960; *m* 1990 *Helen M, er dau of Capt George T Cooper, OBE, RN, of Lilliput, Poole, Dorset

   1 *Belinda; *b* 6 Oct 1957; *m* 19– *– Shaker

2 *Nicola [Mrs John Bampfylde, 56 Ames St, Paekakariki, Wellington, NZ]; *b* 11 Oct 1958; *m* 1st 1981 (*divorce*) 1985 Nigel Iorwerth Stodart Parry, er s of John Stanley Hammond Parry, of Staplegordon, Seale, Surrey; *m* 2nd 1985 — Duffain; *m* 3rd 1990 *John Spencer Warwick Bampfylde (*see* POLTIMORE, B)

Lineage: KENNETH McLEOD, of Swordale, Isle of Skye, had:

Rev NORMAN McLEOD, of Paible, N Uist; *b* 5 Dec 1801; *m* 21 Feb 1838 Julia (*d* 11 June 1901), dau of Dr Alexander McLeod and Mary Campbell, and *d* 5 March 1881, leaving, with five daus and six other sons:

Sir Charles McLeod, 1st Bt (UK), *cr* 22 Jan 1925; *b* 19 June 1858; sr ptnr: McLeod, Russel & Co,of London, and McLeod & Co of Calcutta, East India Merchants, chm Nat Bank India, V-Pres Roy Empire Soc, KGStJ; *m* 9 June 1892 Mary Louisa (*d* 19 Feb 1951), er dau of Dep Surgn-Gen Henry Cayley, CMG (*see* CAYLEY, Bt), and *d* 2 Oct 1936, leaving:

1 MURDOCH CAMPBELL (Sir), **2nd Bt**

   1 Madeline Joyce; *m* 26 Oct 1929 Hugh Elliot Colvin, s of Sir Elliot Graham Colvin, KCSI, ICS, and *d* 31 Jan 1966, leaving issue

The 1st Bt's s,

  Sir Murdoch Campbell McLeod, 2nd Bt; *b* 17 July 1893; *educ* Winchester; WW I with Seaforth Highrs and Gen Staff, East India merchant, FLS, FRES; *m* 29 Nov 1920 (Annette) Susan (Mary) (*d* 7 Dec 1964), dau of Henry Hammond Whitehead, of S Kensington, and *d* 21 April 1950, leaving:

1 Roderick Campbell; *b* 4 Oct 1921; *educ* Winchester; Lt Scots Gds WW II; *ka* Salerno 11 Sept 1943

2 Sir CHARLES HENRY McGRIGOR, **3rd and present Bt**

McLintock

Arms: Azure a book expanded or, leaved gules, over all a writing pen palewise proper. **Crest:** A lion passant or, holding in his dexter paw a thistle slipped proper. **Motto:** *Virtute et labore* (By virtue and labour'). **Creation:** Bt. (UK) 19 Jan 1934.

SIR MICHAEL WILLIAM McLINTOCK, 4TH BT, of Sanquhar, Co Dumfries; *b* 13 Aug 1958; *s f* 1987

Lineage: Sir William McLintock, 1st Bt (UK), so *cr* 19 Jan 1934, GBE (1929, KBE 1922), CVO (1922) (s of Thomson McLintock, of Glasgow); *b* 26 Sept 1873; sr ptnr Thomson McLintock Co, chartered accountants, memb: Broadcasting Ctee 1935, Bd Referees of Industrial Arbitration Ct, Devpt (Public Utility) Advsy Ctee, Fin Risks Ctee, Roy Commn Income Tax, Ctee Nat Debt and Taxation, Ec Advsy Cncl 1929, Company Law Amendment and Unemployment Insur Ctees, Ctee Civil Research Cotton Industry, Ctee Electrificn of Rlwys and Race-course Betting Control Bd 1928–33; a fin advsr Imp Wireless and Cable Conf; *m* 17 April 1901 Margaret (*d* 5 March 1960), dau of Henry Lyons, of Co Sligo, and *d* 8 May 1947, leaving:

1 THOMSON (Sir), **2nd Bt**

   1 Norah Lyons; *b* 3 Feb 1903; *m* 9 June 1936 Stephen Everest Watson (*d* 6 June 1952), er s of Eric Watson, and had:

     (1) *Eric William; *b* 6 July 1938; *educ* Eastbourne Coll

2 Jean Lyons; *b* 3 June 1907; *m* 4 June 1946 Maj Alexander Culbertson Lyons, Roy Inskilling Fus (ret), est s of Alexander Lyons, and *dsp* 23 Oct 1958

3 *Mary Lyons [Mrs Robert Myles, Coach House, Lees Court, Matfield, Kent]; *b* 7 June 1912; *m* 1st 14 Oct 1937 Capt Malcolm George Lillingston, King's Dragoon Gds (*ka* Nov 1941), s of Canon Arthur Blackwell Goulburn Lillingston, of The College, Durham, and has:

     (1) *Mark Campbell; *b* 29 July 1938; *educ* Eton and Magdalene Coll Cambridge

     (1) *Diane Margaret [Mrs Robin Paterson, Lees Court, Matfield, Kent TN12 7JU]; *b* 19 May 1941; *m* 27 July 1963 *Robin Andrew Paterson, CA, only s of John Leggat Paterson, of Craighouse, Beith, Ayrshire, and has:

       1a *Jamie John Lillingston PATERSON later LILLINGSTON-PATERSON (1987); *b* 6 Aug 1967; *educ* Eton

       1a *Joanna Mary Lillingston; *b* 16 May 1965; *m* 1990 *Michael Richard John Bell, yst s of Lt-Cdr Peter Bell, of Yeabridge Close, S Petherton, Somerset, and has:

         1b *Hollie Mary Ann; *b* 1993

         2b *Camilla Margaret Lucy (twin); *b* 1993

         3b *Tara Polly Francesca; *b* 24 Jan 1997

3 (cont.) Mrs Malcolm Lillingston *m* 2nd 16 Oct 1947 Maj Robert Bradford Myles, MC (*d* 1981), late Roy Inniskilling Fus, yr s of Robert Myles, of Stratherne, Ballyshannon, Co Donegal, and by him has:

     (2) *Nicholas Robert William Bradford; *b* 12 April 1954; *educ* Eton

     (2) *Sarah Louise Bradford [Mrs Michael Robinson, 8 Gorst Rd, London SW11 6JE]; *b* 11 June 1950; *m* 1982 *Michael James Corbett Robinson and has:

       1a *Jonathon Myles; *b* 1986

       1a *Cara Myles; *b* 1984

     (3) *Penelope Jean Bradford [Mrs Anthony Lipscomb, Rosewarne House, Lodge Rd, Bicknacre, Essex CM3 4HG]; *b* 11 Jan 1952; *m* 1979 *Dr Anthony Pitt Lipscomb and adopted:

       *Gemma Jayne; *b* 1991

The 1st Bt's only s,

  Sir Thomson McLintock, 2nd Bt; *b* 30 April 1905; *educ* Loretto and Pembroke Coll Cambridge; chartered accountant; *m* 26 July 1929 (Agnes) Jean Thomson, dau of Robert Traven Donaldson Aitken (*see* BEAVERBROOK, B), and *d* in a car crash 23 Dec 1953, leaving:

1 WILLIAM TRAVEN (Sir), **3rd Bt**

2 +Peter Thomson [Peter McLintock Esq, Springfield, Penicuik, Midlothian]; *b* 20 March 1933; *educ* Harrow; *m* 1st 11 Sept 1954 (*divorce* 1977) Fiona, yst dau

of Gen Sir Philip Christison, 4th Bt, GBE, CB, DSO, MC (see 1970 edn); m 2nd 1986 *Patricia-Anne, dau of —, and by his 1st w has:

(1) +Traven Thomson Christison; b 12 Oct 1957; educ Edinburgh Acad; m 1984 *— and has:

1a *Sarah; b 1987

(1) *Morar; b 7 April 1955; m 1986 *David Honeyman and has:

1a *Ailsa; b 1986

The 2nd Bt's er s,

Sir William Traven McLintock, 3rd Bt; b 4 Jan 1931; educ Harrow; m 1st 8 Nov 1952 (divorce 19–) Andrée, dau of Richard Lonsdale Hands, of Lausanne; m 2nd 1974 *Mrs (Muriel) Heather Homfray Newman, dau of Philip Dennis Homfray-Davies, and d 1987, leaving by his 1st w:

1 Sir MICHAEL WILLIAM McLINTOCK, **4th and present Bt**

2 +ANDREW THOMSON; b 2 Dec 1960; heir presumptive

3 +Kevin Robert; b 21 Sept 1963

McMAHON

Arms: Per saltire or and ermine a lion passant azure between two lions passant-regardant in pale, gules. **Crest:** An arm embowed in armour, holding a sword, blade wavy, all proper, surmounted of a portcullis gules, chained or. **Supporters:** On either side a private of the 10th Foot, habited and accoutred, and holding in the exterior hand a musket proper. **Motto:** Sic nos, sic sacra tuemur ('Thus we defend ourselves and our sacred rights'). **Creation:** Bt. (UK) 7 Aug 1817.

SIR BRIAN PATRICK McMAHON, 8TH BT [Sir Brian McMahon Bt, Oak Ridge, School Rd, Thorney Hill, Bransgore, Dorset BH23 8DS]; b 9 June 1942; s f 1977; educ Wellington and Wednesbury Tech Coll (BSc Engrg Metallurgy 1964); engr, AIM 1967, AInstW 1968; m 1981 (divorce 1991) Kathleen Joan, dau of William Hopwood

Lineage: JOHN McMAHON, Patentee Comptroller Port of Limerick; had by his 1st w:

1 **Sir John McMAHON, 1st Bt** (UK), so cr 7 Aug 1817, with remainder, in default of male issue, to his half bro Thomas, PC (I); Priv Sec and Keeper Privy Purse to GEORGE IV when Prince Regent; dsp 12 Sept 1817

JOHN McMAHON m 2nd July 1771 Mary (d 22 May 1791), dau of James Stackpole, of Cork, and d 22 Dec 1789, having by her had:

2 Sir WILLIAM McMAHON, **1st Bt** (UK), so cr 6 May 1815, PC, of Dublin; b 12 July 1776; barrister, Master Rolls Ireland; m 1st 16 May 1807 Frances (d 9 Feb 1813), dau of Beresford Burston, KC, Irish Bar, and had:

(1) Sir BERESFORD BURSTON McMAHON, **2nd Bt**; b 14 Feb 1808; Capt Scots Fus Gds; m 4 Jan 1838 Maria Catherine (d 6 Aug 1876), sis of 1st Baron Deramore (qv), and d 11 Jan 1873, leaving:

1a Sir WILLIAM SAMUEL McMAHON, **3rd Bt**, JP (Co Clare), DL (Co Tyrone); b 9 Nov 1839; Attaché Br Legation Munich, Capt 2nd Life Gds; d unm 3 June 1905

2a Robert Bateson; b 5 Nov 1840; d unm 9 July 1894

3a Beresford Burston; b 26 July 1849; d unm 27 Nov 1890

4a Gerald Charles; b 3 Sept 1851; d unm 23 April 1894

5a Sir LIONEL McMAHON, **4th and last Bt**, DL (Co Tyrone); b 30 June 1856; High Sheriff 1914, barrister Inner Temple, Lt 58th Regt Zulu War 1879; m 29 Aug 1888 Anne Cecilia Austin-Cooke (d 15 Feb 1923) and dsp 20 Feb 1926, when this btcy expired

1a Catherine Charlotte; m 27 July 1867 Sir Edward Grogan, 1st Bt (d 26 Jan 1891; see 1927 edn), and d 25 Feb 1919, leaving issue

2a Frances Thomasine; m 3 Sept 1863 Joseph Gubbins (d 20 Feb 1895), of Kilfrush, Co Limerick, and d 25 Feb 1909, leaving issue

3a Maria Constance Georgiana; d 2 Sept 1847

4a Nina Gertrude; m 31 July 1871 Rev Arthur Gore Ryder, DD (d 1889), Canon Christ Church and Rector Donnybrook, nr Dublin, and d 31 July 1908, leaving issue

(2) William John; b 3 July 1811; d unm 26 Oct 1861

2 (cont.) Sir WILLIAM m 2nd 9 Sept 1814 Charlotte, sis of Sir Robert Shaw, 1st Bt (qv), of Bushy Pk, Co Dublin, and d 1837, having by her had:

(3) Robert; b 13 Dec 1815; dsp

(4) Augustus; b 15 Aug 1819; d unm 25 May 1853

(5) Charles (Sir); b 10 July 1824; Capt 10th Hus, Speaker Legislative Assembly Victoria; m twice and d 28 Aug 1891

(1) Charlotte Maria; m 29 April 1852 Samuel Edward McGwire, of Clonea Ho, Co Waterford, and d 5 March 1894. He d 1886

(2) Louisa; m 21 Sept 1841 Col Francis Ellis (d 24 Oct 1881) and d 28 Sept 1889, leaving issue

(3) Wilhelmina; m 1844 Maj Henry Shaw (d 1886) and had issue

3 **Sir Thomas McMAHON, 2nd Bt**, GCB; b 27 Dec 1779; Adj-Gen forces India 13 years, Lt-Govr Portsmouth, cmdg SW dist England five years, C-in-C Bombay army seven years, Col 10th Foot; m 27 Aug 1808 Emily Anne (d 11 May 1866), dau of Michael Robert Westropp, and d 10 April 1860, having had:

(1) **Sir Thomas Westropp McMahon, 3rd Bt**, CB; Gen, Col 5th Dragoon Gds, previously Col 18th Hus (medals for Sobraon and Crimea, with three clasps), formerly cdr Cav Bde Aldershot, Inspr-Gen Cav; m 1st 7 Oct 1851 Dora Paulina (d 23 Sept 1852), dau of Evan Hamilton Baillie; m 2nd 13 Jan 1859 Frances Mary (d 14 April 1867), dau of John Holford; m 3rd 14 Aug 1888 Constance Marianne (d 19 Sept 1893), widow of John Bell Brooking, and d 23 Jan 1892, having by his 2nd w had:

1a **Sir Aubrey Hope McMahon, 4th Bt**; b 26 Aug 1862; Lt and Adj Gren Gds; d unm 8 April 1893

2a **Sir Horace Westropp McMahon, 5th Bt**, OBE, DSO; b 28 Oct 1863; Maj Roy Welch Fus, Lt-Col cmdg 9th Bn Roy Welch Fus, T/Col and Group Cdr 1916, T/Lt-Col and Cmdt Corps Sch 1917, served S Africa 1896 (severely wounded, despatches), S African War 1899–1900 (Queen's medal, four clasps) and WW I (despatches, Croix de Guerre avec Palme); m 3 May 1911 Ellie Maude (d 21 Dec 1969), dau of Hon Henry Moses, MLC, of Sydney, NSW, and widow of Capt Charles Edward Bancroft, Roy Welsh Fus, and dsp 9 July 1932

3a Francis Yorke; Capt 1st Dragoons; b 16 Dec 1864; d unm 6 July 1897

4a Norman Reginald, DSO; b 24 Jan 1866; Lt-Col Roy Fus and Brig-Gen and GSO(1) Expdny Force Burma 1886–87 and S Africa 1899–1902 (despatches) and WW I (despatches); ka 11 Nov 1914

1a Frances Mary Holford, OBE (1918); b 25 March 1867; m 3 Jan 1888 Capt John Wreford Julian Hardman (d 30 May 1900), 1st Roy Dragoons, only s of Frederick Hardman, and d 18 June 1926, leaving issue

(2) Frederick Hislop; b 27 Aug 1817; d 30 April 1827

(3) Adolphus; b 14 Aug 1821; d 14 Sept 1829

(4) William; b 3 Dec 1825; m 6 March 1854 Julia (d 1874), dau of James Coster, of Streatham, and widow of Joseph Davies, of Stonecot, Surrey, and d 27 Feb 1916, having had:

1a Vivian Massey; b 2 Nov 1856; dsp

2a KELLERMAN EYRE (Sir), **6th Bt**

3a Bernard William Lynedoch, CMG (1917), CVO (1925); b 10 Oct 1865; Col Durham LI, Equerry to HRH PRINCESS LOUISE, DUCHESS OF ARGYLL; d unm 23 Dec 1928

4a Lionel Westropp; b 31 May 1868; educ Wellington

5a Arthur Beresford; b 20 Sept 1873; Lt 4th Bn Beds Regt; m 1894 Annette Alice (d 3 June 1937), est dau of William C Turner, ICS, and dsp 30 March 1944

1a Emily Anne; d 15 Sept 1864

2a Maude Geraldine; m 1882 Adrian Charles Chamier, barrister, Capt 10th Regt, and d 28 Dec 1913, leaving issue

3a Ida Beatrice; m 20 Dec 1887 Maj-Gen James Spens, CB, CMG (d 19 June 1934), Salop LI, and d 22 Feb 1951, leaving issue

4a Helena Constance; d unm 27 Jan 1933

5a Hamilton Hamilton; m 12 Nov 1891 Arthur Holdsworth Brooking (d c 1932), s of Marmaduke Hart Brooking, of Sussex Gdns, London, and d 21 Nov 1960, leaving issue

6a Ethel Selina Julia; d unm 1 Jan 1950

(1) Jane; d unm 31 Dec 1835

(2) Emily; m 27 April 1839 Sir William Miller, 3rd Bt (d 30 Oct 1861), and d 8 Aug 1892 aged 76, having had issue

(3) Charlotte; m 23 Feb 1843 John Kellermann Wedderburn (d 4 June 1891) and d 4 April 1894, having had issue (see WEDDERBURN, B)

(4) Frederica; m 8 July 1852 Rev Hon Augustus Byron (see BYRON, B), and d 29 March 1903, leaving issue

(5) Georgiana Mary; d unm 14 July 1847

The 5th Bt's cousin,

Sir Kellerman Eyre McMahon, 6th Bt, OBE (1919); b 24 Aug 1860; Lt-Col 2nd Bn King's Salop LI, RTO WW I; m 8 June 1899 Lydia Mary (d 31 Oct 1933), dau of Maj W P Hoey, of Co Wicklow, and widow of Slingsby Cradock, 19th Hus, and d 10 Sept 1935, leaving:

1 **Sir (William) Patrick McMAHON, 7th Bt**; b 24 April 1900; educ Wellington; FLAS, ASI; m 14 Feb 1939 (divorce 1960) Ruth Stella, yr dau of Percy Robert Kenyon-Slaney (see KENYON, B) and formerly w of Lt-Cdr John Francis Crofton Barker Hahlo, RN, and d 5 Jan 1977, leaving:

1 Sir BRIAN PATRICK McMAHON, **8th and present Bt**

2 +SHAUN DESMOND [Shaun McMahon Esq, Dendron, 21 Old Vineyard Rd, Constantia, CP, S Africa]; b 29 Oct 1945; heir presumptive; educ Wellington; m 1st 1971 Antonia Noel, dau of Antony James Adie, of Rowington, Warwicks; m 2nd 1985 *Jill Rosamund, yr dau of Dr Jack Cherry, of Abingdon, Oxon, and has by her:

(1) +Patrick John Westropp; b 7 Feb 1988

(2) +Charles Beresford; b 1989

McNair

Arms: Gu. three barrulets wavy arg. surmounted of a lion rampant or, armed and langued az., between two teasel thistle-heads, stalked and leaved paleways or. **Crest:** An ancient ship under full sail or, flagged az., the sail emblazoned of ensigns armorial as on the escutcheon. **Supporters:** Two Bedlington terriers ppr.
Motto: *Periculum in mora* ('There is danger in delay').
Creation: B. (UK) 4 Aug 1955.

THE 3RD BARON McNAIR, of Gleniffer, Co Renfrew (Duncan James McNair) [The Rt Hon The Lord McNair, House of Lords, London SW1A 0PW]; *b* 26 June 1947; *s* 1989; *educ* Bryanston and Gloucester Tech Coll; *chm:* Emission Control Systems Internat, DMCK Consultants Ltd; *m* 1st 11 Jan 1973 Clodagh Margaret Hawtayne Blake, dau of Dr Eric Alfred Blake Pritchard, and has:

1 *Thomas John; *b* 24 Dec 1972
2 *Victoria Mary; *b* 24 Dec 1972 (twin)

The 3rd BARON also adopted:

*Donnia Anna Charlotte Olive; *b* 1 Jan 1969

The 3rd BARON *m* 2nd 19– Kodikaraarachige Perera, of Sri Lanka; *m* 3rd Dec 1995 *Margaret Elizabeth Hannah —

Lineage: WILLIAM McNAIR; *b* 9 March 1759; had:

JOHN McNAIR, of Paisley, Renfrewshire; mfr; *m* Jennie Grierson and *d* 1834, having had:

DUNCAN McNAIR, of Paisley; mfr; *b* 23 Aug 1828; *m* 18– Catherine Gibb (*b* 1826; *d* 1915) and *d* 1909, leaving:

JOHN McNAIR; *b* 13 April 1855; memb Lloyd's; *m* 11 April 1884 Jeannie (*b* 4 Aug 1858; *d* 1951), dau of John Ballantyne, of Paisley, and had:

1 ARNOLD DUNCAN, **1st Baron**
2 Arthur James; *b* 27 April 1887; *educ* Aldenham and Emmanuel Coll Cambridge (MA), (MB); Surgical Specialist RAMC WW I, Consulting Obstetric Surgn Guy's Hosp, Hon Librarian, V-Pres RCOG, Pres Section of O&G Roy Soc of Medicine, FRCS Eng, FRCOG; *m* 19– *Grace Mary, dau of Maj R N Buist, RAMC, and *d* 30 May 1964, leaving:
  (1) *Mary Dorothy; *b* 13 May 1931; *m* 21 Oct 1955 *George Henry Dickman Coates and has:
    1a *David James; *b* 17 Feb 1959
    1a *Fiona Mary; *b* 20 June 1957
  (2) *Jean Lennox, MB, BS [The Rt Hon The Lady McColl of Dulwich, 12 Gilks Crescent, Dulwich Village, London SE21 7BS]; *b* 20 June 1934; *m* 1960 *Baron McColl of Dulwich (*qv*) and has issue
  (3) *Alison Margaret [Mrs Michael Dredge, 26 Havelock Rd, Southsea, Hants PO5 1RU]; *b* 3 March 1937; *m* 7 Nov 1959 *Michael Jamen [*sic*] Dredge, BDS, LDS, RCS, and has:
    1a *James William Jamen; *b* 27 Aug 1960
    2a *Peter John; *b* 21 Aug 1962
    3a *Andrew Duncan; *b* 21 April 1964
    1a *Catherine Jane; *b* 13 March 1965
3 *John Ballantyne; *b* 23 March 1889; WW I in HAC and Border Regt; *m* 19– *Susie, dau of Albert Vinson, of Belvedere, Kent, and has issue
4 William Lennox (Sir), ktd 1946; *b* 18 March 1892; *educ* Aldenham and Gonville and Caius Coll Cambridge (LLM); Legal Advsr Min of War Tport, WW I as Capt Roy Warwicks Regt, barrister Gray's Inn 1918, High Court Judge 1950–66, Bencher 1938, Treasurer 1951, KC 1950
1 Dorothy; *b* 21 Nov 1895; MD Lond, FFARCS Eng, pres Medical Women's Fedn, emeritus consulting anaesthetist; *d* unm 11 April 1975

JOHN McNAIR's est son,

  ARNOLD DUNCAN McNAIR, **1st Baron McNair**, of Gleniffer, Co Renfrew (UK), so *cr* 4 Aug 1955, CBE (1918); *b* 4 March 1885; *educ* Aldenham and Gonville and Caius Coll Cambridge (BA and LLB 1909, LLM 1913, LLD 1925, Fell 1912); slr 1906, barrister Gray's Inn 1917, Bencher 1936, Treasurer 1947, KC 1945, FBA, Whewell Prof Internat Law Cambridge, Sec Coal Controllers Advsy

Bd 1917–19, Coal Industry (Sankey) Commn 1919, Tagore Prof U Calcutta 1931, V-Chllr U Liverpool 1937–45, memb Hague Permanent Court of Arbitration 1945, Judge Internat Court of Justice 1946–55 (Pres 1952–55), chm: Ctee Supply and Trg of Teachers 1942–44, Ctee Recruitment of Dentists 1955–56, Burnham Ctees 1956–58, Commissary Cambridge U 1955, ktd 1943, Hon LLD Glasgow 1937, Liverpool 1940, Salonica 1948, Birmingham 1949, DCL Oxon 1948, Hon LittD Reading 1949; *m* 28 March 1912 Marjorie (*d* 22 Jan 1971), 2nd dau of Hon Sir Clement Meacher Bailhache, High Court Judge, of Totteridge, Herts, and had:

  1 (CLEMENT) JOHN, **2nd Baron**
1 Oona Elizabeth; *b* 7 Feb 1913; *m* 17 June 1939 G/Capt John Barrett Altham, CBE [G/Capt John Altham CBE, Ivy Cottage, Little Shelford, Cambridge], s of Capt Edward Altham CB, RN, and had:
  (1) *James Edward John [James Altham Esq, 8a Canterbury Close, Cambridge]; *b* 13 Nov 1941; *educ* Eton and Trin Coll Cambridge; *m* 11 Sept 1965 *Patricia Mary Elizabeth, er dau of Robert Gray, of Holm Close, Baslow, Derbys, and has:
    1a *Joseph Robert Edward; *b* 23 Jan 1977
  (2) *David Thomas Wale [David Altham Esq, Ivy Cottage, Little Shelford, Cambridge]; *b* 26 June 1945; *educ* Eton and Trin Coll Cambridge
  (1) *Jane Henrietta [Mrs Philippe Lagesse, 41A Norland Sq, London W11]; *b* 23 March 1940; *m* 2 April 1960 *Philippe Pierre de Marigny Lagesse, s of Philippe Lagesse, of Moka, Mauritius, and has:
    1a *Pierre Arnaud Marc de Marigny; *b* 2 June 1963
    1a *Marie Henriette de Marigny; *b* 27 Jan 1961
  (2) *Elizabeth Georgina; *b* 12 Feb 1955
2 *Sheila Margaret Ramsay [The Hon Mrs Barwell, 33 Fulbrooke Rd, Cambridge CB3 9EE]; *b* 19 Feb 1918; *m* 24 April 1946 John Harold Barwell (*d* 1983) and has:
  (1) *Hugh John [Hugh Barwell Esq, c/o 33 Fulbrooke Rd, Cambridge CB3 9EE]; *b* 24 April 1949; *m* 1973 *Glynis Christine Rolfe and has:
    1a *Guy Harold; *b* 1989
    1a *Leigh Ellen; *b* 1978
  (1) *Alice Marjorie Sheila [Mrs Franklyn Prochaska, 9 Addison Bridge Place, London W14]; *b* 12 July 1947; *educ* Somerville Coll Oxford (BA 1968, MA 1973, PhD 1975); FRHistS 1968; *m* July 1971 *Franklyn Kimmel Prochaska, PhD, FRHistS, and has:
    1a *William Anton Franklin; *b* 1982
    1a *Elizabeth Harriet; *b* 1980
  (2) *Lucy Elizabeth [Mrs Mitch Diamond, 470 Hunting Ridge Rd, Stamford, CT 06903, USA]; *b* 31 May 1951; *m* 1st 1973 (*divorce* 1978) Lloyd Herman Bernstein; *m* 2nd 1990 *Mitch Diamond
  (3) *Claire Bridget [Mrs Gil Aufray, 53c Randolph Ave, London W9]; *b* 29 May 1953; *educ* Somerville Coll Oxford (BA 1975); *m* 1979 *Gil Aufray and has:
    1a *Oliver Daniel; *b* 1988
3 *Elinor Ruth [The Hon Mrs Hanscomb, Powells End, Kempley, Dymock, Glos GL18 2BA]; *b* 25 Feb 1924; *m* 24 March 1955 *Raymond Hanscomb, MRCVS, s of William Hanscomb, of Chapel House, Overthorpe, Oxon, and has:
  (1) *Benjamin Douglas; *b* 39 Aug 1956; *m* 27 March 1993 *Sandra Ellis and has:
    1a *Isobel Rose; *b* 25 Jan 1995
3 (cont.) The Hon Mrs Hanscomb also adopted 15 June 1966 and Nov 1963 respectively:
  *George Sebastian; *b* 21 Dec 1965
  *Emma Frances Mary; *b* April 1963; *m* 4 Nov 1995 *Clive Matthew Gawlik and has:
    1a *Millicent Victoria; *b* 5 March 1997

The 1st BARON *d* 22 May 1975; his only son,

(CLEMENT) JOHN McNAIR, **2nd Baron McNair**; *b* 11 Jan 1915; *m* 16 Nov 1941; *educ* King's Coll Choir Sch Cambridge, Shrewsbury and Balliol Coll Oxford; RA WW II 1940–45, 1940–46 in Tunisia, Italy and Austria (wounded, despatches), Maj, memb Gen Advsy Cncl IBA 1978–89, memb UK Delegn Cncl of Europe on WEU; author: *Wagonload* (1971) and *A Place called Marathon* (1976); *m* 1941 *Vera Frances, dau of Theodore James Faithfull, MRCVS, of Birmingham, and *d* 1989, leaving:

  1 DUNCAN JAMES McNAIR, **3rd and present Baron McNair**
  2 +WILLIAM SAMUEL ANGUS; *b* 19 May 1958; heir presumptive; *m* 1981 (*divorce* 19–) Emma U Procter and has:
    (1) +John Samuel; *b* 1984
    (1) *Emily Harriet; *b* 1982
  1 *Josephine Margaret; *b* 4 April 1949

McNALLY

Creation: B. (LP, UK) Nov 1995.

THE BARON McNALLY, of Blackpool, Co Palatine of Lancaster (Tom McNally) [The Rt Hon The Lord McNally, 30 Cunningham Ave, St Albans, Herts AL1 1JL]; *b* 20 Feb 1943; *educ* Coll of St Joseph Blackpool and UCL; V-Pres NUS 1966–67, Assist Gen Sec Fabian Soc 1966–67; researcher Lab Party 1967–68, Internat Sec 1969–74, political advsr to: For Sec 1974–76, PM 1976–79; MP (Lab) Stockport S 1979–81, (SDP) 1981–83, SDP Spokesman Educn and Sport 1981–83; Lib Dem Ho Lds; memb Select Ctee on Industry and Trade 1979–83; public affrs advsr GEC 1983–84; Dir-Gen Retail Consortium 1985–87, Dir Br Retailers Assoc 1985–87; head public affrs: Hill and Knowlton 1987–93, Shandwick Consultants 1993–; Pres St Albans Lib Dems; FRSA, MIPR, Fell UCL 1995; *m* 1st 1970 (*divorce* 1990) Eileen Powell; *m* 2nd 1990 *Juliet Lamy Hutchinson and by her has:

1 *John; *b* 14 June 1990
2 *James George; *b* 7 Aug 1993
1 *Imogen Alice; *b* 28 Oct 1995

Lineage: JOHN P McNALLY; *m* Elizabeth May McCarthy and had:

TOM, *cr* a **Baron**

MEATH

Arms: Gu. on a bend or three martlets sa. **Crest:** On a mount vert a falcon rising or, belled gold. **Supporters:** Two wyverns or, winged and membered gu., collared and chained gold. **Motto:** *Vota vita mea* ('My life is devoted'). **Creations:** B. (I) 19 July 1616 (Lord Brabazon, Baron of Ardee); E. (I) 16 April 1627; B. (UK) 10 Sept 1831 (Chaworth of Eaton Hall).

THE 14TH EARL OF MEATH, **Lord Brabazon, Baron of Ardee**, and **Baron Chaworth of Eaton Hall**, Co Hereford (Anthony Windham Normand Brabazon) [The Rt Hon the Earl of Meath, Killruddery, Bray, Co Wicklow, Ireland], *b* 3 Nov 1910; *s* f 1949; *educ* Eton and RMC Sandhurst; ADC Govr Bengal 1936, Maj Gren Gds WW II (wounded); *m* 30 July 1940 *Elizabeth Mary, only dau of Capt Geoffrey Vaux Salvin Bowlby, RHG, and has:

1 +JOHN ANTHONY, *Lord Ardee* [Lord Ardee, Ballinacor, Rathdrum, Co Wicklow, Ireland]; *b* 11 May 1941; *educ* Harrow; Page of Honour to HM THE QUEEN 1956–58, served Gren Gds 1959–62; *m* 12 May 1973 *Xenia, yr dau of P Goudime, of Windlesham Park, Surrey, and has:
   (1) +Anthony Jacques; *b* 30 Jan 1977
   (1) *Corinna Lettice; *b* 1974
   (2) *Serena Alexandra; *b* 1979
2 +David Geoffrey Normand [The Hon David Brabazon, North Wing, Killruddery, Bray, Co Wicklow, Ireland]; *b* 9 Oct 1948; *educ* Tabley House; *m* 16 Sept 1972 *Gaye, yr dau of Cdr W (Jock) Whitworth, DSC, RN, of Trudder, Newtownmountkennedy, Co Wicklow, and has:
   (1) +Geoffrey William; *b* 27 Sept 1975
   (2) *Celia Antonia; *b* 1974
   (3) *Diana Elizabeth; *b* 1981
1 *Romayne Aileen [The Lady Romayne Pike, Kidborough House, Danehill, Sussex]; *b* 26 May 1943; *m* 25 March 1968 *Capt (Robert Eben) Neil Pike, Gren Gds, yr s of Lt-Col Godfrey Eben Pike, DSO, MBE, Gren Gds, of Dublin, and has:
   (1) *Harry Eben; *b* 1974
   (1) *Tamsin Lucy; *b* 1972
2 *Lavinia Anne [The Lady Lavinia Jobson, Barnacullia, Kilmacanoge, Co Wicklow, Ireland]; *b* 12 Sept 1945; *m* 1 June 1969 *John Ernest Baron Jobson, s of Robert Ralph Baron Jobson, of Newcastle, Co Kildare, and has:
   (1) *James Robert; *b* 1977
   (1) *Rebecca Catherine; *b* 1971

   (2) *Charlotte Naomi Marya; *b* 1973
   (3) *Suzannah Elizabeth; *b* 1976

Lineage: JACQUES le BRABANCON; had:

JOHN le BRABANCON, of Betchworth, Surrey, *temp* HENRY I and HENRY II; had:

ADAM le BRABAZON, of Betchworth *temp* RICHARD I, JOHN and HENRY III; had:

THOMAS le BRABAZON; living 1236; *m* Amelia, dau and heiress of John Mousley, of Mousley, Leics, and had:

Sir ROGER le BRABAZON, of Mousley and Eastwell, Leics; ktd 1268; *m* Beatrix, dau and coheir of Mansel de Bissett, of East Bridgeford, and had, with another s (Sir Roger, Ch Justice Common Pleas 1313, *m* Beatrix, dau and heiress of Sir John Sproxton, of Sproxton, Leics, and *dsp* 1326):

MATHEW le BRABAZON; *m* Sarah — and had:

Sir WILLIAM BRABAZON, of Galtrop and Sproxton, Leics, 1327, which manors were made over to him by his unc; *m* Joan, dau of Sir William Trussel, of Marston Trussel, Northants, and had, with another s (Sir John, of Sproxton, *m* Agnes, dau of Richard de Whatton, and had a dau Joan, who *m* William de Woodford, thus bearing the Manor of Sproxton away from the BRABAZONs):

THOMAS BRABAZON, of Mousley and Eastwell; *b* 1299; had:

JOHN BRABAZON, of Mousley and Eastwell; cmded troops in Hundred Years War; living *temp* HENRY IV; had:

NICHOLAS BRABAZON, of Mousley and Eastwell, living 1445; had:

JOHN BRABAZON, of Eastwell; *m* Maud, dau and heiress of Nicholas Jervis, of Hardby, Leics, and was *k* Batttle of Bosworth 1485, leaving, with other issue:

JOHN BRABAZON; *m* — Chaworth, of Wiverton, Notts, and had an only s:

Sir WILLIAM BRABAZON; V-Treasurer and General Receiver Ireland 1534–52, Ld Justice Ireland 1543, 1546 and 1550; *m* Elizabeth (*m* 2nd Christopher Blunte, *m* 3rd Capt Humphry Warren, *m* 4th Sir Edward Moore (see DROGHEDA, E)), dau and coheir of Nicholas Clifford, of Holme, Kent, and *d* 1552, having had:

1 EDWARD (Sir)
2 Anthony, of Ballinasloe Castle, ancestor of the BRABAZONs of Brabazon Park, Co Mayo; the last male representative of this family, Sir William John Brabazon, 2nd Bt, *d unm* 24 Oct 1840
1 Anne; *m* 1st Andrew Wise, of Dublin; *m* 2nd William Thwaits, of Kent
2 Elizabeth; *m* 1st John Giffard; *m* 2nd Sir Henry Duke, of Castle Jordan

Sir WILLIAM's er son,

EDWARD BRABAZON, **1st Lord Brabazon, Baron of Ardee**, Co Louth (I), so *cr* 19 July 1616, PC (I 1584); *b c* 1548; MP Co Wicklow 1585 and Bangor, Co Down, 1613–15, High Sheriff Staffs 1606; *m* Mary (*d* 23 Aug 1625), dau of Edward Smith, of Mitcham, Surrey, Clerk of the Green Cloth, and *d* 7 Aug 1625, having had:

1 WILLIAM, **1st Earl**
2 Wallop, of Eaton Garnage, Herefs; High Sheriff 1630; *m* Anne, dau and heiress of Richard Blount, of Grendon, and had issue
3 Anthony (Sir), of Tallaghtstown or Callistown, Co Louth; *m* Margaret (*d* Aug 1636), dau and heiress of Christopher Hovendon, of Chinnor, Oxon, and 1 July 1636, leaving, with four daus (Dorcas, *m* 21 March 1644 1st Viscount Lanesborough (see LANESBOROUGH, E); Anne; Catherine Magdalen; Margaret):
   (1) Edward; *m* Lady Rose Lambart, 3rd dau of 1st Earl of Cavan (*qv*), and *d* 1666, leaving an only dau:
    1a Jane; *m* Sir Thomas Newcomen
   (2) James; Capt in Army; *m* Alice Bates, of N Wales, and was *k* 1676, leaving, with other issue:
    1a William, of Rath House, Louth; *b* 1658; *m* 1st — Bickerton and had an only dau; *m* 2nd Elizabeth, dau of George Lambart, and *d* 1714, leaving:
     1b Wallop; *m* 1730 Vincentia Townley and *d* 1767, leaving:
      1c William, of Rath House; *b* 1732; *m* 1768 his cousin Catherine Frances, dau of Anthony Brabazon, of Carstown, and *d* 1793, leaving:
       1d Wallop, of Rath House; *b* 10 March 1770; *m* 1st 19 March 1796 Jane (*d* 1800), dau of Josias Du Pré, of Wilton Park, and had, with another s (*d unm*):
        1e William (Rev); Rector Syddon, nr Ardee; *b* 6 May 1798; *m* 22 Jan 1827 Georgiana (*d* 1854), dau of William Crane, and *d* 1883, having had issue (*d unm*)
        1e Rebecca; *m* 1827 George Henry Pentland, of Black Hall, Louth
        2e Catherine Frances; *m* 1833 Thomas Knox Armstrong (*d* 1840) and *d* 31 Aug 1871
       1d (cont.) Wallop Brabazon *m* 2nd 1810 Margaret (*d* 4 Nov 1864), dau of William Crane, and *d* 28 Oct 1831, having by her had, with five other daus and another s (all *d unm*):
        2e Arthur Wellesley; *b* 10 Sept 1811; 54th Regt; *d unm* 20 Oct 1833
        3e Wallop, of Rath House; *b* 2 Feb 1813; *m* 1835 Victoria (*d* 2 June 1894), dau of George Cash, and *d* 17 April 1890, having had issue
        4e James Du Pré; *b* 24 Jan 1819; Maj 17th Regt; *m* 2 Aug 1855 Sophia Catherine (*d* 15 Feb 1862), only child of Rev John Courtney, and *d* 19 July 1900, leaving issue
        3e Vincentia; *m* 15 March 1841 Col Charles John Kemeys-Tynte (*d* 16 Sept 1882), of Cefn Mably, and *d* 14 Oct 1894, leaving issue
        4e Maria Georgina; *m* 24 Nov 1842 James Cransbourne Strode (*dsp* 5 Feb 1852) and *d* 11 May 1908
    2a James; *b* 8 March 1661; *m* 12 Dec 1686 Mary, dau of Dudley Colley/Cowley (see WELLINGTON, D), and *d* 15 Jan 1728 leaving:
     1b Anthony; *b* 16 Dec 1688; *m* 24 Nov 1732 Mary, dau of — Donagh, and *d* 6 July 1771, leaving:

1c Philip, of Mornington, Co Meath; *b* 22 Nov 1733; *m* 28 May 1772 Elizabeth (*d* 6 July 1793), dau of George Adams, and *d* 5 Jan 1828, leaving:

1d Anthony; *m* 1st Grace (*d* 1821), dau of James Godsell, and had issue; *m* 2nd Catherine (*d* 18 May 1852), dau of Hardy Eustace and widow of F W Hopkins, and *d* 18–, leaving, with another s (*d* unm):

1e James (Rev); *b* 12 Jan 1800; *m* 25 June 1828 Elizabeth Jane (*d* 1885), dau of Richard Hugh Levinge, of Levington Park, Co Westmeath, and *d* 1884, leaving, with other issue:

1f Samuel Levinge; *b* 22 March 1829; *m* 18– — and had:

1g Gerald Hugh; *b* 18–; *m* 189– Eleanor Murphy and *d* 19–, leaving:

1h Clarence Levinge; *b* 18–

2h Claude Hugh; *b* 18–

3h Edward Alfred; *b* 18–

2f Anthony Godsell; *b* 10 Sept 1841; *m* 24 Oct 1865 Emma Wilson, dau of William Holdsworth, MD, of Ripley, Yorks, and *d* May 1900, having had:

1g Charles James Anthony; *b* 19 Aug 1869; *m* 14 July 1897 Amy Ruby Victoria (*d* 14 March 1947), er dau of William McMillan, of Maneroo Station and later Culparoo Park, nr Longreach, Qld, and *d* 26 Sept 1944, leaving:

1h Anthony Godsell; *b* 28 Sept 1899; *m* 12 Feb 1925 Margaret Victoria, only dau of J A Gibson, of Sydney, and *d* 18 Dec 1982, leaving:

1i *Margaret Ann, JP [Mrs Ian Shevill JP, 1 Boorana St, Jindalee, Brisbane, Qld 4074, Australia]; *b* 12 May 1927; ACIS, FCPA; *m* 1 Aug 1974 Rt Rev Ian Wotton Allnutt Shevill (*d* 3 Nov 1988), Bp Newcastle, NSW

1i Ellen Patricia Brabazon (twin); *d* 2 July 1927

2h Charles Reginald; *b* 23 May 1904; *m* 30 June 1940 *Minnie Isabel [Mrs Charles Brabazon, M53 356 Blunder Rd, Durack, Brisbane, Qld, Australia], dau of James Lennox Arthur, of N Qld, and *d* 1987, leaving:

1i +Charles James Lennox [Mr Justice Brabazon, 48 Tenth Ave, St Lucia, Brisbane, Qld 4067, Australia]; *b* 26 April 1944; *educ* Qld U (BA, LLB) and London U (LLM); Lt Qld U Regt, CMF; *m* 1981 *Michelle May, QC, and has:

1j *Sarah Margaret; *b* 1991

2j *Lucinda Claire (triplet); *b* 1991

3j *Alice Elizabeth (triplet); *b* 1991

2i +Richard Anthony; *b* 16 March 1949; *educ* The Southport Sch; *m* 1975 *Susan Margaret, dau of G Greentree, and has:

1j +Timothy Richard; *b* 1979

1j *Jennifer Amy; *b* 1981

3h Rupert William; *b* 24 Nov 1908; *m* 1 Nov 1952 *Margaret Cecil Pender, dau of Edward Pender Phillott, of Colane Winton, N Qld, and *d* 1979, leaving:

1i +Anthony Edward [Anthony Brabazon Esq, 39 Kincaid Drive, Highland Park, Qld 4211, Australia]; *b* 1954; *m* 1993 *Tracy Clarkson

2i William Robert; *b* 31 Aug 1960; *d* 1982

1i *Wendy Pender [Miss Wendy Brabazon, 19 Edgar St, Newmarket, Brisbane, Qld 4051, Australia]; *b* 1955

2i *Patricia Rain [Miss Patricia Brabazon, 3 Reef Court, Mermaid Waters, Qld 4218, Australia]; *b* 1957

1h Ruby Sylvia May; *b* 1 May 1898; *m* March 1919 William Henry Rudd, of Qld, and had issue

2h Dorothea Millicent; *b* 3 Jan 1902; *m* 3 Jan 1922 Basil Beaufort Brett (*d* 16 Nov 1959) and had:

1i *Basil Brabazon; *b* 24 Nov 1922; *m* 8 Sept 1956 *Helen Mary, only dau of Herbert Arthur Bourne, of Pennant Hills, NSW, and has:

1j *David Arthur; *b* 7 Dec 1960

1j *Jennifer Grace; *b* 9 April 1958

2i *Peter Brabazon [Peter Brett Esq, 12 Banool Ave, St Ives, Sydney, NSW, Australia]; *b* 11 July 1924; *m* 1948 *Gwynneth Allan, 2nd dau of Allan Ewart Jones, of Qld, and has:

1j *James Brabazon; *b* 31 Oct 1956

1j *Barbara Brabazon; *b* 16 July 1949

1i *Victoria Brabazon; *b* 11 Jan 1926; *m* 1959 *Michael Frederick Killeen and has:

1j *Mary Dorothea Killeen; *b* 22 Feb 1961

2i *Dorothea Brabazon [Mrs Clyde Wiley, 9 Edward St, Dalby, Qld, Australia]; *b* 6 April 1928; *m* 1961 *Clyde Newman Wiley and has:

1j *Susan Jane Wiley; *b* 1962

3i *Susan Brabazon [Miss Susan Brett, 106 Highland Terrace, St Lucia, Qld, Australia]; *b* 30 Dec 1930

3h *Kathleen Patricia Brabazon [Miss Kathleen Brabazon, 6/9 Norwood St, Toowong, Brisbane, Qld 4066, Australia]; *b* 19 Jan 1903

4h *Eileen Emma; *b* 3 March 1907; *m* 1929 *Bernard Carr Clark and has had:

1i Michael George; *b* 1930; *d* 1991

2i *Adam Charles [Adam Clark Esq, PO Box 348, Bradshaw Cres, Taroom, Qld 4420, Australia]; *b* 6 May 1933; *m* 8 May 1954 *Dorothy Isabel, dau of John B S Milne, of Dalby, Qld, and has:

1j *Bruce Robert [Bruce Clark Esq, Nunbank, Taroom, Qld, Australia]; *b* 1 May 1955; *m* 1st 4 Jan 1975 (*divorce*

19–) Christine Ann Suter; *m* 2nd 13 June 1987 *Judy Clare, dau of John Bazley, of Ullenhall, Warwicks, and has:

1k *Darryl James Carr; *b* 27 Feb 1993

1k *Nicole Hanna Carr; *b* 7 May 1991

2j Ian Charles; *b* 21 Aug 1956; *m* 19 Aug 1978 (*divorce* 19–) Fiona Elizabeth McKinley and *d* 12 Feb 1997

3j *Owen Mark [Owen Clark Esq, Bimbadeen, Taroom, Qld, Australia]; *b* 12 Jan 1967; *m* 9 Feb 1991 *Helen Marian, dau of Douglas Kimber, of Bowen, Qld, and has:

1k *Emily Kate; *b* 7 Jan 1992

2k *Rachael Louise; *b* 27 Sept 1993

3k *Shelley Marie; *b* 11 June 1996

4j *Kevin Adam [Kevin Clark Esq, PO Box 55, Quilpie, Qld, Australia]; *b* 4 April 1969; *m* 19– *Sandra Robyn, dau of Frank Lamb, of Taroom, and has:

1k *Michael Adam; *b* 24 Dec 1996

1j Karen Ruth; *b* 15 Feb 1959; *d* 4 Sept 1965

2j *Wendy Ann [Mrs Rodney Woodrow, Juandah Plains, Wandoan, Qld 4419, Australia]; *b* 4 Feb 1961; *m* 14 March 1981 *Rodney Hans Woodrow and has:

1k *Rowan Max; *b* 9 Feb 1985

2k *Ryan Wayne; *b* 20 Feb 1990

1k *Megan Rose; *b* 17 Feb 1983

2k *Krystal Lee; *b* 13 April 1988

3i *Robert Anthony [Robert Carr-Clark Esq, Mutation, Clermont, Qld, Australia]; *b* 1936; *m* 14 Dec 1967 *Margot Grant, dau of A F G Cameron, of Brisbane, and has:

1j *Michael Robert; *b* 22 Feb 1969

1j *Ann Laura; *b* 1970

2g Rupert Levinge; *b* 1871; *m* 1904 Grace Eva (*d* 1 May 1948), dau of Campbell Livingstone Macdonald, of Qld, and *d* 25 March 1924, leaving:

1h Guy Levinge; *b* 1905; *d* May 1964

2h Rupert Macdonald; *b* 1907; *m* 1934 Moyra Joy, 4th dau of Edgar Joyce, of Beaudesert, Qld, and has:

1i *Margaret Joy; *b* 1936; *m* 10 Aug 1957 *Desmond Lea Bradley, only s of Denis Bradley, of Edmonton, N Qld, and has:

1j *Peter Donald; *b* 14 Nov 1958

1j *Helen Janette; *b* 14 Jan 1960

2i *Barbara Joan [Mrs Kenneth Maddox, Turana, Cunnamulla, Qld, Australia]; *b* 16 May 1938; *m* 11 May 1963 *Kenneth Arthur Maddox, only s of Arthur Maddox, of Cunnamulla, and has:

1j *Kim Anita; *b* 21 Sept 1965

2j *Kerry Anne; *b* 17 Aug 1967

3i *Patricia Elizabeth [Mrs Harold Bergman, Banksia, 35 Addison Rd, Graceville, Brisbane, Qld, Australia]; *b* 29 June 1940; *m* 7 Jan 1961 *Harold Joseph Bergman, est s of Emil Bergman, and has:

1j *Anthony Michael; *b* 15 Nov 1965

2j *Thomas Joseph; *b* 18 Jan 1967

1j *Patricia Joan; *b* 25 Oct 1961

2j *Coleen Frances; *b* 10 April 1964

3j *Rosemary Joy; *b* 4 Aug 1968

3h +Campbell Anthony; *b* 1910; AIF WW II (wounded); *m* 2 June 1945 *Marjorie Seymour Villiers, dau of Villiers Seymour Brown, of Qld, and adopted:

*Cecily June; *b* 1953

*Jennifer Grace; *b* 1958

4h +Robert Charles; *b* 1912; AIF WW (POW Far East 1942–45); *m* 29 Dec 1950 *Geraldine Hope Gordon, 3rd dau of Robert John Gordon Burrow, of NSW, and has:

1i +Mark Levinge; *b* 4 Nov 1958; *educ* Brisbane Boys' Coll; BA, LLB

1i *Kathleen Grace; *b* 1906

3g Frederick Reginald; *b* 1873; *d* 1963

1g Emily Constance; *b* 1867; *d* 1957

2g Mary Violet; *b* 1875; *m* J A Atkinson and *d* 1948, leaving issue

3g Elsie May; *b* 1897; *d* 1948

1f Thomasine Jane; *m* 16 Feb 1855 John Hall (*d* 25 Aug 1878) and had issue

2f Elizabeth Melesina; *m* 5 Aug 1875 Robert Kearns, MD, of Banagher, and had issue

1e Eliza; *m* 28 Aug 1828 Rev James Crawford, Vicar St Mary's, Drogheda, and *d* 16 Oct 1863, leaving issue

2e Catherine Jane; *m* John Snow (*d* 7 Dec 1863)

2d George (Rev); Rector Painstown; *b* 1780; *m* 22 Dec 1804 Leonora Jane (*d* 1 Jan 1860), dau of Robert Heyland, and *d* 30 March, 1851, leaving, with five daus:

1e Philip Robert Waller (Rev); had, with a dau (*d* unm):

1f George Philip Augustus, JP Co Monaghan; Capt 6th Bn Roy Irish Rifles; *b* 1845; *m* 1886 Rhoda Jane (*d* 30 April 1946), dau of Edmond Nugent, MD, FRCS(I), and *d* 10 Oct 1912, leaving:

1g Cecil George Le Normand; *b* 1887; *m* June 1927 Gladys May, dau of Nathan Wyman Downs, of Chula Vista, California, and had:

1h *Cora Jane; *b* 26 Oct 1934; *m* 1962 *Charles F Ruhr

2g Montague Philip Le Normand; *b* 1890; *m* 7 Aug 1916 Edwina Meston, dau of George T Smith, of Alpine, California, and *d* 1967, leaving:

    1h +Keith Elmer [Keith Brabazon Esq, 5738 Willow Rd, Alpine, CA 92001, USA]; *b* 21 Oct 1917; *m* 1963 *Clara Carolina, dau of Rudolph Wenger, of Max, N Dakota, and has:

        1i +Lee Monte [Lee Brabazon Esq, 5670 Willow Rd, Alpine, CA 92001, USA]; *b* 1964; *m* 19– *Kathleen Lorraine, dau of Barry Hulahan, of San Diego

3g Edmond Charles Heyland; *b* 1893; *m* Feb 1928 Anna Irene, dau of Edward Ward Young, of Salt Lake City

4g Louis Nugent; *b* 1895; *m* Oct 1923 Jessie Etta, dau of William Ross Mealey, of San Diego

5g Anthony Beaufort; *b* 1896; *m* 7 Sept 1954 *Nola Belle, dau of Joseph Franklin Thornley, of Conshatta, Louisiana, and *d* 4 Nov 1961

1g Marian Constance; *b* 1900; *m* 21 March 1936 Howard Jonathan Edwards (*d* 6 March 1950)

2e Anthony Beaufort, MD; *b* 1 Aug 1821; *m* 4 Sept 1849 Eleanor Elizabeth (*d* 4 July 1912), dau of Walter Bourne, and *d* 1896, leaving, with two other sons and a dau (*d* unm):

    1f George Disney, of New Peacock Estate, Ceylon, JP; *b* 3 March 1853; *m* 1903 Mabel Elizabeth Mary, dau of Rev John Forbes St Maur Russell, of Aldborough, York and *d* 26 Sept 1912

    2f William Beaufort; *b* 6 Oct 1860; Lt-Col Naval Ordnance Dept, Capt Essex Regt; *m* 7 June 1894 Mabel (*d* 28 April 1957), dau of Clement Smith Barter, MB, of Bath, and *d* 12 Feb 1936, leaving:

        1g Terrence Anthony Chaworth; *b* 20 Feb 1896; Capt Essex Regt WW I; *d* 3 Aug 1916 of wounds recd in action

        2g Joan Alexandra Mabel; *b* 7 March 1902

    3f Richard Carmichael (Rev); *b* 11 Jan 1864; BA Oxford; *m* 1893 Ida Lambourne; *d* 1901

    4f Anthony Heyland; *b* 8 April 1867; Maj, Staff Offr RMLI Chin-Lushai Campaign 1889–90 (medal with clasp); *m* 1896 Ada Mary, dau of Capt J F Gunning, RN, and widow of Philip Dudgeon, and *dsp* 21 May 1907

    1f Louisa Jane; *m* 1886 F H Kerr, of Rockmount, Eastcourt, Natal, and *d* 1924, leaving issue

    2f Leonora Harriet Jocelyn; *m* 22 Jan 1888 John Semple Dick (*d* 9 Jan 1923) and *d* 11 Nov 1930, leaving issue

    3f Eleanor Isabel May; *m* 27 Oct 1894 H M Knight, of Travancore, and *d* 23 Dec 1894

3d William Philip, of Mornington; *b* 28 Oct 1783; *m* 17 March 1809 Letitia (*d* 20 Dec 1859), dau of Rev John Vignoles, and *d* 13 Dec 1854, leaving, with another s and dau (*d* unm):

    1e James, of Mornington, JP; *b* 7 April 1810; *m* 14 June 1832 Amelia (*d* 6 Dec 1881), only dau of Sir Henry E Austen, of Shalford House, Surrey, and *d* 11 July 1873, leaving:

        1f James Henry, of Mornington, JP; *b* 3 March 1833; Offr 16th Regt; *m* 1st 16 March 1858 Rose Augusta (*d* 24 Feb 1859), dau of George Vandeleur, of Ballynamona, Co Limerick, and had:

            1g Rose Augusta Cecil; *m* 7 Sept 1880 Willoughby Harford Hurt-Sitwell (*d* 28 June 1913) and had issue

        1f (cont) James Brabazon *m* 2nd 14 Nov 1862 Helena, 3rd dau of William P Hodnett, and *d* 1921, having by her had:

            2g Athalie Maria Hervey; *m* 26 April 1895 Giuseppe Antonio Baudoin (*ka* Battle of Adowa March 1896), Maj Roy Bersaglieri Regt, and had issue

        1f Cecil Elizabeth

        2f Louisa Letitia Henrietta; *m* 16 July 1858 Arthur C Innes, of Dromantine, Co Down, and *d* 27 Jan 1886, having had issue

        3f Maria Georgina; *m* 13 July 1878 Ralph Smyth, of Newton House, Drogheda, and *d* 2 Jan 1908

    2e John Vignoles (Rev); *b* 7 April 1811; BA Dublin, RD Ardnurcher; *m* 1st 10 Oct 1837 Mary (*d* 24 May 1855), dau of Thomas Jefferson; *m* 2nd 4 June 1861 Sophia (*d* 1888), dau of Capt William Crow, and *d* 1889, having by his first w had, with other issue:

        1f Thomas Jefferson; *b* 25 March 1844; *m* 16 June 1875 Jane Mary, dau of Daniel Bailey, and *dsp*

        1f Isabella

        2f Mary Louisa; *m* 10 Aug 1867 Alexander Humfrey and had issue

        3f Anna Honoria; *m* 18 Dec 1880 James Shannon, barrister

    3e Philip William; *b* 29 March 1815; *m* 26 May 1836 Maria, dau of Thomas Flood, and *d* 13 Oct 1848, leaving, with another s and a dau (*d* unm):

        1f William Philip, MD, JP Cheshire; *b* 3 March 1838; *m* 19 Dec 1871 Eleanor (*d* 17 Jan 1904), dau of Benhamin Pierpoint, and *d* 30 Sept 1906, leaving:

            1g Charles Pierpoint; *b* 11 Feb 1879; BA Oxon, Capt KOSB; *d* 13 Feb 1927

            1g Frances Kathleen; *d* unm 21 July 1956

            2g Norah Eleanor; *m* 29 April 1902 Henry Ambrose Burrowes (*d* 16 Aug 1925), MBE, MD, s of Rev Henry Burrowes, and *d* 29 Nov 1951

    4e Martin Godfrey; *b* 1826; Capt HEICS; *m* Louisa, dau of Gen — Salter, CB, and *d* 1876, leaving:

        1f Martin; *b* 1853

        1f Letitia; *m* J K Nottenbelt

        2f Julia

        3f Anna

        1e Anne Honoria; *m* 1st June 1831 Robert Ash; *m* 2nd June 1842 Thomas Desvoeux (*d* 8 May 1865) and had issue

        2e Julia; *m* 10 April 1838 John Reilly (*d* 1847)

        3e Letitia; *m* 4 June 1856 Lt-Gen J S Hawkshaw, RE (*d* 1862)

        4e Catherine Maria; *m* 3 Feb 1859 Col Chidley Coote (*see* COOTE, Bt) and *d* 1910

    4d Charles Francis; had issue

    1d Jane; *m* Rev A Ellis

    1a Rose; *m* 1686 William Eccleston, of Drumshallon, Co Louth, High Sheriff Co Louth 1705, and had issue

1 Elizabeth; *m* 1st Rt Rev George Montgomery, DD, Bp Meath; *m* 2nd Sir John Breketon (*d* 1 Oct 1629), of Ashley; *m* 3rd Sir John Bramston, Ld Ch Justice King's Bench, and *d* 7 June 1647

2 Ursula; *m* as his 1st w 1st Viscount Claneboye (*see* DUFFERIN AND CLANEBOYE, B) and *dsp*

The 1st BARON's est son,

WILLIAM BRABAZON, **1st Earl of Meath** (I), so *cr* 16 April 1627, with remainder, in default of direct male issue, to his bro, Sir Anthony Brabazon, and his male heirs; *b c* 1580; ktd Feb 1603/4; *m* Feb 1607 Jane (*bur* 19 Dec 1644), est dau of Rt Hon Sir John Bingley, and was *bur* 19 Dec 1651, leaving an only s:

EDWARD BRABAZON, **2nd Earl of Meath**, PC (I *temp* CHARLES I and 1660–69); *b c* 1610; ktd 1626; MP Athlone 1634–35, royalist Civil War; *m* 1632 Mary (*bur* 14 Sept 1685), yr dau of Calcot Chambré, of Denbigh, Wales, and Carnowe, Co Wicklow, and was drowned 25 March 1675 off Holyhead *en route* to England, having had, with another s (*d* young):

    1 WILLIAM BRABAZON, **3rd Earl of Meath**, PC (I March 1673/4); *b c* 1635; called up to Ho Lds *vp* 30 Oct 1665 in f's Barony; killed a man in a duel but pardoned 1671; *m* by 1671 Elizabeth (*m* 2nd 1686 Hon William Moore (*see* DROGHEDA, E) and *d* 28 Dec 1701), sis of 1st Earl of Sussex (*see* DACRE, B), and was *bur* 1 March 1684/5, having had, with a s (*d* young):

        (1) Elizabeth; *m* 1st Sir Phillips Coote (*see* COOTE, Bt); *m* 2nd Hon Philip Bertie (*see* LINDSEY and ABINGDON, E)

        (2) Catherine; *m* Alonzo Vere

    2 EDWARD BRABAZON, **4th Earl of Meath**, PC (I 1679); *b c* 1638; Capt of Foot 1661 and later of Horse, MP Co Wicklow June–Aug 1666, Ranger Phoenix Park 1675, attainted by JAMES II's Irish Parl May 1689, cmded a Williamite regt Battle of the Boyne 1690 and Siege Limerick; *m* 1st by 1677 Cecilia (*d* 12 July 1704), dau of Sir William Brereton, 1st Bt; *m* 2nd 22 Sept 1704 Dorothea (Swift's 'Countess Doll'; *m* 2nd Dec 1716 Gen Richard Gorges, of Kilbrue, Co Meath), dau of James Stopford (*see* COURTOWN, E), and *dsp* 22 Feb 1707

    3 CHAMBRE, **5th Earl**

    1 Jane; *m* Randal Moore

    2 Mary; *m* Robert Needham

The 4th EARL's bro,

CHAMBRE BRABAZON, **5th Earl of Meath**, PC (I 1710); *b c* 1645; *m* by 1682 Juliana (*bur* 12 Nov 1692), only dau and heiress of 3rd Viscount Chaworth of Armagh, and *d* 1 April 1715, having had:

    1 CHAWORTH BRABAZON, **6th Earl of Meath**; *b* 1686; MP Co Dublin 1713–14, called up to Ho Lds *vp* in f's Barony 9 March 1714/5, Ld Lt Cos Dublin and Wicklow; *m* 1st his aunt's chambermaid but never cohabited with her; *m* 2nd 13 Dec 1731 Juliana (*d* 12 Dec 1758), dau of Sir Thomas Prendergast, 1st and last Bt, of Gort (*see* GORT, V), and *dsp* 14 May 1763

    2 EDWARD, **7th Earl**

    1 Juliana

    2 Mary; *m* Rev William Tisdall, Vicar St James's Dublin

    3 Catharine; *m* T Hallowes, of Bethick Hall, Derbys

    4 Frances; *m* Brig-Gen Henry Ponsonby

The 6th EARL's only bro,

EDWARD BRABAZON, **7th Earl of Meath**; *bapt* 24 Nov 1691; MP Co Dublin 1715–60; *m c* 1720 Martha (*d* 24 April 1762), dau of Rev William Collins, of Warwick, and *d* 24 Nov 1772, having had:

    1 ANTHONY, **8th Earl**

    2 William, of Tara House, Co Meath; *b* Aug 1723; *m* 10 May 1764 Catherine (*d* 11 Feb 1833), dau and sole heiress of Arthur Gifford, of Aghern, and had, with other issue (*dsp*):

        (1) Barbara; *m* 24 May 1788 John Moore, of New Lodge, Herts, and had issue (*see* BRABAZON OF TARA, B)

The 7th EARL's er s,

ANTHONY BRABAZON, **8th Earl of Meath**; *bapt* 17 Feb 1721; MP Co Wicklow 1745–60 and Co Dublin 1761–62; *m* 20 May 1758 Grace (*d* 23 Oct 1812), dau of John Leigh, of Rosegarland, Co Wexford, and *d* 4 Jan 1790, having had, with five daus:

    1 WILLIAM BRABAZON, **9th Earl of Meath**; *b* 6 July 1769; MP Co Dublin 1789–90; *k* in a duel 26 May 1797

    2 JOHN CHAMBRE, **10th Earl**

    1 Arabella; *m* Rev John Scott, of Ballygannon, Co Wicklow, and had issue (*see* VIVIAN, B)

    2 Catherine; *m* 6 Aug 1799 Rev Francis Brownlow (*d* 20 Oct 1847) and *d* 24 Dec 1847, leaving issue

The 9th EARL's bro,

JOHN CHAMBRE BRABAZON, **10th Earl of Meath**, KP (1821), PC (I 1833); *b* 9 April 1772; Ld Lt Co Dublin 1831–51 and custos rotulorum Co Wicklow 1797–1851; *cr* 10 Sept 1831 BARON CHAWORTH OF EATON HALL, Co Hereford (UK); *m* 31 Dec 1801 Lady Melosina Adelaide Meade (*d* 26 March 1866), 4th dau of 1st Earl of Clanwilliam (*qv*), and *d* 15 March 1851, having had, with four other sons:

    1 WILLIAM BRABAZON, **11th Earl of Meath**; *b* 25 Oct 1803; Hon Col 5th Bn Roy Dublin Fus, ADC to HM QUEEN VICTORIA (auxiliary forces), Ld Lt Co Wicklow; *m* 23 Nov 1837 Harriot (*d* 16 July 1898), 2nd dau of Sir Richard Brooke, 6th Bt, of Norton Priory (*qv*), and *d* 26 May 1887, having had:

        (1) Jacques Le Normand; *b* 18 May 1839; *d* Aug 1844

(2) REGINALD, **12th Earl**

(1) Kathleen Harriot; *d* unm 15 Feb 1930

1 Theodosia; *m* 22 June 1832 3rd Earl of Gosford (*qv*) and *d* 13 Feb 1876

The 11th EARL's yr s,

REGINALD BRABAZON, **12th Earl of Meath**, KP (1905), GCVO (1923), GBE (1920), PC (I 1887), JP Cos Wicklow and Dublin; *b* 31 July 1841; HM's Lt Co and City of Dublin, Chllr Roy U Ireland 1902–06, 2nd Sec Dip Serv, Hon Col 5th Bn Roy Dublin Fus, KJStJ; *m* 7 Jan 1868 Lady Mary Jane Maitland (*d* 4 Nov 1918), only surv dau of 11th Earl of Lauderdale (*qv*), and *d* 11 Oct 1929, having had:

1 REGINALD LE NORMAND, **13th Earl**

2 Arthur Lauderdale Le Normand; *b* 28 Sept 1872; Capt 5th Bn Roy Dublin Fus; *d* unm 19 April 1933

3 Claud Maitland Patrick, OBE (1919); *b* 16 July 1874; *educ* Wellington and Trin Hall Cambridge; Maj Irish Gds, Lt-Col RAF, Boer War 1902, WW I; *m* 22 Feb 1915 Kathleen (*d* 14 July 1961), yst dau of Arthur Maitland, of Shudy Camps Park, Cambs, and *d* 14 May 1959, leaving:

(1) *Elizabeth Maitland [Mrs Evered Poole, Robin Hood Cottage, Standford, Hants GU35 8RA]; *b* 9 Dec 1915; *m* 7 Feb 1942 Lt-Col Evered Mansfield Poole (*d* 1982), RA, only s of William Mansfield Poole, of Beckley, Sussex, by his w, dau of 1st Baron Ilkeston (*see* 1940 edn), and has:

1a *Catherin Elizabeth [Mrs James Forrester, Copper Beeches, Sikeside, Cumbria CA6 6DR]; *b* 7 Jan 1953; *m* 1980 *James Keith Forrester and has:

1b *Jack James Everard; *b* 26 Nov 1994

1b *Anne-Marie Catherin; *b* 1983

2b *Charlotte Antonia; *b* 1986

3b *Alice Elizabeth; *b* 1988

(2) Felicity Margaretta; *b* 9 April 1917; *educ* London U (BA 1939); 1st Offr WRNS WW II; *m* 29 June 1948 Gilbert Stanley Hodson and *d* 2 Jan 1985, leaving issue (*see* HODSON, Bt)

4 Ernest William Maitland Molyneux, DSO; *b* 22 March 1884; Capt Coldstream Gds WW I (despatches); *m* 29 Oct 1912 Dorothy Mary (*d* 9 Jan 1970), yst dau of Col Horace Ricardo, CVO, DL, of Bramley Park, Surrey, and was *ka* France 17 June 1915

1 Mary Florence; *b* 16 April 1877; *m* 4 June 1904 Lt-Col Harold Edward Sherwin Holt CBE (*d* 3 Jan 1932), of Sandleford Priory, Berks, only s of Joseph Holt, JP, of Farnborough Grange, and *d* 4 March 1957, leaving issue

2 Violet Constance Maitland; *b* 26 Sept 1886; *m* 27 Oct 1909 4th Earl of Verulam (*qv*) and *d* 21 July 1936, leaving issue

The 12th EARL's est son,

REGINALD LE NORMAND BRABAZON, **13th Earl of Meath**, CB (1915), CBE (1919), DL Co Wicklow; *b* 24 Nov 1869; *educ* Wellington and RMC Sandhurst; Col Irish Gds (Hon Brig-Gen 1919), Boer War 1900–02 (Queen's medal, three clasps, King's medal, two clasps) and WW I (wounded, despatches); *m* 12 Feb 1908 Lady Aileen May Wyndham-Quin (*d* 25 May 1962), yr dau of 4th Earl of Dunraven and Mount-Earl (*qv*), and *d* 10 March 1949, leaving:

1 ANTHONY WINDHAM NORMAND BRABAZON, **14th and present Earl of Meath**

1 Maureen Margaret; *b* 14 Nov 1908; *m* 11 Dec 1950 Hon Laurence Paul Methuen and *d* 1980, leaving issue (*see* METHUEN, B)

2 *Meriel Aileen; *b* 23 Jan 1913; *m* 10 Sept 1947 Maj Ernest Gerald Howarth, MBE (*d* 24 June 1967), and has:

(1) *Sarah Ann; *b* 8 May 1950; *m* 1st 1972 (*divorce* 1982) Robert A H Smeddle (*see* HUGHES, Bt) and has:

1a *William Robert; *b* 1976

1a *Vanessa Mary; *b* 1974

(1) (cont.) Mrs Sarah Smeddle *m* 2nd 1987 *Alastair D M Ritchie, s of Lt-Col C W M Ritchie, of The Grange, Dolphinton, Peeblesshire

(2) *Aileen Jane Howarth [Mrs Michael Oram, 102 Richmond Hill, Richmond on Thames, Surrey TW10 6RJ]; *b* 22 Dec 1951; *m* 26 Feb 1977 *Michael D B Oram, only s of Maj P A Oram, of Washington, DC, and has:

1a *Francesca Louise; *b* 1978

(3) *Elizabeth Meriel [Mrs Patrick White, Dunster Lodge, 1 Bristol Gdns, London SW15 3TG]; *b* 21 May 1953; *m* 1979 *Patrick Frank Alain White and has:

1a *Sebastian Patrick; *b* 1985

2a *Jocelyn Claud Howarth; *b* 1987

3a *Dominic Christian; *b* 1989

1a *Marina Charlotte; *b* 1983

(4) *Penelope Susan [Mrs Timothy Carew, 131 Studlands Park, Newmarket, Suffolk CB8 7AX]; *b* 21 May 1958; *m* 1988 Timothy P G Carew (*d* 1990) and has:

1a Frederick; *b* 1989

Seat: Killruddery, Bray, Co Wicklow, Ireland. A first house on the Kilruddery estate was destroyed during the turbulent 1640s. Its replacement, started the following decade, has proved more durable, though enlargement in the 18th century, substantial remodelling in the early-19th then pruning back in the middle of the 20th has enhanced the original appearance almost beyond recognition. This is not so of the gardens, which largely retain their formal 17th-century layout.

The architects of the early–19th century alterations to the house, one of the first in the neo-Tudor style to be attempted in Ireland, were Sir Richard Morrison and his son William Vitruvius. Later in the century a conservatory was added by William Burn and filled with statuary. It formerly culminated in a glass dome by Richard Turner, who was also responsible for the Dublin Botanical Gardens conservatory. A second decorative item of glass has survived. This is the stained window in the hall showing William the Conqueror's legendary standard bearer Jacques de Brabançon, who is thus implicitly claimed as ancestor by the Earls of Meath. Jacques is also mentioned in the Battle Abbey Roll, a fact which has been adduced to support the legend, but the Roll is worthless as historical evidence, being compiled many centuries after the Conquest by authors who interpolated names more to propitiate their bearers than from scholarship.

In the 1950s dry rot and the difficulty of heating so vast a building forced the **14th** and current **Earl** to knock down much of it. The very substantial recasting of the external layout, to say nothing of the principal rooms inside, was accomplished by his fellow peer the 4th Lord Phillimore (*qv*), a noted architect.

MEDLYCOTT

DAT·CURA·QUIETEM

Arms: Quarterly per fess indented gules and azure three lions rampant argent. **Crest:** Out of a mural crown gules a demi-eagle, wings elevated or. **Motto:** *Dat cura quietem* ('Vigilance ensures tranquillity'). **Creation:** Bt. (UK) 8 Oct 1808.

SIR MERVYN TREGONWELL MEDLYCOTT, 9TH BT, of Ven House, Co Somerset [Sir Mervyn Medlycott Bt, The Manor House, Sandford Orcas, Dorset DT9 4SB]; *b* 20 Feb 1947; *s* unc 1986; *educ* Milton Abbey; Fell Soc Genealogists, memb AGRA, Pres (formerly Fndr and Hon Sec 1975–77, Chm 1977–84, V-Pres 1984–86) Somerset and Dorset Family History Soc 1986–

Lineage: RICHARD MEDLICOTT, of Pontesbury, Salop; *m* Anne (*d* Nov 1606), dau of Richard Wilcocks, of Pontesbury, and *d* May 1603, leaving:

THOMAS MEDLICOTT, of Pontesbury and London, citizen and dyer; *m* 27 June 1593 Lennard (*d* 1618), dau of James Pluck, citizen and fishmonger, of London, and *d* March 1623, having had a 2nd s:

JAMES MEDLICOTT, of London, citizen and dyer; *b* 25 Feb 1628; *educ* Merchant Taylors; Common Councilman Queenhithe Ward City London 1658 and 1660–62; *b* 5 July 1596; *m* 11 Sept 1621 Elizabeth (*d* 1674), dau of Edmund Joyner, of Newbury, Berks, and *d* Jan 1663, having had:

THOMAS MEDLICOTT, of Abingdon, Berks, JP, DL; *educ* Merchant Taylors and Christ's Coll Cambridge; barrister, Govr Christ's Hosp Abingdon 1675–1716, Recorder Abingdon 1687–88, MP Abingdon 1688–89 and Milborne Port, Somerset, 1705–10; *m* Anne, yst dau and coheir of John Whickers, of London, merchant, and *d* 13 Dec 1716, leaving, with other issue:

JAMES MEDLICOTT, JP, of Ven House, Milborne Port; *b* 1658; barrister, Master in Chancery 1706–17, MP Milborne Port 1710–22; *m* 3 July 1695 Ann Howard, of St Clement Danes, London (*d* May 1758), and *d* 12 May 1731, having had, with other issue:

1 Thomas, of Ven House, JP; *bapt* 22 Oct 1697; MP Milborne Port 1734–63, Commr for Licensing Hawkers and Pedlars 1742–47; *m* 1st 16 June 1731 Elizabeth (*d* 15 June 1741), dau of Anthony Ettrick, of High Barnes, Co Durham, and widow of Musgrave Davidson; *m* 2nd 1742 Elizabeth (*d* 1763), widow of Gilbert Dawson, and *d* 24 July 1763, having by his 1st w had:

(1) Thomas, *dsp* 13 July 1741 aged 10

1 Elizabeth; *m* 20 April 1726 John Hutchings, of Sherborne, Dorset, attorney (*d* 3 July 1774), s of Samuel Hutchings, of S Cadbury, Somerset, and *d* 18 June 1757, leaving:

(1) Thomas HUTCHINGS later MEDLYCOTT, of Ven House, JP; barrister, MP Milborne Port 1763–70 and 1780; *b* Sept 1729; *m* 16 Sept 1766 Jane (*d* 18 June 1824), only dau of William Coles, of Salisbury, Wilts and *d* 15 May 1795, having had:

1a WILLIAM COLES (Sir), **1st Bt**

2a Thomas Mervin; *b* 25 Oct 1773; Lt Inniskilling Dragoons; *d* unm 4 July 1793

1a Jane Paget; *m* 22 May 1794 Philip Calard Ainslie, of Lincoln's Inn, barrister (*d* 6 Sept 1833), s of Sir Philip Ainslie, and *dsp* 30 March 1839

THOMAS MEDLYCOTT's est son,

Sir William Coles Medlycott, 1st Bt (UK), so *cr* 8 Oct 1808, of Ven House; *b* 22 Oct 1767; MP Milborne Port 1790–94; *m* 28 Jan 1796 Elizabeth (*d* 31 July 1847), only dau of William Tugwell, of Bradford, Wilts, and *d* 25 May 1835, having had, with other issue (*d* young):

Sir William Coles Medlycott, 2nd Bt, JP, DL; *b* 31 July 1806; *educ* Harrow and Trin Coll Oxford (Hon DCL 1844); Pres Br Architectural Assoc; *m* 16 March 1830 Sarah Jeffery (*d* 13 May 1879), only dau of Rev Edward Bradford, Rector Stalbridge, Dorset, and *d* 23 Dec 1882, having had:

1 **Sir William Coles Paget Medlycott, 3rd Bt**, of Ven House, JP, DL; *b* 6 June 1831; *educ* Rugby; *d* unm 8 Jan 1887

2 **Sir Edward Bradford Medlycott, 4th Bt**, JP; *b* 29 Sept 1832; *educ* Harrow and Merton Coll Oxford (MA); barrister; *m* 2 Sept 1869 Maria Emma (*d* 1 May 1912), dau of Sir John Bell William Mansel, 9th Bt (*qv*), and *d* 17 Feb 1902, having had:

(1) Lilian Mansel; *b*15 April, 1872; *d* unm 8 March 1966

(2) Ethel Emma; *b* 12 April 1874; *d* an inf

3 **Sir Mervyn Bradford Medlycott, 5th Bt**; *b* 20 Sept 1837; *educ* Harrow; FRGS, R-Adml; *d* unm 27 March 1908

4 HUBERT JAMES (Sir), **6th Bt**

1 Sarah Elizabeth; *m* 23 May 1863 Col Joshua Frederick Kemmis Betty, RA (*d* 23 Nov 1909), and *d* 1915, leaving issue

2 Mary Hutchings; *m* 10 Aug 1858 George Sydney Strode (*d* 16 Dec 1874), of Newham Park, Devon, and *dsp* April 1894

3 Jane Mervyn; *m* 27 Nov 1860 Rev Edward Duke, JP, FGS (*d* 1895), of Lake House, Wilts, and *d* Dec 1906, having had issue

4 Florence Caroline; *m* 3 May 1867 John Thomas Medlycott, of Rocketts Castle, Co Waterford, and *d* 30 Jan 1868, leaving issue

The 5th Bt's bro,

Rev Sir Hubert James Medlycott, 6th Bt, of Ven House, later the Manor House, Sandford Orcas, Dorset; *b* 9 Dec 1841; *educ* Harrow and Trin Coll Cambridge (MA); Vicar Milborne Port 1870–83 and Hill, Glos, 1883–86; *m* 11 May 1870 Julia Ann (*d* 16 Nov 1921), dau of Rev Charles Thomas Glyn (*see* GLYN, Bt), and *d* 25 May 1920, having had:

1 HERBERT MERVYN (Sir), **7th Bt**

1 Florence Julia; *b* 28 June 1871; *m* 1st 1896 George Warkins Yardley (*d* 12 Feb 1927), of Belgravia; *m* 2nd 25 April 1929 Maj Edmund S Jackson (*d* 16 Nov 1932), Innskilling Dragoons, and *d* 6 Oct 1952

2 Cicely Glyn; *b* 28 Sept 1892; *m* 20 March 1925 Sir Gavin Rylands de Beer, MA, DSc, FRS (*d* 21 June 1972), and *d* 21 Nov 1973

Sir HUBERT *d* 25 May 1920; his only son,

Sir Herbert Mervyn Medlycott, 7th Bt; *b* 29 Sept 1874; *educ* Harrow and Trin Coll Cambridge (BA 1896); Maj Dorset Yeo, Govr Sherborne Sch (chm Governing Body), Govr Sherborne Sch for Girls, chm Sherborne Yeatman Hosp and Sherborne RDC; *m* 5 June 1906 Nellie Adah (*d* 31 July 1964), est dau of Hector Edmond Monro, of Edmondsham, Dorset, and *d* 2 Sept 1964, leaving:

1 **Sir (James) Christopher Medlycott, 8th Bt**; *b* 17 April 1907; *educ* Harrow and Magdalene Coll Cambridge (BA 1930); *d* unm 1986

2 (Thomas) Anthony Hutchings, FRIBA; *b* 17 Aug 1909; *educ* Harrow; *m* 25 June 1938 *Cecilia Mary [Mrs Anthony Medlycott, Cowleaze, Edmondsham, Dorset BH21 5RE], yr dau of Maj Cecil Harold Eden, of Tregonwell Lodge, Cranborne, Dorset, and *d* following a climbing accident in N Wales 29 May 1970, leaving:

(1) Sir MERVYN TREGONWELL MEDLYCOTT, **9th and present Bt**

(1) *Julia Elizabeth [Mrs Julia Smith, Edmondsham House, Edmondsham, Dorset BH21 5RE]; *b* 22 March 1939; *m* 19 April 1965 (*divorce* 1986) Michael John Bazeley Smith and has:

1a *Timothy John Medlycott; *b* 1 May 1966

2a *Philip Anthony Medlycott; *b* 1971

1a *Catherine Frances Sarah; *b* 9 Nov 1968

(2) *Philadelphia Jane [Mrs Rupert Oliver, The Residence, Kenchester, Herefs HR4 7QJ]; *b* 12 Oct 1941; *m* 8 April 1967 *Rupert OLIVER formerly BROWN (deed poll 1961) and has:

1a *Kim; *b* 1970

2a *Philadelphia Jo; *b* 1972

(3) *Sarah Nell [Mrs Kenneth Ritchey, 112 Wright Rd, Beckley, WV 25801, USA]; *b* 27 June 1944; *m* 1971 *Kenneth Dale Ritchey and has:

1a *Jonathan Dale; *b* 1975

1a *Emily Jane; *b* 1977

3 John Hubert Nicholas; *b* 24 Dec 1920; *d* unm 22 Feb 1948

MELCHETT

Arms: Quarterly, 1st and 4th, gules a demi-lion rampant argent between in chief a decrescent and an increscent and in base a crescent, all or, on a chief argent an eagle displayed between two mullets sable (for MOND); 2nd and 3rd, azure, on a pile between three mullets argent an eagle displayed sable (for LOWENTHAL). **Crest:** A demi-bear rampant proper, holding between the paws a fountain. **Supporters:** Dexter, a doctor of science of the University of Oxford holding in the exterior hand a chemical measure glass; sinister, a labourer holding in the exterior hand a pick resting on the shoulder, all proper. **Motto:** Make yourself necessary. **Creations:** Bt. (UK) 8 July 1910, B. (UK) 15 June 1928.

THE 4TH BARON MELCHETT, of Landford, Co Southampton, and a **Baronet** (Sir Peter Robert Henry Mond, Bt) [The Rt Hon The Lord Melchett, House of Lords, London SW1A 0PW]; *b* 24 Feb 1948; *s* f 1973; *educ* Eton, Pembroke Coll Cambridge (BA) and Keele U (MA); Ld in Waiting 1974–75, Parly U-Sec DTI 1975–76, Min State NI 1976–79, chm: Community Industry 1979–85, Working Party on Pop Festivals 1975–76, Wildlife Link 1981–86 and Greenpeace UK 1986–89, exec dir Greenpeace UK 1989–, pres Ramblers Assoc 1981–84, memb Friends of Release

Lineage: BAER MEYER MOND, of Ziegenhain, Landgravate of Hesse Cassel; *m* Zerlina Weinberg (*d* 20 July 1865) and *d* 20 March 1820, leaving:

MEYER BAER MOND, of Ziegenhain; *b* 16 Nov 1811; *m* 12 Feb 1837 Henrietta (*d* 10 Aug 1878), yst dau and coheir of Aaron Levinsohn, of Cassel, and *d* 16 Dec 1891, leaving, with other issue:

LUDWIG MOND, of The Poplars, Ave Rd, Hampstead; Winnington Hall, Northwich, Cheshire; and Palazzo Zuccari, Rome; *b* 7 March 1839; Hon DSc Oxford, FRS, PhD, Pres Soc Chemical Industry 1888–89, V-Pres Roy Inst 1896–97; *m* 20 Oct 1863 his cousin Frieda (*d* 16 May 1923), only child and heiress of Adolph Meyer Löwenthal, of Cologne, by Johanna, 2nd dau and coheir of Aaron Levinsohn, of Cassel, and *d* 11 Dec 1909, leaving:

1 Robert Ludwig (Sir); ktd 1932, of Cavendish Sq, London; *b* 9 Sept 1867; LLD, DSc, MA Cambridge, FSA, FRS London and Edinburgh, FPhS, FGS, FZS, Messel Medal Soc of Chemical Industries GB, Pres Société de Chemie Industrielle France; *m* 1st 28 July 1898 Helena Edith (*d* 28 Dec 1905), dau of Julius Levis, of Belsize Grove, Hampstead; *m* 2nd 6 Dec 1922 Marie Louise Guggenheim (*d* 21 Nov 1949), dau of Guillaume Jean Le Manach, of Belle-Isle-en-Terre, Brittany, and *d* 22 Oct 1938, having by his 1st w had:

(1) Frieda Helen; *b* 26 Aug 1899; Liveryman Guild of Air Pilots and Air Navigators, Freeman City of London; *m* 27 Sept 1922 A/Cdre Herbert George Brackley, CBE, DSO, DSC (*d* 15 Nov 1948), RAF, and *d* 16 July 1963, leaving issue

(2) Irene Henrietta; *b* 24 March 1901; *m* 1st 1 June 1922 (*divorce* 1931) Bertram Herbert Austin, MBE, MA (*d* 14 March 1966), Maj RPC, and had issue; *m* 2nd 4 June 1932 Maj James William Thursby Dunn (*d* 15 Oct 1969), RFA, yst s of Lt-Col Thomas Duncan William Dunn, and *d* 5 Jan 1972, leaving further issue

2 **Sir Alfred Moritz Mond, 1st Bt**, and **1st Baron Melchett**, of Landford, Co Southampton (both UK), so *cr* 8 July 1910 and 15 June 1928 respectively, PC (1913), DL (Cheshire 1929); *b* 23 Oct 1868; *educ* Cheltenham, St John's Coll Cambridge and Edinburgh U; barrister Inner Temple 1894, MP (Lib) Chester 1906–10, Swansea 1910–23 and Carmarthen (C) 1924–28, 1st Commr of Works 1916–21, Min Health 1921–22, 1st Chm ICI Ltd, chm Mond Nickel Co, Amalgamated Anthracite Collieries Ltd, Nat Fedn of Employers, Cncl Jewish Agency Palestine, jt chm Conference Industrial Re-organisations and Industrial Relations, dir Westminster Bank, Hon LLD St Andrews 1927 and Manchester 1928, Hon DSc Oxford and Paris 1928, Hon DCL Durham 1929, FRS; *m* 16 June 1894 Violet Florence Mabel (*d* 25 Sept 1945), DBE (1920), CStJ, Order of Mercy, Hon Freeman Chelsea 1934, dau of James Henry Goetze, and had:

(1) HENRY LUDWIG, **2nd Baron**

(1) Eva Violet, CBE (1957), JP (Co London 1937); *b* 6 Aug 1895; *m* 28 Sept 1914 2nd Marquess of Reading (*qv*) and *d* 14 Aug 1973, leaving issue

(2) Mary Angela; *b* 20 June 1901; *m* 1st 29 March 1922 (*divorce* 1928) Sir Neville Arthur Pearson, 2nd Bt, of St Dunstan's (*see* 1970 edn), and had issue; *m* 2nd 14 June 1928 Clifford Willoughby Hordern, s of Peter Hordern, of Bury House, Alverstoke, Hants, and *d* 29 Oct 1937, having had further issue

(3) Rosalind Jean Nora; *b* 15 May 1905; *m* 1st 24 July 1926 (*divorce* 1933) Francis John Buckland, ARIBA, and had issue; *m* 2nd 16 Nov 1933 Maj Ernest Arthur Northen (*d* 21 Dec 1965), only s of Lt-Col Arthur Northen, CBE, DSO, and Lady Mayo-Robson, and *d* 27 May 1967, leaving further issue

The 1st BARON *d* 27 Dec 1930; his only son,

HENRY LUDWIG MOND, **2nd Baron Melchett**; *b* 10 May 1898; *educ* Winchester; MP (Lib) Isle of Ely 1923–24 and (C) E Toxteth 1929–30, Hon Col 27th AANn, RE (TA), dir Internat Nickel Co of Canada Ltd, Industl Finance and Investment Corp Ltd, Palestine Plantations Ltd, Barclays Bank and Cncl Jewish Agency Palestine, dep chm ICI Ltd, Tstee Imp War Museum 1931–46 and Ramsay Memorial Fellowship, Fell Nuffield Coll, Jt MFH Tedworth 1927–34 and Oakley 1935–38, served WW I (wounded, 1914–15 star), author: *Thy Neighbour, Modern Money, Why the Crisis?* and *Hunting and Polo*; *m* 28 Jan 1920 (Amy) Gwen (*d* 4 June 1982), dau of Edward John Wilson, of Parktown, Johannesburg, and had:

1 Derek John Henry; *b* 18 Oct 1922; Lt (A) RNVR, WW II; *m* 18 July 1942 *Yvonne Victoria (*m* 2nd 14 Sept 1951 Richard Louis Rowe) [Mrs Richard Rowe, 4133 Marlowe Ave, Montreal H4A 3M3, Canada], only child of Capt T Douglas Searle, of Cheltenham, and was *k* in a flying accident at sea 30 April 1945

2 JULIAN EDWARD ALFRED, **3rd Baron**

1 *Karis Valerie Violet [The Hon Mrs Wallace, Greenways, Lambourn, Berks]; *b* 26 July 1927; *m* 1st 15 Dec 1949 (*divorce* 1956) John Hackman Sumner and has:

(1) *Justin Mark Sumner; *b* 8 June 1953

1 (cont.) The Hon Mrs Karis Sumner *m* 2nd 10 May 1956 *Brian Albert Wallace, s of Peter Daniel Wallace, of Melbourne, Victoria, and by him has:

(1) *Jessica Karis; *b* 8 April 1957

(2) *Arabella Katherine; *b* 7 Sept 1959

The 2nd BARON *d* 22 Jan 1949; his only surv s,

JULIAN EDWARD ALFRED MOND, **3rd Baron Melchett**; *b* 9 Jan 1925; *educ* Eton; Lt (A) RNVR, chm BSC 1967–73, dir: Br Field Products Ltd, Guardian Assur Co Ltd, Orion Ltd, Hill Samuel, Organising Ctee Nat Steel Corp 1966–67, memb Cncl CBI 1968–73 and NEDC 1969–73, memb: Advsy Cncl Export Credits Guarantee Dept, Br Tport Docks Bd and Br memb Cncl Admin Malta Dry-docks; *m* 26 April 1947 *Sonia Elizabeth, novelist, er dau of Lt-Col Roland Harris Graham, RAMC, of The Lodge, Bridge, nr Canterbury, Kent, and *d* 15 June 1973, leaving:

1 PETER ROBERT HENRY MOND, **4th and present Baron Melchett**

1 *Kerena Ann Mond [The Hon Mrs Boulton, 16 Tite St, London SW3]; *b* 17 May 1951; *m* 1st 1980 Richard Moorehead and has:

(1) *Lucy; *b* 1981

1 (cont.) The Hon Mrs Moorehead *m* 2nd 1985 *Adam Boulton and by him has:

(2) *Blaise; *b* 1990

(3) *Hannah; *b* 1987

2 *Pandora Shelley; *b* 11 Sept 1959; *m* 1991 *Nicholas Wesolowski, s of Michael Joseph Wesolowski, of Pelham St, London SW3, and has:

(1) *Ludovic; *b* 199–

(2) *Alexander Jozef; *b* 14 July 1997

MELVILLE

Arms: Arg. a lion rampant gu., armed and langued az., within a bordure az., charged with three boar's heads couped or, armed ppr. and langued gu. **Crest:** A lion's head affronté gu., struggling through an oak bush, all ppr. **Supporters:** Dexter, a leopard regardant; sinister, a stag attired arg., both ppr. **Motto:** *Essayez* ('Keep trying'); *Quod potui perfeci* ('I have done what I could to the best of my ability'). **Creations:** B. and V. (UK) 24 Dec 1802.

THE 9TH VISCOUNT MELVILLE OF MELVILLE, Co Edinburgh, and **Baron Dunira**, Co Perth (Robert David Ross Dundas) [The Rt Hon The Viscount Mel-

ville, 3 Roland Way, London SW7 3RF]; *b* 28 May 1937; *s* unc 1971; *educ* Wellington; Lt Ayrshire Yeo, Capt (Res) Scots Gds, pres Lasswade Civic Soc, memb Lasswade CC and DC; *m* 23 July 1982 *Fiona Margaret, dau of Roger Kirkpatrick Stilgoe, of Derby House, Stogumber, Somerset, and has:

1 +ROBERT HENRY KIRKPATRICK; *b* 23 April 1984

2 +James David Brouncker; *b* 1986

Lineage: This family is a branch of DUNDAS of Arniston, itself a scion of DUNDAS of Dundas.

ROBERT DUNDAS of Arniston (*see* 1970 edn DUNDAS, Bt, of Arniston) had a 4th s:

HENRY DUNDAS, **1st Viscount Melville of Melville**, so *cr* 24 Dec 1802, as also BARON DUNIRA, of Co Perth (both UK), PC (1782–1805 and 1807); *b* 28 April 1742; advocate 1763, Slr-Gen Scotland 1766–75, MP (Tory) Midlothian 1774–80 and 1783–90, Newtown IoW, 1782 and Edinburgh 1790–1802, Ld Pres Court of Session, Ld Advocate Scotland 1775–83, Commr Bd Indian Affrs 1784–93, Treasurer Navy 1782–April 1783 and Dec 1783–1800, a Ld of Trade 1784–86, Home Sec 1791–94, Pres Bd Control India 1793–1801, Sec War 1794–1801, Privy Seal Scotland 1800–11, First Ld Admlty 1804–05, resigning on an H of C motion (216–216, but the Speaker cast his vote against) that he had breached the law and his duty when Treasurer Navy, though the following year when impeached on 10 similar counts by the Ho Lds he was found not guilty; *m* 1st 16 Aug 1765 Elizabeth, dau and coheir of David Rannie, of Melville Castle, Lasswade, Midlothian, and had:

1 ROBERT, **2nd Viscount**

1 Elizabeth; *m* May 1787 Rt Hon Robert Dundas, Ld Ch Baron of Scotland (*see* 1970 edn DUNDAS of Arniston, Bt) and *d* 18 March 1852

2 Anne; *m* 1st 13 Feb 1786 Henry Drummond (*d* 4 July 1794) and had issue (*see* PERTH, E); *m* 2nd 18 Dec 1798 James Strange (*d* 6 Oct 1840) and *d* Jan 1852

3 Montagu; *m* 25 Jan 1799 2nd Baron Abercromby (*see* 1924 edn) and *d* 1837

The **1st Viscount** *m* 2nd 2 April 1793 June (*m* 2nd 1st and last Baron Wallace of Knaresdale (*see* 1844 edn) and *dsp* 9 June 1829), dau of 2nd Earl of Hopetoun (*see* LINLITHGOW, M), and *d* 29 May 1811

His only son,

ROBERT DUNDAS later SAUNDERS-DUNDAS (added under terms of will (proved 14 Dec 1775) of his w's uncle Adml Sir Charles Saunders, KB, whose beneficiary he was), **2nd Viscount Melville of Melville**, KT (1821), PC (1807, I 1809); *b* 14 March 1771; *educ* Edinburgh HS and Emmanuel Coll Cambridge; Priv Sec to his f 1794–1801, MP (Tory) Hastings 1794–96, Rye 1796–1801) and Midlothian 1801–11), Pres Bd Control India 1807–09, 1809–12 and Feb-Sept 1828, Ch Sec Ireland April-Oct 1809, 1st Ld of Admlty 1812–27 and 1828–30 (during his term of office an Arctic expedn which he had supported named the Melville Sound after him), Ld Privy Seal 1814–51, Govr Bank of Scotland 1811–21, Chllr St Andrews U 1814–51, FRS, Lt Gen Roy Co Archers; *m* 29 Aug 1796 Anne (*d* Sept 1841), dau and coheir (with her sis Jane, 2nd w of 10th Earl of Westmorland (*qv*)), of Richard HUCK-SAUNDERS formerly HUCK, MD, of Plymouth, by his w Jane (dau and heiress of Peter Kinsey and his w Anne, sis and heiress of Adml Sir Charles Saunders, KB), and *d* 10 June 1851, having had, with two daus:

1 HENRY DUNDAS, **3rd Viscount Melville of Melville**, GCB (1865, KCB 1849, CB 1839); *b* 25 Feb 1801; MP (Tory) Rochester 1826–30 and Winchelsea 1830–31, ADC to HM QUEEN VICTORIA 1841–42, served Second Sikh War 1849, Govr Edinburgh Castle 1855–60, Col 100th Foot 1858–62 and 32nd Foot 1862–63, Col Cmdt 60th Rifles 1863–76, Gen 1868; *d* unm 1 Feb 1876

2 Richard Saunders (Sir), KCB; *b* 11 April 1802; V-Adml, a Ld Admlty; *d* 3 June 1861

3 ROBERT DUNDAS, **4th Viscount Melville of Melville**; *b* 14 Sept 1803; Dep Comptroller Navy 1830, Storekeeper-Gen Navy 1832–69; *dsp* 18 Feb 1886

4 Charles (Rev); Preb Lincoln, Rector Epworth, Lincs; *b* 11 Sept 1806; *m* 1 Aug 1833 Louisa Maria (*d* 6 Sept 1895), est dau of Sir William Boothby, 8th Bt (*qv*), and *d* 24 Feb 1883, leaving, with other issue:

(1) HENRY DUNDAS, **5th Viscount Melville of Melville**; *b* 8 March 1835; *m* 18 June 1891 Hon Violet Marie Louise Cochrane-Wishart-Baillie (*d* 31 March 1943), dau of 1st Baron Lamington (*see* 1949 edn), and *d* 3 Nov 1904, leaving:

1a Maisie Violet Annabella; *b* 3 May 1892; *m* 30 Nov 1915 Hugo Henry Houstoun and *d* 7 Feb 1929

2a Montagu Lilias Nina; *b* 9 Sept 1893; *d* unm 21 Nov 1946

(2) CHARLES SAUNDERS, **6th Viscount**

(3) William Walter; *b* 20 May 1847; Lt 5th Dragoon Gds; *d* unm 3 Feb 1910

(1) Edith Anne; *m* 5 Feb 1863 Lt-Col John Reeve, Gren Gds (*d* 2 Jan 1897), of Leadenham, Lincs, and *d* 12 Aug 1902, having had issue

(2) Fanny Emma; *m* 20 July 1864 Lt-Col Ellis P F Reeve, Coldstream Gds (*d* 1 June 1930), and *d* 8 July 1892, leaving issue

(3) Alice Caroline (twin with William Walter); *m* 7 June 1870 Capt Joshua Gladwyn Jebb (*d* 22 June 1901), of Barnby Moor House, Notts, and *d* 19 April 1924, leaving issue (*see* GLADWYN, B)

The 5th VISCOUNT's bro,

CHARLES SAUNDERS MELVILLE DUNDAS, **6th Viscount Melville of Melville**, ISO; *b* 27 June 1843; *educ* Rossall; Consul Santos, Brazil, 1869–76, Tenerife 1876–82 and Stettin 1883–85, Consul-Gen Hamburg 1885–97 and Christiania (now Oslo) 1897–1906; *m* 1st Aug 1872 Grace Selina Marion (*d* 16 Jan 1890), only child of William Scully; *m* 2nd 9 Feb 1891 Mary (*d* 29 Oct 1919), dau of George Hamilton, MD, of Falkirk, Scotland; *m* 3rd 8 Dec 1920 Margaret (*d* 2 Feb 1961), dau of William James Todd, and by his 1st w had:

1 HENRY CHARLES CLEMENT, **7th Viscount**

2 Cospatrick Philip Brooke; *b* 30 March 1879; *m* 1913 Isabella (*d* 1968 aged 80), dau of E A W Mackenzie, of Saskatchewan, Canada, and *d* 1954, leaving:

(1) Kenelm Crispin Vivian Douglas, DFC (1941); *b* 1916; S/Ldr RAF WW II 1939–42 (missing), Greek DFC

(1) *Daphne Roseabella Louise; *b* 1923; *m* 1949 *Wilfrid Rankin Hodgin

3 Richard Serle; *b* 14 Nov 1880; Assist Grain Commr Saskatchewan, Boer War with Canadian Forces; *m* 1st 1907 Lydia Catherine (*d* 1922), dau of E A W Mackenzie, of Saskatchewan, and had:

(1) +Hugh Mackenzie [Hugh Dundas Esq, 298 Alfred St, Pembroke, ON K8A 3A6, Canada]; *b* 3 June 1910; *educ* Saskatchewan U (BA 1932); WW II 1943–45; *m* 29 Sept 1939 Catherine Sanderson (*d* 1994), dau of John Wallace, of Edinburgh, and has:

1a +Robert Hugh Sanderson [Robert Dundas, Box 82, Hesperia, CA 92345, USA]; *b* 4 Oct 1943; *educ* Saskatchewan U (BA) and Carleton U (MA); *m* 1980 *Nancy, dau of Kenneth Howard Sullivan, of Montreal

1a *Catherine Marion Wallace [Miss Catherine Dundas, 298 Alfred St, Pembroke, ON K8A 3A6, Canada]; *b* 13 Feb 1948; *educ* Carleton U (BA)

(2) +Richard Serle [Richard Dundas Esq, Box 281, Paradise Hill, SK S0M 2G0, Canada]; *b* 1911; served WW II; *m* 1942 *Marianne, dau of John Semple, of N Battleford, Saskatchewan, and has:

1a +Richard Serle [Richard Dundas Esq, 1300-12th Ave, Williams Lake, BC V2G 3X4, Canada]; *b* 1948; *m* 1970 *Denise Paulette, dau of Frank Dechant, of Manning, Alberta, and has:

1b +Richard Serle; *b* 1971

1b *Kelsi Shannon; *b* 1974

2a +James; *b* 1951

1a *Dianne Mary [Mrs Lyle Winder, Box 301, Paradise Hill, SK S0M 2G0, Canada]; *b* 1947; *m* 1965 *Lyle Merle Winder and has:

1b *Laurie Dianne; *b* 1966

2a *Carolyn Patricia [Mrs Daniel Gervais, 2302-49th Ave, Lloydminster, SK S9V 1M1, Canada]; *b* 1954; *educ* Regina U, Saskatchewan (BEd); *m* 1978 *Daniel Brian Gervais and has:

1b *Aaron Daniel; *b* 1983

1b *Danelle Lindsay; *b* 1979

2b *Whitney Nicole; *b* 1986

(3) Kenneth Brooke; *b* 21 Aug 1913; *educ* Saskatchewan U (BE Civil); RCAF 1936–39 (permanent), RCAF (Res) 1940–45, tech dir R & R Domtar Chemicals Ltd, Montreal; *m* 20 June 1942 Dorothy Helen (*d* 1994), dau of John A Walters, of 427 Seventh St, Saskatoon, and *d* 1988, having had:

1a David Kenneth Glenn; *b* 3 Sept 1943; *d* 29 Aug 1950

2a +Anthony John; *b* 23 April 1946; *educ* Queen's U Ontario (BA) and Duke U (MA); with Roy Bank of Canada; *m* 1972 *Carol Anne, dau of R Brunini, of Pte Claire, Quebec, and has:

1b *Amy Leana; *b* 1978

2b *Kristina; *b* 1982

3a +Peter Melville; *b* 14 Jan 1948; *educ* U of Saskatchewan (BA); with Classics Books, Montreal, Canada; *m* 1973 *Mary Ann, dau of J Thorne, of Ottawa, and has:

1b +Zachary David; *b* 1979

1b *Jennifer Mary; *b* 1975

4a +Christopher Charles; *b* 11 July 1950; *educ* Queen's U (BA) and U of California (MBA); Special Assist to Hon R Andra, Canadian Govt; *m* 1976 *Marie Madeleine Suzanne, dau of Vianney Provencher, of Gentilly, Quebec, and has:

1b *Sarah Daisy; *b* 1977

2b *Carla; *b* 1982

1a *Dorothy Anne [Mrs Dorothy Becker, 101 Lanton Boulevard, Toronto, ON, Canada]; *b* 26 May 1945; with W H Smith & Son; *m* 1977 (*divorce* 19–) R Stephen Becker, of Springfield, Ill., USA

(4) Gerald Alexander; *b* 11 Oct 1916; *m* 1939 *Alice Marjorie [Mrs Gerald Dundas, 3058 Whitmore Ave, Regina, SK, Canada], dau of Richard M Lister, of Pelly, Saskatchewan, and *d* 1966, leaving:

1a +Richard Melville; *b* 1940; RCMP Ottawa, Canada ; *m* 1965 *Dorothy Vivian, dau of Alex Bursey, of St John's, and has:

1b *Karen Anne; *b* 1965

2b *Katherine Dawn; *b* 1969

2a +Gerald James; *b* 1959; *m* 1980 *—

1a *Pamela Marion; *b* 1942; SRN, St Joseph's Sch of Nursing, Victoria BC; *m* 1965 Anthony Braun (*d* 1980)

(5) +Robert Montague [Lt-Cdr Robert Dundas RCN (ret), 5738 Wallace St, Vancouver, BC V6N 2A4, Canada]; *b* 1920; *educ* RMC Kingston (BMilSc) and U of BC (BApp Science 1948, BA, MA); Lt RCNVR WW II; *m* 1953 *Shirley Janet (BA U of BC), dau of Urwin Finch, of Vancouver, and has:

1a +James Urwin; *b* 25 May 1954

2a Hugh Montague; *b* 6 Feb 1959; RC priest; *d* 1993

1a *Janet Glencora Dundas [Mrs Stephen Corbett, 4640 Duncliffe Rd, Richmond, BC V7E 3N1, Canada]; *b* 5 May 1956; *m* 1982 *Stephen Corbett and has:

1b *George Miles; *b* 1984

1b *Madeline Janet; *b* 1987

2a *Patricia Hope; *b* 8 April 1965

(1) Blanche Constance; *b* 1908; *m* 1935 *Robert Norfolk, RCMP, and has issue

(2) Grace Edith Marion; *b* 1918; *educ* Sask U (BHSC)

3 (cont.) Richard Dundas *m* 2nd 1926 Mathilde Mary (*d* 1979), dau of Louis Saxon, of Yorkton, Saskatchewan, and *d* Sept 1968, having by her had:

(2) *Oenone Judith [Miss Oenone Dundas, 786 Island Rd, Victoria, BC, Canada]; *b* 1927; *educ* BC U (BA), London U (MA), Wisconsin (PhD)

(3) *(Iris) Anne Alayne [Mrs Ronald Shepherd, Easter Hill, 110 Ensilwood, Salt Spring Island, BC V8K 1N1, Canada]; *b* 1928; BA; *m* 3 July 1952 *Rt Rev Ronald Francis Shepherd, Dean and Rector All Saints Cathedral, Edmonton, Bp BC (1985–92), s of G H Shepherd, of Victoria, BC, and has:

1b *Jeremy Michael; *b* 1956

2b *Christopher Patrick; *b* 1958

3b *Timothy David; *b* 1962

4b *Peter Andrew Dundas; *b* 1966

1b *Mary Mathilde; *b* 1954

2b *Susan Clare

4 Kenneth Robert; *b* 10 May 1882; DC Br E African Protectorate, Lt RNVR Anson Bn RND; *m* 8 Dec 1909 Anne Claudia Whalley (*m* 2nd 12 April 1922 Lt-Col Auberon Claud Hegan Kennard, of Cromwell House, E Grinstead, Sussex (*d* 1 Nov 1951), est s of Col Edmund Hegan Kennard (*see* KENNARD, Bt), and *d* 11 June 1943), yr dau of Capt Charles Edward Foot, RN, and was *ka* 7 Aug 1915, leaving:

(1) Claud Kenneth Melville; *b* 6 July 1911; *educ* RNC Dartmouth; served WW II; *m* 2 Feb 1939 *Janet [Mrs Claud Dundas, The Haven, Woodlands Dve, Barnston, Cheshire], dau of John Donaldson, of Dumfries, and *d* 1993, having had:

1a +Kenneth Ninian Melville; *b* 11 May 1943; *educ* Trin Coll Glenalmond; *m* 19– *Susan —

5 Kenelm James (twin with Kenneth Robert); *d* an infant 1883

6 Charles Cecil Farquharson (Sir), KCMG (1938), OBE (1922); *b* 6 June 1884; DC Br E Africa 1908–15, Political Offr as Maj German E African Campaign 1915–18, Sr Commr Tanganyika Territory 1921–25, Prov Commr 1926, Ch Sec Tanganyika Territory 1926, Sec Native Affrs 1926, Colonial Sec Bahamas 1929 (Actg Govr May–Nov), Ch Sec N Rhodesia 1934–37, Govr and C-in-C Bahamas 1937–40 and Uganda Protectorate 1940–44, KStJ; *m* 16 Oct 1920 Anne Louise CStJ (*d* 14 Oct 1959), yst dau of Rev Samuel Cox Hay, DD, of NY, and *dsp* 10 Feb 1956

1 Selina Louisa Grace; *b* 23 Oct 1874; *m* 5 Sept 1899 Sir Richard Harington, 12th Bt (*qv*), and *d* 3 Dec 1945, leaving issue

2 Hilda Guilhermina, DGStJ; *b* 19 May 1877; Order of Mercy, v-pres League of Mercy; *m* 22 Sept 1903 William Ingham Whitaker, DL (*d* 10 July 1936), of Pylewell Park, Lymington, Hants, and *d* 18 Dec 1971 leaving issue

The 6th VISCOUNT *d* 21 Sept 1926; his est son,

HENRY CHARLES CLEMENT DUNDAS, **7th Viscount Melville of Melville**; *b* 25 June 1873; *educ* Trin Coll Glenalmond; Sec Consulate-Gen Hamburg 1892–95, Assist Dist Offr Br Centl Africa Protectorate 1896–97, cmded garrisons Fort Lister and Fort Anderson 1896–97, Sec and ADC to Commr Br E Africa 1897–99, V-Consul Zanzibar 1897–08, Tahiti 1908–09, Dep Commr Pitcairn Island 1909–09, Bahia 1909 and Corsica 1909–21, Cmdt POW Camp Port Talbot 1916–17; *m* 20 June 1899 Agnes Mary Florence (*d* 13 Sept 1954), dau of Henry Brouncker, of Beveridge Park, Dorset, and *d* 30 Jan 1935, leaving:

1 HENRY CHARLES PATRIC BROUNCKER DUNDAS, **8th Viscount Melville of Melville**; *b* 5 March 1909; *educ* King's Canterbury; *d* unm 26 March 1971

2 Robert Maldred St John Melville; *b* 25 Nov 1912; Lt 1st Lothian and Border Yeo WW II; *m* 5 March 1936 *Margaret Connell (*m* 2nd 14 Nov 1946 Gerald Bristowe Sanderson, Lanarks Yeo), er dau of Percy Cruden Ross, of Monkwood House, Ayrshire, and was *ka* 5 June 1940, leaving:

(1) ROBERT DAVID ROSS DUNDAS, **9th and present Viscount Melville of Melville**

1 Isobel Mia Douglas Hamilton; *b* 7 March 1900; *d* unm July 1945

2 Diana Pearl; *b* 7 Aug 1902; *m* 15 April 1929 Morogh Wyndham Percy Bernard (*d* 16 Feb 1977), 4th s of Percy Brodrick Bernard, of Castle Hacket, Co Galway, and has issue (*see* 1970 edn BANDON, E)

MENUHIN

Arms: Azure, four bendlets between as many violin bridges gold. **Crest:** Out of an eastern crown or inscribed on either side with a crotchet rest a sharp a semi-quaver a flat a semi-quaver rest sable, a pair of cubit arms proper supporting a terrestrial globe the land vert fimbriated or, the sea azure. **Supporters:** On either side a representation of a Firebird à la Benois, wings elevated and addorsed gules, beaked and membered with wings tipped or, the tail bleu celeste, that to the dexter gorged with a chain or, pendant therefrom a hurt fimbriated and charged with a Menorah or, the candles argent enflamed proper, that to the sinister gorged with a like chain pendant therefrom a bezant charged with a representation of the Gypsy Flag mon proper, the compartment a grassy mound with bluebells and blue poppies growing therefrom all proper, with at the centre thereof a plough gold. **Motto:** צדקה תקוה אמונה ידע הבנה חכמה ('Wisdom, understanding, knowledge, faith, hope, charity'). **Creation:** B. (LP, UK) 19 July 1993.

THE BARON MENUHIN, of Stoke d'Abernon, Co Surrey (Sir Yehudi Menuhin, OM (1987), KBE (1965)) [The Rt Hon The Lord Menuhin OM KBE, c/o SYM Music Company, PO Box 6160, London SW1W 0XJ]; *b* 22 April 1916; *educ* privately; fndr Music Festivals: Gstaad 1957, Bath 1959–68, fndr Yehudi Menuhin Sch of Music Surrey 1963, Jt Artistic Dir Windsor Festival 1969–72, Fndr and Pres Internat Menuhin Music Acad Gstaad 1976, fndr Live Music Now 1977, Pres: Trin Coll Music 1971, UK Internat Music Cncl UNESCO, European String Teachers' Assoc, Young Musicians' Symphony Orchestra 1989–, Musicians' Internat Mutual Aid Fund; took UK nationality 1985; Pres and Assoc Conductor: Royal Philharmonic Orchestra 1982–, Hallé Orchestra 1992–; Pncpl Guest Conductor English String Orchestra 1988–; Fndr and Conductor Asian Youth Orchestra; Goodwill Ambassador UNESCO 1992; Hon DMus: Oxford 1962, Cambridge 1970, Sorbonne 1976, Toronto 1984, Virginia Commonwealth U 1987, Hartford CN 1987, Santa Clara CA 1988; Hon LLD Liverpool, St Andrews, Sussex, Bath; Hon DLit Warwick; FRCM; Sr Fell RCA; Hon Fell: Trin Coll Music, St Catharine's Coll Cambridge 1970, Fitzwilliam Coll Cambridge 1991; Cobbett Medal Musicians' Co 1959, Gold Medal Roy Philharmonic Soc 1962, Mozart Medal 1965, Sonning Music Prize Denmark 1972, Gold Medal Canadian Music Council 1975, Albert Medal RSA 1981, Una Vita Nella Musica Italy 1983, Brahms Medal Hamburg 1987, Brahms Orden Hamburg 1988, Gold Medal Cordoba U 1990, Glenn Gould Prize Canada 1990, Yehudi Menuhin and Luciano Berio Wolf Prize 1991; Jawaharlal Nehru Award for Internat Understanding 1970, Grand Offr Legn Hon 1986, Cdr Order Arts and Letters France, Cross of Lorraine France, Cdr Order Leopold Belgium, Offr Order Crown Belgium, Kt Cdr and Grand Cross Order Merit Germany, Order Merit Republic Italy, Roy Order Phoenix Greece, Cdr Orange-Nassau Netherlands; Freeman Edinburgh, Bath; Hon Swiss Citizenship 1970; author: *The Violin* (1971), *Theme and Variations* (1972), *Violin and Viola* (1976), *Sir Edward Elgar* (essay, 1976), *Unfinished Journey* (autobiography, 1977), *The Music of Man* (with Christopher Hope, 1980), *The King, the Cat and the Fiddle* (1983), *Life Class* (1986); *m* 1st 1938 Nola Ruby, dau of George Nicholas, of Melbourne, Australia, and had:

  1 *Krov Nicholas [The Hon Krov Menuhin, Mas de la Baleine, 13210 St Rémy de Provence, France]; *b* 1940; *m* 1967 *Elizabeth Ann, dau of Herbert Christoffers, and has:

    (1) *Aaron Nicholas; *b* 1982

  1 *Zamira [The Hon Mrs Benthall, 212 Hammersmith Grove, London W6 7HG]; *b* 1939; *m* 1st 1960 (*divorce* 1969) Fou Ts'ong, concert pianist, and has:

    (1) *Lin Menuhin (son); *b* 1964

  1 (cont.) The Hon Mrs Zamira Fou Ts'ong *m* 2nd 1975 *Jonathan Charles Mackenzie Benthall, s of Sir (Arthur) Paul Benthall, KBE, of Benthall Hall, Broseley, Salop, and by him has:

    (1) *Dominic Gabriel Menuhin; *b* 1976

    (2) *William Jonathan Menuhin; *b* 1981

THE BARON MENUHIN *m* 2nd 1947 *Diana Rosamond, dau of Gerard L E Gould, of Paris and London, and Lady Harcourt (Evelyn Suart, the pianist), and by her has:

  1 *Gerard [The Hon Gerard Menuhin, PO Box 55, CH-3780, Gstaad, Switzerland]; *b* 1948; *m* 1983 (*divorce* 19–) — and has:

    (1) *Maxwell Duncan; *b* 1990

  2 *Jeremy; *b* 1951; *educ* Eton; *m* 1983 (*divorce* 19–) Hon Brigid Gabriel Forbes-Sempill, yst dau of 19th Lord Sempill (*qv*), and has issue

Lineage: MOSHE MNUCHIN later MENUHIN; Head Jewish Educn Bd San Francisco; *m* 1914 Marutha Sher (*d* 1996 aged 100) and *d* 1988, leaving:

  1 YEHUDI, *cr* a **Baron**

  1 Yalta; *b* 1920

  2 Hepzibah; *b* 1921; keyboard player; *d* 1984

MERLYN-REES

Creation: B. (LP, UK) 1992.

THE BARON MERLYN-REES, of Morley and S Leeds, Co W Yorks, and of Cilfynydd, Co Mid Glamorgan (Merlyn Merlyn-Rees, PC (1974)) [The Rt Hon The Lord Merlyn-Rees PC, 51 West Sq, London SE11 4SP]; *b* 18 Dec 1920; *educ* Harrow Weald GS, Goldsmiths' Coll London, LSE and London U Inst of Educn; S/Ldr RAF WW II; sch master 1949–60, organiser Festival of Labour 1960–62, Lecturer Economics Luton Tech 1962–63, MP (Lab) S Leeds 1983–83, Morley and Leeds S 1983–92, PPS to Chllr Exchequer 1964, Parly U-Sec: MOD (Army) 1965–66, (RAF) 1966–68, Home Office 1968–70, memb Shadow Cabinet and Oppn Spokesman NI 1972–74, NI Sec 1974–76, Home Sec 1976–79, Shadow Home Sec 1979–80, Oppn Spokesman Energy 1980–83; Memb: Franks Ctee Official Secrets Act 1971, Franks Ctee Falklands 1982; Chm S Leeds Groundwork Tst 1987 (memb Bd Groundwork Fndn 1990–96); Pres Video Standards Cncl 1990–; Chllr Glamorgan U 1994, Freeman City of Leeds 1993; Hon Fell Goldsmiths' Coll 1984; Hon LLD: Wales U 1987, Leeds 1992; author: *The Public Sector in the Mixed Economy* (1973), *Northern Ireland: a personal perspective* (1985); *m* 26 Dec 1949 *Colleen Faith, dau of Henry F Cleveley, of Kenton, Middx, and has:

  1 *Patrick Merlyn; *b* 1954; slr; *m* — and has a s and dau

  2 *Gareth David; *b* 1956; barrister; *m* — and has a s and two daus

  3 *Glyn Robert; *b* 1960; *m* — and has a s and dau

Lineage: LEVI DANIEL REES, of Cilfynydd, S Wales; *m* Edith Mary Williams and had:

MERLYN REES later MERLYN-REES (deed poll 1992), *cr* a **Baron**

MERRIVALE

Arms: Argent an anchor fouled sable between three chaplets, all within a bordure engrailed azure. **Crest:** Issuant from a chaplet fesswise argent a demi-griffin, holding between the claws a fasces erect or. **Supporters:** On either side a griffin or, the dexter gorged with a chain sable, pendant therefrom an escutcheon argent charged with a saltire vert between four castles sable, the sinister gorged with a like chain, suspended therefrom an escutcheon per pale gules and sable, charged with a triple-towered castle or. **Motto:** *Gradatim vincimus* ('We conquer by degrees'). **Creation:** B. (UK) 19 Jan 1925.

THE 3RD BARON MERRIVALE, of Walkhampton, Co Devon (Jack Henry Edmond Duke) [The Rt Hon The Lord Merrivale, 16 Brompton Lodge, 9–11 Cromwell Rd, London SW7 2JA]; *b* 27 Jan 1917; *s f* 1951; *educ* Dulwich, abroad and Ecole des Sciences Politiques Paris; FRSA 1964, F/Lt RAF WW II (despatches 1944), pres: Inst Traffic Admin 1953–70 and Rlwy Devpt Assoc, chm Anglo-Malagasy Soc 1961, v-chm Travel and Tourist Bureau and Olympos Ltd, chm Grecian Investments (Gibraltar) Ltd 1990– and Scotia Investments, Chevalier Nat Order Malagasy 1968, Cdr Nat Order Lion Senegal 1992; *m* 1st 30 Sept 1939 (*divorce* 1974) Colette, dau of John Douglas Wise, of Bordeaux, France; *m* 2nd 16 Sept 1975 *Betty, widow of Paul Baron, and by his 1st w has:

  1 +DEREK JOHN PHILIP; *b* 16 March 1948; *educ* Arcachon, French Lycée London, Lycée de Sailly Paris and Faculté de Sciences d'Orsay Paris; *m* 19– *— and has issue

  1 *Elizabeth Anne Marie Violet; *b* 24 Nov 1939

Lineage: SOLOMON DUKE, of Plymouth, Devon, clockmaker, had:

WILLIAM EDWARD DUKE, of 22 Richmond St, Plymouth; accountant; *b* 1828; *m* 20 June 1850 Elizabeth Ann, dau of George Lord, of 18 Richmond St, Plymouth, and *d* 1898, leaving:

HENRY EDWARD DUKE, **1st Baron Merrivale**, of Walkhampton, Co Devon (UK), so *cr* 19 Jan 1925, PC (GB 1915, I 1916), QC (1899); *b* 5 Nov 1855; barrister Gray's Inn 1885, Recorder Plymouth 1897–1900 and Devonport 1897–1914, Bencher 1899, Treas 1908 and 1927, MP (C) Plymouth 1900–06 and Exeter 1910–18, arbitrator by jt appt of GWR Co and its employees under Rlwy Conciliation Scheme 1907, V-Treas 1928, Chm Devon QS 1927, Hon Freedom Plymouth 1924, Chm Roy Commn Defence of Realm Losses 1915, Attorney-Gen and memb Cncl Duchy of Cornwall 1915, Ch Sec Ireland 1916–18, Ld Justice Appeal 1918–19 and Pres Probate, Divorce and Admlty Div High Court 1919–33, ktd 1918; *m* 1876 Sarah (*d* 1914), dau of John Shorland, of Shrewsbury, and *d* 20 May 1939, leaving:

  1 EDWARD, **2nd Baron**

  1 Violet; *m* 1st 1912 Maj Frederick John Stockham Davis (*das* 4 Nov 1918), Devonshire Regt; *m* 2nd 1922 Rev Marcus Ethelbert Atlay (*d* 30 July 1934), Canon Residentiary Gloucester and Treasurer Gloucester Cathedral, and *d* 8 May 1958

The 1st BARON MERRIVALE's only s,

  EDWARD DUKE, **2nd Baron Merrivale**, OBE (1918), JP Devon; *b* 22 May 1883; *educ* Dulwich Coll and Neuchâtel; barrister Gray's Inn 1908, Capt Devonshire Regt, Boer War 1900–02 and WW I, Sec to Pres Probate, Divorce and Admlty Div High Court 1919–33, Dep Chm Devon QS 1947; *m* 1st 1912 (*divorce* 1939) Odette, dau of Edmond Roger, of Paris; *m* 2nd 5 April 1939 Meta Therese Amelia, dau of Joseph Herman Wolczon, of Danzig, and *d* 8 June 1951, leaving by his 1st w:

  1 JACK HENRY EDMOND DUKE, **3rd and present Baron Merrivale**

  1 *Elizabeth Suzanne [The Hon Mrs Bechmann, La Charité, 60500 Chantilly, France]; *b* 27 Aug 1921; *m* 1st 22 Oct 1942 (*divorce* 1953) Capt Jean Pompei, French Air Force, s of Louis Pompei, and has:

    (1) *François [M François Pompei, 18 rue Ferdinand Duval, 75004 Paris]; *b* 24 Sept 1944; *m* 1973 (*divorce* 1992) Elizabeth, dau of Christian Dupuy, and has:

      1a *Antoine; *b* 1975

      2a *Louis; *b* 1977

3a *Philippe; *b* 1978

1a *Marie; *b* 1980

(1) *Nicole Elizabeth [Mme Bouchard, 43 rue de Boulainvilliers, 75016 Paris]; *b* 22 March 1946; *m* 28 June 1968 (*divorce* 1980) Jean-Louis Bouchard, s of Gen Robert Bouchard, and has:

    1a *Robert; *b* 1971

    1a *Alexandra Jacqueline; *b* 9 March 1969; *m* 1991 *Laurent Rousseau and has:

      1b *Marie; *b* 1993

1 (cont.) The Mrs Elizabeth Pompei *m* 2nd 30 Sept 1955 Jacques Bechmann (*d* 1985), banker, s of René Bechmann, and by him has:

    (2) *Pierre; *b* 18 Jan 1957

MERSEY

Arms: Per bend dancettée azure and or a bend invected between three crosses patée in chief and as many horseshoes in base, all counterchanged. **Crest:** A horse per pale or and sable, charged on the body with three horseshoes fessways counterchanged, and resting the dexter foreleg on a cross patée gules. **Supporters:** On either side a mermaid proper crowned with a naval crown gules, the dexter supporting with the exterior hand an anchor or, the sinster an oar argent. **Motto:** *J'avance* ('I advance'). **Creations:** L (S) 27 Jan 1680/1, B. (UK) 16 March 1910, V. (UK) 22 Jan 1916.

THE 4TH VISCOUNT MERSEY, of Toxteth, Co Lancaster, **Lord Nairne** and **Baron Mersey**, of Toxteth, Co Lancaster (Richard Maurice Clive Bigham, DL (Sussex 1977)) [The Rt Hon The Viscount Mersey DL, Bignor Park, Pulborough, Sussex RH20 1HG]; *b* 8 July 1934; *s* f 1979 in the UK peerages, mother 1995 in Lordship of Nairne; *educ* Eton and Balliol Coll Oxford; served Irish Gds 1952–54, documentary film-maker, pres: SIESO 1987–91 and Combined Heat and Power Assoc 1989–92, Hon FRAM 1996, author: *The Hills of Cork and Kerry* (1987); *m* 6 May 1961 *Joanna Dorothy, er dau of John Arnaud Robin Grey Murray, MBE, of Hampstead and Mayfair, and has had:

    1 A son; *b* and *d* 30 June 1964

    2 +EDWARD JOHN HALLAM, *Master of Nairne*; *b* 23 May 1966; *educ* Eton and Balliol Coll Oxford; *m* 1994 *Claire L, dau of David Haigh

Lineage (of Bigham): The BIGHAMs were originally settled on the Templetown estate in Co Antrim.

ANDREW BIGHAM, Kirkcudbrightshire; grazier; *b* 1742; had:

SAMUEL BIGHAM; cloth manufacturer Wigan, Lancs; *b* 1777; *m* 15 June 1813 as his 2nd w Catherine (*d* 1854), dau of John Hughes, of Chester, and *d* 22 Aug 1830, leaving:

JOHN BIGHAM; Liverpool merchant and shipowner, memb Liverpool City Cncl and Mersey Docks and Harbour Bd; *b* 5 April 1814; *m* 16 Oct 1834 Helen (*d* 12 Aug 1904), dau of John East, of Liverpool, and *d* 5 Oct 1880, having had:

    1 Henry, of New York; *b* 29 July 1835; *m* 4 Feb 1871 Helen (*d* 1914), dau of John Numan, and *d* 4 July 1873, leaving issue (now extinct)

    2 JOHN CHARLES, **1st Viscount**

    1 Catherine; *d* young

    2 Agnes Maria; *b* 3 July 1842; *m* 10 Sept 1868 Thomas Brough (*d* 2 Oct 1892), of Liverpool, and *d* 7 Aug 1919, leaving issue

JOHN BIGHAM's 2nd s,

    JOHN CHARLES BIGHAM, **1st Viscount Mersey**, of Toxteth, Co Lancaster, so *cr* 22 Jan 1916, as also earlier 16 March 1910 BARON MERSEY, of Toxteth, Co Lancaster (both UK), PC (1909), QC (1883); *b* 3 Aug 1840; barrister Middle Temple 1870, MP Liverpool Exchange 1895–97, Justice High Court 1897–1909, a Roy Commr revision martial law sentences S Africa 1902 and Civ Serv 1914, Pres: Rlwy and Canal Commn 1904–07 and Probate, Divorce and Admlty Div High Court 1909–10, Wreck Commr UK 1912–14, ktd 1897; *m* 17 Aug 1871 Georgina Sarah (*d* 9 Jan 1925), dau of John Rogers, of Liverpool, and *d* 3 Sept 1929, having had:

    1 CHARLES CLIVE, **2nd Viscount**

    2 John Trevor Buckley; *b* 27 Nov 1873; *d* 23 Jan 1875

3 (Frank) Trevor Roger (Sir), KBE (1929), CB (1919), JP (London); *b* 22 May 1876; *educ* Eton and Magdalen Coll Oxford (MA); barrister Middle Temple 1901, Ch Constable Metropolitan Police 1909–14, Assist Commr 1914–31 and Dep Commr 1931–34; *m* 1st 17 Dec 1901 Frances Leonora (*d* 10 Jan 1927), 2nd dau of John Leonard Tomlin, of Richmond, Yorks; *m* 2nd 2 Sept 1931 Edith Ellen, OBE (1926) (*d* 1985), dau of Lt-Col David Drysdale, and *d* 23 Nov 1954, leaving by his 1st w:

    (1) Veronica Beatrice Mary; *b* 8 Jan 1905; *m* 21 Sept 1935 James Carew O'Gorman Anderson (*d* 19 Nov 1946), s of Brig-Gen Sir Francis Anderson, of Ballydavid, Co Waterford, and had:

      1a *Ben; *b* 19–

      2a *Rory; *b* 19–

      1a *Melanie; *b* 19–

    (2) Celia Hermione Margaret; *b* 9 Aug 1909; *d* unm 14 April 1997

The 1st VISCOUNT MERSEY's er surv s,

    CHARLES CLIVE BIGHAM, **2nd Viscount Mersey**, CMG (1901), CBE (1919), PC (1946), DL London; *b* 18 Aug 1872; *educ* Eton and RMC Sandhurst; Dip Serv 1896–1900 (Br delegate Thessaly 1897–98), served Peking Expdn 1900 (despatches), Mil Intell Dept War Office 1901–04, BOT, Sec to Roy Commns 1905–52, Bde Maj Bde of Gds 1914, Lt-Col Gren Gds, Provost Marshal Dardanelles and Mil Attaché Egypt 1915, GSO(1) cmdg Mil Mission French War Office 1916–19 (despatches), attached Paris Peace Conf 1919, Br Delegate Burma Round Table Conf 1931, Dep Speaker and Dep Chm Ctees Ho of Lds, Ch Lib Whip 1944–49, dir Nat Provident Instn, V-Pres Roy Westminster Ophthalmic Hosp (Chm 1935–46), Chm Westminster (St George's) Bench 1935–47, Tstee Nat Portrait Gallery 1941–49, KStJ, Offr Legion Honour and Crown Italy, also Turkish, China and European War medals; *m* 1 June 1904 Mary Gertrude, JP (*d* 1 May 1973), 2nd dau of Sir Horace Alfred Damer Seymour, KCB (*see* HERTFORD, M), and *d* 20 Nov 1956, leaving:

    1 EDWARD CLIVE, **3rd Viscount**

    2 Roger Claude; *b* 16 Sept 1908; *educ* Eton and RMA; Lt-Col RA, GSO(1) Br Mil Mission Greece 1949–51; *d* unm 5 Dec 1958

    3 Ralph John; *b* 3 Aug 1913; *educ* Eton; OStJ; *m* 3 Aug 1954 Cicely Ruth, yst dau of Percy Johnson, of Douglas, IoM

    1 Elizabeth Mary; *b* 17 April 1905; *m* 5 Dec 1929 2nd Baron Ponsonby of Shulbrede (*qv*) and had issue

The 2nd VISCOUNT MERSEY's est s,

    EDWARD CLIVE BIGHAM, **3rd Viscount Mersey**; *b* 5 June 1906; *educ* Eton and Balliol Coll Oxford (BA 1927); Capt Irish Gds WW II 1940–45, memb LCC Paddington 1955–65, CC 1966 W Sussex; *m* 24 July 1933 Lady Katherine Evelyn Constance Petty-Fitzmaurice, **Lady Nairne** in her own right (*d* 20 Oct 1995), er dau of 6th Marquess of Lansdowne (*qv*), and *d* 2 Aug 1979, leaving:

    1 RICHARD MAURICE CLIVE BIGHAM, **4th and present Viscount Mersey**

    2 +David Edward Hugh [The Hon David Bigham, Hurston Place, Pulborough, W Sussex RH20 2EW]; *b* 14 April 1938; *educ* Eton; late 2nd Lt RHG, dir Tryon Gallery; *m* 2 Jan 1965 *Anthea Rosemary, est dau of Capt Leo Richard Seymour (*see* HERTFORD, M), and has:

      (1) *Charles Richard Petty; *b* 21 April 1967; *m* 18 May 1996 *Claire, dau of Col John Worthington, and has:

        1a +Caspar Patrick Ronan; *b* 5 June 1997

      (2) +Patrick David Hugh; *b* 21 Aug 1969

      (3) +James Edward Conway; *b* 12 March 1973

      (1) +Lucinda Emma (in remainder to Lordship of Nairne only); *b* 3 Nov 1965

    3 +Andrew Charles [The Hon Andrew Bigham, High Mill, Coverham, N Yorks DL8 4RN]; *b* 26 June 1941; *educ* Eton and Worcester Coll Oxford; Teacher's CertEd Lond U (1967); late 2nd Lt Irish Gds, sch master Aysgarth Sch, Bedale, Yorks 1968–89, Sunningdale Sch, Berks, 1989–94

Lineage (of Nairne): ROBERT NAIRNE, of Athurd; advocate; *m* Catherine, dau of Sir John Preston of Penicuik, Ld Pres Court of Session 1609–16, and *d* Feb 1652, leaving an est s:

ROBERT NAIRNE, **1st Lord Nairne** (S), so *cr* 27 Jan 1680/1, with remainder to heirs male of his body and in default of such to Lord George Murray (his s-in-law), yst s of the Marquess of Atholl (*see* ATHOLL, D), and future heirs begotten of him and Margaret Nairne (the **1st Lord Nairne**'s only dau) and in default of such to any other of the Marquess of Atholl's sons she might happen to marry and heirs begotten by them; *b c* 1620; advocate 1644, captured by English under Gen Monck 1651 and imprisoned as royalist Tower of London 1651–60, ktd 1661, Ld of Session Feb 1660/1, Ld Commr Justiciary 1671; *m* by 1669 Margaret (*bur* 3 May 1704), dau of Patrick Graham of Inchbraco, and *d* 30 May 1683, when the Lordship of Nairne entered into a state of suspension by reason of the later Lord's dau not yet having *m*, leaving:

MARGARET NAIRNE; *b* 16 Dec 1669; *m* between 18 Jan and 28 Feb 1690/1 Lord William Murray, who accordingly became **2nd Lord Nairne** (*b* 10 Dec 1664; served RN from *c* Jan 1683, subsequently a cavalry offr; Jacobite involved in the 1715 Rising but captured Battle of Preston 14 Nov 1715, imprisoned Tower of London and sentenced to death for high treason, also attainted and the Lordship of Nairne forfeited, he meanwhile being reprieved a bare hour before sentence was due to be carried out; *d* 3 Feb 1725/6), 4th s of 1st Marquess of Atholl by Lady Amelia Stanley, dau of 7th Earl of Derby (*qv*), and *d* 14 Nov 1747, having had, with other issue (all of whom seem to have taken the surname NAIRNE):

    1 John, *Master of Nairne*, titular Earl of Nairne, so *cr* 24 June 1721, as also Viscount Stanley (both S) by the titular James III; *b c* 1691; Lt-Col in his unc Lord Charles Murray's regt on Jacobite side 1715 Rising; along with his f captured at Preston, imprisoned in the Tower, found guilty of high treason, attainted and sentenced to death then reprieved; remained a Jacobite, holding a colonelcy of foot in a Jacobite regt 1719, assumed f's title of LORD NAIRNE 1726 on, Master St John's Masonic Lodge Dunkeld, Perthshire, 1741–48, fought as Jacobite 1745 Rising at Battles of Prestonpans, Falkirk and Culloden, again attainted, but escaped to Sweden; *m c* 3 Nov 1712 his cousin Lady Catherine Murray, dau of 1st Earl of Dunmore (*qv*), and *d* Sancerre, France, 11 July 1770, leaving, with two yst sons (*d* unm):

      (1) James; *dsp* 1737

      (2) William; *dsp* 1729 or 1730

(3) John; Ensign Regular Army 1742, Capt 1st Foot 1747, later Lt-Col, Ld Provost St Andrews by 1782; *m c* 1756 Brabazon, dau of Richard Wheeler, of Leyrath, Co Kilkenny (*see* 1934 edn WHEELER-CUFFE, Bt), and *d* 7 Nov 1782, having had:

   1a John; offr Fraser's 71st Regt; *d unm* America 1781

   2a WILLIAM MURRAY NAIRNE, as which restored by Act of Parl 17 June 1824; *b* 1757 or 1758; Maj and Assist Inspr Barracks Scotland; *m* 2 June 1806 his cousin Caroline, authoress of romantic Jacobite ballads, 3rd dau of Laurence Oliphant of Gask, titular Lord Oliphant, by Margaret, est dau of Duncan Robertson of Strowan, and *d* 9 July 1830, leaving an only s:

     1b WILLIAM MURRAY NAIRNE, **4th Lord Nairne**; *b* 1808; *d unm* 7 Dec 1837

2 ROBERT NAIRNE later MERCER; fought as a Jacobite in 1745 Rising; *m* 16 Aug 1720 Jean (*d* 1 Dec 1749), dau and heiress of Sir Laurence Mercer, of Aldie, Perthshire, and was *ka* Battle of Culloden 16 April 1746, leaving:

   (1) William, of Aldie; *m* 3 April 1762 Margaret, dau of William Murray and heiress of Pitkeathly, and *d* 19 Jan 1790, leaving an est surv dau:

     1a Jane; *m* 9 April 1787, as his 1st w, 1st and last Viscount Keith (*see* ELPHINSTONE, L) and *d* 12 Dec 1789, leaving an only dau:

       1b MARGARET, *de jure* LADY NAIRNE in her own right (the decision of the Ho of Lds of 1874 allowing her the succession occurring after her death); *s f* in his Baronies of Keith, which had been *cr* with special remainders to her, and her maternal cousin in the right to the Lordship of Nairne; *b* 12 June 1788; *m* 20 June 1817 Auguste Charles Joseph, Count de Flahault de la Billardrie, ADC to NAPOLEON and later French Amb Austria and UK, and *dspm* 11 Nov 1867, when her two Baronies expired, having had, with three other daus (*d unm*):

         1c EMILY JANE, **Lady Nairne**

         2c Georgiana Gabrielle; *m* 2 Feb 1871 Marquis de Lavalette and *dsp* 16 July 1907. He *d* 1881

MARGARET the *de jure* LADY NAIRNE's est surv dau,

EMILY JANE MERCER ELPHINSTONE De FLAHAULT, **Lady Nairne**, as which recognised by Ho Lds 4 Aug 1874; *b* 16 May 1819; *m* 1 Nov 1843 4th Marquess of Lansdowne (*qv*) and *d* 25 June 1895, leaving an est s:

HENRY CHARLES KEITH PETTY-FitzMAURICE, **7th Lord Nairne** and 5th MARQUESS OF LANSDOWNE; *b* 14 Jan 1845; *d* 3 June 1927, leaving, with other issue:

HENRY WILLIAM EDMUND PETTY-FitzMAURICE, **8th Lord Nairne** and 6th MARQUESS OF LANSDOWNE; *b* 14 Jan 1872; *d* 5 March 1936, having had, with other issue:

   1 CHARLES HOPE PETTY-FitzMAURICE, **9th Lord Nairne** and 7th MARQUESS OF LANSDOWNE; *b* 9 Jan 1917; *ka* 20 Aug 1944

   1 KATHERINE EVELYN CONSTANCE, *s* bro as **Lady Nairne** in her own right; *b* 22 June 1912; *m* 24 July 1933 3rd Viscount Mersey and *d* 20 Oct 1995, leaving issue (*see above*)

   2 +Elizabeth Mary; *b* 16 March 1927; *m* 27 June 1950 *Maj Charles William Lambton (*see* DURHAM, E) and has issue, who are in remainder to the Lordship of Nairne

MERTHYR

Arms: Sa. a lion rampant arg., over all a fess or charged with three bees volant ppr. **Crest:** An eagle displayed az., charged on the breast with a bee volant or and holding in the beak a roll of paper arg. **Supporters:** On either side a lion rampant sa., charged on the shoulder with a bezant, thereon a bee volant ppr (*see below*, however). **Mottoes:** 1 *Gwna a ddylit doed a ddel* ('Do thy duty come what may'), 2 *Hirbarhad* ('Perseverance'). **Creations:** Bt. (UK) 15 Feb 1896, B. (UK) 24 June 1911.

Trevor Oswin Lewis, CBE (1983) [Trevor Lewis Esq CBE, Hean Castle, Saundersfoots, Dyfed SA69 9AL]; *b* 29 Nov 1935; *s f* 5 April 1977 as 4th Baron Merthyr, disclaimed barony for life 26 April 1977 (hence does not use armorial supporters) and does not use btcy title; *educ* Eton and Magdalene Coll Cambridge; JP

Dyfed 1969–94; memb Countryside Commn 1973–83, dep chm 1980–83 and chm of Ctee for Wales 1973–80; *m* 18 April 1964 *Susan Jane, yr dau of Arthur John Birt-Llewellin, of Boulston Manor, Haverfordwest, Pembs, and has:

   1 +DAVID TREVOR; *b* 21 Feb 1977

   1 *Lucy Delia [The Hon Mrs Bradnam, The Old Rectory, The Street, Hullavington, Chippenham SN14 6DU]; *b* 10 April 1967; Lt RN 1987–94; *m* 1990 *Harvey John Bradnam and has:

     (1) *Benjamin Arthur John; *b* 3 Oct 1994

     (2) *James Cameron; *b* 28 Feb 1997

   2 *Elizabeth Anne; *b* 1970

   3 *Jessamy Jane; *b* 1972; *m* 1996 *Capt Charles Marcus Ross Elmhirst, Scots Gds

Lineage: THOMAS WILLIAM LEWIS, of Cwm Taf, Vaynor, Breconshire, later of Merthyr Tydfil, Glam; *b* 1765; *m* 19 Dec 1789 Gwenllian Llywelyn (*bur* 1843), and *d* 1828, having had, with other issue:

WILLIAM THOMAS LEWIS, of Merthyr Tydfil; *b* 1792; *m* 22 April 1817 Margaret (*d* 6 Feb 1854), dau of John Thomas, of The Wern, Llanybyther, Carmarths, and *d* Dec 1836, having had, with other issue:

THOMAS WILLIAM LEWIS, of Abercanaid House, Merthyr Tydfil; *b* 20 March 1818; *m* 14 Oct 1834 Mary Anne (*d* 18 May 1887), dau of Watkin John, and *d* 7 Feb 1900, leaving, with other issue:

Sir William Thomas Lewis, 1st Bt, and **1st Baron Merthyr**, of Senghenydd, Co Glamorgan (both UK), so *cr* 15 Feb 1896 and 24 June 1911 respectively, GCVO, JP (Glam, Pembs, Brecon and Mon), DL (Glam); *b* 5 Aug 1837; High Sheriff Breconshire 1884, Pres Inst of Mining Engrs, Mining Assoc of GB and S Wales Inst of Engrs, V-Pres Iron and Steel Inst and Inst of Mech Engrs, memb Cncl Inst Civ Engrs, fndr and chm Monm and S Wales Coal Assoc, S Wales Sliding Scale Ctee and S Wales Miner's Provident Fund, KGStJ, ktd 16 Dec 1885; *m* 1 March 1864 Anne (*d* 2 Oct 1902), est dau of William Rees, of Llettyshenkin, Glam, and had:

   1 HERBERT CLARK, **2nd Baron**

   2 Trevor Gwyn Elliot; *b* 4 Jan 1871; *educ* Trin Coll (MA); barrister; *m* 21 Nov 1903 Sara Winston (*d* 17 Dec 1961), only child of C C Scales, of Kentucky, USA, and *d* 19 April 1927

   1 Katharine Mary; *m* 18 Jan 1899 Most Rev Charles Alfred Howell Green (*d* 7 May 1944), DD, DCL, Archbp Wales, 74th Bp Bangor, and *d* 8 Feb 1950

   2 Annie Lucy; *d unm* 9 Sept 1951

   3 Lilian Tydfil; *d unm* 15 June 1964 aged 95

   4 Gwendolen Halliburton; *d unm* 1 Jan 1944

   5 Marie Spencer; *m* 2 June 1898 Lt-Col William Forrest (*d* 1 Nov 1921), DSO, 3rd Bn Welch Regt, of Greenwood, St Fagan's, Cardiff, and *d* 29 Aug 1951, having had issue

   6 Margaret Menelaus; *m* 18 Sept 1901 William Francis Parry de Winton (*d* 2 April 1962), of Slwch House, Brecon, and *d* 27 July 1949, leaving issue

The 1st BARON *d* 27 Aug 1914; his er son,

HERBERT CLARK LEWIS, **2nd Baron Merthyr**, JP, DL Pembs, High Sheriff Pembs 1907 and Radnorshire 1914; *educ* Clifton; civil and mining engr; *b* 3 July 1866; *m* 5 Oct 1899 Elizabeth Anna (*d* 10 May 1925), er dau of Maj-Gen Richard Short Couchman, Madras SC, and had:

   1 WILLIAM BRERETON COUCHMAN, **3rd Baron**

   1 Anne Elizabeth Mary Llewelyn; *b* 17 April 1902; *m* 30 March 1941 Brig Arthur George Hewson, MC, RHA, 2nd s of George Rawdon Maurice Hewson, DL, of Dromahaire, Co Leitrim, and *d* 7 Feb 1963, leaving issue

The 2nd BARON *d* 20 March 1932; his son,

WILLIAM BERETON COUCHMAN LEWIS, **3rd Baron Merthyr**, KBE (1969), TD, PC (1964); *b* 7 Jan 1901; *educ* Eton and Magdalen Coll Oxford (BA 1923, MA 1926); barrister Inner Temple 1927, Maj Pembroke Heavy Regt RA (TA) WW II (POW), JP (Pembs 1925), V Lt Pembs 1959 (DL 1932–59), Chm: Magistrates Assoc, Pembs QS and Dyfed-Powys Police Authority, CC Pembs 1928–39, Departmental Ctee on The Rag Flock Acts 1938, Nat Marriage Guidance Cncl 1951–57, Deptl Ctee on Hedgerow and Farm Timber 1953, RSPCA 1953–57, Constituency Delineation Commn Malaya 1954 and Nigeria 1957–58, Ctees (and Dep Speaker) Ho Lds 1957–65; memb: Roy Commn on Local Govt on Tyneside 1936, Deptl Ctee on Justices' Clerks 1938, Roy Commn on JPs 1948, Nat Parks Commr 1950–53; Pres: Roy Forestry Soc of England and Wales 1948–50, Nat Assoc Parish Cncls; V-Pres FPA, Nat Marriage Guidance Cncl, chm: Chm, Hon Treas NSPCC 1952–57, CStJ; *m* 10 Nov 1932 *Violet [The Rt Hon Violet Lady Merthyr, Churchton, Saundersfoot, Dyfed SA69 9BB], yst dau of Brig-Gen Sir Frederick Charlton Meyrick, 2nd Bt (*qv*), and *d* 5 April 1977, leaving:

   1 TREVOR OSWIN LEWIS, **briefly 4th Baron Merthyr**

   2 +Peter Herbert [Lt-Col The Hon Peter Lewis, The Old Rectory, Chilfrome, Dorchester DT2 0HA]; *b* 25 March 1937; *educ* Eton; Lt-Col 9th/12th R Lancers (PWO) (ret); *m* 26 Oct 1974 *Caroline Monica, er dau of Erik Cadogan (*see* CADOGAN, E), and has:

     (2) *Amanda Caroline; *b* 28 Aug 1977

   3 +John Frederick [The Hon John Lewis, 1 Cedar Hill, Carisbrook, IoW PO30 1DN]; *b* 30 Dec 1938; *educ* Eton and St John's Coll Cambridge; *m* 23 July 1966 *Margaret Dilys Rachel (Gretl), twin dau of Lt-Col James William Lewis-Bowen, of Dyfed, and has:

     (1) +Paul William; *b* 1979

     (1) *Deborah; *b* 1 Feb 1967

     (2) *Sarah; *b* 12 May 1968

     (3) *Hannah; *b* 1983

   4 +Robin William, OBE (1988) [The Hon Robin Lewis OBE, The Cottage, Cresswell Quay, Kilgetty, Dyfed SA68 0TE]; *b* 7 Feb 1941; *educ* Eton and Magdalen Coll Oxford; chm and md The Magstim Co Ltd, dep chm Welsh Devpt Agency, chm Nat Tst Ctee for Wales 1994–97, Gen Advsy Cncl IBA 1989–90, High Sheriff Dyfed 1987; *m* 28 April 1967 *Judith Ann, only dau of Vincent Charles Arthur Giardelli, MBE, of Carmarths, and has:

     (1) +Christopher William; *b* 6 April 1970; *m* 2 Aug 1997 *Julia, only dau of Gisilot von Rohr, of Isernhagen, Germany

     (1) *Katharine Ann; *b* 1972

5 +Antony Thomas [The Hon Antony Lewis, The Skreen, Erwood, Builth Wells, Powys LD2 3SJ]; *b* 4 June 1947; *educ* Eton; *m* 17 April 1974 *Mary Carola Melbon, yr dau of Rev Humphrey John Paine, of Fressingfield Vicarage, Diss, Norfolk

MESTON

Arms: Argent a palm tree eradicated proper, on a chief azure an eastern crown between two thistles slipped and leaved or.
Crest: An angel proper, habited argent, holding in the dexter hand a crown as in the arms. **Supporters:** Dexter, a demoiselle crane proper; sinister, a stag proper, charged on the shoulder with a saltire argent. **Motto:** *In Deo fides* (In God is my trust').
Creation: B. (UK) 29 Nov 1919.

THE 3RD BARON MESTON, of Agra and of Dunottar, Co Kincardine (James Meston, QC (1996)) [The Rt Hon The Lord Meston QC, Queen Elizabeth Building, Temple, London EC4Y 9BS]; *b* 10 Feb 1950; *s f* 1984; *educ* Wellington, St Catharine's Coll Cambridge (MA) and Leicester U (LLM); barrister Middle Temple 1973, jr counsel Queen's Proctor 1992–96, Recorder 1997–; *m* 20 April 1974 *(Jean Rebecca) Anne, yr dau of John Carder, of Stud Farm House, Chalvington, Sussex, and has:

1 +THOMAS JAMES DOUGALL; *b* 21 Oct 1977; *educ* Eton and Edinburgh U
1 *Laura Anne Rose; *b* 1980
2 *Elspeth Mary; *b* 1988

Lineage: JAMES MESTON, of Oldmacher, Aberdeenshire; *m* Jane Greig (*d* 1901), 3rd dau of James Scorgie, of Aberdeen, and had:

JAMES SCORGIE MESTON, 1st Baron Meston, of Agra and Dunottar, Co Kincardine (UK), so *cr* 29 Nov 1919, KCSI (1911, CSI 1908), VD (1914); *b* 12 June 1865; *educ* King's Coll Aberdeen and Balliol Coll Oxford; joined ICS 1883, Fin Sec Govt Utd Provinces 1899–1903, advsr Govts Cape Colony and Transvaal on CS Reform 1904–06, Sec Finance Dept Govt India 1906–12, T/Fin Memb Cncl Govr-Gen India 1908, memb Imp Legislative Cncl 1909, Lt-Govr UP Agra and Oudh 1912–18, rep India Imp War Cabinet and Conf 1917, Fin Memb Cncl Govr-Gen 1918–19, Hon Fell UCL, Chllr Aberdeen U 1928–43, V-Chm Supervisory Commn League Nations Geneva, KGStJ, Hon LLD Aberdeen and Edin, Hon MD Zurich, FRGS, FRSL, Freedom Cities London 1917, Manchester 1917 and Aberdeen 1935; *m* 10 Dec 1891 Jeanie, CBE, DGStJ (*d* 23 Dec 1946), only dau of James McDonald, of Mossat, Aberdeenshire, and *d* 7 Oct 1943, leaving:

1 DOUGALL MESTON, 2nd Baron Meston; *b* 17 Dec 1894; *educ* Charterhouse and RMA Woolwich; barrister Lincoln's Inn 1924, Capt RA WW I, Afghan War 1919 and Waziristan 1919–20, Hon Memb IAAS; *m* 12 July 1947 *Diana Mary Came [The Rt Hon Diana Lady Staplehurst, High St, Mistley, Essex CO11 1HD], only dau of Capt Otto Sigismund Doll, ARIBA, of Chelsea, and *d* 2 Jan 1984, leaving:

(1) JAMES MESTON, 3rd and present Baron Meston
(2) +William Dougall [The Hon William Meston, 11 The Green, Mistley, Essex CO11 1EU]; *b* 17 May 1953; *educ* Wellington; *m* *Elizabeth, yst dau of Dr Peter Dawes, of Mayfair and Mijas, Spain, and has:

1a +Dougall William; *b* 1985
2a +Felix Peter; *b* 1987
1a *Louise Elizabeth Joan; *b* 29 March 1996

METHUEN

Arms: Argent three wolf heads erased proper, borne on the breast of an imperial eagle with two heads displayed sable. **Supporters:** On either side two fiery lynxes regardant proper, collared and lined or.
Motto: *Virtus invidiæ scopus* ('Virtue is the target of envy').
Creation: B. (UK) 13 July 1838.

THE 7TH BARON METHUEN OF CORSHAM, Co Wilts (Robert Alexander Holt Methuen) [The Rt Hon The Lord Methuen, Knobb Hall, Two Dales, Matlock, Derbys DE4]; *b* 22 July 1931; *s bro* 1994; *educ* Shrewsbury and Trin Coll Cambridge; electrical engr, with Rolls-Royce to 1994; *m* 1st 10 May 1958 (*divorce* 1993) Mary Catherine Jane, only dau of Ven Charles German Hooper, Archdeacon Ipswich; *m* 2nd 1994 *Margrit Andrea, dau of Friedrich Karl Ernst Hadwiger, of Vienna, and by his 1st w has:

1 *Charlotte Mary; *b* 15 Feb 1964
2 *Henrietta Christian; *b* 15 Oct 1965; *m* 1990 *Robert Llewelyn JONES later METHUEN-JONES, er s of D L Jones, of Reigate, Surrey, and has:

(1) *Teresa Mary; *b* 1990
(2) *Keziah Lynne; *b* 1992
(3) *Miriam Lucy; *b* 1997

Lineage: The METHUENs or METHVENs allegedly took their name from the territorial Barony of Methven, Perthshire.

JOHN METHUEN/METHVEN; Scots Protestant; migrated to England; had:

Rev PAUL METHUEN; Preb Wells; *m* Ann Rogers (*bur* 7 June 1610), of Cannington, Somerset, and *d* by 23 Jan 1606/7, leaving:

Rev ANTHONY METHUEN; *b* 1575; *educ* Queen's Coll (BA 1599) and St Edmund Hall (MA 1601, BD 1609) Oxford; Canon Lichfield, Vicar Frome Selwood, Rector Lamyat, Somerset, 1614; *m* Jane (*d* 2 March 1640/1), dau and heir of Thomas Taylor, of Bristol, and *d* 6 July 1640, having had:

1 PAUL
2 Anthony (Rev); Canon Wells, Rector Lamyat, Preb Bath and Wells; *b* 1601; *educ* Oxford (BA 1621, MA 1624); *m* Marian — and had issue
3 Francis; *m* Dorothy — and had issue

The est s,

PAUL METHUEN, of Bradford and Bishop's Cannings, Wilts; clothier; *m* 1st Sarah —; *m* 2nd *c* 1650 Grace, dau of John Ashe, of Freshford, Somerset, and *d* 1667, having had, with other issue (*dsp*):

1 John, PC; *b c* 1650; ancestor in the female line of the Methuen Bts (*see* 1924 edn); *educ* St Edmund Hall Oxford 1665; barrister Inner Temple 1674, Master Chancery 1685, MP Devizes 1690–1705, Envoy Portugal 1691 and 1702, Ld Chllr Ireland 1697–1703, Amb Extrdy Portugal 1703, concluded Methuen Treaty 1703, which one commentator suggested had as its chief effect the drinking by Englishmen of dear port instead of cheap claret; *m c* 16 Feb 1671/2 Mary, clothier, dau of Seacole Chivers (*d* 1723), of Comerford, Wilts, and *d* 13 July 1706, having had, with other issue (*d* young or unm):

(1) Paul (Sir), KB (1725), PC (1714); *b* 1672; Dip Serv from 1690, Envoy Portugal 1697–1705, Min Turin 1705, Amb Portugal 1706–08, MP Devizes 1708–10 and Brackley 1713–47, Ld Admlty 1709 and Treasury 1714–17, Amb Spain and Morocco 1714, Sec State 1716, Comptroller Household 1720 and Treasurer 1725–30; *d* unm 11 April 1757; Methuen, Mass, N America, was named after him

2 Anthony, of Bradford-on-Avon; *b c* 1651; *m* 17 April 1683 Gertrude (*d* 20 July 1699), dau and coheir of Thomas Moore, of Spargrove, Somerset, and Elizabeth, er dau of Sir John Bampfield, Bt (*see* POLTIMORE, B), and *d* 10 May 1717, leaving:

(1) Thomas, of Bradford-on-Avon; *m c* 20 May 1720 Anne (*b* 1696; *d* 15 May 1733), dau and sole heir of Isaac Selfe, of Benacre, Wilts, by Penelope, dau of 2nd Baron Lucas of Shenfield (*see* LUCAS OF CRUDWELL, B), and *d* 2 Jan 1737/8, leaving:

1a Paul, of Corsham, Wilts (which he inherited from his cousin Rt Hon Sir Paul Methuen); *b* 16 May 1723; *educ* Winchester; MP Warwick 1762 and 1768 and Gt Bedwin 1774 and 1780; *m* 25 June 1749 Christian (*b* 1723; *d* 21

May 1779), dau and coheir of Sir George Cobb, 3rd and last Bt, of Adderbury, and *d* 22 Jan 1795, having had:

  1b PAUL COBB

  2b Thomas; *b* 2 Feb 1754; *educ* Winchester; *d* 27 April 1774

  1b Christian; *m* 15 May 1755 2nd Baron Boston (*qv*) and *d* 9 May 1832, leaving issue

PAUL METHUEN's er s,

PAUL COBB METHUEN, of Corsham; *b* 15 June 1752; *educ* Winchester; MP Gt Bedwin 1781, Sheriff Wilts 1780; *m* 20 April 1776 Matilda (*b* 28 April 1754; *d* 6 Dec 1826), dau of Sir Thomas Gooch, 3rd Bt (*qv*), of Benacre, Suffolk, and *d* 14 Sept 1816, having had:

  1 PAUL, **1st Baron**

  2 Thomas Anthony (Rev); *b* 23 May 1781; *educ* Eton; Rector All Cannings, Wilts, 1809; *m* 5 June 1810 Eliza Maria (*d* 16 April 1835), est dau of Rev Henry Plumptre, and *d* 15 June 1869, leaving issue

  3 Charles Lucas; *b* 11 June 1791; Capt; *d* unm 1826

  4 John Andrew (Rev); *b* 25 Aug 1794; *educ* Ch Ch Oxford (BA 1817, MA 1826); Vicar Corsham, Wilts; *m* 25 June 1822 Louisa (*d* 18 May 1871), dau of John Fuller, of Neston Park (*see* FULLER, Bt), and *dsps* 19 June 1869

  1 Matilda; *m* 10 May 1804 3rd Baron Walsingham (*qv*) and *d* 26 April 1831

  2 Gertrude; *m* 11 April 1815, as his 2nd w, Lord Edward O'Brien (*see* INCHIQUIN, B) and *d* 1 May 1817, leaving issue

  3 Catherine; *m* 2 April 1818 John Pemberton Plumptre (*d* 7 Jan 1864), MP Fredvile, Kent, and *d* 2 Dec 1886 aged 98, leaving issue

  4 Cecilia Penelope; *m* 24 Aug 1822 Rev Hon Francis J Noel and *d* 27 June 1885 aged 87, leaving issue (*see* GAINSBOROUGH, E)

PAUL METHUEN's est s,

PAUL METHUEN, **1st Baron Methuen of Corsham**, Co Wilts (UK), so *cr* 13 July 1838; *b* 21 June 1779; *educ* Eton and Ch Ch Oxford; MP (Whig) Wilts 1812–19 and N Wilts 1833–37, High Sheriff Wilts 1833–32; *m* 31 July 1810 Jane Dorothea (*b* 11 April 1788, *d* 15 March 1846), est dau of Sir Henry Paulet St John Mildmay, 3rd Bt, MP (*see* 1970 edn), and *d* 11 Sept 1849, having had:

  1 Paul Mildmay; *b* 31 Jan 1814; *educ* Eton; Dip Serv; *d* unm 16 July 1837 *en poste* in Russia

  2 FREDERICK HENRY PAUL, **2nd Baron**

  3 St John George Paul, of Shaftesbury House, Weston-super-Mare; *b* 23 Nov 1819; *m* 12 Sept 1854 Anne (*d* 26 Nov 1923), dau of Preb William Thomas Sergison, Rector Slaugham, Sussex, and *d* 17 June 1899, having had:

    (1) St John Frederick Charles (Rev); *b* 27 July 1862; *educ* Sherborne and Pembroke Coll Cambridge (BA 1884); Rector Vange Essex 1897–1930; *m* 1st 19 Jan 1892 Louisa Elizabeth (*d* 7 Jan 1933), dau of Maj-Gen James Hyde Champion; *m* 2nd 3 Dec 1940 Millicent Emma Fosket (*d* 1970), dau of Samuel George Wittey, of The Abbey, Penzance, Cornwall, and *d* 1 June 1953, having by his 1st w had:

      1a St John Arthur Paul; *b* 19 Nov 1892; served FA 1st Contingent; *ka* 20 July 1918

      2a Charles Leslie, MCG 1919; *b* 4 March 1901; RAF 1922, F/Lt WW II; *d* unm 20 Aug 1967

      1a Margaret Dorothea; *b* 17 May 1894

      2a Kathleen Louisa Mildmay; *b* 25 Aug 1896

      3a Frances Mary Hyde; *b* 29 July 1899; *d* unm 26 July 1970

      4a Beatrice Ethel Gertrude; *b* 28 April 1905

    (1) Janette Catherine Kemeys; *d* unm 4 June 1947

    (2) Annie Mildmay; *d* unm 29 May 1938

    (3) Mary Georgiana; *m* 10 Aug 1893 Rev Canon Leonard Hugh Evans, Rector Smarden, Kent, s of Rev H Evans, Vicar Scremerton, Berwick-on-Tweed, and *d* Nov 1945, having had issue

    (4) Lucy Charlotte; *d* 2 Oct 1863

  1 Jane Matilda; *b* 1816; *m* 1 Dec 1849 David Lewis (*d* 23 Jan 1895) and *d* 9 Aug 1881

The 1st BARON's 2nd s,

FREDERICK HENRY PAUL METHUEN, **2nd Baron Methuen of Corsham**, JP, DL; *b* 23 Feb 1818; *educ* Harrow and RMA Woolwich; army offr to 1842, Militia ADC to HM QUEEN VICTORIA 1860–91, Ld-in-Waiting (Lib) 1859–66, 1868–74, 1880–85 and Feb–Aug 1886, Hon Col 3rd Bn Wilts Regt; *m* 14 Oct 1844 Anna Horatia Caroline (*b* 1824, *d* 3 March 1899), only child of Rev John Sanford, of Nynehead, and *d* 26 Sept 1891, having had, with other issue:

  1 PAUL SANFORD, **3rd Baron**

  2 Frederick George Paul; *b* 10 Dec 1851; *d* July 1931

  1 Georgiana Horatia Sanford; *b* 9 July 1846; *d* 3 July 1926

  2 Jane Charlotte; *b* Nov 1847; *m* 18 Oct 1870 Col Hon Richard Southwell Stapleton-Cotton (*d* 24 Nov 1925), s of 2nd Viscount Combermere (*qv*), and *d* 10 Aug 1924, leaving issue

The 2nd BARON's est s,

PAUL SANFORD METHUEN, **3rd Baron Mehtuen of Corsham**, GCB (1902, KCB 1900, CB 1882), GCMG (1919, CMG 1886), GCVO (1910, KCVO 1897), JP, DL; *b* 1 Sept 1845; *educ* Eton; served Gold Coast 1873, Ashanti War 1874 (medal with clasps), Assist Mil Sec to C-in-C Ireland 1877, Lt-Col Scots Gds 1876–81 (Col 1904), Maj-Gen 1890, Lt-Gen 1898, Gen 1904, Mil Attaché Berlin 1877–80, QMG Home Dist 1881–84, Commandant Egypt Expdn 1882 (mentioned despatches, medal with clasp, Osmanieh 3rd Cl and Khedive's Star), Bechuanaland 1885, DAG S Africa 1888–91, OC Home Dist 1892–97, Afridi Expdn 1897, NW Frontier 1897–98 and Boer War 1899–1902 (despatches), GOC Eastern Cmd 1904–08 and S Africa 1908–12, FM 1911, Govr and C-in-C Malta 1915–19, Constable Tower 1920, Hon Col 3rd Bn Wilts Regt, KGStJ, Grand Offr Order Crown Italy, Grand Cross Legion Honour, Hon LLD Malta; *m* 1st 18 June 1878 Evelyn (*dsp* 2 June 1879), dau of Sir Frederick Bathurst, 3rd Bt (*see* 1949 edn); *m* 2nd 9 Jan 1884 Mary Ethel, CBE (*d* 11 May 1941), dau of William Ayshford Sanford by Sarah Ellen (dau of Henry Seymour of Knoyle House, Wilts), and *d* 30 Oct 1932, having had:

1 PAUL AYSHFORD METHUEN, **4th Baron Methuen of Corsham**; *b* 29 Sept 1886; *educ* Eton and New Coll Oxford (BA 1910, MA 1914); RA 1959 (ARA 1951), RWS, PRWA, FSA, Hon ARIBA, painter and zoologist, Assist Transvaal Museum Pretoria 1910–14, Livestock and Marketing Offr Min Ag 1924–31, Dip Ag 1920, Maj Scots Gds (SR) WW I and WW II 1940–45 as Staff Capt London Dist, AEF, Memb Roy Fine Art Commn, Tstee: Nat Gallery 1938–45 and Tate Gallery 1940–45, Chev Legion Honour, author *Normandy Diary* (1952), Hon LLD Bristol; *m* 6 July 1915 Eleanor (Norah) (*d* 17 Dec 1958), dau of William John Hennessy, of Rudgwick, Sussex, and *dsp* 7 Jan 1974

2 ANTHONY PAUL METHUEN, **5th Baron**

3 Laurence Paul METHUEN later METHUEN-CAMPBELL still later METHUEN again (deed poll June 1969), JP (Argyll 1943); *b* 18 Sept 1898; *educ* privately and Magdalene Coll Cambridge; memb Roy Co Archers, Lt Res Offrs Scots Gds, ADC to GOC Malta 1918; *m* 1st 23 Feb 1927 Hon Olive Douglas Campbell (*b* 1896, *d* 8 March 1949), only child of 4th Baron Blythswood, KCVO (*see* 1940 edn), and *d* 1970, having had:

  (1) Christopher Paul Mansel Campbell; *b* 23 March 1928; *educ* Eton and Magdalene Coll Cambridge; Scots Gds 1945–48, High Sheriff Glamorgan 1971; *m* 1st 31 Oct 1950 (*divorce* 1973) Oona Cicely, only dau of John Dalrymple Winn Treherne (*see* SLIGO, M), of Otley High House, Otley, Suffolk, and had:

    1a +JAMES PAUL ARCHIBALD [James Methuen-Campbell Esq, Corsham Court, Corsham, Wilts SN13 0BF]; *b* 25 Oct 1952; heir presumptive; *educ* Stowe

    1a *Joanna Olive [Mrs Edward Martin, Oak Tree Farm, Finborough Rd, Hitcham, Suffolk IP7 7LS]; *b* 9 Sept 1951; *educ* Cobham Hall, Bristol U (BA 1974) and Darwin Coll Cambridge (PhD 1978); genealogist and historian; *m* 9 July 1977 *Edward Ashley Martin

    2a *Lucinda Sheelah; *b* 28 Feb 1959; *educ* Cobham Hall Kent and Swansea U; has:

      1b *Poppy Evelyn; *b* 23 May 1984

    3a *Catherine Alice Mansel; *b* 12 Oct 1965; *educ* Ipswich High Sch and has:

      1b *Gulliver James; *b* 29 Sept 1985

      2b *Orlando David; *b* 1 Nov 1988

      3b *Alexander; *b* 8 May 1991

  (1) (cont.) Christopher Methuen-Campbell *m* 2nd 28 Nov 1975 *Judith Anne [Mrs Christopher Methuen-Campbell, Penrice Castle, Reynoldston, Swansea SA3 1LN], only dau of Joseph Crowther and formerly w of David Basset, and *d* 8 Jan 1998, leaving by her:

    2a +Thomas Rice Mansel; *b* 4 March 1977; *educ* Eton and Peterhouse Cambridge

  (2) +David Archibald James [David Methuen-Campbell Esq, 45 Redcliffe Rd, London SW10; Stembridge Cottage, Reynoldston, Swansea, Glam]; *b* 23 Aug 1929; *educ* Eton; painter; *m* 1978 *Elizabeth Ann, dau of James Fletcher Martin, of Egdon Cottage, Swanage, Dorset

  (1) *Diana Evelyn [Lady McNair-Wilson, 5 Kelso Place, London W8; Godfreys Farm, Beaulieu, Hants]; *b* 25 July 1932; *m* 11 April 1953 *Sir Patrick Michael Ernest David McNair-Wilson, MP New Forest 1968–97, er s of Robert McNair-Wilson, MB, ChB, of Broadley House, Sway, and has:

    1a *Guy Patrick Adam Campbell; *b* 20 March 1968

    1a *Jennifer Jean; *b* 26 Jan 1954

    2a *Arabella Jane Campbell [Mrs Nicholas Ashley, Flat 8, 50 Cornwall Gdns, London SW7; *b* 23 Jan 1959; *m* 1984 *(David) Nicholas Ashley, s of Sir Bernard Albert Ashley

    3a *Patricia Ann Campbell; *b* 20 Jan 1964

    4a *Kate Campbell; *b* 16 April 1974

  (2) *Daphne Mary Jean; *b* 29 Sept 1935; *m* 22 Feb 1957 *Hon Cecil Towry Henry Law, yr s of 7th Baron Ellenborough (*qv*), and has issue

3 (cont.) Laurence Methuen *m* 2nd 11 Dec 1950 Lady Maureen Margaret Brabazon (*d* 2 April 1980), er dau of 13th Earl of Meath (*qv*), and *d* 18 April 1970, having by her had:

  (3) *Caroline Aileen [Mrs Charles Fox, Tredrea Barn, Perranarworthal, Cornwall TR3 7QE]; *b* 27 Sept 1952; took by deed poll 1969 name METHUEN; *m* 1988 *Charles Lloyd Fox, 2nd s of Philip Hamilton Fox, of Glendurgan, Falmouth, Cornwall, and has:

    1a *Meriel Sophia; *b* 25 May 1990

    2a *Stella Caroline; *b* 11 March 1992

    3a *Roselle Viola; *b* 6 Nov 1994

1 Ethel Christian; *b* 7 March 1889; *m* 15 May 1915 Hon Geoffrey William Algernon Howard (*d* 20 June 1935), s of 9th Earl of Carlisle (*qv*), and *d* 26 April 1932, leaving issue

2 Ellen Seymour; *b* 23 Nov 1893; *m* 1 Nov 1924 Capt Cyril Gwynne Sedley Barnes (*d* 22 Dec 1954), s of Robert Barnes, of Harley St, London W1, and had issue

The 4th BARON's bro,

ANTHONY PAUL METHUEN, **5th Baron Methuen of Corsham**; *b* 26 June 1891; *educ* Wellington and New Coll Oxford; Capt Scots Gds (SR) WW I 1916–18 (wounded), chartered architect; *m* 22 July 1920 Grace Durning, JP (Wilts 1942) (*d* 7 Aug 1972 aged 74), est dau of Sir Richard Durning Holt, 1st Bt (*see* 1940 edn), and *d* 21 June 1975, having had:

  1 Anthony Richard Paul; *b* 14 May 1923; *d* 8 Dec 1934

  2 ANTHONY JOHN METHUEN, **6th Baron Methuen of Corsham**; *b* 26 Oct 1925; *educ* Winchester and RAC Cirencester; served Scots Gds and Roy Signals 1943–47, lands offr Air Min 1951–62, QALAS 1954, ARICS; *d* unm 24 Aug 1994

3 ROBERT ALEXANDER HOLT METHUEN, **7th and present Baron Methuen of Corsham**

1 *Elizabeth Penelope [The Hon Mrs Fraser, Southbank House, Lacock Rd, Corsham, Wilts SN13 9HS]; *b* 4 July 1928; *m* 8 Dec 1956 *Malcolm Henry Alastair Fraser, er s of (Hugh) Alastair Hamilton Fraser, JP, of Mill Place, Stanton Drew, Somerset and has:

  (1) *Elizabeth Mary Alexandra; *b* 16 Oct 1957; *m* 23 Oct 1982 *Mark Geoffrey Sewell, 2nd s of Geoffrey Sewell, of Tysoe Manor, Warwicks, and has:

1a *Emma Lucy Alexandra; *b* 6 Sept 1985

2a *Rosanna Mary Alice; *b* 27 Oct 1988

3a *Lucinda Charlotte Anne; *b* 21 Sept 1993

(2) *Anne Catriona Hamilton; *b* 12 July 1961; *m* 31 May 1997 *William May Somerville, only s of Michael May Somerville, of Lamerhooe, Devon

Seat: Corsham Court, Corsham, Wilts. One Thomas Smythe built the manor house at Corsham in the local honey-coloured stone in 1582. The existing south face, stable block and riding school remain from that time. Fifteen years after Paul Methuen bought the place in the mid-18th century he employed 'Capability' Brown to alter the house as well as lay out the grounds. The result was the present east wing, the gem of which is the the picture gallery, with window seats by Chippendale, a plaster ceiling originally designed for Burton Constable, Yorks, and crimson silk wall coverings. At the end of the century the north front and entrance were gothicised by Nash, though this part of the house was later remodelled by Thomas Bellamy in 1845 and little of the original Nash work remains. Humphrey Repton was also involved in landscaping the grounds.

MEXBOROUGH

Arms: Arg. on a bend sa. three owls of the field. **Crest:** An owl as in the arms. **Supporters:** Two lions ppr., collared and chained or. **Motto:** Be fast. **Creations:** B. (I) 8 Nov 1753, E. and V. (I) 11 Feb 1766.

THE 8TH EARL OF MEXBOROUGH OF LIFFORD, Co Donegal, **Viscount Pollington of Ferns** and **Baron Pollington of Longford**, Co Longford (John Christopher George Savile) [The Rt Hon The Earl of Mexborough, 14 Lennox Gdns Mews, London SW1X ODP; Arden Hall, Hawnby, Yorks YO6 5LS]; *b* 16 May 1931; *s f* 1980; *educ* Eton and Worcester Coll Oxford; late 2nd Lt Gren Gds; *m* 1st 30 May 1958 (*divorce*1972) Lady Elizabeth Hariot Grimston (*d* 1987), est dau of 6th Earl of Verulam (*qv*), and has had:

1 +JOHN ANDREW BRUCE, *Viscount Pollington*; *b* 30 Nov 1959

1 Alethea Frances Clare; *b* 3 June 1963; *d* 16 Sept 1994

The 8th EARL *m* 2nd 5 June 1972 *Catherine Joyce, yst dau of James Kenneth Hope, CBE, DL, LMA, of West Park, Lanchester, Co Durham, and formerly w of Lt-Col Hon Nicholas Crespigny Vivian (*see* VIVIAN, B), and by her has:

2 +James Hugh Hope John; *b* 21 Aug 1976

2 *Lucinda Sarah Catherine; *b* 3 April 1973

Lineage: Sir JOHN SAVILE, of Savile Hall, Yorks; *m* —, dau of Sir Simon de Rockley, and had:

Sir JOHN SAVILE, of El(l)and, Yorks; Sheriff Yorks 1380 and 1388, MP Yorks 1384–85; had a yst s:

HENRY SAVILE; *m* Elizabeth, dau and heiress of Simon Thornhill, of Thornhill, and had, with a dau (Jennett):

1 Thomas (Sir), of Thornhill; MP Yorks *temp* HENRY IV; ancestor of the Saville [*sic*] Marquesses of Halifax

2 Henry; *m c* 1403 Helen, dau and heiress of Thomas Copley, of Copley, Yorks, and had, with other issue:

(1) John (Sir); ancestor of:

1a John, of Copley, Yorks; *m* Anne, dau of Sir George Palmer, of Naburn, Yorks, and *d c* 1644, leaving:

1b Sir JOHN SAVILE, 1st and last Bt (E), so *cr* 24 July 1662; *b c* 1640; *m* by 1663 Mary, dau of Clement Paston, of Barningham, Norfolk, and *dspm* 1689, when the btcy expired, leaving:

1c Elizabeth Mary; *b c* 1663; *m* Lord Thomas Howard and had:

1d THOMAS HOWARD, 8th DUKE OF NORFOLK (*qv*)

(2) Thomas, of Hullinedge, Elland, Yorks; *m* Anne, dau of John Stansfield, and had, with three er sons:

2a Nicholas, of New Hall, Yorks; *m* Margaret/Margery, dau of William Wilkinson, and had, with other issue:

1b John, of New Hall; *m* Margery, dau of John Gleadhill, and had, with two est sons, a yst son and four daus:

1c Henry, of Bradley Hall, nr Halifax; *m* Elizabeth/Ellen, dau of Robert Ramsden, and had, with five daus:

1d JOHN (Sir), for whom *see* further below

2d Henry (Sir); *b* 30 Nov 1549; Warden Merton Coll Oxford, Provost Eton 1596; tutored ELIZABETH I in Greek, Envoy to Low Countries, ktd 1604; *m* Margaret, dau of George Dacres, of Cheshunt, Herts, and *dspms* 19 Feb 1621/2, leaving:

1e Elizabeth; *m* 1613 Sir John Sedley, 2nd Bt, of Aylesford, Kent, and had, with two er sons:

1f Sir Charles Sedley, 5th Bt, of Southfield, Kent; *b c* 1640; *m* 23 Feb 1657 Lady Catharine Savage, dau of John, Earl Rivers, and *dspml* 20 Aug 1701, when the btcy expired, having had:

1g CATHERINE SEDLEY, COUNTESS OF DORCHESTER, Co Dorset, so *cr* 20 Jan 1685/6, as also BARONESS OF DARLINGTON, Co Durham (both E), both in her own right but for life only; *b* 21 Dec 1657; mistress of JAMES II, by whom she had, with other issue (*d* young):

1h Catherine, styled 'Lady Catherine Darnley'; *b* 1681; *m* 1st 28 Oct 1699 (*divorce* 12 June 1701) James Annesley, 3rd Earl of Anglesey of the 1661 *cr* (*see* VALENTIA, V), and had:

1i Catherine; *m* William Phipps and had issue (*see* NORMANBY, M)

1h (cont.) Catherine Countess of Anglesey *m* 2nd 16 March 1705/6 1st Duke of the County of Buckingham and of Normanby (*see* SHEFFIELD, Bt), and *d* 17 March 1743, having had further issue

1g (cont.) The COUNTESS OF DORCHESTER *m c* Aug 1696 1st Earl of Portmore and *d* 26 Oct 1717, leaving:

1h CHARLES COLYEAR, 2nd EARL OF PORTMORE

HENRY SAVILE's est son,

Sir JOHN SAVILE, of Bradley Hall, Yorks; MP Newton 1572–83, Baron Exchequer 1598–1606; *m* 1st Jane, dau of Richard Garth, of Morden, Surrey, and had:

1 Sir HENRY SAVILE, 1st and last Bt (E), so *cr* 29 June 1611, of Methley Hall, Yorks; *b* 1579; ktd 1603, MP Aldborough 1604–11 and York 1629; *m* Mary (*m* 2nd 23 Sept 1634 Sir William Sheffield), dau and coheir of John Dent, of London, and *dsps* 23 June 1632, when the btcy expired

1 Jane; *m* Sir Henry Goodrich, of Ribston, Yorks

2 Elizabeth; *m* Sir John Jackson, of Hickleton, Yorks

Sir JOHN *m* 2nd Elizabeth, dau of Thomas Wentworth, of Elmshall, Yorks, and widow of Richard Tempest, of Bowling, and by her had issue; *m* 3rd Dorothy, dau of 1st Lord (Baron) Wentworth of the 1529 *cr* (*see* LYTTON, E) and widow of (a) Sir Paul Widmerpool/Withypoole and (b) Sir Martin Frobisher; *m* 4th Margery, dau of Ambrose Peake and widow of Sir Jerome Weston, and *d* 2 Feb 1606/7; his s by his 2nd w:

2 John, of Methley Hall; *m* 1st Mary, dau of John Robinson, of Ryther; *m* 2nd Margaret, dau of Sir Henry Garraway, Ld Mayor London, and *d* 1651, having by her had issue:

(1) JOHN

(1) Margaret; *m* Sir William Ingleby, 2nd Bt, of Ripley (*see* 1854 edn), and *d* 9 Nov 1697, leaving issue

(2) Elizabeth; *m* Leonard Wastell

(3) Catherine; *m* 1st April 1657 Sir William Cholmley, 2nd Bt, of Whitby; *m* 2nd 1665 Sir Nicholas Strode, of Chipsted House, Kent, and *d* 1710

(4) Dorothy; *b* 1 May 1647; *m* 15 Sept 1663 John Clavering, est s of Sir James Clavering, 1st Bt, and had issue

JOHN SAVILE's son,

JOHN SAVILE, of Methley Hall and Thrybergh; *b* 1644; *m* Sarah, dau of Peter Tryon, of Harringworth, and Bulwich, Northants, and had:

1 John; *m* Mary (*d* Nov 1740), dau and coheir of Sir John Banks, Bt, of Aylesford, Kent, and *dvp* 1717, having had, with two sons:

(1) Elizabeth; inherited Thrybergh; *m* 30 April 1726 John, yr s of 1st Earl of Aylesford (*qv*)

2 Charles, of Methley Hall; *b* 1676; *m* Alathea (*d* 24 June 1759), dau and coheir of Gilbert Millington, of Felley Priory, Notts, and *d* 5 June 1741, having had:

(1) JOHN, **1st Earl**

3 James, of Wakefield; had an only dau and heiress (Sarah, *m* Rev Joseph Leech)

4 Samuel, of Darrington, Yorks; had an only dau and heiress (Sarah, *m* William Sotherton)

1 Sarah; *m* 12 April 1692 Sir Thomas Slingsby, 4th Bt, of Scriven (*see* 1869 edn)

JOHN SAVILE's gs,

JOHN SAVILE, **1st Earl of Mexborough of Lifford**, Co Donegal, so *cr* 11 Feb 1766, as also VISCOUNT POLLINGTON OF FERNS and earlier 8 Nov 1753 BARON POLLINGTON OF LONGFORD, Co Longford (all I), KB (1749); *b* Dec 1719; MP (Whig) Heydon 1747–54 and Shoreham 1761–68; *m* 20 Jan 1760 Sarah (*m* 2nd 4 May 1780 Rev Sandford Hardcastle and *d* 9 Aug 1821), dau of Francis Blake Delaval and sis of 1st Baron Delaval of Seaton Delaval (*see also* HASTINGS, B), and *d* 17 Feb 1778, leaving, with two yr sons (Henry, *b* 17 Sept 1763, *d* 1828; Charles, *b* 27 April 1774, *m* 27 Aug 1803 Annabella Wilson, *dsp* 18 Feb 1807):

JOHN SAVILE, **2nd Earl of Mexborough**; *b* 8 April 1761; MP (Tory) Lincoln 1808–12; *m* 30 Sept 1782 Elizabeth (*d* 7 June 1821), only dau and heiress of Henry Stephenson, of E Burnham, Bucks, and Cox Lodge, nr Newcastle-on-Tyne, and *d* 3 Feb 1830, having had, with a dau (Sarah Elizabeth, *m* 1st 30 Oct 1807 4th Baron Monson (*qv*), *m* 2nd 21 Oct 1816 3rd Earl of Warwick (*see* WARWICK, BROOKE and, E) and *d* 30 Jan 1851):

JOHN SAVILE, **3rd Earl of Mexborough**; *b* 3 July 1783; *educ* Eton and Trin Coll Cambridge; MP (Tory) Pontefract 1807–26 and 1831–32; *m* 20 Aug 1807 Anne (*d* 17 July 1870), est dau of 3rd Earl of Hardwicke (*qv*), and had:

1 JOHN CHARLES GEORGE, **4th Earl**

2 Henry Alexander; *b* 12 Dec 1811; Army Offr; *m* 17 Aug 1840 Catherine (*d* 1 Jan 1843), 3rd dau of Kingsmill Pennefather, of New Park, Co Tipperary, and *d* 1 March 1850, leaving:

(1) William, DL (Cards); *b* 8 Oct 1841; Capt 9th Lancers; *m* 12 June 1865 Emily (*d* 28 Jan 1909), dau of Capt Delme Seymour Davies, of Highmead, Cards, and *d* 4 April 1903, leaving:

1a John Herbert Drax; *b* 29 March 1866; *d* 2 Oct 1912

1a Beatrice Anne Louisa; *m* 11 June 1908 Francis Henry Tristram Jervoise, TD, JP, DL, FSA (*d* 27 May 1959), of Herriard Park, Basingstoke, Hants, and 13 Hertford St, London W1, and *dsp* 26 Oct 1944

3 Philip Yorke (Rev); *b* 23 Aug 1814; Rector Methley, Yorks, MA Cantab; *m* 20 Jan 1842 Emily Mary Brand (*d* 9 Aug 1881), est dau of William Hale, of King's Walden, Herts, and *d* 23 July 1897, having had, with other issue:

(1) George; *b* 26 April 1847; *m* 1 June 1876 Charlotte Maria (*d* 13 May 1879), 2nd dau of Henry Baker, of Stoke, Devon, and gdau of Adml Sir Henry Leake, KCB, and *d* 4 Sept 1904, leaving:

1a Beatrice Mary; *b* 3 June 1877; *m* 3 July 1897 George Lowsley-Williams (*d* 1 Sept 1937), of Tetbury, Glos, and *d* 18 Oct 1952, leaving issue (*see* MAKINS, Bt)

(2) Henry William; *b* 9 March 1850; Cdr RN; *d* 8 Jan 1932

(3) William Hale (Rev); *b* 31 Dec 1859; Rector St Swithun, Winchester; *m* 21 July 1888 Mabel (*d* 16 July 1947), only dau of Maj Count (of HRE) Hippolyt Victor Alexander von Bothmer (naturalized 1857), and *d* 5 Feb 1925, leaving:

1a Venetia Mary Stanley Errington; *m* 1st 17 Feb 1916 (*divorce* 1926) Everard Noel Rye Trentham, CMG; *m* 2nd 10 Feb 1930 Capt Cecil Hunter Boyd Gowan, RN (*d* 28 July 1941); *m* 3rd 5 April 1955 Lt-Col Valentine Leathley Armitage, TD, MA (*d* 1964), s of Rev Allan Leathley Armitage, of Newbury, Berks

2a Violet Irene; *m* 1st 6 April 1921 (*divorce* 1924) Gordon Brooke Willoughby Hamilton-Gay; *m* 2nd 18 Jan 1930 (*divorce* 1947) William Francis Egginton Briggs, only surv s of Col W E Briggs, of Winchester, and had issue; *m* 3rd 6 Sept 1956 Col Christopher Pemberton Worsfold, MC, RE, s of Edward Mowll Worsfold, JP, of Dover

3a Veronica Yorke Hélène Cecilia; *m* 24 April 1926 Willem Karel Marie de Bruijn van Gouderack (*d* 1984), only s of Eduard Rudolf Marie de Bruijn, of Dordrecht, Holland

4 Charles Stuart; *b* 24 Feb 1816; Attaché Legation Prussia, author: *Karah-Kaplang* (an oriental romance); *m* 11 June 1864 Paulina Mary Ann (*m* 2nd 5 Oct 1871 Wallace James Harding, barrister), only dau of Maj William John King, 21st Fus, and *d* 1 March 1870, having had:

(1) Marie Alice Paulina; *d* young 1869

5 Frederick; *b* 17 March 1817; Lt RA; *m* 27 May 1839 Antonia (*d* 23 March 1869), dau of Rev William Archdall, Rector Tintern, and *d* 3 April 1851, leaving:

(1) Philip Alexander; *b* 1 April 1843; *d* 14 Nov 1869

(1) Louisa; *d* unm 9 Feb 1920

(2) Agnes Yorke; *d* unm 17 May 1904

(3) Sarah Elizabeth; *d* unm 24 Sept 1912

6 Arthur (Rev); *b* 20 Dec 1819; Rector Fowlmere, Cambs; *m* 13 July 1852 Hon Lucy Georgina Neville (*d* 25 May 1919), 3rd dau of 3rd Baron Braybrooke (*qv*), and *d* 23 April 1870, leaving:

(1) Arthur Cornwallis; *b* 6 Oct 1865; *d* unm 19 Aug 1922

(2) Latimer; *b* 9 Sept 1868; *d* unm 27 Dec 1916

(1) Elizabeth Jane; *b* Sept 1853; *d* unm 13 May 1925

(2) Mirabel Anne; *b* 8 Dec 1854; *m* 15 Aug 1877 William Marsland Francis Schneider (*d* 3 May 1918), of S Kensington, and *d* 10 Aug 1938, leaving issue

(3) Alethea Maude; *b* 11 March 1856; *d* unm 11 Feb 1947

(4) Georgina Lucy; *b* 11 May 1859; *d* unm 28 Aug 1936

(5) Vere Philippa; *b* 1 Jan 1861; *m* 17 Nov 1887 William Blackburn (*d* 13 May 1927), of Roshven, Inverness-shire, and *d* 19 Nov 1932

(6) Blanche Audley; *b* 16 Feb 1862; *d* unm 13 April 1950

(7) Florence Augusta; *b* 2 May 1863; *d* unm 18 Dec 1954

(8) Octavia Louisa; *b* 20 July 1864; *d* unm 4 Dec 1939

1 Sarah Elizabeth; VA, Woman Bedchamber to HM QUEEN VICTORIA; *m* 6 Nov 1845 Gen Hon Sir James Lindsay, KCMG, and *d* 16 Dec 1890 aged 77, leaving issue (*see* CRAWFORD and BALCARRES, E)

The 3rd EARL *d* 25 Dec 1860; his est son,

JOHN CHARLES GEORGE SAVILE, **4th Earl of Mexborough**; *b* 4 June 1810; *educ* Eton and Trin Coll Cambridge; MP (Tory) Gatton 1831–32 and Pontefract 1835–37 and 1841–47; *m* 1st 24 Feb 1842 Rachel Katherine (*d* 21 June 1854), est dau of 3rd Earl of Orford (*see* WALPOLE, B), and had:

1 JOHN HORACE SAVILE, **5th Earl of Mexborough**, JP, DL (W R Yorks), JP (Berks, Middx, London and Westminster); *b* 17 June 1843; *educ* Eton and Trin Coll Cambridge; High Sheriff W R Yorks 1877, Cornet W R York Yeo; *m* 1st 24 April 1867 Venetia Stanley (*dsps* 13 Nov 1900), 3rd dau and coheir of Sir Rowland Stanley Errington, 11th Bt (*see* 1970 edn); *m* 2nd April 1906 Sylvia Cecilia Maria (*d* 20 Aug 1915), dau of the Nobile Carlo de Ser-Antoni of Lucca and widow of Capt Claude Clerk, CIE; *m* 3rd 28 Jan 1916 Anne (*d* 11 Feb 1943) (*m* 3rd 1 June 1920 (*divorce* 1926) Alfred Charlemagne Lambart, *see* CAVAN, E), dau of Rev Andrew Holmes Belcher and formerly w of George Bainbridge Ritchie, and *dsps* 8 June 1916

The **4th Earl** *m* 2nd 27 July 1861 Agnes Louisa Elizabeth (*d* 23 Dec 1898), dau of John Raphael, and *d* 17 Aug 1899, having by her had:

2 JOHN HENRY, **6th Earl**

3 George, JP N R Yorks; *b* 24 Nov 1871; Lt 3rd Bn Yorks Regt, Capt and 1st Assist Supt Remount Serv 1915–17, attd Intell GHQ Italy 1918; *m* 22 Sept 1920 Lady Margaret Forbes (*d* 19 May 1965), yst dau of 7th Earl of Granard (*qv*), and *d* 15 July 1937

1 Mary Louisa; *m* 11 July 1898 (*divorce* 1905) Walter B Harris (*d* 4 April 1933) and *d* 25 July 1945

2 Anne; *m* 15 April 1897 HSH PRINCE LUDWIG KARL Zu LOEWENSTEIN WERTHEIM FREUDENBERG (*dsp* 25 March 1899), of Castle Litznitz, Frankfort-on-the-Oder; lost trying to cross the Atlantic on a solo flight *c* 31 Aug 1927

The 5th EARL's half-bro,

JOHN HENRY SAVILE, **6th Earl of Mexborough**, JP, DL (W R Yorks), JP (N R Yorks); *b* 27 Sept 1868; Hon Capt Army, T/Capt Remount Serv and Lt 2nd Life Gds; *m* 15 July 1905 Hon Margaret Eva de Burgh Knatchbull-Hugessen (*d* 26 Jan 1957), er dau of 2nd Baron Brabourne (*qv*), and had:

1 JOHN RAPHAEL WENTWORTH, **7th Earl**

1 Agnes Marjorie Alice; *b* 26 Oct 1907; *m* 23 Oct 1930 Capt Thomas More Eyston, DL (*d* of wounds recd in action 31 May 1940), Roy Berks Regt, and had issue

2 Beatrice Anne; *b* 25 June 1910; *m* 14 June 1934 Ralph Henry Scrope, 2nd s of Henry Scrope, of Danby, and *d* 29 Dec 1973, leaving issue

3 (Mary Elspeth) Sylvia; *b* 29 May 1914; *m* 4 Feb 1937 Andrew Ramon Dalzell de Bertodano (*d* 1957), est s of 8th Marquis del Moral, and *d* 25 Oct 1948, leaving issue

4 (Anne) Sarah Alethea Marjorie Savile; *b* 17 Sept 1919; *m* 4 Aug 1955 *Ld Justice (Sir James Roualeyn) Cumming-Bruce, 3rd (twin) s of 6th Baron Thurlow (*qv*), and *d* 1991, leaving issue

The 6th EARL *d* 16 Sept 1945; his only son,

JOHN RAPHAEL WENTWORTH SAVILE, **7th Earl of Mexborough**, JP (N R Yorks 1947), JP (W R Yorks 1935–47), DL (N R Yorks 1967); *b* 11 Oct 1906; *educ* Downside and Pembroke Coll Cambridge (BA 1930, MA 1938); Capt Intell Corps WW II, ADC to Govr Bihar 1944–45; *m* 23 July 1930 Josephine Bertha Emily (*d* 1992), dau of Andrew Mansel Talbot Fletcher, of Saltoun, and *d* 15 July 1980, leaving:

1 JOHN CHRISTOPHER GEORGE SAVILE, **8th and present Earl of Mexborough**

2 +(Charles) Anthony [The Hon Anthony Savile, Youngsbury, Ware, Herts SG12 0TZ]; *b* 28 June 1934; *educ* Eton and Trin Coll Cambridge; late 2nd Lt Gren Gds; *m* 5 Nov 1966 *Zita Loretta, yr dau of Leslie White, and has:

(1) +Henry Charles; *b* 15 Sept 1970

(2) +Andrew David; *b* 5 Feb 1973

1 Anne Sarah Elizabeth; *b* 10 Sept 1938; *m* 30 Oct 1964 *Charles Hynman Allanby, only s of Maj Ronald Hynman Allanby, of Balblair, Nairn, and *d* 1980, leaving:

(1) *Henry Hynman; *b* 11 Oct 1965

MEYER

RAST · NICH · ROST · NICH

Arms: Sa. a key, wards downwards or, between four bezants. **Crest:** A cock sa., armed, combed and wattled or, holding in the dexter claw a key, as in the arms. **Motto:** *Rast nich rost nich* ('Rest not rust not'). **Creation:** Bt. (UK)18 July 1910.

SIR ANTHONY JOHN CHARLES MEYER, 3RD BT, of Shortgrove, Newport, Essex [Sir Anthony Meyer Bt, 9 Cottage Place, Brompton Sq, London SW3 2BE]; *b* 27 Oct 1920; *s f* 1935; *educ* Eton and New Coll Oxford; Lt Scots Gds WW II 1941–45 (wounded), For Serv 1946, 1st Sec Paris 1951–56 and Moscow 1956–58, FO 1958, MP (C): Eton and Slough 1964–66, W Flint 1970–83, Clwyd NW 1983–1992, CRD 1968, fndr/dir *Solon*, political journal, 1969, Jt Hon Sec Br Cncl European Movement 1970–, PPS to Sec State Employment 1972–74, chm Franco-Br Party Rels Ctee 1979–, v-chm C Euro Affrs Ctee 1979–83, Policy dir European Movement 1992–, Dep Chm Franco-British Cncl (UK section), Tstee Shakespeare Memorial Nat Theatre, author: *A European Technological Community* (1966), *Stand Up and Be Counted* (1990), *A Federal Europe: Why Not* (1992), Offr Legn Hon 1983; *m* 30 Oct 1941 *Barbadee Violet, only child of Athro Charles Knight, JP, of Lincoln's Inn, London WC2, and Herne Place, Sunningdale, Berks, and has:

1 +(ANTHONY) ASHLEY FRANK [Anthony Meyer Esq, Flat 9 156 West Hill, London SW15 3SR]; *b* 23 Aug 1944; *educ* Eton; *m* 12 May 1966 (*divorce* 1980) Susan Mathilda, dau of John Freestone, and has:

(1) *Sophie Matilda Barbadee; *b* 1972

1 *Carolyn Clare Barbadee [Mrs Carolyn Sands, 7 Cottage Place, Brompton Sq, London SW3 2BE]; *b* 13 March 1943; *m* 19 Nov 1965 (*divorce* 1988) Charles Francis Sands, yr s of Arthur Langdale Sands, of The Mill House, Woodborough, Wilts, and has:

(1) *Robert Charles; *b* 24 Aug 1970

(2) *David Francis; b 5 Feb 1974

2 *Tessa Violet [Mrs David Murdoch, 3 Luxemburg Gdns, London W6]; b 28 Aug 1955; m 1977 *David Peter Murdoch and has:

  (1) *Iona Dorothy; b 1984

  (2) *Frances Evelyn; b 1986

  (3) *Sienna Rose Adèle; b 1992

3 *Sally Minette [Mrs Marcus Vergette, Coombe Farm, Highampton, Beaworthy, Devon]; b 3 Aug 1961; m 1989 *Marcus John Vergette

Lineage: SIEGMUND MEYER, of Hamburg; b 14 Feb 1815; m 16 Nov 1845 Elise Rosa (d 5 March 1855), dau of Reuben Hahn, of Hamburg, and d 3 July 1882, having had, with an er s (Ernest Friedrich, of Hamburg, b 20 Aug 1849, m and dsp Jan 1927):

Sir Carl Ferdinand Meyer, 1st Bt (UK), so cr 18 July 1910, JP (Co London); b Hamburg 23 Dec 1851; Lt City London, naturalized UK subject 10 Nov 1877, dir Nat Bank Egypt; m 14 March 1883 Adèle (d 17 Jan 1930), est dau of Julius Levis, of Belsize Grove, Hampstead, and d 18 Dec 1922, leaving, with a dau (Elsie Charlotte, b 17 Feb 1885, m 1st 25 Nov 1909 St John Murray Lambert (d 8 Dec 1926) and had issue, m 2nd 27 Oct 1927 Capt Harry Hulbert, OBE, and d 19 June 1954):

Sir Frank Cecil Meyer, 2nd Bt; b 7 May 1886; educ New Coll Oxford (BA 1908); barrister Inner Temple 1910, Lt Essex Yeo 1906–12 and 1914–19 WW (despatches), MP Gt Yarmouth 1924–29; m 11 Feb 1920 Marjorie Amy Georgina (m 2nd 28 April 1938 Carl Bendix (d 5 Feb 1945) and d 11 March 1961), 2nd dau of Frederick Seeley, of Hale, Cheshire, and d 19 Oct 1935, leaving:

Sir ANTHONY JOHN CHARLES MEYER, **3rd and present Bt**

MEYRICK

HEB·DHU, HEB·DHIM, DHU·A·DIGON

Arms: Quarterly, 1st and 4th, sable on a chevron argent, between three brands erect, raguly or, inflamed proper, a fleur-de-lys gules between two Cornish choughs, respectant, also proper (for MEYRICK); 2nd and 3rd, or a lion rampant gules, sinister quarter quarterly, 1st and 4th, gules, ten besants, 2nd and 3rd, argent, on a mount vert a lion passant guardant or (for CHARLTON).
Crests: 1 A tower argent, thereon upon a mount vert a Cornish chough proper, holding in the dexter claw a fleur-de-lys gules (for MEYRICK), 2 Issuant out of an Eastern coronet or a leopard's head gules (for CHARLTON). **Motto:** Heb dhu, heb dhim, dhu a digon ('Without God, without anything: God is enough').
Creation: Bt. (UK) 5 May 1880.

SIR DAVID JOHN CHARLTON MEYRICK, 4TH BT, of Bush, Pembs [Sir David Meyrick Bt, Bush House, Gumfreston, Dyfed SA70 8RA]; b 2 Dec 1926; s f 1983; educ Eton and Trin Hall Cambridge (BA 1948, MA 1956); FRICS, FCLAS 1948; m 29 Sept 1962 Penelope Anne, er dau of Cdr John Bertram Aubrey Marsden-Smedley, RN, of Chelsea, and has:

1 +TIMOTHY THOMAS CHARLTON; b 5 Nov 1963; educ Eton and Bristol U

2 +Simon Edward; b 20 Sept 1965; educ Shrewsbury and RAC Cirencester; m 1989 *Jennifer Amanda, yr dau of J B Irvine, of Thornton, Fife

3 +Christopher John; b 11 Dec 1967; educ Eton and Trin Hall Cambridge

Lineage (of Charlton): Sir ALAN CHARLTON, of Apley Castle, nr Wellington, Salop, yr bro of Sir John de Cherleton, ancestor of the Barons Charleton or Cherleton (cr 1313, abeyant March 1420/1); m Margery, heiress of Hugh Fitz Aer, and acquired Witherford and Aston Aer; Govr Montgomery and Wigmore Castles c 1312; had:

THOMAS CHARLTON, of Apley Castle; had, with a s Thomas (dsp):

ANNE; m William KNIGHTLEY, of the family of Knightley, Bts, of Fawsley, Northants, and had:

KNIGHTLEY CHARLTON, of Apley; had:

ROBERT CHARLTON, of Apley; Sheriff Salop 1472; ancestor in the 8th generation of:

FRANCIS CHARLTON, of Apley Castle; Sheriff Salop 1665; m Dorothy, dau and coheir of 5th Baron St John of Bletso (qv); ggf of:

ST JOHN CHARLTON, JP and DL, of Apley Castle; Sheriff 1757; b 1733; m 26 Jan 1759 Mary Tampsit, of Goudhurst (d 1767), and d 27 Jan 1776, leaving:

  1 St John, of Apley Castle; b April 1760; High Sheriff 1790; m 22 Dec 1781 Charlotte (d 31 Oct 1814), dau of James Payne, of Hayes, Surrey, and d 3 Oct 1802, leaving two daus

  2 WILLIAM

  3 Philip, of Wytheford Hall, Salop; b 26 Jan 1767; m 4 April 1796 Jane Brady (d 20 Aug 1843), dau of Hon William Barnett, of Arcadia, Jamaica, and d 30 July 1843, leaving issue

The 2nd s,

WILLIAM CHARLTON, of Apley Castle; b 1 May 1761; Lt-Col, High Sheriff 1807; m 22 April 1796 Catharine (d 12 Feb 1839), widow of Dr Thomason, of York, and d 14 Jan 1838, having had:

  1 ST JOHN CHIVERTON

  1 Charlotte Anne; m 4 April 1818 Rev Arthur Charles Verelst, of Aston Hall, Yorks, and d 14 Jan 1838

  2 Elizabeth; m 11 June 1822 Harry Croft (d 30 June 1853), of Stillington Hall, Yorks

  3 Louisa; m 21 July 1828 William Garforth, of Wiganthorpe, Yorks

Lt-Col WILLIAM CHARLTON's s,

ST JOHN CHIVERTON CHARLTON, JP and DL, of Apley Castle; b 29 May 1799; High Sheriff 1825; m 1st 7 Sept 1820 Jane Sophia (d 26 March 1837), only dau and heiress of Thomas Meyrick (see below), of Bush, Pembs, and had, with a dau (d unm):

  1 St John William; b 18 Aug 1831; Capt 1st Royals Crimea; d 30 Oct 1864

  2 THOMAS CHARLTON (Sir), **1st Bt**

  1 Catherine Jane; m 11 July 1846 F W Coe

  2 Louisa Catherine Sophia; m 9 July 1851 Clement Swetenham (d 26 Nov 1886), of Somerford Booths, Cheshire, and d 27 Dec 1900, leaving issue

  3 Jane Sophia; m 24 Jan 1849 Robert Davies Pryce (d 1891), of Cyfronydd, Montgomeryshire, and d 28 Dec 1913, having had issue

  4 Dorothea; m 23 Nov 1859 Arthur Robert Naghten (d 7 Aug 1881), of Blighmont, Millbrook, Hants, MP Winchester 1874–80

ST JOHN CHARLTON m 2nd 24 Feb 1842 Anne, 3rd dau of Philip Charlton, of Wytheford Hall, Salop, and d 3 Feb 1873, leaving by her:

  5 Mary Eleanor; m 1 Oct 1868 14th Viscount Mountgarret (qv) and d 12 May 1900, leaving issue

ST JOHN CHIVERTON CHARLTON's 2nd s,

Sir THOMAS CHARLTON later MEYRICK (roy licence 31 March 1858), **1st Bt** (UK), so cr 5 May 1880, KCB, JP, DL; b 14 March 1837; High Sheriff Salop 1877, Hon Col, formerly Lt-Col cmdg 3rd Bn KSLI, MP Pembroke 1868–74; m 10 April 1860 Mary Rhoda (d 4 Oct 1924), 2nd dau of Col Richard Frederic Hill, of Prees Hall, Salop, and n of 2nd Viscount Hill (qv), and d 30 July 1921, having had:

  1 FREDERICK CHARLTON (Sir), **2nd Bt**

  2 St John; b 4 Aug 1866; BA Cantab; Capt Gordon Highrs; ku Boer War 29 May 1900

  3 Rowland Francis, JP (Salop); b 10 Sept 1867; educ Eton; Boer War 1900 (Queen's medal, four clasps), Travelling Inspr Bd Ag 1890–94; m 15 June 1901 Eleanor Georgiana (d 12 Nov 1966 aged 93), yst dau of Hon Ralph Pelham Nevill (see ABERGAVENNY, M), and d 18 March 1953, having had:

    (1) Gerald Ralph; b 24 June 1902; d 22 July 1916

    (1) Honor Mary; b 25 Nov 1907; m 25 Sept 1943 Charles Eade, MC, land agent, 2nd s of Rev Charles John Aylmer Eade, Vicar Aycliffe, Co Durham, and d 26 April 1965, leaving two daus

  4 Herbert Cheverton; b 18 Oct 1874; Boer War 1900–01; d unm 19 May 1909

  5 Walter Thomas, JP (Lindsey, Lincs); b 11 Jan 1882; educ Eton; served WW I, Chev du Mérite Agricole; m 1st 21 July 1914 (divorce 1935) Mabel Violet Blanche (d 12 Jan 1957), est dau of Col Arthur Hill Sandys Montgomery, Rifle Bde, and widow of Percy Downes; m 2nd 1935 *Mary Jocelyn, 2nd dau of Sir James Ernest Thorold, 14th Bt (qv), and d 27 Sept 1953, having by her had:

    (1) +Walter James Charlton [Walter Meyrick Esq, 310 North Buildings, Starco, Beirut, Lebanon]; b 22 July 1936; educ Eton; m 30 Jan 1965 *Gillian, yr dau of W Macduff Urquhart, of Edinburgh, and has:

      1a +St John James Charlton; b 16 Nov 1969

      2a +William Andrew; b 17 Sept 1976

      1a *Louisa Mary; b 17 Feb 1966

      2a *Sophia Rachel; b 17 Feb 1966

    (2) +Michael Alan Charlton; b 7 Oct 1937; educ Gordonstoun

    (3) Christopher Thomas Charlton; b 25 July 1946; m 1975 *Caroline Mary [Mrs Julian Freeland, Green Close, Combe, Oxon OX7 2N5] (m 2nd 1985 Julian Richard Freeland, yst s of Maj P K Freeland, of Ipplepen, Devon), er dau of Iain Hugh Webster, of Forest Row, Sussex, and d 1979

    (1) *(Mary) Rhoda Charlton; b 6 May 1944; m 2 Jan 1971 *Colin A Matheson, yr s of W/Cdr W R A Matheson, RAF, and Lady Williams-Wynn (qv), and has:

      1a *Nicholas Simon; b 1973

      2a *Patrick William Christopher; b 1979

      1a *Camilla Karen; b 1976

  1 Dora Rhoda; d unm 13 Feb 1939

  2 Alice Maude; m 28 Nov 1903 Col Robert Francis Peel and d 21 March 1957, leaving issue (see PEEL, E)

  3 Eva Mary; m 1 Aug 1903 John Henry Weatherby (d Feb 1948), s of Edward Weatherby, and d 2 Jan 1961

  4 Rachel Cicely; m 19 July 1904 Henry George Atkinson-Clark, JP (d 13 Aug 1948), est surv s of George Dixon Atkinson-Clark, JP, DL, of Belford Hall, Northumberland, and d 9 July 1959, leaving issue (see SUFFIELD, B)

Sir THOMAS's est s,

Sir Frederick Charlton Meyrick, 2nd Bt, CB (1900), CMG (1918), JP and DL (Pembs); b 7 July 1862; educ Trin Hall Cambridge (BA); High Sheriff Pembs 1926,

Hon Brig-Gen, formerly Col cmdg S Wales Mtd Bde, Maj 15th Hus, Col cmdg Pembs Yeo, Hon Col 1928, Bde Cdr 1916, Cmdt Remount Depot 1917, Boer War as Cmdt 5th Bn Imp Yeo 1899–1901 (wounded, despatches, medal and clasps), WW I (despatches); *m* 16 Oct 1897 Mary Emma, OBE (1960), JP (Pembs) (*d* 26 Aug 1970 aged 92), dau of Major Oswin Cumming Baker Cresswell, of Cresswell, Northumberland, and *d* 23 Feb 1932, having had:

1 THOMAS FREDERICK (Sir), **3rd Bt**

1 Mary Cicely; *m* 28 June 1921 Giles Fendall Newton, MBE, BA, only s of William Latham Newton, of Goldington, Bedford, and had issue

2 *Rachel Eva Meyrick [Mrs Rachel Lithgow, The Old House, Great Barton, Suffolk]; *m* 30 April 1929 Laurence Lithgow, JP (*d* 1972), 15th Hus, yr s of Samuel Lithgow, CBE, of N Kensington, and has:

   (1) *James Frederick; *b* 1933

   (1) *Esther Mary; *b* 1930; *m* 19– *— Nicholson

   (2) *Ruth; *b* 1934

3 *Violet [The Rt Hon Violet Lady Merthyr, Churchton, Saundersfoot, Dyfed SA69 9BB], SSStJ; *m* 10 Nov 1932 3rd Baron Merthyr (*qv*) and has issue

Sir FREDERICK's only s,

Sir Thomas Frederick Meyrick, 3rd Bt, TD, JP (1928), DL (1936); *b* 29 Nov 1899; *educ* Eton and RMC Sandhurst; High Sheriff 1938, Maj 102nd Pembroke and Cardigan Field Bde RA (TA), Capt 15th/19th Hus, Hon Col 302 (Pembroke Yeo) Field Regt RA (TA) 1954–59, Pres Roy Welsh Ag Soc 1955, MFH: Pembrokeshire 1934–35 and 1945–57 and S Pembrokeshire 1935–39; *m* 1st 5 Jan 1926 Ivy Frances (*d* 29 May 1947), dau of Lt-Col Frederick Charles Pilkington, DSO, of Sweethay Court, Trull, Taunton, and had:

1 Sir DAVID JOHN CHARLTON MEYRICK, **4th and present Bt**

2 (Frederick) Rowland; *b* 20 Aug 1928; *educ* Eton; Maj 15th/19th King's Roy Hus (ret); *m* 1985 (*divorce* 1993) Patricia Anne Busswell-Dewitte, est dau of Dennis William Busswell, KRRC, of Lisbon, and *d* 19–

3 +Richard Eric [Richard Meyrick Esq, Lower Helland, Helland Bridge, Cornwall PL30 4QP]; *b* 14 May 1936; *educ* Monkton Combe and RAC Cirencester; FRICS 1962; *m* 11 May 1962 *Catherine Ann, er dau of Col Vivian Joseph French Popham, S Wales Borderers, of Begelly, Kilgetty, Pembs

1 Mary Joan; *b* 29 Jan 1930; *m* 21 April 1954 *Ian Marshall Lang [Ian Lang Esq, Whitewick Farm, Stogursey, Somerset], yr s of David Marshall Lang, MRCS, LRCP, and *d* 21 Dec 1995, leaving:

   (1) *Patrick John; *b* 25 Oct 1957

   (2) *Edward Nicholas; *b* 29 July 1959; *m* 1989 *Louise Costin and has:

     1a *Frederick Thomas Meyrick; *b* 27 Nov 1995

     2a *Hugh Alexander Simon; *b* 18 Sept 1997

   (1) *Ivy Frances; *b* 30 Aug 1960; *m* 1992 *David P C Tennick, of Pretoria, S Africa, and has:

     1a *Anthony Paul Marshall; *b* 12 Sept 1996

     1a *Gemma Louise; *b* 18 March 1995

2 *Susan Ethel [Mrs Roland Owen-George, Hillside, Garway, Herefs HR2 8RL]; *b* 9 Dec 1932; *m* 7 Sept 1954 *Roland Owen-George, yst s of John Owen George, of Bryncyon, Hirwaun, Glam

3 *Penelope Ann [Mrs Michael McGarvie, 19 Styles Hill, Frome, Somerset BA11 5JG]; *b* 23 June 1939; *m* 23 April 1966 *Michael McGarvie, yst s of Edward McGarvie, of East Calder, Edinburgh, and Mrs R E Oram, of Blandford Forum, Dorset, and has:

   (1) *Emma Louise; *b* 30 May 1969

   (2) *Victoria Grace; *b* 23 March 1971

   (3) *Alice Katherine; *b* 4 Sept 1974

Sir Thomas *m* 2nd 4 Dec 1951 (Gladice) Joyce (*d* 22 Oct 1977), only dau of Bertram Wedgwood Allen, of Cilrhiw, Narbeth, Pembs; *m* 3rd 5 May 1978 Suzanne (*d* 14 July 1979), yst dau of D A Evans, formerly of Bristol, and *d* 23 Dec 1983, having by his 2nd w had:

4 +John Herbert [John Meyrick Esq, 63 Dawson Drive, Trimley St Mary, Ipswich, Suffolk]; *b* 24 Sept 1952; *educ* Abbotsholme; *m* 1982 *Sandra Dawn, only dau of L V Blackman, of Lewes, E Sussex, and has:

   (1) +Matthew Thomas; *b* 1986

   (2) +Alistair Charles; *b* 1988

Lineage (of Meyrick): The MEYRICKs of Bush are a branch of the MEYRICKs of Goodrich Court, being descended from:

Rt Rev ROWLAND MEYRICK; Bp Bangor 1559; *m* Catherine, dau of Owen Barrett, of Gellyswick, Pembs, and had a 2nd s:

Sir FRANCIS MEYRICK, of Monkton; had:

Sir JOHN MEYRICK, of Monkton; Serjeant-Maj-Gen Parly Army Civil War, MP Newcastle-under-Lyne Long Parl 1641; *m* 1st Alice, dau of Sir Edward Fitton, 1st Bt, of Gawsworth; *m* 2nd Jane, widow of Sir Peter Wyche and dau of William Meredith, of Wrexham; ancestor of:

THOMAS MEYRICK, of Bush, had an only dau:

JANE SOPHIA Meyrick; *m* 7 Sept 1820 St John Chiverton CHARLTON, of Apley Castle (*see above*)

MEYSEY-THOMPSON

Arms: Quarterly, 1st and 4th, per fess arg. and sa. a fess counter-embattled between three falcons counterchanged, belled and jessed or (for THOMPSON); 2nd and 3rd, arg. a fess between three cinquefoils sa. (for MEYSEY). **Crests:** 1 An arm embowed in armour quarterly or and az., the gauntlet ppr., holding a truncheon of a broken lance of the first (for THOMPSON), 2 A dragon's head couped at the neck quarterly or and az. (for MEYSEY). **Motto:** *Je veux de bonne guerre* ('I wish for fair fight'). **Creation:** Bt. (UK) 26 March 1874.

SIR (HUMPHREY) SIMON MEYSEY-THOMPSON, 4TH BT, of Kirkby Hall, York [Sir Simon Meysey-Thompson Bt, 10 Church St, Woodbridge, Suffolk IP12 1DH]; *b* 31 March 1935; *s* cousin 1967

Lineage: JONAS THOMPSON, of Thornton and Pickering Leigh; living 1460; *m* Eleanor Philips, of Brickwell, and had, with a yr s (Richard, of Haughton, *m* Bridget, sis of Sir F Fleming, Master Ordnance to EDWARD VI):

HENRY THOMPSON; *m* —, dau of — Wellburne, and had, with an er s:

RICHARD THOMPSON; *m* Anne, dau of William Langland, of Scarborough, and had, with a yr s:

WILLIAM THOMPSON, of Humbleton, Yorks; *m* —, dau and heiress of John Barker, of Scarborough Castle, and *d* 1637, having had, with an er s (Francis, of Humbleton, gf of William Thompson, MP Scarborough, and ancestor twice over of the Barons Hotham, *qv*):

RICHARD THOMPSON, of Kilham; *b* 1580; *m* Anne, dau of Edward Nelthorpe, and *d c* 1650, having had:

1 Jonas, of Kilham; *m* Frances, dau of William Beilby, of Killerby, Yorks, and had issue

2 Henry (Sir), of Marston; gf of 1st Earl Cowper (*see* LUCAS OF CRUDWELL, B), ggf of Gen Wolfe (*k* taking of Quebec 1759); also ancestor of the Barons Wenlock (*see* 1932 edn)

3 STEPHEN (Sir)

4 Edward; MP Yorks; ancestor of the THOMPSONs of Sheriff Hutton Park, Yorks

5 Richard, of Kilham; *b* 1637; ancestor of Thompson, Bt, of Hartsbourne (*qv*)

The 3rd son,

Sir STEPHEN THOMPSON, of Kirby Hall, Yorks; *b* 1635 ; *m* Mary (*d* 9 Feb 1731/2), dau of Leonard Thompson, of York, and *d* 22 Feb 1692/3, having had, with other issue, including a dau (Anne, *m* Rev Charles Palmer and issue; *see* HALIFAX, E):

HENRY THOMPSON, of Kirby Hall; *b* 1677; *m* Catherine, dau and heiress of Rev J Mawhood, DD, and *d* 1760, leaving, with an est s (Stephen, *b* 1699, *m* Jane (*m* 2nd Sir Richard Heron, 1st Bt; *see* 1854 edn), dau and coheir of Abraham Hall, MD, and *dsp* 1763):

JOHN THOMPSON, of Kirby Hall; *b* 1701; *m* 1st Elizabeth Croft (*d* Oct 1753), of Stillington, and had a s and two daus (Eliza Catherine, *m* Sir John Eden, 4th Bt (*see* EDEN OF WINTON, B); Mary, *m* Childers Walbanke, of Carr House); *m* 2nd Mildred, widow of William Walbanke, of Kirkbridge, and dau of Leonard Childers, of Carr House; his s by his 1st w:

HENRY THOMPSON, of Kirby Hall; *b* 1743; *m* 30 Jan 1769 Mary (*d* 23 April 1843), only child and heiress of Thomas Spence, of Harts Hall, Suffolk, and had, with three daus:

   1 RICHARD JOHN

   2 Henry, of Burton; *b* 21 Sept 1774; *m* Caroline, dau of Thomas Stafford, of Stafford Barton, and *d* 26 June 1854, leaving issue

   3 Robert Stephen (Rev); Vicar Askham-Bryan and Myton, Yorks; *b* 11 Oct 1778; *m* Harriet (*d* 18 Sept 1858), dau of Walbanke Childers, of Cantley, and *d* 7 Jan 1862, having had issue

   4 Charles; *b* 19 Jan 1781; *m* Jane, dau of John Turton, of Sugnall Hall, Staffs, and *d* 1829, having had issue

HENRY THOMPSON was *bur* 10 March 1814; his est son,

RICHARD JOHN THOMPSON, of Kirby Hall; Capt 4th Dragoons, Maj Yorks Hus Yeo; *b* 24 Jan 1771; *m* 5 Aug 1803 Elizabeth (*d* 20 Feb 1840), dau of John Turton, of Sugnall Hall, by Mary, dau and coheir of Richard Meysey, of Shakenhurst, Worcs (descended from the de Meyseys who came to England from Meysey, Britanny, with WILLIAM I (THE CONQUEROR), and were long seated at Meysey Hampton and Marston Meysey, Glos), and had, with four other daus (*d* unm):

1 HARRY STEPHEN (Sir), **1st Bt**

2 Thomas Charles (Rev); Rector Ripley, Yorks; *b* 13 Nov 1811; *d* unm 16 Feb 1885

3 Frederick William; *b* 10 Oct 1816; *m* April 1848 Gertrude Elizabeth, est dau of John Dalton, of Sleningford Park, Yorks, and Fillingham Castle, Lincs, and had issue

1 Eliza Mary; *m* 27 Sept 1828 Rev Thomas Hutton Croft, Vicar Hutton Bushel and Stillington, Canon York, RD, and *d* Oct 1884, leaving issue. He *d* 23 June 1873

2 Henrietta; *m* 6 April 1848 Frederick Richard Saye, of Upton Park, Slough, and *d* 4 May 1872, leaving issue

RICHARD THOMPSON *d* 3 Aug 1853; his est son,

Sir HARRY STEPHEN THOMPSON later MEYSEY-THOMPSON, **1st Bt** (UK), so *cr* 26 March 1874, of Kirby Hall, JP, DL Yorks, High Sheriff 1856, MP (Lib) Whitby 1859–65; *b* 11 Aug 1809; *m* 26 Aug 1843 Elizabeth Anne (*d* 28 March 1910), 2nd dau of Sir John Croft, 1st Bt, of Cowling Hall (*qv*), and *d* 17 May 1874, leaving:

1 **Sir Henry Meysey Meysey-Thompson, 2nd Bt**, and 1st and last BARON KNARESBÓROUGH, of Kirby Hall, Co York (UK), so *cr* 26 Dec 1905, JP, DL Yorks; *b* 30 Aug 1845; *educ* Eton and Trin Coll Cambridge; MP (Lib) Knaresborough 1880, Brigg, Lincs, 1885–86 (Lib to 1886, Lib U thereafter) and Handsworth 1892–1905, Hon Maj Yorks Hus Yeo; *m* 21 April 1885 Ethel Adeline (*d* 18 Aug 1922), only child of Sir Henry Pottinger, 3rd and last Bt (*see* 1902 edn), and *dspms* 3 March 1929, when the Barony expired, having had:

(1) Claude Henry Meysey; *b* 5 April 1887; *educ* RMC Sandhurst; Capt Rifle Bde; *d* 17 June 1915 from wounds recd at Ypres

(1) Violet Ethel; *b* 15 Feb 1886; *m* 1st 3 Nov 1910 Capt Alexander Moore Vandeleur, 2nd Life Gds (missing presumed *ka* 30 Oct 1914), only surv s of Capt Hector Stewart Vandeleur, of Kilrush, Co Clare, and had issue; *m* 2nd 11 Oct 1921 Maj Sir Algar Henry Stafford Howard, KCB, KCVO, MC, TD (*see* NORFOLK, D), and *d* 29 Feb 1960, leaving further issue

(2) Helen Winifred; *b* 14 June 1889; *m* 28 Jan 1914 3rd Baron Newton (*qv*) and *d* 28 Dec 1958, leaving issue

(3) Doris Mary Pottinger; *b* 26 April 1899; *m* 1st 7 Feb 1921 Capt Francis Egerton, 17th Lancers Res (*see* SUTHERLAND, D), and had issue; *m* 2nd 1 March 1938 Maj John Humphrey Allison Seed, TD, DL, JP, MA, Yorks Hus Yeo, only s of Benjamin Shaw Seed, of Everthorpe Hall, Brough, E Yorks, and *d* 27 March 1953, leaving further issue

(4) Gwendolen Carlis; Ldy-in-Waiting to HRH THE DUCHESS OF GLOUCESTER 1938–44; *b* 10 April 1903; *m* 20 Nov 1951 (*divorce* 1968), as his 2nd w, Sir Charles Frederick Richmond Brown, 4th Bt (*qv*), and *d* 1 Sept 1977

2 Richard Frederick; Col Rifle Bde and 4th Bn W Yorks Regt, Ashanti War 1873–74 (medal), Boer War 1900–02 as Remount Purchaser, WW I as 2ic 14th Regt Dist 1914 and Mil Adviser Recruiting Area (raised five Brigades RFA and six Batteries RGA), Roy Humane Soc medal, author: *The Course, the Camp, the Chase, The Fishing Catechism* and other works; *b* 17 April 1847; *m* 14 July 1879 Charlotte (*d* 3 March 1935), yst dau of Sir James Walker, 1st Bt, of Sand Hutton (*qv*), and *d* 1 Sept 1926, leaving:

(1) **Sir Algar de Clifford Charles Meysey-Thompson, 3rd Bt**; *b* 9 Nov 1885; *educ* Eton and Trin Coll Cambridge (MA); Assoc (late Professional Assoc) Surveyors' Instn, Capt 7th Bn Rifle Bde and RFA, atdt 3rd Cav Bde, WW I (Star, GS and Victory Medals); *d* unm 11 Jan 1967

(1) Violet Ileene Cassandra; *m* 17 Oct 1905 Maj Charles William Cuff Knox, Rifle Bde (*d* 25 Jan 1910), est s of Col Charles Howe Cuff Knox, DL, of Creagh, Co Mayo, and *d* 17 Feb 1917

3 Albert Childers, QC; *b* 13 July 1848; *m* 9 Aug 1882 Mabel Louisa (*d* 24 Dec 1941), dau of Rev Hon James Walter Lascelles (*see* HAREWOOD, E), and *d* 20 March 1894, leaving:

(1) Hubert Charles, CBE (1950); barrister Inner Temple 1907, Capt KRRC WW I, Legal Chancery Visitor Lunatics 1928; *b* 9 June 1883; *educ* Marlborough and Trin Coll Cambridge (BA 1905); *m* 12 Aug 1936 Millicent Mary (*d* 18 May 1970) Edmund Wallace Blake, of Cheltenham, and *dsp* 9 Nov 1956

4 Charles Maude (Rev); Rector Claydon, Bucks; *b* 5 Dec 1849; *educ* Trin Coll Cambridge (MA); *m* 28 April 1874 Emily Mary (*d* 18 Dec 1937), 2nd dau of Sir James Walker, 1st Bt, of Sand Hutton (*qv*), and *d* 12 Sept 1881, leaving, with a dau (*d* young):

(1) Harold James; Capt Rifle Bde, Munshi Expdn, N Nigeria 1906 and WW I 1917–18 (GS and Victory Medals); *b* 24 Sept 1876; *m* 22 Dec 1911 Louise, only child of Francois Peccoud, of Grenoble, and *d* 15 March 1926

5 Arthur Herbert, JP (W R Yorks); *b* 5 Oct 1852; *educ* Eton; Lt Yorks Hus, MInstCE; *m* 1 June 1896 Horatia Dorothy (*d* 4 April 1949), 2nd dau of Sir Hedworth Williamson, 8th Bt (*qv*), and *d* 5 Feb 1950, leaving:

(1) Guy Herbert; *b* 21 Sept 1901; *educ* Eton; Lt RNVR; *m* 26 June 1934 Miriam Beryl (Betty) (*d* 1985), dau of Sidney Hand, of Mayfair and York Ho, Hendon, and *d* 10 May 1961, leaving:

1a Sir (HUMPHREY) SIMON MEYSEY-THOMPSON, **4th and present Bt**

1a *Sarah Horatia [Mrs Charles Paterson, 31 Ranelagh Grove, London SW1W 8PA]; *b* 28 Aug 1944; *m* 9 April 1969 *Charles William Spencer Paterson, s of Dr Arthur Spencer Paterson, of Chelsea and Ely Hill, Suffolk, and has:

1b *Charles Joseph Alexander; *b* 1983

(1) Sylvia Dorothy; *m* 12 July 1921 Capt Aubrey Leo Kennedy, MC, Scots Gds (*see* AILSA, M), and *d* 29 June 1968, leaving issue

(2) *Diana Elizabeth; *m* 15 Aug 1932 Roderick Le Mesurier, only s of Maj Eugene Le Mesurier, and has:

1a *Jeremy John; *b* 1934; *educ* Eton and Grenoble U; *m* 14 Oct 1960 his cousin *Elisabeth Dorothy, formerly w of Charles Russell Scarr and est dau of Capt Aubrey Leo Kennedy

6 Ernest Claude, JP (N and W R Yorks); *b* 18 Feb 1859; *educ* Eton and Trin Coll Cambridge; Lt-Col RFA, raised five bdes RFA and six heavy batteries RGA WW I, cmded 175th Bde RFA and 5th DAC, Maj Yorks Hus Yeo, MP Handsworth 1906–22 (chm H of C Remounts Ctee), sheep and cattle farmer NZ, Extra ADC to Govr-Gen NZ, Pres Yorkshire Coach-horse Soc, author: *India of To-day* and *A Treatise on Grassland*; *m* 1 Nov 1894 Alice Jane Blanche (*d* 17 July 1960 aged 89), dau of Col John Joicey, DL, of Newton Hall, Northumberland, MP N Durham, and *d* 28 Feb 1944, leaving:

(1) Onslow Victor Claude; *b* 1 June 1897; *educ* Eton, RMA Woolwich, and Corpus Christi Coll Cambridge (BA 1924, MA 1931); Lt-Col RA WW I (wounded), Iraq 1920, WW II (despatches), Liveryman Merchant Taylors' Co 1933; *d* unm 18 May 1965

(1) Alice Hildegarde Eva; *b* 13 Sept 1895; *d* unm 31 Aug 1977

1 Elizabeth Lucy; *m* 23 Sept 1868 2nd Earl of Iddesleigh (*qv*) and *d* 17 April 1928, leaving issue

2 Mary Caroline; *m* 2 July 1878 William Henry Bond, Roy Scots Regt, of Tyneham, Dorset, and *d* 1 Jan 1949, leaving issue. He *d* 11 Jan 1935

MIDDLETON, Baron

Arms: Quarterly, 1st and 4th, or fretty azure (for WILLOUGHBY of Eresby); 2nd and 3rd, or on two bars gules three water-bougets argent, two and one (for WILLOUGHBY of Middleton, formerly BUGGE). **Crest:** The bust of a man, couped at the shoulders and affrontée proper, ducally crowned or. **Supporters:** Dexter, a pilgrim or grey friar in his habit proper, with his beads, cross and staff in his right hand, argent; sinister, a savage with a club in his exterior hand, wreathed about the temples and middle with laurel, all proper, each supporter holding a banner gules, fringed or, ensigned with an owl argent, gorged with a ducal coronet, collared and chained gold, the owl being the crest of WILLOUGHBY of Middleton. **Motto:** *Verité sans peur* ('Truth without fear').
Creation: B. (GB) 1 Jan 1711/2, Bt. (E) 7 April 1677.

THE 12TH BARON MIDDLETON OF MIDDLETON, Co Warwick, and a **Baronet** (Sir (Digby) Michael Godfrey John Willoughby, Bt, MC (1945), JP (1958), DL (E R Yorks 1963)) [The Rt Hon The Lord Middleton MC JP DL, Birdsall House, Malton, N Yorks YO17 9NR]; *b* 1 May 1921; *s f* 1970; *educ* Eton and Trin Coll Cambridge (BA 1950, MA 1958); Coldstream Gds WW II (despatches, Croix de Guerre), land agent 1951, memb: E R CC 1964–77 and N Yorks CC 1974–77, Yorks and Humberside Ec Planning Cncl 1968–79, Hon Col 2nd Bn Yorks Vols 1976, Dep Pres CLA 1979; *m* 14 Oct 1947 *Janet, JP (N Yorks), only surv dau of Gen Sir James Handyside Marshall-Cornwall, KCB, CBE, DSO, MC, of Knightsbridge, and has:

1 +MICHAEL CHARLES JAMES [The Hon Michael Willoughby, North Grimston House, Malton, N Yorks YO17 8AX]; *b* 14 July 1948; *educ* Eton; Coldstream Gds 1967–71, Queen's Own Yeo; *m* 26 Jan 1974 *Hon Lucy Corinna Agneta Sidney, yst dau of 1st Viscount De L'Isle (*qv*), and has:

(1) +James William Michael; *b* 8 March 1976; *educ* Eton

(2) +Charles Edward Henry; *b* 27 July 1986

(1) *Charlotte Jacqueline Louise; *b* 20 Sept 1978

(2) *Emma Coralie Sarah; *b* 7 Sept 1981

(3) *Rose Arabella Julia; *b* 25 Sept 1984

2 +(John) Hugh Francis [The Hon Hugh Willoughby, 4 Westmorland Terr, London SW1]; *b* 13 July 1951; *educ* Eton; late Capt Coldstream Gds

3 +Thomas Henry Richard; *b* 20 Nov 1955; *educ* Harrow and Manchester U (BSc)

Middleton, earlier creation: An Earldom of Middleton in the peerage of Scotland was held by a family of the same name between 1660 and 1695. John Middleton, a Scot, served in the Parliamentary army in the south of England during the Civil War and was the second in command of a Parliamentarian force when it beat the chief Royalist one in Scotland under the Marquess of Montrose (*see*

MONTROSE, D) at the Battle of Philiphaugh in 1645. He later became a Royalist and fought for that party at the Battles of Preston 1648 and Worcester 1651, following which he was imprisoned in the Tower of London. From there he managed to escape *en travestie*, deceiving the guards by walking out in his wife's clothes despite having a red face and high nose. (The Tower of London turnkeys cannot have been very bright, or perhaps were too gentlemanly to strip search whatever passed by in skirts on its way out, for nine years earlier Daniel O'Neill (*see* O'NEILL, B) had brought off the same trick and 60 years later Lord Nithsdale (*see* HERRIES OF TERREGLES, L) was to do so as well.) Back in Scotland again he led a Royalist army in the Highlands but was beaten by General Monck, who was also later to turn Royalist, at the encounter of Lochgarry in 1654. After the Restoration he was made Earl of Middleton with precedence of 1656 and Commander-in-Chief Scotland. His son the 2nd Earl remained loyal to JAMES II after the Glorious Revolution, was attainted 1695 and his titles forfeited, but was created titular Earl of Monmouth by the Old Pretender in 1701.

Lineage: Sir CHRISTOPHER WILLOUGHBY, *de jure* 10th LORD (Baron) WILLOUGHBY DE ERESBY (*qv*); *d* between 1 Nov 1498 and 13 July 1499, leaving, with other issue:

Sir THOMAS WILLOUGHBY; Ld Ch Justice Common Pleas *temp* HENRY VIII; *m* Bridget, dau and heiress of Sir Robert Read, of Bore Place, Kent, Judge Common Pleas, and *d* 1545, leaving:

ROBERT WILLOUGHBY, of Bore Place; *m* Dorothy, dau of Sir Edward Willoughby, of Wollaton, Notts (of a wholly different family, called Bugge till the early 14th century), and had:

THOMAS WILLOUGHBY; *m* Catherine, dau of Sir Percival Hart (ancestor of the (Hart) DYKE Bts, *qv*), of Lullingstone Castle, Kent, and had, with six yr sons and three daus:

Sir PERCIVAL WILLOUGHBY, of Blore Place, Wollaton Hall, Notts, and Middleton Hall, Warwicks; MP Notts 1603; *m* his cousin (through the marriage two generations back with the dau of Sir Edward Willoughby, of Wollaton, not through his male grandpaternal line) Bridget, est dau and coheir of Sir Francis Willoughby, of Wollaton, thereby acquiring the Wollaton and Middleton estates, and *d c* 1642, having had, with other issue (including four other sons):

1 Francis (Sir); *m* Lady Cassandra Ridgeway, dau of 1st Earl of Londonderry of the 1622 *cr* (*see* LONDONDERRY, M, preliminary remarks), and *d* 17 Dec 1665, having had an only s:

  (1) Francis; *b* 1635; *educ* Trin Coll Cambridge; astronomer, mathematician, naturalist (said to have been the first such to classify birds scientifically, laying the groundwork on which Linnaeus later built; the genus of rubber plants called *Willughbeia* and the leaf-cutting bee *Megachile Willulbuella* are named after him), FRS 1663 (one of the original band), author posthumously: *The Ornithology of Francis Willughby* (1678) and other works; *m* Emma (*m* 2nd Sir Josiah Child), 2nd dau and coheir of Sir Henry Bernard, Turkey merchant, and *d* 3 July 1672, leaving:

    1a **Sir Francis Willoughby, 1st Bt** (E), so *cr* 7 April 1677 in infancy in recognition of his f's services to science, with remainder to his bro Thomas; *d* unm 1688

    2a THOMAS, **1st Baron**

    1a Cassandra; *m* 4 Aug 1713 her first cousin 1st Duke of Chandos (*see* KINLOSS, L) and *dsp* 16 July 1735

2 Percival(l); *b* 1596; *educ* Rugby, Eton and Magdalen Coll Oxford; obstetrician and writer on obstetrics; *d* 1685

1 Bridget; *m* 14 Oct 1610 Henry Cavendish (*see* WATERPARK, B)

The 1st Bt's bro,

Sir Thomas Willoughby, 2nd Bt, and **1st Baron Middleton of Middleton**, Co Warwick (GB), so *cr* 1 Jan 1711/2, PC (1702–11 and 1714–29), DL (Notts 1694); *b c* 1670; High Sheriff Notts 1695–96, MP (Tory) Notts 1698–1702 and 1705–10 and Newark 1710–12, FRS 1693; *m* 9 April 1691 Elizabeth, dau and coheir of Sir Richard Rothwell, Bt, of Stapleford, Lincs, and *d* 2 April 1729, having had, with other issue:

1 FRANCIS WILLOUGHBY, **2nd Baron Middleton of Middleton**; *b* 29 Sept 1692; *educ* Eton; MP (Tory) Notts 1713–22 and Tamworth 1722–27; *m* 25 July 1723 Mary (*d* 12 March 1762), 2nd dau and coheir of Thomas Edwards, of Filkins, Oxon, and *d* 4 Aug 1758, having had, with a dau:

  (1) FRANCIS WILLOUGHBY, **3rd Baron Middleton of Middleton**; *b* 25 Jan 1725/6; *d* unm 16 Dec 1774

  (2) THOMAS WILLOUGHBY, **4th Baron Middleton of Middleton**; *b* 19 Dec 1728; *m* 7 April 1770 Georgiana (*m* 2nd 14 June 1788, as his 2nd w, Edward Miller Mundy, MP, of Shipley Hall, nr Ilkeston, Derbys (*d* Oct 1822), and *d* 29 June 1789, leaving further issue), dau of Evelyn Chadwick, of West Leake, Notts, and *dsp* 2 Nov 1781

2 Thomas; *b* 11 June 1694; MP Cambridge U 1720 and 1721–27 and Tamworth 1727–30; *m* Elizabeth (*d* 25 April 1752), dau and heiress of Thomas Southby, of Birdsall, Yorks, and *d* 2 Dec 1742, with four daus:

  (1) HENRY WILLOUGHBY, **5th Baron Middleton of Middleton**; *b* 19 Dec 1726; *m* 25 Dec 1756 Dorothy (*d* 18 Sept 1808), dau and coheir of George Cartwright, of Ossington, Notts, and *d* 14 June 1800, having had:

    1a HENRY WILLOUGHBY, **6th Baron Middleton of Middleton**; *b* 24 April 1761; *m* 21 Aug 1793 Jane, dau of Sir Robert Lawley, 5th Bt (*see* 1932 edn WENLOCK, B), and *dsp* 19 June 1825

    1a Dorothy; *m* 24 Nov 1784 Richard Langley, of Wykeham Abbey, and *d* 13 April 1824

    2a Henrietta; *m* 25 May 1787 6th Earl of Scarbrough (*qv*) and *d* March 1846

  (2) Francis, of Hesley, Notts; *b* 1727; *m* 25 May 1762 Octavia, dau and coheir of Francis Fisher, of The Grange, Grantham, Lincs, and had, with other issue:

    1a DIGBY WILLOUGHBY, **7th Baron Middleton of Middleton**; *b* 26 Nov 1769; *d* unm 5 Nov 1856

  (3) James (Rev); *b* 1731; Rector Guiseley, Yorks; *m* Eleanor, dau and coheir of James Hobson, of Kirkby Moorside, and *d* 1816, leaving:

    1a Henry, of Birdsall and Settrington, Yorks; *b* 15 Dec 1780; *m* 1815 Charlotte (*d* 1845), est dau of Ven Archdeacon John Eyre, of Babworth, and *d* 1849, leaving:

      1b HENRY, **8th Baron**

2b Francis Digby; *b* 17 Jan 1819; Capt 9th Lancers; *d* Meerut, India, 27 April 1846

3b Charles James (Rev); *b* 5 Feb 1822; granted with his siblings rank of baron's daus/yr s; Rector Wollaton-with-Cossall, Notts; *m* 7 Aug 1845 Charlotte Payne (*d* 13 Jan 1892), est dau of Henry John Hyde Seymour (*see* SOMERSET, D), and *d* 6 Nov 1875, having had:

  1c Adolphus Henry; *b* 14 June 1846; *d* 4 Aug 1859

  2c Hugh St Maur (Rev); *b* 13 June 1847; Vicar Fawley, Berks, Rector Trowell, Notts; *m* 22 Sept 1874 Anne Blanche (*d* 1931), dau of George Thomas Davy, of Colston Basset, Notts, and *d* 3 Sept 1904, having had:

    1d Magdalen; *m* 14 Nov 1901 Hugh Ker Colville (*d* 22 Feb 1930), of Bellaport Hall, Salop, 2nd s of Thomas Colville, of Annfield, Stirlingshire, and *d* 12 Aug 1965, leaving issue

    2d Bridget; *m* 28 July 1910 Hammett Drake (*d* 4 Sept 1915), 4th s of Maj-Gen John Mervyn Cutcliffe Drake, CB, RE, and had issue

  3c Charles Stuart Percival; *b* 13 Aug 1848; Maj 96th Foot; *m* 2 Dec 1880 Elizabeth (*d* 1939), 3rd dau of Frederick A Wiggins, of Bayswater, and *d* 6 Dec 1909, leaving:

    1d Geoffrey St Maur; *b* 11 Nov 1881; Maj 2nd/9th Bn Hants Regt; *m* 1st 3 May 1910 Julia Henrietta Cave (*d* 18 June 1946), dau of Rev Edmund Joseph Francis Johnson, Rector Sarsden-cum-Churchill; *m* 2nd 30 Aug 1947 Gwyneth Preston (*d* 1981), only dau of Arthur Henry Willmore, of Oak Ridge, Chandlers Ford, Hants, and *d* 11 Dec 1954, having by his 1st w had:

      1e *Julia Hermione [Mrs Richard Chamberlen, Little Pitt, Wonston, Hants SO21 3LR; Edificio Portanova 310, Palma Nova, Majorca, Spain]; *b* 9 Aug 1913; Naval cypher staff Gibraltar 1940–42; *m* 1936 *Lt-Cdr (S) Richard William Chamberlen, RNR, and has had issue

    4c Cecil Edward; *b* 2 Feb 1851; Lt RN; *m* 26 July 1883 Harriet Maud (*d* 16 June 1951), dau of Sir Thomas Birkin, of Ruddington, Notts, and *d* 28 Jan 1930, leaving:

      1d Gladys Maude; *b* 24 April 1884; *d* unm 27 Jan 1946

      2d Hilda St Maur; *b* 16 Sept 1885 *m* 1st 12 Nov 1913 (*divorce* 1922) Lt-Col George Albert Jessop Cantrell-Hubbersty, DSO (*d* 11 Feb 1928), Notts Hus, of Alsop Hall, Ashbourne, Derbys, 2nd s of Col Albert Cantrell-Hubbersty, of Ragdale Hall, Leics; *m* 2nd 22 June 1922 Brig-Gen Rupert Farquhar Riley, CMG, DSO (*d* 12 Oct 1941), and *d* 1 Feb 1964, leaving issue

  5c Gerard Francis; *b* 28 June 1853; *d* 18 April 1928

  6c Henry Somerset; *b* 1 July 1854

  7c James Frederick Digby, OBE (1920), JP (Notts); *b* 19 May 1856; MRCS Eng, LRCP London; *m* 26 Oct 1881 Mary Elizabeth (*d* 29 Jan 1927), dau of Rev Edward J Randolph, Canon York, and *d* 17 Dec 1947, having had:

    1d Ronald James Edward; *b* 7 May 1884; Cdr RN; *m* 19 June 1930 Constance Louisa (*d* 1977), yst dau of Rev (Henry) Nevile Sherbrook (*see* WESTMORLAND, E), and *d* 1971, leaving:

      1e +Christopher Ronald [Christopher Willoughby, 5340 Falmouth Rd, Bethesda, MD 20816, USA]; *b* 24 Feb 1938; *educ* Marlborough and Balliol Coll Oxford; IBRD Washington, DC; *m* 1972 *Marie-Anne, er dau of Emile Normand, of Charmalières, Clermont-Ferrand, France

      1e *Josephine Cicely Alice [Miss Josephine Willoughby, 45 Templar Rd, Oxford OX2 8LS]; *b* 21 June 1931; SRN

      2e *Nina Mary [Mrs David Lines, Ewens Farm, W Chelborough, Dorset DT2 0PY]; *b* 11 June 1933; *m* 4 April 1959 *Cdr David Harold Lines, OBE, RN, s of Harold Thomas Lines, of Alresford, Hants, and has:

        1f *Charles Willoughby; *b* 21 Aug 1960; *m* 1986 *Catherine, dau of Brian Campbell and has:

          1g *Jonathan Richard; *b* 1992

          1g *Jessica Mary; *b* 1987

        2f *Patrick Simon; *b* 13 Sept 1963

        3f *James Michael; *b* 18 July 1965; Lt-Cdr RN; *m* 1995 *Christine, dau of Harry Haddon, and has:

          1g *Samuel Toby; *b* 1997

        4f *Rupert Martin; *b* 6 July 1969

        1f *Vanessa Jane; *b* 8 Nov 1961; *m* 1988 *Richard Harold Davison, s of Eric Davison, and has:

          1g *Edward Henry; *b* 1990

          1g *Harriet Lucy; *b* 1991

          2g *Sarah Constance Louisa; *b* 1994

          3g *Elizabeth Alice; *b* 1997

    2d Archibald Macdonald; *b* 20 May 1887; Cdr RN; *m* 1st 27 July 1912 (*divorce* 1935) Mabel Doris (*d* 5 June 1956), dau of Sir William Norton Hicking, 1st Bt (*see* NORTH, Bt); *m* 2nd 28 Sept 1935 *Elizabeth [Mrs Charles Smyth, Flat 11, 68 Elm Park Gdns, London SW10] (*m* 2nd 21 March 1951 Capt Charles Devaynes Smyth (*d* 11 Feb 1962), s of Devaynes Smyth, of Bray Head, Co Wicklow), dau of Maj-Gen Sir John Hanbury-Williams, GCVO, KCB, CMG, and *das* 8 Nov 1943, having by his 1st w had:

      1e *Doris Barbara; *b* 3 June 1913; *m* 14 June 1937 Lancelot Roger Percival, MBE, TD, JP (*d* 1 Sept 1964), s of Preb Lancelot Jefferson Percival, KCVO, and has:

        1f *David William; *b* 17 Aug 1945; *educ* Milton Abbey

        1f *Gillian Barbara [Mrs Richard Hagen, Yew Tree House, Broadway, Worcs]; *b* 17 June 1938; *m* 1971 *Richard Llewellyn Whitley Hagen, s of Lawrence Arthur Hagen, of Norton, Presteigne, Radnorshire, and has issue

      2e *Pamela Mary Norton [Mrs Ronald Parkinson, Flat 5, 21 Osberton Rd, Oxford]; *b* 11 Nov 1916; *m* 12 Sept 1952 Rev Ronald Curnow Parkinson (*d* 1984), er s of William Parkinson, of Petergate, York

3e *Prudence Joan Mabel [Mrs John Hannay, Hill Cottage, 11-13 The Hill, Gt Walsingham, Norfolk]; *b* 22 April 1918; *m* 14 Dec 1949 *John Alexander Hannay, s of Howard Hannay, of Notting Hill, and has:

   1f *Johnathan Howard; *b* 24 July 1951; *educ* Lancing

   1f *Philippa Catherine; *b* 18 July 1953

4e *Sheila Katherine [Mrs Frederick Astley-Jones, Church Farm, Garway, Herefs]; *b* 9 Feb 1921; *m* 17 July 1952 *Cdr Frederick Edward Astley-Jones, RN, s of Capt A Astley-Jones, of Tenbury Wells, and Mrs Piet van der Byl, of S Africa, and has:

   1f *Hugh Edward Arthur; *b* 26 March 1953; *educ* Bradfield

   1f *Hilary Margaret Doris; *b* 21 Feb 1958

5e *Anne Rosemary [Mrs George Rothwell, Little Breach, Moulsford, Oxon OX10 9JN]; *b* 17 Jan 1926; *m* 25 Aug 1956 *George Frederick Rothwell, s of Richard Hornsby Rothwell, of Wallingford, and has:

   1f *James Peter; *b* 19 Oct 1958

   2f *Gerald Charles; *b* 24 April 1963

   3f *Charlotte Jane; *b* 25 Aug 1964

   4f *Frances Elizabeth; *b* 12 June 1966

3d Bernard Digby (Rev); *b* 8 April 1896; *educ* Wellington; Rector Ballinrobe, Co Mayo 1950, Canon Tuam Cathedral 1963–73, Maj IA; *m* 5 Sept 1944 *Ruth, dau of Walter Browne Barber, of Beacon Hill, Hucknall, Notts, and *d* 21 March 1997, leaving:

   1e +Colin James; *b* 20 Nov 1949; *educ* Portora Royal Sch; *m* 1976 *Bridget, dau of Brig Philip Henry Cecil Hayward, CBE, of the Old Mill House, Roughton, Norwich, and has:

      1f +Philip Mark Digby; *b* 1993

      1f *Georgia Violet; *b* 14 June 1996

   1e *Elisabeth Grace [Mrs Thomas Ormsby, Milford, Cloghans Hill, Tuam, Co Galway, Ireland]; *b* 8 June 1945; *m* 31 Oct 1964 *Thomas Miller Ormsby, only s of Lt-Col John Yeadon Ormsby, RA, of Milford, Cloghans Hill, Tuam, and has:

      1f *Thomas Anthony Bowen Miller; *b* 1969; *m* 1993 *Amanda Lex Edgley and has:

         1g *Ellen Catherine; *b* 14 Aug 1997

      2f *John Charles; *b* 1971

      1f *Lucy Anne [Mrs Geoffrey Tottenham, Cloragh, Ashford, Co Wicklow, Ireland]; *b* 9 Aug 1966; *m* 1992 *Geoffrey Tottenham and has:

         1g *Thomas Edward Charles; *b* 10 Feb 1997

         1g *Joanna Elisabeth Lucy; *b* 22 June 1994

      2f *Catherine; *b* 1973

1d Katherine Mary Seymour; *b* 20 Sept 1883; *m* 23 Oct 1915 John Gilbert Kennedy (*ka* Flanders 1916)

8c Leonard Broke; *b* 24 Nov 1860; Maj 14th Foot, Capt 3rd Bn Lancs Fus 1894, Maj 2ic 17th (service) Bn W Yorks Regt 1914–15, cmded 19th (Res) Bn 1915–17, Maj Staff 1917, Inspr QMG's Servs Northern Cmd 1917–19, Ch Govt Area Disposal Offr Treasury Northern and Western Cmds 1919–22; *m* 18 July 1888 Ada Mary (*d* 17 May 1960), dau of Charles Baxter Cousens, and *d* 1932, leaving:

   1d Charles d'Eresby; *b* 12 Sept 1889

   2d Gilbert de Bec; *b* 15 May 1894; *m* 7 Oct 1923 Queenie Kathleen Lillian (*d* 1978), dau of Charles William Henry Butts

1c Julia Mary; *m* 1st 9th June 1878 Rev Gordon Heslop (*d* 1894), Rector Levisham, Yorks; *m* 2nd 29 Sept 1898 Benjamin Day and *d* his widow 24 March 1931

2c Mildred Cassandra; *b* 25 July 1857; *m* 5 June 1881 Granville Walter Randolph, s of Rev Canon Randolph, Rector Dunnington, Yorks, and *d* 27 Nov 1936, leaving issue

3c Evelyn; *b* 16 March 1864; *m* 20 Nov 1884 Rev Robert John Thorp, Rector Armthorpe, Yorks, and *d* 21 Oct 1934, leaving issue

4b Percival George (Rev); *b* 1 March 1827; MA Cantab, Rector Durweston-cum-Bryanston, Dorset; *m* 20 April 1852 Sophia (*d* 15 Jan 1898), est dau of Edward Blackett Beaumont, of Woodhall, Yorks (*see* ALLENDALE, V), and *d* 8 July 1913, leaving:

   1c Herbert Percival; *b* 19 Jan 1853; Col RA; *m* 20 July 1875 Mary Louisa, 3rd dau of T Allen Brown, of Allahabad, and *dvp* 5 April 1913, having had:

      1d Cecil Percival; *b* 28 May 1876; *d* 17 Feb 1877

      2d Nesbit Edward; *b* 4 July 1878; Lt East Surrey Regt; *ka* 19 Nov 1916

      3d Percival Francis; *b* 16 Oct 1882; Cdr RN

      4d John Herbert; *b* 13 April 1896; Capt RM; *m* 19– Dorothy Mary — and *d* 1975, having had:

         1e *Lois Ann Mary; *b* 19–

      1d Eva Mary; *b* 1877; *d* unm 24 Nov 1960

      2d Mabel Isabel; *b* 1880; *d* unm

   2c Nesbit Edward (Rev); *b* 5 April 1854; Vicar Bickington, Devon, 1916–19; *m* 1st 18 June 1889 Florence Mary (*dsp* 15 Sept 1897), dau of Rev E Lowe; *m* 2nd 29 Oct 1901 Marjorie Helen, dau of John E Kaye, and *d* Feb 1919, leaving:

      1d Guy, CB (1955); *b* 7 Nov 1902; served WW II, R-Adml, Dir Air Warfare and Training Admlty 1945–46, memb Australian Cwlth Navy Bd 1948–50, Flag Offr Flying Training 1953–56; *m* 10 July 1923 Mary (*d* 1990), dau of James George Wilcox Aldridge, AMICE, and *d* 1987, having had:

         1e +Hugh Nesbit; *b* 24 Aug 1925; *educ* Monckton Combe Sch; ARIBA, Dip AA, RAF WW II and RE 1943–47

         1e Anthea Joan; *b* 14 Dec 1929; *m* *Richard Alan Cornelius, s of W C V Cornelius, of E Coker, Somerset, and adopted:

         *Stuart William Guy; *b* 9 Nov 1963

         *Philippa Mary; *b* 22 April 1965

   2d Lawrence; *b* 5 May 1908; MB, ChB Bristol 1940, MRCOG 1951, Surgn-Cdr RNVR; *m* 1st 1936 Mrs Dorothy Hughes (*d* 16 July 1956); *m* 2nd 1 Aug 1957 Elizabeth (*d* 1987), dau of Alexander Sadowski, of Rosko, Poland, and *d* 1980, having by her had:

      1e +Guy Alexander [Guy Willoughby Esq, 11823-83rd St, Edmonton, Alberta, Canada]; *b* Oct 1958

      2e Digby Edward; *b* Dec 1959

      1e *Veronica Anne (twin); *b* Oct 1958

3d Anthony; *b* 28 Feb 1911; *m* 1942 *Olive Andrews

4d Bernard; *b* 7 May 1914; Lt (A) RN; *m* 14 July 1940 *Elizabeth Jane Delves (*m* 2nd Anthony Pim; *m* 3rd 1948 Kenneth Philipps (*d* 1950); *m* 4th Bruce Clark), er dau of Lt-Col Geoffrey Delves Broughton (*see* BROUGHTON, Bt), and was missing believed *ka* over Java March 1942

1d Veronica; *b* 4 Dec 1903; *m* 1935 George Alexander Scott and had issue

2d Gwendolen Mary; *b* 11 Sept 1905; RRC (1959), Lt-Col QARANC

3c Aubrey Frederick; *b* 1 July 1857; slr; *m* 11 July 1907 Kathleen Alice (*m* 2nd 22 June 1912 Luigi Canepa, of Sestri, Italy, and was *k* by enemy action *c* 1941), yr dau of Cdr George Purcell, RN, and *dsp* 7 Jan 1911

4c Sydney Beaumont; *b* 29 March 1859; *m* 7 June 1887 Hon Margaret Katherine Erskine (*d* 25 July 1940), dau of 4th Baron Erskine of Restormel (*see* BUCHAN, E), and *d* 5 Aug 1921, leaving:

   1d Horace Lancelot; *d* 28 June 1950

   2d Christopher John; *b* 4 Sept 1889; Lt Welsh Gds; *m* 16 Aug 1942 Mary Hastings (*d* 30 Dec 1965), dau of P G Edgar, and *d* 19–

1c Edith Louisa; *b* 7 Feb 1856; *d* unm 17 Oct 1890

2c Mabel Eleanor; *b* 4 Oct 1860; *d* unm 4 June 1931

3c Ethel Mary; *b* 29 June 1862; *d* unm 10 Sept 1945

4c Alice Lilian; *b* 16 Feb 1865; *d* unm 16 May 1880

1b Charlotte Henrietta; *m* 26 Oct 1839 H Willoughby Legard and *d* 25 Jan 1844, leaving issue (*see* LEGARD, Bt)

2b Emma; *m* April 1850 Rev Richard Beverley Machell, MA (*d* 18 Aug 1898), Canon York, Rector Roos, and *d* 10 June 1915, leaving issue

3b Harriet Cassandra; *m* 5 July 1864 Godfrey Wentworth Bayard Bosville, *de jure* 13th Bt, and *d* 28 Sept 1903, leaving issue (*see* BOSVILLE MACDONALD, Bt)

1a Elizabeth; *m* 30 Oct 1798 J S Foljambe (*d* 14 Jan 1805), of Alwarke, and *d* 25 Sept 1858, leaving issue (*see* LIVERPOOL, E)

2a Emma; *d* 11 May 1859

The 7th BARON's cousin,

HENRY WILLOUGHBY, **8th Baron Middleton of Middleton**; *b* 28 Aug 1817; *educ* Eton and Trin Coll Cambridge; *m* 3 Aug 1843 Julia Louisa, only dau of Alexander William Bosville, *de jure* 12th Bt (*see* BOSVILLE MACDONALD, Bt), and *d* 20 Dec 1877, having had:

1 DIGBY WENTWORTH BAYARD WILLOUGHBY, **9th Baron Middleton of Middleton**, JP (E and N Ridings, Yorks), DL (Ross-shire and Notts); *b* 24 Aug 1844; CA E R Yorks, Capt Scots Fus Gds, Hon Col 1st Yorks Vol Brig RA (Vol Offrs decoration); *m* 5 Aug 1869 Eliza Maria Gordon (*d* 27 April 1922), only dau of Sir Alexander Penrose Gordon-Cumming, 3rd Bt (*qv*), and *dsp* 28 May 1922

2 GODFREY ERNEST PERCIVAL, **10th Baron**

3 Francis Henry Stirling; *b* 13 Aug 1848; *d* unm 23 June 1900

4 Rothwell James Bosville; *b* 26 May 1850; RN; *d* 1867

5 Leopold Vincent Harold; *b* 19 Nov 1851; MA Oxon; *d* 22 March 1924

6 Tatton Lane Fox, JP and DL (N R Yorks); *b* 29 Dec 1860; ADC to Govr Victoria 1890–91, Lt-Col York Regt 1915–16, Hon Col 5th Bn Green Howards, formerly Lt Yorks Hus; *m* 18 June 1898 Esther Ann, OBE (1920), JP (*d* 23 May 1940), only dau of Sir Charles William Strickland, 8th Bt (*see* STRICKLAND-CONSTABLE, Bt), and *dsp* 10 July 1947

7 Claude Henry Comaraich, CVO; *b* 1 July 1862; Lt-Col and Brev Col 9th Lancers, Groom-in-Waiting to HM GEORGE V, Mil Sec to Govr-Gen Australia, Boer War 1899–1900, cmded a Bde TF 1908–11, Dep Ranger Windsor Gt Park 1916–29; *m* 24 Aug 1893 Sybil Louise (*d* 8 Oct 1957), only dau of Charles James Murray (*see* DUNMORE, E), and *d* 22 Sept 1932, having had:

   (1) Henry Douglas; *b* 14, *d* 27 March 1908

   (1) *Mary Bridget [Lady Howard-Vyse, Town Farm Cottage, Langton, Malton, Yorks]; *b* 26 Oct 1910; *m* 20 July 1940 Lt-Gen Sir Edward Dacre Howard-Vyse, KBE, CB, MC, DL (*d* 1992), yr s of Col Cecil Howard-Vyse, JP, of Langton Hall, Malton, and has:

      1a *Richard Edward, TD, DL (N Yorks) [Richard Howard-Vyse Esq TD JP DL, Town Farm, Langton, Malton, Yorks YO17 9QP]; *b* 1941; *m* 1965 *Sally Rosemary, dau of Cdr R R Whalley, RN, and has:

         1b *Thomas Norcliffe; *b* 1971

         1b *Mary Elizabeth; *b* 1975

         2b *Alice Joan Lucy; *b* 1978

      2a *John Cecil [Lt-Col John Howard-Vyse, Old Vicarage, Burneston, Bedale, N Yorks DL8 2HP]; *b* 1947; Lt-Col RA; *m* 1972 *Jennifer Anne, er dau of Maj-Gen Geoffrey de Egglesfield Collin, CB, MC, DL, of Roecliffe, Boroughbridge, and has:

         1b *James Edward; *b* 1977

         1b *Georgina; *b* 1975

         2b *Victoria; *b* 1980

      1a *Elizabeth [Mrs George Perera, St Hilda's Vicarage, 7 Kingsmead Drive, Hunts Cross, Liverpool L25 0NG]; *b* 1945; *m* 1983 *Rev George A Perera, er s of J K P Perera, FRCS, of Blundellsands, Liverpool, and has:

         1b *Timothy Mark Grant; *b* 1985

         2b *Christopher John Kenneth; *b* 1987

         3b *Robert; *b* 1989

(2) Joan Lavinia; *b* 18 June 1913; *m* 1960 Harry Nettleton (*d* 1996) and *dsp* 23 Nov 1989

8 Alexander Hugh; *b* 18 Sept 1863; Capt 3rd Bn Princess of Wales's Own Yorks Regt, ADC to GOC E Yorks Bde; *m* 14 Aug 1889 Mary Selina Honoria (*d* 12 Jan 1925), dau of Gen Hon James Bosville-Macdonald, CB (*see* MACDONALD, B), and *d* 5 Dec 1927, leaving:

(1) James Alexander; *b* 31 July 1890; Capt Northants Regt WW I (wounded), WW II as W/Cdr RAF (despatches); *m* 1st 10 Aug 1918 (*divorce*1926) Dorothea Maryon, est dau of Richard Hilton Burbrook, and had:

1a *Diana Evelyn Mary [Mrs John Martens, 1 Tower House, London Rd, Arundel, W Sussex BN18 9BH]; *b* 1 April 1919; *m* 9 Aug 1941 John Erwin Martens (*d* 1984), F/Capt ATA, er s of Erwin Gustav Martens

2a *Susan Clara; *b* 2 July 1922; *m* 1963 Maj Robert Bellord, Irish Gds (*d* 1970), and has:

1b *Sarah Mary [Mrs Richard Astell, 60 Clarewood Court, Crawford St, London W1H 5DF; Shaggs Cottage, E Lulworth, Dorset]; *b* 1st 1969 (*divorce* 1984) Martin Charles Neale Thompson, s of Lt-Col Sir Edward Hugh Dudley Thompson, MBE, TD, DL, of Culland Hall, Brailsford, Derbys; *m* 2nd 1986 *Richard William Godfrey Astell, of Putney, and has:

1c *Rupert Alexander Robert Neale; *b* 1973

2c *Edward Charles Neale; *b* 1974

1c *Miranda Mary; *b* 1971

(1) (cont.) James Willoughby *m* 2nd 1926 Jill (*d* 1977), yr dau of David Denton, FRCO, of Newport Pagnell, Bucks, and *d* 22 Nov 1955, having by her had:

3a *Griselda Mary Honoria [Mrs Paul Gifford, Holly Lodge, Weathercock Lane, Woburn Sands, Bucks]; *b* 26 May 1931; *m* 18 March 1955 *Lt Paul Julian David Gifford, RN, s of Dr Alexander Harold Gifford, and has:

1b *Mark Richard Alexander; *b* 1960

1b *Nicola Jane; *b* 1965

(2) Joe Henry Claude; *b* 25 Jan 1892; Capt RN, WWs I and II (Haakon VII Liberty Medal Norway); *m* 14 March 1919 Enid Mary (*d* 1980), dau of Harry J Clements, of Somerville Ho, Sutton Coldfield, and *d* 1966, leaving:

1a *Ann Honoria Mary [Mrs Wayne Etive, 3184 Pioneer Rd, Medford, OR, USA]; *b* 10 May 1920; *m* 1st 1940 S/Ldr P Campbell-Canney, RAF (*ka* 1942), s of R Campbell-Canney, MD, of Cambridge, and has:

1b *Josephine; *b* 1942

1a (cont.) Mrs P Campbell-Canney *m* 2nd 8 Jan 1944 (*divorce*) John Dean, of Vancouver, BC; *m* 3rd 19– *Wayne Etive

(3) Ernest Hugh; *b* Nov 1893; *d* 7 March 1894

1 Alexandrina Henrietta Matilda; *m* 3 Feb 1869 Sir John Thorold, 12th Bt (*qv*), and *d* 11 Dec 1931, leaving issue

2 Leila Louisa Millicent; *m* 10 Feb 1876 Rev Henry Charles Russell and *d* 24 Feb 1886, leaving issue (*see* BEDFORD, D)

3 Hylda Maria Madeline, MBE (1919); *m* 20 April 1882 William Henry Garforth (*d* 15 June 1931) and *d* 1 Feb 1944, leaving issue

4 Lettice Hermione Violet; *m* 18 April 1895 Col William Gordon-Cumming, ISC (*see* GORDON-CUMMING, Bt) and *d* Aug 1922

5 Mairi Myrtle; *m* 1 Jan 1880 William Bethell (*d* 13 Aug 1926), of Rise, Yorks, and *d* 13 Nov 1900, leaving issue

The 9th BARON's bro,

GODFREY ERNEST PERCIVAL WILLOUGHBY, **10th Baron Middleton of Middleton**; *b* 18 June 1847; Midshipman RN and Capt 9th Lancers; *m* 15 June 1881 Ida Eleonora Constance (*d* 7 March 1924), yst dau of George W H Ross, of Cromarty, and *d* 11 Nov 1924, having had:

1 Henry Ernest Digby Hugh; *b* 1 July 1882; Cdr RN; *ka* off Jutland 31 May 1916

2 MICHAEL GUY PERCIVAL, **11th Baron**

3 Francis George Godfrey; *b* 29 Aug 1890; Capt 9th Bn Rifle Bde, *ka* 9 Aug 1915

4 (Rothwell) Charles Wentworth; *b* 13 Feb 1896; Lt-Cdr RN; *m* 3 July 1939 Violet Ivy (*d* 21 Nov 1972), formerly w of John Geoffrey Frere and only dau of Maj James Douglas Sparks, Roy Fus, and *dsp* 27 Sept 1960

1 Adelaide Daphne Hermione; *b* 20 Nov 1883; *m* 3 Nov 1909 R-Adml Laurence Richard Oliphant, CBE (*d* 6 Dec 1950), 2nd s of Arthur Craigie Oliphant, and *d* 6 March 1954, leaving issue

2 Leila Myrtle Dorothea; *b* 21 June 1886; *m* 26 Sept 1931 Thomas Alexander Ballard (*d* 3 Dec 1931), s of Thomas Ballard, of Walton-on-Thames, resumed by deed poll maiden name WILLOUGHBY 1947 and *dsp* 17 March 1961

3 Ida Mary Hazel; *b* 30 Aug 1889; *m* 31 Aug 1910 Capt Henry Strickland, OBE, RN (*d* 2 Sept 1934), yst s of Sir Charles William Strickland, 8th Bt (*see* STRICKLAND-CONSTABLE, Bt), and *d* 12 July 1965, leaving issue

4 Julia Violet Monica Louise; *b* 8 Dec 1893; *d* unm 5 May 1926

The 10th BARON's er surv s,

MICHAEL GUY PERCIVAL WILLOUGHBY, **11th Baron Middleton of Middleton**, KG (1957), MC, TD (1942), JP (E R Yorks 1925); *b* 21 Oct 1887; *educ* Wellington and RMC Sandhurst; Col late 5th Bn Green Howards (TA), Maj 10th Lancers IA WW I (despatches), cmded 5th Bn Green Howards (TA), and WW II (cmded 5th and 30th Bns E Yorks Regt), Pres U Coll Hull 1931–70, Ld Lt E R Yorks 1936–68, Chllr Hull U 1954–70, Pres E R Yorks TA&AFA, Hon Freeman Hull 1968, KStJ, Hon LLD Leeds 1955 and Hull 1955; *m* 28 April 1920 Angela Florence Alfreda (*d* 11 Jan 1978), est dau of Charles Oswin Hall, of Eddlethorpe, Malton, Yorks, and *d* 16 Nov 1970, leaving:

1 (DIGBY) MICHAEL GODFREY JOHN WILLOUGHBY, **12th and present Baron Middleton of Middleton**

2 +(Henry Ernest) Christopher [Brig The Hon Christopher Willoughby, Somerleyton House, White Hart St, E Harling, Norfolk NR16 2NE]; *b* 12 June 1932; *educ* Eton and RMA Sandhurst; Lt-Col Coldstream Gds, Brig, Def Attaché Ankara; *m* 1st 7 May 1955 (*divorce*1990) Jean Adini, er dau of Lt-Col John David and Lady Rosemary Hills (*see* CROMER, E); *m* 2nd 1990 *J Elizabeth, dau of Robert Philip Sidney Bache, OBE, of Himbleton, Worcs, and by his 1st w has:

(1) +Guy Nesbit John [Guy Willoughby Esq, Gilchristland House, Thornhill, Dumfriesshire DG3 5HN]; *b* 2 June 1960; *educ* Eton and RMA Sandhurst; Lt Coldstream Gds, dir The HALO Trust; *m* 1990 *Fiona K, dau of Patrick Stewart-Blacker, of Blairgowrie, Perthshire, and has:

1a *Louisa Ariana Rose; *b* 2 Nov 1992

1b *Eritrea Isabella; *b* 20 Jan 1996

(1) *(Angela) Jane; *b* 5 Feb 1956; *m* 4 June 1976 *Denis Patrick Antony Critchley-Salmonson and has issue (*see* HOWARD DE WALDEN, B)

(2) *Caroline Rosemary; *b* 22 May 1957

1 *Angela Hermione Ida [The Hon Mrs Charles Wynn, Bunkersland, Withleigh, Tiverton, Devon]; *b* 5 May 1924; *m* 16 Dec 1947 *Lt-Cdr Hon Charles Henry Romer Wynn, RN, yr s of Lt-Col 6th Baron Newborough (*qv*), and has issue

2 *Jean Elizabeth Mary [The Hon Lady Matheson, Hedenham Old Rectory, Bungay, Norfolk NR35 2LD]; *b* 26 Jan 1928; *m* 17 May 1952 *Maj Sir Fergus John Matheson, 7th Bt (*qv*), and has issue

MIDDLETON, Bt

Arms: Quarterly gu. and or, in the first quarter a cross flory arg.
Crest: A wild man arg., holding in bend an oak tree eradicated bendways or. **Creation:** Bt. (E) 24 Oct 1662.

SIR LAWRENCE MONCK MIDDLETON, 10TH BT, of Belsay Castle, Northumberland [Sir Lawrence Middleton Bt, Estate Office, Belsay Castle, Newcastle-upon-Tyne NE20 0DY]; *b* 23 Oct 1912; *s* bro 1993; *educ* Eton and Edinburgh U (BSc Forestry 1939); *m* 1984 *Mrs Primrose Westcombe, dau of Lawrence Haynes Adams, of Shrubland House, Soham, Cambs

Lineage: Sir JOHN de MIDDLETON, of Belsay Castle, Northumberland; *m* Christian, eventual coheir of 1st and last Lord (Baron) Stryvelyn (*i.e.*, Stirling), a leading military man in EDWARD III's wars against the Scots, for which services he was granted the reversion of the Manor of Belsay 1335, and had:

Sir JOHN de MIDDLETON; MP Northumberland *temp* HENRY V; ancestor of:

ROBERT MIDDLETON, of Belsay Castle; *m* as his 2nd w Mabell, dau of John Ogle, of Ogle Castle, Northumberland, and had, with other issue:

RALPH MIDDLETON, of Trewick, Northumberland; *m* Isabel, dau of Ambrose Fenwick, of West Matfen, and had, with other issue:

Sir William Middleton, 1st Bt (E), so *cr* 24 Oct 1662, of Belsay Castle; Sheriff Northumberland 1666; *m* 1st Mary (*d* 16 Sept 1667), 2nd dau of Sir Thomas Wentworth, of Elmsall, Yorks, and had issue (*d* unm); *m* 2nd Elizabeth (*bur* 23 Feb 1680), dau of John Mundy, of Markeaton, Derbys, and was *bur* 22 March 1690, having by her had, with an er s (William, *dsp*) and four daus (of whom Elizabeth *m* Sir James Clavering, Bt):

Sir John Middleton, 2nd Bt; *b* 1678; *m* Frances, dau and sole heiress of John Lambert, of Calton, Yorks (est s of Maj-Gen Lambert, Parly General), and *d* 1717, leaving, with other issue:

1 **Sir William Middleton, 3rd Bt**; MP Northumberland 1722–57; *m* Anne, dau and coheir of William Ettrick, of Silkworth, Co Durham, and *dspm* 28 Sept 1757

2 JOHN LAMBERT (Sir), **4th Bt**

3 Thomas; *m* Rebecca Guy and had:

(1) Barbara; *m* Rev Hugh Nanny

Sir WILLIAM's bro,

Sir John Lambert Middleton, 4th Bt; *b* 14 June 1705; *m* 1737 Anne (*d* 1762), dau of Sir Nathaniel Hodges and widow of Warner Perkins, and had, with other issue:

1 WILLIAM (Sir), **5th Bt**

2 John, of Bickington, Devon; *m* Catherine, dau of Amos Thorne, and *d* Nov 1778, leaving, with other issue:

(1) John; *b* 25 Jan 1771; *m* Martha — and had, with a dau (*d* unm):

1a John Clement (Rev); Rector Greenford, Middx; *m* 1877 Emily, dau of Robert Miller, Serjeant-at-law, and *d* 13 Dec 1899

1 Elizabeth; *m* Jacob Reeson and *dsp*

2 Frances Jory; *m* 1770 Sir George Cooke, 7th Bt (*qv*), of Wheatley Hall, nr Doncaster

Sir JOHN *d* 22 March 1768; his est son,

Sir William Middleton, 5th Bt; *b* 6 June 1738; Capt RHG (Blues), severely wounded Battle of Minden 1 Aug 1759, MP Northumberland 1774; *m* 20 April 1774 Jane (*d* June 1794), only surv dau and heiress of Lawrence Monck, of Caenby, Lincs, and had, with other issue:

1 William Lawrence; *dsp* 29 Nov 1789

2 Thomas Ogle; *dspm* 10 March 1784

3 CHARLES MILES LAMBERT (Sir), **6th Bt**

1 Isabella Cecilia Viviana; *m* 8 April 1823 Sir William B K Cooke, 8th Bt, of Wheatley Park, nr Doncaster (*qv*), and *d* 26 Nov 1869

Sir WILLIAM *d* 7 July 1795; his only surv son,

Sir CHARLES MILES LAMBERT MIDDLETON later MONCK (1799 under terms of will of maternal gf Lawrence Monck), **6th Bt**; *b* 7 April 1779; MP Northumberland 1812–20; *m* 1st 11 Sept 1804 Louisa (*d* 5 Dec 1824), 2nd dau of Sir George Cooke, 7th Bt (*qv*); *m* 2nd 26 July 1831 Mary Elizabeth (*d* 27 Feb 1851), dau of 4th Earl of Tankerville (*qv*), and by his 1st w had, with other issue:

1 Charles Atticus; *b* 17 July 1805; Offr Coldstream Gds; *m* 2 May 1835 Laura (*d* 29 April 1873), dau of Sir Matthew White Ridley, 3rd Bt (*see* RIDLEY, V), and *d* 12 Dec 1856, leaving, with other issue:

(1) ARTHUR EDWARD (Sir), **7th Bt**

(2) Henry Nicholas MONCK later MIDDLETON (12 Feb 1876), JP (Northumberland and Roxburghs), DL (Northumberland); *b* 27 July 1845; Lt Rifle Bde, V-Chm Northumberland CC; *m* 7 March 1872 Sophia Elizabeth (*d* 28 Jan 1927), er dau of Ch Justice Sir William Colles Meredith, DCL, of Quebec, and *d* 6 Dec 1928, leaving:

1a Lambert William; *b* 29 April 1877; *m* 21 Sept 1922 Lady Sybil Grey, OBE (1918) (*d* 4 June 1966), 2nd dau of 4th Earl Grey (*qv*), and *d* 10 Dec 1941, leaving:

1b +HENRY (HARRY) LAMBERT [Henry Middleton Esq, Enbrook House, Ball Hill, Berks RG15 0NU]; *b* 26 Aug 1923; heir presumptive; *educ* Eton and New Coll Oxford; joined BBC 1943, announcer 1944, Assist Head Outside Broadcasts Sound 1955–59, Assist Head Outside Broadcasts TV 1959–63, Head Events Dept Outside Broadcasts Gp 1963–65, Ch Assist and Dep to Gen Manager TV Outside Broadcasts 1965; *m* 8 Jan 1964 (*divorce* 19–) (Susan) Jenifer, er dau of William Arthur Fearnley Whittingstall, TD, QC, JP, of The Old Manor House, Milbourn, Cambs, and widow of Hon Rodney Mathias Berry (*see* CAMROSE, V), and has:

1c *Laura Sybil Rose; *b* 7 July 1969; *m* 30 Aug 1997 *Peter de Wesselow, yst s of Ian de Wesselow, of Shurlock Row, Berks

1b *Mary Sybil [Mrs John Boyd, Whiterigg, Melrose, Roxburghshire TD6 9HE]; *b* 4 July 1925; *m* 20 Feb 1948 *Capt John Brooke Boyd, KOSB, only s of Cdr John Gordon Boyd, RN, of Whiterigg, and has:

1c *Simon John [Simon Boyd Esq, 34 Kimberley Rd, Cambridge]; *b* 1949; *educ* Eton and New Coll Oxford; *m* 1979 *Julia Mary Seiber

2c *James Lambert [James Boyd Esq, Rue Rotselaerlaan 13, 3180 Tervuren, Belgium]; *b* 1952; *educ* Eton

1c *Caroline Elizabeth (twin); *b* 1952

2c *Diana Mary [Mrs Neil Braithwaite, Aydon Grange, Corbridge, Northumberland]; *b* 1952; *m* 1990 *Neil Braithwaite

1a Laura Beatrice; *b* 16 Jan 1874; *m* 5 Feb 1902 Maj William Barnett, KRRC (*d* 16 July 1912), and *d* 27 Nov 1967, leaving issue

2a Harriett Constance; *b* 21 Aug 1875; *m* 6 Dec 1910 Adml William Henry Baker Baker, OBE, JP, DL (*d* 7 Aug 1932), yst s of Henry John Baker Baker, of Elemore Hall, Durham, and had issue

3a Dorothy; *b* and *d* 1894

(1) Alice Louisa; *b* 29 June 1841; *m* 17 July 1862 Sir John William Powlett Campbell-Orde, 3rd Bt (*qv*), and *d* 7 Jan 1883, leaving issue

2 William (Rev); *b* 13 July 1809; *d* 19 May 1845

1 Julia; *m* 1 May 1830 Sir Edward Blackett, 6th Bt (*qv*), and *d* 25 June 1846, leaving issue

Sir CHARLES *d* 20 July 1867; his gs,

Sir ARTHUR EDWARD MONCK later MIDDLETON (12 Feb 1876), **7th Bt**, JP (Northumberland); *b* 12 Jan 1838; *educ* Trin Coll Cambridge (BA); High Sheriff 1884, MP Durham 1874–80; *m* 8 Nov 1871 Lady Constance Harriet Amherst (*d* 7 Oct 1879), dau of 2nd Earl Amherst (*see* AMHERST OF HACKNEY, B, preliminary remarks), and *d* 1 April 1933, having had:

1 Gilbert William; *b* 23 Aug 1872; *d* 1 Jan 1896

2 **Sir Charles Arthur Middleton, 8th Bt**; *b* 22 Oct 1873; *d* unm 22 Feb 1942

3 Hugh Jeffery; *b* 1 Oct 1879; Lt RN, Cdr RNVR; *m* 22 July 1905 Mary Katharine, OBE (1920), JP (Northumberland) (*d* 23 Aug 1949), er dau of R-Adml Samuel Long, and *d* 10 Aug 1914, leaving:

(1) John Arthur Tournay, JP (Northumberland); *b* 1 July 1906; Lt Northumberland Hus; *d* unm 11 May 1939

(2) **Sir Stephen Hugh Middleton, 9th Bt**; *b* 20 June 1909; *educ* Eton and Magdalene Coll Cambridge; *m* 21 May 1962 *Mary E Robinson and *dsp* 1993

(3) Sir LAWRENCE MONCK MIDDLETON, **10th and present Bt**

(1) Katharine Elinor; *b* 15 Sept 1907; *d* unm 11 Oct 1947

1 Gertrude Mary; *b* 24 May 1875; *d* unm 16 June 1909

2 Elinor Isabel, JP (Northumberland); *b* 2 Nov 1876; *d* unm 5 Oct 1942

Seat: Belsay Castle, Northumberland. Belsay is a combination of medieval tower house and Georgian mansion annexe more usual in Ireland than England. The former dates back to the 14th century and is now completely uninhabitable. The latter, erected by the **6th Baronet**, who dropped the name Middleton for that of Monck, is neo-classical in design. The grounds extend over 30 acres and are famous for the unusual species of flowering trees to be found in the section known as the Quarry Gardens. These too were Sir Charles Monck's contribution.

MIDLETON

A · CUSPIDE · CORONA

Arms: Argent, on a chief vert two spears' heads erect of the field, the points embrued gules. **Crest:** Out of a ducal coronet or, a spear argent, embued gules. **Supporters:** Two men in complete armour, each holding in his exterior hand a spear, all proper.
Motto: *A cuspide corona* ('From the spear a crown').
Creations: V. (I) 15 Aug 1717, B. (Brodrick of Midleton) (I) 13 April 1715 and (Brodrick of Peper Harow) (GB) 11 June 1796.

THE 12TH VISCOUNT MIDLETON OF MIDLETON, Co Cork, **Baron Brodrick of Midleton**, Co Cork, and **Baron Brodrick of Peper Harow**, Co Surrey (Alan Henry Brodrick) [The Rt Hon The Viscount Midleton, 2 Burrell's Orchard, Westley, Suffolk IP33 3TH]; *b* 4 Aug 1949; *s* unc 1988; *educ* St Edmund's Canterbury; Keeper Horology John Gershom Parkington Collection of Time Measurement Instruments, Bury St Edmunds, 1986–, Br Horological Inst: Fell, memb Cncl 1993–, chm Museum and Library Ctee 1994–; *m* 1978 Julia Helen, dau of Michael Pitt, of Lias Cottage, Compton Dundon, Somerset, and has:

1 +ASHLEY RUPERT; *b* 25 Nov 1980

2 +William Michael; *b* 1982

1 *Charlotte Helen; *b* 1983

Lineage: WILLIAM BRODRICK, of Wandsworth (where he settled *temp* ELIZABETH I) and Richmond, Yorks; *d* 1620; f of:

Sir THOMAS BRODRICK, of Wandsworth; *b c* 1596; Lt-Govr Tower of London, ktd 1625; *m* Katharine (*bur* 4 Dec 1678), dau of Robert Nicholas, of Manningford Bruce, Wilts, by Jane, dau of Nicholas St John, of Lydiard Tregoze, Wilts, and *d* 1642, having had, with other issue (including two middle sons):

1 Alan (Sir); *b* 28 July 1623; ktd 1660, Surveyor, Estimator and Extensor-Gen Ireland 1660; *d* unm 25 Nov 1680

2 St John (Sir), of Midleton, Co Cork; *b* 3 Dec 1627; settled in Ireland during the troubles of 1641, obtained large tracts of land in Co Cork *c* 1680; *m* Alice (*bur* 21 April 1696), sis of Sir Randal Clayton, of Thelwall, Cheshire, and dau of Laurence Clayton, of Mallow, Co Cork, and *d* Jan 1711/2, having had:

(1) Thomas (Sir), PC (1714), of Ballyanan Castle, Midleton; *b* 4 Aug 1654; MP (I) Cork 1703, Jt Comptroller Army Accounts 1708, MP (GB) Stockbridge 1713 and Guildford 1722; *m* Anne (*d* 3 May 1731), dau of Alexander Pigott, of Inishannon, Co Cork, and *dsp* 3 Oct 1730

(2) ALAN, **1st Viscount**

(3) St John, of Lamb's Buildings, Middle Temple, London; Serjeant-at-law, *d* unm 13 June 1707

(4) William; Attorney-Gen Jamaica 1692, Justice King's Bench Ireland 1721; had a son

(5) Laurence (Rev), of Islip, Oxford, DD; Chaplain H of C 1708, Preb Westminster 1710; *m* 27 April 1710 Anne Humphrys and *d* 19 July 1748, leaving, with a dau:

1a Laurence (Rev); *educ* Ch Ch Oxford (MA 1742); Rector Callan, Co Tipperary, 1745 and Stradbally, Queen's Co, 1774; *m c* 24 April 1748 his cousin Jane, dau of Rt Hon St John Brodrick, and had issue

Sir ST JOHN's 2nd s,

ALAN BRODRICK, **1st Viscount Midleton of Midleton**, so *cr* 15 Aug 1717, as also earlier 13 April 1715 BARON BRODRICK OF MIDLETON, Co Cork (both I), PC (I 1703–11 and 1714–28); *b c* 1656; *educ* Inner Temple and Magdalen Coll Oxford; attainted by JAMES II's I Parl 1689 as a Williamite, Recorder Cork 1690, Serjeant-at-Law Feb 1690/1, MP (Whig) Cork 1692–1704 and Co Cork 1713–14, Speaker I H of C 1703–10 and 1713–14, Slr-Gen I 1695–1704, Attorney-Gen I 1710–09, Ch Justice Queen's Bench I 1709–11, Ld Chllr I 1714–25, MP (GB Parl) Midhurst 1717–28; *m* 1st Catherine, dau of Redmond Barry, of Rathcormick, Co Cork, and had an only s:

1 St John, PC (1724), of Ballyanan; MP Midleton; *m* Anne (*d* 25 April 1752), sis of 1st Viscount Hillsborough (*see* DOWNSHIRE, M), and *dvp* 21 Feb 1728, having had:

(1) Katherine; *d* unm (*bur* 2 Nov 1713)

(2) Anne; *m* James Jeffreyes and *d* May 1762, having had issue (*see* COLTHURST, Bt)

(3) Alice; *m* Charles O'Neill and had issue (*see* O'NEILL, B)

(4) Mary; *m* Sir John Redmond Freke, 3rd Bt, of Castle Freke (*see* CARBERY, B)

(5) Jane; *m* her kinsman Rev Laurence Brodrick (*see above*)

The **1st Viscount** *m* 2nd *c* 16 Oct 1693 Lucy (*bur* 30 June 1703), dau of Sir Peter Courthope, of Little Island, Co Cork, and by her had:

2 ALAN, **2nd Viscount**

3 Courthoe; *bapt* 25 March, *d* Dec 1700

1 Alice; *b* 31 May 1697; *m* 3 March 1736 Rev John Castleman, Fell All Souls' Coll Oxford, and *d* 1780

The **1st Viscount** *m* 3rd 1 Dec 1716 Anne (*d* 5 Jan 1747), dau and heiress of Sir John Trevor, of Brykinalt, Denbighs, Master Rolls and Speaker H of C, and widow of Michael Hill, PC, of Hillsborough, Co Down, and *d* Aug 1728

His only surv s,

ALAN BRODRICK, **2nd Viscount Midleton of Midleton**; *bapt* 31 Jan 1701/2; *educ* Clare Coll Cambridge and Inner Temple; Commr Customs 1727–30, Jt Comptroller Army accts 1730–47; *m* 7 May 1729 Lady Mary Capell (*d* 12 Nov 1762), yst dau of 2nd Earl of Essex (*qv*), and *d* 8 June 1747, having had, with a yr s (Courthope, *bur* 1 Sept 1733):

GEORGE BRODRICK, **3rd Viscount Midleton of Midleton**; *b* 3 Oct 1730; *educ* Eton; MP (Whig) Ashburton 1754–61 and Shoreham 1761–65; *m* 1 May 1752 Albinia (*d* 18 Sept 1808), est dau of Hon Thomas Townshend (*see* TOWNSHEND, M) and *d* 22 Aug 1765, leaving:

1 GEORGE BRODRICK, **4th Viscount Midleton of Midleton**; *b* 1 Nov 1754; *educ* Eton and St John's Coll Cambridge; MP Whitchurch 1774–96, *cr* 11 June 1796 BARON BRODRICK OF PEPER HAROW, Co Surrey (GB), with limitation in default of male issue of his body to heirs male of the body of his f; *m* 1st 5 Dec 1778 Lady Frances Pelham (*d* 23 June 1783), dau of 1st Earl of Chichester (*qv*), and had:

(1) Frances Anne; *m* 24 Aug 1808 Inigo Thomas, of Ratton, Sussex, and *d* his widow 19 Feb 1858, leaving issue

1 (cont.) The **4th Viscount** *m* 2nd 13 June 1797 Maria (*d* 14 Jan 1852), dau of Richard Benyon, of Englefield Ho, Berks, and *d* 12 Aug 1836, having by her had, with four other daus:

(1) GEORGE ALAN BRODRICK, **5th Viscount Midleton of Midleton**; *b* 10 June 1806; *m* 14 May 1833 Ellen (*m* 2nd 28 April 1859 Richard Quain, FRS, of Cavendish Sq, and *d* 13 Nov 1886) and *dsp* 1 Nov 1848

(1) Harriet; *b* 10 Aug 1804; *m* 31 March 1829 **7th Viscount Midleton of Midleton** (*see* below) and *d* 13 Aug 1893

2 Thomas; *b* 17 April 1756; U-Sec Home Dept; *d* unm 13 Jan 1795

3 Charles (Rt Rev); *b* 3 May 1761; DD, Archbp Cashel; *m* 8 Dec 1786 Mary, dau of Rt Rev Richard Woodward, DD, DCL, Bp Cloyne, and *d* 6 May 1822, leaving, with other issue:

(1) CHARLES BRODRICK, **6th Viscount Midleton of Midleton**; *b* 14 Oct 1791; *educ* St John's Coll Cambridge; barrister Lincoln's Inn; *m* 5 May 1825 Hon Emma Stapleton (*d* 29 Dec 1879), 3rd dau of 12th Lord (Baron) Le Despenser (*see* FALMOUTH, V), and *d* 2 Dec 1863, having had:

1a Mary Emma; *b* 20 Feb 1826; *m* 5 Sept 1865 3rd Earl of Enniskillen (*qv*) and *d* 25 May 1896

2a Albinia Frances; *b* 5 May 1831; *m* 30 Sept 1858 Alexander Samuel Leslie Melville (*see* LEVEN and MELVILLE, E) and *d* 18 March 1918, leaving issue

(2) WILLIAM JOHN, **7th Viscount**

(1) Mary Susan; *m* 13 March 1809 2nd Earl of Bandon (*d* 31 Oct 1856; *see* 1970 edn) and *d* 23 April 1870, leaving issue

(2) Albinia; *m* 18 Oct 1817 Hon Sir James Ashley Maude, CB, KCH (*see* HAWARDEN, V), and *dsps* 20 April 1863

4 John; *b* 3 Nov 1765; Gen; *m* 6 Sept 1809 Anne (*d* 3 May 1852), dau of Robert Graham, of Fintry, Scotland, and *d* 9 Oct 1842, having had:

(1) John Robert; *b* 11 Nov 1815; *d* unm 18 Feb 1848

(1) Anne; *m* 28 May 1846 Rev William Pennefather (*d* 1870), Rector Callan, Co Tipperary, 2nd s of Rt Hon Edward Pennefather

(2) Mary Elizabeth; *m* 1 Jan 1858 Rt Rev Edmund Hobhouse, DD (*d* 20 April 1904), Bp Nelson, NZ, 2nd s of Rt Hon Henry Hobhouse, and *d* 12 Oct 1864, leaving issue

(3) Maria Albinia; *m* 10 June 1851 William Dundas Cloete and *d* 16 July 1877

The 6th VISCOUNT's bro,

WILLIAM JOHN BRODRICK, **7th Viscount Midleton of Midleton**; *b* 8 July 1798; *educ* Balliol Coll Oxford; Dean Exeter 1863–67, Chaplain to HM QUEEN VICTORIA 1847; *m* 1st 16 March 1824 Lady Elizabeth Anne Brudenell (*dsp* 21 Nov 1824), widow of Hon John Perceval (*see* EGMONT, E) and est dau of 6th Earl of Cardigan (*see* AILESBURY, M); *m* 2nd 31 March 1829 Harriet, dau of his uncle **4th Viscount**, and *d* 29 Aug 1870, having by her had, with other issue:

1 WILLIAM BRODRICK, **8th Viscount Midleton of Midleton**, JP (Co Cork); *b* 6 Jan 1830; *educ* Eton and Balliol Coll Oxford; barrister, High Steward Kingston-on-Thames 1873–93, MP (C) Mid-Surrey 1868–70, Ld Lt Surrey 1896–1905; *m* 25 Oct 1853 Augusta Mary (*d* 1 June 1903), 3rd dau of 1st Baron Cottesloe (*qv*), and *d* 18 April 1907, having had:

(1) WILLIAM ST JOHN FREMANTLE BRODRICK, **9th Viscount Midleton of Midleton** and 1st EARL OF MIDLETON, as which *cr* 2 Feb 1920, as also VISCOUNT DUNSFORD OF DUNSFORD, Co Surrey (both UK), KP (1916), PC, JP and DL (Surrey); *b* 14 Dec 1856; *educ* Eton and Balliol Coll Oxford; MP: W Surrey 1880–85 and SW Surrey 1885–1906, Fin Sec to War Office 1886–92, U-Sec War 1895–98 and For Affairs 1898–1900, Sec State: War 1900–03 and India 1903–05, Cdr Order Leopold Belgium, Hon LLD Dublin, Alderman LCC 1907–13, Hon Col 98th Surrey and Sussex Yeo Bde RFA (TA), Govr Charterhouse, High Steward Kingston-upon-Thames 1930–42; *m* 1st 4 Dec 1880 Lady Hilda Charteris (*d* 1 Aug 1901), 3rd dau of 9th Earl of Wemyss (*qv*), and had:

1a GEORGE ST JOHN BRODRICK, **10th Viscount Midleton of Midleton** and 2nd EARL OF MIDLETON, MC, JP (Kent 1936); *b* 1 Feb 1888; *educ* Eton and Balliol Coll Oxford; Capt Surrey Yeo, ADC to GOC Mediterranean Expdny Force 1915, GSO(2) 1918 WW I (despatches, Legion Honour), re-

employed 1939 (ADC to C-in-C Home Forces); *m* 1st 23 June 1917 (*divorce* 1925) Margaret, dau of J Rush, of Cromer, Norfolk; *m* 2nd 28 July 1925 (*divorce* 1975) Guinevere (*d* 20 Feb 1978), dau of Alexander Sinclair, of Dublin, and widow of George Jay Gould; *m* 3rd 24 April 1975 Irene Creese (Rene Ray, actress; *d* 1993) and *d* 2 Nov 1979, when the Earldom and Viscountcy of Dunsford expired but the Viscountcy of Midleton and Barony of Brodrick of Midleton passed to his cousin

1a Muriel; *b* 23 Nov 1881; *m* 30 Nov 1901 3rd Baron Tweedmouth, CMG, DSO, MVO (*d* 23 April 1935; *see* 1935 edn), and *d* 7 Sept 1966, leaving issue

2a Sybil; *b* 9 March 1885; Maid of Honour to HM QUEEN MARY 1911–12, Grand Cordon Order El Kemal Egypt; *m* 17 Jan 1912 Sir Ronald William Graham, GCB, GCMG, GCVO, PC (*d* 26 Jan 1949), s of Sir Henry John Lowndes Graham, KCB, and *dsp* 3 April 1934

3a Aileen Hilda; *b* 13 Aug 1890; *m* 27 Sept 1913 Charles Francis Meade and *d* 30 Sept 1970, leaving issue (*see* CLANWILLIAM, E)

4a Moyra; *b* 11 Jan 1897; *m* 29 July 1922 Gen Sir (Henry) Charles Loyd, GCVO, KCB, DSO, MC, DL (*d* 11 Nov 1973), Coldstream Gds, s of Edward Henry Loyd, of Langleybury, Herts, and had:

1b *Julian St John (Sir), KCVO (1991, CVO 1979), DL (Norfolk 1983) [Sir Julian Loyd KCVO DL, Perrystone Cottage, Burnham Market, Norfolk PE31 8HA]; *b* 25 May 1926; *educ* Eton and Magdalene Coll Cambridge; Coldstream Gds 1944–45, FRICS 1955, agent to HM THE QUEEN at Sandringham 1964–91; *m* 20 Oct 1960 *(Philippa) Mary Emma, twin dau of Sir Christopher Eden Steel, GCMG, MVO, of Southrop Lodge, Lechlade, Glos, and has:

1c *Charles Anthony; *b* 20 March 1963; *m* 14 Sept 1996 *Jenny, er dau of Julian Cartwright, of Godalming

1c *Alexandra Mary; *b* 14 Oct 1961; *m* 11 Feb 1995 *Duncan Byatt, yr s of Sir Hugh Byatt, KCVO

2c *Mary Rose; *b* 8 June 1967; *m* 29 April 1995 *Ellis Whitcomb, s of Maj Stuart Whitcomb

1b Lavinia Gertrude Georgiana; *b* 21 Dec 1923; *m* 3 Jan 1946 Maj Thomas Anthony Gore-Browne (*d* 1988), late Gren Gds, yr s of Col Sir Eric Gore-Browne, DSO, OBE, TD, of Glaston House, Rutland, and *d* 12 Dec 1995, leaving issue

(1) (cont.) The **9th Viscount** *m* 2nd 5 Jan 1903 Madeleine Cecilia Carlyle, JP Surrey (*d* 2 June 1966), est dau of Col Hon John Constantine Stanley (*see* STANLEY OF ALDERLEY, SHEFFIELD and, B), and *d* 13 Feb 1942, having by her had:

2a Francis Alan BRODRICK later STEWART-MACKENZIE OF SEAFORTH (1935); *b* 27 Feb 1910; *educ* New Coll Oxford (BA 1932); Maj 98th (Surrey and Sussex Yeo) Field Bde, RA (TA), WW II; *m* 23 Jan 1937 *Margaret Letitia [Mrs Charles Gifford, 1 Wyndham House, Aldeburgh, Suffolk] (*m* 2nd 6 June 1944 Charles Henry Pearson Gifford, OBE, er s of T J Carlyle Gifford, of Edinburgh), only dau of Maj Hon Charles Henry Lyell (*see* LYELL, B), and was *ka* Italy Sept 1943

3a Michael Victor, MC; *b* 25 Feb 1920; Maj Coldstream Gds WW II; *ka* Italy Sept 1943

(2) Laurence Alan, JP (Denbighs); *b* 24 Jan 1864; BA Oxon; *m* 5 Feb 1896 Anne Gwendolyn (*d* 8 Sept 1929), dau of Hugh Robert Hughes, of Kinmel, and widow of Maj-Gen Edward William Lloyd Wynne, DL (Coed Coch, N Wales), and *d* 30 March 1915, leaving:

1a Margaret, JP (Denbighs 1947), of Plas Llewelyn, Abergele, N Wales; *b* 10 March 1897; served Croix Rouge Française 1916–19, Women's Transport Service (FANY) and ATS 1939–46 as Capt and Jr Cdr Middle East, Italy and India, French Croix de Guerre and Medaille de la Reconaissance; *d* unm 20 Dec 1962

(3) Arthur Grenville, DL (Surrey); *b* 2 June 1868; Col TA, Lt-Col cmdg 5th Bn Roy W Surrey Regt Mesopotamia, CA Surrey, Chm Surrey TAA, Extra ADC to HM GEORGE V 1920–21; *m* 29 April 1912 Lesley Venetia (*d* 21 May 1954), only dau of Lt-Col Edward Harrison Clough-Taylor, Roy Welch Fus, by Lady Elisabeth Campbell, dau of 8th Duke of Argyll (*qv*), and *d* 18 Sept 1934, leaving:

1a *Elisabeth Venetia Marian; *b* 4 June 1914

(1) Augusta Louisa; *m* 3 Jan 1884 Sir Cuthbert Edgar Peek, 2nd Bt (*qv*), and *d* 3 Nov 1934, leaving issue

(2) Evelyn Harriet; *b* 21 Nov 1855, *d* 30 Jan 1856

(3) Helen Anna; *m* 14 April 1885 Rt Rev Archibald Ean Campbell (*d* 18 April 1921), Bp Glasgow and Galloway, and *d* 18 Sept 1937, leaving issue

(4) Edith Mary, Ldy Manors Hopton, Carsington, and Midleton; *m* 25 July 1889 Philip Lyttelton Gell, JP, MA (*d* 29 May 1926), Fell King's Coll London, of Hopton Hall, Derbys, and *d* 17 April 1944

(5) Albinia Lucy, JP (Co Kerry); CC Co Kerry; *d* unm 16 Jan 1955 aged 93

(6) Marian Cecilia; *m* 15 April 1896 Sir James Beethom Whitehead, KCMG (*d* 19 Sept 1928), of Efford Park, Lymington, Hants, Min Belgrade 1906–10, s of Robert Whitehead, of Fiume, and *d* 28 April 1932, leaving issue

2 George Charles, JP (Oxon); *b* 5 May 1831; MA Oxon, DCL, barrister, Hon Fell and Warden Merton Coll Oxford; *d* unm 8 Nov 1903

3 Henry; *b* 11 Feb 1838; 60th Rifles; *m* 1st 10 Sept 1862 Kathleen Henrietta Frances (*d* 31 July 1867), dau of Richard Brouncker, of Boveridge, Dorset; *m* 2nd 1 June 1869 Alice (*m* 2nd 3 July 1883 Rev James Meaburn Staniland; *d* July 1892), dau of Capt Alfred Chapman, and *dsp* 31 Oct 1877

4 Alan (Rev); *b* 1 Jan 1840; MA Oxon; Master St Cross Hosp, Rector Alverstoke, Hon Canon Winchester, RD; *m* 18 June 1867 Emily Hester (*d* 2 Aug 1906), dau of Philip Melvill and gdau of Sir James Cosmo Melvill, KCB, and *d* 6 May 1909, leaving:

(1) Alan Melvill; *b* 30 April 1868; Lt 2nd Vol Bn W Surrey Regt; *m* 1st 27 April 1898 (*divorce* 1901) Beatrice, dau of Henry Ernst Hall, of Godalming; *m* 2nd 25 June 1912 Diana (*d* 26 Nov 1930), widow of Thomas Davies Peacey, and *d* 14 July 1933, having by his 1st w had:

1a Beatrice Mary Alleyne; *b* 7 Aug 1899; *m* 1945 F/O Alban Churton Roe, RAFVR

(2) William John Henry, OBE (1917); *b* 25 Jan 1874; *educ* Charterhouse and Corpus Christi Coll Oxford (BA 1897, MA 1930); barrister Lincoln's Inn 1899, Recorder Bournemouth 1924–28, Met Police Magistrate 1928–44, Chev Order Crown Belgium; *m* 7 June 1902 Blanche Sophia Emily (*d* March 1944), er dau of F A Hawker, of Woodend, Wickham, Hants, and *d* 28 Oct 1964, leaving:

1a TREVOR LOWTHER BRODRICK, **11th Viscount Midleton of Midleton**; *b* 7 March 1903; *educ* privately; *m* 12 Aug 1940 Sheila Campbell (*d* 17 Dec 1995), dau of Charles Campbell MacLeod, of Cawthorpe House, Bourne, Lincs, and *d* 1988

2a (Alan) Rupert; *b* 19 March 1904; *educ* Sherborne; *m* 6 Dec 1941 *Alice Elizabeth [Mrs Rupert Brodrick, 104 Fitzjohn's Ave, Hampstead, London NW3 6NT], dau of George R Roberts, of Purley, Surrey, and *d* 16 Oct 1972, leaving:

1b ALAN HENRY BRODRICK, **12th and present Viscount Midleton of Midleton**

1b *Susan Margaret [Mrs Robert Swann, 44 Munster Rd, Teddington, Middx]; *b* 1945; *m* 1971 *Robert Andrew Swann and has:

1c *Benedick Rupert Christopher; *b* 1976

1c *Tabitha Mary; *b* 1972

2c *Jessica Araminta May; *b* 1978

2b *Elizabeth Ann [Mrs Stephen Kershaw, 1 Westbourne Rd, London N7 8AR]; *b* 1947; *m* 1974 *Stephen James Kershaw

3a Melvill Seymour; *b* 17 Sept 1906; *educ* privately; *m* 25 Feb 1961 Elizabeth Vaughan, dau of Lt-Col Philip Vaughan Holberton, and *d* 19–

4a Norman John Lee, QC (1960), JP (Hants 1967); *b* 4 Feb 1912; *educ* Charterhouse and Merton Coll Oxford (BA 1933, MA 1951); barrister Lincoln's Inn 1935, Recorder: Penzance 1957–59, Bridgwater 1959–62, Plymouth 1962–64 and Portsmouth 1964–67, additional Judge Central Criminal Court (Circuit Judge) 1967–82, Chm IoW QS 1964–67 (Dep Chm 1967–71), Chm Departmental Ctee on Certification of Death and Coroners 1964, Regnl Chm Mental Health Review Tbnl (Wessex) 1960–63, Dep Chm Middx QS 1961–65, Bencher Lincoln's Inn 1965; *m* 2 July 1940 *Ruth Severn, dau of Sir Stanley Unwin, and *d* 1992, leaving:

1b +Michael John Lee; *b* 12 Oct 1941; *educ* Charterhouse and Merton Coll Oxford (BA 1964, MA 1968); barrister Lincoln's Inn 1965, Western Circuit, Senate Inns of Court and Bar 1979–82, Recorder 1981–87, Memb Wine Ctee W Circuit 1982–86, Judicial Memb Tport Tbnl 1986–, Circuit Judge 1987–, Liaison Judge SE Hants Magistrates 1989–93, IoW magistrates 1989–94, Memb Ld Chllr's Advsy Ctee Appointment Magistrates Portsmouth 1990–93 and SE Hants 1993–, Counsellor Dean and Chapter Winchester Cathedral 1993–; *m* 27 Sept 1969 *Valerie Lois, yr dau of Gerald Max Stroud, JP, of Pond Ho, Rogate, Hants, and has:

1c +Robert John Lee; *b* 1972; *educ* Charterhouse and Roy Holloway Coll London

1c *Tessa Elizabeth; *b* 14 Nov 1975

2b +Christopher David [Christopher Brodrick Esq, 30 Wroxton Terrace, Christchurch, New Zealand]; *b* 10 Feb 1953; *educ* Gordonstoun; *m* 1975 *Kirsty Margaret, yst dau of Hon Sir Ian Macarthur, of Christchurch, and has:

1c +Peter Hannay; *b* 12 March 1978

1c *Katherine Ruth; *b* 1980

3b +Peter Matthew [Peter Brodrick Esq, Hillcroft, Midcross Lane, Chalfont St Peter, Bucks SL9 0LF]; *b* 10 Aug 1954; *educ* Charterhouse and Charing Cross Hosp Medical Sch London (MB, BS); LRCP, MRCS, FRCA; *m* 1982 (*divorce* 1993) Melanie Jean, dau of Lloyd Forbes, of Swansea, and adopted:

*James Christopher; *b* 6 April 1988

*Camila Alice; *b* 7 April 1989

1b *Frances Mary Severn [Mrs Pedro Prá-Lopez, 59 Twyford Ave, London N2]; *b* 27 Dec 1947; *m* 17 June 1972 *Pedro, only s of P Prá-Lopez, of Kilburn, and has:

1c *Nicholas Norman Pedro; *b* 19–

2c *Thomas Severn; *b* 30 Aug 1977

(3) George Trevor; BA Oxon; *b* 4 June 1877; *d* unm 26 Dec 1902

(1) Mabel Emily; *m* 12 Jan 1892 Adml Sir William Lowther Grant, KCB, JP (*d* 30 Jan 1926), s of William Grant, of Monckton House, Alverstoke, and *d* 24 Dec 1956, leaving issue

(2) Dorothea Mary; *m* 22 July 1914 Lt-Col Hugh Gildart Worsley (*d* 7 Feb 1968), RA, est s of Lt-Col Henry Gildart Worsley, of Belleisle, Richmond, Yorks, King's Own Regt, and *dsp* 21 Feb 1953

MILBANK

Arms: Gu. a saltire arg. gutté de poix between two lion's heads couped in pale and as many roses in fess of the second. **Crest:** A lion's head couped arg. gutté de poix, charged with a pale gu., thereon three roses also arg. **Creation:** Bt. (UK) 16 May 1882.

SIR ANTHONY FREDERICK MILBANK, 5TH BT, of Well, Co York, and of Hart, Co Durham [Sir Anthony Milbank Bt, Barningham Park, Richmond, N Yorks DL11 7DW]; *b* 16 Aug 1939, *s f* 1984; *educ* Eton; late 2nd Lt Coldstream Gds, High Sheriff Durham 1991–92; *m* 4 Feb 1970 *Belinda Beatrice, yr dau of Brig Adrian Clements Gore, DSO (*see* GORE, Bt), and has:

1 +EDWARD MARK SOMERSET; *b* 9 April 1973

2 +Toby Adrian Jamieson; *b* 1977

1 *Alexina Victoria; *b* 1971

Lineage: WILLIAM MELVILLE later MILBANK (roy warrant 17 May 1792) (possibly illegitimate s of Mark Milbank (*d* after a fall from a haystack at harvest time 23 July 1775), of Thorp Perrow, Yorks (himself s of John Milbank (*d* 22 Aug 1759), of Thorp Perrow, by his cousin Dorothy (*d* 1741), dau of Sir Mark Milbanke, 4th Bt, of Halnaby (*see* 1949 edn), John being s by Mary (dau and heiress of Timothy Robson, of Newcastle-on-Tyne) of another John Milbank (*d* 13 March 1713), of Thorp Perrow, who was 4th s of Sir Mark Milbanke, 1st Bt, of Halnaby), of Thorp Hall, Thorp Perrow, and Barningham Park, which estates he inherited from his putative f's sisters; *b* 15 Jan 1768; *educ* Bedale GS; *m* 1792 Dorothy, dau of John Wise, of Woolston, Devon, and *d* Feb 1802, leaving:

MARK MILBANK, of Thorp Perrow and Barningham Park, JP, DL (Yorks); *b* 2 May 1795; High Sheriff Yorks 1837, MP Camelford; *m* 2 June 1817 Lady Augusta Henrietta Vane (*d* 13 Sept 1874), 2nd dau of 1st Duke of Cleveland (*see* BARNARD, B), and *d* 21 Oct 1881 having had, with three daus:

1 Mark William Vane, JP and DL (N R Yorks); *b* 5 April 1819; *m* 24 March 1845 Barbarina Sophia (*d* 30 Oct 1850), dau of Sir Thomas Harvie Farquhar, 2nd Bt (*qv*), and *d* 6 Oct 1883, having by her had, with a s (*d* an infant):

(1) Sybil Augusta; *m* 31 Nov 1871 Gen Hon William Henry Herbert (*d* 29 Jan 1909), of Winsley Hall, Shrewsbury, yst s of 2nd Earl of Powis (*qv*), and *d* 28 Oct 1926, leaving issue

(2) Edith Dorothy; *d* 27 June 1935

2 FREDERICK ACCLOM (Sir), **1st Bt**

3 Henry John, of Newsham, Yorks, JP and DL; *b* 22 June 1824; *m* 1st 6 Oct 1846 Lady Margaret Henrietta Maria (*d* 7 March 1852), sis and heiress of 7th Earl of Stamford (*see* 1970 edn), and had, with a s (*d* an infant):

(1) Katherine Henrietta Venezia; *m* 12 June 1869 Arthur GREY formerly DUNCOMBE (*see* FEVERSHAM, B), and *d* 31 Oct 1926, leaving issue

(2) Louisa Elizabeth Jane; *m* 2 June 1868 Francis Arkwright (*d* 1 March 1915), MP E Derbys, and *d* 6 May 1873, leaving issue

3 (cont.) Henry Milbank *m* 2nd 22 June 1864 Lady Susan Georgiana Godolphin Osborne (*d* 14 Nov 1903), est dau of 8th Duke of Leeds (*see* 1963 edn), and *d* 4 June 1872, having by her had:

(1) Godolphin Henry Vane; *b* 24 May 1865; *m* 20 Aug 1890 Sybil Jessie, dau of Sir Alfred Hughes, 9th Bt (*qv*), and *dsp* 8 Aug 1947

(2) Darcy Francis Mark; *b* 20 Feb 1867; *m* 1891 Eleanor (*d* July 1914), dau of James Lord, barrister, and widow of Capt Henry Charles Hardinge (*see* HARDINGE, V), and *d* 20 Sept 1937

(3) Ralph Schomberg MILBANK later MILBANK-LESLIE-MELVILLE (deed poll 25 May 1908); *b* 28 June 1872; *m* 20 Aug 1907 Elizabeth Harriet (*d* 11 Aug 1938), er dau of Thomas Robert Brook Leslie-Melville-Cartwright, DL, of Newbottle Manor, Banbury, by Lady Elizabeth Jane Leslie Melville, dau and heiress of line of 7th Earl of Leven and (4th Earl of) Melville (*qv*), and *d* 14 Dec 1930

(1) Harriet Caroline; *d* unm

4 Augustus Sussex, JP and DL (Co Durham), JP (N R Yorks); *b* 2 Oct 1827 (HRH THE DUKE OF SUSSEX stood sponsor)

MARK MILBANK's 2nd son,

Sir Frederick Acclom Milbank, 1st Bt (UK), so cr 16 May 1882, DL; *b* 21 April 1820; Lt 79th Highrs, MP N Yorks 1865–85; *m* 18 Sept 1844 Alexina Harriet

Elizabeth (*d* 22 Feb 1919 aged 93), dau of Sir Alexander Don, 6th Bt (*see* DON-WAUCHOPE, Bt), and had:

1 William Harry Vane; *b* 28 Dec 1848; Lt RHG; *m* 1 March 1871 Alice Sidonie Vandenburg (*d* 26 April 1916), dau of Desiré Baruch, of Brussels, and widow of Edward Charles Belleroche, of Swansea, and *dsp* 24 Oct 1892

2 POWLETT CHARLES JOHN (Sir), **2nd Bt**

1 Alice Frederica Milbank; *m* 2 Aug 1888, as his 2nd w, Sir David Dale, 1st Bt (*d* 28 April 1906; see 1902 edn), and *dsp* 25 Nov 1902

2 Wilhelmina Louisa; *d* unm 3 March 1903

Sir FREDERICK *d* 28 April 1898; his only surv son,

Sir Powlett Charles John Milbank, 2nd Bt, JP and DL (Yorks); *b* 1 May 1852; Radnorshire: Ld Lt, custos rotulorum, Pres TFA, MP 1895–1900; *m* 3 June 1875 Edith Mary (*d* 1 March 1928), dau of Sir Richard Green-Price, 1st Bt (*qv*), and had:

1 FREDERICK RICHARD POWLETT (Sir), **3rd Bt**

1 Aline Laura; *m* 10 April 1894 Capt Francis William Forester (*see* FORESTER, B) and *d* 6 March 1962, leaving issue

2 Sybil May; *m* 16 Feb 1904 Lt-Col Sir Murrough John Wilson KBE, JP, DL (*d* 30 April 1946), of Cliffe Hall, Yorks, and *d* 19 Sept 1930, leaving issue

3 Gladys Mary; *m* 1st 18 Oct 1906 Col Vivian Henry, CB (*d* 22 Sept 1929), Roy Fus, of Oakfield, Hay, Herefs, 2nd s of Col Francis Henry, of Elmstree, Glos, and had issue (*see* SUDELEY, B); *m* 2nd 20 Jan 1931 Reginald Akroyd

Sir POWLETT *d* 30 Jan 1918; his only son,

Sir Frederick Richard Powlett Milbank, 3rd Bt, JP Radnorshire and N R Yorks; *b* 7 Sept 1881; *educ* Eton; Maj 5th Bn Yorks Regt, formerly Lt Yorks Hus, WW I (despatches twice, Croix de Guerre Belgium); *m* 12 July 1904 (Harriet Anne) Dorothy (*d* 1 May 1970 aged 93), est dau of Col John Gerald Wilson, CB, of Cliffe Hall, Yorks, and had:

1 MARK VANE (Sir), **4th Bt**

2 John Gerald Frederick; *b* 17 April 1909; *educ* Eton; Maj Green Howards WW II (despatches); *m* 9 June 1938 Louisa Harriet (*d* 1974), only dau of Edward Beaumont Cotton Curtis, of Caynham Cottage, Ludlow, Salop (*see* CURTIS, Bt), and *d* 1991, having had:

  (1) +David John [David Milbank Esq, Gayles Fields, Dalton, Richmond, Yorks DL11 7HR]; *b* 12 June 1940; *educ* Gordonstoun; *m* 1971 *Clarissa Mary, dau of Capt S L Bigge, of Langdale, Melsonby, Yorks, and has:

    1a +James John; *b* 16 Jan 1974

    2a +Nicholas Charles; *b* 24 July 1975

  (2) +Charles Gerald; *b* 3 Aug 1942; *educ* Eton; racehorse trainer; *m* 1973 Mrs Wendy Wright, dau of E N Hohnson, of Newton Firs, Newton, by Frodsham, Cheshire, and has:

    1a +Philip Augustus; *b* 1974

    1a *Camilla; *b* 1975

    2a *Sophie Kathleen; *b* 1977

3 +Denis William Powlett, TD [Major Denis Milbank TD, Southbrook, Galphay, Ripon, N Yorks HG4 3NJ]; *b* 6 July 1912; *educ* Radley; Maj RA (TA) WW II (despatches); *m* 5 July 1934 Doreen Frances (*d* 1991), yr dau of Sir Richard Pierce Butler, 11th Bt, of Cloughgrenan (*qv*), and has:

  (1) +Mark Richard [Mark Milbank Esq, Chirume Ranch, (Box 767), Marondera, Zimbabwe]; *b* 9 Sept 1937; *educ* Duke of York Sch, Nairobi; served Kenya Regt as Dist Offr against Mau Mau; *m* 1st 17 Sept 1966 (*divorce* 1989) Frances Elizabeth, 2nd dau of R V Holme, of Marandellas, Rhodesia; *m* 2nd 1993 *Mrs Nicola Mary Sclater, dau of Antony Cropper, of Tolson Hall, Kendal, Cumbria, and by his 1st w has:

    1a +Robert Frederick; *b* 13 July 1968

    2a +Henry Mark Thomas; *b* 1970

    3a +Jack Patrick; *b* 1979

  (1) *Penelope Ann [Mrs Hougham Mills, Box 628, Umtentweni, 4235 Natal, S Africa]; *b* 21 May 1935; *m* 1st 6 Aug 1955 John Frederick de Vere Shaw (*see* SHAW, Bt) and has issue; *m* 2nd Hougham Robert Mills, s of R N Mills, of Somerset E, CP

  (2) *Susan Fiona Milbank [Mrs Antony Pelly, Common Gate, Holnest, Dorset]; *b* 25 Feb 1942; *m* 7 Sept 1963 Antony Roger Pelly and has issue (*see* PELLY, Bt)

Sir FREDERICK *d* 29 April 1964; his est son,

Sir Mark Vane Milbank, 4th Bt, KCVO (1962, CVO 1958, MVO 1953), MC (1944); *b* 11 Jan 1907; *educ* Eton; ADC Govr Bombay 1933–38, Maj Coldstream Gds WW II, Comptroller to Govr-Gen Canada 1946–52, Master HM's Household 1953–67 (Dep Master 1952–53), Extra Equerry to HM THE QUEEN 1954–84; *m* 1st 20 Oct 1930 (*divorce* 1933) Angela Isabel Nellie, only dau of 4th Marquess of Abergavenny (*qv*); *m* 2nd 12 Feb 1938 Hon Verena Aileen (*d* 29 May 1995), dau of 11th Baron Farnham (*qv*) and widow of Charles Lambart Crawley, and *d* 4 April 1984, having by her had:

1 (Sir) ANTHONY FREDERICK MILBANK, **5th and present Bt**

2 +(Arthur) John [John Milbank Esq, The Old Laundry House, Smeeth, Kent TN25 6ST]; *b* 2 Dec 1940; *educ* Gordonstoun; *m* 1 March 1969 *Rosalind Eleanor Lucy, only dau of G E L Townsend, of Plettenberg Bay, S Africa, and has:

  (1) +Robert Andrew; *b* 1972

  (1) *Lucy Verena; *b* 30 Nov 1970; *m* 29 April 1995 *Alexander Graham Hunn

MILBORNE-SWINNERTON-PILKINGTON

Arms: Quarterly, 1st and 4th, arg. a cross flory, voided gu. (for PILKINGTON); 2nd, arg. a cross formé fleuretté sa., surmounted by a bend engrailed gu. (for SWINNERTON); 3rd, per pale arg. and gu. a cross patonce between in the sinister chief and dexter base two leopard's faces counter-changed (for MILBORNE).
Crests: 1 A mower with his scythe ppr., habited per pale arg. and sa. (for PILKINGTON), 2 On a mount vert a boar passant arg., charged with a cross formé fleuretté sa. (for SWINNERTON), 3 A demi-lion per fess arg. and gu., holding between the paws a leopard's face of the first (for MILBOURNE). **Motto:** Now thus, now thus.
Creation: Bt. (NS) 29 June 1635.

SIR THOMAS HENRY MILBORNE-SWINNERTON-PILKINGTON, 14TH BT, of Stanley, Co York [Sir Thomas Milborne-Swinnerton-Pilkington Bt, King's Walden Bury, Hitchin, Herts SG4 8JU]; *b* 10 March 1934; *s f* 1952; *educ* Eton; late 2nd Lt Roy Scots Greys; *m* 17 Nov 1961 *Susan, est dau of Norman Stewart Rushton Adamson, of Durban, and has:

1 +RICHARD ARTHUR; *b* 4 Sept 1964; *educ* Eton and RAC Cirencester; *m* 1994 *Katya T, dau of Terence J Clemence, of Belgravia

1 *Sarah Elizabeth; *b* 7 Oct 1962; *m* 1993 *James B Anderson, s of Ian Anderson, of La Goulée, France

2 *Joanna; *b* 19 Feb 1967

Lineage: ALEXANDER de PILKINGTON, of Pilkington, Salford Hundred, Lancs; had, with another s (William):

Sir ALEXANDER de PILKINGTON; held the Manor of Pilkington *temp* JOHN and possibly as early as *temp* HENRY II, also six oxgangs of land in Rivington; one of 17 'trusty Knights' apptd Commrs 1212, a juror on the Roll of Eyre 1225; *m* allegedly Ursula, dau of Geoffrey de Workedleigh, and *d* between 1231 and 1242, leaving:

1 ROGER

2 Robert; living 21 Sept 1247; had:

  (1) Robert; *k* Salford 1291 by an arrow shot by Nicholas de Dogwero

  (2) Adam; *k* by a fall from an oak tree in Pilkington

3(?) John (either s of Sir Alexander or of his bro William); had:

  (1) Alexander; pardoned 23 July 1292 for having *k* Adam del Wode in self defence; had:

    1a Richard; *m* 1309 Joan, widow of Adam de Pennington

Sir ALEXANDER's est son,

Sir ROGER de PILKINGTON; Ld Manor Pilkington by 1242, held 1/4 of a kt's fee in Pilkington from Thomas de Grelly by 1242/3; *d c* 1270, leaving:

Sir ALEXANDER de PILKINGTON, of Pilkington; *b c* 1225; *m* Alice (*d* 1274), probably dau of Henry de Chetham and sis of Sir Geoffrey de Chetham, Ld Manor Cheetham and Crompton, and *d* by 1291, leaving:

1 ROGER

2 Richard; ancestor of the PILKIMNGTONs of Rivington

3 John (Sir); MP Lancs 1316; *b c* 1265; *m c* 1291 Margery, dau of William de Anderton, of Anderton and Rumworth, and had:

  (1) John

  (2) Thomas, of Salford; living 1332

  (3) Henry; held three burgages in Salford 1323

4 Adam, of Bolton and Sharples; held in right of his w 1284 the Manor of Wickleswick in Barton, disposing of his life-interest to William de Penulbury (his w's unc) 1291; *m* Matilda/Maud (*d* 1290), dau of Elias de Penulbury, feudal Ld of Wickleswick and Pendlebury, and *d* 1298 of a wound inflicted by Henry del Wode, having had a dau (Cicely, *d* an infant)

Sir ALEXANDER's est son,

Sir ROGER de PILKINGTON; Ld Manors of Pilkington, Cheetham and Cromp-ton; served under EDWARDs I and II Gascony and Scotland, fought Battle of Ban-nockburn 1314, MP Lancs 1316; *b c* 1255; *m* 1st Amery (*d* 1294/5), dau of Sir Gilbert de Barton, feudal Ld of Barton, through whom he acquired 1/6 of the Manor of Barton, and had two sons (including a yr, William, Rector Swillington 1344); *m* 2nd by 6 April 1295 Alice, dau of Sir Ralph de Otteby (who settled the Manor of Otteby upon them and their issue) and by her had a s (Alexander, Ld Manor Otteby, Lincs, contributed money for knighting EDWARD III's est s 1346); *m* 3rd *c* 1310 Margery de Middleton (*m* 2nd by May 1323 Sir Adam de Swilling-ton) and *d* after 11 July 1322, having by her had two sons (Richard; Adam); his er s by his 1st w:

Sir ROGER de PILKINGTON; Ld Manors of Pilkington, Cheetham and Cromp-ton; served Guienne under EDWARD II; *b c* 1291; *m* Alicia (*d c* 1374), heir of her bro Henry de Bury and dau of Henry de Bury, feudal Ld of Bury, by Margery, dau of Richard de Radclyffe, and *d* 1343, leaving:

1 ROGER

2 Robert; campaigned France, Spain and Scotland; *b c* 1329; *d* probably unm *c* 1399

3 Henry; went abroad with Sir Edward le Despenser 1374; *m* — and had:

  (1) John; Rector Bury

  (2) Richard

4 Richard; Rector Prestwich 1361; *d* 1400

1 Jane; *m* John del More, of Liverpool

2 Margaret; *m* 1st Sir John de Arden (*d* 1408), s of Sir Thomas de Arden, of Elford, Staffs, and had issue; *m* 2nd as his 2nd w Sir Robert Babthorp and *d* 1423

3 Isabel; *m* Nicholas de Prestwich

Sir ROGER's est son,

Sir ROGER de PILKINGTON; Ld Manors of Pilkington, Cheetham and Cromp-ton, JP Lancs 1350, MP Lancs in six Parls; *b c* 1325; *d* 2 Jan 1406/7, leaving, with two daus (Isabel, *m* 1st Thomas de Lathom, s of Sir Thomas de Lathom, and had issue, and 2nd Sir John de Dalton and had furthur issue; Lora, *m* 1398 Laurence de Standish, of Standish, s of Ralph de Standish by Cecilia, dau of Roger de Brad-shagh):

Sir JOHN de PILKINGTON; Ld Manors of Pilkington, Bury, Cheetham and Crompton; Sheriff Nottingham 1419, fought Battle of Agincourt 1415; *b c* 1363/4; *m* 1383 Margaret (*d* 24 Nov 1436), widow of Hugh de Bradshagh and dau and heir of Sir John de Verdon, and *d* 16 Feb 1420/1, leaving:

1 John (Sir); Ld Manors of Pilkington, Cheetham and Crompton; fought Agin-court; *b c* 1394; *m* 1435 Elizabeth (*m* 2nd *c* 10 Oct 1451 Sir Piers Legh, of Lyme, Cheshire, and *d* 4 April 1474), dau of Sir Edmund de Trafford (*see* DE TRAF-FORD, Bt), and *dsp* 23 Feb 1451

2 Edmund; ancestor of the PILKINGTONs of Pilkington

3 ROBERT

4 Henry; *d* young

5 Roger; *dsp*

1 Katherine; *m* Sir Henry Scarisbrick, of Scarisbrick Hall, Lancs, and had issue

2 Elizabeth; *m* Sir William Atherton, s of Sir William Atherton, feudal Ld Ath-erton, and had issue

3 Margaret; *m* 1st Nicholas Griffin (*d* 1437) and had issue; *m* 2nd 1442 Sir Tho-mas Savile, of Thornhill, Yorks, and had further issue

4 Hannah; *m* Sir Francis Bernard, of Acorn Bank, Westmorland

Sir JOHN's 3rd son,

ROBERT PILKINGTON, of Bury, Lancs, and later Sowerby, Yorks; *b c* 1398; *m* Joan (? Rawson) and *d c* 1460, leaving, with other issue:

Sir JOHN PILKINGTON, Kt Banneret (1471 or 1475), of Sowerby and later Pilk-ington Hall, Wakefield; Constable Chester Castle for life 1461, Commr of Array Northants 1461–64 and W R Yorks 1464–78, Chamberlain Exchequer 1477; *b c* 1420; *m* Joan (*m* 2nd Sir Thomas Wortley and *d* on or after 2 Jan 1497), dau and heiress of William de Balderston, and *d* by 30 June 1479, having had a s (*d* young); by Elizabeth, dau of Darcy Lever, he had an illegitimate s:

ROBERT PILKINGTON, of Bradley Manor, Nether Bradley, Yorks; Freeman City of York 1494; *m* 1st Alice (*dsp*), dau of James Burrell; *m* 2nd Alice, dau and heir-ess of William Bernard, of Knaresborough, and *d* 31 Jan 1497/8, leaving, with a dau:

ARTHUR PILKINGTON, of Bradley; *b* 1482; *m* Alice (*d* his widow), dau of Nicho-las Savile, of Newhall, Yorks, and *d* by 29 June 1537, leaving, with other issue:

ROBERT PILKINGTON, of Bradley; *b c* 1514; *m* Rosamund, dau of Sir Thomas Waterton, of Walton, nr Wakefield, and *d* 1541, leaving:

THOMAS PILKINGTON, of Nether Bradley; Bowbearer to ELIZABETH I; *m* Bar-bara, dau of Lionel Reresby, of Thriberg, nr Rotherham, and *d* 1565, leaving:

FREDERICK PILKINGTON, of Nether Bradley; *m* 1st Grace, dau of Edward Beau-mont, of Whitley, and had a s (*dsp*); *m* 2nd Frances, dau of Francis Rodes, of Barl-borough, Derbys, Justice Ct Common Pleas, and by her had, with at least one other s and a dau (Mary, *m* 1609 Sir Ferdinando Lee, of Middleton):

Sir Arthur Pilkington, 1st Bt (NS), so *cr* 29 June 1635, of Stanley, nr Wakefield, and Nether Bradley, also Yorks; *m* by 1613 Ellen (*bur* 5 Feb 1646/7), dau of Henry Lyon, of Roxby, Lincs, and Twyford in Willesden, Middx, and was *bur* 5 Sept 1650, leaving, with other issue:

Sir Lyon Pilkington, 2nd Bt; *bapt* 14 Nov 1613; *m* 1st allegedly 31 Dec 1639 — (*dsp*) of Sir Thomas Newton; *m* 2nd (licence 15 Aug 1650) Phoebe (*d* 20 June 1686), dau of Capt Robert Moyle, of Buckwell, Kent, and was *bur* 5 Nov 1684, leaving:

Sir Lyon Pilkington, 3rd Bt; *b c* 1660; *m* 1st by 1683 Amy (*d* 4 April 1695), dau and heiress of Thomas Eggleton, of Grove-in-Ellesborough, Bucks, and had issue; *m* 2nd *c* 18 March 1698 Lennox (*dsp*), widow of George Smith, of Osgodby, Yorks, and only dau and heiress of Cuthbert Harrison, of Acaster Selby, Yorks, and *d* 7 Aug 1714; his est s by his 1st w:

Sir Lyon Pilkington, 4th Bt; *bapt* 5 June 1683; *m* 3 Feb 1704/5 Anne (*m* 2nd Sir Charles Dalston, 3rd Bt; *m* 3rd 1 Dec 1730 John Maude, of Alverthorpe Hall, and *d* 5 Aug 1764), dau of Sir Michael Wentworth, of Wolley, Yorks, and was *bur* 26 June 1716, leaving, with other issue:

1 **Sir Lionel Pilkington 5th Bt**, of Stanley, later Chevet in Royston, Yorks; *bapt* 20 Jan 1706/7; *educ* Ch Ch Oxford; High Sheriff Yorks 1740–41, MP Horsham 1748–68; *d* unm 11 Aug 1778

2 **Sir Michael Pilkington, 6th Bt**, of Lupset in Wakefield; *bapt* 25 May 1715; *m* 1st 7 Dec 1738 Judith (*dsp* 29 Jan 1772), dau and coheir of Rev Charles Nettle-ton, Rector Bulwick, Northants; *m* 2nd 11 Nov 1772 Isabella (*m* 2nd April 1791 Maj Thomas Hewetson and *d* 25 Feb 1823), dau of William Rawstorne, Vicar Badaworth, Yorks, and *d* 6 Feb 1788, having by her had, with two daus:

1 **Sir Thomas Pilkington, 7th Bt**, of Chevet; *b* 7 Dec 1773; *educ* Merton Coll Oxford, Sheriff Yorks 1798–99; *m* 1 Aug 1797 Elizabeth Anne (*m* 2nd William Mules and *d* Nov 1842), dau of William Tufnell, of Langley, Essex, and *dspm* 9 July 1811, leaving:

  (1) Elizabeth Anne; *m* 19 May 1819 (*divorce*) Sir John Tyrell, 2nd Bt, of Bore-ham (*see* 1877 edn)

  (2) Anne; *m* 1822 Philip Bennet, of Rougham, MP Suffolk (*d* 17 Aug 1866)

  (3) Louisa; *m* 1st 4 Aug 1830 Rev George Augustus Dawson (*d* 1848), of Gro-ton, Suffolk; *m* 2nd 15 Feb 1849 Sir Henry Charles Blake, 4th Bt, of Langham (*see* 1970 edn), and *d* 28 Dec 1881

  4 Catherine; *m* 1 Nov 1831 James Bunbury Blake, s of Sir James Henry Blake, 3rd Bt, of Langham, and *d* 1899

2 **Sir William Pilkington, 8th Bt**, of Chevet, which he bought from his nieces on inheriting the btcy; *bapt* 14 Nov 1775; *m* 25 June 1825 Mary (added MIL-BORNE SWINNERTON to PILKINGTON by Act of Parl 1836–37; *d* 11 Dec 1854), 2nd dau and coheir of Thomas Swinnerton, of Butterton Hall, Tren-tham, Staffs, by Mary, dau and heir of Charles Milborne, of Wonastow, Mon, and the Priory, Abergavenny, and *d* 30 Sept 1850, having had, with three daus:

  (1) **Sir Thomas Edward Pilkington, 9th Bt**, of Chevet; *b* 19 March 1829; *educ* Univ Coll Oxford; *d* unm 7 Feb 1854

  (2) Sir WILLIAM PILKINGTON later MILBORNE-SWINNERTON (Act of Parl 1836–37) later still MILBORNE-SWINNERTON-PILKINGTON (Act of Parl 1854), **10th Bt**, of Chevet; *b* 8 June 1831; Lt Staffs Yeo 1854; *d* unm 12 Nov 1855

  (3) Sir LIONEL PILKINGTON later MILBORNE-SWINNERTON (roy licence 15 Feb 1856) later still MILBORNE-SWINNERTON-PILKINGTON, **11th Bt**, DL Yorks; *b* 7 July 1835; *educ* Charterhouse; Cornet 1st W Yorks Yeo Cav, High Sheriff Yorks 1859; *m* 3 Feb 1857 Isabella Elizabeth Georgiana (*d* 8 Jan 1894), only child and heiress of Rev Charles Kinleside, Rector Poling, Sus-sex, and had:

    1a THOMAS EDWARD (Sir), **12th Bt**

    2a Ernest Milborne; *b* 30 Dec 1858; *educ* Trin Coll Cambridge (BA); *d* 17 June 1925

    3a Claude William Egerton; *b* 11 May 1863; *educ* Ch Ch Oxford (MA); Capt 4th Bn Argyll and Sutherland Highrs; *m* 31 Oct 1889 Frances Julia (*d* 12 July 1936), er dau of William Wright, of Wollaton, Notts, and *d* 4 Jan 1932

    1a Renée Elizabeth; *m* 28 April 1881 William Frederick Lee (*d* 6 March 1930), of Grove Hall, Knottingley, and *d* 28 Nov 1922

    2a Ida Mary; *m* 15 April 1890 John Montague Spencer-Stanhope, DL (*d* 10 July 1944), of Cannon Hall, Barnsley, Yorks, and *d* 21 March 1920, leaving issue

    3a Aimée; *m* 12 July 1899 Sir George Ayscough Armytage, 7th Bt (*qv*), and *d* 24 Sept 1955, leaving issue

    4a Veronica; *d* unm 22 April 1929

Sir LIONEL *d* 25 June 1901; his est son,

Sir Thomas Edward Milborne-Swinnerton-Pilkington, 12th Bt, JP W R Yorks; *b* 9 Dec 1857; *educ* Ch Ch Oxford (MA); Maj KRRC (60th) 1898, Transvaal 1881, Tel-el-Kebir 1882, Lt-Col (Hon Col 1904) 6th Bn KRRC 1903–08, cmded 14th Bn KRRC 1914–16, Special Serv France 1917–19 High Sheriff Yorks 1911–12; *m* 23 July 1895 Lady Kathleen Mary Alexina Cuffe, DGStJ (*d* 5 Oct 1938), only child of 4th Earl of Desart (*see* 1934 edn), and had:

1 ARTHUR WILLIAM (Sir), **13th Bt**

2 Ulick O'Connor; *b* 5 Feb 1903; *educ* privately; *m* 28 March 1951 *Angela Mary Purcell [Mrs Edward Eborall, Tally Ho House, Castletownshend, Co Cork, Ireland] (*m* 2nd 1981 Cdr Edward Alfred Eborall, FIEE, RNVR), only dau of Dr Gerald de Purcell Cotter (*see* COTTER, Bt), and *d* 14 June 1979, leaving:

  (1) +Lionel Ulick [Lionel Milborne-Swinnerton-Pilkington Esq, 62 Manor Court, Knocknacarra, Salthill, Co Galway, Ireland]; *b* 6 Dec 1956; *educ* Univ Coll Cork (MA) and Toronto U (PhD); *m* 1990 *Elizabeth Susan, PhD, dau of Col Hugh Tilley, of Ottawa, and has:

    1a +Colin Patrick; *b* 1993

  (2) +Michael Gerald; *b* 12 May 1959; *educ* Trin Coll Dublin (MSc)

1 Phyllis; *m* 18 Dec 1919 Maj Gordon Bentley Foster, DL (*d* 1 April 1963), of Leysthorpe, Oswaldkirk, Yorks, and *d* 2 Jan 1938, leaving issue

2 Pamela Irene; *m* 25 Sept 1926 Jermyn Moorsom (*d* 11 Feb 1951), of Hyndlee, Hawick, Roxburghshire, and *d* 10 March 1967, leaving issue

Sir THOMAS *d* 17 Feb 1944; his er son,

Sir Arthur William Milborne-Swinnerton-Pilkington, 13th Bt, MC (1918); *b* 7 April 1898; *educ* Eton and RMC Sandhurst; Maj 16th/5th Lancers WW I (des-patches) and WW II (despatches); *m* 10 Nov 1931 (*divorce* 1950) Elizabeth Mary (*m* 2nd 1950 Maj Patrick Henry Anthony Burke, Gren Gds (*d* 1964)), est dau of Col John Fenwick Harrison, DL, JP, of King's Walden Bury, Hitchin (*see* BURN-HAM, B), and *d* 24 July 1952, leaving:

1 Sir THOMAS HENRY MILBORNE-SWINNERTON-PILKINGTON, **14th and present Bt**

1 *Sonia Margery; *b* 29 Aug 1937; *m* 1st 30 Oct 1965 Capt Anthony Dyke Darby Rogers (*d* 1984), est s of Capt T D (Darby) Rogers, of Rathbride, Co Kildare; *m* 2nd 1990 *I B Jorgensen, of Airlie, Lucan, Co Dublin, and by her 1st husb has:

  (1) *John Dyke Darby; *b* 17 Dec 1968

  (2) *Anthony Patrick; *b* 10 Feb 1971

2 *Carole Mary [Mrs James Daly, Brainge, Putley, Herefs]; *b* 29 Jan 1942; *m* 14 June 1962 James Bowes Daly (*d* 1989), only s of Maj Dermot Ralph Daly (*see* McGOWAN, B), and has:

    (1) *Dermot Christopher; *b* 19 Oct 1964

    (2) *Henry Duncan James; *b* 15 Oct 1966

3 *Moira Elizabeth [Mrs Banjamin Hanbury, Green Man House, Cowlinge, Newmarket, Cambs]; *b* 25 July 1943; *m* 31 May 1969 *Benjamin Hanbury, 2nd s of Capt Thomas Francis Jeune Hanbury, MC, of Downs Ho, Letcombe Bassett, Berks, and has:

    (1) *Emma Jane; *b* 1970

    (2) *Amanda Aline; *b* 1973

Seat: Kings Walden Bury, Herts. A former Victorian mansion on the site was demolished a few years ago. The present structure is one of Quinlan Terry's most successful creations, avoiding the too-obvious pastiche with which he has been charged in some of his other works. The front elevation is of five central bays of high semi-circular-topped windows with two wings jutting forward at either end, of two bays (with rectilinear windows) each. A pediment with finials over two storeys concentrates the eye on the main entrance, the door of which is perhaps a shade small for such a grandiose surround. Tall chimneys, almost Venetian in their prominence, surmount a ridge-tiled roof, whose cornice rises sufficiently high above the windows on the wings to complete the Provençal or Tuscan appearance framing the pure classicism of the centre. The rear elevation is symmetrical to the front, giving an H-block shape to the whole. Internally the ceilings reach up 15 feet (the bane of so any of Terry's buildings, especially the Richmond riverside development, is the inadequacy of the room sizes compared with the exterior) so as to allow the huge chandeliers from the old house to hang freely. It is a triumph of eclecticism.

MILBURN

Arms: Per fess or and gules a pale counterchanged, between two bear's heads erased or in chief sable, muzzled of the first, and as many bear's hands also erased and muzzled in base. **Crest:** In front of a bear's head, erased sable, muzzled or, four mascles interlaced fessways of the last. **Badge:** On a millrind sable an escallop shell argent. **Motto:** *Dum spiro spero* ('While I breathe I hope'). **Creation:** Bt. (UK) 30 Dec 1905.

SIR ANTHONY RUPERT MILBURN, 5TH BT, of Guyzance, Parish of Shilbottle, Northumberland [Sir Anthony Milburn Bt, Guyzance Hall, Acklington, Northumberland NE65 9AG]; *b* 17 April 1947; *s* unc 1985; *educ* Eton and RAC Cirencester; ARICS, MRAC; *m* 1977 *Olivia (Livy) Shirley, yst dau of Capt T N Catlow, CBE, DL, RN, of Tunstall, Lancs, and has:

1 +PATRICK THOMAS; *b* 4 Dec 1980

2 +(Edward) Jake; *b* 1987

1 *Lucy Camilla Anne; *b* 11 Aug 1982

Lineage: The MYLBORNEs were one of four powerful families in N Tynesdale and Redesdale before the Union of English and Scottish crowns 1603. Till the 16th century they occupied lands around the Comb on Tarset Burn, Roses Bower on the Warks Burn and the Leam in Redesdale; a century later their lands were at Birtley.

THOMAS MILBURN, of Broomhope in Birtley, parish of Chollerton, Northumberland; *b c* 1639; *m c* 1665 Jane (*d* 8 Dec 1724) and *d* 13 Nov 1702, leaving, with a yr s and two daus:

GEORGE MILBURN, of Birtley; *bapt* 20 Jan 1667; *d* 4 Nov 1720, leaving, with a dau and er s:

WILLIAM MILBURN, of Birtley; weaver; *bapt* 18 Sept 1709; *m* 1736 Dorothy, dau of George Urwin by Anne Dinning, and had, with four other sons and three daus:

GEORGE MILBURN, of Birtley; *bapt* 24 Aug 1740; weaver; *m* 1st 1763 Mary (*b* 7 March 1743; *d* 5 April 1767), dau of George Charlton, of Birtley, and had a s and dau; *m* 2nd Ann (*b* 27 July 1735; *d* 8 June 1810) and *d* Oct 1823, having had two further sons; his s by his 1st w:

THOMAS MILBURN, of Birtley and Chollerton, later of Ashington Farm, parish of Bothal; *b* 1765; *m* 10 Oct 1804 Elizabeth, dau of Thomas Turner, of Chester-le-

Street, Co Durham, by Elizabeth Buckham, and *d* 2 Nov 1850, having had two sons and three daus; his illegitimate s:

GEORGE MILBURN, of Sparrow House and later Newsham Park, Blyth, Northumberland; *b* July 1804; *m* 10 Aug 1826 Mary, dau and eventual heir of Stephen Watson, of Sparrow House, Ashington, and W Sleekburn, by Mary, dau of Thomas Lawson, of Longhirst Grange, Morpeth, and *d* 1 April 1866, having had, with five yr sons and three daus:

WILLIAM MILBURN, of Wardrew House, Gilsland, N Seaton Hall, Northumberland, and Rosedale Abbey, Pickering, Yorks, JP (N R Yorks); *b* 5 Dec 1826; *m* 23 Oct 1850 Mary (*d* 22 Aug 1909), er dau of John Davison, of Link House, Blyth, shipowner, by Catharine, dau of John Crow, of Bog Hall, and Bellasis, and *d* 12 Nov 1903, having had:

1 JOHN DAVISON (Sir), **1st Bt**

2 William, of E Grinstead, Sussex, JP (Sussex); *b* 1856; *m* 1882 Edith Jane (*d* 14 Oct 1951), dau of Richard Hewlins, of St Ives, Hunts, and *d* 16 June 1908, leaving:

    (1) William Hewlins; *b* 14 May 1883; *educ* Uppingham and Jesus Coll Cambridge; Maj Yorks Regt; *m* 1 March 1910 Gladys Constance, dau of George Edward Griffin, and *d* 14 Jan 1949, leaving:

        1a *Frederick Michael Hewlins [Lt-Cdr Frederick Milburn RN, Bocaddon, Lanreath, Looe, Cornwall; 3 Fawcett St, London SW10]; *b* 17 Feb 1923; *educ* RNC Dartmouth; WW II (despatches), FLAS 1961; *m* 30 July 1949 *Elspeth Georgina, only dau of Maj Thomas William Farquhar-Spottiswood, of Aberdeenshire, and has:

            1b *Bruce Michael Spottiswood; *b* 11 May 1950

            2b *Laurence Hew Spottiswood; *b* 18 Aug 1955

            3b *Benedict William Spottiswood; *b* 14 July 1959

            4b *Hugh Basil Spottiswood; *b* 31 Oct 1962

            1b *Catherine Mary; *b* 12 Aug 1953

        2a *William; *b* 8 Feb 1927; *educ* Stowe; *m* 1 June 1957 *Patricia Carroll, dau of Cdr Sir Thomas Butler, 2nd Bt, of Old Park (*qv*), and has:

            1b *Peter William Hewlins; *b* 9 July 1958

            2b *Christopher; *b* 11 Nov 1961

        1a *Gladys Patience Jane; *b* 17 Oct 1916; *m* 1st June 1940 Edward Godwin Brown (*d* March 1942) and has:

            1b *Gabrielle Elizabeth; *b* March 1941

        1a (cont.) Mrs Edward Brown *m* 2nd Oct 1946 *Alan James Bowyer, ROI, s of John Bowyer

        2a *(Heather) Elizabeth [Mrs Herbert King-Hedinger, Primavera 26–27, Bosques de San Isidro, Zapopan, Jalisco, Mexico]; *b* 11 Feb 1919; *m* 10 May 1952 Herbert King-Hedinger, MA, (*d* 3 Oct 1998) and has:

            1b *(Marton) Lucretia [Sra Lucretia King-Hedinger, Castello 120 (7-Izq), 28006 Madrid, Spain]; *b* 9 March 1953; *m* 31 Jan 1976 (*divorce* 1983) Manuel Fernandez-Aldao, Marqués de la Pedrosa, and has:

                1c *Sandra Isabel; *b* 15 Feb 1977

                2c *Patricia Victoria, *b* 23 Dec 1978

            2b *Aurora Elizabeth [Mrs Aurora Thurmond, Shelburne, Burlington, Vermont, USA]; *b* 23 May 1954; *m* 17 May 1979 (*divorce* 1998) Bruce Thurmond and has:

                1c *Edward Talbot; *b* 11 Sept 1984

        3a *Felicity Ann, MB, BS; *b* 12 April 1925

    (2) Booker, DSO, MC; *b* 1888; Capt Coldstream Gds; *m* 1st 7 Oct 1924 (*divorce* 1932) Violet Alice, er dau of Adml Hon Sir Victor Stanley, KCB, MVO (*see* DERBY, E); *m* 2nd 19 July 1933 *Betty (*m* 2nd 12 March 1942 Lt James Duff McCulloch, Argyll and Sutherland Highrs, er s of G D McCulloch), only dau of Capt Walter Henry Calthrop Calthrop, OBE, AM, RN, of Woking, and *d* 11 March 1941, having by her had:

        1a *Hector Iain Calthrop; *b* 15 April 1939

        2a *Donald; *b* 20 May 1940; *educ* Trin Coll Glenalmond and Jesus Coll Cambridge; *m* 14 Sept 1963 *Marjorie L E, dau of Thomas C Burns

    (3) Gerald Richard; *b* 1893; Lt E Surrey Regt; *ka* nr Ypres 1915

    (1) Edith Winifred Rhoda; *m* 1918 Brev-Maj Ellis George Whately, MC, Herts Regt (*d* 4 Sept 1969 aged 87), and had:

        1a *Gerald Arthur [Gerald Whately Esq, The Manor House, Holybourne, Alton, Hants]; *b* 23 Aug 1919; Roy Signals WW II; *m* 19 July 1947 *Nina Abigail, dau of Alexander MacArthur Finlayson, and has:

            1b *Julian Richard; *b* 10 Aug 1949; *educ* Eton

            1b *Miranda Nina; *b* 19 May 1952

        2a *(Thomas) David, MC [David Whately Esq MC, 6 Montpelier Sq, London SW7]; *b* 4 March 1924; 9th Roy Lancers WW II; *m* 30 July 1952 *Belinda, dau of Anthony Seymour Bellville, of IoW, and has:

            1b *Sophia Louise; *b* 29 Aug 1955

            2b *Victoria Mary; *b* 2 May 1959

            3b *Polly Maria; *b* 30 May 1967

        1a *Daphne Estelle [Mrs Douglas Finlayson, The Knapp, Sutton Veny, nr Warminster, Wilts]; *b* 11 July 1921; *m* 23 Nov 1946 *Col Douglas Ian MacArthur Finlayson, RA, and has:

            1b *Alexander Ian; *b* 15 Nov 1953

            2b *Robert George; *b* 27 Nov 1956

            1b *Jane Daphne; *b* 3 Feb 1950

        2a *Angela Joan; *b* 9 Sept 1927

    (2) Estelle Mary; *m* 1926 John Francis Edwin Goad, OBE, and *d* 11 Feb 1957, leaving a dau

    (3) Muriel Rose; *m* 1924 Col Maurice James Hartley Wilson, OBE, QOCH, only surv s of Lord Ashmore (Scottish Ld of Session), and had:

        1a *Philip John Maurice [Philip Wilson Esq, Rycroft House, Rycroft Lane, Bolney, Sussex]; *b* 5 Nov 1927; dir Chevron Internat Oil; *m* 29 Oct 1956 *Valerie, dau of Arthur Bibby (*see* BIBBY, Bt), and has:

            1b *Richard Peter Philip; *b* 9 May 1958

            1b *Virginia Valerie; *b* 1 Feb 1960

2a *Malcolm Richard Milburn (Rev); b 6 May 1930; Deacon Scottish Episcopal Ch 1959, Priest 1960, late Lt QO Cameron Highrs; m 30 April 1960 *Jean Carle, dau of Rev Canon Robert Denholm, and has had:

  1b John Robert Malcolm; b 19 Nov 1962; d 8 May 1963

  2b *David William James; b 24 July 1964

  3b *Robert Patrick Malcolm; b 18 March 1968

  1b *Catriona Jean; b 4 Feb 1961

1a *Pamela Muriel [Mrs Peter Carmichael, Arthurstone, Perthshire]; b 11 Nov 1925; m 1948 *Peter Oliphant Carmichael of Arthurstone, JP, DL, s of James Louis Carmichael of Arthurstone by Ethel, dau of Sir John George Smyth Kinloch, 2nd Bt, of Kinloch (qv), and has:

  1b *Ralph Peter Kinloch; b 20 April 1950

  2b *Alastair James Milburn; b 1 Dec 1952

  3b *Malcolm Drummond Alexander; b 8 Sept 1955

  1b *Madeleine Pamela; b 5 Sept 1960

2a *Lillias Diana [Mrs Donald Fairclough, The Old Parsonage, Tankersley, Yorks]; b 29 July 1933; m 13 April 1957 *Dr Donald James Fairclough, only s of Dr James Fairclough, and has:

  1b *James David MacDonald; b 1 June 1958

  2b *Simon Maurice Lytton; b 1 July 1961

3 Charles Thomas, JP (Hants), of Compton Manor, Kings Somborne, Hants; b 1 Aug 1860; m 1 Dec 1921 *Elsie Barbara, JP (Hants), dau of R N G Baker, and d 23 Nov 1922

4 Frederick; b 29 April 1862; FZS; d 19 April 1944

1 Mary Watson; b 17 March 1853; m 24 Feb 1876 James Smith Clark (d 1922), of Newcastle, and d 1936, leaving issue

2 Catherine; b 8 May 1866; m John Henry Hancock and d 3 Feb 1899, leaving issue

WILLIAM MILBURN's est s,

Sir John Davison Milburn, 1st Bt (UK), so cr 30 Dec 1905, of Guyzance and Wardrew Northumberland, JP; b 4 Aug 1851; m 24 Aug 1876 Clara Georgiana (d 29 Dec 1936), dau of William Charles Stamp, of Mayfair, and had:

1 Sir Charles Stamp Milburn, 2nd Bt; b 5 Dec 1878; educ Christ's Coll Cambridge (MA); d unm 16 July 1917

2 LEONARD JOHN MILBURN (Sir), **3rd Bt**

3 John Davison; b 9 Jan 1886; educ Rugby and Trin Coll Cambridge (BA 1908, MA 1911); barrister Middle Temple 1911, Lt Roy Highrs WW I; m 10 Oct 1922 Grace Emily (d 24 July 1934), only dau of Stuart MacRae, and d 11 May 1972, having had:

  (1) Nigel William Stuart; b 8 Aug 1923; d 8 Nov 1924

  (1) *Angela Mary [Miss Angela Milburn, Highcliff, Little Switzerland, Douglas, IoM]; b 16 Jan 1925

  (2) *Sybil Pauline [Miss Sybil Milburn, Highcliff, Little Switzerland, Douglas, IoM]; b 20 May 1926

4 Archibald William, JP (Northumberland); b 14 April 1887; educ Rugby and Trin Coll Cambridge (BA 1910, MA 1912); High Sheriff 1936, Capt Northumberland Hus WWs I (despatches) and II HG, chm N of England Shipowners' Assoc 1935; m 7 Jan 1931 Eleanor Lilias (d 24 Sept 1983 aged 86), only dau of Maj Nevill Arthur Charles de Hirzel Tufnell, of Langleys, Essex, and d 19 Dec 1965, leaving:

  (1) +Mark Anthony William [Maj Mark Milburn, Apart 164, Arrecife de Lanzarote, Canary Islands]; b 16 Nov 1932; educ Eton, Le Rosey and RMA Sandhurst; Maj SAS (RARO), late Lt RSG, French Brevet Militaire; m 2 Feb 1968 (divorce 1976) Angela Margaret Cromwell, dau of Lt-Col Geoffrey Stephen Carmac Weigall, King George's Own Bengal Lancers, of Eldoret, Kenya, and formerly w of David Francis Brugham Maitland Edye, and has:

    1a +Francis Shahid; b 11 Nov 1969; educ Millfield; BSc

  (1) *Sarah Caroline Georgiana [Mrs David Micklem, Langleys, Gt Waltham, Essex CM3 1AH]; b 11 April 1935; m 14 April 1956 *David Robert Micklem, only s of Cdr Sir (Edward) Robert Micklem, CBE, RN, and has:

    1a *Alexander David Robert; b 11 March 1965; m 9 June 1990 *Jennifer Jane, er dau of Dr Maurice Healy, and has:

      1b *Oliver David; b 6 Aug 1991

      2b *Henry James; b 21 Oct 1993

      3b *Charles Nicholas; b 23 Aug 1995

    1a *Lucy Victoria Cornelia; b 7 June 1958; m 14 April 1984 *Peter John Bradford Gibson and has:

      1b *Archibald John Peter; b 8 March 1991

      1b *Olivia Emily Victoria; b 21 Feb 1987

      2b *Alice Emma Louise; b 4 April 1989

    2a *Anna Caroline; b 2 June 1960; m 12 April 1987 *Jonathan James Grew and has:

      1b *James Edward; b 8 May 1988

      2b *Jeremy Charles; b 28 Feb 1993

      3b *Richard David; b 1 March 1985

      1b *Louisa Sarah; b 2 Nov 1990

5 Anthony; b 28 Sept 1891; educ Harrow and Trin Coll Cambridge (BA 1914); Capt Yorks Hus Yeo; m 1st 28 Nov 1916 (divorce 1930) Dorothy Lilian, er dau of Maj William Fairbairn Wailes-Fairbairn, of Askham Grange, York, and had:

  (1) Peter Bronwyn; b 7 Nov 1917; educ Harrow; Pte Yorks and Lancs Regt WW II; m 2 Sept 1939 *Ivy Maude Allan and was ka Normandy 12 Aug 1944, leaving:

    1a +Anthony Bronwyn; b 21 Feb 1942; m 27 July 1963 *Mary Millicent Beatrice Murray and has:

      1b +Peter Bronwyn; b 17 Jan 1966

5 (cont.) Anthony Milburn m 2nd 8 March 1932 *Vera Doris Madeline (m 2nd 7 April 1953 Lt-Gen Sir Colin Muir Barber, KBE, CB, DSO, DL (d 5 May 1964)), yr dau of Robert Bell Barrett, JP, of Skipton Castle, Yorks, and d 5 Oct 1941

1 Rosalind Mary; m 23 April 1903 Sir William Whytehead Boulton, 1st Bt (qv), of Braxted Park, Essex, and d 11 Dec 1969, leaving issue

Sir CHARLES's bro,

Sir Leonard John Milburn, 3rd Bt, JP (Northumberland); b 14 Feb 1884; High Sheriff 1928, FZS, Lt Reserve Regt RHG, WW I and WW II; m 18 April 1917 Joan Katherine Anne Paula Anson, yr dau and eventually coheir of Henry Anson Horton, MA, JP, of Catton Hall, Derbys, and d 17 Sept 1957, having had:

1 Sir John Nigel Milburn, 4th Bt; b 22 April 1918; educ Eton and Trin Coll Cambridge; Capt Northumberland Hus Yeo (TARO) WW II (POW), Jt MFH W Percy; m 23 Oct 1940 *Dorothy Joan [Dorothy Lady Milburn, Brainshaugh, Acklington, Morpeth, Northumberland], est dau of Leslie Butcher, and d 1985, having had:

  (1) Nigel John; b 19 June 1946; d 9 Oct 1954

2 Rupert Leonard Everseley, JP (Northumberland 1951); b 8 May 1919; educ Eton and RMC Sandhurst; RSG Palestine 1939 and WW II (despatches); m 1 April 1944 Anne Mary, only dau of Maj Austin Scott Murray, MC, of Heckfield Place, Basingstoke, and d 16 March 1974, leaving:

  (1) Sir ANTHONY RUPERT MILBURN, **5th and present Bt**

  (2) +Michael Richard; b 21 June 1950; educ Eton

  (1) *Caroline Anne [Lady Renwick, Whalton House, Whalton, Morpeth, Northumberland]; b 12 May 1945; m 11 June 1966 *Sir Richard Eustace Renwick, 4th Bt (qv)

  (2) *Diana Rosemary [Mrs Diana Wilson, 34 Salcott Rd, London SW11]; b 15 March 1949; m 12 Dec 1970 (divorce 1980) Richard Murrough Wilson, only s of Gerald Richard Powlett Wilson, JP, of Cliffe Hall, Piercebridge, Darlington, and has:

    1a *Nicholas Rupert Gerald; b 1974

1 *Darea Joan [Mrs Michael Sankey, Shackerley Hall, Albrighton, Staffs WV7 3AB]; b 18 Dec 1923; m 21 Dec 1950 Maj (George Harold) Michael Sankey, Staffs Yeo (d 1993), est s of Col Harold Bantock Sankey, CBE, MC, TD, DL, of Whiston Hall, Albrighton, and has:

  (1) *Christopher Michael David [Christopher Sankey Esq, Rosedale, Church Lane, Pritton, Salisbury, Wilts SP5 1DJ]; b 7 Jan 1952; educ Shrewsbury; m 22 April 1995 *Sarah Elizabeth, est dau of Ronald Gilbert Frost, of Ham Farm, Brent Knoll, Highbridge, Somerset, and has:

    1a *Hannah Elizabeth; b 2 Feb 1996

  (2) *Peter William Richard [Peter Sankey Esq, Cranmere, Worfield, Salop WV15 5LP]; b 1953; educ Shrewsbury; m 1991 *Mrs Sarah Caroline Aileen Davenport Greenshields, only dau of John Sydney Birch Lea (see LEA, Bt), and has:

    1a *Edward Philip George; b 1994

    1a *Georgina Elisabeth Joan; b 1992

  (1) *Nicola Mary Joan; b 1 Feb 1955

  (2) *Virginia Karen Margaret; b 19 Aug 1957

2 *Susan Ann [Lady Farr, Shortwood House, Lamport, Northants NN6 9HN]; b 21 Nov 1937; m 26 Aug 1960 Sir John Arnold Farr, MP (C) Harborough 1959–92 (d 25 Oct 1997), er surv s of Capt John Farr, JP, of Worksop Manor, Notts, and has:

  (1) *Jonathan Leonard; b 28 July 1962; m 1996 *Caroline, dau of DC Barton, of Liverpool and has:

    1a *William John; b 18 June 1997

  (2) *George Nelson; b 21 Oct 1967; m 1992 *Jane F, dau of C R Lachlan, of Melbourne, and Mrs David Gape, of Caxton, Cambs, and has:

    1a *Oliver George Tebbitt; b 10 Sept 1997

    1a *Harriet Philippa Joan; b 1994

    2a *Katherine Elizabeth; b 8 Jan 1996

MILES

Arms: Azure a chevron paly of six ermine and or between three lozenges argent, each charged with a fleur-de-lys sable. **Crest:** A dexter arm embowed in armour proper, garnished or, supporting with the hand an anchor, also proper. **Motto:** *Labora sicut bonus miles* ('Work as a good soldier'). **Creation:** Bt. (UK) 19 April 1859.

SIR WILLIAM NAPIER MAURICE MILES, 6TH BT, of Leigh Court, Somerset [Sir William Miles Bt, Old Rectory House, Walton-in-Gordano, Clevedon, Avon BS21 7AW]; *b* 19 Oct 1913; *s f* 1966; *educ* Stowe and Jesus Coll Cambridge (BA); *m* 31 Aug 1946 *Pamela, yr dau of Capt Francis Michael Dillon, and has:

1 +PHILIP JOHN; *b* 10 Aug 1953; *educ* Northease Manor Lewes

1 *Catherine Anne Elizabeth [Mrs Peter Beloe, Madam's End Farm, Hardwicke, Glos GL2 3SQ]; *b* 10 June 1947; *m* 6 Sept 1974 *Peter Charles Beloe and has:

  (1) *William Alexander Peter; *b* 1977

  (1) Sophie Elizabeth Pamela; *b* 1975; *d* 1982

  (2) *Phoebe Caroline; *b* 1983

2 *Lorraine; *b* 19 March 1950; *m* 1972 *Martin Hugh Sessions-Hodge and has:

  (1) *James Anthony; *b* 1975

  (2) *Henry George Patrick; *b* 1977

  (1) *Abigail Theodora; *b* 1980

Lineage: WILLIAM MILES, of a family originally settled at Ledbury, Herefs, but himself of Jamaica and Bristol; merchant; *m* Ann Barrow and had:

PHILIP JOHN MILES, of Leigh Court, Somerset, and King's Weston, Glos; merchant, MP Bristol; *m* 1st 1795 Maria (*d* 22 June 1811), dau of Very Rev Arthur Whetham, Dean Lismore; *m* 2nd 11 May 1813 Clarissa (*d* 22 June 1868), dau of Samuel Peach Peach, and by his 1st w had:

1 WILLIAM (Sir), **1st Bt**

1 Sarah Agatha; *m* 1828 John Ogle, est s of Rev John Savile Ogle, of Kirkley Hall, Northumberland

2 Elizabeth; *m* Rev Henry Lloyd

3 Millicent; *m* Rev Henry Mirehouse

PHILIP MILES *d* 24 March 1845; his est son,

Sir William Miles, 1st Bt (UK), so *cr* 19 April 1859, of Leigh Court; *b* 13 May 1797; *chm* Somerset QS 35 years, MP E Somerset, Chippenham and Romney; *m* 12 Sept 1823 Catherine (*d* 23 March 1869), dau of John Gordon, and *d* 17 June 1878, having had:

1 **Sir Phillip John William Miles, 2nd Bt**; *b* 2 Sept 1825; MP E Somerset 1878–85; *m* 17 Oct 1848 Frances Elizabeth (*m* 2nd 1904 Dr John Nicholls, of St Louis, Mo., and *d* 18 Dec 1908), dau of Sir David Roche, 1st Bt (*qv*), and *d* 5 June 1888, having had:

  (1) William John; *b* 13 March 1852; *d* 2 April 1859

  (2) **Sir Cecil Miles, 3rd Bt**; *b* 7 Aug 1873; *m* 1896 Minnie (*m* 2nd 17 Dec 1904 Frederick Hilton Gibbes and *d* 24 Oct 1929), dau of James Spire, of Innsworth, Glos, and *dsp* 25 Oct 1898

  (1) Alice Catherine; *m* 1st 17 Dec 1870 George Duppa, JP (*d* 5 Jan 1888), of Hollingbourne House, Kent, and had issue; *m* 2nd 20 Feb 1889 Lt-Col Gerard Vivian Ames (*d* 27 April 1899), 1st Dragoons, of The Hyde, Ayot St Lawrence, and *d* 3 April 1926, leaving further issue

  (2) Edith Clare; *m* 20 July 1875 Charles William Mansel Lewis, DL (*d* 13 March 1931), of Stradey, Llanelly, Carmarths, and *d* 9 June 1934, leaving issue

  (3) Mabel Constance; *m* 2 Feb 1884 Casamaijor William Gaussen (*d* 14 April 1923), of Howlands, Hatfield, Herts, and *d* 30 Oct 1944, leaving issue

  (4) Violet Bessie Ellin; *d* 14 April 1883 aged 16

2 William Henry; *b* 7 Sept 1830; *m* 24 April 1862 Mary Frances (*d* 10 Sept 1909), only dau of Rev John Kynaston Charleton, Vicar Elberton, Glos, and *d* 15 Jan 1888, leaving issue

3 Charles John William; *b* 16 Jan 1832; Capt 5th Fus; *m* 26 Jan 1866 Elizabeth Maria, only dau of Rev Henry Lloyd, of Selattyn, Salop, and *dsp* 2 June 1874

4 Arthur John William Whetham; *b* 1841; *d* 1853

5 HENRY ROBERT WILLIAM (Sir), **4th Bt**

1 Maria Catherine; *m* 3 March 1846 Robert Charles Tudway (*d* 20 March 1855), of The Cedars, Wells, Somerset, MP Wells, and *d* 26 May 1909, leaving issue

2 Agatha; *m* 13 Sept 1849 Gen Edward Arthur Somerset, CB, and *d* 13 Aug 1912, leaving issue (*see* BEAUFORT, D)

3 Emma Clara; *m* 31 July 1856 Rev Hon James Walter Lascelles and *d* 30 April 1911, leaving issue (*see* HAREWOOD, E)

4 Catherine; *m* 5 Nov 1856 Gen Sir Robert Onesiphorous Bright, GCB (*d* 15 Nov 1896), and *d* 5 Feb 1911, leaving issue

5 Frances Harriett; *m* 4 Sept 1862 Sir William Augustus Ferguson-Davie, 3rd Bt, CB (*qv*), and *d* 18 June 1923, leaving issue

6 Harriott Ellin; *m* 4 Sept 1862 1st Baron Cranworth (*qv*) and *d* 7 April 1864, leaving issue

7 Florence Louisa; *m* 8 June 1859 5th Earl of Strafford (*qv*) and *d* 14 Feb 1862, leaving issue

The 3rd Bt's unc,

Sir Henry Robert William Miles, 4th Bt; *b* 6 Jan 1843; Lt 5th Fus; *m* 12 Sept 1882 Mary (*d* 12 Feb 1938), dau of Frederick Neame, of Luton, Selling, Kent, and had:

1 CHARLES WILLIAM (Sir), **5th Bt**

2 William Henry; *b* 27 March 1888; *educ* Uppingham and Pembroke Coll Cambridge; Capt Somersetshire LI WW I (wounded, despatches); *m* 1 Feb 1913 Lilian (*d* 1972), yst dau of Sir Hartley Williams, of Knightsbridge, and *d* 6 Dec 1975, leaving:

  (1) Charles Robert; *b* 27 March 1919; *educ* Rugby and Pembroke Coll Cambridge; F/O RAF WW II; *ka* 7 Oct 1941

  (1) *(Lilian) Mary [Mrs Alan Maby, 64 Bishops Mansions, Bishops Park Rd, London SW6]; *b* 1914; *m* 17 June 1939 Alan Grant Maby (*d* 5 Dec 1965) and has:

    1a *Michael Robin Patrick; *b* 9 March 1944; *educ* Wellington; *m* 17 May 1969 *Miranda Jane, 2nd dau of Charles Marrow, of Kingsdon, Somerton, Somerset

    2a *Keith Alan; *b* 24 April 1946; *educ* Wellington and Ch Ch Oxford

  (2) *Pamela [Mrs Daniel Goedhuis, Ossington House, Newark, Notts NG23 6LJ]; *b* 1916; *m* 1st 25 April 1947, as his 2nd w, Lt-Col (William) Maxwell Evelyn Denison, JP, DL (*d* 15 Aug 1972); *m* 2nd 1974 Prof Daniel Goedhuis, Netherlands Embassy (*d* 10 Oct 1995), and by her 1st husb has:

    1a *Georgina Jane; *b* 1 March 1948

Sir HENRY *d* 7 Feb 1915; his er son,

Sir Charles William Miles, 5th Bt, OBE (1919), DL (Somerset 1932); *b* 7 July 1883; *educ* Uppingham; Lt-Col Somerset LI WW I (wounded, despatches), Adj 4th Bn 1912–16, DAAG GHQ India, Assist Mil Sec to C-in-C India 1916–19, AAG GHQ 1919; *m* 1 Oct 1912 Favell Mary (*d* 3 Jan 1969), er dau of Charles Gathorne Hill, of Claverton Manor, Bath, and *d* 28 Dec 1966, having had:

1 Sir WILLIAM NAPIER MAURICE MILES, **6th and present Bt**

2 +Charles William Noel, CBE (1980) [Professor Charles Miles CBE, Wheelers, Hound Green, Hants RG27 8LE]; *b* 3 Nov 1915; *educ* Stowe, and Jesus Coll Cambridge (MA); Reading U: Prof Estate Management, Dean Urban and Regnl Studies 1970–75, Professor Emeritus 1981; FRICS; *m* 16 March 1940 *Jacqueline (Dickie), yr dau of Robert Singlehurst Cross, and has had:

  (1) Anthony William; *b* 2 Dec 1946; *educ* Stowe; *d* unm 28 Feb 1969

  (1) *Phinola Jane Miles; *b* 19 Aug 1943; *m* 30 Sept 1967 *Anthony McCandlish Smith, s of Dr David Smith, of E London, S Africa

MILFORD

Arms: Arg. a lion rampart sa., ducally gorged and chained or. **Crest:** A lion as in the arms. **Supporters:** On either side a horse arg., charged on the neck with bars wavy az. **Motto:** *Ducit amor patriæ* ('Patriotism guides me'). **Creations:** Bt. (UK) 22 Sept 1919, B. (UK) 2 Feb 1939.

THE 3RD BARON MILFORD, of Llanstephan, Co Radnor, and a **Baronet** (Sir Hugo John Laurence Philipps, Bt) [The Rt Hon The Lord Milford, Llanstephan House, Llanstephan, Powys LD3 0YR]; *b* 27 Aug 1929; *s f* 1993; *educ* Eton and

King's Coll Cambridge; High Sheriff Powys 1976–77; *m* 1st 1951 (*divorce*1958) Margaret, only dau of Capt Ralph Heathcote, DSO, RN, of Gressingham, Lancs, and has:

  1 *Anna Margaret [The Hon Mrs Woodhouse, 14 Crescent Grove, London, SW4]; *b* 1954; *m* 1975 *Christopher Richard James Woodhouse and has issue (*see* TERRINGTON, B)

The 3rd BARON *m* 2nd 1959 (*divorce* 1984) Hon Mary Makins, twin dau of 1st Baron Sherfield (*qv*); *m* 3rd 1989 *Mrs Felicity Leach, dau of Murray Ballantyne, of Montreal, and by his 2nd *w* has:

  1 +GUY WOGAN [The Hon Guy Philipps, 68 Westbourne Park Rd, London W2 5PJ]; *b* 25 July 1961; *educ* Eton and Magdalen Coll Oxford (BA); barrister Inner Temple 1986; *m* 1st 1988 Rebecca, yr dau of Nigel Nicolson (*see* CARNOCK, B); *m* 2nd 1996 *Alice, dau of Dr Archie Sherwood, of London, and has by her:

    (1) +Archie Sherwood; *b* 12 March 1997

  2 +Roland Alexander [The Hon Roland Philipps, 231 Westbourne Park Rd, London W11 1EB]; *b* 1962; *educ* Eton and Trin Coll Cambridge (MA); *m* 1991 *Felicity Kate, dau of Hilary Harold Rubinstein, and has:

    1a +Nathaniel Alexander; *b* 19 Dec 1996

  3 +Ivo Laurence; *b* 1967; *educ* Eton and Bristol U

  2 *Katherine Nina; *b* 1964

Lineage: The Rev Sir JAMES ERASMUS PHILIPPS, 12th Bt (*see* ST DAVIDS, V); had, with other issue:

Sir Laurence Richard Philipps, 1st Bt, and **1st Baron Milford,** of Llanstephan, Co Radnor (both UK), so *cr* 22 Sept 1919 and 2 Feb 1939 respectively, JP (Radnorshire 1918 and Hants 1910); *b* 24 Jan 1874; *educ* Felsted and Roy Sch of Mines; High Sheriff Hants 1915, chm: Court Line Ltd, Kia-Ora Ltd and Northern Securities Tst; dir Schweppes Ltd and Ilford Ltd (ret 1949), memb Lloyd's, Govr U Coll of Wales (Hon LLD 1939); *m* 10 April 1901 Ethel Georgina, JP (Radnorshire) (*d* 30 June 1971 aged 91), only dau of Rev Benjamin Speke, Rector Dowlish Wake, Somerset, and had:

  1 WOGAN, **2nd Baron**

  2 (Richard) Hanning, MBE (1945), JP; *b* 14 Feb 1904; *educ* Eton; Maj Welsh Gds WW II, Hon Col Pembroke Yeo 1959, Ld Lt Pembs 1958–74 (V-Lt 1957–58, previously DL) and Dyfed 1974–79, memb Civic Tst Wales and memb London Stock Exchange, Hon Pres Schweppes Ltd (chm 1940–69, dir 1930–69), chm: Northern Securities Tst Ltd, Dun and Bradstreet Ltd and Milford Haven Conservancy Bd, CStJ; *m* 10 June 1930 Lady Marion Violet Dalrymple, JP (Pembs 1965), FRAgS 1963–76 (*d* June 1995), yr dau of 12th Earl of Stair (*qv*), and *d* 29 Jan 1998, leaving:

    (1) +Jeremy Hew [Jeremy Philipps Esq, Peach House, Picton Castle, Haverfordwest, Pembs SA62 4AS]; *b* 2 April 1931; *educ* Eton; Lt Pembroke Yeo (TA), chm Laurence Philipps Hldgs, Laurence Philipps Ltd 1969–; *m* 30 Sept 1959 *Susan, yr dau of Henry Edward Bowden Gundry, of Grange, Honiton, Devon, and has:

      1a *Clare Marion; *b* 9 Nov 1961

      2a *Nicola Jane; *b* 27 Aug 1964

  2 (cont.) The Hon Hanning and Lady Marion Philipps also adopted:

    *Louise; *b* 29 April 1946; *m* 27 March 1971 *Hugh Simon Fetherstonhaugh, er s of David Henry Fetherstonhaugh, JP (*see* GALWAY, V)

  3 James Perrott, TD; *b* 25 Nov 1905; *educ* Eton and Ch Ch Oxford; High Sheriff Suffolk 1955, memb Lloyd's and Horserace Totalisator Bd, dir Racecourse Assoc, Maj TAR WW II (despatches); *m* 24 June 1930 *Hon Elizabeth Joan Kindersley [The Hon Mrs James Philipps, Dalham Hall, Newmarket, Suffolk], dau of 1st Baron Kindersley (*qv*), and *d* 1984, having had:

    (1) +Peter Anthony [Peter Philipps Esq, Parsonage Farm, Ugley, Herts]; *b* 14 Dec 1933; *educ* Eton and Trin Coll Cambridge; Lt RNR, memb Stock Exchange; *m* 5 April 1957 (*divorce*1981) Susannah Margaret, est dau of Sidney Wilfred Eaton, of Luddesdown Court, Luddesdown, Kent, and has:

      1a +Charles Edward Laurence; *b* 20 Jan 1959

      2a +James Anthony Hanning; *b* 23 May 1961

      3a +Gavin Piers Alexander; *b* 19 Dec 1963

    (1) Penelope Doune; *b* 9 March 1931; *m* 30 March 1950 *Capt Anthony Walsham Neville Lake [Capt Anthony Lake, Higham's Farm, Wimbish, Essex], er s of Capt Henry Neville Lake, DSO, DSC, RN, of Tinker's Hill Farm, Furneaux Pelham, Herts, and *d* 1985, having had:

      1a *David Anthony; *b* 20 Jan 1953; *educ* Eton

      2a *Simon Neville; *b* 20 Feb 1956; *educ* Eton

      3a *Mark Philip; *b* 30 May 1958

    (2) *Daphne Deirdre [Mrs Daphne Lewes, Springfield Maltings, Stogumber, Somerset TA4 3SY]; *b* 20 April 1940; *m* 25 July 1963 Robin Hugh Lewes, TD (*d* 15 April 1969), yr s of Capt John Hugh Lewes, CBE, DSC, RN, of Bittescombe Manor, Wiveliscombe, Somerset, by Lilla Muriel Moss, only dau of Robert Curzon Henry Moss King, of Harcourt House, Camberley, and has:

      1a *James Hugh; *b* 30 June 1967

      1a *Katherine Mary; *b* 18 Sept 1968

      2a *Sarah Jane; *b* 18 Sept 1968

  4 Geoffrey; *b* 17 Sept 1908; *d unm* 18 April 1930

  5 William Speke, CBE (1957); *b* 17 Sept 1908; *educ* Eton; Capt RA (TA) WW II (despatches), High Sheriff Pembs 1968, chm Br Nat Life Insur Soc and Court Line Ltd, Liveryman Shipwrights' Co, Freeman City London; *m* 31 Aug 1939 *Lady Jean Meriel McDonnell [The Lady Jean Philipps, Slebech Park, Haverfordwest, Dyfed; 40 Hill St, London W1], yr dau of 7th Earl of Antrim (*qv*), and *d* following an accident 5 Sept 1975, having had:

    (1) +Geoffrey Mark [Geoffrey Philipps Esq, Slebech Park, Haverfordwest, Dyfed; 48 Pembridge Villas, London W11]; *b* 9 Nov 1948; *educ* Eton; *m* 1984 Georgina Bridget, dau of R-Adml J G B Cooke, CB, DSC, of Downstead House, Morstead, Hants, and has:

      1a +Alexander Gervaise; *b* 1985

      1a *Lara Helen; *b* 1986

      2a *Leonora Isabel Jean; *b* 1989

    (2) +David William [David Philipps Esq, South Lodge, Pentre, Dyfed]; *b* 4 April 1952; *m* 11 Sept 1971 *Stella Katharine Anne, only dau of A W Fordham, of Newcastle Emlyn, Dyfed, and has:

      1a +Frederick William; *b* 1973

    (1) *Georgina Rose [Mrs David Lloyd, 41 Pembroke Sq, London W8]; *b* 13 Jan 1942; *m* 14 Jan 1967 *David Llewellyn Pryse Lloyd, only s of Llewellyn Pryse Lloyd, of Carmarths, and has had:

      1a *Huw Llewellyn; *b* 1971

      2a *Jonathan; *b* 1973

      1a Isobel Rose; *b* 14 Jan 1969; *d* 1989

      2a *Juliet Ann; *b* 8 July 1970

    (2) *Theresa Margaret Philipps [Mrs Christopher Payne, New House, Burdett St, Ramsbury, Wilts]; *b* 6 Oct 1946; *m* 8 April 1972 *Christopher John Payne and has:

      1a *Joseph Vernon William; *b* 1975

      2a *Benjamin Christopher John; *b* 1978

      1a *Harriet Sarah Jean; *b* 1982

      2a *Charlotte; *b* 19 June 1986

  1 *Gwenllian, OBE (1962), JP (Radnorshire 1951) [The Hon Gwenllian Philipps, The Old Rectory, Boughrood, Llyswen, Brecon]; *b* 13 Aug 1916; WW II as Subaltern ATS, CC Radnorshire 1959–64, High Sheriff 1970–71, Commr Girl Guides

The 1st BARON *d* 7 Dec 1962; his est son,

  WOGAN PHILIPPS, **2nd Baron Milford**; *b* 25 Feb 1902; *educ* Eton and Magdalen Coll Oxford; sat as Communist Ho Lds; *m* 1st 21 Nov 1928 (*divorce* 1944) Rosamond Nina (*d* 1990), the novelist, dau of Rudolph Chambers Lehmann, of Fieldhead, Bourne End, Bucks, and had:

  1 HUGO JOHN LAURENCE MILES PHILIPPS, **3rd and present Baron Milford**

  1 Sarah Jane; *b* 14 Jan 1934; *m* 28 Feb 1956 *Patrick J G Kavanagh and *d* 22 June 1958

The **2nd Baron** *m* 2nd 17 Jan 1944 Cristina (*d* 22 March 1953), dau of Marchese Casati, of Palazzo Barberini, Rome, and formerly *w* of 15th Earl of Huntingdon (*qv*); *m* 3rd 20 May 1954 *Tamara, dau of — Kravetz and widow of William Rust, ed *Daily Worker*, and *d* 1993

MILFORD HAVEN

Arms: Quarterly, 1st and 4th, az. a lion rampant double-queued barry of ten arg. and gu., armed and langued of the last, crowned or, within a bordure company of the second and third; 2nd and 3rd, arg. two pallets sa., charged on the honour point with an escutcheon of the arms of the late PRINCESS ALICE (*viz.*, the Royal Arms differenced by a label of three points arg., the centre point charged with a rose gu., barbed vert, and each of the other points with an ermine spot sa.) **Crests:** 1 Out of a ducal coronet or two horns barry of ten arg. and gu., issuing from each three linden leaves vert and from the outer side of each horn four branches barwise, having three like leaves, pendant therefrom of the last (for HESSE), 2 Out of a ducal coronet or a plume of four ostrich feathers alternately arg. and sa. (for BATTENBERG). **Supporters:** On either side a lion double-queued and crowned all or. **Motto:** In honour bound. **Creations:** V., E. and M. (all UK 17 July 1917).

THE 4TH MARQUESS OF MILFORD HAVEN, **Earl of Medina**, Co Southampton, and **Viscount Alderney**, Co Southampton (George Ivar Louis Mountbatten) [The Most Hon The Marquess of Milford Haven, House of Lords, London SW1A 0PW]; *b* 6 June 1961; *s f* 1970; *educ* Gordonstoun; *m* 1st 1989 (*divorce* Feb 1996) Sarah Georgina, er dau of George Alfred Walker, financier, and n of the boxer Billy Walker, and has:

  1 +HENRY (HARRY) DAVID LOUIS, *Earl of Medina*; *b* 19 Oct 1991

  1 *Tatiana Helen Georgia; *b* 1990

The 4th MARQUESS *m* 2nd 20 Aug 1997 *Clare, formerly *w* of Nick Wentworth-Stanley and dau of Annie Reiner, of Nantucket, Mass.

Lineage: YDULF; held rank of *Dux* ('Duke', at this stage still predominantly a term denoting a military leader rather than title of honour) in what is now Belgium and Luxembourg during the 6th century; had:

BRUNULF; had:

AUBRI II; had:

WALTER I; had:

WALTER II; had:

ALBO; had:

MAINIER; had:

GAINFROI, of Sens; had:

GISELBERT, Count of the Masau; a fully documented history starts with his son:

GISELBERT, Count in the valley of the Meuse, ruling Masau/Maasgau in what is now Belgium 841; *m* 846 Irmgard, dau of the HOLY ROMAN EMPEROR LOTHAIR (gs of CHARLEMAGNE), who granted his s-in-law the Countship of Darnau 863, and had:

   1 REGINAR I

   2 Albert; perhaps Count of the Southern Ardenne

   3 Richwin; Bp Strasbourg; *d* 933

   4 Sigard, Count over Luihgau, Hainault and Hesbaye

GISELBERT's er son,

   REGINAR/REGNIER I, Margrave between the Meuse and the Scheldt, also Count of Hainault, the Hesbaye and several other areas in Lotharingia (modern Lorraine); lay Abbot or temporal guardian of the Abbeys of St Servais de Maestricht, St Maximin, Chevremont, Echternach and Stavelot; *m* Alberada — and *d* 915, leaving, with a dau (*m* Berenger, Count of Namur and Count in the Lommagau and Maifeld):

   1 GISELBERT, DUKE OF LORRAINE; *b c* 890; *m* 929 the Saxon princess Gerberga (*m* 2nd LOUIS IV OF FRANCE), dau of HENRY (THE FOWLER), KING OF THE EAST FRANKS, and was drowned 939 attempting to ford the Rhine in armour after his defeat nr Andernach while in rebellion against his bro-in-law OTTO THE GREAT (later HOLY ROMAN EMPEROR), leaving:

      (1) HENRY, DUKE OF LORRAINE, *b c* 931; *dsp c* 944

   2 REGINAR II

   3 Balderic; Bp Utrecht; *d* 977

   4 Frederick; Prince Archbp of Mainz; *d* 954

GISELBERT's 2nd son,

   REGINAR II, COUNT OF HAINAULT; *b* between 891 and 901; *m* Adelaide, dau of RICHARD, DUKE OF BURGUNDY, and *d c* 932, leaving:

   1 REGINAR III

   2 Rudolph, Count of La Hesbaye; attended Diet of Nijmwegen 947

   3 Liechard; *d* by 944

   1 A dau; *m* Nevelon, s of Ricfrid, Count in the Betau, and had:

      (1) Balderic; made Bp of Liège by his unc REGINAR III

REGINAR II's er son,

   REGINAR III, DUKE OF UPPER LORRAINE 954, called 'Long Neck'; *m* Adèle (*d* 961), dau of Lambert, Count of Toxandrie, and *d* in exile in Bohemia 973, leaving:

   1 REGINAR IV, COUNT OF HAINAULT; *m c* 997 Hathuide, dau of HUGH CAPET, KING OF FRANCE (987–996), and *d* 1013, leaving with a dau (Beatrice; *m* Eble I, Count of Roucy):

      (1) REGINAR V, COUNT OF HAINAULT; *m* 1015 Maud, dau of Hermann of Lorraine, Count of Eenham, and *d c* 1039, leaving:

         1a HERMANN, last COUNT OF HAINAULT of his line; *m* Richilde (*m* 2nd Baldwin VI, Count of Flanders; *m* 3rd William Fitz Osbern, Earl of Hereford and Jt Viceroy England, and *d* 1086), perhaps dau of Roger or Reginar, bro of Arnoul, Count of Valenciennes, and *d* by 1051, leaving, with a dau (Gertrude, Benedictine nun):

            1b Roger; Bp Châlons-sur-Marne 1066; *dsp* 1093

   2 LAMBERT, COUNT OF LOUVAIN, called 'The Bearded'; *m* Gerberge (*d* 1008), dau of CHARLES, DUKE OF LORRAINE, bro of LOTHAIR, KING OF FRANCE, and was *k* 12 Sept 1015 at the Battle of Florennes defending his nephew's County of Hainault against the newly created Duke Godfrey of Brabant, leaving:

      (1) Henry I, Count of Louvain; *k* Louvain 1038, leaving:

         1a Otto, Count of Louvain; *dsp* 1041

      (2) LAMBERT II

      (1) Maud; *m* Eustace I, Count of Boulogne, and had issue

LAMBERT I's yr son,

   LAMBERT II, COUNT OF LOUVAIN, called 'The Belted'; *m* Oda, dau of GOZEL I, DUKE OF LORRAINE, and *d c* 1063, leaving, with a dau (Adèle, *m* 1st Otto, Margrave of Meissen, and 2nd 1069 Dedo II, Margrave of Eilenberg and the Saxon Ostmark):

HENRY II, COUNT OF LOUVAIN; *m* Adèle, dau of Eberhard, Count in the Betau, and *d* 1078, leaving:

   1 HENRY III, COUNT OF LOUVAIN; *d* 1095

   2 GODFREY I

   3 Auberon; Bp Liège 1122; *d* 1128

   1 Ida; *m* Baldwin VI, Count of Hainault, and *d c* 1139

HENRY II's yr son,

   GODFREY I, DUKE OF BRABANT from 1106, also MARQUIS OF ANTWERP and COUNT OF LOUVAIN, called 'The Bearded', deposed from his Duchy 1127 but continued styling himself Duke and was so succeeded by his son; *m* 1st Ida, dau of Albert III, Marquis of Namur, and had:

   1 GODFREY II

   2 HENRY, COUNT OF LOUVAIN; *d* 1141

   1 Adela; *m* 1st 2 Feb 1121, as his 2nd w, HENRY I OF ENGLAND (*d* 1135); *m* 2nd 1138 William d'Aubigny, Earl of Arundel (*see* NORFOLK, D); both *d c* 1157

GODFREY I *m* 2nd Clemence, widow of Robert II, Count of Flanders, dau of Count William I of Burgundy and sis of POPE CALIXTUS II, and *d c* 1140, having by her had:

   3 Jocelin/Josceline, of Louvain; *m* Agnes, 2nd dau but eventual heiress of William de Percy (*see* NORTHUMBERLAND, D) and had issue, the 1st Duke of Northumberland of the 1766 *cr* choosing the title 'Lord Lovaine, Baron of Alnwick' when also given a Barony 1784 in commemoration of this ancestral connection

GODFREY I's er son,

   GODFREY II, DUKE OF BRABANT; *b c* 1095; *m* Luitgard, dau of Berenger I, Count of Sulzbach, and *d* 1142, leaving:

GEOFFREY III, DUKE OF BRABANT, called 'The Baby'; *b c* 1141; *m* 1st Margaret, dau of Henry II, Count of Limbourg, and had:

   1 HENRY I

   2 Albert; Bp, Cardinal and Saint; *d* 1192

GODFREY III *m* 2nd Imaine, dau of Louis, Count of Loos, abdicated 1183 in favour of his er s, and *d* 1190, having by her had:

   3 William, of Louvain, Lord of Perwez; *d c* 1224

   4 Godfrey, of Louvain or in Anglo-Norman French 'de Lovaine'; custodian of his half-bro DUKE HENRY I's lands in England (chiefly the Castle and Honour of Eye in Suffolk), which came to the latter by his w (*see* below); joined the Baronial party opposed to KING JOHN; *m c* 1199 Alice, dau of Robert de Hastings and widow of Ralph de Cornhill, and *d* by 26 April 1226, leaving:

      (1) Matthew; *m* Muriel — and *d* by June 1258, leaving, with a yr s (John):

         1a Matthew; *b c* 1237; campaigned intermittently 1258–March 1300/1 in service of HENRY III and EDWARD I OF ENGLAND against the French, Scots and Welsh; *m* 1st by 31 May 1268 Helisant, a relative of HENRY III; *m* 2nd Maud Poyntz and *d* by 24 May 1302, leaving (probably by his 2nd w):

            1b Thomas (Sir); *b* 11 July 1291; fought for EDWARD II Battle of Boroughbridge 16 March 1321/2 against the rebels opposed to the King's favourites the Despensers (*see* FALMOUTH, V) under EDWARD II's cousin Thomas Earl of Lancaster; ktd by 1324; *m* Joan — and *d* 9 April 1345, leaving:

               1c John (Sir); *b c* 1318; *m* 1st Joan —and had a dau (Isabel, *d* young); *m* 2nd Margaret, dau of Sir Thomas de Weston, and *dspm* 30 Jan 1346/7, leaving by her:

                  1d Alianore/Eleanor; *b* 27 March 1345; *m* by June 1359 Sir William de Bourg(h)chier and *d* 5 Oct 1397, leaving:

                     1e WILLIAM BOUR(G)CHIER, *cr* 10 June 1419 COUNT OF EU (as part of HENRY V's policy of bestowing French fiefs on English subjects to consolidate his hold on English-occupied territory in France); *m* by 20 Nov 1405 Anne, est dau and ultimate heir of Thomas of Woodstock, Duke of Gloucester (EDWARD III's yst s), by Alianore/Eleanor, er dau and coheir of Humphrey de Bohun, Earl of Hereford, Essex and Northampton, and *d* 28 May 1420, leaving issue; (*see* BERNERS, B, and HEREFORD, V, preliminary remarks)

GODFREY III's est son,

   HENRY I, DUKE OF BRABANT, called 'The Warrior'; *b* 1165; a leader Third Crusade; *m* 1st 1179 Maud, dau of Matthew of Flanders, Count of Boulogne, and gdau of KING STEPHEN OF ENGLAND, and had:

   1 HENRY II

   2 Godfrey, of Louvain; *b* 1209; Lord of Baucignies, Leeuwe and Gaesbeck; *m* 1243 Mary of Baucignies, dau of Arnulf IV, Lord of Audenarde, and *d* 1253

   1 Mary; *b c* 1191; *m* 1214 THE HOLY ROMAN EMPEROR OTTO IV and *d c* 1260

   2 Margaret; *m* Gerard III, Count of Gelderland, and *d* 1231

   3 Maud; *m* 1st 1212 Henry II of the Palatinate; *m* 2nd 1224 Florence IV, Count of Holland and Zeeland, and *d* 1267

HENRY I *m* 2nd 1213 Mary, dau of PHILIP AUGUSTUS OF FRANCE, and *d* 1235, having by her had two daus (Elizabeth; Mary); his est s:

HENRY II, DUKE OF BRABANT, called 'The Magnanimous'; *b c* 1207; *m* 1st 1215 Mary of Hohenstaufen, dau of PHILIP OF SWABIA, KING OF THE ROMANS, and had:

   1 HENRY III, DUKE OF BRABANT; *b* after 1225; gf of:

      (1) JOHN, DUKE OF BRABANT; *m* Margaret, dau of EDWARD I OF ENGLAND, and *d* 1261; his male-line descendants became extinct on the death 1355 of JOHN III, DUKE OF BRABANT, called 'The Triumphant'

   1 Maud; *m* 1237 Robert I, Count of Artois (*k* Mansourah 1288), bro of St LOUIS IX OF FRANCE, and *d* 1250

   2 Beatrice; *b c* 1225; *m* 1241 HENRY RASPE, KING OF THE GERMANS and Landgrave of Thuringia (*d* 1247, leaving Thuringia to his bro-in-law and great-nephew Henry, *see* below)

HENRY II *m* 2nd *c* 1240 Sophia, dau of Louis IV, Landgrave of Thuringia, by St Elizabeth, dau of ANDREW II, KING OF HUNGARY, and *d* 1248, having by her had:

   2 HENRY I, 1st LANDGRAVE OF HESSE, called 'The Child'; *b* 1244; bequeathed Thuringia 1247 by his great-uncle KING HENRY RASPE, but as he was then only 3 years old the HOLY ROMAN EMPEROR FREDERICK II granted the succession instead to Henry, Margrave of Meissen, called 'The Illustrious' (ancestor of the Br Roy House of Windsor); after a war of succession 1256–63 HENRY I managed to wrest from the Margrave of Meissen only Hesse out of all the Thurigian domains and proclaimed himself first Landgrave of Hesse, being recognised as a Prince of the Holy Roman Empire; *m* 1st 1263 Adelaide, dau of Otto I, Duke of Brunswick, and had:

      (1) Henry; *b c* 1266; *d* 1298

      (2) OTTO I

   2 (cont.) HENRY I *m* 2nd Maud (*d* 1309), dau of Dietrich VI, Count of Cleves, and *d* 1308 having by her had:

(3) John, Landgrave of Lower Hesse; *b c* 1280; *d* 1311

(4) Louis; Bp Munster; *b* 1282; *d* 1357

3 Elisabeth; *b* 1243; *m* 1254 Albert I, Duke of Brunswick, called 'The Great', ancestor of the Br Roy House of Hanover, and *d* 1261

The 1st LANDGRAVE's surv son,

OTTO I, 2nd LANDGRAVE OF HESSE; *b* 1272; *m* 1297 Adelaide, dau of Otto III, Count of Ravensberg, and *d* 1328, having had:

1 HENRY II, 3rd LANDGRAVE OF HESSE; *b c* 1300; *d* 1376, having had:

(1) Otto; Co-Regent Hesse 1340; *b c* 1322; *dsp* 1366

2 Otto; Archbp Magdeburg; *b* 1301; *d* 1361

3 Louis, called *Der Junker* ('The Squire'); *b c* 1302; *m* 1340 Elizabeth, dau of Simon II, Count of Sponheim, and *d* 1345, having had:

(1) HERMANN II

4 Hermann; Canon Wurzburg, Lord of Nordeck and Grebenstein; *d c* 1369

The 3rd LANDGRAVE's nephew,

HERMANN II , 4th LANDGRAVE OF HESSE, called 'The Learned'; *b c* 1342; Co-Regent Hesse 1366; *s* unc as ruler 1376, called first Parliament of Hesse; *m* 1st 1377 Joan (*d* 1383), dau of John I, Count of Nassau-Weilburg; *m* 2nd Margaret of Hohenzollern, dau of Frederick V, Burgrave of Nuremberg, and *d* 1413, having by his 2nd w had:

LOUIS , 5th LANDGRAVE OF HESSE, called 'The Peaceful'; *b* 1402; acquired the Counties of Ziegenhain and Nidda 1450; *m* 1436 Anne, dau of Frederick I, Elector of Saxony, and *d* 1458, having had:

1 LOUIS II

2 Henry III, Landgrave of Hesse-Marburg; *b* 1441; *d* 1483, leaving:

(1) William III, Landgrave of Hesse-Marburg; *b* 1471; *d* 1500, when Marburg reverted to the sr line

3 Hermann; Prince Archbp Cologne; *b* 1449; *d* 1508

The 5th LANDGRAVE's est son,

LOUIS II, 1st LANDGRAVE OF HESSE-CASSEL, called 'The Frank'; *b* 1438; *m* 1454 Mathilda, dau of Louis I, Count of Württemberg, and *d* 1471, having had, with an er s (William I, Landgrave of Hesse-Cassel 1471–93, *b* 1466, *d* 1515):

WILLIAM II, 5th LANDGRAVE OF HESSE, called 'The Intermediate'; *b* 1469; Co-Regent Cassel 1483, of which he became Landgrave on his bro's abdication 1493; also inherited Marburg 1500 and acquired the Counties of Dietz and Katzenelnbogen, including Darmstadt and Rheinfels 1479; *m* 1st 1496 Yolande (*d* 1500), dau of Frederick VI, Duke of Lorraine; *m* 2nd 1500 Anne, dau of Magnus II, Duke of Mecklenburg, and *d* 1509, having by her had:

PHILIP I, 6th LANDGRAVE OF HESSE, called 'The Magnanimous'; *b* 1504; famous promoter of the Reformation; signed the 'Protest' (hence 'Protestant') presented by the reforming states of the Holy Roman Empire in 1529 against an edict of the Diet of Spier that the religious status quo was to be preserved (in effect that no further proselytising by reformers could take place); fndr League of Protestant Princes, defeated Catholic Imperial Forces; *m* 1st 1523 Christina (*d* 1549), dau of George, Duke of Saxony, and had:

1 WILLIAM IV, LANDGRAVE OF HESSE-CASSEL, called 'The Wise'; *b* 1532; fndr Cassel line; *m* 1566 Sabina, dau of Christopher, Duke of Württemberg, ancestor of the TECKs (*see* Royal Family), and *d* 1592

2 LOUIS, LANDGRAVE OF HESSE-MARBURG, called 'The Elder'; *b* 1537; *d* 1604

3 PHILIP , LANDGRAVE OF HESSE-RHEINFELS, called 'The Younger'; *b* 1541; *d* 1583

4 GEORGE I

PHILIP I *m* 2nd 1540 (bigamously but with the public support of Martin Luther) Margaret, dau of Hans von der Saale, and by her had, with other issue, the Counts of Dietz; *d* 1567, when Hesse was partitioned amongst the four sons of his 1st w

The 6th LANDGRAVE's yst son,

GEORGE I, 1st LANDGRAVE of HESSE-DARMSTADT, called 'The Pious'; *b* 1547; recd as his share of the family territory the County of Katzenelnbogen, whose capital he established at Darmstadt; *m* 1st 1572 Madeleine (*d* 1587), dau of Bernard IX, Count of Lippe, and had:

1 LOUIS V

2 PHILIP, LANDGRAVE OF HESSE-BUTZBACH; *b* 1581; *dsp* 1643

3 FREDERICK I, LANDGRAVE OF HESSE-HOMBURG; *b* 1585; *d* 1638; his line died out 1866

GEORGE I *m* 2nd 1589 Eleanor (*d* 1618), dau of Christopher, Duke of Württemberg (ancestor of the Marquesses of Cambridge (*see* 1970 edn) and Earls of Athlone (*see* 1956 edn)), and *d* 1597, having by her had:

4 Henry; *d* an infant

The est son,

LOUIS V, 2nd LANDGRAVE OF HESSE-DARMSTADT, called 'The Steadfast'; *b* 1577; *m* 1598 Madeleine, dau of John-George I, Elector of Brandenburg, and *d* 1626, having had:

1 GEORGE II

2 JOHN, LANDGRAVE OF HESSE-BRAUBACH; *b* 1609; *dsp* 1651

3 Henry; Rector Marburg U; *b* 1612; *dsp* 1629

4 Frederick; scholar-administrator, Adml, Gen and Cardinal, Capt-Gen cmdg the galleys of the Knights of Malta against Turks 1640; *b* 1616; *dsp* 1682

The est son,

GEORGE II, 3rd LANDGRAVE OF HESSE-DARMSTADT, called 'The Learned'; *b* 1605; *m* 1627 Sophia Eleanor, dau of John-George I, Elector of Saxony, and *d* 1661, having had, with a yr s (GEORGE III, LANDGRAVE OF ITTER ZU VOHL; *b* 1632, *d* 1678):

LOUIS VI, 4th LANDGRAVE OF HESSE-DARMSTADT; *b* 1630; *m* 1st 1650 Mary Elisabeth (*d* 1665), dau of Frederick, Duke of Schleswig-Holstein-Gottorp, and had:

1 LOUIS VII, 5th LANDGRAVE OF HESSE-DARMSTADT; *b* 1655; *dsp* 1678

2 Frederick; *b* 1659; Rector Giessen U; *dsp* 1676

LOUIS VI *m* 2nd 1666 Elisabeth Dorothea, dau of Ernest I, Duke of Saxe-Gotha, called 'The Pious' (ancestor of the Br Roy House of Windsor), and *d* 1678, having by her had:

3 ERNEST LOUIS

4 George; *b* 1669; cmded Br Roy Marines capture Gibraltar; 1st Br Govr Gibraltar 1704; *d* 1705

5 Philip; *b* 1671; fought in Br Army as Col of the Regt which bore his name; Imperial Govr Mantua; *d* 1714

6 Henry; *b* 1674; served with his bro George; *d* 1741

7 Frederick; *b* 1677; Canon Breslau; entered Russian Imperial Serv, *k* fighting Swedes 1708

The 5th LANDGRAVE OF HESSE-DARMSTADT's yr bro,

ERNEST LOUIS, 6th LANDGRAVE of HESSE-DARMSTADT; *b* 1667; added the County of Hanau-Lichtenberg to his family possessions 1736; *m* 1st 1687 Dorothea Charlotte (*d* 1705), dau of Albert V, Margrave of Brandenburg-Ansbach, and had a s; *m* 2nd morganatically 1727 Louise Sophie, *cr* Countess of Epstein, dau of Hermann William von Spiegel, and *d* 1739; his s by his 1st w:

LOUIS VIII, 7th LANDGRAVE OF HESSE-DARMSTADT; *b* 5 April 1691; *m* 5 April 1717 Charlotte Christiana Magdalena Johanna, dau and heiress of Johann Reinhard II, last Count of Hanau-Lichtenberg, through whom the family inherited Hanau-Lichtenberg 1736, and *d* 17 Oct 1768, having had:

1 LOUIS IX

2 George William; *b* 11 July 1722; *m* 6 March 1748 Marie Louise Albertine (*d* 11 March 1818), dau of Christian Carl Reinhard, Count of Leiningen-Dachsburg-Heidesheim, and *d* 21 June 1782, having had, with other issue:

(1) LouiseHenriette Karoline; *b* 15 Feb 1761; *m* 19 Feb 1777 her cousin LOUIS I, GRAND DUKE OF HESSE (*see* below), and *d* 24 Oct 1829, having had issue

1 Carolina Louisa; *b* 11 July 1723; *m* 28 Jan 1751, as his 1st w, Charles Frederick, Margrave (later first Grand Duke) of Baden-Durlach, and *d* 8 April 1783, having had issue

The er son,

LOUIS IX, 8th LANDGRAVE OF HESSE-DARMSTADT; *b* 15 Dec 1719; Corps Cdr under FREDERICK THE GREAT in Prussian serv; *m* 1st 12 Aug 1741 (Henriette) Caroline Chrstiana Louisa (*d* 30 March 1774), called 'The Great Landgravine' (patroness of such literary figures as Goethe, Grimm and Herder), dau of Christian II of Wittelsbach, Count Palatine of Zweibrücken-Birkenfeld; *m* 2nd morganatically 1775 Marie Adelaide de Cheirouze, *cr* Countess of Lemberg, and *d* 6 April 1790, having had by his 1st w, with other issue:

1 LOUIS X and I

2 Frederick; *b* 1759; *dsp*

1 Caroline; *b* 1746; *m* Frederick Louis, Landgrave of Hesse-Homburg, and *d* 1821

2 Frederica Louise; *b* 1751; *m* 1769 FREDERICK WILLIAM II OF PRUSSIA and *d* 1805

3 Amelia; *b* 1754; *m* Charles Louis, Hereditary Prince of Baden, and *d* 1882, having had, with other issue:

(1) Louise (Elisabeth); *b* 1779; *m* 1801 TSAR ALEXANDER I OF RUSSIA and *d* 1826, leaving issue

(2) Frederica; *b* 1721; *m* 1797 GUSTAVUS IV ADOLPHUS OF SWEDEN and *d* 1826

(3) Wilhelmina; *b* 1788; *m* 1804 LOUIS II, 2nd GRAND DUKE OF HESSE AND THE RHINE (*see* below); *d* 1836

4 Wilhelmina (Natalie); *b* 1755; *m* 1773 TSAREVITCH PAUL OF RUSSIA and *d* 1776

The est son,

LOUIS X, 9th LANDGRAVE OF HESSE-DARMSTADT later I, GRAND DUKE OF HESSE AND BY RHINE, a title he assumed 7 July 1816, having previously joined NAPOLEON's puppet Germanic organisation the Confederation of the Rhine and assumed the title Grand Duke of Hesse 13 Aug 1806; *b* 14 June 1753; in the turmoil of the French Revolutionary and Napoleonic Wars acquired territories on the right bank of the Rhine 1803 in compensation for rather smaller ones lost to France on the left bank 1801; *m* 19 Feb 1777 his cousin Louise (*see* above) and *d* 6 April 1830, having had, with other issue, including three yr sons (George, *b* 1780, *d* 1856; Frederick, *b* 1788, *d* 1867; Emil, *b* 1790, *d* 1856):

LOUIS II, 2nd GRAND DUKE OF HESSE AND BY RHINE; *b* 26 Dec 1777; *m* 19 June 1804 his cousin Wilhelmina Luise, dau of Charles Louis, Hereditary Prince of Baden (*see* above), and *d* 16 June 1848, having had, with other issue:

1 LOUIS III, 3rd GRAND DUKE OF HESSE AND BY RHINE, KG (1865); *b* 9 June 1806; *m* 1st 26 Dec 1833 Mathilde Caroline Friederike Wilhelmine Charlotte (*d* 25 May 1862), dau of LOUIS I OF BAVARIA; *m* 2nd 20 June 1868 morganatically Anne Magdalene, *cr* Baroness von Hochstädten, dau of Johann Heinrich Appel, and *dsp* 13 June 1877

2 Charles William Louis; *b* 23 April 1809; *m* 22 Oct 1836 (Marie) Elisabeth Caroline Victoria, dau of PRINCE WILLIAM OF PRUSSIA, s of FREDERICK WILLIAM II OF PRUSSIA, and *d* 20 March 1877, having had, with other issue:

(1) LOUIS IV, 4th GRAND DUKE OF HESSE AND BY RHINE, KG (1862); *b* 12 Sept 1837; *m* 1st 1 July 1862 HRH PRINCESS ALICE MAUD MARY (*d* 14 Dec 1878), 2nd dau of HM QUEEN VICTORIA, and had issue; *m* 2nd morganatically 30 April 1884 (annulled) Alexandrine, *cr* Countess von Romrod (*m* 3rd 22 Jan 1893 Vassiliy Romanovitch Bacheracht, Russian Min Berne, and *d* 8 May 1941), dau of Count Adam Hutten-Czapski and formerly w of Alexander Kolemin, Russian Chargé d'Affaires Darmstadt, and *d* 13 March 1892, had no issue by her; among his children by his 1st w were:

1a ERNEST LOUIS, 5th GRAND DUKE OF HESSE AND BY RHINE, KG, GCB; *b* 1868; deposed 1918; *m* 1st 1894 (*divorce* 1901) PRINCESS VICTORIA MELITA (*d* 1936), dau of HRH ALFRED DUKE OF EDINBURGH, KG, s of HM QUEEN VICTORIA; *m* 2nd 1905 Eleanore, dau of Hermann, 5th Prince of Solms-Hohensolms-Lich, and *d* 1937, having by her had:

1b George Donatus, Hereditary Grand Duke of Hesse; *b* 1906; *m* 1931 Cecile, dau of PRINCE ANDREW OF GREECE, GCVO, sis of HRH

PRINCE PHILIP, DUKE OF EDINBURGH, and was *k* with his mother, *w* and children in a flying accident 1937

2b Louis, Grand Duke of Hesse; *b* 1908; *m* 17 Nov 1937 Hon Margaret Campbell Geddes (*d* 26 Jan 1997), only dau of 1st Baron Geddes (*qv*), and *dsp* 30 May 1968

1a Victoria Alberta Elizabeth Mathilde Marie, VA; *b* 5 April 1863; *m* 30 April 1884 her cousin **1st Marquess of Milford Haven** (*see* below) and *d* 24 Sept 1950, leaving issue

2a Elizabeth Alexandra Louise Alice later Elizabeth Feodorovna on undergoing baptism in Russian Orthodox Church, VA; *b* 1 Nov 1864; *m* 15 June 1884 GRAND DUKE SERGEI ALEXANDROVITCH OF RUSSIA (assassinated 17 Feb 1905) and was murdered by Bolsheviks night of 17/18 July 1918

3a Irene Luise Marie Anna; *b* 11 July 1866; *m* 24 May 1888 PRINCE HENRY OF PRUSSIA (*d* 20 April 1929), 2nd s of EMPEROR FREDERICK III OF GERMANY, and *d* 11 Nov 1953, having had issue

4a (Victoria) Alix Helena Louise Beatrice later Alexandra Feodorovna on undergoing baptism in Russian Orthodox Church, VA; *b* 6 June 1872; *m* 26 Nov 1894 TSAR NICHOLAS II OF RUSSIA, KG, and was shot with her husband and apparently all her children by Bolsheviks on the night of 16/17 July 1918

3 ALEXANDER

1 Maximiliane Wilhelmine Auguste Sophie Marie later Maria Alexandrovna on undergoing baptism in Russian Orthodox Church; *b* 8 Aug 1824; *m* 28 April 1841 TSAR ALEXANDER II OF RUSSIA, KG (assassinated 13 March 1881), and *d* 3 June 1880, having had issue

The 3rd son,

PRINCE ALEXANDER LOUIS GEORGE FREDERICK EMIL OF HESSE AND BY RHINE, GCB; *b* 15 July 1823; Gen Russian and Austrian servs; *m* morganatically 28 Oct 1851 Julie Therese (*b* 12 Nov 1825; *d* 19 Sept 1895), *cr* 5 Nov 1851 Countess of Battenberg in Hesse and 26 Dec 1858 Princess of Battenberg, dau of Count Maurice von Hauke, Polish Min War, and *d* 15 Dec 1888, leaving:

1 LOUIS ALEXANDER, **1st Marquess**

2 ALEXANDER I, PRINCE OF BULGARIA 1879–86, later Count of Hartenau in Hesse; *b* 1857; *m* 6 Feb 1889 Johanna Marie Louise Loisinger (Countess Hartenau) (*d* 1951) and *d* 17 Nov 1893, leaving:

(1) Assène Ludwig Alexander, Count Hartenau; *b* 16 Jan 1890; *m* 1934 Bertha (*d* 4 Nov 1971), dau of Dr Josef Hussa and formerly w of (a) Alois Polaczek and (b) Max Ritter Riedl von Riedenau, and *d* 15 March 1965, having adopted his w's s by her 1st husb

(1) Marie Therese Vera Zwetana; *b* 24 Oct 1893; *m* 29 Dec 1924 Charles Hercule Boissevain (*d* 19 Oct 1946) and *dsp* 24 Nov 1935

3 HENRY MAURICE (HRH, so *cr* 23 July 1885), KG, PC; *b* 5 Oct 1858; naturalised UK subject; Govr and Capt IoW and Carisbrooke Castle; served Ashanti Expdn but *d* of malaria 20 Jan 1896 homeward bound aboard HMS *Blonde*; *m* 23 July 1885 HRH PRINCESS BEATRICE (*d* 26 Oct 1944), yst dau of HM QUEEN VICTORIA, and had:

(1) ALEXANDER ALBERT (HH), PRINCE OF BATTENBERG later MOUNTBATTEN (renounced title of prince etc, also changed surname 14 July 1917), 1st and last MARQUESS OF CARISBROOKE, so *cr* 18 July 1917, as also EARL OF BERKHAMSTED and VISCOUNT LAUNCESTON, Co Cornwall (all UK), GCB (1927), GCVO (1911); *b* 23 Jan 1886; Cadet and Midshipman RN, later Gren Gds WW I, RAF WW II; *m* 19 July 1917 Lady Irene Frances Adza Denison, GBE, DJStJ (*d* 16 July 1956), dau of 2nd Earl of Londesborough (*see* LONDESBOROUGH, B), and *d* 23 Feb 1960, when his peerages expired, leaving:

1a Iris Victoria Beatrice Grace; *b* 13 Jan 1920; *m* 1st 15 Feb 1941 (*divorce* 1946, resumed maiden name by deed poll 1949) Capt Hamilton O'Malley, Irish Gds, est s of Lt-Col Middleton O'Malley-Keyes, RHA, of Ross House, Westport, Co Mayo; *m* 2nd 5 May 1957 (*divorce* 1957) Michael Kelly Bryan, of Memphis, Tenn.; *m* 3rd 11 Dec 1965 William Alexander Kemp (*d* 12 Dec 1991), Canadian TV announcer, and *d* 1 Sept 1982, leaving by her 2nd husb:

1b *Robin Alexander; *b* 20 Dec 1957

(2) LEOPOLD ARTHUR LOUIS (HH), PRINCE OF BATTENBERG later MOUNTBATTEN (roy licence 14 July 1917, rank of marquess's yr s by roy warrant 11 Sept 1917), GCVO; *b* 21 May 1889; Capt KRRC, formerly 8th Bn Hants Regt, ADC Personal Staff 1917, WW I, also IoW Rifles and 60th Rifles; *d* unm 23 April 1922

(3) MAURICE, PRINCE OF BATTENBERG; *b* 1891; WW I in 60th Rifles; *k* 28 Oct 1914 in retreat from Mons

(1) VICTORIA EUGENIE, PRINCESS OF BATTENBERG, VA; *b* 24 Oct 1887; *m* 31 May 1906 ALFONSO XIII OF SPAIN, KG, GCVO (*d* 28 Feb 1941), and *d* 15 April 1969, having had issue

4 Francis Joseph, GCVO, KCB; *b* 24 Sept 1861; Lt-Col Hessian Inf and 1st Bulgarian Cav, PhilD, Kt Italian Order Annunciation; *m* 18 May 1897 HRH PRINCESS ANNA (*d* 22 April 1971 aged 96), dau of NICHOLAS I OF MONTENEGRO, and *dsp* 31 July 1924

1 Marie Caroline; *b* 15 July 1852; *m* 29 April 1871 Gustav, Prince of Erbach-Schönberg (*d* 29 Jan 1908), and *d* 20 June 1923, leaving issue

PRINCE ALEXANDER's est son,

PRINCE LOUIS ALEXANDER OF BATTENBERG (HSH) later MOUNTBATTEN (roy licence 14 July 1917, having renounced for self and issue all German styles and titles), **1st Marquess of Milford Haven**, so *cr* 17 July 1917, as also EARL OF MEDINA and VISCOUNT ALDERNEY, Co Southampton (all UK), GCB (Mil 1921, Civil 1887), KCB 1909, GCVO (1901), KCMG (1905), PC (1914), JP and DL (IOW), JP (Hants); *b* 24 May 1854; naturalised UK subject and joined RN 31 Oct 1868, Egyptian Campaign 1882, Capt 1891, Naval Advsr to Inspr-Gen Fortifications 1892–94, Hon ADC to HM QUEEN VICTORIA 1897–1901, Assist Dir Naval Intell 1899–1901, Personal Naval ADC to TM EDWARD VII 1901–10 and GEORGE V 1910–21, Cdre 2nd Cl Mediterranean 1901–02, Dir Naval Intell 1902–05, R-Adml 1904, cmded 2nd Cruiser Sqdn 1905–07, 2ic Mediterranean Fleet 1907–08, V-Adml 1908, C-in-C Atlantic Fleet 1908–10, cmded 3rd and 4th Div Home Fleet 1911, 2nd Sea Ld 1911–12, Adml 1912 (ret 1919), 1st Sea Ld

1912–14, Adml of the Fleet 1921, KJStJ, Er Bro Trin House, Hon LLD Cantab 1918, FRGS, FRNS; *m* 30 April 1884 his cousin PRINCESS VICTORIA ALBERTA ELIZABETH MARIE IRENE, VA (*d* 24 Sept 1950), est dau of HRH LOUIS IV, GRAND DUKE OF HESSE, KG, by HRH PRINCESS ALICE, dau of HM QUEEN VICTORIA, and *d* 11 Sept 1921, having had:

1 GEORGE LOUIS VICTOR HENRY SERGIUS, **2nd Marquess**

2 LOUIS FRANCIS ALBERT VICTOR NICHOLAS MOUNTBATTEN, *cr* EARL MOUNTBATTEN OF BURMA (*qv*)

1 (Victoria) Alice (Elizabeth Julia Marie), RRC; *b* 25 Feb 1885; *m* 7 Oct 1903 HRH PRINCE ANDREW OF GREECE, GCVO (*d* 3 Dec 1944), and *d* 5 Dec 1969, leaving issue (*see* ROYAL FAMILY)

2 Louise Alexandra Marie Irene, RRC; *b* 13 July, 1889; *m* 3 Nov 1923 GUSTAF VI ADOLF OF SWEDEN, KG, GCB, GCVO (*d* 15 Sept 1973), and *d* 7 March 1965

The 1st MARQUESS's er son,

GEORGE LOUIS VICTOR HENRY SERGIUS MOUNTBATTEN, **2nd Marquess of Milford Haven**, GCVO (1932, KCVO 1916); *b* 6 Nov 1892; *educ* RNC Osborne; RN: Midshipman 1910, acting Sub-Lt 1912, Sub-Lt 1913, Lt 1914, Lt-Cdr 1922, Cdr 1927, ret 1932 (Capt ret list 1937), served Battle Cruiser Fleet WW I, present Battles of Heligoland 1914, Dogger Bank 1915 and Jutland 1916; chm and md Sperry Gyroscope Co, dir Electrolux; Order St Vladimir 4th Cl Russia, Mil Order Savoy 4th Cl Italy, Grand Cross Order Isabella the Catholic Spain, Grand Cross Polar Star Sweden, Freeman City London; *m* 15 Nov 1916 Nadejda (Nada) (*d* 22 Jan 1963), yr dau of HIH GRAND DUKE MIKHAIL MIKHAILOVITCH OF RUSSIA, and *d* 8 April 1938, having had, with a dau (Tatiana Elizabeth; *b* 16 Dec 1917):

DAVID MICHAEL MOUNTBATTEN, **3rd Marquess of Milford Haven**, OBE (1943), DSC (1943); *b* 12 May 1919; *educ* RNC Dartmouth; memb Inst Electronic and Radio Engrs, Lt RN WW II (despatches twice), Freeman Shipwrights' Co; *m* 1st 4 Feb 1950 (*divorce* Mexico 1954, UK 1960) Romaine Dahlgren, only dau of Vinton Ulric Dahlgren Pierce, of USA, and formerly w of William Simpson; *m* 2nd 17 Nov 1960 *Janet Mercedes, only dau of Maj Francis Bryce, OBE, KRRC, of Hamilton, Bermuda, and *d* 14 April 1970, having by her had:

1 GEORGE IVAR LOUIS MOUNTBATTEN, **4th and present Marquess of Milford Haven**

2 +Ivar Alexander Michael [The Lord Ivar Mountbatten, Bridwell Park, nr Tiverton, Devon]; *b* 9 March 1963; *educ* Gordonstoun; *m* 1994 *Penelope A V, dau of Colin Thompson, of Warminster, Wilts, and has:

(1) *Ella Louise Georgina; *b* 20 March 1996

(2) *Alexandra Nora Victoria; *b* 8 May 1998

MILLAIS

Arms: Per bend sinister or and az. an estoile of eight points between three fleurs-de-lys, two in fess and one in base, all counterchanged. **Crest:** In front of a dexter hand, gauntleted and couped gu., an estoile of eight points or. **Motto:** *Ars longa, vita brevis* ('Art endures, life is short'). **Creation:** Bt. (UK) 16 July 1885.

SIR GEOFFROY RICHARD EVERETT MILLAIS, 6TH BT, of Palace Gate, Kensington, Co Middlesex, and of St Ouen, Jersey; *b* 27 Dec 1941; *s f* 1992; *educ* Marlborough

Lineage: GEOFFROY MILAYES, of a family of Norman origins but settled in Jersey, held land from the Crown 1331; presumably f of:

JOHN MILLAYS; living 1381; apparently ancestor of:

JOHN MYLAYS; *m c* 1540 Perrine Le Jarderay, a sole heiress, thus acquiring the Tapon estate, and had an est s:

JOHN MILAYS; *b* 1542; *m* Catherine Falle and had, with other issue:

JOHN MYLAIS; *m* Elizabeth Poingdestre and had:

JOHN MILAYS; *m* 1st Mary, dau of John Bisson; *m* 2nd Jane, dau and heiress of Benjamin Bertram, and had, with other issue:

EDWARD MILLAYS; *m* 1st 1671 Margaret, dau and eventual heiress of Rev Joshua Pallot; *m* 2nd Judith (*dsp*), dau and eventual heiress of Amice de Carteret, and by his 1st w had:

EDWARD MILLAYS; *b* 1672; *m* 1696 Mary, dau of John Mourant, and had:

EDWARD MILLAIS; *b* 1710; *m* 1728 Rachael le Geyt, an heiress, and had, with other issue:

EDWARD MILLAIS; *b* 1729; *m* 1752 Elizabeth, dau of Edward Falle, and had, with other issue:

JOHN MILLAIS; *b* 1769; Capt Roy Jersey Artillery; *m* Sarah Mary, dau of William Matthews, and had, with other issue:

JOHN WILLIAM MILLAIS; *m* Mary Emily (*d* 22 April 1864), dau of Richard Evamy and widow of Enoch Hodgkinson, and *d* 28 Jan 1870, having had, with three daus and an er s (William Henry, of Ward Hill, Farnham, Surrey, *b* 1828, *m* 1st 1860 Judith Agnes (*d* 6 April 1862), dau of Rev Charles Boothby (*see* BOOTHBY, Bt), and had issue; *m* 2nd 7 June 1866 Adelaide Jane (*d* 24 April 1924), yst dau of John Farquhar Fraser, and *d* 27 March 1899):

Sir John Everett Millais, 1st Bt (UK), so *cr* 16 July 1885, DCL; *b* 8 June 1829; the painter, Offr Legion Honour, Prussian Order Merit, Order Leopold Belgium, PRA 1896; *m* 3 July 1855 Euphemia (Effie) Chalmers (*d* 23 Dec 1897), est dau of George Gray, of Bowerswell, Perthshire, and formerly w of John Ruskin, the author, and *d* 13 Aug 1896, having had:

1 **Sir Everett Millais, 2nd Bt**; *b* 30 May 1856; *m* 10 April 1886 Mary St Lawrence, JP (Kent) (*d* 10 Nov 1948), only dau of William Edward Hope-Vere (*see* LINLITHGOW, M), and *d* 7 Sept 1897, having had:

  (1) **Sir John Everett Millais, 3rd Bt**, JP (Kent); *b* 28 Nov 1888; Lt-Cdr RN; *d* unm 30 Sept 1920

  (1) Euphemia Doris Mary; *b* 23 Dec 1889; *d* 8 Dec 1893

  (2) Perrine, JP; *b* 8 Feb 1893; *m* 3 June 1914 Capt Malcolm Matthew Moncrieff, MBE, 6th Dragoon Gds, s of Sir Alexander Moncrieff, KCB, FRS, of Barnhill, Perthshire, and *d* 1979, leaving issue

  (3) Mary Amice de Carteret; *b* 4 July 1897; *m* 16 Jan 1924 (*divorce* 1940) Sydney Hewitt Pitt, MC (*d* 22 March 1964), and *d* 4 Dec 1978, leaving issue

2 George Gray; *b* 19 Sept 1857; *d* 30 Aug 1878

3 GEOFFROY WILLIAM (Sir), **4th Bt**

4 John Guille; *b* 24 March 1865; Lt-Cdr RNVR, Lt Seaforth Highrs; *m* 31 Oct 1894 Fanny Margaret (*d* 1 May 1960), yr dau of Philip George Skipwith, of Hundleby, Lincs, and *d* 24 March 1921, having had:

  (1) Geoffroy de Carteret; *b* 2 Dec 1896; Capt 1st Beds Regt; *d* 22 Aug 1918 of wounds recd in action

  (2) +(Hesketh) Raoul le Jarderay [Raoul Millais Esq, Westcote Manor, Kingham, Oxon]; *b* 4 Oct 1901; Capt Scots Gds; *m* 1st 28 April 1926 Elinor Clare (*d* 1953), yst dau of Allan Ronald Macdonell, of Montreal, and has:

    1a +John Ronald Raoul MILLAIS later LEES-MILLAIS, JP (Northants 1955, Wilts 1965) [John Lees-Millais Esq JP, Rockley Manor, nr Marlborough, Wilts]; *b* 25 April 1927; *m* 1952 *Lavinia Charlotte, dau of Capt Geoffrey William Martin Lees, of Falcutt House, Brackley, Northants, and has had:

      1b +David John Geoffroy; *b* 26 Jan 1953; *m* 1980 *Jane V H, er dau of Kenneth J Forder, of Fulham, and has:

        1c +Edward; *b* 1982

        1c +Rosie; *b* 1987

        2c *Catherine; *b* 1991

      2b +Colin Everett [Colin Lees-Millais Esq, Coldthorn, Whittlebury, Northants NN12 8XL]; *b* 12 April 1957; *m* 1991 *Frances Maria Loftus, only dau of Humphry Stuart Loftus Tottenham (*see* ARCHDALE, Bt), and has:

        1c *Sophie Frances Margery; *b* 1994

        2c *Emily Grace; *b* 1997

      3b +Patrick James; *b* 23 July 1958; *m* 1987 *Fiona Astrid, yst dau of Maj John Edward Joicey, MC, and has:

        1c +Marcus John; *b* 1989

        2c +Rory; *b* 1990

      4b Simon; *b* 8 Oct, *d* 10 Oct 1963

      5b Stephen; *b* 8 Oct, *d* 10 Oct 1963

      1b *Joanna Clare; *b* 29 Dec 1954; *m* 1981 *Thomas Hornby Graham Cooper, of East Markham Hall, Newark, Notts, s of Brig Thomas Cooper, of Bottom Farm, Eaton, Lincs, and has:

        1c *Alexander Thomas; *b* 1986

        1c *Louisa Clare; *b* 1983

        2c *Emma Lavinia; *b* 1985

      2b *Fiona Katherine; *b* 1964; *m* 1996 *Richard Henry Charles Nourse

    2a +Hugh Geoffroy [Hugh Millais Esq, The Stables, Kirtlington Park, Oxon OX5 3JN]; *b* 23 Dec 1929; *m* 1st 1957 (*divorce* 19–) Suzy Falconnet; *m* 2nd 1988 *Anne Mary Sheffield and by his 1st w has:

      1b +Ian; *b* 1958

      2b +Joshua; *b* 1961

      1b *Tara Romaney; *b* 24 July 1967

  (2) (cont.) Raoul Millais *m* 2nd *Katherine Edith, yr dau of Frank Bibby, CBE, JP, DL (*see* BIBBY, Bt), and formerly w of Maj-Gen George Erroll Prior-Palmer, CB, DSO, and by her has:

    3a +Hesketh Merlin; *b* 31 Oct 1950; *educ* Milton Abbey; Capt R Hussars (PWO); *m* 1981 *Amanda W, dau of James Fletcher, of W Kensington, and has:

      1b +Raoul Edward; *b* 1981

      1b *Iona Effie; *b* 1983

      2b *Katherine Alice; *b* 1986

1 Yvonne Daphne; *b* 28 Aug 1895; *d* 6 Aug 1906

2 Natalie Rosamond Sophia; *b* 25 Dec 1903; *m* 20 June 1930 Richard Gerald Coghlin, MBE (*d* 16 April 1959), and *dsp* 26 Oct 1948

1 Effie Gray; *b* 28 Nov 1858; *m* 28 Nov 1879 Maj William Christopher James (*d* Dec 1894), RSG, and *d* 24 April 1911, leaving issue

2 Mary Hunt; *b* 13 May 1860; *d* unm 17 Jan 1944

3 Alice Sophia Caroline; *b* 10 April 1862; *m* 6 Jan 1886, as his 2nd w, 1st and last Baron Stuart of Wortley (*see* WHARNCLIFFE, E) and *d* 1 Jan 1936, leaving issue

4 Sophia Margaret Jameson; *b* 15 June 1868; *m* 9 Dec 1891 Capt Douglas Lilburn MacEwen, Cameron Highrs, and *d* 1 May 1907, having had issue

The 3rd Bt's unc,

Sir Geoffroy William Millais, 4th Bt; *b* 8 Sept 1863; *m* 15 May 1901 Madeline Campbell (*d* 7 Feb 1963 aged 86), dau of Col Charles Hallyburton Grace, IA, of W Malling, Kent, and had:

1 RALPH REGNAULT (Sir), **5th Bt**

2 +EDWARD GRAY ST HELIER [Edward Millais Esq, Crosswater Farm, Churt, Surrey GU10 2JN]; *b* 15 March 1918; heir presumptive; *educ* Radley; late Capt AA Regt RA; *m* 8 Feb 1947 *Rosemary Barbara, yr dau of Brig-Gen Frederick George Lucas, CB, CSI, CIE, DSO, 5th Roy Gurkha Rifles, and has:

  (1) +Andrew Michael; *b* 13 April 1948; *educ* Clayesmore

  (2) +John Frederick; *b* 17 Sept 1949; *educ* Radley; *m* 19– *Susan Clayton and has:

    1a *Rosie Grace; *b* 13 Nov 1992

    2a *Ella Rose; *b* 5 March 1995

  (3) +Peter William; *b* 17 July 1951; *educ* Radley; *m* 19– *Heather Hunt

  (4) +David Gray; *b* 29 Aug 1959; *educ* Monkton Combe; *m* 1993 *Susanna M, dau of Dr Patrick Maybin and Dr Maureen Maybin, of Ballylesson, Co Down, and has:

    1a +Patrick David; *b* 19 June 1995

  (1) *Fiona Mary; *b* 24 Dec 1960

1 Esmé Edith; *b* 2 Oct 1902; *m* 28 June 1930 (*divorce* 1940) Charles Anthony Stanley Prowse, only s of Brig-Gen Charles B Prowse, and *d* 31 Dec 1987, leaving:

  (1) *Althea Hermione; *b* 30 Nov 1931; *m* 27 April 1968 *Rev Desmond John Parsons and has issue (*see* ROSSE, E)

Sir GEOFFROY *d* 7 Nov 1941; his er son,

Sir Ralph Regnault Millais, 5th Bt; *b* 4 March 1905; *educ* Marlborough and Trin Coll Cambridge (BA 1926, MA 1930); W/Cdr RAFVR WW II; *m* 1st 4 Sept 1939 (*divorce* 1947) Felicity Caroline Mary Ward (*d* 3 Nov 1994), dau of Brig-Gen William Ward Warner, CMG, and formerly w of Maj John Peyton Robinson, 8th Hus, and had:

1 Sir GEOFFROY RICHARD EVERETT MILLAIS, **6th and present Bt**

1 *Caroline Mary Felicity; *b* 17 July 1940; *m* 31 Aug 1963 *David Anthony Campbell-Jones and has:

  (1) *Henry David Mervyn; *b* 1972; *educ* Radley

  (1) *Serena Caroline Mary; *b* 14 Feb 1969; *educ* Royal Naval Sch Haslemere

Sir Ralph *m* 2nd 22 Oct 1947 (*divorce* 1971) Irene Jessie, er dau of Edward Albert Stone, Jersey and the Bahamas, and formerly w of Stephen Eric Alley; *m* 3rd 18 Feb 1975 *Babette Irene [Babette Lady Millais, Elizabeth Court, 27 Elizabeth Court, 47 Milmans St, London SW10 0DA], yr dau of Maj-Gen Harold Francis Salt, CB, CMG, DSO, RA (*see* SALT, Bt, of Weeping Cross), and formerly w of (a) Maj John de Gray Tatham Warter, MC, 2nd Dragoon Gds, and (b) Victor William Henry Sefton-Smith, and *d* 14 May 1992

MILLER of Chichester

Arms: Arg. a fess wavy az. between three wolf heads erased gu.
Crest: A wolf's head erased gu., gorged with a collar wavy azure.
Creation: Bt. (E) 29 Oct 1705.

SIR HARRY MILLER, 12TH BT, of Chichester, Sussex [Sir Harry Miller Bt, 53 Koha Rd, Taupo, New Zealand]; *b* 15 Jan 1927; *s* bro 1995; *m* 1954 *Gwynedd Margaret, dau of R P Sherriff, of St Anthony, Paraparaumu, NZ, and has:

1 +ANTHONY THOMAS [Anthony Miller Esq, 261 Kohimarama Rd, Auckland 5, New Zealand]; *b* 4 May 1955; *m* 1990 *Barbara Battersby, and has issue

1 *Sara Margaret; *b* 1957; *m* 1986 *Garth Laing and has:

  (1) *Maggie Eleanor; *b* 1992

2 *Judith Christine; *b* 1960

Lineage: MARK MILLER, Alderman; m Mary, sis and coheir of John Comber, and had:

Sir Thomas Miller, 1st Bt (GB), so cr 29 Oct 1705; Chichester: MP 1688–90, Mayor; m Hannah — (d 11 Jan 1706) and d 2 Dec 1705, leaving:

Sir John Miller, 2nd Bt; MP Chichester 1698–1713; m 1st Margaret (d 23 Sept 1701), dau of John Peachy, of Chichester; m 2nd Ann (dsp 6 May 1709), dau of William Ellson, of Groves, Sussex; m 3rd 2 May 1710 Elizabeth (dspm 22 April 1756), est dau of Sir William Meux, 2nd Bt, of IoW, and had by his 1st w:

1 THOMAS (Sir), **3rd Bt**
2 John; m Mary, only dau and heiress of Richard Challen, of Oving, Sussex, and d 1735, leaving:
　(1) Charles, of Shopwick, Sussex
　(2) John, of Gravellingwell, Sussex
1 Elizabeth; m 10 Jan 1737 Sir Edward Worsley, of Gatcombe, and d March 1774
2 Anne; d unm
3 Jane; m Capt — Bockland
4 Hannah; m Thomas Gooch, DD, Bp Norwich
5 Mary; m Rev John Buchshell, LLD, and d 2 May 1738
6 Margaret; m Thomas Yates

Sir JOHN d 29 Nov 1721; his est son,

　Sir Thomas Miller, 3rd Bt; MP Chichester 1715–27; m Jane, dau of Alderman Francis Gother, of Chichester, and d 1733, having had an est s:

Sir John Miller, 4th Bt; m Susan (d 26 June 1788), dau of Matthew Combe, MD, of Winchester, and had:

1 THOMAS (Sir), **5th Bt**
2 George; d unm 1755
3 Combe (Very Rev); Dean Chichester; m Joan, dau and sole heiress of Rev — Green, of Eccles, Norfolk, and dsp 1814
4 Charles; had a dau (Eleanor, m John Herberden, MD)
1 Mary; m Henry William Wilson and had issue (see BERNERS, B)
2 Margaret; m 15 May 1766 George Garnier (bur 2 Nov 1819), of Rookesbury, Hants, and d 22 Dec 1807, having had issue
3 Anne; m 3rd Earl of Albemarle (qv)

Sir JOHN d 19 April 1772; his est son,

　Sir Thomas Miller, 5th Bt; MP Lewes 1774–78 and Portsmouth 1806–16; m 1st Hannah, dau of Alderman Black, of Norwich, and had two daus (Susannah, m Nathaniel Lee Acton, of Livermere Park, Suffolk; Hannah, m Sir St Leger Gilman, 1st and last Bt (d 1815), of Curaheen, Co Cork, and had issue); m 2nd Elizabeth Edwards, heiress, and d 4 Sept 1816, having had, with three daus and an er s (John, d unm 22 April 1804):

Rev Sir Thomas Combe Miller, 6th Bt; b 1780; educ St John's Coll Cambridge (LLB); Vicar Froyle, Hants; m 5 May 1824 Martha (d 28 June 1877), est dau of Rev Thomas Holmes, of Bungay Suffolk, and d 29 June 1864, had:

1 **Sir Charles Hayes Miller, 7th Bt**; b 6 Feb 1829; m 9 April 1856 Katherine Maria (d 11 Dec 1909), 2nd dau of James Winter Scott (see SCOTT, Bt, of Rotherfield), and d 12 Jan 1868, leaving:
　(1) **Sir Charles John Hubert Miller, 8th Bt**, JP (Hants); b 12 Sept 1858; Capt Coldstream Gds; d unm 4 Oct 1940
　(2) Cecil Walter Nicholson; b 9 July 1860; Lt S Staffs Regt; m 30 July 1903 Emily Mary, dau of John Roberts, and dsp 27 March 1912
　(1) Margaret Katherine; d unm 6 Feb 1879
　(2) Gertrude Teresa; m 3 Jan 1888 Sir John Evelyn Gladstone, 4th Bt (qv), and d 14 March 1937, leaving issue
　(3) Constance Caroline; m 18 Aug 1896 Herbert William D'Arcy Vertue, of Chelsea, and d 31 Aug 1914
2 Henry John (Sir), JP NZ; b 9 Sept 1830; MLC NZ 1865–1917 (Speaker 1892–1903, MEC July–Sept 1872); ktd 1901; m 15 Dec 1864 Jessie (d 23 July 1920), dau of John Orbell, of Hawkesbury, Waikonati, NZ, and d 7 Feb 1917, leaving:
　(1) HENRY HOLMES (Sir), **9th Bt**
　(2) William Nicholson; b 1868; m 1906 Edith Mary (d 1956), dau of J C Forsyth, and d 21 Aug 1950, leaving:
　　1a +William Maxwell [William Miller Esq, Unit 10/14–18 Chesterville Rd, Cheltenham, VIC 3192, Australia]; b 1913; MICE Aust, chartered civ engr (ret), MNZIE; m 1938 Marjory, dau of L M Bell, MICE, and has:
　　　1b +Leonard Maxwell [Leonard Miller Esq, c/o LMA Ptnrship, Level, 31 Queen St, Melbourne, VIC 3000, Australia]; b 26 July 1948; BCEng, MIE Aust, chartered civ engr; m 1975 *Ruth Annette Vile and has:
　　　　1c +Daniel James; b 1976
　　　　1c *Katherine Rachel (twin); b 1976
　　　　2c *Rebecca Sarah; b 1977
　　　1b *Diana Marjory [Mrs Jeremy Pope, 42 Madrid Rd, Barnes, London SW13 9PG]; b 1940; BA, DipArch; m 1963 *Jeremy Pope, barrister and slr, NZ, and has:
　　　　1c *Adam Quentin; b 1969
　　　　2c *Samuel William; b 1974
　　　　1c *Jemima Mary; b 1971
　　　2b *Mary Nicholson [Mrs Faizal Khan, 43-31 223rd St, Bayside, NY 11361, USA]; b 29 Jan 1947; MBA, BA, Dip Soc Studies; m 1st 1976 Yoram Zamir, of NYC; m 2nd 1989 *Faizal Khan and by her 1st husb has:
　　　　1c *Talor Miller; b 1981
　　　3b *Robyn Elizabeth [Mrs Geoffrey Collis, 4 Sherwood Ct, Lindisfarne, Tasmania 7015, Australia]; b 28 Jan 1951; BA, DipEd; m 1973 *Geoffrey Collis, BA, DipEd, and has:
　　　　1c *Matthew William; b 1980
　　　　1c *Jacqueline Louise; b 1983
　　1a *Margaret May [Mrs Margaret Zohrab, Waiapu House, Havelock North, New Zealand]; b 1907; m 1937 Edward Ernest Zohrab (d 1970) and has:

1b *Margaret Ann; b 1938; m 1964 *Jerome Glazebrook Whyte, of Clive, Hawkes Bay, New Zealand, and has issue
2b *Jenny Elizabeth [Mrs John Ewart, 33 Portland Rd, Remuera, Auckland, New Zealand]; b 1940; m 1964 *John Mundell Ewart and has issue
3b *Patricia Joan [Mrs Bryan Moore, Wharemoa, Otoroa, Kaeo, Northland, New Zealand]; b 1947; m 1970 *Bryan Gifford Moore and has issue
2a Helen Frances; b 1911; m 1940 *John Robert Shorter, s of A V Shorter, of Lower Hutt, Wellington, NZ, and d 1984, leaving:
　1b *Richard John; b 15 Oct 1943
　1b *Judith Dorothy; b 6 April 1945; m 1967 *Dr Kevin Shannon
　2b *Margaret Helen; b 1 April 1950
3a Geraldine Edith; b 1915; m 19– *Jack Reid and d 1978
4a Rosemary Alice; b 1919; m May 1947 *Douglas Balfour Zohrab, s of F Zohrab, of Silverstream, Wellington, NZ, and d 1989, leaving issue
(3) George Ralph, DSO (1919); b 23 Dec 1874; Lt-Col SA, Boer War 1899–1901 and WW I (despatches three times, twice wounded); m 21 Feb 1916 Violet Mary (d 1981), 3rd dau of W H Teschemaker, of Kauro Hill, Otago, NZ, and d 1948, leaving:
　1a +Cecil Ralph, TD [Maj Cecil Miller TD, 70 Ballabrooie Way, Douglas, IoM]; b 13 Nov 1917; Maj Parachute Regt (TA); m 1981 *Marie, dau of Stephen Sumner and widow of Maj Robert Thomas Williamson, The Cameronians, of Edinburgh
　2a +Anthony John [Arthur Miller Esq, Shadwell Cottage, High Hurstwood, E Sussex TN22 4AB]; b 21 May 1920; m 1952 *Sheila Doreen, dau of Lt-Col L Harvey, of Clare Glen, High Hurstwood, and widow of S/Ldr M Savage, and has:
　　1b +Richard Charles Cecil; b 3 Feb 1956; m 1984 *Eileen Joy, dau of E R Odey, of Norfolk, and has:
　　　1c +Mark George Ralph; b 1987
　　　2c +Matthew Anthony Edward; b 1989
　　2b +Timothy John; b 17 Dec 1957
　　1b *Jennifer Anne; b 1 Oct 1952; m 1st 1976 Peter Antony Twist (d 1979); m 2nd 1988 *Warren Sullivan, of Sydney, NSW, and by him has:
　　　1c *Luke Anthony; b 1989
　　　1c *Françoise Alice; b 1989
(4) Arthur Edmund; b 1877; d unm 1 Aug 1966
(5) John Charles; b 1880; m 9 April 1910 Ellina (d 3 May 1937), dau of Julius Mendleson, and d 2 April 1967
(1) Katherine Helen; b 1870; d 2 Aug 1894
(2) Frances May; b 1875; m 1st 14 June 1899 St John McLean Buckley and had issue; m 2nd 19 April 1930 Sir Alfred Karney Young, KC (d 5 Jan 1942), and d 4 Oct 1952
3 Thomas Edmund; b 16 Feb 1832; Maj 12th Regt; m 1868 Katherine Margaret (d 1 Sept 1912), dau of J Douglas, and d 29 Aug 1920, having had:
　(1) Alfred Richard; b 8 June 1870; d Sept 1912
　(2) Ernest Combe, RD; b 5 May 1872; Cdr RNR
　(3) Thomas Valentine; b 14 Feb 1875; d 12 Aug 1936
　(1) Mabel Helen; b 30 Nov 1873; d 3 April 1919
　(2) Mary Ann Francis; b 26 Feb 1883
4 George, CB; b 7 July 1833; Assist Sec Bd Educn; m 25 July 1865 Mary Elizabeth (d 27 March 1904), est dau of Rev Peter Aubertin, Rector Chipstead, Surrey, and d 29 Dec 1909, having had:
　(1) John Combe (Rev); b 1869; educ Haileybury and New Coll Oxford (BA 1892, MA 1918); English Chaplain Zurich 1922–36 and 1938–50; m 1893 Annie Louise (d 29 Dec 1910), dau of James Francis Maguire, of Australia, and widow of Dr C E Wyer
　(2) William Edmund; b 1872
　(1) Katharine Mary Frances; m 31 Jan 1893 William Calthorpe Mallaby (d 1912) and had issue
5 William Uvedale; b 5 Aug 1835; Capt 38th Regt; d 1868
6 Richard Combe, JP Sussex, JP and DL Kent; b 19 April 1841; Sheriff Kent 1897, twice Mayor Chichester; m 11 Oct 1870 Elizabeth (dsp 22 Oct 1901), est dau of William Aldworth, of Frilford, Berks, and d 26 April 1916
1 Charlotte Elizabeth; m 4 Aug 1849 Capt William Smith Nicholson, 26th Foot, 2nd s of George Thomas Nicholson, of Waverley Abbey, Surrey, and d 8 March 1874, leaving issue
2 Marianne; d unm 11 Jan 1910
3 Frances Margaret; d unm 24 Oct 1909
4 Georgina Emily; m 1st 3 May 1866 Henry Thomas Lambert (d 1879), of Bletchingley, Surrey, and had issue; m 2nd 15 Jan 1898 Walter James Marshall (d 6 Feb 1899), of Patterdale Hall, Westmorland, and d 23 April 1902

The 8th Bt's cousin,

Sir Henry Holmes Miller, 9th Bt; b 15 Dec 1866; educ Christ's Coll NZ; sheepfarmer; m 1895 Caroline Matilda, dau of Henry Joseph Greville, of Pahiatua, NZ, and had:

1 ERNEST HENRY JOHN (Sir), **10th Bt**
2 Charles Holmes; b 1905; m 1st 1936 Hester Amelia (d 1974), dau of E J Wilde; m 2nd 1975 *Pauline Rochfort [Mrs Pauline Miller, 2/26 Clyde Rd, Napier, New Zealand] and d 1984, having by his 1st w had:
　(1) +Patrick Holmes; b 1941
　(2) +Paul Greville; b 1943
　(1) *Monica Jane; b 1938
　(2) *Elizabeth Hope; b 1940
1 Jessie Martha; b 1896; m 1921 Gerard James Wilde and had issue
2 Alice Helen; b 1906; m 1928 John Palmer Tylee and had issue
3 Joan Frances; b 1908; m 1946 Ronald David Buchanan and had issue

Sir HENRY d 13 Nov 1952; his er son,

Sir Ernest John Miller, 10th Bt; b 8 May 1897; m 1920 Mahalah Netta Bennett and d 22 April 1960, leaving:

1 **Sir John Holmes Miller**, **11th Bt**; *b* 1925; *m* 1950 *Jocelyn Edwards, of Wairoa, NZ, and *d* 1995, leaving:

   (1) *Roslyn Mary; *b* 1955

   (2) *Diana; *b* 1958; *m* 19– *Murray John Telford, of Paraparaumu, NZ

2 Sir HARRY HOLMES MILLER, **12th and present Bt**

1 *Hilary [Mrs John Nisbet, 10 Weka Rd, Taupo, New Zealand]; *b* 1921; *m* 1945 *John Alexander Nisbet and has issue

2 *Norah Jessie [Mrs Roy Gardiner, 68A Wakeman St, Pahiatua, New Zealand]; *b* 1933; *m* 1949 *Roy Galloway Gardiner and has issue

MILLER of Glenlee

Arms: Arg. a cross-moline az., the base wavy vert, in chief a lozenge between two mullets of the second. **Crest:** A dexter hand couped at the wrist, two first fingers pointing upwards ppr. **Supporters:** On either side a roebuck ppr. **Motto:** *Manent optima coelo* ('The best things remain to be enjoyed in heaven'). **Creation:** Bt. (GB) 3 March 1788.

SIR STEPHEN WILLIAM MACDONALD MILLER OF GLENLEE, 8TH BT, Kirkcudbrightshire [Sir Stephen Miller of Glenlee Bt, The Lawn, Shebbear, Beaworthy, Devon EX21 5RU]; *b* 20 June 1953; *s f* 1991; *educ* Rugby and Bart's Hosp; MB, BS, FRCS 1981, FRCGP 1995; *m* 1st 1978 Mary Carolyn (*d* 1989), only dau of Gwynedd Bulkeley Owens, of Huddersfield, and has:

1 +JAMES STEPHEN MACDONALD; *b* 25 July 1981

1 *Katherine Helen; *b* 1983

Sir STEPHEN *m* 2nd 1990 *Caroline Mary Clark, dau of Leslie A E Chasemore, of Shebbear, and widow of Harold Frederick Clark

Lineage: MATTHEW MILLER of Glenlee, Stewartry of Kirkcudbright; *m* Agnes, dau of Rev William Guthrie, Minister Fenwick, and had:

1 John; *m* Grizel, dau of Sir Hugh Cathcart, 1st Bt (*see* 1850 edn), and *dsp*

2 WILLIAM

3 Patrick; Army Offr; *m* Lucy Webb, of Ireland, and had issue

MATTHEW MILLER's 2nd s,

WILLIAM MILLER, WS; *m* Janet, est dau of Thomas Hamilton, of Shield Hall, and *d* 1753, having had:

1 John; Prof Law Glasgow U; *d unm* 28 Nov 1780

2 THOMAS (Sir), **1st Bt**

3 Patrick, of Dalwinston, Dumfriesshire; *b* 1731; *m* Lindsay — and *d* 1815, leaving:

   (1) Patrick; Capt 12th Lancers, MP Dumfriesshire 1790–96; *m* 1804 Matilda, dau of Thomas Cuming, and had issue

   (2) William; Maj RHG (Blues); *m* Frances (*d* 1824), dau of Sir Edward Every, 8th Bt (*qv*), and had issue

   (3) Thomas Hamilton; advocate; *m* Mary Anne, dau of Abel Ram, of Clonattin, Co Wexford, and had issue

   (1) Janet; *m* 17 March 1795 8th/24th Earl of Mar (*qv*) and had issue

   (2) Jean; *m* Col — Johnson, 1st Foot Gds, and had issue

1 Martha; *m* John Davidson of Stewartfield, Roxburghs

2 Grizell; *m* George Chalmers of Pittencrieff, Fife

WILLIAM MILLER's 2nd s,

Sir Thomas Miller of Glenlee, 1st Bt (GB), so *cr* 3 March 1788; *b* 3 Nov 1717; Ld Pres Court of Session; *m* 1st 16 April 1753 Margaret, est dau of John Murdoch, of Rose Bank, Provost Glasgow; *m* 2nd Anne, dau of John Lockhart, of Castle Hill, and *d* 27 Sept 1789, having by his 1st w had, with a dau (Jessy, *m* John Dunlop):

Sir William Miller of Glenlee, 2nd Bt; Ld of Session as Lord Glenlee; *b* 12 Aug 1755; *m* 5 Nov 1777 his cousin Grizel, dau of George Chalmers, and had:

1 Thomas; *m* 1814 Edwina (*d* 18 March 1857), dau of Sir Alexander Penrose Gordon Cumming, 1st Bt (*qv*), and *dvp* 1827, leaving:

   (1) WILLIAM MILLER (Sir), **3rd Bt**

   (2) Alexander Penrose; *b* 1817; Maj 92nd Gordon Highrs; *m* Julia Monica (*d* 9 Feb 1888), dau of S Shiel, of Ballyshannon, and *d* 18 Sept 1880, leaving:

      1a Alice Edwina; *m* 16 Jan 1883 Col Clement Richard Johnson (*d* 4 April 1892), 50th Queen's Own Regt, and *d* 31 March 1883

      2a Julia Griselda; *d unm* 28 June 1895

      3a Martha Maud Mary; *m* 28 Nov 1896 Col Charles Richard Tierney-Davidson, RE (*d* 1915)

   (3) George Cuming; Maj 54th Regt; *m* 1850 Lucy, dau of John Masterson, and *dsp* 29 Oct 1868

   (4) Thomas, JP (Co Dublin); Adml, FRGS; *b* 28 Nov 1819; *m* 1st 26 June 1856 Anne Julia (*dsp* 12 May 1874), dau of Dr — Miller, of Exeter; *m* 2nd 5th Sept 1878 Eliza Mary Anne (*d* 3 Oct 1902), dau of Capt — Forster, RA, of The Wilderness, Dartmouth, and widow of Robert John Henry, of Drumlamph, Co Derry, and *dsp* 22 April 1899

   (5) Matthew; *d* 1860

2 William; Lt-Col 1st Foot Gds; *d* 17 June 1815 of wounds recd Quatre Bras 16 June 1815

3 John, WS, of Stewartfield; *b* 28 Dec 1789; *m* 15 March 1828 Mary (*d* 9 Sept 1875), est dau of Nicholas Sutherland, and *d* 24 Sept 1863, leaving:

   (1) William; *b* Nov 1831; Lt 92nd Regt; *dsp*

   (2) James; *b* 26 Oct 1835; Maj-Gen IA; *m* 28 Aug 1873 Elinot Katharine (*d* 30 Sept 1914), dau of T L Robinson, DL, of Croydon, and *d* 20 March 1929, having had:

      1a John Lockhart; *b* 3 Oct 1883; Lt 8th Bn London Regt; *ka* 21 May 1916

   (3) Arthur Wellesley; *b* 2 July 1839; *m* Sept 1896 Edith Maude, dau of Richard Fisher Hamilton, of Carisbrook House, Dublin, and widow of George Augustus Cuming Eliott, and *d* 12 Feb 1899, leaving:

      1a John Leslie Wellesley; *b* 1897; Lt The Buffs; *ka* 1916

   (1) Mary; *m* 17 Aug 1864 Robert Berry, LLD, DL (*d* 17 Jan 1903), advocate, and *d* 22 Jan 1917, leaving issue

1 Grizel; *m* 1808 William MacDonald (*d* 1841), advocate

2 Martha; *m* Adml Sir Houston Shaw-Stewart, GCB (*see* SHAW-STEWART, Bt), and *d* 17 April 1870

Sir WILLIAM *d* 9 May 1846; his gs,

Sir William Miller of Glenlee, 3rd Bt; *b* 12 Sept 1815; Lt 12th Lancers; *m* 27 April 1839 Emily (*d* 8 Aug 1892), 2nd dau of Lt-Gen Sir Thomas McMahon, 2nd Bt, KCB (*qv*), and *d* 30 Oct 1861, having had, with two daus (*d unm*) and a yr s (William Stewart, *b* Jan 1853, *d* 29 Aug 1913):

Sir Thomas Macdonald Miller of Glenlee, 4th Bt; *b* 1 Jan 1846; *m* 1863 Isabella Freeman Seton (*d* 10 Oct 1915) (*m* 2nd 1880 Evan Baillie Grant, 3rd Hus (*d* 22 Aug 1903)), dau of William Anderson, and had:

1 William Frederic; *b* 1863; *d* in a fire 31 Aug 1868

2 WILLIAM FREDERIC (Sir), **5th Bt**

3 Thomas George Alexander; *b* July 1869; served Matabeleland, Bechuanaland, Boer War 1901 and WW I (severely wounded); *m* 28 June 1939 Martha Clara (*d* 9 June 1945), est dau of Robert Berry, LLD, DL, advocate, Sheriff Lanarks, and *dsp* 14 Nov 1955

4 Francis Macdonald; *b* 23 March 1870; AIF WW I; *ka* 4 July 1918

1 Emily Agnes; *d unm* 31 Oct 1958

2 Constance Frances; *m* 1st 8 July 1888 (*divorce* 1904) Charles Edward Bexley Vansittart and had issue; *m* 2nd Maj Ernest de Lannony Hayes (*ka* 12 March 1915), The Cameronians, and *d* 7 May 1940, having had further issue

Sir THOMAS *d* 4 Sept 1875; his est surv son,

Sir William Frederick Miller of Glenlee, 5th Bt; *b* 7 April 1868; *educ* Harrow; Hon Capt Army, Lt 3rd Bn Princess of Wales's Own Yorks Regt, served Imp Yeo Boer War 1900–01, Staff Capt 17th Corps WW I (wounded); *m* 17 May 1890 Mary Augusta (*d* 10 March 1946), yst dau of Charles John Manning by Louise Augusta, dau of Rev Sir Augustus Henniker, 3rd Bt (*qv*), and *d* 20 Dec 1948, having had, with an er s (Frederick William Joseph Macdonald, *b* 21 Dec 1891, Lt Gren Gds, *ka* 23 Oct 1914) and a dau (Cynthia Mary Grizelda):

Sir Alastair George Lionel Joseph Miller of Glenlee, 6th Bt; *b* 5 March 1893; *educ* Beaumont; Capt Irish Gds and F/Cdr RFC WW I; *m* 1st 16 Oct 1919 (*divorce* 1926) Kathleen Daisy, yr dau of Maj Stephen Goodwin Howard, CBE, JP, DL, of The Moat, Upend, Newmarket, and *d* 1 April 1964, having had:

1 (FREDERICK WILLIAM) MACDONALD (Sir), **7th Bt**

Sir Alastair *m* 2nd 1 Dec 1927 (*divorce* 1933) Margaret May, dau of Frederick Shotter, and by her had:

1 *Pamela Ann Mary [Mrs John Nicholson, Crag View Farm, North Rigton, nr Huby, Yorks]; *b* 15 Aug 1928; *m* 9 Aug 1950 *John Ward Randolph Nicholson, s of Maj Randolph Nicholson, DSO, MC, of Willoughton Manor, Gainsborough, Lincs, and has:

   (1) *Mark John Anthony; *b* 1952

   (2) *Martin Euan Thomas; *b* 1955

   (3) *Moray John Fergus; *b* 1962

   (4) *Myles Ian Vaughan; *b* 1964

   (5) *Magnus Francis Benedict; *b* 1966

   (6) *Mungo Patrick Lee; *b* 1969

   (1) *Annette Mary Ward; *b* 1951

   (2) *Philippa Mary Randolph; *b* 1954

   (3) *Iona Frances Marianne; *b* 1957

   (4) *Alexandra Mary Elizabeth; *b* 1959

2 Elizabeth Margaret Mary Cynthia; *b* 24 Jan 1931; *m* 12 May 1956 *Sir Filmer Courtenay William Honywood, 11th Bt (*qv*), and *d* 25 Dec 1996, leaving issue

Sir Alastair *m* 3rd 3 Jan 1938 (*divorce* 1957) Cynthia Rosemary, dau of Frederick Edward Huish, of Cardiff, and by her had:

2 +Graham Frederick Alastair; *b* 19 Sept 1938; *educ* Pangbourne; *m* 1968 Gaynor (*d* 2006), dau of Tudor Whitcombe, of Cardiff, and has:

   (1) +Alastair; *b* 1971; B Eng

   (1) *Penelope; *b* 1969; *educ* U of Wales at Cardiff (BSc)

3 +George Edward John; *b* 8 May 1946; *m* 1970 *Merrill, dau of T G Morris, and has:

   (1) +Christopher Carl Edward; *b* 1980

(1) *Stephanie Claire; *b* 1971; *educ* U of Wales at Swansea (BSc)
3 *Teresa Rosemary Ann; *b* 26 Sept 1939; *m* 1961 (*divorce* 1976) Grenfell King
and has:
  (1) *Julian Grenfell; *b* 1972
Sir ALASTAIR *d* 1 April 1964; his est son,
  Sir (Frederick William) Macdonald Miller of Glenlee, 7th Bt; *b* 21 March 1920; *educ* Tonbridge; WW II 1939–43: Beds and Herts Regt 1940, Black Watch 1941–42 and RAC 1943, C Agent: Whitehaven 1947–50, Wembley N 1950–52, N Norfolk 1952–65 and Lowestoft 1965; *m* 2 Sept 1947 *Marian Jane Audrey [Audrey Lady Miller of Glenlee, Ivy Grange Farm, Westhall, Suffolk IP19 8RN], only dau of Richard Spencer Pettit, of Chilton, Suffolk, and *d* 1991, leaving:
1 Sir STEPHEN WILLIAM MACDONALD MILLER OF GLENLEE, **8th and present Bt**
1 *Alison Hilary Miller [Mrs John Freeman, Holly Farm, Bergh Apton, Norfolk NR15 1BT]; *b* 3 Aug 1951; *m* 1976 *John Glover Freeman and has:
  (1) *William Griffin Henry; *b* 1981
  (2) *Thomas Michael Percy; *b* 1984

MILLER OF HENDON

Arms: Vert on a fess between in chief a windmill of four sails in the form of stylised petals or and in base the tree sorbus, torminals erased, three sparrows close proper. **Supporters:** Dexter, a female figure habited in blouse and skirt *temp* 1905, wearing from right shoulder to left hip a sash of the suffragette movement, holding in the dexter hand a pole, thereon a placard with the words 'Votes for Women' all proper; sinister, a female figure also habited in a day dress rose, decorated with silver grey, hatted sable, feathered argent, all *temp* 1905, holding by the interior hand against dexter shoulder a scroll of the law proper and by the other a torch azure flamed gules. **Motto:** *Quare non?* ('Why not?'). **Creation:** B. (LP, UK) 1993.

THE BARONESS MILLER OF HENDON, of Gore in the London Borough of Barnet (Doreen Feldman, MBE (1989), JP Brent (1970)) [The Rt Hon The Baroness Miller of Hendon, House of Lords, London SW1A 0PW]; *b* 13 June 1933; *educ* Kilburn High Sch and LSE; chm and md: Universal Beauty Club Ltd (UK), Cosmetic Club Int GmbH (Germany) and Universal Beauty Club (Pty) Ltd (Australia)1971–88; nat chm and exec dir The 300 Gp 1985–88; chm Women into Public Life Campaign 1987–; Human Rights Advsr Soroptimist Internat 1987–90; Tstee Menerva Educnl Tst 1992–; Chm Barnet FHSA 1990–94; Crown Agent 1990–94; Jt Treasurer Gtr London Area Nat Union of C and U Party 1990–93 (Chm 1993–96); Memb Monopolies & Mergers Commn 1992–93; Baroness-in-Waiting 1994–97; author: *Let's Make Up* (1995); *m* 1955 *Henry Lewis Miller, s of Ben Miller, and has:
1 *Michael Steven; *b* 1956
2 *Paul Howard; *b* 1959; *m* 1992 *Sharon Hunt
3 *David Philip; *b* 1962
Lineage: BERNARD HENRY FELDMAN; *m* Hetty — and had:
DOREEN, *cr* a **Baroness**

MILLS, Viscount

Arms: Per chevron az. and arg., in chief two millrinds of the last and in base a balance sa. **Crest:** A bear's gamb erased or, supporting a flint lock ppr. **Supporters:** On either side a lion or collared and chained az., pendant from the collar an escutcheon of the last, charged with a sun in splendour gold. **Motto:** Balance and control.
Creations: Bt. (UK) 1 July 1953, B. (UK) 22 Jan 1957, V. (UK) 22 Aug 1962.

THE 3RD VISCOUNT MILLS , of Kensington, Co London, **Baron Mills**, of Studley, Co Warwick, and a **Baronet** (Sir Christopher Philip Roger Mills, Bt) [The Rt Hon The Viscount Mills, House of Lords, London SW1A 0PW]; *b* 20 May 1956; *s f* 1988; *educ* Oundle and London U (BSc, MSc); *m* 1980 *Lesley Alison, er dau of Alan Bailey, of Lichfield, Staffs

Lineage: D MILLS, of Stockton-on-Tees, had:
Sir Percy Herbert Mills, 1st Bt, and **1st Viscount Mills**, of Kensington, Co London, so *cr* 1 July 1953 and 22 Aug 1962 respectively, as also 22 Jan 1957 BARON MILLS, of Studley, Co Warwick (all UK), KBE (1946), PC (1957); *b* 4 Jan 1890; *educ* N Co Sch Barnard Castle; Controller-Gen Machine Tools Min Supply 1940–44, ktd 1942, Head Production Div Min Production 1943, Pres Ec Sub-Commission CCG (BE) 1944–46, chm NRDC 1949, pres Birmingham Chamber Commerce 1947–48, Hon Advsr Housing Min Housing and Local Govt 1952, chm W and T Avery Ltd 1955–57, Min Power 1957–59, Paymaster Gen 1959–61, Min without Portfolio 1961–64, Master Gunmaker's Co 1957 and 1965; *m* 7 Aug 1915 Winifred Mary (*d* 26 Feb 1974), dau of George C Conaty, of Birmingham, and had:
1 ROGER CLINTON, **2nd Viscount**
1 *Beatrice Margaret [The Hon Mrs Davis, Chantry House, Sheep St, Stow-on-the-Wold, Glos]; *b* 21 July 1916; *m* 20 Dec 1941 *Walter Goodwin Davis and has:
  (1) *Patrick Walter Goodwin; *b* 9 April 1947
  (2) *Andrew Christopher Goodwin; *b* 2 Dec 1950
  (1) *Jane Winifred; *b* 22 Dec 1957
The 1st VISCOUNT *d* 10 Sept 1968; his only son,
  ROGER CLINTON MILLS, **2nd Viscount Mills**; *b* 14 June 1919; *educ* Canford and Jesus Coll Cambridge; Maj RA WW II, Admin Offr Colonial Serv Kenya, barrister Middle Temple 1958; *m* 6 Oct 1945 *Joan Dorothy [The Rt Hon Joan Viscountess Mills, Whitecroft, 24 Abbey Rd, Knaresborough, N Yorks HG5 8HY], dau of James Shirreff, of London, and *d* 1988, leaving:
1 CHRISTOPHER PHILIP ROGER MILLS, **3rd and present Viscount Mills**
1 *Felicity Jane [The Hon Mrs Pickford, Heddfan, Ffawyddog, Crickhowell, Powys]; *b* 21 June 1947; *m* 20 June 1970 *Roger B Pickford, est s of Dr Steven Pickford, of Wisbech, Cambs
2 *Philippa Susan [The Hon Mrs Arthurton, 253 Riversdale High St, Boston Spa, Yorks]; *b* 25 Feb 1950; *m* 10 Oct 1970 *Russell Scott Arthurton, yst s of R I D Arthurton, of the Anchorage, Shiplake, Oxon

MILLS, Bt

Arms: Sa. three mill-rinds in pale or between two swords erect ppr., pommelled and hilted of the second. **Crest:** A peewit's head, the neck encircled by a serpent nowed, both ppr. **Motto:** *Forte nihil difficile* ('Nothing tough is difficult'). **Creation:** Bt (UK) 21 Jan 1921.

SIR PETER FREDERICK LEIGHTON MILLS, 3RD BT, of Ebbw Vale, Co Monmouth [Sir Peter Mills Bt, PO Box A474, Avondale, Harare, Zimbabwe]; *b* 9 July 1924; *s f* 1955; *educ* Eastbourne Coll, Cedara Ag Coll Natal and U of Natal (BSc Ag 1952); Roy Corps Signals 1943–44, Lt 5th Roy Gurkha Rifles 1946–47, CS Fedn Rhodesia and Nyasaland 1953, with Rhodesia Min Ag 1964, Zimbabwe Min Ag 1980–90; *m* 11 Dec 1954 *Pauline Mary, dau of Lionel Raymond Allen, of Calverton, Notts, and has:

1 +MICHAEL VICTOR LEIGHTON, *b* 30 Aug 1957; *m* 1981 *Susan, dau of J Doig, of Harare

Lineage: JOHN MILLS, of Exeter; had:

PETER MILLS, of Sunderland; *b* 1896; had:

LEIGHTON MILLS; *b* 31 March 1836; *m* 1864 Jane Ann (*d* Jan 1937), dau of A Gilbert Dalziel, and *d* 18 Oct 1898, leaving:

Sir Frederick Mills, 1st Bt, JP and DL Mon; High Sheriff 1912, MP (C) E Leyton 1931–45, chm Ebbw Vale Steel, Iron and Coal Co; *b* 23 April 1865; *m* 1st 19 Aug 1889 Edith Mary (*d* 14 Nov 1916), est dau of George Marshall Topham, of Tynemouth, Northumberland, and had:

1 (FREDERICK LEIGHTON) VICTOR (Sir), **2nd** Bt

1 Grace; *b* 26 Dec 1890; *m* 22 May 1915 Engr-Lt-Cdr Stanley John Reed, RNVR (*k* Sheerness 28 May 1915), and *dsp* 2 Jan 1969

2 Hilda; *b* 22 June 1895; *d* 26 Sept 1903

Sir Frederick *m* 2nd 10 April 1918 (Mary) Kathleen (*d* 8 Sept 1973), only child of Ernest Dawkins, of St Albans, Herts, and *d* 22 Dec 1953

His only son,

Sir (Frederick Leighton) Victor Mills, 2nd Bt, MC and bar; *b* 14 March 1893; *educ* Cheltenham and RMA Woolwich; Lt RFA WW I (despatches, Belgian Croix de Guerre), Colonial CS 1922–47, Assist Dir Public Works Nigeria 1936–39, Dir Public Works Freetown, Sierra Leone, 1939–45 and Uganda 1945–47; *m* 11 Dec 1923 Dorian (Doris), Pres Natal Soc Artists, dau of Louis Armitage, of Eastbourne, and *d* 21 April 1955, having had:

1 Sir PETER FREDERICK LEIGHTON MILLS, **3rd and present Bt**

2 Michael Victor; *b* 24 Feb 1926; *d* 21 May 1929

MILMAN

DEUS NOBISCUM QUIS CONTRA

Arms: Az. a snake nowed or between three sinister gauntlets open arg. **Crest:** A hart lodged per pale erm. and erminois, attired and unguled or, charged on the body with two hurts fessways. **Motto:** *Deus nobiscum, quis contra* ('With God on our side, who can stand against us?'). **Creation:** Bt (GB) 28 Nov 1800.

SIR DEREK MILMAN, 9TH BT, of Levaton-in-Woodland, Co Devon, MC [Lt-Col Sir Derek Milman Bt MC, Forge Cottage, Wilby Rd, Stradbroke, Suffolk IP21 5JN]; *b* 23 June 1918; *s* bro 1990; *educ* Bedford Sch and Sandhurst; Unattached List IA 1938, 3rd/2nd Punjab Regt 1939, WW II Eritrea (despatches), N Africa, Burma; Pakistan Army 1947–50; 1st Bn Beds and Herts Regt 1950, Instr RMA Sandhurst 1957, 5th Beds TA 1959–61, Instr CD Staff Coll 1963–68; London Business School 1970–83, Lt-Col (ret) 3rd E Anglian Regt; *m* 21 Nov 1942 *Margaret Christine, dau of Alfred Whitehouse, of Sutton Coldfield, and has:

1 +DAVID PATRICK [David Milman Esq, 71 Camden Rd, Sevenoaks, Kent]; *b* 24 Aug 1945; *educ* London U (BEd 1969, MA); *m* 9 Aug 1969 *Christina, dau of John William Hunt, of Leigh-on-Sea, Essex, and has:

  (1) +Thomas Hart; *b* 1976

  (1) *Katharine Jane; *b* 1975

1 +Terence Martin [Terence Milman Esq, 98 New Dover Rd, Canterbury, Kent]; *b* 13 April 1947; *educ* Bedford Sch, UCL and RADA; *m* 1976 *Sandra Wendy Elizabeth, dau of Frederick Garrett, of Canterbury, Kent, and has:

  (1) +William Frederick; *b* 1984

  (1) *Alexandra Elizabeth; *b* 1979

Lineage: THOMAS MILMAN, of South Brent, Devon; had:

Rev FRANCIS MILMAN; Vicar Paignton, Devon, 1692–1719, Rector Marldon, Devon; *b c* 1666; *educ* Exeter Coll Oxford (BA Oriel Coll 1687); *d* 1719, having had:

Rev FRANCIS MILMAN; Rector E Ogwell, Vicar Abbotskerswell, Devon; *b c* 1704; *educ* Exeter Coll Oxford (BA 1722); *m* Sarah, dau and eventual coheir of Richard Dyer, of Levaton, Devon, and *d* 1773, having had, with three daus (Mary, *d unm* 1799; Anne; Sarah):

Sir Francis Milman, 1st Bt (GB), *cr* 28 Nov 1800, of Levaton in Woodland, Co Devon; *b* 31 Aug 1746; *educ* Exeter Coll Oxford (BA 1764, Fell 1765–80, MA 1767, BMed 1776, BD 1778); MD, FRS, Physician to Roy Household 1785 and GEORGE III 1806, Pres Coll Physicians 1811–13; Physician to Middx Hosp 1771–79, FCP 1778, inherited estate of his unc John Dyer, of Levaton; *m* 20 July 1779 Frances (*d* 1836), dau and heiress of William Hart, of Stapleton, Glos, by Frances, sis of William Miles, of The Grove, Pinner, Middlesex, and had:

1 WILLIAM GEORGE (Sir), **2nd Bt**

2 Francis Miles; Lt-Gen, Col 82nd Foot; *b* 22 Aug 1783; *m* 8 March 1817 Maria Margaretta (*d* 15 May 1875), est dau of Sir Charles Morgan, 2nd Bt (*see* 1963 edn TREDEGAR, B), and *d* 9 Dec 1856, having had, with other issue:

  (1) Egerton Charles William Miles; Coldstream Gds, Maj-Gen cmdg forces Mauritius; *b* 6 Feb 1819; *m* 8 May 1866 Isabella Anne (*m* 2nd 3 Oct 1872 Hon William Frederick Barton MASSEY later MASSEY-MAINWARING (*d* 12 March 1907), 4th s of 3rd Baron Clarina (*see* 1949 edn), and *d* 16 Oct 1905), only dau of Charles Benjamin Lee-Mainwaring, and *d* 23 Oct 1869, leaving:

    1a Charles Egerton Forbes MILMAN later MILMAN-MAINWARING (roy licence 1874); *b* 20 Feb 1867; *educ* Magdalen Coll Oxford (BA); 4th Bn W R Regt; *m* 7 July 1915 Marguerite Doris Roper (*d* 1965), dau of Lt-Col Francis Washington Lethbridge, DSO, W R Regt, and gdau of Sir Roper Lethbridge, KCIE, and *d* 28 April 1951, leaving:

      1b Rosamund Irene; *b* 15 May 1916; *m* 14 Dec 1946 (divorce 1966) Mulford Albert Colebrook, Consul US For Serv, s of Albert S Colebrook, of Rochester, NY

    1a Alice Sophia Mary; *m* 26 April 1897 George Forbes, JP (*d* 22 Feb 1915), of Inverernan, Strathdon, est s of Gen Sir John Forbes, GCB, and had issue

  (2) Henry Salusbury; barrister; *b* 1821; *m* 6 Aug 1857 Matilda Jane (*d* 23 Oct 1861), widow of Eliot Warburton and yr dau of Edward Grove, of Shenstone Park, Staffs, and *d* 22 Dec 1893, having had:

    1a Margaret Anne; *d unm* 4 Feb 1954 in her 96th year

2a Bertha Mary; *d* unm 3 Sept 1931

3a Matilda Julia; *m* 9 April 1888 Lt-Col James Lowry Cole Acton, Connaught Rangers, of Glenageary, Kingstown, Co Dublin, and *d* 21 March 1938, leaving issue. He *d* 3 Sept 1914

(3) (George) Bryan (Sir), KCB, JP Middx and London; *b* 30 Dec 1822; served Indian Mutiny, Col 5th Northumberland Fus, Maj Tower London 1870–1909, Lt-Gen; *m* 15 May 1861 Mary Rose (*d* 1885), yst dau of Lt-Gen William Lovelace Walton, and *d* 28 Jan 1915, having had:

1a Angelena Frances; *m* 19 Nov 1908 Edward Ashley Walrond Clarke, Agent and Consul-Gen Zanzibar, and *d* his widow 16 Jan 1914

(4) Gustavus Hamilton Lockwood; *b* 6 Dec 1824; Maj-Gen RA; *m* 3 April 1872 Louisa Mary, Baroness Berkeley in her own right (*qv*), and *d* 28 March 1915, having had issue

(5) Everard Stepney, JP; *b* 2 Nov 1832; Lt-Col RA, FRGS, Govr Holloway and Newgate Prisons; *m* 1st 25 May 1865 Frances Elizabeth (*d* 10 July 1870), 2nd dau of Thomas Clarke, Madras CS, and had:

1a Francis Robert Everard; *b* 4 April 1869; *d* 9 May 1891

1a Ethel Frances; *m* 29 July 1899 Col Charles Hay, of Robin's Croft, Chilham, Canterbury, Bombay SC and Warden Christ's Hosp, and was *k* by enemy action 11 Oct 1940. He *d* 10 Feb 1912

2a Helen Margaret; *d* 25 Aug 1924 following a boating accident

3a Leonora Maria; *d* unm 24 April 1970 aged 102

4a Mildred Charlotte; *m* 7 Sept 1912 Eustace Henry Lipscomb, JP, MB, BCh (*d* 25 Aug 1924 in same boating accident as sis-in-law), of St Albans, and *d* 14 Feb 1934, leaving issue

(5) (cont.) Everard Milman *m* 2nd 8 Sept 1874 Grace Henrietta Hamilton (*d* 6 Dec 1909), yst dau of William Bell, and *d* 13 Feb 1912, having by her had:

2a Edmund Wilbraham Everard; Lt IA; *b* 19 Jan 1880; *d* unm 16 Feb 1909

3a Octavius Rodney Everard, DSO (1917); Lt-Col RA WW I (despatches, brevet), Fell and Bursar Keble Coll Oxford (Hon MA 1930); *b* 23 April 1882; *educ* RMA Woolwich; *m* 30 Nov 1911 Mary Freya (*d* 1979), dau of Rev William Edward Haigh, Hon Canon Bristol, and *d* 19 June 1971, leaving:

1b *Joanna Woolstone [Mrs Denys Bulkeley, Little Orchard, Bracken Road, Seaford, Sussex]; *b* 7 Dec 1912; *m* 28 Oct 1939 Major Denys Paul Bulkeley RA (*d* 1981), s of John Pierson Bulkeley, CIE, and has:

1c *Richard Milman [Richard Bulkeley Esq, Lane End, 9 St Botolph's Lane, Orton Longueville, Peterborough]; *b* 28 July 1940; *m* 14 Oct 1967 *Elizabeth, dau of Charles Mahoney, RA Elect, of Oak Cottage, Wrotham, Kent, and has:

1d *Thomas William; *b* 1971

2d *Joanna Louise; *b* 1971 (twin)

2b *Patricia Freya [Mrs Lionel Woolf, 7B Bedford Towers, Cavendish Place, Brighton BN1 2JG]; *b* 17 Nov 1920; *m* 5 Jan 1942 *Lionel Noel Woolf, s of Julian Woolf, of Buckland House, Gerrards Cross, and has:

1c *Inigo Rodney Milman; *b* 7 Sept 1946; *m* 1970 *Susan Rebecca Davis and has:

1d *Bethia Fearne Milman; *b* 1974

2c *Christopher Patrick Milman; *b* 6 Nov 1947; *m* 2 Oct 1969 *Linda, dau of John Boyd Johnston, of Welwyn, Herts, and has:

1d *Simon Justin; *b* 1970

2d *Jonathan Marcus; *b* 1973; *m* 1997 *Soumhya Venkatesan

3c *Nicholas David Milman; *b* 1 Jan 1953; *m* 1973 (*divorce* 1996) Ann Elizabeth March and has:

1d *Benjamin Douglas; *b* 1978

5a Elsie Hamilton; *d* unm 9 Sept 1968 aged 90

6a Phyllis Grace Ida; *d* unm 15 April 1960 aged 72

3 Henry Hart (Very Rev), DD; Dean St Paul's, writer; *b* 10 Feb 1791; *m* 11 March 1824 Mary Anne (*d* 1 July 1871), dau of Lt-Gen William Cockell, and *d* 24 Sept 1868, having had, with other issue:

(1) William Henry (Rev), MA Oxon; Rector St Augustine and St Faith, Minor Canon St Paul's, Librarian Sion Coll; *b* 25 April 1825; *m* 1884 (*divorce*) Julia Margaret, dau of Sir George Campbell, KCSI, MP, and *dsp* 9 June 1908

(2) Arthur; *b* 10 Jan 1829; *educ* Ch. Ch. Oxford (MA); LLD, barrister, Registrar London U; *m* 6 April 1872 Frances Mary (*d* 22 April 1886), 2nd dau of John Lawrence Tatham, barrister, of Highgate, and *d* 23 Jan 1913, leaving:

1a Ida Mary; *d* unm 21 Sept 1950

2a Sylvia Frances; *m* 1916 John Mills Whitham and *d* 7 Feb 1957. He *d* 28 July 1956

3a Enid Alice; *d* unm 3 Sept 1966

4a Maud

(3) Archibald John Scott (Sir), KCB; *b* 2 Feb 1834; MA Cantab; Clerk H of C; *m* 28 Dec 1871 Susan Augusta Carter (*d* 16 Sept 1928), est dau of Robert Hanbury, of Bolehall, Tamworth, and *d* 14 Feb 1902, leaving:

1a Lilian Mary Hart; *m* 20 April 1901 Edward Mellish Clark (*d* 1949), s of J W Clark, Registrar Cambridge U, and had issue

2a Margarita Harriet Hart; *m* 23 Dec 1907 Rev Richard Swann Swann-Mason, OBE, MA, Vicar Ch Ch, Albany St, and *d* 23 Sept 1955, leaving issue. He *d* 21 Sept 1942

3a Violet Eveline Hart; *d* unm Oct 1944

4a Rosalind Louisa Hart; *m* unm 22 Jan 1956

5a Eglantine Olive Hart; *d* unm 3 May 1917

6a Daphne Ellen Dianora Hart; *d* unm Dec 1949

1 Frances Emily; *d* unm 26 July 1835

Sir FRANCIS *d* 24 June 1821; his est son,

Sir William George Milman, 2nd Bt; *b* 19 April 1781; *m* 23 Oct 1809 Elizabeth Hurry (*d* 13 Dec 1853), only dau of Robert Alderson, Recorder Ipswich, and had, with three other daus (*d* unm):

1 Francis; *b* 21 July 1811; *dsp*

2 WILLIAM (Sir), **3rd Bt**

3 Robert (Rt Rev), DD; Bp Calcutta; *b* 25 Jan 1816; *d* unm 15 March 1876

4 Edward Augustus; 33rd Regt; *b* 19 Aug 1817; *d* 21 Dec 1850

5 George Alderson; Col RA; *b* 11 Oct 1830; *m* 6 May 1858 Frances Edith (*d* 27 Dec 1930), 2nd dau of Rt Rev James Chapman, DD, Bp Colombo, and *d* 29 Dec 1898, leaving, with two sons:

(1) Gertrude Ellen; *m* 25 Jan 1898 Rev Col Leonard Julius Shadwell, OBE, Vicar Woolacombe, N. Devon, Lancs Fus, and *d* 3 Aug 1934, leaving issue. He *d* 30 Jan 1930

1 Emily Matilda; *m* 3 Oct 1844 Rev Charles Augustus Fowler, Rector Walton-in-Gordano, Somerset, s of Adml R Fowler

Sir WILLIAM *d* 21 Aug 1857; his est surv s,

Sir William Milman, 3rd Bt; barrister; *b* 21 Nov 1813; *m* 26 Oct 1841 Matilda Frances (*d* 24 May 1890), est dau of Rev John Pretyman, Rector Sherington, Bucks, and had, with three other sons and two other daus:

1 FRANCIS JOHN (Sir), **4th Bt**

2 Hugh Miles, RN; Govr Thursday Island, Qld; *b* 3 Aug 1845; *m* 15 June 1871 Katharine Maule (*d* 1947), yst dau of John Jardine, Commr Goldfields Rockhampton (*see* JARDINE, Bt, of Applegirth), and *d* 23 Sept 1911, having had:

(1) Helen Isabella Maule

(2) Cecil Maule; *m* 7 Jan 1899 Robert Sewers Berry, MD, of Southport, Qld, and *d* 26 Sept 1928

(3) Edith Mary; *m* 1903 David W Crombie, and *d* 1906, leaving issue

3 Walter Charles Gordon; Schs Inspr; *b* 3 Oct 1853; *educ* King's Coll Cambridge (MA); *m* 10 June 1886 Edie Helen Blythe (*d* 21 Nov 1955), dau of John Alexander Radcliffe, of Ordsal, Cobham, Surrey, and *d* 3 April 1907, leaving:

(1) Humphrey Radcliffe; served WW I; *b* 23 March 1895; *m* 2 Aug 1923 Edith Mary, dau of Rev Henry Elias Mocatta, of Clive House School, Prestatyn, Flints, and had:

1a John Walter Francis; *b* 7 Dec 1928; *m* 27 Aug 1955 Jean Margaret (*d* 1984), dau of G C Till, of IoW, and *d* 1984, having had:

1b *Pamela Rosemary; *b* 10 June 1961

2b *Laura Frances; *b* 1965

1a Petronella Anne; *d* an infant 13 Nov 1925

(1) Mary Frances

(2) Norah Helen; *m* 23 April 1927 Capt Lancelot Milman Shadwell, RN (*d* in an accident 5 June 1960), er s of Rev Col Leonard Julius Shadwell, OBE, Vicar Woolacombe

(3) Isabel Joan; *b* 1898; *m* 10 June 1922 Maj William Martineau Martineau, MC, RASC (*d* 1983), only s of Streiff Martineau, and has:

1a *Josephine Helen; *b* 1923; *m* 1959 *John Van Valkenburg

1 Isabella Frances; *m* 4 Jan 1870 Alexander Anderdon Weston and *d* 19 Aug 1922, leaving issue. He *d* 1 Nov 1901

2 Helen Rose Anne; *m* 9 April 1890 Maj Caldwell Henry Crofton, RA, of Tilford, Surrey, and *d* 2 Jan 1937, leaving issue. He *d* 22 Sept 1947

3 Constance Angelena, MBE (1920), JP Hants; *m* 6 June 1899 Sir Alexander John Arbuthnot, KCSI, CIE, s of Bp of Killaloe, and *d* 20 Feb 1936. He *d* 10 June 1907

Sir WILLIAM *d* 17 June 1885; his est son,

Sir Francis John Milman, 4th Bt; Maj 2nd Bde Welsh Div RA; *b* 10 Aug 1842, *m* 25 Aug 1870 Katharine Grace (*d* 31 Dec 1924), 2nd dau of Stephen Charles Moore, DL, of Barne, Clonmel, Co Tipperary, and *d* 2 June 1922, leaving:

1 **Sir Francis Milman, 5th Bt**; *b* 27 Oct 1872; *m* Nov 1898 Georgina Maude Emma (*d* 7 May 1964), only dau of Thomas Ripon Wallis, and *d* 10 Oct 1946

2 **Sir William Ernest Milman, 6th Bt**, MM; *b* 11 Aug 1875; served WW I, in Oslo throughout WW II; *m* 8 Sept 1934 Elder Wilse (*d* June 1960), dau of George Samson, of Oslo, and *d* 30 Aug 1962

3 LIONEL CHARLES PATRICK (Sir), **7th Bt**

4 Stephen Walter; *b* 15 Nov 1879; *m* 1st 6 Jan 1907 Ethel (*d* 17 May 1914), 4th dau of William Dowdeswell Horsley, ICS, and had:

(1) Gerald Stephen; Lt Welsh Gds WW II; *b* 10 Feb 1908; *educ* Harrow; *m* 1944 *Noreen [Mrs Gerald Milman, El Venado, Casilla de Correo 27, La Cumbre, Sierras de Cordoba, Argentina], dau of Thomas Johnston Elliot, and *d* 1987, having had:

1a +Ian Stephen; *b* 1946; *m* 1978 *Gloria Wassermann

1a *Stephanie Rosalind; *b* 1949; *m* 1975 *Robert Albert Christopher Lovell and has:

1b *Andrew Christopher; *b* 1979

2b *Mark Stephen; *b* 1982

2a Angela Caroline; *b* 1952; *m* 1974 *Peter Scott Kirkwood and *d* 1991 in an air crash, leaving:

1b *Catriona Alexandra; *b* 1979

2b *Melanie Jane; *b* 1980

3b *Caroline Louise; *b* 1989

3a *Geraldine Stella; *b* 1956; *m* 1988 *Marcelo di Tomasi and has:

1b *Stephen George; *b* 1992

2b *Patrick Gerald; *b* 1993

(1) Lavender Grace; *b* 30 Sept 1913; *d* 2 March 1914

4 (cont.) Stephen Milman *m* 2nd 1917 his dead w's sis Hilda (*d* 5 May 1964 aged 90), dau of William Dowdeswell Horsley, ICS, and *d* 12 July 1957

5 Henry Augustus, OBE (1943); Cdr (S) RN, Somaliland 1902–04, WWs I and II (A/Capt (S) Staff Combined Ops), on Internat Danube Commn 1920–27; *b* 2 Oct 1882; *m* 1912 Genevieve (*d* 1984), dau of Capt John Irving, of Victoria, BC, and *d* 8 April 1952, leaving:

(1) John Alexander Ralph, OBE (1943); *b* 22 Nov 1912; *educ* Haileybury and RMC Sandhurst; Maj (ret) Highland LI, Mohamand Campaign 1934 and WW II (wounded, despatches), Actg Lt-Col Middle East, Burma and Courmes, Alpes Maritimes, Mil Attaché Budapest 1953–55; *m* 3 Jan 1943 *Daphne Mary, formerly w of G E E Webster and dau of Alexander Andrew Bisset, and *d* 1996, leaving:

1a +John Andrew Francis Pretyman; *b* 11 March 1945

1a *Anne Isabel Jane; *b* 17 Sept 1943; *m* 11 Dec 1965 *William Frederick Hempsall

6 Hugh, OBE (1919); Maj RE (SR), AMICE; *b* 1884; *m* 8 June 1914 Marjorie (*d* 10 Aug 1964), only dau of Malcolm McCulloch Paterson, MICE, of The Croft, Pannal, Yorks, and *d* 1959, having had:

(1) Hugh Bruce; P/O RAFVR WW II; *b* 4 Nov 1918; *d* of wounds recd in action 1941

(1) Stephanie Grace, BA; *b* 21 April 1915; *d* 1994

(2) *Diana Constance [Mrs John Merry, Tunnel Cottage, Knapp Lane, Ledbury, Herefs HR8 1JD]; *b* 29 June 1920; *m* 9 March 1942 *Capt John Michael Merry, RA, s of Robert Naylor Merry, of Holbeach, Lincs, and has:

  1a *Bruce Carmichael; *b* 3 July 1944; *educ* King Edward's Sch Birmingham, Corpus Christi Coll Oxford and Stanford U California; *m* 21 Nov 1964 *Serenella, dau of Elio Papi, of Spoleto, Italy, and has:

    1b *Ludovica; *b* 13 Jan 1965

  2a *David Paul Nicholas [David Merry Esq, 59A Crimsworth Rd, London SW8 4RJ]; *b* 20 Oct 1945; *educ* Hereford Cathedral Sch and Manchester Business Sch (HCITB); gen manager Milburn's Restaurants Ltd; *m* 1979 *Anna-Mai [Mrs Anna-Mai Merry, 24 Longford Close, Hampton Hill, Hampton, Middx TW12 1AB] and has:

    1b *Louise Sarah; *b* 1984

  1a *Tessa Michele; *b* 20 June 1947

  2a *Miranda Diana; *b* 26 May 1951

  3a *Dilys Ruth; *b* 29 Dec 1956

1 Violet Grace; WW I as nursing sister (despatches); *d* unm 11 July 1965 aged 91

The 6th Bt's bro,

Sir Lionel Charles Patrick Milman, 7th Bt, CMG (1917); *b* 23 Feb 1877; Maj, Brevet Lt-Col RA, Hon Brig-Gen 1919, Controller Gun Ammunition Min Munitions and Dir Min Supply WW II; *m* 30 Dec 1911 Marjorie Aletta (*d* 1980), dau of Col Arthur Harry Clark-Kennedy, and *d* 2 Nov 1962, leaving:

1 **Sir Dermot Lionel Kennedy Milman, 8th Bt**; *b* 24 Oct 1912; *educ* Uppingham and Corpus Christi Coll Cambridge; Maj RASC WW II (despatches), Liaison Offr Hostel Development Br Cncl; *m* 23 Nov 1941 *Muriel [Muriel Lady Milman, 7 Old Westhall Close, Warlingham, Surrey CR6 9HR], only dau of John Edward Scott Taylor, of King's Lynn, and *d* 13 Jan 1990, leaving:

  (1) *Celina Anne [Ms Celina Milman, 4147 Burkehill Pl, W Vancouver, BC V7V 3M8, Canada]; *b* 16 Jan 1945; *m* 1st 20 Jan 1968 (*divorce* 1980) John Springett Appleby, s of Arthur Appleby, of W Vancouver; *m* 2nd 16 Sept 1995 *Paul Leslie Hammond, of Vancouver, and by her 1st husb has:

    1a *Tristan Dermot Springett; *b* 1968

    2a *Tremayne Robert; *b* 1974

2 Malcolm Douglas; *b* 18 May 1915; *educ* Canford and Worcester Coll Oxford; Capt RA WW II; *m* 1940 (*divorce* 1949) Sheila Maud, dau of Albert Maurice Dudeney, and *d* 1987, having had:

  (1) *Felicity Ann [Mrs Peter Flockton, RR# 1 Apple Hill, Ontario KOC 1BO, Canada]; *b* 1941; *m* 1965 *Peter Robin Flockton and has:

    1a *Phyllida Fiona; *b* 1969; *m* 1994 *Michael Gerald Gillissie, of Ottawa

    2a *Vanessa; *b* 1971; *m* 1995 *Michael John Low, of Vancouver

  (2) *Penelope Fiona; *b* 1943; *m* 1964 *Anthony Stuart Darroch, of Witham-on-the-Hill, Lincs, and has:

    1a *Ian George; *b* 1965; *m* 1989 *Victoria — and has:

      1b *Oliver; *b* 1995

      2b *George; *b* 1997

    2a *James Anthony; *b* 1967; *m* 1997 *Sally —

3 Sir DEREK MILMAN, **9th and present Bt**

1 Joy Beatrice; *b* 18 Dec 1920; *d* unm 27 May 1969

MILNE

Arms: Or a cross moline pierced lozengeways of the field between four mullets az. **Crest:** A dexter hand holding up an open book ppr., leaved or. **Supporters:** Dexter, an officer of the Royal Horse Artillery; sinister, an officer of the Greek Evzone Guard, both in full dress uniform. **Motto:** *Efficiunt clarum studia* ('Study makes for fame'). **Creation:** B. (UK) 26 Jan 1933.

THE 2ND BARON MILNE, of Salonika, and Rubislaw, Co Aberdeen (George Douglass Milne, TD) [The Rt Hon The Lord Milne TD, 33 Lonsdale Rd, London SW13 9JP], *b* 10 Feb 1909; *s f* 1948; *educ* Winchester and New Coll Oxford; Maj RA (TA) WW II Norway and Middle East (wounded, despatches, POW), memb Lambeth Hosp Management Ctee 1947–51, ptnr Arthur Young McClelland Moores 1954–73, MICA Scotland, Master Grocers' Co 1961–62, dir London & Northern Gp 1973–87 (dep chm 1982–87); *m* 2 April 1940 *Cicely, 3rd dau of Ronald Leslie, late of Buenos Aires, and has:

1 +GEORGE ALEXANDER [The Hon George Milne, 188 Broom Rd, Teddington, Middx]; *b* 1 April 1941; *educ* Winchester; Liveryman Grocers' Co 1971

2 +Iain Charles Luis [The Hon Iain Milne, Carlos Condell, 27 San Felipe, V Region, Chile]; *b* 16 Sept 1949; *educ* Oundle; FCA, Liveryman Grocers' Co; *m* 1987 *Berta (Ita), dau of Enrique Urzua Guerrero, of San Felipe, Chile, and has:

  (1) +Iain Eduardo Alexander; *b* 1990

  (2) +Leslie Axel Fernando; *b* 1993

1 *Ann Geraldine [The Hon Mrs Straker, Hever Warren, Hever, Kent], *b* 29 March 1946; *educ* Queen's Gate Sch; Freeman City London 1967, Liveryman Grocers' Co 1984; *m* 15 March 1969 *Ian Frederick Lawrence Straker, s of Graham Straker, of S Kensington, and has:

  (1) *Ross Alexander Lawrence; *b* 1977; *educ* Millfield

  (2) *Frances Georgina; *b* 1980

Lineage: GEORGE MILNE, of Rosehearty, Aberdeenshire (3rd s of James Milne, of Rosehearty, by Elizabeth Grey); *b* 1777; *m* Margaret (*d* 1855), dau of William Milne, and *d* 1832, leaving an est s:

GEORGE MILNE, of Westwood, Aberdeenshire; *b* 26 Sept 1825; *m* 20 Sept 1862 Williamina (*d* 22 Jan 1924), dau of John Panton, of Knockiemill, Aberdeenshire, and *d* 20 Sept 1890, leaving, with two daus (Edith Alexa, *m* 20 Sept 1888 Capt T W M Georges and *d* Oct 1945; Elizabeth Mary, *d* unm 19 April 1961):

GEORGE FRANCIS, **1st Baron Milne**, of Salonika and of Rubislaw, Co Aberdeen (UK), so *cr* 26 Jan 1933, GCB (1927, KCB 1918, CB 1912), GCMG (1919, KCMG 1919), DSO (1902); *b* 5 Nov 1866; *educ* privately, Aberdeen U and RMA Woolwich; joined RA 1885, Nile Expdn 1898 (two medals, six clasps), Brevet Lt-Col 1902, Brevet Col 1905, Col 1909, WW I (despatches): Maj-Gen 1915, Lt-Gen 1917; Gen 1920, FM 1928, DAQMG HQ 1903–07, GSO(2) N Cmd 1908–09, GSO(1) 6th Div 1909–13, cmdg 4th Div E Cmd 1913–14, cmdg 27th Div 1915, GOC-in-C Salonika Army 1916 and Army of Black Sea 1919–20, Lt Tower London 1920–23, GOC-in-C E Cmd 1923–26, CIGS and 1st Mil Memb Army Cncl 1926–33, Constable Tower London 1933–38, ADC Gen to HM GEORGE V 1923–27, Col Cmdt RA, Col Cmdt Pioneer Corps 1940–44, Master Gunner St James's Park 1929–46, Hon LLD Aberdeen and Cantab, Hon DCL Oxon, Hon Freeman Aberdeen, Gd Pres Br Emp Serv League, Chm Empire Socs War Hospitality Ctee, Pres Lond Fever Hosp, Chm Exec Ctee Roy Cancer Hosp, Patron Salonika Reunion Assoc, Old Contemptibles, Grand Cross Orders of Allied Nations, KGStJ; *m* 3 June 1905 Claire Marjoribanks, MBE, DGStJ (*d* 15 Dec 1970), only dau of Sir John Nisbet Maitland, 5th Bt (*qv*), and *d* 23 March 1948, leaving:

1 GEORGE DOUGLASS MILNE, **2nd and present Baron Milne**

1 Joan Claire Florence; *b* 12 March 1907; *m* 16 March 1937 Lt-Cdr James Hart Rutland, RNVR (*d* 17 May 1954), only s of Archibald Hart Rutland, and *d* 19 Jan 1997

MILNE-WATSON

Arms: Argent on a mount vert an oak tree proper, fructed or, over all a chevron azure charged with two mullets gold.
Crest: A demi-griffin sable, gorged with an antique crown and charged on the body with two mullets palewise or.
Motto: *Deo et patriae omnia debeo* ('I owe all to God and country').
Creation: Bt. (UK) 11 June 1937.

SIR MICHAEL MILNE-WATSON, 3RD BT, of Ashley, Longbredy, Co Dorset, CBE (1953) [Sir Michael Milne-Watson Bt CBE, The Stables, Oakfield, Mortimer, Berks RG7 3AP]; *b* 16 Feb 1910; *s* bro 1982; *educ* Eton and Balliol Coll Oxford (MA); Sub-Lt RNVR WW II; md Gas Light and Coke Co 1933, Govr 1946–49; chm N Thames Gas Bd 1949–64, Richard Thomas and Baldwins Ltd 1964–67, William Press Gp 1969–74; dep chm BSC 1967–69; Pres Soc Br Gas Industries 1970–71; Pres Pipelines Industries Guild 1971–72; Dir Finance for Industry 1974–80 and Commercial Union Assur 1968–81; Memb Cncl Reading U 1972–80 (Pres 1975–80); Govr BUPA 1975 (chm 1976–81, v-pres 1981–), Nuffield Nursing Homes Tst 1975–80; ktd 1969, Liveryman Grocers' Co 1947; *m* 27 March 1940 Mary Lisette (*d* 1993), yr dau of Harold Carleton Bagnall, of Auckland, NZ, and has:

1 +ANDREW MICHAEL [Andrew Milne-Watson Esq, 22 Musgrave Crescent, London SW6 4QE]; *b* 10 Nov 1944; *educ* Eton; *m* 1st 3 April 1970 (*divorce* 1981) Beverley Jane Gabrielle, er dau of Philip Cotton, of Majorca, and has:

(1) +David Alistair; *b* 24 Aug 1971

(1) *Emma Victoria; *b* 3 Jan 1974

1 (cont.) ANDREW MILNE-WATSON *m* 2nd 1983 *Mrs Gisella Stafford, dau of Hans Tisdall, of Chelsea, and by her has:

(2) +Oliver; *b* 1985

Lineage: DAVID WATSON, of Edinburgh; *b* 1 April 1807; *m* 2 Oct 1867 Anne Carnegie (*d* 13 Oct 1901), dau of William Milne, and *d* 13 Jan 1884, leaving, with a dau (Charlotte Playfair, *m* 24 July 1895 Rev George Dodds and *d* by 1939):

Sir DAVID WATSON later MILNE-WATSON, **1st Bt** (UK), so *cr* 11 June 1937, DL (London); *b* 10 March 1869; *educ* Merchiston, Edin U and Balliol Coll Oxford (MA, LLB); barrister Middle Temple 1896, Hon Col The Rangers (KRR Corps) TA, memb London TAA; govr and md Gas Light and Coke Co, Pres Nat Gas Cncl; chm Jt Industl Cncl Gas and Govt Mkt Supply Ctee Industry, memb Nat Fuel and Power Ctee, Advsy Cncl Govt Dept of Scientific and Industrial Research; Birmingham Medal 1938, Chief Scottish Clans Assoc London, Hon LLD Leeds 1926, ktd 1927; *m* 27 June 1899 Olga Cicely (*d* 20 March 1952), dau of Rev George Herbert, and *d* 3 Oct 1945, leaving:

1 **Sir (David) Ronald Milne-Watson, 2nd Bt**, of Ashley, Parish of Longbredy, Dorest; *b* 15 July 1904; *educ* Trin Coll Glenalmond and Balliol Coll Oxford (MA); WW II as Capt 2nd/5th Roy Gurkha Rifles (FF) (despatches); *d* umn 1982

2 Sir MICHAEL MILNE-WATSON, **3rd and present Bt**

1 *Gabriel Olga Margaret [Mrs Christian Reed, Fox and Hounds Farm, Bolney, Sussex]; *b* 1901; *m* 10 April 1929 Christian William Lawrence Peel Reed (*d* 1984), s of Leicester Morgan Reed, and has:

(1) *Laurence Cecil [Laurence Reed Esq, Hookhams, Lurgashall, W Sussex GU28 9EW]; *b* 27 Jan 1930; *educ* Eton and Worcester Coll Oxford (MA 1953); *m* 21 April 1956 *Georgina, dau of Thomas St John Alston, of Petworth, and has:

1a *Nicholas William; *b* 30 April 1958

2a *Charles Christian Thomas; *b* 8 Nov 1959

3a *Andrew Laurence; *b* 14 March 1962

(2) *Martin David [Martin Reed Esq, Standgates Farm, Kirdford, W Sussex RH14 0LH]; *b* 30 May 1932; *educ* Eton; *m* 1 June 1957 *Shirley, dau of Charles C Naumann, of Rudgwick, Sussex

(3) *Denys Christian [Denys Reed Esq, 22 West St, Corfe Castle, Dorset BH20 5HD]; *b* 11 Aug 1935; *educ* Eton; *m* 1st 19 Sept 1959 (*divorce* 1972) Tessa Caroline, dau of Stephen Cannon, of Belgravia, and has:

1a *Christopher Stephen; *b* 1961

2a *Jeremy Matthew; *b* 1962

---

(3) (cont.) Denys Reed *m* 2nd 1973 (*divorce* 1997) Angela Frances Croft and has:

1a *James Christian; *b* 1975

MILNER

Arms: Per pale or and sa. a chevron between three horse's bits counterchanged. **Crest:** A horse's head couped sa., bridled and maned or, between two wings gold. **Motto:** *Addit frena feris* ('He puts bridles on brute beasts'). **Creation:** Bt (GB) 26 Feb 1716/7.

SIR TIMOTHY WILLIAM LYCETT MILNER, 10TH BT, of Nun Appleton Hall, Co York [Sir Timothy Milner Bt, Oude Natte, Valleij, Klapmuts, Cape Province, S Africa]; *b* 11 Oct 1936; *s* f 1995; *educ* Michaelhouse Natal

Lineage: WILLIAM MILNER, of Nun Appleton Hall, Easington Hall, Beeston Manor and Bolton Percy, Yorks, Mayor Leeds 1697; *b* 1662; *m* Mary, dau of Joshua Ibbetson, Mayor Leeds, and *d* 23 Dec 1740, leaving an est s:

Sir William Milner, 1st Bt (GB), so *cr* 26 Feb 1716/7, of Nun Appleton Hall; MP York 1722–34, Grand Master Freemasons England; *m* 5 Dec 1716 Elizabeth (*d* 9 March 1782), dau of Sir William Dawes, Bt, DD, Archbp York, and *d* 23 Nov 1745, leaving, with a dau (Mary, *m* 19 Sept 1768 R-Adml Sir John Lindsay, KB (*dsp* 4 June 1788), s of Sir Alexander Lindsay, 3rd Bt, of Evelick, and *d* 24 Oct 1799):

Sir William Milner, 2nd Bt; *b* 1719; High Sheriff Yorks 1747, Receiver-Gen Excise; *m* 30 April 1747 Elizabeth (*d* 1785), yst dau and coheir of Rev Hon George Mordaunt (*see* MORDAUNT, Bt), and had, with four daus:

1 WILLIAM MORDAUNT (Sir), **3rd Bt**

2 George, of Mickleham, Surrey; Scots Fus Gds, Gen; *b* 1760; *m* 1786 Charlotte (*d* 19 Feb 1844), widow of Robert Evance FitzGerald and dau of — Colombier, and *dsp* 13 May 1836

3 Henry Stephen (Rev); DCL; *b* 1764; *d* unm

Sir WILLIAM *d* 8 Nov 1774; his est son,

Sir William Mordaunt Milner, 3rd Bt; MP York 1790–1811, Mayor 1787 and 1790; *b* 6 Oct 1754; *m* 1776 Diana (*d* 15 Jan 1805), est dau of Humphrey Sturt, of More Crichel, Dorset, and had:

1 WILLIAM MORDAUNT STURT (Sir), **4th Bt**

2 Charles William, of Mickleham; Col; *b* 20 May 1788; *m* 10 Oct 1843 Mary Jane (*d* 16 May 1881), dau of R Moore, of Hampton Court Palace, and *dsp* 31 May 1847

3 George William Thomas; Rector Larling; *b* 27 June 1790; *m* 4 Sept 1816 Sarah Georgina, 2nd dau of Rev George Buckston, of Ashbourne, Derbyse, and *dsp* 1824

1 Diana Elizabeth; *m* 2 June 1804 Sir Francis Hastings Doyle, 1st Bt (*d* 6 Nov 1839; *see* 1970 edn), and *d* 14 Jan 1828

2 Mary Emilia; *d* unm 3 April 1855

Sir WILLIAM *d* 9 Sept 1811; his son,

Sir William Mordaunt Sturt Milner, 4th Bt; High Sheriff Yorks; *b* 21 Oct 1779; *m* 1st 13 July 1803 Selina (*d* 28 May 1805), only dau of Rt Hon Theophilus Clements (*see* 1953 edn LEITRIM, E), and had:

1 Selina Catherine Diana; *d* unm 1834

2 Catherine Frances Nannette; *m* 30 Aug 1827 Rev David Markham, Canon Windsor, Vicar Stillingfleet, and *d* 7 May 1876, having had issue

Sir William *m* 2nd 28 May 1809 Harriet Elizabeth (*d* 31 Dec 1862), dau of Lord Edward Charles Cavendish-Bentinck (*see* PORTLAND, E), and *d* 24 March 1855, having by her had:

1 **Sir William Mordaunt Edward Milner, 5th Bt**; MP York 1848–57; *b* 20 June 1820; *m* 16 April 1844 Lady Georgiana Anne Lumley (*d* 2 Feb 1877), sis of 9th Earl of Scarbrough (*qv*), and *d* 12 Feb 1867, leaving:

(1) **Sir William Mordaunt Milner, 6th Bt**; *b* 10 May 1848; *d* unm 14 April 1880

(2) **Sir Frederick George Milner, 7th Bt**, GCVO (1930), PC (1900), JP, DL (W R Yorks); MP York 1883–85 and Bassetlaw 1890–1906, KJStJ; *b* 7 Nov 1843; *m* 19 Oct 1880 Adeline Gertrude Denison (*d* 6 July 1902), dau of William Beckett, MP (*see* GRIMTHORPE, B), and *d* 8 June 1931, having had:

1a **Sir William Frederick Victor Mordaunt Milner, 8th Bt**; *b* 2 Oct 1893; *educ* Wellington and Ch Ch Oxford (BA 1919, MA 1934); FRIBA, FSA, ptnr Milner and Craze, architects, London, Lt 2nd/1st Lothians and Border Horse 1915–19, Offr-in-charge Signals Clyde Garrison 1918–19, memb Coll Gdns Nat Shrine Our Lady of Walsingham; *d* unm 19 March 1960

1a Violet Helen; *b* 7 June 1883; *m* 10 May 1906 Lt-Col Edward York, JP, DL, of Hutton Hall, Yorks, and *d* 28 Nov 1919, leaving issue (*see* NUTTALL, Bt). He *d* 11 Dec 1951

2a Doreen Maud, CI, DGStJ; *b* 20 May 1886; Kaisar-i-Hind gold medal; *m* 19 April 1911 2nd Marquess of Linlithgow (*qv*) and *d* 2 Aug 1965, leaving issue

(3) Granville Henry; *b* 28 Dec 1851; *d* 1911

(4) Dudley Francis; *b* 9 March 1854; *d* 9 April 1882

(5) Edward Carolus; Lt Coldstream Gds; *b* 1 Feb 1858; *d* 23 April 1878

(1) Edith Harriet; *d* 16 May 1921

(2) Evelyn Selina; *m* 14 April 1869 Lt-Col Thomas Ferdinand Fairfax, Gren Gds, of Steeton and Newton Kyme, and *d* 11 Feb 1900, leaving issue. He *d* 6 Feb 1884

2 Henry Beilby William, of W Retford House, Notts, JP; *b* 17 Dec 1823; *m* 16 Aug 1853 Charlotte Henrietta (*d* 15 Sept 1884), dau of Most Rev Marcus Beresford, Archbp Armagh (*see* WATERFORD, M), and *d* 7 June 1876, having had:

(1) Edward, JP Notts; Maj Scots Gds and KRRC, Egypt, Boer War and WW I, ADC to Govrs Hong Kong 1890–91 and S Australia 1892–95, memb Gentlemen-at-Arms 1905–33; *b* 30 Jan 1858; *m* 19 Jan 1897 Evelyn Augusta (*d* 7 Aug 1932), dau of Col Hercules Rowley (*see* LANGFORD, B), and *d* 28 April 1937

(2) George Francis, CMG (1918), DSO (1902); Col 5th Lancers, Hon Brig-Gen 1919, Boer War 1899–1902; *b* 10 July 1862; *m* 21 April 1910 Phyllis Mary Lycett (*d* 7 Sept 1954), yr dau of Sir Edward Lycett Green, 2nd Bt (*qv*), and *d* 20 June 1921, leaving:

1a **Sir (George Edward) Mordaunt Milner, 9th Bt**; *b* 7 Feb 1911; *educ* Oundle and Leeds U; Capt RA WW II, Stipendiary Steward Jockey Club S Africa 1954–59, Steward 1977–80, Steward Milnerton Turf Club 1959, Steward Cape Turf Club 1960–76, memb Cncl Thoroughbred Breeders Assoc 1975–82, author: *Inspired Information, Vaulting Ambition, The Last Furlong, Thoroughbred Breeding* and *The Godolphin Arabian*; *m* 1st 17 April 1935 Barbara Audrey (*d* 17 Jan 1951), 3rd dau of Henry Noel Belsham, of Hunstanton, Norfolk, and had:

1a Sir TIMOTHY WILLIAM LYCETT MILNER, **10th and present Bt**

2a +CHARLES MORDAUNT [Charles Milner Esq, PO Box 41, Klapmuts, Cape, S Africa]; *b* 18 May 1944; heir presumptive; *educ* St Andrew's Grahamstown; *m* 19 June 1965 *Lady Charlene Mary Olivia French, est dau of 3rd Earl of Ypres (*see* 1970 edn), and has:

1b +Marcus Charles Mordaunt; *b* 6 Jan 1968

2b +Patrick Edward French Mordaunt; *b* 7 Oct 1969

3b +Alexander George French Mordaunt; *b* 1981

1a *Georgina (Georgie) Madeleine Mary [Mrs Bertie Grattan-Bellew, Hole Farm, Gt Waldingfield, Suffolk]; *b* 3 Sept 1939; *m* 20 June 1961 *(Arthur Henry) Bertram Grattan-Bellew (*see* GRATTAN-BELLEW, Bt) and has issue

1a (cont.) **Sir Mordaunt** *m* 2nd 10 Jan 1953 *Katherine Moodie Bissett, dau of David Henderson Hoey, of Dunfermline, Fifeshire, and *d* 18 Dec 1995

2a Henry George; RAF WW II; *b* 27 Oct 1912; *educ* Oundle and Magdalene Coll Cambridge (BA 1934); *m* 8 Aug 1952 Florence, dau of William Tai Chung, of Kingston, Jamaica

(3) Marcus Henry, DSO, MVO; Maj (Gen List), Capt 2nd Co London Yeo, ADC Personal Staff 1916, Boer War 1900–01 (medal) and WW I, Croix de Guerre Belgium; *b* 16 April 1864; *m* 27 July 1888 Caroline Agnes (*d* 16 Nov 1894), widow of 4th Duke of Montrose (*qv*) and dau of 2nd Baron Decies (*qv*), and *dsp* 16 Jan 1939

(1) Mary Emmeline Laura; *b* 5 Nov 1854; *m* 7 Aug 1877 2nd Baron Gerard (*qv*) and *d* 19 Feb 1918, leaving issue

(2) Ethel Elizabeth Louisa; *b* 4 Sept 1860; *m* 28 Oct 1882 3rd Earl of Durham (*qv*) and *d* 28 Oct 1931

(3) Emily Constantia Fredrica; *b* 26 Sept 1866; *m* 1886 her cousin Edward Beresford and *d* 30 Oct 1889, leaving issue (*see* WATERFORD, M)

3 Harriet Emily Mary; *m* 9 Dec 1828 George Savile Foljambe, of Osberton, Notts, and *d* 28 Dec 1830, leaving issue

4 Charlotte Caroline, *m* 13 Dec 1836 Rev Thomas Egerton, Rector Dunnington, Salop, bro of 1st Baron Egerton of Tatton (*see* 1956 edn), and *d* 1894, leaving issue. He *d* 17 Sept 1847

5 Caroline Elizabeth Mary, *m* 23 July 1844 Sir John Craven Carden, 4th Bt, of Templemore (*qv*), and *d* 5 Nov 1850

6 Fanny Frederica Sophia; *d* 12 April 1876

7 Georgina Selina Septima; *m* 19 Feb 1850 Sir Charles William Strickland, 8th Bt, and *d* 13 June 1864, leaving issue (*see* STRICKLAND-CONSTABLE, Bt)

8 Louisa Diana; *d* unm Aug 1875

9 Laura Emma; *m* 8 Dec 1859 Egerton Vernon Harcourt and *d* 5 Feb 1889, aged 63. He *d* 19 Oct 1883

MILNER OF LEEDS

Arms: Gu. on a chevron erm. between in chief two bits or and in base a rose arg., barbed and seeded ppr., a teazel sa. **Crest:** Perched on a sword with point to the dexter ppr. and hilt and pomel or an owl, also ppr., gorged with a collar sa., thereon three mullets arg., pendant therefrom a pair of scales and resting on the dexter claw a portcullis, chained or. **Supporters:** On either side an owl ppr. gorged with a collar sa., thereon three mullets arg., pendant therefrom a portcullis chained or. **Motto:** Do right and fear nothing. **Creation:** B. (UK) 20 Dec 1951.

THE 2ND BARON MILNER OF LEEDS, of Roundhay, in the City of Leeds ((Arthur James) Michael Milner, AE) [The Rt Hon The Lord Milner of Leeds AE, 2 The Inner Court, Old Church St, London SW3 5BY]; *b* 12 Sept 1923; *s f* 1967; *educ* Oundle and Trin Hall Cambridge (BA, 1949, MA 1951); slr 1951, ptnr Milner's, Curry and Gaskell, London (subsequently Gregory, Rowcliffe & Milner's) and J H Milner & Son, Leeds; F/Lt RAFVR and RAF WW II, F/Lt 609 (W R) Sqdn RAuxAF 1947–52, AEA 1952, Oppn Whip Ho Lds 1971–74, memb Jt Ctee Consolidation Bills 1982–92, Select Ctees Private Bills 1990–96, Hon Treas Soc Yorkshiremen London; *m* 31 March 1951 *Sheila Margaret, dau of Gerald Hartley, of Weetwood Lane, Headingley, Leeds, and has:

1 +RICHARD JAMES; *b* 16 May 1959; *educ* Charterhouse and Surrey U (BSc); assoc fin dir Chelgate PR, Freeman City London, Liveryman Clothworkers 1988; *m* 25 June 1988 *Margaret Christine, yst dau of Gerald Francis Voisin, of Jersey, CI, and has:

(1) *Charlotte Emma; *b* 8 May 1990

(2) *Nicola Louise Christine; *b* 1992

1 *Geraldine Jane [The Hon Mrs Fenton, 3 Darnley Rd, Leeds LS16 5JF]; *b* 24 Nov 1954; *m* 1978 *Mark Anthony Fenton and has:

(1) *Harry James Oliver; *b* 1982

(2) *Alexander Philip Guy; *b* 1992

(1) *Kate Emma Jane; *b* 1984

2 Meredith Ann; *b* 28 Sept 1956; *d* unm Dec 1993

Lineage: JAMES HENRY MILNER, of Mount Farm, Alwoodley, Leeds; slr, Coroner Leeds; *b* 28 Feb 1863; *educ* Wortley GS; *m* 11 Oct 1888 Elizabeth (*d* 26 Dec 1939), dau of Robert Tate, of Colliery House, Garforth, Yorks, and *d* 10 Dec 1948, leaving:

1 JAMES, **1st Baron**

2 Eric Henry; MB, ChB, Divnl Surgn and Hon Life Memb St John Ambulance Assoc, Chm E R Yorks Nat Health Exec Cncl, Chm E R Yorks Local Medical Ctee, OStJ; *b* 3 June 1901; *educ* Leeds GS, Leeds U (MB, ChB 1925) and UCL; *m* 14 July 1927 Adela Scotson (*d* 23 March 1957), and *d* 19 Sept 1975, leaving:

(1) Eric Peter Gerard; *b* 30 July 1929; *educ* Sedbergh; *m* 13 Sept 1960 *Myra Grace, dau of John Francis Binington, and *dsp* 1979

(1) Gillian Elizabeth; *b* 21 April 1935; MSR 1955; *d* unm 22 Nov 1979

3 Alan; MB, ChB, Assist Res MO Leeds Maternity Hosp, House Surgn Leeds Gen Infirmary; *b* 31 May 1904; *educ* Leeds GS and Leeds U (MB, ChB 1928); *m* 25 April 1934 Enyd Gibson (*d* 1950) and *d* 4 Nov 1957, leaving:

(1) *Patrick Daniel Russell [Patrick Milner Esq, 57 Old Park Rd, Leeds LS8 1JX]; slr 1966; *b* 14 Oct 1941; *educ* Rugby and Leeds U (LLB 1964); *m* 9 Sept 1967 *Gillian Patricia, dau of Alec Fuller Foulds, of Harrogate, and has:

1a *Richard Russell; *b* 17 Jan 1969; *educ* Leeds GS and Nottingham U (BA)

2a *David Russell; *b* 25 July 1971; *educ* Leeds GS, Essex U (BA) and Newcastle U (MA)

1 Joyce Eleanor Margaret, JP; *b* 21 Sept 1906; *m* 12 June 1940 Maj Brian Brook Gardner, TD, s of Maj Wilson Gardner, of Leeds

The est son,

JAMES MILNER, **1st Baron Milner of Leeds**, of Roundhay, in the City of Leeds (UK), so *cr* 20 Dec 1951, MC, TD (1925), PC (1945), DL (W R Yorks 1939); *b* 12 Aug 1889; *educ* Leeds Modern, Easingwold GS and Leeds U (LLB 1911); slr 1911, sr ptnr J H Milner & Son, memb Cncl Law Soc and Court and Council Leeds U, served WW I, Hon Maj, memb Leeds CC 1923–29, chm Improvements Ctee, Dep

Ld Mayor 1928–29, MP S E Leeds 1929–51, PPS Min Ag 1930–31, T/Chm Standing Ctees 1935–43, Chm Ways and Means and Dep Speaker 1943–45 and 1945–51, Dep Speaker 1943–45 and 1945–51, Dep Speaker Ho Lds 1951, Chm Select Ctee Revision Standing Orders Private Bills 1945 and Ctee Standing Orders Public Bills 1948, memb: History Parl Tst, Select Ctee Capital Punishment 1931, Indian Franchise Ctee 1932, Cncl Inter-Parly Union Geneva; chm Br Inter-Parly Union, v-pres Assoc Muncpl Corps and Building Socs Assoc, pres Health Offrs Assoc 1952–55, Hon Memb Leeds Chamb Commerce, Pres Leeds Law Soc, Leeds Civic Tst and Leeds Flower Show, Hon Fell Valuers' Inst, Jr Grand Warden Utd Grand Lodge England 1953–54, Pres Soc Yorkshiremen London 1957–58, Hon LLD Leeds 1953; *m* 10 Feb 1917 Lois Tinsdale (*d* 16 April 1982), dau of Thomas Brown, of Roundhay, Leeds, and *d* 16 July 1967, leaving:

1 (ARTHUR JAMES) MICHAEL MILNER, **2nd and present Baron Milner of Leeds**

1 Lois Elizabeth Florence Zaidée; *b* 9 Jan 1919

2 *Shelagh Mary Margaret [The Hon Mrs Grimshaw, High Barn, Thorner, Yorks]; *b* 8 March 1925; *m* 2 Oct 1948 (*divorce* 1965) Harry Barker Grimshaw, of Bardsley, Yorks, and has:

  (1) *John Sherwood; *b* 18 June 1950
  (1) *Miranda; *b* Sept 1952

MILNES COATES

Arms: Per fess or and arg. three pallets sa. two flaunches gu., the dexter charged with a rose of the second, barbed and seeded ppr., the sinister with a lion passant, also of the second. **Crest:** Upon a rock ppr. a cock or, charged on the breast with a quatrefoil gu. and resting the dexter leg on an escarbuncle arg. **Motto:** *Dum spiro dimicabo* ('While I breathe I will struggle'). **Creation:** Bt. (UK) 29 June 1911.

SIR ANTHONY ROBERT MILNES COATES, **4TH BT**, of Helperby Hall, Helperby, Co York, JP (N R Yorks) [Prof Sir Anthony Milnes Coates Bt, Helperby Hall, Helperby, York; Hereford Cottage, 135 Gloucester Rd, London SW7 4TH]; *b* 8 Dec 1948; *s f* 1982; *educ* Eton and St Thomas Hosp London (BSc, MRCS 1973, MB, BS 1973, MRCP 1978, MD); Sr Lecturer (Hon Consultant) Dept of Medical Microbiology London Hosp 1984–90, Prof and Chm Dept Medical Microbiology St George's Hosp Med Sch London 1990–; *m* 28 Sept 1978 *(Dr) Harriet Ann, yr dau of Raymond M Burton, of Bunythorpe, Yorks, and has:

1 +THOMAS; *b* 19 Nov 1986

1 *Sara; *b* 1981
2 *Sophie; *b* 1984

Lineage: RICHARD COATES, of Thornton-le-Beans (s of Richard Coates, of Thornton-le-Beans (*d* by 1558)); *m* Dorothy — (*bur* 13 Feb 1611/2) and was *bur* 25 Dec 1592, leaving an est s:

ROBERT COATES, of Pasture House, Thorton-le-Beans; *m* Dorothy — and was presumably f of:

WILLIAM COATES, of Thornton-le-Beans; *m* Isabel — (*bur* 10 Jan 1627/8) and was *bur* 18 March 1621/2, having had:

1 John, of Thornton-le-Beans; *m* 24 June 1610 Isabel Clarkson and had issue
2 JAMES
3 Valentine, of Thornton-le-Beans; *bapt* 11 July 1596; *m* 13 Nov 1621 Jane Waide and *d c* 1664, leaving issue
4 Christopher; *bapt* 25 Feb 1598/9
5 George, of Thornton-le-Beans; *bapt* 12 March 1602/3; *m* 8 May 1624 Margaret Kendrew (*bur* 5 June 1641) and was *bur* 12 May 1641, leaving issue

The 2nd son,

JAMES COATES, of Thornton-le-Beans; *m* 19 May 1618 Margaret Cuthbert (*bur* 17 May 1644) and was *bur* 12 May 1651, having had, with two daus:

1 WILLIAM
2 John; *bapt* 11 Nov; *bur* 22 Nov 1621
3 James, of Thornton-le-Beans; *bapt* 14 Feb 1630/1; living 1679
4 Christopher, of Thornton-le-Beans; *bapt* 10 March 1632/3; living 1664
5 George, of Thornton-le-Beans; *bapt* 30 April 1637; living 1664

6 John, of Thornton-le-Beans; *bapt* 3 Feb 1637/8; *m* Dinah — (*bur* 7 Nov 1689) and *d* in or after 1664, leaving issue

The est son,

WILLIAM COATES, of Thornton-le-Beans; *bapt* 18 April 1624; *bur* 30 March 1673, having had, with other issue:

JAMES COATES, of Thornton-le-Beans and Thornton-le-Moor; *bapt* 17 Dec 1655; *m* by licence 25 March 1699 Anne Walker and was *bur* 6 March 1717/8, having had an est surv s:

JAMES COATES, of Thornton-le-Beans; *m* 9 Nov 1727 Mary Langley (*bur* 19 May 1781) and was *bur* 7 Jan 1788 aged 87, having had a yst s:

JOSEPH COATES, of N Otterington; *bapt* 27 June 1743; *m* 30 April 1767 Mary Smith (*bur* 18 Jan 1826 aged 78) and was *bur* 20 Feb 1804, having had, with four daus and three er sons:

JONATHAN COATES, of Thornton-le-Beans and The Grange, Helperby, Yorks, JP; *b* 5 Jan 1784; *m* 1812 Anne (*d* 21 Feb 1862), dau of Thomas Cooper, of Kirkbridge, Yorks, and *d* 15 July 1863, having had:

1 JAMES
2 Thomas, of Helperby; *bapt* 29 Dec 1817; *d* 14 April 1867
3 Joseph; *b* 9 April 1821; *m* 30 April 1846 Sarah Farrar (*d* 8 May 1906) and *d* 10 July 1889, leaving issue
4 Richard; *b* 31 July 1823; *m* 22 May 1852 Sarah Jane (*d* 17 Aug 1877), dau of Thomas Percy, of Stockton, Co Durham, and *d* Nov 1904, leaving issue

The est son,

JAMES COATES, of Helperby Hall, JP, DL N R Yorks; *b* 12 Jan 1816; *m* 21 April 1852 Elizabeth (*d* 10 March 1912), only dau of William Sayer, of Yarm, Yorks, and *d* 27 May 1905, having had:

1 EDWARD FEETHAM (Sir), **1st Bt**
2 William James, OBE, JP (N R and W R Yorks and Liberty of Ripon), DL (N R Yorks); *b* 9 Dec 1855; Capt W Yorks Regt, Co Commr N R Yorks Scouts 1919, memb: Church Assembly and Ripon Diocesan Bd Finance, Exec Ctee Corp Sons Clergy and Nat Cncl YMCA; *d* unm 15 Aug 1948
3 Charles Hutton (Rev); Rector Burton Agnes with Harpham 1898, RD Bridlington 1904, Chaplain RN; *b* 5 April 1857; *educ* Trin Coll Cambridge (MA); *m* 21 April 1892 Frances Mary (*d* 31 Dec 1943), dau of Joseph Richardson, of Potto Hall, Yorks, MP SE Durham, and *d* 15 Feb 1922, leaving:

  (1) Annie Elizabeth Hutton; *b* 9 Feb 1893; *d* unm 1 July 1959

1 Margaret Anne
2 Elizabeth Augusta

The est son,

Sir Edward Feetham Coates, 1st Bt (UK), so *cr* 29 June 1911; Capt and Hon Maj 3rd Bn Duke of Wellington's W R Regt, MP (C) Lewisham 1903–18 and W Lewisham 1918–23; *b* 13 July 1853; *m* 30 April 1878 Edith (*d* 7 Jan 1930), er dau and coheir of Capt Philip Woolley, of Gravenhurst, Bolney, Sussex, and *d* 14 Aug 1921, leaving, with a dau (Dorothy Anne):

Sir (EDWARD) CLIVE COATES later MILNES COATES (deed poll March 1946), **2nd Bt**, OBE (1919); *b* 21 May 1879; *educ* Charterhouse and Exeter Coll Oxford; Capt (RO) 15th/19th Hus WW I (despatches); *m* 8 Oct 1906 Lady Celia Hermione Crewe-Milnes, JP, dau of 1st and last Marquess of Crewe, KG (*see* 1935 edn), and had:

1 ROBERT EDWARD JAMES CLIVE (Sir), **3rd Bt**
2 Anthony Richard Milnes; Lt Coldstream Gds WW II (despatches); *b* 20 March 1920; *ka* 6 Aug 1944
1 *Bridget Sibyl [Mrs Seton Dearden, Hill House, W Witton, Leyburn, N Yorks]; Ldy-in-Waiting to HRH PRINCESS MARY THE PRINCESS ROYAL 1953–63; *b* 13 July 1910; *m* 1st 15 Oct 1931 (*divorce* 1944) Harold David Cuthbert (*d* 2 July 1959), of Beaufront Castle, Hexham, Northumberland, and has:

  (1) *(John) Aidan [Aidan Cuthbert Esq, Beaufront Castle, Hexham, Northumberland]; *b* 10 March 1934; *educ* Eton; *m* 1975 *Lady Victoria Lucy Diana Percy, 2nd dau of 10th Duke of Northumberland (*qv*), and has issue
  (1) *Belinda Jane Elizabeth [The Hon Mrs Matthew Beaumont, Bearl House, Stocksfield, Northumberland NE43 7AJ]; *b* 6 Aug 1932; *m* 13 Oct 1973, as his 2nd w, *Hon Matthew Henry Beaumont, 4th s of 2nd Viscount Allendale (*qv*)
  (2) *Caroline Alice Celia [Mrs Caroline Raban, 42 Eland Rd, London SW11]; *b* 31 March 1940; *m* 1985 (*divorce* 1992) Jonathan Mark Hamilton Priaulx Raban, author
1 (cont.) Mrs Bridget Cuthbert *m* 2nd 21 Aug 1962 *Seton Hedley Dearden, MBE (*d* 1989), s of Percy Dearden, of Lytham Hall, Lancs
2 *Elizabeth Hermione [Mrs William Harris, Moatlands, East Grinstead, Sussex RH19 4LL; 29 Barkston Gdns, London SW5]; *b* 4 Jan 1914; *m* 15 July 1937 *William Barclay Harris, QC, only s of William Cecil Harris, of Kensington and Moatlands, and has:

  (1) *Jonathan William [Jonathan Harris Esq, 9 Lower Addison Gdns, London W14 8BG]; *b* 30 May 1940; *educ* Harrow and Trin Coll Cambridge (MA 1962); *m* 26 April 1966 *Nabila Fares, yr dau of Fares Sarofim Bey, OBE, of Cairo
  (1) *Jessica Elizabeth [Mrs Peter Tcherepnine, 1192 Park Ave, New York, NY 10128, USA]; *b* 14 May 1938; *m* 1973 *Peter Tcherepnine
  (2) *Hermione Mary [Mrs Marc Karlin, 80 Highbury Hill, London N5 1AP]; *b* 17 April 1943; *educ* St Hilda's Coll Oxford (BA) and LSE; *m* 1982 *Marc Karlin

Sir CLIVE *d* 4 Sept 1971; his only surv son,

Sir Robert Edward James Clive Milnes Coates, 3rd Bt, DSO (1945), JP (N R Yorks 1960); *b* 27 Sept 1907; *educ* Harrow, RMC Sandhurst and Queens' Coll Cambridge; Lt-Col Coldstream Gds, Transjordan Frontier Force 1937–40 (despatches) and WW II (despatches); *m* 4 Sept 1945 *Lady (Ethel) Patricia, widow of Lt-Col Charles Thomas Milnes-Gaskell, Coldstream Gds, and er dau of 4th Earl of Listowel (*qv*), and *d* 9 May 1982, leaving:

1 Sir ANTHONY ROBERT MILNES COATES, **4th and present Bt**
1 *Mary Freda, JP [Mrs Peter Brodrick JP, 25 Wandle Rd, London SW17 7DL]; *b* 15 Aug 1947; *educ* St Mary's Wantage, U Hall Buckland and Sheffield U (BA, CQSW); *m* 1977 *Peter Gordon Brodrick and has:

(1) *Robert Cumberland; *b* 1983
(1) *Frances Celia; *b* 1979
(2) *Emma Charlotte; *b* 1981

MILVERTON

MINTO

Arms: Arg. three lozenges conjoined in fess gu. between two barrulets sa., all within two flaunches of the second, both charged with a spear head of the field. **Crest:** A Malay tiger's head erased ppr., gorged with a collar lozengy arg. and gu. **Supporters:** On either side a Malay tiger ppr., gorged with a collar lozengy and gu. **Motto:** *Mens cujusque id est quisque* ('The mind makes the man'). **Creation:** B. (UK) 10 Oct 1947.

THE 2ND BARON MILVERTON, of Lagos, and of Clifton, City of Bristol (Rev Fraser Arthur Richard Richards) [The Rev The Rt Hon The Lord Milverton, 2 Benjamin Rd, Barton Park, Marlborough, Wilts SN8 1TL]; *b* 21 July 1930; *s* f 1978; *educ* Ridley Coll Ontario, Clifton, Egerton Ag Coll Njoro, Kenya, and Bishop's Coll Cheshunt, Herts; Roy Signals 1949–50, Kenyan Police Reserve 1952–53, Deacon 1957, Priest 1958, Curate St George's Beckenham, Kent, 1957–63, Assist Priest St John the Baptist Sevenoaks 1959–60, Curate and Assist Priest St Nicholas Gt Bookham 1960–63, Vicar Okewood with Holy Trinity Forest Green, Surrey, 1963–67, Rector Christian Malford with Sutton Benger and Tytherton Kellaway 1967–93, formerly Roy Army Chaplain's Dept TA&VR Wilts, Army Cadet Force 1969; *m* 10 Aug 1957 *Mary Dorothy, BD King's Coll London, only dau of Leslie Fly, ARCM, of Corsham, Wilts, and has:

1 *Susan Mary; *b* 23 Jan 1962; *m* 1991 *Robert Adam Brisbane Cross, er s of Diarmid A Cross, of Tavistock, Devon, and has:

  (1) *Alice Rose; *b* 1993

  (2) *Lucy Mary Belinda; *b* 3 May 1995

2 *Juliet Elisabeth; *b* 8 Nov 1964; *m* 1992 *Maurice Charles Steuart-Corry, yr s of William Steuart-Corry, of Helensburgh, Dunbartonshire, and has:

  (1) *Sophie; *b* 1993

  (2) *Emma; *b* 1993 (twin)

  (3) *Katie Mary; *b* 22 Feb 1996

Lineage: WILLIAM RICHARDS, of Bristol (descended from John Richards, of Milverton, *b* 1677, *d* 1734); had, with a yr s (Maurice John, OBE, MC, *b* 7 May 1894, *d* 16 Sept 1969, leaving a son):

Sir ARTHUR FREDERICK RICHARDS, **1st Baron Milverton**, of Lagos and of Clifton, in the City of Bristol (UK), so *cr* 10 Oct 1947, GCMG (1942, KCMG 1935, CMG 1933); *b* 21 Feb 1885; *educ* Clifton and Ch Ch Oxford (BA 1907, MA 1950); Malayan CS 1908, Actg 1st Assist Col Sec Straits Settlements 1921, Actg U-Sec Fedtd Malay States 1926, U-Sec 1927–29, Actg Gen Advsr Johore 1929–30, Govr N Borneo 1930–33, Govr and C-in-C Gambia 1933–36, Govr and C-in-C Fiji and HC W Pacific 1936–38, Capt-Gen and Govr-in-C Jamaica 1938–43, Govr and C-in-C Nigeria 1943–47, KStJ, US Medal Freedom with Silver Palm; *m* 6 Sept 1927 *(Noelle) Benda, CStJ [The Rt Hon Benda Lady Milverton, Flete, Ermington, S Devon], dau of Charles Basil Whitehead, of Torquay, and *d* 27 Oct 1978, leaving:

1 FRASER ARTHUR RICHARD RICHARDS, **2nd and present Baron Milverton**

2 +MICHAEL HUGH [The Hon Michael Richards, Windrush Lodge, Middleton Park, Bicester, Oxon]; *b* 1 Aug 1936; heir presumptive; *educ* Ridley Coll Ontario, Heatherdown Ascot, Clifton and RMA Sandhurst; Capt Rifle Bde Malaya 1957 (despatches), seconded to Roy Nigerian Army 1962, memb UN Congo Force 1963–65, ret 1965, md Imperial Tobacco Co 1965, md Philip Morris Nigeria Ltd 1972–77, dir Africa Carreras Rothmans Ltd 1978–82, md Murray Sons & Co 1982–87, personnel dir Rothmans International Tobacco 1987–93, md Rothmans of Pall Mall (NZ) Ltd 1993–; *m* 18 Aug 1960 *(Edna) Leonie, yst dau of Col Leo Stevenie, OBE, MC, IA, and has:

  (1) +Arthur Hugh; *b* 10 Jan 1963; *educ* Hurn Court Sch Christchurch

1 *Diana Benda [The Hon Mrs Clement, The Bell House, Kewstoke Rd, Worle, Somerset]; *b* 9 Aug 1928; *educ* Nga Tawa Coll, NZ, Havergal Coll Toronto, Cheltenham Ladies' Coll, London U (BA) and the Sorbonne; *m* 1 Sept 1960 *S/Ldr Glyn Jones Clement, RAF, s of Sydney Joseph Clement, of Dunraven, Gower, Glam, and has:

  (1) *Paul Nicholas Arthur; *b* 24 Oct 1961

  (1) *Caroline Benda; *b* 1966

Arms: Quarterly, 1st and 4th grand quarters, quarterly 1st and 4th, argent a hunting-horn sable, stringed gules, on a chief azure three mullets of the field (for MURRAY of Melgund); 2nd and 3rd, azure a chevron argent between three fleurs-de-lys or (for KYNYNMOUND of that Ilk); 2nd and 3rd grand quarters, gules within a bordure vair, a bend engrailed or, thereon a baton azure (for ELLIOT of Minto); over all a chief of augmentation argent, charged with a Moor's head sable, couped in profile proper (arms of Corsica). **Crest:** A dexter arm embowed, issuant from clouds, throwing a dart, all proper. **Supporters:** Dexter, an Indian sheep; sinister, a fawn, both proper. **Mottoes:** 1 (over crest) *Non eget arcu* ('He needs not the bow'), 2 (below arms) *Suaviter et fortiter* ('Mildly but firmly'). **Creations:** Bt. (NS) 19 April 1700, B. (GB) 20 Oct 1797, E. and V. (UK) 24 Feb 1813.

THE 6TH EARL OF MINTO, Co Roxburgh, **Viscount Melgund**, of Melgund, Co Forfar, **Baron Minto of Minto**, Co Roxburgh, and a **Baronet** (Sir Gilbert Edward George Lariston Elliot-Murray-Kynynmound, Bt, OBE (1986, MBE 1955), JP (Roxburghshire 1961), DL (Borders 1983)) [The Rt Hon The Earl of Minto OBE JP DL, Minto, Hawick, Roxburghshire]; *b* 19 June 1928 (HM QUEEN MARY and HRH THE PRINCE OF WALES (later DUKE OF WINDSOR) stood sponsors); *s* f 1975; *educ* Eton and RMA Sandhurst; Capt Scots Gds (Res), ADC to: C-in-C FARELF 1951, CIGS 1953–55 and C-in-C Cyprus 1955; memb Roy Co Archers, Regnl Cncllr Hermitage Div Borders Regn 1974–, Chm Scottish Cncl Alcoholism 1973–; *m* 1st 26 Nov 1952 (*divorce* 1965), as her 1st husb, Lady Caroline Child-Villiers, er dau of 9th Earl of Jersey (*qv*), and has:

1 +(GILBERT) TIMOTHY GEORGE LARISTON, *Viscount Melgund* [Viscount Melgund, Upper Ham Farm, Thornhill, Wilts SN4 7RZ]; *b* 1 Dec 1953; *educ* Eton and NE London Poly (BSc 1983); Lt Scots Gds, memb Roy Co Archers; *m* 30 July 1983 *Diana Barbara, yr dau of Brian Trafford by Hon Audrey Taylor, dau of Baron Taylor of Hadfield (LP, *d* 1995), of Rudgwick, W Sussex, and has had:

  (1) +Gilbert Francis; *b* 15 Aug 1984

  (2) Lorne David; *b* and *d* 1986

  (3) +Michael Timothy; *b* 1987

  (1) *Clare Patricia; *b* 1991

1 *Laura [The Lady Laura Palmer, The New House, Carlton Curlieu, Leics LE8 0PH]; *b* 11 March 1956; *m* 23 Feb 1984 *John Reginald David Palmer, yr s of William Palmer, and has:

  (1) *Sam; *b* 1985

  (2) *Nicholas; *b* 1987

The 6th EARL *m* 2nd 10 July 1965 Mary Elizabeth (*d* 24 Jan 1983), dau of Peter Ballantine, of Gladstone, NJ; *m* 3rd 1991 *Caroline Jane, dau of Stanley Godfrey, of Ruislip, Middx, and formerly w of Christopher Larlham

Lineage: GAVIN ELLIOT of Grange and Midlem, Roxburghs (4th s of Gilbert Elliot [*sic*] of Stobs, Kirkton and Horsliehill; *see* ELLIOTT, Bt); had a 2nd s:

Sir Gilbert Elliot, 1st Bt (NS), so *cr* 19 April 1700, of Headshaw and later Minto, Roxburghshire; MP Roxburghshire 1702–07, Ld of Session as Lord Minto 1705; *m* 1st Helen, dau of Andrew Stevenson, of Edinburgh, and had:

1 Mary; *m* 23 Aug 1703 Sir John Elphinstone, 2nd Bt, of Logie (*qv*), and *d* 18 May 1767, leaving issue

Sir Gilbert *m* 2nd 17 March 1692 Jean, dau of Sir Andrew Carre of Cavers, Roxburghshire, and *d* 1 May 1718, having by her had, with a yr s (Andrew, drowned aged 16 sailing to Holland):

1 **Sir Gilbert Elliot, 2nd Bt**; MP Roxburghshire 1722–26, Ld of Session as Lord Minto 1726, Ld of Justiciary 1733, Ld Justice Clerk 1763; *m* 1720 Helen (*d* 22 June 1774), dau of Sir Robert Stewart, 1st Bt, of Allanbank (*see* 1850 edn), and *d* 16 April 1766, having had, with other issue:

  (1) GILBERT (Sir), **3rd Bt**

  (2) Andrew; Lt-Govr New York; *m* Elizabeth Plumstead and *d* May 1797, leaving:

1a Eleanor; *m* 1st James Jauncy (*dsp c* 1783), of New York; *m* 2nd 19 Aug 1784 Adml Hon Robert Digby (*see* DIGBY, B) and *d* 28 July 1830

2a Elizabeth; *m* 10 April 1779 1st Earl Cathcart (*qv*) and *d* 14 Dec 1847

3a Agnes Murray; *m* 30 April 1783 Sir David Carnegie, 4th Bt (*see* FIFE, D), and *d* 9 June 1860

(3) John; Adml the Red; MP Cockermouth 1766–68; *d* 1809

The 2nd Bt's est son,

Sir Gilbert Elliot, 3rd Bt, PC (1762); *b* 1722; MP Selkirkshire 1753–65 and Roxburghshire 1765–77, Treasurer RN 1770–77; *m* 14 Dec 1746 Agnes (*s* to her f's estates and *d* 30 Dec 1778), dau of Hugh Dalrymple-Murray-Kynynmound formerly Dalrymple, of Melgund, Forfarshire, and Kynynmound, Fifeshire (2nd s of Hon Sir David Dalrymple, 1st Bt, of Hailes; *see* STAIR, E), and *d* 11 Feb 1777, having had:

1 GILBERT, **1st Earl**

2 Hugh, PC; *b* 6 April 1752; Govr Madras; *m* 1st 1778 (*divorce* 1783) Charlotte, dau of Friedrich von Kraut, and had:

(1) Isabella; *m* 1810 George Payne and *d* 1826

2 (cont.) The Rt Hon Hugh Elliot *m* 2nd Margaret Jones (*d* 2 March 1819) and *d* 10 Dec 1830, having by her had, with other issue:

(1) Edward Francis; *b* 1796; *m* Isabella, dau of Cdr Hardie, RN, and *d* 11 June 1866, leaving:

1a Frederick Augustus Hugh, CIE; *b* 1847; *m* 1872 Constance Alice (*d* 1931), dau of Surgn-Maj Elijah Impey, and *d* 16 March 1910, leaving:

1b Edward Halhed Hugh, DSO and bar (1918); *b* 18 Dec 1876; Lt-Col RFA WW I (despatches, Order Nile 3rd Cl); *m* 16 Feb 1911 Ethel Winifred, yst dau of John Fair, of Bournemouth, and *d* as a result of enemy action 19 Feb 1944, leaving:

1c +Frederick John Hugh; *b* 4 Feb 1914

1c Margaret Elizabeth; *b* 20 April 1912; *m* 26 Sept 1936 Sub-Lt Robert Percival Lawrence, RNVR (*ka* 1 Sept 1940), 2nd s of E A Lawrence, of Guildford, and had issue

1b Isabella Margaret Impey; *b* 1873; *d* unm 12 Oct 1956

2b Winifred Alice; *b* 24 March 1875; *m* 1st 1894 Rev James Arthur Beaumont (*d* 1920); *m* 2nd May 1925 John Godolphin Bennett, Capt RE, and *d* 25 July 1958

1a Georgina Isabella; *m* 19 Dec 1861 Rev Henry Montagu Butler (*d* 14 Jan 1918), Master Trin Coll Cambridge, and *d* 11 Feb 1883, leaving issue

2a Emma Margaret Elphinstone; *m* 1868 Rev J A Cruikshank, of Herga, Woking, and *d* 29 Aug 1921

(2) Gilbert (Very Rev); *b* 17 March 1800; MA Cantab, DD, Dean Bristol; *m* 1st 20 Aug 1825 Williamina (*d* 1853), dau of Patrick Brydore, and had:

1a Gilbert; RN; lost at sea

1a Margaret; *d* unm 11 Jan 1901

2a Emma Mary; *m* 4 Sept 1862 Montagu Blackett (*dsp* 28 May 1866)

(2) (cont.) The Very Rev Gilbert Elliot *m* 2nd Nov 1863 Frances, dau of Charles Dickinson, and widow of J E Geiles, and *d* 11 Aug 1891

(3) Charles (Sir), KCB; *b* 1801; Adml; Govr St Helena; *m* 1828 Clara Genevieve (*d* 1885), dau of Robert Harley Windsor, and *d* 9 Sept 1875, leaving:

1a Hugh; *d* unm

2a Gilbert Wray; *b* 1833; Bombay CS; *m* 1st — and had:

1b Charles Arthur Powell; *b* 1855; lived USA; *m* twice

2a (cont.) Gilbert Elliot *m* 2nd Fanny, dau of Charles Staunton Cahill, of Lahinch, Co Galway, and by her had:

1b Hattie, OBE (1919); *m* 22 Jan 1889 Maj-Gen Sir George Vero Kemball, KCMG, DSO, RA (*d* 8 Jan 1941), and *d* 2 Sept 1943, leaving issue

2a (cont.) Gilbert Elliot *m* 3rd Ann (*d* 27 March 1939), dau of William Mason, and *d* 7 Oct 1910, having by her had:

2b Launceston; *b* 1874; *m* 1897 Rose Emelia Kathleen (*d* 1945), dau of Rev F W Helder, of Lee, Kent, and *d* 8 Aug 1930, leaving:

1c Kathleen Marguerite; *b* 6 April 1898; *m* 1st 1927 (*divorce*) John Hill Longhurst; *m* 2nd 1936 Reginald Malcolm Halsey and *dsp* in an accident 1944

2c Nancy Maud; *b* 5 May 1901; lived NZ; *m* 1929 Capt William Lewis Renwick, Welsh Horse Yeo (*d* 1957), s of William Henry Renwick, JP, and had:

1d *Ann Elliot; *b* 3 Feb 1940; *m* 1962 (*divorce* 1972) Garry Eric Smith and has:

1e *Ian Lewis Elliot; *b* 24 Dec 1966

3c Constance Joan; *b* 8 Oct 1905; *d* 29 Dec 1922

3a Frederick Eden; *b* 9 Oct 1837; BCS 1858–94; *m* 20 Aug 1861 Marcia Cordelia (*d* 10 Jan 1914), dau of Lt-Col John Ouseley, RA, and *d* 30 May 1916, leaving:

1b Hugh; *b* 22 Oct 1863; Maj King's Regt; *m* 1888 Alicia Lucy (*d* 1954), dau of Rev William Percy Robinson, DD, Warden Glenalmond, and was *ka* 26 July 1915, leaving:

1c Walter; *b* 21 Aug 1889; Indian Police

2c Frederick Eden; *b* 4 Feb 1892; Lt-Col RA, Queen's Messenger; *m* 22 July 1936 Elizabeth Anne, dau of William Christian Symonds

3c Hugh; *b* 28 May 1896; Lt 1st Bn King's Regt; *das* Salonika 24 June 1916

4c Gilbert Percy; *b* 3 Nov 1898; Maj RA

5c Charles Francis Desmond; *b* 25 Dec 1908; Maj Gurkha Regt

1c Margaret; *b* 31 May 1894

2c Clare Lucy; *b* 9 Sept 1900

2b Ernest Ousely; *b* 15 Feb 1865; *d* 1925

1b Beatrice Ellen; *b* 14 Nov 1867; *d* unm 28 Aug 1957

2b Emily Agnes; *b* 14 Nov 1867; *m* 1894 Lt-Col John McConaghey, IMS, Inspr-Gen Civ Hosps India, and *d* 2 April 1914

1a Harriet Agnes; *m* 31 March 1853 23rd Lord (Baron) De Clifford (*qv*) and *d* 17 Feb 1896, leaving issue

2a Emma Clara; *m* 8 June 1864 Rev G B Pennell and *d* 27 May 1865, leaving issue

(4) Hugh Maximilian; *b* 1802; 17th Lancers; *m* 1825 Mary (*d* 1838), dau of George Lys, Judge Madras, and *d* Jan 1826, leaving:

1a Hugh Maximilian; *b* 11 April 1826; R-Adml; *m* 28 Nov 1850 Mary Jane, dau of Edward Jennings, and *dsp* 30 April 1900

(5) Thomas Frederick (Sir), KCMG; *b* July 1808; U-Sec Colonies; *m* 1st 15 May 1833 Jane (*dsp* 4 Jan 1850), dau of James Perry; *m* 2nd 4 Jan 1869 Elizabeth (*d* 8 Feb 1880), dau of Adml Sir Robert Howe Bromley, 3rd Bt (*qv*), and *dsp* 12 Feb 1880

(2) Emma; *m* 3 Oct 1823 Gen Sir Thomas Hislop, 1st Bt, GCB (*d* 3 May 1843; *see* 1834 edn), and *d* 10 Aug 1866, leaving issue

3 Alexander Kynynmound; *b* 8 April 1754; EICS; *d* 12 Sept 1778

4 Robert (Rev); *b* 4 April 1755; Rector Wheldrake, Yorks; *m* 9 April 1788 Mary, dau of Rev Edmund Garforth, of Askham, Yorks, and *d* 1824 leaving, with other issue:

(1) Edward Eden; *b* 1797; Accountant-Gen Bombay; *m* 1826 Anne, dau of Capt Harrison, and *d* 4 Dec 1872, leaving:

1a Minto, CB; *b* 26 Sept 1833; Maj-Gen RA; *m* 2 Feb 1857 Amelia (*d* 12 Feb 1871), dau of Thomas George Martin, and *dsp* 14 March 1909

1a Mary; *m* 14 Oct 1868 Charles Woollam, JP (*d* 1915), of St Albans, Herts

(1) Isabella Lucy; *m* 21 April 1830 Gilbert Eliott (*d* 30 June 1871), and *d* 1871, leaving issue (*see* ELIOTT, Bt)

1 Eleanor; *m* 26 Sept 1776 1st Baron Auckland (*qv*) and *d* 18 May 1818, leaving issue

The 3rd Bt's est son,

Sir GILERT ELLIOT later ELLIOT-MURRAY-KYNYNMOUND (roy licence 2 Oct 1797), **4th Bt**, and **1st Earl of Minto**, Co Roxburgh, so *cr* 24 Feb 1813, as also VISCOUNT MELGUND of Melgund, Co Forfar (both UK), and earlier 20 Oct 1797 BARON MINTO OF MINTO, Co Roxburgh (GB), PC (1793); *b* 23 April 1751; *educ* La Pension Militaire Fontainebleau and Ch Ch Oxford; barrister Lincoln's Inn 1774, MP Morpeth 1776–77, Roxburghshire 1777–84, Berwicks 1786–90 and Helston 1790–95), Min Italians States March-May 1794, Viceroy Corsica 1794–96 on its being ceded to GB in return for protection, Envoy Vienna 1779–1801, Pres Bd Control India Feb–July 1806, Govr-Gen India 1806–13 (where he was said to have built up a fortune of £245,000 (something over £5,000,000 in late-1990s terms) while in office); *m* 3 Jan 1777 Anna Maria (*d* 8 March 1829), est dau of Sir George Amyand, 1st Bt (*see* 1959 edn CORNEWALL, Bt), and *d* 21 June 1814, having had:

1 GILBERT, **2nd Earl**

2 George (Sir), KCB; *b* 1 Aug 1784; Adml; Gen Mint Scotland, a Ld Admlty; *m* Dec 1810 Eliza Cecilia (*d* 23 May 1848), yst dau of James Ness, of Osgodby, Yorks, and *d* 24 June 1863, having had:

(1) George (Sir), KCB; *b* 1812; Adml; Naval ADC 1856–58, Naval C-in-C Portsmouth 1875–78; MP Chatham 1874–75; *m* 1 Aug 1842 Hersey Susan Sydney (*d* 11 Dec 1893), only dau of Lt-Col Wauchope, of Niddrie, Marischal, Edinburgh, and *d* 13 Dec 1901, leaving:

1a George Edmund Lyons; *b* 5 April 1849; *d* Feb 1917

1a Elizabeth Georgina Frances; *m* 28 Feb 1865 her cousin 9th Earl of Northesk (*qv*) and *d* 2 May 1933, leaving issue

2a Nina Helen; *m* 12 July 1877 Capt Sir Thomas Dacres Butler, KCVO, JP (*d* 29 Dec 1937), of Hambledon, Hants, Yeoman Usher Black Rod Ho Lds, est s of Col Thomas Butler, 53rd Regt, and *d* 7 March 1947, leaving issue

3a Hersey Eliza Cecilia; *m* 20 July 1876 Lt-Cdr Gerald Rivers Maltby, MVO, RN (*d* 3 April 1922), and *d* 17 May 1918, leaving issue

4a Anna Maria Olivia; *m* 17 June 1873 Charles Windham R Kerr and *d* 20 Jan 1937, leaving issue (*see* LOTHIAN, M)

(2) Gilbert John; *b* 25 July 1818; 47th Regt; *m* 27 Nov 1849 Isabella Elizabeth (*d* 20 Feb 1902), 2nd dau of Rev Thomas Gore (*see* GORE, Bt), and *d* 20 Aug 1852, leaving issue, an only dau who *d* unm

(3) Horatio Foley; Lt RN; *d* 1845

(4) Alexander James Hardy (Sir), KCB; *b* 23 Feb 1825; Maj-Gen 5th Dragoon Gds, Col 21st Lancers; *m* 5 June 1855 Gertrude Mary Wilmot (*d* 5 May 1909), 2nd dau of James Wilmot Williams, of Herringston, Dorset, and *dsp* 1 July 1909

(5) Frederick Boileau; *b* 23 Oct 1826; HEICS; *m* 17 Dec 1868 Lady Charlotte Carnegie (*d* 15 Jan 1880), sis of 9th Earl of Southesk (*see* FIFE, D) and widow of Thomas Frederick Scrymsoure Fothringham of Pourie, and *d* 23 Dec 1880, leaving:

1a Gilbert Compton; *b* 28 June 1871; Lt 3rd Bn Black Watch Roy Highrs; *m* 25 Aug 1910 Marguerita (*d* 16 Oct 1955), dau of Henry I Barbey, of New York, and *d* 1 Jan 1931, leaving:

1b Gilbert George; *b* 24 June 1911; P/O RAFVR WW II; *ka* 10 Oct 1940

2b Alexander Henry; *b* 22 Dec 1913; *educ* Eton and Ch Ch Oxford; WW II as Maj RA; *m* 8 June 1937 *Lady Ann Child-Villiers, yr dau of 8th Earl of Jersey (*qv*), and *d* 1986, leaving:

1c +Gilbert Francis; *b* 26 March 1949

1c *Victoria Cynthia [Mrs John Hunter, Minto, Mount Rankin, Bathurst, NSW, Australia]; *b* 9 Feb 1938; *m* 29 Jan 1960 *Lt John Robert Hunter, RN, only s of Kenneth Max Hunter, of S Woodford, Essex, and has:

1d *David John; *b* 9 July 1961

2d *James Max; *b* 29 Sept 1963

3d *Michael Alexander; *b* 7 Oct 1965

4d *Andrew William; *b* 1976

2c *Patricia Joan; *b* 2 Jan 1940; *m* 25 July 1964 *F/Lt David John Curry, RAF, only s of Cecil John Curry, of Vowchurch, Herefs, and has:

1d *Alexander David Ian; *b* 1974

1d *Georgina Sophie Gay; *b* 13 Dec 1967

1b *Cynthia Sophie, BEM (1944) [Mrs Ian Major BEM, c/o Chase Manhattan Bank, Tortola, Br Virgin Islands]; *b* 12 March 1916; WW II Red Cross, nursing POWs while herself a POW Germany 1940–44; *m* 1st 22 June 1944 1st and last Baron Hore-Belisha, PC (*d* 16 Feb 1957; *see* 1956 edn);

m 2nd 17 Dec 1957 Maj Ian Victor Major, DSC, RM (*d* 1973), er s of William Albert Major

(1) Georgiana Maria; *m* 14 Feb 1843 8th Earl of Northesk (*qv*) and *d* 23 Feb 1874, leaving issue

(2) Eliza; *m* 21 Aug 1844 4th Marquess of Northampton (*qv*) and *d* 4 Dec 1877, leaving issue

(3) Catherine Frances; *m* 5 Feb 1856 Adml Hon Sir James Robert Drummond, GCB, and *d* 20 April 1914, leaving issue (*see* PERTH, E)

(4) Cecilia Mary; *m* 11 Oct 1866 Hon William Nassau Jocelyn, CB (*see* RODEN, E), and *d* 1 Jan 1894

3 John Edmund, MP; *b* 30 March 1788; *m* 3 Oct 1809 Amelia (*d* 23 July 1872), 3rd dau of James Henry Casamaijor, of Madras, and *d* 4 April 1862, having had:

(1) Edmund James; *b* 6 Aug 1813; Lt-Col 79th Foot; *m* 5 Oct 1853 Matilda (*m* 2nd 17 Dec 1881 Maj G W W Carpenter and *d* 1887), est surv dau of Charles Halkett Craigie Inglis of Cramond, and *d* Varna 12 Aug 1854, leaving:

1a Edmund Halbert (Sir), MVO; *b* posthumously 7 Nov 1854; Maj RA, Ensign Yeomen Gd; *m* 22 Feb 1898 Isabella (*d* 10 Nov 1927), dau of Chevalier de Colquhoun and widow of 3rd Earl of Limerick (*qv*), and *d* 20 Sept 1926

(2) William Brownrigg, JP (Roxburghs); *b* 6 Oct 1820; barrister; *m* 2 Jan 1858 Mary Geraldine (*d* 22 June 1904), dau of Justin McCartie, of Carrignavar, and widow of Thomas Morton, and *d* 14 July 1900, having had:

1a William Gerald; *b* 9 Nov 1858; BA Cantab; barrister; *d* unm 30 Aug 1930

2a Cyril Herbert John; *b* 6 Oct 1861; *d* 2 Sept 1868

(3) Amyand Powney Charles; *b* 18 June 1823; Capt Bengal Army; *m* 6 Oct 1842 Anna Maria (*d* 6 Nov 1857), est dau of Lt-Col Alexander, and *d* 5 Jan 1869, having had:

1a Amyand; *b* 18 March 1849; *m* 1885 Rose Ellen, dau of H Borde, and *dsp*

2a William Alexander; *b* 19 Nov 1851; RN; *m* 1887 Louisa Margaret (*d* 20 June 1890), dau of Charles Russell, MD, and *d* 1894, having had:

1b Charles Amyand Alexander; *b* 13 June 1890; *educ* Cheltenham; Lt Argyll & Sutherland Highrs, Col RASC, WW I (despatches); *m* 1st 23 April 1918 Doreen Stuart (*d* 1941), dau of Adml George Lydiard Sullivan; *m* 2nd 1944 Lillian Jean, dau of William Henry Harrell, and *dsp* 26 Nov 1961

1b Amy Millicent; *m* 1st 27 July 1907 (*divorce* 1915) Cdr Eric Marsland Groves, RN (*d* 28 June 1949), 5th s of James Grimble Groves, JP, DL, of Cheshire, and IoM, and had:

1c Colin Eric; *b* 17 Aug 1908; Maj HLI; *m* 1937 Dorothea Mary Blamey (*d* 18 Jan 1998) and *d* 1985, leaving:

1d *Mary Fay Sylvia [Mrs Andrew Douglas-Bate, Alwyn Lawn House, Stone, nr Aylesbury, Bucks HP17 8RZ]; *b* 2 Nov 1940; *m* 12 May 1961 *Andrew Sandys Douglas-Bate and has:

1e *Rupert Louis Elliot; *b* 7 Sept 1963; *m* 10 Oct 1987 *Janet Ratcliffe Duffin and has:

1f *Samuel George; *b* 22 Aug 1990

2f *Tobias Alexander; *b* 10 Dec 1996

1f ^Laura Elizabeth; *b* 1 Oct 1988

1e *Sophie Louise; *b* 19 July 1965

2e *Harriet Mary; *b* 25 Nov 1966; *m* 1992 *Edward Barnwell Parker and has:

1f *Jack Andrew; *b* 19 March 1997

1b (cont.) Mrs Amy Groves *m* 2nd 1 Jan 1916 (*divorce* 1932) Lt-Cdr Paris Graham Singer, RN (*d* 12 Dec 1953); *m* 3rd 15 March 1948, as his 3rd w, William Henry Gill

3a Charles Sinclair; *b* 26 Sept 1853; Cdr RN; Ch Magistrate Norfolk Island; *m* 20 Feb 1889 Florence Louisa (*d* 29 Dec 1950), est dau of Frederick Leacroft Dudley, and *d* 30 March 1915, leaving:

1b Dudley Sinclair; *b* 14 Jan 1890, Lt AIF; *m* 28 Aug 1913 Annie Caroline (*d* 7 July 1962), dau of William Hammett Howard, of Sydney, and was *ka* 12 Oct 1917, leaving:

1c +Dudley Charles Howard [Dudley Elliot Esq, PO Box 84, Murwillumbah, NSW 2484, Australia]; *b* 2 March 1918; *educ* Sydney U (LLB); WW II in RAAF; *m* 26 June 1943 *Rosalie Yvonne, dau of Francis Walter Vizard, of S Australia, and had:

1d +Gilbert Dennis [Gilbert Elliot Esq, 19 Wilga St, Concorde West, NSW 2138, Australia]; *b* 17 Jan 1947; *educ* U of NSW (Dip Hosp Admin); *m* 1973 *Jane, dau of John Guinane, of NSW, and has:

1e +Robert Gilbert Sinclair; *b* 1979

2e +Gerard Charles Cameron; *b* 1982

1e *Lenore Elizabeth; *b* 1977

2d +Victor Roderick; *b* 3 May 1950

3d +Hugh Kent; *b* 16 Oct 1953

1d *Roslyn Kristin; *b* 17 Nov 1944; *m* 1966 *Dr Ronald Charles Newland, and has issue

2b John Amyand; *b* 6 April 1891; *ka* 1915

3b Alban Charles, MC; *b* 7 June 1892; Capt and Adj AIF France WW I (despatches), Silver Jubilee Medal 1935, WW II as Maj AIF; *m* 14 May 1919 Fanny Compton (*d* 1974), dau of Francis Henry Atherton, of Taunton, and Gympie, Qld, and had:

1c +Charles Atherton [Charles Elliot Esq, Pathfield, Bells Line of Rd, Bilpin, NSW 2758, Australia]; *b* 25 Aug 1921; *educ* Sydney U (LLB); WW II with AIF New Guinea; *m* 23 May 1955 *Doris May Pritchard, of Llansannan, and has:

1d +Timothy Charles; *b* 1960

2d +Owen Francis; *b* 1963

1c *Eileen; *b* 17 June 1924; WW II with AWAS New Guinea; *m* 1947 Alasdair David Thomson (*d* 1993) and has:

1d *Peter David; *b* 20 Jan 1948

2d *Ian Charles; *b* 19 Jan 1953

3d *John Elliot; *b* 8 Oct 1958

1d *Patricia Eileen; *b* 8 March 1951

2c *Hilary [Mrs Denys Head, 6 Greenacres, Crooksbury Rd, Dunfold, Surrey GU10 1QU]; *b* 11 April 1927; WW II with AWAS; *m* 15 Nov 1952 *Denys Eric Head, only s of Eric Burton Head, of Guildford, and has:

1d *Roger Denys; *b* 26 June 1957

1d *Lynette Ann; *b* 27 March 1954

2d *Gillian Margaret; *b* 20 Oct 1955

4b William Alexander; *b* 10 June 1896; Lt-Cdr RN, WWs I and II (despatches), Order Sacred Treasure Japan; *m* 20 Dec 1920 Jean Maud Bennett, MBE (*m* 2nd 11 July 1950 Sir Allan George Mossop (*d* 1965)), dau of A B Paton, and was *ka* at sea 28 May 1941

5b Gerald Augustus, MC; *b* 3 Feb 1900; F/O RAF, WW II 1940–46 as Capt SAAF; *m* 5 Oct 1938 Margery Lutley, dau of A L Barrett

1b Florence Grace; *m* 1922 Reginald Joslyn Buckingham and had issue

2b Margaret Mildred Norfolk Hope; *m* 1 Aug 1928 ACM Sir Basil Edward Embry, GCB, KBE, DSO, DFC, AFC (*d* 1977), s of Rev James Embry, of Dover, and had:

1c *Keith Elliot; *b* 9 June 1929; *m* 1968 *Georgina Methven and has:

1d *Katherine; *b* 1969

2c *Mark Elliot; *b* 27 Sept 1935; *m* 1959 *Joan Douglas, dau of Air Cdre Bright, and has:

1d *Paul Douglas; *b* 1956

2d *Andrew; *b* 1963

1d *Anne Margaret; *b* 1958

2d *Sarah; *b* 1960

3d *Jill; *b* 1961

3c Andrew Elliot; *b* 9 Dec 1936; *d* 1940

4c *Patrick Paul Elliot; *b* 19 Oct 1943

1c *Bridget Elliot; *b* 22 May 1931; *m* 9 May 1953 *Vivian Jenner Mackereth, est s of Dr J G Mackereth, of Matamata, NZ, and has:

1d *James; *b* 1956

2d *Neil; *b* 1959

1d *Susan Embry; *b* 4 Nov 1954

2d *Wendy; *b* 1958

1a Amy Amelia; *m* 20 March 1866 Albert Champion Mangles, BCS (*d* 1891), and *d* 25 Feb 1923

2a Grace; *m* 8 April 1874 Henry Alexander Lane, est s of Col Henry Lane, of Bexhill, Sussex, and *d* Dec 1928, leaving issue

3a Augusta Helen; *d* young 6 March 1862

(4) Augustus John; *b* 27 Aug 1824; BCS, memb Cncl of India; *m* 1st 19 Jan 1855 Helen (*d* 29 April 1866), dau of John Lowis, of Plean, Stirling, and had:

1a Guy Patton; *b* 5 Nov 1855; *m* 2 April 1929 Blanche Isabel, widow of Edward Leonard Holmes-Leigh, of Moyard, Co Clare, and *d* 5 Feb 1937

2a Edmund Colville; *b* 6 May 1857; *m* 1888 Edith Mary, dau of John Cadenhead, HEICS, and *dsp*

3a Ninian Lowis; *b* 4 April 1861; Imp Yeo Boer War 1900, WW I in Bihar Light Horse; *m* 1st 25 March 1896 Æmilia Margaret (*d* 5 July 1924), dau of J A Guthrie, of Craigie, Forfar, and had:

1b Archibald Guthrie; *b* 17 Feb 1898; Lt-Cdr RN, F/Lt RAF; *m* 7 Jan 1929 Evelyn Agnes (*m* 2nd Lt Maurice Carmichael Niven, 11th Hus (*d* 1942), and *d* 16 Sept 1965), only dau of Alexander Buchanan, of Nova Scotia, and *d* in flying accident 2 Oct 1931, leaving:

1c +John Alexander Ninian [John Elliot Esq, Portmans Bridge, Box 6, Gilgil, Kenya]; *b* 1 April 1930; *m* 1962 *Jean Patricia, dau of Arthur Willis Winfield Sale, of Pulborough, Sussex

1c *Margaret Dolores [Mrs Timothy Matthews, 7 Chislehurst Rd, Richmond, Surrey]; *b* posthumously 9 Nov 1931; *m* 1953 *Timothy Romer Matthews, er s of Dr Ronald Matthews, of Crawley, and has:

1d *Sophia Elizabeth; *b* 1955; *m* 1982 *William Gerald Kelly

1b Helen Alice; *b* 5 Sept 1899; *m* 1st 10 Nov 1924 (*divorce* 1928) Capt Guy Fife Earle (*see* EARLE, Bt); *m* 2nd 9 May 1928 Malcolm Douglas Lyon, LLB, barrister, RM Tanganyika, and *d* Nov 1967, leaving issue

3a (cont.) Ninian Elliot *m* 2nd 19 Oct 1926 Flora Cecil (*d* 12 Nov 1971), dau of Alexander Cochran, of Ashkirk, and *d* 1 May 1935

4a Archibald Campbell; *b* 20 Aug 1864; WW I in Bihar Light Horse; *m* 1899 Harriet Newcome (*d* 3 Sept 1951), dau of J M Lowis, ICS, of Alton, Hants, and *d* 15 Oct 1921, leaving:

1b Augustus John; *b* 5 Aug 1901; Lt-Col IA; *m* 1st 15 Sept 1930 (*divorce* 1946) Theodora Dorothy (*d* 1982), dau of Engr-Cdr T G J Harvey, RIN, and had:

1c +Archibald Keith [Archibald Elliot Esq, 78 Howard Rd, Queens Pk, Bournemouth BN8 9ED]; *b* 11 Feb 1932; late Ch Technician RAF; *m* 1957 *Pauline Mary, dau of Cecil Edward Pierman Parker, of Watford, Herts, and has:

1d +Ross Ian; *b* 1 April 1958

2d +Clive Graham; *b* 30 Dec 1960; *m* 1993 *Helena Mary, dau of Denis Martin Prendergast, of Co Kerry, and has:

1e *Jasmine Portia; *b* 26 Oct 1994

2c +Angus Ian [Angus Elliot Esq, Gorse Cottage, 82 Coleshill Rd, Marston Green, Birmingham 37]; *b* 22 Feb 1938; late RAF; *m* 12 Dec 1959 *Carol Ann, only dau of William Henry Evans, of Birmingham, and has:

1d +Mark Keith; *b* 24 Sept 1960

2d +Jamie Ian; *b* 10 Jan 1964

1c *Betty Anne [Mrs Jeffrey Browning, The Grange, Worlingworth, Woodbridge, Suffolk]; *b* 10 Nov 1933; *m* 23 June 1956 *Capt Jeffrey Edward Power Browning, 8th King's Roy Irish Hus, only s of Richard Samuel Power Browning, and has:

1d *Charles Richard Power; *b* 1957; *m* 1993 *Kate Borwick

2d *Alastair Jeffrey Power; *b* 15 Oct 1960

1d *Philippa Anne Campbell; b 22 Feb 1963; m 1994 *Timothy John Inskip

2d *Joanna Elizabeth Newcombe; b 1967

1b (cont.) Col Augustus Elliot m 2nd 22 Oct 1946 Ilona, dau of Frederic Charles Wilson Bindley, of Eastbourne, and d 1979

1a Helen; d unm 17 Jan 1870

(4) (cont.) Augustus Elliot m 2nd 23 Nov 1869 Katharine (d 22 May 1912), dau of Ross Donelly Mangles, memb Cncl of India, and d 29 June 1889, having by her had:

5a Gilbert Augustus; b 17 March 1873; Boer War 1899–1900, WW I (7th Vol Bn W Yorks Regt), FLAS; m 11 Jan 1905 Phyllis Baret (d 1972), 2nd dau of Maj Edward William Stokes, 4th King's Own Regt, and d 26 Jan 1959, leaving:

1b +Gilbert Cecil Ninian [Gilbert Elliot Esq, 2 Earswick Village, Yorks YO3 9SL]; b 15 May 1907; AMICE, ChE; m 10 Oct 1942 Esther Rosamond (d 1987), yr dau of Capt Hugh Alfred Cholmley, of Yorks, and has:

1c +Gilbert Hugh Cholmley [Gilbert Elliot Esq, 22 Limewood Cl, St Johns, Woking, Surrey]; b 15 Sept 1947; educ St Peter's York; m 1979 *Beryl Breakspear and has:

1d +Jonathan; b 1983

1d *Rebecca; b 1981

2c +Rowland George Cholmley [Rowland Elliot Esq, 2 Earswick Village, York YO3 9SL]; b 12 July 1949; educ St Peter's York; RAF; m 1986 *Ruth Skovgaard, of Bornholm, Denmark, and has:

1d +Samuel Gilbert; b 1990

1d *Hanna Rosamond; b 1988

2d *Marianne Esther; b 1995

1c *Jane [Mrs David Ewart, Court Hill House, Potterne, Wilts SN10 5PN]; b 23 Sept 1943; m 9 Jan 1963 (divorce 1985) Maj Iain Alastair McKay, Scots Gds, s of G F McKay, and has:

1d *Alastair James Mark; b 19 Oct 1963; m 1991 *Susan Lee and has:

1e *Peter James; b March 1997

1e *Eleanor; b Aug 1995

2d *Andrew Simon Charles; b 1970

1d *Catriona Jane; b 6 March 1966; m 1995 *Philip Littlehales and has:

1e *Matilda; b Aug 1996

2d *Arabella Charlotte; b 12 April 1968

1c (cont.) Mrs Jane McKay m 2nd 1994 *David Ewart

2c *Lorna [Mrs L Clive, Foxhanger Cottage, Priorsfield Rd, Godalming, Surrey GU7 2RG]; b 19 April 1945; m 23 Sept 1967 (divorce 1991) John Edward Clive, s of Edward Clive, of Swanmore, Hants, and has:

1d *Simon John David; b 1970

2d *Edward Thomas; b 1974

1d *Sarah Margarita; b 1968

1b *Daphne Patricia [Mrs Godfrey Royle, Home Farm, Balscote, Oxon OX15 6JP]; b 26 Feb 1917; m 12 Nov 1949 *Capt Godfrey Carrington Royle, RA (TA), 3rd s of Vernon P Royle, of Lancaster

(1) Amelia Jane; m 1830 Thomas Campbell Robertson (d 5 July 1863) and d 19 June 1837

(2) Anna Maria Elizabeth; m 18 May 1865 Pierce G E Taylor, of Devon, and d 8 Nov 1883

1 Anna Maria; m 1832 Lt-Gen Sir Rufane Shawe Donkin, KCB, GCH (d 1841), and d 18 Oct 1855

2 Harriet Mary Frances; d July 1825

3 Catherine Sarah; m 14 Nov 1825 Sir John Peter Boileau, 1st Bt (qv), and d 25 June 1862, leaving issue

The 1st EARL's est son,

GILBERT ELLIOT-MURRAY-KYNYNMOUND, **2nd Earl of Minto**, GCB (1834), PC (1832); b 16 Nov 1782; educ Eton and Edinburgh U; MP (Whig) Ashburton 1806–07 and Roxburghshire 1812–14, Envoy Extrdy and Min Plen Berlin 1832–34, 1st Ld Admiralty 1835–41, Ld Privy Seal 1846–52, Envoy Sardinia 1847–48, Govr Naval Coll Portsmouth, Tstee Br Museum; m 4 Sept 1806 Mary (d 21 July 1853), est dau of Patrick Brydone, of Lennel House, Berwicks, and d 31 July 1859, having had:

1 WILLIAM HUGH, **3rd Earl**

2 Henry George (Sir), GCB, PC; b 30 June 1817; Sec Legation The Hague 1848 and Vienna 1853, Envoy and Min Plen Copenhagen 1858, Naples 1859, Italy 1863–67, Amb Constantinople 1867 and Vienna 1877–84; m 9 Dec 1847 Anne, 2nd dau of Sir Edmund Antrobus, 2nd Bt (qv), and d 30 March 1907, having had:

(1) Francis Edmund Hugh (Sir), GCMG, GCVO; b 24 March 1851; educ Balliol Coll Oxford (MA); Dip Serv 1874, Sec Legation Athens 1890–95, Agent and Consul-Gen Bulgaria 1895–1903, Envoy Extrdy and Min Plen Greece 1903–17; m 26 Oct 1881 Henrietta Augusta Mary (d 26 Feb 1938), only dau of Sir Francis Clare Ford, GCB, GCMG, PC, and d 20 Jan 1940, leaving:

1a Katharine; b 8 Nov 1882; m 21 Nov 1911 William J Moloney, Offr Order Orange-Nassau, King Haakon VII Liberty Cross, and d 11 Nov 1964, leaving issue

2a Frances Clara; b 3 March 1885; m 18 July 1908 Sir Charles Alban Young, 9th Bt, KCMG, MVO, of North Dean (qv), and d 28 Nov 1967, leaving issue

3a Dorothy; b 30 Oct 1888; m 29 Oct 1914 Henry Montesquieu Anthony, CBE, Egyptian CS (d 8 May 1949), s of Joseph Montesquieu Anthony, of Clifton, and had:

1b *Lydia Margaret Elliot; b 1918

4a Violet Marie; b 17 March 1896; m 3 June 1920 Lt Edmond Henry O'Conor, RN (d 29 June 1924), 2nd s of Capt Edmond O'Conor, JP, DL, of Dunleer, Co Louth

(1) Gertrude; b 17 Aug 1855; d unm 23 Dec 1947

3 Charles Gilbert John Brydone (Sir), KCB; b 12 Dec 1818; Adml Fleet, C-in-C The Nore 1870–73; m 1st 8 Dec 1863 Louisa (d 17 July 1870), est dau of Sir Edward Blackett, 6th Bt (qv), and had:

(1) Gilbert Edward; b 2 Feb 1865; d 23 June 1870

(2) Walter Charles; b 8 Dec 1866; d 19 Feb 1867

(3) Bertram Charles; b 5 Dec 1867; m 29 Oct 1901 Norah Kathleen (d 23 Dec 1937), dau of Walter Raleigh Trevelyan (see TREVELYAN, Bt, of Nettlecombe), and d 14 Jan 1933

(4) Julian Arthur; b 8 March, d 18 Oct 1870

3 (cont.) Adml of the Fleet Sir Charles Elliot-Murray-Kynynmound m 2nd 4 Feb 1874 Lady Harriette Emily Liddell (d 6 Feb 1913), dau of 1st Earl of Ravensworth (see RAVENSWORTH, B), and d 21 May 1895, having by her had:

(1) Sybil Harriett; b 29 May 1875; m 3 Nov 1903 Frederick Oswald Durell Durell, 2nd s of Frederick Thomas Durell Durell, and d 24 Dec 1953, leaving issue

(2) Rachel Mira Horatia; b 26 June 1876

4 George Francis Stewart; b 9 Oct 1822; MA Cantab; barrister; d unm 14 Feb 1901

5 Gilbert; b 23 May 1826; Lt-Col Rifle Bde; m 17 Aug 1858 Katharine Anne (m 2nd 12 April 1879 Hugh C E Childers, PC, MP (d 29 Jan 1896), and d 30 May 1895), 6th dau of Rt Rev Dr Gilbert, Bp Chichester, and d 25 May 1865

1 Mary Elizabeth; m 1838 Ralph Abercromby, 2nd and last Baron Dunfermline, KCB (dspm 12 July 1868), and d 10 April 1874, leaving issue

2 Frances Anna Maria; m 20 July 1841 1st Earl Russell (qv) and d 17 Jan 1898

3 Elizabeth Amelia Jane; m 29 Nov 1848 Lt-Col Frederick Romilly, of Barry, Glam (d 6 April 1887), and d 18 Jan 1892, leaving issue

4 Charlotte Mary; m 9 Oct 1855 Melville Portal and d 3 June 1899, leaving issue (see PORTAL, Bt)

5 Harriet Anne Gertrude; dvp 9 Feb 1855

The 2nd EARL's est son,

WILLIAM HUGH ELLIOT-MURRAY-KYNYNMOUND, **3rd Earl of Minto**, KT (1870), DL (Roxburghshire); b 19 March 1814; educ Eton and Trin Coll Cambridge; MP (Lib) Hythe 1837–41, Greenock 1847–52 and Clackmannan 1857–59, Chm Lunacy Commn 1857; m 20 May 1844 his cousin Emma Eleanor Elizabeth (d 21 April 1882), only dau of Gen Sir Thomas Hislop, 1st Bt, GCB (see 1834 edn), and d 17 March 1891, having had:

1 GILBERT JOHN, **4th Earl**

2 Arthur Ralph Douglas, MP; b 17 Dec 1846; MA Cantab; barrister; MP Roxburghs 1880–92 and Durham 1898–1906, Fin Sec Treasury 1903; ed Edinburgh Review 1895–1912, Hon DCL Durham; m 14 Feb 1888 Madeleine Harriet Dagmar (d 1 Jan 1906), dau of Sir Charles Lister Ryan, KCB, and d 12 Feb 1923, leaving:

(1) Robert Douglas; b 19 Sept 1889; d 23 Dec 1894

(2) Hubert William Arthur Elliot; b 20 Feb 1891; educ Eton and Trin Coll Cambridge (BA 1912); Capt 4th Bn Wilts Regt WW I; m 1st 27 Feb 1919 Mary Hester (d 16 Feb 1945), 2nd dau of Hon Sir Langer Owen, CBE, Ch Judge Divorce Supreme Court, Sydney, NSW, and had:

1a +John William Owen [John Elliot-Murray-Kynynmound Esq, Old House Farm, Cockfield, Suffolk]; b 3 July 1921; educ Eton and Trin Coll Cambridge; Capt 3rd Bn Scots Gds WW II; m 1 April 1944 *Mary Norah, er dau of Hon John Mulholland (see DUNLEATH, B), and has:

1b +Hugh John [Hugh Elliot-Murray-Kynynmound Esq, 1361 E Street SE, Washington DC, USA]; b 24 Sept 1946; educ Eton and Gonville and Caius Coll Cambridge (MA); m 1987 *Mary Anna, dau of John Portner, of Washington

2b +Timothy David [Timothy Elliot-Murray-Kynynmound Esq, Green House, Timworth, nr Bury St Edmunds, Suffolk]; b 23 March 1952; educ Eton and Bristol U; m 1975 *Helen Margaret, dau of Michael Lacey, of Bideford, N Devon, and has:

1c +Robert John; b 1977

2c +Michael David; b 1982

1c *Rebecca Frances; b 1979

1b *Susan Mary [Mrs Patrick del Cassero-Nisbett, Wood Hall, Little Waldingfield, Suffolk]; b 5 April 1948; educ Goldsmiths' Coll London U (DipEd); m 6 Aug 1969 *Patrick Gilbert Dominic Toriglioni del Cassero-Nisbett, Gren Gds, est s of Hugh Nisbett, and has:

1c *Dominick Gilbert; b 16 March 1972

2c *Hugo Alexander; b 1977

3c *Edmund Dudley; b 1982

1c *Olivia Eleanora; b 1975

1a Anne Madeleine; b 28 April 1920; m 25 May 1940 Maj David Gerald Bevan, MC, Northants Yeo, er s of Maurice Bevan, and d 13 Oct 1954, leaving issue

(2) (cont.) Hubert Elliot m 2nd 15 Jan 1955 Pamela Violet, er dau of Patrick Douglas Stirling, OBE, MC, JP, of Perthshire, and formerly w of Charles Frederick Cathcart (see CATHCART, E), and d 13 Dec 1967

3 Hugh Frederick Hislop; b 23 Feb 1848; BA Cantab; MP N Ayr 1885–92; m 15 July 1879 Mary Euphemia (d 4 Oct 1934), 2nd dau of Col Samuel Long, of Bromley Hill, Kent, and d 30 April 1932, leaving:

(1) Hugh Samuel Roger; b 3 April 1881; Lt Coldstream Gds Boer War; author; m 26 July 1906 Rosa Maud (d 14 June 1937), dau of N Chesterfield, and d air crash 6 May 1930, leaving:

1a Herbert Hugh; b 3 June 1909; educ Trin Coll Cambridge (BA); P/O RAF WW II; m 14 Dec 1939 Kate Marjorie (d 1972), dau of Rev Vernon Iles, of Swindon, Wilts, and was ka 13 June 1942, leaving:

1b *Patricia [Mrs Ieuan Davies, Fistral, Southway Windmill, Padstow, Cornwall PL28 8RZ]; b 27 Nov 1940; m 20 March 1964 *Maj Ieuan Davies, 11th Hus (PAO), s of Evan Richard Davies, of Aberystwyth

(1) Nina Emily; b 4 July 1882; m 12 Sept 1907 Sir (Charles) Lennox Somerville Russell (d 31 Jan 1960), 2nd s of Capt Stuart Russell, and d 19 July 1976, having had:

1a Stuart Hugh Minto; b 18 Jan 1909; educ Rugby and Trin Coll Cambridge; MP Darwen 1935–43, PPS to: U-Sec Air 1937, Chllr Exchequer 1937–39; Capt Coldstream Gds WW II; das 30 Oct 1943

2a Raymond Lennox Somerville; b 11 April 1913; educ Eton and Trin Coll Cambridge; Lt RA WW II; das 17 July 1941

(2) Mabel Victoria; *b* 16 June 1884; Red Cross 1915–16, memb RSW 1930–50; *m* 1st 1916 Hugh Monro (*d* 28 July 1928); *m* 2nd 9 Oct 1929 William Stewart McGeorge, RSA (*d* 9 Nov 1931), of Gifford, E Lothian, and *d* 13 March 1960

4 William Fitzwilliam; *b* 14 Sept 1849; Lt-Col Princess Louise's Argyll & Sutherland Highrs, DAA Gen Dublin Dist 1881–84, War Off 1884–89 and NE Dist 1889–92, Zulu War 1879 (despatches, medal and clasp); *m* 1880 Elizabeth Fanny (*d* 4 Feb 1929), dau of John Rutherford, of Halifax, Nova Scotia, and *d* 16 Nov 1928, leaving:

(1) John Augustus Gilbert; *b* 26 Jan 1881; Lt Roy Scots Fus and Roy Scots Fus Boer War 1900–01 (severely wounded, medal and four clasps); Dist Offr Kenya Colony and E Africa Protectorate 1909–29; Freeman City London; *m* 5 Jan 1921 Ann Barbara, MBE (*d* 16 Jan 1970), dau of F Berkeley Matthews, of Langholm, Dumfriesshire, and *d* 3 June 1938, leaving:

1a John Martin; *b* 16 June 1922; *educ* Wellington; Maj Roy Scots Fus WW II; *ka* 6 April 1945

(1) Mary Adelaide; *b* 14 Nov 1883; *m* 27 Aug 1907 Sir John Hepburn Milne-Home, JP, DL (*d* 28 April 1963), 3rd s of Col Milne-Home, of Wedderburn, and *d* 8 Feb 1970, leaving issue

(2) Margaret Cecil Anne; *b* 17 March 1886; *m* 15 Nov 1904 Maj Frederick Adrian Cathcart and *d* 2 March 1956, leaving issue (*see* CATHCART, E)

The 3rd EARL's est son,

GILBERT JOHN ELLIOT-MURRAY-KYNYNMOUND, **4th Earl of Minto**, KG (1910), GCSI (1905), GCMG (1898), GCIE (1905), VD, PC (1902), DL (Selkirk and Roxburghshire); *b* 9 July 1845; *educ* Eton and Trin Coll Cambridge (BA, Hon LLD 1911); Lt Scots Gds, Capt Res of Offrs, Col Vols, Col and Brig-Gen cmdg Scottish Bdrs Vol Inf Bde, war correspondent *Morning Post* Carlist War Spain 1873–76, attd Turkish Army Russo-Turkish War 1877 (medal), Afghanistan 1879 (medal), Priv Sec to C-in-C S Africa 1881, Mounted Inf Egypt 1882 (wounded), cmded Mounted Inf Cairo (despatches, medal, 4th Cl Medjidie), NW Rebellion Canada as COS 1885 (despatches, medal with clasp), Mil Sec to Govr-Gen Canada 1883–86; Convener Roxburghshire CC, Ld Rector Edinburgh U 1911, Hon LLD Queen's U, Govr-Gen Canada 1898–1904, Viceroy India 1905–10 (as which partly responsible for Morley-Minto reforms which allowed a native memb onto the Viceroy's Exec Cncl), Brig Roy Co Archers, Br Del Internat Conf Rome 1905, KJStJ; rode five times in Grand National; *m* 28 July 1883 Mary Caroline (*d* 14 July 1940), CI, DJStJ, Extra Ldy Bedchamber to HM QUEEN MARY, dau of Gen Hon Charles Grey (*see* GREY, E), and *d* 1 March 1914, having had:

1 VICTOR GILBERT LARISTON GARNET, **5th Earl**

2 Gavin William Esmond; *b* 25 April 1895; Lt Scots Gds; *ka* 6 Aug 1917

1 Eileen Nina Evelyn Sibell; *b* 13 Dec 1884; *m* 11 Feb 1915 Lord Francis George Montagu-Douglas-Scott (*see* BUCCLEUCH and QUEENSBERRY, D) and *d* 29 May 1938, leaving issue

2 Ruby Florence Mary; *b* 26 Sept 1886; DGStJ, V-Pres OStJ London 1944–49; *m* 4 April 1908 2nd Earl of Cromer (*qv*) and *d* 5 Nov 1961, leaving issue

3 Violet Mary; *b* 28 May 1889; Controller Co of London ATS; CC Kent 1946–51, Hon Freedom Dover, DStJ; *m* 1st 20 Jan 1909 Lord Charles George Francis Mercer Nairne (*ka* 30 Oct 1914), yr s of 5th Marquess of Lansdowne (*qv*), and had issue; *m* 2nd 28 Aug 1916 1st Baron Astor of Hever (*qv*) and *d* 3 Jan 1965, having by him had further issue

The 4th EARL's er son,

VICTOR GILBERT LARISTON GARNET ELLIOT-MURRAY-KYNYNMOUND, **5th Earl of Minto**, JP (1924), DL (Roxburghshire 1942); *b* 12 Feb 1891; *educ* Eton; Capt Scots Gds (Res of Offrs), ADC to Govr-Gen Canada 1918–19, memb Roy Co Archers, FRCS; *m* 19 Jan 1921 Marion, OBE (1956) (*d* 16 Jan 1974), dau of George William Cook, of Westmount, Montreal, and *d* 11 Jan 1975, leaving:

1 GILBERT EDWARD GEORGE LARISTON, **6th and present Earl**

2 +(George Esmond) Dominic [The Hon Dominic Elliot, 88 St James's St, London SW1A 1PW]; *b* 13 Jan 1931; *educ* Eton and Madrid U; late Lt Scots Gds; *m* 1st 4 May 1962 (*divorce* 1970) Countess Marianne, only child of Count Maria Thomas Paul Esterhazy, of Geneva, and has had:

(1) Alexander; *b* 13 Feb 1963; *d* 1985

(2) +Esmond; *b* 8 Sept 1965

2 (cont.) The Hon Dominic Elliot *m* 2nd 25 June 1983 *Jane Caroline, dau of Laurence Alick Roger Reeve, of Bromham, Wilts, and by her has:

(3) +George William Hugh; *b* 1990

(1) *Violet Elizabeth Marion; *b* 1988

1 *Bridget [The Lady Bridget Miller Mundy, The Dower House, Crow Hall Farm, Denver, Norfolk PE38 0DG]; *b* 7 Dec 1921; *m* 1st 19 April 1944 (*divorce* 1954) Lt-Col James Averell Clark Jr, DFC, USAAF (*d* 1990), er s of James Averell Clark, of Long Island, and has issue; *m* 2nd 13 April 1954 (*divorce* 1963) Maj Henry Claude Lyon Garnett, CBE (*d* 1990), only s of Capt Claude Lyon Garnett, RA, of Lancaster; *m* 3rd 7 Oct 1966 (*divorce* 1970) Maj Edward Peter Godfrey Miller Mundy, MC (*d* 1981), only s of Maj Godfrey Edward Miller Mundy, of Derbys and Andover, Hants, and by her 1st husb has:

(1) *Christopher [Christopher Clark Esq, Crow Hall Farm, Denver, Norfolk PE38 0DG]; *b* 1949; *m* 1986 *Alice, only dau of Thomas Auckland Hall, of Rockland St Mary, and has:

1a *Thomas Averell; *b* 1987

2a *James Auckland; *b* 1994

1a *Scarlett Alexandra; *b* 1989

2 *Willa [The Lady Willa Chetwode, Swiss Farm House, Upper Slaughter, Glos GL54 2JP]; *b* 21 March 1924; *m* 9 Oct 1946 *Maj (George) David Chetwode (*see* CHETWODE, B) and has issue

MISHCON

Arms: Per pale argent and azure, between in chief and in base bar gennel wavy counterchanged a tent per pale azure and argent lined gules. **Crest:** Upon a wreath argent and azure a lion or and a lamb proper rampant, supporting between them a sword erect gules, the pommel resting on a book, bound azure, edged and garnished gold. **Supporters:** Dexter, a lamb regardant proper, gorged with a collar gules with flames issuing above and below proper; sinister, a lion regardant or, gorged with a Saxon crown azure. **Motto:** Dwell in peace. **Creation:** B. (LP, UK) 1978.

THE BARON MISHCON, of Lambeth, Greater London (Victor Mishcon, DL (Greater London)) [The Rt Hon The Lord Mishcon DL, House of Lords, London SW1A 0PW]; *b* 14 Aug 1915; *educ* City of London Sch; slr 1937; memb: Lambeth Borough Cncl 1945–49 (chm Fin Ctee 1947–49), LCC Brixton 1946–65, Standing Jt Ctee Co London Sessions 1950–65 (v-chm 1959–61), Govt Ctee Enquiry London Tport 1953–54, Deptl Ctee Homosexual Offences and Prostitution 1954–57, GLC Lambeth 1964–67 (Chm Gen Purposes Ctee 1964–67), ILEA 1964–67, Exec Ctee LTB 1965–67; V-Chm Cncl Christians and Jews 1976–77; V-Pres: Bd Deputies Br Jews 1967–73, Assoc Jewish Youth; Consultant Mishcon De Reya 1992– (sr ptnr 1988–92); Memb Bd: Nat Theatre 1965–90, London Orchestra 1966–67, South Bank Theatre 1977–82; Memb Ho Lds: EC Ctee Law Sub-Ctee 1978–86, Select Ctee Procedure 1981–83; Standing Jt Ctee with Commons Consolidation Bills 1983–85, Select Ctee Medical Ethics 1983–94, Select Ctee Medical Ethics 1993; V-Chm Lds and Commons Slrs' Gp 1983–; Oppn Spokesman: Home Affairs 1983–90, Legal Matters 1983–92; Pres Br Cncl Shaare Zedek Hospital Jerusalem; Chm Govrs: Cormont and Loughborough Secondary Schs 1947–60, Stockwell Manor Sch 1960–67 and 1970–78 (Govr 1960–78); Govr JFS Comprehensive Sch 1970–85, Phillipa Fawcett Coll of Ed 1970–80; Hon LLD Birmingham 1991; Hon QC 1992; Hon Fell UCL 1993; Cdr Roy Swedish Order of North Star 1954; Star of Ethiopia 1954; *m* 1st 1940 Jean Marie (*d* 1943), dau of L J Hydleman, JP; *m* 2nd 1945 (*divorce* 1959) Beryl Honor, dau of J E Posnansky, and has:

1 *Peter Arnold [The Hon Peter Mishcon, 89 Elgin Crescent, London W11 2JF]; *b* 1946; architect; *m* 1967 *Penny Green and has:

(1) *Oliver; *b* 1968

(1) *Anna; *b* 1972; documentary producer

(2) *Kate; *b* 1973

(3) *Eliza; *b* 1977; *educ* Godolphin and Latymer; singer

2 *Russell Orde [The Hon Russell Mishcon, Wick Lodge, Englefield Green, Surrey TW20 0HJ]; *b* 1948; *educ* City of London Sch; *m* 1975 *Marcia Regina Leigh and has:

(1) *Joel; *b* 1977

(1) *Portia; *b* 1979

(2) *Honor Meg; *b* 1991

1 *Jane Malca; *b* 1950; *m* 1st 1971 (*divorce*1979) Anthony Jay and has:

(1) *Adam; *b* 1972

(1) *Lucy, *b* 1974

1 (cont.) The Hon Mrs Jane Jay *m* 2nd 1990 *Edward Landau

The BARON MISHCON *m* 3rd 1976 *Joan Estelle, dau of Bernard Monty

Lineage: Rabbi ARNOLD MISHCON; *m* Queenie — and had:

VICTOR, *cr* a **Baron**

MOIR

MOLESWORTH

Arms: Arg. a span of a bridge enarched, embattled and in perspective, chequy or and az., between three Moor's heads couped sa., each banded of the second and third and distilling three drops of blood ppr. **Crest:** Upon a span of a bridge as in the arms a Moor's head affrontée, couped at the shoulders sa., banded or and az., collared chequy of the same. **Motto:** *Virtute non aliter* ('By virtue, not otherwise'). **Creation:** Bt. (UK) 11 July 1916.

SIR ERNEST IAN ROYDS MOIR, 3RD BT, of Whitehanger, Fernhurst, Sussex [Sir Ernest Moir Bt, Three Gates, 174 Coombe Lane West, Kingston-upon-Thames, Surrey KT2 7DE]; *b* 9 June 1925; *s f* 1957; *educ* Rugby, Gonville and Caius Coll Cambridge (BA 1949); RE WW II; *m* 24 July 1954 *Margaret Hanham, dau of George Eric Carter, of Cranbrook, Netheroyd Hill, Huddersfield, and has:

1 +CHRISTOPHER ERNEST [Christopher Moir Esq, 77 Dora Rd, London SW19 7JT]; *b* 22 May 1955; *educ* King's Coll Sch Wimbledon; *m* 1983 *Vanessa, yr dau of Victor Alfred Crosby, of Wimbledon, and formerly w of Joseph William Kirtikar, and has:

  (1) +Oliver Royds; *b* 1984

  (2) +Alexander Victor; *b* 1984 (twin)

2 +Timothy James; *b* 19 June 1959

3 +Nicholas Ian (Rev); *b* 7 June 1961; *m* 17 April 1998 *Rosalind, er dau of John Love, of Llangybi, Gwent

Lineage: ALEXANDER MITCHELL MOIR, of Hampstead; *d* 1907, leaving a 3rd s:

Sir Ernest William Moir, 1st Bt (UK), so *cr* 11 July 1916; *b* 9 June 1862; civil engr, Pres Jr Instn Engrs 1929, Capt RE (T), Min Munitions Rep US and Comptroller Munitions Inventions WW I, Offr Legion Honour, headed Ernest William Moir & Co, dir S Pearson and Sons, contractors, MICE, MAmSocCE, MAI, Fell UCL; *m* 1 June 1887 Margaret Bruce, OBE (1920) (*d* 5 Oct 1942), dau of John Pennycook, of Ravelston and Dalmeny, Midlothian, and had:

1 Reginald; *b* 1 Jan 1893; *educ* Caius Coll Cambridge (BA); Lt RE; *das* 9 Nov 1915

2 ARROL (Sir), **2nd Bt**

3 Edward; *b* and *d* 25 Sept 1907

Sir ERNEST *d* 14 June 1933; his only surv s:

Sir Arrol Moir, 2nd Bt; *b* 16 Sept 1894; *educ* Repton and Gonville and Caius Coll Cambridge (BA 1919); Capt RE WW I, MICE, V-Pres Inst Patentees, Hon Memb Br IRE (Past Pres), MRI; *m* 21 June 1922 *Dorothy Blanche (*m* 2nd 8 June 1960 Dr Robert William Nichol, est s of Dr F E Nichol, of Margate, Kent), dau of Adml Sir Percy Royds, CB, CMG, and *d* 8 Aug 1957, leaving:

1 Sir ERNEST IAN ROYDS MOIR, **3rd and present Bt**

1 June Pamela; WRNS WW II; *b* 22 Nov 1923; *m* 18 June 1949 Ian Colin Wetherell (Ian Colin, actor), s of Marmaduke Arundel Wetherell, of Rhodesia and Richmond, Surrey, and *d* 1984, leaving:

  (1) *Peter Arrol Royds; *b* 29 July 1953

2 Joy Yvonne; *b* 13 Aug 1927, *m* 1st 4 Sept 1948 (*divorce* 1954) Sir Baldwin Patrick Walker, 4th Bt, of Oakley House (*qv*); *m* 2nd 2 July 1954 (*divorce* 19–) Michael Haggerty, s of Charles Haggerty, of Vancouver, and *d* 1996, leaving:

  (1) John Wyeth; *b* 1957; *d* 199–

  (1) *Susan Bret; *b* 1955

  (2) *Gillian Ruth; *b* 1958

Arms: Gules an escutcheon vair between eight cross-crosslets in orle or. **Crest:** A dexter arm embowed in armour proper, holding a cross-crosslet or. **Supporters:** Dexter, a pegasus argent, wings elevated or; sinister, a pegasus, wings elevated gules, semé of cross-crosslets, winged, crined and tailed or. **Motto:** *Vincit amor patriæ* ('Patriotism prevails'). **Creation:** V. (I) 16 July 1716.

THE 12TH VISCOUNT MOLESWORTH OF SWORDS, Co Dublin, and **Lord Molesworth, Baron of Philipstown,** in King's County (Robert Bysse Kelham Molesworth) [The Rt Hon The Viscount Molesworth, 22 Miranda Rd, London N19 3RB]; *b* 4 June 1959; *s f* 1997; *educ* Cheltenham and Sussex U (BA)

Lineage: Sir ROGER MOLESWORTH, of Huntingdon, had:

JOHN MOLESWORTH, of Helpeston, Northants; Escheator (roy official implementing escheats, or reversions to the Crown of property held from it on death of tenant) Rutland; *d* 1542, leaving:

JOHN MOLESWORTH; *b* 1516; *m* Margaret, dau and heiress of William Westcott, of Hansacre, Staffs, and had, with other issue, including a yr s (John, of Pencarrow, had issue; see MOLESWORTH-ST AUBYN, Bt):

ANTHONY MOLESWORTH; *m* Cicely, dau and heiress of Thomas Hurland, of Fotheringhay, Northants, which he thus acquired but which he was forced to sell when in debt; his er s:

WILLIAM MOLESWORTH; *m* Mary, dau of Sir Francis Palmes, of Ashwell, Rutland, and had, with two er sons (Guy, royalist Col of Horse Civil War; Edward, Capt of Foot 1642, Maj-Gen, *m* — Hatbean and had three daus (Mary; Jane; Frances)):

ROBERT MOLESWORTH; Offr in Civil War in Ireland, where he later subscribed £1,500 (some £54,000 in late-1990s terms) for 2,500 acres in the (territorial) Baronies of Moghergallin and Lune, Co Meath; also a Dublin merchant; *m* Judith (*m* 2nd Sir William Tichborne, of Beaulieu, Co Louth), est dau and coheir of John Bysse, Ld Ch Baron Exchequer Ireland, and *d* 3 Sept 1656, leaving:

ROBERT MOLESWORTH, **1st Viscount Molesworth of Swords,** Co Dublin, so *cr* 16 July 1716, as also LORD MOLESWORTH, BARON OF PHILIPSTOWN, King's County (both I), PC (I 1679, 1702–13/4 and 1715); *b* 7 Sept 1656; *educ* Trin Coll Dublin; Williamite 1689 (when attainted by JAMES II's Irish Parl 7 May), Envoy Denmark 1689–92, MP (Whig) Camelford (E Parl) 1695–98, Dublin (I Parl) 1695–99, Swords 1703–14, Lostwithiel (E Parl) 1705–06, E Retford (E and GB Parls) 1706–08 and St Michael 1715–22, Commr Trade and Plantations 1714–15; *m* 16 Aug 1676 Laetitia, 3rd dau of Richard Coote, 1st Baron Coote of Coloowney, and sis of 1st Earl of Bellomont (see COOTE, Bt), and *d* 22 May 1725, having had 17 children, including (*d* unm):

1 JOHN MOLESWORTH, **2nd Viscount Molesworth of Swords**; *bapt* 4 Dec 1679; Commr Stamp Office 1706, Commr Trade and Plantations 1715–20, Min Florence, Venice and Genoa, Envoy Turin 1720–25; *m* Sept 1718 Mary, dau and coheir of Thomas Middleton, of Stanstead Hall, Stanstead Mountfichet, Essex, and *dspm* 17 Feb 1725/6, leaving:

  (1) Mary; *b* posthumously 8 May 1726; *m* 1751 Frederick Gore, MP (see GORE, Bt)

2 RICHARD MOLESWORTH, **3rd Viscount Molesworth of Swords**, PC (I 1733); Offr 1702, Ensign and Capt Roy Regt of Foot, Capt Coldstream Gds, ADC to 1st Duke of Marlborough (*qv*) at Battle of Ramillies 1706, raised a regt (19th Light Dragoons) for suppression 1715 Uprising (wounded Preston), Lt Ordnance 1714–18, Col Molesworth's Foot (later Roy Inniskilling Fus) 1725–32, 9th Dragoons 1732–37 and 5th Dragoons 1737–58, Maj-Gen 1735, Lt Gen 1739, Gen 1746, Gen of Horse 1741, C-in-C Ireland 1751, FM 1757, MP (I Parl) Swords 1715–26; *m* 1st Jane Lucas (*d* 1 April 1742) and had:

  (1) Mary; *m* 1 Aug 1736 1st Earl of Belvidere (*d* 13 Nov 1774)

  (2) Letitia; *m* 2 Oct 1753 Lt-Col James Molesworth and *d* 1787

  (3) Amelia; *d* unm 30 Jan 1758

2 (cont.) The **3rd Viscount** *m* 2nd 7 Feb 1743/4 Mary (*d* in a fire with her daus, Melosina and Mary, 6 May 1763), dau of Ven William Ussher, Archdeacon Clonfert, and *d* 12 Oct 1758, having by her had:

(1) RICHARD NASSAU MOLESWORTH, **4th Viscount Molesworth of Swords**; *b* 4 Nov 1748; *d* unm 3 June 1793

3 William; Capt in the wars with Spain, MP Philipstown, Commr Trade and Plantations; *m* 1726 Anne, est dau of Robert Adair, of Holybrook, Co Wicklow, and had, with six daus:

(1) ROBERT MOLESWORTH, **5th Viscount Molesworth of Swords**; *bapt* 22 Dec 1729; *m* 18 Aug 1761 Mary Anne Bushe (*d* 2 Aug 1819), widow, dau of Israel Alleyne, of Cork, and *d* 29 Jan 1813, having had:

1a WILLIAM JOHN MOLESWORTH, **6th Viscount Molesworth of Swords**; *b* 18 Aug 1763; Maj-Gen, Lt-Col 95th Foot; *m* — and was lost with her on board the *Arniston* near the Cape of Good Hope on their passage from Ceylon 30 May 1815

2a Walter; *d* 1783

3a Robert; *b* 16 April 1768; *m* 27 Sept 1793 Hon Mary Jones (*d* 25 Feb 1814), est dau of 4th Viscount Ranelagh, and *d* April 1814, leaving:

1b Henrietta Sarah; *d* 9 Feb 1834

2b Mary Annette; *d* 27 Feb 1831

4a Richard; *d* 19 Sept 1793

1a Anne; *m* 1st 27 Dec 1792 John Foster Hill; *m* 2nd 1807 Baron de Mallet and had issue

2a Jane; *m* John Stephenson

(2) John; *d* unm

(3) Richard; *b* 1737; *m* Catherine, dau of Francis Cobb, of Twickenham, and *d* 29 Sept 1799, leaving:

1a RICHARD PIGOTT MOLESWORTH, **7th Viscount Molesworth of Swords**; *b* 23 July 1786; *d* unm 20 June 1875

2a Francis; Lt RN; *dsp* 23 May 1812

3a John; Capt RN; *m* 6 Feb 1828 Louisa (*d* 11 Aug 1873), dau of Rev Dr Tomkyns, and *d* 14 Aug 1858, leaving:

1b SAMUEL, **8th Viscount**

1b Margaret Letitia; *m* 4 April 1866 Rev Charles Richard de Havilland (*d* 6 Feb 1901), and *d* 27 Jan 1910, leaving issue

2b Mary Louisa; *m* 8 Nov 1876 Rev Canon Edward Carr, LLD, Vicar St Helens, and *d* 30 March 1914. He *dsp* 1886

4a Anthony Oliver, Capt RA; *b* 23 Oct 1793; *m* 1st 26 April 1827 Jane, dau of John Potter; *m* 2nd 7 July 1835 Grace Jane (*d* 12 April 1897), dau of Morgan Crofton (*see* CROFTON, Bt, of Mohill), and *d* 9 July 1848, having by her had:

1b Richard; Maj Roy Dragoons; *b* 3 May 1836; *m* 24 July 1861 Mary Louisa (*d* 20 July 1921), est dau of Charles Augustus Stewart, of High Leigh, Cheshire, and *d* 2 April 1900, leaving, with a s (*d* an infant) and two daus (*d* unm):

1c Richard Bevil; *b* 10 Nov 1870; *d* unm 13 March 1898

2c Lionel Charles; *b* 18 March 1873; *m* 10 Nov 1896 Saba Maud (*d* 25 April 1956), yst dau of Sir Henry Delves Broughton, 9th Bt (*qv*), and *d* 23 Dec 1916, leaving:

1d Roger Bevil; Col RA NW Frontier India 1929–30, Waziristan 1942 (despatches); *b* 7 May 1901; *m* 28 Feb 1929 Iris Alice (*d* 26 March 1977), dau of Lt-Col Roger Lloyd Kennion CIE, of Tullecombe, Rogate, and *d* 14 July 1974, leaving:

1e +Allen Henry Neville [Allen Molesworth Esq, 31 Norland Square, London W11 4PU]; *b* 20 Aug 1931; *educ* Cambridge (MA); Lt Shropshire Yeo (RAC); *m* 1970 *Gail Cheng Kwai, LRMM, ARCM, LGSM, dau of L C Chang, of Singapore

2d Hender Delves; *b* 10 Feb 1907; Keeper Dept Architecture and Sculpture V&A 1946–54, Keeper Dept of Woodwork 1954; *m* 14 March 1935 Evelyn Carnegy Helena (*d* 24 March 1995), dau of Malcolm Galloway, of Shelley Hall, Ongar, Essex, and *d* 20 April 1978

1d Violet Saba; *b* 6 Aug 1897; *m* 7 Dec 1925 Ernest Godfrey Mills and had issue. He *d* 1964

1c Mary Cicely Caroline; *m* 29 July 1893 James Charles Prinsep, s of Charles Robert Prinsep, of Calcutta, and *d* 19 Jan 1950, leaving issue

2c Louisa Juliet Marion; *m* 15 Dec 1898 Julian Grant Duff AINSLIE later GRANT DUFF (deed poll 22 Nov 1927) and *d* 31 March 1925, leaving issue. He *d* 16 April 1937

2b Morgan Crofton; Capt RE; *b* 3 May 1837; *m* 30 April 1862 Georgina (*d* 4 Sept 1906), only child of Abraham Duke, FRCS, of The Hollies, Rugby, and *d* 10 July 1867, leaving:

1c Herbert Crofton St George; *b* 1 Feb 1863; Maj RA WW I; *m* 31 Jan 1891 Adeline Stella (*d* 26 Dec 1959), dau of Charles Edward Hutton, and *d* 26 Aug 1933, leaving:

1d Adrienne Cicely Monica; *m* Capt A W P Phillips, of Vancouver, BC, and *d* 10 March 1955

2d Vivienne Yseulte Doreen, MBE (1958); 1st Sec Visa Dept UK Embassy Istanbul; *d* unm 30 Jan 1968

3d Georgina Evelyn Hutton; *d* unm 11 May 1990

1c Lilian Mary Grace; *d* unm 11 June 1951

2c Georgina Beatrice; *m* 20 Oct 1904 Hugh Perronet Thompson, est s of Gen C W Thompson, 14th Hus, of Wethersfield Place, Braintree, Essex, and *d* 2 Dec 1916. He *d* 18 Jan 1937

3b Anthony Oliver; Lt-Col RA; *b* 14 Aug 1839; *m* 23 March 1865 Anne Elizabeth (*d* 13 April 1910), yr dau of Maj William Hope Smith, HEICS, of Cruicksfield, Berwicks, and *d* 11 March 1917, leaving:

1c William, CIE (1914), CBE (1918); *b* 30 Dec 1865; *educ* Bristol and Durham Us; Col IMS, MB, BS, MRCS, LRCP, Surgn to Govr Madras 1899–1904 and 1905–08 and Viceroy India 1904, Dep Dir Medical Serv HQ India 1916, served Wuntho Field Force Burma 1891 (medal with clasp); *m* 9 March 1893 Winifred Anne (*d* 9 July 1960), dau of Thomas Earle Weeks, JP, of Hazlesdean, Monkstown, Co Cork, and *d* 27 Feb 1951, leaving:

1d William Earle, MC (1917) and bar (1918); *b* 14 March 1894; *educ* Marlborough; Lt-Col Roy Tank Regt, Roy Munster Fus, RFC, and RAF, WW I (despatches, Silver Medal Italy), SEO WW II, Min Supply

1941–54; *m* 1 June 1918 Dorothy Loftus (*d* 1985), dau of Col St George Loftus Steele, CB, and *d* 22 Oct 1955, leaving:

1e *Pamela [Mrs Robert Langham, 19 Alexandra Rd, Reading, Berks]; *b* 14 March 1919; *m* 15 Dec 1950 Robert Anthony Langham, yr s of Capt Clement Arthur Langham, of Stamford Lodge, Reading, and has:

1f *Peter Anthony [Peter Langham Esq, Silverdale, Woodmead Rd, Lyme Regis, Dorset]; *b* 28 April 1953; *m* 1983 *Cynthia Maynard and has:

1g *Catherine; *b* 1984

1f *Susan Marie [Mrs Raymond Purdy, 100 Upper North St, Brighton, Sussex]; *b* 1 Nov 1951; *m* 1982 *Raymond Purdy and has:

1g *Daniel; *b* 1982

1g *Lara; *b* 1985

2d Kathleen Winifred; *m* 1919 Alfred Allyson Fennell Minchin, Indian Forest Service, of Berwicks, s of Henry Paul Minchin, of Greenhills, Co Tipperary, and Ensleigh, Bath, and had issue. He *d* 10 June 1973

2c Hugh Wilson, CBE (1922); *b* 9 Sept 1870; *educ* Cooper's Hill Coll; Assist U-Sec Min Public Works Cairo (3rd Cl Medjidie, 4th Cl Osmanieh, 2nd Cl Order Nile), Lt-Col Suez Canal Defences WW I (despatches); *m* 7 July 1903 Dora Hanbury (*d* 26 Feb 1972), only dau of Maj Sir Hanbury Brown, KCMG, RE, and *d* 5 Jan 1959, leaving:

1d (Hugh) Mervyn, FCA (1931), of Broad Oak, Copthorne, Sussex; *b* 19 July 1907; *educ* Marlborough and Sidney Sussex Coll Cambridge (BA 1928); *m* 1st 16 March 1934 (*divorce* 1936) Mary Langhorne, yr dau of Henry Langhorne Johnson, CBE, MA, of Hurst, Copthorne; *m* 2nd 24 Nov 1939 Enid Mary (*d* 22 Oct 1969), dau of John Utrick Roger Grave, AMICE, of Kersal Bank, Manchester, and Shanghai, China, and *d* 1980, having by her had:

1e +Roger Molesworth Esq, Little Jordans, Colgate, Sussex]; *b* 6 Oct 1945; *educ* Marlborough; *m* 1974 *Pauline Fay, dau of Philip Hunt, of Wood Green, London N22

2e +Donald [Donald Molesworth Esq, Balmoral, Benenden, Kent]; *b* 26 June 1948; *educ* Embley Park Sch; *m* 1982 *Charlotte Rosalie Penelope, dau of J W K Cox, of Green Lane Farm, Challock, Kent

2d Denys Hope, MC, of Rory Cottage, Forest Row, Sussex; Lt-Col RA WW II (wounded, POW) and Malaya 1951 (despatches); *b* 12 Aug 1910; *educ* Marlborough; *m* 22 June 1945 Dorothy May (*d* 1984), yr dau of William Connell Johnston, of Calcutta, and *d* 1989, leaving:

1e *(Gillian) Tessa [Mrs Juan Molesworth de Planells, Barrio Ses, Torres 61, Jésus, Ibiza 07819, Balearic Islands]; *b* 24 Aug 1946; *m* 5 Jan 1972 *Juan Planells, of Ibiza, and has:

1f *Nicolas Juan; *b* 29 March 1973

1f *Emma Maria; *b* 15 April 1976

2f *Sara Luisa; *b* 8 Aug 1980

2e *Jennifer Margaret [Mrs Farad Azima, 9 Orchard Gate Barn, Wittington Green, Bucks SL7 2ES]; *b* 6 July 1948; *m* 1984 *Farad Azima and has:

1f *Cyrus Alexander; *b* 2 Jan 1985

1f *Artemis Natasha; *b* 10 Dec 1986

1d Eileen Rose; *b* 30 June 1904; *m* 15 Oct 1931 *Lt-Col Basil Woods Ballard, CIE, MBE, Indian Political Serv, s of Frederick George Ballard, and *d* 1980 leaving:

1e *Timothy John, MICE (1962) [Timothy Woods Ballard Esq, Harpsden Way, Henley, Oxon RG9 1NX]; *b* 24 July 1932; *educ* Marlborough and Sidney Sussex Coll Cambridge (BA 1955, MA 1968), FICE; *m* 5 Sept 1964 *Helen Mary, only dau of John Clifford Christopherson, and has:

1f *Patrick Robert; *b* 10 March 1975

1f *Bridget Anne; *b* 15 March 1970

2f *Jennifer Clare; *b* 14 Nov 1971

2e *William Richard [William Woods Ballard Esq, Olivers Cottage, 101 The Street, Capel St Mary, Suffolk IP9 2EH]; *b* 23 Dec 1933; *educ* Marlborough and Coll of Aeronautics Cranfield (MSc 1958); CEng, MIMechE, MRAeS; *m* 1 April 1967 *Marianne Jean Elspeth, yr dau of Lt-Col Hugh Arbuthnott (*see* ARBUTHNOTT, V), and has:

1f *Hugh William; *b* 22 Nov 1968

2f *Andrew James; *b* 1976

3c Ernest Kerr; Maj RE Tibet Expdn (medal); *b* 28 March 1878; *m* 31 May 1905 Hilda Rosalie (*d* 16 Aug 1943), yst dau of Lt-Gen Henry Alexander Brownlow, RE, and was accidentally *kas* 31 Dec 1914, leaving:

1d Brownlow David, of Hunthay, Axminster, Devon; *b* 10 Feb 1913; *educ* Emmanuel Coll Cambridge (BA 1934, MB and BChir 1937); Colonial Med Service Malaya, MRCS, IRCP; *m* 15 July 1939 Rosemary Katharine (*d* 1989), dau of Lt-Col A W Moore, RAMC, and *d* 1986, leaving:

1e +Patrick David [Patrick Molesworth Esq, 5 Mervyn Road, Bristol BSY 9EL]; *b* 7 Oct 1946; *m* 1974 *Shelia Doreen Cooling and has:

1f *Peter Patrick; *b* 1983

2f *Ian David; *b* 1985

2e +Anthony Simon; *b* 10 Sept 1955

1e *Jenifer Rosemary [Mrs Peter Rohde, 84 Burbage Rd, London SE24]; *b* 14 June 1940; *m* 1961 *Dr Peter David Rohde, FRC Psych, FRCP Ed, er s of Lt-Col Robert Hawkins Rohde, and has:

1f *Simon Peter; *b* 22 June 1962; *m* 1988 *Juliette Ann Louise Hinchliff and has:

1g *Florence Rebecca; *b* 1992

1f *Katherine Leslie; *b* 3 Nov 1963; *m* 1991 *Paul Simon Bogan and has:

1g *Raphael David; b 1993

2e *Sheila [Mrs Jeremy Harvey, Obridge House, Obridge Rd, Taunton, Somerset TA2 7QA]; b 6 June 1942; m 29 July 1967 *(Charles) Jeremy Harvey, s of Reginald Charles Harvey, and has:

1f *Benjamin David; b 1972

1f *Rachel Claire; b 25 April 1969

2f *Joanna Elizabeth; b 1970

1d Mollie Rosalie; b 11 March 1907; m 1 Oct 1935 Arthur Durnford Iliff, OBE, MRCS, LRCP, s of Rev A Iliff, and d 12 Oct 1935 following a car crash

4c Francis Crofton; b 26 July 1880; Col RE, WW I, South Persia 1918–19 and Afghan War 1919 (despatches), FRGS, FRAS; m 4 Feb 1913 Eileen (d 27 May 1951), est dau of Lt-Col Richard Denny (see DENNY, Bt, of Castle Moyle), and d 27 June 1955, leaving:

1d +Richard Denny [Richard Molesworth Esq, 25 Naunton Way, Cheltenham, Glos]; b 17 Dec 1919; AInstPI; m 1972 *Eva Emily Elizabeth Bowler

2d +Stephen Lindsay [Stephen Molesworth Esq, 42 Chalcot Crescent, London NW1]; b 27 Jan 1925; served WW II 1944 (wounded, despatches), ARIBA; m 1959 *Eve Lovie and has:

1e +Ivan Alexander; b 1964

1e *Anna Cordelia; b 1960

2e *Polly; b 1967

1d *Beatrix; b 23 Aug 1917

5c Anthony Oliver (Rev); b 21 Jan 1882; public preacher Exeter Diocese 1932, civil engr, PWD Burma; m 12 Feb 1907 Melita (d 29 Dec 1931), 2nd dau of Harry Lindsay Tilly, Burma Commn, and d 21 Sept 1953, having had:

1d Anthony Oliver; b 7 Aug 1908; G/Capt RAF WW II; m 8 Aug 1933 *Noelle, yst dau of John Richard Holmes, of Newton Abbot, Pres District Court Cyprus, and was kas 15 Aug 1944, leaving:

1e *Dawn Noëlle [Mrs Simon Muirhead, 61 Merton Hall Road, London SW19 3PR]; b 4 July 1934; m 12 Nov 1955 *Simon Jerrard Findlay Muirhead, only s of L Russell Muirhead, and has:

1f *Anthony Oliver Molesworth [Anthony Muirhead Esq, 3777 Caribeth Drive, Encino, CA 91436, USA]; b 29 May 1957; educ Edinburgh U (MA); m 1985 *Cora Ann, only child of Martin D Seiler, of Studio City, Calif., and has:

1g *Molly Laura; b 1991

2f *Lauriston Philip [Lauriston Muirhead Esq, 409 Nowland Avenue, Lavington, NSW 2641, Australia]; b 21 Oct 1959; educ Newcastle U (BSc); m 1984 *Katherine Barbara, dau of John Rutty, of Kuantan, Malaya, and has:`

1g *Dauntie Claire; b 1989

1f *Imogen Jane; b 10 Dec 1962; educ Edinburgh U (MA, MSc)

1d *Elizabeth Melita [Mrs Elizabeth Lawson, Rock House, Yetminster, Dorset DT9 6LL]; b 10 Oct 1911; m 20 May 1933 (divorce 1962) Robert James Neale Lawson, s of R-Adml Robert Neale Lawson, CB, and has:

1e *Neale Anthony [Neale Lawson Esq, Caerlaverock House, Bank End, Dumfries DE1 4RL]; b 31 Dec 1935; educ King's Sch Bruton; CEng, DipEE, MIEE; m 12 Dec 1964 *Jennifer Jill, yr dau of Brig J M C Hoblyn, of Manor Farm, Ashmore, Wilts, and has:

1f *Susanna Joy [Mrs Mark Bedford, 6 The Green, Malshanger, Hants RG23 7EU]; b 23 Dec 1965; m 21 Dec 1991 *Mark David Wyatt Bedford, 3rd s of Peter Wyatt Bedford, and has:

1g *David Benedict James; b 9 July 1993

1g *Matilda Isabelle Wyatt; b 22 April 1995

2f *Elizabeth Ann [Miss Elizabeth Lawson, 61 Fauldburn, East Craigs, Edinburgh EH12 8YQ]; b 18 April 1968; MEng

1e *Priscilla Joy [Mrs Henry Moule, Horders, Compton Abbas, Dorset SP7 0NQ]; b 21 June 1938; m 1st 21 Sept 1957 John Patrick Charles Rucker (d 20 March 1967), s of Charles Edward Rucker, MC, of South's Farm, Ashmore; m 2nd 19– *Henry Moule, MA, s of Edward Christopher Moule, of Sherborne and by her 1st husb has:

1f *Prudence Elizabeth [Mrs Richard Bell Davies, Crossways, Denmead, Portsmouth, Hants]; b 18 July 1958; educ Kingston U (BA); m 7 Aug 1993 *Cdr Richard William Bell Davies, RN, s of V-Adml Sir Lancelot Bell Davies, KBE, of Hamble, Hants, and has:

1g *Camilla Sophie Rucker; b 16 Feb 1995

2g *Miranda Charlotte Rucker; b 5 July 1996

2f *Nancy Jane [Mrs Benjamin Thompson, 10 Walton Cres, Oxford]; b 21 June 1960; educ Clare Coll Cambridge (MA); m 14 Sept 1985 *Dr Benjamin John Thompson, s of Rt Rev Hewlett Thompson, Bp Exeter, and has:

1g *Humphrey John Rucker; b 26 May 1995

1g *Hermione Elizabeth Rucker; b 26 Oct 1990

2g *Eleanor Clare Rucker; b 17 Aug 1992

3f *Venetia Frances [Ms Venetia Rucker, 55 York Rd, Montpelier, Bristol]; b 31 May 1963; educ Liverpool Art Coll (BA)

4f *Sophia Damaris [Mrs David Brown, c/o Hordere, Compton Abbas, Shaftesbury, Dorset]; b 24 Sept 1965; educ Goldsmith's Coll London U (BA); m 14 Dec 1991 *Maj David Alfred John Brown, Glosters, s of Alan Brown, of Godalming, Surrey

2e *Melita Frances [Mrs Patrick Moule, Ryall's Ground, Yetminster, Dorset DT9 6LL]; b 22 April 1943; m 11 Sept 1971 *Patrick Fenton Moule, 2nd s of Edward Christopher Moule, of Sherborne, and has:

1f *Christopher Andrew Fenton; b 2 Dec 1974; educ Winchester and Cambridge (BA)

2f *Timothy James Neale; b 19–; educ Winchester

1c Evelyn; m 1892 Maj Harry E Harington Rice, IA, and d Nov 1939, leaving issue

2c Maud St George; m 17 Aug 1898 Lt-Col Walter Rothney Battye, DSO, IMS, s of Maj Legh Richmond Battye, and d 9 May 1958, leaving issue. He d 27 April 1943

3c Winefred Grace; m 1896 Lt-Col James Hanson William Tapp, DSO, RA, and d 9 March 1958, leaving issue. He d May 1951

4c Rose Miriam; m 29 Jan 1935 Lt-Col Kennedy de la Poer Beresford (see WATERFORD, M) and d 27 Nov 1951

4b William Robert, Lt RA; b 1841; d 15 Sept 1864

1b Mary; m 15 Jan 1863 Rev William Sykes and d 7 Sept 1918, leaving issue (see SYKES, Bt, of Cheadle)

2b Kate Charlotte Eleanor; m 21 July 1880 Thomas Duke and d 12 Jan 1929, leaving issue. He d May 1916

3b Grace Jane Sarah; m 27 July 1869 Rev John Marshall Collard, Vicar W Fordington, Dorchester, 4th s of Rev John Marshall Collard, of Tuffley, Glos, and d 17 Sept 1924, leaving issue (see STARKEY, Bt). He d 25 May 1917

4b Amelia Frances; m 30 Aug 1881 Rev Walter Oswald Wait, BCL, Vicar Titley, Herefs, and d 15 Dec 1928

5a James Thomas; d 13 July 1872

1a Wilhelmina; m 5 May 1804 Bartholomew Jeffery and d 7 May 1866. He d 1842

2a St George Catherine; d 4 May 1858

3a Salome Letitia; m Rev John Boucher and d 1829

4 Edward, Maj; m 1st Sept 1718 Catherine (dsp Jan 1731), dau and coheir of Thomas Middleton, of Stansted, Essex; m 2nd Catherine — (dsp 15 Feb 1748); m 3rd 26 March 1750 Mary Renouard and d 29 Nov 1768, having by her had:

(1) John; bapt 14 Feb 1751; m 13 June 1786 Frances (d 17 Jan 1848), est dau of Matthew Hill, and d 24 April 1791, leaving:

1a John Edward Nassau (Rev); DD, Vicar Rochdale; b 5 Feb 1790; m 1st 28 Nov 1815 Harriet (d 7 Dec 1850), dau of William Mackinnon, and had:

1b William Nassau (Rev); LLD Cantab, Hon Canon Manchester, Vicar Spotland, Lancs; b 8 Nov 1816; m 3 Sept 1844 Margaret (d 2 Nov 1913), dau of George Murray, of Ancoats Hall, and d 19 Dec 1890, having had, with other issue:

1c James Murray, JP (Warwicks); b 19 Jan 1849; FRGS,Warwicks: CA and memb TFA, Mayor Leamington 1899–1900; m 11 Nov 1891 Emily Maria (d 19 May 1945), dau of Robert Leech, and d 3 Dec 1924, leaving:

1d Robert Murray Nassau; b 11 June 1895; educ Haileybury and RMC Sandhurst; Lt Res of Offrs 2nd Bn Gordon Highrs WW I (wounded); m 1st 4 Feb 1916 (divorce 1925) Lucie Amy Gertrude (d 1971), 2nd dau of Edward Lawrence, of Clifton, Bristol; m 2nd 4 April 1926 Nora Madalene, dau of William John Connell, of Sparkhill, Birmingham, and by her had:

1e *Emily Patrica; b 20 Jan 1927; m — Reid

1d (cont.) Robert Molesworth m 3rd 1955 *Clare, widow of T W Price, and d 1976

2c Alexander, of Hamer Hall, Lancs, JP, slr; b 8 Sept 1851; d 12 May 1924

3c William Nassau; b 28 Oct 1853; m 1882 Clara (d 22 April 1914), dau of Thomas Healey, of Howarth Cross, Rochdale, and d 2 Dec 1929, leaving:

1d William Nassau, MC; b 1888; educ Haileybury; Maj 6th Bn Manchester Regt WW I (twice wounded, despatches twice); m 24 Nov 1917 Hester Winifred (d 11 Sept 1966), dau of Alfred Watkin, JP, of Dane Bank, Lymm, and d 15 Nov 1959, leaving:

1e +Anthony Edward Nassau (Rev Canon) [The Rev Canon Anthony Molesworth, 3 Barrow Hill, Stourton Caundle, Dorset DT10 2LD]; b 23 June 1923; educ Haileybury, Pembroke Coll Cambridge (BA 1945, MA 1948) and Coll Resurrection Mirfield; Mission Priest Swaziland, Rector St Anne's Pigg's Peak and Mission District Mhohho 1960, Canon Pro-Cathedral St Michael and All Angels Eshowe Diocese of Zululand 1963–68 and Swaziland 1968–71, Canon Diocese of Swaziland 1968, Canon Emeritus 1971; m 15 Aug 1969 *Susan, SRN, SCM, RN, MTD, yr dau of Prof Harold Robert Backwell Fenn, of Weald, Sevenoaks, and has:

1f +Hugh William Nassau; b 1972

1f *Anna Margaret; b 1970

1e *Gwendolen Clara Nassau [Lady Lloyd, 90 Carrington St, Macedon, Victoria 3440, Australia]; WAAF WW II; b 24 March 1919; m 1947 Maj Sir (John) Peter Daniel Lloyd, RA (d 1996), s of David Lloyd, of Menai Bridge, Anglesey, and has:

1f *David William Molesworth; b 20 Oct 1950; m 1977 Deborah Armstrong (d 1994) and has:

1g *Carson James; b 1978

1g *Zoë; b 1980

2f *John Peter Anthony; b 27 Oct 1956

1f *Judith Mary; b 24 Oct 1947; m 1st 1968 (divorce 1975) Robert Anthony Hyndes, of Sydney, NSW; m 2nd 1977 (divorce 1984) John Paul Kent and by her 1st husb has:

1g *Anthony Peter; b 1968

2f *Angela Hester Olwyn; b 20 June 1949; m 1st 1971 M J G Knox-Knight (d 1979) and has:

1g *Lucy Charlotte; b 1974

2g *Emily Sarah; b 1976

2f (cont.) Mrs Knox-Knight m 2nd 1983 *David Robert Langley and by him has:

3g *Jessica Penelope; b 1984

3f Penelope; b 17 Feb 1953; m 1976 *Adam Thomson and d 1996, leaving:

1g *Edward William; b 1986

2g *Hugh Lloyd; *b* 1988

1g *Alice Clara Margaret; *b* 1992

4f *Sarah Jane; *b* 25 April 1955; *m* 1978 (*divorce* 1981) Robert Sheehy and has:

1g *Nicholas; *b* 1979

1d Dorothy Nassau; ARRC WW I; *b* 1883; *m* 20 Nov 1930 her cousin Eric Nassau Molesworth (*see below*)

4c Murray Crompton; *b* 14 March 1856; *d* 6 Feb 1897

5c Robert Francis Stuart; *b* 19 May 1858

6c Arthur Henry; *b* 14 Dec 1863

1c Margaret; *m* 8 Oct 1891 Rev Samuel Edmond Clarke, Vicar St Matthew's Burnley, Lancs, and *d* 25 April 1939, leaving issue. He *d* 18 Aug 1919

2b John; *b* 22 April 1818; *m* 5 Oct 1847 Mary (*d* 7 Sept 1878), dau of Laurence Newall, of Littleborough, and *d* 21 Dec 1886, having had:

1c Edward Newall MOLESWORTH later MOLESWORTH-HEPWORTH; *b* 1 July 1848; *m* 20 April 1880 Marion (*d* 23 Nov 1927), dau of Rev Francis Ley Bazeley, Rector Bideford, N Devon, and *d* 1 Jan 1918

2c Frederick Nassau; slr, Coroner Lancs; *b* 25 Oct 1850; *m* 14 Aug 1877 Emma Louisa (*d* 6 Dec 1908), dau of John Henry Davenport, and *d* 11 Oct 1920, leaving:

1d Eric Nassau; Coroner Lancs, 6th Bn Lancs Fus WW I (wounded); *b* 8 June 1878; *m* 1st 28 April 1909 Harriet Cicely (*d* 25 March 1928), yst dau of Rev Canon Harry Mitchell; *m* 2nd 20 Nov 1930 his cousin Dorothy Nassau Molesworth (*see above*) and *dsp* 26 Oct 1952

2d Henry Talbot; *b* 1 Feb 1880; *d* unm 3 May 1908

3d John Davenport Newall, MC; Maj Roy Signals, Capt 6th Bn Lancs Fus, WW I (despatches twice), memb Sussex TAA; *b* 7 Sept 1884; *m* 1st 1 June 1909 (*divorce* 1927) Mary (*d* 14 Feb 1970 aged 84), yst dau of A Blake Norman, of Oakham, Rutland, and had:

1e +John Henry Nassau, DSO (1945), DFC, AFC [Wing Commander John Molesworth DSO DFC AFC, Beehive Cottage, Eltisley, Cambs PE19 4TH]; W/Cdr RAFVR WW II (wounded, despatches); *b* 24 Sept 1913; *m* 1 June 1946 *Pamela Joan, dau of Frederick William Guildford, of Ramsgate, Kent, and has:

1f +Peter John Norman [Peter Molesworth Esq, 20 Elgin Park, Bristol BS6 6RX]; *b* 7 Jan 1956; *educ* Oakham Sch and Newcastle U (BSc); late Capt Green Howards, Capt Yorks Vols; *m* 1990 *Julie A, dau of Vince Wicks, of Cairns, Australia, and has:

1g +John Henry; *b* 1994

1g *Frances Jane; *b* 1992

3d (cont.) John Molesworth *m* 2nd Frances Blake (*d* 1964) and *d* 29 Feb 1952

1d Emma Freda Margaret; *b* 27 Oct 1888; *m* 20 Aug 1912 Wyndham D'Arcy Madden, CBE, only s of Wyndham Madden, and *d* 20 Sept 1968, leaving issue. He *d* 3 June 1968

3c John; *b* 24 Feb 1858; *m* 1885 Emily Maude (*d* 1941), dau of Rev Henry Mitchell, FSA, Vicar and RD Bosham, Sussex, and *d* 1947, leaving:

1d John; *b* 30 April 1894; *m* 1927 *Dorothy Josephine Mudge [Mrs John Molesworth, 205 Foley St, Junction, TX 76849, USA] and *d* 1971, leaving:

1e +John Mudge [John Molesworth, PO Box 104, Junction, TX 76849, USA]; *b* 19 March 1928; *m* 1951 *Joanne Hill, of New York, and has:

1f +John; *b* 21 July 1952

2f +Lynn Hill; *b* 12 Dec 1955

1f *Cynthia; *b* 5 Oct 1953

2e +Fred [Fred Molesworth, Route 3, Box 437B, Amarillo, TX, USA]; *b* 3 Sept 1931; *m* 14 Sept 1962 *Ann Spoon, of Memphis, Tex., and has:

1f +Fred Vance; *b* 22 Nov 1963

1e *Dorothy Patricia [Mrs William Craft, Drawer M, Clarendon, TX, USA]; *b* 23 Aug 1929; *m* 26 Nov 1949 *William Eugene Craft, only s of George Dewey Craft, of Brice, Tex., and has:

1f *William Patrick; *b* 27 July 1951

2f *John Robert; *b* 5 Oct 1962

1f *Catharine *b* 5 Dec 1950; *m* 1974 *John Throckmorton Keene and has:

1g *Kathleen; *b* 1977

2f *Christine; *b* 29 Jan 1957

1d Helen; *b* 1 Sept 1886; *m* 1921 Loyd Brown, of Clarendon, Tex.

2d Mary; *b* 16 Sept 1889; *d* 18 Jan 1910

3d Charlotte; *b* 21 Jan 1902; *m* 16 Dec 1952 William James Adams, of Clarendon, Tex.

4c Lawrence Teesdale; *b* 16 Feb 1864; *m* 10 Oct 1893 Annie Marie Wallace (*d* 25 April 1933), dau of George S Bournes, of Rossport, Co Mayo, and *d* 1 Nov 1941, leaving:

1d Elizabeth Wallace; *b* 6 Oct 1894; *m* 3 Dec 1918 Rev Edward Noel Mellish, VC, MC, CF 1915–19, of The Court House, S Petherton, Somerset, s of Edward Mellish, and *d* 27 Dec 1982, leaving:

1e *Patrick Molesworth [Patrick Mellish Esq, Flaxlands Farm, Merriot, Crewkerne, Somerset]; *b* 9 Dec 1921

2e *Richard Wallace Paul [Richard Mellish, 123 Spartina Court, Kiawah Island, SC, USA]; *b* 9 Dec 1923; *m* 1956 *Veronica Finetta, dau of Col Charles Edward Kirwan Bagot, MC, of Greengates, Painswick, Glos, and has:

1f *Martin Christopher Bagot; *b* 18 Sept 1957

2f *Nicholas Charles; *b* 6 May 1961

1f *Fiona Molesworth; *b* 29 June 1964

3e *Robin Hugh [Robin Mellish Esq, Church Cottage, Burcombe, Wilts]; *b* 21 May 1924; *m* 18 Sept 1954 Leonie Maria (*d* 3 Aug 1992), dau of Henry Knibbler, and has:

1f *Nicholas Noel; *b* 18 Feb 1960; *m* 7 Oct 1989 *Joanne, dau of Geoffrey Poulton, of Northend House, Woodford, Glos, and has;

1g *Elizabeth Leonie Anne Maria; *b* 20 Aug 1995

2g *Claire Alice Victoria; *b* 22 May 1997

1f *Elizabeth Leonie Anne; *b* 23 Sept 1956; *m* 9 June 1990 *Robert Wheeler, s of Kenneth Wheeler, of The Parsonage, Udimore, Rye, E Sussex, and has:

1g *Simon Kenneth; *b* 11 Sept 1991

2g *Philip Robin; *b* 1 June 1994

1g *Emily; *b* 1 June 1994

2g *Tabitha Heather; *b* 15 Sept 1997

1e *(Margaret Elizabeth) Claire [Miss Claire Mellish, The Court House, S Petherton, Somerset]; *b* 4 Dec 1935

2d Margaret Patricia Newall; *b* 17 March 1904; *m* 1st 11 Sept 1928 Theophilus Rhys Jones, Headmaster St Peter's Sch, Harefield, Exmouth, Devon (*d* 29 Dec 1959), and had:

1e *Theophilus Molesworth [Theophilus Rhys Jones Esq, Ash Cottage, Upper Framilode, Glos GL2 7LH]; *b* 21 Sept 1929; *m* 5 Sept 1964 *Jyllian, dau of John De Vic Carey, of The Old School House, Frampton-on-Severn, Glos, and has:

1f *Cressida Helen; *b* 12 Aug 1971

2e *Christopher Bournes [Christopher Rhys Jones Esq, Church Cottage, Brenchley, Kent TN12 7BH]; *b* 19 June 1931; *m* 24 June 1961 *Mary, dau of C T O'Sullivan, and has:

1f *David Bournes; *b* 19 Feb 1963; *m* 28 Sept 1996 *Zara Louise, dau of Hugh Spencer Freeland, of Woodlands, Beckley, Kent

2f *Sophie Helen; *b* 20 Jan 1965

1e Helen Tait; *b* 17 Feb 1936; *d* unm 23 March 1960

2d (cont.) Mrs Jones *m* 2nd 20 Nov 1965 *Howard John Bettany, of Sutton, Surrey and *d* 20 March 1985

5c William Mackinnon; *b* 27 April 1867; *m* 24 Aug 1893 Jane Emily Charlotte (*d* 1952), est dau of Rev Richard Galbraith, of Montell Uvalde, Tex., and *d* 1956, leaving:

1d +Edward William [Edward Molesworth Esq, 606 West Hervey Drive, Roswell, NM, USA]; *b* 6 Dec 1901; *m* 1935 *Minella, dau of Adolph A Stadler, of Kent, Ohio

1d Kathleen; *b* 7 Dec 1895

2d Hilda Margaret; *b* 14 April 1898; *m* 4 Feb 1935 Ashley Green Classen, BSc (Civil Eng), of El Paso, Tex., and *d* 26 Jan 1960, leaving two sons and a dau

3d Frances Emily; *b* 1904; *m* 1st 1927 Nelson Anderson Sims (*d* 1956), of Austin, Tex., and had:

1e *Kathleen Molesworth [Mrs David Donaldson, 1915 Brecken Hobbs, NM, USA]; *b* 5 Dec 1936; *m* 15 Aug 1956 *David Alan Donaldson

3d (cont.) Mrs Nelson Sims *m* 2nd 15 March 1959 Ernest L Long, of San Benito, Tex.

1c Mary Frances; *b* 8 Aug 1852; *d* unm

2c Sarah Emma; *b* 24 June 1854; *d* unm 29 July 1948

3c Harriet Eleanor; *b* 11 May 1856; *d* unm 16 June 1927

4c Margaret Elise; *m* 1885 Edward Ashwell Mitchell, of California, and *d* 1946, leaving issue

5c Marion Patricia; *m* 30 April 1900 Lionel R Stert, of Isleworth, Middx, and *d* 26 June 1930, leaving issue

6c Flora Hill; *m* 22 Feb 1900 Vincent John Rigg, MRCS, of Littleborough, and *d* 22 June 1911, leaving issue

3b Daniel; *b* 3 June 1821; *dsp*

4b George Mill Frederick, JP Devon and Lancs, of Northdown Hall, Bideford, Devon; Capt RN; *b* 14 Sept 1825; *m* 19 Aug 1851 Sarah (*d* 14 Nov 1896), dau of Lawrence Newall, of Littleborough, and *d* 11 Nov 1913, having had, with a dau (*d* an infant):

1c Reginald Balfour; *b* 6 Nov 1852; *m* 19 April 1888 Marian (*d* 8 Oct 1921), yst dau of Edmund Thomson, and *d* 1895, leaving:

1d Gilbert Edmund Nassau (Rev); *b* 26 April 1895; *educ* Queens' Coll Cambridge (BA 1922, MA 1925); Area Dir SW Industl Church Fellowship 1957, Vicar Castle Cary Somerset 1952–57, Capt IA, Devonshire Regt; *m* 17 Oct 1923 Florence Edith Mary, dau of Rev Canon Thomas Fisher Maddrell, and *d* 12 Aug 1976, leaving:

1e +Michael Nassau [Michael Molesworth Esq, Greystones House, Alvescott, Oxon]; *b* 8 Sept 1924; *educ* King Edward VI Sch Birmingham and Sidney Sussex Cambridge (BA 1948, MA 1951); Sub-Lt RNVR WW II (despatches); *m* 8 Jan 1951 Heather (*d* 24 May 1965), dau of Adml Sir Henry Daniel Pridham-Wippell, KCB, CVO, of Kingsdown, Deal, Kent, and has:

1f +William Martin Nassau; *b* 5 Aug 1957

2f +Peter Timothy Nassau; *b* 24 Nov 1959

1f *Susan Claire; *b* 26 Nov 1961; *m* 19– *Stephen Horton and has:

1g *Richard John; *b* 16 March 1995

1g *Tessa Katherine; *b* 16 March 1995

2e +John Edmund Nassau [John Molesworth Esq, c/o Lloyds Bank Ltd, Okehampton, Devon]; *b* 28 April 1926; *educ* King's Sch Bruton, Sidney Sussex Coll Camb, Middle East Centre Arab Studies U of London and St Luke's Coll Exeter; F/Lt RAF, ADC to Air C-in-C Middle East Air Force, Sqdn Cdr Aden Protectorate Levies 1948–55; *m* 30 Sept 1952 *Pamela Anne, dau of Harold Richard Summers MacMullen, of Hall Gate, Ash Priory, Somerset, and has:

1f +David Reginald Nassau; *b* 31 Aug 1953; *educ* Arborfield Coll Reading

1f *Carol Anne; *b* 11 March 1956

2f *Elizabeth Stephanie; b 13 Dec 1958; m 1983 *Martin C Rees

3f *Hilary; b 8 July 1964

3e +Richard Mark Nassau [Richard Molesworth, 9 Webb Farm Rd, Monroe, NY 10950, USA]; b 4 May 1930; educ King Edward VI Sch Birmingham and Birmingham U (BSc); 2nd Lt E Lancs Regt; m 1958 *Margaret Elizabeth, dau of Dr George Thomas Alexander Hastings, MD, of Birmingham, and has:

1f +Philip Nassau; b 2 Sept 1960

2f +Richard Nassau; b 8 April 1962

3f +John Nassau; b 13 Dec 1963

4f +William Nassau; b 1971

1f *Jennifer Ann; b 8 April 1959

2f *Elizabeth Mary; b 1975

1e *Elizabeth Raphael [Mrs Duncan Urquhart, Grays Hills, Fairlie, NZ]; b 7 May 1934; m *Duncan Urquhart and has:

1f *Mark Alexander; b 28 July 1967

2f *Roger David; b 1970

1f *Lorna Mary; b 2 June 1966

2f *Joanna; b 24 Dec 1968

1d Katharine Sarah Newall; b 12 Oct 18 91; d 14 Jan 1898

2c George Nassau; b 4 June 1856; d unm 13 April 1879

3c Arthur Hill; b 25 Oct 1857; d 1936

1c Mary Capel; m 3 Dec 1901 James Foyster Bowen, s of James Hill Bowen, of Leweston, Chislehurst, and d 26 Dec 1943. He d 26 Sept 1935

2c Jessie Fitzgerald; m 3 Oct 1889 her cousin Henry Bridges Molesworth and d 6 Aug 1928, leaving issue (see below)

5b Rennell Francis Wynn (Rev); b 17 Jan 1827; MA Oxon, Rector Washington, Co Durham; m 1st 17 June 1851 Eleanor Jane (d 12 March 1862), only dau of Rev John Hilton, and had:

1c Francis Hilton; Public Analyst Sydney, NSW; b 24 Jan 1854; m 1891 Cecilia Michaeliene (d 1963), yst dau of N Buczkowski, of Seven Hills, S Australia, and d 3 Feb 1934, leaving:

1d Reginald Howard Wynn, of Sydney; Lt RAE WW II; b 1899; educ King's Sch Canterbury

1d Cecilia Frances; m 30 Dec 1918 Rev Thomas Quigley (d 1964), of Ipswich, and had:

1e *Thomas Molesworth (Rev); BD London 1945, Curate Accrington, served Malayan Campaign 1952 (despatches); b 9 Dec 1919

2e *John Molesworth [John Quigley Esq, 18 Ashburton Road, Birkenhead, Cheshire]; b 8 Nov 1921; educ BNC Oxford (BA 1944, MA 1947); m 3 Sept 1948 *Betty Spafford, dau of Hubert Armstrong, MD, of Liverpool, and has:

1f *Mark Andrew; b 11 April 1952

2f *Hugh; b 11 March 1956

3e *Philip Molesworth; RN WW II; b 26 Sept 1923; educ St Peter's Hall Oxford (BA); m 1958 *Janine Marie Mirouse and has:

1f *Sophie Anne; b 29 Feb 1960

4e *David Francis Molesworth; b 16 Oct 1926

1e *Cicely Ruth Molesworth [Mrs Desmond Campion, Lower Farm House, Westerfield, Ipswich, Suffolk]; b 1925; m 7 Dec 1946 Desmond Campion, s of Frederick Herbert Campion, and has:

1f *Stephen Charles [Stephen Campion Esq, Lower Farm House, Westerfield, Ipswich, Suffolk]; b 13 June 1950

2f *Nicholas Paul [Nicholas Campion Esq, Lower Farm House, Westerfield, Ipswich, Suffolk]; b 4 March 1953

2e *Kathleen Mary Molesworth; lecturer Vancouver Coll, Capt WRAC; b 28 April 1928; educ Trin Coll Dublin (MA 1948) and U of BC (MA)

3e *Margaret Winifred Molesworth; b 4 Dec 1931

2c John Hilton (Rev); Rector Feltwell, Norfolk, MA Oxon; b 14 March 1856; m 11 Feb 1908 Everilda Hamer (d 1 Oct 1928), est dau of Rev Canon James Hamer Rawdon, and d 4 Aug 1921, leaving:

1d *Rachel Frances Hilton [Mrs Neil Mackinnon, The Old Fox, Lewknor, Oxon]; b 15 Oct 1912; m 17 Jan 1936 Cdre Neil Alexander Mackinnon (d 19–), RAN, 2nd s of Donald de Burgh D'Arcy Mackinnon, and has:

1e *Peter William Alexander [Peter Mackinnon Esq, The Old Fox, Lewknor, Oxon]; b 27 Feb 1938

2e *John Hugh Molesworth [John Mackinnon Esq, 19 The Croft, Richmond, Victoria 3121, Australia]; b 7 Jan 1941; educ Worcester Coll Oxford (BA)

1e *Fiona Margaret [Mrs Jan Horsley, Gundillawah, Adelong, NSW, Australia]; b 19 June 1946; m 1970 *Jan Horsley

2d *Cecilia Margaret [Lady Mogg, Church Close, Watlington, Oxon OX9 5QR]; b 20 Sept 1914; m 29 June 1939 *Gen Sir (Herbert) John Mogg, GCB, CBE, DSO and bar, DL, Dep SACEUR 1973–76, s of Capt H B Mogg, MC, of Watlington, and has:

1e *John Nigel Ballard; Brig 1st Royal Green Jackets; b 15 May 1940; MA Cantab; m 29 July 1967 *Tessa Elizabeth, dau of Frank D Wright, of Brightwell Park, Brightwell Baldwin, Oxon, and has:

1f *John Peter Francis; b 1969; BA

2f *Richard Julian Charles; b 1971; BSc

2e *Patrick Henry Molesworth; b 28 April 1942

3e *Timothy David (Rev); b 22 Oct 1945; educ St John's Coll Durham (BA); m 1981 *Rachel Mary, dau of Ven D I T Eastman, of Beaminster, Dorset, and has:

1f *Christopher James David; b 1984

2f *John Charles Timothy; b 1984

1f *Alice Mary; b 1982

3c Ernest Hilton (Rev); MA Cantab, FRGS, Vicar Bures Suffolk 1916–23, Boer War (medal with three clasps); b 11 June 1858; m 1st 6 July 1886 Adeline (d 2 July 1908), dau of Rev Charles King, Canon Salisbury, and had:

1d Charles Ernest Wynn; Assist Cmdt Police Rangoon; b 20 Aug 1888; ka 24 March 1918

2d Eric Mackinnon; Surgn-Lt RN; b 16 Oct 1890; educ Fettes and Edinburgh U (MB and ChB 1914); m March 1916 Ethel (d 1984), dau of Isaac Clark Griffin, of The Chace, Eastbourne, and d 15 July 1963, having had:

1e +Selwyn Hilton [Selwyn Molesworth Esq, Trevelen, Cot Hill, Stratton, Cornwall EX23 9DN]; b 6 Feb 1917; educ Epsom Coll and Manchester U; Lt RA, MRCS, LRCP 1951; m 5 Nov 1949 *Margaret Seymour, yr dau of Percy Arthur Smith, of Bridlington, E Yorks, and has had:

1f Christopher Roger; b 1 Aug 1951; educ Lancaster Roy GS and Nottingham U (BA); m 20 Nov 1976 *Annette Caroline [Mrs Christopher Molesworth, 44 Olivers Battery Rd North, Winchester, Hants SO22 4JB], only dau of G C Holliday, and d 12 Dec 1988, leaving:

1g +Steven Richard; b 21 Dec 1981

1g *Caroline Patricia; b 6 May 1980

2f +(William) Hugh [Hugh Molesworth Esq, Old Park Cottage, 19 Walnut Avenue, Bryanston, Dorset DT11 0PT]; b 9 Nov 1952; educ Lancaster Roy GS, St Peter's Coll Oxford and OU (BA Hons); m 12 March 1977 *Angela Jane Walker, only dau of Mrs Doreen Smith, of Oxford, and has:

1g +Thomas Edward Alexander; b 23 Oct 1978; educ Bryanston and Warwick U

2g +Benjamin James; b 6 Sept 1985

1g *Emma Catherine Seymour; b 21 Nov 1981; educ Millfield

3f +(Arthur) David [David Molesworth Esq, 82 Bishopthorpe Rd, York YO2 1JS]; b 10 Feb 1956; educ Shebbear Coll, Bristol U and London U (MSc); m 22 June 1996 *Emma Ruth, dau of Angus Mackinnon, of Kettering, Northants, and has:

1g *Daniel Thomas Mackinnon; b 29 March 1986

2g *George Edward Mackinnon; b 15 Jan 1989

3g *Joshua William Mackinnon; b 10 Feb 1993

1f *Elizabeth Anna; b Feb 1968; m 18 April 1992 *Michael Gregan and has

1g *Sian Catherine; b 11 Oct 1996

2e Richard Charles Victor; Lt RN WW II; b 20 March 1919; m 15 May 1940 *Doreen Mary (m 2nd 1967 Bruce Page, of Hobart, Tasmania), only dau of Joseph Greenwood, of Plymstock, Devon, and das 25 Nov 1941, leaving:

1f +Eric Richard [Eric Molesworth Esq, 54 Swan St, Bagdad, Tasmania 7030, Australia]; Master Mariner Merchant Navy; b 24 Jan 1942; educ Christ's Hosp and Southampton U

3e +Robert Mackinnon [Robert Molesworth Esq, RD4 Whangarei, NZ]; b 14 July 1923; educ Oundle, Magdalene Coll Cambridge (BA 1950, MA 1962) and Roy West of England Academy Sch of Architecture; Lt RNVR WW II, ARIBA, chartered architect; m 1st 4 Jan 1947 (divorce 1967) Ursula, only dau of Alwin Julius Jaeger, chemical engr, of Thalwill-Zürich, Switzerland, and has:

1f +Stephen James; b 23 Feb 1961

3e (cont.) Robert Molesworth m 2nd 11 March 1967 *Mary Craig, er dau of V-Adml Sir Maxwell Richmond, KBE, CB, DSO, of NZ, and by her has:

1f +Peter Maxwell; b 1974

1f *Elizabeth Anna; b 23 Feb 1968

2f *Catherine Julia; b 18 June 1969

4e +David William [David Molesworth Esq, 37 Lacy Drive, Wimborne Minster, Dorset BH21 1DG]; b 13 March 1930; educ King's Sch Canterbury and RAF Coll Cranwell; late S/Ldr RAF; m 19 March 1955 *Doreen Joyce, 3rd dau of George Hunter, of Lincoln, and has:

1f *Caroline Shona [Mrs David Martin, 22 Chemin des Tieulières, Mont Peyroux 34150, France]; b 7 May 1956; educ St Helen's Sch Abingdon and U Coll Hosp (SRN); m 1979 *David R B Martin and has:

1g *Daniel Russell; b 1982

1g *Anna Catherine; b 1986

2f *Melanie Susan [Mrs Martin Dennis, 34 Thornton Ave, London W4 1QG]; b 20 Oct 1958; educ St Helen's Sch; m 1987 *Martin Gerald Wesley Dennis, est s of J G W Dennis, of Malaga, Spain, and has:

1g *George Wesley; b 1988

2g *Ralph Wesley; b 1992

3f *Diana Louise; b 6 Aug 1964; educ Pipers Sch High Wycombe and St Mary's Hosp (RGN, RSCN); m 1989 *Roy M Kirby, est s of T M Kirby, of Wimborne, Dorset, and has:

1g *Jack William Michael; b 1992

3d Selwyn Francis; Lt Middx Regt WW I (wounded), Paymaster Sub-Lt RNVR 1918–19; b 13 Dec 1894; educ Haileybury and London U; d unm 30 Dec 1965

1d Dorothea; b 21 May 1893; m 13 April 1917 Bernard Winthrop Swithinbank, CBE, ICS (d 1968), s of Rev Herbert Spenser Swithinbank, and d 28 Oct 1991, leaving issue

3c (cont.) The Rev E H Molesworth m 2nd 1909 Hilda (d 1940), dau of James Cramp, JP, of Coventry, and d 20 Oct 1931

4c Arthur Hilton Wynn; barrister Inner Temple, FRAS; b 1 June 1860; educ Balliol Coll Oxford (BA); d unm 25 March 1943

1c Mary Agnes; d unm

2c Eleanor Jane; *d* 25 May 1928

5b (cont.) The Rev R F W Molesworth *m* 2nd 27 July 1864 Frances Elizabeth (*d* 1892), dau of Adml George Henderson, and *d* 6 Jan 1906, having by her had:

5c Rodney Henderson; *b* 2 June 1865; *m* 10 Nov 1909 Elonora (*d* 31 July 1979), est dau of Charles Blair, JP, DL, of Tillicoultry, and *d* 22 Oct 1944, leaving:

1d +Wynn Blair [Wynn Molesworth Esq, White House, Bonnington, Kent]; late RAF; *b* 3 March 1911; *educ* King's Sch Canterbury

6c Theodore Henderson; *b* 22 June 1872; *educ* Gonville and Caius Coll Camb and St Bartholomew's Hosp (MB, BCh 1896, FRCS 1903); Boer War 1900–02; *m* 6 June 1906 Ethel Alexandra (*d* 24 Jan 1955), yst dau of Edward Upton, and *d* 1955, leaving:

1d +Michael Henderson; *b* 18 June 1914

2d +Peter Rennel Henderson [Peter Molesworth Esq, 61 Sinah Lane, Hayling Island, Hants]; *b* 31 Oct 1923; *educ* St Lawrence Coll Ramsgate and St Bartholomew's Hosp; MRCS Eng, LRCP Lond 1956; *m* 7 March 1953 *Rosemary Ann, er dau of Cdr Roy Alfred Gould, OBE, RN, of Hayling Island, and has:

1e +Simon Peter Henderson [Simon Molesworth Esq, 19 The Avenue, Hambrook, W Sussex PO18 8TZ]; *b* 5 Oct 1954; *m* 1975 *Joan Lesley Anderson and has:

1f +Alexis Ralph Henderson; *b* 1975

2f +Jason Oliver Henderson; *b* 1978

2e +David Rennell Henderson; *b* 18 Dec 1955; *educ* Dauntsey's Sch; *m* 1984 *Debra C Dixon

3e +Nigel Piers Henderson; *b* 28 July 1960; *educ* All Hallows Lyme Regis; MB, BS

1d Mary Wynne; *m* 15 Sept 1934 Gerald Dorrett Baxter, ISE

2d Elizabeth Theodora; *m* 5 Nov 1938 Capt Allan Dunn MacConachie, 7th Gurkha Rifles, and had issue

3d Margaret Ethel; *b* 1910

4d *Joan Frances [Mrs Lancelot Shutte, 1 Sea View Cottages, St Margaret-at-Cliffe, Dover, Kent]; *b* 1918; *m* 9 Dec 1944 *Lt Lancelot Mitchell Shutte, RM, and has:

1e *Susan Frances [Mrs J Van Der Walt, PO Box 248, Gweru, Zimbabwe]; *b* 1952; *m* 1st 1972 Peter Derek Lapage, BSA Police, and has:

1f *Sally Frances; *b* 1975

1e (cont.) Mrs Lapage *m* 2nd 1986 *J J Van Der Walt and by him has had:

1f Andrew Mitchell; *b* 1990; *d* 1991

2e *Mary Jane [Mrs Selwyn Danielson, 18 Bredell St, Edenglen Ext 40, Edenvale 1610, Transvaal, S Africa]; *b* 1959; *m* 1980 *Selwyn Ronald Danielson and has:

1f *Kyle Bruce; *b* 1982

1f *Megan Nicole; *b* 1986

7c Walter Henderson; MIEES, MIME, MPhS; *b* 3 Aug 1873; *educ* Durham Sch and Berlin Coll of Science; *m* 12 Jan 1910 Theodosia Maud (*d* 28 Dec 1920), 2nd dau of John Chapman, and *d* 18 March 1952, leaving:

1d +Ernest Walter [Ernest Molesworth Esq, Little Orchard, Hinton St George, Somerset TA17 8SE]; *b* 13 Jan 1911; *educ* Dover Coll and London U; served WW II (POW Japanese-Singapore and Siam Burmah Railway); *m* July 1946 *Irene, dau of Rev S F Whitehead, of Aston Somerville, Glos

2d +Richard Nassau [Richard Molesworth Esq, c/o 14 Blue Coat Pond, Horsham, W Sussex]; *b* 9 Nov 1913

1d Kathleen Janet; *d* 6 Sept 1997

2d *Margery Evelyn [Mrs Phineas Jackson, 14 Blue Coat Pond, Horsham, W Sussex]; *m* 1st 23 April 1946 Anthony Orde; *m* 2nd 1974 *Maj Phineas Arthur Jackson, FCIS, FCII

3c Bertha; *d* unm 16 Dec 1949

4c Dora; *d* unm 18 Dec 1950

6b Guilford Lindsey (Sir), KCIE (1888); India PWD, consulting engr Govt India for State Rlwys 1871–89; *b* 3 May 1828; *m* 22 Aug 1854 Maria Elizabeth (*d* 22 Feb 1919), dau of John Thomas Bridges and gdau of Sir Robert Affleck, 4th Bt (*see* 1939 edn), and *d* 21 Jan 1925, having by her had:

1c Henry Bridges; *b* 7 July 1855; *m* 3 Oct 1889 his cousin Jessie FitzGerald (*d* 9 Aug 1928), 2nd dau of Capt George Mill Frederick Molesworth, RN (*see* above), and *d* 8 Feb 1916, leaving:

1d George Noble, CSI (1941), CBE (1958, OBE 1950); Lt-Gen IA WW I (despatches), Dep Dir Mil Ops and Intell India 1936–38, Dir Mil Ops and Intell 1938–41, Dept CGS India 1941–43, Mil Sec India Office 1943–45, Col 4th/15th Punjab Regt 1941–60, Hon Col 12th Punjab Regt 1961, memb Nat Savings Ctee S Regn 1949–60, author: *History of the Somerset Light Infantry 1919–46* (1951), *A Soldier's War* (1958), *Three Centuries of Parish Life* (1960), *Sancta Cruce de Dwile* (1961), *Afghanistan 1919* (1964), *Curfew on Olympus* (1966); *b* 14 July 1890; *educ* Bradfield and RMC Sandhurst; *m* 17 March 1927 Marjorie Frances (*d* 7 April 1974 aged 83), yr dau of Benjamin F Simpson, of Little Friston, E Dean, Sussex, and *dsp* 7 Jan 1968

1d Mary Newall; *b* 18 April 1896

2c Robert Bridges; MA Cantab, MICE; *b* 31 May 1863; *d* 29 Nov 1897

3c Guy Layard Nassau; civil engr Mooi River Natal; *b* 24 Sept 1865; *d* 12 Dec 1920

4c Percy Braybrook; Maj RE; *b* 2 April 1867; *d* Dec 1908

1c Amy Frances; *m* 1879 Charles Blair, CE, and *d* 9 Nov 1896, having had issue

2c Eva; *d* unm

3c Louisa Mary; *m* 28 Dec 1881 Edward Augustus Dennys, 4th s of Gen Julius Bentall Dennys, Bengal Army, of Sidmouth, Devon, and *d* 16 Jan 1956, having had issue. He *d* Nov 1930

1b Harriet; *m* 1 Jan 1856 Samuel Crompton, MD, and *d* 24 Nov 1910. He *d* 1891

2b Emma Frances; *m* 20 Sept 1850 George Poulden, Recorder Portsmouth, and *d* 26 June 1911. He *dsp* 12 June 1868

3b Louisa; *m* 1 Sept 1846 Rev John Edwards and had issue. He *d* 1864

1a (cont.) The Rev John Molesworth *m* 2nd 31 Oct 1854 Harriet Elizabeth (*d* 1897), widow of John Thomas Bridges and dau of Sir Robert Affleck, 4th Bt (*see* 1939 edn), and *d* 21 April 1877

(2) Robert; *m* 17 Nov 1773 Elizabeth, dau of John Tuke, and had:

1a Edward; Maj 10th Dragoon Gds; *b* 7 July 1775; *m* 1st Elizabeth Dorothea (*d* 8 Oct 1812), dau of Redmond de Montmorency (*see* DE MONTMORENCY, Bt) and had:

1b John Charles Villiers; Capt 8th Regt; *b* 18 Oct 1800; *m* 17 June 1827 Maria Catherine, only child of Rev Roger Ford, and *d* 2 Feb 1832, leaving:

1c Elizabeth Maria Frederica; *m* Oct 1852 William Willans

1b Elizabeth Dorothea; *m* 4 June 1818 Theophilus Boileau and *dsp* 8 May 1870. He *d* 5 Nov 1845

2b Margaret Letitia; *m* Col John Hope, RE, and *d* 22 July 1854, leaving issue (*see* HOPE, Bt, of Craighall)

1a (cont.) Maj Edward Molesworth *m* 2nd Mary, widow of Gen Joseph Trueman and dau of F Crane, and *d* 14 June 1842, having by her had:

2b Edward Nassau; Maj 27th Regt; *b* 17 Feb 1818; *m* 14 Aug 1852 Mary Anne (*d* 24 March 1912), dau of John Hunt, and *d* 30 April 1868, having had:

1c Edward Hogarth, CB; Brig-Gen IA, Bde Cdr 1915, cmdg Assam Bde, Afghan War, Akha, Abor and Mishmi Expdns, WW I; *b* 2 May 1854; *d* unm 17 March 1943

2c William John; *b* 7 May 1856; *m* 26 Nov 1892 Anne Brunette (*d* 23 June 1948), dau of Robert Boyd, MD, of Mayfair, and *d* 6 May 1937, leaving:

1d Mary Nassau; *b* 27 Sept 1897; *m* 10 April 1924 Maj Alfred Charles Stuart Smith, RA (*d* 1973), only s of Stuart Alfred Smith, of Hall Place, Ropley, and *d* 3 Jan 1997, leaving:

1e *Anthony Molesworth Stuart [Anthony Stuart Smith Esq, Whitsend Cottage, Tebay Lane, Ulverston, Cumbria LA12 7SG]; *b* 29 July 1928; *educ* Charterhouse and Trin Coll Oxford (MA); *m* 20 March 1952 *Dorothy, dau of Nestor Bennett, and has:

1f *Christopher John Stuart; *b* 3 Jan 1953; *educ* Cranleigh

2f *Peter Martin Stuart; *b* 26 Feb 1954; *educ* Cranleigh

1f *Gillian Eleanor Mary Stuart; *b* 31 May 1958; *m* 10 Sept 1983 *Peter Anthony Lonsdale and has:

1g *Gemma Ann; *b* 31 Jan 1984

2g *Natalie Louise; *b* 13 Oct 1987

1e *Bridget Mary Stuart [Mrs Maurice Collins, Old Wheatsheaf, Privett, Hants GU34 3NX]; *b* 19 Aug 1927; *m* 6 Sept 1952 *Rev Maurice Arthur Reily Collins, s of Arthur Collins, of Waverley Court, Camberley, Surrey, and has:

1f *Jonathan Stuart Reily; *b* 24 June 1955; *educ* Cranleigh; *m* 1985 (*divorce* 1991) Mary Randall; *m* 2nd 1991 *Christine Barber and by her has:

1g *Erin Elizabeth Stuart; *b* 1993

2f *Edward Charles Reily; *b* 30 Sept 1957

1c Amy Ellen Mary; *d* unm 24 Sept 1925

3b Emma; *d* unm 9 June 1877

2a Arthur, Capt RM; *b* 24 March 1786; *m* 21 Aug 1809 Eleanor (*d* 3 Jan 1869), only dau of Lazarus Steele Roberts, MD, and *d* 30 Jan 1850, leaving:

1b Arthur John; Lt RM; *b* 16 July 1810; *m* 1840 Sarah, est dau of John Parks, and *d* 23 Aug 1857, having had:

1c Sarah Mary

2c Alice

3c Letitia Jane

2b Thomas Hooper, RN; *b* 5 Aug 1823; *m* 1st 29 Dec 1847 Harriet Morphitt (*dsp*), dau of John Parks; *m* 2nd Rosa Carlotta, dau of Lt Henry Walker, RN, and *d* 21 Nov 1876, having by her had:

1c Isabel

3b Robert Sackville, Lt RN; *b* 24 Jan 1825; *m* Marianne — (*m* 2nd J L Soubeiran; *d* 1900) and *d* 5 April 1864, leaving:

1c Constance Florence Emma Sackville; *m* 27 Nov 1883 Sydney Knowles Muspratt, JP, and *d* 28 June 1948, leaving issue. He *d* 1 Dec 1923

4b Erasmus William Gray; *b* 12 Feb 1830; *d* 3 Dec 1863

1b Ellen Mary; *m* 1 Jan 1837 Peter Lund Simmonds and *d* 15 Aug 1868, leaving issue

2b Julia Caroline; *d* 7 Oct 1893 aged 73

3b Clara; *m* 24 Oct 1854 Robert Bruce Walker and *d* 9 June 1873, leaving issue

3a Richard Carr; Maj-Gen RA; *b* 23 April 1789; *m* 24 May 1810 Marianne (*d* 24 March 1858), dau of Thomas Tuke, MD, and *d* 11 Feb 1859, having had:

1b Thomas Edward; MD, Surgn RN; *b* 5 July 1813; *m* 3 Dec 1850 Marianne (*d* 2 June 1867), dau of Dover Farrant, RMA, and *d* 11 April 1873, leaving:

1c Richard Farrant; *b* 3 Dec 1851; *d* 9 May 1856

2c Charles Edward; *b* 26 Sept 1853; *m* 1st 19 Aug 1882 Anne Ellen (*d* 24 April 1886), dau of John Terry; *m* 2nd 19 Sept 1887 Katherine Marianne (*d* 18 April 1936), dau of Rev Robert Airey, Vicar of Santon, IoM, and *d* 27 July 1935

3c Dover Nassau O'Dwyer; *b* 29 Sept 1860; *m* 18 May 1882 Margaret, dau of George Tierney Ferguson, BA Oxford, and *d* 11 June 1897 as the result of a boating accident

2b Henry Orlebar; *b* 10 June 1817; *d* unm Oct 1881

3b Robert; *b* 17 Jan 1819; *d* unm March 1858

1b Mary Eliza; *d* unm 30 June 1881

1a Elizabeth; *d* unm

1a Letitia; *m* Sackville Hamilton Eaton, 62nd Regt

5 Hamilton Walter; *m* Sarah Maria, only dau of John Skrine, of Warleigh and Middle Temple, and *dsp* 1773

6 Coote, MD, FRS; *m* Mary, dau of William Palmer (*see* SELBORNE, E), and *dsp* 29 Nov 1782, aged 85

7 Bysse; MP Swords; *m* 7 Dec 1731 Elizabeth (*d* Jan 1770), widow of Edward Archdale, of Castle Archdale, Co Fermanagh, and sis of 1st Baron Mountflorence of Florence Court (*see* ENNISKILLEN, E), and *d* 1779, leaving:

(1) Arthur; Maj, of Fairlawn, Co Armagh; *m* 1st Sept 1764 Catherine, dau of Sir Walter Fletcher Vane, Bt (*see* 1934 edn), and had:

1a Elizabeth; *m* Richard Reynell, of Reynella, Co Westmeath

(1) (cont.) Arthur Molesworth *m* 2nd Henrietta (*dsp*), widow of — Blackett; *m* 3rd Elizabeth Ledgingham (*d* 14 Dec 1816) and *d* 20 Aug 1803, having by her had:

1a Arthur Nepean, of Fairlawn, *b* 27 Aug 1799; *m* 18 Jan 1820 Harriet (*d* 6 Oct 1880), 2nd dau of Capt Charles Hawkins, 3rd Foot, and *d* 25 May 1877, leaving, with a dau (*d* unm):

1b Arthur, of Fairlawn; *b* 11 Oct 1821; *m* July 1855 Elizabeth Urquhart (*d* 1889), dau of Dr King, RN, and *d* 1892, leaving:

1c Arthur Nepean, of Fairlawn; *b* 28 Nov 1856; *m* 5 Oct 1898 Kathleen (*d* 1934), dau of John De la Cour Cornwall, of Janeville, Bandon, Co Cork, and *d* 1929, leaving:

1d Arthur William Bysse Nepean; *b* 30 Jan 1902; *m* Feb 1923 Ruth Patricia (*d* 1971), dau of Thomas Gracey, of Moy, Co Armagh, and *d* 1958, leaving:

1e +Guilford Bysse Nepean [Guilford Molesworth Esq, 64 Hill Parade, Clontarf, Qld 4019, Australia]; Petty Officer RN; *b* 28 Dec 1923

2e +John Robert [John Molesworth Esq, 527 Crumlinside Rd, London, Ontario, Canada]; late Black Watch Regt of Canada; *b* 1930; *m* 1954 *Mary, dau of Alexander Rodgers, of Montreal, and has:

1f *Deborah; *b* 1957

2f *Kathryn; *b* 1962

3f *Sandra; *b* 1964

1e *Kathleen Violet; *b* 1927

2e *Ann; *b* 1928; *m* 1961 *Dr Herman Gelber [Mrs Herman Gelber, Centennia Hospital, Scarborough, Ontario, Canada] and has:

1f *Sean Roderick [Sean Gelber Esq, 589 Jamaica Court, London, Ontario N6K 1N2, Canada]; *b* 18 June 1968

1c Frances Elizabeth Ives; *b* 10 Sept 1858

2b Thomas Nepean; *b* 24 June 1824; *m* 11 Oct 1846 Sarah Georgina, dau of William Kertland, and had:

1c Arthur Nassau; *b* 14 Aug 1851; *m* 1st 17 Jan 1878 Sophia (*d* 1892), dau of Hon John Sifton, of Canada, and had:

1d Kate; *d* unm 27 Feb 1963

1c (cont.) Arthur Molesworth *m* 2nd 1894 Edith (*d* 17 July 1963), dau of William B Whiteside, of Johnson City, Tenn., and *d* 23 April 1925

2c Balfour Nepean; *b* 6 Dec 1853; *m* 1882 Louisa Agnes (*d* May 1938), dau of H H Thompson, and *d* Nov 1896, leaving:

1d Henry Balfour; *b* 1883; *d* 1919

2d Herbert Nepean; *b* 1888; *m* 1912 Marjorie Kittredge (*d* 1976), dau of W M Thompson, of Penetanguishene, Ontario, and *d* 1978, leaving:

1e +William Herbert [William Molesworth Esq, 1850 Des Cheneaux Street, Trois Riviéres, P Québec, Canada]; *b* 1915; *m* 10 Sept 1938 *Joan Anne, dau of Charles Percival Rudman, of Grand-Mère, Québec, and has:

1f +Michael Herbert [Michael Molesworth Esq, 101–6th St, Grand-Mere, Québec, Canada]; *b* 2 July 1944; *m* 1982 *Sylvie Desbiens and has:

1g +David Alexander Hamilton; *b* 1986

1g *Allison Louise; *b* 1983

1f *Patricia Anne [Mrs Stephen Osterman, 12 Terrasse St, Maurice, Cap-de-la-Madeleine, Québec, Canada]; *b* 1 April 1942; *m* 1st 26 Sept 1964 (*divorce* 1978) Clifford Hastings Laurence and has:

1g *William Hastings; *b* 22 Sept 1966, BA, LLB

1g *Kelly Anne; *b* 26 July 1965, BCom

1f Mrs Patricia Laurence *m* 2nd 1978 *Stephen Alexander Osterman, BSc, DipEd, and by him has:

2g *Michael Alexander; *b* 1979

3g *Stephen Bradley; *b* 1980

2g *Jennifer Joan; *b* 1982

2e +Robert Nepean [Robert Molesworth Esq, 11285 Greenhill Drive, RR2 Ladysmith, BC VOR 2EO, Canada]; *b* 1922; *m* 4 June 1943 *Cecily Elizabeth, dau of Lt-Cdr Cecil Alexander Wade, RN, of Edgeley, Whitchurch, Salop, and has:

1f +Robert Alexander; *b* 15 Nov 1946; *m* 1973 *Rosalind Anne Stacey and has:

1g +Ryan Jason; *b* 1977

2g +Brent Russell; *b* 1979

2f +Gregory Daniel; *b* 6 May 1951; *m* 1st 1975 Claire Marie Deschambeault; *m* 2nd 1985 *Terri Kazemir and by her has:

1g *Danielle Elizabeth; *b* 1988

1f *Susan Elizabeth [Mrs Fraser Sibbald, 721–19th St, Pacific Grove 93950, CA, USA]; *b* 10 April 1944; *m* 1st 1965 (*divorce* 19–) Robert J Black; *m* 2nd 12 July 1970 (*divorce* 1973) Troy Lee Roper II, s of Troy Lee Roper, of Los Angeles; *m* 3rd 1983 *Fraser Thomas Sibbald and by her 2nd husb has:

1g *Troy Lee III; *b* 18 Sept 1971

1e *Marjorie Julia Kittridge [Mrs John Ellis, Ross Ferry Rd, Boulardarie Bras d'Or, Cape Breton, Nova Scotia, Canada]; *b* 1919; *m* 1948 *John MacLeod Ellis and has:

1f *Marnie MacLeod [Mrs Peter Crosby, 23 Addison Place, Dartmouth, NS, Canada B2U 1G9]; *b* 1951; *m* 1987 *Peter Douglas Adair Crosby, MD, and has:

1g *Alexander Douglas Judson; *b* 1992

2g *William Russel Arthur; *b* 1993

1d Lucy Darling

2d Muriel; *m* 1926 Dighton Wynans Baxter (*d* 1949)

3d Violet Maud

3c William Ponsonby; *b* 11 May 1856; *m* 1883 Bathurst Georgina (*d* March 1938), dau of Edward FitzGerald, QC, of Toronto, and *d* 19 Aug 1937, leaving:

1d George Nepean; Maj Canadian Forces WW I, architect; *b* 1885; *m* 1916 Helen Nelles (*d* 27 Jan 1954), dau of Sydney Bellingham Sykes, of Toronto, and *d* 14 Aug 1958, leaving:

1e +John Sydney [John Molesworth Esq, 74 Second St, Oakville, ONT L6J 3T3, Canada]; Lt Roy Canadian Artillery WW II; *b* 1919; *m* 1946 *Barbara Caroline, dau of Dr Carswell Marshall, of Sawley, Clitheroe, Lancs, and has:

1f +William Marshall [William Molesworth Esq, 4616 Route 620, Limekiln Rd, NB E0H 1T0, Canada]; *b* 1949; *m* 1992 *Susan Irene Newell, of Whitby, Ontario

2f +Hugh Carswell [Hugh Molesworth Esq, PO Box 622, Shelburne, ONT L0N 1S0, Canada]; *b* 10 Feb 1952; *m* 1975 *Rosemary Druscilla, dau of A Ulch, of Simcoe, Ontario

3f +James Colin [James Molesworth Esq, 310-8th Ave W, New Westminster, BC V3L 1Y2, Canada]; *b* 26 Oct 1959; *m* *Patricia Cameron

1f *Helen Mary [Mrs David Weiser, 6488 Bay St, W Vancouver, BC V7W 2H1, Canada]; *b* 16 June 1954; *m* 1985 *David Weiser, of Houston, Tex.

2e +David Hugh George [David Molesworth Esq, 156 Collier, Street, Toronto, ONT M4W 1M3, Canada]; *b* 1927; *educ* Toronto U (B Arch); *m* 1952 *Ann De Veber, dau of Maj Alfred Clarence Larter, of Toronto, and has:

1f +Ian De Veber [Ian Molesworth Esq, 4 Sydenham St, Guelph, Ontario, Canada]; *b* 13 Aug 1956

2f +ANTHONY later TONY Nelles [Tony Molesworth Esq, 49 Lawloa Av, Toronto, Ontario M4E 3L8, Canada]; *b* 4 Aug 1958

1e Margaret Jean; *b* 1921; *d* 1983

2d John Christian Ponsonby; *b* 1888; *d* 1909

3d FitzGerald William; *b* 1892; *d* 1972

1d Margaret Louisa; *m* 1927 Raymond Tyrwhitt, of Oakville, Ontario, and *d* 30 Jan 1957, leaving issue. He *d* 1947

1c Ellen Harriett; *d* 3 Jan 1903

2c Lucy Mary; *d* 13 April 1925

3c Eva Sarah; *d* Feb 1944

4c Maud Marion; *m* 1896 James Hastings Carter and *d c* 1939. He *d* 1924

1b Caroline; *m* 21 May 1873 Ralph McGeough Bond Shelton, JP, DL, of The Argory, Moy, Co Armagh, and *dsp* 27 Nov 1907. He *d* 8 March 1916

2b Harriet; *m* 1st 3 Jan 1850 Rev Richard Wrightson, Vicar Lusk (*d* 10 July 1875), and had issue; *m* 2nd 27 Nov 1877 William Symms

2a Thomas William Ponsonby; *b* 10 Dec 1800; *m* 16 April 1827 Anne, yst dau of Rev Thomas Fawcett, Rector Greens Norton, Northants, and *d* 11 Jan 1881, leaving, with four daus (*d* unm):

1b Thomas (Rev); MA Cantab, CF; *b* 31 Dec 1828; *m* 13 June 1854 Caroline Mary (*d* 16 Jan 1922), dau of William Bowles, of Abingdon, and *d* 12 May 1915, having had:

1c Montague Pulteney; Maj Royal Guernsey Art, Capt 7th Bn City of London Regt; *b* 4 June 1856; *d* 14 March 1921

2c Hugh Thomas (Rev); Rector St Philip's, Thompson Estate, S Brisbane, Queensland; *b* 30 March 1860; *m* 1889 Alice Marian, dau of Edward Deshon, CMG, Auditor-Gen Qld, and *d* 1930, leaving:

1d Bevil Hugh, of Sydney; *b* 1891; *m* 1918 Maud Margaret, dau of A Mutch, School Inspr, and had:

1e Hugh Bevil Alec; *b* 1925; *m* 1959 *Patricia [Mrs Ian Martin, 40 Carlyle Rd, E Lindfield, NSW 2070, Australia] (*m* 2nd 1963 Dr Ian Martin, dau of Clive Quinton, of Wahroonga, NSW), and *d* April 1960, leaving:

1f +Hugh Bevil Clive [Hugh Molesworth Esq, 176 Parnassus Avenue, San Francisco, CA 94117, USA]; *b* posthumously 20 Aug 1960; *m* 1989 *Karen Roberta, dau of Irwin David Staller, of Stockton, Calif., and has:

1g *Maude Clara Felice; *b* 1994

2g *Talia Ruby Camille; *b* 23 Sept 1997

2d Hilton Edward; *b* 1892; *d* young

3d +Guilford Bysse [Guilford Molesworth Esq, 27 Marriott Street, Cooparoo, Brisbane, Qld, Australia]; *b* 14 March 1907; *m* 30 June 1931 *Catherine Maud, dau of Edward Charles Woodward, of Cooparoo, and has:

1e +William Guilford Hugh [William Molesworth Esq, 39 Newman Ave, Camp Hill, Brisbane, Qld, Australia]; *b* 3 Aug 1943; *educ* U of Qld (BPharm 1966); *m* 20 Nov 1968 *Helen, dau of John Edward McCaskie, and has:

1f +Mark William; *b* 1975

2f +Peter John; *b* 1979

3c Arthur Bysse, Capt West India Regt; *b* 22 Feb 1867; *d* unm 17 Oct 1902

1c Constance Maude Caroline; *d* unm 1 Nov 1940

2c Agnes Mary; *d* 16 June 1930

3c Alice Sophia; *d* unm 22 Jan 1941

2b Walter (Rev); MA Cantab, Vicar Bishopsworth, Bristol; *b* 6 Feb 1831; *d* unm 11 Feb 1912

(2) Robert; Capt 38th Regt; *m* 1770 Elizabeth, dau of Hickman Rose, of Limerick, by Elizabeth, er dau of Jonah Pratt, of Castlemartyr, Co Cork, and had, with other issue:

1a Arthur; Maj-Gen HEICS; *m* Mary (*d* 3 Feb 1860), dau of Matthew Kearney, and *d* 7 Jan 1843, having had, with six daus:

1b Hickman Thomas, of Kenwith, Abbotsham, Devon; Maj-Gen RA; *b* 7 Aug 1820; *m* 15 April 1857 Marianne, dau of Robert Lindsay (*see* CRAWFORD and BALCARRES, E), and *d* 27 Jan 1896, having had:

1c Hickman Crawford; Lt-Col RA; *b* 12 Feb 1858; *m* 1st 1883 Margaret Amelia (*d* 27 March 1915), widow of Surgn-Maj — McLean and dau of John Hopper, and had:

1d Arthur Crawford Valentine; Lt 5th Bn Royal Dublin Fus; *b* 1885; *m* and had a s

2d Guy Lindsay; Lt Cork RGA; *b* 1887

1d Violet Marguerite

2d Ivy Frederica; *b* 1891; *m* 1922 Donald Henry Alexander (*d* 1975) and had:

1e *Douglas Gundry [Douglas Alexander Esq, 4453 Torquay Drive, Victoria, BC, Canada V8N 3L3]; *m* 1954 *Margaret Lindsay Wilson and has:

1f *Brian Douglas; *b* 1955; *m* 1978 *Carol Martin and has:

1g *Lindsay Kathleen; *b* 1984

1f *Carol Margaret; *b* 1957; *m* 1984 *James Keith Collins

2f *Janice Eileen; *b* 1962

3f *Heather Louise; *b* 1965

2e *Ralph Molesworth [Ralph Alexander Esq, 141 Hampton Rd, Victoria, BC, Canada]; *b* 1929; *m* 1951 *Shirley Margaret Boulton and has:

1f *Ross Wayne; *b* 1954; *m* 1976 *Merry Louise McKinnon

2f *Glen Darryl; *b* 1955; *m* 1st 19– Cindy Barry; *m* 2nd 1989 *Barbara Anne Whiteley and by his 1st w has:

1g *Shaun Michael; *b* 1980

3f *Dean Murray; *b* 1970

1f *Laraine Merrill; *b* 1960; *m* 1989 *Grant Richard McTaggart, of Melbourne

2f *Julie Marlaine; *b* 1965; *m* 1989 *David Frederick McCormick

1c (cont.) Col Hickman Molesworth *m* 2nd 2 Dec 1920 Charlotte Anne (*d* 1977), QAIMNSR, dau of Alfred Thomas, of Robin Hood House, Hall Green, Birmingham, and *d* 1939

2c Arthur Ludovic, CMG (1918); Col RA; *b* 18 July 1860; *m* 1896 Beatrice Emma (*d c* 1946), dau of Fourney Adams, of Augusta, Ga., and *dsp* 14 Sept 1939

3c Robert Everard; MRCS, LRCP, Lt-Col RAMC; *b* 7 July 1861; *m* 1st 1889 Katharine Isabella (*dsp* 1907), dau of W G Allan, Conservator India Woods and Forests; *m* 2nd 1908 Gladys (*d* 1976), dau of Louis Otto Law, and *d* 1941, having by her had:

1d +Robert Louis; Lt IA; *b* 1910

2d *Marianne Sheila Lindsay; *b* 1914; *m* 18 March 1935 *Thomas Bogue Alder, s of Thomas Bogue Alder, of Orchard, Hawick, Roxburghs, and has:

1e *Lucinda Ann; *b* 1936

2e *Hermione Sarah; *b* 1941

4c George Nassau; Lt Royal Irish Fus; *b* 5 Feb 1865; *dsp*

5c Thomas Charles Underwood (Rev); MA Cantab, Chaplain India Govt; *b* 27 Oct 1866; *m* 23 Nov 1895 Mary Rosamond (*d* 12 Oct 1962, aged 90), dau of Rev John Richard Turner Eaton, Hon Canon Worcester, and *d* 8 Oct 1907, having had:

1d Richard Cecil, of Orchard Farm House, St Catherine, nr Bath, Somerset; Lt-Col 8th Gurkha Rifles, IA, 3rd Cl Order Star Nepal, WW I, MEF 1917–18, Chin Hill Rebellion 1919–20, NWF India 1939–40, WW II Egypt 1941–42, NWF India 1942–44, Assam 1944–45; *b* 31 May 1898; *educ* Wellington; *m* 16 Dec 1933 *Susan, only dau of Harry Bazeley, of Bideford, and *d* 31 Aug 1974, leaving:

1e *Gillian Ann [Mrs John Dupré, 72 Sherwood Av, London, Ontario, Canada]; *b* 2 Jan 1935; *m* 1959 *Dr John Dupré, only s of W E Dupré, of Montreal, and has:

1f *Matthew; *b* 15 April 1961

2f *Luke; *b* 1972

1f *Louisa; *b* 12 Nov 1962

1d Margaret Theodora; *b* Nov 1896; *m* 17 April 1922 Brig Alfred Edmund Barlow, MC, Royal Garhwal Rifles, s of C E Barlow, of Rhosneigr, Anglesey, and New York, and *d* 30 Nov 1960, leaving issue. He *d* 31 Dec 1945

6c Richard Piggot, CMG; Lt-Col and Brevet Col RA, Waziristan Expdn 1894–95 (medal with clasp), NWF India 1897–98 (medal with clasp), WW I (despatches, brevet, Legn Honour); *b* 25 Jan 1868; *m* 27 Oct 1904 Madeleine (*d* 1 May 1959), 3rd dau of Dr Otho Galgey, of Co Cork, and *d* 24 Feb 1946, leaving:

1d Ralph Gerard Lindsay; Maj RA, 2nd Lt Roy Berks Regt, WW II; *b* 19 July 1910; *educ* Downside; *m* 1st 15 Feb 1933 *Eleanor (*m* 2nd — McColl), dau of G Rooke, and had:

1e +Christopher Ralph; *b* 7 April 1934

2e *Anthony John Lindsay, MBE (1972); *b* 10 March 1936; Col

1d (cont.) Ralph Molesworth *m* 2nd 1948 *Valerie St Claire [Mrs Ralph Molesworth, 10 Richmond Hill, Clifton, Bristol], dau of Charles Francis Earle, and *d* 1960, leaving by her:

3e +Richard Charles Lindsay [Richard Molesworth Esq, 1 Town Mills, Church St, Dawlish, Devon; 8 Gloucester Rd, Teignmouth,

Devon]; *b* 1950; *educ* Belmont Abbey and U Coll Wales, LLB (London)

7c Herbert Ellicombe, CMG (1919), DSO (1917); Col RA WW I (despatches), Greek Mil Cross; *b* 15 Dec 1872; *m* 24 Feb 1914 Eileen Mary (*d* 14 March 1969), 3rd dau of Col Henry Waugh Renny-Tailyour (*see* POWERSCOURT, V), and *d* 24 Dec 1941, leaving:

1d *Phyllis Eileen; *m* 21 July 1956 *Cyril Pickard, yst s of F Pickard, of Cambridge

2d *Betty Lindsay [Mrs Frederick Craswell, Rising Sun, Boutport St, Barnstaple, Devon]; *m* 3 June 1946 Frederick Augustus Craswell, s of William Augustus Craswell, of Hitchin, Herts, and has:

1e *Lindsay; *b* 1951

8c Walter Guy; Pub Works Dept Madras; *b* 18 Feb 1874; *m* 18 Feb 1903 Ethel Vernon (*d* 8 Feb 1973), dau of Thomas Richard Jessop, FRCS, of Leeds and *d* 16 Jan 1941, leaving:

1d Peter Guy Lindsay; *b* 1908; *educ* Lancing; *m* 1937 *Nina Veronica, dau of Lt-Col William Lockhart Maxwell, IA, and *d* 30 April 1954

9c Alec Lindsay Mortimer, CIE (1937); Col 8th Gurkha Rifles, IA, T/Brig and Bde Cdr 1933–37, Hon Brig 1937, Makaware Expdn 1910–11, Abor Expdn 1911–12 (despatches, medal with clasp), Mishmi 1912–13, WW I (wounded), 3rd Afghan War 1919, NWF India 1930, 3rd Cl Order Star Nepal; *b* 24 March 1881; *m* 1st 26 July 1915 Esther Alice (*d* 14 Aug 1935), yst dau of W H Taylor, of Buenos Aires, and had:

1d *Lindsay Diana [Mrs Reginald Porter, Old Pound Cottage, Chertsey Road, Chobham, Surrey]; *b* 1916; *m* 25 Nov 1940 Cdr (S) Reginald Nevill Da Costa Porter, MBE, RN, only s of Adolphus Reginald Zouch Porter, of Hurtmore, Surrey, and has:

1e *Jeremy Nevill; *b* 29 July 1948

1e *Valerie Lindsay; *b* 25 Oct 1942

9c (cont.) Brig Alec Molesworth *m* 2nd 1936 *Hilda [Mrs Alec Molesworth, 50 Courtfield Gardens, London SW7], dau of Alfred Henry Miles, OBE, of Wellington, NZ, and *d* 28 July 1939

1c Gertrude; *m* 15 July 1885 Rev Robert Walpole Sealy, Vicar Abbotsham, Devon, and had issue

2c May; *m* 3 June 1891 Charles John Didham, RN, and *d* 24 June 1915, leaving issue

2b Robert Francis (Rev); Rector Coston, Leics, and St Mary, March, Cambs, Capt 5th Regt Madras NI (Burma medal, Pegu clasp); *b* 30 June 1826; *m* 7 Feb 1852 Gertrude Maria Le Normand (*d* 11 March 1915), est dau and coheir of Capt George Bagot Gosset, 4th Dragoon Gds, and *d* 8 May 1877, having had:

1c George Bagot Gosset Francis Richard Pigot (Rev); barrister, Curate St Nicholas, Stamford, 1917; *b* 23 Jan 1853; *educ* King's Coll Cambridge (MA); *d* 20 July 1919

2c Henry Lempriere; Lt 6th West York Militia; *b* 26 Sept 1862; *m* 10 June 1878 Katherine Barstow and *d* 22 June 1881, leaving:

1d Hugh; *b* 19 June 1879; *d* 14 Feb 1932

3c Algernon Francis; *b* 26 June 1873; *d* unm 2 Sept 1912

2a Hickman Blayney; attorney; *b* Oct 1773; *m* 1st 30 Jan 1806 Wilhelmina Dorothea (*d* 5 Dec 1814), yst dau of Brindley Hone, of Usher Quay, Dublin, and had:

1b Robert (Sir); Judge Supreme Court Victoria, Australia, 1856–86; *b* 3 Nov 1806; *m* 2 Jan 1840 Henrietta (*d* 1879), dau of Rev Joseph England Johnson, and *d* 1890, leaving:

1c Hickman; Puisne Judge Supreme Court Victoria; *b* 23 Feb 1842; *m* 1st 9 July 1868 Eliza Emily (*d* 6 July 1881), dau of William Rutledge, and had:

1d Robert Arthur; *b* 6 July 1870; *m* Margaret —, and *dsp* 1917

2d William Farnham; *b* 7 March 1873; *m* Nellie Smith, and *d* 1923 leaving issue

1d Enid Josephine; *b* 1869; *d* unm 1953

2d Emily Maud; *b* 1871; *d* unm 1957

1c (cont.) Hickman Molesworth *m* 2nd 15 June 1882 Alice Henrietta (*d* 1 Sept 1927), dau of Dr Ffloyd Minter Peck, of Sale, Gippsland, Australia, and *d* 18 July 1907, having by her had:

3d Hickman Walter Lancelot, JP; FRCS, Surgn-Lt RN WW I, EMS (CD) WW II; *b* 23 Jan 1892; *m* 15 Dec 1923 Caryl Margaret (*d* 10 July 1997), dau of Stanley Hoare, of London, and *d* 7 April 1969, leaving:

1e Robert Stanley Hickman; *b* 8 Dec 1934; *educ* Sherborne and Ch Ch Oxford (MA); slr; *m* 23 Oct 1965 *Ann [Mrs Robert Molesworth, 23 Pavenham Rd, Carlton, Beds], er dau of Anthony Metcalfe Gibson, of Greenside Head, Ravenstonedale, Westmorland, and *d* 4 May 1998, leaving:

1f +William Metcalfe; *b* 26 Feb 1968

2f +Philip Hoare; *b* 5 May 1970

1f *Catherine Jessie; *b* 14 Oct 1966

2e +Richard Baxter [Richard Molesworth Esq, 4 Fromfield Place, Fromfield, E Sussex TN22 5QH]; *b* 26 Aug 1939; *educ* Sherborne and Trin Coll Dublin; *m* 23 April 1966 *Ann Kathleen Duncan, er dau of Frederick N H Pexton, of Le Jardin Renaut, St Saviours, Guernsey, CI, and has:

1f +Edward James Hickman; *b* 25 Sept 1967

1f *Rachel Jane; *b* 5 Nov 1970; *m* 1996 *Gavin Robin Cunningham Manger

2f *Victoria Bridget; *b* 1975

1e *Bridget Margaret [Mrs John Heyworth, 1 Wesley Close, Park Lane, Reigate, Surrey RH2 8JS]; *b* 20 July 1931; *m* 25 Sept 1954 *John Ormerod Heyworth, yr s of Lawrence Heyworth, and has:

1f *James Hickman Frederick; *b* 11 Jan 1958; *m* 1993 *Julie Caroline, dau of John Bannister, of Frampton, Lincs, and has:

1g *George Marshall John; *b* 9 Aug 1995

2g *Thomas James Oliver; *b* 13 April 1997

2f *Peter Lawrence Ormerod; *b* 28 May 1963; *m* 1994 *Susan Kathleen, yst dau of John Gill, of Vessy, Geneva, Switzerland

1f *Caroline Margaret; *b* 14 July 1956; *m* 1st 1981 Richard Neil Burnard, s of Victor Burnard, and has:

    1g *Olivia Rose Victoria; *b* 29 Sept 1988

1f (cont.) Mrs Burnard *m* 2nd 1995 *Stuart Holder, s of Mark Holder, and has by him:

    1g *Toby Heyworth; *b* 20 Sept 1997

3d Margaret Alice Elaine; *m* 23 Feb 1907 Maj-Gen William George Walker, VC, CB, IA, and *d* 19 May 1973, leaving issue. He *d* 16 Feb 1936

4d Lynette Emily Ffloyd; *m* 27 April 1910 John Lee Matheson, est s of John Matheson, of Moranghukr, Victoria, and *dsp* 13 June 1949

5d Oenone Florence Mary; *m* 1st 7 June 1911 Capt Francis Buchanan Lefroy, Leinster Regt (*d* 26 Sept 1913), yr s of Capt Robert Lefroy, JP; *m* 2nd 25 May 1921 Geoffrey H Palmer (*see* PALMER, B) and *d* 11 Jan 1977

2c Robert Arthur; *b* 15 April 1843; *m* 10 June 1874 Flora Macdonald (*d* 13 Feb 1911), 2nd dau of John Matheson, and *d* 1 Nov 1920, having had:

1d John Matheson; *b* 16 Feb 1878; *m* 6 Dec 1906 Elizabeth Flora Frances Hill (*d* 12 Feb 1951), er dau of Edwin M James, MRCSE, and *d* 27 Aug 1942, leaving:

1e +Richard William Edwin [Richard Molesworth Esq, Cowl-Cowl, Linacre Road, Hampton, Victoria, Australia]; *b* 4 Dec 1908; *m* 17 Dec 1937 *Dirleen Muriel, 2nd dau of Leslie Sprague, of Geelong, and has had:

    1f +Michael John Leslie; *b* 1941, BSc, MSc; *m* 1st 1967 (*divorce* 1984) Caroline Carse Hay (BA) and has:

        1g *Tamsin Louise; *b* 1972

        2g *Amanda Frances; *b* 1976

        3g *Charlotte Marie Louise; *b* 1981

    1f (cont.) Michael Molesworth *m* 2nd *19– Annette Rilton and by her has:

        1g +Christopher James Michael; *b* 1981

        2g +Timothy Mark Richard; *b* 1985

        4g *Louise Annette Marie; *b* 1988

    2f +Simon Richard [Simon Molesworth Esq, 9 Loller St, Brighton, Victoria, Australia]; *b* 1954; barrister; *m* 1983 *Rosalind Marie Cochrane (BSc) and has:

        1g +Lachlan James Simon; *b* 1984

        1g *Anika Genevieve Fleur; *b* 1989

    1f Frances Dirleen; *b* and *d* 1943

    2f *Corinne Dirleen; *b* 9 June 1949, BA; *m* 1981 *David Ross Fraser (BA) and has:

        1g *Hamish Ross Molesworth; *b* 1985

        2g *Edwina Ross Molesworth; *b* 1983

2e +John Robert Nassau, DFC [John Molesworth Esq DFC, Ballark, Morrisons, Victoria, Australia]; S/Ldr RAAF WW II; *b* 30 April 1910; *m* 27 July 1940 *Sheila Morrell, dau of Charles Armytage, of The Wilderness, Coleraine, Victoria, Australia, and has:

    1f +Robert John Armytage [Robert Molesworth Esq, Lindavale, Morrisons, Elaine, Victoria, Australia]; *b* 29 Dec 1941; *m* 1967 *Amanda Grage and has:

        1g +Charles John Matheson; *b* 1968

        2g +Edward Paul; *b* 1971

        3g +Peter Robert; *b* 1976

        1g *Katrina Mary; *b* 1974

    2f +John Peter Armytage [John Molesworth Esq, Ballark, Morrisons, Elaine, Victoria 3334, Australia]; *b* 19 Nov 1944; *m* 1st 1970 (*divorce* 1987) Georgina Mary Pierrepont and has:

        1g +James Robert Beiri; *b* 22 May 1975

        1g *Emma Pamela Pierrepont; *b* 27 Nov 1972

    2f (cont.) John Molesworth *m* 2nd June 1989 *Elizabeth Eddy and by her has:

        2g *Kate Elizabeth; *b* 25 Feb 1993

    1f *Morrell Frances Armytage; *b* 16 Nov 1945; *m* 1967 *Michael Earle and has issue (*see* EARLE, Bt)

    2f *Jackalyn Armytage [Mrs Barry Lazarus, 21 Dwyer St, Sunshine Beach, Qld 4567, Australia]; *b* 1949; *m* 1974 *Barry Lazarus and has:

        1g *James Albert; *b* 1982

        1g *Georgina Armytage; *b* 1979

3e John Bysse, of Abbington, Gordon, Victoria, Australia; WW II as Pte AIF; *b* 15 Sept 1912; *m* 21 June 1941 *Jessie Martha, dau of W Thomas, of Chartres Towers, Qld, and *d* 1977, leaving:

    1f +David John [David Molesworth Esq, 25 Meigs Cres, Stuart Park 5790, NT, Australia]; *b* 7 April 1942; *m* 1965 (*divorce* 1976) Diana Lynette, dau of Thomas E Mann, of Caulfield S, Melbourne, and has:

        1g +Nicolas Andrew; *b* 1973

    1f *Judith Hill; *b* 1 June 1946, BA; *m* 1st 1969 (*divorce* 1981) Roger John Young (BEng) and has:

        1g *Tristan Samuel; *b* 1972

    1f (cont.) Mrs Judith Young *m* 2nd 1981 *Peter Fleming Terracall and by him has:

        1g *Mikaila Hill; *b* 1981

4e +Edwin Noel Walter [Edwin Molesworth Esq, Mittagong, 31 Governor's Drive, Mt Macedon, Victoria 3441, Australia]; *b* 6 Jan 1916; *m* 3 July 1940 *Alison Mary, dau of Alexander Dalrymple, of Glenluce, Gisborne, Australia, and has:

1f +William Anthony Hill; *b* 5 June 1941; *educ* Geelong C of E GS and U of Melbourne (BAgSci); *m* 1973 *Merran Sutherland and has:

    1g +Stephen Alexander; *b* 1975

    1g *Amy Merran Hill; *b* 1979

2f +Richard Matheson; *b* 7 Jan 1948; BAgSc; *m* 1977 *Janet Elaine McIntyre and has:

    1g *Louise Elizabeth; *b* 1980

    2g *Katherine Wendy; *b* 1982

1e *Flora Roma Maroa; *b* 22 Oct 1907; *m* 16 May 1939 *Frank Hobill-Cole and has:

    1f *Robert Molesworth; *b* 9 Feb 1940; *educ* Melbourne C of E GS

    2f *Frank Molesworth; *b* 13 Aug 1948; *educ* Melbourne C of E GS

    1f *Letitia Molesworth [Mrs William Shelton, Little Mittagong, 6 Hawksburn Rd, South Yarra SE1, Vict, Australia]; *b* 10 Dec 1941; *m* 22 July 1964 *William Geoffrey Shelton, 2nd s of Capt John Thomas Shelton, and has:

        1g *Lucile Matheson; *b* 18 April 1966

        2g *Sophie Letitia; *b* 9 June 1968

    2f *Rowena Molesworth; *b* 6 Sept 1943

2e *Mary Margaret Hill [Mrs Richard Hope, Burlendi, Coleraine, Vict, Australia]; *b* 26 Oct 1921; *m* 9 March 1943 Richard Sladen Hope (*d* 1981), s of R E H Hope, of Wolta-Wolta, Clare, S Australia, and has:

    1f *Christopher Sladen [Christopher Hope Esq, 71 Canterbury Rd, Middle Park, Vict, Australia]; *b* 10 Aug 1947; MIE, Polar Medal; *m* 1982 *Wendy (TPCT, Dip Ed), dau of Patrick Jones, and has:

        1g *Richard Francis Sladen; *b* 1984

        2g *David William; *b* 1986

    2f *Roland Molesworth; *b* 12 Oct 1949

    3f *Linden Kenny [Linden Hope Esq, Wolta Wolta, Bungower Rd, Moorooduc, Vict, Australia]; *b* 18 Aug 1954; *m* 1977 *Priscilla Jane (BA, LLB), dau of Ross Boaden, MSc, of Mt Eliza, Victoria, and has:

        1g *Edward Charles Kenney; *b* 1984

        1g *Emily Jane Kenney; *b* 1981

2d Robert Hickman; *b* 24 Nov 1879

3d William Edwin; *b* 19 Sept 1884; *d unm* 7 Aug 1907

1c Elizabeth Josephine; *m* 10 March 1869 George Edmeades Tolhurst

2a (cont) Hickman Molesworth *m* 2nd 1822 Maria (*dsp* 18 Jan 1861), 3rd dau of George Studdert, and *d* 3 May 1844

(3) St George; had:

    1a William St George

(4) Richard

(5) Ponsonby; Army Offr; *m* Susannah, sis of Sir R H Sheaffe, Bt (*see* 1851 edn)

(6) William

(7) John Cole

(1) Caroline; *m* Thomas Walker

(2) Florence; *m* as his first w Rev Thomas Colcough, DD, of Kilinagee, Co Kildare, 6th s of Caesar Colclough, of Tintern Abbey, Co Wexford, and had issue

(3) Alice

(4) Caroline Amelia

1 Mary; *m* George Monck, of Dublin

2 Charlotte Amelia; *m* Capt William Tichburne

3 Letitia; *m* Edward Bolton, of Brazeel, Co Dublin

4 Henrietta; *m* 10 Oct 1774 John Staples, PC

5 Louisa; *m* 1st 26 Dec 1769 1st Baron Ponsonby of Imokilly (*see* BESSBOROUGH, E) and had issue, *m* 2nd 21 July 1823 4th Earl Fitzwilliam (*d* 8 Feb 1833; *see* 1970 edn) and *d* 1 Sept 1824

6 Elizabeth; *m* James Stewart, of Killymoon, Co Tyrone, and *d* 30 April 1835

7 Charlotte

The 7th VISCOUNT's nephew,

SAMUEL MOLESWORTH, **8th Viscount Molesworth of Swords**; *b* 19 Dec 1829; *educ* Cambridge (MA); Rector St Petrock, Cornwall, 1876–98; *m* 1st 6 May 1862 Georgina Charlotte Cecil (*d* 22 Jan 1879), yst dau and coheir of George Bagot Gosset, 4th Dragoon Gds, by Charlotte Douglas, afterwards Marchesa di Vinchiaturo, and had:

1 **GEORGE BAGOT MOLESWRTH**, **9th Viscount Molesworth of Swords**; *b* 6 June 1867; *educ* Wellington; Maj Army Pay Dept, Capt DCLI; *m* 6 Feb 1894 Nina Alida (*d* 25 March 1958), dau of Col H D Faulkner, and *d* 20 March 1947, having had:

(1) Charles Willoughby Murray; 2nd Lt DCLI; *b* 21 Nov 1897; *d* 15 April 1917 of wounds recd in action

(1) Irene Evelyn Beatrice; *b* 22 Sept 1895; *m* 1st 14 Oct 1917 Capt Charles Donovan Rowley, MBE (*see* ROWLEY, Bt); *m* 2nd 8 March 1941 Francis Henry Ash, of Narborough Hall, King's Lynn, Norfolk, s of Arthur Edward Ash, of Kensington, and *d* 7 Sept 1949

(2) Cicely Sylvia; *b* 25 July 1902; *m* 15 Oct 1927 (*divorce* 1937) Guy Haylett Walker Ramsey (*d* 11 Oct 1959), s of Cecil Ramsey, of Hampstead, and *d* 11 July 1986, leaving:

    1a *Valentine Bagot Rudolph Haylett Walker [Valentine Ramsey Esq, 12 Parkfield, Horsham, W Sussex RH12 2BG]; *b* 8 May 1928; *m* 5 Sept 1959 (*divorce* 1972) Shirley Mary Clare Esterre, only dau of Reginald E Jex, of Barton-on-Sea, Hants, and has:

        1b *Guy Dominic Jex Haylett; *b* 11 Oct 1960

        1b *Michelle Elizabeth d'Esterre; *b* 22 March 1963

2 **CHARLES RICHARD**, **10th Viscount**

3 Arthur Ernest Parnell; *b* 1 May 1870; *educ* Clifton; *m* 28 Nov 1910 Nellie Maud, JP Dominion of NZ (*d* 2 Jan 1956), widow of Dr George Watson, of S America, and dau of George W Banks, of Wellington, NZ, and *d* 2 Sept 1951, leaving:

(1) Frank Ernest Bysse; *b* 15 Dec 1911; *educ* Auckland GS and Auckland U; *m* 1st Aug 1934 (*divorce* 1940) Phyllis Margaret Patrick, dau of George Wells, of Auckland; *m* 2nd 1943 (*divorce* 1957) Joan, JP (1949), dau of Alfred George Lethbridge, of Thames Valley, and Taranaki, NZ; *m* 3rd 1961 Nellie Verdun, dau of Edward Hughes, of Hikurangi, NZ; *m* 4th 1982 *Bernice Sheila Polden Bell, 7th dau of George Augustus Hawkes, of NZ, and *d* 19–, leaving by his 3rd w:

1a *Helen Deirdre Velvet; *b* 1962

(1) *Betty Eleanor Gosset [Mrs Frank Allen, Villa Coca, Los Barrios, Prov Cadiz, Andalusia, Spain] *b* 21 July 1913; *m* 1 May 1948 Frank Geoffrey Harald Allen, W/Cdr RAFVR (*d* 1985)

4 Samuel Percy; *b* 29 July 1873; *d* 29 Jan 1897

1 Andalusia Louisa Charlotte Georgina; *m* 30 April 1887 John Athelstan Laurie Riley, of Kensington, and *d* 29 Feb 1912, leaving issue. He *d* 17 Nov 1945

2 Charlotte Elizabeth; *m* 16 Oct 1883 Rev Henry Edward James Bevan, Rector Chelsea, and *d* 8 Aug 1931, leaving issue. He *d* 11 July 1935

3 Gwen Gertrude Mary; *m* 9 May 1906 Col Julius Dyson Dyson-Laurie, Border Regt, and *d* 12 March 1951, leaving issue. He *d* 19 Dec 1909

The **8th Viscount** *m* 2nd 23 Jan 1883 Agnes (*dsp* 20 Jan 1905), dau of Dugald Dove, of Nutshill, Renfrewshire, and *d* 7 June 1906

The 9th VISCOUNT's bro,

CHARLES RICHARD MOLESWORTH, **10th Viscount Molesworth of Swords**; *b* 3 Jan 1860; *educ* Cheltenham; *m* 4 Dec 1906 Elizabeth Gladys, (*d* 27 May 1974), dau of Edward Martin Langworthy, and *d* 24 Feb 1961, having had:

1 RICHARD GOSSET MOLESWORTH, **11th Viscount Molesworth of Swords**; *b* 31 Oct 1907; *educ* Lancing; RAF WW II, Freeman City London 1978; *m* 29 Aug 1958 *Ann Florence, MA [The Rt Hon The Viscountess Molesworth, Garden Flat, 2 Bishopswood Rd, London N6 4PR], and *d* 15 Oct 1997, leaving:

(1) ROBERT BYSSE KELHAM MOLESWORTH, **12th and present Viscount Molesworth of Swords**

(2) +WILLIAM JOHN CHARLES; *b* 20 Oct 1960; heir presumptive; *educ* Cheltenham and Trin Coll Cambridge (MA); LTCL

2 James Vernon Crispin; Lt DCLI and Commandos (attached Chindits) WW II; *b* 24 Oct 1917; *d* a POW Burma 1943

1 Joan; *b* 4 July 1919

MOLESWORTH-ST AUBYN

Arms: Quarterly, 1st and 4th, erm. on a cross sa. five bezants (for ST AUBYN); 2nd and 3rd, gu. an escutcheon vair between eight cross-crosslets in orle arg. (for MOLESWORTH). **Crest:** A rock, thereon a Cornish chough rising, all ppr.
Creation: Bt. (E) 19 July 1689.

SIR WILIAM MOLESWORTH-ST AUBYN, 16TH BT, of Pencarrow, Cornwall [Sir William Molesworth-St Aubyn Bt, Pencarrow, Bodmin, Cornwall PL30 3AG; 8 St Stephen's Rd, London W12]; *b* 23 Nov 1958; *s* f 1998; *educ* Harrow; late Capt RGJ; *m* 1988 *Carolyn M, er dau of William H Tozier, of Chelsea, and has:

1 +ARCHIE; *b* 27 March 1997

1 *Jemima; *b* 28 Oct 1995

Lineage: JOHN MOLESWORTH; *b* 1516 (see MOLESWORTH, V); had a 4th s:

JOHN MOLESWORTH; Auditor Cornwall; settled at Pencarrow by 1620; *m* 1st Catherine, est dau and coheir of John Hender, of Botreaux Castle, Cornwall; *m* 2nd Philippa, dau of Henry Rolle, of Heanton, Devon, and by his 1st w had, with a yr s (John, *b* 1601, *k* expdn to Ile de Rhé 1627):

HENDER MOLESWORTH, of Pencarrow, Cornwall; *b* 1597; *m* Mary, est dau of John Spark, of The Friary, Plymouth, and *d* 1647, having had, with a yst s, also a 2nd s (**Sir Hender Molesworth, 1st Bt** (E), so *cr* 19 July 1689 with remainder to

his er bro, settled at St Katherine's, Jamaica, where Pres Cncl and Lt-Govr 1684; *m* 1st Grace, widow of Thomas Tottle, of Jamaica, and dau of Capt George Mangye, of Jamaica; *m* 2nd 12 Feb 1688/9 Mary (*d* 11 July 1721), widow of Sir Thomas Lynch, Govr Jamaica, and dau and coheir of Thomas Temple, of Franckton, Warwicks, and was *bur* 12 Aug 1689):

Sir John Molesworth, 2nd Bt; ktd, V-Adml N Cornwall, MP Bossiney 1701 and Lostwithiel 1702; *bapt* 27 May 1635; *m* 1st 7 Oct 1663 Margery (*d* 19 June 1671), est dau of Thomas Wise, of Sydenham, Devon; *m* 2nd Margaret (*dsp* 12 Feb 1682), dau of Sir Nicholas Slanning, and was *bur* 1 Oct 1716, leaving:

Sir John Molesworth, 3rd Bt; *bapt* 23 June 1668; *m* 19 Sept 1699 Jane (*bur* 6 May 1719), dau of John Arscott, of Tetcott, Devon, and was *bur* 20 June 1723, leaving:

Sir John Molesworth, 4th Bt; MP Newport, Cornwall, 1734 and Cornwall 1744–61; *bapt* 28 Feb 1705; *m* 1728 Barbara (*d* 17 May 1755), 2nd dau and coheir of Sir Nicholas Morrice, 2nd Bt, of Werrington, Devon, and had:

1 JOHN (Sir), **5th Bt**

2 William, of Wembury, Devon; *m* Anne, dau and coheir of James Smyth, of St Audries, Somerset, and *d* 9 Feb 1762, leaving:

(1) Frances; *m* 31 Dec 1785 1st Marquess Camden (*qv*) and *d* 7 July 1829, leaving issue

Sir JOHN *d* 4 April 1766; his est s,

Sir John Molesworth, 5th Bt; Col Cornwall Militia, MP Cornwall 1765–75; *b* 12 March 1729; *m* 1st 28 Sept 1755 Frances (*d* 1 July 1758), dau and coheir of James Smyth, of St Audries, and had:

1 **Sir William Molesworth, 6th Bt**; MP Cornwall 1784–90; *b* 30 June 1758; *m* 27 May 1786 Caroline Treby (*d* 10 Dec 1842), dau of Paul Henry Ourry, and *d* 22 Feb 1798, having had, with two daus:

(1) **Sir Arscott Ourry Molesworth, 7th Bt**; *b* 1789; *m* 7 July 1809 Mary (*d* 16 April 1877), est dau of Patrick Brown, of Edinburgh, and *d* 30 Dec 1823, having had, with other issue:

1a **Sir William Molesworth, 8th Bt**; MP (Lib) Cornwall 1832–37, Leeds 1837–41, Southwark 1845–55, 1st Commr Works 1852, Sec State Colonies 1855; *b* 23 May 1810; *m* 9 July 1844 Andalusia Grant (*d* 16 May 1888), widow of Temple West, of Mathon Lodge, Worcs, and only dau of Bruce Carstairs, and *dsp* 22 Oct 1855

1a Mary; *m* 12 June 1851 Richard Ford, of Heavitree, Devon, writer and patron of the arts, and *d* 4 March 1910. He *d* 1 Sept 1868

(2) William (Rev); Rector St Breoke, Cornwall; *b* 5 Nov 1792; *m* 1st 6 Nov 1817 Katherine (*d* 26 May 1823), est dau of Paul Treby, of Plympton, Devon, and had:

1a **Rev Sir Hugh Henry Molesworth, 9th Bt**; Rector St Petroc-Minor, Cornwall; *b* 13 Oct 1818; *m* 15 July 1856 Beatrice Anne (*d* 3 March 1902), yst dau of Charles Prideaux Brune, of Prideaux Place, Cornwall, and *d* 6 Jan 1862, having had:

1b Hugh Prideaux; *b* 17 June 1857; *d* an infant

2a Montague Treby; Lt RN; *k* by natives off Madagascar coast March 1844

3a **Sir Paul William Molesworth, 10th Bt**; *bapt* 13 Jan 1821; *m* 25 Sept 1849 Jane Frances (*d* 17 Feb 1912), est dau of Gordon William Francis Gregor, of Trewarthenick, Cornwall, and *d* 23 Dec 1889, having had, with other issue:

1b **Sir Lewis William Molesworth, 11th Bt**; JP, DL Cornwall; High Sheriff 1899, MP Bodmin 1900–06, FRGS; *b* 31 Oct 1853; *m* 3 June 1875 Jane Graham (*d* 21 Sept 1913), 2nd dau of Brig-Gen Daniel Marsh Frost, US Army, of St Louis, and *dsp* 29 May 1912

1b Mary Letitia; *b* 11 Nov 1858; *m* 15 June 1882 Henry Acton Welman and *d* 12 March 1936, leaving issue. He *d* 19 May 1928

2b Katharine Maud Morwenna; *b* 30 July 1860; *m* 5 Sept 1888 Gerard Wilfrid Welman, of Torquay, Devon, and *d* 12 March 1925, leaving issue. He *d* 2 Aug 1913

4a Walter Hele; *b* 26 May 1823; *m* 10 March 1840 Frances Mary (*d* 17 July 1892), only dau of Adml Henry Duncan Twysden (see 1970 edn TWYSDEN, Bt), and *d* 11 Jan 1885, leaving:

1b Katherine Twysden; *m* 3 July 1871 Rev John Dene (*d* 1922), Rector Horwood, Devon, and *d* 1 March 1932, leaving issue (see WREY, BT)

2b Blanche Mary Twysden; *m* 15 Jan 1878 Arthur Bowen Richards Myers, Bde-Surgn-Lt-Col Bde of Gds, and *d* 18 Oct 1919, leaving issue. He *d* 6 Aug 1921

3b Cordelia Twysden; *m* 15 Jan 1873 Col Hon Edward Henry Legge and *d* 19 March 1915, leaving issue (see DARTMOUTH, E)

4b Imogen Isabella Twysden; *m* 26 July 1881 Rev Richard Johnstone, Rector Stone, Staffs, and *d* 20 Jan 1931, leaving issue. He *d* 1894

(2) (cont.) The Rev William Molesworth *m* 2nd 10 Feb 1820 Frances Susanna, dau of James Buller, of Downes, Devon, and *d* 28 March 1851, having by her had:

5a James; Lt Roy Fus; *d* Malta 5 Oct 1854

1a Frances; *m* 6 Oct 1863 Edward H J Craufurd, MP Ayr Burghs, and *d* 26 Sept 1899, leaving issue. He *d* 29 Aug 1887

Sir John *m* 2nd 22 July 1762 Barbara (*d* 14 Aug 1814), yst dau of Sir John St Aubyn, 3rd Bt, of Clowance, Cornwall, and *d* 20 Oct 1775, having by her had, with two daus:

2 John (Rev); LLB; *b* 3 Sept 1763; *m* 18 June 1790 Catherine (*d* 21 Oct 1836), 2nd dau and eventually coheir of Sir John St Aubyn, 4th Bt (see SAINT LEVAN, B), and *d* 18 Sept 1811, leaving, with two daus:

(1) John MOLESWORTH later MOLESWORTH-ST AUBYN (roy licence 15 Nov 1839) (Rev), of Clowance, Cornwall; *b* 21 April 1791; MA Oxon; *dsp* 28 Jan 1844

(2) Hender MOLESWORTH later MOLESWORTH-ST AUBYN (roy licence 14 March 1844) (Rev), of Clowance, JP, BA Oxon; *b* 12 March 1798; *m* 1 Jan 1829 Helen Matilda Isabella (*d* 28 March 1877), dau of Rev Timothy Napleton, and *d* 13 Dec 1867, leaving:

1a Hender John, of Clowance, JP, DL; *b* 21 Dec 1829; *m* 1 Jan 1856 Kythe Catherine (*m* 2nd 26 April 1881 Edward Maurice Greenway, of Haines Hill, Taunton; *d* 2 April 1905), dau of Christopher Wallis Popham, of Trevarno, Cornwall, and *dsp* 26 June 1868

2a ST AUBYN HENDER (Sir), **12th Bt**

3a Walter Napleton MOLESWORTH; barrister, MP Helston 1880–85; *b* 18 Oct 1838; *educ* Ch Ch Oxford (MA); *m* 21 Jan 1880 Anne (*d* June 1914), widow of Charles Gaddon Mitchell Smith and dau of George Coles, and *dsp* 29 June 1895

(3) St Aubyn, Col RE; *b* 27 April 1800; *m* 15 Jan 1833 Isabella Margaretta (*d* 28 March 1887), dau of Richard Waring, and *d* 19 Sept 1858, leaving, with a dau (*d* unm):

1a St Aubyn; Col RA; *b* 26 March 1843; *m* 12 Feb 1874 Jane Emily (*d* 27 June 1916), dau of J P Magor, and *d* 18 Aug 1914, having had:

1b Edward Algernon, DSO; Maj 1st Bn Roy Dublin Fus Boer War 1899–1902 (Queen's medal with five clasps, King's medal with two clasps) and WW I (wounded, despatches); *b* 9 May 1875; *m* 9 Aug 1916 Ruth, 3rd dau of Leslie Creery, of Co Dublin, and *d* 2 July 1939, leaving:

1c +St Aubyn; Ch Engr S African Marine Corps; *b* 1917

2b Arthur St Aubyn; Capt DCLI; *b* 7 June 1878; *d* unm 22 Dec 1911

2a St John; *b* 4 Dec 1847; *d* 23 Nov 1919

1a Catherine; *m* 8 Aug 1861 Lt-Col James Herne Wade, 90th LI and 35rd Regt, and *d* 19 April 1911, having had issue. He *d* 22 Sept 1908

2a Isabella; *m* 29 Oct 1872 Capt Arthur George Fullerton, RN, and *dsp* 7 Nov 1906. He *d* 9 Sept 1930

The 11th Bt's cousin,

Rev Sir St Aubyn Hender Molesworth-St Aubyn, 12th Bt, JP Cornwall; *b* 27 Dec 1833; *educ* Ch Ch Oxford (MA); Vicar Collingham Yorks 1868–74; *m* 1st 3 June 1862 Caroline (*d* 8 June 1899), 3rd dau of Rev Charles Wheler, of Ledstone Hall, Yorks (*see* WHELER, Bt), and had:

1 HUGH (Sir), **13th Bt**

2 Beville; *b* 4 Feb 1871; *educ* Ch Ch Oxford (BA); chartered surveyor, PASI, FLAS, Hants Inf Yeo Boer War 1899–1901; *m* 22 Oct 1902 Georgiana Mary (*d* 6 Feb 1946), widow of Sir Walter George Barttelot, 2nd Bt (*qv*), and only dau of George Edmond Balfour, of Sidmouth, and *dsp* 24 Sept 1946

1 Helen Flora; *m* 20 Aug 1891 Rev Charles Rowland Wynne de Cerjat, Rector Gt Hallingbury, Herts, and *d* 9 March 1930, leaving issue. He *d* 29 March 1917

2 Annie Caroline; *m* 19 Oct 1897 Edward Harvey Williams (*see* WILLIAMS, Bt, of Tregullow) and *d* 10 Feb 1943

Sir St Aubyn *m* 2nd 2 Sept 1902 Ingeborg Alfhild, OBE (1920) (*d* 11 Dec 1928), dau of Johan Viggo Sigvald Muller, of Beaucliffe, Newquay, Cornwall, and *d* 18 May 1913

His est son,

Sir Hugh Molesworth-St Aubyn, 13th Bt, JP (Cornwall 1903–42); *b* 8 Jan 1865; *educ* Charterhouse and Ch Ch Oxford (BA 1890); Cornwall CC 1910–19, High Sheriff 1922–23, Capt DCLI WW I Depot DCLI Bodmin; *m* 26 June 1894 Emma Sybil (*d* 4 April 1929), dau of Adml Charles Wake (*see* WAKE, Bt), and had:

1 JOHN (Sir), **14th Bt**

2 Hender Charles, TD; *b* 5 Jan 1901; *educ* Eton; Maj Roy Pioneer Corps, Capt Roy Devon Yeo Art (Res Offrs) WW II Iceland, France and Germany; *m* 26 Oct 1935 (*divorce* 1946) Dulcebella Joy, er dau of Lt-Col John Cayzer Medlicott-Vereker (*see* GORT, V), and *d* 1986, leaving:

(1) *(Caroline) Gay [Mrs Simon Foord, Hill Farm House, Bures, Suffolk]; *b* 15 Feb 1940; *m* 27 July 1963 *(Edward) Simon Foord, only s of Brig Edward John Foord, CBE, and has:

1a *Edward Richard; *b* 4 July 1965

1a *Nicola Samantha; *b* 24 July 1967; *m* 1995 *Paul Richard Sercombe, 3rd s of John Sercombe, and has:

1b *Alice Olivia; *b* 31 Oct 1996

2a *Annabel Jane; *b* 12 July 1971

3 Guy Kemyel; *b* 7 July 1904; *educ* Eton and Ch Ch Oxford; *m* 6 June 1931 Catherine, JP (Herts 1951) (*d* 1979), yst dau of Richard Tattersall Hargreaves, of Benington Park, Herts, and *d* 1981, leaving:

(1) +Anthony William [Anthony Molesworth-St Aubyn Esq, Cobbs, Howe St, nr Chelmsford, Essex CM3 1BT]; *b* 19 Dec 1936; *educ* Eton; *m* 3 April 1964 *Mary Evelyn, only dau of Kenneth Matthew Meiklejohn, and has:

1a +Charles Hugh [Charles Molesworth-St Aubyn Esq, Grooms Cottage, Ashby Folville, Leics]; *b* 18 April 1966; *educ* Eton; late Capt RGJ; *m* 1992 *Zoë, dau of J J Prow, and Mrs F M Gibson, of Notts, and has:

1b +Samuel Guy; *b* 3 Nov 1994

1b *Alexandra Frances; *b* 6 Dec 1992

1a *Anna Victoria [Countess Peter Krasinsky, VI Czarnieckieeo 50m I Warsaw, Poland]; *b* 24 March 1970; *m* 1997 *Count Peter Krasinsky

(2) Simon Guy; *b* 24 June 1944; *educ* Eton; Maj 60th Rifles; *m* 3 June 1977 *Amanda Juliet, er dau of George B Walker, and *d* 1995, leaving:

1a +Thomas Kemyel; *b* 1981

1a *Cressida Juliet; *b* 1988

(1) *Felicity Sybil [The Hon Lady Butler, The Old Rectory, Lighthorne, Warwicks]; *b* 6 May 1932; High Sheriff Warwicks 1997–98; *m* 21 Oct 1955 *Hon Sir Adam Courtauld Butler, PC, 2nd s of Baron Butler of Saffron Walden (LP; *see* 1970 edn), and has issue

1 Guinevere May; *b* 4 May 1895; *m* 16 July 1921 Charles Edward Honoratus Lloyd, s of Edward Honoratus Lloyd, KC, and *d* March 1966

Sir HUGH *d* 5 Jan 1942; his est son,

Sir John Molesworth-St Aubyn, 14th Bt, CBE (1968), JP (Devon 1941 and Cornwall 1942); *b* 12 Jan 1899; *educ* Eton and Ch Ch Oxford (BA 1920); F/Lt RAFVR WW II, Cornwall: CA, High Sheriff 1948, chm Ag Exec Ctee, local dir Lloyds Bank Ltd; *m* 12 Jan 1926 Celia Marjorie (*d* 11 Oct 1965), est dau of Lt-Col Valentine Vivian, CMG, DSO, MVO, by Aline Mary, dau of 5th Earl of Portarlington (*qv*), and *d* 1985, having:

1 **Sir (John) Arscott Molesworth-St Aubyn, 15th Bt**, MBE (1963), JP (Devon 1971), DL (Cornwall 1971); *b* 15 Dec 1926; *educ* Eton; 2nd Lt KRRC 1946, Malaya 1961–63, RGJ 1966, Lt-Col 1967, ret 1969, High Sheriff Cornwall 1975–76, Co Commr Scouts Cornwall 1969–79, Pres Roy Cornwall Ag Assoc 1976, memb Cncl Devon Co Ag Assoc 1979–82; *m* 2 May 1957 *Iona Audrey

Armatrude [Iona Lady Molesworth-St Aubyn, Pencarrow, Bodmin, Cornwall PL30 3AG], dau of Adml Sir Francis Tottenham, KCB, CBE, and *d*, apparently by his own hand, 22 April 1998, leaving:

(1) Sir WILLIAM MOLESWORTH-ST AUBYN, **16th and present Bt**

(2) +James Francis [James Molesworth-St Aubyn Esq, Garden Cottage, Pencarrow, Cornwall PL30 3AG]; *b* 7 Oct 1960; *educ* Harrow

(1) *Emma Jane; *b* 10 Feb 1971; *m* 28 Sept 1996 *Maj Simon David Oliver, Roy Scots Dragoon Gds, yr s of Lt-Col M D Oliver, of Pimperne, Dorset

2 Christopher Mark; *b* 10 Jan 1933; *d* 17 July 1935

1 *Johanna Katherine [The Rt Hon The Countess of Morley, Pound House, Yelverton, Devon PL20 7LJ]; *b* 22 Jan 1929; *m* 15 Oct 1955 *6th Earl of Morley (*qv*) and has issue

2 *Prudence Aline [Mrs Joseph Cooke-Hurle, Long Ash, Buckland Monachorum, Devon PL20 7LL]; *b* 26 May 1937; *m* 27 Sept 1969 *Joseph Robertson Cooke-Hurle, only child of Lt-Col Reginald Joseph Cooke-Hurle, RA (*see also* ROSSE, E), and has:

(1) *Celia Hermione; *b* 12 Aug 1970

(2) *Penelope Joy; *b* 30 Sept 1971

Seat: Pencarrow, Washaway, Bodmin, Cornwall. When in the mid-18th century **Sir John Molesworth, 4th Bt**, commissioned a new house he chose to design the plans a man from almost the other end of the country, Robert Allanson, of York. Not that the earlier house was entirely swept away: remains of it are still visible on the western elevation. But the principal facade, that to the south, is a lusciously harmonious Palladian creation of three storeys with two bays either side of a three-bay break-front centre. The middle storey has triangular pediments above the windows in the outer bays, low-pitched curvilinear D-shaped ones to those in the three central bays. A dentillated cornice above supports a classical pediment ornamented with a blind oculus in the centre. The creamy pinkish-buff stucco adds warmth. The triangular pediment atop the portico surmounts a door of four glazed panels. The gardens are very fine, being laid out so as to show the rhododendra and azaleas to best advantage, while the drive up to the house winds through thick woods. Inside the chief attractions are the music room and library, although these are later than Allanson's contribution, dating from the **8th Bt**'s time just prior to the mid-19th century. They are the work of George Wightwick, a pupil of Soane's who had built up a large West Country practice and whose essay on Wren won an RIBA medal in 1858–59.

MOLLOY

JUSTICE·AND·COMPASSION·

Arms: Vert on a rounded mount or an oak tree proper, leaved and fructed also or, and in base two barrulets wavy argent, all within a bordure ermine. **Crest**: Upon rocks thereon oyster shells proper a representation of the Mumbles Lighthouse at Swansea diffusing light from its lantern all proper. **Supporters**: Dexter, on a grassy mount proper a dragon passant, its tail looped gules, tongue and claws or; sinister, on a like mount a swan, wings displayed, inverted and addorsed, all proper. **Motto**: Justice and compassion. **Creation**: B. (LP, UK) 1981.

THE BARON MOLLOY, of Ealing in Greater London (William John Molloy) [The Rt Hon The Lord Molloy, House of Lords, London SW1A 0PW; 2a Uneeda Drive, Greenford, Middx UB6 8QB]; *b* 26 Oct 1918; *educ* St Thomas Swansea and Swansea Coll Wales U; memb TGWU 1936–46; RE WW II; memb: Civ Serv Union 1947–52 (ed *Civil Service Review*), Co-op and USDAW 1952; FO Staff-Side: Lecturer 1946–52, Chm Germany/Austria Sections Whitley Cncl 1948–52; Leader Fulham Borough Cncl 1959–62 (memb 1954–62); MP (Lab) Ealing N 1964–79; V-Chm PLP Gp for Common Market and European Affrs; Chm PLP Soc Servs Gp 1974; Parly Advsr: London Trades Cncl Transport Ctee 1968–70, COHSE 1974 (Sponsored MP 1972), Civ Serv Union 1974–79; PPS to Min Posts and Telecommunication 1969–70; Memb: Cncl Europe and WEU 1969–73, European Parl 1976–79; Memb: H of C Estimates Ctee 1968–70, CPA 1964, IPU 1964 (memb exec 1984–), Parly and Scientific Ctee 1982 and Saudi Arabia, Kuwait, Abu Dhabi, Bahrein, Iraq and Dubai Parly Gps; Political Consultant: COHSE 1979–, Br Library Assoc 1984–; Consultant and Advsr Arab League 1982–88; Pres Disabled Drivers' Assoc 1969–; Chm Br Tunisia Soc 1987–; Nat V-Pres Roy Br Legion 1994– (Chm Met Area 1985–93); Hon Life Pres: London U Debating Soc 1970, London U Union Soc 1983–; V-Pres and Tstee Health Visitors' Assoc

1987–; Fell World Assoc Arts and Sciences 1982; Hon Associate Br Veterinary Assoc 1988–; Hon Fell U Coll Swansea 1987; FRGS 1967; *m* 1st 1946 Eva Lewis (*d* 1980) and has:

1 *Marion Ann [The Hon Mrs Laurence Motl, 6225 Idylwood Lane, Edina, MN 55436, USA]; *b* 1947; *m* 1974 (*divorce* 1987) Laurence George Motl and has:

    (1) *Julia Mation; *b* 1976

    (2) *Ann Lillian; *b* 1979

The BARON MOLLOY *m* 2nd 1981 (*divorce* 1987) Doris Paines

Lineage: WILLIAM JOHN MOLLOY; had:

WILLIAM JOHN, *cr* a **Baron**

MOLONY

Arms: Gu. six arrows in saltire between two bows erect to dexter and sinister or, a chief erm. **Crest:** A dexter arm embowed in armour ppr., charged with a fleur-de-lys gu., the hand in a gauntlet holding a sword of the first. **Motto:** *In domino et non in arcu meo sperabo* ('In God and not in my bow will I put my trust'). **Creation:** Bt. (UK) 21 Jan 1925.

Thomas Desmond Molony, 3rd Bt [Desmond Molony Esq, 33 Ernest St, Leichardt, Qld 4305, Australia]; *b* 13 March 1937; *s* f 1976 but does not use title; *educ* Ampleforth and Trin Coll Dublin; P/O RAF (RO); *m* 16 June 1962 *Doris, dau of E W Foley, of Cork, and has:

1 *Jennifer Mary; *b* 1963

2 *Grace Ann; *b* 1964

3 *Daphne Julia; *b* 1965

4 *Lynda Jacqueline Rose; *b* 1967

Lineage: JAMES MOLONY, of Harcourt St, Dublin; *m* Jane, yst dau of Nicholas Sweetman, of New Bawn, Co Wexford, and had, with other issue:

Sir Thomas Francis Molony, 1st Bt (UK), so *cr* 21 Jan 1925, PC (I 1913), of Dublin; *b* 31 Jan 1865; *educ* Trin Coll Dublin (BA and LLB 1886, MA 1902, Hon LLD 1922); barrister King's Inn 1887, Bencher 1911, QC (I) 1899, barrister Middle Temple 1900, Crown Counsel Co Carlow 1906, Dublin City and County 1907; Ireland: 2nd Serjeant-at-law 1911, Slr-Gen 1912–13, Attorney-Gen 1913, High Court Judge 1913–15, Ld Justice Appeal 1915–18, Ld Ch Justice 1918–24, Commr Educn 1907–25, memb Intermediate Educn Bd 1914–23, pres Statistical and Social Inquiry Soc 1920–24; Visitor Trin Coll Dublin 1918–31, V-Cllr U of Dublin 1931, chm Home Office Ctee treatment juvenile offenders 1925 and Deptl Ctee Veterinary Educn 1936, Hon LLD Queen's U Belfast 1945, KGStJ, pres Irish Centre St John Ambulance Assoc, Hon Bencher Middle Temple 1933, dir Nat Bank Ltd; *m* 3 Jan 1899 Pauline (*d* 16 July 1951), only child of Bernard Rispin, of Eccles Street, Dublin, by Thomasina, dau of James Macken, of Palmerston, Co Dublin, and had:

    1 HUGH FRANCIS (Sir), **2nd Bt**

    2 Joseph Thomas (Sir), KCVO (1970), QC (1955); *b* 8 Dec 1907; *educ* Downside and Trin Coll Cambridge (BA 1929, LLB 1930, MA and LLM 1933); barrister Inner Temple 1930 (Bencher 1961), S/Ldr RAF WW II, Recorder Devizes 1951–54, Exeter 1954–58, Southampton 1960–64 and Bristol 1964–78, Commr Assize Midland and S Eastern Circuits 1958, Commr Assize NE Circuit 1960 and Western Circuit 1968, Attorney-Gen Duchy Cornwall 1960–69, *ktd* 1967, Chm Gen Cncl Bar 1963–66, Leader Western Circuit 1964–78; *m* 15 Aug 1936 Carmen Mary, only dau of Frankland Dent, PhD, FIC, MSc, and *d* 28 May 1978, leaving:

        (1) +PETER JOHN [Peter Molony Esq, Rock House, Great Elm, Somerset BA11 3NY]; *b* 17 Aug 1937; heir presumptive; *educ* Downside and Trin Coll Cambridge (MA); FCA, v-pres Sea Containers Inc 1968–73, dir: Post Office 1973–75, Scottish and Newcastle Breweries plc 1975–79, Rolls Royce plc 1979–86, Allied Leisure plc 1994–, Chemming Gp plc 1997–; *m* 28 Nov 1964 *Elizabeth Mary, est dau of Henry Clervaux Chaytor, of Cambridge, and has:

            1a +(James) Sebastian; *b* 2 Sept 1965

            2a +(John) Benjamin; *b* 19 Oct 1966

            3a +(Simon) Benedict; *b* 1972

            4a +(Thomas) Francis; *b* 1975

        1a *(Carmen) Jane; *b* 19 Dec 1967

        (2) +John Fernando [John Molony Esq, Clematis Cottage, St Ann's Lane, Godmanchester, Cambs PE18 8JF]; *b* 17 June 1949; *educ* Downside and Trin Coll Cambridge; *m* 1985 *Caroline Christine, yst dau of Brig Wilfred Ponsonby, OBE, of West Burton, N Yorks, and has:

            1a *Nicola Carmen; *b* 1986

            2a *Catherine Elizabeth; *b* 1988

        (1) *Mary Carmen [Mrs Martin Wells, 34 Beeleigh Rd, Maldon, Essex CM9 7QH]; *b* 26 Aug 1939; *m* 30 Nov 1963 *Martin Noble Wells, er s of William Thomas Wells, QC, MP, and has:

            1a *Nicholas Thomas Clinton; *b* 4 Sept 1964

            2a *Adrian Francis; *b* 4 Feb 1966

            3a *Jonathan Patrick; *b* 17 Nov 1968

            1a *Joanna Kate; *b* 1971

        (2) *Angela Carmen [Mrs Philip Vincent, Taverners, Woodeaton, Oxon OX3 9TH]; *b* 30 Sept 1942; MB, BS 1966, MSc 1969; *m* 27 May 1967 *Philip Morse Vincent, 3rd s of Peter Alan Clarke Vincent, and has:

            1a *Patrick Henry Morse; *b* 27 May 1970

            2a *Bruno Charles; *b* 1979

            1a *Antonia Louise; *b* 24 May 1968

            2a *Katherine Eleanor; *b* 1974

    3 John Bernard; *b* 30 Oct 1912; Sgt Pilot RAF WW II; *m* 27 April 1940 *Marjory (*m* 2nd Trevor Thomas) [Mrs Trevor Thomas, The Vice-Chancellor's Lodge, Sefton Park Rd, Liverpool], yst dau of Samuel Higgs, of Reading, and was *ka* 23 April 1941

    1 Eileen Mary

    2 Ita Mary Doreen; *m* 6 June 1942 Frederick William Hunt, DFC (*d* 19 Nov 1959), s of Lt-Cdr John Hunt, DSO, RN, and *d* 8 Dec 1959, leaving issue

    3 Marie Etienne

Sir THOMAS *d* 3 Sept 1949; his est son,

Sir Hugh Francis Molony, 2nd Bt; *b* 2 Sept 1900; *educ* Trin Coll Dublin (BA 1921, MA 1945, B Eng 1922, Master 1927); MICE, MICEI, MConsEI, consulting engr 1954, Engineering Inspr Mins Health 1938 and Housing and Local Govt 1938–54; *m* 13 June 1936 Alexandra Campbell (*d* 17 Sept 1983 aged 80), dau of John Alexander Todd, MRCVS, of Glasgow, and formerly w of Myles Cooper, of Argentina, and *d* 1976, leaving:

Sir (THOMAS) DESMOND MOLONY, **3rd and present Bt**

MOLYNEAUX OF KILLEAD

Arms: Gyronny of eight or and azure a cross moline between four alder leaves slipped inwards all counterchanged. **Crest:** A wolf statant or holding in the dexter forepaw a flax flower azure slipped and leaved or. **Supporters:** On either side a wolf argent regardant, unguled and langued gules, gorged with a collar or, therefrom pendant a chain also or. **Motto:** *In hoc signo vinces* ('In this sign thou shalt conquer') **Creation:** B. (LP, UK) 1997.

THE BARON MOLYNEAUX OF KILLEAD, of Killead in the County of Antrim (Sir James Henry Molyneaux, KBE (1996), PC (1983)) [The Rt Hon The Lord Molyneaux of Killead KBE PC, Aldergrove, Crumlin, Co Antrim BT29 4AR]; *b* 27 Aug 1920; *educ* Aldergrove Sch; RAF WW II, Hon Sec S Antrim U Assoc 1964–70, MP (UU) Antrim S 1970–83 and Lagan valley 1983–97, memb (UU) S Antrim NI Assembly 1982–86, Leader UU Party H of C 1974–95, JP Co Antrim 1957–87

Lineage: WILLIAM MOLYNEAUX, of Seacash, Killead; *m* Sarah Gilmore and had:

JAMES HENRY, *cr* a **Baron**

MONCK

Arms: Gu. a chev. between three lion's heads erased arg.
Crest: A dragon passant, wings elevated sa. **Supporters:** Dexter, a dragon, wings elevated arg., langued gu., holding over the dexter shoulder a laurel branch fructed ppr.; sinister, a lion arg., langued gu., holding over the sinister shoulder a laurel branch fructed ppr.
Motto: *Fortiter, fideliter, feciliter* ('Boldly, faithfully, successfully').
Creation: B. (I.) 23 Nov 1797 and (UK) 12 July 1866, V. (I) 5 Jan 1801.

THE 7TH VISCOUNT MONCK OF BALLYTRAMMON, Co Wexford, **Baron Monck of Ballytrammon**, Co Wexford, and **Baron Monck of Ballytrammon**, Co Wexford (Charles Stanley Monck) [Mr Charles Monck, c/o The Viscount Monck, House of Lords, London SW1A 0PW]; *b* 2 April 1953; *s f* 1982 but does not use title; *educ* Eton and Loughborough U

Lineage: WILLIAM le MOYNE; Ld Manor Potheridge, Devon; ggf of:

PETER le MOYNE; *m* Maud, dau and heiress of — Coffin, of Beacombe; gggf of:

HUGH le MOYNE; *fl c* 1275; *m* —, dau of Aulambe, of Ro(w)borough, Devon, and was gf of:

HUGH le MOYNE; *m* Alicia, dau of Robert Crues, feudal Ld of Torringon; gggf of:

WILLIAM le MOYNE; *fl temp* HENRY VI; *m* Christina, dau and coheir of John Crukerne, of Chelday, Dorset, and had:

1 John, of Potheridge; ancestor of:
  (1) Thomas; *m* 1st —; *m* 2nd, as her 2nd w, Frances, dau and coheir of 1st and last Viscount Lisle of the 1523 *cr* by Elizabeth, dau of 1st Viscount Lisle of the 1483 *cr* by Elizabeth, dau of 1st Viscount Lisle of the 1451 *cr* (*see* DE L'ISLE, V, preliminary remarks), s of 1st Earl of Shrewsbury and Waterford (*qv*) by Margaret, dau of Richard Beauchamp, Earl of Warwick (*see* WARWICK, BROOKE and, E) and 1st Earl of Aumale (hence his descendant's choice of ducal title, Albemarle being a corruption of Aumale) of the 1419 *cr*, by Elizabeth, maternal gdau of Warin, Lord (Baron) Lisle, gs of Warin de Lisle by Alice, dau of Henry, Lord (Baron) Teyes/Tyas (hence their descendant GEORGE MONCK's choice of Barony title); gf of:
    1a Thomas (Sir); *m* Elizabeth, dau of Sir George Smith or Smythe, of Madford or Madeworthy, Devon (*see* SMITH-MARRIOTT, Bt), and had, with an er s (*d* young):
      1b GEORGE MONCK, 1st DUKE OF ALBEMARLE, so *cr* 7 July 1660, as also BARON MONCK OF POTHERIDGE, BEAUCHAMP AND TEYES, and EARL OF TORRINGTON (all E), KG (1660), PC (I 1660); *b* 6 Dec 1608; MP Devon 1653 and 1660, memb also of CROMWELL's 'Upper House', C-in-C all Forces and Jt-Gen of the Fleet for Parl 1660, as which changed sides and brought about the Restoration; Capt Gen and Master of the Horse 1660, Ld Lt: Ireland 1660–62, Devon 1660, Middx 1662, Actg Ld High Adml March–June 1666, 1st Ld Treasury 1667–70; *m* 23 Jan 1652/3 Anne, dau of John Clarges, farrier, of London, and widow or possibly separated w of Thomas Radford/Redford, and *d* 3 Jan 1669/70, leaving:
        1c CHRISTOPHER MONCK, 2nd and last DUKE OF ALBEMARLE, KG (Feb 1669/70), PC 1675; *b* allegedly 14 Aug 1653; MP Devon 1667–70, Gentleman Bedchamber 1670, Col of Horse 1679 and 1st Horse Gds 1679–85, Ld Lt Devon 1675–85, Govr Jamaica 1686; *m* 30 Dec 1669 Elizabeth (*m* 2nd 8 Sept 1692 1st Duke of Montagu; *see* MANCHESTER, D), est dau of 2nd and last Duke of Newcastle-upon-Tyne (*see* DEVONSHIRE, D), and *dsps* 6 Oct 1688, when his titles expired
    1a Frances; *m* Sir Lewis Stucley, of Affeton, Devon (*see* STUCLEY, Bt)
2 Robert MONCKE, of Hatherby, Devon; *m* Elizabeth, dau and heiress of William Eure, and had:
  1a John; *m* Christian, dau of — Kelly, of Kelly, Devon, and had:
    1b Richard MONCK, of Iver, Bucks, and Lever, Devon; *m* 2nd Blanche, dau of Richard Ansham, of Heston, Middx, and had:
      1c Henry; *m* Jo(h)an, dau of William Heathcock, and had:
        1d Charles; Jt Surveyor-Gen Customs Ireland 1627, bought estates in Co Westmeath; MP Coleraine 1639; *m* Elizabeth, est dau of Sir John Blennerhassett, Ld Ch Baron Exchequer I, and had:

1e Henry; attainted by JAMES II but restored by WILLIAM III; *m* 1673 Sarah, dau and heiress of Sir Thomas Stanley, of Grange Gorman, Co Dublin, and had, with other issue:
  1f George; *m* Mary, dau of 1st Viscount Molesworth (*qv*), and had issue
  2f CHARLES
  3f William; *m* Dorothy, sister of 1st Earl of Darnley (*qv*), and was ggf of:
    1g John Bligh, of Coley Park, Berks
  1f Rebecca; *m* John Foster, Ch Justice Common Pleas, and had, with a s and yr dau:
    1g Sarah; *m* the philosopher George Berkeley, DD, Bp Cloyne

HENRY MONCK's 2nd son,
CHARLES MONCK; barrister, inherited the Stanleys' Grange Gorman estate; *m* 23 Oct 1705 Agneta (heir to her brother's estate of Charleville, Co Wicklow), dau of MajWalter Hitchcock by Agneta, dau of Sir John Stephens, of Finglas, and *d* 1752, having by her had:
1 Henry, of Charleville and Grange Gorman, *m* 8 Nov 1739 Isabella (*d* 1783), 2nd dau of 1st Duke of Portland (*see* PORTLAND, E), and *d* 1787, having had:
  (1) Elizabeth; *m* 1st Marquess of Waterford (*qv*)
2 Thomas; barrister, MP Old Leighlin; *m* 15 Oct 1753 Judith (*d* 14 Oct 1814), dau of Robert Mason, of Mason Brook, and *d* 1772, leaving:
  (1) CHARLES STANLEY, **1st Viscount**
  (2) Thomas Stanley (Rev); *b* 1762; *m* 1792 Jane (*d* 14 Oct 1814), dau of Rev Alexander Staples (*see* STAPLES, Bt), and *d* 4 March 1842, leaving issue
  (3) William Domville; MP Coleraine 1797; *b* 1763; *m* Elizabeth Penelope, dau of Col Monck Mason, and *d* Aug 1840, leaving issue
  (1) Anne Isabella; *m* 3 June 1777 1st Viscount Hawarden (*qv*) and *d* 26 July 1851, leaving issue
1 Anne; *m* Henry Quin, MD, and had issue

HENRY MONCK's n,
CHARLES STANLEY MONCK, **1st Viscount Monck of Ballytrammon**, Co Wexford, so *cr* 5 Jan 1801, as also earlier 23 Nov 1797 BARON MONCK OF BALLYTRAMMON, Co Wexford (both I); *b c* 1754; *educ* Eton and Trin Coll Dublin; MP (I Parl) Newborough (Gorey, Co Wexford) 1790–97; *m* 1784 his cousin Anne (*m* 2nd Sir John Craven Carden, 1st Bt, of Templemore (*qv*), and *d* 1823), dau of Henry Quin, MD, and *d* 9 June 1802, having had:
1 HENRY STANLEY MONCK, **2nd Viscount Monck of Ballytrammon** and 1st and last EARL OF RATHDOWNE (I), so *cr* 12 Jan 1822; *b* 26 July 1785; *educ* Eton; *m* 28 July 1806 Frances (*d* 22 Nov 1843), dau of 1st Earl of Clancarty (*qv*), and *d* 22 Nov 1843, when the Earldom expired, having had, with five other daus:
  (1) Frances Isabella; *m* 25 Aug 1834 Owen Blayney Cole, DL Co Monaghan (*d* 26 Nov 1886), High Sheriff 1835, and *d* 9 June 1871, leaving issue
  (2) Elizabeth Louise Mary; *m* 22 July 1844 **4th Viscount Monck of Ballytrammon** (*see* below) and *d* 16 June, leaving issue
  (3) Emily; *m* 7 Feb 1837 William Barlow Smythe, of Barbavilla, Co Westmeath, and *d* 22 Nov 1837
  (4) Georgiana Ellen; *m* 17 May 1841 Edward Croker, of Ballynagarde, Co Limerick, and *d* 20 March, 1887, leaving issue
2 CHARLES JOSEPH KELLY, **3rd Viscount**
1 Anne Wilhelmina; *m* 1812 Daniel James Webb
2 Isabella; *m* 6 Sept 1815 Thomas Maunsell Wilson and *d* 1830

The 2nd VISCOUNT's bro,
CHARLES JOSEPH KELLY MONCK, **3rd Viscount Monck of Ballytrammon**; *b* 12 July 1791; *educ* Rugby; Lt 43rd LI (fought Battles of Vittoria, Nive, Nivelle, Pyrenees and Toulouse (medal of five clasps)); *m* 29 Nov 1817 Bridget (*d* 1843), dau of John Willington, of Killoskehane, Co Tipperary, and had:
1 CHARLES STANLEY, **4th Viscount**
2 William; Capt 7th Fus; *b* 28 Feb 1823; *ka* Battle of the Alma 20 Sept 1854
3 Richard; Lt-Gen Coldstream Gds; *b* 23 Oct 1829; *m* 13 Aug 1861 Frances Elizabeth Owen (*d* 31 July 1919), est dau of Owen Blayney Cole, of Brandrum, Co Monaghan, and *d* 7 Oct 1904, having had, with two other sons and a dau:
  (1) Cecil Stanley Owen; *b* 24 July 1863; Hon Brig-Gen, Col Coldstream Guards, Boer War 1899–1900 (Queen's medal and three clasps); *m* 15 Aug 1914 Violet (*d* 12 May 1969 aged 96), widow of Henry Dawson-Greene, of Whittington Hall, Lancs, and dau of J H Ley, of Trehill, Exeter, and *dsp* 4 Dec 1940
1 Anne; *m* May 1841 her cousin James Napier Webb and *d* 23 Sept 1853
2 Henrietta; *m* 18 Nov 1848 Francis Richard Brooke and *d* May 1911, having had issue (*see* BROOKE, Bt, of Summertown)

The 3rd VISCOUNT *d* 20 April 1849; his est s,
CHARLES STANLEY MONCK, **4th Viscount Monck of Ballytrammon**, GCMG (1869), PC (1869); *b* 10 Oct 1819; Commr Church Temporalities Ireland, Ld Lt Co Dublin 1874–92, Capt Gen and Govr-in-Ch Canada, Govr-Gen Br America 1861, Govr-Gen Canada 1867–68; *cr* 12 July 1866 BARON MONCK OF BALLYTRAMMON, Co Wexford (UK), DCL, LLD; *m* 23 July 1844 his cousin Lady Elizabeth Louise Mary Monck (*d* 16 June, 1892), 4th dau of Earl of Rathdowne (*see* above), and had:
1 HENRY POWER CHARLES STANLEY, **5th Viscount**
2 Richard Charles Stanley Mountjoy; *b* 2 Aug 1858; Lt Northants Regt; *m* 15 Nov 1879 Alice Ann (*d* 11 April 1905), yst dau of T E Lymer, of Wolverhampton, and *dsp* 13 Dec 1892
1 Frances Mary; *m* 26 April 1888 Rev Richard Aslatt Pearce (*d* 1928), est s of R S Pearce, and *d* 30 Oct 1930
2 Elizabeth Louise Mary; *m* 25 Sept 1875 John Macdonald Royse, JP (*d* 25 Aug 1910), 2nd s of T H Royse, of Nanteenan, Co Limerick, and *d* 16 May, 1913, having had issue

The 4th VISCOUNT *d* 29 Nov 1894; his er son,
HENRY POWER CHARLES STANLEY MONCK, **5th Viscount Monck of Ballytrammon**, JP (Co Dublin); *b* 8 Jan 1849; *educ* Ch Ch Oxford (BA); V-Lt Co Wick-

low, High Sheriff 1887, Capt Coldstream Gds, Egypt 1882, E Sudan 1885 (medal with two clasps and bronze star); m 23 July 1874 Lady Edith Caroline Sophia Scott (d 1 Aug 1929), yst dau of 3rd Earl of Clonmell, and had:

1 Charles Henry Stanley; b 9 Nov 1876; Capt Coldstream Gds, Boer War 1899–1902 (Queen's medal with seven clasps, King's medal with two clasps), WW I; m 16 Feb 1904 Mary Florence (d 12 Feb 1918), yr dau of Sir William Wyndham Portal, 2nd Bt (qv), and was ka 21 Oct 1914, having had:

(1) HENRY WYNDHAM STANLEY, 6th Viscount

(1) Elisabeth Noel; granted by roy warrant 23 April 1928 with her sister Mary Patricia rank of viscount's dau; b 25 Dec 1908; m 12 July 1928 William Frederick Batt, MBE, JP, DL, Maj Coldstream Gds, est s of Lt-Col Reginald Crossley Batt, CBE, MVO, of Gresham Hall, Norwich, and had issue

(2) Mary Patricia; b 20 June 1911; m 28 Nov 1935 Brig (Charles) Hilary Vaughan Vaughan Pritchard, DSO, JP, DL, Roy Welch Fus (d 28 March 1976), only s of Lt-Col Charles Hamerton Pritchard, CSI, and d 14 Nov 1996, leaving:

1a *Susan Katharine Vaughan [Mrs David Muirhead, Shuckburgh House, Naseby, Northants]; b 10 Dec 1936; m 14 Dec 1957 David Spencer Muirhead (d 1977), only s of Brig James Muirhead, MC, of Boath, Auldearn, Nairnshire

2a *Molly Cecilia Vaughan; b 18 Jan 1941; m 28 July 1962 *His Honour Judge Ian (Hewitt) Davies TD, er s of Rev John Robert Davies of Birmingham

3a *Patricia Nesta Vaughan; b 18 Jan 1941; m 1984 George Engel (d 1987), only s of Max Engel

4a *Jane Arabella Vaughan [Mrs David Allen, The Old Rectory, Pen Selwood, Wincanton BA 9 8LS]; b 8 Nov 1945; m 26 Sep 1970 *David Patrick M Allen, er s of P M Allen, of Linden, Sutton, Dublin

2 George Scott Stanley; Lt 2nd Bucks VRC; b 3 Nov 1888; d unm July 1912

1 Annette Louise, GBE; b 23 May 1875; DGStJ; m 27 July 1897 2nd Earl of Liverpool (qv) and dsp 25 May 1948

The 5th VISCOUNT d 18 Aug 1927; his gs,

HENRY WYNDHAM STANLEY MONCK, 6th Viscount Monck of Ballytrammon, OBE (1961), JP (Hants 1944), DL (Hants 1973); b 11 Dec 1905; educ Eton and RMC Sandhurst; Lt Coldstream Gds, memb Southern Gas Board 1965–72, V-Chm Nat Assoc Boys' Clubs 1938–78; m 1st 7 July 1937 (divorce 1951) Baroness Eva Maria Vreto, 2nd dau of Professor Zaunmuller-Freudenthaler, of Vienna; m 2nd 14 Dec 1951 *Brenda Mildred (m 2nd 1985, as his 2nd w, Brig Gerald (Ged) Michael Palmer, MC) [Mrs Gerald Palmer, Pilgrims Farm, Overton, Hants], only dau of George William Adkins, of Bowers Close, Harpenden, Herts, and d 21 June 1982, leaving:

1 CHARLES STANLEY MONCK, 7th and present Viscount Monck of Ballytrammon

2 +GEORGE STANLEY [The Hon George Monck, Yew Tree House, Lea, Wilts SN16 9PA]; b 12 April 1957; heir presumptive; educ Eton and Ch Ch Oxford (BA 1980); m 1986 *Camilla E V, 2nd dau of John Naylor, of The Mill House, Bramley, Hants, and has had:

(1) Henry; b and d 1991

3 +James Stanley; b 5 July 1961; educ Eton and Queen Mary's Coll Basingstoke

MONCKTON OF BRENCHLEY

Arms: Quarterly, 1st and 4th, sa. on a chevron between three martlets or three mullets sa. (for MONCKTON); 2nd and 3rd, or a chevron gu., a chief vair (for ST QUINTIN). **Crest:** A martlet or. **Supporters:** On either side a horse arg., crined and unguled or, gorged with a chain gold, pendant therefrom an escutcheon sa., charged with a rose also arg., barbed and seeded ppr. **Badge:** Within an annulet a martlet or. **Motto:** Famam extendere factis ('Spreading fame by deeds'). **Creation:** V. (UK) 11 Feb 1957.

THE 2ND VISCOUNT MONCKTON OF BRENCHLEY, of Brenchley, Co Kent (Maj-Gen Gilbert Walter Riversdale Monckton, CB (1966), OBE (1965), MC (1940), DL (Kent 1970)) [Maj-Gen The Rt Hon The Viscount Monckton of Brenchley CB OBE MC DL, Runhams Farm, Runham Lane, Harrietsham, Kent ME17 1NJ]; b 3 Nov 1915; s f 1965; educ Harrow and Trin Coll Cambridge (BA

1939, MA 1942); idc, psc, 5th Roy Inniskilling Dragoon Gds WW II and Korea 1951–52, Bde Maj Armoured Bde 1942, Gen Staff Coll USA 1943, Instructor Middle East Staff Coll 1943, GSO(2) 7th Armoured Div 1949–51, GSO(1) Mil Ops War Office 1953–55, Mil Advsr Br Delegn Geneva Conf Korea and Indo-China 1954, Lt-Col cmdg 12th Roy Lancers 1956–58, Cdr RAC 3rd Div 1958–60 Roy Yeo (Vols) TAVR 1974, Dep Dir Personnel Admin 1962, Dir PR War Office 1960–65, Ch Staff HQ BAOR 1965–67, Col 9th/12th Roy Lancers (Prince of Wales's) 1967–73, Maj-Gen, Hon Col Kent and Sharpshooters Yeo Sqdn 1974–79, dir: U dg and Gen Tst, Anglo-Portuguese Bank, Burberrys, H St G Ralling, Monckton Equities Ltd and Country Bldg Soc, Ransom, Hoffmann Pollard, Modern Investments, Sahsmarez Carey S Harris 1973–, Liveryman Broderers' Co (Master 1978–79), Grand Cross Merit SMO 1980 (Chllr Br Assoc 1961–66, V-Pres 1967, Pres 1974–83), KJStJ (Chm Cncl Kent 1969–75), Bailiff Grand Cross Justice Constantinian Order St George 1975, Cdr Order Crown Belgium 1965, Grand Off Order Leopold II 1978, Pres: Kent Assoc Boys' Clubs 196578, Inst Heraldic and Genealogical Studies 1965, Kent Archaeological Assoc 196875, Medway Productivity Assoc 1968–72, Maidstone & Dist Football League 1968, Anglo-Belgium Union 1973–83, Chm Thurnham Parish Cncl 1968–70, FSA 1987, V-Chm Scout Assoc Kent 1968, m 30 Dec 1950 *Marianna Laetitia, High Sheriff Kent 1981–82, Dir Allied Malta Newspapers and Progress Press, Dame Honour and Devotion and Offr Merit SMO Malta, pres St John's Ambulance Kent 1975–80, OStJ, 3rd dau of Cdr Robert Tatton Bower, RN, of Putney, and has:

1 +CHRISTOPHER WALTER, DL (Greater London 1988) [The Hon Christopher Monckton DL, Crimonmogate, Lonmay, Fraserburgh, Aberdeenshire AB43 8SE]; b 14 Feb 1952; educ Harrow, Churchill Coll Cambridge (BA 1973, MA 1977) and U Coll Cardiff (Dip Jrnlsm Studies 1974); jnlst Yorkshire Post Newspapers Ltd Leeds 1974–77, Press Offr C Centl Office 1977–79, ed The Universe 1979–81, Sec Ec Accounting Study Gp CPS 1980, managing ed Sunday Telegraph Magazine 1981–82, memb PM's policy unit 1983–86, assist ed Today 1986–87, consulting ed Evening Standard 1987–92, dir Christopher Monckton Ltd 1987– and Beechwood Clothing Co 1993–, Liveryman Broderers' Co, Freeman City London, OStJ 1973, Kt Honour and Devotion SMO Malta; m 1990 *Juliet Mary Anne, elder dau of Jørgen Malherbe Jensen, of Bloomsbury

2 +Timothy David Robert; b 15 Aug 1955 (HRH THE late DUKE OF WINDSOR stood sponsor); educ Harrow and RAC Cirencester; Kt Honour and Devotion SMO Malta; m 21 Jan 1984 *Jennifer, 2nd dau of Brendan Carmody, of Ealing and late of Sydney, and has:

(1) +Dominic Walter; b 1985

(2) +James Timothy; b 1988

(3) +William Henry; b 1992

3 +Jonathan Riversdale St Quintin [The Hon Jonathan Monckton, 90 Innes Gdns, London SW15 3AD]; b 15 Aug 1955; educ Worth; Benedictine monk Worth Abbey 1975–89, m 1992 *Carina Therese, dau of Brian Beeson, OBE

4 +Anthony Leopold Colyer [The Hon Anthony Monckton, c/o FCO, King Charles St, London SW1A 2AH; b 25 Sept 1960 (HM LEOPOLD III of the Belgians stood sponsor); educ Harrow, Magdalene Coll Cambridge (MA) and RMA Sandhurst; 2nd Lt 9th/12th Roy Lancers 1982, Capt 1984 (ret 1987), 1st Sec FCO 1993–; m 1985 *Philippa Susan, yr dau of Gervase Christopher Brinsmade Wingfield (see POWERSCOURT, V), and has:

(1) +Edward Gervase Colyer; b 1 June 1988

(1) *Camilla Mary; b 6 Sept 1989

1 *Rosamond Mary; b 26 Oct 1953; md Tiffany, London; Freeman Goldsmiths' Co; m 1991, as his 2nd w, *Hon Dominic Ralph Campden Lawson, s of Baron Lawson of Blaby (qv), and has issue

Lineage: THOMAS MONCKTON, of Swine, Yorks (2nd s of William Monckton, of Caril, Yorks; see GALWAY, V); m Margery, 5th dau and coheir of John St Quintin, of Ganstead, and d 4 July 1584, having had, with an est and yst s and a dau:

Rev CHRISTOPHER MONCKTON; educ St John's Coll Cambridge (BA 1585, MA 1600, MD 1617); ordained 1604, Rector Hayes 1619 and Orpington with St Mary Cray, Kent, 1620; b 28 March 1578; m 1st Ann — (d 20 March 1637) and had a s (John); m 2nd 18 Sept 1641 Sarah Stearle (d March 1654), of Hayes, Kent, and d 26 June 1652, leaving:

Rev JOHN MONCKTON; educ St John's Coll Cambridge (BA 1641, MA 1645); Vicar Brenchley, Kent, 1651; m 1st Sarah, dau of Rev Samuel Fisher, Vicar Naverstock, and had issue; m 2nd Eleanor Kitchenham and had issue; m 3rd Joan Kitchenham (d Feb 1730), of Leigh, Kent, and d 1708, having by her had:

TIMOTHY MONCKTON, of Porto Bello House, Brenchley; b 11 Jan 1684; surgn; m Ann (d 13 Dec 1751), dau of John Hooker, of Broadoak, Brenchley, and d 18 Aug 1751, having had, with three er sons and a yst one:

EDWARD MONCKTON, of Catt's Place, Brenchley; bapt 28 May 1727; m 31 March 1762 Rosamond (d 1 Jan 1847), dau of Stephen Walter, of Marden, Kent, and d 14 April 1812, having had, with two er sons:

EDWARD MONCKTON, of Hale Place, East Peckham, Kent; bapt 13 Jan 1768; m 30 Aug 1790 Sarah, dau of Thomas Mills, of Tatlingbury, Capel, Kent, and d 21 Oct 1851, having had, with three other sons and nine daus:

1 Stephen, of Tudeley Grange; b 2 Feb 1793; m 20 March 1821 Fanny (d 4 Dec 1878), dau of John Maddoks, and d 16 Aug 1855, leaving a 2nd s:

(1) Frederick; settled NZ 1883; b 23 Sept 1827; m 22 Feb 1863 Anne (d 14 June 1912), dau of Thomas Martin, of E Peckham, and d 1904, leaving, with other issue:

1a Edward Martin, of Gisborne, NZ; b 1878; m 20 Jan 1915 Grace Lane and had:

1b *Christopher Martin; b 27 Jan 1916; m *Janet Jefferd, of Hylands, Ngatapa, Gisborne, and has:

1c *John; b Sept 1946

1c *A dau; b 1948

2a John Martin; b 1883; m Dorothy Rutledge

2 Jonathan, of Porto Bello Ho; b 21 Sept 1796; surgn; m 16 Sept 1823 Ann Elizabeth, dau of Robert Wicksteed, of London, and d 16 Feb 1853, having had, with other issue:

(1) Stephen, JP; MD, FRCS, FRCP; b 21 Sept 1824; m 21 June 1855 Maria, dau of Lancelot Holland, of Beckenham, and had a 3rd s:

1a Stephen Lancelot; Town Clerk Maidstone, sr pntr Monckton, Son & Collis, slrs; *b* 30 July 1861; *m* 20 Sept 1891 Elizabeth, dau of Rev T G Headley, of Petersham, and *d* 19 May 1931, having had an only child:

  1b Lancelot Richard Stephen, JP Kent; *b* 29 Sept 1895; *educ* Eton; sr pntr Monckton, Son & Collis; Capt QO Roy W Kent Regt; *m* 17 Sept 1925 *Mary Seymour, dau of Sir Seymour Tritton, KBE (*see* TRITTON, Bt), and had:

    1c *June Seymour; *b* 3 June 1931; *m* 18 Sept 1954 Peter Sydney Morrish, QALAS, of Castlemaine, Horsmonden, Kent, s of Sydney Victor Morrish, of Hove, and has:

      1d *Lancelot Peter; *b* 19 Oct 1956

      1d *Annabel June; *b* 24 Feb 1959

(2) Robert; *b* 21 Sept 1831; *m* Jan 1877 Ellen Magdalen Giraud (*d* 17 Dec 1932) and *d* 5 Nov 1901, leaving:

  1a Robert Vernon Giraud; MD, BS; *b* 21 March 1878; *m* Elizabeth (*d* 13 March 1956), dau of Timothy Jones, and *d* 28 April 1958, leaving:

    1b Robert Timothy; *b* 15 July 1918; *educ* Rugby and London U; *m* 19 June 1943 *Marjorie Helen Gage and *d* 28 Sept 1983, leaving:

      1c *Joanna; *b* 30 June 1944

      2c *Angela; *b* 19 Aug 1946

    2b David, MC, TD; *b* 16 April 1920; *educ* Malvern; late Major QO Roy W Kent and Parachute Regts; *m* March 1947 *Vera Kathleen Boorman Jolliffe and *d* 29 June 1995, leaving:

      1c *David Robert Charles; *b* 8 Nov 1950; *m* 11 Aug 1979 *Pamela Joyce Cox and has:

        1d *Timothy Charles; *b* 7 Sept 1981

      1c *Elizabeth Anne; *b* 2 June 1948

    3b *John [John Monckton Esq, 40 College St, Bury St Edmunds, Suffolk IP33 1NL]; *b* 17 Sept 1923; *educ* Rugby, London U and St Bartholomew's Hosp; MRCS, FRC Ophth, ophthalmic surgn; *m* March 1950 *Millicent James and has:

      1c *Christopher John; *b* 23 March 1954

      1c *Jennifer Jane; *b* 1 Nov 1952

3 EDWARD

4 John; *b* 6 Nov 1802; fndr and sr pntr Monckton, Son & Collis; Town Clerk Maidstone 36 years; *m* 30 June 1829 Eliza Whitmore, dau of John Braddick, of Boughton Mount, and *d* 3 July 1886, having had, with four other sons and five daus:

(1) John Braddick (Sir); *b* 6 July 1832; ktd 1880, FSA; *m* Maria Louisa (*b* 10 April 1837; *d* 24 Sept 1920), dau of Peter B Long, of Ipswich, and *d* 1902, leaving, with two other sons and a dau:

  1a John Lionel Alexander; *b* 18 Dec 1861; composer; *m* 1902 Gertrude (*m* 2nd 30 April 1924 2nd Earl of Dudley (*qv*) and *d* 25 April 1952), dau of John Millar, and *d* 25 Feb 1924

  2a Charles Falkland; *b* 28 Aug 1863; slr; *m* Anne Maude Emily (*b* 3 Dec 1870; *d* 8 Sept 1954), dau of H Rockingham Gill, and *d* 10 June 1947, leaving:

    1b John Falkland; *b* 5 July 1901; *educ* Sherborne; LRIBA, architect, Maj RE WW II; *m* 21 Oct 1939 *Anne, dau of Francis Cornwall Weldon, of Charleville, Co Cork, and *d* 25 Oct 1958, leaving:

      1c *Oonagh Karolyn Anne; *b* 29 Sept 1940; *m* 13 Jan 1968 *F/Lt Kenneth Charles H Simpson, RAF, s of Charles Simpson, of Teignmouth, Devon

      2c *Diana Jane [Miss Diana Monckton, Flat 3, 17 St. John's Road, Eastbourne, Sussex]; *b* 11 July 1942

    2b Charles Henry; *b* 23 Aug 1904; *educ* Tonbridge; civ serv, F/O RAF Regt WW II; *m* 20 June 1936 *Kathleen Mollie, dau of Reginald Brandon Trye, of Weybridge, and *dsp* 7 March 1969

    1b (Anne) Dorothy; *b* 17 July 1897; *m* 7 Oct 1919 Maj Charles Leonard Miskin, OBE (*d* 18 Aug 1969), s of William Thomas Miskin, of Courtyard House, Eltham, Kent, and had:

      1c *Nigel Monckton [Nigel Miskin Esq, 37 Melton Court, London SW7]; *b* 10 April 1921; *educ* Charterhouse and New Coll Oxford (MA); barrister, Capt RA WW II; *m* 28 Oct 1950 Hilda Meryl (*d* 26 July 1962), widow of F/O Gerald Stark-Toller, RAFVR, and dau of George Knight, CIE, and has:

        1d *Charles James Monckton; *b* 29 Nov 1952; *educ* Charterhouse; *m* 1982 *Karen (Kass) Elizabeth, dau of Ronald Booth, of Whorton, Co Durham, and has:

          1e *Henry Charles Monckton; *b* 7 Feb 1983

        1d *Rosamond Anne Elizabeth Monckton; *b* 3 Oct 1954

      1c Dorothy Brenda; *b* 30 March 1925; *d* unm 24 May 1964

    2b Ellen Joan; *b* 27 Oct 1898; *m* 16 March 1921 Douglas Donovan Smith (*d* 13 Aug 1945), s of William Oliver Smith, of Blackheath, and had:

      1c *Desmond Guy Donovan [Desmond Smith Esq, 36 The Lawns, London SE3]; *b* 16 Jan 1922; *educ* Tonbridge; Staff-Sgt Roy Tank Regt and The Buffs WW II, with BICC 1946

(2) Herbert; *b* 1839; Town Clerk Maidstone, sr pntr Monckton, Son & Collis; *m* 1877 Jessie Emily, dau of Rev J F Baynham, and *d* 1926, leaving, with other issue:

  1a Philip Marmaduke; *b* 17 Dec 1885; *m* 17 Jan 1906 Lydia Jane (*d* 26 Aug 1968), dau of W Turner, MSBA, and *d* 28 Jan 1932, leaving:

    1b *John [John Monckton Esq, 10 Groom Place, London SW1; Abberley, Sittingbourne Rd, Maidstone, Kent]; *b* 23 Nov 1913; barrister Lincoln's Inn 1936; *m* 1st 19 Aug 1944 Mary Matilda Ellis (*d* 22 Feb 1949); *m* 2nd 28 March 1953 *Emily Mary Husband Steiner and by her has:

      1c *John Victor; *b* 13 Oct 1955

      1c *Anne Whittington; *b* 29 Sept 1954

    2b *Francis Philip, DSC; *b* 30 Dec 1915; Croix de Guerre 1945, CA

    3b *George [Dr George Monckton, 9214 117th Street, Edmonton, Alberta, Canada]; *b* 9 Feb 1920; Consultant Neurologist U Hosp Edmonton, MD, MRCP; *m* 31 July 1951 *Jean Jenkins and has:

      1c *Stephen George; *b* 11 Feb 1955

      2c *Simon Philip; *b* 21 Jan 1963

      1c *Elizabeth Alice; *b* 27 Aug 1952

  1b *Dorothy [Miss Dorothy Monckton, 93 Harestone Valley Rd, Caterham, Surrey]; *b* 19 Aug 1917

  2d *Kathleen Jessie [Mrs Christopher Johnson, East Cliff Cottage, Marazion, Cornwall]; *b* 4 June 1927; *m* 1950 *Christopher Coventry Johnson and has a s and three daus

2a Francis Guy; *b* 1891; *m* Jessica Hamilton (*d* 1979), dau of Richard Herbert Townsend Bland, and *d* 2 Nov 1965, leaving:

  1b *(Herbert) Anthony; *b* 13 July 1923; *educ* Malvern; Lt RM 1942–45, assist md Flower & Sons 1955–68, Whitbread E Pennines Ltd 1968–80, chm and md Publishing and Literary Services Ltd 1981–88, memb Inst of Brewing 1949–, dir Laing & Co, William Hickling & Son, Wiley & Co, author: *A History of English Ale and Beer* (1966) and *A History of the English Public House* (1969); *m* 11 Sept 1948 *Peggy, dau of Fred Bunting, of Luton, Beds, and has two daus

  2b *Peter Gerald; *b* 8 Sept 1925, *educ* Shrewsbury; pntr Monckton, Son & Collis; Ensign Irish Gds 1944–47; *m* *Barbara Royle, dau of Ernest Harry Soar, of Epsom, and has:

    1c *Timothy Charles; *b* 12 Sept 1953

    1c *Julie Anne; *b* 9 March 1955

The 3rd son,

EDWARD MONCKTON, of Parsonage House, Brenchley, and Borough Green House, Wrotham, Kent; *b* 22 Jan 1798; *m* 14 April 1826 Ann (*d* 4 Nov 1883), dau and coheir of Ambrose Gibbons, of Parsonage House, Brenchley, and *d* 4 Oct 1883, having had, with four other sons and three daus:

1 WALTER

2 Ambrose Gibbons, of Park Farm, Brenchley; *b* 1833; *m* Emily, dau of George Oyler Thirkell, and *d* 4 Feb 1921, having had, with five yr sons:

  (1) Ambrose Gibbons; *b* 22 Sept 1863; *m* Minnie Hogwood (*d* 5 May 1940) and *d* 26 Dec 1909, leaving an est s:

    1a Henry Charles, of Nightingale Farm, Yalding, Kent; *b* 1896; *m* 1st Mabel Jessie Taylor (*d* 5 March 1951) and had:

      1b *Anthony Gibbons; *b* 15 Nov 1930; *m* 2 March 1951 *Janet Bowes and has:

        1c *Caroline Lesley; *b* 21 Sept 1960

    1a (cont.) Henry Monckton *m* 2nd *Elsie Hollason and *d* 1962

The est son,

WALTER MONCKTON, of Basted and Ightham Warren, Ightham, Kent, JP Kent; *b* 6 Feb 1827; *m* 10 April 1851 Caroline Backshell (*d* 13 June 1901), dau of John Shaw, of Battle, Sussex, and *d* 1 April 1900, having had, with four er and two yr sons and six daus:

FRANK WILLIAM MONCKTON, of Ightham Warren; *b* 24 June 1861; *m* 8 April 1890 Dora Constance (*d* 15 June 1915), dau of William Golding, of Leavers, Hadlow, Kent, and *d* 3 July 1924, having had:

1 WALTER TURNER, **1st Viscount**

2 Frank Leslie, of Tudor Cottage, Ightham; *b* 4 Feb 1896; *educ* Harrow; Lt Roy W Kent Regt; *d* unm 28 March 19–

1 Dora Golding; *b* 26 June 1892; *m* 20 Aug 1924 Brig Robert Denis Keane, RE, s of Denis Keane, and *d* 15 Aug 1969, leaving a son and two daus

The er son,

WALTER TURNER, **1st Viscount Monckton of Brenchley**, of Brenchley, Co Kent (UK), so *cr* 11 Feb 1957, GCVO (1964, KCVO 1937), KCMG (1945), MC, PC (1951), KC (1930); *b* 17 Jan 1891; *educ* Harrow and Balliol Coll Oxford (BA and MA 1918, Hon Fell 1957, Visitor 1957); barrister Inner Temple 1919 (Bencher 1937, Dep Treasurer 1961–65), Chllr Diocese Southwell 1930–36, St George's Hosp 1945–51 and Sussex U 1961–65, served WW I (despatches), Recorder Hythe 1930–37, Attorney-Gen Duchy Cornwall 1932–47 and 1948–51, Standing Counsel to Oxford U 1938–51, Dir-Gen Min Info and Dep U-Sec For Affrs 1940, Head Propaganda and Info Servs Cairo 1941, Commr Assize Midland Circuit 1943, Slr-Gen May–July 1945, MP Bristol W 1951–57, Min Labour and Nat Serv 1951–55, Min Def 1955–56, PMG 1956–57, UK Del Allied Reparations Commn, Pres MCC 1956–57 and Surrey CC 1950–52 and 1959–65, chm Midland Bank 1957–64, Iraq Petroleum 1958–65 and Advsy Commn Centl Africa 1960, Hon DCL Oxford 1951, Hon LLD Bristol 1954 and Sussex 1936; *m* 1st 18 July 1914 (*divorce* 1947) Mary Adelaide Somes (*d* 30 April 1964), dau of Sir Thomas Colyer Colyer-Fergusson, 3rd Bt (*qv*), and had:

1 GILBERT WALTER RIVERSDALE MONCKTON, **2nd and present Viscount Monckton of Brenchley**

1 *Valerie Hamilton [Senator The Hon Lady Goulding, Dargle Cottage, Enniskerry, Co Wicklow, Ireland]; *b* 1918; Subaltern WRAC (Reserve), Senator Republic of Ireland, chm and md Centl Remedial Clinic Dublin 1951, fndr memb National Rehabilitation Bd 1955 and Union of Voly Orgnsns for Handicapped, a Govr St Patrick's Hosp, memb Management Ctee Mater Hosp, Southern Movement for Peace, Hon LLD 1968 Nat U Ireland, Dame of Honour and Devotion SMO Malta; *m* 28 Aug 1939 Sir (William) Basil Goulding, 3rd Bt (*qv*), and has issue

The **1st Viscount** *m* 2nd 13 Aug 1947 Bridget Helen, CBE (*d* 17 April 1982 aged 85), Lady Ruthven of Freeland in her own right (*see* CARLISLE, E), formerly w of 11th Earl of Carlisle (*qv*), and *d* 9 Jan 1965

MONCREIFF

Arms: Quarterly, 1st and 4th, argent a lion rampant gules, armed and langued azure, a chief ermine; 2nd and 3rd, argent an oak tree issuing out of a well in base, proper. **Crest:** A demi-lion rampant as in the arms. **Supporters:** Two men armed cap-à-pie, holding in the exterior hand a spear resting on the shoulder, all proper, the breast-plate charged with a crescent gules. **Motto:** *Sur espérance* ('On hope'). **Creations:** Bt. (NS) 22 April 1626 and (UK) 23 May 1871, B. (UK) 9 Jan 1874.

THE 5TH BARON MONCREIFF OF TULLIEBOLE, Co Kinross, and a **Baronet** (Sir Harry Robert Wellwood Moncreiff, Bt) [The Rt Hon The Lord Moncreiff, Tulliebole Castle, Fossoway, Kincross-shire KY13 7QN]; *b* 4 Feb 1915; *s f* 1942; *educ* Fettes; Maj RASC WW II (despatches), ret 1958 as Hon Lt-Col; *m* 19 Jan 1952 Enid Marion Watson (*d* 1985), only dau of Maj Henry Watson Locke, of Belmont, Dollar, Clackmannanshire, and has:

1 +RHODERICK HARRY WELLWOOD [The Hon Rhoderick Moncreiff, c/o Tulliebole Castle, Fossoway, Kincross-shire KY13 7QN]; *b* 22 March 1954; *educ* Holt Sch, Norfolk; *m* 1982 *Alison Elizabeth Anne, dau of James Duncan Alastair Ross, of West Mayfield, Dollar, and has:

  (1) +Harry James Wellwood; *b* 12 Aug 1986

  (2) +James Gavin Francis; *b* 1988

Lineage: WILLIAM MONCREIFF; *b c* 1526; had, with other issue (*see* ERROLL, E):
1 WILLIAM MONCREIFF OF THAT ILK, 11th Laird; had:

  (1) William; *dvp* unm

  (2) **Sir John Moncreiff, 1st Bt** (NS), so *cr* 22 April 1626, with remainder to his heirs male whatsoever, of that Ilk; sat as Minor Baron in Scottish Parl 1605, MP Perths 1639–41; *m* 1st Anne, dau of David Beaton of Creich, and had issue; *m* 2nd *c* 1635 Lady Mary Murray (*d* Dec 1650), dau of 2nd Earl of Tullibardine (*see* ATHOLL, D), and *d c*1651, having by her had, with a s by his 1st w (*d* young):

    1a **Sir John Moncreiff, 2nd Bt**, of that Ilk; *b* 1635; Offr Scots Gds; forced by his mother's extravagance to sell first 1657 his Fifeshire estate of Carnbee and then 1663 the Barony of Moncreiffe, doing so in the latter case to his cousin Sir Thomas Moncreiff, 1st Bt, of the 1685 *cr* (*see* ERROLL, E); *d* unm 1674

    2a **Sir David Moncreiff, 3rd Bt**; Lt Scots Gds, *d* unm 26 July 1692

    3a William; *d* young

    4a Henry; *d* unm

    5a **Sir James Moncreiff, 4th Bt**; Col Moncreiff's Regt 1693–97, wounded Tangier and Sedgemoor; *dsp* 1698

    1a Margaret; *m* 1667 Lt-Col Hon George Murray, 5th s of 1st Lord Elibank (*qv*)

  (3) Robert, of Craigie; *dsp*

  (4) Hugh; living 12 Oct 1666; *m* Isabel, dau of Hay of Megginch, and had:

    1a **Sir John Moncreiff, 5th Bt**, of Tippermalloch (for whose acquisition by the family *see* ERROLL, E); *b c* 1628; physician; *m c* 1680 his cousin Nicola, dau of John Moncreiff of Easter Moncreiff, and *d* 27 April 1714, having had an only surv s:

      1b **Sir Hugh Moncreiff, 6th Bt**; *d* unm 1744, when the btcy for a while became dormant

    1b Bethia; *m* Rev William Moncreiff, Min Methven, and had:

      1c John; *s* to Tippermalloch

2 Archibald (Rev); had a 2nd s:

  (1) George (Rev); Min Arngask; *m* Katherine Murray of Fosterseat and *d* by 1665, leaving:

    1a William (Rev); Min Monzie, Fifeshire; *m* 1st his cousin Nicola Moncreiff; *m* 2nd Eupheme Alexander and *d c* 1711, leaving:

      1b Archibald (Rev); Min Blackford 1697–1739; *m* Catherine, dau of John Halliday of Tulliebole, Kinross-shire, and *d* 1739, leaving, with 15 other children:

        1c **Rev Sir William Moncreiff, 7th Bt**, which title he assumed *c* 1750; Min Blackford; *m* by 1749 Catherine, est dau of Robert Wellwood of

Garvock and niece of Henry Wellwood of Garvock (who 1749 bought the Tulliebole estate from the creditors of John Halliday's (*see* above) gs Robert and made it over 1752 to his niece's s the future **8th Bt** with the stipulaton that the latter take the name Wellwood), and *d* 9 Dec 1767, having had, with other issue:

  1d HENRY (Sir), **8th Bt**

  2d William; HEICS; had an only dau (*m* 20 Oct 1817 James Corbet Porterfield, of Renfrewshire)

  1d Susan; *b* Sept 1752; *m* 7 April 1783 Rev William Paul, Chaplain in Ordinary to GEORGE III, and *d* 21 Nov 1828, having had issue

The er son,
Rev Sir HENRY MONCREIFF later WELLWOOD-MONCREIFF (according to terms of his great-uncle's deed of gift; *see* above), **8th Bt**; *b* 7 Feb 1750; *educ* Glasgow Coll; Min Blackford 1771 and St Cuthbert's Edinburgh 1775, Moderator Gen Assembly Ch Scotland 1785, Chaplain to PRINCE OF WALES (later GEORGE IV) 1785, DD Glasgow 1785; *m* 16 Nov 1772 Susan Robertson (*d* 1826), est dau of James Robertson Barclay of Keavil, Fifeshire, and *d* 9 Aug 1827, having had, with other issue:

  1 William; *educ* Balliol Coll Oxford (MA, DCL); barrister, King's Advocate Admlty Court Malta; *d* unm 5 Sept 1813

  2 JAMES (Sir), **9th Bt**

  1 Isabella; *m* Sir John Stoddart, Ch Justice and Judge Admlty Court Malta; *d* Feb 1846, having had issue

The 2nd son,
Sir James Wellwood-Moncreiff, 9th Bt; *b* 13 Sept 1776; *educ* Balliol Coll Oxford (BCL); advocate 1799 (as which acted as defence counsel for the 'Resurrectionists' Burke and Hare), a Ld Session as Lord Moncreiff 1829–51; *m* 19 June 1808 Ann (*d* 28 May 1843), dau of Lt George Robertson, RN, and *d* 4 April 1851, having had, with other issue:

  1 **Rev Sir Henry Wellwood-Moncreiff, 10th Bt**; *b* 12 May 1809; *educ* Edinburgh HS, Edinburgh U (DD) and New Coll Oxford (BA); Min Baldernock, Stirling, 1836–37, E Kilbride 1837–43 and St Cuthbert's Edinburgh 1852–83, Moderator Free Ch Gen Assembly 1861; *m* 1st 8 March 1838 Alexina Mary (*d* 12 April 1874), dau of George Bell, of Edinburgh; *m* 2nd 19 Aug 1875 Lucretia (*d* 10 Sept 1885), yst dau of Andrew Murray, of Murrayshall, Perths, Sheriff Aberdeenshire, and *dsp* 3 Nov 1883

  2 JAMES, **1st Baron**

  3 William; *b* 28 Sept 1813; *m* 26 April 1860 Susan Ballantine (*d* 24 Oct 1905), yst dau of Joseph Dykes Ballantine Dykes, of Dovenby Hall, Cumberland, and *dsp* 31 Aug 1895

  4 George Robertson (Rev), MA; *b* 29 Jan 1817; Schs Inspr 1850–84; *m* 13 Oct 1858 Martha (*d* 1893), 2nd surv dau of William Home, of Tattenhall, Cheshire, and *dsp* 1897

The 10th Bt's bro,
Sir James WELLWOOD-MONCREIFF later MONCREIFF, **11th Bt**, and **1st Bt** (UK), so *cr* 23 May 1871, of Kilduff, Co Kinross, also **1st Baron Moncreiff of Tulliebole**, Co Kinross (UK), PC (1869); *b* 29 Nov 1811; *educ* Edinburgh HS and U; advocate 1833, MP (Lib) Leith 1851–59, Edinburgh 1859–68, Glasgow and Aberdeen Us 1868–69, Ld Advocate 1851–March 1852, Dec 1852–March 1858, 1859–66 and 1868–69, Dean Faculty Advocates 1858–59, Ld Justice Clerk 1869–88, LLD Glasgow 1879; *m* 12 Sept 1834 Isabella (*d* 19 Dec 1881), only dau of Robert Bell, Procurator Ch of Scotland and Sheriff Berwicks and Haddington, and *d* 27 April 1895, having had:

  1 HENRY JAMES MONCREIFF, **2nd Baron Moncreiff of Tulliebole**; *b* 24 April 1840; *educ* Harrow and Trin Coll Cambridge (BA, LLB); advocate 1863, Sheriff Renfrew and Bute 1881–88, Ld of Session as Lord Wellwood and as Lord Moncreiff 1888–1905, Ld Lt Kinross 1901–09; *m* 1st 3 April 1866 Susan Whilhelmine (*dsp* 29 Oct 1869), 3rd dau of Sir William Henry Dick-Cunyngham, 8th Bt (*see* 1940 edn STEWART-DICK-CUNYNGHAM, Bt); *m* 2nd 26 March 1873 Millicent Julia (*dsp* 6 Jan 1881), er dau of Col Frederick Daniel Fryer, of Newmarket, and *dsp* 3 March 1909

  2 ROBERT CHICHESTER, **3rd Baron**

  3 James William, WS, DL Kinross-shire; *b* 16 Sept 1845; *m* 19 March 1872 Mary Lillias (*d* 29 Dec 1910), est dau of George Mitchell Innes of Bangour, and *d* 30 Jan 1920, leaving:

    (1) James Frederick, WS; *b* 1872; *m* 1922 Elizabeth Jane (*d* 5 Feb 1941), dau of Peter William Souter, of Edinburgh, and *dsp* 5 July 1948

    (2) Henry Wellwood; *b* 21 July 1876; Lt 3rd Bn Salop LI; *m* 25 May 1921 Ivy St John Muir

    (3) Edwin Robert; *b* 30 June 1877; stockbroker, memb Roy Co Archers; *m* 20 April 1904 Mary (*d* 1953), 2nd dau of Matthew Montgomerie Bell, WS, of Edinburgh, and *d* 1962, having had issue

      1a George James Wellwood; *b* 30 Sept 1912; Capt RASC WW II; *m* 30 April 1937 (*divorce* 1939) Marina Isobel, only child of Frank Rowland Eustace, and *d* 5 Feb 1942

      1a *Mary Eileen; *b* 1909; *m* 1st 9 Oct 1929 Maj John Roy Oakley, Roy Scots (*ka* Palestine Aug 1938); *m* 2nd 8 Sept 1939 Capt Charles Philip McLaughlan, architect, and by him has:

        1b *Ian Wellwood; *b* 1940; Maj Scots Gds

        1b *Ann Wellwood; *b* 1944; *m* 1965 *David Godfrey-Faussett and has:

          1c *Katherine Sarah; *b* 1971

    (4) William Francis; *b* 1882

  4 Frederick Charles; *b* 15 Oct 1847; barrister Middle Temple, Puisne Justice Supreme Court Mauritius 1895–1900 and Ceylon 1900–05; *m* 14 July 1892 Mary Ann (*d* 1943), dau of Charles Seymour Brook, and *d* 1 Jan 1929

  5 Francis Jeffrey; *b* 27 Aug 1849; chartered accountant; *m* 1st 2 Aug 1871 Frances Ramsay (*d* 8 Jan 1875), est dau of James Hamilton Lawson, and had:

    (1) James Hamilton; *b* 1872; *m* 1905 Elizabeth Lilian (*d* 1950), dau of Charles Harvey, and *d* 5 June 1923, leaving:

      1a Francis Hamilton (Most Rev); *b* 29 Sept 1906; *educ* Shrewsbury and St John's Coll Cambridge (BA 1927, MA 1931); Rector St Salvator's Edinburgh 1947–50, Canon St Mary's Cathedral Edinburgh 1950–52, Bp Glasgow and Galloway 1952, Primus Scottish Episcopal Ch 1962

2a Frederick Henry Wellwood; *b* 13 Feb 1909; *educ* Shrewsbury and Pembroke Coll Cambridge (BA); F/Lt RAF; *m* 11 Dec 1939 *Gwendolen Alma [Mrs Frederick Moncreiff, Box 98, Haenertsburg, Transvaal, S Africa], dau of Patrick Gifford, of Forneath, Castle Douglas, and had:

1b +Andrew Malcolm [Andrew Moncreiff Esq, Crossways House, Vann Rd, Fernhurst, W Sussex GU27 3PH]; *b* 12 April 1944; *educ* Pembroke Coll Cambridge; *m* 9 Oct 1971 *Jennifer Margaret, dau of John Chapman, of Johannesburg, and has:

1c +Michael Patrick; *b* 14 July 1974

2c +Robert James; *b* 8 Aug 1977

1b *(Patricia) Jane [Miss Jane Moncreiff, 4 Blandford House, Fentiman Rd, London SW8 1LB]; *b* 16 June 1941

(2) Frederick Charles; *b* 1873; *d* 18 March 1877

5 (cont.) Francis Moncreiff *m* 2nd 29 Oct 1880 Mildred (*d* 24 Jan 1943), 4th dau of Lt-Col Richard Henry FitzHerbert (*see* FitzHERBERT, Bt), and *d* 30 May 1900, having by her had:

(3) Richard Henry FitzHerbert, TD; *b* 10 March 1882; *educ* Fettes; Maj Roy Scots (Roy Regt) WW I (wounded, two medals, 1914/15 Star), WW II 1939–41, memb Roy Co Archers; *d unm* 12 July 1966

(4) Francis Beresford; *b* 18 June 1883; Lt 9th Bn Roy Scots WW I (wounded); *m* 8 Sept 1911 Winifred, dau of Arthur S Laxon, of Coventry, and *d* 18 Dec 1928

(5) Adrian Wellwood; *b* 22 March 1885; *educ* Fettes; memb Roy Co Archers, WW I 1917–18 with Canadian Expdny Force; *d unm* 23 Sept 1968

(6) Norman Halliday; *b* 19 Sept 1886; Maj 2nd Canadian Mtd Rifles; *m* 20 June 1912 Lucy Anna (*m* 2nd 8 Feb 1921 Maj Guy Fletcher Luther, Sherwood Foresters (*d* 18 June 1953), and *d* 14 Dec 1964), yst dau of Rev Edward William Collinson, of Berrynarbor, N Devon, and *das* 18 Nov 1916, leaving:

1a Margaret Mildred; *b* 17 March 1913

2a Betty later Elizabeth (deed poll 1947) Cleather; *b* 10 March 1915

1 Eleanora Jane Ross; *m* 3 Dec 1873 Patrick Blair (*d* 30 Nov 1910) and *dsp* 25 April 1996

2 Marianne Eliza; *m* 6 April 1877 1st Baron Kinross (*qv*) and *d* 25 Sept 1913, leaving issue

The 2nd BARON's bro,

ROBERT CHICHESTER MONCREIFF, **3rd Baron Moncreiff of Tulliebole**; *b* 24 Aug 1843; *educ* Cambridge (BA); Vicar Tanworth-in-Arden Warwicks 1885–1913; *m* 4 Jan 1871 Florence Kate (*d* 23 Nov 1926), 3rd dau of Col Richard Henry FitzHerbert (*see* FitzHERBERT, Bt), and *d* 14 May 1913, having had:

1 JAMES ARTHUR FITZHERBERT, **4th Baron**

1 Daisy Isabel; *b* 1874; *m* 12 Dec 1900 her cousin Arthur FitzHerbert Wright (*d* 6 Jan 1952), of Wootton Court, Warwicks and Aldercar Hall, Derbyshire, and *d* 2 July 1957, having had issue

2 Lilian Mary Susan; *b* 11 March 1876; *m* 21 July 1914 Donald Crawford, KC, LLD (*d* 1 Jan 1919), s of Alexander Crawford, of Aros, Argyll, and *d* 22 Feb 1950

3 Gladys Nora May; *b* 17 Sept 1878; *d unm* 4 Dec 1969

The 3rd BARON's only son,

JAMES ARTHUR FitzHERBERT WELLWOOD MONCREIFF, **4th Baron Moncreiff of Tulliebole**; *b* 19 July 1872; *educ* New Coll Oxford (BA); *m* 16 Dec 1909 (Lucy) Vida (*d* 2 Dec 1973), est dau of David Lechmere Anderson, LRCP, of Inveresk, Doncaster, and *d* 8 Dec 1942, having had:

1 HARRY ROBERT WELLWOOD MONCREIFF, **5th and present Baron Moncreiff of Tulliebole**

2 Donald Graham FitzHerbert; *b* 1919; *educ* Dollar Acad; Capt Argyll & Sutherland Highrs; *m* 17 Aug 1955 *Catriona Sheila, dau of James MacDonald, of Devonshaw House, Dollar, and *d* 1993, leaving:

(1) +Ranald Patrick MacDonald; *b* 31 July 1965

(1) *Barbara Jane; *b* 21 Sept 1957

(2) *Frances Catriona FitzHerbert; *b* 19 July 1959

(3) *Theresa Madeleine FitzHerbert; *b* 25 Feb 1961; *m* 1987 *James Stephen Hanna and has:

1a *A dau; *b* 1988

3 +Robert Frederick Arthur [The Hon Robert Moncreiff, 26 Croft St, Galashiels, Selkirk TD1 3BJ]; *b* 1924; *m* 11 Jan 1951 Aileen Marr (*d* 16 June 1996), est dau of Robert Marr Meldrum, LDS, PhD, and has:

(1) +Richard Gerard Arthur; *b* 24 April 1964

(1) *Gillian Nicola Ann; *b* 15 June 1954; *m* 1981 *Norman Alexander Stewart and has:

1a *Rory Alexander; *b* 1989

1a *Rebecca Jane; *b* 1986

1 Katherine Moira; *b* 1910; *m* 20 April 1940 S/Ldr Archibald Cyril Wilkie, BDS, FDS, RCS Edinburgh, and *d* 20 Aug 1969, leaving issue

2 *Lilian Vida Lechmere [The Hon Mrs Young, Tanworth, Fossoway, Kinross-shire]; *b* 1912; *m* 10 June 1942 *David Robert Young, s of Robert S Young, JP, of Duncroft, Kinross, and has:

(1) *Robert Arthur Moncreiff [Robert Young Esq, 11 Coulston Place, Dalgety Bay, Fife]; *b* 2 July 1944; *educ* Fettes; *m* 8 June 1968 *Fiona Margaret, only dau of Dr William Hugh Finlayson, of Stirling, and has issue

(1) *Caroline Vida Rosemary; *b* 25 Feb 1951

3 *Nicola Gladys [The Hon Mrs Renny, Greenways, Montville Rd, St Peter Port, Guernsey, CI]; *b* 1917; *m* 1st 9 April 1940 Capt Frederick William Gifford, RA (*ka* 23 March 1943), s of Frederick William Gifford, of Dunfermline, Fife, and has:

(1) *James Alexander Moncreiff [James Gifford Esq, Fernlee, 9 High Shore, Banff AB45 1DB]; *b* 6 Sept 1942; *educ* Stowe; *m* 1967 *Patricia Anne Dalton and has:

1a *Robert James Moncreiff; *b* 1974

1a *Lucinda Felicity Moncreiff; *b* 1971

2a *Samantha Louise Moncreiff; *b* 1985

3 (cont.) The Hon Mrs Gifford *m* 2nd 20 July 1946 Lt (Charles John) Derek Renny, RNVR (*d* 22 May 1970), and by him has:

(2) *Nicholas Charles Moncreiff; *b* 7 May 1954; *m* 1982 *Carol, dau of Neil R Ashman, of Guernsey, and has:

1a *Alicia Nicola Rose; *b* 1985

2a *Emily Ellen Miranda; *b* 1987

3a *Abigail Eloise Mateldy; *b* 1988

4a *Felicity Alice Prudence; *b* 1990

(1) *Susan Miranda Fitzherbert [Mrs Anthony O'Donnell, Le Veux Rouvet, St Saviours, Guernsey]; *b* 3 July 1950; *m* 1972 *Anthony John O'Donnell, MB, BS, and has:

1a *Nicholas John Renny; *b* 1975

2a *Alexa Caroline; *b* 1973

3a *Abigail Kate; *b* 1978

(2) *Prudence Jane Fitzherbert; *b* 21 Feb 1952; *m* 1977 *Paul Lynch and has:

1a *James Patrick Moncreiff; *b* 1980

2a *Harry John Renny; *b* 1983

4 *Pamela Anne [The Hon Mrs Epps MB ChB, 13 Bartongate Ave, Edinburgh 4], MB, ChB (Edin) 1949; *b* 1927; *m* 1st 24 Sept 1951 Edward James White; *m* 2nd 1979 Ernest Frederick Epps (*d* 1987) and by her 1st husb has:

(1) *Nicholas Alan; *b* 1953

(2) *Douglas Andrew; *b* 1959

(1) *Vivienne Lucy; *b* 1957

Seat: Tulliebole Castle, Fossoway, Perth and Kinross. The year of Tulliebole's construction tends to be given as 1608 since this is the date inscribed on a stone over the principal door. But records show that some kind of fortified dwelling stood on the site as far back as the early 14th century and JAMES VI often stayed there before he went south to take up the Crown of England in 1603, so it seems likely that what is now the west wing was originally a tower of the peile type and was extended in the early years of the 17th century. Indeed the east wing also shows signs of pre-1608 construction work. The Hallidays acquired Tulliebole in 1598, when John Halliday, a lawyer from Edinburgh, purchased the property. He and his son carried out the alterations and extension associated with the date 1608. For the manoeuvres whereby the property came to the Moncreiffs *see* above against the **7th** and **8th Bts**.

MONK BRETTON

Arms: Arg. on a fess raguly plain cotised, between six fleurs-de-lys all gu., a sword fesswise, point to the dexter ppr., pommel and hilt or. **Crest:** Two lion's gambs erased and in saltire gu., entwined by a serpent, head to the dexter ppr. **Supporters:** On either side a female figure ppr., vested arg., mantle az., each resting the exterior hand on an antique shield, also az., adorned gold, that on the dexter charged with a balance suspended, and that on the sinister with a staff erect entwined by a serpent, all or. **Motto:** *Benigno numine enisus* ('Successful by the favour of Providence').
Creation: B. (UK) 4 Nov 1884.

THE 3RD BARON MONK BRETTON, of Conybro and Hurstpierpoint, Sussex (John Charles Dodson DL (E Sussex 1983)) [The Rt Hon The Lord Monk Bretton DL, Shelley's Folly, Cooksbridge, Sussex BN8 4SU]; *b* 17 July 1924; *s f* 1933; *educ* Westminster and New Coll Oxford (MA); late C Whip Ho Lds; *m* 29 Jan 1958 *Zoë Diana Mary Alicia, only dau of Ian Douglas Murray Scott, and has:

1 +CHRISTOPHER MARK; *b* 2 Aug 1958; *educ* Eton and U of S California (MBA); *m* 1988 *Karen L, only dau of B J McKelvain, of Fairfield, Conn., and has:

(1) +Ben; *b* 1989

(2) +James; *b* 1994

(1) *Emma; *b* 1990

2 +Henry George Murray; *b* 11 Feb 1960; *educ* Eton; BSc 1983 CNAA, ARICS 1986

Lineage: Rev JEREMIAH DODSON; Vicar Wye, Rector St Katherine Coleman, London, 1665–92 (cousin of Sir William Dodson, Common Councilman and Alderman City London, ktd 1680); had:

Rev JEREMIAH DODSON; Rector Broadwater, Sussex, and Hurstpierpoint 1701; *d* 1744, leaving:

Rev CHRISTOPHER DODSON, DD; Rector Hurstpierpoint 51 years; *d* 1784, leaving:

Rev JOHN DODSON, DD; Rector Hurstpierpoint; *m* 1776 Frances, dau of Rev — Dawson, of Stapenhill House, Derbys, and *d* 1807, leaving, with other issue:

Sir JOHN DODSON, PC; LLD, advocate Admlty 1829, King's Advocate-Gen 1834, Master Faculties 1841, Vicar-Gen Province of Canterbury 1849, Dean Arches and Judge Prerogative Court of Canterbury 1852, MP Rye 1819–23; *m* 1822 Frances Priscilla, dau of George Pearson, MD, chemist and doctor, and *d* 27 April 1858, leaving an only s:

JOHN GEORGE DODSON, **1st Baron Monk Bretton**, of Conybro and Hurstpierpoint, Co Sussex (UK), so *cr* 4 Nov 1884, PC (1872); *b* 18 Oct 1825; *educ* Eton and Ch Ch Oxford; MP (Lib) Sussex 1857–74, Chester 1874–80 and Scarborough 1880–84, Dep Speaker H of C 1865–72, Fin Sec Treasury 1873–74, Pres Local Govt Bd 1880–82, Chllr Duchy Lancaster 1882–84; *m* 3 Jan 1856 Florence (*d* 17 Feb 1912), 2nd dau of William John Campion, of Danny, Sussex, by Harriet, est dau of Thomas Kemp, of Kemptown, Brighton, and *d* 25 May 1897, leaving, with three daus (Florence Harriet, *d* unm 8 June 1907; Ethel Millicent, *d* unm 22 Oct 1938; Mildred Augusta, *d* unm 18 June 1951):

JOHN WILLIAM DODSON, **2nd Baron Monk Bretton**, CB, JP, DL (Sussex and London); *b* 22 Sept 1869; Attaché Dip Serv 1894–97, Vicar-Gen to For Sec, PPS to Colonial Sec 1900–03, CA London 1911–15, Maj Sussex Yeo 1918, memb LCC 1922–33 (Chm 1929–30); *m* 19 Aug 1911 Ruth (*d* 5 Aug 1967), 2nd dau of Hon Charles Brand (*see* HAMPDEN, V), and *d* 29 July 1933, leaving:

1 JOHN CHARLES DODSON, **3rd and present Baron Monk Bretton**

1 Priscilla; *b* 20 July 1914; *m* 7 Jan 1935 Maj Claude Thorburn Knight, Coldstream Gds (*d* 1993), s of Ernest Knight, of Syon House, S Devon, by Isabel, dau of Sir Walter Thorburn, of Glenbeck, and *d* 1995, leaving:

(1) *(Christopher) William [William Knight Esq, 82 Lansdowne Rd, London W11 2LS]; *b* 10 April 1943; *educ* Eton; *m* 6 Sept 1969 *Jonkvrouwe Sylvia Caroline van Lennep, 2nd dau of Jonkheer Emile van Lennep, of The Hague, and has:

1a *Christopher Thorburn; *b* 1973

1a *Alexa Isobel; *b* 1971

2a *Louisa Jane; *b* 1977

(1) *(Caroline) Jane [Mrs Jerome Fane de Salis, Bourne House, East Woodhay, Berks]; *b* 3 Dec 1935; *m* 14 April 1956 Maj Jerome Otway Fane de Salis, Welsh Gds (*d* 1989), only s of Lt-Col Edmund William Fane de Salis, MC, of Bourne House, and has:

1a *Nicholas Charles; *b* 21 Nov 1957; *m* 1988 *Felicity Anne, dau of David Stewart, FRCOG, of Axmouth, Devon, formerly of Harare, Zimbabwe, and has:

1b *Alexandra Claire; *b* 19 Sept 1991

2b *Katharine Elisabeth Jane; *b* 14 Aug 1994

3b *Sophie Rebecca; *b* 17 May 1997

2a *Rodolph William [Rodolph Fane de Salis Esq, Bourne House, East Woodhay, Berks]; *b* 4 Nov 1970; *educ* Eton, UEA (BA) and SIHE

1a *Henrietta Jane; *b* 8 June 1960; *m* 1982 *Nigel Ronald Graham (*see* GRAHAM, Bt, of Norton Conyers)

(2) *Patricia Susan; *b* 4 Oct 1938; *m* 26 July 1962 *Sir Timothy Lewis Achilles Daunt, KCMG, only s of Leslie Henry Graeme Daunt, and has:

1a *Achilles James; *b* 18 Oct 1963; *m* 1994 *Katherine, dau of Rev Alan Steward

1a *Eleanor; *b* 23 April 1965; *m* 1990 *Dr Marco Puccioni, only s of Dr Marco Puccioni, of Florence, and has:

1b *Emma; *b* 1991

2b *Olivia; *b* 1993

2a *Alice Louise; *b* 23 Nov 1969

(3) *Georgiana Sarah Ann; *b* 28 Nov 1945; *m* 12 Dec 1970 *R-Adml Timothy Michael Bevan, CB, only s of Thomas Richard Bevan, of Annes, Hadlow Down, Sussex, and has:

1a *Thomas Loraine; *b* 1973

2a *Michael David; *b* 1975

3a *Richard John; *b* 1977

MONKSWELL

Arms: Arg. on a chevron az. between in chief two demi-unicorns courant and in base an elephant's head erased gu., three oak branches, slipped, leaved and fructed or. **Crest:** A demi-man affrontée ppr., holding in the dexter hand an oak branch, slipped and leaved ppr., fructed or, and resting the sinister hand on an escutcheon az., charged with two keys saltirewise or. **Supporters:** Two druids, vested arg., wreathed about the temples with laurel leaves vert, each resting the exterior hand on an escutcheon az., charged with a balance suspended or. **Motto:** Persevere. **Creation:** B. (UK) 1 July 1885.

THE 5TH BARON MONKSWELL OF MONKSWELL, Co Devon (Gerard Collier) [The Rt Hon The Lord Monkswell of Monkswell, 513 Barlow Moor Rd, Chorlton cum Hardy, Manchester M21 8AQ]; *b* 28 Jan 1947; s f 1984; *educ* George Heriot's Sch Edinburgh, Portsmouth Poly (BSc Mech Eng 1971), Slough Poly (Cert in Works Management 1972); product quality engr 1972 and serv admin manager 1984 Massey Ferguson, memb (Lab) Manchester CC 1989–94, Parly Consultant 1990–, chm Campaign Against Bullying at Work; *m* 1974 *Ann Valerie, dau of James Collins, of Liverpool, and has:

1 +JAMES ADRIAN; *b* 29 March 1977

2 +Robert William Gerard; *b* 1979

1 *Laura Jennifer; *b* 1975

Lineage: JOHN COLLIER, JP, DL, of Grimstone and Monkswell, Devon; *b* 1769; MP Plymouth 1832–41; *m* 1816 Emma, dau of Robert Porrett, of North Hill, Devon, by —, dau of Thomas Mortimer, author, and *d* 1849, having had:

1 ROBERT PORRETT, **1st Baron**

2 William Frederick, JP, of Woodtown and Sampford Spiney, Devon; *b* 1824; *m* 1854 Cycill Christiana, dau of Charles Biggs Calmady, DL, of Langdon Court, Devon, and *d* 9 Feb 1902, leaving issue

3 Mortimer John, VD; *b* 1825; Lt-Col 2nd Devon Rifle Vols; *m* 1st Mary Elizabeth, dau of Sir William Snow Harris, FRS; *m* 2nd Sophia Luddington (*d* 30 Oct 1913), dau of J Whipple, of Plymouth, and *d* 28 Oct 1916, leaving issue

4 John Francis, JP Lancs; *b* 19 June 1829; Judge County Court 1873–1907; *m* 1 Feb 1870 Frances Ann Jane (*d* 17 July 1900), dau of Robert F Jenner, DL, of Wenvoe Castle, Glam, and *d* 1911, leaving issue

5 Arthur Bevan, JP Cornwall; *b* 1832; Maj and Hon Lt-Col 2nd Vol Bn DCLI; *m* Eliza, dau of Elfred Blaker, and *d* Feb 1908, leaving issue

1 Elizabeth Anne; *m* Col — Pipon, of Noirmont Manor, Jersey, and had issue

The est son,

Sir ROBERT PORRETT COLLIER, **1st Baron Monkswell of Monkswell**, Co Devon (UK), so *cr* 1 July 1885, PC (1871), QC (1854); *b* 21 June 1817; *educ* Trin Coll Cambridge (BA 1841); barrister 1843, Recorder Penzance, Judge Advocate the Fleet and Counsel Admlty 1859–63, MP Plymouth 1852–71, Slr-Gen 1863–66, Attorney-Gen 1868–71, Judge Common Pleas 1871, Judge Judicial Ctee PC, ktd 1863; *m* 14 April 1844 Isabella Rose (*d* 10 April 1886), dau of William Rose Rose, of Wolston Heath, Warwicks, and had:

1 ROBERT, **2nd Baron**.

2 John, OBE (1920); *b* 27 Jan 1850; *m* 1st 30 June 1879 Marian (*d* 18 Nov 1887), dau of Thomas Henry Huxley, PC, LLD, PRS, the biologist and champion of Darwinianism, and had:

(1) Joyce; portrait miniaturist, memb Roy Soc Miniature Painters; *m* 1st 27 April 1906 (*divorce* 1918) Leslie Crawshay Williams (*d* 22 Feb 1945), 2nd s of Arthur John Williams, DL, MP, of Coed-y-Mwstwr, Glam, and had:

1a Rupert; *b* 23 Feb 1908; *educ* Repton and Queen's Coll Oxford; *m* March 1932 Elizabeth Joyce Violet, dau of Lt-Col Henry George Powell, of The Red House, Aldermaston, Berks

1a Gillian (Jill); *b* 11 April 1910; *m* 1 June 1940 Baron Greenwood of Rossendale (LP; *d* 1982), only s of Arthur Greenwood, PC, CH, MP, and *d* 19 July 1995, leaving:

1b *Susanna Catherine Crawshay; *b* 25 Aug 1943; *m* 1970 (*divorce* 1991) Christopher Gardiner and has:

1c *Thomas Keir; *b* 1982

2c *Anna Kathryn; b 1980

2b *Dinah Karen Crawshay [Dr The Hon Mrs Murray, 42 Cheverton Rd, London N19]; b 27 May 1946; PhD; m 1970 *David Murray and has:

 1c *Bruno; b 1974

 2c *Leo, b 1976

 3c *Fergus, b 1978

(1) (cont.) Mrs Joyce Williams m 2nd 2 Nov 1918 Drysdale Dilburn (d 13 March 1940), 2nd s of Nicholas Dilburn, JP, MusD, and d 21 Nov 1972, leaving by him:

2a *(Nicholas) John Drysdale [John Dilburn Esq, 43 Westgate Road, St Anne's-on-Sea, Lancs]; b 1925; m 6 Nov 1954 *Bette, dau of Claude Seal, and has:

 1b *Howard John; b 4 June 1956

 1b *Wendy Suzanne; b 25 July 1957

2 (cont.) The Hon John Collier m 2nd 1 April 1889 his deceased w's sis Ethel Gladys (d 11 May 1914), 5th dau of Thomas Huxley, and d 11 April 1934, having by her had:

(1) Laurence (Sir), KCMG (1944); b 13 June 1890; educ Bedales and Balliol Coll Oxford; Clerk FO 1913, 2nd Sec Tokyo 1919–21, Counsellor FO 1932–41, Min to Norwegian Govt in London 1941, Amb Extrdy and Plen Oslo 1945, ret 1951; m 31 May 1917 Eleanor Antoinette (d 7 Aug 1975 aged 83), only dau of William Luther Watson, S Lancashire Regt, and d 1976, leaving:

1a +William Oswald [William Collier Esq, 34 Berwyn Rd, Richmond, Surrey]; b 26 Nov 1919; educ Bradfield and Balliol Coll Oxford (MA); FSA, FRHistS; m 1st 29 Aug 1947 (divorce 1957) Hon Muriel Joan Lamb, yst dau of 1st Baron Rochester (qv), and has had:

 1b Francis Robert; b 10 July, d 14 July 1949

 1b *Sylvia Antoinette; b 3 Sept 1952; m 1985 *Stephen Kenneth Godfrey

1a (cont.) William Collier m 2nd 2 April 1958 *Ina Mary Grace, only dau of Charles W Crowne, of Littlehampton, Sussex, and by her has:

 2b +Jonathan Charles Laurence; b 3 June 1959

 2b *Lucy Eleanor Mary; b 19 May 1961; m 1988 *David William Hewitt

 3b *Stella Catherine Juliet; b 24 May 1965

(2) Joan; b 12 Feb 1893; m 2 Aug 1911 Brig-Gen Frank Anstie Buzzard, DSO, RFA (see BUZZARD, Bt), and had issue

1 Margaret Isabella; m 1873 Count Arturo Galletti di Cadilhac, Lt-Col Italian Artillery, and d 1928, leaving issue. He d 1912

The 1st BARON d 27 Oct 1886; his er s,

ROBERT COLLIER, **2nd Baron Monkswell of Monkswell**, JP, DL Middx; b 26 March 1845; educ Cambridge (BA, LLB); barrister Inner Temple 1869, Ld-in-Waiting 1892–95, U-Sec War 1895, Chm Roy Commn Health and Safety Miners 1906, memb LCC 1889–1907 (V-Chm 1902–03, Chm 1903–04); m 21 Aug 1873 Mary Josephine (d 14 May 1930), dau of Joseph Alfred Hardcastle, MP Bury St Edmunds, and d 22 Dec 1909, leaving:

1ROBERT ALFRED HARDCASTLE COLLIER, **3rd Baron Monkswell of Monkswell**; b 13 Dec 1875; educ Eton and Trin Coll Cambridge; Attaché Dip Serv 1900, 3rd Sec 1902–05, 2nd Sec 1905, Clerk FO 1905–10, 2nd Lt B Bn 63rd Bde RFA, Hon 2nd Lt 1918, WW I; m 1st 7 Oct 1908 Ursula Mary (d 29 Jan 1915), dau of Hugh Gurney Barclay, MVO of Colney Hall, Norwich, and had:

(1) Lorna Evelyn; b 24 Jan 1915

1 (cont.) The **3rd Baron** m 2nd 22 Jan 1925 Katharine Edith (d 1985), er dau of William Shaw Harriss Gastrell, of Rockbeare Grange, Devon, and d 14 Jan 1964, having by her had:

(1) Robert Douglas; b 8 April 1926; Lt Hants Regt; accidentally drowned Cyprus on active service 5 Aug 1946

2 Gerard; b 17 Oct 1878; MA Oxon; m 21 July 1910 Lily Ermengarde Fanny, novelist (d 16 July 1956, having m 2nd 22 March 1928 William John Anderson, of Montrose), 3rd dau of Sir Mountstuart Elphinstone Grant Duff, GCSI, PC, and d 26 April 1923, having had:

(1) Paul Robert Gerard; b 16, d 22 June 1912

(2) WILLIAM ADRIAN LARRY, **4th Baron**

(3) +Perceval Gerard; b 17 Jan 1915, educ Faraday House; FHDip, REME WW II; m 1st 26 Dec 1940 (divorce 1947) Lorraine Walker and has:

1a +Anthony Gerard [Anthony Collier Esq, W/5 Water Rat, T/O Entrepotdok 55, 1018 AD, Amsterdam, Holland]; b 28 June 1942; educ Leicester U

(3) (cont.) Perceval Collier m 2nd 8 July 1949 Sheila (d 1975), formerly w of S/Ldr Robert Francis Doe, DSO, DFC and bar, RAF, and er dau of Capt Stuart Mackintosh Macpherson, OBE, RAMC, and by her has:

2a +Gavin Gerard [Gavin Collier Esq, 113 Mesa Vista 3, Santa Fe, NM 87501, USA]; b 25 Nov 1951; educ Stowe

1a *Tessa Jill [Ms Tessa Collier, 22 Courtland Drive, Chigwell, Essex]; b 27 June 1950

(3) (cont.) Perceval Collier m 3rd 1977 *Brenda Mary, dau of Nathaniel Victor Fortescue and formerly w of Geoffrey Dacre Carpenter

(4) John Bernard; b 15 May 1920; m Aug 1947 *Elsie [Mrs John Collier, 12 Argyle Crescent, Edinburgh EH15 2QG], dau of James Dunbar, of Edinburgh, and d 1993, having had:

1a *(Anna) Lee [Mrs Lee Gates, 90 Charterhall Rd, Edinburgh EH9 3HS]; b 1948; m 19– (divorce 19–) Michael Gates and has:

 1b *Catherine; b 1973; educ Edinburgh and Aberdeen Us (MB, ChB 1997)

2a *Sarah [Mrs John Bett, East Lodge, Balbirnie, Markinch, Fife KY7 6JT]; b 1950; educ Glasgow U (MA 1972); m 1987 *John Bett and has:

 1b *Leo Mark Sean Collier; b 1988

(4) (cont.) John Collier also had issue by Barbara Oriel Markham:

1a *Piers Markham [Piers Collier Esq, 11 Northbank Walk, Didsbury, Manchester]; b 1947; m 1973 (divorce 1993) Susan Margaret Robinson and has:

 1b *Matthew John Samuel; b 1978

 1b *Esmé Lorraine; b 1976

(1) *Anna Evangeline [Mrs Elvin Thorgerson, 19 Earl St, Cambridge]; b 24 April 1918; Land Army WW II; m 1940 Elvin Thorgerson and has:

1a *Storm Elvin; b 1944

3 Eric Cecil Frederick; b 2 Sept 1882; educ Eton; Lt 16th Bn London Regt Queen's Westminster Rifles WW I, Assist Priv Sec to Govr Mauritius 1905 and Ch Sec Ireland 1906; m 1st 15 Oct 1912 Dorothea Gertrude Agnes (d 4 March 1952), dau of Phillip Lawrence, of Sydney, NSW; m 2nd 11 Dec 1953 *Lena Victoria (Queenie), dau of James Kennedy, of Forfar, and dsp Dec 1968

The 3rd BARON's n,

WILLIAM ADRIAN LARRY COLLIER, **4th Baron Monkswell of Monkswell**, disclaimed peerage for life 7 April 1964; b 25 Nov 1913; educ Switzerland, Summerhill, George Heriot's Sch and Edinburgh U (MB, BCh 1943); RAMC WW II, DPH Lond 1947, memb: Halstead UDC 1954–67 and Essex River Authority; m 1st 21 Sept 1939 (divorce 1945) Erika, dau of Dr Edward Kellner, of Vienna; m 2nd 9 July 1945 (divorce 1950) Helen (m 2nd 1954 Edward Edmund Kemp), dau of James Dunbar, of Edinburgh, and by her had:

1 GERARD COLLIER, **5th and present Baron Monkswell of Monkswell**

2 +Neil Adrian José [The Hon Neil Collier, 1335 Peralta Ave, Berkeley, CA 94702, USA]; b 20 Aug 1948; educ George Heriot's Sch Edinburgh, UEA (BSc) and Leicester U (CertEd); m 1st 1975 (divorce 1985) Frances Myra Chapman; m 2nd 1987 *Judith Bosca Brandes, dau of Rico G Bosca

The **4th Baron** m 3rd 1951 *Nora Selby [Mrs William Collier, 6 Corona Rd, Cambridge] and d 1984, having by her had:

3 +Benjamino; b 2 Feb 1958; m 1984 *Clare Maria Murphy and has:

(1) +Daniel James William Paulo, b 1987

1 *Tiaré Penelope Katharine [The Hon Tiaré Collier, The Clatterway, Bonsall, Derbys]; b 5 Sept 1952

2 Cressida; b 4 Oct 1953, d 1955

MONRO OF LANGHOLM

Creation: B. (LP, UK) 1997.

THE BARON MONRO OF LANGHOLM, of Westerkirk, Dumfries and Galloway (Sir Hector Seymour Peter Monro, AE (1953), PC (1995), JP (1963), DL (Dumfries 1973)) [The Rt Hon The Lord Monro of Langholm AE PC JP DL, Williamwood, Kirtlebridge, Dumfriesshire DG11 3LN]; b 4 Oct 1922; educ Canford Sch and King's Coll Cambridge; RAF 1941–46, F/Lt RAuxAF 1946–53; memb: Dumfries CC 1952–67 (Chm Planning Ctee, Police Ctee), Dumfries T&AFA 1959–67; Chm Dumfriesshire U Assoc 1958–63, MP (C) Dumfries 1964–97, Scottish Ch Whip 1967–70, Ld Commr Treasury 1970–71, Parly U-Sec: Scottish Office 1971–74 and 1992–95, DOE 1979–81, Oppn Spokesman: Scottish Affrs 1974–75, Sport 1974–79, memb Select Ctee: Scottish Affrs 1983–86, Def 1987; Chm: Scottish C Members Ctee 1983–92, C Parly Ctee Sport 1984–85; V-Chm C Members Ag Ctee 1983–87, ktd 1981; memb: Area Exec Ctee NFU Scotland, Nature Conservancy Cncl 1982–91, Cncl Nat Tst Scotland 1983–92; Pres: Auto-cycle Union 1983–90, NSRA 1987–92, Scottish Rugby Union 1976–77 (memb 1958–77, V-Pres 1975); Hon Air Cdre No 2622 RAuxAF Regt Sqdn 1982–, Hon Inspr Gen RAuxAF 1990–; memb Roy Co Archers; m 1st 4 March 1949 (Elizabeth) Anne (d 1994), dau of Maj Harry Welch, of Longstone Hall, Derbys, and has:

1 *Seymour Hector Russell Hale; b 7 May 1950

2 *A son; b 19–

BARON MONRO OF LANGHOLM m 2nd 1944 *Mrs Doris Kaestner, of Baltimore

Lineage: CHARLES J HALE MONRO, of Ingsdon Manor, S Devon; had:

SEYMOUR CHARLES HALE MONRO, CB (1903); b 22 July 1856; Army: joined 1876, served Afghan War 1878–80 (severely wounded, despatches, medal with four clasps, bronze decoration), Egypt 1882 (medal with clasp, Khedive's Star), S Africa 1884 (despatches), Capt and Maj 1888, Hazara Expdn 1891 (medal with clasp), Chitral Relief Force 1895 (despatches, medal with clasp), Brevet Lt-Col 1896, NWF India 1897–98 (two clasps), S Africa 1899–1908 (despatches, Brevet Col, medal with six clasps, King's Medal with two clasps), Col 1900, Brig-Gen cmdg Ahmednagar Bde 1905; m 4 Dec 1886 Lady Ida Constance Vaughan, est dau of 5th Earl of Lisburne (qv), and d 30 Sept 1906, leaving, with another s and a dau:

IAN ALASTAIR SEYMOUR MONRO; Capt QO Cameron Highrs; m 22 April 1919 Marion Frances, dau of Lt-Gen Sir John Spencer Ewart of Craigcleuch, KCB, JP, and had:

1 HECTOR SEYMOUR PETER (Sir), cr a **Baron**

2 *Jean Marion Pamela; b 2 May 1920; m 6 Oct 1942 *Capt Douglas Stamp Denis Brisbane-Jones-Stamp, Duke of Wellington's Regt

MONSON

Arms: Or two chevronels gu. **Crest:** A lion rampant ppr., supporting a column or. **Supporters:** Dexter, a lion or, gorged with a collar and having a line reflexed over the back az., the collar charged with three crescents of the first; sinister, a griffin, wings elevated arg., beaked and membered az., collared and lined as the dexter. **Motto:** *Prest pour mon pais* ('Ready for my country'). **Creations:** Bt (E) 29 June 1611, B (GB) 25 May 1728.

THE 11TH BARON MONSON OF BURTON, Co Lincoln, and a **Baronet** (Sir John Monson, Bt) [The Rt Hon The Lord Monson, The Manor House, South Carlton, Lincs LN1 2RN]; *b* 3 May 1932; *s f* 1958; *educ* Eton and Trin Coll Camb (BA 1954); Pres Soc for Individual Freedom; *m* 2 April 1955 *Emma, only dau of Anthony Devas, ARA, RP, and has:

1 +NICHOLAS JOHN [The Hon Nicholas Monson, 24 Fentiman Rd, London SW8 1LS]; *b* 19 Oct 1955; *educ* Eton; jnlst, fndr and ed *The Magazine* 1982–84, dir Strategic Solutions (PR) 1985–87, md Grenfell Communications Ltd (PR), non-exec dir The Organiser Co (Publishing); *m* 1981 (*divorce* 1996) Hilary, only dau of Kenneth Martin, of Mombasa, Kenya, and has:

  (1) +Alexander John Runan; *b* 1984

  (1) *Isabella; *b* 1986

2 +Andrew Anthony John [The Hon Andrew Monson, 7A Melrose Gardens, London W6]; *b* 12 May 1959; *educ* Eton and Merton Coll Oxford (BA); barrister Middle Temple 1983; *m* 1993 *Emily C, yr dau of Richard Clement Wheeler-Bennett, of The Mill House, Calstone Wellington, Wilts

3 +Stephen Alexander John; *b* 5 Jan 1961

Lineage: JOHN MONSON, of Owersby and E or Market Rasen, Lincs; living 1378; had:

JOHN MONSON; accompanied HENRY V's French campaign 1418; had:

JOHN MONSON; merchant of the Staple (group involved in restrictive trading practice in wool) 1441; had, with other issue:

JOHN MONSON, of South Kelsey; *m* 1st —; *m* 2nd Elizabeth (*d* 8 Dec 1473), dau of Sir Richard Hansard, and had, with three daus:

Sir JOHN MONSON, of S Carlton and S Kelsey; Escheator (roy official implementing escheats, or reversions to the Crown on a Crown tenant's death) Lincs 1505–06, ktd 1541; *b* 1467; *m* 1st Beatrice, dau of John Hurst/Thirsk, of Burton-on-Stather, Lincs, merchant, and had:

1 Thomas, of S Kelsey; *m* Elizabeth (*d* May 1573), dau of Sir Robert Sheffield, of Butterwick, and had issue

Sir JOHN *m* 2nd Dorothy Meres, of The Marsh, Lincs, and by her had:

2 George (Rev); Rector Clayworth, Notts; Chaplain to ANNE OF CLEVES; living 19 July 1557

3 Robert, of Belton, Isle of Axholme; *m* Margaret (*d* July 1570), dau and heiress of Sir Francis Belwood, of Belton, Lincs, and *d* Aug 1555, leaving issue

4 WILLIAM

1 Anne; *m* Thomas Rygge, of Boothby

2 Frances; *m* Sir Christopher Ayscough, of Ashby

Sir JOHN *d* 26 May 1542; his 4th son,

WILLIAM MONSON, of S Carlton; High Sheriff Lincs 1553, MP Totnes 1547; *m* Elizabeth (*d* 8 Oct 1546), dau of Sir Robert Tyrwhitt, of Kettleby, Lincs, and had:

1 John, of Beckenham and Boyle, Notts; *m* Mary (*m* 2nd Simon Hall; *d* 4 March 1572/3), dau of Sir Robert Hussey, of Linwood, and coheir of her mother Anne, dau of Sir Thomas Say, and *dvp* 17 Nov 1552, having had, with other issue:

  (1) JOHN (Sir)

2 Robert; MP Lincoln *temp* EDWARD VI, MARY and ELIZABETH, Recorder Lincoln 1567, Justice Common Pleas 1572; *m* 12 Sept 1559 Elizabeth, dau and heiress of John Dyon, of Tathwell, and *dsp* 25 Sept 1583

3 Gilbert (Rev); Preb Lincoln; *d* 1555

4 George (Rev); Preb Lincoln; *m* 15 Sept 1565 Eleanore (*m* 2nd Francis Yarborough, of Weston), dau and heiress of George Farmery, of Northorpe, and *d* 21 March 1578/9, leaving issue

WILLIAM MONSON *d* Nov 1558; his grandson,

Sir JOHN MONSON, of S Carlton; *b* 1546; High Sheriff Lincs 1577, ktd 1586; *m* Jane (*d* Oct 1624), dau of Robert Dighton, of Little Sturton, and had, with other issue:

1 THOMAS (Sir), **1st Bt**

2 William (Sir); Adml, ktd Cadiz; *m* 1593 Dorothy, widow of Richard Smith, of Shelford, Warwicks, and dau of Richard Wallop, of Bugbrooke, and was *bur* 13 Feb 1642/3, leaving, with two daus (one of whom, Jane, *m* Sir Francis Howard; see EFFINGHAM, E):

  (1) John, of Kinnersley, Horley, Surrey; *b* 1604; *m* Anne (*d* 29 Aug 1667), dau of James Mayne, and had:

    1a Anne; *m* Sir Francis Throgmorton, 2nd Bt (*d* 1680), of Coughton (see 1970 edn THROCKMORTON, Bt), and *d* 23 July 1728

  (2) WILLIAM MONSON, 1st and last VISCOUNT MONSON OF CASTLEMAINE, Co Kerry, so *cr* 23 Aug 1628, as also BARON MONSON OF BELLINGUARD (both I); *b* 1598 or 1599; ktd Feb 1622/3, MP Reigate 1626 and 1640–53, royalist Civil War till *c* 1646 but Parliamentarian thereafter, one of the judges who voted to execute CHARLES I Jan 1648/9, consequently deprived of his honours 12 July 1661 after the Restoration and sentenced to be drawn in a sledge with a rope round his neck from The Tower to Tyburn and back again, then to life imprisonment in The Tower; *m* 1st 23 Oct 1625 Margaret (*d* 4 Aug 1639), widow of 1st Earl of Nottingham of the 1597 *cr* (see EFFINGHAM, E) and dau of 2nd Earl of Moray (*qv*), and had a s (Stewart, *d* young); *m* 2nd May 1646 Frances (*d* Jan 1650/1), dau of Thomas Alston, of Portshead, Suffolk, and had a s and dau (both *d* young); *m* 3rd Elizabeth (restored to a viscountess's rank after her 3rd husb's death; *m* 4th 1676 Sir Adam Felton, 3rd Bt; *d* 26 Dec 1695), widow of (a) Sir Francis Foljambe, Bt, and (b) Edward Horner, of Mells, Somerset, and dau of Sir George Rearsby, of Thrybergh, Yorks, and *d* 1673, having had by her (who had Monson tied naked to a bedpost and horsewhipped him for his heterodox political opinions):

    1a Elizabeth; *m* 1st Sir Philip Hungate, Bt; *m* 2nd Lewis Smith

3 Robert (Sir), of North Carlton; ktd 1603, MP Lincoln 1625; *m* Sarah, dau of William Clayton, of Wakefield, and widow of Thomas Saville, and *d* 15 April 1638, having had, with other issue:

  (1) SARAH Monson; *b c* 1624; *cr* 23 Oct 1679 VISCOUNTESS CORBET OF LINCHLADE, Co Buckingham (E), for life; *m* 1st by 1642 Sir Vincent CORBET, 1st Bt, of Mor(e)ton Corbet, Salop (*d* 28 Dec 1656; see 1970 edn); *m* 2nd 18 Dec 1679 Sir Charles Lee, of Billesley, Warwicks, and *d* 5 June 1682, when the Viscountcy expired

Sir JOHN *d* 20 Dec 1593; his eldest son,

Sir Thomas Monson, 1st Bt (E), so *cr* 29 June 1611, of Carlton; Master of the Armoury, Master Falconer to JAMES I, MP Lincs 1597–98, Castle Rising 1604–11 and Cricklade 1614, ktd; *m* July 1590 Margaret (*bur* 3 Aug 1630), dau of Sir Edmund Anderson, Ch Justice Common Pleas, and *d* 25 May 1641, having had, with a yr s:

Sir John Monson, 2nd Bt, KB; *b* 1597; DCL Oxford, MP Lincs 1626; *m* 1627 Ursula (*d* Dec 1692), dau and heiress of Sir Robert Oxenbridge, of Hasborne, by Elizabeth, widow of Thomas West and dau and coheir of Sir Henry Cock, of Broxbourne, Herts, and was *bur* 29 Dec 1683, having had:

1 John (Sir); MP Lincoln 1660; *m* Judith, est dau of Sir Thomas Pelham, 2nd Bt (see CHICHESTER, E), and *dvp* 1674, having had, with seven other sons and a dau:

  (1) **Sir Henry Monson, 3rd Bt**; MP Lincoln; *m* 4 March 1674/5 Elizabeth, dau of Charles Cheyne, Viscount Newhaven, and was *bur sp* 6 April 1718

  (2) **Sir William Monson, 4th Bt**; *m* Letitia, sister of Earl Poulett (see 1970 edn), but *dsp* 7 March 1727

  (3) George; *b* 27 Feb 1657/8; *m* Anne (*d* 16 Oct 1726), dau of Charles Wren, of the Isle of Ely, and had, with four other sons:

    1a **Sir John Monson, 5th Bt** and **1st Baron Monson of Burton**, Co Lincoln (GB), so *cr* 28 May 1728, KB (1725), PC (1737); *b c* 1693; *educ* Ch Ch Oxford; MP (Whig) Lincoln 1722–28, Capt Gentlemen Pensioners 1733, 1st Commr Trade 1737–48; *m* 8 April 1725 Lady Margaret Watson, yst dau of 1st Earl of Rockingham (see 1970 edn SONDES, E), and had:

      1b JOHN, **2nd Baron**

      2b Lewis MONSON later WATSON (roy licence 31 Jan 1750/1 on inheriting estates of his cousin, 3rd and last Earl of Rockingham (*d* 26 Feb 1745/6)), 1st BARON SONDES OF LEES COURT

      3b George; Brig-Gen; *m* Lady Anne Vane, dau of 1st Earl of Darlington (see BARNARD, B) and previously w of Charles Hope-Vere (see LINLITHGOW, M), and *dsp* 1777

The 1st BARON *d* 1748; his eldest son,

JOHN MONSON, **2nd Baron Monson of Burton**; *b* 23 July 1727; *m* 23 June 1752 Theodosia (*d* 20 Feb 1821), dau of John Maddison, of Harpswell, Lincs, and *d* 1774, having had:

1 JOHN MONSON, **3rd Baron Monson of Burton**; *b* 25 May 1753; *educ* Eton; *m* 18 July 1777 Lady Elizabeth Capell (*d* 23 Feb 1834), dau of 4th Earl of Essex (*qv*), and *d* 20 May 1806, leaving, with two daus:

  (1) JOHN GEORGE MONSON, **4th Baron Monson of Burton**; *b* 1 Feb 1785; *educ* Harrow and Ch Ch Oxford; *m* 30 Oct 1807 Lady Sarah Savile (*m* 2nd 21 Oct 1816 3rd Earl of (Brooke and 3rd Earl of) Warwick (*qv*), est dau of 2nd Earl of Mexborough (*qv*), and *d* 14 Nov 1809, leaving an only s:

    1a FREDERICK JOHN MONSON, **5th Baron Monson of Burton**; *b* 3 Feb 1809, *m* 21 June 1832 Theodosia (*d* 3 July 1891), yst dau of Latham Blacker, of Newent, Glos, and *dsp* 7 Oct 1841

2 George Henry; *b* 17 Oct 1755; *m* 15 March 1784 Susanna, widow of Thomas Smith, of Hawkesworth, and dau of George Johnson, and *d* 17 June, 1823, leaving an only dau:

  (1) Georgiana Theodosia; *d* 22 Nov 1858

3 Charles; Maj-Gen; *b* 11 March 1758; *d* 11 Jan 1800

4 William; Col, MP Lincoln; *b* 15 Dec 1760; *m* 10 Jan 1786 Anne (*d* 1841), yst dau of John Debonnaire, and *d* 26 Dec 1807, leaving an only s:

(1) WILLIAM JOHN, **6th Baron**

5 Thomas John (Rev); Rector Bedale; *b* 10 May 1764; *m* 1st 29 July 1790 Anne Shipley (*d* 8 Sept 1818), dau of Joseph Greene, and had:

(1) John Joseph Thomas (Rev); Chaplain to HM QUEEN VICTORIA; *b* 7 July 1791; *m* 26 Aug 1813 Elizabeth Anne (*d* 21 Jan 1859), dau of Rev Christopher Wyvill, of Constable Burton, Yorks, and *dsp* 31 July 1861

5 (cont) The Rev Thomas Monson *m* 2nd 11 Aug 1824 Sarah (*d* 25 June 1865), dau of the above-mentioned Rev Christopher Wyvill, and *d* 3 April 1843, having by her had:

(2) Thomas John (Rev); Canon York, RD, Rector Kirby-under-Dale, Yorks; *b* 28 April 1825; *m* 25 March 1856 Caroline Isabella (*d* 9 April 1922), yst dau of 5th Viscount Galway (*qv*), and *d* 23 July 1887, leaving:

1a George John; AMICE; *b* 28 Jan 1857; *educ* Eton

2a Charles John; MIEE; *b* 9 May 1858; *d* unm 7 June 1902

3a Alfred John; *b* 30 May 1860; *m* 27 Oct 1881 Agnes Maude (*d* 1942), 3rd dau of William Day, of Eversley Garth, Yorks, and had:

1b Philip Evelyn John; DD, PhD, *b* 1887; *m* 1st 1920 Doris Murray (*d* 1942), of Leeds, and had:

1c +Philip John; *b* 2 March 1928

1c *Margaret Enid; *b* 5 Feb 1922

1b (cont.) Philip Monson *m* 2nd 1956 *Catherine A — and *d* 1965

1b Florence Edome; *m* — Potter and *d* 1918, leaving two sons and a dau

2b Margaret Rosamond

3b Violet Theodosia

4b Mildred Grace

5b Constance Lilian; *m* 1st Rupert Worrell (*d* 19–); *m* 2nd 1941 George Reeves (presumed drowned 1941)

4a Henry John; *b* 24 Sept 1862; *m* 21 Aug 1901 Theodosia Anne Emily (*d* 17 Jan 1951), only dau of Rev George Howard Wright, of White Hill House, West Liss, Hants, and *d* 11 March 1930, leaving:

1b +Thomas Debonnaire John; *b* 14 Feb 1905, *educ* Haileybury, *m* 1936 (*divorce* 1959) Anna Philippe Bois Clements

1b Edomé Theodosia; *b* 3 May 1903; *m* 1st 24 April 1924 (*divorce* 1935) Leonard Oswald Johnson and had issue; *m* 2nd 3 May 1947 James Brandeth Warden and *d* 22 Aug 1965. He *d* Dec 1959

2b Patricia Alexandrina; *b* 3 May 1906; *m* 23 Aug 1947 Hugh Stewart Gray, LDS, DSc, of Beaconsfield, Bucks, yst s of William Gray, BSc, Pncpl Presbyterian Ladies' Coll Melbourne, Australia

5a Gilbert John MONSON later MONSON-FitzJOHN (added 1909); *b* 17 Sept 1872; BSc, FRHistS, FRSL, Capt 5th Border Regt and T/Maj RAF, formerly E Yorkshire Regt, WW I 1915–16 (despatches, twice wounded); *m* 14 Jan 1909 Ellen, dau of William J Sanderson, of Stainton, Yorks, and *d* 28 June 1936

1a Elizabeth Theodosia; *d* unm 2 Dec 1889

2a Charlotte Henrietta; *d* unm 3 May 1883

3a Beatrice Grace; *m* April 1908 Joseph Nixon and *d c* 1927. He *d* 22 Nov 1924

4a Caroline Alexandrina; *d* unm 18 Jan 1901

5a Florence Mary; *d* unm 28 May 1934

6a Alice Edomé; *m* 23 May 1906 Edward Cecil Gordon Maddock, Capt RIAMC, s of Canon — Maddock, and *dsp* April 1908

7a Constance Adelaide; *d* unm 13 Aug 1928

(1) Henrietta Anne Theodosia; *m* 2 March 1848 Henry William de la Poer Beresford-Peirse (*see* BERESFORD-PEIRSE, Bt) and *d* 28 Oct 1921, leaving issue

1 Catharine; *d* unm

2 Charlotte Grace; *m* Henry Peirse, of Bedale, and *d* 1793

3 Theodosia Margaret; *m* 9 March 1782 Sir John Gregory Shaw, 5th Bt (*see* BEST-SHAW, Bt), and *d* 24 Oct 1847

The 5th BARON's cousin,

WILLIAM JOHN MONSON, **6th Baron Monson of Burton**; *b* 14 May 1796; *educ* Eton and Ch Ch Oxford; *m* 8 May 1828 Eliza (*d* 22 Jan 1863), dau of Edmund Larken, of Bloomsbury, and *d* 17 Dec 1862, leaving, with three daus (*d* young or unm):

1 WILLIAM JOHN MONSON, **7th Baron Monson of Burton** and 1st and lst VISCOUNT OXENBRIDGE OF BURTON (UK), so *cr* 13 Aug 1886, KCVO (1896), PC (1874), DL, JP; *b* 18 Feb 1829; *educ* Eton and Ch Ch Oxford; MP (Lib) Reigate 1858–62, Treasurer Household 1874, Capt Yeomen Gd 1880–86, Dep Speaker Ho Lds 1882, Hon Col 3rd Bn Lincs Regt and 2nd Bn Queen's Vols (Roy W Surrey Regt), Militia ADC to HM QUEEN VICTORIA 1886–96, Master of the Horse 1892–94; *m* 7 Aug 1869 Maria Adelaide (*d* 24 Dec 1897), widow of 2nd Earl of Yarborough (*qv*) and sister of 1st and dau of 3rd Viscount Hawarden (*qv*), and *dsp* 16 April 1898, when the Viscountcy expired

2 DEBONNAIRE JOHN, **8th Baron**

3 Charles Edmund John; *b* 29 May 1831; *d* 18 April 1832

4 Sir EDMUND JOHN MONSON, 1st Bt, so *cr* 1905 (*see* 1949 edn MONSON, Bt)

5 Charles John; *b* 10 Aug 1836; *d* 30 March 1846

6 Evelyn John (Rev); Vicar Croft, Lincs; *b* 7 May 1838; *m* 10 July 1872 Anne Grace Hynde (*d* 30 Aug 1919), dau of James Kinncar, WS, of Edinburgh, and *d* 13 Sept 1892, leaving:

(1) William John; *b* 12 Sept 1873; *educ* Eton and Magdalen Coll (BA 1896, MA 1911); Ch Assist Sec to Govt E Africa as Hon Col 1916; *d* unm 18 March 1956

(2) Charles Evelyn John; *b* 4 May 1878; *educ* Winchester; Capt 2nd/4th Bn Lincs Regt; *m* 23 April 1924 *Mabel Gertrude, dau of Edwin Benjamin Pritchard, of Lincoln, and *d* 17 Oct 1953, leaving:

1a *Rachel Anne [Miss Rachel Monson, 123 Yarborough Road, Lincoln]; *b* 2 Nov 1926

(3) Christopher John; *b* 8 Oct 1881; Ag Dept Br E Africa Protectorate; *m* 1930 *Joan Eileen, dau of Cdr R M Reynolds, and *d* 10 Jan 1932

(1) Rachel Mary Eliza; *b* 21 March 1875; *d* unm 21 Feb 1910

The 7th BARON's bro,

DEBONNAIRE JOHN MONSON, **8th Baron Monson of Burton**, CVO (1896), JP Kent; *b* 7 March 1830; Serjeant-at-arms to HM QUEEN VICTORIA 1873–98, Comptroller Household to Duke of Saxe-Coburg and Gotha, Capt 52nd Regt; *m* 25 Dec 1861 Augusta Louisa Caroline (*d* 21 May 1936), Ldy-in-Waiting to the Duchess of Saxe-Coburg and Gotha, yst dau of Lt-Col Augustus Frederick Ellis (*see* HOWARD DE WALDEN, B), and had:

1 William John; *b* 20 June, *d* 8 Aug 1864

2 AUGUSTUS DEBONNAIRE JOHN, **9th Baron**

1 Edomé Eliza Theodosia; *m* 14 June 1890 Capt Walter Hill Chetwynd and *d* 30 May 1950, leaving issue (*see* CHETWYND, Bt)

2 Mary Evelyn Milna; *d* unm 1 Jan 1942

3 Adelaide Violet Cicely; *m* 8 June 1898 Sir George Granville Leveson-Gower, KBE, and *d* 21 April 1955, leaving issue (*see* GRANVILLE, E)

The 8th BARON *d* 18 June 1900; his only surv son,

AUGUSTUS JOHN DEBONNAIRE MONSON, **9th Baron Monson of Burton**, JP, DL (Lincs); *b* 22 Sept 1868; Attaché and Priv Sec to Amb Paris 1897–1900, Assist Comptroller Household and Equerry to Duke of Saxe-Coburg and Gotha 1900, Commr BRCS Italy, Hon Lt-Col, Grand Offr Order Crown Italy, KJStJ; *m* 1 July 1903 Romaine, DGStJ (*d* 1 Jan 1943), widow of Laurence Turnure, of New York, and *d* 10 Oct 1940, leaving:

JOHN ROSEBERY MONSON, **10th Baron Monson of Burton**, JP (Lindsey, Lincs); *b* 11 Feb 1907; *educ* Eton and Ch Ch Oxford (BA 1929); barrister Inner Temple 1931, Maj Gen List, CStJ; *m* 4 Aug 1931 *Bettie Northrup (*m* 2nd 12 Feb 1962 Capt James Arnold Phillips (*d* 1983)) [Mrs James Phillips, La Corderie, Rue St Pierre, St Peter in the Wood, Guernsey, CI], dau of Col E Alexander Powell, of Conn., USA, and *d* 7 April 1958, leaving:

1 JOHN MONSON, **11th and present Baron Monson of Burton**

2 +Jeremy David Alfonso John [Maj The Hon Jeremy Monson, Keeper's Cottage, Hare Hatch, Berks RG10 9TL]; *b* 29 Sept 1934; *educ* Eton and RMA Sandhurst; 2nd Lt Grenadier Gds 1954, Cyprus, Malta, BAOR, Br Guiana, Maj 1964 (ret 1967), Mil Assist Def Servs Sec 1964–66, OStJ 1992, CC Berks 1981–93, High Sheriff Berks 1994–1995; *m* 4 Dec 1958 *Patricia Mary, yst dau of Maj George Barker, MFH, and has:

(1) +(John) Guy Elmhirst; *b* 11 Sept 1962; *m* 17 March 1995 *Lady Rose FitzRoy, dau of 11th Duke of Grafton (*qv*), and has:

1a *Olivia Effie Fortune; *b* 8 Dec 1995

(1) *Antonia Debonnaire; *b* 3 Sept 1959

3 +Anthony John; *b* 27 April 1944; *educ* Malvern

1 *Sandra Debonnaire [The Hon Mrs Sandra Patterson, 23 Lamont Rd, London SW10 OHR]; *b* 16 Dec 1937; *m* 24 June 1958 (*divorce* 1971) Maj (William) Garry Patterson, Life Gds, s of William Norman Patterson, of Hove, and has:

(1) *James William John; *b* 20 April 1970

(1) *Debonnaire Jane; *b* 19 Aug 1959; *m* 1984 *Count Leopold von Bismarck, yst s of Prince Otto von Bismarck, of Friedrichsruh, W Germany, and has:

1a *Nikolai Leopold Archibald; *b* 29 Dec 1986

2a *Tassilo Valentine Christian; *b* 14 Feb 1989

3a *Caspar Maximilian Otto; *b* 20 Dec 1991

4a *Carl Alexander Ludwig John; *b* 4 Feb 1995

(2) *Juliet Mary; *b* 9 Feb 1963; *m* 1995 *Richard Julian Western Milliken

(3) *Annabel Kate [The Rt Hon The Lady Rayleigh, Terling Place, Chelmsford, Essex]; *b* 12 July 1965; *m* 1991 *6th Baron Rayleigh (*qv*) and has issue

Montagu of Beaulieu

SPECTEMUR AGENDO

Arms: Quarterly of four, 1st and 4th grand quarters, 1st and 4th, arg. three lozenges conjoined in fess gu., a bordure sa. (for MONTAGU), 2nd and 3rd, or an eagle displayed vert, beaked and membered gu. (for MONTHERMER); 2nd, or on a bend az. a mullet of six points between two crescents of the field (for SCOTT); 3rd grand quarterly, 1st and 4th, arg. a human heart gu., crowned with an Imperial crown or, and on a chief az. three mullets of the field (for DOUGLAS), 2nd and 3rd, a bend between six cross-crosslets fitchée or (for MAR), the whole of this quarter within a bordure or, charged with a double tressure flory counterflory gu. (for SCOTLAND). **Crests:** 1 A gryphon's head couped or, beaked and wings addorsed sa. (for MONTAGU), 2 A stag trippant ppr., attired and unguled or (for SCOTT), 3 A heart gu., winged and ensigned with an imperial crown or (for DOUGLAS). **Supporters:** Two gryphons or, winged, beaked and membered sa., each charged on the shoulder with a chapeau az., doubled erm. **Motto:** *Spectemur agendo* ('Let us be judged by our actions'). **Creation:** B. (UK) 29 Dec 1885.

THE 3RD BARON MONTAGU OF BEAULIEU, Co Southampton (Edward John Barrington Douglas-Scott-Montagu) [The Rt Hon The Lord Montagu of Beaulieu, Palace House, Beaulieu, Hants SO42 7ZN; Flat 11 Wyndham House, 24 Bryanston Sq, London W1H 7FJ]; *b* 20 Oct 1926; *s f* 1929; *educ* Ridley Coll St Catharine's Ontario, Eton and New Coll Oxford; Lt Gren Gds 1945–48, fndr Montagu Motor Museum Beaulieu, ed and publisher *The Veteran and Vintage* magazine 1956–79, author motoring books, Chm Nat Motor Museum Tst 1972– and English Heritage 1984–92, fndr pres Hist Houses Assn 1973–78, Pres: Museums Assoc 1982–84, Union of European Historic Houses 1978–81, Southern Tourist Bd and Assoc of Brit Trnspt and Engrg Museums, Historic Commercial Vehicle Soc, Disabled Drivers' Motor Club, Fedn Br Historic Vehicle Clubs and UK Vineyards Assoc, Devpt Commr 1980–84, Chllr Wine Guild of UK, Hon Fell Museums Assoc, FRSA, Cdre Beaulieu River Sailing Club, Nelson Boat Owners' Club, V-Cdre Ho Lds Yacht Club, Cdre Roy Southampton Yacht Club 1983–86, V-Pres Inst Motor Industry; *m* 1st 11 April 1959 (*divorce* 1974) (Elizabeth) Belinda, only dau of Capt Hon John de Bathe Crossley, JP (*see* SOMERLEYTON, B), and has:

1 +RALPH; *b* 13 March 1961

1 *Mary Rachel; *b* 16 Nov 1964; *m* 21 June 1997 *Rupert SCOTT later MONTAGU-SCOTT, s of Christopher Scott of Gala, in Scotland

The 3rd BARON *m* 2nd 26 Sept 1974 *Fiona Margaret, only dau of Richard D L Herbert, of Clymping, Sussex, and by her has:

2 +Jonathan Deane; *b* 11 Oct 1975; *educ* Eton and New Coll Oxford

Montagu (creations by the name of): The name Montagu derives from the Latin *mons acutus* ('pointed peak'), or, when applied to a person associated with the place which took its name from the phrase, *de Monte Acuto*. A cone-shaped hill stands behind the Somerset village of Montacute in Somerset to this day. (The mansion there is Elizabethan, however, and has no connection with the early Lords Montagu).

A family called de Montagu, descended from a Domesday tenant (*i.e*, who was living 1086), held land in the area of Somerset where Montacute is situated throughout the 12th and 13th centuries and Simon de Montagu, the then head of the family, is deemed by later doctrine to have been created Lord (Baron) Montagu by writ of summons in 1299. His grandson, the 3rd Lord (Baron) Montagu, was promoted Earl of Salisbury (*see* SALISBURY, M, preliminary remarks) in March 1336/7. The Barony of Montagu created in 1299 became forfeited along with the Earldom on the attainder of John de Montagu, 3rd Earl of Salisbury, in Jan 1399/1400 but was revived for John's son, Thomas de Montagu, in 1421. On Thomas's death without surviving male issue in 1428 it is deemed by later doctrine to have passed to his daughter Alice, and from her to her son Richard Nevill(e), Earl of Warwick (the 'Kingmaker'; *see* ABERGAVENNY, M). Warwick too died without male issue and the Barony would therefore have passed to his daughter Isabel's son Edward Plantagenet. Although Edward was attainted and

his honours forfeited in 1504 (posthumously, since he had had his head struck off back in 1499), it is possible, and was certainly so argued by the House of Lords Privileges Committee in 1928, that his sister Margaret had the Barony of Montagu of 1299 restored to her by the Act of 1513 that revived the Earldom of Salisbury in her favour.

Meanwhile the youngest son of the 2nd Lord (Baron) Montagu mentioned above was by later doctrine deemed to have been created Lord (Baron) Montagu, also by writ of summons, in 1348. This Barony would have fallen into abeyance on the death of the grantee's infant son in 1361. Only a few years later, in 1357, another member of the de Montagu family, John, a younger son of the 1st Earl of Salisbury of the 1336/7 creation, was called to Parliament by writ, thereby becoming according to later doctrine Lord (Baron) Montagu. When John's son inherited the Salisbury title in 1397 he must be deemed also to have inherited the original (1299) Barony of Montagu along with the one of 1357 that had come to him from his father. To confuse matters further John Nevill(e), a brother of the Richard Earl of Warwick (the 'Kingmaker') aleady noted, was created Lord (Baron) Montagu by writ of summons in 1461 and later advanced to the Marquessate of Montagu (*see* also NORTHUMBERLAND, D, preliminary remarks). John Nevill(e)'s son and heir George had his titles confiscated for being too poor and they therefore expired. Nevertheless in 1357 there were according to later doctrine no fewer than three members of the then House of Lords holding the title Lord (Baron) Montagu. The absurdity of this is one of the strongest arguments for supposing that early writs of summons did no more than create a lordship of Parliament for the duration of that Parliament.

The Margaret Plantagenet mentioned already who had the Earldom of Salisbury revived in her favour in 1513 had a son Henry by Sir Richard Pole who was apparently created Lord (Baron) Montagu in 1514 by the unusual but not unique method of the King's word of mouth, or even general hearsay (*par parole*). Henry was attainted and his titles forfeited, however.

The 1st Marquess of Montagu's daughter Lucy had married Sir Anthony Browne. Their grandson, another Anthony, was created Viscount Montagu in 1554, a title which continued till 1797. In 1621 one Edward Montagu, whose family have claimed kinship with the medieval family but for which claim there is only scanty evidence (his 15th-century ancestor who changed his name from Ladde to Montagu probably had some connection with the medieval family through inheritance of property however), was made Baron Montagu of Boughton (*see* also MANCHESTER, D, and SANDWICH, E). His grandson was promoted Earl of Montagu in 1689 and Duke of Montagu 16 years later, having begged WILLIAM III in vain for a dukedom but having finally won round QUEEN ANNE through the good offices of Sarah Duchess of Marlborough, his son John's mother-in-law. He had long been rich enough to support the rank, having won the hand of the mad but enormously wealthy Dowager Duchess of Albemarle (heiress also of her father the Duke of Newcastle) by passing himself off as the Emperor of China — in her deluded state she had pledged herself to marry no one beneath the rank of sovereign. He built Boughton, now one of his descendant the Duke of Buccleuch's properties (*qv*). The Dukedom of 1705 expired on the 2nd Duke's death in 1749, following which his son-in-law George Montagu, formerly Brudenell, 4th Earl of Cardigan, was made Duke of Montagu in a fresh creation in 1762 (*see* AILESBURY, M). On the latter's death without surviving male issue in 1790 this Dukedom too expired.

Two further Baronies of Montagu of Boughton were created. The first in 1762 for the last-mentioned Duke of Montagu's son John. This survived only till 1770, when on the grantee's death unmarried it expired. The second, created in 1786 for the last-mentioned Duke of Montagu's younger grandsons by his daughter Elizabeth, wife of the 3rd Duke of Buccleuch (*qv*), expired in 1845. The **1st Baron Montagu of Beaulieu** was a great-grandson of the 3rd Duke of Buccleuch and Elizabeth.

Lineage: The 5th DUKE OF BUCCLEUCH and (7th DUKE OF) QUEENSBERRY had a 2nd s—

Lord HENRY JOHN MONTAGU-DOUGLAS-SCOTT later DOUGLAS-SCOTT-MONTAGU, **1st Baron Montagu of Beaulieu** (UK), so cr 29 Dec 1885, DL and JP (Hants and Selkirk), JP (Midlothian); *b* 5 Nov 1832; *educ* Eton; CA Hants, Hon Col 4th Vol Bn Hants Regt, MP (C) Selkirkshire 1861–68 and S Hants 1868–84; *m* 1 Aug 1865 Cecily Susan (*d* 2 May 1915), yst dau of 2nd Baron Wharncliffe (*see* WHARNCLIFFE, E), and had:

1 JOHN WALTER EDWARD, **2nd Baron**

2 Robert Henry; Lt 3rd Bn Roy Scots; *b* 30 July 1867; *m* 12 Jan 1904 Alice (*d* 13 Aug 1944), widow of Oscar Davy-Davies, and *d* 1 Feb 1916

3 James Francis; *b* 6 Feb 1873; *d* 2 March 1874

1 Rachel Cecily, GBE (1926), DGStJ; *m* 3 June 1890 1st and last Baron Forster, GCMG, PC, and *d* 12 April 1962, leaving issue. He *d* 15 Jan 1936

The 1st BARON *d* 4 Nov 1905; his est son,

JOHN WALTER EDWARD DOUGLAS-SCOTT-MONTAGU, **2nd Baron Montagu of Beaulieu**, KCIE (1919), CSI (1916), VD, JP, DL (Hants); *b* 10 June 1866; *educ* Eton and New Coll Oxford; motoring pioneer as well as engr and steam engine driver on the railways (LSWR), FRMetS, CIMechE, CA Hants, MP (C) New Forest 1892–1905, correspondent *The Times* Matabele War 1896, fndr ed *Car Illustrated*, Lt-Col cmdg and Hon Col 7th Bn Hants Regt, Brig-Gen 1918; *m* 1st 4 June1889 Lady Cecil Victoria Constance Kerr (*d* 18 Sept 1919), dau of 9th Marquess of Lothian (*qv*), and had:

1 Helen Cecil; *b* 7 March 1890; *m* 1916 (*divorce* 1925) Arthur John Clark-Kennedy, yr s of Col John Clark Kennedy, CB, of Knockgray, Kirkcudbrightshire, and *d* 21 May 1969. He *d* 26 Nov 1926

2 *Elizabeth Susan [The Hon Mrs Varley, The Mill Race, Beaulieu, Hants SO42 7YF]; *b* 26 Sept 1909; *m* 29 Aug 1962 Col Arthur Noel Claude Varley, CBE (*d* 1985), only s of Rev John Edwin Varley, Vicar Long Ashton

The **2nd Baron** *m* 2nd 10 Aug 1920 (Alice) Pearl (*d* 10 April 1996 aged 101, having *m* 2nd 2 May 1936 Capt Hon Edward Pleydell-Bouverie, MVO, RN (*d* 5 May 1951), 2nd s of 6th Earl of Radnor, *qv*), est dau of Maj Edward Barrington Crake, Rifle Bde, by his 2nd w Clara Alice, er dau of George William Plunkenett Woodroffe, RHG, and by her had:

1 EDWARD JOHN BARRINGTON DOUGLAS-SCOTT-MONTAGU, **3rd and present Baron Montagu of Beaulieu**

3 *Anne Rachel Pearl, JP (Hants 1968) [The Hon Lady Chichester JP, Battramsley Lodge, Lymington, Hants SO41 8PT]; *b* 4 Oct 1921; *m* 1st 2 March 1946 Maj Howel Joseph Moore-Gwyn, Welsh Gds (*d* 20 Sept 1947), only s of Maj Joseph Gwyn Moore-Gwyn, of Dyffryn, Glamorgan, and Abercrave, Brecknock, and has:

  (1) *David John Howel [David Moore-Gwyn Esq, 7 Phillimore Terr, London W8 6BJ]; *b* 21 April 1947; *educ* Winchester and Trin Coll Cambridge; barrister Lincoln's Inn 1972; *m* 1974 *Alison Frances, yr dau of Clifford G White, and has:

    1a *Henry John Howel; *b* 1975

    2a *George Augustus Joseph; *b* 1987

    1a *Alice Beatrice Rachel; *b* 1978

3 (cont.) Mrs Howel Moore-Gwyn *m* 2nd 23 Sept 1950 Sir (Edward) John Chichester, 11th Bt (*qv*), and has further issue

4 *Caroline Cicely; *b* 13 Feb 1925; *m* 15 Feb 1950 (*divorce* 1987) George Grainger Weston, est s of (Willard) Garfield Weston, of Chester House, Clarendon Place, London, W1, and has had:

  (1) *Galvin; *b* 14 June 1951; *m* 1st 1976 (*divorce* 1979) Lori Lipsey; *m* 2nd 17 May 1997 *Michelle Louise, yr dau of S/Ldr David Evans, of Canford Cliffs, Dorset

  (2) *Gregg; *b* 29 Aug 1956; *m* 1988 Monique de Gagné, of Toronto, and has:

    1a *Charlotte; *b* 1995

    2a *Isabella; *b* 1998

  (3) Glenn; *b* 30 Aug 1961; *d* 14 June 1965

  (4) *Graham; *b* 4 March 1964; *m* 24 April 1995 *Elizabeth Cluck, of San Antonio, Tex., and has:

    *1a *Glenn; *b* 1997

  (1) *Sarah; *b* 28 Jan 1953; *m* 1975 *Dr Mark Eidson, of Weatherford, Tex., and has:

    1a *Weston; *b* 1980

    2a *Beau; *b* 1982

    3a *Barrett; *b* 1986

5 *Mary-Clare [The Hon Mrs Horn, Chapel House, Builth Wells, Powys]; *b* 9 June 1928; *m* 1st 31 Oct 1953 (*divorce* 1968) Viscount Garnock (later 15th Earl of Lindsay, *qv*); *m* 2nd 1979 Timothy Charles Austin Horn and by her 1st husb has issue

The **2nd Baron** *d* 30 March 1929, having also had by Eleanor Thornton, assist ed of his magazine and model for The Spirit of Ecstasy displayed on the bonnet of Rolls-Royces:

6 Joan; *b* 5 April 1903; *m* 5 Aug 1936 Surgn-Cdr Leslie Moorby, RN, and *d* 23 June 1979, leaving:

  (1) *John; *b* 14 Oct 1939; *m* 20 Apr 1968 *Margaret Elizabeth Loomes and has two sons

  (2) *Richard; *b* 26 Nov 1944; *m* 4 Oct 1969 *Margaret Ann Woodrow Johnson and has a dau

Seat: Palace House, Beaulieu, Hampshire. The present structure consists of two contrasting arcitectural styles: the imposing late 13th-century Great Gatehouse of Beaulieu Abbey, which was founded by KING JOHN in 1204, joined to a Victorian wing added by the **1st Baron** in the 1870s. The Gatehouse is largely intact, having been retained for domestic purposes together with two other major monastic buildings by Thomas Wriothesley, 1st Earl of Southampton of the 1547 creation, who had acquired Beaulieu in 1538 following the dissolution of the Monasteries. The Gatehouse was only intermittently used by the Wriothesleys, however.

The **4th Earl's** daughter, Elizabeth, married at the end of the 17th century Ralph, 1st Duke of Montagu, whose family thus acquired Beaulieu. The 2nd and last Duke of Montagu of the 1705 creation carried out extensive improvements and repairs, including the construction of a moat. Later in the 18th century Beaulieu passed to the Dukes of Buccleuch when the 3rd Duke married a Montagu heiress, Elizabeth. For the next century or so it was little used, until being given to Lord Henry Scott as a wedding present by his father, the 5th Duke of Buccleuch. On being created a peer in 1885 Lord Henry changed the family surname from Montagu-Douglas-Scott to Douglas-Scott-Montagu to commemorate Beaulieu's long history as a Montagu property.

Before that, back in the 1870s the Gatehouse was restored in the Gothic Style. The Victorian wing, to designs by Sir Arthur Blomfield, is Scottish Baronial, reflecting the **1st Baron's** upbringing in various Buccleuch houses in the Borders. Today the National Motor Museum in the grounds is a celebrated and highly successful tourist attraction.

MONTAGU-POLLOCK

Arms: Quarterly, 1st and 4th, azure three fleurs-de-lys within a bordure embattled or, and (as honourable augmentation, for the 1st Bt's servs Afghan war) on a chief of the second an eastern crown gules superscribed 'Khyber', and on a canton ermine three cannons fessways in pale sable (for POLLOCK); 2nd and 3rd, per pale argent and gules four lozenges conjoined in fess counterchanged (for MONTAGU). **Crests:** 1 A lion rampant guardant argent, adorned with an eastern crown or, holding in his dexter paw in bend an Afghan banner displayed gules, bordered or and vert, the staff broken in two, and in his sinister paw a part of the broken staff (for POLLOCK), 2 A boar passant quartered embattled or and vert, pierced through the sinister shoulder with an arrow proper and 3 A griffin's head couped erminois, wings addorsed, gorged with a collar lozengy (for MONTAGU). **Supporters:** Dexter, a heraldic tiger sable, maned, tufted and gorged with an Eastern crown, chain reflexed over the back or, pendant by a chain from the crown an escutcheon also or, charged with a bomb fired proper; sinister, a talbot sable, gorged, chained as the dexter and pendant from the crown a like escutcheon. **Mottoes:** 1 Afghanistan, 2 *Audacter et strenue* ('Boldly and strenuously'), 3 *Spectemur agendo* ('Let us be regarded by our conduct'). **Creation:** Bt. (UK) 26 March 1872.

SIR GILES HAMPDEN MONTAGU-POLLOCK, 5TH BT, of the Khyber Pass [Sir Giles Montagu-Pollock Bt, The White House, 7 Washington Rd, London SW13 9BG]; *b* 19 Oct 1928; *s f* 1985; *educ* Eton and De Havilland Aeronautical Tech Sch; De Havilland Enterprise 1949–56, Bristol Aeroplane Co Ltd 1956–59, Bristol Siddeley Engines Ltd 1959–61, J Walter Thompson 1961–69, C Vernon and Sons Ltd 1969–71, Acumen Mktg Gp Ltd 1971–74, 119 Pall Mall Ltd 1972–78, John Stork and Partners Ltd 1980–89, management consultant 1974–, Associate Korn/Ferry Internat 1989–; *m* 13 June 1963 *Caroline Veronica, yr dau of Richard Francis Russell, of Westminster, and has:

  1 +GUY MAXIMILIAN; *b* 27 Aug 1966; *educ* Eton and Hatfield Poly

  1 *Sophie Amelia; *b* 15 Aug 1969

Lineage: DAVID POLLOCK, bro of Sir Frederick Pollock, 1st Bt (*qv*), had a 5th s:

Sir George Pollock, 1st Bt (UK), so cr 26 March 1872 (with thanks of Parl), GCB (1842), GCSI (1861); *b* 4 June 1786; captured Kabul in Afghan War, FM, Constable Tower of London; *m* 1st 6 Aug 1810 Frances Webb (*d* 12 Sept 1849), dau of — Barclay, Sheriff of Tain, and had, with a dau (*d* unm):

  1 FREDERICK (Sir), **2nd Bt**

  2 George David; *b* 18 Oct 1817; FRCS, Surgn St George's Hosp; *m* 4 June 1850 Marianne Charity (*d* 6 Feb 1910), dau of Robert Saunders, BCS, and *d* 14 Feb 1897, having had, with two daus (*d* unm):

    (1) Barclay; *b* 28 March 1851; *d* 18 Nov 1882

    (2) Hugh; *b* 15 Jan 1859; *educ* Trin Coll Cambridge (MA); barrister, Assist Registrar Land Registry 1898–1921; *m* 8 June 1898 Alice (*d* 19 Oct 1971), dau of Cdr Cornwallis Wykeham-Martin, RN, of Purton, and *d* 1944, leaving:

      1a Hugh Wykeham David, JP (Westmorland 1957); *b* 27 June 1900; *educ* Harrow and Trin Coll Cambridge (BA 1922); High Sheriff Westmorland 1960–62; *m* 17 Jan 1934 Barbara (*d* 1993), er dau of Sir Philip Bealby Reckitt, 3rd Bt, OBE (*see* 1940 edn), and *d* 1972, leaving:

        1b *Bridget Wykeham [Mrs Bridget Marshall, Lowlands Farm, Shrewley, Warwicks]; *b* 6 Jan 1935; *m* 17 Jan 1959 (*divorce* 1977) Michael John Marshall, er s of Sir Arthur Gregory George Marshall, OBE, DL, of Horseheath Lodge, Linton, Cambridge, by Rosemary Wynford, 2nd dau of Marcus Southwell Dimsdale, and has:

          1c *Robert David; *b* 21 July 1962; *m* 1992 *Julia Kathleen, yr dau of Timothy Patrick Hamilton-Russell (*see* ASHBOURNE, B), and has:

            1d *Bethany Finn; *b* 1996

          2c *James Gregory; *b* 29 Aug 1964

          1c *Belinda Louise; *b* 17 Dec 1960; *m* 1988 *Adrian Richard Hill

2c *Cressida Michal; *b* 5 June 1967

2b *Catherine [Miss Catherine Pollock, Coshandrochaid, Tayvallich, Argyll PA3 8PQ]; *b* 30 Aug 1938

3b *Jane [Miss Jane Pollock, Winderwath, Penrith, Cumbria]; *b* 4 Sept 1945

1a Frances Alison; *m* 17 Oct 1923 Sir Edward Reynell Anson 6th Bt (*qv*) and *d* 29 April 1997, leaving issue

(3) Evelyn, CBE (1916); *b* 28 Jan 1861; *educ* Harrow; Lt-Col and Brevet Col RFA, Lt-Col cmdg Jersey Artillery, Cmdt Lines of Communication 1914, WW I (despatches); *m* 16 July 1890 Mary (*d* 12 Aug 1936), dau of Henry Jefferd Tarrant, and *d* 31 Dec 1951, having had:

1a Ronald Evelyn (Sir); *b* 17 April 1891; *educ* Harrow and Pembroke Coll Cambridge (MA); barrister Gray's Inn, ICS, Judge High Court Nagpur 1936–48, Actg Ch Justice 1947, ktd 1947, Chm Medical Appeal Tbnl S Regn 1948–63; *m* 1st 7 July 1921 Margery (*d* 28 Feb 1959), 2nd dau of Samuel Fitze, of Eastbourne, and *d* 9 March 1974, leaving:

1b *Anne Margery [Mrs Richard Parsons, Fiddlers Green, 9 Grenehurst Way, Petersfield, Hants GU31 4AZ]; *b* 1924; WW II in WRNS; *m* 1st 1 March 1958 (*divorce* 1979) Clive Robert Basche, er s of Sidney Basche, of Kearton Close, Kenley, and has:

1c *Timothy James; *b* 9 Sept 1961; *m* 1988 (*divorce* 1997) Melanie Jane Lawson and has:

1d *Charlotte Louise; *b* 1990

2d *Sophie Elizabeth; *b* 1993

1c *Clare Nicola; *b* 22 July 1959; *m* 1983 *Jonathan Gordon Drew and has:

1d *James Newcombe; *b* 1983

2d *Robert Edmund; *b* 1986

3d *Christopher Gordon; *b* 1987

1b (cont.) Mrs Anne Basche *m* 2nd 1981 *Lt-Cdr Richard Holman Parsons, RN

1a (cont.) Sir Ronald Pollock *m* 2nd 10 May 1963 Pamela Margaret Anstice (*d* 1989), widow of Percy John Hodsall Stent, CIE, ICS, and only dau of Francis Winckworth Anstice Prideaux, OBE

2a George Henry; *b* 21 Dec 1893; Lt 4th S Staffs Regt; *d* 18 June 1915 from wounds recd on active service

3a Sidney Geoffrey; *b* 18 Oct 1895; Lt Gloucester Regt; *d* 19 Nov 1918

4a Vincent David, Lt IA; *b* 6 Sept 1899; *d* unm 3 May 1949

5a Philip John; *b* 6 Nov 1903; *educ* Haileybury, and Pembroke Coll Cambridge (BA 1925, MA 1953); *d* 9 May 1993

1a Gwyneth Mary; *m* 18 Dec 1923 Lt-Col Boughey Burgess (*d* 1954), RE, and *d* 14 Nov 1970, leaving issue

2a *Jean [Mrs Paul Gomez, Las Gaviotas 3°-5A, Paseo San Pedro, Altea, Alicante, Spain]; *m* 1st 2 Aug 1940 Major Gerard Joseph McCann, RM (*ka* 10 July 1943), s of L D McCann, of Onslow, Guildford, and has:

1b Peta Jean Madeline; *b* 15 Dec 1941; *d* 9 Oct 1996

2a (cont.) Mrs Gerard McCann *m* 2nd 14 Sept 1951 G/Capt Paul Slocombe Gomez, CBE, RAF (*d* 1972), s of F J Gomez, MD, of S Petherton, Somerset, and by him has:

1b *Nicholas David [Nicholas Gomez, Carretera de Boadilla del Monte, 52–7°B, Madrid 24, Spain]; *b* 14 July 1952; *educ* Sherborne; *m* 1976 *Felicidad Mediavilla and has:

1c *Karen Alexandra; *b* 1978

2c *Gillian; *b* 1982

(1) Lilian; *d* unm 29 June 1957

3 Robert Henry; *b* 1 Aug 1822; Lt Bengal HA; *k* Mudkee 1845

4 Archibald Reid Swiney; *b* 12 June 1829; Bengal CS; *m* 2 Oct 1852 Janet Justina (*d* 27 June 1919), dau of John Davidson, and *d* 3 Oct 1877, leaving:

(1) Frederick George; *b* 19 Jan 1855; Lt-Col ISC; *m* 1 Aug 1882 Jane (*d* 28 Oct 1923), widow of Lt Robert St George Harding Hamilton, 65th Regt (*see* HAMILTON, Bt, of Silverton Hill), and dau of Gen Harry Smith Obbard, and *d* 18 Sept 1914, leaving:

1a Harry Clement, MBE (1944); *b* 5 Oct 1883; Lt-Col RE, WWs I (1914–15 star, two medals) and II; *m* 1st 17 Oct 1914 (*divorce* 1928) Dorothy Beatrice, dau of Hon Sir Theodore Caro Piggott, Puisne Judge NWP India, and had:

1b George Frederick; *b* 27 Aug, *d* 21 Sept 1915

2b *John Basil [John Pollock Esq, 224A Connaught Rd, Brookwood, Surrey GU24 0AH]; *b* 19 April 1920; *educ* Lond U (BSc Eng (metallurgy) 1942); ARSM (metallurgy) 1942; *m* 12 April 1949 *Betty Angela, dau of H A Lusher, of Sevenoaks, Kent, and has:

1c +Christopher Robert; *b* 28 April 1954

1c *Anne Patricia; *b* 26 June 1951

2c *Sarah Gillian; *b* 15 March 1957

1a (cont.) Lt-Col Harry Pollock *m* 2nd 2 Oct 1929 Constance Ferne (*d* 15 Dec 1943), dau of Alfred Russell, of Rushall, Staffs; *m* 3rd 1944 *Winifred Eileen [Mrs Harry Pollock, 14A Queens Rd, Royston, Herts], dau of W T C Macgregor, of Wick, Caithness, and *d* 1971, having by her had:

3b *Martin Donald; *b* 21 May 1948; *educ* Hertford GS and Churchill Coll Cambridge (BA 1969)

2a Archibald Frederick; *b* 27 Jan 1885; *m* 3 Oct 1922 Ada Gertrude (*d* 1979), 3rd dau of Albert Imossi, of Gibraltar, and *d* 26 May 1941, leaving:

1b +David Francis [Major David Pollock RA, 126 Grovedale Rd, Floreat Park, Perth, W Australia 6014]; *b* 8 Sept 1928; *educ* Exeter Sch and RMA Sandhurst; Maj RA, dep exec dir Austn Red Cross Soc (W Aust Div); *m* 1 Aug 1959 *Diana Mary, dau of Maj Francis John Andrews, of Cheam, Surrey, and has:

1c +James Robert; *b* 26 July 1962; *educ* U of W Australia (BCom)

1c *Gillian Mary [Mrs David Hill, 44 Needlewood St, Kambalda, W Australia]; *b* 22 June 1960; *m* 1983 *David Ian Hill, s of Ian Hill, of Auckland, NZ

1b *Mary [Mrs Bryan Epsom, c/o PO Box 40026, Nairobi, Kenya]; *b* 16 Sept 1924; *m* 21 Dec 1946 *Capt Bryan L B Epsom, QO Roy W Kent Regt, and has:

1c *Hugh David; *b* 10 June 1949; *educ* St Mary's Sch, Nairobi, and Loughborough U

2c *Guy Bryan; *b* 20 Feb 1954; *educ* King's Coll Taunton

3c *Paul Robert; *b* 14 Oct 1956

3a William Hamilton; *b* 7 Sept 1887; *m* 10 Sept 1915 Sara Amanda (*d* 1981), dau of Jose Santos Tello, of Chile, and *d* 1976, leaving:

1b Edward Alexander; *b* 14 Sept 1919; F/Lt RAF WW II; *ka* 1945

2b Richard Douglas; *b* 22 Dec 1924; *educ* U Tecnica Federico Santa Maria, Valparaiso, Chile; chemical engr; *m* 22 Dec 1956 *Maria Helia Veloso Campos, dau of Ceferino Veloso Carrasco and Olga Campos de Veloso, of Santiago, and *d* 1990, leaving:

1c +William Douglas; *b* 16 July 1957; industl engr Chile U; *m* 1990 *Agnes Joyce, dau of Richard Sharman Claude, of Viña del Mar, Chile, and has:

1d +Michael Douglas; *b* 1993

1d *Agnes Marianne; *b* 1990

2c +James Edward; *b* 23 Jan 1959; *educ* Chile U; electrical engr; *m* 1986 (*divorce* 1992) Macarena, dau of Claudio Mas Ferret, of Santiago, Chile, and has:

1d +Benjamin Edward; *b* 1988

2d +Vincent; *b* 1991

1d *Macarena Sofía; *b* 1987

3c +Philip Andrew; *b* 23 Nov 1962; *educ* Chile U; industl engr; *m* 1988 *María Gabriela, dau of Juan Lasnibat Aninat, of Santiago, and has:

1d +Philip Anthony; *b* 1990

1d *Anne Mary; *b* 1991

1c *Maureen Elizabeth; *b* 9 Aug 1960; *m* 1986 *Pablo Emanuel Quiñones de León, of Santiago, and has:

1d *Luis Felipe; *b* 1987

2d *Juan Pablo; *b* 1989

3d *José Antonio; *b* 1992

(2) John Archibald Henry, CB (1903), JP Stewartry of Kirkcudbright; *b* 1 Dec 1856; *educ* Haileybury and RMC Sandhurst; Jowaki Expdn 1877–78, Afghan War 1878–79 (despatches), Mahsood Waziri Expdn 1881 (despatches), Samana Expdn 1891, Waziristan 1894–95, NWF India 1897 (despatches) and China 1900 (despatches), Maj-Gen IA, Hon Col 1st/12th PWO Sikhs FF; *m* 8 Dec 1898 Lillian Forrester (*d* 8 July 1954), est dau of John Fortune, of Bengairn, Kirkcudbrightshire, and *d* 27 Feb 1949, leaving:

1a Frederick Arthur; *b* 26 Aug 1899; *educ* Wellington; WW I 1918 in RE

1a *Justina Lillian (Pansy); *b* 15 Nov 1902; *m* 15 Jan 1926 Frederic Whigham McConnel, 2nd s of James Irving McConnel, of Compton, Surrey, and has:

1b *James Frederic Whigham [James McConnel Esq, Whitehouse, Newcastle, Monmouth, Gwent NP5 4NF]; *b* 1929; *m* 1984 *Judith Marian, dau of Cyril Jackson Hannaford, banker

2b *John William [John McConnel Esq, Lettrick, Dunscore, Dumfriesshire DG20UX]; *b* 1931; *m* 19– *Lois Christine Lyon and has:

1c *James Archibald Robert; *b* 1958; *m* 19– *Sarah Helen Walker and has:

1d *James Archibald Frederic Whigham; *b* 1994

2c *John Andrew Douglas; *b* 1961

3c *William Kennedy; *b* 1962; *m* 19– *Susan Mary, dau of Edward Alfred Heycock (*see* HALSEY, Bt), and has:

1d *Jennifer Kathryn Halsey; *b* 1993

1c *Fiona Mary; *b* 1957; *m* 19– *Ian Macpherson and has:

1d *Morag Fiona; *b* 1988

2d *Katherine Anne; *b* 1989

2a *Daphne Victoria Catherine; *b* 1 Dec 1907; *m* 5 April 1934 Alan Reginald Cathcart (*d* 26 April 1967), er s of Maj Frederick Adrian Cathcart (*see* CATHCART, E), and has issue

(3) Alexander; *b* 30 Dec 1865; *educ* Trin Coll Cambridge (MA); slr; *d* unm 13 Nov 1944

(4) Robert Gordon; *b* 30 Dec 1865 (twin with his brother Alexander); *educ* Trin Coll Cambridge (BA); slr; *m* 16 June 1908 Evelyn Lucy, yst dau of Rev W Coxe Radcliffe, Rector Fonthill Gifford, Wilts, and *dsp* 8 Dec 1942

(5) Richard David; *b* 17 Jan 1875; *d* 7 Aug 1878

(1) Louisa Amelia; *m* 21 Oct 1875 Col Geoffrey Craythorne Hall (*d* 27 Oct 1923) and *d* 29 Sept 1876, leaving issue

(2) Helen Frances; *m* 20 July 1887 Col Archibald Boyd Maxwell (*d* 9 Oct 1941), Manchester Regt, and *dsp* 13 Aug 1904

(3) Georgiana Maud; *m* 23 April 1889 Lt-Col John Thomas Edward Flint (*d* 12 May 1912), 1st Dragoon Gds, and *d* 1 Oct 1913

(4) Anna Julia; *m* 27 July 1887 H F Horne (*dsp* 28 Oct 1890), LRCS, and *d* 28 April 1888

(5) Nora Josephine; *d* unm 29 March 1946

(6) Adelaide Laura; *d* unm as the result of enemy action 16 April 1941

1 Annabella Homeria; *m* 1st 8 Nov 1832 John Harcourt (*k* 12 Jan 1842), 44th Regt; *m* 2nd 27 Feb 1847 John Binnie Key (*d* 19 May 1873) and *d* 1 Nov 1873, leaving issue

Sir George *m* 2nd 15 Jan 1852 Henrietta (*d* 14 Feb 1873), dau of George Hyde Wollaston, and *d* 6 Oct 1872

His est son,

Sir FREDERICK POLLOCK later MONTAGU-POLLOCK (roy licence 1873), **2nd Bt**; *b* 27 Feb 1815; *m* 9 July 1861 Laura Caroline (*d* 26 May 1900), only surv dau of Henry Seymour Montagu, of Westleton Grange, Suffolk, and *d* 17 June 1874, leaving, with a yr s (Perceval William, *b* 6 March 1871, *d* 18 Jan 1891) and three daus (Louisa Constance, *b* 25 Aug 1862, *d* unm 23 Aug 1929; Eleanor

Spencer, *b* 4 Aug 1865, *d* unm 27 Dec 1946; Beatrice Laura, *b* 15 Feb 1868, *d* unm 8 Sept 1932):

Sir Montagu Frederick Montagu-Pollock, 3rd Bt; *b* 31 Jan 1864; *educ* Trin Coll Cambridge; *m* 4 Oct 1899 Margaret Angela (*d* Feb 1959), dau of William Abraham Bell, of Pendell Court, Bletchingley, and had:

1 GEORGE SEYMOUR (Sir), **4th Bt**

2 Hubert Vernon; *b* 13 March 1902; *educ* Charterhouse and Edinburgh U; Lt-Cdr RNVR WW II; *m* 12 June 1945 Delia Florence Alice (*d* 22 Feb 1977), widow of Capt Harold Edward Pearce, RA, and dau of Herbert Snowden, and *d* 23 Feb 1970, leaving:

  (1) +Jonathan David [Jonathan Montagu-Pollock Esq, Bridge Cottage, Winterbourne Stoke, Wilts SP3 4SW]; *b* 3 July 1947; *educ* Charterhouse; late 2nd Lt RGJ; *m* 1979 *Deirdre Clare, yr dau of John Edward Binding, of Rock, N Cornwall, and has:

    1a +Thomas George; *b* 1983

    2a +Archer William; *b* 1986

3 William Horace (Sir), KCMG (1957, CMG 1946); *b* 12 July 1903; *educ* Marlborough and Trin Coll Cambridge (BA 1925, MA 1959); Dip Serv: Amb Syria 1952–53, Peru 1953–58, Switzerland 1958–60 and Denmark 1960–62 (ret), Dir Br Nat Ctee for Cultural Co-operation in Europe, Govr Br Inst of Recorded Sound, Treas Soc for Promotion of New Music; *m* 1st 16 May 1933 (*divorce* 1945) Francis Elizabeth Prudence (*d* 1985), dau of Sir John Fischer Williams, CBE, KC, of Lamledra, Gorran Haven, Cornwall, and had:

  (1) +Hubert George Murray [Dr Hubert Montagu-Pollock, Low Beckfoot, Barbon, Carnforth, Cumbria LA6 2LE]; *b* 20 March 1935; *educ* Winchester and Trin Coll Cambridge (MA, PhD); Reader Surface Physics at Lancaster U, past Fell of Trin Coll, late 2nd Lt Royal Signals; *m* 17 Sept 1960 *Emmerentia Johanna, yr dau of J B De Jong Cleyndert, of Palegate Farm, Henham, Essex, and has:

    1a *Harriet Marthe; *b* 12 Oct 1961

    2a *Catherine Juliet; *b* 26 April 1963

    3a *Annabel Frances; *b* 26 March 1966; *m* 22 March 1997 *Stewart McWilliam

  (1) *Fidelity Juliet [Mrs Alan Dean, Balgone House, N Berwick, E Lothian EH39 5PB]; *b* 4 July 1940; *m* 15 Sept 1962 *Alan Charles Barclay Dean, MB, FRCS, s of William Dean, of Dunromyn, Insh, Aberdeenshire, and has:

    1a *Marcus William Fischer; *b* 14 Sept 1963; RIBA, RIAS

    1a *Juliet Angusta Carolyn; *b* 5 July 1965

    2a *Corinna Lucy; *b* 20 June 1967

3 (cont.) Sir William *m* 2nd 22 July 1948 *Barbara (*m* 3rd 19– *R E Hodgkin), formerly w of Thomas Josceline Gaskell and dau of Percy Hague Jowett, CBE, RWS, of Chelsea, and *d* 26 Sept 1993, having by her had:

  (2) +Matthew John [Matthew Montagu-Pollock Esq, No 7 Yap Compound, Bauhinia Drive, Banilad, Cebu City, Philippines]; *b* 3 Jan 1951; *educ* Westminster and Ch Ch Oxford; *m* 1984 *Aliaa, dau of Abdel Rahman Zayed, and has:

    1a +Gabriel; *b* 10 Sept 1994

    1a *Sasha; *b* 7 Dec 1991

  (2) A dau; *b* 14 March, *d* 16 March 1953

4 John Gathorne; *b* 7 Nov 1911; *educ* Oundle; ARIBA; *m* 13 March 1943 Elizabeth Metcalf (*d* 1989), dau of Carl Herbert Coston, of S Hadley Falls, Mass., and *d* 21 June 1995, leaving:

  (1) +Stephen Hull; *b* 25 Sept 1945; *m* 1979 *Barbara Ann, dau of Ralph J Betschart

  (2) +Christopher James; *b* 17 Sept 1952; *m* 1980 *Dianne Kristen, dau of Eugene M Spear, and has:

    1a +Toby William; *b* 1986

    1a *Jennifer Ann; *b* 1982

  (1) *Margaret Bell; *b* 26 April 1948; *m* 1972 Robert Lewis Merkow (*d* 1989), of Hartland, Wisconsin, and has:

    1a *Sarah Ellen; *b* 1981

    2a *Carla Lauren; *b* 1984

1 Cara Elizabeth; *b* 4 May 1913; *d* unm 25 Jan 1945

Sir MONTAGU *d* 14 Aug 1938; his est son,

Sir George Seymour Montagu-Pollock, 4th Bt ; *b* 14 Sept 1900; *educ* RNCs Osborne and Dartmouth; Lt-Cdr RN, with Unilever 1920–64, King Haakon VIII Liberty Cross, US Medal of Freedom (with Bronze Palm); *m* 15 Dec 1927 Karen-Sofie (*d* 1991), only child of Hans Ludvig Dedekam, of Oslo, and *d* 1985, leaving:

1 Sir GILES HAMPDEN MONTAGU-POLLOCK, **5th and present Bt**

1 *Karen Aagot Georgina [Mrs Richard Hodgkin, 42 Dellers Court, Dellers Wharf, Taunton, Somerset TA1 1DX]; *b* 26 May 1931; *m* 13 Sept 1952 *Richard Eliot Hodgkin, OBE, MC, of Stanton House, Norton, Suffolk, and has:

  (1) *Harry John; *b* 10 May 1961; *educ* Radley and Ealing College (LLB); barrister; *m* 1990 *Karen Lesley Pearce and has:

    1a *John Eliot; *b* 1994

    2a *George Harry; *b* 1997

    1a *Polly Grace; *b* 1992

  (2) *Edward Eliot; *b* 7 Aug 1963; *educ* Radley and Jesus Coll Oxford (MA, DPhil); assoc dir Wyeth-Ayerst Research Princeton, USA; *m* 1993 *Karen Lesley Jones and has:

    1a *Amy Beatrice; *b* 1995

    2a *Lucy Margaret; *b* 1997

  (1) *Georgina Elizabeth; *b* 29 May 1954; *m* 1st 1975 (*divorce* 1979) Nicholas David Douro Hoare and has:

    1a *Caspar Michael Douro; *b* 1977

  (1) (cont.) Mrs Georgina Hoare *m* 2nd 1997 *David Francis Clift Peace and by him has:

    2a *Philip Louis Clift; *b* 1997

MONTAGUE OF OXFORD

Arms: Gules, on a fess wavy between two bulls' heads cabossed argent armed or a bull's head cabossed gules armed or. **Crest:** A demi-yale sable, armed, tusked, unguled and supporting with the hooves a key wards downwards and inwards or. **Supporters:** On either side a red crested cardinal reguardant proper, in the beak a chrysanthemum argent, seeded slipped and leaved or.
Motto: Endless endeavour. **Creation:** B. (LP, UK) 1 Nov 1997.

THE BARON MONTAGUE OF OXFORD, of Oxford, Co Oxon (Michael Jacob Montague, CBE (1970)) [The Rt Hon The Lord Montague of Oxford CBE, 5 Clareville Grove, London SW7 5AU]; *b* 10 March 1932; *educ* High Wycombe Roy GS and Magdalen Coll Sch Oxford; fndr Gatehill Beco Ltd 1958, md Yale and Valor plc 1963 (chm 1965–91); chm: Asia Ctee BNEC 1968–71, Superframe, English Tourist Bd 1979–84, Nat Consumer Cncl 1984–87, Montague Multinational Ltd 1991–, Henley Festival Ltd 1992–94; memb: BTA 1979–84, Ordnance Survey Advsy Bd 1983–85, Millennium Commn 1994–; Pres BAIE 1983–85, Ec and Industl Research Soc 1990–; dir: Pleasurama 1985–88, Jarvis Hotels 1990–, Williams Hldgs 1991–92; V-Pres Roy Albert Hall 1992–94 (memb Cncl 1985–)

Lineage: DAVID ELIAS MONTAGUE; *m* Eleanor Stagg and had:

MICHAEL JACOB, *cr* a **Baron**

MONTEAGLE OF BRANDON

Arms: Quarterly, 1st and 4th, quarterly 1st and 4th, per pale indented arg. and gu. (for RICE), 2nd and 3rd, az. a lion rampant or (for MEREDYTH), 2nd, or on a chevron sa., between three mascles, as many mullets arg.; 3rd, paly of six arg. and az. a bend sa. **Crest:** A leopard's face affrontée gu., ducally crowned or. **Motto:** *Fides non timet* ('Faith does not fear'). **Creation:** B. (UK) 5 Sept 1839.

THE 6TH BARON MONTEAGLE OF BRANDON, of Brandon, Co Kerry (Gerald Spring Rice) [The Rt Hon The Lord Monteagle of Brandon, 242A Fulham Road,

London SW10 9NA; Templemore, Fermoy, Co Cork, Ireland]; *b* 5 July 1926; *s* f 1946; *educ* Harrow; Capt Irish Gds (ret 1955), served Palestine, memb: Gentlemen-at-Arms 1978–96, London Stock Exchange 1958–76 and Lloyd's 1978–; *m* 28 May 1949 *Anne, only dau of Col Guy James Brownlow, DSO, DL, Rifle Bde, of Ballywhite, Portaferry, Co Down, and has:

1 +CHARLES JAMES [The Hon Charles Spring Rice, 26 Malvern Rd, London E8 3LP]; *b* 24 Feb 1953; *educ* Harrow; *m* 1987 *Mary Teresa Glover and has:

(1) *Helena Maire; *b* 1987

(2) *Charlotte Etain; *b* 1988

(3) *Agnes Imogen; *b* 1991

(4) *Thea Teresa; *b* 22 March 1995

1 *Elinor [The Hon Mrs Elliott, 41 Ravenscourt Rd, London W6 0UJ]; *b* 23 April 1950; *m* 1 June 1974 *Myles Clare Elliott, s of N E Elliot, of Cuckney House, Cuckney, Notts, and has:

(1) *Thomas Emerson; *b* 1977

(2) *Nina Anne; *b* 1980

(3) *Emma Clare; *b* 1983

2 *Angela [The Hon Mrs Ottewill, 24 Marney Rd, London SW11 5EP]; *b* 23 April 1950; *m* 1st 20 Oct 1973 (*divorce* 1982) Christopher Richard Seton Sheppard, er s of Lt-Cdr Sheppard, MBE, RN, of Kensington; *m* 2nd 1991 *Peter Alan Kirby Ottewill, s of Maj W K Ottewill, of Rafford, Moray, and by her 1st husb has:

(1) *Catherine Christy Seton; *b* 11 Feb 1976

3 *Fiona [The Hon Mrs Garber, 88 Drakefield Rd, London SW17]; *b* 10 April 1957; *m* 26 March 1982 *Andrew Louis Garber, yst s of S Garber, of St John's Wood, and has:

(1) *Rose Anne; *b* 1985

(2) *Eliza Kate; *b* 1987

(3) *Alice Finola; *b* 1991

Barony of Monteagle: A peerage of this degree under the title Monteagle or Mounteagle was conferred in 1514 on Edward Stanley, a younger son of the 1st Earl of Derby (*qv*), seemingly by the curious means of creation called *par parole* (*see* MONTAGU OF BEAULIEU, B, preliminary remarks). 'Seemingly' because although the creation was not by writ of summons, there is no record of letters patent being issued either. (The form of creation is important because it determined whether a female descendant and her issue could inherit the barony.) The creation itself, as opposed to the form it took, was a reward for Stanley's important contribution the previous year to the English victory over the Scots at Flodden, where he had led the left wing of the army.

HENRY VIII himself chose the title. It referred to the hill Stanley had won possession of, and from which he attacked JAMES IV of Scotland's rear, and to the eagle on the Stanley crest. On the death in 1581 of Stanley's grandson the Barony might be supposed to have expired but William Parker, the grandson's own grandson by a daughter, was known as Lord Monteagle from at least 1595 (14 years after the 3rd Baron's death) and was called to Parliament as Lord Mo(u)nteagle in Jan 1603/4, giving rise to the assumption that some new creation under that title must have taken place but the record of it been lost. It is this Lord Monteagle who is famous as the legislator warned about the imminent Gunpowder Plot in 1605. Yet only a few years before he had been involved in a plot against the sovereign too (the Essex conspiracy; *see* ESSEX, E, preliminary remarks) and had even been imprisoned in The Tower. His grandson the 3rd or 6th Lord Mo(u)nteagle died childless in 1697 and the Barony expired or fell into abeyance.

A Sir Stephen Rice, Chief Baron of the Exchequer in Ireland, was allegedly supposed to be created Lord Monteagle by JAMES II in or about 1690, but this never came to pass. And the Thomas Spring Rice created Baron Monteagle of Brandon in 1839 was allegedly some relation, hence his choice of title.

Lineage: STEPHEN EDWARD RICE, of Mount Trenchard, Co Limerick (s of Thomas Rice by Mary, widow of Robert Collins and dau of Maurice FitzGerald, 14th Knight of Kerry; *see* FitzGERALD, Bt, of Valencia), *m* 10 Aug 1785 Catherine, only child and heiress of Thomas Spring, of Castlemaine, Co Kerry, and *d* 1831, having had, with two daus (Catherine Ann, *d* unm 1829; Mary, *m* Sir Aubrey de Vere, Bt):

THOMAS SPRING RICE, **1st Baron Monteagle of Brandon** (UK), so *cr* 5 Sept 1839, PC (I 1831, UK 1834); *b* 8 Feb 1790; *educ* Trin Coll Cambridge; MP (Whig) Limerick 1820–32 and Cambridge 1832–39, U-Sec Home Affrs 1827–30, Sec Treasury 1830–34, Sec State War and Colonies July–Nov 1834, Chllr Exchequer 1835–39, Comptroller Gen Exchequer 1839–65, FRS 1841; *m* 1st 11 July 1811 Lady Theodosia Pery (*d* Dec 1839), 2nd dau of 1st Earl of Limerick (*qv*); *m* 2nd 13 April 1841 Mary Anne (*d* 11 April 1889 aged 89), dau of John Marshall, of Hallsteads, Cumberland, and *d* 7 Feb 1866, having had by his 1st w:

1 Stephen Edmond; *b* 31 Aug 1814; Dep Chm Bd Customs; *m* 11 March 1839 Ellen Mary (*d* 23 March 1869), est dau of William Frere, DCL, Serjeant-at-law, Master Downing Coll Cambridge, and *d* at sea 9 May 1865, leaving:

(1) THOMAS SPRING RICE, **2nd Baron Monteagle of Brandon**, KP (1885), DL Co Limerick; *b* 31 May 1849; *educ* Harrow and Trin Coll Cambridge (BA); *m* 26 Oct 1875 Elizabeth (*d* 27 April 1908), est dau of Most Rev Samuel Butcher, DD, Bp Meath, and *d* 24 Dec 1926, having had:

1a Stephen Edmond; *b* 23 July 1877; *d* unm 7 April 1900

2a THOMAS AUBREY SPRING RICE, **3rd Baron Monteagle of Brandon**, CMG (1926), MVO (1922); *b* 8 Nov 1883; *educ* Eton and Balliol Coll Oxford (BA); Dip Serv 1907–34: Attaché St Petersburg 1908, 3rd Sec 1910 there and Washington 1913, 2nd Sec 1917, 1st Sec Paris 1920 and Brussels 1921, FO 1924, Offr Order Leopold of Belgium; *d* unm 11 Oct 1934

1a Mary Ellen; *b* 14 Sept 1880; *d* unm 1 Dec 1924

(2) FRANCIS, **4th Baron**

(1) Theodosia; granted 1870 with her sisters and er bro Francis before he inherited the title rank of baron's dau/yr s; *m* 30 April 1872 Rev Edward William Chapman, Hon Canon Carlisle, est s of W G Chapman, of Paul's Cray Hill, Kent, and *d* 6 July 1926, leaving issue. He *d* Feb 1919

(2) Mary; *m* 8 Sept 1863 Edward O'Brien, of Cahirmoyle, Co Limerick, and *d* 25 April 1868, leaving issue (*see* INCHIQUIN, B)

(3) Aileen; *m* 6 Oct 1864 John Rayner Arthur, Bombay CS, 6th s of Sir George Arthur, 1st Bt (*qv*), and *d* 15 June 1916, leaving issue

(4) Lucy; *m* 23 Aug 1866 Octavius Newry Knox and *d* 10 May 1884, leaving issue (*see* RANFURLY, E)

(5) Alice; *d* unm 23 Dec 1929

(6) Frederica; *m* 24 Oct 1893 Rev Walter Edward Hamilton Sotheby, formerly Vicar Gillingham, Dorset, and *d* 8 April 1924. He *d* 24 Jan 1933

(7) Catherine Ellen; *d* unm 22 Sept 1930

(8) Amy; 13 June 1920

2 Charles William Thomas; *b* 10 Jan 1819; Assist U-Sec For Affrs; *m* 26 April 1855 Elizabeth Margaret (*d* 11 Jan 1883), est dau of William Marshall, MP, of Hallsteads and Patterdale Hall, Cumberland, and *d* 13 July 1870, having had:

(1) Stephen Edward, CB; *b* 28 March 1856; *educ* Trin Coll Cambridge (MA, Fell); Auditor Civil List, Pncpl Clerk Treasury; *m* 12 Jan 1888 Julia Emma Isabella (*d* 9 May 1936) (*m* 2nd 11 Sept 1935 **4th Baron Monteagle of Brandon** (*see* below) and *d* 9 May 1936), 6th dau of Sir Peter George FitzGerald, 1st Bt, of Valencia (*qv*), Knight of Kerry, and *d* 6 Sept 1902, leaving:

1a Edward Dominick; *b* 3 June 1891; Fin Advsr Br Mission Russia 1918–19; *m* 1st 26 July 1919 (*divorce* 1936) Margaret Lois, widow of Capt Charles Edward Coursolles Jones, Warwicks Regt, and dau of Samuel Garrett, JP, of Gower House, Aldeburgh, Suffolk, and had:

1b Stephen Edward; *b* 24 Feb 1920; *educ* Eton and King's Coll Cambridge; T/Lt RNVR WW II; missing presumed *ka* Mediterranean Jan 1943 while serving in HM Submarine P48

2b *Theodosia Cecil [Mrs Charles Robertson, Sheepstead House, Abingdon, Berks]; *b* 23 April 1921; *educ* Girton Coll Cambridge (BA 1942); *m* 4 Sept 1942 Prof Charles Martin Robertson, FBA, MA, er s of Prof Donald Struan Robertson, FBA, FSA, MA, of Trin Coll Cambridge, and has:

1c *Stephen Edward [Stephen Robertson Esq, 72 Lyndhurst Grove, London SE15]; *b* 6 April 1946; *educ* Trin Coll Cambridge (BA 1967, MSc 1968); *m* 25 July 1966 *Judith Anne, dau of Edwin Donald Kirk, of Sheffield

2c *Matthew Nicolas; *b* 27 Feb 1949

3c *Dominick Henry; *b* 12 June 1952

4c *Thomas Morgan; *b* 14 Oct 1958

1c *Lucy Petica; *b* 24 Sept 1943; *educ* Girton Coll Cambridge (MA 1969)

2c *Catherine Julie; *b* 24 Aug 1950

1a (cont.) Edward Spring Rice *m* 2nd 30 Oct 1936 Margaret Angela, MRCS, LRCP (*m* 2nd 21 June 1957 Prof Hugh Owen Meredith, OBE, MA, MCom, s of Thomas Meredith), dau of Gerald Ritchie, BCS, and *d* 11 Nov 1940

1a Mary Honora; *b* 21 Aug 1896; *m* 30 July 1919 Charles Zachary Macaulay Booth, 3rd s of Charles Booth, PC (*see* BOOTH, Bt), and had issue

(2) Cecil Arthur (Sir), GCMG, GCVO, PC (1913); *b* 27 Feb 1859; Envoy Extrdy and Min Plen Teheran 1906–08, Stockholm 1908–12, Amb Washington 1913–18, Grand Cordon Medjidie; composed the hymn *I Vow to Thee My Country*; *m* 1 June 1904 Florence Caroline (*d* 9 Dec 1961), only dau of Sir Frank Lascelles, PC (*see* HAREWOOD, E), and *d* 14 Feb 1918, leaving:

1a Anthony Theodore Brandon; *b* 15 Sept 1908; *d* unm 23 July 1954

1a Mary Elizabeth, MBE (1950); *b* 1 May 1906; *m* 8 May 1935 Sir (Oswald) Raynor Arthur, KCMG, CVO (*see* ARTHUR, Bt), and *d* 1994, leaving issue

(3) Gerald, DL Cumberland; *b* 13 Sept 1864; Lt 11th (Lonsdale) Bn Border Regt; *m* 21 June 1905 Mary Isabella (*d* 24 June 1937), yr dau of John Bush, of Beauthorn, Penrith, and was *ka* 27 May 1916, having had:

1a Stephen; *b* and *d* 14 Oct 1906

2a John Herbert; *b* 5 April, *d* 13 May 1908

(4) Bernard Wilfred Charles, JP and CA Sussex; *b* 4 May 1869; *educ* Eton; *m* 21 Feb 1906 Cicely Henrietta (*d* 1 March 1932), 2nd dau of William Cleverly Alexander, of Heathfield Park, Sussex, and *d* 4 May 1953

(1) Agnes; *d* unm 5 Nov 1928

(2) Margaret; *m* 26 July 1894 Aubrey Henry Birch-Reynardson, 3rd s of Henry Birch-Reynardson, JP, of Adwell House, Tetsworth, Oxon, and *d* 22 July 1930, leaving issue. He *d* 3 Aug 1935

(3) Evelyn Mary; *m* 27 July 1892 2nd Baron Farrer (*d* 12 April 1940) and *d* 22 April 1898, leaving issue (*see* 1963 edn)

(4) Georgiana Ellen; *d* unm 17 July 1942

3 Edmond Henry Francis Louis; *b* 31 March 1821; *m* 23 Dec 1870 Margaret Jane, dau of James Little, of Caledonia, Canada, and *d* 16 Jan 1887, leaving:

(1) Thomas Aubrey Edmond; *b* 3 June 1872; *d* unm 1899

(1) Theodosia Mary Ann

4 Aubrey Richard (Rev); *b* 15 Aug 1822; Vicar Netherbury, Dorset; *m* 15 June 1852 Anne Maria Jane (*d* 3 June 1872), est dau of Paulet St John-Mildmay, of Hazlegrove, Somerset, MP (*see* ST JOHN-MILDMAY, Bt), and *dsp* 29 Nov 1897

5 William Cecil; *b* 1 Nov 1823; barrister, Registrar Court Bankruptcy, Sec Lunacy Commn; *dsp* 11 Aug 1880

1 Mary Alicia Pery; Maid of Honour to HM QUEEN VICTORIA; *m* 9 Feb 1841 James Garth Marshall, of Headingley House, Yorks, and Monk Coniston, Lancs, and *d* his widow 11 May 1875

2 Catherine Anne Lucy; *m* 1837 Henry Cowper Marshall, of Weetwood, Yorks, and The Island, Derwentwater, Cumberland, and *d* 23 July 1853

3 Theodosia Alicia Ellen Frances Charlotte; *m* 17 Oct 1839 Sir Henry Taylor, KCMG, and *d* 2 Jan 1891, leaving issue. He *d* 27 March 1886

The 3rd BARON's unc,

FRANCIS SPRING RICE, **4th Baron Monteagle of Brandon**; *b* 1 Oct 1852; Cdr RN; *m* 1st 28 Sept 1882 Elizabeth Ann (*d* 11 Dec 1922), dau of Sir Peter George FitzGerald, 1st Bt, of Valencia (*qv*), Knight of Kerry; *m* 2nd 11 Sept 1935 Julia Emma Isabella (*d* 9 May 1936), widow of Stephen Edward Spring Rice, CB (*see* above), and *d* 22 Dec 1937, having had by his 1st w:

1 Francis Peter; *b* 13 Aug, *d* 2 Dec 1883

2 CHARLES SPRING RICE, **5th Baron Monteagle of Brandon**; *b* 28 Jan 1887; *educ* Harrow and Trin Coll Cambridge; Capt RASC WW I; *m* 14 April 1925 Emilie de Kosenko (*m* 2nd 12 Nov 1954 Col Courtenay Fergus Ochoncar Grey

Forbes, Coldstream Gds (see FORBES, L) and d 1981), dau of Mrs Edward Brooks, of New York, and d 9 Dec 1946, leaving:

(1) GERALD SPRING RICE, **6th and present Baron Monteagle of Brandon**

(2) +Michael [The Hon Michael Spring Rice, Fosseway House, Nettleton Shrub, Wilts SN14 7NL]; b 18 Feb 1935; educ Harrow; Lt Irish Gds 1954–56; m 28 Aug 1959 *Fiona, yr dau of James Edward Kenneth Sprot, of Natal, S Africa, and has:

  1a +Jonathan; b 30 Oct 1964; m 16 Aug 1997 *Natalie Lara, er dau of Anthony Rivett Robinson, of Bracknell, Berks

  1a *Kerry, b 30 March 1962

(1) *Joan [The Hon Mrs Payne, Scotlands Farm, Cockpole Green, nr Wargrave, Berks]; b 16 Aug 1928; m 15 May 1953 *Michael Shears Payne, MC, only surv s of Rawdon Shears Payne by Sylvia, dau of Maj Charles Batson Harvey (see 1931 edn HARVEY, Bt), and has:

  1a *Ashley Desmond; b 20 Aug 1956

  1a *Karina; b 1 April 1954

MONTGOMERY

Arms: Quarterly, 1st and 4th, az. three fleurs-de-lys or; 2nd and 3rd, gu. three annulets or, stones az.; over all dividing the quarters a cross waved of the second, charged with three cinquefoils in fess erm. **Crest:** A dexter hand issuing out of the wreath holding a sword indented on the back like a saw, ppr. **Motto:** *Fideliter* ('Faithfully').
Creation: Bt (UK) 16 July 1801.

SIR (BASIL HENRY) DAVID MONTGOMERY, 9th Bt, of Stanhope, Co Peebles, JP (Kinross-shire 1966) [Sir David Montgomery Bt JP, Home Farm, Kinross KY13 7EU]; b 20 March 1931; s unc 1964; educ Eton; Black Watch 1949–51, Kinross-shire: V-Lt 1966–74 (DL 1960), Perth and Kinross: Ld-Lt 1995– (DL 1975–95); memb: Nature Conservancy Cncl 1973–79, Tayside Regnl Authority 1974–79, Mental Welfare Commn Scotland 1990–91, Tstee Municipal Mutual Insur 1980–96, Hon LLD Dundee 1977; m 5 April 1956 *Delia, only dau of Adml Sir (John) Peter Lorne Reid, GCB, CVO (see REID, Bt, of Ellon), and has had:

1 +JAMES DAVID KEITH [James Montgomery Esq, Kinross House, Kinross KY13 7ET]; b 13 June 1957; educ Eton and Exeter U; Capt Black Watch RHR 1976–86; m 24 Sept 1983 *Elizabeth Lynette, est dau of E Lyndon Evans, of Tyla Morris Farm, Pentyrch, Mid-Glam, and has:

  (1) +Edward Henry James; b 1986

  (1) *Iona Rosanna; b 1988

2 Andrew Peter; b 26 July 1967; d 15 Aug 1971

1 *Caroline Jean [Mrs Nicholas Liddle, Carsehall, Wester Balgedie, Kinross, KY13 7HE]; b 27 March 1959; m 1983 *Nicholas J K Liddle, est s of Alan Liddle, and has:

  (1) *Alexander Alan Kessel; b 1988

  (1) *Lucy Delia; b 1986

  (2) *Harriet Susan; b 1991

2 *Davina Lucy; b 15 Dec 1961; m 198– *Humphrey Martin Butler, est s of Geoffrey Butler, of Cheveney Cottage, Stetchworth, Newmarket, and has:

  (1) *Bertie James; b 1991

  (2) *Hector Charles; b 1993

3 *Iona Margaret; b 1972

4 *Laura Elizabeth; b 1974

Lineage: ROBERT MONTGOMERIE, yr bro of 1st Lord Montgomerie (see EGLINTON and WINTON, E), had a charter 9 March 1413/4 confirming a grant by his f Sir John Montgomerie of Ardrossap, Giffen and other lands in Ayrshire, and was ancestor of a line of MONTGOMERYs of Giffen. From them the MONTGOMERYs of Stanhope claim descent through a cadet branch who owned the lands of Macbethhill, or Magbiehill, Ayrshire.

WILLIAM MONTGOMERY bought c 1712 the lands of Coldcoat, Peeblesshire, which he called Magbiehill, and had:

WILLIAM MONTGOMERY, of Magbiehill; advocate; m Barbara, dau of Robert Rutherford of Bowland, and d 1768, having had:

1 Sir WILLIAM MONTGOMERY, 1st Bt (GB), so cr 29 Oct 1774, of Magbiehill, MP (I Parl); b 19 Nov 1717; m 1st 1 July 1750 Hannah, 2nd dau and coheir of Alexander Tomkyns, of Prehen, Co Londonderry, and had:

(1) William Stone; Capt 9th Regt; b Aug 1754; d unm 8 July 1777

(1) Elizabeth; m 3 July 1773 1st Viscount Mountjoy and d 7 Nov 1783, leaving issue. He d 5 June 1798

(2) Barbara; m 4 June 1774 John Beresford, bro of 1st Marquess of Waterford (qv), and d 2 Dec 1788, leaving issue

(3) Anne; m 19 May 1773 1st Marquess Townshend (qv) and d 29 March 1819, leaving issue

1 (cont) Sir WILLIAM m 2nd 9 Jan 1762 Anne (d 19 June 1777), dau of Humphry Evatt, of Mount Louise, Co Monaghan, and d 23 Dec 1788, having had:

(2) Sir GEORGE MONTGOMERY, 2nd and last Bt; MP Peeblesshire; d unm 9 July 1831, when the btcy expired

(3) Robert; Col 19th Regt; b 26 Feb 1767; k in a duel with Capt Macnamara 6 April 1803

(4) Jane; m 1791 William Reynell (d 3 May 1829), of Castle Reynell, and had issue

(5) Harriet; m George Byng, MP Middx (see STRAFFORD, E), and dsp

(6) Amelia; m 22 Nov 1795 Rev Charles Cobbe Beresford (see WATERFORD, M) and d 14 March 1839, leaving issue

2 **Sir James Montgomery, 1st Bt** (UK), so cr 16 July 1801; Ld Advocate Scotland 1766, MP Peebles 1768, Ch Baron Exchequer Scotland 1775–81; m Margaret, dau and heiress of Robert Scott, of Killearn, Stirling, and had:

(1) William, Lt-Col 43rd Regt; dsp Oct 1800

(2) JAMES (Sir), **2nd Bt**

(3) Archibald Charles, of Whim, Peeblesshire; Judge Rungpore; b 25 June 1771; m Maria Rausch (d Feb 1854) and d 1845, having had:

  1a James, of Lillington, Warwicks; 3rd Dragoon Gds; b 7 Dec 1809; m 19 June 1835 Eleanor (d 8 Jan 1878), dau of John Anstruther-Thomson of Charleton (see ANSTRUTHER, Bt), and d 1894, having had:

    1b Archibald; b 22 May 1837; d unm 7 Feb 1857

    2b James Frederick; b 11 March 1839; dsp

    3b John Conrad; b 14 Sept 1843

    1b Clementina Margaret; d unm

    2b Emily Harriet; d unm 22 June 1854

  2a Charles William; b 11 June 1818; m Jane Caroline (m 2nd 1855 Capt Robert Peel Floyd (see FLOYD, Bt), d 24 July 1885), dau of Richard Rennard, and d 23 Sept 1849, leaving:

    1b Emily Emma; m 15 Sept 1871 Sir (Andrew) Charles Howard, KCB, and d 26 Feb 1929, leaving issue. He d 11 June 1909

  3a Conrad; b 19 Oct 1824; d unm 1859

  1a Emily Maria; m 6 Aug 1838 9th Lord Elibank (qv) and d 3 June 1879, leaving issue

(4) Robert; barrister; b 5 June 1775; m 24 April 1817 Elizabeth (d 29 March 1870), dau of Bryant Mason, of Bushey, Herts, and d 2 Dec 1854, having had:

  1a James Francis (Rev); DD, advocate 1840, later ordained, Dean Edinburgh 1873; b 10 July 1818; m 17 Jan 1860 Elizabeth Mary, sis of 15th Lord Elphinstone (qv), and dsp 21 Sept 1897

  2a Robert; b 27 Nov 1820; m 1st Jan 1855 Helen (dsp March 1857), dau of Robert Spankey; m 2nd Nov 1869 Emily, dau of T T Draper

  3a William; b 20 March 1822; m 31 Aug 1860 Elizabeth Maxwell (d 1928), dau of Colin McEachern, of Oatfield, and d 1888, leaving:

    1b Robert Hamilton; b 26 July 1863; m 9 Aug 1898 Evelyn Mary (d 10 Nov 1951), dau of Rev Frederick Vernon, Vicar Shawbury, and d 31 March 1943, leaving:

      1c Ian Stuart; b 1900; m 1942 *Neva, dau of Ogden Minton, of Greenwich, Conn., and d 1984, having had:

        1d +Brian Stuart; b 17 April 1952; m 1976 *Patty —, of Warrenton, Va.

        1d *Ann Vernon; b 1945; m 24 June 1967 *James R Egan, s of James H Egan, of Wallaston, Mass., and has:

          1e *Cheryl Ann; b 1970

          2e *Mischell; b 1974

        2d *Sheila Minton; b 3 March 1949; m 1972 *Mervin J Marles, of New York, and has:

          1e *Mervin John; b 1978

          2e *Ian Stuart; b 1978 (twin)

      2c Alan Robert; Adml USN; b 1905; m 1st 27 July 1928 (divorce 1940) Josephine Marie, dau of Edward J Strain, of Philadelphia, and had:

        1d +Robert Edward; b 1932

        1d *Doris Marie; b 1929

      2c (cont) Alan Montgomery m 2nd 1941 *Mary Helen, dau of George E Kohlhaas, of San Bernardino, Calif., and d 17 April 1964

      3c +Colin Tassie [Colin Montgomery, 7813 Ellenham Avenue, Ruxton, MD, USA]; b 1911; m 1941 *Carol, dau of Dr Joseph Kant Worthington, of Baltimore, and adopted:

        *Robert Hamilton; b 3 Jan 1947

        *Mary Lindsay; b 24 May 1949

      1c *Dorothy Vernon [Mrs William Rust, Magbie Hill, Warenton, VA, USA]; b 1909; m 7 April 1952 *William Smoot Rust, s of David N Rust, Jr, of Leesburg, Va., and has:

        1d *William Montgomery; b 1952

    2b Colin Francis (Rev); MA Cantab, Vicar Shapwick with Ashcott, Somerset; b 28 July 1867; m 1894 Evelyn (d 1948), dau of Henry Webb, of Worcester, and d 21 March 1906, leaving:

      1c James Colin (Rev); Vicar St George's, Dean Prior, Devon, F/O RAF; b 1894; d unm 11 Aug 1948

      2c Robert Maxwell; Lt RHA and RFC, S/Ldr RAF WWs I (wounded twice) and II; b 1897; m 1st 8 Nov 1924 (divorce 1936) Eleanor Pierce (d 1957), 2nd dau of J P D Adams, of Chilton House, Chilton Polden,

Bridgewater; m 2nd 9 May 1936 Audrey Winifred (d 1980), only dau of C Field, and d 1977, having by her had:

  1d +Andrew John [Andrew Montgomery Esq, Farthingham House, Farthingham Lane, Ewhurst, Surrey]; b 8 Feb 1937; m 6 March 1965 *Maureen Patricia, dau of M J Roberts, and has:

    1e +Robert Maxwell [Robert Montgomery Esq, Heath Cottage, Holmbury St Mary, Surrey]; b 16 July 1968

    2e +Michael Andrew; b 1971

3c Andrew Graham; 2nd Lt Cameron Highrs; b 22 June 1899; ka 6 Sept 1918

1c Evelyn Ruth; b 1902; m 27 Jan 1926 Ven Richard Hamilton Babington (d 1984), Archdeacon Exeter, only s of Rev Richard Babington, Dean Cork, and had:

  1d Richard Andrew; b 1927; Vicar Blandford, Dorset; d 1993

  2d *Gervase Hamilton; b 1930; Canon

  1d *Susan Mary; b 1933

  2d *Felicity Ruth; b 1939

3b William Harold, JP E Lothian; b 19 Aug 1869; m 7 Oct 1908 Dorothea Godiva (d 9 March 1968), dau of William John Mann, and d 30 Dec 1937, leaving:

  1c +James Graham [James Montgomery Esq, 9 Ravelston House, Grove, Edinburgh]; b 17 Aug 1913; educ Rugby; m 1st 29 April 1952 (annulled 1955) Andreena Nora, dau of John Forest Menelaws; m 2nd 13 May 1961 *Nancy Melville Blyth, of Juniper Green, Midlothian

  1c *Elizabeth Margaret [Mrs William Gary-Muir, 42 Dick Place, Edinburgh]; b 7 Aug 1909; m 23 June 1932 William Edgar Gary-Muir, WS, memb Roy Co Archers, s of Andrew Gray-Muir, WS, and has issue. He d 20 Jan 1959

  2c Dorothea Jean; b 28 Nov 1910; d unm 30 Nov 1943

1b Elizabeth Annabella; m 1896 Maj William S Anderson, 60th Rifles, and d 23 Feb 1937, leaving issue

2b Margaret Seton Stewart; m 10 Feb 1891 Arthur Bruce Dundas, 3rd s of Maj Joseph Dundas (see ZETLAND, M), and d 28 Jan 1912

3b Mary Alice

4b Jane Ethel

4a George Finch; b 30 Aug 1829; m 16 April 1874 Marianne Hooper, dau of J Wilkins

1a Elizabeth; m 2 Dec 1852 Sir Henry James Seton-Steuart, 3rd Bt, of Allanton (see 1930 edn), and d Jan 1901, leaving issue. He d 6 Dec 1884

2a Margaret

  (1) Margaret; m Robert Campbell of Kailzie

  (2) Barbara; m Brig-Gen Alexander Walker

  (3) Anne; m Thomas Hart, of Castlemilk, Dumfriesshire

Sir JAMES d 2 April 1803; his son,

Sir James Montgomery, 2nd Bt; advocate 1787, Ld Advocate 1804–06, MP Peeblesshire 1800–31; b 9 Oct 1766; m 1st 1 Aug 1804 Elizabeth (d 28 Oct 1814), dau of 4th Earl of Selkirk (qv), and had:

1 James; b 28 April 1811; d 16 July 1833

1 Helen Anne; m 1830 William Forbes Mackenzie, MP, of Portmore, and d 1870. He d 25 Sept 1862

2 Elizabeth; m 3 Jan 1834 James Ker Williamson of Cardrona and d 15 Sept 1874. He d 1847

Sir James m 2nd 1816 Helen (d 1828), yr dau of Thomas Graham, MP, of Kinross, and d 27 May 1839, having by her had:

2 Sir GRAHAM MONTGOMERY later GRAHAM-MONTGOMERY, **3rd Bt**; b 9 July 1823; MA Oxon, MP Peebles 1852–68 and Selkirk and Peeblesshire 1868–80, Jr Ld Treasury 1866–68 and 1880, Ld Lt Kinross-shire, V-Lt Peeblesshire, Lt-Gen Roy Co Archers; m 10 April 1845 Alice (d 16 Dec 1890), yst dau of John James Hope-Johnstone, MP (see LINLITHGOW, M), and d 2 June 1901, leaving:

  (1) **Sir James Gordon Henry Graham-Montgomery, 4th Bt**, DL Peeblesshire and Kinross-shire; b 6 Feb 1850; Maj and Lt-Col Coldstream Gds; accidentally k 8 Nov 1902

  (2) **Sir Basil Templer Graham-Montgomery, 5th Bt**; b 1 March 1852; Hon Lt-Col Kinross Vol Regt, Lt 60th Rifles; m 1st 26 Oct 1880 (divorce 1905) Mary Katherine (d 30 July 1910), dau of Sir Thomas Moncreiffe of that Ilk, 7th Bt (see ERROLL, E), and had:

    1a Walter Basil, OBE (1920), DL Kinross-shire; b 1881; Hon Attaché Dip Serv; m 2 Nov 1912 (divorce 1914) Fanny, only child of Theodore M Zarifi, of Bayswater, and d 23 March 1928

    1a Lena; b 1882

  (2) (cont.) **Sir Basil** m 2nd 6 June 1905 Theresa Blanche (d 24 June 1936), est dau of Lt-Col Henry William Verschoyle, Gren Gds, of Kilberry, Co Kildare, and dspm 4 Oct 1928

  (3) **Rev Sir Charles Percy Graham-Montgomery, 6th Bt**; b 6 Sept 1855; educ Emmanuel Coll Cambridge (MA); Vicar St John's Taunton; m 1st 1887 Minnie Gertrude Compton (d 13 Feb 1922), dau of Maj-Gen Chamberlain Walker, Bombay SC, and had:

    1a Graham John Early; b 1894; Capt Hants Regt; ka 24 April 1917

    2a Percy Cecil; b 6 Sept 1898; d 21 April 1915

  (3) **Sir Charles** m 2nd 1923 Rose Kathleen, widow of Charles Wilfrid Blunt and dau of Peter John Sullivan, of Dublin, and dsps 1 April 1930

  (4) Arthur Cecil; Lt HLI; b 3 Jan 1858; d 1887

  (1) Alice Anne; DGStJ, Médaille de la Reine Elisabeth; m 1st 17 Feb 1885 3rd Duke of Buckingham and Chandos (see TEMPLE OF STOWE, E); m 2nd 8 Aug 1894 1st and last Earl Egerton of Tatton (see 1956 edn EGERTON OF TATTON, B) and d 15 Sept 1931. He d 16 March 1909

  (2) Helen Mabel; m 29 Dec 1870 4th Earl Temple of Stowe (qv) and d 21 Nov 1919, leaving issue

  (3) Lucy Aline Campbell; d unm 6 May 1881

---

  (4) Evelyn Henrietta; m 22 April 1893 Sir Robert Dundas, 2nd Bt, of Arniston (see 1956 edn), and d 29 Aug 1930, leaving issue. He d 12 Dec 1910

3 John Basil Hamilton, of Newton, Lanarks; Commr Supply Lanarks; b 11 Sept 1824; d unm 22 Feb 1911

4 Thomas Henry; Capt 42nd Highrs; b 21 Aug 1828; m 4 March 1857 Hon Anna Maria (d 20 March 1914), sis of 15th Lord Elphinstone (qv), and d 20 Jan 1879, leaving:

  (1) HENRY JAMES (Sir), **7th Bt**

  (2) Herbert Elphinstone; b 2 May 1861; m 5 Dec 1899 Janet Katharine Olive (d 22 June 1937), yst dau of Sir John William Hamilton Anson, 2nd Bt (qv), and d 24 Feb 1943, having had:

    1a Ernest John, CB (1953), CBE (1950, OBE 1945, MBE 1940), JP Argyllshire; b 24 March 1901; educ Rugby and RMC Sandhurst; Brig Highland LI WW II (despatches twice) and Malaya 1951–54, memb Roy Co Archers; m 11 March 1931 Rosemary Elizabeth, er dau of Sir John Noble, 1st Bt, of Ardkinglas (qv), and d 10 Oct 1972, having adopted:

      *Elizabeth Jean; b 12 Jan 1946; m 6 Aug 1970 *Douglas Cotton, s of — Cotton and Mrs John Scrutton, of 31 Eaton Sq

    2a Arthur Herbert, OBE (1945), TD; b 17 Nov 1902; educ Wellington and Hertford Coll Oxford; Brig RA (TA) WW II, FICA; m 23 Sept 1939 Feodora Kathleen Alice (Jane Baxter, actress; d 1996), widow of Clive Dunfee and 2nd dau of Henry Bligh Forde, and d 1978, having had:

      1b +James Henry Anson [James Montgomery Esq, Wellow Mead, Sherfield English, Romsey, Hants SO51 6DU]; b 16 Sept 1945; educ Wellington and Magdalen Coll Oxford; TV/radio presenter/producer; m 1st 1972 (divorce 1977) Carolyn Winifred Finlay; m 2nd 1984 *Julia Rosamund (Fiona Richmond, actress), dau of Rev John Harrison, of Cornwall, and by her has:

        1c *Tara Féodora; b 1984

      1b *Rachel Janet [Mrs Max Monsarrat, Le Tournier, Latouille-Lentillac, St Céré, Lot 46400, France]; b 14 July 1940; m 1972 *Max Monsarrat

      2b *Sylvia Mary [The Rt Hon The Lady Crathorne, Crathorne House, Yarm, N Yorks TS15 0AT]; b 3 March 1942; m 8 Jan 1970 *2nd Baron Crathorne (qv)

    1a Janet Elizabeth Anna; b 22 Oct, d 10 Nov 1909

  (1) Violet Anna; d unm 31 Oct 1944

3 Anne; d unm 30 June 1835

4 Margaret Fleming; d unm 28 Feb 1840

The 6th Bt's cousin,

Sir HENRY JAMES MONTGOMERY later PURVIS-RUSSELL-MONTGOMERY (1906) later still PURVIS-RUSSELL-HAMILTON-MONTGOMERY (1933), **7th Bt**, JP Kinross-shire; b 6 Sept 1859; educ Trin Coll Glenalmond and Jesus Coll Cambridge; Ld Lt Kinross-shire 1934–37; m 1882 Mary Maud, MBE (d 6 Oct 1947), dau of T Purvis-Russell, of Warroch, Kinross-shire, and d 6 Aug 1947, having had:

1 **Sir Basil Purvis-Russell Montgomery, 8th Bt**; b 25 Sept 1884; educ Uppingham and Trin Hall Cambridge; NZ Forces WW I; m 1915 Amelia A Richards, of Timaru, NZ, and d 28 Jan 1964, having had:

  (1) Rachel; WAAC 2nd NZ Expdy Force 1945–46; b 1916

  (2) *Sheila [Mrs Desmond Widgery, Warroch, Newstead, RD, Hamilton, NZ]; b 1923; WAAF (Radar) WW II; m 1st 1945 (divorce 1959) John Martin Griffith and has:

    1a *Andrea Suzanne; b 4 May 1946; m 1975 *Alexander Palmarczuk

    2a *Gael Virginia; b 1 May 1949; m 1982 S/Ldr Gordon Graham, RAF (kas 1990)

  (2) (cont.) Mrs Sheila Griffith-Montgomery (augmented by deed poll) m 2nd 16 Jan 1967 Desmond Widgery, MIEE, MNZIE, chartered electrical engr (d 1989), s of Herbert Widgery, of Hamilton, NZ

2 Henry Keith, OBE (1944); b 1896; educ Rugby and Jesus Coll Cambridge; Ld Lt Kinross-shire 1944 (DL 1937), Lt-Col Black Watch (TA), Capt Black Watch Roy Highrs WW I Salonika (wounded), dir Kinross Estate Co; m 23 April 1930 *Cynthia Louisa Winifred [Mrs Henry Purvis-Russell-Montgomery, Kinross House, Kinross], only dau of John Allan Maconochie-Welwood, of Kirknewton, Midlothian, and Garvock, Fife, and d 1 Oct 1954, leaving:

  (1) Sir (BASIL HENRY) DAVID MONTGOMERY, **9th and present Bt**

  (2) *Veronica Mary Anthea [Miss Veronica Montgomery, Kinross House, Kinross]; b 20 Feb 1935

1 Mary Gertrude; d unm 1912

2 Ethel Anna; b 1887; m 7 Aug 1913 (divorce 1919) George Balfour-Kinnear, WS, only s of James Balfour-Kinnear, WS, and d 16 Feb 1968, leaving issue

3 Clementina Helen Maud Purvis-Russell; b 1900

MONTGOMERY OF ALAMEIN

Arms: Azure two lions passant guardant between three fleur-de-lys, two in chief and one in base, and two trefoils in fess, all or. **Crest:** Issuant from a crescent argent an arm embowed in armour, the hand grasping a broken tilting spear in bend sinister, the head pendant proper. **Supporters:** Dexter, a knight in chain armour and surcoat, resting his exterior hand on his sword; sinister, a soldier in battle dress, all proper. **Motto:** *Gardez bien* ('Watch well'). **Creation:** V. (UK) 31 Jan 1946.

THE 2ND VISCOUNT MONTGOMERY OF ALAMEIN, of Hindhead, Co Surrey (David Bernard Montgomery, CBE (1975)) [The Rt Hon The Viscount Montgomery of Alamein CBE, 54 Cadogan Sq, London SW1X 0JW]; *b* 18 Aug 1928; *s f* 1976; *educ* Winchester and Trin Coll Cambridge (MA); late Lt RTR; Shell Int 1951–62, memb Ctee Exports to Latin America 1964; dir: Yardley Int Ltd 1963–74, Korn Ferry Int 1977–93, NEI 1981–87, md Terimar Servs (Overseas Trade Consultancy) 1974–, chm: Antofagasta (Chile) and Bolivia Rlwy Co 1980–82, Ec Affs Ctee Canning Ho 1973–75, Hispanic and Luso Brazilian Cncl 1978–80 (pres 1987–94), Brazilian Chamber Commerce Britain 1980–82, European Atlantic Gp 1992–94 (pres 1994–97), Baring Puma Fund; edtl advsr Vision Interamericana 1974–94; pres: Br Industrial Exhibition Sao Paulo 1974, Anglo-Argentine Soc 1977–87, Redgrave Theatre Farnham 1977–87, Restaurateurs Assoc GB 1982–90 (patron 1991–), Centre for Int Briefing Farnham Castle 1985–, Anglo-Belgian Soc 1994–, Academy of Food and Wine Service 1995–; exec ctee Inter-Parly Union Br Gp 1987–; deleg OSCE Parly Assembly 1992, Patron: D-Day and Normandy Fellowship 1980-, 8th Army Veterans Assoc 1985–, Grand Offr Orders: Bernardo O'Higgins Chile 1989, Libertador San Martin Argentina 1992, Nacional Cruzeiro do Sul Brazil 1993, Isabel la Catolica Spain 1993, Aguila Azteca Mexico 1994, Leopold II Belgium 1997; Cdr's Cross Order Merit Germany 1993, Aguila Azteca Mexico 1994, Leopold II Belgium 1997; author (with Alistair Horne) *The Lonely Leader: Monty 1944–45*; *m* 1st 27 Feb 1953 (*divorce* 1967) Mary Raymond, yr dau of Sir Charles Connell, of Craigallan, Milngavie, Dunbartonshire, and has:

> 1 +HENRY DAVID [The Hon Henry Montgomery, The Manor House, All Stretton, Salop SY6 6JU]; *b* 2 April 1954; *educ* Wellington and Seale Hayne Ag Coll; *m* 21 June 1980 *Caroline Jane, er dau of George Richard Odey, of Hotham Hall, York, and has:

>> (1) *Alexa Maud; *b* 30 Aug 1984
>> (2) *Flora Veronica; *b* 4 May 1988
>> (3) *Phoebe Matilda; *b* 4 Feb 1990

> 1 *Arabella Clare [The Hon Mrs Stuart-Smith, Pie Corner, Millhouse Lane, Bedmond, Herts WD5 0SG]; *b* 21 Nov 1956; *educ* North Foreland Lodge and York U; *m* 25 Sept 1982 *Jeremy Hugh Stuart-Smith (*see* VERULAM, E) and has:

>> (1) *Edward Murray; *b* 6 May 1988
>> (2) *Samuel Nicholas; *b* 6 Dec 1990
>> (3) *Luke David; *b* 19 Jan 1993
>> (1) *Emma; *b* 6 Oct 1984
>> (2) Laura; *b* 1986; *d* 1987

The 2nd VISCOUNT *m* 2nd 30 Jan 1970 *Tessa, er dau of Lt-Gen Sir Frederick Arthur Montague Browning, GCVO, KBE, CB, DSO, and Lady Browning (Dame Daphne du Maurier DBE, author), of Menabilly, Par, Cornwall, and formerly w of Maj Peter Paul John de Zulueta, Welsh Gds

Lineage: In 1628 a branch of the MONTGOMERYs of Scotland settled at Killaghtee, near Dunkineely, S W Donegal; from them descended:

SAMUEL MONTGOMERY; *b* 1723; Londonderry merchant; bought 1,000 acres on the north bank of Lough Foyle, Co Donegal, 1773 and built New Park (sold *c* 1950 by Harold Robert Montgomery, CMG, s of Rt Rev H H Montgomery, *see* below); had:

Rev SAMUEL LAW MONTGOMERY; had a 2nd s:

Sir ROBERT MONTGOMERY, GCSI (1866), KCB (1859), of New Park; *b* 2 Dec 1809; Memb Cncl of India, Lt-Govr Punjab 1859–65, took control of Lahore in Indian Mutiny, for which ktd and voted thanks of Parl; LLD; *m* 1st 17 Dec 1834 Frances Mary (*d* 23 March 1842), dau of Rev T T Thomason; *m* 2nd 2 May 1845 Ellen Jane, dau of William Lambert, of Woodmansterne, Surrey, and *d* 28 Dec 1887, having by her had a 2nd s:

Rt Rev HENRY HUTCHINSON MONTGOMERY, KCMG (1928), of New Park; *b* 3 Oct 1847; *educ* Harrow and Trin Coll Cambridge; Vicar Kennington 1879–89; Bp Tasmania 1889–1901, Sec SPG 1901–18, Preb St Paul's and Prelate Order St Michael and St George; Hon DD Oxon 1908, Hon DCL Durham 1908; *m* 28 July 1881 Maud (*d* 9 July 1949), 3rd dau of Very Rev Frederic William Farrar, DD, FRS, Dean Canterbury, and *d* 25 Nov 1932, having had:

> 1 Harold Robert, CMG (1936); *b* 8 May 1884; *educ* King's Sch Canterbury; Ch Native Commr Kenya 1934–37; *m* 1st 10 Nov 1926 Ursula (*d* Oct 1937), dau of Gardner Johnson, of Vancouver; *m* 2nd 1941 Betty (*m* 3rd 19 May 1960 Lt-Col F C G Stratton, of Nairobi, and *d* 19–), dau of J M Sandy, of Sydney, NSW, and widow of L D Galton Fenzi, and *d* 17 May 1958, leaving by his 1st w:
>> (1) *Gardner; *b* 11 April 1931
> 2 Donald Stanley, MC (1917), QC (BC Bar 1911); *b* 2 May 1886; *educ* Cambridge (BA); barrister, served WW I; *m* 20 April 1920 Dorothy Frances, dau of James Rawlinson Waghorn, of Vancouver, and had:
>> (1) *James Henry; *b* 14 Nov 1921
>> (2) *John Desmond; *b* 14 May 1928
> 3 BERNARD LAW, **1st Viscount**
> 4 Desmond; *b* 6 May 1896; *d* 26 Nov 1909
> 5 Colin Roger (Rev), TD (1951); *b* 27 June 1901; Vicar St John, Wallasey, Cheshire, 1932–42, CF TA 1935 and Educn Corps 1939–46, Vicar Ladysmith Natal 1946–48, Rector Aklavik Cathedral Canada 1948–52, Rector Vryburg CP 1952–59; *m* 19– Margaret, 3rd dau of John W Drennan, of Carse Hall, Limavady, Co Londonderry, and *d* 28 Aug 1959
> 6 Brian Frederick, MBE (1942); *b* 18 Oct 1903; *educ* St Paul's and RMC Sandhurst; Lt-Col (ret) Roy Warwicks Regt 1923, KAR 1927–33, Baluch Regt 1935 (ret 1947), WW II (despatches twice), Dip Serv 1947–70, author *A Field Marshal in the Family* (1973), *Shenton of Singapore* and *Monty's Grandfather* (1984); *m* 1 April 1944 *Mrs Barbara Peggy (Bunty) MacNeece, est dau of Mrs Grace Hincks, of Folkestone, Kent, and *d* 14 May 1989
> 1 Sybil Frances (Queenie); *b* 27 Sept 1882; *d* 18 Nov 1889
> 2 Una; *b* 12 May 1889; *m* 31 Jan 1912 Andrew Holden, CBE, Egyptian CS, s of Lonsdale Holden, MRCS, and *d* 26 May 1936, leaving a s and four daus
> 3 Maud Winifred (Winsome); *b* 14 Feb 1895; *m* 1st 30 Jan 1924 Lt-Col William Holderness, MC, Roy Sussex Regt (*d* 1958), s of Robert Fitzroy Holderness, of Cashel St, Christchurch, NZ; *m* 2nd 2 Jan 1971 Maj Gen Sir (William) Godwin Michelmore, KBE, CB, DSO, MC, TD, JP, DL (*d* 29 Oct 1982), s of Henry William Michelmore, of Grove Hill, Topsham, Devon, and *d* 5 Jan 1989

The Rt Rev HENRY MONTGOMERY's 3rd s,

BERNARD LAW MONTGOMERY, **1st Viscount Montgomery of Alamein**, of Hindhead, Co of Surrey (UK), so *cr* 31 Jan 1946, KG (1946), GCB (1945, KCB 1942, CB 1940), DSO (1914), DL (Hants 1959); *b* 17 Nov 1887; *educ* St Paul's (later Govr) and RMC Sandhurst; joined Roy Warwicks Regt 1908, WW I on Staff (severely wounded, despatches, Brevet Maj), DAAG Staff Coll 1926–29, GSO Staff Coll Quetta 1934–37, Col 1934, cmded: 9th Inf Bde 1937–38, 8th Div 1938–39, 3rd Div 1939 (despatches), 5th Corps and 12th Corps 1940, GOC-in-C SE Cmd 1941–42, cmded 8th Army 1942–43, 21st Army Gp 1944, FM 1944, C-in-C BAOR and Br Memb Allied CCG 1945–46, CIGS 1946–48, Chm C-in-C Ctee W Union 1948–51, Dep Supreme Cdr Allied Powers Europe 1951–58, Col Cmdt Army Physical Training Corps 1946–60, Col Roy Warwicks Regt 1947–63, Silver Jubilee Medal 1935 and Coronation Medal 1937, author *Memoirs* (1958), *The Path to Leadership* (1961), *A History of Warfare* (1968), Ch Cdr US Legion Merit, US DSM, Orders Suvorov and Victory USSR, Grand Cross Legn Hon and Croix de Guerre France (twice), Medaille Militaire France 1958, Grand Cordon Order Leopold and Croix de Guerre Belgium, 1st Cl Order Elephant Denmark, Grand Cross Order Lion Netherlands, Grand Cross Order White Lion, Star of Victory and Croix de Guerre Czechoslovakia, 1st Cl Order Virtuti Militari Poland, Grand Cross George I Greece and Medal for Gallantry, Order Couronne de Chêne and Medaille Militaire Luxembourg, 1st Cl Order Ouissam-Alaouite Morocco, 1st Cl Order Nicham-Iftikhar Tunisia, Grand Cross Seal of Solomon Ethiopia, Hon DCL: Oxon, Edin, Dalhousie Halifax and U of BC; Hon LLD: Cantab, Columbia U NY, Glasgow, Queen's U Belfast, St Andrews and Toronto; Hon DSc; McGill, Louvain and Liège; Freeman: Mercers' Co, Fletchers' and Bonnetmakers' Co, Carpenters' Co and Dyers' Co; *m* 27 July 1927 Elizabeth (*d* 19 Oct 1937), dau of Robert Thompson Hobart, ICS, of Tunbridge Wells, and widow of Capt Oswald Armitage Carver, and *d* 24 March 1976, leaving:

DAVID BERNARD MONTGOMERY, **2nd and present Viscount Montgomery of Alamein**

MONTROSE

Arms: Quarterly, 1st and 4th, or on a chief sable three escallops of the field (for GRAHAM); 2nd and 3rd, argent three roses gules, barbed and seeded proper (for MONTROSE). **Crest:** An eagle, wings hovering, or, preying upon a stork on its back proper. **Supporters:** Two storks argent, beaked and membered gules. **Motto:** *N'oubliez* ('Forget not'). **Creations:** L. (S) between 20 June 1432 and 28 June 1445 (Graham); E. (S) between 7 July and 20 Nov 1503 (Montrose); Bt. (NS) 28 Sept 1625; M. (Montrose), E. (Kincardine) and L. (Graham and Mugdock) (S) 6 May 1644; D., M (Graham and Buchanan), E. (Kincardine), V. (Dundaff) and L. (Aberuthven, Mugdock and Fintrie) (S) 24 April 1707; E. (Graham) and B. (GB) 23 May 1722.

THE 8TH DUKE OF MONTROSE, Marquess of Montrose, Marquess of Graham and Buchanan, Earl of Montrose, Earl of Kincardine (twice), **Earl Graham, Viscount (of) Dundaff, Lord Graham, Lord Graham and Mugdock, Lord Aberuthven, Mugdock, and Fintric, Baron Graham of Belford**, Co Northumberland, and a **Baronet** (Sir James Graham, Bt) [His Grace The Duke of Montrose, Auchmar, Drymen, Glasgow G63 0AG]; *b* 6 April 1935; *s f* 1992; *educ* Loretto; Brig Roy Co Archers 1986– (memb 1965–), Area Pres Scottish NFU 1981–86 (memb Cncl 1982–86 and 1987–90), OStJ 1978; *m* 31 Jan 1970 *Catherine Elizabeth MacDonell, dau of Capt Norman Andrew Thompson Young, QO Cameron Highrs, of Ottawa, and has:

1 +JAMES ALEXANDER NORMAN, *Marquess of Graham*; *b* 16 Aug 1973; *educ* Eton, Edinburgh U and Cape Town U (MSc)

2 +Ronald John Christopher; *b* 13 Oct 1975; *educ* Eton and Edinburgh U

1 +Hermione Elizabeth; *b* 20 July 1971; *educ* Oxford

Montrose, earlier Dukedom: *See* CRAWFORD and BALCARRES, E, against the 4th Earl of Crawford.

Lineage: WILLIAM de GRAHAM of Abercorn and Dalkeith, which he was granted by DAVID I (1124–53); living 1139; had:

1 Peter, of Dalkeith, part of which he granted to Newbottle Abbey; had, with a yr s (William):

  (1) Henry, of Dalkeith; confirmed his f's grant to Newbottle Abbey; had:

    1a Henry, of Dalkeith; confirmed his f's and gf's grants; a leading MP 1284; acknowledged MARGARET, THE MAID OF NORWAY, as heiress to the throne; *m* —, dau and heiress of Roger Avenel (*d* 1243), who brought him the AVENELs' estate in Eskdale; had:

      1b Nicholas (Sir); of Dalkeith; MP 1290 (a nominee of ROBERT BRUCE 1292), but swore fealty to EDWARD I OF ENGLAND 1296; *m* Mary, who inherited property from (hence may have been kin to) Marjory de Muschamp, 1st w of 5th Earl of Strathearn, and had:

        1c John (Sir) of Dalkeith and Abercorn; confirmed predecessors' grants to Melrose Abbey; had:

          1d John, of Dalkeith; granted Elvyston, Co Edinburgh, to John, s of Richard Graham (roy charter of confirmation 1362); *dsp*

          1d A dau; *m* William More, who thus acquired the (territorial) Barony of Abercorn

          2d Margaret; *m* William Douglas of Lugton (who thus acquired the (territorial) Barony of Dalkeith) and had issue (*see* MORTON, E)

2 John; *fl* 1170–1200; had:

  (1) William; living 1200; had:

    1a David, of Kinnabar, Forfarshire, which was granted him, with other lands nr Montrose, by WILLIAM I (THE LION) (1165–1214); also acquired lands in Midlothian from his cousin Henry de Graham of Dalkeith (*see* above); had:

      1b DAVID (Sir)

      2b Patrick (Sir); living 1248

      3b Thomas (Sir); living *temp* ALEXANDER II (1214–49)

      4b William

The est son,

  Sir DAVID de GRAHAM of Dundaff; of which, with Strathcarron (formerly the King's Forest), had charters *temp* ALEXANDER II; a guarantor of an Anglo-Scots treaty 1244; *m* Agnes — and had:

  Sir DAVID GRAHAM of Dundaff; Sheriff Berwicks; acquired roy charter of all his lands between 1249 and 1286 and from 5th Earl of Strathearn (*see* above) the lands of Kincardine, Perths; *m* Annabella, dau of 4th Earl of Strathearn, and *d c* 1270, having had:

  1 PATRICK (Sir)

  2 John (Sir), of Dundaff; rose against English with Sir William Wallace June 1289; *ka* at Scottish defeat by English of Falkirk 22 July 1289

  3 David (Sir); supported John Balliol for the Crown of Scotland 5 June 1292 but swore fealty to EDWARD I 3 Aug 1292, nevertheless made EDWARD's prisoner 1296, released 1297 provided he served in EDWARD's wars against France; acquired lands of Loveth, Inverness-shire

The est son,

  Sir PATRICK GRAHAM of Kincardine; sent 1281 to negotiate the marriage of PRINCE ALEXANDER, s of ALEXANDER III (1249–86), with Margaret, dau of Guy, Earl of Flanders; MP 1284, when MARGARET, THE MAID OF NORWAY, acknowledged heiress to the Crown; nevertheless swore fealty to EDWARD I 12 July 1292, called 1 Sept 1294 to attend EDWARD to France; *ka* fighting on English side at victory over Scots of Dunbar 28 April 1296, leaving, with a yr s (Sir John, living 1317):

  Sir DAVID GRAHAM of Kincardine; imprisoned England 1296–30 July 1297 (released on condition he served in EDWARD I's foreign wars); granted by ROBERT I (THE BRUCE) various lands; exchanged with ROBERT the estate of Cardross, Dunbartonshire, for the lands of Old Montrose, Forfarshire; a guarantor of the Anglo-Scots treaty 1322; had, with a dau (alleged to have been Margaret, *m* by 1329, apparently as his 2nd w, Hugh de Ross, 4th Earl of Ross), an only s:

  Sir DAVID GRAHAM of Kincardine and Old Montrose; one of the Scottish magnates who negotiated ransom by English of DAVID II (1329–71) following latter's capture at Scottish defeat of Durham 17 Oct 1346; MP (S Parl) 1357, when treaty for release of DAVID II approved; swore fealty to ROBERT II 27 March 1371; witnessed 2nd Act of Settlement of Crown of Scotland 4 April 1373; had, with other issue, including a 3rd s (John, 1st of Auchencloich and Tamrawer, had issue), an est s:

  Sir PATRICK GRAHAM of Kincardine and Dundaff, KB; one of the hostages exchanged with the English for DAVID II; a Commr to treat with the English 30 Aug 1394; *m* 1st Matilda — and had:

  1 WILLIAM (Sir)

  1 Matilda; *m* Sir John Drummond of Concraig

  Sir PATRICK *m* 2nd Eupheme, dau of Sir John Stewart of Ralston (bro of ROBERT II, *see* MORAY, E), and *d c* 1404, having by her had:

  2 PATRICK GRAHAM (Sir), EARL OF STRATHEARN in right of his w, of Kilpont and Illieston, W Lothian; *m* by 24 Aug 1406 Eupheme, Countess Palatine of Strathearn and Countess of Caithness (*d* allegedly Oct 1415), only dau and heiress of David Stewart, 1st Earl of Strathearn of the 1371 *cr* (5th s of ROBERT II by his 2nd w Eupheme, dau of Hugh, 4th Earl of Ross), and was *k* 10 Aug 1413 by his bro-in-law Sir John Drummond of Concraig (*see* above), leaving:

    (1) MALISE GRAHAM (S), 1st EARL OF MENTEITH (S), so *cr* 6 Sept 1427 (with remainder to heirs male of his body) as compensation for being deprived of the title of Earl of Strathearn (as which he had styled himself from the date of his f's death in 1406), JAMES I having stripped him of the latter on the pretext that it was heritable only through males; *b c* 1407; imprisoned Pontefract Castle 1427–53 as hostage for payment of ransom of JAMES I; *m* 1st Janet — and had three sons; *m* 2nd Marion (*m* 2nd by 17 May 1491 John Drummond), possibly dau of Sir Colin Campbell of Glenorchy (*see* ARGYLL, D, and BREADALBANE AND HOLLAND, E), and *d* between 8 Dec 1485 and 17 May 1491, having by her had, with an er s (*d* young):

      1a Patrick; *m* 24 Jan 1465/6 Isobel, dau of 2nd Lord Erskine (*see* MAR and KELLIE, E), and *dvp* after 3 March 1481/2, leaving:

        1b ALEXANDER GRAHAM, 2nd EARL OF MENTEITH; *b c* 1472; *m* Margaret, dau of Walter Buchanan, and *d* between 27 Feb 1536/7 and 16 May 1537, leaving:

          1c WILLIAM GRAHAM, 3rd EARL OF MENTEITH; *m* by 16 June 1521 Margaret, dau of John Moubray of Barnbougle and widow of John Cornwall of Bonhard, and was allegedly *k* in a clan feud with the Tutor (*i.e.*, Guardian for a minor [of the Stewarts?]) of Appin, whose retinue had eaten up a wedding breakfast at which the 3rd EARL OF MENTEITH was a guest, this apparently constituting the *casus belli*, leaving:

            1d JOHN GRAHAM, 4th EARL OF MENTEITH, PC (S by late June 1545); captured by the English at their victory of Solway Moss 24 Nov 1542 and held prisoner till July 1543, when ransomed; one of the Lds of Congregation (anti-French, pro-Protestant body) 1558; *m c* 8 Oct 1548 Marion (*m* 2nd, as his 3rd w, 11th Earl of Sutherland, *qv*), est surv dau of 4th Lord Seton (*see* EGLINTON and WINTON, E), and *d* Jan 1564/5, leaving, with at least one other s (George, Tutor (Guardian) to his n 6th EARL) an est s:

              1e WILLIAM GRAHAM, 5th EARL OF MENTEITH, PC (S 1577/8); *m c* 16 May 1571 Margaret, dau of Sir James Douglas of Drumlanrig by his 2nd w and widow of 7th Lord Crichton of Sanquhar (*see* BUTE, M), and *d* Sept 1578, leaving an only s:

                1f JOHN GRAHAM, 6th EARL OF MENTEITH; *b c* 1573; *m c* 22 Oct 1587 Mary, 5th dau of Sir Colin Campbell of Glenorchy (*see* 1970 edn BREADALBANE AND HOLLAND, E), and *d* Dec 1598, leaving:

                  1g WILLIAM GRAHAM, 7th EARL OF MENTEITH, PC (S Jan 1626/7, E 1630); *b* after July 1589; Ld Justice Gen 1628, Extra Ld of Session 1628–33, Ld Pres Cncl Scotland 1628–33 and 1639 on; initially took steps to establish his right to the Earldom of Strathearn but waived his claim 13 Aug 1629 (though reserving one to the purely genealogical lineage and the Kilbride estate, the Crown having taken into its ownership much of the lands that had formerly gone with the Earldom of Stratearn); served heir of line to the 1st Earl thereof 25 May 1630 yet 11 June 1630 granted £3,000 (some £120,000 in late-1990s terms) for his renunciation of the claim to the Earldom and its lands; repeated the renunciation 22 Jan 1630/1 yet paradoxically it was officially ordained 31 July 1631 (following a charter of 21 July 1632) that he be in future known as 'Earl of Stratearn and Menteith etc', an action the Court of Session rescinded by depriving him of any such title as Earl of Stratearn 22 March 1633, alleging (falsely) that the 1st Earl had *dsp*, but the charter of 21 July 1632 was annulled and he *cr* instead EARL OF AIRTH (S) 21 Jan 1632/3; the reason behind these twists and turns was the strong claim of the Menteith line of descendants of ROBERT II to the throne, especially if ROBERT's descendants by his 1st wife should be shown to be illegitimate, a consideration which had increased in importance following the death of JAMES V 1542 since with him had died the sr heir male of ROBERT II; was regranted the Earldom of Menteith 11 Jan 1643/4 to himself, with remainder to his *s* and his heirs male whomsoever; *m* after 30 March 1612 Agnes, dau of 6th Lord Gray (*qv*) by his 2nd *w*, and *d* after 13 April 1661, having had:

1h John, *Lord (Graham of) Kinpont*; *b c* 1613; *m c* 11 April 1632 Mary (*d* in or after 1663, having been disordered in her wits ever since her husb's death; *see* below); est dau of 5th Earl Marischal (*see* KINTORE, E), and *dvp*, being murdered by James Stewart of Ardvoirlich 1 Sept 1644 while in the royalist camp with his distant cousin the **1st Marquess of Montrose** at Collace, Perths, leaving:

1j WILLIAM GRAHAM, 2nd EARL OF AIRTH and 8th EARL OF MENTEITH; *b c* 1634; Capt Perth Militia 1669, Commr Excise 1680; *m* 1st Nov 1661 (*divorce* 19 July 1684 on grounds of her adultery (evidence for which was tendentiously cobbled together) with Robert Ross, Yr. of Auchlossen) Anne Hewes; *m* 2nd 4 April 1685 Catherine, dau of Thomas Bruce of Blairhall, Perths, and *dsp* 12 Sept 1694, when his titles expired or became dormant

1h Margaret; *m* 1st 15 July 1633, as his 2nd *w*, Alexander, Lord Garlies, *s* of 1st Earl of Galloway (*qv*); *m* 2nd 16th Earl of Crawford (*see* CRAWFORD and BALCARRES, E)

(1) Eupheme; *m* 1st by 26 April 1425 5th Earl of Douglas; *m* 2nd *c* 25 Feb 1440/1, as his 1st *w*, 1st Lord Hamilton (*see* ABERCORN, D) and *d* autumn 1468, having had issue

(2) Elizabeth; *m* Sir John Lyon of Glamis (*see* STRATHMORE AND KINGHORNE, E) and had issue

3 Robert (Sir), of Kilpont; assassinated JAMES I at Perth 21 Feb 1437, for which executed 1437; had issue

4 David

5 Alexander

Sir PATRICK GRAHAM's est son,

Sir WILLIAM GRAHAM of Kincardine; had roy charter 12 Feb 1407 containing an entail of the lands of Old Montrose; *m* 1st allegedly Mariot, dau of Sir John Oliphant of Aberdalgy, and had:

1 Alexander; hostage 1408 in England for Murdoch, *s* of the Regent Robert, Duke of Albany; *dvp* between 14 March 1415/6 and 8 Jan 1421/2, leaving:

(1) PATRICK, **1st Lord**

(2) Alexander

(1) Catherine; *m* Sir Humphrey Moray of Ogilvy and 4th of Abercairny (*d* 1503) and had issue

2 John; living 8 Jan 1421/2

1 Elizabeth; *m* 1414 Sir John Stewart (*see* MORAY, E), illegitimate *s* of ROBERT II

Sir WILLIAM *m* 2nd 13 Nov 1413 Lady Mary Stewart (*m* 4th Sir William Edmonstone; *see* EDMONSTONE, Bt), 2nd dau of ROBERT III and widow of (a) 1st Earl of Angus (*see* HAMILTON and BRANDON, D) and (b) Sir James Kennedy of Dunure (*see* AILSA, M), and *d* 1424, having by her had, with two other sons (*d* young):

3 Robert, of Strathcarron; ancestor of the GRAHAMs of Fintry and GRAHAMs of Claverhouse

4 William; ancestor of the GRAEMEs of Garvock (*see* also 1842 edn LYNEDOCH, B)

5 Walter, of Wallacetown; ancestor of the GRAHAMs of Knockdolian

Sir WILLIAM GRAHAM's gs,

PATRICK GRAHAM, **1st Lord Graham**, so *cr* between 20 June 1432 and 28 June 1445; a Ld of Regency in minority of JAMES II; *m* Christian (*m* 2nd 1476 William Charteris of Kinfauns), yr dau of 1st Lord Erskine (*see* MAR and KELLIE, E), and *d* after 24 June 1466, having had, with other issue:

WILLIAM GRAHAM, **2nd Lord Graham**; *m* by 1460 Elene/Helen, dau of 2nd Earl of Angus (*see* HAMILTON and BRANDON, D), and *d* 1472, having had:

1 WILLIAM, **1st Earl**

2 George, of Callander; *m* Elizabeth Oliphant and was *ka* Flodden 9 Sept 1513, leaving:

(1) William, of Callander; had:

(1) John; *d c* 1597, leaving:

1a Laurence; had:

1b Agnes; *m* John Bonar of Kilgraston

1 Jean; *m* 2nd Lord Ogilvy of Airlie (*see* AIRLIE, E)

2 Christian; *m* 1st James Haldane of Gleneagles; *m* 2nd Sir Thomas Maule of Panmure

3 —; *m* Walter, 15th Of Buchanan

The 2nd LORD's er son,

WILLIAM GRAHAM, **1st Earl of Montrose**, so *cr* between 7 July and 20 Nov 1503; *b* 1463/4; *m* 1st 25 Nov 1479 Annabel, dau of John, Lord Drummond (*see* PERTH, E), and had:

1 WILLIAM, **2nd Earl**

2 Walter; ancestor of the GRAHAMs of Cairnie

The **1st Earl** *m* 2nd by 3 March 1504 Janet, dau of Sir Archibald Edmonstone (*see* EDMONSTONE, Bt), and had:

1 Margaret; *m* (contract 10 July 1510) Sir John Somerville of Cambusnettan

2 Elizabeth; *m* Feb 1513/4 Walter, Master of Drummond, gs of 1st Lord Drummond (*see* PERTH, E)

3 Helen; *m* (dispensation 13 July 1509) Humphrey Colquhoun, Yr. of Luss (*see* COLQUHOUN, Bt)

The **1st Earl** *m* 3rd by 12 July 1509 Christian, dau of Thomas Wawane of Stevinston and widow of (a) Andrew Mowbray, of Edinburgh, and (b) 5th Lord (Haliburton of) Dirletoun, and was *ka* Flodden 1513, having by her had:

3 Patrick, of Inchbrakie by charter 20 June 1513; ancestor of the GRAHAMs of Inchbrakie

4 Jean; *m* David Graham of Fintry

The 1st EARL's est son,

WILLIAM GRAHAM, **2nd Earl of Montrose**; *m* Dec 1515 Lady Janet Keith (*d c* 25 Aug 1547), dau of 2nd Earl Marischal (*see* KINTORE, E), and *d* 24 May 1571, having had:

1 Robert, *Lord Graham*; *m* Margaret (*m* 2nd Thomas, Master of Erskine, 2nd *s* of 5th Lord Erskine (*see* MAR and KELLIE, E); *m* 3rd 4th Earl of Atholl), dau of 3rd Lord Fleming, and *dvp* Battle of Pinkie 10 Sept 1547, leaving:

(1) JOHN, **3rd Earl**

2 Alexander, of Cambuskenneth; *m* Mariot, dau of 3rd Lord Seton and widow of 2nd Earl of Eglinto(u)n (*see* EGLINTON and WINTON, E), and *dsp*

3 Mungo; had charter of Rathernis, Perths, from his *f* 25 Aug 1547 and of Orchill 8 Dec 1560; *m* (contract 26 March 1571) Marjory (*m* 2nd (contract 17 Sept 1592) Sir John Maxwell, of Pollok), est dau of Sir William Edmonstone (*see* EDMONSTONE, Bt), and was ancestor of the extinct GRAHAMs of Orchill

4 William; Rector Killearn; had charter of Killearn from his *f* 7 Jan 1560

1 Margaret; *m* Robert, *Master of Erskine*, est *s* of 5th Lord Erskine (*see* MAR and KELLIE, E), and *dsp*

2 Elizabeth; *m* 4th Earl of Caithness (*qv*) and had issue

3 Agnes; *m* 15 April 1547 Sir William Murray of Tullibardine (*see* ATHOLL, D) and had issue

4 Janet; *m* 1st 28 Sept 1542 Sir Andrew Murray of Balvaird; *m* 2nd Sir Harrie Graham of Morphie and *d* Aug 1547

5 Christian; *m* 7 May 1552 Robert Graham of Knockdolian and had issue

6 Nicholas; *m* (contract 11 Feb 1539/40) her cousin John Moray, 6th of Abercairny (*ka* Battle of Pinkie 1547), and had issue

The 2nd EARL's gs,

JOHN GRAHAM, **3rd Earl of Montrose**, PC (S 1569, 1571 and March 1577/8); *b* 1548; Extrdy Ld Session 1584–86 and 1591–96, High Treas Scotland 1584–85, High Chllr Scotland Jan 1598/9–1605, Viceroy Scotland 1604; *m* (contract 24 Aug 1563) Jean (*d* March 1567/8), est dau of 2nd Lord Drummond (*see* PERTH, E), and *d* 9 Nov 1608, having had:

1 JOHN, **4th Earl**

2 **Sir William Graham, 1st Bt** (NS), so *cr* 28 Sept 1625, with remainder to his heirs male whatsoever, of Braco, Muthill, Perths; *m* Mary, dau of Sir James Edmonstone (*see* EDMONSTONE, Bt) and widow of John Cunningham of Cunninghamhead, Ayrshire, and *d* by 1636, leaving:

(1) **Sir John Graham, 2nd Bt**, of Braco; royalist Civil War; *m* Margaret, dau of Sir Dugald Campbell, 1st Bt, of Auchinbreck (*qv*), by his 1st *w*, and *d* by 1647, leaving:

1a **Sir William Graham, 3rd Bt**, of Braco; *m* Mary, dau of John Cowan of Tailzartoun, Stirling, and *d* by 1685, leaving:

1b **Sir James Graham, 4th Bt**, of Braco; *b c* 1661; *d unm*, when the btcy became dormant until assumed by the line of the Dukes of Montrose

3 Robert (Sir), of Scotstoun; *dsp* by Oct 1617

1 Lilias; *m* 1st Earl of Wigtoun and had issue

The 3rd EARL's est son,

JOHN GRAHAM, **4th Earl of Montrose**, PC (S 1604), JP (Stirlingshire 1610); *b* 1573; a Commr Treasury Scotland 1625, Pres PC Scotland March-Nov 1626; *m* (contract 12 Dec 1593) Lady Margaret Ruthven, est dau of 1st Earl of Gowrie (*see* CARLISLE, E), and *d* 14 Nov 1626, having had:

1 JAMES, **1st Marquess**

1 Lilias; *m* Sir John Colquhoun of Luss, 1st Bt (*qv*), and had issue

2 Margaret; *m* 1st Lord Napier (*see* NAPIER and ETTRICK, L) and had issue

3 Dorothea; *m* 24 April 1628, as his 1st *w*, 2nd Lord Rollo (*qv*) of Duncrub and *dsp* 16 May 1638

4 Beatrix; *m* 3rd Lord Maderty (*d* 1684) and had issue (*see* PERTH, E)

5 Katherine

The 4th EARL's only son,

JAMES GRAHAM, **1st Marquess of Montrose**, so *cr* 6 May 1644, as also EARL OF KINCARDINE and LORD GRAHAM AND MUGDOCK (all S), KG (nominated Jan 1649/50 by CHARLES II but not installed due Interregnum); *b* 1612; *educ* Glasgow and St Andrews; initially a Covenanter but imprisoned by Covenanters in Edinburgh Castle June–Nov 1641 for maintaining links with CHARLES I, at whose HQ of Oxford he arrived Aug 1643 after withdrawing from public life for a while following his release from prison; Lt-Gen royalist forces Feb 1643/4, Capt-Gen and C-in-C royalist forces Scotland from May 1645, winning against heavy odds victories of Tippermuir and Aberdeen Sept 1644, Inverlochy Feb 1644/5, Auldearn May 1645, Alford July 1645 and Kilsyth Aug 1645, following which Edinburgh and Glasgow capitulated, but defeated at Philiphaugh 13 Sept 1645; settled for a while on the Continent, where made FM by the EMPEROR FERDINAND III; returned to Scotland via the Orkneys 1649 with a scratch force of foreign troops, was defeated at Carbisdale, Ross and Cromarty, but remained at large for a while until handed over by Macleod of Assynt to the authorities, by whom he was hanged, drawn and quartered at Edinburgh 21 May 1650, his quartered remains being exposed then buried under the gallows (they were reinterred in St Giles's Cathedral 14 May 1661); author of the celebrated lines 'He either fears his fate too much/Or his deserts are small,/Who dares not put it to the touch,/To gain or lose it all.'; m c 10 Nov 1629 Lady Magdalen Carnegie, dau of 1st Earl of Southesk (see FIFE, D), and had, with two other sons and a dau:

1 John, *Earl of Kincardine; b* 1630; accompanied his f in his campaign 1645; *dvp* at the Bog of Gicht March 1645

2 JAMES GRAHAM, **2nd Marquess of Montrose**, called 'The Good', PC (S Feb 1660/1); *b* 1633; Extrdy Ld of Session 1668; *m c* Nov-Dec 1656 Isabel (*d* 16 Jan 1650), 5th dau of 7th Earl of Morton (*qv*) and widow of 1st Earl of Roxburghe (*see* ROXBURGHE, D), and *d* Feb 1669, having had:

  (1) JAMES, **3rd Marquess**

  (2) Charles; *dsp* 25 Feb 1674

  (1) Anne; *m* 3rd Earl of Callendar and had issue

  (2) Jane; *m* Jonathan Urquhart of Cromarty and had issue

  (3) Grizel; *m* William, yr bro of 2nd Earl of Dundonald (*qv*), and *d* 30 June 1726, leaving issue

The 2nd MARQUESS's er son,

JAMES GRAHAM, **3rd Marquess of Montrose**, PC (S 1678); *b* 20 Oct 1657; *educ* Glasgow U; Pres PC Scotland 1682–84; *m* (articles 9 June 1681) Christian (*m* 2nd May 1687 Sir John Bruce, 2nd Bt, of Balcaskie and Kinross, and *d* 21 April 1710), dau of Duke of Rothes (*see* ROTHES, E), and *d* 25 April 1684, leaving an only s:

JAMES GRAHAM, **1st Duke of Montrose**, so *cr* 24 April 1707, as also MARQUESS OF GRAHAM and BUCHANAN, EARL OF KINCARDINE, VISCOUNT OF DUNDAFF and LORD ABERUTHVEN, MUGDOCK AND FINTRY, PC (S 1707 and GB 1717); *b* 1682; Commr Treasury Scotland 1705–07, High Adml Scotland 1705–06, Pres PC Scotland 1706, Ld Privy Seal Scotland 1709–13, Pncpl Sec State Scotland 1714, rep S peer 1707–10 and 1715–34; regranted Marquessate of Montrose 5 Aug 1706 with remainder to heirs female and of nomination (the + against living females and their issue hereafter referring to their status as in remainder to this title alone of all those borne by the Dukes of Montrose); *m* (contract 31 March 1702) Christian (*d* 25 May 1744), dau of 3rd Earl of Northesk (*qv*), and *d* 7 Jan 1742, having had, with an est s (*d* an infant):

1 DAVID GRAHAM, **1st Earl Graham**, so *cr vp* 23 May 1722, as also BARON GRAHAM OF BELFORD, Co Northumberland (both GB), with remainder to his bros; *b* 8 June 1705; *educ* Eton; *dvp* unm 30 Sept 1731

2 WILLIAM, **2nd Duke**

3 George; MP Stirling; *b* 26 Sept 1715; Capt RN; *d* unm 2 Jan 1747

The 1st DUKE's er surv son,

WILLIAM GRAHAM, **2nd Duke of Montrose**; *b* 27 Aug 1712; *educ* Eton; *m* 28 Oct 1742 Lucy (*d* 18 June 1788), dau of 2nd Duke of Rutland (*qv*), and *d* 23 Sept 1790, having had:

1 JAMES, **3rd Duke**

1 Lucy; *b* 28 July 1751; *m* 13 July 1771, as his 1st w, Archibald, 1st Baron Douglas of Douglas (*see* HAMILTON and BRANDON, D), and *d* 13 Feb 1780, leaving issue

The 2nd DUKE's only son,

JAMES GRAHAM, **3rd Duke of Montrose**, KG (1812), KT (1793–1812), PC (1789); *b* 8 Sept 1755; *educ* Eton and Trin Coll Cambridge; MP (Tory) Richmond 1780–84 and Gt Bedwyn 1784–90, a Ld Treasury 1783–89, V-Pres BOT 1789–90, Master of the Horse 1790–95 and 1807–21, Jt Paymaster-Gen 1791–1800, a Commr Indian Affrs 1791–1803, Ld Justice Gen Scotland 1795–1836, Pres BOT and Jt PMG 1804–06, Ld Lt: Hunts 1790–93, Stirlingshire 1794–1836 and Dunbartonshire 1813–36, Ld Chamberlain 1821–27 and 1828–30, Capt-Gen Roy Co Archers 1824–30, Chllr Glasgow U; *m* 1st 3 March 1785 Jemima Elizabeth (*d* 17 Sept 1786), dau of 2nd Earl of Ashburnham (*see* 1924 edn), and had a s (*d* in infancy); *m* 2nd 24 July 1790 Lady Caroline Maria Montagu (*d* 25 March 1847), dau of 4th Duke of Manchester (*qv*), and *d* 30 Dec 1836, having by her had:

1 JAMES, **4th Duke**

2 Montagu William; *b* 2 Feb 1807; Capt Coldstream Gds; MP Grantham and Hereford; *m* 14 Feb 1867 Harriet Anne (*d* 18 April 1884), est dau of 1st Baron Bateman (*see* 1931 edn) and widow of George Astley Charles Dashwood (*see* DASHWOOD, Bt, of Kirtlington Park), and *dsp* 21 June 1878

1 Georgiana Charlotte; *m* 26 July 1814 10th Earl of Winchilsea and (5th Earl of) Nottingham (*qv*) and *d* 13 Feb 1835, leaving issue

2 Caroline; *d* unm 24 March 1875

3 Lucy; *m* 9 Feb 1818 2nd Earl of Powis (*qv*) and *d* 16 Sept 1875, leaving issue

4 Emily; *m* 16 Aug 1832 Edward Thomas Foley (*see* FOLEY, B) and *dsp* 1 Jan 1900

The 3rd DUKE's er son,

JAMES GRAHAM, **4th Duke of Montrose**, KT (1845), PC (1821); *b* 16 July 1799; *educ* Eton and Trin Coll Cambridge; V-Chamberlain Household 1821–27, MP (Tory) Cambridge 1825–32, Commr Indian Affrs 1828–30, Ld Lt Stirlingshire 1843–74, Ld Steward Household 1852–53, Chllr Duchy Lancaster 1858–59, PMG 1866–68, Maj-Gen Roy Co Archers; *m* 15 Oct 1836 Caroline Agnes (*m* 2nd 22 Jan 1876 William Stuart Stirling-Crawfurd of Milton (*d* 23 Feb 1883); *m* 3rd 26 July 1888 Marcus Henry Milner (*see* MILNER, Bt) and *d* 16 Nov 1894), yst dau of 2nd Baron Decies (*qv*), and *d* 30 Dec 1874, having had:

1 James John, *Marquess of Graham; b* 7 Feb 1845; *d* 31 Jan 1846

2 James, *Marquess of Graham; b* 22 June 1847; Lt 1st Life Gds; *d* unm 3 April 1872

3 DOUGLAS BERESFORD MALISE RONALD, **5th Duke**

1 Agnes Caroline; *m* 15 Sept 1759 Lt-Col John Murray, Gren Gds (*d* 11 Aug 1903), of Touchadam and Polmaise, Stirling, and *dsp* 8 May 1873

2 Beatrice Violet; *m* 15 Dec 1863 2nd Baron Greville (*d* 2 Dec 1909; *see* 1970 edn) and *d* 29 Feb 1932, having had issue

3 Alma Imogen Leonora Carlotta, DGStJ; *m* 27 July 1872 7th Earl of Breadalbane and Holland (*qv*) and *dsp* 10 May 1932

The 4th DUKE's only surv son,

DOUGLAS BERESFORD MALISE RONALD GRAHAM, **5th Duke of Montrose**, KT (1879); *b* 7 Nov 1852; *educ* Eton; Lt Coldstream Gds 1872–74 and 5th Lancers 1874–78, Gen Roy Co Archers, Ld Lt Stirlingshire 1885–1925, Ld Clerk Register Scotland 1890–1925, Hon Brig-Gen, Col Cmdt 3rd Bn Argyll & Sutherland Highrs, Col Lanarks Yeo Cav, Chllr Order Thistle 1921–25, Militia ADC to TM QUEEN VICTORIA, EDWARD VII and GEORGE V, served Boer War and WW I, Ld HC Gen Assembly Ch Scotland 1916; *m* 24 July 1876 Violet Hermione, GBE (1918), JP (Stirling), Hon LLD Glasgow (*d* 21 Nov 1940), 2nd dau of Sir Frederic Graham, 3rd Bt, of Netherby (*qv*), and *d* Dec 1925, having had:

1 JAMES, **6th Duke**

2 (Douglas) Malise, CB (1936), DSO (1917), MC (1915); *b* 14 Oct 1883; *educ* Cheltenham and RMA Woolwich; ADC WW I (despatches), Assist Dir Artillery WO 1931, T/Brig and Cmdt Sch Artillery 1934–36, Mil Attaché Paris 1940, Mil Liaison Offr to Regnl Commr Western Cmd 1942–45; *m* 29 July 1919 Hon Rachael Mary Holland (*d* 6 June 1977), 2nd dau of 2nd Viscount Knutsford (*qv*), and *d* 20 Nov 1974, leaving:

  (1) +Ivar Malise [Ivar Graham Esq, The Glen, Coombe Kea, Truro, Cornwall]; *b* 11 Aug 1920; *educ* Eton and Trin Coll Cambridge (BA 1947, MA 1950), Archives Diploma (Lond) 1949; Assist Archivist Herts CC 1948–50, Middx CC 1950–55, Archivist to Govts of N Rhodesia and Zambia 1955–65, Ch Asst Archivist Herts CC 1965–; *m* 1 Aug 1958 (*divorce* 1973) Isabel Mary, yst dau of C B Ewart, of Limpsfield, Surrey, and formerly w of A W Carpenter, and has:

    1a +Alistair David; *b* 1 Oct 1959

    1a +Lucy Helen; *b* 1 Feb 1963; *m* 4 Jan 1997 *Jeremy Charles Hawes, s of John Hawes, of New Yatt, Oxon

  (2) +Euan Douglas, CB (1985); *b* 29 July 1924; *educ* Eton and Ch Ch Oxford (MA); *m* 1st 3 June 1953 (*divorce* 1972) Pauline Laetitia, est dau of Hon David Pax Tennant (*see* GLENCONNER, B) and formerly w of Capt Julian Lane-Fox-Pitt-Rivers, and adopted:

    *Andrew Douglas; *b* 13 May 1964

  (2) (cont.) Euan Graham *m* 2nd 1972 *Caroline Esther, dau of Sheriff W B Middleton, of Ledwell, Oxon, and by her has:

    1a +Sarah Caroline; *b* 1973

    2a +Alexandra Katherine; *b* 1976

3 Alastair Mungo; *b* 12 May 1886; Capt RN WW I (wounded); *m* 1st 4 May 1916 Lady Meriel Olivia Bathurst (*d* 18 Jan 1936), only dau of 7th Earl Bathurst (*qv*), and *d* 1976, leaving:

  (1) +Ian James [Ian Graham Esq, Chantry Farm, Campsey Ash, Suffolk IP13 0PZ]; *b* 12 Nov 1923; *educ* Winchester and Trin Coll Dublin (BA 1951); RNVR 1943–47 (Sub-Lt 1945–47), Assist Curator Peabody Museum Harvard, Mass.

  (2) +Robin Angus [Robin Graham Esq, Stone Farm, Blaxhall, Woodbridge, Suffolk IP12 2DF]; *b* 27 Nov 1926; *educ* Winchester, Trin Coll Cambridge and Exeter U

  (1) +Lilias Violet, MBE [Miss Lilias Graham MBE, 68 High St, Dunblane, FK15 0AY]; *b* 6 March 1917

  (2) +Margaret Christina [Mrs Thomas Campbell-Preston, 1 Bishop's Way, Stradbroke, Suffolk IP21 5JR]; *b* 3 July 1919; *m* 18 June 1960 *Maj Thomas Colin Ernest Campbell-Preston, MC, TD, Argyll and Sutherland Highrs, yst s of Col Robert William Pigott Clarke Campbell-Preston, JP, DL, of Ardchattan Priory, Connel, Argyllshire, and adopted:

    *Patrick [Patrick Campbell-Preston Esq, 123 Ross St, Cambridge CB1 3BS]; *b* 6 May 1964; *educ* Eton and Trin Coll Cambridge

3 (cont.) Lord Alastair Graham *m* 2nd 24 Oct 1944 Sheelah Violet Edgeworth (*d* 1985), dau of Essex Edgeworth Reade and Sheelah, Lady Ruggles-Brise (*see* RUGGLES-BRISE, Bt), and *d* 1976

1 Helen Violet, DCVO; *b* 1 July 1879; Woman Bedchamber to HM QUEEN MARY; Pres YWCA of GB; *d* unm 27 Aug 1945

2 Hermione Emily; *b* 22 Feb 1882; *m* 29 March 1906 Col Sir Donald Walter Cameron of Lochiel (*d* 11 Oct 1951), 25th Chief of Clan Cameron, and had issue

The 5th DUKE's est son,

JAMES GRAHAM, **6th Duke of Montrose**, KT (1947), CB (1911), CVO (1905), VD, JP (Bute), JP and DL (Stirlingshire); *b* 1 May 1878; *educ* Eton; Cdre RNVR, Lt 5th Vol Bn Roy Highrs, Lt ASC Boer War 1900, attd Naval Bde WW I; ADC to HM GEORGE V 1919–22, Ld Lt Bute 1920–53, Assist Priv Sec to Chllr Exchequer 1905, Chm Scots Nat Party 1924–34, Ldr Scottish Trade Mission Canada 1932, Ld High Commr Gen Assembly Ch Scotland 1942 and 1943, memb Roy Co Archers, Yr Bro Trin House, Pres: BIME 1911–12, Jr Inst Engrs 1914–16, Scottish Travel and Tourist Assoc, Hon Treasurer Incorpn Master Mariners, Treasurer RNLI GB 1947, V-Pres Inst Naval Architects, Cdre Sea Cadets Scotland 1940–41, Hon LLD Glasgow U; *m* 14 June 1906 Lady Mary Louise Douglas Hamilton (*see* HAMILTON and BRANDON, D) and *d* 20 Jan 1954, having had:

1 JAMES ANGUS, **7th Duke**

2 Ronald Malise Hamilton, JP (St Ann Parish Jamaica 1961); *b* 20 Sept 1912; *educ* Stowe and Trin Coll Cambridge; Lt-Cdr RNVR, SBStJ; *m* 16 Sept 1938 Nancy Edith, dau of Edgar Morris Baker, of Dawlish, Devon, and formerly w of Dudley Claude Douglas Ryder (*see* HARROWBY, E), and *dsp* 11 June 1978

1 +Mary Helen Alma [The Lady Mary Dunn, 8 Wheatfield Road, Ayr]; *b* 11 April 1909; *m* 1st 21 April 1931 Maj John Perceval Townshend Boscawen and has issue (*see* FALMOUTH, V); *m* 2nd 15 Dec 1975 Brig Leslie Colville Dunn, TD, DL (*d* 1990)

2 Jean Sibyl Violet, DL (Ayr and Arran); *b* 7 Nov 1920; *m* 8 Oct 1947 (*divorce* 1957) Col John Patrick Ilbert Fforde, Commr Police N Rhodesia, yr s of Maj Charles Annesley Wilbraham Fford, IA, and *d* 1993, leaving:

  (1) +Charles John Graham; *b* 4 Nov 1948; *educ* RAC Cirencester

The 6th DUKE's er son,

JAMES ANGUS GRAHAM, **7th Duke of Montrose**; *b* 2 May 1907; *educ* Eton and Ch Ch Oxford (MA 1964); Lt-Col RNVR; MP Hartley-Gatooma Fedl Parl Rhodesia and Nyasaland 1958–62, Min Ag and Lands S Rhodesia 1962–63, Rhodesia (under UDI): Min Ag 1964–65, Min External Affrs and Def 1966–68; *m* 1st 20 Oct 1930 (*divorce* 1950) Isobel Veronica, BA (*d* 1990), yr dau of Lt-Col Thomas Byrne Sellar, CMG, DSO, and had:

1 JAMES GRAHAM, **8th and present Duke of Montrose**
1 +Fiona Mary [The Lady Fiona Hannon, The Fort House, Dundooan, Coleraine, Co Derry BT52 2PX]; *b* 1 Jan 1932; author: *The Castle Kitchen* (cook book 1994); *m* 1 Oct 1966 *Peter Alexander O'Brien Hannon, 2nd s of Ven Archdeacon Gordon Hannon, of Ardreigh House, Cultra, Co Down, and has:
(1) +Catherine Mary; *b* 15 July 1968; *m* 1991 *Mark Tremayne Boobbyer (*see* RENNELL, B) and has issue
(2) +Veronica Maeve; *b* 12 Aug 1971; *m* 1992 *Jasper E Bark, s of Roy Bark, of Dalton-in-Furness, Cumbria

The **7th Duke** *m* 2nd 17 April 1952 *Susan Mary Jocelyn [Her Grace The Dowager Duchess of Montrose, Nether Tillyrie, Milnathort, Kinross-Shire KY13 7RW], dau of Dr John Mervyn Semple, of Gilgil, Kenya (by Anne Gladys, est dau of David Miller Steen, barrister, of Mountsandel, Carrickmines, Co Dublin, and widow of Lt Arthur George Cronhelm), and widow of Michael Raleigh Gibbs, of Nakuru, Kenya, and *d* 1992, having by her had:
2 +Donald Alasdair [The Lord Donald Graham, Nether Tillyrie, Milnathort, Kinross-shire KY13 7RW]; *b* 28 Oct 1956; *educ* St Andrew's Grahamstown S Africa, St Andrews U Scotland (BSc) and INSEAD (MBA); *m* 1981 his 2nd cousin *Bride Donalda Elspeth, yst dau of Maj Allan John Cameron, of Allangrange, Ross and Cromarty, and has had:
(1) Alasdair John Cameron; *b* 1986; *d* 1988
(1) +Caitriana Mary Alice; *b* 1984
(2) +Violet Elizabeth Helen; *b* 1992
(3) +Jennie Alexandra Cameron; *b* 1993
3 +Calum Ian [The Lord Colum Graham, Montrose Estate, Drymen, Glasgow G63 0BQ]; *b* 22 July 1958; *educ* St Andrew's Grahamstown, Cape Town U (BSc) and INSEAD (MBA); *m* 1991 *Catherine Beatrice, yst dau of John Peter Fraser-Mackenzie (*see* SCOTT, Bt, of Witley), and has:
(1) +Iain Angus; *b* 21 Feb 1995
(2) +Euan Douglas; *b* 24 May 1996
2 +Cairistiona (Kirstie) Anne [The Lady Kirstie Saggers, 42 Cook St, Randwick, NSW 2031, Australia]; *b* 7 Jan 1955; *educ* Ruskin Sch of Fine Art Oxford; *m* 1982 *Philip Patrick Saggers, son of Gordon F Saggers, of NSW, and has:
(1) +Susanna Mary; *b* 1984
(2) +Marina Lilias; *b* 1986
(3) +Georgina Frances; *b* 1989
3 +Lilias Catriona Maighearad [The Lady Lilias Bell, c/o Ngaiana, Masterton, New Zealand]; *b* 16 Feb 1960; *educ* St Andrews U; *m* 1990 *Jonathan Dillon Bell and has issue (*see* BORTHWICK, Bt)

MOON of Copsewood

VINCIT · OMNIA · VERITAS

Arms: Arg. an eagle displayed gu. and two flaunches of the last, each charged with a fleur-de-lys of the field, on a chief of the second three crescents of the first. **Crest:** A demi-eagle displayed gu., in front thereof a fleur-de-lys arg. and charged on the breast with an escutcheon of the last, thereon a crescent also gu.
Motto: *Vincit omnia veritas* ('Truth conquers everything').
Creation: Bt. (UK) 22 July 1887.

SIR ROGER MOON, 6TH BT, of Copsewood, Stoke, Co Warwick [Sir Roger Moon Bt, The Barn House, Wykey, Ruyton XI Towns, Salop SY4 1JA]; *b* 17 Nov 1914; *s* bro 1988; *educ* Sedbergh; served with Johore Vol Engrs in Malaya and Singapore, POW in Thailand 1942–45; coffee planter Kenya 1933–35, rubber planter Malaya 1939–41 and 1946–63, Oil Palm Planter Malaya 1963–67; *m* 16 Dec 1950 *Meg, yr dau of Arthur Mainwaring Maxwell, DSO, MC, of Moss Vale, NSW, and gdau of Maj-Gen Sir William Throsby Bridges, KCB, CMG, fndr AIF, and has:
1 *Sarah Corinna; *b* 14 Oct 1951
2 *Gillian Adèle; *b* 21 Aug 1954; *m* 1986 *William Andrew Johnston, yr s of Brian Johnston, CBE, and has:
(1) *Harry Edward Duff; *b* 1987
(1) *Emily Rose; *b* 1988
(2) *Georgia Grace; *b* 1990

3 *Patricia Isolda [Mrs Peter Hogg, House 6, Pacific View, 22 Cape Rd, Hong Hom Kok, Hong Kong]; *b* 12 Sept 1955; *m* 1982 *Peter W A Hogg, only s of Lt-Col A G Hogg, OBE, of Ibthorpe House, Hurstbourne Tarrant, Hants, and has:
(1) *Anthony Oliver Richard; *b* 1985
(1) *Camilla Adèle; *b* 1983
(2) *Arabella Louisa Daphne; *b* 1987

Lineage: This family was settled at Newsham, Woodplumpton, Lancs, *temp* ELIZABETH I.
ROBERT MOON, of Catterall; *m* wife Ann, dau of Rev James Fisher, Rector Garstang, and had:
1 James; gf of:
(1) Anna; *m* Hercules Scott, of Brotherton, Forfarshire, and had:
1a Edward; Liverpool merchant; *dsps* 10 Aug 1880
2 RICHARD
3 Edward
4 John; had issue
5 William; had issue
6 Henry; *k* unm Lisbon 1826
1 Isabella; *m* Samuel Martin

The 2nd s,
RICHARD MOON; Liverpool merchant; *b* 1783; *m* 1808 Elizabeth, dau of William B Frodsham, and *d* 1842, leaving:
1 RICHARD (Sir), **1st Bt**
2 Robert; barrister Inner Temple 1844; *b* 7 July 1817; *educ* Queens' Coll Cambridge (BA 1838, MA 1841, Hon Fell); *m* 1857 Mary Jane (*d* 12 Nov 1932 aged 101), dau of Robert Pacy, of Rio de Janeiro and Liverpool, and *d* April 1889, having had:
(1) Edward Robert Pacy; *b* 4 Feb 1858; *educ* Winchester and New Coll Oxford (MA); barrister Inner Temple 1884, MP N St Pancras 1895–1906, V-Pres Br and For Bible Soc and CMS; *m* 21 Nov 1900 Frideswide, OStJ (*d* 5 April 1951), yst dau of Sir Arthur Kekewich, PC, Judge High Court, and *dsp* 11 Sept 1949
(2) Arnold William; *b* 26 July 1859; *educ* Oriel Coll Oxford (MA); Capt W India Regt; *d* unm 14 Oct 1921
(3) Robert Oswald, JP London; *b* 17 March 1865; *educ* Winchester and New Coll Oxford (MA, MD); Maj RAMC WW I, FRCP; *m* 8 July 1901 Ethel Rose Grant (*d* 6 Oct 1933), 3rd dau of Gen — Waddington, and *d* 28 July 1953, leaving a son and three daus
(1) Eliza Rosalie; *d* unm 1886
(2) Constance Mary; *m* 10 July 1889 Rev Charles Moor, DD Oxon, FSA, FRHistS, Canon Lincoln, and had issue
(3) Mary Jane; *m* 9 July 1890 11th Earl Ferrers (*qv*) and *d* 10 Jan 1944, leaving issue
1 Eliza Ann; *m* 4 Oct 1836 Ralph Brocklebank, DL, JP, of Childwall Hall, Lancs, and *d* 26 Jan 1885, leaving issue. He *d* 2 Feb 1892
2 Anne Jane; *m* 20 Feb 1844 Walter Fergus MacGregor and *d* 26 March 1892, leaving issue. He *d* 11 June 1863
3 Isabella; *m* W B Aspinall
4 Mary Elizabeth; *m* James Templeton Wood, barrister, and had issue
5 Alice Mary; *m* Rev William D Lamb

The er son,
Sir Richard Moon, 1st Bt (UK), so *cr* 22 July 1887, of Copsewood Grange, Co Warwick; *b* 23 Sept 1814; Chm LNWR 1861–91; *m* 27 Aug 1840 Eleanor (*d* 31 Jan 1891), yst dau of John Brocklebank, of Hazelholm, Cumberland, and *d* 17 Nov 1899, having had, with another s and a dau (both *d* unm):
1 Edward, of Cassiobury, Watford, Herts; *b* 4 June 1841; *m* 25 Sept 1866 Jessie (*d* 19 Jan 1918), dau of Benjamin Darbyshire, of Kenyon Mount, Cheshire, and *dvp* 12 April 1893, leaving:
(1) **Sir Cecil Ernest Moon, 2nd Bt**; *b* 2 Sept 1867; *m* 1st 1888 (*divorce* USA 1910) Kate, dau of P Grattan Lawder, of The Grove, Co Wicklow; *m* 2nd 8 June 1912 Lilian Mary (*d* 20 Sept 1950), widow of Dr W James Preston, of Mosborough, Derbys, and 2nd dau of Rev B S Darbyshire, of Birkdale, Lancs, and *dsp* 22 Feb 1951
(2) Lawrence Darbyshire; *b* 10 Sept, *d* 18 Nov 1869
(3) Hubert Charles; *b* 21 April 1871; *k* by enemy action Sept 1940
(1) Muriel Eleanor; *b* 11 Oct 1873; *d* unm 16 March 1954
2 Richard, JP, of Pen-y-voel House, Llanymynech, Salop; *b* 14 July 1843; *m* 9 Sept 1868 Sarah (*d* 18 Nov 1928), dau of Edward Hugh Blakeney, MD, Staff Surgn, and gn of FM Sir Edward Blakeney, GCB, PC, and *d* 9 Sept 1922, having had, with other issue:
(1) Reginald Blakeney; *b* 9 April 1873; *m* 1900 Lucy Annie (*d* 1 March 1935), dau of Joseph Edward Crowther, of Huddersfield, and *d* 17 Feb 1927, leaving:
1a **Sir Richard Moon, 3rd Bt**; *b* 12 April 1901; *educ* Shrewsbury; *m* 1st 2 Jan 1929 (*divorce* 1954) Bertha Mae, dau of J H Edward, Mayor Govan, Saskatchewan, and had:
1b Lucy Beverly; *b* 23 Nov 1929; *m* 26 May 1952 John Douglas McPhail, yst s of Alfred Donald McPhail, of Oregon, and had:
1c *Suzanne Beverley; *b* 15 Jan 1962
2c *Barbara Robin; *b* 12 Sept 1963
2b *Lila Colleen [Mrs George Little, 4132 Balkan Street, Vancouver 10, BC, Canada]; *b* 17 Nov 1931; *m* 30 June 1953 George Garroway Little (*d* 1992), only s of Robert Little of Vancouver, and has:
1c *Gregory Robert; *b* 19 April 1959
1c *Sharon Colleen; *b* 14 Dec 1961
1a (cont.) **Sir Richard** *m* 2nd 19 Oct 1954 *Mary Gertrude, dau of Herbert E Waggoner, of Bowen, Ill., and *dspm* 23 Feb 1961
2a Joseph Edward; *b* 10 March 1904; *m* 16 Nov 1932 *Joan Anges Rea and *dsp* 18 July 1958
3a **Sir John Arthur Moon, 4th Bt**; *b* 27 Oct 1905; *educ* Cottesmore Sch; Master Merchant Navy, Roy Humane Soc's Bronze Medal; *m* 6 Dec 1939 Renée

Henriette Maria Dolores (d 6 Jan 1949), only dau of Joseph Amedée Amedet, of Le Mans, France, and d 2 Feb 1979

4a Robert Blakeney; b 3 March 1908; T/Maj RASC, 2nd Lt 89th (W Lancashire) Field Bde RA (TA) WW II (despatches); m 1st 7 March 1936 (divorce 1941) Margaret, est dau of W H Law, of West Kirby; m 2nd 24 Oct 1945 (divorce 1968) Helen Everard Collier, dau of Col Charles Henry Willey, VD, MD, CM, DSc, RE; m 3rd 2 Nov 1968 *Dorothy Mary, dau of Walter Hill, of Sheffield

(2) Jasper; b 17 Oct 1881; m 19 April 1910 Isabel (d 8 April 1961), yst dau of Edward Logan, of Upton, Chester, and d 26 Feb 1975, leaving issue

1a **Sir Edward Moon, 5th Bt**; b 23 Feb 1911; educ Sedburgh; Maj KAR WW II and Kenya 1934–62; m 23 April 1947 *Mary [Mary Lady Moon, Heath House, Crickheath, Oswestry, Salop SY10 8BN], only child of Capt B D Conolly, RAMC, and dsp 1988

2a Sir ROGER MOON, **6th and present Bt**

3a +HUMPHREY [Humphrey Moon Esq, 22 Brewitt Rd, Estcourt, Natal, S Africa]; b 9 Oct 1919; heir presumptive; Capt; m 1st 1955 (divorce 1964) Diana Marion, dau of F Basil Hobson, of The Homestead, Freshwater Bay, IoW, and has:

1b *Susan Caroline; b 1957

2b *Vicki Georgina; b 1960

3a (cont.) HUMPHREY MOON m 2nd 1964 Elizabeth Anne Drummond (d 1994), widow of Henry James Butler, of Lusaka, and dau of George Archibald Drummond Angus, of Pietermaritzburg, Natal, and by her has:

3b *Jennifer Claire; b 22 Feb 1966

1a *Ursula [Mrs Peter Joscelyne, White Rock, Llanymynech, Montgomeryshire]; b 1912; m 9 Aug 1945 Peter Harry Joscelyne (d 1958), est s of Dr F P Joscelyne, of Shallowpool, nr Looe, and has had:

1b Hugh Anthony; b 1947; d 1990

2b *Nigel Townshend; b 1949

2a *Mary [Miss Mary Moon, White Rock, Llanymynech, Montgomeryshire]; b 1913

3a *Gwyneth Elinor [Miss Gwyneth Moon, White Rock, Llanymynech, Montgomeryshire]; b 1916

(1) Cicely; m 4 June 1913 Raoul Hector Fôa, of Holywell Park, Wrotham, Kent, and dsp 19 March 1963. He d 2 May 1935

(2) Sarah Katherine; m 5 Aug 1903 Cecil Everard Haines and d 28 Sept 1954 leaving issue. He d 18 May 1935

(3) Morfydd

3 Ernest Robert (Sir), KCB, KC (1902); b 21 June 1854; educ Trin Coll Cambridge (LLB); barrister Inner Temple 1878, Bencher 1910, Counsel to Speaker H of C 1907; m 9 Aug 1881 Emma Henrietta Penelope (d 16 Dec 1947), dau of J de Villers Lamb, of Sydney, NSW, and d 31 May 1930, leaving:

(1) Arthur, MC, KC (1928); b 1882; educ Eton and New Coll Oxford (BA 1906); barrister Inner Temple 1907, Bencher 1935, Capt London Regt WW I, Chm Gen Claims Tbnl 1945; m 11 April 1912 Marjorie Isabel (d 15 Nov 1966), est dau of Charles Lancelot Andrews Skinner (see BESSBOROUGH, E), and d 4 April 1961, leaving:

1a John Richard Philip, OBE (1966); b 30 Jan 1915; educ Eton and New Coll Oxford (BA 1936, MA 1949); Lt Black Watch WW II, Registrar RCA; m 25 May 1945 *Ann (m 2nd 1980 W A Beare, of Ledgeland, St Margaret's Bay), dau of R P Melhuish, of White Cliffe, St Margaret's Bay, and d 1978, having had:

1b +Richard; b 8 Jan 1954; educ Westminster

1b *Susan Katharine [Mrs George Keelan, The Stables, Cargill, Perth]; b 25 Jan 1947; m 1st 1969 (divorce 1980) Cameron Murray and has:

1c *Jamie; b 1972

1c *Pollyanna; b 1973

1b (cont.) Mrs Susan Murray m 2nd 1980 *Lt-Col George Douglas Birdwood Keelan

2b *Elizabeth Anne [Mrs Matthew Gloag, Hillockhead, Airlie, Angus]; b 28 Jan 1949; m 1971 *Matthew Gloag and has:

1c *Emma; b 1972

2c *Sorcha Ann; b 1974

3b *Sarah [Mrs Peter Cutts, Yewtree Cottage, Foster Green, Biddenham, Kent TN7 8ER]; b 12 July 1956; m 1989 *Peter Cutts and has:

1b *Richard Adam Moon; b 1991

2b *Alexander Charles Famin; b 1992

1a *Penelope Kathleen [Countess Thomas Lubienski, 60 Thorpe Rd, Peterborough PE3 6BZ]; b 5 March 1924; m 9 Sept 1950 *(Count) Thomas Andreas Constantine Lubienski, only child of Count Michael Lubienski, of Ealing, and has:

1b *Andrew; b 26 Oct 1952; educ Stonyhurst; m 1990 *Louise King

2b *Henry Roger; b 24 April 1960; m 1991 *Petra Limberg and has:

1c *Jonathon; b 1991

1c *Helen; b 1993

3b *Michael Arthur; b 11 Nov 1962

1b *Clare Barbara; b 1 Aug 1955; m 1988 *Christopher Hamilton and has:

1c *Patrick Thomas; b 1989

2c *Alex; b 1992

2a *Christine Marjorie [Mrs John Watson, The Red House, Hambledon, Hants PO7 6RX]; b 9 Sept 1925; m 2 Nov 1962 Lt-Cdr John Bertram Watson, RN (ret), only s of V-Adml Bertram Chalmers Watson, CB, DSO, of The Court House, Hambledon, Hants, and has:

1b *Robin Bertram Stephen; b 1967

2b *Rupert Philip; b 1971

1b *Rosamund Isobel; b 1965

(2) Basil Oliver; b 1884; 2nd Lt PO Rifles London Regt; ka 24 May 1915

(1) Edith May; d unm 17 Dec 1947

MOON of Portman Square

Arms: Arg. an eagle displayed gu., charged on the breast with two swords in saltire ppr., on a chief nebuly az. a fasces erect or between two crescents arg. **Crest:** A crescent arg. in front of a fasces in bend or, surmounting a sword in bend sinister ppr. **Motto:** *Æquam servare mentem* ('Keeping a calm mind'). **Creation:** Bt. (UK) 4 May 1855.

SIR PETER WILFRED GILES GRAHAM MOON, 5TH BT, of Portman Square, London [Sir Peter Moon Bt, c/o The Red Lion, Bradenham, Bucks]; b 24 Oct 1942; s f 1954; educ Lancing; md Riton Inns Ltd, chm Trans Continental Corp 1990–; memb Brit Inst Innkeepers; m 1st 21 April 1967 (divorce 1992) Sarah Gillian, est dau of Lt-Col Michael Carson Lyndon Smith, MC (see SMITH, Bt, of Stratford Place), and formerly w of Maj Antony Gibbon Chater, 9th/12th Roy Lancers, and has:

1 +RUPERT FRANCIS WILFRED GRAHAM; b 29 April 1968; educ Marlborough and Exeter U

2 +Thomas Edward Bradshaw; b 19 Feb 1972; educ Dean Close, Cheltenham

Sir PETER m 2nd 1993 *Mrs Terry Lynn de Vries, dau of W Coetzee, of Brackenfell, Cape Town

Lineage: CHRISTOPHER MOON; had:

Sir Francis Graham Moon, 1st Bt (UK), so cr 4 May 1855, JP, DL; b 28 Oct 1796; Sheriff City London 1843, Alderman 1844, Ld Mayor 1854–55, Chev Legn Hon; m 28 Oct 1818 Anne (d 24 May 1870), dau of John Chancellor, of Kensington, and had, with other issue:

1 EDWARD GRAHAM (Sir), **2nd Bt**

2 John Francis, JP Middx; b 31 Dec 1826; Lt City London; d 1 July 1915

1 Mary Anne; m 28 Dec 1844 William Butler Langmore and d 3 Sept 1900, leaving issue. He d 1893

2 Ellen; m 1847 William Bosville James and d 17 Aug 1897, leaving issue. He d 1885

3 Louisa; m 6 Sept 1846 John Andrew Clarke and d 16 June 1903, leaving issue. He d 1882

Sir FRANCIS d 13 Oct 1871; his est son,

Rev Sir Edward Graham Moon, 2nd Bt; b 25 March 1825; MA Oxon, Rector Fetcham, Surrey; m 3 July 1851 Ellen (d 29 Sept 1906), only child of Thomas Sidney, of Leyton House, Essex, Alderman London, MP Stafford, and d 21 Feb 1904, having had:

1 Edward Sidney Moon; d in infancy

2 **Sir Francis Sidney Graham Moon, 3rd Bt**; b 4 May 1855; Maj and Hon Lt-Col 4th Bn E Surrey Regt Boer War 1902 (Queen's medal with two clasps); d unm 30 Jan 1911

3 Arthur Graham; b 16 Jan 1857; d unm 1 Aug 1895

4 Wilfred Graham; b 17 Sept 1864; Maj Seaforth Highrs, served Hazara 1888 and 1891, Chitral 1895, Boer War 1899–1902; m 1 March 1892 Mary Frances (d 14 Nov 1946, having m 2nd 7 July 1910 Col Arthur Lionel Crisp Clarke, DSO, who d 15 Feb 1935), dau of Gen Sir Alexander Frederick Bradshaw, KCB, and d 14 April 1909, leaving:

(1) ARTHUR WILFRED GRAHAM (Sir), **4th Bt**

(1) Muriel Doris; m 1st 1920 (divorce 1936) Capt Richard Michael Trevethan, MC; m 2nd 1936 (divorce 1949) W F B McLellan and had issue

(2) *Evelyn Lorna Elliot; m 1st 31 May 1928 (divorce 1933) Edward Sydney Hogg, s of J S Hogg, of Westhouse, Pinner; m 2nd 20 July 1939 (divorce 1947) Robert Barry-Chambers

5 Cecil Graham (Rev); b 7 June 1867; educ Eton and Magdalen Coll Oxford (BA, 1890, MA 1893); Rector Westcote 1898–1906 and Heythrop 1906–14, Vicar Nether Swell 1914–22, CF France 1917, Mem Chaplain 4th Cl 1918; m 13 July 1898 Mary Andalusia (d 18 May 1970 aged 92), 2nd dau of John Barnard Hankey, of Fetcham Park, Surrey, and d 13 Aug 1948, leaving:

(1) Arthur Graham; *b* 28 Oct 1901; *educ* Rugby; F/O RAF; *m* 1st 1 Aug 1931 (*divorce* 1936) Nancy Dorothy, dau of Allen Paull, of Shipton Moyne, Glos; *m* 2nd 30 July 1936 Elizabeth Helen, dau of Ian Alistair Ewing, of Mounthooly, Jedbergh

(2) Edward Horace Graham; *b* 15 Sept 1904; *educ* Eton and Magdalen Coll Oxford (BA); Lt-Col 15th/19th Hus WW II; *m* 8 Oct 1931 Cynthia Rosamond (*d* 1989), only dau of Maj L Avery, DSO, of Mayfair, and *d* 1990, having had:

  1a +John Jeremy Edward Graham, MBE (1985) [Lt-Col John Moon MBE, Thrintoft House, Thrintoft, Northallerton, N Yorks]; *b* 4 Nov 1932; *educ* Sherborne and RMA Sandhurst; Maj 15th/19th Hus (ret), Lt-Col Army Legal Corps; *m* 1st 8 Oct 1958 (*divorce* 1964) Jane Mary, dau of T J Cundy, of White Grange, Brant Broughton, Lincs, and Mrs John Thornton Hildyard, of Bankwood Farm, Southwell, Notts, and has:

    1b +; *b* 15 June 1962; *m* 1986 *Lorraine, est dau of Michael Willoughby, of Hinton Waldrist, Oxon, and has:

      1c *Camilla Sarah Jane; *b* 1992

    1b *Caroline Rachel Graham; *b* 8 April 1960; *m* 1987 *Charles Nicholas Frank, s of Charles Frank, of Standlake, Oxon, and has:

      1c *Georgina Rachel; *b* 1990

      2c *Elizabeth Jane; *b* 1992

  1a Lt-Col John Moon *m* 2nd 10 Dec 1966 *Dorrit, est dau of Gert Anderson, of Copenhagen, and by her has:

    2b +Christian Graham; *b* 5 Sept 1967

    3b +Thomas Edward Graham; *b* 9 May 1969

  1a Vanessa Mary Graham; *b* 14 May 1936; *d* 28 Jan 1939

  2a *Camilla Mary Graham; *b* 7 Sept 1939; *m* 1972 *Clinton Bourdon and has:

    1b *Jeremy Edward Currier; *b* 1979

    2b *Timothy Francis Avery; *b* 1981

(3) +John Cecil Graham [Maj John Moon, Springfield Mews, Corbridge, Northumberland NE45 5LG]; *b* 7 Sept 1919; *educ* Eton; Maj 15th/19th King's Roy Hus WW II; *m* 7 July 1952 *Susan Mary Milburn, yr dau of Edward Reed, of Ghyllheugh, Longhorsley, Northumberland, and has:

  1a *Belinda Mary Graham; *b* 3 May 1954; *m* 1977 *Marek William Kwiat-kowski and has issue (*see* DARTMOUTH, E)

  2a *Amanda Jane Graham; *b* 6 April 1958; *m* 1985 *Thomas G Bowring, est s of Geoffrey Bowring, of Halton Park, Lancs, and has:

    1b *Cynthia Mary Elizabeth; *b* 13 March 1991

    2b *Flora Katharine Louise; *b* 17 June 1994

  3a *Philippa Ann Graham; *b* 24 Nov 1959

1 Ada Sidney; *d* in infancy

2 Evelyn Sarah; *m* 4 Sept 1878 Herbert Webb Bonsor, of York House, Worcester Park, Surrey, and *d* 11 Aug 1928

3 Ellen Gertrude; *m* 28 April 1888 John Barnard Hankey, JP, DL, of Fetcham Park, Surrey, and *d* 14 April 1946, leaving issue. He *d* 24 May 1914

4 Beatrice Graham; *d* 14 Sept 1884

The 3rd Bt's nephew,

Sir (Arthur) Wilfred Graham Moon, 4th Bt; *b* 24 June 1905; *educ* Eton and Magdalen Coll Oxford; ADC to Govr Fiji 1929–31; *m* 1st 18 Sept 1928 (*divorce* 1934) Constance, dau of John William Abbott, of Wellington, NZ, and had:

1 Diana Patricia; *b* 12 Nov 1929; *d* 1942

Sir Wilfred *m* 2nd 11 Dec 1934 (*divorce* 1947) Doris Patricia Baron (*d* 30 Nov 1953), yr dau of Thomas Baron Jobson, of Dublin, and by her had:

1 Sir PETER WILFRED GILES GRAHAM MOON, **5th and present Bt**

Sir Wilfred *m* 3rd 14 Dec 1951 Theodora (*d* 17 May 1956), widow of Capt Michael Greaves and dau of Cdr — Montagu, RN, and *d* 25 Feb 1954

MOORE of Hancox

Arms: Arg. on a fess between two garbs az. three mullets or (for MOORE); on an inescutcheon az. between three fleur-de-lys erminois, two and one, a sword in pale, point upwards ppr., pommel and hilt or (for BURROWS). **Crest:** In front of a Moor's head ppr. a garb barwise or. **Motto:** *Nitor in adversum* ('I strive against adversity'). **Creation:** Bt (UK) 28 May 1919.

Norman Winfrid Moore [Dr Norman Moore, The Farm House, 117 Boxworth End, Swavesey, Cambs CB4 5RA]; *b* 24 Feb 1923; *s f* 1959 and has established right to title but does not use it; *educ* Eton, Trin Coll Cambridge (BA 1943) and Bristol U (PhD 1954); Lt RA WW II (wounded, POW), sr scientific offr Nature Conservancy 1953– (pncpl sci offr 1958–65, sr pncpl offr 1965–83), Visiting Prof Environmental Studies Wye Coll London 1979–83, chm Farming and Wildlife Advsy Gp 1983–84, author: *The Bird of Time* (1987); *m* 14 July 1950 *Janet, PhD, only dau of Paul Singer, and has:

  1 +PETER ALAN CUTLACK; *b* 21 Sept 1951; *educ* Eton and Trin Coll Cambridge (BA 1973), DPhil (Oxon) 1980; *m* 1989 *Pamela Edwardes and has:

    (1) +Paul Edwardes; *b* 1990

    (1) *Esther Edwardes; *b* 1993

  1 *Caroline Mary Phyllis; *b* 7 May 1953; barrister; *m* 1982 *Richard Anthony Cohen and has:

    (1) *Toby Benedict: *b* 1983

    (2) *Guy Peter Gillachrist: *b* 1988

    (1) *Mary Beatrix: *b* 1986

  2 *Helena Meriel; *b* 15 Feb 1957; *m* 1986 *David Alexander and has:

    (1) *Rose Maribel; *b* 1990

    (2) *Catherine Janet; *b* 1990 (twin)

    (3) *Harriet Alannah; *b* 1994

Lineage: This family claims to be a branch of the MUREs or MOOREs of Rowal-lan.

WILLIAM MOORE; *b* 1784; *m* Anne Rowan (*d* 1830) and *d* 1858, leaving:

ROBERT ROSS ROWAN MOORE, of Garden Hill, Kilmainham, Dublin; *b* 23 Dec 1811; barrister; *m* 1 Jan 1845 Rebecca, dau of Benjamin Clarke Fisher, of Lifford, Co Tipperary, and *d* 6 Aug 1864, leaving:

Sir Norman Moore, 1st Bt (UK), so *cr* 28 May 1919; *b* 8 Jan 1847; LLD, Hon Fell St Catharine's Coll Cambridge. (BA 1869), MA and MB 1872, MD 1876, FRCP 1877, Hon FRCPI 1912, assist physician St Bartholomew's Hosp 1883–1902 (lecturer 1893–1911, physician 1902–11, Consultant and Emeritus Lecturer 1911–22), Pres Roy Coll Physicians 1918–22; *m* 1st 30 March 1880 Amy (*d* 25 Aug 1901), dau of William Leigh Smith, of Crowham, Sussex, and had:

  1 ALAN HILARY (Sir), **2nd Bt**

  2 Gillachrist; *b* 22 March 1894; 2nd Lt Roy Sussex Regt; *ka* Ypres 7 Nov 1914

  1 Ethne Philippa, MBE (1918), BEM (1946); *b* 1886; served WWs I and II; *m* 12 Oct 1910 Lt-Col Walter Marlborough Pryor, DSO and bar, DL, only s of Marlborough Robert Pryor, JP, DL, of Weston Park, Herts, and *d* 29 March 1968, leaving issue. He *d* 28 March 1962

Sir Norman *m* 2nd 1 Sept 1903 Milicent (*d* 9 Feb 1947), yr dau of Maj-Gen John Ludlow, and *d* 30 Nov 1922

His only surv s,

Sir Alan Hilary Moore, 2nd Bt; *b* 23 Jan 1882; *educ* Eton and Trin Coll Cambridge (MB, BCh 1911); DPH, RCPS Eng 1914, MOH Battle RD 1934 and Rye 1941, Assist Sch MO E Sussex (ret 1947), T/Surgn RN WW I, memb Soc Nautical Research (V-Pres 1951), memb Battle RDC 1949–58, Govr Bexhill E Sussex County GS for Boys (chm 1953–58) and for Girls 1953–57; *m* 26 April 1922 Hilda Mary (*d* 12 Aug 1959), dau of Rt Rev Winfrid Oldfield Burrows, Bp Chichester, and *d* 13 June 1959, leaving:

  1 Sir NORMAN WINFRID MOORE, **3rd and present Bt**

  2 +Richard Gillachrist [Richard Moore Esq, 16 Thornhill Sq, London N1 1BQ]; *b* 20 Feb 1931; *educ* Trin Coll Cambridge (BA 1955, Pres Union Lent 1955); jnlst *News Chronicle*, Political Sec to Leader Lib Party 1967 and Fedn of Lib and Dem Parties EC, Sec-Gen Lib Internat 1961–64; *m* 25 June 1955 *Ann Hilary,

only child of W/Cdr Charles Cleaver Miles, MC, RAF, of Old Mill House, East Bergholt, Suffolk, and has:
(1) +Charles Hilary [Charles Moore Esq, c/o Daily Telegraph, 1 Canada Sq, Canary Wharf, London E14 5DT]; *b* 31 Oct 1956; *educ* Eton and Trin Coll Cambridge; ed: *Spectator* 1984–90 (assist ed 1983–84), *Sunday Telegraph* 1992–95, *Daily Telegraph* 1995– (leader-writer 1981–83, dep ed 1990–92); *m* 1981 *Caroline Mary, er dau of Ralph Lambert Baxter, and has:
  1a +William; *b* 1990
  1a *Katharine; *b* 1990 (twin)
(2) +Ronan William Gillachrist; *b* 22 March 1961; *m* 1991 *Elizabeth Triep
(1) *Charlotte Sydney [Mrs Mark Smith, Hancox, Whatlington, Battle, Sussex TN33 0NX]; *b* 1 April 1959; *m* 1987 *Mark V E Smith and has:
  1a *George; *b* 1990
  2a *Samuel; *b* 1991
1 Hilary Mary; *b* 10 Nov 1927; teacher; *d* Dec 1996
2 *Meriel Edith Milicent [Mrs John Oliver, The Bishop's House, The Palace, Hereford HR4 9BN]; *b* Dec 1936; *m* 16 Sept 1961 *Rt Rev John Keith Oliver, Bp Hereford 1990–, er s of William Keith Oliver, of Eaton Lodge, E Leake, Notts, and has:
(1) *Thomas Hilary; *b* 18 April 1964
(2) *Henry Caspar William; *b* 1968
(1) *Mary Philomena; *b* 1971

MOORE of
Moore Lodge

Arms: Az. on a chief indented or a spur sa. between two mullets pierced gu. **Crest:** Out of a ducal coronet or a blackamoor's head, face to dexter ppr., wreathed about the temples arg. and az. **Motto:** *Fortis cadere cedere non potest* ('The brave may fall but cannot yield'). **Creation:** Bt. (UK) 20 June 1932.

SIR WILLIAM ROGER CLOTWORTHY MOORE, 3RD BT, of Moore Lodge, Co Antrim, TD (1962), DL (Co Antrim 1990) [Sir William Moore Bt DL TD, Moore Lodge, Ballymoney, Co Antrim BT53 7NT]; *b* 17 May 1927; *s f* 1978; *educ* Marlborough and RMC Sandhurst; Lt Roy Inniskilling Fus 1945, Maj NI Horse 1950–63, High Sheriff Co Antrim 1964, chm Bd Visitors Prisons NI 1971, BBC broadcaster 1963–66; *m* 17 May 1954 *Gillian, dau of John Brown, of Lisburn, Co Antrim, and has:

1 +RICHARD WILLIAM; *b* 8 May 1955; *educ* Portora Roy Sch and RMA; Lt Roy Scots 1974; *m* 1985 *Karen Furness and has:
(1) *Charlotte; *b* 27 Dec 1988
(2) *Sophie; *b* 5 July 1990
(3) *Fenella; *b* 14 May 1993
1 *Belinda Jane; *b* 3 Dec 1956; *m* 1978 *Timothy James Bryce Duncan, of Castlehill, Kirkmahoe, Dumfries, yst s of Sir Arthur Bryce Duncan, and has:
(1) *Sally; *b* 31 Jan 1980
(2) *Gemma; *b* 9 March 1981
(3) *Harriet; *b* 10 April 1983

Lineage: JAMES MOORE; migrated to NI from Cumberland *temp* JAMES I and settled at Ballinacreemore, Ballymoney, Co Antrim; gf of:

JAMES MOORE, of Ballinacree; *b* by 1675; Quaker; *d* after 29 Dec 1727, leaving:
1 William; settled 1702 at Killead, Co Antrim; High Sheriff Co Antrim 1718; *m* — Clotworthy and had:
(1) John, of Moore's Grove; High Sheriff Co Antrim 1732; gf of:
  1a Roger, of Killead; High Sheriff Co Antrim 1750, Capt, led 173 volunteers 1760 to oppose a landing by the French at Carrickfergus
2 James, of Ballinacree
3 Jodeph, of Cullytrumin House and Rosnashane, Co Antrim; *m* 1706 Susan Brady/Breddy, of Grange, Co Antrim, and had:
(1) WILLIAM
(2) James, of Desertderrin; ancestor of the MOOREs of Moore Fort
(3) John; *b* 1712; ancestor of the MOOREs of Lishceihan

(4) Joseph, of Ahoghill; *b* 1716; had issue, now extinct
(5) Samson, of Moore Lodge; High Sheriff Co Antrim 1767; *d* 1775
(6) George

The est son,
WILLIAM MOORE, of Cullytrumin House and Rosnashane; *b* 4 Aug 1708; *m* Elizabeth Courtenay, of Glenburn, and had, with three daus:
1 JOSEPH
2 William, of Killagan, Co Antrim; High Sheriff 1778; *m* — dau of Rev J Warren, Rector Kilrea, Co Londonderry, and had:
(1) Samson, of Moore Lodge, later Ballinacree; Capt Antrim Regt, High Sheriff 1809; *m* Sarah, dau of William Warren, and *dsp*
(2) William, of Moore Lodge; 3rd Dragoons, Capt Antrim Regt, High Sheriff 1808; *m* 3 Sept 1789 Elizabeth, dau of Richard Rothe, of Mount Rothe, Co Kilkenny, and had:
  1a George; *d unm*

The er son,
JOSEPH MOORE, of Cullytrumin House and Rosnashane; barrister; *m* Susan, dau of Joseph Courtenay, of Glenburn, and had, with two er sons (*d* young) and two daus:

SAMSON MOORE, of Cullytrumin House and Rosnashane; Capt Finvoy Yeo; *m* 1787 Jane Ramadge, of Mullens, and *d* 1832, leaving:

ALEXANDER MOORE, of Cullytrumin House and Rosnashane; MD; *m* 1821 Mary (*d* 1897), dau of Rev B Mitchell, and *d* 1840, leaving with a yr s (Courtenay (Rev), Rector Mitchelstown, Co Cork, Canon Cloyne, gf of Maureen, Lady Dunbar of Hempriggs, *qv*):

WILLIAM MOORE, of Moore Lodge, JP; *b* 13 Nov 1826; MD, High Sheriff Co Antrim 1890, Pres King and Queen's Coll Physicians Ireland 1883–1904, King's Prof Medicine Trin Coll Dublin, Physician-in-Ordinary Ireland to HM QUEEN VICTORIA 1885; *m* 3 Sept 1863 Sidney Blanche (*d* 1919), dau of Capt Abraham Fuller, of Woodfield, King's Co, by Anna, dau of Edmund Bigoe Armstrong, of Castle Armstrong, King's Co, and *d* 17 April 1901, leaving, with other issue:

1 **Sir William Moore, 1st Bt** (UK), so *cr* 20 June 1932, PC (I 1921, NI 1922), QC (1899), JP, DL (Co Antrim); *b* 22 Nov 1864; *educ* Marlborough and Trin Coll Dublin (MA, LLD); called Irish Bar 1887, barrister Lincoln's Inn, 1899 (Bencher King's Inns 1910 and Inns of Court NI, Hon Bencher Inner Temple 1926), MP Antrim N 1899–1905 and Armagh N 1906–07, Sr Crown Prosecutor Belfast 1915–17, Justice King's Bench 1917–21, Ld Justice Appeal NI 1921, Ld Ch Justice NI 1925–37, Chllr Diocese of Down 1921, Hon LLD Queen's U Belfast; *m* 15 Sept 1888 Helen Gertrude (*d* Feb 1944), 4th dau of Joseph Wilson, DL, of Westbury, Stillorgan, Co Dublin, and had:
(1) WILLIAM SAMSON (Sir), **2nd Bt**
(2) Joseph Roger; *b* 25 March 1895; *educ* Shrewbury; Capt Roy Irish Rifles WW I, Co Inspr RUC; *m* 2 Nov 1920 Amy Florence (*d* 7 Sept 1948), dau of Col John Patrick, DL, of Dunminning, and *d* 15 Sept 1951, leaving:
  1a William, MC; *b* 16 Sept 1924; Irish Gds WW II; *d unm* 10 Oct 1950
  1a *Jean Florence Helen [Mrs Robert Young, Falcon Cottage, S Warnborough, Hants]; *b* 4 Sept 1923; *m* 25 Feb 1949 *Robert Andrew Young, s of William Alexander Young, of Cheltenham, Glos, and has:
    1b *Timothy David; *b* 26 Sept 1950; *m* 1979 *Sarah Elizabeth Armorel Leng
    1b *Alexandra Louise; *b* 13 Sept 1952; *m* 1984 *John Crawford Cone
(1) Nina Mary Adelaide; *m* 17 Aug 1911 Norman Colum Patrick, Ch MO NI, 3rd s of John Patrick, of Dunminning (*see* above), and *d* 19 Oct 1965, leaving issue. He *d* 24 March 1937

Sir WILLIAM *d* 28 Nov 1944; his er son,
Sir William Samson Moore, 2nd Bt, JP, DL (Co Antrim); *b* 17 April 1891; *educ* RN Acad Gosport and Marlborough; served WW I, High Sheriff Co Antrim 1944; *m* 4 March 1915 Ethel Cockburn Gordon (*d* 1973), 2nd dau of Walter Livingstone Wheeler, of Lennoxvale, Belfast, and *d* 27 July 1978, having had:

1 Sir WILLIAM ROGER CLOTWORTHY MOORE, **3rd and present Bt**
1 Nina Pamela; *b* 19 Oct 1916; *m* 1st 10 June 1939 W/Cdr John Anthony Hustler Tuck, DFC, RAF (*d* 12 Dec 1951), only s of Col Charles Harold Amys Tuck, CIE, Gurkha Regt, IA, of Brook House, Rickinghall, Norfolk, and had two daus; *m* 2nd 27 Aug 1962 Francis Edward John Barry Jackson, s of Herbert John Jackson, of Frant, Sussex, and *d* 21 March 1968

Seat: Moore Lodge, Ballymoney, Co Antrim. The house was built 1603/4, bought by the MOOREs 1676 and added to from 1759 on by Samson Moore, who was High Sheriff of the county 1767 (*see* above) and great-great-great-great-uncle of the **1st Bt**.

MOORE OF LOWER MARSH

Arms: Azure a dolphin naiant argent between three bunches of grapes stalked and leaved gold. **Crest:** A griffin statant erect azure, billety or and bezanty, beak, forelegs and wings also or, holding in the dexter foreclaw a double-warded key, wards upward gold. **Supporters:** On either side a griffin statant erect azure, that to the dexter bezanty, that to the sinister billety or, the beak, forelegs and wings of each also or, the compartment comprising two grassy mounts with marshland between them all proper. **Motto:** Live free or die. **Creation:** B. (LP,UK) 1992.

THE BARON MOORE OF LOWER MARSH, of Lower Marsh in the London Borough of Lambeth (John Edward Michael Moore, PC (1986)) [The Rt Hon The Lord Moore of Lower Marsh PC, 85 Church Rd, London SW19 5AL]; *b* 26 Nov 1937; *educ* Licensed Victuallers' Sch Slough and LSE (BSc); offr Roy Sussex Regt Korea 1955–57; Memb Cncl London Borough of Merton 1971–74, MP (C) Croydon Centl 1974–92, V-Chm C Party 1975–79, Parly U-Sec Energy 1979–83, Ec Sec Treasury 1983, Fin Sec 1983–86, Sec State: Tport 1986–87, DSS 1987–88, DHSS 1988–89; chm: Dean Witter Internat 1975–79 (dir 1968–79), Energy Saving Tst 1992–95 (Pres 1995–), Credit Suisse Asset Management 1992–, Monitor European Exec Ctee 1992–; dir: Monitor Inc 1990–, Gartmore Investment Management 1990–92, Swiss American Corp 1992–, GTECH Corp 1992–, Blue Circle Industries 1993–, Camelot 1994– (dep chm 1996–), Rolls Royce plc; Memb: Court Govrs LSE 1977–, Lloyd's 1978–92, Cncl IoD 1991–, TIG (USA) 1996–, Advsy Bds: Sir Alexander Gibb & Ptnrs 1990–96, Marvin & Palmer Assocs Inc; *m* 1962 *Sheila Sarah, dau of Richard Tillotson, of Ill., and has:

1 *Martin; *b* 1970

2 *Richard; *b* 1972

1 *Stephanie Jane; *b* 1968; *m* 1994 *David Mortimer Man, s of William Mortimer Man (*see* 1956 edn JOWITT, E)

Lineage: EDWARD O MOORE, of Brighton; had:

JOHN EDWARD MICHAEL, *cr* a **Baron**

MOORE OF WOLVERCOTE

MORIBUS·ET·CONSILIO·

Arms: Gules on a fess, between two lions passant guardant or, three moorcocks sable crested gules. **Crest:** A moorcock proper, gorged with a crown or, holding in its dexter claw a quill pen proper. **Supporters:** Dexter, a wolf proper crowned or, gorged with a collar argent, fimbriated or, thereon roses gules, barbed and seeded proper, and cross crosslets sable; sinister, a stag proper, attired and unguled or, crowned also or, gorged with a collar argent fimbriated or, thereon cross crosslets sable and roses gules, barbed and seeded proper, therefrom a chain reflexed behind the back ending in a ring gold, the compartment comprising a grassy mount, growing therefrom on each side between a thistle and a shamrock, both proper, a rose gules, stalk and leaves vert, barbed and seeded to the front thereof; dexter, a rugby football and similarly on the sinister side a cricket ball proper. **Motto:** *Moribus et consilio* ('By character and counsel'). **Creation:** B. (LP,UK) 1986.

THE BARON MOORE OF WOLVERCOTE, of Wolvercote, City of Oxford (Sir Philip Brian Cecil Moore, GCB (1985, KCB 1980, CB 1973), GCVO (1983, KCVO 1976), CMG (1966), QSO (1986), PC (1977)) [The Rt Hon The Lord Moore of Wolvercote, GCB GCVO CMG QSO PC, Apt 64 Hampton Court Palace, E Molesey, Surrey KT8 9AU]; *b* 6 April 1921; *educ* Cheltenham and BNC Oxford (Hon Fell 1981); F/Lt Bomber Command RAF WW II; Pncpl Priv Sec to First Ld Admlty 1957–58 (Assist Priv Sec 1950–51); Dep UK Commr Singapore 1961–63 (Br Dep HC 1963–65); Ch PRO MOD 1965–66; Priv Sec to HM THE QUEEN and Keeper Roy Archives 1977–86 (Assist Priv Sec 1966–72, Dep Priv Sec 1972–77), Perm Ld in Waiting and Extra Equerry 1990–; dir Gen Accident Fire and Life Assur 1986–91; V-Pres SPCK; Chm King George VI and Queen Elizabeth Fndn of St Catharine's Columbia Lodge 1986–96; *m* 1945 *Joan Ursula, dau of Capt M E Greenop, DCLI, and has:

1 *Sally Jane [The Hon Mrs Sally Leachman, 20 Marlborough Buildings, Bath, Avon]; *b* 1949; *m* 1980 (*divorce* 1984) Richard Gerald Grindon Leachman and has:

(1) *Lucinda; *b* 1980

2 *Jill Georgina; *b* 1951; *m* 1971 (*divorce* 1990) Peter Gabriel and has:

(1) *Anna Marie; *b* 1974

(2) *Melanie; *b* 1976

Lineage: CECIL MOORE, ICS; had:

PHILIP BRIAN CECIL, *cr* a **Baron**

MORAN

Creation: B. (UK) 8 March 1943.

THE 2ND BARON MORAN, of Manton, Co Wilts (Sir (Richard) John McMoran Moran Wilson, KCMG (1981, CMG 1970)) [The Rt Hon The Lord Moran KCMG, House of Lords, London SW1A 0PW]; *b* 22 Sept 1924; *s f* 1977; *educ* Eton and King's Coll Cambridge; Sub-Lt RNVR 1943–45, F(C)O 1945–84, 3rd Sec Ankara 1948–50 and Tel Aviv 1950–53, 2nd Sec Rio de Janeiro 1953–56, 1st Sec FO 1956–59 and 1961–65 and Washington 1959–61, Counsellor Pretoria and Cape Town 1965–68, Head W African Dept FCO 1968–73, Amb Chad 1970–73, Hungary 1973–76 and Portugal 1976–81, High Commr Canada 1981–84, Ho Lds: memb Environment Sub-ctee 1986–91, Chm All Party Parly C Gp 1992– (V-Chm 1989–92), V-Chm Atlantic Salmon Tst 1988–95 (memb Management Ctee 1984–), chm Wildlife and Countryside Link, Fisheries Advsy Ctee Welsh Regn Nat Rivers Authority 1989–94, memb Regnl Fisheries Advsy Ctee Welsh Water Authority 1987–89, pres Welsh Salmon and Trout Angling Assoc 1988– and Radnorshire Wildlife Tst 1994–, memb cncl RSPB 1989–94 (V-Pres to 1997), Grand Cross Order Infante Portugal 1978, author: *CB, A Life of Sir Henry*

Campbell-Bannerman (1973), *Fairfax* (1985); *m* 29 Dec 1948 *Shirley Rowntree, est dau of George James Harris, MC, of Bossall Hall, YorkS, and has:

1 +JAMES McMORAN [The Hon James Wilson, 65 Upland Rd, Brookline, MA 02146, USA]; *b* 6 Aug 1952; *educ* Eton and Trin Coll Cambridge; *m* 1980 *Hon (Mary) Jane Hepburne-Scott, yst dau of 10th Lord Polwarth (*qv*), and has:

   (1) +David Andrew McMoran; *b* 6 Nov 1990

   (2) +Alistair Thomas Hay; *b* 1993

2 +William Edward Alexander; *b* 16 Dec 1956; *educ* Eton and Inns of Court Sch of Law; barrister; *m* 1989 *Juliette E C, dau of Maj Jonathan Mungo Palmes Walker (*see* WALKER, Bt, of Sand Hutton)

1 *Juliet [The Hon Mrs Evans, 5 Campden House Court, 42 Gloucester Walk, London W8 4HU]; *b* 29 Sept 1950; *educ* St Mary's Sch Calne and Newnham Coll Cambridge; *m* 1 July 1972 *Hon Jeffrey de Corban Richard Evans, yr s of 2nd Baron Mountevans (*qv*), and has issue

Lineage: WILLIAM WILSON; *b c* 1770; Trooper Louisa (Muff) Cav 1800 and 1808, living at Dirtagh 1841 and Gortnamoney, Co Derry, 1851; *m* Jan 1808 Elizabeth, dau of Lt John Lurting, of Tamlaghtard, RM, and *d* 14 March 1857, having had:

1 James, of Gortnamoney; *b* 1811; *m* 1829 Agnes, dau of Alexander Hopkins, of Artikelly, and *d* Dec 1882, having had:

   (1) Alexander Hopkins; *b* 1840; *d unm* 9 April 1863

   (2) William; *b* 1845; *d unm* 1911

   (1) Anna; *b* 1830; *m* James Shannon and *d c* 1900, leaving issue

   (2) Eliza; *b* 1833; *d unm* 11 Sept 1870

   (3) Jane; *b* 1835; *m* Marcus Doherty, of Limavady, and *d* 1 May 1883, leaving issue. He *d* 12 May 1863

   (4) Susan; *b* 1848; *d* young

2 ALEXANDER LURTING

1 Jane; *m* Joseph Wallace and had issue

The 2nd son,

ALEXANDER LURTING WILSON, of Gortmore, Co Derry; *b* 1812; *m* 12 Jan 1841 Susan (*d* 19 Aug 1895 aged 85), dau of Jacob Forsythe, of Gortmore, and *d* 25 Jan 1883, leaving:

1 William; *b* 10 Aug 1846; *d unm* 25 Feb 1896

2 James; *b* 10 Aug 1848; *d unm* in Chicago

3 JOHN FORSYTHE

1 Jane Eliza; *b* 29 July 1844; *m* March 1866 Hugh Cumming Fisher, of the Northern Bank, Belfast, and *d* 12 April 1894, leaving issue

The 3rd son,

JOHN FORSYTHE WILSON; *b* 20 Oct 1850; *educ* Coleraine Academical Inst, Queen's U Belfast and Dublin; MD, MCh, LM 1873, NZ Govt Emigration Serv 1874–78, GP Skipton-in-Craven, Wolston, Warwicks, and Barrow-in-Furness, Hon Surgn N Lonsdale Hosp Barrow 1898–1909, served under LCC at Bexley and Hanwell Asylums 1915–19 and Bootham Park, Yorks; *m* 20 Aug 1878 Mary Jane (*d* 1 June 1923 aged 74), dau of Rev John Hanna, Presbyterian Min Clogher, by Matilda, dau of John McMorran, MD, of Co Monaghan, and *d* 2 Dec 1931, leaving:

1 Lorton Alexander; *b* 10 Aug 1879; *educ* Epsom Coll and Owen's Coll Manchester; MRCS, LRCP 1907, Hon MO Barrow War Memorial Convalescent Home to 1941, Medical Referee Min Pensions, Hon Sec Barrow Panel Ctee to 1946, Hon Sec Furness Div BMA 1922–46 (Chm 1930), Pres N Lancs and S Westmorland Branch 1931, Capt RAMC (TA) attd 2nd/5th Border Regt, 2nd/6th King's Regt and 4th King's Own (Roy Lancaster) Regt, WWs I and II (Maj HG), memb Soc Genealogists, a fndr and Fell Irish Genealogical Research Soc; *m* 4 Dec 1909 Kathleen Emily (*d* 15 Jan 1951), est dau of Rev William Berry, of Eglish, King's Co, Vicar St Paul's, Barrow, and *d* 15 Sept 1958, leaving:

   (1) Kathleen Moira; *b* 5 May 1911; higher certificate National Froebel Union; *d* 1996

   (2) *Ethne Patricia [Mrs James Button, 49 Merrydown Country Club, Private Bag XII, Bryanston 2021, S Africa]; higher Froebel certificate, assist mistress St Columba's Kilmalcolm and Kingsmead, Melrose, Johannesburg; *b* 23 June 1912; *m* 1 Jan 1942 James Button, s of James Button, of Machadodorp, formerly of Caistor, Lincs, and has:

     1a *James [Dr James Button Esq, PO Box 128, Prince Alfred Hamlet, Cape 6840, S Africa]; *b* 18 Nov 1942; *educ* Natal U (PhD Ag 1972, MSc Ag 1968); *m* 17 Feb 1973 *Sylvia Jean, dau of L W Clarke, of Pietermaritzburg, Kwa Zulu, Natal

     2a *Christopher [Dr Christopher Button Esq, 675 Deptford Rd, Bairnsdale, VIC 3876, Australia]; *b* 9 Feb 1945; *educ* U of Pretoria (BVetSc 1969, PhD Texas A&M U 1979); *m* 23 Jan 1971 *Mary Ann Hofmeyr and has:

       1b *Victoria Jane; *b* 28 July 1972

       2b *Catherine Gail; *b* 8 April 1974

       3b *Jillian Leonie; *b* 30 Nov 1981

     3a *Andrew [Dr Andrew Button Esq, 2 Alastair Court, Surrey Hills, Melbourne, VIC 3127, Australia]; *b* 9 Feb 1954; *educ* U of Witwatersrand (BSc Geology 1967, MSc 1969, PhD 1971); *m* 20 Dec 1967 *Brenda Maud, only dau of E E Collins, of Belfast, Transvaal, and has:

       1b *Matthew James; *b* 30 June 1976

       2b *James Edward; *b* 20 Feb 1980

       1b *Caroline Wendy; *b* 28 Feb 1970

       2b *Lisa Ann; *b* 22 Dec 1972; *m* April 1997 *Gavin McLaven

     1a *Kathleen Ann [Mrs Garth Anderson, 11 Wexford Avenue, Westcliff, Johannesburg 2193, Gauteng, S Africa]; *b* 9 Nov 1954; *educ* U of Natal (BA HEd, H DipLib 1977); *m* 11 Dec 1976 *Garth Elsworth Anderson, s of M K Anderson, of Pretoria, Gauteng, and has:

       1b *Michael James; *b* 26 Oct 1984

       1b *Sarah Leigh; *b* 3 Nov 1981

2 CHARLES McMORAN, **1st Baron**

1 Matilda McMoran; *b* 13 Dec 1880; *d unm* Feb 1961

JOHN WILSON *d* 2 Dec 1931; his 2nd s,

CHARLES McMORAN WILSON, **1st Baron Moran**, of Manton, Co Wilts (UK), so *cr* 8 March 1943, MC (1916); *b* 10 Nov 1882; *educ* Pocklington GS and St Mary's Hosp London (MB, BS Lond 1908, MD (gold medal) 1913); MO Roy Fus and as Maj RAMC WW I (despatches three times, Italian Silver Medal Valour), MRCS England, LRCP Lond 1908, MRCP 1913, FRCP Lond 1921 (Treasurer, Pres 1914–50), Hon FRCP (Edin) 1946, Hon Fell American Coll Physicians, Roy Australian Coll Physicians and Roy Faculty Physicians and Surgns Glasgow, Casualty Physician, Medical Registrar, Assist Physician and Physician St Mary's Hosp (Dean Medical Sch 1920–45), Consultant Physician Paddington and Queen Charlotte's Hosps, Advsr Min Health 1941, Hon Sec Faculty Medicine Lond U, memb GMC 1945, personal physician to Winston Churchill WW II and thereafter, author: *The Anatomy of Courage* (1945) and *Winston Churchill, The Struggle for Survival* (1966), ktd 1938; *m* 15 July 1919 Dorothy (*d* 12 July 1983 aged 88), MBE (1918), dau of Samuel Felix Dufton, MA, DSc, and had:

1 (RICHARD) JOHN McMORAN WILSON, **2nd and present Baron**

2 +Geoffrey Hazlitt, CVO (1989); *b* 28 Dec 1929; *educ* Eton and King's Coll Cambridge (BA 1952); FCA, FCWA, late 2nd Lt RHG, chm Southern Electric plc 1993–96, dep chm Johnson Matthey 1994–, dir Blue Circle Industries 1980–97 and Drayton English and Internat Tst 1978–95, chm Delta plc 1982–94, dep Pres Engineering Employers Fedn, chm 100 Group of Fin Dirs 1979–80 and Nat West Bank 1990–92; *m* 19 Oct 1955 *(Barbara) Jane, only dau of William Edward Hilary Hebblethwaite, of Itchen Stoke, Hants, and has:

   (1) *Nicholas Charles Hazlitt; *b* 9 Oct 1957

   (2) +Hugo William Hazlitt; *b* 17 May 1963

2 (cont.) The Hon Geoffrey and Mrs Wilson also adopted:

   *Laura Jane; *b* 12 March 1986

   *Jessica Harriet; *b* 1967; *m* 1st 1992 *Simon C Newson, yr s of J A Newson, of Bury, W Sussex; *m* 2nd 1997 *Nicholas C G Strachwitz Hamilton, er s of C Strachwitz Hamilton, of Dorset

MORAY

Arms: Quarterly, 1st and 4th, a lion rampant within a double tressure flory counterflory gules (royal arms of Scotland), surrounded with a bordure compony argent and azure (for MORAY); 2nd, or a fess chequy azure and argent (for STEWART of Doune); 3rd, or three cushions, two and one, within a double tressure flory counterflory gules (for RANDOLPH, EARL OF MORAY). **Crest:** A pelican in her piety feeding her young, proper. **Supporters:** Two greyhounds argent, collared gules. **Motto:** *Salus per Christum Redemptorem* ('Salvation through Christ the Redeemer'). **Creations:** E. and L. (S) 30 Jan 1561/2 (Abernethy) (new charter 17 April 1611), L. (S) 1563 (Strathdearn), L. (S) 24 Nov 1581 (Doune), L. (S) 26 Feb 1619/20 (St Colme), B. (GB) 4 June 1796 (Stuart of Castle Stuart).

THE 20TH EARL OF MORAY, **Lord Abernethy**, **Lord Strathdearn**, **Lord Doune**, **Lord St Colme** and **Baron Stuart of Castle Stuart**, Co Inverness (Douglas John Moray Stuart, JP (Perthshire 1968)) [The Rt Hon The Earl of Moray JP, Doune Park, Doune, Perthshire FK16 6HA; Darnaway Castle, Forres, Moray IV36 0ST]; *b* 13 Feb 1928; *s f* 1974; *educ* Hilton Coll Natal and Trin Coll Cambridge (BA); FLAS 1948; *m* 27 Jan 1964 *Lady Malvina Dorothea Murray, er dau of 7th Earl of Mansfield and Mansfield (*qv*), and has:

1 +JOHN DOUGLAS, *Lord Doune* [Lord Doune, Doune Park, Doune, Perthshire FK16 6HA; Darnaway Castle, Forres, Morayshire]; *b* 29 Aug 1966; *educ* Loretto and UCL (BA Hist of Art)

1 *Louisa Helena; *b* 18 Aug 1968

Moray, Earldom of: The district of Moray remained for a long time separate from both the area of Scotland occupied by the Northern Picts and that of the Southern Picts, but its rulers were not strictly speaking Earls. It was finally conquered by the Scots proper in 1130 and thereafter held by the Kings of Scots as a royal possession till 1312. In that year Thomas Randolph, whose mother was sister of ROBERT I (THE BRUCE), was created Earl of Moray. He led the left wing of the Scottish army to the victory over the English at Bannockburn in 1314, having a few months before retaken Edinburgh Castle from its temporary English captors. The year after Bannockburn he was declared Guardian of the Realm in the event of the crown descending to a minor. He accordingly became Regent on ROBERT I's death in 1329.

His successor the 3rd Earl of Moray of the 1312 creation was also Regent, though jointly with Robert Stewart, but was killed at the shattering defeat by the English of Neville's Cross in 1346. Since he died without issue the Earldom expired.

About 1332 the same Henry Beaumont who was looked on by the English as Earl of Buchan (qv) seems to have been created Earl of Moray, at any rate for a short time, at a moment when right to confer the title lay with Edward Balliol, a puppet King of Scotland installed by the English, in the absence of DAVID II, the properly constituted one. Henry Beaumont is certainly so referred to in a contemporary document in which, as Earl of Buchan and Moray as well as Constable of Scotland, he was a benefactor to Bridlington Priory.

From 1346, the year of the last Randolph Earl of Moray's death, to 1367, Patrick, 8th Earl of Dunbar (see DUNBAR, Bt, of Mochrum), who had married Lady Agnes Randolph, daughter of the 1st Earl of Moray of the 1312 creation, extorted from DAVID II recognition of him as Earl of March and Moray. DAVID, being imprisoned by the English for much of the time, was in no position to argue. By an Act of Renunciation of 1367 the territory of the Earldom of Moray called a comitatus was taken back into the hands of the Crown and in 1359 DAVID, for reasons which remain mysterious, conferred the Earldom on an Englishman of royal blood, Henry Duke of Lancaster (great-great-grandson of HENRY III). On Henry's death without male issue in March 1360/1, the Earldom expired. It was revived in March 1371/2 for John de Dunbar, great-nephew of the Patrick created Earl of March and Moray some 35 years earlier. John's mother Isabel was the younger of the two daughters of Thomas Randolph, 1st Earl of Moray of the 1312 creation, so there was a double blood link with the earliest holders of the title.

The blood link was maintained after the death of Elizabeth, Countess of Moray, John de Dunbar's great-great-granddaughter. She had married Archibald Douglas, a younger son of the 7th Earl of Douglas (see QUEENSBERRY, M). The Douglases at that time wielded complete supremacy in Scotland and Archibald sat in the Scottish Parliament as Earl of Moray even though his wife was not Countess of Moray in her own right. On his rebelling against JAMES II the latter bestowed the Moray title on James Crichton (see BUTE, M); but James's wife Janet was sister to Elizabeth, Archibald's Countess, so the choice of title was not entirely arbitrary.

Archibald was subsequently attainted and his Earldom forfeited, though he himself had already been killed in a renewed revolt against the Crown. But a direct line of James and Janet Crichton's heirs survived till the late 17th century, almost exactly two and a half centuries after the death of James in 1454, and would have been entitled to the Earldom of Moray. Nevertheless the Stewart Kings appear to have regarded it as a family dignity of their own from now on, with a single and short-lived exception in the mid-16th century (see below). Doubtless this was a harking back to earlier times, when the comitatus of Moray had been held directly by the Crown rather than through tenants. JAMES II conferred the Earldom of Moray on his infant third son David Stewart in 1456, who died the next year. And JAMES IV conferred it on his illegitimate son James Stewart by Janet (2nd w of 5th Earl of Angus; see HAMILTON and BRANDON, D) around 1500 (he died without legitimate issue in about 1544/5).

True, the Earl of Huntly (see HUNTLY, M) was briefly granted the title in February 1548/9, but he renounced it six years later. Finally, JAMES V created his illegitimate son James Stewart Earl of Moray in January 1561/2. In that family it has remained to the present day.

Lineage: ALAN; Breton noble living c 1045; hereditary Steward of Dol in Britanny; had:

1 Alan; a leader of the First Crusade 1097, during which he probably died without direct heirs

2 FLEALD

3 Rhiwallon; monk of St Florent at Saumur

The 2nd son,

FLAALD or FLEALD; living 1080; active on the Welsh border c 1101; had:

ALAN fitz FLEALD; feudal Baron of Oswestry, Sheriff Salop 1101; fndr Sporle Priory Norfolk by 1122; m Aveline, dau of Arnulf or Ernulf, Seigneur of Hesdin, Picardy, a large land-holder in England 1086, and had:

1 Jordan FitzAlan; living 1130; m Mary — and had:

  (1) Jordan

  (2) Alan; living 1167; held land in Britanny, Lincs, Notts and Norfolk; m Joan — and had:

    1a Jordan; dsp

    1a Olive; heiress of Tuxford, Notts, and Sharrington, Norfolk; living 1227; m 1st Robert de St John, Seigneur of St Jean-le-Thomas; m 2nd c 1200 Roger de Monbegon

    2a Alice; heiress of lands in Britanny; m William Epine or Spina, s of Hamo, and left issue, who inherited the Stewardship of Dol

2 William FitzAlan; feudal Baron of Oswestry, Sheriff Salop and Castellan Shrewsbury 1138; besieged there as an adherent of the EMPRESS MAUD by KING STEPHEN; restored to his lands by HENRY II 1155 and set about recovering the Barony of Oswestry, by now in Welsh hands; fndr Haughmond Abbey; m 1st Christian, possibly a niece of Robert FitzRoy, 1st Earl of Gloucester of the 1122 cr, illegitimate s of HENRY I, and had a dau (Christian, m Hugh Pantulf); m 2nd Isabel (m 2nd c 1166 Geoffrey de Vere, m 3rd c 1188 William Boterel, d c 1199), dau and heir of Ingram de Say, feudal Lord of Clun, Salop, and d 1160, having by her had:

  (1) William FitzAlan, of Clun and Oswestry; dsp 1216

  (2) John FitzAlan; feudal Baron of Oswestry; one of the magnates opposed to KING JOHN; m 1st Isabel d'Aubigny, sis and coheir of Hugh, 5th Earl of Arundel, and d 1240, being with her ancestor of the FitzAlan Earls of Arundel (see NORFOLK, D)

3 Walter FitzAlan; made hereditary Gt Steward of Scotland by DAVID I (1124–53), fndr Paisley Priory c 1163; lay bro Benedictine Order; repelled an invasion of Renfrewshire by the Islesmen 1164; m Eschyne de Molle (widow of Robert de Croc), probably dau of Thomas of the Lundins and sis of Malcolm, 1st hereditary Doorward of Scotland, and d 1177, leaving:

  (1) Alan Fitz Walter, 2nd Gt Steward Scotland; allegedly Crusader with RICHARD I; m Eve, possibly dau of Sweyn Thor's son, overlord of Crawford (see CARLISLE, E), and d 1204, having had:

1a WALTER

2a David; living 1220

3a Leonard; benefactor to Convent of Durham

1a Aveline; abducted 1200 by (and probably m) Duncan mac Gilbert, afterwards 1st Earl of Carrick (d 13 June 1250; see also CARRICK, E, preliminary remarks)

The 2nd Great Steward's son,

WALTER STEWART (first to assume the surname), 3rd Gt Steward of Scotland; raised Paisley Priory to rank of Abbacy c 1219, Justiciar Scotland north of Forth 1230; m Beatrix, dau of Gilchrist, 3rd Earl of Angus, and d 1241, having had:

1 ALEXANDER

2 John; went on Crusade with St LOUIS (LOUIS IX of France) and was k at Damietta in Egypt fighting the Saracens 1249

3 WALTER STEWART, EARL OF MENTEITH, so invested in right of his w c 1260; called Ballach or Bailloch ('Freckled'); allegedly also accompanied St LOUIS 1248; Sheriff Ayrshire 1264 and Dunbartonshire 1289; m Mary, Countess of Menteith in her own right, yr dau and coheir of Maurice, 3rd Earl of Menteith, and d by 28 April 1296, having had:

  (1) ALEXANDER STEWART, 6th EARL OF MENTEITH; invaded England with other Scottish earls 1296, besieged Carlisle, was defeated and captured at Dunbar and imprisoned in the Tower of London until he did homage to EDWARD I; m Maud — and d c 1300, leaving:

    1a ALAN STEWART, 7th EARL OF MENTEITH; supported ROBERT (THE) BRUCE; m Marjorie —, was imprisoned by the English and d in captivity c 1308, leaving:

      1b MARY Stewart, COUNTESS OF MENTEITH in her own right from 1332; m Sir John GRAHAM, 9th EARL OF MENTEITH in right of his w (see MONTROSE, D), and d c 1360, leaving:

        1c MARGARET Graham, COUNTESS OF MENTEITH in her own right, carried the title with its caput or chief seat of Doune Castle to her 4th husb, Robert Stuart, Duke of Albany (see below), with whom she was ancestor of the Earls Castle Stewart (qv) and of Moray

    2a Piers; accompanied EDWARD I to Flanders and campaigned in France 1297

    3a MURDOCH STEWART, 8th EARL OF MENTEITH; m probably Alice, possibly of the family of Ferrers (of Groby), and was k fighting the Balliol claimant to the Scottish throne at the Battle of Dupplin 12 Aug 1332

    4a Alexander; bore the surname Menteith

  (2) John (Sir), of Menteith; Sheriff Dunbartonshire owing fealty to EDWARD I 1304 and as such captured the Scottish national hero Sir William Wallace, whom he took in chains to London; named Earl of Lennox by EDWARD I but joined ROBERT (THE) BRUCE, for whom he fought in the War of Scottish Independence and acted as Guardian of the Earldom of Menteith 1320; ancestor of the MENTEITHs of Rusky and Kerse (including some of the DALYELL of the Binns Bts (qv); see also STUART-MENTETH, Bt)

1 Eupheme; m c 1213 5th Earl of Dunbar (see DUNBAR, Bt, of Mochrum)

2 Margaret; m Neil, 2nd Earl of Carrick (d 1256)

3 Elizabeth; m Maldouen, 3rd Earl of Lennox (d c 1250)

4 A dau; m Donald, Lord of the Isles, and had issue (see BOSVILLE MACDONALD, Bt)

The est son,

ALEXANDER STEWART, 4th Gt Steward of Scotland; Crusader, Jt Regent of Scotland 1255; as leader of the pro-English party helped kidnap the young ALEXANDER III from Edinburgh Castle; commanded the right wing at the victory over invading Norsemen at Largs 1263, when the Hebrides were brought under Scottish sway, in reward for which was granted Garlies by ALEXANDER III; m Jean, heiress of the Isles of Bute and Arran, dau of James (who with his f and bros was k 1210 by the men of Skye), s of Angus, Lord of Bute and Arran (yr s of Somerled, King of the South Isles), and had:

1 JAMES

2 John (Sir), of Bonkyl; led his Islesmen from Bute and his w's Border archers in the fight for Scottish independence; m Margaret, dau and heiress of Sir Alexander Bonkyl of that Ilk, and was k fighting for Sir William Wallace at the Battle of Falkirk 1298, leaving, with other issue:

  (1) Alexander (Sir), of Bonkyl; d 1319; had:

    1a JOHN STEWART, 1st EARL OF ANGUS, so cr 1329, probably because of his marriage (papal dispensation 24 Oct 1328) to Margaret, Lady of Abernethy (living 1370), er dau and coheir of Alexander Abernethy of that Ilk (see SALTOUN, L), and d 9 Dec 1331, leaving:

      1b THOMAS, 2nd EARL OF ANGUS; captured Berwick 1355; Great Chamberlain of Scotland 1357/8; imprisoned for alleged complicity in the murder of DAVID II's mistress Catherine Mortimer; m (papal dispensation 3 June 1353) Margaret (m 2nd Sir John de St Clair of Herdmanston; see SINCLAIR, L), dau of Sir William de St Clair or Sinclair of Rosslyn, and d of the plague while captive in Dumbarton Castle 1361, leaving:

        1c THOMAS STEWART, 3rd EARL OF ANGUS; dsp young 1377

        1c MARGARET Stewart, COUNTESS OF ANGUS in her own right; m 9th Earl of Mar (qv) and d 1417, having as mistress of her sis-in-law's husb William, 1st Earl of Douglas (see QUEENSBERRY, M), had an illegitimate s (to whom she resigned the Earldom 1389):

          1d GEORGE DOUGLAS, EARL OF ANGUS; ancestor of the Dukes of Hamilton and Brandon (qv)

        2c Elizabeth; m Sir Alexander Hamilton of Innerwick and with him was ancestor of the Earls of Haddington (qv)

  (2) Alan (Sir), of Dreghorn; k at Scottish defeat by English of Halidon Hill 1333, leaving, with other issue:

    1a John (Sir), of Darnley and Crookston; d c 1369, having had two sons (John; Robert; dsp)

    2a Walter; dspm c 1371

    3a Alexander (Sir), of Darnley; had:

      1b Alexander (Sir), of Darnley; m 1st possibly a sis of Sir John Turnbull of Minto and had five sons and a dau; m 2nd c 1381 Janet (living 1406), dau of Sir William Keith of Galston and widow of Sir David Hamilton of Cadzow (see ABERCORN, D), and *d c* May 1404, having by her had, with a 6th *s* (William, *k* Battle of Rouvray 12 Feb 1428/9 fighting with the French in the Hundred Years War against the English in the defence of Orleans 1429):

1c Sir JOHN STUART (first to use that French version), 1st Seigneur d'Aubigny and Concressault and COUNT d'EVREUX, so *cr* by the grateful French 1426/7 with the right to quarter the Royal Arms of France 1427/8; took over 4,000 Scots to fight the English in France at the Dauphin's special request 1421; Constable of the Scots in command of all Scottish troops in France from 1424; Jt French Amb to Scotland 1428; held Orleans against the English; *m* (papal dispensation 23 Sept 1406) Elizabeth (*d* Nov 1429), yr dau and coheir of Duncan, 8th Earl of Lennox (beheaded 1425), and was *k* Rouvray 12 Feb 1428/9, leaving:

1d Alan (Sir), of Darnley; 2nd Seigneur d'Aubigny; Constable of the Scots troops in France; present Siege and capture of Montereau 1437 but then resigned his French fiefs and returned to Scotland; *m* Catherine (*m* 2nd 1st Lord Maxwell; see MAXWELL, Bt), sis of 1st Lord Seton (see EGLINTON and WINTON, E), and was *k* by Sir Thomas Boyd of Kilmarnock (see KILMARNOCK, B) in a feud 1439, leaving, with a yr *s* (Alexander, ancestor of Frederick Stewart, *cr* Lord Pittenweem 1609):

1e JOHN STUART, 10th EARL OF LENNOX, *cr* EARL OF DARNLEY *c* 1460; Lord Warden W March 1481, one of the lords who seized JAMES III 1482 but was pardoned; retoured heir to the Earldom of Lennox 1473 but only became so effectively after compensating the coheirs 1488; Jt Keeper Dumbarton Castle with his *s* 1488; rebelled but defeated by JAMES IV 1489, though soon pardoned; *m* (indenture 15 May 1438) Margaret, dau of 1st Lord Montgomerie (see EGLINTON and WINTON, E), and *d* Sept 1495, leaving:

1f MATTHEW STUART, 11th EARL OF LENNOX; *m* 1st Margaret, dau of Robert, Lord Lyle; *m* 2nd (contract 9 April 1494) Elizabeth, dau of James, 1st Lord Hamilton, by Mary, sis of JAMES III, and was *k* Battle of Flodden 9 Sept 1513, having by her had, with three daus and a yr *s* (Mungo, one of the three officers of the King of France's Scots Guard 1521/2):

1g JOHN STUART, 12th EARL OF LENNOX, PC; Ld Warden E March, a Ld of Regency 1524; captured Battle of Manuel trying to rescue JAMES V from the Douglases; *m* (papal dispensation 29 Jan 1511/2) Elizabeth Stewart, dau of John, 1st Earl of Atholl, and was murdered by Sir James Hamilton of Finnart for being a potential rival to the Hamiltons as eventual heir presumptive to the throne, having had:

1h MATTHEW STUART, 13th EARL OF LENNOX, Regent of Scotland; *b* 21 Sept 1516; campaigned in Provence for FRANCIS I against CHARLES V 1536; lived in exile in England, invading Scotland with 18 ships as English Ld Lt of northern England and southern Scotland 1544; his title forfeited for treason after invading Scotland again 1545; burnt the town of Annan 1547; raided Scotland again 1548; was restored 1564; Regent for his gs JAMES VI and I from 1570; *m* 29 June 1544 Margaret Douglas (*d* 9 March 1577/8), dau and heir of Archibald, 6th Earl of Angus, by MARGARET TUDOR, QUEEN DOWAGER OF SCOTLAND and sis of HENRY VIII, was mortally wounded while a prisoner during an attack on his Parliament at Stirling and *d* after rescue 4 Sept 1571, leaving:

1i HENRY STUART, KING CONSORT OF SCOTS, so proclaimed the day before his marriage 29 July 1565 to MARY QUEEN OF SCOTS, though styled *Lord Darnley* (under which name he is best known to history) by courtesy while brought up in exile in England, also EARL OF ROSS, so *cr* May 1565 and DUKE OF ALBANY (both S), so *cr* July 1565; *b* 7 Dec 1545; murdered 10 Feb 1566/7, leaving:

1j JAMES VI of Scotland and I of England and Ireland

2i CHARLES STUART, 1st EARL OF LENNOX of the 1572 *cr*; *b c* 1556; *m* 1574 Elizabeth Cavendish (*d* Jan 1581/2), sis of 1st Earl of Devonshire (see DEVONSHIRE, D), and *d* 1576, leaving:

1j Arabella; *b c* 1577; centre of intrigues as potential heir to the throne; *m* secretly 22 June 1610 William Seymour (later 2nd Duke of Somerset; *qv*), was imprisoned by her cousin JAMES I, escaped 1611 but was retaken at sea and imprisoned for life in the Tower of London, where she *d* insane 27 Sept 1615

2h ROBERT STUART, Bp Caithness 1543, attainted with his er bro and exiled for 20 years; restored to the revenues of his bishopric 1563 and became a Protestant, *s* as 2nd EARL OF LENNOX 1578/9 but resigned the Earldom and was *cr* instead EARL OF MARCH 1579/80; *m* 6 Dec 1578 (*divorce* for his impotence 19 May 1581) Elizabeth (*m* 3rd 6 July 1581 James Stuart, Earl of Arran (see ARRAN, E, preliminary remarks), and *d* Sept 1595), dau of 4th EARL OF ATHOLL of the 1457 *cr* (see below) and widow of 5th Lord Lovat (*qv*), and *dspl* 29 Aug 1586

3h John, 6th Seigneur d'Aubigny; offr King of France's Body Guard of Scots Archers 1531; imprisoned Bastille 1544–47 when his bro *m* the King of England's niece; cmded a company of men-at-arms in Italy 1550; captured at French defeat of St Quentin by Spaniards 1557 but ransomed; supported MARY QUEEN OF SCOTS' claim to the English throne, unsuccessfully claimed the hereditary command of the Archer Gd which had passed into the hands of his Montgomerie cousins and resigned his own company in pique, but was given command of the privileged Gendarmes Ecossus 1565; *m c* 1542 Anne (*d c* 1579), 4th dau and coheir of François,

Seigneur de la Queuille, by his 2nd *w* Anne de Rohan, and *d* 31 May 1567, leaving:

1i ESME STUART, 1st DUKE OF LENNOX, so *cr* 5 Aug 1581, as also earlier 5 March 1579/80 EARL OF LENNOX (both S), 7th Seigneur d'Aubigny; *b c* 1542; made hereditary Gt Chamberlain of Scotland 1580, Capt of the King's Gd 1581, worked for the restoration of MARY QUEEN OF SCOTS but exiled 1582; *m* Catherine de Balsac (*d c* 1631), dau of Guillaume, Seigneur d'Entragues, and *d* of fever at Paris 26 May 1583, leaving, with three daus (Henrietta Marchioness of Huntly (*qv*); Mary Countess of Mar (*qv*); Gabrielle, a nun):

1j LUDOVICK STUART, 2nd DUKE OF LENNOX and 1st DUKE OF RICHMOND, Co York, and EARL OF NEWCASTLE-UPON-TYNE, so *cr* 17 May 1623, as also earlier 6 Oct 1613 EARL OF RICHMOND and BARON OF SETTRINGTON, Co York (all E), KG; *b* 29 Sept 1574; Gt Chamberlain of Scotland; Pres PC 1589; Jt Lt of Scotland during absence of JAMES VI 1589–90, Ld Chamberlain Household 1590, Ld High Adml Scotland 1591, Amb France 1601, 1604–05 and 1613; naturalised in England 1603; King's Alnager (official supervisor of cloth standards in England) 1605, Ld High Commr to S Parl 1607, Dep Earl Marshal England 1614, Ld Steward Household 1615–24, Alnager Ireland 1618–24, Ld Lt Kent 1620; *m* 1st *c* 1586 Sophia Ruthven (*dsp c* 1590), dau of William, 1st Earl of Gowrie (see CARLISLE, E); *m* 2nd 1598 Jean (*d* Dec 1610), sis of 1st Lord Campbell of Loudoun (see LOUDOUN, E) and widow of the Master of Eglinton (see EGLINTON and WINTON, E), and by her had a *s* and dau (*d* young); *m* 3rd 16 June 1621 Frances Howard (*dsp* 8 Oct 1639), dau of Thomas, 1st Viscount Howard of Bindon, and widow of 1st Earl of Hertford (see SOMERSET, D), and *dspl* 16 Feb 1624, when the Dukedom of Richmond expired, leaving:

1k John (Sir), of Methven; Keeper Dumbarton Castle 1620

2j ESME STUART, 3rd DUKE OF LENNOX and 1st EARL OF MARCH (E), so *cr* 1619, 8th Seigneur d'Aubigny, KG; *b* 1579; Gt Chamberlain Scotland; Sheriff Dunbartonshire; naturalised in England 1603; *m* 1609 Katherine, Baroness Clifton (of Leighton Bromswold) in her own right (*m* 2nd *c* 1632 James, 2nd Earl of Abercorn (see ABERCORN, D), and *d* 21 Aug 1637), dau and heiress of Gervase, 1st Baron Clifton (of Leighton Bromswold), and *d* of spotted fever 30 July 1624, leaving, with three daus (Elizabeth Countess of Arundel (see NORFOLK, D), Anna Countess of Angus (see HAMILTON and BRANDON, D), Frances Countess of Portland; see PORTLAND, E):

1k JAMES STUART, 4th DUKE OF LENNOX and 1st DUKE OF RICHMOND, Co York (E), so *cr* 8 Aug 1641, KG; *b* 6 April 1612; Gt Chamberlain and High Adml of Scotland, *cr* a Grandee of Spain 1st Cl 1632, Ld Warden of the Cinque Ports 1640, Ld Steward of the Household 1642; royalist Civil War, fought Naseby 1645, spent £40,000 (over £1,600,000 in late-1990s terms) in CHARLES I's cause, one of four peers who offered themselves to the Commons to be executed in place of CHARLES I 1649; *m* 3 Aug 1637 Lady Mary Villiers (*m* 3rd 'Northern Tom' Howard, duellist, Lt Yeomen Gd and bro of 1st Earl of Carlisle (*qv*), and *d* Nov 1685), dau of 1st Duke of Buckingham (see JERSEY, E) and widow of Charles, Lord Herbert of Shurland (see PEMBROKE and MONTGOMERY, E), and *d* 30 March 1655, leaving, with a dau (Mary, Baroness Clifton (of Leighton Bromswold) in her own right, *m* Richard Butler, 1st Earl of Arran (see MOUNTGARRET, V), and *dsp* July 1667 aged 17):

1l ESME STUART, 2nd DUKE OF RICHMOND and (5th DUKE OF) LENNOX; *b* 2 Nov 1649; Great Chamberlain of Scotland; *dsp* 10 Aug 1660

2k Henry; 9th Seigneur d'Aubigny; *b* 1616; *dsp* Venice 1632

3k Francis; *d* young

4k George; 10th Seigneur d'Aubigny; raised 300 Horse for CHARLES I, all gentlemen of fortune; *m* secretly 1638 Lady Catherine Howard (*m* 2nd *c* 1649 1st Earl of Newburgh (*qv*) and *d* in exile at The Hague 1650), dau of 2nd Earl of Suffolk (see SUFFOLK and BERKSHIRE, E), and was *ka* Battle of Edgehill 22 Oct 1642, leaving:

1l CHARLES STUART, 3rd and last DUKE OF RICHMOND and 6th and last DUKE OF LENNOX, also 1st and last EARL OF LICHFIELD and BARON STUART OF NEWBURY (both E), so *cr* 10 Dec 1645, also 1st and last BARON OF COBHAM (E), so *cr* 28 May 1666, 12th Seigneur d'Aubigny, KG (1661), PC (S Feb 1660/1); *b* 7 March 1639; Gt Chamberlain and Ld High Adml Scotland, Ld Lt Dorset 1660, Keeper Dumbarton Castle 1661, Jt Ld Lt Kent 1668, Amb Denmark 1672; *m* 1st Elizabeth (*d* in childbirth 21 April 1661 aged *c* 17), dau and coheir of Richard Rogers, of Bryanston, Dorset, and widow of Charles Cavendish, Viscount Mansfield; *m* 2nd 31 March 1662 Margaret (*dsp* 6 Jan 1667), dau of Laurence Banaster and widow of William Lewes, of the Vann; eloped with and *m* 3rd March 1667 (to the great displeasure of CHARLES II who was deeply in love with her) Frances Theresa, 'La Belle Stuart' (depicted as Britannia on penny coins; *d* 15 Oct 1702, leaving her cousin Alexander Stuart, 5th Lord Blantyre (*see* 1900 edn), a fortune to buy an estate which he named Lennoxlove (*see also* HAMILTON and BRANDON, D, section **Seat**), hence the Scottish country dance 'Lennoxlove to Blantyre'), dau of Walter Stuart, yr s of Walter, 1st Lord Blantyre, and *dsps* 12 Dec 1672 after dining aboard an English man-of-war off Elsinore but slipping between the ship and his boat and drowning, when all his titles bar the Barony of Clifton expired

 1l CATHERINE Stuart, BARONESS CLIFTON (of Leighton Bromswold) in her own right; *bapt* 5 Dec 1640; *m* twice and *d* 1702; by her 1st husb, Henry O'Brien, Lord Ibrackan, est s of Henry, 6th Earl of Thomond (*see* INCHIQUIN, B), she left issue and in 1725 John Bligh (who had *m* her gdau) was *cr* Earl of Darnley (*qv*)

 5k Ludovic; 11th Seigneur d'Aubigny, Cardinal; *b* 14 Oct 1619; RC priest, Grand Almoner to QUEEN HENRIETTA MARIA; *d* at Paris 3 Nov 1665 shortly after the arrival of his Cardinal's hat from Rome

 6k John; *b* 23 Oct 1621; royalist Gen of Horse Civil War; *k* Battle of Alresford 29 March 1644

 7k Bernard; *b c* 1623; intended Earl of Lichfield (*see* above) but *k* cmdg King's Troop of Life Gds Battle of Rowton Heath 26 Sept 1645

 1h Helen; mistress of JAMES V, by whom she had an illegitimate s (Adam Stuart, Prior of Charterhouse); *m* 1st 6th Earl of Erroll (*qv*); *m* 2nd 1549 11th Earl of Sutherland (*qv*) and *d c* 25 Nov 1564

2f William (Sir); Seigneur d'Oizon and de Grey; fought for France in the Italian campaign 1495, became Capt of the whole privileged Company of Scots Men-at-Arms and Archers in the French service; *dsp c* 1503

3f Alexander; *d c* 1508

4f Robert (Sir); 5th Seigneur d'Aubigny; Marshal of France, Count of Beaumont-le-Roger; *b c* 1470; Lt of the Scots men-at-arms in France 1498, Seigneur de St Quentin in right of his 1st w *c* 1499; took part in the French invasion of Lombardy 1499; cmded the garrison in Milan, distinguishing himself in LOUIS XII's tournaments there 1507; cmded vanguard Battle of Agnadel 1508; *s* in-law as Count of Beaumont-le-Roger and Seigneur d'Aubigny 1508; held Brescia against the Venetians until forced by famine to capitulate with the honours of war; Capt of the King of France's Body Guard of Scottish Archers 1512–42; secured special concessions for Scots living in France, also Marshal's baton 1514 at LOUIS XII's dying request; defeated and captured Prospero Colonna Battle of Villafranca 1515; fought Battle of Marignano 1515; was captured with FRANCIS I Battle of Pavia (French defeat by Imperial forces) 1525; regranted the County of Beaumont-le-Roger after his 1st w's death 1527; drove EMPEROR CHARLES V out of Provence 1536; *m* 1st *c* 1499 his cousin Anne Stuart, Countess of Beaumont-le-Roger and Dame d'Aubigny (*dsp c* 1527) and heiress of Bernard, 4th Seigneur d'Aubigny, Duke of Terranuova and Marshal of France; *m* 2nd Jacqueline, dau and coheir of François, Seigneur de la Queulle, and *dsp* 1543

5f John (Sir); Seigneur d'Oizon; campaigned in Italy from 1499, saved his bro Bernard's life at the battle of Terina, Premier Homme d'Armes of France 1505–08, Capt King of France's Body Guard of Scottish Archers 1508–12, Chamberlain and Cncllr to LOUIS XII from 1508; *m* 1st *c* 1486 Mary Sempill; *m* 2nd Anne Monypenny (*m* 2nd Jean de Montferrand; *m* 3rd Antoine de la Roche Chandre), dau and heir of Alexander, Seigneur de Concressault, and *d* 1512

 1f Elizabeth; *m* Archibald, 2nd Earl of Argyll (*see* ARGYLL, D)

 2f Marion; *m* (contract 8 May 1472) Robert Crichton of Kinnoull, s of 1st Lord Crichton of Sanquhar (*see* BUTE, M)

 3f Janet; *m* Ninian, 3rd Lord Ross (*d* Feb 1555/6)

 4f Elizabeth; *m c* 1480 Sir John Colquhoun of Luss (*see* COLQUHOUN, Bt)

 5f Elizabeth; *m* John Maxwell of Pollok (*see* HERON-MAXWELL, Bt)

2d John (Sir); 3rd Seigneur d'Aubigny and de Concressault; a Fndr Kt Order of St Michael instituted by LOUIS XI 1469; *m* 1446 Beatrice, dau of Bérault, Seigneur d'Apchier, and had:

 1e Bernard (christened Bérault), 3rd Seigneur d'Aubigny, DUKE OF TERRANUOVA, so *cr* by the King of France following French conquests in Italy, as also MARCHESE Di GIRACE, COUNT OF VANASSAC and BARON De ST GEORGE, also *cr* MARCHESE Di SQUILAZZO and COUNT Di ACRI 1495; Marshal of France, Kt of St Michael; *b c* 1447; French Amb to Scotland 1483 to announce the CHARLES VIII's accession, cmded the Franco-Scottish troops who fought for HENRY VII at Bosworth 1485, became COUNT OF BEAUMONT-LE-ROGER in right of his 2nd w after 1487, Capt of the King of France's personal Body Gd of Scottish Archers 1493–1508, Cncllr and Chamberlain to CHARLES VIII and LOUIS XII, Amb to the Pope to claim the Two Sicilies for France 1494; led 1,000 horse over the Alps into Lombardy and took part in the conquest of Romagna 1494; Govr of Calabria 1495, routed Gonsalvo de Cordoba and the King of Naples at Seminara 1495, campaigned with LOUIS XII in Italy 1499, Govr of Milan and C-in-C of the French army of occupation in Italy 1500, Viceroy of Naples, which he conquered 1501; defeated the Spaniards at Terranuova Christ-

mas Day 1502 and again at Girace; Great Constable of Sicily and Naples; defeated by Gonsalvo de Cordoba at Seminara and after a siege was forced to surrender at Angistola 1503; Amb to Scotland; *m* 1st Guillemette de Boucard and had:

  1f Guyonne, heiress of his Neapolitan fiefs; *m* Philip de Brague, Seigneur de Luat, and had issue

 1e (cont) The DUKE OF TERRANUOVA *m* 2nd *c* 1487 Anne, COUNTESS OF BEAUMONT-LE-ROGER in her own right, dau of Guy de Maumont, Seigneur de St Quentin, by Jeanne, *cr* Countess of Beaumont-le-Roger 1470, illegitimate dau of Jean II, Duc d'Alençon, and *d* 15 June 1508, having by her had a 2nd dau:

  2f ANNE, COUNTESS OF BEAUMONT-LE-ROGER, Dame d'Aubigny and de St Quentin; *m c* 1499 her cousin Robert Stuart, 4th Seigneur d'Aubigny and Marshal of France (*see* above), but *dsp c* 1527

3d Alexander; avenged his est bro's murder by killing Sir Thomas Boyd of Kilmarnock in private battle 9 July 1439; *dspm*

2c William (Sir); possibly the person of that name who was 'of Jedworth' (*see* GALLOWAY, E) and who was put to death by Harry 'Hotspur' while his prisoner 1402, in which case had:

 1d John (Sir); had:

  1e William (Sir), of Garlies; sat in S Parl as a feudal Baron 1467; alleged ancestor of the Stewart Bts of Ramelton (*qv*); had:

   1f Alexander (Sir); had issue (*see* GALLOWAY, E)

   2f Thomas, of Minto; Squire of the Body to JAMES III 1476; Provost of Glasgow; *m* Isabel, dau and coheir of Walter Stewart of Arthurlie, and *d* 1500, leaving, with other issue:

    1g John (Sir), of Minto; Provost of Glasgow; *m* Janet Fleming and *d* 1512; ancestor of the STEWARTs of Minto, Provosts of Glasgow throughout the 16th century, and the Lords Blantyre (*see* 1900 edn)

    2g William; Bp Aberdeen 1532, Ld High Treasurer Scotland 1530–37, Jt Amb to England 1534; *d* April 1545

  2e John; Provost of Glasgow; left issue

(3) Walter (Sir), of Dalswinton, which granted for servs to ROBERT I (THE BRUCE); also granted other lands forfeited by the COMYNs; *s* to (territorial) Barony of Garlies (which his sis had inherited) from his n (her s) John Randolph, 3rd Earl of Moray; had:

 1a John (Sir), of Garlies and Dalswinton; captured Battle of Neville's Cross 1346; had:

  1b Walter (Sir), of Garlies and Dalswinton; had:

   1c Marion; *m* her cousin Sir John Stewart (*see* above) and had issue

(4) James (Sir), of Perston and Warwickhill, Ayrshire, which granted by ROBERT (THE BRUCE); *k* fighting the English Battle of Halidon Hill 1333; had:

 1a Robert (Sir), of Innermeath (Invermay), Perthshire; sat in S Parl as a feudal Baron; one of the magnates who personally took the oath to observe the succession to the Crown 1373; granted lands of Durrisdeer 1374; *d c* 1388, leaving, with a yr s (Robert, ancestor of the STEWARTs of Rosyth) and a dau (Catherine; *m* John Beatoun of Balfour):

  1b John (Sir), Lord of Lorn in right of his w (her sis and coheir having *m* his yr bro Robert, who resigned his share of Lorn in exchange for the lands of Durrisdeer 1388); *s* f as feudal Baron of Innermeath; Jt Amb to England and France 1412; *m* Isabel of Argyll, dau and coheir of Eoin, Lord of Lorn, Chief of Clan Dougall (heir of the local dynasts of Argyll), and *d* 26 April 1421, having had, with three daus (Christian, *m* James Dundas of that Ilk; Isabel, *m* 1st Sir William Oliphant of Aberdalgy and 2nd Sir David Murray of Tullibardine (*see* ATHOLL, D); Jean, *m* Sir David Bruce of Clackmannan):

   1c ROBERT STEWART, 1st LORD LORN (S), so *cr* by 5 Sept 1439 as one of the new Lds of Parl following the 1428 Act distinguishing Lords from the ordinary lairds in the Scots Baronage; a Commr to England for the release of JAMES I 1421 and hostage for latter's ransom 1424, one of the peers who tried and condemned the ex-Regent Albany 1425; *m* (papal dispensation 27 Sept 1397) Joan Stewart, dau of Robert, 1st Duke of Albany, Regent of Scotland, and *d c* 1449, leaving, with other issue:

    1d JOHN STEWART, 2nd LORD LORN; called *Muireach* ('The Leper'); *m* 1st — and had:

     1e Janet; *m c* 1448 Sir Colin Campbell of Glenorchy (*d* Sept 1475; *see* 1970 edn BREADALBANE AND HOLLAND, E)

     2e Isabel; *m c* 9 April 1465 1st Earl of Argyll (*see* ARGYLL, D)

     3e Marion; *m* Arthur Campbell of Ottar

    1d (cont) The 2nd LORD LORN allegedly *m* 2nd on his deathbed (a marriage not recognised) a dau of the MacLaren chieftain of Ardveich and in any case was surprised and mortally wounded by some of the Clan Dougall led by the 10th Chief's wild son Black Alan MacDougall (against whom an Act of Parliament was afterwards passed) and *d* of wounds in his Castle of Dunstaffnage 20 Dec 1463, leaving by his putative 2nd w:

     1e Dugald, of Appin; tried to enforce his claim to the Lordship of Lorn by force of arms and in 1469 made a compromise with his unc Walter, retaining the Appin district of Upper Lorn and becoming the 1st Chief of the Clan Stewart of Appin; *k* in battle *c* 1498 supporting the MacLarens against the Macdonells of Keppoch, whose cattle the former had raided

    2d WALTER STEWART, 3rd LORD LORN (resigned Lorn to his niece's husb Colin Campbell 1st Earl of Argyll (*see* ARGYLL, D), retaining his peerage and precedence but altering its style so that he became 1st LORD INNERMEATH (Invermay) 1469/70; allegedly *m* Margaret, dau of 1st Lord Lindsay of the Byres (*see* LINDSAY, E), and *d c* 1489, leaving:

     1e THOMAS STEWART, 2nd LORD INNERMEATH; *m* 1481 Janet, dau of 1st Earl Marischal (*see* KINTORE, E), and widow of the Master of Rothes (*see* ROTHES, E); *k* Battle of Flodden 9 Sept 1513, leaving, with other issue (including a dau, Mariota, *m* as his 1st w Patrick Ogilvy of Inchmartine; *see* SEAFIELD, E):

1f RICHARD STEWART, 3rd LORD INNERMEATH; *m* Margaret (*m* 2nd Sir James Stuart of Beath, *k* 1544), dau of John, 3rd Lord Lindsay of the Byres (*see* LINDSAY, E), and *d* 1532, leaving, with other issue:

1g JOHN STEWART, 4th LORD INNERMEATH; Sheriff of Forfar, Extrdy Ld of Session 1541–44; *m c* 1540 JAMES V's mistress Elizabeth (*m* 2nd James Gray (*k* Dundee 1585/6), 4th s of 4th Lord Gray (*qv*), but divorced him for adultery with her niece Isabel Beaton 1581), dau of Sir John Beaton of Creich, Hereditary Keeper of Falkland, and *d* Jan 1569/70, leaving, with other issue:

1h JAMES STEWART, 5th LORD INNERMEATH; one of the peers offered as hostages for MARY QUEEN OF SCOTS 1569, a Cncllr Extraordinary 1577/8, Commr for quieting the public troubles within the realm; *m* 1554 Helen, dau of James, 4th Lord Ogilvy of Airlie (*see* AIRLIE, E), and *d* 14 Feb 1585/6, leaving, with four yr sons and six daus (one of whom, Jean, *m* 1st, as his 2nd w, Sir Walter Rollo (*see* ROLLO, L); *m* 2nd Sir Alexander Jardine of Applegarth:

1i JOHN STEWART, 1st EARL OF ATHOLL, so *cr* 1595/6 on the extinction of the cadet branch which had previously held the title (*see* below); with a band of his highlanders raided the Spaldings of Ashintully and besieged the House of Morcleuch, capturing its owner (Walter Leslie) 1597; *m* 1st (contract 6 Oct 1580) Margaret, dau of 9th Earl of Crawford (*see* CRAWFORD and BALCARRES, E), and had five sons and a dau; *m* 2nd (contract 31 March 1596) Mary, Dowager Countess of Atholl (*m* 3rd James Stewart, s of James, Master of Buchan; *see* below), dau of William, 1st Earl of Gowrie (*qv*), and widow of 5th EARL OF ATHOLL of the 1457 *cr* (*see* below), and *d* 1603, leaving no issue by her; his est s by his 1st w:

1j JAMES STEWART, 2nd EARL OF ATHOLL; *b* 1583; imprisoned for misrule in Atholl and undertook to sell the Earldom but escaped from the custody of Walter Stuart, Lord Blantyre, 1609; *m* (contract 12 Sept 1603) his cousin Mary Stewart (*m* 2nd Capt Peter Rollo; *see* ROLLO, L), dau and coheir of 5th EARL OF ATHOLL of the 1457 *cr* (*see* below), and *dsp* 1625, when the Earldom of Atholl and it would seem the Lordship of Innermeath expired

2h John, of Redcastle, which he took by force and defended against his step-f James Gray 1579; poet; *m* Catherine, dau of Andrew Gray of Duninald, and *d c* 1607; ancestor of the STEWARTs of Laitheris

3d Alan; *d* in prison *c* 1463

2c Archibald; named in the entail of Lorn 1452

3c James (Sir); 'the Black Knight of Lorn'; *m* (papal dispensation 21 Sept 1439) JANE/JOAN BEAUFORT, QUEEN DOWAGER OF SCOTLAND (*d* 15 July 1445), dau of John, Marquess of Dorset and Earl of Somerset (s of John of Gaunt and gs of EDWARD III; *see* BEAUFORT, D, and SOMERSET, D, preliminary remarks), and widow of JAMES I, and was captured at sea by a Flemish ship and put to death, having had:

1d JOHN STEWART, 1st EARL OF ATHOLL (S), so *cr* 1457; *b c* 1440; granted the Castle and Lordship of Balvenie (forfeited by his 1st w's family) 1460, defeated and captured the last Lord of the Isles (*see* MACDONALD, B) 1475; Amb to England 1484; *m* 1st 1459/60 Margaret, 'the Fair Maid of Galloway', Dowager Countess of Douglas (*d* by 1475), dau of 5th Earl of Douglas, widow of her cousin 8th Earl of Douglas and divorced w of another cousin 9th Earl of Douglas and sis and heiress of 6th Earl of Douglas (for all of whom *see* QUEENSBERRY, M), and had, with a yr dau:

1e Janet; *m* (contract 14 Oct 1474) 3rd Earl of Huntly (*see* HUNTLY, M) and *d* 27 Oct 1510, leaving issue

1d (cont) The 1st EARL *m* 2nd *c* 27 April 1475 Eleanor (*d* 21 March 1518), dau of 1st Earl of Caithness (*qv*), and *d* 15 Sept 1512, having by her had, with nine more daus (including Margaret, *m* Sir William Murray of Castleton; *see* ATHOLL, D); Catherine, *m* as his 1st w 6th Lord Forbes; *qv*) and a yr s (Andrew, Bp Caithness 1518–42):

1e JOHN STEWART, 2nd EARL OF ATHOLL; said to have forcibly seized Rattray Castle after Flodden, where the Rattray chief had fallen, and carried off the heiress; *m* Janet (*d* Feb 1545/6), dau of 2nd Earl of Argyll (*see* ARGYLL, D), and *d* 1521, leaving, with three other daus:

1f JOHN STEWART, 3rd EARL OF ATHOLL; *m* 1st *c* 1521 Grizel, heiress of the Barony of Rattray and of extensive lands in Atholl, er dau and coheir of John Rattray, Yr. of Rattray (*dvp*), s of Sir John Rattray of that Ilk (*k* at Flodden), and had seven daus (including Margaret, *m* as his 1st w John Grant, 4th of Freuchie; *see* STRATHSPEY, B) and a s; *m* 2nd (shortly before he *d* 1542) Jean (*m* 2nd Alexander Hay of Delgaty; *m* 3rd William Leslie of Balquhain (*see* LESLIE, Bt), by whom she was grandmother of Count Leslie, the killer of the Imperial warlord Count Wallenstein in the Thirty Years War), dau of 6th Lord Forbes (*qv*), but by her had no issue; his s:

1g JOHN STEWART, 4th EARL OF ATHOLL; PC; Catholic, helped MARY QUEEN OF SCOTS win Battle of Corrichie 1562, Ld Lt of the North 1565, nominated provisional Regent 1567, Chllr Scotland 1578; *m* 1st *c* 26 May 1547 Elizabeth, dau of 4th Earl of Huntly (*see* HUNTLY, M), and had:

1h Elizabeth; *m* 1st 24 Dec 1567 5th Lord Lovat (*qv*); *m* 2nd 6 Dec 1578 2nd EARL OF LENNOX of the 1572 *cr* (later 1st EARL OF MARCH; *see* above); *m* 3rd 6 July 1581 1st Earl of

Arran of the 1581 *cr* (*see* CASTLE-STEWART, E), Chllr of Scotland and Lt of the Realm, who had been attainted since 1585 and was murdered 5 Dec 1595, and *d* Sept 1595

2h Margaret; *m* by 3 Aug 1574 7th Lord Saltoun (*qv*) of Abernethy

1g (cont.) The 4th EARL *m* 2nd (contract 1 April 1557) Margaret, dau of Malcolm, 3rd Lord Fleming (by Jean Stuart, illegitimate dau of JAMES IV and mistress of HENRY II of France), and widow of (a) the Master of Montrose (*see* MONTROSE, D) and (b) the Master of Erskine (*see* MAR and KELLIE, E), and *d* (possibly poisoned) 24 April 1579, having by her had:

1h JOHN STEWART, 5th EARL OF ATHOLL, PC; *b* 22 May 1563; Commr to pursue the Clan Gregor 1589/90; *m* 24 Jan 1579/80 Mary (*m* 2nd 1596 1st EARL OF ATHOLL of the 1595/6 *cr* (*see* above); *m* 3rd James Stewart, s of James, Master of Buchan (*see* below), dau of 1st Earl of Gowrie (*see* CARLISLE, E), and *dspm* 28 Aug 1595, having had:

1i Margaret; *d* young

2i Dorothea; *m* Sept 1604 2nd Earl of Tullibardine and had issue (*see* ATHOLL, D)

3i Mary; *m* 1st 1603 her cousin 2nd EARL OF ATHOLL of the 1595/6 *cr* (*see* above); *m* 2nd *c* 1626 Capt Peter Rollo (*see* ROLLO, L)

4i Jean; *m* 1st 1603 1st LORD SAINT COLME of the March 1610/1 *cr* (*see* below); *m* 2nd Nicol Bellenden of Standenflat and *d* 19 July 1623

5j Anne; *m* 1604 Andrew Stuart, Master of Ochiltree, afterwards 2nd Lord Castle Stewart (*d* 30 March 1639, *see* below and CASTLE STEWART, E), and *d* Oct 1635

3h Jean; *m* (contract 18 Nov 1573) Sir Duncan Campbell of Glenorchy (*d* 23 June 1631; *see* BREADALBANE AND HOLLAND, E) and *d* Sept 1593

4h Grizel; *m* 1581 11th Earl of Crawford (*see* CRAWFORD and BALCARRES, E)

5h Mary; *m* 1586/7 9th Earl of Erroll (*qv*) and *d c* 1588

1f Janet; *m* 1st *c* 16 June 1520 Alexander, Master of Strathnaver (*see* SUTHERLAND, Countess of); *m* 2nd by 13 May 1532 Sir Hew Kennedy of Girvanmains; *m* 3rd by 4th Nov 1544 her cousin 1st Lord Methven (*see* below); *m* 4th 3rd Lord Ruthven (*see* CARLISLE, E)

2d JAMES STEWART, 1st EARL OF BUCHAN (*see* separate article); had:

1e ALEXANDER STEWART, 2nd EARL OF BUCHAN; had, with a yr s and two daus:

1f JOHN STEWART, 3rd EARL OF BUCHAN; had:

1g John, *Master of Buchan*; had:

1h CHRISTIAN Stewart, COUNTESS OF BUCHAN in her own right; *m* Robert DOUGLAS, 4th EARL OF BUCHAN in right of his w, and had issue

2g James, *Master of Buchan* from 1547 until his niece had a child; *m* Christian, dau of John Strang of Balcaskie, and had, with two daus:

1h James; served heir male to the Buchan branch of the STEWARTs 1618

2h Alexander

2d (cont) The 1st EARL OF BUCHAN also had by his mistress, Margaret Murray (widow of William Murray), with other illegitimate issue:

2e James, 1st of Traquair, which lands he recd from his f 1491 legitimated 20 Feb 1488/9; *m* (papal dispensation 9 Nov 1505) Catherine, sis and coheir of Richard Rutherford of that Ilk, and was *k* Flodden 1513, having had, with two daus:

1f William, 2nd of Traquair; living 1538; *m* Christian, dau of 2nd Lord Hay of Yester (*see* TWEEDDALE, M), and had, with two daus:

1g Robert, 3rd of Traquair; *dsp* 9 Sept 1548

2g John (Sir), 4th of Traquair; Capt of the Gd to MARY QUEEN OF SCOTS 1566; *m* Janet Knox and *dsp* 28 April 1591

3g William (Sir), 5th of Traquair, PC; Gentleman of the Bedchamber to JAMES VI, Keeper Dumbarton Castle 1582, MP Peeblesshire 1593–1604; *d* 20 May 1605

4g James, 6th of Traquair; Lt of the Gd under his bro Sir John; *m* Catherine Kerr and *d* 9 March 1605/6, having had, with three yr sons and five daus:

1h John, Yr. of Traquair; *m* Margaret, dau of Andrew, Master of Ochiltree (*see* CASTLE STEWART, E), and *dvp*, leaving:

1i JOHN STEWART, 1st EARL OF TRAQUAIR, LORD LINTON AND CABERSTON, so *cr* 23 June 1633, with remainder to his heirs male bearing the name and arms of Stewart, as also earlier LORD STEWART OF TRAQUAIR (all S), with identical remainder, PC (S 1628); *b c* 1600; MP (S Parl) Peeblesshire 1621, ktd by Feb 1621/2, Keeper Dumbarton Castle Dec 1627–Feb 1627/8, Burgess Edinburgh 1630, Treasurer Depute Scotland 1630, Extrdy Ld of Session 1630–41, a Commr Exchequer 1631 and 1640, Ld High Treasurer Scotland 1636–41, as which attempted to follow a moderate path between on the one hand CHARLES I and his insistence on foisting the Laudian church service on the Scots, and on the other hand the Covenanters, who opposed it; royalist Civil War in England, but later signed the Covenant; Commr War Peebles 1647 and Roxburghs and Selkirkshire 1648; fought for CHARLES II against CROMWELL 1647 (taken prisoner following royalist defeat of Preston 1648 and held at Warwick Castle till 1651); *m c* 14 Sept 1620 Catherine, dau of 1st Earl of Southesk (*qv*), and *d* 27 March 1659 after having been forced to beg in the Edinburgh streets following the sale of his estates to meet debts and fines levied on him for his royalism in the Civil War, leaving:

1j JOHN STEWART, 2nd EARL OF TRAQUAIR; *b* after 8 March 1623/4; taken with his f following Preston 1648 but shortly afterwards set free; *m* 1st 1649 Henrietta (*d* in childbirth 1651, having had no issue by him), dau of 2nd Marquess of Huntly (*qv*) and widow of George, Lord Seton (*see* EGLINTON and WINTON, E); *m* 2nd April 1654 Anne, half-sis of his former f-in-law and dau of 3rd Earl of Winton (*see* EGLINTON and WINTON, E), and *d* April 1666, leaving:

1k WILLIAM STEWART, 3rd EARL OF TRAQUAIR; *b* 18 June 1657; *d* unm by 23 Dec 1673

2k George; *dvp*

3k CHARLES STEWART, 4th EARL OF TRAQUAIR, PC (1686 and 1687–88); *b* 1659; *educ* St Andrews; remanded in custody Edinburgh Castle and interrogated London March 1707/8–June 1708 for suspected involvement in the abortive French descent on Scotland to help the Jacobites; *m* 9 Jan 1693/4 Mary, only dau of 4th Earl of Nithsdale (*see* HERRIES OF TERREGLES, L), and *d* 13 June 1741, having had, with two est daus (Lucy; Anne) and two yst ones (Barbara; Margaret):

1l CHARLES STEWART, 5th EARL OF TRAQUAIR; *b* 31 March 1697; *educ* Paris; co-fndr of the Scottish Jacobite Association 1739 (*see also* LOVAT, L), but despite preparing for the 1745 Uprising he did not participate in it; nevertheless held in Tower of London Aug 1746–Feb 1747/8 on suspicion of complicity in Uprising, after which he was set free, having not been brought to trial, on bail of £30,000 (over £1,720,000 in late-1990s terms); *m* (contract 30 Oct 1745) Theresa, yst dau of Sir Baldwin Conyers, 4th Bt, of Horden, Co Durham, and *dsp* 24 April 1764

2l William; *b* 27 Feb 1697/8; *d* young

3l JOHN STEWART, 6th EARL OF TRAQUAIR; *b* 3 Feb 1698/9; *educ* in Paris; also co-fndr Scottish Jacobite Association; also took no part in 1745 Uprising itself; *m* 1740 Christian, dau of Sir Philip Anstruther of Anstrutherfield (*see* ANSTRUTHER, Bt) and widow of Sir William Weir, 2nd Bt, and *d* 28 March 1779, leaving, with three daus:

1m CHARLES STEWART/STUART, 7th EARL OF TRAQUAIR; *b* spring 1744; *m* 19 Aug 1773 Mary, yr dau of George Ravenscroft, of Wykeham, Lincs, and *d* 14 Oct 1827, leaving:

1n CHARLES STEWART/STUART, 8th and last EARL OF TRAQUAIR; *b* 31 Jan 1781; *d* apparently unm 2 Aug 1861 when it would seem that all his titles expired

1n Louisa; *b* 20 March 1776; *d* unm 6 Dec 1875

4l Robert; *b* 9 Feb 1709/10; *d* young

1l Mary; *m* titular 5th Duke of Perth (*see* PERTH, E)

2l Catherine; *m* 27 June 1731, as his 1st w, her cousin William Maxwell, self-styled 6th Earl of Nithsdale (*see* HERRIES OF TERREGLES, L), and *d* 16 June 1765

1j Margaret; *m* 2nd Earl of Queensberry and had issue (*see* QUEENSBERRY, M)

2j Elizabeth; *m* 2nd Lord Elibank (*qv*) and had issue

3j Anne; *m* Sir John Hamilton of Redhouse and had issue

4j Catherine; *m* John Stewart and had two sons and a dau

1e Agnes; mistress of JAMES IV (*see* below); *m* 1st 1511 Adam Hepburn, 2nd Earl of Bothwell (*k* Flodden 1513); *m* 2nd *c* 1513 3rd Lord Home (*see* HOME, E); *m* 3rd 4th Lord Maxwell (*see* MAXWELL, Bt); *m* 4th Cuthbert Ramsay and *d* Feb 1557

3d Andrew; Bp Moray 1483–1501

4c Alexander; ancestor of the STEUARTs and STEUART FOTHRINGHAMs of Murthly and Grandtully

(5) John (Sir), of Daldar; *dsp*(?; for an alternative account *see* GALLOWAY, E), *k* Battle of Halidon Hill 1333

(1) Isabel, Lady of Garlies; *m* Thomas Randolph, 1st Earl of Moray (*see* above, preliminary remarks)

1 Elizabeth; *m* Sir William Douglas of that Ilk, called 'The Bold' (*d* a prisoner of the English in the Tower of London 1298)

The 4th GREAT STEWARD *d* 1283; his est son,

JAMES STEWART, 5th Gt Steward of Scotland; *b c* 1243; Jt Regent of Scotland as one of the six Guardians of the Realm 1286, supported the claims of the er ROBERT (THE BRUCE) to the throne, opposed EDWARD I's attempts to dominate Scotland and ratified the treaty with France 1295; forced to submit to EDWARD I 1297 and sent by the English to negotiate with Sir William Wallace but joined him instead and fought for him at the rout of the English at Stirling Bridge 1297, supported ROBERT (THE BRUCE) and attended his Parl at St Andrews; *m* Jill du Bourg (Egidia de Burgo), dau of Walter, 1st Earl of Ulster, and *d* 16 July 1309, leaving:

1 Andrew; *dvp*

2 WALTER

3 John (Sir); *k* Battle of Dundalk 1318

4 James (Sir), of Durrisdeer; *dsp*

1 Jill; *m* Alexander of Menzies

The 2nd son,

WALTER STEWART, 6th Gt Steward of Scotland; *b* 1292; Regent of Scotland during ROBERT I (THE BRUCE)'s absence in Ireland 1316, defended Berwick

against an English army, made a raid with Douglas that nearly kidnapped EDWARD II from Yorkshire 1322; *m* 1st 1315 MARJORIE, LADY OF SCOTLAND (*d* 1316), dau of ROBERT I (THE BRUCE), and had issue; *m* 2nd Isabel, dau of Sir John Graham of Abercorn (*see* MONTROSE, D), and *d* 9 April 1327, having by her had two more sons (Sir John, of Railston; Sir Andrew) and a dau (Jill, *m* 1st Sir James Lindsay of Crawford (*see* CRAWFORD and BALCARRES, E), *m* 2nd Sir Hugh de Montgomerie, *m* 3rd Sir James Douglas of Dalkeith; his est s by his 1st w:

ROBERT II, KING OF SCOTS; *b* 2 March 1315/6; *s* f as 7th Gt Steward of Scotland 1327; fought Halidon Hill 1333, cmdg the retreat after his uncle DAVID II was captured at Neville's Cross 1346, Regent or Guardian of Scotland 1346–57, *s* DAVID II 1370/1; *m* 1st (papal dispensation 22 Nov 1347) Elizabeth, dau of Sir Adam Muir of Rowallan, and had, with other issue:

1 JOHN; ascended the throne as ROBERT III

2 WALTER STEWART, EARL OF FIFE in right of his w Isabel; *dsp c* 1362

3 ROBERT STEWART, 1st DUKE OF ALBANY (S), so *cr* 1398 (Albany being the Gaelic for Scotland north of Forth), the same day as his n, the heir apparent to the throne, they being the first two dukes ever *cr* in Scotland; also EARL OF MENTEITH in right of his w and EARL OF FIFE by entail 1371; *b c* 1340; Gt Chamberlain of Scotland 1382–1408, invaded England with Douglas 1385, Regent 1388–1420; imprisoned his n, who *d* mysteriously 1402; invaded England 1417; rebuilt Doune Castle; *m* 1st (papal dispensation 9 Sept 1361) Margaret (*d c* 1380), COUNTESS OF MENTEITH in her own right (through whom he inherited Doune Castle), dau of John Graham, Earl of Menteith (*see* MONTROSE, D), and widow of (a) Sir John Murray, (feudal) Lord of Bothwell, (b) 9th Earl of Mar (*qv*), and (c) Sir John Drummond of Concraig, and *d* 2 Sept 1420, having had, with at least two daus (Beatrice, may have *m* 7th Earl of Douglas (*see* QUEENSBERRY, M); another dau *m* William Abernethy, 6th of Saltoun; *see* SALTOUN, L) an est s:

(1) MURDACH STEWART, 2nd DUKE OF ALBANY; *b c* 1362; Justiciar of Scotland north of Forth 1389, captured by the Percys (*see* NORTHUMBERLAND, D) Homildon Hill 1402 but released in exchange for the Earl of Northumberland 1415; Regent of Scotland 1420; secured JAMES I's release from captivity in England and (as Earl of Fife, hence heir of the Clan MacDuff) enthroned him at Scone 1424, but was considered over-powerful, arrested with his family, tried and beheaded 25 May 1425, having *m* (indenture 17 Feb 1391/2) Isabel, Countess of Lennox in her own right (*d c* 1458), dau, and coheir of Duncan, 8th Earl of Lennox (beheaded with the Albany family 1425), and left, with a dau (Isabel, *m* Sir Walter Buchanan of that Ilk):

1a Robert, *Master of Fife* (possibly s of an earlier marriage); *dvp* unm by July 1421

2a Walter (Sir), *Master of Fife, Lennox and Menteith*; arrested and imprisoned on the Bass Rock 1424 then beheaded at Stirling 24 May 1425; said to have *m* unlawfully (presumably uncanonically for want of a papal dispensation for consanguinity) a dau of Duncan, 1st Lord Campbell, and (since the marriage was null) had illegitimate issue:

1b ANDREW STEWART, 1st LORD AVANDALE (S), so *cr* 1456, PC; ktd in England *c* 1437; Ld Warden of the Marches 1456–60, Ld High Chcllr Scotland 1460–82, Keeper Stirling Castle 1467, Amb Denmark 1468, Jt Amb France 1484; built the Castle of Strathaven; granted a life-rent of the lands of the Earldom of Lennox 1471; obtained letters of legitimation 1472 and 1479 for himself and his bros Arthur and Walter; *m* a noblewoman but *dsp* July 1488

2b Alexander; *d c* 1472

2a (cont) The *Master of Fife* also had illegitimate issue (by which mother is uncertain):

3b Murdoch (Sir); ktd in England *c* 1437; *d c* 1472

4b Arthur; legitimated 1472 and 1479; *d c* 1488

2a (cont) The *Master of Fife* had a papal dispensation (24 April 1421) to *m* Janet, dau of Robert, 1st Lord Erskine (*see* MAR, E), and (probably by her) had:

5b Walter, feudal Baron of Morphie (*see also* CASTLE STEWART, E); officially legitimated with his er half-bros 1472 and 1479; allegedly *m* Elizabeth Arnot, dau of the Laird of Arnot, Fifeshire, and *d c* 1488, leaving, with a yr s (John):

1c Alexander, of Avandale, to whom that feudal Barony was resigned by his unc 4 Jan 1485/6; a Lord Auditor Jan 1488/9; *d* 1489 before taking up title to the Lordship, to which he may have *s* in 1488; his s:

1d ANDREW STEWART, 1st (by *cr* by 4 Feb 1497/1500/2nd LORD AVANDALE (by inheritance from his unc); First Usher of the King's Chamber 1502–09, a Lord Auditor 1512; *m* by 4 Feb 1499/1500 Margaret, sis of 1st Earl of Cassillis (*see* AILSA, M), and was *ka* Flodden 9 Sept 1513, having had:

1e ANDREW STEWART, *s* as 2nd/3rd LORD AVANDALE 1513 but exchanged the feudal Barony with Sir James Hamilton of Finnart for that of Ochiltree 1534 and changed his peerage style by Act of Parl 1542/3 to that of 1st LORD (STEWART OF) OCHILTREE; Master Usher of the King's Chamber 1524, Sheriff Dunbartonshire 1527; *m c* 22 Aug 1515 Margaret Hamilton, illegitimate dau of James, 1st Earl of Arran, by Beatrix, dau of John, 1st Lord Drummond (*see* PERTH, E), and *d* 1548, having had, with a yr s (Walter) and a dau (Isabel, *m* Duncan Macfarlane of that Ilk):

1f ANDREW STEWART, 2nd LORD (STEWART OF) OCHILTREE, called 'The Good Lord Ochiltree', though this seems to be no more than a reference to his enthusiastic Protestantism, PC; *b c* 1521; one of the Lds of the Congregation who led the Reformation in Scotland 1559/60, refused his consent to MARY QUEEN OF SCOTS' marriage to Lord Darnley (*see* above) and fled to England 1565; severely wounded fighting against MARY QUEEN OF SCOTS Battle of Langside 1568; Warden W Marches 1586; Commr to suppress Jesuits 1589/90; *m* 1st by 27 Oct 1549 Agnes, sis of William Cunningham, 5th of Caprington (High Commr to Gen Assembly Ch Scotland 1581); *m* 2nd between Aug 1570 and Feb 1572/3 Lady Margaret Cunningham, dau of 5th Earl of Glencairn (*see* CUNINGHAME, Bt) and widow of John Wallace of

Craigie, and *d* 1591, leaving issue by his 1st w (*see* CASTLE STEWART, E)

2e HENRY STEWART, 1st LORD METHVEN(S), so *cr* 17 July 1528; *b c* 1495–1500; *m* 1st 'The Lady Leslie' and had a s (*dvp* 1547); *m* 2nd March 1527/8 MARGARET, dau of HENRY VII of ENGLAND and widow of JAMES IV of Scots, and had a dau (*d* an infant); *m* 3rd by 4 Nov 1544 Janet Stewart (*m* 4th 3rd Lord Ruthven *see* CAR-LISLE, E), est dau of 2nd Earl of Atholl (*see* above) and formerly w of (a) Sir Hugh Kennedy of Girvanmains and (b) Alexander Gordon, Master of Sutherland, and *d* shortly after 10 Oct 1551, having by her had, with three daus:

1f HENRY STEWART, 2nd LORD METHVEN PC (*s* 1571); *b* (like his sisters) before his parents' marriage but legitimated 1551; *m* in or after March 1568 Jean (*m* 2nd *c* Oct 1573, as his 2nd w, 5th Earl of Rothes; *qv*), est dau of his stepf, 3rd Lord Ruthven, and was *k* by a cannon ball fired from Edinburgh Castle (then held by the pro-English party) 3 March 1571/2, leaving:

1g HENRY STEWART, 3rd and last LORD METHVEN; *m* —, dau of Henry Stewart, 2nd s of James Stewart, Earl of Arran (*qv*, preliminary remarks) of the 1581 *cr*, and *dsp* apparently *c* 1580, when the title expired

3e James (Sir), of Beath; Gentleman Bedchamber to JAMES V; Capt and Constable Doune Castle 1528, Commendator of St Colme's Inch, Steward Menteith by 1538; *m* Margaret, dau of John, 3rd Lord Lindsay of the Byres (*see* LINDSAY, E), and widow of 3rd LORD INNERMEATH (*see* above), and was *k* at Dunblane Whitsunday 1547 by Sir William Edmonstone of Duntreath (*see* EDMON-STONE, Bt) and his bros, leaving:

1f JAMES STEWART, **1st Lord Doune**, so *cr* 24 Nov 1581, with remainder to his heirs male whatsoever, PC; *b c* 1529; Commendator (lay proprietor, drawing revenues but undertaking no spiritual duties, following religious houses' dissolution) St Colme; Constable Doune Castle; joined the Protestant Lords of the Congregation at the Reformation 1560, Jt Amb France 1560, ktd 1565, Extrdy Ld of Session 1584–86; *m* 11 Jan 1563/4 Margaret Campbell (*d* Feb 1571/2 of injuries from a fire), dau of 4th Earl of Argyll (*see* ARGYLL, D), and *d* 20 July 1590, having had:

1g JAMES, **2nd Lord** and **2nd Earl of Moray** (*see* below)

2g HENRY STEWART, 1st LORD SAINT COLME (S), so *cr* 7 March 1610/1, JP (Fife and Kinross 1610); had the lands of the dissolved Abbey of St Colme made over to him by his f 1581, Constable Doune Castle after er bro's death but deprived for supporting Bothwell 1593; *m* (contract Dec 1603) Jean (*m* 2nd Nicol Bellenden of Standenflat and *d* 19 July 1623), dau and coheir of 5th EARL OF ATHOLL of the 1457 *cr* (*see* above), and *d* 12 July 1612, leaving:

1h JAMES STEWART, 2nd and apparently last LORD SAINT COLME; Col in Swedish service under GUSTAVUS ADOL-PHUS in Germany during Thirty Years War; *dsp c* 1620, when it would appear his Lordship of Parl expired

3g Archibald; living 1579

4g John; sentenced to beheading *c* 1609 for murdering one John Gibb 1608

1g Mary; *m* (contract Aug 1581) Sir John Wemyss of Wemyss (*see* WEMYSS, E)

2g Margaret; *d* young

3g Jean; *m* 4 April 1596 6th Lord (Fraser of) Lovat (*qv*) and *d* 1 July 1622

2f Archibald; Provost Edinburgh 1578; *dsp*

3f Henry, of Buchlyvie; *m* (contract 27 Jan 1566/7) Elizabeth, dau of John Robertson, and had, with 2 yr sons (William; Robert):

1g James, of Burray in Orkney; *m* Janet, dau of Torquil (s of Ruaridh MacLeod, 10th Chief of Lewis, by his 2nd w Barbara Stuart, owner of the island of Burray in Orkney and dau of the 2nd LORD AVANDALE), and had:

1h Barbara, heiress of Burray; *m* William Stewart of Mains, yr bro of 1st Earl of Galloway (*qv*), and had issue

1f Majory; *m* 1st James Ross of Craighton; *m* 2nd John Lindsay of Dowhill (*see* LINDSAY, Bt)

2f Margaret; *m* (contract 6 Feb 1553/4) James Ogilvie of Balfour

3f Elizabeth; *m c* 22 May 1558 Robert Crichton of Cluny, Lord Advocate and a Ld of Session

4e Alexander; living 1541

5e William; living 1548; *m* Isabel Kerr

1e Barbara; acquired the island of Burray in Orkney; *m* 1st *c* 1535 Sir James Sinclair of Sanday, Govr of Kirkwall in Orkney; *m* 2nd 1541 Ruaridh MacLeod, 10th Chief of Lewis

2e Agnes; *m* John Boswell of Auchinleck

3e Anne; *m* Bartholomew Crawford of Carse

3a Alexander (Sir); ktd 1424; *m* after *c* 1 Feb 1420/1 Algidia/Egidia/Jill, dau of Sir William Douglas of Nithsdale and widow of 2nd Earl of Orkney of the 1379 *cr* (*see* CAITHNESS, E); beheaded at Stirling 25 May 1425

4a James (Sir), called *Seumas Mor* ('Big James'), 1st of Baldorran; only s of the Regent Albany to escape the general liquidation of the family in 1425; avenged his family by burning Dumbarton at the head of a band of Highlanders, killing its Keeper (JAMES I's uncle) then fleeing to England; settled Ireland, where he *d* 1451, having had by a Macdonald (with another illegitimate child Matilda; *m* Sir William Edmonstone of Duntreath; *see* EDMONSTONE, Bt):

1b James, called *Seumas Beg* ('Little James'), 2nd of Baldorran; *m* Annabel, dau of Patrick Buchanan, 14th of that Ilk, and was ancestor of the STEWARTs in Balquhidder

3 (cont.) The 1st DUKE *m* 2nd (papal dispensation May 1380) Muriel (*d* May 1449), dau of Sir William Keith, Marshal of Scotland (*see* KINTORE, E), and by her had, with two yr sons (Andrew, *dsp c* 1413; Robert, living 1431):

(2) JOHN STEWART, EARL OF BUCHAN (*see* BUCHAN, E, preliminary remarks)

ROBERT II *m* 2nd (papal dispensation 2 May 1355) Eupheme (*d* 1387), dau of Hugh, 4th Earl of Ross, and widow of John, 3rd Earl of Moray (*k* Neville's Cross 1346), and *d* 19 April 1390, having by her had further issue and by another woman at least one illegitimate s (*see* BUTE, M):

His est son,

ROBERT III; *b c* 1337; *m c* 1367 Annabella, dau of John Drummond of Stobhall (*see* PERTH, E), and *d* 4 April 1406, leaving, with other issue:

JAMES I; *b* Dec 1394; *m* 2 Feb 1433/4 Joan Beaufort (*m* 2nd 1439 Sir James Stewart, 'The Black Knight of Lorn' (*see* above) and *d* 15 July 1445), ggdau of EDWARD III, and was assassinated 21 Feb 1436/7, having had:

JAMES II; *b* 16 Oct 1430; *m* 3 July 1449 Mary (*d* 1 Dec 1463), dau of Arnold, Duke of Gueldres, and was *k* by the bursting of one of his own cannon while besieging the English in Roxburgh Castle 3 Aug 1460, leaving, with other issue:

1 JAMES III

3 DAVID STEWART, 1st and last EARL OF MORAY, so *cr* 12 Feb 1455/6; *d* in infancy by 18 July 1457

JAMES II's est lawful son,

JAMES III; *b* 10 July 1451; *m* 13 July 1469 Margaret (*d* 14 July 1486), dau of CHRISTIAN I of Denmark, and was stabbed to death 11 June 1488 after being thrown from his horse on leaving the battlefield of Sauchieburn following his defeat by the rebellious lords under the Earl of Angus and Lord Home (*see* HOME, E), having had, with two other sons:

JAMES IV; *b* 17 March 1472/3; *m* 8 Aug 1503 MARGARET (*m* 2nd 6 Aug 1514 (*divorce*) Archibald Douglas, 6th Earl of Angus; *m* 3rd March 1527/8, as his 2nd w, 1st Lord Methven (*see* above) and *d* 18 Oct 1541), dau of HENRY VII, and was *k* Flodden 9 Sept 1513, leaving, with other issue:

JAMES V; *b* 10 April 1512; *m* 1st 1 Jan 1536/7 Madeline (*dsp* 7 July 1537), dau of FRANCIS I of France; *m* 2nd June 1538 Mary of Lorraine (Regent of Scotland after his death; *d* 10 June 1560), dau of Claude, Duke of Guise, and widow of Louis d'Orleans, Duke of Longueville, and had, with other issue:

1 MARY, QUEEN OF SCOTS

JAMES V *d* 14 Dec 1542, leaving, with other illegitimate children by various women, but in this case by Margaret Erskine, sis of 18th Earl of Mar (*qv*):

1 JAMES STEWART, **1st Earl of Moray**, so *cr* 30 Jan 1561/2 as also LORD ABERNETHY (new charter of Earldom 1563, when granted also Ldships of Abernethy and Strathdearn, so becoming LORD STRATHDEARN; a new charter altering the remainder to heirs general was ratified by Parl 1567) and briefly EARL OF MAR (so *cr* 7 Feb 1561/2; resigned it 1562 and it granted to his unc; *see also* MAR, E) (all S); *b c* 1531; *educ* St Andrews; Prior St Andrews and Pittenweem 1538, legitimated 7 Feb 1550/1, Prior Mâcon in France (with papal dispensation to hold three benefices) 1555, Jt Amb France 1558; joined the Protestant Lds of the Congregation 1559/60; chief adviser to his half-sis MARY QUEEN OF SCOTS, cmdg her forces victory of Corrichie over her opponents under Earl of Huntly (*see* HUNTLY, M); exiled for his opposition to the Queen's marriage to Lord Darnley (*see* above) 1565/6, returned to Scotland after consenting to Rizzio's murder 1566, withdrew to France before the Queen's marriage to the Earl of Bothwell 1567, returned again after the Queen's abdication and became Regent at her request, restoring order on the Borders, where he hanged or drowned many reivers (marauders) 1567, but opposed the Queen after her escape from Lochleven, defeating her army at Langside and driving her into exile 1568; ruled Scotland 1567–70; *m* 8 Feb 1561/2 Agnes Keith (*m* 2nd Feb 1571/2 6th Earl of Argyll (*see* ARGYLL, D) and *d* 16 July 1588), dau of 4th Earl Marischal (*see* KINTORE, E), and was assassinated at Linlithgow by James Hamilton of Bothwellhaugh (whose family he had wronged) 21 Jan 1569/70, being *bur* in the Moray aisle of St Giles's Cathedral in Edinburgh (though his skull was disinterred some centuries later and kept by his descendants at Darnaway Castle, mounted as a drinking-cup on silver acorns — the Stuart plant-badge being oak), having had, with two yr daus (Annabel, *d* young *c* Nov 1572; Margaret, *m c* 27 June 1584 9th Earl of Erroll (*qv*) but *dsp* 1586):

(1) ELIZABETH Stewart, **Countess of Moray** in her own right; *m* 23 Jan 1580/1 JAMES STUART (later **2nd Lord Doune**; *see* above), who seems to have been regarded as **2nd Earl of Moray** from the moment he married her (called the 'Bonny Earl'; was attacked one night at Donibristle, which was set on fire by his hereditary enemy George, 6th Earl and afterwards 1st Marquess of Huntly (*qv*), who had been authorised by JAMES VI to arrest those suspected of involvement in a raid on Holyroodhouse by Francis Stuart, Earl of Bothwell; Lord Moray, making his way to the seashore in darkness, was espied from the flames on a silken tassel that had caught fire in his cap and slashed to death 7 Feb 1591/2; a contemporary portrait at Darnaway shows the wounds on his naked corpse and his murder is lamented in the old ballad 'the Bonny Earl of Moray') and *d* 18 Nov 1591, leaving:

1a JAMES, **3rd Earl**

2a Francis (Sir), KB; memb of Sir Walter Raleigh's club at the Mermaid Tavern

1a Margaret; *m* 1st Sept 1603 2nd Baron Howard of Effingham (*see* EFFINGHAM, E); *m* 2nd 1st and last Viscount Monson of Castlemaine (*see* MONSON, B, preliminary remarks), and *d* 4 Aug 1639

2a Elizabeth; *m* 1605 8th Lord Saltoun (*qv*) of Abernethy

3a Grizel; *m* (contract 18 Dec 1611) Sir Robert Innes, 1st Bt, of that Ilk (*see* ROXBURGHE, D)

The er son,

JAMES STUART, **3rd Earl of Moray** also 1st LORD ST COLME (S), so *cr* 26 Feb 1619/20, even though his cousin the 2nd and apparently last LORD SAINT COLME of the March 1610/1 *cr* (*see* above) was still living; *b* between 1581 and 1583; requested by JAMES VI not to pursue his f's murderer, whose dau he eventually married; 1st Earl's charter of 1566 ratified in his favour 1599 but he resigned his titles and was granted 17 April 1611 a new charter of them in favour of himself and the heirs male of his body, with remainder to his bro Francis and the heirs male of his body, whom failing, to his nearest heirs and assignees; *m* (contract 2 Oct 1607) Anne, est dau of 1st Marquess of Huntly (*qv*), and *d* 6 Aug 1638, having had, with at least one dau (Mary, *m* 24 April 1640 James Grant, 7th of Freuchie; *see* STRATHSPEY, B) an er s:

JAMES STUART, **4th Earl of Moray**, PC (Feb 1637/8); subscribed to the Covenant; *m* (contract 18 Oct 1627) Margaret, er dau of 1st Earl of Home (*qv*), and *d* 4 March 1653, having had:

 1 James, *Lord Doune, dvp unm*

 2 ALEXANDER, **5th Earl**

 3 Francis, of Cullelo, Fife; *dsp*

 4 Archibald, of Dunearn, Fife; Govr Stirling Castle; *m* Anne, dau of Sir John Henderson of Fordel, and *d* Feb 1688, having had, with other issue:

 (1) Charles, of Dunearn; Offr 3rd Foot Gds, Master of Works Tower of London; *m* 1st 1697 Christian, dau of Sir William Bennet, of Grubbet, and had:

 1a Alexander, of Dunearn; Capt 11th Dragoons, ADC to Lord Mark Ker Battle of Culloden 1746, Keeper Ludlow Castle; *m* Christian Boterel and *dsp* 13 Feb 1786

 (1) (cont.) Charles Stuart *m* 2nd 24 Aug 1700 his cousin Jean, dau of Alexander Hamilton of Dalziel, and *d* 1732, having by her had, with other issue:

 2a James; Provost Edinburgh 1764–65 and 1768–69; *m* 1st Elizabeth, dau and heiress of Adam Drummond of Binnend, s of Adam Drummond of Megginch (*see* PERTH, E), and had:

 1b Charles, of Dunearn, MD; *s* 1786; Pres RS Edinburgh 1807–09 and RCP Edinburgh 1806–09; *m* 1st 29 Oct 1773 Mary (*d* 15 April 1817), dau of John Erskine, DD, of Carnock, and had, with other issue:

 1c John Alexander, of Carnock; *b* 4 Nov 1787; *m* 13 May 1824 Margaret (*d* 11 March 1865), dau of Thomas Murray, and *d* 3 Nov 1869, leaving, with other issue:

 1d Charles, of Hillside, Chirnside; MD Edin; *b* 30 March 1825; *m* 28 Oct 1851 Georgina Logan (*d* 26 March 1904), dau of Rev John L Edgar, and *d* 12 Feb 1902, leaving:

 1e John Alexander Erskine; LRCS, LRCP; *b* 30 April 1855; *m* 31 Oct 1881 Margaret Maude Marion (*d* 15 Jan 1931), dau of William Blackburn, and *d* 26 Dec 1927, having had:

 1f Charles Drummond Erskine; *b* 7 Nov 1883; *d* 4 Oct 1925

 2f Henry Erskine; *b* 29 Jan 1885; *d unm* 2 Nov 1955

 1f Sylvia Georgina Maude; *b* 5 July 1890; *d unm*

 2f Marjorie Violet; *b* 13 July 1900; *m* 2 Sept 1930 Rev John Edmund Simpson, s of William Edward Simpson, and had issue

 2e Charles; MB (Edin); *b* 20 March 1858; *d* 21 July 1923

 3e Edgar Francis; *b* 29 March 1864; *m* Oct 1885 Margaret Jones (*d* 1935), having had, with three daus:

 1f Charles; *ka* 7 July 1916

 2f Edgar Archibald; *ka* 1916

 3f Herbert; *b* 1893

 4f Francis Gerald; *b* 1896

 5f Alan Bruce; *b* 1897

 4e James; *b* 21 Jan 1866; *m* 5 Sept 1900 Elizabeth, dau of Peter Duff, of Macduff, Banffshire and *d* 1929, leaving:

 1f Charles Edward; *b* 27 Jan 1902; *m* 23 Dec 1931 Blanche Wilma Bouvett (*d* 29 Nov 1965) and *d* 1982, having had:

 1g +James Henry; *b* 23 April 1934; *m* 16 July 1965 *Anna Frances Ebl and has:

 1h +Charles Allan; *b* 8 Jan 1964

 1h *Heather Marie; *b* 8 Feb 1961

 2h *Sheila Christine; *b* 3 Dec 1962; *m* 1983 *John Steven Beliveau

 5e Archibald; *b* 13 Jan 1868; *m* 25 Nov 1896 Josephine, dau of John Walker Wooley, of Frankfort, Ky., and *d* 5 March 1937, leaving:

 1f Sylvia Georgina; BA; *b* 21 June 1905

 6e Richard Edgar; *b* 1869; *m* 1 Feb 1892 Mary (*d* 1939), dau of William Evans, of Santa Cruz, Calif., and *d* 1942, having had:

 1f Charles William; *b* 15 April 1895; *m* 22 Sept 1920 Bessie Lee, dau of Walter W Cook, of Milford, Utah, and *d* 13 Sept 1921, leaving:

 1g *Maxine Charles [*sic*]; *b* posthumously 19 Jan 1922; *m* 1944 *Charles Maxwell Letz and has:

 1h *Vicki Diane; *b* 1947

 2f Arthur Wellesley (twin); *b* 8 July 1899; *d* 1934

 1f Evelyn Edgar (twin); *b* 8 July 1899; *m* 1931 Claude L Smithwick (*d* 1954) and has issue

 1e Jessie Logan; *b* 4 Sept 1860; *d* 3 Aug 1923

 2e Christian Erskine; *b* 17 April 1862; *d* 1950

 3e Georgina Logan Edgar; *b* 1872; *d unm* 11 June 1937

 4e Mary Erskine Carmichael; *b* 1875; *d unm* 17 July 1928

 5e Katherine Elizabeth; *b* 1879; *m* 20 June 1907 John Taylor Craw (*d* 10 March 1934) and *dsp* Oct 1940

 1d Alice; *m* 11 Aug 1870 her cousin George Burnett (*d* 24 Jan 1890), LLD, Lord Lyon King of Arms, and had issue

 1b (cont.) Charles Stuart *m* 2nd Margaret Parlane (*d* 10 Nov 1821) and *d* 1826

 2a (cont.) James Stuart *m* 2nd Alison, dau of James Spittal of Leuchit

 1a Mary; *m* Col Hon John Erskine of Carnock and had issue (*see* BUCHAN, E)

 (1) Margaret; *m* 1st Sir Archibald Stewart of Burray, Bt; *m* 2nd 4th Lord Lindores (*see* ROTHES, E)

 1 Mary; *m* 1650 9th Earl of Argyll (*see* ARGYLL, D)

 2 Margaret; *m* Alexander, 1st Lord Duffus

 3 Henrietta; *m* 1662 Sir Hugh Campbell of Cawdor (*see* CAWDOR, E)

 4 Anne; *m* 1666 David Ross of Balnagowan and *d* 1719

The 4th EARL's 2nd son,

ALEXANDER STUART, **5th Earl of Moray**, KT (1687), PC (Feb 1660/1); *bapt* 8 May 1634; fined £3,500 (over £140,000 in late-1990s terms) as a royalist 1654, Ld Justice Gen of Scotland 1675/6, opposed Convenanters, raised a Regt of Highlanders 1678, a Ld Treasury 1678, Sec State and Extrdy Ld of Session 1680, Ld High Commr to Parl of Scotland 1686, deprived of his offices 1688 and imprisoned as a suspected Jacobite 1690; *m c* 1658 Emilia (*d* Jan 1683), dau of Sir William Balfour of Pitcullo, Lt Tower London, and *d* 1 Nov 1700, having had:

 1 James, *Lord Doune*; *m* 1st Katherine, dau of Sir Lionel Tollemache, 3rd Bt (*see* DYSART, E), and *dspm & vp c* 1693, leaving:

 (1) Elizabeth; *m* Alexander Grant 2nd of Grant (*see* STRATHSPEY, B), and *dsp*

 (2) Amelia; *m* 1st Alexander Fraser, 5th of Strichen (*see* LOVAT, L); *m* 2nd 19th Earl of Crawford (*see* LINDSAY, E)

 2 Sir CHARLES STUART, 1st and last Bt (NS), so *cr* 23 Sept 1681, **6th Earl of Moray**, KT (1731); *b c* 1660; imprisoned as a suspected Jacobite 1707–08; *m* Anne, widow of 4th Earl of Lauderdale (*qv*) and dau of 9th Earl of Argyll (*see* ARGYLL, D), and *dsp* 7 Oct 1735, when the btcy expired

 3 John; *dsp*

 4 FRANCIS STUART, **7th Earl of Moray**; *b* 4 Sept 1673 or 1674; *s* suspected Jacobite 1715; *m* 1st early Sept 1698 Elizabeth (*dsps*), dau of Sir John Murray of Drumcairn, a Ld of Session, bro of 4th Viscount Stormont (*see* MANSFIELD and MANSFIELD, E); *m* 2nd *c* late July 1730 Jean (*d* 1739), dau of 4th Lord Balmerinoch (*see* ELPHINSTONE, L), and *d* 11 Dec 1739, having by her had, with other issue:

 (1) JAMES, **8th Earl**

 (2) Francis, of Pittendriech; *m* 1st 4 Jan 1745 Helen Montgomerie (*d* 1747), 6th dau of 9th Earl of Eglinto(u)n (*see* EGLINTON and WINTON, E), and had:

 1a Francis; *d* 1766

 (2) (cont.) The Hon Francis Stuart *m* 2nd and left a dau (*m* 1 Nov 1783 Thomas Lewis O'Beirne, DD, Bp of Meath)

 (1) Amelia; *m* Sir Peter Halkett, 2nd Bt (*see* ROSSLYN, E)

The 7th EARL's est son,

JAMES STUART, **8th Earl of Moray**, KT (1741); *b* 1708; rep S peer 1741–67; *m* 1st Dec 1734 Grace (*d* 17 Nov 1738), dau of George Lockhart of Carnwath by the widow of 3rd Earl of Aboyne (*see* HUNTLY, M), and had, with a dau:

 1 FRANCIS, **9th Earl**

The **8th Earl** *m* 2nd Margaret (*d* 1779), dau of 3rd Earl of Wemyss (*see* WEMYSS and MARCH, E), and *d* 5 July 1767, having by her had:

 2 James; Lt-Col, Dep-Govr Fort George; *d unm* 4 May 1808

 3 David; Lt RN; *m* Elizabeth Begg and *d* 1784, having had issue (all *d unm*)

The 8th EARL's est son,

FRANCIS STUART, **9th Earl of Moray**; *b* 11 Jan 1737; rep S peer 1784–96; *cr* 4 June 1796 BARON STUART OF CASTLE STUART (GB); Ld Lt Morayshire 1794–1810; *m* 28 June 1763 Jean (*d* 19 Feb 1786), est dau of 11th Lord Gray (*qv*), and *d* 28 Aug 1810, having had, with other issue:

 1 FRANCIS STUART, **10th Earl of Moray**, KT (KT 1827); *b* 2 Feb 1771; *m* 1st 26 Feb 1795 Lucy (*d* 3 Aug 1798), 2nd dau of Gen John Scott of Balcomie, Fife, and had:

 (1) FRANCIS STUART, **11th Earl of Moray**; *b* 7 Nov 1795; *d unm* 6 May 1859

 (2) JOHN STUART, **12th Earl of Moray**; *b* 25 Jan 1797; Capt Army; *d unm* 8 Nov 1867

 1 (cont.) The **10th Earl** *m* 2nd 7 Jan 1801 his 1st cousin Margaret Jane (*d* 3 April 1837), dau of Sir Philip Ainslie of Pilton, Edinburgh, and *d* 12 Jan 1848, having by her had, with other issue:

 (3) ARCHIBALD GEORGE STUART, **13th Earl of Moray**; *b* 3 March 1810; Lt-Col; *d unm* 12 Feb 1872

 (4) GEORGE PHILIP STUART, **14th Earl of Moray** and 18th LORD GRAY (*qv*, in which he *s* his cousin Margaret 27 May 1878), DL (Inverness-shire); *b* 14 Aug; *d unm* 16 March 1895

 (1) Jane; *m* 1st 25 Jan 1832 Sir John Archibald Drummond Steuart of Grandtully, 6th Bt (*dsp* 20 May 1838); *m* 2nd 25 Aug 1838 Jeremiah Lonsdale Pounden, of Brownswood, Co Wexford (*d* 3 March 1887), and *d* 14 March 1880, leaving an only child:

 1a EVELEEN, **LADY GRAY** in her own right (*see* GRAY, L)

 2 Archibald; twin with his er bro; *m* 17 March 1793 Cornelia (*d* 1 March 1830), yst dau of Edmund Morton Pleydell, of Milbourne St Andrew, Dorset, and *d* 30 Oct 1832, leaving, with other issue:

 (1) Edmund Luttrell (Rev); *b* 21 Feb 1798; Rector Winterbourne Houghton, Dorset; *m* 2 Sept 1834 Elizabeth (*d* 28 March 1885), 2nd dau of Rev J L Jackson, Rector Swanage, Dorset, and *d* 5 Nov 1869, leaving:

 1a EDMUND ARCHIBALD STUART, **15th Earl of Moray**, JP and DL (Perthshire and Inverness-shire); *b* 5 Nov 1840; *educ* Exeter Coll Oxford (MA); barrister; *m* 6 Sept 1877 Anna Mary (*d* 20 Jan 1915), dau of Rev George J Collinson, Vicar St James, Clapham, and *dsp* 11 June 1901

 2a FRANCIS JAMES STUART, **16th Earl of Moray** (Perthshire), JP (Dorset and Fife); *b* 24 Nov 1842; Lt-Col Liverpool Regt; *m* 24 June 1879 Gertrude Floyer (*d* 15 March 1928), dau of Rev Francis Smith (*see* SMITH-MARRIOTT, Bt), and *dsp* 20 Nov 1909

 3a MORTON GRAY, **17th Earl**

 1a Cornelia; granted rank of earl's dau 10 April 1897; *m* 29 July 1873 Rev William Henry Augustus Truell, of Clonmannon, Co Wicklow (*d* 27 Jan 1934), Vicar Wall, Staffs, and *d* 24 May 1933, leaving issue

 (2) Douglas Wynne; *b* 8 May 1801; *m* 4 Feb 1842 Marcia — (*d* 13 Feb 1870) and *d* 10 Dec 1855, having had:

 1a Douglas Moray; *b* 22 Jan 1843; *d unm* 26 Nov 1863

The 16th EARL's bro,

MORTON GRAY STUART, **17th Earl of Moray**; *b* 16 April 1855; *educ* Cambridge (MA); *m* 17 Dec 1890 Edith Douglas (*d* 17 April 1945), dau of R-Adml George Palmer, and *d* 19 April 1930, having had:

 1 FRANCIS DOUGLAS STUART, **18th Earl of Moray**, MC; *b* 10 July 1892; Capt Scottish Horse and RAF WW I (wounded); Ld Lt Morayshire 1935–43; *m* 21

June 1924 Barbara (*d* 16 April 1996), dau of John Archibald Murray, of New York, and *d* 9 July 1943, having had:

(1) *Mary Anne; *b* 23 June 1926; *m* 1st 20 Sept 1945 (*divorce* 1960) Leonard Harold Robert Byng, ARBS (*d* 2 Sept 1974), only s of Frederick Gustav Byng, and has:

1a *Rupert Wingfield; *b* 5 June 1946; *educ* Harrow and New Coll Oxford; *m* 1987 *Francesca Stewart-Liberty

2a *Francis John Stuart; *b* 19 Feb 1956; *educ* Eton; *m* 1986 *Caroline Margaret, only dau of G E Stevenson of Lymington, Hants, and has:

1b *Toby James Findhorn; *b* 1986

2b *Maximillian Rupert Stuart; *b* 1989

1a *Charlotte Victoria; *b* 27 July 1947; *m* 1991 *Julian L C de Wette

2a *Elizabeth [Countess Hervé le Bault de la Morinière, Knoyle Place, E Knoyle, Wilts SP3 6AF]; *b* 5 July 1949; *m* 1st 1970 George Sulimirski, s of Prof Tadeusz Sulimirski; *m* 2nd 1983 *Count Hervé le Bault de la Morinière, s of Jean le Bault de la Morinière, and by him has:

1b *Louis Jean Victor; *b* 1987

2b *John Hervé; *b* 1990

1b *Camilla; *b* 1985

3a *Lucy Anne [Mrs Francis Stickney, Stoke Farthing House, Broad Chalke, Salisbury SP5 5EE]; *b* 25 Feb 1954; *m* 1st 1975 (*divorce* 1984) Isidore Brandel and has had:

1b Rebecca; *b* and *d* 1975

2b *Lara Rebecca; *b* 1977

3a (cont.) Mrs Lucy Brandel *m* 2nd 1990 *Francis Robin Christopher Stickney, only s of Richard Currier Stickney, and has by him:

1b *Jasper Oliver; *b* 1994

(1) (cont.) Lady Mary Anne Byng *m* 2nd 24 March 1961 Lt-Col John Bovill Denham, Scots Gds (*d* 1990), only s of Sir Edward Brandis Denham, GCMG, KBE, and Mrs Ralph Beresford Turner, and by him had:

3a *Charles Edward; *b* 28 July 1966; *educ* Harrow and U of Kent

4a *Harriet; *b* 9 Nov 1963

(2) *Sarah Gray [The Lady Sarah Stuart, 62 Pembridge Villas, London W11 3ET]; *b* 23 Sept 1928; *m* 9 Aug 1947 (*divorce* 1977, resumed maiden name) 4th Baron Hillingdon (*qv*) and has issue

(3) *Arabella [The Lady Arabella Stuart, 44 Elm Park Rd, London SW3 6AX]; *b* 11 July 1934; author: *First Slice Your Cookbook*, etc; *m* 9 Dec 1956 (*divorce* 1981, resumed maiden name) (Charles) Mark Edward Boxer, MSSIA, cartoonist and publisher (*d* 1988), s of Lt-Col Harold Stephen Boxer, of Bushey Heath, Herts, and has:

1a *Charles Stephen; *b* 3 May 1961; *m* 1984 *Katie, dau of Peter Forshall

1a *Henrietta Sophia; *b* 3 Aug 1958

2 ARCHIBALD JOHN MORTON, **19th Earl**

3 JAMES GRAY STUART, *cr* VISCOUNT STUART OF FINDHORN (*qv*)

1 Hermione Moray; *b* 13 Oct 1899; *m* 23 April 1919 Adml Sir Henry Tritton Buller, GCVO, CB (*d* 29 Aug 1960), s of Adml Sir Alexander Buller, GCB, of Erle Hall, Devon, and had:

(1) Alexander John Stuart; *b* 10 March 1920; P/O RAF WW II; *ka* 6 June 1940

(2) Robin Francis; *b* 16 Jan 1923; *educ* RNC Dartmouth; Cdr RN, served WW II (despatches); *d* unm 15 Nov 1956

(3) Peter Henry; *b* 26 Sept 1926; *educ* Eton; WW II in RNVR; *m* 16 June 1956 *Elizabeth, yr dau of W H P Landon, and had:

1a *Charles Peter William; *b* 12 May 1959

1a *Alexandra Clare; *b* 29 June 1957

2a *Susannah Louise; *b* 24 Sept 1960

(1) *Patricia Moray [Lady Ashmore, Netherdowns, Sundridge, Kent TN14 6AR]; *b* 13 July 1929; *m* 18 Oct 1952 *V-Adml Sir Peter William Beckwith Ashmore, KCB, KCVO, DSC, yr s of V-Adml Leslie Haliburton Ashmore, CB, DSO, of Sevenoaks, Kent, and has:

1a *John Peter; *b* 2 Feb 1964; *m* 7 Oct 1989 *Sally, yst dau of George Teacher Dunlop, of Corran, Ormsary, Argyll

1a *Jane Kyra; *b* 21 Feb 1957

2a *Alison Elizabeth; *b* 4 July 1958

3a *Catherine Patricia; *b* 10 Nov 1960

The 18th EARL's bro,

ARCHIBALD JOHN MORTON STUART, **19th Earl of Moray**, DL (Morayshire 1949); *b* 14 Nov 1894; *educ* RNCs Osborne and Dartmouth; Lt-Cdr RN WWs I and II; *m* 28 Jan 1922 (May) Mabel Helen Maud (*d* 1 Oct 1968), only child of Benjamin 'Matabele' Wilson, of Battlefields, S Rhodesia, and *d* 27 March 1974, having had:

1 DOUGLAS JOHN MORAY STUART, **20th and present Earl of Moray**

2 +Charles Rodney Stanford [The Hon Charles Stuart, 6 Lynch Rd, Farnham, Surrey; Delupes Mill, Dunphail, Moray IV36 0QL]; *b* 30 May 1933; *educ* Stowe and McGill (BCom); late 2nd Lt The Queen's Bays; *m* 1st 8 July 1961 (*divorce* 1986) Sasha Ann, er dau of Lt-Col Richard George Lewis, of Stow-on-the-Wold, Glos, and has:

(1) +James Benjamin; *b* 22 Sept 1962

(2) +Justin Nicholas Moray; *b* 19 Jan 1964

(3) +Duncan Douglas; *b* 13 March 1967

2 (cont.) The Hon Charles Stuart *m* 2nd 1986 *Frauke, only dau of Hans Stender, of Marne, Schleswig-Holstein

3 +James Wallace Wilson [The Hon James Stuart, 67 Cloncurry St, London SW6; Dunphail, Moray]; *b* 30 May 1933; *educ* Stowe and McGill (BA); late 2nd Lt 13th/18th Hus; *m* 28 Nov 1958 *Jane Scott, only dau of G/Capt Henry Gordon Richards, of Louisville, Ky., and has:

(1) *Elizabeth May; *b* 1967; *educ* Westminster and Yale U

1 Hermione Mary Morton; *b* 2 March 1925; *m* 1st 16 June 1950 (*divorce* 1960) Cdr John Oliver Roberts, RN, er s of John Vaughan Roberts, of Llangurig, Montgomeryshire, and had a dau; *m* 2nd 13 Dec 1961 HRH PRINCE FRIEDRICH KARL OF PRUSSIA, only s of HRH PRINCE FRIEDRICH SIGISMUND OF PRUSSIA, and *d* as the result of a riding accident 2 Sept 1969

MORDAUNT

Arms: Arg. a chevron between three estoiles sa. **Crest:** A blackamoor's head affrontée couped at the shoulders ppr., banded with a wreath round the temples or and gu. **Motto:** *Ferro comite* ('The sword my companion'). **Creation:** Bt. (E) 29 June 1611.

Richard Nigel Charles Mordaunt [Richard Mordaunt Esq, 1/12 Marattia Place, Suffolk Park, NSW 2481, Australia]; *b* 12 May 1940; *s* f 1979 but does not use title; *educ* Wellington; *m* 1964 *Myriam Atchia and has:

1 +KIM JOHN; *b* 11 June 1966

1 *Michele; *b* 1965

Lineage: OSBERT, of Radwell, Beds; had:

OSBERT; had:

EUSTACHE MORDAUNT; *m* Alice, est dau and coheir of Sir William de Alneto, who brought him the feudal Lordship of Turvey, Beds, and had:

WILLIAM MORDAUNT; feudal Ld of Turvey, Radwell and Asthull; had:

WILLIAM MORDAUNT; granted permission 1297 to enclose a park at Turvey, later the chief seat of the Peterborough branch of his descendants; *m* Rose, dau of Sir Ralph Wake, and had an est s:

ROBERT MORDAUNT, of Turvey; MP Beds *c* 1342; had:

EDMUND MORDAUNT, of Turvey; *m* Helen, dau and coheir of Ralph Brock, and had:

ROBERT MORDAUNT, of Turvey; *m* Agnes, dau and heiress of John le Strange, of Ampton Tynmouth, Suffolk, and had:

ROBERT MORDAUNT; MP Beds *c* 1422; *m* Elizabeth, dau of John Holdenby, of Holdenby, Northants, and had:

WILLIAM MORDAUNT, of Turvey; living *c* 1472; *m* Margaret, dau of John Peeke, of Cople, Beds, and had, with other issue:

1 John (Sir), of Turvey, KC; cmded detachment of HENRY VII's troops in victory of Stoke 1487 over Lambert Simnel and remnants of the Yorkist party; Speaker H of C 1487, Serjeant-at-law 1495, Justice Chester 1500, Chllr Duchy Lancaster, ktd Feb–March 1503/4; *m* Edith, dau and coheir of Nicholas Latimer, of Duntish, Dorset, and had an est s:

(1) JOHN MORDAUNT, 1st LORD (Baron) MORDAUNT (E), so *cr* 5 March–4 May 1532, KB (Feb 1502/3); *b c* 1480–85; Sheriff Beds and Bucks 1509–10, granted arms Feb 1512/3; *m* 21 March–2 Sept 1499 Elizabeth, er dau and coheir of Sir Henry Vere, of Gt Addington, Northants, and *d* 18 Aug 1562, leaving, with three other sons and six daus:

1a JOHN MORDAUNT, 2nd LORD (Baron) MORDAUNT, KB (1533), PC (1553); Sheriff Beds and Bucks 1537 and Essex and Herts 1538, MP Beds 1553–55; *m* 1st by 24 Feb 1526 Ela, dau of John FitzLewis, of W Horndon, Essex; *m* 2nd *c* 3 Dec 1545 Joan, dau of Sir Richard Fermo(u)r, of Easton Neston, Northants (*see* HESKETH, B), and widow of Robert Wilford, of London, and *d* April-Oct 1571, having had no issue by her; had by his 1st w, with other issue:

1b LEWIS MORDAUNT, 3rd LORD (Baron) MORDAUNT; *b* 21 Sept 1538; *educ* Middle Temple; MP Beds 1563–67, ktd 1568, High Sheriff Beds 1570–71; *m* Elizabeth, dau of Sir Arthur Darcy (*see* DARCY DE KNAYTH, B), and *d* 16 June 1601, leaving:

1c HENRY MORDAUNT, 4th LORD (Baron) MORDAUNT; *b c* 1568; fined 10,000 marks (well over £350,000 in late-1990s terms) and imprisoned Tower of London 15 Nov 1605–3 June 1606 on suspicion of involvement in Gunpowder Plot; *m* by 1 Oct 1593 Margaret, sis of 1st Earl of Northampton (*see* NORTHAMPTON, M), and *d* 13 Feb 1608/9, having had, with other issue:

1d JOHN MORDAUNT, 1st EARL OF PETERBOROUGH, Co Northampton (E), so *cr* 9 March 1627/8, KB (1616); *bapt* 18 Jan 1598/9; Ld Lt Northants 1640–42 and (Parly appointment) 1642–43, Col Infantry, Capt of Cavalry and Gen Artillery Parly Army 1642; *m* by 7 April 1621 Elizabeth, *de jure* Baroness Beuachamp (of Bletso) according to later doctrine, dau of 3rd Baron Howard of Effingham (*see* EFFINGHAM, E) by Anne (also *de jure* Baroness Beauchamp (of Bletso) according to later doctrine), dau of 2nd Baron St John of Bletso (*qv*), and *d* 19 June 1644, leaving:

1e HENRY MORDAUNT, 2nd EARL OF PETERBOROUGH, KG (1685), PC (1674–79 and Feb 1682/3–Feb 1688/9); *bapt* 18 Oct 1623; *educ* Eton and in France; initially Parliamentarian Civil War (cmdg his f's troop of horse), but changed to royalists April 1643, fighting wiith them at Newbury (wounded), Cropredy Bridge and Lotwithiel 1644 and being present at Sieges of Bristol and Glouces-ter; also took part in a royalist rising 1648; Govr, Capt-Gen forces and Col Tangier Regt Tangier 1661–63, Capt of Horse 1666 and Duke of York's Regt of Horse 1678–79, Col of Foot 1673–74 and 2nd Dragoon Gds 1685–88, Capt in Navy Second and Third Dutch Wars 1665 and 1672 respectively; Jt Ld Lt Northants 1666–73, Ld Lt: W Northants 1673–78, Northants entire 1678–88 and Rutland Jan-Dec 1688, Recorder Northampton 1671–72 and 1682–88; Groom Stole and First Gentleman Bedchamber 1685–88, High Steward and Ch Bailiff to JAMES II's w MARY Jan 1685/6; turned RC (which his family had remained after the Reformation till his f was con-verted to Anglicanism *c* 1625, apparently after hearing Archbp Henry Ussher of Armagh (the same who famously put the date of the Creation at 4004 BC) get the better of Father Oswald Tesimond, *alias* Philip Beaumont, a Catholic priest, in a theological disputa-ton), attempted to fly the country at the Glorious Revolution of 1688 but was held in the Tower of London 24 Dec 1688–7 Oct 1690 and proceedings for impeachment initiated against him 1689, though they were not proceeded with; *m* winter 1644–45 Penelope, dau of 5th Earl of Thomond (*see* INCHIQUIN, B), and *dspm* 19 June 1697, leaving:

1f MARY Mordaunt, *de jure* BARONESS MORDAUNT in her own right (assuming the Barony of 1532 to have been *cr* by writ of summons, which it was declared to have been by a Ho of Lds rul-ing 1928 although no documentary evidence to that effect had been found); *m* 1st 8 Aug 1677 (separated 1685, *divorce* 11 April 1700 for which the Duke was awarded 100 marks damages (some £2,840 in late-1990s terms) in the Court of King's Bench) with the man who became her 2nd husb) Henry HOWARD, 7th Duke of Norfolk (*qv*); *m* 2nd *c* 15 Sept 1701, as his 1st w, Sir John GERMAINE, 1st and last Bt (*m* 2nd Lady Elizabeth Berkeley, dau of 2nd Earl of Berkeley (*see* BERKELEY, B), and *dsp* 11 Dec 1718), and *dsp* 17 Nov 1705, having left the Drayton Manor estate and other property to him, who in turn left those properties to his 2nd w, who left them to Lord George Sackville later Germaine (*see* SACKVILLE, B)

2e JOHN MORDAUNT, 1st VISCOUNT MORDAUNT OF AVA-LON, Co Somerset, so *cr* 10 July 1659, as also BARON MOR-DAUNT OF RYEGATE (*i.e.*, Reigate), Co Surrey (both E); *b* 18 June 1626; participated in several royalist conspiracies during the Inter-regnum, hence tried for treason 1658 but acquitted by the presid-ing judge's casting vote; ktd 1660, Capt of Horse, Col of Foot, High Steward Windsor, Govr and Capt Windsor Castle 1660–68, Ranger Windsor Forest and Keeper Windsor Gt Pk 1660–68, Lt Lt Surrey 1660–75; *m* apparently *c* 1656 Elizabeth, dau of Thomas Carey (2nd s of 1st Earl of Monmouth of the Feb 1625/6 *cr*; *see* FALK-LAND, V), and *d* 5 June 1675, leaving, with other issue:

1f CHARLES MORDAUNT, 1st EARL OF MONMOUTH, so *cr* 9 April 1689, also EARL OF PETERBOROUGH, as which *s* unc 1697, and 8th LORD (Baron) MORDAUNT, as which *s* his cousin MARY 1705, PC (Feb 1688/9–Jan 1696/7 and 1705–07), KG (1713); *b c* 1658; *educ* Westminster and Ch Ch Oxford; partici-pated in campaign against Dey of Algiers and in garrison at Tang-ier 1678–80, Capt of a Man of War 1681, Col of Foot 1688–94, Gentleman Bedchamber 1689–97, Ld Lt Northants 1689–97 and 1702–15, First Commr Treasury 1689–90, held in Tower of Lon-don Jan-March 1697 for opposition to the Govt, non-resident Govr Jamaica 1702, Gen Allied Forces Spain and Jt Adml and Ch Cdr Fleet 1705, as which was instrumental in bringing about the capture of Barcelona Oct 1705 and the ejection of a French army from Spain 1706, Col Dragoons 1706–07, Gen Marines 1707 and all Marine Forces 1722, Amb Vienna and Turin 1710–11 and Sic-ily 1713–14, Col Roy Regt Horse Gds 1712–15, Govr Minorca April-Oct 1714; *m* 1st *c* 1678 Carey, dau of Sir Alexander Fraser, 1st and last Bt, of Durris; *m* 2nd 1722 or 1735 (probably latter) Anastasia, singer and stage performer (thought to have been the first British peer ever to have selected a bride from this class of person, later to become such a fecund supply of peeresses, who had for some time previously been under his protection, dau of Thomas Robinson, a portraitist, and *d* 25 Oct 1735, having had, with other issue:

1g John, *Lord Mordaunt*; *b c* 1681; *educ* Ch Ch Oxford; MP Chippenham 1701–05 and 1705–08, Lt-Col Gren Gds, served Blenheim 1704 (wounded), Col N Br Fus (later 21st Foot) 1704–06 and 1709–10, 28th Foot 1706–09; *m c* 1707 Frances, dau of 7th Marquess of Winchester (*qv*), and *dvp* 6 April 1710, leaving:

1h CHARLES MORDAUNT, 4th EARL OF PETERBOROUGH and 2nd EARL OF MONMOUTH; *b c* 12 Oct 1708; *educ* West-mister and Balliol Coll Oxford; *m* 1st by 1735 Mary (*dspm* or *dspms* 18 Nov 1755), dau of Thomas Cox, a Quaker whols-esale grocer in Aldgate, and had, with an er dau:

1i MARY ANASTASIA GRACE, *de jure* BARONESS MOR-DAUNT in her own right, as which *s* half-bro 1814; *b* 5 June 1738; *d* unm 22 June 1819, when right to the Barony of Mordaunt, and possibly to that of Beauchamp (of Bletso), passed to her cousin 7th Marquess of Huntly (*qv*)

1h (cont.) The 4th and 2nd EARL *m* 2nd 5 Dec 1755 Robini-ana Browne and *d* 1 Aug 1779, leaving by her:

1i CHARLES HENRY MORDAUNT, 5th and last EARL OF PETERBOROUGH and 3rd and last EARL OF MON-MOUTH; *b* 16 May 1758; *educ* Harrow, Westminster and Ch Ch Oxford; *d* unm 16 June 1814, when all his titles bar the Barony of Mordaunt expired, litigation over his funeral expenses constituting a milestone in English case law on burial (*see* Charles Mosley, *Debrett's Guide to Bereavement*, 1995)

2h John; *m* 9 Oct 1735, as her 2nd husb, Mary, dau of 1st Vis-count Howe (*see* HOWE, E) and widow of 8th Earl of Pem-broke and (5th Earl of) Montgomery (*qv*)

1g Henrietta; *m* 5th Marquess of Huntly (*qv*) and had issue

2f Harry; MP, Lt Gen, Treasurer Ordnance 1699; *m* 1st Margaret, dau of Sir Thomas Spencer, Bt, of Yarnton, Oxon (*see* MARL-BOROUGH, D, **Lineage (of Spencer)**), and had, with other issue:

1g John (Sir), KB ; Gen

1g Elizabeth Lucy; *m* 14 March 1723/4 Sir Wilfrid Lawson, 3rd Bt, of Isell, Cumberland, and was *bur* 29 Nov 1765, having had issue (*see* 1959 edn LAWSON, Bt, of Brayton)

2f (cont.) Gen Harry Mordaunt *m* 2nd Penelope, dau of William Tipping, of Ewelme, Oxon, and had:

2g Penelope; *m* Sir Monnoux Cope, 7th Bt, of Hanwell, Oxon, and Dec 1737, leaving issue (*see* 1970 edn)

3f Lewis; Brig Gen; *m* 1st —; *m* 2nd Mary, dau of Lt-Col Collyer, Lt-Govr Jersey, and *d* 2 Feb 1712/3, having by her had:

1g Anne Maria; a celebrated beauty of her day, praised by the minor poet Samuel Croxall in 'The Fair Circassian'; *m* Feb 1732/3 Stephen Poyntz, PC, diplomat, of Midgham, Berks, and *d* 14 Nov 1771, having had, with two sons and another dau:

1h Margaret Georgiana; *m* 1st Earl Spencer (*qv*) and had is-sue

2g Sophia; *m* 6 June 1739, as his 1st w, Sir Roger Martin, 3rd Bt (*see* 1854 edn), and *d* 22 Dec 1752, leaving issue

4f George (Rev); *m* 1st —; *m* 2nd Elizabeth, dau of Sir John D'Oyly, Bt, and had issue; *m* 3rd Elizabeth, dau of Col Collyer, and by her had, with an er dau:

1g Elizabeth; *m* 30 April 1747 Sir William Milner, 2nd Bt (*qv*), and *d* 1785, having had issue

1e Elizabeth; *m* 21 July 1646, as his 1st w, 2nd Baron Howard of Estrick (*see* SUFFOLK and BERKSHIRE, E) and was *bur* 12 Aug 1716

1d Frances; *m* 1st Sir Thomas Nevill(e), KB (*see* ABERGAVENNY, M); *m* 2nd Sir Basil Brooke, of Madeley, Salop

1b Ursula; *m* Edward, yr s of Sir Nicholas Fairfax by his 2nd w Jane (*see* FAIRFAX OF CAMERON, L)

2 William; Prothonotary Common Pleas 1495; *m* 1495 Anne, 2nd dau and coheir of Thomas Huntington, of Hempsted, Essex, and had an est s:

(1) Robert, of Hempsted; *m* Barbara, dau and heiress of John L'Estrange, of Massingham Parva or Little Massingham, Norfolk, who brought him the estates of Massingham and Walton D'Evile, Warwicks; his yst s:

1a Henry, of King's Lynn; *m* Anne Poley, of Beds, and had:

1b **Sir L'Estrange Mordaunt, 1st Bt** (E), so *cr* 29 June 1611, of Little Mass-ingham, Norfolk; mil cdr *temp* ELIZABETH I Low Countries and Ireland; *b* 1572; *m* 1st Margaret, dau of Peter de Charles, of Antwerp, and had:

1c ROBERT (Sir), **2nd Bt**

2c Henry; *m* Barbara, dau of James Calthorpe, and had:

1d L'Estrange Mordaunt; *m* Barbara, sis of Sir Nevil Catlin, and had:

1e Henry

1e Barbara; *m* Capt John Brown

1b (cont.) **Sir L'Estrange** *m* 2nd Frances, widow of Thomas Sotherton, of Norwich, and dau of Robert Cheeke, and *d* by 1 Oct 1627

1 Joan; *m* Giles Strangways, of Melbury, Dorset

2 Elizabeth; *m* Sir Whiston Browne

The er son,

Sir Robert Mordaunt, 2nd Bt; ktd 1618; *m* 1614 Amy (*m* 2nd 18 June 1639 Bas-set Cole and was *bur* 26 March 1668), dau of Sir Austin Sotherton, and *d* 23 Aug 1638, having had an est s:

1 **Sir Charles Mordaunt, 3rd Bt**; *m* Catherine (*m* 2nd Sir Charles Lee, of Billeslee, Warwicks), sis of Sir Lionel Tollemache, 3rd Bt (*see* DYSART, E), and *d* 10 July 1648, having had, with two other sons and three daus (all *d* unm):

(1) **Sir Charles Mordaunt, 4th Bt**; *m c* 18 Dec 1663 Elizabeth (*m* 2nd Francis Godolphin, of Colston, Wilts), dau and coheir of Nicholas Johnson, and *dsp* 24 April 1665

(2) **Sir John Mordaunt, 5th Bt**, of Walton D'Evile; MP Warwicks; *m* 1st 13 June 1678 Anne (*d* June 1692), dau and heiress of William Risley, and had:

1a Penelope; *d* young

(2) (cont.) **Sir John** *m* 2nd *c* 8 June 1695 Penelope, dau of Sir George Warbur-ton, 1st Bt, of Arley, Cheshire, and by her had:

1a CHARLES (Sir), **6th Bt**

2a John; fought against the Moors of Tangier; *d* unm Sept 1723

1a Penelope; *m* Joseph Herne

2a Catherine; *m* Dr — Dobson, Warden of Winchester

(2) (cont.) **Sir John** *m* 3rd 1 July 1715 Elizabeth (*d* 1734), widow of — Floyd, and *d* 6 Sept 1721

His est son,

Sir Charles Mordaunt, 6th Bt; DCL Oxon, MP Warwicks; *m* 1st 1 Dec 1720 — (*d* March 1725/6), dau of John Conyers, and had two daus (*d* unm); *m* 2nd 7 July 1730 Sophia (*d* April 1738), only dau of Sir John Wodehouse, 4th Bt (*see* KIM-BERLEY, E), and by her had:

1 JOHN (Sir), **7th Bt**

2 Charles (Rev); Rector Massingham; m 1774 Charlotte, dau of Sir Philip Musgrave, 6th Bt (see MUSGRAVE, Bt, of Hartley Castle), and d 22 Jan 1820, leaving, with other issue:

(1) Charles (Rev); Rector Badgworth, Somerset, m 1812 Frances Harriet (d 1866), yst dau of James Sparrow, of Flax Bourton, Somerset, and had:

1a Charles (Rev); Rector Badgworth; m and dsp 1861

2a John; 17th Lancers; m 1st 1843 Harriet Maria (d 1849), yst dau of Capt — Cumberlege, RN, and had:

1b James Sparrow; Lt-Col Leinster Regt; b 14 Nov 1843; m 1872 Harriet Theresa (d 1925), dau of Rev Joseph Gibbs (see ALDENHAM and HUNSDON OF HUNSDON, B), and d 19 Dec 1927, leaving:

1c John Francis Cumberlege, MC; Maj 3rd Somerset LI, Boer War 1901–02 and WW I (wounded, despatches, star, two medals); b 15 Feb 1881; d 27 May 1936

2c Charles Stanley; Lt RA (TA); b 4 June 1886; m 1915 Edith Violet Wood and dsp 4 May 1946

1c Harriet Emily; d unm 19 March 1956

2c Mildred Dorothea; m 1915 Capt Robert Wyndham Humphrey Marciel Bland, 18th Roy Irish Rifles (d 18 July 1942), and dsp 23 March 1949

3c Helen Mary; d unm 24 Jan 1958

2b Francis Lionel; 23rd Roy Welch Fus; b 1845; m 1889 Sara Elliot (d 1939), dau of William St John Elliot Marshall, of Natchez, Miss., and d 16 May 1918, leaving:

1c Elizabeth Morris; b 5 Feb 1891; m 2 April 1918 D Drayton Burrill and had:

1d *Gerald Drayton; b 1921

1d *Helena Van Cortlandt; b 1924

2c Mildred Cumberlege; b 31 Oct 1893; m 1st 29 June 1916 David Ogden Rogers, of Hyde Park, New York (d 14 May 1928), and had:

1d *Francis Lionel Mordaunt [Francis Rogers, Laurel Lane, Darien, CT, USA]; b 1917; late V-Pres American Airlines; m 1942 *Elizabeth Lesure Culver and has:

1e *Nathaniel Pendleton; b 1950

1e *Susan Farnum; b 1945

1d *Nathalie Pendleton; b 1921; m 1948 *Lt-Cdr J James Spurr III, USN, and has:

1e *J James IV, USN; b 1949

2e *Peter Stuyvesant; b 1954

1e *Deborah Mordaunt; b 1951

2c (cont) Mrs David Rogers m 2nd 19 June 1929 Arthur Spencer Kittle (d 16 May 1953), of New York

3b John; b 19 April 1848; RN; d 1899

1b Mildred; b 1846; m 3 Sept 1868 Rev George Henry Gibbs (see ALDENHAM and HUNSDON OF HUNSDON, B) and d 22 Sept 1926

2a (cont.) John Mordaunt m 2nd Isabel, dau of Maj Fletcher Norton Balmain, Madras Cav, and d 15 Nov 1801, having by her had:

4b Harry; b 1852; m 1875 Annie (d 26 April 1928), dau of Rev J Cautley, of Thorney Abbey, Cambs, and d 22 July 1929, having had:

1c Osbert Cautley, DSO; Col Roy Signals, Somerset LI, Boer War 1899–1903 (two medals, four clasps), WW I (despatches, Brevet Lt-Col 1918, Croix de Guerre with Palm, Order SS Maurice and Lazarus Italy); b 26 May 1876; m 1906 Constance Katherine (d 1964), dau of Capt R N Young, RHA, of Orlingbury, Northants, and d 1949, leaving:

1d Anthony Osbert; Maj Somerset LI; b 1907; educ Malvern

2c Christopher John; b 11 Dec 1879; m 1st 24 Aug 1907 his sis-in-law Helena Charlotte, dau of Capt R N Young, RHA, and had:

1d Richard John, VRD (1963); Lt-Cdr RNR WW II, Sec Berkeley Hunt 1957–65; b 10 June 1908; educ Woodbridge Sch; m 1st 16 July 1930 Gertrude Anna Katherine (Nancy) (d 1986), dau of Major Thomas Clayton Toler, DL, JP, of Swettenham Hall, Congleton, and had:

1e +(Thomas) Christopher John [Christopher Mordaunt Esq, Brawby Lodge, Brawby, N Yorks]; Capt 9th/12th Roy Lancers; b 15 Dec 1934; m 7 Nov 1959 *Belinda Madeline, yr dau of Thomas Cecil Gouldsmith, of Coneysthorpe, Malton, York (see 1956 edn LAURIE, Bt, of Sevenoaks), and has:

1f *(Sarah) Camilla [Mrs William Shuttleworth, Brook House, Stanton Lacy, Salop]; b 19 Sept 1961; m 1985 *William Richard Ashton Shuttleworth (see CROSS, V) and has:

1g *Tom William Ashton; b 1990

1g *Alexandra Sophie Ashton; b 1987

2f *Sophie Jane; b 18 March 1967

1e *Rosemary Jane [Mrs Lyndon Bolton, Arrat's Mill, by Brechin, Angus]; b 10 May 1931; m 18 Dec 1957 *Lyndon Bolton, only s of Brig Lyndon Bolton, DSO, of Denwick House, Alnwick, Northumberland, and has:

1f *Lyndon; b 1958

2f *Timothy William; b 1963

2e *Nicola Anna Mary b 1944

1d (cont.) Lt-Cdr Richard Mordaunt m 2nd 1988 *Sarah (Sally) Anne, dau of W/Cdr E Seymour Williams, and d 17 Feb 1998

2c (cont.) Christopher Mordaunt m 2nd 25 April 1916 Mary Patricia (d 1975), dau of Lt-Col John Cumberledge Cautley, Roy W Kent Regt, and d 5 July 1954, having by her had:

2d Guy Michael; WW II in RAFVR; b 2 March 1917; d 23 Jan 1945

3d +Barry Stephen Clare [Barry Mordaunt Esq, Horseshoe House, 51 Sydney Bldgs, Bath BA2 6DB]; Master Mariner, Capt P&O (ret); b 13 May 1925; m 18 Feb 1950 *Joan, 2nd dau of Louis Henry Poppleton, of Nightingale Villa, Batheaston, Bath, and has:

1e +Guy Roger; b 21 Feb 1952; educ Grenville Coll Bideford; m 1980 *Deborah Anne, yst dau of B A G Norton, and has:

1f +Simon Richard Stephen; b 1988

1f *Sally Jane; b 1985

2f *Elizabeth Muriel; b 1990

1e *Ann Patricia; b 28 Jan 1956; m 1978 *John Quartly and has:

1f *Amy; b 1979

2f *Ruth; b 1981

3f *Emma; b 1982

1d *Katherine Patricia [Mrs David Isard, Wyke Croft, 36 Brandy Hole Lane, Chichester, Sussex]; b 27 Nov 1918; m 21 March 1950 David Isard (d 1980), s of Jean Isard, of Fareham, Hants, and has:

1e *John David; b 6 Nov 1951; educ Cranleigh and Leicester U

3c Harry Cumberlege; b 1882; m 27 June 1914 Ruth, dau of Harry Thompson

4c Julian Musgrave; m 12 Oct 1910 Zoë (d 19 Feb 1951), dau of John Burton Barrow, of Ringwood Hall, Chesterfield, and dsp

1c Penelope Catherine; m 1903 Charles Pell Hall, of Bedford, and had:

5b Charles; b Feb 1854; m and d Feb 1931

6b Philip Musgrave; b Feb 1858; m M Matthew and d 21 Oct 1935

2b Harriet Isabel; m William Foord Kelcey and d 13 May 1953, having had issue. He d 1922

3b Katherine; m Albert Edward Masters and d 6 June 1953, leaving issue. He d 1901

3a James; d unm

4a Henry; Lt 46th Foot; d unm 1842

1a Charlotte; m Rev John Matthew, Rector Chelvey, and had issue

Sir CHARLES d 11 March 1778; his son,

Sir John Mordaunt, 7th Bt; Groom Bedchamber, MP Warwicks, LLD; bapt 9 May 1734; m 3 Jan 1769 Elizabeth (d 5 Oct 1826), dau and coheir of Thomas Prowse, of Axbridge, Somerset, and had, with other issue:

1 CHARLES (Sir), **8th Bt**

2 John; Rector Wicken, Bucks; d 1806

1 Mary; m 1802 John Erskine, bro of 2nd Earl of Rosslyn (qv), and d 17 July 1821, leaving issue

2 Catherine; m 26 Oct 1811 Rev Francis Mills, of Barford, Warwicks, 4th s of Rev John Mills, Rector Barford and Oxhill, Warwicks, and d 7 May 1852, leaving issue. He d 23 April 1851

3 Charlotte; m 15 April 1800 Richard Hippisley Tuckfield, of Fulford, Devon, and d a widow May 1848

4 Susan; m 30 Aug 1814 2nd Earl of St Germans (qv) and dsp 5. Feb 1830

Sir JOHN d 18 Nov 1806; his only surv son,

Sir Charles Mordaunt, 8th Bt; b c 1771; educ Eton and Ch Ch Oxford (BA); MP Warwicks 1804–20; m 30 June 1807 Marianne (d 9 June 1842), est dau of William Holbech, of Farnborough, Warwicks, and d 30 May 1823, having had, with other issue:

1 **Sir John Mordaunt, 9th Bt**; b 24 Aug 1808; educ Eton and Oxford; MP S Warwicks 1835–45; m 7 Aug 1834 Caroline Sophia (m 2nd 25 April 1853 Capt Gustavus Thomas Smith, Queen's Bays (d 6 Jan 1875), of Goldicote, Worcs, and d 28 March 1913), 2nd dau of Rt Rev George Murray (see ATHOLL, D), and d 27 Sept 1845, having had:

(1) **Sir Charles Mordaunt, 10th Bt**, DL; b 28 April 1836; educ Eton and Ch Ch Oxford; Hon Lt-Col Warwicks Yeo, MP S Warwicks 1859–68, High Sheriff 1879; m 1st 7 Dec 1866 (divorce 1875) Harriet Sarah (d 9 May 1906), 4th dau of Sir Thomas Moncreiffe of that Ilk, 7th Bt (see ERROLL, E), and had:

1a Violet Caroline; m 19 April 1890 5th Marquess of Bath (qv) and d 29 May 1928, leaving issue

(1) (cont.) **Sir Charles** m 2nd 24 April 1878 Mary Louisa (d 10 June 1947), dau of Rev Hon Henry Pitt Cholmondeley (see DELAMERE, B), and d 15 Oct 1897, having by her had:

1a **Sir Osbert L'Estrange Mordaunt, 11th Bt**; b 27 Jan 1884; d unm 23 Feb 1934

2a Adela; b 27 Jan 1879; m 8 June 1916 Brig-Gen John Cecil Macrae, CB, DSO, DL (d 20 Aug 1940), 1st/14th Punjab Regt, of Orkney, s of John Macrae, Procurator-Fiscal Orkneys

3a Irene; b 27 Dec 1880; m 24 July 1907 Maj Sir Robert Caradoc Hamilton, 8th Bt, of Silverton Hill (qv), and d 24 Oct 1969, leaving issue

4a Lilian; b 8 Jan 1882; m 21 June 1904 Rev Mildmay Francis Hall, s of Rev Charles Hall, of Scopwick Rectory, Lincs, and d 18 March 1969, leaving issue. He d 21 Nov 1948

5a Cicely; medal of Queen Elisabeth of Belgium; b 4 June 1889

6a Winifred, JP (Warwicks 1936), Croix de Guerre; b 5 March 1891; m 31 Jan 1923 John Wilding Arundel Geare, of Blarich, Rogart, Sutherland, s of Edward Arundel Geare, of Lincoln's Inn, and had issue

(2) John Murray, JP, DL (Warwicks); b 30 Dec 1837; m 15 May 1866 Elizabeth Evelyn (d 15 Sept 1914), 3rd dau of John Cotes, of Woodcote, and d 21 Dec 1923, having had:

1a **Sir Henry John Mordaunt, 12th Bt**; b 12 July 1867; Bd Educn 1898–1904, Ch Clerk Educn Dept LCC 1904–24; d unm 15 Jan 1939

2a Eustace Charles; b 6 Sept 1870; m 12 June 1906 Cicely Marion (d 13 Nov 1974 aged 91), 2nd dau of Henry Tubb, of Bicester, and d 21 June 1938, leaving:

1b NIGEL JOHN (Sir), **13th Bt**

2b Henry Caryl Charles; b 12 Dec 1921; educ Radley and E Sussex Sch of Ag; m 18 April 1964 *Doris Ellen (Helen) [Mrs Henry Mordaunt, Cleavers Mead, Etchingham, Sussex], yst dau of Edward Cruchley, of Hurst Green, Sussex, and d 19 Jan 1973 following a car crash

1b Evelyn Margarette; b 17 Sept 1908; m 3 Dec 1936 Lt-Col George William Anthony Tufton and has issue (see HOTHFIELD, B)

2b *Ursula Marion [Mrs Charles Awdry, The Old Vicarage, Bowden Hill, Lacock, Wilts]; b 7 April 1913; m 2 Nov 1933 Maj Charles Edwin Awdry, TD, JP, Roy Wilts Yeo (d 16 Nov 1965), est s of Maj Charles Selwyn Awdry, DSO, of Notton, Lacock, and has issue

3b *Cynthia Violet [Miss Cynthia Mordaunt, Court Farm, Burwash, Sussex]; *b* 8 April 1918

3a Gerald John; *b* 20 Jan 1873; *educ* Wellington and Univ Coll Oxford; *m* 8 Feb 1900 Grace Adeline (*d* 11 April 1965 aged 94), yst dau of Col Edward Charles Impey, and *d* 5 March 1959, leaving:

1b Eustace John; *b* 27 May 1901; *educ* Wellington and Univ Coll Oxford; *m* 25 Jan 1934 Anne Frances (*d* 27 Nov 1976), only dau of Alastair Gilmour, and *d* 1988, having had:

1c +David John [David Mordaunt Esq, Mondhuie, Nethy Bridge, Inverness-shire PH25 3DF]; *b* 24 July 1937; *educ* Wellington; Roy Northumberland Fus 1955–57, assist master Wellington 1963–86, housemaster 1968–79, former Sussex cricketer; *m* 1990 *Catharine Hilary, PhD, dau of John Mayne, CB

2c +Gerald Charles [Gerald Mordaunt Esq, 55 Melody Rd, London SW18]; *b* 16 July 1939; *educ* Wellington; *m* 18 Sept 1965 (*divorce* 1981) Carol Elspeth, yst dau of Brig Richard Montagu Villiers, DSO (*see* CLARENDON, E), and has:

1d +James Richard John; *b* 3 Dec 1967

2d +Christopher Charles; *b* 23 Dec 1969

1d *Tanya Alexandra; *b* 4 March 1974

2d *Harriet Georgia; *b* 1980

1c *Angela Mary [Mrs David Carr, The Lodge, Little Haywood, Staffs ST18 0TS]; *b* 4 Nov 1934; *m* 18 Aug 1955 *David Neil Carr, 2nd s of Lt-Col John Lillingston Carr, Royal Berks Regt, of Bridgeford House, Bridge, Canterbury, and has:

1d *Philip Donald Mordaunt; *b* 15 May 1959; *m* 1989 *Katherine Jane Hubbord and has:

1e *Charles David; *b* 16 March 1994

1e *Susannah Clare; *b* 10 Feb 1992

1d *Sally Jane; *b* 9 Dec 1956; *m* 1st 1977 (*divorce* 1987) Anthony Mitchell and has:

1e *Andrew David; *b* 1982

1d (cont.) Mrs Sally Mitchell *m* 2nd 1989 *Andrew Simms

2d *Judith Anne; *b* 4 Jan 1961; *m* 1983 (*divorce* 1989) Patrick Dickinson; *m* 2nd 1989 *Geoffrey Teather and has by him:

1e *James Alexander; *b* 17 June 1997

1e *Victoria Anne; *b* 16 Dec 1990

2e *Charlotte Philippa; *b* 15 May 1993

3e *Annie Louise; *b* 3 May 1995

2b +Robin Charles [Robin Mordaunt Esq, 89B Winchester St, Christchurch, New Zealand]; *b* 22 Feb 1909; *educ* Wellington and Univ Coll Oxford; *m* Jan 1939 *Mrs Brita Grose, dau of H Thoren, of Stockholm, and has:

1c +Timothy John [Timothy Mordaunt Esq, 60 Karina Terrace, Palmerston North, New Zealand]; *b* 22 Sept 1949; *m* 1976 *Heather Gowing and has:

1d +Guy John; *b* 1977

2d +Anthony Charles; *b* 1979

3d +Samuel John; 1986

1d *Rebecca Jean; *b* 1982

1c *Kristina Birgitta [Mrs Christopher McVeigh, 26 Innes Rd, Christchurch, New Zealand]; *b* 4 Oct 1946; *educ* Canterbury U NZ (BA); *m* 15 Dec 1967 *Christopher Ardagh McVeigh, LLM, and has:

1d *Brita; *b* 1970

2d *Carlotta; *b* 1971

3d *Anna; *b* 1974

4d *Juliet; *b* 1978

1b Catherine Evelyn; *b* 30 Oct 1903; *m* 20 Aug 1947 Maj Samuel Geirnaert, RE, of The Cottage, Newtown, Leominster, Herefs, s of Oscar Geirnaert, of Southport

2b *Joan Helen; *b* 26 May 1905

1a Mabel Louisa; *m* 10 Nov 1904 Rupert Palmer Colomb, CB, only s of Sir John Colomb, KCMG, PC, MP, of Droquinna, and *d* 4 Aug 1958, leaving issue. He *d* 24 May 1955

2a Gertrude Catherine; *m* 9 May 1911 Lt-Gen. Leonard Thales Pease, CB, RMA, s of Sir Thales Pease, KCB, and *d* 1 Oct 1938, having had issue. He *d* 24 July 1936

(3) Osbert (Rev); *b* 4 Dec 1842; *educ* Ch Ch Oxford (MA); Rector Hampton Lucy, Warwicks; Hon Canon Worcester; *m* 14 Oct 1879 Jessie Louisa (*d* 27 Jan 1933), dau of Rev Henry Snow, Vicar Bibury, and *d* 25 Sept 1923, having had:

1a David Osbert; *b* 16 June 1892, *d* 1894

1a Caroline; *m* 11 Sept 1906 Roderick Pryor, yst s of Arthur Pryor, of Hylands, Essex, and *d* 1 July 1918. He *d* 26 July 1930

2a Bridget; *d* unm 7 Feb 1958

(4) Henry; *b* 12 April 1845; *d* 1853

(1) Mary Augusta; *m* 23 Dec 1879 Rev Humphrey Farran Hall, Rector Pylle, and *d* 1 July 1924. He *d* 1910

(2) Alice; *m* 5 Oct 1864 Rev Hon Walter Berkeley Portman and *d* 25 July 1917, leaving issue (*see* PORTMAN, V)

1 Mary; *m* 14 March 1841 Sir Thomas Dyke Acland, 11th Bt, of Columb John (*qv*), and *d* 11 June 1851, leaving issue

The 12th Bt's n,

Sir Nigel John Mordaunt, 13th Bt, MBE (1954); *b* 9 May 1907; *educ* Wellington and Ch Ch Oxford; Lt-Col RA WW II (despatches); *m* 7 Feb 1938 Anne (*d* 1990), 2nd dau of Arthur Francis Tritton (*see* TRITTON, Bt), and *d* 4 Aug 1979, leaving:

1 Sir RICHARD NIGEL CHARLES MORDAUNT, **14th and present Bt**

2 +David Arthur John; *b* 17 Dec 1942; *educ* Radley; *m* 14 Jan 1969 *Elizabeth Aske, dau of William Edgel Luke, of Belgravia, and has:

(1) *Katherine Elizabeth Aske; *b* 7 July 1970

(2) *Alexandra Caroline Aske; *b* 27 Oct 1972

---

3 +Peter Anthony Charles [Peter Mordaunt Esq, 9 Napier Ave, London SW6]; *b* 6 Sept 1946; *educ* Wellington; *m* 4 Dec 1972 *Angela Mary (Badge), formerly w of (Luke Edward) Timothy Hue Williams and yr dau of Ralph Arthur Hubbard (*see* ADDINGTON, B), and has:

(1) +Alastair Nigel Charles; *b* 16 Jan 1974

(1) *Anna Rose; *b* 1981

1 *Tessa Anne [Mrs David Nutting, Newhouse, Terling, Essex]; *b* 10 Oct 1947; *m* 25 April 1974 *David Anthony Nutting (*see* NUTTING, Bt) and has issue

MORLEY

Arms: Sa. a stag's head cabossed between two flaunches arg.
Crest: A cubit arm, erect, couped below the elbow, the sleeve az., cuffed and slashed arg., the hand grasping a stag's attire gu.
Supporters: Dexter, a stag arg., collared or, therefrom suspended an escutcheon vert, charged with a horse's head, couped arg., bridled or; sinister, a greyhound sa., collared or, therefrom suspended an escutcheon gu. charged with a ducal coronet or. **Motto:** *Fideli certa merces* ('Reward is sure to the faithful'). **Creations:** B. (GB) 18 May 1784, E and V. (UK) 29 Nov 1815.

THE 6TH EARL OF MORLEY, Co Devon, **Viscount Boringdon of North Molton**, Co Devon, and **Baron Boringdon of Boringdon**, Co Devon (Sir John St Aubyn Parker, KCVO (1998), JP (Plymouth 1972)) [The Rt Hon The Earl of Morley KCVO JP, Pound House, Yelverton, S Devon PL20 7LJ]; *b* 29 May 1923; *s* unc 1962; *educ* Eton; Ld Lt Devon 1982– (V-Ld Lt 1978–82, DL 1973–78), Lt-Col Roy Fus WW II and Palestine 1945–46, KRRC –1974, tfd to Roy Fus, Korea 1952–53, Middle East 1953–55 and 1956, cmded 1st Bn 1965–67, GSO(1) E Midlands Dist 1967–70, Hon Col Devon ACF 1978–87 and 4th Bn Devonshire & Dorset Regt 1987–92, memb Devon and Cornwall Bd Lloyds Bank 1972–89 (chm 1974), chm: Farm Industries Ltd Truro 1970–85, Plymouth Sound Ltd 1974–, govr Plymouth Poly 1975–82, memb Devon and Cornwall Regnl Ctee Nat Tst 1969–84, Pres: Plymouth Incorporated Chamber Trade & Commerce 1970–, W Country Tourist Bd 1971–89, Fedn Chambers Commerce and Traders Assoc Cornwall 1972–79, Govr Seale-Hayne Ag Coll 1973, Hon Fell Plymouth Poly, Hon LLD Exeter; *m* 15 Oct 1955 *Johanna Katherine, er dau of Sir John Molesworth-St Aubyn, 14th Bt (*qv*), and has:

1 +MARK LIONEL, *Viscount Boringdon* [Viscount Boringdon, Pound House, Yelverton, Devon PL20 7LJ]; *b* 22 Aug 1956; *educ* Eton; Capt Roy Green Jackets; *m* 12 Nov 1983 *Carolyn Jill, dau of Donald McVicar, of Meols, Wirral, Cheshire, and has:

(1) *Alexandra Louise; *b* 1985

(2) *Olivia Clare; *b* 1987

(3) *Helena Georgia; *b* 1991

1 *Venetia Katherine; *b* 5 Feb 1960; *m* 20 Sept 1997 *Francis Jonathan Longstreth Thompson, s of Prof Francis Michael Longstreth Thompson, of Wheathampstead, Herts

Other peerage(s) under the title Morley: A Barony by writ of summons was held between 1299 and 1697 (or conceivably by investiture or some other mode of recreation from the early 16th century on) by members of a family who originally took their name from territorial possessions in Morley, Norfolk. By the middle of the 15th century, however, the male line of Morleys or de Morleys had died out and right to the Barony passed by marriage of the heiress (according to later doctrine) to a member of the Lovel family which held the Barony of Lovel. Soon afterwards this new line ended in an heiress too. She then married a knight of the name of Parker. Parker's origins are obscure and no known connection exists between him and the family who hold the current Earldom. From the late 16th century the Barony of Morley seems either to have been held with that of Monteagle (*qv*) or to have been recreated under a title that embraced both names. On the death of the notional 15th Baron Morley in 1697 the title is deemed to have fallen into abeyance.

In the late 19th and early 20th century a woollen mill engineer by the name of Thorne called himself Lord Morley, claiming a descent from the medieval holders of the title, and even managed very briefly to get into the House of Lords wearing a peer's robes, but was swiftly ejected. His claim was bogus in any case. The 1st Earl of Morley of the current creation had bought an estate at Moreleigh or

Morley in Devon just before being ennobled but this has no more connection with the place in Norfolk from which the original Morleys took their name than did the two sets of Parkers with each other.

Lineage: THOMAS PARKER, of N Molton, Devon; *m* Elizabeth, dau and coheir of John Frye, of Fryhall, Devon, and *d* 1464, leaving:

THOMAS PARKER, of N Molton; *b* c 1465; *m* C (probably Catherine) Stokes and *d* 1545, leaving:

THOMAS PARKER; *bur* 1566, leaving, with a yr s (William, ancestor of the PARKER Bts of Long Melford, *qv*):

JOHN PARKER, of N Molton; High Sheriff Devon 1571; *m* Elizabeth, dau and heiress of Thomas Elycott, of Bratton Clovelly, Devon, and had, with six daus:

EDMUND PARKER, of N Molton; High Sheriff Devon 1600; *m* Dorothy, dau of Sir Clement Smith, of Little Baddow, Essex, Ch Baron Exchequer, and *d* by 18 May 1611, having had, with four daus:

JOHN PARKER; *m* Frances, dau of Jeronemy Mayhew, of Boringdon, Devon, and *dvp* 1610, leaving, with other issue:

EDMUND PARKER, of N Molton; *b* c 1593; High Sheriff Devon 1621; *m* Amy, dau of Sir Edward Seymour, Bt, of Berry Pomeroy, Devon (*see* SOMERSET, D), and *d* between 6 Nov 1642 and 1 Nov 1649, having had an est s:

EDMUND PARKER, of Boringdon, later N Molton; High Sheriff Devon 1647–75; *d* Oct 1691, having had, with other issue, including a yr s (Edmund, had four sons):

GEORGE PARKER, of Boringdon; High Sheriff Devon 1702; *m* 1st Elizabeth, dau of Sir John Fowell Bt, of Fowellscombe, Devon, but had no surv issue; *m* 2nd Anne, dau of John Buller, of Morval, Cornwall, and by her had:

1 JOHN

2 Francis, of Blagdon, Devon; had:

  (1) Anne, *m* 24 Nov 1757 John Baring, of Mount Radford, Devon (*see* NORTHBROOK, B)

  (2) Elizabeth; *m* 1st 24 Aug 1758 Thomas Fowler Baring; *m* 2nd John Spicer, of Wear

  (3) A dau; *m* John Fryer, of Exeter

GEORGE PARKER *d* 1743; his er son,

  JOHN PARKER, of N Molton; *m* 26 June 1725 Catharine (*d* 16 Aug 1758), dau of 1st Earl Poulett (*see* 1970 edn), and had, with another dau (*d unm*):

1 JOHN

2 Montagu Edmund, of Whiteway, Devon; High Sheriff; *m* 1775 Charity, dau of Adml Paul Ourry, and *d* Jan 1813, leaving:

  (1) Montagu Edmund, of Whiteway; *m* 1806 Harriet, dau of John Newcombe, of Starcross, and *d* March 1830, leaving:

    1a Montagu Edmund, of Whiteway; MP S Devon, High Sheriff 1849; *b* 22 Jan 1807; *dsp* 1 July 1858

    2a John; Capt 66th Regt; *m* 1841 Lady Catherine Leslie (*d* 11 Jan 1844), yst dau of Countess of Rothes (*qv*), and *d* 1847

    1 Harriet Sophia, of Whiteway; *m* 1st William Coryton, of Pentillie Castle, Cornwall; *m* 2nd 1842 her cousin **2nd Earl of Morley** (*see* below) and *d* 15 Feb 1897

  1 Catherine; *m* Henry Lambert, of Hope End, Herefs

  2 Bridget; *m* Lt-Col Redmond Kelly

JOHN PARKER *d* 1768; his er son,

  JOHN PARKER, **1st Baron Boringdon of Boringdon**, Co Devon (GB), so *cr* 18 May 1784; *b* c 1737; *educ* Ch Ch Oxford; MP (Whig to 1783, Pittite thereafter) Bodmin 1761–62 and Devon 1762–84; *m* 1st 10 Jan 1764 Frances (*dsp*), dau of Rt. Rev Josiah Hort, DD, Archbp Tuam; *m* 2nd 1769 Hon Theresa Robinson, dau of 1st Baron Grantham (*see* LUCAS OF CRUDWELL, B), and *d* 27 April 1788, leaving by her, with a dau (Theresa, *m* 17 April 1798 Hon George Villiers (*see* CLARENDON, E) and was *bur* 10 Jan 1856):

JOHN PARKER, **1st Earl of Morley**, so *cr* 29 Nov 1815, as also VISCOUNT BORINGDON OF NORTH MOLTON, Co Devon (both UK); *b* 3 May 1772; *educ* Ch Ch Oxford; FRS 1795; *m* 1st 20 June 1804 (*divorce* 14 Feb 1809) Augusta (*m* 2nd Sir Arthur Paget; *see* ANGLESEY, M), 2nd dau of 10th Earl of Westmorland (*qv*), but had no surv issue; *m* 2nd 23 Aug 1809 Frances (*d* 7 Dec 1857), only dau of Thomas Talbot, allegedly an apothecary, of Gonville, Norfolk, and *d* 14 March 1840, leaving:

EDMUND PARKER, **2nd Earl of Morley**; *b* 10 June 1810; *educ* Eton and Ch Ch Oxford; Ld in Waiting (Lib) 1846–52; *m* 1 March 1842 his cousin Harriet Sophia Parker and *d* 28 Aug 1864, leaving, with a dau (Emily Katherine, *d unm* 9 Oct 1910):

ALBERT EDMUND PARKER, **3rd Earl of Morley**, PC (1886), JP, DL Devon; CA Devon; *b* 11 June 1843; *educ* Eton (Fell 1871–1905) and Balliol Coll Oxford; Ld-in-Waiting (Lib) 1868–74, Sec Local Govt Bd 1873–74, U-Sec War 1880–85, First Commr Works Feb-April 1886, Chm Ctees and Dep Speaker Ho Lds 1889–1905; *m* 17 June 1876 Margaret (*d* 9 Feb 1908), est dau of Robert Stayner Holford, MP, of Westonbirt, Glos, and *d* 26 Feb 1905, leaving:

1 EDMUND ROBERT PARKER, **4th Earl of Morley**, JP, CA Devon; *b* 19 April 1877; *educ* Eton and Trin Coll Cambridge (BA); Capt TFR, Roy 1st Devon Yeo, WW I at XI Corps HQ; *d unm* 10 Oct 1951

2 MONTAGU BROWNLOW PARKER, **5th Earl of Morley**; *b* 13 Oct 1878; *educ* Eton; Capt Gren Gds, ADC to GOC Germiston Dist S Africa 1902 and GOC Home Dist 1903, Boer War 1900–02 (wounded) and WW I (despatches five times, Croix de Guerre), V-Cdre Roy Western Yacht Club; *d unm* 28 April 1962

3 John Holford; *b* 22 June 1886; *educ* Eton and Trin Coll Cambridge (BA); RE WW I; *m* 27 Nov 1919 Marjory Katharine Elizabeth Alexandra St Aubyn, dau of 2nd Baron St Levan (*qv*), and *d* 27 Feb 1955, leaving:

  (1) JOHN ST AUBYN PARKER, **6th and present Earl of Morley**

  (2) +Robin Michael [Brig The Hon Robin Parker, Saltram, Plympton, Devon PL7 3UH]; *b* 12 Aug 1925; *educ* Eton; granted 6 May 1963 with yr bro rank of earl's yr s; Lt-Col KRRC 1967, commissioned 1944, served Palestine 1946–48 (despatches), cmded 2nd Bn RGJ 1967–69, Col 1972, Brig 1977 (ret 1980)

(3) +Nigel Geoffrey [The Hon Nigel Parker, Combe Lane Farm, Wormley, Surrey GU8 5TA]; *b* 18 Nov 1931; *educ* Eton and Trin Coll Cambridge (BA); Gren Gds 1955–52, with Shell Petroleum 1955–91; *m* 23 April 1965 *Georgina Jane, est dau of Sir Thomas Gordon Devitt, 2nd Bt (*qv*), and has:

  1a +Edward Geoffrey; *b* 15 Oct 1967; *educ* Eton and BNC Oxford; *m* 1992 *Alice Victoria, dau of Thomas Elliott, of Ivy House, Slawston, Leics

  1a *Theresa Hilaria; *b* 5 March 1966; *educ* Homerton Coll Cambridge; *m* 1994 *Simon Maurice William Latham, est s of Robert Sidney Latham, of The Old Granary, Reigate, Surrey

1 Mary Theresa; *b* 13 Dec 1881; *m* 18 March 1915 Capt Hon Lionel Michael St Aubyn, MVO, and *d* 2 Nov 1932, leaving issue (*see* ST LEVAN, B)

MORRIS, Baron

Arms: Barry wavy of eight arg. and az., two cod-fish naiant ppr., on a chief of the second a two-masted schooner in full sail, also ppr. **Crest:** A caribou's head couped at the neck ppr., charged on the neck with a trefoil or. **Supporters:** On either side a caribou ppr. charged on the shoulder with a trefoil or. **Motto:** *Semper fidelis* ('Always faithful'). **Creation:** B. (UK) 15 Jan 1918.

THE 3RD BARON MORRIS, of St John's in the Dominion of Newfoundland, and of the City of Waterford (Michael David Morris) [The Rt Hon The Lord Morris, House of Lords, London SW1A 0PW]; *b* 9 Dec 1937; *s f* 1975; *educ* Downside; FCA; *m* 1st 11 Nov 1959 (*divorce* 1961) Denise Eleanor, only dau of Morley Richards; *m* 2nd 4 Sept 1961 (*divorce* 1969) Jennifer, only dau of S/Ldr Tristram Gilbert, of The Cranhams, Cirencester, and Mrs E N Hastings, of Malta, and has adopted:

*Anna Maria; *b* 23 Dec 1962

*Michaela Mary; *b* 8 Sept 1965

The 3rd BARON *m* 3rd 25 Jan 1980 *Juliet Susan, twin dau of Anthony Buckingham, of The Shaugh, Upper Hartfield, Sussex, and has:

1 +THOMAS ANTHONY SALMON; *b* 2 July 1982

2 +James; *b* 1 Aug 1983

2 *Lucy Juliet; *b* 18 Jan 1981

Lineage: EDWARD PATRICK MORRIS, **1st Baron Morris**, of St John's in the Dominion of Newfoundland, and of the City of Waterford (UK), so *cr* 15 Jan 1918, KCMG (1913), PC (1911), QC (1896); *b* 8 May 1858 (s of Edward Morris (*d* 5 July 1898), of Waterford and later St John's Newfoundland); slr Supreme Court Newfoundland 1884, barrister 1885, MP St John's Newfoundland 1885–1919, memb Cabinet 1889–97 and 1900–07, Actg Attorney-Gen 1890–95, dir Newfoundland Savings Bank 1893–1906, Del Ottawa on Confedn 1895 and Colonial Office 1897 and 1901 on French Shore, Ldr Ind Lib Party 1898–1900, Attorney-Gen and Min Justice 1903–07, Ldr People's Pty 1908, PM 1909–18, Newfoundland rep Imp Confs 1909, 1911 and 1917, Br Counsel Hague Arbitration 1910, memb War Cabinet 1916–18, ed *Morris's Newfoundland Law Reports* (1820–1905), ktd 1904, LLD Ottawa, Hon DCL Oxon, Hon LLD: Cantab, Edin and Glasgow; *m* 19 Jan 1901 Isabel Langrishe (*d* 1 July 1934), widow of Hon James P Fox and dau of Rev William Wellman Le Gallais, of Jersey and Newfoundland, and *d* 24 Oct 1935, leaving:

MICHAEL WILLIAM MORRIS, **2nd Baron Morris**; *b* 12 April 1903; *educ* Downside and Trin Coll Cambridge (BA 1925, MA 1929); barrister Inner Temple 1925, disbarred at own request and admitted slr 1931, S/Ldr WW II 1939–43, legal staff offr Middle East, Mil Prosecutor Palestine 1940–42, chm Solicitors' Benevolent Assoc, memb Sub-Ctee Reforms Admin Justice, sr ptnr Blout Petre & Co; *m* 1st 18 April 1933 (*divorce* 1946) Jean Beatrice (*m* 2nd 1946 Lord Salmon; *d* 1989), er dau of Lt-Col David Maitland-Makgill-Critchton (*see* LAUDERDALE, E), and has:

1 MICHAEL DAVID MORRIS, **3rd and present Baron Morris**

2 +(Edward) Patrick [The Hon Patrick Morris, Dormer Cottage, Petham, Kent]; *b* 9 Dec 1937 (twin); *educ* Downside; *m* 27 July 1963 *Mary Beryl, est dau of Lt-Col Dick Harry George Thrush, of Canterbury, and has:

  (1) +Edward Patrick; *b* 23 Feb 1965; *educ* The Harvey GS Folkestone

  (1) *Elizabeth Mary; *b* 8 June 1968

1 *Aislinn Mary Katherine [The Hon Mrs Hildyard JP, Goxhill Hall, Goxhill, Barrow upon Humber, N Lincs DN19 7LZ]; *b* 22 April 1934; *m* 5 Jan 1954 Capt

Angus Jeremy Christopher HILDYARD formerly DUNLOP (deed poll 1945, plus arms by roy licence 1964), DL, RA (*d* 20 March 1995), only surv *s* of Maj Donald Maxwell Dunlop, of Eastbourne, and has:

(1) *Nicholas Alexander Cyril [Nicholas Hildyard Esq, The Elms, Roos, Kingston upon Hull, E Yorks]; *b* 5 Dec 1954; *educ* Westminster; *m* 1981 *Philippa Clare, only dau of Lt-Col Anthony Gillett, TD, DL, of Northfield House, Swanland, E Yorks, and has:

  1a *Christopher Charles D'Arcy; *b* 1984
  2a *William George Alexander; *b* 1987

(1) *Charlotte [Lady Tyrwhitt, 51 Whitecross St, Barton-on-Humber, N Lincs DN18 5EU]; *b* 21 March 1958; *m* 1984, as his 2nd w, *Sir Reginald Thomas Newman Tyrwhitt, 3rd Bt (*qv*), and has issue

2 *Clodagh Mary [The Hon Mrs Farrell, 22 Wood Lane, Beverley, N Yorks HU17 8BS]; *b* 8 Nov 1936; *m* 2 May 1964 *Lt-Col Thomas Hugh Francis Farrell, CBE, TD, only *s* of Hugh Farrell, of N Ferriby, Yorks, and has:

(1) *James Thomas Hugh; *b* 12 Aug 1966; *m* 10 Aug 1996 *Caroline Juliet, dau of James Ford, of Jarnac, France

(1) *Sophia Mary; *b* 30 March 1965; *m* 21 Oct 1995 *Marco Betti-Berutto, *s* of Carlo Betti-Berutto, of Rome, and Mrs Marilena Scala Leon, of Newington, Oxon, and has:

  1a *Thomas Federico Alexis; *b* 18 May 1997

The **2nd Baron** *m* 2nd 12 July 1960 Mary (*d* 1991), formerly w of Anthony Robert Agate, MRCS, LRCP, and yr dau of Rev Alexander Reginald Langhorne, of Halstead, Neston, Cheshire, and *d* 11 March 1975

MORRIS, Bt

Arms: Sa. on a saltire engrailed erm. a bezant, charged with a cross couped gu. **Crest:** A lion rampant or, charged on the shoulder with a cross couped gu., within a chain in the form of an arch or.
Motto: *Scuto fidei* ('By the shield of faith').
Creation: Bt. (UK) 12 May 1806.

SIR ROBERT BYNG MORRIS, 10TH BT, of Clasemont, Co Glamorgan [Sir Robert Morris Bt, 10885 15th Sideroad, RR3, Georgetown, ONT L7G 4SG, Canada]; *b* 25 Feb 1913; *s* cousin 1982; *m* 1947 *Christina Kathleen, dau of Archibald Field, of Toddington, Glos, and has:

1 +ALLAN LINDSAY [Allan Morris Esq, 10885 15th Sideroad, RR3, Georgetown, ONT L7G 4SG, Canada]; *b* 27 Nov 1961; *m* 1986 *Cheronne Denise, est dau of Dale Whitford, of Par, Cornwall, and has:

(1) +Sennen John; *b* 5 June 1995
(2) +Chace James; *b* 18 Sept 1997
(1) *Chelsea Alana; *b* 29 Aug 1992

1 *Geraldine Ann; *b* 1948; *m* 1st 1969 (*divorce* 1981) Gilbert Baxter Jr, of Vancouver, and has:

(1) *Jennifer Carly; *b* 1975

1 (cont.) Mrs Geraldine Baxter *m* 2nd 1984 *Thomas Millard, of Vancouver
2 *Gillian; *b* 1950; *m* 1972 (*divorce* 19–) Andrew Jamieson, of Quebec
3 *Roberta Crystal; *b* 1965; Canadian Jr Dressage Champion 1983

Lineage: ROBERT MORRIS, of Bishop's Castle and Cleobury Mortimer, Salop; *m* Mary, dau of Richard Tristam, of More Hall, Worcs, and had:

ROBERT MORRIS, of Tredegar, Glam; *m* Margaret, dau and heiress of David Jenkins, of Machynlleth, Montgomeryshire, by Bridget, dau of John Parry, and *d* 1768, leaving:

1 Robert; barrister Lincoln's Inn; *dsp* 1797
2 JOHN (Sir), **1st Bt**
1 Bridget; *m* Thomas Lockwood.
2 Margaret; *m* Noel Desenfans, Consul-Gen for Poland
3 Jane; *m* Edward King, of Marino, Glam

The 2nd son,

Sir John Morris, 1st Bt (UK), so *cr* 12 May 1806, of Clasemont; *b* 15 July 1745; *m* 26 May 1774 Henrietta (*d* 16 June 1812), dau of Sir Philip Musgrave, 6th Bt, of Eden Hall, Cumberland (*qv*), and had, with two daus (*d* unm):

1 JOHN (Sir), **2nd Bt**

2 Thomas; MA
1 Henrietta; *m* Sir Nathaniel Levitt Peacocke, Bt (*see* 1875 edn), and *d* 4 June 1825
2 Matilda; *m* 13 Nov 1807 Edward Jesse, of W Bromwich, Staffs, and *d* 5 July 1850
3 Caroline; *m* 6 Sept 1824 Rev George Lillie Wodehouse Fauquier and *d* 26 Jan 1883

Sir JOHN *d* 25 June 1819; his son,

Sir John Morris, 2nd Bt; *b* 14 July 1775; *m* 5 Oct 1809 Lucy Juliana (*d* 27 Nov 1881), yst dau of 5th Viscount Torrington (*qv*), and *d* 24 Feb 1855, having had, with other issue:

1 **Sir John Armine Morris, 3rd Bt**, DL; *b* 13 July 1813; *m* 1847 Catherine (*d* 16 March 1890), dau of Ronald MacDonald, and *d* 8 Feb 1893, leaving:

(1) **Sir Robert Armine Morris, 4th Bt**, JP, DL (Glam); High Sheriff 1900, Maj Welch Regt; *b* 27 July 1848; *m* 12 Feb 1885 Lucy Augusta (*d* 15 Nov 1902), dau of Thomas Cory, of Nevill Court, Tunbridge Wells, and *d* 20 Feb 1927, having had:

  1a **Sir Tankerville Robert Armine Morris, 5th Bt**, MC; Capt 1st Bn Glos Regt WW I (despatches, two medals); *b* 9 June 1892; *d* unm 29 Sept 1937
  2a John Torrington; 2nd Lt RWF; *b* 6 June 1896; *ka* 15 or 16 May 1915
  1a Lucy Gwladys; *m* 3 June 1911 Cecil Francis Milsom, DSO, Maj RASC, and *d* 21 April 1948, leaving issue. He *d* 3 July 1963
  2a Valerie Ermyntrude; *m* 1st 20 Feb 1917 Capt Eric Belfield, Middx Regt (*ka* 31 July 1917); *m* 2nd 12 Oct 1922 Maj Thomas Chalmers Bowie, MB, RAMC, of Lindisfarne, Gullane, E Lothian
  3a Dulcie Elaine; *m* 27 Feb 1913 Charles FitzRoy Bruce, 8th *s* of Alan Cameron Bruce-Pryce, of Monknash, Glam, and *d* 27 March 1967, leaving issue. He *d* 3 Jan 1951
  4a Sibyl Rowena; *m* 1st 4 Feb 1918 (*divorce* 1925) Capt Harold Dare, MC, RFA, and had:

    1b *George Harold Armine [George Dare Esq, 9 Launceston Place, London W8 5RL]; *b* 2 Nov 1918; *m* 25 May 1957 *Penelope Constance, dau of Capt Hon Ivan Josselyn Lumley Hay, MBE (*see* ERROLL, E), and has issue
    1b Sonia Ione; *b* 3 Nov 1919; *d* 198–

  4a (cont.) Mrs Sibyl Dare *m* 2nd 21 July 1925 William Edridge Yockney, of The Manor Farm, Milborne Wick, Dorset, and *d* Dec 1972

(2) John; Hon Lt-Col Welsh Div RA; *b* 9 Sept 1850; *m* 1881 Jessie (*d* 1941), dau of William Fowler, and *d* 28 March 1916, having had:

  1a John Armine Robert (Rev); BA Durham, Curate St Columba, Leytonstone; *b* 1882; *d* unm 16 May 1908
  1a Jessie Harriett Amy Blanche; *m* 1923 Capt Bertram Wellington Parker, QO Roy W Kent Regt (*d* 19 Feb 1966)
  2a Beryl Violet; *d* 1894

(3) **Sir George Cecil Morris, 6th Bt**; *b* 10 April 1852; *m* 1 Jan 1873 Mary Jane Hunt and *d* 17 July 1940, having had:

  1a Armine Cecil Edward George; *b* 1885; *m* 23 Dec 1911 *Adelaide, dau of Thomas Nangle, of Redfern, NSW, and *d* 19 March 1934, leaving:

    1b *Nancy Gwynne; *b* 1915; *m* Leonard Clement McAlry
  1a Gwladys; *b* 1890

(4) Arthur Ronald; *b* 18 Nov 1855; *d* 20 July 1931
(5) Herbert; *b* 17 June 1858; *m* 25 July 1880 Margery Rachel, dau of John Barron, and *d* 12 Sept 1931, leaving:

  1a John Barron; *b* 5 March 1882; *d* 1912
  2a **Sir Herbert Edward Morris, 7th Bt**; *b* 4 July 1884; Bailiff Swansea County Court; *m* 4 June 1938 *Olive Irene, dau of William Davies, of Swansea, and *dsp* 15 Aug 1947

  1a Katherine Daisy; *m* 1904 George Rollings and had a dau

(1) Henrietta Ellen; *m* 10 Oct 1876 Felix Hussey Webber and *d* 1 Nov 1935, leaving issue. He *d* 19 April 1905
(2) Amy Blanche Caroline; *m* 1885 Maj Robert Bowen Robertson, 2nd Bde Welsh Div RA, of Berkeley House, Limpley Stoke, and *d* 14 Aug 1907, leaving issue

2 George Byng, JP, DL (Glam); High Sheriff; *b* 25 March 1816; *m* 23 Oct 1852 Emily Matilda (*d* 9 July 1913), dau of Charles H Smith, of Derwen Fawr, Glam, and *d* 3 Dec 1899, leaving:

(1) Robert Townsend; *b* 9 July 1853; *d* unm 5 June 1939
(2) Charles Smith; *b* 12 Dec 1854; *m* 7 Feb 1888 Maud Mary (*d* 5 Jan 1936), dau of Rev George Alston, Rector Studland, and *d* 27 May 1933, having had:

  1a Charles Alan Smith; Capt 3rd Bn Beds Regt WW I (wounded three times); *b* 15 May 1895; *d* 7 May 1917 of wounds recd Battle of Arras
  1a Mabel Travers; *d* 10 Dec 1983
  2a Daisy Emily Smith; *m* 30 April 1930 Brig Geoffrey William Auten, OBE, Welch Regt, of Castle House, Knockholt, Kent, *s* of William Blee Auten, of Plymouth, and had:

    1b *Mary Morris [Mrs James Carpenter, Holbeache House, Trimpley, Worcs DY2 1PA]; *b* 8 March 1933; *m* 4 March 1961 *James Montagu Carpenter, *s* of Edward Harry Osmund Carpenter, of Trimpley, and has:

      1c *Charles James; *b* 29 Dec 1961; *m* 1 March 1997 *Fiona Louise Lockwood Forbes
      2c *Peter Edward; *b* 7 Nov 1963
      3c *Henry William Hugh; *b* 4 Sept 1971

  3a Lucy Maud; *m* 8 Jan 1930 Lt-Col Francis John Nugee, MC, TD, Headmaster Eastbourne Coll (*d* 29 Jan 1966), *s* of Canon F E Nugee, and *d* 20 Dec 1977, leaving:

    1b *Lucy Frances Mary [Mrs Keith Walker, Holly Lodge, 14 Billett Avenue, Waterlooville, Hants PO7 7SZ]; *b* 17 Sept 1932; *m* 24 Sept 1955 *Keith William Scutts Walker, TD, FRICS, *s* of William Scutts Walker, and has:

      1c *Julian Francis Scutts, TD; *b* 2 Sept 1956; BSc, FRICS; *m* 14 April 1984 *Phillipa Xanthe Lane
      2c *Nicholas Charles William; *b* 2 April 1961

1c *Sally Henrietta; *b* 4 April 1958
2c *Lucy Victoria; *b* 17 Oct 1962
3c *Judy Belinda; *b* 23 March 1965
2b *Patricia Ruth [Miss Patricia Nugee, 55 Walham Grove, Fulham, London SW6]; *b* 29 Aug 1937
(3) **Sir George Lockwood Morris, 8th Bt**; *b* 29 Jan 1859; Lt Roy Mon Engrs Militia; *m* 1889 Wilhelmina Elizabeth (*d* 8 Oct 1948), dau of Thomas Cory, of Sketty House, nr Swansea, and *d* 23 Nov 1947, having had:
1a **Sir Cedric Lockwood Morris, 9th Bt**; *b* 11 Dec 1889; *educ* Charterhouse, Paris and Rome; served WW I, artist, Pncpl E Anglian Sch of Painting; *d* unm 8 Feb 1982
1a Muriel Emily; *d* young
2a Nancy Wilhelmina Lockwood; *b* 1893
(4) Musgrave; *b* 18 Nov 1864; *m* 1892 Edith Marion, dau of K Lockhart, of Manitoba, and *dsp*
(5) Thomas Byng; *b* 24 July 1866; *m* 24 Aug 1898 Edith Amy (*d* 4 Aug 1965), dau of F S Bishop, of Glanyafon, Glam, and *d* 23 April 1951, leaving:
1a *Rosamond Byng; *m* 14 Jan 1933 *Walter Edgar Aylwin, MC, s of C R Aylwin, of Berkhamsted, Herts, and has:
1b *Charles Byng; *b* 5 June 1934; *educ* Emmanuel Coll Cambridge (MA); *m* 2 Feb 1963 *Lesley Dorothy, yr dau of L V Taylor, of Cobham, Surrey, and has:
1c *Simon John Byng; *b* 19 Oct 1965
2c *Antony Charles Barton; *b* 19 Oct 1969
2b *John Morris; *b* 23 July 1942; *educ* Emmanuel Coll Cambridge (BA); *m* 1970 *Angela, yr dau of C D Phillips, of California, and has:
1c *Michael Deryk Morris; *b* 1972
2c *Christopher John; *b* 1974
1b *Anne Elizabeth; *b* 17 July 1936; *m* 7 Nov 1964 *Bradford Gary Siegrist, of W Vancouver, and has:
1c *William Peter; *b* 4 June 1965
1c *Susan Elizabeth; *b* 5 June 1969
2a *Betty Byng; *m* 15 June 1928 A Alan Connell (*d* 19–), s of W G Connell, and has:
1b *Thomas Alan Byng; *b* 1936; *m* 1959 *Sylvia Hudson and has:
1c *Christopher Byng; *b* 1960
1c *Debbie Jane; *b* 1963
1b *Joan Ursula; *b* 1929; *m* 1954 *John Murray and has:
1c *Francis Patricia; *b* 1955
2c *Jane Penelope; *b* 1958
(6) Frank Hall MORRIS later BYNG-MORRIS (deed poll 1927); *b* 16 July 1869; *m* 29 Oct 1913 Irene Catherine (*d* 11 Feb 1968), dau of Lt-Col — Rogers-Harrison, of Cheltenham, and *d* 21 Oct 1954, leaving:
1a *Daphne Veronica [Mrs Norman Halfhead, Beech House, Wildernesse Ave, Seal, Kent]; *b* 1914; *m* 10 Oct 1942 Norman Halfhead (*d* 1988), s of R N Halfhead, of Godden Grange, Sevenoaks, and has:
1b *Christopher Norman; *b* 1946; *m* 1984 *Francesca Waterhouse and has:
1c *Michael Christopher; *b* 1986
1c *Lucy Christina; *b* 1985
(1) Edith Charlotte; *m* 1887 Francis Montagu Lloyd, of The Grange, Newnham-on-Severn, and *d* 29 May 1939, having had issue. He *d* 14 July 1922
(2) Fanny Matilda; *m* 16 Sept 1882 Harry Bathurst Christie and *d* 19 June 1926, leaving issue
(3) Lucy Emily; *m* 1887 Maj Henry Selwyn Goodlake, Lancs Fus, and *d* 29 May 1936. He *d* 1917
(4) Rose Herbert; *d* unm 9 Sept 1952
3 Frederick; Cdr RN, Syria and bombardment St Jean d'Acre 1840; *b* 25 Jan 1819; *m* 28 Jan 1854 Agnes (*d* 4 Dec 1909), dau and heiress of Charles Brandford Lane, of Castle Grant and Clermont, Barbados, and *d* 23 Jan 1903, leaving:
(1) Frederick; Maj Roy Welch Fus; *b* 20 Dec 1854; *m* 1884 Sybil (*d* May 1942), dau of John Rowland, BCS, and *dsp* 3 Jan 1915
(2) Charles Lane; Lt 1st Warwicks Militia; *b* 29 March 1857; *m* 1903 Mabel Emily, only dau of Rev Augustus Cooper, of Upper Norwood and Syleham Hall, Suffolk, and *dsp* 22 March 1922
(3) Percy Byng; Lt WW I; *b* 13 Nov 1871; *educ* Kelly Coll Tavistock; *m* 25 March 1912 Ethel Maud (*d* 16 March 1923), only dau of William Morley Glascott, of Melbourne, Australia, and had:
1a Sir ROBERT BYNG MORRIS, **10th and present Bt**
4 Charles Henry, CB; Gen, Offr Legn Hon; *b* 27 Feb 1824; *m* 16 Sept 1869 Lady Blanche Godolphin-Osborne (*d* 13 Feb 1917), yst dau of 8th Duke of Leeds (see 1963 edn), and *d* 12 Oct 1887, leaving:
(1) Ethel Harriet; *m* 2 Dec 1905 Gerald Cloete, RM Frankfort, Orange River Colony, and *dsp* 31 March 1947. He *d* 1939
(2) Lilia Gwendolen; *m* 16 March 1907 Henry Ralph Champion Partridge, only s of Henry Thomas Partridge, JP, of Hockham Hall, Norfolk, and *d* 9 April 1941, leaving issue. He *d* 7 Sept 1962
1 Henrietta Juliana; *m* 2 March 1938 Albert Lascelles Jenner, s of Robert Jenner, of Wenvoe Castle, and *d* 7 Oct 1871, leaving issue. He *d* Oct 1864

MORRIS OF CASTLE MORRIS

Creation: B. (LP,UK) 1990.

THE BARON MORRIS OF CASTLE MORRIS, of St Dogmaels, Co Dyfed (Brian Robert Morris) [The Rt Hon The Lord Morris of Castle Morris, The Old Hall, Foolow, Derbys S32 1QR]; *b* 4 Dec 1930; *educ* Cardiff HS and Worcester Coll Oxford (MA, DPhil); 1st Bn Welch Regt 1949–51, 4th Bn Welch Regt (TA) 1951–56; Fell Shakespeare Inst Birmingham U 1956–58; Assist Lecturer Reading U 1958–60 (Lecturer 1960–65); Lecturer York U 1965–67 (Sr Lecturer 1967–71); Prof English Lit, Dep Dean and Public Orator Sheffield U 1971–80; Pncpl St David's U Coll Lampeter 1980–91; Chm: Museums and Galleries Commn 1985–90 (memb 1975–), Cncl Prince of Wales's Inst of Architecture 1993–96; V-Pres: Cncl Nat Parks 1985–, Museums Assoc 1985–, Prayer Bk Soc 1990–; Tstee: Nat Portrait Gallery 1977–, Nat Heritage Memorial Fund 1980–91, Welsh Advsy Ctee Br Cncl 1983–, Anthony Panizzi Fndn 1987–, Museum of Empire and Cwlth 1991–, CPRW 1991–; Memb: Archbps' Cncl Evangelism 1971–75, Cncl Yorks Art Assoc 1973–81, Yr Academi Gymreig 1979–, Welsh Arts Cncl 1983–86, Cncl Poetry Soc 1980– (V-Pres 1990–), Br Library Bd 1980–91, Cncl Nat Library Wales 1981–91; Pres Welsh Historic Gdns Tst 1990–; Oppn Dep Ch Whip Ho Lds 1992–97; gen ed: *New Mermaid Dramatists* 1964–86, *New Arden Shakespeare* 1974–82; Hon LittD Sheffield 1991; Hon LLD Wales 1992; author: *Ford's The Broken Heart* (ed, with Roma Gill, 1965), *John Cleveland: a Bibliography of his Poems* (1967), *The Poems of John Cleveland* (with Eleanor Withington, 1967), *Ford's 'Tis Pity She's a Whore* (ed, with Roma Gill, 1968), *New Mermaid Critical Commentaries I–III* (ed, 1969–72), *Mary Quant's London* (1973), *Tourneur's The Aetheist's Tragedy* (ed, 1976), *Tide Race* (1976), *Stones in the Brook* (1978), *Ritual Murder* (ed, 1980), *Shakespeare's The Taming of the Shrew* (ed, 1981), *Dear Tokens* (1987), *Harri Webb* (1993); *m* 1955 *Sandra Mary, dau of Percival Samuel James, and has:
1 *Christopher Justin Robert; *b* 1959
1 *Lindsay Alison Mary; *b* 1957; *m* 19– *- Boxall

Lineage: WILLIAM ROBERT MORRIS, of Cardiff; Capt RN; *m* Ellen Elizabeth Shelley and had an only s:

BRIAN ROBERT, *cr* a **Baron**

MORRIS OF KENWOOD

Creation: B. (UK) 11 July 1950.

THE 2ND BARON MORRIS OF KENWOOD, of Kenwood, in the City of Sheffield (Philip Geoffrey Morris, JP (Inner London 1967)) [The Rt Hon The Lord Morris of Kenwood JP, 35 Fitzjohn's Ave, London NW3 5JY]; *b* 18 June 1928; *s f* 1954; *educ* Loughborough Coll; F/O RAF 1946–49 and 1951–55, tstee Stonham Meml Tst 1995–; *m* 9 Sept 1958 *Hon Ruth Joan Gertrude Rahle (memb Gen Advsry Cncl IBA 1987–), only dau of Baron Janner (see JANNER OF BRAUNSTONE, B), and has:
1 +JONATHAN DAVID; *b* 6 Aug 1968; *m* 30 July 1996 *Melanie, only dau of Rubin Klein
1 *Diane Susan [The Hon Mrs Zitcer, 2 Sidmouth Rd, London NW2 5JX]; *b* 25 Jan 1960; *educ* St Paul's and Central Sch of Speech and Drama (Dip Stage Management); *m* 22 Sept 1981 *Cary Haskell Zitcer, er s of C J Zitcer, and has:
(1) *Natasha Esther; *b* 1986
(2) *Emily Margaret; *b* 1988
2 *Caroline Harriet; *b* 23 April 1961
3 *Linda Jane [The Hon Mrs Gelernter, 5 Manor Park Crescent, Edgware, Middx HA8 7NL]; *b* 28 April 1965; *m* 1991 *Paul M Gelernter, s of David Gelernter and Mrs Jeanne Canning, and has:
(1) *Theo Saul; *b* 3 Dec 1994
(2) *Jake Oliver; *b* 25 July 1997

Lineage: JACOB SAMUEL MORRIS; *m* Fanny — (*d* Nov 1904) and *d* Feb 1923, leaving, with six er sons (Isaac; Samuel, Alderman Doncaster; Hyman, Alderman Leeds, *d* 1956; William, *d* June 1958; Simon; Nathan) and two daus (Minnie, *m* Abraham Rosen, of Harrogate; Eva, *m* Leo Josephs, of Harrogate):

HARRY MORRIS, **1st Baron Morris of Kenwood**, of Kenwood, in the City of Sheffield (UK), so *cr* 11 July 1950; *b* 7 Oct 1893; *educ* Tivoli House Sch Gravesend and privately; memb Sheffield City Cncl 1920–26 and 1929–37, York and Lancs Regt and Capt Roy Fus WW I (despatches), WW II as Lt-Col KOYLI; slr 1920 and 1952, barrister 1936, MP Sheffield Centl 1945–50 and Sheffield Neepsend Feb–March 1950; *m* 11 June 1924 Florence (*d* 1982), dau of Henry Isaacs, of Leeds, and *d* 1 July 1954, having had:
1 Roger James; *b* 17 Aug 1925; *d* 3 June 1938
2 PHILIP GEOFREY MORRIS, **2nd and present Baron Morris of Kenwood**
1 *Hilary Zara [The Hon Mrs Lewis, Zaraz, Littlewick Green, Maidenhead, Berks]; *b* 24 June 1932; *m* 6 Oct 1964 *Ronald Graham Lewis, s of Arthur Spencer Lewis, of London

MORRIS OF MANCHESTER

Creation: B. (LP, UK) 2 Aug 1997.

THE BARON MORRIS OF MANCHESTER, of Manchester, Co Gtr Manchester (Alf(red) Morris, PC (1979), QSO (1989)) [The Rt Hon The Lord Morris of Manchester QSO PC, House of Lords, London SW1A 0PW]; *b* 23 March 1928; *educ* Ruskin Coll Oxford, St Catherine's Coll Oxford and Manchester U; office worker Manchester 1942–46; Nat Serv 1946–48; Nat Chm Labour League of Youth 1950–52; Observer Cncl Europe 1952–53; teacher and lecturer Manchester 1954–56; iIndustl rels offr Electricity Cncl London 1956–64; ed Nat Jt Advsy Cncl Electricity Supply Industry Jnl 1959–61; MP (Lab) Manchester Wythenshawe 1964–97, PPS to MAFF 1964–67, memb Parly Delegn UN Gen Assembly 1966, Ld Pres Cncl and Leader H of C 1968–70, Oppn Spokesman Social Servs and Disabled People 1970–74 and 1979–92, Parly U-Sec DHSS 1974–79; memb: Gen Advsy Cncl BBC 1968–74 and 1983–, Exec Ctee Nat Fund Research Crippling Diseases 1970–74; Parly Advsr Police Fedn 1971–74; Chm: PLP Food and Ag Gp 1971–74, Co-op Parly Gp 1971–72 and 1983–85; Patron: Disablement Income Gp 1970, Motability 1978–; Pres N of England Regnl Assoc for Deaf 1980–; Tstee Crisis at Christmas 1982–; Hon Fell Manchester Metropolitan U 1990; Hon AO 1991; author: *Human Relations in Industry* (ed, 1958), *Value Added Tax* (1970), *The Growth of Parliamentary Scrutiny by Committee* (1970), *No Feet to Drag* (with A Butler, 1972); *m* 1950 *Irene Jones and has two sons and two daus

Lineage: GEORGE HENRY MORRIS; *m* Jessie Murphy and had:

ALF(RED), *cr* a **Baron**

MORRISON

Creation: B. (UK) 16 Nov 1945.

THE 2ND BARON MORRISON (Dennis Glossop Morrison), of Tottenham, Co Middlesex [The Rt Hon The Lord Morrison, 7 Ullswater Ave, Felixstowe, Suffolk IP11 9SD]; *b* 21 June 1914; *s f* 1953; *educ* Tottenham Co Sch; mfacturing exec Metal Box Co Ltd 1957–72, Ld Lt's Rep Tottenham 1955–, FSS 1953–37, V-Pres Acton Chamber Commerce 1972 (memb exec ctee 1962), Hon Pres Robt Browning Settlement 1967–; *m* 1st 1 March 1940 (*divorce* 1958) Florence Alice Helena, dau of Augustus Hennes, of Tottenham; *m* 2nd 21 March 1959 (*divorce* 1975) Joan Eleanor, dau of William Richard Meech, of Ealing

Lineage: JAMES MORRISON, of Aberdeen; had:

ROBERT CRAIGMYLE MORRISON, **1st Baron Morrison**, of Tottenham in the County of Middlesex (UK), so *cr* 16 Nov 1945, PC (1949), JP, DL (Middx); *b* 29 Oct 1881; *educ* elementary and higher grade schs Aberdeen; handicrafts teacher, served WW I, memb Wood Green Cncl 1914–19, CC Middx 1919–24, Alderman Tottenham 1935, MP (Lab) Tottenham N 1922–31 and 1935–45, PPS to PM 1929–30, memb Met Water Bd 1938–47, chm Food Waste Bd Min Supply 1941–49 and Nat Juvenile Employment Cncl 1946, Parly Sec Min Works 1949–51, Ld-in-Waiting 1947–48; *m* 27 July 1910 Grace (*b* 26 Feb 1888; *d* 1983), est dau of Thomas Glossop, and *d* 25 Dec 1953, having had:

  1 DENNIS GLOSSOP MORRISON, **2nd and present Baron Morrison**

  2 Douglas; *b* 1 April 1920; *educ* Tottenham GS; *d unm* 31 April 1946

MORRISON-BELL

Arms: Quarterly, 1st and 4th, sa. on a fess erm. between three bells arg. a falcon close between two crescents of the field (for BELL); 2nd and 3rd, arg. on a fess az. between three moor's heads couped at the neck ppr., the turbans vert doubled arg., three roses or (for MORRISON). **Crests:** 1 A falcon close ppr., belled or, holding in the beak a bell as in the arms (for BELL), 2 In front of a moor's head couped at the shoulders as in the arms, three roses gu. (for MORRISON). **Motto:** *Perseverantia* ('Perseverance'). **Creation:** Bt. (UK) 18 Dec 1905.

SIR WILLIAM HOLLIN DAYRELL MORRISON-BELL, 4TH BT, of Otterburn Hall [Sir William Morrison-Bell Bt, Highgreen, Tarset, Northumberland NE48 1RP; 106 Bishop's Rd, London SW6 7AR]; *b* 21 June 1956; *s f* 1967; *educ* Eton and St Edmund Hall Oxford; slr; *m* 1984 *Cynthia Hélène Marie, yr dau of Teddy White, of Kensington, and has:

  1 +THOMAS CHARLES EDWARD; *b* 13 Feb 1985

  1 *Emily Prudence Collette; *b* 12 Dec 1996

Lineage: JOHN BELL, of Blackbank and later Nether Steele, both Allendale, Northumberland; *m* 31 Jan 1744 Elizabeth Kirk, of Allendale, and had an er s:

WILLIAM BELL, of the Steele, Allendale, and later Anfield House, Lanchester, Co Durham; *b* 24 Sept 1744; *m* 19 July 1778 Jane (*d* 20 July 1823), est dau of John Kirsopp, of Conside, Medowsley, Co Durham, and *d* 11 May 1818, having had a 2nd s:

WILLIAM BELL, of Ford Hall, Sunderland, Co Durham, JP; V-Adml Co Durham, Paymaster Royal Yacht *Victoria and Albert* 1843–56; *b* 11 April 1779; *m* 20 May 1828 Mary Wilhelmina (*d* 26 May 1850), 2nd dau and in her issue heir of John Morrison, RN, of Alston, Cumberland, and *d* 16 Dec 1856, having had an est s:

Sir CHARLES WILLIAM BELL later MORRISON-BELL (roy licence 16 Oct 1905), **1st Bt** (UK), so *cr* 18 Dec 1905, of Otterburn Hall, Elsdon, Northumberland, JP (Cos Durham, Sussex, Wilts, and Northumberland), DL Co Durham; *b* 18 March 1833; *educ* St John's Coll Cambridge; FGS, Lt 15th Hus, Lancs Hus Yeo and Durham Artillery Militia and Maj 3rd Admin Bn Durham Rifle Vols; *m* 1 Sept 1863 Louisa Maria (*d* 15 Dec 1920), 2nd dau of William Henry Dawes, JP, of The Hall, Kenilworth, Warwicks, and had:

  1 CLAUDE WILLIAM HEDLEY (Sir), **2nd Bt**

  2 Sir (ARTHUR) CLIVE MORRISON-BELL, 1st and last Bt (UK), so *cr* 18 July 1923, of Harpford, Devon; *b* 19 April 1871; Maj Scots Gds, Boer War 1899–1900 (medal, three clasps, despatches) and WW I, MP (C) Honiton 1910–31, PPS to: 1st Ld Admlty 1920–23, Ld Privy Seal 1923 and Chllr Exchequer 1924–26; *m* 21 Nov 1912 Hon Lilah Katherine Julia Wingfield (*d* 20 Oct 1981 aged 93) dau of 7th Viscount Powerscourt (*qv*), and *dspm* 16 April 1956, when the btcy expired, having had:

    (1) *Shelagh Jocelyn; *m* 1st 17 April 1943 (*divorce* 1951) William Cooper Moore, est s of William Arthur Moore, of New Rochelle, NY, and has:

      1a *David Anson Clive [David Moore, 373 Marion St, Denver, CO 80218, USA]; *b* 10 Feb 1944; US Army (Inf); health care finance; *m* 1978 *Christiane Hyde, dau of Casper Citron, of New York, and has:

      1b *Cornelia Wingfield; *b* 26 Sept 1986

    (1) (cont.) Mrs Shelagh Moore *m* 2nd 20 Jan 1968 Sir Ralph Abercromby Campbell (*d* 1989), Ch Justice Bahamas, 2nd s of Maj William Orr Campbell, MC, of Burton Hall, Christchurch, Hants

    (2) Deirdre Pamela Clare; *d* 6 Jan 1916

    (3) *Patrica Louisa; *m* 1st 7 Jan 1941 (*divorce* 1956) Maj John Nevile Wake Gwynne (see WAKE, Bt) and has:

      1a *(Nevile) Martin [Nevile Gwynne Esq, Woodbrook House, Killanne, Enniscorthy, Co Wexford, Ireland]; *b* 5 Nov 1941; *educ* Eton and Trin Coll Oxford (BA); ACA; *m* 1st 1972 Charlotte, dau of Sir Cyril Hugh Kleinwort (see KLEINWORT, Bt), and formerly w of Richard Lawrence Baillieu; *m* 2nd 19– *Frederica Rosana Gale Lennox and by his 1st w has:

      1b *Chloe Patricia; *b* 7 Oct 1973

1a *Jessica Violet [Mrs Rodney Leach, 63 Hillgate Place, London W8]; *b* 7 Feb 1944; *m* 1st 28 Jan 1966 Charles Cospatrick Douglas-Home (*see* HOME, E); *m* 2nd 1993 *Rodney Leach and by her 1st husb has issue

3 Ernest Fitzroy, OBE (1919), JP, DL (Glos); *b* 19 April 1871; Lt-Col Res Offrs 9th Lancers, Boer War 1899–1902 (despatches) and WW I, MP Ashburton 1908–Jan 1910 and Dec 1910–18; *m* 12 Nov 1902 Maud Evelyn (*d* 12 March 1960), dau of Lt-Col Francis Henry, JP, 9th Lancers, and *d* 20 Oct 1960, leaving:

(1) *(Louisa) Monica [Mrs Cecil Grenville-Grey, Long Cottage, Davis St, Hurst, Berks]; *b* 1903; *m* 24 Sept 1929 Col Cecil Everard Montague Grenville-Grey, CBE, KRRC (*d* 5 June 1973, s of Grenville Grenville-Grey, OBE, of St Aldhelms, Blandford, and has:

1a *Wilfrid Ernest; *b* 1930; *m* 1963 *Edith Dlamini and has:

1b *Wilfrid Jonathan; *b* 1964

2b *Peter Thulani; *b* 1967

1b *Susan Thandi (twin); *b* 1964

1a *Susan Monica; *b* 1932; *m* 26 May 1951 *10th Duke of Richmond and (5th Duke of) Gordon (*qv*)

(2) Ruth Evelyn; *d* 1993

(3) *Claire Wilhelmina Maud [Mrs Robert Moubray, The Glebe House, Maxton, St Boswells, Roxburghshire]; *b* 1907; *m* 8 Nov 1928 Maj Robert Moubray, DL (*d* 21 Dec 1961), 16th Lancers, and has:

1a *John Robert Fitzroy [John Moubray Esq, Glencairn, Castlegate, Jedburgh, Roxburghshire TD8 6B]; *b* 1945; *m* 1972 (*divorce* 1990) Patricia Maeve MacLeod and has:

1b *Belinda Mary Claire; *b* 1973

1a *Evelyn Mary; *b* 1929; *m* 1979 *6th Duke of Sutherland (*qv*)

2a *Anne Catherine Wilhelmina; *b* 1931

3a *Gillian Claire; *b* 1933; *m* 1976 Sir Richard James Boughey, 10th Bt (*qv*)

(4) *Mary Ernestine; *b* 1910; Sr Cdr ATS; *m* 30 Sept 1946 Brig Geoffrey William Goschen, DSO, MC and bar, and has issue (*see* GOSCHEN, V)

4 Eustace Widdrington ; *b* 10 Feb 1874; CC W Marylebone Dist, Lt-Col TFR, Capt Rifle Brigade, NWF India 1897–98, Boer War 1901–02, WW I (despatches) *m* 4 Aug 1914 Hon Harriet Margaret Hepburn-Stuart-Forbes-Trefusis (*d* 2 Feb 1975), dau of 20th Baron Clinton (*qv*), and *d* 13 Dec 1947, leaving:

(1) Anthony Eustace, DFC; *b* 23 Dec 1916; *educ* Eton; Actg W/Cdr RAFVR WW II; *d* 19 June 1982

(1) *Pamela Elizabeth; *b* 7 April 1918

(2) *Sylvia Morwenna [Mrs Arthur Chamberlayne, Clouds Garden Lodge, E Knoyle, Wilts]; *b* 14 Jan 1922; *m* 21 June 1941 *Maj Arthur Thomas Chamberlayne, Roy Fus, s of Arthur Chamberlayne, of Suffolk, and has:

1a *Michael Thomas (later changed to Trefusis by statutory declaration), LVO [Michael Trefusis Esq LVO, Lower Hearn, Headley, Hants]; *b* 14 Aug 1943; *educ* Wellington; CA 1967, ch exec Baring Asset Management (client div), Chm Cncl Tstees Clinton Devon Estate, memb RNLI Fin Ctee

1 Evelyn Beatrice; *m* 10 Dec 1924 Henry Dixon, s of John Dixon, and *d* 24 July 1927

2 Muriel Blanche Gwendoline; *m* 10 May 1899 Col John Middleton Rogers, DSO, JP, DL, 1st Roy Dragoons, and *d* 25 Dec 1919, leaving issue. He *d* 11 Aug 1945

Sir CHARLES *d* 21 Oct 1914; his est son,

Sir Claude William Hedley Morrison-Bell, 2nd Bt, JP Northumberland; *b* 5 May 1867; *educ* Eton; Capt Argyll and Sutherland Highrs (93rd Regt), NWF India 1897–98 and WW I; *m* 11 Nov 1903 Frances Isabel (*d* 12 March 1966), dau of Lt-Col Charles Atkinson Logan, JP, RSG, and had:

1 CHARLES REGINALD FRANCIS (Sir), **3rd Bt**

1 *Kathleen Frances, TD, JP (Northumberland 1957) [Maj Kathleen Morrison-Bell TD JP, Charlton, Tarset, Northumberland]; *b* 12 Dec 1906; CC 1952, CA 1957, Maj WRAC

2 Daphne Frances; *b* 24 April 1908; *m* 12 May 1950 *Brig Brian Mortimer Archibald, CBE, DSO, RE, est s of Dr Thomas Dickson Archibald, of Toronto, and *d* 1993, leaving:

(1) *Elizabeth Frances [Miss Elizabeth Archibald, 2566 Penrhyn St #1, Victoria, BC V8N 1G1; *b* 18 June 1951

3 *Veronica Frances [Mrs John Stonborough, Glendon, Brog St, Corfe Mullen, Dorset BH21 3HB]; *b* 27 Feb 1911; *m* 17 July 1942 *John Jerome Stonborough, Maj Canadian Army, yr s of Jerome Stonborough, of New York, and has:

(1) *Jerome Claude; *b* 1 July 1943; *educ* Stowe

(2) *John Tarret Christian; *b* 20 May 1948; *educ* Gordonstoun; *m* 1987 *Jane, only dau of Louis Berger and widow of Charles Tallents, and has:

1a *Eloise Charlotte India; *b* 1988

(1) *Margaret Isabella; *b* 29 Sept 1944; *educ* Benenden

Sir CLAUDE *d* 22 Nov 1943; his only son,

Sir Charles Reginald Francis Morrison-Bell, 3rd Bt; *b* 26 June 1915; *educ* Eton and Trin Coll Cambridge; High Sheriff Northumberland 1955, Capt 12th Lancers (RAC) WW II (wounded); *m* 18 June 1955 *Prudence Caroline [Prudence Lady Morrison-Bell, 70 Doneraile St, London SW6 6EP] (*m* 2nd 19 Sept 1969 (*divorce* 19–) Peter Gillbanks), only dau of Lt-Col Wyndham Dayrell Davies, 60th Rifles, and *d* 22 Dec 1967, having had:

1 Sir WILLIAM HOLLIN DAYRELL MORRISON-BELL, **4th and present Bt**

2 +Julian Francis Tarret; *b* 14 Feb 1959; *m* 1st 1984 Penelope Josephine, dau of Lt-Col Richard Ian Griffith Taylor, DSO, MC, JP, DL, of Chipchase Castle, Wark-on-Tyne, Northumberland, and formerly w of Robert John Elkington (*see* WOLVERTON, B), and has:

(1) +Charles Richard Francis; *b* 17 Nov 1986

2 (cont.) Julian Morrison-Bell *m* 2nd 1991 *Karenina A, dau of Nigel O'Flaherty, of Dublin, and by her has:

(2) +Francis William Doyle; *b* 8 July 1995

(1) *Alice Ursula Grace; *b* 1992

MORRISON-LOW

Arms: Quarterly, 1st and 4th, argent two wolves counter-passant sable, armed and langued gules, on a chief gules three fleurs-de-lys of the first (for LOW); 2nd and 3rd, per chevron or and ermine three Saracen's heads couped at the neck proper, turbaned vert (for MORRISON). **Crests:** 1 An eagle's head couped between two thistles slipped proper (for LOW), 2 A Saracen's head proper, turbaned vert (for MORRISON). **Mottoes:** *Aspera me juvant* ('I rejoice in hardships') and *Prudentia praestat* ('Prudence before everything').
Creation: Bt. (UK) 27 Nov 1908.

SIR JAMES RICHARD MORRISON-LOW, 3RD BT, of Kilmaron, Co Fife, DL (Fife 1978) [Sir James Morrison-Low Bt DL, Kilmaron Castle, nr Cupar, Fife KY15 4NE]; *b* 3 Aug 1925; *s f* 1955; *educ* Harrow, Merchiston and Faraday Ho Eng Coll; Capt Roy Corps Signals WW II 1943–47, electrical engr Osborne and Hunter Ltd, Glasgow, 1952– (dir 1956–89), pres Electrical Contractors Assoc of Scotland 1982–84, memb Roy Scottish Pipers Soc (Hon Pipe-Maj 1981–83), DFH, CEng, MIEE; *m* 13 June 1953 *Ann Rawson, yr dau of A/Cdre Robert Gordon, CB, CMG, DSO, and has:

1 +RICHARD WALTER; *b* 4 Aug 1959

1 *Alison Dorothy; *b* 18 June1955

2 *Jean Elspeth; *b* 20 May 1957

3 *Susan Elizabeth [Mrs Graham Latham, 1 Meadow Cottages, Church St, Sturminster Marshall, Dorset BH21 4BU]; *b* 5 March 1963; *m* 1989 *Graham William Latham, est s of K O E Latham, of Poole, Dorset

Lineage: WILLIAM LOW, of Kirriemuir, Angus; *m* Janet, dau of Alexander Morrison, of Kirriemuir, and had:

1 JAMES LOW (Sir), **1st Bt**

2 William, of Belbo, Fife, JP (Fife and City of Dundee); *b* 1858; *m* 1884 Isabella Sands, dau of John Alexander, and *d* 22 Sept 1936, having had issue

1 Mary; *m* 5 Jan 1897 Sir John Leng, DL, MP, LLD (*d* 13 Dec 1906), and *d* 12 June 1938

2 Annie; *m* William Rettie, of Connonsythe

WILLIAM LOW's er son,

Sir James Low, 1st Bt (UK), so *cr* 27 Nov 1908, JP, DL; *b* 10 Feb 1849; Ld Provost Dundee 1893–96, ktd 1895; *m* 21 May 1890 Katherine Mary Duff (*d* 12 Sept 1931), 4th dau of William Munro, of Dundee, and *d* 30 June 1923, having had:

1 James Morrison; *b* 14 Oct 1891; Lt Seaforth Highrs; *ka* 1 July 1916

2 WALTER JOHN LOW (Sir), **2nd Bt**

1 Katherine Mary; *b* 1893; *d* unm 9 Nov 1969

2 Emily; *b* 1895

The 1st Bt's only surv son,

Sir WALTER JOHN LOW later MORRISON-LOW (deed poll 1 Sept 1924), **2nd Bt**, JP (Fifeshire); *b* 27 May 1899; *educ* Harrow; Scots Gds WWs I (Spec Res) and II (Res of Offrs), Hon Maj 1943; *m* 1st 23 Sept 1924 Dorothy Ruth de Quincey (*d* 8 June 1946), er dau of Richard de Quincey Quincey, of Chislehurst, Kent; *m* 2nd 13 Oct 1948 *(Henrietta) Wilhelmina Mary [Dowager Lady Morrison-Low, Kingsbarns House, 6 The Square, Kingsbarn, Fife KY16 8SS], only dau of Maj Robert Walter Purvis, of Gilmerton, Fife, and *d* 19 July 1955, leaving by his 1st w:

1 Sir JAMES RICHARD MORRISON-LOW, **3rd and present Bt**

2 +(Colin) John [John Morrison-Low Esq, Route 1, Box 302, Easton, MD 21601, USA]; *b* 8 April 1928; *m* 1st 11 July 1953 Susan Désirée MacDougall (*d* 4 March 1977), only dau of Patrick Campbell MacDougall Watson, of Heriot, George, S Africa; *m* 2nd 1980 *Mrs Anne de Clerk and by his 1st w has :

(1) Walter Patrick; *b* 22 July 1961; *d* 5 Feb 1962

(1) *Katherine Dorothy; *b* 12 Oct 1955; *m* 1978 *Peter Jarman, of Australia

(2) *Corinna Helen; *b* 17 Nov 1959; *m* 1984 (*divorce* 1989) Mark Brettel, s of Ray Brettel, of Alicante, Spain

MORTON

Arms: Quarterly, 1st and 4th, argent a man's heart gules, ensigned with an Imperial crown proper, on a chief azure three mullets of the field (for DOUGLAS); 2nd and 3rd, argent three piles issuing from the chief gules, and in chief two mullets of the field (for DOUGLAS of Lochleven). **Crest:** A wild boar proper sticking in the cleft of an oak-tree, fructed vert, with a lock holding the clefts of the tree together azure. **Supporters:** Two savages, wreathed with laurel about their temples and waists, each holding a club in his exterior hand, all proper. **Motto:** (over the crest) *Lock sicker* ('Held fast').
Creation: E. (S) 14 March 1457/8.

THE 21ST EARL OF MORTON and **Lord Aberdour** (John Charles Sholto Douglas, DL (W Lothian 1982)) [The Rt Hon The Earl of Morton DL, Dalmahoy, Kirknewton, Midlothian EH27 8EB]; *b* 19 March 1927; *s* cousin 1976; *educ* Bryanston and Cranford; md Dalmahoy Country Club, Scot Dir Bristol and West Bldg Soc, Ptnr Dalmahoy Farms, Chm Edinburgh Polo Club; *m* 20 Sept 1949 *Sheila Mary, only dau of Rev Canon John Stanley Gibbs (*see* ALDENHAM and HUNSDON OF HUNSDON, B), and has:

1 +(JOHN) STEWART SHOLTO, *Lord Aberdour* [Lord Aberdour, Haggs Farm, Kirknewton, Midlothian]; *b* 17 Jan 1952; *educ* Dunrobin Castle and Aberdeen U; Ptnr Dalmahoy Farms; *m* 1985 *Amanda Kirsten, yr dau of David John Macfarlane Mitchell, of Kirkcudbright, and has:

    (1) +John David Sholto, *Master of Aberdour*; *b* 28 May 1986

    (1) *Katherine Florence; *b* 1989

    (2) *Jennifer Mary; *b* 1991

2 +(Charles) James Sholto [The Hon James Douglas, Warriston, Currie, Midlothian]; *b* 14 Oct 1954; *educ* Edinburgh Acad, Dunrobin Castle and RAC Cirencester; ptnr Dalmahoy Farms; *m* 1981 *Anne, dau of William Gordon Morgan, of Neapuke, Waikato, NZ, and has:

    (1) +James William Sholto; *b* 1984

    (1) *Rebecca Katherine; *b* 1982

    (2) *Jillian Rosamond Florence; *b* 1986

1 *Mary Pamela [The Lady Mary Callander, Saughland House, Pathhead, Midlothian]; *b* 12 Nov 1950; *m* 7 April 1973 *Richard Callander, yr s of Maj John David Burn Callander, MC, of Prestonhall, Midlothian, and has:

    (1) *James Edward; *b* 10 April 1979

    (1) *Sarah Mary; *b* 19 Dec 1977

    (2) *Emma Louise; *b* 8 April 1981

Lineage: ARCHIBALD DOUGLAS, 2nd Chief of the DOUGLASes (*see* QUEENSBERRY, M); had a yr s:

Sir ANDREW DOUGLAS of Hermiston, Midlothian; living 1259; had:

WILLIAM DOUGLAS of Hermiston; living 1277; swore fealty 1296 to EDWARD I of England for his lands in W Lothian; had, with a yr s (Andrew, of Creswell, Lanarks; living 1351):

JAMES DOUGLAS of Lothian; granted Kincavil and Calderclere by ROBERT I (THE BRUCE) 1315; *m* Joan — and *d* by 20 April 1323, having had:

1 Sir WILLIAM DOUGLAS, 1st and last EARL OF ATHOLL (S), so *cr* 18 July 1341, though he resigned the title soon afterwards in favour of Robert Stewart, gs of ROBERT I (*see* MORAY, E, also ATHOLL, D, preliminary remarks), of Liddesdale; acquired the feudal Lordship of Dalkeith from the Grahams (*see* MONTROSE, D), also the (territorial) Barony of Aberdour, Fife, and lands in Tweeddale, Liddesdale, Eskdale and Ewesdale which had been forfeited by the SOULISes and LOVELs and which he entailed 1351 on his nephews (his yr bro John's sons); known as the 'Flower of Chivalry'; allegedly (?)*m*(?) 1st(?) Margaret, sis and coheir of John Graham of Dalkeith and Abercorn (*see* MONTROSE, D); *m* (?)2nd(?) Elizabeth — (*m* 2nd 4th Lord (Baron) Dacre, *qv*) and *dspm* Aug 1353, *k* by his relative William Douglas, 1st Earl of Douglas (*see* QUEENSBERRY, M), having by her had:

    (1) Mary; *m* 1st 1361 (*divorce* 1365) Reginald More of Abercorn; *m* 2nd Thomas Erskine and *dsps c* 30 June 1367

2 JOHN (Sir)

3 James; *k* in battle 1335

1 Elizabeth; *m* Sir Thomas Somerville

The 2nd s,

Sir JOHN DOUGLAS; *m* Agnes, allegedly widow of John Monfode, and was *k* by order of Sir David Barclay of Brechin (himself *k* in revenge 25 Jan 1350 shortly afterwards), leaving, with other issue:

1 James (Sir), of Dalkeith; *m* 1st 21 Nov 1372 Lady Agnes Dunbar, dau of 8th Earl of Dunbar/2nd Earl of March (*see* DUNBAR, Bt, of Mochrum), through whom he acquired Whittinghame, E Lothian; *m* 2nd 1378 Egidia, half-sis of ROBERT II and widow of (a) Sir James Lindsay of Crawford (*see* CRAWFORD and BALCARRES, E) and (b) Sir Hugh Eglinton, and *d* 1420, having by his 1st w had:

    (1) James (Sir), of Dalkeith; ktd between Sept 1390 and 18 Jan 1391/2; had a charter 24 March 1381/2 of the (territorial) Barony of Morton in Nithsdale with Mordlingtoun and Whittinghame and allegedly had conferred on him the new title of a Ld of Parl as 'Lord Dalkeith', though evidence for this is nugatory; *m* 1st between 24 March 1381/2 and 10 March 1387 Lady Elizabeth Stewart, dau of John Stewart, Earl of Carrick, later ROBERT III, and had:

        1a William; *b* 1390; *m* (dispensation 9 Dec 1420) Margaret, dau of William Borthwick, and *dsp & vp*

        2a James, (?)2nd Lord Dalkeith(?); of unsound mind, so declared by Act of Parl 22 May 1441, a circumstance which his step-mother and brothers seem to have taken material advantage of to the detriment of his infant son's interests; *m* Elizabeth, dau of James Gifford of Sheriffhall, and *d* between 8 Sept 1456 (when he resigned his lands in favour of his s) and 14 March 1457/8, leaving:

            1b JAMES DOUGLAS, **1st Earl of Morton** (S), so *cr* 14 March 1457/8 in anticipation of his becoming the King's son-in-law; Envoy to France and Castile 1491; *m* by 15 May 1459 Joan, deaf mute dau of JAMES I, and *d* between 22 June and 22 Oct 1492, having had, with a dau (Janet; *m* 1st Earl of Bothwell; *see* BUCHAN-HEPBURN, Bt):

            1c JOHN DOUGLAS, **2nd Earl of Morton**; *b* by 1466; ktd by 1474, Envoy to England 1494; *m* by summer 1493 Janet, dau of Patrick Crichton of Cranstonriddel, and *d* between 8 Nov 1511 and 26 Nov 1513, having had:

                1d JAMES DOUGLAS, **3rd Earl of Morton**, PC (S 1526); Envoy England 1516; coerced by JAMES V 17 Oct 1540 into resigning his Earldom and lands in favour of his cousin Robert Douglas of Lochleven, under reservation of his life rent; after JAMES's death the Court of Session nullified (29 March 1542) the charter benefitting Sir Robert as having been procured under duress; on 22 April 1543 the Earl of Morton executed a conveyance of his Earldom (confirmed by Royal Charter the same day) to his yst dau's husb, James Douglas, and whoever outlived the other and their issue male, with further remainder to James Douglas's er bro David, 7th Earl of Angus; *m* by 10 Dec 1507 Catherine Stewart, illegitimate dau of JAMES IV by Margaret Boyd, and *dspm* Dec 1548, having had:

                    1e Margaret; *m* 2nd Earl of Arran, Duke of Chatelherault, and Regent of Scotland

                    2e Beatrix; *m* 6th Lord Maxwell (*see* MAXWELL, Bt) and had, with an er s (7th Lord Maxwell):

                        1f 8th JOHN MAXWELL, 8th Lord Maxwell and 1st EARL OF MORTON (S), so *cr* 5 June 1581, though on the attainder of the **4th Earl of Morton**'s being reversed the Earldom must be regarded as reverting to the heir of entail (*see* below)

                  3e Elizabeth; *m* 1543 JAMES DOUGLAS, **4th Earl of Morton** (right to title confirmed in a grant of 2 June 1564), PC (S 1552 and 1578) (*b c* 1516; Protestant, Ld Chllr Scotland 1562/3–66; after playing a leading role in the murder of MARY QUEEN OF SCOTS' secretary Rizzio (9 March 1566) he was forced to flee the country; nevertheless Chllr again 1567–73, a Commr for the QUEEN's renunciation of the throne and JAMES VI's Coronation 1567, cdr JAMES VI's forces Battle of Langside 1568, Adml of Scotland Feb 1569/70 and Gt Adml 1570–80, Regent 1572–8 March 1577/8, after which, his strict methods of government having made him unpopular, he was tried for high treason (specifically involvement in Darnley's assassination), found guilty and executed 2 June 1581, when his estates and honours were forfeited; JAMES VI conferred the Earldom of Morton on John, Lord Maxwell, gs of 3rd Earl of Morton, but later revoked this grant; the attainder of the **4th Earl of Morton** was formally reversed 29 Jan 1585/6 and the Earldom reverted to the heir of entail), bro of 7th Earl of Angus (*see* HAMILTON and BRANDON, D), and had three surv daus whose names are unknown; the **4th Earl**'s nephew:

                    1f ARCHIBALD DOUGLAS, **5th Earl of Morton** (in which he *s* his unc under terms of special remainder of 22 April 1543, confirmed 2 June 1564) and 8TH EARL OF ANGUS (*b c* 1555; *m* 1st 13 June 1573 Lady Mary Erskine (*dsp* 3 May 1575), dau of John, Earl of Mar (*qv*); *m* 2nd 25 Dec 1575 (*divorce* 1587) Lady Margaret Leslie, dau of 4th Earl of Rothes (*qv*); *m* 3rd (contract 29 July 1587) Jean, dau of 8th Lord Glamis (*see* STRATHMORE AND KINGHORNE, E) and widow of Robert Douglas, Yr., Master of Morton, and *dspm* 4 Aug 1588, having by her had a dau Margaret (*d* unm)

                2d Richard; *m* and had issue

              1d Elizabeth/Beatrice; *m* Robert, Lord Keith

              2d Agnes; *m* 5th Lord Livingston

        3a Henry (sometimes styled 'of Dalkeith'); had from his f a charter of Borg and other lands in Galloway; *m* Margaret, dau of 7th Earl of Douglas, and had:

            1b Hugh of Borg; in 1474 renounced to his cousin the **1st Earl of Morton** all right to Dalkeith except what might accrue to him as heir male of the family

    (1) Sir James Douglas *m* 2nd between 1411 and Oct 1439 Janet (*m* 2nd Sir George Crichton, Earl of Caithness, *qv*), dau of Sir William Borthwick (*see*

BORTHWICK, L), and *d* between Feb 1439/40 and May 1441, having by her had:

4a William (Sir), of Morton and Whittinghame, though in 1474 he renounced his right to Morton in favour of his n, **1st Earl of Morton**; his descendants the DOUGLASes of Whittinghame ended in an heiress Elizabeth, who *m c* 1661, as his 2nd w, 1st Viscount of Kingston (*see* EGLINTON and WINTON, E); through their dau the lineal representation of this branch passed to the HAYs of Drummelzier; the male line of DOUGLAS of Whittinghame was continued in Sweden by the descendants of a yr bro

(2) William, of Mordingtoun; living 1406

(1) Agnes; *m* 1st (contract 15 Aug 1381) John Livingstone of Callendar (*d* 1402); *m* 2nd John Gordon of Gordon

(2) Jacoba; *m* 1st (contract 1 Nov 1388) Sir John Hamilton of Cadzow (*see* ABERCORN, D) and had issue; *m* 2nd (dispensation 12 June 1410) Sir William Douglas of Drumlanrig

(3) Margaret; *m* as his 2nd w Philip de Arbuthnott (*see* ARBUTHNOTT, V)

2 William (Sir); living 1406; had issue

3 John; living 1351; *m* Mariota (*m* 2nd John Keith), dau and coheir of Reginald de Chene, and *d c* 1366, leaving issue

4 Henry (Sir), of Lugton and Lochleven; *m* Marjory (*d* 1438), dau of Sir John Stewart of Ralston (half-bro of ROBERT II) and widow of Sir Alexander Lindsay of Glenesk, and had, with a dau (Margaret, *m* Sir John Wallace of Craigie):

(1) William (Sir), of Lochleven; acquired Ralston from his uncle Sir Walter Stewart; *m* Elizabeth, dau of 1st Earl of Crawford (*see* CRAWFORD and BALCARRES, E), and was *k* in battle 1421, having had:

1a Henry (Sir), of Lochleven; *m* Elizabeth, dau of Sir Robert Erskine of Erskine, and *d c* 1469, having had:

1b Robert (Sir), of Lochleven; *m* 1st (contract 10 April 1445) Elizabeth, dau of David Boswell of Balmuto, and had:

1c Robert (Sir), of Lochleven; *m* 1st Margaret, dau of David Balfour of Burleigh (*see* BALFOUR OF BURLEIGH, L); *m* 2nd 1500 Margaret, dau of 1st Earl of Erroll (*qv*) and widow of (a) Alexander Fraser of Philorth and (b) Sir Gilbert Keith of Inverugie, and had:

1d Thomas; *m* Elizabeth, dau of Archibald Boyd (*see* KILMARNOCK, B) and *dvp*, having had, with other issue:

1e Robert (Sir), of Lochleven, of which he had a charter 20 Feb 1539/40; *m* (contract 11 July 1547) Margaret (*d* 5 May 1572), dau of 4th Lord Erskine and *de jure* 15th Earl of Mar (*qv*), and was *k* Battle of Pinkie 10 Sept 1547, having had:

1f WILLIAM (Sir), **6th Earl**

2f ROBERT DOUGLAS; *m* Christian Stewart, Countess of Buchan in her own right and by virtue of the marriage became 4th EARL OF BUCHAN (*qv*); *d* 18 Aug 1580, leaving issue

3f George (Sir); arranged MARY QUEEN OF SCOTS' escape from Lochleven; *m* 1st Janet, dau of John Lindsay of Dowhill (*see* LINDSAY, Bt) and widow of (a) Andrew Lundie and (b) Sir William Scott; *m* 2nd Margaret Durie, widow of William Scott of Abbotshall, and had:

1g Margaret; *m* 1st Lord Ramsay of Dalhousie (*see* DALHOUSIE, E)

1f Euphemia; *m* 1545 6th Lord Lindsay of the Byres (*see* LINDSAY, E)

2f Janet; *m* Sir James Colville of Easter Wemyss (*see* COLVILLE OF CULROSS, V), and had issue

3f Catherine; *m* 1557 David Durie of Durie

2d Henry; living 1520

1d Margaret; *m* 1516 Henry Stewart, Yr. of Rosyth

1c Agnes; *m* Thomas Hamilton of Raploch

2c Margaret; *m* 1st Sir David Stewart of Rosyth; *m* 2nd Henry Mercer of Meikleour

1b (cont.) Sir Robert Douglas *m* 2nd Isobel, dau of Sir John Sibbald of Balgonie and widow of 4th Earl of Angus (*see* HAMILTON and BRANDON, D); *m* 3rd Marion, dau of Sir William Baillie of Lamington and widow of 3rd Lord Lindsay of the Byres (*see* LINDSAY, E), and was *k* Battle of Flodden 9 Sept 1513

2b David; living 1494; allegedly ancestor of the DOUGLASes of Tilquhillie

3b Thomas; living 1494

2a James (Sir), of Ralston; *m* Janet, dau and coheir of Walter Fenton of Baky, and had:

1b Henry, of Culbirny

3a Alexander; living 1488

1a Elizabeth; Maid of Honour to JANE/JOAN, w of JAMES I; *m* Richard Lovel of Ballumby

5 Nicholas; *m c* Sept 1373 Janet, yr dau of William Galbraith (*see* STRATHCLYDE, B); living 1392, ancestor of the DOUGLASes of Mains

1 Margaret; allegedly *m* Sir Adam de Glendonwyne of that Ilk and *d c* 1 Aug 1377

The 5th EARL's distant cousin,

Sir WILLIAM DOUGLAS, **6th Earl of Morton**, PC (S Jan 1593/4), of Lochleven; *b* 1539/40; had custody of MARY QUEEN OF SCOTS during her imprisonment at Lochleven Castle 1567–68; *m* by 1565 Lady Agnes Leslie, dau of 4th Earl of Rothes (*qv*), and *d* 22, 24 or 27 Sept 1606, having had:

1 Robert; *m* (contract 19 March 1582/3) Jean (*m* 2nd 1587 8th Earl of Angus (*see* HAMILTON and BRANDON, D); *m* 3rd 1593 1st Lord Spynie; *see* CRAWFORD and BALCARRES, E), dau of 8th Lord Glamis (*see* STRATHMORE AND KINGHORNE, E), and *dvp* March 1584/5, being killed by pirates, leaving:

(1) WILLIAM, **7th Earl**

2 James; Commendator (lay proprietor in wake of dissolution of religious houses, receiving revenues but undertaking no spiritual duties) of Melrose; *m* 1st (contract 6 Nov 1587) Mary, dau of Sir Thomas Ker of Ferniehirst (*see* LOTHIAN, M); *m* 2nd (contract 7 Nov 1598) Helen, dau of William Scott, of

Abbotshall; *m* 3rd 1609 Jean, dau of Sir James Anstruther (*see* ANSTRUTHER, Bt), and had issue by all three

3 Archibald (Sir), of Keillor; *m* Barbara, dau of 7th Lord Forbes (*qv*) and widow of (a) Robert Allardyce, Yr. of Allardyce, and (b) Alexander Hay of Dalgaty, and *d* 1649, leaving issue

4 George (Sir), of Kirkness; ancestor of the DOUGLASes of Kirkness and Douglas Bts, of Carr; *m* 1597 Margaret, dau of Thomas Forrester of Strathendry, and *d c* 9 Dec 1609, leaving issue

1 Margaret; *m* (contract 17 April 1574) Sir John Wemyss of Wemyss (*see* WEMYSS and MARCH, E)

2 Christian; *m* 1st (contract 17 Feb 1575/6) Laurence, Master of Oliphant; *m* 2nd 9 Jan 1586 1st Earl of Home (*qv*)

3 Mary; *m* 1582, as his 3rd w, 1st Lord Ogilvy of Deskford (*see* SEAFIELD, E)

4 Eupheme; *m* 1586 Sir Thomas Lyon of Baldukie, Master of Glamis (*see* STRATHMORE AND KINGHORNE, E)

5 Agnes; *m* 24 July 1592 7th Earl of Argyll (*see* ARGYLL, D) and *d* 3 May 1607

6 Elizabeth; *m* 9th Earl of Erroll (*qv*)

7 Jean; *d unm*

The 6th EARL's gs,

WILLIAM DOUGLAS, **7th Earl of Morton**, KG (1633), PC (S 1621, E 1627); *b c* 1584; Ld High Treas Scotland 1630–36, Capt Yeoman Gd 1635–44; granted a charter 16 March 1638 of the lands, Earldom and Barony of Morton, his title thus becoming Earl of Morton and Lord Aberdour; before the Civil War one of the richest subjects in either Kingdom but as a royalist he raised £100,000 (Scots) by parting with the Dalkeith and other estates, though in compensation he was granted by roy charter 15 June 1643 the Orkney and Shetland Islands, redeemable by the Crown on payment of £30,000 sterling (over £1,300,000 in late-1990s terms); *m* (contract between 5 and 28 March 1604) Lady Anne Keith (*d* 30 May 1648), est dau of 5th Earl Marischal (*see* KINTORE, E), and *d* 7 Aug 1648, having had:

1 ROBERT DOUGLAS, **8th Earl of Morton**; *b* by 1616; *m c* 28 April 1627 Anne (*d* Dec 1654), dau of Sir Edward Villiers (*see* JERSEY, E), and *d* 12 Nov 1649, having had:

(1) WILLIAM DOUGLAS, **9th Earl of Morton**; PC (S Feb 1660/1); obtained a fresh grant of the Orkney and Shetland Islands in 1662 but it and the original grant were later declared invalid by Act of Parl 27 Dec 1669; resigned 9 Sept 1672 any right he possessed to the Lordship of Dalkeith in favour of James, Duke of Buccleuch (*see* BUCCLEUCH and QUEENSBERRY, D) and Monmouth; *m* 1st 12 June 1662 Lady Grizel Middleton, est dau of 1st Earl of Middleton; *m* 2nd Marjory Foulis and *dsps* by 1 Nov 1681

(2) Robert; Master of the Horse to Henrietta, Duchess of Orleans; *dsp* 1661

(1) Anne; *m* 1654 6th Earl Marischal (*see* KINTORE, E) and *dsp*

(2) Mary; *m* 24 July 1662 Sir Donald Macdonald of Sleat, 3rd Bt (*see* BOSVILLE MACDONALD, Bt)

2 Sir JAMES DOUGLAS, **10th Earl of Morton**; ktd 1635; *m* 10 Feb 1649 Anne, dau and coheir of Sir James Hay, 1st Bt, of Smithfield, Peeblesshire (*see* 1963 edn), and *d* 25 Aug 1686, having had, with two other sons:

(1) JAMES DOUGLAS, **11th Earl of Morton**; PC (S 1690); obtained the repeal of the Act of 1669 and recovered the Orkney and Shetland Islands; a Commr for the Union; *d unm* 7 Dec 1715

(2) ROBERT DOUGLAS, **12th Earl of Morton**; MP (Whig) Wick Burghs 1709–10; *d unm* 22 Jan 1730

(3) GEORGE DOUGLAS, **13th Earl of Morton**; *b* 1662; Lt-Col; MP (S Parl) Kirkall 1792–07 and (Whig, GB Parl) Linlithgow Burghs 1708–13 and 1715–22 and Orkney and Shetland 1713–15 and 1722–30, rep S peer 1730–38; *m* 1st a dau of Alexander Muirhead of Linhouse, Co Edinburgh, but by her had no surv issue; *m* 2nd by 1702 Frances, dau of William Adderly, of Halsgow, Kent, and *d* 4 Jan 1738, having by her had:

1a JAMES, **14th Earl**

2a Robert; MP Orkney; Col; *k* Battle of Fontenoy 30 April 1745

3 John; *k* Battle of Carbisdale 27 April 1650

4 George; in Dutch sevice; *dsp*

1 Anne; *m* (contract 7 Sept 1622) 2nd Earl of Kinnoull (*qv*)

2 Margaret; *m* 7 Aug 1626 Archibald, Marquess of Argyll (*see* ARGYLL, D)

3 Mary; *m* (contract 9 Nov 1632) 2nd Earl of Dunfermline (*see* EGLINTON and WINTON, E) and *d c* 1659, having had issue

4 Jean; *m* (contract 13 July 1640) 3rd Earl of Home (*qv*)

5 Isabel; *m* 1st 1st Earl of Roxburghe (*see* ROXBURGHE, D); *m* 2nd 2nd Marquess of Montrose (*see* MONTROSE, D)

The 13th EARL's est son,

JAMES DOUGLAS, **14th Earl of Morton**, KT (1738); *b* 1709; rep S peer 1739–68; obtained an Act of Parliament 16 March 1741/2 granting him the Lordship of Orkney and Shetland but sold the rights in 1766 to the DUNDASes (*see* ZETLAND, M) for £63,000 (over £3,200,000 in late-1990s terms); Pres Roy Soc 1764–68; *m* 1st Agatha (*d* 12 Dec 1748), dau and heiress of James Halyburton of Pitcur, Forfar, and had:

1 SHOLTO CHARLES DOUGLAS, **15th Earl of Morton**; *b* 1732; *m* 19 Nov 1758 Katherine (*d* 25 April 1823), dau and coheir of Hon John Hamilton, gdau of 6th Earl of Haddington (*qv*), and *d* 25 Sept 1774, having had:

(1) GEORGE DOUGLAS, **16th Earl of Morton**, KT (1797); *b* 3 April 1761; *educ* Eton; rep S peer 1784–90, *cr* 11 Aug 1791 BARON DOUGLAS OF LOCHLEVEN, Co Kinross (GB); *m* 13 Aug 1814 Susan Elizabeth Buller-Yarde-Buller (*m* 2nd 17 Sept 1831 Edward Godfrey, of Old Hall, Suffolk), sis of 1st Baron Churston (*qv*), and *dsp* 17 July 1827, when the Barony expired

(2) Hamilton DOUGLAS later DOUGLAS-HALYBURTON of Pitcur; *b* 10 Oct 1763; lost at sea off New York 30 Dec 1783

1 Mary; *m* 14 May 1774 4th Earl of Aboyne (*see* HUNTLY, M) and *d* 25 Dec 1816

The **14th Earl** *m* 2nd 31 July 1755 Bridget (*d* 2 March 1805), dau of Sir John Heathcote, 2nd Bt, of London (*qv*), and *d* 12 Oct 1768, having by her had:

2 John; *b* 1 July 1756; *m* 4 Oct 1784 Lady Frances Lascelles (*d* 31 March 1817), est dau of 1st Earl of Harewood (*qv*), and *d* 1 May 1818, leaving, with other issue:

(1) GEORGE SHOLTO, **17th Earl**

(2) Charles (Rev); granted with his yr siblings 28 Aug 1835 rank of earl's dau/yr s; *b* 10 March 1791; *m* 1st 2 March 1816 Isabella (*d* 30 Nov 1838), dau of 2nd Earl of Arran (*qv*), and had:

1a William Grant; *b* 25 Feb 1824; Capt RN; *m* 1st 16 Dec 1851 Elizabeth (*d* 1865), dau of William Inglis, and had:

1b Bessie Henrietta; *m* 1st 17 Feb 1875 Claud William Leslie Ogilby (*d* 1894), of Altnachree Castle, Co Tyrone; *m* 2nd 1895 Hugo Bartels and *d* 12 Oct 1938

2b Ada Charlotte; *m* 1st 1886 Harris St John Dick (*d* 1886); *m* 2nd 1892 Frederick Gray Maturin (*d* 1912)

3b Mary Louisa; *m* 17 Jan 1877 Colin Bent Phillip (*d* 8 July 1932), only s of John Phillip, RA, and *dsp* 1940

4b Margaret Caroline; *m* 1883 Rev Edward Douglas Prothero (*d* 5 Oct 1907) and *d* 25 April 1921

5b Maud Isabel Gore; *m* 23 April 1895 Adml Cuthbert E Hunter, s of John Hunter, of Whickham, Co Durham, and *d* 2 Feb 1934

1a (cont) Capt William Douglas *m* 2nd 6 June 1867 Elizabeth Frances (*d* 10 Jan 1919), dau of Thomas Agmondesham Vesey, of Cookstown, Co Tyrone, and *d* 16 Dec 1898, having by her had:

1b Sholto Osborne Gordon; *b* 14 Sept 1873; *educ* Oxford (BA); *d* 27 Jan 1937

2a Charles Edward; *b* 1825; *d* 1842

3a Gordon James; *b* 27 Aug 1835; *m* 12 Aug 1858 Louisa (*d* 26 Jan 1923), dau of James Turbett, of Owenstown, Co Dublin, and *d* 1905, having had, with another dau (*d* unm):

1b Isabelle Sophia Frances; *m* 20 Sept 1883 Capt Belford Randolph Wilson (*d* 1897), 4th Roy Irish Dragoons, and had issue

1a Jane; *m* 3 Jan 1843 Frederick R Surtees and *d* 10 Jan 1868

2a Augusta Frederica; *m* 15 Dec 1842 Henry Poore Cox (*d* 1876)

3a Julia Mary; *m* 20 July 1848 Lt-Col George James Montgomery (*d* 1860), Bengal SC

4a Caroline; *m* 17 Dec 1844 Lt-Col Edward Prothero (*d* 1887), 14th Regt, s of Thomas Prothero, of Monmouth, and *d* 9 April 1908, having had issue

5a Georgiana Frances; *d* 20 June 1844

6a Adelaide Charlotte; *m* 30 Jan 1851 William Ogilby, of Altnachree Castle (*d* 1 Sept 1873), and *d* 1903, having had issue

7a Louisa Emma; *m* 29 Sept 1857 Charles Fox and had issue

(2) (cont.) The Rev and Hon Charles Douglas *m* 2nd 28 Dec 1852 Agnes Julia (*m* 2nd Oct 1862 Lt-Col Wills Croft Gason, of Kilteelagh, Co Tipperary (*d* 3 Nov 1887), and *d* 4 Nov 1916), 4th dau of Capt John S Rich, of Woodlands, Co Limerick, and *d* 28 Jan 1857

(3) Edward Gordon DOUGLAS later DOUGLAS-PENNANT (roy licence), 1st BARON PENRHYN (*qv*)

(1) Frances; *m* 21 April 1804 Lt-Gen Hon Sir William Stewart, GCB (*see* GALLOWAY, E) and *d* 6 Aug 1833

(2) Harriet; *m* 1st 25 Nov 1809 Viscount Hamilton (*see* ABERCORN, D); *m* 2nd 8 July 1815 4th Earl of Aberdeen (*see* ABERDEEN AND TEMAIR, M) and *d* 26 Aug 1833

(3) Elizabeth Emma; *m* 10 July 1827 William Hamilton Ash, of Ashbrook, Co Londonderry, and *d* 2 Feb 1857

(4) Caroline; *m* 31 Dec 1817 William Augustus Lane Fox (*d* 11 Feb 1832) and *d* 7 Nov 1873, having had issue

2 Bridget; *m* Hon W H Bouverie (*see* RADNOR, E) and *d* 1842

The 16th EARL's cousin,

GEORGE SHOLTO DOUGLAS, **17th Earl of Morton**; *b* 23 Dec 1789; *educ* Trin Coll Cambridge; rep S peer 1828–58; *m* 3 July 1817 Frances Theodora (*d* 12 July 1879), dau of Rt Hon Sir George Henry Rose, GCH, and *d* 31 March 1858, having had:

1 SHOLTO JOHN, **18th Earl**

2 George Henry; *b* 5 Oct 1821; Adml; *m* 18 July 1850 Charlotte Martha (*d* 20 Dec 1909), dau of Adml Sir William Parker, 1st Bt, GCB, of Shenstone (*qv*), and *d* 19 June 1905, leaving:

(1) George Sholto, JP Herts; *b* 27 April 1858; Capt 1st Bn Cameronians, 4th Bn Beds Regt; *m* 30 April 1889 Lady Laura Mary Wentworth-Fitzwilliam (*d* 2 March 1936), sis of 7th Earl Fitzwilliam (*see* 1970 edn), and *d* 10 Feb 1916, leaving:

1a Archibald Sholto George, CBE (1943); *b* 17 March 1896; *educ* Eton and RMC Sandhurst; psc, Brig Rifle Bde WW I (despatches), WW II, Order Kutuzov 2nd Cl USSR; *m* 2 Feb 1928 Violet Patricia (*d* 1989), 4th dau of Arthur Pearson Davison, TD, and *d* 1981, leaving:

1b +Colin Sholto Archibald [Colin Douglas Esq, 18 Upshire Gdns, The Warren, Bracknell, Berks RG12 9YZ]; *b* 20 July 1932; *educ* Eton; *m* 1st 25 July 1958 (*divorce* 1971) Jean (*d* 1978), er dau of Brig George Streynsham Rawstorne, CBE, MC, of Sutherland, and adopted:

+Malcolm Sholto Colin; *b* 9 Feb 1966

*Laura Jean; *b* 1 July 1968

1b (cont) Colin Douglas *m* 2nd *Sally Anne, only dau of D C H Townsend, of Wolviston, Teeside, and has:

2c +Archie Sholto James; *b* 26 Dec 1972

3c +Euan Sholto David; *b* 20 July 1975

2b +James Sholto Arthur [James Douglas Esq, Good Mondays Farm, Dauntsey, Wilts SN15 4HL]; *b* 2 Jan 1935; *educ* Eton; late Capt 15th/19th Hus; *m* 1st 23 April 1966 (*divorce* 1979) Tedda Ann (*m* 2nd 1979 David Reid and has issue by him; *see* REID, Bt of Ellon), est dau of Albert Charles Webber, of Dorset, and has had, with another s (*d* an infant):

2c +Harry Sholto Gavin; *b* 9 Oct 1974

2b (cont.) Mr James Douglas also adopted:

*Justin Sholto James; *b* 23 Aug 1972

*Camilla Patricia Ann; *b* 30 March 1971

2b (cont.) James Douglas *m* 2nd 22 Aug 1979 *Elizabeth Ann, dau of Maj Montague Howard Crocker, of Malmesbury, and has:

3c +Toby Sholto Arthur; *b* 7 May 1982

3b +Gavin Sholto George [Gavin Douglas Esq, Heiton Mill, nr Kelso, Roxburghshire TD5 8LA]; *b* 7 Sept 1945; *educ* Gordonstoun; *m* 1982 *Amanda Jane, er dau of Capt Christopher Evelyn Twiston Davies, 4th/7th Roy Dragoon Gds, and has:

1c *Alice Violet; *b* 1983

2c *Charlotte Rose; *b* 1985

1b *Joanna Patricia Margaret [Mrs R Day, Newcotts Farm, N Newton, Bridgwater, Somerset TA7 0DQ]; *b* 11 May 1948; *m* 1972 *Roger D Day and has:

1c *Gregory Laramy; *b* 1972

1c *Lorna Elizabeth; *b* 1974

2a David Sholto William; *b* 26 Aug 1899; *educ* Eton; Capt Rifle Bde WW II; *m* 25 May 1940 *Elizabeth Sarah Ione [Mrs David Douglas, c/o Lynwick House, Rudgwick, W Sussex], only dau of Maj George Edward Capel Cure, of Blake Hall, Ongar, Essex, and *d* 1980, leaving:

1b *Sheena Elizabeth [Mrs Richard Wright, Lynwick House, Rudgwick, W Sussex]; *b* 5 May 1948; *m* 1973 *Richard James Wright, only s of George W J Wright, of N Yorks, and has:

1c *Charles Anthony; *b* 1979

2a (cont) Capt and Mrs David Douglas also adopted:

*Ione Lavinia Margaret; *b* 2 June 1946; *m* 1983 (*divorce* 1994) Richard Zatloukal

3a John Sholto Henry, OBE (1950); *b* 16 June 1903; *educ* Eton and RMA Sandhurst; Lt-Col Seaforth Highrs Palestine 1936 (despatches), Shanghai 1937–40, WW II (despatches), Malaya 1948–50 (despatches); *m* 2 June 1955 *Celia [Mrs John Douglas, Fir Tree Cottage, Yarrowford, Selkirk], only dau of Maj James Hay McInnes Skinner, of Norfolk, and widow of Roderick Christopher Musgrave, and *d* 15 Oct 1960, leaving:

1b +Robin Sholto John [Robin Douglas Esq, 18 Shandon St, Edinburgh EH11 1QH]; *b* 30 April 1956; *m* 1983 *Ann Elisabeth Forssell and has:

1c +James Sholto Edward; *b* 18 Jan 1989

1c *Anna Louisa Victoria; *b* 22 May 1991

2c *Olivia Laura Elisabeth; *b* 6 Feb 1996

2b +John Sholto James; *b* 18 Nov 1959; *m* 14 April 1997 *Mieke Elisabeth van den Bergh

1a Margaret Laura; *m* 23 April 1924 Maj Thomas Hunter Cecil Cox, JP, 3rd Bn Black Watch, s of James Cox-Cox, of Invertrossachs, Callendar, and *d* 2 Oct 1933, leaving issue

2a Katharine Charlotte; *m* 7 Feb 1921 Brig Sir Henry Walter Houldsworth, KBE, DSO and bar, MC, TD (*d* 9 Oct 1963), Ld Lt Morayshire, yr s of James Hamilton Houldsworth, JP, DL, of Coltness, Lanarks, and had issue

(1) Blanche; *m* 29 Sept 1887 George Ponsonby Talbot (*see* SHREWSBURY and WATERFORD, E) and *d* 19 March 1922

3 Henry (Rev); *b* 17 Dec 1822; *educ* Durham U (MA) and U of the South USA (BLC); Hon Canon Worcester, Rector Hanbury, Worcs, 1855–77, Vicar St Paul's Worcester 1877–1904; *m* 7 June 1855 Lady Mary Baillie (*d* 29 March 1904), dau of 10th Earl of Haddington (*qv*), and *d* 4 Oct 1907, leaving:

(1) Mary; *d* 26 Nov 1921

4 Edward William, JP, DL Hants; *b* 19 Oct 1825; *m* 1st 16 July 1857 Augusta Anne (*dsp* 6 May 1880), yst dau of George Bankes, PC, MP, 7th of Kingston Lacy and Studland Manor, Dorset; *m* 2nd 27 Sept 1881 Hon Evelyn Anne Trefusis (*d* 28 Feb 1911), dau of 19th Baron Clinton (*qv*), and *d* 7 May 1918, leaving:

(1) Gertrude Evelyn Augusta; *b* 19 Jan 1883; *d* unm 2 Feb 1966

5 Arthur Gascoigne (Rt Rev), DD; *b* 5 Jan 1827; Bp Aberdeen and Orkney 1883–1905; *m* 17 April 1855 Anna Maria Harriet (*d* 13 May 1915), yst dau of Richard Richards, DL, of Caerynwch, Merioneths, and *d* 19 July 1905, having had:

(1) Sholto James; *b* 21 Aug 1866; *m* 22 June 1909 Grace Elizabeth (*d* 25 March 1968), 3rd dau of Sir James Henry Gibson-Craig, 3rd Bt (*see* GIBSON-CRAIG-CARMICHAEL, Bt), and *d* 8 Nov 1950, leaving:

1a +Archibald Sholto (Rev Canon), TD (1950) [The Rev Canon Archibald Douglas TD, Monks Heath Hall Farm, Chelford Rd, Nether Alderley, Cheshire SK10 4SY]; *b* 22 April 1914; *educ* Brighton Coll and Selwyn Coll Cambridge (MA); CF, Maj 4th Bn KOSB (TA), Vicar Capesthorne and Siddington, Cheshire, 1955, Chaplain to High Sheriff Cheshire 1960–61

2a +Hugh Alastair [Hugh Douglas Esq, Broadlands House, Brockenhurst, Hants]; *b* 3 Aug 1915; *educ* Trin Coll Glenalmond and Worcester Coll Oxford (BA 1937); Conservator Forests Ghana; *m* 27 Oct 1955 *Elizabeth, dau of Col John Meredith Hulton, CBE, DSO, of Larges Orchard, Bracknell, Berks, and has:

1b *Angela Elizabeth; *b* 26 Dec 1956; PhD; *m* 1984 *Jeremy Byron Searle

2b *Coleena Jane; *b* 29 Oct 1958; *m* 1978 *Nicholas Hutson Reid

(2) Arthur Hugh, JP; *b* 14 Sept 1867; FSI; *m* 7 July 1909 Helen (*d* 29 Oct 1948), est dau of Wilton Allhusen, of Pinhay, Lyme Regis, and *d* 28 May 1936

(3) Archibald William (Rev Canon); *b* 8 June 1870; *educ* Keble Coll Oxford (MA 1897); Chaplain RN WW I; Rector Tankersley, Hoyland Common, Yorks, 1918–41, Hon Canon Sheffield Cathedral 1932–41 (Canon Emeritus 1941), RD Ecclesfield 1921–41; *m* 23 Oct 1902 Ursula Helen (*d* 28 Feb 1962), 2nd dau of Capt Robert Watts Davies, RN, of Bloxham, Oxon, and *d* 23 March 1955, having had:

1a Helen St Bride; *b* 14 June 1904; *m* 12 Aug 1931 Cdr Killingworth Richard Utten Todd, RN (*d* 13 April 1950), s of Canon Richard James Utten Todd, of Woolverstone, Ipswich, and *d* 18 Dec 1948, leaving issue

2a Joanna Katharine; *b* 24 March 1912; *m* 20 Nov 1937 James Utten Todd, MA (*d* 1981), s of Canon Richard James Utten Todd, of Woolverstone, Ipswich, and *d* 19 April 1984, leaving:

1b *James Donald Utten; *b* 1 March 1939; *educ* Ipswich Sch; *m* 10 March 1962 *Susan Mary, yr dau of Robert Townley Briscoe, of Hilton, Natal, and has:

1c *Robert Alastair Utten; *b* 30 Sept 1966

1c *Katie Elizabeth; *b* 10 March 1971

2b *William Utten [William Todd Esq, 17 Talbot Rd, Twickenham Green, Middx]; *b* 5 March 1947; *educ* Gresham's; *m* 1976 *Frances Margaret Warren and has:

    1c *Dylan Utten; *b* 1977

1b *Helen Patricia Utten; *b* 28 Feb 1941; *m* 2 June 1962 *David Brian Wentworth, s of F A Wentworth, of Orange, Calif., and has:

    1c *Shaun David; *b* 12 June 1963

    2c *James Douglas; *b* 29 March 1968

    3c *Richard Benning; *b* 1974

    1c *Jennifer Louise; *b* 12 July 1965

(1) Helen; *d* unm 11 May 1955

(2) Margaret St Bride; *d* unm 6 April 1909

(3) Ela; *m* 10 Feb 1892 Rev Charles Rowland Fowke (*see* FOWKE, Bt) and *d* 13 March 1941, leaving issue

(4) Cecil; *d* unm 5 Dec 1916

(5) Annie Lilla; *m* 19 Oct 1887 Maj Henry Bayly (*d* 1 Dec 1891), Gordon Highrs, and *d* 1 Nov 1931, having had issue

(6) Beatrice Mary; *m* 1 May 1909 Philip Beagley le Despencer Tree (*d* June 1965), s of Philip Tree, and *d* 25 Sept 1962, leaving a s

1 Frances Harriet; *m* 10 Sept 1838 6th Earl Fitzwilliam (*qv*) and *d* 15 June 1895, leaving issue

2 Ellen Susan Anne, VA; *m* 15 July 1851 Rev Hon Douglas Hamilton-Gordon (*see* ABERDEEN AND TEMAIR, M) and *d* 22 Jan 1914, having had issue

3 Harriett Bridget Emily; *d* unm 25 March 1832

4 Alice Louisa; *m* 26 June 1862 Rt Rev Alexander Ewing, DCL, LLD (*d* 22 May 1873), Bp Argyll and the Isles, and *d* 2 March 1913

5 Gertrude Jane; *m* 6 Oct 1860 Hon Mark George Kerr Rolle, 2nd s of 19th Baron Clinton (*qv*), and *d* 21 March 1924, leaving issue

6 Agnes Charlotte; *m* 9 Aug 1883 Maj-Gen Sir Owen Tudor Burne, GCIE, KCSI (*d* 3 Feb 1909), s of Rev Henry Thomas Burne, and *dsp* 7 July 1907

The 17th EARL's est son,

SHOLTO JOHN DOUGLAS, **18th Earl of Morton**; *b* 13 April 1818; rep S peer 1859–84; Lt 11th Hus; *m* 1st 24 Jan 1844 Helen (*d* 23 Dec 1850), dau of James Watson, of Saughton, Midlothian, and had issue; *m* 2nd 7 July 1853 Lady Alice Anne Caroline Lambton (*dsp* 15 Jan 1907), Extra Ldy Bedchamber to HM QUEEN ALEXANDRA, 6th dau of 1st Earl of Durham (*qv*), and *d* 24 Dec 1884; his s by his 1st w:

SHOLTO GEORGE DOUGLAS, **19th Earl of Morton**, JP and DL (Argyllshire), JP (Midlothian); *b* 5 Nov 1844; rep S peer 1886–1935; Lt Midlothian Yeo, Head Coast Watcher RN at sea 1914–16; *m* 25 July 1877 Hon Helen Geraldine Ponsonby (*d* 5 Jan 1949), 4th dau of 2nd Baron de Mauley (*qv*), and *d* 8 Oct 1935, having had:

1 Sholto Charles, *Lord Aberdour*; *b* 4 Dec 1878; Capt Leics Yeo and 4th Bn Oxfords LI; *m* 5 June 1905 Minnie Christina Brenda (*d* 27 Aug 1954), dau of Adml of the Fleet Lord John Hay, GCB (*see* TWEEDDALE, M), and *dvp* 20 Sept 1911, leaving:

  (1) SHOLTO CHARLES JOHN HAY DOUGLAS, **20th Earl of Morton**; *b* 12 April 1907; *educ* Magdalen Coll Oxford (MA 1936); F/Lt RAFVR, WW II; RHS Victoria Medal of Honour 1967, Fell Linnean Soc; *d* unm 13 Feb 1976

  (1) (Helen Christina) Joanna; *b* 28 April 1909; granted rank of earl's dau 23 March 1937; *m* 16 Oct 1934 Maj Hubert Trench Crane, Roy Norfolk Regt, only s of Hubert William Crane, and *d* 2 Aug 1965, leaving issue

2 Charles William Sholto; *b* 19 July 1881; Lt RNVR, Lt 4th Bn Oxon LI, WW I; *m* 1st 11 Dec 1920 Alice Agnes (*d* 19 Jan 1924), only dau of Lt-Col William Augustus Lane Fox-Pitt, of Presaddfed, Anglesey, and had:

  (1) Thomas William; *b* 10 Jan 1924; Black Watch, attd Scottish Paratroop Regt WW II; *ka* Dec 1943

  (1) *Helen Alice [The Rt Hon The Lady de Mauley, Langford, Little Faringdon, Lechlade, Glos]; *b* 7 Oct 1921; *m* 1st 20 Oct 1947 Lt-Col Bryan Leslie Lynch Abdy Collins, OBE, MC, RE (*d* 22 Dec 1952), only s of Bernard Abdy Collins, CIE, ICS, and had:

    1a *Thomas Abdy [Thomas Abdy Collins Esq, PO Box 39664, Nairobi, Kenya]; *b* 1948; *m* 1982 *Anna Mary, est dau of Col Ian Critchley, OBE, of Greenden, Farnell, Breckin, and has:

      1b *Alice Susanna Abdy; *b* 1983

      2b *Eleanor Katherine Abdy; *b* 1986

      3b *Phoebe Helen Abdy; *b* 1988

    2a *(Brian) James Douglas [James Abdy Collins Esq, Church Farm, Little Faringdon, Glos]; *b* 1952; *m* 1st 1976 (*divorce* 1988) Philippa Martha Gausel, dau of Sir Rowland John Rathbone Whitehead, 5th Bt (*qv*), and has:

      1b *Henry James Abdy; *b* 1980

      1b *Rose Alice Louise; *b* 1978

    2a (cont.) James Abdy Collins *m* 2nd 1989 *Emma Charlotte, dau of Sir Neill Cooper-Key (*see* ROTHERMERE, V), and by her has:

      2b *Esmond Gerald Beau; *b* 17 June 1997

      2b *Elspeth Peggy; *b* 1990

      3b *Cicely Violet; *b* 1992

      4b *Christabel Lily; *b* 1993

  (1) (cont.) Mrs Bryan Collins *m* 2nd 16 Nov 1954 *6th Baron de Mauley (*qv*)

2 (cont.) The Hon Charles Douglas *m* 2nd 15 April 1926 Florence (*b* 25 May 1897), er dau of Maj Henry Thomas Timson, of Lyndhurst, and *d* 10 Oct 1960, having by her had:

  (2) JOHN CHARLES SHOLTO DOUGLAS, **21st and present Earl of Morton**

3 (Archibald) Roderick Sholto; *b* 11 Sept 1883; Lt RNVR, Lt Leics Imp Yeo, and 1st Lovat Scouts, WW I, WW II as Staff Capt Scottish Cmd, i/c Lothian's Border Dist (Army Ag); *m* 22 Oct 1907 Winona Constance De Maraisville (Nonie) (*d* 26 July 1951), dau of Col Walter Ancell Peak, DSO, of Melton Mowbray, and *d* 29 Dec 1971, leaving:

  (1) Roderick Walter Sholto; *b* 16 July 1908; Maj RAC (TA) WW II; *m* 1st 7 Nov 1935 (*divorce* 1949) Elizabeth Margaret (*d* 1977), est dau of Stephen Clement Paston Cooper (*see* COOPER, Bt, of Gadebridge), and had:

1a +Alastair Sholto; *b* 15 Jan 1949; *m* 1974 *Diane Adams and has:

    1b +Michael Bruce Sholto; *b* 1979

    1b *Chantal Bernadine; *b* 1974

    2b *Fay Robyn; *b* 1977

1a *Anna Winona [Mrs Thomas Bushby, 53A Bannister Rd, Braeside, Harare, Zimbabwe]; *b* 28 July 1936; *m* 6 Feb 1965 *Thomas Charles Bushby and has:

    1b *Lucinda Irene; *b* 8 Aug 1966

2a *Juliet Elizabeth [Mrs Graham Peters, 40 Parel Vallei Rd, Somerset West, S Africa]; *b* 12 June 1941; *m* 1975 *Graham Peters

(1) (cont.) Maj Roderick Douglas *m* 2nd 13 Feb 1950 *Margaret [Mrs Roderick Douglas, Buckstone, Banket, Zimbabwe], er dau of J M Tennent, of Troon, Ayrshire, and *d* 1990, having by her had:

  2a +Bruce Sholto; *b* 17 July 1951

(2) Patrick Sholto, MC and bar; *b* 13 April 1912; Brig Black Watch, RHR, WW II (wounded, despatches); memb Roy Co Archers; *m* 1st 22 Feb 1940 (*divorce* 1959) Maude Carol Hermione, yst dau of George Orr, of Drem, E Lothian; *m* 2nd 21 Jan 1963 *Alexa Granger [Mrs Patrick Douglas, Tanyard Cottage, Fernhurst, Surrey], yst dau of Adml John Ewen Cameron, CB, MVO, JP, of Northumberland, and widow of Capt George Howard Usher Crookshank, King's Own Hus, and *d* 16 June 1977, leaving by his 1st w:

  1a *Katharine Diana [Mrs Peter Hendriks, 2 Russell Place, Edinburgh]; *b* 14 Aug 1942; *m* 7 June 1969 *Peter R C Hendriks, s of Brig N Hendriks, and has:

    1b *Timothy Ivan Mark; *b* 1970

    1b *Alice Sophie; *b* 1973

(3) Peter Frederic Sholto, DSO (1941); *b* 23 Aug 1916; *educ* Uppingham; Maj Argyll & Sutherland Highrs, WW II (wounded, despatches), King Haakon VII of Norway Freedom Cross, US Certificate of Merit 1945, MSM Rhodesia 1976; *m* 6 June 1942 Ursula (*d* 23 Feb 1998), yr dau of Henry Somers Rivers, of Sawbridgeworth, Herts, and *d* 8 Oct 1989, leaving:

  1a (Roderick) Gavin Sholto; *b* 24 June 1944; *educ* U Coll of Rhodesia and Nyasaland, UCL (Sch for Library, Archive & Info Studies), Dip Lib, ALA; Ch Archivist Nat Archives, Zimbabwe; *d* 16 Oct 1995

  1a *Sara [Mrs Peter Newbery, Giwonde, PO Box 119, Centenary, Zimbabwe]; *b* 14 June 1947; *m* 1974 *Peter David Newbery and has:

    1b *Nicholas David; *b* 1982

    1b *Eloise; *b* 1987

(1) *Rosemary [Mrs Winfred Curtis, 27 Sefton St, London SW15]; *b* 6 Feb 1915; *m* 23 Feb 1944 Capt Winfred Marlet Curtis, RM (*d* 1960), s of William Curtis, of Kobe, Japan, and has:

  1a *Winona Penelope [Mrs Richard Peddar, 12 Lower Richmond Rd, London SW15]; *b* 1951; *m* 1973 *Richard Granville Peddar and has:

    1b *Adam Winfred Richard; *b* 1985

    2b *Alexander David Roderick; *b* 1987

    1b *Theresa Adelina Alice; *b* 1980

4 William Sholto; *b* 11 June 1886; Lt RNVR, WW I; *m* 26 Nov 1914 Hon (Ethel) Georgiana Frances Somerset (*d* 1981), dau of 3rd Baron Raglan (*qv*), and *d* 16 Nov 1932, leaving:

  (1) +Ian FitzRoy Sholto [Ian Douglas Esq, Dalwhat Cottage, Moniaive, Dumfriesshire]; *b* 22 Jan 1916; *educ* Bryanston; *m* 1st 15 June 1946 Heather Joan, JP, CC (Kirkcudbright) (*d* 1985), 4th dau of Lt-Col Alexander John Hew Maclean of Ardgour, and has:

    1a +William Hew Sholto [Maj William Douglas, 21 Moor Rd, Balfron, Stirlingshire G63 0BD]; *b* 5 April 1947; *educ* Harrow; Maj 1st Bn Argyll & Sutherland Highrs; *m* 1986 *Frances Mary, dau of Brig William Riddle, of Blyth Bridge, Peeblesshire, and has:

      1b +Peter Sholto; *b* 1987

      2b +Charles Robert; *b* 1989

      3b +Andrew William; *b* 1993

      1b *Kerry Ann Heather; *b* 1991

    2a +(Peter) James [James Douglas Esq, Allandale, High St, New Galloway, by Castle Douglas, Kirkcudbrightshire]; *b* 13 April 1952; *educ* Gordonstoun

    1a *Elizabeth Heather Winifred [Mrs Paul Brown, 118 Spirea Drive, Oakwood, Dayton, OH, USA]; *b* 6 Oct 1948 *m* 1st 3 April 1971 (*divorce* 1983) Edward Inman, er s of John Inman, and has:

      1b *James Michael; *b* 1974

      1b *Heather Louise; *b* 1977

    1a (cont.) Mrs Elizabeth Inman *m* 2nd 1985 *Paul William Alexander Brown

    2a *Jane Charlotte Georgiana [Miss Jane Douglas, Knolklae, Steading, Balmaclellan, Castle Douglas, Kirkcudbrightshire]; *b* 22 Feb 1950

(1) (cont.) Ian Douglas *m* 2nd 1988 *Hester Kathleen Lyndon, dau of Maurice Lyndon White and widow of David McCall-McCowan, of Dumfriesshire

(2) Maurice William Sholto; *b* 31 Dec 1919; *d* 2 Jan 1920

(3) Ronald George Sholto; *b* 17 Oct 1926; *educ* Lancing; Lt Roy Pioneer Corps 1946–48; *m* 1st 9 Aug 1952 (*divorce* 1957) Margaret Jean Gai Eliott-Drake, only dau of Ivor Herbert McClure, DSO, of Montreal, and had:

  1a +Roderick Olaf William Sholto [Roderick Douglas Esq, 8 Old Sopwell Gdns, St Albans, Herts AL1 2BY]; *b* 24 Aug 1953; *m* 1997 *Margaret, dau of Alan Pickles

  2a +Malcolm David Sholto [Malcolm Douglas Esq, 25 Culver Rd, Newbury, Berks]; *b* 27 Feb 1955; *m* 1979 *Barbara Elizabeth, dau of Charles Hughes, and has:

    1b +James Robert Sholto; *b* 24 July 1982

    2b +Michael Charles Sholto; *b* 2 March 1984

  1a *Fiona Anne Georgiana [Mrs Robert Somerville, 16 Grange Rd, Edinburgh EH9 1UJ]; *b* 17 Feb 1956; BSc; *m* 1981 *Dr Robert Anderson Somerville, s of Charles Somerville, and has:

    1b *Ian Douglas; *b* 25 June 1986

    1b *Anne Margaret; *b* 25 May 1985

2b *Catherine Mary; b 1 Sept 1988

(3) (cont.) Ronald Douglas m 2nd 23 June 1960 Valerie, yr dau of William Quarterman, of Birmingham, and by her has:

    2a *Shona Fay [Mrs Roderick Johnstone, 66 The Lanes, Over, Cambs CB4 5NQ]; b 13 May 1962; m 1983 *Dr Roderick McDiarmid Johnstone, only s of Dr Robert Douglas Johnstone, of Pitlochry, Perthshire, and has:

        1b *Peter William Douglas; b 6 Oct 1993

        2b *Tristan James Douglas; b 19 July 1996

        1b *Victoria Katherine; b 22 Feb 1995

(3) (cont.) Ronald Douglas m 3rd 1983 *Heather Grey [Mrs Ronald Douglas, c/o Linton, Linton's Rd, Maungaturoto, Northland, New Zealand], dau of James Philip Law, of NZ, and d 8 May 1996

(1) *Jean Georgiana Ethel, OBE [Mrs Peter Heneage OBE, North Carlton Old Hall, N Carlton, Lincs]; b 5 July 1922; m 5 March 1949 *Capt Peter Edward Findlay Heneage, RA, 2nd s of Lt-Col Sir Arthur Pelham Heneage, DSO, JP, DL (see 1967 edn HENEAGE, B), and has:

    1a *Thomas Peter William; b 1950; m 1980 (divorce 1990) Shaunagh Anne Henrietta (m 2nd 2 Aug 1995 Hon Crispin Money-Coutts; see LATYMER, B), est dau of (George Silver) Oliver Annesley Colthurst (see COLTHURST, Bt), and has:

        1b *Henry Robert; b 1983

        1b *Elizabeth Anne Sophia; b 1981

    2a *Charles Arthur [Charles Heneage Esq, Bailes Hill House, Birdbrook, Essex CO9 4BY]; b 1952; m 1978 *Sarah Elizabeth, yst dau of Col Arthur Harold Newmarch Reade, LVO, of Ipsden, Oxon, and has:

        1b *Frederick Rory Winwood; b 1990

        1b *Sophia Georgiana; b 1980

        2b *Alice Rose; b 1983

    3a *Robert John [Robert Heneage Esq, Newport House, North Carlton, Lincs]; b 1956; m 1984 *Maryann Louise, dau of J N Milne, of Ledbury, and has:

        1b *William; b 1986

        1b *Georgiana; b 1988

    1a *Katherine Julia [Mrs Malcolm Moir, 31 Poplar Grove, London W6 7RF]; b 1960; m 1991 *Malcolm Moir, er s of Nigel Moir, of Bacton, Suffolk, and has:

        1b *Jemima Mary; b 1994

        2b *Mathilda Rose; b 1996

5 Ronald John Sholto, OBE (1919); b 22 April 1890; Lt RNVR WW I; m 28 June 1920 Alexandra Albertha Jean (d 2 March 1974), dau of Adml Sir Frederick Tower Hamilton, GCVO, KCB (see BELHAVEN AND STENTON, L), and d 31 Jan 1922, leaving:

(1) *Victoria Maria [Mrs Gillachrist Campbell, Mendham Lodge, Harleston, Norfolk]; b 25 March 1921; m 4 Feb 1956, as his 2nd w, Lt-Col Gillachrist Campbell, RA (d 1975), est s of Joseph Campbell by Nancy, only dau of Lt-Col Aubrey Maurice Maude (see HAWARDEN, V), and has:

    1a *Maria; b 1956

    2a *Sophia Frances [Ms Sophia Campbell, Chestnut Cottage, St Margarets, Harleston, Norfolk]; b 1958

    3a *Catherine; b 1959; m 1986 *Michel Jean Jerôme Corby-Tuech and has:

        1b *Jacques Max Gillachrist; b 1988

        1b *Poppy Colette; b 1987

MOSTYN, Baron

Arms: Quarterly, 1st and 4th, per bend sinister erm. and ermines a lion rampant or (for MOSTYN); 2nd and 3rd, gu. a Saracen's head affrontée, erased at the neck ppr., wreathed about the temples sa. and arg. (for LLOYD). **Crests:** 1 On a mount vert a lion rampant or, 2 A Saracen's head as in the arms, 3 A stag trippant ppr., charged on the back with an escutcheon of the second, thereon a chevron of the first, between three human heads in profile, couped at the neck, also ppr. **Supporters:** Dexter, a stag ppr., attired or, charged on the shoulder with an escutcheon gu., thereon a chevron arg., between three human heads couped in profile ppr.; sinister, a lion or charged on the shoulder with an escutcheon arg., thereon a cross engrailed and fleurettée sa., between four Cornish choughs ppr.
Motto: Auxilium meum a domino ('My help is from the Lord').
Creations: Bt. (GB) 29 Aug 1778, B. (UK) 10 Sept 1831.

THE 5TH BARON MOSTYN OF MOSTYN, Co Flint, and a **Baronet** (Sir Roger Edward Lloyd Lloyd-Mostyn, Bt, MC (1943)) [The Rt Hon The Lord Mostyn MC, Mostyn Hall, Mostyn, Flintshire]; b 17 April 1920; s f 1965; educ Eton and RMC Sandhurst; Capt 8th Queen's Roy Lancers 1939, WW II France, N Africa and Italy (wounded 1940 and 1942, despatches 1940), T/Maj 1946, race horse trainer; m 1st 3 April 1943 (divorce 1957) Yvonne Margaret, yst dau of Arthur Stuart Johnson, JP, of Henshall Hall, Congleton, Cheshire, and has:

    1 +LLEWELLYN ROGER LLOYD [The Hon Llewellyn Mostyn, 9 Anderson St, London SW3]; b 26 Sept 1948; educ Eton; late Capt Army Legal Servs, barrister Middle Temple 1973; m 18 July 1974 *Denise Suzanne, dau of Roger Louis Duvanel, of Gaillard, France, and has:

        (1) +Gregory Philip Roger; b 31 Dec 1984

        (1) *Alexandra Stefanie; b 19 May 1975

    1 *Virginia Yvonne Lloyd, b 24 March 1946; m 1st 13 Dec 1973 (divorce 1983) John Robert Hodgkinson, barrister, s of Lt-Col Reginald Bradsheigh Hodgkinson, MC, JP, of Shennington House, Ettington, Warwicks, and has:

        (1) *Dominic Edward; b 10 Nov 1974

        (2) *Thomas William; b 5 May 1976

    1 (cont.) The Hon Mrs Virginia Hodgkinson m 2nd 30 March 1983 *James R K Price, barrister

The 5th BARON m 2nd 6 May 1957 *Sheila Edmondson, OBE, DL, formerly w of Henry English Shaw and only child of Maj Reginald Fairweather, of Stockwell Manor, Silverton, Devon

Lineage (of Lloyd): RHYS Ap EDRYD (descended from MARCHUDD Ap CYNAN, of Uwch Dulas, Denbighs, ancestor through another branch of the TUDOR Dynasty) had, with two er sons (David; Cyndelw, ancestor of that William Hughes, Bp St Asaph, whose dau Anne m Thomas Mostyn, see below):

GWILLIM Ap RHYS; had:

DWYWG Ap GWILLIM; ggggf of:

EDNYFED Ap TUDUR; had:

DAFYDD LLWYD Ab EDNYFED; m Alswn, dau of Gruffudd ab Einion Dew ('The Fat'), and had:

GRUFFUDD GETHIN Ap DAFYDD LLWYD; m Alswn, dau of Jenkin (d 1476) ap Hywel Pigot, and had:

GRONWY Ap GRUFFUDD GETHIN; m Isabel, dau of Gruffudd ap Einion, incumbent Llanefydd, Denbighs, and had:

MAREDUDD Ap GRONWY, of Llansannan, Denbighs; m Agnes, dau of Robert Fychan ap Tudur, of Berain, Llanefydd, and d between 8 and 14 Feb 1567/8; his (probably yst) s:

DAFYDD Ap MAREDUDD; m Jane, dau of William Wyn ap John ap William, of Dyffryn Melai, Llanfair Talhaearn, Denbighs, and had:

WILLIAM LLOYD, of The Forest, Llansannan; m Mary, dau of Hugh Dryhurst, s of John Dryhurst, and had, with two est sons (John, of The Forest; William, London clothworker) and several daus:

ROBERT LLOYD; *m* —, of Llys-faen, and had:

WILLIAM LLOYD, of The Forest; *m* —, dau of (Robert?) Lloyd, of Dolygleyn, Corwen, Merioneths, and had:

JOHN LLOYD, of Pontruffudd, Flint, which he bought 1688; *m* Rebecca, dau and heiress of William Owen, of Plas Isa, and *d* 1729, having had, with an est *s* (*d* young, having had two sons, who *dsp*):

1 William; *m* 1726 Frances, dau and heiress of Bell Jones, of Plasmawr, Flint, and *d* 1730, leaving (with a dau, Lumley, *d* unm 1804):

(1) Bell, of Pontriffith; *b* 25 Aug 1729; *m* 13 Dec 1758 Anne, dau and heiress of Edward Pryce, of Bodfach, Montgomeryshire, and *d* 6 May 1773, having had:

1a EDWARD, **1st Baron**

2a Bell, of Crogan, Merioneths, *m* 20 Dec 1792 Anne (*d* 25 May 1822), sis of 1st Viscount Anson (*see* LICHFIELD, E), and *d* July 1845, leaving, with other issue (*d* unm):

1b Edward Bell; Lt 16th Lancers; *b* 3 May 1794; *m* 1819 Lowry (*d* 14 Feb 1878), dau of Robert Morris, and *d* 8 May 1864, leaving:

1c Edward; *b* 4 Oct 1819; *m* Jane Adams and *dsp* 1 Jan 1841

2c William; *b* 7 Jan 1824; *m* 1854 Anne (*d* 1908), dau of C Stuke, and *d* 28 Nov 1878, leaving:

1d William Anson; *b* 27 April 1859; *d* 1890, leaving:

1e Ernest William; *d* 1897

1e Violet Anson

2d St George Llewellyn; *b* 31 March 1861; *m* 7 Feb 1886 Ellen (*d* 16 Feb 1946), dau of James Bateson, and *d* 1 Jan 1894, leaving:

1e Llewellyn Bateson; *b* 13 May 1887; *m* 28 Sept 1910 Mabel Ellen (*d* 23 Feb 1961), dau of William French, and *d* 10 Sept 1952, leaving:

1f George Llewellyn; *b* 12 Nov 1911; *m* 22 Jan 1948 *Marianne, dau of Pierre Marcelli, and *d* 1978

2e Frederick George; *b* 22 March 1889; *m* 5 April 1913 Ethel May, dau of James Jackson, and was *k* with her in a car crash 22 May 1931

3e Mostyn William; *b* 4 March 1891; *ka* 16 Nov 1916

4e Charles Anson; *b* 16 Nov 1892; *d* 21 April 1893

3d Edward Bell; *b* 22 Dec 1862; *m* 1888 Alice Maud Mary (*d* 1954), dau of — Awbery, and *d* 1922, leaving:

1e Dorothy Alice; *d* aged 10 days

2e Alice Anson; *b* 1891; *d* unm

3e Beatrice Alice; *b* 1893; *d* unm

4e Clarice Audrey; *b* 1897

4d Thomas Mostyn; *b* 9 March 1865

5d Frederick Victor; Capt, Inspr S African Police Pretoria; *b* 14 Feb 1867; *m* 1902 Dorothy Omagh and *d* 1954, having had:

1e James Mostyn; Br S Africa Police; *b* 1906; *m* 1937 (*divorce* 1956) Elsie, dau of N S L Coltzee, of Sutherland, CP

1e Gladys Anson; *d* unm 23 May 1918

6d Charles Anson; *b* 1 Feb 1869; *d* 1900

7d Constantine Cynric; *b* 8 May 1874

1d Constance Ellen; *b* 15 March 1856; *m* 27 Sept 1887 Rev James Silvester, FRHistS, Vicar Gt Clacton, and *d* 6 Feb 1939, leaving issue

2d Laura Letitia; *b* 23 Oct 1857; *m* 11 April 1886 Charles Midlane Welsh and *d* 8 Aug 1939, leaving issue

3d Ellen Anson; *b* 6 March *d* 8 July 1873

4d Eleanor Arabella; *b* 1 Sept 1876; *m* 1901 George D Haring

1c Mary Elizabeth; *d* unm

2c Anne Anson; *d* unm

2b William Henry Cynric (Ven); Archdeacon Durban; *b* 13 Jan 1802; *m* 1st 3 July 1832 Lucy Anne (*d* 1843), dau of Rev John Jeffreys, and had, with three other daus:

1c Jemima Charlotte; *b* 23 May 1837; *m* 1862 Dr W H Bleek, Librarian Greys Library, Cape Town, and *d* 6 Oct 1909, having had issue. He *d* 1878

2b (cont.) The Ven William Mostyn *m* 2nd 23 May 1844 Ellen (*d* 12 Sept 1903), dau of Rev Henry Norman, and *d* 3 Jan 1881, having by her had, with two other sons and six other daus:

1c Albert Charles George; *b* 5 June 1851; *m* 1882 (*divorce* 1904) Eleanor, widow of Swainston Harrison, and *d* 19 Jan 1916

2c Alfred Norman Mostyn; Registrar Deeds Pietermaritzburg; *b* 28 Sept 1868; *m* 1st 29 April 1895 Harriet (*d* 28 Feb 1904), dau of Rev Canon Crompton, and had:

1d Theodore Cynric; BSc S Africa, MSc Lond, PhD Columbia; *b* 24 March 1901; *m* 31 July 1937 *Stella Patience, dau of Alfred William McLaren

1d Gwynedd; *b* 18 July 1899; *m* 18 June 1934 Victor Holmes McNaghten Barrett, BSc, Inspr Mines Natal (*d* 1 May 1966), and had:

1e *David McNaghten [David Barrett Esq, 5 Burne Crescent, Athlone Park, Umbogintwini, South Coast, Natal, S Africa]; BSc S Africa; *b* 3 Sept 1937; *m* 22 July 1961 *Barbara Leone, er dau of Benjamin van der Hoven, of Pietermaritzburg, and has:

1f *James McNaghten; *b* 7 July 1965

2c (cont.) Alfred Mostyn *m* 2nd 30 June 1910 Alice Rivière (*d* 7 Aug 1944), dau of Henry Ainsworth Condron, and *d* 26 Aug 1941, having by her had:

2d Norman Mostyn, RD; Cdr RNR WW II; *b* 27 April 1911; *m* 2 April 1941 Ethel Kathleen (*d* 1986), dau of Edward Crouch, and *d* 1986, having had:

1e +Edward Mostyn [Edward Lloyd Esq, 125A Ashley Gdns, London SW1P 1HL]; *b* 15 Jan 1943

1e *Margaret Gwynedd; *b* 12 April 1944; *m* 24 June 1966 *Capt Douglas Havers

3d +Alfred Anson [Alfred Lloyd Esq, 12 Humber Cres, Durban North 4051, S Africa]; *b* 27 Feb 1914; *educ* Michaelhouse Natal; CA (SA), Capt SA Artillery WW II, Instr Artillery Sch Potchefstroom 1941–43, Troop Cdr and Adj 4/22 Field Regt SA Artillery Egypt and Italy, Chm S Africa Sugar Assoc, V-Chm S Africa Sugar Millers' Assoc, dir Huletts' Sugar Corp, Hon DEc; *m* 5 March 1941 *Elanie Ivy Maud, dau of Horace Vivian Burdon, and has:

1e *Patricia Burdon; *b* 31 Jan 1943; *educ* Maris Stella Convent, Durban

2e *Barbara Ann [Mrs Robert Slater, 24 Burleigh Crescent, Duban North 4051, S Africa]; *b* 11 Feb 1948; *educ* St Anne's Diocesan Coll Natal; *m* 7 Sept 1971 *Robert John Kendall Slater and has:

1f *Kendall Lloyd; *b* 26 June 1972

2f *Stuart James; *b* 25 Oct 1974

2d Mary Rivière; *b* 16 Jan 1916; *m* 29 March 1941 Lt-Cdr Charles Frederick Joshua Finch, RNR, s of Charles Samuel Finch, and *d* 20 March 1956, leaving issue

2c Adelaide Octavia Susan; *m* Feb 1883 Robert Treiss Nimmo, of Durban, and *d* 22 May 1908, leaving issue

3c Eva Alexandra Georgiana; *b* 25 Oct 1863; *m* Rev C L Garde and *d* 6 Oct 1888, leaving issue

3a Griffith (Rev); Rector Christleton, Cheshire; *d* unm 25 Jan 1843

4a Cynric; *m* 6 March 1809 Martha (*m* 2nd 27 Jan 1829 Lt-Col Sir Henry Wyatt; *d* 9 April 1839), sis of 1st Baron Dinorben of Kinmel Park, and *dsp* 1822

5a Llewellyn; *b* 14 Nov 1806 Jane, dau of Edward Falkner, of Fairfield Hall, Lancs, and *d* 29 July 1866, having had:

1b Llewelyn Falkner Lloyd, JP, DL, of Cilcen Hall and Plas-yn-Llan, Flints; High Sheriff 1847; *b* 8 July 1809; *m* 28 July 1841 Mary Susan (*d* 26 April 1883), only dau of Rev William Wickham Drake, Rector Malpas, Cheshire, and *d* 27 Aug 1873, leaving:

1c Mary Frances, of Cilcen Hall

2b Cynric; barrister; *d* unm

3b Thomas Henry (Rev); Fellow All Souls; *d* unm 26 July 1850

4b Banastre Pryce; Maj-Gen Bengal Army; *b* 1824; *m* Anna Maria Grimes (*d* 1907), dau of Col L R Stacy, CB, FEICS, and *d* 1882, leaving:

1c Llewelyn Henry; *k* Zulu War 8 March 1879

2c Charles Banastre; *m* Ellen Rymer (*d* 1944) and *d* 23 July 1929, leaving:

1d Henry Charles Stacy; *b* 1880; *m* 23 June 1930 Ruth (*d c* 1964), 2nd dau of Frederick Meanwell, and *d c* 1964

2d Llewelyn; *b* 1883; *m* 12 May 1920 Jessie Elizabeth, dau of James Thomas Forrester, and *d* 1960, having had:

1e Valentine Mostyn; *b* 28 Nov, *d* 3 Dec 1925

1e *Daphine Ellen Kate [Mrs Read, Buxton House, 132 Long Market St, Pietermaritzburg, S Africa]; *b* 5 April 1921; *m* 19– (*divorce* 1949) — Read, of Johannesburg, and has:

1f *Arland Everard; *b* 1944

1f *Susan; *b* 1946

1d Ethel Margaret; *m* 5 July 1923 Lt-Col Granville Pennefather-Evans, CBE, IA, s of Mathew Pennefather-Evans, and *dsp* Dec 1965. He *d* 1963

2d Gladys Amy; *m* 9 Jan 1914 (*divorce* 1937) Francis Harold Wroughton

3c Hugh Wroughton; *b* 1885; *m* 1890 Juliana Acutt and *d* 26 July 1911, leaving:

1d Lewis John; *b* 1892

4c Bell George; *m* 1893 Lilias (*d* 1929), dau of Rev W O Newnham, and *d* 8 Dec 1936

1c Anne Stacy; *m* 1880 Lt-Col Sir Marshal James Clarke, KCMG, RA, and *d* 15 June 1933, having had issue. He *d* 1 April 1909

2c Mary Elizabeth; *m* Edward Brewster Stainbank, 3rd s of R H Stainbank, of Waldron, Sussex, and had issue. He *d* 19 Jan 1927

3c Frances Charlotte; *m* Lewis Wroughton and *d* 17 Nov 1928, leaving issue. He *d* 1912

4c Margaret Jane; *d* unm 8 Feb 1955

5b Griffith Clayton; Cdr RN

6b George Charles; Col Bengal Army

1b Anne Bridget; *d* 11 July 1854

2b Elizabeth Lumley Frances

3b Jane

2 Sir Edward Lloyd, 1st Bt (GB), so *cr* 29 Aug 1778, with remainder to his n BELL LLOYD (who, however, *d* 6 May 1773 in his unc's lifetime) and the latter's heirs male; Sec of War; *m* 1st Anna Maria, dau and heiress of Edward Lloyd, of Pengwern, Flint; *m* 2nd 3 July 1774 Amelia (*d* 1831) dau of Sir William Yonge, Bt, PC, of Escot, Devon, and *dsp* 26 May 1795

1 Margaret; *m* J Morrall, of Plas Yolyn

Sir EDWARD's great-nephew,

Sir Edward Pryce Lloyd, 2nd Bt, and **1st Baron Mostyn of Mostyn**, Co Flint (UK), so *cr* 10 Sept 1831, MP (Whig) Flint Burghs 1806–07 and 1812–31 and Beaumaris 1808–12, Sheriff Flint 1796–97, Caernarvonshire 1797–98, Merionethshire 1804–05 and Cards 1825–26; *b* 17 Sept 1768; *m* 11 Feb 1794 Elizabeth (*d* 8 Nov 1842), 3rd dau of Sir Roger Mostyn, 5th Bt, and sis and coheir of Sir Thomas Mostyn, 6th and last Bt, of Mostyn (*see below*), and had:

1 EDWARD, **2nd Baron**

2 Thomas Pryce; *b* 4 Aug 1800; *d* 11 March 1874

1 Elizabeth; *d* 22 July 1873

2 Essex; *d* 26 April 1857

The 1st BARON *d* 3 April 1854; his est son,

EDWARD MOSTYN LLOYD later LLOYD-MOSTYN (roy licence 9 May 1831 under terms of will of maternal uncle Sir THOMAS MOSTYN, 6th and last Bt),

2nd Baron Mostyn of Mostyn; *b* 13 Jan 1805; MP (Whig) Flints 1831–37, 1841–42 and 1847–54 and Lichfield 1846–47, Ld Lt Merioneths 1840–84, V-Adml N Wales 1854–84; *m* 20 June 1827 Harriet Margaret (*d* 3 June 1891), est dau of 2nd Earl of Clonmell (*see* 1935 edn), and had:

1 Thomas Edward; *b* 23 Jan 1830; MP Flintshire 1854–56; *m* 19 July 1855 Lady Henrietta Augusta Nevill (*d* 25 Jan 1912), 2nd dau of 4th Earl of Abergavenny (*see* ABERGAVENNY, M), and *dvp* 8 May 1861, leaving:

  (1) LLEWELYN NEVILL VAUGHAN, **3rd Baron**

  (2) Henry Richard Howel, JP, DL Caernarvs, of Bodysgallen, Llandudno; *b* 6 April 1857; *educ* Eton and RMC Sandhurst; 23rd Foot, Lt-Col and Hon Col cmdg 4th Bn RWF 1903–08, Lt-Col and Hon Col cmdg 3rd Bn Cheshire Regt 1909–12, helped raise and cmded 17th RWF 1915, granted rank of baron's yr s 13 Oct 1884; *m* 20 Sept 1883 Hon Pamela Georgina Douglas-Pennant, MBE (*d* 20 July 1949), dau of 2nd Baron Penrhyn (*qv*), and *d* 3 Sept 1938, leaving:

    1a Ieuan; *b* 14 Nov 1884; *educ* Eton; Lt 6th Bn KRRC WW I; *d* unm 29 Aug 1966

    2a Morys Lancelot; *b* 20 Feb 1887, *educ* Eton; Lt-Col and Brevet Col 6th Bn Roy Welch Fus (TAR), GSO(3) 1917 WW I (wounded), Bronze Medal Roy Humane Soc, OStJ; *m* 22 Nov 1917 Marjorie Eleanor (*d* 4 April 1974), est dau of Henry Tubb, of Chesterton, Bicester, and *d* 3 Dec 1968, having had:

      1b Henry Pyers Ronald; *b* 16 Dec 1918; *educ* Eton; 2nd Lt 15th/19th Hus WW II; *ka* 1940

2 Roger; *b* 1 May 1831; Lt-Col Scots Gds; *m* 1896 Adeline Frances Brereton, dau of James Ashley, and *dsp* 27 Feb 1899

3 Savage (Sir), KCB, DL Denbighs; *b* 27 March 1835; Maj-Gen, Col Roy Welch Fus (formerly cmdg), served Crimea, Indian Mutiny and Ashanti; *m* 22 April 1891 Emily (*d* 28 May 1956), dau of Rev George Earle Welby (*see* WELBY, Bt), and *d* 2 June 1914, leaving:

  (1) Rhona Felicia Bridget; *m* 28 Oct 1929 Lt-Col Edward Percy Aymer des Graz, Rifle Bde, s of Maurice des Graz, of The Firs, Wimbledon, and had issue. He was *ka* Libya 6 June 1942

4 Ieuan Lloyd Vaughan; Lt RN; *b* July 1836; *d* unm 13 Aug 1872

5 Hugh Wynne (Rev); Rector Buckworth, Hunts, 1863–1908, Hon Canon Ely; *b* 25 Jan 1838; *m* 19 June 1866 Ellen Grey (*d* 6 Oct 1923), dau of James Duberly, of Gaynes Hall, Hunts, and *d* 8 Dec 1930, leaving:

  (1) Edward Hugh; *b* 25 Aug 1871; *m* 13 May 1902 Ella (*d* 22 Nov 1928), yr dau of Thomas Grant, and *d* 16 Nov 1922, leaving:

    1a Hugh Wynne; *b* 16 Nov 1903; *m* 17 Jan 1933 Eileen Grace (*d* 1985), only dau of Arthur Walsh Titherley, DSc, PhD, FRIC, of Itchen Abbas Manor, nr Winchester, and *d* 1975 having had:

      1b +Roger Hugh [Roger Lloyd-Mostyn Esq, 42 Lichfield Lane, Mansfield, Notts]; *b* 1 Dec 1941; *educ* Lancing and Westminster Hosp Med Sch (MB, BS Lond 1965, LRCP, MRCS 1965, FRCP Lond 1969); *m* 21 Jan 1967 *Mary Frances, dau of Capt Edward Fothergill Elderton, AFRaeS, ACGI, of IoW, and has:

        1c +Christopher Edward; *b* 25 May 1968

        2c +James William; *b* 23 April 1970

        3c +David Thomas; *b* 1981

      1b *Rosemary Eleanor; *b* 3 Oct 1933; *m* 1974 *Rev J D Thorp and has:

        1c *Simon Robin Hugh; *b* 1975

      2b *Jean Grant [Mrs John Matthews, 792 Victoria Rd, Ryde, Sydney, NSW 2112, Australia]; *b* 11 June 1935; *m* 20 Aug 1956 *John Harold Matthews, film and TV dir and producer, 2nd s of Harold Matthews, of Melbourne, Australia, and has:

        1c *Nicholas Stuart; *b* 1958; *m* 1980 *Debra Young and has:

          1d *Michael Lloyd; *b* 1984

          2d *Daniel James; *b* 1989

        1c *Sarah Jo; *b* 1964; *m* 1988 *Dennis Brian Heape

(2) James Pryce; *b* 17 Feb 1879; *educ* Marlborough and RMC Sandhurst; Lt-Col Norfolk Regt, served India, E Africa (KAR), Somaliland 1902, Egypt and Sudan (Egyptian Army) 1910–16, WW I (despatches, brevet), cmded 1st Bn Norfolk Regt 1925–29 and WW II (cmded 11th (HD) Bn Queen's Roy Regt 1939–41, Army Cadet Force 1942–45), Order Nile 4th Cl; *m* 6 Aug 1915 Alix Doreen Inigo (*d* 17 Dec 1956), dau of Maj-Gen Inigo Richmund-Jones, CVO, CB, of Kelston Park, Somerset, and *d* 26 Jan 1968, leaving:

    1a Edwyn Inigo, MC , of Dissiford House, Bishop's Lydeard, Somerset; *b* 20 Jan 1921; *educ* St Edward's Sch Oxford; Maj Scots Gds WW II and Malaya (despatches); *m* 1st 30 May 1942 (*divorce* 1963) Avice Louise Trevor, 2nd dau of Cdr Sir Hugh Dawson, 2nd Bt, RN, of Rede Hall, Burstow, Surrey (*see* 1970), and had:

      1b +James Michael; *b* 30 March 1952; *m* 1974 *Susan Patricia, dau of J A Hough, of Nantwich, Cheshire, and has:

        1c +Neil James; *b* 29 Sept 1982

        1c *Sarah Louise; *b* 1977

        2c *Joanna Mary; *b* 1979

      1b *Caroline Anne; *b* 10 April 1954; *m* 1979 *John J Baggerman, s of K J Baggerman, of Twyford, Hants

      2b *Louise Avice; *b* 9 Dec 1955; *m* 12 Nov 1977 *Francis D Foster, s of H F Foster, of Park House, Drumoak, Aberdeenshire

      3b *Annabelle Alix; *b* 19 July 1957

    1a (cont.) Maj Edwin Lloyd-Mostyn *m* 2nd 1964 *Janet Hope, formerly w of — Rutherford and est dau of Eric Cecil Barnes, CMG, of Palmear, Frogham, Fordingbridge, Hants; *m* 3rd 1975 *Angela, widow of Ralph Leyland, and *d* 1978

    2a +David Henry [David Lloyd-Mostyn Esq, 41 Marion Way, Gooseberry Hill, W Australia 6076]; *b* 26 April 1923; *educ* St Edward's Sch Oxford; Rifle Bde and Queen's Roy Regt (invalided) WW II; *m* 25 Feb 1956 *Betty, only dau of James Francis O'Connor, of Applecross, W Australia, and has had:

      1b Christopher James; *b* 20 Oct, *d* 28 Oct 1964

    1a Sydna Alix; Jr Cdr ATS WW II; *b* 18 July 1917; *d* 24 May 1983

  (1) Maria Bridget; *m* 12 April 1898 Sir Anthony Alfred Bowlby, 1st Bt (*qv*), and *d* 12 Sept 1957, leaving issue

  (2) Essex; *d* unm 27 Jan 1950

  (3) Katharine Ellen Grey; *m* 16 April 1903 Rev Austin le Strange, Rector Ringstead, Norfolk, 2nd s of Hamon le Strange, of Hunstanton Hall, Norfolk, and *d* 11 Feb 1954, leaving issue. He *d* 11 Feb 1936

  (4) Harriot Emily; *m* 5 April 1910 Rev Henry Bromley Maling, Vicar Woodbastwick, Norwich, est s of T J Maling, of Christchurch, NZ, and *d* 26 May 1954, leaving issue. He *d* 2 Sept 1946

  (5) Elizabeth Margaret Wynne; *m* 28 Feb 1922 Sir Geoffrey Edmund Cator, CMG, yst s of Robert Cator, of Bath, and *d* 2 Sept 1967, leaving issue. He *d* 21 April 1973

1 Harriot Margaret; *d* unm 10 Aug 1914

2 Elizabeth; *m* 3 Nov 1868 Nathaniel Weekes, of Guillards Oak, Sussex, and *dsp* 14 March 1887

3 Essex; *d* unm 21 Oct 1916

4 Charlotte; *d* 19 Nov 1851

5 Katherine; *d* unm 15 April 1927

The 2nd BARON *d* 17 March 1884; his grandson,

LLEWELYN NEVILL VAUGHAN LLOYD-MOSTYN, **3rd Baron Mostyn of Mostyn**, JP, DL Caernarvs; *b* 7 April 1856; Flintshire and Kent, V-Adml N Wales and Carmarths 1898, Hon Col cmdg 3rd Bn Roy Welch Fus, KJStJ; *m* 1 May 1879 Lady Mary Florence Edith Clements, OBE (*d* 9 Feb 1933), sis of 4th Earl of Leitrim (*see* 1953 edn), and had:

1 Thomas Edward Llewelyn; *b* 26 May 1880; *d* 27 May 1882

2 EDWARD LLEWELYN ROGER, **4th Baron**

3 Roderick Clements; Lt Gren Gds; *b* 11 Aug 1887; *d* unm 26 Feb 1968

1 Gwynedd Mary; *b* 11 Aug 1889; *d* unm 26 June 1968

The 3rd BARON *d* 11 April 1929; his er surv son,

EDWARD LLEWELLYN ROGER LLOYD-MOSTYN, **4th Baron Mostyn of Mostyn**, JP, DL Flints, *b* 16 March 1885; *educ* Eton; High Sheriff 1928, Lt Gds MG Regt, formerly Irish Gds, CStJ; *m* 14 May 1918 (Constance) Mary (*d* 14 Feb 1976), only child of Walter Hugh Reynolds, of Aldeburgh, Suffolk, and *d* 2 May 1965, having had:

1 ROGER EDWARD LLOYD LLOYD-MOSTYN, **5th and present Baron Mostyn of Mostyn**

2 John Llewelyn Lloyd; *b* 19 Feb 1922; Midshipman RN; *d* following an accident 10 Jan 1940

3 Richard Lloyd; *b* and *d* 22 Oct 1925

4 Thomas Nevill Lloyd; *b* 28 Jan 1933; *d* following a car crash 16 Nov 1954

1 *Elizabeth Mary Gwenllian [The Hon Mrs Russell, Pitillock House, Freuchie, Fife KY15 7JQ]; *b* 18 Aug 1929; *m* 1st 14 Sept 1950 (*divorce* 1957) Capt David Nicholas Goldsmith Duckham, Welsh Gds, yst s of Thomas Henry Duckham, of Mulberries, Guilfail, Lewes, and has:

  (1) *Kiloran Mary; *b* 22 June 1953

1 (cont.) The Hon Mrs Elizabeth Duckham *m* 2nd 25 May 1957 John Henry Russell, er s of Lt-Col George Gray Russell, DSO, King Edward's Horse, of Northenby, East Woodhay, nr Newbury

Lineage (of Mostyn): THOMAS Ap RICHARD (*see* MOSTYN, Bt, for previous generations), of Mostyn, Flintshire; *b c* 1483; took the name MOSTYN, High Sheriff Anglesey 1553–54; *m* on or after 6 May 1517 Jane, dau of Sir William Griffith, of Penrhyn, Caernarvs, and *d* 30 Aug 1558, having had, with eight yr sons and five daus:

WILLIAM MOSTYN, of Mostyn; served Horse Gds 1553–54, MP Flints 1553–54 and Caernarvs 1576, High Sheriff Flints 1560–61, 1565–66, 1570–71 and Caernarvs 1556–57; *m* 1st by 10 April 1541 Margaret Wen ('The White'), dau of Robert ap Hywel, of Park, Whittington, Salop, and had three sons and two daus; *m* 2nd on or after 4 Oct 1556 Margaret (*dsp* between 5 Oct 1592 and 26 Feb 1594/5), dau of Sir William Brereton and widow of William Goodman, Alderman Chester, and *d* 9 Sept 1576, leaving an est s by his 1st:

Sir THOMAS MOSTYN, of Mostyn; *b c* 1535; MP Flints 1576–77, High Sheriff Anglesey 1574–75, 1587–78, 1586–87 and Caernarvs 1583–84, memb Cncl of Marches of Wales, ktd 1599; *m* on or after 4 Oct 1556 Ursula (*d* 1578), dau of William Goodman, Alderman Chester (his stepmother's former husb's dau); *m* 2nd on or after 6 Feb 1581/2 his cousin Catherine (*dsp*), dau of Piers Mostyn, of Talacre (*see* MOSTYN, Bt), and widow of Sir Rhys Griffith, of Penrhyn, and *d* 28 Feb 1617/8, having had by his 1st w:

1 William, *d* unm

2 ROGER (Sir)

3 Thomas, of Rhyd, Flints; *m* Anne, dau and heiress of William Hughes, Bp St Asaph (*see* above **Lineage (of Lloyd)**), and had issue

1 Margaret; *m* Pierce Griffith, of Penrhyn, and had issue

2 Catherine, *m* Sir Thomas Hanmer (*d* 18 April 1619; *see* HANMER, Bt), and had issue

The 2nd son,

Sir ROGER MOSTYN, of Mostyn; *b* 1559/60; High Sheriff Anglesey 1589–90 and Flints 1608–09 and 1626–27, ktd 1608, MP Flints 1621–22; *m* 1596 Mary, dau of Sir John Wynn, of Gwydir, and *d* 18 Aug 1642, having had:

1 Thomas (Sir); *b c* 1598; admitted Lincoln's Inn 1620, ktd 1623; *m* May 1623 Elizabeth (*m* 2nd Owen Wynn, s of Sir John Wynn, of Gwydir), dau of Sir James Whitlock, Ch Justice Chester, and *dvp* 12 Nov 1641, leaving:

  (1) ROGER (Sir), 1st Bt

  (2) Thomas; ancestor of the MOSTYNs of Kilken

2 John, of Maesmynan; *dsp* 1671

3 William, Archdeacon Bangor; *m* Elizabeth (*d* 10 April 1647), dau and coheir of Richard Aldersey, of Chester, and was ancestor of the MOSTYNs of Brongwyn

4 Richard; Capt Army; *k* at La Rochelle 1627

5 Robert; *m* Margaret, dau and heiress of Henry Conway, of Nant, Flint, and had issue

6 Roger; of the Inns of Court

7 Edward; *d* young

1 Sydney; *m* 1628 Sir Richard Grosvenor, 2nd Bt (*see* WESTMINSTER, D)

2 Catherine; *m* Col Richard Bulkeley, s and heir of 1st Viscount Bulkeley

The grandson,

Sir ROGER MOSTYN, 1st Bt (E), so *cr* 3 Aug 1660, of Mostyn; *b c* 1620; admitted Inner Temple 1637, royalist Govr Flint Civil War, ktd 5 June 1660, High Sheriff Montgomerys 1660–61, Flints 1665–66 and Caernarvs 1666–67; *m* 1st 1642 Prudence, dau of Sir Martin Lumley, 1st Bt, of Gt Bradfield, Essex, and had (with two sons *dsp*):

1 Jane; *m* 1st Roger Puleston, of Emeral, Flint, and had issue; *m* 2nd Sir John Trevor (*see* TREVOR, B)

2 Mary; *m* William Salisbury, of Rug, and had issue

Sir ROGER *m* 2nd by 1651 Mary (*d* 16 Oct 1662), dau of 1st Viscount Bulkeley of Cashel, and by her had, with other issue:

1 THOMAS (Sir), 2nd Bt

2 Richard, of Penbeddw, MA Oxon; *m* Charlotte Theophilia, dau of John Digby, of Gothurst, Bucks, and had two daus

Sir ROGER *m* 3rd Lumley (*dsp*), dau of — Coytmore, of Coytmore, Caernarvs, and *d* 4 Oct 1690

His est s,

Sir THOMAS MOSTYN, 2nd Bt; *b c* 1651; MP Caernarvon 1679–81, *m* Bridget, dau and heiress of Darcy Savage, of Leighton, Cheshire, through whom he acquired that estate, and *d* 1700, having had:

1 ROGER (Sir), 3rd Bt

2 Thomas; MP Flint, *m* Margaret, dau and heiress of William Mostyn, of Rhud, Flint, and *dsp* 21 Dec 1737

3 John; MA Oxon; *d* unm 24 Dec 1720

The est son,

Sir ROGER MOSTYN, 3rd Bt; MP Flint; *m* 20 July 1703 Essex (*d* 23 May 1721), dau of 7th Earl of Winchilsea and (2nd Earl of) Nottingham (*qv*), and *d* 5 May 1739, having had, with other issue:

1 Daniel; *dvp* 1733

2 THOMAS (Sir), 4th Bt

1 Essex; *m* 16 June 1739 2nd Duke of Roxburghe (*qv*) and *d* 7 Dec 1764, leaving issue

The est surv son,

Sir THOMAS MOSTYN, 4th Bt; MP Flint 1734–58; *m* 1735 Sarah (*d* 28 May 1740), dau and coheir of Robert Western, and *d* 24 March 1758, having had an er s:

1 Sir ROGER MOSTYN, 5th Bt; MP Flint 1758–96; Ld Lt Flint; *m* 19 May 1776 Margaret (*d* 14 Oct 1792), dau and heiress of Rev Hugh Wynne, LLD, Preb Salisbury, and *d* 26 July 1796, having had:

(1) Sir THOMAS MOSTYN, 6th Bt; MP Flint 1799–1831; *d* unm 17 April 1831, when the btcy expired and his estates passed to the LLOYDs (*see* above)

(1) Essex; *d* unm

(2) Charlotte; *m* 21 April 1792 Sir Thomas Swymmers Mostyn Champneys, 2nd Bt, and *dsp*

(3) ELIZABETH; *m* 11 Feb 1794 **Sir Edward Pryce Lloyd, 2nd Bt**, who was *cr* **Baron Mostyn of Mostyn** (*see* above)

(4) Anna Maria; *m* Sept 1801 Sir Robert Williames Vaughan, 2nd Bt (*see* 1850 edn), and had issue

(5) Catherine

(6) Bridget

MOSTYN, Bt

Arms: Per bend sinister erm. and ermines a lion rampant or.
Crest: A lion rampant or. **Mottoes:** 1 *Auxilium meum a Domino* ('My help is from the Lord'), 2 *Morte leonis vita* ('Life by the death of the lion'). **Creation:** Bt. (E) 28 April 1670.

SIR WILLIAM BASIL JOHN MOSTYN, 15TH BT, of Talacre, Co Flint [Sir William Mostyn Bt, The Coach House, Church Lane, Lower Heyford, Oxon]; *b* 15 Oct 1975; *s* f 1988

Lineage: TUDUR TREFOR (*see also* KENSINGTON, B); *b c* 900; *m* Angharad, dau of HYWEL *Dda* ('The Good'), KING OF WALES, and had:

LLUDDICA Ap TUDUR TREFOR; had:

LLYWARCH *Gam* ('The Lame') Ap LLUDDICA; had:

EDNYFED Ap LLYWARCH *Gam*; had:

RHYS SAIS; held the Manor of Whittington, Salop; also held some of the territory around Oswestry, Salop, and Maelor Gymraeg; *m* Efa, dau of Gruffudd *Hir* ('The Tall'), and had:

TUDUR Ap RHYS SAIS; *fl* 1078–86; held Nanheudwy from Roger Earl of Shrewsbury in 1086; also held Whittington till the Normans wrested it from him; had:

BLEDDYN Ap TUDUR; had:

OWAIN Ap BLEDDYN, of Pen-gwern, Llangollen; had:

YR *Hen* ('The Old') IORWERTH, of Pengwern; *b c* 1170; Steward N Powys; *m* Angharad, dau of Gruffudd ap Meilir Eutun, and was living 1236; had:

IORWERTH FYCHAN/GOEG; Steward N Powys; *m* Catherine, dau of Gruffudd ap Llywelyn, Prince of Gwynedd, and *d* by 1270, leaving:

IORWERTH FOEL, of Pengwern; rose against the English 1295 and 1300; *m* Gwladus, dau and heir of Iorwerth ap Griffri, and was living 1313; had:

EDNYFED GAM Ab IORWERTH FOEL; *m* Gwladus, dau of Llywelyn ap Madog, and was living 1341 (when he made over land at Halghton to his est s Llywelyn); had a yr s:

IORWERTH *Ddu* ('The Black'), of Pengwern; living 1332; *m* Angharad, dau and coheir of Adda *Goch* ('The Red') ab Ieuaf ab Adda, of Trefor, and had:

ADDA Ab IORWERTH *Ddu* ('The Dark'), of Pengwern; *m* Isabel, sister of OWEN GLENDOWER and dau of Gruffudd Fychan, and had:

IEUAN Ab ADDA, of Pengwern; living 1419; *m* Angharad, dau and heir of Ednyfed ap Tudor ap Gronwy, paternal uncle of Owen Tudor and yr s of Sir Tudor ap Grono, thus acquiring the Trecastell estate and other lands in Anglesey, and *d* probably by 1437, having had:

IEUAN FYCHAN Ab IEUAN, of Pengwern; Esq to Thomas Earl of Arundel 1415, served France 1421, Steward Ldship of Mostyn 1437; *m* Angharad, dau and coheir of Hywel ap Tudur, Sheriff Flints 1390, and had:

HYWEL Ap IEUAN FYCHAN, of Mostyn, Pengwern and Tregarnedd; living 1464; *m c* 1457 Margaret (*m* 2nd Henry Salesbury, of Llanrhaeadr-yng-Nghinmeirch, Denbighs), dau and heir of Gruffudd ap Rhys, of Gloddaith, Eglwys-rhos, and had:

RICHARD Ap HYWEL Ab IEUAN, of Mostyn, of which Steward 1502; *m* Catherine, dau of Thomas Salusbury Hen, of Lleweni, Henllan, Denbighs, and *d* 7 Feb 1539/40, having had, with two er sons (including Thomas; *see* MOSTYN, B):

PI(E)RS Ap RICHARD, of Talacre, Llanasa, Flints; *b c* 1495; took surname MOSTYN, High Sheriff Flints 1552; *m* Elen, dau of Thomas Griffith, of Pantyllongdy, Llanasa, and *d* by 13 June 1580, having had, with an er s (Pi(e)rs, of Talacre, *m* Lowri, dau of John Conwy, of Bodrhyddan (*see* LANGFORD, B), and *dsp*), five yst sons and seven daus (including Jane, *m* John Egerton, *see* GREY EGERTON, Bt):

WILLIAM MOSTYN, of Cornist 1558, afterwards of Maes-glas (*i.e.*, Greenfield), Holywell, Flints; High Sheriff Flints 1563 and 1575; *m c* 1540 Anne, dau and coheir of Harry ap Thomas Parry, of Maes-glas, with whom he acquired the houses and lands in the neighbourhood of Basingwerk Abbey, and *d* 1605, having had, with four yr sons and five daus:

EDWARD MOSTYN, of Talacre and Basingwerk; *b c* 1569; *m c* 1600 Elizabeth, dau of Edward Morgan, barrister, of Gwylgre or Gouldgreave, Llanasa, and *d* in or after 1632, havinghad, with a yr s and three daus:

JOHN MOSTYN, of Maes-glas; *m* 1st Ann, dau of Henry Fox, of Le Hurst, Salop, and had three sons and four daus; *m* 2nd — Peters and *d* 19 July 1634; his est s by his 1st w:

Sir Edward Mostyn, 1st Bt (E), so *cr* 28 April 1670, of Talacre; *b c* 1628 *m* 1st Elizabeth, dau of Robert Downes, of Bodney, Norfolk, and had, with other issue, a s and dau (Margaret, *m* —Fettiplace); *m* 2nd Eleanor (*dsp* 1685), widow of Thomas Poole, of Poole, Cheshire, and dau of Francis Draycott, of Staffs; *m* 3rd Mary (*dsp* and *bur* 28 Jan 1697/8), widow of Sir George Selby, of Wentingdon, Co Durham, and dau of 1st Viscount Molyneux of Maryborough (*see* 1970 edn SEFTON, E), and *d* 3 Nov 1706; his est surv s by his 1st w:

Sir Pyers Mostyn, 2nd Bt; *b c* 1655; *m* his cousin Frances, dau and coheir of Sir George Selby, 1st Bt, by Mary, dau of 1st Viscount Molyneux of Maryborough, and *d* 15 Nov 1720, leaving, with other issue:

1 **Sir Pyers Mostyn, 3rd Bt**; *d* unm 1735

2 **Sir George Mostyn, 4th Bt**; *m* 1st Mary (*dsp*), dau of Thomas Clifton, of Lytham, Lancs; *m* 2nd Theresa (*d* 27 March 1766), 1st dau of Charles Towneley, of Towneley, Lancs (*see* O'HAGAN, B), and by her had:

(1) EDWARD (Sir), **5th Bt**

(2) Pyers; *b* 1 Jan 1727

(3) Charles; *d* young

(4) Thomas; *b* 2 March 1732; *m* 1773 Mary Catharine, est dau of 10th Baron Teynham (*qv*)

(1) Mary; *m* 1752 Charles, 2nd s of 14th Earl of Shrewsbury and Waterford (*qv*)

(2) Elizabeth; *m* Henry Blundell and *d* 1767

Sir GEORGE *d* 30 Sept 1746; his est son,

Sir Edward Mostyn, 5th Bt; *b* 27 April 1725; *m* June 1748 Barbara (*m* 2nd Edward Gore), only dau and heiress of Sir George Browne, last Bt, of Kiddington,

Oxon, by Lady Barbara Lee, yst dau of 1st Earl of Lichfield of the 1674 cr (see LICHFIELD, E, preliminary remarks, also JERSEY, E), and had:

1 PYERS (Sir), **6th Bt**

2 Charles MOSTYN later BROWNE-MOSTYN (added under terms of will of Sir George Browne); b 21 Nov 1753; m 1st 1 July 1755 Elizabeth (dsps), dau of Henry Witham; m 2nd — Tucker, and d 19 Sept 1844, having by her had:

(1) Charles BROWNE-MOSTYN later MOSTYN; m 17 May 1801 Mary Lucinda (d 2 Dec 1831), dau and heiress of George Butler, of Ballyraggett, Co Kilkenny, and d 11 March 1821, leaving:

1a GEORGE CHARLES MOSTYN, 6th BARON VAUX OF HARROWDEN (qv)

1a Barbara Maria; m 1st 6 Oct 1825 Carl, Baron von Krober; m 2nd 23 Dec 1833 Sir Frederick William Slade, 2nd Bt (qv), and d 15 April 1885, leaving issue

(2) Henry, of Usk, Mon; b 1799; m 4 April 1825 Jane Caroline (d 9 Feb 1849), dau of William Bower, of Weymouth, and d 1 Aug 1845, leaving:

1a Charles; b 24 April 1840; m 22 Sept 1864 Jane (d 5 Nov 1934), dau of William Warren, of Cheltenham, and d 28 March 1922, leaving:

1b Charles, JP Somerset; b 1865; m 8 Oct 1913 Lilian Elaine (d 2 Feb 1962 aged 87), dau of Col Trevenen James Holland, CB, DL, and dsp 13 July 1935

2b Henry; b 1867; m 1901 Virginia (d 27 Nov 1953), dau of Thomas J McLain, US Consul Bahamas, and d 17 April 1946, having had:

1c Thomas Mervyn; b June 1904; m 1948 *Ella Aurora, dau of Gustaf Larson, of Washington, DC, and d 1988

1c Ruth Mary; b 3 Jan 1902; m 5 June 1931 Hughes Adams Shank (d 1968), s of James Nelson Shank, of College Park, Md., and d 1988, leaving:

1d *David Hughes; b 24 Oct 1941; m 18 April 1966 *Elaine Christina Furs and has:

1e *Michael Aaron; b 16 Nov 1969

2e *Jacob Adams; b 1981

1d *Margaret Elizabeth [Mrs Patrick Jarboe, PO Box 55, 17721 Rosecroft Rd, St Mary's City, MD 20686, USA]; b 14 Aug 1936; m 23 Aug 1958 *(James) Patrick Jarboe, MD, and has had:

1e Christopher Scott; b 7 Dec 1962; d an inf

2e *Thomas Hughes; b 15 July 1969; m 16 June 1990 *Shannon K Smith and has:

1f *Nicholas Killian; b 4 Feb 1993

1f *Christian Hunter; b 7 May 1995

1e *Karen Elizabeth; b 6 July 1959; m 25 July 1981 *Donald L Mumbert and has:

1f *David Noah; b 30 April 1985

2f *Daniel Reuben; b 14 Oct 1990

1f *Rachel Nicole; b 1 Dec 1986

2f *Hannah Elizabeth; b 11 Sept 1993

2e *Barbara Gail; b 31 Dec 1960; m 8 Sept 1984 *Robert K Brunner and has:

1f *Steven Matthew; b 2 Sept 1993

1f *Kelly Christina; b 16 Dec 1990

3e *Mary Kathleen; b 16 Feb 1965; m 22 July 1989 *Christopher David Cantwell and has:

1f *Camden Scott; b 27 Nov 1991

2f *Kent Thomas; b 17 Sept 1994

1f *Corene Ruth; b 28 Jan 1997

4e *Jessica Rose; b 5 Sept 1972; has:

1f *Alexander Christopher; b 4 Feb 1996

2c Myfanwy; b 1903; d 10 Nov 1925

3b Edward (Rev); b 1870; d unm 23 Feb 1936

4b Francis Llewellyn; b 1873; m 21 Dec 1901 Sarah Thornton (d 1925) and d 1959, leaving:

1c +Charles Francis Llewellyn; b 26 Sept 1904; m 20 Dec 1933 *Marion, dau of Angus McKay, and has had:

1d +Francis Llewellyn; Cpl RCAF; b 8 March 1935; m 1958 *Yvonne Brown and has:

1e +Douglas William Francis; b 10 May 1959

1e +Donald Mayne; b May 1960

1e *Patricia; b 13 March 1964

2d Edward Donald, RCAF; b 16 March 1936; d 4 April 1959

3d +Trevor Angus; b 21 Aug 1946; m 1966 *Doris De Rosier and has:

1e *Laurie Irene Grace; b 19 Sept 1966

2e *Dianna Lyn Carolyn; b 17 Oct 1967

1d *Gwendolyn Grace; b 1937; m 1958 *Leonard Alexander Gyulai, s of Alexander Gyulai, of Lethbridge, Alberta, and has had:

1e *Edward Llewellyn Alexander; b 28 July 1959

2e *Donald Leonard Trevor; b 8 Sept 1966

1e *Sarah Teresa Marion; b 12 Nov 1960

2e *Sandra Agnes Grace; b 19 Dec 1961

3e *Susan Julianne Gladys; b 15 March 1964

5b George William; Maj AIF; b 3 Aug 1875; m 2 Feb 1898 Isobel Almond and d 29 April 1939, having had:

1c +Vaux Almond [Maj Vaux Mostyn, 17 Frederick St, Glengowrie, S Australia]; b 1 April 1906; Maj AIF; m 1st 24 March 1933 Mavis Marshall (d 1958); m 2nd 1964 Monica Lewsey Jackson (d 1985)

1c Winifred May; b 22 Nov 1898; m 18 Feb 1922 Frederick Vincent Nelson (d 1954), of Black Forest, S Australia, and d 21 May 1984 leaving:

1d *Jack Mostyn; b 18 Nov 1925; m 28 Jan 1950 *Bernadine Creek and has:

1e *Warren John; b 23 April 1954; m 27 Oct 1984 *Robyn Kay Marker and has:

1f *Kate Jessica; b 30 Oct 1987

1f *Rachel Eileen; b 9 Dec 1994

1e *Jacqueline; b 16 April 1957; m 1st 16 April 1977 (divorce 19–) Malcolm Donald Cameron; m 2nd 5 Feb 1981 (divorce 19–) Brent James Farquhar and has by him:

1f *Gemma Blair; b 19 June 1984

2d Ronald O'Dea; b 15 June 1927; m 17 Sept 19– *Marjorie Catharine Edmonds and d 16 March 1988, leaving:

1e *Rodney Edmond; b 8 April 1954; m 18 Dec 1976 *Gloria Ruth Rautamara and has:

1f *Mahalia Catherine; b 3 March 1980

1e (cont.) Mr and Mrs Rodney Nelson also adopted:

*Vanessa Fay; b 14 Jan 1971

2e *Gary Francis; b 31 May 1963; has:

1f *Alexander Zavier; b 12 Nov 1992

3d Nelson Peter, MBE, BA; b 26 April 1931; m 7 Nov 1953 *Marjorie Jackson and d 2 Feb 1977, leaving:

1e *Alan; b 28 May 1961; m 3 Sept 1988 *Jeannie Shand and has:

1f *Andrew; b 8 March 1991

1e *Sandra; b 24 Oct 1957; m 1st 19– (divorce 19–) Desmond Corcoran and has:

1f *Dale; b 25 Sept 1982

2f *Stephanie Jeanette; b 19 Nov 1985

3f *Mardi Anne; b 1 Sept 1987

1e (cont.) Mrs Sandra Corcoran m 2nd 7 June 1997 *Dennis John Freeman

2e *Anne; b 15 March 1964; m 30 Sept 1995 *Bruno Wrzeszcynski and has:

1f *Jordan Tyler; b 16 April 1997

4d *Lindsay Frederick; b 25 Oct 1941; m 3 Nov 1962 *Marlies Elizabeth van der Linden and has had:

1e *Anthony John; b 24 July 1964; m 12 Jan 1985 *Raelene Hutchinson and has:

1f *Brent Tyler; b 20 Aug 1988

2f *Jake Conner; b 23 Jan 1995

1f *Dayna Bree; b 17 March 1988

2e *Ian Andrew; b 4 Aug 1966; m 23 Jan 1988 *Sonia Maria Fiocco and has:

1f *Kieren James; b 28 April 1994

1f *Monique Elise; b 27 March 1996

3e *David Mostyn; b 13 July 1967; m 26 Nov 1988 *Eileen Patricia O'Regan

4e Scott Lindsay; b 6 June 1972; d in an accident 18 July 1991

1d *Laurel Rosemary [Mrs Michael Brady, 2/1 Edinburgh St, Prospect, SA 5082, Australia]; b 12 Aug 1924; m 24 June 1944 Michael Francis Brady (d 17 Aug 1989) and has:

1e *Michael John Nelson; b 29 Jan 1946; m 4 Jan 1969 *Patricia Mary Browne and has:

1f *Matthew Michael O'Callahan; b 15 Jan 1970; m 17 Sept 1994

2f *Benjamin Thomas O'Callahan; b 22 Aug 1972

3f *Daniel Gerard O'Callahan; b 9 Nov 1973

4f *Joseph Terrence O'Callahan; b 20 Dec 1978

5f *John Christopher O'Callahan; b 18 Aug 1984

6f *Mark Samuel O'Callahan; b 30 May 1986

1f *Pamela Jennifer Morson; b 17 Aug 1970

2f *Patricia Michelle O'Callahan; b 5 June 1977

1e *Mariwyn Nelson; b 20 June 1948; m 17 Jan 1970 (divorce 19–) Richard Hoddle Gough and has:

1f *Catherine Tessa; b 9 Dec 1970

2e *Bernadette Nelson; b 19–

3e *Laurel-Frances Nelson; b 17 Dec 1964; m 26 Nov 1994 *Wesley Anthony Hosking and has:

1f *William Arthur; b 24 Jan 1998

2c Marjorie Frances; b 3 March 1902; m 1920 Norman Sanders and d 6 Dec 1930, leaving:

1d *Mostyn George; b 18 May 1928; m 19 Sept 1950 *Rae Grace Josling and has:

1e *Debra Rae; b 19 Feb 1953; m 19– *Michael Cain and has:

1f *John Corey Johnson; b 20 July 1973; m *Linder Harrison and has:

1g *Zachary Peter Johnson; b 16 Oct 1995

1g *Michell Mostyn Johnson; b 4 June 1997

2e *Vicki Lee; b 17 July 1959; m *Mervyn James Curtis and has:

1f *Bluey James; b 24 Feb 1980

2f *Dustin James; b 28 July 1984

1f *Libby Jo; b 7 Oct 1986

1d Betty Emerson; b 18 Feb 1926; m 16 July 1949 Frederick Edward Myers (d 18 Nov 1955) and has:

1e *Frederick Mostyn Myers; b 13 April 1950; m 3 July 1976 *Diana Cameron Whitehouse and has issue

2e *Russell Graham Myers; b 5 June 1951; m 17 Aug 1974 *Judith Isabel Godson and has issue

1d (cont.) Mrs Frederick Myers m 2nd 29 March 1960 (divorce 19–) Joseph Bock and has by him:

1e *Christopher James; b 14 Feb 1963

1e *Dallas Michelle; b 24 Dec 1961; m Oct 1987 *Anthony Ray Faull and has issue

2e *Kathryn Jane; b 2 April 1964

6b Arthur (Rev); RC priest; b 1876; d 25 Dec 1969

7b Iltyd Edward; *b* 1881; *m* 27 Nov 1901 Lily Humphrey (*d* 1984) and *d* 1958, leaving:

1c Iltyd Humphry; *b* 24 Sept 1907; *m* 2 Nov 1934 Joan Athol (*d* 1989), dau of Charles J Radwell, and *d* 1982, leaving:

1d +(David) Pyers [Pyers Mostyn Esq, 744 Lilac Drive, Parksville, BC V9P 1E6, Canada]; *b* 26 March 1938; *m* 9 Feb 1963 *Susan Wallace Johnson and has:

1e +Richard Pyers [Richard Mostyn Esq, 9 Magpie Rd, Whitehouse, Yukon YIA 5X5, Canada]; *b* 23 Dec 1963; *m* 1990 *Shona Sugrue and has:

1f +Richard Thomas; *b* 1994

2f +Liam Alexander; *b* 26 April 1996

2e +David Wallace; *b* 4 Feb 1967

1e +Peter Llewellyn; *b* 10 Aug 1968

2d +Richard Clive [Richard Mostyn Esq, 2510 W 1st Ave, Vancouver, BC V5M 1A3, Canada]; *b* 28 Aug 1945; *m* 1986 *Ursula Anna Schmiing

2c +Charles Gerard [Charles Mostyn Esq, 305-8840 No1 Rd, Richmond, BC V7C 4C1, Canada]; *b* 30 Oct 1910; *m* 12 Sept 1936 Ruth Winona (*d* 1988), dau of William Brown, and has:

1d +Trevor Illtyd [Trevor Mostyn Esq, 380 Hidhurst Pl, W Vancouver, BC V7S 1K1, Canada]; *b* 6 Oct 1940; *m* 1979 *Sarah Katherine Ford

1c Gwendolyn Mary; *b* 12 Jan 1905; *m* 1939 *Charles Allen Higginson and *d* 1996, leaving:

1d *Brenda Lynne [Mrs Kirby O'Donaughy, DDS, Box 276, Rossland, BC, Canada]; *b* 2 Oct 1940; *m* Aug 1963 *Kirby Michael O'Donaughy and has:

1e *Denise Margaret; *b* 1964

2e *Theresa Lynne; *b* 1967

3e *Kelly Corinne; *b* 1969

2d *Kathleen Mary [Mrs Lorne Simpson, 5900 Unsworth Rd, Sardis, BC V2R 4P5, Canada]; *b* 5 Sept 1942; *m* Sept 1962 *Lorne Richard Simpson and has:

1e *Thomas Allen [Thomas Simpson Esq, 10121-172nd Street, Surrey, BC V4N 4W6, Canada]; *b* March 1968; *m* Sept 1992 *Christina Ann Reyna

1e *Barbara Kathleen [Mrs Robert Taylor, 8517 Jellicoe St, Vancouver, BC V5S 4T5, Canada]; *b* Dec 1964; *m* July 1995 *Robert Dennis Taylor

1b Mary; *d* 1932

2b Margaret Emma

3b Frances Mary (twin); *d* unm 16 May 1957

4b Winifred; *d* 1934

1a Caroline; *m* 7 Sept 1847 Llewelyn Mostyn (*see* below) and *d* 1897, leaving issue

(3) Francis (Rt Rev); RC Bp; *d* 11 Aug 1847

(1) Winefred; *m* 15 Feb 1821 Hugh O'Connor, of Dublin, and *d* 13 March 1852, leaving issue

(2) Louisa; *d* unm

Sir EDWARD was *bur* March 1775; his er son,

Sir Pyers Mostyn, 6th Bt; *b* 23 Dec 1749; *m* 1780 Barbara Slaughter (*d* 2 Oct 1815), of Ingatestone, Essex, and *d* 29 Oct 1823, leaving:

Sir Edward Mostyn, 7th Bt; High Sheriff Flints 1837; *b* 10 April 1785; *m* 1st 20 Oct 1808 Frances (*d* 25 Jan 1825), dau of Nicholas Blundell, of Crosby Hall, Lancs, and had, with other issue:

1 PYERS (Sir), **8th Bt**

2 Edward Henry, JP, DL Flints; Capt 8th Hus; *b* 14 Jan 1813; *m* 16 May 1848 Anastasia Elizabeth (*d* 23 Nov 1893), widow of Edward Joseph Smythe and dau of Sir John Fenton Boughey, 2nd Bt (*qv*), and *d* 23 Feb 1895, having had:

(1) Edward Henry Joseph, JP Sussex; Lt-Col 4th Bn Royal Sussex Regt; *b* 27 Feb 1857; *m* 21 July 1886 Mary Cecily (*d* 22 Nov 1916), dau of John Reginald Francis George Talbot (*see* TALBOT OF MALAHIDE, B), and *das* 1 Aug 1916, having had:

1a Joseph Edward Hubert, TD; *b* 14 Dec 1888; *educ* Downside; FLAS, Capt 4th Royal Sussex Regt TA WW I; *m* 1 June 1920 (Gertrude) Clare, dau of John Hutchinson, of Appleton, Lancs, and *d* 18 Dec 1960, leaving:

1b +Edward John, TD [Edward Mostyn Esq TD, Rosemary Cottage, Chapel Row, Bucklebury, Berks RG7 6P3]; *b* 3 Jan 1922; *educ* Ampleforth; QALAS, Capt RA (TA), F/Lt RAFVR WW II (despatches), Hon Research Fell Reading U; *m* 15 June 1945 *Dorothy Brady and has had:

1c +Francis Edward Terence; *b* 24 May 1946

2c +Stephen John; *b* 24 July 1949

1c Sara Juliet; *b* 1955; *d* 19–

2a Joseph Cecil Mary, MC; *b* 2 May 1891; *educ* Downside; Maj RA WW I (despatches), NW Frontier Prov 1931 and WW II; *m* 27 Feb 1924 Joan Wake (*d* 21 July 1975), 2nd dau of Guy Shorrock, of Sandford Orleigh, Newton Abbot, and *d* 11 July 1971, having had:

1b Michael Joseph James; *b* 29 Sept 1925; *d* 1926

2b +Jerome John Joseph [Jerome Mostyn Esq, c/o Lloyds Bank plc, 4 Dean Stanley St, London SW1P 3HU]; *b* 21 July 1933; *educ* Downside; *m* 1st 29 Sept 1956 (*divorce* 1971) Mary Anna Bridget Ghislaine, est dau of Ronald Francis Medlicott, of Lane House, King's Walden, Hitchin, Herts, and has issue:

1c +Nicholas Anthony Joseph Ghislain [Nicholas Mostyn Esq, 10 Regents Parks Terr, London NW1 7EE]; *b* 13 July 1957; *educ* Ampleforth; barrister 1980, QC 1997, Assist Recorder 1997; *m* 25 April 1981 *Lucy Joanna, yst dau of John Hodgson Willis, of Wressle House, Brigg, Lincs, and has:

1d +Henry Francis Joseph Ghislain; *b* 17 May 1987

2d +Gregory Thomas Joseph Ghislain; *b* 7 April 1985

1d *Daisy Catherine Mary Ghislaine; *b* 24 July 1989

2c +Mark Francis Joseph Ghislain [Mark Mostyn Esq, 49 Wandsworth Bridge Rd, London SW6 2TB]; *b* 9 Nov 1959

3c +Giles Patrick Joseph Ghislain; *b* 6 March 1967

1c *Joanna Charlotte Mary Ghislaine; *b* 4 May 1963

2b (cont.) Jerome Mostyn *m* 2nd 29 June 1972 Ana Julia (*d* 29 Jan 1980), yst dau of Dr Julio Oscar Novoa, of San Salvador, El Salvador, and by her has:

4c +Philip Anthony Julio Jerome; *b* 31 May 1978

2c *Anna Teresa Joan; *b* 7 July 1973

2b (cont.) Jerome Mostyn *m* 3rd 16 April 1981 Margaret Joyce Cullen (*neé* Plowright); *m* 4th 1988 *Rosemary Joy Hamilton, widow of (Alan) Ross McWhirter and dau of Leslie C H Hamilton Grice

1b *Philomena Mary Cecilia [Mrs Hugh Symon, 8 Upper Brook St, Oswestry, Salop SY11 2TB]; *b* 6 Nov 1926; *m* 18 June 1949 Hugh Dudley Symon (*d* 1980), MA, MRCS, LRCP, only s of Canon Dudley James Symon, of The Mount, Felixstowe, and St Anne's House, Soho, and has:

1c *Anthony Nicholas Dudley; *b* 11 Sept 1950

2c *Neil Anthony; *b* 10 July 1953; *m* 1981 *Victoria Alison Edwards

3c *Pyers Hugh; *b* 4 May 1957; U of Wales (BSc); *m* 1986 *Patricia Mary Roberts

2b *Charmian Mary [Mrs Guy Cooper, c/o Nat Westminster Bank, 39 The Borough, Farnham, Surrey GU9 7NR]; *b* 16 April 1938; *m* 10 Sept 1966 Guy Hipsley Cooper (*d* following an accident 1986) and has:

1c *Tarquin Rupert Christopher Mostyn; *b* 10 April 1975

1c *Sophie Maria; *b* 22 Dec 1968

2c *Jonquil Kate; *b* 27 Jan 1971

3c *Alice Teresa Mostyn; *b* 1972

3a Joseph Philip David; Lt Roy Sussex Regt; *b* 2 June 1894; *m* 31 Jan 1928 Mary Catherine (*m* 2nd 1931 Brig James Desmond Seymour Keenan (*d* Feb 1996) and *d* Jan 1995), dau of Richard Cecil Moss, and *d* 17 Jan 1929, leaving:

1b +(Joseph) David Frederick (Sir), KCB (1983), CBE (1974, MBE 1961) [Gen Sir David Mostyn KCB CBE, c/o Lloyds Bank, Broad St, Lyme Regis, Dorset DT7 3QR]; *b* 28 Nov 1928; *educ* Downside and RMA Sandhurst; Gen RGJ, despatches Brunei 1963, GOC Berlin 1980–83, Mil Sec 1983–86, Adj Gen MOD 1986–88, Col Cmdt Light Div 1983–86, Army Legal Corps 1983–88, Kt SMO Malta 1995, Aide de Camp Gen to HM THE QUEEN 1987–89; *m* 13 Dec 1952 *Patricia Diana Patricia, dau of Col Bertrand Cecil Owens Sheridan, MC, and has:

1c +Philip Joseph; *b* 3 Sept 1955; *educ* Downside; Lt-Col; *m* 1985 *Helen Catharine Stewart, dau of Maj George Stewart Nickerson, of Cour, by Campbeltown, Argyll, and has:

1d *Isobel Mary; *b* 1987

2d *Alice Mary; *b* 1989

3d *Rosanna Mary; *b* 1990

4d *Clare Mary; *b* 1993

2c +(David) Mark Joseph; *b* 19 March 1960; *m* 1989 *Jane Carolyn, dau of J W Rhodes, of Melbourne, Australia, and has:

1d +Joshua Marcus Joseph; *b* 1991

2d +William Joseph; *b* 1992

3d *Georgia Mary; *b* 15 Sept 1995

3c +Rupert Joseph Sheridan; *b* 31 May 1961

4c +Matthew Anthony; *b* 11 July 1971

1c *Celia Mary; *b* 8 Nov 1953

2c *Katherine Mary; *b* 1973

4a Joseph John Reginald Henry (Most Rev); Prothonotary Apostolic, DCL Rome 1929, Canon St Peter's Rome 1953, Kt SMO Malta, Cdr Order Leopold II Belgium; *b* 5 Jan 1903; *educ* Downside and Fribourg U (PhD 1925); *d* 1982

1a Mary Philomena; *m* 17 Oct 1933 Capt Thomas Tyrrhitt-Drake (*d* 22 March 1956), MC, 52nd LI, of Shardeloes, Amersham, and *dsp* 4 Nov 1953

2a Mary Anastasia Elizabeth; *m* 18 Nov 1920 R-Adml James Sacheverell Constable Salmond (*d* 1958), only s of Lt-Col Albert Louis Salmond, and *dsp* 2 March 1946

3a Mary Clare, twin with Anastasia; *m* 26 June 1929 Capt Stephen Francis Gaisford-St Lawrence, RN (*d* 30 Sept 1957), 2nd s of Julian Charles Gaisford-St Lawrence, of Howth, Co Dublin, and *d* 27 May 1985, leaving issue

4a Mary Margaret; *m* 20 April 1922 (*divorce* 1930) Lt-Cdr Lionel Carol Ansdell, RN, and *d* following an accident at sea 6 May 1953, leaving issue

5a Mary Teresa, twin with her sister Margaret; *m* 1st 27 Feb 1919 (*divorce* 1929) Cdr Christopher Dalrymple-Hay, DSC, RN, and has issue (*see* DALRYMPLE-HAY, Bt); *m* 2nd 26 Jan 1939 Capt Charles Hugh Fletcher, 60th Rifles, s of Arthur Charles Fletcher, of Dale Park, Slindon, Sussex, and by him had:

1b *Sarah Anne; *b* 29 Oct 1940; *m* 26 June 1964 *Robin Cursham, s of Capt Miles Cursham, RN, of Tremlett Hall, Greenham, Wellington, Somerset

(1) Mary Josephine; nun; *b* 16 May 1849

(2) Frances Barbara; *b* 25 Sept 1850; *d* 15 Jan 1922

(3) Teresa Anastasia; *b* 6 Feb 1855; *d* 1 Nov 1876

3 Llewelyn; *b* 22 June 1816; *m* 7 Sept 1847 Caroline, only dau of Henry Mostyn, of Usk (*see* above), and *d* 1897, leaving issue

4 William; *b* 2 Aug 1823; *m* 6 June 1861 Clementina (*d* 7 Dec 1925), 4th dau of Edmund William Jerningham (*see* STAFFORD, B), and *d* 1909

1 Barbara; *m* 22 Oct 1829 Charles Stanley Massey Stanley, bro of Sir Thomas Stanley, 9th Bt

2 Frances; *m* 17 June 1844 Edward Slaughter (*d* 1862) and *d* 26 March 1859

Sir Edward *m* 2nd 2 Aug 1826 his cousin Constantia (*d* 12 Dec 1872), 3rd dau of Henry Slaughter, of Furze Hall, Essex, and had, with other issue:

5 Roger Joseph; *b* 1840; *m* 12 Jan 1870 Mary (*d* 1885), est dau of Thomas Aloysius Perry, of Bitham House, Warwicks, and *d* 31 Jan 1911, leaving:

(1) Roger Joseph Francis; *b* 1871; *m* 1899 Mary Catherine Frances, dau of Lawrence John Macnamara, MD, of Moyriesk, Torquay, and *d* 27 Jan 1924

(2) Charles Aloysius; *b* 1873; *d* 1877

3 Winifred; *m* 10 July 1851 William Simpson (*d* 1888) and *d* 3 April 1898

4 Teresa; *m* 18 Sept 1853 Francis Whitgreave, JP, DL, of Burton Manor, Staffs, and *d* 17 Aug 1873, leaving issue

5 Mary Pauline; *m* 7 Oct 1862 Richard Lerins de Bary (*d* 1891), of Weston Hall, Nuneaton, Warwicks, and had issue

6 Agnes; nun

7 Catherine; nun

Sir EDWARD *d* 18 July 1841; his est son,

Sir Pyers Mostyn, 8th Bt, High Sheriff Flintshire 1843; *b* 27 Sept 1811; *m* 9 May 1844 Hon Frances Georgiana Fraser (*d* 25 Dec 1899), 2nd dau of 14th Lord (Fraser of) Lovat (*qv*), and *d* 14 May 1882, having had:

1 **Sir Pyers William Mostyn, 9th Bt**, JP, DL Flints; High Sheriff 1893; *b* 14 Aug 1846; *m* 4 Nov 1880 Anna Maria (*d* 11 June 1916), 5th dau of Thomas Aloysius Perry, DL, of Bitham House, Warwicks, and *d* 10 May 1912, leaving:

(1) **Sir Pyers Charles Mostyn, 10th Bt**; *b* 13 Aug 1895; *d* unm 16 Jan 1917

(1) Helen Mary Winefride; *d* unm 1 April 1946

(2) Clementina Mary; *d* unm 18 Sept 1960

(3) Agnes Margaret Mary; *m* 3 Oct 1911 Col Percy Reginald Worrall (*d* 29 Nov 1950), CBE, DSO, MC, Devonshire Regt, s of William Henry Worrall, of Eastcombe House, Barnstaple, and had issue

2 George Trevor Basil; Lt HLI; *b* 13 June 1857; *m* 1st 12 May 1891 Augusta Mary Geraldine (*d* 28 Sept 1893), est dau of Capt William Gerard Walmesley, 17th Lancers, and had:

(1) **Sir Pyers George Joseph Mostyn, 11th Bt**, MC, JP; Capt Roy Welch Fus WW I (despatches, wounded, 2nd Cl Order St Anne Russia); *b* 28 Aug 1893; *m* 29 Nov 1927 Margery (*d* 15 May 1982 aged 86), only dau of Alfred Stanley Marks, of Sydney, NSW, and *d* 28 Feb 1937, leaving:

1a **Sir Pyers Edward Mostyn, 12th Bt**; *b* 12 July 1928; *k* in a car crash 11 Feb 1955

1a *Margaret Claire; *b* 9 Sept 1931

(1) Geraldine Mary Frances; *m* 10 June 1920 (*annulled* 1927) Capt Simon Edwin Henry Orde (*d* 23 April 1953), RAF

2 (cont.) George Mostyn *m* 2nd 30 April 1901 Mary Hermione (*d* 14 March 1955), dau of Augustus Henry de Trafford (*see* DE TRAFFORD, Bt), and *d* 16 April 1913, having by her had:

(2) BASIL ANTHONY TREVOR (Sir), **13th Bt**

(3) George Augustus Francis; *b* 9 June 1911; *educ* The Oratory Sch; Maj Roy Welch Fus WW II (despatches)

(2) Miriam; *b* 14 July 1904; *m* 16 June 1931 George Moorhead (*d* 18 July 1965), 3rd s of Henry Moorhead, JP, MD, of Moate, Co Westmeath, and had issue

(3) *Hermione Mary Josephine; *b* 18 March 1906; *m* 1942 Col Joseph TUZINKIEWICZ later MOSTYN (deed poll on naturalisation 1949), Polish Army (*d* 11 April 1969), and has:

1a *Richard Jan Joseph [Richard Mostyn Esq, Old Manor Farm, Broughton, Aylesbury, Bucks]; *b* 11 Aug 1942; *m* 10 Sept 1966 *Annette, dau or Maj Miles Alfred Garrick, of Kennel Cottage, Herriard, Hants, and has:

1b *Suki Hermione; *b* 22 April 1968

2b *Melissa Bernadette; *b* 18 Aug 1970

3b *Chloe Mary; *b* 1975

2a *Paul [Paul Mostyn Esq, Mill Hook Farm, Granborough, Bucks]; *b* 8 Oct 1945; *m* 1971 *Elizabeth Catherine Bernadette, dau of Peter Northcote Lunn, CMG, OBE, of Lebanon Park, Twickenham, by Hon Eileen Antionette Mary, only dau of 15th Viscount Gormanston (*qv*), and has:

1b *Toby Joseph; *b* 1975

1b *Theresa Antionette; *b* 23 May 1973

2b *Olivia Mary; *b* 1977

3a *Simon Edward Basil [Simon Mostyn Esq, Kings Court, Talley, Dyfed]; *b* 14 June 1947; *m* 1973 *Alison Mary Bridget, dau of Capt J Thomas, RN, and has:

1b *Samuel John Savage; *b* 1975

2b *Freddy Joseph George; *b* 1980

3b *Harry Edward Llewelyn; *b* 1987

1b *Polly Elizabeth Hermione; *b* 1973

2b *Meg Joan Elizabeth; *b* 1983

1a *Wanda Krystyna Hermione; *b* 11 Aug 1942; *m* 4 April 1964 *Terence Percyvall Hart Dyke, Roy Dragoons (*see* DYKE, Bt), and has issue

(4) Evelyn Margaret Mary; *b* 19 Aug 1909; *m* 24 Oct 1934 Capt Richard Somers Angus Hardy, Gren Gds, and had issue

3 Thomas Alexander Joseph; *b* 7 March 1859; *m* 1904 Marguerite, dau of Reynolds Probasco

4 Francis Edward (Most Rev); RC priest, Vicar Apostolic Wales, Bp Ascalon 1895–98, Menevia 1898-1921, Archbp Cardiff 1921-38; *b* 6 Aug 1860; *d* 25 Oct 1939

5 Nicholas Joseph; *b* 17 June 1865; *d* 9 Aug 1888

1 Charlotte Mary Barbara; *m* 24 Aug 1871 4th Viscount Southwell (*qv*) and *d* 4 Feb 1929, leaving issue

2 Margaret Elizabeth; *m* 4 Oct 1882 Henry McKenna and *d* 13 Feb 1925

3 Mary Louisa; *d* unm 2 April 1933

4 Clementina Frances; *m* 20 Nov 1879 Sigismund Cathcart de Trafford (*see* DE TRAFFORD, Bt) and *d* 4 June 1937, leaving issue

5 Gertrude Winefride; nun; *d* 16 Feb 1933

The 12th Bt's uncle,

Sir Basil Anthony Trevor Mostyn, 13th Bt; *b* 6 Feb 1902; *educ* Stonyhurst and Pembroke Coll Cambridge; Lt RASC; *m* 1st 10 June 1931 (*divorce* 1949) Anita

Mary, 2nd dau of Lt-Col Rowland Charles Feilding, DSO (*see* DENBIGH and DESMOND, E), and had:

1 JEREMY JOHN ANTHONY (Sir), **14th Bt**

2 +TREVOR ALEXANDER RICHARD [Trevor Mostyn Esq, 39B Elgin Crescent, London W11 2JD]; *b* 23 May 1946; heir presumptive; *educ* Oratory Sch and Edinburgh U; with EC Directorate Gen of External Rels; *m* 1986 (*divorce* 1988) Elizabeth, dau of Peter Dax

1 *Sara Ann [Mrs Ranjit Banerji, 7 London Place, Oxford OX4 1BD]; *b* 6 June 1932; *m* 4 March 1957 *Ranjit Banerji and has:

(1) *Bijoya [Mrs Ian Chisholm 10 Molescroft Park, Beverley, Humberside HU17 7EA]; *b* 1957; *m* 1983 *Ian Chisholm and has:

1a *Rory; *b* 1989

1a *Anna; *b* 1987

(2) *Sabita [Ms Sabita Banerji, 87 Lytton Rd, Oxford OX4 3NY]; *b* 1961; *m* 1989 Arild Bergh (*divorce* 1997) and has:

1a *Maia; *b* 1994

(3) *Juthika [Mrs David Slaughter, Penny Cottage, London Rd, Henfield, W Sussex BN5 9JJ]; *b* 1963; *m* 1987 *David Nicholas Slaughter

2 *Joanna Mary Patricia [Mrs Hugh Griffith, La Mariscala 315, San Isidro, Lima 27, Peru]; *b* 2 April 1939; *m* 4 Jan 1960 *Hugh Edward Sarne Griffith, er s of Hugh O Griffith, of Chaclacayo, Peru, and has:

(1) *Hugh Pyers Sarne [Hugh Griffith Esq, 5 St Dunstan's Rd, London W6]; *b* 1962

(1) *Isolde Gemma Sarne [Mrs Ian Georgeson, Flat 3, 355 Argyle St, Glasgow G2 8LT]; *b* 1961; *m* 1988 *Ian Aitken Georgeson

(2) *Bronwen Anita; *b* 1963

(3) *Samantha Joanna; *b* 1967

(4) *Phoebe Abigail; *b* 1976

Sir Basil *m* 2nd 1949 Elizabeth Margaret (*m* 3rd 1959 (*divorce* 1966; resumed maiden name by deed poll 19 Dec 1967) David George Longman), formerly w of Maj Roderick Walter Sholto Douglas (*see* MORTON, E) and est dau of Stephen Clement Paston Cooper (*see* COOPER, Bt, of Gadebridge), and *d* 19 March 1956

Sir BASIL's er son,

Sir Jeremy John Anthony Mostyn, 14th Bt; *b* 24 Nov 1933; *educ* Downside and St George's Coll Salisbury, Rhodesia; *m* 23 June 1963 *Cristina Beatrice Maria [Lady Mostyn, The Coach House, Church Lane, Lower Heyford, Oxon OX6 3NZ], dau of Marchese Pier Paolo Orengo, of La Mortola di Ventimiglia, Italy, and *d* 1988, leaving:

1 Sir WILLIAM BASIL JOHN MOSTYN, **15th and present Bt**

1 *Casimira Anita Maria; 3 Dec 1964

2 *Rachel Joanna Maria; *b* 26 Aug 1967

MOTT

Arms: Sa. four crescents in cross, the horns turned inwards arg.
Crest: An estoile of eight points arg. encircled by an annulet or.
Badge: A leopard's head erased affrontée ppr., holding in the mouth a crescent arg. and enfiled with a circlet or. **Motto:** *In periculis audax* ('Bold in dangers'). **Creation:** Bt. (UK) 25 June 1930.

SIR JOHN HARMAR MOTT, 3RD BT, of Ditchling, Co Sussex [Sir John Mott Bt, Staniford, Brookside, Kingsley, Cheshire WA6 8BG]; *b* 21 July 1922; *s* f 1964; *educ* Radley, New Coll Oxford (MA 1948, BM and BCh 1951) and Middx Hosp (MRCGP 1958); F/O RAF 1943–46, Regnl MO DHSS 1969–84, House Physician Middx Hosp 1951 (House Surgn 1952); *m* 24 Nov 1950 *Elizabeth, only dau of Hugh Carson, FRCS, of Harborne, Birmingham, and has:

1 +DAVID HUGH; *b* 1 May 1952; *educ* Shrewsbury, Sussex U (BSc), Birkbeck Coll London U (MSc) and Queen Mary Coll London U (PhD); *m* 1980 *Amanda Jane, only dau of Lt-Cdr D W P Fryer, RN, and has:

(1) +Matthew David; *b* 1982

(2) +Jonathan William; *b* 1984

1 *Jennifer; *b* 5 May 1954; *m* 1977 *Robert Alexander Buckey and has:

(1) *Mark Robert; *b* 1981

(2) *James John; *b* 1983

2 *Alison Mary; *b* 13 June 1958; *educ* Southampton U (BM); MRCP; has:

(1) *Jack Lewis Mott KINNERSLEY; *b* 1993

(1) *Anna Morag Mott KINNERSLEY; *b* 1995

Lineage: JULIUS MOTT, of Shellthorpe Cottage, nr Loughborough, *d* 11 Nov 1859, leaving:

FREDERICK THOMPSON MOTT, of Birstall Hill, Leics; *b* 24 March 1825; *m* 1850 Elizabeth Ann (*d* 14 Feb 1861), dau of Isaac Dobell, and *d* 14 March 1908, leaving:

1 Herbert Henry; *b* 19 May 1851; *m* 8 Jan 1880 Amelia Anne, dau of John Cornish, and had:

(1) Percival; *b* 11 June 1890; *educ* Boston U; *m* Annie Louise Hopkins, of Boston

2 Frederick Blount; *b* 3 May 1856; *m* 1886 Maud Pentecost and had issue

3 BASIL (Sir), **1st Bt**

1 Mary Eliza; *m* 10 April 1877 Maj Horace Walter Plant, *s* of Benjamin Plant

The 3rd son,

Sir Basil Mott, 1st Bt (UK), so *cr* 25 June 1930, CB (1918); *b* 16 Sept 1859; consulting civil engr, MICE (sometime Pres), ARSM, FRS, Fell Imp Coll Sci and Technology 1933; *m* 9 April 1887 Florence Harmar (*d* 21 July 1923), dau of William Parker, and had:

1 ADRIAN SPEAR (Sir), **2nd Bt**

2 Mark Dobell; civil engr; *b* 15 July 1892, *m* 1st 4 April 1916 (*divorce* 1936) Mary Coryndon, dau of James Henry Greathead; *m* 2nd 21 March 1936 *Martha Lewis, 2nd dau of Arthur Willis, of Witton Gilbert, Co Durham, and *d* 1975, having by her had:

(1) +Peter Lewis; *b* 21 Aug 1944; *educ* Ellesmere Coll Salop, Manchester U (BA 1966) and U of California (MA 1967)

(1) *Diana Dobell; *b* 30 Aug 1947

Sir BASIL *d* 7 Sept 1938; his er son,

Sir Adrian Spear Mott, 2nd Bt; *b* 5 Oct 1889; *educ* Radley and Merton Coll Oxford (BA 1912, MA 1930); barrister Inner Temple 1915, publisher, Capt RFA WW I; *m* 23 July 1914 Mary Katherine (*d* 13 May 1972 aged 88), est dau of Rev Alfred Herbert Stanton, Vicar St Peter-in-the-East, Oxford, and *d* 23 May 1964, leaving:

1 Sir JOHN HARMAR MOTT, **3rd and present Bt**

1 *Anne Lawrence [Mrs David Hodges, Kerensa, 3 Chute Lane, Gorran Haven, St Austell, Cornwall]; *b* 2 Aug 1915, *educ* St Anne's Coll Oxford (MA), *m* 1st 23 Nov 1939 W/Cdr Anthony Dockray Phillips, DSO, DFC, RAF (*ka* 4 July 1944), *s* of Christopher James Phillips, of Oxford, and has:

(1) *Anthony Adrian [Anthony Phillips Esq, Teddington House, Warminster, Wilts]; *b* 27 Aug 1942, *educ* Shrewsbury and Merton Coll Oxford (BA), *m* 1970 *Lucinda Aris and adopted:

*Anthony Julian; *b* 1980

*Katherine Mary; *b* 1979

1 (cont.) Mrs Anthony Phillips *m* 2nd 19 Jan 1946 (*divorce* 1961) F/Lt Wilfred Robert Peasley, DFC, *s* of Hugh Wilfred Peasley, of London, and by him has:

(1) *Patricia Mary Anne [Mrs Peter Crowe, Tregarth, 28 Chute Lane, Gorran Haven, Cornwall PL26 6NU]; *b* 12 March 1947; *m* 1 June 1968 *Peter James Crowe, *s* of George Albert Crowe, of W Ewell, Surrey, and has:

1a *Tasman Peter; *b* 11 Nov 1968

2a *James Aylwyn; *b* 1971

3a *Matthew Tristan George; *b* 1973

1a *Elena Catherine; *b* 1975

(2) *Julia Jane; *b* 2 June 1950; *m* 5 July 1969 (*divorce* 1988) Alan Nigel Clark, *s* of Lawrence William Clark, of Walton-on-Thames, Surrey, and has:

1a *Alexander Edward; *b* 1977

2a *Dominic; *b* 1979

3a *Justin; *b* 1982

(3) *Lydia Elizabeth; *b* 4 March 1953; *m* 1973 (*divorce* 1988) David Charles Whetter and has:

1a *Timothy Andrew; *b* 1978

2a *Thomas Charles; *b* 1985

1a *Donna Marie; *b* 1980

1 (cont.) Mrs Anne Peasley *m* 3rd 1983 *David John Hodges

2 Monica Mary; *b* 22 Sept 1919; *m* 1st 17 April 1948 (*divorce* 1978) Robert Milne Sellar, *s* of Robert Thomson Sellar, of Hamewith, Huntly, Aberdeenshire, and *d* Oct 1994, leaving:

(1) *Robert John; *b* 8 Dec 1950; *educ* Rugby and St Thomas's Hosp Medical Sch

(1) *Mary Milne [Mrs Robin Webb, Hill House, Holcombe, nr Bath BA3 5EF]; *b* 4 April 1949; *m* 1970 *Robin Edward Austin Webb and has:

1a *William Austin; *b* 1972

2a *Robert; *b* 1975

3a *George; *b* 1978

1a *Rachael Frances; *b* 1971

2a *Julia; *b* 1984

2 (cont.) Mrs Monica Sellar *m* 2nd 1978 *John Linfield

3 Elizabeth Fettiplace; *b* 25 April 1930; *d* 19 Nov 1939

MOTTISTONE

Arms: Az. three ears of wheat, banded or, between two martlets in pale, and as many chaplets of roses in fess arg. **Crest:** In front of three ears of wheat, banded or, the trunk of a tree fesswise eradicated, and sprouting to the dexter, ppr. **Supporters:** On either side a sea horse az., gorged with a mural crown and charged on the shoulder with a maple leaf or. **Motto:** *In Deo spero* ('I put my hope in God'). **Creation:** B. (UK) 21 June 1933.

THE 4TH BARON MOTTISTONE, of Mottistone, Co Southampton (David Peter Seely, CBE (1984) [Capt The Rt Hon The Lord Mottistone CBE RN, The Old Parsonage, Mottistone, IoW PO30 4EE]; *b* 16 Dec 1920 (HRH THE late DUKE OF WINDSOR stood sponsor); *s* half-bro 1966; *educ* RNC Dartmouth; Capt RN (ret at own request 1967), served WW II, cmded HMS *Cossack* Far East Fleet 1958–59, Dep Dir Signal Div Admlty 1961–63, cmded 24th Escort Sqdn and HMS *Ajax* Far East Fleet 1964–65, served Malaysian anti-confrontation ops 1964–65 (despatches), RN Liaison Offr Ottawa 1965, Dir Distributive Industry Trg Bd 1969–75 and Cake & Biscuit Alliance 1975–82, Ld Lt IoW 1985–95 (DL 1981–85), Govr IoW 1992–95, FIMgt, FIEE, FIPM, FRCSoc, chm Bureau Applied Sciences 1987–91, Dir Associated Info Servs 1987–90, Hon DLitt Bournemouth U 1993, KStJ 1989; *m* 16 Sept 1944 *Anthea Christine, er dau of (Thomas) Victor Wallace McMullan, of Bangor, Co Down, and has had:

1 +PETER JOHN PHILIP [The Hon Peter Seely, Alendale, Uckfield Lane, Hever, Kent TN8 7LJ]; *b* 29 Oct 1949 (HRH THE DUKE OF EDINBURGH stood sponsor); *educ* Uppingham; *m* 1st 26 May 1972 (*divorce* 1975) Joyce, dau of Robert Cairns, of Stirling, and has:

(1) +Christopher David Peter; *b* 1 Oct 1974

1 (cont.) The Hon PETER SEELY *m* 2nd 1982 *Linda, dau of W Swain, of Judds House, Bulphan Fen, Upminster, Essex, and by her has:

(2) +Richard William Anthony; *b* 1988

(1) *Penelope Jane; *b* 1984

(2) *Jennifer Elizabeth; *b* 1986

(3) *Caroline Mary; *b* 1990

2 +Patrick Michael [The Hon Patrick Seely, The Old Rectory, Brook, IoW PO30 4EU]; *b* 12 Oct 1960; *educ* Harrow and Trin Coll Cambridge; *m* 1984 *Susannah Shelley, dau of Cdr J C Q Johnson, RN, of Brook, IoW, and has:

(1) +Thomas Charles Rupert; *b* 1989

(1) *Clementine Mary; *b* 1991

1 Penelope Caroline; *b* 20 June 1947; *d* 30 Nov 1955

2 *Diana Mary [The Hon Mrs Nicholson, Staple Ash House, Froxfield Green, Hants, GU32 1DH]; *b* 30 July 1954; *m* 19 Nov 1977 *Edward Anthony Spours Nicholson, only *s* of Anthony John Nicholson, of Bickerton, Cheshire, and has:

(1) *Alexander James Edward; *b* 1988

(2) *Zoë Mary Louisa; *b* 1990

(3) *Henrietta; *b* 1994

3 *Victoria Ann [The Hon Mrs Russell, Ningwood Manor, Ningwood, IoW PO30 4NJ]; *b* 23 Dec 1957; *m* 1984 *Christopher Russell, *s* of John Russell, and has:

(1) *John Hugh; *b* 1987

(1) *Emily; *b* 1985

(2) *Kate; *b* 1989

(3) *Alice; *b* 1991

Lineage: Sir CHARLES SEELY, 1st Bt (*see* SHERWOOD, B), had a 4th *s*:

JOHN EDWARD BERNARD SEELY, **1st Baron Mottistone**, of Mottistone, Co Southampton (UK), so *cr* 21 June 1933, CB (1918), CMG (1918), DSO (1900), TD, PC (1909), JP Hants and IoW; *b* 31 May 1868; *educ* Harrow and Trin Coll Cambridge (BA 1890); barrister Inner Temple, served Boer War 1900 (despatches, medal with four clasps), MP (Lib) IoW 1900–06 and 1923–24, Liverpool Abercromby 1906–10 and Ilkeston 1910–22, U-Sec Colonies 1908–11 and War 1911–12, Sec State War 1912–14, WW I: Special Serv Offr and cmdg Canadian Cav Bde (despatches five times, wounded, Order Crown Belgium, Croix de Guerre, Legion Honour, 1914 star, two medals), Parly U-Sec Min Munitions and Dep Min Munitions 1918, U-Sec Air 1919, Chm Nat Savings Ctee 1926–43

(V-Pres 1943), Hon Maj-Gen, Col TA, Hon Col 72nd (Hants) AA Bde RA (TA), Hon A/Cdr AAF, V-Pres RNLI; Ld Lt Hants, KJStJ; *m* 1st 9 July 1895 Emily Florence (*d* 9 Aug 1913), dau of Col Hon Sir Henry George Louis Crichton, KCB (*see* ERNE, E), and had:

1 Frank Reginald; 2nd Lt Hants Regt, ADC Personal Staff; *b* 26 June 1896; *ka* April 1917

2 HENRY JOHN ALEXANDER SEELY, **2nd Baron Mottistone**, OBE (1961), DL; *b* 1 May 1899; *educ* Harrow and Trin Coll Cambridge; architect, Surveyor St Paul's Cathedral, Chm London Soc, FSA, FRIBA; RFA WW I Italy, F/Lt AAF WW II and Emergency Works Offr Min Works; with his ptnr Paul Paget restored Eltham Palace, Lambeth Palace, Deanery and Canon's Houses Westminster Abbey, Fulham Palace, Charterhouse (London), Eton, All Hallows by the Tower, St Andrew Holborn Viaduct, St Mary Islington, St Mary W Kensington and Tower of Ch Ch Greyfriars, also new bldgs at Oxford, Cambridge, Bristol, St George's Stevenage New Town, Chapel for Order Br Empire St Paul's Cathedral; Lay Canon Portsmouth Cathedral 1961–63; *d* unm 18 Jan 1963

3 (ARTHUR) PATRICK WILLIAM SEELY, **3rd Baron Mottistone**, TD; *b* 18 Aug 1905; *educ* Harrow and Trin Coll Cambridge; Lt-Col 5/7th (Wessex) AA Bde RA (TA), CC IoW 1934–38; *m* 2 Sept 1939 (*divorce* 1949) Josephine Wilhelmina Philippa, only dau of Jonkheer Frans Izaak van Haeften, of The Hague, and *dsp* 4 Dec 1966

1 Emily Grace; CC IoW 1956–67; *b* 18 Jan 1898; *m* 28 Aug 1937 Lt-Col Archibald Ogilvie Lyttelton Kindersley, CMG, DL, of Hamstead Grange, IoW, s of Capt Henry Wasey Sextus Kindersley, of Tranmere, Lymington, Hants. He *d* 19 June 1955

2 Irene Florence; *b* 22 June 1902; *m* 11 June 1924 Capt Mason Hogarth Scott, RN, and had issue (*see* SCOTT, Bt, of Beauclerc)

3 Kathleen (Kitty) Mary; *b* 14 Nov 1907; *m* 20 March 1946 (Clement) Maxwell Winton Haydon (*d* 1981), only s of Clement John Haydon, of Greencroft, Cartmel, Grange-over-Sands, and Bournemouth

4 Louisa Mary Sylvia; *b* 9 Aug 1913; *m* 24 Oct 1941 Prof Charles Montague Fletcher, CBE, MD, FRCP (*d* Dec 1995), only s of Sir Walter Morley Fletcher, KBE, CB, MD, FRS, of 15 Holland St, London W8, and *d* 14 Jan 1998, leaving:

(1) *Mark Walter [Mark Fletcher Esq, 30 Musgrave Cres, London SW6]; *b* 1942; *m* 1st 1968 Amelia Henrietta Rose, yr dau of RichardTyler, of Meesden Hall, Buntingford, Herts; *m* 2nd 1988 *Mrs Lindy Jones, dau of Brig Michael Harbottle, OBE, of Chipping Norton, Oxon, and by his 1st w has:

1a *Benjamin Charles; *b* 14 July 1971

1a *Ellen Maisie Madeleine; *b* 1973

(1) *Susanna Mary [Lady Lyell, Hill Farm, Markyate, Herts AL3 8AU]; *b* 1945; *m* 2 Sept 1967 *Sir Nicholas Walter Lyell, QC, MP, Attorney Gen 1992–97, s of Sir Maurice Legat Lyell, and has:

1a *Oliver; *b* 1 July 1971

2a *Alexander; *b* 8 Dec 1981

1a *Veronica; *b* 8 May 1970; *m* 21 June 1997 *Robert Paul Byrne

2a *Mary-Kate; *b* 5 March 1979

(2) *Caroline Anne [Mrs Christopher Clarke, 42 The Chase, London SW4 0NH]; *b* 1949; *m* 1974 *Christopher Simon Courtenay Stephenson Clarke, QC, s of Rev John Stephenson Clarke, and has:

1a *Edward; *b* 1981

1a *Henrietta; *b* 1977

2a *Louisa; *b* 1979

The **1st Baron** *m* 2nd 31 July 1917 Hon Evelyn Izme Murray, JP, widow of George Crosfield Norris Nicholson (*see* NICHOLSON, Bt) and dau of 10th Lord Elibank (*qv*), and *d* 7 Nov 1947, leaving by her:

4 DAVID PETER SEELY, **4th and present Baron Mottistone**

MOUNT

Arms: Or on a mount vert a lion rampant az., ducally crowned or, between in chief two roses gu., barbed and seeded ppr. **Crest:** Upon a mount vert a fox salient ppr., supporting a ragged staff erect sa. **Motto:** *Prudenter et constanter* ('Prudently and constantly'). **Creation:** Bt. (UK) 21 June 1921.

(William Robert) Ferdinand Mount [Ferdinand Mount Esq, 17 Ripplevale Grove, London, N1 1HS]; *b* 2 July 1939; *s* unc 1993 but does not use title; *educ* Eton, Vienna U and Ch Ch Oxford (BA); former CRD desk offr (home affairs, health and social security), former ch ldr writer *Daily Mail*, columnist *The Standard* 1980–82, political correspondent *The Spectator* to 1982, head PM's Policy Unit 1982–83, lit ed *The Spectator* 1984–85, columnist *Daily Telegraph* 1985–90, ed *Times Literary Supplement* 1991–, author: *Very Like a Whale* (1967), *The Theatre of Politics* (1972), *The Man who Rode Ampersand* (1975), *The Clique* (1978), *The Subversive Family* (1982), *The Selkirk Strip* (1987), *Of Love and Asthma* (1991), *The British Constitution Now* (1992), *Umbrella* (1994) and *The Liquidator* (1995, 4th in the novel sequence *A Chronicle of Modern Twilight*); *m* 20 July 1968 *Julia Margaret, twin dau of Archibald Julian Lucas (*see* GRENFELL, B), and has had:

1 +WILLIAM ROBERT HORATIO; *b* 12 May 1969; *educ* Westminster and Magdalen Coll Oxford; *m* 20 Dec 1997 *Deborah, er dau of Colin Gray, of Oxshott, Surrey

2 Francis Ferdinand; *b* 27 Sept, *d* 18 Nov 1970

3 +Henry Francis; *b* 1971; *educ* Westminster and Magdalen Coll Oxford

1 *Mary Julia; *b* 1972; *educ* Westminster and Worcester Coll Oxford

Lineage: RALPH MOUNT, of Chislehurst, Kent; *m* 31 Jan 1653/4 Mary Court and *d* 1668, leaving an est s:

RICHARD MOUNT, of Tower Hill, London; Master Stationers' Co 1717–19; *b* 1654; *m* 3 Oct 1682 Sarah (*d* 1717), dau of William Fisher, of London, and *d* 29 June 1722, leaving an est s:

WILLIAM MOUNT, of Tower Hill; Master Stationers' Co 1733–36; *m* 1st 3 June 1708 Mary (*d* 26 June 1745), dau of Thomas Huckell, of St Martin-le-Grand; *m* 2nd 20 March 1745/6 Elizabeth (*d* 1785), dau of John Girle, MD, surgn St Thomas's Hosp, and *d* 23 Feb 1769, having by his 1st w had, with three daus:

JOHN MOUNT, of Tower Hill and Wasing Place, Berks; High Sheriff 1770; *b* 24 July 1725; *m* 1st 21 July 1748 Jane (*d* 5 April 1772), dau of Thomas Fletcher, of Cheapside, and had issue; *m* 2nd 23 Aug 1773 Christian (*m* 2nd 11 Aug 1794 Robert Heysey, *d* 11 Aug 1882), dau of John Hyett, of Epsom, Surrey, and *d* 12 July 1786; his est s by his 1st w:

WILLIAM MOUNT, of Wasing Place; *b* 3 Jan 1753; *m* 4 Oct 1781 Jenny (*d* 11 Oct 1843), dau of Thomas Page, of E Sheen and Poynters, Surrey, and *d* 15 June 1815, leaving an only s:

WILLIAM MOUNT, DL Berks, of Wasing Place; MP Yarmouth, IoW, 1818–20 and Newport 1831–32, High Sheriff Berks 1826; *b* 21 Nov 1787; *m* 27 June 1818 Charlotte (*d* 17 Jan 1879), dau and coheir of George Talbot (*see* SHREWSBURY and WATERFORD, E), and *d* 10 April 1869, leaving an est s:

WILLIAM GEORGE MOUNT, DL Berks, of Wasing Place; High Sheriff Berks 1877, MP S Berks 1885–1900; *b* 18 July 1824; *m* 28 Aug 1862 Marianne Emily (*d* 19 Sept 1928), dau of Robert Clutterbuck, of Watford House, Herts, and *d* 14 Jan 1906, leaving an est s:

Sir William Arthur Mount, 1st Bt (UK), so *cr* 21 June 1921, CBE, JP, DL Berks; *b* 3 Aug 1866; BA Oxon, barrister Inner Temple 1893, MP S Berks 1900–06 and 1910–22, PPS to Chllr Exchequer 1896–1903, memb Cncl Duchy Lancaster 1912–22, civil memb Br Claims Commn France 1916–17, 2nd Church Estates Commr 1919–23, Ecclesiastical Commr 1923, Chm Berks CC 1926–30, Offr Legn Hon; *m* 9 Nov 1899 Hilda Lucy Adelaide, OBE (1920), JP, CA Berks (*d* 3 April 1950), yr dau of Malcolm Low, of Clatto, Fife, and *d* 8 Dec 1930, leaving:

1 **Sir William Malcolm Mount, 2nd Bt**, TD (1942), of Wasing Place; *b* 28 Dec 1904; *educ* Eton and New Coll Oxford; Berks: CC 1938 (Chm 1960), High Sheriff 1947, V-Lt 1960–93 (DL 1946); Lt-Col Reconnaissance Corps (wounded) WW II; *m* 17 Oct 1929 Elizabeth Nance (*d* 199–), only dau of Owen John Llewellyn, of The Thatched House, Moulsford, Berks, and *d* 1993, leaving:

(1) *Cecilia Mary [Lady Dugdale, Blyth Hall, Coleshill, Birmingham B46 2AD]; *b* 15 Jan 1931; *m* 17 Oct 1967 *Sir William Stratford Dugdale, 2nd Bt (*qv*), and has issue

(2) *Mary Fleur [Mrs Ian Cameron, The Old Rectory, Peasemore, Berks]; *b* 22 Oct 1934; *m* 20 Oct 1962 *Ian Donald Cameron, only s of Ewen Donald Cameron (*see* MANTON, B), and has:

1a *(Allan) Alexander; *b* 27 Aug 1963; *m* 1990 *Sarah Louise, 2nd dau of (William) George Fearnley-Whittingstall, of Springhill, Eastington, Glos, and Mrs Douglas Montagu Douglas Scott, of Halford, Warwicks, and has:

1b *Imogen Clare; *b* 1992

2a *David William Donald; *b* 9 Oct 1966

1a *Tania Rachel; *b* 7 March 1965

2a *Clare Louise; *b* 1971

(3) *(Viola) Clare [Mrs John Currie, 6 Dakota Road, Claremont, Cape Town, S Africa]; *b* 14 Feb 1938; *m* 20 Aug 1960 *John Robert Blyth Currie, MB, DPM, 2nd s of Reginald Michael Currie, of Angels Copse, Woolhampton, Berks, by Marjorie Rhona Cecilia, 3rd dau of Sir Robert James Black, 1st Bt (*qv*), and has:

1a *Thomas Mark; *b* 18 July 1966

1a *Mary Teresa; *b* 3 May 1962

2a *Anna Magdalene; *b* 8 March 1964

2 Robert Francis; *b* 7 June 1907; *educ* Eton and Magdalen Coll Oxford; *m* 1st 5 March 1938 Lady Julia Agnes Cynthia Pakenham (*d* 10 Sept 1956), yst dau of 5th Earl of Longford (*qv*), and had:

(1) (Sir) (WILLIAM ROBERT) FERDINAND MOUNT, **3rd and present Bt**

(1) *Frances Leone [Miss Frances Mount, 1 Steps Farm, Polstead, Colchester, Essex]; *b* 19 Sept 1941

2 (cont.) Robert Mount *m* 2nd 1965 *Constance Mercer Stearns [Mrs Robert Mount, 23 Cadogan Lane, London SW1], formerly w of Emerson Muschamp Bainbridge and dau of Leo S de Pinna, and *d* 22 Aug 1969

3 George Richard; *b* 25 June 1911; *educ* Eton; *m* 3 Dec 1936 Patricia Elizabeth (*d* 19–), dau of John Anthony Baring, of New York, and *d* 1991, leaving:

(1) *(Serena) Georgeanne [Mrs Claude Johnson, 26 Devonshire Place, London W1]; *b* 16 Oct 1941; *m* 9 July 1969 *Claude Royston Johnson, s of Capt (S) Royston Henry Johnson, CBE, RN, of Old Barn House, Wootton, Boar's Hill, Oxford

MOUNT EDGCUMBE

Arms: Gules on a bend ermines cotised or three boar's heads argent. **Crest:** A boar statant argent, gorged with a wreath of oak vert, fructed or. **Supporters:** Two greyhounds argent, guttée de poix and gorged with a collar, dovetailed gules. **Motto:** *Au plaisir fort de Dieu* ('At the disposal of God'). **Creations:** B. (GB) 20 April 1742, V. (GB) 5 March 1781, E. (GB) 31 Aug 1789.

THE 8TH EARL OF MOUNT EDGCUMBE, Viscount Mount Edgcumbe and Valletort and **Baron Edgcumbe of Mount-Edgcumbe** (Robert Charles Edgcumbe) [The Rt Hon The Earl of Mount Edgcumbe, Empacombe House, Cremyll, Mount Edgcumbe, Cornwall PL10 1HZ]; *b* 1 June 1939; *s* unc 1982; *educ* Nelson Coll, NZ; farm manager 1960– (NZ Lands and Survey 1975–84, Cornwall 1984–); *m* 1960 (*divorce* 1988) Joan Ivy, dau of Ernest Wall, of 3 RD Otorohanga, NZ, and has:

1 *(Valerie) Denise; *b* 1960
2 *Megan Frances [The Lady Megan Edgcumbe, 14 Grey St, Kawerau, Bay of Plenty, New Zealand]; *b* 1962; horticulturalist
3 *Tracy Anne; *b* 1966; *m* 1988 *Colin Rush, of Opotiki, Bay of Plenty, NZ, and has:
  (1) *Shaun; *b* 1987
  (1) *Jamie Lee; *b* 1989
4 *Vanessa Erina Michelle [The Lady Vanessa Edgcumbe, 2 Anderton Quay Cottages, Millbrook, Torpoint, Cornwall PL10 1DU]; *b* 1969; has by *Ralph Winsor:
  (1) *Tobias Richard; *b* 1989
  (1) *Coral Erina; *b* 1991
5 *Alison Nicole; *b* 1971

Lineage: WILLIAM de EGGCOMB; *m* Hillaria, dau and heiress of William de Cotehele, of Cotehele, Cornwall, and lived there as his principal residence; *d* 1380, leaving:

WILLIAM EDGCOMB; granted *c* 1419 custody of Devon lead mines and silver ore in them; *m* —, dau and heiress of — Denset, and had:

PETER EDGCOMBE; *m* Elizabeth, dau and heiress of Richard Holland, and had:

Sir RICHARD EDGCOMBE, of Cothele; MP Tavistock *c* 1468, Escheator (roy official implementing escheats, or reversion to feudal lord of land holdings on death of tenant) Cornwall, joined Duke of Buckingham's rising against RICHARD III and narrowly escaped with his life, later fought Battle of Bosworth 1485 under Earl of Richmond (HENRY VII), by whom ktd and to whom was Comptroller Household; granted Totnes Castle, Manor of Cornworthy and other lands in Devon; Sheriff Devon 1487; *m* Joan, dau of Thomas Tremayne, of Colacomb, and *d* 1489, having had:

1 PIERS (Sir)
1 Margaret; *m* as his 1st w Sir William ('The Great') Courtenay, of Powderham, and had issue (see DEVON, E)
2 Agnes; *m* Sir William Trevanion, of Cornwall
3 Elizabeth; *m* Weymond Raleigh, of Raleigh

Sir RICHARD's s,

Sir PIERS EDGCOMBE, KB (*c* 1513); Sheriff Devon *c* 1495 and *c* 1498; with HENRY VIII's French expedition 1513, present Sieges Thérouanne and Tournai and Battle of the Spurs; *m* Jane, dau and heiress of Stephen Durnford, of East Stonehouse, Devon, and *d* 1539, leaving an est s:

Sir RICHARD EDGCOMBE; Sheriff Devon *c* 1542 and 1553; built the family seat at W Stonehouse called Mount Edgcumbe (altered 18th century, when it attracted the praise of the actor David Garrick: 'This Mount all the Mounts of Great Britain surpasses.'/'Tis the haunt of the Muses, the Mount of Parnassus.'; rebuilt following WW II); *m* 1st —; *m* 2nd Winifred, dau of William Essex, of Berks, and *d* 1539, leaving an est s by her:

PETER EDGCUMBE; MP Cornwall and Sheriff Devon *temp* ELIZABETH I; *m* Margaret, dau of Sir Andrew Luttrell, of Dunster Castle, Somerset, and *d* 1607, leaving an est s:

Sir RICHARD EDGCUMBE; *m* 1st Anne, dau of George Cary, of Cokington, Devon; *m* 2nd Mary, dau and heiress of Sir Thomas Cottle or Coteel, of London, and *d* 1638, leaving an est s by her:

PIERS EDGCUMBE, of Mount Edgcumbe; MP Newport and Chelmsford *temp* CHARLES I; royalist Civil War; *m* Mary, dau of Sir John Glanvil, of Broad Hinton, Wilts, and *d* 1660, leaving, with a dau (Winifred, 1st w of 1st Earl of Coventry, *qv*):

Sir RICHARD EDGCUMBE, KB 1661; FRS 1678; *m* Lady Anne Montagu, 2nd surv dau of 1st Earl of Sandwich (*qv*), and *d* 1688, leaving, with two er sons (*d* young):

RICHARD EDGCUMBE, **1st Baron Edgcumbe of Mount-Edgcumbe** (GB), so cr 20 April 1742, PC (I 1727; *bapt* 23 April 1680; *educ* Trin Coll Cambridge; MP (Whig) Cornwall 1701, St Germans 1701–02, Plympton 1702–34 and 1741–42 and Lostwithiel 1734–41, a Ld Treasury 1716–17 and 1720–24, Maj-Gen 1755, Ld Lt Cornwall 1742–58 (DL 1702), Chllr Duchy Lancaster 1743–58; *m* 12 March 1715 Matilda, dau of Sir Henry Furnese, 1st Bt, of Waldershare, Kent, and *d* 22 Nov 1758, leaving:

1 RICHARD EDGCUMBE, **2nd Baron Edgcumbe of Mount-Edgcumbe**, PC (1756); *b* 2 Aug 1716; *educ* Eton; MP (Whig) Plympton 1742–47, Lostwithiel 1747–54 and Penryn 1754–58, Ld Commr Trade and Plantataions 1754–55, Comptroller Household 1756–61, Ld Lt Cornwall 1759–61; *d* unm 1761
2 GEORGE EDGCUMBE, **1st Earl of Mount Edgcumbe**, Co Devon, so cr 31 Aug 1781, as also earlier 5 March 1781 VISCOUNT MOUNT EDGCUMBE AND VALLETORT (both GB), PC (1765); *b* 3 March 1720; served RN, Adml the White 1782, MP (Whig) Fowey 1746–61, Ld Lt Cornwall 1761–95, Treasurer Household 1765–66; FRS 1784, FSA 1775; *m* 16 Aug 1761 Emma, only dau and heiress of Most Rev John Gilbert, DD, Archbp York, and *d* 4 Feb 1795, leaving an only s:

(1) RICHARD EDGCUMBE, **2nd Earl of Mount Edgcumbe**, PC (1808); *b* 13 Sept 1764; *educ* Harrow and Ch Ch Oxford; MP (Tory) Lostwithiel 1790–91 and Fowey 1791–95, Ld Lt and V-Adml Cornwall 1795–1839, FRS 1808, FSA 1808; *m* 21 Feb 1789 Sophia (*d* 17 Aug 1806), 3rd dau and coheir of 2nd Earl of Buckinghamshire (*qv*), and *d* 26 Sept 1839, having had:

1a William Richard, *Viscount Valletort*; *b* 19 Nov 1794; *dvp* unm 29 Oct 1818
2a ERNEST AUGUSTUS EDGCUMBE, **3rd Earl of Mount Edgcumbe**; *b* 1797; Militia ADC to TM WILLIAM IV and QUEEN VICTORIA; Col Cornwall Militia; DCL; *m* 6 Dec 1831 Caroline Augusta, VA (2nd Cl) (*d* 2 Nov 1881), est dau of R-Adml Charles Feilding (see DENBIGH and DESMOND, E), and *d* 3 Sept 1861, having had:

1b WILLIAM HENRY EDGCUMBE, **4th Earl of Mount Edgcumbe**, GCVO (1897), PC (1879), JP and DL (Devon); *b* 5 Nov 1833; *educ* Harrow and Ch Ch Oxford; MP (C) Plymouth 1859–61, Ld Chamberlain Household 1879–80, Ld Steward Household 1885–86 and 1886–92, ADC to HM QUEEN VICTORIA 1887–97, Chm Cornwall CC 1895–1917, memb Cncl Duchy Cornwall 1901–07 (Keeper Privy Seal 1907–17), Ld Lt and V-Adml Cornwall, pres Cornwall TFA, Dep Warden Stannaries, Hon Col 5th Bn Devonshire Regt; *m* 1st Lady Katherine Elizabeth Hamilton (*d* 3 Sept 1874), dau of 1st Duke of Abercorn (*qv*), and had:

1c PIERS ALEXANDER HAMILTON EDGCUMBE, **5th Earl of Mount Edgcumbe**, JP (Cornwall), DL (Cornwall and Devon); *b* 2 July 1865; Lt-Col 3rd Bn DCLI Boer War (medal with 3 clasps), Hon Col Special Reserve, Hon Capt Army, Dep Warden Stannaries 1913–14, KStJ; *m* 15 May 1911 Lady Edith Villiers (*d* 1 Aug 1935), only dau of 5th Earl of Clarendon (*qv*), and *dsp* 10 April 1944
1c Victoria Frederica Caroline; *m* 3 Aug 1880 Lord Algernon Malcolm Arthur Percy, 2nd s of 6th Duke of Northumberland (*qv*), and *d* 20 Feb 1920, leaving issue
2c Alberta Louisa Florence; *m* 10 Oct 1891 1st Baron Roborough (*qv*) and *d* 25 March 1941, leaving issue
3c Edith Hilaria; *m* 23 June 1892 2nd Baron Saint Levan (*qv*) and *d* 3 April 1931, leaving issue
1b (cont.) The **4th Earl** *m* 2nd 21 April 1906 Caroline Cecilia (*dsp* 23 Feb 1909), dau of Hon George Edgcumbe (see below) and widow of 3rd Earl of Ravensworth (see RAVENSWORTH, B), and *d* 25 Sept 1917
2b Charles Ernest, JP (Cornwall and Devon); *b* 23 Oct 1838; Lt-Col Gren Gds, Hon Col 6th Bn Roy Fus, City of London Regt; *d* 14 Sept 1915
1b Ernestine Emma Horatia; *d* 20 May 1925
3a George; *b* 23 June 1800; Chargé d'Affaires; *m* 19 May 1834 Fanny Lucy (*d* 11 May 1899), est dau of Sir John Shelley, 6th Bt (*qv*), and *d* 18 Feb 1882, leaving:

1b Richard John Frederick, MVO (1921), JP; *b* 12 Aug 1843; Lt 52nd LI, Capt Roy Bucks Militia; Serjeant-at-Arms to TM QUEEN VICTORIA 1880–1901, EDWARD VII 1901–10 and GEORGE V 1910–21; *m* 1st 26 Nov 1872 Mary Louisa (*d* 2 Sept 1923), 2nd dau of John Bligh Monck, of Coley Park, Berks, and had:

1c KENELM WILLIAM EDWARD EDGCUMBE, **6th Earl of Mount Edgcumbe**, TD, JP, DL (Cornwall 1961); *b* 9 Oct 1873; MICE, pres and hon memb IEE, Fell UCL, Lt-Col RE (TA); *m* 19 July 1906 Lilian Agnes (children's author; *d* 28 Sept 1964), only dau of Col Arthur Chandos Arkwright, of Hatfield Place, Witham, Essex, and *d* 10 Feb 1965, having had:

1d Piers Richard; *b* 22 Oct 1914; Lt 12th Roy Lancers WW II; *ka* nr Wormhout 27 May 1940
1d *Hilaria Agnes [The Lady Hilaria Gibbs, Aldenham, Deer Park Lane, Tavistock, Devon]; *b* 16 Jan 1908; *m* 17 Oct 1933 Lt-Col Denis Lucius Alban Gibbs (see ALDENHAM and HUNSDON OF HUNSDON, B) and has had:

1e Jillianne Bridget; *b* 11 July 1935; *m* 1st 18 April 1959 (*divorce* 1973) Maj Martin John Minter-Kemp, RWF, and had:
  1f *Robin John Edgcumbe; *b* 11 Dec 1963; *m* 19– *Penelope Garner and has:
    1g *William; *b* 19–
    1g *Louisa; *b* 19–

2g *Georgia; b 1996

1f *Emma Hilaria; b 10 Nov 1960

2f *(Penelope) Claire; b 11 Dec 1963; m *Thomas Dickins and has:

   1g *Merlin; b 19–

   2g *Oscar; b 1997

   1g *Hebe; b 19–

1e (cont.) Mrs Jillianne Minter-Kemp m 2nd 19– *Anthony Alan Russell Cobbold, of The Vineyard, Weston-under-Redcastle, Salop, and d 20 Jan 1994

2e *(Margaret) Hilaria [Mrs Hilaraia Thornewill, Yonder Cottage, 9701 Covered Bridge Prospect, KY 40059, USA]; b 26 Aug 1937; m 11 Feb 1961 (divorce 1989) Rev Mark Lyon Thornewill, Lt Cdr RN, and has:

   1f *(John-Mark) Judah; b 3 Nov 1961; m 5 Oct 1985 *Araby Jane Wedekind and has:

     1g *Benjamin Aaron; b 4 Aug 1985

     1g *Alice Hilaria; b 11 Dec 1988

   2f *Luke Thomas; b 3 Nov 1961; m 23 Aug 1997 *Caroline Stewardson

   3f *Jeremy Lyon; b 4 Nov 1970

   1f *Joanna Lilian; b 5 June 1965; m 23 May 1987 *Taylor Hay

2e (cont.) The Rev and Mrs Thornewill also adopted:

   *(Christopher) Shane Kenelm; b 1968; m 9 May 1992 *Wendy Bissett

3e *Rosamund Lucia [Lady Woodard, Restormel Manor, Lostwithiel, Cornwall PL22 0HN]; b 1 April 1941; m 20 July 1963 *R-Adml Sir Robert Nathaniel Woodard, KCVO, est s of Rev F A Woodard, and has:

   1f *Rupert Piers Nathaniel; b 1964; m 1990 *Anna Culley and has:

     1g *Oliver; b 1992

     2g *Benjamin; b 1994

     3g *Harry; b 1997

   2f *Jolyon Robert Alban; b 1969

   1f *Melissa Lucia Rosamund; b 1967

4e *Penelope Mary [Mrs Timothy Douglas-Riley, 2 Marryat Gdns, Manadon, Plymouth PL5 3DT]; b 25 March 1949; m 1st 1970 (divorce 1983) Douglas Arthur Dale; m 2nd 28 Sept 1985 *Surg Capt Timothy Roger Douglas-Riley, RN, and has:

   1f *Henrietta Lucia; b 19 Feb 1987

   2f *Venetia Louise; b 15 Dec 1988

2d Katherine Lilian; b 1 May 1910; m 1 Aug 1936 (divorce 1957) G/Capt Francis Campbell de la Poer Beresford-Peirse, RAF (see BERESFORD-PEIRSE, Bt); m 2nd 19– Cdr R Gabbett Mulhallen, CBE, RN, and d 19–, having had by her 1st husb:

1e Jeremy Edgcumbe de la Poer; b 7 Sept 1937; d 16 Feb 1940

1e *Susan Katherine; b 7 Sept 1940; m 19– *Myles Fleetwood Bird and has:

   1f *Justyn; b 19–

   1f *Tiffany; b 19–

2e *Philippa Jane; b 4 April 1944; m 19– *Nigel Hope and has:

   1f *A dau

   2f *A dau

3d Margaret Louisa; b 21 March 1912; m 6 June 1932 Lt-Col Conolly Robert McCausland, Irish Gds (d 22 April 1968), only s of Rt Hon Maurice Marcus McCausland, and d 19–, leaving:

1e Marcus; b 19–; m *June — (m 2nd 19– —) and d 19–, having had:

   1f *Conolly Patrick; b 19–

   2f *Shane; b 19–

   1f *Marianne; b 19–

2e *Antony Richard; b 1941; m 1964 (divorce 1975) Priscilla Cornwallis, er dau of E S Vernon-Jones, and has:

   1f *Richard Cornwallis; b 1969

   1f *Henrietta Elisabeth; b 1965

2e *Piers Conolly; b 1949; m 1970 *Elizabeth, dau of Dr James Duff, of Hampstead Hall, Derry, and has:

   1f *Cuillean Benjamin; b 1972

   2f *Simon; b 19–

   3f *Alexander; b 19–

   1f *Athaena; b 19–

1e *Mary Fania; b 1936; m 1958 *Capt Denis Mahony, Irish Gds, of Bessborough, Balrath, Co Meath, and has had:

   1f *Justin; b 19–; d 19–

   2f *Edmond Conolly; b 1960

   3f *Dominick Denis Martin; b 1962; m 19– *Africa —

   1f *Maria Louisa Siobhan; b 1968

2e *Caroline Anne; b 1944; m 1964 Simon Maxwell Weatherby (see BANGOR, V) and has:

   1f *Max; b 19–

   2f *Dicken; b 19–

   1f *Rebecca; b 19–

1b (cont.) Richard Edgcumbe m 2nd 21 July 1926 Henrietta Constance, er dau of John Jones, of Mere Ho, Newton-le-Willows, and d 3 Nov 1937

2b Edward Mortimer; b 30 Aug 1847; Lt NZ Militia; m 30 Jan 1868 Constance Bevin (d 1922), yst dau of Rev Robert Burrowes, of Auckland, NZ, and d 29 June 1890, leaving:

1c George Valletort; b 26 Jan 1869; m 1897 Georgina Mildred (b 9 April 1867; d 27 Oct 1941), dau of Thomas Aubrey Bell, of Auckland, NZ, and d 6 Aug 1947, leaving:

1d EDWARD PIERS EDGCUMBE, **7th Earl of Mount Edgcumbe**; b 13 July 1903; m 27 Dec 1944 (Victoria) Effie (d 29 Nov 1979), yr dau of Robert Campbell, of N Ireland and NZ, and widow of John Warbrick, and dsp 9 Dec 1982

2d George Aubrey Valletort; b 15 Sept 1907; m 1st 6 April 1935 (divorce 1943) Meta, dau of Charles Robert Lhoyer, of Nancy, France, and had:

   1e Richard Valletort; b 3 Jan 1936; d May 1943

   2e ROBERT CHARLES EDGCUMBE, **8th and present Earl Mount Edgcumbe**

2d (cont.) George Edgcumbe m 2nd 15 Feb 1944 *Una Pamela (m 2nd 1989 Kenneth Baron) [Mrs Kenneth Baron, 77 Arapiki Rd, Stoke, Nelson, NZ], dau of Edward Lewis George, of Perth, W Australia, and d 1977, leaving by her:

3e +PIERS VALLETORT [Piers Edgcumbe Esq, 23 Chamboard Pl, Nelson, New Zealand]; b 23 Oct 1946; heir presumptive; m 1971 (divorce 19–) Hilda Warn and has:

   1f *Prudence; b 1972

   2f *Angela; b 1975

4e +Christopher George Mortimer; b 1950; m 1985 (divorce 1991) Marian Frances, dau of Murray Stevenson, and has:

   1f +Douglas George Valletort; b 1985

4e (cont.) Christopher Edgcumbe adopted his step-dau:

   *Emma Louise; b 1983

1d Erina Shelley; b 1898; m 1930 John Richard Sutton, MICE, and d 19–, having had:

   1e *Gillian Mary Edgcumbe; b 1941

2d Ernestine Cecilia; b 8 Aug 1899; m 4 April 1929 Edwin Clay, 4th s of Thomas Benjamin Clay, of Sowerby Bridge, Yorks, and Auckland, NZ, and had:

1e *Howard Edgcumbe; b 1931; m 1961 *Helen Muriel Jenner and has:

   1f *Simon Edgcumbe; b 1964

   1f *Sarah Georgina; b 1966

   2f *Rebecca Jane; b 1969

2e *Roger Edgcumbe [Roger Clay Esq, 2 Everett Ave, Dulich, Adelaide, S Australia]; b 1939; PhD, BAgSc; m 1978 *Jennifer Margaret Launy

1e *Geraldine Ann; b 1935; m 1959 *Emlyn Donald Jones and has:

   1f *Richard Edwin Lewis; b 1964

   1f *Catherine Louise; b 1966

   2f *Joanna Elizabeth; b 1972

3d Frances Huia; m 1920 Harold Stott and had:

   1e *Frank Ernest; b 1921

   1e *Georgina Amy; b 1923

2c Ernest Athole Valletort; b 25 July 1870; m 19 Nov 1896 Louisa Charlotte (d 1949), dau of William Martin, of Auckland, NZ, and d 2 Oct 1937, leaving:

1d Florence Maye; b 1900; m 28 April 1925 Charles Richard Howard (d 1972) and d 19–

2d *Jessie Hilaria [Mrs Leslie Reeves, 4A Chelsea Place, Hamilton, New Zealand]; b 1911; m 1934 Leslie Reeves (d 1986) and has:

1e *Gaynor Hilaria Ann [Mrs Arthur Lidington, 20 Chelsea Pl, Hamilton, New Zealand]; b 1936; m 1957 *Arthur Herbert Lidington and has:

   1f *Brett Arthur; b 1961; m 1987 *Sonia Jane Haines and has:

     1g *Reid Arthur; b 30 June 1992

     2g *Fraser Oliver; b 25 June 1994

   1f *Janine Lesley; b 1959; m 1979 *Graeme William Pickering and has:

     1g *Samuel Thomas; b 25 Dec 1987

     1g *Hannah Louise; b 21 Dec 1991

3c Richard Gerald Valletort; b 15 Aug 1871; m 2 Oct 1900 Annie (d 1964), yst dau of Maj Broughton, and d 3 Nov 1908, leaving:

1d Edward Mortimer; b 11 April 1904; m 23 Aug 1941 *Mary MacArthur [Mrs Edward Mortimer, 27 Tuhaere St, Orakei, Auckland, New Zealand], dau of John Stone, and d 1983, having had:

1e +Richard John; b 22 Oct 1946

1e *Margaret Ann [Mrs William Smithyman, 66 Alton Ave, Northcote, Auckland, New Zealand]; b 17 May 1942; m 1981 *William Kendrick Smithyman

1d Constance Joyce; b 10 July 1901; m 1922 Cecil Vincent Haysom and had:

1e *Bevan Valletort; b 1923; m 1949 *Rae Florence, dau of Leopold Valentine Landman, of Hamilton, Waikato, NZ, and has:

   1f *David Valletort; b 1951

   1f *Elizabeth Jane; b 1952

   2f *Sally Anne; b 1955

2d Caroline Vivienne; b 29 June 1902; d 19–

3d Acushla Bevin; b 11 Oct 1906; d 1918

1c Florence Violet

1b Emma Frances; d 13 May 1854

2b Caroline Cecilia; m 1st 19 May 1866 3rd Earl of Ravensworth (see RAVENSWORTH, B); m 2nd 21 April 1906 **4th Earl of Mount Edgcumbe** (see above) and dsp 23 Feb 1909

3b Elizabeth Catherine; m 1 July 1874 Col Albert Thornton Wodehouse, RA (see KIMBERLEY, E), and dsp 5 Oct 1918

4b Emily Fanny Georgiana; m 1st 13 April 1871 George Edward Earle (see EARLE, Bt); m 2nd 4 June 1879 Lt-Gen James Sinclair Thomson (d 1893) and dsp 8 June 1915

1a Emma Sophia; *m* 24 July 1828, as his 3rd w, 1st Earl Brownlow (*see* BROWNLOW, B) and *dsp* 28 Jan 1872

2a Caroline; *m* 13 Feb 1812 Reginald George Macdonald, 19th of Clanranald, JP, DL (*d* 11 March 1873), and *d* 10 April 1824, leaving issue

MOUNTAIN

Arms: Erm. a fess az. between three lions rampant guardant sa., each holding between the fore-paws an escallop gu., three cross-crosslets arg. **Crest:** Issuant from the battlements of a tower ppr. a demi-lion guardant arg., holding between the paws an escallop gu. **Motto:** *Cum cruce salus* ('Safety with the Cross'). **Creation:** Bt. (UK) 23 Jan 1922.

SIR DENIS MORTIMER MOUNTAIN, 3RD BT, of Oare Manor, Co Somerset, and Brendon, Co Devon [Sir Denis Mountain Bt, The Manor, Morestead, Hants SO21 1LZ; 12 Queens Elm Sq, Old Church St, Chelsea SW3 6ED]; *b* 2 June 1929; *s f* 1977; *educ* Eton; late Lt RHG, Pres Eagle Star Hldgs 1958–93, Chm: City London Insur, Eagle Star Assur America 1978–85, Australian Eagle Insur 1977–85, S African Eagle Insur 1977–85, Pres Compagnie de Bruxelles Risques Divers SA d'Assurances (Belgium) 1977–85, dir: Threadneedle Insur, Midland Assur, Masters Ltd (Bermuda), Winston Estates, Daejan Hldgs, Met Properties and Scotiabank (UK) Ltd 1997, chm and md Eagle Star Insur 1974–85, Eagle Star Hldgs 1979–85, Rank Organisation 1968–94, Grovewood Securities 1969–85 (dep chm), Philip Hill Investment Tst 1967–86, Bank of Nova Scotia (Toronto) 1978–, BATT Industries 1984–85, Allied London Properties 1986–; *m* 18 Feb 1958 *(Hélène) Fleur Mary Kirwan, dau of (William) John Kirwan-Taylor, OBE (*see* GRANTCHESTER, B), and has:

1 +EDWARD BRIAN STANFORD; *b* 19 March 1961; late Maj Blues and Royals; *m* 24 Oct 1987 *Charlotte Sarah Jesson, dau of His Honour Judge (Henry) Pownall, and has:

  (1) +Thomas Denis Edward; *b* 14 Aug 1989

  (2) +Harry Brian Pownall; *b* 1991

  (1) *Camilla; *b* 1993

2 +William Denis Charles; *b* 18 Nov 1966; *m* 1994 *Emma V G, dau of Cdr Patrick Mitchell, of Chorleywood, Herts

1 *Georgina Lily Fleur; *b* 1 Aug 1959; *m* 1986 *Nigel Charles Blake Macpherson, only s of Ian Macpherson, of The Old Hall, Blofield, Norfolk, and has:

  (1) *Charles Edward Ian; *b* 1989

  (1) *Lara Alexandra Fleur; *b* 1991

  (2) *Katie Victoria Lily; *b* 1994

Lineage: JOHN MOUNTAIN, of N Tuddenham, Norfolk; *m* Mary (*d* June 1718) and *d* Oct 1732, leaving:

JOHN MOUNTAIN, of N Tuddenham, *b* 1687; *m* Mary (*d* March 1760) and *d* Jan 1747, leaving:

THOMAS MOUNTAIN, of Mattishall, Norfolk, *b* 1723, *m* 28 Aug 1748 Ann (*d* Sept 1804), dau of Gabriel Scott, of Mattishall, and *d* July 1805, leaving:

FRANCIS MOUNTAIN, of Mattishall; *b* Sept 1748; *m* 25 Oct 1771 Frances, dau of Christopher Bishop, and had:

THOMAS MOUNTAIN, of Bury St Edmunds; *b* April 1772; *m* Harriott Mortimer and *d* 5 June 1858, leaving:

HENRY MOUNTAIN, of Bury St Edmunds; *b* 24 April 1808; *m* 1831 Elizabeth Smith (*d* 12 Nov 1844) and had:

STANFORD HENRY MORTIMER MOUNTAIN, of Dulwich, Kent; *b* 15 Sept 1834; *m* 22 Dec 1858 Louisa (*d* 24 Feb 1916), dau of George Eve, of Chislehurst, Kent, and *d* 11 March 1890, leaving:

Sir Edward Mortimer Mountain, 1st Bt (UK), so *cr* 23 Jan 1922; *b* 24 Nov 1872; *educ* Dulwich Coll; Chm Eagle Star Insur, Second Covent Garden Property Co and Philip Hill Investment Tst; *ktd* 1918; *m* 6 Jan 1897 Evelyn Ellen Regina (*d* 13 Jan 1950), dau of August Seiglé, and *d* 22 June 1948, leaving:

Sir Brian Edward Stanley Mountain, 2nd Bt; *b* 22 Aug 1899; *educ* Charterhouse and RMC Sandhurst; Lt-Col RARO WW I with 9th Lancers and WW II, dir Utd Dominions Tst, Midland Assur, Bank of Nova Scotia (Canada), chm Eagle Star Insur, Hampstead and Suburban Properties Ltd, Second Covent Garden Property

Ltd, Trent Insur, Utd Racecourses, Br Crown Assur, Bernard Sunley Investment Tst, Ashdale Land & Property, chm and md Threadneedle Insur, pres Bernard Sunley Bldg (Bahamas) and Sceptre Tst (Bahamas), memb Cncl Racehorse Owners Assoc; *m* 8 June 1926 *Doris Elsie [Doris Lady Mountain, 75 Eaton Sq, London, SW1], est dau of Eric Charles Edward Lamb, of 2 Queen St, London W1, and *d* 17 Feb 1977, leaving:

1 Sir DENIS MORTIMER MOUNTAIN, **3rd and present Bt**

2 +Nicholas Brian Edward [Nicholas Mountain Esq, 17 Hollywood Rd, London SW10 9HT]; *b* 15 Feb 1936; *educ* Eton and St Catharine's Coll Cambridge; late Lt RHG; *m* 30 July 1965 *Penelope, yr dau of Maurice H Shearme, of Chelsea, and has:

  (1) +Henry Nicholas; *b* 29 Nov 1967

  (1) *Nathalie Frances; *b* 6 July 1970

1 *Fleur Caroline [Mrs Dane Douetil, Busbridge Lakes House, Hambledon Rd, Godalming, Surrey]; *b* 22 Feb 1933; *m* 21 July 1955 *Dane Peter Douetil, yr s of Capt Philip Victor Douetil, of Wonersh, Surrey, and has had:

  (1) *Dane Jonathan; *b* 28 July 1960

  (2) *Guy William; *b* 27 Feb 1963

  (3) *William Walton; *b* 28 Oct 1966

  (1) Nicola Fleur; *b* 7 June 1957; *d* 19–

MOUNTBATTEN OF BURMA

Arms: Quarterly, 1st and 4th, azure a lion rampant double-queued barry of ten, argent and gules, armed and langued of the last, crowned or, within a bordure compony of the 2nd and 3rd; 2nd and 3rd, argent two pallets sable charged on the honour point with an escutcheon of the arms of the late Princess Alice, namely: the Royal Arms differenced by a label of three points argent, the centre point charged with a rose gules barbed vert, and each of the other points with an ermine spot sable. **Supporters:** On either side a lion double-queued and crowned all or. **Motto:** In honour bound. **Creations:** B. and E. (UK) 28 Oct 1947, V. (UK) 23 Aug 1946.

THE COUNTESS MOUNTBATTEN OF BURMA, Viscountess Mountbatten of Burma, of Romsey, Co Southampton, and **Baroness Romsey**, of Romsey, Co Southampton (Patricia Edwina Victoria Knatchbull, CBE (1991), CD (1976), JP (Kent 1971), DL (Kent 1973)) [The Rt Hon The Countess Mountbatten of Burma CBE CD JP DL, Newhouse, Mersham, Kent TN25 6NQ; 39 Montpelier Walk, London SW7 1JH]; *b* 14 Feb 1924 (HRH THE DUKE OF WINDSOR and Lady Patricia Ramsay stood sponsor); *s f* 1979; WRNS WW II, V-Lt Kent 1984–, Col-in-Ch Princess Patricia's Canadian LI 1974–; pres: SOS Children's Villages (UK), Friends of Cassel Hosp, Friends of William Harvey Hosp, Shaftesbury Homes and *Arethusa*, Kent branches NSPCC, Save the Children Fund and Marriage Guidance Cncl; chm Sir Ernest Cassel Educn Tst; v-pres: SSAFA 1981–, BRCS 1984–, Family Planning Assoc, Natural Childbirth Tst, RLSS, Shaftesbury Soc, Nat Soc Cancer Relief, Kent Vol Serv Cncl, RCN, Roy Nat Coll for the Blind; hon pres: Soc Nautical Research, Br Maritime Charitable Fndn; patron: Commando Assoc, HMS *Cavalier* Tst, Legion Frontiersmen of Cwlth, *Foudroyant* Tst, HMS *Kelly* Reunion Assoc, Nuclear Weapons Freeze, VADs (RN), Compassionate Friends, Nurses' Welfare Tst; v-patron Burma Star Assoc, govr Ashford Sch, DStJ 1981; *m* 26 Oct 1946 *7th Baron Brabourne (*qv*) and has had:

1 +NORTON LOUIS PHILIP, *Lord Romsey* [Lord Romsey, Broadlands, Romsey, Hants SO51 9ZD]; *b* 8 Oct 1947 (HM THE QUEEN OF SWEDEN and HRH THE DUKE OF EDINBURGH stood sponsor); *educ* Gordonstoun and U of Kent (BA 1969); High Steward Romsey 1980–, chm: Jawaharlal Nehru Memorial Tst; *m* 20 Oct 1979 *Penelope Meredith, only dau of Maj Reginald Wray Eastwood, of Son Vida, Palma de Mallorca, and has had:

  (1) +Nicholas Louis Charles Norton; *b* 15 May 1981

  (1) *Alexandra Victoria Edwina Diana; *b* 5 Dec 1982

  (2) Leonora Louise Marie Elizabeth; *b* 25 June 1986; *d* 22 Oct 1991

2 +Michael-John (Joe) Ulick; *b* 24 May 1950 (HM THE QUEEN and HRH PRINCE LOUIS OF HESSE stood sponsor); *educ* Gordonstoun and Reading U

(BSc 1971); *m* 1 June 1985 (*divorce* 12 March 1997) Melissa Clare, actress, only dau of Judge Sir John Owen (*see* SECOMBE, B), of Bickerstaff Ho, Idlicote, Warwicks, and has:

·(1) *Kelly Louise Doreen; *b* 30 March 1988

3 +Philip Wyndham Ashley [The Hon Philip Knatchbull, 41 Montpelier Walk, SW7 1JH]; *b* 2 Dec 1961 (HRH PRINCESS LOUIS OF HESSE stood sponsor); *educ* Gordonstoun, Kent U and London Internat Film Sch; *m* 16 March 1991 *Atalanta, dau of John Cowan and formerly w of Hugo Dominic Charles Medlicott Vereker (*see* GORT, V), and has:

(1) *Daisy Isadora; *b* 5 Oct 1992

4 Nicholas Timothy Charles; *b* 18 Nov 1964 (HRH THE PRINCE OF WALES stood sponsor); *educ* Gordonstoun; assassinated 27 Aug 1979 by IRA bomb

5 +Timothy Nicholas Sean; *b* 18 Nov 1964 (HRH THE PRINCE OF WALES stood sponsor); *educ* Gordonstoun, Atlantic Coll and Christ's Coll Cambridge; *m* 11 July 1998 *Isabella, dau of David Norman, of Burkham, Hants

1 *Joanna Edwina Doreen; *b* 5 March 1955 (HM THE KING OF SWEDEN and HRH PRINCE GEORGE OF HANOVER stood sponsor); *educ* Benenden, Atlantic Coll, Kent U (BA 1976) and Columbia U USA; *m* 1st 3 Nov 1984 (*divorce* 1995) Baron Hubert Henry François du Breuil, yr s of Baron Bertrand Pernot du Breuil; *m* 2nd 19 Nov 1995 *Azriel Zuckerman and by her 1st husb has:

(1) *Eleuthera Roselyne Patricia; *b* 13 May 1986

2 *Amanda Patricia Victoria; *b* 26 June 1957 (HRH PRINCE GEORGE OF HANOVER stood sponsor); *educ* Benenden, Gordonstoun, Kent U (BA 1979), Peking U and Goldsmith Coll London; *m* 31 Oct 1987 *Charles V Ellingworth, est s of William Ellingworth, of Laughton, Leics, and has:

(1) *Luke John William; *b* 27 Jan 1991

(2) *Joseph Louis Vincent; *b* 2 Dec 1992

Lineage: (*See* MILFORD HAVEN, M); the 1st MARQUESS OF MILFORD HAVEN's 2nd s:

LOUIS FRANCIS ALBERT VICTOR NICHOLAS MOUNTBATTEN, **1st Earl Mountbatten of Burma**, so *cr* 28 Oct 1947, as also BARON ROMSEY, of Romsey, Co Southampton, and earlier 23 Aug 1946 VISCOUNT MOUNTBATTEN OF BURMA, of Romsey, Co Southampton (all UK), with remainder to the heirs male of his body, in default of which to his er dau and the heirs male of her body, and to every other dau by primogeniture and to the heirs male of their bodies, KG (1946), GCB (1955, KCB 1945, CB 1943), OM (1965), GCSI (1947), GCIE (1947), GCVO (1937, KCVO 1922, MVO 1920), DSO (1941), PC (1947); *b* 25 June 1900 (HM QUEEN VICTORIA and TSAR NICHOLAS II stood sponsor); *educ* RNCs Osborne and Dartmouth and Christ's Coll Cambridge (Hon Fell 1946); Cadet RN 1913, Midshipman 1916, served Grand Fleet WW I 1916–18, Sub-Lt 1918, Lt 1920, Naval ADC to HRH THE PRINCE OF WALES 1920–22, Lt-Cdr 1928, Cdr 1932, Capt 1937, WW II: cmded: 5th Destroyer Flotilla in HMS *Kelly* 1939–41 (despatches twice), HMS *Illustrious* 1941, Cdre Combined Ops 1941–42, Ch Combined Ops and memb Br Chs Staff Ctee 1942–43 (Actg V-Adml 1942), SACSEA 1943–46 (Actg Adml 1943), R-Adml 1946, last Viceroy India Feb-Aug 1947, Govr-Gen India Aug 1947–June 1948, Flag Offr Cmdg 1st Cruiser Sqdn 1948–49, V-Adml 1949, Ld Commr Admlty, Fourth Sea Ld and Ch Supplies and Tport 1950–52, C-in-C Mediterranean 1952–54, C-in-C Allied Forces Mediterranean 1953–54, Adml 1953, Adml of the Fleet 1956, First Sea Ld and Ch Naval Staff 1955–59, CDS and Chm Chs Staff Ctee 1959–65; Govr IoW 1965–79, Gold Stick and Col Life Gds and Col Cmdt RM 1965–79, Personal Naval ADC to TM EDWARD VIII 1936, GEORGE VI 1937–52 and THE QUEEN March 1953–79, Ld Lt IoW 1974–79, Hon Lt-Gen and Hon Air Marshal 1942, Hon Col 289 Parachute Regt RHA 1956, Hon Col Calcutta Light Horse 1947, Hon Col 4/5 Bn Roy Hants Regt (TA) 1964; AMIEE 1927, Hon MIEE and Hon MIERE 1965; grand pres: Br Cwlth Ex-Servs League and Roy Life Saving Soc and Roy Overseas League; pres: SSAFA, Inst Electronic and Radio Engrs, chm and fndr Nat Electronics Res Cncl, pres Roy Naval Film Corp, Roy Naval Polo Assoc, Br Computer Soc, Soc of Film and Television Arts, Sailors' Home and Red Ensign Club (London), Gordon Smith Inst Liverpool and Soc of Genealogists; Er Bro Trin House, pres RAC and Hants Aeroplane Club, chm cncl Atlantic Colls 1968–79, Cdre Roy Thames Yacht Club, V-Adml Roy Motor Yacht Club, Cdre Sea Scouts, Past Prime Warden Shipwrights' Co, memb Mercers', Vintners' and Grocers' Cos, hon memb Co Master Mariners, memb Roy Swedish Naval Soc, Freeman City of London with Sword of Honour 1946, High Steward 1940 and First Freeman 1946 Romsey, Freeman Edinburgh 1954, KStJ 1943, Gd Cross Order of Isabela La Catolica Spain and Crown and Star Romania, MC Greece, Grand Cross Order George I Greece, US Legion Merit and DSM, Grand Cross Legn Hon and Croix de Guerre, Special Grand Cordon Cloud and Banner China, Grand Cross Order Star Nepal, White Elephant Siam, Lion Netherlands, Seraphim Sweden, Grand Cross Mil Order Aviz Portugal, Agga Maha Thiri Thuddhamma Burma, Kt Grand Cross Dannebrog Denmark, Grand Cross Solomon of Ethiopia; FRS, Hon LLD: Cantab 1946, Leeds 1950, Edinburgh 1954, Southampton 1955, Sussex 1963; Hon DCL Oxon 1946, Hon DSc Delhi and Patna 1948; *m* 18 July 1922 Hon Edwina Cynthia Annette Ashley, CI (1947), GBE (1947, CBE 1943), DCVO (1946), GCStJ (*d* 21 Feb 1960), er dau of 1st and last Baron Mount Temple (*see* SHAFTESBURY, E) and was assassinated by an IRA bomb 27 Aug 1979, leaving:

1 PATRICIA EDWINA VICTORIA, **present Countess Mountbatten of Burma**

2 +Pamela Carmen Louise [The Lady Pamela Hicks, Albany, Piccadilly, London W1V 9RP; The Grove, Brightwell Baldwin, Oxon OX9 5PF]; *b* 19 April 1929 (HM KING ALFONSO XIII OF SPAIN and HRH THE DUKE OF KENT stood sponsor); bridesmaid to HM THE QUEEN 20 Nov 1947, Ldy-in-Waiting to HM THE QUEEN (when Princess Elizabeth during her visit to Kenya 1952) and Cwlth Tour 1953–54; *m* 13 Jan 1960 David Nightingale Hicks (*d* 29 March 1998), designer, s of Herbert Hicks, of The Hamlet, Coggeshall, Essex, and has:

(1) +Ashley Louis David; *b* 18 July 1963 (HM THE KING OF SWEDEN and HRH THE DUKE OF EDINBURGH stood sponsor); *m* 1990 *Allegra Marina, er dau of Dr Carlo Tondato, of Turin, and has:

1a *Angelica Margherita Edwina; *b* 1992

(1) *Edwina Victoria Louise [Mrs Jeremy Brudenell, Parson's Piece, Roke, Wallingford, Oxon OX9 6JE]; *b* 24 Dec 1961 (HM THE QUEEN and THE QUEEN OF SWEDEN stood sponsor); *m* 1984 *Jeremy A R Brudenell, actor, 2nd s of (John) Michael Brudenell, FRCS, FRCOG, of Hever, Kent, and has:

1a *Maddison May; *b* 1994

2a *Jordan Anne; *b c* July 1995

3a *Ambrosia Maria Elizabeth; *b* 1997

(2) *India Amanda Caroline; *b* 5 Sept 1967 (TRH THE PRINCE OF WALES and THE DUCHESS OF KENT stood sponsor)

MOUNTEVANS

Arms: Arg. two bars wavy az. between three boar's heads erased sa. **Crest:** Between two cross crosslets fitchée sa. a demi-lion erased regardant or, holding between the paws a boar's head erased, also sa. **Supporters:** On either side a king penguin ppr. **Motto:** *Libertas* ('Liberty'). **Creation:** B. (UK) 12 Nov 1945.

THE 3RD BARON MOUNTEVANS, of Chelsea, Co London ((Edward Patrick) Broke Andvord Evans) [The Rt Hon The Lord Mountevans, House of Lords, London SW1A 0PW]; *b* 1 Feb 1943; *s f* 1974; *educ* Rugby and Trin Coll Oxford (BA 1965); Lt (ret) 74 MC Regt AER (TAVR), manager: Consolidated Goldfields 1966–72, BTA: Sweden and Finland 1972–73, Head Promotion Servs London 1976, Marketing Manager 1982–89 (Advsr 1989–); *m* 26 July 1973 *Johanna Maria, er dau of Antonius Franciscus Keyzer, of The Hague

Lineage: FRANK EVANS, barrister, of 5 New Sq, Lincoln's Inn, London WC2; *d* 1921, leaving:

EDWARD RATCLIFFE GARTH RUSSELL EVANS, **1st Baron Mountevans**, of Chelsea, Co London (UK), so *cr* 12 Nov 1945, KCB, DSO; *b* 28 Oct 1881; *educ* Merchant Taylor's and HMS *Worcester*; 2nd Offr Relief Ship *Morning* Nat Antarctic Expdn 1902–04 (Antarctic Medal), 2ic Br Expdn 1910–13, Dover Patrol cmdg HMS *Broke* and Sr Naval Offr Ostend (despatches) WW I, cmded HMS *Carlisle* 1920–22, Capt Patrol, Mine-sweeping and Fishery Protection Flotilla 1923–25, cmded HMS *Repulse* 1926–27, Naval ADC to HM GEORGE V 1928, R-Adml 1928, V-Adml 1932, cmded RAN 1929–31, C-in-C Africa Station 1933–35, Actg HC S Africa 1933–35, C-in-C The Nore 1935–39, Adml 1936, Head Factories Def Sect Min Aircraft Prodn 1940, Jt Regl Commr CD London Regn 1939–45, Rector Aberdeen U 1936–42 (LLD 1936), KStJ, Freedom Calgary 1914, Dover 1938, Chatham 1939 and Chelsea 1945, Admlty's Shadwell Testimonial Prize 1907, Livingstone Gold Medal of Roy Scottish Geographical Soc 1913, Lloyd's Gold Medal 1922, BOT Silver Medal Gallantry at Sea 1923, Cdr Order St Olaf Norway, Cavalier Mil Order Savoy, Legn Hon, Croix de Guerre, Orders Leopold and Crown Belgium, Tower and Sword Portugal, US Navy Cross, Norwegian War Medal; *m* 1st 13 April 1904 Hilda Beatrice (*d* 18 April 1913), dau of Thomas Gregory Russell, barrister, of Christchurch, NZ; *m* 2nd 22 Jan 1916 Elsa (*d* 21 Oct 1963), dau of Richard Andvord, of Oslo, and by her had:

1 RICHARD ANDVORD, **2nd Baron**

2 +Edward Broke, VRD [Cdr The Hon Edward Evans VRD RNR, 15 York Mansions, Prince of Wales Dve, London SW11]; Cdr (E) RNR, with ICI; *b* 21 Aug 1924; *educ* Simonstown S Africa and Wellington; *m* 15 July 1947 *Elaine Elizabeth, dau of Capt (S) William Wilson Cove, RN, of The Clock House, Bodenham, Wilts, and has:

(1) +Julian Phillip Broke; *b* 25 April 1956

(2) +William Garth; *b* 2 April 1959

(1) *Rosemary Broke; *b* 18 Oct 1948

The 1st BARON *d* 20 Aug 1958; his er son,

RICHARD ANDVORD EVANS, **2nd Baron Mountevans**; *b* 28 Aug 1918; *educ* Cranbrook Sch Sydney and Stowe; Lt (S) RNVR WW II, with ICI 1946–61, Dir Internat Fedn Periodical Press, Chm Anglo-Swedish Parly Gp and Norwegian Export Centre, V-Chm Anglo-Norwegian Parly Gp, Kt Cdr Vasa Sweden; *m* 6 Sept 1940 Deirdre Grace (*d* 16 Sept 1997), dau of John O'Connell, of Buxton House, Buxton Hill, Co Cork, and *d* 12 Dec 1974, leaving:

1 (EDWARD PATRICK) BROKE EVANS, **3rd and present Baron Mountevans**

2 +JEFFREY RICHARD De CORBAN [The Hon Jeffrey Evans, 5 Campden House Court, 42 Gloucester Walk, London W8 4HU]; *b* 13 May 1948; heir presumptive; *educ* Nautical Coll Pangbourne and Pembroke Coll Cambridge (BA 1971); dir H Clarkson & Co, Liveryman Shipwrights' Co; *m* 1 July 1972 *Hon Juliet Wilson, dau of 2nd Baron Moran (*qv*), and has:

(1) +Alexander Richard Andvord; *b* 23 July 1975

(2) +Julian James Rowntree; *b* 20 Sept 1977

1 *Lucinda Mary Deirdre; *b* 8 Jan 1951 (retains maiden name); jnlst; *m* 1980 *John E Hooper

MOUNTGARRET

Depressus · extollor

Arms: Quarterly: 1st and 4th, per fess sa. and az. a quadrangular castle with four towers between three martlets, all arg. (for RAWSON); 2nd and 3rd, or a chief indented az., a crescent for difference (for BUTLER). **Crests:** 1 An eagle's head per fess sa. and az. gouttée d'or, holding in the beak two annulets interlaced paleways or (for RAWSON); 2 Out of a ducal coronet or a plume of five ostrich feathers arg., therefrom a falcon rising of the last (for BUTLER). **Supporters:** Dexter, a falcon, wings inverted arg., beak membered or; sinister, a male griffin arg., armed, beaked, forelegged, rayed, collared and chained or. **Motto:** *Depressus extollor* ('Adversity makes me only the more keyed up'). **Creations:** V. (I) 23 Oct 1550, B. (UK) 20 June 1911.

THE 17TH VISCOUNT MOUNTGARRET, Co Wexford, and **Baron Mountgarret of Nidd**, West Riding of Yorkshire (Richard Henry Piers Butler) [The Rt Hon The Viscount Mountgarret, Stainley House, South Stainley, Yorks HG3 3LX; 42 Ebury Bridge Rd, London SW1W 8PZ]; *b* 8 Nov 1936, *s* f 1966; *educ* Eton and RMA Sandhurst; 2nd Lt 1956, Sub Capt (ret 1964) Irish Gds, Pres Yorks CC 1984–90; *m* 1st 20 May 1960 (*divorce* 1969) Gillian Margaret (*m* 2nd, as his 2nd w, 9th Baron Howard de Walden, *qv*), only dau of Cyril Francis Stuart Buckley, of Chelsea, and has:

1 +PIERS JAMES RICHARD; *b* 15 April 1961; *educ* Eton; *m* 2 Sept 1995 *Laura Brown Gary, dau of Albert Dickens Williams Jr, of Lake Forest, Ill.

2 +Edmund Henry Richard; *b* 1 Sept 1962; *educ* Stowe; *m* 1988 *Adelle I, only dau of M Lloyd, of New York

1 *Henrietta Elizabeth Alexandra; *b* 4 Nov 1964; *m* 1991 *Robert Cluer, only s of Henry Cluer, of S Africa

The 17th VISCOUNT *m* 2nd 29 April 1970 (*divorce* 1983) Jennifer Susan Melville, yr dau of (Walter) Douglas Melville Wills, CBE, of Barley Wood, Wrington, nr Bristol, and formerly w of David William Fattorini, of Sawley Hall, Ripon, Yorks; *m* 3rd 25 May 1983 *Angela Ruth, dau of Maj Thomas G Porter, of The Croft, Church Fenton, Tadcaster, Yorks, and formerly w of John Waddington

Lineage: RICHARD BUTLER, **1st Viscount Mountgarrett** (I), of Co Wexford, so *cr* 23 Oct 1550 (2nd/3rd s of 8th Earl of Ormonde and (1st Earl of) Ossory; *see* 1970 edn); ktd 1546/7; *m* 1st Catherine, dau and heiress of Peter Barnewall, of Stackallan, Co Meath, and had a s (*d* young and unm); *m* 2nd 1541 (*divorce* 1546) Anne Plunket (*m* 2nd William Fleming), dau of 4th Lord Killeen (*see* 1970 edn FINGALL, E) by his 1st w Margaret, dau of 2nd Viscount Gormanston (*qv*); *m* 3rd (*divorce* 1546) Eleanor, (*m* 3rd John *Og* ('The Younger') FitzGibbon, the white knight), dau of Sir John FitzGerald, styled Earl of Desmond (*see* DENBIGH and DESMOND, E, preliminary remarks; his right to the title was disputed) and widow of Thomas Tobin, of Killaghy, feudal Ld of Compshinagh, Co Tipperary; *m* 4th his cousin Ellen/Evelyn (living 4 June 1575), dau of Theobald Butler, of Neigham, Co Kilkenny (whose f was an illegitimate bro of the 8th Earl of Ormonde and (1st Earl of) Ossory), and *d* 20 Dec 1571, leaving by her:

1 EDMUND, **2nd Viscount**

2 Piers; *m* Margaret, dau of Sir Nicholas Devereux, of Balmagir, Co Wexford and had issue

3 Thomas; *m* and had issue

4 John; *m* and had issue

1 Margaret; *m* Sir Nicholas Devereux, the younger, of Ballymagin, Co Wexford, and *dsp*

2 Ellice; *m* Walter Walsh, of Castlehoel, Co Kilkenny, and had issue

3 Eleanor; *m* 1st Thomas Tobin, of Campshinagh, Co Tipperary; *m* 2nd Gerald Blanchville, of Blanchevillstown, Co Kilkenny; *m* 3rd by Oct 1598 Thomas Butler, 2nd Baron of Caher, and had:

   (1) Margaret; *b c* 1606; *m* by 1627, as his 1st w, 3rd Baron Dunboyne (*qv*) and *d* 1632, leaving issue

4 Catherine; *m* Marcus FitzHarris, of Macmine, Co Wexford

5 Ellen; *m* as his 1st w Sir Oliver Shortall, of Ballylarkin, Co Kilkenny, and had:
   (1) James

The est son,

EDMUND BUTLER, **2nd Viscount Mountgarret**; Dep and Sheriff Co Kilkenny 1576; *m* Grizel/Grany FitzPatrick, dau of 1st Baron of Upper Ossory by his 3rd w Elizabeth O'Connor and had:

1 RICHARD, **3rd Viscount**

2 James, of Tinnahinch, Co Carlow, and Ballyboro, Co Wexford; cmded Confederate Horse Ulster 1664; *m* Catherine Fleming, dau of Thomas, 10th Lord Slane, and mother by Pierce Butler of 1st Viscount of Galmoye, and had:

   (1) Edward; *m* Susan Luttrell and *d* 1637, leaving two daus

3 Edward; fought alongside his est bro 1600

4 Thomas; *m* a dau of 2nd Baron Dunboyne (*qv*)

5 Theobald; *m* Lettice FitzGerald, of Queen's Co, and had four sons

6 John; Gen Confederate Horse Leinster 1641

7 Gilbert; living 1631

8 Piers; of Killagheen, Co Tipperary; living 1631

1 Helen; *m* her distant cousin 11th Earl of Ormond and (4th Earl of) Ossory and *d* 28 Jan 1631/2, leaving issue

2 Eleanor; *m* Morgan MacBryan Kavanagh, of Co Carlow, and had 16 children

3 Ellen; *m* Sir Lucas Shee, of Upper Court, Co Kilkenny, and was greatgrandmother of the 2nd w of the **5th Viscount** (*see* below)

4 Mary; *m* 1st Piers Butler, s of Sir Edmond Butler, of Cloughgrenan; *m* 2nd Brian O'Connor (*d* 1621); *m* 3rd Calvach O'Molloy

5 Margaret; *m* Oliver Grace, of Carney, Co Tipperary

6 Anne; *m* 1st Viscount of Galmoye and had issue

7 Joan; *m* William O'Farrell, of Ballintober, Co Longford

8 Ellice/Elizabeth; *m* Walter Dalton, of Killmodalin, Co Kilkenny

The 2nd VISCOUNT *d* 24 Nov 1602; his est son,

RICHARD BUTLER, **3rd Viscount Mountgarret**; *b c* 1578; Jt Govr Co Kilkenny at start of uprising by Confedn of Kilkenny 1641 but soon went over to the Confedn, cmdg Irish forces at Battle of Kilrush 15 April 1642, where his cousin Lord Ormond led the opposing side to victory, also at Battles of Liscarrol 3 Sept 1642 (another victory for the Crown forces), Pres Supreme Cncl Confedn of Kilkenny 1642–48, negotiating peace 28 March 1646; *m* 1st by 8 Oct 1596 Margaret, dau of 3rd and last Earl of Tyrone (*see* O'NEILL, B), by his 2nd w and had:

1 EDMUND ROE, **4th Viscount**

2 Edward; cmded Confederate garrison Urlingford Castle 1642; *m* Mary, dau of Edmund FitzPatrick, and was executed by a Cromwellian offr at Kilkenny 1652

3 Richard; cmded Confederate garrison Kilkenny Castle 1646

1 Elizabeth; *m* Sir Walter Butler, 1st Bt, of Poolestown (*see* ORMONDE, M), and *d* 26 Aug 1636, leaving issue

2 Ellice; *m* Andrew FitzPatrick, bro of Mary (*see* above)

3 Margaret; *m* July 1631 Sir Richard Belling, Sec to Supreme Cncl Confedn Kilkenny; *d* 6 Aug 1635, leaving, with six yr sons:

   (1) Richard; sec to QUEEN CATHERINE OF BRAGANZA, CHARLES II's consort

4 Ellen; *m* Philip Purcell, of Ballyfoile, and had issue

5 Joan; *m* 1st Sir Richard Masterston, of Ferns; *m* 2nd Sir Philip Paulet, of Carrylough, Co Wexford, and *d* 1633, leaving issue

The **3rd Viscount** *m* 2nd by 1617/8 Thomasine Elizabeth (*dsp* 1625), dau of Sir William Andrews, of Newport Pagnell, Bucks; *m* 3rd by 23 July 1631 Margaret (*d* 16 Dec 1655), widow of Sir Thomas Spencer, Bt, of Yarnton, and dau of Richard Branthwaite, Serjeant-at-law, and *d* 1651

His est son,

EDMUND ROE BUTLER, **4th Viscount Mountgarret**; *b c* 1595; joined his f in the 1641 uprising, Govr Kilkenny 1646, Capt in army of exiled CHARLES II, by whom pardoned 1660 and given back his estates; *m* 1st Lady Dorothy Touchet (*d* 10 Feb 1635), 2nd dau of 2nd Earl of Castlehaven (*see* 1970 edn AUDLEY, B), and had:

1 RICHARD, **5th Viscount**

2 James; *d* young

1 Margaret; *d* unm

2 Elizabeth; *m* — Sutton, of Co Wexford, and *dsp*

The **4th Viscount** *m* 2nd 1635 Anne (*d* 1636), widow of William Thatcher and dau of Sir Thomas Tresham; *m* 3rd 1637 Elizabeth (*d* 18 Feb 1674), widow of Sir John Conyers and dau of Sir George Simeon (*see* VAUX OF HARROWDEN, B), and by her had:

3 Edward, of Ballyraggett, Co Kilkenny; *m* Elizabeth, dau of George Mathew, of Thomastown, Co Tipperary, and had issue (*see* VAUX OF HARROWDEN, B)

3 Elizabeth

The 4th VISCOUNT *d* 5 April 1679; his est son,

RICHARD BUTLER, **5th Viscount Mountgarret**; Captain French Army *temp* CHARLES II and Jacobite army Siege of Londonderry 1689; *m* 1st Sept 1661 Emilia (*d* 1682), dau of William Blundell, of Crosby, Lancs, and had:

1 EDMUND, **6th Viscount**

2 Richard; *b* 1666; *m* 1690 Lady Hamilton, widow, and left issue abroad

3 James; *b* 1675; in Flanders 1694; had issue abroad

The **5th Viscount** *m* 2nd his 3rd cousin Margaret, widow of Gilbert Butler, of Tynehinch, and dau of Richard Shee, of Shee's Court, and *d* 27 Feb 1707

His est son,

EDMUND BUTLER, **6th Viscount Mountgarret**; Lt-Col Horse in JAMES II's Irish army, taken prisoner Siege Londonderry 1689; *b* 17 July 1663; *m* 1st by 15 Feb 1691 Mary Buchanan, of Londonderry; *m* 2nd 2 Aug 1715 Elizabeth (*d* 13 June 1736), widow of Oliver Grace and dau of John Bryan, of Bawnmore, Co Kilkenny, and *d* 25 July 1735, having by his 1st w had:

1 RICHARD BUTLER, **7th Viscount Mountgarret**; *b* by 15 Feb 1691; *m* 19 Oct 1711 Catherine (*d* 15 April 1739), dau of John O'Neill, of Shane's Castle (*see* O'NEILL, B), and *dsp* 14 May 1736

2 JAMES BUTLER, **8th Viscount Mountgarret**; served Austrian Army of HRE CHARLES VI 1735; *m* Jan 1736 Margaret (*d* June 1764), 2nd dau of 11th Baron Trimlestown (*qv*), and *dsp* 13 May 1749

3 EDMUND, **9th Viscount**

1 Emilia; *m* 1712 Hugh Reilly, of Ballinlough, Co Meath, and *dsp*

The 8th VISCOUNT's yr bro,

EDMUND BUTLER, **9th Viscount Mountgarret**; *m* Anne (*d* Oct 1773), dau of Toby Purcell, of Ballymartin, Co Kilkenny, and *d* 6 March 1750/1, having had:

1 EDMUND BUTLER, **10th Viscount Mountgarret**; *educ* Trin Coll Dublin and Middle Temple; barrister 1749; *m* 1744 Charlotte (*d* 27 March 1778), 2nd dau of Sir Simon Bradstreet, 1st Bt, and had:

(1) EDMUND, **11th Viscount**

(2) Richard; in holy (C of I?) orders, Rector Tullophelin, Co Carlow; *d* unm Aug 1795

(3) Simon; barrister; *m* 18 Jan 1795 Eliza, dau of Edward Lynch, of Hampstead, Co Dublin, and *d* 19 May 1797 aged 48, leaving:

  1a Edward Lynch; *b* 1796

(1) Elinor; *d* unm 18 April 1762 aged 15

(2) Anne Emilia; *m* Lt-Col William Jephson, of The Castle, Mallow, Co Cork, and *d* 1786

The 10th VISCOUNT *d* 9 Feb 1779; his est son,

EDMUND BUTLER, **11th Viscount Mountgarret**; MP Co Kilkenny 1776–79; *b* 27 July 1745; *m* 7 Oct 1768 Lady Henrietta Butler (*b* 15 Aug 1750; *d* 16 June 1785), 2nd dau of 1st Earl of Carrick (*qv*), and *d* 16 July 1793, having had:

1 EDMUND BUTLER, **12th Viscount Mountgarret** and 1st and last EARL OF KILKENNY (I), so *cr* 2 Dec 1793; *b* 6 Jan 1771; *m* 8 June 1793 Mildred (*dsp* 30 Dec 1830), est dau of Most Rev Robert Fowler, Archbp Dublin, and *d* insane (which he had been from 1799) 16 July 1846, when the Earldom expired

2 Somerset Richard; *b* Dec 1771; *m* Jane, widow of Daniel Kelly and est dau of Arthur French, of French Park, Co Roscommon, and *dsp* 18 April 1826

3 Henry, of Linton, Yorks; *b* 16 Feb 1773; *m* 3 Sept 1811 Anne (*d* 19 May 1857), yst dau and coheir of John Harrison, of Newton House, Yorks, and *d* 6 Dec 1842, leaving:

(1) HENRY EDMUND, **13th Viscount**

(1) Anne Henrietta; granted with her sisters rank of viscount's daus 30 Nov 1855; *m* 26 Aug 1863 Capt James Little, JP, of Bovennet House, Co Down, and Cliff Castle, Co Dublin, and *dsp* 15 May 1866

(2) Juliana Jemima; *m* 20 Sept 1842 Thomas Clifton Wilkinson, of Newall Hall, Yorks, and *d* 19 Feb 1873, leaving issue. He *d* 1889

(3) Charlotte; *m* 20 June 1865 John Stedman Christie, of Newton House, Lanarks, and *dsp* 23 Oct 1894

4 Pierce; Col Kilkenny Militia, MP; *b* 6 May 1774; *m* 1800 Anne (*d* 1872), dau of Thomas March of Lisburne, and *d* 13 June 1846, having had, with three daus (*d* unm):

(1) Pierce Somerset; *b* 26 Jan 1801; *m* 3 Feb 1835 Jessy Anne (*d* 4 April 1888), widow of Poole Abel Warren, of Lodge Park, Co Kilkenny, and *d* 28 July 1865, having had two daus (*dvp* unm)

(2) Edmund John (Rev); *b* 8 July 1804; *m* 11 Aug 1832 Eliza (*d* 23 Aug 1836), dau of Maj-Gen John Wilson Kettlewell, RA, and *d* 3 April 1873, leaving:

  1a Anne; *m* 22 Dec 1880 John Hewson, of Cambridge

  2a Eliza; *d* unm

(3) Henry; Capt 59th Regt; *b* 21 June 1805; *m* 16 April 1846 Clara (*d* 28 Dec 1901), est dau of John Taylor, of The Newarke, and *d* 13 April 1881, having had:

  1a Pierce Henry; *b* 25 July, *d* 12 Aug 1847

  2a Somerset James, of Kilmurry, Thomastown, Co Kilkenny, DL Co Kilkenny; High Sheriff 1893, Lt-Col Roy Berks Regt; *b* 2 Feb 1849; *d* 10 Aug 1922

  3a Henry; Capt 31st Regt; *b* 11 Oct 1850; *dsp* 9 Aug 1884

  4a Walter Theobald, of Kilmurry; Maj 5th Bn Roy Irish Regt; *b* 11 Feb 1853; *d* 16 Oct 1931

  1a Isabel Harriet; *d* 1 April 1935

  2a Mildred Anne; RWS (exhibited RA and elsewhere); *d* unm 11 Oct 1941

(4) Somerset, of Belvedere House, Sandymount, Dublin; *b* 1808; *dsp* 21 Jan 1850

(5) Thomas; *b* 1810; *dsp* 1848

(6) William; Lt RN; *b* 8 Aug 1814; *m* 15 April 1841 Catherine (*d* Dec 1844), 2nd dau of John Walsh, and *d* 24 May 1847, leaving:

  1a Walter; *b* Dec 1842; *d* 1850

(7) Walter; *b* 10 Feb 1821; *m* Sept 1852 Maria Emily (*d* 21 April 1902), dau of Michael Farrell, and *d* 22 Oct 1900, leaving:

  1a Theobald; *b* 22 Oct 1853; *m* 1st 15 April 1882 (*divorce*) Jane (*d* 30 Jan 1931), est dau of William Edward Stuart, and had:

    1b Theobald Stuart; MICE, Maj RE, Regnl Tech Advsr: Min Home Security WW II and Ch Engr's Branch Home Office, ret 1952; *b* 26 June 1884; *m* 4 Sept 1919 *Edith Sarah, only dau of Joseph Chilton, of Southgate, and *d* 19–, having had:

      1c James Stuart; *b* 28 March 1928; *d* 12 Aug 1937

    1b Kathleen Dorothea; *b* 20 Feb 1883; *m* 2 April 1913 Capt Stephen Percy Groves, RGA, s of Col John Percy Groves, and *d* 24 June 1950, leaving issue. He *d* 15 Dec 1947

  1a (cont) Theobald Butler *m* 2nd 1894 Elizabeth Marie Terese (*d* 1953), dau of Hermann Frazscher, of Sweden, and *d* 1917, having by her had:

    2b Pierce Cyril Somerset; MD, pioneer geriatric research; *m* 31 March 1923 Kerstein Maria (*d* 21 April 1967), est dau of Carl Samuelson, of Sweden, and *d* 14 April 1906, leaving:

      1c +Pierce Torsten [Pierce Butler Esq, Raketgatob 18, 22357, Lund, Sweden]; *b* 24 Nov 1927; *m* 4 June 1952 Dagmar (*d* 7 July 1968), dau of Richard Hakansson, of Sweden, and has:

        1d +Pierce Richard; *b* 8 Feb 1962

        1d *Jenny Maria; *b* 8 Nov 1953

        2d *Anne Kerstin; *b* 17 June 1956

      2c +Carl Somerset [Carl Butler Esq, Rorstrandsgaten 11, 113, 40, Stockholm, Sweden]; *b* 16 Feb 1929

      3c +Lars Theobald [Lars Butler Esq, Hagagaten 1 113 48, Stockholm, Sweden]; *b* 24 Nov 1939; *m* 18 June 1959 *Ulla, dau of A Bergh, of Sundsvall, and has:

        1d +Pierce Anders; *b* 11 Oct 1963

        1d *Anna Christina; *b* 15 April 1962

      1c *Kerstin Ellen Lisbeth; *b* 1923

    2b Dorothea Beatrice; *b* 1897; *m* 1928 Edward de Fine Sucht and had a dau. He *d* 1957

    2a Walter; *b* 22 Sept 1855; *d* 1919

  1a Beatrice Amelia; *d* unm Oct 1928

  2a Isabella Lily, CBE (1920); vol worker Paris WW I; *d* unm

(1) Charlotte Juliana; *b* 6 Aug 1778; *m* 7 Aug 1799 Capt John Carrington Smith and *d* 26 Oct 1830, leaving a son and dau

The 12th VISCOUNT's nephew,

HENRY EDMUND BUTLER, **13th Viscount Mountgarret**, JP, DL Co Kilkenny; *b* 24 Jan 1816; *educ* Worcester Coll Oxford (MA); *m* 11 March 1844 Frances Penelope (*d* 19 Oct 1886), only child of Thomas Rawson, of Nidd Hall, Yorks (*see* LONDONDERRY, M), through whose aunt Lord Moungarret inherited 1891 £561,300 (nearly £30m in late-1990s terms) in cash and securities while his s inherited much real estate, and had:

1 HENRY EDMUND, **14th Viscount**

1 Frances Sarah; *b* 20 Nov 1845; *m* 29 Sept 1892 Edward Arthur Whittuck, of Claverton Manor, nr Bath, s of Whittuck Whittuck, of Hanham, Glos, and *dsp* 23 Feb 1916. He *d* 10 March 1924

The 13th VISCOUNT *d* 26 Aug 1900; his only son,

HENRY EDMUND BUTLER later RAWSON-BUTLER (roy licence 26 May 1891) later still BUTLER again, **14th Viscount Mountgarret**, JP (W R Yorks), DL (W R Yorks, Co Kilkenny); *b* 18 Dec 1844; *educ* Eton and Ch Ch Oxford; High Sheriff Yorks 1895, Lt 1st Life Gds, *cr* 20 June 1911 BARON MOUNTGARRET OF NIDD, W Riding Co York (UK); *m* 1st 1 Oct 1868 Mary Eleanor (*d* 12 May 1900), yst dau of St John Chiverton Charlton, of Apley Castle, Salop (*see* MEYRICK, Bt), and had:

1 EDMUND SOMERSET BUTLER, **15th Viscount Mountgarret**; *b* 1 Feb 1875; *m* 1 June 1897 Cecily (*m* 2nd 12 July 1919 Lt-Col Charles Hervey GREY formerly HOARE, DSO (*d* 24 July 1955), of Earlybank House, Stalybridge, and W Lodge, Malton; *d* 8 April 1961), dau of Arthur GREY formerly DUNCOMBE (*see* FEVERSHAM, B), and *dsp* 22 June 1918

1 Elinor Frances; *b* 25 Nov 1869; *m* 1st 28 Feb 1889 Andrew Sherlock Lawson, DL, of Aldborough Manor, Yorks, and had issue (*see* LAWSON-TANCRED, Bt); *m* 2nd Jan 1918 Alfred James Bethell, 82nd Regt, of The Abbey, Storrington, and *d* 8 Dec 1943. He *d* 28 Oct 1920

2 Ethel Mary; *b* 11 June 1871; *m* 2 March 1897 Henry Rimington Wilson, 2nd s of James Rimington Wilson, of Bromhead Hall, Yorks, and *d* 27 Jan 1926, leaving issue. He *d* 17 May 1915

3 Kathleen Grace; twin with Edmund; *d* 30 Aug 1875

The **14th Viscount** *m* 2nd 5 Feb 1902 Robina Marion, OBE (1920), DGStJ (*d* 13 Dec 1944), er dau of Col Edward Hanning Hanning-Lee, of Bighton Manor, Alresford, Hants, and *d* 2 Oct 1912, having by her had:

2 PIERS HENRY AUGUSTINE BUTLER, **16th Viscount Mountgarret**, JP W R Yorks 1928–65; *b* 28 Aug 1903; *educ* RNCs Osborne and Dartmouth and Trin Coll Cambridge; MFH N Yorks and Ansty 1929–37, OStJ; *m* 1st 15 Oct 1931 (*divorce* 1941) (Eglantine Marie) Elizabeth (*m* 2nd 1956 R-Adml Patrick Vivian McLaughlin, CB, DSO (*d* 1969), est dau of William Lorenzo Christie, of Jervaulx Abbey, Middleham, Yorks, and had:

(1) RICHARD HENRY PIERS BUTLER, **17th and present Viscount Mountgarret**

(1) *Sarah Elizabeth Ann [The Hon Mrs Sarah Raynar, 52 St Anne's Rd, Headingley, Leeds L6 3NX]; *b* 26 Dec 1932; *m* 5 Nov 1955 (*divorce* 1976) Geoffrey Kenneth Sefton Raynar, 2nd s of Joseph Percival Raynar, of Bilton Hall, Yorks, and has:

  1a *Rupert James Geoffrey; *b* 28 Jan 1957

  2a *James Augustine; *b* 4 July 1962

2 (cont.) The **16th Viscount** *m* 2nd 14 Nov 1941 Elise Margarita (*d* 8 Aug 1968), only dau of Sir John Nicholson Barran, 2nd Bt (*qv*), and *d* 2 Aug 1966

MOWBRAY

Arms: Quarterly, 1st and 4th, gu. a lion rampant erm., two flaunches or, each charged with three billets in pale az. (for MOWBRAY); 2nd and 3rd, per pale az. and sa. a chevron embattled between in chief two roses and in base a cross-pattée or (for CORNISH). **Crests:** 1 An oak tree or, therefrom pendant an escutcheon gu. charged with a lion's head erased arg. (for MOWBRAY); 2 Between two branches of laurel a Cornish chough rising ppr., charged on the breast with a cross-pattée or (for CORNISH). **Mottoes:** 1 *Suo stat robore virtus* ('Virtue stands by its own strength') (for MOWBRAY), 2 *Deus pascit corvos* ('God feedeth the ravens') (for CORNISH). **Creation:** Bt (UK) 3 May 1880.

SIR JOHN ROBERT MOWBRAY, 6TH BT, of Mortimer, Berks, and Bishopwearmouth, Co Durham, DL (Suffolk 1993) [Sir John Mowbray Bt DL, The Hill House, Duffs Hill, Glemsford, Suffolk CO10 7PP]; *b* 1 March 1932; *s* f 1969; *educ* Eton and New Coll Oxford; *m* 3 July 1957 *Lavinia Mary, only dau of Lt-Col Francis Edgar Hugonin, OBE, JP, RA (*see* WALKER, Bt, of Sand Hutton), of Stainton House, Stainton-in-Cleveland, Yorks, and has:

1 *Mary Clare; *b* 8 June 1959; *m* 12 May 1984 *James D Delevingne, only s of E N Delevingne, and has:

  (1) *Benjamin James; *b* 1984

  (2) *Oliver Guy; *b* 1988

2 *Teresa Jane; *b* 7 April 1961

3 *Katherine Diana; *b* 23 Dec 1965; *m* 1993 *David Norman Chastel de Boinville, s of Gerard Nicolas Pyemont Chastel de Boinville, MC, TD, of Walkern Hall, Herts, and has:

  (1) *William Mowbray; *b* 1997

Lineage: TEASDALE MOWBRAY, of Wolsingham, Co Durham; *m* 1738 Anne, dau and heir of Thomas Reid, of Bishopswearmouth, and had:

GEORGE MOWBRAY, of Ford, Co Durham; *m* Elizabeth, dau of Anthony Wilkinson, of Crossgate, Co Durham, and *d* 1791; his only surv child:

GEORGE MOWBRAY, of Ford and Mortimer, Berks; *m* Jane, dau and heir of Oliver Coghill, of Coghill Hall, Yorks, and *d* 1798, leaving:

1 GEORGE ISAAC

2 Thomas, of Grange Wood House, Overseale, Leics; Capt RN; *b* 28 Aug 1793; *m* 22 April 1823 Anne (*d* 1 July 1869), dau of Richard Thomas Streatfeild, of Gawthorpe, Lancs, and *d* 16 June 1864, leaving:

  (1) George Thomas, of Grange Wood House, JP (Derbys and Leics), DL (Leics); *b* 29 April 1824; *educ* Cambridge (MA); Derbys: High Sheriff 1879, Maj Militia; *d* unm 29 Feb 1892

  (2) Sydney Richard; *d* in infancy

  (1) Georgina Anne, of Grange Wood House; *m* 15 Feb 1858 Pierre Richard de Preville, of Orthes, France, and had issue

The er son,

GEORGE ISAAC MOWBRAY, of Bishopwearmouth and Mortimer; *m* Nov 1821 Elizabeth, est dau of Rt Rev Robert Gray, DD, Bp Bristol, and *d* 25 June 1823, leaving an only dau:

1 ELIZABETH Mowbray; *m* 19 Aug 1847 Sir JOHN ROBERT CORNISH later MOWBRAY (roy licence 26 July 1847), **1st Bt** (UK), so *cr* 3 May 1880, PC, JP, DL Co Durham, JP, CA Berks, MA and DCL Oxon (*b* 3 June 1815; MP (C) Durham 1853–68 and Oxford U 1868–99, JAG 1858–59 and 1866–68; *d* 22 April 1899), only s of Robert Stribling Cornish, of Exeter, by Marianne, dau and heiress of John Powning, of Hills Court, Exeter, and *d* 16 Feb 1899, having had:

  (1) **Sir Robert Gray Cornish Mowbray, 2nd Bt**, JP, DL and CA Berks; *b* 21 May 1850; *educ* Eton and Balliol Coll Oxford (MA); Fell All Souls, Chm Berks QS and CC, MP Prestwich 1886–95 and Lambeth 1900–06, barrister Inner Temple; *d* unm 23 July 1916

  (2) **Sir Reginald Ambrose Mowbray, 3rd Bt**; *b* 5 April 1852; *educ* Ch Ch Oxford (MA); *d* unm 30 Dec 1916

  (3) EDMUND GEORGE LIONEL (Sir), **4th Bt**

  (1) Annie Maud; *m* 5 Aug 1884 Rev Charles Thomas Cruttwell, Rector Ewelme and Canon Residentiary Peterborough, and *d* 29 Oct 1926, leaving issue. He *d* 4 April 1911

  (2) Edith Marian; *d* unm 27 March 1933

The 3rd Baronet's yr bro,

Rev Sir Edmund George Lionel Mowbray, 4th Bt; *b* 26 June 1859; *educ* New Coll Oxford (MA); ordained 1883, Rector Durley Hants 1890–92, Vicar St Bartholomew, Charlton-in-Dover, 1892–1906, Freeland Oxford 1908–09 and St Michael and All Angels Brighton 1909–17; *m* 27 Jan 1891 Caroline Elwes (*d* 18 March 1941), dau of Lt-Gen George T Field, RA, and *d* 2 Feb 1919, leaving:

Sir George Robert Mowbray, 5th Bt, KBE (1957), JP (1925), DL (1967); CA Berks 1938, High Sheriff 1930, Chm CC 1944–46 and 1960–65 (V-Chm 1957–60); *b* 15 July 1899; *educ* Charterhouse and New Coll Oxford (BA 1929, MA 1945); Pres Cncl Reading U 1933–66 (Treas 1931–33), Lt RFA WWs I and II (CD, ARP Controller Berks), V-Chm CCs Assoc 1946–47 and 1949–50 (Chm 1950–56), memb Roy Commn Civil Service 1953–55, Warden Bradfield Coll 1945–46; *m* 1 Nov 1927 Diana Margaret (*d* 18 Oct 1996), yst dau of Sir Robert Heywood Hughes, 12th Bt (*qv*), and *d* 9 Nov 1969, leaving:

1 Sir JOHN ROBERT MOWBRAY, **6th and present Bt**

1 *Carolyn Mary [Mrs Stamford Vanderstegen-Drake, The Old Tannery, Ecchinswell, Berks]; *b* 2 March 1930; *m* 14 June 1952 *Stamford Robert Francis Vanderstegen-Drake, yr s of Maj John Hughes Drake, of Inshriach, Aviemore, Inverness-shire, and has:

  (1) *John Peter; *b* 8 July 1955; *m* 1986 *Charlotte Susannah, dau of Brian Gunn, of Quarry Close, Winscombe, Avon, and has:

    1a *John William; *b* 1988

  (2) *Mark Stamford; *b* 7 May 1959; *m* 1986 *Susan, dau of Cdr Alan Dickie, of Bowdown House, Rodborough Common, Stroud

  (1) *Clare Rosdew [Mrs Christopher Bromfield, The Old Coaching House, Lacock, Wilts]; *b* 21 Aug 1953; *m* 1st 1978 (*divorce* 1984) William Gerald Cheyne and has issue (*see* CHEYNE Bt); *m* 2nd 1984 *Christopher J B Bromfield, est s of Dr F B Bromfield, of The Blue House, Rodborough Common, and has:

    1a *George Frank; *b* 1985

    1a *Alice Mary; *b* 1987

2 *Elizabeth Rose [Mrs Patrick Glennie, The Old Mill House, Clanfield, Waterlooville, Hants PO8 0RP]; *b* 15 July 1936; *m* 26 Sept 1964 *Capt Patrick Hector Raymond Glennie, RN, yst s of Arthur Glennie, of The Granary, E Ogwell, Devon, and has:

  (1) *Christopher Arthur John; *b* 20 Oct 1966; *m* 1991 *Christina Marie, dau of Cyril Steiner, of Stevensville, Michigan, and has:

    1a *Lucinda Rose; *b* 23 Jan 1998

  (2) *Alexander Patrick; *b* 11 March 1970

  (1) *Sarah Fiennes; *b* 30 Aug 1965; *m* 1997 *Robert John Mathews, s of Richard Mathews, of Shroton, Dorset

MOWBRAY, SEGRAVE and STOURTON

Arms: Quarterly of six, 1st, sa. a bend or between six fountains (for STOURTON); 2nd, gu. on a bend between six cross crosslets arg. an escutcheon or, charged with a demi-lion rampant, pierced through the mouth by an arrow, within a double tressure flory counter-flory of the first (for HOWARD); 3rd, gu. a lion rampant arg. (for MOWBRAY); 4th, sa. a lion rampant arg., ducally crowned or (for SEGRAVE); 5th, gu. three lions passant guardant in pale or, a label of three points arg. (for THOMAS OF BROTHERTON); 6th, gu. a lion rampant or, a border engrailed of the last (for TALBOT).

Crest: A demi-monk ppr., habited in russet, his girdle or, and wielding in his dexter hand a scourge also or, thereon five knotted lashes. **Supporters:** Dexter, a lion arg. ducally crowned or; sinister, a sea-dog sa., scaled and finned or. **Motto:** *Loyal je serai durant ma vie* ('I will be loyal during the whole of my life'). **Badge of the Barons Stourton:** A drag (or sledge) or. **Creations:** B. (E) 28 June 1283/24 June 1295 (Mowbray), 28 June 1283/24 June 1295 (Segrave), 13 May 1448 (Stourton).

THE 26TH LORD (BARON) MOWBRAY, 27TH LORD (BARON) SEGRAVE AND 23RD BARON STOURTON, of Stourton, Wilts (Charles Edward Stourton, CBE (1982)) [The Rt Hon The Lord Mowbray Segrave and Stourton CBE, 23 Warwick Sq, London SW1V 2AB; Marcus by Forfar, Angus DD8 3QH]; *b* 11 March 1923; *s f* 1965; *educ* Ampleforth and Ch Ch Oxford; WW II 1943–44 in Gren Gds, Lt 2nd Armoured Bn (wounded, invalided 1945), memb: Lloyd's 1952 and Nidderdale RDC 1954–59, Oppn Whip Ho Lords 1967–70 and 1974–78, Ld in Waiting 1970–74 and 1979–80, Dep Ch Whip (C) 1978–79, Kt of Honour and Devotion SMO Malta 1947, Kt Sacred and Mil Constantinian Order St George; *m* 28 June 1952 Hon Jane Faith de Yarburgh-Bateson (*d* 2 April 1998), only child of 5th Baron Deramore (*qv*), and has:

1 +EDWARD WILLIAM STEPHEN [The Hon Edward Stourton, The Stables, Allerton Park, nr Knaresborough, N Yorks]; *b* 17 April 1953; *educ* Ampleforth; *m* 12 July 1980 *Penelope Lucy (Nell), est dau of Dr Peter Cameron Jamieson Brunet, MA, DPh, of 4 Rawlinson Rd, Oxford, and has:

(1) +James Charles Peter; *b* 12 Dec 1991

(1) *Sarah Louise; *b* 28 Feb 1982

(2) *Isabel Laura *b* 13 Nov 1983

(3) *Camilla Charlotte; *b* 1987

(4) *Francesca Jane; *b* 1988

2 +James Alastair [The Hon James Stourton, 21 Moreton Place, London SW1V 2NL]; *b* 3 July 1956; *educ* Ampleforth and Magdalene Coll Cambridge; V-chm Sotheby's 1997–, proprietor The Stourton Press, Kt of Honour and Devotion SMO Malta; *m* 1993 (*divorce* 1996) Hon Sophia Ulla Stonor, yst dau of 7th Baron Camoys (*qv*)

Lineage (of Stourton): ROBERT de STOURTON; living 1166; *d* in or after 1177; possibly f of:

WILLIAM de STOURTON; possibly kin to:

Sir MICHAEL de STOURTON; of age by 1199; ktd by 1208; collector of the Fortieth (tax) for Wilts 1232; seems to have *m* — de Bere and *d* in or after 1242–43, leaving:

EUDES de STOURTON; *d* in or after 1257, leaving:

RALPH de STOURTON; of age by 1284; *d* in or after 1303, possibly leaving, with another s (Eudes):

WILLIAM; possibly f of:

JOHN; Sheriff (Wilts? Somerset?) 1377; possibly f of:

WILLIAM de STOURTON; living 1325; *m* Joan — and *d* in or after 1343, leaving an est s:

JOHN de STOURTON, JP Somerset 1355–78; fndr of a chantry for his family 1374; Escheator (royal official implementing reversions of properties without heirs to the Crown) Somerset and Dorset 1377–79; *m* 1st Lettice —; *m* 2nd Alice — and had, probably by his 1st w, with at least one dau (Edith, *m* John Beauchamp, of Bletso; *see* SAINT JOHN OF BLETSO, B, and BEAUFORT, D):

WILLIAM de STOURTON, JP 1382–1413; MP Somerset and Wilts 1401, Speaker-elect H of C 1413 (did not take up post due to physical incapacity); *m* by 1398 Elizabeth, dau and heir of Sir John Moigne, of Maddington, Wilts, and Easton, Essex, and *d* 18 Sept 1413, having had, with a dau:

JOHN STOURTON, **1st Baron Stourton**, of Stourton, Wilts (E), so *cr* 13 May 1448, PC (1437); *b c* 1399; MP Wilts 1421 and Dorset 1423, Sheriff Wilts 1426–27, 1433 and 1437, Somerset and Dorset 1428, Glos 1432 and 1439 and Welsh Marches 1432; ktd by late 1432, Treasurer Household by late 1446, Jt Guardian Calais 1450–55; *m* Margery, dau of Sir John Wadham, of Merrifield, Somerset, Puisne Judge Court Common Pleas, by his 2nd w Joan Wrottesley, and had, with two sons (*dsp*):

1 WILLIAM, **2nd Baron**

2 Reginald (Sir); *m* Margaret, widow of Sir Alexander Hody, of Bowen, Somerset, and had a dau (*m* Oliver Carminow)

1 Margaret; *m* Sir George Darrel, of Littlecote, Wilts, and had a dau (Elizabeth, *m* Sir John Seymour, of Wolfhall, gf by her of JANE SEYMOUR, HENRY VIII's 3rd w)

2 Joan; *m* Richard Warre (*d* 1462), of Hestercombe, Somerset

The 1st BARON *d* 25 Nov 1462; his est son,

WILLIAM STOURTON, **2nd Baron Stourton**, JP (Dorset 1451–61); *b c* 1430; MP Dorset Jan 1446/7, ktd by autumn 1450; *m* by 18 May 1450 Margaret (*m* 2nd 1st and last Lord (Baron) Cheyne of the 1487 *cr*), dau and coheir of Sir John Chidiock by Katherine, dau of Sir Ralph Lumley, and *d* 18 Feb 1477/8, leaving, with other issue:

1 JOHN STOURTON, **3rd Baron Stourton**, KB (1475); *b c* 1454; *m* by 20 Feb 1473/4 Katherine (*m* 2nd by 21 July 1486 Sir John Brereton), dau of Sir Maurice Berkeley, of Beverstone, Glos, and *d* 6 Oct 1485, having had, with a dau (Anna, *d* unm):

(1) FRANCIS STOURTON, **4th Baron Stourton**; *d* an inf 18/27 Feb 1486/7

2 WILLIAM STOURTON, **5th Baron Stourton**, KB (1489); *b c* 1457; allegedly *m* 1st Catherine, dau of John de la Pole, 2nd Duke of Suffolk, by Elizabeth, sis of EDWARD IV and RICHARD III; *m* 2nd(?) Thomasine, dau of Sir Walter Wrottesley (*see* WROTTESLEY, B), but *dsp* 17 Feb 1523/4

3 EDWARD, **6th Baron**

1 Katherine; *m* Sir William Berkeley (*d c* 1486), of Beverstone; *m* 2nd, as his 3rd w, 7th Lord (Baron) Grey (of Codnor) (*qv*); *m* 3rd probably 1497 her bro's bro-in-law Lord William de la Pole, 5th s of 2nd Duke of Suffolk, and *d* 25 Nov 1521

2 Margaret; *m* James Chudleigh, of Ashton, Devon

3 Alice; *m* John Philpot, Sheriff Hants *c* 1501

4 Amy; *m* Sir Henry Rogers, of Bryanston, Dorset

The 5th BARON's bro,

EDWARD STOURTON, **6th Baron Stourton**; *b c* 1463; ktd by late Feb 1502/3; *m* Agnes, dau of John Fauntleroy, of Marsh, Dorset, and *d* 13 Dec 1535, having had, with a dau (*d* unm) and three other sons (including an est, Peter, *dvp*, and two yst ones: Roger, of Ruston, *m* Joan Bures and *dsp*; Christopher, of Little Langford, *m* Elizabeth Dennis and had issue):

WILLIAM STOURTON, **7th Baron Stourton**; *b* by 1505; ktd 1523, MP Somerset 1529–35, served against Scots 1544–45, Dep Gen Ambleteuse, nr Boulogne, 1546–48; *m* Elizabeth, dau of Edmund Dudley and sis of John, Duke of Northumberland (*see* DUDLEY, B), and *d* 16 Sept 1548, having had, with other issue (including by his mistress Agnes, dau of Rhys ap Gruffudd (*see* DINEVOR, B), an illegitimate dau Mary, who *m* Richard Gore, of Alderton, Wilts):

1 CHARLES, **8th Baron**

2 Andrew; *dsp*

3 Arthur, of Over Moigne, Dorset; MP Westminster 1555, Master King's Jewels and Keeper Westminster Palace; *m* Anne, dau of Henry Mackwilliams, and had, with other issue:

(1) Philip, of Over Moigne; *m* Joan St John and had, with other issue:

1a Henry, of Over Moigne; *m* Frances, dau of John Best, of Alington Castle, Kent, and had, with other issue:

1b John; *m* — dau of John Bennett, of Abingdon, Berks, and had, with three sons:

1c Elizabeth *m* her cousin **14th Baron Stourton** (*see below*)

1 Ursula *m* 1st Earl of Lincoln (*qv*)

2 Dorothy; *m* Sir Richard Brent

The 7th BARON's est son,

CHARLES STOURTON, **8th Baron Stourton**; *b* 1518–24; ktd 1547, Ld Lt Wilts, Somerset and Dorset 1553, author: *A Remarkable Treatise On The Sacrament*; *m c* 10 Feb 1548/9 Lady Anne Stanley (*m* 2nd Sir John Arundell, of Lanherne, Cornwall), dau of 3rd Earl of Derby (*qv*), and was hanged 6 March 1556/7 for murdering with four servants his father's steward, having had issue:

1 JOHN STOURTON, **9th Baron Stourton**; *b* Jan 1552/3; *educ* Exeter Coll Oxford; *m c* 1580 Frances Brooke (*m* 2nd Sir Edward Moore, of Odiham, Hants), dau of 10th (Baron) Lord Cobham (*see* COBHAM, V, preliminary remarks), but *dsp* 13 Oct 1588

2 EDWARD, **10th Baron**

3 Charles

1 Mary; *m* Thomas Treglan, of Cornwall

2 Anne; *m* Edward Rogers, of Feltham, Somerset

3 Katherine; *m* Richard Sherborne, of Stonyhurst, Lancs, Capt IoM

The 9th BARON's yr bro,

EDWARD STOURTON, **10th Baron Stourton**; *b c* 1555; *educ* Exeter Coll Oxford; imprisoned Tower London 1605–06 and fined £4,000 (over £240,000 in late-1990s terms) for suspected complicity in the Gunpowder Plot; *m* by 1588 Frances, sis of Sir Lewis Tresham, 1st Bt, and Francis Tresham, one of the Gunpowder conspirators (hence the suspicions as to Lord Stourton), and had:

1 WILLIAM, **11th Baron**

2 Francis; *b* 1599; *m* Elizabeth, dau of Henry Norton, of Chediston, Suffolk, and *d* 1638, leaving:

(1) Frances; *m* Francis Rockley

1 Margaret; *m* Sir Thomas Sulyard, of Wetherden, Suffolk

2 Mary; *m* Walter Norton, of Sibsay, Norfolk

The 10th BARON *d* 7 May 1633; his er son,

WILLIAM STOURTON, **11th Baron Stourton**, KB (1616); *b* by 1594; royalist Civil War hence estates sequestrated by Parl and Stourton House plundered by Gen Ludlow Sept 1644; *m* 2 July 1615 his cousin Frances (*d* 5 Jan 1662), dau of Sir Edward Moore, of Odiham, and had, with other issue:

1 Edward; *b* 1617; royalist Civil War; *m* after 28 Oct 1638 Mary (*d* 1672), dau of 3rd Baron Petre (*qv*), and *dvp* Jan 1643/4, leaving, with a dau (*d* unm):

(1) WILLIAM, **12th Baron**

2 William; *m* Margaret, dau of George Morgan, of Penrith, Cumberland, but *dsp*

3 Thomas; a monk; *d* Paris 1684

1 Mary; *m* 1649 Sir John Weld, of Compton Bassett, Wilts, and Lulworth Castle, Dorset, and *d* 1650, leaving issue

2 Frances; nun at Cambrai

The 11th BARON *d* 25 April 1672; his gs,

WILLIAM STOURTON, **12th Baron Stourton**; RC, hence excluded from Parl by Test Act 1678; *b c* 1644; *m c* 1664 Elizabeth (*d* April 1688), dau of Sir John Preston, 1st Bt, of Preston Patrick and Nether Levens, Westmorland, and *d* 7 Aug 1685, leaving, with other sons (two of whom *d* in infancy):

1 EDWARD STOURTON, **13th Baron Stourton**; *bapt* 24 June 1665; sold 1714 the family estates (including Stourton House) for £19,400 (just under £1,030,000 in late-1990s terms; six years later the property was bought by Henry Hoare, the banker, who demolished Stourton House and constructed a new mansion, which he called Stourhead; the grounds remain to this day); allegedly imprisoned May 1692 for Jacobitism; accompanied JAMES II to France; *m* Teresa, dau of Robert Buckenham, Equerry to JAMES II and the titular James III, and *dsp* Paris 6 Oct 1720

2 THOMAS STOURTON, **14th Baron Stourton**; *bapt* 14 June 1667; *educ* St Gregory's Coll Douai; bought the manor of Bonham; *m* his cousin Elizabeth (*d* 1749), dau of John Stourton, of Over Moigne, and *dsp* 24 March 1743/4

3 Charles; Capt Gds *temp* JAMES II; *bapt* 4 Nov 1669; *m* 1699 Catherine (*d* 1736), dau and coheir of Richard Frampton, of Moreton, Dorset, and *d* 18 Sept 1739, leaving, with other issue:

(1) CHARLES STOURTON, **15th Baron Stourton**; *b* 2 March 1701/2; *educ* St Gregory's and Gray's Inn; *m* 2 April 1733 Catherine (*d* 31 Jan 1785), widow of 7th Baron Petre (*qv*) and dau of Bartholomew Walmsley, of Dunkenhalgh, Lancs, and *dsp* 11 March 1753

(2) WILLIAM, **16th Baron**

(1) Mary; *m* by 1721 Jordan Langdale, of Cliffe, Yorks, and *d* 21 Nov 1764, having had issue

(2) Katherine; nun at Liége; *d* 1777

(3) Jane; *b* 7 Jan 1708; *m* Anthony Kemp, of Slindon, Sussex, and *dsp* Liége 21 Dec 1769

(4) Elizabeth; nun at Liége; *d* 1741

4 John; priest and monk at St Gregory's Douai, Prior Winchester and St Benedict, Flanders; *b* 1673; *d* Antwerp 3 Oct 1748

The 15th BARON's bro,

WILLIAM STOURTON, **16th Baron Stourton**; *b* Aug 1704; *educ* St Gregory's and Gray's Inn; *m* 11 Oct 1749 Winifred (*d* 9 July 1753), est dau of Philip Howard, of Buckenham, Norfolk (on whom his bro the 9th Duke of Norfolk (*qv*) settled the Rothwell Haigh estate) and *d* 3 Oct 1781, having had, with two daus (both nuns at Liége):

CHARLES PHILIP STOURTON, **17th Baron Stourton**; *b* 22 Aug 1752; *educ* St Gregory's; sold 1785 the Manor of Bonham, Stourton, to Henry Hoare, who already owned the bulk of the Stourton estate (*see* above), for £7,288 (a little over £334,000 in late-1990s terms); bought the Allerton Mauleverer estate, Yorks, 1805 and 1810 for £193,315 (some £5,375,000 in late-1990s terms); *m* 12 July 1775 Hon Mary Langdale (*d* 12 April 1841), 2nd dau and eventually sole heiress of 5th and last Baron Langdale of Holme, and had, with two sons (*d* young), and three daus (*d* young or unm):

1 WILLIAM JOSEPH, **18th Baron**

2 Sir EDWARD MARMADUKE JOSEPH STOURTON later VAVASOUR (roy licence 27 Feb 1826), 1st Bt (*qv*)

3 Charles Joseph STOURTON later LANGDALE (roy licence 24 Dec 1814 under terms of will of his cousin Philip Langdale, of Houghton, Yorks), JP, DL; MP Beverley 1828–34 and Knaresborough 1837–41, Capt Yorks Hus; published memoirs of Mrs FitzHerbert (his 1st cousin) 1856; *b* 19 Sept 1787; *m* 1st 27 Jan 1817 Charlotte Mary (*d* 31 March 1819), 5th dau of 6th Baron Clifford of Chudleigh (*qv*), and had, with a dau (*d* unm):

(1) Charlotte Mary; *m* 19 Jan 1846 John Vincent Hornyold (*d* 31 March 1902), 13th Marquess Gandolfi (Genoa *cr* 29 Aug 1529), and *d* 15 Jan 1907, leaving, with other issue:

1a THOMAS CHARLES GANDOLFI-HORNYOLD, 1st DUKE GANDOLFI (Papal *cr* 6 May 1899, as also earlier 29 March 1895 MARQUIS GANDOLFI, with remainder to heirs male), JP (Herefs and Worcs), DL (Worcs), of Blackmore Park and Hanley Castle, Worcs; *b* 22 Dec 1846; Kt Grand Cross Pontifical Order Holy Sepulchre and Kt SMO Malta; *m* 19 Feb 1878 Maria Teresa Luisa (*d* 1918), est dau of Ramon Cabrera, Count de Morella and Marquis del Ter, of Spain, and *d* 27 Feb 1906, having had:

1b ALFONSO OTTO GANDOLFI-HORNYOLD, 2nd DUKE GANDOLFI, also 14th MARQUIS GANDOLFI, 11th MARQUIS OF MELASSI and MONTCRESCENTE (1616) and COUNT OF RICALDONI (1620 both Mantua), 10th COUNT OF GAZELLI and CHIOSANICA (1626 Sardinia); *b* 20 June 1879 (ALFONSO XII OF SPAIN stood sponsor); *m* 8 Jan 1909 Francesca (*d* 3 May 1967), dau of Count Piero Po di Nerviano, and *d* 11 May 1937, leaving:

1c Maria Teresa; *b* 8 Jan 1910; *m* 30 April 1932 Luigi Acchiappati (*d* 1972) and *d* 1988, leaving:

1d *Gianantonio [Gianantonio Acchiappati, 33 rue George Sand, 75016 Paris]; *b* 1933; *m* 1966 *Pierrille, dau of Count Alfred de Bertier de Sauvigny, and has:

1e *Ugo; *b* 1968

1e *Gaîa Francesca; *b* 1971

2d *Pierluigi [Pierluigi Acchiappati, 15 via Zenale, 20121 Milan, Italy]; *b* 1934; *m* 1968 *Chiara, dau of Giorgio Bicchi

1d Elena; *b* 1936; *m* 1964 *Jean-Francis Buck [Jean-Francis Buck, 18 rue Brasseur, Luxembourg 1258] and *d* 1977, having had:

1e Laurent; *b* 1965; *d* 1976

2e *Nicolas; *b* 1968

3e *Frédérique; *b* 1973

2d *Nicoletta [Nicoletta Acchiappati, 33 via Dei Serragli, Florence, Italy]; *b* 1937

2b RALPH VINCENT GANDOLFI-HORNYOLD, 3rd DUKE GANDOLFI; *b* 4 May 1881; Lt 5th Bn Worcs Regt; *m* 14 Dec 1928 Beatrix Purdey (*m* 2nd 7 March 1940 Lt-Col (Cuthbert) Euan Charles Rabagliati (*d* 1978), MC, DFC, KOYLI, of Villa Valentine, Domaine de la Roseraie, Mougins, France AM, and *d* 1992), dau of Frederick Scott Oliver, of Edgerston, nr Jedburgh, Roxburghshire, and *d* 1938, leaving:

1c *ANTONY FREDERICK GANDOLFI-HORNYOLD, 4th DUKE GANDOLFI [Antony Hornyold Esq, Blackmore House, Hanley Swan, Worcs WR8 0EF]; *b* 20 June 1931; *educ* Ampleforth and Trin Coll Cambridge; late 2nd Lt KOSB, FO: 3rd Sec Baghdad 1958, Ankara 1959, FO 1961–62, 2nd Sec Accra 1962–64, FO 1964–66, 1st Sec Rawalpindi 1966–67, MOD 1967, Kt SMO Malta; *m* 1993 *Caroline Mary Katherine, MVO, dau of Maj Patrick Dudley Crichton-Stuart (*see* BUTE, M)

2c *Simon Ralph [Simon Hornyold Esq, 271 Sandycomb Rd, Kew, Richmond, Surrey]; *b* 1933; *educ* Ampleforth; late Lt 16th/5th Lancers; *m* 1965 *Catherine, dau of John Charles Roberts, and has:

1d *Anthony Vincent; *b* 1964

1b CHARLOTTE MARY; *b* 1 Jan 1885; *cr* 6 May 1899 COUNTESS GANDOLFI by POPE LEO XIII, with remainder to the heir to be designated by her; *m* 15 Aug 1921 Henry Spalinger, s of Herman Spalinger, of Carouge, Geneva

2a Alfred Joseph; had:

1b Henry GANDOLFI-HORNYOLD later HORNYOLD-STRICKLAND (roy licence 1932), FSA; *m* 1920 Hon Mary Constance Elisabeth Christina, CBE, est dau of 1st Baron Strickland (*see* 1970 edn), and had:

1c Thomas Henry, DSC; Lt-Cdr RN; *b* 1921; *s* maternal gf as 7th Count della Catena (*cr* 1745; *see* 1956 edn Maltese Nobility Section); quartered by roy licence 1938 the arms of Matthews with his own, High Sheriff Westmorland 1973–74; *m* 1951 *Angela Mary, OBE, DL (Cumbria) [Mrs Thomas Hornyold-Strickland OBE DL, Sizergh Castle, Kendal, Cumbria LA8 8AE], est dau of Francis Henry Arnold Engleheart, of The Priory, Stoke-by-Nayland, Suffolk, and *d* 1983, leaving:

1d *Henry Charles, 8th Count della Catena [Count della Catena, 56 Ladbroke Rd, London W11 3NW]; *b* 1951; *educ* Ampleforth, Exeter Coll Oxford (BA) and INSEAD (MBA); Kt Honour and Devotion SMO Malta; *m* 1979 *Claudine Thérèse, dau of Clovis Poumirau, of Hossegor, France, and has:

1e *Hugo; *b* 1979

2e *Thomas; *b* 1985

2d *Robert Francis Michael [Robert Hornyold-Strickland Esq, 74 Honeywell Rd, London SW11 6EF; Villa Parisio, Lija, Malta BZN 10]; *b* 31 Oct 1954; *educ* Ampleforth; Kt Honour and Devotion SMO Malta; *m* 1983 (*divorce* 1996) Teresa Mary, dau of Richard Fawcett, and has:

1e *Francis Richard; *b* 18 Sept 1986

2e *Rollo Michael; *b* 27 Oct 1988

1e *Zöe Clementine; *b* 24 March 1991

3d *John Jarrard [John Hornyold-Strickland Esq, Hunters Cottage, 315 The Star, Holt, Trowbridge, Wilts BA14 6QB]; *b* 1956; *educ* Ampleforth; Kt Honour and Devotion SMO Malta; *m* 1996 *Jane Elizabeth Fothergill and has:

1e *Katherine Alice; *b* 7 Sept 1996

4d *Edward Thomas; *b* 1960; *educ* Ampleforth

1d *Clare Edeline [Mrs Anthony Prince, 26 Abingdon Court, Abingdon Villas, London W8 6BT]; *b* 1953; *m* 1981 *Anthony Prince

2d *Alice Mary [Mrs Charles Loftie, Bowerbank, Pooley Bridge, Cumbria CA10 2NG; Les Places, Les Arques 46250, Cazals, France]; *b* 1959; *m* 1988 *Charles Loftie, and has:

1e *William Thomas Crozier; *b* 1991

2e *Alexander Edward Henry; *b* 28 June 1996

1e *Eleanor Sophie; *b* 1992

1c Edeline Winifred; *b* 1922; *m* 1943 Norman Coppock (*d* 1982) and *d* 1981, leaving:

1d *Michael Thomas [Michael Coppock Esq, 13 Saunders St, Southport, Lancs PR9 0HP]; *b* 1949; *educ* More House Sch; *m* 1975 *Susan Ann, dau of John B Davies, of Southport, Lancs, and has:

1e *David Michael; *b* 1978

2e *Andrew Joseph; *b* 1983

1e *Sarah Louise; *b* 1976

1b Dorothy Hornyold; *b* 1892; *m* 1917 11th Baron Clifford of Chudleigh (*qv*) and *d* 1918, leaving issue

1a Mary; *m* 29 Nov 1871 Hubert Aloysius Tichborne Hibbert and had:

1b Washington Charles Thomas, of Pitt Manor, Hants; *b* 7 July 1875; *educ* The Oratory; KOR Boer War and WW I; *m* 10 Jan 1906 (*divorce* 1944) Mary Elizabeth, est dau of Sir William Nelson, 1st Bt (*qv*), and *d* 6 April 1950, leaving:

1c Hugh Washington; *b* 1911; Maj The Queen's Bays; *m* 1st 1938 (*divorce* 1949) Lady Patricia Margery Kathleen Mackay (*d* 1973), er dau of 2nd Earl of Inchcape (*qv*); *m* 2nd 1952 *Angela Mary, est dau of Peter Haig Thomas (*see* NORMANTON, E), formerly *w* of Richard Miles Backhouse (*see* BACKHOUSE, Bt) and previously widow of Capt Count Richard Dudley Melchior Gurowski, Scots Gds, and *d* 1985, leaving by his 1st *w*:

1d *Michael Washington; *b* 1946; *educ* Ampleforth; *m* 1972 *Gisela, dau of Paul Thomsen, of Odense, Denmark, and has:

2e *Peter Michael Washington; *b* 1974

2e *Jasper Erik Washington; *b* 1978

1d Bridget Anne; *b* 1939; *m* 1966 *Edward Alan Mervyn Molyneux Herbert and *d* 1976, leaving issue (*see* CARNARVON, E)

2d *Elizabeth Caroline [Mrs Kenneth Anderson, Gifford Hall, Broughton Gifford, Wilts SN12 8LY]; *b* 1943; *m* 1st 1965 Capt Jeremy Michael Porter, RN (*d* 4 May 1985), and has issue (*see* CHARLEMONT, V); *m* 2nd 9 March 1991 *Kenneth Rouse Anderson

1c Violet Margaret; *b* 1907; *m* 1936 Lt-Cdr Llewellyn Somerset Edward Llewellyn, RN (*d* 1940), and *d* 1986, leaving:

1d *Virginia Mary [Miss Virginia Llewellyn, 77 Cadogan Gdns, London SW3]; *b* 1937

1b Marguerite Mary Julia; *b* 1872; *m* 1899 Capt Francis ffrench Davis and *d* 1964, leaving:

1c Francis Holdsworth; *b* 1907; *m* 1940 *Ingrid Margaret Mary (*m* 2nd 1948, as his 2nd *w*, Maj Edmond Myles Pery-Knox-Gore; *see* LIMERICK, E), dau of Maj Henry MacDermot, KC, of Dublin, and was *ka* 1944, leaving:

1d *Francis Conor [Francis ffrench Davis, Knockharley, Brownstown, Navan, Co Meath, Ireland]; *b* 1941; *m* 1962 *Prudence Mary Fiona, dau of John Evelyn Smith Wright, of Javea, Alicante, Spain, and has:

1e *Francis Dermot; *b* 1964

2e *Dominic John; *b* 1965

3e *Stephen Luke; *b* 1967

4e *Michael James; *b* 1969

1e *Nicola Marguerite; *b* 1977

2e *Sarah Jane Victoria; *b* 1985

2c *Peter Charles [Peter ffrench Davis Esq, Flat 34, 77 Hallam St, London W1N 5LR]; *b* 1912; *educ* Ampleforth and Trin Coll Cambridge (BA), late memb London Stock Exchange, Capt Welsh Gds WW II

1c Marguerite Elizabeth Josephine; *b* 1913; *m* 1944 Frederick Michael Selmes Jackson (*d* 1968), and *d* 1995

2b Angela Mary; *b* 1877; *m* 1st 1905, as his 2nd *w*, Brig-Gen Paul Aloysius Kenna, VC, DSO (*ka* 1915); *m* 2nd 1919 Col Allen Victor Johnson (*d* 1939), DSO, and *d* 1972, leaving by her 1st husb:

1c Kathleen; *b* 1906; *m* 1936 Lt-Cdr Lionel Rupert Knyvett Tyrwhitt, DSO, DSC, RN (*ka* 1942), bro of Vera Ruby, Baroness Berners in her own right (*qv*)

2c Celia Mary Ethel; *b* 1909

3 (cont.) The Hon Charles Langdale *m* 2nd 1 May 1821 Mary (*d* 25 Sept 1857), est dau of Marmaduke William Constable-Maxwell (*see* HERRIES OF TERREGLES, L), and *d* 1 Dec 1808, having by her had, with a *s* (*d* young):

(1) Charles Joseph, of Houghton Hall, Brough, Yorks, JP, DL; *b* 7 March 1822; *m* 4 Aug 1852 Henrietta (*d* 12 March 1898), est dau and coheir of Henry Grattan, MP, of Celbridge Abbey, Co Kildare, and *d* 12 April 1895, leaving:

1a Henry Joseph, of Houghton Hall, JP, DL; Capt 4th Bn Roy Irish Fus; *b* 2 June 1853; *d* 11 Sept 1923

2a Marmaduke Joseph (Rev), OSB; *b* 25 Oct 1861; *d* 17 Jan 1934

3a Philip Joseph, OBE (1919), TD, JP, DL (Yorks), of Houghton Hall; Lt-Col TFR cmdg E R Yorks Yeo, Capt 8th Hus; *b* 8 May 1863; *educ* Stonyhurst and RMC Sandhurst; *m* 18 July 1895 Gertrude Lysley (*d* 15 Nov 1939), dau of Adml Samuel Hoskins Derriman, CB, by Caroline Gertrude, dau of William Luard Lysley, MP, of Pewsham, Wilts, and Mimwood Park, Herts, and *d* 15 April 1950, leaving:

1b *Joyce Elizabeth Mary; *b* 25 April 1898; *m* 1st 9 May 1922 (*divorce* 1956) 2nd Viscount FitzAlan of Derwent, OBE, and had issue (*see* NORFOLK, D); *m* 2nd 3 April 1956 10th Earl Fitzwilliam (*see* 1970 edn)

2b Alathea Pauline Mary Alys; *b* 23 May 1902; *m* 18 April 1923 (*divorce* 1936) 2nd Baron Manton (*qv*) and *d* 1979, leaving issue

3b Ursula Dorothy Mary; *b* 14 Sept 1903; *m* 3 Nov 1931 Lt-Col Norman Birch (*d* Oct 1960), E R Yeo, and *d* 18 Jan 1969, leaving:

1c *Michael Edward Stafford [Michael Birch Esq, Walkington Park, Beverley, E Yorks]; *b* 1933

2c *Timothy Malcolm Stafford [Timothy Birch Esq, 1 Little Weighton Rd, Walkington, Beverley, E Yorks]; *b* 1937

4a Francis Joseph; *b* 19 July 1866; *m* 6 July 1802 Teresa Mary (*d* 24 Nov 1929), widow of John Duncuft and dau of James Bruno Pilley, of Mawfield, Herefs, and *dsp* 23 May 1944

1a Mary; nun; *b* 11 Sept 1856; *d* 1 Dec 1935

2a Pauline Mary; *b* 19 June 1858; *m* 20 Sept 1887 Lt-Col Horace Walpole (*d* 4 April 1919), KRRC, of Heckfield Place, Basingstoke, Hants, and *d* 10 Dec 1944, leaving:

1b Dorothy Mary Paula; *m* 1st 1919 Maj Austin Edward Scott Murray, MC; *m* 2nd 1945 *Col Colin Kayser Davy, MC, and by her 1st husb had:

1c Anne Mary Scott; *b* 1920; *m* 1944 Maj Rupert Leonard Eversley Milburn (*d* 1974) and *d* 1991, leaving issue (*see* MILBURN, Bt)

2b Maude Mary Winifred; *b* 1897; *m* 1st 1921 Cyril James Wenceslas Torr (*d* 1940), For Serv; *m* 2nd 1946 Vicomte Théophile de Lantsheere, CVO (*d* 1958), and *d* 1968, leaving by her 1st husb:

1c *Jean Rosita Mary, MBE (1984) [Lady Nevil MBE, Aubourn Hall, Lincs LN5 9DZ]; *b* 1923; VAD WW II; *m* 1944 Capt Sir Henry Nicholas Nevil, KCVO (*d* 20 Oct 1996), Ld Lt Lincs 1975–95, JP, and has:

1d *Christopher James [Christopher Nevil Esq, Manor Farm, Aubourn, Lincs]; *b* 1954; *m* 1981 *Sarah Caroline, yr dau of Sir Peter William Youens, KCMG, OBE, and has:

1e *Charles Cato; *b* 1990

1e *Zita Stephanie; *b* 1984

2e *Nyasa Jane; *b* 1986

2d *Hugh Simon [Hugh Nevil Esq, 23 Cromwell Grove, London W6]; *b* 1960; *m* 1989 *Joanna Mary, er dau of Timothy Seymour Bathurst (*see* BATHURST, E), and has:

1e *Max Henry; *b* 1994

2e *Thomas Michael; *b* 1996

1d *Sarah Rosita Mary [Mrs Roger Hudson, 38 Kensington Place, London W8 7PR]; *b* 1945; *m* 1968 *Roger Hudson and has:

1e *Toby; *b* 1970

2e *George; *b* 1972

2d *Elizabeth Jane Mary [Lady Arnold, 74 Ashley Gdns, Thirleby Rd, London SW1]; *b* 1947; *m* 1st 1970 Robin Irwin Smithers (*d* 1979) and has:

1e *Christian Alexander Langley; *b* 1971

2e *Lucian James Angelo; *b* 1974

2d (cont.) Mrs Robin Smithers *m* 2nd 1984 (*divorce* 1993) Sir Thomas Richard Arnold, MP (C) Hazel Grove 1974–97, V-Chm C Party 1983–92, and by him has:

1e *Emily Minna Mary; *b* 1986

3d *Jill Gabriel Anne Mary [Mrs David Hughes, Hop Hill, Aubourn, Lincs LN5 9DZ]; *b* 1950; *m* 1982 *David Hughes and has:

1e *Anthony James Alleyne; *b* 1983

2e *Ralph Nicholas Alleyne; *b* 1985

(2) William Joseph; *b* 28 March 1826; *m* 8 Jan 1863 Emily Elizabeth Russell Crawford (*d* 28 Dec 1904) and *dsp* 13 Feb 1897

(3) Henry (Rev); priest Redemptorist Order; *b* 8 May 1837; *d* 23 March 1871

(4) Arthur Joseph; memb London School Bd; *b* 12 July 1838; *m* 6 Aug 1872 Catherine Agnes Eleanor (*d* 13 Sept 1927), dau of Adrian de Bruyn, of Zevenbergen, N Brabant, and *d* 24 Nov 1893, leaving:

1a Charles Adrian Joseph; Maj W R Regt WW I; *b* 14 Aug 1874; *m* 8 March 1934 Josephine Mary Everilda Pia (*d* 8 Jan 1946), widow of Alfred Harrison and dau of Edmund Waterton, of Walton Hall, Wakefield, and Deeping Waterton, Lincs, and *dsp* 17 Nov 1960

2a Edward Francis Joseph; T/Lt RE; *b* 21 Oct 1884; *ka* France 5 Oct 1916

1a Cecilia Mary; *b* 23 Jan 1876; *d* unm 23 April 1924

2a Mary Agnes; *b* 2 Dec 1877; *d* unm 9 Feb 1917

3a Gertrude Pietrina Josephine Mary; *b* 1 March 1882; *m* 23 Dec 1907 Capt James Ughtred Farie, RN (*d* 1957), and *d* 26 Aug 1915, leaving:

1b *Margaret Jean Mary; *b* 1912; Benedictine Nun

4 Philip Henry Joseph, of Holme Hall, JP, DL; *b* 14 Jan 1793; *m* 28 July 1829 Catherine (*d* 27 Jan 1874), est dau of Henry Howard, of Corby (*see* NORFOLK, D), and *d* 3 Aug 1860, leaving, with other issue:

(1) Henry Joseph, of Holme Hall, JP; BA Oxon, Capt and Hon Maj Yorks Hus; *b* 4 July 1844; *m* 19 Sept 1870 Lydia Anne Tichborne (*d* 27 Feb 1888), dau of Capt John Hubert Washington Hibbert, of Bilton Grange, Warwicks, and *d* 19 Oct 1896, leaving:

1a Violet Mary Annette, OBE (1919); *b* 3 Jan 1873; *m* 19 Sept 1893 Francis Joseph Siltzer (*d* 28 Aug 1924), and *d* 10 April 1961, leaving:

1b Derek Henry; *b* 1897; *educ* Oratory Sch; *m* 1938 *Merlyn Seaforth, dau of William Densham, of Melbourne, Australia, and widow of Keith Poulton

2a Amy Mary Josephine; *b* 22 Nov 1874; *m* 29 Sept 1896 Frederic Dundas Harford (*d* 28 April 1931), CVO, JP, DL, Envoy Extrdy Venezuela, and *d* 14 March 1954, leaving:

1b Joan Mary; *b* 1897; *m* 1920 Lt-Col Sir Alexander Bannerman, 11th Bt (*qv*), and *d* 1983, leaving issue

(1) Blanche Mary; *b* 20 Sept 1834; *m* 25 June 1856 Sir James George D'Alton Fitzgerald, 9th Bt (*dsp* 16 Jan 1867), of Castle Ishen, became a nun and *d* 1 June 1875

1 Mary; Canoness Holy Sepulchre; *b* 11 Feb 1780; *d* 27 Dec 1850

2 Charlotte Mary; *b* 7 March 1782; *m* 22 Nov 1802 Joseph Weld, of Lulworth Castle, Dorset, and *d* 16 Jan 1864, leaving issue

3 Apollonia Mary; *b* 4 Jan 1785; *m* 20 Jan 1812 Thomas Davison Bland (*d* 6 Dec 1847), of Kippax Park, Yorks, and *d* 2 Nov 1868, leaving issue

4 Juliana Mary; *b* 12 May 1789; *m* 23 July 1812 Peter Middelton (*d* 3 June 1866), of Stockeld Park and Myddelton Lodge, Yorks, and *d* 27 Nov 1861, leaving issue

The 17th BARON *d* 29 April 1816; his est son,

WILLIAM JOSEPH STOURTON, **18th Baron Stourton**; *b* 6 June 1776; *educ* St Gregory's; took seat in Ho Lords 1 May 1829 following Catholic Emancipation; *m* 1 Oct 1800 Catherine Winifred (*d* 27 Dec 1862), dau of Thomas Weld, of Lulworth Castle, Dorset, and had, with five daus (nuns):

1 CHARLES, **19th Baron**

2 William Joseph, of Folkestone; *b* 13 July 1810; *m* 16 Oct 1838 Catherine Alicia (*d* 27 July 1907), dau of Edmond Scully, of Bloomfield, Co Tipperary, and *d* 21 Nov 1873, leaving, with other issue:

(1) Marmaduke William Joseph; Capt 63rd Regt; *b* 14 Jan 1840; *m* 7 Jan 1870 Mary (*d* 12 Dec 1876), yst dau of William Franks, and *d* Natal 18 April 1879, having had:

1a William; *b* 7 *d* 15 Aug 1875

(2) Arthur Joseph; served 78th Highrs; lived Australia, served Australian Sudan Contingent 1885; *b* 21 Feb 1841; *m* 6 Oct 1875 Adeline Constance, MBE, only dau of Donald Cameron, MLC, of Tasmania, and *d* 26 Oct 1908, having had:

1a Frederick Joseph; *b* 3 Oct 1876; *d* 11 Jan 1887

2a Reginald Norman Joseph, JP Tasmania; Lt Tasmanian Forces Boer War (Queen's medal with five clasps); *b* 4 Oct 1877; *d* 1943

(3) Jeremias Joseph (Rt Rev Mgr); RC priest, Domestic Prelate to HH BENEDICT XV 1918, Order Crown Belgium; *b* 23 March 1845; *d* 17 March 1921

3 John Joseph; served 96th Regt; *b* 22 March 1816; *m* 4 May 1846 Caroline Emma (*m* 2nd 5 July 1856 (*divorce* 1866) William Lonergan and *d* 11 May 1898), dau of Patrick MacNulty, and *d* 23 May 1847, leaving:

(1) John Marmaduke Joseph; *b* posthumously 31 May 1847; *d* 30 Aug 1899

4 Marmaduke; *b* 14 Aug 1818; *d* 14 Sept 1848

1 Theresa; *b* 21 March 1812; *m* 19 June 1838 11th Baron Arundell of Wardour (*see* 1940 edn) and *d* 26 Oct 1878, leaving issue

2 Eleonora Mary; *b* 1 Jan 1820; *m* 23 Jan 1844 Lt Richard Peter Carrington Smythe (*dsp* 14 Sept 1853), 8th Hus, 2nd *s* of Sir Edward Joseph Smythe, 6th Bt, and *d* 7 Sept 1899

The 18th BARON *d* 4 Dec 1846; his est son,

CHARLES STOURTON, **19th Baron Stourton**, DL Yorks; *b* 13 July 1802; Lt Yorks Hus 1824–26; *m* 1 Aug 1825 Mary Lucy (*d* 30 Sept 1872), 6th dau of 6th Baron Clifford of Chudleigh (*qv*), and had, with three other sons (*d* young):

1 ALFRED JOSEPH, **20th Baron**

2 Everard Joseph; Capt 10th Hus Crimean War and Indian Mutiny; *b* 18 Feb 1834; *m* 7 May 1862 Fermina Maria Magdalena (*d* 29 Feb 1932), yst dau of 1st Baron Bellew (*qv*), and *d* 20 Feb 1869, having had, with other issue:

(1) Everard Joseph; Boer War 1900–02 in 2nd Bn Imp Yeo, Lt 2nd Bn QOCH, T/Capt Yorks Yeo; *b* 28 Dec 1864; *m* 18 Feb 1903 Ethel Maude (*d* 25 May 1964), dau and heir of Lt-Col James Swinburne, of Marcus, Forfar (*see* 1949 edn SWINBURNE, Bt), and *d* 2 May 1932, having had:

1a Everard Botolph; *b* 20 July 1905; *educ* Beaumont; *d* 198–

2a Conyers Joseph; *b* 3; *d* 17 Aug 1906

3a Athelstan Claud Edward; Capt 3rd/7th Gurkha Rifles WW II; *b* 18 Dec 1907; *ka* Burma 11 Feb 1942

1a Enid Mary; *b* 26 March 1904; *d* unm 25 March 1954

3 Albert Joseph; *b* 20 Dec 1835; *m* 25 April 1866 Elizabeth Laura Caroline (*d* 8 Jan 1927), yst dau of Sir Robert George Throckmorton, 8th Bt (*see* 1970 edn), and *d* 16 Aug 1902, having had:

(1) Auberon Joseph; *b* 28 April 1867; *m* 9 July 1896 (*divorce* 1906) Gwladys Jessie (*d* 10 Jan 1949), dau of George William Thomas, of Ystrad Mynach, Glam, and *d* 21 Nov 1923, leaving:

1a Eudo Philip Joseph; Capt 58th AA Bn RE (TA) WW II; *b* 24 Oct 1900; *educ* Eton and Christ's Coll Cambridge; *m* 14 July 1927 Cicely Frances (*d* 11 July 1982 aged 78), yst dau of Henry Hyman Haldin, KC, of Marylebone, and *d* 27 Feb 1975, leaving:

1b *Veronica Philippa [Mrs Biden Ashbrooke, La Grande Maison, La Grande Route St Jean, Jersey, CI JE3 4FN]; *b* 31 Oct 1929; *m* 23 Oct 1954 (Philip) Biden Derwent Ashbrooke (*d* 1993), barrister, Capt 8th Hus, only *s* of Philip Ashbrooke, of Doveray Place, Porlock, Somerset, and has:

1c *Auberon Francis Biden; *b* 4 Aug 1956 *educ* Ampleforth and St John's Coll Cambridge; Lt-Col KRH

1c *Sophia Mary Veronica [Viscountess Stormont, Scone Palace, Perthshire PH2 6BD]; *b* 22 Jan 1959; *m* 1985 *Alexander David Mungo, Viscount Stormont, er *s* of 8th Earl of Mansfield and Mansfield (*qv*)

(2) Herbert Marmaduke Joseph, OBE (1919), Maj RASC, Lt Oxon Hus, French Medaille d'Honneur, Greek Order Merit; *b* 30 Dec 1873; *m* 7 June 1898 Hon Frances Mary Winifred (*d* 7 March 1950), only dau of 4th Viscount Southwell (*qv*), and *d* 20 Aug 1932, leaving:

1a Ivo Herbert Evelyn Joseph (Sir), CMG (1951), OBE (1939), KPM (1949); *b* 18 July 1901; *educ* Stonyhurst; joined Colonial Police 1921: Mauritius 1921–33, Commr Police Bermuda 1933–39, Aden 1940–45, Uganda 1945–50, Inspr-Gen Nigeria 1951–53, Dep Inspr-Gen Colonial Police 1953–57, Inspr-Gen 1957–66, ktd 1961; *m* 1st 9 Feb 1926 Lilian Marguerite (*d* as the result of enemy action Dec 1942), dau of George Dickson, of Mauritius, and had:

1b +Nigel John Ivo, OBE (1981) [Nigel Stourton Esq OBE, Arbour Hill, Patrick Brompton, Bedale, N Yorks DL8 1JX]; *b* 29 July 1929; Kt SMO Malta; *m* 1 Sept 1956 *Rosemary Jennifer Rushworth, yr dau of Hon Mr Justice (Sir Myles John) Abbott, Ch Justice Bermuda, and has:

1c +Ed(ward) John Ivo [Edward Stourton Esq, The Old Rectory, Compton Bassett, Wilts SN11 8RE]; *b* 24 Nov 1957; BBC newscaster, Kt SMO Malta; *m* 1980 *Margaret, est dau of Sir James Napier Finnie McEwen, 2nd Bt (*qv*), and has:

1d +Ivo James Benedict; *b* 1982; *educ* Eton

2d +Thomas Edward Alexander; *b* 1987

1d *Eleanor Mary Elizabeth; *b* 1984

2c +Julian Nicolas [Julian Stourton Esq, 25 Lower Addison Gdns, London W14 8BG]; *b* 23 Sept 1959; *m* 1992 *Margaret A, dau of A J Barsham, of Broadwater, Weybridge, Surrey, and has:

1d +Frederick John Nigel; *b* 9 Sept 1994

3c +Christopher Nigel Paul [Christopher Stourton Esq, 37 Patience Rd, London SW11]; *b* 28 May 1965; *m* 1992 *Melissa, yr dau of Hon Sir Richard Storey, 2nd Bt (*qv*), and has:

1d *Oria; *b* 8 May 1998

1c *Lavinia Margaret Grace; *b* 1 Oct 1962; *m* 1986 *Frank D Nicholson and has issue (*see* LAWSON-TANCRED, Bt)

2b +Simon Nicolas [Simon Stourton Esq, Humehall, Kelso, Roxburgh TD5 7TW]; *b* 12 June 1932; *m* 1975 *Pamela, dau of Charles James Baker, of Letcombe Manor, Wantage Berks, widow of Maj Alexander James Scratchley, MC, and formerly w of 3rd Viscount Bridport (*qv*)

1b *Felicity Magdalen [Miss Felicity Stourton, 40 East Witton, Leyburn, N Yorks]; *b* 25 Dec 1927

1a (cont.) Sir Ivo Stourton *m* 2nd 26 Jan 1945 *Virginia (*m* 2nd 1986 W Hilary Young CMG) [Mrs Hilary Young, The Old Bakery, Kimpton, nr Andover, Hants], late 3rd Offr WRNS, er dau of Sir Horace James Seymour, GCMG, CVO (*see* HERTFORD, M), and *d* 1985, leaving by her:

2b *(Barbara) Jane [Mrs Graham Buchanan-Dunlop, Broughton Place, Broughton, Biggar, Lanarks]; *b* 16 April 1947; *m* 1 Dec 1974 *Maj (Archibald) Graham Buchanan-Dunlop, late Royal Highland Fus, only *s* of Brig Archibald Ian Buchanan-Dunlop, DSO, OBE, of The Coach House, Colinton, Edinburgh, and has:

1c *(Archibald) Roderick; *b* 1979

2c *David Erskine; *b* 1981

1a Magdalen Mary Charlotte; *b* 19 Feb 1899; *m* 1st 7 Oct 1925 (*divorce* 1936) Maj Archibald Ashworth Bailie Hay, DSO, MC, RA (*d* 7 Jan 1965), and *d* 1981, leaving:

1b James Douglas; Lt 11th Hus; *b* 22 Nov 1926; *d* unm 6 Dec 1961

1a (cont.) Mrs Magdalen Hay *m* 2nd 22 April 1936 (*divorce* USA 1943) Robert Ducas (*d* 1978), *s* of Robert Ducas, of New York, and by him had:

2b *Robert Ivo [Robert Ducas Esq, Flat 10, 24 Lowndes St, London SW1 9JE]; *b* 20 Jan 1937; jnlst; *m* 1963 Patricia (*d* 19–), yr dau of P Provatoroff, of Crippenden Manor, Cowden, Kent, and has:

1c *Annoushka; *b* Jan 1966; *m* 1990 *John A C Ayton, est *s* of Antony Ayton, of Jordans End, Jordans, Bucks, and has:

1d *Marina Isobel Provatoroff; *b* 1993

1b *Magdalen June Ruth; *b* 2 June 1938; *m* 2 July 1959 *Hon James Donald Diarmid Ogilvy, yst *s* of 9th Earl of Airlie (*qv*), and has issue

1a (cont.) Mrs Magdalen Ducas *m* 3rd 20 June 1947 (*divorce* 1956) (William) Brian Buchel, er *s* of Charles Buchel

2a Barbara Bertha Mary; *b* 11 April 1900; *m* 1st 29 March 1924 (*divorce* 1929) Maj Eric Charlton Tunnicliffe (*d* 11 Oct 1953), Roy Welch Fus, Govr Winchester Prison, and had:

1b Nigel Arthur; Capt Gren Gds; *b* 13 Feb 1928; *m* 1957 (*divorce* 1980) Diana Edith, formerly w of Hon Jeremy John Cubitt (*see* ASHCOMBE, B) and er dau of Cdr Peter Du Cane, OBE, RN, of E Hoe Manor, Hambledon, Hants (*see* POLE, Bt), and *d* 28 April 1982, leaving:

1c *Joanna; *b* 2 April 1958

2c *Brigid Serena [Mrs Richard Pavry, 19 Dalby Rd, Wandsworth, London SW18 1AW]; *b* 7 Jan 1963; *m* 1990 *Richard L Pavry

1b *Elizabeth Anne [Mrs William Mackenzie, Lower Hendre Farm, St Weonards, Herefs, HR2 8PD]; *b* 14 April 1926; *m* 1 Nov 1947 *William Alexander Mackenzie, yr son of Lt-Col Douglas William Alexander Dalziel Mackenzie, CVO, DSO, DL, JP, of Farr, Inverness-shire, and has:

1c *Michael Alexander Edward [Michael Mackenzie Esq, Chapel House, Kettlebridge, Cupar, Fife]; *b* 23 Aug 1949; *educ* Stanbridge Earls Sch; *m* 27 Oct 1973 *Louise Lees Baugh and has:

1d *Edward Alexander; *b* 2 Jan 1976; *educ* Rannoch Sch; 1st Bn Highrs (Seaforth, Gordons and Camerons)

2d *Christopher James; *b* 8 Nov 1977; *educ* Glenalmond Coll and Aberdeen U

3d *Frederick Thomas; *b* 18 Aug 1981; *educ* Wellington

1c *Margaret-Anne [Mrs George Streatfeild, Denmark House, Longtown, Herts]; *b* 9 April 1955; *m* 1975 *George Champion Streatfeild

2a (cont.) Mrs Tunnicliffe *m* 2nd 15 Aug 1929 Frank Ashton Bellville (*d* 22 July 1937) and by him had:

2b *Patricia Barbara [Mrs Charles Gladitz, Sadlers House, Hardington Mandeville, Somerset BA22 9PQ]; *b* 1931; *m* 31 Dec 1965 *(Alfred) Charles Gladitz and has:

1c *Rupert Ivo Charles; *b* 10 Dec 1969; *educ* Ampleforth and Gonville and Caius Coll Cambridge (BA)

2a (cont.) Mrs Frank Bellville *m* 3rd 20 Sept 1946 Capt Henry Steuart Harrison-Wallace (*d* 1963), DSO, RN (ret), and *d* 2 May 1980

3a Gytha Mary Dorothy; *b* 20 March 1904; *m* 23 Aug 1934 Frederick Ramón de Bertodano, 8th Marqués del Moral (Spain) (*d* 25 Feb 1955), and *d* 12 March 1992, leaving:

1b *Alfonso Michael George de Bertodano, 9th Marqués del Moral [Marqués del Moral, Ferraz 73, Madrid 28008, Spain]; *b* 7 Dec 1937 (HM ALFONSO XIII stood sponsor); *m* 28 June 1968 *Carolina García de la Riva, dau of Abel García Sirera, of Murcia, Spain, and has:

1c *Miguel Ramón Marcus [Sr D Miguel de Bertodano, San Luis Gon Zaga 3, 11500 Puerto de Santa María, Cádiz, Spain]; *b* 25 April 1969

2c *Ignacio José Roberto; *b* 25 Oct 1970

3c *Gonzalo Alberto; *b* 16 March 1974

4c *Jaime Felipe; *b* 13 Jan 1982

1c *Carolina Isabel; *b* 12 June 1978

1b *Helen Gytha May [Mrs Jean le Goaëc, Mas de la Condamine, 83570 Cotignac, France]; *b* 30 May 1935; *m* 7 May 1957 *Jean Charles le Goaec, *s* of Col Charles le Goaec, of Les Murons, Parame, Brittany, and has:

1c *Yann Charles Ramon; *b* 29 May 1959

2c *Michel Patrick Roland; *b* 23 April 1962

1c *Annik Marie Nicole; *b* 28 Feb 1958; *m* 1982 *Bruno Gaschet and has:

1d *Guillaume; *b* 1986

1d *Astrid; *b* 1984

2c *Katarina Nancy Gytha [Mrs Mark de Caestecker, 5 Ravenoak Rd, Cheadle Hume, Cheshire]; *b* 12 May 1960; *m* 1981 *Dr Mark de Caestecker and has:

1d *Sebastian; *b* 1986

2d *Christian; *b* 1990

1d *Cassandra; *b* 1983

3c *Sophie Marie-Helena; *b* 1971

4c *Isabelle Marie-Anne; *b* 1974

4a (Mary) Jeanne; *b* 22 May 1913; *m* 14 July 1938 6th Baron Camoys (*qv*) and *d* 1987, leaving issue

(3) Ernest Joseph William Basil; *b* 14 June 1875; *d* unm 8 Oct 1941

(4) Rudolph Henry Philip Joseph; Gren Gds WW I (wounded); *b* 7 April 1881; *d* unm 11 June 1953

(1) Mabel Mary Lucy; *b* 13 Nov 1868; *d* 5 Aug 1879

(2) Beatrice Mary; b 23 Feb 1870; d unm 2 March 1959

(3) Elizabeth Mary Alberta; nun; b 15 Sept 1871; d 1945

(4) Bertha Mary Phillippa; b 14 Sept 1872; m 29 Aug 1894 Maj Frederick Bartholomew Joseph Stapleton-Bretherton (d 13 Oct 1938) and d 1958, having had:

  1a Osmond Frederick; b 1898; Lt 9th Lancers ka 1918

  1a Ruth Mary; b 1897; m 1st 1914 Ronald Bodley; m 2nd 19– George Piggott-Moodie and d 1956, leaving by her 1st husb:

    1b Mark Courtney; b 1918; Lt RSG; kas 1942

  2a Mary Henrietta; b 1906; m 1940 (divorce 1953; resumed maiden name by deed poll 1960) Col John Pell Archer-Shee, MC, 10th Hus, s of Lt Col Sir Martin Archer-Shee, CMG, DSO, and d 1995, leaving:

    1b *Mary Pauline Daphne Thérèse [Miss Mary Archer-Shee, 44 Cornwall Gdns, London SW7 4AA]; b 1941

(5) Florence Winifred Pauline Mary; nun Franciscan Convent, Taunton; b 30 June 1877

(6) Eleanora Isabella Berardine Ursula Mary; b 22 Oct 1883; d 17 Oct 1964

The 19th BARON d 23 Dec 1872; his son,

ALFRED JOSEPH STOURTON, **20th Baron Stourton** and **23rd Lord** (Baron) **Mowbray** and **24th Lord** (Baron) **Segrave** on termination of abeyance in those baronies (which unlike that of Stourton are heritable by heirs general, hence the + against living female issue hereafter) in his favour 3 and 18 Jan 1878 respectively, JP, DL; b 28 Feb 1829; Lt Yorks Hus 1853–65; m 13 Sept 1865 Mary Margaret (d 26 Nov 1925), only child of Matthew Elias Corbally, DL, MP Corbalton Hall, Co Meath, by Matilda, yr dau of 12th Viscount Gormanston (qv), and had:

1 CHARLES BOTOLPH JOSEPH, **24th/25th Lord and 21st Baron**

2 Alfred Edward Corbally Joseph, Maj 4th Bn King's Own Loyal Lancaster Regt, Capt 3rd (Mil) Bn Border Regt, served Boer War 1900–01 and WW I; b 24 Oct 1872; d 4 Nov 1926

3 Nigel Roger Plantagenet Joseph; Lt 1st Dragoon Gds; b 9 Feb 1879; m 26 Sept 1901 Florence Anne (d 8 July 1961), dau of Jonathan Piggott, and dsp 23 Jan 1908

4 Edward Plantagenet Joseph STOURTON later CORBALLY STOURTON (added 1927), DSO (1917); b 24 March 1880; educ Ampleforth and Beaumont; KOYLI Boer War 1900–02 and WW I (wounded twice, despatches four times), cmded 1st Bn KOYLI 1929–32, Col 1933; m 14 July 1934 *Beatrice Cicely [The Hon Mrs Edward Corbally Stourton, Arlonstown, Dunsany, Co Meath, Ireland], only dau of Harold Ethelbert Page, of Wragby, Lincs, and Tichwell, Norfolk, and d 6 March 1966, leaving:

  (1) +Nigel Edward [Nigel Corbally Stourton Esq, 41 St Mary Abbots Court, Warwick Gdns, London W14 8RB]; b 9 March 1937; educ Ampleforth and RMA Sandhurst; late Capt 2nd Bn Gren Gds, served 1955–65, with IBM (UK) Ltd; m 1st 22 Oct 1960 (divorce 1975) Frances Deirdre Morton, dau of Maj Patrick Lancaster, of Wapsbourne Manor, Sheffield Park, Sussex, and has:

    1a +Edward Richard Plantagenet; b 14 Sept 1961

    2a +Nicholas Simon; b 10 May 1963

    3a +Patrick Henry; b 14 Aug 1965

  (1) (cont.) Nigel Corbally Stourton m 2nd Sept 1995 *Lavinia, widow of 5th Baron Fermoy (qv) and dau of Capt John Pitman

  (1) +Vanessa Mary [Miss Vanessa Corbally Stourton, 2 Camden Studios, Camden St, London NW1]; b 13 May 1935; educ UCL, Slade Sch of Art

1 Mary Lucy Agnes; m 4 Oct 1894 Cecil Henry Maxwell Lyte (d 26 Jan 1926) and d 11 Oct 1950

2 Edith Matilda Mary; d unm 6 Oct 1924

3 Hilda Mary; d unm 6 Dec 1958

4 Alison Mary; d unm 24 Aug 1957

5 Ethel Mary Josephine; d unm 21 March 1948

6 Matilda Margaret Mary Josephine m 24 Nov 1910 Baron Herbert Alexander von Metzsch-Reichenbach (d 8 Aug 1932), Gentleman-in-Waiting to HRH PRINCESS MATHILDE OF SAXONY, Lt-Col Saxon Army, yst s of Baron Gustav von Metzsch-Reichenbach, of Schloss Friesen, Reichenbach, by Emily, sis of 1st Viscount Goschen (qv)

The 20th BARON d 18 April 1893; his est son,

CHARLES BOTOLPH JOSEPH STOURTON, **24th Lord** (Baron) **Mowbray**, **25th Lord** (Baron) **Segrave** and **21st Baron Stourton**, JP, DL (W R Yorks); b 23 May 1867; Lt 3rd Bn E Yorks Regt (Militia) 1887–89; claim to Earldom of Norfolk (cr 1312) rejected 27 Nov 1906; m 26 July 1893 Mary (d 9 Dec 1961), only child of Thomas Angus Constable (see NORFOLK, D), and had:

1 WILLIAM MARMADUKE, **25th/26th Lord and 22nd Baron**

2 John Joseph, TD; Maj 5th Bn Roy Norfolk Regt (TA), Lt 10th Roy Hus, MP S Salford 1931–45, served N Russian Relief Force 1919 and WW II 1939–43; b 5 March 1899; educ Downside; m 1st 18 Dec 1923 (divorce 1933) Kathleen Alice (d 1986), er dau of Robert Louis George Gunther, of Englefield Green, Surrey; m 2nd 14 May 1934 (divorce 1947) Gladys Leila (d 3 June 1953), dau of Col Sir William James Waldron, of Winkfield and S Kensington, and d 1992, leaving by his 1st w:

  (1) +Michael Godwin Plantagenet [Maj Michael Stourton, The Old Rectory, Great Rollright, Chipping Norton, Oxon OX7 5RX]; b 7 Dec 1926; educ Eton and Coll of Estate Management Kensington; Maj Gren Gds (ret 1959), ADC to Cmdt RMA Sandhurst 1952, Adj 1st Bn Gren Gds 1953–55, Staff Capt HQ London Dist 1955–57, served Palestine 1948, Libya 1949–51 and Cyprus 1958, ACLAS 1963, FRICS 1965, land agent to HRH THE late DUKE OF GLOUCESTER for the Barnwell Manor estate Northants 1966–71, ptnr Curtis and Henson 1966–68, ptnr Savills 1966–94; m 3 Nov 1955 *Lady Joanna Lambart, yr dau of 10th Earl of Cavan (qv), and has:

    1a +Thomas Michael John; b 16 May 1965

    2a +Henry Matthew; b 25 June 1971

    1a +Julia; b 7 May 1958; m 1987 *Sir Simon Anthony Carne Rasch, 4th Bt (qv), and has issue

    2a +Clare Elizabeth; b 30 Sept 1962; m 1993 *Charles Francis Houghton Beckford, FCO, 2nd s of Maj Adrian Beckford, of Hook Norton, Oxon, and has:

      1b +Jack Michael; b 22 March 1997

      2b +Joseph Patrick; b 22 March 1997

(2) +John Ralph, JP (Co Fermanagh 1977) [John Stourton Esq JP, The Malthouse Granary, Poulton, Cirencester, Glos GL7 5HN]; b 25 March 1930; educ Eton and Magdalene Coll Cambridge (MA); late Lt Gren Gds; m 1st 11 Dec 1958 (divorce 1965) Virginia, twin dau of Basil Colin Shrubra Hordern, of The Old Rectory, Fernhurst, Sussex, and has:

  1a +Lucilla Mary; b 15 Sept 1959; m 1989 *John Michael Joseph Royden, er s of Sir Christopher John Royden, 5th Bt (qv), and has issue

(2) (cont.) John Stourton m 26 July 1967 *Caroline Honor, yr dau of Col J C O'Dwyer, of Magheracross, Ballinamallard, Co Fermanagh, and by her has:

  2a +Georgina Caroline; b 28 June 1969

  3a +Jemima Nicola; b 25 May 1971; m 1992 Marcelo Novoa (d 1997) and has:

    1b +Oscar; b 24 Nov 1995

(1) +Mary [The Rt Hon The Countess of Gainsborough, Horn House, Exton, Leics LE15 7QU]; b 24 Sept 1925; m 23 July 1947 *5th Earl of Gainsborough (qv) and has issue

(2) +Monica Kathleen [Lady Greig, Brook House, Fleet, Hants GU13 8RF]; b 18 Jan 1928; m 23 Sept 1955 *Sir Henry Louis Carron Greig, KCVO, CBE, DL, Gentleman Usher to HM THE QUEEN 1961–, only s of G/Capt Sir Louis Greig, KBE, CVO, DL, of Binsness, Forres, Morayshire, and has:

  1a +Louis Stourton; b 12 July 1956; educ Eton and St Edmund Hall Oxford; Page of Honour to HM THE QUEEN 1970–73

  2a +Jonathan; b 6 Aug 1958; educ Eton and Downing Coll Cambridge

  3a +George Carron; b 16 Dec 1960; educ Eton and St Peter's Coll Oxford; m 25 Nov 1995 *Kathryn Elizabeth, dau of Don Dewitt Terry, of Texas

  1a +Laura Monica; b 16 Dec 1960; Ldy-in-Waiting to DIANA PRINCESS OF WALES 1989–97; m 18 July 1984 *James Leopold Somerset Lonsdale and has issue (see RAGLAN, B)

1 Winifred Mary; b 21 Aug 1894; d 2 Dec 1904

2 +Charlotte Mary [The Hon Charlotte Stourton, 2 Arthington Ave, Harrogate, Yorks]; b 20 Jan 1904

The 25th BARON d 29 July 1936; his est son,

WILLIAM MARMADUKE STOURTON, **25th Lord** (Baron) **Mowbray**, **26th Lord** (Baron) **Segrave** and **22nd Baron Stourton**, MC, JP (W R Yorks); b 31 Aug 1895; educ Downside and RMC Sandhurst; Capt Gren Gds, Lt 8th (King's Roy Irish) Hus, WW I (despatches); m 6 Dec 1921 Sheila (d 19 Feb 1975), er dau of Hon Edward Walford Karslake Gully, CB (see SELBY, V), and d 7 May 1965, leaving:

1 CHARLES EDWARD STOURTON, **26th and present Lord** (Baron) **Mowbray**, **27th Lord** (Baron) **Segrave** and **23rd and present Baron Stourton**

1 +Patricia Winifred Mary [The Hon Mrs Crowder, 8 Quarrendon St, London SW6 3SV]; b 2 Nov 1924; FO; m 12 July 1948 *(Frederick) Petre Crowder, QC, MP 1950–79, only s of Capt Sir John Frederick Ellenborough Crowder, MP, of Belgravia, by Florence Gertrude, est dau of Alfred William Ralph Glynn Petre (see PETRE, B), and has:

  (1) +Richard John [Richard Crowder Esq, Candie House, Candie St, St Peter Port, Guernsey, CI]; b 28 March 1950; educ Eton; m 1st 1 March 1973 (divorce 19–) Belinda Jane, er dau of Matthew Page Wood (see PAGE WOOD, Bt); m 2nd 1984 *Lucy E, est dau of Michael Charlesworth, and has:

    1a +George; b 1997

    1a +Louisa Ann; b 1995

  (2) +John George [John Crowder Esq, Polmear Lodge, Sausmarez Rd, St Martin's Guernsey CI]; b 16 July 1954; educ Eton; m 2 June 1984 *Caroline C, dau of Donald Griffiths, of Craigforth, Elie, Fife, and has:

    1a +Charles Petre Gordon; b 1990

    1a +Anna Jane; b 1992

Lineage (of Segrave): HEREWARD of Segrave (later Seagrave), Leics; had:

GILBERT de SEGRAVE; held half a fee of William, Earl of Warwick (see WARWICK, BROOKE and, E) in 1166; d apparently by autumn 1201, leaving:

STEPHEN de SEGRAVE; of age by 1200; Keeper: Sauvey Castle June 1220, Essex and Herts Nov 1220, the Honour of Boulogne Dec 1220, Lincs March 1221/2, Hedingham Castle, Essex, March 1221/2, Lincoln Castle and Lincs Dec 1223, Hertford Castle Jan 1223/4, Northampton Castle 1229; appointed a guardian of England in HENRY III's absence in France 1230; Sheriff: Beds, Bucks, Leics, Northants and Worcs 1230; Commr to negotiate with LLEWELYN PRINCE OF N WALES 1232; Keeper: Kenilworth Castle May 1232, Northampton Castle July 1232 and Beds, Bucks, Leics, Northants and Warwicks for life for life; Justiciar of England 1232; a pncpl advsr to HENRY III 1233; m 1st Rohese, sis of Hugh Despenser; m 2nd Ida, sis of Henry de Hastings, and d 1241, leaving, with an er s (dvp):

GILBERT de SEGRAVE; Keeper Newcastle-under-Lyme Castle 12321 and Bolsover Castle Feb 1232/3; Justice Forest below Trent 1242, Judge King's Bench 1251; m by 30 Sept 1231 Amabil [sic], dau and coheir of Robert de Chaucombe, and d by 8 Oct 1254, leaving, with perhaps at least one dau (Alice, m 8th Earl of Warwick (see WARWICK, BROOKE and, E) of the 1088 cr):

NICHOLAS de SEGRAVE, **1st Lord** (Baron) **Segrave** (E), so cr (according to later doctrine) by writ of summons to Parl 24 June 1295; b c 1238; apparently ktd 1 Aug 1263; with others of the magnates opposed to HENRY III laid siege to Rochester April 1264; also cmded the London contingent at Battle of Lewes 14 May 1264; in addition fought Battle of Evesham 1265 (wounded and captured, subsequently seeking pardon 1266 and receiving it 1267); called up for mil service against Welsh 1276, 1277, 1282 and 1283; attended 1283 a meeting at Shrewsbury which in a Ho Lds decision 1877 was deemed to be a Parliament, hence to have been capable of creating peerages by writ, though this decision is now held to be flawed; m Maud, possibly dau of — Lucy, and d by 12 Nov 1295, leaving, with at least two other sons (Henry, Sheriff Norfolk and Suffolk and Constable Norwich Castle; Stephen):

1 JOHN de SEGRAVE, **2nd Lord** (Baron) **Segrave**; b c 1256; undertook mil service Wales by 1285, Ireland by 1287 and Scotland by 1291, also 1297–1322; Keeper Scotland by Feb 1302/3 (and again March 1308/9), when briefly taken

prisoner by Scots; Keeper Nottingham Castle c 1308; Keeper marches with Scotland in Cumberland 1313, captured by the Scots at their victory over the English of Bannockburn 1314; m 1269/70 Christian, dau of Hugh de Plessis, and d by 4 Oct 1325, leaving, with a dau (Christiane):

(1) STEPHEN de SEGRAVE, **3rd Lord** (Baron) **Segrave**; had ceased to be a minor by time of his f's death; undertook mil service against Scots 1305, 1307 and 1322; ktd by autumn 1307; Constable Tower London Feb 1322/3; m Alice, allegedly dau of — Arundell and d by 12 Dec 1325, leaving:

1a JOHN de SEGRAVE, **4th Lord** (Baron) **Segrave**; b c 1315; m by 15 Dec 1338 Margaret, cr 29 Sept 1397 Duchess of Norfolk for life and de jure Countess of Norfolk in her own right (m 2nd Walter, Lord (Baron) Mauny, and dspm 24 March 1398/99, when the Duchy expired but the Earldom of Norfolk passed to her gs **7th Lord** (Baron) **Mowbray**, see below), dau and eventually sole heiress of Thomas of Brotherton, Earl of Norfolk, 5th s of EDWARD I, and dspm 1 April 1353, leaving:

1b ELIZABETH, **Baroness Segrave** in her own right according to later doctrine; b 25 Oct 1338; m c 1349 **4th Lord** (Baron) **Mowbray** and d before him, leaving issue (see below)

2 NICHOLAS de SEGRAVE, 1st LORD (Baron) SEGRAVE (of Barton Segrave and Stowe) (E), so cr (according to later doctrine) by writ of summons (made out to 'Nicholas de Segrave junior') 24 June 1295; Marshal of England March 1307/8, Constable Northampton Castle March 1307/8, served against Scots from 1308; m Alice — and d 25 Nov 1321, leaving:

(1) MAUD de Segrave, BARONESS SEGRAVE in her own right according to later doctrine; b c 1296; m Edmund De BOHUN and dsp by 20 March 1334/5, when such Barony as may be deemed to have been cr by the writ of summons of 1295 expired

Lineage (of Mowbray): WILLIAM d'AUBIGNY, Seigneur of Aubigny (subsequently Saint-Martin d'Aubigny), Normandy; m by 1048 —, sis of Grimald de Plessis, and had:

ROGER d'Aubigny; m Amice — and had, with another s (Rualoc):

1 William; living Norfolk temp WILLIAM II; Butler to HENRY I; fndr Wymondham Priory, Norfolk, by 1207; m Maud, dau of Roger le Bigod by his 2nd w Alice, dau of Robert de To(s)ny, and had:

(1) WILLIAM, EARL OF ARUNDEL (see NORFOLK, D)

2 Nele; closely associated with HENRY I, who made over to him following his victory of Tinchebrai 1106 the possessions in England of Robert de Stuteville, a follower of HENRY's defeated er bro ROBERT, DUKE OF NORMANDY; m 1st after 1107 (but later repudiated) Maud, formerly w of Robert de Mowbray (originally Mon(t)brai, in Normandy), Earl of Northumberland, her marriage to the latter having been previously declared null due to their kinship (Robert, it has been suggested, may have been 1st cousin to Nele through the latter's mother, sis of Roger de Mowbray, f of Robert); m 2nd June 1118 Gundred, dau of Gerard de Gournay by Edith, dau of William de Warenne, 1st Earl of Surrey (see NORFOLK, D, preliminary remarks), and d 21/26 Nov 1129, leaving by her:

(1) Roger De MOWBRAY; helped defeat invading Scots Battle of the Standard 1138; supported KING STEPHEN in period of the Anarchy, fighting on his behalf Battle of Lincoln Feb 1140/1; joined Second Crusade 1147; rebelled against HENRY II 1173 and allegedly escaped to Scotland following rebels' defeat, but submitted 1174; again went on crusade 1186, captured by Saracens 1187 Battle of Hittin but ransomed; m Alice, dau of Walter de Gant and widow of Ilbert de Lacy, and d 1188 in the Holy Land when on the point of returning to England, leaving, with another s (Robert):

1a Nele; associate of his f in 1173 Uprising; went with RICHARD I on crusade 1189; m by autumn 1170 Mabel — and d at Acre in the Holy Land 1191, leaving:

1b William; supporter of KING JOHN at time of latter's loss of Normandy to the French 1204–05, whereby the original Montbrai possessions were alienated; accompanied JOHN to Ireland 1210 but joined baronial opposition to JOHN over Magna Carta 1215, to enforce which he was one of the 25 magnates appointed; excommunicated by INNOCENT III at JOHN's request after prolonged opposition to him, his estates being confiscated also; captured Battle of Lincoln May 1217 fighting for the French King against HENRY III but submitted to latter Oct 1217 and got back his estates; m Avice — and d by March 1223/4, leaving:

1c Nele; m Maud — (m 2nd by 2 Jan 1233/4 John de Courtenay) and dsp 1230

2c Roger; seemingly took HENRY III's part in Barons' War in 1260s; m Maud (m 2nd, as his 1st w, 1st and last Lord (Baron) Strange (of Ellesmere), see SAINT DAVIDS, V), est dau of William de Beauchamp, and d c Nov 1266, leaving, with three daus (including Joan, m c 1261 Robert de Mohaut and had by him Roger de Mohaut, 1st and last Lord (Baron) Mohaut of the 1295 cr):

1d ROGER de MOWBRAY, **1st Lord** (Baron) **Mowbray** (E), so cr by writ of summons to Parl 24 June 1295 according to later doctrine, although in a Ho Lds decision of 1877 (now generally held to be flawed) a date of 28 June 1283 was assigned as the valid Parl to which ROGER's summoning created him a peer; called up for mil serv against Welsh 1282 and 1283 and against Scots 1291, also in Gascony 1294; m 1270 Roese [sic], dau of Richard de Clare, Earl of Gloucester and Hertford (see HERTFORD, M, preliminary remarks) by his 2nd w Maud, dau of John de Lacy, Earl of Lincoln (see LINCOLN, E, preliminary remarks), and d by 21 Nov 1297, leaving:

1e JOHN de MOWBRAY, **2nd Lord** (Baron) **Mowbray**; allegedly b 4 Sept 1286; ktd 1306; served regularly against Scots 1308–19, Keeper City and Co of York 1312, Warden Marches towards Carlise 1313 and Jan 1314/5, Capt and Keeper Newcastle-upon-Tyne and Northumberland March 1314/5, Keeper town and castle of Scarborough and manor and castle of Malton 1317; joined Thomas, Earl of Lancaster, in rebellion against EDWARD II; m 1298 Aline de Braose/Brewes, dau and coheir of 1st and apparently last Lord (Baron) Brewes, and after being taken prisoner at the Battle of Boroughbridge 16 March 1321/2 was hanged 23 March at York, his

corpse allegedly being kept dangling in chains for around three years, leaving:

1f JOHN de MOWBRAY, **3rd Lord** (Baron) **Mowbray**, JP (Lincs 1351); b 29 Nov 1310; incarcerated Tower of London 26 Feb 1321/2, presumably for complicity in his f's rebellion; Keeper Berwick-on-Tweed 1340–41, a cdr English victory over Scots of Neville's Cross 1346; m 1st 1325 Joan, 6th and yst dau of 3rd Earl of Lancaster, gs of HENRY III, and had issue; m 2nd Elizabeth, dau of 7th Earl of Oxford (see SAINT ALBANS, D) and widow of Hugh de Courtenay, s of 2nd Earl of Devon (qv) of the Feb 1334/5 cr, and d 4 Oct 1361, leaving by his 1st w:

1g JOHN de MOWBRAY, **4th Lord** (Baron) **Mowbray**; b 25 June 1340; ktd 1355; m c 1349 Elizabeth, **Baroness Segrave** (see above) in her own right, dau of **4th Lord** (Baron) **Segrave** (see above), and was k by Saracens nr Constantinople on his way to the Holy Land 9 Oct 1368, leaving:

1h JOHN de MOWBRAY, **5th Lord** (Baron) **Mowbray**, also **6th Lord** (Baron) **Segrave** (as which s mother before 9 Oct 1368), also 1st and last EARL OF NOTTINGHAM (E), so cr 16 July 1377; b 1 Aug 1365; ktd 1377; d unm just prior to 12 Feb 1382/3, when the Earldom expired

2h THOMAS de MOWBRAY, **6th Lord** (Baron) **Mowbray** and **7th Lord** (Baron) **Segrave**, also 1st DUKE OF NORFOLK, so cr 29 Sept 1397, as also earlier 12 Feb 1382/3 EARL OF NOTTINGHAM and 12 Jan 1385/6 Earl Marshal; in addition 3rd EARL OF NORFOLK (as which s grandmother 24 March 1398/9), KG (c 1383); b 22 March 1365/6; Marshal of England 1385; served against Scots 1385 and a Franco-Hispanic-Flemish fleet off Margate March 1386/7; a Ld Appellant (clique of nobles opposed to RICHARD II's favourites) Feb 1387/8; Keeper Berwick and Roxburgh and Warden E March 1389; Capt Calais Feb 1390/1–95/6; King's Lt Artois, Calais, Flanders and Picardy 1392; Jt Amb France Feb 1396/7 and Rhine Palatinate June 1397; quarrelled with the Duke of Hereford (later HENRY IV), each accusing the other of treason; both banished 1398; after his old enemy had usurped the throne as HENRY IV the conferring of the Dukedom of Norfolk was annulled by Parl 6 Oct 1399; m 1st 15 March 1382/3 Elizabeth (dsp 23 Aug 1383), dau and heiress of 1st Lord (Baron) Strange of the 1360 cr (see SAINT DAVIDS, V); m 2nd July 1384 Elizabeth (m 3rd by 19 Aug 1401 Sir Robert Goushill (by whom she was mother of Elizabeth, who m Sir Robert Wingfield, of Letheringham; see POWERSCOURT, V) and 4th by 3 July 1414 Sir Gerard Usflete and d 8 July 1425, leaving further issue), widow of Sir William de Montagu (dsp), est s of Earl of Salisbury (see SALISBURY, M, preliminary remarks), and dau of 11th/4th Earl of Arundel (see NORFOLK, D), and d of plague in Venice 22 Sept 1399, leaving:

1i THOMAS de MOWBRAY, **7th Lord** (Baron) Mowbray and **8th Lord** (Baron) **Segrave**, also 2nd EARL OF NOTTINGHAM, 4th EARL OF NORFOLK and Earl Marshal; b 17 Sept 1385; ktd by 22 Sept 1399; m by 1 June 1402 Constance (m 2nd by 24 Feb 1412/3 Sir John Grey, KG), daughter and heiress of John Holand, Duke of Exeter, by Elizabeth, dau of John of Gaunt, Duke of Lancaster and s of EDWARD III, and dsp, being beheaded without trial 8 June 1405 for involvement in a plot against HENRY IV

2i JOHN de MOWBRAY, **8th Lord** (Baron) **Mowbray** and **9th Lord** (Baron) **Segrave**, also 3rd EARL OF NOTTINGHAM, 5th EARL OF NORFOLK and Earl Marshal, KG (1421), PC (1422); b 1392; served last phase of Hundred Years War; restored as 2nd DUKE OF NORFOLK 30 April 1425; m 12 Jan 1411/2 Lady Katharine Nevill(e), daughter of 1st Earl of Westmorland (see ABERGAVENNY, M), and d 19 Oct 1432, having had:

1j JOHN de MOWBRAY, **9th Lord** (Baron) **Mowbray** and **10th Lord** (Baron) **Segrave**, also 3rd DUKE OF NORFOLK etc, KG (1451), PC (by April 1437); b 12 Sept 1415; ktd 1426; soldier and diplomat in struggles against Scotland and France; Lancastrian c 1455–Feb 1460/1, Yorkist thereafter, fighting for EDWARD IV Battle of Towton 29 March 1460/1; m 1424 Eleanor Bourchier (d Nov 1474), sis of 1st Earl of Essex (see BERNERS, B), and d 6 Nov 1461, leaving:

1k JOHN de MOWBRAY, **10th Lord** (Baron) **Mowbray** and **11th Lord** (Baron) **Segrave**, also 4th DUKE OF NORFOLK etc, in addition 1st and last EARL OF SURREY AND WARENNE (E), so cr 24 March 1450/1 vp, KG (1472), KB (1461); b 18 Oct 1444; Yorkist Wars of Roses; m by 27 Nov 1448 Lady Elizabeth Talbot, dau of 1st Earl of Shrewsbury and Waterford (qv), and dspm 16/17 Jan 1475/6, when the Dukedom and all his Earldoms bar that of Norfolk expired, leaving:

1l ANNE de Mowbray, **Baroness Mowbray** and **Baroness Segrave** (according to later doctrine), also COUNTESS OF NORFOLK, all in her own right; b 10 Dec 1472; m (aged 5) 15 Jan 1477/8 RICHARD DUKE OF YORK (2nd s of EDWARD IV), cr 7 Feb 1476/7 DUKE OF NORFOLK and EARL WARENNE, as also earlier 12 June 1476 EARL OF NOTTINGHAM, all in anticipation of his match with the Mowbray heiress, and murdered c 23 June 1483 (with his er bro EDWARD V, they being the two Princes in the Tower), when all his titles expired; she dsp a minor 25 Jan–10 Nov 1481, when the Earldom of Norfolk appears to have become dormant, while her Baronies fell into abeyance between the heirs of her great-great-aunts Margaret and Isabel (*see* imediately below)

1i Margaret; *m* Sir Robert Howard (*see* NORFOLK, D) and had, with two daus:

1j JOHN HOWARD, *ex post facto* 12th/13th LORD

2i Isabel; *m* 1st Henry Ferrers (*dvp*), s and heir of 5th Lord (Baron) Ferrers (of Groby), and had issue; *m* 2nd 1423 1st Lord (Baron) Berkeley (*qv*) and by him had further issue

ANNE BARONESS MOWBRAY and SEGRAVE's 1st cousin twice-removed,

JOHN HOWARD, declared by Ho Lds 1877 to have been 12th LORD (Baron) MOWBRAY and 13th LORD (Baron) SEGRAVE by virtue of letters of RICHARD III which referred to him thus, in what has later been generally recognised as a mistaken belief that these letters were evidence that RICHARD had called the Baronies out of abeyance, also 1st DUKE OF NORFOLK (*see* separate article), so *cr* 28 June 1483; posthumously attainted 7 Feb 1485 but attainder reversed 1489; had:

THOMAS HOWARD, regarded as 2nd DUKE OF NORFOLK by virtue of the re-creation of 1 Feb 1513/4 which assigned him precedence of the 1483 *cr*, but though his and his f's attainder was reversed 1489 only the Earldom of Surrey was restored to him, so that the Baronies of Mowbray and Segrave should for the time being be regarded as still subject to forfeiture; had:

THOMAS HOWARD; 3rd DUKE OF NORFOLK; had:

HENRY HOWARD, 1st EARL OF SURREY; had:

THOMAS HOWARD, *ex post facto de jure* 13th LORD (Baron) MOWBRAY and 14th LORD (Baron) SEGRAVE, also 4th DUKE OF NORFOLK; restored in honours as well as blood 1553 but attainted afresh Jan 1571/2, when all his titles were once more forfeited; had:

PHILIP HOWARD, EARL OF ARUNDEL (*see* NORFOLK, D); had:

THOMAS HOWARD, *ex post facto de jure* 14th LORD (Baron) MOWBRAY and 15th LORD (Baron) SEGRAVE; restored 18 April 1604 in blood both to the Earldoms of Arundel and Surrey and to the Baronies his gf had held, which was taken in 1877 to include those of Mowbray and Segrave; *cr* 6 June 1644 EARL OF NORFOLK; had:

HENRY FREDERICK HOWARD, *ex post facto de jure* 15th LORD (Baron) MOWBRAY and 16th LORD (Baron) SEGRAVE, also 1st BARON MOWBRAY (E), so *cr* April 1640 after being called up to Ho Lds *vp* in his f's supposed Barony of Mowbray, although since the latter was only coheir to it such writ must be held to have instituted a fresh title, albeit under the same designation as that of (1283/)1295; nevertheless he was given precedence as the premier Baron; was also 2nd EARL OF NORFOLK, as well as EARL OF ARUNDEL and SURREY (as which *s f*); had:

1 THOMAS HOWARD, *ex post facto de jure* 16th LORD (Baron) MOWBRAY and 17th LORD (Baron) SEGRAVE, also 2nd BARON MOWBRAY of the 1640 *cr* and 5th DUKE OF NORFOLK (as which restored 1660) etc; *d unm* 13 Dec 1677

2 HENRY HOWARD, *ex post facto de jure* 17th LORD (Baron) MOWBRAY and 18th LORD (Baron) SEGRAVE, also 3rd BARON MOWBRAY of the 1640 *cr* and 6th DUKE OF NORFOLK etc, in addition *cr* 27 March 1669 BARON HOWARD OF CASTLE RISING and 19 Oct 1672 EARL OF NORWICH; had:

(1) HENRY HOWARD, *ex post facto de jure* 18th LORD (Baron) MOWBRAY and 19th LORD (Baron) SEGRAVE, also 4th BARON MOWBRAY of the 1640 *cr* (as which was called up to Ho Lds *vp* 14 Jan 1677/8) and 7th DUKE OF NORFOLK etc; *dsp* 1701

(2) Thomas, of Worksop, Notts; *m* Mary Elizabeth, dau of Sir John Savile, Bt, and had:

1a THOMAS HOWARD, *ex post facto* 19th LORD (Baron) MOWBRAY and 20th LORD (Baron) SEGRAVE, also 5th BARON MOWBRAY of the 1640 *cr* and 8th DUKE OF NORFOLK etc; *dsp* 23 Dec 1732

2a EDWARD HOWARD, *ex post facto* 20th LORD (Baron) MOWBRAY and 21st LORD (Baron) SEGRAVE, also 6th BARON MOWBRAY of the 1640 *cr* and 9th DUKE OF NORFOLK etc; *dsp* 20 Sept 1777, when the two Baronies of Mowbray (of the (1283/)1295 and 1640 creations) and that of Segrave fell into abeyance between his nieces (as did various other Baronies or representations thereto; *see* NORFOLK, D, PETRE, B, and 1970 edn FURNIVALL, B), while the Dukedom of Norfolk passed to his cousin (*see* NORFOLK, D)

3a Philip, of Buckenham, Norfolk; *b* 24 Jan 1687/8; *m* 1st 7 Jan 1723/4 Winifrede (*d* 3 Feb 1730/1), dau of Thomas Stonor (*see* CAMOYS, B), and had:

1b Thomas; *b* 4 Feb 1727/8; *d unm* 9 Jan 1763

1b WINIFRED Howard; *m* 11 Oct 1749 **16th Baron Stourton** (*see* above **Lineage (of Stourton)**) and had issue

3a (cont.) Philip Howard *m* 2nd 8 Nov 1739 Henrietta (*d* 26 March 1782), widow of Petre Proli and dau and coheir of Henry Blount, of Blagdon, Devon, and *d* 23 Jan 1749/50, having by her had:

2b Edward; *b* 22 Jan 1743/4; *d unm* 7 Feb 1767

2b Anne; *m* 19 April 1762 9th Baron Petre (*qv*) and had issue

MOYNE

Arms: Per saltire gules and azure, a lion rampant or; on a chief ermine two ducal coronets each enfiling as many arrows in saltire of the third. **Crest**: A boar passant quarterly or and gules, charged with a mullet counterchanged. **Supporters**: On either side a Cingalese macaque sejant proper. **Motto**: *Noli judicare* ('Judge not'). **Creation**: B. (UK) 21 Jan 1932.

THE 3RD BARON MOYNE, of Bury St Edmunds, Co Suffolk (Jonathan Bryan Guinness) [The Rt Hon The Lord Moyne, House of Lords, London SW1A 0PW]; *b* 16 March 1930; *s f* 1992; *educ* Eton and Trin Coll Oxford; sometime jnlst with Reuters, dir: Arthur Guinness, Son & Co 1961–88, Leopold Joseph & Sons 1963–91, Leopold Joseph (late Dir) Mattson Guinness Securities, Access to Justice 1995–97 and Introcan, chm and dir Trustor, chm Monday Club 1970–72, contested (C) Lincoln and Coventry NW by-elections March 1973 and 1976 respectively and latter seat in gen election Oct 1974, CC Leics 1970–74, author *Requiem for a Family Business* (1997); *m* 1st 25 July 1951 (*divorce* 1963) Ingrid Georgia Olivia Kelvedon; *qv*), yr dau of Maj Guy Richard Charles Wyndham, MC (*see* EGREMONT, LECONFIELD and, B), and has:

1 +JASPER JONATHAN RICHARD [The Hon Jasper Guinness, 96 Cheyne Walk, London SW10 0DQ; Arniano, Murlo, Siena, Italy]; *b* 9 March 1954; *educ* Eton and Ch Ch Oxford; *m* 1985 *Camilla Alexandra, dau of Robie David Corbett Uniacke, and has:

(1) *Amber; *b* 1989

(2) *Claudia; *b* 1989

2 +Valentine Guy Bryan [The Hon Valentine Guinness, 87 Hereford Rd, London W2 5BB]; *b* 9 March 1959; *educ* Eton and Ch Ch Oxford; sometime lead singer with pop group The Panic; *m* 1986 *Lucinda (Lulu) Jane, only dau of Cdr Miles James Rivett-Carnac, RN (*see* RIVETT-CARNAC, Bt), and has:

(1) *Tara Victoria; *b* 29 Nov 1991

(2) *Madeleine Rose; *b* 16 Jan 1997

1 *Catherine Ingrid [The Hon Mrs Hesketh, Meols Hall, Southport, Lancs PR9 7LZ; 36 Porchester Terrace, London W2 3TP]; *b* 1 June 1952; *m* 1st 16 July 1983 (*divorce* 1988) Lord Neidpath, s of 10th Earl of Wemyss and (5th Earl of) March (*qv*); *m* 2nd 1990 *Rob(ert) (Fleetwood) Hesketh (*see* SCARBROUGH, E) and by him has:

(1) *Francis Roger Fleetwood; *b* 1992

(1) *Violet Ingrid; *b* 1991 (twin)

(2) *Anna Mary ; *b* 1991

(3) *Mary Olivia Charteris; *b* 23 April 1997

The 3rd BARON MOYNE *m* 2nd 10 Jan 1964 *Suzanne, dau of Harold William Denis Lisney, of Cadaques, Gerona, Spain, and formerly w of Timothy Phillips, and has:

3 +Sebastian Walter Denis [The Hon Sebastian Guinness, La Ermita de San Sebastian, Cadaques, Gerona, Spain]; *b* 15 Feb 1964; *educ* Eton; *m* 1st 1987 (*divorce* 1991) Silvie Dominique, dau of Eric A Fleury, of Geneva; *m* 2nd 18 Nov 1995 *Peggy Stephaich

2 *Daphne Suzannah Diana Joan [The Hon Mrs Niarchos, 41 Park St, London W1]; *b* 9 Nov 1967; *m* 1987 *Spyros Niarchos, 2nd s of Stavros Niarchos, of St Moritz, and has:

(1) *Nicolas Stavros; *b* 1989

(2) *Alexis Spyros; *b* 1991

The 3rd BARON MOYNE has by *Susan ('Shoe') Mary, dau of Ronald Taylor, of Oldham, Lancs:

4 *Thomas Julian William Jon TAYLOR; *b* 1986

3 *Diana Gloria Isolde Rose Dimilo TAYLOR; *b* 1981

4 *Aster Sophia Mary TAYLOR; *b* 1984

Lineage: The 1st EARL OF IVEAGH (*qv*) had a 3rd s:

WALTER EDWARD GUINNESS, **1st Baron Moyne**, of Bury St Edmunds, Co Suffolk (UK), so *cr* 21 Jan 1932, DSO (1917) and bar (1918), TD, PC (20 Feb 1924); *b* 29 March 1880; *educ* Eton (rowed three yrs in The Eight and was Capt of Boats); Capt Imp Yeo Boer War 1900–01 (wounded, despatches, Queen's Medal, four clasps) and Bde Maj cmdg 10th Bn London Regt Gallipoli and GSO2 Flanders (despatches thrice) WW I, Lt-Col Suffolk Yeo, MP (U) Bury St Edmunds 1907–31 (also fought Stowmarket 1906), U-Sec War 1922–23, Fin Sec Treasury 1923–Jan 1924 and Nov 1924–Nov 1925, Min Ag and Fisheries Nov 1925–June 1929, Financial Mission to Kenya 1932, chm: Deptl Ctee Housing 1933, Roy Commn U of Durham 1934, Deptl Ctee Cinematograph Films Act 1936 and W Indies Roy Commn 1938–39, Jt-Parly Sec Min of Ag 1940–41, Sec State Colonies and Ldr Ho Lds 1941–42, Dep Min State Middle East 1942–44, Resident Min Middle East Jan-Nov 1944, memb LCC (N Paddington) 1907–10, author: *Walkabout. A journey in lands between the Pacific and Indian Oceans* (1936) and *Atlantic Circle* (1938); *m* 24 June 1903 Lady Evelyn Hilda Stuart Erskine (*d* 21 July 1939), dau of 14th Earl of Buchan (*qv*), and was assassinated in Cairo by membs of the Stern Gang 6 Nov 1944, leaving:

1 BRYAN WALTER, **2nd Baron**

2 +Murtogh David [The Hon Murtogh Guinness, 117 E 80th St, New York, NY 10021, USA]; *b* 7 May 1913; *m* 15 Nov 1949 Nancy Vivian Laura (*d* 1975 following a car crash), only dau of Cyril Edward Tarbolton, of Hampstead

1 *Grania Maeve Rosaura [The Most Hon The Dowager Marchioness of Normanby, Lythe Hall, Whitby, N Yorks; Argyll House, 211 King's Rd, London SW3]; *b* 14 April 1920; Sectn Offr WAAF WW II, Hon LLD Trin Coll Dublin 1953, JP N Yorks 1971–83, Pro Chlr Dublin U 1985–; *m* 10 Feb 1951 4th Marquess of Normanby (*qv*) and has issue

The 1st BARON's er s,

BRYAN WALTER GUINNESS, **2nd Baron Moyne**; *b* 27 Oct 1905; *educ* Eton and Ch Ch Oxford (BA 1928, MA 1931); barrister Inner Temple 1930, Maj Roy Sussex Regt Middle East and France WW II, v-chm Arthur Guinness, Son & Co 1947–79, tstee Iveagh Housing Tst Dublin and Guinness Housing Tst London, Govr Nat Gallery of Ireland 1955–92, Hon LLD Trin Coll Dublin 1958, Hon Fell Trin Coll Dublin and Nat U of Ireland 1961, FRSL, novelist (as Bryan Guinness): *Singing Out of Tune* (1933), *Landscape with Figures* (1934), *A Week by the Sea* (1936), *A Fugue of Cinderellas* (1956), *The Giant's Eye* (1964), *The Girl with the Flower* (1966) and *Helenic Flirtation* (1978), playwright: *The Fragrant Concubine* (1938) and *A Riverside Charade* (1954) and poet: *23 Poems* (1931), *Under the Eyelid* (1935), *Reflexions* (1947), *Collected Poems* (1956) and *The Clock* (1973), memb Irish Acad of Letters 1968; *m* 1st 30 Jan 1929 (*divorce* 1934) Hon Diana Freeman-Mitford (*m* 2nd Sir Oswald Mosley, 6th Bt; *see* RAVENSDALE, B), 3rd dau of 2nd Baron Redesdale (*qv*), and had:

1 JONATHAN BRYAN GUINNESS, **3rd and present Baron Moyne**

2 +Desmond Walter [The Hon Desmond Guinness, Leixlip Castle, Co Kildare, Ireland]; *b* 8 Sept 1931; *educ* Eton, Gordonstoun and Ch Ch Oxford (MA 1958); Lt 7th Hus, pres Irish Georgian Soc 1958–91, Hon LLD Trin Coll Dublin, author: *A Portrait of Dublin* (1967), *Georgian Dublin* (1979), *Irish Houses and Castles* (jt author, 1971), *Mr Jefferson, Architect* (jt author, 1973), *Palladio – A Western Progress* (jt author, 1976), *The White House* (1980), *Newport Restored* (1981) and *Great Irish Houses and Castles* (with Jacqueline O'Brien, 1992); *m* 3 July 1954 (*divorce* 1981) Princess Hermione Marie-Gabrielle ('Mariga') Petronella Sophie Devota Elizabeth Albertine (*d* 9 May 1989), est dau of HSH Prince Albrecht Eberhard Karl Gero-Maria von Urach, Count of Württemberg, and has:

  (1) +Patrick Desmond Karl Alexander [Patrick Guinness Esq, Furness, Naas, Co Kildare, Ireland]; *b* 1 Aug 1956; *educ* Winchester and Trin Coll Dublin (BA Mod); *m* 1st 19– (*divorce* 1989) Felicity Casey and has:

    1a *Jasmine; *b* 28 Sept 1976

  (1) (cont.) Patrick Guinness *m* 2nd 25 March 1990 *Louise Arundel and by her has:

    1a +Tom; *b* 2 Dec 1991

    2a *Celeste; *b* 6 July 1990

    3a *Lily; *b* 6 April 1995

  (1) *Marina; *b* 16 Aug 1957; *educ* Cranborne Chase; has issue by *Perry Ogden, photographer:

    1a *Violet; *b* 19–

2 (cont.) The Hon Desmond Guinness *m* 2nd 1985 *Penelope ('Penny'), dau of Graham Cuthbertson

The **2nd Baron** *m* 2nd 21 Sept 1936 *Elisabeth [The Rt Hon The Dowager Lady Moyne, Biddesden House, Andover, Hants; Knockmaroon House, Castleknock, Co Dublin, Ireland], 3rd dau of Capt Thomas Arthur Nelson, of Achnacloich, Connel, Argyll, and *d* 1992, having had:

3 Diarmid Edward; *b* 23 Sept 1938; *educ* Winchester and St Catharine's Coll Cambridge (BA 1963, MA 1965); Lt QOH, dir Guinness Overseas Ltd; *m* 8 Dec 1962 *Felicity [The Hon Mrs Diarmid Guinness, 2 Keats Grove, London NW3 2RT], only dau of Sir Andrew Hunter Carnwath, KCVO, of The Old Vicarage, Ugley, nr Bishop's Stortford, Herts, and *d* 15 Aug 1977, having had:

  (1) +Ewan Diarmid; *b* 6 Oct 1965; *educ* Eton; *m* 20 Oct 1995 *Claire Elizabeth, dau of Alan Perry by his w Patricia, of East Horsley, Surrey, and has:

    1a +Aidan Diarmid; *b* 21 April 1997

  (1) *Camilla; *b* 1 Dec 1963

  (2) *Lorna; *b* 12 Dec 1967; *educ* Edinburgh U

  (3) *Harriet; *b* 16 Feb 1970

4 +Finn Benjamin [The Hon Finn Guinness, Chute Forest House, Chute, Andover, Hants SP11 9DS]; *b* 26 Aug 1945; *educ* Winchester, Ch Ch Oxford (BA 1968, MA1972) and Inst of Animal Genetics Edinburgh U (PhD 1973); biologist, pres Arab Horse Soc 1976; *m* 25 March 1989 *Mary Wilson, dau of Benjamin Wilson Price, of Baltimore, Md., and formerly 2nd w of J(ames) P(atrick) ('Mike') Donleavy, the author

5 +Kieran Arthur [The Hon Kieran Guinness, Knockmaroon House, Castleknock, Co Dublin, Ireland]; *b* 11 Feb 1949; *educ* Winchester and Ch Ch Oxford (BA 1971, MA); botanist; *m* 4 Nov 1983 *Mrs Vivienne Halban, dau of André-Jacques van Amerongen, DFC, MB, BCh, MRCOG, FRCOG, of Grafton House, Blisworth, Northants, and has:

  (1) +Malachy; *b* 1985

  (2) +Lorcan; *b* 1989

  (1) *Kate; *b* 1985

6 +Erskine Stuart Richard [The Hon Erskine Guinness, Fosbury Manor, Marlborough, Wilts SN8 3NJ]; *b* 16 Jan 1953; *educ* Winchester and Edinburgh U;

farmer, Wilts CC 1979–81, Tstee Guinness Housing Tst 1979–90, MFH Tedworth 1981–84, Govr Chadacre Ag Inst 1982–88; *m* 26 April 1984 *Louise Mary Elizabeth, ed *Fathers, An Anthology* (1996), only dau of Patrick (Paddy) Dillon-Malone and Mrs John (Ann) Reihill, of Deepwell, Blackrock, Co Dublin, and has:

  (1) +Hector Erskine Patrick; *b* 1986

  (2) +Arthur Paris; *b* 1991

  (3) +Matthew Richard; *b* 1992

  (4) +Samuel Hugo; *b* 26 June 1995

  (1) *Molly Louise; *b* 1985

1 *Rosaleen Elisabeth [The Hon Mrs Mulji, 150 Malcha Marg, New Delhi 110021, India]; *b* 7 Sept 1937; *educ* St Anne's Coll Oxford (BA 1960, MA 1965); *m* 12 June 1965 *Sudhir Jayantilal Mulji, only s of Jayantilal Mulji, of Bombay, and has:

  (1) *Sachin Sudhir; *b* 6 March 1967

  (2) *Kabir Jayantilal Bryan; *b* 1 June 1970

  (1) *Sangita Rosaleen; *b* 19 Feb 1966

  (2) *Gopali Sharda Elizabeth; *b* 9 June 1975

2 *Fiona Evelyn [The Hon Fiona Guinness, Isle of Rhum, Inner Hebrides, Scotland]; *b* 26 June 1940; *educ* Cranborne Chase, Millfield and McGill U Montreal; zoologist, jt author: *Red Deer, Behaviour and Ecology of Two Sexes*

3 *Thomasin Margaret [The Hon Thomasin Guinness, Biddesden House, Andover, Hants SP1 9DN]; *b* 16 Jan 1947; *educ* Cranborne Chase, Dublin Coll of Art Dublin and Farnham Coll of Art; potter and painter; has:

  (1) *Luke Colm; *b* 10 Feb 1979

4 *Catriona Rose [The Hon Catriona Guinness, Biddesden Farm, Andover, Hants]; *b* 13 Dec 1950; *educ* Cranborne Chase, Winchester Co High Sch and LMH Oxford (BA 1973, MA 1977); botanist and farm manager

5 *Mirabel Jane [The Hon Mrs Helme, Mount Orleans, Collingbourne Ducis, Marlborough, Wilts SN8 3EF]; *b* 8 Sept 1956; *educ* Cranborne Chase and UEA (BA 1978); equestrienne, MFH Tedworth 1986–, author *Biddesden Cookery* (1987); *m* 10 Aug 1984 *Patrick Ian ('Tom') Helme, interior decorator, s of A R Helme, of Danehill, E Sussex, and has:

  (1) *Toby Anthony Bryan; *b* 1992

  (1) *Alice Mirabel; *b* 1987

  (2) *Tyga Elisabeth; *b* 1990

  (3) *Lily Pauline; *b* 1994

MOYNIHAN

Arms: Az. a chevron between in chief three mullets arg. and in base a rose, also arg., barbed and seeded ppr. **Crest:** A demi-knight in armour affrontée, resting the sinister hand on the hip ppr. and supporting with the dexter hand a spear, also ppr., flowing therefrom a forked pennon arg. charged with a Maltese cross sa. **Supporters:** On either side an owl arg., gorged with a baron's coronet or. **Motto:** *Spiandact tapeir neill* ('Sunshine after rain'). **Creations:** Bt. (UK) 26 June 1922, B. (UK) 19 March 1929.

THE 4TH BARON MOYNIHAN, of Leeds, Co York, and a **Baronet** (Sir Colin Moynihan, Bt) [The Rt Hon The Lord Moynihan, 28 Nicosia Rd, London SW18 3RN]; *b* 13 Sept 1955; *s* half-bro on termination of dormancy 1997; *educ* Monmouth Sch and Univ Coll Oxford (BA 1977, Pres Union 1976, double blue rowing 1976, boxing 1977); mktg exec Tate & Lyle 1983–87, political assist to For Sec 1983, MP (C) Lewisham E 1983–92, PPS to Sec State DHSS 1985 and Paymaster-Gen 1985–87, Parly U-Sec (Min Sport, having won gold medal 1978 Internat Rowing Fedn lightweight rowing, Olympic Silver Medal Rowing 1980 and World Silver Medal rowing 1981) DOE 1987–90 and Energy 1990–92; dir Ranger Oil and Gas 1995–, Rowan Cos Inc 1996–, fnr ptnr CMA Consultants 1994–, Pres Br Wind Energy Assoc 1995–, Chm Sydney Olympic UK Business Task Force 1995–, Freeman City London 1978, Liveryman Haberdashers' Co 1981; *m* 1992 *Gaynor(-Louise), only dau of Paul G Metcalf, of S Humberside, and has:

1 +NICHOLAS EWEN BERKELEY; *b* 31 March 1994

2 +George Edward Berkeley; *b* 4 June 1995

1 *India Isabella; *b* 2 Sept 1997

Lineage: ANDREW MOYNIHAN, of Sefton Park, Liverpool; *d* 1837, leaving:

ANDREW MOYNIHAN, VC; Capt 8th King's Regt; *m* Ellen Anne, dau of John Parkin, JP, of W Derby, Liverpool, and *d* 19 May 1867, leaving, with a dau (Ada Augusta, *m* Rev Canon Arthur Needham Claye):

Sir Berkeley George Andrew Moynihan, 1st Bt, and **1st Baron Moynihan**, of Leeds, Co York (both UK), so *cr* 26 June 1922 and 19 March 1929 respectively, KCMG (1918), CB (1917), DL (W R Yorks); *b* 2 Oct 1865; *educ* RN Sch New Cross; MB and LRCP Lond 1887, FRCS Eng, BS 1889, MS Gold Medal 1893, consulting surgn: Leeds Gen Infirmary 1907, BEF 1914–16, Hon MD Ghent, Hon DCL Oxon and Durham, Hon LLD Leeds, Edin, St Andrews, Bristol, Manitoba, Toronto, Montreal, Hon DSc Belfast, MCh Trinity Coll Dublin, Hon MS Egypt, FZS, FRGS, Hon Col RAMC (TA), T/Maj-Gen 1917, Emeritus Prof Surgery Leeds U, PRCS (MCRCS 1912), ktd 1912, Grand Cordon Nile, Chev Legn Honour, KJStJ; author: *Abdominal Operations* (1905); *m* 17 April 1895 Isabella Wellesley (*d* 31 Aug 1936), dau of Thomas Richard Jessop, FRCS, JP, of Roundhay Mount, Leeds, and had:

1 PATRICK BERKELEY MOYNIHAN, **2nd Baron Moynihan**, OBE (1945), TD; *b* 29 July 1906; *educ* Winchester and Univ Coll Oxford (BA 1928); barrister Lincoln's Inn 1929, ptnr Montagu Stanley then Stokes, Priest & Co, of Cheapside, served WW II, Lt-Col 53rd (City London) HAA Regt RA 1947–52, Chm NW Met Regnl Hosp Bd 1960–65, *m* 1st 8 April 1931 (*divorce* 1952) Ierne Helen, only dau of Maj Cairnes Derrick Carrington Candy, of W Australia, and had:

  (1) ANTONY PATRICK ANDREW CAIRNES BERKELEY MOYNIHAN, **3rd Baron Moynihan**; *b* 2 Feb 1936; *educ* Stowe; 2nd Lt Coldstream Gds 1954–56; *m* 1st 25 May 1955 (*divorce* 1958) Ann, dau of Reginald Stanley Herbert, of Greenfield Cottage, Therfield, Herts; *m* 2nd 1958 (*divorce* 1967) Shirin Roshan Berry, snake charmer and fire-eater's assist, dau of late Ahmed Quereshi, of Malaya, and by her had:

    1a *Miranda Dorne Ierne; *b* 25 Feb 1959; *m* 1977 (*divorce* 1985) Horace Harry O'Garrow Omowale X and has:

      1b *Saskia Beulegh Ierne; *b* 1979

    1a (cont.) The Hon Mrs Miranda Omowale X has:

      2b *Ayisha; *b c* 1991

  (1) (cont.) The **3rd Baron** *m* 3rd May 1968 (*divorce* 1980) Luthgarda Maria Beltran del Rosa, dau of Alfonso Fernandez, of The Philippines, and by her had:

    2a *Antonita Maria Carmen Fernandez; *b* 31 March 1969

    3a *Aurora Luzon Maria Dolores; *b* 22 Jan 1971

    4a *Kathleen Maynila Helen Imogen Juliet; *b* 9 April 1974

  (1) (cont.) The 3rd Baron *m* 4th Feb 1981 (went through a form of divorce 1990, declared null and void in the British courts 31 July 1996) *Editha Eduarda, dau of Maj-Gen Eduardo Ruben, of Bulacan, The Philippines; went through a form of marriage 2 Dec 1990 with *Jinna Sabiaga and *d* 24 Nov 1991, when the titles became dormant, having by her had:

    1a *Daniel; *b* Jan 1991

  (1) *Imogen Anne Ierne; *b* 12 April 1932; *m* 1st 3 Sept 1953 (*divorce* 1965) Michael Edward Peter Williams, only s of W/Cdr Gwyn Herschell Jones Williams, MRCS, RAF, of Bayswater; *m* 2nd 23 April 1965 *Charles Ivan Vance, est s of Eric Goldblatt, of NI, and by him has:

    1a *Jacqueline Belinda Ierne; *b* 1 Sept 1963

  (2) *Juliet Jane Margaretta; *b* 18 April 1934; *m* 1st 25 July 1958 Thomas Edwin Bidwell Abraham (*d* 1976), only s of Maj-Gen William Ernest Victor Abraham, CBE, of Kencot Manor, Lechlade, Glos, and has:

    1a *James Bidwell; *b* 21 July 1959

    2a *John Richard; *b* 1 Oct 1960

  (2) The Hon Mrs Abraham *m* 2nd 1978 *Harry Hougham Sparks

1 (cont.) The **2nd Baron** *m* 2nd 28 Nov 1952 *June Elizabeth (*m* 2nd 23 June 1967 Neville Barton Hayman (*d* 1994), s of Frank Stanley Hayman, of Sutton, Surrey), yr dau of Arthur Stanley Covacic Hopkins, of Woodford Green, Essex, and *d* 30 April 1965, leaving by her:

  (2) COLIN BERKELEY MOYNIHAN, **4th and present Baron Moynihan**

  (3) *Melanie June [The Hon Mrs Corbett, Cedar Cottage, Ludlow Green, Glos GL6 6DH]; *b* 19 Aug 1957; *m* 1983 *Peter-John Stewart Corbett and has:

    1a *Edward John Patrick; *b* 1990

    1a *Poppy Ann; *b* 1986

    2a *Daisy Angelica Jak; *b* 1988

MOYOLA

Arms: Quarterly, 1st, gules three swords erect in pale proper, hilts and pommels or, a canton argent, charged with a trefoil vert (for CLARK); 2nd, chequy or and gules, a chief vair (for CHICHESTER); 3rd azure fretty argent (for ETCHINGHAM); 4th, azure on a bend or three daws gules (for DAWSON). **Crest:** Out of a mural crown an arm embowed in armour, the hand holding a dagger, all proper, charged with a trefoil vert. **Supporters:** On either side a heron's wing addorsed and gorged with a baron's coronet proper. **Motto:** *Virtute et labore* ('By labour and exertion'). **Creation:** B. (LP, UK) 1971.

THE BARON MOYOLA, of Castledawson, Co Londonderry (James Dawson Chichester-Clark, PC (1967)) [The Rt Hon The Lord Moyola PC, Moyola Park, Castle Dawson, Co Derry BT45 8ED]; *b* 12 Feb 1923; *educ* Eton; 2nd Lt Irish Gds WW II; ADC to Govr-Gen Canada 1947–49, psc 1956, Maj 1960; NI Parl: MP (U) S Derry 1960–72, Assist Whip 1963, Ch Whip 1963–67, Leader House 1966–67, Min Ag 1967–69, PM 1969–71, V-Lt Co Derry 1975–93 (DL 1954–75); *m* 1959 *Moyra Maud, dau of Brig Arthur de Burgh Morris, CBE, DSO, and widow of Capt T G Haughton, and has:

1 *Fiona; *b* 1960; *m* 1994 *William Rodney David Fisher, s of Leonard Fisher, of Lurgan, Co Armagh

2 *Tara Olivia; *b* 1962; *m* 1984 *Edward Thomas Whitley, s of John Whitley, of Hamsey Lodge, Lewes, Sussex

Lineage: *See* DONEGALL, M

MUIR

Arms: Per chevron arg. and or on a chevron cotised az. a redbreast ppr. between two mullets of the first, in chief as many fleurs-de-lys of the third. **Crest:** A Saracen's head couped, wreathed with laurel ppr., charged on the neck with a mullet az. **Motto:** *Duris non frangor* ('I am not broken by hardships'). **Creation:** Bt.(UK) 20 Oct 1892.

Richard James Kay Muir [Richard Muir, Park House, Blair Drummond, Perthshire]; *b* 25 May 1939; *s* f 1994, but does not use title; *educ* Trin Coll Glenalmond; m 1st 22 May 1965 (divorce 1974) Susan Elizabeth, only dau of George Albert Gardener, of Leamington Spa and Calcutta, and has:

1 *Louisa Jane; b 30 May 1967

2 *Catherine Elizabeth; b 2 Sept 1968

Richard Muir m 2nd 29 Aug 1975 *Lady Linda Mary Cole, only dau of 6th Earl of Enniskillen (qv), and by her has:

3 *Daisy Mary; b 5 July 1977

4 *Anna Charlotte; b 21 March 1979

Lineage: WILLIAM MUIR; Glasgow merchant; b 1739; m 1773 Catherine Scott and had an est s:

JOHN MUIR; merchant; b 17 March 1774; m Margaret (d 22 Oct 1858 aged 85), dau of Matthew Gardiner, of Glasgow, and had, with other issue:

1 James; b 9 March 1801; m 20 Dec 1827 Elizabeth (d 25 Sept 1864), dau of Andrew Brown, of Glasgow, and had:

(1) JOHN (Sir), **1st Bt**

(2) Andrew Brown; b 2 Sept 1830; d 3 June 1834

2 Matthew Andrew, of Ardenvior Row, Dunbartonshire; b 5 Oct 1812; m 1851 Agnes Clark, est dau of James Bunten, of Glasgow, and d Feb 1880, having had issue

JOHN MUIR d 18 April 1851; his gs,

Sir John Muir, 1st Bt (UK), so cr 20 Oct 1892, of Deanston, Perthshire, and Park Gdns, Glasgow, JP Perthshire and Lanarks, DL Lanarks, Ayrshire and Glasgow; Ld Provost Glasgow 1889–92, Hon Col 4th Vol Bn Cameronians (Scottish Rifles), merchant and mill owner; b 8 Dec 1828; m 26 July 1860 Margaret Morrison (d 28 Aug 1929), est dau of Alexander Kay, of Cornhill, Lanarks, and d 6 Aug 1903, having had:

1 **Sir (Alexander) Kay Muir, 2nd Bt**, JP Perthshire and Glasgow; High Sheriff Co Waterford 1919, memb Roy Co Archers; b 20 April 1868; m 1st 25 July 1910 Grace Frances (d 31 July 1920), widow of Henry Charles Villiers-Stuart (see BUTE, M) and only dau of John Adam Richard Newman, DL, of Newbury Manor, Co Cork; m 2nd 17 March 1924 Nadejda (d 15 April 1957), est dau of Dimitri Stancioff, GCVO, late Bulgarian Min London, and dsp 4 June 1951

2 James Finlay, of Braco Castle, Perthshire, JP; chm J Finlay & Co; b 17 Dec 1870; m 25 Aug 1909 Charlotte Escudier (d 1 Feb 1967), 2nd dau of Joseph Harling Turner, CBE, JP, and d 7 Sept 1948, having had:

(1) JOHN HARLING (Sir), **3rd Bt**

(2) Gerald Robin, OBE (1941), JP Kirkcudbrightshire; Lt-Cdr (S) RN, co dir, Polish Gold Cross 1942; b 18 July 1917; educ RNC Dartmouth; m 1st 2 Jan 1940 Doreen Margaret (d 1982), yr dau of Col Charles Wanford Watney, of Devon; m 2nd 1983 *Margaret Claire, dau of Llewellyn Arthur Hugh-Jones, OBE (see AUCKLAND, B), and widow of (a) Philip Muir Hutton Worthington, MBE, and (b) Lt-Cdr Thomas Mervyn Smith Dorrien Smith, of Tresco Abbey, Scilly, and d 1991, having by his 1st w had:

1a +Hugh James Robin [Hugh Muir Esq, PO Box 521, Malanda, N Qld 4885, Australia]; b 17 Oct 1944; educ Trin Coll Glenalmond; m 1969 *Maureen Yearsly and has:

1b +Andrew James; b 1970

2b +Jeremy Kim; b 1973

2a +Nicholas John [Nicholas Muir Esq, Dunduff, Braco Castle Farm, by Dunblane, Perthshire]; b 18 May 1953; m 1st 1975 Janet Mary Bain (dsp 1978), dau of Sir Colin Campbell, 8th Bt, of Aberuchill (qv); m 2nd 1980 *Angela Cramp and has:

1b +David Stuart; b 1981

1a *Sarah Nadéjda [Mrs Sarah Williams, Blaenau Dwr Farm, Froncysyllte, Llangollen, Clwyd]; b 17 Nov 1940; m 1965 (divorce 1982, took name WILLIAMS) Alexos Katsikidis, of Athens, and has had:

1b Simion; b 1966; d 1987

1b Maria; b 1967; d 1976

2a *Anne Catriona [Mrs John Gibb, Glenisla House, by Blairgowrie, Perthshire PH11 8QL]; b 10 April 1943; m 7 Feb 1970 *Maj John Philip Ogilvy Gibb, Scots Gds, er s of John Henry Creasy Gibb, and has:

1b *Alastair John Richard; b 1972

2b *Nicholas James Harry; b 1975

1b *Catriona Mary; b 25 Jan 1971

3a *Jean Charlotte [Mrs Alexander Gregory, Duncryne House, Gartocharn, by Alexandria, Dunbartonshire]; b 17 July 1946; m 1970 *Lt Alexander Michael Gregory, RN, and has:

1b *Charlotte Clare; b 1971

2b *Katherine Jane; b 1973

3b *Helen Veronica; b 1979

4b *Sarah Rachel; b 1982

4a *Diana Rachael; b 9 Oct 1949; m 1985 *James Lonergan, of New Inn, Co Tipperary, and has:

1b *James Robin; b 1986

1b *Rosanna Rachel; b 1988

2b *Clare Charlotte; b 1989

(1) *Margaret Vivian [Mrs Eric Hayes, Craigdhu, Barbreck, Lochgilphead, Argyll]; b 8 March 1912; m 8 Sept 1938 Capt Eric Gerald Hayes (d 1959), s of George Whitley Hayes, of Upton Grey House, Basingstoke, and has:

1a *David Richard [David Hayes Esq, Muir of Knock, Pityoulish, Aviemore, Inverness-shire]; b 1939; m 1968 *Hon Sarah Maclay, dau of 2nd Baron Maclay (qv)

1a *Helen Jane [The Hon Mrs Robert Younger, Old Leckie, Gargunnock, Stirling]; b 1941, m 1971 *Hon Robert Edward Gilmour Younger (see YOUNGER OF LECKIE, V)

(2) Helen Hamilton; b 18 July 1915; d 4 May 1921

3 John Buchanan; b 17 May 1876; m 5 Dec 1911 his cousin Agnes Heather Gardiner (d 14 May 1961), dau of John Gardiner Muir, DL, of Farmingwoods Hall, Northants, and d 1956, having had:

(1) Marguerite Judith; d 16 June 1936

(2) *Diana Heather [Mrs John Binny, Kiftsgate Court, Chipping Campden, Glos]; b 12 March 1915; m 15 April 1950 *John Anthony Francis Binny, s of Lt-Col Stewart Scott Binny, DSO, and has:

1a *Anne Heather [Mrs Jonathan Chambers, Kiftsgate Court, Chipping Campden, Glos]; b 30 Nov 1951; m 1st 1979 (divorce 1982) David Child; m 2nd 1983 *Jonathan Guy Chambers and has:

1b *Robert Edward; b 1983

2b *Patrick William Jack; b 1987

1b *Clare Heather; b 1983

2a *(Katherine) Emma; b 9 Nov 1953; m 1976 *Philip Austin George Mackenzie (see GRAFTON, D) and has issue

(3) *Bettine Clara [Miss Bettine Muir, Hidcote Vale, Chipping Campden, Glos]; b 1917

4 Matthew William; b 18 Sept 1878; m 12 Oct 1912 his cousin Clara Gardiner (m 2nd 14 April 1925 Maj David Johnstone Mitchell, MC, KRRC (d following car crash 25 Dec 1954), 2nd s of Arthur Charles Mitchell, of High Grove, Tetbury, Glos; d 25 June 1952), yst dau of John Gardiner Muir, DL, of Farmingwoods Hall, Northants, and d 9 Feb 1922 following a hunting accident, leaving:

(1) Ian Kay; Lt 10th Hus WW II; b 23 June 1916; ka France 27 May 1940

(1) *Gillian Rachel [Mrs Evan Williams, Ballyvolane Stud, Bruff, Co Limerick, Ireland]; b 23 Sept 1914; m 16 July 1940 *Evan Morgan Williams, s of Frederick Williams, of Bear Hotel, Cowbridge, Glam, and has:

1a *Ian Muir [Ian Williams Esq, Ballykisteen Stud, Tipperary, Co Tipperary, Ireland]; b 20 June 1942; educ Eton

2a *Hugh Frederick; b 10 July 1943; educ Eton

1 Jean Miller; m 22 Feb 1887 Gen Sir Ian Standish Monteith Hamilton, GCB, GCMG, DSO, Gordon Highrs, est s of Col Christian Monteith Hamilton by Hon Corinna, dau of 3rd Viscount Gort (qv), and dsp 23 Feb 1941. He d 12 Oct 1947

2 Elizabeth Brown; m 30 Aug 1883 Thomas George Harry Moncreiffe (see ERROLL, E) and d 20 Feb 1947, having had issue

3 Margaret Anne Kay, OBE (1919); m 3 Nov 1886 Alexander McGrigor, of Cairnock, Stirling, and d 9 Jan 1940, having had issue

4 Agnes Bunten; m 9 Oct 1888 William Allan Coats, 4th s of Thomas Coats, of Ferguslie, Paisley (see 1970 edn GLENTANAR, B), and d 13 March 1894, leaving issue. He d 31 Aug 1926

5 Edith Mary Kay; d unm 28 April 1909

6 Catherine Hetherington; m 7 March 1905 Lt-Col Stephen Hungerford Pollen, CMG, and d 11 July 1954, leaving issue (see POLLEN, Bt)

Sir KAY's n,

Sir John Harling Muir, 3rd Bt, TD, DL (Perthshire 1966), of Deanston; b 7 Nov 1910; educ Stowe; Maj and Actg Lt-Col Staff and 25th Dragoons and 3rd Carabiniers WW II, memb Roy Co Archers, chm James Finlay & Co, dir Scottish Utd Investors, National and Grindlays Bank, London and Lancashire Insur, Royal Insur, Vickers, chm Forth River Bd and Forth River Purificn Bd; m 24 Oct 1936 *Elizabeth Mary [Dowager Lady Muir, Bankhead, Blair Drummond, Perthshire FK9 4UX], est dau of Frederick James Dundas (see ZETLAND, M), and d 1994, leaving:

1 RICHARD JAMES KAY, **4th and present Bt**

2 +IAN CHARLES [Ian Muir Esq, Well Cottage, Poulner, Ringwood, Hants BH24 3LB]; b 16 Sept 1940; heir presumptive; educ Gordonstoun, m 7 Oct 1967 *Fiona Barbara Fiona (er dau of Maj (Douglas) Stuart Malcolm Mackenzie, of Rose Cottage, Charlton All Saints, Salisbury, and has:

(1) *Sophie Amanda Nöel; b 25 Dec 1969

(2) *Lisa Jane Fiona; b 13 Aug 1973

(3) *Juliet Sara Kirstie; b 14 Dec 1978

3 +Andrew Hugh John [Andrew Muir Esq, Itchen Lodge, Itchen Abbas, Hants]; b 28 Aug 1943; educ Gordonstoun; m 1st 3 May 1969 (divorce 1993) Primrose Jean Onslow How (see ONSLOW, E), and has:

(1) *Philip John Frederick; b 18 June 1974

(1) *Alexandra Julie; b 2 July 1971

3 (cont.) Andrew Muir m 2nd 1993 *Ann Mary, dau of — Corbally and formerly w of Timothy Jenkins

4 +James Francis [James Muir Esq, Underhill, Muthill, Crieff, Perthshire PH5 2BZ]; b 11 Aug 1948; educ Gordonstoun; m 29 Jan 1975 *Griselda Catherine, est dau of Sir Anthony Nathaniel Stainton, KCB, QC, of Bethersden, Kent, and has:

(1) +John Alexander Hector; b 5 Jan 1976; educ Gordonstoun

(2) +William Anthony Nathaniel; b 5 June 1979; educ Winchester

5 +Robert William; b 29 Dec 1950; educ Tabley House

1 *Fiona Mary [Mrs Walter Goetz, 19 Alexander Place, London SW7 2SG]; b 23 Jan 1938; m 25 Nov 1968 Walter Goetz (d Sept 1995), s of Alfred Goetz, of Bayswater, and has:

(1) *Sebastian; b 30 June 1970

(2) *Dominic; b 1971

2 *Margaret Elizabeth [Lady Aird, Grange Farm, Evenlode, Moreton-in-Marsh, Glos]; b 1 Aug 1946; m 31 Aug 1968 *Sir John Aird, 4th Bt (qv), and has issue

MUIR MACKENZIE

Arms: Quarterly, 1st and 4th, arg. on a fess az. three mullets or (for MUIR of Cassencarrie); 2nd and 3rd, az. a stag's head cabossed or (for MACKENZIE of Delvine), all within a bordure nebuly quarterly gu. and arg. **Crests:** 1 A palm branch in bend dexter, surmounted of a sword in bend sinister, all ppr. (for MUIR); 2 A dexter hand grasping a dart ppr (for MACKENZIE). **Mottoes:** *In utrumque paratus* ('Ready for anything') and *Recte ad ardua* ('Straight at difficulties'). **Creation:** Bt. (UK) 9 Nov 1805.

SIR ALEXANDER ALWYNE HENRY CHARLES BRINTON MUIR MACKENZIE, **7TH BT**, of Delvine, Co Perth [Sir Alexander Muir Mackenzie Bt, Stones Farm, Hilfield, Dorset DT2 7BA]; *b* 8 Dec 1955; *s f* 1970; *educ* Eton and Trin Coll Cambridge; *m* 1984 *Susan Carolyn, yst dau of John David Henzell Hayter, of Adbury Court, nr Newbury, Berks, and has:

1 +ARCHIE ROBERT DAVID; *b* 17 Feb 1989

1 *Georgina Mary; *b* 1 March 1987

Lineage: GEORGE MUIR of Cassencarrie, Kirkcudbrightshire; *m* Margaret, dau of Alexander Mackenzie of Delvine, Perthshire (*see* MACKENZIE, Bt, of Coul) and had:

Sir ALEXANDER MUIR later MUIR MACKENZIE (added on inheriting his great-uncle John Mackenzie of Delvine's estates), **1st Bt** (UK), so *cr* 9 Nov 1805; *b* 2 March 1764; *m* 6 Sept 1787 Jane, est dau of Sir Robert Murray, 6th Bt, of Clermont (*see* MURRAY, Bt, of Dunerne), and *d* 11 March 1835, having had, with eight daus (including Susan, *m* Robert Smythe, of Methven, and *d* 1852; Georgina, *b* 1833, *m* 24 Nov 1871 Sir Charles Sebright, Consul Corfu, and *d* 24 Jan 1874):

Sir John William Pitt Muir Mackenzie, 2nd Bt; *b* 1806; *m* 28 Aug 1832 Sophia Matilda (*d* 29 Jan 1900), 5th dau of James Raymond Johnstone (*see* JOHNSTONE, Bt), and *d* 1 Feb 1855, leaving:

1 **Sir Alexander Muir Mackenzie, 3rd Bt**, DL Perthshire; Maj Highland Borderers Inf Mil, Capt 78th Highrs; *b* 6 July 1840; *m* 21 Feb 1871 Frances Rose (*d* 7 July 1923), 6th dau of Sir Thomas Moncreiffe of that Ilk, 7th Bt (*see* ERROLL, E), and *dsp* 25 June 1909

2 ROBERT SMYTHE (Sir), **4th Bt**

3 Cecil Cholmeley; Lt RE, *b* 28 Sept 1843; *d* 2 Nov 1863

4 KENNETH AUGUSTUS, 1st and last BARON MUIR MACKENZIE, of Delvine, Co Perth (UK), so *cr* 29 June 1915, GCB (1911, KCB 1898, CB 1893), PC (1924), QC (1887), JP London; *b* 26 June 1845; *educ* Charterhouse and Balliol Coll Oxford (BA 1868, MA 1873); barrister Lincoln's Inn 1873, Bencher 1891, Perm Sec to Ld Chllr 1880–1915, Clerk to Crown in Chancery 1885–1915, Govt Whip, High Bailiff Westminster 1912–30, Warden Winchester Coll 1904–15; *m* 26 Feb 1874 Amelia (*d* 18 Dec 1900), dau of William Graham, DL, MP Glasgow, and *dspms* 22 May 1930, when the Barony expired, having had:

(1) William Montague; barrister; *b* 12 May 1876; *d* unm 18 July 1901

(1) Margaret Mary; *b* 29 May 1879; *m* 3 Jan 1907 Donnell Post, 2nd s of Frederick Post, of Pimlico, and *d* 19 Aug 1958, leaving issue. He *d* 15 July 1937

(2) Dorothea Frances; *b* 4 April 1881; *m* 5 March 1907 Mark Hambourg, of St John's Wood, pianist, s of Prof Michael Hambourg, and had issue. He *d* 26 Aug 1960

(3) Magdalen; *b* 26 April 1884; *m* 10 July 1905 Sir Robert Henry Clive, GCMG, PC, yst s of Charles Meysey Bolton Clive, JP, of Whitfield, and *d* 14 Oct 1971, leaving issue. He *d* 13 May 1948

5 Montague Johnstone, JP Glos; barrister, Bencher Middle Temple, Fell Hertford Coll Oxford, BA, Official Referee Supreme Court, Recorder Sandwich and Deal; *b* 29 Sept 1847; *m* 17 Aug 1888 Hon Sarah Napier Bruce (*d* 21 Dec 1931), dau of 1st Baron Aberdare (*qv*), and *d* 18 April 1919, leaving:

(1) Enid; *b* 25 June 1889; *d* unm 17 Nov 1952

6 John William Pitt (Sir), KCSI; ICS 1874–1910, Commr Sind 1904, memb Cncl Bombay 1905–10, Actg Govr Bombay 1907; *b* 19 March 1854; *m* 1st 2 Aug 1876 Fanny Louisa (*d* 24 Sept 1895), 2nd dau of Lt-Gen Montague Cholmeley Johnstone (*see* JOHNSTONE, Bt), and had:

(1) Montague Ronald Alfred; barrister, Dep Serjeant-at-Arms Ho Lds to 1916, Reading Clerk Ho Lds 1916–34, Clerk Assist Parls 1934; *b* 1881; *m* 17 March 1910 Constance Felicity (*d* 3 Aug 1975 aged 91), yst dau of Samuel Henry Romilly, DL, of Huntingdon Park, Herefs, and *dsp* 4 May 1937

(2) Kenneth James; barrister, Capt 5th Bn Royal Munster Fus, Attorney-Gen Fiji 1922, Actg Ch Justice 1922–23, MLC Fiji 1927, Judge High Court Tanganyika 1927; *b* 1882; *m* 24 July 1915 Phyllis (*m* 2nd 6 Feb 1932 Lt-Cdr William Oswald Rees Millington, RN; *d* 1938), yr dau of Henry Howard Taylor, of Thurnscoe Hall, and *d* 3 June 1931, leaving:

1a Hamish, DSC; Lt-Cdr RN WW II; *b* 20 Oct 1917; *das* following a flying accident 18 June 1947

1a *Susan [Mrs Gerald Whyte, The Mill Farm, Tinwell, nr Stamford, Lincs]; twin with her brother; *m* 1st 28 March 1939 (*divorce* 1947) Lt-Col George David Garforth-Bles, QVO Corps Guides, Cav IA, est s of Capt George Marcus Garforth-Bles, of Manchester and Knutsford, and has:

1b *George William [George Garforth-Bles Esq, Little Tor, 1 Longdown Close, Lower Bourne, Farnham, Surrey]; Capt Black Watch (RHR); *b* 7 Oct 1941; *educ* Rugby, RMA Sandhurst and Downing Coll Cambridge (BA)

1b *Suzanna Mary [Mrs Anthony Birley, 49 Main Street, Shadwell, Leeds 17, Yorks]; *b* 30 March 1943; *m* 1 Aug 1963 *Anthony Richard Birley, FSA, yr s of Prof Eric Barff Birley, MBE, FSA, of Carvoran House, Greenhead, Cumbria, and has:

1c *Paul Hamish Aurelius; *b* 8 March 1966

1c *Ursula Ann; *b* 5 March 1964

1a (cont) Mrs George Garforth-Bles *m* 2nd 22 Nov 1947 *Lt-Col Gerald Owen Whyte, 2nd/10th Gurkha Rifles, s of Percy Horatio Marnfred Whyte, and by him has:

2b *Belinda Jane; *b* 5 Oct 1948

3b *Lucinda Enid; *b* 18 Nov 1951

(1) Mary Louisa; *m* 1904 Brev Lt-Col William Drysdale, DSO, Roy Scots, and *d* 11 Oct 1946, leaving issue. He *d* 1916 of wounds recd in action

(2) Susanne Frances Maud; *m* April 1910 Arthur Swinburne and *d* 17 Dec 1927

(3) Georgina Margaret Alice; *d* young

6 (cont) John Muir Mackenzie *m* 2nd 16 July 1898 Rhoda (*dsp* 15 May 1900), dau of William Watson, of Caversham Rise, Oxford; *m* 3rd 16 Feb 1904 Mary Therese, Kaisar-i-Hind gold Medal, LGStJ (*d* 9 March 1926), est dau of Henry Windsor Villiers-Stuart (*see* BUTE, M), and *d* 25 Oct 1916

1 Georgiana Mary; *m* 24 Nov 1871 Sir Charles Sebright, KCMG, and *d* 24 Jan 1874

2 Lucy Jane Eleanor; *m* 20 Oct 1859 Bentley Murray, yst s of William Murray, of Monkland, and *d* 22 Sept 1874, leaving issue

3 Susan Anne Eliza; *d* unm 22 Aug 1908

The 2nd Bt's yr bro,

Sir Robert Smythe Muir Mackenzie, 4th Bt; Lt-Col RA; *b* 27 Nov 1841; *m* 17 Oct 1872 Anne Elizabeth Augusta (*d* 29 April 1908), 2nd dau of Capt Charles Kinnaird Johnstone-Gordon (*see* JOHNSTONE, Bt), and had:

1 ROBERT CECIL (Sir), **5th Bt**

1 Geraldine; *d* unm 5 March 1903

2 Cecily Emmeline; *m* 14 Sept 1908 Rev Theodore Catton, Rector Crayke, Easingwold, s of Rev John William Catton, and *d* 30 July 1961, leaving issue. He *d* 17 Feb 1953

3 Sophia Helen; *d* unm 5 April 1966 aged 80

Sir ROBERT *d* 2 Feb 1918; his only son,

Sir Robert Cecil Muir Mackenzie, 5th Bt, MC; *b* 17 Oct 1891; *educ* Jesus Coll Cambridge (BA 1913); Lt 5th Bn Durham LI; *m* 20 Oct 1914 Kate Brenda Blodwen, DGStJ (*m* 2nd 15 Aug 1929 Maj John Campbell Holberton (*d* 2 Sept 1962), Devon Regt, only s of Campbell Scott Holberton; *d* 23 Nov 1958), yr dau of Henry Jones, of Cardiff, and was *ka* 12 April 1918, leaving:

Sir Robert Henry Muir Mackenzie, 6th Bt; *b* 6 Jan 1917; *educ* Marlborough and New Coll Oxford (BA 1938); Capt RA and GSO(3) WW II (despatches, wounded); *m* 1st 24 April 1947 Charmian Cecil de Vere (*d* 28 March 1962), widow of Brig Walter Glencairn Glencairn-Campbell, OBE, and only dau of Col Cecil Charles Brinton, OBE, JP, of Yew Tree House, Belbroughton, Worcs, and had:

1 Sir ALEXANDER ALWYNE HENRY CHARLES BRINTON MUIR MACKENZIE, **7th and present Bt**

1 *(Charmian) Miranda [Mrs Robert Smyly, Sunderland Hall, Galashiels, Selkirkshire TD1 3PG]; *b* 4 Nov 1948; *m* 7 Nov 1968 *Robert Dennis Smyly, yst s of Col Dennis Douglas Pilkington Smyly, DSO, of Hill House, Hartpury, Glos, and has:

(1) *(Henry) Richard; *b* 16 Nov 1972

(1) *Henrietta Miranda; *b* 10 July 1970; *m* 24 May 1997 *Edward Timothy Gimlette

Sir Robert *m* 2nd 25 July 1963 *Mary Teresa [Mary Lady Muir Mackenzie, 51 Elizabeth Court, Milmans St, London SW10 0DA], widow of John Geoffrey Turner, of Lower Old Park, Farnham, Surrey, and er dau of Dr James Mathews, and *d* 4 Dec 1970

MUNRO of
Foulis-Obsdale

Arms: Or an eagle's head erased gu., langued az., a label of three points of the second, charged with three lion's heads, erased arg., and in dexter chief a canton of a baronet of Nova Scotia. **Crest:** An eagle displayed ppr., charged across his breast and wings with a label of three points gu. charged with three lion's heads erased arg. **Motto:** I dread God. **Creation:** Bt. (NS) 7 June 1634.

SIR KENNETH ARNOLD WILLIAM MUNRO 16TH BT, of Foulis-Obsdale [Sir Kenneth Munro Esq, 3 Courtrai Rd, London SE23]; *b* 26 June 1910; *s* cousin 1994 but has not established claim; *m* 26 Oct 1935 *Olive Freda, dau of Francis Broome, and has:

1 +IAN KENNETH [Ian Munro Esq, Foulis, Gold Cup Lane, Ascot, Berks SL5 8NP]; *b* 4 April 1940

1 *Christine Freda [Mrs K Bridle, Timbers, Barclay Park, Aboyne ABE SJP]; *b* 20 Oct 1944; *m* 1971 *Capt K Bridle and has:

  (1) *Christopher; *b* 1972

  (2) *Andrew; *b* 1975

Lineage: The MUNROs, originally vassals of the Earls of Ross, held lands lie on the north shore of the Cromarty Firth.

DONALD; living 1025; had:

GEORGE; living 1101; had:

HUGH; had:

ROBERT; *d* 1164, leaving:

DONALD; *d* 1192, leaving:

ROBERT; *d* 1239, leaving:

GEORGE; *d* 1282, leaving:

ROBERT; had:

GEORGE; *d* 1333, leaving:

ROBERT; *k* 1369, leaving:

HUGH; had:

GEORGE; *k* 1454, leaving, with a dau (*m* Angus Roy; *see* REAY, L):

JOHN; had;

WILLIAM; *k* 1505, leaving:

HECTOR MUNRO of Foulis; *m* 1st Katherine, dau of Kenneth Mackenzie of Kintail (*see* CROMARTIE, E); *m* 2nd Margaret, dau of Roderick Macleod of Harris and widow of Donald *Grumach* Macdonald, 4th of Sleat (*see* BOSVILLE MACDONALD, Bt), and *d* 1541, leaving by his 1st w:

ROBERT MUNRO of Foulis; *m* Margaret, dau of Sir Alexander Dunbar of Westfield (*see* DUNBAR, Bt, of Mochrum), and was *ka* Battle of Pinkie 8 Sept 1547, having had, with a yr s (Hector, of Contulloch and Kilermory, *m* —, dau of Mackenzie of Gairloch, and had issue; *see* INGLIS, Bt):

ROBERT MUNRO of Foulis; *m* 1st Margaret, dau of James Ogilvy of Cardell and aunt of 1st Lord Ogilvy of Deskford, and *d* 4 Nov 1588, having had, with two daus:

1 Robert, of Foulis; *m* four times and *dspm*, leaving:

  (1) Margaret; *m* Robert Munro of Assynt

2 Hector, of Foulis; *m* 1st Anne, dau of 5th Lord (Fraser of) Lovat (*qv*); *m* 2nd Janet, dau of Andrew Munro, and *d* 14 Nov 1603, leaving by his 1st w:

  (1) Robert, of Foulis; Col; *m* 1st Margaret, dau of William Sutherland of Duffus; *m* 2nd Mary Haynes and *d* in foreign serv at Ulm 1633, having had:

    1a Margaret; *m* 1634 Kenneth Mackenzie of Scatwell (*see* MACKENZIE, Bt, of Scatwell)

    2a Florence

  (2) **Sir Hector Munro, 1st Bt** (NS), so *cr* 7 June 1634, with remainder to his heirs male whatsoever; Col; *m* 1619 Mary, sis of 1st Lord Reay (*qv*), and *d* April 1635, leaving with two daus:

    1a **Sir Hector Munro, 2nd Bt**; *dsp* Holland Dec 1651

    1a Jean; *m* **Sir Robert Munro, 3rd Bt** (*see* below)

ROBERT MUNRO of Foulis *m* 2nd Katherine, dau of Alexander Ross of Balnagowan, and by her had, with two other sons:

3 George, of Obsdale; *m* Catherine, dau of Andrew Munro of Milnton and Newmore, and *d* 1589, having had:

  (1) John, of Obsdale; *m* Catherine, dau of John Gordon of Embo (*see* 1956 edn GORDON, Bt, of Embo), and *d* 1633, having had, with other issue:

    1a **Sir Robert Munro, 3rd Bt**; MP Inverness-shire 1649 and Ross-shire 1649–50; *m* Jean, dau of **Sir Hector Munro, 1st Bt**, and *d* 14 Jan 1668, having had, with other issue:

      1b **Sir John Munro, 4th Bt**; MP Ross-shire 1689–97; *m* Agnes, dau of Sir Kenneth Mackenzie, 1st Bt, of Coul (*qv*), and *d c* 29 Sept 1697, having had, with other issue:

        1c **Sir Robert Munro, 5th Bt**; MP Ross-shire 1697–1701, Sheriff Ross and Cromarty 1725; *m c* 1684 Jean, dau of John Forbes of Culloden by Anne, dau of Alexander Dunbar of Grange (*see* DUNBAR, Bt, of Durn), and *d* 11 Sept 1729, leaving, with other issue, including a yr s (George, of Culcairn):

          1d **Sir Robert Munro, 6th Bt**; *b c* 1684; MP Wick Burghs 1710–41, Lt-Col of a Highland Regt Battle of Fontenoy 1745; *m* Mary (*d* 24 May 1732), dau of Henry Seymour, of Woodlands, Dorset, and was *ka* fighting the Jacobites Battle of Falkirk 17 Jan 1745/6, leaving:

            1e **Sir Harry Munro, 7th Bt**; MP Ross-shire 1746–47 and Wick Burghs 1747–61; *m c* 1762 Anne, dau of Hugh Rose of Kilravock, Nairn, and *d* 12 June 1781, having had, with a yr s (George, *d* 22 April 1802):

              1f **Sir Hugh Munro, 8th Bt**; *b* 1763; *m* Jane (drowned bathing in the Cromarty Firth 1 Aug 1803), dau of Alexander Law, and *dspms* 2 May 1848

2a George (Sir); C-in-C royalist army Ireland; *m* as his 2nd w Christian, sis of 1st Viscount Boyne (*qv*), and *d* 1690, having had:

  1b George, of Culraine; *m* 1st Catherine (*dsps*), dau of — Dunbar of Grange (*see* DUNBAR, Bt, of Durn); *m* 2nd Anne, dau of Sir John Cunninghame of Enterkin, Ayrshire; *m* 3rd —, dau of Hugh Wallace of Ingleston, and *d* 1724, having by his 2nd w had, with two daus:

    1c Gustavus, of Culraine; *m* Mary, dau of Munro of Newmore, and *dsps*

    2c James, of Culraine; had:

      1d Charles, of Culraine; *m* Mary Anne, dau of Charles Ross of Inverchassley, and *d* 1783, leaving:

        1e George, of Culraine; *m* 1792 Margaret, dau of John Montgomery of Millmount House, Ross, and *d* 19 Dec 1845, leaving:

          1f CHARLES (Sir), **9th Bt**

          2f John; *d* unm 1847

          1f Mary; *m* 1st Owen Lindsey; *m* 2nd Alexander Simpson and *d* 1 Nov 1863

  1b Helen; *m* William Sinclair of Stemster (*see* SINCLAIR, Bt)

The 8th Bt's cousin,

Sir Charles Munro, 9th Bt, of Culraine, later of Foulis; *b* 20 May 1794; served Peninsular War 1811 on (wounded storming of Badajoz, medal and six clasps for Rodrigo, Badajoz, Salamanca, Nive, Orthes and Toulouse); cmded a div of the Colombian Army of independence under Simon Bolivar against Spaniards in S America; *m* 1st 20 June 1817 Amelia (*d* 14 Sept 1849), dau of Frederick Browne, 14th Dragoons; *m* 2nd 14 Jan 1853 Harriette (*d* 17 July 1886), dau of Robert Midgley, of Essington, Yorks, and *d* 12 July 1886, having by his 1st w had:

1 **Sir Charles Munro, 10th Bt**, of Foulis, JP, DL; *b* 20 Oct 1824; *m* 19 March 1847 Mary Anne (*d* 3 Oct 1903), dau of John Nicholson, of Camberwell, and *d* 29 Feb 1888, having had:

  (1) **Sir Hector Munro, 11th Bt**; *b* 13 Sept 1849; Col cmdg 3rd Bn Seaforth Highrs, ADC to HM GEORGE V, Ld Lt and Pres TAA Ross and Cromarty; *m* 7 April 1880 Margaret Violet (*d* 20 Feb 1946), est dau of John Stirling of Fairburn, and *dspms* 15 Dec 1935, having had:

    1a Robert Ian; *b* March 1887; *d* 12 May 1888

    2a Hector Charles Seymour, MC (1918); *b* 30 March 1895; Capt Seaforth Highrs WW I (despatches, Mons star); *ka* 23 Oct 1918

    1a Eva Marion, took name MUNRO of Foulis 1935 under terms of f's will but dropped it 1938; *b* 28 April 1881; *m* 27 Oct 1904 Lt-Col Cecil Claud Hugh Orby Gascoigne, DSO (*d* 5 July 1929), Seaforth Highrs, of Muirton, Blairgowrie, Perths, 3rd s of Col Clifton Gascoigne, Gren Gds, and *d* 1976, leaving:

      1b Patrick GASCOIGNE later MUNRO of Foulis (Lyon Court decree 1937, also recognised as Chief of Clan Munro), TD; *b* 1912; *educ* ISC and RMC; Capt Seaforth Highrs WW II (POW); V-Lt Ross and Cromarty 1969–95 (previously DL); *m* 1946 *Eleanor Mary, dau of Capt Hon William Joseph French (*see* DE FREYNE, B), and *d* 24 Feb 1995, leaving:

        1c *Hector William; *b* 1950; *m* 1974 *Sarah Katharine, dau of Henry George Austen de l'Etang Herbert Duckworth (*see* CHATFIELD, B), and has:

          1d *Finnian George; *b* 1975

          1d *Isabella Katharine; *b* 1978

          2d *Aline Angela; *b* 1981

         2c *Harry Robert Gascoigne; *b* 1954; *m* 1976 *Lynda, dau of Cecil Cranton, of Nova Scotia, and has:

          1d *Eva Marian; *b* 1983

          2d *Fiona; *b* 1986

          3d *Monica Bernice; *b* 1988

        3c *John Alexander Seymour; *b* 1959; *m* 1979 *Silvia Charlotte Maria, 4th dau of Knud Johan Ludvig, Count von Holstein-Ledreborg, of

Ledreborg, Denmark by his w HRH PRINCESS MARIA GABRIELLE OF LUXEMBURG, and has:

  1d *Alexander; b 1985

  1d *Tatiana Angela Marie; b 1983

  2d *Charlotte Angela Marie; b 1990

  3d *Angela Charlotte Marie; b 1992

1c *Charlotte Eva [Mrs Robin Hunt, Keirhill, Balfron, Stirlingshire G63 0LG]; b 1947; m 1st 1975 John William Betts Donaldson (d 1985), s of Norman Fraser Graham Donaldson of Ballindalloch, Balfron, Stirlingshire; m 2nd 1992 *Col Robin Chester Vaughan Hunt, s of Gen Sir Peter Mervyn Hunt, GCB, DSO, OBE, and has by her 1st husb:

  1d *William Betts; b 1980

  2d *Robert John; b 1983

  1d *Joanna Eva; b 1977

2b Robert Clifton; b 1915; Maj Seaforth Highers; m 1st 1940 (divorce 1954) Sylvia Rapozo and has:

  1c *Robert Hugh; b 1941

  1c *Caroline Orby; b 1946; m 1st 1968 Michael Robarts; m 2nd 1973 *Andrew Gordon-Duff and by him has issue (see BAIRD, Bt, of Newbyth)

2b (cont.) Maj Robert Gascoigne m 2nd 1954 *Margaret [Mrs Robert Gascoigne, 2 Hampton Pl, Edinburgh EH12 5JA], dau of N E Douglas Menzies, of Newtonairds, Dumfries, and d 2 Nov 1994, leaving by her:

  2c *Matilda Anne [Mrs Michael Bevan, Sothenbury Farm, Scaynes Hill, W Sussex RH17 7PE]; b 1955; m 1979 *Michael Charles Bevan, only s of Maj T H Bevan, of Milton Grange, Co Louth, and has:

    1d *Conor Thomas Hector; b 1983

    1d *Georgina Kathleen; b 1991

3b Cecil Alastair Hector; b 1916; educ ISC; m 1947 Jean Muller (d 1959) and d 1993, leaving:

  1c *Michael Neil Clifton [Michael Gascoigne Esq, Grove Cottage, Aberlady, E Lothian EH32 0RB]; b 1949; m 1975 *Anna Jennifer, dau of John Milne, of Dumfries, and has:

    1d *James Neil Crispin; b 1979

    2d *Peter John Hector; b 1987

    1d *Gemma Eva Pamela; b 1981

  2c *Patrick Edward Cecil; b 1950; Lt-Col Scots Gds; m 1979 *Penny, er dau of Maj Alastair K MacGeorge, of The Glebe House, Cockpen, Bonnyrigg, Midlothian, and has:

    1d *Cecily; b 1991

1b *Marion Erica; b 1906; m 1934 Brig George Des Champs Chamier, OBE, KOYLI (d 1987), s of Sir Edward Maynard Des Champs Chamier, KCSI, KCIE, and has:

  1c *Anthony Edward Des Champs [Anthony Chamier Esq, Achandunie House, Ardross, Ross and Cromarty IV17 0YB]; b 16 Aug 1935; m 1962 *Anne-Carole Dalling and has:

    1d *Daniel William Des Champs; b 28 April 1964

    1d *Amy Louise Des Champs; b 12 Dec 1962

  2c *George Washington Des Champs; b 1947; m 1974 *Janet Michele St Claire

  1c *Antoinette Des Champs; b 1938; m 1973 *Angus Buchan Gordon, FRCS, and has:

    1d *James Buchan; b 1974

    1d *Madeleine Claire; b 1976

  2c *Georgiana Des Champs; b 1949; m 1979 *Adrian Gruzman and has:

    1d *Angus Michael; b 1982

    1d *Alice Freyer; b 1980

    2d *Amelia Anastasia; b 1989

2b *Joan Orby; b 1910; m 1st 1937 Alastair Gordon-Ingram, Colonial Police, and has:

  1c *Donald Alexander; b 1938

2b (cont.) Joan Orby m 2nd 1947 His Honour Harold William Paton, DSC (d 1986), and by him has:

  1c *Mary Joanne Letitia; b 1948

2a Isobel Euphane; b 23 April 1883; m 29 Sept 1915 Capt Malcolm Bedford Duncan, 3rd Bn Roy Scots, and d 14 May 1917, leaving:

  1b *Marjorie V I [Mrs Ian Robertson of Brackla, Gardeners Cottage, Brackla, Nairn IV12 5QY]; b 7 May 1917; m 1939 *Maj-Gen Ian Argyll Robertson of Brackla, CB, MBE, and has:

    1c *Susan Argyll; b 27 Oct 1942; m 19– *Col David G B Saunders and has:

      1d *Mark; b 13 Dec 1964

      2d *Hector; b 1 Dec 1966

    2c *Sarah Elisabeth; b 16 Oct 1945; m *Archibald Hugh Duberly and has:

      1d *James Grey; b 24 Sept 1968

      2d *Harry Grey; b 9 Oct 1975

      1d *Kate Saffron; b 2 May 1970

3a Violet Florence; b 10 Sept 1889; d unm 31 Oct 1969

4a Aline Margaret; b 22 Oct 1892; m 8 Sept 1915 Adml Sir Lionel Victor Wells, KCB, DSO (d 22 April 1965), and d 31 May 1977, leaving issue

(2) Charles Frederick; b 8 Dec 1851; m 8 Oct 1907 Ethel Salkeld (d 1949), dau of Edward Budd, SC, of Leatherhead, and d 1 Dec 1933

(3) George Montgomery; b 12 Aug 1853; Capt 1st Bn Black Watch, and d 13 Oct 1896

(1) Amelia; m 22 Jan 1889 Col John Alfred Wyllie, IA, and d 17 Oct 1929

(2) Maud Mary; d 1939

2 Harry; b 30 Aug 1830; m 11 July 1862 Julia Dutton (d 31 Oct 1906), dau of John Chambers, Lt RM, and d 23 Feb 1876, leaving:

(1) **Sir George Hamilton Munro, 12th Bt**; b 10 May 1864; FRCA; m 22 Nov 1891 Amelia Sarah (d 12 Sept 1946), er dau of John Chapple, of Peckham, and dsp 20 Feb 1945

(2) Walter Ross; b 4 June 1865; d unm 2 May 1919

(3) **Sir Arthur Talbot Munro, 13th Bt**; b 26 July 1866; m 21 Feb 1893 Frances Emily Emmeline, dau of William March, of Peckham, and d 16 Feb 1953, having had:

  1a **Sir Arthur Herman Munro, 14th Bt**; b 10 Sept 1893; educ Wilson's GS Camberwell; WW I with 47th Div; m 1919 Violet Beatrice, dau of Henry Powles, and dspms 27 March 1972, having had:

    1b Hector Charles Seymour; b 7 Aug 1923; Ldg Torpedoman RN WW II; das 1945

    1b Doreen Violet; b 25 July 1922; d unm 10 May 1945

    2b *Audrey Muriel [Mrs Donald Fifield, Greystones, Malling Rd, Teston, Maidstone, Kent]; b 9 Sept 1924; m 1946 *Donald Ernest Fifield and has:

      1c *Richard Donald; b 19 Nov 1947

      1c *Rowena Susan; b 26 June 1950

    3b *Betty Millicent; b 6 Jan 1926; m 12 June 1950 *Brian Leslie Wright and has:

      1c *Gail Louise; b 6 April 1951

      2c *Linda Ann; b 7 Jan 1953

  1a Beatrice Maud; b 1891; m 10 Oct 1919 William Lidyard Bligh, of Hounslow, Middx (d 1978), and had:

    1b *Beatrice Olive Joan [Mrs Kenneth Hansford, Ashcombe, 11a Links Rd, Ashtead, Surrey]; b 24 July 1920; m 22 July 1944 *Lt Kenneth Sidney Hansford, RNVR, of Thames Ditton, and has:

      1c *Anthony Nicholas; b 1950; m 1981 *Gillian Barbara Crouch and has:

        1d *Caroline Victoria; b 1983

      2c *Colin Gordon; b 1956

    2b *Molly Dora [Mrs Philip Bunker, 7 Crumnock Close, Bramcote, Nottingham]; b 15 Feb 1925; m 18 July 1953 *Philip George Bunker, AMInstT, of Croxley Green, Herts, and has:

      1c *Timothy John; b 1956

      2c *Nicholas Philip; b 1958

  2a Lilian Julia; b 19 Jan 1895; m 1st 1915 Stanley Cruse (ka 1916) and had issue; m 2nd 26 Oct 1918 Sub-Lt Alfred Edward Collis, RNVR, and had further issue

  3a Florence Elizabeth; b 18 May 1896; m 1st 10 Oct 1918 Robert Cameron, of Glasgow (d 4 July 1928), and had:

    1b *Donald Marsh; b 19 Dec 1922; m 3 Sept 1943 *Caroline Cunningham, of Liverpool, and has:

      1c *Keith; b 6 July 1945

      2c *Ian; b 10 April 1947

      3c *Craig; b 2 Feb 1951

      1c *Michelle; b 24 Jan 1949

      2c *Zhan; b 27 July 1953

  3a (cont.) Mrs Robert Cameron m 2nd 16 Aug 1931 (divorce 1963) Leonard Frederick Burnett; m 3rd 1964 *Jack Maddock and by him had:

    2b *Roy Beech; b 16 Aug 1932

    3b Antony Peter; b 9 Aug 1944; d 15 March 1946

    1b *Zhan Jacqueline; b 3 Sept 1935

    2b *Sonia Christine; b 30 Dec 1936; m 18 Dec 1954 *Joseph le Pare, of New York

  4a *Grace [Mrs William Price, 119 Crystal Palace Rd, London SE22]; b 29 July 1903; m Dec 1931 *William Price and has:

    1b *Jean; b 19–

    2b *Sylvia; b 19–

    3b *Barbara; b 19–

  5a Gladys; b 4 Aug 1908; m 1st 1 Oct 1932 M F Cooke and had issue; m 2nd 1953 Thomas Sheron

  6a *Minne Isabel; b 23 Oct 1914; m 10 Feb 1935 *M Ernest Price and has:

    1b *Ernest Talbot; b 1939; m 1965 *Patricia, dau of Albert Edward Green

    1b *Jacqueline; b 1935; m 1967 *George James Fox and has:

      1c *Dawn Leslie; b 1959

(4) Charles, FAA, FLAA; b 1 March 1869; m 1st 26 July 1896 Phyllis, 2nd dau of Henry Cross, of New York; m 2nd 1931 *Maude Wilmie Primrose, dau of Robert Whyte, and d 1959, leaving by his 1st w:

  1a Robert Hector; b 5 Sept 1898; m 1st 1928 (divorce 1938) Ethel Amy Edith, dau of Harry Hudson; m 2nd 1950 *Simone [Mrs Robert Munro, 24 Bramcote, York Rd, Weybridge, Surrey], dau of Louis Jean Bareau and widow of Rudolph Lancaster Fisk, and d 2 Sept 1965, leaving by his 1st w:

    1b **Sir Ian Talbot Munro, 15th Bt**; b 28 Dec 1929; educ Bradfield; d unm 15 Dec 1996

  2a Malcolm; b 24 Feb 1901; m 22 July 1931 *Constance [Mrs Malcom Munro, Whitegates, Rock, Wadebridge, Cornwall PL27 6JZ], dau of William Carter, of London, and d 25 June 1994, having had, with a s (d an infant):

    1b *Mary Lee [Mrs David Denny, Shalmar Hollow, Rock, Wadebridge, N Cornwall PL27 6JY]; b 1 April 1935; m 23 July 1955 *David Rex Denny, of Windsor, Berks, and has:

      1c *Sally Louise [Mrs Stephen Mably, Dinham Farm, St Minver, Cornwall]; b 13 Oct 1961; m 1st 1989 (divorce 1995) Robert Gerald Leeds Scovell; m 2nd 5 June 1996 *Stephen Bennett Mably

      2c *Felicia Mary [Mrs Richard Jones, Merryfield Cottage, Rock, Cornwall]; b 4 Feb 1965; m 1987 *Richard Michael Latham Jones and has:

        1d *William David Studley; b 1994

        1d *Lucy Mary Studley; b 1992

        2d *Amy Louise; b 11 May 1996

  3a Colin; b 17 March 1903; m 20 June 1928 Muriel Esther, dau of Edgar Llewellyn Jones, of Cardiff; d 19 May 1984

4a Donald; *b* 28 July 1906; *m* 16 Dec 1944 Doreen, dau of Harold Weston, of Hendon

(5) Percy; *b* 29 March 1870; *m* 1909 Annie Louisa (*d* 1963), dau of William Henderson Pearson, of Kennington, and *d* 1953, leaving:

1a Hector George Hamilton; *b* 25 July 1912; Army 1931–45; *m* 12 April 1947 (*divorce* 1975) Clare Amelia Emily, dau of Herbert Pitcher, of Norfolk, and *d* 25 July 1988, leaving:

1b *Desirée Yvonne [Mrs Othman Merichan, 32 Jalan Maktob, Kuala Lumpur, Malaysia]; *b* 7 Feb 1944; *m* 1962 *Othman Merichan

2b *Wendy Amelia; *b* 12 Aug 1945; *m* 1961 *Ray Williams

1a Ivy Susannah; *b* 1910; *m* Dec 1948 Arthur Noel Lloyd, of Hendon, and *d* March 1973, leaving issue

2a Irene Louisa; *b* 1915; *m* 1940 William Archer Lawrence and had:

1b *Michael; *b* 1943

2b *Iain; *b* 1944

(6) Arnold Harry; *b* 13 May 1871; *m* 1st 21 Sept 1895 Matilda Ethel, only dau of Samuel Long, of Camberwell, and had:

1a Margory Ethel; *b* 24 Nov 1897

(6) (cont.) Arnold Munro *m* 2nd 12 June 1909 Hilda Marion (*d* 5 Jan 1961), yst dau of William Smith, and *d* 24 Feb 1968, having by her had:

1a Sir KENNETH ARNOLD WILLIAM MUNRO **16th and present Bt**

2a +Roland Alec Wilfred [Roland Munro Esq, Maycroft, 223 Crookston Rd, London SE9 1YE]; *b* 4 Nov 1911; IA WW II, co dir; *m* 15 May 1937 *Queenie May Johnson, dau of Ernest Rose Johnson, and has:

1b +Godfrey Roland [Godfrey Munro Esq, 184 Greenvale Rd, London SE9 1PQ]; *b* 1 July 1938; *m* 13 April 1985 *Julie Pamela Munro, dau of R Gosling, of N Cheam, Surrey, and has:

1c +Rupert Roland; *b* 6 Feb 1987

2c +Lawrence Godfrey; *b* 29 Jan 1990

1c *Victoria Ella May; *b* 13 April 1993

1b *Yvonne May; *b* 29 Oct 1943; *m* 30 Sept 1967 *Kenneth B Parkes, of Sidcup, Kent, and has:

1c *Alexander James; *b* 7 Oct 1977

(7) Hermann Vezin; *b* 22 Dec 1875; *m* 23 March 1898 Lilian Augusta (*d* 1944), dau of William Percy, of Camberwell, and *d* 16 July 1959, having had:

1a George Hermann; *b* 20 July 1899; *ka* 15 April 1918

(1) Lilian; *b* 16 June 1872; *m* 27 Nov 1897 James Edward Andrews, of Brighton, and had issue

3 Frederick Ledsum; *b* 15 Oct 1832; *d* 25 Aug 1905, leaving issue

4 Gustavus Francis; *b* 19 Oct 1834; Lt-Gen RMLI; *m* 8 Aug 1865 Edith Thomasine, only dau of John William Hampton, and *d* 19 March 1908

5 Arthur; *b* 5 May 1836; *d* 1888

1 Mary Anne Ross; *b* 8 July 1846 Joseph Theodore Trekell (*d* 1899), of Ryde, IoW, and *d* 16 Jan 1908, leaving issue

2 Amelia Agnese; *m* 28 Sept 1860 Rev Wollaston Goode, Vicar Holy Trinity, Barnstaple, and *d* July 1916, having had issue

MUNRO of Lindertis

Arms: Or an eagle's head erased gu., encircled by a branch of laurel on the dexter and oak on the sinister ppr., on a chief arg. the representation of an Indian hill-fort and beneath in letters of gold the word BADAMY; on a canton gu. a representation of a silver medal presented by the East India Co to the first Bt for his services in Seringapatam 1799. **Crest:** An eagle close ppr., having a representation of the medal above-mentioned pendant from its neck by a ribbon, the dexter claw resting on an escutcheon gu. charged with a representation of the first of BADAMY as in the arms, and in the beak a sprig of laurel. **Motto:** Dread God. **Creation:** Bt. (UK) 6 Aug 1825.

SIR ALASDAIR THOMAS IAN MUNRO OF LINDERTIS, 6TH BT, Forfarshire [Sir Alasdair Munro of Lindertis Bt, River Ridge, Box 940, Waitsfield, VT 05673, USA]; *b* 6 July 1927; *s f* 1985; *educ* Landon Sch Bethesda Md., Georgetown U

Washington DC (BSS 1946), Wharton Sch Pennsylvania U (MBA 1951) and IMEDE Lausanne Switzerland; 2nd Lt USAF (Res) 1946–53, Sr V-Pres McCann-Erickson NY 1952–69, Pres Jennings Real Estate Waitsfield 1970–83, Fndr Dir St Andrew's Soc Vermont 1972–, Ch-Chm Assoc Bd of Directors Howard Bank Waitsfield 1974–84, Chm Munro Jennings and Doig 1983–90, Highland Devpt Gp 1987–91; *m* 6 March 1954 *Marguerite Lillian, dau of Franklin R Loy, of Dayton, Ohio, and has:

1 +KEITH GORDON; *b* 3 May 1959; *educ* Cardigan Mount Sch, Kimball Union Acad and U of New Hampshire; *m* 1989 *Jada Louise, dau of Adrian Elwell, of Waitsfield, and has:

(1) +Zachary Adrian; *b* 1992

(2) *Mackenzie Carmen; *b* 1996

1 *Karen Fiona; *b* 1956; *m* 1980 (*divorce* 1988) Robert David Macmichael, Jr, of New London, NH, s of Robert David Macmichael, of New London, and has:

(1) *Josh Munro; *b* 1981

(2) *Blake Thomas Ian; *b* 1984

Lineage: HUGH MUNRO, 9th of Foulis, Ch of the MUNROs; fought Battle of Harlaw 1411; *d* 1424, leaving a yr s:

JOHN MUNRO, 1st of Milntown; ggf of:

ANDREW MUNRO, 5th of Milntown; had a yr s:

ANDREW MUNRO of Kincraig; had a yr s:

JOHN MUNRO, 1st of Culcraggie, which he bought from his cousin; ggf of:

WILLIAM MUNRO, 5th of Culcraggie; sold it and settled in Glasgow; had:

DANIEL MUNRO; Glasgow merchant; had:

ALEXANDER MUNRO; Glasgow merchant; *m* Margaret, dau of Thomas Stark, and *d* 1809, leaving:

1 Daniel; *d* 1800, leaving:

(1) John; writer (legal practitioner) Madras; *d* unm

2 THOMAS (Sir), **1st Bt**

3 Alexander, of Edinburgh; *m* Anne, dau of Capt Patrick Brown, of Edinburgh, and had issue (now extinct)

4 William; *d* unm

5 James; surgn Madras; *d* unm

1 Erskine; *m* 1st Sir James Turnbull, of Edinburgh; *m* 2nd Hon Henry Erskine (*see* BUCHAN, E)

2 Margaret; *m* George Harley Drummond and had issue (*see* PERTH, E)

The 2nd son,

Sir Thomas Munro, 1st Bt (UK), so *cr* 6 Aug 1825, KCB; Maj-Gen, Govr Madras; *m* 30 March 1814 Jane (*d* 21 Sept 1850), dau of Richard Campbell of Craigie, Ayrshire, and *d* Madras 6 July 1827, leaving:

1 **Sir Thomas Munro, 2nd Bt**, JP, DL Forfar; Capt 10th Hus; *b* 30 May 1819; *d* unm 28 Oct 1901

2 **Sir Campbell Munro, 3rd Bt**, JP, DL Forfar and Dorset; Capt Gren Gds; *b* 7 Sept 1923; *m* 4 April 1853 Henrietta Maria (*d* 28 Aug 1912), dau of John Drummond, of Redenham, Hants (*see* PERTH, E), and had:

(1) HUGH THOMAS (Sir), **4th Bt**

(2) Edward Lionel MUNRO later WALKER-MUNRO (roy licence 1887); Lt-Cdr RN, Khartoum Expdn 1895 (wounded, despatches, medals and star), WW I; *b* 26 Jan 1862; *m* 30 June 1887 Mabel Zoe (*d* 7 Sept 1934), only child and heiress of Thomas Walker, of Eastwood Hall, Notts, and *d* 2 July 1920, leaving:

1a Ian Charles Ronald; Lt Gren Guards, KAR Br E Africa WW I (despatches twice); *b* 9 Oct 1889; *m* Oct 1919 his cousin Morna Violet (*d* 1988), dau of **Sir Hugh Thomas Munro, 4th Bt** (*see* below), and *d* 1 July 1952, leaving:

1b (Thomas Ian) Michael; *b* 1 Oct 1922; *educ* Eton and Trin Coll Cambridge; RNVR 1942–46; *m* 15 Jan 1947 *Hon Marjorie Amy (Molly) Biddulph, er dau of 3rd Baron Biddulph (*qv*), and *d* 31 Dec 1965, leaving:

1c +Thomas Malcolm; *b* 10 March 1948; *educ* Milton Abbey and RAC Cirencester

1c *Sarah Amy; *b* 31 Oct 1950; *m* 1973 *Brig Melville Stewart Jameson, CBE, Roy Scots Dragoon Gds, and has:

1d *Melville Harry Stewart; *b* 1977

2d *Michael Andrew Stewart; *b* 1980

2b Patrick Angus; *b* 8 July 1924; *educ* Canford; *m* 2 May 1950 Mary Barnett (*d* 1980), only child of Richard Youel Phillips, of Kenya, by Isabel Fernandez, later Lady Torphichen (*qv*), and *d* 1993, leaving:

1c +Ian David Torquil [Ian Walker-Munro Esq, 8 Nixon Place, Lennoxhead 2478, NSW, Australia]; *b* 10 July 1951; *educ* Trin Coll Glenalmond; *m* 1982 *Mrs Suellan Lough, of Sydney, and has:

1d +Brenton Neil Patrick; *b* 1985

2d +Alaisdair John Torquil; *b* 1988

1d *Catherine; *b* 1983

2c +(Charles Michael) Angus [Angus Walker-Munro Esq, 34 Forest End, Fleet, Hants GU13 9XE]; *b* 29 Sept 1953; *educ* Trin Coll Glenalmond; *m* 1981 (*divorce* 19–) Christine Margaret, dau of Albert Arthur Humphrey, of Bexleyheath, Kent, and has:

1d +Peter Michael Angus; *b* 1985

3b +Lionel Malcolm [Lionel Walker-Munro Esq, 64 Bourne St, London SW1]; *b* 5 Sept 1929; *educ* Eton and Wadham Coll Oxford

4b +(Roderick) Hugh [Hugh Walker-Munro Esq, Kinnettles House, Forfar, Angus DD8 1TR]; *b* 5 Sept 1929 (twin); *educ* Eton and Le Rosey; *m* 1st 1 Sept 1964 Irene Margaret (*d* 1976), yst dau of Robert Watt Edgar, of Dundonald House, Dundonald, Fife, and has:

1c +Euan Torquil Drummond; *b* 21 Sept 1965; *m* 1993 *Susan, dau of Keith Howman, of Shepperton, Middx

2c +Geordie Roderick Hamish; *b* 27 April 1968; *m* 1993 *Lorraine Rose, only dau of Patrick Orchard, of Carandain, Perths

4b (cont.) Hugh Walker-Munro *m* 2nd 1993 *Brenda, dau of Donald Wheelton

3a Philip Harvey, Lt RN; *b* 31 July 1866; drowned HMS *Victoria* 22 June 1893

(1) Annie Katharine; *d* unm 2 Aug 1955 aged 97

(2) Ethel Dora; *m* 8 July 1886 Charles Henry Labouchere and *d* 7 May 1955 aged 95. He *d* 5 March 1916

(3) Georgina Evelyn; *d* unm 27 March 1951

(4) Mabel Ida; *m* 25 July 1891 Maj-Gen Hugh Clement Sutton and *d* 29 March 1896, leaving issue (*see* SUTTON, Bt)

(5) Blanche Margaret; *d* unm 1883

(6) Louisa Olive; *m* 18 June 1910 V-Adml Ian Edmund Drummond (*see* PERTH, E) and *d* 4 Oct 1965 aged 93

The 3rd Bt *d* 13 June 1913; his eldest son,

Sir Hugh Thomas Munro, 4th Bt, JP, DL Forfarshire; served Basuto Campaign 1880–81 (medal with clasp); *b* 16 Oct 1856; *m* 29 Aug 1892 Selina Dorothea (*d* 13 May 1902), dau of Maj-Gen Thomas Edmond Byrne, RA, and had:

1 (THOMAS) TORQUIL ALPHONSO (Sir), **5th Bt**

1 Sheila Mable Judith; *b* 20, *d* 25 Sept 1893

2 Morna Violet; *b* 4 Jan 1895; *m* Oct 1919 her cousin Ian Charles Ronald Walker-Munro and *d* 1988, leaving issue (*see above*)

3 Carmen Ida Constance; *b* 2 Dec 1896; *d* 8 Jan 1973

Sir HUGH *d* 19 March, 1919; his only son,

Sir (Thomas) Torquil Alphonso Munro, 5th Bt, of Lindertis, Forfarshire, JP (Angus 1932); *b* 7 Feb 1901; *educ* Winchester and Magdalene Coll Cambridge; 2nd Lt Gren Gds; *m* 1st 16 April 1925 (*divorce* 1932) Beatrice Maude, dau of Robert Sanderson Whitaker, of Villa Sofia, Palermo, and *d* 1985, leaving:

1 Sir ALASDAIR THOMAS IAN MUNRO OF LINDERTIS, **6th and present Bt**

Sir Torquil *m* 2nd 27 Oct 1934 *Averil Moira Katharine, er dau of Kenneth Owen Hunter, of Perths and S Kensington, and by her had:

2 +James Kenneth Torquil; *b* 7 Jan 1941; *educ* Bradfield; *m* 1970 (*divorce* 19–) Camilla Ann, yr dau of Cdr J Nigel Ball, DSC, RN, and has:

(1) *Iona Katharine; *b* 1973

(2) *Flavia Isla; *b* 1975

(3) *Camilla Morna; *b* 1977

1 Fiona Margaret; *b* 31 May 1937; *m* 10 Aug 1957 Hon Nicholas Henry Eno Hopkinson (*d* 1991), only s of 1st Baron Colyton (*qv*), and *d* 15 May 1996, leaving issue

MUNSTER

Arms: The arms of WILLIAM IV minus the escutcheon of the Arch Treasurer of the Holy Roman Empire and the crown of Hanover, debruised by a baton sinister az. charged with three anchors or. **Crest:** On a chapeau gu., doubled erm., a lion statant guardant, crowned with a ducal coronet or and gorged with a collar az., charged with three anchors or. **Supporters:** Dexter, a lion guardant, ducally crowned or; sinister, a horse arg., each gorged with a collar az., charged with three anchors or. **Motto:** *Nec temere nec timide* ('Neither rashly nor fearfully'). **Creation:** E, V. and B. (UK) 4 June 1831.

THE 7TH EARL OF MUNSTER, Viscount Fitz-Clarence and **Baron Tewkesbury**, Co Gloucester (Anthony Charles Fitz-Clarence) [The Rt Hon The Earl of Munster, 611 Howard House, Dolphin Sq, London SW1V 3PG]; *b* 21 March 1926; *s* f 1983; *educ* St Edward's Sch Oxford; served RN 1942–47, graphic designer 1950–79 (Daily Mirror Newspapers 1957–66), IPC Newspapers Div (*Sun*) 1966–69, freelance 1971–79, stained glass conservator Burrell Museum 1979–83, conservator with Chapel Studio 1983–89, FRSA 1987; *m* 1st 28 July 1949 (*divorce* 1966) Louise Margaret Diane, dau of Louis Delvigne, of Liège, Belgium, and has issue:

1 *Tara Francesca [The Lady Tara Heffler, 146 Ramsden Rd, London SW12 8RE]; *b* 6 Aug 1952; dir Sotheby's; *m* 1979 *Ross Jean Heffler and has:

(1) *Leo Edward Michael; *b* 1985

(1) *Alexandra Louise; *b* 1982

2 *Finola Dominque [The Lady Finola Poynton, 1660 Lyon St, San Francisco, CA 94116, USA]; *b* 6 Dec 1953; *m* 1981 *Jonathan Terence Poynton, yr s of D R Poynton, of Woodford, Cheshire, and has:

(1) *Oliver Maximilian Christo; *b* 1984

(1) *Chloë Nona; *b* 1982

The 7th EARL *m* 2nd 18 June 1966 (*divorce* 1979) Mrs Pamela Margaret Hyde, dau of Arthur Spooner, and by her has:

3 *Georgina [The Lady Georgina Fitz-Clarence, 27 Heather Mead, Frimley, Surrey GU16 5QA]; *b* 1966

The 7th EARL *m* 3rd 1979 (Dorothy) Alexa, MusB (Edin), LRAM (*d* 13 June 1995), yst dau of Lt-Col Edward Boyd Maxwell, OBE, MC; *m* 4th May 1997 *Dr Halina Winska, MD, PhD (Warsaw), snr lecturer/consultant rheumatology UCH London

Lineage: WILLIAM IV had by Dora or Dorothy ('Mrs Jordan' the comic actress; *b* 22 Nov 1761; never *m* ('Mr Jordan' having no more reality than her compatriot Oscar Wilde's Bunbury) but had two daus and a son by Sir Richard Ford, police magistrate, and one by Richard Daly, manager of the Theatre Royal, Cork, besides those by WILLIAM; *d* 5 July 1816), yr dau of Francis Bland, actor and stage heroine (3rd s of Nathaniel Bland, Irish Judge):

1 GEORGE AUGUSTUS FREDERICK, **1st Earl**

2 Henry Edward; *b* 27 March 1795; *d* unm Sept 1817

3 Frederick, GCH; Lt-Gen, Col 36th Foot, cmded forces Bombay; *b* 9 Dec 1799; granted 24 May 1831 with his yr siblings bar the Countess of Erroll and Viscountess Falkland (who had *m* husbs of higher rank) rank of a marquess's dau/yr s; *m* 19 May 1821 Lady Augusta Boyle (*d* 28 July 1876), dau of 4th Earl of Glasgow (*qv*), and *d* 30 Oct 1854, having had a dau (*d* unm)

4 Adophus, GCH; R-Adml, Naval ADC to HM QUEEN VICTORIA, Ranger Windsor Home Pk; *b* 18 Feb 1802; *d* unm 17 May 1856

5 Augustus (Rev); Rector Maple Durham, Oxon, Chaplain to HM QUEEN VICTORIA; *b* 1 March 1805; *m* 2 Jan 1845 Sarah Elizabeth Catherine (*d* 23 March 1901), est dau of Lord Henry Gordon (*see* HUNTLY, M), and *d* 14 June 1854, having had:

(1) Augustus; *b* 13 Feb 1849; *d* unm 16 Oct 1861

(2) Henry Edward; *b* 19 Jan 1853; *m* 11 June 1879 Mary Isobel Templer (*d* 17 July 1932), only dau of John Parsons, and *d* 19 Feb 1930, having had:

1a Augustus Arthur Cornwallis; Capt 2nd Bn Roy Fus, Adj Civil Service Rifles; *b* 16 March 1880; *m* 7 April 1910, as her 1st husb, Lady Susan Yorke, only dau of 7th Earl of Hardwicke (*qv*), and was *ka* 28 June 1915

1a Cynthia Adela Victoria; *b* 7 Feb 1887; *m* 11 June 1908 Maj Roland George Orred, MC, Coldstream Gds (*d* 20 June 1963), s of Maj John Cavendish Orred, 12th Lancers, of Tranmere, Runcorn, Cheshire, and had:

1b Diana Susan; *b* 4 May 1909; *d* unm 5 Dec 1932

2b *Angela; *b* 12 March 1915

(1) Dorothea; *m* 17 March 1863 Capt Thomas William Goff, DI, of Oakport, Co Roscommon, and *d* 15 May 1870, leaving issue. He *d* 3 June 1876

(2) Eva; *d* unm 2 March 1918

(3) Beatrix; *d* unm 18 March 1909

(4) Mary; *d* an infant 14 March 1858

1 Sophia; *b* Aug 1796; *m* 13 Aug 1835 1st Baron De L'Isle and Dudley and *d* 10 April 1837, leaving issue (*see* DE L'ISLE, V)

2 Mary; *b* 19 Dec 1798; *m* 19 June 1824 Gen Charles Richard Fox, MP, Col 57th Foot, Receiver-Gen Duchy Lancaster, illegitimate s of 3rd Baron Holland (*see* ILCHESTER, E), and *d* 13 July 1864

3 Elizabeth; *b* 17 Jan 1801; *m* 4 Dec 1820 18th Earl of Erroll (*qv*) and *d* 16 Jan 1856, leaving issue

4 Augusta; *b* 17 Nov 1803; *m* 1st 5 July 1827 Hon John Kennedy-Erskine, of Dun, Forfar, 2nd s of 1st Marquess of Ailsa (*qv*), and had issue; *m* 2nd 24 Aug 1836 Lord John Frederick GORDON later HALYBURTON, 3rd s of 9th Marquess of Huntly (*qv*), and *d* 8 Dec 1865

5 Amelia; *b* 21 March 1807; *m* 27 Dec 1830 10th Viscount Falkland (*qv*) and *d* 2 July 1858, leaving issue

The est son,

GEORGE AUGUSTUS FREDERICK Fitz-CLARENCE, **1st Earl of Munster**, so *cr* 4 June 1831, as also BARON TEWKESBURY, Co Gloucester, and VISCOUNT Fitz-CLARENCE (all UK), with special remainder in default of his own male issue to his bros by WILLIAM IV in order of birth and their male descendants, PC (1833); *b* 29 Jan 1794; *educ* Roy Mil Coll Marlow; Maj-Gen, ADC to his f 1830–37 and HM QUEEN VICTORIA 1837–41, Lt the Tower 1831–33, Constable Windsor Castle 1833–42; *m* 18 Oct 1819 Mary Wyndham (*d* 3 Dec 1842), illegitimate dau of George, Earl of Egremont (*see* EGREMONT, LECONFIELD and, B), and *d* 20 March 1842, having had:

1 WILLIAM GEORGE Fitz-CLARENCE, **2nd Earl of Munster**, DL Middx; Capt 1st Life Gds; *b* 19 May 1824; *m* 17 April 1855 his 1st cousin Wilhelmina (*d* 9 Oct 1906), dau of Hon John Kennedy-Erskine (*see above*), and *d* 30 April 1901, leaving:

(1) Edward, *Viscount Fitz-Clarence*; *b* 29 March 1856; *d* 1870

(2) Lionel Frederick Archibald; *b* 24 July 1857; *d* 1863

(3) GEOFFREY GEORGE GORDON Fitz-CLARENCE, **3rd Earl of Munster**, DSO; Maj 3rd Bn Lothian Regt, Capt 2nd Bn KRRC, Afghan War 1879–80, 1st Boer War 1881, 2nd Boer War 1899–1902; *b* 18 July 1859; *d* unm S Africa 2 Feb 1902

(4) Arthur Falkland Manners; *b* 1860; *d* 1861

(5) AUBREY Fitz-CLARENCE, **4th Earl of Munster**; Gentleman Usher-in-Ordinary to TM QUEEN VICTORIA 1885–1901 and EDWARD VII 1901–02; *b* 7 June 1862; *d* unm 1 Jan 1928

(6) William George; *b* 17 Sept 1864; *m* 1887 Charlotte Elizabeth Aline (*d* 5 Sept 1902), dau of Richard Williams, and *d* 4 Oct 1899, leaving:

1a Dorothy Margaret Aline; *b* 23 Sept 1888; *m* 11 Sept 1909 Cecil Cadogan Elborough, yst s of Alfred Louis Elborough, of Lancing, Sussex, and had issue

2a Wilhelmina Violet Eileen; *b* 17 July 1894; *m* 19 Jan 1918 Maj Cecil John Cokayne Maunsell, JP, RA, of Thorpe Malsor Hall, Kettering, Northants, and had issue. He *d* 11 Feb 1948

(7) Harold Edward, MC; Govr Manchester Prison, T/Maj, Govr 1st Cl Mil Prisons in the Field 1918, Lt 3rd Bn Yorks LI and S African Constabulary, Boer War 1900–01, WW I (despatches); *b* 15 Nov 1870; *m* 14 May 1902 Frances Isabel Eleanor (*d* 1 Feb 1951), er dau of Lt-Col William Henry Augustus Keppel (*see* ALBEMARLE, E), and *d* 28 Aug 1926, leaving:

1a GEOFFREY WILLIAM RICHARD HUGH Fitz-CLARENCE, **5th Earl of Munster**, KBE (1957), PC (1954); *b* 17 Feb 1906; *educ* Charterhouse; T/Maj Gren Gds, Capt RASC (TA), ADC to FM Viscount Gort 1939–42 (despatches), Govt Whip 1932–38, Paymaster-Gen 1938–39, Parly U-Sec War and V-Pres Army Cncl Jan–Sept 1939, Parly U-Sec: India and Burma 1943–44, Home Office 1944 and May–July 1945 and Colonial Office Nov 1951–Oct 1954, Min without Portfolio Oct 1956–June 1957, Ld Lt Surrey 1957–73, memb LCC (MR) N Paddington 1931–37, Chm Assoc C Clubs 1948–61 and Uganda Relationships Commn 1960–61, Grand Cross Order Crown Belgium, KStJ; *m* 9 July 1928 Hilary, only child of Edward Kenneth Wilson, of Cannizaro, Wimbledon, and Tranby Croft, Yorks, and *dsp* 27 Aug 1975

1a (Wilhelmina) Joan Mary; *b* 17 Nov 1904; granted rank of earl's dau 1928; *m* 1st 21 April 1928 Col Oliver Birkbeck (*d* 13 May 1952), er s of Edward Lewis Birkbeck, and had:

1b *Edward Harold [Edward Birkbeck Esq, Skeffington Hall, Leics]; *b* 2 May 1929; *educ* Eton and RMC Sandhurst; *m* 11 June 1958 *Sarah Ann, only dau of Capt Edward William Brook, 20th Hus, of Kinmount, Annan, and 2 Mansfield St, London W1, and has:

1c *George Charles Edward; *b* 8 Dec 1964

1c *Elizabeth Mary; *b* 17 Oct 1960

2c *Nicola Susan; *b* 2 Dec 1962

2b *John Oliver Charles [John Birkbeck Esq, Litcham Hall, King's Lynn, Norfolk PE32 2QQ]; *b* 22 June 1936; *educ* Gordonstoun; *m* 2 May 1964 *Hermione Ann, only dau of Maj D'Arcy Armytage Dawes, of Leacon Hall, Warehorne, Kent, and has:

1c *Lucy Claire; *b* 7 Oct 1966

1b *Mary Joan; *b* 13 Sept 1931

1a (cont.) Lady Joan Birkbeck *m* 2nd 28 April 1961 Lt-Col Henry John Cator, MC, JP, DL, only s of John Cator, JP, DL, of Woodbastwick Hall, and Beckenham, Kent

(1) Lilian Adelaide Katherine Mary; *b* 10 Dec 1873; *m* 17 Jan 1893 Capt William Arthur Edward Boyd, 2nd Life Gds, only surv s of Curwen Boyd, DL, JP, of Merton Hall, Wigtownshire, and *d* 15 July 1948, having had issue. He *d* 6 Dec 1931

(2) Dorothea Augusta; *b* 5 May 1876; *m* 20 Nov 1899 Maj Chandos Brydges Lee-Warner, JP, of Tyberton Court, Herefs, and *d* 28 Jan 1942, leaving issue. He *d* 1 Oct 1944

2 FREDERICK CHARLES GEORGE Fitz-CLARENCE later Fitz-CLARENCE-HUNLOKE (1865), of Wingerworth Hall, Derbys, DL Derbys; Capt 10th Hus, *b* 1 Feb 1826, *m* 2 Dec 1856 his 1st cousin Adelaide Augusta Wilhelmina (*d* 20 Sept 1904), est dau of 1st Baron De L'Isle and Dudley (*see* DE L'ISLE, V) and gdau of Sir Henry Hunloke, 4th Bt, of Wingerworth Hall, Derbys; *dsp* 17 Dec 1878

3 George; Capt RN, Kt Medjidie; *b* 15 April 1836; *m* 5 July 1864 Lady Maria Henrietta Scott (*d* 27 July 1912), est dau of 3rd Earl of Clonmell (*see* 1935 edn), and *d* 24 March 1894, leaving:

(1) Charles, VC and bar (1900); Boer War 1899–1901 and WW I, Brig-Gen cmdg Irish Gds Regtl Dist 1913–14; *b* 8 May 1865; *m* 20 April 1898 Violet (*d* 22 Dec 1941), dau of Lord Alfred Spencer Churchill (*see* MARLBOROUGH, D), and was *ka* leading 1st Gds Bde 12 Nov 1914, leaving:

1a EDWARD CHARLES, **6th Earl**

1a Joan Harriet; *m* 30 March 1933 Lt-Cdr Francis Barchard, RN (*ka* 25 Nov 1941), only s of Francis Barchard, JP, of Horsted Place, Sussex, and *d* 6 Jan 1971, leaving:

1b *Jane Ann Violet [Mrs Geoffrey Martin, Old Stores Curload, Stoke St Gregory, Somerset]; *b* 5 Nov 1935; *m* 10 March 1962 *Geoffrey Ewart Martin, s of Milton Ewart Martin, of Twickenham House, Abingdon, and has:

1c *Lucinda Katharine; *b* 20 Oct 1966

2b *Elizabeth Mary [Mrs David Scott, Mynals Woodlands House, Mildenhall, Wilts]; *b* 18 April 1939; *m* 13 July 1967 *David Leslie Scott, 2nd s of Thomas Leslie Scott, of Troy, Old Bosham, Sussex, and has:

1c *Juliet Caroline; *b* 23 Nov 1968

(2) Edward; Capt 1st Dorsetshire Regt (twin with Charles); *b* 8 May 1865; *k* Abu-Hamed 7 Aug 1897

(3) William Henry; Capt RN; *b* 17 Feb 1868; *m* 11 Aug 1908 Hilda Charlotte (*d* 3 Jan 1959), dau of Richard Sankey, of South Hill, Hastingleigh, Kent, and *d* 24 Nov 1921

(4) Lionel Ashley Arthur; Cape Mounted Rifles Boer War 1899–1902; *b* 30 Nov 1870; *m* 16 July 1913 Theodora Frances Maclean (*d* 12 April 1948), dau of Evan A Jack, of S Kensington, and *d* 19 Dec 1936, leaving:

1a *Mary Theodora Annette [Mrs Adam Gluszkiewicz, 14 Ellesmere Orchard, Westbourne, Hants PO10 8TR]; *b* 10 May 1914; *m* 1948 *Adam Gluszkiewicz and has:

1b *Anna Judita [Miss Anna Gluszkiewicz, Flat 4, The Glen, Church Path, Emsworth, Hants]; *b* 28 Oct 1949

(1) Annette Mary; *b* 15 June 1873; *d unm* 7 July 1970

(2) Mary; *b* 7 Aug 1877; *m* 5 Oct 1905 Maj-Gen Frederick Drummond Vincent Wing, CB, RHA, only s of Maj Vincent Wing, 95th Regt, by Gertrude Elizabeth, only dau of Sir Francis Fletcher Vane, 3rd Bt (*see* 1934 edn), and *d* 19 Feb 1939, having had issue. He was *ka* France 2 Oct 1915

4 Edward; Lt 7th Fus; *b* 8 July 1837; *d* 23 July 1855 of wounds recd in attack on the Redan during Crimean War

1 Adelaide Georgiana; *d unm* 11 Oct 1888 aged 62

2 Augusta Margaret; *m* April 1844 Philip, Baron Knut de Bonde, and *d* 5 Sept 1846, leaving issue. He *d* 1871

3 Mary Gertrude; *d* an infant 1834

The 5th EARL's cousin,

EDWARD CHARLES Fitz-CLARENCE, **6th Earl of Munster**; *b* 3 Oct 1899; *educ* Eton and RMC Sandhurst; Capt Irish Gds, SBStJ; *m* 1st 30 July 1925 (*divorce*

1930) Monica Sheila Harrington (*d* 5 Oct 1958), 4th dau of Lt-Col Sir Henry Mulleneux Grayson, 1st Bt, KBE (*qv*), and had:

1 ANTHONY CHARLES Fitz-CLARENCE, **7th and present Earl of Munster**

1 Mary Jill; *b* 6 Feb 1928; *m* 1st 4 June 1953 (*annulled* 1960) Melvin Flyer; *m* 2nd 28 March 1968 John Walter, Jr, er s of John Walter, of Hove, Sussex, and *d* 19–

The **6th Earl** *m* 2nd 28 Sept 1939 *Mrs Vivian Schofield [The Rt Hon Vivian Countess of Munster, 1 Arundel Court, Jubilee Place, Chelsea Green, London SW3], yst dau of Benjamin Schofield, JP, of Greenroyde, Rochdale, Lancs, and stepdau of Judge A J Chotzner, MP, and *d* 1983

MURRAY of Blackbarony

Arms: Or a fetterlock az., on a chief of the last three mullets arg. **Crest:** A dexter hand holding a scroll fessways ppr. **Motto:** *Deum time* ('Fear God'). **Creation:** Bt. (NS) 15 May 1628.

SIR NIGEL ANDREW DIGBY MURRAY, 15TH BT, of Blackbarony, Co Peebles [Sir Nigel Murray Bt, Establecimiento Tinamú, CC 67, 2624 Arias, Prov de Córdoba, Argentina]; *b* 15 Aug 1944; s f 1978; *educ* St Paul's Sch Argentina, Salesian Ag Tech Sch Argentina and RAC Cirencester; arable, bee- and cattle- farmer; *m* 1980 *Diana Margaret, yr dau of Robert Campbell Bray, of Sarmiento, Argentina, and has:

1 +ALEXANDER NIGEL ROBERT; *b* 1 July 1981

1 *Rachel Elisabeth Vanda Digby; *b* 1982

2 *Evelyn Caroline Digby; *b* 1987

Lineage: JOHN MURRAY of Falahill, had charter of the lands of Philiphaugh, Selkirkshire, 20 July 1461; *d c* 20 Feb 1477; appears to have had three sons:

1 Patrick, of Falahill; ancestor of the MURRAYs of Philiphaugh

2 William, of Sundhope; *d* by Feb 1505/6

3 A son; f of:

(1) John; Burgess Edinburgh; had charter 4 May 1507 of the (territorial) Barony of Blackbarony or Halton; *m c* 31 Jan 1503/4 Isobel (*m* 2nd *c* 27 May 1519 Sir Archibald Douglas of Kilspindie), dau of Richard Hoppar, of Edinburgh, and was *ka* Battle of Flodden 9 Sept 1513, having had, with two daus (including Isabel, *m* Patrick Scott of Tanlawhill; *see* NAPIER and ETTRICK, L):

1a Andrew, of Blackbarony; *m* 1st Elizabeth (*d c* 26 May 1533), dau and heiress of William Lockhart, of Edinburgh, and *d* 1 Sept 1572, having had:

1b Marion; *m* (contract 14 Dec 1566) James Pringle of Whitebank and *d* May 1585, leaving issue

1a (cont.) Andrew Murray *m* 2nd (contract 8 Feb 1551/2) Grissel (*d* 18 Aug 1579), dau of John Beaton of Creich and widow of Sir William Scott of Kirkurd, and by her had:

1b JOHN (Sir)

2b Andrew; *d* by 2 June 1587

3b Gideon (Sir); had issue (*see* ELIBANK, L)

4b William; had issue (*see* MURRAY, Bt, of Dunerne)

2b Elizabeth; *m* 1st (contract 20 April 1572) James Borthwick of Glengilt (*d* April 1574) and had issue; *m* 2nd Thomas Hamilton of Priestfield

3b Agnes; *m* (contract 9 April 1580) her cousin Patrick Murray of Falahill (*d* 1601) and had issue

ANDREW MURRAY's est son,

Sir JOHN MURRAY of Blackbarony; ktd 1594, MP Peeblesshire 1608 and 1609; *m* 1st Margaret, dau of Sir Alexander Hamilton of Innerwick; *m* 2nd Margaret, dau of — Wauchope of Keckmure, and by her had two daus (including Isabel, Patrick Scott of Tanlawhill; *see* NAPIER and ETTRICK, L); his issue by his 1st w (which included five others sons):

1 ARCHIBALD (Sir), **1st Bt**

2 John (Sir), of Ravelrig

1 Margaret; *m* Sir Robert Halket of Pitfirran

2 Agnes; *m* Sir John Riddell of that Ilk, 1st Bt (*qv*), and had issue

3 Elizabeth; *m* 1st Earl of Ancram (*see* LOTHIAN, M)

4 Grizel; *m* Sir William Douglas of Cashgole

5 Christian; *m* Sir William Veitch of Dawick

Sir JOHN's est surv son,

Sir Archibald Murray, 1st Bt (NS), so *cr* 15 May 1628, with remainder to heirs male whatsoever; ktd when a young man, MP Peeblesshire 1617 and 1625; *m* by 1617 Margaret Maule, of the house of Panmure, and *d c* 1634, having had:

1 ALEXANDER (Sir), **2nd Bt**

2 Walter, of Halmire

3 Robert; had:

  (1) Robert, of Murray's Hall

1 Margaret; *m* Sir John Hope, 2nd Bt (*qv*), of Craighall

2 Bethia; *m* 1st Sir William Forbes, 1st Bt, of Craigievar (*qv*); *m* 2nd Sir Alexander Forbes of Tolquhone

3 Helen; *m* Sir John Carstairs of Kilconquhar

Sir ARCHIBALD'S s est son,

Sir Alexander Murray, 2nd Bt; MP Peeblesshire 1639–41, royalist Civil War period (for which fined 1646) but Cromwellian-appointee as Sheriff Peeblesshire 1657; *m* 1st Margaret, dau of Sir Richard Cockburn of Clerkington, and had:

1 **Sir Archibald Murray, 3rd Bt**; MP Peeblesshire Selkirk and Peebles 1659 and Peeblesshire 1661–63, 1663, 1667, 1669–74, 1678, 1681–82, 1683–86 and 1689–1700; Lt-Col Linlithgowshire and Peeblesshire Militia 1669, Master of the Works 1689; *m* Lady Mary Keith, dau of 6th Earl Marischal (*see* KINTORE, E) and widow of Sir James Hope of Hopetoun (*see* LINLITHGOW, M), and had, with three other sons:

  (1) **Sir Alexander Murray, 4th Bt**; Peeblesshire: MP 1700–02, Sheriff Depute 1732; *m* 28 July 1687 Margaret, dau of William Wallace of Helington, and *dsp* 31 Dec 1741, having left his estates first to his n Margaret (*see* below) and then to the MURRAYs of Elibank (*see* ELIBANK, L):

  (2) Archibald; Army Capt; *m* Naomi, dau of James Hamilton, a cadet of the Earl of Clanbrassil's family, and had an only dau:

    1a Margaret; *m* John STEWART later MURRAY of Ascog and *dsp* 5 April 1771

  (1) Jane; *m* Col James Cranston of Glen

  (2) Elizabeth; *m* Samuel Semple, Min Liberton

2 Richard, of Spittlehaugh; Lt-Col Linlithgow and Peebles Militia; *m* 1st Mary (*dsp*), dau of George Browne of Coalston; *m* 2nd Jean, dau of James Davidson, writer (legal practitioner) Edinburgh, and by her had:

  (1) WILLIAM (Sir), **5th Bt**

  (2) Archibald

1 Margaret; *m* Sir John Gilmore of Craigmillar, Ld Pres of the Session

2 Helen; *m* Andrew Fletcher, s of Sir Andrew Fletcher of Aberlady or Innerpeffer

The **2nd Bt** *m* 2nd Margaret, dau of John Murray of Halmyre and sis of Sir David Murray of Stanhope, and *d* between 1667 and 1669, having by her had, with five daus:

3 John, of Cringletie, Peeblesshire; *m* —, dau of Drummond of Hawthornden, and *dsp*

4 Alexander, of Cringletie; *m* Susan, dau of John Douglas of Mains, and had:

  (1) Alexander, of Cringletie; MP and Sheriff Peeblesshire; *m* Katherine, dau of Sir Robert Stewart of Tillicoultry, and had, with other issue:

    1a Alexander, of Cringletie; Lt-Col 48th Foot, served Louisberg and Quebec; *m* 1749 Marion, dau of Sir James Stewart, Bt, of Goodtrees, and *d* Martinique 1762, leaving, with a dau (*d* unm):

      1b Alexander; Maj regular Army and Fifeshire Fencibles, Capt 13th Light Dragoons; *d* 1822

      2b James Wolfe, of Cringletie; *b* 5 Jan 1759; *educ* Edinburgh HS; Ld of Session as Lord Cringletie; *m* 7 April 1807 Isabella Katherine (*d* 25 Dec 1847), only dau of James Charles Edward Stuart Strange, and *d* 29 May 1836, leaving, with another s and two daus (*d* unm):

        1c James, of Cringletie and Westshields, Lanarks, JP, DL; *b* 11 May 1814; Brig-Gen Roy Co Archers; *m* 1st 25 March 1852 Elizabeth Charlotte (*d* 4 Oct 1857), dau of John Whyte Melville, of Bennochie and Strathkinness, by Lady Catherine Osborne, dau of 5th Duke of Leeds (*see* 1963 edn), and had:

        1d James Wolfe (Sir), KCB, of Cringletie and Westshields, JP, DL Peeblesshire; *b* 13 March 1853; Lt-Gen RA, QMG India 1903–04, Commr Supply, Master-Gen Ordance HQ 1904–07, cmded Secunderabad Div 1907–11, GOC Scottish Cmd 1913–14, GOC-ic S Africa 1914, CIGS 1914–15, GOC-ic Eastern Cmd 1916–18, Ashanti and S Africa, WW I, Order St Anne Russia 1st Cl with swords, White Eagle Russia, Grand Cordon Sacred Treasure Japan; *m* 1st 14 May 1875 Arabella (*d* 25 July 1909), dau of W Bray; *m* 2nd 30 April 1913 Fanny Worswick (*d* 29 March 1953), yst dau of James Scott Robson, of Pontefract, and widow of Sir Donald Horne Macfarlane, and *d* 17 Oct 1919, having by his 1st w had:

          1e George Wolfe, JP, DL Peeblesshire; *b* 27 June 1876; *educ* Harrow and RMC Sandhurst; Lt Seaforth Highrs and T/Capt RASC 1914–16; Transvaal CS; *m* 21 Dec 1910 Louisa Catherine (*d* 10 June 1955), est dau of Rev Thomas Jones, Rector Llanbedr-cum-Partrishow, and *d* 31 Jan 1955, having had:

            1f +Thomas Wolfe [Thomas Murray Esq, Hycroft, Hatton Rd, Kinnoull, Perths]; *b* 19 May 1913; *educ* St Bees and Faraday House; *m* 3 June 1946 *Violet May, dau of Alexander Scott, of Vancouver, and has:

              1g +Alexander James Wolfe; *b* 1 Feb 1949; *educ* Perth High Sch and U of BC Canada (BA)

              2g +Robin Wolfe; *b* 31 July 1951; *educ* Perth Academy and St Andrews (BSc (Hons), PhD)

              1g *Patricia Ann Wolfe; *b* 7 Aug 1947

              2g *Susan May Wolfe; *b* 26 Nov 1958

            1f *Katherine Jean Wolfe; *b* 14 Nov 1911; *m* 15 July 1958 *James Gordon Fyfe, TD, WS, DL, s of Alex Fyfe, of Kendalmere, Peebles

2f *Miriam Arabella Elizabeth Wolfe [Mrs Albert Baker, Inglenook, Winsor Lane, Winsor, Southampton]; *b* 13 Feb 1916; *m* 13 July 1950 *Albert Victor Baker and has:

  1g *Victor George; *b* 13 April 1954; *m* 1975 *Christine Mary Hollis

  1g *Katherine; *b* 2 Oct 1951

3f Patricia Grace Margaret Wolfe; *b* 27 July 1917; *d* 17 June 1935

2e James Wolfe, DSO (1919); *b* 9 June 1880; Capt RN WW I (despatches, Czechoslovak Croix de Guerre); *d* 16 Nov 1930

1e Lilian Ann Wolfe; *m* 30 June 1897 (*divorce* 1908) Maj Charles Hamlyn Agnew (*d* 31 March 1928), and *d* 15 Dec 1937, having had issue (*see* AGNEW, Bt, of Lochnaw)

2e Grace Catherine Wolfe; *m* 9 Feb 1901 Maj Sholto William Douglas, CBE, DSO (*d* 12 April 1959), RA, Ch Constable Lothians and Peebles, s of Maj G M Douglas, 33rd Regt, and *d* 8 March 1942

3e Arabella Elizabeth Wolfe; *m* 16 Feb 1904 Sir George Henry Sutherland, JP, DL (*d* 11 May 1937), Commr Supply, and *d* 27 March 1930, leaving issue

2d Francis D'Arcy Osborne Wolfe; *b* 10 April 1854; Indian CS; *m* 21 Sept 1881 Frances Henrietta (*d* 15 Sept 1925), dau of Maj-Gen Henry Rhodes Morgan, and *d* May 1914, having had:

  1e Harold Osborne Wolfe; *b* 1884; *educ* Wellington; ADC to Govr Br Honduras; *m* 31 July 1908 Yvonne, er dau of Gabriel Saint René Taillandier, of Saint Remy de Provence, France, and *dsp* 25 June 1956

  1e Stella Claire Hilda Wolfe; *m* 3 Jan 1929 Philip Francis Sulley, est s of Philip Sulley, Inspr Taxes Edinburgh, and *d* 24 Aug 1935

3d Sidney George Wolfe; *b* 2 March 1855; *dsp*

4d Philip Charles Knightley Wolfe; *b* 20 April 1856; Cdr RN; *m* 6 Jan 1886 Ellie Blanch (*d* 25 June 1938), dau of Capt Robert Henry de Winton, JP, DL, of Graftonbury, and *d* 5 Nov 1932, leaving:

  1e Robert Alexander Wolfe, DSO (1918), MC; *b* 2 June 1889; Lt-Col S Lancs Regt, Gordon Highrs and Seaforth Highrs 1910–46, WW I (wounded, despatches twice, brevet, A/Lt-Col cmdg 1st Gordon Highrs), WW II (POW, escaped from Japanese at Singapore); *m* 1 June 1923 Isobel Mary (Isma) (*d* 1970), yr dau of Edward Armitstead Baxter, JP, DL, of Kincaldrum, Forfar, and *d* Nov 1973, leaving:

    1f +James Wolfe [James Murray Esq, House of Daviot, Daviot, Inverness-shire]; *b* 22 July 1931; *educ* Harrow; Capt QO Highrs, memb Roy Co Archers; *m* 1st 6 Feb 1961 (*divorce* 1969) Baroness Catherina Ingrid Madelaine von Stedingk, dau of Baron Eugen Fredrik Christer von Stedingk, of Sweden, and gdau of Charles, Duke of Otranto, Master of the Horse to GUSTAV V OF SWEDEN, and has:

      1g *Chanette Pauline Catharina; *b* 6 Nov 1964

      2g *Tatjana Thesy Isma; *b* 13 Aug 1965

    1f (cont.) James Murray *m* 2nd 1976 *Sally Ann, only dau of Eric Gordon Bean, of Burnside, Struy, Inverness-shire, and by her has:

      1g +James Wolfe; *b* 1978

    1f *Sibyl Pauline Wolfe [Mrs Frank Carson, 8 Kingsburgh Rd, Murrayfield, Edinburgh]; *b* 28 Sept 1924; *m* 25 Sept 1951 *Lt-Col Frank Derek Carson, OBE, Seaforth Highrs (*d* 16 March 1997), only s of Francis Samuel Carson, MC, MD, MCh, DPH, of Knockupworth Hall, Cumberland, and has:

      1g *Philip Derek Murray; *b* 2 Aug 1955; *educ* Shiplake Coll and Napiers' Tech Coll Edinburgh; *m* 1993 *Alison Marguerite, dau of Cdr Graham Creedy, LVO, RN, and has:

        1h *Marguerite Anne Murray; *b* 26 Jan 1998

      1g *Rachel Isma Ann; *b* 7 Aug 1957; *m* 1st 1979 (*divorce* 1984) Capt Christopher Glyn-Jones and has:

        1h *Caroline Mary; *b* 1980

        2h *Alexandra Pauline; *b* 1982

      1g (cont.) Mrs Rachel Glyn-Jones *m* 2nd 1987 *Timothy Horrox and by him has:

        3h *Charlotte Julia; *b* 1988

        4h *Olivia Julia; *b* 1990

      2g *Iona Fairlie Edith; *b* 25 Aug 1959; *m* 1996 *Richard Jones

2e Philip George Wolfe; *b* 5 July 1891; Lt RNVR, WW I; *das* Oct 1916

3e (David Knightley) Wolfe; *b* 11 Sept 1897; *educ* Shrewsbury and RMA Woolwich; Lt-Col RA; *m* 19 Jan 1920 Ivry Cordelia (*d* 1984), yr dau of Montague Townsend, of Chichester, and *d* 12 July 1970, leaving:

  1f +(Christopher) Michael Wolfe [Michael Murray Esq, Easter Slap, Dirleton, E Lothian EH39 5ET]; *b* 6 April 1929; *educ* Oundle; memb London Stock Exchange, Capt Gordon Highrs; *m* 1st 11 Oct 1955 (*divorce* 1980) Jacqueline, yr dau of Col Sir John Turnbull Usher, 4th Bt (*qv*); *m* 2nd 1980 *Alison Isabel Rowe, dau of James Boyd, TD, DL, of Carradale, Helensburgh, and by his 1st w had:

    1g *Dorinda Mary [Mrs Murray Hancock, 280 Amess St, N Carlton, Melbourne, Australia]; *b* 12 Oct 1957; *m* 1984 *Murray Ross Maclean Hancock and has:

      1h *Sam Fergus; *b* 1991

      2h *Benjamin Rory; *b* 1993

    2g *Erica Jacqueline [Mrs Malcolm Brinkworth, The Malt House, St Mary Bourne, Hants]; *b* 21 July 1959; *m* 1986 *Malcolm Brinkworth and has:

      1h *Alexander; *b* 1989

      2h *Christopher Rory; *b* 1993

      1h *Faye Tamsin; *b* 1988

3g *Serena Jean [Mrs Justin Varcoe, The Long Barn, Par, Cornwall]; *b* 25 June 1964; *m* 1989 *Justin J B Varcoe, er s of Beaumont Varcoe, of Nanscawen, Cornwall

1f Pamela Ann Wolfe; *b* 30 Oct 1920; *d* 1 April 1936

2f *Ivri Patricia Wolfe; *b* 10 June 1922; *m* 20 Dec 1951 *Charles Mailert Wormser, s of Moritz Wormser, and has:

    1g *Andrew Charles; *b* 25 Jan 1953

    1g *Nina Carolyn; *b* 1 April 1955

4e Christopher Charles Wolfe; *b* 25 April 1903; *educ* Loretto; Sub-Lt East Scot Div RNVR 1922–26, T/Lt RNVR 1939–47, Flag Lt to FOEAZ 1942; *m* 26 Oct 1933 Hester Mary, er dau of Newton Charles Ogle, JP, DL, of Kirkley, Northumberland

1e Blanch Heather Wolfe; *d* unm 1 Dec 1966

2e Maud Elaine Wolfe

1d Elizabeth Catherine Mary Wolfe; *m* 1886 Hugh Edward Hoare, MP (*d* 15 July 1929), and *d* 14 April 1905, leaving issue

1c (cont.) James Murray *m* 2nd 27 Nov 1862 Louisa Grace (*d* 7 May 1883), 3rd dau of Sir Adam Hay, 7th Bt, of Haystoun, and *d* 1890, having by her had:

5d Arthur Alexander Wolfe, CB; *b* 22 May 1866; Brig-Gen, Lt-Col HLI, Assist Mil Sec to GOC Scottish Cmd 1909–12, T/Brig-Gen cmdg a Bde 1915, Boer War (wounded, despatches twice, two medals with three clasps), WW I (despatches); *m* 12 Nov 1904 Evelyn Mary Hay, JP (*m* 2nd 7 Feb 1920 Archibald Robert Craufurd Pitman, est s of Frederick Pitman, of Edinburgh, and *d* 6 March 1955), 2nd dau of Colin James Mackenzie, of Portmore, and *d* 7 Dec 1918, leaving:

1e Malcolm Victor Alexander Wolfe, DL (Peeblesshire 1959); *b* 16 Dec 1908; *educ* Eton and Ch Ch Oxford (MA); Lt-Col Black Watch (RHR) WW II, memb Roy Co Archers; *m* 1st 23 April 1935 Lady Grizel Mary Boyle (lost at sea in enemy action 26 Sept 1942), est dau of 8th Earl of Glasgow (*qv*), and had:

1f +James Archibald Wolfe [James Murray Esq, 13 Howards Lane, London SW15]; *b* 25 April 1936; *educ* Eton and Worcester Coll Oxford (BA); *m* 1st 8 June 1963 (*divorce* 1976) Lady Diana Lucy-Douglas Home, yst dau of 14th Earl of Home (*qv*), and has:

1g +Rory Murray [Rory Murray Esq, 57 Broughton Rd, London SW6]; *b* 28 March 1965; *m* 1987 *Marion J, dau of Dr Philip Arthur Zorab, of Golden Hill, Chepstow, and has:

    1h +Harry; *b* 1990

    1h *Flora Jessica; *b* 1992

1g *Fiona Grizel Wolfe; *b* 12 March 1964; *m* 1991 *Andrew M Shufflebotham, s of David Shufflebotham, of Mijas, Spain, and has:

    1h *Molly Rita; *b* 1994

2g *Clare Elizabeth; *b* 6 March 1969; 19– *John Flett

1f (cont.) James Murray *m* 2nd 1978 *Amanda Felicity, er dau of Anthony Street, and by her has:

2g +Andrew Alexander Wolfe; *b* 1978

2f +Angus Malcolm Wolfe; *b* 20 May 1937; *educ* Eton; author: *The End of Something Nice*; *m* 11 Nov 1961 *Stephanie Vivian, yr dau of Maj Hadden Royden Todd, and has:

1g +Kim Alexander Wolfe; *b* 1 June 1962

2g +Rupert Hamish Wolfe; *b* 24 Sept 1963

3g +Gavin Scott Wolfe; *b* 20 March 1966

4g +Magnus Wolfe; *b* 27 Aug 1968

1e (cont.) Malcolm Murray *m* 2nd 10 June 1947 Zofia Cecilia (*d* 26 July 1968), er dau of Jaxa Chamiec, of Warsaw, and formerly w of Count Stanislas Tarnowski, and *d* 1985, having by her had:

1f *Teresa Mary Wolfe; *b* 7 Jan 1950

2d Hilda Louisa Janey Wolfe; *m* 1 Aug 1894 1st and last Baron Murray of Elibank (see ELIBANK, L) and *dsp* 27 Sept 1929

2c Alexander; Col cmdg 87th Regt; *m* 1853 Eugenia Grace, est dau of Col — Curtis, CB, and *dsp* 24 Dec 1865

3c Thomas Andrew Lumsden; *b* 1 March 1825; Maj-Gen RE; *m* 1849 Elizabeth (*d* 10 Nov 1906), est dau of John Charlton Fisher, LLD, Queen's Printer, Canada, and *d* 3 Oct 1893, leaving, with a dau (*d* unm):

1d Thomas; *dsp*

2d Dennistoun; *dsp*

1d Elizabeth Charlotte; *m* 30 Aug 1880 Col Henry Champernowne (see HARINGTON, Bt) and *d* 7 Aug 1928

1c Isabella Katherine; *m* 1834 James Dennistoun of Dennistoun (*dsp* 13 Feb 1855), author: *The History of the Dukes of Urbino*, etc, and *d* April 1864

2c Marianne Lloyd; *m* 1836 Edmund Ironside (*d* 14 Oct 1840), only s of Edmund Ironside, of Tannochside, Lanarks, and *d* 1862, leaving issue

3c Margaret Elizabeth; *m* 1848 Victor Robert de Cussac and *d* 17 May 1856

4c Louise Anne; *m* 1st 1839 Edmond Jeannin (*d* 1872) and had issue; *m* 2nd 27 Dec 1873, as his 2nd w, Hon Peter Campbell Scarlett, CB (see ABINGER, B), and *d* 19 March 1900

5c Amelia Jane; *m* 1848 Philippe Angrand, Sous-Préfet Gex, France, and *d* Dec 1877

6c Sophia Carolina; *m* 1849 Leopold Isoard, Préfet Saône Inférieure, France, and *d* 25 Dec 1877

7c Frances Octavia; *m* 19 Dec 1849 Charles Greenstreet Addison (*d* 19 Feb 1866), barrister, and *d* 22 Jan 1910, leaving issue

(2) Archibald; Sheriff Depute Peeblesshire, a Commr Edinburgh; acquired the Nisbet estate, nr Edinburgh, later called Murrayfield; *m* Jean, dau of Lord William Hay (see TWEEDDALE, M), and had issue (see also CAMPBELL, Bt, of Succoth)

(1) Margaret; *m* James Justice, Pncpl Clerk of Session, s of Sir James Justice, of Justice Hall

The 4th Bt's cousin,

Sir William Murray, 5th Bt, DL (Peeblesshire); sold 1738 the Spittlehaugh estate he had inherited from his f; *m* Jean, dau of — Allan, of Southland, and had with a dau (*d* unm):

1 **Sir Richard Murray, 6th Bt**; *d* unm 4 Oct 1781

2 Alexander; *dsp*

3 Robert; *dspm*

4 ARCHIBALD (Sir), **7th Bt**

1 Barbara; *m* Christopher Bannatyne, of Lanark, Baillie, and *d* 10 Aug 1786

2 Margaret; *m* Alexander Nicholson, of Edinburgh

Sir RICHARD's yr bro,

Sir Archibald Murray, 7th Bt; *m* 1st 4 May 1760 Mary Moorhead (*d* 8 Dec 1779); *m* 2nd 27 May 1784 Mrs Barry, widow, and *d* 23 June 1794, having by his 1st w had, with another s and two daus (*d* young):

1 JOHN (Sir), **8th Bt**

2 William; *b* 28 Feb 1768; EICS; *dsp*

1 Mary; *m* 19 June 1781 John B Swann, RN

2 Jean; *m* 4 July 1780 Andrew Atkinson, 25th Regt

Sir ARCHIBALD's er surv son,

Sir John Murray, 8th Bt; *b* 1766; Offr 46th Regt; *m* 3 Nov 1791 Anne (*d* 31 May 1818), dau of John Digby, of Cork (3rd s of John Digby, of Landenstown, Co Kildare), and *d* 30 Aug 1809, having had:

1 **Sir Archibald John Murray, 9th Bt**; *b* 3 Aug 1792; Lt-Col Scots Fus Gds; *m* 6 Nov 1856 Eliza Hope (*d* 26 Oct 1899), dau of Samuel Unwin, and *dsp* 22 May 1860

2 John William; *dsp*

3 JOHN DIGBY (Sir), **10th Bt**

4 William Augustus; *dsp*

1 Anne Maria; *m* 22 Feb 1851 Filippo, Duke of Lanté Monte Feltro della Rovere, Grandee of Spain 1st Cl, and *d* 12 Oct 1884

Sir ARCHIBALD's yr bro,

Sir John Digby Murray, 10th Bt; *b* 17 April 1798; Lt-Col Scots Fus Gds; *m* 1st 1 April 1823 Susannah (*d* 3 Dec 1823), dau of John Cuthbert, and had:

1 John Cuthbert; *b* Dec 1823; *dsp* Sandhurst, Australia, 11 May 1861

The **10th Bt** *m* 2nd 14 June 1827 Frances (*d* 17 June 1885), dau and coheir of Peter Patten Bold, MP, of Bold Hall, Lancs, and *d* 8 May 1881, having by her had, with three daus (*d* unm):

2 DIGBY (Sir), **11th Bt**

3 Archibald John; *b* 14 Feb 1831; *d* Feb 1840

4 Kenelm Digby, DSO; *b* 6 Feb 1839; Col Roy Irish Fus Egypt and Sudan; *m* 23 May 1870 Caroline (*d* 13 Feb 1927), only dau of Lt-Col George Thomson, CB, Bengal Engrs, and *d* 19 Feb 1915, leaving:

(1) Archibald Digby, DSO (1919); *b* 30 April 1878; *educ* Haileybury; Lt-Col RA, Waziristan 1901–02, WW I (wounded, despatches), WW II, Legn Hon and Croix de Guerre; *m* 2 Oct 1905 Rosamund (*d* 1980), yst dau of Thomas Davey, of Leigh Woods, Somerset, and *d* 21 Aug 1949, having had:

1a +Archibald John [Lt-Col Archibald Murray, Woodford, Dartmouth, Devon TQ6 9PA]; *b* 22 Nov 1907; *educ* Harrow; Lt-Col Black Watch WW II (wounded); *m* 1st 3 Sept 1935 Nancy (*d* 30 April 1974), er dau of Philip George, of Barrow Gurney, Somerset; *m* 2nd 1977 *Phyllis Walker, dau of Surgn R-Adml David Walker Hewitt, CB, CMG, MD, BCh, FRCS, and widow of Capt P G Burgess, MVO, RN, and by his 1st w has:

1b +John Archibald Digby, JP [John Murray Esq JP, Churchill Court, Churchill, Avon BS19 5QW]; *b* 4 Aug 1941; *educ* Harrow; *m* 1975 *Janet, dau of Adam Johnstone, OBE, of Temple Wood, Capel, Surrey, and has:

    1c +Angus John Digby; *b* 1976

    1c *Nicola Rosamund; *b* 1979

    2c *Alice; *b* 1982

1b Grania Joan; *b* 28 March 1938; *m* 20 April 1963 *Charles Richard Thurlow Laws and had:

    1c *Mathew Thurlow; *b* 20 Feb 1964

    1c *Antonia Mary; *b* 3 Nov 1965

    2c *Jessica Susan; *b* 3 Feb 1968

2b *Gillian Claire; *b* 9 Aug 1946; *m* 1978 *Roger Philip Latham

2a Ian Digby; *b* 9 Aug 1912; *educ* Harrow; Maj Argyll & Sutherland Highrs WW II; *m* 16 May 1944 Pamela (*d* 1988), only dau of Claud Parbury, of Sussex, and *d* 1974, leaving:

1b +Julian Charles Digby; *b* 21 Dec 1949; *educ* privately; *m* 1974 *Gillian Frazer

1b *Petrina Rosamund; *b* 16 Oct 1947; *m* 1970 *Manuel Moran, of Madrid, and has:

    1c *Mark; *b* 1977

    1c *Sophia; *b* 1976

    2c *Ania (twin); *b* 1977

2b *Charlotte Davey; *b* 1 May 1954; *m* 1977 *Grahame Royds Gordon Nicholson and has:

    1c *Ian Royds Gordon; *b* 1981

    2c *Rupert Grahame Murray; *b* 1983

    3c *Sabrina Pamela; *b* 1989

3a Stanley Digby; *b* 8 Nov 1920; FO, RAFVR, WW II; *ka* Far East 17 April 1943

(2) Kenelm Digby Bold, CB (1933), DSO (1917); *b* 30 Oct 1879; *educ* Haileybury; Col BA WW I (wounded, despatches); Hon MA Cantab 1934; *m* 25 Nov 1911 Gwendolen (*d* 1979), dau of Thomas Andrew de Wolf, of Sydney, NSW, and *d* 3 Feb 1947, leaving:

1a +Andrew Digby; *b* 26 April 1916; Lt-Col RA; *m* 14 Feb 1947 *Joan Roberts, only dau of Maj A Nelson Allen, of Leigh, Surrey, and has:

    1b *Anna Teresa; *b* 1947

1a Joan Digby; *b* 1 Dec 1912; *m* 10 April 1937 Lt-Col Bernard William de Courcy-Ireland, DSC, RM, yst s of Rev Magens de Courcy-Ireland by Elizabeth Mildred, dau and eventual heiress of Rev William Graham-Foster-Pigott, of Abington Pigotts Hall, Cambs, and had:

  1b *David Graham; *b* 22 July 1938

  1b *Philippa Ann; *b* 27 June 1946

  (1) Frances Anne; Dame Juliana Murray OSB; *d* 9 June 1962

  (2) Constance Digby; *d* unm 2 July 1965

5 Alan; *b* 28 Feb 1840; Maj-Gen Bengal SC; *d* unm 20 Jan 1919

1 Marion Jane; *m* 12 Nov 1867 Sir Spencer Walpole, KCB, and *d* 9 May 1912, leaving issue (see WALPOLE, B)

Sir JOHN's est surv son,

  Sir Digby Murray, 11th Bt, RN; *b* 31 Oct 1829; Marine Dept BOT; *m* 7 May 1861 Helen Cornelia (*d* 8 Aug 1888), dau of Gerry Sanger, of Utica, USA, and *d* 5 Jan 1906, having had:

1 Digby; *b* 16 April 1862; *d* young

2 Archibald John; *b* 10 July 1863; *d* 26 April 1864

3 **Sir John Murray, 12th Bt**; *b* 12 Jan 1867; Lt Scottish Horse; *m* 7 April 1896 Edith Mary (*d* 18 July 1925), dau of George Raby, of Valparaiso, and *d* 15 Sept 1938, having had:

  (1) **Sir Kenelm Bold Murray, 13th Bt**; *b* 26 May 1898; Lt MGC WW I; *d* unm 16 Aug 1959

  (1) Helen Mary Edith; *m* 22 Feb 1930 James Millie Wodehouse (see KIMBERLEY, E) and had issue

  (2) Vanda Digby; *m* 6 June 1929 Edward Cecil Cutler, MBE, MC (*d* 1955), s of E I Cutler, of Littlehampton, Sussex, and had:

    1a *John Leslie; *b* 4 July 1940; *educ* Eton

4 Alan Digby; *b* 20 June 1870; *m* 19 Nov 1907 Eileen Muriel (*d* 18 March 1931), dau of Arthur E Shaw, MICE, and *d* 17 Oct 1954, leaving:

  (1) ALAN JOHN DIGBY (Sir), **14th Bt**

  (1) *Eileen Charmian Digby [Mrs David Hinchcliff-Mathew, Estancia Los Flamencos, Sancti Spiritu, Prov Sta Fé, Argentina]; *b* 11 Oct 1910; *m* 19 Feb 1930 David Hinchcliff-Mathew (*d* 1974) and has:

    1a *Murray Alan; *b* 29 Nov 1933; *m* Feb 1958 *Marilyn Nazabal Chapman, dau of Evaristo Nazabal, of Rufino, Argentina, and has:

      1b *David; *b* 19–

      2b *Andrew; *b* 19–

      1b *Marjory Charlotte; *b* 30 June 1959

      2b *Carol; *b* 1961

      3b *Rose Ann; *b* 19–

      4b *Alexandra; *b* 19–

    2a *John Gervase; *b* 1 May 1947; *m* 1984 *Susan Penelope, dau of Donald Maxwell Jack, and has:

      1b *Daniel; *b* 1985

      1b *Vanessa; *b* 1987

5 Danvers Ismay; *b* 4 Aug 1882; *d* 13 Feb 1883

1 Helen; *m* 17 Sept 1889 Edward Hallmann (*d* 26 June 1906) and had issue

2 Marion Louise; *m* Nov 1897 Frank Oliver Quennel and *d* Oct 1920

Sir KENELM's cousin,

  Sir Alan John Digby Murray, 14th Bt; *b* 22 June 1909; *educ* Brighton Coll; *m* 28 Aug 1943 *Mabel Elisabeth, dau of Arthur Bernard Schiele, of Arias, Argentina, and *d* 9 May 1978, having had:

1 Sir NIGEL ANDREW DIGBY MURRAY, **15th and present Bt**

2 +Kenelm Gerald Digby [Kenelm Murray Esq, Crofts, Woodside Rd, Chiddingfold, Surrey]; *b* 9 June 1946; *educ* St Paul's Sch Argentina and Birmingham U (BSc elec); *m* 1973 *Jolandë Grazyna Maria St Clare Byrne, and has:

  (1) +Alan James Digby; *b* 1980

  (1) *Olivia Lucile Caroline Digby; *b* 22 June 1977

3 +Peter Francis Digby; *b* 6 July 1947; *educ* St Paul's Sch Argentina, Shuttleworth Ag Coll (NDA) and Bangor U (BSc Ag Econ)

4 +Denis Jermyn Digby [Denis Murray Esq, The Farmyard, Upper Llandwrog, Fron, Gwynedd]; *b* 5 July 1949; *educ* St Paul's Sch Argentina and Bangor U (BSc Forestry); *m* 1980 Christine Baars (*d* 1993) and has:

  (1) +David Christopher; *b* 1981

  (2) +Lawrence Stephen; *b* 1986

  (1) *Teresa Mabel; *b* 1983

MURRAY of Dunerne

Creation: Bt (NS) 20 April 1630.

SIR ROWLAND WILLIAM MURRAY, 15TH BT, of Dunerne, Co Fife [Sir Rowland Murray Bt, 4363 E Brookhaven Dve, Atlanta, GA 30319, USA]; *b* 22 Sept 1947; *educ* Georgia State U; Pres Southern Furniture Galleries, V-Pres Ball-Stalker Inc; *m* 1970 *Nancy Diane, dau of George C Newberry, of Orlando, Fla., and has:

1 +ROWLAND WILLIAM IV; *b* 31 July 1979

1 *Ryan McCabe; *b* 1974

Lineage: ANDREW MURRAY of Blackbarony (see MURRAY, Bt, of Blackbarony); had by his 2nd w Grissel (*d* 1579) a yst s:

WILLIAM MURRAY; acquired the Dunerne estate, Fifeshire; *m* 1st Marjorie Schaw (*d* 29 May 1626) and had a s and dau (Anas, *m c* 9–18 Nov 1618 Sir William Hay of Linplum, see TWEEDDALE, M); *m* 2nd *c* 1627 Margaret Colvill and *d* 25 Dec 1638, having by her had a s (John, *b* 17 April 1628); his s by his 1st w:

Sir William Murray, 1st Bt (NS), so cr 20 April 1630, of Dunerne; also bought 1628 the lands and territorial Barony of Newton, Midlothian; *m* 27 July 1620 Lady Margaret Alexander, dau of 1st Earl of Stirling, and *d* by 1641, leaving:

1 **Sir William Murray, 2nd Bt**, of Newton; *m* (contract 3 Feb 1644) his 2nd cousin, Jean, dau of 1st Lord Elibank (*qv*), and had:

  (1) **Sir William Murray, 3rd Bt**; *m* Marion Crichton and had an est s:

    1a **Sir William Murray, 4th Bt**; *dsps*

2 Patrick (Sir); had issue

3 Charles; had issue

4 James, of Outerston; *m* Magdalen, dau and heiress of John Johnston of Polton, and had, with other issue:

  (1) **Sir James Murray, 5th Bt, of Hilhead**; Gen Receiver Customs Scotland; *m* Marion, dau of James Nairn, and *dsp* 14 Feb 1769

  (2) William; Col in Dutch service; *m* Anne, dau of Hosea Newman or Schurmann, and had, with other issue:

    1a ROBERT (Sir), **6th Bt**

5 Archibald

6 Anthone

7 Henry; bought Dunerne from his bro; had issue

The 5th Bt's nephew,

  Sir Robert Murray, 6th Bt, of Clermont; *m* 1st 22 June 1750 Janet (*d* 9 Aug 1759), dau of 4th Lord Elibank (*qv*), and had, with a dau:

1 Sir JAMES MURRAY later MURRAY-PULTENEY, **7th Bt**, PC (1807); joined Army 1771, served America 1775, assisted at taking of St Lucia 1778, Adj-Gen Br forces Flanders 1793–94, Col 18th Foot 1794, Lt-Gen 1799, MP Weymouth 1790–1811, Sec at War 1807–09; *m* 23 July 1794 Henrietta (*dsp* 14 July 1808), Countess of Bath in her own right (see BATH, M, preliminary remarks) and dau and heiress of Sir William JOHNSTONE later PULTENEY, 5th Bt, and *dsp* 26 April 1811

Sir Robert *m* 2nd Susan, dau of John Renton of Lamerton, by Lady Susan Montgomerie, dau of 9th Earl of Eglinto(u)n (see EGLINTON and WINTON, E), and *d* 21 Sept 1771, having had by her, with five daus:

2 **Sir John Murray, 8th Bt**, GCH; *b c* 1768; Col 56th Foot 1818, Gen 1825, MP Wootton Bassett 1807–11 and Weymouth 1811–18; *m* 25 Aug 1807 Anne Elizabeth Cholmondeley (*d* 10 April 1848), only dau and heiress of 2nd Baron Mulgrave (see NORMANBY, M), and *dsp* 15 Oct 1827

3 **Rev Sir William Murray, 9th Bt**; *b c* 1769; *educ* Westminster and Ch Ch Oxford; Rector Lavington Wilts 1795, Lofthouse Yorks 1802–42; *m* 1809 Esther Jane Gayton (*d* 6 Feb 1875) and *d* 14 May 1842, having had, with other issue (*d* unm):

  (1) **Sir James Pulteney Murray, 10th Bt**; *b c* 1814; *d* unm 22 Feb 1843

  (2) ROBERT (Sir), **11th Bt**

  (3) Arthur; Army Capt; *b* May 1816; *m* Margaret, est dau of Dr Wardrop, and *dsp*

  (4) John; *b* 17 Nov 1817; *m* 14 Aug 1843 Caroline Atkinson, 2nd dau of Joseph James Swaby, of Jamaica, and *d* 25 June 1879, having had five sons and two daus

  (5) William; Maj-Gen Bengal SC; *d* 10 March 1886 aged 65

  (6) Horace; Lt Madras Army; *d* 6 May 1852

  (1) Sophia; *m* 19 May 1846 James Edward Jerningham (see STAFFORD, B)

  (2) Madeline; *m* 28 March 1846 Charles Roderick Mackenzie (see MACKENZIE, Bt, of Scatwell)

  (3) Esther Jane; *m* 29 Jan 1853 John de Monte Arbuthnot (*d* 1886), 3rd s of George Arbuthnot of Elderslie, and had issue

The 10th Bt's bro,

  Sir Robert Murray, 11th Bt; *b* 1 Feb 1815; *m* 1st 21 Aug 1839 Susan Catherine Sanders (*d* 21 April 1860), widow of Adolphus Cottin-Murray and 2nd dau and coheir of John Murray, of Ardeley Bury, Herts, and had a s and dau (Emily Mary, *m* 16 March 1875 Robert Alexander Douglas Lithgow, LLD, FSA, of Wisbech, Cambs, and *d* 15 March 1895, leaving issue); *m* 2nd 1 Dec 1868 Laura (*d* 5 March 1893), widow of Rev W H Crawford, of Haughley Park, Suffolk, and yst dau of Rev Charles Taylor, Rector Biddesham, Somerset, and *d* 15 April 1894; his only s:

Sir William Robert Murray, 12th Bt; *b* 19 Oct 1840; *m* 1st 1868 Lastania (*dspm* 1873), dau of J Fontanilla, of La Plata, and had:

1 Emily Marguerite; *d* 1872

Sir William *m* 2nd 1874 Esther Elizabeth (*d* 1884), widow of John Rickard, of London, and dau of J Body, and by her had:

1 **Sir Edward Robert Murray, 13th Bt**, DSO (1900); Hon Lt-Col 10th Bn Imp Yeo Boer War 1899–1902 (despatches); *b* 22 June 1875; *m* 1st 1904 Elsie Innes Macgeorge (*d* 14 July 1935), er dau of W A Brown, Sheriff Aberdeen and Kincardine, and had a dau (Rachel Mary Gertrude Charlotte, *b* 26 Dec 1908, *d* 4 Feb 1915); *m* 2nd 16 April 1938 *Ruby, dau of S Hearn, of Helmdon, Northants, and *d* 14 Jan 1958

2 Rowland William; *b* 5 June 1877; served Boer War 1901–02; *m* 1907 Gertrude Frances, dau of Patrick McCabe, of Belfast, and *d* 28 July 1946, leaving:

  (1) **Sir Rowland William Patrick Murray, 14th Bt**; *b* 26 Oct 1910; *educ* Georgia State U; Maj US Army WW II (Bronze Star Medal); *m* 1st 1944 Josephine Margaret, dau of Edward D Murphy; *m* 2nd 1991 *Sarah Jane Wikle [Sarah Lady Murray, 2820 Peachtree Rd NE, Apt 1312, Atlanta, GA 30305, USA], dau of Walter W Lafevre, and *d* 1994, leaving by his 1st w:

    1a Sir ROWLAND WILLIAM MURRAY, **15th and present Bt**

    2a +Edward George [Edward Murray, 635 Creekwood Crossing, E Rowswell, GA 30076, USA]; *b* 1951; mktg consultant; *m* 1975 *Glenda Sharon, dau of John Foutes, and has:

      1b +Michael Betton; *b* 1971

    3a +Robert Michael [Robert Murray, 6819 Brewster Court, Columbus GA 31904, USA]; *b* 1953; *educ* Young Harris Coll Ga., Columbus Coll Ga. (BS) and Troy State U (MBA); Lt-Col US Army; *m* 1981 *Vickie, dau of Helen Kent, of Augusta, Ga., and has:

      1b +Robert Michael; *b* 1985

1b *Ashley Kathren; *b* 1989

4a +Christopher Joseph [Christopher Murray, 11 Plumosa Dve, Cassell-berry, FL, USA]; *b* 1957; *m* 1984 *Kimberly Ann, dau of James Johnson, and has:

1b +Nicholas Christopher; *b* 1986

1b *Jessica Kirsten; *b* 1988

1a *Helen Brooke [Mrs Ronald Reppert, 1322 Andover Rd, Richmond, VA 23229, USA]; *b* 1945; *m* 1st Clinton S Ferguson and has:

1b *Clinton S; *b* 1970

1b *Julia H; *b* 1971

1a (cont.) Mrs Ferguson *m* 2nd 1980 *Capt Ronald Grant Reppert, US Army, and has:

2b *Stephen Harris; *b* 1984

2a *Patricia Marie [Mrs Edward Scoloro, 3303 Decatur Ave, Tampa, FL 33603 USA]; *b* 28 July 1949; *m* 1977 *Edward A Scolavo and has:

1b *Anthony Edward; *b* 5 April 1985

1b *Nina Murray; *b* 7 Dec 1988

(1) Gertrude Jane; Capt Army Med Specialists' Corps USA; *b* 13 Feb 1909; *educ* Oglethorpe U Ga. (BA 1931)

3 Robert Lithgow; served Boer War 1900–02 (wounded twice); *b* 1 Feb 1881; *m* 13 March 1908 *Harriet Pope and *d* 1942, leaving:

(1) +Vernon Robert William; *b* 24 May 1909; *m* 1934 *Elizabeth Camberne Kirkwood and has:

1a +Vernon Kirkwood; *b* 1945; BA Hardwick Coll; *m* Jan 1966 *Linda Tischler and has:

1b *Christine Lynn; *b* 1966

1a *Harriet Elizabeth; *b* 1937; *educ* State U NY (BS 1958) and Longsland U (MS 1967); *m* 7 April 1958 *Dale Aldrich Edwards, s of Olin M Edwards, of Southampton, NY, and has:

1b *Daniel Vernon; *b* 25 April 1962

1b *Susan Dale; *b* 22 May 1959

2b *Carolyn Kirkwood; *b* 16 Feb 1968

2a *Phyllis Vernon; *b* 20 June 1939; *m* 1st 21 Sept 1957 (*divorce* 1978) Adrian Cecil Stanley and has:

1b *Kenneth William; *b* 23 March 1960

2b *Edward Murray; *b* 11 May 1966

1b *Janet Elizabeth; *b* 9 June 1958

2b *Alice Camberne Stanley; *b* 1970

(2) James Edward; *b* 8 Oct 1911; *m* 1934 *Dorothy Elizabeth Holley [Mrs James Murray, 38–38 217th Street, Bayside, NY, USA] and *d* 29 Oct 1963, leaving:

1a +Donald MacLean; *b* 1945; *educ* MIT

1a *Elizabeth Anne [Mme Louis Cabrol, Route de Maraussan, Beziers, Herault, France]; *b* 1938; *m* 9 Nov 1957 *Louis H Cabrol and has:

1b *Jean Louis; *b* 27 Nov 1964

2b *Jacques; *b* 1970

1b *Marie Thérèse; *b* 19 Oct 1958

2b *Danielle; *b* 15 June 1960

3b *Alice; *b* 23 July 1961

4b *Hélène; *b* 28 Aug 1963

2a *Susan Eleanora; *b* 1939; *m* 1st 6 Sept 1958 (*divorce* 1982) James A Kowalski and has:

1b *Glenn R; *b* 29 Jan 1960

2b *Gary W; *b* 7 Dec 1962

3b *James Edward; *b* 27 Feb 1964

1b *Melissa Jill; *b* 16 July 1969

(3) +Robert Atholl; *b* 26 Aug 1914; *m* 1935 *Mary Ellen Guinan and has:

1a +Robert Atholl; *b* 1937

2a +James Ivor; *b* 1947

1a *Diane; *b* 1942

2 Marguerite Emily Frances; *d unm* 25 Sept 1924

Sir William *m* 3rd 22 Sept 1885 Magdalen Agnes (*d* 30 Dec 1926), dau of Gerard Gandy, of Oaklands, Windermere, and *d* 21 Jan 1904, leaving by her:

4 William Gerard Pulteney; *b* 6 May 1891; *m* 1919 Frances Swartz and *d* 1 April 1953, leaving:

(1) +Alan Gerald; *b* 1928; *m* *Penny Phillips and has:

1a +William

1a *June Ann

2a *Gail

3 Laura Magdalen Irving; *b* 1887; *m* 2 May 1907 Gerald Alexander Marlowe King, est s of Alexander I King, of Tunbridge Wells, and had issue

4 Marie Eugenie; *d unm* 21 Jan 1952

MURRAY of Ochtertyre

Arms: Az. three mullets arg., in the centre a cross of the second surmounted of a saltire gu., both couped. **Crest:** An olive branch ppr. **Motto:** *Ex bello quies* ('Out of war, peace'). **Creation:** Bt. (NS) 3 or 7 June 1673.

SIR PATRICK IAN KEITH MURRAY, 12TH BT, of Ochtertyre [Sir Patrick Murray Bt, Sheephouse, Hay-on-Wye, Powis; 12 Burgos Grove, London SE10 8LL]; *b* 22 March 1965; *s f* 1977; *educ* Christ Coll Brecon and LAMDA

Lineage: Sir DAVID MURRAY of Tullibardine (*see* ATHOLL, D); had a yr s:

PATRICK MURRAY; had charters of Dollerie and Ochtertyre, Perths; *m* Katherine, dau of Michael Balfour of Montguhanie, and *d* 1476, leaving, with a yr s (Anthony, 1st of Raith, ancestor of the MURRAYs of Dollerie):

DAVID MURRAY, 2nd of Ochtertyre; *m* Margaret, dau of Henry Pitcairn of Pitcairn and Forthar, and *d c* 4 Feb 1509/10, leaving:

PATRICK MURRAY, 3rd of Ochtertyre, of which had a confirmatory charter 4 Feb 1509/10; *m* Elizabeth, dau of Charteris of Kinfauns, and was *k* Flodden 1513, leaving:

DAVID MURRAY, 4th of Ochtertyre; *m* Agnes, dau of Hay of Megginch, and *d* 1547, leaving, with other issue:

PATRICK MURRAY, 5th of Ochtertyre; *m* Nicola, dau of Graham of Inchbrakie, and *d* 1589, leaving, with other issue:

WILLIAM MURRAY, 6th of Ochtertyre; *m* Bethia, dau of Murray of Letterbannochy, and *d* 1647, leaving, with other issue:

PATRICK MURRAY, 7th of Ochtertyre; *m* Mary, only dau of Sir William Moray of Abercairney, and *d* 1677, leaving, with other issue:

Sir William Murray, 1st Bt (NS), so *cr* 3 or 7 June 1673, of Ochtertyre; *m* 7 June 1649 Isabel (*d* 6 April 1683), dau of John Oliphant of Bachiltoun, and *d* 18 Feb 1681, leaving surv issue:

1 PATRICK (Sir), **2nd Bt**

2 Mungo; *b* 1662; *m* 1st Janet, dau of Arnott of Mugdrum; *m* 2nd Martha, dau of Andrew Forester, of Dundee, and *d* 1719, leaving, with a yr s (Alexander, *m* Lilias, dau of James Steuart of Alantin, and had, with other issue (*d unm*), Amelia, *m* James Guthrie, Yr. of Craigie):

(1) John, of Lintrose, Perths; *b* 1706; *m* 1731 his cousin Amelia, dau of **Sir William Murray, 3rd Bt** (*see* below), and *d* 1771, leaving, with a yr s (William, Col 27th Regt, *d* 1778):

1a Mungo, of Lintrose; *b* 1735; *m* Cecilia, dau of John Lyon of Brigton, and *d* 1805, having had, with another s (William, *m* —, widow of Nisbet of Cairnhill, and *d* 1808, leaving, with three sons and three other daus (*d unm*), Euphemia, *m* David Smythe, Ld of Session as Lord Methven):

1b John, of Lintrose; *b* 11 July 1763; *m* 12 Feb 1802 Anne (*d* 3 Nov 1846), 2nd dau of John Gray of Baledgarno, Forfarshire, and *d* 31 Oct 1831, having had:

1c Mungo, of Lintrose, DL Perths; *b* 4 Dec 1802; *m* 27 Oct 1831 Anne, dau of Thomas Willing, of Philadelphia, and *dsp* 1890

2c John Gray, twin with Mungo; *d unm* March 1866

3c David Smythe; *b* 30 April 1807; *m* Elizabeth, dau of John Davis, of W Australia, and *d* 1866, leaving, with four daus (*d unm*):

1d John Gray; *b* 1840; *d unm* 1884

2d David Smythe, of Lintrose; *b* 1850; *d unm* 1901

3d George William; *b* 1852; *d unm* 1901

4c Mackenzie; *b* 8 Feb 1810; HEICS; *m* 13 Jan 1870 Eliza Margaret, est dau of Edward James Jackson, of The Priory, St Andrews, by Elizabeth (sis of Margaret Seton, w of John Buchanan Hamilton of Leny, Callendar, Perths), and *d* 14 Feb 1876, leaving:

1d Edward Mackenzie MURRAY later MURRAY-BUCHANAN of Leny (1919 on inheriting the Leny estate from his cousin John Hamilton-Buchanan), JP, DL; *b* 3 June 1874; *educ* Rugby and Oriel Coll Oxford; *m* 9 Oct 1913 Jean Isabella Shaw (*d* 9 Dec 1952), dau of

James Carmichael of Arthurstone, Meigle, Perthshire, and *d* 22 Dec 1956, leaving:

1e *Euphemia Cecilia [Mrs John Hay-Young, West Lodge, 3a Glen Rd, Bridge of Allen, Stirlingshire FK9 4PP]; *b* 1915; *m* 1st 24 April 1940 Maj Francis William Clark (*ka* Italy 1944), Argyll & Sutherland Highrs, of Ulva, Argyll; *m* 2nd 7 May 1956, as his 2nd w, Lt-Col John Hay-Young, DSO, MC (*d* 1979), s of Charles Cornelius Cardew Young, of Inverness, and by her 1st husb has:

1f *Francis Malcolm; *b* 22 June 1942; *educ* Fettes and RAC Cirencester; *m* 1971 *Georgina Jane, dau of Maj F J Swinton Lee, Seaforth Highrs, and has:

1g *John Francis; *b* 1971

2g *Michael James; *b* 1972

1g *Fiona Janet; *b* 1980

2e Margaret Avril; *m* 16 June 1946 Albert Fairfield, of Acklam, Middlesbrough, Yorks, and had issue

3e *Phoebe Aeonie [Mrs James Inglis, Inglisfield, Gifford, E Lothian, EH41 4JH]; *b* 1922; *m* 25 July 1952 *James Craufuird Roger Inglis, WS, only s of Lt-Col John Inglis, CMG, DSO, of Grangemuir, Pittenweem, Fife, and has:

1f *Richard David [Richard Inglis Esq, Cardrona, 5 Hamilton Rd, N Berwick, E Lothian]; *b* 15 Nov 1953; *educ* Rugby; *m* 1980 *Pauline Goldie and has:

1g *Crawford; *b* 1986

1g *Zoe; *b* 1982

2g *Charlotte; *b* 1984

2f *John (Jack) Edward [Jack Inglis Esq, 25 Halsey St, London SW3 2PT]; *b* 24 Dec 1961; *m* 1st 1991 (*divorce* 1994) Marina Lloyd; *m* 2nd 19 Oct 1996 *Victoria Helen Rose Mellstrom

1f *Jean Helen [Mrs Christopher Smith, 1 Wester Coates Terr, Edinburgh]; *b* 4 Aug 1955; *m* 1980 *Christopher Smith and has:

1g *Jeremy Gordon; *b* 1983

1g *Camilla Helen; *b* 1985

2f *Fiona Ann; *b* 3 June 1957; *m* 1993 *Mark A Ramsay and has:

1g *Jamie; *b* 1 Dec 1996

3f *Sheena Mary [Mrs Michael Crerar, 3 Gordon Rd, Edinburgh]; *b* 4 Nov 1960; *m* 1986 *Michael Crerar and has:

1g *Gordon; *b* 1993

1g *Katherine; *b* 1991

4f *Susan Patricia; *b* 13 Aug 1964

1 Ann; *m* (contract 6 April 1675) as his 1st w Henry Cheape, 2nd of Rossie, and had issue

Sir WILLIAM's est son,

Sir Patrick Murray, 2nd Bt; *m* 15 Feb 1681 Margaret (*d* 17 Feb 1722), est dau of Mungo Haldane of Gleneagles, and *d* 25 Dec 1735, having had:

1 WILLIAM (Sir), **3rd Bt**

2 Patrick, of Ayton, Fife; *b* Feb 1856; *m* 16 Sept 1709 Anne (*d* 18 July 1773), dau of Duncan of Lundie, and *d* Nov 1773, leaving:

(1) Alexander; *m* Martha, dau of Joseph Williamson, and had:

1a Alexander, of Ayton; *m* 23 Aug 1780 Mary (*d* Dec 1789), dau of 7th Lord Banff, and *d* 1829, leaving, with other issue:

1b Joseph, of Ayton; *b* 25 April 1786; *m* 1823 his cousin Grace (*d* 29 July 1876), dau of Sir George Abercromby, 4th Bt (*qv*), and *d* 17 June 1876, leaving surv issue:

1c George Joseph, of Wootton Court, Kent, JP; *b* 22 June 1833; *m* 3 Sept 1861 Augusta Anne (*d* 1910), dau of Rev George Deane, Rector Bighton, Hants, and *d* 3 Dec 1913, leaving:

1d Alexander Penrose; *b* 13 July 1863; Capt Gordon Highrs, Consul St Pierre 1911–26, Consul-Gen Haiti, T/Maj, Pioneer Depot 1915; *m* 1st 1891 Nina (*d* 1894), dau of Col Alexander Solovtsoff, Russian Engrs, and had:

1e Alexander Gordon; *b* 30 June 1892; Lt RN; *ka* Battle of Jutland 27 May 1916

1d (cont.) Alexander Murray *m* 2nd 1895 Ethel Chorley, dau of Maj-Gen Arthur Hill, and *d* 18 March 1926, having by her had:

1e Charles; *b* 1895

2d George Henry Lygon; *b* 25 May 1871; *educ* Radley and Keble Coll Oxford (BA 1892); Dist Offr Br E Africa, V-Consul Seattle 1918–27; *m* 2 April 1908 Helen Marion, yst dau of Thomas B Illingworth, of Shipley, Yorks

1d Mary Grace; *b* 17 Sept 1865; *m* 24 Aug 1898 Rt Rev Edward Ralph Johnson, DD (*d* 11 Nov 1911), Bp Calcutta 1876–98

2d Margaret Beatrice; *b* 31 May 1868

3d Amelia Augusta; *b* 9 Oct 1873

3 George, MD; *m* Mary, dau and heiress of David Clayhills, of Invergowrie, and *d* 1777, leaving issue

4 John; Sheriff-Depute Perths, Pncpl Clerk of Session 1723; *d* 1755, leaving issue

1 Isabel; *m* 1702 Alexander Duncan and had issue (*see* 1933 edn CAMPERDOWN, E)

2 Mary; *m* 1703 Sir John Murray, Bt, of Glendoick, and had issue

Sir PATRICK's est son,

Sir William Murray, 3rd Bt; *m* 25 July 1706 Katherine Fraser (*d* 4 March 1771), 3rd dau of 9th Lord (Fraser of) Lovat (*qv*), and *d* 20 Oct 1739, having had, with other issue:

1 PATRICK (Sir), **4th Bt**

2 Edward; *b* 20 April 1730; Offr 57th Regt; *m* Henrietta Maria Alice Goodall and had:

(1) Henry John, of Woodbrook, Trinidad; *b* 1777; Inspr-Gen Militia, memb Cncl Trinidad; *m* 1 April 1799 Louise Rose (*d* 1799), dau of Louis Alexander,

Marquis and Count de Rochard, and 3rd cousin of EMPRESS JOSEPHINE, and had:

1a Edward; *b* 24 June 1800; Prefect Trinidad; *m* 7 Oct 1822 Catherine Josephine Adelaide, est dau of Pierre Auguste Roget de Belloquet and great-niece of Gen Baron Roget de Belloquet, and had:

1b Henry Augustus; *b* 3 Sept 1823; Lt 79th Regt; *m* 23 Aug 1859 Adelaide Jane, dau of Gen Edmund Wilford, RA, Cmdt RMA Woolwich, and had:

1c Arthur Harris; *b* 16 May 1860

2b Edward; *b* 3 March 1825; Capt Militia; *m* 5 March 1846 Grace (*d* 13 Jan 1898), only child of Sir Thomas Elmsley Croft, 7th Bt, of Croft Castle (*qv*), and *d* 1893, leaving:

1c Edward Croft; *b* 5 Oct 1847; Maj 9th Regt; *m* 16 Jan 1879 Julia Elizabeth, yst child of Maj George Willock, KLS, Madras Cav

2c Denman Croft, of Ryde, IoW; *b* 11 June 1849; Lt-Col Roy Warwicks Regt; *m* 17 Dec 1885 Mary Margaret, est dau of Henry Davis Willock, Bengal CS, and had:

1d William Raymond Croft; *b* 1887; *educ* Eton; Capt Gren Gds WW I; *m* 24 Sept 1912 Mary Agneta Frances (*d* 17 Oct 1973), est dau of Lt-Col Lionel Richard Cavendish Boyle (*see* CORK and ORRERY, E), and *das* 25 Feb 1971, leaving:

1e Mary Janet Croft; *b* 9 June 1915; *m* 9 Jan 1946 Alwyne Douglas Home, Consul Ethiopia, of Natal, yr s of Rev J D Home, Rector Bagthorpe, Norfolk, and had:

1f *Nichola Anne Mary; *b* 26 May 1947

2f *Josephine Georgiana Janet; *b* 8 June 1948

3f *Mariota Eleanor Croft; *b* 28 July 1951

3c Bernard Croft; *b* 8 March 1858; *m* Amy James, of Otterburn Tower, Northumberland, and had:

1d Edward Frederick Croft, CBE (1966), of Croft Castle, Leominster; *b* 1 Sept 1907; *educ* Lancing and Magdalen Coll Oxford (BA), FSA (1940); WW II: Admlty 1939–40, Civilian Offr, Mil Intell WO 1940–43, Maj Allied Control Commn (Monuments and Fine Arts Section) Italy and Austria 1943–46; Assist Keeper Dept Prints and Drawings Br Museum 1933–53, Dep Keeper 1953–54, Keeper 1954, Tstee Cecil Higgins Museum Bedford, memb (rep Oxford U) Br Instn Fund; *m* 1st Contessina Giovanna, dau of Count Zaffi, of Rome, and had:

1e *Tatiana Camilla

2e *Mary Croft

1d (cont.) Edward Murray *m* 2nd 1960 *Rosemary Jill, dau of Capt E H Whitford-Hawkey, and by her had a dau

1 Amelia; *m* 1731 her cousin John Murray, of Lintrose

2 Katherine; *m* (elopement) 2 June 1730 Sir Thomas Moncreiffe of that Ilk, 3rd Bt, and *d* 24 June 1735, leaving issue (*see* ERROLL, E)

3 Margaret; *m* 1735 Robert Graham of Fintry

Sir WILLIAM's est son,

Sir Patrick Murray, 4th Bt; *b* 21 Aug 1707; *m* 18 Feb 1741 Helen (*d* 18 July 1773), est dau of John Hamilton, and *d* 9 Sept 1764, having had:

1 WILLIAM (Sir), **5th Bt**

1 Helen; *m* 1765 her distant cousin Anthony Murray of Crieff and had issue

2 Joan; *m* 1769 Col Charles Churchill and had issue

The 4th Bt's only son,

Sir William Murray, 5th Bt; *b* 23 Oct 1746; *m* 6 March 1770 Augusta (*d* 20 Jan 1809), yst dau of 3rd Earl of Cromarty (*see* CROMARTIE, E), and *d* 6 Dec 1800, having had:

1 PATRICK, (Sir), **6th Bt**

2 George (Sir), GCB, PC; *b* 6 Feb 1772; Col 1st Royals, Gen, Govr Fort George; *m* 1826 Louisa, sis of 1st Marquess of Anglesey (*qv*) and widow of Lt-Gen Sir James Erskine, Bt, of Torrie, Fife (*d* 1825; *see* 1834 edn), and *d* 28 July 1846, leaving:

(1) Louisa; *m* H G Boyce, 2nd Life Gds (*dsp* 1840)

3 William; *b* 7 June 1791; HEICS; *dsp*

1 Isabella; *m* 1808 James Glassford and *d* 1809

2 Augusta; *m* 14 May 1808 Gen Duncan Campbell of Lochneil (*d* 9 April 1837) and *d* 1846, leaving issue

The 5th Bt's est son,

Sir Patrick Murray, 6th Bt; *b* 3 Feb 1771; advocate 1793, Baron Court Exchequer Scotland 1820; *m* 13 Dec 1794 Mary Anne (*d* 21 Feb 1838), yst dau of 2nd Earl of Hopetoun (*see* LINLITHGOW, M), and *d* 1 June 1837, having had:

1 WILLIAM KEITH (Sir), **7th Bt**

2 John MURRAY later MURRAY-GARTSHORE, of Ravelston, Midlothian; *b* 5 Oct 1804; *m* 1st 11 Aug 1836 Mary (*d* March 1851), 4th dau of Gen Sir Howard Douglas, 3rd Bt, and had:

(1) John; *dsp* Aug 1857

(1) Mary Anne Georgiana, of Ravelston, Midlothian; *b* 1840; *d* unm 4 June 1914

2 (cont.) John MURRAY-GARTSHORE *m* 2nd 29 June 1852 Augusta Louisa (*d* 14 May 1915), only child of Rev George Frederick Tavel by Lady Augusta FitzRoy, dau of 3rd Duke of Grafton (*qv*), and widow of Rev William Casaubon Purdon, of Tinneranna, Co Clare, Vicar Loxley, Warwicks, and *d* 22 June 1884

3 Peter; advocate; *d* 18 Feb 1889

4 George; Army Capt, Ch Constabulary Force Corfu; *d* 24 Feb 1866

5 Henry Dundas; *b* 8 April 1818; Stipendiary Magistrate Gwaler, S Australia; *m* 16 Dec 1857 Jane (*d* 2 March 1867), dau of Robert Travers Lewis, and *d* 1882, leaving:

(1) William Tullibardine; *b* 11 Jan 1863; *m* 1886 May Elizabeth Margaret, dau of James Bell, MD, of Kaipara, NZ, and *d* 1923, leaving:

1a Henry Lamont; *b* 1891

1a Yolande; *b* 1887

(1) Mary Isabel; *m* 8 Jan 1880 Robert Kinloch, WS, of Perth, yst s of Alex John Kinloch of Park, Aberdeenshire, and had issue

1 Mary; m 11 Sept 1839 James Bonar (d 2 March 1867), of Kimmerghame, Berwicks, and d 4 July 1886

2 Georgiana; m 19 Oct 1829 her distant cousin Anthony Murray of Dollerie and d 18 April 1877, having had issue

3 Charlotte Elizabeth; m 29 Oct 1840 Rev Arthur Isham and d 29 Jan 1892, leaving issue (see ISHAM, Bt)

The 6th Bt's est son,

Sir WILLIAM MURRAY later KEITH-MURRAY, 7th Bt; b 19 July 1801; m 1st 28 Nov 1833 Helen Margaret Oliphant (d 28 Oct 1852), only child of Sir Alexander Keith of Dunnottar, Kt Marischal Scotland; m 2nd 8 July 1854 Lady Adelaide Augusta Lavinia Hastings (d 6 Dec 1860), dau of 1st Marquess of Hastings (see LOUDOUN, E), and by his 1st w had, with other issue:

1 PATRICK (Sir), 8th Bt

2 William; b 25 Sept 1837; Offr 60th Rifles; d 7 Sept 1864

3 Alexander; b 28 Oct 1843; m 12 Nov 1889 Helen Mary (d 28 Nov 1931), dau of Maj Alexander Patrick Orr, and d 29 May 1903, leaving, with a dau (d an infant):

(1) Alastair William; b 10 June 1894; 2nd-Lt Black Watch; ka Balkans 8/9 May 1917

4 Henry Arthur; b 7 July 1846; Lt-Cdr RN; m 3 Oct 1872 Rosina Uniacke (d 2 Jan 1899), dau of Hon Edmund Murray Dodd, Judge Supreme Court, Nova Scotia, and d 23 Sept 1918, leaving, with a dau (d an infant):

(1) Harry Edmund Colquhoun; MD, LRCP, LRCS, Edinburgh; b 17 Aug 1873; m 2 June 1903 Dora Amy (d 21 Feb 1956), er dau of C H Barclay, and d 22 March 1922, leaving:

1a Thomas Whitney Uniacke (Rev); b 2 March 1904; educ Haileybury; Vicar Dudley 1951–66, Hon Canon Worcester; m 6 May 1944 Edith Monica (d 23 Jan 1969), dau of Rev Canon W G Mosse, of Sapcote, Leics

2a John Graeme; b 15 July 1906; d 22 Dec 1927

(1) Caroline Mary; m 17 Oct 1912 Rev Canon Bernard Keble Kissack, of Monmouth, s of Rev Canon Edward William Kissack, of Chillenden Rectory, Kent, and d 7 Aug 1954, leaving issue

5 David; b 30 March 1849; m 8 April 1875 Amy Louise (d 18 Nov 1933), dau of Col Phillip Goldney, Bengal Army, and had:

(1) Helen Louise; b 13 April 1876; d 14 June 1877

6 Archibald Lamont; b 6 Aug 1852; m 30 April 1884 Mary Ida Ellen (d 26 Oct 1944), dau of James Hughes, civil surgn, of Nowgong, Assam, and d 18 Dec 1911, having had:

(1) Archie; b 8 July 1886; m 3 Sept 1928 Inez Mary Josephine (d 27 Feb 1938), dau of Maj F G Fox, Indian Police

(2) Walter Herbert; b 7 June 1889; Lt NZEF; ka 26 June 1915

(3) David; b 30 Sept 1900; m 26 Oct 1932 *Nancy May [Mrs David Keith-Murray, 126 Mount Baker Crescent, Salt Spring Island, BC V8K 2J7, Canada], dau of Henri Gautschi, of Vancouver, BC, and d 1968, leaving:

1a +PETER [Maj Peter Keith-Murray, 895 Brentwood Heights, Brentwood Bay, BC V8M 1A8, Canada]; b 12 July 1935; heir presumptive; ret Maj Canadian Forces; m 1960 *Judith Anne, dau of William Andrew Tinsley, of Sarnia, Ont, and has:

1b +(David) Andrew; b 7 Dec 1965

1b *Leslie Anne; b 1961; m 1989 *Paul Joseph Lascelle

2a +(David) Mark [Mark Keith-Murray Esq, 525 Bayliss Rd, Qualicum Beach, BC V9K 2G2, Canada]; b 1939; m 1960 (divorce 1984) Hazel, dau of Amos Pineau, of Prince Edward Island, and has:

1b +David Wayne; b 1961

2b +Christopher Mark; b 1964

1a *Marnie; b 20 Aug 1937; m 1958 (divorce 1979, having resumed maiden name 1978) Douglas Tufts, of Madoc, Ontario, and has:

1b *Paul Anthony; b 1960

2b *Colin Douglas; b 1964

1b *Andrea Dee; b 1959

(1) Georgina Mary; b 20 June 1887

(2) Adelaide Emily; b 4 July 1891

(3) Millicent Ethel; b 25 March 1893

(4) Maude Louisa; d young 13 July 1903

(5) Jean Helen; b 18 Jan 1898

1 Mary Anne Charlotte; m 29 Nov 1888 Rev Edward William Kissack, MA (d 29 April 1901), Rector Chillenden, and dsp 12 June 1927

The 7th Bt d 16 Oct 1861; his est son,

Sir Patrick Keith-Murray, 8th Bt; b 27 Jan 1835; Capt Gren Gds; m 1st 23 Aug 1870 his distant cousin Frances Amelia Jemima (d 7 Oct 1874), 6th dau of Anthony Murray of Dollerie, and d 10 Jan 1921, having had:

1 Sir William Keith-Murray, 9th Bt; b 8 April 1872; educ Harrow and Trin Coll Cambridge (BA 1895); Capt 3rd Bn Black Watch; d unm 4 Feb 1956

2 George; b 6 July 1873; m 5 Oct 1899 Agnes Hunter (d 24 Feb 1967), yr dau of James Richmond, 1st of Kincairney, Murthly, and d 20 Aug 1938

3 Frances Keith; b 3 Sept 1874; d 6 Nov 1875

The 8th Bt m 2nd 30 March 1876 Ione Campbell Penney (d 6 March 1881), dau of Lord Kinloch, Ld of Session, and by her had:

4 Patrick Keith, WS; b 28 Nov 1878; m 15 July 1903 Cecilia Mary Dorothea (d 3 Nov 1964), 2nd dau of Lt-Gen John Sprot, JP, DL, of Riddell, and d 11 June 1937, having had:

(1) PATRICK IAN (Sir), 10th Bt

(2) Robert Malise; b 15 Sept 1906; educ Ardvreck, Bradley Ag Coll and RMC Sandhurst; ADC and Priv Sec to Govr Nyasaland 1939, Maj (Hon Lt-Col) Argyll & Sutherland Highrs WW II, memb Roy Co Archers; m 1st 1940 (divorce 1945) Joan Margaret, er dau of Maj Hugh Kettles-Roy, of London and Nairobi; m 2nd 24 July 1952 Joan Hepburn, er dau of Lt-Col Harold Thompson, DSO, and Mrs Irwin, of Bridge of Allan, Perthshire

(1) *Bethia Ioné [Mrs Bethia Harding-Edgar, 1 Hillpark Ave, Edinburgh 4]; b 30 July 1911; m 25 Aug 1939 (divorce 1966) Paul Nicholas Robert Harding-Edgar, WS (d 1989), s of Paul Harding-Edgar, of Edinburgh, and has:

1a *John George Keith [John Harding-Edgar Esq, 10 Ormidale Terr, Edinburgh EH12 6EQ]; b 13 May 1949; educ Trin Coll Glenalmond and Aberdeen U; m 1976 *Jennifer Kyles and has:

1b *Caroline Julia; b 1982

2b *Louisa Clare; b 1985

3b *Georgina Liska (twin); b 1985

1a *Amanda Elizabeth [Mrs George Hogg, 12 Glencairn Cres, Edinburgh EH12 5BS]; b 26 April 1944; m 1st 24 Aug 1968 John Murray Byers (d 1985); m 2nd 1991 *Capt George Hogg and by her 1st husb has:

1b *James Paul Edward Murray; b 1973

1b *Katharine Lucy Victoria; b 1971

2a *Susan Nicola [Mrs Douglas Lowe, 11 Warriston Cres, Edinburgh 3]; b 19 Aug 1954; m 30 March 1968 *(Ian) Douglas Lowe, MA, Dip Ag, MBA, yr s of John Jamieson Lowe, of St Michael's, Musselburgh, and has:

1b *Cecilia Jean; b 1973

5 John; b 2 March 1881; educ Harrow; d unm 13 Nov 1954

1 Ioné; b 20 Jan 1877; d unm 20 Feb 1937

Sir WILLIAM's nephew,

Sir Patrick Ian Keith-Murray, 10th Bt; b 28 Aug 1904; educ Harrow; tech advsr Mutron Ltd 1947–62, with BBC and PID FO; m 1929 Liska, dau of A T Creet, of Chusick, Kaliphari, India, and d 18 June 1962, leaving:

Sir William Patrick Keith Murray, 11th Bt; b 7 Sept 1939; m 1st 26 April 1963 (divorce 1973) Susan Elizabeth [Mrs James Hudson, Flat 6, 16 Harcourt Terrace, Lonson SW10; Old Ffordfawr, Hay-on-Wye, Herefs] (m 2nd 1976 James Carr Hudson), dau of Stacey Jones, of Hay-on-Wye; m 2nd 1975 *Deirdra (folk singer as Dee Dee Woods), dau of Norman Wood, of Crail, Fife, and d by his own hand 2 Nov 1977, leaving by his 1st w:

Sir PATRICK IAN KEITH MURRAY, 12th and present Bt

MURRAY OF EPPING FOREST

Creation: B. (LP,UK) 1985.

THE BARON MURRAY OF EPPING FOREST, of Telford, Co Shropshire (Lionel (Len) Murray, OBE (1966), PC (1976)) [The Rt Hon The Lord Murray of Epping Forest OBE PC, 29 The Crescent, Laughton, Essex IG10 4PY]; b 2 Aug 1922; educ Wellington (Salop) GS, London U, NCLC and New Coll Oxford; TUC: Ec Dept 1947 (Head Dept 1954–69), Assist Gen-Sec 1969–73, Gen-Sec 1973–84; memb NEDC 1973–84; V-Pres: ICFTU 1973, European Trade Union Confedn 1974; V-Pres: Hearing and Speech Tst, Br Heart Fndn, Ironbridge Museum Tst, Wesley's Chapel; Tstee: Carnegie UK Tst, NUMAST, Crisis at Christmas, Prison Service Tst; V-Chm Nat Childrens' Home; Govr Nat Youth Theatre; Fell QMW 1988; Hon Fell: New Coll Oxford 1975, Sheffield City Poly 1979; Hon DSc: Aston 1977, Salford 1978; Hon LLD: St Andrews 1979, Leeds 1985; m 1945 *Heather Woolf and has:

1 *Stephen William; b 1959

2 *David Paul, MBE (1996); b 1960; S/Ldr RAF; m 1984 *Moira Denise, dau of Fl/Lt Patrick Joseph Roche, of Stillorgan, Dublin, and has:

(1) *Joseph; b 1987

(1) *Elizabeth; b 1985

1 *Nicola Ruth; b 1954

2 *Sarah Isobel [The Hon Mrs Cook, 88 Beamish Close, Northweald, Essex]; b 1959; m 1983 *Ian Cook and has:

(1) *Georgia; b 1987

(2) *Jodie; b 1990

MURTON OF LINDISFARNE

Arms: Argent a lion tricorporate sable, on a chief sable three crosses of St Cuthbert argent. **Crest:** In front of a blackcock, drumming proper, three crosses of St Cuthbert argent. **Supporters:** Dexter, a lion guardant sable, langued and armed gules, gorged with a circlet of St Cuthbert crosses linked argent, pendant therefrom an escallop or; sinister, a like lion similarly gorged, pendant therefrom a portcullis gold, the compartment comprising a grassy mount proper surrounded by water barry wavy azure and argent.
Motto: *Quo eas voca* ('Call things how you will').
Creation: B. (LP, UK) 1979.

THE BARON MURTON OF LINDISFARNE, of Hexham, Co Northumberland (Henry Oscar Murton, OBE (1946),TD (1947 clasp 1951), PC (1976), JP (Poole 1963)) [The Rt Hon The Lord Murton of Lindisfarne OBE TD PC JP, 49 Carlisle Mansions, Carlisle Place, London SW1P 1HY]; *b* 8 May 1914; *educ* Uppingham; commissioned TA 1934, Staff Capt 149 Inf Bde (TA) 1937–39, WW II: Roy Northumberland Fus, Lt-Col Gen Staff 1942–46; md Henry A Murton Ltd 1949–57; memb: Poole Borough Cncl 1961–63, Herrison (Dorchester) Hosp Gp Management Ctee 1963–74; MP (C) Poole 1964–79, Sec C Parly Ctee Housing, Local Govt and Land 1964–67 (V-Chm 1967–70), Chm C Parly Ctee Public Building and Works 1970, PPS to Min Local Govt and Devpt 1970–71, Assist Govt Whip 1971–72, Ld Commr Treasury 1972–73, Second Dep Chm Ways and Means Ctee H of C 1973–74, (First Dep Chm 1974, Chm 1976–79), Dep Speaker 1976–79, Dep Chm Ctees Ho Lds 1981, Dep Speaker Ho Lds 1983; Memb: Exec Ctee Inter-Party Union Br Gp 1970–71, Panel Chm Standing Ctees 1970–71, Jt Select Ctee Lords and Commons Private Bill Procedure 1987–88; Pres Poole C Assoc 1983–95; V-Pres Assoc Municipal Corps; Chllr Primrose League 1983–88; Govr Canford Sch 1972–76; Freeman City London 1977, Wax Chandlers' Co; Past Master Clockmakers' Co; *m* 1st 1939 Constance Frances (*d* 1977), er dau of Fergus O'Loughlin Connell, of Low Fell, Co Durham, and has had:

1 *(Henry) Peter John Connell; *b* 1941; *m* 1962 (*divorce* 1972) Louisa, dau of Maj Percy Montagu Nevile, of Skelbrooke Park, Yorks

1 Melanie Frances Isobel Connell; *b* 1946; *m* 1971 *Ian Lee Vickery, of Amersham, Bucks, and *d* 1986, leaving issue

The BARON MURTON OF LINDISFARNE *m* 2nd 1979 *Pauline Teresa, yst dau of Thomas Keenan, JP, of Johannesburg

Lineage: HENRY EDGAR CROSSLEY MURTON, of Hexham, Northumberland; *m* E M Renton and had an only s:

HENRY OSCAR, *cr* a **Baron**

MUSGRAVE of Hartley Castle

Arms: Az. six annulets or, three, two and one. **Crest:** Two arms embowed in armour ppr., the hands grasping an annulet or.
Motto: *Sans changer* ('Without changing').
Creation: Bt. (E) 29 June 1611.

SIR CHRISTOPHER PATRICK CHARLES MUSGRAVE, 15TH BT, of Hartley Castle, Westmorland [Sir Christopher Musgrave Bt, Ranvilles Cottage, 29 Ranvilles Lane, Fareham PO14 3DX]; *b* 14 April 1949; *s f* 1970; *m* 1978 (*divorce* 1992) Megan, dau of Walter Inman, of Hull, and has:

1 *Helena; *b* 1981

2 *Antonia; *b* 1987

Sir CHRISTOPHER *m* 2nd 1995 *Carol, dau of Geoffrey Lawson, of Winchester

Lineage: THOMAS de MUSGRAVE; held land in and around Musgrave, Westmorland, 1235; *m* Alice, dau and heiress of William de Sandford, of Askham, Cumberland, and *d c* 1246, leaving:

1 Thomas; yeoman 1256; kt by 1265; by 1273 held manors of Musgrave, Sandford and Murton; *m* Sibyl — and *dspm* by 1287, leaving:

(1) Avice; *m* by Oct 1289 Thomas de Hellebek and had:

1a Isabel; *m* Richard de Blencansoppe

2a Margaret; *m* Robert de Swinburne

2 RICHARD

3 Hugh

The 2nd s,

RICHARD de MUSGRAVE; kt; Sheriff Westmorland 1261, Coroner Westmorland to 1297, jt collector tax Cumberland 1297; (?*m* 1st(?)) — and had a dau Alice (*m* Thomas de Neuton); *m* (2nd(?)) by 1292 Christian — and *d* by Jan 1301, leaving by her:

THOMAS de MUSGRAVE; *m* by 1301 Sarah (*m* 2nd Sir Robert de Leyburn, Sheriff Lancs 1322 and 1326, Adml of the North), sis of Sir Andrew de Har(t)cla, 1st and last Earl of Carlise of the March 1321/2 *cr*, through whom the manor of Har(t)cla or Hartley came to the Musgraves, and *d* by 21 Aug 1314, leaving:

THOMAS de MUSGRAVE, 1st LORD (Baron) MUSGRAVE, so *cr* (according to later doctrine) by writ of summons to Parl 25 Nov 1350, although none of his successors were called to Parl by that title or by writ of summons at all; Westmorland: Dep Sheriff 1339, MP 1340–44; a Keeper W March of Scotland March 1345/6, a cdr English Army victory over Scots of Nevill(e)'s Cross Oct 1346, Govr Berwick 1377; *m* 1st Margaret, dau and coheir of William de Ros, of Youlton and S Holme, Yorks; *m* 2nd Isabel, widow of Robert 3rd Lord (Baron) (de) Clifford (*qv*) and dau of 2nd Lord (Baron) Berkeley (*qv*), and *d c* 1385, leaving by his 1st w:

Sir THOMAS de MUSGRAVE ktd by 1372; *dvp* 1372, having had:

Sir THOMAS de MUSGRAVE, JP Westmorland 1390 and Cumberland 1392; ktd 1377, Sheriff Cumberland 1391–92; *m* (1st?) by 1372 Mary, dau of Alan de Strother; *m* (?)2nd(?) and *d c* 1407, leaving issue (probably by his 2nd(?) w):

Sir RICHARD de MUSGRAVE, JP 1410; ktd by 1418, Under-Sheriff Westmorland 1423; *m* Elizabeth, dau of Sir Thomas Beetham, and *d* 9 Nov 1464, having had, with a yr s (Richard, *m* as her 2nd husb Mariota/Mary, widow of William Hilton/Hylton):

THOMAS MUSGRAVE; *m* Joan, er dau and coheir of William Stapilton, of Edenhall (she brought that property to the Musgraves, who subsequently made it their principal seat), and *dvp* by Oct 1457, leaving:

RICHARD MUSGRAVE; *m* Joan, dau of 8th Lord (Baron) Clifford (see DE CLIFFORD, B), and *d* 10 Aug 1491, leaving:

Sir EDWARD MUSGRAVE; *b c* 1461; ktd after victory over Scots of Flodden 1513, at which he fought; *m* 1st *c* 10 Jan 1483/4 Alice, dau of Thomas Radcliffe, and had two daus; *m* 2nd *c* 27 Oct 1496 Joan, dau and ultimate coheir of Sir Christopher Ward, of Givendale, Yorks, and *d* 23 May 1542, leaving:

1 William (Sir); *b c* 1509; ktd 1523; Keeper Bewcastle Castle Cumberland 1531; *m* Elizabeth, widow of Thomas Tamworth and dau of Sir Thomas Curwen, of Workington, and *d* 18 Oct 1544, leaving:

(1) Richard (Sir); *b* Aug 1524; ktd 15–; Keeper Carlisle Castle 1553; *m* Anne Wharton, dau of 1st Lord (Baron) Wharton (*qv*), and *d* 10 or 11 Sept 1555, leaving:

  1a Thomas; *b c* Jan 1546/7; *d c* 1567

  1a Eleanor; *b c* 1546; *m* as his 2nd w Robert Bowes, of Aske, Yorks, and *dsp* 25 July 1623

2 Simon (Sir); *m* Julian, dau of William Ellerker, and *d* 30 Jan 1596/7, leaving:

(1) Christopher; *m* Jane, dau of Sir Henry Curwen, and had:

  1a **Sir Richard Musgrave, 1st Bt** (E), so *cr* 29 June1611, KB 1603; *m* Frances, dau of 3rd Lord (Baron) Wharton (*qv*), and *d* 1615, leaving:

    1a **Sir Philip Musgrave, 2nd Bt**; *b* 21 May 1607; Govr Carlisle, fought royalist side Civil War Battles of Marston Moor 1644, Worcester 1651 and IOM; CHARLES II signed a warrant 1650 to *cr* him BARON OF MUSGRAVE but this was never effected; *m* Julian, yst dau of Sir Richard Hutton, of Goldsborough, Yorks, Judge Court Common Pleas, and *d* 7 Feb 1677/8, leaving:

      1c **Sir Richard Musgrave, 3rd Bt**; *b* June 1635; *m* Margaret, dau of Sir Thomas Harrison, of Allerthorpe, Yorks, by Margaret, dau of 4th Lord (Baron) Darcy and (7th) Conyers (of Knayth) (*see* YARBOROUGH, E), and *dspm* 27 Dec 1687, leaving (with two er children, *dsp*):

        1d Mary; *b* 5 April 1661; *m c* 1680 John Davison, s of Alexander Davison, of Blakiston, Norton, Co Durham, and had issue

      2c **Sir Christopher Musgrave, 4th Bt**; Teller Exchequer 1702; *m* 1st Mary, dau and coheir of Sir Andrew Cogan, Bt, and had, with other issue:

        1d Philip; Clerk Cncl to JAMES II; *m* 1685 Mary (*m* 2nd John Crawford), dau of 1st Baron Dartmouth (*see* DARTMOUTH, E), and *d* 1689, leaving:

          1e CHRISTOPHER (Sir), **5th Bt**

          1e Barbara; *m* Thomas Howard, of Corby Castle (*see* NORFOLK, D)

      2c (cont.) **Sir Christopher** *m* 2nd 15 April 1671 Elizabeth, dau of Sir John Franklin, of Willesden, and had, with other issue:

        2d George, Keeper Ordnance Chatham; had:

          1e George; MP Carlisle; gf of:

            1f George Musgrave (Rev), of Borden, Kent, and Shillington Manor, Beds; *b* 1798; translated Homer's *Odyssey*, author: *Travels in France*; had, with two er daus:

              1g Clare; *m* 12 Dec 1853 Rev John FitzGerald, Vicar St Stephen's Camden Town, and had issue

Sir CHRISTOPHER *d* 1704; his gs,

Sir Christopher Musgrave, 5th Bt; MP Carlisle, Clerk Cncl 1710; *m* 1711 Julia, dau and heiress of Sir John Chardin, of Kempton Park, Middx, whose s made it over to **Sir Philip Musgrave, 6th Bt**, 1746, and had, with three other children:

1 PHILIP (Sir), **6th Bt**

2 Christopher; Fell All Souls, Rector Barking, Essex; *m* 1757 Mrs Perfect, of Hatton Gdn

3 Hans; Lt-Col

4 Chardin; Provost Oriel Coll Oxford

1 Mary; *m* 1st Hugh Lumley; *m* 2nd John Pigot

2 Julia; *m* Edward Hasell, of Dalemain, Cumberland

3 Barbara; *m* 1st John Hogg; *m* 2nd Ch Baron of the Exchequer Idle

4 Anne; *m* Henry Aglionby

Sir CHRISTOPHER *d* 1735; his est son,

Sir Philip Musgrave, 6th Bt; MP Westmorland 1741; *m* 24 June 1742 Jane, dau of John Turton, of Orgreave, Staffs, and had:

1 JOHN CHARDIN (Sir), **7th Bt**

2 Christopher; *m* Elizabeth Anne, 2nd dau and coheir of 2nd and last Lord Archer, Baron of Umberslade, and had two sons and two daus

1 Jane; *m* Joseph Musgrave, of Kypler

2 Elizabeth; *m* Heneage Legge, of Idlicote (*see* DARTMOUTH, E)

3 Charlotte; *m* Rev Charles Mordaunt, of Massingham (*see* MORDAUNT, Bt)

4 Henrietta; *m* Sir John Morris, 1st Bt (*see* MORRIS, Bt, of Clasemont), and *d* 16 Jan 1812

5 Dorothy; *d* unm

Sir PHILIP *d* 5 July 1795; his est son,

Sir John Chardin Musgrave, 7th Bt; *m* 1791 Mary (*d* 1838), dau of Rev Sir Edmund Filmer, Bt, of E Sutton Place, Kent, and *d* 1806, leaving:

1 **Sir Philip Christopher Musgrave, 8th Bt**; MP Carlisle; *b* 1794; *m* 21 Oct 1824 Elizabeth (*d* 21 Aug 1861), 3rd dau of George Fludyer, of Ayston, by Lady Mary Fane, dau of 9th Earl of Westmorland (*qv*), and *d* July 1827, having had:

  (1) Elizabeth Mary; *d* 3 Dec 1844

2 **Rev Sir Christopher John Musgrave, 9th Bt**; *m* Sept 1825 Mary Anne, dau of Edward Hasell, of Dalemain, and *dspm* 11 May 1834, leaving:

  (1) Georgiana; *m* 29 July 1847 Hon Frederick Petre and *d* 11 April 1868, having had issue (*see* PETRE, B)

  (2) Augusta; *m* 1st 27 Aug 1850 Col H F Bonham, 10th Hus; *m* 2nd 26 May 1857 2nd Earl of Stradbroke (*qv*) and *d* 11 Oct 1901, leaving issue

  (3) Edith; *d* 23 March 1849

  (4) Harriet; *m* 28 April 1851 Sir Walter Barttelot, 1st Bt (*qv*), and *d* 29 July 1863

  (5) Fanny; *d* unm 26 Sept 1853

3 GEORGE (Sir), **10th Bt**

4 Thomas; *b* 1802; *d* 1822

1 Julia; *d* 1815

The 9th Bt's bro,

Sir George Musgrave, 10th Bt; *b* 14 June 1799; *m* 26 June 1828 Charlotte (*d* 26 June 1873), dau of Sir James Graham, 1st Bt, of Netherby (*qv*), and had:

1 Philip; *b* 1833; *d* 16 May 1859

2 RICHARD COURTENAY (Sir), **11th Bt**

1 Caroline; *m* 8 March 1859 William Stanley, of Dalegarth and Ponsonby Hall, Cumberland, and *d* 21 Feb 1919, having had issue. He *d* 15 Dec 1881

2 Agnes; *m* 19 June 1862 Rev Malise Richard Graham and *d* 12 March 1901, leaving issue (*see* GRAHAM, Bt, of Netherby)

3 Sophia; *m* 3 Aug 1869 Samuel Steuart Gladstone, JP, 2nd s of Thomas Steuart Gladstone, JP, of Capenoch, Dumfriesshire, and *d* 5 Dec 1922, leaving issue. He *d* 6 May 1909

Sir GEORGE *d* 29 Dec 1872; his 2nd son,

Sir Richard Courtenay Musgrave, 11th Bt, JP; Ld Lt Westmorland, 71st HLI, MP E Cumberland; *b* 21 Aug 1838; *m* 17 Jan 1867 Adora Frances Olga (*m* 2nd 18 April 1882 3rd Baron Brougham and Vaux (*qv*); *d* 17 Dec 1925), only dau of Peter Wells by Adora Julia, dau of Sir John Lethbridge, 3rd Bt (*qv*), and *d* 13 Feb 1881, having had:

1 **Sir Richard George Musgrave, 12th Bt**, DL Cumberland, of Edenhall, Cumberland; Lt 4th Bn Argyll and Sutherland Highrs; *b* 11 Oct 1872; *m* 9 Feb 1895 Hon Eleanor Harbord, Ldy-in-Waiting to HRH PRINCESS VICTORIA (*d* 12 July 1939), 6th surv dau of 5th Baron Suffield (*qv*), and *d* 21 May 1926, having had:

  (1) **Sir (Nigel) Courtenay Musgrave, 13th Bt**; *b* 11 Feb 1896; *educ* Charterhouse; Lt Gren Gds; *d* unm 19 Feb 1957

  (2) Christopher; Cadet RN; *b* 4 May 1899; *ka* off Chile 1 Nov 1914

2 Philip Richard; Lt 3rd Bn Roy Sussex Regt; *b* 26 Nov 1873; *m* 1906 Ellen Watson and *d* 13 June 1929

3 Thomas Charles; *b* 28 Nov 1875; *m* 31 Dec 1810 Ethel (*d* 13 May 1966), dau of Arthur Charles Frost, of Melbourne, Australia, and *d* 30 June 1934, leaving:

  (1) CHARLES (Sir), **14th Bt**

  (1) Dorothy; *b* 9 Nov 1913, VAD WW II; *m* 1 Sept 1959 Albert John Manley, est s of John Manley, of Axminster, Devon

1 Dorothy Anne; *b* 25 June 1869; *m* 12 June 1895 Henry Francis Compton, MP, of Minstead Manor, Lyndhurst, Hants, and *d* 18 June 1944, leaving issue. He *d* 11 April 1943

2 Zoe Caroline; *b* 12 Oct 1871; *m* 16 Jan 1893 Alexander Haldane Farquharson of Invercauld, Aberdeenshire, and *d* 23 Dec 1929, leaving issue. He *d* 17 March 1936

3 Joan; *b* 8 June, *d* 18 Aug 1879

The 13th Bt's cousin,

Sir Charles Musgrave, 14th Bt, of Hartley Castle; Rifle Bde 1934–43, RE 1943–45; *b* 9 Nov 1913; *educ* Thurlestone Coll; *m* 5 June 1948 (*divorce* 1961) Olive Louise Avril (*m* 2nd 1961 Peter Charles Nelson, of Tans End, Wells-on-Sea, Norfolk), dau of Patrick Cringle, of Holme-on-Sea, Hunstanton, and *d* 26 July 1970, leaving:

1 Sir CHRISTOPHER PATRICK CHARLES MUSGRAVE, **15th and present Bt**

2 +JULIAN NIGEL CHARDIN, *b* 8 Dec 1951; heir presumptive; *educ* S Wymondham Coll and Queen Mary Coll London (BSc), *m* 1975 *Gulshanbanu Buddrudin and has:

  (1) *Anar; *b* 1980

  (2) *Ruth; *b* 1983

MUSGRAVE of Tourin

Arms: Az. six annulets or, three, two and one. **Crest:** Two arms in armour, the hands gauntletted ppr. and grasping an annulet or. **Motto:** *Sans changer* ('Without changing'). **Creation:** Bt (I) 2 Dec 1782.

SIR RICHARD JAMES MUSGRAVE, 7TH BT, of Tourin, Co Waterford [Sir Richard Musgrave Bt, Knightsbrook House, Trim, Co Meath, Ireland; Komito, PO Box Syros, Greece]; *b* 10 Feb 1922; *s f* 1956; *educ* Stowe; Capt IA with Poona Horse (17th QVO Cavalry) WW II; *m* 5 Feb 1958 *Maria, only dau of Col Mario Cambanis, of Athens, and has:

1 +CHRISTOPHER JOHN SHANE; *b* 23 Oct 1959; *educ* Cheltenham

2 +Michael Shane; *b* 30 Jan 1968; *educ* Cheltenham

1 *Olivia Mirabel; *b* 30 Nov 1958

2 *Anastasia Maria; *b* 3 Jan 1961; *m* 1980 *Robert Michael Wilson-Wright and has:

(1) *Michael Almroth; *b* 1983

(1) *Sophie Margaret; *b* 1980

3 *Charlotte Elizabeth; *b* 16 Sept 1963; *m* 1989 *James Hanly and has:

(1) *Jack Alexander; *b* 1991

4 *Alexandra Victoria; *b* 19 May 1965

Lineage: RICHARD MUSGRAVE, of Wortley, Yorks; settled in Ireland; *m* Jane Proctor and had:

1 Richard, of Salterbridge, Co Waterford; *d* 1782, having had two daus (*m* Anthony Chearley, of Springfield; the other *m* Richard English, of Littlebridge)

2 Christopher, of Tourin, Co Waterford; *m* Susanah, dau of James Usher, of Ballyntaylor, and *d* Aug 1787, having had:

(1) **Sir Richard Musgrave, 1st Bt** (I), so *cr* 2 Dec 1782, with remainder to the issue male of his father Sir Richard; MP; *m* 10 Nov 1782 Deborah, dau of Sir Henry Cavendish, 2nd Bt (*see* WATERPARK, B), and *dsp* 6 April 1818

(2) John, of Ballylin, Co Waterford; *m* Frances, dau of Richard Kelly, and *dsp* May 1800

(3) **Sir Christopher Frederick Musgrave, 2nd Bt**; *b* 11 Sept 1758; *m* 1st 20 Dec 1781 Jane (*d* 12 April 1795), dau of John Beere, of Ballyboy, Co Tipperary, and had:

1a RICHARD (Sir), **3rd Bt**

2a John; *b* 26 Nov 1792; *d* Nov 1837

1a Anne; *m* 27 April 1801 John Garde, of Ballinacurra, Co Cork, and *d* June 1843

(3) (cont.) **Sir Christopher** *m* 2nd 15 Dec 1797 Elizabeth (*dsp* 28 July 1798), dau of William Nicholson, of Wilmer, Co Tipperary; *m* 3rd 10 May 1801 Catherine (*d* 14 July 1832), dau of Pierce Power, of Affane, Co Waterford, and by her had:

3a Christopher Frederick; *b* 2 March 1802; *d unm* March 1840

Sir CHRISTOPHER *d* Sept 1826; his est son,

Sir Richard Musgrave, 3rd Bt; MP Waterford; *b* 6 Jan 1790; *m* 29 July 1815 Frances (*d* 23 Sept 1875), dau of William Newcome, Archbp Armagh, and *d* 7 July 1859, leaving:

1 **Sir Richard Musgrave, 4th Bt**; *b* 24 Aug 1820; Ld Lt Co Waterford; *m* 30 April 1845 Frances Mary (*d* 7 July 1895), dau of John Ashton Yates, and *d* 8 July 1874, having had:

(1) **Sir Richard John Musgrave, 5th Bt**, JP, DL Co Waterford; High Sheriff 1880; *b* 10 Dec 1850; *m* 23 Sept 1891 Jessie Sophia (*d* 16 Feb 1946), dau of Hon Robert Dunsmuir, of Victoria, BC, and *dspm* 4 March 1930, leaving:

1a Joan Moira Maud; *b* 4 Oct 1892; *m* 11 June 1920 Capt Thomas Ormsby Jameson, Rifle Bde, 2nd s of James Ormsby Jameson, of Dolland, Clonsilla, Co Dublin, and *d* 22 Sept 1953, leaving issue. He *d* 6 Feb 1965

2a Dorothy Frances; *b* 1 Nov 1894; *m* 29 March 1933 Edmund Glen Browne, RN, and Lt RA, of the Hermitage, Glanmire, Co Cork

(1) Maria; *m* 19 June 1873 Hon Cosby Godolphin Trench (*see* ASHTOWN, B) and *d* 4 Nov 1938, leaving issue

(2) Anna Frances; lost at sea 10 Oct 1918

(3) Florence Sophia; lost at sea 10 Oct 1918

(4) Edith Melesina Lovett; *m* 29 Jan 1919 Edward Philips Thompson, JP, of Paulsmoss, Whitchurch, Salop, and *d* 19 Dec 1955. He *d* 1924

2 Christopher; *b* 23 April 1823; *d* 12 Nov 1872

3 Robert; *b* 14 June 1830; *d* 1878

4 Edward, JP Waterford; *b* 13 Oct 1834; *m* 10 June 1858 Anastasia Letitia (*d* 30 Jan 1902), dau of James Gee, of Cappagh, Co Waterford, and *d* 5 Jan 1911, leaving:

(1) James; MICE; *b* 13 Oct 1860; *m* 8 July 1891 Kathleen Const (*d* 31 Jan 1940), dau of Francis Const Barker, of Blackrock, Dublin, and *d* 28 Jan 1930, leaving:

1a CHRISTOPHER NORMAN (Sir), **6th Bt**

2a Francis Edward, MC and bar; Maj RE WW I (despatches) and Indian Rlwys 1920–48; *b* 22 Jan 1894; *educ* Trin Coll Dublin (BAI, BM), *m* 12 June 1919 Kathleen Ethel (*d* 12 Oct 1966), only child of Lt-Col Charles William Grey, RASC, and *d* 1975, having had:

1b *Patricia Kathleen [Mrs David Bay, 11 East Common, Harpenden, Herts]; *b* 11 July 1921; *m* *David Michael Bay and has:

1c *Nicholas Michael [Nicholas Bay Esq, 1 New Cottages, Bendish, Hitchin, Herts]; *b* 1948; *m* 1975 *Jane Lilly

2c *Anthony David; *b* 1951

2b *Shelagh Monica; *b* 8 Feb 1927; *m* 1956 *Michael R P Boyd-Moss and has:

1c *Robin James; *b* 1959

1c *Nicola Margaret; *b* 1958

1a Dorothy Maude; *m* 1 Oct 1936 Thomas Harold Nash-Peake, s of Thomas Nash-Peake, of Watcombe House, Watcombe, nr Torquay

2a Kathleen Joyce; *m* 20 April 1927 Edmund Savile Monckton (*see* GALWAY, V) and *d* 2 Feb 1975, leaving issue

(2) John; *b* 2 June 1868; *m* 19 Aug 1924 Constance Louise (*m* 3rd 13 Nov 1943 Sir Henry Lumley Drayton, KC, PC (*d* 29 Aug 1950), and *d* 14 Sept 1969 aged 89), widow of Francis Wright and dau of James Merrick Gavin, and *d* 10 March 1942

(3) Robert; *b* 28 Aug 1870; *m* 27 March 1905 Amy Lindsay (*d* 28 Aug 1939), dau of Brig-Surgn F Lindsay Dickson, of Vancouver, and *d* 1940, leaving:

1a +Robert John; *b* 1905; *m* 1934 Marjorie Winifred Chinneck (*d* 1973) and has:

1b *Jean Marjorie Frances; *b* 1935

2b *Daphne Edith Amy; *b* 1936

2a Edward Lindsay; *b* 1907; *m* 1949 *Judith Bradfield Stevens [Mrs Edward Musgrave, 2931 Seaview Drive, Victoria, BC, Canada] and *d* 1985, having had:

1b +Anthony Richard; *b* 1955; *m* 1984 *Celia Lydia Mary Lane and has:

1c +Alexander Anthony John; *b* 1991

2b +Robert Lindsay; *b* 1958; has by *Theresa Mary Killoran:

1c *Patrick James Musgrave; *b* 1994

1b *Susan Patricia [Mrs Stephen Reid, PO Box 2421, Sidney, BC, Canada V8L 3Y3]; *b* 1951; *m* 1st 19– *— Nelson and has:

1c *Charlotte Amelia Musgrave; *b* 1989

1b (cont.) Mrs Nelson *m* 2nd 1986 *Stephen Douglas Reid and by him has:

2c *Sophie Alexandra Musgrave; *b* 1989

2b *Mary Kathleen; *b* 1961; *m* 1982 *William Arthur Broughton and has:

1c *Christopher William; *b* 1984

2c *Marcus Edward; *b* 1990

1c *Jennifer Kathleen; *b* 1987

1a Frances Kathleen; *b* 1907; *m* 1936 Ian James Montagu Scott and had issue

(4) Edward Christopher, DSO (1916); Maj KRRC WW I (despatches); *b* 17 Dec 1872; *m* 9 Oct 1901 Louise Muriel Menteith (*d* 22 Dec 1904), 2nd dau of Clermont Livingston, of Cowichan Bay, Vancouver Is, and *d* 19 Nov 1951, leaving:

1a Anastasia Ellen; *d unm* 14 Jan 1965

(5) William Newcome; Capt RASC; *b* 16 Nov 1878; *m* 1914 Madge Violet, dau of Allan Emerson Francis, of Newton, Montgomeryshire, and *d* 4 Aug 1932

(1) Frances Newcome; *b* 13 Oct 1862; *m* 9 Nov 1888 Maj Frederick Dundas Elderton, RAMC

(2) Anastasia Rose; *m* 11 Oct 1911 Capt Harry de Moleyns Mellin, Rifle Bde, of Gordon Head, Victoria, BC, and *d* 18 Feb 1936

5 John; *b* 10 Sept 1840; *d* 1870

Sir RICHARD's cousin,

Sir Christopher Norman Musgrave, 6th Bt, OBE (1952); T/Capt RE WW I (despatches), Lt-Col Staff and OC Signal Coy WW II, Ch Commr Scouts NI; *b* 19 Oct 1892; *m* 3 Jan 1918 Kathleen (*d* 2 May 1967), 3rd dau of Robert Spencer Chapman, of Dartrey Lodge, Moy, Co Tyrone, and *d* 12 May 1956, having had:

1 Sir RICHARD JAMES MUSGRAVE, **7th and present Bt**

2 Christopher Michael; Lt Irish Gds WW II; *b* 19 Feb 1923; *ka* Feb 1944

3 John Anthony Newcome; *b* 30 May 1926; *d* 7 Feb 1929

1 *Elizabeth Anne [Mrs Elizabeth Bates, Pagos 85, Syros, Greece]; *m* 1 June 1955 (*divorce* 1980) Thomas Aydon Bates, only s of Capt Edward Giles Bates, MC, of Aydon, Northumberland, and has:

(1) *Giles Langley [Giles Bates Esq, 44 Peakefield Rd, London SW17 8RP]; *b* 19 March 1963; *educ* Ampleforth; *m* 1994 *Emily Knott and has:

1a *Hester; *b* 17 Dec 1993

21 *Domenica; *b* 9 March 1996

(2) *Benedict Loftus [Benedict Bates Esq, Wayside Cottage, Haydon Bridge, Northumberland NE47 6BZ]; *b* 23 Nov 1964; *educ* Ampleforth, *m* 1993 *Alison Kilner and has:

1a *Dominic Michael; *b* 1990

2a *William Thomas; *b* 1992

3a *Edward; *b* 1994

(1) *Annabelle Carol Elizabeth; *b* 25 Dec 1955; *m* 1980 (*divorce* 1991) Samuel Rodd Morshead, yr s of Maj Christopher Morshead, of Bellewstown House, Co Meath, and has:

1a *Charles Christopher Thomas; *b* 1981

2a *Samuel Harry; *b* 1983

(2) *Belinda Anne [Mrs Robin Erskine, East Dean Row, Langley-on-Tyne, NE47 5LY]; *b* 1 Jan 1957; *m* 1st 1981 David W Pulford, yr s of Rev Walter William Pulford; *m* 2nd 1985 (*divorce* 1997) Robin David Erskine and has issue (*see* MAR and KELLIE, E)

(3) *Corrinne Lucy [Mrs Fawzard Shooshterri, Esp Hill, Haydon Bridge, Northumberland]; *b* 30 March 1958; *m* 1st 1976 (*divorce* 1982) Athanasios Komninos; *m* 2nd 1992 *Fawzard Saffari Shooshterri and has by him:

1a *Sebastian Thomas Dariush; *b* 1985

2a *Felix Ferrydon; *b* 13 March 1995

1a *Francesca Elizabeth; *b* 1988

(4) *Teresa Astrid [Mrs Nicholas Somerville, 63B Elizabeth St, London SW1W 9PP]; *b* 19 July 1959; *m* 1981 *Nicholas C H Somerville, only s of Maj A J Somerville, of Bury St Edmunds, Suffolk, and has:

1a *Fedora Isabella Charlotte; *b* 1989

MUSKERRY

Arms: Arg. two bars gu. **Crest:** Out of a ducal coronet or a demi-sea-otter ppr. **Supporters:** Two angels, habited and winged az., holding in their exterior hands medallions ppr. **Mottoes:** 1 (above crest) *Honor et virtus* ('Honour and virtue'), 2 (under arms) *Forti et fideli nihil difficile* ('Nothing is difficult to the strong and faithful'). **Creations:** Bt. (I) 10 March 1709/10, B. (I) 5 Jan 1781.

THE 9TH BARON MUSKERRY, Co Cork and a Baronet (Sir Robert FitzMaurice Deane, Bt) [The Rt Hon The Lord Muskerry, 725 Ridge Rd, Beren, 4001 Durban, S Africa]; *b* 26 March 1948; *educ* Sandford Park Sch Dublin and Trin Coll Dublin (BA, BAI); md Elgin Brown & Hamer (Pty) Ltd; dir: Port Marine Ltd, Electro Marine Ltd; *m* 1975 *Rita Brink, of Pietermaritzburg, and has:

> 1 +JONATHAN FitzMAURICE; *b* 7 June 1986
>
> 1 *Nicola; *b* 1976
>
> 2 *Catherine; *b* 1978

Viscountcy of Muskerry: In 1628 a title under this name was conferred on Cormac (*alias* Charles) *Og* ('The Younger') Maccarty. His father held a territorial Barony of Muskerry in Co Cork, as had several gnerations of ancestors before him. His son was promoted Earl of Clancarty (*see* CLANCARTY, E, preliminary remarks) but both titles were forfeited by attainder in 1691.

Lineage: Sir **Matthew Deane**, 1st Bt (I), so *cr* 10 March 1709/10; *b* 1626; bought large estates at Dromore, Co Cork; *m* 1st Mary, dau of Thomas Wallis, of Somerset; *m* 2nd Martha, widow of Lt-Col John Nelson and dau of Richard Boyle, Archbp Tuam; *m* 3rd Dorothy, widow of 2nd Earl of Barrymore and dau of John Ferrer, of Dromore, Co Down, and *d* 10 Jan 1710/1, leaving by his 1st w:

Sir **Robert Deane**, 2nd Bt; *m* Anne, dau and coheir of Col William Bettridge, Cromwellian offr, and *d* 14 Sept 1714, leaving:

Sir **Matthew Deane**, 3rd Bt; MP Co Cork; *m* Jane, only dau of Rev William Sharpe, s of Archbp St Andrews, and *d* 11 March 1746/7, having had:

> 1 Sir **Matthew Deane 4th Bt**; MP Cork; *m* Salisbury (*d* 14 Nov 1755), dau and sole heiress of Robert Davis, of Manley Hall, Cheshire, and *dspm*
>
> 2 Sir **Robert Deane**, 5th Bt, PC (I); barrister, MP; *m* 24 Aug 1738 Charleton, 2nd dau of Thomas Tilson, of Dublin, and had, with an est s:
>
>> 1 ROBERT TILSON, **1st Baron**
>>
>> 2 Jocelyn; MP Helston, Cornwall, and Baltimore, Ireland; *b* 1749; *d* Nov 1780
>
> 1 Frances; *m* 1st Col John Hodges, only s of Sir James Hodges; *m* 2nd Jan 1819 Rev Thomas Leman, of Bath

The 5th Bt *d* Feb 1770; his est surv s,

Sir **Robert Tilson Deane**, 6th Bt, and **1st Baron Muskerry** (I), Co Cork, so *cr* 5 Jan 1781, PC (I 1777); Custos Rotulorum Co Limerick 1780–1818, also Govr, MP (I Parl) Carysfort 1771–76 and Co Cork 1776–80; *b* 19 Oct 1745; *m* 7 June 1775 Anne (*d* 30 July 1830), dau of John FitzMaurice and sole heiress (to the tune of £30,000, or over £1,500,000 in late-1990s terms) of her gf John FitzMaurice (*see* LANSDOWNE, M), and *d* 25 June 1818, having had, with two other sons:

> 1 JOHN THOMAS FitzMAURICE DEANE, **2nd Baron Muskerry**, CB (1815); Maj-Gen 1821; *b* 27 Sept 1777; *m* 17 Jan 1815 Sarah (*m* 2nd 1826 Frederick Dundas Radford; *m* 3rd James Dawson; *d* 2 Aug 1852), 2nd dau of M Haynes, of Bishop's Castle, Salop, and *dsp* 24 Dec 1824
>
> 2 MATTHEW FitzMAURICE DEANE, **3rd Baron Muskerry**; *b* 29 March 1795; *m* 1st 13 Aug 1825 Louisa Dorcas (*d* 25 Sept 1846), 2nd dau of Henry Deane Grady, of Lodge, Co Limerick, and had:
>
>> (1) Robert Tilson FitzMaurice DEANE later DEANE-MORGAN (roy licence 14 Dec 1854); *b* 30 June 1826; *educ* Eton; *m* 11 Dec 1847 Elizabeth Geraldine, dau and coheir of H K Grogan-Morgan, of Johnstown Castle, MP, and *d* 28 Feb 1857, leaving an only s:
>>
>>> 1a HAMILTON MATTHEW TILSON FitzMAURICE DEANE later DEANE-MORGAN, **4th Baron Muskerry**, DL Co Limerick; *b* 18 May 1854; served RN, rep peer I 1892; *m* 1st 23 Nov 1872 Flora Georgina (*d* 20 Dec 1902), 3rd dau of Hon Chichester Thomas Foster Skeffington (*see* MASSEREENE and FERRARD, V); *m* 2nd 24 Jan 1905 Lydia (*dsp* 12 July 1915), only dau of G L

Booth; *m* 3rd 1 Aug 1916 Adeline (*d* 14 March 1950), dau of Patrick Ryan, of The Turrets, Charville, and *d* 9 June 1929, having had by his 1st w:

>>> 1b Hamilton Robert Tilson Grogan FitzMaurice; Lt Roy Irish Regt Boer War 1900; *b* 21 Nov 1873; *m* 5 Jan 1904 Eva Susan (*m* 2nd 15 Feb 1911 Godfrey William Edward Massy (*d* 1 June 1923) and *d* 12 March 1958), er dau of William Bolton, of The Island, Co Wexford, and *d* 30 July 1907, leaving:
>>>
>>>> 1c *Eileen; *b* posthumously 14 Aug 1907
>>>
>>> 2b ROBERT MATHEW FitzMAURICE DEANE-MORGAN, **5th Baron Muskerry**; *b* 14 Nov 1874; *m* 1906 Charlotte Jane (*d* 27 July 1960 aged 88), yr dau of John William Henry Irvine, of Mervyn, Co Wexford, and *dsp* 12 July 1952
>>>
>>> 3b MATHEW CHICHESTER CECIL FitzMAURICE DEANE-MORGAN, **6th Baron Muskerry**; *b* 3 Nov 1875; *m* 8 June 1915 Helen Henrietta Blennerhassett (*d* 11 Sept 1952), only surv dau of Surg-Lt-Col Rodolph Harman, AMS, and *dsp* 3 May 1954
>>>
>>> 4b Cormac FitzMaurice; Assist Engr RNR; *b* 1892; accidentally *k* in HMS *Princess Irene* 27 May 1915
>>
>> 1b Flora FitzMaurice; *b* 27 April 1882; *m* 1st 31 Oct 1906 (*divorce* 1915) Edward St George Tottenham Irvine, 16th Lancers, only s of Capt Edward Tottenham Irvine, DL, 16th Lancers, of St Aidan's, Co Wexford, and had issue; *m* 2nd 19 Aug 1918 Capt William R S Harman, RN, s of Surg-Lt-Col Rodolph Harman, AMS, and *d* 10 March 1929. He *d* 5 Aug 1947
>
> (2) Henry Standish FitzMaurice; RN; *b* 29 Aug 1829; *d* 10 Jan 1869
>
> (3) Matthew James Hastings FitzMaurice; Offr 4th Dragoon Gds; *b* 16 Sept 1831; *m* 27 Sept 1871 Maria (*d* Feb 1879), widow of Henry Bagge, of Sholt Castle, Co Cork, and dau of Rev William Banbury, of Shandrum, Co Cork, and *d* 1907, leaving:
>
>> 1a MATTHEW FitzMAURICE TILSON, **7th Baron**
>
> 2 (cont.) The **3rd Baron** *m* 2nd 13 April 1864 Lucy (*d* 16 Jan 1867), widow of Col Aldrich, RE, and *d* 19 May 1868

The 6th BARON's cousin,

MATTHEW FitzMAURICE TILSON DEANE, **7th Baron Muskerry**; *b* 30 July 1874; *m* 1st 6 Oct 1879 Mabel Kathleen Vivienne (*d* 15 Aug 1954), dau of Charles Henry Robinson, MD, FRCSI, and had:

> 1 Matthew FitzMaurice Tilson, MM; 87th Bn Canadian Gren Gds WW I, Merchant Navy WW II; *b* 31 July 1898; *m* 12 May 1936 *Dorothy (*m* 2nd 1968 James Edward Anderton) [Mrs James Anderton, 24 Elm Rd, Windsor, Berks], dau of Charles George Cook, of Kensington, Liverpool 6, and *dsp* 7 July 1956
>
> 2 Victor Leslie FitzMaurice; *b* 26 June 1904; *d* unm 29 Oct 1928
>
> 3 HASTINGS FitzMAURICE TILSON DEANE, **8th Baron Muskerry**; *b* 12 March 1907; *educ* Sandford Park Sch Dublin and Trin Coll Dublin (MA, MB, ChB, DMR); Capt RAMC WW II, consultant radiologist E Transvaal Hosps 1949, radiologist Limerick RHA 1961; *m* 29 Jan 1944 Betty Fairbridge (*d* 1988), dau of Wilfred George Reckless Palmer, of Glenstone, Grahamstown, S Africa, and *d* 14 Oct 1988, leaving:
>
>> (1) ROBERT FitzMAURICE DEANE, **9th and present Baron Muskerry**
>>
>> (1) *Betty Charlotte; *b* 3 July 1951; BA; *m* 1974 *Jonathan Dugdale Sykes and has:
>>
>>> 1a *Daniel Jonathan; *b* 1990
>>>
>>> 1a *Karen Betty; *b* 1985
>
> 1 Marjorie Maria FitzMaurice; *b* 9 April 1900; *m* 16 April 1955 Anthony Deane, s of William Frederick Barker, and *d* 2 Feb 1977

The **7th Baron** *m* 2nd 12 June 1964 Muriel Doreen Sellers, dau of Arthur Gibson Simpson, of Sheffield, and *d* 2 Nov 1966

MUSTILL

Creation: B. (LP, UK) 1992.

THE BARON MUSTILL, of Pateley Bridge, Co N Yorks (Sir Michael John Mustill, PC (1985)) [The Rt Hon The Lord Mustill PC, 42 Lawrier Rd, London NW5 1SJ]; *b* 10 May 1931; *educ* Oundle and St John's Coll Cambridge (Hon Fell 1992); served RA 1949–51; barrister Gray's Inns 1955, QC 1968, Dep Chm Hants QS 1971, Recorder 1972–78, Bencher 1976, High Court Judge Queen's Bench 1978–92, ktd 1978, Presiding Judge NE Circuit 1981–84, Ld Justice Appeal 1985–92, Ld Appeal in Ordinary 1992–97; Chm: Civ Serv Appeal Tbnl 1971–78, Judicial Studies Bd 1985–89, Deptl Ctee Law of Arbitration 1985–90; Pres: Br Maritime Law Assoc and Chartered Inst of Admin, CIArb; LLB Cantab 1992, FBA 1996; author: *The Law and Practice of Commercial Arbitration in England* (with S C Boyd QC, 1982, 2edn 1989), *Anticipatory Breach of Contract* (1990), *Scrutton on Charterparties and Bills of Lading* (jt ed), *Arnould on Marine Insurance* (jt ed); *m* 1st 1960 (*divorce* 1983) Beryl Reid, dau of John Alban Davies, of Chandlers Ford, Hants; *m* 2nd 1991 *Mrs Caroline Phillips and has by his 1st w two sons and a stepdau

Lineage: CLEMENT WILLIAM MUSTILL, of Sandholme Cottage, Pateley Bridge, Yorks; *m* Marion — and had an only s:

MICHAEL JOHN, *cr* a **Baron**

MYNORS

Arms: Sa. an eagle displayed or, beaked and membered gu., on a chief az., bordured arg., a chevron between two crescents in chief and a rose in base of the second. **Motto:** *Spero ut fidelis* ('I hope I may be faithful'). **Creation:** Bt. (UK) 24 Jan 1964.

SIR RICHARD BASKERVILLE MYNORS, 2ND BT, of Treago, Co Hereford [Sir Richard Mynors Bt, Treago, St Weonards, Herefs HR2 8QB]; *b* 5 May 1947; *s f* 1989; *educ* Marlborough, RCM (ARCM 1966, ARCO 1967) and Corpus Christi Coll Cambridge (BA 1969); musician, Assist Dir Music King's Sch Macclesfield 1970–73, Dir Music Wolverhampton GS 1973–81, Merchant Taylors' 1981–88, Belmont Abbey 1988–89; *m* 18 July 1970 *Fiona Bridget, dau of Rt Rev George Edmund Reindorf, DD, Bp Guildford, and has:

1 *Alexandra Fiona; *b* 9 July 1975

2 *Frances Veronica; *b* 3 July 1978

3 *Victoria Jane; *b* 1983

Lineage: PHILIP MYNORS, of Treago, *m* Alice, dau of Gwillim John ap Jenkin, of Llanfair Kilgoed, Mon, and had:

RICHARD MYNORS, of Treago; Sheriff Herefs 1500, Gentleman Usher of the Chamber; *b c* 1450; *m* 1st Joan, dau of William ap Thomas; *m* 2nd 1514 Sybil, dau of Sir James Baskerville, and *d* March 1528, having had, with two er sons (Roger (Sir), of Treago and Windley Hill, Derbys, Serjeant of the Cellar to HENRY VIII, Sheriff Notts and Derbys 1513, ktd 1527; *b c* 1478, *m* 1501 Alice (*d* 19 Jan 1540), widow of Nicholas Knyveton, of Myrcaston, Derbys, and dau of Sir William Myll, of Harescombe, Glos, and *dsp* 1536; Reginald, *d* unm) and five daus:

THOMAS MYNORS, of Treago; *m* 1st Joan, dau of Watkin Vaughan, of Hergest, Radnorshire, and had issue; *m* 2nd Elizabeth, dau of Thomas Dethick, of Newhall, Derbys, and *d* by his own hand 4 July 1539; his only *s*:

RICHARD MYNORS, of Treago; *m* 28 Oct 1538 Anne (*d* Sept 1592), dau of Thomas Burgh, of Guildford, Surrey, and *d* 1550, leaving an est *s*:

RICHARD MYNORS, of Treago; *m* Catherine (*d* Feb 1601), dau of Sir Roger Vaughan, of Porthamel, Breconshire, and *d* Jan 1592, leaving an est *s*:

ROGER MYNORS, of Treago; *m* Jane (*d* Dec 1598), dau of John Harley, of Brampton Bryan, Herefs, and *d* Dec 1615, leaving an est *s*:

ROWLAND MYNORS, of Treago; *m* 1610 Theodosia (*d* Nov 1630), dau of Sir Percival Willoughby, MP, of Middleton, Warwicks (*see* MIDDLETON, B), and *d* April 1651, leaving an est *s*:

ROBERT MYNORS, of Treago; *b* 23 Sept 1616; *m* 21 Feb 1650 Elizabeth (*d* 1727), dau of James Oswald, of St Weonards, Herefs, and *d* 23 Aug 1672, leaving, with nine other children:

1 Crompton, of Treago; *b* 1650; *m* 3 March 1678 Anne, dau of Richard Reed, of Lugwardine, Herefs, and *d* April 1687, leaving a dau (*d* young)

2 Robert, of Treago; *b* 1654; *m* Elizabeth, dau of William Adams, of Monmouth, and *d* June 1710, leaving an er *s*:

(1) Robert, of Treago; High Sheriff Herefs 1735; *b* 1692; *m* 1717 Thomasin, dau and heir of Thomas Gouge, London merchant, and *d* 10 June 1742, leaving an only *s*:

  1a Robert MYNORS later MYNORS GOUGE (by Act of Parl 1756 under terms of his unc Nicholas Gouge's will), of Treago; High Sheriff Herefs 1758; *b* 1721; *m* his 1st cousin Mary (*m* 2nd 19 March 1767 Charles Morgan, of Ruperra, Mon, MP, Ld Lt Breconshire; *d* 24 June 1779), dau and heir of Thomas Parry, of Arkston, Herefs, and *dsp* 7 Feb 1765

1 Theodosia, *b* 1652, *m* 1st 16 June 1670 Roger Boulcott, mercer, of Hereford, and had, with three sons (*dsp*):

(1) Theodosia, *b* 1675, *m* 16 July 1698 Peter Rickards, of Evenjobb, Radnorshire, and *d* March 1724, leaving, with other issue:

  1a Peter, of Evenjobb; High Sheriff Radnorshire 1742; *b* 21 Jan 1716; *m* 30 Sept 1751 his 1st cousin Catherine Witherston and *d* 23 June 1780, leaving:

    1b PETER

1 (cont.) Mrs Roger Boulcott *m* 2nd Richard Witherston, of Burghill, Herefs, and *d* Dec 1700, leaving by him:

(2) Edward; High Sheriff Herefs 1720; *b* May 1684; *m* 1708 Anne, dau of Thomas Barrett, of Jamaica, and had, with several sons:

  1a Catherine; *m* Peter Rickards (*see* above)

PETER and CATHERINE RICKARDS's *s*,

PETER RICKARDS later MYNORS (roy licence 14 Sept 1787), of Treago and Evenjobb; *b* 15 March 1754; *m* 26 Feb 1787 Meliora (*m* 2nd 1819 Capt Jasper Farmar, RM, of Sunnybank, Herefs, DL, JP; *d* 12 Oct 1829), dau and heir of Rev John Powell, of Penland and Clyro Courts, Radnorshire, by the only dau and heiress of Thomas Baskerville, of Aberedw Court, Radnorshire, and *d* 4 Aug 1794, leaving:

1 PETER

2 Thomas Baskerville MYNORS later BASKERVILLE

1 Meliora, *b* 1 Jan 1789, *m* 12 Jan 1815 Hugh Hovell Farmar, JP, of Dunsinane, and *d* 11 Nov 1854, leaving issue. He *d* 26 March 1828

The er son,

PETER RICKARDS MYNORS, of Treago and Evancoyd, Radnorshire, DL, JP; High Sheriff Radnorshire 1825; *b* 27 Nov 1787; *educ* Merton Coll Oxford; *m* 20 Feb 1817 Mary Elizabeth (*b* 9 May 1795; *d* 29 April 1882), dau of Edmund Trowbridge Halliday, of Chapel Cleeve, Somerset, and *d* 20 Jan 1866, having had:

1 ROBERT BASKERVILLE RICKARDS

2 Edmund Baskerville (Rev); Rector Ashley, Wilts; *b* 11 March 1823; *educ* Eton and Balliol Coll Oxford (MA); *m* 19 Feb 1855 Horatia Charlotte Campbell (*d* 13 March 1883), dau of John Crawfurd, of Blackbrook House, Mon, Govr Singapore, and *d* 28 June 1906, having had:

(1) Roland Crawfurd Baskerville; *b* Nov 1855; *d* Aug 1863

(1) Alice Eleanor; *b* 15 Nov 1857; *m* 21 June 1877 Charles William Jervis SMITH later CRAWFURD (roy licence 13 Sept 1909 on death of his w's uncle J O Crawfurd), of Great Fenton, Staffs, and *d* 30 Jan 1927, leaving issue. He *d* 2 March 1918

(2) Sybil Agnes; *b* 10 Sept 1860; *m* 1st 23 Oct 1888 Arthur Hoare (*d* 26 Jan 1919), of Trull, Glos; *m* 2nd 6 Sept 1923, as his 2nd w, Lt-Col Henry George Ricardo, DSO, RA (*d* 15 Dec 1940), of Gatcombe Park, Glos, and *dsp* 14 Oct 1947

(3) Margaret Beatrice; *b* 25 Feb 1864; *m* 31 Jan 1888 Very Rev Charles Edward Thomas Griffith (*d* 25 June 1934), of Braich-y-Celyn, Merioneths, Dean Llandaff, and *d* 17 Nov 1934, having had issue

(4) Violet Mary; *b* 21 Aug 1866; *m* 2 June 1892 Robert Wake Pretor-Pinney, 2nd *s* of Frederick Wake Pretor-Pinney, of Somerton-Erleigh, Somerset, and *d* 14 May 1938, leaving issue. He *d* 29 May 1950

3 Walter Baskerville (Rev), JP; Rector Llanwarne, Herefs; *b* 28 Aug 1826; *educ* Eton and Oriel Coll Oxford (BA); *m* 3 April 1856 Caroline (*b* 10 March 1831; *d* 3 Oct 1922), er dau of Henry Clay, of Foremark Hall, Derbys, and Piercefield Park, Mon, and *d* 11 Feb 1899, having had:

(1) Harry Walter Baskerville (Rev); Rector Llanwarne with Llandinabo, Herefs; *b* 28 Oct 1857; *educ* Repton and BNC Oxford (BA); *m* 11 Jan 1906 Edith Katharine (*d* 20 Oct 1937), 3rd dau of William Henry Barneby, of Longworth, Herefs, and *dsp* 6 June 1938

(2) Nigel Baskerville; *b* 22 Aug 1862; *educ* Repton; drowned there 12 June 1880

(3) Aubrey Baskerville (Rev); Rector Langley Burrell, Wilts, Vicar St John Evangelist Clifton, Stratfield Mortimer, Berks, Kempsford with Whelford, Glos, and Bridstow, Herefs; *b* 13 April 1865; *educ* Repton and Oriel Coll Oxford (MA); *m* 11 April 1901 Margery Musgrave (*d* 28 July 1974), yst dau of Rev Charles Musgrave Harvey (*see* HARVEY, Bt), and *d* 11 April 1937, leaving:

  1a Roger Aubrey Baskerville (Sir); *b* 28 July 1903; *educ* Eton and Balliol Coll Oxford (BA 1926, MA 1929); Fell and Classical Tutor Balliol Oxford 1926–44, Visiting Lecturer Harvard 1938, T/Pncpl Treasury 1940–45, Kennedy Prof Latin Cambridge and Fell Pembroke Coll 1944–53, Corpus Christi Prof Latin Language and Lit Oxford and Fell Corpus Christi Coll 1953, FBA 1944, Hon LittD Cantab, Hon DLitt Durham and Edin, Hon Fell Balliol Coll Oxford and Pembroke Coll Cambridge, ktd 1963; *m* 12 Dec 1945 *Lavinia Sybil, MB, BS (Lond), 3rd dau of Very Rev Cyril Argentine Alington, Dean Durham; *d* 17 Oct 1989

  2a HUMPHREY CHARLES BASKERVILLE (Sir), **1st Bt**

  3a *Thomas Halliday Baskerville [Thomas Mynors Esq, Ashlea, Stone Cross Rd, Wadhurst, E Sussex TN5 6LR]; *b* 1 Aug 1907; *educ* Marlborough and Oriel Coll Oxford (BA); Sudan Political Serv 1930–54, Chm E Sussex CC 1975 and Cncl Sussex U 1980–85, Hon LLD; *m* 15 May 1938 Dagmar, er dau of Carl Elinar Sjogren, of Sweden, and has had:

    1b *Peter Thomas Baskerville [Peter Mynors Esq, Saddlers, Cousley Wood, Wadhurst, E Sussex TN5 6EF]; *b* 2 Jan 1943; *educ* Marlborough and Oriel Coll Oxford (MA), ptnr Coopers & Lybrand 1975; *m* 5 Sept 1970 *Rosemary Anne, yr dau of Lt-Col Oscar Leslie Boord, MC (*see* BOORD, Bt), and has:

      1c *Robert Thomas Baskerville; *b* 5 Aug 1976; *educ* Marlborough and Oxford Brook's U

      1c *Camilla Greta Baskerville; *b* 24 Aug 1974; *educ* Downe House and Southampton U

    1b Margaret Dagmar Baskerville; *b* 16 Feb 1941; *m* 3 June 1967 Michael Edward Randall Lambert, yr *s* of Ven Charles Edmund Lambert, Rector St James's, Piccadilly, and *d* 18 July 1970, leaving:

      1c *Charles Michael; *b* 4 May 1969; *educ* Stowe and Ch Ch Oxford

    2b *Charlotte Birgitta Baskerville [Mrs Timothy Frost, The Manor House, Ogbourne St George, Wilts SN8 1SU]; *b* 21 Dec 1946; *m* 28 Sept 1968 *Timothy Oliver Frost, only *s* of Oliver Harry Frost, MBE, MC, of The Manor House, Ogbourne St George, Wilts, by Hon Joyce Ida Jessie, only dau of 2nd Baron Swaythling (*qv*), and has:

      1c *Samuel Timothy Einar; *b* 20 Oct 1973; *educ* Marlborough

      2c *Zachary Oliver Gustav; *b* 30 Aug 1975; *educ* Marlborough

3c *Roger Harry Gosta; *b* 26 July 1978; *educ* Marlborough and Southampton U

4a *David Rickards Baskerville, OBE [Maj David Mynors Esq OBE, The Old Vicarage, Moulsford, Wallingford, Oxon OX10 9JB]; *b* 16 Sept 1915; *educ* Eton and New Coll Oxford (MA); Maj Scots Gds M East and Italy WW II (despatches, US Bronze Star), with Courtauld's 1937–67 (dir 1955), dir Nat Provident Instn 1957–87 (dep chm 1968–87), Imperial Tobacco 1967–71, RFD Gp 1972–86 (chm 1974–83), Beresfords Gp 1976–87 (chm 1980–87), HP Bulmer 1974–83, memb Oxon HA 1974–85 (v-chm 1979–85), memb Ct of Assists Weavers' Co 1955 (Upper Bailiff 1968–69); *m* 6 July 1938 *Mary Laurence, est dau of Charles Leslie Garton, of Great Oaks, Goring Heath, Oxon, and has:

1b *Robert David Baskerville [Robert Mynors Esq, Gorehill House, nr Petworth, W Sussex GU28 0JJ]; *b* 28 May 1939; *educ* Eton and New Coll Oxford (BA 1962); chartered accountant, 2nd Lt Welsh Gds 1957–59; *m* 19 Sept 1970 *Jane Elizabeth Charlotte Pike, dau of Bp of Sherborne, and adopted:

*Harry Robert Baskerville; *b* 11 Aug 1975; *educ* Eton and Magdalen Coll Oxford

*Sibella Elizabeth Baskerville; *b* 31 Dec 1977; *educ* Wycombe Abbey and Edinburgh U

2b *Peter Leslie Baskerville [Peter Mynors Esq, 25 Hillcroft Crescent, London W5 2SG]; *b* 9 July 1941; *educ* Marlborough and New Coll Oxford; FICE, FIHT, consulting engr Travers Morgan and Symonds Gp; *m* 1 Feb 1968 *Angela Elles, dau of Lt-Col Evelyn Arundel Medows Norie, DSO, and has:

1c *Rowland Peter Baskerville; *b* 1 April 1972; *educ* Latymer Upper and Southampton U

1c *Geraldine Angela Baskerville; *b* 22 July 1969; *educ* Notting Hill and Ealing High School and New Coll Oxford; *m* 16 Sept 1995 *Dr Iain Alexander McNeish, s of Prof Alexander McNeish of Glasgow and Birmingham

3b *Edward Baskerville [Edward Mynors Esq, High Copse, Forestside, Rowlands Castle, Hants PO9 6ED]; *b* 11 Nov 1946; *educ* Winchester and Birmingham U; *m* 31 Jan 1970 *Janet Elizabeth, dau of Bernard Crompton Bischoff, of Churt, Surrey and adopted:

*Philip Edward Baskerville; *b* 17 March 1980; *educ* Milton Abbey

*Sophie Elizabeth Baskerville; *b* 4 Dec 1984; *educ* Godolphin Sch Salisbury

4b *James Baskerville [The Rev James Mynors, The Rectory, High St, Fowlmere, Royston, Herts SG8 7SU]; *b* 5 April 1949; *educ* Marlborough, Peterhouse Cambridge and Ridley Hall Cambridge; *m* 22 Jan 1977 *Helen, dau of Geoffrey Taylor, of Pinner, Middx, and has:

1c *Thomas Baskerville; *b* 7 Aug 1989

5b *Charles Baskerville [Charles Mynors Esq, 16 Elm Crescent, London W5 3JW]; *b* 27 Aug 1953; *educ* Eton and Corpus Christi Coll Cambridge; FRTPI, ARICS, barrister Middle Temple (planning and ecclesiastical law), Dep Chllr Dioces of Worcester 1998–; *m* 18 Nov 1978 *Janet Lennox, dau of Francis Wardrop, of Johannesburg, and has had:

1c *David Francis Rickards; *b* 25 June 1997

1c Katherine Janet Rickards; *b* 13 Oct 1982; *educ* Notting Hill and Ealing High Sch; *d* 20 Feb 1996

2c *Elizabeth Lavinia Rickards; *b* 20 Feb 1985; *educ* Notting Hill and Ealing High Sch

1b *Eleanor Mary Baskerville [Mrs Peter Davies, Conway, Croft Drive West, Caldy, Wirral L48 2JQ]; *b* 5 Dec 1950; *educ* St Mary's Calne; *m* 29 March 1975 *Dr Peter D O Davies, only s of Rev H L O Davies, of The Rectory, Bourton-on-the-Hill, and has:

1c *Richard Peter Owen; *b* 1 Nov 1976; *educ* Birkenhead Sch and Edinburgh U

2c *Edward John; *b* 12 Dec 1978; *educ* Birkenhead Sch

3c *Michael David Owen; *b* 21 Oct 1985

1c *Mary Elizabeth; *b* 17 Aug 1982; *educ* Moreton Hall

1a Winifred Mary Baskerville; *b* 22 May 1902; *m* 8 April 1931 Thomas Francis Vivian Matthews, MC, JP, Capt Worcs Regt, and S/Ldr RAFVR, s of Thomas Gadd Matthews, of Newport Towers, Glos, and *d* 5 Oct 1992, leaving three sons

(1) Evelyn Baskerville; *b* 9 Dec 1860; *m* 30 Aug 1894 Francis Lloyd Oswell, yst s of Rev Henry Lloyd Oswell, and *d* 4 Dec 1915, leaving issue. He *d* 19 Jan 1940

4 Thomas Baskerville, of Pontshony, Aberedw, Radnorshire, JP; *b* 10 Dec 1834; *educ* Eton and Ch Ch Oxford; *m* 1 Aug 1865 Constance Mary (*d* 29 May 1889), est dau of Sir Richard Green-Price, 1st Bt (*qv*), and *dsp* 11 March 1906

1 Mary Meliora; *b* 16 Aug 1821; *d* 9 April 1822

2 Mary Philippa; *b* 17 Sept 1832; *m* 14 Aug 1856 Col George Henry Warrington Carew, King's Dragoon Gds, of Carew Castle, Pembs, and Crowcombe Court, Somerset, est s of Thomas George Warrington Carew, and *d* 17 March 1913, having had issue. He *d* 24 Jan 1874

The est son,

ROBERT BASKERVILLE RICKARDS MYNORS, of Treago and Evancoyd, DL, JP Radnorshire; *b* 1 July 1819; *educ* Eton and Ch Ch Oxford (MA); High Sheriff Radnorshire 1856, Capt Herefs Militia, barrister; *m* 30 Sept 1852 Ellen Gray (*d* 1 June 1910), only child of Rev Edward Higgins, of Bosbury House, Herefs, and *d* 21 Sept 1889, having had:

1 Willoughby Baskerville, of Treago, Evancoyd and Bosbury, JP, DL (Radnorshire); *b* 25 Nov 1854; *educ* Eton and Ch Ch Oxford; Radnorshire: CC, High Sheriff 1891, Lt 7th Hus and 4th Dragoons, Maj Salop Yeo Cav; *m* 2 Sept 1884 Mabel Katherine (*d* 25 April 1928), est dau of William Stevenson, of Boquhan, Stirlingshire, and *dsp* 14 Aug 1914

2 Arthur Clynton Baskerville; Lt 60th Rifles; *b* 17 Aug 1856; *educ* Eton and RMC Sandhurst; *d* unm 25 April 1879

3 Charles Baskerville; *b* 9 Aug 1859; *d* 13 June 1863

4 Audley Baskerville; *b* 28 Nov 1861; *d* unm Queensland 8 Dec 1892

---

1 Beatrice Eleanor; *b* and *d* 16 Dec 1857

2 Eleanor Mary, of Treago and Barland, Radnorshire; *b* 6 Aug 1864; *d* unm 1 June 1940; *s* by her first cousin once-removed

The Rev AUBREY MYNORS's 2nd s,

Sir Humphrey Charles Baskerville Mynors, 1st Bt (UK), so *cr* 24 Jan 1964; *b* 28 July 1903; *educ* Marlborough and Corpus Christi Coll Cambridge (BA 1925, MA 1929); Hon DCL Durham 1955, Hon Fell Corpus Christi Coll Cambridge 1926–33, Hon Fell 1953, with Bank of England 1933–64, Dir 1949–54, Dep Govr 1954–64; *m* 14 Oct 1939 Lydia Marian (*d* May 1992), MA (Camb), only dau of Sir Ellis Hovell Minns, Disney Prof Archaeology Cambridge, LittD, FSA, FBA, and *d* 25 May 1989, having had:

1 John Humphrey Baskerville, *b* 3 Oct 1942; *d* 29 Aug 1943

2 Sir RICHARD BASKERVILLE MYNORS, **2nd and present Bt**

1 *Elizabeth Baskerville [Mrs Jeremy Russell, Batch Cottage, Almeley, Hereford HR3 6PT]; *b* 21 Aug 1940; *educ* Downe House Newbury and Newnham Coll Cambridge (BA 1961); *m* 24 Feb 1962 *Jeremy Longmore Russell, 2nd s of Harold George Bedford Russell, and has:

(1) *Thomas Lancelot; *b* 26 Feb 1965; *educ* Eton and Swansea U

(1) *Jennifer Frances; *b* 2 Jan 1969; *educ* Godolphin & Latimer, Marlborough and Warwick U

2 *Catherine Baskerville [Mrs Christopher Richards, 4 St Ronan's Ave, Redland, Bristol BS6 6EP]; *b* 2 May 1944; *m* 30 July 1966 *Christopher Mordaunt Richards, er s of Dr Arthur Hubert Mordaunt Richards, TD, of Munstead Lawn, Godalming, and has:

(1) *Benedict William Mordaunt; *b* 3 Feb 1972

(1) *Sophia Janet; *b* 19 Oct 1969

(2) *Clare Eleanor; *b* 28 Nov 1974

3 *Philippa Baskerville [Mrs Alan Duce, 2 Temple Gdns, Lincoln]; *b* 30 July 1950; *m* 28 May 1977 *Rev Alan Duce and has:

(1) *Patrick Richard; *b* 1984

(1) *Eleanor Rachel; *b* 1 July 1979

(2) *Catherine Veronica; *b* 1 Dec 1981

4 *Jane Margery Baskerville [Mrs Nicholas King, 12 Whiteford Rd, Mannameads, Plymouth PL3 5LX]; *b* 3 Oct 1952; *m* 27 April 1974 *Nicholas Kersteman King, yr s of Edmund King, of Bristol, and has:

(1) *Hugh Samuel; *b* 26 Aug 1982

(1) *Theresa Jane; *b* 30 Dec 1977

(2) *Jennifer Vivien; *b* 16 Jan 1980

NAIRN

Arms: Per fess arg. and sa., on a chaplet four escallops all counterchanged. **Crest:** Three thistles conjoined in stalk, entwined with two roses, all slipped ppr. **Motto:** *Usque conabor* ('I shall strive to the limit'). **Creation:** Bt. (UK) 16 Dec 1904.

SIR MICHAEL NAIRN, 4TH BT, of Rankeilour, Collessie, and Dysart House, Dysart, Co Fife, DL (Perth and Kinross 1996) [Sir Michael Nairn Bt DL, PO Box 55, Dundee DD1 9JJ]; *b* 1 July 1938; *s f* 1984; *educ* Eton and INSEAD; *m* 1st 23 Sept 1972 Diana Gordon (*d* 1982), er dau of Leonard Bligh, of Pejar Park, Woodhouselee, NSW, Australia, and has:

1 +MICHAEL ANDREW; *b* 2 Nov 1973

2 +Alexander Gordon; *b* 11 Aug 1975

1 *Emma Helen Beatrice; *b* 16 Sept 1980

Sir MICHAEL *m* 2nd 1986 *Sally Jane, yr dau of Maj William P S Hastings, of Brandy Well, Eglingham, Alnwick, Northumberland, and formerly w of Maj Ivan Charles Straker

Lineage: MICHAEL NAIRN (s of James Nairn, of Kirkcaldy, Fife), of The Priory, Kirkcaldy; fndr Scottish floorcloth industry; *b* 4 April 1804; *m* 15 Dec 1834 Catherine (*d* 3 May 1891), dau of Alexander Ingram, of Kirkcaldy, by Euphemia Burt, and *d* 18 Jan 1858, having had:

1 MICHAEL BARKER (Sir), **1st Bt**

2 Robert; *d* unm 6 June 1886

3 John, of Kirkcaldy; *b* 4 April 1853; *m* 1st Mary Macdonell Methven; *m* 2nd 8 Oct 1889 Gertrude (*d* 30 Sept 1927), dau of Roderick Allison Couper, and *d* 12 March 1928, leaving issue

1 Isabella Barker; *d unm* 12 March 1882

2 Euphemia; *d* 23 Nov 1921

The eldest son,

Sir Michael Barker Nairn, 1st Bt (UK), so *cr* 16 Dec 1904, of Rankeilour, Springfield, Fife, JP; *b* 29 May 1838; Hon Fell Educnl Inst Scotland, Chm Kirkcaldy Sch Bd and Michael Nairn & Co, Nairn Linoleum USA, Compagnie Française de Linoleum Nairn Orly and Germania Linoleum-Werke; *m* 7 June 1866 Emily Frances (*d* 1 June 1939), dau of Alfred Rimington Spencer, of Byfleet, Surrey, and had:

1 MICHAEL (Sir), **2nd Bt**

2 Sir ROBERT SPENCER-NAIRN, 1st Bt (*qv*)

3 Alfred Douglas; *b* 23 May 1882; *d* 12 Nov 1895

1 Catherine Ann; *b* 27 March 1867; *m* 7 Sept 1892 William Black, of St Mary's Priory, Kirkcaldy, and Chapel, Kingskettle, Fife, s of William Black, of Monkshill, Foveran, Aberdeenshire, and *d* 6 Sept 1955, leaving issue. He *d* 23 Sept 1922

2 Emily Frances; *b* 24 Nov 1868; *d unm* 16 May 1958

3 Edith Blanche; *b* 18 Feb 1871; *m* 24 June 1916 James Harry Sinclair Holroyd, JP, 5th s of George Barron Holroyd, of W Byfleet, Surrey, and *dsp* 1 April 1965. He *d* 11 July 1959

4 Euphemia; *b* 23 Aug 1872; *m* 5 Dec 1899 Harry Oliphant Nicholson, MD, FRCP, s of Henry Alleyne Nicholson, MD, FRS, of Aberdeen, and *d* 12 March 1942, leaving issue. He *d* 26 May 1941

5 Isabella; *b* 1 Oct 1875; *m* 19 Jan 1909 Sir John William Thomson-Walker, OBE, MB, FRCS, DL, 2nd s of John Henry Walker, JP, of Fife, and had issue. He *d* 5 Oct 1937

6 Mary; *b* 25 Dec 1876; *m* 12 March 1910 William Keir Balfour (*see* BALFOUR OF BURLEIGH, L) and *d* 29 Sept 1952

7 Lucy; *d young* 29 April 1881

8 Dorothy Clare; *b* 7 May 1884; *m* 20 Aug 1921 Bruce B Thomas (*d* 5 Jan 1965) and had:

(1) *David Bruce; *b* 1924; *m* 1948 *Betty, dau of Joseph W Milligan, of Manchester, and has:

1a *Alison Edith; *b* 1952

2a *Patricia Dorothy; *b* 1958

(1) *Emily Jocelyn [Mrs Athol Robertson, Clovelly, Bonalbo, NSW, Australia]; *b* 29 March 1930; *m* 6 April 1957 Athol Bruce Robertson (*d* 1967), only s of Samson Bruce Robertson, of Scarborough, Qld, and has:

1a *Duncan Bruce; *b* 7 April 1958

1a *Elspeth Clare; *b* 24 Aug 1960

2a *Fiona Frances; *b* 4 March 1962

The 1st Bt *d* 24 Nov 1915; his est s,

Sir Michael Nairn, 2nd Bt, DL and JP Fife; Dir Bank of Scotland, chm Michael Nairn and Greenwich Ltd; *b* 19 Feb 1874; *educ* Edin Acad, Sherborne and Marburg U Germany; *m* 12 June 1901 Mildred Margaret (*d* 16 Oct 1953), est dau of George Watson Neish, and had:

1 (MICHAEL) GEORGE (Sir), **3rd Bt**

1 Rachel Emily; *b* 13 June 1902; *m* 2 June 1925 Maj Arthur Frederic Purvis, MC, Scots Gds, est s of William Herbert Purvis. He *d* 20 March 1955

2 Constance Jane; *b* 20 Aug 1904; *m* 12 Jan 1928 John Inglis (*d* 27 July 1960), est s of William Inglis, of Granton House, Edinburgh, and had:

(1) *Sally Elizabeth Jane [Mrs Peter Loyd, Towersey Manor, Thame, Oxon]; *b* 18 Jan 1931; *m* 4 March 1958 *Maj Peter Wyndham Loyd, Coldstream Gds, yr s of William Lewis Brownlow Loyd, of Upper House, Shamley Green, Surrey, and has:

1a *Andrew Wyndham; *b* 1 Nov 1962

1a *Henrietta Jane Rachel; *b* 31 Jan 1959

(2) *Constance Mary Teresa [Mrs Ronald Cunningham-Jardine, Fourmerkland, Lockerbie, Dumfriesshire]; *b* 14 Aug 1936; *m* 19 Sept 1959 *Capt Ronald Charles Cunningham-Jardine, RSG, s of Charles Cunningham-Jardine, of Fourmerkland, and Woodend, Banchory, Kincardineshire, and has:

1a *John Charles; *b* 11 Nov 1961

1a *Rachel Mary; *b* 28 Dec 1963

3 Mildred Brenda; St Olaf medal Norway 1957; *b* 20 Oct 1906; *m* 4 Nov 1930 Lt-Col Sir William Giles Newsom Walker, TD, DL, Fife and Forfar Yeo (*d* 26 March 1989), est s of Harry Giles Walker, of Over Rankeillour, Cupar, Fife, and *d* 11 Sept 1983, leaving

(1) *Michael Giles Neish [Michael Walker Esq, Shanwell, Milnathort, Kinross-shire]; *b* 28 Aug 1933; *educ* Shrewsbury and St John's Coll Cambridge; Maj Fife and Forfar Yeo; *m* 27 Jan 1960 *Margaret Ruby, yr dau of Lt-Col John David Hills, MC, MA (*see* CROMER, E), and has:

1a *Simon Giles David; *b* 9 March 1961

2a *Geordie Michael; *b* 6 July 1966

1a *Nicola Margaret; *b* 17 July 1965

(1) *Margaret Elizabeth Bluebell [Mrs John Williams-Ellis, Backnamullogh House, Dromore, Co Down BT25 1QP]; *b* 11 Aug 1931; *m* 1st 29 July 1954 (*divorce* 1980) John Kay Pringle Mackie, est s of John Pringle Mackie, CBE, DL, of Ringdufferin, Toye; *m* 2nd 10 Dec 1983 *John Richard Baldwyn Williams-Ellis, DL, FLAS, only s of Martyn Ivor Williams-Ellis, OBE, DL, of Porthmadoc, Gwynedd, and by her 1st husb has:

1a *James William Pringle; *b* 28 Nov 1956; *m* 27 July 1983 *Andrea Jane, est dau of James Innes, of Denia, Spain, and has:

1b *Nicolas John Giovani; *b* 16 Dec 1989

1b *Alexandra Lynette; *b* 2 Feb 1988

1a Charlotte Rose; *b* 18 May 1959; *d unm* 22 Jan 1994

2a *Sara Georgina; *b* 10 Sept 1964; *m* 19 June 1996 *Dimitri Zarlas, s of Andreas Zarlas, of Athens, and has:

1b *Katerina Charlotte; *b* 11 April 1996

(2) *Angela Rachel; *b* 22 May 1938; *m* 18 July 1958 *Jeremy Hugh Dewhurst, only s of Lt-Col Hugh Littleton Dewhurst, RA (*see* FORTEVIOT, B), and has:

1a *Charles Hugh; *b* 21 Feb 1961

2a *James Edward; *b* 2 Jan 1963

4 Elizabeth Barbara; *b* 15 Jan 1915; *m* 1st 5 Aug 1938 (*divorce* 1947) Maj Alexander Oliphant Hutchison, Fife and Forfar Yeo, est s of Alexander Hutchison, and had:

(1) *Roderick Alexander Oliphant [Roderick Hutchison Esq, Chalet La Bernoise, Coriengy, 74450 St Jean de Sixt, France]; *b* 24 Aug 1943; *educ* Fettes; *m* 8 Aug 1970 *Gillian Mary, dau of Lt-Cdr R L Boddy, RN, of Roshven, Lochaillort, Inverness-shire

(2) *Edward Anthony Oliphant [Edward Hutchison Esq, 19 Dover Park Dve, London SW15 5BT]; *b* 17 June 1946; *educ* Eton; *m* 1971 *Polly Matilda Saunders and has:

1a *Jeremy George Oliphant; *b* 1979

1a *Daisy Frances Alexandra; *b* 1977

(1) *Caroline Victoria Oliphant [Lady Marshall, Old Inn House, Slindon, W Sussex]; *b* 10 Oct 1941; *m* 1st 6 July 1963 (*divorce* 1970) George Charles Caswell Cornelius, s of C C C Cornelius, of Malton, Yorks, and has:

1a *Deborah Caswell Oliphant; *b* 25 Feb 1965

2a *Katherine Caswell Oliphant; *b* 20 Jan 1967

(1) (cont.) Mrs Caroline Cornelius *m* 2nd 1973 *Sir (Robert) Michael Marshall, MP (C) Arundel Feb 1974–97

4 (cont.) Mrs Elizabeth Hutchison *m* 2nd 11 March 1948 (*divorce* 1958) Leon Robert de Notto, s of Anthony de Notto-Izycki, of Cracow, Poland; *m* 3rd 19 Oct 1961 *(John) Michael Wentworth [Michael Wentworth Esq, Gainsborough House, 69 High St, Odiham, Hants RG29 1LB], and *d* 8 April 1997

Sir MICHAEL *d* 24 Sept 1952; his only son,

Sir (Michael) George Nairn, 3rd Bt, TD, DL (1955); *b* 30 Jan 1911; *educ* Trin Coll Glenalmond; Maj Black Watch WW II (wounded), Chm Nairn & Williamson Hldgs 1957, Kirkcaldy and Dist TSB; *m* 5 Nov 1936 *Helen Louise [Helen Lady Nairn, Wester-Pitcarmick, Bridge of Cally, Blairgowrie, Perthshire PH10 7NW], yr dau of Maj Ernest James Webster Bruce, MC, RFA, of Melbourne, Australia, by Mrs Leonard Ware Graham Clarke, and *d* 1984, leaving:

1 Sir MICHAEL NAIRN, **4th and present Bt**

2 +Charles Bruce; *b* 17 Sept 1942; *educ* Eton and McGill U Montreal (BA 1965); *m* 1973 *Carol Ann, dau of Lt-Col Sidney Clive Blaber (*see* HARTWELL, Bt), and has:

(1) *Amy; *b* 1985

NALL

Arms: Per chevron barry of six gu. and or and of the first, in chief two stag's heads cabossed ppr., and in base a lion rampant guardant of the second. **Crest:** Within a leathern garter buckled gu. a bee or. **Motto:** Be ready. **Creation:** Bt. (UK) 25 Jan 1954.

SIR MICHAEL JOSEPH NALL, 2ND BT, of Hoveringham, Co Notts [Lt-Cdr Sir Michael Nall Bt RN DL, Hoveringham Hall, Notts NG14 7JR]; *b* 6 Oct 1921; *s f* 1958; *educ* Wellington; RN WW II (Lt-Cdr 1950–61); Notts: High Sheriff 1971–72, V-Ld Lt 1989–91 (DL 1970); dir Singer & Friedlander, Pres Nottingham Chamber Commerce 1972–74; *m* 3 April 1951 *Angela Loveday Hanbury, est dau of Air Ch Marshal Sir (William) Alec Coryton, KCB, KBE, MVO, DFC, of S Kensington and Dorset, and has:

1 +EDWARD WILLIAM JOSEPH; *b* 24 Oct 1952; *educ* Eton; late Maj 13th/18th Roy Hussars (QMO) Light Dragoons

2 +Alexander Michael JP (Notts 1996) [Alexander Nall Esq JP, Hockerton Manor, Hockerton, Notts NG25 0PP]; *b* 3 July 1956; *educ* Eton; late Capt 2nd RGJ; *m* 1982 *Caroline Jane, yr dau of Anthony L à Court Robinson (*see* HEYTESBURY, B), and has:

(1) +William Alexander Coryton; *b* 1985

(1) *Katharine Caroline; *b* 1986

Lineage: STEPHEN NALL, of St Mary's, Nottingham; *m* Mary (*d* Oct 1709) and *d* by 1709, leaving:

EDWARD NALL, of Nottingham; *b* 1693; *m* Anne — and had:

JOSEPH NALL, of Nottingham; *m* 26 Sept 1743 Ruth Shaw (*d* 1788) and *d* 1795, having had, with other issue:

JOSEPH NALL, of Nottingham; *m* 23 April 1772 Ann Barnet and had, with other issue:

JOSEPH NALL, of Northenden, Cheshire; *b* 1789; *m* Elizabeth, dau of Jeffrey Etchells, of Newark, Notts, and had:

1 Robert, of Hoylake, Cheshire

2 JOSEPH

3 William, of Kegworth, Leics; *b* 8 May 1816; *m* 4 April 1850 Ann Peet and *d* 16 Aug 1883, having had:

  (1) William; *b* 26 Dec 1854; *d* 1 March 1859

  (2) William Herbert; *b* 23 March 1859; *d* 3 Dec 1886

  (1) Alice Ann; *d* 25 March 1859

  (2) Mary Elizabeth; *m* 27 July 1876 Peter Sullins

  (3) Ellen; *m* 13 Sept 1877 Charles Bower Fernihough

  (4) Jane; *d* 16 March 1859

  (5) Florence; *m* 13 Sept 1888 1st Baron Brocket (*qv*) and *d* 21 Oct 1927, leaving issue

The 2nd son,

JOSEPH NALL, of Hoveringham Hall, Notts (which he bought 1858); *b* 26 Nov 1810; *m* 1st 7 Sept 1829 Elizabeth (*d* 13 April 1861), dau of William Waite, of Melton Mowbray, Leics; *m* 2nd Cordelia Maria (*d* 1900), widow of Frank Beardsall, and *d* 10 Nov 1890, leaving by his 1st w:

WILLIAM NALL, of Hoveringham Hall; *b* 11 Sept 1830; *m* 1st 7 Sept 1854 Lucy Isabella (*d* 14 Sept 1871), dau of John Woollam, of Manchester, and had a s and four daus; *m* 2nd Mary Jane Webster (*dsp* 18 Oct 1912) and *d* 23 Oct 1900, leaving:

JOSEPH NALL, of Hoveringham Hall, Worsley, Lancs, and Broom Cottage, High Legh, Cheshire; *b* 1 July 1863; *m* 31 March 1886 Annie (*d* 28 June 1942), dau of Charles Bower Fernihough, of Todmorden and Southport, Lancs, and *d* 5 March 1936, leaving:

1 JOSEPH (Sir), **1st Bt**

2 William, of Grotto House, Over Peover, Cheshire; *b* 5 Jan 1892; *m* 25 June 1919 Gladys (*d* 3 June 1953), dau of Henry Pickthall, of Bowden, Cheshire, and *d* 23 Dec 1937, leaving:

  (1) *Audrey [Mrs Joseph Butler, 14 Nile Street, Crewe, Cheshire]; *b* 17 June 1921; RNVAD WW II; *m* 1st 3 Nov 1950 (*divorce* 1960) Thomas Henry Goodwin, s of Thomas Henry Goodwin, of Nantwich, and has:

    1a *William Henry, *b* 14 June 1951; *educ* Crewe Co GS

    2a *Robert Michael; *b* 21 Sept 1954; *educ* Crewe Co GS

  (1) (cont.) Mrs Audrey Goodwin *m* 2nd 6 Feb 1962 *Joseph Butler, s of Albert Butler, of Wheelock, Cheshire

1 Annie; *b* 8 Nov 1889; *m* 28 Nov 1914 John William Cherry, s of John William Cherry, of Worsley, and *d* 25 Oct 1966, having had two sons and a dau. He *d* 19 Aug 1955

2 Mary Rigby; ARCM 1925; *b* 15 Nov 1896; *d* 27 Feb 1991

The elder son,

Sir Joseph Nall, 1st Bt (UK), so *cr* 25 Jan 1954, DSO (1918), TD, JP (Notts 1932), DL (1941), DL (Lancs 1931); *b* 24 Aug 1887; served WW I (wounded, despatches), Col Res of Offrs, ret 1948, MP (U) Hulme 1918–29 and 1931–45, PPS to Parly Sec Min Labour and Min Mines 1919–21, Pres Inst Tport 1925–26, ktd 1924, dir Trafford Pk Estates, High Sheriff Notts 1952; *m* 17 Aug 1916 Edith Elizabeth (*d* 25 Jan 1963), yst dau of John Liell Francklin, of Gonalston, Notts, and *d* 2 May 1958, leaving:

1 Sir MICHAEL JOSEPH NALL, **2nd and present Bt**

2 +(William) George Joseph [George Nall Esq, Farm House, Wellow, Notts NG22 0EA]; *b* 21 Sept 1926; *educ* Wellington; AMInstTA, BBSI, Lt 13th/18th Roy (QMO) Hus 1945–48; *m* 6 May 1961 *Jennifer Jane, er dau of Leo Aylwin Richardson, FRCS, LRCP, of Minstead, Hants, and has:

  (1) +Charles William Joseph; *b* 23 April 1965; *educ* Rugby, BA, ACA

  (2) +Richard George Aylwin; *b* 16 Sept 1966; *educ* Rugby; BA, DipM; *m* 1993 *Sarah Helen, er dau of B J Wood, of Ablington, Glos

  (1) *Olivia Jane Caroline; *b* 20 March 1970; *m* July 1997 *Neil Reynolds

1 *Elizabeth Josephine , TD, JP (Notts) [Miss Elizabeth Nall TD JP, Hall Close, Hoveringham, Notts NG14 7JR]; *b* 3 May 1920; ATS WW II

2 *Rosemary Alice Anne [Mrs Peter Inchbald, Holdfast Manor, Upton-on-Severn, Worcs]; *b* 21 Oct 1923; WW II: Army Remount Depot Melton Mowbray 1939–41, Admlty Ops Sigs 1942–45; *m* 26 April 1947 *Capt Peter Bingham Inchbald, RA, er s of Maj Pierre Eliott Inchbald, MC, of Wraxall Manor, Dorset, and has:

  (1) *Peter Joseph Nicholas; *b* 3 Feb 1951; *educ* Bryanston

  (2) *Guy William Benjamin; *b* 18 June 1952; *educ* Bryanston; *m* 1981 *Hazel Brenda, yst dau of E Trant, of Esk Bank, Dalkeith, Midlothian, and has:

    1a *Robin Peter Guy; *b* 1991

    1a *Joanne Elizabeth; *b* 1982

    2a *Jenny Anne; *b* 1984

3 *Diana Christian Isabella [Mrs Sidney Watson, Ballingarrane, Clonmel, Co Tipperary, Ireland]; Mobile Red Cross attd RN WW II; *b* 17 Dec 1924; *m* 3 June 1950 *Col Sidney John Watson, MBE, MA, RE, only s of Wilfred Francis Herbert Watson, of Ballingarrane (*see* DULVERTON, B), and has:

  (1) *John Wilfred; *b* 3 Feb 1952; *educ* Eton and RAC Cirencester; ARICS, World Three-Day-Event Championship Silver Medal 1978; *m* 1977 *Julia Morrish and has:

    1a *Samuel James; *b* 1985

    1a *Suzannah Irene; *b* 1980

    2a *Rosalind Sara; *b* 1982

  (1) *Elizabeth Sandra; *b* 22 Oct 1953; SRN; *m* 1975 *Richard Vincent Craik-White and has:

    1a *James Richard; *b* 1977

    2a *Henry William; *b* 1979

NAPIER of Merchistoun

Arms: Quarterly, 1st and 4th, argent a saltire engrailed between four roses gules, the roses barbed vert (for NAPIER of Merchistoun); 2nd, azure a lion rampant argent, crowned or (for MacDOWALL of Garthland); 3rd, argent a fess azure, voided of the field, between three demi-lions crowned gules (for MILLIKEN of that Ilk). **Crests:** Dexter, an arm grasping an eagle's leg proper, talons expanded gules (for NAPIER of Merchistoun); sinister, a demi-lion rampant gules holding in his dexter forepaw a dagger or (for MILLIKEN of Culcreuch). **Supporters:** Two eagles with their wings closed proper. **Mottoes:** 1 *Fides servata secundat* ('Faith preserved renders prosperous'), 2 *Regarde bien* ('Look well'), 3 *Sans tache* ('Without stain'). **Creation:** Bt. (NS) 2 March/May 1627.

SIR JOHN ARCHIBALD LENNOX NAPIER OF MERCHISTOUN, 14TH BT [Sir John Napier of Merchistoun Bt, Merchistoun, PO Box 65177, Benmore 2010, S Africa]; *b* 6 Dec 1946; *s f* 1990; *educ* St Stithian's Coll Johannesburg and Witwatersrand U (MSc, PhD); *m* 9 Dec 1969 *Erica, dau of Kurt Kingsfield, of Johannesburg, and has:

  1 +HUGH ROBERT LENNOX; *b* 1 Aug 1977

  1 *Natalie Ann; *b* 1973

Lineage: ALEXANDER NAPIER of Merchistoun, nr Edinburgh, which he acquired 1434, though originally pledged him as a crown debt; Provost Edinburgh 1436; *d* 1454, leaving, with an er s (Robert, apparently passed over as heir or perhaps *dsp* & *vp*):

Sir ALEXANDER NAPIER of Merchistoun; Provost Edinburgh 1452–55 and 1457; tried to help JOAN (*see* BEAUFORT, D), widow of JAMES I, when in 1439 she was imprisoned by a faction led by the LIVINGSTON family, for which he was granted 1449 the lands of Philde, Perthshire; Comptroller Royal Household 1449; also diplomat and businessman; *m* Elizabeth, dau of Lauder of Hatton, and *d c* 15 Feb 1475, leaving:

JOHN NAPIER of Merchistoun; *m* Elizabeth, dau and coheir of Murdoch Menteith of Rusky (s of Robert Menteith of Rusky by Margaret, dau of Duncan, 8th Earl of Lennox), and *d c* 3 Nov 1487, leaving:

ARCHIBALD NAPIER of Edinbellie and Merchistoun; *m* 1st Katherine, dau of William Douglas of Whittinghame (*see* MORTON, E), and had issue; *m* 2nd Elizabeth Crichton and by her had issue; *m* 3rd Margaret, dau of Sir Colin Campbell of Glenorchy (*see* 1970 edn BREADALBANE AND HOLLAND, E), and *d* 1521, having had further issue; his s by his 1st w:

Sir ALEXANDER; ktd *c* 1507; had a charter of Merchistoun in free barony 1512; *m* Janet (*m* 2nd Sir Ninian Seton of Touch (*see* SETON, Bt, of Abercorn) and 3rd Sir James Towers of Inverleith), dau of Edmund Chisholm of Cromlix, and was *k vp* at the English victory over the Scots of Flodden 9 Sept 1513, having had, with two daus (Helen, *m* Sir John Melville of Raith; Janet, *m* 1st Andrew Bruce of Powfoulis and 2nd Robert Bruce):

ALEXANDER NAPIER of Merchistoun; *m* 1533 Annabella (*m* 2nd Robert Fairlie), dau of Sir Duncan Campbell of Glenorchy (*see* 1970 edn BREADALBANE AND HOLLAND, E), and was *k* at the English victory over the Scots of Pinkie 1547, having had:

Sir ARCHIBALD NAPIER of Merchistoun; *b c* 1534; Master of the Mint 1576; *m* 1st 1549 Janet (*d* 20 Dec 1563), dau of Sir Francis Bothwell, Provost Edinburgh, by Katherine Bellenden, of Auchinoule, and had:

  1 JOHN

  2 Francis; *d* 1664

Sir ARCHIBALD *m* 2nd Elizabeth, dau of John Moubray of Barnbougle, and *d* 15 May 1608, having by her had, with other issue:

  3 Alexander (Sir), of Lauriston; a Ld of Session; *d* 1629, leaving issue

  1 Elizabeth; *m* 1st 6th Lord Ogilvy (*see* AIRLIE, E); *m* 2nd Alexander Auchmoutie

The est son,

JOHN NAPIER of Merchistoun; invented logarithms; *b* 1550; *m* 1st (contract 23 Feb 1571/2) Elizabeth (*d* 1579), dau of Sir James Stirling of Keir, and had:

1 **Sir Archibald Napier, 1st Bt** (NS), so *cr* 2 March (or May) 1627, with remainder to his heirs male whatsoever, as also 4 May 1627 LORD NAPIER OF MERCHISTOUN (S), with remainder to the heirs male of his body, PC (S) 1617; *b c* 1575; *educ* Glasgow U; Gent Privy Chamber to JAMES VI and I; ktd 1616; Treasurer Depute Scotland 1622–31, Ld Justice Clerk Scotland 1623–24, a Ld Session 1623–26 (Extra Ld Session 1626–28); Covenanter by 1638 though imprisoned by Covenanters 1641 on eve of Civil War, in which he was a royalist, and placed under house arrest till 1645; *m c* 15 April 1619 Lady Margaret Graham, dau of 4th Earl of Montrose (*see* MONTROSE, D), and *d* Nov 1645, leaving a 2nd but only surv s:

(1) **Sir Archibald Napier, 2nd Bt**, and 2nd LORD NAPIER OF MERCHISTOUN; *b c* 1625; royalist Civil War; *m c* May-June-July 1641 Lady Elizabeth Erskine, dau of 19th/3rd Earl of Mar (*qv*), and *d* 4 Sept 1658, leaving:

1a **Sir Archibald Napier, 3rd Bt**, and 3rd LORD NAPIER OF MERCHISTOUN, which latter title he resigned 20 Nov 1676, obtaining a double regrant 7 and 17 Feb 1677 (apparently to make doubly sure of the continuation of the title) with remainder, failing heirs male of his body, to his est sis and the heirs male of her body, failing whom to the eldest heir female of her body, failing whom to his other sisters by primogeniture in the same way, failing whom to the heirs male of Archibald Lord Napier (an ambiguous piece of wording since all three Lords of Parl had been called Archibald), with remainder to heirs and assigns whatsoever; *d* unm a little while prior to 7 Aug 1683, when the Ldship passed to his est sister's s, while the btcy became dormant till 1817

1a Jean; *m* Sir Thomas Nicolson, 3rd Bt (*see* CARNOCK, B), and had:

1b Sir THOMAS NICOLSON, 4th LORD NAPIER OF MERCHISTOUN; *b* 14 Jan 1669; *d* unm and under age 9 June 1686

2a MARGARET; *s n* as LADY NAPIER OF MERCHISTOUN in her own right (*see* NAPIER and ETTRICK, L)

3a Mary; *d* unm Sept 1680

1 Joan

JOHN NAPIER of Merchistoun *m* 2nd Agnes (*m* 2nd William Cunningham of Craigends), dau of Sir James Chisholm of Cromlix, and *d* 3 April 1617, having by her had:

2 John, of Easter Torrie; *m* 1613 Mary, dau of Sir James Foulis; his issue died out

3 Robert, of Culcreuch, Stirling; *b* 1580; edited his f's works; *m* 1st — and had:

(1) Archibald, of Boquhapple, Menteith; had issue

(2) John; *dsp*

3 (cont.) Robert Napier *m* 2nd Anna, dau of Sir William Drummond of Riccartoun, and *d* 1655, leaving, with three daus:

(3) William, of Culcreuch (which he sold to his yr bro (Sir) Alexander 1675) and Culnagrein, Menteith; *m* 1659 Elizabeth, dau of Sir Ludovick Houstoun of Houstoun, Renfrewshire, and was *k* at Inverary 1685 during Argyll's abortive uprising in support of the Duke of Monmouth and a Protestant succession, leaving issue

(4) (Sir) Alexander Napier, *de jure* 4th Bt; *m* 1st Marion (*dsp*), dau of Sir Ludovick Houstoun; *m* 2nd Margaret Lennox of Woodhead or Lennox Castle, Stirling, and *d* 1702, leaving by her an est s:

1a (Sir) John Napier of Culcreuch, *de jure* 5th Bt; *b* 1686; *m* Margaret Lennox and had a yr s:

1b (Sir) William Napier of Culcreuch, *de jure* 6th Bt; under age at his f's death; *m* Jean, er dau of James Milliken of Milliken by Joan, dau of Alexander McDowall of Garthland, and had, with a dau (Jean, *b* 1771) an only s:

1c (Sir) Robert John NAPIER later MILLIKEN NAPIER (under terms of maternal gf's will) of Culcreuch, *de jure* 7th Bt; *b* 1765; sr Col in the Army, cmded at Siege of Mangalore, East Indies; *m* 1786 Anne, dau of Robert Campbell of Downie, Argyllshire, and *d* 1808, leaving, with other issue:

1d **Sir William John Milliken Napier, 8th Bt**; *b* 1788; assumed btcy on being served 17 March 1817 heir male general of **Sir Archibald Napier, 3rd Bt**; *m* 11 Nov 1815 Eliza Christian (*d* 3 March 1860), 5th and yst dau of John Stirling of Kippendavie, Perthshire, and had:

1e ROBERT JOHN MILLIKEN (Sir), **9th Bt**

2e John Stirling; DL Renfrewshire; *b* 7 May 1820; *m* 4 March 1845 Janet (*d* Oct 1913), only child of Andrew Brown, of Auchintorlie, Renfrewshire, and *d* 17 April 1891, having had, with other issue:

1f John Stirling; *b* 22 June 1856; Lt-Col Res of Offrs and Maj Argyll & Sutherland Highrs; *m* 17 Sept 1902 Caroline Charlotte (*dsp* 1908), yr dau of Col Keith Ramsay Maitland (*see* MAITLAND, Bt), and *d* 1913

1f Mary Elizabeth; *m* 9 June 1902 Capt Charles Lisle Stirling-Cookson (*d* 17 Oct 1919), RA, of Renton House, Grants House, Berwickshire, and *d* 29 April 1925

1e Mary; *m* 6 June 1839 Robert Speir (*d* 18 Feb 1853), of Culdees Castle, Perthshire, and had issue

4 Alexander, of Gillets, *dspm* Oct 1652

5 William; ancestor of the NAPIERs of Craiganet

6 Adam; ancestor of the NAPIERs of Blackstoun

2 Jane; *m* 1620 George Hamilton of Kilbrachmont

3 Elizabeth; *m* 1622 William Cunningham of Craigends

4 Anne; *m* 1620 George Drummond of Balloch

5 Helen; *m* 1629 Matthew Brisbane

6 Margaret; *m* James Steward of Rosyth

The 8th Bt *d* 4 Feb 1852; his est son,

Sir Robert John Milliken-Napier, 9th Bt; *b* 7 Nov 1818; Hon Col 4th Bn Princess Louise's Argyll & Sutherland Highrs; *m* 4 April 1850 Anne Salisbury Meliora (*d* 5 Jan 1902), only surv dau of John Ladeveze Adlercron, of Moyclare, Co Meath, and *d* 4 Dec 1884, having had:

1 ARCHIBALD LENNOX (Sir), **10th Bt**

2 Robert Francis Ladeveze; *b* 3 Dec 1856; Maj QO Cameron Highrs, 4th Cl Medjidie; *m* 25 July 1887 Emily Norrie (*d* 17 April 1961), dau of George Louis Augustus Moke, of New York (*see* NORRIE, B), and *das* Atbara, Egypt, 23 May 1898, leaving:

(1) Lennox Robert Murray; *b* 1 Sept 1890; Capt 2nd Bn QO Cameron Highrs WW I (wounded twice); *das* 28 July 1916

(2) Gerald Francis George; *b* 23 Dec 1891; *d* unm 1 Aug 1911

(3) Ivan Robert; *b* 9 Nov 1893; Lt 3rd Bn QO Cameron Highrs WW I (despatches); *m* 3 July 1919 Evelyn Mary (*d* 21 July 1965), yr dau of John Williams Horton Bolitho, of Alverne-Haye, Penzance, Cornwall, and *dsp* 2 Jan 1975

(1) Noreen Mary Hay; *b* 6 Feb 1895; *m* 18 April 1914 Hon Charles Paulet St John (*see* SAINT JOHN OF BLETSO, B) and *dsp* 28 Aug 1977

3 William Edward Stirling; *b* 2 May 1858; *m* 12 April 1884 Janet Catherine (*d* 14 Oct 1945), dau of W M Reid, and *d* 25 Sept 1900, leaving:

(1) William Edward Stirling, MC, TD, DL (Peeblesshire 1954); *b* 24 May 1893; Lt-Col RA (TA), Maj Lothians and Border Horse, WW I and WW II (POW); *m* 4 March 1919 Audrey (*d* 1986), only dau of William Houlding, of Kerfield, Peebles, and Arcachon, France, and *d* 1983, having had:

1a William Ian Houlding Lennox; *b* 5 Nov 1927; *d* Kenya 1986

1a *(Elizabeth) June Houlding [Mrs Patrick Gardner-Brown, Culcrench Cottage, Milton St, Bowral, NSW 2576, Australia]; *b* 13 June 1920; *m* 1 May 1947 Lt-Col Gerald Patrick Gardner-Brown (*d* 1994), RHA, s of Prof John Gerald Gardner-Brown, and has had:

1b *Elspeth Susan; *b* 22 April 1948

2b Vivien Patricia; *b* 22 Jan 1951; *m* 11 Dec 1974 *John Grant Pagan, only s of Brig Sir John Pagan, CMG, MBE, TD, FRGS, and *d* 1987, leaving:

1c *Jonathan Edward; *b* 1981

2c *Peter Napier; *b* 1983

2a *Lavinia [Mrs Lavinia Czarkowski-Napier, 30 Beatrice Terrace, Ascot, Qld 4007, Australia]; *b* 14 July 1924; *m* 4 Jan 1947 *Capt C Czarkowski-Golijeiwski, 14th Polish Lancers, of The Bauhinias, Yamala, Qld, Australia, and has issue; they assumed the surname CZARKOWSKI-NAPIER

3a *Elspeth Mary [Mrs Denbigh Harding, 7 Lodersfield, Lechlade, Glos GL7 3DJ]; *b* 26 April 1933; *m* 16 Feb 1957 *Denbigh Hamilton Harding, est s of George Trevor Hamilton Harding, CIE, of Wimbledon, and has:

1b *Caroline; *b* 9 Dec 1958

2b *Fiona; *b* 24 March 1960

3b *Unity; *b* 1 June 1962

(2) Alec Douglas; *b* 17 July 1894; T/Lt RASC; *m* 1929 Doris Mary Clara, dau of Victor Hide Hill, and *d* Nov 1965, leaving:

1a +Alexander Colin; *b* 18 Oct 1930

2a +John Stirling; *b* 1935

(1) Lola Lillias Daphne; *b* 12 Dec 1891; *m* 17 May 1928 Col Algernon Cantley Jeffcoat, CB, CMG, DSO (*d* 1964), s of Surgn-Gen James Henry Jeffcoat, and had issue

1 Anne Salisbury Mary Meliora (Lola); *m* 10 March 1881 Sir John Adam Robert Hay, 9th Bt (*d* 4 May 1895), and *d* 13 May 1941, leaving issue

2 Aymee Elizabeth Georgina; *m* 4 Jan 1876 Sir George Douglas Clerk, 8th Bt (*qv*), and *d* 8 May 1947, leaving issue

3 Theodora Evelyn; *d* unm

The 9th Bt's est son,

Sir Archibald Lennox Milliken-Napier, 10th Bt; *b* 2 Nov 1855; Lt Gren Gds; *m* 1st 16 Dec 1880 (*divorce*) Mary Alison Dorothy (*d* 7 Nov 1936), yst dau of Sir Thomas Fairbairn, 2nd Bt (*qv*), and had:

1 **Sir Alexander Lennox Milliken-Napier, 11th Bt**; *b* 30 May 1882; Capt Gren Gds Boer War, ADC to Govr-Gen Australia 1910–12, ADC Personal Staff WW I (wounded twice); *m* 14 June 1913 Joan Alice Ashurst (*d* 9 May 1962), only child of Edward Ashurst Moris, and *d* 15 July 1954, having had:

(1) (Mary) Marjory; *b* 17 April 1915

2 ROBERT ARCHIBALD (Sir), **12th Bt**

Sir Archibald *m* 2nd 12 July 1904 Charlotte Louise (*d* 11 July 1962), only dau of Hon Henry William Austin, of Montreal, Ch Justice Bahamas, and *d* 18 Jan 1907

The 11th Bt's bro,

Sir Robert Archibald Napier, 12th Bt; *b* 19 July 1889; *educ* Eton; WW I as Trooper, City of London Yeo (Rough Riders) and Lt 1st Roy E Kent Yeo, WW II as F/Lt RAF; *m* 1st 1914 (*divorce* 1929) Violet, dau of E Payne, and had issue; *m* 2nd 9 Nov 1929 Margaret Ann Searle, MBE (*d* 24 Jan 1962), only surv dau of Thomas James Hinton, of Horwell Lodge, Copplestone, Devon, and *d* 25 June 1965; his s by his 1st w:

Sir William Archibald Napier, 13th Bt; *b* 19 July 1915; *educ* Stowe; FIMH, AMIME (SA), AMICertE; WW II as Capt S African Engrs; *m* 1942 Kathleen Mabel (*d* 14 Oct 1994), dau of Reginald Henry Greaves, of Tafelberg, CP, and *d* 1990, leaving:

Sir JOHN ARCHIBALD LENNOX NAPIER, **14th and present Bt**

NAPIER of
Merrion Square

Arms: Arg. on a saltire engrailed between four roses gu. five escallops or. **Crest:** A dexter cubit arm erect ppr., the hand grasping a crescent arg., the arm charged with a rose as in the arms.
Motto: *Sans tâche* ('Without blemish').
Creation: Bt. (UK) 9 April 1867.

SIR CHARLES JOSEPH NAPIER, 6TH BT, of Merrion Square, Dublin [Sir Charles Napier Bt, Woodlands, Martyr Worthy, Hants SO21 1AT]; *b* 15 April 1973; *s f* 1994; *educ* Eton and Edinburgh U (MA); fundraising exec Scottish European Aid 1995–96, MIND 1996–

Lineage: JOSEPH NAPIER, of St Andrews, Co Down (s of William Napier, of Templecron, by Mary Moore); *m* Mary Macpherson (*d* 1805) and *d c* 1812, having had, with two yr sons (*dsp*):

WILLIAM NAPIER, of St Andrews; merchant Belfast; *m* 1798 Rosetta MacNaghten (*d* 30 June 1836), of Ballyreagh House, Co Antrim, and had, with other issue:

1 William; *b* 17 Jan 1801; *m* 17 May 1826 Mary Ramsay (*d* Oct 1846), est dau of Arthur Birnie, and *d* March 1864, having had issue

2 JOSEPH (Sir), **1st Bt**

1 Mary; *m* Echlin Molyneux, QC, and *d* 29 April 1831

2 Rosetta; *m* July 1833 James Whiteside, PC, Ld Ch Justice Ireland

WILLIAM NAPIER *d* 25 May 1830; his 2nd son,

Sir Joseph Napier, 1st Bt (UK), so *cr* 9 April 1867, PC (1852), QC (1844), DCL Oxford; *b* 26 Dec 1804; *educ* Trin Coll Dublin (MA, LLD); barrister 1831, MP Dublin U 1848 (V-Chllr 1867–80), Attorney-Gen Ireland, Ld Chllr Ireland 1858; *m* 20 Aug 1831 Charity (*d* 4 March 1901), 2nd dau of John Grace, of Dublin, and had:

1 William John; barrister; *b* 30 Oct 1837; *d* unm 3 Dec 1874

2 JOSEPH (Sir), **2nd Bt**

1 Cherry; *m* 13 March 1860 Rev Paulus Aemilius Singer, 5th s of Most Rev Joseph Henderson Singer, PC, DD, of Mount Anville Park, Co Dublin, Bp Meath and Primate Ireland, and *d* 7 Nov 1915. He *d* 25 Oct 1901

2 Rosetta; *m* 6 Aug 1863 Col Henry Grey MacGregor, CB, 3rd s of Gen Sir Duncan MacGregor, KCB, and *d* 17 Sept 1891, leaving issue

3 Grace Anne Marie Louise; *m* 4 Nov 1868 John William Gardiner, JP, BCS, and *d* 3 Aug 1919, leaving issue

Sir JOSEPH *d* 9 Dec 1882; his only surv son,

Sir Joseph Napier, 2nd Bt; Capt 23rd Royal Welch Fus; *b* 28 May 1841; *m* 10 Nov 1864 Maria Octavia (*d* 10 April 1918), 2nd dau of Joseph Mortimer, of Weymouth, Dorset, and *d* 13 Nov 1884, leaving, with a yr s (Joseph Duncan Mortimer, *b* 13 Aug 1871, *d* unm 3 Jan 1900):

Sir William Lennox Napier, 3rd Bt; barrister Inner Temple 1894, slr 1902, Maj 4th Bn S Wales Bdrs, Lt-Col 7th Bn Roy Welch Fus, WW I; *b* 12 Oct 1867; *m* 5 Aug 1890 Mabel Edith Geraldine (*d* 24 July 1955), 2nd dau of Rev Charles Thornton Forster, Vicar Hinxton, Cambs, and was *ka* Gallipoli 13 Aug 1915, leaving:

1 JOSEPH WILLIAM LENNOX (Sir), **4th Bt**

2 Charles Macnaughton; Maj RA WW I, Staff Capt and DAAG WW II; *b* 10 Dec 1896; *m* 7 Nov 1923 (*divorce* 1939) Dorothy Constance (*d* 30 Jan 1960), dau of Col Reginald Hawkins Hall-Dempster, DSO, of Dunnichen, Angus, and *d* 9 March 1967, leaving:

  (1) +Lennox Alexander Hawkins, CB (1983), OBE (1970, MBE 1965), MC (1958) [Maj-Gen Lennox Napier CB OBE MC, Osbaston Farm, Monmouth, Gwent NP5 4BB]; *b* 28 June 1928; *educ* Radley and RMC Sandhurst; Maj-Gen Roy Regt Wales, Gwent: High Sheriff 1988, Ld Lt 1995– (formerly DL); chm Centl Tport Consultative Ctee, Inspr Public Inquiries, memb Br Tport Police Ctee, OStJ; *m* 25 July 1959 *Jennifer Dawn, dau of Basil Brees Wilson, of Medlicott, Neston, Cheshire, and Mrs Oliver Charles Gregson, of Osbaston, Mon, and has:

    1a +Philip Martin Lennox; *b* 29 Dec 1964; Capt RRW; *m* 1990 *Philippa (Pippa) N, er dau of James Rawson, of Clitheroe, Lancs, and has:

    1b +Harry James Lennox; *b* 4 Dec 1996
    1b *Phoebe Henrietta; *b* 1992
    2b *Louisa Rodier; *b* 1994
  1a *Joanna Dawn; *b* 28 Sept 1962; *m* 1987 *Lt-Col Robert Hanbury Tenison Aitken, RRW, only s of Capt Harry Kerr Aitken, MC, Argyll and Sutherland Highrs
  2a *Sally Vanessa; *b* 21 April 1967

(1) *Audrey Lennox [Mrs Henry Harding, Furzey Lodge, Furzey Lane, Beaulieu, Hants SO42 7WB]; *b* 5 April 1926; *m* 1st 8 Oct 1949 (*divorce* 1955) Thomas Eric Sampson, s of Thomas George Sampson, of Tunbridge Wells; *m* 2nd 21 Nov 1958 *Lt-Col Henry Christian Ewart Harding, MC, RA, s of Col George Harding, of Borris-in-Ossory, Co Laois, and has:

  1a *William George Charles; *b* 30 Jan 1964
  1a *Sarah Constance Hope; *b* 5 Feb 1961; *m* 1992 *Oliver Dacres Wise, er s of Derek Wise, of Barcombe, Sussex, and has:

    1b *Henry Gerard Dacres; *b* 4 Jan 1993
    1b *Eleanor Lucy Constance; *b* 27 March 1995
  2a *Susan Jane Napier; *b* 12 June 1966

3 Vivian John Lennox, MC (1919); V-Lt Breconshire 1964– (DL 1958), Brig S Wales Bdrs, Lt-Col cmdg 1st Bn Welch Regt, served WWs I and II (despatches, POW), Brig cmdg Mombasa Area 1948–49; *b* 13 July 1898; *educ* Uppingham and RMC; *m* 12 Feb 1958 Marion Avis, OBE (1955), dau of Lt-Col Sir John Conway Lloyd

1 Marjorie Lennox; *b* 25 April 1894; *d* unm 2 May 1973

2 (Gwendolyn Mabel) Shelagh; *b* 4 Nov 1900; *m* 1st 27 June 1929 (*divorce* 1934) Clive Norman Burnett, only s of Walter Burnett, of Embleton, Northumberland; *m* 2nd 14 July 1949 Thomas Tettrell Phelps (*d* 1963)

Sir WILLIAM's est s,

Sir Joseph William Lennox Napier, 4th Bt, OBE (1944); *b* 1 Aug 1895; *educ* Rugby and Jesus Coll Cambridge; Lt Res Offrs RFA (TA), Capt 4th Bn S Wales Bdrs WW I Gallipoli and Mesopotamia (wounded three times, POW) and WW II (Lt-Col (AQMG) HQ Staff Eastern Cmd and in Italy), memb Lloyd's; *m* 12 Feb 1931 *Isabelle Muriel [Isabel Lady Napier, 17 Cheyne Gdns, London SW3 5QT], yr dau of Maj Henry Siward Balliol Surtees, JP, DL, of Redworth Hall, Darlington, and *d* 1986, leaving:

1 Sir ROBERT AUBONE SIWARD NAPIER later Sir ROBERT SURTEES NAPIER, **5th Bt**; *b* 5 March 1932; *educ* Eton; 2nd Lt Coldstream Gds 1950–52, chm Standard Fireworks plc 1980–86, dir: Charterhouse Japhet 1967–83, Brickhouse Dudley 1981–86, Marlar Internat 1983–89, Dane & Co 1987–, UK rep Rothschild Bank AG 1983–94; *m* 1971 *Jennifer Beryl [Lady Napier, Woodlands, Martyr Worthy, Hants SO21 1AT], formerly w of Mark R Palmer, of Houston, Tex., and only dau of H Warwick Daw, of Henley-on-Thames, and *d* 1994, leaving:

  (1) Sir CHARLES JOSEPH NAPIER, **6th and present Bt**

2 +John Lennox [John Napier Esq, 86 Ennerdale Rd, Kew, Surrey]; *b* 25 Jan 1934; *educ* Eton; memb Stock Exchange 1962–96; *m* April 1967 *Cecily Mary, est dau of Arthur Mortimer, of Malta, and has:

  (1) +James Alexander; *b* 5 March 1969; *educ* Oundle and Edinburgh U (MB, ChB)

  (1) *Jessica; *b* 1971; *m* 26 July 1997 *Dr Tobias George Sykes, PhD, yr s of Richard Sykes, of Chelsea

NAPIER and ETTRICK

Arms: Quarterly, 1st and 4th, argent a saltire engrailed, between four roses gules, barbed vert (for NAPIER); 2nd and 3rd, or on a bend azure a mullet pierced between two crescents of the field, within a double-tressure flory-counterflory of the second (for SCOTT OF THIRLESTANE); below the shield on a compartment the top of an embattled tower argent, masoned sable, issuant therefrom six lances disposed saltirewise proper, three and three, with pennons azure (for SCOTT). **Crest:** A dexter arm erect, couped below the elbow proper, grasping a crescent argent (for NAPIER). **Supporters:** Dexter, an eagle, wings expanded, proper; sinister, a chevalier in coat of mail and steel cap, all proper, holding in the exterior hand a lance with a pennon azure. **Mottoes:** (above crest) *Sans tache* ('Without stain'), (below arms) Ready, aye ready. **Creations:** L. (S) 4 May 1627, Bt. (NS) 22 Aug 1666, B. (UK) 16 July 1872.

THE 14TH LORD NAPIER OF MERCHISTOUN, 5th Baron Ettrick of Ettrick, Co Selkirk, and a **Baronet** (Sir (Francis) Nigel Napier Bt, KCVO (1992, CVO 1985, LVO 1980), DL (Selkirk 1974–75, Ettrick and Lauderdale 1975)) [The Rt Hon The Lord Napier and Ettrick KCVO DL, Nottingham Cottage, Kensington Palace, London W8 4PU]; *b* 5 Dec 1930; *s* f 1954, also as Chief of the Name of Napier; *educ* Eton and RMA Sandhurst; commissioned 1950; Maj Scots Gds (Res Offrs) Malaya 1950–51 (invalided), Adj 1st Bn Scots Gds 1955–57; Priv Sec, Comptroller and Equerry to HRH THE PRINCESS MARGARET, COUNTESS OF SNOWDON 1973–98 (Treas 1998–), Equerry to HRH THE 1st DUKE OF GLOUCESTER 1958–60; Dep Ceremonial and Protocol Sec CRO 1962–66, Purple Staff Offr funeral of Sir Winston Churchill 1966, C Whip Ho Lds 1970–71, memb: Roy Co Archers, Exec Ctee Standing Cncl Btage 1985– and Standing Cncl Scottish Chiefs, Pres St John Ambulance Assoc and Bde Co of London 1975–83, Freeman City London, Liveryman Grocers' Co, Hon DLitt Napier U 1993, KStJ 1991 (CStJ 1988); *m* 30 Oct 1958 *Delia Mary, yr dau of Maj Archibald David Barclay Pearson, of Upper Sattenham, Milford, Surrey, and has:

1 +FRANCIS DAVID CHARLES, *Master of Napier* [The Master of Napier, 23 Poyntz Rd, London SW11 5BH]; *b* 3 Nov 1962; *educ* Stanbridge Earls Sch, S Thames Coll Wandsworth (City and Guilds Computer Dip); with a Lloyd's agency 1984–92, Heath Bloodstock Ltd 1992–97; *m* 1993 *Zara Jane, only dau of Hugh Dermot McCalmont, and has:

  (1) +William Alexander Hugh; *b* 10 June 1996

2 +Nicholas Alexander John; *b* 27 Feb 1971; *educ* Milton Abbey

1 +Louisa Mary Constance [The Hon Mrs Morrison, Yew Tree Cottage, Kingston Lisle, Wantage, Oxon OX12 9QL]; *b* 5 Feb 1961; *m* 1987 *Alexander Morrison, Maj Scots Gds (Res), er s of Peter Morrison, and has:

  (1) +Oliver Charles Francis; *b* 1989

  (2) +Hugo Peter Alexander; *b* 1992

2 +Georgina Helena Katherine; *b* 21 Feb 1969; *m* 15 Sept 1995 *Capt Jonathan Walker, only s of Sir David Walker, exec chm Morgan Stanley Gp, and has:

  (1) +Amelia Rose Katherine; *b* 1 Sept 1997

Lineage (of Napier): (For preceding generations *see* NAPIER, Bt, of Merchistoun).

MARGARET Napier, **Lady Napier of Merchistoun** in her own right (5th holder of the title); *m* 1676 John BRISBANE (*d* 1684), Sec to the Admiralty *temp* CHARLES II, and *d* Sept 1706, having had, with two sons (Charles, *d* an infant 1678; John, *Master of Napier*; RN; *d* unm 1704):

ELIZABETH Brisbane, *Mistress of Napier*; *m* by contract 15 Dec 1699 **Sir William Scott, 2nd Bt**, of Thirlestane (*see* Lineage (of Scott) below), and *dvm* 11 Aug 1705, leaving, with a dau (Agnes, whose issue *dsp*) an only surv s:

Sir FRANCIS SCOTT later NAPIER (1706), **3rd Bt**, as which *s* f 1725, and **6th Lord Napier of Merchistoun**, as which *s* grandmother; *b c* 1702; Commr Police Scotland 1761–73; *m* 1st *c* 14 March 1729 Lady Henrietta Hope, dau of 1st Earl of Hopetoun (*see* LINLITHGOW, M), and had:

1 WILLIAM, **7th Lord**

---

2 Charles, of Merchistoun Hall, Stirling; *b* 19 Nov 1731; Capt RN; *m* 1st 19 Dec 1763 Grizel (*dsp* 15 Nov 1774), dau of Sir John Warrender, Bt, of Lochend (*see* BRUNTISFIELD, B); *m* 2nd 2 July 1777 Christian, dau of Gabriel Hamilton, of Westburn, Lanarks, and *d* 9 Dec 1807, having by her had, with three daus:

  (1) Charles (Sir), KCB, of Merchistoun House, Hants; *b* 6 March 1786; Adml the Blue, Count of Cape St Vincent and Grandee 1st Cl Portugal; MP; *m* Eliza (*d* 19 Dec 1857), dau of George Younghusband and widow of Lt Edward Elers, RN, and *d* 5 Nov 1860, leaving an only child:

    1a Eloise Fanny; *m* 19 Oct 1843 Rev Henry Jodrell (*d* 1896), n of Sir Richard Paul Jodrell, 2nd Bt (*see* 1929 edn), and *d* 20 Aug 1915, leaving issue

  (2) Thomas Erskine (Sir), KCB; *b* 10 May 1790; Gen, Col 71st Foot, Govr Edinburgh Castle; *m* Margaret (*d* 18 Oct 1885), dau and coheir of Alexander Falconer, of Woodcot, and *d* 5 July 1863, leaving:

    1a Matilda; *d* 1849

3 Francis; Lt-Col RM; *m* Elizabeth, dau of John Greenway, of Portsmouth, and *dsp* 1779

4 John; *d* unm 1759

5 Mark; *b* 30 Dec 1738; Maj-Gen; *m* 1st 24 Feb 1761 Anne, dau of John Nelson, of Craigcaffie; *m* 2nd Margaret (*d* 8 Aug 1829), dau of Alexander Simpson of Concraig, and *d* 10 June 1809, having by her had, with a dau (*d* unm):

  (1) Francis, WS; *b* 20 Aug 1770; *m* 30 March 1796 Mary Elizabeth Jane Douglas, est dau of Col Archibald Hamilton, and had:

    1a Mark; Sheriff Dumfries and Galloway; *b* 24 July 1798; *m* 29 Dec 1842 his cousin Charlotte (*d* 14 April 1883), dau of Alexander Ogilvy (*see* OGILVY, Bt) and widow of W D Macfarlane, and *d* 22 Nov 1879, leaving, with two other daus (*d* young):

      1b Francis John Hamilton Scott; *b* 20 Dec 1850; Lt-Cdr RN; *m* 1909 Anne (*d* 17 Dec 1916), dau of William Ward, and *d* 17 Nov 1929

      1b Frances Anne; *b* 12 June 1848; *m* 5 Dec 1866 Lt-Col Cecil Rice (*d* 6 May 1917), 72nd Highrs, s of Edward Royds Rice, of Dane Court, Kent, and *d* 5 July 1884, leaving issue

    1a Alicia Colden

  (2) Mark; *b* 14 Feb 1779; Lt-Gen; *d* 1843

  (1) Isabella; *m* 28 April 1797 Charles Maitland and *d* 11 Dec 1805

  (2) Marcia Anne Sympson; *m* 2 Jan 1804 Alexander Ogilvy and *d* his widow 1 April 1861

  (3) Maria; *m* June 1823 Rev Thomas Henry Yorke, Vicar Bishop-Middleham, Durham, bro of John Yorke, of Bewerley Hall, Yorks, and *d* 1 Feb 1868

The **6th Lord** *m* 2nd 1750 Henrietta Maria, dau of George Johnston, of Dublin, and *d* 1773, having by her had:

6 George; *b* 11 March 1751; Col, Comptroller Army Accounts Ireland; *m* 1st 22 Jan 1775 Elizabeth, dau of Capt Robert Pollock, and had an only dau:

  (1) Louisa Mary; *d* 26 Aug 1856

6 (cont.) Col The Hon George Napier *m* 2nd 27 Aug 1781 Lady Sarah Lennox (*see* RICHMOND and GORDON, D) and *d* 13 Oct 1804, having by her had, with two daus (*d* unm):

  (1) Charles James (Sir), GCB; *b* 10 Aug 1782; Lt-Gen, Col 22nd Regt, C-in-C India; *m* 1st April 1827 Elizabeth (*dsp* 31 July 1833), dau of Thomas Oakeley and widow of Francis John Kelly; *m* 2nd 1835 Frances (*d* 22 June 1872), dau of William Philipps, of Court Henry, Carmarths, and widow of Richard Alcock, RN, and *dsp* 29 Aug 1853

  (2) George Thomas (Sir), KCB; *b* 30 June 1784; Gen, Col 1st West India Regt; *m* 1st 28 Oct 1812 Margaret (*d* 1810), dau of John Craig, of Glasgow, and had:

    1a George Thomas Conolly, CB; *b* 1816; Maj-Gen, Col 96th Foot; *d* 5 May 1873, leaving:

      1b Maria Aletta; *m* 1862 John F Bell

    2a John Moore; *b* 1817; Capt 62nd Foot; *m* July 1843 Maria (*d* 1 Oct 1906), dau of Capt Richard Alcock, RN, and *d* Sind 7 July 1846, leaving:

      1b Sarah (posthumous); *m* 23 June 1872 Lord Albert Seymour and *d* 30 April 1901, leaving issue (*see* HERTFORD, M)

    3a William Craig Emilius, JP (Hants); *b* 18 March 1818; Gen, Col KOSB, 3rd Buffs, Govr RMC Sandhurst 1875–82; Kt Medjidie; *m* 21 April 1845 Emily Cephalonia Napier (*d* 29 Feb 1908) and *d* 23 Sept 1903, leaving, with other issue:

      1b Charles James; *b* 2 Aug 1858; Maj E Surrey Regt and 3rd Bn Cameronians, Legn Hon; *m* 1887 Ellen Frederica, dau of Frederick Thompson, CE, and *d* 12 June 1938, leaving:

        1c Cecil Charles James; *b* 1890; *m* 19 March 1907 Marie de Geneville Goodbirn

      1b Susan Frances; *m* 12 Feb 1873 Col Cecil Bunbury (*see* BUNBURY, Bt) and *dsp* 6 Nov 1878

      2b Georgiana Anne Emily; *m* 21 April 1909 Henry James Lionel Oakes (*d* 11 Nov 1944), est s of Lt-Col Orbell Henry Oakes, of Nowton Court, Suffolk, and *d* 24 Feb 1933

      3b Hester Johnston

      4b Emily Caroline, MBE (1918); *d* 25 Nov 1919

      5b Margaret Cephalonia

      6b Sarah Lennox

      7b Violet Bunbury

    1a Sarah; *m* Thomas Clarke and *d* 29 April 1850

    2a Cecilia; *m* 30 Nov 1852 Col Henry William St Pierre Bunbury, CB (*see* BUNBURY, Bt) and *d* 5 June 1896, leaving issue

  (2) (cont.) Sir George *m* 2nd 1839 Frances Dorothea (*d* 11 July 1881), est dau of R W Blencose and widow of William Peere Williams Freeman, of Fawley Court, Oxon, and *d* 8 Sept 1855

  (3) William Francis Patrick (Sir), KCB; *b* 17 Dec 1785; Gen, Col 22nd Foot, author: *History of the Peninsular War*; *m* 14 March 1812 Caroline Amelia (*d* 26 March 1860), 2nd dau of Gen Hon Henry Edward Fox (*see* ILCHESTER, E), and *d* 12 Feb 1860, having had, with two daus (*d* unm):

    1a John Moore; *b* 4 Nov 1816; *m* 22 June 1847 Elizabetha Amelia Henrietta (*d* 19 Oct 1888), 3rd dau of Col Charles Alexander, RE, and *d* 24 April 1867, having had, with another dau (*d* unm):

1b William Charles; *b* 7 April 1854; *d* 23 June 1935

2b Charles Arthur Wellington; *b* 26 Dec 1861; *d* unm 2 Aug 1904

1b Louisa Blanche; *b* 30 July 1850; *m* Arthur Gordon Schneider and *d* 1878

2b Rose Leslie; *b* 13 April 1852; *m* 17 Jan 1878 Edward Robert Portal (*see* PORTAL, Bt) and had issue

1a Elizabeth Marianne; *m* 1888 4th Earl of Arran (*qv*), and *d* 27 April 1899, leaving issue

2a Louisa Augusta; *m* 15 July 1844 Col Patrick Leonard McDougall, s of Sir Duncan McDougall, and *d* 8 Sept 1856

3a Pamela Adelaide; *m* 21 Dec 1846 Philip William Skynner Miles, of Kingsweston, Glos (*d* 1 Oct 1881), MP Bristol, and *d* 21 Feb 1910, leaving issue

4a Nora Creina Blanche; *m* 17 Aug 1854 1st Baron Aberdare (*qv*) and *d* 27 April 1897, leaving issue

(4) Richard; *b* 1787; barrister; *m* 1817 Anna Louisa (*d* 30 March 1867), dau of Sir J Stewart, Bt, and widow of Capt Staples, RN, and *d* 13 Jan 1868

(5) Henry Edward; *b* 5 March 1789; Capt RN, FRS; *m* Caroline Bennett (*d* 5 Sept 1836) and *d* 13 Oct 1853, leaving:

1a Charles George; *b* 20 July 1829; FGS, CE; *m* 13 Dec 1860 Susanna Juliana Ricarda (*d* 25 Aug 1927), dau of Samuel John Carolin, and *d* 2 Sept 1882, leaving:

2b Henry Edward; *b* 21 Sept 1861; T/Brig-Gen cmdg 2nd Bn Roy Irish Rifles, Col 1st Bn Cheshire Regt, Boer War, WW I; *m* 1887 Mary Ada (*d* 27 Oct 1949), dau of Capt W F Stewart, BSC, and *das* 25 April 1915, leaving:

1c Charles Lee; *b* 19 Feb 1895; *d* unm 5 Jan 1970

1c Lilias Mary; *b* 25 July 1892

2c Hester Caroline; *b* 22 Oct 1896; *m* 9 Aug 1928 Harmond Victor Carruthers Johnstone, OBE (*d* 25 Dec 1945), s of Carruthers Charles Johnstone, and *d* 15 April 1970, leaving:

1d +Charles Napier Carruthers; *b* 1 July 1929; *educ* Shrewsbury; Overseas Civ Serv; *m* 1958 *Patricia Mary Elmes, and has:

1e +Clive Charles Carruthers; *b* 6 Sept 1963

1e +Sally Caroline; *b* 1 Dec 1959

2e +Louise Elizabeth; *b* 15 Dec 1960

2d +Henry Walcot Carruthers; *b* 21 June 1931; *educ* Shrewsbury

3d +Edward Townshend Carruthers; *b* 3 Feb 1937; *educ* Shrewsbury and St John's Coll Cambridge; *m* 28 April 1962 *C Mälzer and has:

1e +Christopher Michael Carruthers; *b* 27 Feb 1965

1b Lilias Juliana; *m* 1902 Ernest Stanley Stork, DSO, MC (*d* 27 Nov 1949), and *d* 16 Jan 1954

2b Mable Christiana; *m* 16 Nov 1897 John Peere Williams Freeman, JP, MD (*d* 20 Dec 1943), yst s of Frederick Peere Williams Freeman, of Greatham, Sussex, and *d* 27 March 1969, leaving issue

2a Richard Henry; *b* 11 March 1836; V-Adml; *m* 1st 1861 Mary (*d* 6 Sept 1871), dau of Frederick Dyer; *m* 2nd 1883 Mary Teresa (*d* 31 Jan 1930), est dau of Robert Priest, and *d* 1 March 1903

1a Emily Louisa Augusta; *m* 22 Sept 1830 Sir Henry Edward Bunbury, 7th Bt (*qv*), and *d* 18 March 1863

2a Augusta Sarah; *m* 6 Oct 1853 Frederick Peere Williams-Freeman (*d* 17 Jan 1870), of Greatham, Sussex, and *d* 3 May 1897, leaving issue

7 James; *d* 1760

8 Patrick; Capt RN; *d* June 1801

9 James John; Lt Marines; *k* aboard the frigate *Fox* 1776

10 Stewart; Lt RM; *d* 1778

1 Hester; *m* Alexander Johnston, HEICCS, of Carnsalloch, and *d* his widow 1819, leaving issue

2 Mary; *d* 1765

The 6th LORD's est son,

WILLIAM NAPIER, **7th Lord Napier of Merchistoun**; Lt-Col and DAG Forces Scotland; *m* 16 Dec 1754 Marie Anne, dau of 8th Lord Cathcart (*see* CATHCART, E), and *d* 1775, having had, with four daus:

FRANCIS NAPIER, **8th Lord Napier of Merchistoun**; *b* 23 Feb 1758; rep S peer 1796–1806 and 1807–23, Ld Lt and Sheriff Pncpl Selkirkshire, 1st Ld HC to Gen Assembly Ch of Scotland 1802–16, Grand Master Mason Scotland, DCL; *m* 13 April 1784 Maria Margaret (*d* 29 Dec 1821), est dau of Lt-Gen Sir John Clavering, KB, and *d* 1 Aug 1823, having had, with a dau (*d* unm):

1 WILLIAM JOHN, **9th Lord**

2 Charles, of The Woodlands, Taunton; *b* 24 Oct 1794; Maj; *m* 1st 1824 Alice Emma (*d* 16 May 1834), dau of Roger Barnston, and had, with another s (*d* young) and two daus (*d* unm):

(1) Francis Roger Barnston; *b* 5 Oct 1828; Bombay Army; *d* 15 Nov 1849

(2) John Warren NAPIER later NAPIER-CLAVERING (roy licence 8 Feb 1894) (Rev); *b* 16 Sept 1832; *educ* Cambridge (BA); Vicar Stretton, Staffs; *m* 30 Sept 1857 Anna Maria Margaret Helen (*d* 2 Feb 1900), dau of Col Francis Hunter, HEICS, and *d* 9 June 1906, leaving, with a dau (*d* unm):

1a Charles Warren, JP; *b* 19 Aug 1858; Col Somerset LI, Burmese Expdn 1885–87 (medal with clasp); *m* 24 Oct 1899 Margaret Nevile (*d* 4 Feb 1950), 5th dau of Nevile Reid, of Ross-shire, and *d* 22 Oct 1931, leaving:

1b Hélène Margaret; *b* 6 Oct 1900; Kaisar-i-Hind Medal; *m* 30 June 1927 Maj-Gen Christopher Michael Maltby, CB, MC, DL, IA, est s of Christopher James Maltby, of Felmersham, Beds, and had:

1c +Ann Margaret; *b* 7 April 1928; *educ* Newnham Coll Cambridge (BA 1952); *m* 29 May 1958 John Hallam

2c +Barbara Helen Jessie; *b* 25 April 1931; *m* 7 Aug 1954 *Brian Wilfred Hastilow, MA, 2nd s of Cyril Alexander Frederick Hastilow, CBE, MSc, FRICS, of Birmingham, and has:

1d +Alexander Michael; *b* 4 Sept 1955; *educ* Malvern

2d +David Napier; *b* 8 May 1959

2a Francis; *b* 22 Nov 1859; *educ* Cambridge (MA); *m* 11 Jan 1888 Elizabeth (*d* 1 June 1941), dau of Thomas Cowan, and *d* 1 March 1937, leaving:

1b Noel Warren, CB (1944), CBE (1941), DSO (1917); *b* 24 Dec 1888; *educ* Clifton and RMA Woolwich; WW I (despatches, Brevet Maj, Chevalier du Mérite d'Agricole), Maj-Gen RE, T/Col and Ch Engr Br Forces Palestine 1936–37, AA and QMG 4th Div 1937–39; Brig ic Admin BTE 1939–41, DAG GHQ Middle East 1941–42 and Ch Br Mil Mission to Egyptian Army 1942–45, WW II (despatches twice); *m* 14 July 1921 Margaret (*d* 1983), only dau of Thomas William Vigers, of Guernsey, and *d* 30 Sept 1964, having had:

1c James Francis Warren; *b* 25 Feb, *d* 18 July 1931

1c +Diana Margaret [Mrs John Todd, Dressors, Eversley, Hants]; *b* 24 Jan 1926; *m* 21 Oct 1950 Lt John Evelyn Gray Todd, RN (*d* 1978), er s of Lt-Col Alfred John Kennett Todd, of Bath, and has:

1d +Michael John Clavering; *b* 10 Oct 1951; *educ* Nautical Coll Pangbourne; *m* 1983 *Eileen Margaret Nemoy, of Los Angeles, and has:

1e +Jenna Lauren; *b* 1984

2d +David Matthew; *b* 20 Nov 1953; *educ* Sherborne

3d +Philip Napier; *b* 29 Sept 1956; *educ* Sherborne

4d +Brian William; *b* 13 March 1958

2b Francis Donald, MC; *b* 28 April 1892; *educ* Clifton; MICE, MIChemE, ACGI; Maj RE Spec Res, WW I (despatches), Dep Dir Roy Ordnance Factories Min Supply WW II, Lt-Col cmdg 10th Bn Denbigh HG, Roy Welch Fus 1942–43; *m* 1 Sept 1920 Dorothy Avison (*d* 1979), only dau of Victor Avison Holroyd, of Leamington Spa, and *d* 28 Dec 1969, leaving:

1c +Jean Margaret Avison, JP, DL [Mrs James Hartridge, The White House, Groby, Leics]; *b* 14 June 1922; *m* 14 Dec 1943 *Capt James Gordon Hartridge, TD, RA, s of James Stanley Hartridge, of Richmond, Rothley, Leics, and has:

1d +David John; *b* 14 Dec 1944; *educ* Oundle; *m* 27 April 1968 *Deborah Jane, dau of Thomas Robson, of Newtown Linford, Leics, and has:

1e +Andrew Charles Napier; *b* 1974

1e +Anthea Frances; *b* 15 Aug 1969

2e +Jessica Mary; *b* 1972

1d +Susan Margaret Anne; *b* 27 Aug 1950; MCSP; *m* 1980 *David Peter Hadfield, MICE, of Johannesburg, and has:

1e +Christopher John; *b* 1984

2e +Alastair David; *b* 1987

2c +Anne Katherine [Mrs Eric Wood-Hill, 7 The Garden, N Woodchester, Glos GL5 5PU]; *b* 20 Jan 1924; *m* 25 Sept 1948 *Eric George Wood-Hill, late RHG (Blues), only s of Cyril Wood-Hill, CBE, and has:

1d +Geoffrey Napier [Geoffrey Wood-Hill Esq, New House Farm, Dorsington, Warwicks]; *b* 30 April 1951; *educ* St Edmund's Sch Canterbury (MBA, BSc); *m* 1980 *Jennifer Margaret Hilton and has:

1e +Joanna Claire; *b* 1981

2e +Eve Katherine; *b* 1984

1d +Heather Anne; *b* 23 Sept 1953; *m* 1st 1978 (*divorce* 1983) Robert David William Roddall, of Barnes, London; *m* 2nd 1987 *Michael Harley and by him has:

1e +Timothy James Alexander; *b* 1987

1e +Victoria Louise; *b* 1989

3c +Frances Alison Eve; *b* 7 April 1929; *m* 23 June 1951 (*divorce* 1988) Maj Richard Mansel Colvile, 1st Bn RGJ (43rd and 52nd), only surv s of Cdr Mansel Brabazon Fiennes Colvile, DSO, RN, and has:

1d +Julia Francis; *b* 7 Dec 1955; *m* 1977 *Nicholas Stephen Gallop, MSc, and has:

1e +Katherine Anna; *b* 1981

2e +Georgina Claire; *b* 1983

2d +Philippa Katherine [Mrs George Sampson, The Cottage, Hall Lane, Taddington, Derbys]; *b* 8 Sept 1957; *m* 1982 *George Edward Sampson, s of D N Sampson, of Grindleford, Derbys, and has:

1e +Elizabeth Jill; *b* 1986

2e +Claire Joanna; *b* 1988

3e +Caroline Louisa; *b* 1990

3d +Joanna Caroline [Mrs Michael Watkiss, Row Farm, Keysoe, Beds]; *b* 21 Dec 1959; BSc; *m* 1980 *Michael Christopher Watkiss and has:

1e +Benjamin Michael; *b* 1984

2e +Alistair James; *b* 1987

3e +Edward George; *b* 1990

4e +Robert David; *b* 1993

4d +Fiona Patricia; *b* 1 May 1966

1b Edith Margaret; *b* 8 Sept 1890; *m* 1st 9 Nov 1911 Lt-Col William Hamilton Kenrick, IMS (*d* 7 May 1927), 3rd s of William Kenrick, of Wynn Hall, Ruabon, and had issue; *m* 2nd 12 June 1928 Rev Alwin Corden Larmour, of Wellington Coll, Berks (*d* 1 Nov 1946)

3a Henry Percy (Rev); *b* 7 July 1861; *educ* Cambridge (MA); Vicar Tetsworth, Oxon; *m* 23 Feb 1909 Clarissa Katie Elizabeth, est dau of Francis Gedge, of Redhill, Surrey, and *d* 14 Aug 1935

4a Arthur Lenox NAPIER-CLAVERING later NAPIER, OBE, DL Northumberland; *b* 3 Dec 1863; Capt Yorks Regt, Sec TAA; *m* 1st 15 Oct 1890 Marianne (*d* 2 Sept 1931), dau of Louis Valentine, and had:

1b John Lenox Clavering, CBE (1944); *b* 9 Dec 1898; *educ* Wellington and RMA Woolwich; Brig RTR, WW I, NWF India (Mohmand Ops 1933), WW II (despatches twice), US Legn Merit; *m* 15 April 1925 Grace Edythe Muriel, only dau of Col Charles Augustus Young, CB, CMG, and *d* 27 May 1966, leaving:

1c +Charles John Lenox (Rev) [The Rev Charles Napier, The Rectory, Drewsteignton, Devon]; *b* 24 April 1929; *educ* Radley and Univ Coll Oxford (BA 1952, MA 1957); late 2nd Lt RTR; Lecturer London Coll Divinity 1966; *m* 3 Oct 1964 *Jane Noel, dau of Rev Gerard Noel Davidson, of Drewsteignton Rectory, and has:

1d +William John Noel; *b* 18 Aug 1965; *m* 1990 *Lynne Margaret, yr dau of Geoffrey Wright, of Folkstone, Kent

2d +Henry Lenox Charles; *b* 19 June 1967

1d +Anna Clare; *b* 1970

2c +Gerald William Alastair [Col Gerald Napier, Dunterton Glebe House, Tavistock, Devon PL19 0QJ]; *b* 23 Nov 1932; *educ* Radley, RMA Sandhurst and Gonville and Caius Coll Cambridge (MA); Col RE; *m* 23 April 1962 *Marjorie Currie, dau of Robert Torrance, of Peebles, and has:

1d +Alexander John Robert [Alexander Napier Esq, 730 Meyersville Rd, Gillette, NJ 07933, USA]; *b* 7 July 1963; *m* 1988 *Nicola, dau of John Sykes, of Stanstead, Essex, and has:

1e +Jack Alexander Luke; *b* 1992

2e +Sam Augustus James; *b* 21 Aug 1994

1e +Molly Rose; *b* 16 Aug 1997

2d +Mark [Mark Napier Esq, 34 Meadow Rd, London SW8]; *b* 19 May 1964; *m* 1994 *Fiona, dau of Michael King, OBE, of Cambridge

3d +George [George Napier Esq, Lista de Carreos, 07620 Llucmajor, Mallorca, Spain]; *b* 27 May 1967; *m* 1995 *Helen, dau of John Brown, of Eltham, London

1c +Jean Elizabeth Alison [Mrs Jean Seivwright, 46 Causewayend, Coupar Angus, Blairgowrie PH13 9DX]; *b* 18 April 1931; *educ* Roedean; MSCP; *m* Aug 1970 (*divorce* 1988) John Seivwright

1b Lilias Edith; *b* 3 Jan 1892; *m* 30 July 1912 Sir Eyre Gordon, CSI, CIE, ICS (*d* 28 July 1972), 2nd s of Alexander Hamilton Miller Haven Gordon, of Florida Manor and Delamount, Co Down, and *d* 3 June 1933, having had issue

2b Marian Ellen; *b* 9 Oct 1893; *m* 27 Oct 1917 Capt James Westoll (*d* 27 July 1969), Durham LI (TF), only s of James Westoll, JP, of Darlington, and *d* Aug 1969, leaving two sons and a dau

4a (cont.) Arthur Napier *m* 2nd 9 April 1941 *Mary Adelaide, dau of K E Landsdale, of Sidcup, Kent, and *d* 13 Dec 1945

5a Alan Bertram NAPIER-CLAVERING later NAPIER; *b* 1 Oct 1867; *educ* Rossall and Trin Coll Cambridge (BA 1889); ICS, Kaisar-i-Hind medal; *d* unm 20 Aug 1950

6a Claude Gerald; *b* 3 Feb 1869; *m* 31 July 1897 Millicent Mary (*d* 26 March 1932), dau of Rt Hon William Kenrick, and *d* 29 May 1938, leaving:

1b Mark NAPIER-CLAVERING later NAPIER (deed poll 27 May 1924); *b* 5 May 1898; *educ* Clifton; *m* 1st 23 July 1921 (*divorce* 1945) Elizabeth (*d* 1974), er dau of Sir (Samuel) Squire Sprigge, MD, FRCS, FRCP, novelist, author: *Castle in Andalusia* and *The Raven's Wing*, biographer of Gertrude Stein and Dame Sybil Thorndike, and had:

1c +Julyan [Mrs Cawthra Mulock, Falconfield, RR2 Stn Main, Newmarket, Ontario L3Y 4V9, Canada]; *m* 3 Dec 1946 *Cawthra Falconbridge Mulock, only s of Cawthra Mulock, of Toronto, and has:

1d +Richard Cawthra [Richard Mulock Esq, Camphill Village, Angus, Ontario L0M 1B0, Canada]; *b* 3 Aug 1948; *educ* New Sch, Kings Langley

2d +Julian Napier [Julian Mulock Esq, 4 Chester Hill Rd, Toronto, Ontario M4K 1X3, Canada]; *b* 3 May 1950; *educ* Michael Hall, Forest Row; *m* 1993 *Andrea Risk

3d +Mark Ettrick [Mark Mulock Esq, Makarios, 17902 St Croix Isle Dve, Tampa, FL 33647, USA]; *b* 29 June 1951; *educ* Michael Hall; *m* 1982 *Miranda Ramsay and has:

1e +Jonathan; *b* 1990

2e +Geoffrey; *b* 1992

4d +Nigel Falcon [Nigel Mulock Esq, 27 Stadium St, London SW10 0PU]; *b* 4 June 1955; *educ* Sussex U (BA)

2c +Ruth [Mrs Timothy Lumley-Smith, The Old School House, Fawley, Wantage, Oxon]; *m* 12 Feb 1944 Capt Timothy Algernon Lumley-Smith (*d* 1979), 17th/21st Lancers, er s of Maj Sir Thomas Gabriel Lumley-Smith, DSO, of Kintbury, Berks, and has:

1d +Elizabeth; *b* 1947

2d +Sarah; *b* 1949

3d +Jane; *b* 1951

1b (cont.) Mark Napier *m* 2nd 1946 *Frances Alice [Mrs Mark Napier, 14 William Morgan Dve, Toronto, Canada], dau of Dr Henry Allen Turner, of Millbrook, Ontario, and *d* 1983

2b Alan William NAPIER-CLAVERING later Alan NAPIER (1952 on taking US citizenship); *b* 7 Jan 1903; *educ* Clifton; film actor; *m* 1st 1930 (*divorce* 1944) Nancy Bevill (*d* 27 March 1970), dau of Frank Pethybridge, and had:

1c +Jennifer Mary; *b* 25 March 1931; *m* 1 Oct 1950 *Robert E Nichols, of California, and has:

1d +David; *b* 1954

1d +Christie Catherine; *b* 10 Jan 1952

2b (cont.) Alan Napier *m* 2nd 1944 Aileen Dickens Bourchier (*d* 12 Feb 1961), yr dau of Ernest Bourchier Hawksley, and *d* 1988

1b Mary Helen; *b* 14 May 1900; *educ* St Anne's Coll Oxford (BA 1925); adopted 1942:

Colin POWELL later POWELL NAPIER (deed poll 1959); *b* 17 Dec 1937

2 (cont.) Maj The Hon Charles Napier *m* 2nd 2 July 1840 Annabella Jane (*d* 6 March 1885), only dau of Edward Gatacre, JP, DL, of Gatacre, Salop, and *d* 15 Dec 1874, having by her had, with a dau (*d* young):

(4) Edward; *b* 12 June 1841; Col, cmded Cav Depot, Canterbury; *m* 12 June 1866 Marthe Louise (*d* 25 May 1918), est dau of William Barber Buddicom, of Penbedw Hall, Flintshire, and *d* 15 April 1922, having had, with another dau (*d* young):

1a Egbert; *b* 12 Aug 1867; Maj 3rd Bn Gordon Highrs, Ch Constable Norfolk 1909–16; *m* 20 Sept 1901 Evangeline Senechal (*d* 11 Oct 1936), dau of J G Dreyer, of Valsschrivierdrift, Orange River Colony, SA; *ka* 13 Nov 1916, leaving:

1b Evangeline Mary; *b* 25 April 1904; *m* 22 June 1925 Percy Henry Vincent-Fosbery, s of Percy Henry Vincent-Fosbery, of Clifton, Bristol, and had:

1c +Napier; *b* 1926

2c +Anthony Vincent; *b* 1929

2b Esmé Georgiana; *b* 1 July 1905; *m* 28 Sept 1931 Stephen Napier Bax, est s of Rev Canon Arthur Nesham Bax, of Sherborne, Dorset, and had issue

2a Owen Lloyd Hownam; *b* 1 Aug 1869; *educ* Winchester; India Forest Service; *m* 21 Oct 1898 Eliza Davidson (*d* 1918), dau of Gen David Pott, CB, of Todrig, Selkirk, and *dsp* 1948

3a George Charles; *b* 20 Aug 1873; Lt RNR; *d* unm 27 Nov 1949

1a Phyllis Louise; *b* 4 Aug 1868; *m* 23 Jan 1899 Sir Henry Staveley Lawrence, KCSI, ICS (*d* 29 June 1949), s of George Henry Lawrence, Bengal CS, and *d* July 1912, leaving issue

2a Diana Caroline Marie; *b* 3 March 1875; *m* 17 June 1899 Rev Arthur Nesham Bax (*d* 18 March 1960), Vicar Long Benton, Newcastle, and *d* 1 Dec 1912, leaving issue

3a Jane Rosamond; *b* 19 July 1879; *m* 14 March 1914 her bro-in-law Sir Henry Staveley Lawrence, KCSI, ICS, and *d* 16 Feb 1976, leaving issue

(5) William Archibald; *b* 25 March 1845; *m* 30 April 1879 Mabel (*d* 2 April 1943), yst dau of William Edward Royds, of Greenhill, Rochdale, and *d* 13 Aug 1901, leaving:

1a Charles; *b* 14 Feb 1880; Boer War, WW I, Chev Order Leopold Belgium; *m* 1909 Lillie (*d* 2 Feb 1961), dau of J Mills, of Frome, Somerset, and *d* 22 Sept 1930, leaving:

1b +Marcelle; *b* 31 May 1910

2a Alan; *b* 9 July 1881; V-Consul Naples 1909–21, Consul Bologna 1921–22, Fiume 1922–24 and Venice 1924–40, FO 1940–41; *m* 21 Nov 1911 Dorothy Emily Austin (*d* 16 May 1960), yr dau of James Robertson-Walker, JP, of Distington, Cumberland, and *dsp* 14 Dec 1960

3a Lenox, CE; *b* 26 Aug 1887; Maj RE; *m* 11 Nov 1916 Florence Kathleen, 3rd dau of Alexander Abercrombie, of Rusholme, Lancs, and *dsp* 13 July 1925

1a Esmé; *b* 9 July 1884; *m* 25 July 1905 Frank Douglas Montgomerie (*d* 3 April 1951), est s of Capt Frederick Montgomerie, of Fittleworth, Sussex, and had issue

(6) Lenox; *b* 17 Sept 1846; Cdr RN; *m* 21 June 1873 Ellin (*d* 6 March 1933), 2nd dau of William Barber Buddicom, of Penbedw Hall, Flints, and *d* 21 Jan 1886, leaving:

1a Henry Lenox; *b* 18 June 1876; Maj 11th Bn Sherwood Foresters, Notts and Derbyshire Regt, Boer War (two medals and five clasps); *m* 1 Feb 1911 Dorothy Alyn Louise, yst dau of James Mathias, of Fareham, Hants, and *das* aboard hospital ship *Anglia* 17 Nov 1915

2a William Rawdon, CB (1927), CMG (1919), DSO (1917); *b* 13 June 1877; Adml, Naval ADC to HM GEORGE V 1923, First Naval memb Cwlth Naval Board 1926–29, WW I (despatches); *m* 22 July 1902 Florence Marie (*d* 13 Dec 1965), est dau of James O'Reilly Nugent (see NUGENT, Bt, of Ballinlough), and *d* 8 April 1951, leaving:

1b Mark; *b* 10 May 1911; *educ* Beaumont; Lt-Cdr RN; *m* 28 June 1945 *Hon Jean Astley, yst dau of 21st Baron Hastings (*qv*), and *d* 8 Feb 1962, leaving:

1c +Brian Mark Lenox [Brian Napier Esq, 119 Kingsmead Ave, Worcester Park, Surrey KT4 8UT]; *b* 28 May 1946; *educ* Hamilton Lodge Sch, Brighton; *m* 11 Sept 1970 *Melinda, er dau of James Prideaux, of Finchley, and has:

1d +Mark Anthony Rawdon; *b* 1975

1d +Jemina Melinda Sarah; *b* 1972

1b +Ellin Ruth Veronica; *b* 22 June 1916

3a Patrick Ronald; *b* 3 April 1879; Capt ASC Boer War (medal with two clasps); *m* 6 Oct 1903 his er bro's sis-in-law Kathleen Hilda Mary (*d* 1 April 1948), 2nd dau of James O'Reilly Nugent, and *d* 30 May 1911, leaving:

1b +Patricia Marion Barbara [Reverend Mother (Patricia Napier), La Rameé 5902, Jauchelette, Belgium]; *b* 27 July 1904; nun, formerly at Bangalore, India

1a Barbara; *b* 5 May 1874; *d* 7 July 1878

2a Ellin Winifred; *b* 12 March 1881; nun; *d* 24 Nov 1968

(7) Alfred; *b* 13 May 1848; *m* 20 July 1886 Mary Louisa (*d* 10 Oct 1928), dau of Gen Charles Vanbrugh Jenkins, of Cruckton Hall, Salop, and *d* 29 Jan 1916, leaving:

1a Donald Charles; *b* 1893; 2nd Lt Sherwood Foresters WW I (wounded); *d* 17 Jan 1963

1a Mary Katherine; *d* unm 8 Sept 1969

(1) Annabella Jane; *m* 5 Aug 1869 Thomas W Gill, of Trewerse, Oswestry, and *dsp* 6 Jan 1902

(2) Lilias; *m* 5 Aug 1874 Sir Thomas Wilmot Peregrine Blomefield, 4th Bt, CB (*qv*), and *d* 6 Aug 1933, leaving issue

3 Henry Alfred (Rev); *b* 20 June 1797; Rector Swyncombe, Oxon; Master Ewelme Hosp; author: *Historical Notices of Swyncombe and Ewelme*; *d* 20 Nov 1871

1 Maria Margaret; *m* 29 Aug 1816 Rev Orfeur William Kilvington, Vicar Brignall, Yorks, and *d* his widow 19 July 1861

2 Anne; *m* 13 June 1816 Sir Thomas Gibson-Carmichael, 10th Bt, and *d* 7 Dec 1862, leaving issue (see GIBSON-CRAIG-CARMICHAEL, Bt)

3 Caroline; *m* 9 April 1825 Nevile Reid and *d* his widow 9 Nov 1844, leaving issue

The 8th LORD's est son,

WILLIAM JOHN NAPIER, **9th Lord Napier of Merchistoun**; *b* 13 Oct 1786; Capt RN Battle of Trafalgar; rep S peer 1824–32, Ld Bedchamber to WILLIAM IV, Special Trade Commr and Ch Resident Canton, China, 1833; *m* 28 March 1816 Elizabeth (*d* 6 June 1883), only dau of Hon Andrew James Cochrane Johnstone (see DUNDONALD, E), and *d* 11 Oct 1834, having had, with two daus (*d* unm):

1 FRANCIS, **10th Lord**

2 William; *b* 27 July 1821; *m* 3 May 1854 Louisa May (*d* 13 Oct 1908), dau of John H Lloyd, QC, and *d* 21 Jan 1876, having had, with a dau (*d* unm):

(1) Francis Horatio, OBE (1919); *b* 7 Feb 1861; BS Lond, MB, FRCS Eng, LLD Witwatersrand, Maj S African Med Corps (Res), MLA Transvaal; *m* 1st 26 April 1893 (*divorce* 1923) Margaret Elizabeth Horatio (*d* March 1947), dau of Lt-Col William Hope, VC (*see* LINLITHGOW, M), and had:

1a Archibald John Robert; *b* 19 March 1894; *educ* Charterhouse and RMC Sandhurst; WW I as Capt Cheshire Regt and RFC (wounded), WW II as Maj RAOC; PWD Tanganyika Territory; *m* 12 Nov 1926 Lilian Grey Delphin (*d* 1979), dau of Christopher Delphin Petersen, of Oslo, and *d* 5 April 1967, leaving:

1b +William Francis André [William Napier Esq, 22 Ruston Terrace, Mt Masura, Perth, Western Australia 6112]; *b* 10 Nov 1927; *educ* France; *m* 6 Nov 1954 *Rosemary, dau of Charles William Jacobs, BEM, research engr, and has:

1c +Stephen Charles Edward; *b* 1 Aug 1955

1c +Anne-Marie; *b* 27 Dec 1956

2b +Robert Anthony Peter [Robert Napier Esq, 162 Boldmere Rd, Sutton Coldfield, W Midlands B73 5UD]; *b* 17 July 1940; *educ* Cotton Coll; *m* 1983 *Teresa Dent

1b +Charlotte Esmé Mary-Rose [Mrs Richard Rose, 7 Church Lane, E Huntspill, Highbridge, Somerset TA9 3PJ]; *b* 5 Jan 1930; MCSP; *m* 31 Aug 1956 *Richard Harry Rose, only s of Donald Henry Barker Rose, of Birmingham, and has:

1c +Nicholas Henry Napier [Nicholas Rose Esq, Clearwater Estate, Zimbabwe]; *b* 9 May 1957; *m* 1989 (*divorce* 199–) Laure Anne, dau of Alain Legréau, of Draguigan, France, and has:

1d +Dominic Henry; *b* 3 May 1991

2d +Pierre Anthony; *b* 26 Oct 1992

2c +Alistair Donald; *b* 8 March 1964

1c +Yvonne Charlotte [Mrs Hugh Norman, 15 Hay St, Marshfield, Wilts SN14 8NL]; *b* 23 May 1958; *m* 1988 *Hugh Alexander Norman and has:

1d +Alexander Henry; *b* 24 Nov 1988

2d +Thomas Martin; *b* 9 Sept 1990

2c +Mary Eleanor; *b* 12 March 1961

2a Laurence Egerton Scott, DSO (1920); *b* 1896; Cdr RN WW I (despatches); *m* 1st 1921 (*divorce*) Nora Creina, dau of Owen Christian, of Port Elizabeth, S Africa; *m* 2nd 27 June 1930 (*divorce*) Florence Silvia Jack (*m* 2nd C Tizzard, of Cape Town), and *d* 19 Aug 1969, having by her had:

1b +Patricia [Mrs Robert Moseley, 1 De Klerks Drive, De Klerkshof, Edenvale, Transvaal, S Africa]; *b* 13 April 1931; *m* 1952 *Robert Louis Moseley

3a Basil Hope; *b* 6 Aug 1911; lost in the bush near Babi, Tanganyika, 10 Oct 1932

(1) (cont.) Francis Napier *m* 2nd 2 Oct 1923 Isoline Richards, only dau of Frederick Barriff Shotter, of Shotover, Surrey, and *d* 10 Sept 1949

(2) Charles Frederick; *b* 24 Feb 1862; *educ* Oxford (BA); barrister, High Court Judge Madras; *d* 21 July 1932

(3) William John, CB (1917), CMG (1916); *b* 10 Nov 1863; Maj-Gen RA, Boer War (medal with clasps), WW I (wounded, despatches), Order Crown Italy, Offr Legn Hon; *m* 4 Sept 1889 Maud Denison Gooch (*d* 10 Nov 1941), only dau of Col Edward Nicol William Holbrook, RMLI, and *d* 18 Nov 1925, leaving:

1a Arthur Francis Scott; *b* 20 Sept 1890; *educ* Wellington; served WW I, Brig RA, Brevet Lt-Col 1933, Brevet Col 1937, Ch Instr Mil Coll Science 1936–38, Memb Ordnance Ctee 1938–39, Mil Adviser Min Supply 1940–46 (ret 1946), Memb Dorset CC 1949–55, Memb W Dorset Hosp Management Ctee 1956–60; *m* 15 Nov 1915 Phyllis Grace (*d* 1978), er dau of Edward Fleming, and *d* 1971, having had:

1b Charles John Scott; *b* 12 Oct 1917; *d* unm 24 April 1948

1b +Margaret Esmé [Mrs John Whittingdale, Runnymede, 69 Newland, Sherborne, Dorset DT9 3AG]; *b* 30 Dec 1920; *m* 1st 18 May 1942 (*divorce* 1946) Capt Ephraim Stewart Cook Spence, Argyll & Sutherland Highrs, s of A T G Spence, of Ardvreck Gardens, Crieff; *m* 2nd 21 Sept 1946 her cousin Maj Alexander Napier (*d* 31 Aug 1954), Indian Political Service, s of Archibald Scott Napier (*see below*) and has issue; *m* 3rd 30 Dec 1957 John Whittingdale, FRCS (*d* 1974), s of John Flasby Lawrance Whittingdale, BA, MB, of Wharton, Sherborne, and by him has:

1c +John Flasby Lawrance, OBE (1990) [John Whittingdale Esq OBE MP, House of Commons, London SW1A 0AA]; *b* 16 Oct 1959; *educ* Winchester and U Coll London (BSc Econ); Political Sec to PM 1988–90, MP (C) S Colchester and Maldon 1992–97 and Maldon and Chelmsford East 1997–, Oppn Whip 1997–98, Oppn Treasury Spokesman 1998–; *m* 1990 *Ancilla Campbell Murfitt and has:

1d +Henry John Flasby; *b* 1993

1d +Alice Margaret Campbell; *b* 20 Dec 1995

(4) Archibald Scott; *b* 9 June 1865; MInstCE; *m* 16 March 1889 Katherine Edith (*d* 20 Dec 1942), est dau of Robert Liveing, MD, and *d* 22 Dec 1934, leaving:

1a Charles Scott, CB, CBE; *b* 3 Feb 1899; *educ* Wellington; Maj-Gen RE WW II, Ch Movements and Tportn Branch 6–4 Div, Supreme HQ, Allied Expdny Force 1943–45, Legn Hon, Cdr US Legn Merit; *m* 8 Aug 1927 Ida Kathleen (*d* 1979), dau of Victor Napoleon Douétil, and *d* 16 June 1946, leaving:

1b Michael Scott (Rev); *b* 15 Feb 1929; *educ* Wellington and Trin Hall Cambridge (MA 1955); RC priest (Oratorian); *d* 22 Aug 1996

2a Alexander; *b* 7 Sept 1904; *educ* Wellington; Maj IA and Indian Political Service, V-Consul Khoramshahr 1939, Sec to Resident Eastern States Calcutta 1946, ret 1947; *m* 21 Sept 1946 *Margaret Esmé Scott (Spence) (*m* 3rd 30 Dec 1958 John Whittingdale, FRCS), dau of Brig Arthur Francis Scott Napier (*see above*), and *d* 31 Aug 1954, leaving:

1b +Charles Scott; *b* 1 July 1947; *educ* Wellington and Exeter U (BA 1969)

(1) Lilias; *m* 1st 27 July 1881 William Rose Robinson (*d* 1885), est s of Sir William Rose Robinson, KCSI; *m* 2nd 18 Oct 1893 Henry Alfred Constant Bonar, CMG (*d* 5 Aug 1935), Consul-Gen Seoul, Korea, and *d* 20 July 1938

1 Maria Margaret; *m* 19 April 1837 1st Baron Addington (*qv*) and *d* 18 April 1896, having had issue

2 Eliza; *m* 18 Aug 1847 Sir John Charles Dalrymple-Hay, 3rd Bt (*qv*), and *d* 2 April 1901, leaving issue

3 Anne Carmichael; *m* 29 April 1847 Capt Hon George Hope, RN, and *d* 28 May 1877, leaving issue (*see* LINLITHGOW, M)

4 Ellinor Alice; *m* 10 Nov 1853 Hon George Grey Dalrymple and *d* 11 May 1903, leaving issue (*see* STAIR, E)

The 9th LORD's est son,

FRANCIS NAPIER, **10th Lord Napier of Merchistoun** and **1st Baron Ettrick of Ettrick**, Co Selkirk (UK), so *cr* 16 July 1872, KT (1864), PC (1861); *b* 15 Sept 1819; LLD, Harvard, Glasgow and Edinburgh Us; Envoy Extrdy and Min Plen USA 1857–59 and Netherlands 1859–61, Amb Russia 1861–64 and Prussia 1864–66, Govr Madras 1866–72, Actg Viceroy India 1872; *m* 2 Sept 1845 Anne Jane Charlotte, CI (*d* 24 Aug 1911), only dau of Robert Manners Lockwood, and *d* 19 Dec 1898, having had:

1 WILLIAM JOHN GEORGE, **11th Lord and 2nd Baron**

2 John Scott, CMG; *b* 13 Nov 1848; Col Gordon Highrs, Inspr Army Gymnasia 1897–1905, served Afghanistan 1878–80 at Battle of Kandahar (despatches three times), S Africa 1881 and 1900 (despatches); *m* 1st 6 April 1876 Isabella (*d* 12 Nov 1928), yst dau of Thomas Shaw, of Ditton, Lancs, and Hyde Park Sq, London, and widow of Maj James Leith, VC (*see* BURGH, B), and had:

(1) Lilias Dorothea Scott; *m* 18 Oct 1913 Reginald Evan Wynne-Roberts, Coldstream Gds, er s of Maj Reginald Wynn Wynne, DSO, and had issue

2 (cont.) Col The Hon John Napier *m* 2nd Dec 1928 Eva Ingledew (*d* 18 April 1946), est dau of Charles Selby Davidson, of Newcastle, and *d* 9 March 1938

3 Basil; *b* 3 July 1850; Lt RN; *d* 21 Feb 1874

4 Mark Francis; *b* 21 Jan 1852; *educ* Cambridge (BA); barrister, MP Roxburgh 1892–95; *m* 30 May 1878 Emily Jones (*d* 20 Oct 1922), illegitimate dau of 7th Viscount Ranelagh, and *d* 19 Aug 1919, leaving:

(1) Basil; *b* 16 March 1879; Imperial Yeo S Africa, where *ka* 28 Dec 1900

(2) Claude Inverness, JP (Hants); *b* 1 April 1880; Maj RASC; *m* 5 Jan 1917 Lilian (*d* 1972), er dau of Lt-Cdr Alfred Francey, RN, of Ballymena, Co Antrim, and *d* 14 March 1946, leaving:

1a +Mark Francis [Mark Napier Esq, Northfield House, Northfield, Somerton, Somerset]; *b* 10 May 1925; *m* 1951 *Mary Frances, only dau of Prof A W Ling, of Parkstone, Dorset, and has:

1b +Charles Algernon [Charles Napier Esq, 3 Manor Close, Kingsdon, Somerton, Somerset]; *b* 28 Aug 1953; *m* 1977 *Heather, est dau of Dennis Harding, and has:

1c +Sebastian Charles Bruce; *b* 1979

1c +Sophie Ann Frances; *b* 1982

2b +Robert Bruce [Robert Napier Esq, 37 King Ina Rd, Somerton, Somerset]; *b* 28 Feb 1959; *m* 1980 *Susan Ellen, yst dau of Ceril Parsley, and has:

1c +Matthew Victor Mark; *b* 1988

1c +Gemma Marie; *b* 1984

1b +Claudia Frances; *b* 5 Sept 1962

1a +Margaret Emily [Mrs Peter Hincks, The Hatch, Upton, Langport, Somerset]; *b* 4 Sept 1919; *m* 1954 *Peter Hincks, of Berks

2a +Eleanor Rosemary Jean; *b* 18 March 1921; *m* 4 April 1942 Capt Frank Wilson, s of William Wilson, of Greyfriars, Chapel-en-le-Frith, nr Stockport

(3) Philip Henry; *b* 17 April 1884; *educ* Trin Coll Cambridge (BA 1905); Egyptian CS; *m* 7 Sept 1909 Gabrielle Jean (*d* 3 Feb 1936), yst dau of Sir Charles Harvey, 2nd Bt (*see* HARVEY OF TASBURGH, B), and *d* 11 March 1965, having had:

1a Basil Mark; *b* 2 Feb 1911; *educ* Magdalene Coll Cambridge (BA 1933); *m* 21 Dec 1935 *Elizabeth Jean, er dau of Col Reginald John Armes, CMG, and *dsp* 27 May 1961

2a Nigel Claude Oliver; *b* 28 Aug 1913; *educ* Trin Coll Cambridge; Maj RA WW II (despatches); *m* 1st 14 April 1945 Lucy Margaret (*d* 1980), only dau of Capt Arthur Walter Brown, MBE, JP, of Thackley, nr Bradford; *m* 2nd 1983 *Hazel Therese, est dau of Joseph Dolan, and *d* 1994, having had by his 1st w:

1b +Alastair Denis; *b* 12 July 1946; *educ* Stowe

The 10th LORD/1st BARON's est son,

WILLIAM JOHN GEORGE NAPIER, **11th Lord Napier of Merchistoun** and **2nd Baron Ettrick of Ettrick**, DL (Selkirk); *b* 22 Sept 1846; Sec Legation Stockholm 1887–88, Chargé d'Affaires Tokyo 1888–91; *m* 1st 5 Jan 1876 Harriet Blake Armstrong (*d* 5 June 1897), yst dau of Edward Lumb, of Wallington Lodge, Surrey, and Buenos Aires, and had:

1 FRANCIS EDWARD BASIL, **12th Lord and 3rd Baron**

2 Frederick William Scott; *b* 10 May 1878; Lt 3rd Bn KOSB, Capt 7th SW Bdrs, Boer War 1902, WW I; Toronto City Constabulary 1905–08; *d* 16 May 1935

The **11th Lord/2nd Baron** *m* 2nd 19 July 1898 Grace (*d* 29 Jan 1928), 2nd dau of James Cleland Burns, and *d* 6 Dec 1913, having by her had:

3 Archibald Lenox Colquhoun William John George; *b* 11 Dec 1899; *educ* RNCs Osborne and Dartmouth; Cdr RN; *m* 1st 3 July 1924 Barbara Fountayne (*d* 8 Aug 1926), only child of Rev Reginald William WILBERFORCE later PULESTON (deed poll 15 Oct 1924), of Bittering Hall, Norfolk, and had:

(1) William Puleston Scott; *b* 22 Jan 1923; *educ* Eton; WW II with Roy Norfolk Regt; *m* 28 May 1949 *Rosemary Heather, yr dau of Capt R H A McLaren, of Thetford, Norfolk, and *d* 1986, leaving:

1a +Lenox Scott; *b* 26 Nov 1953; *educ* Rugby; *m* and has a son

3 (cont.) Cdr Archibald Napier *m* 2nd 8 Sept 1928 Marianne Irene (*d* 1958), yst dau of John Russell-Cox, JP, of Manor House, Beaminster, Dorset, and gdau of Rev Charles Marriott Leir, of Ditcheat Priory, Somerset, and *d* 6 June 1951, having by her had:

(2) Archibald; *b* 14 Sept, *d* 15 Sept 1929

The 11th LORD/2nd BARON's est s,

FRANCIS EDWARD BASIL NAPIER, **12th Lord Napier of Merchistoun** and **3rd Baron Ettrick of Ettrick**, JP (Selkirk); *b* 19 Nov 1876; memb Roy Co Archers; Capt 7th KRRC and RAF WW I; *m* 12 Dec 1899 Hon Clarice Jessie Evelyn (*d* 11 May 1951), dau of 9th Lord Belhaven and Stenton (*qv*), and *d* 22 March 1941, having had:

1 WILLIAM FRANCIS CYRIL JAMES HAMILTON, **13th Lord** and **4th Baron**

2 Neville Archibald John Watson Ettrick; *b* 25 Jan 1904; *educ* RNCs Osborne and Dartmouth; Cdr RN, Flag Lt to C-in-C E Indies and Adml cmdg HF Destroyers WW II, Gold Staff Offr Coronation 1953; *m* 1st 1 May 1937 Eileen (*d* 18 Jan 1965), est dau of Hubert Prangley Thorne, of Alleyne's House, Stevenage, Herts; *m* 2nd 6 June 1967 *(Helen) Catherine [The Hon Mrs Neville Napier, Kippilaw, St Boswells, Roxburghshire TD6 9HF], yr dau of John Martin Sanderson, of Linthill, Melrose, and *dsp* 8 Oct 1970

3 Alastair John George Malcolm, TD (1947); *b* 9 June 1909; *educ* Merchiston and Sherborne; Maj RE WW II, Kenya Min Works 1950–65; *m* 6 May 1933 Geraldine (*d* 1983), yr dau of James Dunlop, of The Bield, Ayr, and *d* 1984, having had:

(1) +Diana Elizabeth [Mrs Robin Harris, Eden Croft, Wetheral, Carlisle, Cumbria CA4 8HA]; *b* 26 May 1939; *m* 8 July 1967 *Maj Robin Edward Doveton Harris, MBE, MC, 14th/20th King's Hus, er s of Capt Cuthbert Harris, of Thirsk, Yorks, and has:

1a +Gerald Neville Napier; *b* 21 Aug 1975

1a +Serita Catherine; *b* 21 April 1968; *m* 24 July 1993 *Nicholas David Mark Sleep and has:

1b +Jessica Catherine; *b* 8 Jan 1997

2a +Meralynn Elizabeth; *b* 8 March 1970

3a +Chania Rozanthe; *b* 28 Dec 1973

1 Augusta Caroline Georgina Harriet Mary; *b* 28 Nov 1901; *m* 27 Sept 1922 Col James Hebblethwaite Martin Frobisher, OBE, MB, RAMC, s of William Frobisher, MD, of Leeds, a descendant of Sir Martin Frobisher, the Elizabethan sea-dog, and *d* 11 Oct 1962, leaving issue

The 12th LORD/2nd BARON's est s,

WILLIAM FRANCIS CYRIL JAMES HAMILTON NAPIER, **13th Lord Napier of Merchistoun** and **3rd Baron Ettrick of Ettrick**, TD, JP, DL; *b* 9 Sept 1900; *educ* Wellington and RMC Sandhurst; Lt-Col KOSB WW II cmdg a Bn of his Regt and on Staff, AAG War Office 1943–44; memb Roy Co Archers, CC Selkirk (1946–48); *m* 28 Sept 1928 (Violet) Muir (*d* 1992), Nat Pres YWCA of Scotland, er dau of Sir Percy Wilson Newson, 1st and last Bt (*see* 1949 edn), and *d* 23 Aug 1954, leaving:

1 (FRANCIS) NIGEL NAPIER, **14th and present Lord Napier of Merchistoun** and **4th and present Baron Ettrick of Ettrick**

2 +(Charles) Malcolm [The Hon Malcolm Napier, Bardmony House, Alyth, Perthshire; 1 Newton Spicer Dve, Highlands, Harare, Zimbabwe, SA]; *b* 8 June 1933; *educ* Canford; Capt Lothian and Border Horse (TA), formerly Lt 1st Roy Dragoons, Egypt 1952–53; memb Roy Co Archers, chm and md Inyati Gold Mining Co (Pty Ltd), fndr memb Cncl Anglo-Rhodesian Soc, dir Caravan Mfrs Ltd, Viking Travel Ltd and General Belting (PVT Ltd); *m* 25 Jan 1969 *Lady Mariota Cecilia Murray, yr dau of 7th Earl of Mansfield and Mansfield (*qv*), and has:

(1) +Eloise Dorothea; *b* 10 March 1970

(2) +Maryel Cecilia; *b* Sept 1973

(3) +Cecilia Frances Stephanie; *b* 18 Dec 1976

3 (John) Greville; *b* 3 Jan 1939; *educ* Fettes; md Napier Antiques Ltd; with Christie, Manson and Woods, and H W Kell Ltd; *m* 27 March 1968 *Juliet Elizabeth Hargreaves [The Hon Mrs Greville Napier, Underhill, Treyford, Midhurst, W Sussex GU29 0LD], only dau of Sir Alexander Charles Durie, CBE, of The Garden House, Windlesham, Surrey, Dir-Gen AA 1964–77, and *d* 1988, having had:

(1) +Lucilla Fleur Scott; *b* 14 July 1969; *m* 12 March 1994 *Richard Anthony Agace Ferard, er s of James Ferard, of Ewdness, Bridgnorth, Salop

(2) +Araminta Elizabeth Muir; *b* 3 Oct 1972; *m* 30 Aug 1997 *Andrew Perham, est s of Dr Geoffrey Perham, of Plymouth

4 (Hugh) Lenox; *b* 18 July 1943; *educ* privately; *d unm* 17 Sept 1996

Lineage (of Scott): Sir WALTER SCOTT, of Branxholme (*see* BUCCLEUCH and QUEENSBERRY, D), had a yr s:

ALEXANDER SCOTT; had, with other issue, including an er s (Walter, of Howpaslot):

ROBERT SCOTT; probably f of:

JOHN SCOTT; acquired Thirlestane *c* 1535; granted by JAMES V a royal tressure around his coat of arms; had:

ROBERT SCOTT of Thirlestane; *m* Margaret, dau of Sir Walter Scott of Buccleuch, and had:

1 Robert (Sir), of Thirlestane; *m* 1st a dau of Cranston of that Ilk and had:

(1) Robert (Sir); *m* Lady Mary Lyon, dau of the Earl of Strathmore (*see* STRATHMORE AND KINGHORNE, E), and *dsp*

1 (cont) Sir Robert *m* 2nd Katherine, dau of Sir Alexander Jardine of Applegirth, and by her had:

(2) John (Sir), whose male issue died out

2 WALTER

3 William, of Fingland

The 2nd son,

WALTER SCOTT of Gamescleuch; *m* Janet Porteous and was *k* in a duel 1609, leaving:

PATRICK SCOTT of Tanlawhill; bought up Thirlestane; *m* Isabel, dau of Sir John Murray, 1st Bt, of Blackbarony (*qv*), and *d* 21 June 1666, having had, with other issue (including a dau Jean, *m* Sir James Hay, 1st Bt, of Linplum; *see* TWEEDDALE, M):

Sir Francis Scott, 1st Bt (NS), so *cr* 22 Aug 1666, of Thirlestane; *b* 11 May 1645; *m* (contract 27 Nov 1673) Lady Henrietta Kerr (*d* 30 June 1741), 6th dau of 3rd Earl of Lothian (*see* LOTHIAN, M), and *d* 7 March 1712, leaving:

Sir William Scott, 2nd Bt; *m* 1st 15 Dec 1699 Elizabeth, *Mistress of Napier* (*see* above); *m* 2nd (contract 30 June 1710) Jane, dau of Sir John Nisbet of Dirleton and widow of Sir William Scott of Harden, but by her had no issue, and *d* 8 Oct 1725, leaving by his 1st w an only child:

Sir FRANCIS SCOTT later NAPIER, **3rd Bt**, and **6th Lord Napier of Merchistoun**

NAPIER OF MAGDALA

Arms: Gu. on a saltire, between two mural crowns in pale and as many lions passant in fess or a rose of the field. **Crest:** On a mount vert, a lion passant or, gorged with a collar gu., and a broken chain reflexed over the back, gold, supporting with the sinister forepaw a flagstaff in bend sinister ppr., therefrom flowing a banner arg., charged with a cross couped gu. **Supporters:** Dexter, a soldier of the Royal Engineers; sinister, a Sikh Sirdar; both habited, and each holding in his exterior hand a musket, all ppr. **Motto:** *Tu vincula frange* ('Break thou the chains'). **Creation:** B. (UK) 17 July 1868.

THE 6TH BARON NAPIER OF MAGDALA in Abyssinia and of **CARYNGTON**, Co Palatine of Chester (Robert Alan Napier) [The Rt Hon The Lord Napier of Magdala, The Coach House, Kingsbury St, Marlborough, Wilts SN8 1HU]; *b* 6 Sept 1940; *s* f 1987; *educ* Winchester and St John's Coll Cambridge (BA 1962, MA 1966); *m* 1964 *Frances Clare, est dau of Alan Frank Skinner, OBE, of Monks Close, Woolpit, Suffolk, and has:

1 +JAMES ROBERT; *b* 29 Jan 1966; *educ* Winchester and Edinburgh U; *m* 1992 *Jacqueline, est dau of A Stephen, of Inverkeithing, Fife

1 *Frances Catherine [The Hon Mrs Cholerton, 5 Prince St, N Parramatta, NSW 2151, Australia]; *b* 2 July 1964; *m* 1992 *Simon Andrew Cholerton and has:

(1) *Nicholas Geoffrey; *b* 1991

(1) *Frances Barbara Clare; *b* 1990

Lineage: Maj CHARLES FREDERICK NAPIER, RA; *m* Catherine, dau of Codrington Carrington, of The Chapel and Carrington, Barbados, and Gt Missenden Abbey, Bucks, and *d* March 1812, leaving:

ROBERT CORNELIS NAPIER, **1st Baron Napier of Magdala** in Abyssinia and of **Caryngton** in the County Palatine of Chester (UK), so *cr* 17 July 1868, GCB (1868, KCB July 1858, CB March 1858), GCSI (1867); *b* Ceylon 5 Dec 1810; joined Bengal Engrs 1826, Bde Maj Sutlej Campaigns 1845–46, Siege Moultan 1848, Gujerat 1849, Lt-Col Siege Lucknow and Battle of Powree 1858, thanked by Parl 1858 and 1861 following capture Peking in China War, memb Cncl India 1861–65, C-in-C Bombay Army as Gen 1865–69, Maj-Gen 1861, Lt-Gen 1867, Gen 1874, cmded Abyssinian Expdn 1867, granted annual pension of £2,000 (over £80,000 in late-1990s terms) to him and next surv male heir male for life 1868, C-in-C India 1870–76, Govr Gibraltar 1876–82, Col RE 1874–90, FM 1883, Constable Tower London 1887–90, Lt Tower Hamlets, FRS 1869, Grand Cross Charles III of Spain 1879; *m* 1st 3 Sept 1840 Anne Sarah (*d* 30 Dec 1849), est dau of George Pearse, MD, HEICS, and had:

1 ROBERT WILLIAM NAPIER, **2nd Baron Napier of Magdala**; *b* 11 Feb 1845; Col IA; *m* 27 Jan 1885 Eva Marie Louisa (*d* 7 Feb 1930), widow of Capt Henry Algernon Langham, Gren Gds (*see* LANGHAM, Bt), and dau of 4th Baron Macdonald (*qv*), and *d* 11 Dec 1921, leaving:

(1) Eva Lilian Cecilia, *m* 16 Oct 1906 6th Baron Wynford (*qv*) and *d* 23 March 1974, leaving issue

2 George Campbell, CIE; *b* 11 Feb 1845; Col IA; *m* 7 Feb 1882 Alice Mary (*d* 23 March 1926), only dau of James Beech, of Brandon Hall, Warwicks, and *d* 10 March 1914, leaving:

(1) Rupert George Carrington; *b* 10 Dec 1885; Lt Gren Gds, Capt Warwickshire Yeo; *d* 2 Aug 1917 of wounds recd in action

(1) Sibyl Esther; *d unm* 28 Oct 1962

3 JAMES PEARSE NAPIER, **3rd Baron Napier of Magdala**; *b* 30 Dec 1849; *educ* Cheltenham and Jesus Coll Cambridge (BA 1872); Col 10th Roy Hus, Bde Maj 1887–90, DAAG NE Dist 1890–97, AAG Southern Dist 1900–03, served Afghan

War 1879–80 (medal); *m* 25 July 1876 Mabel Ellen (*d* 16 July 1907), yr dau of Lt-Col Windsor Parker, of Clopton Hall, Suffolk, and had:

(1) James Windsor; *b* 17 Oct 1882; *d* 11 Jan 1883

(1) Gertrude Carrington; *d* unm 24 June 1937

(2) Mabel Alice; *d* unm 15 Aug 1938

1 Catherine Anne Carrington; *b* 12 Oct 1841; *m* 12 March 1863 Henry Robert Dundas and *d* 3 Jan 1929, leaving issue. He *d* 12 Aug 1912

2 Anne Amelia; *b* 11 Nov 1842; *m* 15 March 1864 Henry Robarts Madocks, BCS, and *d* 22 March 1932, leaving issue. He *d* 29 Dec 1902

3 Clara Frances; *b* 19 Dec 1843; *d* June 1846

The **1st Baron** *m* 2nd 2 April 1861 Mary Cecilia, CI (*d* 18 Dec 1930), dau of Maj-Gen Edward William Smyth Scott, RA, and *d* 14 Jan 1890, having by her had:

4 EDWARD HERBERT SCOTT, **4th Baron**

5 Henry Dundas, CMG (1907); *b* 16 Feb 1864; Special Serv offr China Expdny Force 1900 (Brevet Maj), Lt-Col KGO Centl India Horse, Lt KOSB, Mil Attaché Teheran 1901–02, St Petersburg 1903–07, Sofia and Belgrade 1908–11 and Sofia and Bucharest 1914, POW Austria 1916–17, Br Mil Rep Sofia 1918–19; 2nd Cl Order St Anne Russia,*m* 11 Nov 1897 Sybil (*d* 14 Aug 1944), dau of John Gurney, of Sprowston Hall, Norwich, and *d* 13 Nov 1941, leaving:

(1) Arthur Henry Gurney, OBE (1942); *b* 17 May 1900; *educ* Wellington; Col RE WW II; *m* 15 April 1937 Rosemary Evelyn (*d* 1993), 2nd dau of Charles George Lumley Cator (*see* BLOIS, Bt), and *d* 1978, leaving:

1a *Mary-Rose [Miss Mary-Rose Napier, 22 Morrison St, London SW11 5LR]; *b* 3 Feb 1938

2a *Angela Marina; *b* 23 Oct 1940; *m* 1979 *James Denis Merrik Naper, of Newtown House, Loughcrew, Oldcastle, Co Meath, est s of Capt Nigel William Ivo Naper, MC (*see* VALENTIA, V), and has:

1b *Merrik Henry Nigel; *b* 1980

2b *Alexander Denis James; *b* 1981

1b *Isabel Carola Rosemary; *b* 1983

3a *Belinda Jane [Mrs Michael Leather, Heath Farm House, Heath Lane, Childer Thornton, Wirral, Cheshire]; *b* 1 Oct 1946; *m* 5 Oct 1968 Michael Alan Fishwick Leather, yr s of Alan Guy Fishwick Leather, of Heswall, Cheshire, and has:

1b *James Napier Fishwick; *b* 22 March 1971

2b *Giles Napier Fishwick; *b* 1973

(1) Margaret Laura Evelyn; *m* 1st 8 Nov 1922 Richard Samuel Lancelot Worsley (*d* 19 Sept 1937), s of Richard Worsley, of Broxmead, Cuckfield, Sussex, and had:

1a *Richard Henry Napier; *b* 16 March 1924; *educ* Eton and Trin Coll Cambridge (BA Econ, MA 1968); RAF 1942–47; *m* 28 Jan 1954 *Juliet Anne, dau of Henry Herbert Nash, of Cove House, Ashton Keynes, Glos, and has:

1b *Caroline Patricia; *b* 5 Dec 1960

2b *Philippa Jane; *b* 4 Sept 1965

3b *Joanna Rachel; *b* 24 April, 1967

2a *Michael Robert; *b* 23 May 1926; *educ* Stowe and Trin Coll Cambridge; *m* 5 Feb 1964 *Jane Elizabeth, yr dau of Major Percy Arthur Love, and has:

1b *Robert Napier; *b* 26 Nov 1966

2b *Charles Roderick; *b* 2 Jan 1969

1b *Elizabeth Frances; *b* 21 Jan 1965

3a *John Bertrand [John Worsley Esq, Furlong House, Hurstpierpoint, Sussex BN6 9QA]; *b* 7 Jan 1929; *educ* Eton and Trin Coll Cambridge (MA, LLB); *m* 18 July 1956 *Jennifer Jane, barrister Inner Temple 1955, er dau of Sir Andrew Edmund James Clark, 3rd Bt, of Cavendish Sq (*see* 1970 edn), and has:

1b *James Jonathan; *b* 20 Nov 1957; *m* 1987 *Marion Coratte and has issue

1b *Harriet Laura; *b* 25 Oct 1960; *m* 1986 *Mark Thornycroft Vernon (*see* VERNON, Bt) and has issue

2b *Alison Margaret; *b* 24 Sept 1963; *m* 1992 *Christian Holstein and has issue

3b *Victoria Mary; *b* 19 March 1966

(1) (cont) Mrs Richard Worsley *m* 2nd 14 May 1946 Lt-Col Victor Robert Jones, QC, OBE, ED, s of Ernest Jones, of Calgary, Alberta. He *d* 24 July 1979

6 Arthur Fullarton; *b* 4 June 1865; Capt IA; *d* unm 17 July 1898

7 Charles Frederick Hamilton; *b* 19 March 1872; *educ* RMC Sandhurst; Lt-Col RAPC, Capt Rifle Bde, served Tochi Valley 1897 (medal), Boer War 1901–02 (medal, two clasps) and WW I (medal); *m* 23 Oct 1902 Helen Mary Campbell (*d* 15 March 1960), yst dau of Col Sir Alexander Brook-Morgan, KCB, and *d* 15 June 1963, leaving:

(1) Charles Campbell; *b* 16 Aug 1903; *m* 3 Feb 1931 Violet Mushla (*d* 1992), dau of — Burnie, and *d* 1989, leaving:

1a +Peter Charles Cornelis [Peter Napier Esq, Flat 6, 30 Smith Sq, London SW1]; *b* 5 July 1936; dir Tambrands Ltd; *m* 1 April 1962 (*divorce* 1970) Sylvia Walker, dau of Charles Kimball Fitts, of Lincoln, Mass., and has:

1b *Arianne Campbell; *b* 1 Nov 1962

2b *Tanya Kimball; *b* 11 April, 1968

(1) Helen Margaret; *b* Oct 1911; *m* 1st 26 March 1938 Capt Charles Richard Tucker, York and Lancaster Regt (*d* 10 Aug 1941 of wounds recd in action), only s of Rev Alfred Richings Tucker, Rector Leasingham, Lincs, and had:

1a *Rosalind Helen Morgan [Mrs Daniel Guinard, 26 Ave Rue de la Plage, La Hume, 33470 Gujan Mestras, France]; *b* 28 May 1939; *m* *Daniel Guinard

(1) (cont.) Mrs Charles Tucker *m* 2nd 14 July 1944 (*annulled* 1958) Maj Geoffrey Charles Reid, S Staffs Regt, yr s of Lt-Col Charles Savile Reid, DSO, JP, of Wolverley, Yalding, Kent, and *d* 199–

8 Cecil Scott; *b* 13 April 1876; *d* unm 17 Oct 1908

9 Albert Edward Alexander (Sir), KCB (1945), KCVO (1954), KC (1947); *b* 4 Sept 1881; *educ* Eton and New Coll Oxford (BA 1904, MA 1932); barrister Inner Temple 1909 (Master Bench 1949), Priv Sec to Ld Chllr 1915–19, Ld Chllr's

Dept: Assist Sec 1944–54, Dep Clerk Crown 1919–44, Clerk Crown in Chancery 1944–54; *m* 29 Aug 1917 Gladys (*d* 1978), dau of FM Sir George Stuart White, VC, GCB, OM, GCSI, GCMG, GCIE, GCVO, and *d* 18 July 1973, leaving:

(1) George Robert Edward; *b* 26 Aug 1920; *educ* Eton and New Coll Oxford; 2nd Lt KRRC WW II; *das* 23 March 1942

(1) *Patricia Mary Stuart [Mrs Philip English, 14 Milborne Grove, London SW10 9SN]; *b* 18 June 1918; *m* 2 June 1948 *Philip Ernest Ricardo English, s of Cecil Rowe English, of Khami, S Rhodesia, and has:

1a *Georgina Frances; *b* 13 Feb 1958

2a *Philippa Katharine; *b* 31 Aug 1962

4 Mary Grant; *b* 15 Dec 1862; *m* 21 May 1889 North More Nisbett, of Midlothian and Bayswater, and *d* 6 Jan 1940. He *d* 5 Jan 1939

5 Emilia Herbert Fullarton; *b* 18 July 1870; *m* 25 May 1899 Col Edward John Mounsey Gore and *d* 6 April 1932, leaving issue (*see* ARRAN, E)

6 Alice Maude; *b* 29 Dec 1874; *d* 17 July 1875

The 3rd BARON *d* 2 May 1935; his half-brother,

EDWARD HERBERT SCOTT NAPIER, **4th Baron Napier of Magdala**; *b* 16 Dec 1861; *educ* Cooper's Hill Coll; MInstCE, Indian State Rlwys, E Yorks Vol and Admlty WW I; *m* 11 July 1900 Florence Martha (*d* 1 Dec 1946), dau of Gen John Maxwell Perceval, CB, and had:

1 (ROBERT) JOHN, **5th Baron**

1 Kathleen Marion; *m* 22 Feb 1930 James Robert Bargrave Armstrong (*d* 3 July 1980), barrister, of Fellows Hall, Killylea, Co Armagh, 4th s of Henry Bruce Armstrong, PC, and *d* 14 Sept 1986, having had:

(1) *Henry Armstrong Esq DL [Henry Armstrong Esq DL, Fellows Hall, Killylea, Co Armagh BT60 4LU]; *b* 28 Feb 1936; *educ* Winchester and Trin Coll Cambridge (MA); Lt RE (TA), barrister Inner Temple 1961, Advocate High Court Kenya and Tanzania; *m* 25 Feb 1967 *Rosemarie, dau of Harold White, OBE, and has:

1a *Bruce William; *b* 18 April 1970; *educ* Glenalmond and Edinburgh U; B Mech Engr; with African Mining Servs, Accra, Ghana

2a *Mark Harold Napier; *b* 1 June 1978; *educ* Loretto and Newcastle U

1a *Antonia Kathleen; *b* 7 Jan 1974; *educ* St Leonard's Sch and RAC Cirencester (BSc)

(2) *John Fortescue [John Armstrong Esq, Cawthorne Hall, Bourne, Lincs PE10 0AB]; *b* 28 Feb 1936; *educ* Eton, Univ Coll Oxford and U of BC (BSc); civ engr; *m* 4 March 1967 *Chantal, dau of Claude de Chazal, of Funchal, Madeira, and has:

1a *Philip Raymond; *b* 9 May 1968

2a *Eric Napier; *b* 30 Aug 1969

(1) Frances Evelyn; *b* 27 Dec 1930; *educ* Girton Coll Cambridge (BA); *m* 5 Jan 1957 *Reginald West, Scots Gds and Overseas CS, of Teffont, Wilts, s of William Albert West, Hampshire Regt, and *d* 3 Jan 1969, leaving a s and dau

(2) *Kathleen Mary Perceval [Mrs Michael Armstrong, 34 College Hill, Armagh BT61 9DF]; *b* 15 Nov 1932; *educ* Trin Coll Dublin; *m* 7 Jan 1954 her cousin Michael Henry Armstrong, DL, MBE (*d* 29 Jan 1982) only s of Maj William Fortescue Armstrong, DSO, MC, and has:

1a *Edward James Maxwell; *b* 1 Feb 1958; *educ* Glenalmond; *m* 3 Aug 1991 *Jill J O'Dowd and has:

1b *William Edward O'Dowd; *b* 9 Sept 1993

1b *Madeleine Margaret O'Dowd; *b* 1 Sept 1995

2a *Robert William Fortescue; *b* 12 March 1960; *educ* Glenalmond and Aberdeen U

1a *Anne Helen Madeleine; *b* 29 Oct 1954; *m* 29 Dec 1983 *Michael John Alexander Coole and has issue

2a *Florence Kathleen Margaret; *b* 12 March 1956; *educ* St Andrew's U; *m* 12 Sept 1981 *James Hume Walter Mieville Stone and has issue

3a *Jane Elizabeth Alice; *b* 5 Jan 1967; *educ* Aberdeen U

(3) Florence Margaret; *b* 26 May 1934; *educ* Trin Coll Dublin (Dip Soc Sci) and Bible Training Inst Glasgow; *d* unm 23 Aug 1981

2 Evelyn Rose; *m* 5 Oct 1935 Desmond Walter Molony, Maj Kenya Def Force and E African Pioneer Corps, of Gillitts, Natal, er s of Col Walter William Molony, DSO, of Kiltanon, Kenya, and *d* 22 Aug 1952, leaving issue

3 (Ermine) Maude; *b* 25 Jan 1907; *d* 21 Feb 1995

The 4th BARON *d* 20 July 1948; his only son,

(ROBERT) JOHN NAPIER, **5th Baron Napier of Magdala**, OBE (1944); *b* 16 June 1904; *educ* Wellington; Col RE Waziristan 1936–37 and WW II (despatches) Brig (retd 1959); *m* 20 Sept 1939 *Elizabeth Marian [The Rt Hon The Dowager Lady Napier of Magdala, 51 Moorside Rd, Brookhouse, Lancs LA2 9PJ], yst dau of Edmund Henderson Hunt, FRCS, of Surrey, and *d* 1987, leaving:

1 ROBERT ALAN NAPIER, **6th and present Baron Napier of Magdala**

2 +Andrew Perceval [The Hon Andrew Napier, 17 The Groves, Driffield, Yorks YO25 7XZ]; *b* 22 Oct 1947; *educ* Winchester and Imp Coll London

3 +Michael Elibank ; *b* 25 April 1953; *educ* Trin Coll Glenalmond, St John's Coll Cambridge (MA) and Newcastle U (PhD)

1 *Jane Elizabeth [The Hon Mrs Butler-Cole, The Old Manse, Carlops, Penicuik, Midlothian EH26 9NH]; *b* 13 May 1942; *m* 7 Aug 1964 *Christopher Thomas Butler-Cole, s of Michael Bernard Butler-Cole, of Eskmeals, Cumberland, and has:

(1) *Thomas Falcon; *b* 6 Nov 1967

(1) *Emma [Mrs Phillip Aiken, 447 Gilmerton Rd, Edinburgh EH17 7JJ]; *b* 21 April 1966; *m* 1988 *Phillip Stephen Aiken and has:

1a *Amanda Joy; *b* 1990

2a *Melanie Louise; *b* 1992

2 *Ruth Kathleen (twin) [The Hon Mrs Self, 20 Moorside Rd, Brookhouse, Lancaster LA2 9PJ]; *b* 22 Oct 1947; *m* 1972 *John Arthur Self, PhD, and has:

(1) *Martin David; *b* 1974

(1) *Pamela Clare; *b* 1976

NASEBY

Creation: B. (LP, UK) 2 Aug 1997.

THE BARON NASEBY, of Sandy, Co Beds (Michael Wolfgang Laurence Morris, PC (1994)) [The Rt Hon The Lord Naseby PC, Caesar's Camp, Sandy, Beds SG19 2AD]; *b* 25 Nov 1936; *educ* Bedford Sch and St Catharine's Coll Cambridge; Nat Serv RAF pilot 1955–57, management trainee Reckitt and Coleman 1960–63; Service Advertising Ltd 1964–68; mktg exec Horniblow Cox-Freeman Ltd 1968–71 (dir 1969–71); dir Benton and Bowles Ltd 1971–81; proprietor AM Internat 1980–92; memb Islington Cncl 1968–70 (Chm Housing 1968, Leader 1969–71, Alderman 1970–74); MP (C) Northampton S 1974–97, PPS to Min State NI 1979–81, memb: Public Accounts Ctee 1979–82, Select Ctee Energy 1982–85, Chm's Panel 1984–92, Chm Ways and Means and Dep Speaker H of C 1992–97, Memb Cncl Europe and WEU 1983–91, Sec: Br-Venezuela Ctee, C Housing and Local Govt Ctee 1974–76, C Trade Ctee 1974–76, C Environment Ctee 1977–79; Treas Br ASEAN and Thai Ctee; V-Chm: Br Indonesia Ctee, C Energy Ctee 1981–92; Chm: Br-Sri Lanka Ctee 1979–92, Br-Singapore Ctee 1985–92, Br-Malaysia Ctee 1987–92, Br-Burma Ctee 1989–92; Fndr Parly Food and Health Forum; Capt Parly Golf Soc 1988–91; Chm Govrs Bedford Sch 1989– (Govr 1982–); author: *Helping the Exporter* (jt author, 1967), *The Disaster of Direct Labour* (1978); *m* 1960 *Dr Ann Appleby, MB, BS, MRCS, MCRP, and has two sons and a dau

NATHAN

Arms: Or a fess cotised sa. over all a sword erect gu., on a canton of the second a roll of parchment ppr. **Crest:** A kiln inflamed ppr. **Supporters:** Dexter, a lion; sinister, a hind arg., each charged on the shoulder with a grenade sa., fired ppr. **Motto:** *Labor nobilitat* ('Toil ennobles'). **Creation:** B. (UK) 28 June 1940.

THE 2ND BARON NATHAN, of Churt, Co Surrey (Roger Carol Michael Nathan) [The Rt Hon The Lord Nathan, Collyers Farm, Lickfold, W Sussex GU28 9DU]; *b* 5 Dec 1922; *s f* 1963; *educ* Stowe and New Coll Oxford (BA 1947, MA 1948); slr 1950, sr ptnr Herbert Oppenheimer Nathan & Vandyk (ret 1986), Renter Warden Gardeners' Co (Master 1963), Capt 17th/21st Lancers WW II (twice wounded, despatches), Hon Life Assoc Memb Bar Assoc New York, Chm Ho Lds Select Ctee Murder and Life Imprisonment 1988–89, Pres Jewish Welfare Bd 1967–71, Hon Pres Centl Br Fund Jewish Relief and Rehabilitation (Chm 1970–77), Chm RSA 1975–77 (V-Pres 1977–), V-Chm Cancer Research Campaign 1987– (Chm Exec Ctee 1970–75, Treasurer 1979–87), memb Roy Commn Environmental Pollution 1979–89 and 1989–92 and Ho Lds Select Ctee EC 1983–88, Chm Environment Sub-Ctee 1983–87 and 1989–92, Pres UK Environmental Law Assoc 1987–92, Nat Soc Clean Air 1987–89 and V-Pres 1992–, Soc Sussex Downsmen 1987–1992, Chm: Animal Procedures Ctee 1990–93 and Sussex Downs Conservn Bd 1992–, Memb Ho Lds Select Ctee Sci and Technology 1994–, Hon LLD Sussex, FSA, FRSA, FRGS; *m* 14 Nov 1950 *Philippa Gertude, er dau of Maj Joseph Bernard Solomon, MC, of Shortland, Sutton, W Sussex, and has:

1 +RUPERT HARRY BERNARD; *b* 26 May 1957; *educ* Charterhouse and Durham U (BA); *m* 1st 1987 (*divorce* 1997) Ann, dau of A S Hewitt, of Aldingbourne, Sussex; *m* 2nd 26 May 1997 *Jane, dau of David Cooper, of Llanon, Swansea

  1 *Jennifer Ruth; *b* 4 June 1952

2 *Nicola Janet Eleanor; *b* 18 May 1954; *educ* St Mary's Coll Durham U

Lineage: MICHAEL van NOORDEN later NATHAN, of 18 Pershore St, Birmingham, general dealer, settled in England during the Napoleonic wars; *b* Holland *c* 1782; *d* 1842, leaving:

HENRY NATHAN, of Manchester; *b* 1812; *m* 2 Sept 1846 Matilda (*d* 1888), dau of Joseph Jacobs, of Manchester, and *d* 1865, leaving, with two yr sons (Maurice; Joseph, emigrated to New Zealand, *m* Minna Possenniskie and had issue) and two daus:

MICHAEL HENRY NATHAN, JP, of Manchester and London; *b* 1852; *m* 14 July 1887 Constance (*d* 20 Feb 1949 aged 84), yst dau of Louis Beaver (formerly Bibergeil), of Manchester, by Rachel Mayer, of Hanley, Staffs, and had, with a yr s (Cyril, *b* 1891, *educ* St Paul's, *m* and had issue):

HARRY LOUIS NATHAN, **1st Baron Nathan**, of Churt, Co Surrey (UK), so *cr* 28 June 1940, TD (1945), PC (1946), JP, DL Co London; *b* 2 Feb 1889; *educ* St Paul's; slr 1913, an original offr TF, Maj (T/Lt-Col) 1st London Regt WW I (severely wounded), Hon Col, Welfare Offr Eastern Cmd 1939–41 and London Dist 1941–43, Hon Col 300 LAA Regt RA 1937–63 and Hon A/Cdre No 906 (Middx) Balloon Sqdn AAF 1939–45, Sr hon Col Roy Regt Artillery 1961–63, sr ptnr Herbert Oppenheimer, Nathan and Vandyk, MP Bethnal Green NE 1929–35 and Wandsworth Centl 1937–40, memb Min Pensions Centl Advsy Ctee 1942–45, Parly U-Sec War and V-Pres Army Cncl 1945–46, Min Civil Aviation 1946–48, Chm PM's Ctee Law and Practice Charitable Tsts 1949–52, Dep Chm Chllr Exchequer's Ctee Law and Customs and Excise 1951, Chm: Exec Ctee Br Empire Cancer Campaign 1954–63 and Westminster Hosp 1948–63, Crown Nominee Lay Memb GMC 1949–59, FBA, FRGS (Pres 1958–61), FRSA (Chm 1961), FSA (Council), Fell Roy Ec Soc, Fell Roy Statistical Soc and St George's Soc, Govr St Paul's Sch and St Paul's Girls' Sch, Tstee and memb Bd Deps Br Jews, memb Co of London TA&AF Assoc 1942–45, KStJ, Coronation Medals 1937 and 1953, Freeman and Lt City London, Pres London and Middx Archaeologists Soc 1947–49, Master Pattenmakers' Co 1951–52 and 1952–53 and Gardeners' Co 1955–56, Liveryman Gold and Silver Wyre Drawers' Co (Court), Bakers, Coach Makers and Harness Makers, Chm Wolfson Fndn, author: *Free Trade To-day* (1929), *Medical Negligence* (1957); *m* 27 March 1919 Eleanor Joan Clara, MA, JP Co London, memb LCC 1928–34 and 1937–49 (Chm 1947–48), Alderman 1951–65 (*d* 6 June 1972 aged 79), dau of Carl Stettauer, and *d* 23 Oct 1963, leaving:

1 ROGER CAROL MICHAEL NATHAN, **2nd and present Baron Nathan**

1 *Joyce Constance Ina [The Hon Lady Waley-Cohen, Honeymead, Simonsbath, Somerset TA24 7JX]; *b* 20 Jan 1920; *educ* St Felix Sch and Girton Coll Cambridge (BA 1941, MA 1950); JP Middx 1949–59 and Somerset 1959–87, memb Bd Govrs Westminster Hosp Group 1952–68, Chm: Westminster Children's Hosp 1952–68, Gordon Hosp 1961–68, Governing Bodies Girls' Schs Assoc 1974–79 (memb 1963–), memb ISIS Cncl and Management Ctee 1972–86, Chm Ind Schs Jt Cncl 1977–80, Pres ISIS 1981–86, Govr: Taunton Sch 1978–90, Wellington Coll 1979–90 and St Felix Sch Cambridge 1945–83 (Chm 1970–83); *m* 21 Dec 1943 Sir Bernard Nathaniel Waley-Cohen, 1st Bt (*qv*), and has issue

NAYLOR-LEYLAND

Arms: Quarterly, 1st and 4th, erm. on a fess engrailed sa. between nine ears of barley, three, three and three vert, banded or in chief, and three like ears in base, a lion passant of the last between two escallops arg. and for distinction a canton gu. (for LEYLAND); 2nd and 3rd, per pale or and arg. a pale sa. fretty of the first between two lions rampant of the third, a canton gu. for distinction (for NAYLOR). **Crests:** 1 A mount vert, thereon an escallop arg., surmounted by a demi-eagle erminois, wings addorsed azure bezantée, in the mouth three ears of barley vert, a cross crosslet gu. for distinction (for LEYLAND), 2 A lion passant sa., charged on the body with two saltires or, resting the dexter forepaw on a shield charged with the arms of Naylor and charged further for distinction with a cross crosslet also or (for NAYLOR). **Motto:** *Fidus et audax* ('Faithful and bold'). **Creation:** Bt. (UK) 31 Aug 1895.

SIR PHILIP VYVIAN NAYLOR-LEYLAND, 4TH BT, of Hyde Park House, Albert Gate, London [Sir Philip Naylor-Leyland Bt, Nantclwyd Hall, Ruthin, N Wales LL15 2PR; The Ferry House, Milton Park, Peterborough, Cambs PE6 7AB]; *b* 9 Aug 1953; *s f* 1987; *educ* Eton, RMA Sandhurst, NY U Business Sch and RAC Cirencester; late Lt Life Gds, V-Chm Peterborough Roy Foxhound Show Soc, 1988–95 (Chm 1995), Pres Nat Coursing Club 1988–, Jt MFH Fitzwilliam 1987–; *m* 1980 *Lady Isabella Lambton, yst dau of Lord (Antony Claud Frederick) Lambton (*see* DURHAM, E), and has:

1 +THOMAS PHILIP; *b* 22 Jan 1982

2 +George Antony; *b* 1989

3 +Edward Claud; *b* 1993

1 *Violet Mary; *b* 1983

Lineage: TOM NAYLOR-LEYLAND, of Nantclwyd Hall; Lt-Col Denbighs Yeo; *m* 25 March 1862 Mary Anne Scarisbrick (*d* 15 June 1902), dau and heiress of Charles Scarisbrick, of Scarisbrick Hall, Lancs, and *d* 26 Aug 1886, leaving, with a dau (Florence Mary, *m* 8 Jan 1889 (*divorce* 1900) Hon Richard Walter Chetwynd and *d* 28 April 1955, leaving issue; *see* CHETWYND, V):

Sir Herbert Scarisbrick Naylor-Leyland, 1st Bt (UK), so *cr* 31 Aug 1895, of Hyde Park House, Albert Gate, London; *b* 24 Jan 1864; Capt 2nd Life Gds Res of Offrs, MP Colchester 1892–95 and Southport 1898–99, FRAGS, FZS; *m* 5 Sept 1889 Jeannie Willson (*d* 10 March 1932), 2nd dau of William S Chamberlain, of Cleveland, Ohio, and *d* 7 May 1899, leaving, with a yr s (George Vyvyan, of Brynyffynon Park, Denbighs, *b* 11 March 1892 (TRH THE DUKEs OF CAMBRIDGE and YORK stood sponsor), Lt RHG WW I, *d* of wounds recd in action 21 Sept 1914):

Sir Albert Edward Herbert Naylor-Leyland, 2nd Bt, JP (Denbighs), High Sheriff 1921; *b* 6 Dec 1890 (HRH THE PRINCE OF WALES stood sponsor); *educ* Eton and Ch Ch Oxford; Hon Attaché Berne and Paris; *m* 10 April 1923 Marguerite (*d* 26 Jan 1945), 2nd dau of Baron de Belabre, French Ministry For Affrs, and had:

1 VIVIAN EDWARD (Sir), **3rd Bt**

2 +Michael Montague George, MC [Michael Naylor-Leyland Esq MC, The Red House, Lacock, Chippenham, Wilts SN15 2LB]; Capt Life Gds WW II; *b* 21 Feb 1926; *m* 8 April 1953 *Jacqueline Marie Françoise, yst dau of Maj Ides Floor, DSO, MBE, of E Grinstead, and has had:

  (1) +David George Edward; *b* 13 Oct 1955; *educ* Eton and RMA Sandhurst; Lt LG, proprietor Egerton House, Franklin and Duke's Hotels, London; *m* 1978 *Jane, est dau of Lt-Col John Monsell Christian, MC, KRRC, of Clifferdine House, Rencomb, Glos, and has:

    1a +John; *b* 1984

    2a +Frederick George; *b* 1987

    1a *Victoria; *b* 1982

  (1) Atalanta Mary Margaret; *b* 22 March 1954; *d* 15 March 1972

  (2) *Joanna Rosemary Jane [Mrs Philip Lambert, 8 Soudan Rd, London SW11 4HH]; *b* 18 Jan 1961; *m* 1st 1985 (*divorce* 1989) Nigel James Norman, er s of Sir Mark Annesley Norman, 3rd Bt (*qv*); *m* 2nd 1989 *Philip S O Lambert, yr s of Capt Richard Lambert, of Garthgwynion, Machynnleth, and by him has:

    1a *Jack; *b* 4 Sept 1990

    2a *Thomas; *b* 30 Aug 1994

    1a *Laura; *b* 15 Sept 1992

3 (Alick) David Yorke, MVO (1952); Lt Gren Gds; *b* 20 May 1929; *educ* Eton; *m* 1st 9 Dec 1953 (*divorce* 1961) Diana Elizabeth Lea (*m* 2nd 1962 7th Earl of Wilton; *qv*), only dau of Roy Galway, of St Ronans, Winkfield Row, Berks, and had:

  (1) +Michael Alexander Robert [Michael Naylor-Leyland Esq, 10 Wallgrave Rd, London SW5 0RL]; *b* 14 July 1956; *m* 1st 1984 (*divorce* 19–) Lucy C, dau of Henry Potts, of Eglingham Hall, Alnwick, Northumberland; *m* 2nd 1990 *HRH PRINCESS TANIA SASKIA VIKTORIA-LUISE OF HANOVER, only child of HRH PRINCE WOLF ERNST AUGUST ANDREAS PHILIPP GEORG WILHELM LUDWIG BERTHOLD OF HANOVER, and by her has:

    1a +Jake John; *b* 1993

  (1) *Amanda Jane; *b* 1954; *m* 28 June 1977 (*divorce* 1982) Thomas Skiffington, jockey, s of Col T J Skiffington, of Middleburgh, Va.

3 (cont.) David Naylor-Leyland *m* 2nd 1961 (*divorce* 1969) Dita Amory, dau of J Gordon Douglas, Jr, of Prince's Neck, Newport, RI, and by her has:

  (2) +Nicholas Edward; *b* 1962

3 (cont.) David Naylor-Leyland *m* 3rd 5 April 1973 Carolyn S Neilson (*d* Jan 1989) and *d* 1991, leaving by her:

  (3) +Edward Frederick; *b* 23 Nov 1975

1 *Veronica Rosemary [Mrs Veronica Munster, 3 Queens Gate Place Mews, London SW7 5BG]; *b* 22 March 1932; *m* 20 Oct 1955 (*divorce* 1975) Count Peter Cyril Alexander Munster (*see* DUDLEY, E), only surv s of Count Paul William Alexander Munster, of The Manor House, Bampton, Oxon, and has:

  (1) *Alexander Paul; *b* 24 Oct 1961

  (1) *Sarah Hélène; *b* 9 June 1957

  (2) *Marina Claire; *b* 5 Jan 1960

Sir ALBERT *d* 23 Sept 1952; his est son,

Sir Vivian Edward Naylor-Leyland, 3rd Bt, of Hyde Park House, Albion Gate, London; *b* 5 March 1924; *educ* Eton, Ch Ch Oxford and RAC Cirencester; Lt Gren Gds; *m* 1st 17 Jan 1952 (*divorce* 1960) Hon Elizabeth Anne Fitzalan-Howard, yr dau of 2nd Viscount Fitzalan of Derwent (*see* NORFOLK, D), and had:

1 Sir PHILIP VYVYAN NAYLOR-LEYLAND, **4th and present Bt**

Sir Vivian *m* 2nd 17 Nov 1967 (*divorce* 1975) (Noreen) Starr, only dau of W/Cdr Peter Anker Simmons, DFC, RAF, and Countess Noreen Raben (*see* BAILEY, Bt), and by her had:

1 *Cleonie Mary Veronica; *b* 23 June 1968

Sir Vivian *m* 3rd Jameina Flora [Mrs David Scarisbrick, Domaine de Montmoreau, 24300 La Chapelle Montmoreau, France] (*m* 2nd David Scarisbrick), dau of James Freeman Reid, and *d* 1987, leaving by her:

2 *Virginia; *b* 16 April 1983

3 *Jessica Pamela; *b* 27 March 1987

NEAVE

Arms: Arg. on a cross sa. five fleurs-de-lys or. **Crest:** Out of a ducal coronet gold a lily stalked and leaved vert, flowered and seeded or. **Motto:** *Sola proba quæ honesta* ('Those things only are becoming which are honourable'). **Creation:** Bt. (GB) 13 May 1795.

SIR PAUL ARUNDELL NEAVE, 7TH BT, of Dagnam Park, Essex [Sir Paul Neave Bt, Queen's House, Monk Sherborne, Hants RG26 5HH]; *b* 13 Dec 1948; *s f* 1992; *educ* Eton; memb Stock Exchange 1980, dir Henderson Crosthwaite Ltd; *m* 8 May 1976 *Coralie Jane Louise, est dau of Sir Robert (Robin) George Caldwell Kinahan, ERD, JP, DL, of Castle Upton, Templepatrick, Co Antrim, and has:

1 +FREDERICK PAUL KINAHAN; *b* 25 Jan 1981

2 +Julian Robin Kinahan; *b* 1983

Lineage: ROBERT le NEVE, of Tivetshall, Norfolk; living *c* 1399; had an est s:

JOHN le NEVE, living *c* 1420; had issue, with a yr s (John):

ROBERT le NEVE, of Tivetshall; *d* 1486, leaving, with other issue (including Jeffry, of Aslacton, Norfolk, *m* Alice, dau of Roger Brett, and *d* 1539, ancestor of Sir William Le Neve, Clarenceux King of Arms 1660):

JOHN le NEVE, of Tivetshall, living *c* 1546; had an est s:

ROBERT le NEVE or NEAVE, of Ringland, Norfolk; *m* Alice, dau of Thomas Delamere, of Ringland, and *d* 1558, having had, with other issue:

1 John, of N Tuddenham, Norfolk; had a s Thomas (*d* unm)

2 THOMAS

3 Firmian, of Ringland; *m* Mary, dau of Thomas Watts, of Mateshall, and had issue

1 Mary; *m* Robert Tylney, of E Tuddenham

2 Alice; *m* John Laverock, of Ringland, and had issue

ROBERT's 2nd son,

  THOMAS le NEVE or NEAVE, of Ipswich; living *c* 1566; had an est s:

JOHN le NEVE; *d* 1597, leaving, with three yr sons:

EDWARD NEAVE; *d* 1617, leaving, with two yr sons (Richard; Edward, *d* 1617) and a dau:

JOHN NEAVE; *m* Martha Beaumont and had:

RICHARD NEAVE, of London; *b* 25 July 1666; *m* Elizabeth, dau of Samuel Bradford, and *d* 1741, having had, with a yr s (Edward):

JAMES NEAVE, of London and Walthamstow, Essex; *b* 7 Aug 1700; *m* Susanna (*d* 1766 aged 73), dau of Thomas Truman, of Nottingham, and *d* 1764, having had, with a yr s (James, *m* H Hervey and *d* 1796, leaving issue) and a dau (Susanna, *b* 1732, *m* William Wells (*d* 1805), of Bickley Hall, Kent, and *d* 17 April, 1810, leaving issue):

Sir Richard Neave, 1st Bt (GB), so *cr* 13 May 1795, of Dagenham Park, Essex; *b* 22 Nov 1731; Govr Bank of England 1780, High Sheriff Essex 1794; *m* 16 Feb 1761 Frances (*d* 18 Jan 1830), 4th dau of John Bristow, of Quidenham Hall, Norfolk, and had, with other issue:

1 THOMAS (Sir), **2nd Bt**

2 John; Judge Tirhoot, Ch Judge Benares; *b* 2 Jan 1763; *m* 9 Sept 1798 Catherine (*d* 3 May 1822), dau of Col — Smith, of Ireland, and *d* 18 May 1835, leaving:

  (1) John; *b* 11 July 1799; *d* 1840

  (2) Robert; HEIC CS, Sessions Judge Aizmgurh, Bengal; *b* 11 March 1805; *m* 14 Jan 1834 Sabrina Marianna (*m* 2nd G Offord), 2nd dau of Lt-Col George Bristow, and *d* 23 Dec 1848, leaving:

    1a Robert John Bristow; *b* 2 Feb 1835; drowned 13 Sept 1855

    2a Spencer Le Neve; *b* 31 Aug 1838; *m* —

    3a Arthur Montagu; *b* 7 May 1842; *m* —

    1a Katherine Frances; *m* 1st 11 Aug 1857 John David Hay Hill, 12th Lancers, Consul Brest (*d* 26 May 1868); *m* 2nd 29 Oct 1870 Maj Trevor Andrews (*d* 23 Feb 1787); *m* 3rd 29 Aug 1889 Dep Surg-Gen A G Elkington and *d* 20 Jan 1894

  (3) Edgar; *b* 30 Dec 1810; *m* — and *d* 1880, leaving issue

(1) Anna Frances; *m* 30 March 1843, as his 2nd w, Ludovic James Grant (*see* GRANT, Bt, of Dalvey) and *d* 27 Dec 1867

(2) Caroline Mary; *m* June 1819 Rev William Cookson, Vicar Hungerford, and *d* 22 Sept 1888. He *d* 1870

(3) Eliza; *m* 16 Dec 1817 J Milford, of Exeter, and *d* 2 May 1865

3 Richard; barrister, Dep Paymr Forces, Sec and Registrar Roy Hosp Chelsea 1816; *b* 18 Dec 1773; *m* 2 July 1807 Sarah (*d* 31 Aug 1826), dau of Alexander Irvine, and *d* 13 Jan 1858, leaving, with other issue:

(1) Richard; *b* 31 May 1808; *m* 6 Oct 1838 Anna Maria Dorothea (*d* 1888), yst dau of Rev John Eyton, Rector Eyton, Salop, and *d* 12 Sept 1877, leaving:

1a Richard Lewis Irvine (Rev); RC priest, Hon Canon St George's Cathedral Southwark; *b* 3 July 1851; *d* 8 June 1925

1a Barbara Frances; *m* 1886 Count Roger de Courson, of Bayeux, France (*d* 29 June 1919)

2a Mary Rose; *m* 4 April 1883 Edouard de St Jullien, of Montreuil-sur-Mer, Pas de Calais, only surv s of Capt de St Jullien, and *d* 13 Feb 1916, leaving issue

(2) George Peters; *b* 18 Nov 1809; *m* 23 Sept 1845 Maria (*d* 21 Dec 1879), dau of Richard Pinder, of Newnham, Glos, and *d* 19 Dec 1887, leaving:

1a Richard Irvine; *b* 21 Sept 1849; *m* 10 July 1872 Harriet, dau of William White, of Upcerne House, Dorset, and had:

1b Arundell Francis Robert; *b* 1 Sept 1874; *m* 1902 Mona Lewis (*d* 1958) and had:

1c Leslie Francis; *b* 1903; *d* 1965

2c Arundell Richard York Irvine, DSC; Lt-Cdr Nigerian Navy WW II; *b* 1915; *m* 18 Feb 1941 *Barbara Marie, only dau of Frederick Charles Evelyn Liardet, of Beech Park, Newton Abbot, S Devon, and *d* 1977, leaving:

1d +Guy Richard Irvine; *b* 27 Dec 1941; *educ* King's Sch Worcester and Queen Mary's Coll London (BA 1964, PhD); research memb Inst d'Education, Fondation Européenne de la Culture, Université Dauphine, Paris

1d *Penelope Gaye; *b* 3 April 1945; *m* 1966 (*divorce* 1977) Duncan Edward McBarnett and has:

1e *Justin Guy; *b* 1970

2e *Alasdair Mathew; *b* 1972

1c *Muriel Catherine; *b* 1907; *m* 1928 Graham Thorpe, of Lyndhurst, Hants

1b Violet Maria; *d c* 1906

2b Harriet Gladys Irvine; *b* 5 Feb 1883

2a George Howard; *b* 21 Jan 1851; *m* 24 June 1875 Isabella Augusta, dau of Samuel Chapman, and had:

1b Cecil Howard; *b* 1877; *m* 10 March 1903 Daisy Dolores Scales (*d* 1945) and *d* 3 May 1937, leaving:

1c Geoffrey Howard; *b* 30 June 1917; *m* 1946 *Mary Therese Jeanette [Mrs Geoffrey Howard, 21 Cornell Avenue, Rumford, RI, USA], dau of Joseph Adelard Voyer, and *d* 1983, leaving:

1d *Bernadette Blanche Dolores; *b* 1947; *m* 1968 *Arvid C Nelson, US Marines, and has:

1e *Michael Shawn; *b* 1969

2e *Robert David; *b* 1973

1c Sybil Isabella Herschell; *b* 5 April 1904; *m* 1st 15 Sept 1925 (*divorce* 1942) Cdr (S) Stanley Albert Wiggett, RN (*d* 1956), s of Albert Wiggett, and had issue; *m* 2nd Aug 1942 Lt-Col Charles Greig-Edwards, Devonshire Regt and RASC, s of Rev Charles Greig-Edwards, of Devon

2c Iris Olga; *b* 20 May 1906; *m* 17 June 1932 Lt (S) Frederick James, RN, s of Frederick James, of Peverell, Plymouth, and had issue

2b George Reginald; *b* 1886; *d* 14 March 1909

1b Minnie; *m* 21 June 1907 Peter White, of Cape Town

(1) Elizabeth; *m* 4 April 1839 Alexander Middleton and *d* 25 May 1879. He *d* 24 July 1846

1 Frances Louisa; *m* 10 July 1786 Beeston Long, Govr Bank of England, and *d* 30 Dec 1841

2 Catherine Mary; *m* 18 March 1793 Henry Howard (*see* NORFOLK, D) and *d* 16 Jan 1849

Sir RICHARD *d* 28 Jan 1814; his est s,

Sir Thomas Neave, 2nd Bt; *b* 11 Nov 1761; FRS, FAS, High Sheriff Essex 1820; *m* 13 June 1791 Frances Caroline (*d* 14 April 1835), dau of Very Rev Hon William Digby (*see* DIGBY, B), and had, with other issue:

1 RICHARD DIGBY (Sir), **3rd Bt**

2 Henry Lyttelton (Rev); Vicar Epping, Essex; *b* 21 March 1793; *m* 31 Aug 1824 Agnes Anne, est dau of Sir Robert Sheffield, 3rd Bt (*qv*), and *dsp* 4 Aug 1873

3 Sheffield; Dir Bnk of England; *b* 11 April 1799; *m* 1 Oct 1851 Mary Henrica (*d* 11 July 1884), dau of David Richard Morier, Plen Switzerland, and *d* 24 Sept 1868, leaving:

(1) Sheffield Henry Morier; *b* 13 Oct 1853; *educ* Eton and Balliol Coll Oxford; Capt RAMC; *m* 30 April 1878 Gertrude Charlotte Margaret (*d* 6 Aug 1935), est dau of Julius Talbot Alrey, of Frognal Hall, Hampstead, and *d* 24 Oct 1936, leaving:

1a Sheffield Airey, CMG (1941), OBE (1933); *b* 20 April 1879; *educ* Eton and Magdalen Coll Oxford (MA and BSc 1906, DSc 1918); Assist Dir Imp Inst Entomology 1913–42 (Dir 1942–46), Sec ZS London 1942–52, Hon Sec Roy Entomolgical Soc London 1918–33 and Pres 1934–35; *m* 1st 29 April 1915 Dorothy (*d* 3 Feb 1943), dau of Lt-Col Arthur Thomson Middleton, JP, 13th Hus, of Ayshe Court, Horsham, and had:

1b Airey Middleton Sheffield, DSO (1945), OBE (1947), MC (1942), TD (with first clasp 1950); *b* 23 Jan 1916; *educ* Eton and Merton Coll Oxford (BA 1938, MA 1955); barrister Middle Temple 1943, Lt-Col RA (TA) WW II (wounded, despatches, POW), Assist Sec Internat Mil Tbnl Nuremberg 1945–46, Commr Tbnl Criminal Orgns 1946; MP (C) Abingdon 1953–79, PPS to: Min Tport and Civil Aviation Feb 1954, Sec State Colonies Aug 1954–July 1956; Jt Parly Sec Tport and Civil Aviation 1957–59, Parly

U-Sec Air Jan-Oct 1959; dir John Thompson Gp, Govr Imp Coll Sc and Technology 1963, Dawson and Barfos 1972, author: *They Have Their Exits* and *Saturdays at MI9*, Croix de Guerre, American Bronze Star, Offr Orange Nassau Netherlands; *m* 29 Dec 1942 Diana Josceline Barbara (*cr* Baroness Airey of Abingdon 1979; *d* 1992), er dau of Thomas Arthur Giffard, MBE, of Chillington Hall, Wolverhampton (*see* TROLLOPE, Bt), and was assassinated by the INLA 1979, leaving:

1c +(Richard) Patrick Sheffield [The Hon Patrick Neave, 16 Maze Rd, Kew, Richmond, Surrey]; *b* 12 Nov 1947; *educ* Eton and City of London Poly; *m* 1980 *Elizabeth Mary Catherine, yr dau of Cuthbert Edward Alphonso Riddell, of Hermeston Hall, Worksop, Notts, and has:

1d +James Riddell Airey; *b* 1983

2d +Thomas Edward Riddell Airey; *b* 1985

3d +Matthew Robert Riddell Airey; *b* 1993

2c +William Robert Sheffield [The Hon William Neave, 20 Kirkstall Rd, London SW2]; *b* 13 Aug 1953; *educ* Eton; *m* 1986 *Joanna Mary Stuart, 2nd dau of James Stuart Paton, of The Old Vicarage, Gt Hockham, Norfolk, and has:

1d +Richard Digby Stuart; *b* 1987

2d +Sebastian Airey Stuart; *b* 1989

1c *Marigold Elizabeth Cassandra [The Hon Mrs Webb, Barbers, Martley, Worcs WR6 6QA]; *b* 5 May 1944; *m* 8 June 1968 *William Richard Broughton Webb, DL, er s of Lt-Cdr William Frank Broughton Webb, DSC, RN, of Caulin Court, Droitwich, Worcs, and has:

1d *Edward Alexander Broughton; *b* 1974

1d *Katherine (Kate) Angela Mary; *b* 26 Nov 1970; *m* 2 Dec 1995 *Christian Holland, s of Rodney Holland and has:

1e *Luke William Airey; *b* 29 Sept 1997

2b +Digby John Sheffield [Digby Neave Esq, 1 rue Champflour, 78160 Marly-le-Roi, Seine-et-Oise, France]; *b* 17 July 1928; *educ* Eton and Merton Coll Oxford; late 2nd Lt Life Gds; *m* 1st 6 Oct 1958 Ulla (*d* 19 March 1963), dau of A B Schmidt, of Gilleleje, Denmark, and has:

1c *Victoria Janet [The Hon Mrs Hugh Fairfax, 50 Streathbourne Rd, London SW17 8QX]; *b* 1959; *m* 1984 *Hon Hugh Nigel Thomas Fairfax, 2nd s of 13th Lord Fairfax of Cameron (*qv*), and has issue

2c *Philippa; *b* 1960

2b (cont.) Digby Neave *m* 2nd 1966 *Christiane, dau of E J Corty, of L'Etang-la-Ville, France, and by her has:

1c +Lionel Digby Sheffield; *b* 12 July 1966; *educ* Eton; *m* 1992 *Hon Victoria Alice, 2nd dau of Baron McAlpine of West Green (*qv*), and has:

1d +Digby; *b* 11 Sept 1996

1d +Alice Artemis; *b* 1994

1b Iris Averil; 2nd Offr WRNS; *b* 2 April 1918; *m* 4 Feb 1954 Sir Frank Milton, of Riverside, Hewish, nr Crewkerne, Somerset, and adopted two sons

2b *Rosamund Malua; *b* 22 May 1921; *m* 9 Sept 1939 *Capt Edward Noble Sheppard, Essex Yeo, s of Edward Byas Sheppard, of St Leonard's, Ingatestone, Essex, and has two adopted daus

3b Viola Dorothy; *b* 8 Aug 1925

1a (cont.) Sheffield Neave *m* 2nd 18 Oct 1946 Mary Irene (*d* 1993), dau of Henry Hodges, of Broadway Hall, Churchstoke, Montgomery, and *d* 31 Dec 1961

2a Richard; *b* 9 July 1881; *educ* Eton; Col Essex Regt, Assist Instr Musketry NZ Mil Forces 1916, served Boer War 1901–02 (medal with four clasps) and WW I (1914 star, two medals); *m* 9 Oct 1912 Helen Elizabeth Mary (*d* 1976), est dau of Robert Miller, of Ingatestone, Essex, and *d* 14 Dec 1962, leaving:

1b Robert Morier Sheffield, MC; *b* 12 June 1917; *educ* Sherborne and London U; MRCVS, Maj 13th/18th Hus (SR) WW II (wounded), Colonial Serv 1948–56 E Africa, Kenya 1948–53, Ch Vet Offr Cyprus 1953–56; *m* 13 Sept 1952 *Philippa (Pip) Elizabeth, only dau of Lt-Col (Vincent) Basil Ramsden, DSO, MC (*see* ST DAVIDS, V), and *d* 21 Sept 1995, leaving:

1c *Julia Helen; *b* 29 May 1953; *m* 1976 *Jonathan Bennett Walker, of Westport, Conn., and has:

1d *Bennett Neave; *b* 1984

1d *Megan Philippa; *b* 1980

2d *Lydia Joy; *b* 1982

2c *Lucinda (Lucy) Philippa [Mrs Michael Muller, Tithe Farmhouse, Hitcham Lane, Burnham, Bucks SL1 7DP]; *b* 25 Oct 1954; *m* 1983 *Michael Philip Muller, er s of Dr Walter Muller, of Cheltenham, and has:

1d *Thomas Robert; *b* 1992

1d *Katharine Elise; *b* 1985

2d *Jessica Philippa; *b* 1986

3d *Rebecca Madeleine; *b* 1989

3c *Harriet Elise Bunty; *b* 19 Feb 1957

2b +Julius Arthur Sheffield, CBE (1978, MBE 1945), JP, DL (Essex) [Maj Julius Neave CBE JP DL, Mill Green Park, Ingatestone, Essex CM4 0JB]; *b* 17 July 1919; *educ* Sherborne; Maj 13th/18th Hus WW II (despatches), OStJ 1988; *m* 25 April 1951 *Helen Margery, yst dau of Col Percy Morland Acton-Adams, DSO, of Clarence Reserve, Kaikoura, NZ, and has:

1c *(Helen) Penelope; *b* 5 March 1952; *m* 1981 *Michael Wilson and has:

1d *Esme Beatrice; *b* 1983

2d *Julia Rose; *b* 1985

2c *(Joan) Miranda Mary [Mrs Anthony Bowles, Holmhead, Corsock, Castle Douglas, Kirkcudbrightshire DG7 3DT]; *b* 27 March 1954; *m* 1979 *(George) Anthony John Bowles (*see* 1970 edn BARWICK, Bt) and has:

1d *Richard Anthony Julius; *b* 1981

2d *Humphrey John Edward; *b* 1984

1d *Georgina Helen Diana; *b* 1987

3c *Venetia Beatrice; *b* 18 April 1958; *m* 1982 *William Lebus, yr s of Oliver Lebus, of Kensington, and has:

1d *Frederick Oliver; *b* 1985

2d *Henry William; *b* 1991

1d *Tomasina Olivia; *b* 1987

1b *Beatrice Honoria Sheffield [Mrs Eustace Robinson, Garden Cottage, Drinkstone Park, Bury St Edmunds, Suffolk]; *b* 28 June 1916; *m* 5 June 1952 Eustace Blewitt Robinson (*d* 1992), only s of Eustace Harold Robinson, of Millgreen House, Ingatestone, Essex, by Ellen, 5th dau of William Blewitt, of Dove House, Pinner, Middx, and has:

1c Eleanor Mary; *b* 27 March 1953; *m* 1977 *Julian Richard Edwards and *d* 1992, leaving:

1d *Alexander Julian; *b* 1981

2d *James Blewitt; *b* 1984

1a Beatrice; *m* 22 March 1897 Lt-Col Walter S Brindle, Worcs Regt, of Littlestone, Kent, and S Kensington, and *d* following an accident 25 April 1957

2a Violet; *m* 5 Sept 1919 Col Norman Holmes Stone, RTC, s of F H Stone, of Kensington

(2) Edward Strangways; *b* 11 Nov 1857; *m* 4 Nov 1882 Evelyn Jane (*d* 23 Aug 1934), dau of Col Robert Vansittart, Coldstream Gds (*see* 1956 edn VANSITTART, B), and *d* 25 Jan 1935, having had:

1a Edward Arthur; *b* 2 Aug 1883; Natal Police and S African Mounted Riflemen, served Boer War 1901–02 (medal, three clasps), Native Rebellion 1906 (medal) and WW I SW Africa (1914–15 star, two medals); *m* 7 Oct 1916 Evelyn Margaret (*d* 7 Jan 1966), dau of George Augustus Lamb, of Rye, Sussex, and *d* 4 Aug 1960, leaving:

1b +Digby Seymour; *b* 7 April 1921; FRICS, sr ptnr Neave, Tinworth & Nuan, chartered quantity surveyors, Lt RA WW II; *m* 28 Dec 1948 Chrystel (*d* 19 March 1963), authoress, only dau of Prof Poul Outzen-Boisen, OBE, Kt Dannebrog, of Rungsted Kyst, Denmark

2a Gerald Vansittart; T/Capt Oxon and Bucks LI WW I (despatches, wounded); *b* 2 Oct 1884; *ka* 16 Aug 1917

3a Guy Morier; *b* 21 Oct 1886; *m* 20 Aug 1925 Dorothy (*d* 26 April 1961), only dau of J E Ponsonby-Steel, of Ealing, and *d* 15 Nov 1950, leaving:

1b *June Violet [Mrs Bryan Blake, 115 Meadvale Rd, London W5 1NB]; *b* 15 Jan 1928; *m* 8 Dec 1956 *Bryan Francis Blake, s of Sidney Horace Blake, of Portsmouth, and has:

1c *Stephen Guy; *b* 23 July 1958

1c *Judith Clare [Mrs Bernard Greatbatch, First Tower, St Helier, Jersey, CI]; *b* 2 Dec 1960; *m* 1987 *Bernard Carl Greatbatch and has:

1d *Toby William; *b* 1990

2d *Robin Stephen; *b* 1991

1d *Chloë Ruth; *b* 1988

2b *Rose Ann [Mrs Robert Jackman, 6 Overwood Drive, King's Park, Glasgow S4]; *b* 12 Dec 1930; *m* 10 Sept 1955 *Robert Arthur Jackman, LLB, (*d* 16 July 1997) s of William Arthur Jackman, of Southampton, engr offr Merchant Marine, and has:

1c *Scott Robert; *b* 4 May 1963; *m* 1991 *Eileen Jane, dau of Robert Trail, of Paisley, Renfrewshire

1c *Lindsey Ann; *b* 2 Feb 1961; *m* 1984 *Stuart Alan Horton, F/Sgt RAF, s of H A Horton and has:

1d *Sarah Ann; *b* 1985

2d *Michelle Ashley; *b* 1989

3d *Philippa Abigail; *b* 1990

4a Hugh Alexander; Mechanical Tport Flanders WW I; *b* 1 June 1893; *m* 10 March 1931 Clarice (*d* 1956), only dau of Clayton C Lee, and *dsp* 9 Sept 1957

5a Eric Lloyd Strangways; *b* 1898; *m* 14 June 1934 Lucy Mary, dau of Josiah Charles Roberts; *d* 10 July 1990

1a Evelyn Henrica; *m* 27 Feb 1935 Ernest Morison (*d* 1955), s of H G Morison, merchant Madras, and *d* 4 Aug 1979

(3) Arthur Thomas Digby, of Hutton Hall, Brentwood, Essex, JP, DL; *b* 24 Aug 1859; Lt-Col cmdg and Hon Col 3rd Bn Essex Regt, Capt S Wales Borderers; *m* 17 July 1883 Harriet (*d* 25 Jan 1947), dau of Pandely Ralli (*see* RALLI, Bt), and *dsp* 8 March 1902

(1) Anna Charlotte; *m* 23 Dec 1878 Reginald James Mure, barrister, and *d* 1946, leaving issue. He *d* 23 Dec 1908

(2) Cecilia Louisa; *m* 27 July 1876 Charles William Matthews and had issue. He *d* 1921

(3) Nora; *m* 1885 William Arrow. He *d* 1921

(4) Alice Henrica Dora; *m* 31 Oct 1888 John Newton Hayley, of The Tower, Bognor, and had issue. He *d* 1 Dec 1929

4 William Augustus; *b* 5 Feb 1802; Madras CS; *m* 18 Aug 1838 Anne Elizabeth (*d* 12 Feb 1892), est dau and coheir of Alexander Black, of Gidea Hall, Essex, and *d* 3 Oct 1844, leaving, with a dau:

(1) William Alexander (Rev); Curate Branston, Lincs; *b* 8 Feb 1841; *m* 29 July 1868 Frances Mary (*d* 22 May 1928), est dau of Charles Saunders, of Carr Hall, Whitby, and *d* Oct 1879, leaving:

1a Charles Alexander, OBE (1919); Lt-Col 3rd Bn Somerset LI, Tport Offr Nairobi 1914, Assist Dir Tport 1916, Lt RA Boer War 1899–1902, Nandi Expdn 1905–06 and WW I; *b* 29 July 1869; *m* 1891 Klara Elizabeth, dau of Richard Schur, of Vienna, and *d* 9 June 1942, having had:

1b Alexander Lionel William; Capt IA; *b* 19 June 1894; *ka* 20 Sept 1918

2b Harold Digby; *b* 1897

1b Frances Lilian; *m* Maj A Roy Bingley and *d* 1923, leaving issue

2a Lionel Digby; *b* 15 Nov 1873; *educ* Marlborough, Bath Coll and Merton Coll Oxford (BA 1896); MRCSEng and LRCP London 1906; *m* 15 Nov 1909 Winifred (*d* 11 May 1956), dau of Michael Burke, and *d* 17 Nov 1951, leaving:

1b +Nelson Digby [Nelson Neave Esq, Flat 3, 32 Fitzwilliam St, Kew, Victoria 3101, Australia]; F/Lt RAFVR WW II; *b* 7 Oct 1914; *m* 1936 *Betty Ross, of Liverpool, and has:

1c *Marilyn Kathryn [Mrs Anthony Challinor, 29 Hestercombe Ave, London SW6 5LL; Le Bosc, Sauveterre, 82110 Lamzerte, Tarn et

Garonne, France]; *b* 1938; *m* 1st 1958 (*divorce* 1974) Dr Samuel Shub, MB, BS, MRACP, of Victoria, Australia, and has:

1d *Martin David Neave [Martin Shub Esq, Flat 1, 24 Gardyne St, Bronte, Sydney, Australia]; *b* 11 Feb 1959; *m* 1991 *Helen Bongiorno

1d *Caroline Leanne [Mrs James Ford, 166 Ormond Rd, Elwood, Melbourne, Australia]; *b* 24 Aug 1960; *m* 1987 *James Ford and has:

1e *Charles James; *b* 1988

2e *Oliver; *b* 1990

2d *Melissa Louise; *b* 3 Dec 1965

1c (cont) Mrs Marilyn Shub *m* 2nd 1983 *Dr Anthony Challinor, BSc, PhD (Cantab), FGS

2b +John Alexander [John Neave Esq, 17 Netheredge Drive, Knaresborough, N Yorks HG5 9DA]; *b* 21 Feb 1919; *m* 29 Aug 1946 *Jacqueline, only child of F Ranger, of Holyhead, Anglesey, and has:

1c +David John; *b* 8 Feb 1954; *m* 1976 *Jacqueline Irene, dau of Peter Flack, of Haughley, Suffolk

1c *Judith Marion [Mrs James Brame, Highwood, Topcliffe, N Yorks]; *b* 2 March 1948; *m* 1969 *James Brame and has:

1d *James Kenneth; *b* 1969

1d *Danielle; *b* 1980

2d *Kimberley; *b* 1982

2c *Margaret Alison [Mrs Alan Parnham, 17 Western Rd, Lancing, Sussex]; *b* 1950; *m* 1st 1969 (*divorce* 1981) Jean-Claude Estripeau and has:

1d *Natalie Isabelle; *b* 1970

2d *Tamsin Jane; *b* 1976

2c (cont.) Mrs Margaret Estripeau *m* 2nd 1983 *Alan Parnham

3c *Catherine Mary [Mrs Hartwig Nicolaus, 5 Rose Rd, Rochester, NY 14624, USA]; *b* 1951; *m* 1971 *Hartwig Waldemar Nicolaus and has:

1d *Heidi Marie; *b* 1971

3b +Geoffrey Lionel [Geoffrey Neave Esq, Flat 1, 1 Marmara Drive, Elsternwick, Vic 3185, Australia]; *b* 2 March 1920; *educ* Ascham Coll and Co High Sch Clacton-on-Sea; Roy Hants Regt WW II; *m* 1964 *Freda Mary Walmsley, yst dau of G H Hobson, of Lincoln

1b Mary Winifred; *b* 10 May 1913; *m* 10 May 1933 Rev Dennis Victor Wright, AKC (*d* 1982), and *d* June 1994, leaving:

1c *Stephen John Neave [Stephen Wright Esq, 4 Langdale Mansions, Thornton Rd, London SW12 0LN]; *b* 21 Aug 1934; *educ* Brentwood Sch and County High Sch, Buckhurst Hill, Essex; *m* 29 Oct 1960 *Jennifer Anne, SRN, dau of Arthur John Carter, of Chingford, and has:

1d *Christopher Jonathan Neave [Christopher Wright Esq, 3 School Rd, Silver End, Witham, Essex CM8 3RZ]; *b* 2 Sept 1961

2d *Nigel Robin Neave [Nigel Wright Esq, 11 School Rd, Silver End, Witham, Essex CM8 3RZ]; *b* 26 Sept 1962; *m* 31 July 1986 (*divorce* 1992) Julie Darkins and has:

1e *Danny James Neave; *b* 27 Sept 1987

1d *Samantha Jane [Mrs Anthony Bocks, 3605 Wosley Drive, Fort Worth, TX 76133, USA]; *b* 27 Jan 1966; *m* 6 July 1985 *Anthony Glenn Bocks and has:

1e *Ryan; *b* 2 Sept 1989

2e *Nicholas; *b* 3 Jan 1997

1e *Chelsea; *b* 19 May 1988

2c *Martin Neave (Rev) [The Rev Preb Martin Wright, The Bishop's Palace, Wells, Somerset BA5 2PD]; *b* 25 April 1937; *educ* Brentwood Sch, King's Coll London and St Boniface Coll Warminster (AKC 1st Cl honours 1961); RPC 1955–57, Suez 1956 (GS Medal), ordained Peterborough 1962, Assist Curate St Columba and the Northern Saints Corby, Northants, 1962–65, Industl Chaplain to Bp Peterborough 1965, Bp Coventry's Offr for Social Responsibility; Chaplain to Bp of Bath & Wells

1c *Ruth Mary [Miss Ruth Wright, Flat 11, 2 Dashwood Rd, Banbury, Oxon OX16 8HD]; *b* 16 Nov 1943; SRN, CertEd

1a Ethel Mary; *d* unm 27 Jan 1953

2a Florence Katherine; *m* 1899 George Herbert Martin, MA, FCS, and *d* 14 Oct 1950. He *d* Oct 1951

3a Gertrude Atherton; *m* 4 June 1907 Lawrence Middleton Brettingham, of Milverton, Somerset, and had issue. He *d* 21 Sept 1952

4a Frances Eveline; *m* 2 Nov 1906 Stephen Wilkinson, AFC, FRIBA, county architect, RAF, and *d* 3 Oct 1952, leaving issue. He *d* 1 Jan 1962

(2) Francis Digby Spencer; *b* 20 April 1842; *educ* Ch Ch Oxford (BA); *m* 21 Oct 1869 Eliza Marianne (*d* 16 Nov 1922), est dau of Henry Cormack, of Bombay, and *d* 7 Oct 1913, having had:

1a Henry Everard; Capt Roy Warwicks Regt; *b* 14 Oct 1872; *d* 9 Sept 1902

2a Francis Digby; *b* 4 Aug 1874; *m* 20 Sept 1910 Ethelberta (*d* 1970), only child of Edward Washbourne, of St Albans, Christchurch, NZ, and *d* 9 Sept 1943, having had:

1b Francis Edward; *b* 1914; *d* unm 5 Feb 1943

2b John Digby; *b* 1916; ch instr Canterbury Aero Club; *m* 21 June 1939 Martha Dorothy (*d* 1985), dau of R T Francis, of Christchurch, and *d* 4 Feb 1995, leaving:

1c +Richard Francis [Richard Neave Esq, 54 Norrie St, Northcote, Christchurch, New Zealand]; *b* 12 Dec 1941; *educ* St Andrews Coll Christchurch; *m* 1962 *Patricia Lorraine McGuire and has:

1d +Roger John Francis; *b* 22 Sept 1962

1d *Deborah Michelle; *b* 7 July 1965

2d *Amanda Gaye; *b* 1969

1c *Barbara Alice [Mrs Ramon Saunders, 54 Holland Avenue, Hillcrest, Auckland 10, New Zealand]; *b* 4 Sept 1940; *m* 10 Feb 1962 *Ramon Juan Saunders, s of Ronald James Saunders, of Westport, NZ, and has:

1d *David John; *b* 21 Nov 1968

2d *James Richard Neave; *b* 1972

1d *Rachael Louise; *b* 1974

2c *Eleanor Elizabeth [Mrs Bruce Anderson, 32 James St, Glenfield, Auckland, New Zealand]; *b* 29 Sept 1943; *m* 28 March 1964 *Bruce Peter Anderson and has:

  1d *Thomas Digby; *b* 1970

  2d *Philip Richard; *b* 1972

3b +Henry Washbourn [Henry Neave Esq, 8 Merepark Place, Ham, Christchurch 4, New Zealand]; *b* 1918; *m* 1st 18 April 1945 (*divorce* 1949) Doreen Melba, only child of J W Wright, of Spreydon, Christchurch, NZ; *m* 2nd 1953 *Sheila Duncan, dau of R H Bennetts Halswell, of Christchurch, and by her has:

  1c +Alistair Dudley Digby [Alastair Neave Esq, 1351 Whangaparaoa Rd, Hibiscus Coast, New Zealand]; *b* 1956; *m* 1978 *Lorraine Mary, dau of J Irvine, of Auckland

  2c +Richard Henry Digby [Richard Neave Esq, 71 Deepdale St, Burnside, Christchurch 5, New Zealand]; *b* 1960

  1c *Diana Sheila [Mrs Brett Russell, 10 Lynmouth Ave, Karori, Wellington, New Zealand]; *b* 23 June 1954; *m* 1979 *Brett Michael Russell

4b +Arthur Kenelm; *b* 1924; *m* 1st 16 April 1951 Mrs Elizabeth Marie Doyle (*d* 1983), only dau of George C T Brady, of Riccarton, Christchurch; *m* 2nd 1984 (*divorce* 1993) Winifred Emma Bates, dau of Roy Stiggants

1b *Elizabeth Marjorie [Mrs Grgo Franicevic, 5 Tui St, Fendalton, Christchurch, New Zealand]; *b* 1911; *m* 23 Dec 1941 Grgo Franicevic (*d* 1981), s of Visko Franicevic, of Riccarton, and has had:

  1c Vincent Peter Ivan; *b* 16 Sept 1942; *educ* St Andrew's Coll Christchurch and U of Canterbury; md Marisa Knitwear Ltd; *m* 26 Dec 1963 (*divorce* 1972) Maritza Ann Frances, est dau of Mate Glucina, of Christchurch, and *d* 23 July 1994

  2c *Edward John Grgo; *b* 18 Dec 1946; *m* 1967 (*divorce* 1986) Margaret Anne Blay and has:

    1d *Lisa Marie; *b* 1967

    2d *Anita Margaret; *b* 1969; *m* 19– *A G Bigwood

    3d *Terry; *b* 1974

  3c *Paul Francis Anton; *b* 29 May 1949; *m* 1983 *Shona Lorna Mitchell and has:

    1d *Scott Anton; *b* 1989

    1d *Kim Marie; *b* 1991

  1c Lois Ethel Yurka; *b* 16 June 1944; *m* 1st 1966 (*divorce* 1988) Geoffrey Herbert Heath and had:

    1d *Michael Geoffrey; *b* 1969

    2d *Thomas James; *b* 1970

    1d *Katrina Louise; *b* 1973

  1c (cont.) Mrs Lois Heath *m* 2nd 1990 *Robert Basil Thombs Colley

  2c *Mara Elizabeth; *b* 9 March 1948; *m* 1978 *Peter Charles Abrams and has:

    1d *Anna Marza; *b* 1979

    2d *Sarah Katherine Louise; *b* 1981

2b Nancy Mary; *b* 2 Sept 1921; *m* 15 Sept 1945 *Maxwell Milner, s of William Milner, of Christchurch, and had:

  1c *Bruce Digby; *b* 15 Oct 1948

  1c *Judith Adrienne [Mrs L Wilson-Parr, 29a Chepstow Ave, Christchurch 4, New Zealand]; *b* 29 July 1946; *m* 19– *L E Wilson-Parr and has issue

3a Kenelm; barrister; *b* 20 Nov 1875; *educ* NZ U (LLB); *d* unm 5 Feb 1931

4a Arthur Cormack; 2nd Lt 1st Bn Yorks Regt; *b* 4 June 1877; *ka* Paardeberg S Africa 18 Feb 1900

5a Everard Aldigus; *b* 1879; *m* Dec 1900 Nora Cottell (*d* 1953) and *d* Sept 1954, leaving:

  1b Digby Everard; Roy Ordnance Corps; *b* 31 March 1911; *d* unm 19–

  1b Nina Elisabeth; *b* 13 Jan 1908; *d* unm 19–

1a Adelaide Constance; *d* unm 24 April 1949

2a Anne Eleanor; *d* unm 10 Nov 1943

3a Alice Mary; *m* 6 April 1904 Col Percy Morland Acton-Adams, DSO, of Clarence Reserve, Walau, NZ, and *d* 27 March 1937, leaving issue. He *d* 23 Nov 1927

(3) Everard Strangways; Lt-Col 18th Bengal Cav; *b* 21 Aug 1844; *m* 1st 11 Nov 1876 Annie Laura (*d* 18 Oct 1877), est surv dau of Alfred Douglas Hamilton (*see* HAMILTON and BRANDON, D), and had:

  1a Everard Reginald NEAVE later HAY-NEAVE (roy licence 1910); *b* 31 July 1877; *educ* Balliol Coll Oxford (BA 1900); ICS, Dist and Sessions Judge UP 1923, Actg Judge High Court Allahabad 1924–26; *m* 25 Oct 1910 Amy Charlotte Balfour Hay (*d* 1971), of Leys and Carpow, Perthshire, and Randerstone and Mugdrum, Fifeshire, dau and coheir of Peter Hay Paterson and n and coheir of Edmond de Hay Paterson-Balfour-Hay of Leys, Carpow, Randerstone and Mugdrum, and *d* 1951, having had:

    1b David Reginald Hay NEAVE HAY OF LEYS (Lyon Court decree 1954); *b* 5 Sept 1912; *educ* Blundells; Assist Supt Br Guyana Colonial Police 1937–40, Capt IA 12th–13th Frontier Force Burma 1940–43, Assist Resident Chin Hill Burma 1945–58, For Serv 1948–58: Persia, Nepal, Indonesia and Siam; *d* unm 1 Jan 1961

    2b Peter Arundell; F/O RAFVR WW II; *b* 2 June 1923; *ka* 11 Nov 1943

    1b *Beatrice Rosemary; *b* 1911; SRN; *m* 26 Aug 1939 Capt Colin Napier Christie, Black Watch, of Sheelyn, Leven, Fife, s of Robert Maitland Christie of Durie, Fife, and has:

      1c *Mary Helen [Mrs James Marshall, Ormlie, Bankend Rd, Bridge of Weir, Renfrewshire]; *b* 27 May 1941; *m* 1970 *James Beaton Marshall

      2c *Anna Margaret [Mrs Derek O'Shea, 49 Woodfield Crescent, London W5]; *b* 25 May 1943; *m* 1970 *Derek O'Shea and has:

        1d *Catherine Janet; *b* 1972

        2d *Linda Margaret; *b* 1975

    2b Anne Elizabeth; *b* 31 May 1916; *d* 30 Aug 1919

  3b *Diana Hope [Mrs Ryszard Habdank-Kolaczkowski, 280 Easy St, 515 Mountain View, CA 94043, USA]; *b* 1918; late WRNS; *m* 1st July 1940

P/O David James Reoch Ritchie, RAFVR (*kas* 1943); *m* 2nd 1950 *Lt Ryszard Habdank-Kolaczkowski, RA and Polish AF, and by him has:

  1c *Anita Marya Star [Mrs Piotr Moncarz, 3255 Emerson St, Palo Alto, CA 94306, USA]; *b* Sept 1951; *m* 1976 *Piotr Daniel Moncarz and has:

    1d *Sylvana Marya; *b* 1981

  4b *Griselda Nancy [Mrs Henry Jascoll, 28 Ravensbourne Gdns, London W13]; *b* 1920; late ATS; *m* 23 Nov 1943 *Henry Feliks JASCOLL formerly JASZCZOLT, late 10th Polish Mounted Rifles, and has:

    1c *Dominic Peter; *b* 14 Oct 1945; took name HAY OF LEYS by Lord Lyon decree 1986

    2c *John Henry David [John Jascoll Esq, 2633 Hazelwood Rd, Lancaster PA 17601, USA]; *b* 17 Dec 1949; *educ* LSE (MSc Econ); *m* 1974 *Dorothy (Dorie) Ann, dau of Homer K Luttringer, and has:

      1d *Jennifer Elizabeth; *b* 1983

(3) (cont.) Col Everard Neave *m* 2nd 7 Dec 1887 Julia Anne (*d* 15 Jan 1915), dau of William Ashwell, of Chetwode Priory, Bucks, and *d* 1896

Sir THOMAS *d* 11 April 1848; his est s,

  Sir Richard Digby Neave, 3rd Bt; *b* 9 Dec 1793; *m* 7 Aug 1828 Hon Mary Arundell (*d* 30 Aug 1849), yst dau of 9th Baron Arundell of Wardour (*see* 1940 edn), and had, with other issue:

1 ARUNDELL (Sir), **4th Bt**

1 Venetia; *m* 5 Jan 1860 Rev John Whittaker Maitland, Rector Loughton, Essex, and *d* 30 June 1901, leaving issue. He *d* 28 Nov 1909

2 Cicely; *m* 10 Feb 1863 Wyndham Slade and *d* 11 May 1920, leaving issue (*see* SLADE, Bt)

3 Mariquita; *m* 6 Aug 1874 Alexander George Middleton and *d* 31 Oct 1938. He *d* 15 Nov 1875

Sir RICHARD *d* 10 March 1868; his est s,

  Sir Arundell Neave, 4th Bt, DL Essex; *b* 5 June 1829; Capt 3rd Dragoon Gds; *m* 26 Sept 1871 Hon Gwyn Gertrude Hughes (*d* 30 Sept 1916), yst dau of 1st Baron Dinorben of Kinmel Park (*see* 1851 edn), and had:

1 THOMAS LEWIS HUGHES (Sir), **5th Bt**

2 Arundell; Maj 16th Lancers Boer War 1900–02 and WW I (despatches, Legn Honour); *b* 2 July 1875; *ka* 21 Feb 1915

1 Mary Gertrude Catherine; *b* 24 Sept 1872; *d* unm 10 Feb 1951

Sir ARUNDELL *d* 21 Sept 1877; his er s,

  Sir Thomas Lewis Hughes Neave, 5th Bt, JP, DL Anglesey, JP Essex; *b* 26 June 1874; Maj and Cmdt Roy Def Force, Hon Lt-Col 1st Vol Bn Roy Welch Fus, Maj Roy Anglesey Militia; *m* 26 Nov 1908 Dorina Lockhart (*d* 26 Dec 1955), dau of George Henry Clifton, of Nottingham, and had:

1 ARUNDELL THOMAS CLIFTON (Sir), **6th Bt**

2 +Kenelm Digby [Kenelm Neave Esq, Saunders Farm, Camden Hill, Kent TN17 2AR]; *b* 4 July 1921; *educ* Harrow; Capt Welsh Gds WW II NW Europe 1944–45 (wounded); *m* 1st 29 June 1949 *Venetia, only child of Harold Digby Neave (*see* above), and has:

  (1) *Nicola Venetia [Mrs Robert Reagan, Cowley Close, Cheltenham, Glos]; *b* 15 March 1956; *m* 1976 *Robert Reagan and has:

    1a *Paul; *b* 1979

    2a *Jonathan; *b* 1984

    1a *Louise; *b* 1982

  (2) *Dorinda May; *b* 1958; *m* 1985 *Barry Shell and has:

    1a *Samuel; *b* 1987

    1a *Davina; *b* 1991

2 (cont.) Kenelm Neave *m* 2nd 1970 *Marian Rosamond, dau of Gerald Hartley Lees

1 *Dorina Mary Eileen [Mrs Frederick Parsons, Wren House, 32 Vicarage St, Warminster, Wilts]; *b* 7 March 1911; *m* 1 July 1936 Brig Frederick Gillespie Austin Parsons, CBE (*d* 1992), Roy Northumberland Fus, only s of Col Frederick George Parsons, DSO, Queen's Regt, of Bath, and has:

  (1) Anthony Frederick Arundell, MBE (1976); *b* 4 Sept 1937; *educ* Wellington and RMC Sandhurst; Lt-Col Roy Regt Fus; *m* 1965 *(Elizabeth Margaret) Jane, only dau of John C Llewellin, of Long Compton, Warwicks, and *d* 1982 of wounds recd on active service NI, leaving:

    1a *Charles William Anthony; *b* 27 Aug 1968

    2a *James; *b* 1971

  (2) *Robert Gillespie [Robert Parsons Esq, Chapel House, Church Path, Purton, Wilts]; *b* 29 April 1942; *educ* Wellington and RMC Sandhurst; Capt Roy Regt Fus; *m* 1st 9 Aug 1969 (*divorce* 1976) Anne Penelope Stanton, only dau of Maj John Prestwich, of Highlands Farm, Ossington, Notts, and has:

    1a *Rollo Crispin Gillespie; *b* 22 Jan 1971

    1a *Eugénie Sophia Gillespie; *b* 1972

  (2) (cont.) Robert Parsons *m* 2nd 1983 (*divorce* 1986) Nicola, dau of Patrick Dyas, OBE, of Broadbridge Heath, Sussex

2 Renée Arundell; *b* 1 Nov 1913; *m* 8 June 1938 Lt-Col Sir Richard Harry David Williams-Bulkeley, 13th Bt (*qv*), and *d* 1994, leaving issue

Sir THOMAS *d* 12 May 1940; his er s,

  Sir Arundell Thomas Clifton Neave, 6th Bt; *b* 31 May 1916; *educ* Eton; Maj Welsh Gds WW II; *m* 24 April 1946 Richenda Alice Ione (*d* 1994), only child of Sir Robert Joshua Paul, 5th Bt (*see* 1956 edn), and *d* 1992, leaving:

1 Sir PAUL ARUNDELL NEAVE, **7th and present Bt**

2 +Robert Joshua; *b* 16 April 1951; *educ* Eton

1 *Dilys Richenda [Mrs Timothy Hobson, Harvard Farm, Halstock, Somerset BA22 9SZ]; *b* 6 July 1947; *m* 22 June 1968 *Timothy Hayward Hobson, 2nd s of John Hobson, of Ringshall, Herts, and has:

  (1) *Jake Timothy; *b* 1971

  (2) *Barnaby John; *b* 1974

  (3) *Samuel Jeffrey; *b* 1979

  (1) *Richenda Eveline; *b* 16 Sept 1969

2 *Serena Mary; *b* 22 March 1955

NEILL OF BLADEN

Creation: B. (LP, UK) 1997.

THE BARON NEILL OF BLADEN, of Briantspuddle, Co Dorset (Sir (Francis) Patrick Neill) [The Rt Hon The Lord Neill of Bladen, House of Lords London SW1A 0PW]; *b* 8 Aug 1926; *educ* Highgate Sch and Magdalen Coll Oxford (U V-Chllr 1985–89, Hon DCL 1987); Rifle Bde 1944–47, Capt GSO (3) Egypt 1947; All Souls: Fell 1950–77, Sub-Warden 1972–74, Warden 1977–95; barrister Gray's Inn 1951 (Bencher 1971, V-Treas 1989, Treas 1990), lecturer air law LSE 1955–58, QC 1966, Chm: Bar Cncl 1974–75 (memb 1967–71, V-Chm 1973–74), Senate Inns of Court and bar 1974–75 and All Souls Ctee Review Admin Law 1978–87, Crown Court Recorder 1975–78, Judge Courts Appeal Guernsey and Jersey 1977–94; ktd 1983; Chm: Press Cncl 1978–83, DTI Ctee Inquiry Lloyd's Regulatory Arrangements 1986–87, Lloyd's Feltrum Loss Review Ctee 1991–92, Cncl Securities Industry 1978–85 and Ctee on Standards in Public Life 1998–; ind dir Times Newspapers Hldgs 1988–98, Hon Prof Legal Ethics Birmingham 1983–84, Hon LLD Hull 1978, Buckingham 1994; author: *Administrative Justice: some necessary reforms* (1988); *m* 1954 *Caroline Susan, dau of Sir Piers Debenham, 2nd Bt (*qv*) and has issue

Lineage: Sir THOMAS NEILL, JP; *m* Annie Strachan Bishop and had:

(FRANCIS) PATRICK, *cr* a **Baron**

NELSON, Earl

Arms: Or a cross flory sable, a bend gules surmounted by another engrailed of the field, charged with three bombs fired proper, on a chief (of honourable augmentation) undulated argent waves of the sea from which a palm tree issuant between a disabled ship on the dexter, and a battery in ruins on the sinister, all proper. **Crests:** 1 (honourable augmentation) On a naval crown or the chelenk or plume of triumph presented to Horatio, Viscount Nelson, by the Grand Signior Sultan Selim III, 2 Upon waves of the sea the stern of a Spanish man-of-war, all proper, thereon inscribed 'San Josef' (with motto over 'Faith and Works'). **Supporters:** Dexter, a sailor armed with a cutlass and a pair of pistols in his belt, proper, the right hand supporting a staff thereon hoisted a commodore's flag gules, and in his left a palm branch proper; sinister, a lion rampant regardant, in his mouth two broken flagstaffs, proper, flowing from one a Spanish flag or and gules, and from the other a French flag, in his dexter paw a palm branch, proper. **Motto:** *Palmam qui meruit ferat* ('Let him wear the palm who has deserved it'). **Creations:** E. and V. (UK) 20 Nov 1805, B. (UK) 18 Aug 1801.

THE 9TH EARL NELSON OF TRAFALGAR and **OF MERTON, VISCOUNT MERTON OF TRAFALGAR** and **OF MERTON**, Co Surrey, and **BARON NELSON OF THE NILE** and **OF HILBOROUGH**, Co Norfolk (Peter John Horatio Nelson) [The Rt Hon The Earl Nelson, House of Lords, London SW1A 0PW]; *b* 9 Oct 1941; *s* unc 1981; former police detective sgt, pres RN Commando Assoc and Nelson Soc, v-pres Jubilee Sailing Tst, dir Br Navy Pusser's Rum, chm Retainacar Ltd, patron Int Fingerprint Soc and Clapton Assoc Football Club, memb Ctee of Friends of Nat Maritime Museum; *m* 1st 1969 (*divorce* 19–) Maureen Diana, dau of Edward Patrick Quinn, of Kilkenny, and has:

1 +SIMON JOHN HORATIO, *Viscount Merton*; *b* 21 Sept 1971

1 *Deborah Jane Mary; *b* 19 June 1974

The 9th EARL *m* 2nd 1992 *Tracy Cowie and by her has:

2 +Edward James Horatio; *b* 23 March 1994

Lineage: RICHARD NELSTON, of Mawdesley, Lancs; *fl* 1377; ancestor of:

RICHARD NELSON, of Mawdesley, living 1508; had:

THOMAS NELSON, of Fairhurst; *m* Cecilia, dau of Ralph Maxey, and had, with three er sons and a dau:

WILLIAM NELSON, of London; *m* Judith Clinton and had, with two er sons (Michael; William):

THOMAS NELSON, of London and Norfolk; *b* 1580; *m* Elizabeth — and was *bur* 28 July 1654, leaving, with two daus (Elizabeth, *b* 1601, *m* John Green; Anne, *m* William Williams):

EDMUND NELSON, of Wendling, Norfolk; *m* 1st Joann — and had:

1 Edmund, of Wendling and Scarning, Norfolk; *bapt* 29 Nov 1629; *m* 16– Mary — and was *bur* 1 Nov 1711, leaving issue; his descendants were settled at Holme-next-the-Sea, Norfolk, from 1750

1 Joan; *bapt* 29 June 1636

2 Anna; *bapt* 28 May 1637

EDMUND NELSON *m* 2nd Alice — and by her had:

2 WILLIAM

3 John; *bapt* 2 Feb 1656

3 Bridget; *bapt* 24 Feb 1653

EDMUND NELSON's 2nd s,

WILLIAM NELSON, of Scarning, later Dunham Parva, Norfolk; *bapt* 24 March 1654; *m* Mary (*d* 2 Jan 1731), dau of Thomas Shene, of Dunham Parva, and *d* 7 Jan 1713, leaving:

1 Thomas, of Sporle; *b* 19 July 1683; had:

(1) Edmund (Rev); Rector Conyham, Norfolk; had:

1a James (Rev); Rector Conyham

2a Charles; Post Capt RN; *d* 22 April 1762

2 William, of Dunham Parva and Curds Hall, Fransham, Norfolk; *b* 18 Feb 1688; *d* 29 Jan 1773, leaving:

(1) William (Rev), of Curds Hall; Rector Hillington and Hilgay, Norfolk; had three daus, the est of whom inherited his estates

3 Edmund (Rev); *b* 1693; MA, Vicar Sporle, Rector and Patron of living Hilborough, Norfolk; *m* Mary (*d* 4 July 1789 aged 91), dau of John Bland, baker in Petty Cury, Cambridge, and *d* 23 Oct 1747, having had, with a yr s and a dau (*d* unm):

(1) EDMUND

1 Alice; *m* Rev Robert Rolfe, Rector Hilborough, and had:

(1) Monsey (Rev); Rector Cranworth, Norfolk; *m* Jemima, dau of William Alexander, and had:

1a ROBERT MONSEY ROLFE, 1st and last BARON CRANWORTH, of Cranworth, Norfolk (UK), so *cr* 20 Dec 1850, PC (1850); *b* 18 Dec 1790; *educ* Bury GS, Winchester and Trin Coll Cambridge (17th Wrangler and BA 1812, Fell Downing Coll and MA 1815); barrister Lincoln's Inn 1816, Recorder Bury 1832, KC 1832, MP (Lib) Penryn 1832–39, Slr-Gen 1834 and 1835–39, ktd 1825, a Baron of Exchequer 1839–50, a Commr Gt Seal June–July 1850, a V-Chllr 1850, a Ld Justice Appeal 1851, Ld Chllr 1852–58 and 1865–66; *m* 9 Oct 1845 Laura, yst dau of Thomas William Carr, of Frognal and Esholt Heugh, Northumberland, and *dsp* 26 July 1868, when the Barony expired

2 Thomasine; *m* John Goulty, of Norwich

The Rev EDMUND NELSON's er s,

Rev EDMUND NELSON; *b* 1722; MA, Rector Hilborough and Burnham Thorpe, Norfolk; *m* 11 May 1749 Catherine (*d* 26 Dec 1767), only dau of Rev Maurice Suckling, DD, Preb Westminster, by Mary (dau of Sir Charles Turner, 1st Bt (*cr* 1727; *extinct* 1780), of Warham, Norfolk, by his 1st w Mary, sis of Sir Robert Walpole, KG, PM, 1st Earl of Orford (*see* WALPOLE, B)) and *d* 26 April 1802, having had, with four other sons and a dau (*d* young or unm):

1 Maurice; *b* 24 May 1753; clerk Navy Office; *dsp* 24 April 1801

2 Rev WILLIAM NELSON, **1st Earl Nelson of Trafalgar** and **of Merton**, and **Viscount Merton of Trafalgar** and **of Merton**, Co Surrey (both UK), so *cr* (for his bro's heroic services to the nation) 20 Nov 1805 (with similar special remainder to that of the Barony of Nelson of the Nile and of Hilborough in his bro's case; *see* below), also **2nd Baron Nelson of the Nile** and **of Hilborough** and **2nd Duke of Brontë** (*see* below); *b* 20 April 1757; *educ* Norwich GS and Christ's Coll Cambridge (BA, MA, DD); Rector Brandon Parva Norfolk 1784, Hilborough 1797, Preb Canterbury 1803–35; (by Act of Parl 1806 Earl Nelson and his successors in the title were granted £5,000 a year (nearly £150,000 in late-1990s terms) plus a lump sum of £90,000 (well over £2,600,000 in late-1990s terms) to buy an estate; the manor house of Standlynch (subsequently Trafalgar House then Trafalgar Park), Downton, nr Salisbury, which had been built by the banker Sir Peter Vandeput in 1733 to the design of John James, was chosen and was owned by the family till 1948; the pension was discontinued, without compensation, on the death of the **5th Earl** 1951; by the 1806 Act the surname NELSON was to be taken by every inheritor of the title); *m* 1st 9 Nov 1786 Sarah (*d* 13 April 1828), dau of Rev Henry Yonge, and had:

(1) Horatio, *Viscount Trafalgar*; *b* 26 Oct 1788; *educ* Eton and Cambridge; *dvp* unm 17 Jan 1808

(2) Charlotte Mary, **Duchess of Brontë** in her own right; *m* 2nd Baron Bridport (*d* 6 Jan 1868) and *d* 29 Jan 1874, leaving issue (*see* BRIDPORT, V)

2 (cont.) The **1st Earl** *m* 2nd 26 March 1829 Hilare (*m* 3rd 7 Feb 1837 George Thomas Knight; *d* 22 Dec 1857), 3rd dau of Adml Sir Robert Barlow, GCB, sis of Viscountess Torrington (*qv*) and widow of her cousin Capt George Ulric Barlow, 4th Light Dragoons (*d* 1824), and *dspms* 28 Feb 1835, when the UK titles passed to his n and the Neapolitan/Sicilian Dukedom to his dau

3 HORATIO NELSON, **1st Baron Nelson of the Nile** and **of Hilborough** (UK), so *cr* 18 Aug 1801, with remainder, failing heirs male of his own body lawfully begotten, to his f and his f's heirs male, and failing them to the heirs male of the bodies of (a) his sis Mrs Bolton and (b) his other sis Mrs Matcham, KB (1797); *b* 29 Sept 1758 at Parsonage House, Burnham Thorpe, Norfolk, and christened Horatio after his godfather and maternal grandmother's 1st cousin Horatio, 2nd Baron Walpole of Wolterton (*see* WALPOLE, B) and 1st Earl of Orford (of the second creation); *educ* Norwich High Sch and a sch at North Walsham; entered RN 1770, joined 1771 HMS *Raisonnable*, 64 guns, commanded by his uncle Capt Maurice Suckling, Col of Marines 1795–97, R-Adml 1797 and 1799,

V-Adml 1801 and 1804; cmded at Battles of the Nile 1798 (French defeat), Copenhagen 1801 (Danish defeat) and Trafalgar 1805 (Franco-Spanish defeat), *cr*: 6 Nov 1798 BARON NELSON OF THE NILE and OF BURNHAM THORPE, Co Norfolk (UK) (voted thanks and £2,000 (over £72,000 in late-1990s terms) a year for life and the lives of his two immediate successors in the title by GB Parl, £1,000 a year by I Parl and £10,000 by the HEIC), 9 Jan 1801 DUKE OF BRONTË (Br roy licence Sept 1801 to accept for himself and his heirs this title; *see* BRIDPORT, V), with the fief of the Duchy annexed, by FERDINAND IV OF NAPLES AND SICILY (whose restoration Nelson had brought about June 1799) and 22 May 1801 VISCOUNT NELSON OF THE NILE and OF BURNHAM THORPE, Co Norfolk (UK), Kt Grand Cross St Ferdinand and Merit Naples 1801, Kt Crescent Ottoman Empire 1st Cl 1802, Grand Cdr St Joachim Leiningen 1802, DCL Oxon 1802; *m* 11 March 1787 (WILLIAM IV being best man) Frances (Fanny) Herbert (*b* St Nevis 1758; £2,000 a year settled on her by Parl 1806; *d* 6 May 1831), dau of William Woolward, sr Judge St Nevis, and widow of Josiah Nisbet, MD, of St Nevis, and *dspl*, *ka* 21 Oct 1805 (state funeral 9 Jan 1806 St Paul's London), when the Barony and Viscountcy of the 1798 and 1801 creations respectively expired, but the Barony of the 1801 *cr* and the Neapolitan/Sicilian Dukedom passed to his er bro, leaving illegitimate issue by Lady (Emma) Hamilton (*see* HAMILTON and BRANDON, D):

(1) Horatia Nelson THOMPSON (pseudonym adopted by her f when writing to Lady Hamilton) later NELSON (roy licence 30 Sept 1806); *b* 29 Oct 1800; *m* 1822 Rev Philip Ward (*d* 1859), Curate, of Burnham Market, Norfolk, and *d c* 1880, having had nine children (including two sons, Horatio and Nelson)

4 Suckling (Rev); *b* 5 Jan 1764; *d unm* 1799

1 Susanna; shop assistant in Bath; *m* 5 Aug 1780 Thomas Bolton, dealer in corn, malt and coals, of Wells, Norfolk (*d* 17 Oct 1834), and *d* 16 July 1813, having had, with a dau (*d unm*):

(1) THOMAS, **2nd Earl**

(2) George; *b* 10 Nov 1787; *d* at sea 1799

(1) Jemima Susanna; *d* 10 Aug 1864

(2) Catherine (twin with Jemima); *m* 18 May 1803 Capt Sir William Bolton, RN (*d* 1 Dec 1830), and *d* 22 April 1857

(3) Elizabeth Anne; *m* Rev Henry Hirdlestone, Rector Landford, Wilts, and Colton St Andrew, Norfolk

2 Catherine; *m* 26 Feb 1787 George Matcham (*d* 3 Feb 1833), of Ashfold Lodge, Slaugham, Sussex, and *d* 28 March 1842, having had, with four other sons (*d* under age):

(1) George Nelson; *b* 7 Nov 1789; DCL; *m* 20 Feb 1817 Harriet, est dau and heiress of William Eyre, of Newhouse, Wilts, and *d* 15 Jan 1877, having had:

1a Horatio Nelson Eyre; *b* 16 April 1819; *d* 1845

2a George Simon Eyre; *b* 3 Jan 1822; *d* 5 Nov 1833

3a William Eyre MATCHAM later EYRE-MATCHAM (deed poll 11 April 1889), of Newhouse, Wilts, JP, DL; *b* 10 April 1823; *m* 3 Jan 1861 Mary Elizabeth (*d* 24 March 1902), 4th dau of H L Long, of Hampton Lodge, Surrey, and *d* 11 July 1906, leaving:

1b George Henry Eyre, of Newhouse, Wilts, JP; *b* 21 Feb 1862; Capt 3rd Bn Wilts Regt; *m* 5 June 1889 Constance Gertrude (*d* 12 April 1933), est dau of Hon St Leger Richard Glyn, 2nd s of 1st Baron Wolverton (*qv*), and *d* 28 June 1939, leaving:

1c John St Leger; *b* 28 March 1890; *educ* Charterhouse and Corpus Christi Coll Oxford; *m* 23 Nov 1949 *Norah Olivia Alice, dau of Clement Albert Privett, of Ascot, and widow of John Spencer Spear, of Imperial Airways, Athens, and *d* 19–

1c Florence Ellery Mary; *b* 7 Feb 1893; *d unm* 9 July 1967

2c Joyce Horatia; *b* 4 Oct 1895; *d* 16 April 1954 following an accident

3c Constance Valentine; *b* 14 Feb 1897; *m* 7 July 1923 Cdr Edmund Valentine Jeffreys, RN, yst s of John Jeffreys, of Canterton Manor, and *d* 1984, having had:

1d *George William Eyre [George Jeffreys Esq, Newhouse, Redlynch, Wilts]; *b* 20 April 1931; *educ* Radley; *m* 18 June 1960 *June, yr dau of Alexander Bennett, of Fordingbridge, and has:

1e *Sarah Kezia Eyre; *b* 17 July 1963

2e *Elizabeth Jemima Eyre; *b* 9 July 1964

3e *Rachel Jane Eyre; *b* 9 May 1968

1d *Catharine Elizabeth Eyre [Mrs Anthony Lane, Over Silton Manor, nr Thirsk, Yorks]; *b* 25 May 1933; *m* 22 Aug 1953 Anthony William Lane (*d* 1992), only s of Eric William Lane, of Midhurst, Sussex, and has:

1e *Harriet Elizabeth; *b* 12 July 1954; *m* 1974 *David Geoffrey Crusher, of Northallerton, N Yorks

2e *Caroline Mary; *b* 5 April 1956; *m* 1986 *Gordon Smith, of Leighton Buzzard, Beds, and has:

1f *Daniel Harry; *b* 1989

1f *Sarah Valentine; *b* 1987

3e *Georgina Margaret; *b* 14 April 1959; *m* 1981 *David Owen Bowe, of Northallerton, and has:

1f *William David; *b* 1983

2f *Matthew George; *b* 1990

1f *Emily Jane; *b* 1985

2f *Jessica Elizabeth; *b* 1987

4e *Victoria Anne Michell; *b* 22 Feb 1962

5e *Florence Sophia; *b* 23 June 1967

2b William Eyre, DSO; *b* 16 May 1865; Col Duke of Edinburgh's Wilts Regt Boer War 1900–02 (despatches, two medals, five clasps) and WW I Remount Depot; *m* 23 Jan 1906 Edith Evelyn (*d* 27 Nov 1952), yr dau of Henry Inman Betterton, of Woodville, Leics (see 1949 edn RUSHCLIFFE, B), and *dsp* 13 Sept 1938

1b Mary Harriet Eyre; *b* 2 May 1869; *d unm* 19 Oct 1944

1a Catherine Eyre; *m* 1848 Rev Henry Blackstone Williams (*d* 1879), Rector Bradford Peverel, Dorset, and had issue

2a Louisa Harriet Eyre; *m* 2 Feb 1860 Rev Fortescue Richard Purvis (*d* 1885), est s of Rev Richard Fortescue Purvis, Vicar Whitsbury, Hants, and had issue

(2) Charles Horatio Nelson; *b* 1806; *d* Australia 1844

(3) Nelson; *b* 1811; barrister, LLD; *d* 1886

(1) Catherine; *m* 10 Aug 1820 Lt John Bendyshe, RN (*m* 2nd 21 Oct 1833 Anna Maria, est dau of Sir Charles Watson, 1st Bt), of Barrington, Cambs, and *d* Nov 1831, having had five sons and four daus

(2) Elizabeth; *m* 6 May 1824 Arthur Davies, Post Capt RN, and *d* Nov 1851, leaving issue

(3) Harriet; *m* 1810 Edward Blanckley, Capt RN

(4) Horatio; *m* 1826 Lt Henry William Mason, RN, of Beel House, Bucks, and *d* 31 Dec 1869

(5) Susanna; *m* 24 April 1832 Alexander Montgomery Moore, of Garvey, Co Tyrone

The 1st EARL's nephew,

THOMAS BOLTON later NELSON (took latter name on inheriting title 1835), **2nd Earl Nelson of Trafalgar** and **of Merton**; *b* 7 July 1786; *educ* High Sch Norwich and Peterhouse Coll Cambridge (BA, MA); High Sheriff Wilts 1834; *m* 21 Feb 1821 Frances Elizabeth (*d* 28 March 1878), dau and heiress of John Maurice Eyre, of Landford and Brickworth, Wilts, and *d* 1 Nov 1835, having had:

1 HORATIO, **3rd Earl**

2 John Horatio (Rev); *b* 15 Jan 1825; MA Cantab, Rector Shaw-cum-Donnington, Newbury, 1872–1909; *m* 27 Aug 1857 Susan (*d* 2 Feb 1898), est dau of Lord Charles Spencer-Churchill (*see* MARLBOROUGH, D), and *d* 28 Sept 1917, having had:

(1) John Eyre; *b* 1 Oct 1858; *m* 14 Feb 1899 Kathryn Cornelia, dau of A J Kell, of Battle Creek, Michigan, and *d* 9 Jan 1913

(2) Horatio Spencer; *b* 6 June 1860; *d* 8 May 1935

3 Maurice Horatio; *b* 2 Jan 1832; R-Adml, Kt Medjidie; *m* 21 April 1863 Emily (*d* 24 Sept 1906), 4th dau of Adml Sir Charles Burrard, 2nd Bt, of Lymington (*see* 1963 edn), and *d* 6 Sept 1914, having had:

(1) Maurice Henry Horatio, CBE (1919); *b* 17 Nov 1864; Capt RN; *d unm* 23 Dec 1942

(2) Edward John (Rev); *b* 4 Oct 1867; MA Oxon, Rector Blendworth, Hants, 1902–28; *m* 4 Oct 1898 Katherine Elizabeth (*d* 2 Jan 1936), dau of Frederick Robert Knollys, of Chobham, and *dsp* 1940

(3) Charles Burrard; *b* 27 Nov 1868; Lt 3rd Bn Wilts Regt; *m* 10 Feb 1904 Emma Geraldine Kitson (*d* 10 Jan 1969 aged 89), dau of Rev Ernest Henry Glencross, Vicar Morval, Cornwall, and *d* 2 Aug 1931, leaving:

1a +John Charles Horatio; *b* 11 May 1905; *m* 28 April 1934 *Alice Helen [Mrs John Nelson, Forestgate, Landford, Salisbury, Wilts], 3rd dau of Col Robert Maximilian Rainey-Robinson, CB, CMG, of Upwey, Weymouth, and *d* 20 June 1994, having had:

1b +Antony Burrard Horatio [Antony Nelson Esq, Westbury Estate, Masinagudi PO, Nilgiris 643 223, S India]; *b* 5 July 1935; Lt RN; *m* 1st 2 April 1960 (*divorce* 1989) Judith Constance, yst dau of Brig Thomas Farquharson Ker Howard, DSO, RA, of Goldenhayes, Woodlands, Hants, and has:

1c +Thomas Antony Horatio; *b* 18 June 1963

2c +Edward Maximilian; *b* 1971

1c *Teresa Helen; *b* 12 April 1962; *m* 19– *Giles P D Ormerod, s of Brig D Ormerod, of Kent, and has:

1d *Maurice; *b* 19–

2d *Robin; *b* 19–

1d *Eden; *b* 19–

2c *Rebecca Anne [Mrs Oliver Crosthwaite-Eyre, Warrens, Bramshaw, Lyndhurst, Hants]; *b* 1975; *m* 19– *Oliver Crosthwaite-Eyre and has:

1d *George Douglas Oliver; *b* 14 Oct 1996

1b (cont.) Antony Nelson *m* 2nd 6 Dec 1990 *Vasanthi Muriel, dau of Charles Vedanyakam, of Cooke Town, Bangalore, India and has:

3c *Antonia Kavitha Hannay; *b* 22 Aug 1996

Mr and Mrs Nelson have also adopted:

*Jayanna Bridget Hannay NELSON; *b* 3 Dec 1980

2b David Rainey; *b* 30 Sept 1938; *d* 18 Oct 1939

1b *Joanna Elizabeth [Mrs Henry Milne, Domerfield, Longbredy, Dorset]; *b* 23 July 1940; *m* 6 Jan 1962 *Henry Bruce Milne, yst s of Henry Philip Manfield Milne, of Knightsbridge, and has:

1c *Robert Henry; *b* 19 Feb 1968

1c *Emma Alice; *b* 1970

2c *Sarah Elizabeth; *b* 1973

3c *Kate Mary; *b* 1978

1a (Emily Geraldine) Morval; *b* 1 Nov 1906; *m* 1st 5 June 1928 (*divorce* 1944) Jocelyn Panizzi Preston (*d* 1970), s of Sir Frederick George Panizzi Preston, KBE, JP of Landford Manor, Salisbury, and had:

1b *Simon Douglas Nelson [Simon Preston Esq, Bohemia, The Old Kennels, Eridge Park, Eridge Green, Kent TN3 9HA]; *b* 1933; *m* 1962 *Celia Mary, dau of Francis Bodenham Thornley, and has:

1c *Rupert Robin Nelson; *b* 1963

2c *Adam Bodenham Nelson; *b* 1966

3c *John Simon Nelson; *b* 1975

4c *Charles Frederick Nelson; *b* 1975

1c *Emma Frances Morval; *b* 1965

1a (cont.) Mrs Morval Preston *m* 2nd 26 July 1946 Cdr Arthur Roland Thomas Kirby, OBE, RNR (*d* 1971), s of Arthur Kirby, of London, and *d* 1995, leaving by him:

2b *Ben Martin [Ben Kirby Esq, Bishop's Quay, St Martin, Helston, Cornwall TR12 6DF]; *b* 1948; *m* 1970 *Katharine Alice Mary, dau of Alan A C Jackson, and has:

1c *Henry Rowland; *b* 1974

2c *Robin Gerald; *b* 1978

1c *Samantha Jane Alice; 1972

(4) Horatio William; *b* 18 June 1871; BA Cantab; Registrar Supreme Ct Ceylon; *d* unm 6 Aug 1910

(1) Maud Mary; *b* 20 Nov 1865; *d* unm 15 July 1943

(2) Emily Frances; *b* 22 March 1870; *m* 6 Dec 1898 Charles Menzies McCausland (*dsp* Nov 1899), of Templestowe, Watawala, Ceylon, and *d* 21 July 1961

(3) Alice; *b* 30 April 1876; *d* 19—

4 Edward Foyle (Rev); *b* 11 Nov 1833; MA; *d* 8 Sept 1859

5 Henry; *b* 28 July 1835; *k* by a fall from his horse 28 Nov 1863

1 Frances Catherine; *m* 25 Jan 1855 Robert John Pettiward (*d* 3 Feb 1908), of Great Finborough, Suffolk, and *d* 14 April 1877, leaving issue

2 Susanna; *m* 27 June 1865 Rev Alexander Colvin Blunt (*d* 1 April 1920), Canon Winchester (*see* BLUNT, Bt), and *dsp* 8 April 1900

The 2nd EARL's est s,

HORATIO NELSON, **3rd Earl Nelson of Trafalgar** and **of Merton**, JP and DL (Wilts); *b* 7 Aug 1823; *educ* Eton and Trin Coll Cambridge (MA 1844); *m* 28 July 1845 Lady Mary Jane Diana Agar (*d* 8 May 1904), only dau of 2nd Earl of Normanton (*qv*), and *d* 25 Feb 1913, having had:

1 Herbert Horatio, *Viscount Trafalgar*, JP (Glos), JP and DL (Wilts); *b* 19 July 1854; Capt Roy Wilts Militia, High Sheriff Wilts 1877; *m* 5 Aug 1879 Eliza Blanche (*d* 24 May 1938), est dau of Frederick Gonnerman Dalgety, JP, DL, of Lockerley Hall, Hants, and *dsp* & *vp* 4 May 1905

2 Charles Horatio; *b* 28 June 1856; *educ* Radley; *m* 12 Jan 1887 Ellen (*d* 12 Dec 1900), dau of G W Petty, and *dsp* & *vp* 28 March 1900

3 THOMAS HORATIO NELSON, **4th Earl Nelson of Trafalgar** and **of Merton**; *b* 21 Dec 1857; *d* unm 30 Sept 1947

4 EDWARD AGAR HORATIO, **5th Earl**

5 Albert Horatio; *b* 12 Sept 1862; *d* 8 Jan 1868

1 Alice Mary Diana; *d* 18 Aug 1919

2 Constance Jane; *m* 21 April 1870 Rev Hon Bertrand Pleydell-Bouverie (*see* RADNOR, E) and *d* 27 Jan 1922

3 Edith; *m* 5 July 1870 Charles Clement Tudway (*d* 7 Sept 1926), of Wells, Somerset, and *d* 24 Aug 1877, leaving issue

4 Mary Catherine; *m* 21 Oct 1890 Richard Shaw, of Audlem, Cheshire, and *d* 14 Nov 1901

The 4th EARL's bro,

EDWARD AGAR HORATIO NELSON, **5th Earl Nelson of Trafalgar** and **of Merton**; *b* 10 Aug 1860; Lt 3rd Bn Wilts Regt Nile Expdn 1885–86; *m* 7 Aug 1889 Geraldine (*d* 20 July 1936), dau of Henry H Cave, of Rugby, Warwicks, and *d* 30 Jan 1951, leaving:

1 ALBERT FRANCIS JOSEPH HORATIO NELSON, **6th Earl Nelson of Trafalgar** and **of Merton**; *b* 2 Sept 1890; *educ* Downside and Maredsous, Belgium; lecturer astronomy and anthropology; AIF WW I, Maj Home Def Force WW II; FRAS, FRGS, FRHS, FRSA, FZS; *m* 1st 16 Jan 1924 (*divorce* 1925) Amelia (*d* 1937), 4th dau of George Buchanan Cooper, of Sacramento City, Calif., by Elizabeth, dau and coheir of Jean de Beverley Mackenzie (*see* STRABOLGI, B), and widow of John C Scott, of Bayswater; *m* 2nd Scotland 1927 and England 1942 Marguerite Helen (*d* 6 Feb 1969), dau of Capt J M O'Sullivan, of Dublin and Tipperary, and *dsp* 23 June 1957

2 HENRY EDWARD JOSEPH HORATIO NELSON, **7th Earl Nelson of Trafalgar** and **of Merton**; *b* 22 April 1894; *educ* Maredsous Belgium; AIF WW I, Merchant Navy and Maj IA WW II; *d* unm 8 Aug 1972

3 Charles Sebastian Joseph Horatio; *b* 26 April 1896; *educ* Stonyhurst; Lt-Col Roy Pioneer Corps WW I with AIF (Inf) and WW II (despatches); *m* 29 Nov 1916 Kathleen Cook (*d* 1980) and *d* 18 Jan 1964, having had:

  (1) James Berkeley Horatio; *b* 19 Nov 1917; S African forces WW II, 3rd Bn Roy Australian Regt Korea 1951 (severely wounded, blinded through enemy action); *b* 21 Sept 1924; *d* unm 30 May 1958

  (1) Mary Teresa Muriel; *b* 19 Nov 1917; SAAF WW II; *m* Jan 1946 Cornelius Johannes Erasmus (*d* 4 Feb 1985, having had:

    1a *Anthony Charles; *b* 28 Sept 1953

    1a *Martina Kathleen; *b* 19 Jan 1947

4 GEORGE JOSEPH HORATIO NELSON, **8th Earl Nelson of Trafalgar** and **of Merton**; *b* 20 April 1905; *educ* Ampleforth; ACA; *m* 29 Dec 1945 *Mary Winifred [The Rt Hon Mary Countess Nelson, 9 Pwlldu Lane, Bishopston, Swansea], dau of G Bevan, of Swansea, and *d* 21 Sept 1981, leaving:

  (1) *Sarah Josephine Mary [The Lady Sarah Nelson Robert, Long Acre, Riverside Rd, Dittisham, Devon TQ6 0HS]; *b* 7 Jan 1947; *m* 21 May 1978 *Dr John Clive Robert, MB, BS, FFARCS

5 John Marie Joseph Horatio; *b* 21 July 1908; *educ* Ampleforth; Capt RA WW II; *m* 1941 *Kathleen Mary [The Hon Mrs John Nelson, 306 Chartleigh Ho, Beach Rd, Sea Point, Cape Town 8001, S Africa], dau of William Burr, of Torquay, and *d* 1970, having had:

  (1) PETER JOHN HORATIO NELSON, **9th and present Earl Nelson of Trafalgar** and **of Merton**

  (2) +Francis Edward Horatio; *b* 1947; *m* 1973 — and has:

    1a +William; *b* 1975

    1a *Emma; *b* 1974

  (1) *Jane Priscilla [Mrs Roy Hannant, 17 Fairways, Mouille Point, Cape Town, S Africa]; *b* 1944; *m* 1968 *Roy Hannant and has:

    1a *David John Charles; *b* 1972

    2a *Richard Roy; *b* 1974

    1a *Sally Kathleen; *b* 1974

1 Edith Mary Josephine; *m* 6 Sept 1921 Capt Henry Charles Coulston, 1st Bn KORR (Lancaster), Capt Warwicks Yeo (*ka* France 14 June 1940), 3rd s of Henry Joseph Coulston, JP, of Carnforth, Lancs, and *d* 28 July 1978, having had:

  (1) *John Alban Horatio Nelson [John Coulston Esq, 3 Blake Hill Crescent, Parkstone, Poole, Dorset]; *b* 9 Aug 1927; Merchant Navy 1944–50; *m* 1st 1956 (*divorce* 1966) Sheelagh Alston, dau of Herbert V Gartlan, and has:

    1a *Jonathan Charles Nelson; *b* 5 July 1957; BA, MPhil, PhD, lecturer St Andrews U

(1) (cont.) John Coulston *m* 2nd 1966 *Patricia Rose, dau of Guy Neville, of Poole, Dorset, and by her has:

  2a *Andrew Peter James; *b* 15 Feb 1971; Lt Roy Corps Signals NI 1994–95, Bosnia 1996

  1a *Catherine Mary Anne; *b* 26 June 1966; *m* 28 May 1994 *Dean Rodney Morgan and has:

    1b *Danielle Grace; *b* 14 Feb 1996

  2a *Helen Christina; *b* 9 Dec 1967

2 Mary Winifred; *b* 3 July 1899; *d* 14 June 1984

3 (Geraldine Mary) Diana; *b* 23 Oct 1900; nurse, PMRAFNS WW II; *d* 4 Sept 1982

NELSON, Baronet

Arms: Quarterly, 1st and 4th, gu. on a fess between three daggers, points downwards, or, two sinister hands couped of the field (for NELSON); 2nd and 3rd, arg. a pile engrailed ermines between two lion's heads erased in base gu., langued az., a chief vair, all within a bordure vert (for HOPE). **Crests:** 1 In front of a sun rising or a sinister arm embowed in armour ppr., the hand grasping a dagger point downwards as in the arms (for NELSON), 2 Issuant from clouds ppr., charged with three mullets az., a globe fracted at the top under a rainbow with clouds at each end ppr. (for HOPE). **Motto:** *Per se confidens* ('Confident in oneself'). **Creation:** Bt. (UK) 5 Feb 1912.

SIR JAMIE CHARLES VERNON HOPE NELSON, 4TH BT, of Acton Park, Acton, Co Denbigh [Sir Jamie Nelson Bt, 39 Montacute Rd, Tintinhull, Somerset BA22 8QD]; *b* 23 Oct 1949; *s* f 1991; *educ* Redrice; *m* 1983 *Maralynn Pyatt, dau of Albert Pyatt Hedge, of Audenshaw, Lincs, and has:

  1 *Liam Chester; *b* 1982

Lineage: JOHN NELSON, of Orastown, Kells, Co Meath, *b c* 1725; *bur* 5 Sept 1773, having had:

HUGH NELSON, of Orastown; *b c* 1736; *m* Anne (*d* 1840 aged 81) and *d* between 25 Sept 1834 and 31 Dec 1835, having had, with four yr sons and a dau:

WILLIAM NELSON, of Kells; *bapt* 21 Dec 1792; *m* 1813 Jane Allan and *d* 19 March 1872, having had, with two er sons and six daus:

JAMES NELSON, of Liverpool; *b* Kells 6 Oct 1821; *m* 15 April 1849 Elizabeth (*d* 26 Nov 1893), dau of William McCormick, of Glenidan, Collinstown, Co Westmeath, and *d* 22 Dec 1896, having had:

1 Hugh; *b* 10 Jan 1851; *dvp* unm 26 Jan 1893

2 WILLIAM (Sir), **1st Bt**

3 Thomas Cormac; *b* 20 Nov 1857; *m* 17 April 1901 Margaret (*d* 4 Sept 1954), dau of Thomas L'Estrange, of Woodlands, Banagher, King's Co, and had:

  (1) Thomas L'Estrange; *b* 26 Jan 1902

  (2) Edward Hugh; *b* 20 Nov 1904; *m* 29 Aug 1933 Eileen, yst dau of John J Keane, of Dublin, and *d* 10 Dec 1937 following a rlwy accident at Castlecary

  (1) Elizabeth Oswaldina

  (2) Margaret Mary

4 John; *b* 21 April 1859; *m* 12 Nov 1889 Jane Louisa, dau of Thomas Duggan, of Buenos Aires, and *d* 10 Sept 1931, leaving:

  (1) John James; *b* 26 May 1891

  (2) Louis Thomas; *b* 19 Jan 1894

  (1) Mary Marcella

  (2) Olive Isabel

5 James; *b* 18 Aug 1860; *m* 22 June 1887 Susanna Mary, dau of Richard McCormack, of Ballynock House, Co Westmeath, and *d* 17 Sept 1912, leaving:

  (1) James Edward Cormack; *b* 28 April 1890

  (2) Richard Cormack; *b* 16 Dec 1891

  (3) Hugh Francis Cormack; *b* 11 July 1893

  (4) Thomas Cormack Oswin; *b* 11 April 1895

  (1) Rosanna Elizabeth; *m* 6 April 1910 Edward McHugh and had issue

6 Edward; *b* 8 July 1862; *m* 30 April 1901 Esther Mary (*d* 3 July 1912), dau of John Eyres, of Fawleigh, Totton, Hants

1 Rebecca Louisa; *m* 8 Sept 1875 Richard Bobbett, of Cooldrinagh, Leixlip, Co Kildare, and had issue

2 Oswaldina; *m* 1st 4 Sept 1878 Maurice Hegarty (*d* 28 Aug 1885), of Bally-healy, Co Westmeath, and had issue; *m* 2nd 30 Aug 1898 Sir Joseph Michael Redmond, MD, FRCPI, of Dublin. He *d* 25 Nov 1921

3 Kathleen Concepta

The 2nd son,

Sir William Nelson, 1st Bt (UK), so *cr* 5 Feb 1912; *b* 8 Dec 1851; *m* 16 July 1879 Margaret (*d* 6 April 1932), dau of Michael Hope, of Gartlandstown, Co West-meath, and *d* 7 July 1922, having had:

1 **Sir James Hope Nelson, 2nd Bt**; *b* 26 Feb 1883; *m* 1st 26 Sept 1913 (*divorce* 1921) Mary Isabel, dau of Dr Jules F Vallel, MD, of St Louis, Mo.; *m* 2nd 24 Sept 1923 Annie Cathleen Elizabeth, yr dau of Lt-Col Loftus Bryan, DL, of Borr-mount Manor, Co Wexford, and *dsp* 5 May 1960

2 William Hope; *b* 23 Jan 1885; *m* 23 Nov 1910 Dora Violet Venables (*d* 4 Dec 1966), dau of Col Arthur Venables Kyrke, of Staplegrove, Taunton, and *d* 14 April 1953, leaving:

(1) WILLIAM VERNON HOPE (Sir), **3rd Bt**

(1) Noelle Marguerite Mary; *b* 30 Dec 1912; *m* 29 July 1949 Maj Neville Ger-ald Fitzgerald Dunne, 8th King's Roy Irish Hus, only s of Capt Gerald Fitzger-ald Dunne, of Donacomper, Celbridge, Co Kildare, formerly of Black Hall, Sallins, Co Kildare, and had:

1a *Marguerite Vivien; *b* 3 Feb 1953

3 Hugh Hope; *b* 9 June 1886; *m* 12 Jan 1918 Alice, widow of Capt Alexander F Todd, Norfolk Regt, and 4th dau of Michael Crean, barrister, of Dublin, and *d* 8 June 1937

1 Mary Elizabeth; *m* 1st 10 Jan 1906 (*divorce* 1944) Maj Washington Charles Thomas Hibbert, KORL (*d* 6 April 1950), and had issue; *m* 2nd Lt-Col Charles Barker and *d* 24 Feb 1957. He *d* 1960

2 Josephine Mary Margaret; *m* 1st 11 June 1909 (*divorce* 1923) Maj Morgan Grainger Jones, DL, Roy Welch Fus (*d* 4 July 1943), and had issue; *m* 2nd 28 Nov 1923 Henry Thomas Loud Young, yst s of Charles Florence Young, and *d* 15 Oct 1965. He *d* 27 Sept 1957

3 Leonie Mabel Mary; *m* 20 Jan 1910 Lt-Col Codrington Howard Rees Craw-shay, DSO, Roy Welch Fus, and *d* 18 Dec 1948, leaving issue. He *d* 15 Feb 1937

4 Gladys Mary; *m* 1st Oct 1916 (*divorce* 1924) Capt Keld Robert George Fen-wick (*see* MANCHESTER, D) and had issue; *m* 2nd 30 June 1928 Lt-Cdr Colin Buist, CVO, RN (ret), est s of Col Frederick Braid Buist, of Scone, Perthshire

5 Violet Mary, *m* 1st 20 April 1914 (*divorce* 1920) George Richard Francis Rowley, Coldstream Gds, and had issue; *m* 2nd 26 Nov 1920 (*divorce* 1926) 2nd Duke of Westminster (*qv*); *m* 3rd 8 Oct 1927 (*divorce* 1951) 3rd Baron Parmoor (*qv*) and *d* 1983, having had further issue

The 2nd Bt's nephew,

Sir William Vernon Hope Nelson, 3rd Bt, OBE (1952), of Acton Park; *b* 25 May 1914; *educ* Beaumont; Maj 8th KRI Hus Palestine 1936–39 (despatches, medal with clasp) and WW II; *m* 21 Nov 1945 *Hon Elizabeth Ann Bevil Cary, er dau of 14th Viscount Falkland (*qv*), and *d* 1991, leaving:

1 Sir JAMIE CHARLES VERNON HOPE NELSON, **4th and present Bt**

2 +DOMINIC WILLIAM MICHAEL HOPE [Dominic Nelson Esq, Barretts Mill, Corton Denham, Sherborne, Dorset]; *b* 13 March 1956; *heir presumptive*; *educ* St Edward's Malta; *m* 1981 *Sarah, est dau of John Neil Hylton Jolliffe (*see* HYLTON, B), and has:

(1) +Barnaby John; *b* 1982

(2) +Thomas Dudley; *b* 1984

(3) +George Marcus; *b* 1986

3 +Declan Hugh Plantagenet; *b* 16 Oct 1968

1 *Deirdre Elizabeth Ann [Mrs John Macguire, Bently Cottage, 12 The Highlands, Cuckfield, Sussex RH17 5HL]; *b* 22 May 1947; *m* 1st 1980 (*annulled* 1985) Martin Thomas and has:

(1) *Peter; *b* 1981

1 (cont) Deirde Nelson *m* 2nd 19– *Dr John Dillow Macguire

2 *Cary Georgina [Miss Cary Nelson, 2 Court Barton, Crewkerne, Somerset]; *b* 2 Dec 1952

3 *Sophie Lucia; *b* 1971

NELSON OF STAFFORD

Arms: Arg. a cross flory sa., a chief gu., thereon between a Stafford knot and a rose arg., barbed and seeded ppr., a pale also arg., charged with a sword erect gu. **Crest:** An arm embowed, resting on the elbow in armour ppr., the gauntlet grasping a cross flory fitchée sa. between two roses gu., barbed and seeded, also ppr. **Supporters:** Dexter, a lion guardant or, charged on the shoulder with a thunderbolt az.; sinister, a grey horse ppr., gorged with a coronet composed of four fleurs-de-lys with chain affixed thereto and reflexed over the back also or, and charged on the shoulder with a Stafford knot gold. **Motto:** Who leads serves. **Creations:** Bt. (UK) 11 July 1955, B. (UK) 20 Jan 1960.

THE 3RD BARON NELSON OF STAFFORD of Hilcote Hall, co Stafford, and a **Baronet** (Sir Henry Roy George Nelson, Bt) [The Rt Hon The Lord Nelson of Staf-ford, Eastlands, Tibthorpe, E Yorks YO25 9LD]; *b* 26 Oct 1943; *s f* 1995; *educ* Ampleforth and King's Coll Cambridge (MA); CEng, FIMechE, MIEE, dir TIB plc; *m* 8 June 1968 *Dorothy, yr dau of Leslie Caley, of Tibthorpe Manor, and has:

1 +ALISTAIR WILLIAM HENRY; *b* 3 June 1973

1 *Sarah Jane; *b* 1981

Lineage: JOHN DAVID NELSON; *m* Mary Ann Taylor and had:

GEORGE NELSON, of Muswell Hill, London; *b* 29 Feb 1860; *m* 24 April 1886 Emily Walsh (*d* 21 Dec 1943), dau of William Edward Lewis, of London, and *d* 15 Oct 1938, leaving:

1 GEORGE HORATIO, **1st Baron**

2 Lewis Archibald, MC; Army Capt; *b* 23 Dec 1888; *m* 7 July 1917 Kate (*d* 16 Nov 1965), only dau of W M Still, of London, and *d* 7 May 1961, leaving:

(1) *Mary Gwendoline [Mrs Norman Neale, Little Stubbings, Burchetts Green, Maidenhead, Berks]; *b* 1 Dec 1918; *m* 21 Aug 1945 *Norman Harry Neale and has:

1a *Andrew John; *b* 17 Feb 1953

1a *Sarah Elizabeth; *b* 6 July 1949

(2) *Kate Emily; *b* 2 Jan 1921; *m* 19– John Freke

1 Gwendoline Alexandra; *b* 30 June 1901; *d* 15 Oct 1990

GEORGE NELSON's er son,

Sir George Horatio Nelson, 1st Bt, and **1st Baron Nelson of Stafford**, of Hilcote Hall, Co Stafford (both UK), so *cr* 11 July 1955 and 20 Jan 1960 respectively; *b* 26 Oct 1887; *educ* City and Guilds Technical Coll London; md English Electric Co 1930–56 (chm 1933–62), Marconi's Wireless Telegraph Co Ltd 1946–61 (dir 1961), D Napier and Son 1943–61, The Vulcan Foundry Ltd 1955, Robert Ste-phenson and Hawthorns Ltd 1957; dir: Lloyds Bank 1950, John Inglis Co Toronto 1951 and English Electric Co of Canada 1951, memb BOT Advsy Cncl 1938 and Air Min Heavy Bomber Gp Ctee 1939–45, Pres Fend Br Industry 1943–44 and 1944–45, Chm Census of Pro-duction Advsy Ctee 1945, Hon Fell Queen Mary Coll London 1947, Prime War-den Goldsmiths' Co 1960, Pres: IEE 1955–56 (hon memb 1961), IMechE 1957–58, Br Electrical and Allied Research Assoc 1952, BEAMA 1950–53, Br Electrical Power Convention 1957–58 and Locomotive and Allied Mfrs' Assoc 1958, memb Governing Body Imperial Coll Science and Technology 1955 (Hon Fell 1955), Memb Court Govrs Manchester Coll Science and Technology 1956–61, Hon Freeman Stafford 1956, V-Pres City and Guilds Inst 1958, ktd 1943, Hon LLD Victoria U Manchester 1957, Hon DSc Engrg London 1961, FCGI 1944, DIC 1955, MIMechE 1941, MIEE 1918; *m* 17 July 1913 Florence Mabel (Jane) (*d* 14 Dec 1962), only dau of Henry Howe, JP, of Leicester, and *d* 16 July 1962, leaving:

1 (HENRY) GEORGE NELSON, **2nd Baron Nelson of Stafford**; *b* 2 Jan 1917; *educ* Oundle and King's Coll Cambridge (BA 1937, MA 1941); FEng, FICE, Hon DSc (Aston, Keele and Cranfield), Hon Fell City and Guilds, CEng, Hon FIMechE, FIEE (Pres 1971), FRAeS, Hon LLD Strathclyde, Fell Imperial Coll Science & Tech, md D Napier & Son 1942–49, dir GEC 1968–87 (chm 1968–83) (dep md English Electric 1949–56, md 1956–62, chm and ch exec 1962–68, chm 1968), jt dep chm BAC 1960–77, dir Nat Bank Australasia Ltd (London Bd of Advice) 1950–81, chm Roy Worcester Gp 1978–83, Dir Bank of England 1961–87, Inco Ltd (Canada) 1966–88 and Enserch Corp USA 1984–89, memb:

Govt Advsy Cncl on Scientific Policy 1955–58, Advsy Cncl Middle E Trade 1958–63 (Industrial Leader and V-Chm 1959–63), Advsy Cncl Technology 1964–70, Engrg Advsy Cncl 1958–61 and Exec Ctee Br Nat Ctee World Energy Conf 1957–87 (chm 1971–74); Chm Def Industs Cncl 1971–77, Pres Sino-Br Trade Research Assoc 1973–83, Tstee Civic Tst 1962–72, Pres: Electrical Research Assoc 1963–64, Orgalime (Organisme de Liaison des Industries Métallique Européennes) 1966–70, Br Electrical & Allied Mfrs Assoc 1966–67, Locomotive & Allied Mfrs Assoc 1964–66, Br Electric Power Convention 1967 and Soc of Br Aircraft Constructors 1961–62, V-Pres Engrg Employers' Fedn 1963–82, 1st Chllr Aston U, Birmingham 1966–79, Govr Cwlth Inst 1972–74, memb Ho Lds Select Ctee Science and Technology 1984–90, Ld High Steward Stafford 1966–71, Liveryman Goldsmiths' Co (Memb Court 1974, Prime Warden 1983–84) and Coachmakers' and Coach Harness Makers' Co (Assist to Court 1959–62), Freeman City London; *m* 8 June 1940 *Pam(ela) Roy [The Rt Hon Pamela Lady Nelson of Stafford, 244 Cranmer Court, Whiteheads Grove, London SW3 3HD], yr dau of Ernest Roy Bird, MP Skipton, Yorks, and *d* 19 Jan 1995, leaving:

(1) HENRY ROY GEORGE NELSON, **3rd and present Baron Nelson of Stafford**

(2) +James Jonathan [The Hon James Nelson, 82 Tachbrook St, London SW1V 2NB]; *b* 17 June 1947; *educ* Ampleforth and McGill; md Foreign & Colonial Ventures Ltd 1985–; *m* 1977 *Lucy Mary, er dau of Roger Gopsill Brown, of Chestnut House, Albrighton, Salop, and has:

1a *Camilla Amy; *b* 1982
2a *Lara Kitty; *b* 1986
3a *Eloise Violet; *b* 2 Aug 1987

(1) *Caroline Jane [The Hon Mrs Ford, Lower Moorhayne Farm, Yarcombe, nr Honiton, Devon EX14 9BE]; *b* 11 Jan 1942; *m* 2 April 1964 *Michael John Henry Ford, s of Lt-Col Mortimer Noel Ford, TD, DL, of The Cross House, Alphington, Devon, and has:

1a *James Mortimer Henry; *b* 12 Feb 1965
2a *Andrew Michael Felix; *b* 8 Aug 1967
1a *Annabel Emma Jane; *b* 14 July 1972

(2) *Sally Louise [The Hon Mrs Tritton, Weasel Cottage, Brent Pelham, Herts SG9 0HH]; *b* 20 Oct 1955; *m* 9 Sept 1975 *Peter Robert Jolliffe Tritton, yr s of Lt-Col John Tritton, of Powers Hall, Witham, Essex, and has:

1a *Jonathan James Hedley; *b* 25 July 1981
1a *Emma Pamela Louise; *b* 19 Dec 1986

1 Margaret Joan, JP (1960) Warwicks; *b* 20 Nov 1915; *m* 13 Sept 1941 Edward Michael Price, AM, MIME, MIEE (*d* 1992), est s of Dr Bernard Price, OBE, DSc, FCGI, MICE, MIEE, of Johannesburg, and *d* 15 March 1997, leaving:

(1) *Elizabeth Joan; *b* 14 May 1943; *m* 1st (*divorce*) —
(2) *Susan Jane; *b* 10 May 1944
(3) *Anne Waldegrave; *b* 28 May 1947

NEPEAN

Arms: Gu., a fess wavy erminois between three mullets arg.
Crest: On a mount vert a goat passant sa., charged on the side with two ermine spots in fess or, collared, attired and unguled gold, the collar charged with two mullets gu. **Motto:** *Respice* ('Look back').
Creation: Bt. (UK) 16 July 1802.

SIR EVAN YORKE NEPEAN, 6TH BT, of Bothenhampton, Dorset [Lt-Col Sir Evan Nepean Bt, Allwyns, 43 Queens Rd, Devizes, Wilts SP10 5HR]; *b* 23 Nov 1909; *s f* 1953; *educ* Winchester and Downing Coll Cambridge (BA 1931, MA 1947); Lt-Col Roy Signals NW Frontier (Mohmand) 1935, GSO(3) War Office WW II, Staff Southern Cmd 1947, MOD 1950–53, SO1 (Tels) GHQ FARELF 1953–54, CEng, MIEE; *m* 6 Jan 1940 *(Georgiana) Cecily, only dau of Maj Noel Edward Grey Willoughby, Middx Regt, of Heytesbury, Wilts, and has:

1 *Susan Cicely [Mrs James Hall, 1 Partridge Down, Olivers Battery, Winchester, Hants]; *b* 23 July 1941; *m* 26 Aug 1961 *James Martin Norman Aylmer Hall, s of Lt-Col James Aylmer Hall, OBE, of Dinton, Salisbury, and has:

(1) *Richard John Nepean Aylmer; *b* 12 Sept 1964; *m* 1988 *Tracy-Jane Boal

(2) *Patrick Robert Aylmer; *b* 30 Jan 1966; *m* 1995 *Elizabeth Woods

(1) *Katherine Mary Aylmer; *b* 27 April 1963; *m* 1986 *Russell Wheeldon and has:

1a *Christopher Andrew; *b* 1989
1a *Helen Rebecca; *b* 1996

(2) *Carole Margaret Aylmer; *b* 20 March 1967; *m* 1997 *Robert Robotham

2 *Judith Sarah [Mrs Noel Goldthorp, Black Sheep House, Healey, N Yorks HG44 LH]; *b* 3 June 1946; *m* 1993 *(Edgar) Noel Goldthorp

3 *Gillian Helen [Mrs Paul Stevens, 74 Queens Rd, Devizes, Wilts SP10 5HR]; *b* 27 Dec 1950; *m* 1982 *Paul Stevens and has:

(1) *David Yorke; *b* 1986
(2) *Jonathan Edward; *b* 1988

Lineage: The NEPEANs come from St Just, Cornwall. The name derives from the Cornish words *nans pedn* (head of the valley) and was variously spelt Nanspean, Nanpaen and in 1660 Nepean.

NICHOLAS NEPEAN, of Saltash (est s of Nicholas Nepean); *m* Margaret, dau of Evan Jones, of Aallagadno, Glam, and had:

1 Thomas; Lt-Gen RE; *d* unm 25 Nov 1816
2 EVAN (Sir), **1st Bt**
3 Nicholas; Lt-Gen; *m* April 1783 Francina, only dau of Maj — Wedikind, 11th Hanoverian Regt, and *d* 1823, leaving issue

The 2nd son,

Sir Evan Nepean, 1st Bt (UK), so *cr* 16 July 1802, PC, of Bothenhampton and Loders, Dorset; MP Queensborough and Bridport, Sec Admlty, Sec State Ireland, a Ld of Admlty, Govr Bombay; *m* 6 June 1782 Margaret (*d* 26 Dec 1833), only dau of Capt William Skinner, and *d* 2 Oct 1822, having had:

1 **Sir Molyneux Hyde Nepean, 2nd Bt**, of Loders Court; *b* 20 Sept 1783; Ld Manor, Patron Living and Lay Rector Loders, Clerk Crown Jamaica; *m* 1st 20 Aug 1813 Charlotte (*d* 26 June 1838), yst dau of Philip Tighman, and had, with other issue:

(1) **Sir Molyneux Hyde Nepean, 3rd Bt**, of Codnus Court, DL; *b* 2 July 1814; *m* 30 April 1841 Isabel (*d* 17 March 1895), only dau of Col Gells, of Dumbuck, Dunbartonshire, and *dsp* 13 March 1895

(2) Evan Philip Tighman; *b* 17 Feb 1818; Capt 38th Bengal Native Inf Sikh war (medal and two clasps); *d* E Indies

1 (cont.) **Sir Molyneux** *m* 2nd 30 May 1852 Lydia (*m* 2nd 14 Jan 1863 Dr Montague Kirkman), dau of William Wright, of Wallsend, Northumberland, and *d* 4 June 1856, having by her had a dau (*d* in infancy)

2 Frederick; Commercial Resident Patna;, *b* 4 March 1794;, *m* 20 Nov 1816 Harriet Martina, dau of Capt William Becher, and *d* 17 Sept 1833, leaving two daus

3 William;, Maj-Gen; *b* 20 Sept 1795;, *m* 1820 Emilia (*d* 26 June 1861), dau of Col — Yorke, and *d* 8 Dec 1864, having had:

(1) EVAN YORKE (Sir), **4th Bt**

(1) Anna Maria; *m* 8 June 1865 Gen Sir William Parke, KCB, and *d* 27 April 1900, leaving issue. He *d* 29 March 1897

4 Evan (Rev Canon); MA, Rector Heydon, Norfolk, Canon Westminster, Min Grosvenor Chapel S Audley Street, Chaplain-in-Ordinary to IIM QUEEN VICTORIA; *b* 20 April 1800; *m* 5 Sept 1832 Anne (*d* 6 Sept 1871), 2nd dau of Sir Herbert Jenner Fust, of Hill Court, Glos, and *d* 13 March 1873, having had, with other issue:

(1) Evan Colville (Sir), CB; *b* 7 Dec 1836; *m* 9 Nov 1864 Elizabeth Anne (*d* 17 Oct 1928), dau of Edward Francis Jenner, and *d* 14 May 1908, leaving:

1a Evan Alcock; BA Oxon, barrister; *b* 13 Sept 1865; *m* 11 Jan 1892 Evelyn Maud (*d* 7 Nov 1931), er dau of Cecil Frederick Reid, and *d* 20 Jan 1906, leaving:

1b Evan Cecil; Lt 3rd Bn Roy Scots Fus; *b* 31 July 1893; *ka* 4 Oct 1918

2a Molyneux Edward; manager Nat Provincial Bank; *b* 22 Jan 1870; *m* 27 Feb 1899 Mary Edith, novelist, Meritul Cultural Romania (*d* 23 March 1960), dau of John Bellis, of Llandudno, and *dsp* 5 Nov 1948

3a Arthur Frederick; Registrar Bristol, Gloucester and Hereford Probate Courts; *b* 30 Jan 1871; *m* 9 July 1908 Muriel Helena Osborne (*d* 12 Jan 1947), dau of Capt Hugh Osborne Bateman, Oxon LI, and *dsp* 3 Oct 1945

4a Charles Stuart; *b* 28 Oct 1872; *d* 28 March 1896

5a Richard Colville; *b* 16 March 1878; *d* 15 Feb 1927

6a Nicholas Herbert Jenner Fust; *b* 22 Oct 1882; *d* unm 1 March 1955

1a Emily Margaret; *m* 14 Jan 1896 Felton George Randolph, barrister, est s of Rev Cyril Randolph, Rector Riverhead, Surrey, by Frances Selina, dau of Col Lionel Charles Hervey, yst bro of Col Sir Felton Elwell Hervey-Bathurst, 1st Bt (*qv*), and *d* 21 Aug 1950, leaving issue. He *d* 29 Dec 1906

2a Catherine Mansel; *d* unm 8 Oct 1942

3a Olive Wilmot; *d* unm 9 Oct 1961

4a Gladys Adelaide Beauchamp; *m* 14 April 1903 Capt John Alfred Roy Eliot, MBE, s of Very Rev Philip Frank Eliot, KCVO, DD, Dean Windsor, and *d* 21 Jan 1959, leaving issue. He *d* 5 May 1956

5a Edith Cicely; *m* 1 June 1918 Julius Ernest Mumm, only s of Robert Julius Mumm, of London, and *d* 22 July 1946, leaving issue. He *d* 23 March 1960

6a Dorothy; *m* 25 Oct 1913 Reginald William Clifford-Smith, s of A Clifford-Smith, and *d* 2 Sept 1959, leaving issue. He *d* Sept 1960

(2) Frederick Augustus Tierney; Col IA; *b* 17 April 1839; *m* 1st 10 Nov 1864 (*divorce* 1878) Alice, dau of Maj-Gen James Walker Bayley, and had:

1a Herbert Evan Charles Bayley, CB (1921), CSI (1919), CMG (1917); *b* 10 Oct 1865; Cmdt 123rd Outram's Rifles IA, Admin Cmdt and T/Brig-Gen and Bde Cdr MEF 1916–21, Hon Brig-Gen 1922; *m* 1st 1892 Alice Maud (*d* 6 March 1950), dau of Surgn-Maj Hamilton Ross, of Ballynacrae House, Ballymoney, Co Antrim, and had:

1b Herbert Dryden Home Yorke, CIE (1945), DSO (1918); *b* 27 Nov 1893; *educ* Tonbridge and RMC Sandhurst; Col 5th Roy Gurkha Rifles (FF) and 9th Gurkha Rifles IA, Dep Mil Advsr-in-Ch Indian States Forces 1942–46, served WW I (wounded, despatches) and Afghan War 1919, Roy Humane Soc's Bronze Medal; *m* 21 April 1927 Edith Florence (*d* 16 Aug 1962), dau of Edward Patrick Woods, of Waterford, and *dsp* 25 Jan 1956

2b Leslie Norman Molyneux; *b* 1897; *d* young

1b Clare Agnes Betty; *b* 1905

1a (cont.) Herbert Nepean *m* 2nd Oct 1950 *Muriel, dau of Rev R Butler Faulkner, of Oak Park House, Dawlish, Devon, and *d* 28 March 1951

2a Francis Molyneux Yorke; Capt 7th Bn Somerset LI; *b* 31 March 1868; *ka* 10 Sept 1915

1a Alice Mary Blanchette; *m* 17 Sept 1902 James Curle, of Priorwood, Melrose, and *d* leaving issue

(2) (cont.) Col Herbert Nepean *m* 2nd 9 Aug 1894 Agnes Louisa (*d* 9 Aug 1943), dau of John More Nisbett, of Cairnhill, Lanarks, and The Drum, Midlothian, by Lady Agnes, dau of 9th Earl of Stair (*qv*), and *d* 10 Dec 1924

(3) St Vincent, MVO; Cdr RN, Ch Inspr Lifeboats; *b* 23 July 1844; *m* 16 July 1872 Anne Julia (*d* 15 Jan 1935), dau of Gustavus William Blanch, MD, and *d* 28 March 1915, having had:

1a Nicholas St Vincent; *b* 18 March 1876; *m* 24 Dec 1915 (*annulled* 1923) Maria Gladys (resumed maiden name), only dau of Edward Lee-Warner, of Denton House, Norfolk, and *d* 28 Jan 1950

2a Charlton St Vincent; *b* 8 June 1878; *d* unm 18 May 1914

3a Leonard Percyval St Vincent; Capt 6th Bn Manchester Regt, Imp Yeo S Africa 1902, N Nigeria 1903–04 and WW I; *b* 2 Feb 1879; *m* 26 May 1909 Ellen Mary (*d* 10 Dec 1957), dau of Mathew E Edwards, of St Petersburg, and *d* 20 July 1932, leaving:

1b *Anne Camilla Catherine [Mrs John McQuade, Calle Nuñes de Arce 4-1 Interior, 35005 Las Palmas, Gran Canaria, Canary Islands, Spain]; *b* 18 July 1910; *m* 1st 9 March 1932 (*divorce* 1947) Alfred Lingley Bennett, s of Gordon Charles Bennett, of Kikwetu Estate, Lindi, Tanzania, and has:

1c *Gordon Lingley Nepean; *b* 13 March 1934; *m* 1st 1958 (*divorce* 1972) Faith Merritt (*d* 1988) and has:

1d *Lingley Graham Nepean; *b* 1959; *m* 1989 *Fiona, dau of — Eccleston, and has:

1e *Harry Lingley Nepean; *b* 1992

2d *Robert; *b* 1966; *m* 1993 *Valerie Anderson

1d *Sally Jacqueline Nepean; *b* 1957; *m* 1980 (*divorce* 1991) Duncan Edward Sibbald and has:

1e *Kieran; *b* 1982

1e *Kimberley; *b* 1981

2d *Angela; *b* 1961; *m* 1984 *Ian Bowerman and has:

1e *Andrew; *b* 1991

1e *Amy Samantha; *b* 1989

1c (cont.) Gordon Bennett *m* 2nd 1979 *Christine Stephanie Barbara Maria Whipps and has:

3d *Christian; *b* 1980

2c *Roger Lingley Nepean; *b* 13 June 1935; *m* 1966 *Diana Jacqueline Westcob and has:

1d *Nicola; *b* 1967; *m* 1991 *Simon Bush

2d *Tasmin; *b* 1970

2d *Justine; *b* 1978

1b (cont) Mrs Bennett *m* 2nd 1948 John Herbert McQuade (*d* 1980)

2b Evelyn; *b* 2 April 1917; *m* 16 Aug 1939 Percival William Singleton, 2nd s of Patrick William Singleton, Rangoon Customs, and had:

1c *Gregory St Vincent Nepean; *b* 7 May 1951

2c *John Dominic St Vincent Nepean; *b* 15 May 1956

1c *Mary Catharine [Mrs Michael O'Connor, The Meadows, Loughborough Rd, Thringstone, Leics]; *b* 28 May 1940; *m* 11 Feb 1961 *Michael Villers Forbes O'Connor, only s of Leo Forbes O'Connor by Daphne Mary, sister of 11th Baron Byron (*qv*), and has:

1d *Dominic Rupert; *b* Nov 1961

2d *Christopher Rupert; *b* 5 Jan 1963

3d *Gregory; *b* 5 Nov 1964

4d *Benedict; *b* 13 Nov 1967

2c *Ruth Angela [Mrs Robin Driver, 2 St John's St, Duxford, Cambs]; *b* 10 Oct 1941; *m* 4 April 1961 *Robin Driver, only s of Albert Driver, of Duxford, and has:

1d *Elizabeth Anne; *b* 10 Jan 1962

2d *Lucy-Clare; *b* 31 March 1964

3d *Sarah Magdalen; *b* 8 April 1966

4d *Anne-Marie; *b* 4 Oct 1968

3c *Margaret Elizabeth; *b* 25 Oct 1949

4c *Cecilia Teresa; *b* 21 April 1953

5c *Bernadette Lucy; *b* 17 April 1958

6c *Felicity Maud; *b* 15 June 1960

4a Evelyn Charles Yorke St Vincent, MC; Clerk Bank of England, Lt RFA WW I (despatches); *b* 24 Nov 1880; *d* 23 Feb 1937

1a Elinor Augusta Heather; *d* unm 22 Dec 1963 aged 89

2a Annie Blanch, MBE (1946); *m* 6 Nov 1915 Sir Hugh Byard Clayton, CIE, ICS, Chm Public Services Commn Bombay and Sind, Kaisar-i-hind gold medal, 2nd s of R B B Clayton, of Beaulieu, Hants, and *d* 28 July 1968, having had issue. He *d* 27 Sept 1947

(1) Frederica Sophia; *d* unm 23 Oct 1946

(2) Ellen Georgiana; *d* 20 April 1853

1 Harriet; *d* 8 May 1875

The 3rd Bt's cousin,

Rev Sir Evan Yorke Nepean, 4th Bt; *b* 1825; MA Oxon; Vicar Appleshaw, Hants; *m* 3 Aug 1865 Maria Theresa (*d* 1875), 2nd dau of Rev F Morgan Payler, and *d* 15 June 1903, leaving:

Sir Charles Evan Molyneux Yorke Nepean, 5th Bt; *b* 24 March 1867; *educ* Winchester; Capt and Hon Maj 3rd Bn Roy Berks Regt; *m* 3 Nov 1896 Mary Winifred (*d* 30 Dec 1958 aged 88), only dau of Rev William John Swayne, Vicar Heytesbury, and *d* 1 Jan 1953, leaving:

1 Sir EVAN YORKE NEPEAN, **6th and present Bt**

1 Winifred Diana; *m* 27 May 1936 Christopher Pennycuick Bartlett and *d* 12 April 1966. He *d* 30 Jan 1957

2 Mary Theresa, Kaisar-i-Hind Medal; *m* 3 April 1934 Arthur Geoffrey Tindall Glaisby, OBE, only s of Arthur Glaisby. He *d* 19 Sept 1966

3 Sylvia; *m* 1924 Richard Ivor Stratton and had issue

4 Olivia; WRNS WW II, 1st Offr WRNR 1947–56

NETHERTHORPE

Arms: Arg. on a cross gu. between four garbs vert five millrinds erect or, a chief of stone masonry ppr. **Crest:** A lion passant guardant gu., gorged with a collar sa. charged with bezants, supporting with the dexter paw a cornucopia inverted or, the fruit ppr. **Supporters:** Dexter, a bull; sinister, a ram, both arg., horned and unguled or and gorged with a collar sa. charged with bezants. **Motto:** *Juvat ipse labor* ('Work itself is pleasing'). **Creation:** B. (UK) 10 March 1959.

THE 3RD BARON NETHERTHORPE, of Anston, W Riding of Yorkshire (James Frederick Turner) [The Rt Hon The Lord Netherthorpe, 65 Westover Rd, London SW18 2RF]; *b* 7 Jan 1964; *s* f 1982; *educ* Harrow; dir UBS London; *m* 10 Dec 1989 *(Elizabeth) Curran, dau of Edward William Fahan, of Redding, Conn., and has:

1 +ANDREW JAMES EDWARD; *b* 24 March 1993

1 *Megan Anna Curran; *b* 19 Nov 1994

2 *Nell Katherine Elizabeth; *b* 10 June 1997

Lineage: JAMES TURNER, JP, of Anston, W R Yorks; *b* 6 Jan 1845; *m* Sarah (*d* 9 April 1883), dau of Thomas Mann, of Walesby, Notts, and *d* 24 Jan 1924, leaving:

1 ALBERT EDWARD MANN

2 Percival John Mann; *b* 5 Nov 1875; *educ* Woodhouse Grove Sch, Apperley Bridge

3 James William Mann; *b* 23 Jan 1878; *educ* Woodhouse Grove Sch

4 George Henry Mann; *b* 6 Feb 1880; *educ* Woodhouse Grove Sch

The est son,

ALBERT EDWARD MANN TURNER, of Anston, JP; *b* 8 May 1870; *educ* Ollerton and Newark, Notts; *m* 19 May 1898 Lucy, dau of Henry Helliwell, of Hoad's Farm, Woodsetts, Worksop, Notts, and *d* 11 July 1948, leaving:

1 Stanley, DFC (1918), TD, JP; *b* 16 March 1899; *educ* King Edward Sch Sheffield and Sheffield U; *m* 13 June 1929 Vera, dau of H Alfred Bealby, of Worksop, and had:

(1) *David John [David Turner Esq, Needham Hall, Gazeley, Newmarket, Suffolk]; *b* 4 Aug 1930; *educ* Kingswood; *m* 21 Oct 1954 *Elizabeth Ann, dau of Jeffrey Phillip Forrest, of Worksop, Notts, and has:

1a *Nicholas Mark; *b* 23 July 1962

1a *Penelope Ann; *b* 11 Sept 1959

(2) *James Albert; *b* 30 Dec 1932; *educ* Rydal Sch and Clare Coll Cambridge (MA); *m* 20 Sept 1958 *Marjory Ruth, dau of William Arnold Morphy, of Westmorland, and has:

1a *Michael Jonathan; *b* 10 Nov 1959

1a *Patricia Jane; *b* 9 Jan 1962

2a *Wendy Lynn; *b* 24 July 1964

(3) *Michael Stanley [Michael Turner Esq, Little Bredbury, Bishops Down Park Rd, Tunbridge Wells]; *b* 3 Oct 1935; *educ* The Leys

(1) *Susan Margaret [Mrs Oswald Brewis, Little Swinton, Coldstream, Berwickshire TD12 4HH]; *b* 2 May 1939; *educ* Reading U (BSc Ag 1960); *m* 24 June 1961 *Oswald Brewis, only s of Thomas William Brewis, of Little Swinton, Coldstream, and has:

1a *Thomas Michael; *b* 27 May 1964

2a *Robert Oswald; *b* 21 April 1967

1a *Deborah Jane; *b* 2 May 1962

2 JAMES, **1st Baron**

3 *Albert Henry; *b* 30 May 1911; *educ* Woodhouse Grove Sch; *m* 1st 20 Sept 1944 (*divorce* 1948) Joan, dau of — Forgan, of Banstead, Surrey; *m* 2nd 20 March 1953 *Kathleen Margaret, dau of John Johnstone Dewhurst, of Boyton Manor, Warminster, Wilts

4 *John, JP [John Turner Esq JP, The Elms, Lound, nr Retford, Notts DN22 8RH]; *b* 11 Sept 1915; *educ* Woodhouse Grove Sch and Reading U; *m* 28 Jan 1943 *Margaret Grace, dau of Bruce Collard, of Canterbury, Kent, and has:

(1) *Nicholas John [Nicholas Turner Esq, South Lodge, Ropsley, N Grantham, Lincs NG33 4AS]; *b* 1 Aug 1945; *educ* Wrekin and RAC Cirencester; MFH

(2) *Richard Patrick [Richard Turner Esq, Barleythorpe House, Barleythorpe, Rutland LE15 7EG]; *b* 2 July 1949; *educ* Millfield and RAC Cirencester

(1) *Susan Margaret [Mrs Michael Sutton, West Bank, Gamston, Notts DN22 0QD]; *b* 1 Feb 1946; *m* 24 July 1971 *Michael Sutton, er s of Philip Sutton, of Worksop, Notts

1 *Winifred Mary; *b* 29 May 1901; *m* 29 Oct 1929 *Wilfred Fisher Wyatt, s of Henry Wyatt, of Anston, and has two sons and a dau

2 *Edith Muriel; *b* 20 March 1903; *m* 15 Oct 1930 *Charles Naish, s of Alfred Naish, of Edwinstowe, Notts, and has two sons and a dau

3 *Jessie; *b* 20 April 1906; *m* 6 Dec 1945 *Hugh Snell, s of Joseph Snell, of Whitwell, Notts, and has a s

ALBERT TURNER's 2nd s,

JAMES TURNER, **1st Baron Netherthorpe**, of Anston, West Riding Co York (UK), so *cr* 10 March 1959; *b* 6 Jan 1908; *educ* Knaresborough and Leeds U (BSc Ag 1928); chm Fisons, dep chm Richard Costain Ltd, dir Lloyds Bank, Abbey Nat Bldg Soc, Steetly Co, Liveryman Painters-Stainers' Co and Farmers' Co, Pres NFU 1945–60, Internat Fedn Ag Producers 1946–48, memb NEDC, Pay Bd, v-chm Unigate 1976, ktd 1949, Hon LLD Leeds 1952 and Birmingham 1959; *m* 3 Oct 1935 Margaret Lucy (d 5 March 1995), dau of James Arthur Mattock, of Sheffield, and had:

1 (JAMES) ANDREW, **2nd Baron**

2 Richard Anthony; *b* 3 Oct, *d* 5 Oct 1939

3 +(Edward) Neil [The Hon Neil Turner, The Limes, Crowgate, Yorks S25 5AL]; *b* 27 Jan 1941; *educ* Rugby, RAC Cirencester and London U; FRICS, QALAS, Dip FBA (Lond), FBIM, Sheffield Regnl Advsr Samuel Montagu & Co 1973, chm Edward Turner Cos and Lazard Smaller Equities Investment Tst, memb Yorks and Humberside Regnl Ec Planning Cncl 1975–79, S Yorks Residuary Body 1985–89, Cutlers Hallamshire Co, Cncl BIM 1976–81, 1982–88, Gen Commr Tax 1973, High Sheriff S Yorks 1983; *m* 12 Oct 1963 *Gillian Mary, est dau of Christopher John King, of Abbots Leigh, Somerset, and has:

(1) +Charles James; *b* 3 May 1966; *m* 1992 *Sarah Eastwood and has:
  1a +Edward Nicholas; *b* 1995
  2a +Henry James; *b* 1997
(1) *Sara Jane; *b* 4 Feb 1971

4 +(Philip Noel) Nigel [The Hon Nigel Turner, Parsonage House, Helions Bumpstead, Suffolk]; *b* 8 May 1949; *educ* Rugby and Worcester Coll Oxford; V-Pres Northern Tst 1970–82, md Barclays Merchant Bank 1983–85, Lazard Bros 1985–; *m* 1st 1973 *Anne Rachel, dau of R Brown, of Somerton, Oxon, and has:

(1) *Lucy Victoria; *b* 1977
(2) *Catherine Louise; *b* 1979
(3) *Georgina Anne; *b* 1983

4 (cont.) The Hon Nigel Turner *m* 2nd 1988 *Mrs Jennifer (Annie) Goodwin, yst dau of Capt David Armstrong, of Morpeth, Northumberland

The 1st BARON *d* 8 Nov 1980; his er s,

(JAMES) ANDREW TURNER, **2nd Baron Netherthorpe**; *b* 23 July 1936; *educ* Rugby and Pembroke Coll Cambridge (BA 1958); dep chm and ch exec Dalgety Ltd, dir NZ Loan, Lazard Bros, Babcock Int, Commercial Bank of Anston, Bank of Australia, memb Br Nat Export Cncl Australia Ctee; *m* 3 Sept 1960 *Belinda [The Rt Hon Belinda Lady Netherthorpe, Boothby Hall, Boothby Pagnell, Lincs NG33 4DQ], only dau of Frederick Hedley Nicholson, of Firbeck, Notts, and *d* 4 Nov 1982, leaving:

1 JAMES FREDERICK TURNER, **3rd and present Baron Netherthorpe**
2 +Patrick Andrew; *b* 4 June 1971
1 *Anna Elizabeth; *b* 17 Dec 1961; *m* 1986 *Simon M Edwards, er s of Roland Edwards
2 *Kate Belinda; *b* 12 Oct 1967; *m* 1993 *Rupert J Ivey, 3rd s of John Ivey

NEWALL

Arms: Per pale az. and gu. two lions passant guardant in pale or, on a chief erm. a rose of the second barbed and seeded between a lotus flower and a sprig of New Zealand fern, all ppr. **Crest:** Issuant from an astral crown or an eagle, wings elevated sa., breathing flames ppr. **Supporters:** On either side a pegasus arg. gorged with an astral crown or. **Motto:** *Deo juvante* ('With God's approval'). **Creation:** B. (UK) 18 July 1946.

THE 2ND BARON NEWALL, of Clifton-upon-Dunsmoor, Co Warwick (Francis Storer Eaton Newall, DL (Gtr London 1988)) [The Rt Hon The Lord Newall DL, 18 Lennox Gdns, London SW1X 0DG; Wotton Underwood, Aylesbury, Bucks HP18 ORZ]; *b* 23 June 1930; *s f* 1963; *educ* Eton and RMA Sandhurst; 11th Hus (PAO): 2nd Lt 1950, Capt.1955, ret 1961, served Germany, Malaya, Singapore, Adj Roy Glos Hus 1956–58, with Schweppes (USA), md Neilson McCarthy 1972–, C Whip Ho Lds 1976–79, Upper Renter Warden Merchant Taylors's Co 1977–78 (Master 1985–86), chm and dir Br Greyhound Racing Bd 1985–97; *m* 29 Sept 1956 *Pamela, er dau of Edward Hugh Lee Rowcliffe, TD (*see* FARRINGTON, Bt), and has:

1 +RICHARD HUGH EATON [The Hon Richard Newall, 17 Manchuria Rd, London SW1 6AF]; *b* 19 Feb 1961; *m* 24 Aug 1996 *Keira, 2nd dau of Robert Glen, of Forest Hill
2 +David William Norton [The Hon David Newall, The Power House, Cromwell Grove, London W6 7RQ]; *b* 2 July 1963; *educ* Eton and RMA Sandhurst; *m* 5 Dec 1998 *Georgina, yr dau of Peter Lee, of How Caple Court, Herefs
1 *Miranda Jane [The Hon Mrs Lawson, Long Acre, Honeycombe Leaze, Fairford, Glos]; *b* 25 Feb 1959; *m* 1986 *Timothy Guy Lawson, s of Derek C Lawson, of Bradford Abbas, Dorset, and has:

(1) *George Thomas Guy; *b* 1987
(2) *Sam Frederick Guy; *b* 1989
(1) *Eliza Daisy; *b* 1991

Lineage: Lt-Col WILLIAM POTTER NEWALL, IA; had:

CYRIL LOUIS NORTON, **1st Baron Newall**, of Clifton-upon-Dunsmoor, Co Warwick (UK), so *cr* 18 July 1946, GCB (1938, KCB 1935, CB 1929), OM (1940), GCMG (1940, CMG 1919), CBE (1919), AM; *b* 15 Feb 1886; *educ* Bedford Sch and RMC Sandhurst; 2nd Lt Roy Warwicks Regt 1905, served Zakka Khel Expdn 1908, tfd IA 1909, RFC 1914 and RAF 1918, WW I (despatches three times, Brevet Maj) and WW II, Dep Dir Personnel Air Min 1919–22, Air ADC to HM GEORGE V 1923–24, Air Offr Cmdg Special Reserve and AAF 1925, Dir Ops and Intell Air Min and Dep Ch Air Staff 1926–31 (memb Air Cncl 1930–31 and 1935–37), Air Offr cmdg RAF Middle East 1931–34, AVM 1930, Air-Marshal 1935, Air Ch Marshal 1937, Marshal RAF 1940, Ch Air Staff and 1st and Sr Memb Air Cncl 1937–40, Govr-Gen and C-in-C NZ 1941–46, KStJ, Order Leopold and Croix de Guerre Belgium, Order Crown Italy, Offr Legion Honour, Pres RAF Assoc; *m* 1st 18 Jan 1922 Mary Dulcie Weddell (*d* 1924); *m* 2nd 18 April 1925 Olive Tennyson Foster, DStJ (*d* 1988), only dau of Horace Tennyson Foster and Mrs Francis Storer Eaton, of Boston, USA, and *d* 30 Nov 1963, having by her had:

1 FRANCIS STORER EATON NEWALL, **2nd and present Baron Newall**
1 Georgiana; *b* 22 Jan 1926; *d* 1985 following a road accident
2 *Diana Olive [The Hon Mrs Diana Joly, Tower House, Reybridge, Chippenham, Wilts]; *b* 12 June 1927; *m* 16 Oct 1956 (*divorce* 1967) John Leonard Joly, only s of Kenneth Henry Joly, OBE, of Beirut, and has had:

(1) Susan Rosemary; *b* 6 Aug 1957; *d* 19–
(2) *Harriet Diana; *b* 6 March 1960

NEWBOROUGH

Arms: Sa. three fleurs-de-lys arg. **Crest:** A dexter cubit arm erect in armour holding in the hand ppr. a fleur-de-lys or. **Supporters:** Two lions gu., the dexter gorged with a collar or, charged with three fleurs-de-lys sa.; the sinister, with a collar arg., charged with three crosses-patée gu. **Motto:** *Suaviter in modo, fortiter in re* ('Gentle in manner, vigorous in action'). **Creations:** Bt. (E) 25 Oct 1742, B. (I) 23 July 1776.

THE 7TH BARON NEWBOROUGH, and a **Baronet** (Sir Robert Charles Michael Vaughan Wynn, Bt, DSC (1942), JP (Merioneths 1948)) [The Rt Hon The Lord Newborough DSC JP, Rhug, Corwen, Clwyd LL21 0EH]; *b* 24 April 1917, *s f* 1965; *educ* Oundle; High Sheriff Merioneths 1963, 2nd Lt 9th Lancers Supp Res 1935–39 and Lt 16th/5th Lancers WW II till invalided out of Army 1940, Lt RVNR cmdg MTB 74 St Nazaire raid (wounded, despatches, POW Colditz 1942–44, escaped); *m* 1st 1 Dec 1945 (*divorce* 1971) Rosamund Lavington, yst dau of Maj Robert Barbour, of Bolesworth Castle, Tattenhall, Cheshire, and has:

1 +ROBERT VAUGHAN [The Hon Robert Wynn, Peplow Hall, Peplow, Market Drayton, Salop]; *b* 11 Aug 1949; *educ* Milton Abbey; *m* 1st 1981 (*divorce* 1988) Mrs Sheila Christine Wilson, dau of William A Massey, of Corsley, Wilts, and has:

     (1) *Lucinda Rosamond; *b* 1982

1 (cont.) The Hon Robert Wynn *m* 2nd 1988 *Mrs Susan E Hall, dau of Andrew Lloyd, of Malta

1 *(Anne) Patricia Rosamund [The Hon Mrs Budgen, Boreatton House, Baschurch, Salop SY4 2EP]; *b* 14 Sept 1947; *m* 8 Aug 1970 *Anthony George Budgen and has:

     (1) *Mark George; *b* 1972

     (1) *Nadine Patricia Mary; *b* 1975

2 *Diana Heather Marion [The Hon Mrs Carmichael, The Old Rectory, Wooltaston, Church Stretton, Salop]; *b* 3 March 1951; *m* 1979 *Capt Ralph Peter Kinloch Carmichael, Roy Scots Dragoon Gds (ret), and has:

     (1) *William Ralph; *b* 1983

     (1) *Sophie Emma; *b* 1980

The 7th BARON *m* 2nd 1971 *Jennifer Caroline Acland, yst dau of Capt Cecil C A Allen, RN

Lineage: GOLLWYN Ap TANGNO; a chieftain in Eifionydd, Carnarvs; *b c* 1025; had:

MERWYDD GOCH ('The Red'); living 1094; had:

GWGON Ap MERWYDD GOCH; had:

CARADOG Ap GWGON; had:

EINION Ap CARADOG, of Penychen, Llanor, Caernarvs; *d* 1210?, leaving:

MAREDUDD Ab EINION; had:

HYWEL, of Bron-y-foel, Ystum-llyn, Caernarvs, Ap MAREDUDD Ab EINION; *m* Gwellian, dau of Gruffudd ab Ednyfed Fychan, steward to Llywelyn ap Gruffudd, Prince of Wales; had:

GRUFFUDD Ap HYWEL; *m* Angharad, dau of Tegwared y Balswen ('of the white coat'), allegedly illegitimate s of LLYWELYN THE GREAT, and had, with another s (Sir Hywel y Fwyall ('of the battle-axe'), fought at Crécy and Poitiers, Constable Cricieth Castle, *d c* 1381)::

EINION Ap GRUFFUDD; Sheriff Caernarvs 1354–56; *m* Nest, dau of Gruffudd, of Dyffryn Ardudwy, Merioneths, ab Adda Foel, and had:

IEUAN Ab EINION; living 1366; Sheriff Caernarvs 1389; *m* 1st Gwenhwyfar, dau of Einion abp Ynyr Fychan, of Nannau, Llanfachreth, Merioneths; *m* 2nd Rhegau, dau of Gruffudd ap Maredudd, and had, probably by his 1st w:

MADOG, of Pennarth, Llanystumdwy, Caernarvs; living 1416; *m* Gwerful, dau of Rhys of Erddreiniog (*d* 1412), ap Tudur ap Gronwy, of Penmynydd, and uncle of Owen Tudor, and had:

HYWEL Ap MADOG, of Pennarth; *m* 1st Margaret, dau of Rhys (living 1410) ap Gruffudd ap Madog Gloddaith, and had a s (Rhys) and dau (Gwerful); *m* 2nd Erd-

dylad, dau of Gruffudd ap Hywel Coetmor, of Coetmor, Betws-y-coed, Caernarvs, and had two sons (Gruffudd; MADOG) and three daus; *m* 3rd Elen, dau of Dafydd ap Gruffudd, of Llanwnda, Caernarvs, and by her had three daus; his yr s by his 2nd w:

MADOG Ap HYWEL Ap MADOG; *m* Ellyw, dau of Morgan ab Ieuan, of Penllech, Caernarvs, and had:

JOHN Ap MADOG, of Bodfel, Llannor, Caernarvs; *m* Jonet, dau of Gruffudd ap Llywelyn, of Chwaen, Llantrisaint, Anglesey, and had:

HUGH Ap JOHN Ap MADOG, of Bodfel; *m* Catherine, dau of Henry Salesbury, of Llanrhaeadryng-Nghinmeirch, Denbighs, and had, with a yr s (Harry, of Pistyll, Dinllaen, Caernarvs, *m* Mawd, dau of Sir William Herbert, of Coldbrook, Abergavenny, Mon) and two daus:

JOHN WYNNE Ap HUGH, of Bodfel; High Sheriff Caernarvs 1551 and 1561; standard-bearer roy forces suppressing Kett's rebellion Norwich 1549, for which granted Bardsey Island; *m* Elizabeth, dau of Sir John Puleston, Chamberlain N Wales and Constable Caernarvon, and *d* between 11 Oct and 3 Nov 1576, leaving:

   1 Hugh Gwyn BODFEL; had:

     (1) John BODFEL/BODVILE, of Bodfel/Bodvile; had:

       1a John; *d unm*

       1a Sarah; her bro's sole heiress; admired as a beauty by Samuel Pepys; *m* by 1658 John Robartes, Viscount Bodmyn (*b* 1633; MP Cornwall 1660 and Bossinney 1661–79; *dvp* and *bur* 12 Feb 1681/2), s of 1st Earl of Radnor of the 1679 *cr* (*see* RADNOR, E, preliminary remarks); she was granted 25 Jan 1685/6 rank of an earl's widow, as if her late husb had *s* his *f*; *bur* 20 Sept 1720

   2 Thomas GWYN or WYNN, of Bodvean, *m* Elizabeth, dau of Owain ap Gruffudd ap Morus, of Plas Du, Llanarmon, Caernarvs, and *d* between 14 Nov 1593 and 23 March 1594, having had, with four daus (two *dsp*):

     (1) Hugh GWYNNE, of Chelsea; *dsp* on or after 28 March 1599

     (2) JOHN

     (3) Fowk

     (4) Charles; *dsp*

THOMAS GWYN/WYNN's 2nd s,

JOHN WYNN, of Boduan, Buan, Caernarvs; *m* Elin, dau of Edward Rowland, of Mellteyrn, Caernarvs, and *d* 6 June 1635, having had, with two yr sons (Hugh, *dsp* and *bur* 27 April 1682; Frederick) and four daus:

THOMAS WYNNE, of Boduan; *b c* 1602; Surveyor Crown property N Wales 1636, Clerk of Cheque Gentlemen Pensioners 1637, Parliamentarian Civil War; *m* between 8 Dec 1637 and 28 March 1638 Susan, dau of Francis Dayrell and sis of Sir Thomas Dayrell, of Lillingstone Dayrell, Bucks, and *d* 14 Feb 1673, leaving, with three daus:

GRIFFITH WYNN, of Boduan; *b c* 1646; *m* Catherine (*m* 2nd Hugh Nanney, of Nannau, Llanfachreth, Merioneths), dau of William Vaughan, of Corsygedol, Llanddwywe, Merioneths, and had, with a yr s (Sir William, *bapt* 11 march 1678, Capt Band of Gentlemen Pensioners, *d* 20 May 1754):

Sir Thomas Wynn, 1st Bt (GB), so *cr* 25 Oct 1742, of Boduan/Bodvean; *bapt* March 1677; MP Caernarvon 1713–49, Equerry to GEORGE II; *m c* 1700 Frances (*d* Oct 1709), dau and eventual heiress of John Glynne, of Glyn-llifon, Llandwrog, Merioneths, and *d* 13 April 1749, having had, with four daus (Catherine; Elizabeth; Dorothy, *m* William Thomas, of Coedhelen; Frances):

Sir John Wynn, 2nd Bt; *b* 1701; MP Caernarvonshire 1740–41 and 1754–61 and Caernarvon 1761–68, Surveyor King's Mines Wales; *m* 1736 Jane (*d* 24 April 1784), dau and heiress of John Wynne, of Melai, Denbighs, and Maenan, Caernarvs, and had:

   1 THOMAS (Sir), **1st Baron**

   2 Glynn; Lt-Col, MP Caenarvon; *m* 11 Jan 1766 Bridget, est dau of Edward Philip Pugh, of Penrhyn and Coytmer, and had:

     (1) John Glynn; *b* Oct 1766

     (2) William WYNN later COTYMORE (under terms of grandmother's will) (Rev); DD; *b* 1767; *m* Eliza, widow of — Bellingham, of Castle Bellingham, Co Louth, and gdau and heiress of Thomas Tenison, Ch Justice Common Pleas Ireland

     (3) Thomas Edward WYNN later BELASYSE-WYNN, of Newborough Hall, Yorks; *m* Lady Charlotte Belasyse (*b* 10 Jan 1767; *dsp* 1825), est dau and coheir of 2nd and last Earl Fauconberg of Newborough

     (4) Glynn; *b* 1766; *m* 1793 Elizabeth, 6th dau of Rev Hon George Hamilton (*see* ABERCORN, D)

     (1) Bridget; *m* 16 March 1792 4th Earl of Egmont (*qv*) and *d* 24 Jan 1826

   1 Frances; *m* Henry Soame

   2 Dorothea

Sir JOHN *d* 16 Feb 1773; his er s,

THOMAS WYNN, **1st Baron Newborough** (I), so *cr* 23 July 1776, of Bodvean; *b* 1736; *educ* Queens' Coll Cambridge; MP (Tory) Carnarvs 1761–74, St Ives 1775–80 and Beaumaris 1796–1807, Ld Lt Caernarvs 1761–81; *m* 1st 15 Sept 1766 Lady Catherine Perceval (*d* June 1782), est dau of 2nd Earl of Egmont (*qv*), and had:

1 John; *b* 27 April 1772; *m* Oct 1793 Lena (*m* 2nd Rev Dr Werninck; *d* 27 April 1834), dau of Tillas Vanerdauky, and *dsp* 18 Oct 1800

The **1st Baron** *m* 2nd 10 Oct 1786 (she being then 13) Maria Stella Petronilla (*b* 16 April 1773; *m* 2nd 11 Sept 1810 Baron Edward Ungern-Sternberg; *d* 28 Dec 1843), dau of Lorenzo Chiappini, innkeeper and gaoler, of Modigliana, Italy, and *d* 12 Oct 1807, having by her had:

2 THOMAS JOHN WYNN, **2nd Baron Newborough**; *b* 3 April 1802; *educ* Rugby and Ch Ch Oxford; MP (Tory) Caernarvs 1826–30; *d unm* 15 Nov 1832

3 SPENCER BULKELEY WYNN, **3rd Baron Newborough**; *b* 23 May 1803; *educ* Rugby and Ch Ch Oxford; High Sheriff Anglesey 1847; *m* 10 May 1834 Frances Maria (*d* 18 Nov 1857), est dau of Rev Walter de Winton, and *d* 1 Nov 1888, having had:

(1) Thomas John; *b* 31 Dec 1840; *m* 11 July 1871 Sybil Anna Katherine (*d* 7 Jan 1911), est dau of Edwin Corbett, Min Athens, and *dvp* 25 Aug 1878, having had:

1a WILLIAM CHARLES WYNN, **4th Baron Newborough**; *b* 4 Nov 1873; T/Lt Welsh Gds, formerly Denbighshire Yeo, High Sheriff Denbighshire 1902; *m* 7 Nov 1900 Grace Bruce (*d* 26 Nov 1939), dau of Col Henry Montgomery Carr, of Kentucky, and *dsp* 19 July 1916

2a Spencer Perceval; *b* 16 May, *d* 15 Aug 1876

3a THOMAS JOHN WYNN, **5th Baron Newborough**, JP Merionethshire; *b* 22 Nov 1878; T/Lt RNVR; *m* 1st 30 Jan 1907 (*divorce* 1938) Vera Evelyn Mary (*d* 30 April 1940), widow of Henry L Winch (*see* FALKLAND, V) and dau of Capt Philip Montagu, 12th Lancers, of Down Hall, Dorset, and had:

1b Stella Maria Glyn; *b* 23 Jan 1908; *m* 1st 9 June 1932 Charles Vivian Jackson (*d* 30 Dec 1936), er s of Sir Charles Jackson, and had issue; *m* 2nd 23 Oct 1942 (*divorce* 1963) Lt-Col Derek Cardiff, Scots Gds, 2nd s of Col Richard Henry Wingfield Cardiff, of Easton Court, Ludlow, and *d* 6 Nov 1977

3a (cont.) The **5th Baron** *m* 2nd 23 March 1939 (*divorce* 1947) Denisa Josephine, formerly w of Jean Malpuech, Govr Laos, and dau of Lazar Braun, of Subotica, Yugoslavia, and by her had:

2b *(Blanche-Neige) Juno Palma Odette Denisa [The Hon Mrs Wolfe-Parry, 5 Braemar Ave, Wimbledon Pk, London SW19]; *b* 14 Feb 1940; *m* 23 Sept 1963 *Philip Wolfe-Parry, LDS, RCS Eng, er s of Reginald George Wolfe-Parry, of Grayshott, Surrey, and has:

1c *Edward Thomas Wilton; *b* 2 June 1972

3a (cont.) The **5th Baron** *m* 3rd 7 Aug 1947 Katherine Rudkin (*d* 1979), dau of Henry Stephen Murray, of Melbourne, Australia, and *dspm* 27 April 1957

1a Mabel; *b* 19 July 1872; granted 14 May 1889 with her sisters rank of baron's daus; *m* 19 Nov 1896 Francis Charles Cowper Annesley (*see* ANNESLEY, E) and *dsp* 14 Feb 1970

2a Stella Frances; *b* 15 Dec 1874; *d* 12 Jan 1875

3a Dorothy Beatrix; *b* 18 July 1877; *m* 1 Feb 1905 R-Adml Cuthbert Godfrey Chapman, MVO (*d* 17 March 1931), est s of Peter Godfrey Chapman, and *d* 5 March 1974, leaving issue

(2) William Perceval; *b* 19 Aug 1845; *d* 2 Aug 1851

(3) Charles Henry, of Rhug, Corwen, Merioneths, JP; CA, High Sheriff 1873; *b* 22 April 1847; *m* 31 Aug 1876 Frances Georgiana (*d* 27 Oct 1919), 2nd dau of Lt-Col Romer, 5th Regt, of Bryncelyn, Merioneths, and *d* 14 March 1911, having had:

1a ROBERT VAUGHAN, **6th Baron**

2a William; *b* 3 Aug, *d* 6 Aug 1878

3a Charles William; *b* 4 May, *d* 4 Aug 1884

4a Arthur William, JP Merioneths; Lt Welsh Gds; *b* 22 June 1885; granted with surv bros rank of baron's yr sons 9 Jan 1958; *m* 4 Sept 1915 Gladys Catherine (*d* 1988), dau of Richard Hanbury Joseph Gurney, of Northrepps Hall, Norfolk, and *d* 14 Aug 1964, leaving:

1b +John Christopher Watkin [John Wynn Esq, No 1 Margaret Lilly Way, Aldbrough, Norwich NR11 7PA]; Capt RA WW II India and Burma; *b* 17 July 1917; *m* 9 March 1946 *Cynthia Maureen, only dau of William Dodwell, of Wolverhampton, and has:

1c +Nicholas Romer; *b* 7 Dec 1952; *m* 1980 *Julie-Ann, er dau of David Turrell, of Pietermartizburg, S Africa

2c +Gareth Rowland; *b* 12 Dec 1958; *m* 1982 *Karen, only dau of Kenneth Lake, of Lilongwe, Malawi

1c *Ann Richenda Dodwell; *b* 24 May 1947; *m* 1973 (*divorce* 1983) Thomas William Everett

2b (Dennis) Gurney; *b* 31 July 1922; *m* 6 July 1950 *Joan Edith [Mrs Gurney Wynn, The Mount, Ketton, Lincs PE9 3TE], dau of Alfred Pearman Bentley, of St Mary's Hall, King's Lynn, Norfolk, and *d* 1983, leaving:

1c +Simon Charles [Simon Wynn Esq, 80 Chevening Rd, London NW6 6EA]; *b* 22 Dec 1952; *educ* Soham GS and Roy Sch Mines Imp Coll; ARSM, MIMM; *m* 1984 *Alison Rona, only dau of Frank Cropper, of Kirkcudbrightshire, and has:

1d *Victoria Rona; *b* 1987

2d *Fiona Emily; *b* 1991

2c +Mark Gurney [Mark Wynn Esq, 52 The Drive, Henley-on-Klip, Gauteng, S Africa]; *b* 29 Sept 1957; *educ* Soham GS and Cardiff U; *m* 1990 *Donna, dau of Gyula Lennert of Vanderbjit Park, Gauteng, and has:

1d +Alexander Anthony; *b* 19 Sept 1993

1c *Sarah Frances [Mrs Philip Knight, Post Cottage, Farnsfield, Notts]; *b* 4 Nov 1954; *m* 1994 *Philip Knight and has:

1d *Paul A Wynn; *b* 1994

1d *Emma Joanna; *b* 24 Nov 1997

2c *Rebecca Helen [Miss Rebecca Wynn, c/o The Mount, Ketton, Lincs PE9 3TE]; *b* 30 Dec 1956

1b Rosemary Vera Georgiana [Mrs Edward Record, 53 Cromer Rd, Overstrand, Cromer, Norfolk NR27 0NT]; *b* 7 Oct 1919; *m* 1st 11 Jan 1941 (*divorce* 1966) John Richard Boydell, s of George Henry Farmer Boydell, of Lower Haynards, Tixall, Stafford, and had:

1c *John Richard Wynn; *b* 29 March 1942

2c *Gerald Romer; *b* 6 Aug 1943; *m* 3 April 1965 *Susan Jane, 2nd dau of Frederick Donald Hay, and has:

1d *Gillian Elizabeth; *b* 22 Nov 1967

2d *Angela Susan; *b* 6 April 1969

3c *Christopher Henry Robert; *b* 6 Feb 1945

1b (cont.) Mrs Rosemary Boydell *m* 2nd 1966 (*divorce* 1969) John Leicester Goldsmith; *m* 3rd Dec 1996 *Edward Record

5a John Salisbury; *b* 29 April 1887; *d* unm 4 Feb 1946

6a Charles Watkin Meredith; Queen's Messenger, Capt 9th Lancers, ADC; *b* 24 Oct 1890; *d* unm 27 March 1967

7a Rowland Tempest Beresford, CBE (1949); *b* 31 Jan 1898; *educ* Uppingham and Trin Hall Cambridge (MA); FIEE, chartered engr Designs Dept Marconi 1922–26, BBC 1926–60, Ch Engr BBC 1952–60, RFC and RAF WW I; *m* 2 April 1943 Eleanor Mary Tydfil (*d* 20 Aug 1997), yst dau of Arthur Edmund Smith-Thomas, and *d* 24 April 1977

1a Gwendoline Frances; *b* 23 Aug 1879; *m* 15 Oct 1808 Griffith Lloyd Roberts, MD, of Green Bank, Caernarvon, er s of Very Rev Griffith Roberts, Dean Bangor, and *d* 10 July 1954, leaving issue. He *d* 23 June 1941

2a Dorothy Mary; *b* 30 April 1881; *d* unm 14 Jan 1940

3a Margaret Constance; *b* 27 March 1883; *d* unm 31 Dec 1934

(4) Frederick George, of Glynllivon Park, Bodvean Hall and Fort Belan, Caernarvonshire, DL; High Sheriff 1894; CA 1889–1904; *b* 17 Jan 1853; *d* unm 20 Jan 1932

(1) Frances Maria; *d* unm 5 Jan 1886

(2) Emily Annina; *m* 29 Sept 1874 Murray Gladstone, RN, s of Murray Gladstone, JP, and *d* 18 Aug 1927. He *d* 5 Nov 1928

(3) Ellen Glyn; *d* unm 17 March 1917

(4) Catherine; *d* unm 10 Dec 1885

(5) Isabella Elizabeth; *m* 29 April 1875 3rd Viscount Hill (*qv*) and *d* 29 July 1898, leaving issue

(6) Mary Georgiana; *d* 1851

The 5th BARON's cousin,

ROBERT VAUGHAN WYNN, **6th Baron Newborough**, OBE (1944), JP, DL; *b* 17 July 1877; Capt 9th Lancers, Maj Montgomeryshire Yeo (TF), Boer War 1899–1902 (despatches), WW I (despatches four times, once for exceptional gallantry, brevet) and WW II as Sector Cdr; *m* 16 Dec 1913 Ruby Irene (*d* 6 Nov 1960), yst dau of Edmund Wigley Severne, of Thenford, Northants, and Wallop, Salop, and *d* 27 Oct 1965, leaving:

1 ROBERT CHARLES MICHAEL VAUGHAN WYNN, **7th and present Baron Newborough**

2 +Charles Henry Romer [Lt-Cdr The Hon Charles Wynn RN, Bunkersland, Withleigh, Tiverton, Devon EX16 8JN]; *b* 25 May 1923; *educ* Canford; RN WW II; *m* 16 Dec 1947 *Hon Angela Hermione Ida Willoughby, er dau of 11th Baron Middleton (*qv*), and has:

(1) +Antony Charles Vaughan [Antony Wynn Esq, 46 Crescent Lane, London SW4 9PU]; *b* 2 May 1949; *educ* Eton and Balliol Coll Oxford; *m* 1st 1 Dec 1973 (*divorce* 1986) Jane Slane Sloan, er dau of Rev William Thompson, of Oxnam Manse, Jedburgh, Roxburghshire; *m* 2nd 1996 *Victoria Somenge

(2) +Andrew Guy, LVO (1984) [Cdr Andrew Wynn LVO RN, The Bursary, Eton College, Windsor, Berks SL4 6AJ]; *b* 26 Nov 1950; *educ* Eton and Gonville and Caius Coll Cambridge; Cdr RN (ret), Equerry to HRH THE DUKE OF EDINBURGH 1982–84, Bursar Eton; *m* 1st 22 April 1978 (*divorce* 1986) Susan-Jane, er dau of Selwyn Willis Fraser-Smith, CBE, MC, of Stove Cross Cottage, Crowborough, Sussex, and has:

1a +Alexander Charles Guy; *b* 9 June 1980; *educ* Pangbourne

(2) (cont.) Cdr Wynn *m* 2nd 1988 *Shelagh Jean Macsorley, yr dau of Prof I K M Smith, of Welwyn Garden City, Herts

1 Pamela Rosamund; *b* 25 Jan 1916; *d* 15 Aug 1932

NEWBURGH

Creations: E., V. and L. (S) 31 Dec 1660; Prince (Rospigliosi) (HRE) 6 June 1668 and (Papal) 1854), (Castiglione) (Kingdom of Two Sicilies) 1602, Italy 1897; D. (Papal) 1668); M. (Two Sicilies) 1543 and (Italy) 1897; Count (Two Sicilies) 1553 and (Italy) 1897; B. (Two Sicilies) 1780 and (Italy) 1897; Signore (Lord) and Roman Noble 1854; Patrician (Venice) 1667 and (Genoa) 12 April 1786.

THE 12TH EARL OF NEWBURGH, Viscount of Kynnaird and **Lord Levingston of Flacraig**, also 11th (HRE) and 7th (Papal) Prince Rospigliosi, 14th (Two Sicilies) and 5th (Italy) Prince Castiglione, 11th Duke of Zagarolo, Marquis of Giuliana, Count of Chiusa, Baron of Valcorrente and La Miraglia, Lord of Aidone, Burgio, Contessa and Trappeto, also conscribed Roman Noble and Patrician of Ferrara, Genoa, Pistoia, Ravenna and Venice (Don Filippo Giambattista Francesco Aldo Maria Rospigliosi) [The Rt Hon The Earl of Newburgh, Piazza St Ambrogio 16, 20123 Milan, Italy]; *b* 4 July 1942; *s f* 1986; *m* 15 July 1972 *Baroness Donna Luisa, dau of Count Annibale Caccia Dominioni, and has:

1 +BENEDETTA FRANCESCA MARIA, *Mistress of Newburgh*; *b* 4 June 1974

Lineage: The LIVINGSTONs of Kinnaird, Fifeshire, probably descended from Robert, 2nd s of Sir John Livingston of Callendar (*k* Battle of Homildon 14 Sept 1402; ancestor by his est s of the Earls of Linlithgow (*see* LINLITHGOW, M, preliminary remarks) and Callendar).

HENRY LIVINGSTON of Falkirk; Provost Stirling 1553; *m* Margaret, dau of Sir James Forrester of Torwood and had a 4th s:

Sir JOHN LIVINGSTON of Abercorn; Master Stabler to MARY QUEEN OF SCOTS and JAMES VI; *m* (contract 15 Oct 1567) Elizabeth Carmichael and *d c* 1610, leaving a 3rd s:

Sir JOHN LIVINGSTON, 1st Bt (NS), of Kinnaird, Co Fife, so cr 29 June 1627, with remainder to his heirs male whatsoever; Groom Bedchamber to JAMES VI, Clerk Market to CHARLES I; had charter of (territorial) Barony of Kinnaird 26 March 1613; *m* 7 Feb 1618/9 Jane (*m* 3rd by 1645, as his 2nd w, 1st Baron Gorges of Dundalk and was *bur* 15 May 1665), dau of Richard Sproxto(u)n(e), of Wakefield, Steward Star Chamber, and widow of William Marwood, and was *bur* 12 March 1627/8, having had, with a dau (Dorothy, *m* 28 Nov 1641 2nd and last Baron Stanhope of Harrington):

Sir JAMES LIVINGSTON, 2nd Bt, and **1st Earl of Newburgh**, VISCOUNT OF KYNNAIRD and LORD LEVINGSTON [*sic*] OF FLACRAIG, so cr 31 Dec 1660, with remainder to heirs whomsoever, as also earlier VISCOUNT OF NEWBURGH (all S), so cr 13 Sept 1647, with remainder to heirs male of his body, PC

(S Feb 1660/1); *b c* 1622; *educ* Merton Coll Oxford; royalist Civil War (tried to free CHARLES I during latter's transfer under guard between Hurst and Windsor Castles Dec 1648); with CHARLES II at The Hague by 1650, accompanying him to Scotland later that year; fought Battle of Worcester 3 Sept 1651, following which fled to Paris; cmded Middleton's Regt in Low Countries 1656–57; Capt King's Body Gd and Col 4th Horse Gds 1660–70; MP Cirencester 1661–70, V-Adml Scotland 1666; *m* 1st by Dec 1648 Catherine (*dspm* 1650), dau of 2nd Earl of Suffolk (*see* SUFFOLK and BERKSHIRE, E) and widow of Lord George Stuart (*see* MORAY, E); *m* 2nd probably after April 1660 Anne (*bur* 26 May 1692), dau of Sir Henry Poole, of Saperton, Glos, and *d* 4 Dec 1670, leaving by her, with a yr s (James):

Sir CHARLES LIVINGSTON, 3rd Bt, and **2nd Earl of Newburgh**; *b c* 1662–66; served heir to his f 25 Jan 1684; *m* by licence 12 Sept 1692 Frances (*m* 2nd 1695 3rd Baron Bellew of Duleek (*see* BELLEW, B) and *d* 23 Feb 1736), dau of Francis, Lord Brudenell (*see* AILESBURY, M), and *dspm* 6 April 1694, when the btcy became dormant and the 1647 Viscountcy expired, leaving a posthumous and only dau:

CHARLOTTE MARIA Livingston, **Countess of Newburgh** in her own right; *b* 1694; *m* 1st *c* 22 Dec 1713 Thomas CLIFFORD (*d* 21 Feb 1718/19), er surv s of 2nd Baron Clifford of Chudleigh (*qv*), and had:

1 ANNE Clifford; *m* 1st 22 Dec 1739, as his 2nd w, James Joseph MAHONY, Count Mahony in France and Lt-Gen in the Neapolitan serv (*bapt* 5 Nov 1699; *d* on or after 10 April 1757), est s of Lt-Gen Count Daniel O'Mahony, Count of Castile, known in France as 'le fameux Mahoni', and *d* 1 April 1793, having had:

(1) CECILIA CARLOTTA FRANCESCA ANNA Mahony, COUNTESS MAHONY; *b* Naples 27 Dec 1740; *m* 18 May 1757 Benedetto GIUSTINIANI, 5th Prince Giustiniani (*d* 26 Feb 1793; his family reigned in Chios till 1364 and was expelled from there by the Turks 1566; the title of Prince was bestowed 22 Nov 1644 by INNOCENT X on his gggf Andrea, Marquis Giustiniani), and *dvm* 18 Feb 1789, having had, with two er sons (*d* young):

1a VINCENZO GIUSEPPE FILIPPO GRAZILIANO GIACOPO GASPARO BALDASSARO MELCHIOR DOMENICO GIUSTINIANI, *de jure* 6th EARL OF NEWBURGH, as which, however, took no proceedings to establish his right; also 6th Prince Giustiniani; *b* 2 Nov 1762; *m* 21 May 1789 Maria Nicoletta Giuseppa Francesca Raffaela Cornelia Teresa Melchiorra Gaspara Baldassara Angela Giovanna Lyuisa Giudetta, dau and heiress of Domenico Grillo, Duke of Mondragone (*cr* of Kingdom of Two Sicilies), and *d* 13 Nov 1826, leaving:

1b MARIA CECILIA AGATA ANNA JOSEFA LAURENZIA DONATA MELCHIORRA BALDASSARA GASPARA Giustiniani, **Countess of Newburgh** in her own right, as which recognised by Ho Lds 30 July 1858, also Princess Giustiniani; *bapt* 5 Feb 1796; *m* 21 Sept 1815 Carlo BANDINI, 4th Marquis Bandini, of Lanciano and Rustano, Papal States (*d* 5 June 1850; the Bandini family, originally from Umbria, established themselves in Rome in the 16th century, Carlo's ggf Alessandro having a papal marquisate conferred on him 30 May 1753), and *d* 8 Jan 1877, leaving:

1c SIGISMONDO NICCOLO VENANZIO GAETANO FRANCISCO, **8th Earl**

1c Nicoletta; *m* 1835 Don Carlo Manca, Marquis of Santa Croce and Villahermosa, and *d* 1836

2c Elizabetta; *m* 1841 Marquis Agostino Trionfi, of Ancona

3c Cristina; *m* 1845 Count Marcello Marcelli Fiori and *d* 9 July 1865

4c Maria; *m* 1851 Count Federico Pucci Boncambi, of Perugia

2a Lorenzo (Chevalier Giustiniani); renounced right of succession to the Princely title and the Giustiniani estates; *d unm* 22 March 1843

3a James, 7th and last Prince Giustiniani; Cardinal-Bp Albano; *d* 24 Feb 1843

1a Maria Isabella; *m* 1781 Francesco, Prince Ruspoli, and *d* 1783

2a Catherine; *m* 1777 Balthazar, Prince Odescalchi, and *d* 1813, leaving issue

1 (cont.) Lady Anne Mahony *m* 2nd (licence 13 April 1773) Don Carlo Severino and *d* Ischia 28 April 1793

2 Frances; *d* 1771 either unm or having *m* 20 Sept 1738 William Middleton, of Yorks

The **Countess of Newburgh** *m* 2nd 24 June 1724 Charles RADCLYFFE (*b* 3 Sept 1693; involved in Jacobite Uprising 1715; attainted accordingly; broke out of Newgate with 13 other Jacobites 11 Dec 1716; was Sec to the titular Prince Charles Edward; after his n John *d unm* 1731 styled himself 5th Earl of Derwentwater; was taken in a ship off Deal, presumably *en route* to Scotland though this was never proven, just prior to the 1745 Uprising and was beheaded 11 Dec 1746 on Tower Hill, his death sentence at the time of the earlier insurrection being held good notwithstanding the general pardon of 1716; 3rd s of 2nd Earl of Derwentwater by Lady Mary Tudor (illegitimate dau of CHARLES II by the singer Mary Davies) and bro of 3rd Earl of Derwentwater (attainted and beheaded 24 Feb 1715/6 for involvement in previous year's Jacobite Uprising), and *d* 4 Aug 1755, having by him had, with three other daus:

1 JAMES BARTHOLOMEW RADCLYFFE, **4th Earl of Newburgh**; *b* Vincennes 23 Aug 1725 (the titular James III stood godfather); captured with his f 1745 but quickly set free; claimed the Derwentwater estates on grounds that his f had been made tenant of them for life (hence his attainder did not militate against their being inherited by the son); an Act of Parl of 1749 set aside the estates for the benefit of Greenwich Hosp but assigned £30,000 (over £1,700,000 in late-1990s terms) to him and his siblings; *m* 11 Nov 1749 Barbara (*d* 12 Sept 1797), dau and eventually sole heiress of Anthony Kemp, of Slindon, Sussex, and *d* 2 Jan 1786, having had, with a dau (Anne, *b* 1758, *d unm* 18 Nov 1785):

(1) ANTHONY JAMES RADCLYFFE, **5th Earl of Newburgh**; *b* 20 June 1757; granted 1788 by Parl £2,500 p.a. (£112,000 in late-1990s terms) out of the Derwentwater estates to him and the heirs male of his body; *m* 30 June 1789 Anne (*dsp* 3 Aug 1861 aged 99), sis of Sir Thomas Webb, 6th Bt (*see* 1874 edn), and *dsp* 29 Nov 1814

2 James Clement; *b* Rome 5 Nov 1727; Maj-Gen in French serv; *m* but *dsp* 1788

3 Maria Francesca Giulielma; *b* Rome 1 April 1732; *m* 11 Feb 1755 Francis Eyre, of Warkworth Castle, Northumberland (*s* his nephew in the Hassop estates 1792 and *d* 7 Oct 1804), and *d* 27 Aug 1798, leaving, with other issue (*dsp*):

(1) Francis EYRE later RADCLYFFE-LIVINGSTONE-EYRE, of Warkworth and Hassop Hall, Notts; *b* 10 Feb 1762; from 1814 styled himself Earl of Newburgh in the mistaken belief that a foreign citizen (*see* against *de jure* 6th EARL) could not inherit a British peerage; *m* 29 Aug 1787 Dolly/Dorothy (*d* 2 Nov 1838), 4th and yst dau and coheir of John Gladwin, of Mansfield, Notts, Steward to the Duke of Portland, and *d* 23 Oct 1827, leaving, with a yst s and four other daus (all *d unm*):

1a Thomas, of Hassop; *b* 21 Oct 1790; also styled himself Earl of Newburgh, petitioning for recognition as such 1830, though no further proceedings taken; *m* 14 Nov 1817 Lady Margaret Kennedy (*d* 3 Sept 1889), 3rd dau of 1st Marquess of Ailsa (*qv*), and *dsp* 22 March 1833

2a Francis, of Hassop; *b* 7 July 1794; also styled himself Earl of Newburgh; Offr Coldstream Gds; *d unm* 18 Oct 1852

1a Maria Dorothea; *b* 13 July 1788; styled herself Countess of Newburgh in her own right; *m* 21 July 1836, as his 2nd w, Col Charles Leslie, 26th of Balquhain, KH (*d* 11 Jan 1870; *see also* LESLIE, Bt) and *dsp* 22 Nov 1852

(2) James, of Metz; *m* Thérèse Josephine de Chinancourt and *d* 1816, leaving an only dau (*d unm*)

The COUNTESS's only son,

SIGISMONDO NICCOLO VENANZIO GAETANO FRANCISCO BANDINI later GIUSTINIANI-BANDINI (added 1850), **8th Earl of Newburgh**, also 1st Prince Bandini-Giustiniani, so *cr* by PIUS IX 28 Jan 1863, with precedence of the old Princes Giustiniani (title confirmed by King of Italy 9 June 1893), Duke of Mondragone (as which *s* mother 1878, she having inherited the title from her gf) and 5th Marquis Bandini; *b* 30 June 1818; naturalised a Br subject 17 Aug 1857, Kt SMO Malta; *m* 14 Sept 1848 Maria Sofia Angelica (*d* 15 Dec 1898), dau of Cavaliere Giuseppe Maria Massani, of Rome, and *d* 3 Aug 1908, having had:

1 Charles; *b* 29 April 1860; *d* 2 Sept 1861

2 CHARLES GIUSTINIANI-BANDINI, **9th Earl of Newburgh**, also 2nd Prince Giustiniani-Bandini; *b* 1 Jan 1862; *m* 8 Aug 1885 Donna Maria Lanza di Trabia (*d* 22 Jan 1949), dau of Giuseppe, Prince of Trabia and Butera, of Palermo, and *d* 1941, having had:

(1) Sigismondo Maria Bandino Giuseppe, *Viscount Kynnaird* and *Duke of Mondragone*; *b* 20 June 1886; *m* 4 April 1910 Teresa (*m* 2nd 25 Aug 1921 Ferenc Adamacz, Hungarian Min Brussels, and *d* 1 May 1969), dau of Prince Ugo Boncompagni Lodovisi, est s of Rodolfo, Prince of Piombino, and *dvp* 4 Nov 1918

(2) Giuseppe Maria; *b* 3 Sept 1896; served Italian Army WW I; *ka* Monfalcone, *bur* 14 Aug 1916

(3) Lorenzo Maria; *b* 14 April 1898; *d* an infant

(1) MARIA SOFIA GIUSEPPINA Giustiniani-Bandini, **Countess of Newburgh** in her own right, also Princess Giustiniani-Bandini; *b* 4 May 1889; *m* 3 May 1922 Count Manfredi GRAVINA Di RAMACOS, High Commr Danzig (*d* 19 Sept 1932), and *d* 30 April 1977

1 Nicoletta Maria; *d* young 15 May 1855

2 Carolina Maria Elena Gioacchina; *b* 10 June 1851; *m* 8 April 1872 Guardino, Count dei Colleoni Porto and Count di Solza of Venice, and *d* 4 Nov 1918

3 Elena Maria Concetta Isabella Gioacchina Giuseppa; *b* 8 June 1853; *m* 25 June 1876 Camillo, Prince Rospigliosi (*d* 6 June 1915), Cdr Guardia Nobile, and *d* 1 May 1950, having had:

(1) Giambattista Pio Sigismondo Francesco; *b* 5 May 1877; *m* 1st 16 May 1903 Ethel Julia (*d* 5 Nov 1924), dau of Isaac Bronson, of New York; *m* 2nd 12 Feb 1926 Princess Flaminia (*d* 29 Jan 1948), dau of Prince Baldassare Odescalchi, and *d* 5 April 1956, having by his 1st w had:

1a GIULIO CESARE TADDEO COSIMO, **11th Earl**

1a Elena Maria Alice; *b* 21 Feb 1904; *m* 25 Nov 1926 Antonio, Duke Lante Montefeltro della Rovere (*d* 1954), and *d* 1974, having had:

1b +Pietro [Don Pietro, Duke Lante della Rovere, Fundo Millaray, Casella 176, Rengo, Chile]; *b* 22 Dec 1928; Roman Noble and Noble of Foligno; *m* 1st 6 Dec 1953 Marianne La Fourcade Ithuralde; *m* 2nd 1989 his cousin *Donna Livia, 6th dau of Don Filippo, Prince Lancellotti, of Rome, and by his 1st w had:

1c +Marcantonio Maria Francesco; *b* 1957

1c +Angela Maria; *b* 1956

2c +Patrizia; *b* 1959

3c +Livia Francesca; *b* 1963

2b Lodovico; *b* 10 April 1931; *m* 1958 *Lya Marquez Mendez [Donna Lodovico Montefeltro della Rovere, Calle Los Cortijos, Edificio Country Suites, Urbanization Campoalegro, Caracas, Venezuela] and *d* 1986, leaving:

1c +Federico Maria; *b* 1959

1c +Alessandra; *b* 1963

2c +Elena

3b +Francesco; *b* 15 May 1933; *m* 4 Sept 1957 *Carla, dau of Marquis Franco Spinola di Pasturana and Countess Maria Laura Floresi Dondini Casana, and has:

1c +Antonio; *b* 1962

1c +Silvia; *b* 1965

4b +Alessandro; *b* 27 July 1936; *m* *Marina Punturieri and has had:

1c Francesco; *b* 1966

1c +Lucrezia

5b +Federico [Don Federico Montefeltro della Rovere, Calle Rengo 550, Los Angeles, Chile]; *b* 11 Dec 1938; *m* 1965 *Marcella Sandrez and has:

1c +Francesco René Maria Baltazar; *b* 1966

2c +Pietro Alessandro Maria Gaspar; *b* 1971

1b +Anna Vittoria [Sister Maria Carmela del Bambino Gesu, Carmelo delle Tre Madonne, Rome, Italy]; *b* 8 Dec 1927; Carmelite nun

2b +Angela [Donna Angela Igliori, via Bitossi 34, Rome, Italy]; *b* 1 Feb 1930; *m* 26 April 1950 *Massimo Igliori and has:

    1c +Ulisse Maria; *b* 1961

    2c +Alessandro; *b* 1963

    1c +Paola; *b* 17 Sept 1952

    2c +Benedetta; *b* 7 Nov 1954

    3c +Maria Gaia; *b* 1959

2a Margherita Maria Francesca; *b* 4 Feb 1909

3a Giovanna Ethel; *b* 9 Jan 1911; *m* 27 Oct 1937 Baron Umberto Duranti Valentini

(2) Tommaso Clemente Francesco; *b* 28 June 1879; *m* 5 June 1930 Beatrice dei Marchesi Viti-Mariani (*d* 1964) and *d* 21 April 1958

(3) Francesco Luigi Giuseppe; *b* 8 July 1880; *m* 30 June 1914 Laura Macdonald Stallo (*d* 1972), of Cincinnati, USA, and *d* 1943, leaving:

1a +Francesca [Princess Francesca Rospigliosi, 4000 Cathedral Ave NW, Apt 12B, Washington DC 20016, USA]; *b* 15 March 1921; *m* 12 Dec 1949 Alexander Clausen Schmidt (*d* 1972), has resumed her maiden name and has:

    1b +William Francis [William Schmidt, 4000 Cathedral Ave NW, Apt 518, Washington DC 20016, USA]; *b* 21 Sept 1950

    2b +Camillo Alexander; *b* 26 Oct 1953

    1b +Laura Maria [Mrs Joseph Pizzarello, 8507 Fountain Valley Drive, Gaithersburg, MD 20879, USA]; *b* 7 July 1952; *m* 1988 *Joseph Pizzarello

2a Camilla; *b* 31 Aug 1922; *m* 1st 1945 John Eden Grace; *m* 2nd 1960 *Sam Fry Jr and *d* 1992

(4) Lodovico Guardino Carlo Francesco; *b* 16 Oct 1881; *m* 14 April 1904 (*judicial separation* 1912) Mildred, dau of William Stanley Haseltine, of Rome and New York, and *d* 30 Oct 1917, leaving:

1a Guardino Guglielmo Francesco Oberto Maria Giuseppe; *b* 17 Dec 1906; *d* unm 14 Oct 1956

2a Guglielmo Camillo Carlo; *b* 19 Sept 1908; *m* 6 July 1933 (*divorce* 1959) Hon Helen Lyon-Dalberg-Acton, 3rd dau of 2nd Baron Acton (*qv*), and *d* 26 Oct 1990, leaving:

    1b +Ludovico Giulio Francesco Maria [Prince Ludovico Rospigliosi, 116 via del Seminario, OD186 Rome, Italy]; *b* 30 June 1934; Kt Hon and Devotion SMO Malta (Historian to the Order), Kt Justice Constantinian Order of St George, Offr Order Ad Merito Melitensi; *m* 19 Dec 1960 *Giovanna Sallier de la Tour, yr dau of 8th Marquis of Cordon and Combloux Sallier de la Tour, and has:

        1c +Camillo Carlo Felice Francesco Maria; *b* 13 June 1969

        1c +Maria Lucrezia Elena Francesca Carolina Margherita Vittoria; *b* 11 May 1966

        2c +Olimpia Francesca Maria; *b* 6 Jan 1975

    2b +Guardino Ricardo Carlo Francesco Maria [Prince Guardino Rospigliosi, 119 Whitchurch Rd, Tavistock, Devon]; *b* 6 Sept 1940; Kt Justice Constantinian Order of St George; *m* 1st 22 March 1961 (*divorce* 1975) Veronica Shan, yr dau of Lt-Col Wilfred York Price, of Chepstow, and has:

        1c +Pericles Stephen Guardino Francesco Maria; *b* 29 Dec 1961; *m* 1987 *Pauline Cheriou Lyzette, dau of Lloyd Power, and has:

            1d +Caspian Guglielmo Francesco Maria; *b* 1988

        2c +Saladin Gabriel Charles Francesco Maria; *b* 1964

        3c +Joseph Darius Francesco Maria; *b* 1970

    2b (cont.) Prince Guardino Rospigliosi *m* 2nd 1976 *Patricia Harvey, dau of Robert Campbell, of Langley, Bucks, and by her has:

        1c +Elissa Alicia Elena Francesca Maria; *b* 1977

        2c +Ezinna Margherita Barbara Francesca Maria; *b* 1979

    1b +Giovanna Maria Carolina Annunziata [Princess Giovanna Rospigliosi, 47 Josephine Ave, London SW2 2JL]; *b* 16 June 1935; *m* 15 Sept 1961 (*divorce* 1989) Giles Frere Wordsworth (*d* 1992), 2nd s of Andrew Wordsworth, and has:

        1c +Andrew Guardino Theodore; *b* 23 Aug 1962

        1c +Catherine Columbine Maria Annunziata; *b* 25 Jan 1964

        2c +Anne Lucy Susannah; *b* 1966

(5) Ferdinando Carlo Nicola Francesco; *b* 24 July 1883; *m* 1st 23 July 1910 (*annulled* 1937) Baroness Yvonne Leonie Pauline Marie Ghislaine (*d* 23 May 1946), dau of Baron Albert de Villenfagne de Sorinnes; *m* 2nd 23 Feb 1938 Maria Teresa Montanucci and *d* 24 May 1950, having had by his 1st w:

1a Camilla Tatiana; *b* 12 Jan 1914; *d* 19 Feb 1921

(6) Clemente Giambattista Francesco; *b* 23 Nov 1893; *m* July 1922 Clara Weil, of Boston, USA

(1) Ottavia Maria Francesca; *b* 27 May 1878; *m* 2 Oct 1898 Roberto Vimercati Sanseverino, Count of Castel Palazzo (*d* 1945), and had:

1a Ottaviano; *b* 13 July 1899

2a Lionello; *b* 1 April 1911; *m* 15 June 1936 *Oretta dei Conti Ceriana Mayñeri and had:

    1b +Lodovico; *b* 10 May 1940; *m* 1964 *Donna Agnesa Tosti dei Duchi di Valminuta and has:

        1c +Ottaviano; *b* 1966

        2c +Giralamo

    1b +Roberta; *b* 5 Sept 1942

1a +Francesca; *b* 5 Aug 1917; *m* June 1937 *Enrico Budini Gattai and has:

    1b +Antonello; *b* 7 June 1940

    2b +Leopoldo; *b* 18 Sept 1942

    3b +Roberto; *b* 25 July 1946

    4b +Federico; *b* 16 April 1948

    5b +Francesco; *b* 19 Oct 1949

    6b +Ferdinando; *b* 13 May 1951

    7b +Ruggero; *b* 18 Jan 1955

    8b +Rodolfo; *b* 21 Feb 1957

    1b +Giulia; *b* 8 July 1938

2b +Maria Vittoria; *b* 1 Nov 1944

3b +Nicoletta; *b* 21 March 1953

4b +Cristina; *b* 21 Feb 1957

2a +Laura; *b* 15 July 1923; *m* 21 July 1945 *Livio Calenda dei Baroni di Tavani, S/Ldr Italian Air Force, and has:

    1b +Landolfo; *b* 20 April 1946

    2b +Michelangelo; *b* 19 Sept 1953

    1b +Maria Nuvola; *b* 1 Sept 1947

    2b +Maria Gloria; *b* 2 April 1951

    3b +Maria Luce; *b* 2 April 1951

    4b +Benedetta; *b* 19 June 1955

    5b +Candida; *b* 1962

(2) Maria Camilla Giulia Francesca; *b* 23 Feb 1886; *d* unm 9 May 1953

(3) Maria Maddalena Clementina; *b* 8 May 1889; *m* 26 Sept 1909 Ardicino della Porta, Count of Carpine, Biscina and Frontone, and *d* 1966, leaving:

1a Giovanni Ubaldo; *b* 8 May 1914; *m* *Emma Brugliese and *d* 1967, leaving:

    1b +Ferdinando; *b* 23 March 1951

    2b +Carlo; *b* 7 Sept 1956

    1b +Giuliana; *b* 6 Sept 1947

2a +Carlo [Count Carlo della Porta, Le Carpini, Montone, Perugia, Italy]; *b* 30 May 1920; *m* 9 June 1949 *Laura, Countess Pignatti Morano and Countess of Custozza, and has had:

    1b +Giammaria; *b* 13 April 1950

    2b Lodovico; *b* 21 Oct, *d* 28 Oct 1952

    3b +Roberto; *b* 5 April 1955

    4b +Giulio; *b* 6 April 1956

    1b +Anna Barbara; *b* 25 July 1951

    2b +Maria Camilla; *b* 3 May 1962

    3b +Maria Veronica; *b* 1964

3a +Enzo Maria; *b* 9 Sept 1922

1a +Laura; *b* 25 Feb 1911; *m* 20 Jan 1951 Lorenzo Scotti Douglas, Count of Vigoleno (*d* 1965)

2a +Lucia; *b* 29 April 1912; *m* 2 Oct 1938 Prof Dr Gaetano Gentile and has:

    1b +Giovanni; *b* 20 Sept 1939; *m* 1964 *Giovanna Ferragamo

    2b +Fortunato; *b* 21 June 1945

    1b +Maddalena; *b* 5 Nov 1940; *m* 1966 *Giuseppe Passetti

    2b +Lodovica; *b* 5 Oct 1943

3a +Maria; *b* 25 March 1917; *m* 15 June 1940 *Giuseppe, Count Forni, and has:

    1b +Carlo Francesco Giuseppe Gaetano Ardicino; *b* 19 March 1941

    2b +Giulio Maria Giuseppe Pietro Canisio Gaetano Anastasio; *b* 27 April 1946

    1b +Anna Maria Maddalena dei Pazzi Giulia Francesca dei Paolo Giuseppina Antonia Gaetana; *b* 2 April 1942

    2b +Teodolinda Maria Assunta Laura Antonia Giuseppina Gioacchina; *b* 16 Aug 1943

    3b +Maria Cristina Beatrice Paola Giuseppina Antonia Gaetana; *b* 12 Sept 1944

    4b +Elena Maria Teresa; *b* 15 Oct 1949

(4) Carolina; *b* 14 Oct 1891; *d* unm 13 Oct 1961

4 Nicoletta Maria Nazarena Gioacchina Margherita; *b* 23 Oct 1863; *m* 20 Feb 1881 Mario, Duke Grazioli, of Rome (*d* 12 Dec 1936), and *d* 26 Aug 1938, leaving:

(1) Pio; *b* 29 Aug 1886; *m* 1st 23 Jan 1908 Donna Rufina (*d* 30 Jan 1942), dau of Don Filippo Massimo, 1st Prince Lancelotti, and had, with other issue:

1a Mario; *b* 29 Nov 1908

2a Massimiliano; *b* 4 Aug 1911; *m* 11 July 1942 Isabella Perrone (*d* 1988) and was kidnapped (presumed *d*) 1977, leaving:

    1b +Giulio [Duke Grazioli, Palazzo Grazioli, via del Plebiscito 102, 00186 Rome, Italy]; *b* 10 June 1943

1a +Caterina [Countess Gabriele Emo, via del Plebiscito 102, 00186 Rome, Italy]; *m* 15 June 1940 Count Gabriele Emo Capodilista Maldura (*d* 1983) and has:

    1b +Giorgio [Count Giorgio Emo, 45 Brunswick Gdns, London W8]; *b* 30 April 1941; *m* 1976 *Christiane Hoberg and has issue:

        1c +Alvise Luca; *b* 1981

        2c +Pietro Antonio; *b* 1990

        1c +Rufina; *b* 1978

        2c +Beatrix; *b* 1984

    2b +Giovanni [Count Giovanni Emo, 48 Cheyne Walk, London SW3]; *b* 16 Feb 1944; *m* 1st 1981 (*divorce* 1988) Lady Arabella Avice Diana Sackville, only dau of 10th Earl De La Warr (*qv*); *m* 2nd 1989 *Madeleine Maria, yst dau of C J de Jong, of Glassenbury Pk, Kent, and by her has:

        1c +Gabriele Filippo; *b* 1990

        1c +Olimpia; *b* 1992

2a +Anna; *b* 1916; *m* 1942 Don Francesco, Marquis di Caravita, Prince of Sirignano, Neapolitan Patrician, and *d* 1987, leaving:

    1b +Giuseppe; *b* 1944

    2b +Alvaro Pietro; *b* 1945

    1b +Nila [Donna Nila Pintado, Palazzo Grazioli, via S Nicola del Lesarini 3, 00186 Rome, Italy; Villa Castello, Capri, Naples, Italy; Paseo de la Reforma 1670, 11000 Mexico DF]; *b* 1951; *m* 1975 *Ricardo Pintado Rivero and has:

        1c +Ricardo Pintado Caravita di Sirignano; *b* 1975

        2c +Tazio Pintado Caravita di Sirignano; *b* 1978

        3c +Diego Pintado Caravita di Sirignano; *b* 1983

(1) (cont.) The Duke Grazioli *m* 2nd 1948 *Cleo Conversi and *d* 1 Sept 1954, having by her had:

3a +Ricardo [Duke of Magliano, via Ginepro 10, Orbetello Scalo, Grosseto, Toscana, Italy]; *b* 1943; Baron of Castelporziano, Nobile di San Marino and Duke of Magliano; *m* 1st Clara Randaccio; *m* 2nd *Donna Patrizia Musso di Peralta and by her has:

  1b +Giorgiana Pia Olimpia; *b* 1986

5 Maria Cristina Isabella Agnese Gioacchina; *b* 20 Feb 1866; nun; *d* Dec 1959
6 (Maria) Isabella Giovanna Teresa Gioacchina; *b* 17 April 1867; *m* 17 Nov 1898 1st Baron Howard of Penrith (*qv*) and *d* 20 Jan 1963, leaving issue
7 Maria Cecilia Pia Anna Gioacchina; *b* 20 Nov 1871; *m* 8 Dec 1920 Gen Count Paolo Pielia (*d* 1 April 1952)
8 Anna Maria; *b* 19 July, *d* 29 July 1874

The 9th EARL's great-nephew
  GIULIO CESARE TADDEO COSIMO ROSPIGLIOSI, **11th Earl of Newburgh**, also 10th Prince Rospigliosi, 10th Duke of Zagarolo, etc; *b* 26 Oct 1907; *m* 25 Nov 1940 *Donna Giulia Visconti di Modrone [Giulia Princess Rospigliosi, via Corridoni 3, 20122 Milan, Italy], and *d* 1986, leaving:

1 FILIPPO GIAMBATTISTA FRANCESCO ALDO MARIA ROSPIGLIOSI, **12th and present Earl of Newburgh**
1 +Francesco Guido Carlo Antonio Maria [Prince Francesco Rospigliosi, viale Elvezia 24, Milan 20154, Italy]; *b* 8 Jan 1947; *m* *Clothilde, dau of Henri Rival de Rouville, and has:

  (1) +Alessandro Guilio Enrico Francesco; *b* 1978

The ROSPIGLIOSI family, originally of Pistoia, are first heard of in the 13th century. Among its members have been Giovanni, a condottiere in the service of POPE MARTIN V, and Giovanni, a general in the papal armies of PAUL III. Giulio di Girolamo Rospigliosi was made a Cardinal in 1637 and elected Pope as CLEMENT IX in 1667. Giacomo, the latter's nephew, was made Cardinal by his uncle in 1667.

Giovanni Battista Rospigliosi, a general in the papal armies, acquired from the Ludovisi family the Duchy of Zagarolo. He also married Camilla Pallavicini, niece of Cardinal Sforza Pallavicini, last of the Roman branch of that family (who were originally Genoese) and heir to the Lordships of Colonna and Gallicano. Cardinal Lazzaro Pallavicini made Giovanni Battista Rospigliosi his heir, the latter accordingly assuming the titles of Prince of Gallicano and taking the surname Pallavicini. The line died out in 1835, however.

Newby

Creation: B. (LP, UK) 2 Aug 1997.

THE BARON NEWBY, of Rothwell, Co W Yorks (Richard Mark Newby, OBE (1990)) [The Rt Hon The Lord Newby OBE, 4 Rockwells Gdns, London SE19 1HW]; *b* 14 Feb 1953; *educ* Rothwell GS and St Catherine's Coll Oxford; Customs and Excise: admin trainee 1974, Priv Sec to Perm Sec 1977–79, Pncpl Planning Unit 1979–81, Sec to SDP Parly Ctee 1981, Staff SDP HQ 1981, Nat Sec SDP 1983–88; dir of Corporate Affairs Rosehaugh plc 1991– (exec 1985–90), dir Matrix Communications Consultancy Ltd 1992–; Chm Reform Publications Ltd 1993–; dir External Communication Lib Dem Election Team 1996–97; *m* 1978 *Ailsa Ballantyne, yr dau of Baron Thomson of Monifieth (*qv*), and has issue

Lineage: FRANK NEWBY; *m* Kathleen — and has:

RICHARD MARK, *cr* a **Baron**

NEWMAN of Cecil Lodge

LABORE · ET · HONORE

Arms: Arg. an ostrich ppr., on a chief az. a lozenge of the field between two bezants. **Crest:** Out of an antique coronet or a springbok's head ppr. **Motto:** *Labore et honore* ('With toil and honour'). **Creation:** Bt. (UK) 6 Feb 1912.

SIR FRANCIS HUGH CECIL NEWMAN, 4TH BT, of Cecil Lodge, Newmarket, Co Cambridge [Sir Francis Newman Bt, Burloes Hall, Royston, Herts SG8 9NE]; *b* 12 June 1963; *s f* 1987; *educ* Eton and Pennsylvania U; *m* 1990 *Katharine M, yr dau of (Cecil Ralph) Timothy Edwards, of Grendon Court, Upton Bishop, Herefs, and has:

1 +THOMAS RALPH GERARD; *b* 7 Jan 1993
2 +Arthur Guy Hugh; *b* 28 April 1996
1 *Lily May Violet; *b* 1994

Lineage: GUSTAV NEUMANN, of Fuerth, Bavaria; merchant and banker; *b* 12 May 1819 (s of Simon Neumann, of Baden); *m* 12 July 1853 Babette (*d* 20 Dec 1895), dau of Hirsch Marx Goldscheider, of Fuerth, and *d* 2 March 1876, having had:

1 Hugo; *b* 16 Dec 1855
2 SIGMUND (Sir), **1st Bt**
3 Ludvig; *b* 13 Aug 1859; *m* 1888 Rose (*dsp* 1895), dau of Martin Lillenfield, and *d* 14 Aug 1934
1 Betty; *m* 1886 Julius Kahnweiler and *d* 1908

The 2nd son,
  Sir SIGMUND NEUMANN later NEWMAN (deed poll 9 March 1936), **1st Bt** (UK), so *cr* 6 Feb 1912; *b* Bavaria 25 May 1857; ptnr S Neumann & Co, merchants, of Salisbury House, London EC, and Newmann, Luebeck & Co, bankers, dir African Banking Corp and London Jt Stock Bank; *m* 25 Aug 1890 Anna Allegra (*d* 14 June 1951), est dau of Jacques Hakim, and had:

1 CECIL GUSTAVUS JACQUES (Sir), **2nd Bt**
2 Guy Arthur NEUMANN later NEWMAN (deed poll 9 March 1936), JP (Co London 1940); *b* 24 March 1904; *educ* Eton and Univ Coll Oxford (BA, MA 1934); memb LCC E Islington 1934–37, dir Woodcote Grove Estate and Stanners Ltd, Capt RA WW II; *m* 19 Dec 1930 Hon Jean Sybil Loch (*d* 1994), 2nd dau of 2nd Baron Loch (see 1970 edn), and *d* 1982, leaving:

  (1) *Mary Ella [Mrs Mary Edgedale, 34 Edna St, London SW11]; *b* 3 Oct 1931; *m* 19 July 1954 (*divorce* 19–) Maj William Richard Edgedale, Life Gds, only s of His Honour Judge Samuel Richard Edgedale, QC (see ALDENHAM and HUNSDON OF HUNSDON, B), and has:

    1a *James William; *b* 14 Jan 1963; *m* 1993 *Sarah Louise Jenkinson
    1a *Mirabel Jean Elaine; *b* 13 June 1955
    2a *Emma Margaret [Mrs Emma dos Santos, 55 Rowena Crescent, London SW11 2PT]; *b* 20 Aug 1956; *m* 1993 (*divorce* 1997) Orlando dos Santos and has:

      1b *Frederick Andrew William; *b* 1986
      1b *Ella Clementine; *b* 1989
      2b *Charlotte Maria Elizabeth; *b* 1993
    3a *Sarah Jane; *b* 12 Dec 1965

  (2) *Diana Margaret Anna [Miss Diana Newman, 23 Glebe Place, London SW3 5LD]; *b* 30 April 1934
  (3) *Ann Elizabeth [Mrs Richard MacDonnell, Ivy Lodge, Front St, Churchill, Somerset BS25 5NB]; *b* 22 April 1937; *m* 6 Feb 1965 *Richard James Randal MacDonnell, er s of Edward Geoffrey Randal MacDonnell, of Pixeycombe, Meavy, Devon, and has:

    1a *Simon Guy Randal; *b* 16 May 1968; *m* 1996 *Sarah Catrin Evans
    2a *Crispin Paul Geoffrey Randal; *b* 1974
    1a *Tania Alice; *b* 17 Sept 1966

1 Sybil Rose; *m* 1st 17 Feb 1920 (*annulled* 1921) Capt Victor Malcolm Wombwell, Scots Gds, est surv s of Graham Menzies of Hallyburton; *m* 2nd 24 Oct 1923 1st Baron Grimston of Westbury (*qv*) and *d* 19 Nov 1977, leaving issue
2 Rosie Violet Nina Millicent; FRGS
3 Ella Julie; *d unm* 15 Feb 1925

Sir SIGMUND *d* 13 Sept 1916; his er s,
  Sir CECIL GUSTAVUS JACQUES NEUMANN later NEWMAN (roy licence 23 Jan 1936 for himself and issue), **2nd Bt**, JP and CC Herts, High Sheriff 1939; *b* 9 June 1891; *educ* Eton and Balliol Coll Oxford; Capt 1st Norfolk Yeo 1911–20, Staff Capt 1917–20, served WW I, Pres Nat Assoc Fishery Bd 1946–51, dir Woodcote Grove and Haling Down Estates; *m* 31 Jan 1922 Joan Florence Mary, CBE (1964), SStJ, Pres N Herts C Assoc (*d* 15 Sept 1969), er dau of Canon Hon Robert Grimston (see VERULAM, E), and had:

1 Cecil Hugh Grimston; *b* 19 Feb 1924; *d* 8 Nov 1928
2 GERARD ROBERT HENRY SIGISMUND (Sir), **3rd Bt**
3 +John Francis [John Francis Newman Esq, Compton Park, Compton Chamberlayne, Wilts SP3 5DE]; *b* 25 Jan 1930; *educ* Eton and RMC Sandhurst; late Lt RHG, dir Rom River Co, Blick plc, Galloway Gp; *m* 17 April 1963 *Caroline Henrietta, yr dau of Lt-Col Angus John Campbell Rose, of Comrie, Perthshire, and Mrs Robert James Stephen, of Jersey, and has:

  (1) +Anthony John Cecil; *b* 27 June 1966; *educ* Harrow and RAC Cirencester
  (1) *Henrietta (Hetty) Mary Alison; *b* 23 Jan 1964; *m* 1989, as his 2nd w, *7th Earl of Caledon (*qv*)
  (2) *Sarahjane Caroline; *b* 20 April 1968; *educ* Bristol U

1 *Annabel Cecilia Mary [Mrs Peter Beckwith-Smith, Bishopstone House, Salisbury, Wilts SP5 4AS]; *b* 1922; *m* 9 Dec 1947 Maj Peter Merton Beckwith-Smith (*d* 1984), er s of Maj-Gen Merton Beckwith-Smith, DSO, MC, of Aberarder, Strathnairn, Inverness-shire, and has:

  (1) *James Merton; *b* 1948; *educ* Tabley House, Knutsford
  (1) *Anne Honor Mary, LVO (1990) [Miss Anne Beckwith-Smith LVO, Bishopstone House, Salisbury, Wilts SP5 4AS]; *b* 1951; Ldy-in-Waiting to HRH THE (later DIANA) PRINCESS OF WALES 1981
2 *Lynette Johanna Violet; *b* 1927
3 *Rosalind Cynthia [Mrs Francis Watson, Chestnut Brow, Church Rd, Bramshott, Hants]; *b* 24 Sept 1936; *m* 28 June 1969 Francis Albert John Watson (*d* 1973), s of Albert Elijah Watson, of Kingswood, Surrey, and has:

  (1) *Jeremy John Albert; *b* 2 Nov 1970
  (1) *Joanna Clare Elizabeth; *b* 1972

Sir CECIL *d* 21 May 1955; his er surv s,

Sir Gerard Robert Henry Sigismund Newman, 3rd Bt; b 19 July 1927; educ Eton and Jesus Coll Oxford (BA 1951); dir Rom River Co, chm Galloway Gp, High Sheriff Herts 1981–82; m 15 Dec 1960 Caroline Philippa (m 2nd 17 July 1996 Andrew F B Crawshaw), only child of Brig Alfred Geoffrey Neville, CBE, MC, DL, JP (see BRAYBROOKE, B), and d 1987, leaving:

1 Sir FRANCIS HUGH CECIL NEWMAN, **4th and present Bt**
2 +Geoffrey John; b 12 Dec 1966; educ Eton and Bristol U
3 +Christopher George; b 5 May 1969; educ Eton and Napier U Edinburgh
1 *Susanna Philippa Helen [Mrs Julian Gorst, Oxcombe Manor, Horncastle, Lincs LN9 6LU]; b 9 Jan 1962; m 1985 *Julian Eldon Gorst, est s of Sir John Michael Gorst, MP (C) Hendon N (later Hendon) 1970–97, and has:
  (1) *Henry Eldon Geoffrey; b 1991
  (2) *Edward John; b 1997
  (1) *Rose Philippa Tatiana; b 1990

NEWMAN of Mamhead

Arms: Az. three demi-lions rampant couped arg., semée of cross-crosslets sa., langued gu. **Crest:** A lion rampant per chevron az. gutté-de-l'eau and arg. gutté de sang. **Motto:** *Probitas verus honos* ('Honesty is the true honour'). **Creation:** Bt. (UK) 17 March 1836.

SIR GEOFFREY ROBERT NEWMAN, 6TH BT, of Mamhead, Co Devon [Sir Geoffrey Newman Bt, Blackpool House, Dartmouth, S Devon TQ6 0RG]; b 2 June 1947; s f 1968; educ Heatherdown Ascot, Kelly Coll Tavistock; Lt 1st Bn Gren Gds 1967–70, Lt SAS (TAVR) to 1979, dir Blackpool Sands (Devon) Utilities, FRGS; m 1980 *Mary Elizabeth, yr dau of Col Sir Martin St John Valentine Gibbs, KCVO, CB, DSO, TD (see ALDENHAM and HUNSDON OF HUNSDON, B), and has:

1 +ROBERT MELVIL; b 4 Oct 1985
1 *Frances Joyce; b 11 Nov 1983
2 *Elsie Laura; b 1987
3 *Louisa Bridget; b 1990

Lineage: RICHARD NEWMAN; m Anne — and had:
1 THOMAS
2 John, of Dartmouth; b 7 Sept 1593; m 12 Feb 1616 Ellen (d 8 April 1662), dau of Zacharie Irish, and d 1640, leaving issue
3 George; m —
1 Mary; m 26 June 1585 John Parr
2 Judith; m Christopher Strange

The est s,
THOMAS NEWMAN, of Exeter; m Zabian (d 2 Nov 1643 aged 66), dau of Gilbert Staplehill, merchant privateer, of Dartmouth, and d c 1650, leaving:
1 Thomas
2 Richard, of Exeter; b 1607
3 Edward; b 1610; d 1611
4 Edward (Rev); Vicar Loddiswell, Devon
5 ALEXANDER
1 Zabian; b 7 March 1605; m John Holder, of Exeter

The yst s,
ALEXANDER NEWMAN; b 26 Dec 1614; m Blanch (d 1647 aged 36), dau of Thomas Irish, and had, with a yr s and dau:

RICHARD NEWMAN, of Dartmouth; bapt Dec 1607; m 12 April 1666 Elizabeth, dau of Robert Holdsworth, of Modbury, and had, with other issue:
1 ROBERT
1 Elizabeth; m Robert Holdsworth, of Modbury, and had an only child:
  (1) Mary; m 1733 her cousin R Newman, of Dartmouth (see below)

RICHARD NEWMAN d 20 Jan 1679; his s,
ROBERT NEWMAN, of Dartmouth; bapt 11 June 1674; m 1st Joyce, dau of J Lydstone, of Townstall, and had:
1 Richard; bapt 11 Nov 1701; m — Mason, of Gloucester, and d 1741
2 ROBERT

1 Joyce; m Ambrose Weston, of Poole, Dorset
2 Elizabeth; m Nathaniel Terry, of Dartmouth
ROBERT NEWMAN m 2nd 1715 his cousin Elizabeth, dau of Robert Holdsworth, of Modbury, and d 1739

His 2nd s,
ROBERT NEWMAN, of Dartmouth; bapt 31 March 1704; m 1733 his cousin Mary, only child of Robert Holdsworth, and had, with other issue:
1 Robert, of Dartmouth and Stoke Fleming, Devon, JP; bapt 9 Dec 1735; m 1766 Anne, sis of Arthur Holdsworth, Govr Dartmouth Castle, and dsp
2 Richard; d young
3 Thomas, of Dartmouth; b 1740; m Oporto 1774 Sarah, dau of John Page, of London, and had, with other issue:
  (1) ROBERT WILLIAM (Sir), **1st Bt**
  (1) Harriet; m 1802 Thomas Holdsworth Hunt, JP, of Dartmouth, and d 1808, having had issue. He d 5 Jan 1845

THOMAS NEWMAN d 3 Dec 1802; his s,
Sir Robert William Newman, 1st Bt (UK), of Mamhead, so cr 17 March 1836; b 18 Aug 1776; MP Exeter, High Sheriff Devon 1827; m 21 Sept 1813 Mary Jane (d 28 July 1834), 3rd dau of Richard Denne, of Mariteau House, Winchelsea, Sussex, and d 24 Jan 1848, having had:
1 **Sir Robert Lydston Newman, 2nd Bt**; b 19 Feb 1822; Capt Gren Gds; ka Battle of Inkerman 5 Nov 1854
2 **Sir Lydston Newman, 3rd Bt**, JP, DL Devon; High Sheriff 1871, Capt 7th Hus; b 14 Nov 1823; m 28 Feb 1867 Emma (d 17 Nov 1911), dau of Field E D Dudley, and d 29 Dec 1892, leaving:
  (1) **Sir Robert Hunt Stapylton Dudley Lydston Newman, 4th Bt**, and 1st and last BARON MAMHEAD (UK), of Exeter, Co Devon, so cr 5 Dec 1931, JP, DL; CC Devon, MP (U) Exeter 1918–29 and (Ind) 1929–31; b 27 Oct 1871; d unm 2 Nov 1945, when the Barony expired
  (1) Lily Lydston; b 12 Sept 1862; m 12 Dec 1882 Maj Edward Murphy, 5th Dragoon Gds, est s of Patrick Edward Murphy, of Ballinacloon, Co Westmeath, and d 30 Aug 1894, leaving issue
  (2) Mary Jane Cosens Lydston; b 15 Nov 1868; m 8 June 1904 Frederick Robert Lumley, s of B Lumley, and d 17 Aug 1918. He d 20 Feb 1948
3 Thomas Holdsworth, JP; Capt Devon Yeo Cav; b 6 Feb 1825; m 21 April 1864 Elizabeth Laura (d 7 June 1909), est dau of Martin Tucker Smith, MP, and d 27 Jan 1894, leaving:
  (1) Robert Lydston, JP Devon; Lt City London, High Sheriff Co London 1907, Dir Bank of England 1896–1936, Lt Roy 1st Devon Yeo Cav; b 30 March 1865; m 18 Oct 1899 Alfreda Ernestine Albertha (d 3 May 1939), dau of Sir George Ferguson Bowen, GCMG, PC, and d 24 Oct 1937, leaving:
  1a RALPH ALURED (Sir), **5th Bt**
  2a Thomas; b 29 May 1906; educ Eton and Ch Ch Oxford (BA 1928, MA 1961); Capt Gren Gds WW II (wounded), Liveryman Fishmongers' Co, Freeman City London, Ld Manor Coryton; m 24 June 1938 Helen (d 1972), er dau of Sir Charles Alban Young, 9th Bt, of N Dean (qv), and d 1980, leaving:
    1b +Peter Thomas Lydston [Peter Newman Esq, The Manor House, Coryton, Okehampton, Devon]; b 23 Jan 1944; educ Eton and Ch Ch Oxford (MA); FCA; m 1981 *Catherine Jane, dau of Alistair James Lilburn, of Coull, Aboyne, Aberdeenshire (see REID, Bt), and has:
      1c +Rupert Thomas Lydston; b 1984
      2c +William Alistair; b 1988
      1c *Harriet Joan; b 1986
    1b *Priscilla Helen [Mrs Charles Stuart-Menteth, Woodchester House, Woodchester, Glos GL5 5NY]; b 1 April 1939; m 12 June 1963 *Charles Granville Stuart-Menteth, yr s of Sir William Frederick Stuart-Menteth, 5th Bt (qv), and has issue
    2b *Elizabeth Clare [Mrs Robert MacDonnell, 17 Malbrook Rd, London SW15]; b 19 July 1941; m 18 April 1964 *(Robert Myles) Randal MacDonnell, late 9th/12th Roy Lancers, yr s of Edward Geoffrey Randal MacDonnell, of Pixeycombe, Meavy, Yelverton, Devon, and has:
      1c *Julian Sorley Randal; b 1 March 1967; m 1992 *Sophia Helen, dau of David Reed, of Bath, and has:
        1d *Amity Catherine; b 1993
      2c *Natasha Clare; b 21 March 1965
      3c *Louisa Helen; b 1 May 1971
  1a Joyce Alfreda; b 3 April 1904; m 26 Nov 1928 Maj-Gen Sir Julian Alvery Gascoigne, KCMG, KCVO, CB, DSO, Gren Gds, Govr Bermuda, est s of Brig-Gen Sir Ernest Frederick Orby Gascoigne, KCVO, CMG, DSO, and had issue (see VERNON, B)
  (2) Ralph Denne; b 4 March 1871; m Oporto Dec 1894 Mabel (m 2nd 24 Aug 1898 C R Johnson), dau of Frederick Blake, of Oporto, and dsp 23 Nov 1896
  (3) Lionel Ernest; b 1875; d unm 15 Aug 1902
  (1) Lilian Louisa; b 14 Aug 1866; m 29 Sept 1894 James Fortescue Crichton Stuart and d 27 April 1950, leaving issue (see BUTE, M)
  (2) Helen Beatrice; b 3 Dec 1867; m 16 May 1895 Lt-Col William Vere Reeve FANE later KING-FANE (roy licence Sept 1920) and d 8 March 1962, leaving issue (see WESTMORLAND, E)
  (3) Adeline; b 19 July 1869; m 4 Aug 1897 Sir Henry Augustus Ferguson-Davie, CB, 2nd s of Sir William Augustus Ferguson-Davie, 3rd Bt (qv), and d 23 March 1951, leaving issue
4 Alured; b 19 Feb 1831; m 1880 Ida Leonora Adalina Beatrice Arlington (d 1904) and d Feb 1904, leaving:
  (1) Edward Devon; b 25 Oct 1885; educ Trin Hall Cambridge; Maj Lincs Yeo WW I (wounded); m 1st 18 Nov 1909 (divorce 1926) Violet Ethel, dau of Rev D Morgan-Kirby, and has:
  1a +John Edward Alured [John Newman Esq, PO Box 1216, Pinetown, Natal 3600, S Africa]; b 13 Dec 1915; educ Radley; m 1st 1947 (divorce 1958) Katherine Dolores, dau of Frank Bazette, of Newbury, Berks, and formerly w of Stephen Townsend, and has:

1b *Priscilla Elizabeth [Mrs Priscilla de Pau, Maestro Perez Cabrero 62A, 08021 Barcelona, Spain]; *b* 1949; *m* 1969 (*divorce* 1989) Eugene de Pau and has:

    1c *Gregory; *b* 1972

1a (cont.) Edward Newman *m* 2nd 1964 *Winifred Betty, dau of Charles Rowe, of Wellington, NZ, and formerly w of Eric Paull

1a *Myra Beatrice Bellona [Mrs William Bagnall, Upper Brook House, Marchington, Uttoxeter, Staffs]; *b* 20 July 1914; *m* 16 March 1946 Lt-Col William Bagnall, OBE (*d* 1984), s of Rev William Bagnall, and has:

    1b *William Edward Hampshire [William Bagnall Esq, 2 Brook House, New Pond Rd, Compton, Surrey]; *b* 18 July 1947; *m* 1969 *Bridget, dau of Kenneth Charles Pearce, and has:

       1c *William Richard; *b* 1978

       1c *Jessica Jane; *b* 1976

    1b *Felicity Jane [Mrs Nicholas Mills, Bank House Farm, Hyde Lea, Stafford]; *b* 10 Feb 1951; *m* 1977 *Nicholas John Sutton Mills

(1) (cont.) Maj Edward Newman *m* 2nd 4 Aug 1926 Hilda (*d* 1970), 3rd dau of Leonard Norman Barrow, JP, of Normanton Hall, Southwell, Notts

1 Mary Ann; *b* 31 July 1816; *m* 21 March 1844 William Erving Smith Clark, of Mooreland, est s of William John Clark, of Buckland Toussaints, and *d* 30 Dec 1889, leaving issue

2 Charlotte; *b* 7 July 1818; *d* unm 21 Dec 1839

3 Caroline; *b* 10 Nov 1819; *m* 16 April 1861 1st Baron Churston (*qv*) and *dsp* 27 Nov 1866

4 Louisa; *b* 28 May 1826; *m* 25 Aug 1874 Sir Massey Lopes, 3rd Bt (*see* ROBOROUGH, B), and *dsp* 27 April 1908

5 Harriet; *b* 18 June 1828; *m* 19 May 1863, as his 2nd w, Charles Langton Massingberd, of Gunby Hall, Lincs, and *dsp* 21 April 1908. He *d* 9 Feb 1887

The 4th Bt's cousin,

Sir Ralph Alured Newman, 5th Bt; *b* 23 April 1902; *educ* Eton and Corpus Christi Coll Cambridge (BA 1923, MA 1927); Lt RASC WW II, Liveryman Fishmonger's Co, Freeman City London; *m* 12 June 1946 *Ann Rosemary Hope [The Hon Lady Newman, Blackpool House, Dartmouth, S Devon TQ6 ORG], est dau of Hon Claude Hope Hope-Morley (*see* HOLLENDEN, B), and *d* 20 July 1968, leaving:

1 Sir GEOFFREY ROBERT NEWMAN, **6th and present Bt**

2 +Richard Claude; *b* 2 May 1951; *educ* Dawlish Coll; *m* 1992 *Louise Dorothy Catherine, only child of Gordon Alexander Egerton Ruck (*see* BRAYBROOKE, B), and has:

    (1) +Henry Ralph Gordon; *b* 31 July 1997

    (1) *Georgina Dorothy Catherine; *b* 1995

1 *Zabian Carlotta Annette Alfreda; *b* 28 Nov 1948

2 *Louisa Ann [Mrs Louisa Smith, Melverley, Ravensbourne Lane, Stoke Fleming, Dartmouth TQ6 0QR]; *b* 23 Oct 1955; *m* 1st 1977 (*divorce* 1992) Andrew William Kingsley Thomas and has:

    (1) *William Lydston; *b* 1983

    (1) *Rachael Elizabeth Ann; *b* 1987

2 (cont.) Mrs Louisa Thomas *m* 2nd 1997 *Michael Clive Bowker Smith

NEWSON-SMITH

Arms: Gu. on a chevron or, between in chief two bezants and in base a cross patée fitchée of the second, a pellet between two crosses patée fitchée sa. **Crest:** Issuant from a mural crown or a goat's head arg., armed and bearded or, eared sa. and charged with a sword erect gu. **Motto:** *Integritas et industria* ('Integrity and industry'). **Creation:** Bt. (UK) 1 Dec 1944.

SIR PETER FRANK GRAHAM NEWSON-SMITH, 3RD BT, of Totteridge, Co Hertford; *b* 8 May 1947; *s f* 1997; *educ* Dover Coll and Trin Coll of Music; *m* 1974 *Mary-Ann, dau of Cyril C Collins, of Marnhull, Dorset, and formerly w of Anthony Owens, and has:

1 +OLIVER NICHOLAS PETER; *b* 1975

1 *Emma; *b* 1977

Lineage: HENRY NEWSON-SMITH, DL, CA, of London; *b* 14 May 1856; *m* Elizabeth Caroline Louise (*d* 17 Oct 1898), dau of William Henry Powning, of Truro, and *d* 28 April 1898, leaving,

Sir Frank (Edwin) Newson-Smith, 1st Bt (UK), so *cr* 1 Dec 1944; *b* 25 March 1879; *educ* St Lawrence Coll Ramsgate and U Coll Sch London; memb London Stock Exchange 1900 and Court Common Cncl 1911–38, Dep for Broad St Ward 1928, Ch Commoner 1930, Alderman 1938–68, Lt City London 1929, Sheriff 1939–40, Ld Mayor 1943–44, memb Court Assistants HAC, Master Turners' Co 1933 and Spectacle Makers' Co 1947–48, pres London Chamber Commerce 1946–49, chm Govt Ctee Training for Business Admin 1945; Hon MA Oxford 1941, Hon DCL Oxford 1944; ktd 1941; *m* 7 July 1904 Lilian Dorothy (*d* 3 Jan 1955), dau of Sir Henry Tozer, of Exeter, and *d* 1971, having had:

1 **Sir John Kenneth Newson-Smith, 2nd Bt:** DL (City of London 1947); *b* 9 Jan 1911; *educ* Dover Coll and Jesus Coll Cambridge (BA 1933, MA 1946); Lt RNVR WW II, memb Court of Common Cncl 1945, Deputy 1961–78, Lt City London 1947, Master Turners' Co 1969–70; *m* 1st 17 March 1945 (*divorce* 1971) Vera Margaret, er dau of Dr Greenhouse Allt, CVO, CBE, Pncpl Trin Coll Music, London; *m* 2nd 1972 Annie (*d* 1987), dau of Harold Burns; *m* 3rd 1988 *Mrs Sarah Lucretia Wimberley Ramsay [Sarah Lady Newson-Smith, 67 East St, Warminster, Wilts BA12 9BZ], dau of Robert Bicknell, and *d* 11 Nov 1997, leaving by his 1st w:

    (1) Sir PETER FRANK GRAHAM, **3rd and present Bt**

    (1) *Susan Rosemary [Mrs Charles Reiss, 91 Belsize Lane, London NW3 5AU]; *b* 11 Jan 1946; *m* 1978 *Charles Reiss, est s of Dr J C Reiss, and has:

       1a *Rowan Susannah Charlotte; *b* 1978

       2a *Holly Clare; *b* 1980

       3a *Bryony; *b* 1986

    (2) *(Elizabeth) Jane; *b* 16 June 1953; *m* 1978 *Kenneth Hall and has:

       1a *Katherine Louise; *b* 1979

       2a *Rachel Helen; *b* 1980

2 Peter Henry; *b* 6 Nov 1914; *educ* Dover Coll and Wadham Coll Oxford; Capt RA WW II; *m* 3 Sept 1939 Gertrude Irene (*m* 2nd 1948 Bertrand Walker, dau of Frederick Lester Walker, of Georgia, USA), and was *kas* Italy 7 July 1944, leaving:

    (1) *Carole Irene; *b* 26 Aug 1943

1 Doris Enid; *b* 7 Aug 1905; *m* 2 Sept 1948 *Maj Stanley Thomas Woodruff, TD, s of John Gravener Woodruff, of Deal, Kent, and had:

    (1) *Peter Miles; *b* 8 Sept 1946; *m* July 1969 *Deborah Mascall

2 Mary Sharland; *b* 30 June 1907; *m* 20 July 1935 Maj Claude Morrison (*d* 4 April 1967), s of Percy George Morrison, of Otterleigh, St Albans, and *d* 10 July 1997, leaving:

    (1) *John Anthony (Ven) [The Ven The Archdeacon of Oxford, 60 Wendover Rd, Aylesbury, Bucks HP21 9LW]; *b* 11 March 1938; *educ* Haileybury and Jesus Coll Cambridge (BA 1960, MA 1964); Chaplain Lincoln Coll Oxford 1968–74, Archdeacon Oxford 1998–; *m* 20 July 1968 *Angela, er dau of Jonathan Eric Bush, of Fetcham, Surrey, and has:

       1a *Dominic; *b* 1970

       2a *Nicholas; *b* 1974

       1a *Philippa; *b* 1972

    (2) *Michael Bruce [Michael Morrison Esq, The White Horse, 9 Place Luxembourg, Brussels]; *b* 80 Dee 1939; *educ* Haileybury; *m* 1st 17 June 1960 (*divorce* 1972) Anne Margaret, dau of Dr Archibald Hew Grace, of Cooden, Sussex, and has:

       1a *Bruce Anthony; *b* 29 Dec 1961

       1a *Clare Fiona; *b* 22 Sept 1964

    (2) (cont.) Michael Morrison *m* 2nd 1972 *Mary, dau of Lt-Col William Pollock, and by her has:

       2a *Samantha Lois; *b* 1978

    (1) *Jennifer Mary [Mrs Peter Daniel, Heatherly Cottage, Ladbrook Lane, Gastard, nr Corsham, Wilts SN13 9PE]; *b* 26 June 1943; *m* 3 April 1965 *Peter Robert Daniel, s of Leslie Henry Daniel, of Burton-on-Trent, and has:

       1a *Mark Leslie; *b* 1970

       2a *Paul Gavin; *b* 1974

       1a *Karen Jane [Mrs John Walton, 4 Laurel Place, Staple Street, nr Faversham, Kent]; *b* 9 March 1966; *m* 1990 *John Walton, s of Eric Walton, of Maidstone, Kent, and has:

          1b *Thomas Eric; *b* 1993

          1b *Megan Jane; *b* 1997

       2a *Tracey Emma [Mrs Peter Lewis, Flat 2, 99 Stanley Rd, Carshalton, Surrey]; *b* 17 April 1968; *m* 1993 *Peter Lewis, s of John Lewis, of Walton-on-Thames

NEWTON, Baron

Arms: Gu. a cross engrailed arg., in the chief point on an inescutcheon sa. semée of estoiles an arm in armour embowed of the second, the hand ppr., holding a pennon silver, all within a bordure wavy or. **Crest:** Out of a ducal coronet or a ram's head arg, armed or, in the mouth a slip of laurel proper, over all a pallet wavy az. **Supporters:** On either side a mastiff-dog ppr., collared sa.
Motto: *En Dieu est ma foi* ('My faith is in the Lord').
Creation: B. (UK) 27 Aug 1892.

THE 5TH BARON NEWTON, of Newton-in-Makerfield, Co Lancaster (Richard Thomas Legh) [The Rt Hon The Lord Newton, Laughton Park Farm, Laughton, E Sussex BN8 6BU]; *b* 11 Jan 1950; *s* f 1992; *educ* Eton and Ch Ch Oxford; slr; *m* 19 May 1978 *Rosemary Whitfoot, yr dau of Herbert Clarke, of Eastbourne, and has:

1 +PIERS RICHARD; *b* 25 Oct 1979

1 *Alessandra Mary; *b* 1978

Lineage: THOMAS PETER LEGH, of Giolborne Park, Lancs; MP Newton, Col Lancs Fencible Cav; inherited the Lyme estate, nr Macclesfield, Cheshire, from his unc Piers (*dspm* 20 May 1792), and willed most of it to his illegitimate sons:

1 Thomas, JP, of Lyme Park, Cheshire, Haydock Lodge and Golborne Park; MP Newton 1819–31, LLD, FAS; *m* 14 Jan 1829 Ellen (*d* 1831), dau of William Turner, of Shrigley Park, Cheshire, MP Blackburn, and *d* 8 May 1857, leaving:

(1) Ellen Jane; *m* 1847 Brabazon Lowther, JP, of Shrigley Park (*d* 1877), and *d* 22 Nov 1906, having had issue

2 William, of Brymbo, Denbighs; *m* Mary, dau and heiress of John Wilkinson, of Ratcliffe Hall, Leics, and had:

(1) WILLIAM JOHN LEGH, **1st Baron Newton**, of Newton in Makerfield, Co Lancaster (UK), so *cr* 27 Aug 1892, JP, DL Cheshire and Lancs; *b* 19 Dec 1828; *educ* Rugby; Capt 21st Fus, served Crimea, Lt-Col Lancs Hus, MP (C) S Lancs 1859–65 and E Cheshire 1868–85; *m* 29 May 1856 Emily Jane (*d* 17 April, 1901), dau of Ven Charles Wodehouse (*see* KIMBERLEY, E), and had:

1a THOMAS WODEHOUSE, **2nd Baron**

2a Gilbert; *b* 21 April 1858; Maj Gren Gds; *m* 28 June 1894 Louisa Marie (*d* 22 Nov 1932), widow of Col Hon George Villiers (*see* CLARENDON, E) and dau of George Disney Maquay, and *d* 23 Dec 1939, having had:

1b Peter; F/Cdr RNAS; *b* 4 Sept 1896; *d* 3 May 1919 following a flying accident

3a Piers William; *d* an infant 12 March 1862

1a Dulcibella Jane (Sybil); *b* 22 Nov 1859; *d* unm 5 March 1960

2a Mabel Maud; *b* 16 Sept 1863; *m* 25 July 1889 6th Baron Langford (*qv*) and *d* 12 May 1966

The 1st BARON *d* 15 Dec 1898; his er surv s,

THOMAS WODEHOUSE LEGH, **2nd Baron Newton**, JP, DL Cheshire; *b* 18 March 1857; *educ* Eton and Ch Ch Oxford (BA); Attaché Dip Serv 1880–86, Lt-Col Lancs Hus Imp Yeo, MP (C) Newton 1886–98, Paymaster-Gen 1915–16, Assist U-Sec For Affrs 1916, author: *Life of Lord Lyon*; *m* 24 July 1880 Evelyn Caroline (*d* 13 Sept 1931), est dau of William Bromley Davenport, MP, of Capesthorne, Cheshire, and Baginton Hall, Warwicks, and had:

1 RICHARD WILLIAM DAVENPORT, **3rd Baron**

2 Piers ('Joey') Walter (Sir), GCVO (1948), KCB (1953), CMG (1925), CIE (1922), OBE (1919), JP Berks and Co of London; *b* 12 Dec 1890; *educ* Eton; Lt-Col Gren Gds, Equerry in ordinary to HRH THE PRINCE OF WALES 1919–36, Equerry to TM EDWARD VIII 1936 and GEORGE VI 1937–46 (Extra Equerry 1946–55), Master Household to TM GEORGE VI 1941–52 and THE QUEEN 1952–53, Mil Sec WW I (despatches), Croix de Guerre, Order St Maurice and St Lazarus Italy; *m* 15 Nov 1920 Sarah Polk (*d* 17 Oct 1955), widow of Capt Hon Alfred Thomas Shaughnessy (*see* SHAUGHNESSY, B; also Section Polk, AMERICAN PRESIDENTIAL FAMILIES, 1994, Morris Genealogical Books SA) and dau of Judge James C Bradford, of Woodstock, Nashville, Tenn., and *d* 16 Oct 1955, leaving:

(1) *Diana Evelyn [Mrs Norman Colville, Penheale Barton, Launceston, Cornwall; 11 Kensington Sq, London W8; *b* 28 March 1924; High Sheriff Cornwall 1988–89; *m* 1st 27 Oct 1945 (*divorce* 1948) 4th Earl of Kimberley

(*qv*); *m* 2nd 1 June 1951 Lt- Col Norman Robert Colville, MC (*see* CLYDESMUIR, B) and by him has:

1a *James Charles David; *b* 1952; *educ* Eton; Page of Honour to HM THE QUEEN 1966–68; *m* 1983 *Fiona, dau of John Gaylor, of Bromley, Kent, and has:

1b *Robert John James; *b* 1984

1b *Sarah Elizabeth Rose; *b* 1986

2b *Lucy Isabelle Amy; *b* 1988

1 Lettice, JP Hants; *b* 7 Nov 1885; *m* 1st 11 June 1908 Capt John Egerton-Warburton, Scots Gds, of Arley, Cheshire, and had issue (*see* GREY EGERTON, Bt); *m* 2nd 6 Feb 1919 Lt-Col John Dallas Waters, CB, DSO, DL, s of John Michael Waters, of Hill House, Farnham, Surrey, and *d* 30 April 1968. He *d* 31 Jan 1967

2 Hilda Margaret; *b* 23 June 1892; *d* unm 6 Feb 1970

3 Phyllis Elinor; *b* 9 Dec 1895; *m* 31 Jan 1918 Henry Gerard Walter Sandeman (*d* 19 Jan 1953), Gren Gds, of The Old Mill House, Melton, Woodbridge, Suffolk, 2nd s of Walter Sandeman, of Morden House, Royston, Herts, and had issue (*see* STRABOLGI, B)

The 2nd BARON *d* 21 March 1942; his est s,

RICHARD WILLIAM DAVENPORT LEGH, **3rd Baron Newton**, TD, JP, DL Cheshire; *b* 18 Nov 1888; *educ* Eton and Magdalen Coll Oxford; Hon Attaché Constantinople and Vienna 1912–14, Capt Lancs Hus WW I, War Office 1940–43, Hon Col 7th Bn Cheshire Regt; *m* 28 Jan 1914 Hon Helen Winifred Meysey-Thompson (*d* 28 Dec 1958), 2nd dau of 1st and last Baron Knaresborough (*see* MEYSEY-THOMPSON, Bt), and had:

1 PETER RICHARD LEGH, **4th Baron**

2 Hugo Claude; *b* 27 Aug 1916; *d* 21 Dec 1933

3 Francis Michael (Sir), KCVO (1968); *b* 2 Aug 1919; *educ* Eton and RMC Sandhurst; Maj Gren Gds, GSO(2), Mil Mission Greece (despatches) WW II, Assist Priv Sec and Equerry to HM QUEEN ELIZABETH THE QUEEN MOTHER 1956–59, Equerry 1956–84, Priv Sec to HRH PRINCESS MARGARET 1959–71, Priv Sec and Treas 1962–84; *m* 16 Nov 1948 Ruadh Daphne (*d* 6 Sept 1973), only child of Alan Holmes Watson and Mrs Jack Mason, and *d* 1984, leaving:

(1) +Nicholas Charles; *b* 16 Dec 1951; *educ* Eton; 2nd Lieut RGJ; *m* 1980 *Annabel G, dau of Peter Hawkings, of Greywell, Hants, and has:

1a *Lucy Henrietta; *b* 1982

2a *Alice Sophia; *b* 1985

(1) *Laura Helen; *b* 16 May 1954; *m* 1979 Hon Simon Andrew Weinstock (*d* 8 May 1996), s of Baron Weinstock (*qv*), and has:

1a *Pamela Helen; *b* 1982

2a *Celia Rose; *b* 1985

3a *Laetitia Anne Daphne; *b* 1990

The 3rd BARON *d* 11 June 1960; his est s,

PETER RICHARD LEGH, **4th Baron Newton**, JP Hants 1951; *b* 6 April 1915; *educ* Eton and Ch Ch Oxford (BA 1937, MA 1947); CC Hants 1949–52 and 1954–55, MP (C) Petersfield 1951–60, PPS to Fin Sec Treasury 1952, Assist Govt Whip 1953–55, Govt Whip (Ld Commr Treasury) 1955–57 and (V-Chamberlain Household) 1957–60, Dep Govt Ch Whip H of C ('Treasurer Household) 1959–60, Dep Govt Ch Whip Ho Lds (Capt Yeomen Gd) 1960–62, Parly Sec Health 1962–64, Min State Educn and Sci April–Oct 1964, Maj Gren Gds WW II; *m* 6 July 1948 *Priscilla (*m* 2nd, as his 2nd w, Frederick Charles Horace Fryer; *see* PEEL, E) [Mrs Frederick Fryer, Vernon Hill House, Bishop's Waltham, Hants], widow of Viscount Wolmer (*see* SELBORNE, E) and yr dau of Capt John Egerton-Warburton (*see* GREY EGERTON, Bt), and *d* 1992, leaving:

1 RICHARD THOMAS LEGH, **5th and present Baron Newton**

2 +David Piers Carlis [The Hon David Legh, Cubley Lodge, Ashbourne, Derbys DE6 2FB]; *b* 21 Nov 1951; *educ* Eton and RAC Cirencester; FRICS; *m* 20 July 1974 *Jane Mary, er dau of John Roy Wynter Bee, of West End, Surrey, and has:

(1) +Hugo Peter David; *b* 1979

(2) +Thomas John Rowland; *b* 1984

(1) *Charlotte Mary; *b* 10 Aug 1976

(2) *Katherine Anna; *b* 1991

NEWTON, Bt, of Beckenham

Arms: Arg. on a chevron between three eagles displayed az. as many garbs or. **Crest:** A bear's head couped arg., muzzled gu., charged on the neck with three crescents interlaced az. **Motto:** *Faveat fortuna* ('May fortune show favour'). **Creation:** Bt. (UK) 27 Oct 1924.

SIR KENNETH GARNAR NEWTON, 3RD BT, OBE (1969, MBE 1944), TD [Sir Kenneth Newton Bt OBE TD, Oaklands, Harborough Gorse, W Chiltington, W Sussex RH20 2RU]; *b* 4 June 1918; *s f* 1971; *educ* Wellington; Lt-Col 1st AA Divl RASC (TA) WW II, Gen Commr Income Tax 1961, pres Br Leather Fedn 1968–69, Internat Cncl Tanners 1972–78, chm Garnar Booth plc 1972–87 (md 1961–83), Liveryman and Memb Ct Assists Leathersellers' Co (Master 1977–78) and Feltmakers' Co (Master 1983–84), chm Govrs Colfe's Sch 1983; *m* 1st 11 March 1944 Margaret Isabel (*d* 1979), dau of Rev Dr George Blair, of Dundee, and has:

  1 +JOHN GARNAR [John Newton Esq, North House, Wyboston, Beds]; *b* 10 July 1945; *educ* Reed's Sch Cobham; *m* 27 May 1972 *Jacynth Anne Kay Miller and has:

   (1) +Timothy Garnar; *b* 4 Sept 1973

   (2) +Alistair Blair; *b* 4 Sept 1973

   (3) +Andrew Robert; *b* 2 July 1975

  2 +Peter Blair [Peter Newton Esq, Park House, Souldern, nr Bicester, Oxon]; *b* 18 Aug 1950; *educ* Wellington; *m* 16 Dec 1983 *Fiona S, only dau of W Q FitzGerald, of Penny Broom, Burnham Market, Norfolk, and has:

   (1) +Alex Blair; *b* 4 Sept 1988

   (2) +Rory James; *b* 26 May 1990

Sir KENNETH *m* 2nd 1980 (*divorce*) Pamela Sidney, widow of F T K Wilson

Lineage: REUBEN NEWTON, of Macclesfield; had:

Sir Louis Arthur Newton, 1st Bt (UK), so *cr* 27 Oct 1924; *b* 17 Dec 1867; Hon Col RASC, Lt and Alderman City London (Sr Sheriff 1917), ktd 1917, Ld Mayor London 1924, Govr Irish Soc 1928–33, memb LCC 1931–34, Govr Roy Hosp, Commr Income Tax City London, memb Coal Mines Nat Industl Bd, Master Loriners', Feltmakers' and Needlemakers' Cos, Grand Warden Freemasons, Fell Auctioneers' Inst, Orders Crown Italy, Leopold Belgium and White Lion Czechoslovakia; *m* 1st 29 Aug 1891 Eleanor Jane (*d* 27 Feb 1929), dau of George Faulder, and had:

1 EDGAR HENRY (Sir), **2nd Bt**

2 Sidney Arthur; *b* 23 Sept 1901; slr 1923, consultant Nash, Field & Co, Master Distillers', Parish Clerks' and Loriners' Cos, Donation Govr Christ's Hosp, Under Sheriff City London 1930, 1931 and 1933; *m* 27 April 1933 Oonagh (*d* 1990), yst dau of John Fleming, of Dublin, and *d* 1978, leaving:

   (1) +Hedley John [Hedley Newton Esq, Moat Farm House, Kettle Green, Herts]; *b* 24 March 1936; *educ* Charterhouse and Trin Hall Cambridge (MA, LLB); slr 1960, ptnr Nash, Field & Co and Duffield, Bruty & Co, Liveryman Vintner's Co; *m* 27 Feb 1964 *Virginia, only dau of James Archibald Baiss, of Ringle Oast, Sandhurst, Kent, and has:

     1a +Marcus James; *b* 28 Jan 1966

     2a +Charles Benedict; *b* 5 Aug 1968

     3a +Caspar John; *b* 18 May 1971

   (1) *Shane; *b* 24 Aug 1934; *m* 26 April 1960 *3rd Baron Gisborough (qv) and has issue

   (2) *Gaidagh [Mrs Martin Strong, West Bradley, Templeton, Devon]; *b* 26 Feb 1947; *m* 1 Nov 1968 *(James) Martin Strong, only s of Walter Strong, of Cork

1 Elsie Louise Marion; *m* 1st 4 June 1921 (*divorce*) Sydney Ewart Tucker, s of William Ewart Tucker, of Farningham, Kent; *m* 2nd —

2 Winifred Emily; *m* 11 Feb 1926 Desmond Arthur Wright, s of Arthur Wright, of Grey Friars, Edgbaston, and *d* 10 June 1972, leaving two daus. He *d* 5 April 1942

Sir Louis *m* 2nd 7 June 1930 Florence E H (*d* 17 Feb 1955), widow of Albert David Wheatley and only dau of William Yates Baker, and *d* 17 April 1945

His er s,

  Sir Edgar Henry Newton, 2nd Bt; *b* 6 May 1893; *educ* Merchant Taylors; slr 1919, Master Feltmakers' Co, memb Court Common Cncl City London, Col 1st AA Divnl RASC (TA), memb TA&AFA Co London, served WW I (despatches) and WW II; *m* 1st 17 Feb 1917 Gladys Maud (*d* 18 Nov 1966), dau of Sir James Wilson Garnar, and had:

   1 Sir KENNETH GARNAR NEWTON, **3rd and present Bt**

   1 Daphne Mary; *b* 27 Oct 1921

Sir Edgar *m* 2nd 12 March 1968 *Alice Mary [Alice Lady Newton, 14 Castle Hill View, Sidford, Sidmouth, Devon], widow of Glynn Rosser and dau of Henry Barber, of Surbiton, Surrey, and *d* 4 Feb 1971

NEWTON, Bt, of The Wood

Arms: Az. two shin bones in saltire, the sinister surmounted by the dexter or, between as many roses in fess arg., barbed and seeded ppr., on a chief of the second a lotus-flower leaved and slipped of the last. **Crest:** Out of the battlements of a tower or a cubit arm erect in chain armour, the hand grasping a sword in bend sinister ppr., pommel and hilt or, suspended from the blade of the sword a banner arg., charged with a dagger erect gu., within two branches of oak, slipped and saltirewise also ppr. **Motto:** *Faveat fortuna* ('May fortune show favour'). **Creation:** Bt. (UK) 18 May 1900.

SIR (HARRY) MICHAEL REX NEWTON, 3RD BT, of The Wood, Sydenham Hill, Lewisham, Kent, and Kottingham House, Burton-on-Trent, Co Stafford [Sir Michael Newton Bt, Cliff House, Old Lyme Rd, Charmouth, Dorset DT6 6BW]; *b* 7 Feb 1923; *s f* 1951; *educ* Eastbourne Coll; KRRC (wounded) WW II N Africa and Middle East, Past Master Girdlers' Co, Freeman City London, dir Thomas Parsons & Sons; *m* 3 July 1958 *Pauline Jane, only dau of Richard John Frederick Howgill, CBE, of Sullington Warren, Sussex, and has:

  1 +GEORGE PETER HOWGILL (Rev) [The Rev George Newton, 8 Collingwood Ave, Blackpool FY3 8BZ]; *b* 26 March 1962; *educ* Sherborne and Pembroke Coll Cambridge (MA); Curate St Thomas's Blackpool 1993–, Freeman City London; *m* 30 Jan 1988 *Jane L, twin dau of John Rymer, and has:

   (1) *Sarah Rebecca; *b* 4 Jan 1991

   (2) *Kate Evangeline; *b* 11 Nov 1992

Sir MICHAEL and Lady NEWTON also adopted:

  *Lucinda Jane; *b* 24 Nov 1964; *m* 21 April 1990 *Peter A Cliff, only s of Cyril E Cliff, of Manchester

  *(Julia) Kate; *b* 27 Feb 1967; *m* 1994 *Daryn K Hufton-Rees, only s of Kenneth Rees, of Manchester

  *Jennifer Anne; *b* 27 Feb 1967; *m* 10 April 1993 *John I T Hardy

Lineage: GEORGE NEWTON, of Drypool, Hull; *b* 1773; *m* Elizabeth Beeforth (*d* 29 Oct 1854) and *d* 29 Jan 1845, leaving:

GEORGE BEEFORTH NEWTON, of Kottingham, Hull; *b* 5 May 1810; *m* 8 Oct 1834 Helen (*d* 14 Oct 1893), dau of Philip Rowe, of Liverpool, and *d* 27 Feb 1889, leaving, with two er sons:

Sir Alfred James Newton, 1st Bt (UK), so *cr* 18 May 1900 on formation City of London Imp Vols; *b* 18 Nov 1845; Lt City London, last Sheriff London and Middx 1888–89, Govr Irish Soc, Alderman Bassishaw Ward, Ld Mayor London 1899–1900, Chm City Police Ctee 1906–11, Orders Lion and Sun Persia (highest grade), Leopold Belgium, Polar Star Sweden and Norway, Tirkova Serbia, Grand Cordon Medjidie, Hon Freeman Scarborough and City of Londonderry; *m* 24 June 1874 Elizabeth Jane (*d* 27 Oct 1945), est dau of Joseph Watson, of Mill House, Mitcham Common, and had:

1 HARRY KOTTINGHAM (Sir), **2nd Bt**

1 Muriel Prudhoe; *m* 21 Oct 1902 George Parons, s of Thomas Parons, of Baron Grove, Mitcham, and had issue

Sir ALFRED *d* 20 June 1921; his only son,

  Sir Harry Knottingham Newton, 2nd Bt, OBE (1919); *b* 2 April 1875; *educ* Rugby and New Coll Oxford (BA 1898, MA 1901); barrister Lincoln's Inn 1899, Lt City London, v-chm Harrods, MP Harwich 1910–22, Hon Sec City Imp Vols serving Boer War 1900, Maj RASC 1914, Offr cmdg Chatham Adminve Dist, Dep

Assist Dir Tport and Supplies E Cmd 1915; *m* 5 June 1920 Myrtle Irene (*d* 18 Sept 1977), er dau of William Wilson Grantham, KC, of Balneath Manor, nr Lewes, and *d* 22 June 1951, leaving:

 1 (Alfred) Jeremy Grantham; *b* 20 July 1921; Lt RA WW II; *ka* Italy 8 Feb 1944
 2 Sir (HARRY) MICHAEL REX NEWTON, **3rd and present Bt**
 3 +Christopher Wynne (Rev) [The Rev Canon Christopher Newton, 24 Slade Court, Watling St, Radlett, Herts WD7 7BT]; *b* 23 July 1925; *educ* Eastbourne Coll and Trin Hall Cambridge (BA 1946, MA 1948); Urban Dean Milton Keynes, Vicar Hemel Hempstead, Ecumenical Offr, Oxford Diocese 1979–83, Priest-in-charge St Peter and St Paul Little Gaddesden Herts 1983–85 (ret); *m* 22 July 1950 *Margaret, yst dau of John Ormerod, of Accrington, and has:

 (1) +(John) Jeremy; *b* 13 May 1952; *educ* Bryanston and Trin Coll Cambridge (MA); *m* April 1974 *Anne Patricia Royle and has:

 1a +(Michael) David; *b* 16 May 1989
 1a *Fiona Elizabeth; *b* 3 May 1978
 2a *Alison Mary; *b* 15 July 1980
 (2) +Peter Michael; *b* 26 July 1953; *educ* Bryanston and St Bartholomew's Hosp; *m* Feb 1975 *Susan Valerie Love and has:

 1a +Richard James Grantham; *b* 29 June 1979
 1a *Claire Louise; *b* 1 March 1978
 2a *Joanne Elizabeth; *b* 24 July 1980

NEWTON OF BRAINTREE

Creation: B. (LP, UK) 1997.

THE BARON NEWTON OF BRAINTREE, of Coggeshall, Co Essex (Tony (Antony) Harold Newton, OBE (1972), PC (1988)) [The Rt Hon The Lord Newton of Braintree OBE PC, House of Lords, London SW1A 0PW]; *b* Aug 1937; *educ* Friends Sch Saffron Walden and Trin Coll Oxford; V-Chm Fedn University C and U Assocs 1959, CRD: Head Ec Section 1965–70, Assist Dir 1970–74, Chm Coningsby Club 1965–70, MP (C) Braintree 1974–97, Assist Govt Whip 1979–81, Ld Commr Treasury 1981–82, Parly U-Sec DSS 1982–84, Min for Disabled 1983–84, Min State: DSS 1984–86, Health 1986–88, Chm NHS Mgmt Bd DHSS 1986–88, Chllr Duchy Lancaster 1988–89, Min Trade and Industry 1988–89, Sec State DSS 1989–92, Ld Pres Cncl and Leader H of C 1992–97; Govr Felsted Sch; *m* 1st 1962 (*divorce* 1986) Janet Huxley; *m* 2nd 1986 *Mrs Patricia Gilthorpe and has by his 1st w:

 1 *Polly Jane; *b* 19–; political reporter *The Times*; *m* 4 April 1998 *Roger Adam Blitz, s of Mrs Paul Newnham and steps of Paul Newnham, of Hampstead
 2 *Jessica; *b* 19–; *m* 19 Dec 1998 *John Mounteney-Smith, s of John Mounteney-Smith, of Boundway, Hants

NICHOLLS OF BIRKENHEAD

Arms: Sable two bars, each between two cotises, set on the outer edge with birch leaves or. **Crest:** A demi-mole sable, holding between the paws a daffodil slipped and leaved or, mantled sable, doubled or. **Supporters:** On either side a cormorant, wings displayed and inverted sable, beaked and legged or. **Motto:** Let equity prevail. **Creation:** B. (LP, UK) 3 Oct 1994.

THE BARON NICHOLLS OF BIRKENHEAD, of Stoke D'Abernon in the County of Surrey (Sir Donald James Nicholls, PC (1980)) [The Rt Hon The Lord Nicholls of Birkenhead PC, House of Lords, London SW1A 0PW]; *b* 25 Jan 1933; *educ* Birkenhead Sch, Liverpool U (LLB, Hon LLD 1987), Trin Hall Cambridge (BA, LLB, Hon Fell 1986); barrister Middle Temple 1958 (Bencher 1981), QC 1974, High Court Judge Chancery 1983–86, ktd 1983, Ld of Appeal 1986–91, V-Chllr Supreme Court 1991–94, Ld Appeal in Ordinary 1994–, non-perm Judge Hong Kong Court Final Appeal 1998–; *m* 1960 *Jennifer Mary, yr dau of W E C Thomas, JP, MB, Bch, MRCOG, and has two sons and a dau

Lineage: WILLIAM GREENHOW NICHOLLS; *m* Eleanor Jane — and had:

DONALD JAMES, *cr* a **Baron**

NICHOLSON

Arms: Per pale nebuly az. and gu., two bars arg. guttée de poix, in chief two suns in splendour ppr. **Crest:** A lion's head couped, sa., guttée d'eau, before a sun in splendour ppr. **Creation:** Bt. (UK) 7 Feb 1912.

SIR CHARLES CHRISTIAN NICHOLSON, 3RD BT, of Harrington Gardens, Royal Borough of Kensington [Sir Charles Nicholson Bt, Turners Green Farm, Elvetham, Hants RG27 8BE]; *b* 15 Dec 1941; *s f* 1993; *educ* Ampleforth and Magdalen Coll Oxford; *m* 20 Jan 1975 *Martha (Martie) Rodman, dau of Col Stuart Warren Don, of 1 Hyde Park St, London W1, and widow of Niall Hamilton Anstruther-Gough-Calthorpe (*see* ANSTRUTHER-GOUGH-CALTHORPE, Bt)

Lineage: THOMAS NICHOLSON, of Kirkoswald, Cumberland; had:

ISAAC NICHOLSON, of Staffield, Kirkoswald; *b* 1663; *m* Isabel — (*d* 1727) and *d* 1744, leaving:

GEORGE NICHOLSON; *b* 1714; *m* 6 Oct 1737 Hannah (*d* 1 March 1798), dau of Samuel Lothian, and had, with an er s:

ISAAC NICHOLSON, of Staffield and Whitehaven, Cumberland; *b* 1740; *m* Mrs — Elliot and *d* 1818, leaving, with two er sons:

ISAAC NICHOLSON, of Clapham Common and Gordon Sq, London; official assignee in bankruptcy; *b* 1780; *m* 22 Feb 1814 Leonora, dau of William Norris, and *d* 25 Jan 1860, leaving an est s:

WILLIAM NORRIS NICHOLSON, of 43 Phillimore Gdns, Kensington; *b* 27 Oct 1815; *educ* Trin Coll Cambridge (MA); barrister Lincoln's Inn, Master in Lunacy 1878; *m* 1st 2 Sept 1856 Emily (*d* 28th Feb 1873), er surv dau of James Stock Daniel, of Ramsgate, and had:

 1 CHARLES NORRIS (Sir), **1st Bt**
 2 Lothian Demain; *b* 5 Oct 1858; *m* 4 July 1882 Frances Laura (*d* 5 Sept 1952), dau of William Square, of Feltham Hill, Middx, and *d* July 1931
 3 Robert Isaac; *b* 12 March 1860; *d* 31 July 1873
 4 William Henry; Capt RN; *b* 13 Nov 1861; *m* Sibyl Wigham and *d* 8 Feb 1932, leaving:

 (1) Ethel Ruth; *m* 1st 15 March 1934 John Lambton (*ka* 11 Aug 1941; *see* DURHAM, E) and had issue; *m* 2nd E Ballard, of USA, and by him had:

 1a *Dana H; *b* 15 Oct 1946; *m* 31 May 1969 *Jane Michalke, of Rice Lake, Wisconsin
 1a *Frances S; *b* 23 March 1949
 5 Frederick; *b* 20 Aug 1864; *m* and had issue
 6 Godfrey John; *b* 1 July, *d* 16 July 1868
 7 Reginald, MBE, JP W Sussex; MP Doncaster 1918–22; *b* 15 July 1869; *m* 15 Feb 1915 Natalie, only dau of Frederick Stark Pearson, of Coombe House, Kingston Hill, Surrey, and Gt Barrington, Mass.
 1 Bessie Agnes; *b* 7 May 1863; *d* 25 June 1864
 2 Mildred Alice; *b* 31 Dec 1865; *m* Rev Frederick William Hodgson, Rector Stedham, Sussex, and *d* 24 Sept 1930, having had issue. He *d* 21 July 1939
 3 Gertrude; *b* 21 Feb 1871; *d* 2 Sept 1872
 4 Hilda; *b* and *d* 22 Feb 1873

WILLIAM NICHOLSON *m* 2nd 25 July 1876 Charlotte Alice, dau of Charles Mathew Clode, CB, FSA, and by her had:

 8 Walter Norris, CMG (1924), DSO (1916); *b* 10 June 1877; *educ* Charterhouse and Trin Coll Cambridge; served Boer War 1899–1902 (Queen's medal, three clasps, King's medal, two clasps) and WW I (despatches), AQMG N Cmmd India 1929–33, Col Suffolk Regt 1939–47; *m* 12 March 1924 Una Phyllis (*d* 27 April 1965), dau of Philip Higgs, of Kidlington, Oxon, and *d* 5 April 1964, leaving:

 (1) *Sarah Lothian [Mrs Stephen Bolton, Norney Rough, Shackleford, Surrey GU8 6AE]; *b* 27 July 1931; *m* 11 April 1953 *Maj Stephen Duncan Bolton, MA, DipEd Oxon, 11th Hus (PAO), yst s of Rev Julius Duncan Bolton, of Moonsfield, Brenchley, Kent, and has had:

1a *Robert Lothian Stephen; *b* 24 March 1958; BA Oxon, Maj TA RGJ; *m* 17 Nov 1984 *Hazel Margaret, dau of Alan East, of Charlton Kings, Glos, and has:

  1b *Richard Ashley Lothian; *b* 26 May 1990

  2b *Edward Alan George; *b* 1 Feb 1996

2a Mark Ashley; *b* 5 July 1961; *d* 21 Dec 1965

1a *Jacqueline Charlotte Matilda; *b* 1 May 1968

(2) *Susan Norris [Mrs Susan Cole, Royal Farm House, Elstead, Surrey GU8 6LA]; *b* 27 July 1936; *m* 28 July 1956 (*divorce* 19–) John Vernon Cole, er s of Kenneth Davey Cole, of Beech Hill Cottage, Hambledon, Surrey, and has:

1a *Simon Lawrence Vernon; *b* 22 Nov 1958

2a *Marcus John Davey; *b* 11 Sept 1961

3a *Dominic Andrew Mitchell; *b* 25 Oct 1965

1a *Miranda Jane Norris; *b* 25 May 1963; *m* 15 Oct 1988 *Paul Cooke and has:

  1b *Samuel Davey; *b* 11 Oct 1997

  1b *Kate Emily; *b* 25 June 1992

  2b *Poppy Elizabeth; *b* 18 Aug 1994

5 Lilian Maud; *b* 15 Sept 1878; *d* unm 1 April 1948

WILLIAM NICHOLSON *d* 29 Jan 1889; his eldest son,

Sir Charles Norris Nicholson, 1st Bt (UK), so *cr* 7 Feb 1912; *b* 30 July 1857; *educ* Trin Coll Cambridge (MA, LLM); barrister Lincoln's Inn, Second Church Estates Commr 1910–18, MP (Lib) Doncaster 1906–18; *m* 26 Jan 1882 Amy Letitia (*d* 20 Feb 1937), dau and heiress of George Crosfield, of Walton Lea, Warrington, Lancs, by Isabella, er dau of Henry Ashworth, of Turton, Lancs, and had:

1 George Crosfield Norris; *b* 19 Nov 1884; Asst Priv Sec to Parly Sec Admlty 1907–08 and U-Sec War 1908–12, Pncpl Priv Sec to Sec State War 1912–14, Capt RFC; *m* 18 Oct 1906 Hon Evelyn Izme Murray (*m* 2nd 31 July 1917 1st Baron Mottistone (*qv*); *d* 1976), yst dau of 1st Viscount Elibank (*see* ELIBANK, L), and was *kas* 11 March 1916, leaving:

  (1) JOHN NORRIS (Sir), **2nd Bt**

1 Dorothea Marian Norris; *b* 8 Oct 1887; *m* 8 July 1913 Maj Joseph Basil Lawrence Monteith, CBE, DL, JP, Gordon Highrs, of Carstairs, Lanarks, and *d* 16 April 1958, leaving issue. He *d* 20 Nov 1960

2 Olivia Joyce Norris; *b* 25 March 1895; *m* 1st 15 Nov 1917 (*divorce* 1932) Capt Herbert Sanford Ward, RAF, est s of Herbert Ward, of Paris, and had issue; *m* 2nd 25 May 1932 Lionel Jackson Mars, of Chelsea, er s of William Mars, and had further issue

Sir CHARLES *d* 29 Nov 1918; his gs,

Sir John Norris Nicholson, 2nd Bt, KBE (1971), CIE (1946), JP; *b* 19 Feb 1911; *educ* Winchester and Trin Coll Cambridge; Capt Cheshire Regt (TA), Lt Princess Beatrice's (IoW Rifles) Heavy Bde RA (TA) WW II (despatches), with Min Shipping 1941, Min War Tport rep Delhi, Chm Ocean Steamship Co 1957–71, dir and chm Martins Bank, Lt Lt IoW 1980–86 (V Ld Lt 1974–80); *m* 15 Oct 1938 Vittoria Vivien (*d* 1991), yst dau of Alfred Percy Trewhella, of Taormina, Sicily, and *d* 1993, leaving:

1 Sir CHARLES CHRISTIAN NICHOLSON, **3rd and present Bt**

2 +JAMES RICHARD LOTHIAN [James Nicholson Esq, The Stableyard, Kirtlington Park, Oxford]; *b* 24 Oct 1947; heir presumptive; *educ* Ampleforth and Churchill Coll Cambridge; *m* 1st 1974 (*divorce* 1980) Charmian Joy, dau of Maj Harcourt Michael Scudamore Gold, MC; *m* 2nd 1980 *Sarah Hazel, dau of Richard Alan Budgett, of Kirtlington, Oxford, and by her has:

  (1) +Edward; *b* 1983

  (1) *Lara; *b* 1986

1 *Tessa Mary [Mrs Piers Phipps, Trerose Manor, Mawnan, Falmouth, Cornwall]; *b* 14 April 1944; *m* 30 June 1967 *Piers Anthony Constantine Howard Phipps, only s of S/Ldr Francis Constantine Phipps and Mrs Patrick Anthony Ormond McGrath, of Southwater, Sussex

2 *(Mary) Louise Petronella [Mrs Adam Smail, Spring Hill, Compton Abdale, Glos GL54 4DU]; *b* 28 April 1950; *m* 2 June 1973 *Adam Trevor Kelly Smail, 2nd s of Lt-Col Adam Trevor Smail, DSO, of Edgeworth Manor, Stroud, Glos

NICHOLSON OF WINTERBOURNE

Creation: B. (LP, UK) 1997.

THE BARONESS NICHOLSON OF WINTERBOURNE, of Winterbourne, Roy Co of Berks (Emma Harriet Nicolson) [The Rt Hon The Baroness Nicholson of Winterbourne, House of Lords, London SW1A 0PW]; *b* 16 Oct 1941; *educ* St Mary's Sch Wantage and RAM; computer programmer, instructor and systems analyst ICL 1962–66, computer consultant John Tyzack and Ptnrs 1967–69, consultant gen management and computers McLintock Mann and Whinney Murray 1969–74; Dir Fund Raising Save The Children 1977–85); MP (C to 1996, Lib Dem 1996–97) Devon W and Torridge 1987–97; PPS to: Min State Home Office 1992–93, MAFF 1993–95, Fin Sec Treasury 1995–97, Fndr/Jt-Chm All Party Parly Gp Romanian Children; alternate memb UK Delegn WEU and Cncl Europe, Chm: All Party Parly Gp for Iraqi-Shias, C Backbench Environment Ctee 1991 (Sec 1990–91), Advsy Ctee Carnegie UK Tst Venues Improvement Programmes, V-Chm All Party Parly Gp Penal Affrs 1992, C Party 1983–87, memb: Select Ctee Employment 1990–91, Parly Panel RCN 1990–92, Exec Bd UNICEF UK, MRC, Cncl Europe Movement, European Union of Women, POW Advsy Tst Disability, Cncl PITCOM, CPS, RIIA, V-Pres: C Technology Forum, C Disability Gp, Western Area YCs, Small Farmers' Assoc, Assoc DCs; Dir Shelter; Visiting Parly Fell St Antony's Coll Oxford 1995; V-Moderator Movement for Ordination of Women 1991–; Pres: Plymouth and W Devon Cassette Talking Newspaper, W Regnl Assoc Deaf; Patron: Hospice Care Tst N Devon, CRUSAID; Devon Care Tst; Tstee Ross McWhirter Fndn; author: *Why does the West Forget?* (1993); *m* 1987, as his

2nd w, *Sir Michael Harris Caine, s of Sir Sydney Caine, KCMG, and has an adopted s and a stepson and stepdau

Lineage: Lineage: JOHN NICHOLSON, of Great Corby, Cumberland; *d* 1728, leaving, with three daus:

JAMES NICHOLSON, of Southwaite, Hesket-in-the-Forest, Cumberland; *m* 1731 Ann, dau of William Bowman, of Burdoswald, Lanercost Abbey, Cumberland, and *d* 1755, leaving, with two yr sons and two daus:

JOHN NICHOLSON, of Southwaite, Cumberland; *d* 1732; *m* 1771 Ann (*d* 1835), dau of James Graham, of Kirkoswald Parks, and *d* 1805, having had, with two est sons, five yst sons and two daus:

JOHN NICHOLSON, of Upper Clapton, Middx; *b* 20 Feb 1778; *m* 1811 Ellen (*d* 12 July 1863), yr dau of Richard Payne, of Rochester, and *d* 24 Nov 1846, having had, with three er sons and four daus:

WILLIAM NICHOLSON, of Basing Park, Hants (which he bought 1863), JP, DL Hants; *b* 2 Sept 1824; MP (Lib) Petersfield 1866–74 and 1880–85, High Sheriff Hants 1878; *m* 1858 Isabella Sarah (*d* 26 Sept 1934 aged 99), only dau of John Meek, of Camberwell, and *d* 25 July 1909, having had:

1 William Graham, PC (1925), of Basing Park, JP, DL Hants; *b* 11 March 1862; *educ* Harrow and Trin Coll Cambridge (BA); CA Hants, Lt-Col and Hon Col cmdg 3rd Bn Hants Regt, MP (C) E Hants 1897–1935; *m* 19 July 1890 Alice Margaret (*d* 8 May 1935), only dau of William Wither Bramston Beach, PC, MP (*see* ST ALDWYN, E), and *d* 29 July 1942, leaving:

  (1) Otho William, TD (1942), DL (Middx 1942); *b* 30 Nov 1891; *educ* Harrow and Magdalene Coll Cambridge; Lt 5th Bn Rifle Bde WW I, Hon Col 1st AA Div Signals (TA), cmded 40th AA Group (TA) 1938–41, 54th AA Bde 1941–42, Assist Cmdt Sch AA Artillery 1942, V-Chm Middx TA&AFA, Brig, memb LCC 1922–25, Mayor Finsbury 1923–24, MP (C) Westminster Abbey 1924–32, CStJ; *m* 12 Jan 1927 (*divorce* 1932) Elisabeth, er dau of Frederick C Bramwell, of Hythe, Kent, and had:

    1a *Diana Mary; *b* 29 May 1928; *m* 12 May 1955 *Maj Jonathan Mungo Palmes Walker (*see* WALKER, Bt, of Sand Hutton) and has issue

    2a *Ursula Isabel; *b* 3 Feb 1931; *m* 8 July 1961 *Lt-Cdr Anthony Ainger Browne, RN, only s of Lt-Col Cuthbert Garrard Browne, CMG, DSO, of Shamley Green, Surrey, and has:

      1b *Nicholas Ainger; *b* 15 Nov 1962

      1b *Caroline Jane; *b* 8 June 1964

  (2) (John) Humphrey, MC; *b* 14 Sept 1893; *educ* Marlborough and Trin Coll Cambridge (BA); Lt-Col Roy Wilts Yeo WW I; *m* 9 Oct 1929 (Elizabeth) Anne, only dau of Sir Henry Floyd, 4th Bt (*qv*)

2 John Sanctuary, CB (1902), CMG (1905), CBE (1918), DSO (1897); *b* 19 May 1863; *educ* Harrow; Matabele Campaign 1896 (despatches), Boer War (despatches), WW I (despatches), Inspr-Gen SA Constabulary 1903–05 , Hon Brig-Gen, Lt-Col and Brevet Col 7th Hus, MP Westminster Abbey 1921–24, Grand Offr Order Avis Portugal; *d* unm 21 Feb 1924

3 Arthur Carleton, TD, JP, DL, of Hartham Park, Corsham, Wilts; *b* 2 July 1864; *educ* Winchester and Ch Ch Oxford (BA 1885); Lt-Col Hants Yeo, Boer War, WW I, High Sheriff Wilts 1929; *m* 31 Aug 1909 Agnes Susan Elizabeth (*d* 30 April 1966), dau of William Alexander Dumaresq, of NSW, and *d* 11 Feb 1945, leaving:

  (1) *Arthur Wilfrid, of Hartham Park; *b* 8 Oct 1913; *educ* Winchester and Ch Ch Oxford (MA); Civ Serv Dept Overseas Trade 1938 and 1945–47, Min Ec Warfare 1930–43, FO 1943–45; *m* 1st 26 June 1948 (*divorce* 1959) Jean Elinor Mary, er dau of Lt-Col Donald James Handford, of Guyers, Corsham, Wilts, and has:

    1a *Anthony Arthur; *b* 19 Feb 1950; *educ* Bryanston

    2a *Charles Dumaresq; *b* 13 Dec 1952; *educ* Winchester

  (1) (cont.) Arthur W Nicholson *m* 2nd 11 Nov 1959, as her 2nd w, *Margaret, formerly w of Edward Hugh Lee Rowcliffe, TD, and only dau of Sir Henry Anthony Farrington, 6th Bt (*qv*)

  (1) Ruth Isabel Agnes; *b* 3 April 1912; *d* unm 29 Sept 1968

4 Richard Francis, of Woodcott House, Whitchurch, Hants; *b* 7 Oct 1865; *educ* Harrow and Trin Coll Cambridge (MA 1894); *m* 31 Aug 1897 Helen Violet, er dau of Rev George Raymond Portal (*see* PORTAL, Bt), and *d* 6 May 1940, leaving:

  (1) Claude, CB; *b* 2 July 1898; *educ* Winchester; Brig, Lt-Col 16th/5th Lancers, Defence Calais May 1940; *m* 31 Dec 1935, as her 1st husb, Hon Ursula Katherine Hanbury-Tracy (*see* SUDELEY, B) and *d* a POW in Germany 26/27 June 1943, leaving:

    1a *Richard Hugh; *b* 17 Nov 1936; *educ* Winchester; T/Capt 16th/5th Queen's Roy Lancers 1955–60 [Woodcott House, Whitchurch, Hants]; *m* 23 June 1960 *Margaret Jane, yr dau of Lt-Col Henry Charles Minshull Stockdale (*see* STOCKDALE, Bt), and has:

      1b *James Alexander; *b* 3 Sept. 1965

      1b *Camilla; *b* 19 Oct 1962

    1a *Sylvia Mary Victoria; *b* 20 Nov 1939; *m* 20 Feb 1965 her bro's bro-in-law Christopher Minshull Stockdale (*d* 12 May 1970) and has issue

  (2) Sir GODFREY NICHOLSON, 1st and last Bt, so *cr* 21 March 1958, of Winterbourne, Berks; *b* 9 Dec 1901; *educ* Winchester and Ch Ch Oxford (MA 1925); Roy Fus and Commandos WW II 1939–42, MP (Nat C) Morpeth 1931–35 and (C) Farnham 1937–66, Chm Estimates Ctee 1961–64, FSA; *m* 30 June 1936 Lady Katharine Constance Lindsay, 5th dau of 27th Earl of Crawford and (10th Earl of) Balcarres (*qv*), and *d* 14 July 1991, when the btcy expired, leaving:

    1a *Rose Helen; *b* 13 May 1937; *m* 5 April 1961 *Sir Richard Napier Luce, PC, MP (C) Arundel and Shoreham 1971–74 and Shoreham 1974–92, only s of Sir William Henry Tucker Luce, GBE, KCMG, of Brook House, Fovant, Wilts, and has:

      1b *Alexander Richard; *b* 18 July 1964

      2b *Edward Godfrey; *b* 1 June 1968

    2a *Laura Violet; *b* 18 Jan 1939; *m* 9 Sept 1964 *Sir John Christopher Foggo Montgomery Cuninghame, 12th Bt, and has issue (*qv*)

    3a EMMA HARRIET, *cr* a **Baroness**

4a *Harriet Mary; *b* 29 June 1946; *m* 25 Sept 1969 *Charles Hamilton Flower (*see* ABERCORN, D)

5 Hugh Blomfield, DSO (1918), JP (Dorset); *b* 13 Nov 1866; *educ* Harrow and New Coll Oxford; Maj KRRC WW I (despatches twice), Dorset: CA, High Sheriff 1926; *m* 1st 17 Dec 1902 Kathleen Laura, DGStJ (*d* 9 Aug 1936), 2nd dau of Ulick John Burke, of Newton Valence Manor, Hants; *m* 2nd 28 Feb 1940 Eileen Dorothy (*d* 29 Oct 1968), only child of Capt Frank William Northey, 36th Regt, of Box, Wilts, and *d* 10 Dec 1958

6 Reginald, TD, JP (Hants 1926); *b* 26 Nov 1867; *educ* Winchester and Trin Coll Cambridge (MA 1894); High Sheriff Hants 1939, Maj Hants Yeo; *m* 7 June 1904 Lady (Laura) Margaret, widow of Alfred Millington Knowles and yr dau of 9th Earl Waldegrave (*qv*), and *d* 13 Oct 1952, leaving:

(1) Gerald Hugh, of The Round House, Bayford, Herts; *b* 24 April 1905; *educ* Harrow and Magdalene Coll Cambridge; Lt-Col; *m* 21 Oct 1930 Margaret Evelyn, only dau of Nigel Hanbury, and *d* 11 May 1970, leaving:

1a *John Gerald [John Nicholson Esq, Benefield House, Lower Benefield, Peterborough PE8 5AF]; *b* 26 Aug 1937; *educ* Eton; *m* 11 April 1964 *Priscilla Faith, only dau of Michael Francis Berry, of Benefield House, and has:

1b *Andrew William; *b* 27 Feb 1966; *educ* Eton

2b *Henry Michael Hugh; *b* 6 Nov 1969; *educ* Eton

1b *Clare Fenella; *b* 4 March 1967

2a *Christopher Nigel [Christopher Nicholson Esq, Wootton Farm, Stoke Darcy, Herefs]; *b* 13 June 1939; *educ* Haileybury and RAC Cirencester; QALAS; *m* 12 July 1969 *Sandra Valerie, yr dau of Nestonna Ord Capper, of Lower Hope, Ullingswick, Herefs, and has:

1b *A son; *b* 17 April 1974

3a *Robin Alaster [Robin Nicholson Esq, 7 Highbury Place, London N5 1QZ]; *b* 27 July 1944; *educ* Eton and Magdalene Coll Cambridge; *m* *Fiona Bird (*see* VAVASOUR, Bt) and has:

1b *A son; *b* 7 March 1971

2b *A son; *b* 13 Sept 1974

1a *Mary Joan; *b* 23 Nov 1931

2a *Jean Fenella; *b* 25 May 1934; *m* 15 July 1961 *Maj Douglas Christopher Prior, Scots Gds, s of C L Prior, of Gingley Stock, Essex, and has:

1b *James Douglas; *b* 10 Jan 1965

1b *Lucinda Jane; *b* 8 Oct 1962

(2) David John Stafford; *b* 15 Jan 1907; *educ* Winchester and Magdalene Coll Cambridge (MA); barrister Inner Temple 1932, Capt Roy Hants Regt WW II; *m* 18 April 1950 *Rosemary Christian [Mrs David Nicholson, Marks Barn, Crewkerne, Somerset], dau of Lt-Col Frank Melvin Matthews, MBO, OBE, of W Meon, and *d* 28 Dec 1965, having adopted:

*Alan John Melvin; *b* 29 March 1952; *educ* Malvern

*Iain Reginald; *b* 11 Jan 1954 (HRH PRINCES ALICE, COUNTESS OF ATHLONE, stood sponsor); *educ* Malvern

*Christian Iona Margaret; *b* 12 Sept 1955

(3) *William Reginald, DSO, OBE; *b* 29 Dec 1909; *educ* Harrow and RMC Sandhurst; Col cmdg 2nd Lothian and Border Horse and 16th/5th Lancers WW II (despatches); *m* 25 Jan 1939 *Diana Mary, dau of Maj Charles Nelson, DSO, of Brockenhurst, Hants, and had:

1a *Michael William; *b* 11 April 1941; *educ* Harrow; ACA; *m* 29 April 1967 *Jane Rose, er dau of John Young, of East End Farm, Ringstead, Norfolk, and has:

1b *Victoria Louise; *b* 11 Dec 1969

2a *Nigel Richard; *b* 7 Dec 1946; *educ* Harrow

(1) *Joan Margaret; *b* 19 May 1912; *m* 7 July 1934 Sir Peter Curtis, 6th Bt (*qv*), and has issue

7 Godfrey Maule; *b* 31 March 1872; *educ* Winchester and Ch Ch Oxford; Lt Hants Artillery Militia; *d* unm 12 July 1901

8 Clement Octavius Edward; *b* 7 Aug 1874; *educ* Harrow and Trin Coll Cambridge; Lt RSG and Scottish Horse, Boer War, WW I (despatches twice, Brevet Maj), Offr Order Redeemer Greece; *m* 30 Dec 1913 Judith Lilian (*d* 13 Oct 1951 aged 89), 6th dau of Thomas Frederick Burnaby-Atkins, and *d* 4 Jan 1930

1 Ellen Isabel; *m* 4 Sept 1878 Rev Preb Edward Russell Bernard (*d* 22 April 1921), Canon and Chllr Salisbury, Chaplain in Ordinary to HM GEORGE V 1911–21, s of Rev Thomas Dehany Bernard, and *d* 27 Oct 1953 aged 94, leaving issue

2 Edith Mary; *m* 25 Oct 1898, as his 2nd w, Col Sir Edward Ridley Colborne Bradford, 1st Bt (*qv*), and *d* 28 March 1951 aged 89

3 Isabel Winifred Maud; *d* unm 27 June 1959 aged 90

4 Mary Stephanie, OBE (1918); *m* 5 Sept 1891 Lt-Col Henry Matthew Ridley (*see* RIDLEY, V) and *dsp* 22 March 1948 aged 78

5 Gertrude Ann; *m* 10 Jan 1912 Lt-Col George Wemyss Anson (*see* LICHFIELD, E) and *d* 30 Jan 1961 aged 89

6 Marion Theodora; *m* 26 Sept 1899 Maj Edward Frederick Talbot-Ponsonby and *d* 1 Jan 1970 aged 96, leaving issue (*see* SHREWSBURY and WATERFORD, E)

NICKSON

Arms: Azure, a cross flory or between four bezants, on a chief argent a wolf's head erased proper. **Crest:** A lion rampant proper supporting a tilting spear argent point downwards. **Supporters:** Two salmon proper each charged with a hurt thereon a cross flory or. **Motto:** (above crest) *Pedem prolatum refero nunquam* ('Having put my foot forward, there I keep it'). **Creation:** B. (LP, UK) 1994.

THE BARON NICKSON, of Renagour, in the District of Stirling (Sir David Wigley Nickson, KBE (1987, CBE 1981)) [The Rt Hon The Lord Nickson KBE DL, Renagour House, Aberfoyle, Stirling FK8 3TF]; *b* 27 Nov 1929; *educ* Eton and RMA Sandhurst; Coldstream Gds 1949–54, dir: William Collins plc 1959–76 (v-chm and gp md 1976–83), Radio Clyde 1981–85, Scottish & Newcastle 1981–95 (dep-chm 1982, chm 1983–89), Edinburgh Investment Tst 1981–94, Hambro's 1989– and National Australia Bank Ltd 1991–, chm: Clydesdale Bank 1991– (dir 1981–, dep-chm 1990–91), Countryside Commn Scotland 1983–85 and Atlantic Salmon Tst 1988–95, dep-chm Gen Accident 1993– (dir 1981–), Pres CBI 1986–88 (Chm Scotland 1979–81), memb: Scottish Ec Cncl 1980–94, NEDC 1985–88, Sr Salaries Review Body 1989–95, Scottish Devpt Agency 1989–91 and Scottish Enterprise 1990–93, Brig Roy Co Archers, Chllr Glasgow Caledonian U 1993–, V-Lt Stirling and Falkirk 1997– (DL 1982–97), Hon DUniv Stirling 1986, Hon DBA Napier Poly 1990, Hon Fell U of Paisley 1992, CIMgt (CBIM 1980), FRSE 1987; *m* 18 Oct 1952 *(Helen) Louise, dau of Lt-Col Louis William La Trobe Cockcraft, DSO, MVO, and has:

1 *Felicity; *b* 1955; *m* 1980 *James Lewis and has:

(1) *Emily; *b* 1984

(2) *Sophie; *b* 1986

(3) *Harriet; *b* 1989

2 *Lucy; *b* 1959; *m* 1983 *Melfort Campbell and has:

(1) *Iona; *b* 1986

(2) *Araminta; *b* 1988

(3) *Alice; *b* 1990

3 *Rosemary; *b* 1963; *m* 1986 (*divorce* 1992) George Petronanos and has:

(1) *Andrew; *b* 1988

3 (cont.) Mrs Rosemary Petronanas *m* 2nd 1992 *Maj Alexander Campbell and has:

(2) *Alexander Nickson; *b* 1995

Lineage: GEOFFREY WIGLEY NICKSON; *m* Janet Mary Dobie and had:

DAVID WIGLEY NICKSON, *cr* a **Baron**

NICOL

Creation: B. (LP, UK) 1982.

THE BARONESS NICOL, of Newnham, Co Cambridge (Olive Mary Wendy Rowe-Hunter) [The Rt Hon The Baroness Nicol, House of Lords, London SW1A 0PW]; *b* 21 March 1923; *educ* Cahir Sch Co Tipperary Ireland; Civ Serv 1943–48; Tstee Utd Charities 1967–86; Cncllr Cambridge City 1972–82; memb: Cncl Granta Housing Soc 1975–; Supplementary Benefits Tbnl 1976–78, Careers Serv Consultative Panel 1978–81; Oppn Whip 1983–87, Oppn Dep Ch Whip 1987–89; JP Cambridge 1972–86, FRGS 1990; *m* 1947 *Alexander Douglas Ian Nicol, CBE, s of Alexander Nicol, and has :

1 *Adrian Timothy; *b* 4 March 1949; *m* 1st 1973 (*divorce* 1984) Valerie Joan, dau of Alan Gilbert, of Mobberley, Cheshire, and has a s and dau; *m* 2nd 1991 *Christine Susan, dau of Herbert John Barnes, of Paignton, Devon, and by her has:

(1) *Thomas Alexander; *b* 1988

(2) *James Edward Jack; *b* 1991

2 *Colin Douglas; *b* 1950; *m* 1992 *June, dau of Donald Alexander Smith, of Hull

1 *Jane Lesley; *b* 1954; *m* 1984 *Edward John, only s of J E John, of Margam, Port Talbot, W Glam

Lineage: JAMES ROWE-HUNTER; *m* Harriet Hannah — (*d* 1932) and *d* 1962, leaving:

OLIVE MARY WENDY, *cr* a **Baroness**

NIGHTINGALE

Arms: Per pale erm. and gu. a rose counterchanged. **Crest:** An ibex sejant arg., tufted, armed and maned or. **Motto:** *Pro rege et patria* ('For king and country'). **Creation:** Bt. (E) 1 Sept 1628.

SIR CHARLES MANNERS GAMALIEL NIGHTINGALE, 17TH BT, of Newport Pond, Co Essex [Sir Charles Nightingale Bt, 16 Unity Grove, Harrogate, N Yorks HG1 2AQ]; *b* 21 Feb 1947; *s* f 1977; *educ* St Paul's and OU (BA 1990); DHSS: exec offr 1969, higher exec offr 1977, sr exec offr 1989, grade 7 1996

Lineage: GEOFFREY NIGHTINGALE (descended from William Nightingale (*d* 1474), of Brentwood, Essex), of Newport Pond, Essex; Double Reader Gray's Inn; *m* Katharine, dau and heiress of John Clamps, of Huntingdon, and *d* 22 Feb 1619, leaving:

Sir Thomas Nightingale, 1st Bt (E), so *cr* 1 Sept 1628, of Newport Pond and Kneesworth, Cambs; High Sheriff Essex 1627; *m* 1st Millicent, dau of Sir Robert Clerk, and had:

1 Robert; *m* Theodosia, dau of Sir Robert Chester, and *dvp* 30 April 1639, having had:

(1) **Sir Thomas Nightingale, 2nd Bt**; *b* 15 Oct 1629; *m* Jane (*d* 1705), dau of George Shires, of Slyfield Hall, Surrey, and heiress of her n, Sir George Shires, Bt, and was *bur* 19 Oct 1702, having had:

1a Robert (Sir); Sheriff Norfolk 1685–86, ktd 1685; *m* Sarah Cock (*m* 2nd John Burkin; *d* 19 Aug 1724) and dsp & *vp* 3 July 1697

(2) Geoffrey, of Enfield; *m* Anne, dau of John Bridges, of London, and was *bur* 23 July 1690, having had:

1a **Sir Bridges Nightingale, 3rd Bt**; *d* unm

2a **Sir Robert Nightingale, 4th Bt**; Dir HEIC; *d* unm by 24 July 1722, when his estates passed to his gn, Robert Gascoyne (*see* below), while the btcy became dormant

1a Anne; *m* Francis Theobald, of Barking, Suffolk, and had:

1b Joseph Gascoyne (Rev); Vicar Enfield; had:

1c Robert Gascoyne; *s* to the Nightingale estates

Sir Thomas, 1st Bt, *m* 2nd his niece by marriage Catherine, dau of Sir Robert Chester, and *d* Jan 1644, having by her had, with other issue (*d* unm):

2 Geoffrey, of Kneesworth, *m* Elizabeth, dau of Sir William Luckyn, and *d* 9 May 1681, leaving:

(1) EDWARD NIGHTINGALE, *de jure* 5th Bt, of Kneesworth; did not assume the title; *bapt* 27 Aug 1658; *m* Anne Charlotte, dau of Sir Arthur Slingsby, 1st Bt, of Bifrons, and *d* 2 July 1723; his e s:

1a GAMALIEL NIGHTINGALE, *de jure* 6th Bt; did not assume the title; *d* unm in or after 1722

2a EDWARD NIGHTINGALE, *de jure* 7th Bt; did not assume the title; *b* 1696; *m* Eleanora (*d* 14 Sept 1771), dau of Charles Ethelston, and *d* 20 Oct 1750; his e s:

1b EDWARD NIGHTINGALE, *de jure* 8th Bt; did not assume the title; *b* 4 Sept 1726; *d* unm July 1782

2b GAMALIEL NIGHTINGALE, *de jure* 9th Bt; did not assume the title; *b* 15 Feb 1731; Capt RN; *m* Narua (*d* 20 Feb 1789), dau of Peter Clossen, of Hamburg, and *d* Jan 1791, leaving:

1c **Sir Edward Nightingale, 10th Bt**; established right to and assumed the title 1797; *b* 14 Oct 1760; *m* 28 Dec 1782 his cousin Eleanor (*d* 20 Jan 1825), dau and heiress of his unc Robert Nightingale, of Kneesworth (s of EDWARD NIGHTINGALE, *de jure* 7th Bt), and had, with three other sons and a dau:

1d CHARLES ETHELSTON (Sir), **11th Bt**

2d Alexander Malcolm; *b* 30 Nov 1792; *m* 1818 Marianne (*d* 17 Feb 1847), dau of Maj Herbert Beaver, 19th Regt, and *d* 11 Jan 1826, having had:

1e Edward Herbert; *b* 15 April 1821; Capt 23rd Regt Madras LI; *m* Sophia (*m* 2nd 18 Oct 1865 Lt-Col J W Carter), dau of Lt-Gen Robert Blackall, Bengal Army, and *d* 5 May 1856, leaving:

1f Emily Grace; *m* —

2e Manners Randolph; *b* 30 April 1823; Lt-Col Bengal SC; *m* 15 May 1851 Elizabeth Ann (*d* 1889), 2nd dau of Bryan William Stevens, of Weston, Northants, and *d* 25 July 1892, having had, with a dau (*d* unm):

1f Charles Alexander Malcolm; *b* 12 May 1853; *m* 1878 Caroline (*d* 18 Jan 1927), dau of W Johnson, of Richmond, Surrey, and *d* May 1905, leaving:

1g Grace Caroline; *m* 2 Dec 1903 Harry R Mackeson and *d* 12 Oct 1944, leaving issue. He *d* 1909

2g Elizabeth Anne; *m* 3 Dec 1913 Archibald J Baker and *d* 9 Sept 1921

3e Charles William, JP Devon; *b* 15 May 1825; Lt-Col Bengal SC; *m* 4 Feb 1858 Martha (*d* 22 April 1921), 2nd dau of Maj James Winfield, Bengal Army, and *d* 28 Oct 1912, leaving:

1f Marianne Florence; *d* unm 15 Oct 1952 aged 94

3d Leonard; *b* 9 Feb 1794; *m* — Perry and had issue

4d Geoffrey; *b* 2 March 1799; *m* 29 June 1822 Mary (*d* 15 April 1873), only dau of Thomas Knowlys, of Stockwell, and *d* 15 Jan 1864, having had:

1e Geoffrey; *b* 1823; Lt-Col Madras Army; *m* 25 Feb 1858 Anna Maria Martha (*d* 28 April 1911), 3rd dau of Thomas John Knowlys, DL, of Heysham Tower, Lancs, and *d* 5 Oct 1868, leaving two daus (*d* unm)

2e Frederic Charles; *b* 29 Aug 1835; *m* 10 Sept 1868 Katherine Jane (*d* 2 Nov 1918), only dau of Francis Hamilton, of Friar's Place, Middx, and *d* 18 Feb 1916, having had:

1f Philip Geoffry; *d* an infant 7 Aug 1877

2f Claud Robert, MC; *b* 18 June 1878; *educ* Radley; Capt RASC WW I (despatches); *m* 18 Jan 1912 Eleanor Maude (*d* 19 Jan 1977), yr dau of Sir William Percival Rivett-Carnac, 5th Bt (*qv*), and *d* 11 Feb 1954, leaving:

1g Christopher Carnac; *b* 2 Oct 1913; *educ* Marlborough; Lt RNVR WW II, FIA; *m* 25 Oct 1941 *Muriel de Lissa, dau of F B Philips, of Leatherhead, and *d* 15 April 1970, leaving:

1h +Nicholas John [Nicholas Nightingale Esq, Woodnorton, Oakwood, Northumberland]; *b* 29 Aug 1942; *educ* Trin Coll Dublin (BA, LLB 1964); slr 1968; *m* 27 Dec 1968 *Susan Kay, BA (Keele), Dip Soc Sci, dau of Philip Lyth, of Park Hill, Southwell, Notts, and has:

1i +Thomas James; *b* 1977

1i *Rebecca Jane; *b* 1972

2i *Elizabeth Jane; *b* 14 March 1976

1h *Anne Christine [Mrs Kenneth Murchison, 21 Calvert Ave, Killara, NSW 2071, Australia]; *b* 18 Dec 1944; *m* 1972 *Kenneth Ian Murchison and has:

1i *Scott Timothy; *b* 1973

2i *Hamish Charles; *b* 1977

1i *Emma Georgina; *b* 1974

2h *Patricia Ruth [Mrs Ian Christie, 131 Mount View Rd, London N4]; *b* 16 April 1950; *m* 1979 *Ian Christie and has:

1i *Edward Nightingale; *b* 1987

1i *Beatrice Nightingale; *b* 1980

2i *Laura Nightingale; *b* 1982

3i *Isabel Nightingale; *b* 1985

2g Robert Forbes; *b* 4 Sept 1917; *educ* Stowe; ACCA, Lt RA WW II; *m* 1st 1 Nov 1940 (*divorce* 1956) Lesley Phyllis, dau of S Kenneth West, and *d* 1993, leaving:

1h +Peter Robert [Peter Nightingale Esq, Meadowbank, The Avenue, Godalming, Surrey]; *b* 15 Jan 1947; *educ* Lucton Sch Leominster, OU (BA 1986) and Keele U (MA 1987); *m* 20 April 1968 *Joan Anne, dau of James Alexander Kerr, and has:

1i +James Peter [James Nightingale Esq, 35 Bridgefield Close, Holmbush Way, Midhurst, W Sussex]; *b* 5 Sept 1974

1i *Andrea Jane [Mrs Andrew Hurley, 34 Kingsfield Cres, Newland, Witney, Oxon]; *b* 13 April 1969; *m* 1994 *Andrew Hurley and has:

1j *Megan Anne; *b* 14 March 1997

2i *Helen Mary [Miss Helen Nightingale, 3 Windrush Close, Bramley, Surrey]; *b* 17 June 1971

2h +Richard John [Richard Nightingale Esq, Blackdown Cottage, Denbigh Rd, Haslemere, Surrey]; *b* 6 Dec 1948; *m* 1971 *Frances Catherine, dau of C B Green, and has:

1i *Catherine; *b* 1972

2g (cont.) Robert Nightingale *m* 2nd 2 Aug 1956 Dora (*d* 1992), dau of George Henry Kirkpatrick, and *d* 1993

3f Dudley Arthur; *b* 4 Dec 1880; *educ* Harrow and Trin Coll Cambridge (BA 1902); Lt Roy Def Corps WW I; *m* 10 July 1912 Sylvia Dorothea Bold Hesketh (*d* 6 Dec 1949), dau of Louis Arthur Goodeve, and *dsp* 13 July 1954

3e Arthur Collett; *b* 1 March 1837; Col and Lt-Col Cmdt 2nd Bn Princess Louise's Argyll and Sutherland Highrs; *d* 10 Jan 1899

1d Leonora; *m* 16 April 1808 James Markland, 63rd Regt

2d Julia; *d* 11 March 1815

3d Elizabeth Sophia; *m* 8 March 1811 Hon Charles Ewan Law, s of 1st Baron Ellenborough (*qv*), and *d* 25 Jan 1864

Sir EDWARD d 4 Dec 1804; his est s,

Sir Charles Ethelston Nightingale, 11th Bt; b 1 Nov 1784; Lt 3rd Foot Gds; m 9 Dec 1805 Maria (d 8 Dec 1847), dau of Thomas Lacy Dickonson, of W Retford, Notts, and d 8 Dec 1846, having had, with three sons (d young) and a dau (d unm):

1 **Sir Charles Nightingale, 12th Bt**; b 30 April 1809; m 2 Feb 1829 Harriet Maria (d 22 Dec 1881 aged 81), dau of Edward Broughton Foster, of Ayleston, Leics, and d 17 Sept 1876, having had:

(1) **Sir Henry Dickonson Nightingale, 13th Bt**; b 15 Nov 1830; Lt-Col Army Pay Dept, 21st Fus, 80th Foot, 45th Foot and RM, served Burmese War 1852; m 12 Feb 1856 Mary Anne (d 7 May 1924), dau of Capt Thomas Spark, RN, and d 17 July 1911, having had:

1a Edward Henry; b 17 June 1856; educ St John's Coll Cambridge (MA); barrister; m 9 July 1887 Lily Maitland (d 6 Dec 1916), est dau of Capt Charles Daniel Addison, 39th Regt, and dvp 26 Jan 1895, leaving:

1b **Sir Edward Manners Nightingale, 14th Bt**; b 30 Dec 1888; Capt RAOC (TAR) WW I (two medals); m 11 Dec 1923 Alice Duncan (d 14 Jan 1975), est dau of Robert Mackay Sutherland, of Solsgirth, Kinross-shire, and dsp 26 Aug 1953

2a Valentine Charles; b 3 Feb 1859; m 16 May 1894 Alice Mary (m 3rd 19 Feb 1916 Robert Symmons Clifton; d 23 Aug 1928), widow of Edgar Vaux-Huggett and dau of Rev Henry Eastfield Bayly, Rector Fiddington, Somerset, and dsp 11 May 1914

3a Harry Ethelston; b 15 March 1860; m 17 May 1881 Coralie Louise Pauline Jeanne (d 18 May 1935), yr dau of Louis Charles d'Harcourt Mary, of Monconrour, Côtes du Nord, France, and d 23 Jan 1933, leaving:

1b Naomi Coralie; m 6 June 1914 Lt-Cdr Sir Griffith Wilfred Norman Boynton, 13th Bt, RN (d 10 March 1966; see 1949 edn)

1a Florence Muriel; m 30 June 1879 Maj-Gen Arthur Robert Macdonnell, RE, and d 14 Sept 1888

2a Emily Frances Mary; m 1 Jan 1886 Mansfeldt Henry Mills, 2nd s of Mansfeldt Forster Mills, of Tapton Grove, Chesterfield, and d 25 Feb 1940, leaving issue

3a Violet Harriet; RRC; m 24 Nov 1894 Col Charles Herbert Clay, 8th Gurkhas, IA, and d 1938, leaving issue

(1) Rosalind Agnes; m 22 Sept 1857 Lt-Col Edward Smyth Mercer, 5th Regt, and d 10 Nov 1896

2 Thomas Henry; b 18 April 1810; RN, Port Capt Simon's Bay, Cape of Good Hope; m 22 Nov 1830 Hannah Elizabeth (d 8 Aug 1879), est dau of John H Parry, and d 12 Dec 1865, having had:

(1) Percy; b 10 Jan 1836; Inspecting Commr Cape Good Hope; m 3 July 1860 Frances Emma (d 9 May 1905), est dau of Peter Brophy, and d 24 May 1895, leaving:

1a Thomas Slingsby, CMG (1915), CBE (1918); b 29 Jan 1866; Official Sec Office of HC Union S Africa 1911–18; m 21 April 1900 Doris Elizabeth (d 3 Sept 1959), yst dau of Charles Stoughton Collison, of E Bilney, Norfolk, and d 20 June 1918, leaving:

1b **Sir Geoffrey Slingsby Nightingale, 15th Bt**; b 24 Nov 1904; educ Marlborough and London Hosp; MRCS Eng, LRCP Lond, DPM 1934, Lt-Col RAMC WW II: Psychiatrist SE and Western Commands, OC Div 32nd Gen Hosp BLA, Physician Supt Warley Hosp 1946–69, consulting psychiatrist Oldchurch and Barking Hosps; m 18 Jan 1936 Mary Madeleine (d 27 Dec 1970), dau of Richard Doyle, of Tramore, Co Waterford, and adopted:

*Jeremy Roger; b 27 Feb 1945; educ Beaumont; slr Essex

2b Roger Chester; b 8 Jan 1909; educ Blundell's; Maj RA, formerly Devonshire Regt and HAC WW II (despatches); ka France 1 Sept 1944

1b Ihone Doris; b 8 June 1911; d unm 5 Nov 1956

2a Percy Athelstan, JP; b 7 Oct 1867; Dist Surgn and MO Victoria, S Rhodesia, DM (Edin); m 7 Jan 1899 Muriel Stoughton (m 2nd 21 May 1919 Lt-Col Richard Philip Aremberg de Moleyns (see VENTRY, B); d 12 July 1955), 3rd dau of Charles Stoughton Collison, of E Bilney, and d 17 Oct 1918, leaving:

1b CHARLES ATHELSTAN (Sir), **16th Bt**

3a Lacy Gamaliel, KC; b 25 March 1869; educ Univ Coll Oxford (MA, BCL); barrister Inner Temple, Advocate Supreme Court Union S Africa, Attorney-Gen Transvaal and CP; m 24 Oct 1906 Katie (d 25 Nov 1930), only dau of J M Wagner, of Johannesburg, and d 22 Feb 1934, leaving:

1b Manners Percy; b 28 Jan 1908; educ St John's Coll Johannesburg and St Thomas's Hosp; MRCS Eng, LRCP Lond 1937, SBStJ; m 12 Dec 1936 Mary Ursula (d 1983), er dau of Rev George Sanders Gilbert, Vicar Groombridge, Sussex, and d 30 Sept 1974, leaving:

1c +EDWARD LACY GEORGE [Edward Nightingale Esq, Kneesworth, Hollerday Drive, Lynton, N Devon EX35 6HQ]; b 11 May 1938; heir presumptive; educ Exeter Sch; Master Mariner

1c *Jane Elizabeth; b 20 Feb 1940

2b Neville Gascoyne; b 20 May 1911; educ Diocesan Coll Cape Town and St John's Coll Cambridge (BA 1933); barrister Inner Temple 1936, Lt Middx Regt WW II (wounded); m 21 Aug 1946 *Nancy Esther [Mrs Neville Nightingale, 56 Shelfanger Rd, Diss, Norfolk], dau of Godfrey James Whistler, of Ross-on-Wye, Herefs, and d 29 Sept 1989, leaving:

1c +Thomas (Tommy) Lacy Manners [Thomas Nightingale Esq, 102 Denmark St, Diss, Norfolk]; b 23 May 1947; educ Sandon House Sch; m 1993 *Lois Allison, only dau of Rev Thomas Oswald Welch Glass, of Roydon, Norfolk

4a Manners Ralph Wilmott, CB (1923), CMG (1918), CIE (1919), DSO (1915); b 15 April 1871; served Tirah Campaign 1898 (medal), China Expdn 1900–01 (medal), WW I (despatches, wounded, three medals), Bde Cdr 1917, Kurdistan 1919 (medal and clasp), Iraq 1920 (clasp), T/Col Cmdt 1921, Bde Cdr 1923, Waziristan 1923–24 (medal and clasp), Maj-Gen IA 1924 (ret 1929), Col 5th Roy Gurkha Rifles (FF) IA 1937–45, CD WW II, Coronation Medal 1937; m 1st 1 Aug 1907 Anna (d 15 Sept 1924), dau of Arthur George Forestier-Walker, ICS (see FORESTIER-WALKER, Bt), and had:

1b George Manners, MC (1943); b 17 Dec 1913; educ Wellington; Lt-Col 5th Roy Gurkha Rifles FF and RA WW II (wounded, despatches twice) and Malaya 1953–55 (despatches); m 20 March 1946 *Alison Cornwallis [Mrs George Nightingale, Wits End, Grayshott Rd, Headley Down, Hants], formerly w of Stanley William Vernon Sutton and dau of Col James Cameron, RE, and d 1992, leaving:

1c +Christopher George Manners; b 23 March 1949; educ Kelly Coll and RMA Sandhurst; Capt 1st Bn Staffs Regt; m 1st 1971 Marie-Claudette, dau of Marc Roger Tenermont; m 2nd 1978 *Anna Sorina, dau of Christian Niels Fischer, and by her has:

1d +Edward George Manners; b 1985

2c +Jeremy John Charles; b 21 Jan 1952; educ Wellington

1b *Tessa Frances Moyra; b 1 Oct 1908; m 24 April 1930 Brig Harold Gordon Fowler, OBE, IA, s of Rev Harold Metcalfe Fowler, of Hereford, and has:

1c *Patricia Jacqueline [Mrs Ian Ross, Rajmaji Tea Estate and PO, Sibsager District, Assam, India]; b 11 Feb 1931; m 1st 1959 Capt Richard Tobias, RE (kas 1960), and has a dau; m 2nd 1962 *Ian Galsworthy Ross and has a further dau

2c *Veronica Jane [Mrs Robert Ferguson, 33 Farnborough Rd, Heath End, Farnham, Surrey]; b 12 Jan 1935; m 2 Jan 1960 *Robert Ferguson, sn of Thomas Willem Ferguson, of The Hague, and has:

1d *Ian William; b 13 Dec 1962

1d *Carol Ann; b 27 Nov 1960

2d *Wendy Joanna; b 26 Aug 1966

3d *Belinda Tessa; b 25 Oct 1968

3c *Tessa Pauline; b 25 Nov 1938; educ Sacred Heart Convent Hove; m 4 June 1960 *Anthony Grove, s of Eric Hereward Grove, of Cranleigh, Surrey, and has:

1d *Jonathan Gordon; b 12 Aug 1961

2d *Simon James; b 8 May 1963

3d *Patrick Nigel; b 30 Jan 1967

1d *Virginia Louise; b 21 May 1965

4a (cont.) Maj-Gen Manners Nightingale m 2nd 2 Oct 1930 Violet Marion (d 1972), widow of Capt Charles Albert Glentworth Cunningham, 12th Scottish Rifles and N Staffs Regt, and dau of Lt-Col Howard Molyneux Edward Brunker, The Cameronians, and d 9 April 1956

1a Blanche Esther; m 17 Dec 1891 Petrus Cornelis van der Poel Hiddingh and d 10 Dec 1940, leaving issue

2a Beatrice Marian; m 1889 Edward Bromley, CE, and d 20 June 1936. He d 1900

3a Ethel Lempriere; m 1887 W H Ross, MD. He d 1912

(2) James Edward; b 23 March 1838; Dist Forest Offr Cape Good Hope; m 1st Feb 1861 Louisa Short (d 29 Dec 1869) and had, with two daus (d unm):

1a Geoffrey Edward; b 5 Feb 1862; m 1882 Emily Christina, dau of John Austen, and d 12 Sept 1929, leaving:

1b Winifred Florence

2a Ernest Albert; b 30 April 1867; m 15 Nov 1893 Sarah Annette Thornton (d 15 Nov 1947), dau of John Austen, and d 11 March 1945, leaving:

1b Alfred James; b 1905; m 1944 *Peter Adrianne, dau of M D Van Niekerk, of Ladybird, Orange Free State, and had:

1c Ernest Alfred; b 1945; m *Rosa, dau of T G Vsagie, of Durban

2c Peter Austen; b 1946

1c Carol Ann; b 1956

1b Ida Frances; m 2 Sept 1933 Robert Gordon Cocks, of Basutoland, and d 7 Feb 1947, leaving issue

2b Irene Mary; b 1899; m 30 Sept 1926 Norman Owen Halse (d 1966) and had:

1c *Norma Renee; b 18 Aug 1928

2c *Varney Marren; b 28 Aug 1935

3c *Rosemary Joy; b 18 Aug 1943

3a Frank Leopold; b 27 Dec 1869, m three times

(2) (cont.) James Nightingale m 2nd Aug 1881 Adriana Josina (d 1932), dau of Michael van Niekerk, and d 9 Dec 1908, having by her had:

4a Thomas Cecil Parry; b 1885; m 1911 Anita Adendorff (d 1954) and d 1949, leaving:

1b *Joy Thelma [Mrs Cornie Liesching, 9 Kinnerset Court, 76 Brand Rd, Durban, Natal, S Africa]; b 1913; m 13 Nov 1936 Cornie Hugo Liesching and has:

1c *Frederick Jabris; b 1937

2c *Cornie; b 1940

1c *Anita Lorraine; b 1945

2c *Margaret; b 1947

2b Edna Nita; m 1945 Dennis Williams, of Johannesburg, and d 1954, leaving issue

5a James Percy; b 1889; d unm 1920

1a Eleanor Adeline; m 10 July 1907 Bertram Owen Reed, of Alexandria, CP, S Africa, and d 24 Jan 1946, leaving issue. He d 11 June 1946

2a Effie Edith

3a Julia Venning

4a Ida Nellie, of Alexandria, CP

(3) Arthur; b 26 Nov 1841; m 11 Dec 1909 Helena Hester, widow of Capt Harmer Hardy, 18th Hus, and dau of J J Cruysvagen, of Newlands, and d 1 Feb 1919

(4) Lionel Brydges; MD; b 29 June 1843; m 30 Aug 1876 Julia Stewart (d 4 Dec 1909), dau of William Henry Grenelle, of Brooklyn, USA, and d 1889, leaving, with a dau (d unm):

1a Lionel Grenelle; b 29 Feb 1881; educ Cornell (BA and MechEng); Maj US Army; m 10 June 1917 Mildred, MA, dau of David Thomas Clark, of Denver, and d 1932

1a Eleanor Mary; PhM

2a Julia Huntington Grenelle; m 1903 Harrison Bennet Perkins and had issue

   3a Lucy Magoun; nun

   4a Ida Ethelstone; BA

(5) Geoffrey Ethelstone; b 17 Sept 1852; m 4 Nov 1911 Margaret, dau of John Humphrevs Parry, Serjeant-at-law, and d 7 Jan 1920

(1) Eleanor Maria; m 1 Aug 1872 Robert Robinson, of Jamaica, and d 20 Feb 1015. He d 1876

(2) Mary Julia; m 1866 John Tucker Ross, MRCS, RN, and d 3 May 1915. He d 1866

(3) Ida Sophia; d unm

3 Edward; b 3 May 1811; m 3 June 1841 Elizabeth (d 6 May 1848), est dau of — Price, of Ramsbury, Wilts, and d 21 Dec 1847

4 Manby; b 1 April 1813; BDJ, Assist Surgn Bengal; m 4 May 1844 Frederica Helen (m 2nd 9 Feb 1856 Gen Charles Lionel Showers, 14th Bengal NI; d 1895), only dau of George P Hurst, and d 1850, having had:

   (1) Manby Lindsay; d unm 30 Oct 1870

   (2) George Ewan; b 1847; m 10 Aug 1871 Blanche Cecile (d 20 Sept 1899), 2nd dau of Louis Enouf, advocate Pondicherry, and d 1916, leaving:

      1a Lilian Marie; b 1873

      2a Clarice Marie; b 1875; m 1st 1900 James Morison (d 1917), civ surgn Berar, and had issue; m 2nd 1934 Justin Glynn Ryan (d 1939)

      3a Violet Marie; b 1880; m 1906 Arthur Ball, of Cawnpore, and d 1920, leaving issue. He d 1941

         (1) Ethel

5 George Lacy; b 8 May 1815; m 29 Jan 1842 Martha Ann, dau of Sylvester Fellows, of New York, and d 31 May 1859, leaving, with other issue:

   (1) Henry Dickinson; b 23 Sept 1843

   (2) James Wilson; b 7 Aug 1845; m 26 Nov 1869 Elizabeth, dau of Enoch R Lumbert, and had:

      1a George Lacy; b 17 June 1877

      1a Eleanor Alison

      2a Bessie Barclay

   (3) Charles Ethelston; b 26 Nov 1858

   (1) Mary Mills

   (2) Julia Bissul

6 Ernest; b 5 June 1821; m 22 Oct 1842 Helen Louisa, dau of Francis Evans, of Dublin, and d 24 Sept 1868, leaving:

   (1) Frederick Hamilton; b 6 Jan 1847; k 27 Oct 1864

   (1) Louisa Maria; m 13 June 1866 François Duquet, of Montreal, and d 3 Dec 1916. He d 1878

   (2) Emily Ernesta; m 1st 19 Nov 1867 (divorce 1889) Benjamin George Ballard (d 1925); m 2nd Horace Rogers, of Australia, and d 1912

Sir GEOFFREY d 3 Sept 1972; his cousin,

Sir Charles Athelstan Nightingale, 16th Bt; b 23 July 1902; educ Harrow; m 1932 Nadine (d 6 Aug 1995), dau of (Charles) Arthur Diggens, and d 7 March 1977, leaving:

1 Sir CHARLES MANNERS GAMALIEL NIGHTINGALE, **17th and present Bt**

1 *Nadine Mary Rosalie [Mrs Derek Curtis, 54 Willow Close, Quintrell Downs, Newquay, Cornwall TR8 4NQ]; b 13 April 1938; m 1st 12 Sept 1959 (divorce 1972) Peter Maurice Edmunds, s of Maurice Edmunds, of Bexhill, Sussex, and has:

   (1) *Thomas Charles; b 5 Dec 1961

   (2) *David Michael; b 22 Feb 1963

   (3) *Jeremy John; b 18 March 1964

   (1) *Jane Elizabeth; b 20 June 1965

1 (cont.) Mrs Nadine Edmunds m 2nd 1972 *Derek Frederick Curtis and by him has:

   (4) *James; b 1972

2 *Clothilde Muriel Frances [Mrs Derek Glenister, 2 Albany Close, Ickenham, Middx]; b 7 Sept 1939; m 31 Aug 1964 *Derek Edward Glenister, s of Sidney William Glenister, of Vine House, Vine Grove, Hillingdon, Middx, and has:

   (1) *Frances Mary; b 23 May 1966

   (2) *Clare Julia; b 4 March 1968

NIXON

TOUJOURS·PRET

Arms: Az. on a chevron engrailed between three frets couped or as many trefoils vert, on a chief indented of the second a cat passant between two fleams of the field. **Crest:** A leopard rampant az. bezantée holding in the dexter paw a fleam or. **Motto:** Toujours prêt ('Always ready'). **Creation:** Bt. (UK) 14 July 1906.

SIR SIMON MICHAEL CHRISTOPHER NIXON, 5TH BT, of Roebuck Grove, Milltown, Co Dublin, and Merrion Square, City of Dublin, MC [Sir Simon Nixon Bt, Salt Winds, Torridge Rd, Appledore, N Devon]; b 20 Jun 1954; s unc 1997

Lineage: CHRISTOPHER WILLIAM NIXON, of Dublin; m Mary Anne, dau of William James Hackett, of Kildare, and d 1849, leaving:

Sir Christopher John Nixon, 1st Bt (UK), so cr 14 July 1906, PC (I 1914), JP, DL Co Dublin; b posthumously 29 June 1849; BA, MB, LLD Dublin U, MD, Hon FBIPM, Hon ARCVS, PRCPI 1900, Physician-in-Ordinary to Ld Lt Ireland 1880, 1892 and 1905, 1st PRVCI, V-Chllr Nat U Ireland, Sr Physician Mater Misericordiae Hosp Dublin, ktd 1895; m 6 Nov 1871 Mary Agnes (d 11 Jan 1924), 3rd dau of Dominick Edward Blake, s of Joseph Blake, of Castlegrove, Co Galway, and Anna Josephine, dau of Joseph Bourke, of Carrowkeale, Co Mayo, and had:

1 CHRISTOPHER WILLIAM (Sir), **2nd Bt**

2 Dominick Edward Francis; b 3 Sept 1883; d 23 July 1890

1 Elizabeth Mary Blake; d an infant

2 Josephine Anna Mary; d an infant

3 Mary Christina; m 17 Aug 1912 Col William John Phelim Preston, DSO, OBE, IA, s of Surgn-Gen A F Preston, of Co Meath, and d 30 April 1952, leaving issue. He d 18 Jan 1943

4 Josephine Francesca; m 12 Aug 1930 18th Baron Trimlestown (qv) and d 15 June 1945

5 Catherine Elizabeth; m 8 June 1951, as his 2nd w, 6th Baron ffrench (qv) and dsp 25 July 1960

Sir CHRISTOPHER d 19 July 1914; his est s,

Sir Christopher William Nixon, 2nd Bt, DSO (1918), DL; b 19 Nov 1877; MA, BL, Maj RA WW I (despatches), chm and md Clery & Co Dublin; m 7 July 1917 Louise (d 27 March 1949), yr dau of Robert Clery, JP, of The Glebe, Athlacca, Co Limerick, and Moorefield, Co Dublin, and d 21 April 1945, leaving:

1 **Sir Christopher John Louis Joseph Nixon, 3rd Bt**, MC (1944); b 21 March 1918; educ Beaumont; Pres Br Assoc Soc Occupnl Therapists; Maj Roy Ulster Rifles WW II attd IA (despatches), Palestine and Korea 1950–51 (wounded, despatches); m 26 Nov 1949 *Joan Lucille Mary [Lady Nixon, c/o Lloyds Bank, 3 St George's Rd, London SW19], dau of Robert Felix Mervyn Brown, of Rangoon, and dspm 31 Jan 1978, leaving:

   (1) *Anne Louise Catherine; b 14 Sept 1954; MB, BSc, FRCP, FRC (Path); m 1980 *Jonathan Anthony Miller, MB, BCh, FRCP, and has:

      1a *David Christopher; b 1988

      2a *Nicholas Johnathan; b 1989

   (2) *Mary Joan Teresa; b 16 Nov 1957; MCSP, SRP; m 1988 *Eric Olivier Léchere and has:

      1a *Jeremy; b 1989

      2a *Samuel; b 1992

   (3) *Sally Veronica Rose; b 5 Feb 1961; BDS, FDS (RCS); m 1989 *Andrew Kenneth Robson, MB, BS, FRCS, est s of Dr Angus Robson, of Princes Risborough, Bucks, and has:

      1a *Lucy Dorothy; b 1990

      2a *Rosie Esme; b 1992

2 **Rev Sir Kenneth Michael John Basil Nixon, 4th Bt**, SJ; b 22 Feb 1919; educ Beaumont and Heythrop Coll, Oxford; ordained 1952; d 2 June 1997

3 Cecil Dominic Henry Joseph, MC; b 5 Feb 1920; educ Beaumont; Maj Roy Ulster Rifles attd IA; m 12 Sept 1953 *Brenda, widow of Maj M F McWhor and only dau of Samuel Lycett-Lewis, and d 22 Oct 1994, leaving:

   (1) Sir SIMON MICHAEL CHRISTOPHER NIXON, **5th and present Bt**

   (2) +MICHAEL HUGH DAVID; b 19 May 1957; heir presumptive

   (3) +(Kenneth Philip) Guy; b 9 Sept 1959

(1) *Susan Penelope; *b* 28 July 1955
1 *Christine Mary Agnes Reginalda; *m* 7 July 1947 John Gerard Counihan (*d* 1 Feb 1956), yr s of Patrick Joseph Counihan, of The Hall, Kilkenny, and has:
  (1) *Niall Christopher John; *b* 19 Feb 1948
  (1) *Louise Mary Christine; *b* 16 Oct 1949
  (2) *Vivienne Christine Kathleen; *b* 3 Feb 1953

NOBLE of Ardkinglas

Arms: Per pale arg. and vert three bay leaves counterchanged. **Crest:** A bay tree vert, trunked sa., ensigned by an estoile arg. **Motto:** *Folium non defluet.* ('The leaf does not drop'). **Creation:** Bt. (UK) 26 July 1923.

SIR IAIN ANDREW NOBLE, 3RD BT, of Ardkinglas, Co Argyll (OBE 1988) [Sir Iain Noble Bt OBE, An Lamraig, Eilean Iarmain, Isle of Skye IV43 8QR]; *b* 8 Sept 1935; *s f* 1987; *educ* Eton and Univ Coll Oxford (MA); exec Scottish Cncl (Devpt and Industry) Edinburgh 1964–69, jt fndr and md Noble Grossart 1969–72, jt fndr and chm Seaforth Maritime 1972–77, chm Noble & Co, merchant bankers, Edinburgh, 1980–, dir Adam & Co 1983–93, dir: Independent Insur Gp plc 1986–, Premium Investment Tst 1993–, proprietor Fearann Eilean Iarmain and Barony of MacDonald Isle of Skye 1972–, chm Pràban Ltd (whisky distillers) 1977–, fndr 1st chm and tstee Coll of Sabhal Mor Ostaig 1974–84, memb Edinburgh U Court 1970–73, dep chm Traverse Theatre Club Edinburgh 1966–69, tstee Nat Museums Scotland 1987–91, Tstee Nat Museum of Scotland Charitable Tst 1990–, chm Scots Australian Cncl 1990, pres Saltire Soc 1993–96; *m* 27 Oct 1990 *Lucilla Charlotte James, dau of Col Hector Andrew Courtney Mackenzie, OBE, MC, TD, JP, DL, of the House of Rosskeen, Invergordon, Ross-shire

Lineage: Sir ANDREW NOBLE, 1st Bt, of Ardmore (*qv*); had a 3rd s:

Sir John Henry Brunel Noble, 1st Bt (UK), so *cr* 26 July 1923; *b* 18 May 1865; MA Oxon; Order Sacred Treasure Japan 2nd Cl; *m* 15 July 1902 Amie, Belgian Order Queen Elisabeth (*d* 5 Aug 1973 aged 94), widow of Hedworth Herbert Grogan and 6th dau of Samuel Abraham Walker-Waters, JP, of Stillorgan, Co Dublin, and had:
1 ANDREW NAPIER (Sir), **2nd Bt**
2 John Samuel Brunel; *b* 19 May 1909; *educ* Eton and Magdalen Coll Oxford (BA); *m* 15 May 1934 Elizabeth Virginia (*d* 1983), only dau of Maj William Louis Lucas by Beatrice, dau of Sir Julian Goldsmid, 3rd Bt, PC (*see* 1970 edn D'AVIGDOR-GOLDSMID, Bt), and *d* 1972, leaving:
  (1) +Simon John [Simon Noble Esq, Ardkinglas, Cairndow, Argyll PA26 8BH]; *b* 31 Oct 1936; *educ* Eton and Oxford; chm Wine Imports Edinburgh Ltd and Loch Fyne Oysters Ltd, dir Noble & Co and Edinburgh Tapestry Co
  (1) *Sarah [Mrs Peter Sumsion, Bachie Barn House, Cairndow, Argyll]; *b* 8 June 1935; *m* 7 Aug 1957 *Peter Whitton Sumsion, 2nd s of Dr Herbert Sumsion, of 20 College Green, Gloucester, and has:
    1a *David Peter; *b* 26 June 1958
    2a *Daniel; *b* 19 June 1967
    1a *Virginia; *b* 10 Feb 1960
    2a *Lucy; *b* 2 Sept 1963
  (2) *Christina Campbell [Mrs Kranti Singh, 66 Hungerford Rd, London N7 9LP]; *b* 10 June 1942; *m* 1980 Kranti Singh (*d* 1992) and has:
    1a *Rahul John; *b* 1976
    1a *Tara Anastasia; *b* 1977
3 MICHAEL ANTONY CRISTOBAL NOBLE, BARON GLENKINGLAS, of Cairndow, Co Argyll (LP, UK), so *cr* 1974, PC (1962); *b* 19 March 1913; *educ* Eton and Magdalen Coll Oxford; MP (C) Argyll 1958–74, Govt Whip 1960–61, Ld Commr Treasury 1961–62, Sec State Scotland 1962–64, Chm U Pty Scotland 1962–63 and Assoc Fisheries 1966–84, Min State DTI 1970–72, S/Ldr RAFVR WW II; *m* 11 Sept 1940 *Anne [The Rt Hon The Lady Glenkinglas, 7 Egerton Gardens, London SW3 2BP], dau of Sir Neville Arthur Pearson, 2nd Bt, of St Dunstan's (*see* 1970 edn), and *d* 1984, leaving:
  (1) *Catharine Gina Amita; *b* 19 Jan 1943; *m* 1st 8 Sept 1964 (*divorce* 1987) Peter Conrad Hamilton Vey, only s of David Christopher Leslie Vey, of Ewshot, Surrey, and has:
    1a Rupert; *b* 15 June 1971; *d* 1979

1a Tessa Atlanta Louise; *b* 22 Feb 1969; *d* 1977
  (1) (cont.) The Hon Mrs (Catharine) Vey *m* 2nd 1989 *Denzil Robert Onslow How (*see* ONSLOW, E)
  (2) *Marya Anne [The Hon Mrs Peter Egerton-Warburton, Mulberry House, Bentworth, Hants GU34 5RB]; *b* 10 Dec 1944; *m* 6 June 1969, as his 3rd w, *Maj Peter Egerton-Warburton (*see* GREY EGERTON, Bt) and has issue
  (3) *Anastasia Diana [The Hon Mrs Delap, Little Armsworth, Alresford, Hants]; *b* 17 Jan 1948; *m* 7 Oct 1967 *Jonathan Sinclair Delap, s of William Frederick Delap, of Kalou, Kenya, by Mrs Rodney Archibald Douglas-Pennant (*see* PENRHYN, B), and has:
    1a *James Robert Onslow; *b* 1969
    2a *Michael Jonathan Sinclair; *b* 1972
  (4) *Rebecca Juliet [Viscountess Dungarvan, Lickford House, Petworth, Sussex GU28 9EY]; *b* 20 Jan 1950; *m* 2 June 1973 *Viscount Dungarvan and has issue (*see* CORK and ORRERY, E)
1 Rosemary Elizabeth; *b* 25 June 1903; *m* 11 March 1931 Brig Ernest John Montgomery, CB, CBE (*see* MONTGOMERY, Bt) and adopted a dau
2 *Anastasia Mary Elizabeth [Miss Anastasia Noble, The Square, Ardkinglas, Cairndow, Argyll]; *b* 25 Dec 1911

Sir JOHN *d* 8 Jan 1938; his est s,
  Sir Andrew Napier Noble, 2nd Bt, KCMG (1954, CMG 1947), of Ardkinglas, Co Argyll; *b* 16 Sept 1904; *educ* Eton and Balliol Coll Oxford (BA); Dip Serv: Counsellor Buenos Aires 1945–47, Assist U-Sec FO 1949, Min Helsinki 1951–54, Amb Warsaw 1954–56, Mexico 1956–60 and The Hague 1960–64, Ethiopian Order Trinity; *m* 16 Oct 1934 *Sigrid [Sigrid Lady Noble, Galsworthy House, 177 Kingston Hill, Kingston-upon-Thames KT2 7LX], 2nd dau of Johan Michelet, Min Norwegian Dip Serv, and *d* 1987, leaving:
1 Sir IAIN ANDREW NOBLE, **3rd and present Bt**
2 +TIMOTHY PETER [Timothy Noble Esq, Ardnahane, Barnton Ave, Edinburgh EH4 6JJ]; *b* 21 Dec 1943; heir presumptive; *educ* Eton, Univ Coll Oxford (MA), INSEAD Fontainebleau (MBA) 1970; barrister Gray's Inn, exec dir Lyle Shipping Glasgow 1976–84 and ch exec Noble Gp 1984–, dir Waverley Mining Finance 1988–, Br Ski Fedn 1993–, Hardy Underwriting Gp, Br Ski & Snowboard Fedn, chm Br Ski Academy & RSNO Endowment Tst; *m* 18 Dec 1976 *Elizabeth Mary, only dau of Alexander W Aitken, of Edinburgh, and has:
  (1) +Lorne Andrew Wallace; *b* 13 July 1980; *educ* Edinburgh Acad
  (2) +Andrew Iain Brunel; *b* 10 March 1984; *educ* Edinburgh Acad
  (1) *Sasha Heidi Elizabeth; *b* 27 Dec 1978; *educ* St Leonards Sch and Bristol U
1 *Laila Ilona [Mrs George Embleton, 15 Millicent Ave, Toorak, 3142 VIC, Australia; Flat 7, 53 Kensington Ct, London W8 5DE]; *b* 8 Sept 1937; *m* 1st 26 Sept 1958 Kenneth Magnus Spence (*d* 1989), s of Col Patrick Magnus Spence, MC; *m* 2nd 20 July 1995 *George Embleton, of Melbourne, Australia and by her 1st husb has:
  (1) *Magnus Andrew; *b* 5 Sept 1959; *educ* Radley and LSE; *m* 23 Oct 1993 *Sarah, 2nd dau of FM Sir Nigel Bagnall, GCB, CVO, MC
  (2) *Patrick Matthew; *b* 14 Oct 1967; *educ* St Paul's and Exeter U
  (1) *Melanie Jane; *b* 13 May 1961

NOBLE of Ardmore and Ardardan Noble

Arms: Arg. three bay leaves vert slipped ppr. **Crest:** A dexter hand couped holding a dagger all ppr. **Supporters:** On either side a wild man wreathed around the head and waist with bay leaves, supporting with the exterior hand a holly tree eradicated and resting the exterior foot on the roots thereof, all ppr. **Motto:** *Virtute et valore* ('By virtue and valour'). **Creation:** Bt. (UK) 25 July 1902.

SIR DAVID BRUNEL NOBLE, 6TH BT, of Ardmore and Ardardan Noble, Cardross, Co Dumbarton [Sir David Noble Bt, 3 Oast Cottages, Breach Lane, Upchurch, Sittingbourne, Kent ME9 7PH]; *b* 25 Dec 1961; *s f* 1991; *educ* Eton; sales exec Gabriel Communicns 1986–88, sales consultant Allied Maples Gp 1989–; *m* 1st 1987 (*divorce* 1993) Virginia Ann, yr dau of Roderick Lancaster Wetherall, MBE, of Platt Oast, St Mary's Platt, Kent, and has:

1 +RODERICK LANCASTER BRUNEL; *b* 12 Dec 1988

2 +Alexander David; *b* 1990

Sir DAVID *m* 2nd 1993 *Stephanie Digby and by her has had:

3 +A son

4 A son; *d* 19–

1 *A dau

Lineage: JOHN NOBLE, living *temp* ROBERT III (1390–1406); had:

ROBERT NOBLE; Baillie (magistrate) Dumbarton 1449; had, with an er s (Walter, of Ferme, Lanarks, *m* Janet Macfarlane, *dsp* 1490):

ROBERT NOBLE of Ferme and Stuckendow; Baillie Dumbarton 1486; *m* Margaret Lauche (*m* 2nd William Douglas of Ledcameroch) and had:

ROBERT NOBLE of Ferme; Sheriff Depute Dunbartonshire; *m* — Cunninghame, of Drumquhassil, and had:

JAMES NOBLE of Ardardan Noble, Ardmore and Stuckendow 1563; *m* Katherine Stirling and had:

WILLIAM NOBLE of Ardardan Noble and Ardmore; *m* Janet (*d* 1616), dau of John Sempill of Fulwood, and had an est s:

HUMPHREY NOBLE of Ardardan Noble and Ardmore; *m* 1st 1601 Mary, dau of David Cunningham of Robertland; *m* 2nd Isabella Gwen; his only s by his 1st w:

WILLIAM NOBLE of Ardardan Noble and Ardmore; *m* 1629 Janet, dau of — Hay of Renfield; his only s:

JOHN NOBLE of Ardardan Noble and Ardmore; Commr Supply Dunbartonshire 1665; *m* 1653 Elizabeth Scott and had an est s:

WILLIAM NOBLE of Ardardan Noble and Ardmore; Commr Supply, Lt Dunbartonshire Fencibles, granted 1705 charter erecting his lands into (territorial) Barony of Noble; *m* 1707 Lillias, dau of Patrick Maxwell of Newark, and had an est s:

JOHN NOBLE of Ardardan Noble and Ardmore; Capt Roy N Br Fus and 81st Foot; *m* Isobel, est dau of James Duncanson of Garshake, and had:

1 William; sold the family property; *m* Isabella, dau of Andrew Geils, and had, with other issue:

(1) John, CB; Lt-Col Madras Horse Artillery (which he formed); *d* unm 16 July 1827 aged 48

(2) James; Lt-Col HEICS; *dsp* 1837

2 James; *m* Mary Reid and *dsp*

3 George; settled Jamaica; *m* Agnes (*d* 26 Aug 1804), dau of John Somerville of Park, Renfrewshire, and *d* 1791, having had:

(1) GEORGE

(1) Anna Isabella; *m* her cousin James Dennistoun Brown, Madras Artillery, and had issue

The only son,

GEORGE NOBLE, of Springbank, Greenock, Renfrewshire; Lt RN; *b* 11 Oct 1791; *m* 18 Sept 1821 Georgina Moore (*d* 4 Jan 1863), only dau of Andrew Donald, of Ottercaps, Va., and *d* 30 Sept 1847, having had, with five daus (*d* unm):

1 George; *b* 1826; *d* unm India 1842

2 ANDREW (Sir), **1st Bt**

3 Benjamin; *b* 13 May 1834; *m* 1871 Margaret, dau of A Blair, of Perth, and *d* 22 Sept 1924

4 James; *b* 1843; lost at sea 1859

1 Georgina Geils Donald; *m* 21 Jan 1864 Isambard Brunel, barrister, est s of Isambard Kingdom Brunel, the engr, and *d* 17 May 1911. He *d* 21 March 1902

2 Isabella Jane; *m* 1858 William Darling Campbell, of Quebec, and *d* 28 Jan 1928 aged 90

The est surv son,

Sir Andrew Noble, 1st Bt (UK), so cr 25 July 1902, KCB (1893, CB 1881), JP, DL Northumberland, of Ardmore, Ardardan Noble and Jesmond Dene House, Northumberland; *b* 13 Sept 1831; *educ* RMA Woolwich; Sec Ctees on: Rifled Cannon 1858 and Plates and Guns 1859, Assist Inspr Artillery 1860, Assoc Memb Ordnance Select Ctee; Sir W G Armstrong: joined 1860, later chm, memb 1st Ctee Explosives to 1880, assoc memb 2nd Explosives Ctee, memb last Ctee Explosives and Ordnance Bd, RA, High Sheriff Northumberland 1896, FRS (Roy Medal), FCS (Gold Medal Soc Chemical Industry), DSc Oxon and Cantab, Hon DCL Durham, FRAS, Roy Albert Medal Soc of Arts, Grand Cordon Osmanieh, Medjidie and Rose Brazil, Sacred Treasure and Rising Sun Japan 1st Cl, Double Dragon China, Grand Cross Crown Italy, Kt Cdr Jesus Christ Portugal, Companion Order Charles III Spain; *m* 15 Nov 1854 Margery Durham (*d* 23 July 1929), dau of Archibald Campbell, of Quebec, and *d* 22 Oct 1915, leaving:

1 **Sir George John William Noble, 2nd Bt**, JP Northumberland; High Sheriff 1918, Maj Northumberland Hus and Capt 13th Hus Boer War 1900–01 (medal with two clasps); *b* 3 March 1859; *m* 29 July 1896 (*divorce* 1916) Mary Ethel, dau of Samuel Abraham Walker-Waters, JP, of Chute Hall, Co Kerry, Ch Insp RIC, and had:

(1) Veronica Margaret, JP Argyllshire; *b* 3 March 1900; *m* 3 Feb 1921 2nd Baron Gainford (*qv*) and *d* 7 Nov 1995, leaving issue

2 SAXTON WILLIAM ARMSTRONG (Sir), **3rd Bt**

3 Sir JOHN HENRY BRUNEL NOBLE, 1st Bt, of Ardkinglas (*qv*)

4 Philip Ernest, of Glendoe, Fort Augustus, and Newcastle; *b* 23 Nov 1870; High Sheriff Northumberland 1922; *m* 15 Oct 1895 Mabel (*m* 2nd 26 Nov 1936 Capt Frank Buddle-Atkinson, JP, MFH, s of B Atkinson, of Woolley Grange, Bradford-on-Avon), dau of Percy Graham Buchanan Westmacott, JP, of Benwell Hill, Newcastle, and Rosemount, Ascot, and *d* 18 July 1931 following a flying accident, leaving:

(1) Graham Philip; *b* 5 Jan 1898; *educ* Eton; S/Ldr RAFVR; *m* 1st 15 April 1926 (*divorce* 1933) Pamela Susan, yst dau of Basil Hoare, of Sutton Veny House, Wilts, and Belgravia; *m* 2nd 1936 Joan (*d* 14 Oct 1955), widow of F/Lt Charles Henry Godwin Bembridge, RAF

(2) Horace Westcott; *b* 7 March 1899; *educ* Eton, RMC Sandhurst and New Coll Oxford; Maj Scots Gds; *m* 1st 29 April 1929 (*divorce* 1934) Joan Marion, only child of H R Miller, of Mayfair and New York, and had:

1a +Philip Ralph; *b* 27 Jan 1930; *educ* Eton

(2) (cont) Maj Horace Noble *m* 2nd 1946 *Mrs Edna Louise Malone, dau of Charles Johnson, of Chicago, and *d* 1980

(1) Dorothy Agnes; *m* 1918 Cdr James Lawrence Boyd, DSC, RN, and had issue. He *d* 1930

(2) Yseult Joan; *m* 25 April 1922 her aunt's bro-in-law Wilfred Theodore Claude Cochrane, yst s of Rev David Crawford Cochrane, Vicar Ettwall, Derbys, and had issue. He *d* 4 Jan 1955

1 Lilias Hilda Geils; *d* unm 16 Dec 1937

2 Ethel Isobel Virginia, MBE (1910); *d* unm 16 Dec 1937

2 Ethel Isobel Virginia, MBE (1910); *m* 25 July 1895 Alfred Henry John Cochrane, 2nd s of Rev David Crawford Cochrane, and *d* 9 Jan 1961. He *d* 1948

Sir GEORGE *dspm* 29 July 1937; his bro,

Sir Saxton William Armstrong Noble, 3rd Bt; *b* 13 Feb 1863; MInstCE, FSA, of Armstrong, Whitworth, dir Mond Nickel and Whitehead Torpedo Cos, Orders Sacred Treasure Japan 2nd Cl and Rising Sun 4th Cl; *m* 23 July 1891 Celia Brunel (*d* 23 May 1962), dau of Arthur James, of Eton College, and gdau of Isambard Kingdom Brunel (*see above*), and had:

1 HUMPHREY BRUNEL (Sir), **4th Bt**

2 Marc Andrew Patrick; *b* 19 May 1897; Lt RFA WW I; *d* 1 July 1917 of wounds recd in action

1 Marjorie Florence; *m* 20 Nov 1919 Capt Geoffrey Spencer Madan, s of Falconer Madan, of BNC Oxford, and had issue. He *d* 6 July 1947

2 Cynthia; *m* 22 Jan 1929 1st Baron Gladwyn (*qv*) and *d* 1990, leaving issue

Sir SAXTON *d* 12 Oct 1942; his only surv s,

Sir Humphrey Brunel Noble, 4th Bt, MBE (1946), MC; *b* 9 May 1892; *educ* Eton and King's Coll Cambridge (BA 1914, MA); Maj Northumberland Hus WW I (despatches twice, Order Leopold Belgium, Croix de Guerre) and WW II, High Sheriff Northumberland 1956, FRSA; *m* 28 Jan 1926 Celia, JP (Northumberland 1950, *d* 6 June 1982), only dau of Capt Stewart Carnac Weigall, RN, and had:

1 MARC BRUNEL (Sir), **5th Bt**

2 +Peter Saxton Fitzjames, CBE (1977) [Peter Noble Esq CBE, Flax Cottage, Ham Common, Surrey TW10 7JB]; *b* 22 May 1929; *educ* Eton and Magdalene Coll Cambridge; *m* 1st 7 Aug 1954 (*divorce* 1966) Elizabeth Emmeline, yr dau of Launcelot Williams Gregory Eccles, CMG, MC, of Salisbury, S Rhodesia, and has:

(1) +Simon-Peter Saxton Fanshaw; *b* 22 July 1958

2 (cont.) Peter Noble *m* 2nd 18 June 1966 (*divorce* 1980) Helen Margaret, formerly w of David Anthony Harries and dau of Thomas Essery Rose-Richards, and by her has:

(2) +James Essery Brunel; *b* 6 Oct 1968

2 (cont.) Peter Noble *m* 3rd 1980 *Penelope Margaret, dau of Leslie Landeau

1 *Lilias Mulgrave [Mrs Robin Sheepshanks, The Rectory, Eyke, Woodbridge, Suffolk]; *b* 13 Jan 1931; *m* 29 Nov 1951 *Capt Robin John Sheepshanks, CBE, DL, King's Dragoon Gds, only s of Maj Richard Hasell Sheepshanks, DSO, MVO, IA (*see* CHELMSFORD, V), and has:

(1) *David Richard; *b* 30 Oct 1952; *educ* Eton

(2) *Richard John; *b* 4 Dec 1955; *educ* Stanbridge Earls Sch

(3) *Andrew Charles; *b* 7 Aug 1960

(4) *Christopher James; *b* 10 Oct 1964

Sir HUMPHREY *d* 14 Aug 1968; his er s,

Sir Marc Brunel Noble, 5th Bt; *b* 8 Jan 1927; *educ* Eton; Maj Roy Dragoons (ret 1966, King's Dragoon Gds 1947–58, tfd Roy Dragoons on amalgamation 1958); *m* 27 Jan 1956 *Jennifer Lorna Jane [Dowager Lady Noble, Deerleap House, Knockholt, Kent TN14 7NP], yr dau of John Mein-Austin, of Flint Hill, W Haddon, Northants, and Mrs Richard Barry Butler, of Castle Carrock, Cumberland, and *d* 1991, having had:

1 Sir DAVID BRUNEL NOBLE, **6th and present Bt**

2 +Charles Richard Austin [Charles Noble Esq, Deerleap House, Knockholt, Kent TN14 7NP]; *b* 6 Aug 1963; *educ* Harrow

1 *Anna Margaret [Mrs John Porter, Deerleap House, Knockholt, Kent TN14 7NP]; *b* 20 Sept 1957; *m* 1984 John Edward Llewellyn Porter (*d* 1987), s of Stephen Porter, and has:

(1) *George Edward; *b* 1986

2 Katherine Louise; *b* 16, *d* 26 Dec 1960

NOEL-BUXTON

Arms: Arg. a lion rampant, tail elevated and turned over the head sa., between two mullets of the second. **Crest:** A buck's head couped gu., attired or, gorged with a collar of the last, therefrom pendant an escutcheon arg., charged with an African's head sa. **Motto:** Do it with thy might. **Creation:** B. (UK) 17 June 1930.

THE 3RD BARON NOEL-BUXTON, of Aylsham, Co Norfolk (Martin Connal Noel-Buxton) [The Rt Hon The Lord Noel-Buxton, Little London, Hingham, Norfolk]; *b* 8 Dec 1940; *s f* 1980; *educ* Bryanston and Balliol Coll Oxford (BA 1962, MA); slr 1966–85, dir Central Wagon 1975, ptnr Speedily Bircham, slrs; *m* 1st 21 July 1964 (*divorce* 1968) Miranda Mary (*d* 1979), er dau of Maj Hugo Atherton Chisenhale-Marsh, of Gaynes Park, Epping, Essex, by Lady Buxton (*see* BUXTON, Bt); *m* 2nd 1972 (*divorce* 1982) Sarah Margaret Surridge, only dau of Neil Charles Wolseley Barrett, TD, of Twickenham Rd, Teddington, and has by her:

1 +CHARLES CONNAL; *b* 17 April 1975; *educ* Eton; trainee insur broker

1 *Lucy Margaret; *b* 1977

The 3rd BARON *m* 3rd 1986 *Mrs Abigail Marie Granger, dau of Eric Philip Richard Clent, and by her has:

2 *Antonia Helen; *b* 1989

Lineage: Sir THOMAS FOWELL BUXTON, 3rd Bt (*qv*), had a 2nd s:

NOEL EDWARD BUXTON later NOEL-BUXTON, **1st Baron Noel-Buxton**, of Aylsham, Co Norfolk (UK), so *cr* 17 June 1930, PC (1924); *b* 9 Jan 1869; *educ* Harrow and Trin Coll Cambridge (MA), MP (Lib) Whitby 1905–06 and N Norfolk 1910–18 and 1922–30, Min Ag and Fisheries 1924 and 1929–30; *m* 30 April 1914 Lucy Edith, MP N Norfolk 1930–31 and Norwich 1945–50 (*d* 9 Dec 1960), est dau of Maj Henry Pelham Burn, of S Kensington, by Janet Edith, dau of Sir Archibald Orr Ewing, 1st Bt (*qv*), and had:

1 RUFUS ALEXANDER, **2nd Baron**

2 Christopher Arthur Noel; *b* 18 Feb 1918; 2nd Lt 12th Roy Lancers SR; *d* following a riding accident 17 Sept 1940

3 Michael Barnett Noel; *b* 4 Jan 1920; *educ* Harrow and Balliol Coll Oxford; Capt RA WW II, Colonial CS Gold Coast 1947–59; *d* 26 July 1995

1 Lydia Victoria Noel; *b* 4 Feb 1922; *d* unm 10 Oct 1955

2 *Jane Elizabeth (Noel) [The Hon Jane Buxton, Maddison Farm, Long Load, nr Langport, Somerset TA10 9LA]; *b* 22 May 1925; dropped Noel by public declaration 1957; has:

(1) *Rachel Susan; *b* 18 Jan 1967

3 *Sarah Edith Noel [The Hon Mrs Hogg, Old Broad Oak, Brenchley, Kent]; *b* 23 Jan 1928; *m* 2 June 1955 *John Goldsborough Hogg, er s of Francis Goldsborough Hogg, of Oddington, Glos, and has:

(1) *Sarah Jane [Mrs Sarah Houldsworth, 11 Astell St, London SW3 3RT]; *b* 27 Dec 1956; *m* 1981 (*divorce* 1993) David Henry Houldsworth (*see* MORTON, E)

(2) *Joanna Wynfreda; *b* 20 March 1960

The 1st BARON *d* 12 Sept 1948; his est son,

NOEL ALEXANDER NOEL-BUXTON later RUFUS ALEXANDER BUXTON (deed poll 1944), **2nd Baron Noel-Buxton**; *b* 13 Jan 1917; *educ* Harrow and Balliol Coll Oxford (BA 1938); research assist Ag Ec Inst Oxford 1940–43, lecturer HM Forces 1943–45, producer BBC Overseas Serv 1946–48, edtl staff *Farmer's Weekly* 1950–52, WW II 1939–40 with Artist's Rifles (invalided), author *Westminster Wader* (1957); *m* 1st 22 Sept 1939 (*divorce* 1947) Helen Nancy (*d* 16 June 1949), yr dau of Col Kenneth Hugh Munro Connal, CB, OBE, TD, JP, DL, of Monktonhead, Monkton, Ayrshire, and had:

1 MARTIN CONNAL BUXTON later NOEL-BUXTON (deed poll Nov 1964), **3rd and present Baron Noel-Buxton**

2 +Simon Campden [The Hon Simon Buxton, The Orchard, High St, Bathford BA1 7TG]; *b* 9 April 1943; *educ* Bryanston and Balliol Coll Oxford; *m* 1981 *Alison D, dau of S J Liddle, of Exmouth, Devon, and has:

(1) +Christopher John Noel; *b* 1988

(1) *Katherine Helen; *b* 1983

The **2nd Baron** *m* 2nd 25 Sept 1948 *Margaret Elizabeth (*d* 3 June 1978), er dau of Stephanus Abraham Cloete, of Pretoria, S Africa, and *d* 1980, having by her had:

3 +Richard Christopher [The Hon Richard Noel-Buxton, Strechney, Diptford, Totnes, S Devon TQ9 7NN]; *b* 15 Feb 1950; *educ* Bryanston; *m* 1988 *Annabel, dau of Peter Hawker (*see* RAVENSDALE, B), and has:

(1) *Sarah; *b* 1990

(2) *Rosie; *b* 1993

1 *Clare Elizabeth Anne [The Hon Mrs Inskip, Park Farm, Shipton Moyne, Glos GL8 8PR]; *b* 19 April 1954; *m* 8 Oct 1977 *Owen Hampden Inskip (*see* CALDECOTE, V) and has issue

NOLAN

Creation: B. (LP, UK) 1994.

THE BARON NOLAN, of Brasted, Co Kent (Sir Michael Patrick Nolan, PC (1991)) [The Rt Hon The Lord Nolan PC, Tanners, Brasted, Kent TN16 1NH]; *b* 10 Sept 1928; *educ* Ampleforth and Wadham Coll Oxford; RA 1947–49, TA 1949–55; barrister Middle Temple 1953, QC 1968, Bencher 1975, Memb: Bar Cncl 1973–74, Senate Inns of Court and Bar 1974–81 (Treasurer 1977–79); barrister (NI) 1974, QC (NI) 1974; Recorder 1975–82; High Court Judge Queen's Bench 1982–91, ktd 1982, Presiding Judge Western Circuit 1985–88, Ld Justice Appeal 1991–93, Ld of Appeal in Ordinary 1993–98; Chm Ctee Standards in Public Life 1994–97; Govr: Convent of Sacred Heart Woldingham 1973–83 and Combe Bank Sch 1974–83, Chllr Essex U 1997–; *m* 1953 *Margaret, yr dau of Alfred Noyes, CBE, the poet, by Mary Mayne, and has:

1 *Michael Alfred Anthony [The Hon Michael Nolan, 18 Girdlers Rd, London W14 0PS]; *b* 1955; *educ* Ampleforth, St Benet's Hall Oxford (MA) and City U (Dip Law); barrister Middle Temple 1981; *m* 1984 *Adeline Mei Choo, dau of Henry S H Oh, of Singapore, and has:

(1) *Hugh; *b* 1986

(2) *Felix; *b* 1992

(1) *Sophia; *b* 1989

1 *Patricia Margaret; *b* 1954; *m* 1979 *Col Richard John Morris and has:

(1) *Henry John Richard; *b* 1982

(2) *Benjamin Michael Joseph; *b* 1985

(1) *Alice Rose; *b* 1988

2 *Sheila Mary; *b* 1957; *m* 1981 *Charles William Edward Hume and has:

(1) *Thomas Charles; *b* 1982

(2) *Joshua Michael; *b* 1986

(3) *Samuel Donald; *b* (twin) 1986

(1) *Lucy Margaret; *b* 1984

3 *Anne Teresa; *b* 1959; *m* 1997 *Simon Yorke

4 *Clare Elizabeth; *b* 1965

Lineage: JAMES THOMAS NOLAN, of London; *m* Jane Walsh and had a yr s:

MICHAEL PATRICK, *cr* a **Baron**

NORBURY

Arms: Quarterly, 1st and 4th, arg. a cross-fleury gu. charged with a plain cross coupled of the field between four oak leaves slipped ppr. (for TOLER); 2nd and 3rd, arg. a trefoil slipped vert, on a chief sa. three escallop shells or (for GRAHAM). **Crest:** On a ducal coronet a fleur-de-lys or. **Supporters:** Dexter, a horse or. bridled gu.; sinister, a fawn ppr. **Motto:** *Regi et patriæ fidelis* ('Faithful to king and country'). **Creations:** B. (I) 24 Nov 1797 (Norwood) and (I) 27 Dec 1800, E. and V. (I) 23 June 1827.

THE 6TH EARL OF NORBURY, *Viscount Glandine*, of Glandine, King's Co, **Baron Norbury of Ballycrenode**, Co Tipperary, and **Baron Norwood of Knockalton** (Noel Terence Graham-Toler) [The Rt Hon The Earl of Norbury, The Woodlands, Seer Green, Bucks HP9 2UL]; *b* 1 Jan 1939; *s f* 1955; *educ* HMS *Conway* and privately; *m* 28 Oct 1965 *(Rosamund Margaret) Anne, 2nd dau of Francis Mathew, of S Kensington, and has:

1 +RICHARD JAMES, *Viscount Glandine*; *b* 5 March 1967

1 *Patricia Margaret; *b* 22 Feb 1970; *m* 19– *Michael Gaca and has:

(1) *Edward Walenty; *b* 26 April 1997

Lineage: NICHOLAS TOLER, of Graige otherwise Beechwood, Co Tipperary; had a 3rd s:

DANIEL TOLER, of Graige; *m* 1st *c* 9 Jan 1721 Helena Maria, dau of Symon Purdon, of Tinerana, Co Clare, and had, with a dau (*d* unm):

1 Nicholas; *d* unm *vp* after 1744

1 Helena Maria; *m* 18 June 1745 Richard Maunsell, of Ballywilliam, Co Limerick, and had issue. He *d* 1790

DANIEL TOLER *m* 2nd *c* 12 Oct 1732 Letitia (*d* 17 Feb 1794), dau of Thomas Otway, of Castle Otway, Co Tipperary, and *d* between 5 Dec 1754 and 30 Aug 1756, having by her had, with other issue:

2 Daniel, of Beechwood; *b* 1739; MP Co Tipperary 1783–90, High Sheriff 1766; *m* Nov 1760 Rebecca (*d* Sept 1800), dau of Paul Minchin, of Bogh, Co Carlow, and *d* June 1796, having had:

(1) Daniel Minchin; High Sheriff Co Tipperary 1794; *d* unm *vp*

(1) Harriet; *m* Sir Henry Osborne, 11th Bt (*qv*)

(2) Sarah; *m* 1786 Robert Curtis, of Inane, Co Tipperary

(3) Eliza; *m* 1798 Thomas Taylor, of Maperath, Co Meath

3 JOHN, **1st Earl**

1 Catherine; *m* 30 June 1758 John Greene, of Old Abbey, and *d* 8 Oct 1798, leaving issue. He *d* 2 March 1784

2 Phoebe; *m* John Head, of Ashley Park, Co Tipperary, and had issue. He *d* 23 June 1817

DANIEL TOLER's 3rd s,

JOHN TOLER, **1st Earl of Norbury**, so *cr* 23 June 1827, as also VISCOUNT GLANDINE, of Glandine, King's Co, with special remainder to his 2nd s (*see* below), and earlier 27 Dec 1800 BARON NORBURY OF BALLYCRENODE, Co Tipperary (all I), KC 1781; *b* 3 Dec 1745; *educ* Trin Coll Dublin; barrister King's Inn 1770, MP Tralee 1776–83, Philipstown 1783–90 and Gorey/Newborough 1790–99, Bencher 1781, Slr-Gen 1789–98, Attorney-Gen 1798–99 (in which capacity he prosecuted many of those involved in the 1798 Uprising; he had been challenged to a duel back in 1792 by James Napper Tandy, he of the United Irishmen and *The Wearing of the Green*) and Ch Justice Common Pleas 1800–27; *m* 2 June 1778 Grace (*cr* 24 Nov 1797 **Baroness Norwood of Knockalton**, Co Tipperary (I); *d* 21 July 1822), dau of Hector Graham, Secondary Common Pleas (I), and *d* 27 July 1831, having had:

1 DANIEL TOLER; *b c* 1780; *s* mother as **2nd Baron Norwood of Knockalton** and *f* as **2nd Baron Norbury of Ballycrenode**; *d* insane & unm 30 Jan 1832

2 HECTOR JOHN, **2nd Earl**

1 Isabella

2 Letitia; *m* 8 March 1813 William Browne, of Browne's Hill, Co Carlow

The 1st EARL's 2nd s,

HECTOR JOHN TOLER later GRAHAM-TOLER (roy licence 26 Nov 1825), **2nd Earl of Norbury**, as which *s f* 1831, also **3rd Baron Norwood of Knockalton**

and **3rd Baron Norbury of Ballycrenode**, as both of which *s er bro* 1832, DL Queen's Co; *b* 27 June 1781; *m* 1 Jan 1808 Elizabeth (brought her husb the Phibbs estates in Cos Leitrim, Mayo and Sligo; *d* 25 Aug 1859), only child of William Brabazon (yr bro of Sir Anthony Brabazon, 1st Bt, of New Park, Co Mayo; *see* MEATH, E), by Elizabeth, dau and heiress of John Phibbs, of Lisconny, Co Sligo, and was shot dead by his butler (who it is thought may have been associated with the Ribbonmen) in the grounds of his house, Durrow Abbey, Tullamore, King's Co (now Co Offaly), 3 Jan 1839, having had, with two other sons (*d* young) and two daus (*d* unm):

1 HECTOR JOHN GRAHAM later GRAHAM-TOLER, **3rd Earl of Norbury**, DL King's Co; *b* 17 Sept 1810; High Sheriff King's Co 1835; *m* 7 Nov 1848 Stewart (*d* 5 March 1904), dau of Sir Henry Bethune, 1st Bt, *de jure* 9th Earl of Lindsay (*qv*), and *d* 26 Dec 1873, having had:

(1) WILLIAM BRABAZON LINDSAY GRAHAM-TOLER, **4th Earl of Norbury**; *b* 2 July 1862; *educ* Harrow and Ch Ch Oxford; *m* 28 July 1908 Lucy Henrietta Katharine (*d* 26 May 1966), er dau of Rev Hon William Charles Ellis (*see* HOWARD DE WALDEN, B), and *dsp* 20 April 1943

(1) Mary Catherine; *m* 13 Oct 1884 Sir Charles John Stewart, KBE, and *d* 5 Feb 1930, leaving issue. He *d* 4 March 1932

(2) Elizabeth; *m* 9 Oct 1884 4th Earl of Caledon (*qv*) and *d* 6 Oct 1939, leaving issue

(3) Margaret Albinia Grace; *m* 18 March 1880 Edward Boycott Jenkins, barrister, est s of the Countess of Lovelace (*qv*) and Edward Jenkins, and *d* 8 Sept 1926. He *d* 1915

(4) Charlotte Emily Alexina; *d* unm 13 Dec 1932

2 Otway Fortescue TOLER later GRAHAM-TOLER; *b* 1 Nov 1824; 5th Dragoon Gds; *m* 28 July 1846 Hon Henrietta Elizabeth Scarlett (*d* 4 March 1895), dau of 2nd Baron Abinger (*qv*), and *d* 23 April 1884, having had, with another s and two daus (*d* unm):

(1) Hector Robert, of Durrow Abbey, DL King's Co; High Sheriff 1893, Capt 2nd Life Gds; *b* 17 June 1847; *m* 16 May 1884 Alice (*m* 2nd 18 Feb 1909 Maj Arthur Lockwood Trevor Boothe, 4th Hus, only s of Rev John Edmund Boothe, and *d* 29 June 1933, dau of Charles Steer, Judge High Court Calcutta, and *d* 10 July 1899, having had:

1a Otway Scarlett, of Durrow Abbey, DL King's Co; High Sheriff 1911, Lt Irish Gds; *b* 1886; *educ* Wellington; *m* 5 July 1923 Mona Marian, yst dau of Lt-Col John Maxwell Low, of Sunvale, Co Limerick, and *dsp* 18 Nov 1941

1a Muriel Alma; *b* 28 Sept 1885; *m* 4 April 1906 Lt-Cdr John Gunnell, USN, and *d* 6 Dec 1943, leaving issue

(2) James Otway, of Beechwood Park, Nenagh, Co Tipperary; Lt-Col 4th Bn Highland LI; *b* 12 Jan 1849; *m* 3 Feb 1885 Emily Alexina (*d* 9 Feb 1921), dau of Robert Balfour Wardlaw Ramsay, of Whitehill, Midlothian, Tillicounty, Clackmannanshire, and Balcurvie, Fifeshire, and *d* 27 July 1913, leaving:

1a Leopold James, MC (1919), of Beechwood Park; Capt 6th Bn Middx Regt SR WW I, Hon Maj 1933; *b* 1888; *d* unm 9 June 1938

2a RONALD IAN MONTAGU, **5th Earl**

1a Lilian Frances; granted with her yr sis Jan 1944 rank of earl's dau; *m* 4 Oct 1923 George Nicholas Hardinge and had issue (*see* HARDINGE, V)

2a Clementine Ivy; *m* 31 July 1916 Capt Rodulph Cole Metge, 3rd s of Robert Henry Metge, MP, of Athlumney, Co Meath, and *d* 9 Jan 1951, leaving issue. He *d* 1919

(3) George John Scarlett; *b* 17 Aug 1850; *m* 17 Oct 1892 Maria del Carmen, 3rd dau of Antonio Monteverde del Castillo, and *d* 31 Aug 1929

1 Elizabeth; *m* May 1836 Hon Lawrence Parsons, 2nd s of 2nd Earl of Rosse (*qv*), and *d* 9 Dec 1844

2 Grace; *m* 23 April 1832 Col Crofton Moore Vandeleur, JP, DL, of Kilrush House, Co Clare, and *d* 2 June 1872, leaving issue. He *d* 8 Nov 1881

3 Helen; *m* 18 Dec 1837 John Vandeleur Stewart, DL, of Rock Hill, Co Londonderry, and *d* 22 April 1883, leaving issue. He *d* 24 June 1872

4 Georgina; *m* 2 Dec 1845 John Gurdon Rebow, MP, of Wivenhoe Park, Essex, and *d* 23 Jan 1900, leaving issue. He *d* 12 Oct 1870

5 Charlotte; *m* 1st 27 Jan 1852 4th Baron Braybrooke (*qv*); *m* 2nd 6 Nov 1862 Frederic Hetley, MD, of Upper Norwood, and *d* 4 Feb 1867

6 Isabella Rebecca; *m* 17 May 1851 Alexander John Robert Stewart, DL, of Ards, Co Donegal, and *d* 12 July 1914, leaving issue. He *d* 30 July 1904

The 4th EARL's cousin,

RONALD IAN MONTAGU GRAHAM-TOLER, **5th Earl of Norbury**; *b* 11 Jan 1893; Capt Roy Inniskilling Fus WW I, Rlwy Traffic Offr 1917, attd Inter-Allied Mission 1919, Fndr UNRRA, Regnl Dir Yugo-Slav Mission UNRRA Cairo 1944–45; *m* 1st 7 Oct 1919 (*divorce* 1933) Simone Evangeline Julie Caroline, dau of Hans Apenes, Norwegian Consul France, of Calais; *m* 2nd 24 May 1933 Margaret (*d* 1984), dau of John Kevan Greenhalgh, of Hoylake, Cheshire, and *d* 24 May 1955, having by her had:

1 *John Patrick; *b* 16 April 1932

2 Shaun Dermot; *b* 25 May, *d* 22 Nov 1936

3 NOEL TERENCE GRAHAM-TOLER, **6th and present Earl of Norbury**

NORFOLK

Arms: Quarterly, 1st, gu. a bend between six cross crosslets fitchée arg. (for HOWARD) and on the bend (honourable augmentation granted by HENRY VIII after Flodden) an escutcheon or charged with a demi-lion rampant, pierced through the mouth by an arrow, within a double tressure flory counterflory of the first (referring to the Royal Scottish Arms); 2nd, gu. three lions passant guardant in pale or, in chief a label of three points arg. (for BROTHERTON); 3rd, chequy or and az. (for WARENNE); 4th gu. a lion rampant or (for Fitz ALAN); behind the shield two gold batons in saltire, enamelled at the ends, sa. (Earl Marshal's insignia). **Crests:** 1 Issuant from a ducal coronet or a pair of wings gu. each charged with a bend, between six cross crosslets fitchée arg., 2 On a chapeau gu., doubled erm., a lion statant guardant, tail extended or, gorged with a ducal coronet arg., 3 On a mount vert a horse passant arg., holding in the mouth a slip of oak fructed ppr. **Supporters:** Dexter, a lion; sinister, a horse, both arg., the latter holding in his mouth a slip of oak vert, fructed ppr. **Motto:** *Sola virtus invicta* ('Virtue alone is unconquerable'). **Creations:** E. (Arundel) 1189 (feudal honour as adjudged by Parl 8 July 1433, held by possession of Arundel Castle), B. (Beaumont) 4 March 1308/9 but allowed precedence only of 1432 when abeyance terminated 1840; D. 28 June 1483, E. (Surrey) 1 Feb 1513/4, (Norfolk) 6 June 1644 and (Marshal) 19 Oct 1672 (all E); B. (FitzAlan and Maltravers) 1627 (but *see* below for discussion of date of *cr*) (E) and (Howard of Glossop) (UK) 9 Dec 1869.

THE 17TH DUKE OF NORFOLK, Earl of Arundel, Earl of Surrey, **Earl of Norfolk**, **Lord** (Baron) **Beaumont**, **Baron FitzAlan**, **Baron Maltravers** and **Baron Howard of Glossop** (Sir Miles Francis Stapleton Fitzalan-Howard, KG (1983), GCVO (1986), CB (1966), CBE (1960), MC (1944), DL W Sussex (1977)) [His Grace The Duke of Norfolk KG GCVO CB CBE MC DL, Arundel Castle, Arundel, W Sussex BN18 9AB; Carlton Towers, Goole, Yorks DN14 9LZ; Bacres, Hambleden, Oxon RG9 6RY]; *b* 21 July 1915; *s* mother as 12th Lord (Baron) Beaumont 1971 (to which title her female issue are in remainder), *f* as 4th Baron Howard of Glossop 1972, and cousin in other titles 1975, also as premier Duke and Earl of England and Earl Marshal; *educ* Ampleforth and Ch Ch Oxford (MA, Hon Student 1983); WW II in France, N Africa, Sicily, Italy and NW Europe (despatches), Maj-Gen (ret), late Gren Gds, Kt SMO Malta, Head Br Mil Mission to Russian Forces Germany 1957–59, cmdg 70th Bde KAR Kenya 1961–63, GOC 1st Div BAOR 1963–65, MOD: Dir Management and Support Intell 1965–66, Dir Serv Intell 1966–67; chm Arundel Castle Tstees Ltd; Hon Master Bench Inner Temple 1984–, Hon Jt Treasurer (with Duchess of Norfolk) Help The Aged 1987–, Prime Warden Fishmongers' Co 1985–86, Hon Fell St Edmund's Coll Cambridge 1983, Kt Grand Cross Order of Pius IX; *m* 4 July 1949 *Anne Mary Teresa, CBE, dau of W/Cdr Gerald Joseph Constable-Maxwell, MC, DFC, AFC (*see* HERRIES OF TERREGLES, L), and has:

1 +EDWARD WILLIAM, *Earl of Arundel* [Earl of Arundel, Arundel Castle, Sussex BN18 9AB]; *b* 2 Dec 1956; *educ* Ampleforth and Lincoln Coll Oxford (MA); *m* 27 June 1987 *Georgina Susan, yr dau of John Temple Gore (*see* EGLINTON and WINTON, E), and has:

  (1) +Henry Miles, *Lord Maltravers*; *b* 3 Dec 1987

  (2) +Thomas Jack; *b* 14 March 1992

  (3) +Philip; *b* 14 July 1996

  (1) +Rachel Rose; *b* 10 June 1989

  (2) +Isobelle Serena; *b* 7 Feb 1994

2 +Gerald Bernard [The Lord Gerald Fitzalan-Howard, Carlton Towers, Goole, Yorks DN14 9LZ]; *b* 13 June 1962; *educ* Ampleforth; *m* 1 Dec 1990 *Emma Georgina Egerton, dau of Dr Desmond James Cecil Roberts, of Woodhill, Mayfield, Sussex, and has:

  (1) +Arthur; *b* 23 Oct 1991

  (1) +Florence; *b* 15 Jan 1993

  (2) +Grace; *b* 31 Dec 1994

1 +Tessa Mary Isabel [The Lady Tessa Balfour, Burpham Lodge, Burpham, Arundel, Sussex]; *b* 30 Sept 1950; *m* 14 July 1971 *Roderick Francis Arthur Balfour and has issue (*see* BALFOUR, E)

2 +Carina Mary Gabrielle [The Lady Carina Frost, 5 St Mary Abbots Place, London W8 6LS]; *b* 20 Feb 1952; *m* 19 March 1983 *Sir David Paradine Frost, OBE, author and broadcaster, s of Rev W J Paradine Frost, of Tenterden, Kent, and has:

  (1) +Miles Paradine; *b* 2 June 1984

  (2) +Wilfred Paradine; *b* 7 Aug 1985

  (3) +George Paradine; *b* 23 April 1987

3 +Marcia Mary Josephine [The Lady Marcia Ryecart, Stable Cottage, Bacres House, Hambleden, Oxon RG9 6RY]; *b* 10 March 1953; actress as Marsha Fitzalan; *m* 4 July 1977 (*divorce* May 1995) Patrick Geoffrey Ryecart, actor, yr s of Rev John Reginald Ryecart, of Dovercourt, Essex, and has:

  (1) +Fred(erick) William Hamlet; *b* 12 April 1987

  (1) +Mariella Celia; *b* 24 March 1982

  (2) +Jemima Carrie; *b* 11 Feb 1984

Norfolk, other creations: For the early post-Conquest Earldom of Norfolk, which was held with that of Suffolk, *see* SUFFOLK and BERKSHIRE, E, preliminary remarks.

In the winter of 1140–41 Hugh Bigod or le Bigod, who seems to have come from a Norman family settled in England soon after the Conquest and whose sister was mother of William, Earl of Arundel (*see* below and MOWBRAY, SEGRAVE and STOURTON, B), was made Earl of Norfolk. This Earldom too was looked on by contemporaries as including that of Suffolk. Hugh was an associate of HENRY I, particularly during that King's expedition to Normandy to crush rebellion there in 1130, but was less wholehearted a supporter of KING STEPHEN. Hugh was created by HENRY II Earl of Norfolk afresh in 1155, despite an agreement before the King's accession between the latter and STEPHEN which is thought to have recognised Hugh's prior possession of the Earldom. Hugh rebelled against HENRY II also and died shortly after being reconciled to that King.

His son Roger was not immediately recognised as 2nd Earl of Norfolk but was so invested in 1189, some 12 years after Hugh's death. Yet Roger was more loyal than Hugh, fighting against his own father on HENRY II's side at the Battle of Fornham in 1173, when Hugh and an army of invading Flemings were defeated. Roger later served as one of the baronial guarantors of the liberties extorted from KING JOHN at the signing of Magna Carta, however, and evidently fell out with JOHN such that the latter confiscated his lands. He died in 1221, having been reconciled to the Crown from 1217, by which time HENRY III had ascended the throne.

Hugh (le) Bigod, the 3rd Earl of Norfolk of this creation, was present with his father the 2nd Earl at the signing of Magna Carta and was also one of the guarantors of its provisions. He died only a few years after his father, whereupon his widow Maud, eldest daughter of William Marshal, Earl of Pembroke and hereditary Master Marshal of the household, married William de Warenne, Earl of Surrey. This concatenation of three dignities — the hereditary marshalcy, Earldom of Norfolk and Earldom of Surrey — foreshadowed their simultaneous possession by the present Dukes of Norfolk.

The 5th and last Earl of Norfolk of this 1140/1 or 1189 creation, another Roger (le) Bigod, also served as Marshal at EDWARD I's coronation but was stripped of the office by the King on refusing to take an army to Gascony in early 1297. After a long-standing dispute with the King over the confirmation of his charters and Magna Carta itself he in 1302 surrendered the Earldom for regrant together with a life interest in additional territorial possessions bringing him an annual income of £1,000 (over £24,000,000 in late-1990s terms). On his dying childless in late 1306 the Earldom and Marshalcy reverted to the Crown, whereas if he had not made the surrender four years earlier the former at any rate would have passed to his brother.

The latter had male issue which certainly survived till the mid–16th century and may well have done so to the present day. In 1906 the then Lord Mowbray claimed the Earldom of Norfolk as senior coheir of Thomas of Brotherton, who was created Earl of Norfolk six years after the death of the 5th and last Bigod holder of that title. His claim was rejected by the House of Lords on the grounds that the 1302 surrender by Bigod had been invalid. Those grounds have been attacked since and would certainly appear unsound. Such surrenders as Bigod's did in fact occur throughout the medieval period, though not often. But the Bigod-held Earldom of Norfolk was in effect snuffed out, albeit legitimately, by an exercise in royal legerdemain which a recent doctoral thesis has suggested was a deliberate policy by EDWARD I of reducing overmighty subjects.

The Thomas of Brotherton created Earl of Norfolk in 1312 was a younger brother of EDWARD II, who gave the new Earl and another brother of his, Edmund, nearly all the large territorial possessions of the old Bigod Earls. Thomas was also made Marshal of England but on his death without male issue in 1338 the latter office reverted to the Crown whereas the Earldom passed to his elder daughter Margaret. She in the same year, or possibly the preceding one, was promoted Duchess of Norfolk for life. On her death over 60 years later the Earldom descended to her grandson Thomas de Mowbray, for whom *see* MOWBRAY, SEGRAVE and STOURTON, B.

Baronies of FitzAlan and Mautravers: Sir Brian Fitz Alan, of Bedale, Yorks, descended from a younger son of Alan Count of Brittany (died 1146), fought in EDWARD I's wars against the Welsh in 1277 and 1287 and held high positions in relation to EDWARD's policy of containing and if possible controlling the Scots. He fought at the Battle of Falkirk in 1298, for instance, and assisted at the Siege of Carlaverock two years later. He was summoned to Parliament by writ in 1295 whereby according to later doctrine he would have become Lord (Baron) Fitzalan. He died without surviving male issue in 1306, whereupon, again according to later doctrine, any Barony created by the writ of summons of 1295 would have fallen into abeyance between his two daughters Agnes and Katherine and ultimately between their representatives. In Agnes's case, oddly enough, such representatives included the Stapletons of Ingham, Yorkshire, who for some generations also carried the representation of the Barons Beaumont (*see* below against **Lineage (of Beaumont)**). But by the turn of the 15th–16th centuries one of the coheiresses had married Sir Edward Howard, the celebrated Admiral (*see* below). He, however, died without issue. The assumption of the Barony by the 17th-century Howards was therefore unjustifiable in terms of descent.

The Mautraverses had held land in the West Country from the Counts of Eu since shortly after the Conquest, but it has not been possible to start tracing a detailed ancestry till about a century later. The Sir John Mautravers who murdered EDWARD II by forcing a red-hot poker up him was a member of this family and by writ of summons to Parliament of January 1329/30 is deemed according to later doctrine to have been created Lord (Baron) Mautravers. He was also directly responsible for the judicial murder of Edmund, Earl of Kent, EDWARD II's younger brother, and when QUEEN ISABELLA (EDWARD II's widow) and her lover Roger de Mortimer were overthrown and EDWARD III came into his own he lost his lands and high positions and would have lost his life had he not fled to Germany. Even as it was, he did so with a price on his head and a sentence of execution by both hanging and beheading. He later acted as a secret agent for the English government in Flanders. Shortly after mid-century his outlawry was revoked. He outlived both his son and grandson so that after his death in 1364 the Barony passed according to later doctrine to his granddaughter Eleanor. She married John d'Arundel (*see* below), who probably as a result was created a Baron by writ of summons to Parliament (according to later doctrine), though as Lord (Baron) Arundel.

Lineage (of Howard): Sir WILLIAM HOWARD, of East Winch, Norfolk, where he bought land 1277 and the manor house 1298; Counsel to King's Lynn Corporation 1285; Justice of Assize for the Northern Counties 1293, MP 1295, Judge Common Pleas 7 Oct 1297; *m* 1st Alice (*dsp*), dau of Sir Robert de Ufford, of Ufford, Suffolk, Justiciar Ireland; *m* 2nd Alice, dau of Sir Edward Fitton, of Wiggenhall St Germans, and *d* July or Aug 1308, leaving by her, with another s (Sir William, Sheriff Cambs and Hunts, *m* Joan, widow of Baldwin Dakeni, of Holkham, Norfolk, and *dsp* by 22 Sept 1328):

Sir JOHN HOWARD, of Wiggenhall and E Winch; Gentleman of the Bedchamber to EDWARD I; Sheriff Norfolk and Suffolk 3 Oct 1317–12 June 1323; *m* Joan (*m* 3rd John Avenel, of Gunthorpe, Norfolk), widow of Sir Thomas Peche, MP Cambs 1307, and dau of Sir Richard de Cornwall (illegitimate s of Richard, Earl of Cornwall, 2nd s of KING JOHN; *see* GREY, B), and *d* 1333, leaving:

Sir JOHN HOWARD; Adml North Seas 1335, Sheriff Norfolk 1345; *m* Alice, sis and heiress of Sir Robert de Boys, of Fersfield, nr Diss, Norfolk, and *d* in or after 1388, having had:

Sir ROBERT HOWARD; *m* Margery, dau of 3rd Lord (Baron) Scales by Lady Catherine de Ufford, sis and coheir of 2nd Earl of Suffolk of the March 1336/7 *cr*, and *dvp*, leaving:

Sir JOHN HOWARD; *b c* 1357; Sheriff Essex and Herts *temp* HENRYs IV and V, MP Cambs; *m* 1st Margaret (*d* 1381), dau and heiress of Sir John Plaiz, of Tofte, Norfolk, and Stansted Mountfichet, Essex, and had:

1 John (Sir); *m* Joan, dau of Sir Richard Walton and sis and heiress of John Walton, of Wivenhoe, Essex, and *dvp* 1409, leaving:

(1) Elizabeth; *b* 1410; *m* 1425 12th Earl of Oxford and had issue (*see* SAINT ALBANS, D)

1 Margaret; *m* 1st Constantine Clifton, of Buckenham Castle, Norfolk; *m* 2nd Sir George Talbot

Sir JOHN *m* 2nd 1383 Alice, dau and heiress of Sir William Tendring, of Tendring Hall, Stoke by Nayland, Suffolk, and by her had:

2 ROBERT (Sir)

3 Henry; Ld Manors of Buckenham, Terringhampton, W Walton and Wiggenhall, Norfolk; *m* Mary, dau of Sir Henry Hussey, and had:

(1) Elizabeth; *m* Henry Wentworth, of Codham, Essex

Sir JOHN *d* on pilgrimage at Jerusalem 17 Nov 1437; his er surv s,

Sir ROBERT HOWARD; cmded English fleet in Channel at time of Agincourt Campaign 1415; *b c* 1385; *m c* 1420 Lady Margaret de Mowbray, er dau of 1st Duke of Norfolk of the 1397 *cr* (*see* MOWBRAY, SEGRAVE and STOURTON, B) by his 2nd w Elizabeth Fitz Alan (*see* below against **Lineage (of Fitz Alan)**), and had, with two daus (Margaret, *m* Thomas Daniel, of Rathwire, Co Meath, s of William Daniel, of Daresbury, Cheshire; Catherine, *m* as his 2nd w 1st Lord (Baron) Bergavenny; *see* ABERGAVENNY, M):

JOHN HOWARD, **1st Duke of Norfolk**, as also Marshal and EARL MARSHAL of England, so *cr* 28 June 1483 (by RICHARD III, who seems illegally to have stripped his own nephew EDWARD, DUKE OF YORK (one of the two Princes in the Tower) of an identically worded dignity (*see* MOWBRAY, SEGRAVE and STOURTON, B), as also by writ of summons 15 Oct 1470 (though previous references to him as Lord Howard are to be found as early as Nov 1467) LORD (Baron) HOWARD (all E), KG (1472), PC (1483); *b* 1421/2; served Hundred Years War in France 1452–53, MP Norfolk 1455, Yorkist in Wars of Roses, ktd by EDWARD IV at Yorkist victory of Towton 29 March 1461; Sheriff Norfolk and Suffolk 1461 and Oxon 1467; Constable Colchester and Norwich Castles 1461; Treasurer Household 1467–74; Govr Calais early 1470s; cmded English fleet in naval victory over Scots in Firth of Forth 1482; Adml of England, Ireland and Aquitaine 1483, Steward Duchy Lancaster 1483; *m* 1st *c* 1443 Katherine (*d* 1465), dau of Sir William de Moleyns, and had, with three other daus:

1 THOMAS, **2nd Duke**

1 Anne; *m* Sir Edmund Gorges, KB, of Wraxall, Somerset

The **1st Duke** *m* 2nd by 22 Jan 1467 Margaret, dau of Sir John Chedworth and widow of (a) John Norreys, of Bray, Berks, and (b) Nicholas Wyfold, Ld Mayor London, and was *k* leading RICHARD III's archers at the front of the army at the Battle of Bosworth 22 Aug 1485, having by her had:

2 Katherine; *m* 2nd Lord (Baron) Berners (*qv*) and had issue

His only son,

THOMAS HOWARD, **2nd Duke of Norfolk**, KG (1483–85 and 1491), KB (Jan 1477/8), PC (1483–85, 1501); *b* 1443/4; *educ* Ipswich and Thetford GSs; yeoman in EDWARD IV's household from *c* 1466; fought Battle of Barnet 14 April 1471, Esq of the Body to EDWARD IV; Sheriff Norfolk and Suffolk 1476; MP Norfolk 1478; *cr* 28 June 1483 EARL OF SURREY (E) but attainted (as was his f posthumously) by HENRY VII's 1st Parl 1485; attainder reversed 1489 as regards Earldom only; Steward Household 1483–84; Warden E and Middle Marches; Ld High Treasurer 1501–22; *cr* 10 July 1510 EARL MARSHAL of England for life; as Lt-Gen in North won the Battle of Flodden 9 Sept 1513 over the Scots, for which he was rewarded by being *cr* 1 Feb 1513/4 DUKE OF NORFOLK with precedence of any previous Duke of Norfolk (*i.e.*, including that of 1397) — effectively, therefore, a restoration of his f's principal title — meanwhile making over the Earldom of Surrey to his est s for the latter's life; *m* 1st 30 April 1472 Elizabeth (*d* 4 April 1497), widow of Sir Humphrey Bourchier (*see* BERNERS, B) and dau of Sir Frederick Tylney, and had, with five other sons and two other daus:

1 THOMAS, **3rd Duke**

2 Edward, KG (1513); *b c* 1477; ktd *c* 1497; King's Standard Bearer for life 1509, Adml of England, Ireland and Aquitaine 1512, Ld Adml of England 1513; *m* 1st after 28 July 1500, as her 3rd husb, Elizabeth (*d* 18 Feb 1504/5), coheiress to the Barony of Fitzalan abeyant since 1306 (*see* preliminary remarks above), dau of Sir Miles Stapleton and widow of (a) Sir William Calthorpe and (b) Sir John Fortescu; *m* 2nd by Jan 1505/6 Alice, *de jure* Baroness Morley and Baroness Marshal in her own right according to later doctrine, dau of William Lovel, 7th Lord (Baron) Morley (in right of his w Eleanor, *de jure* Baroness Morley in her own right according to later doctrine; *see* also MORLEY, E, preliminary remarks) and widow of Sir William Parker, but *dsp*, *k* in a cutting-out expedn against French galleys off Brest 25 April 1513

3 Edmund; Marshal of Horse at Flodden 1513; *m* 1st Joyce, dau and coheir of Sir Richard Culpepper; *m* 2nd Dorothy (*dsp*), dau of Thomas Troyes, and *d* 1538, having had by his 1st w, with other issue:

(1) Henry; *m* Anne — and was attainted with QUEEN CATHERINE HOWARD

(1) Margaret; *m* Sir Thomas Arundell, of Wardour

(2) CATHERINE; *b c* 1521/2; *m* 28 July 1540, as his 5th w, HENRY VIII and was beheaded 13 Feb 1542/3

1 Elizabeth; *m c* 1500 Thomas Boleyn, 1st and last Earl of Ormond and Wiltshire, and had issue

2 Marcella/Muriel; *m* 1st John Grey, 4th Lord and Baron of Lisle and 2nd and last Viscount Lisle (*dspm* 9 Sept 1504; *see* also DE L'ISLE, V, preliminary remarks), and had:

(1) ELIZABETH, BARONESS LISLE in her own right; *b* posthumously *c* 25 March 1505; *m* after June 1515, as his 1st w, 2nd and last Earl of Devon (*qv*) of the 1511 *cr*, but *dsp* between 31 March and 12 May 1519

2 (cont.) Viscountess Lisle *m* 2nd by 9 July 1506 Sir Thomas Knyvet(t), KB (*k* off Brest in a sea battle against the French Aug 1512), of Buckenham, Norfolk, and *d* in childbirth 14 Dec 1512, leaving, with two other sons and a dau:

(1) Edmund (Sir), of Buckenham

(2) Henry (Sir), of Charlton, Wilts

The **2nd Duke** *m* 2nd 8 Nov 1497 Agnes (*d* May 1545), dau of Hugh Tilney and sis and heiress of Sir Philip Tilney, of Skirbeck and Boston, Lincs, and had, with another s and dau:

4 WILLIAM HOWARD, 1st BARON HOWARD OF EFFINGHAM (*see* EFFINGHAM, E)

5 Thomas; tried to marry Lady Margaret Douglas, dau of MARGARET, Dowager QUEEN OF SCOTS, and n of HENRY VIII, hence attainted and *d* a prisoner in Tower of London 1536

3 Elizabeth; *m* 11th Lord (Baron) FitzWalter (*qv*) and *d* 18 Sept 1534, leaving issue

4 Katherine; *m* 1st Rhys ap Gruffudd (*see* DYNEVOR, B); *m* 2nd 1st and last Earl of Bridgwater (*dsp* 12 April 1548) and was *bur* 11 May 1554

5 Anne; *m* 14th Earl of Oxford (*see* SAINT ALBANS, D) and *dsp* by 22 Feb 1958/9

The 2nd DUKE *d* 21 May 1524; his est son,

THOMAS HOWARD, **3rd Duke of Norfolk**, KG (1510, Lt Order Garter 1525), PC (by May 1516); *b* 1473; ktd 1497, Lt-Gen in reversion of English Army in Spain 1512, Ld High Adml 1513–25, served as Capt in the forward position at Battle of Flodden 1513, hence *cr* 1 Feb 1513/4 EARL OF SURREY for life, also 28 May 1533 EARL MARSHAL of England (attainted 27 Jan 1546/7, when his honours were forfeit, and was due to be executed the next morning but was saved by HENRY VIII's death a few hours earlier; restored 3 Aug 1553, having spent all EDWARD VI's reign under confinement in the Tower); Ld Lt Ireland 1522, Ld High Treasurer 1522–Feb 1546/7, Lt Gen English Army against Scots Feb 1522/3, Envoy France 1525–27, Ld Pres Cncl 1527–30, High Steward Cambridge 1529, Kt of St Michael of France 1532; played leading role in suppressing Pilgrimage of Grace 1536–37; Lt-Gen English Army in France 1544; *m* 1st Feb 1494/5 PRINCESS ANNE (*dsps* 23 Nov 1511), 5th dau of EDWARD IV; *m* 2nd by 8 Jan 1512/3 (separated 1534) Lady Elizabeth Stafford, dau of 3rd and last Duke of Buckingham of the 1444 *cr* (*see* STAFFORD, B), and by her had:

1 Henry, *Earl of Surrey*, KG (1541), KB (1536–41); *b* 1516–18; Steward Duchy Lancaster 1543, Govr Guisnes Aug 1545 and Boulogne Sept 1545–March 1545/6; poet who with Sir Thomas Wyatt perfected the (Shakespearian) sonnet form in English (drawing on the Petrarchian sonnet to do so) and was a pioneer in blank verse (especially his translation of Books II and IV of the *Aeneid*); some 40 of his poems were published in *Tottel's Miscellany* (1557); *m* 1532 Lady Frances Vere (*m* 2nd Thomas Staynings, of E Soham, Suffolk, and *d* 30 June 1577), dau of 15th Earl of Oxford (*see* SAINT ALBANS, D) by his 2nd w, and was beheaded for treason 19 Jan 1546/7, having imprudently remarked that his f would be a good choice of guardian for the young Prince Edward (later EDWARD VI) and having quartered the 'arms' of Edward the Confessor with his own, leaving:

(1) THOMAS, **4th Duke**

(2) HENRY HOWARD, 1st and last EARL OF NORTHAMPTON, so *cr* 13 March 1603/4, as also BARON OF MARNHULL, Co Dorset (both E), KG (1605), PC (1603); *b* 24 Feb 1539/40; *educ* King's Coll and Trin Hall Cambridge (MA 1566, MA Oxon 1568); restored in blood (following f's attainder) 8 May 1559, Constable Dover Castle and Ld Warden Cinque Ports Jan 1603/4–14, Jt Commr for Earl Marshal Feb 1603/4 and Feb 1604/5; Ld Lt Herts June-Aug 1605 and Norfolk 1605, Ld Privy Seal 1608–14, First Commr Treasury 1612–14; built Audley End and Northampton (later Northumberland) House in the Strand, London; *d* unm 16 June 1614, when his titles expired

(1) Jane; *m* 6th and last Earl of Westmorland of the 1397 *cr* (*see* ABERGAVENNY, M)

(2) Catherine; m 7th Lord (Baron) Berkeley (qv) and had issue

(3) Margaret; bapt 30 June 1543; m by 10 Sept 1565, as his 2nd w, Henry, 9th Lord (Baron) Scrope (of Bolton), KG, and d 17 March 1590/1, leaving issue

2 THOMAS HOWARD, 1st VISCOUNT HOWARD OF BINDON, Co Dorset (E), so cr 13 Jan 1558/9; b c 1520; ktd 1547, restored in blood (following f's attainder) 1553; m 1st between 1526 and 1542 Elizabeth Marney, yr dau of 2nd Baron Marn(e)y by his 1st w Christian, dau of Sir Roger Newburgh; m 2nd after 1565 Gertrude, dau of William Lyte, of Lillesdon, Somerset; m 3rd 7 June 1576 Mabel, dau of Nicholas Burton, of Carshalton, Surrey; m 4th Margaret, dau of Henry Manning, Marshal Household to HENRY VIII, EDWARD VI, MARY and ELIZABETH I, and d 28 Jan 1581/2, leaving by his 3rd w at least one dau (Frances, m as his 3rd w, 2nd Duke of Lennox and (1st Duke of) Richmond of the 1623 cr; see MORAY, E) and by his 1st w, with other issue b before their marriage:

(1) Charles LYTE alias HOWARD; m Roberta, dau of William Webb, and had:

1a Catharine; m Sir Thomas Thynne (see BATH, M)

2a Elizabeth; m Sir James Murray

(2) HENRY HOWARD, 2nd VISCOUNT HOWARD OF BINDON; b c 1542; m c 10 Feb 1565/6 Frances, dau of Sir Peter Meautys, of Westham, Essex, English Amb to France, and dspm by 16 Jan 1590/1, leaving:

1a Douglas [sic]; bapt 24 Jan 1591/2; m Sir Arthur Gorges (d Oct 1625) and had:

1b Ambrosia; d umn 1606

(3) THOMAS HOWARD, 3rd and last VISCOUNT HOWARD OF BINDON, KG (1606); Dorset: MP 1562–67, Ld Lt 1606–07; m by 10 Jan 1580 Grace, dau of Bernard Duffield, and dsp 1 March 1610/11, when the Viscountcy expired

1 Mary; Ldy in Waiting to ANNE OF CLEVES; m (dispensation 28 Nov 1533) Henry Fitzroy, 1st and last Duke of Richmond (dsp 22 July 1536, having failed to consummate the marriage, sole illegitimate s of HENRY VIII (by Elizabeth Blount, Maid of Honour to CATHERINE OF ARAGON), and dsp 9 Dec 1557

The 3rd DUKE d 25 Aug 1554; his gs,

THOMAS HOWARD, **4th Duke of Norfolk**, having been restored in blood 2 Sept 1553, KG (1559), KB (1553), PC (1562); b 10 March 1537/8; First Gentleman Bedchamber to KING PHILIP (husb of MARY) July–Aug 1554, Ld Lt Norfolk and Suffolk 1558, Lt-Gen in North 1559–60, V-Pres the Cncl, Kt of St Michael France Jan 1565/6; m 1st by 30 March 1555 Lady Mary Fitz Alan (d 25 Aug 1557), 2nd dau and in her issue eventual sole heiress of **19th/12th Earl of Arundel** (see below, **Lineage (of FitzAlan)**), and had:

1 St PHILIP HOWARD, **20th/13th Earl of Arundel**, as which s maternal gf 24 Feb 1579/80 if the Earldom be viewed as a heritable title and his mother's sister's husb 1st and last Baron Lumley (see SCARBROUGH, E) of the 1547 cr (who the same day made over to him the Castle and Honour of Arundel) if the Earldom be viewed as being by tenure of Arundel Castle; b 28 June 1557 (PHILIP II OF SPAIN stood sponsor); educ Cambridge; restored in blood 15 March 1580/1; turned RC Sept 1584 and on trying to leave the country without permission was imprisoned in the Tower 25 April 1585 and held there till his death, in addition being fined £10,000 (over £870,000 in late 1990s terms) and attainted for treason, when he was stripped of all his honours; canonised 1970; m 1571 Anne, dau of his stepmother Elizabeth, Duchess of Norfolk, by her 1st husb 4th Lord (Baron) Dacre (of Gilsland) (see DACRE, B), and d 19 Oct 1595, leaving:

(1) THOMAS HOWARD, **21st/14th Earl of Arundel** and **3rd Earl of Surrey**, as both of which restored 18 April 1604, also **1st Earl of Norfolk**, as which cr 6 June 1644 (E), with remainder, in default of heirs male of his body, to those of his half-uncles Thomas and William; also procured an Act of Parl 1627 'for the annexing of the Castle, etc., of Arundel, with the titles and dignities of the Baronies of FitzAlan, Clun and Oswaldestre and Maltravers [i.e., Mautravers] and with divers other lands, etc., being now parcels of the possessions of Thomas, Earl of Arundel and Surrey, etc., to the same title, name, and dignity of Earl of Arundel', an extraordinary instrument which may just possibly have had the effect of converting the feudal lordships of Clun and Oswaldestre (i.e., Oswestry) to peerages of Parliament although the weight of evidence and expert opinion militates against such an interpretation, if only because it has been argued that no such form of creation is known in Constitutional Law; the situation is complicated by the fact that the Parliamentary peerage titles of FitzAlan and Mautravers had previously existed as Baronies; accordingly THOMAS HOWARD, **21st/14th Earl of Arundel**, **3rd Earl of Surrey** and **1st Earl of Norfolk** may be considered to have been cr 1627 **BARON FitzALAN** and **BARON MALTRAVERS** even if the other 'Baronies' are held not to have been so cr; KG (1611), PC (1616); b 7 July 1585; Jt Ld Lt Sussex 1608 and Cumberland, Northumberland and Westmorland 1633, Ld Lt Norfolk 1615 and Cumberland 1639; built up in Italy from c 1613 the collection of statuary dating from classical antiquity called the Arundel Marbles; turned Protestant 1615 but was reconciled to Catholicism on his deathbed; Earl Marshal for life 1621, Ld Steward Household 1640–41; m Sept 1606 Lady Alathe(i)a Talbot (d 24 May 1654), 3rd dau and eventually sole heiress of 7th Earl of Shrewsbury and Waterford (qv), and d 4 Oct 1646, having had:

1a James, Lord Maltravers, KB (1616); bapt 17 July 1607; d umn 1624

2a HENRY FREDERICK, **22nd/15th, 4th and 2nd Earl**

3a WILLIAM HOWARD, 1st and last VISCOUNT STAFFORD (E), so cr 11 Nov 1640, KB (Feb 1625/6); b 30 Nov 1612; educ St John's Coll Cambridge; m c 11 Oct 1637 MARY (cr also 5 Oct 1688 Countess of Stafford (E) for life; d 13 Jan 1693/4), sis of 5th Baron Stafford (qv) of the 1547 cr, with whom he was jointly cr 12 Sept 1640 BARON and BARONESS STAFFORD, Co Stafford (E), with remainder first to the heirs male of their bodies and in default to the heirs of their bodies, with precedence of 1299, and was attainted 7 Dec 1680 for high treason (falsely, his accuser being Titus Oates), viz., participation in the so-called 'Popish Plot', when he was stripped of his titles, and was beheaded 29 Dec 1680, leaving issue (see STAFFORD, B); his attainder reversed 1838

The **4th Duke** m 2nd between 10 Dec 1558 and 2 March 1558/9 Margaret (d 10 Jan 1563/4), dau and heiress of 1st and last Baron Audley of Walden and widow of Lord Henry Dudley (yr s of 1st and last Duke of Northumberland of the 1553 cr;

see NORTHUMBERLAND, D, preliminary remarks), and by her had, with a dau (Margaret; m 2nd Earl of Dorset; see SACKVILLE, B):

2 THOMAS HOWARD, 1st EARL OF SUFFOLK (see SUFFOLK and BERK-SHIRE, E)

3 William; b 19 Dec 1563; m 28 Oct 1577 Elizabeth, dau of 4th Lord (Baron) Dacre (of Gilsland) (see DACRE, B), thus acquiring Naworth Castle, Cumberland, and Henderskelfe, the site of the present Castle Howard, and d 7 Oct 1640, having had, with other issue, including an er s (see CARLISLE, E) and at least two daus (Mary, m Sir John Wintour and had issue (see POWERSCOURT, V); Elizabeth, m as his 1st w Sir Henry Bedingfeld, see PASTON-BEDINGFELD, Bt):

(1) Francis (Sir), of Corby Castle, Cumberland; royalist Col Civil War; b 29 Aug 1588; m 1st Margaret (d 7 Sept 1625), dau of John Preston, of The Manor of Furness, Lancs, and had:

1a Thomas; royalist Col Civil War; ka Atherton Moor 1643

1a Elizabeth; m Edward Standish, of Standish

(1) (cont.) Sir Francis m 2nd Mary (d 22 July 1672), dau of Sir Henry Widdrington, of Widdrington, and d 11 April 1660, having by her had, with four daus:

2a Francis, of Corby Castle; Army Capt, Govr Carlisle; b 29 June 1635; m 1st Frances (d 1679), dau of Sir William Gerard, 3rd Bt (see GERARD, B), and had two daus; m 2nd Mary Ann Dorothy, dau of Richard Towneley, of Towneley (see O'HAGAN, B), and d 1702, having by her had, with another dau (d unm):

1b Ann; m Marmaduke Langdale, of Houghton

3a William, of Corby Castle; m Jane, dau of John Dalston, of Acornbank, Westmorland, and d 1708, leaving:

1b Thomas, of Corby Castle; m 1st c 1703 Barbara (d 1716), dau of 1st Viscount Lonsdale (see LONSDALE, E), and had a s and three daus; m 2nd Barbara, sis of Sir Christopher Musgrave, 5th Bt, of Hartley Castle (qv); m 3rd 1734 Mary (dsp 1735), sis of Francis Carrington Smith, and d 1740, leaving by his 2nd w:

1c Philip, of Corby Castle; b 1730; m 1754 Ann (d 1794), est dau of Henry Witham, of Cliffe, Yorks, and d 8 Jan 1810, leaving, with other issue:

1d Henry, of Corby Castle; High Sheriff Cumberland 1832; b 2 July 1757; m 1st 4 Nov 1788 Maria (dsp 9 Nov 1789), 3rd dau and coheir of 2nd Lord Archer, Baron of Umberslade; m 2nd 18 March 1793 Catherine Mary (d 16 Jan 1849), 2nd dau of Sir Richard Neave, 1st Bt (qv), and d 1 March 1842, leaving:

1e Philip Henry, of Corby Castle, JP, DL; High Sheriff 1860, MP Carlisle 1830–47 and 1848–52, FSA; b 22 April 1801; m 16 Nov 1843 Eliza Minto (d 11 Feb 1865), est dau of Maj John Canning, HEIC, and d 1 Jan 1883, having had, with three daus (d unm):

1f Philip John Canning, of Corby Castle and Foxcote, Warwicks, JP Cumberland, Glos, Warwicks and Worcs; b 14 March 1853; m 4 Feb 1875 Alice Clare (d 22 May 1941), yst dau of Peter Constable-Maxwell (see HERRIES OF TERREGLES, L), and d 22 April 1934, leaving:

1g Ursula Mary; b 11 Sept 1879; m 1st 22 Nov 1899 Sir Henry Joseph Lawson, 3rd Bt (see HOWARD-LAWSON, Bt), and had issue; m 2nd 27 April 1949 *Lt-Col Hugh Levin, OBE, The Green Howards, s of Maj Lionel Henry Levin, Yorks Regt, and d 5 Jan 1960

2e Henry Francis (Sir), GCB; Envoy Extrdy and Min Plen Brazil, Portugal, Hanover and Bavaria; b 3 Nov 1809; m 1st 23 Dec 1830 Sevilla (d 12 March 1835), 3rd dau of 2nd Baron Erskine of Restormel (see BUCHAN, E), and had:

1f Isabella; Dominican nun at Stone; d 9 July 1905

2f Adela; Benedictine nun at St Scholastica's Priory, Atherstone; d 17 Jan 1914

2e (cont.) Sir Henry m 2nd 30 Aug 1841 Maria Ernestine (d 25 Dec 1897), 4th dau of Wilhelm Leopold von der Schulenburg, of Priemern, Prussia, and d 28 Jan 1898, having by her had:

1f Henry (Sir), GCMG, KCB; Dip Serv 1865 on: Sec of Embassy St Petersburg 1890 and Paris 1894, Envoy Extrdy and Min Plen Holy See 1914–16, Grand Cross Netherlands, Order House of Orange, Luxemburg Order of Oak Crown; b 11 Aug 1843; m 2 Oct 1867 Cecilia (d 3 Dec 1907), dau of George Washington Riggs, of Washington, DC, and d 4 May 1921, leaving:

1g George; b 26 Nov 1869; m 5 Nov 1902 Mary Allen (d 8 Feb 1946), widow of Clifford Perrin, of Cincinnati, Ohio, and dau of William Henry Clagett, of Washington, DC, and d 22 Jan 1919, leaving:

1h Henry; Capt Quartermaster Corps US Army WW II; b 4 May 1907; m 1st 26 Nov 1928 (divorce 1930) Vara, dau of William Doherty, of Houston, Tex.; m 2nd 22 March 1941 Natalie Bayard (m 2nd 16 Dec 1956 Capt Kenneth Douglas Robertson, USNR (ret) and d 5 June 1996), dau of Rev George Grenville Merrill, of Newport, RI, and d 22 Aug 1955, leaving:

1i +George [George Howard, PO Box 1522, Manchester Center, VT, USA]; b 8 May 1944; m 1977 *Ilse Bay Tarafa, of Hamburg

1i +Natalie Bayard [Mrs William Baker, 49 E 86th St, New York, NY 10028, USA]; b 16 Nov 1942; m 1st 8 May 1968 Peter Alan Gordon, s of Alan Stark Gordon, of Montreal; m 2nd 19– *William Thompson Baker and by her 1st husb has:

1j +Jonathan Kingman; b 11 Feb 1970

2i +Mary Mowbray [Mary Mowbray Howard, 160 W 16th St, New York, NY 10011, USA]; b 14 Oct 1948; m 1978 *Robert Charczuk and has:

1j +William George Howard; b 1984

2g Henry Mowbray, OBE (1919); Cdr RNVR, WW I and WW II, Legn Hon, Orders Crown Italy and Sacred Treasure Japan; *b* 1 June 1873; *m* 24 April 1917 Norah Florence Annie (*d* 1974), only child of Maj John Dunlop-Watson, and *d* 16 Jan 1953, leaving:

  1h +Henry Edmund, DSC [Capt Henry Howard DSC RN, 16 Normandy Ct, Station Close, Wickham, Hants PO17 5JZ]; *b* 3 March 1923; Capt RN, WW II; *m* 6 Jan 1945 *Sheila, yr dau of Colin McNab Heys Brown, of Paisley, Renfrewshire, and has:

    1i +Henry Colin Francis, MBE [Maj Henry Howard MBE, Greenway, Green Lane, Exton EX3 0PW]; *b* 30 Sept 1947; *educ* Nautical Coll Pangbourne; Maj RM; *m* 9 Aug 1975 *Katherine, yr dau of Kenneth Charles Harold Rowe, MBE, JP, of Clyst St Mary, Exeter, and has:

      1j +Thomas William; *b* 1977

      2j +Charles Philip; *b* 1979

      1j +Jane; *b* 1982

    1i *Catherine Jane [Mrs Edward Williams, North Corner, Ashford Hill, Berks]; *b* 28 July 1950; *m* 19 May 1973 *Edward Bruce Williams, yr s of Brigadier Edward Stephen Bruce Williams, of Bramdean, Hants, and has:

      1j +Alasdair Edward Bruce; *b* 1 Nov 1975

      2j +Peter Henry Bruce; *b* 1978

      3j +Simon Bruce; *b* 1982

  1h +Joan Cecilia [Mrs Brent Hutton-Williams, 4 Lansdowne House, Lansdowne Rd, London W11]; *b* 15 Dec 1917; *m* 30 Oct 1942 Capt Brent Elworthy Hutton-Williams, MBE (*d* 1989), Intell Corps, s of Capt William Hutton-Williams, FRGS, and has:

    1i +Christopher Brent; *b* 10 Oct 1948; *m* 1974 *Caroline Oppenheimer and has:

      1j +Beatrice Rose; *b* 1980

    1i +Charlotte Fiona Janet [Mrs John Mather, 74 Oakley St, London SW3]; *b* 12 Jan 1944; *m* 1st 1 March 1969 (*divorce* 1975) David Dennis Fennell, s of Rev Alfred Charles Dennis Fennell, of Birmingham, and has:

      1j +Benedict Nicholas; *b* 1971

    1j (cont.) Mrs Charlotte Fennell *m* 2nd 1975 (*divorce* 19–) Michael Harrison; *m* 3rd 1990 *John Mather and has by him:

      2j +Toby Lawrence Brent; *b* 1978

  1g Marie Ernestine; *b* 22 Aug 1868; *m* 5 Sept 1894 Maj-Gen Rudolf Heinrich, Baron von Recum (*d* 14 March 1944), and *d* 21 Jan 1954, leaving issue

  2g Janet Madeleine Cecilia; *b* 11 July 1871; *d* unm 9 July 1960

  3g Alice Lawrason; *b* 21 April 1876; *d* unm 15 July 1942

2f Francis (Sir), KCB, KCMG, JP, DL Glos; Maj-Gen, Col Glos Regt 1912–13, Col Cmdt Rifle Bde 1913–22, ADC to HM; Jowaki Expdn 1878, Afghan War, Bazaar Valley and Lughman Expdns 1878–79, Burma 1888–89, Sudan 1898, Crete 1898, Boer War 1899–1900, Inspr-Gen Inf WW I; *b* 26 March 1848; *m* 23 April 1895 Gertrude Jane (*d* 6 Oct 1953), dau of Hugh Conyngham Boyd, of Torquay and Ballycastle, Co Down, and *d* 21 March 1930, having had:

  1g Francis; *b* 2 Feb 1896; *d* 16 June 1903

  1g Marjorie; *b* 9 Aug 1903; *m* 16 Sept 1931 George John Theodore Hyde Villiers (*see* CLARENDON, E) and *d* 3 Aug 1982, having had issue

3f Sevilla Catherine; *d* young 1846

4f Catherine Mary; *m* 17 July 1873 Ernest Count von Rechberg (*d* 6 Dec 1913) and *d* 15 Feb 1905, leaving issue

5f Mary Louisa; *m* 27 June 1872 Ludwig Baron von Aretin, of Haidenburg, Bavaria (*d* 5 Feb 1884), and *d* 10 Sept 1940, leaving issue

1e Catherine; *m* 28 July 1829 Hon Philip Henry Joseph Stourton (*see* MOWBRAY, SEGRAVE and STOURTON, B) and *d* 27 Jan 1874, leaving issue

2e Emma Agnes; *m* 14 April 1823 11th Baron Petre (*qv*) and *d* 10 Feb 1861

3e Adeliza Maria; *m* 20 April 1830 her cousin Henry W Petre (*see* PETRE, B) and *d* 9 Sept 1833

1d Maria; *m* 1st Hon George Petre (*see* PETRE, B); *m* 2nd Henry Espinasse

The **4th Duke** *m* 3rd 29 Jan 1566/7 Elizabeth (*dsp* 4 Sept 1567), widow of 4th Lord (Baron) Dacre (of Gilsland) (*see* DACRE, B) and 2nd dau of Sir James Leyburne, of Cunswick, Westmorland, and was attainted of high treason for involvement in the Ridolfi Plot (of which he was probably innocent), exacerbated by his communicating clandestinely with MARY QUEEN OF SCOTS (of which he was guilty), who he had hoped to marry, and beheaded 30 Sept 1572, when his titles were forfeited

The 4th DUKE's ggs,

HENRY FREDERICK HOWARD, 22nd/15th Earl of Arundel, 4th Earl of Surrey and **2nd Earl of Norfolk**, KB (1616), PC (I 1634); called up to Ho Lds 21 March 1639/40 *vp* in his f's supposed Barony of Mowbray (*see* MOWBRAY, SEGRAVE and STOURTON, B); *b* 15 Aug 1608; royalist Civil War, fighting at Edgehill Oct 1642; *m* 7 March 1625/6 Lady Elizabeth Stuart (*d* 23 Jan 1673/4), est dau of 3rd Duke of Lennox (*see* MORAY, E), and *d* 17 April 1652, leaving, with other issue:

1 THOMAS HOWARD, **5th Duke of Norfolk**, as which restored 29 Dec 1660 (confirmed 20 Dec 1661), with remainder to heirs male of his body, in default of which to the heirs male of the body of (a) his f, (b) his paternal gf, (c) his male-line ggf, (d) the latter's half-bro Thomas, Earl of Suffolk, (e) the latter's yr bro Lord William and (f) Charles, 1st Earl of Nottingham (*see* EFFINGHAM, E; Charles Earl of Nottingham's yr bro, from whom the current Earls of Effingham

descend, was, rather strangely, excluded), also **23rd/16th Earl of Arundel, 5th Earl of Surrey** and **3rd Earl of Norfolk** etc, as which *s* f 1652, also 14th LORD (Baron) FURNIVALL(E) (*see* PETRE, B, for subsequent history), 12th/15th LORD (Baron) STRANGE (of Blackmere) and 15th LORD (Baron) TALBOT, as which *s* paternal grandmother 1654; *b* 9 March 1626/7; *educ* Utrecht and Padua; *d* unm 13 Dec 1677, having been insane since 1645

2 HENRY HOWARD, **6th Duke of Norfolk**; *b* 12 July 1628; *cr* 27 March 1669 BARON HOWARD OF CASTLE RISING, Co Norfolk (E), and 19 Oct 1672 EARL OF NORWICH and EARL MARSHAL of England, with identical remainder to that of the restored Dukedom of 1660 apart from the exclusion of his er bro; Amb Morocco 1669; *m* 1st just prior to 21 Oct 1652 Lady Anne Somerset (*d* 1662), est dau of 2nd Marquess of Worcester (*see* BEAUFORT, D); *m* 2nd just prior to 23 Jan 1677/8 his mistress Jane (*m* 2nd Col Thomas Maxwell and *d* 28 Aug 1693), dau of Robert Bickerton, Gentleman of the Royal Wine Cellar, and *d* 13 Jan 1683/4, leaving by his 1st w, with two other daus:

  (1) HENRY HOWARD, **7th Duke of Norfolk**, KG (1685), PC (Feb 1688/9); *b* 11 Jan 1654/5; *educ* Magdalen Coll Oxford; called up to Ho Lds 14 Jan 1677/8 *vp* in f's Barony of Mowbray; conformed to C of E; Steward HAC 1682, Constable and Govr Windsor Castle 1682, Ld Lt Berks and Surrey 1682–1701 and Norfolk 1683–1701, Col 12th Foot 1685–86 and 22nd Foot March–-Sept 1689, Capt-Gen Artillery 1690, Ranger Windsor Forest 1700–01; *m* 8 Aug 1677 (*separation* 1685, *divorce* 1700), as her 1st husb, Lady Mary Mordaunt, Baroness Mordaunt in her own right from 1697, dau and heiress of 2nd Earl of Peterborough (*see* MORDAUNT, Bt), and *dsp* 2 April 1701

  (2) Thomas, of Worksop, Notts; *educ* Magdalen Coll Oxford; Lt King's Life Gds(?), Master Robes 1687, Ld Lt W R Yorks 1687, Amb Holy See 1688; *m* Mary Elizabeth (*d* 10 Dec 1732), dau and sole heiress of Sir John Savile, 1st and last Bt (*see* MEXBOROUGH, E), and *d* 9 Nov 1689, lost at sea off Brest while travelling to France from Ireland on the exiled JAMES II's behalf, having had, with other issue:

    1a THOMAS HOWARD, **8th Duke of Norfolk**; *b* 11 Dec 1683; *m* 26 May 1709 Maria Winifreda Francisca (allegedly *m* 2nd Nov 1733 Hon Peregrine Widdrington (with whom she certainly lived after her (1st?) husb's death), yr bro of 4th and last Baron Widdrington of Blankney, and *d* 25 Sept 1754), dau and sole heiress of Sir Nicholas Shireburn, 1st and last Bt, of Stonyhurst, Lancs, and *dsp* 23 Dec 1732

    2a Henry; apptd Bp of Utica *in partibus infidelium* but *d* 1720 before consecration

    3a EDWARD HOWARD, **9th Duke of Norfolk**; *b* 5 June 1686; took part in Jacobite Uprising 1715 but escaped punishment through his er bro's interceding for him and the absence of hostile witnesses at his trial for high treason; rearrested 1722 on suspicion of further Jacobite intrigues but released on bail after six months in custody; *m* 26 Nov 1727 Mary (*d* 27 May 1773), 2nd dau and coheir of Edward Blount (*see* GUISE, Bt), and *dsp* 20 Sept 1777, when the Baronies of Mowbray, Furnivall(e), Strange (of Blackmere) and Talbot fell into abeyance between the daus and coheirs of his yr bro Philip (*see* MOWBRAY, SEGRAVE and STOURTON, B, also PETRE, B), while the Earldom of Norwich and Barony of Howard of Castle Rising expired

    4a Richard; Canon of St Peter's Rome as Mgr Howard de Norfolk

    5a Philip, of Buckenham, Norfolk; *b* 24 Jan 1687/8; *m* 1st 7 Jan 1723/4 Winifrede (*d* 3 Feb 1730/1), est dau of Thomas Stonor (*see* CAMOYS, B) and had:

      1b Thomas; *b* 4 Feb 1727/8; *d* unm 9 Jan 1763

      1b Winifrede; *m* 11 Oct 1749 16th Baron Stourton and *d* 19 July 1753, leaving issue (*see* MOWBRAY, SEGRAVE and STOURTON, B)

    5a (cont.) Philip Howard *m* 2nd 8 Nov 1739 his er bro's sis-in-law Henrietta (*d* 26 March 1782), widow of Peter Proll, of Antwerp, and dau and coheir of Edward Blount, and *d* 23 Jan 1749/50, having by her had, with another s:

      2b Edward; *d* 1767 aged 24

      2b Anne; *m* 19 April 1762 9th Baron Petre (*qv*) and *d* 15 Jan 1787, leaving issue

    1a Mary; *m* 1 Oct 1698 Walter, 4th Lord Aston of Forfar, and *d* 23 May 1723, leaving issue

  (1) Philippa; *m* Ralph Standish, of Standish, and had:

    1a Cecilia; *m* William Towneley (*see* O'HAGAN, B) and had issue

3 Philip; *b* 1629; *educ* St John's Coll Cambridge; took vows as a Dominican (under name Thomas, after St Thomas Aquinas) 1645, ordained priest 1652, 1st Prior of the English Dominican House at Bornem, Flanders, 1658; First Chaplain to CATHERINE OF BRAGANZA, w of CHARLES II; Grand Almoner 1665; Cardinal 1675, Cardinal Protector of England 1679; fndr English Dominican Coll of St Thomas Louvain, Vicar-Gen of the revived English Dominican Province 1694; *d* 16 June 1694

4 Charles, of Greystoke, Cumberland, and Deepdene, Dorking, Surrey; *m* Mary (*d* 7 Nov 1695), est dau and coheir of George Tattershall, of West Court, Finchampstead, Berks, and *d* 31 March 1713, having had, with other issue:

  (1) Henry Charles, of Greystoke; *m* Mary (*d* 7 Oct 1747), dau of John Aylward, London merchant, and *d* 10 June 1730, having had, with two other sons (*d* unm):

    1a CHARLES HOWARD, **10th Duke of Norfolk**; *b* 1 Dec 1720; author: *The Memorial of Charles Howard Esq. Of Greystock [sic], and Miss Frances Howard of the Family of Norfolk of England* (1763), *Considerations on the Penal Laws against Roman Catholics in England and the new-acquired Colonies in America* (1764), *Thoughts, Essays and Maxims, chiefly Religious and Political* (1768) and *Anecdotes of the Howard Family* (1769); *m* 8 Nov 1739 Catherine (*d* 21 Nov 1784), dau and coheir of John Brockholes, of Claughton, Lancs, and *d* 31 Aug 1786, leaving, with a dau (*d* young):

      1b CHARLES HOWARD, **11th Duke of Norfolk**, KG; *b* 14 or 15 March 1746; abjured Catholicism during Gordon Riots 1780; MP (Whig) Carlisle 1780–86, Dep Earl Marshal 1782, Ld Lt W R Yorks 1782–98, a Ld Treasury April–Dec 1783, Pres Soc Arts 1793–1815, Ld Lt Sussex 1807–15, Mayor Gloucester 1810; *m* 1st 1 Aug 1767 Mariana (*d* giving birth to a stillborn child 28 May 1768), only dau of John Coppinger, of Ballyvolane, Co Cork; *m* 2nd 2 April 1771 Frances (shut away as insane from shortly after her marriage till her death 1820), dau and sole heir of Charles

FitzRoy Scudamore (*see* BEAUFORT, D), and *dspl* 16 Dec 1815, having by the most long-staying of his mistresses Mary Gibbon, a cousin of the historian Edward Gibbon, had:

1c Matthew Charles HOWARD-GIBBON; *b* 1796; Richmond Herald; *d* 1873

2c Edward Howard HOWARD-GIBBON; *b* 1799; successively Mowbray Herald, York Herald and Norroy Herald, also Earl Marshal's Sec; *d* 1849

3c Richard HOWARD-GIBBON

1c Mary Eliza HOWARD-GIBBON; *b* 1802

2c Caroline HOWARD-GIBBON; *b* 1806

1b (cont.) The **11th Duke** also had by other mistresses:

4c William WOODS (Sir); *b* 1785; *d* 1842

5c Henry Frederick STEPHENSON; *b* 1790; *d* 1858

3c Mary WARING

5 Bernard, of Glossop, Derbys, DL (Wilts); *b* 16 Oct 1641; *educ* Douai; Col Horse Gds; thrice imprisoned Tower of London on suspicion of Jacobitism; *m* 14 June 1672 his er bro's sis-in-law Catherine (*d* 8 April 1727), widow of Sir Richard Lichford, of Dorking, and 2nd dau of George Tattershall, and *d* 21 Oct 1717, leaving, with three daus (all Dominican nuns at Brussels):

(1) Bernard, of Glossop; *b* 14 March 1674; Jacobite; *m* 24 June 1710 Hon Anne Roper (*d* 1744), dau of 4th Baron Teynham (*qv*), and *d* 22 April 1735, leaving:

1a Bernard; *bapt* St Germain-en-laye 27 March 1711; *dsp*

2a Henry, of Glossop; *bapt* St Germain-en-Laye 9 April 1713; *educ* Douai, St Omer and English College Rome; vintner in Dublin, where he failed, his debts being paid by his his cousin the **9th Duke**, who also appointed him agent for the Sheffield estate; *m* 30 Oct 1764 Juliana (*d* 12 June 1808), 2nd dau of Sir William Molyneux, 6th Bt, of Teversall, Notts, and *d* 11 Nov 1787, leaving:

1b BERNARD EDWARD, **12th Duke**

2b Henry Thomas HOWARD later HOWARD-MOLYNEUX (roy licence 1812) later still HOWARD-MOLYNEUX-HOWARD (roy licence 1817); *b* 7 Oct 1766; granted rank of duke's yr s 1817; *m* 12 Sept 1801 Elizabeth (*d* 24 May 1834), dau of Edward Long, Ch Judge V-Admiralty Court Jamaica, and *d* 17 June 1824, leaving:

1c Henry HOWARD-MOLYNEUX-HOWARD later HOWARD, of Greystoke Castle and Thornbury Castle, Glos; *b* 25 July 1802; *m* 6 Dec 1849 Charlotte Caroline Georgiana (*d* 24 July 1896), est dau of Henry Lawes Long, of Hampton Lodge, Surrey, by Lady Catherine Walpole (*see* WALPOLE, B), and *d* 7 Jan 1875, having had:

1d Henry Charles, of Greystoke Castle, JP, DL Westmorland and Cumberland; High Sheriff 1879, Chm Cumberland CC, MP Penrith 1885–86, BA Cantab; *b* 17 Sept 1850; *m* 6 June 1878 Lady Mabel McDonnell, CBE (*d* 31 Dec 1942), 2nd dau of 6th Earl of Antrim (*qv*), and *d* 4 Aug 1914, leaving:

1e Bernard Henry Esmé, MC, of Greystoke Castle; *b* 15 Sept 1880; *educ* Harrow and Trin Coll Cambridge; Capt 3rd Bn Manchester Regt, WW I in RFC (wounded, POW, escaped); *m* 10 Feb 1934 Glory Evelyn, only dau of Hon Gilbert de Ste Croix Rollo (*see* ROLLO, L), and *dsp* 5 Oct 1949

1e Joan Mabel; *b* 11 Nov 1879; *d* unm 13 Dec 1963

2d Edward Stafford (Sir), KCB, of Thornbury Castle and Cilymaenllwyd, Carmarths, JP, DL Glos, JP Carmarths; *b* 28 Nov 1851; *educ* Cambridge; Ld Manor Thornbury, barrister Inner Temple 1875, MP E Cumberland 1876–85 and S Glos 1885–86, U-Sec India 1886, Commr Woods and Forests 1893–1912, Ecclesiastical Commr 1914–16, Mayor Llanelly 1915–16; *m* 1st 21 Sept 1876 Lady Rachel Campbell (*d* 6 Oct 1906), yst dau of 2nd Earl Cawdor (*qv*), and:

1e Algar Henry Stafford (Sir), KCB (1951, CB 1937), KCVO (1944), MC (1918), TD, JP (Glos 1906), DL (1936); *b* 7 Aug 1880; *educ* Harrow; barrister Inner Temple 1905, Fitzalan Pursuivant 1911, Rouge Dragon Pursuivant 1911–19, Maj Glos Yeo WW I (wounded), Windsor Herald 1919–31 (Registrar 1928–35), Norroy King of Arms 1931–44, Ulster King of Arms and Knight Attendant Order St Patrick 1943–44, Garter King of Arms 1944–50, Extra Gentleman Usher to TM GEORGE VI 1950 and THE QUEEN 1952, Genealogist Order Bath 1946–50, KStJ; *m* 11 Oct 1921 Hon Violet Ethel (*d* 29 Feb 1960), widow of Capt Alexander Moore Vandeleur, JP, 2nd Life Gds, of Kilrush and Cahiracon, Co Clare, and dau and coheir of 1st and last Baron Knaresborough (*see* MEYSEY-THOMPSON, Bt), and *d* 14 Feb 1970, leaving:

1f +Anne Violet [Mrs John Cahill, Dooneen, Castleisland, Co Kerry, Ireland]; *b* 21 March 1923; *m* 19 May 1952 *John Cahill, s of John Cahill, of Knockrom West, Cartaglon, Co Kerry, and has:

1g +John Anthony; *b* 24 Aug 1956

2g +Colin Algar; *b* 8 April 1958

3g +Peter Francis; *b* 23 May 1960

1g +Elizabeth Mary; *b* 10 April 1953

2g +Alice; *b* 27 April 1962

3g +Angela Violet; *b* 15 Jan 1964

4g +Rosemary; *b* 5 Dec 1966

2f +Elizabeth Helen [Mrs Harold Walker, Camrose, Stockton, Beccles, Suffolk]; *b* 22 Nov 1924; *m* 28 June 1958 *Harold William Norman Suckling Walker, est s of Col James Coulthard Walker, IA, and has:

1g +Penelope Anne; *b* 16 Dec 1959

1e Ruth Evelyn; *b* 10 Dec 1877; *m* 1st 5 Jan 1903 Gardner Sebastian Bazley (*see* BAZLEY, Bt) and had issue; *m* 2nd 2 Sept 1913 Cdr Francis Charles Cadogan, RN, and *d* 14 March 1962, leaving further issue (*see* CADOGAN, E)

2e Alianore Rachel; *b* 25 May 1886; *m* 24 July 1913 Maj Arthur Hugh Brabazon Talbot-Ponsonby and *d* 29 May 1974, leaving issue (*see* SHREWSBURY and WATERFORD, E)

2d (cont.) Sir Edward *m* 2nd 21 Sept 1911 Catharine Meriel (*d* 8 June 1952), MBE, JP, CC Carmarths (added STEPNEY by roy licence 9 March 1922 for self and issue), dau and heiress of Sir Arthur Cowell Stepney, 2nd Bt (*see* 1877 edn), and *d* 8 April 1916, having by her had:

2e Stafford Vaughan STEPNEY HOWARD later HOWARD (deed poll 12 Aug 1950); *b* 3 Sept 1915; *educ* Eton and Magdalen Coll Oxford; Capt Coldstream Gds RARO, WW II (despatches) N Africa, Italy and Burma; CC Cumberland 1966; *m* 1st 15 July 1936 (*divorce* 1940) Ursula Priscilla Maria Gabrielle, yr dau of Col Sir James Nockells Horlick, 4th Bt (*qv*), and has:

1f +Nicholas Stafford [Nicholas Howard, Esq, Johnby Hall, Penrith, Cumbria CA11 0UU]; *b* 20 July 1937; *educ* Eton, Magdalen Coll Oxford and Churchill Coll Cambridge; *m* 26 July 1966 *(Phyllis) Bethan, adopted dau of Lewis Duckett, of Essex House, Dursley, Glos, and has:

1g +Henry James Stafford; *b* 31 Dec 1972

1g *Cecilia Charlotte; *b* 3 April 1968

2e (cont.) Stafford Howard *m* 2nd 24 Oct 1940 *(Mary) Gracia [Mrs Stafford Howard, Blind Cottage, Challock Lees, Kent TN25 4AU], dau of George Wilder Neville, of Portsmouth, Va., and *d* 6 Oct 1991, leaving by her:

2f +(Murray Bernard) Neville Cyprian, OBE (1985) [Lt-Col Neville Howard OBE, Greystoke Castle, Penrith, Cumbria CA11 OTG]; *b* 9 Dec 1942; *educ* Eton and RMA Sandhurst; Lt-Col Coldstream Gds, Capt 22 SAS Regt; *m* 11 Oct 1969 *Lavinia Zara, dau of Lt-Col Philip Lewis (*see* DARTMOUTH, E), and has:

1g +Alexander Philip Wilde; *b* 1971

1g +Catherine Anne Cardwell; *b* 1972

1f +Amanda Arianwen Cecilia [Mrs Michael Cottrell, Laurenden Forstal, Challock Lees, Kent TN25 4AU]; *b* 22 Sept 1941; *m* 4 Feb 1967 Michael Noel Cottrell (*d* Nov 1996), yr s of Sir Edward Baglietto Cottrell, CBE, JP, of Gibraltar, and has:

1g +Edward Stafford Cyprian; *b* 10 May 1969; *educ* Sandhurst

2g +Philip Howard Edward; *b* 25 June 1971

1g +Camilla Mary Josephine; *b* 1973

2g +Charlotte Lucinda Gracia; *b* 1981

2f +Arianwen Catharine Cardwell [Mrs Christopher Neve, 16 Pembroke Place, London W8]; *b* 9 Dec 1942; *m* 14 Sept 1968 *Christopher Neville Neve and has:

1g +Thomas Wilder Neville; *b* 1 Jan 1971

1g +Eleanor Marged Deborah; *b* 1972

3e Margaret (Marged) Catharine; *b* 20 Jan 1913; *m* 1st 9 Dec 1933 (*divorce* 1938) Patrick Wyndham Murray-Threipland, of Dale and Toftingall, Caithness, Dryburgh Abbey, St Boswells, and New House, Llanishen, Cardiff (*d* 1 April 1957), s of Col William Murray-Threipland, DSO, and had issue; *m* 2nd 17 Nov 1938 (*divorce* 1948, took name HOWARD-STEPNEY 1952) Alan Francis Welch, and *d* 22 Jan 1953

3d Robert Mowbray, of Ignors, Compton, Guildford, and Bluemire, Threlkeld, Penrith, JP, DL Surrey; *b* 23 May 1854; BA Cantab; *m* 1st 6 Oct 1881 Louisa Georgina (*d* 30 June 1910), dau of Rev Walter Sneyd, JP, of Keele Park, Staffs; *m* 2nd 12 Sept 1912 Audrey Cecilia Campbell (*d* 28 Jan 1926), 3rd dau of Charles Hallyburton Campbell, BCS (n of 1st Baron Stratheden; *see* STRATHEDEN and CAMPBELL, B), by Evelyn, dau of Henry Stuart (*see* BUTE, M); *m* 3rd 28 April 1927 Louisa Felicia (*d* 13 Oct 1956), only child of William Earle Welby (*see* WELBY, Bt), and *d* 2 Oct 1928, leaving by his 1st w:

1e Henry Ralph Mowbray HOWARD later HOWARD-SNEYD (roy licence 27 April 1950), OBE (1918); *b* 18 June 1883; *educ* Harrow; Maj Rifle Bde WW I 1914–16; *m* 1st 8 June 1911 (*divorce* 1931) Helen Millicent (*d* 15 Aug 1967), est dau of William Dodge James, CVO, DL, of W Dean Park, Sussex (*see* FORBES, Bt, of Newe), and had:

1f +Diana Katharine [Mrs Richard Beresford, Walnut House, Benefield Rd, Oundle, Northants PE8 4EU]; *b* 4 May 1913; *m* 29 July 1938 Richard Marcus Beresford (*d* 19 Aug 1968), only s of R A A Beresford, of Lydgate House, Hunstanton, Norfolk, and has:

1g +Christopher Charles Howard [Christopher Beresford, Dryden House, Burtons Way, Chalfont St Giles, Bucks HP8 4BW]; *b* 9 July 1946; *educ* Rugby; *m* 5 May 1973 *Philippa Susan Yates, and has:

1h +Nicholas Charles Marcus; *b* 26 Aug 1979

1h +Antonia Charlotte; *b* 9 May 1975

2h +Fiona Caroline; *b* 25 Oct 1977

1g +Patricia Mary [Mrs Cyril Lea, 59 Ember Lane, Esher, Surrey KT10 8EF]; *b* 10 March 1941; *m* 1st 4 April 1964 (*divorce* 1977) Christopher Arthur Rollo Wells; *m* 2nd 1978 *Cyril Godfrey Lea and by her 1st husb has:

1h +Gavin Marcus; *b* 17 Feb 1965

1h +Amanda Clare; *b* 17 Sept 1967

2g +Katherine Anne [Mrs Osman Streater, 16 Upstall St, London SE5 9JE]; *b* 22 March 1943; *m* 1st 26 June 1965 (*divorce* 1969) Robert Noel Hutchings, yst s of Sir Robert Noel Hutchings, KCIE, CMG, and has issue; *m* 2nd 22 March 1969 *(Jeffrey) Osman Streater, only s of Jasper Sidney Streater, OBE, of Hampstead, and by him has:

1h +Olivia Katherine Nermin; *b* 22 Nov 1974

2f +Pamela Evelyn [Mrs Ian Karslake, Oakfield Cottage, Guildford Rd, Cranleigh, Surrey GU6 8PF]; *b* 5 Oct 1914; *m* 15 Sept 1939 Ian Reginald Gilfrid Karslake (*d* 1982), only s of Capt William Reginald Karslake, of Moorend Court, Mathon, Herefs, and has:

1g +David Ian Howard [David Karslake Esq, 6 rue Victor Chevreuil, 75012 Paris, France]; *b* 9 June 1944; *educ* Shrewsbury and Trin Coll Cambridge (BA 1967); *m* 1988 *Claire Marie, dau of Antoine Bonhomme, and has:

  1h +Charlotte Cordelia Geraldine Leila; *b* 1989

  2h +Emma Caroline Adeliza Howard; *b* 1994

1g +Sarah Vivien [Mrs Peter Matthews, The Old Vicarage, Richmond Rd, Lansdown, Bath]; *b* 11 Nov 1941; *educ* St Anne's Coll Oxford (BA); *m* 1976 *Peter Fraser Matthews and has had:

  1h Rupert Charles Oliver; *b* 1980; *d* 1982

  2h +Guy William Rupert; *b* 1983

  1h +Alexandra Howard; *b* 1978

2g +Elizabeth Ann [Mrs Jeremy Hosking, Frogs Hill Farm, Newenden, Kent TN18 5PX]; *b* 28 Aug 1948; *m* 1993 *Jeremy John Hosking and has:

  1h +Thomas Frederick Karslake; *b* 1992

  2h +Luke Roger Howard; *b* 1996

3f Audrey Elizabeth; *b* 25 Jan 1916; *m* 18 March 1940 (*divorce* 1984) Lt-Col Ronald John Henry Kaulback, OBE, er s of Col Henry Albert Kaulback, and *d* 14 Aug 1994, leaving:

1g +Bryan Henry [Bryan Kaulback Esq, c/ Alexandre Bóveda No 12, 1ºA, Ogrobe 36980, Pontevedra, Spain]; *b* 19 July 1948; *educ* Redrice; *m* 1970 *Maria — and has:

  1h +Bryan; *b* 6 Sept 1971

  2h +Jago; *b* 19–

2g +Peter John [Peter Kaulback Esq, 108 Byron Ave, Ottawa, Ont K1Y 3J2, Canada]; *b* 19 July 1948; *educ* Gordonstoun and U of Saskatchewan; *m* 1973 *Elizabeth Jane, dau of Major Douglas Peter Scopes, of Rectory Cottage, Barnwell, Northants, and has:

  1h +Simon Peter Howard; *b* 7 Jan 1980

  2h +Marcus Ronald Oliver; *b* 25 March 1983

  1h +Caroline Victoria Margaret; *b* 15 June 1978

1g +Sonia Elizabeth [Mrs Robert Waddell, 26 Thicket Rd, Tilehurst, Berks RG3 4TY]; *b* 19 March 1941; *m* 16 Dec 1967 *Robert Erskine Waddell and has:

  1h +Nicholas Henry; *b* 4 Oct 1975

  2h +Alexander John; *b* 18 June 1980

2g +Susan Georgina [Mrs Mark Hatt-Cook, Mascalls, Broad Chalke, Salisbury SP5 5HP]; *b* 9 Aug 1942; *m* 18 Oct 1969 Col Mark Edward Hatt-Cook, OBE, RD, ADC, RMR, s of Lt-Col John Edward Hatt-Cook, MC, of Broad Chalke, and has:

  1h +Catherine Emma Kaulback; *b* 13 Aug 1974

  2h +Georgina Alice Kaulback; *b* 13 June 1977

4f Rosemary Millicent; *b* 22 Sept 1917; *m* 1st 3 Feb 1939 Guy Michael Craigie Anderson (*ka* 30 Jan 1944); *m* 2nd 17 Aug 1946 *Michael Frederick Lilly and *d* 26 April 1986, leaving an adopted son

5f +Joan Margery [Mrs Hubert Sturges, Springmount, Berwick St John, Dorset SP7 0HQ]; *b* 7 Sept 1921; *m* 21 Dec 1945 *Hubert Murray Sturges, s of Francis William Murray Sturges, of Rainham Hall, Essex, and has:

1g +William Henry [William Sturges Esq, Lower Tytherly Farm, Hinton Charterhouse, Bath BA3 6AF]; *b* 19 Feb 1949; *educ* Aiglon Coll Switzerland; *m* 1973 *Virginia Mary, dau of Cdr R FitzGerald DSC, RN, of Petworth, W Sussex, and has:

  1h +Tom Woody; *b* 1979

  1h +Robin Millie; *b* 1977

1g +Rosemary Jane [Mrs Timothy Minett, Ty-Uchaf, Hebron, Whitland, Dyfed SA34 0XU]; *b* 29 Sept 1946; *m* 1st 1971 (*divorce* 1975) Alastair William MacDonald; *m* 2nd 1977 (*divorce* 1988) Simon John Harley Quantock Shuldham; *m* 3rd 1993 *Timothy Joseph Minett and by her 2nd husb has:

  1h +Lucinda Clare; *b* 1979

  2h +Catherine Emma; *b* 1981

1e (cont.) Maj Henry Howard-Sneyd *m* 2nd 9 Feb 1931 *Janet Emma Jameson, formerly w of Lt-Col Samuel Edward Hibbert, RA, and only dau of John Duthie, of Cults House, Aberdeenshire, and *d* 12 Aug 1950, having by her had:

1f +Thomas Henry Gavin [Thomas Howard-Sneyd Esq, 35 Furscroft, George St, London W1]; *b* 15 Oct 1940; *educ* Milton Abbey; *m* 2 Feb 1963 *Serena Patience, yr dau of Thomas Henry Waldore Lumley, of Ashcombe House, Lewes, and has:

1g +Henry Lyulph [*b* 24 Feb 1965; *m* 199– *Ursula McCarthy and has:

  1h +Chiara Zuleika; *b* 28 Nov 1997

2g +Justin Andrew; *b* 27 Oct 1966

1g +Antonia Caroline; *b* 25 May 1969

2e Lyulph Walter Mowbray; Lt 7th Roy W Surrey Regt; *b* 21 Nov 1885; *ka* 15 Sept 1915

1e Muriel Isabel Catherine; *b* 28 June 1882; *m* 24 Oct 1912 Tudor Ralph Castle, Roy W Surrey Regt (*ka* 31 Aug 1916), and *d* 19 Nov 1959, leaving issue

4d ESME WILLIAM HOWARD, *cr* BARON HOWARD OF PENRITH (*qv*)

1d Elisabeth Catharine; *b* 29 March 1856; *m* 26 Dec 1878, as his 2nd w, 4th Earl of Carnarvon (*qv*) and *d* 1 Feb 1929, leaving issue

2d Maud Isabel; *b* 26 May 1858; *m* 12 Nov 1890 Francis William Leyborne-Popham, of Littlecote (*dsp* 15 July 1907), and *d* 12 Nov 1929

1c Henrietta Anne; *m* 4 Aug 1830 3rd Earl of Carnarvon (*qv*) and *d* 26 May 1876, leaving issue

2c Isabella Catherine; *m* 2 Sept 1829 17th Earl of Suffolk and (10th Earl of) Berkshire (*qv*) and *d* 20 June 1891, leaving issue

3c Charlotte Juliana Jane; *m* 5 Oct 1831 James Wentworth Buller, JP, DL, MP, of Downes, Devon (*d* 13 Dec 1865), and *d* 15 Dec 1855, having had issue

4c Juliana Barbara; *m* 7 July 1831 Sir John Ogilvy, 9th Bt (*qv*), and *d* 27 Dec 1833, leaving issue

3b Edward Charles; *b* 28 May 1774; *m* Elizabeth (*d* Jan 1811), dau of William Maycock, and *d* 27 Sept 1816, leaving:

1c Edward Giles; Army Capt; *b* 15 June 1805; *m* 11 Nov 1826 Frances Anne, er dau of George Robert Heneage, of Hainton Hall, Lincs, and *d* 17 June 1840, leaving:

1d Edward Henry; *b* 13 Feb 1829; *educ* Oscott; Offr 2nd Life Gds till early 1850s, following which he was ordained an RC priest; missionary in India; Archbp Neocaesaria *in partibus infidelium* 1872; Cardinal, Protector English Coll Rome and Archpriest St Peter's 1877; *d* 16 Sept 1892

1d Charlotte Frances; *m* 14 Aug 1855 Sir John William Cradock-Hartopp, 4th Bt (*qv*), and *d* 17 Nov 1889, leaving issue

2d Mary Isabella; *d* unm 10 June 1867

3d Catherine Arabella; *m* 4 Feb 1862 Richard MYDDELTON formerly MYDDELTON-BIDDULPH, of Chirk Castle, Denbighs (*d* 7 Jan 1913), and *d* 18 June 1899, leaving issue

4d Adelaide Laura; *m* 16 Dec 1861 Lt-Gen Sir Frederick Marshall, KCMG, 2nd Life Gds (*d* 8 June 1900), and *d* 15 March 1916, leaving issue

1c Elizabeth; *m* 31 May 1822 Hon Charles Petre and *d* 6 Sept 1835, leaving issue (*see* PETRE, B)

2c Julia; *m* 12 Feb 1829 3rd Baron Stafford (*qv*) and *dsp* 19 Nov 1856, leaving issue

1b Mary Bridget; *m* 14 Feb 1786 10th Baron Petre (*qv*) and *d* 30 May 1843, leaving issue

2b Juliana Barbara *m* 16 Jan 1788, as his 2nd w, 9th Baron Petre (*qv*) and *d* 16 April 1833, leaving issue

3a Thomas; Canon St Peter's Collegiate Church Douai; *bapt* St Germain-en-Laye 13 June 1714

4a Philip; *bapt* St Germain-en-Laye 14 Sept 1715

5a Antony; *bapt* St Germain-en-Laye 19 Aug 1716; *bur* there 23 Oct 1716

6a Charles; DD, Rector English Seminary of St Gregory Paris; *bapt* St Germain-en-Laye 2 Nov 1717

1a (Mary) Anne; *bapt* St Germain-en-Laye 20 April 1712; *bur* there 28 April 1712

2a Anne Bridget; Abbess of English (Blue) Nuns at Bastille, Paris; *bapt* St Germain-en-Laye 12 Nov 1719; *d* a prisoner in her own convent during the French Revolution

1 Catherine; *m* John Digby, s and heir of Sir Kenelm Digby

The 11th DUKE's cousin,

BERNARD EDWARD HOWARD, **12th Duke of Norfolk**, KG (1834), PC (1830); *b* 21 Nov 1765; *m* 24 April 1789 (*divorce* May 1794 for her adultery with 2nd Earl of Lucan (*qv*), with whom she is said to have been in love before her arranged marriage with the Duke but from whom she was separated after ten years of the marriage that immediately followed her divorce from the Duke; it was also Canonically annulled 1800) Lady Elizabeth Belasyse, 3rd dau of 2nd and last Earl Fauconberg of Newborough, and *d* 16 March 1842, leaving:

1 HENRY CHARLES HOWARD, **13th Duke of Norfolk**, KG (1848), PC (1837); *b* 12 Aug 1791; MP (Lib) Horsham 1829–32 and W Sussex 1832–41, Treasurer Household 1837–41, Capt Yeomen Gd July–Sept 1841; called up to Ho Lds 16 Aug 1841 *vp* in f's Barony of Maltravers; Master Horse 1846–52, Steward Household 1853–54; forsook Catholicism for C of E 1851 in protest at the restoration by PIUS IX of the Catholic hierarchy in England, which he considered injudicious; nevertheless died fortified by the last sacramaents of his ancestral faith; *m* 26 Dec 1814 Charlotte Sophia (*d* 7 July 1870), dau of 1st Duke of Sutherland (*qv*), and *d* 18 Feb 1856, leaving:

(1) HENRY GRANVILLE HOWARD later FITZALAN-HOWARD (which he added, as did his siblings, by roy licence 26 April 1842), **14th Duke of Norfolk**; *b* 7 Nov 1815; *educ* Eton and Trin Coll Cambridge; zealous Catholic who funded among other projects the building of the Little Oratory chapel at Brompton; author: *A Few Remarks on the Social and Political Condition of the British Catholics* (1847), *Observations on Diplomatic Relations with Rome* (1848) and *The Lives of Philip Howard, Earl of Arundel, and of Anne Dacres* [sic] *his wife* (ed, 1857); Capt RHG, MP (Lib) Arundel 1837–51 and Limerick 1851–52; *m* 19 June 1839 Augusta Mary Minna Catherine (*d* 22 March 1886), yst dau of Adml 1st Baron Lyons of Christchurch, GCB, KCH, C-in-C forces Black Sea (*see* 1887 edn), and *d* 25 Nov 1860, having had, with other issue:

1a HENRY FITZALAN-HOWARD, **15th Duke of Norfolk**, KG (1886), GCVO (1902), VD, PC (1895), JP (W Sussex); *b* 27 Dec 1847; *educ* Oratory Sch Edgbaston; CC W Sussex, fndr memb and First Pres English Catholic Union 1870, memb LCC 1892–96, Pres and Chm Sussex TFA, PMG 1895–1900, Mayor: Sheffield 1895–97, Westminster 1900, Arundel 1902–03, Hon Capt Army, Boer War 1900, Chm Roy Commn on Army Reform 1903, Ld Lt and custos rotulorum Sussex 1905–17, Pres London Municipal Reform Assoc, Kt 1st Cl Noble Order of Christ and of the Golden Spur, Lt-Col and Hon Col cmdg 4th Bn Royal Sussex Rgt (ret 1913 after 42 years' serv); *m* 1st 21 Nov 1877 Lady Flora Paulyna Hetty Barbara Abney-Hastings (*d* 11 April 1887), er dau of Edith, Countess of Loudoun (*qv*), and had:

1b Philip Joseph Mary, *Earl of Arundel and Surrey*; *b* 7 Sept 1879; *d* unm 8 July 1902

1a (cont.) The **15th Duke** *m* 2nd 15 Feb 1904 Gwendolen Mary, Lady Herries of Terregles (*qv*), and *d* 11 Feb 1917, leaving by her:

2b BERNARD MARMADUKE FITZALAN-HOWARD, **16th Duke of Norfolk**, KG (1937), GCVO (1946), GBE (1968), TD (1969), PC (GB 1936), JP (W Sussex 1936); *b* 31 May 1908; *educ* Oratory Sch; Ld Lt Sussex 1949–74 (DL 1945), W Sussex 1974, CC Sussex 1937, V-Chm W Sussex CC; Maj 4th Bn Roy Sussex Regt TA, Hon Col 5th (Vol) Bn Queen's Regt TAVR 1972, Lt Res of Offrs RHG, WW II in France 1940, Chm Cncl

T&AVRA 1956–69, Pres 1969, Jt Parly Sec Min Ag Feb 1941–July 1945, Mayor Arundel 1935, Liveryman and Memb Court the Ironmongers' Co 1946 (Liveryman 1929), manager English Cricket Team 1962–63 tour of Australia and NZ, Er Bro Trin Ho 1965, Pres AA 1961 and MCC, Sr Steward Jockey Club, HM's Rep Ascot, Hon V-Pres Land Agents Soc, Order Pius IX, KStJ, Roy Victoria Chain 1953; *m* 27 Jan 1937 Hon Lavinia Mary Strutt, LG (1990), CBE (1971), Ld Lt W Sussex 1975–90 (*d* 10 Dec 1995), only dau of 3rd Baron Belper (*qv*), and *d* 30 Jan 1975, leaving:

  1c +ANNE ELIZABETH, LADY HERRIES OF TERREGLES (*qv*)

  2c +Mary Katharine, DCVO (1995, CVO 1982, MVO 1974) [The Lady Mary Mumford DCVO, North Stoke Cottage, North Stoke, W Sussex BN18 9LS; Lantonside, Glencaple, Dumfries DG1 4RQ]; *b* 14 Aug 1940; Ldy-in-Waiting to HRH PRINCESS ALEXANDRA 1964–; *m* 1986 *G/Capt Anthony Mumford, CVO, OBE, RAF

  3c +Sarah Margaret [The Lady Sarah Clutton, The Dover, Poling, Arundel, Sussex BN18, 9PX]; *b* 28 Sept 1941; *m* 1988 *Nigel Hugh Clutton

  4c +(Theresa) Jane; *b* 24 Jan 1945; *m* 7 June 1975 *Michael Andrew Foster Jude Kerr, Earl of Ancram, est s of 12th Marquess of Lothian (*qv*), and has had issue

1b (Mary) Rachel, DCVO (1968, CVO 1954); *b* 27 June 1905; Ldy-in-Waiting to HRH PRINCESS MARINA, DUCHESS OF KENT, 1943–68; Order of Mercy; *m* 1st 31 July 1939 Lt-Col Colin Keppel Davidson, CIE, OBE, RA (*ka* Tunisia 2 March 1943), only surv s of Col Leslie Davidson, CB, JP; *m* 2nd 9 Nov 1961 Brig Anthony Hilton Pepys, DSO (*d* 31 Jan 1967), s of Col Walter Pepys, DSO, OBE, of Avon House, Stratford-on-Avon, Warwicks, and *d* 17 Aug 1992, leaving by her 1st husb:

  1c +Duncan Henry [Duncan Davidson Esq, Lilburn Tower, Alnwick, Northumberland NE66 4PQ]; *b* 29 March 1941; *educ* Ampleforth; Page of Hon to HM THE QUEEN 1955–57; RSG 1959–63; *m* 1965 *Sarah, dau of Maj Robin Filmer Wilson, and has:

    1d +Camilla Mary; *b* 1968

    2d +Natasha Anne; *b* 1969

    3d +Flora Rachel; *b* 1975

    4d +Rose Patricia; *b* 1979

  1c +Harriet Mary [Mrs Michael Sefi, Highfield House, Arundel, Sussex BN18 9PQ]; *b* 28 Nov 1942; *m* 29 June 1968 *Michael Richard Sefi and has:

    1d +Charles Antony; *b* 23 Aug 1974

    1d +Clare Louise; *b* 9 Feb 1970

    2d +Laura Mary [Mrs Guy Sturgess, The Boathouse, Llanfoist Wharf, Abergavenny, Mon]; *b* 31 March 1972; *m* 7 Sept 1996 *(Richard) Guy Sturgess and has:

      1e +Samson Oscar; *b* 2 Jan 1998

2b +Katherine Mary [The Lady Katherine Phillips, Field House, Church Rd, Aldingbourne, W Sussex PO20 6TT]; *b* 25 March 1912; Order of Mercy; *m* 7 June 1940 Lt-Col (Joseph) Anthony Moore Phillips, DSO, MBE, DL, King's Dragoon Gds (*d* 16 June 1990), est s of John Henry Phillips, of Oldbury Grange, Nuneaton, Warwicks, and has had:

  1c Anthony Bernard Moore; *b* 26 Jan 1953; lost at sea 1989

3b +Winefride Alice, JP (1965) [The Lady Winefride Freeman JP, St Catherine's Cottage, Aldingbourne, W Sussex PO20 6TQ]; *b* 31 Oct 1914; *m* 7 May 1943 Lt-Col John Edward Broke Freeman, Oxon and Bucks LI (*d* 1986), er s of Sir Philip Horace Freeman, KCVO, KBE, and has:

  1c +Charles Philip Broke [Charles Freeman Esq, Buxhall Vale, Stowmarket, Suffolk IP14 3DH]; *b* 11 Oct 1947; *educ* Eton and Trin Coll Cambridge (BA); *m* 1982 *Hilary Jane, yr dau of Val Faker, of Brentwood, Essex, and has had:

    1d +Thomas; *b* 1988

    1d +Isabella; *b* 1983

    2d Julia; *b* 1986; *d* 1989

    3d +Cordelia Mary Antonia; *b* 1989

  1c +Mary Gwendolen [Mrs Martin de Laszlo, 57 Coniger Rd, London SW6]; *b* 1 Feb 1945; *m* 7 Feb 1967 *Martin Richard de Laszlo, s of John A de Laszlo, of Cob Orchard, Plaxtol, Kent, and Mme Peggy Hennessy, of Paris, and has:

    1d +Rupert John Richard; *b* 2 Oct 1968

    2d +Oliver; *b* 27 Jan 1971

    1d +Lydia; *b* 1980

  2c +Virginia Phyllis Theresa [Mrs Ian Hope Henderson, 20 Westbourne Park Rd, London W2 5PH]; *b* 24 Oct 1949; *m* 28 Oct 1978 Ian Ramsay Hope Henderson (*see* FARINGDON, B)

2a EDMUND BERNARD FITZALAN-HOWARD later TALBOT (roy licence 19 July 1876 under terms of will of 17th Earl of Shrewsbury and Waterford; *qv*) later FITZALAN-HOWARD again (roy licence 9 June 1921), 1st VISCOUNT FITZALAN OF DERWENT, of Derwent, Co Derby (UK), so *cr* 28 April 1921, KG (1925), GCVO (1919), DSO, PC (1918), JP Sussex; *b* 1 June 1855; Dep Earl Marshal 1917–29, Lt-Col 11th Hus, MP (U) Chichester 1894–1921 (fought Burnley 1883 and Sheffield Brightside 1883 and 1886), Priv Sec to Sec State War 1896–98 and U-Sec For Affrs 1898–99, Assist Sec to Sec State War 1900–03 and Sec State India 1903–05, Jr Ld Treasury 1905, Ch U Whip 1913–21, Jt Parly Sec Treasury 1915–21, Ld Lt Ireland 1921–22, Col 11th Hus and DAAG Boer War 1899–1901 (despatches, medal); *m* 5 Aug 1879 Lady Mary Caroline Bertie, JP London (*d* 21 April 1938), est dau of 7th Earl of Abingdon (*see* LINDSEY and ABINGDON, E), and *d* 18 May 1947, leaving:

1b HENRY EDMUND FITZALAN-HOWARD, 2nd and last VISCOUNT FITZALAN OF DERWENT, OBE (1922); *b* 30 Oct 1883; *educ* Oratory Sch and New Coll Oxford; Capt 11th Hus WW I (wounded), Assist Priv Sec to Ld Lt Ireland 1921; dir: National Bank, Pullman Car Co and Br Centl Africa Co; *m* 9 May 1922 (*divorce* 1955) Joyce Elizabeth Mary, est dau of Col Philip Joseph Langdale, OBE, JP, DL (*see* MOWBRAY, SEGRAVE and STOURTON, B), and *dspm* 17 May 1962, when the title expired, leaving:

1c +Alathea Gwendolen Alys Mary; Dame of Honour and Devotion SMO of Malta; *b* 24 Nov 1923; *m* 2 July 1953 G/Capt Hon Edward Frederick Ward, RAF (*d* 1987), twin s of 2nd Earl of Dudley (*qv*)

2c Elizabeth-Anne Marie Gabrielle, DL (Cambs 1994); High Sheriff Cambs 1993; *b* 26 Jan 1934; MFH Fitzwilliam; *m* 17 Jan 1952 (*divorce* 1960) Sir Vivian Edward Naylor-Leyland, 3rd Bt (*qv*), and had issue; *m* 2nd Sept 1975 *Sir Stephen Lewis Edmonstone Hastings, MC, MP (C) Mid Beds 1960–83 [Sir Stephen Hastings MC, Stibbington House, Wansford, Peterborough PE8 6JS], only s of Maj Lewis Aloysius MacDonald Hastings, MC, and *d* 20 March 1997

  1b (Mary Caroline) Magdalen; *b* 24 Aug 1880; *d unm* 24 Nov 1974

1a Victoria Alexandrina; *b* 3 July 1840; *m* 7 Jan 1861 James Robert Hope-Scott and *d* 20 Dec 1870, leaving issue (*see* LINLITHGOW, M)

2a Philippa; *b* 13 Aug 1852; *m* 18 Oct 1888 Sir Edward Stewart, KBE, MD (*d* 4 Dec 1948), of Bullards, E Grinstead, and *d* 1 Sept 1946, having had issue

3a Anne, OBE (1918); *b* 24 April 1878 Maj-Gen Lord Ralph Drury Kerr and *d* 7 Jan 1931, leaving issue (*see* LOTHIAN, M)

(2) EDWARD GEORGE HOWARD later FITZALAN HOWARD (roy licence 26 April 1842), **1st Baron Howard of Glossop**, Co Derby (UK), so *cr* 9 Dec 1869, PC; *b* 20 Jan 1818; MP Horsham 1848–52 and Arundel 1853–68, Dep Earl Marshal 1861–68, V-Chamberlain to HM QUEEN VICTORIA 1846–52, Chm Catholic Poor Sch Ctee; *m* 1st 22 July 1851 Augusta (*d* 3 July 1862), only dau of Hon George Henry Talbot (*see* SHREWSBURY and WATERFORD, E); *m* 2nd 16 July 1863 Winifred Mary (*dsp* 7 Dec 1909), 3rd dau of Ambrose Lisle March Phillipps de Lisle, of Garendon Park, Leics, and *d* 1 Dec 1883, having had by his 1st w, with other issue:

1a FRANCIS EDWARD FITZALAN HOWARD, **2nd Baron Howard of Glossop**, JP Derbys, DL Inverness-shire; *b* 9 May 1859; *m* 1st 24 April 1883 Clara Louisa (*d* 17 April 1887), dau of John Greenwood, of Swarcliffe Hall, and had:

1b BERNARD EDWARD FITZALAN HOWARD, **3rd Baron Howard of Glossop**, MBE (1920); *b* 10 May 1885; *educ* Oratory Sch and Trin Coll Cambridge; Capt Lovat Scouts Yeo WW I, Bailiff Grand Cross SMO Malta; *m* 5 Sept 1914 Mona Josephine Tempest Stapleton, **Baroness Beaumont** (*d* 1971) in her own right (whose descendants are in remainder to that title, hence the + against each living female and her issue hereafter and in this article's opening section), OBE (*d* 31 Aug 1971; *see* Lineage (of Beaumont) below), and *d* 24 Aug 1972, leaving:

1c MILES FRANCIS FITZALAN HOWARD later STAPLETON FITZALAN HOWARD (deed poll 1975), **17th and present Duke of Norfolk and 4th and present Baron Howard of Glossop**

2c +Michael, KCVO (1971), CB (1968), CBE (1962, MBE 1949), MVO (1952), MC (1944), DL Wilts 1974–93 [Maj-Gen The Lord Michael Fitzalan Howard KCVO CB CBE MVO MC DL, Fovant House, Fovant, Wilts SP3 5LA]; *b* 22 Oct 1916; *educ* Ampleforth and Trin Coll Cambridge (BA 1938); WW II (despatches) NW Europe, Palestine 1945–46, Malaya 1948–49, Maj-Gen late Scots Gds, Cdr Mobile Force Allied Cmd Europe 1964–66, Ch Staff Southern Cmd 1967–68, GOC London Dist and Maj-Gen cmdg Household Div 1968–71, Marshal Dip Corps 1972–81, Hon Col Cambridge U OTC 1968–71, Col Queen's Lancs Regt 1970–78, Col Life Gds and Gold Stick HM 1979–, Chm Cncl TA&VRA 1973–81, Pres 1981–84, Patron 1984–93, Hon Recorder Br Cwlth Ex-Serv League 1992–, chm Bow Valley Petroleum-UK 1980–, Kt SMO Malta, Freeman City London 1985; *m* 1st 4 March 1946 Jean Marion (*d* 28 July 1947), yr dau of Sir Hew Clifford Hamilton-Dalrymple, 9th Bt (*qv*), and has:

  1d +Jean Mary [Mrs Max Pike, 12 Alexandra Ave, London SW11 4OZ]; *b* 28 July 1947; Extra Ldy-in-Waiting to HRH THE PRINCESS OF WALES 1986–91, Ldy-in-Waiting 1991–96; *m* 1976 *Max Eben Lecky Pike and has:

    1e +Molly Ann; *b* 9 June 1979

    2e +Amy Mary; *b* 2 Dec 1981

2c (cont.) Lord Michael *m* 2nd 20 April 1950 Jane Margaret (*d* 25 Dec 1995), yr dau of Capt William Patrick Meade Newman, of Hope Cottage, Henley-on-Thames, and by her has:

  1d +Thomas Michael; *b* 11 Feb 1952; *educ* Ampleforth and Oxford (MA); Col Scots Gds; *m* 1st 1977 (*divorce* 1992) Penelope Jan, dau of Capt David Christopher Richard Walters, RN, and has:

    1e +Edward Michael; *b* 1979

    1e +Flora Eleanor Meg; *b* 1982

  1d (cont.) Col Thomas Fitzalan Howard *m* 2nd 7 Dec 1996 *Joanna Mary, dau of Robin Don, of N Elmham, Norfolk

  2d +Richard Andrew; *b* 15 July 1953; *educ* Ampleforth and Oxford; *m* 1990 *Josephine Nina, dau of Peter Johnsen, and has:

    1e +Frederick Peter; *b* 20 July 1996

    1e +Lydia Nina; *b* 1991

    2e +Artemis Cecilia Maria; *b* 1993

  3d +Henry Julian Nicholas [Henry Fitzalan Howard Esq, 103 Abingdon Rd, London W8 6QU]; *b* 7 July 1954; *educ* Ampleforth and Oxford; *m* 1987 *Claire Louise, er dau of Georg Wilhelm von Mallinckrodt (*see* DARELL, Bt), and has:

    1e +George Henry; *b* 10 April 1991

    2e +Luke Valentine; *b* 17 July 1996

    3e +Milo Nicholas; *b* 17 July 1996

    1e +Marina Katherine; *b* 12 Feb 1994

  4d +Alexander Rupert; *b* 29 Feb 1964; *educ* Ampleforth and Magdalen Coll Oxford; *m* 1992 *Hon Joanna Elizabeth Venables-Vernon, yr dau of 10th Baron Vernon (*qv*), and has had:

    1e +William John; *b* 4 March 1995

    2e +Edmund Alexander; *b* 23 April 1998

    1e Helena Katharine; *b* and *d* 24 Jan 1997

  2d +Isabel Margaret [Mrs Peter Bickmore, The Old Rectory, Cuxham, Oxon OX9 5NQ]; *b* 30 Jan 1951; *m* 1975 *Peter Christopher Bickmore and has:

1e +Andrew Ralph; *b* 1979

2e +Rupert Nicholas; *b* 1985

1e +Fiona Clare; *b* 1981

2c (cont.) Lord Michael *m* 3rd 2 July 1997 *Victoria Winifred, widow of Sir Mark Baring, KCVO (*see* CROMER, E)

3c +Martin, JP (N R Yorks 1966), DL (1982) [The Lord Martin Fitzalan Howard JP DL, Brockfield Hall, York YO3 9XJ]; *b* 22 Oct 1922; *educ* Ampleforth and Trin Coll Cambridge; Capt Gren Gds WW II (wounded), Palestine 1945–46, High Sheriff N Yorks 1979–80; *m* 5 Oct 1948 *Bridget Anne, 4th dau of Lt-Col Arnold Ramsay Keppel (*see* ALBEMARLE, E), and has:

1d +Philip Bernard Arnold Richard [Philip Howard Esq, 3 Rutland Sq, Edinburgh EH1 2AS]; *b* 27 May 1963

1d +Clare Launa [Mrs Simon Wood, Brockfield Farmhouse, York YO3 9XJ]; *b* 6 Oct 1949; *m* 1970 *Simon Richard Browne Wood, s of Lt-Col B W Wood, KOYLI, and has:

1e +Charles Browne Martin; *b* 1973; *educ* Eton

1e +Alethea Launa Rose; *b* 1975

2e +Miranda Bridget Sarah; *b* 1978

2d +Sarah Anne [Mrs Francis Roos, 11 Ennismore Gdns, London SW7 1AA]; *b* 19 Aug 1951; *m* 1985 *Francis Jacques Roos, only s of Jean Jacques Roos, and has:

1e +Theodore Martin; *b* 1985

2e +Maximilian Augustus; *b* 1985

3d +Amanda Josephine Margaret [Mrs Robert Pascall, 11 Vaughan Ave, London W6 0XS]; *b* 2 Dec 1953; *m* 1985 *Robert C Pascall and has:

1e +Laurence Blaise Philip; *b* 1989

2e +Joshua Ralph Joseph; *b* 1992

4d +Rose Bridget [Mrs Nicholas Woodhead, The Cottage, Holtby, York]; *b* 11 Sept 1957; *m* 1979 *Nicholas ffolliott Woodhead, est s of Col Michael ffolliott Woodhead, OBE, and has:

1e +Christopher Archie ffolliott; *b* 1985

2e +Frederick Michael Martin; *b* 1986

3e +Hubert Nicholas Philip; *b* 1989

4c +Mark, OBE (1994) [The Lord Mark Fitzalan Howard OBE, 13 Campden Hill Sq, London W8 7LB]; *b* 28 March 1934; *educ* Ampleforth; late 2nd Lt Coldstream Gds, dir Nat Mutual Life Assur Soc 1972–, chm Association of Investment Tst Cos 1981–83, dir Robert Fleming Holdins Ltd 1971–94, Treas Scout Assoc 1986–96; *m* 17 Nov 1961 *Jacynth Rosemary, only dau of Sir Martin Alexander Lindsay, 1st Bt, of Dowhill (*qv*), and has:

1d +Amelia; *b* 9 March 1963

2d +Eliza [Mrs Timothy Bell, 59 Tabor Rd, London W6 0BN]; *b* 17 Nov 1964; *m* 1987 *Timothy Francis Bell and has:

1e +Tamara Alexandra; *b* 1992

2e +Leonora Ianthe; *b* 10 June 1995

1c +Mariegold Magdalene [The Lady Mariegold Jamieson, 226 Cranmer Court, Whiteheads Grove, London SW3 3HD]; *b* 29 Aug 1919; *m* 27 Feb 1957 Gerald (Jerrie) [James Auldjo Jamieson (*d* 1992), yr s of Sir Archibald Auldjo Jamieson, KBE, MC, and has:

1d +Simon David; *b* 8 July 1959; *m* 1 July 1995 *Lady Laura Margaret Fortescue, 2nd dau of 7th Earl Fortescue (*qv*) and has:

1d +Hugh Archibald; *b* 8 Sept 1997

1d +Jerry Jocelyn; *b* 1 June 1996

2d +James Gerrard; *b* 15 May 1963

2c Miriam, DL (Suffolk 1995); *b* 12 Dec 1924; *m* 19 April 1952 *Lt-Cdr Theodore Bernard Peregrine Hubbard, RN (ret) [Lt-Cdr Theodore Hubbard RN, The Flat, Horsecroft Hall, Horsecroft Rd, Bury St Edmunds, Suffolk IP29 5NY], er s of Theodore Stephen Hubbard by Lavinia May, 2nd dau of Rev Hon Alberic Edward Bertie, and *d* 1 Feb 1996, leaving issue (*see* LINDSEY and ABINGDON, E)

3c +Miranda Mary [The Lady Miranda Emmet, The Stables, Seabeach House, Halnaker, W Sussex PO18 0LX]; *b* 21 June 1927; *m* 22 July 1947 Hon Christopher Anthony Robert Emmet, JP (*see* RENNELL, B) and has issue

4c +Mirabel Magdalene [The Lady Mirabel Kelly, 109 Studdridge St, London SW6 3TD]; *b* 25 Oct 1931; *m* 11 July 1952 *Bernard Noël David George Terrence Kelly, er s of Sir David Victor Kelly, GCMG, MC, of Tara House, Co Wexford, and has:

1d +Dominic Noël David Miles Charles [Dominic Kelly Esq, Romden Cottage, Smarden, Kent TN27 8RA]; *b* 1953; *m* 1981 *Miranda, dau of Lance Macklin, and has:

1e +Sabine Mirabel Jemima Noëlle; *b* 1983

2e +Alice Beatrice Noëlle; *b* 1985

3e +Celina; *b* 1987

2d +Anthony Noël Francis [Anthony Kelly Esq, 144 Clapham Manor St, London SW4 6BX]; *b* 1955

3d +Crispin Bernard Noël [Crispin Kelly Esq, 1 Ranelagh Ave, London SW6 3PJ]; *b* 1956; *m* 1982 *Frances, yr dau of Sir Charles William Richards Pickthorn, 2nd Bt (*qv*), and has had:

1e +Alexander; *b* 1985

2e Christian; *b* and *d* 1987

3e +Rowan; *b* 22 Aug 1998

1e +Jessica; *b* 1975

4d +David Mark Noël [David Kelly Esq, 43 Bradbourne St, London SW6 3TF]; *b* 1959; *m* 1992 *Alexandra Mary Romana, 3rd dau of Joseph Czernin (*see* HOWARD DE WALDEN, B), and has:

1e +Frederick David Joseph; *b* 6 March 1996

1e +Natasha Mary Gabriella; *b* 16 Feb 1994

5d +Benedict Bernard Noël d'Arenberg [Benedict Kelly Esq, Knockwood House, Nether Wallop, Hants SO20 8EL]; *b* 1960; *m* 1988 *Elizabeth A, yr dau of Alexander Eaglestone, of Oxford, and has:

1e +Thomas Alexander Noël; *b* 1990

2e +Humphrey Martin Noël; *b* 1992

3e +Marcus Benedict Noël; *b* 1995

4e +Joseph Francis Noël; *b* 27 June 1998

6d +Sebastian Charles Noël [Sebastian Kelly Esq, 332 Wandsworth Bridge Rd, London SW6 2TZ]; *b* 1972

7d +Justin Ghislain Octavius Noël [Justin Kelly Esq, 507d Fulham Rd, London SW6 1HH]; *b* 1974

1d +Anne-Louise Marie-Noële Miranda Josephine [Mrs Charles Arkwright, 55 Perrymead St, London SW6 3SN]; *b* 1962; *m* 1987 *Charles Richard Francis Arkwright, er s of Col Peter Arkwright, OBE, of Willersey House, nr Broadway, Worcs, and has:

1e +Arabella; *b* 1988

2e +Rebecca; *b* 1990

3e +Harriet Marguerita; *b* 1994

4e +Charlotte Mirabel; *b* 1994

1b Muriel Augusta Mary; *b* 26 Feb 1884; *d* unm 1 June 1962

1a (cont.) The **2nd Baron** *m* 2nd 9 April 1891 Hyacinthe (*d* 4 Dec 1930), dau of William Scott-Kerr, of Chatto and Sunlaws, and *d* 22 Sept 1924, having by her had:

2b Philip Granville James; *b* 15 April 1895; Lt Welsh Gds WW I 1915 (wounded); *m* 3 Aug 1915 Gladys Cecily Clara (*m* 2nd 27 Oct 1920 (*divorce* 1931) Capt Henry James Fosbery Mills, KRRC, only s of Sir James Mills, KCMG; *m* 3rd 1931 Maj Philippe Gilbey Riviere and *d* 26 April 1966), dau of Lt-Col Charles Edward Norton, CMG, RE, and *d* 24 May 1918 of wounds recd in action, leaving:

1c +Philippa Gwendolen Mary [Mrs Edward Tyler, Hedsor Farm House, Wooburn Green, Bucks HP10 0JG]; *b* posthumously 29 July 1918; *m* 26 April 1940 *Maj Edward Guy Tyler, MC, Irish Gds, er s of Capt Guy A F Tyler, MC, of Upper Redpits, Marlow, Bucks, and has:

1d +Peter Edward; *b* 16 Oct 1944; *educ* Ampleforth

1d +Virginia Anne; *b* 16 Oct 1941; *m* 29 Oct 1965 *Carlos J Mejia, 2nd s of Pedro Mejia, of Cali, Colombia, and has:

1e +Carlos-Felipe; *b* 31 Dec 1967

1e +Mariana Luisa; *b* 30 April 1971

2e +Elena Isabel; *b* 1975

2b Frances Alice Mary Fitzalan; *b* 29 Feb 1892; *m* 19 Oct 1920 (*divorce* 1936) Maj George Metheun Greaves, RHG (*d* following a shooting accident 2 Aug 1953), s of Edward Seymour Greaves, of Glenetive, Argyll, and has issue

1a Gwendolen Mary Anne; *m* 16 April 1872 3rd Marquess of Bute (*qv*) and *d* 15 Jan 1932, having had issue

2a Angela Mary Charlotte; *m* 14 April 1875 11th Lord Herries of Terregles (*qv*) and *d* 1 March 1919, leaving issue

3a Alice Mary Elizabeth; *m* 4 Feb 1880 11th Earl of Loudoun (*qv*) and *d* 10 May 1915

4a Constance Mary Germana; *m* 4 March 1889 Lt-Col Charles Lennox Tredcroft, JP (*d* 20 Dec 1917), of Glen Ancrum, nr Guildford, only s of Rev Robert Tredcroft, of Tangmere, Sussex, and *d* 30 Jan 1933, leaving issue

5a Winifrede Mary; *m* 30 Oct 1888 William Wilfred Middleton (*d* 7 Jan 1935), of Eastbourne, and *d* 26 Jan 1937, leaving issue

(3) Bernard Thomas HOWARD later FITZALAN HOWARD (roy licence 26 April 1842); *b* 30 Dec 1825; *d* 21 Dec 1846

(1) Mary Charlotte; *b* 13 Dec 1822; *m* 16 July 1849 4th Baron Foley (*qv*) and *d* 8 April 1897, leaving issue

(2) Adeliza Matilda; *b* 14 Aug 1829; *m* 4 Oct 1855 Lord George John Manners and *d* 7 Feb 1904, leaving issue (*see* RUTLAND, D)

Lineage (of FitzAlan): The Earldom of Arundel, like the Barony of Bergavenny (*see* ABERGAVENNY, M, preliminary remarks), has been asserted as going with possession of Arundel Castle, *i.e.*, whoever holds the Castle is Earl of Arundel. Thus when Edmund Earl of Kent, EDWARD I's sixth son, was granted Arundel Castle and its demesne lands in about 1327 during the temporary eclipse of the Fitz Alan Earls of Arundel he is considered to have become Earl of Arundel by virtue of that possession rather than formal investiture. So also the Duke of Exeter in similar circumstances during the 1390s. One effect of this, however, is to make the numbering of Earls of Arundel problematical. For if the Earldom is one by tenure all holders from the very first proceed in successive numerical order. But if it is a personal dignity recreated after each line of holders dies out (as with the Dukedom of Norfolk between Mowbrays and Howards), the numbering starts afresh with each dynasty.

It is in any case an open question whether the original Earls of Arundel were not Earls of a wider territory. (*See* CHICHESTER, E, preliminary remarks.) For instance Roger de Montgomery (*see* SHREWSBURY and WATERFORD, E, preliminary remarks) was at Christmastide 1067 granted among other tracts of land the portion of Sussex that included both Arundel Castle (which he in fact built) and Chichester. Yet although he is often referred to in contemporary sources as Earl of Arundel he is from time to time called Earl of Chichester and by later sources Earl of Sussex. He seems definitely to have been an Earl, but of what or where it is harder to say, not least because an Earl at that time was primarily an official rather than possessor of a personal title of honour, and as such was not in the designation he bore tied to one particular place. Any Earldom of Arundel held by Roger de Montgomery's family ceased with the disgrace and exile of his elder son, another Roger, in 1102. Arundel Castle and the feudal territorial holding of which it was chief place accordingly reverted to the Crown.

In 1138 one William d'Aubigny married Adela, widow of HENRY I, and through her acquired Arundel Castle and its demesne. He became known as Earl of Arundel, although in some contemporary sources he is also described as Earl of Chichester, Earl of Lincoln and Earl of Sussex. His mother was Maud (le) Bigod, aunt of the 1st Earl of Norfolk of the 1140–41 creation (*see* **Norfolk, other creations** above). After his death his son was known as Earl of Arundel from as early as 1189, even though Arundel Castle was retained by the Crown till midsummer 1190. This calls in question the declaration of 1433 (*see* below against **14th/7th Earl**) that the Earldom of Arundel was held by possession of the Castle of the same name. The d'Aubigny male line died out by 1243, whereupon the huge family estates were parcelled out between the last d'Aubigny Earl of Arundel's sisters. Isabel, the second eldest, was wife of John Fitz Alan, who through her came into possession of Arundel Castle but, perhaps significantly, did not style himself Earl of Arundel and was not so referred to by third parties. A contributory factor here seems to have been the longevity of the last d'Aubigny Earl of Arundel's widow, who survived her husband almost forty years and who may in some sense therefore have been regarded as Countess of Arundel in her own right.

JOHN Fitz ALAN (for whose ancestry *see* MORAY, E); *m* 1st Isabel d'Aubigny and had issue; *m* 2nd Hawise de Blancminster (*i.e.*, Whitchurch, Salop) and *d* 1240; his s by his 1st w:

JOHN Fitz ALAN, 6th(?) EARL OF ARUNDEL (if by tenure), though never so referred to either by contemporaries or posterity; on the other hand he is called Lord (*i.e.*, feudal possessor) of Arundel by 1258; feudal Ld of Clun and Oswestry, Salop; came into possession of Arundel Castle by late Nov 1243; fought on HENRY III's side at Battle of Lewes 1264, where captured by Simon de Montfort's forces (*see* LEICESTER, E, preliminary remarks); *m* Maud, dau of Theobald le Botiller (*see* 1970 edn ORMONDE, M), and d by 10 Nov 1267, leaving an only s:

JOHN Fitz ALAN, 7th(?) EARL OF ARUNDEL, though also never so referred to by contemporaries; *b* 14 Sept 1246; feudal Ld of Clun and Oswestry; *m* Isabel, dau of Roger de Mortimer, of Wigmore, Herefs, and *d* 18 March 1271/2, leaving an only s:

RICHARD Fitz ALAN, **8th/1st Earl of Arundel** and/or possibly 1st EARL OF SUSSEX (E), so *cr* 1289, though this may simply be an alternative name for the Earldom of Arundel; served against Welsh and Scots and in Gascony; *m* by 1285 Alasia, dau of Tommaso I, Marquis of Saluzzo (Piedmont), and *d* 9 March 1301/2, leaving, with apparently another dau:

1 EDMUND, **9th/2nd Earl**

2 John (Sir); priest

1 Margaret; *m* William le Botiler, seemingly *de jure* 2nd Lord (Baron) Le Botiller (though never called to Parl) and had issue

The er s,

EDMUND Fitz ALAN, **9th/2nd Earl of Arundel**; *b* 1 May 1285; ktd 1306, Capt Gen north of Trent 1316; having originally opposed EDWARD II and his favourite Piers Gaveston changed sides and was one of only a handful of magnates who stayed loyal to EDWARD; Ch Justiciar N and S Wales 1323, Warden Welsh marches 1325; *m* 1305 Alice, sis and in her issue eventual heir of John de Warenne, 8th Earl of Surrey of the 1088 *cr* (*see* SAINT ALBANS, D), and was summarily beheaded at Hereford 17 Nov 1326, after being taken prisoner by adherents of QUEEN ISABELLA (w but opponent of EDWARD II), following which he was posthumously stripped of his lands and titles, leaving:

1 RICHARD, **10th/3rd Earl**

1 Alice; *m* 1325, as his 1st w, 5th Earl of Hereford of the 1200 *cr* (*dsp*)

2 Al(a)ine; *m* by 1338 5th Lord (Baron) Strange (of Knokyn) (*see* SAINT DAVIDS, V)

The s,

RICHARD Fitz ALAN, **10th/3rd Earl of Arundel**, as which restored 1331 (confirmation 1351 and 1354), getting Arundel Castle back also Dec 1330–31 from the widow of Edmund Earl of Kent (*see* above); after death of his maternal uncle 8th Earl of Surrey's widow 31 Aug 1361 assumed additional title of (9th) EARL OF SURREY; known as 'Copped Hat'; *b c* 1313; Justiciar N Wales for life 1334, Govr Carnarvon Castle 1339, Sheriff Salop for life 1345; Adml of the West 1340–41 and 1345–47; cmded 2nd division at Crécy 1346 and assisted at taking of Calais 1347; *m* 1st 9 Feb 1320/1 (*annulled* 4 Dec 1344) Isabel, dau of 1st Lord (Baron) le Despenser of the 29 July 1314 *cr* (*see* FALMOUTH, V), and had issue (bastardised by the papal annulment of 1344):

1 Edmund; ktd 1352; *m* by July 1349 Lady Sibyl de Montagu, dau of 1st Earl of Salisbury of the March 1336/7 *cr*, and *d* in or after 1377, leaving:

(1) Alice; *m* Sir Leonard Carew and had issue (*see* CAREW, Bt)

1 Philippa; *m* Sir Richard Sergeaux (*d* 30 Sept 1393) and had:

(1) Richard

(1) Alice; *m* 1st Guy St Aubyn; *m* 2nd *c* 1406–07 11th Earl of Oxford (*see* ST ALBANS, D); *m* 3rd by 13 Oct 1421 Nicholas (later Sir Nicholas) Thorley and *d* 18 May 1452

2 Mary; *m* 1st Lord (Baron) Strange of the 1360 *cr* and *d* 29 Aug 1396, leaving issue (*see* SAINT DAVIDS, V)

The **10th/3rd Earl** *m* 2nd 5 Feb 1344/5 his mistress Eleanor, dau of 3rd Earl of Lancaster (ggs of HENRY III) of the 1267 investiture (by his 1st w Maud de Chaworth) and widow of **2nd Lord** (Baron) **Beaumont** (*see* BEAUMONT, Bt), and *d* 24 Jan 1375/6, leaving:

2 RICHARD Fitz ALAN, **11th/4th Earl of Arundel** and 11th EARL OF SURREY, KG (1386); *b* 1346; Adml of West and South 1377, and of all England 1386; fought in Hunded Years War, defeating a Franco-Spanish-Flemish fleet off Margate 1387; Govr Brest 1388; one of the Lds Appellant (clique of nobles opposed to RICHARD II's favourites) 1388; *m* 1st *c* 28 Sept 1359 Elizabeth, dau of William Bohun, 1st Earl of Northampton of the March 1336/7 *cr*, and had with another s (presumably but not necessarily by her), Sir Edmund de Arundel, later bastardised (owing to his f's attainder?), whose dau Philippa was mother of Avice, w of the 11th Earl of Oxford; *see* SAINT ALBANS, D):

(1) THOMAS Fitz ALAN, **12th/5th Earl of Arundel** and 12th EARL OF SURREY, as which restored Oct 1400, KG (1400), KB (1399); *b* 13 Oct 1381; adherent of HENRY IV even before latter's usurpation, following which he was apptd Govr Tower London; High Treasurer and Ld Warden Cinque Ports March 1412/3; *m* 26 Nov 1405 Beatrice, illegitimate (but probably legitimated) dau of JOHN I OF PORTUGAL by Inez Perez, and *dsp* 13 Oct 1415 shortly after the capture of Harfleur at the outset of the Agincourt Campaign, when the Earldom of Surrey is deemed to have reverted to the Crown

(1) Elizabeth; *m* 1st by Dec 1378 Sir William de Montagu (*dsp* & *vp* 6 Aug 1382, accidentally *k* jousting in the lists at Windsor, allegedly by his own f), only s of 2nd Earl of Salisbury of the March 1336/7 *cr*; *m* 2nd 1384, as his 2nd w, Thomas de Mowbray, 6th Lord (Baron) Mowbray and 7th Lord (Baron) Segrave (*see* MOWBRAY, SEGRAVE and STOURTON, B), later 1st Duke of Norfolk of the 1397 *cr* (*d* 1399), and had issue; *m* 3rd by 19 Aug 1401 Sir Robert Goushill and had issue (*see* POWERSCOURT, V); *m* 4th by 3 July 1414 Sir Gerard Usflete and *d* 8 July 1425, leaving further issue

(2) Joan; *b* 1375; *m* Sir William Beauchamp, 1st Lord (Baron) Bergavenny, KG, and *d* 14 Nov 1435, leaving issue (*see* ABERGAVENNY, M)

(3) Margaret; *m* Sir Rowland Lenthall, of Hampton Court, Herefs

(4) Alice; *m* by March 1392 4th Lord (Baron) Cherleton (*dsp* 19 Oct 1401)

2 (cont.) The **11th/4th Earl** *m* 2nd 15 Aug 1390 Lady Philippa Mortimer, dau of 3rd Earl of March by Philippa, only dau of LIONEL DUKE OF CLARENCE (2nd s of EDWARD III), and widow of 5th Lord (Baron) Hastings (*qv*), and was attainted, his titles and lands being forfeited, and beheaded 21 Sept 1397 for his opposition to RICHARD II, having had no issue by her

3 JOHN d'ARUNDEL, 1st(?) LORD (Baron) ARUNDEL (E), as which called to Parl by writ 4 Aug 1377, probably as a result of his marriage (in which case it may be held to be identical with the Barony of Mautravers); Marshal of England 1377 and 1378; cmded a naval force which won a victory over the French off Cornwall; *m* 17 Feb 1358/9 Eleanor, Baroness Mautravers in her own right according to later doctrine (*m* 2nd *c* 9 Sept 1384 2nd Lord (Baron) Cobham (of Sterborough) and *d* 10 Jan 1404/5), yr dau of Sir John Mautravers and gdau of 1st Lord (Baron) Mautravers (*see* above against **Baronies of Fitzalan and Mautravers**), and was lost at sea between Ireland and England 15 or 16 Dec 1379, leaving, with apparently three yr sons and a dau:

(1) John; never called to Parl (perhaps because his mother was still living; if so it would strengthen the supposition that his f was called to Parl as a peer in right of his w; *see* also below against **17th/10th Earl** where the Barony of Arundel and Mautravers are amalgamated); *b* 30 Nov 1364; served against Scots by land 1383 and at sea (against the French?) 1388; *m* by 1387 Elizabeth, dau of 1st Lord (Baron) Le Despenser (*see* FALMOUTH, V), and *d* 14 Aug 1390, leaving, with apparently two yr sons:

1a JOHN d'ARUNDEL, **13th/6th Earl of Arundel**, as which *s* cousin 1415 and was perhaps summoned to Parl 1416 though not thereafter (it is thought because of Mowbray hostility to his claims, that family being heirs general of the previous Earls of Arundel), and *de jure* 3rd LORD (Baron) MAUTRAVERS, as which *s* grandmother Jan 1404/5 (though never summoned to Parl by that title; nevertheless he was frequently referred to as Lord Mautravers prior to 1415), KB (1399); *b* 1 Aug 1385; served Agincourt Campaign 1415; *m* by 1407, as her 1st husb, Eleanor (*m* 2nd Sir Richard Poynings and 3rd by 8 May 1439 1st Lord (Baron) Hungerford; *see* SAINT DAVIDS, V), dau of Sir John Berkeley, of Beverstone, Glos, and *d* 21 April 1421, leaving:

1b JOHN d'ARUNDEL, **14th/7th Earl of Arundel**, as which he was not immediately recognised though he claimed the title 1433 by virtue of his ancestors' continuous occupation of Arundel Castle and its demesne (an unsustainable claim had it been examined) 'for time whereof memory of man [a legal expression meaning the reign of RICHARD I, *i.e.*, not before 1189] was not to the contrary'; claim admitted, the judgement declaring that 'Richard Fitz Alan was seized of the Castle, Honour and Lordship in fee; that, by reason of his possession thereof, he was, without other reason or creation, Earl of Arundel, etc.', previously summoned to Parl 12 July 1429 as 2nd(?) LORD (Baron) ARUNDEL, KG (1432), KB (1426); *b* 14 Feb 1407/8; served Hundred Years War in France; Capt Rouen Castle Feb 1431/2; *cr* 1434 DUKE OF TOURAINE (part of a policy by HENRYs V and VI of granting French-based fiefs and titles to English subjects to strengthen their hold of English-occupied France); *m* 1st Constance Cornwall (*dsp* & *vp* 1429), dau of 1st and last Baron of Fanhope and Baron of Milbroke by Elizabeth (dau of JOHN OF GAUNT, s of EDWARD III); *m* 2nd by May 1429 Maud, dau of Robert Lovel (yr s of 5th Lord (Baron) Lovel (of Titchmarsh)) and widow of Sir Richard Stafford, and *d* 12 June 1435 of wounds recd at Siege of Gerberoy the previous month, leaving by her:

1c HUMPHREY Fitz ALAN, **15th/8th Earl of Arundel** and 2nd and last DUKE OF TOURAINE; *b* 30 Jan 1429; *d* unm 24 April 1438, when the Dukedom expired

2b WILLIAM Fitz ALAN, **16th/9th Earl of Arundel**, KG (1471); *b* 23 Nov 1417; Yorkist, fought at Lancastrian victory of 2nd Battle of St Albans 17 Feb 1461, Constable Dover Castle and Ld Warden Cinque Ports 1471 and 1483–87; fndr 'Arundel Mass' at Magdalen Coll Oxford; *m* after 17 Aug 1438 Lady Joan Nevill(e), dau of 1st/5th Earl of Salisbury (*see* ABERGAVENNY, M), and *d* late autumn 1487, leaving, with apparently three yr sons and a dau:

1c THOMAS Fitz ALAN, **17th/10th Earl of Arundel**, KG (Feb 1473/4), KB (1461); *b* 1450; called up to Ho Lds by 15 Nov 1482 *vp* as LORD (Baron) ARUNDELL [*sic*] DE MAUTRAVERS; Lt Order Garter 1489 and 1517, Warden New Forest 1489; *m* Oct 1464 Lady Margaret Woodville, 2nd dau of 1st Earl Rivers and sis of ELIZABETH, EDWARD IV's w, and *d* 25 Oct 1524, leaving, with apparently a yr s:

1d WILLIAM Fitz ALAN, **18th/11th Earl of Arundel**, KG (1525), KB (1489); *b c* 1476; allegedly *m* 1st Elizabeth, dau of 1st Lord (Baron) Willoughby de Broke (*qv*); *m* 2nd 15 Feb 1510/1 Lady Anne Percy, dau of 3rd Earl of Northumberland of the 1415/6 *cr* (*see* NORTHUMBERLAND, D), and *d* 23 Jan 1543/4, leaving by her an only s:

1e HENRY Fitz ALAN, **19th/12th Earl of Arundel**, KG (1544), PC (1546); *b* 23 April 1512 (HENRY VIII stood sponsor); *educ* Cambridge; Page of Hon to HENRY VIII; called up to Ho Lds 5 Feb 1532/3 *vp* as LORD (Baron) MAUTRAVERS; Dep Govr Calais 1540–44; Marshal of the Field against French in Boulogne Campaign which ended in the capture of that town; Ld Chamberlain 1546–Jan 1549/50; Ld Steward Household 1553; had ambition to marry ELIZABETH I but on her turning him down he threw up all his appointments 1564; abetted his s-in-law **4th Duke of Norfolk**'s designs on the hand in marriage of MARY QUEEN OF SCOTS, for which imprisoned; *m* 1st Lady Catharine Grey, dau of 2nd Marquess of Dorset and aunt of LADY JANE GREY; *m* 2nd 19 Dec 1545 Mary, dau of Sir John Arundell, of Lanherne, Cornwall, and widow of 10th Lord (Baron) FitzWalter (*qv*), and *dspms* 24 Feb 1579/80, when the male line of the Fitz Alans expired, having had no issue by her but having had by his 1st w:

1f Henry, *Lord Mautravers*, KB (Feb 1546/7); *b* 1538; *educ* Queens' Coll Cambridge; *m c* 12 April 1555 Ann, dau of Sir John Wentworth, of Gosfield, Essex, and widow of Sir Hugh Rich, and *dsp* & *vp* of fever at Brussels en route to Bohemia, to which he had been apptd Amb

1f Jane; *m* as his 1st w 1st and last Baron Lumley of the 1547 *cr* (*see* SCARBROUGH, E) and *d* 1576

2f Mary; *m* by 30 March 1555, as his 1st w, **4th Duke of Norfolk** and had issue (*see* above)

1d Margaret; *m* John de la Pole, 1st and last Earl of Lincoln of the March 1466/7 *cr* (*dsp* 1487) and *d* in or after 1493

2d Joan; *m* as his 1st w 3rd Lord (Baron) Bergavenny and had issue (*see* ABERGAVENNY, M)

1a Margaret; *m c* 9 Oct 1394 6th Lord (Baron) De Ros (*qv*) of Helmsley and had issue

4 Thomas; *b* 1353; Archdeacon Taunton and Bp Ely 1373, Ld Chllr 1386–89, 1391–96, 1399, 1407 and 1412, Archbp York 1388–96, Archbp Canterbury 1396–97, as which active against Lollards, banished by RICHARD II 1397 and translated to see of St Andrews but returned with HENRY IV 1399 and reinstated as Archbp Canterbury; *d* 19 Feb 1413/4

3 Alice; *m* a little while after 10 April 1364 2nd/5th Earl of Kent of the 1321/60 *cr* (*see* WAKE, Bt)

Lineage (of Beaumont): JOAN Beaumont (sis of 2nd and last Viscount Beaumont, who was also **7th Lord** (Baron) **Beaumont** of the March 1308/9 *cr*; *see* BEAUMONT, Bt); *m* 1st John LOVEL, 8th Lord (Baron) Lovel, and *d* 5 Aug 1466, having had, with other issue, including a dau (Frideswide, *m* Sir Edward Norreys and had issue; *see* LINDSEY and ABINGDON, E):

JOAN Lovel; *m* Sir Brian STAPLETON, of Carlton, Yorks (*d* 16 Dec 1496), and *d* by 4 Jan 1484/5, leaving:

Sir BRIAN STAPLETON; *m* Elizabeth, dau of 7th Lord (Baron) Scrope (of Bolton), and *d* 2 April 1550, leaving:

RICHARD STAPLETON, of Carlton; *m* Thomasin, dau and heir of Robert Amandas, and *d* 11 Jan 1584/5, leaving:

BRIAN STAPLETON, of Carlton; *d* 13 Dec 1606, having had:

RICHARD STAPLETON, of Carlton; *d c* 1614, leaving:

GILBERT STAPLETON, of Carlton; *m* 1st Katherine, dau of W Hungate; *m* 2nd Eleanor, dau of Sir John Gascoigne, and was *bur* 14 April 1636, having by her had:

1 Sir MILES STAPLETON, 1st and last Bt (E), so *cr* 20 March 1661/2, of Carlton; *bapt* 19 Oct 1626; *m* 1st 1661 Elizabeth (*d* 28 Feb 1683/4), dau of 1st Earl of Lindsey (*see* LINDSEY and ABINGDON, E); *m* 2nd Elizabeth, dau of Sir Thomas Longueville, 2nd Bt, of Wolverton, *dsps* and was *bur* 19 Feb 1706/7, when the btcy expired

1 ANNE; *m* Mark ERRINGTON, of Ponteland, Northumberland, and had:

(1) Nicholas ERRINGTON later STAPLETON; *d* 1715, leaving:

1a Nicholas, of Carlton; *m* 1st — (*dsp*); *m* 2nd — (*dsp*); *m* 3rd Winifred, dau of John White, and *d* 1750, leaving by her:

1b Thomas, of Carlton; claimed Barony of Beaumont 1789; *m* 1st Catherine, dau of Henry Witham, of Cliff; *m* 2nd Anne (*dsp*), dau of Thomas Tuite, and *d* 1821, leaving:

1c Miles, of Carlton; *dsp* 1836

1c Catharine; *m* 29 June 1792 Sir George Throckmorton, 6th Bt (*see* 1970 edn), and *dsp* 22 June 1839

2b Miles, of Drax; *m* 2nd Lady Mary Bertie (*d* 22 July 1826), dau of 3rd Earl of Abingdon (*see* LINDSEY and ABINGDON, E), and *d* 1808, leaving, with other issue:

1c Thomas, of Carlton; *b* 28 April 1778; *m* 1st 3 Nov 1802 Maria Juliana (*d* 9 Feb 1827), dau of Sir Robert Cansfield Gerard, 9th Bt (*see* GERARD, B), and had, with other issue:

1d MILES THOMAS, **8th Lord**

2d Thomas; *b* 1805; antiquary, FSA 1839 (V-Pres 1846); works included studies of the Norman Exchequer and pre-Conquest religious foundations in Yorkshire; a fndr Camden Soc, author: *Historical Memoirs of the House of Vernon* (1855); *d* unm 4 Dec 1849

3d John; *b* 11 April 1816; barrister, MP Berwick; *m* 26 April 1860 Frances Dorothea (*d* 8 May 1899), 2nd dau of Edward Bolton King, of Chadshunt, Warwicks, and *d* 25 Dec 1891, leaving:

1e Gilbert (Rev); *b* 11 May 1862; *educ* Oriel Coll Oxford (MA); Rector Rotherwick Hants 1896–1933; *m* 1st 21 April 1891 Anna Mary Katharine (*dsp* 18 June 1891), est dau of Rev Thomas Langshaw, Rector Silchester, Hants; *m* 2nd 3 Jan 1894 Eleanor Sarah (*d* 18 Jan 1947), only child of Rev Gibbes Jordan, Rector Tunworth, Hants, and *d* 19 July 1949, having had:

1f Katharine Anna; *b* 14 June 1895

2f Margaret Alianora; *b* 20 Aug 1897; *d* unm 6 July 1941

2e Cuthbert; *b* 25 April 1863; *m* 27 Dec 1899 Mrs Amelia Frank (*née* Grainer) and *dsp* 10 July 1906

3e Thomas; 1st Bn Rifle Brigade; *b* 31 May 1869; *ka* Flanders Dec 1914

4e Bryan; PWD State Railways India; *b* 20 Aug 1871; *m* 1st 17 July 1912 Geraldine Emma (*d* 26 Aug 1916), 2nd dau of Col John Henry Crowdy, RE, and had:

1f Miles Henry; *b* 31 Dec 1915; *educ* Emmanuel Coll Cambridge (BA); Lt (A) RNVR WW II; *m* 20 July 1942 *Edna Lyn, Sister QARNNSR (*m* 2nd 2 Jan 1945 Patrick Anthony Swift, dau of William Henry Culshaw, and was *ka* 11 Jan 1943 (posthumous despatches)

1f +Anne Dunscomb [Mrs David Clark, c/o Bryan Stapleton Clark, 412 Murita Rd, Eastbourne, Wellington, New Zealand]; *b* 10 Jan 1914; *m* 23 May 1940 David Edwyn Clark (*d* 1987), s of

William Henry Clark, of Pretoria, S Africa, and has, with an adopted dau:

1g +Anthony Miles Stapleton [Dr Anthony Clark, 2988 Fleet St, Coquitlam, BC V3C 3R8, Canada]; *b* 15 March 1941; PhD Newfoundland; *m* 1970 *Ruth Christine, dau of Rev Frederick Guy Harrison, of Appleton Roebuck, Yorks, and has:

1h +David Crispin Stapleton; *b* 1973; has by *Jennifer Lee, dau of Lloyd King, of Coquitlam:

1i *Aidan Natis Miles King; *b* 1993

1h +Natasha Alexandra; *b* 1971; *m* 1993 *Scott Dean Charpentier

2g +Bryan Stapleton [Bryan Clark Esq, 412 Muritai Rd, Eastbourne, Wellington, New Zealand]; *b* 4 April 1944; *m* 1971 *Nicolien, dau of Leslie Lulofs, of Johannesburg, and has:

1h +Graham Leslie; *b* 1975

1h +Bronwyn; *b* 1972

1g +Geraldine Anne [Miss Geraldine Clark, Apt 1013, 155 Balliol St, Toronto, ONT M45 IC4, Canada]; *b* 13 April 1947

4e (cont.) Bryan Stapleton *m* 2nd 15 Nov 1918 Ruth Jane (*d* 30 Jan 1954), yst dau of Richard James Friel, of Waterford, and *d* 26 March 1941, having by her had:

2f +Thomas [Thomas Stapleton Esq, The Foundry Cottage, Lane End, High Wycombe, Bucks HP14 3JS]; *b* 1 Feb 1920; *educ* Univ Coll Oxford (BA 1941, BM and BCh 1943, MA 1945, DM 1953), FRCP London; late Capt RAMC; Hon MD Sydney

5e Louis Henry; *b* 25 July 1874; 2nd Lt RASC and 19th Hus, Matabele War 1893, Jameson's Raid 1895 (wounded), Boer War 1899–1900, WW I, WW II in Roy Observer Corps; *m* 2 July 1908 Annetta Lima Smith (*d* 24 Jan 1956), er dau of A Perossi, and *d* 9 Feb 1949, leaving:

1f +Diana Enid Violet Dorothea [Mrs Allan Eley, The Cottage, Sonning Common, Oxon RG4 9JR]; *m* 30 Sept 1939 Dr Allan William Vaughan Eley, Maj RAMC (*d* 12 June 1965), and has had:

1g Ian Miles Stanley Vaughan; *b* 18 June 1944; *educ* Oratory Sch; *d* 3 Sept 1983

2g +Nigel Louis Allan; *b* 30 Aug 1949; *educ* Oratory Sch

1g Bridget Diana Lilian Annetta; *b* 25 June 1940; *m* 5 June 1965 *Derek Frank Gardner and *d* 11 Sept 1966

1e Monica; *b* 3 Feb 1681; *d* unm 3 June 1936

2e Frances; *b* 15 May 1864; *m* 21 June 1894 Thomas William St Lawrence Lush (*d* 22 June 1948) and *dsp* 19 Dec 1943

3e Dorothea; *b* 9 April 1867; *d* 17 Jan 1875

4e Georgina Maria; *m* 9 Dec 1891 Rev Edwin John Frayling, Vicar Harwich (*d* 5 Dec 1907), and *d* 8 Sept 1922, leaving issue

5e Joan Henrietta

1d Catherine; *m* 1 July 1830 Edward Widdrington Riddell (*d* 30 Oct 1870) and *d* 27 April 1872

2d Maria; *b* and *d* 1804

3d Monica; nun

1c (cont.) Thomas Stapleton *m* 2nd 29 Sept 1829 Henrietta Lavinia (*d* 14 Nov 1858), 2nd dau of Richard Fitzgerald Anster, HEICS, and *d* July 1839, having by her had:

3d Bryan John, DL Yorks; *b* 6 Jan 1831; *m* 24 June 1857 Mary Helen Alicia (*d* 10 April 1918), only dau of John Thomas Dolman, MD, of Souldern House, Oxon, and *d* 21 March 1903, having had:

1e Thomas Fitzalan; *b* 11 April; *d* 24 Dec 1859

2e Nicholas; Capt 25th Co of London Regt; *b* 30 March 1861; *m* 1st 25 Oct 1887 (*divorce*) Mary Madelaine (*d* 21 July 1945), dau of Lt-Col A A Douglas, RMA, and had:

1f Gwendolyn Lavinia; *m* 1 Dec 1923 (Gustav) Francis S Mann (*d* 5 March 1931), s of Dr Gustav Mann, of New College, Oxford

2f Ruth Madelina; *m* 4 June 1914 Stanley Yates (*d* 1955) and had:

1g Joan Madelaine Dampier; WW II in ATS; *b* 24 Sept 1920; *m* 6 Aug 1965 *Jack Trill

2e (cont.) Nicholas Stapleton *m* 2nd 1 Oct 1906 Mary Jane (*d* 21 May 1939), er dau of Augustus John Abraham, and *d* 6 Dec 1918, having by her had:

1f Nicholas Bryan John, RD; *b* 4 Jan 1909; *educ* Christ's Hosp; Lt-Cdr RNR, Liveryman Master Mariners' Co, Freeman City London, Sr Master RFA Serv; *m* 3 June 1940 Laetitia Frances Mary, dau of Col Charles à Court Repington, CMG

2f Robert Myles Augustus; F/Lt RAFVR WW II 1942–45, Coastal and Tport Cmds, Merchant Navy 1926–36; *b* 26 Oct 1910; *m* 21 June 1947 Aileen Mary, dau of J A Lehni, and *dsp* 2 April 1960

3e Gregory, JP Anglesey; *b* 30 Jan 1864; Cdr RN, Capt Supt Imperial Lighthouse Serv Ceylon 1907, Nautical Assessor Ceylon 1908, cmded Special Armed Constabulary riots Ceylon 1915, Naval Attaché Lisbon 1918, Captain Port of Holyhead 1919–34, Yr Bro Trin Ho, Cdr Portuguese Mil Order of Avis; *m* 29 Feb 1904 Marie Marcella Josephine (*d* 9 July 1947), est dau of Anthony MacDermott, JP, RM, of The Park, Killarney, and *d* 6 June 1938, leaving:

1f Gregory Joseph Kenneth, KPM (1942); *b* 1 Sept 1908; *educ* Ampleforth; FRGS, Maj 1st Kumaon Rifles IA, Master Mariner, Assist Cmdt Burma Frontier Force; *m* 10 Nov 1945 *Margarita, only dau of Henry Fitzroy Chamberlayne, JP, of Stoney Thorpe, Warwick, and *d* 1982, leaving:

1g +Miles Gregory Rowland [Miles Stapleton Esq, Manor Farm, Pengover, Liskeard, Cornwall]; *b* 29 May 1948; *educ* Beaumont; Capt Laker Airways and Cyprus Airways; *m* 1973 *Delia Felicity Mary, dau of Maj Benjamin Harold Dunkey, of Bexhill-on-Sea, and has:

1h +Zoe Yvonne; *b* 1975

2h +Margarita Louisa; *b* 1979

3h +Sarah Jane; *b* 1988

2f (Joseph) Mark Hugh; *b* 29 Nov 1909; Maj Burma Army WW II; *m* 26 June 1948 *Elizabeth [Mrs Mark Stapleton, 28 Cavendish Rd, Woking, Surrey], yst dau of Sidney Martin Vanheems, of Ealing, and *d* 1967, leaving:

  1g +Elizabeth Mary [Mrs Michel Meuret, 35 Impasse Marcel Aymé, 39000 Lons-le-Saunier, France]; *b* 12 June 1949; *m* 1973 *Michel Paul René Meuret and has:

    1h +Nicolas Mark; *b* 1976

    1h +Caroline Anne; *b* 1982

    2h +Anne-Lise Antoinette; *b* 1985

  2g +Anne Mary [Mrs Hendrick Lattul, 29 Moorholme, Guildford Rd, Woking, Surrey GU22 7QZ]; *b* 24 May 1951; *m* 1983 *Hendrick Lattul and has:

    1h +Virginia Helena; *b* 1985

    2h +Tanya Maria; *b* 5 Sept 1989

  3g +Monica Mary [Mrs Thierry Wertheimer, 7 rue du May, 60129 Glaignes, Orrouy, France]; *b* 27 May 1953; *m* 1980 *Thierry René Wertheimer and has:

    1h +Christian Simon; *b* 1982; *educ* Juilly

    2h +Francis Mark; *b* 1985; *educ* Wells Cathedral Sch

    3h +Mark Alastair; *b* 1988

    1h +Claire Monica; *b* 1987

1f Marie Josephine; *m* 18 Feb 1928 Joseph Gregory Littledale (*d* 1993), and *d* 1983, leaving:

  1g +Gregory Bruno [Gregory Littledale Esq, 6B Lyngford Rd, Taunton, Somerset TA2 7EG]; *b* 29 Feb 1932; *educ* Beaumont; late 1st Bn Roy Fus, ret teacher; *m* 1st 6 July 1957 (*divorce* 1968) Patricia Jane, dau of Leonard Howard, of Dover, Kent; *m* 2nd 1969 (*divorce* 1993) Naomi Abigail, dau of G F A Martin, and by her has:

    1h +Mark Gregory; *b* 1976; *educ* Wellington

    1h +Joanna Kerra; *b* 1973

    2h +Tamsyn Greer; *b* 1983

2f Elizabeth Charlotte Josephine; *m* 1st 2 Aug 1941 Maj Francis John Angus Skeet, Roy Dublin Fus (*dsp* 9 Feb 1943); *m* 2nd 4 June 1945 Maj (Casimir Paul Francis) Rowland Blennerhassett (*d* 1993), and *d* 1996, leaving issue (*see* BLENNERHASSETT, Bt)

3f Antonia Marianne Angela Winefrede; *b* 1912; *m* 4 Nov 1939 Guy George Morris Pritchett (*m* 2nd 1972 Katherine Mary Elfrida, dau of Capt John Alick Woodhouse, CBE, RN), s of George William Morris Pritchett, MRCS, LRCP, and *d* 19 July 1969, leaving:

  1g +Malcolm Morris [Malcolm Pritchett Esq, 19 Hare Hill Close, Pyrford, Surrey]; *b* 13 July 1941; *educ* Beaumont and Imp Coll London (BSc); CEng, MSc, ARSM, AMIMM; *m* 12 Oct 1963 *Lamorna Jill, 2nd dau of David Bayly Pike, OBE, and has:

    1h +Clare Marion; *b* 20 Feb 1965; *m* 1987 *Charles Croft, of Brighton

    2h +Karen Fiona; *b* 10 May 1967

    3h +Sally Antonia; *b* 1970

  2g +Roger Morris [Roger Pritchett Esq, Canopus, 7 Bramerton Lodge, Easthill Lane, Bramerton, Norfolk NR14 7EQ]; *b* 18 Aug 1943; *educ* Beaumont; slr; *m* 1st 8 Feb 1969 (*divorce* 1990) Vivien, 2nd dau of Francis H Brothers; *m* 2nd 1990 *Magdelena Joanne Esvyra Sylvyra Margrette, dau of S/Ldr Elbert Bendt Dall, and by his 1st w has:

    1h +Rupert Francis Morris; *b* 1974; *educ* Eton

    1h +Emma Caroline; *b* 1977

  1g +Helen Monica [Mrs Ian Strickland, 2 Kings Rd, Walton-on-Thames, Surrey]; *b* 27 Jan 1945; *m* 15 July 1966 *Ian Strickland, FRCS, and has:

    1h +Alexander Peter; *b* 30 April 1967

    2h +Matthew Douglas; *b* 8 Oct 1968

    3h +Luke Gregory; *b* 1979

    1h +Natasha Jane; *b* 1970

  2g +Antonia Mary [Mrs Philip Wellesley-Davies, Manor Chase, High St, Whitchurch-on-Thames, Oxon RG8 7ET]; *b* 30 May 1947; *m* 1971 *Philip Roger Wellesley-Davies and has:

    1h +William George; *b* 1971

    2h +Edward James; *b* 1978

    3h +Henry Charles; *b* 1980

    1h +Antonia Louise; *b* 1975

4f Anne Penordas Mary Helen; *m* 31 Aug 1946 Xavier Philip Spruyt de Bay (*d* 1983), s of John Box Spruyt de Bay, of Brussels, and *d* 1986, leaving:

  1g +Philip Michael [Philip Spruyt de Bay Esq, 29 Westover Rd, London SW18]; *b* 23 Sept 1950; *m* 1st 1979 (*divorce* 1988) Lucy Therese Frances, yst dau of A/Cdre Noel Holroyd Fresson, DFC, RAF, of Sydenham House, Lewdon, Devon; *m* 2nd 1993 *Elizabeth Jane Stephenson, dau of Lt-Col Anthony Loftus St George Stephenson Clarke, of the Manor House, Seend, Wilts

  1g +Helen Mary [Mrs Jeremy Smithies, 18 Holloway, Bath BA2 4PU]; *b* 1 Sept 1947; *m* 8 May 1971 *Jeremy Smithies, MBA, CEng, MIMechE, MRAeS, and has:

    1h +Roland Jeremy Xavier Spruyt de Bay; *b* 1973

    1h +Frances Mary Barbara; *b* 1976

4e Christopher Robert; PhD, Head English Dept New York City High Schs; *b* 30 May 1870; *m* 29 June 1908 Alice Cicely (*d* 1950), dau of J J Sepple, of Chicago, and *d* 31 July 1929, leaving:

1f +Gwendoline Filumena [Mrs Edward Battell, 515 Helen Rd, Mineola, Long Island, NY, USA]; *b* 1910; *m* 1942 Edward Joseph Battell (*d* 24 Aug 1964)

2f +Alice Veronica Enid; *b* 1912; *m* 7 Oct 1930 *John Tyler Walls, s of Charles Sebastian Walls, of Long Island, and has:

  1g +John Tyler; *b* 21 Nov 1931

  2g +Christopher Stapleton; *b* 5 Aug 1933

  3g +Julian Davis; *b* 9 Dec 1934

  1g +Alice Enid; *b* 9 March 1941; *m* *Charles Jacobs

  2g +Naomi Anne; *b* 12 July 1947; *m* *Arthur Brichielle

  3g +Colette Aurora; *b* 17 June 1948; *m* *Michael Turquime

5e Charles; *b* 29 July 1871; *d* unm 1894

6e Philip (Rev); SJ; *b* 28 Jan 1874; *d* 23 April 1938

7e Mark; *b* 28 April 1879; *d* 19 April 1884

1e Helen; *m* 23 Jan 1893 Wilfrid Ignatius Wilberforce (*d* 14 Jan 1910) and *d* 1958, leaving issue

2e Winifred; Benedictine nun (Mother Mary Frideswide); *b* 1 Sept 1865; *d* 24 Feb 1952

3e Cecily; *d* 3 Dec 1885

4e Sibyl; *m* 27 Feb 1899, as his 1st w, Col Charles Myles O'Reilly, IA (*d* 27 July 1942), 3rd s of Myles William O'Reilly, of Knock Abbey, Co Louth, and was lost in the *Persia* (torpedoed in Mediterranean) 31 Dec 1915, leaving issue

5e Frideswide; *d* 25 Jan 1877

6e Mary Elizabeth; Benedictine nun; *d* 5 Sept 1910

7e Veronica; *m* 9 March 1921 her er sis's widower Col Charles Myles O'Reilly and *d* 23 March 1958

THOMAS STAPLETON *d* 4 July 1839; his s,

  MILES THOMAS STAPLETON, **8th Lord** (Baron) **Beaumont**, as which established claim 16 Oct 1840 but was only given precedence of 1432; *b* 4 June 1805; like the **13th Duke**, forsook Catholicism for C of E *c* 1851 in protest at restoration of Catholic hierarchy in England; *m* 9 Sept 1844 Isabella Anne (*d* 16 March 1910), est dau of 3rd Baron Kilmaine (*qv*), and *d* 16 Aug 1854, leaving:

1 HENRY STAPLETON, **9th Lord** (Baron) **Beaumont**; *b* 11 Aug 1848; Cornet 1st Life Gds 1868–69 and 1st W YorksYeo Cav; forsook C of E for Catholicism 1869; KJStJ, Kt Grand Cross Order Holy Sepulchre, Order Mil Merit Bavaria, Baden and Mecklenburg, attd 17th Lancers Zulu War 1879, fought Battle of Ulundi 1880; *m* 28 July 1888 Violet, OBE (1918) (*d* 13 June 1949), only dau of Frederick Wootton Isaacson, MP, by the Mayfair milliner Mme Elise, and *dsp* 23 Jan 1892

2 MILES STAPLETON, **10th Lord** (Baron) **Beaumont**; *b* 17 July 1850; *educ* Eton; served Staff Canada 1874–75, Malta 1879, Bechuanaland Expdn 1884–85, Egyptian Frontier Field Force 1885–86 (medal and bronze star), Lt-Col cmdg 20th Hus 1891–95; forsook C of E for Catholicism 1880; *m* 9 Nov 1893 Ethel Mary (*d* 19 Jan 1937), only surv child of Sir Charles Henry Tempest, 1st Bt (*see* 1877 edn), and accidentally shot himself dead with his own gun 16 Sept 1895 while climbing a stile in the park at Carlton Towers, having made his will a few hours previously, when the Barony fell into abeyance between his daus, leaving:

(1) MONA JOSEPHINE TEMPEST, **Baroness Beaumont** in her own right, as which recognised on termination of abeyance in her favour 1 June 1896, OBE (1946); *b* 1 Aug 1894; *m* 5 Sept 1914 **3rd Baron Howard of Glossop** and had issue (*see* above)

(2) Ivy Mary; *b* 4 Oct 1895; *m* 9 May 1929 Maj Richard Gerald Mickelthwait (*d* 2 July 1976), ED, of Ardsley House, Barnsley, Yorks, and *d* 31 Jan 1967, leaving:

  1a +Richard Mills [Richard Mickelthwait Esq, Preston Hall, Oakham, Rutland]; *b* 21 Nov 1934; *educ* Ampleforth and Ch Ch Oxford; late Capt Gren Gds; *m* 26 Jan 1961 *Jane Evelyn, est dau of William Melville Codrington (*see* CODRINGTON, Bt, of Dodington Park (1876)), and has:

    1b +Richard John; *b* 11 Aug 1962; *m* 1992 *Fevronia Barnard, only dau of Michael Read

    2b +William James; *b* 13 July 1964

  1a +Mary Imogen [Mrs Macdonald of Tote, Tote House, Skeabost Bridge, Isle of Skye; 50, Chelsea Park Gdns, London SW3 6AB]; *b* 15 Aug 1931; *m* 2 June 1961 *Maj John Lachlan Macdonald of Tote, only s of Lt-Col Kenneth Lachlan Macdonald of Tote, DSO, JP, of Tote House, Isle of Skye, and has:

    1b +Charles Lachlan; *b* 9 July 1964; *m* 1994 *Juliet, dau of John Drysdale, of Brill House, Brill, Bucks, and has:

      1c +Alexander Lachlan; *b* 15 April 1995

      2c +Maximilian John; *b* 14 Dec 1996

    2b +Andrew Kenneth; *b* 29 Nov 1965

    1b +Lisabel Mary; *b* 1969

1 Agnes; *d* unm 14 Feb 1863

Seats: Carlton Towers, Goole, N Yorks; Arundel Castle, Arundel, W Sussex.

The astounding building that is Carlton Towers is now, with the destruction of Eaton and the institutionalising of Scarisbrick, surely the last major example of High Victorian Gothic domestic architecture in the northern part of the United Kingdom. It has only come to the Dukes of Norfolk in the last generation, having hitherto been a Beaumont property. Unusually for such a place its origins are genuinely medieval. Indeed the property on which the house stands is said never to have been bought or sold since the Conquest.

As well as pre-Reformation foundations there is the early 17th-century structure of Carlton Hall, which juts out at right-angles to the Victorian wing to form a huge L. The **9th Lord Beaumont** is responsible for the appearance of that L's larger though more modern arm, commissioning in the 1870s Edward Welby Pugin, Augustus Welby Pugin's less distinguished but far more quarrelsome son. Unfortunately, as might have been expected from E W's temperament, he fell out with his patron and the work had to be completed by John Francis Bentley, better known for a wholly different style of building in the shape of the neo-Byzantine Westminster Cathedral though in fact perfectly competent at Gothic, as a large body of ecclesiastical work testifies. The change of horses in mid-stream was surprisingly successful: the exterior is more or less pure Pugin, the interior predominantly Bentley. The latter's drawing room in the Venetian style (he had ended in Venice when undertaking a grand tour of Mediterranean countries to research styles for Westminster Cathedral) is a tour de force, with murals and heraldic and pictorial panels on the chimney piece by Nathaniel Westlake.

Arundel Castle, which (as has been noted above) was built by Roger de Montgomery, looks like a smaller version of Windsor. And like Windsor it started out as a motte and bailey fortress but was then extended over centuries. The first modification was a keep built on top of the motte in the 12th century with a barbican in place of an earlier archway dating from the end of that century. After the Castle ceased to be a Fitz Alan property and became a Howard one its fortunes declined: it was bombarded by Parliamentary forces in the Civil War of the 17th century then abandoned for a further half century. Indeed despite some minor repairs about the beginning of GEORGE I's reign, which may have been carried out under James Gibbs's direction, and some remodelling of the south-facing apartments and the chapel by James Paine in the 1760s, nothing much was done to look after it till the late 1780s. At that point the **11th Duke**, an amateur but gifted architect, took a hand. He imposed his own brand of Gothick but did not disdain the neo-Norman style, in which he was something of a pioneer. His immediate predecessors, even the **8th Duke** who employed James Gibbs, had at most used Arundel as a shooting lodge, staying there no more than a few weeks in the year. From now on it became increasingly the chief seat of the Howards, though somewhat intermittently. The **12th Duke**, for instance, spent little time there.

The **11th Duke** started by reshaping the park, turning over what had been the demesne to agriculture (it was in any case situated the far side of Arundel town from the Castle) and buying up land to the north of the Castle which was in a state of near scrub but did at least adjoin it. (The **12th Duke** further extended this new territory.) He then turned to the Castle proper, starting with the southeast tower, which he erected in the early 1790s, then remodelling the south front, which contained the chief apartments, from mid-decade on. With the beginning of the new century he started rebuilding the east wing, where the library in particular, over 120 feet in extent with a vaulted ceiling in six sections supported on bunched pillars and copious woodwork in Central American mahogany, is something of a minor masterpiece. As the Napoleonic Wars resumed after the Peace of Amiens he began work on the Barons' Hall. He deliberately left the medieval core of the Castle in a ruinous state, though he took care that it should be embellished with such characteristic Gothick accoutrements as ivy and owls. He inserted some jocose stained glass windows, such as the reception of the Queen of Sheba by Solomon, the latter with the Duke's features, and a depiction of a contortedly reluctant KING JOHN signing Magna Carta under duress, glowered over by Barons, one of whom again displayed the features of the Duke, while the rest were made up of likenesses of his friends. Victorian humourlessness was to balk at these and they have since been removed.

The **12th Duke** carried out various minor improvements to Arundel, using Robert Abraham, a former pupil of Nash who had previously worked on modifications to Lower Regent Street. The **13th Duke** adorned the park with lodges, put up the gatehouse leading into the Castle environs from Arundel High Street and laid out a kitchen garden and parterre in the immediate Castle grounds, placing the latter right up against the north side of the ivy-covered keep. It has since been removed. The **14th Duke**, a nobleman of austerer tastes, installed a private chapel in relatively restrained mid-Victorian neo-Gothic by Matthew Ellison Hadfield. The alterations by the **15th Duke** are much the most elaborate and far-reaching since those in the late-18th-early-19th century. They include such private family apartments as the dining room, a breakfast room and billard room, all in the east wing to designs by Charles Alban Buckler, also the remodelled south and west wings, each with their own large rooms, the main staircase and the chapel. In recent years the castle has been extensively refurbished by the **17th Duke**, Earl of Arundel and Castle Trustees.

NORMAN

Arms: Sa. a thunderbolt and in chief two crosses, patée pierced with the eight symbols of Fhoh-he or the Pa-qua and charged with a roundel containing the eastern symbol known as 'Tae-keigh', all or. **Crest:** Upon a mount vert a spear erect transfixing a saracen's head all ppr. **Supporters:** Two Norsemen ppr. **Motto:** *Vivere nec oblivisci* ('Living but not forgetting'). **Creation:** Bt. (UK) 22 June 1915.

SIR MARK ANNESLEY NORMAN, 3RD BT, of Honeyhanger, Parish of Shottermill, Co Surrey, DL (Oxon 1985) [Air Cdre Sir Mark Norman Bt DL, Wilcote Manor, Wilcote, Oxon OX7 3EB]; *b* 8 Feb 1927; *s f* 1943; *educ* Winchester and RMA; High Sheriff Oxon 1983–84, Lt Coldstream Gds Palestine 1945–47, F/O 601 (County of London) Sqdn RAuxAF 1953–56, Air Cdre 1984, Chm Anglo–US Ctee RAF Upper Heyford 1984–91, with Airwork Ltd 1948–56, Bristol Aircraft 1956–61 (Co Sec Bristol Siddeley Engines 1958, exec assist to md 1959), commercial dir Br Exec and Gen Aviation 1961–63, chm Annesley Maitland & Co 1964–66, Britten-Norman 1968–71, chm IU Europe Ltd 1973–84, dir Gotaas-Larsen Shipping Corp 1979–88, Hon Air Commodore No 4624 (County of Oxford) Movements Sqdn RAAF 1981; *m* 30 May 1953 *Joanna Camilla, dau of Lt-Col Ian James Kilgour, of Bampton, Oxon, by Aura Camilla Desmond, yr dau of Lt-Col Claude Edward Forestier Walker (see FORESTIER-WALKER, Bt), and has:

    1 +NIGEL JAMES; *b* 5 Feb 1956; *educ* Radley; late Maj 13th/18th Roy Hussars (QMO), Sultan of Oman's Armoured Regt, dir Morgan Grenfell Internat Funds Management 1990; *m* 1st 1985 (*divorce* 1989) Joanna Rosemary Jane, dau of Michael Montagu George Naylor-Leyland, MC, of Church Farm, Coates, Cirencester, Glos (see NAYLOR-LEYLAND, Bt); *m* 2nd 1994 *Mrs Juliet Clare Louise Marriott, dau of Richard Lloyd Baxendale, of Aston Park House, Aston Rowant, Oxon, and by her has:

        (1) +Antony; *b* 199–

        (2) +Mark; *b* 199–

        (1) *Sophie Patricia Clare; *b* 11 Sept 1997

    2 +(Antony) Rory; *b* 9 Sept 1963; *m* 3 Oct 1998 *Camilla A C, yr dau of Kenneth Baker, of Taunton

    1 *Lucinda Fay; *b* 7 Dec 1965; *m* 1988 *Stanislas Richard Marie Aubertin, s of Christian Aubertin, of Neuilly-sur-Seine, France, and has:

        (1) *A son; *b* 1991

        (2) *A son; *b* 1994

Lineage: ROGER NORMAN, of Ashby Parva, Leics; *d* between 27 May 1579 and 10 Feb 1580, leaving (with two yr sons, Roger and Thomas):

WILLIAM NORMAN, of Frolesworth and Oadby, Leics; *d* between 27 Aug 1603 and 17 Sept 1603, leaving an est s:

SABINE NORMAN, of Oadby; living 1579 and 1603; *m* Meriall (*d* between 25 March 1642 and 18 Aug 1642) and had:

JAMES NORMAN, of Oadby; Churchwarden 1627–28; *m* Anne (*bur* 9 Jan 1633/4) and *d* between 7 Sept and 24 Oct 1635, having had:

WILLIAM NORMAN, of Oadby; *bapt* 21 July 1633; *m* 1st 28 Oct 1665 Mary Barten (*bur* 29 Nov 1667), of Evington, Leics; *m* 2nd 7 Nov 1668 Frances Smalley and was *bur* 22 Nov 1675, having by her had, with a dau:

THOMAS NORMAN, of Oadby; *b* 22 March 1673, *m* 6 July 1701 Alice Voss and had, with two er and two yr sons:

WILLIAM NORMAN, of Aylestone, later Newtown Linford, both Leics; *bapt* 13 Jan 1703; *m* 10 Nov 1722 Jane Spencer, of Anstey, Leics, and was *bur* 11 Jan 1750, having had, with three other sons and a dau:

JOHN NORMAN, of Newtown Linford; *bapt* 9 Dec 1730; *m* 31 Dec 1754 Barbara Hughes (*bur* 1 Jan 1802), of Quornden, and was *bur* 18 Nov 1804, having had, with three other sons and four daus:

WILLIAM NORMAN, of Newtown Linford; *b* 22 Sept 1762; *m* 1st 8 Jan 1788 Sarah Johnson (*d* 14 Jan 1801) and had a s and two daus; *m* 2nd 19 Sept 1803 Mary Balding (*d* 24 March 1823) and *d* 7 Nov 1844, having by her had:

HENRY NORMAN, of Linford House; cncllr Leicester; *b* 19 April 1814; *m* 22 Nov 1855 Sarah Edna (*d* 26 June 1887), dau of James Riddington, of Hazelbeach, Northants, and *d* 22 Sept 1877, having had, with a dau (Ellen Maude, *b* 28 May 1873, *m* 24 Jan 1896 Robert Duddingstone Herdman, ARSA, of St Bernard's Tower, Edinburgh, and *d* 25 Nov 1915):

Sir Henry Norman, 1st Bt (UK), so *cr* 22 June 1915, PC (1918), JP Surrey, of Honeyhanger; *b* 19 Sept 1858; BA Harvard and Leipzig; BST, FRGS, FAIRE, FIP, AMIEE, MP (Lib) Wolverhampton S 1900–10 and Blackburn 1910–23, Assist PMG 1910, Chm Home Office Industl Paints Ctee, Rent Restriction Act Ctee, memb cncl Soc Authors, Br Assoc Ctee Radio-telegraphic Investign and Inventions Panel Min Munitions 1915, Liaison Offr Min Munitions/Min Inventions Paris as Staff Capt 1916, T/Maj 1917, addnl memb Air Cncl 1918, 1914 Star with bar, two medals, V-Chm Imp Communicns Ctee and Chm Wireless Sub Ctee to 1923, Chm Imp Wireless Telegraphy Ctee 1919–20, dir Sheepbridge Coal & Iron, Yorks Amalgamated Collieries, Cdr Order Saviour Greece, St Maurice and St Lazarus Italy, Offr Legion Honour and Order Crown Belgium, author: *The Real Japan, Peoples and Politics of the Far East, All the Russias, Will No Man Understand?* (play), ktd 1906; *m* 1st 28 Aug 1891 (*divorce* 1903) Menie Muriel (*d* 25 March 1945), dau of James Muir Dowie, and had:

    1 HENRY NIGEL ST VALERY (Sir), **2nd Bt**

Sir Henry *m* 2nd 8 May 1907 Hon Florence Priscilla McLaren, CBE (1917), JP Co London, 1914 Star with bar, two medals, despatches, Tstee Imp War Museum (*d* 1 March 1964), yr dau of 1st Baron Aberconway (*qv*), and by her had:

    2 Willoughby Rollo; *b* 12 Oct 1909; *educ* Eton and Magdalen Coll Oxford (MA); Maj Gren Gds (RARO), underwriting memb Lloyd's, chm Boots Pure Drug Co 1961–72 (v-chm 1954–61), E Regn Nat West Bank, v-chm English China Clays 1968–81, dir GRE Assur and Sheepbridge Engnrg, High Sheriff Leics 1960–61; *m* 1st 26 June 1934 (*divorce* 1973) Hon Barbara Jacqueline Boot, est dau of 2nd Baron Trent (*see* 1956 edn), and had:

        (1) +Jeremy Nicholas [Jeremy Norman Esq, 31 Milner Street, London SW3]; *b* 14 Sept 1935; *educ* Harrow and Harvard; late Gren Gds; *m* 1980 *Danuska Maria Weeks, dau of Mr Grajewski, of Wroclaw, Poland

        (1) *Sarah Jessica [Mrs Peter Rickett, 11 Hyde Park St, London W2]; *b* 16 March 1940; *m* 1st 10 Nov 1960 (*divorce* 1967) Peter Egerton-Warburton (*see* GREY EGERTON, Bt) and has issue; *m* 2nd 19 July 1967 *Peter David Rickett, only s of Harold Rickett, CBE, of Ford's Farm, Pirbright, Surrey, and by him has:

        1a *Nicola Barbara; *b* 4 Feb 1970

        2a *Lucinda Frances; *b* 1971

(2) *(Tessa) Roselle; *b* 26 March 1944; *m* 17 Jan 1968 *George Maurice Pope, late Capt Coldstream Gds, 3rd s of Maj John Pope, of Upton Grove, Tetbury, Glos, and has:

    1a *Edward; *b* 15 Jan 1970
    1a *Emily; *b* 1972
    2a *Arabella; *b* 1975

2 (cont.) Maj Willoughby Norman *m* 2nd 1973 *Anna Caroline [Mrs Willoughby Norman, 28 Ranelagh House, Elystan Place, London SW3; The Grange, South Harting, Petersfield, Hants], dau of William Worthington Worthington, s of William Worthington Worthington (*see* AYLESFORD, E, also FEVERSHAM, B) and formerly w of Oliver Patrick Miller Haskard, and *d* 28 Oct 1997

3 +Antony Charles Wynyard, OBE (1945) [W/Cdr Anthony Norman OBE, Château de la Garoupe, Antibes, AM, France; Lausanne Palace, Lausanne, Switzerland]; *b* 13 March 1912; *educ* Eton and Magdalen Coll Oxford (BA); W/Cdr AAF WW II (despatches), memb Lloyd's; *m* 9 June 1937 *Anne Watson, only dau of John Watson Hughes, of Pontruffydd Hall, Denbighs

1 Laura Rosalind; *b* 20 Feb 1908; *m* 29 Feb 1936 Sir Aubrey Francis Burke, OBE, only s of Andrew Burke, and had:

    (1) *Kevin Aubrey Francis; *b* 15 Nov 1945; *educ* Eton
    (1) *Meriel Colleen [Mrs Theodore Packman, Sliders Farm, Curners Green, Uckfield, Sussex]; *b* 28 Feb 1937; *m* 20 Oct 1961 *Theodore Cyril Vance Packman, only s of Cyril William George Vance Packman, and has:
       1a *Camilla Jane; *b* 29 April 1966
       2a *Nicola Charlotte; *b* 19 Sept 1968
    (2) Merlene Jennifer; *b* 1938; *d* 1942
    (3) *Miranda Rosalind; *b* 14 April 1940; *m* 22 Feb 1963 *Paul Munro Gunn, only s of Sir James Gunn, RA, of Hampstead, and has:
       1a *Munro James; *b* 1 Feb 1966
       2a *Marcus Charles; *b* 6 Sept 1968
       1a *Pauline Miranda; *b* 29 Sept 1964
       2a *Petronella Clare; *b* 24 Aug 1970
    (4) *Melanie Lorna; *b* 21 March 1942

Sir HENRY *d* 4 June 1939; his est son,

Sir Henry Nigel St Valery Norman, 2nd Bt, CBE; *b* 21 May 1897; *educ* Winchester and Trin Coll Cambridge (BA 1921); A/Cdre AAF, chm Airwork Ltd, Dir Misr-Airwork SAE Cairo, served WWs I (despatches) and II; *m* 4 Feb 1926 Patricia Moyra (*m* 2nd 6 Oct 1944 Sir Walter Robert Dempster Perkins, MP, est s of Walter Frank Perkins, of Boldre, Hants; *d* 1986), est dau of Lt-Col James Howard Adolphus Annesley, CMG, DSO, 6th Dragoon Gds (*see* ANNESLEY, E), and was *kas* 19 May 1943, leaving:

1 Sir MARK ANNESLEY NORMAN, **3rd and present Bt**

2 +(Nigel) Desmond, CBE (1971); *b* 13 Aug 1929; *educ* Eton; P/O RAF 1949–51, RAAF 1952–57, dir Britten-Norman 1954 and Crop Culture (Aerial) 1956; *m* 1st 28 April 1956 (*divorce* 1965) Barbara Anne, only child of Capt Mark Fogg Elliot, DSO, RN, of Loose, Kent, and has:

    (1) +Henry Mark Desmond; *b* 13 Feb 1957
    (2) +Alexander Robert; *b* 1 Oct 1959

2 (cont) Desmond Norman *m* 2nd 3 April 1965 *Mrs Boel Elisabeth Holmsen, only dau of Gösta Suenson, of Malmö, Sweden, and by her has:

    (3) +Roderic Peregrine; *b* 28 March 1966
    (4) +Roland; *b* 1971
    (1) *Lisa Jemima; *b* 1969

3 +Torquil Patrick Alexander; *b* 11 April 1933; *educ* Eton; *m* 8 July 1961 *Lady Elizabeth Anne Montagu, 2nd dau of 10th Earl of Sandwich (*qv*), and has:

    (1) +Alexander Jesse; *b* 23 June 1962
    (2) +Casey William; *b* 1 Oct 1963
    (3) +Casper Joe; *b* 11 Aug 1967
    (1) *Lucy Patricia; *b* 28 Feb 1965
    (2) *Amy Jean Mary; *b* 13 Oct 1969

NORMANBY

Arms: Quarterly, 1st and 4th, sa. a trefoil slipped between eight mullets in orle arg. (for PHIPPS); 2nd, paly of six arg. and az., over all a bend gu. (for ANNESLEY); 3rd (granted to Lady Catherine Darnley) the arms of JAMES II within a bordure compony arg. and az. **Crest:** A lion's gamb erased sa., holding a trefoil slipped arg. **Supporters:** Dexter, a unicorn erm.; sinister, a goat erm., each armed and unguled or and gorged with a chaplet of roses ppr. **Motto:** *Virtute quies* ('Rest in virtue'). **Creations:** B. (I) 3 Sept 1767 (Mulgrave of New Ross) and (GB) 13 Aug 1794, E. and V. (UK) 7 Sept 1812, M. (UK) 25 June 1838.

THE 5TH MARQUESS OF NORMANBY, Co York, **Earl of Mulgrave**, Co York, **Viscount Normanby of Normanby**, Co York, **Baron Mulgrave of Mulgrave**, Co York, and **Baron Mulgrave of New Ross**, Co Wexford (Constantine Edmund Walter Phipps) [The Most Hon The Marquess of Normanby, Mulgrave Castle, Whitby, N Yorkshire YO21 3RJ]; *b* 24 Feb 1954; *s f* 1994; *educ* Eton and Worcester Coll Oxford; co dir, author: *Careful with the Sharks* (1985), *Among the Thin Ghosts* (1989); *m* 1990 *Nicola (Nicky), yr dau of Milton Shulman, theatre critic, by Drusilla Beyfus, writer on etiquette, and formerly w of Edward St Aubyn (*see* SAINT LEVAN, B), and has:

1 +JOHN SAMUEL CONSTANTINE, *Earl of Mulgrave*; *b* 26 Nov 1994
2 +Thomas Henry Winston; *b* 3 June 1997
1 *Sibylla Victoria Evelyn; *b* 6 Aug 1992

Earldom of Mulgrave and Marquessate of Normanby: The 3rd Baron Sheffield (of Butterwicke) of the February 1546/7 creation (*see* SHEFFIELD, Bt) was grandson by his mother of the 1st Baron Howard of Effingham (*see* EFFINGHAM, E) and possibly stepson of ELIZABETH I's favourite Robert Dudley, Earl of Leicester, whom his widowed mother may have married in 1573. Whether or not Dudley was Sheffield's stepfather the latter seems to have profited by a connection of some sort with him. Sheffield was both a soldier and sailor, fighting in the Low Countries and at sea, particularly at the time of the Armada. He was a Yorkshireman and served as Lord Lieutenant and Vice-Admiral of the county. At the beginning of CHARLES I's reign he was promoted to the Earldom of Mulgrave. He and his grandson, the 2nd Earl of Mulgrave, were Parliamentarians in the Civil War.

The 3rd Earl's son was promoted Marquess of Normanby and Duke of the County of Buckingham and Normanby in 1694 and March 1702/3 respectively. He is said to have made advances to QUEEN ANNE when she was a girl, hence her making him a duke once she became queen. It is his third wife whose daughter married into the Phipps family (*see* below) and brought them various Sheffield properties, including Mulgrave Castle. He built Buckingham House at the end of the Mall in 1703. His descendant through an illegitimate son Sir Charles Sheffield 1st Bt (*qv*) sold it to GEORGE III in 1761 for £21,000 (over £1.2m in late-1990s terms) and having been much enlarged and altered it became known as Buckingham Palace.

Lineage: ROBERT PHIPPS, of Nottingham; *m* 11 Dec 1570 Isabell Bromley (*d* 1588) and had:

GEORGE PHIPPS, of Edwalton, Notts; *m* 24 Sept 1606 Anne, widow of John Power, of Edwalton, and dau of William Elliott, of Stoke, Notts, and had an er s:

FRANCIS PHIPPS; innkeeper of the Golden Bear at Reading, Berks; imprisoned by Parliamentarians 1643; *m* 2nd Ann Sharpe, of Cirencester, and was *bur* 10 Feb 1667/8, having had a yst s:

Sir CONSTANTINE PHIPPS; Lord Chllr Ireland 1710–14, DCL Oxon, barrister 1684, Bencher 1706, agent for New England 1701–10 and St Kitts 1709, ktd 1710; *bapt* 12 Dec 1658, *m* 10 Oct 1684 Catherine (*d* 30 Oct 1728), dau of George Sawyer, and *d* 9 Oct 1723, having had, with 10 other children:

WILLIAM PHIPPS; *bapt* 11 Oct 1698; *m* 25 Sept 1718 Lady Catherine Annesley (*d* 18 Jan 1735/6), only dau and heiress of 3rd Earl of Anglesey (*see* VALENTIA, V) by Lady Catherine Darnley (*m* 2nd, as his 3rd w, John Sheffield, 1st Duke of Buckingham and Normanby and 3rd Earl of Mulgrave of the Feb 1625/6 cr; *see* above), illegitimate dau of JAMES II by Catherine, dau of Sir Charles Sedley, Bt (*see* MEXBOROUGH, E), and *d* 1 Feb 1729/30, leaving:

CONSTANTINE PHIPPS, **1st Baron Mulgrave of New Ross**, Co Wexford (I), so *cr* 3 Sept 1767, of Mulgrave Castle, Yorks; *bapt* 22 Aug 1722; *m* 26 Feb 1742/3 Lepell (*d* 11 March 1780), est dau of John, Lord Hervey of Ickworth (*see* BRISTOL, M), and *d* 13 Sept 1775, having had issue:

1 CONSTANTINE JOHN PHIPPS, **2nd Baron Mulgrave of New Ross**, PC (1784); *b* 30 May 1744; *educ* Eton; RN: joined 1760, on active service WI 1761–62 under his unc 2nd Earl of Bristol aboard HMS *Oragon* [sic], Lt 1762, Post Capt 1765, undertook expedn to N Pole May–Sept 1773 and discovered the Seven Islands N of Spitzbergen, saw action against French under Adml Keppel 27 July 1778 and off Gibraltar under Lord Howe 26 Oct 1782 when in command of HMS *Courageux*; MP (Whig) Lincoln 1768–74, (Tory) Huntingdon 1776–84 and Newark 1784–90, a Ld Admlty 1777–82, Er Bro Trin House 1778–92, Commr BOT 1784–86 and Bd Control 1784–91, Jt Paymaster-Gen 1784–91, *cr* 7 July 1790 BARON MULGRAVE OF MULGRAVE, Co York (GB), FRS 1771, FSA 1776; *m* 20 June 1787 Anne Elizabeth (*d* 22 May 1788), dau of Nathaniel Cholmondeley, MP, of Howsham and Whitby, and *dspm* 10 Oct 1792, when the GB Barony expired, leaving an only dau:

(1) Anne Elizabeth Cholmondeley; *m* 25 Aug 1807 Lt-Gen Sir John Murray, 8th Bt, of Dunerne (*qv*), and *dsp* 10 April 1848

2 Charles; RN; *b* 1753; *d* unm 1786

3 HENRY, **1st Earl**

4 Edmund; Gen, Col Cmdt 60th Foot; *b* 7 April 1760; *d* unm 14 Sept 1837

5 Augustus; FRS; *b* 1762; *m* Maria, est dau of Peter Thellusson (*see* RENDLESHAM, B), and *d* 1826

1 Henrietta Maria; *b* 1757; *m* 12th Viscount Dillon (*qv*) and *d* 1782, leaving issue

The 2nd BARON's bro,

HENRY PHIPPS, **1st Earl of Mulgrave** Co York, so *cr* 7 Sept 1812, as also VISCOUNT NORMANBY OF NORMANBY, Co York (both UK), and previously 13 Aug 1794 BARON MULGRAVE OF MULGRAVE, Co York (GB), GCB (1820), PC (1804); *b* 14 Feb 1755; *educ* Eton and Middle Temple; Ensign 1st Foot Gds 1775, served War American Independence 1776–78, WI 1780 and Holland, Col 31st Foot 1793–1831, cmded at Toulon 1793, Maj-Gen 1794, Lt-Gen 1801, Gen 1809, MP (Tory) Totnes 1784–90 and Scarborough 1790–94, Commr India Bd 1784–91, Chllr Duchy Lancaster 1804–05, For Sec 1805–06, First Ld Admlty 1807–10, Ld Lt E R Yorks 1807–24; *m* 20 Oct 1795 Sophia (*d* 17 March 1849), dau of Christopher Thompson Maling, of West Herrington, Co Durham, and had, with other issue:

1 CONSTANTINE HENRY, **1st Marquess**

2 Charles Beaumont (Sir), KCB; Col, Keeper Privy Purse, Treas Household to HRH THE PRINCE CONSORT; *b* 27 Dec 1801; *m* 25 June 1835 Margaret Anne (*d* 13 April 1874), 2nd dau of Ven Henry Bathurst, Archdeacon Norwich, and *d* 24 Feb 1866, having had:

(1) Charles Edmund; Maj, Page-of-Honour and Groom-in-Waiting in Ordinary to HM QUEEN VICTORIA; *b* 11 June 1844; *m* 2 June 1868 Susan Stewart (*d* 1930), 2nd dau of Very Rev John Gambie Geddes, DCL, MA, Dean Niagara, and *d* 29 Nov 1906, having had:

1a Charles Stewart; *b* 12 Dec 1871; *m* 1902 Edith Annie Webber (*d* 1946), dau of Capt Francis Douglas, Black Watch, of Edinburgh, and was *ka* 15 Aug 1917, leaving:

1b Charles Francis Douglas; *b* 12 April 1905; *m* 27 April 1935 Katherine Louise Conlan (*d* 1982) and *d* 1984 leaving:

1c +John Douglas Stewart [John Phipps Esq, 1109 London St, New Westminster, BC, Canada V3M 3B9]; *b* 24 July 1936; *m* 13 April 1963 Kathleen May (*d* 1989), dau of James Sinclair Moore, of Cloverdale, BC, and has:

1d *Karleen Louise; *b* 25 April 1964

2d *Kimberly Ann; *b* 23 Feb 1966

3d *Kelly Patricia; *b* 13 Dec 1968; *m* 1989 *Craig Douglas Ervin, s of Douglas Allan Ervin, of New Westminster

1b Katherine Frances Harriet; *b* 1903; *m* 26 April 1930 Alexander Herbert Garvin and had issue. He *d* 1957

2b Edith Sheila Maye; *b* 1906; *m* 15 July 1933 Ronald Kirby Gordon and had issue

3b *Emma Doreen Stewart [Mrs Ian McDiarmid, 3770 East Boulevard, Vancouver, BC, Canada]; *b* 1914; *m* 1st 16 June 1936 (*divorce* 1961) Alvah Robert Hager (*d* 1988) and has:

1c *Robert Stewart [Robert Hager Esq, 2706 West 50th Ave, Vancouver, BC, Canada V6P 1B7]; *b* 1937; *m* 1961 *Judith Frances, dau of Alvin R Brown, of Vancouver, BC, and has:

1d *Leslie Frances [Mrs James Carter, 4489 Harris Place, N Vancouver, V7G 1E9, BC, Canada]; *b* 1965; *m* 1990 *James Gregory Carter, and has:

1e *Taylor Howard; *b* 4 Dec 1992

2e *Jordan Robert; *b* 1 Feb 1995

1e *Alison Frances; *b* 26 Nov 1997

2d *Shelley Bronwyn [Mrs Craig Ferris, 2412 W 49th Ave, Vancouver, V6M 2V3, BC, Canada]; *b* 1967; *m* 1990 *Craig Andrew Boyd Ferris and has:

1e *Jack Brown Hager; *b* 8 April 1995

2e *Alexander Robert Hager; *b* 23 April 1997

1c *Rosemary Douglas [Mrs Roger Thomas, 212 41st St, Manhattan Beach, CA 90266, USA]; *b* 1941; *m* 1966 *Roger Philip Thomas and has:

1d *Lisa Michelle; *b* 1967

2d *Victoria Mary; *b* 1970

3b (cont.) Mrs Emma Hager *m* 2nd 27 March 1964 *Ian Hugh Doughty McDiarmid

2a Albert Edmund; *b* 1 May 1873; *m* 1899 Sydney Florence (*d* 1951), dau of Washington Boultbee, of Ancaster, Ontario, and *d* 11 July 1945, leaving:

1b +Stewart Beaumont [Stewart Phipps Esq, 1535 Despard Ave, Victoria, BC, Canada]; *b* 6 May 1900; Canadian MGC Siberia 1918–19, Capt

Edmonton Fus WW II; *m* 1st 1921 Frances Peacey Brown-Constable (*d* 1951) and has:

1c *Barbara Phyllis [Mrs Thomas Gordon, 10230, 134 St Edmonton, Alberta, Canada]; *b* 1923; *m* 1946 *Thomas H Gordon

2c *Diana Averill [Mrs William Meijer, PO Box 623, Tuxedo Park, NY, USA]; *b* 1937; *m* 1958 *William Otto Jan Groeneveld Meijer

1b (cont.) Stewart Phipps *m* 2nd 1952 *Edith Patricia Allison, dau of Dr Allison Smith, and by her has:

1c +Geoffrey Allison; *b* 22 May 1953; *m* 1973 *Lesley Elizabeth, dau of Douglas D Clarke, of Victoria, BC

2b Geoffrey Edmund; *b* 29 May 1904; *m* 26 Oct 1927 *Eileen — and *dsp* 9 Sept 1967

3b +Norman Ernest, QC (1951) [Norman Phipps Esq QC, 295 Oriole Parkway, Toronto 7, Ontario, Canada]; *b* 22 Feb 1907; *educ* U of Toronto (BA 1929); barrister 1932, Maj Roy Canadian Artillery WW II; *m* 15 Aug 1944 *Dorothy, dau of Albert Edward Kendal-Quarry, and has:

1c +David; *b* 4 Aug 1945

1c *Penelope Ann; *b* 28 Feb 1948; *m* 1972 *Barry E Tobias

1b *Phyllis Lepell; *b* 6 March 1902; *m* 23 April 1925 David Eric Cumberland (*d* 29 Dec 1964) and has:

1c *David Keith; *b* 23 Aug 1930; *m* 19– *Mary Fenn and has had:

1d Peter Phipps; *b* 26 March 1957; *d* 21 May 1958

1c Helen Sydney; *b* 30 Sept 1926; *m* Robert James Loveless

2b *Ruth Audrey; *b* 22 Jan 1910

3a William Henry Gamble; *b* 11 Jan 1880; *m* 4 Dec 1909 Elsie, dau of Edward Scrope Shrapnel, and *d* 11 May 1943, leaving:

1b Mary Louise; *b* 25 Dec 1910; *m* 1 June 1940 Eric Hartley Fearn and *d* 29 May 1963, leaving issue. He *d* 9 Aug 1964

2b Sylvia Grace; *b* 5 Sept 1920; *d* unm 16 June 1954

4a Augustus Henry Constantine; *b* 1882; *m* 1909 Agnes Fraser (*d* 1971), dau of Murdoch MacLachlan, of Kilmun, Scotland, and *d* 1946, leaving:

1b +Charles Norman; *b* 1912; *m* 1940 *Margaret Patricia, dau of George F Saunders, of W Vancouver

1b Adelaide Lepell; *b* 1910; *m* 1935 Thomas Arthur Brown and *d* 1965, leaving two daus. He *d* 1955

2b *Harriet Patricia [Mrs William Brown, 2250 Bowker Ave, Victoria, BC, Canada]; *b* 1914; *m* 1942 William Henry Brown (*d* 1971), of Victoria, and has:

1c *John Arthur; *b* 1943

1c *Margaret Evelyn; *b* 1945; *m* 1965 *Michael Barclay John Shannon and has:

1d *Michael William; *b* 1965

1a Alice Lepell; *b* 26 Sept 1870; *m* 1st 11 Oct 1893 William Johnson-Holt Murison and had issue; *m* 2nd Benjamin Lewis

2a Katherine Mary; *b* 17 Jan 1875; *m* 1897 W F Proctor and *d* 2 March 1958, leaving issue. He *d* 10 March 1915

3a Victoria Alexandrina; *b* 30 March 1877 (HM QUEEN VICTORIA stood sponsor); *d* unm 26 Dec 1959

4a Mary Susan Frances; *b* 26 Aug 1878; *d* 27 Oct 1899

(2) Albert Augustus; *b* 1 July 1847 (HRH THE PRINCE CONSORT stood sponsor); 60th Rifles; *d* unm 16 Jan 1875

(1) Maria Henrietta Sophia; Keeper State Apartments Kensington Palace; *m* 1st 29 Jan 1856 Capt Frederick Sayer, 3rd RWF (*d* 29 Feb 1868), and had issue (*see* SLADE, Bt); *m* 2nd 4 Dec 1872 Lt-Col William Chaine, MVO, 10th Hus, and *d* 21 Dec 1915, leaving further issue. He *d* 3 July 1916

(2) Harriet Lepell (Hon), VA; Bedchamber-Woman in Ordinary to HM QUEEN VICTORIA 1889–1901, Maid-of-Honour 1862–89; *d* 7 March 1922

3 Edmund; *b* 7 Dec 1808; *m* 15 May 1838 Maria Louisa (*d* 1888), widow of Hon Charles Francis Norton (*see* GRANTLEY, B) and est dau of Lt-Gen Sir Colin Campbell, KCB, and *d* 28 Oct 1857, leaving:

(1) Constantine Edmund Henry (Sir), KCMG, CB; Dip Serv 1858–1906, Consul Gen and Sec Legn Budapest 1881–85, Sec Vienna 1885–92, Paris 1892, Min Plen there 1892–94, Envoy Extrdy and Min Plen Rio de Janeiro 1894–1900 and Brussels 1900–06; *b* 15 March 1840; *m* 1st 7 Oct 1863 Maria Jane (*d* 30 Aug 1902), est dau of Alfred Miller Mundy, of Shipley Hall, Derbys, and had:

1a Eric Clare Edmund (Sir), GCB, GCMG, GCVO , PC; Counsellor Brussels 1920–22, Min Plen Paris 1922–28, Envoy Extrdy and Min Plen Vienna 1928–33, Amb Extrdy and Plen Berlin 1933–37, Amb Extrdy and Plen Paris 1937–39, Br Sec Paris Peace Conference 1919, attd Br Delegn Reparations Conferences The Hague 1929 and 1930, Cdr Order Leopold Belgium, Grand Cross Legn Honour France; *b* 27 Oct 1875; *m* 1st 20 July 1907 Yvonne (*dsp* 16 March 1909), yst dau of Count de Louvencourt, of Paris; *m* 2nd 29 April 1911 Frances Georgina (*d* 1988), 2nd dau of Herbert Ward, and *d* 13 Aug 1945, having by her had:

1b Mervyn Constantine Sanford; *b* 26 Feb 1912; *educ* Harrow and New Coll Oxford (BA); Hon Lt-Col 7th Hus WW II (Croix de Guerre avec palme), Mil Attaché Mexico and Centl America 1946–47; *m* 14 Sept 1941 *Joyce Kathleen [Mrs Mervyn Phipps, 1 Stalbridge Rd, Stourton Caundle, Sturminster Newton, Dorset], dau of John Patrick Goode, of Foxhall, Letterkenny, Co Donegal, and *d* 1983, leaving:

1c *Magdalene Frances [Mrs Fergus Rogers, 12 Holly Mount, London NW3]; *b* 2 Dec 1942; *m* 1970 *Fergus Rogers

2c *Caroline Mary [Mrs José López, Sant Pere 15, 4° Caldetes, Barcelona, Spain]; *b* 16 Dec 1943; *m* 1965 *José Vives López, s of Amaranto Vives López, of Tarragona, Spain, and has:

1d *Alexandre Constantine; *b* 1968

2d *Catalina Rosa; *b* 1965

3d *Lucieta Ana; *b* 1967

4d *Marina; *b* 21 July 1974

3c *Elizabeth Helen [Miss Elizabeth Phipps, 74b Queenstown Rd, London SW11]; *b* 31 July 1945

4c *Dorothy Charlotte [Mrs Dorothy O'Boyle, 1 Stalbridge Rd, Stourton Caundle, Sturminster Newton, Dorset]; *b* 10 July 1950; *m* 1979 (*divorce* 1982) Jay Patrick O'Boyle, of Seattle, and has:

  1d *Marlon Orion Sandford; *b* 1982

5c *Mary Ann [Mrs Nicholas Fforde, 104 Stonefall Ave, Starbeck, Harrogate, N Yorks HG2 7NT]; *b* 11 June 1953; *m* 1973 *Nicholas Fforde and has:

  1d *Timothy Constantine; *b* 1977

  1d *Emily Frances; *b* 1973

  2d *Sophie Veronica; *b* 1974

  3d *Sarah Maria; *b* 1980

2b Alan; Lt RN WW II; *b* 1 Oct 1915; *m* 6 Aug 1940 *Hon Veronica Nell Fraser (*m* 2nd 12 Jan 1946 Brig Sir Fitzroy Hew Royle Maclean, 1st Bt, of Dunconnel; *qv*), 2nd dau of 14th Lord Lovat (*qv*), and was *ka* Leros 16 Nov 1943, leaving:

  1c +Jeremy Julian Joseph; *b* 30 June 1942; *educ* Ampleforth and RMA Sandhurst; Brig QOH, with SAS; *m* 12 Oct 1974 *Susan L, only dau of Lt-Cdr Wilfred H Crawford, RN, of Huntington, E Lothian, and has:

    1d +Jake Shimi Alan; *b* 1975

    1d *Jemma Louise Rose; *b* 1977

  1c *Susan Rose [Mrs Nicolas Paravicini, Glyn Celyn House, Brecon, Powys LD3 0TY]; *b* 27 April 1941; *m* 1st 14 Dec 1959 (*divorce* 1968) Richard St Clair de la Mare, s Richard Herbert Ingpen de la Mare, of Much Hadham Hall, Herts, by Amy Catherine, er dau of Rev Stuart Alexander Donaldson, Master Magdalene Coll Cambridge (see 1970 edn DONALDSON OF KINGSBRIDGE, B), by Lady Albinia Hobart-Hampden (see BUCKINGHAMSHIRE, E), and has:

    1d *Casper James; *b* 10 Jan 1962

    2d *Adam John; *b* 15 July 1964; *m* 1993 *Michele Spriggs

    1d *Laura Frances Albinia; *b* 1 July 1960; *m* 1992 *Henry Alexander Boothby (see BOOTHBY, Bt)

    2d *Selina Rose [Mrs Andrew Harley, 290 Portobello Rd, London W10]; *b* 5 Feb 1963; *m* 1991 *Andrew John Harley

  1c (cont) Mrs Susan de la Mare *m* 2nd 1968 (*divorce* 1986) Derek Marlowe and by him has:

    3d *Benjamin; *b* 16 Aug 1969

  1c (cont) Mrs Susan Marlowe *m* 3rd 1986, as his 2nd w, *Nicolas Vincent Somerset Paravicini

3b *John Francis [John Francis Phipps Esq, 59 Rugby Place, Kempton, Brighton BN2 5JB]; *b* 26 Aug 1933; writer; *m* 1st 18 Sept 1956 (*divorce* 1972) Charm Alys, yr dau of Eric Quick, of Recife, Brazil, and has:

  1c +Jonathan Eric; *b* 14 Sept 1957; *educ* Downside

  1c *Anna-Rose; *b* 9 Dec 1959

  2c *Isabel Emma; *b* 30 June 1961

3b (cont) John Phipps *m* 2nd 1975 (*divorce* 1987) Rosemary Carol Anne Tecla (*née* Shirtcliffe) and by her has:

  2c +William Donald; *b* 17 Aug 1978

  3c *Sophie Sarita Mary; *b* 2 May 1976

4b +William Anthony Dominic [William Phipps Esq, 31 Chepstow Villas, London W11 3DR]; *b* 21 April 1936; *educ* Ampleforth and Nautical Coll Pangbourne; silversmith, late Clearance Diver, RCN and Able Seaman; *m* 23 June 1960 *Henrietta Frances, er dau of Henry Taylor Lamb, MC, RA, the painter (see LONGFORD, E), and has:

  1c +Frederick Fabian Aeneas; *b* 8 July 1961

  2c +Samuel Cornelius Dominic [Samuel Phipps Esq, 5 Gillespie St, Edinburgh EH9 9NH]; *b* 9 Oct 1964; *m* 1990 *Clunie Fiona Mary, yst dau of Gen Sir (James) Michael Gow, GCB (see SCOTT, Bt, of Beauclerc, and has:

    1d +Gabriel James William; *b* 12 March 1997

    1d *Stella Phoebe Scarlett; *b* 30 March 1991

  3c +Lucian Percy Denis; *b* March 1966

  1c *Theresa Pansy Frances; *b* 15 April 1963

1b *Mary [Mrs Bonar Sykes, Conock Manor, nr Devizes, Wilts]; *b* 7 May 1923; *m* 28 Sept 1949 Bonar Sykes (*d* 1 June 1998), only s of Maj-Gen Sir Frederick Hugh Sykes, GCSI, GCIE, GBE, KCB, CMG, PC, of Conock Manor, and has:

  1c *Hugh Bonar; *b* 17 Sept 1950; *educ* Eton and The Queen's Coll Oxford; *m* 1983 *Marie-Odile Daulton

  2c *David Eric; *b* 21 Sept 1953; *educ* Eton

  3c *James Richard; *b* 3 June 1956; *educ* Eton

  4c *Alan Geoffrey [Alan Sykes Esq, Talkin Head Farm, Brampton, Cumbria CA8 1LT]; *b* 29 Dec 1960; *m* 1984 *Kate Judith Hughes

2b *Margaret Ann [Mrs Donald Robertson, 2 Richmond Rd, Cambridge CB4 3PU]; *b* 23 March 1925; *m* 1st 23 July 1949 George Anthony Cary (*d* 9 Jan 1953), yst s of Joyce Cary, the writer, and has:

  1c Christopher Alexander George; *b* 23 April 1950; *educ* Westminster and Trin Coll Cambridge; *m* 1973 *Joanna Buczkowska and *d* 1983, leaving:

    1d *Catherine Alexandra Joanna; *b* 1979

2b (cont) Mrs George Cary *m* 2nd 23 Aug 1956 Prof Donald Struan Robertson, FBA, Emeritus Prof Greek Cambridge, s of Henry Robert Robertson. He *d* 5 Oct 1961

(1) (cont) Sir Constantine Phipps *m* 2nd 20 Jan 1904 Alexandra (*d* 7 Nov 1954), widow of Gomes Brandao and dau of Wassili de Schoumaeker, of St Petersburg, and *d* 15 March 1911

4 Augustus Frederick (Rev); Chaplain in Ordinary to HM QUEEN VICTORIA, Hon Canon Ely, RD; *b* 18 Oct 1809; *m* 7 Nov 1837 Lady Mary Elizabeth Emily FitzRoy (*d* 22 Aug 1887), est dau of 5th Duke of Grafton (*qv*), and *d* 27 Jan 1896, leaving, with other issue:

(2) Mary Louisa Sophia; *m* 8 May 1866 Rev Henry Thornton Pearse, Rector Larling, Titchfield, Hants, and *d* 18 May 1913, leaving issue. He *d* 25 Feb 1908

1 Lepell Charlotte; *m* 18 May 1858 John Wallis Alexander, afterwards 4th Bt (see CABLE-ALEXANDER, Bt, of Dublin), and *d* 29 Jan 1869

The 1st EARL *d* 7 April 1831; his est son,

CONSTANTINE HENRY PHIPPS, **1st Marquess of Normanby**, Co York (UK), so *cr* 25 June 1838, KG (1851), GCB (1847), GCH; *b* 15 May 1797; *educ* Harrow and Trin Coll Cambridge; MP (Whig 1818–19, Tory 1819 on) Scarborough 1818–20, Higham Ferrers 1822–26 and Malton 1826–30, Govr Jamaica 1832–34, Ld Privy Seal July–Dec 1834, Ld Lt Ireland 1835–39, Sec State War and Colonies Feb–Aug 1839, Home Sec 1839–41, Amb Paris 1846–52, Min Florence 1854–58; *m* 12 Aug 1818 Hon Maria Liddell (*d* 20 Oct 1882), est dau of 1st Baron Ravensworth (*qv*), and *d* 28 July 1863, leaving:

1 GEORGE AUGUSTUS CONSTANTINE PHIPPS, **2nd Marquess of Normanby**, GCB (1885), GCMG (1877, KCMG 1874), PC (1851); *b* 23 July 1819; Lt-Govr Nova Scotia 1858–63, Govr Queensland 1871–74, NZ 1874–78 and Victoria 1878–84, Capt Gentlemen-at-arms 1869–71, Comptroller Household 1851–52 and Treas 1853–58, offr Scots Fus Gds, MP (Lib) Scarborough 1847–51 and 1852–57; *m* 17 Aug 1844 Laura (*d* 26 Jan 1885), dau of Capt Robert Russell, RN, and n of Elizabeth, Dowager Duchess of Cleveland (see BARNARD, B), and had:

(1) CONSTANTINE CHARLES HENRY, **3rd Marquess**

(2) William Brook; *b* 13 Aug 1847; RN; *m* 31 March 1875 Constance Emma (*d* 1 Oct 1932), yst dau of Alfred Keyser, of Gt Berkhamsted, and *d* 19 Feb 1880, having had, with two sons:

  1a Evelyn Mary; *b* 4 March 1877

(3) Henry George Russell; *b* 26 Jan 1851; *m* 17 Jan 1878 Norma Caroline Georgina (*d* 6 June 1935), 2nd dau of James Leith Hay, 3rd s of Sir Andrew Leith Hay, of Rannes and Leith Hall, and *d* 27 Nov 1905, leaving:

  1a Russell Constantine Charles; Gunner Australian Field Artillery; *b* 14 April 1883; *das* 6 Dec 1916

  2a Vivian Louis Augustus; Australian Medical Corps; *b* 1884; *m* 1921 Marie Elaine (*d* 1974), dau of G E Elliott, and *d* 1971, leaving:

    1b Vivian Henry Blakeney; *b* 1923; AIF WW II; *m* 1944 *Betty Catherine [Mrs Vivian Phipps, 52 Beltana Cres, Buddina, Qld 4575, Australia], dau of Hubert Franklin Blundell, and *d* 1991, leaving:

      1c +Douglas Vivian [Douglas Phipps Esq, 11 Urambi Court, Mooloolaba, Qld 4557, Australia]; *b* 1945; *m* 1st 1968 (*divorce* 19–) Rosemary Florence Tauy and has:

        1d *Justine Danielle; *b* 1969

      1c (cont.) Douglas Phipps *m* 2nd 1980 *Robyn Rayna Temple

      2c +Paul Russell [Paul Phipps Esq, 17 Tallawa Place, Wurtulla, Qld 4575, Australia]; *b* 1953; *m* 1977 *Robyn Faith Binns and has:

        1d +Russell Adam; *b* 1980

        1d *Lauren Elizabeth; *b* 1982

      1c *Catherine Margaret [Mrs Rolf Schnase, Kapilano Cres, Mountain Creek, Mooloolaba, Qld 4557, Australia]; *b* 1948; *m* 1st 1969 (*divorce* 1973) — and has:

        1d *Darren Dupree; *b* 1971

      1c (cont.) Catherine — *m* 2nd 1977 *Rolf Christian Schnase and by him has:

        1d *Kelly Ann; *b* 1978

    2b Harvey Owen; *b* 14 July 1925; RAN WW II; *m* 1947 *Eda Margaret [Mrs Harvey Phipps, 9 Seaview Terr, Moffatt Beach, Caloundra, Qld 4551, Australia], dau of Donald McNab, and *d* 1982, leaving:

      1c +David Owen [David Phipps Esq, 4 Ferrar St, Mt Lawley, Perth, W Australia 6050]; *b* 1948; *m* 1970 *Palma Mary Mammino and has:

        1d +Anthony Owen; *b* 1970

        2d +Paul Ryman; *b* 1972

      2c +John Russell [John Phipps Esq, 13 Seaview Terr, Moffat Beach, Caloundra, Qld 4551, Australia]; *b* 1949; *m* 1972 *Elizabeth Gayle Strickland and has:

        1d *Elaine Ann; *b* 1973

        2d *Melissa Jane; *b* 1974

        3d *Andra Susan; *b* 1979

      1c *Wendy Jane [Mrs Roderick Nash, 6 Greber Rd, Beerwah, Qld 4519, Australia]; *b* 1950; *m* 1st 1969 (*divorce* 1981) Michael George Luland and has:

        1d *Shane Conrad; *b* 1971

        2d *Christopher Michael; *b* 1973

        1d *Katherine Flavelle; *b* 1974

      1c (cont.) Mrs Wendy Luland *m* 2nd 1981 *Roderick Miles Nash and by him has:

        3d *Daniel Owen Miles; *b* 1985

        2d *Emma Jane; *b* 1983

      2c *Susan Margaret [Mrs John Miguel, 38 Peachester Rd, Beerwah, Qld 4519, Australia]; *b* 1950; *m* 1980 *John Francis Miguel and has:

        1d *Benjamin John; *b* 1981

        1d *Anna Jane; *b* 1983

    1b *Maurine Elaine [Mrs James Hunter, 43 Lutzow St, Wellers Hill, Qld 4121, Australia]; *b* 1921; *m* 1944 James Fitz-Gibbon Hunter (*d* 1988) and has:

      1c *Kenneth James [Kenneth Hunter Esq, 18 Soden St, Yeerongpilly, Qld 4105, Australia]; *b* 1955; *m* 1985 *Sally-Anne Jefferies and has:

        1d *James Richard; *b* 1989

        1d *Gabrielle Jane; *b* 1987

      2c *Ross Vivian [Ross Hunter Esq, 30 Hoff St, Mount Gravatt, Qld 4122, Australia]; *b* 1961; *m* 1996 *Nerida Robyn, dau of Harry Small

      1c *Helen Maurine [Mrs Anthony Lewis, 24 Glen St, Hawthorn, Victoria 3122, Australia]; *b* 1945; *m* 1966 *Anthony Beresford Lewis, BEc, ACA, AASA, and has:

        1d *Nicholas Anthony Hunter; *b* 1971; BCom

        1d *Georgia Helen; *b* 1969; *m* 1994 *Christopher Charles Hoelter

2c *Barbara Elaine; *b* 1948; *m* 1st 1969 (*divorce* 1981) Richard Wilfred Armstrong, BEcon; *m* 2nd 1981 *Antonio Ammendola

3c *Julie Margaret [Mrs Roger Harcourt, 1272 Chambers Flat Rd, Chambers Flat, Qld 4133, Australia]; *b* 1952; *m* 1977 *Roger Murray Harcourt and has:

    1d *Andrew Behan; *b* 1979

    2d *David James; *b* 1982

    3d *Anthony Roger; *b* 1984

    4d *Michael Douglas; *b* 1986

2b *Daphne Margaret [Mrs Barry Valttila, 3 Michele Place, Turramurra, NSW 2074, Australia]; *b* 1 Jan 1929; *m* 18 Dec 1948 *Barry Eric Antti Valttila, s of Antti Valttila, of Brisbane, and has:

    1c *Christopher Tony [Christopher Valttila Esq, Lot 1, Currumbin Creek Rd, Currumbin, Qld 4223, Australia]; *b* 2 April 1953; LLB; *m* 1977 *Mirja Karina Heimonen, of Helsinki, and has:

        1d *Eric Antti; *b* 1983

        2d *Esa Christian; *b* 1978

        3d *Elina Carita; *b* 1985

        4d *Emmanita Aleksandra; *b* 1987

    1c *Jane Linda; *b* 5 May 1955

    2c *Gaye Helen; *b* 24 Jan 1964

1a Laura Elizabeth Minnie; *b* 1879; *m* 1897 Arthur Walker (*d* 1944), of Logan, Qld, and had:

    1b Ena Mabel Egerton; *b* 1900; *m* 1924 Roy Richard Burguey and had, with a yr s (Richard Arthur, *b* 1928, *dsp*):

        1c Noel Dudley; *b* 1925; *m* 1950 *Gwynneth Pearl Shelton and had:

            1d *Russell Noel; *b* 1950; *m* 1972 *Nicki Annette Young and has:

                1e *Angelique Rhonell; *b* 1980

            2d *Philip Neil; *b* 1955; *m* 1989 *Jacqueline Kay Mann and has:

                1e *James Dudley; *b* 1989

                2e *Todd William; *b* 1991

                1e *Edwina Elly; *b* 1993

                2e *Philippa Val; *b* 1994

            3d *Roger Shelton; *b* 1960; *m* 1990 *Janice May Quinn and has:

                1e *Elle Louise May; *b* 1992

            1d *Diana Sue; *b* 1953; *m* 1973 *Ross Philip Wilson and has:

                1e *Douglas James; *b* 1980

                1e *Katherine; *b* 1982

                2e *Frances Elizabeth; *b* 1986

2a Katharine Georgina Constance; *b* 2 Nov 1881; *m* 1920 Leslie Brocklebank

3a Norma Cleely Gray; *b* 1887; *m* 1916 Harry Clement Davidson, of Ascot, Brisbane, and had issue. He *d* 1943

4a Mora Margaret Machintyre

5a Beatrice Louisa; *m* 1919 Raymond Nelson Vaughan Ralfe, of Cromer, Yeppoon, Queensland, son of Henry Ralfe

(4) Hervey Lepell; *b* 6 May 1854; *d* unm 21 April 1887

(1) Laura Elizabeth; *m* 2 June 1868 John Vivian Hampton, 2nd s of John Lewis Hampton Lewis, of Henllys and Bodior, Anglesey, and *d* 12 Oct 1934, leaving issue. He *d* 18 Aug 1890

(2) Katherine Louisa; *m* 9 Dec 1868 3rd Earl of Ellesmere and *d* 23 Sept 1926, leaving issue (see SUTHERLAND, D)

(3) Constance Mary; *d* unm 31 Oct 1883

The 1st MARQUESS *d* 3 April 1890; his est son,

CONSTANTINE CHARLES HENRY PHIPPS, **3rd Marquess of Normanby**, JP, DL Yorks; *b* 29 Aug 1846; Vicar Worsley Lancs 1872–90, Canon St George's Chapel Windsor 1891–1907, Hon MA Durham, Lt-Col N R Vol Regt; *m* 30 Dec 1903 Gertrude Stansfeld, OBE (1920), DGStJ (*d* 12 March 1948), yst dau and coheir of Johnston Jonas Foster, of Moor Park, Ludlow, Salop, and had:

1 OSWALD CONSTANTINE JOHN, **4th Marquess**

1 Katharine Mary; *b* 7 Jan 1905; *m* 26 Aug 1949 Roy Amon Harding (*d* 14 April 1960)

2 (Gertrude) Elizabeth; *b* 30 April 1908; *m* 28 April 1934 Adml Sir William Wellclose Davis, GCB, DSO and bar, DL, er s of Walter Stewart Davis, JP, of Coglan House, Longhope, and had issue

The 3rd MARQUESS *d* 25 Aug 1932; his only son,

OSWALD CONSTANTINE JOHN PHIPPS, **4th Marquess of Normanby**, KG, CBE (MBE 1943), JP, DL (N R Yorks 1960); *b* 29 July 1912; *educ* Eton and Ch Ch Oxford; Lt Green Howards WW II (wounded, POW), PPS to Sec State Dominions 1944–45 and Ld Pres Cncl 1945, Ld-in-Waiting May-July 1945, Chm King's Coll Hosp 1948–94 and Nat Library for the Blind, Ld Lt N R Yorks 1965–74 and Lt N Yorks 1974–94 , Hon DCL Durham, Hon Col Green Howards TA&R, Pres Whitby & Dist Beekeepers Assoc, KStJ; *m* 10 Feb 1951 *Hon Grania Maeve Rosaura Guinness [The Most Hon The Dowager Marchioness of Normanby, Argyll House, 211 King's Rd, London SW3 5EH; Lythe Hall, Whitby, N Yorks], OStJ (1975), Hon LLD Trin Coll Dublin (1953), only dau of 1st Baron Moyne (*qv*), and *d* 1994, leaving:

1 CONSTANTINE EDMUND WALTER PHIPPS, **5th and present Marquess of Normanby**

2 +Justin Charles [The Lord Justin Phipps, Cowbridges, Dean, Oxon OX7 3LB]; *b* 1 March 1958; *m* 1985 *Rachel, dau of Charles Stainsby, of Chadlington, Oxon, and has:

    (1) +William David; *b* 5 Feb 1990

    (1) *Elsie Clare; *b* 16 May 1986

    (2) *Anna Matilda; *b* 21 Jan 1988

    (3) *Katherine Maria; *b* 7 Nov 1991

    (4) *Martha Elizabeth; *b* 9 Sept 1996

1 *Lepel Sophia [The Lady Lepel Kornicka, 15 King's Ave, London W5 2SJ]; *b* 12 May 1952; *educ* Wycome Abbey and Oxford; *m* 1975 *Richard Kornicki, yr s of F Kornicki, of Headley Down, Hants, and has:

(1) *Edmund Barnabus; *b* 27 May 1976

(2) *Dunstan Benedick; *b* 8 Dec 1977

(1) *Aniela Eurydice Pelagia; *b* 18 Dec 1979

2 *Evelyn Rose [The Lady Evelyn Buchan, 37 Gloucester Crescent, London NW1 7DL]; *b* 18 Nov 1955; *m* 1986 *Hon James Ernest Buchan, yst s of 3rd Baron Tweedsmuir (*qv*), and has issue

3 *Peronel Katharine [The Lady Peronel Cruz, Claymoor Farm, Kettleness, Whitby, N Yorks YO21 2RY]; *b* 8 Oct 1959; *m* 1990 *Kleber Cruz Jaramillo, s of José Domingo Cruz Sarango, of Ecuador, and has:

(1) *Lucas Oswald; *b* 23 March 1994

(1) *Mariel Katherine; *b* 13 April 1996

4 *Henrietta Laura; *b* 29 Nov 1962; *m* 1982 Adam Charles Sedgwick (*d* 1985), est s of John Humphrey Gerrie Sedgwick, of Fulham

5 *(Anne Elizabeth) Grania; *b* 14 Oct 1965

Seat: Mulgrave Castle, Whitby, N Yorks. A relatively simple house built *c* 1720 by the **1st Baron Mulgrave of New Ross**'s grandmother the Duchess of Buckingham was greatly altered in the 1780s to designs by Sir John Soane, who added two wings. The present Library, Drawing Room and old Dining Room are his work. The house was crenellated in 1802 and further altered and added to by Atkinson.

NORMANTON

Arms: Az. a lion rampant or. **Crest:** A demi-lion rampant or. **Supporters:** Two lions, the dexter per bend and the sinister per bend-sinister or and az., both plain collared and chained gu. and charged on the shoulder with a crescent. **Motto:** *Via trita, via tuta* ('The well-worn path is the safe path'). **Creations:** B. (GB) 1794 (Mendip), (I) 12 June 1795 and (UK) 9 April 1873 (Somerton of Somerley); V (I) 29 Dec 1800; E. (I) 4 Feb 1806.

THE 6TH EARL OF NORMANTON, of Co Kilkenny, **Viscount Somerton**, **Baron Somerton of Somerton**, Co Kilkenny, **Baron Mendip of Mendip**, Co Somerset, and **Baron Somerton of Somerley**, Hants (Shaun James Christian Welbore Ellis Agar) [The Rt Hon The Earl of Normanton, Somerley, Ringwood, Hants BH24 3PL]; *b* 21 Aug 1945; s f 1967 in all titles bar Barony of Mendip, in which last s cousin 1974; *educ* Eton; Lt RARO, late Blues and Royals, formerly RHG; *m* 29 April 1970 *Victoria Susan, dau of John H C Beard, and has:

1 +JAMES SHAUN CHRISTIAN WELBORE ELLIS, *Viscount Somerton; b* 7 Sept 1982

1 *Portia Caroline; *b* 26 Dec 1976

2 *Marisa Charlotte; *b* 1979

Lineage: CHARLES AGAR, of Yorks; *m* Ellis, dau of Peter Blancheville, of Co Kilkenny, and *d* 14 Feb 1696 at Gowran, Co Kilkenny, where he had settled, leaving:

JAMES AGAR, of Gowran Castle; *m* 1st 10 Jan 1692 Susannah, dau of James Alexander, and had issue (*d* young); *m* 2nd Mary (*d* 1771 aged 106), est dau of Sir Henry Wemyss, of Danesfort, Co Kilkenny, and had:

1 HENRY

2 James, of Ringwood, Hants; *b* 7 Sept 1713; *m* 6 July 1741 Rebecca Flower (*d* 3 March 1789), only dau of 1st and Baron Castle Durrow (see ASHBROOK, V), and was k by one Henry Flood in a duel 3 Aug 1769, leaving:

    (1) GEORGE AGAR, 1st and last BARON CALLAN, of Callan, Co Kilkenny (I), so *cr* 4 June 179, PC (I 1789); *b* 4 Dec 1751; MP (I Parl) Callan 1777–90, rep l peer 1801–15; *dsp* 29 Oct 1815

    (2) Charles; *b* 28 May 1755; Archdeacon Emly; *dsp* 5 May 1789

    (1) Mary; *m* 30 Aug 1760 Philip Savage

1 ELLIS Agar, COUNTESS OF BRANDON (LP I), so *cr* 15 Sept 1758; *b c* 1708; *m* 1st March 1726, as his 2nd w, Theobald Bourke, 7th Viscount Mayo of the 1627 *cr* (*dsps* 7 Jan 1741/2); *m* 2nd 17 Aug 1745, as his 2nd w, Francis Bermingham, 14th Baron Athenry (*d* 4 March 1749/50), and *dsp* 11 March 1789, when the life Earldom of Brandon expired

2 Mary; *m* 1742 James Smyth, of Tinny Park, Co Wicklow, MP (I Parl) Antrim 1743–68, yr s of Edward Smyth, DD, Bp Down and Connor, by his 2nd w Mary (5th dau of 2nd Viscount Massereene; see MASSEREENE and FERRARD, V), and had:

(1) Sir EDWARD SKEFFINGTON SMYTH, 1st and last Bt (I), so *cr* 5 Aug 1776, PC (I 1785); *b* May 1745; MP (I) Mullingar 1776–83, Belturbet 1783–90 and Galway 1790–97; *m* 23 Nov 1782 Margaret, only dau of Hyacinth Daly, of Dalystwon, Co Galway and *dspm* 9 Sept 1797, leaving:

    1a Rosetta; *m* March 1811 Michael George Prendergast

    2a Maria; *m* 5 March 1808 James Daly, 1st Baron Dunsandle and Clanconal (*see* 1911 edn), and *d* 2 Nov 1866, leaving issue

JAMES AGAR's er s,

    HENRY AGAR, of Gowran Castle; MP (I Parl) Gowran 1727; *m* 29 May 1733 Anne, dau of Rt Rev Welbore Ellis, Bp Meath, and sis of Welbore Ellis, PC (*b* 15 Dec 1713; *educ* Westminster and Ch Ch Oxford; MP Cricklade 1741–47, Weymouth 1747–61 and 1774–90, Aylesbury 1761–68 and Petersfield 1768–74 and 1791–94, a Ld Admlty 1747–55, Jt V-Treas Ireland 1756–62, 1765–66 and 1770–77, Sec at War 1762–65, Treas Navy 1777–82, Sec State America and Colonies Feb-March 1782; *m* 1st 18 Nov 1747 Elizabeth, dau of Hon Sir William Stanhope (*see* 1967 edn CHESTERFIELD and STANHOPE, E); *m* 2nd 20 July 1765 Anne, dau of George Stanley; *dsp* 2 Feb 1802, having been *cr* 13 Aug 1794 **Baron Mendip of Mendip**, Co Somerset (GB), with special remainder, failing heirs male of his body, to his sis Anne's three er sons or their heirs male, but not to the yst), and *d* 18 Nov 1746, having had:

1 JAMES AGAR, 1st VISCOUNT CLIFDEN (*see* 1970 edn)

2 Welbore; *b* 1735; Commr Customs; *m* 21 Oct 1762 Gertrude, dau of Sir Charles Hotham, 4th Bt (*see* HOTHAM, B)

3 CHARLES, **1st Earl**

4 Henry (Rev); Rector Inniscarra, Co Cork; *m* Mary, dau of Benjamin Tyrrel, and *d* 14 May 1798, leaving, with other issue:

    (1) Charles Welbore (Rev); *d* 1810, leaving issue

    (2) Henry; *m* and had issue

HENRY AGAR's 3rd s,

    CHARLES AGAR, **1st Earl of Normanton**, Co Kilkenny, so *cr* 4 Feb 1806, as also earlier 12 June 1795 BARON SOMERTON OF SOMERTON, Co Kilkenny, and 29 Dec 1800 VISCOUNT SOMERTON (all I); *b* 22 Dec 1736; *educ* Westminster and Ch Ch Oxford; Chaplain to Ld Lt Ireland 1763, Dean Kilmore, Bp Cloyne 1768, Archbp Dublin 1801; *m* 22 Nov 1776 Jane (*d* 25 Oct 1826), est dau of William Benson, of Downpatrick, Co Down, and had:

1 WELBORE ELLIS, **2nd Earl**

2 George Charles; FRS; *b* 1 Aug 1780; *d* unm 24 Jan 1856

3 James, Archdeacon Kilmore (Rev); Rector Carrigallen; *b* 10 July 1781; *m* 7 July 1829 Louisa (*d* 15 March 1885), yst dau of Samuel Thompson, of Greenmount, Co Antrim, and *d* 6 Sept 1866

1 Frances Anne; *m* 14 Dec 1798 2nd Viscount Hawarden (*qv*) and *dsp* 23 May 1839

The 1st EARL *d* 14 July 1809; his est s,

    WELBORE ELLIS AGAR, **2nd Earl of Normanton**; *b* 12 Nov 1778; *m* 17 May 1816 Diana (*d* 2 Dec 1841), dau of 11th Earl of Pembroke and (8th of) Montgomery (*qv*), and had:

1 JAMES CHARLES HERBERT WELBORE ELLIS, **3rd Earl**

2 Herbert Welbore Ellis; *b* 19 Sept 1823; *m* 10 Aug 1871 Helen Millicent (*d* 8 April 1932), er surv dau of James A Gibson, JP, MLA Tasmania, and *d* 9 Aug 1901, leaving:

    (1) Charles Herbert; *b* 25 Sept 1872; *educ* Charterhouse and Trin Coll Cambridge (BA 1897, MA 1900); *d* unm 7 Aug 1959

    (1) Constance Diana; *b* 14 Feb 1874; *m* 6 Nov 1913 Henry Cecil Sutton, s of Sir Richard Sutton, 4th Bt (*qv*), and *d* 14 March 1960, leaving issue. He *d* 24 May 1936

    (2) Laura Mary O'Neill; *b* 13 Sept 1875; *d* unm 23 Jan 1968

3 Charles Welbore Herbert; Capt 44th Foot; *b* 12 Nov 1824; *k* before Sebastopol 18 June 1855

1 Mary Jane Diana; *m* 28 July 1845 3rd Earl Nelson (*qv*) and *d* 8 May 1904, having had issue

The 2nd EARL *d* 26 Aug 1868; his er s,

    JAMES CHARLES HERBERT WELBORE ELLIS AGAR, **3rd Earl of Normanton**, DL Wilts and Hants ; *b* 17 Sept 1818; *educ* Westminster and Trin Coll Cambridge; *cr* 9 April 1873 BARON SOMERTON OF SOMERLEY, Co Southampton (UK); *m* 9 April 1856 Caroline Susan Augusta (*d* 13 Jan 1915), dau of 6th Viscount Barrington of Ardglass (*qv*), and had:

1 Charles George Welbore Ellis, *Viscount Somerton*; *b* 27 April 1858; Lt 7th Hus; *d* unm 17 Jan 1894

2 SIDNEY JAMES, **4th Earl**

3 Henry Augustus Bernard; *b* 21 Nov 1870; *d* 25 April 1885

4 Francis William Arthur; *b* 19 Oct 1873; Lt Sussex Yeo and 4th Bn Bedfordshire Regt; *m* 26 Oct 1897 Laura Astley (*d* 8 May 1960), dau of Henry Steinmetz Kennard (*see* KENNARD, Bt), and *d* 18 Aug 1936, leaving:

    (1) John Herbert; *b* 8 Nov 1907; Capt KOSB WW II; *d* of wounds recd in action on NW Frontier India 29 July 1942

    (1) Muriel Violet Frances; *b* 29 Dec 1899; *m* 30 March 1921 R-Adml William Scott Chalmers, CBE, DSC, s of Quintin Chalmers, JP, of Bloomsbury, and had issue

1 Caroline Elizabeth; *m* 6 Sept 1876 5th Earl of Clarendon (*qv*) and *d* 9 May 1894, leaving issue

2 Mary Beatrice; *b* 10 Aug 1859; *d* unm 20 Dec 1943

3 Margaret Elizabeth Diana; *b* 10 Dec 1863; *m* 23 July 1884 Hon Ivan Campbell, 2nd s of 6th Earl of Breadalbane and Holland (*qv*), and *d* 29 March 1941, having had issue

4 Mary Adelaide; *b* 18 Aug 1869; *m* 14 July 1894 Henry St George Foley and *d* 7 June 1921, having had issue (*see* FOLEY, B)

The 3rd EARL *d* 19 Dec 1896; his son,

    SIDNEY JAMES AGAR, **4th Earl of Normanton**, DL Hants; *b* 9 April 1865; *educ* Eton; *m* 3 Nov 1894 Lady Amy Frederica Alice Byng (*d* 29 March 1961), dau of 4th Earl of Strafford (*qv*), and had:

1 EDWARD JOHN SIDNEY CHRISTIAN WELBORE ELLIS, **5th Earl**

1 Georgina Mary Elizabeth; *b* 1 May 1896; *d* unm 27 Jan 1967

2 Alexandra Henrietta Alice; *b* 23 April 1897 (HM QUEEN ALEXANDRA stood sponsor); *m* 12 April 1917 (*divorce* 1951) Peter Haig Thomas, s of John Howard Thomas, of Yscyborwen, Glam, and *d* 5 Jan 1975, leaving:

    (1) *Reginald Alexander [Reginald Haig Thomas Esq, 91 Valley Rd, Ipswich, Suffolk]; *b* 15 Aug 1919; *educ* Nautical Coll Pangbourne; Offr Oxon and Bucks LI 1937, joined Overseas Prison service in Kenya, mentioned in despatches during Mau Mau Rising 1956; *m* 19 Nov 1942 *Mona, dau of David Meiklejohn Doull, of Ulbster Mains, Ulbster, Caithness, and has:

        1a *Peter Alexander; *b* 30 June 1944; *educ* Gordonstoun

        1a *Elspeth Henrietta; *b* 21 April 1949; *m* 1976 *Col John Richard Bayley, Life Gds, of Halfway House, Suffolk, and has:

            1b *Richard; *b* 19 Jan 1982; *educ* The King's Sch, Canterbury

            1b *Sara; *b* 10 Nov 1978; *educ* Queen Anne's Caversham and Guildhall Sch of Music

    (2) Douglas James Christian; *b* 20 Dec 1920; Maj 3rd QAO Gurkha Rifles; *m* 1st 1944 (*divorce* 1954) Pepita Mary Kathleen Merrill and has:

        1a *David Christian Charles; *b* 9 March 1945

        2a *Hugo Alistair Christian; *b* 22 May 1947; FCO

    (2) (cont.) Maj Douglas Haig Thomas *m* 2nd 1960 (*divorce* 1965) Petronelle Maconochie and *d* 16 Jan 1996, leaving by her:

        3a *William James Christian; *b* 10 Oct 1961

        4a *Rupert Neil Dunbar; *b* 17 June 1964; *m* 19– *Breanda Moodie and has:

            1b *William; *b* 16 Oct 1996

    (2) (cont.) Maj Douglas Haig Thomas *m* 3rd 1966 *Rose Ann Macdonald and by her has:

        1a *Judith Morag Sophie; *b* 17 Oct 1966

    (1) *Angela Mary; *b* 1918; *m* 1st 27 April 1938 Capt 7th Count Richard Dudley Melchior Gurowski, Scots Gds (*kas* Dunkirk 2 June 1940), of Woolhampton Park, Berks, and has a s; *m* 2nd 9 June 1948 (*divorce* 1951) Richard Miles Backhouse (*see* BACKHOUSE, Bt); *m* 3rd 25 Jan 1952 *Maj Hugh Washington Hibbert, Queen's Bays, only s of Washington Charles Thomas Hibbert, of Pitt Manor, Winchester

    (2) *(Jean) Henrietta Rose [Mrs Hugh Haig, Broomy Hall, Dalton, Newcastle-upon-Tyne]; *b* 20 Dec 1920; *m* 12 Feb 1940 Sir Peter McClintock Greenwell, 3rd Bt (*qv*), and has issue; *m* 2nd 1985 *Hugh Kenneth Haig

    (3) *Ruth; *b* 1924; *m* 30 April 1948 (*divorce* 1970) Maj Richard Wellesley, MC, DL (*see* WELLINGTON, D), and has issue

    (4) Alice Alexandra; *b* 1927; *m* 17 Sept 1958 *(Geoffrey) Mark Victor Winn (*see* SAINT OSWALD, B) and *d* 1991, leaving issue

    (5) *Nina Isobel Amy [Mrs Robert Treherne, Hersons Folly, Mayfield, Sussex]; *b* 1930; *m* 21 Aug 1951 *Robert Philip Dalrymple Treherne, late Capt Gren Gds, 3rd s of Edmund Henry Apsley Treherne, JP, Lt Roy Scots, and has issue

3 Caroline Amy Cora; *b* 11 July 1899

4 (Mary) Karen; *b* 14 Nov 1901; *m* 9 Dec 1925 (*divorce* 1945) Lt-Cdr Herbert Ernest Pretyman, RN, 2nd s of Ernest George Pretyman, PC, DL, JP, and *d* 28 Oct 1975, leaving issue

5 Diana Julia; *b* 13 June 1904; *d* unm 18 March 1929

6 Amy Louise; *b* 4 Oct 1905; *m* 21 Oct 1925 3rd Baron Biddulph (*qv*) and *d* 1983, leaving issue

7 Rosemary Beatrice; *b* 3 June 1908; *m* 23 April 1931 Capt Christopher John Darell Jeffreys, MVO, Gren Gds, only s of 1st Baron Jeffreys (*qv*), and *d* 1984, leaving issue

The 4th EARL *d* 25 Nov 1933; his only son,

    EDWARD JOHN SIDNEY CHRISTIAN WELBORE ELLIS AGAR, **5th Earl of Normanton**; *b* 29 March 1910 (HM EDWARD VII stood sponsor); *educ* Eton and Trin Coll Cambridge (BA); Capt RHG WW II; *m* 1st 5 July 1937 (*divorce* 1943) Hon Barbara Mary, formerly w of Brig Otho Leslie Prior-Palmer, DSO, MP, and only dau of Baroness Zouche (*qv*); *m* 2nd 30 Oct 1944 Lady Fiona (*d* 1985), formerly w of Maj Sir (John) Gerard Henry Fleetwood Fuller, 2nd Bt (*qv*), and yr dau of 4th Marquess Camden (*qv*), and *d* 28 Jan 1967, leaving:

1 SHAUN JAMES CHRISTIAN WELBORE ELLIS AGAR, **6th and present Earl of Normanton**

2 +Mark Sidney Andrew [The Hon Mark Agar, Inholmes, Woodlands St Mary, Berks RG17 7SY]; *b* 2 Sept 1948; *educ* Gordonstoun; Lt Blues & Royals; *m* 1st 1973 (*divorce* 1979) Rosemary, dau of Maj Philip Marnham; *m* 2nd 1985 *Arabella Clare, dau of John Gilbert Gilbey (*see* 1970 edn BARWICK, Bt) and formerly w of Thomas Charles Blackwell, and by her has:

    (1) +Max John Andrew; *b* 1986

    (2) +Charles Christopher Edward; *b* 1989

NORRIE

Arms: Quarterly, 1st and 4th, erm. on a pale gu. three helmets arg. (for NORRIE); 2nd and 3rd, or on a chevron az. between two poplar trees eradicated in chief ppr. and a mullet of six points in base of the second a key, the wards downwards, of the first (for MOKE). **Crests:** 1 An elephant's head erased sa., tusked arg., supporting with the trunk a garb or (for NORRIE), 2 A stag's head couped, holding in the mouth a branch of poplar ppr., between the attires a key as in the arms pendent from a chain or. **Supporters:** On either side a dark bay racehorse supporting between the forelegs a frond of New Zealand fern ppr. **Motto:** *Deus nobis providet* ('God provides for us'). **Creation:** B. (UK) 22 Aug 1957.

THE 2ND BARON NORRIE, of Wellington, NZ, and Upton, Co Gloucester (George Willoughby Moke Norrie) [The Rt Hon The Lord Norrie, House of Lords, London SW1A 0PW]; *b* 27 April 1936; *s f* 1977; *educ* Eton and RMA Sandhurst; Maj Roy Hus (ret), ADC to C-in-C Middle East Cmd 1960–61, GSO(3) Intell HQ 4th Gds Bde 1967–69, dir Fairfield Nurseries (Hermitage) Ltd, Internat Garden Centre (UK) 1984–86, Hilliers (Fairfield) Ltd 1989, pres Br Tst for Conservation Vol(s) 1987–, dir Conservation Practice Ltd 1988–92, memb Ho Lds EC Sub Ctee F (Environment) 1988, V-Pres Cncl for Nat Parks 1990–, Tree Cncl 1990–, pres Roy Br Legn Newbury; *m* 1st 10 April 1964 Celia Marguerite, JP (Berks), only dau of Maj John Pelham Mann, MC (*see* MANN, Bt), and has:

1 +MARK WILLOUGHBY JOHN; *b* 31 March 1972; *m* 18 April 1998 *Carol, est dau of Michael Stockdale, of Wetherby, Yorks

1 *Clare Marguerite; *b* 6 May 1966; *m* 6 May 1995 *Richard Stanton and has:

  (1) *Max George John; *b* 1995

2 *Julia Jocelyn; *b* 19 Feb 1968; *m* 12 Sept 1998 *Oliver Skelding, only s of Simon Skelding, of Fulham

The 2nd BARON *m* 2nd 29 May 1997 *Mrs Annie McCaffry (*see* WILMOT, Bt)

Lineage: JAN MOKE; *b* 1498; *m* 1534 Catherine du Voors and *d* 1572, leaving, with other issue:

JAN MOKE, of Thorout, Flanders; *b* 1544; *m* 1575 Ryc Cortyls and *d* 1598, leaving, with other issue:

JAN MOKE, of Wynendale Castle, Thorout; *b* 1588; *m* 1631 Maria Frances Stevens and *d* 8 Feb 1655, leaving, with other issue:

PETER MOKE, of Wynendale Castle; *b* 2 July 1633; *m* 1667 Isabella Eynsaem and *d* 12 Dec 1694, leaving, with other issue:

PETER AMMANUEL MOKE, of Wynendale Castle; *b* April 1671; *m* 1711 Mary Georgina de Broucker and *d* 1734, leaving, with other issue:

JAMES WILLIAM MOKE, of Wynendale Castle, *b* 13 March 1733, *m* 21 May 1765 Marie Anne Mieuls and *d* 22 April 1807, leaving, with other issue:

CHARLES ALEXANDER MOKE; Prof Leyden U (MD), pioneered coffee industry Brazil; *b* 18 Sept 1778; *m* 19 Aug 1808 Martha, dau of Nicholas Masterston, of Cheshire, and *d* 29 Oct 1831, leaving, with other issue:

GEORGE LOUIS AUGUSTUS MOKE, of Prince's Gate, Westminster, and 253 5th Ave, New York; *b* 23 April 1814; *m* 8 Nov 1854 Margaret (*d* Feb 1905), dau of Adam Norrie, of New York, and *d* 17 Jan 1875, leaving:

1 GEORGE EDWARD

1 Harriet; *b* 5 Sept 1859; *d* unm 1942

2 Julia Norrie; *b* 8 April 1864; *m* 19 July 1883 Sir John Rahere Paget, 2nd Bt, of Harewood Place (*qv*), and *d* 31 Oct 1926, having had issue

3 Edith Mary; *b* 1 April 1866; *d* unm 1929

4 Emily Norrie; *b* 9 Jan 1868; *m* 25 July 1887 Maj Robert Francis Ladeveze Napier, QO Cameron Highrs, 2nd s of Sir Robert John Milliken Napier, 9th Bt, of Merchistoun (*qv*), and *d* 17 April 1961, having had issue

5 Helen Gordon Norrie; *b* 6 Aug 1870; *m* June 1889 Charles William Butler, JP, s of Charles Edward Kingstone Butler, DL, and *d* 28 June 1963, having had issue

The only son,

GEORGE EDWARD MOKE later MOKE NORRIE (roy licence 9 June 1893), JP; *b* 1 March 1858; *educ* Haileybury and BNC Oxford (MA); Maj 3rd Bn Duke of

Wellington's W R Regt Boer War, big-game hunter; *m* 6 March 1892 Beatrice, CBE (1921); (*d* 8 July 1933), dau of Andrew Stephen, of S Kensington, and *d* 11 March 1920, having had:

1 (CHARLES) WILLOUGHBY, **1st Baron**

2 George Stuart; Lt Buffs WW I; *b* 13 Nov 1897; *ka* 7 Oct 1916

1 Dorothy Beatrice; *b* 12 Aug 1895; *m* 18 April 1922 Col Percy Macaulay Ashworth Kerans, MC, Carabiniers (*d* 1938), and *d* 8 Sept 1939, leaving a s (*ka* 2 June 1942) and dau

The er son,

Sir (CHARLES) WILLOUGHBY (MOKE) NORRIE, **1st Baron Norrie**, of Wellington, New Zealand, and Upton, Co Gloucester (UK), so *cr* 22 Aug 1957, GCMG (1952, KCMG 1944), GCVO (1954), CB (1942), DSO (1919), MC (1915) and bar (1916); *b* 26 Sept 1893; *educ* Eton and RMC Sandhurst; 11th Hus PAO WW I (wounded four times, despatches twice), Staff Capt 73rd Inf Bde, GSO(3) XVIII Army Corps, Bde Maj 90th Inf Bde, Maj 2nd Tank Bde, GSO(2) Tank Corps, HQ Maj 1924, Bde Maj 1st Cav Bde 1926–30, cmdg 10th Royal Hus 1931–35, Col 1935, 1st Cav Bde 1936–38, 1st Armoured Bde 1939, WW II: GOC 1st Armoured Div 1940, cmdg 30th Corps (ME) (Lt-Gen) 1941–42, GOC RAC 1943, Govr S Australia 1944–52, Col 10th Roy Hus 1947–50, Col 10th Bn (Adelaide Rifles) 1950–77, memb Nat Hunt Ctee 1937–77, Jockey Club (UK), Govr-Gen and C-in-C NZ 1952–57, Pres Combined Cav Old Comrades Assoc 1958–69, Chllr Order St Michael and St George 1960–68, Chm Big Brother Movement 1961–77, KstJ, FRSA; *m* 1st 9 June 1922 Jocelyn Helen (*d* 7 March 1938), dau of Richard Henry Gosling, of Hawthorn Hill, Bracknell, Berks, by Kathleen Maria, yr dau of Sir Swinnerton Halliday Dyer, 10th Bt (*qv*), and had:

1 GEORGE WILLOUGHBY MOKE NORRIE, **2nd and present Baron Norrie**

1 Diana; *b* 7 May 1923; *d* 6 Dec 1932

2 *Rosemary; *b* 28 March 1926; *m* 20 Oct 1959 *3rd Viscount Daventry (*qv*) and has issue

The **1st Baron Norrie** *m* 2nd 28 Nov 1938 *Patricia Merryweather [The Rt Hon Patricia Lady Norrie, The Old Vicarage, Leckhampstead, Newbury, Berks], DStJ, dau of Emerson Muschamp Bainbridge, MP, of Auchnashellach, Ross-shire, by Norah Mossom, and *d* 25 May 1977, leaving by her:

2 +Guy Bainbridge [Lt-Col The Hon Guy Norrie, Old Church Farm, Broughton, nr Stockbridge, Hants SO20 8AA]; *b* 3 May 1940; *educ* Eton; Lt-Col Roy Hus (PWO), HQ 1st (Br) Corps 1966–67, Adj 10th Hus 1967–69, GSO(3) HQ Far East Cmd 1969, GSO(2) MOD (Army Trg) 1973–74, GSO(1) (DS) Staff Coll Camberley 1977–78, memb Gentlemen at Arms 1990; *m* 10 Feb 1968 *Sarah Georgina, only dau of Maj George Rudolph Hanbury Feilding, DSO (*see* DENBIGH and DESMOND, E), and has:

  (1) +Andrew Guy; *b* 1970

  (2) +James Adam George; *b* 1973

3 *Sarah Merryweather [The Hon Mrs Stephenson, The Cottage, Great Longstone, Bakewell, Derbys]; *b* 27 June 1943; *m* Sept 1974 *Charles Lyon Stephenson, TD (*see* STEPHENSON, Bt), and has issue

4 *Annabel Mary Adelaide [The Hon Mrs Malcolm, 19 Lilyville Rd, London SW6 5DP]; *b* 23 Dec 1945; *m* 1988 *Ian Ronald Malcolm, er s of Colin Ronald Malcolm, of Newent, Glos

NORTH, Bt

Arms: Quarterly, 1st and 4th, az. a lion passant or between three fleurs-de-lys arg. (for NORTH); 2nd and 3rd, arg. semée of lozenges vert a bordure gu. (for HICKING). **Crest:** A dragon's head erased sa., ducally gorged and chained or. **Motto:** *Animo et fide* ('With spirit and fidelity'). **Creation:** Bt. (UK) 1 March 1920.

SIR (WILLIAM) JONATHAN FREDERICK NORTH, 2ND BT, of Southwell and Brackenhurst, Co Nottingham [Sir Jonathan North Bt, Frogmore, Weston-under-Penyard, Herefs HR9 5TQ]; *b* 6 Feb 1931; *s gf* 1947; *educ* Marlborough; *m* 19 Oct 1956 *Sara Virginia, only dau of Air Ch Marshal Sir (James) Donald Innes Hardman, GBE, KCB, DFC, RAF, of Lower Baybridge Ho, Owslebury, Hants, and has:

1 +JEREMY WILLIAM FRANCIS; *b* 5 May 1960; *educ* Marlborough; *m* 1986 *Lucy A, dau of G A van der Meulen, of Tunbridge Wells, Kent, and has:

  (1) +Jocelyn Montagu Dudley; *b* 23 March 1989

(2) +Francis Augustus Roderick; *b* 1990

(1) *Polly Antonia; *b* 1992

(2) *Lydia Calypso; *b* 22 Nov 1995

1 *Charlotte Amelia; *b* 19 March 1958; *m* 1989 *Matthew Dufton Tester, yst s of Maurice Tester, of Long Barn House, Cowfold, Sussex

2 *Harriet Cordelia Henrietta; *b* 21 July 1963; *m* 1984 *(Seymour) Thomas Thistlethwayte, s of Seymour Thistlethwayte, of Sheet Mill House, Petersfield, Hants, and has:

(1) *Oliver Seymour; *b* 1990

(2) *Edmund Thomas; *b* 4 March 1996

(1) *Daisy Alexandra; *b* 1988

(2) *Cecily Alice; *b* 1992

Lineage: GEORGE HICKING, of Nottingham, *m* Sarah Norton Hustwayte and *d* 11 March 1902, leaving a yst s:

Sir William Norton Hicking, 1st Bt (UK), so *cr* 5 July 1917 with the usual remainder to heirs male of his body and 1 March 1920 with remainder, failing heirs male of his body, to the heirs male of his daughters successively, of Southwell and Brackenhurst, Notts, JP, DL; High Sheriff 1913–14; *b* 12 Dec 1864; *m* 10 July 1890 Mabel (*d* 29 Jan 1956), dau of William George Eking, of Beeston, Notts, and *d* 18 April 1947, when the Btcy of 1917 expired but that of 1920 passed to his gs, leaving:

1 Mabel Doris; *m* 1st 27 July 1912 (*divorce* 1935) Cdr Archibald Macdonald Willoughby, RN (*das* 8 Nov 1943; *see* MIDDLETON, B), and had issue; *m* 2nd 4 Sept 1935 (Algernon) Peter Warren, yr s of Edward Warren, of Breach House, Cholsey, Berks, and 21 Warwick Sq, London, and *d* 5 June 1956

2 Muriel Norton, *m* 30 April 1927 (*divorce* 1938) Hon John Montagu William North, 2nd s of 8th Earl of Guilford (*qv*), and *d* 1989, leaving:

(1) Sir WILLIAM JONATHAN FREDERICK NORTH, **2nd and present Bt**

(1) *Georgiana Mary [Mrs Esmond Butler, 149 Rideau Terr, Ottawa, Ontario, Canada]; *b* 4 April 1928; *m* 19 March 1960 Esmond Unwin Butler (*d* 1989) CM, CVO, s of Rev Thomas Bertram Butler, of Weston, Ontario, and has:

1a *Mark William; *b* 30 March 1961

1a *Clare Martine; *b* 19 Feb 1963

NORTHAMPTON

Arms: Sa. a lion passant-guardant or between three esquire's helmets arg. **Crest:** On a mount a beacon fired ppr., behind it a ribbon inscribed with the words *Nisi Dominus* ('If not God [nothing]'). **Supporters:** Dexter, a dragon erm., ducally gorged and chained or; sinister, a unicorn arg., horned, maned, hoofed and tufted sa. **Motto:** *Je ne cherche qu'un* ('I seek but one'). **Creations:** E. (E) 2 Aug 1618 (Northampton); B., E. and M. (UK) 7 Sept 1812.

THE 7TH MARQUESS OF THE COUNTY OF NORTHAMPTON, Earl of Northampton, Earl Compton of Compton, Co Warwick, and **Baron Wilmington**, of Wilmington, Co Sussex (Spencer (Spenny) Douglas David Compton, DL (Northants 1979)) [The Most Hon The Marquess of Northampton DL, Castle Ashby, Northampton; Compton Wynyates, Tysoe, Warwicks CV35 0UD]; *b* 2 April 1946; *s* f 1978; *educ* Eton; Assist Grand Master Utd Grand Lodge Freemasons 1995–; *m* 1st 13 June 1967 (*divorce* 1973) Henriette Luisa Maria, only dau of Baron Adolph Willem Carel Bentinck van Schoonheten (*see* PORTLAND, E), and has:

1 +DANIEL BINGHAM, *Earl Compton*; *b* 16 Jan 1973

1 *Lara Katrina; *b* 26 April 1968; *m* 1994 *Peter Falter, mktg exec

The 7TH MARQUESS *m* 2nd 1974 (*divorce* 1977) Annette Marie (*m* 2nd 1983 Hon Simon Howard; *see* CARLISLE, E), dau of Charles Anthony Russell Smallwood; *m* 3rd 1977 (*divorce* 1983) Rosemary Ashley Morritt, only dau of P G M Hancock, of Truro, and formerly w of Hon Lionel John Charles Seymour Dawson-Damer (*see* PORTARLINGTON, E), and by her has:

2 *Emily Rose; *b* 1980; *educ* Westonbirt

The 7th MARQUESS *m* 4th 1985 (*divorce* 1988) Ellen (Fritzi), only dau of Hermann Erhardt, of Munich, and formerly w of Hon Michael Orlando Weetman Pearson (*see* COWDRAY, V), and by her has:

3 *Louisa Cecilia; *b* 1985

The 7th MARQUESS *m* 5th 1990 *Mrs Pamela Martina Raphaela Kyprios, only dau of James Haworth, of Yorks, and formerly w of W A Emmanuel

Northampton, earldom and marquessate of: In the 11th and 12th centuries the Earldom of Northampton seems to have been held with that of Huntingdon (*qv*). Among those recognised as Earls of both counties at this time were Waltheof, son of the Siward who was Earl of Northumberland (*see* NORTHUMBERLAND, D) and DAVID I OF SCOTLAND (*see* again HUNTINGDON, E). Some hundred and fifty years elapsed after the death in 1184 without issue of the last holder of this quasi-dual Earldom of two adjoining East Midlands counties until a fresh creation under the title Northampton alone.

In 1337 EDWARD III conferred the Earldom of Northampton on his cousin and leading adviser William de Bohun, youngest son by a daughter of EDWARD I of Humphrey de Bohun, Earl of Hereford and Essex (*see* HEREFORD, V, and ESSEX, E). The new Earl was occupied in fighting the Scots in the north of England, of which he became Constable in 1338, and the French in the opening stages of the Hundred Years War. William's son Humphrey succeeded him but died without male issue in January 1372/3, when the Earldom expired. It was revived in 1384 for Humphrey's grandson Henry Bolingbroke, although this time it was coupled with that of Hereford. Henry, whose father John of Gaunt had married Earl Humphrey's daughter Mary, later usurped the throne and is better known as HENRY IV. On his succeeding his cousin RICHARD II the Earldom of Northampton merged in the Crown.

In the mid-16th century HENRY VIII's brother-in-law William Parr was created Marquess of Northampton. Being one of the chief members of the Protestant faction throughout EDWARD VI's reign and one of only four peers who did homage to LADY JANE GREY in 1553 he was attainted by MARY, when his titles were forfeited. He outlived that Queen, however, and was recreated Marquess of Northampton by ELIZABETH I in Jan 1558/9 with precedence of the earlier creation of February 1546/7. He died without issue in late 1571, when the title expired.

From 1604 to 1614 a younger brother of the Duke of Norfolk (*qv*) was Earl of Northampton, being so created by JAMES I. He was one of the Commissioners appointed to interrogate the Gunpowder Plot conspirators. He died unmarried and the Earldom expired with him.

Lineage: ROBERT de COMPTON; *d* 1440; had:

EDMUND de COMPTON; had:

Sir WILLIAM COMPTON; Ch Gentleman Bedchamber, Usher Black Rod, Keeper Privy Purse to HENRY VIII, fought Battle of Spurs 1513, Chllr Ireland, at Field of Cloth of Gold; *m* Werburge, widow of Sir Francis Cheyne and dau and heiress of Sir John Brereton by the sis and heiress of Sir William Berkeley, and *d* June 1528, leaving an only s:

PETER COMPTON; *m* Anne Talbot, dau of 4th Earl of Shrewsbury and Waterford (*qv*), and *d* 30 Jan 1538/9, leaving an only s:

HENRY COMPTON, 1st LORD (Baron) COMPTON (E), so *cr* by writ 8 May 1572, of Compton Wynyates, Warwicks; *b* 16 Feb 1537/8; MP Old Sarum 1536–37, ktd Feb 1566/7; *m* 1st Lady Frances Hastings, dau of 2nd Earl of Huntingdon (*qv*), and had:

1 WILLIAM, **1st Earl**

2 Thomas (Sir), KB; *m* after mid-Oct 1606, as her 3rd husb, Mary, *cr* 1 July 1618 Countess of Buckingham (LP) in her own right, dau of Anthony Beaumont, of Glenfield, Leics, and widow of (a) Sir George Villiers (*see* JERSEY, E) and (b) Sir William Rayner, and *d* April 1626

1 Margaret; *m* by 1 Oct 1593 4th Lord (Baron) Mordaunt (*see* MORDAUNT, Bt)

The 1st LORD (Baron) COMPTON *m* 2nd, as her 2nd of three husbs, Anne (*m* 3rd 2nd Earl of Dorset, *see* SACKVILLE, B), widow of William, 3rd Lord (Baron) Mo(u)nteagle, and dau of Sir John Spencer, of Althorp (*see* MARLBOROUGH, D), and by her had:

3 Henry (Sir), KB, of Brambletye, Sussex; *m* 1st Cecily, dau of 2nd Earl of Dorset (*see* SACKVILLE, B); *m* 2nd Mary, widow of Thomas Paston, of Thorpe, and dau of Sir George Browne, and had issue by both ws (*see* SCARBROUGH, E)

The 1st LORD (Baron) COMPTON *d* 1589; his est son,

WILLIAM COMPTON, **1st Earl of Northampton** (E), so *cr* 2 Aug 1618, KG (1628), KB (Jan 1604/5); *b c* 1568; Ld Lt: Warwicks 1603, N and S Wales, Worcs, Herefs and Salop 1617 and Glos 1622, Ld Pres Cncl of Wales 1617–30; *m* after 15 March 1599 Elizabeth, dau and heiress of Sir John Spencer, Ld Mayor London 1594–95, and had:

1 SPENCER, **2nd Earl**

1 Elizabeth

2 Anne; *m* 1st and last Marquess of Clanricarde of the Feb 1645/6 *cr* (*see* SLIGO, M) and *dsp*

The 1st EARL *d* 24 June 1630; his only son,

SPENCER COMPTON, **2nd Earl of Northampton**, KB (1616); *b* May 1601; MP Ludlow 1621–22, called up to Ho of Lds in his f's Barony of Compton *vp* 1626, Master Robes to CHARLES I 1625–30, Ld Lt Warwicks and Glos 1630, Col-Gen royalist forces Northants and Warwicks Civil War, cmdg at royalist victory of Hopton Heath, Staffs, 10 March 1642/3, but *k* there; *m* 1621 Mary, dau of Sir Francis Beaumont (bro of Countess of Buckingham mentioned above), and had:

1 JAMES, **3rd Earl**

2 Charles (Sir); accompanied his f at Battles of Edgehill 1642 and Hopton Heath; *d* Nov 1661, leaving:

(1) Anne; *m c* 1686, as his 3rd w, Sir Thomas Domvile, 1st Bt

3 William (Sir); royalist cdr; *d* 1663

4 Spencer (Sir); accompanied CHARLES II into exile; *d* Bruges unm 1659

5 Francis (Sir); Lt-Gen after Restoration; *d* 20 Dec 1716

6 Henry; Bp London 1675–1712, officiated at coronation of WILLIAM III and MARY since Sancroft, Archbp of Canterbury, had refused the oath of allegiance; *d* 7 July 1713 aged 80

1 Anne; *m* Sir Hugh Cholmley, 4th Bt, of Whitby

2 Penelope; *m* Sir John Nicholas, KB

The 2nd EARL's est son,

JAMES COMPTON, **3rd Earl of Northampton**, PC (March 1672/3); *b* 19 Aug 1622; *educ* Eton and Queens' Coll Cambridge; MP Warwicks 1640–43 (expelled as royalist 1643; imprisoned Tower of London 1659 at time of premature royalist rising), Ld Lt Warwicks 1660–81, FRS 1673, Constable Tower of London 1675–79, a Ld of Trade 1677; *m* 1st 5 July 1647 Lady Isabella Sackville (*d* 22 Aug 1719), dau and coheir of 3rd Earl of Dorset (*see* SACKVILLE, B, and DE CLIFFORD, B), and had one surv dau (Althea, *m* Edward Hungerford, *see* SAINT DAVIDS, V); *m* 2nd by 1664 Mary, dau and heiress of 3rd Viscount Campden (*see* GAINSBOROUGH, E), and by her had, with other issue:

1 GEORGE, **4th Earl**

2 SPENCER COMPTON, 1st and last EARL OF WILMINGTON, so *cr* 14 May 1730, as also VISCOUNT PEVENSEY and previously 8 Jan 1727/8 BARON WILMINGTON, Co Sussex (all GB), KG (1733), KB (1725), PC (1716); *b c* 1674; *educ* St Paul's, Middle Temple and Trin Coll Oxford; MP (Whig) Eye 1698–1710, E Grinstead 1713–15 and Sussex 1715–28, Chm Ctee Privileges 1705–10, Speaker H of C 1715–27, Paymaster Gen 1722–30, Ld Privy Seal May-Dec 1730, Ld Pres Cncl 1730–Jan 1741/2; *dspl* unm (an alleged dau *m* James Glen, Govr S Carolina) 14 July 1743, when his titles expired

1 Mary; *m* 7 March 1685 6th Earl of Dorset (*see* SACKVILLE, B) and *d* 6 Aug 1691, leaving issue

The 3rd EARL *d* 15 Dec 1681; his son,

GEORGE COMPTON, **4th Earl of Northampton**, PC (1702–07); *b* 18 Oct 1664; Ld Lt Warwicks, Constable Tower London; *m* 1st 1686 Jane (*d* 10 June 1721), yst dau of Sir Stephen Fox (*see* ILCHESTER, E), and had:

1 JAMES COMPTON, **5th Earl of Northampton**; *b* 2 May 1687; *educ* Eton; MP (Tory) Warwicks 1710–11, called up to Ho of Lds in f's Barony of Compton *vp* 28 Dec 1711; *m* 3 March 1715/6 Elizabeth, Baroness Ferrers in her own right (*d* 13 March 1740/1), gdau of 1st Earl Ferrers (*qv*), and *dspms* 3 Oct 1754, when the Barony of Compton passed to his only surv dau:

(1) CHARLOTTE Compton, BARONESS COMPTON in her own right, as which *s f*, and BARONESS FERRERS in her own right, as which *s* mother; *m* 19 Dec 1751, as his 1st w, George TOWNSHEND, 1st Marquess Townshend (*qv*) and *d* 3 Sept 1770

2 GEORGE COMPTON, **6th Earl of Northampton**; *b* 1692; *educ* Eton; MP (Tory) Tamworth Jan-July 1727 and Northampton 1727–54, a Ld of Treasury 1742–44; *m* 5 March 1748 Frances (*m* 2nd 26 Nov 1761 Claudius Amyand and *d* 25 Dec 1800), dau of Rev Thomas Payne, and *dsp* 6 Dec 1758

3 Charles; Envoy Portugal, MP Northampton; *m* 13 Aug 1727 Mary, only dau and heiress of Sir Berkeley Lucy, 3rd Bt (*see* RAMSAY-FAIRFAX-LUCY, Bt), and *d* 20 Nov 1755, leaving:

(1) CHARLES COMPTON, **7th Earl of Northampton**; *b* 22 July 1737; *educ* Westminster and Ch Ch Oxford; Amb Venice 1761–63; *m* 13 Sept 1759 Anne, dau of 4th Duke of Beaufort (*qv*), and *dspm* 18 Oct 1763, leaving:

1a Elizabeth; *b* 25 June 1760; *m* 27 Feb 1782 1st Earl of Burlington (*see* DEVONSHIRE, D)

(2) SPENCER, **8th Earl**

(1) Mary; *m* 1st Richard Haddock, RN; *m* 2nd Arthur Scott, RN

(2) Jane; *m* 2 Feb 1753 1st Baron Rodney (*qv*) and *d* Jan 1757, leaving issue

(3) CATHERINE Compton, BARONESS ARDEN of Lohort Castle, Co Cork (I), so *cr* 23 May 1770; *b* 4 June 1731; *m* 26 Jan 1756, as his 2nd w, John PERCEVAL, 2nd Earl of Egmont (*qv*), and *d* 17 June 1784, leaving issue

(4) Elizabeth; *m* 21 March 1761 Hon Henry Drummond (*see* PERTH, E) and *d* 25 March 1819, having had issue

1 Mary; *m* William Gore, of Tring Park, Herts

2 Anne; *m* Sir John Rushout, 4th Bt (*see* 1887 edn NORTHWICK, B)

The **4th Earl** *m* 2nd 3 July 1726 Elizabeth (*dsp* 15 Jan 1749/50), widow of Sir George Thorold, 1st Bt (*qv*), of the 9 Sept 1709 *cr* and dau of Sir James Rushout, 1st Bt, and *d* 15 April 1727

The 7th EARL's brother,

SPENCER COMPTON, **8th Earl of Northampton**; *b* 16 Aug 1738; *educ* Westminster; MP (Tory) Northampton 1761–63; *m* 1st 1758 Jane (*d* 26 Nov 1767), dau of Henry Lawton, and had a s and dau (Frances, *d* unm 1832); *m* 2nd 1769 Anne, dau of Culpeper Hougham, and *d* 7 April 1796; his s by his 1st w:

CHARLES COMPTON, **1st Marquess of the County of Northampton**, so *cr* 7 Sept 1812, as also BARON WILMINGTON, of Wilmington, Co Sussex, and EARL COMPTON OF COMPTON, Co Warwick (all UK); *b* 21 March 1760; *educ* Trin Coll Cambridge; MP (Tory) Northampton 1784–96, Ld Lt Northants 1796–1828, Pres Geological Soc 1820–22; *m* 18 Aug 1787 Maria (*d* 24 March 1843), est dau of Joshua Smith, MP, of Erlestoke Park, Wilts, and *d* 24 May 1828, leaving, with a dau (Frances Elizabeth, *m* 18 Feb 1829 Charles Scrase Dickins, of Coolhurst, and *d* 2 March 1883, leaving issue):

SPENCER JOSHUA ALWYNE COMPTON, **2nd Marquess of the County of Northampton**; *b* 2 Jan 1790; PRS; *m* 24 July 1815 Margaret (*d* 2 April 1830), est dau of Maj-Gen William Douglas-Maclean-Clephane, of Torloisk, Scotland, and *d* 17 Jan 1851, leaving:

1 CHARLES COMPTON later DOUGLAS-COMPTON (roy licence 5 Jan 1831), **3rd Marquess of the County of Northampton**; *b* 26 May 1816; *educ* Eton and Trin Coll Cambridge; *m* 5 July 1859 Theodosia Harriet Elizabeth (*dsp* 18 Nov 1864), dau of Capt and Lady Mary Vyner (dau of 1st Earl de Grey; *see* LUCAS OF CRUDWELL, B), and *dsp* 3 March 1877

2 WILLIAM, **4th Marquess**

3 Spencer Scott; Capt 15th Light Dragoons; *b* 6 March 1821; *d* 21 May 1855

4 Alwyne (Rt Rev); DD, MA Cantab, Bp Ely 1886–1905; *b* 18 July 1825; *m* 28 Aug 1850 Florence Caroline (*d* 24 March 1918), est dau of Rev Robert Anderson by Hon Caroline Dorothea, dau of 1st Baron Teignmouth (*see* 1970 edn), and *dsp* 4 April 1906

1 Marianne Margaret; *m* 10 Feb 1841 John, Viscount Alford, est s of 1st Earl Brownlow (*see* BROWNLOW, B), and *d* 8 Feb 1888 aged 71, having had issue

2 Margaret Mary Frances Elizabeth; *m* 1 June 1853 Hon Edward Frederick Leveson Gower and *d* 22 May 1858, having had issue (*see* GRANVILLE, E)

The 3rd MARQUESS's bro,

WILLIAM COMPTON, **4th Marquess of the County of Northampton**, KG (1885); *b* 20 Aug 1818; RN: joined 1831, served Chinese War, Capt 1866, R-Adml (ret) 1869, Adml 1880, Grand Cross Order Charles III Spain; *m* 21 Aug 1844 Eliza (*d* 4 Dec 1877), 3rd dau of Adml Hon Sir George Elliot, KCB (Isee MINTO, E), and had:

1 Charles John Spencer, *Earl Compton*, DL Northants; *b* 13 July 1849; *d* unm 5 Sept 1887

2 WILLIAM GEORGE SPENCER SCOTT, **5th Marquess**

3 Alwyne Frederick, DSO, DL Argyll; MP Bedford N 1895–1906 and Brentwood 1910–11, Lt-Col Beds Yeo, formerly Lt 10th Hus and Gren Gds, served Sudan 1884 and Boer War 1900; *b* 5 June 1856; *m* 31 July 1886 Mary Evelyn Violet (added by roy licence 30 Sept 1915 name and arms of VYNER; *d* 22 Oct 1957), dau of Robert Charles de Grey Vyner, DL, of Gautby Hall, Lincs, and Newby Hall, Skelton, W R Yorks (*see* LUCAS OF CRUDWELL, B), and *d* 16 Dec 1911, leaving:

(1) Edward Robert Francis, of Newby Hall, Ripon and Torloisk, Isle of Mull, JP (1924), DL (W R Yorks 1926), JP (Ripon 1923 and Argyllshire 1943); Capt RSG and T/Capt MGC WWs I (despatches, wounded) and II, Russian Order St Stanislas 3rd Cl with swords; *b* 14 Dec 1891 (HM EDWARD VII stood sponsor); *educ* Eton and Magdalen Coll Oxford; *m* 1st 3 July 1918 Sylvia (*d* 17 March 1950), 2nd dau of Alexander Haldane Farquharson of Invercauld, and had:

1a +Alwyne Arthur COMPTON later Alwyne Arthur Compton FARQUHARSON OF INVERCAULD , MC, JP (Aberdeenshire 1951) [Capt Alwyne Farquharson of Invercauld MC JP, Invercauld, Braemar, Aberdeenshire AB35 5TS]; *b* 1 May 1919; *educ* Eton; Capt RSG WW II (wounded), memb Aberdeen CC 1949–, recognised in the surname Farquharson of Invercauld and as Ch of Clan Farquharson by warrant of Ld Lyon 1949, uses former surname as 3d forename; *m* 1st 3 Feb 1949 Frances Strickland Lovell (*d* 1991), formerly w of Capt Charles Gordon, widow of Hon James Henry Bertie Rodney, DSO, MC (*see* RODNEY, B), and dau of Robert Pollard Oldham, of Seattle; *m* 2nd 1993 *Patricia Gabriella Estelle, dau of Henry Simms Norman Simms-Adams, of Brancaster Hall, Norfolk, and widow of Nicholas John Dennys Parry de Winton

2a +Robert Edward John, DL (N Yorks) [Maj Robert Compton DL, Newby Hall, Ripon, N Yorks]; *b* 11 July 1922; *educ* Eton; Maj Coldstream Gds WW II (wounded), dir Time Life Internat 1958, High Sheriff N Yorks 1978; *m* 5 July 1951 *Ursula Jane, formerly w of Sir Max Aitken, 2nd Bt (*see* BEAVERBROOK, B), and previously of Peter Lindsay (*see* CRAWFORD and BALCARRES, E), yr dau of Maj Robert Orlando Rodolph Kenyon-Slaney (*see* KENYON, B), and has:

1b +James Alwyne [James Compton Esq, 43A Upcerne Rd, London SW10; Coombe Cottage, Hanging Langford, Salisbury, Wilts SP3 4NW]; *b* 30 May 1953; *educ* Milton Abbey; *m* 1st 1980 (*divorce* 1986) Rebecca, only dau of Sir Alan Lewis Wigan, 8th Bt (*qv*), and formerly w of John Dominic Spearman (*see* SPEARMAN, Bt), and has:

1c +Philip; *b* 1980

2c +Clephane; *b* 1983

1c *Lara Ellen; *b* 1985

1b (cont.) James Compton *m* 2nd 1989 *Lady Tania Frances Meade, yr dau of 7th Earl of Clanwilliam (*qv*), and has:

3c +Frederick Alwyne; *b* 1996

2c *Sophie; *b* 1993

2b +Richard Clephane [Richard Compton Esq, Torloisk House, Isle of Mull, Argyll PA74 6NH; The Manor House, Marton-le-Moor, Ripon, N Yorks HG4 5AT]; *b* 18 April 1957; *educ* Harrow and RAC Cirencester; *m* 1982 *Lucinda Jane Austell, yr dau of Gerald Arthur Hohler (*see* STUCLEY, Bt), and has:

1c +Orlando Edward de Grey; *b* 1986

2c +Ludovic Hugh; *b* 1989

1c *Theodosia Alexandra; *b* 1992

1a Mary; *b* 1 May 1919; *m* 1st 28 Sept 1939 (*divorce* 1947) Bernard Henry Richard van Cutsem (*d* 8 Dec 1975), only s of Henry Harcourt van Cutsem, and has:

1b *Hugh Bernard Edward [Hugh van Cutsem Esq, Anmer Hall, King's Lynn, Norfolk PE31 6RW]; *b* 1941; *educ* Ampleforth; *m* 1971 *Jonkvrouwe Emilie, dau of Jonkheer Pieter Quarles van Ufford, of De Dumdoorn, Aerdenhout, Holland, and has:

1c *Edward Bernard Charles; *b* 1973

2c *Hugh Ralph; *b* 1974

3c *Nicholas Peter Geoffrey; *b* 1977

4c *William Henry; *b* 1979

2b *Geoffrey Neil [Geoffrey van Cutsem Esq, The Old Rectory, Old Somerby, Lincs NG33 4AG; 9a Elm Park Rd, London SW3 6BP]; *b* 1944; *educ* Ampleforth; *m* 1969 *Sally , only dau of Alastair McCorquodale, of Stoke Rochford, Grantham, Lincs, and has:

1c *Sophie; *b* 1975

2c *Zara; *b* 1978

1a (cont) Mrs Mary van Cutsem *m* 2nd 22 Feb 1947 Maj William Dalton Henderson, USAAF, s of Alexander Ogilvy Henderson, of Guerneville, Calif., and *d* 1989, leaving by him:

3b *Alexander William; *b* 1948; *m* 1982 *Penelope Coates and has:

1c *Edward Alwyne; *b* 1985

1b *Mary Clare [Mrs Jonathan Martin, Bentley House, Bentley, Ipswich, Suffolk]; *b* 1951; *m* 1978 *Jonathan Martin and has:

1c *Laura; *b* 1981

2c *Sophie; *b* 1984

(1) (cont.) Edward Compton *m* 2nd 23 Oct 1952 Mary Elizabeth (*d* 23 June 1957), formerly w of Allen Wilson and dau of Sydney Dawson, of Cambridge; *m* 3rd 15 Feb 1958 Sallie Whitney (*d* 1979), widow of 2nd Baron Sysonby (*qv*) and dau of Dr Leonard Cutler Sanford, of New York, and *d* 7 Feb 1977

(2) Clare George COMPTON later VYNER (roy licence 30 March 1912), of Fountains Abbey and Studley Royal, nr Ripon, Yorks; Lt-Cdr RN; *b* 31 March 1894; *m* 10 April 1923 Lady Doris Gordon-Lennox (*d* 1980), 2nd dau of 8th Duke of Richmond and Gordon (*qv*), and *d* 1989, having had:

  1a Charles de Grey; Sub-Lt (A) RNVR WW II; *b* 21 Jan 1926; *ka* off Rangoon 2 May 1945

  2a +Henry [Henry Vyner Esq, Keanchulish, Ullapool, Ross-shire]; *b* 20 April 1932; *m* 1st 13 Oct 1958 *Margaret, formerly w of Hon Hugo John Laurence Phillips (*see* MILFORD, B) and only dau of Capt Ralph Heathcote, DSO, RN, of Hornby, Lancs, and has:

    1b *Harriet de Grey; *b* 18 Aug 1959

    2b *Violet Elizabeth; *b* 21 March 1962

  2a (cont.) Henry Vyner *m* 2nd 1982 *(Charlotte) Claire (Pemberton), dau of Capt Frederick Harold Deming Courtney

  1a Elizabeth; WRNS WW II; *das unm* 3 June 1942

4 Douglas James Cecil, CBE (1918); Col 9th Lancers Boer War 1899–1902 and France WW I; *b* 15 Nov 1865; *m* 22 Feb 1917 Dollie (*d* 14 Sept 1954), 3rd dau of M Woolf, and *dsp* 23 July 1944

1 Katrine Cecilia; *m* 25 Oct 1870 Earl Cowper (*see* LUCAS, B) and *d* 23 March 1913

2 Margaret Georgiana; *m* 30 Dec 1884 Sir Henry John Lowndes Graham, KCB, and *d* 15 Nov 1931, leaving issue. He *d* 5 Dec 1930

3 Alice Elizabeth; *d* 17 June 1862

4 Mabel Violet Isabel; *d unm* 16 Aug 1961 aged 99

The 4th MARQUESS *d* 11 Sept 1897; his est surv son,

WILLIAM GEORGE SPENCER SCOTT COMPTON, **5th Marquess of the County of Northampton**; *b* 23 April 1851; *educ* Eton and Trin Coll Cambridge; Ld Lt Warwicks 1912–13, 2nd Sec Dip Serv Paris, Rome, St Petersburg, KGStJ, MP (Lib) SW Warwicks 1885–86 and Barnsley 1889–97, Hon Col London Heavy Bde; *m* 30 April 1884 Hon Mary Florence Baring (*d* 1 June 1902), dau of 2nd Baron Ashburton (*qv*), and had:

1 WILLIAM BINGHAM, **6th Marquess**

2 Spencer Douglas; Lt RHG; *b* 3 May 1893; *ka* 13 May 1915

1 Margaret Louisa Lizzie; *b* 9 Aug 1886; *m* 6 June 1905 2nd Baron Loch, CB, MVO, DSO (*see* 1970 edn), and *d* 9 April 1970, leaving issue. He *d* 14 Aug 1942

The 5th MARQUESS *d* 15 June 1913; his er son,

WILLIAM BINGHAM COMPTON, **6th Marquess of the County of Northampton**, DSO (1919), JP, DL (Northants 1937, Ross-shire 1936–57); *b* 6 Aug 1885; *educ* Eton and Balliol Coll Oxford (BA 1906); memb Northants CC 1922–55, Chm 1948–55, Maj RHG, Hon Col 11th Bn Lond Regt, Lt-Col Warwicks Yeo (TA) WW I (wounded), author: *History of the Comptons of Compton Wynyates* (1929), Cdr Order Leopold II Belgium, CStJ; *m* 1st 15 Oct 1921 (*divorce* 1942) Lady Emma Margery Thynne, OBE, 2nd dau of 5th Marquess of Bath (*qv*); *m* 2nd 18 June 1942 (*divorce* 1958) Virginia Lucie (*m* 2nd 1958, as his 3rd w, Capt Thomas Andrew Hussey, CBE, RN (*d* 1980)), yst dau of David Rimington Heaton, DSO, of Brookfield, Crownhill, S Devon, and by her had:

1 SPENCER DOUGLAS DAVID COMPTON, **7th and present Marquess of the County of Northampton**

2 +William James Bingham [The Lord William Compton, 50 Bedford Gdns, London W8]; *b* 26 Nov 1947; *educ* Bryanston; *m* 1st 18 Jan 1973 Marlene Frances (*d* 15 Sept 1994), only dau of Francis Hosie, of Brighton House, Australia; *m* 2nd 21 Nov 1996 *Mrs Sarah Langdale and by his 1st w has:

  (1) +James William; *b* 5 Feb 1974

  (1) *Clare Victoria Frances; *b* 1980

1 *Judith; *b* 26 Sept 1943; *educ* RCM and London U; *m* 1970 *Sir Adrian Christopher Swire and has:

  (1) *Merlin Bingham; *b* 1973

  (2) *Samuel Compton; *b* 1980

  (1) *Martha Virginia; *b* 1972; *m* 21 June 1997 *Alexander Allfrey, s of Peter Allfrey (*see* 1959 edn FOX, Bt) and Mrs Susanna Allfrey

2 *Elizabeth, DL (Ross and Cromarty, Skye and Lochalsh 1990) [The Lady Elizabeth Leslie Melville DL, Lochluichart, by Garve, Ross-shire IV23 2PZ]; *b* 7 Dec 1944; *m* 30 March 1968 *Ian Hamish Leslie Melville (*see* LEVEN and MELVILLE, E) and has issue

The **6th Marquess** *m* 3rd 2 Dec 1958 Elspeth Grace (*d* 14 May 1976), formerly w of 19th Baron Teynham (*qv*) and est dau of William Ingham Whitaker, JP, DL, of Pylewell Park, Lymington, Hants, and *d* 30 Jan 1978

Seats: Castle Ashby, Northampton, Northants; Compton Wynyates, Tysoe, Warwicks.

Castle Ashby was started around the last quarter of the 16th century but most of it is 17th-century, including a roof balustrade which seems to have been begun about the beginning of CHARLES I's reign, a linking screen of some 10 years later which may be Inigo Jones's work and a remodelling of the east wing's interior which was probably undertaken about a century after the building of the original structure, that is to say *c* 1675. The attempt in a restoration programme of the 1880s to retain this predominantly 17th-century appearance is not entirely convincing. It was not the only drastic remodelling of the Victorian era. In the 1860s the Capability Brown garden was altered, though his landscaping of the park remained largely untouched.

Compton Wynyates is a cosier affair, though equally a mixture of styles, if not more so. Its front consists of Tudor domestic architecture in rose-tinted brick ornamented with crenellation; only the south-facing tower appears to offer a very sturdy defence. For Compton Wynyates — at least in its elevations — is mock castle, though the castellated elements have a historic value inasmuch as they constitute the chief grounds for assigning a date of origin to some time between the last years of EDWARD IV's reign and the middle ones of HENRY VII's. Its true character is revealed in the skyline: over 40 chimneys, some bar-

ley-sugar twists, many octagonal brick. They make it quite plain that this is a domestic dwelling. The name derives straightforwardly enough as to the first part from the family of its owner. The 'Wynyates' may be a corruption of 'wind-gate', that is to say the cut in the surrounding hills through which alone stormy weather could get at this nestling gem of Renaissance Englishry.

There was a moated high-medieval manor house on the site originally. Edmund Compton began the present structure. His son Sir William added the chapel, the four towers and the handsome main entrance, exploiting Fulbroke Castle, some 20 miles away, as a source of architectural salvage.

Many English houses boast that ELIZABETH I paid a visit. Some, perhaps rather fewer, claim JAMES I as a past house-guest. Compton Wynyates has sheltered both monarchs, also CHARLES 1. They all probably spent the night in the chamber called Henry VIII's Room, where that king slept as well on at least two separate occasions. HENRY's cipher is worked into the plaster of the ceiling along with those of his Stuart successors. The mansion was besieged by Parliamentary forces in 1644 and taken after a 48-hour resistance, despite the continued existence of a double moat. Compton Wynyates as it now stands (the family got it back after the Civil War on condition they filled in the moat) is still less defensible. Actually its very vulnerability saved it. A long-drawn-out siege might have had the disastrous effect that engulfed Basing. So too its neglect in the ensuing 200 years, Compton Wynyates's beauty lies in its being largely unsullied by 'improvements'.

True, the east flank was remodelled in the early 18th century by the 5th Earl and again just after the mid-19th century under the supervision of Sir Digby Wyatt, who archaicised the Georgian additions to make them blend in with the original work. But the essence of the place is summed up behind the outer walls, where lies the courtyard with its splendid bay window dating from the time of the Field of the Cloth of Gold (at which the 1st Lord Compton's grandfather played a conspicuous part). It lends the appearance of an Oxford or Cambridge college but in fact comes from Fulbroke, being arguably the most notable item plundered from there.

NORTHBOURNE

Arms: Gu. a dolphin embowed or. **Crest:** An ostrich arg., beaked and legged or. **Supporters:** Two eagles arg., each gorged with a plain collar gu., pendant therefrom an escutcheon of the arms. **Motto:** *J'ayme a jamais* ('I love forever'). **Creations:** Bt. (GB) 28 July 1791, B. (UK) 5 Nov 1884.

THE 5TH BARON NORTHBOURNE OF BETTESHANGER, Co Kent, **AND OF JARROW GRANGE**, Co Palatine of Durham, and a **Baronet** (Sir Christopher George Walter James, Bt, DL (Kent 1996)) [The Rt Hon The Lord Northbourne DL, 11 Eaton Place, London SW1X 8BN; Coldharbour, Northbourne, Kent CT14 ONT]; *b* 18 Feb 1926; *s* f 1982; *educ* Eton and Magdalen Coll Oxford (MA); QAIS, FAI, late Lt Roy Signals, FRICS, dir Anglo Indonesian Corp 1971–, chm Betteshanger Farms Ltd 1975–, dir Plantation & General plc 1986–, dep chm Centre Parcs plc 1988 (dir 1988–); *m* 18 July 1959 *Aliki Louise Hélène Marie-Sygne, est dau of Henri Charles Walter Claudel, of Chatou, Seine-et-Oise, France, and gdau of Paul Claudel, the poet, and has:

1 +CHARLES WALTER HENRI [The Hon Charles James, Northbourne Court, Northbourne, Kent CT14 OLW; Home Farm, Betteshanger, Kent CT14 OLW]; *b* 14 June 1960; *educ* Eton and Magdalen Coll Oxford; dir Rede Investments and Redesdale Investments; *m* 3 Oct 1987 *Catherine Lucy, only dau of W Ralph Burrows, of Prescot, Lancs, and has:

  (1) +Henry Christopher William; *b* 3 Dec 1988

  (2) +Alexander Oliver Charles; *b* 1996

  (1) *Anastasia Aliki; *b* 1992

2 +Anthony Christopher Walter Paul [The Hon Anthony James, Evistones, Otterburn, Northumberland]; *b* 14 Jan 1963; *educ* Eton and Magdalen Coll Oxford

3 +Sebastian Richard Edward Cuthbert; *b* 11 March 1966; *educ* Eton, Magdalen Coll Oxford and INSEAD Fontainebleau

1 *Ophelia Mary Katherine Christine Aliki; *b* 23 Aug 1969; *educ* St Mary's Ascot, King's Sch Canterbury and Exeter U

Lineage: RICHARD HEAD; m Elizabeth, dau of John Wallis, of Soundness House, Oxon (only s of Dr John Wallis, Savilian Prof Oxford), and had:

RICHARD HEAD, of Langley Hall; had:

1 Thomas (Sir), ktd 1744, High Sheriff Berks 1744; m 1750 Jane, sis of Mary, Countess of Haddington (qv), and dau of Rowland Holt, of Redgrave Hall, Suffolk, and had:

  (1) William HEAD later JAMES (on inheriting 1772 estates of his unc John James, of Denford Court (see below), as did his yr bro on inheriting from him); d unm

  (2) Sir WALTER, **1st Bt**

  (1) Jane; m George Osbaldeston, of Hutton Bushell, Yorks

2 Richard (Rev); d 1789, leaving an only dau:

  (1) Harriet James; m 1788 Rev Morgan Graves, MA, and had issue

1 Elizabeth; m John James, of Denford Court, Berks

Sir THOMAS's yr s,

Sir WALTER HEAD later JAMES, **1st Bt** (GB), so cr 28 July 1791, of Langley Hall and Denford Court, both Berks; m 25 April 1780 Lady Jane Pratt, yst dau of 1st Earl Camden (see CAMDEN, M), and had:

1 Francis; Capt 81st Regt; ka Badajoz April 1812

2 John; Min Plen Netherlands; m 29 June 1814 Lady Emily Jane Stewart (m 2nd 1st Viscount Hardinge (qv); d Oct 1865), dau of 1st Marquess of Londonderry (qv), and d 4 June 1818, having had:

  (1) WALTER CHARLES, **1st Baron**

1 Jane; m 1803 John Trower, of Berkeley Sq, and had issue

2 Mary Anne; m 9 May 1809 1st Earl of Strafford (qv) and d 26 Oct 1845, leaving issue

3 Frances; m 1823 Horatio Davies, only s of Sir John Davies

4 Charlotte Elizabeth; m Francis Frederick de Lerber, memb Sov Cncl Berne, Maj Artillery attd Staff Swiss Confederation, and d Geneva 1820

Sir WALTER d 1829; his gs,

Sir Walter Charles James, 2nd Bt, and **1st Baron Northbourne of Betteshanger**, Co Kent, **and of Jarrow Grange**, Co Palatine of Durham (UK), so cr 5 Nov 1884; b 3 June 1816; educ Westminster and Ch Ch Oxford; MP (C) Hull 1837–47, High Sheriff Kent 1855; m 17 April 1841 Sarah Caroline (d 21 Jan 1890), 5th dau of Cuthbert Ellison, DL, JP, of Hebburn Hall, Co Durham, and had:

1 WALTER HENRY, **2nd Baron**

1 Sarah; m 26 Sept 1871 1st Baron Kilbracken (qv) and d 13 Sept 1921, leaving issue

The 1st BARON d 4 Feb 1893; his son,

WALTER HENRY JAMES, **2nd Baron Northbourne of Betteshanger and of Jarrow Grange**, JP, DL Kent; b 25 March 1846; educ Radley and Ch Ch Oxford (MA); MP (Lib) Gateshead 1874–93, Hon Col 9th Bn Durham LI, T/2nd Lt 3rd Home Counties Bde RFA; m 25 Aug 1868 Edith Emmeline Mary (d 12 March 1929), dau of John Newton Lane, of King's Bromley Manor, Staffs, and had:

1 WALTER JOHN, **3rd Baron**

2 Cuthbert, CBE (1919), JP; b 29 Feb 1872; MP Bromley 1919–30, Lt-Col RM, Maj E Surrey Regt, Assist Fin Sec Egyptian Army, Assist Civil Sec Sudan Govt; m 10 Aug 1905 Florence Marion (d 7 Jan 1933), er dau of Hussey Packe, DL, of Prestwold, Leics (see KIMBERLEY, E), and d 21 July 1930, leaving:

  (1) Thomas; b 10 July 1906; educ Eton and Magdalen Coll Oxford; Maj RASC WW II; m 1st 17 March 1932 (divorce 1940) Lady Germaine Elizabeth Olive Eliot (d 1991), only dau of 8th Earl of St Germans (qv); m 2nd 4 Dec 1940 (divorce 1953) Julia Mary (d 1974), only dau of Charles Solomon, of St John's Wood, and had:

    1a +Nigel Antony [Nigel James Esq, 18 Toorang Ave, N Balwyn, Victoria 3104, Australia]; b 23 Nov 1944; educ Dover Coll and in France; m 1973 *Therese Macormack, of Melbourne, Australia, and has:

      1b +Alexander Robert; b 1974

      2b +Charles Henry Thomas; b 1976

      1b *Francesca Danielle; b 1980

    1a *Georgina Mary [Mrs Christopher Watts, 45 Woodley Lane, Cuppernham, Hants SO5 8JR]; b 15 July 1948; m 25 Jan 1972 *Christopher Watts and has:

      1b *Ian Charles; b 1973

      2b *Mark Andrew; b 1976

  (1) (cont.) Maj Thomas James m 3rd 16 July 1953 Rosemary Heartsease Beare (d 1979), widow of Capt Reginald Dilworth Howard, RN, previously w of Norman Miller and only surv dau of Maj George Frederick Crisp Molineux-Montgomerie, JP, Gren Gds, of Garboldisham Old Hall, Norfolk, and d 6 Feb 1976

  (1) Olivia Mary; b 11 Dec 1909; m 4 July 1934 Stephen Francis Villiers-Smith, MBE, s of Sir Francis Edward James Smith, of Marylebone, and had:

    1a *Timothy Francis; b 11 July 1935; educ Eton; Capt Fife and Forfar Yeo, Scottish Horse (TA); m 25 Jan 1961 (divorce 1969) Cicely Susan Esther, only surv dau of Brig Charles Edward Tryon-Wilson, CBE, DSO (see TRYON, B), and has:

      1b *Charles Francis; b 30 April 1965

      1b *Amy Louise; b 11 Oct 1963

      2b *Rupert Timothy; b 5 April 1967

    1a *Clarissa Mary; b 1 Jan 1938; m 24 July 1957 Sir Geoffrey Christopher John Palmer, 12th Bt, of Carlton (qv), and has issue

    2a Serena Olivia; b 1 April 1940; m 24 April 1963 *Anthony Morden [Anthony Morden Esq, Hunter's Lodge, High Drive, Woldingham, Surrey], only s of Edward Morden, of Kensington, and d 1998, leaving:

      1b *Amanda Serena; b 20 Oct 1965

      2b *Lucinda Antonia; b 21 Oct 1967

  (2) *(Joan) Rosamond [Mrs Launcelot Brydon, 3 Granary Cottages, High St, Kent TN16 1JA]; b 15 Feb 1917; m 21 June 1949 *Maj Launcelot James Francis Brydon, s of Robert Ernest Brydon, and has:

    1a *Robert Alexander [Robert Brydon Esq, 49 Melody Rd, London SW18 2QW]; b 15 Feb 1954; educ Stowe; m 1983 (divorce 1987) Francesca Camilla Roberta Ierne, dau of Henry John William Phillips (see HOTHFIELD, B), and has:

      1b *Lara Daisy Edina Charlotte; b 1984

    1a *Nadia Mary; b 2 April 1952; m 19– (divorce 19–) Sol Alan Saad

3 Robert, JP N R Yorks; b 13 May 1873; educ Harrow and Trin Coll Cambridge; m 1st 18 June 1900 Lady Evelyn Kathleen Wellesley (d 19 Jan 1922), est dau of 4th Duke of Wellington (qv), and had:

  (1) Arthur Walter; b 6 Jan 1904; Maj Res Offrs Gren Gds; m 1st 29 Jan 1929 (divorce 1932) Zita Mary, er dau of Nico Jungman; m 2nd 23 June 1932 *Mary, formerly w of Lionel Cyril Gibbs (see ALDENHAM and HUNSDON OF HUNSDON, B) and yr dau of Albany Hawke Charlesworth, of Ferne, and d 1981, having by her had:

    1a Richard Arthur; b 1 Nov 1935; educ Eton; 2nd Lt Gren Gds; d unm 10 April 1956

    1a *Lucinda Evelyn [Mrs Oliver Steel, Winterbourne Holt, Newbury, Berks RG16 8AP]; b 20 Nov 1933; m 1st 22 July 1953 (divorce 1967) Andrew Duff Tennant (see GLENCONNER, B) and has issue; m 2nd 12 Oct 1967 *(Rupert) Oliver Steel, s of Joseph Steel, of Kirkwood, Lockerbie, and by him has:

      1b *James Oliver; b 26 April 1971

      1b *Emily Jane; b 6 Jan 1970; m 19 Dec 1997 *Edward Henry Duff Andrewes

3 (cont.) The Hon Robert James m 2nd 23 July 1923 *Lady Serena Mary Barbara Lumley, JP (Richmond) [The Lady Serena James JP, St Nicholas, Richmond, N Yorks], DStJ, dau of 10th Earl of Scarbrough (qv), and d 13 Dec 1960, having by her had:

  (1) *Ursula Mary Rose , JP (N R Yorks 1962) [The Rt Hon The Lady Westbury JP, Barton Cottage, Malton, Yorks YO17 0AT]; b 6 May 1924; m 21 Oct 1947 *5th Baron Westbury (qv) and has issue

  (2) *(Serena) Fay [Mrs Serena Campion, St Nicholas Garden Cottage, Richmond, Yorks]; b 2 April 1929; m 19 Feb 1955 (divorce 1963) Colin Griffith Campion, 3rd Carabiniers (POWDG), est s of Maj Herbert Redvers Campion, TD, RA, of Liphook, Hants, and has:

    1a *Marcus Robert Guy; b 1 Oct 1961

    1a *Georgina Serena; b 4 Oct 1955

    2a *Christina Fay; b 4 June 1957

    3a *Meriona Patricia; b 23 Sept 1959

4 Wilfrid; b 7 Dec 1874; m 27 Feb 1900 Margaret Anne (d 30 May 1957), 3rd dau of John Stogdon, and d 10 Jan 1908, having had:

  (1) John Wilfrid; b 30 Dec 1900; d 2 Sept 1934

  (2) +Henry Norman; b 12 Feb 1903; educ Harrow; Roy Observer Corps WW II; m 1st 1 June 1933 (divorce 1946) Constance Margaret, only dau of Capt John Duncan Macdonald, MC, of Bucklebury Place, Woolhampton, Berks; m 2nd 18 July 1946 Kathleen Mary (d 2 Aug 1959), 2nd dau of Charles William Hewtson, of Hull, and by her had:

    1a +John Henry [John James Esq, Woodlands Farm, Adisham, Kent]; b 10 Aug 1947; educ King's Sch Canterbury; m 4 July 1970 *Karen Leslie, dau of F/Lt Leslie A Montgomery, MBE, of Biggleswade, Beds, and has:

      1b *Nicholas John; b 1976

      1b *Lisa Maria; b 1973

    1a *Margaret Anne; b 30 Sept 1950; m 19– *— Speer

  (2) (cont.) Henry James m 3rd 28 Jan 1967 *Marjorie, dau of Charles William Hewtson, of Hull

  (1) Anne Cecilia; b 22 Nov 1907; m 1 June 1931 Maj Hon Godfrey Burdett Money-Coutts, yst s of 6th Baron Latymer (qv), and d 13 April 1969, leaving issue

1 Sarah Agnes; m 21 June 1900 Rev Canon Adolphus Benjamin Parry-Evans, RD, Vicar St Andrews, Bishop Auckland, Co Durham, Hon Canon Durham, Proctor in Convocation, yst s of Maj Samuel Evans, of Bures, Suffolk, and d 19 Oct 1940, leaving issue. He d 8 Feb 1954

The 2nd BARON d 27 Jan 1923; his est son,

WALTER JOHN JAMES, **3rd Baron Northbourne of Betteshanger and of Jarrow Grange**, JP Kent; b 2 Sept 1869; MA Oxon, Lt RNVR WW I; m 4 Oct 1894 Laura Gwenllian (m 2nd 2 Aug 1935 William Curtis Green, RA (d 26 March 1960), s of Frederic Green, barrister; d 29 July 1952), est dau of Adml Sir Ernest Rice, KCB, of Sibertswold Place, Kent, and had:

1 WALTER ERNEST CHRISTOPHER, **4th Baron**

2 Martin Ellison; b 17 Feb 1910; d 22 March 1915

1 Dorothea Gwenllian; b 16 Aug 1897; m 29 Nov 1922 2nd Baron Bicester (qv) and d 21 Aug 1974, leaving issue

2 Mary Beatrix; b 2 March 1902; m 29 June 1926 Nicholas Llewelyn Davies, of Eythorne House, Eythorne, Kent, s of Arthur Llewelyn Davies, barrister, and had issue

3 Jane Margaret; b 19 Jan 1908; m 29 June 1931 Hilary Maurice Bray, of Eythorne House, Kent, er s of Maurice Woodbine Bray, of Rack Close, Shere, Surrey, and d 8 Feb 1966

The 3rd BARON d 22 Dec 1932; his only surv s,

WALTER ERNEST CHRISTOPHER JAMES, **4th Baron Northbourne of Betteshanger and of Jarrow Grange**; b 18 Jan 1896; educ Eton and Magdalen Coll Oxford; Lt 4th Bn The Buffs, Chm Kent Ag Exec Ctee 1947; m 4 March 1925 Katharine Louise, JP (d 1980), yr dau of George Augustus Nickerson, of Boston, Mass., by Hon Lady Hood (see HOOD, V), and d 17 June 1982, leaving:

1 CHRISTOPHER GEORGE WALTER JAMES, **5th and present Baron Northbourne of Betteshanger and of Jarow Grange**

1 *Gwenllian Ellen [The Hon Mrs Hemsley, 10 Denewood Rd, London N6]; b 9 Sept 1929; m 1st 14 June 1952 (annulled 1960) Michael Hugh Rose, 3rd s of Rt Rev Alfred Carey Wollaston Rose, Suffragan Bp Dover; m 2nd 9 Nov 1960 *Thomas Jeffrey Hemsley, s of Sydney William Hemsley, of Hugglescote, Leics, and has:

  (1) *William Thomas James; b 6 March 1962

(2) *Matthew Walter David; *b* 7 Oct 1963

(3) *Michael Richard; *b* 29 Oct 1965

2 *Elizabeth Sarah [The Hon Mrs Fleming, Little Betteshanger, Betteshanger, Kent CT14 0NN]; *b* 9 Feb 1933; *m* 19 March 1960 *Michael Edward Willis Fleming, 2nd s of Col Edward Charles Augustus Willis Fleming, TD, of The Old Farm, Wickhill, Bracknell, Berks, and has:

(1) *John Michael; *b* 24 Oct 1961; *m* 1979 *Rachel, dau of R-Adml Hubert W Hollins, CB, of Llanyfriog, Dyfed

(1) *Penelope Katherine; *b* 18 Jan 1965; *m* 1990 *Jaime Simon Gispert, s of Luis Simon Gispert, of Barcelona

3 *Susan Jane [The Hon Mrs Rose, Le Sirondole, Panzano-in-Chianti, Prov Firenze, Italy]; *b* 10 Feb 1936; *m* 14 Feb 1961 her former bro-in-law *Michael Hugh Rose and has:

(1) *Michael Justin; *b* 22 Dec 1966

(1) *Nell Susanna; *b* 6 Dec 1961

(2) *Emma Katharine; *b* 12 Dec 1963

(3) *Sophy Elizabeth; *b* 15 Sept 1969

4 *Katherine Viola [The Hon Mrs Hersey, Thorneyburn Old Rectory, Tarset, Northumberland]; *b* 25 Jan 1940; *m* 26 Feb 1963 *John Wharton Hersey, yr s of G B Hersey, of Standford, Hants and has:

(1) *Robert Christopher John; *b* 1 Jan 1964

(2) *John Paul; *b* 22 Feb 1966

(3) *Daniel Anthony James; *b* 1971

NORTHBROOK

Arms: Quarterly, 1st and 4th, az. a fess or, in chief a bear's head ppr., muzzled and ringed or (for BARING); 2nd and 3rd, gu. a cross patée fitchée or between three fish hauriant arg. within an orle of eight cross crosslets of the second (for HERRING). **Crest:** A mullet erminois between two wings arg. **Supporters:** On either side a bear ppr., muzzled and charged on the shoulder with a portcullis or.

Motto: *Probitate et labore* ('By uprightness and toil').
Creations: Bt. (GB) 29 May 1793, B. (UK) 4 Jan 1866.

THE 6TH BARON NORTHBROOK, of Stratton, Co Southampton, and a **Baronet** (Sir Francis Thomas Baring, Bt) [The Rt Hon The Lord Northbrook, House of Lords, London SW1A 0PW]; *b* 21 Feb 1954; *s f* 1990; *educ* Winchester and Bristol U (BA 1976); investment manager Smith & Williamson Securities 1993–; *m* 27 June 1987 *Amelia Sarah Elizabeth, er dau of Dr Reginald David Taylor, of Hursley, Hants, and has:

1 *Arabella Constance Elizabeth; *b* 1989

2 *Venetia Harriet Anne; *b* 1991

Lineage: PETER BARING, of Groeningen; *d c* 1536; gggf of:

FRANZ BARING; Lutheran Pastor St Ansgarius, Bremen; had:

JOHANN BARING; *b* 31 Jan 1697; settled 1717 as merchant and cloth manufacturer at Larkbeare or Larkbeer, nr Exeter; naturalised 1723; *m* 1729 Elizabeth (*bur* 16 April 1766), dau of John Vowler, of Bellair, and was *bur* 3 Nov 1748, having had:

1 John, of Mount Radford, Devon; MP Exeter 1776–1800; *b* 5 Oct 1739; *m* 24 Nov 1757 Anne (*bur* 25 Jan 1765), dau of Francis Parker, of Blagdon, Devon, and *d* 1 Feb 1816, having had two sons and four daus

2 Thomas Vowler; *b* 19 Jan 1733; *m* 24 Aug 1758 Elizabeth (*m* 2nd John Spicer, of Wear, Exeter), dau of Francis Parker, of Blagdon, and *dsp* 25 Aug 1758

3 FRANCIS (Sir), **1st Bt**

4 Charles, of Courtland, Devon; *b* 28 Oct 1742; *m* 6 Sept 1767 Margaret (*d* 1812), dau and heiress of William Drake Gould, of Lew Trenchard, Devon and *d* 13 Jan 1829, leaving issue (*see* IDDESLEIGH, E)

1 Elizabeth; *b* 21 July 1744; *m* 31 March 1780 John Dunning (*b* 18 Oct 1731; barrister, MP (Whig) Calne 1768–82, Slr-Gen 1768–70, PC 1782, *cr* 8 April 1782 Baron Ashburton, of Ashburton, Devon (GB); *d* 18 Aug 1783) and *d* 23 March 1809, leaving:

(1) RICHARD BARRE DUNNING, 2nd and last BARON ASHBURTON of the 1782 *cr*; *b* 17 Sept 1782; *m* 17 Sept 1805 Ann, dau of William Cunningham, of Lainshaw, and *dsp* Feb 1823, when the Barony expired

JOHN BARING's 3rd s,

Sir Francis Baring, 1st Bt (GB), so *cr* 29 May 1793; *b* 18 April 1740; London merchant, Dir HEIC 1779 and Chm 1792–93, fndr Baring Bros, bankers, MP Grampound, Wycombe and Calne 1784–1806; *m* 12 May 1767 Harriet (*d* 3 Dec 1804), dau and coheir of William Herring, of Croydon (cousin and coheir of Thomas Herring, Archbp Canterbury), and had, with five daus:

1 THOMAS (Sir), **2nd Bt**

2 ALEXANDER BARING, *cr* BARON ASHBURTON (*qv*)

3 Henry, of Cromer Hall, Norfolk; *b* 18 Jan 1776; *m* 1st 19 April 1802 (*divorce*) Maria Matilda, 2nd dau of William Bingham, of Philadelphia, and had, with another s (*dsp*):

(1) Henry Bingham; *b* 4 March 1804; MP Marlborough 1832–68; *m* 1st 30 June 1827 Augusta (*d* 8 Jan 1853), 5th dau of 6th Earl of Cardigan (*see* AILESBURY, M), and had, with a dau (*d* unm):

1a Charles; *b* 26 June 1829; Lt-Gen Coldstream Gds; *m* 25 Aug 1860 Helen (*d* 17 Jan 1914), yst dau of Sir James Robert George Graham, 2nd Bt, of Netherby, Yorks (*qv*), and *d* 7 Feb 1890, having had:

1b Sir GODFREY BARING, 1st Bt (*qv*)

1b Mabel; *b* 21 June 1861; *m* 3 Sept 1884 Richard Tassell Anthony Grant, of IoW, yst s of Sir Thomas Grant, KCB, and *d* 7 May 1917. He *d* 1 July 1902

2b Olivia; *b* 14 May 1863; *m* 8 July 1886 Sir Richard James Graham, 4th Bt, of Netherby (*qv*), and *dsp* 21 March 1887

2a Henry; *b* 6 Sept 1831; Capt 17th Lancers; *m* 22 March 1888 Harriette Emily (*d* 12 Aug 1950), yr dau of Edward George Cubitt, DL, JP, of Honing Hall, Norfolk, and *d* 13 April 1929, leaving with another s (*d* an infant):

1b Henry; *b* 1893; Capt Roy W Kent Regt and RAF WW I; *d* 14 Sept 1930

2b Francis Guy (Rev); *b* 1893 (twin); *educ* Emmanuel Coll Cambridge (BA 1917, MA 1921); assist master Yardley Court Tonbridge, Kent, 1946–47, Headmaster Earsham Hall Sch, nr Bungay, Suffolk, 1951–62; *d* unm 7 Jan 1962

1b Augusta; *b* 11 May 1889; *m* 1917 Rev Walter Frederick Scott, Vicar New Romney, Kent, and *d* 4 May 1941. He *d* 4 July 1938

3a Francis; *b* 16 March 1833; Adj Yeomen Gd, Lt-Col Scots Gds; *d* unm 21 Feb 1895

1a Mary Emily; *m* 1st 18 May 1857 (*divorce* Nov 1864) Richard Lewis Mostyn Williams Bulkeley, afterwards 11th Bt (*qv*); *m* 2nd 27 July 1867 John Oakley Maund, RMA, s of Herbert Maund, of Ludgershall, Wilts

(1) (cont.) Maj Henry Baring *m* 2nd 1854 Marie de Martinoff (*dsp* 9 Aug 1903) and *d* 25 April 1869

(2) William Frederick; *b* 12 Aug 1822; *m* 12 Nov 1845 Emily, est dau of Sir Richard Jenkins, GCB, of Bicton Hall, Salop, and *d* 10 Dec 1903, having had:

1a Henry Alexander; Lt RN; *dsp* 1902

1a Mary Emily; *m* — Bennett

(1) Anna Maria; *m* William Gordon Coesvelt

(2) Frances Emily; *m* 19 Aug 1830 Henry Bridgeman Simpson, gs of 1st Baron Bradford (*see* BRADFORD, E), and *d* 14 March 1886

3 (cont.) Henry Baring *m* 2nd 9 July 1825 Cecilia Anne (*d* 21 Oct 1874), est dau of V-Adml William Windham, of Cromer Hall, Norfolk, and *d* 13 April 1848, having by her had:

(3) William Windham; *b* 19 April 1826; *m* 2 Jan 1862 Selina Barbara Wilhemina (*d* 22 July 1919), yst dau of Maj-Gen Hon Sir Frederick Cavendish Ponsonby, GCMG, KCB (*see* BESSBOROUGH, E), and *dsp* 20 Nov 1876

(4) EDWARD CHARLES BARING, *cr* BARON REVELSTOKE (*qv*)

(5) Robert; *b* 29 Nov 1833; Col 19th Hus; *d* unm 23 Nov 1915

(6) Richard; twin with Robert; *dsp* 15 Nov 1883

(7) Thomas; *b* 1839; *m* 1901 Constance (*d* 3 July 1948), dau of William Barron, and *d* 4 June 1923, leaving:

1a Richard; *b* 18 Jan 1902; *m* 1st 31 Jan 1922 Violetta Archer (*k* in a flying accident 18 July 1931), n of Lord George Dundas (*see* ZETLAND, M), and had:

1b *Anne Cecilia Maureen [Miss Anne Cecilia Baring, 105 Canfield Gdns, London NW6 3DY]; *b* 16 Oct 1922

1a (cont.) Richard Baring *m* 2nd 15 March 1932 Margaret (*d* 27 Feb 1974), est dau of Dr Henry Thomas Sutton, FACS, of Zanesville, Ohio, and *d* 9 Feb 1940

2a Edward Thomas; *b* 6 Sept 1903; *educ* Eton and Ch Ch Oxford; Maj 1st Derby Yeo WW II (despatches); *m* 1st 16 Oct 1926 (*divorce* 1949) Virginia, dau of John Barry Ryan, of New York, and *d* 1980, leaving:

1b +Thomas Michael, TD (1961) [Lt-Col Thomas Baring TD, Westhay House, Axminster, Devon EX13 5XH]; *b* 24 Oct 1927; Lt-Col Derby Yeo, cmdg Leics and Derbys Yeo; *m* 1st 17 April 1953 (*divorce* 1965) Hon Sarah Katharine Elinor, formerly w of 3rd Viscount Astor (*qv*) and only dau of 6th Baron Grantley (*qv*), and adopted:

*Edward Richard Philip; *b* Sept 1962; *m* 5 July 1996 *Marianne, yst dau of Lawrence Stanton, and has:

1d *James Edward; *b* 11 April 1997

1b (cont.) Lt-Col Thomas Baring *m* 2nd 11 June 1966 *Gillian Ann Rosemary, formerly w of John Graham and dau of Arthur Rupert Woolley, DSO, OBE, of Tisbury, Wilts, and by her has:

1c *Constance Nina; *b* 12 July 1970

2b +(Edward) Patrick [Patrick Baring Esq, Old Rectory, Pimperne, Dorset]; *b* 24 Dec 1932; *m* 1 Oct 1960 *Antonia Miriam, er dau of Anthony Wentworth Guinness (*see* GUINNESS, Bt), and has:

1c +Anthony Shawn; *b* 12 May 1961; *m* 1991 *Kirsty A, yst dau of Sidney Edmond Jocelyn Ackland (the actor Joss Ackland)

2c +Jonathan Patrick Fortune; *b* 17 Dec 1965

1c *Sonya Hermione; *b* 18 March 1963

2c *Lucita Catherine Marianne; *b* 11 Dec 1968

3b +Christopher John; *b* 3 Sept 1939; *m* 1971 *Katherine Gayle, dau of Lee Warren Jones, of Dayton, Ohio

2a (cont.) Edward Baring *m* 2nd 17 Feb 1950 *Pauline Alison, formerly w of Timothy Walter Boden and er dau of Frank Fawcett Copland, of Wagga Wagga, NSW

(8) EVELYN BARING, *cr* EARL OF CROMER (*qv*)

(9) Walter; *b* 22 Oct 1844; Min Res Montevideo, Consul-Gen Uruguay 1893–1906; *m* 1875 Ellen (*d* 21 Jan 1914), dau of Frederick Guarracino, and *d* 3 April 1915, leaving:

1a Oliver; *b* 5 Aug 1879; *m* 27 Feb 1906 Phoebe (*m* 2nd 5 Feb 1946 Lt-Col Frederick Carey Stuckley Samborne-Palmer, CBE, IA (*d* 13 June 1950), s of Rev R L P Samborne, of Timsbury, Somerset; *d* 8 May 1971), only dau of Sir John Winfield Bonser, PC, and *dsp* 1 July 1941

1a Nina Ayesha; *b* 17 April 1876; *m* 27 Sept 1900 3rd Earl Granville (*qv*) and *dsp* 12 June 1955

(3) Cecilia Annetta; Ldy Bedchamber to TM QUEEN VICTORIA and QUEEN ALEXANDRA; *m* 4 April 1854 5th Baron Suffield (*qv*) and *d* 16 Feb 1911, leaving issue

4 William; *b* 8 Dec 1779; MP; *m* 19 July 1810 Frances (*m* 2nd 1824 Arthur Eden; *d* 25 March 1877), 4th dau of J B Paulett Thompson, of Waverley Abbey and sis of 1st and last Baron Sydenham of Sydenham and of Toronto (*see* 1841 edn), and *d* 9 July 1820, leaving, with a dau (*d* unm):

(1) William Henry, of Norman Court, Hants, JP; *b* 1 Dec 1819; Capt Coldstream Gds; *m* 21 April 1849 Elizabeth (*d* 6 Nov 1897), dau of Charles Hammersley, and *d* June 1906, leaving, with a dau (*d* unm):

1a Francis Charles, JP Hants; *b* 1852; Maj 3rd Bn Hants Regt; *m* 5 July 1880 (*divorce* 1899) Isabella Augusta, est dau of Samuel Leo Schuster by Lady Isabella FitzMaurice (*see* ORKNEY, E), and *d* 1 Sept 1926, having had:

1b Thomas Esmé, OBE; *b* 7 May 1882; Maj Rifle Bde WW I (despatches); *m* 2 Oct 1913 Deirdre Mary Hughes (*d* 6 Feb 1973), dau of Hughes Martin, JP, of Tullaghreine, Co Cork, and *d* 9 Dec 1957, leaving:

1c +Maurice Bingham, TD [Maurice Baring Esq TD, Culmer House, Wormley, nr Godalming, Surrey]; *b* 24 July 1916; *educ* Eton and Magdalene Coll Cambridge (MA 1949); Capt Rifle Bde (TA) WW II; *m* 11 Oct 1941 (Loveday) Anne Monica (*d* 22 July 1997), dau of Capt John Tillie Coryton (*see* ST VINCENT, V), and has:

1d *Lynda Anne [Mrs Clive Corke, 16 Cambridge St, London SW1]; *b* 8 July 1944; *m* 15 April 1967 *Clive Edward Theo Corke, s of S G Corke, of Toronto, and Mrs P W M Brindley, of Gidea Park, Essex, and has:

1e *Philip Clive; *b* 1979

1e *Shauna Bingham; *b* 1972

2e *Anthea Lynda; *b* 25 Oct 1973

2d *Shirley Bingham; *b* 28 July 1948

2c +Hugo Charles, MBE (1945), MC [Maj Hugo Baring MBE MC, Koromiko Station, Gladstone, nr Masterton, Wairarapa, New Zealand]; *b* 16 April 1919; *educ* Eton and Magdalene Coll Cambridge; Maj Rifle Bde WW II (despatches) Middle East and Italy, chm Alliance Investment Co 1974; *m* 15 June 1946 Elizabeth Price (*d* 20 Feb 1977), only dau of Maj John Price Wylie, DSO, Sherwood Foresters, and has:

1d +Anthony Hugo [Anthony Baring Esq, No 7, 574 New South Head Rd, Point Piper, NSW 2027, Australia]; *b* 27 March 1947; *educ* Eton; *m* 1976 *Anne Crerar, yr dau of S G McGillivray, of Melbourne, Australia, and has:

1e +Nicholas Anthony; *b* 1979

1e *Jessica Emily; *b* 1977

2e *Eloise Annabelle; *b* 1982

2d +Michael William; *b* 26 Jan 1950; *educ* Eton; *m* 1974 *Faye Smith and has:

1e +Christopher William; *b* 1977

1e *Tanya Elizabeth

2b Arthur Francis Charles; *b* 14 May 1887; *educ* Marlborough; Lt Devonshire Regt; *m* 24 Aug 1906 Margaret McIntryre (*d* 16 Aug 1966), dau of George Moore, of Adelaide, S Australia, and *d* 30 Aug 1964, leaving:

1c Arthur Reginald; *b* 8 May 1909

2c Ian Douglas; *b* 5 Oct 1915; *m* 1937 Doris Mary Emily Luckhurst (*d* 1984) and was *k* in a car crash 28 Nov 1969, leaving:

1d +Douglas Sydney [Douglas Baring Esq, 10 Bennett Ave, Heathmont, Victoria 3135, Australia]; *b* 1938; *m* 1960 *Jean Melville Leslie and has:

1e +David Ian Alan; *b* 1963; *m* 1987 *Lisa Joanne Chapman and has:

1f +Trent Andrew Jesse; *b* 1990

2f +Joshua David; *b* 1992

1e *Jeanette Anne; *b* 1965; *m* 1987 *Keven Anthony Beekman and has:

1f *Ashley Stewart; *b* 1991

1f *Laura Rhiannon; *b* 1991 (twin)

3c Robert Stanley; *b* 15 Oct 1918

4c +Charles Evelyn; *b* 17 Dec 1924; *m* 1951 *Joan Margot Winter and has:

1d +Peter Charles; *b* 1952; *m* 19– *Marie Bernadette Maloney and has:

1e +Eliot Fitzroy; *b* 1985

2e +Alexander St John; *b* 1989

2d +Graham John [Graham Baring Esq, 107 Argyle St, St Kilda, Victoria 3182, Australia]; *b* 1954; *m* 1992 *Ingrid Frances Draeger and has:

1e *Isabella Tess; *b* 1993

3d +Rodney Alan; *b* 1958; has by Fredariki Josephine Alsop:

1e *Oscar Alan; *b* 1989

1c *Jean Margaret [Mrs Arthur Lees, 5/4 Broad St, Labrador, Qld 4215, Australia]; *b* 2 June 1922; *m* 1944 *Arthur Gilmour Lees and has:

1d *Suzanne Leonie Margaret [Miss Suzanne Lees, 23 Scala St, London W1]; *b* 1949; has:

1e *Alexander Lees Fawdrey; *b* 1989

1e *Sophie Serena Lees Fawdrey; *b* 1992

2d *Judith Anne [Mrs Adnan Rashed, 4/72 Burfitt St, Leichhardt, NSW 2040, Australia]; *b* 1951; *m* 1991 *Adnan Rashed

3b Dudley William; *b* 1892; *educ* Wellington; Maj RASC, Capt Hants Regt Res Offrs WW I (two medals), Afghanistan and NW Frontier 1919, WW II; *m* 10 April 1919 Cecilia Mary (*d* Aug 1971), 3rd dau of Lt-Col Michael Rowand Gray-Buchanan, OBE (*see* BUTE, M), and *d* 11 Jan 1952, having had:

1c +Francis William, VRD [Francis Baring Esq VRD, 71 Clarence Gate Gdns, London NW1 6QR]; *b* 17 Feb 1920; *educ* Bradfield; Cdr RNR WW II; *m* 19 May 1967 *Elsie Violet, RD, WRNS 1942–46, dau of William Charles Redding, of Blackheath

2c Michael John; *b* 15 April 1921; Lt-Cdr RN WW II; *m* 19 Jan 1946 *Pamela Anne, late WRNS (*m* 2nd 26 Jan 1959 Capt John Ridgway Berridge Longden, RN, yr s of V-Adml Horace Walker Longden, CMG, and has further issue), yst dau of Lt-Col Frederick Adolphus Fleming Barnardo, CIE, CBE, BSc, MD, MRCP, FRCS, of 19 Cavendish Square, NW1, and *d* following an accident 25 May 1955, leaving:

1d Jeremy Michael Stuart; *b* 28 Sept 1948; *educ* Wellington; *d* unm 1982

1d *(Angela) Jane [Mrs Simon Cox, The Old Rectory Stable House, Farthinghoe, Northants; 29 Rannoch Rd, London W6 9SS]; *b* 26 Dec 1946; *m* 7 Jan 1969 (*divorce* 1991) William George Stirling Home Drummond Moray, 22nd of Abercairny, Crieff, Perthshire, est surv s of Maj James William Stirling Home Drummond Moray, DL, JP, 21st of Abercairny, and has issue (*see* BUCCLEUCH and QUEENSBERRY, D); *m* 2nd 1997 *Maj Simon George FitzHugh Cox

3c David Stuart; *b* 16 Dec 1922; Sub-Lt RNR WW II; *kas* at sea in HMS *Mourne* 15 June 1944

1b Violet Nina; *m* 23 May 1906 William Francis D'Arcy, of Stanmore Hall, Middx, and *d* 25 Nov 1965, leaving issue. He *d* 11 Oct 1919

2a William Bingham; *b* 22 Sept 1859; *m* 2 March 1886 Georgina Margaret (*d* 4 March 1959 aged 95), dau of Charles Hallyburton Campbell, and *d* 9 July 1916, leaving:

1b Evelyn Bingham; *b* 25 June 1893; *educ* Eton; F/Lt RAFVR and Hants Regt WW I (Italian Croce di Guerra), dir Baring Bros, Netherlands Order Orange-Nassau, Cdr Order de Mayo Argentina; *m* 11 Feb 1928 (*annulled* 1929) Joan, yr dau of Percy FitzGerald Campbell (*see* CAMPBELL, Bt), and *dsp* 16 Aug 1966

1b Nina Gladys; *b* 8 Jan 1887; *m* 5 July 1911 Capt William Hollingsworth Agar Hunt, RE (Res), yr s of Maj-Gen Robert Augustus Carew Hunt, IA, of Sid Abbey, Sidmouth, and *dsp* 8 Jan 1970. He *d* 30 June 1975

1a Rosa Frederica; *m* 1st 29 Aug 1878 Capt Frank Wigsell Arkwright, Coldstream Gds, of Sanderstead Court, Surrey; *m* 2nd 25 Nov 1885 Lt-Col George William Adolphus FitzGeorge (*see* 1970 edn CAMBRIDGE, M) and *d* 10 March 1927, having had issue

(1) Fanny; *m* 15 Jan 1839 Rev Francis Charles Massingberd, Rector S Ormsby, Lincs, and *d* 2 April 1891, leaving issue. He *d* 5 Dec 1872

(2) Charlotte Rosa; *m* 23 Oct 1838 Robert Duncombe Shafto, of Whitworth Park, Co Durham, and had issue. He *d* 22 March 1889

5 George; *b* 23 Sept 1781; Lt Col 2nd Lt Bn KGL, Kt of William of Netherlands 1815; *m* 6 March 1806 Harriet Rochfort (*d* 1833), 2nd dau of Sir John Hadley D'Oyly, 6th Bt (*qv*), and *d* 4 Oct 1854, leaving, with four other sons and four daus:

(1) Harriet Frances; *m* 10 March 1827 Thomas Kerrich, 2nd s of John Kerrich, of Harleston, and *d* 6 Nov 1876, leaving issue. He *d* 19 April 1865

(2) Mary; *m* 5 May 1829 'Sir' Grenville Temple, self-styled 10th Bt (*see* 1850 edn), and *d* 10 May 1863, leaving issue. He *d* 7 June 1847

(3) Maynard; *m* R-Adml Henry Algernon Eliot and *d* 15 Jan 1856, leaving issue. He *d* 1903

(4) Marion; *m* 17 Feb 1842 Henry D Storey, RN, and had issue

(5) Emily; *m* C Sneegans and had issue

(6) Augusta Florence; *m* 1828 Rev Robert Louis Koe and *d* 31 March 1916. He *d* 22 Oct 1902

Sir FRANCIS *d* 12 Sept 1810; his est son,

Sir Thomas Baring, 2nd Bt, of Stratton Park, Hants; *b* 12 June 1772; in HEIC's serv 1790–1801, MP Wycombe and Hants; *m* 13 Sept 1794 Mary Ursula (*d* 26 July 1846), dau of Charles Sealy, of Calcutta, barrister, and had, with two daus (*d* unm):

1 FRANCIS THORNHILL, **1st Baron**

2 Thomas; *b* 7 Sept 1799; MP Huntingdon; *d* 18 Nov 1873

3 John, of Oakwood, Sussex; *b* 14 Sept 1801; *m* 1842 Charlotte Amelia (*d* 1846), dau of Rev George Porcher, of Malden Erleigh, and *dsp* 17 April 1888

4 Charles (Rt Rev); *b* 11 Jan 1807; DD, Bp Bristol and Gloucester 1856–61 and Durham 1861–79; *m* 1st 10 June 1830 Mary Ursula (*d* 16 June 1840), only dau of Col Charles Sealy, HEICS, and had, with a dau (*d* unm):

(1) Thomas Charles, of High Beech, Essex, DL; *b* 16 May 1831; MP S Essex 1874–85 and City London 1887–91; *m* 15 Nov 1859 Susan Carter (*d* 11 Jan 1897), dau of Robert Downe Minturn, of New York, and *d* 2 April 1891, having had, with two other sons (*d* young):

1a Harold Herman John, MBE; *b* 4 March 1869; *m* 24 Oct 1898 Mary, dau of John Augustus Churchill, of New York, and *d* 10 Dec 1927

2a Godfrey Nigel Everard; *b* 1 Oct 1870; *m* 14 Oct 1908 Hon Ada Sybil Roche (*d* 15 May 1944), only child of 2nd Baron Fermoy (*qv*), and *d* 22 June 1934, leaving:

1b Desmond Charles Nigel; *b* 5 Jan 1914; *educ* Eton; 3rd Dragoon Gds; *m* 12 Sept 1938 Mary (Mollie) Eileen, JP (*d* 24 March 1998), dau of Benjamin Walter Warner, and *d* 1991, leaving:

  1c +PETER [Peter Baring Esq, Dower Cottage, Ardington, Wantage, Oxon OX12 8PV]; *b* 12 Sept 1939; heir presumptive to btcy only; *educ* Eton; late Gren Gds; *m* 1973 *Rosemary Carol, dau of George Nigel Adams, of Fernham Manor, Faringdon, Oxon, and has:

    1d +Samuel Nigel; *b* 1987

    2d +Mark George; *b* 1990

  2c +Nigel [Nigel Baring Esq, The Lodge, Ardington, Wantage, Oxon OX12 8QA]; *b* 9 Aug 1940; *educ* Eton; *m* 18 July 1968 *Jane Finola, er dau of Francis Byrne, of Fulham, and has:

    1d +Lorne Benjamin Nigel; *b* 28 Aug 1970; *educ* Eton and RMA Sandhurst; Capt Scots Gds 1992–96

    2d +Edward Francis Desmond; *b* 1972; *educ* Eton and Edinburgh U

    1d *Lucinda Anne; *b* 1980; *educ* St Mary's Convent Ascot

  1c *(Margaret) Anne [Mrs Hugh Dalgety, Millards Hill House, Trudoxhill, Frome, Somerset BA11 5DW]; *b* 22 Nov 1944; *m* 1976 *Hugh Barkly Gonnerman Dalgety and has:

    1d *Richard Hugh; *b* 6 Sept 1977

    2d *Thomas Arthur; *b* 3 June 1984

    1d *Katherine Anne; *b* 12 April 1979

1b Cynthia Cecil; *b* 9 Oct 1909; *m* 1st 6 July 1932 (*divorce* 1947) Brig John Theodore de Horne Vaizey, RA, only s of Robert Edward Vaizey, OBE, JP, of Attwoods, Halstead, Essex, and had issue; *m* 2nd 24 Oct 1947 Forest Warren, s of Henry Nathaniel Warren, of Bishop's Caundle, Dorset, and had further issue. He *d* 23 Feb 1954

2b Ursula Doreen; *b* 4 March 1911; *d* 11 Oct 1952

1a Constance Mary; *m* 27 July 1891 Rev William Ewart Beamish Barter and had issue. He *d* 10 Jan 1928

2a Susannah Beatrix; *m* 29 June 1893 Rev Vincent Travera Macy and had issue. He *d* 21 April 1938

3a Muriel Ursula; *m* 25 April 1901 Henry Stephen Brenton, of The Manor House, High Beech, Loughton, Essex, and *d* Nov 1950, leaving issue. He *d* 25 Jan 1926

4 (cont.) Charles Baring *m* 2nd 14 April 1846 Caroline (*d* 9 May 1885 aged 75), dau of Thomas Read Kemp, of Dale Park, Sussex, and *d* 16 Sept 1879, having by her had, with two daus (*d* unm):

  (2) Francis Henry (Rev); *b* 21 Nov 1848; *educ* Trin Coll Cambridge (MA); Rector Eggesford, N Devon; *m* 1st 21 July 1881 Margaret Anne Borthwick (*dsp* 28 July 1882), widow of William Elmslie, FRCS, of Kashmir, India, and dau of Rev William Wallace Duncan, of Peebles; *m* 2nd 27 July 1886 Amy (*d* 19 Feb 1935), dau of Rev John Alexander Stamper, and *d* 22 Sept 1914, leaving:

    1a John Theodore; *b* 18 Aug 1887; Lt RE (T); *m* 16 Aug 1928 Alix McCowan (*d* 14 March 1948), dau of James Milne, of London SW1, and *dsp* 6 April 1967

    2a Ernest; *b* 16 June 1889; AIF WW I; *ka* 2 April 1917

    3a Charles Alexander; *b* 11 Jan 1893; AIF WW I; *ka* 4 Sept 1916

    4a Christopher Cecil; *b* 20 Sept 1897; Lt Roy W Kent Regt; *ka* 21 March 1918

    5a Reginald Arthur; *b* 23 April 1899; Lt RAF; *ka* 9 June 1918

    1a Dorothy Olive; *b* 26 Nov 1890

    2a Amy Rose; *b* 11 April 1894; *m* 1947 Edwin Daniel Doncaster (*d* 1950)

1 Charlotte; *b* 29 May 1805; *m* March 1833 Rev Henry George Wells, RD, of Alresford, Hants, Rector Kingsworthy, 2nd s of John Wells, JP, DL, MP, of Bickley Hall, and *d* 23 April 1871, leaving issue. He *d* 18 Aug 1852

2 Emily; *m* 6 July 1837 Rev William Maxwell Du Pre, Vicar Wooburn, Bucks and *d* 1883, leaving issue. He *d* 16 Oct 1855

3 Frances; *m* 10 April 1840, as his 1st w, her 1st cousin 1st and last Baron Taunton (*see* 1869 edn) and *d* 25 May 1850, leaving issue. He *d* 13 July 1869

Sir THOMAS *d* 3 April 1848; his est s,

Sir Francis Thornhill Baring, 3rd Bt, and **1st Baron Northbrook**, of Stratton, Co Southampton (UK), so cr 4 Jan 1866, PC (1839); *b* 20 April 1796; *educ* Winchester, privately at Cambridge, Ch Ch Oxford (BA and Double First 1817) and Lincoln's Inn 1817; barrister 1823, MP (Lib) Portsmouth 1826–65, a Ld Treasury 1830–34, Jt Sec Treasury June–Nov 1834 and 1835–39, Chllr Exchequer 1839–41, First Ld Admlty 1849–52, FRS 1849; *m* 1st 7 April 1825 Jane (*d* 23 April 1838), yst dau of Hon Sir George Grey, 1st Bt, of Fallodon (*qv*), and had, with another s (*d* an infant) and two daus (*d* unm):

  1 THOMAS GEORGE BARING, **2nd Baron Northbrook** and 1st EARL OF NORTHBROOK, Co Southampton, so cr 10 June 1876, as also VISCOUNT BARING of Lee, Co Kent (both UK), GCSI (1876), PC (1869); *b* 22 Jan 1826; *educ* Ch Ch Oxford (DCL 1876); MP (Lib) Penryn and Falmoutn 1857–66, a Ld Admlty 1857–58, U-Sec India 1859–61 and 1861–64, War 1861 and 1868–72 and Home Dept 1864–66, Sec to Admlty 1866, First Ld Admlty 1880–85, Viceroy India 1872–76, HC Egypt Aug–Nov 1884; Hants: Ld Lt 1892–1904, Chm CC, High Steward Winchester, Hon Col Hants Imp Yeo; ed *Journals and Correspondence of Sir Francis Thornhill Baring, Lord Northbrook* (privately printed 1905); *m* 6 Sept 1848, Elizabeth Harriet (*d* 3 June 1867), dau of Henry Charles Sturt, of Crichel, Dorset (*see* 1940 edn ALINGTON, B), and *d* 15 Nov 1904, leaving:

    (1) FRANCIS GEORGE BARING, **3rd Baron Northbrook** and 2nd EARL OF NORTHBROOK, DL Hants; *b* 6 Dec 1850; *educ* Eton; High Steward Winchester 1906, MP Winchester 1880–85 and N Bedford 1886–92, Lt Rifle Bde and Gren Gds, Orders St Sava Serbia and Crown of Belgium; *m* 1st 26 June 1894 Ada Ethel Sophie (*dsp* 22 July 1894), yst dau of Col C Davidson, CB, and formerly w of Ian Robert James Murray Grant of Glenmoriston, Inverness; *m* 2nd 10 June 1899 Florence Anita Eyre, CBE (*d* 4 Dec 1946), widow of Sir Robert John Abercromby, 7th Bt (*qv*), and dau of Eyre Coote (*see* COOTE, Bt), and *dsp* 12 April 1929, when the Earldom and Viscounty expired

    (2) Arthur Napier Thomas; *b* 3 June 1854; RN; lost at sea in the *Captain* 7 Sept 1870

    (1) Jane Emma, CI, CBE (1920); *m* 29 Jan 1890 Col Hon Sir Henry George Lewis Crichton, KCB, 3rd s of 3rd Earl of Erne (*qv*), and *d* 17 Jan 1936

1 Mary; *m* 21 April 1864 John Bonham Carter, MP, of Adhurst St Mary, Hants, and *d* 7 June 1906, leaving issue. He *d* 26 Nov 1884

The **1st Baron** *m* 2nd 31 March 1841 Lady Arabella Howard (*d* 10 Dec 1884 aged 75), 2nd dau of 1st Earl of Effingham (*qv*), and *d* 6 Sept 1866, having by her had:

  2 Francis Henry; *b* 22 July 1850; High Sheriff Surrey 1888; *m* 13 Feb 1878 Lady Grace Elizabeth (*d* 23 May 1935), dau of 9th Earl of Cork and Orrery (*qv*), and *d* 7 March 1915, having had:

    (1) FRANCIS ARTHUR, **4th Baron**

    (2) John Henry; *b* 3 Dec 1885; *educ* Rugby and Trin Coll Oxford; Capt Roy Irish Regt WW I; *d* unm 3 Dec 1956

    (3) Rupert Alexander; *b* 23 Feb 1891; *d* 3 Aug 1894

The 2nd EARL/3rd BARON's cousin,

FRANCIS ARTHUR BARING, **4th Baron Northbrook**; *b* 20 July 1882; *educ* Eton and Trin Coll Oxford; *m* 1st 30 April 1914 Evelyn Gladys Isabella (*d* 20 Feb 1919), dau of John George Charles by Lady Edith Hester, dau of 5th Marquess of Sligo (*qv*), and had:

  1 FRANCIS JOHN BARING, **5th Baron Northbrook**, JP (Hants 1954), DL (1972); *b* 31 May 1915; *educ* Winchester and Trin Coll Oxford (BA 1937); *m* 27 Jan 1951 *Rowena Margaret, 2nd dau of Brig-Gen Sir William Henry Manning, GCMG, KBE, CB, and *d* 1990, leaving:

    (1) FRANCIS THOMAS BARING, **6th and present Baron Northbrook**

    (1) *Laura Anne [The Hon Mrs Macpherson, The Old Rectory, Aston Sandford, nr Aylesbury, Bucks]; *b* 12 June 1952; *m* 15 May 1982 her sister's bro-in-law *Ewen Cameron Stewart Macpherson, est s of Brig George Philip Stewart Macpherson, OBE, TD, and has:

      1a *James Francis Stewart; *b* 1983

      2a *George Malcolm Stewart; *b* 1985

    (2) *Alexandra Grace [The Hon Mrs Macpherson, Armsworth Park House, Old Alresford, Hants SO24 9RH]; *b* 4 Feb 1957; *m* 1981 *(Philip) Strone Stewart Macpherson, yst s of Brig George Macpherson, OBE, TD, and has:

      1a *Philip Strone Alexander Stewart; *b* 1985

      1a *Temora Anne; *b* 1988

      2a *Clementina Grace; *b* 28 Sept 1989

    (3) *Catherine Margaret [The Hon Mrs Wrey, Pink Cottage, Tawstock, N Devon]; *b* 12 May 1965; *m* 1992 *(Edward) Sherard Bourchier Wrey, yr s of Sir (Castel Richard) Bourchier Wrey, 14th Bt (*qv*), and has issue

  1 *Anne [The Hon Anne Baring, Westwood, West Meon, Petersfield, Hants]; *b* 13 Feb 1917

The **4th Baron** *m* 2nd 1 Dec 1941 Constance Maud (*d* 11 April 1976), dau of Frank Griffin, of Kew, and *d* 15 Dec 1947

NORTHESK

Arms: Quarterly, 1st and 4th, or an eagle displayed azure, armed, beaked and membered sable and (honourable augmentation) charged on the breast with a naval crown of the field; 2nd and 3rd, argent a pale gules (for Earldom of Northesk). **Crests:** 1 The stern of a battleship of the line with three lanthorns, all proper, inflamed gules, 2 Issuant from a naval crown or a demi-leopard proper, holding a rose argent, barbed and seeded vert. **Supporters:** Two leopards regardant proper, gorged of three roses argent, barbed and seeded vert, each leopard sustaining a banner of St George. **Mottoes:** 1 (over 1st crest) Trafalgar, 2 (over 2nd crest) *Britannia victrix* ('Britannia victorious'), 3 (below the compartment) *Tache sans tache* ('Immaculately accomplished task'). **Creations:** L. (S) 20 April 1639, E. (S) 1 Nov 1647.

THE 14TH EARL OF NORTHESK and **Lord Rosehill and Eglismauldie** (David John MacRae Carnegie) [The Rt Hon The Earl of Northesk, Haben Farm House, Rogate, Hants]; *b* 3 Nov 1954; *s f* 1994; *educ* West Hill Park Titchfield, Eton, Brook House, Market Harborough, UCL; estate owner/manager; *m* 1979 *Jacqueline Mary, er adopted dau of David Lorne Dundas Reid (*see* REID, Bt, of Ellon) and has:

  1 +ALEXANDER ROBERT MACRAE, *Lord Rosehill*; *b* 16 Nov 1980

1 *Sarah Louise Mary; *b* 1982

2 *Fiona Jean Elizabeth; *b* 1987

3 *Sophie Margaret Jean; *b* 1990

Lineage: JOHN CARNEGIE, **1st Earl of Northesk**, so *cr* 1 Nov 1647 (originally as EARL OF ETHIE, LORD LOUR AND EGLISMALDIE, but exchanged 25 Oct 1666 for present titles), as also previously 20 April 1639 LORD LOUR AND EGLISMALDIE (originally LORD LOUR till exchanged 1666) (all S), JP (1623); *b c* 1579 (yr bro of 1st Earl of Southesk; *see* FIFE, D); his f made over to him (roy charter 1 March 1595/6) Aithie, Cuickstoun, etc, Forfarshire; ktd 1610 or 1611, Sheriff Forfarshire 1620 and 1634; *m* 1st Magdalen (*d* 10 March 1650), dau of Sir James Halyburton of Pitcur and widow of John Erskine of Dun, and had, with other issue:

1 DAVID, **2nd Earl**

2 John, of Boystack; *m* Margaret, dau of Sir Alexander Erskine of Dun, and had:

(1) John, of Boystack; *m* Jean, dau of David Fothringham of Powrie, and had:

1a John, of Boystack; MP Forfarshire 1708–16; served heir to f 18 Jan 1687; Slr-Gen Scotland 1714–16; *m* 6 Nov 1707 Margaret, dau of Skene of Grange, and *d c* 14 May 1750, having had:

1b James, of Boystack; advocate 1733; *d* 4 Sept 1768, having had:

1c Stewart; *m* her cousin William FULLARTON of that Ilk later LINDSAY of Spynie and *d* 23 May 1765, leaving issue

2b David; *dsp*

1a Margaret; *m* June 1711 John Fullarton of that Ilk

(2) James, of Kinnoull and Braikie; *m* Anne, dau of Sir David Ogilvy of Inverquharity, and *d* Dec 1693, having had:

1a John, of Kinnoull; *m* Anne, dau and heiress of Archibald Auchinleck of Balmanno, and had:

1b Robert; sold Kinnoull 1742

1b Anne; served heiress to her f 10 Aug 1709; *m* Robert Carnegie of Kinnoull, er s of Carnegie of Ballindarg

(1) Margaret; *m* 1673 Sir Charles Ramsay, 3rd Bt (*qv*)

1 Anna; *m* (contract 8 Nov 1684) Patrick Wood, s of Sir Henry Wood of Bonnington, and had issue

2 Marjorie; *m* 1st 1637 James Scott, s of Sir John Scott of Scotstarvit; *m* 2nd (contract 26 March 1652) John Preston, Yr. of Aidrie

3 Jean; *m* 1st Alexander Lindsay (*dsp*), er s of 2nd Lord Spynie (*see* CRAWFORD and BALCARRES, E); *m* 2nd (contract 9 Aug 1647) John Lindsay of Edzell

4 Magdalene; *m* (contract 24 Feb 1645) William Graham of Claverhouse and had issue

The **1st Earl** *m* 2nd 29 April 1652 Marjory (*dsp*), 4th dau of Andrew Maule of Guildie and widow of William Nairn, and *d* 8 Jan 1667 aged *c* 88

His est s,

DAVID CARNEGIE, **2nd Earl of Northesk**; Col Forfarshire 1648, Commr for Supply Forfarshire 1655 and of Excise for Perthshire 1661; *m* (contract 19 Oct 1637 and 12 Jan 1637/8) Lady Jane Maule (*d* Nov 1685), dau of 1st Earl of Panmure, and *d* 12 Dec 1679, having had:

1 DAVID, **3rd Earl**

2 James, of Finhaven; MP Forfarshire; *m* 10 Feb 1674 Anna (*d* 3 Sept 1694), dau of Robert Maitland, and *d* 10 March 1707, having had:

(1) Charles; *dsp* 1712

(2) James, of Finavon; *m* 1st Margaret, dau of William Bennet of Grubbet, and had two daus; *m* 2nd Violet, dau of Sir James Nasmith of Posso, and *d* 1765, having by her had:

1a James, of Finavon; *d* unm 1777

1a Anne; *m* Sir John Ogilvy, 4th Bt, (*qv*), of Inverquharity and had issue

2a Margaret; *m* 1st 29 April 1731 John Foulis of Woodhall; *m* 2nd Charles Lewis and had issue

3a Barbara, of Finavon; *m* Sir Robert Douglas, Bt, of Glenbervie (*see* 1970 edn), author: *Peerage of Scotland*, and *dsps*

(1) Margaret; *m* Patrick Lyon of Auchterhouse (*see* STRATHMORE AND KINGHORNE, E)

(2) Jean; *m* Alexander BLAIR later CARNEGIE of Kinfauns and had issue

3 Patrick, of Lour; *m* 1st 30 Oct 1682 Marjory (*d* 25 May 1701), dau of Sir Patrick Threipland of Fingask, and had eight sons and three daus; *m* 2nd 27 May 1702 Margaret Stewart and *d* 7 Dec 1723, leaving by her, with five yr sons and three daus:

(1) Patrick, of Lour; *b* 14 Jan 1684; *m* Alison, dau of John Watson of Turin, and *d* 8 Sept 1729, having had, with four yr sons and seven daus:

1a Patrick, of Lour; *b* 30 Oct 1720; *m* 1st Elizabeth, dau of John Graham; *m* 2nd Margaret, dau of James Graham, and *d* 11 Nov 1799, having by her had, with two yr sons and three daus:

1b Patrick, of Lour; *b* 25 Feb 1757; *m* 20 April 1789 Margaret St Clair (*d* 21 Feb 1835), dau of Alexander Bower of Kincaldrum, Forfar, and *d* 24 Nov 1819, having had, with three other sons:

1c Patrick CARNEGIE later WATSON-CARNEGY of Lour and Turin; *b* 3 Oct 1791; *m* 23 April 1832 Rachel Ann (*d* 16 Nov 1852), est dau of James Forbes of Echt, Aberdeenshire, and *d* 3 Sept 1838, having had:

1d Patrick Alexander, of Lour, JP, DL; *b* 29 March 1836; Capt 15th Hus, Maj and Hon Lt-Col Forfarshire Light Horse; *m* 5 Jan 1865 Elizabeth Diana (*d* 5 March 1910), dau of Duncan Davidson, of Tulloch Castle, Ross-shire, by Hon Elizabeth Diana, dau of 3rd Baron Macdonald (*qv*), and *dsp* 4 June 1914

2d James Forbes; *b* 11 March 1838; *d* unm 1 May 1855

2c Alexander, CB; *b* 25 Feb 1793; Maj-Gen IA; *m* Sept 1823 Isabella (*d* 20 June 1835), dau of William Don, and *d* 1 Aug 1862, having had:

1d Patrick, CIE; *b* 20 May 1825; FRGS; Commr Indian Serv; *m* 25 Nov 1854 Isabella Grace MacNab (*d* 17 March 1915), dau of Donald Butter, MD, and *d* 1886, having had:

1e Patrick Alexander Donald; *b* 27 Nov 1855; barrister; *d* 27 July 1885

2e Arthur George Clarke; *b* 6 Sept 1857; *d* 7 Sept 1885

3e Robert William Elliott; *b* 20 Sept 1860; Lt RA, ADC to Maj-Gen Alexander Carnegy; *d* 23 April 1887

1e Isabella Eliza Butter; *m* 20 Sept 1881 Francis Edward Joseph (*d* 17 April 1929); *s* her cousin in Lour 1914, took with her husb the name CARNEGY 1915 and *d* 25 Jan 1954 aged 101, leaving:

1f Ughtred Elliott Carnegy, DSO, MC, JP, DL; *b* 1886; *m* 1919 Violet, MBE (*d* 1965), dau of Henry William Henderson (see FARINGDON, B), and had:

1g *ELIZABETH PATRICIA, *cr* BARONESS CARNEGY OF LOUR (*qv*)

2g *Christian Margaret; *b* 1927; *m* 1952 *Sir John Lindsay Eric Smith, CH, CBE, FRIBA, and has:

1h *Adam Carnegy Eric; *b* 1953; *m* 1983 *Katherine, dau of Herbert McDuffee, of Shingle Springs, California

2h *Bartholemew Evan; *b* 1955; *m* 1987 *Catherine Nicola Blanche, dau of Gavin Rowan-Hamilton, of Stenton, E Lothian (*see* BLAKISTON, Bt), and has:

1j *Matthew John Patrick; *b* 1988

1j *Emily (Millie) Blanche Christian; *b* 1989

1h Emma Victoria Eric; *b* 1956; *educ* St Anne's Coll, Oxford; *d* 1983

2h *Serena Mary; *b* 1959; *educ* St Anne's Coll Oxford; *m* 1993, as his 2nd w, *Hon (Arthur) Nicholas Winston Soames, MP (*see* MARLBOROUGH, D)

3h *Clare Elizabeth Dido; *b* 1962; *educ* St Anne's Coll Oxford

2d Alexander, CB; *b* 30 June 1829; Gen Bombay SC; *m* 1st 27 Dec 1853 Frances Jane (*d* 2 Oct 1857), dau of John Whitehead, and had as a s (*d* unm); *m* 2nd 29 Dec 1859 Augusta (*d* 29 Dec 1887), dau of Robert D Ker, and by her had, with two daus (*d* unm):

2e Charles Gilbert, MVO; *b* 29 June 1864; Lt-Col and Brevet Col IA, Burmese Expdn 1886–88 (medal, two clasps), WW I (medal and Russian Order St Stanislas 2nd Cl); *m* 1 March 1892 Evelyn Mary (*d* 30 Dec 1953), dau of Charles Collins Prichard, of Pwllywrach, Glam, and *d* 23 April 1928, leaving:

1f Patrick Charles Alexander (Rev Canon); *b* 1 June 1893; *educ* privately and Hertford Coll Oxford (BA 1915, MA 1918); Vicar Spalding 1945–49, Rector Rugby 1949–51, Canon Coventry 1954–61, Canon Emeritus Coventry 1961; *m* 17 April 1928 *Joyce Eleanor, est dau of William Percy Townsley, of Roundhay, Leeds, and *d* 28 May 1969, leaving:

1g +Patrick Charles [Patrick Carnegy Esq, 5 The Causeway, Elsworth, Cambridge]; *b* 23 Sept 1940; *educ* Rugby and Trin Hall Cambridge (BA 1963, MA 1966); with *TLS* 1969 on

2g +Colin David [Colin Carnegy Esq, The Parsonage, Stapleford, Wilts SP3 4LJ]; *b* 16 Aug 1942; *educ* Rugby and Jesus Coll Oxford (BA 1964, MA 1968); slr 1968; *m* 1 Sept 1973 *Rosemary Frances Deschamps, dau of Saunders Edward Chamier, of Wadhurst, Sussex, and has:

1h +Charles Alexander; *b* 15 Aug 1975

2h +Edward William; *b* 3 Oct 1977

3h +Francis Henry; *b* 10 Oct 1981

1h *Henrietta Claire; *b* 18 Oct 1983

1g *Daphne Joyce [Miss Daphne Carnegy, 4 Ingram Rd, London N2]; *b* 3 March 1947; *educ* Nottingham U (BA 1969)

3e Frederick William (Rev); *b* 20 Oct 1865; *educ* St John's Coll Cambridge (MA); Preb Hereford Cathedral, Rector and RD Ledbury, Hon CF 4th Cl; *m* 9 Nov 1898 Mildred Constance, historical author (*d* 26 Feb 1952), dau of Col Robert Bourne, of Cowarne Court, Ledbury, and *d* 24 Jan 1939, leaving:

1f Hector David; LRAM; *b* 10 Sept 1913; *educ* Wellington and Keble Coll Oxford (BA 1934, MA 1950); *m* 29 July 1942 *Pamela Alice Burnell [Mrs Hector Carnegy, 9 Browning Ave, Bournemouth, Dorset BH5 1NR], dau of Henry Stafford Burnell Tubbs, of Boscombe, Hants, and *d* 1982, leaving:

1g *Alison Sandra Christabel; *b* 19 May 1944

1f Rachel Alexandra; *b* 23 Feb 1912; Order Mercy 1935; *m* 10 Jan 1939 Cyril Herbert Knight, FRCOG, Hon ARCM, s of Mark Knight, of Bournemouth, and had:

1g *Virginia; *b* 11 Nov 1941

2g *Celia Claire; *b* 11 Sept 1945

4e Harry George; *b* 20 Oct 1865; Maj IA; *m* 1 Jan 1891 Rose Marion (*d* 7 June 1948), dau of Maj James Lancaster Bell, RA, and *d* 9 March 1905, having had:

1f Frederick Alexander; *b* 21 July 1895; Lt 10th Glos Regt; *ka* Oct 1915

1f Eileen Augusta; *b* 1 Oct 1898; *m* 7 Feb 1924 (*divorce* 1936) Philip Vaughan Roberts, only s of E O Roberts, of Liverpool, and had issue

1e Augusta Ker; *m* 13 Sept 1879 James T Hathornthwaite (*d* 1911), Pncpl Elphinstone Coll, Bombay, and *d* 14 March 1938, leaving issue

2d (cont.) Gen Alexander Carnegy *m* 3rd 1889 Helen Meta (*d* 4 April 1923), dau of Charles Henry Forbes, DL, of Kingairloch, Argyll, and widow of Maj Robert Graham Mayne, and *d* 25 Oct 1900

1d Mary Anne; *m* 7 Feb 1853 Maj-Gen John Richardson Auldjo (*d* 14 June 1879) and *d* 1899, having had issue

2d Georgina; *m* 26 Dec 1863 Maj Edward Robert Bigsby Barnes, 35th Regt (*d* 1880), and *d* 13 Aug 1900, having had issue

3d Isabella; *m* 27 Sept 1855 James Wilkie (*d* 18 Nov 1871) and had issue

3c James; *b* 19 March 1794; *m* Maria, dau of Adrian Rock, and *d* 27 March 1821, leaving:

1d Patrick Adrian; *b* 4 June 1818; *m* 1856 Catherine (*d* 1876), dau of Michael Chitty, and had:

  1e Charliemine

4c Robert; MD; *b* 2 July 1796; *m* 1st 1 Oct 1821 Amelia Nimmo (*dsp* 1822); *m* 2nd 3 March 1831 Christian (*dsp*), dau of John Ramsay; *m* 3rd Sept 1841 Jane (*dsp* June 1877), dau of Robert Montgomerie

5c William; *b* 31 Aug 1803; Maj HEICS; *m* 16 Sept 1830 Isabella, dau of Edward Newton, and *dsp* 7 May 1880

6c Charles; *b* 8 Jan 1808; HEIC Naval Serv; *m* 27 April 1837 Sophia, dau of Thomas Bell, and *d* 22 March 1874, leaving:

  1d Patrick Thomas; *b* 12 June 1838; DC Assam; *d* unm 21 Jan 1878

  2d Charles William; *b* 31 July 1839; *m* 21 Sept 1880 Margaret, dau of Alexander Smith, MD, of Forfar, and *dsp* 9 April 1905

  3d Alexander St Clair Bower; *b* 18 Feb 1846; *m* 29 Feb 1872 Mary Ann (*d* 15 July 1933), dau of John Lewis Levy, JP Rochester, and *d* 7 Feb 1937, having had:

    1e Patrick Lewis St Clair; *b* 19 Dec 1875; *educ* Cambridge (BA); *d* 19 March 1928

    1e Elizabeth Mary; *d* unm 5 Oct 1958

  4d James Souter; *b* 16 May 1847; *m* 26 Sept 1877 Jeannie (*d* 18 March 1923), dau of Charles Macpherson, of New Brunswick, and *d* 8 Sept 1915, leaving:

    1e Colin Charles Macpherson; *b* 1885; *m* Jan 1922 Mary Teresa Diaz Infante, dau of Michael Diaz Infante, of Leon, Mexico, and *d* Jan 1931, leaving:

      1f +Charles William; *b* 1 Jan 1923

    2e James William Macpherson; *b* 1893

    1e Katie Audrey Macpherson

    2e Marguerite Sophia Macpherson; *m* 1910 James Henry Nelson and had issue

  5d Robert Bower; *b* 19 Nov 1849; *m* 1896 Fanny Jane (*d* 1 March 1949), dau of Dr T A H Dodd, of Newcastle, and *d* 15 Sept 1936, leaving:

    1e Francis Anthony Roberts; *b* 24 May 1900; *educ* London (MA 1923) and Königsberg Us (PhD 1930); F/O RAFVR; *m* 22 Dec 1925 Valentine (*d* 14 Feb 1969), dau of Theodor Taupmann, and had:

      1f Derek Francis; *b* 23 Aug 1928; Lt-Cdr RN Submarine Serv; *m* 24 March 1961 Judith Frances (*d* 1991), only dau of David C Herbert, and *d* 1993, leaving:

        1g +Miles Bower; *b* 13 Oct 1962

        2g [Angus Carnegy Esq, 3 Hickley Cotts, Cheriton, Hants]; *b* 18 Nov 1964; MB, BS; *m* 1992 *Mary-Ann Benson, dau of Ronald Benson Malam

      2f +Julian Roy [Julian Carnegy Esq, 66 Cromford Way, New Malden, Surrey]; *b* 6 Oct 1931; *m* 1957 *Vivien, er dau of Stewart Kay-Menzies, and has:

        1g +Christopher Roy; *b* 9 Dec 1961

        1g *Diana Elizabeth; *b* 1 Jan 1959; *m* 1983 *David John Burchell

  1d Margaret Anne Ogilvy; *d* unm 5 March 1922

  2d Alison Anne; *d* unm 5 Aug 1929

  3d Wilhelmina Sophia; *d* unm 8 Nov 1915

  4d Mary Augusta Hamilton; *m* 30 Nov 1891 Alexander Martin Crichton and *d* 20 Oct 1947, leaving issue

1c Margaret; *d* unm 15 Jan 1864

2c Ann; *m* 3 April 1831 James Sauter and *d* 1870

3c Helen; *m* Jan 1832 Lt-Col James Gardner and *d* 1845, leaving issue

4 Alexander CARNEGIE later BLAIR of Kinfauns; *m* 1st Ann (*d* by 24 May 1638), dau and heiress of Sir William Blair of Kinfauns; *m* 2nd Margaret, dau of John Nairne of Muckarsie, and had issue by both ws

5 Robert; *d* young

1 Jean; *m* 3rd Earl of Balcarres (*see* CRAWFORD and BALCARRES, E)

2 Magdalen; *m* John Moodie of Ardbikie and had issue

The 2nd EARL's est s,

DAVID CARNEGIE, **3rd Earl of Northesk**; *b* Nov 1643; *m* c 9 Sept 1669 Elizabeth, dau of 1st Earl of Lindsay (*qv*) and (17th Earl of) Crawford, and *d* 3 Oct 1668, leaving, with a yr s and four daus (including Christian, *m* 1st Duke of Montrose; *qv*):

DAVID CARNEGIE, **4th Earl of Northesk**, PC (S 1698 and 1702); Sheriff Forfar 1702, Commr Treasury Scotland 1705–08 and Trade and Mfrs 1711, rep S peer 1708–15; *m* c 29 Jan 1697 Margaret, dau of Margaret, Countess of Wemyss in her own right (*see* WEMYSS, E), and *d* 14 Jan 1729, having had, with two other daus (*d* unm):

1 DAVID CARNEGIE, **5th Earl of Northesk**; *b* 11 June 1701; *educ* Edinburgh and St Andrews Us; Sheriff Forfar; *d* unm 24 June 1741

2 GEORGE, **6th Earl**

1 Margaret; *m* George, Lord Balgonie, s of 5th Earl of Leven and (2nd Earl of) Melville (*qv*)

2 Elizabeth; *m* 5th Lord Balmerinoch (*see* ELPHINSTONE, L)

3 Anne; *m* Sir Alexander Hope of Kerse, Stirling

The 5th EARL's bro,

GEORGE CARNEGIE, **6th Earl of Northesk**; *b* 2 Aug 1716; joined RN 1737, Adml the White 1778; *m* 30 April 1748 Anne, est dau of 7th Earl of Leven and (4th Earl of) Melville (*qv*), and *d* 22 Jan 1792, having had, with other issue:

1 David, *Lord Rosehill*; *b* 5 May 1749; Ensign 25th Foot 1765–67; *m* Aug 1768 Christian Cameron or Mary Cheer and *dsp & vp* 19 Feb 1788

2 WILLIAM, **7th Earl**

3 George; *b* 21 Aug 1773; Lt-Col; *m* 1796 Elizabeth, 4th dau of John Swinton, 27th of that Ilk, Ld of Session as Lord Swinton, and *d* 1839, leaving:

  (1) George James; *b* 13 May 1806; *m* 3 Oct 1837 Jacobina Frances, only dau of Alexander Nicholas, and *d* 20 Dec 1837

1 Elizabeth; *m* 16 Aug 1766 3rd Earl of Hopetoun and *d* 19 Aug 1793, having had issue (*see* LINLITHGOW, M)

2 Margaret; *m* Charles Watson, of Saughton, Edinburgh, and *d* 15 March 1793

3 Mary Anne; *m* Rev John Kemp, DD, and *d* 2 June 1798

The 6th EARL's er surv s,

WILLIAM CARNEGIE, **7th Earl of Northesk**, GCB (1815, KB 1806); *b* 10 April 1758; joined RN 1771, Cdr 1780, Post Capt 1782, 3rd i/c as R-Adml the White at Trafalgar, V-Adml the Blue 1808, V-Adml the Red 1810, Adml 1814, R-Adml of the UK 1821–31, C-in-C Plymouth 1827–30; rep S peer 1796–1807 and 1830–31; *m* 9 Dec 1788 Mary (*d* 1836), only dau of William Henry Ricketts, of Longwood, Hants, and n of 1st Earl St Vincent (*qv*), and *d* 28 May 1831, having had:

1 George, *Lord Rosehill*; *b* 3 Nov 1791; *educ* Twyford Sch and Winchester; joined RN; lost at sea while serving in HMS *Blenheim* 2 Feb 1807

2 WILLIAM HOPETOUN, **8th Earl**

3 John Jervis, DL; *b* 8 July 1807; High Sheriff 1862; *m* 1st 13 Feb 1836 Charlotte (*d* 20 May 1874), only dau of David Stevenson, of Dollan, Carmarths, and had a dau; *m* 2nd 8 June 1876 Georgiana (*d* 10 April 1896), dau of Edward Marjoribanks and widow of Elliot Grasett, and *d* 18 Jan 1892

4 Swynfen Thomas, CB; *b* 8 March 1813; *m* 29 Sept 1858 (*divorce* 1872) Louisa Albertina, est dau of Adrian J Hope, and *dsp* 29 Nov 1879

1 Mary; *m* 12 Feb 1810 Walter Long (*d* 1871), of Preshaw, Hants, and *d* 7 March 1875

2 Anne Letitia; *m* 18 Jan 1821 James Cruikshank (*d* 4 May 1842), of Langley Park, Angus, and *d* 25 Feb 1870

3 Elizabeth Margaret; *b* 1798; *m* 21 Nov 1825 Gen Frederick R Thackeray, CB, RE (*d* 19 Sept 1860), and *d* 12 April 1886

4 Jane Christian; *m* 27 Dec 1820 William Fullerton Lindsay Carnegie, of Kinblethmount, Forfar, and *d* 1 Oct 1840

5 Georgina Henrietta; *b* 2 Aug 1811; *d* 7 Nov 1827

The 7th EARL's est surv son,

WILLIAM HOPETOUN CARNEGIE, **8th Earl of Northesk**; *b* 17 Oct 1794; *educ* Winchester; *m* 14 Feb 1843 Georgiana Maria (*d* 23 Feb 1874), est dau of Adml Hon Sir George Elliot, KCB (*see* MINTO, E), and *d* 5 Dec 1878, having had, with a dau (Margaret Mary Adeliza, *d* 27 Sept 1871):

GEORGE JOHN CARNEGIE, **9th Earl of Northesk**, DL (Forfarshire and Hants); *b* 1 Dec 1843; Lt-Col Scots Fus Gds 1873–74; rep S peer 1885–91; *m* 28 Feb 1865 his 1st cousin Elizabeth Georgina Frances (*d* 2 May 1933), dau of Adml Sir George Elliot, KCB (*see* MINTO, E), and *d* 9 Sept 1891, having had:

1 DAVID JOHN CARNEGIE, **10th Earl of Northesk**, JP, DL; *b* 1 Dec 1865; *educ* Eton; Maj and Hon Lt-Col 3rd Bn Glos Regt, ADC to Govr Victoria 1889–91 and 1892–95, rep S peer 1900–21, Lt RNVR WW I; *m* 3 Feb 1894 Elizabeth Boyle (*d* 28 Jan 1950), est dau of Maj-Gen George Skene Hallowes, KOSB, and *d* 5 Dec 1921, having had:

  (1) DAVID LUDOVIC GEORGE HOPETOUN CARNEGIE, **11th Earl of Northesk**; *b* 24 Sept 1901; *educ* Gresham's; 2nd Lt Coldstream Gds Res of Offrs 1921–23, Hon Maj Intell Corps; *m* 1st 19 July 1923 (*divorce* Scottish Court 1928) Jessica Ruth, dau of F A Brown; *m* 2nd 7 Aug 1929 Elizabeth, dau of Anthony Alexander Vlasto, of Binfield Park, Berks, and *d* 7 Nov 1963, having adopted Dec 1962:

    *Phyllida Rosemary [Mrs Marcus Cooke, Welmore Cottage, Hinton Waldrist, Berks]; *b* 4 June 1942; *m* 1st 2 April 1968 Daniel Hurt Palmer Mellen, est s of William Palmer Mellen, of Dunmow, Essex, by Bridget Florida, yst dau of Capt Henry Albert le Fowne Hurt, CMG, RN; *m* 2nd Dec 1973 *Marcus Mervyn Cooke, yr s of (John) Sholto Fitzpatrick Cooke, of Ferry Quarter, Strangford, Co Down (*qv*)

  (1) Katherine Jane Elizabeth; *b* 25 June 1904; *m* 1st 22 Dec 1924 (*divorce* 1945) Lt-Col William Bridgeman Lambert Manley, Gren Gds, er s of Maj William Edward Manley, OBE, and had issue; *m* 2nd 28 April 1945 Brig Edward Leathley Armitage, OBE, RA, s of Col John Leathley Armitage, of Guildford, and *d* 2 April 1949

2 Douglas George; *b* 4 Jan 1870; MP Winchester 1916–18; Hon Lt-Col Labour Corps, Capt and Hon Maj 3rd Bn Glos Regt; *m* 26 April 1894 Margaret Jean (*d* 31 July 1960), 2nd dau of Arthur Henry Johnstone Douglas (*see* QUEENSBERRY, M), and *d* 27 Feb 1937, having had:

  (1) JOHN DOUGLAS, **12th Earl**

  (2) David Alexander; *b* 15 Jan 1897; 2nd Lt RA; *ka* 2 April 1917

  (1) Jean Douglas; *b* 31 Aug 1899; *m* 21 Aug 1928 Lt-Col James David Bibby and had issue (*see* BIBBY, Bt)

  (2) Margaret; *b* 7 June 1901; *d* unm 19 April 1946

3 Ian Ludovic Andrew; *b* 30 Sept 1881; Lt RN; *m* 30 March 1905 Anna Barbara (*m* 2nd 8 Aug 1914 Capt Reginald Dalrymple), yst dau of Col Bradford Atkinson, of Angerton, Northumberland, and *dsp* 4 Jan 1909

1 Helen Alice; *m* 9 April 1890 Sir Francis Eden Lacey (*d* 26 May 1946), barrister, yst s of W C Lacey, and *d* 18 May 1908, having had issue

The 11th EARL's cousin,

JOHN DOUGLAS CARNEGIE, **12th Earl of Northesk**; *b* 16 Feb 1895; *educ* Gresham's and King's Coll Cambridge (BA 1920); T/Maj 95th (Hants Yeo) Bde, FRA (TA), WW I (despatches); *m* 20 July 1920 Dorothy Mary (*d* 29 Aug 1967), est dau of Col Sir William Robert Campion, KCMG, DSO, DL, and *d* 22 July 1975, having had:

1 David John; *b* 4 Dec 1922; *d* 21 Nov 1942

2 ROBERT ANDREW, **13th Earl**

1 Mary Elizabeth; *b* 18 Oct 1921; *m* 1942 (*divorce* 1954) Maj Donald Arthur Knights and had issue

2 *Susan Jean [The Lady Susan Connell, Lower Wreyland, Lustleigh, Devon TQ13 9TS]; *b* 20 Aug 1930; *m* 21 May 1955 *David Blackall Connell, MD, BS, er s of Arthur Blackall Connell, MRCS, LRCP, and has:

  (1) *Timothy Robert Blackall; *b* 10 Sept 1956; *m* 1983 (*divorce* 19–) Susanne Hammer-Jensen, dau of Birthe Jensen, of Hadsund, Denmark; *m* 2nd 1997 *Tepu Heikinheimo, of Tampere, Finland, and by his 1st w has:

    1a *Simon; *b* 1984

    1a *Emilie; *b* 1987

(2) *Alistair Douglas; *b* 25 Jan 1960; *m* 1995 *Karen Ashton, of Upper Hutt, NZ

(1) *Caroline Lisa [Mrs David Wilson, Duchy Home Farm, Broadfield Farm, Tetbury, Glos]; *b* 1 July 1958; *m* 1980 *David John Wilson, est s of Rev John Wilson, of Netherton, Peterborough, and has:

1a *Seth Thomas; *b* 1982

2a *Luke Alexander; *b* 1984

3a *Joshua Peter Arthur; *b* 1987

4a *Benjamin Montague; *b* 1990

The 12th EARL's only surv son,

ROBERT ANDREW CARNEGIE, **13th Earl of Northesk**; *b* 1926; cattle breeder, memb cncl Br Charolais Cattle Soc; author: *Diary of an Island Glen*; *m* 1st 1949 Jean Margaret (*d* 1989), yr dau of Capt John Duncan George MacRae (*see* BRISTOL, M); *m* 2nd 1989 *Brownie Elizabeth Heiman [The Rt Hon The Dowager Countess of Northesk, Springwaters, Ballamodha, IoM], dau of Scot Grimason and widow of Carl Heiman, and *d* 1994, having had by his 1st w:

1 DAVID JOHN MACRAE CARNEGIE, **14th and present Earl of Northesk**

1 *Karen Jean [The Lady Karen Fisher, Kilverstone Hall, Thetford, Norfolk IP24 2RL]; *b* 1951; *m* 1977 *Hon Patrick Vavasseur Fisher and has issue (*see* FISHER, B)

2 *Mary Barbara [The Lady Mary Damerell, Hatchery House, Mill Lane, Barrow, Suffolk IP29 5BT]; *b* 1953; *m* 1977 *William Patrick Stirling Damerell and has:

(1) *Charles; *b* 1980

(2) *Thomas; *b* 1982

(3) *Robert; *b* 1985

NORTHFIELD

Creation: B. (LP, UK) 1975.

THE BARON NORTHFIELD, of Telford, Co Salop ((William) Donald Chapman) [The Rt Hon The Lord Northfield, House of Lords, London SW1A 0PW]; *b* 25 Nov 1923; *educ* Barnsley GS and Emmanuel Coll Cambridge (MA, Sr Scholar); researcher Ag Ec Cambridge 1943–46; CC Cambridge 1945–47; Sec Trades Cncl and Lab Party 1945–57; Gen Sec Fabian Soc 1949–53 (Research Sec 1948–49); MP (Lab) Northfield 1951–70; G Gibbon Fell Nuffield Coll Oxford 1971–73, Visiting Fell Centre Contemporary European Studies Sussex U 1973–; Special Advsr EEC Commn 1978–84; Chm: Devpt Commrs 1973–79, Rural Devpt Commn 1974–80, Telford Devpt Corp 1975–87, Inquiry into acquisition of ag land 1977–79, Consortium Devpts Ltd 1986–92; author: *The European Parliament: the years ahead* (1973), *The Road to European Union* (1975)

Lineage: WILLIAM HENRY CHAPMAN; *m* Norah F E — and had:

(WILLIAM) DONALD, *cr* a **Baron**

NORTHUMBERLAND

ESPERANCE · EN · DIEU

Arms: Quarterly, 1st and 4th grand quarters, counter-quartered 1st and 4th, or a lion rampant azure; 2nd and 3rd, gules three lucies hauriant argent (for LUCY); 2nd and 3rd, azure five fusils conjoined in fess or (for PERCY); 2nd and 3rd, grandquarters quarterly 1st and 4th, or three bars wavy gules, 2nd and 3rd, or a lion's head erased within a double tressure flory counter-flory gules (for HAY of Kinnoull). **Crest:** On a chapeau gules doubled ermine a lion statant, the tail extended azure. **Supporters:** Dexter, a lion rampant azure; sinister, a lion rampant guardant or, ducally crowned of the last, gorged with a collar compony argent and azure. **Motto:** *Esperance en Dieu* ('Hope in God') **Creations:** Bt. (E) 2 Aug 1660; B. (GB) (Percy) 21 Jan 1722/3, (GB) (Warkworth of Warkworth Castle) 2 Oct 1749 and (GB) (Lovaine, of Alnwick) 28 Jan 1784; E. (GB) (Northumberland) 2 Oct 1749, (GB) (Percy) 22 Oct 1766 and (GB) (Beverley) 2 Nov 1790; D. (GB) 22 Oct 1766.

THE 12TH DUKE OF NORTHUMBERLAND, Earl of Northumberland, **Earl Percy**, **Earl of Beverley**, Co York, **Lord Percy**, **Baron Warkworth of Warkworth Castle**, Co Northumberland, **Lord Lovaine**, **Baron of Alnwick**, Co Northumberland, and a **Baronet** (Sir Ralph George Algernon Percy, Bt, DL (Northumberland 1997)) [His Grace The Duke of Northumberland DL, Alnwick Castle, Northumberland NE66 1NG; Chatton Park, Chatton, Northumberland NE66 5RA; Syon House, Brentford, Middx TW8 8JF; Clive Lodge, Albury Park, Guildford, Surrey GU5 9AF]; *b* 16 Nov 1956; *s* bro 1995; *educ* Eton and Ch Ch Oxford; land agent, chartered surveyor and publisher, pres Northumberland Community Cncl; *m* 1979 *(Isobel) Jane M, dau of John Walter Maxwell Miller Richard, stockbroker and coal mine manager, of Edinburgh, and has:

1 +GEORGE DOMINIC, *Earl Percy*; *b* 4 May 1984; Page of Honour to HM THE QUEEN 1996–

2 +Max Ralph; *b* 26 May 1990

1 +Catherine Sarah; *b* 23 June 1982

2 +Melissa Jane; *b* 20 May 1987

Earldom and Dukedom of Northumberland: The pre-Norman Conquest Earls of Northumberland had to begin with ruled their territory as kings. But by the last few generations before 1066 they had come to acknowledge the Saxon kings of England as overlords. Earls of Northumbria, as also rather later of Northumberland, were something like appointed high officials, for example governors, though the office was often held by successive members of the same family, at any rate for a few generations.

Those who held the office wielded enormous devolved power. Because of Northumberland's remoteness its Earls remained something like semi-hereditary governors for a good while after the Conquest. WILLIAM I (THE CONQUEROR) even kept the Saxon Earl, Morcar, on in the post initially, though he was later imprisoned after attempting to rebel.

A subsequent Earl of Northumberland was Gospatric, son and heir of Maldred, who in turn was son of Crinan, Lay Abbot of Dunkeld in what is now Perthshire. Gospatric held the Earldom from *c* Feb 1068/9 to 1072 (*see* ABERGAVENNY, M; also the section Washington in AMERICAN PRESIDENTIAL FAMILIES, 1994, Morris Genealogical Books SA). Gospatric had a hereditary claim to the office of Earl of Northumberland, as did several of his successors. Disloyalty or incompetence in governing could lead to an earl's being deprived of his position, however, and when Gospatric rebelled he was ejected. In 1095, after several such unsatisfactory candidates had ruled as earls, WILLIAM II (RUFUS) took the Earldom into the hands of the crown. There it remained until conferred by DAVID I of Scotland on his only son and heir Henry in 1139. This followed a treaty between DAVID and KING STEPHEN of England whereby the latter made over Northumberland to Scotland as a result of the savage Scottish invasion of the northeast of England, an invasion which was only temporarily halted by the English victory at the Battle of the Standard in 1138 (*see* below).

In 1157 MALCOLM IV of Scotland handed the Earldom back to HENRY II of England, and in 1189 RICHARD I sold it to the Bishop of Durham for 2,000 marks (over £32,000,000 in late-1990s terms) to finance his crusade. What was being sold was not just, indeed hardly at all, a title of honour, but a vast swathe of real estate over which the purchaser would have quasi-sovereign power.

Although the Percys did not become Earls of Northumberland for another two centuries, and then as holders of a peerage creation rather than the quasi-heritable high office it had been earlier, they had been involved with some of the first post-Conquest holders of that Earldom (*see* below).

Even after the Percys became identified with the Earldom of Northumberland it was occasionally bestowed on members of other families, for instance if the Percy of the day was in disgrace. Thus from 1464 to 1470 John Nevill(e) (*see* ABERGAVENNY, M), who was from a rival dynasty in the North of England, held the title of Earl of Northumberland. In 1551 John Dudley, Earl of Warwick, used his ascendancy over the boy King EDWARD VI's council to get himself made Duke of Northumberland. He even tried to instal his daughter-in-law LADY JANE GREY as Queen following EDWARD's death in 1553, but was executed by MARY.

An illegitimate line of Dudleys styled themselves Dukes of Northumberland from 1620, when one of them procured a document from the Holy Roman Emperor FERDINAND II purporting to recognise him as such, till 1728. CHARLES II created one of his bastard sons by Barbara Villiers, Duchess of Cleveland, first Earl of Northumberland then nearly ten years later Duke of Northumberland too. This Duke of Northumberland, who seems from a number of contemporary accounts, including the diarist John Evelyn's, to have been easily the most prepossessing of CHARLES II's bastards though he is surely the least remembered (at any rate of the ennobled ones), died without legitimate issue in 1716.

Lastly The Old Pretender (known to Jacobites as James III) while in exile in Avignon created the then Marquess of Wharton (*see* WHARTON, B) titular Duke of Northumberland in 1716. In the autumn of 1726 this Jacobite Duke of Northumberland was in Rome at the same time as the last of the *soi-disant* Dudley Dukes of Northumberland was living there as a Canon of the Vatican.

Lineage: The family name of Percy allegedly derives from Perci or Percy, in Normandy. Unfortunately several places with that name exist there and it has proved impossible to identify the right one. A descent for the Percys was at one time claimed which went back to Mainfred, a Danish chief who had gone to Normandy before even Rollo the Dane (*c* 846–*c* 932) settled there, Rollo being founder of the line of the Dukes of Normandy who later conquered England and the great-great-great-grandfather of WILLIAM I THE CONQUEROR. But among sources for this claim were the partisan chroniclers of Whitby Abbey in Yorkshire, of which the first Percy known indubitably to have existed was a benefactor, and in later centuries some of the heralds, who were not above concocting fabulous lineages. Twentieth-century research has placed the origin of the Percys no further back than the immediate aftermath of the Norman Conquest, a period in which the Percys first made their mark as successful adventurers, presumably of Norman descent.

This of course is a perfectly respectable date for a family's origins, and compares favourably with those of most other peerage or baronetage families. In any case, the original Percys died out in the male line after only three generations. The grandchildren of the last of the original Percys by his younger daughter then assumed the surname, but their main branch too died out in the male line in 1670. Over the preceding three hundred years or so several acts of attainder had the effect of narrowing down the numbers of branches of the Percy family tree which could inherit the titles. A son-in-law of the 5th and last Earl of Northumberland of the 1557 creation — the most recent in a series of creations that had to be made afresh each time because of acts of attainder — assumed the name Percy but failed to produce an heir. His widow remarried twice and produced a son by her third husband who was erroneously summoned to Parliament as Lord Percy. This gentleman also failed to produce a male heir. His son-in-law then took the surname Percy, the fourth time a connection by marriage or female descent had assumed the full plumage of this historic family. The present Duke descends from the last of these attempts at perpetuating the Percy name.

WILLIAM de PERCY; *b c* 1030; allegedly travelled with Hugh d'Avranches, later Earl of Chester, from Normandy to England, though not necessarily as early as 1066. He seems to have been granted a Barony (at this time a territorial possession rather than peerage) of 30 knight's fees following the Conquest, though 20 years later the Domesday Survey mentions him as holding much more: 80 lordships in Yorkshire and 32 in Lincolnshire, together with other land in Essex, Notts and Hambledon, Hants (the last acquired through his marriage). He helped reconstruct York Castle 1070 after it was destroyed by the Danes and accompanied WILLIAM I THE CONQUEROR on his invasion of Scotland 1072. He was a tenant-in-chief of WILLIAM at the time of Domesday and under-tenant of Hugh, Earl of Chester. It was Hugh, Earl of Chester, who had been granted the lion's share of Gospatric, Earl of Northumberland's lands following the latter's rebellion against WILLIAM in 1069. WILLIAM de PERCY helped Gospatric win forgiveness from WILLIAM THE CONQUEROR, however, and was granted some of the forfeited lands as a sub-tenant by Hugh. WILLIAM de PERCY was known by contemporaries under the sobriquet *als gernons* ('William with the Whiskers'), whence the frequency of the forename Algernon in the family ever since. He refounded the Abbey of St Hilda, Yorkshire, of which his brother Serlo de Percy became first Prior; *m* Emma, sometimes called dau and heiress, but certainly a close relative, of Hugh de Port, feudal lord of Semer, near Scarborough, and a Saxon, and accompanied Duke Robert of Normandy on the First Crusade, during which he *d* 1096 at Montjoie or Mountjoy, nr Jerusalem, a peak so called because it was where Christians on pilgrimage to the Holy City first got a view of their destination, leaving issue (not necessarily in the order given, apart from Alan, who was certainly the est), together with two daus:

1 ALAN

2 Walter; witnessed with his bro William their f s charter to Whitby Abbey

3 William; possibly the Canon of York of the same name who was a witness to charters in *c* 1115–*c* 1125 and 1133–*c* 1144

4 Richard, of Dunsley, nr Whitby, N Yorks; paid tithe with his est bro ALAN to Whitby; *m* Alice, previously or subsequently w of Walter de Argentom, and had issue (again not necessarily in the order given):

(1) William; founded Handale Priory and a hermitage at Mulgrave, N Yorks

(2) Alexander

The est s,

ALAN de PERCY, 'The Great Alan'; seems to have been of age in 1100, when he was party to a dispute with the Bp of Durham which was resolved in the Bp's favour by WILLIAM II (RUFUS); a benefactor to St Peter's Hosp, York; *m* Emma, dau of Gilbert de Gant (himself s of Baldwin, Count of Flanders, and nephew of QUEEN MATILDA or MAUD, w of WILLIAM I THE CONQUEROR) by Gilbert's w Alice, herself dau of Hugh de Montfort, and was probably dead by Dec 1135, having had issue (together with other sons, some of whom may have been illegitimate, *viz.*, Geoffrey, Henry and Robert, and two or more daus):

1 William; fought on KING STEPHEN's side at the Battle of the Standard 1138 against the invading Scots under DAVID I (*see* also above and below); founded Sallay Abbey Jan 1147/8, having presented the Abbey with lands for its upkeep and a site for its physical construction; probably founded also Stainfield Priory, Lincs, and made gifts to Byland and Fountains Abbeys, at the latter of which he was later buried; *m* 1st Alice or Adelaide de Tonbridge (*d* between 1148 and *c* 1166), probably dau of Richard FitzGilbert de (Lord of) Clare by Alice, sis of Ranulph, Earl of Chester; *m* 2nd *c* 1166, as her 2nd of three husbs, Sibyl de Valognes (*d* in or after 1212), widow of Robert de Ros (*see* DE ROS, B), and *dspml* by Easter 1175, leaving by his 1st w, with two daus and coheiresses:

(1) Alan; certainly living *c* 1148 and probably so in 1166; *dvp*, having had an illegitimate s:

1a William; mentioned in a legal transaction involving his aunt Agnes de Percy 20 July 1182

(1) Maud; benefactress of Stainfield Priory and Fountains Abbey, where she was later buried; *m* by 28 Dec 1175, as his 2nd w, William, 3rd Earl of Warwick (*qv*) of the 1088 *cr* (*dsp* in the Holy Land 15 Nov 1184), and *dsp* between Michaelmas 1202 and 13 Oct 1204

(2) Agnes; *m* after 1154 Jocelin or Josceline, of Louvain (thought to have *d* by Michaelmas 1180), of Petworth, Sussex, half-bro of QUEEN ADELA (who presented Jocelin with the Petworth lands), 2nd w of HENRY I, and s of Godfrey I *Barbatus* ('The Bearded'), Duke of Lower Lorraine (*see* MILFORD HAVEN, M), by his 2nd w, and *d* between Michaelmas 1202 and 13 Oct 1204, having had, with other issue:

1a Henry; took the name PERCY; *m* as her 1st husb Isabel (*d* in or after 1230), dau of Adam de Brus, Lord of Skelton, Cleveland (through her he had the Manor of Levington, for which he and his heirs were to repair to Skelton Castle every Christmas Day and lead the lady of the castle from her chamber to the chapel to mass and thence to her chamber again, there to take meat with her, and then withdraw), and *d* by Michaelmas 1198, leaving:

1b WILLIAM

2b Henry, on whom his er bro in 1231 settled the manor of Heyshott, W Sussex; *m* Isabel (survived her husb) and *d* shortly prior to 12 Jan 1245/6; ancestor of the PERCYs of Heyshott

2a Richard (certainly a yr s of Agnes and Jocelin); for some years disputed with his nephew WILLIAM (*see* above) the Percy inheritance; by various agreements and arbitrations from as early as 1212 on, culminating in a hearing before HENRY III himself on 6 July 1234, it came about that Richard got possession of roughly his mother Agnes's half of the Percy inheritance while his nephew WILLIAM had roughly Maud, Countess of Warwick's half, acquiring also the overwhelming part of Richard's share on the latter's death; allegedly one of the 25 magnates nominated to see that KING JOHN honoured Magna Carta (1215) and accordingly excommunicated by Pope INNOCENT III at JOHN's behest 1216; also in 1216 among the Barons of Yorkshire who in rising against JOHN quelled that county in the name of LOUIS VIII of France; *m* 1st Alice, sis of his nephew WILLIAM's guardian Sir William Briwere or Brewer; *m* 2nd, as her 1st husb, Agnes (*d* by 20 July 1239), dau of Geoffrey de Nevill(e), of Raby (*see* ABERGAVENNY, M), and *d* at a great age by Aug 1244, leaving:

1b Henry; given a small portion of the Percy lands held by his f

2b Alexander

1 (cont.) William also had illegitimate issue:

(2) Walter; witness to a charter of his sis Maud, Countess of Warwick; living 1203

(3) Alice; *m* Richard de Morville and had:

1a Alan

(3) (cont.) Alice also had issue by Hugh de or du Puiset or Pudsey, Bp of Durham 1153–95 and Earl of Northumberland 1189–94 by purchase (*see* preliminary remarks):

2a Henry du PUISET; fndr Finchale Priory, Co Durham; *m* 1182, as her 2nd husb, Denise, dau and heiress of Otes de Tilli by Mabel, dau and heiress of William FitzRaven, of Hatfield, Yorks, and *d* in or shortly after 1209

(4) Emma; *m* William Malebise and had:

1a Richard Malebise

2 Walter; received a gift of land from his mother which he presented to Whitby Abbey; *m* by 1153, as her 3rd husb, Avice Meschin, dau of Cecily de Romelli (through whom Avice inherited Rougemont, W Yorks) and widow of (a) William de Curcy and (b) William Paynel

ALAN de PERCY also had an illegitimate s:

3 Alan; fought for DAVID I of Scotland at the Battle of the Standard (*see* above)

AGNES De PERCY's gs and HENRY (I) de PERCY's er s,

WILLIAM De PERCY; attained his majority some time between mid-1212 and mid-1214; was with HENRY III at the taking of William de Forz, titular Count of Aumale's castle of Biham in Lincs 1221 (Aumale being another of the 25 magnates charged with ensuring that Magna Carta was observed but who was now seen as in rebellion against royal authority rather than in understandable opposition to despotism, as had been the case when JOHN was still on the throne five years earlier); *m* 1st Joan (*d* by 12 June 1233), dau of Sir William Briwere or Brewer, his guardian when a minor, and had, with another dau:

1 Joan; *m* — de Ferlington

2 Agnes; *m* Eustace de Balliol and had:

(1) Ingram; *d* by Feb 1298/9

3 Alice; *m* Ralph Bermingham

4 Anastasia; *m* Ralph Fitz Ranulf, of Middleham, Yorks

WILLIAM De PERCY *m* 2nd Ellen (who brought him as dowry Dalton, Co Durham, in consequence called Dalton Percy (it is now in Cleveland), and *d* a short while before 22 Nov 1281), dau of Ingram de Balliol by a dau and heir of Walter de Berkeley, Chamberlain of Scotland, and *d* just before 28 July 1245, having had:

1 HENRY (Sir)

2 Ingram; inherited Dalton Percy from his widowed mother Ellen; *d* just before 24 Oct 1262

3 William; aged 26 in Oct 1262; heir to his er bro Ingram; Canon of York

4 Walter; heir of entail in equal shares with his er bro William to the Dalton Percy property

5 Geoffrey

6 Alan

7 Jocelin

5 Ellen

WILLIAM De PERCY's est s,

Sir HENRY de PERCY; *b c* 1235; ktd by June 1257, served HENRY III's Welsh campaigns 1257 and in Scotland 1258, sided with the Barons against HENRY III but subsequently renewed his allegiance to HENRY III, fighting on the King's side at the Battle of Lewes (1264), where he was taken prisoner and held by Simon de Montfort's party until after the Battle of Evesham (1265), when he was released; *m* 8 Sept 1268 Eleanor or Alianore (*d* in or after 1282), dau of John de Warenne, 7th Earl of Surrey of the 1088 *cr* (*see* NORFOLK, D), and *d* 29 Aug 1272, leaving:

1 John; *b* 1270; *d* by 20 July 1293

2 HENRY de PERCY, 1st LORD (Baron) PERCY (E), so *cr* by writ of summons to Parl (according to later doctrine) 6 Feb 1298/9; *b* posthumously *c* 25 March 1273; served in EDWARD I's Welsh campaign 1294, ktd 1296, fought Battle of Dunbar 27 April 1296, in which his maternal gf the 7th Earl of Surrey beat off an attack by the Scots, Warden of Galloway and Ayrshire Sept 1296, Justiciar Dumfries 1297, Jt Justiciar Cumberland, Lancs and Westmorland 1297, Memb Cncl of Regency during EDWARD I's absence overseas 1297–98, fought English victory of Falkirk over the Scots 1298, at Siege of Carlaverock 1300; accompanied EDWARD I Siege of Stirling 1304, King's Lt and Capt over all men-at-arms of the West Borders 1306, Constable Scarborough Castle March 1307/8; bought 19 Nov 1309 from Anthony Beck or Bek, Bp of Durham, the Barony (here a territorial entity carrying with it certain feudal rights, rather than a title of honour in the modern sense) of Alnwick, Co Northumberland, thus founding the Percy ascendancy there (for the bulk of the lands previously belonging to the family had been further south in Yorkshire, Sussex or Hants); one of the magnates opposed to EDWARD II, took part in the appointment of the Lords Ordainers, an executive committee entrusted with giving specific expression to that opposition; Keeper of the Bishopric of Durham *pro tem* March 1311, Justice of the Forest beyond Trent and Keeper of Bamburgh Castle Dec 1311, Jt Keeper the Marches c 1311; *m* (?)by June 1294 Eleanor (*d* July or

Aug 1328), sis of Richard de Arundel, and *d* between 2 and 10 Oct 1314, leaving:

(1) HENRY, 2nd Lord

(2) William; *d* 1355

HENRY de PERCY, 1st LORD (Baron) PERCY's er s,

HENRY de PERCY, 2nd LORD (Baron) PERCY; *b* 6 Feb 1300/1(?); granted custody of Alnwick Castle 1318, custodian Scarborough Castle 1321–24, ktd 1322, Keeper of the coast: Yorks 1324 and Northumberland 1325, Keeper of the Peace Northumberland 1325, sided with Queen Isabella against her husb EDWARD II's last favourites the Despensers 1326, Keeper Skipton Castle, ch commr to monitor observance of the truce with the Scots and Warden of the Scottish Marches (the last of these till Whitsun that year only) Feb 1326/7, an amb and subsequently ch plen in peace negotiations with the Scots April 1327, being one of only four English nobles not to be deprived of their Scottish possessions under the peace terms; granted by EDWARD III Warkworth Castle 1328, Keeper Bamburgh Castle April 1330, overseer of array (local defence) for northern counties July 1330, envoy to negotiate peace with French Jan 1330/1, Justiciar Eastern March Feb 1330/1, Warden the March 1332, present Siege Berwick (of which subsequently Keeper) and EDWARD III's victory over Scots at Halidon Hill July 1333, ch commr to Scots Parl to ensure Edward Balliol honoured his pledge to do homage to EDWARD III and cede southeast Scotland Oct 1333, memb cncl of regency during EDWARD III's absence overseas 1339 and 1340, commanded 3rd div at English victory of Neville's Cross over Scots 1346, following which DAVID II of Scotland was imprisoned in Bamburgh Castle, commr to negotiate final peace with Scots 1350; *m* Idoine or Idonea de Clifford (*d* 24 Aug 1365), dau of 1st Lord (Baron) Clifford (*see* DE CLIFFORD, B), and *d* late Feb 1351/2, leaving (not necessarily in the order given apart from HENRY, who was indubitably the est s, and Thomas, allegedly the 5th s), with a 6th s:

1 HENRY, 3rd Lord

2 Roger

3 Robert

4 William

5 Thomas; *b* 1333; Bp Norwich 1356–69, restored the Cathedral there; *d* 8 Aug 1369

1 Margaret; *m* 1st (roy licence 20 Jan 1339/40) Sir Robert d'Umfreville (*dvp* & *sp*), est s and heir apparent of 10th Earl of Angus of the putative *cr* of 1115; *m* 2nd by 25 May 1368, as his 2nd w, 3rd Lord (Baron) Ferrers of Groby (*see* TOWNSHEND, M) and *dsp* either 1, 2, 3, 5 or 10 Sept 1375

2 Isabel; *m* by Jan 1326/7 1st Lord (Baron) Aton (*dspms* by March 1388/9) and *d* by 25 May 1368, leaving three daus, among whose representatives the Barony of Aton, if such existed, is abeyant

3 Maud; *m* as his 1st w 3rd Lord (Baron) Nevill(e) (of Raby) and *d* by 18 Feb 1378/9, leaving issue (*see* ABERGAVENNY, M)

4 Alianore/Eleanor; *m* 2nd Lord (Baron) Fitzwalter (*qv*) and *d* before her husb

The 2nd LORD (Baron) PERCY's est s,

HENRY de PERCY, 3rd LORD (Baron) PERCY; *b c* 1320; saw extensive action in the opening phase of The Hundred Years War: served in the 3rd (King's) Div at the confrontation of Flamengerie or La Flamengrie 1339 (battle was not actually joined) and at Battles of Sluys June 1340 (English victory over French), also the failed Sieges of Tournai July 1340 and of Nantes 1342, Crécy 1346 and Winchelsea (naval victory over Spaniards) 1350; *s f* as hereditary Keeper Berwick Castle, Warden Northumberland coast June 1352, Jt Warden the Marches July 1352, commr for peace negotiations with Scots 1353 on, Keeper Roxburgh Castle and Sheriff Roxburghshire 1355, Marshal of Roy Army at Calais 1355; *m* 1st by Sept 1334 Mary (*b c* 1321; *d* 1 Sept 1362), 6th and yst dau of Henry, 3rd Earl of Lancaster of the 1267 *cr* (2nd s of EDMUND CROUCHBACK, 1st EARL OF LANCASTER, 2nd s of HENRY III), and had:

1 HENRY, 1st and last EARL OF NORTHUMBERLAND

2 THOMAS De PERCY, 1st and last EARL OF WORCESTER (E), so *cr* 29 Sept, KG (1375 or 1376), PC (by 4 Dec 1399); *b* 1343; campaigned with the Black Prince and others in France during The Hundred Years War, being present at the engagements of Montauban, Duravel, Purnon, St Savin and Lussac 1369, Montpont 1371 and Soubise 1372 and the Sieges of Roche-sur-Yon 1369, Limoges 1370, Montcontour 1371 and Nantes 1381; also saw military action in the Iberian Peninsula; Seneschal of La Rochelle 1369 and Poitou 1370, Keeper Roxburgh Castle 1376–81, Jt Warden Eastern Marches towards Scotland 1377, 1383 and Jan 1383/4 and Assist Warden All Marches May-June 1384, commr to negotiate/conserve peace with: Scots 1378, (as ch commr) Brittany 1379, the Count of Flanders and the French 1383, the French 1392 and Feb 1392/3 and again 1399 and Feb 1399/1400, also the Scots again Feb 1397/8, Adml of the Fleet towards the North 1378 and Jan 1384/5, Jt Capt of Brest March 1378/9 and Capt outright 1381–Jan 1385/6, helped suppress the Peasants' Revolt 1381, Adml of the Fleet during the Duke of Lancaster's expedition to Spain and Portugal 1386–87, Ch Amb Castile 1389, V-Chamberlain Household Feb 1389/90, Cncllr to RICHARD II's consort QUEEN ANNE OF BOHEMIA till her death in 1394, Justice S Wales 1390, Keeper for life: Newcastle Emlyn 1390–1403 and Haverford Castle Jan 1392/3–1403, Steward Household Feb 1392/3–99 and c 1401–02, Procurator for the clergy in Parl 1397, Constable Jedburgh Castle 1397, Capt of: Calais Jan 1397/8, also Cardigan and Lampeter Castles *c* Nov 1401, Adml of the Fleet for Ireland Jan 1398/9 and again (this time together with responsibility for the North and West of England) 1399–1401, supported 2nd Duke of Lancaster against RICHARD II Aug 1399, thus hastening the latter's deposition, Steward of England at Lancaster's coronation as HENRY IV Oct 1399, guardian of the Prince of Wales (the future HENRY V) 1401/2 and Lt of S Wales 1402, sided with the revolt by his nephew 'Harry Hotspur' against the crown and having been captured at the Battle of Shrewsbury 21 July 1403 was executed by beheading 23 July 1403; he was attainted posthumously, his honours being declared by Parl Feb 1403/4 to be forfeited due to treason, but he was restored in blood and honours by RICHARD III 1483/4 following a request of that date by the 3rd EARL OF NORTHUMBERLAND of the 1415/6 *cr*; *d* unm but apparently had illegitimate issue:

(1) Thomas PERCY; living Aug 1408

The 3rd LORD (Baron) PERCY *m* 2nd by May 1365 Joan, according to later doctrine held to have been Baroness Orreby and Baroness Mare in her own right, dau and heiress of 2nd Lord (Baron) Orreby and 3rd Lord (Baron) Mare or De La Mare (according to the same much later legal judgements), and *d c* 18 May 1368, leaving by her:

3 A son; *d* in infancy

1 Mary; *b* 1367; *m* by 22 June 1385 5th Lord (Baron) Ros of Helmsley (*see* DE ROS, B) and *dsp* 25 Aug 1394

The 3rd LORD PERCY's er s,

HENRY de PERCY, 1st and last EARL OF NORTHUMBERLAND (E) of the 16 July 1377 *cr*, KG (*c* 1366); *b* 10 Nov 1341; ktd Feb 1361/2, jt (his f being among other appointees to this post) surveyor Eastern March of Scotland and keeper of truce with Scots 1367, Jt Warden Eastern March 1369 and 1370, Warden E and W Marches 1372 on and W March 1399, Marshal of England 1376; jt commr to negotiate peace with the Scots 1378, 1393 and Feb 1393/4 and jt amb for the same purpose 1401, Adml the North 1383, Sheriff Northumberland 1384, Capt of Calais 1389, jt amb to negotiate truce with Flanders and France 1390, Keeper Berwick and E March 1391–96; following some two decades of growing dissatisfaction with RICHARD II he played a major role in deposing and probably also in the subsequent murder of the King, as also the process whereby the 2nd Duke of Lancaster ascended the throne as HENRY IV, so that on the latter's coronation day (30 Sept 1399) he was appointed Constable of England for life (forfeited 1403, *see* below) and about the same time was granted the lordship of the Isle of Man; won with his s 'Harry Hotspur' victory of Homildon Hill over Scots 1402 but f and s were not allowed to ransom their prisoners by HENRY IV and what with that and other causes of irritation they conspired to put the 5th Earl of March on the throne, who as a ggs of Lionel Duke of Clarence, 2nd s of EDWARD III, was the candidate of the late RICHARD II's supporters and indeed *de jure* successor to RICHARD; following the Battle of Shrewsbury (1403), in which 'Harry Hotspur' was *k*, the EARL OF NORTHUMBERLAND made his peace with HENRY IV, his actions being adjudged trespass rather than treason; he conspired against HENRY again in 1405 and fled abroad, whereupon he was attainted 1406 and the Earldom of Northumberland and Barony of Percy were forfeited; *m* 1st 12 July 1358 Margaret de Neville (*d* 11, 12 or 13 May 1372), dau of 2nd Lord (Baron) Nevill(e) (of Raby) (*see* ABERGAVENNY, M), and widow of 3rd Lord (Baron) De Ros (*qv*) of Helmsley, and had, with a dau:

1 Henry ('Harry Hotspur') (Sir), KG (1388); *b* 20 May 1364; ktd 1377, accompanied his f in retaking Berwick Castle from the Scots 1378, Jt Warden the Marches with his f 1384, Govr Berwick 1385, served in France in the area around Calais 1386, making raids there on the French; on 5 or 19 Aug 1388 (other sources have 15 Aug, but the latest date seems the most plausible, not least because there was a full moon on 20 August and the English attack came in the evening, with fighting continuing throughout the night) he launched an assault on the encampment of an invading Scottish army at Otterburn, *c* 30 miles northwest of Newcastle; 'Hotspur' and his bro Sir Ralph Percy were made prisoners, but James, 2nd Earl of Douglas (*see* QUEENSBERRY, M), the Scottish general, was slain, a cross supposedly marking the spot being known as Percy's Cross; both sides claimed victory, but modern opinion inclines to the Scots; nevertheless not only were Hotspur and Sir Ralph captured the English popular imagination, keener to celebrate failure than success, and the ballad *Chevy Chase* resulted; the Scots have their own ballad, *Otterburn*; Hotspur was released by midsummer 1389; Warden Carlisle and W March 1389–94 (also E by late 1398), Govr Bordeaux 1393–95, joined forces with the 2nd Duke of Lancaster, afterwards HENRY IV, 1399, as did his f; confirmed as Warden E March and Govr Berwick and Roxburgh by HENRY IV 1399, Justiciar Cheshire, N Wales (1400–01) and Flint, Constable Caernarvon, Chester, Conway and Flint Castles 1400, also granted Anglesey with Beaumaris Castle, together with lordship of Bamburgh Castle, for life 1400, a commr to treat for peace with Scots 1401, a commander at Homildon Hill 1402; turned with his unc and f against HENRY IV and fell at the Battle of Shrewsbury 21 July 1403; *m* by 1 May 1380, as her 1st husb, Lady Elizabeth Mortimer (*b* 12 Feb 1371; *m* 2nd, as his 2nd w, 1st Lord (Baron) Camoys (*qv*) and *d* 20 April 1417), dau of 3rd Earl of March by Philippa, gdau of EDWARD III, and had:

(1) HENRY PERCY, 1st EARL OF NORTHUMBERLAND of the 1415/6 *cr*, for whom *see* further below

(1) Elizabeth; *m* 1st between Aug 1403 and Nov 1412 7th Lord (Baron) Clifford (*see* DE CLIFFORD, B); *m* 2nd 1426, as his 1st w, 2nd Earl of Westmorland (*see* ABERGAVENNY, M) and *d* 26 Oct 1437

2 Thomas (Sir); *m* as her 1st husb Elizabeth (*b* 1361; *m* 2nd by May 1390 Sir John Scrope, 5th s of 1st Lord (Baron) Scrope (of Masham) (*see* YARBOROUGH, E); *m* 3rd Robert de Thorley), er dau and coheir of 12th Earl of Atholl (*see* STRABOLGI, B), and *d* in Spain March 1387, having had:

(1) Henry (Sir), of Atholl; *m* as her 2nd husb Elizabeth (*d* 21 Jan 1440/1), widow of 5th Lord (Baron) Scales (*see* ATHOLL, D), and *d* 25 Oct 1432, leaving:

1a Elizabeth; *m* 1st Thomas Burgh and had issue (*see* BURGH, B); *m* 2nd Sir William Lucy (*dsp*, *k* Battle of Northampton 1460) and *d* 28 Sept or 16 Oct 1455

2a Margaret or Margery; *m* 1st by 5 May 1434 3rd Lord (Baron) Grey (*qv*) (of Codnor) and had issue; *m* 2nd Sir Richard de Vere, 4th s of 12th Earl of Oxford (*see* SAINT ALBANS, D), and *d* 28 Sept 1464

3 Ralph (Sir); captured by the Scots at Otterburn 1388, Warden W March 1393; *m* by 20 March 1376/7 (*annulled*), as her 1st husb, Philippa (aged 15 by 21 March 1376/7; *m* 2nd, as his 1st w, John Halsham, of Coombs, Sussex; *d* 1 or 2 Nov 1395), dau and coheir of 12th Earl of Atholl (*see* STRABOLGI, B), and sis of Elizabeth above, but *dsp* overseas 15 Sept 1397

The 1st and last EARL OF NORTHUMBERLAND of the 1377 *cr m* 2nd by 15 Dec 1381, as her 2nd husb, Maud de Lucy, Baroness Lucy in her own right according to later doctrine (*b c* 1343–45; *m* 1st Gilbert de Umfreville, 10th Earl of Angus; *dsps* 18 Dec 1398), sis and heiress of Anthony, 3rd Lord (Baron) Lucy; in the event of her dying without issue, which is what actually happened, she bequeathed to her stepson Sir Henry ('Harry Hotspur') Percy her estates, including the Honour and Castle of Cockermouth, Cumberland. The 1st and last EARL OF NORTHUMBERLAND of the 1377 *cr* (as it will be convenient still to call him, although he had by now been stripped of his titles), convinced that HENRY IV was widely detested and that the pro-March party would quickly pick up support, headed south with a band of followers into England from the Scottish border in Feb 1408 but was intercepted at Tadcaster, Yorks, 19 Feb 1407/8 and defeated and *k* in battle at Bramham Moor nearby 20 Feb, his head being struck off, removed and fixed on a stake at London Bridge, while his body was divided in four, a separate part being sent to London, Lincoln, Berwick and Newcastle to edify the populace, though HENRY IV later gave the remains to the late Earl's friends for decent burial

The 1st and last EARL OF NORTHUMBERLAND's gs,

HENRY PERCY, 1st EARL OF NORTHUMBERLAND (E), so *cr* 16 March 1415/6, with the same remainder as his gf; *b* 3 Feb 1392/3, had his gf's estates restored to him and was ktd; on mil service in Normandy 1416 and 1417, Warden E March 1417, Memb Cncl Regency on death of HENRY V, commr to negotiate peace with Scots Feb 1423/4 and 1452, jt commr to monitor violations of truce with Scots 1433, Constable England May–Sept 1450; *m* a short while after Oct 1414, as her 2nd husb, Lady Alinaore/Eleanor Nevill(e), dau of Ralph, 1st Earl of Westmorland of the 1397 *cr* (*see* ABERGAVENNY, M), and was *k* fighting on HENRY VI's side at the Battle of St Albans against the Yorkists 22 May 1455, having had, with an est s (*d* young) and five other sons:

1 HENRY PERCY, 2nd EARL

2 Sir THOMAS PERCY, 1st BARON OF EGREMONT (E), so *cr* 20 Nov 1449; *b* 29 Nov 1422; Constable Conisborough Castle 1459; *m* and was *k* fighting for HENRY VI at the Battle of Northampton 10 July 1460, leaving:

(1) JOHN PERCY or EGREMONT, 2nd BARON OF EGREMONT; *b c* 1459; *dsp* or *dspm* by 21 March 1496/7, when his Barony expired

3 Ralph (Sir) (7th s); *b* 1425; a reasonably steadfast supporter of the House of Lancaster in the Wars of the Roses, changing over to EDWARD IV (head of the House of York) only late 1462 to early 1463, a leader of the Lancastrians in their defeat by Yorkists at Hedgeley Moor (Northumberland) 25 April 1464, where he was *k* (another monument called 'Percy's Cross' being erected to commemorate the place where he fell); said to have been unm, but was claimed as ancestor of what purported to be a Worcester/Salop branch of the Percys by Thomas PERCY, Bp of Dromore (*see* below), a branch which it was claimed culminated in:

(1) Arthur Lowe; putative f of Thomas Percy, Bp of Dromore, and if so a grocer in Bridgnorth, Salop; *m* and *d* 1764, having had(?):

1a Thomas PEARCY, PIERCY or PERCY; *b* 13 April 1729; described as the s and gs of grocers in Bridgnorth; *educ* Bridgnorth GS, Ch Ch Oxford (BA 1750, MA 1753) and Emmanuel Coll Cambridge (DD 1770); Vicar Easton Mauduit, Northants, 1753, and simultaneously Rector Wilby, Northants, 1756 onwards, Chaplain to 1st Duke of Northumberland of the 1766 *cr* and to GEORGE III 1769, Dean Carlisle 1778, Bp Dromore (Co Down) 1782, translator, editor and author: *Hau Kiou Choaun, or the Pleasing History* (trans, 1761), *Miscellaneous Pieces relating to the Chinese* (1762), *Five Pieces of Runic Poetry, translated from the Islandic* [sic] *Language* (1763), *A New Translation of the Song of Solomon* (1764), *Reliques of Ancient English Poetry* (compilation with some additions of his own, 1765), *The Household Book of the Earl of Northumberland in 1512, at his Castles of Wressle and Leconfield in Yorkshire* (ed, 1768), *A Key to the New Testament* (1769), *Northern Antiquities, with a Translation of the Edda and other Pieces from the Ancient Islandic* [sic] *Tongue* (trans, 1770) and *The Hermit of Warkworth* (1771); *m* 1759 Anne (nurse 1771 to HRH PRINCE EDWARD, later DUKE OF KENT and f of HM QUEEN VICTORIA; *d* 1806), dau of Barton Gutteridge, of Desborough, Northants, and *d* 1811, having had, with four sons (all *dvp*):

1b Barbara; *m* Ambrose Isted, of Ecton House, Northants

2b Elizabeth; *m* Hon Pierce Meade (*see* CLANWILLIAM, E), Archdeacon of Dromore, and *d* 26 Sept 1823, having had issue

1a (cont.) With the death of Bp PERCY it may well be that the entire male representation of the historic house whose name he bore became extinct

2a Anthony, of Southwark; *m* and had:

1b Thomas; *b* 13 Sept 1768; *educ* Merchant Taylors' and St John's Coll Oxford (BCL and Fell 1792, DCL 1793); Vicar Grays Thurrock, Essex, 1793, ed 4th edn of his unc's compilation *Reliques of Ancient Poetry* 1794; *d* unm 14 May 1808

1 Katherine; *b* 28 May 1423; *m* by Jan 1458/9 Edmund Grey, 1st Earl of Kent (*d* 22 May 1490), and had issue (*see* GREY, B)

The 1st EARL's est surv s,

HENRY PERCY, 2nd EARL OF NORTHUMBERLAND; *b* 25 July 1421; ktd 19 May 1426, Govr Berwick and Warden E Marches 1440 and 1444–61, commr to negotiate with Scots 1451, Justice Forest beyond Trent 1459; *m* by 25 June 1435 Eleanor (*b c* 1422; *d* Feb 1483/4), dau and sole heir of Richard Poynings, who *d* in the lifetime of his f 4th Lord (Baron) Poynings (*see* GREY, B), so that Sir Henry Percy, as he then still was, was summoned to Parliament 1446–55 as LORD POYNINGS in right of his w and in the lifetime of his own f the 1st EARL OF NORTHUMBERLAND; the 2nd EARL OF NORTHUMBERLAND, as he had become by now, fought at the Battle of Wakefield (Lancastrian victory) 30 Dec 1460 but fell leading the van of the Lancastrians against the victorious Yorkists at the Battle of Towton, Yorks, 29 March 1461, and was posthumously attainted 4 Nov 1461, his honours being forfeited, having had:

1 HENRY, 3rd EARL

1 Elizabeth; *m* 6th Lord (Baron) Scrope (of Bolton)

2 Eleanor

3 Anne; *m* 1st by 16 Oct 1460 Sir Thomas Hungerford (attainted and executed 1469), s and h of 3rd Lord (Baron) Hungerford and 1st Lord (Baron) Moleyns (attainted 1461 and beheaded 1464), and had issue (*see* LOUDOUN, E, and SAINT DAVIDS, V); *m* 2nd, as his 2nd w, Sir Laurence Raynsford

4 Margaret; *m* Sir William Gascoigne, of Gawthorpe

The 2nd EARL's only s,

HENRY PERCY, 3rd EARL OF NORTHUMBERLAND, KG (18 Aug 1474), PC (1474); *b c* 1449; confined first in the Fleet Prison then the Tower of London from the date of John Nevill(e)'s *cr* as Earl of Northumberland on 27 May 1464 (*see* introductory remarks above; Nevill(e) later traded in his Earldom for the Marquessate of Montagu; *see* ABERGAVENNY, M) till 27 Oct 1469, when after swearing fealty to EDWARD IV he was freed, although his petition for the reversal of his father's attainder was not granted till the Parl of 1472–73; Warden E and Middle Marches 1470, commr: to negotiate with Scots 1471–73, 1483, 1484 and 1488 and of array in northern counties 1472, Justice Forests North of Trent 1471, Constable: Bamburgh Castle 1471, Dunstanborough and Knaresborough Castles and Newcastle Castle March 1473/4, Sheriff Northumberland for life 1474 and (in HENRY VII's reign) during pleasure Feb 1487/8, Govr Berwick 1483, Ld Gt Chamberlain of England 1483–22 Aug 1485, when he betrayed RICHARD III on the field of the Battle of Bosworth, where he is said to have been entrusted with the command of the right wing of RICHARD's army, though he held them back from action, and despite being captured by the victorious 2nd Earl of Richmond, who later that day, following RICHARD's defeat and death, proclaimed himself HENRY VII, was soon released and had all his northern appointments regranted; Bailiff Tyndale, Northumberland, 1486; *m c* 1476 Lady Maud Herbert, dau of 1st Earl of Pembroke of the 1468 *cr* (*see* POWIS, E), and was *k* 28 April 1489 at one of his Yorkshire residences at the hands of a mob incensed not only by a ten percent income tax imposed to pay for war in defence of Brittany's independence of France, and with which NORTHUMBERLAND as a leading figure of authority was closely identified, but by his betrayal of RICHARD III, who remained popular in Yorkshire, leaving:

1 HENRY ALGERNON, 4th EARL

2 William (Sir)

3 Alan; priest, Preb Dunnington (York Minster) 1513–17, Rector St Anne Aldersgate (London) 1515–18, Master St John's Coll Cambridge 1516–18, Rector St Mary-at-Hill London 1521 and Mulbarton-cum-Keningham Norfolk 1526, Master Holy Trin Coll Arundel 1526–45, Rector Earsham Norfolk 1558; *d* May 1560

4 Jocelyn/Josceline; *m* and *d* 1532, having had:

(1) Edward, of Beverley, Yorks; *b c* 1524; *m* Elizabeth, 5th and yst dau of Sir Thomas Waterton, JP, High Sheriff Yorks *temp* QUEEN MARY, by Joane, dau of Sir Richard Tempest, and *d* 1590 aged 66, having had:

1a Alan; *m* and *d* 1622 or 1632, having had:

1b Joscelyn; *m* and *d* 1652, having had:

1c Alan, of Beverley; *d* 1687

2a Thomas; *b* 1560; *educ* a Protestant but soon turned RC; Constable Alnwick Castle 1594 and agent for his cousin 3rd EARL OF NORTHUMBERLAND of the 1557 *cr* (*see* below); in trouble as a recusant 1598; accused but acquitted of fraud against his cousin and employer 3rd EARL 1602, in contact 1602 with JAMES VI of Scotland (later JAMES I of England) regarding favourable treatment of Catholics in the event of his ascending the throne, JAMES's answer being looked on as hopeful; Gentleman Pensioner 1604; allegedly the Gunpowder Plot conspirator who first suggested assassinating JAMES I as a solution to the persecution of Catholics; was the conspirator who hired the house next door to Parl (foolishly doing so in his own name) 1604; *m* —, sis of John Wright (a fellow Gunpowder Plot conspirator), and *d* 10 Nov 1605 from wounds recd when captured by govt troops nr Holbeach 8 Nov preceding, leaving issue (with two daus, one of whom *m* Robert, s of Percy's fellow conspirator Robert Catesby):

1b Robert; *m* 22 Oct 1615 Emma Mead and had:

1c Francis; *b c* 1616; *m* and *d* 1660 aged *c* 44, having had:

1d Francis; *b c* 1650; *m* and *d* 1717 aged 67, having had:

1e Charles, of Cambridge; *m* and *d* 1743, having had:

1f Josceline (Rev); *dspm* 1755

1 Eleanor; *m c* 14 Dec 1490 3rd and last Duke of Buckingham of the 1444 *cr* (*see* STAFFORD, B) and *d* 13 Feb 1530, leaving issue

2 Anne; *b* by 27 July 1485; *m* 15 Feb 1510/1, as his 2nd w, 18th/11th Earl of Arundel (*see* NORFOLK, D) and *d* 1552, leaving issue

3 Elizabeth; *d* young

The 3rd EARL's est s,

HENRY ('HENRY THE MAGNIFICENT') ALGERNON PERCY, 4th EARL OF NORTHUMBERLAND, KG (1499), KB (1489), JP (Sussex 1515); *b* 14 Jan 1477/8; his sobriquet derived from his profuse expenditure on entertaining (he was also patron of the poet John Skelton, who had in 1489 written an elegy 'On the Death of the Earl of Northumberland', referring to the 3rd Earl's murder by protesting Yorkshiremen earlier the same year, dedicating it to the subject's s, the 4th Earl); helped suppress the uprising of the Cornishmen at Battle of Blackheath 1497, Constable Knaresborough, Steward Lordship of Knaresborough and Master Forester in Forest at Knaresborough 1501, Warden the Marches 1503, commr of array Northumberland and Yorks 1511, Trier Petitions from Gascony and beyond seas Feb 1511/2, commanded 500 Northumbrian light horse at Battle of Spurs against French 1513, commr to enquire into riots in Yorks 1514, Memb Cncl of the North 1522; *m* by 1502 Catherine (*d* between 14 Oct and 9 Nov 1542), dau and coheir of Sir Robert Spencer, of Spencercombe, Devon, by Lady Eleanor Beaufort, 2nd dau of 1st Duke of Somerset of the 1448 *cr* (*see* BEAUFORT, D), and *d* 19 May 1527, leaving:

1 HENRY ('HENRY THE UNTHRIFTY') ALGERNON PERCY, 5th and last EARL OF NORTHUMBERLAND of the 1415/6 *cr*, KG (1531); *b c* 1502; the sobriquet here is undeserved, except insofar as his f's extravagance should have made him even more careful to safeguard his fortune than he actually was, so that by the end of his life he was in real difficulties; ktd 1519, page in youth to Cardinal Wolsey, Memb Cncl the North 1522, Warden-Gen E and Middle Marches 1527–Jan 1536/7, in which capacity he arrested his one time master Wolsey at Cawood Castle, N Yorks, for high treason 4 Nov 1530; Steward Honour of Holderness and Bailiff Tyndale, Sheriff Northumberland 1532, Ld Pres Cncl the North and Vicegerent Order Garter 1536; *m c* Jan 1523/4 Lady Mary Talbot (*d* between 16 April and 6 June 1572), 5th dau of 4th Earl of Shrewsbury and Waterford (*qv*), but *dsp* 30 June 1537, having bequeathed HENRY VIII the major part of his estates, depressed as he was by his bros' rebellion, the recent execution of QUEEN ANNE BOLEYN, with whom he had been desperately in love as a youth in the early '20s and for whom even now he clearly felt tenderness, the concomitant lack of close sympathy between himself and his wife, and actual physical debility; according to the law as it then stood his yr bro Sir Thomas's attainder meant that the Barony of Poynings and Earldom of Northumberland of the 1415/6 *cr* expired, even though his heir was for the last 28 days of his life not Sir Thomas but Sir Thomas's s, another Thomas; this law was changed 1764; accordingly modern writers have sometimes mentioned the latter Thomas as *de jure* 6th Earl

2 Thomas (Sir); executed Tyburn 2 June 1537 for his part in the Pilgrimage of Grace (a traditionalist uprising, mostly in Yorkshire, against enclosures of

common land, the Dissolution of the Monasteries, Thomas Cromwell personally and the role of Parl in forwarding his legislation, particularly that affecting the Church) 1536–37; *m* as her 1st husb Eleanor (*m* 2nd Sir Richard Holland, of Denton, Lancs, and *d* a widow 1567), sis and coheir of George or Guiscard Harbottle, of Beamish, Co Durham, and had:

(1) Blessed THOMAS PERCY, 1st EARL OF NORTHUMBERLAND (E), as which *cr* 1 May 1557 (with the same precedence only that his ancestors as Earls of Northumberland had enjoyed, with the result that he was placed second in the table of precedence for earls, immediately after the Earl of Arundel), as also 30 April 1557 (*i.e.*, the day before) BARON PERCY (both E), with in both cases remainder, failing heirs male of his body, to his bro Henry, in like manner, KG (1563–69); *b* 1528; restored in blood only 14 March 1549, on the understanding that he refrain from putting forward a claim to the property his unc had bequeathed HENRY VIII, including the honours; Keeper Prudhoe Castle 1556, ktd 30 April 1557; High Marshal Army in the North May 1557, Constable Richmond and Middleham Castles July 1557, Jt Warden then Warden E March Aug 1557 and Jan 1558/9, jt commr to negotiate peace with Scots Jan 1557/8; conspired Nov 1569 with 6th and last Earl of Westmorland of the 1397 *cr* (*see* ABERGAVENNY, M) to liberate MARY QUEEN OF SCOTS (by now under house arrest in England, having fled from Scotland) and restore England to what he looked on as the true Church (of Rome) but after taking Barnard Castle, Co Durham, and Hartlepool was forced by advancing govt troops to flee to Scotland, eluding another govt force originally based on the borders one of whose commanders was his own bro Sir Henry Percy; from Scotland he was extradited to England by the Regent Mar (*see* MAR, E) 29 May 1572; leading 20th-century historians tend to minimise the 1st EARL OF NORTHUMBERLAND's religious fervour as a driving force behind the Northern Rebellion, preferring to dwell on such material causes of dissatisfaction as his being deprived of a lucrative Cumberland copper mine by ELIZABETH I, but HH POPE LEO XIII beatified him 13 May 1895 and it was decreed that his feast should be observed in the diocese of Hexham and Newcastle on 14 Nov; moreover by the agents of his contemporary Lord Burghley (*see* EXETER, M), ELIZABETH's chief minister, he was considered 'dangerously obstinate in religion'; *m* 12 June 1558 Lady Anne Somerset (*d* 8 Sept 1591), 3rd dau of 2nd Earl of Worcester (*see* BEAUFORT, D), and was beheaded 22 Aug 1572, following his attainder 1571; as a result of the attainder the Barony of Poynings and Earldom of Northumberland of the 1415/6 *cr* would have expired even if the law as it has stood since 1764 had been in force then (*see* against 5th EARL OF NORTHUMBERLAND), but under a late 13th-century law the fact that his titles *cr* in 1557 were with a special remainder was held to allow their being inherited by his yr bro Henry (*see* below); had:

1a Thomas, *Baron Percy*; *dvp* young and was *bur* 1560

1a Elizabeth; *m* Richard Woodroffe, of Wolley, Yorks, and had issue

2a Mary; fndr Benedictine Convent at Brussels; from it almost all houses of Benedictine nuns in England subsequently descend

3a Lucy; *m* Sir Edward Stanley, KB, of Tong Castle, Salop (*see* DERBY, E), and had issue

4a Jane; *m* Lord Henry Seymour, s of 1st Duke of Somerset of the Feb 1546/7 *cr* (*qv*), and *dsp*

(2) HENRY PERCY, 2nd EARL

3 Ingelram/Ingram (Sir); a leader Pilgrimage of Grace, following which he was imprisoned in the Beauchamp Tower of the Tower of London; *dspl* 1538, leaving at least one dau:

(1) Isabel; *m* 1544 Henry Tempest, of Broughton (*see* LONDONDERRY, M)

3 (cont.) After the death in 1670 *spms* of 5th EARL OF NORTHUMBERLAND (*see* below) of the 1557 *cr*, James Percy (1619–?90), a Dublin trunkmaker, claimed the earldom and associated titles, alleging first descent from the 7th Earl and then descent from Sir Ingelram Percy. He was undoubtedly s of one Henry Percy by a woman called Lydia, dau of Robert Cope, of Horton, Northants, and was generally recognised as gs of another Henry Percy, supposedly of Pavenham, Beds. The House of Lords eventually rejected his petition and sentenced him to be displayed before the four courts in Westminster hall, wearing a piece of paper on his chest, declaring him 'The False and Impudent Pretender to the Earldom of Northumberland'

1 Margaret; *m c* 1516, as his 2nd w, 1st Earl of Cumberland (*see* DE CLIFFORD, B) and was *bur* 25 Nov 1540

The 1st EARL (of the 1557 *cr*)'s bro,

HENRY PERCY, 2nd EARL OF NORTHUMBERLAND; *b c* 1532; predominantly Protestant, perhaps even Presbyterian, in sympathies, nevertheless later supported MARY QUEEN OF SCOTS, while there is also evidence, admittedly extracted under torture from a follower, of his desire towards the end of his life for toleration of Catholics; MP Morpeth 1554 and Northumberland 1571, ktd 1557, commr to treat with the Scottish Lds of the Congregation (Protestant association hostile to the French troops and officials surrounding Marie of Guise when Regent for her young dau MARY QUEEN OF SCOTS) 1559, Capt Gen of Light Horse in attack on French at Leith 1560, commr to negotiate with French 1560, Capt Tynemouth and Norham Castles Feb 1560/1–71, Sheriff Northumberland and commr to put down piracy there 1565, confined Tower London on suspicion of conspiring on behalf of MARY QUEEN OF SCOTS 1571–73, 1582 (on the latter occasion following discovery of the Throckmorton Plot) and Jan 1583/4–85, being ordered to remain at his house at Petworth, W Sussex, for a short time after the first term of imprisonment; *m* by 25 Jan 1561/2, as her 1st husb, Catherine Nevill(e) (*m* 2nd *c* Dec 1587 Francis Fitton, of Binfield, Berks, and *d* 28 Oct 1596), est dau and coheir of 4th Lord (Baron) Latimer (*qv*), and was found dead in bed, shot through the heart by a pistol which had fired three bullets *c* midnight 20/21 June 1585, the subsequent inquest bringing in a verdict of suicide; had:

1 HENRY, 3rd EARL

2 William; *b* 1575; *educ* Gloucester Hall (now Worcester Coll) Oxford; poet: *Sonnets to the Fairest Cœlia* (1594) and playwright (of his six works for the theatre four were unpublished and two published privately); *d* 1648

3 Charles (Sir); soldier Low Countries and Ireland; involved in Essex's Rebellion (*see* below against 3rd EARL OF NORTHUMBERLAND) Feb 1600/1 but pardoned; *m* as her 2nd husb Dorothy, dau of Thomas Cocks (*see* SOMERS, B) and widow of Edmund Hutchens, and *d* 9 July 1628

4 Richard (Sir); soldier in Ireland; *d* 1648

5 Alan (Sir), KB (1604); *d* 1611

6 Jocelyn/Josceline (Sir); involved in Essex's Rebellion; *d* 1631

7 George; *b* 4 Sept 1580; soldier Low Countries; sailed in first settlement of Virginia of JAMES I's reign Dec 1600, an incorporator of Second Co of Virginia 1609 and Dep Govr following John Smith's recall to England 1609–10 and later March-May 1611, memb Cncl of Virginia 1610, returned to Europe 1612 and soldiered in Low Countries against Spaniards 1625–27; *d* 1632

1 Lucy; *m* 1st Sir John Wotton; *m* 2nd Sir Hugh Owen

2 Eleanor; *m* 1st Baron Powis (*see* POWIS, E)

The 2nd EARL's est s,

HENRY ('HENRY THE WIZARD') PERCY, 3rd EARL OF NORTHUMBERLAND, KG (1593), PC (1603), JP (Cumberland, Northumberland, Sussex, Westmorland and all three Ridings of Yorks); *b* just before 27 April 1564; his sobriquet apparently derives from nothing much more sinister — apart from the dabbling in astrology and alchemy indulged in by any man of reasonably scientific bent at that time — than his experiments and patronage of mathematicians, particularly a trio called his 'Three Magi'; soldiered in Low Countries 1585–86 and 1600–01, Capt Gentlemen Pensioners 1603–05, Jt Ld Lt Sussex 1604–05; seems to have been innocent of any complicity in the Gun Powder Plot but was nevertheless imprisoned in the Tower of London (not least because of the involvement of his cousin Thomas Percy, *see* above, though also from the malevolence of Robert Cecil, Earl of Salisbury; *see* SALISBURY, M) 1605–21 and fined £30,000 (just under £4.5 million in late-1990s terms), though he compounded for this by a payment of £11,000 in 1613; obtained from CHARLES I in 1628 a patent giving him precedence of 1299 for the Barony of Percy and of 1377 for the Earldom of Northumberland; *m* 1594 Lady Dorothy Devereux (*d* 3 Aug 1619), sis of QUEEN ELIZABETH's mercurial favourite the 2nd Earl of Essex (instigator of Essex's Rebellion, *see* above, also ESSEX, E, preliminary remarks) and widow of Sir Thomas Perrott, and *d* 5 Nov 1632, having had:

1 Henry, *Baron Percy*; *b* 20 June 1596 (ELIZABETH I stood godmother); *dvp* and was *bur* 31 May 1597

2 Henry, *Baron Percy*; *dvp* and was *bur* 13 Sept 1597

3 ALGERNON, 4th EARL

4 HENRY PERCY, 1st and last BARON PERCY OF ALNWICK (E), so *cr* 28 June 1643; *b c* 1604; *educ* Ch Ch Oxford; MP Marlborough 1628–29, Portsmouth March-May 1640 and Northumberland 1640–41 (expelled from H of C 1641 for his part in the First Army Plot, which opponents represented as a plan by ultra-royalists — this being the eve of the Civil War — to cowe Parl into submission by assembling troops at Westminster), Col of a foot regt in the forces raised for war with the Scots 1639, Master of Horse to PRINCE OF WALES (later CHARLES II) 1639, apptd Capt and Govr Guernsey for life 1640 but only took up appointment *c* Oct 1649–Feb 1649/50; recruited and commanded a cavalry troop for service as CHARLES I's bodygd at York 1640, Col cavalry regt 1643 and Gen Ordnance Royalist Army 1643–44 (seems to have fought at First Battle of Newbury Sept 1643 (Parly victory) and Battles of Cropredy Bridge June 1644 and Lostwithiel Sept 1644 (both Royalist victories)), Memb Cncl of War for 1644 campaign, arrested on CHARLES I's orders 11 Jan 1644/5 either for communicating with the Parliamentarian enemy or for proposing CHARLES treat personally with Parl, but allowed to leave England for Paris; lived in exile till his death; *d* unm 26 March 1659 when the Barony expired

1 Dorothy; *bapt* 20 Aug 1598; *m c* Jan 1615 2nd Earl of Leicester of the 1618 *cr* (*see* DE L ISLE, V) and *d* 20 Aug 1650, leaving issue

2 Lucy; for a while companion to her f in the Tower; *m* 6 Nov 1617 James Hay, 1st Earl of Carlisle (*see* KINNOULL, E) of the 1622 *cr*, and *dsp* 5 Nov 1660

The 3rd EARL's er surv s,

ALGERNON PERCY, 4th EARL OF NORTHUMBERLAND, KG (1635), KB (1616), PC (1636 and again at the Restoration 1660); *b* 29 Sept 1602 (ELIZABETH I stood godmother); *educ* St John's Coll Cambridge (MA 1616); MP Sussex 1624–25 and Chichester 1626, called up to Ho Lds 1626 *vp* as BARON PERCY with precedence of 1299 (although this was premature by two years; *see* above against 3rd EARL), Memb Cncl the North March 1632/3; Adml, Capt-Gen and Govr the Fleet March 1635/6 and during the King's pleasure March 1637/8, Jt Ld Lt Sussex 1636 (Ld Lt 1660) and Northumberland (with his s) 1660, Ld High Adml 1638–42, Gen forces S of Trent and at that time one of the King's principal (and ablest) advisers in matters of state March 1639, Ld Lt Northumberland Aug 1639, Pres Cncl of War and Gen against Scots Feb 1639/40 but from Aug 1640 at least his royalism became less whole-hearted; appointed by Ho of Lds Oct 1642 Ch Commr Admlty and High Adml Jan 1642/3 also Ld Lt Anglesey, Northumberland, Pembroke and Sussex, Ch Commr apptd by Parl to negotiate with CHARLES I Jan 1642/3 and again 1645, indicted by CHARLES I Dec 1643 for high treason; recommended to CHARLES I by H of C Dec 1645 for promotion to Duke; Parly Commr to negotiate agreement of Newport between Parl and CHARLES I 1648, ch peer opposed to ordinance for trial of CHARLES I, Ld High Constable coronation of CHARLES II 18–23 April 1661 and Jt Earl Marshal 26 May 1662; *m* 1st by 1630 Lady Anne Cecil (*bapt* 23 Feb 1612; *d* 6 Dec 1637), dau of 2nd Earl of Salisbury (*see* SALISBURY, M), and had, with three other daus (Catharine, Dorothy and Lucy; all *d* young):

1 Anne; *b* 19 Dec 1633; *m* 21 June 1652, as his 1st w, 2nd Earl of Chesterfield and *dsps* 29 Nov 1654 (*see* 1967 edn CHESTERFIELD and STANHOPE, E)

2 Elizabeth; *b* 1 Dec 1636; *m* 19 May 1653 1st Earl of Essex of the 1661 *cr* (*qv*) and *d* 6 Feb 1717/8, having had issue

The 4th EARL *m* 2nd 1 Oct 1642 Lady Elizabeth Howard (*d* 11 March 1704/5), 2nd dau of 2nd Earl of Suffolk (*see* SUFFOLK and BERKSHIRE, E), through whom the London mansion originally built by Henry Howard, 1st and last Earl of Northampton of the March 1603/4 *cr* (*see* NORFOLK, D), and known as Northampton House came to be owned by the Percys and was renamed Northumberland House (pulled down 1874; Northumberland Avenue runs through its site), and *d* 13 Oct 1668, leaving by her:

1 JOCELINE, 5th EARL

3 Mary; *b* 22 July 1647; *d* 3 July 1652

The 4th EARL's only s,

JOCELINE PERCY, 5th and last EARL OF NORTHUMBERLAND of the 1557 *cr*; *b* 4 July 1644; Jt Ld Lt Northumberland (with his f) 1660 and Ld Lt Sussex 1668; *m* 23 Dec 1662, as her 1st husb, Lady Elizabeth Wriothesley (*m* 2nd, as his 1st w, 24 Aug 1673 1st Duke of Montagu (*see* MANCHESTER, D) and *d* 19 Sept 1690), 6th and yst dau of 2nd Earl of Southampton of the 1603 *cr*, and *d* 21 or 31 May 1670, when all his honours expired, having had:

1 Henry, *Baron Percy*; *b* 2 Feb 1668/9; *dvp* 18 Dec 1669

1 ELIZABETH Percy; *b* 26 Jan 1666/7; *m* 1st 27 March 1679 Henry CAVENDISH later PERCY, Earl of Ogle (*dsp* & *vp* 1 Nov 1680), s and heir of 2nd Duke of Newcastle of the March 1664/5 *cr*; *m* 2nd July(?) 1681 (clandestinely), despite her personal revulsion from him, but cowed into acquiescence by her grandmother the Dowager Countess of Northumberland, Thomas THYNNE, of Longleat, Wilts (*see* BATH, M); Thynne's murder *sp* 12 Feb 1681/2 was promoted by his rival for the great heiress's hand Count Königsmarck, who nevertheless was acquitted at the subsequent trial for being an accessory to murder; Lady ELIZABETH, twice a widow though aged only 15, *m* 3rd, as his 1st w, 30 May 1682 Charles SEYMOUR, 6th Duke of Somerset (*qv*), who had agreed beforehand as part of the marriage settlement to assume the name and arms of PERCY for himself and his children but who was released from this pledge by Lady ELIZABETH on her coming of age; she succeeded Sarah Duchess of Marlborough (*qv*) as Mistress of the Robes and Groom of the Stole to QUEEN ANNE 1711 and *d* 23 Nov 1722, leaving by her 3rd husb (with two other sons):

(1) Charles SEYMOUR, *Earl of Hertford*; *bapt* just before 22 March 1682/3; *dvp* and was *bur* 26 Aug 1683

(2) ALGERNON SEYMOUR, 7th DUKE OF SOMERSET and **1st Earl of Northumberland** of the 1749 and current *cr*, also 1st EARL OF EGREMONT, for whom *see* further below

(1) Elizabeth; *b* 1685; *m* 14 June 1707 7th and last Earl of Thomond of the Jan 1551/2 *cr* (*see* INCHIQUIN, B) and *d* 2 April 1734

(2) Katharine; *m* 21 July 1708 Sir William Wyndham, 3rd Bt, and had, with another s (*see* SOMERSET, D) and two daus:

1a Sir Charles Wyndham, 4th Bt, and 2nd EARL OF EGREMONT (*see* EGREMONT, LECONFIELD and, B)

(3) Anne; *m* 17 Sept 1719, as his 2nd w of three, 3rd Duke of Leeds (*see* 1963 edn) and *dsps* in childbirth 27 Nov 1722

Lady ELIZABETH PERCY's est surv s by the 6th DUKE OF SOMERSET,

ALGERNON SEYMOUR, 7th DUKE OF SOMERSET and **1st Earl of Northumberland**, so *cr* 2 Oct 1749, as also BARON WARKWORTH OF WARKWORTH CASTLE, Co Northumberland, with a special remainder, failing heirs male of his body, to his s-in-law Sir Hugh Smithson, 4th Bt, and the heirs male of the latter's body by his (Sir Hugh's) w Elizabeth, with further remainder to that Elizabeth and the heirs male of her body (which would have had the effect of any children she might have by a subsequent husb being able to inherit the Earldom of Northumberland and Barony of Warkworth if Sir Hugh Smithson had *d* before her), also 3 Oct 1749 BARON COCKERMOUTH and EARL OF EGREMONT, both Co Cumberland (all GB), with special remainder failing heirs male of his body to his nephews, sons of his sis, Lady Katharine Wyndham (*see* above); *b* 11 Nov 1684 (for further biographical details *see* SOMERSET, D); called up to Ho Lds 1722 as LORD (Baron) PERCY in the mistaken belief that the ancient Barony of that name (*cr* 1299) had been inherited by his mother, and by him 23 Nov 1722 from her, though in fact a new Barony of Percy was thereby *cr*; however, this Barony, being *cr* by writ just as if it had been a medieval one, operated as to its descent in a similar way and was thus, according to post-medieval doctrines as to baronies by writ, capable of descending to heirs general, who could be females; thus from now on in this article all females born PERCY or HEBER-PERCY, together with their issue, are marked with + to denote their being in remainder to this Barony only; *m* shortly after 1 March 1714/5 Frances (*d* 7 July 1754), dau and coheir of Hon Henry Thynne (*see* BATH, M), and *dspms* 7 Feb 1749/50, having had, with a s (George Seymour, *Viscount Beauchamp*; *b* 11 Sept 1725; *dvp* unm 11 Sept 1744):

ELIZABETH Seymour, BARONESS PERCY in her own right; *b* 26 Nov 1716; Ldy Bedchamber to QUEEN CHARLOTTE 1761–70; *m* 16 July 1740 Sir Hugh SMITHSON later PERCY, **4th Bt**, KG (1756), PC (1762) (*b* 19 Dec 1714/5; s gf in Btcy 2 March 1733; *educ* Ch Ch Oxford; High Sheriff Yorks 1738, MP (Tory) Middx 1740–50, Tstee Br Museum 1753–86, Ld Bedchamber to GEORGEs II and III 1753–63, Ld Lt: Northumberland 1753–86, Middx 1762–86 and Ireland 1763–65, V-Adml: Northumberland 1755 and N America 1764, Ld Chamberlain to QUEEN CHARLOTTE 1762–68, Master Horse 1778–80, FSA Jan 1735/6, FRS 1736; ten years after his marriage, on the death of his f-in-law, he became **2nd Earl of Northumberland** (and 2nd BARON WARKWORTH OF WARKWORTH CASTLE), assuming also by Act of Parl 12 April 1750 the name and arms of PERCY in place of SMITHSON, *cr* also: 22 Oct 1766 EARL PERCY and **Duke of Northumberland**, and 28 Jan 1784 LORD LOVAINE, BARON OF ALNWICK, Co Northumberland, with special remainder to his 2nd s, Lord Algernon Percy (*see* below); employed Robert Adam and James Paine in gothicising Alnwick Castle and 'Capability' Brown to landscape the grounds, in which a 90–ft high folly, the Brislee Tower, was erected; Adam and Brown also improved Syon House, just outside London; the Duke contributed to the beautification of his estates by planting 1,200 trees a year for twenty years, some with his own hands, as an inscription on Brislee Tower testifies; he was an able manager of his already vast wealth, increasing the rents from his Northumberland estates alone from just over £8,600 a year in 1749 to £50,000 (just under £7.5 million in late-1990s terms) a year in 1778, though much of this was achieved by exploiting mineral deposits; he *d* 6 June 1786, having had illegitimate issue (as well as those mentioned further below by his w): two daus, both bur in Westminster Abbey, and by Elizabeth Hungerford Keate, reputedly a cousin of his w through common kinship to the 6th Duke of Somerset, James Smithson (*b* 1765; fndr of the Smithsonian Institution in Washington, DC; *d* 27 June 1829); Sir Hugh was s of Langdale Smithson, of Stanwick, Yorks, by Philadelphia (*d* 15 May 1764 aged 76), dau of William Reveley, of Newby Wisk, Yorks (*see* REDESDALE, B); Langdale Smithson was in turn yr but only surv s of **Sir Hugh Smithson, 3rd Bt**, by Hon Jane Langdale, er dau of 2nd Baron Langdale of Holme, both the Langdales and Smithsons being recusant families; **Sir Hugh Smithson, 3rd Bt**, was himself est s of **Sir Jerome Smithson, 2nd Bt**, who in turn was est s of **Sir Hugh Smithson, 1st Bt** (E), of Stanwick, Yorks, so *cr* 2 Aug 1660; BARONESS PERCY *d* 5 Dec 1776, having had issue by her husb the **1st Duke of Northumberland**, with a dau Elizabeth (*d* unm):

1 Sir HUGH SMITHSON later PERCY, **5th Bt**, and **2nd Duke of Northumberland**, KG (1788); *b* 14 Aug 1742; s mother as 3rd BARON PERCY 1776; *educ* Eton; served army 1759–1812: fought Seven Years' War at Bergen (victory for France and her allies) April 1759, Minden (victory for Britain and allies) Aug 1759 and possibly Warburg (victory for Britain and allies) 1760, Ensign 24th Foot May 1759, Capt 85th Foot Aug 1759, Capt and Lt-Col Gren Gds 1762, Col and ADC to GEORGE III 1764, Maj-Gen 1775, served War American Independence (especially Lexington and Brooklyn) 1775–77, Lt-Gen 1777, Gen 1793, Col: 11th Foot(?) 1762–63, 5th Foot 1768–84 (where he was so popular the regt asked permission later to change its name to Northumberland Fus), 2nd Troop Horse Gren Gds 1784–88, commanded Percy Yeo Regt 1798 and Col cmdg 1806–12; MP (Tory) Westminster 1763–76, Ld Lt and V-Adml Northumberland 1786–99 and 1802–17, FSA 1787, FRS 1788; *m* 1st 2 July 1764 (*divorce* 16 March 1779 on grounds of her adultery with a Cambridge undergraduate), as her 1st husb, Lady Anne Stuart, dau of 3rd Earl of Bute (*see* BUTE, M); *m* 2nd 25 May 1779 his sis-in-law Frances Julia (*b* 21 Dec 1752; *d* 28 April 1820), 3rd dau of Peter Burrell, of Langley Park, Beckenham, Kent, and sis of 1st Baron Gwydir (*see* 1915 edn), and *d* 10 July 1817, having by her had:

(1) HUGH PERCY, **3rd Duke of Northumberland**, KG (1819), PC (1825); *b* 20 April 1785; *educ* Eton and St John s Coll Cambridge (MA 1805, LLD 1809); MP (Whig, during which time he introduced a bill to abolish slavery in the colonies) Buckingham Aug-Oct 1806, Launceston Nov 1806–07 and Northumberland 1807–12; called up to Ho Lds (where, however, he voted as a Tory moderate, tending, for instance, to avoid opposing outright the proposals for Catholic emancipation if made by men of sense, though as Ld Lt of Ireland he suppressed the Catholic Assoc 1830) 12 March 1812 *vp* in f's Barony of Percy; Ld Lt: Northumberland (and V-Adml there) 1817–47 and Ireland 1829–30, Ld Bedchamber 1821–47, Govr King's Coll London 1831, Roy Tstee Br Museum 1839–47, High Steward Cambridge U 1834–40 and Chllr 1840–47, Constable and High Steward Launceston 1843, FRS and FSA 1823; *m* 29 April 1817 Lady Charlotte Florentia Clive (*d* 27 July 1866), 2nd dau of 1st Earl of Powis (*qv*), and *dsp* 11 Feb 1847

(2) Henry; *b* 1787; *d* 1794

(3) ALGERNON PERCY, **4th Duke of Northumberland**, KG (1853), PC (1852); *b* 19 Dec 1792; *educ* Eton; joined RN March 1805: Midshipman to 1811, when promoted Lt, Cdr 1814, Capt 1815, R-Adml the Blue 1850, Adml 1862, *cr* 27 Nov 1816 BARON PRUDHOE, of Prudhoe Castle, Co Northumberland (UK), First Ld Admlty (C) Feb-Dec 1852, during which short term of office he did much to promote the use of steam in the Navy; briefly Special Dep Warden Stannaries 1852; had an interest in Egyptology and astronomy (hence his DCL Oxford 1841), also funded research for and publication of Edward Lane's *Arabic Lexicon* 1842 to his death (his widow continued the funding); restored Alnwick, employing Anthony Salvin to replace Adam's interiors of the previous century, and kept almost permanent open house there, also erected five churches on his land, subsidised building of five more elsewhere and built six vicarages; in addition he spent some £500,000 on cottages for his tenantry, drainage schemes and road and bridge construction; promoter of life-boat service, being especially active in forwarding RNLI (of which Pres); fndr Tyne Sailors Home and endowed other institutions to help those who gained their living from the sea; FRS 1818, FRAS, FRGS, FSA 1823, LLD Cambridge 1835, Pres: Roy Institution 1842–65 and RUSI; *m* 25 Aug 1842 Lady Eleanor Grosvenor (*d* 4 May 1911), est dau of 2nd Marquess of Westminster (*see* WESTMINSTER, D), and *dsp* 12 Feb 1865, when the Barony of Prudhoe expired, the Barony of Percy passed to his great-nephew and heir-general 7th Duke of Atholl (*see* below), though on the death of the 9th Duke of Atholl in 1957 it passed back to the Dukes of Northumberland, and the Dukedom and all his other hereditary titles passed to his cousin, **2nd Earl of Beverley**

(1) Agnes; *m* 16 Aug 1821 Maj-Gen Frederick Thomas Buller (*d* 5 June 1860; *see* CHURSTON, B), of Pelynt and Lanreath, Cornwall, 2nd cousin twice removed of Gen Sir Redvers Buller, the celebrated late–19th-century soldier, and *dsp* 4 June 1856

(2) Emily; *m* 19 May 1810 Lord James Murray, 2nd s of 4th Duke of Atholl (*qv*), who was *cr* BARON GLENLYON 1821 (*see* 1956 edn), and *d* 20 June 1844, leaving issue; her gs, 7th Duke of Atholl, *s* his great-unc 4th **Duke of Northumberland** in 1865 as 6th LORD (Baron) PERCY

2 ALGERNON SMITHSON later PERCY, **1st Earl of Beverley**, Co York (GB), so *cr* 2 Nov 1790, also 2nd LORD LOVAINE, BARON OF ALNWICK (in which *s* f 1786 under special remainder); *b* 21 Jan 1749/50; *educ* Eton; MP (Tory) Northumberland 1774–86, FSA 1820; *m* 8 June 1775 Isabella Susanna (*see* above against **2nd Duke**; *b* 19 Dec 1750; *d* 24 Jan 1812), 2nd dau of Peter Burrell, of Beckenham, Kent, and *d* 21 Oct 1830, having had, with other issue:

(1) GEORGE, **5th Duke**

(2) Algernon; *b* 1779; Min Plen to Swiss Cantons; *d* 1833

(3) Hugh (Rt Rev); *b* 29 Jan 1784; *educ* Trin Coll Cambridge (MA 1805, DD Cantab 1825 and Oxon 1834); Rector Bishopsbourne and Ivychurch, Kent, 1809, Chllr and Preb Exeter 1810–16, Chllr Salisbury 1812, Preb Canterbury and Finsbury, St Paul's, 1816–56, Archdeacon Canterbury 1822, Dean Canterbury 1825, Bp Rochester July 1827, Bp Carlisle late 1827 or early 1828 to 1856 (during his incumbency of which he would drive four-in-hand in person up and down to London to attend the Ho of Lds); *m* 1st 19 May 1806 Mary (*d* 4 Sept 1831), dau of Most Rev Charles Manners-Sutton, DD, Archbp Canterbury (*see* RUTLAND, D) and had, with seven other daus:

1a Algernon Charles PERCY later HEBER-PERCY (added 1847), of Hodnet Hall, Salop, and Airmyn Hall, Yorks, JP, DL (both Salop); *b* 29 June 1812; *m* 29 July 1839 Emily (*d* 8 Nov 1902), dau of Rt Rev Reginald Heber, DD, Bp Calcutta and hymnographer (author of the celebrated hymn beginning 'From Greenland's icy mountains...'), and niece and heiress of the bibliophile Richard Heber, of Hodnet and Marton, and *d* 24 Jan 1901, leaving:

1b Algernon, of Hodnet and Airmyn Halls, JP, DL (both Salop); *b* 23 Feb 1845; Lt RN, CA Salop, High Sheriff 1908, Maj Shropshire Yeo Cav; *m* 25 Jan 1867 Alice Charlotte Mary (*d* 19 March 1922), only child of Rev F V Lockwood and *d* 11 May 1911, leaving:

1c Algernon Hugh, of Hodnet Hall, JP (Salop); *b* 13 July 1869; Ld Manors of Hodnet, Preston on Weald Moors and Airmyn, Hereditary Seneschal Montgomery Castle and Honour of Montgomery, Lt Shropshire Yeo Cav, ADC to Govr Queensland and Priv Sec to Lt-Govr Br New Guinea; *m* 15 July 1903 Gladys May, MBE (1920) (*d* 18 April 1956), yr dau of William Edward Montagu Hulton-Harrop, DL, of Lythwood Hall, Salop, and Bardsley, Lancs, and *d* 25 Dec 1941, having had:

1d Algernon George William, DSO (1943) and bar (1945); *b* 27 April 1904; *educ* Harrow; ADC to Govr-Gen Union of S Africa 1929–32 and NZ 1935–37, Brig Gren Gds 1942–43 (despatches), OC 158th TA Bde 1947–50, Brig Gen Staff (Inf and Training) Middle East 1950–52, Order King George I Greece with crossed swords; *m* 27 April 1939 (*divorce* 1950) Daphne Wilma Kenyon, dau of Eustace Parker Bowles (*see* MACCLESFIELD, E), and *d* 27 Feb 1961, leaving:

1e +Algernon Eustace Hugh [Algernon Heber-Percy Esq, Hodnet Hall, Market Drayton, Salop TF9 3NN]; *b* 2 Jan 1944; *educ* Harrow; Lt Gren Gds 1962–66, farmer, chm: Mercian Regn Nat Tst 1979–90, Walker Tst, tstee Nat Gdns Scheme, Pines and Lyneal Tst, memb Heart of England HHA and Gdns Ctee, fell Woodard Schs, Salop: High Sheriff 1987, Ld Lt 1996– (V-Lt 1990–96, DL 1986–90); *m* 6 July 1966 *Hon Margaret Jane Lever, yst dau of 3rd Viscount Leverhulme (*qv*), and has:

1f +(Algernon) Thomas Lever; *b* 29 Jan 1984

1f +Emily Jane; *b* 19 Feb 1969; *m* 27 April 1996 *Richard Cave, yst s of Sir Charles Cave, 4th Bt (*qv*), and has issue

2f +Lucy Ann; *b* 29 Dec 1970

3f *Sophie Daphne; *b* 22 Jan 1979 Tait,

1e +Zara Mary; *b* 14 March 1940; *m* 29 June 1961 (*divorce* 1980) Gavin Nicholas Tait, er s of Gordon Tait and Mrs Patricia Richardson, and has:

1f +Lucinda Clare; *b* 15 June 1962; *m* 1983 (*divorce* 1994) James Henderson, s of Lt-Col James B Henderson, and has:

1g +Eliza Jennifer Jane; *b* 1992

2f +Arabella Kate Louise; *b* 31 July 1965

2e +Jane Maude [Mrs Harold Pyman, Windwhistle, Sampford Arundel, Somerset]; *b* 11 Jan 1942; *m* 16 Oct 1965 *Maj Harold Anthony McArthur Pyman, Life Gds, er s of Gen Sir Harold English Pyman, GBE, KCB, DSO, of Chitterwell House, Sampford Arundel, and has:

1f +Richard Anthony; *b* 17 April 1968

1f +Victoria Clare; *b* 9 Nov 1966

2d Cyril Hugh Reginald, DSO, MC; *b* 18 Dec 1905; *educ* Harrow; Lt-Col Welsh Gds WW II (wounded), MFH: Cotswold 1935–42 and Cottesmore 1946–58; *m* 1st 18 Oct 1933 (*divorce* 1944) Anne, yst dau of Charles Tuller Garland, of Moreton Morrell, Warwicks, and had:

1e Alan Cyril; *b* 3 Dec 1935; *educ* Eton; *m* 1st 26 Jan 1962 (*divorce* 198–) Susan Mary, only dau of Michael Charles St John Hornby (*see* DUDLEY, E) and formerly w of 11th Duke of Marlborough (*qv*), and has:

1f +Larissa Anne; *b* 27 April 1968; *m* 28 June 1997 *Justin St Clair Hardy

1e (cont.) Alan Heber-Percy *m* 2nd 1980 *Charlotte [Mrs Alan Heber-Percy, Eyford House, Upper Slaughter, Glos GL54 2JN], 2nd dau of Lt-Cdr Sir Cyril Kleinwort, RNVR (*see* KLEINWORT, Bt), and formerly w of Martin Gwynne (*see* MORRISON-BELL, Bt), and *d* 9 Jan 1998

2e +William David, MBE (1966) [William Heber-Percy Esq MBE, Glawcoed, Talybont-on-Usk, Brecon, Powys LD3 7JR]; *b* 5 March 1939; *educ* Eton; served Colonial Office, Assist Advsr Aden; *m* 18 Jan 1969 *Christine Mary, est dau of Terence Horatio Gates, of Twineham, Sussex, and has:

1f +Peter Hugh; *b* 12 May 1971; *educ* Eton

1f +Robin Virginia; *b* 12 Nov 1969

2d (cont.) Lt-Col Cyril Heber-Percy *m* 2nd 17 Jan 1944 (*divorce* 1959) Diana, only dau of Raymond Augustus Edward Radclyffe, of Lew, Oxon, and by her had:

3e +Cyril Raymond [Cyril Heber-Percy Esq, Folly Farmhouse, Farmington, Northleach, Glos GL54 3NL]; *b* 23 May 1945; *educ* Eton; *m* 1st 27 Nov 1971 Heather Joan, dau of John L Cowland, of Cala Llonga, Ibiza, and formerly w of — Miller, and has:

1f +Tamara Joan; *b* Ibiza 10 Sept 1972

2f +Zara Ana; *b* 7 July 1976

3e (cont.) Cyril Heber-Percy *m* 2nd 1988 *Mrs Ann Elizabeth Francis, dau of John Douglas Rowley, of Bristol

2d (cont.) Lt-Col Cyril Heber-Percy *m* 3rd 11 Nov 1959 *Pamela [Mrs Cyril Heber-Percy, 18 Farmers Ct, Lane End, High Wycombe, Bucks HP14 3LL], er dau of Kinmont Willie Armstrong-Lushington-Tulloch, of Shanbolard, Moyard, Co Galway, and widow of Capt Thomas Ansell Fairhurst, Life Gds, and *d* 1 Aug 1989

3d Alan Charles; *b* 4 May 1907; Lt Welsh Gds; *d* 7 March 1934

4d Robert Vernon; *b* 5 Nov 1911; *educ* Stowe; Lt King's Dragoon Gds (Res); *m* 1st 11 July 1942 (*divorce* 1947) Ann Jennifer Evelyn Elizabeth, only child of Sir Geoffrey Storrs Fry, 1st and last Bt, KCB, CVO (*see* 1956 edn), and had:

1e +Victoria Gala [Mrs Peter Zinovieff, 50 Stevenage Rd, London SW6; Faringdon House, Faringdon, Oxon]; *b* 28 Feb 1943; *m* 25 Nov 1960 *Peter Zinovieff, er s of Maj Leo Zinovieff, RM, and has:

1f +Leo; *b* 3 March 1963; *m* 1988 *Annabelle Charlotte, only dau of Hon Simon Eccles (*see* ECCLES, V) and has:

1g +Kyril; *b* 1991

2g +Alyosha; *b* 1988

2f +Kolinka; *b* 1966

1f +Sofka; *b* 10 Nov 1961; has issue by Vassilis Papadimitriou:

1g *Lara; *b* 17 Aug 1995

4d (cont.) Robert Heber-Percy *m* 2nd 1985 *Lady Dorothy Lygon [The Lady Dorothy Heber-Percy, Lime Tree Cottage, 7 Coach Lane, Faringdon, Oxon SN7 8AB], 4th and yst dau of 7th Earl Beauchamp (*see* 1970 edn) and *d* 1987

2c Josceline Reginald, DL (Warwicks); *b* 2 Sept 1880; Lt Northumberland Fus, Capt 4th Bn Argyll and Sutherland Highrs 1914–19; *m* 15 Sept 1904 his cousin Katharine Louisa Victoria (*d* 10 Jan 1964), only dau of Lord Algernon Malcolm Arthur Percy (*see* below), and *d* 17 Dec 1964, leaving:

1d David Josceline Algernon, DSC; *b* 10 June 1909; Cdr RN WW II (despatches twice); *m* 2 Aug 1942 Olivia Mary (*d* 19 Jan 1996), yr dau of Robert William O'Brien, of Bank of Ireland House, Drogheda, Co Louth, and *d* 2 Oct 1971, leaving:

1e +Michael David [Michael Heber-Percy Esq, Beechenwood Farm, Hillside, Odiham, Hants RG29 1JA]; *b* 10 June 1943; *educ* Eton; architect, AA Dip Hons, ARIBA; *m* 28 Aug 1965 *(Amanda) Sarah, yst dau of Alastair Gilmour, and has:

1f +Colin Michael [Colin Heber-Percy Esq, 4 Hauteville Court Gdns, London W6]; *b* 4 May 1968

2f +Paul David [Paul Heber-Percy Esq, Cottage Farm, Old Milverton, Leamington Spa, Warwicks; 8 Hopgood St, London W12]; *b* 2 May 1970

1e +Carol Margaret Katherine [Mrs Richard Ashby, Empshott Lodge, Empshott, Hants GU33 6HS]; *b* 13 April 1947; *m* 1st 4 April 1970 Robert Ward Woolner, yr s of George Woolner, of Chelsea; *m* 2nd 13 May 1974 *Richard Edward Warcup Ashby, DipArch RIBA, and has:

1f +Sam David Frederick; *b* 29 June 1981

1f +Daisy Katharine; *b* 10 Oct 1974

2f +Poppy Elizabeth Patricia; *b* 8 June 1976

3f +Holly Patricia; *b* 30 June 1979

2e +Angela Mary [Mrs Henry Fawcett, Delmonden Manor, Hawkhurst, Kent TN18 4XJ]; *b* 12 July 1949; *m* 20 June 1970 *Henry Robert Boileau Fawcett, s of Robert Fawcett, of Stocks Green, Hildenborough, Kent, and has:

1f +Joseph Dylan; *b* 18 Jan 1983

1f +Emily; *b* 6 Nov 1972

2f +Kate; *b* 4 April 1975

1d Mary Katharine Victoria; *b* 20 Aug 1906; *m* 9 Oct 1930 Gerald Wellington Williams, JP, of Crockham House, Westerham, Kent, and had issue

2d +(Dorothy) Elizabeth [Elizabeth Lady Walker-Okeover, Park Cottage, Osmaston, Ashbourne, Derbys DE6 1LT]; *b* 23 June 1913; *m* 28 June 1938 Col Sir Ian Peter Andrew Monro Walker-Okeover, 3rd Bt (*d* 1982; *qv*), and has issue

2b Reginald Josceline; *b* 2 May 1849; Lt-Col Rifle Bde; *m* 28 Nov 1894 Johanna Frederica Eugenia Gundreda (*d* 14 Dec 1945), dau of Hardy Eustace, of Castlemore, Co Carlow, and *d* 1 March 1922

3b Hugh Lewis; *b* 7 Jan 1853; FRGS, Capt Shropshire LI; *m* 10 June 1899 Harriet, dau of Henry S Earp, of Dunstall, Staffs, and *d* 1 April 1925

4b Henry Vernon (Rev); *b* 16 April 1858; MA Cantab, Rector Leasingham, Lincs, RD Lafford North Seacombe; *m* 5 Oct 1886 Judith Elizabeth (*d* 7 Sept 1948), dau of Sir Vincent Rowland Corbet, 3rd Bt (*see* 1970 edn), and *d* 1 April 1934, having had:

1c Charles Rowland; *b* 10 Aug 1887; *d* unm 7 Dec 1908

2c Neville Henry; *b* 6 Feb 1891; *educ* Radley; T/Lt RASC; *m* 1 Nov 1912 Violet, dau of Henry Buller Colthurst, of Somerset, and *d* 25 Nov 1966, having had:

1d Charles Henry; *b* 18 Aug 1914; P/O RAF; *d* 22 Jan 1938 following a flying accident

1c Hermione Constance; served WW II; *d* unm 16 Dec 1965

2c Aleen Judith; *m* 6 July 1918 Maj Oliver George Graham Villiers, DSO (*see* CLARENDON, E), and *d* 1976, having had issue

3c Rachel Joan; *m* 10 Oct 1918 her sister's bro-in-law Capt Gerald Berkeley Villiers, OBE, RN, and had issue

4c Hilda Bridget; *m* 11 Oct 1917 Lt-Col James William Garden, DSO (*d* 1957), RFA, advocate, s of James Murray Garden, and *d* 17 Feb 1965, leaving issue

5b Alan William, JP; *b* 27 March 1865; *m* 1st 8 Aug 1893 Hon Susan Alice Portman (*d* 21 Aug 1933), dau of 2nd Viscount Portman (*qv*), and had:

1c Hugh Alan, OBE (1946); *b* 5 Dec 1897; *educ* Charterhouse; Capt 15th/19th Hus WW I (wounded), WW II as Lt-Col S African Staff Corps, Union Def Forces (despatches); *m* 18 June 1926 Monica Violet (*d* 1977), yr dau of Edmond Waterton Coningsby Erskine (*see* MAR and KELLIE, E) and widow of Lt-Col G D Maynard, and *d* 1976, having had:

1d +Robin Erskine [Robin Heber-Percy Esq, Box 1232, Somerset West, CP, S Africa]; *b* 13 Sept 1927; *educ* Hilton Coll Natal; Sapper S African Engr Corps Union Def Forces April-Dec 1945; *m* 1953 *Ann, dau of John Gaw, of Johannesburg

2d +Philip Reginald [Philip Heber-Percy Esq, 14 Edgecliffe Pk, Bartle Rd, Gillitts, Natal 3610, S Africa]; *b* 13 Oct 1929; *educ* Hilton Coll Natal; chartered accountant (UK and S Africa); *m* 6 July 1952 *Cherie, dau of Johannes Van Wyk, of Johannesburg, and has:

1e +Robyn; *b* 21 Sept 1954; *m* 1976 *Anthony David Burgess, s of Roy Burgess, and has:

1f +Trevor; *b* 1983

2f +Bruce; *b* 1985

2e +Julia [Mrs Andries Laubscher, 15 Gavin Ave, Pine Park 2194, S Africa]; *b* 9 Jan 1956; *m* 1993 *Andries Burger Laubscher, s of Nicholaas Laubscher

2d (cont.) Mr and Mrs Philip R Heber-Percy also adopted:

*Renée [Mrs Andrew Scogings, 507 Roper St, Baileys Muckleneuk, Pretoria, S Africa]; b 1959; m 1981 *Dr Andrew Scogings, s of Prof David Scogings

    *Kim; b 21 Oct 1961; m 1985 *Peter Adie, s of Martin Adie

3d +John Kellie [John Heber-Percy Esq, 34 Kingswood Dve, Chirnside Pk, Victoria 3116, Australia]; b 13 June 1935; educ Hilton Coll Natal; m 2 Sept 1961 *Rosalind Marion, dau of Walter Harvey Gathercole, of Port Elizabeth, and has:

    1e +Gillian Dorothy; b 31 May 1965; m 1987 *Michael Alan DIXON later HEBER-PERCY and has:

        1f +Abigail Brianna; b 6 Nov 1996

    2e +Helen Marjorie; b 28 March 1968

2c +Bryan [Bryan Heber-Percy Esq, Hillside, Port Lewaigue Close, Maughold, IoM]; b 29 Nov 1903; Capt RA; m 10 Oct 1936 *Etelka, dau of Istvan Kuiti, of Budapest

3c Peter, OBE (1946); b 3 Nov 1908; educ Wellington; Lt-Col 55th AA Regt RA (TA) WW II; m 1st 27 Sept 1930 (divorce 1946) (Josephine) Sylvia (d 1990), er dau of Brig-Gen Cyril Randall Crofton, CBE, of Trobridge, Crediton, Devon, and had:

    1d +(Sylvia) Venetia [Mrs David Stern, Bednall Hill, Bednall, Staffs ST17 0SA]; b 6 Feb 1932; m 25 April 1953 *David Gerald Stern, yr s of Sir Albert Gerald Stern, KBE, CMG, of Barham Court, Maidstone (see 1970 edn ORR-LEWIS, Bt), and has:

        1e Mark David Robin; b 9 June 1955; d 1981

        1e +Sylvia Louise; b 5 June 1957

    2d +(Susan) Deirdre [Mrs Benedict Fenwick, Sholebrook, Towcester, Northants]; b 10 June 1938; m 28 Nov 1958 *(Anthony) Benedict Xavier Fenwick (see LILFORD, B), and has issue

3c (cont.) Peter Heber-Percy m 2nd 1947 Mrs Elsa Maria Cohen (d 1996), dau of Giacomo Nissim, of Pisa, Italy, and d 29 Jan 1997, having by her had:

    3d +Sandra Caroline; b 19–

4c John; b 18 March 1910; educ Wellington; ADC to HC Egypt 1936, G/Capt RAF 1939–41 (despatches), Air Attaché The Hague 1947–49; m 1st 1 Oct 1940 (divorce 1949) Eve, yr dau of E R Robertson, of Ilkley, Yorks, and had:

    1d +Christopher John (Rev) [The Rev Christopher Heber-Percy, 19 Bellfield Ave, Holderness Rd, Kingston-upon-Hull HU8 9DS]; b 29 July 1941; educ Sedbergh and St John's Coll Cambridge (MA 1967); ordained 1969; m 18 July 1964 *Lyndis Elizabeth, yst dau of Rt Rev John Henry Lawrence Phillips, MA, Bp of Portsmouth, and has:

        1e +William John; b 21 Sept 1965

        2e +Thomas Henry; b 5 Aug 1967

        1e +Anna; b 15 April 1970

    1d +Susan Elizabeth [Mrs Karl Sabbagh, 76 Sheen Pk, Richmond, Surrey TW9 1UP]; b 2 June 1943; educ Girton Coll Cambridge (BA 1964); m 31 July 1965 *Karl John Sabbagh, s of Isa Khalil Sabbagh, of Washington, DC, and Mrs P Edmonds, of London, and has:

        1e +Jonathan Christopher; b 1978

        1e +Lucy Elizabeth; b 13 Jan 1970

        2e +Isabella Mary; b 1972

        3e +Susanna Jane; b 1975

    2d +Josceline Mary [Mrs Richard Newell, 11 Windsor Terrace, Penarth, S Glam CF64 1AA]; b 5 Sept 1946; m 11 Oct 1969 *Richard Leonard Martyn Newell, BSc, MB, BS, FRCS, LRCP, only s of Benjamin Newell, and has:

        1e +Adam Richard Eric; b 14 June 1971

        2e +Benjamin Rhodri; b 1972

        1e +Victoria Claire; b 30 April 1975

        2e +Charlotte Jessica Eve; b 1981

4c (cont.) G/Capt John Heber-Percy m 2nd 6 April 1950 Marie Elise (d 19–), dau of Jonkheer François Edouard Teixeira de Mattos, of The Hague, and d 1975

1c Margaret Eleanor, BEM (1957), JP; b 9 Aug 1894; m 14 Jan 1920 Edward Paget Scholfield, JP (d 10 Aug 1967), est s of Robert Stanley Scholfield, JP, of Sandhall, Yorks, and d 9 Feb 1963, leaving two daus

2c Ida Mary; b 20 March 1900; served WAAF; d unm 2 April 1951

3c Constance Emily; b 14 Nov 1901; d unm 21 July 1938

5b (cont.) Alan Heber-Percy m 2nd 7 Dec 1936 Mabel (d 6 Aug 1953), dau of Sir William Darracott and widow of E Herbert Hinds, and d 19 Oct 1946

1b Blanche Emily; d 29 Jan 1870

2b Ethel Cecilia; m 7 June 1870 Hon Alexander Frederick Gregory, 3rd s of 3rd Viscount Hood (qv), and d 21 Nov 1923, leaving issue

3b Agnes Katherine; d unm 9 Aug 1916

4b Maude Ellen; m 12 Aug 1880 Col Sir Edward Law Durand, 1st Bt (qv), and d 2 June 1953, leaving issue

5b Gertrude Amelia; m 5 Sept 1895 Col John James Hardy Eustace-Duckett (d 26 Dec 1924), of Castlemore, Co Carlow, and d 18 April 1948, leaving issue

6b Evelyn Mary; m 16 July 1889 Francis Monckton and d 17 Nov 1941, leaving issue (see GALWAY, V)

7b Isabel Harriet; m 2 Sept 1891 Andrew Greville Rouse-Boughton-Knight (d 20 Feb 1928) and d 10 Jan 1955, leaving issue (see 1963 edn ROUSE-BOUGHTON, Bt)

2a Henry (Rev); b 5 June 1813; Rector Greystoke, Canon Carlisle, m 1 Feb 1841 Emma Barbara (d Nov 1877), only dau of Capt B B Galbraith, of Old Derrig, Queen's, and d 6 Sept 1870, having had:

    1b Harry; b 19 Jan 1843; d 11 Sept 1856

    2b Hugh William; b 29 March 1844; d unm 30 May 1899

    3b Algernon Payan; b 31 Jan 1847; d unm 25 Nov 1900

4b Alfred, of Laura, S Australia; b 1850; m 1st 5 May 1879 Ada Elizabeth (dsp 1898), dau of Rev Daniel Packard; m 2nd 1899 Mary Hyland (d 7 June 1962) and d 21 Aug 1907, leaving:

    1c Henry; b 13 April 1901; m 6 Oct 1934 Mary Lavinia Mervyn Perry, of Fremantle, W Australia

    1c +Mary; b 28 Feb 1903; m 27 Sept 1930 Hugh Bernard Doherty (d 1974) and has:

        1d +Michael Dominic [Michael Doherty Esq, 104 Beasley St, Torrens, ACT 2607, Australia]; b 1936; m 1960 *Patricia Mary Hassett and has:

            1e +Anthony Michael; b 1961; m 1981 *Narelle Christine Sproule and has:

                1f +Stephen Anthony; b 1992

            2e +Matthew Michael; b 1967; m 1991 *Belinda Maria Hill

            1e +Therese Marie; b 1964; m 1st 1985 (divorce 1992) Neil Morgan and has:

                1f +Nicholas James; b 1985

                1f +Alice Marie; b 1988

            1e (cont.) Mrs Therese Morgan m 2nd 1993 *Scott Alan Boyd McCrohon

            2e +Noeline Elizabeth; b 1965; m 1983 *Colin Andrew Jacob and has:

                1f +David Keith; b 1983

                2f +Michael Patrick; b 1985

                3f +Philip John; b 1991

                1f +Naomi Margaret; b 1988

                2f +Rebecca Mary; b 1993

            3e +Louise Geraldine; b 1968; m 1993 *Peter Wilhelm Merkel

            4e +Catherine Majella; b 1971

        2d +Brian Hugh [Brian Doherty Esq, 34 Lutana Crescent, Mitchell Pk, SA 5043, Australia]; b 1938; m 1961 *Margaret Anne Curran and has:

            1e +Andrew Bernard; b 1962; m 1992 *Lynn Paul Kemmett and has:

                1f +Elizabeth Michele; b 1994

            2e +Michael James; b 1965; m 1991 *Moira Teresa Richardson and has had:

                1f Mary Teresa; b and d 1993

            3e +Joseph Brian; b 1968

            4e +Paul Vincent; b 1973

            5e +Christopher Philip; b 1975

            1e +Catherine Mary; b 1969; m 1990 *Robert Leslie Maher and has:

                1f +Patrick Leslie; b 1991

                1f +Carmel Margaret; b 1993

        1d +Maire Rosaleen [Mrs John Sunners, 6 Travers St, Sturt, S Australia 5047, Australia]; b 1931; m 1957 *John William Sunners and has:

            1e +John Bernard; b 1958; m 1980 *Helen Maree O'Neill and has:

                1f +Damien John; b 1981

                1f +Kylie Maree; b 1980

            2e +Timothy Peter; b 1959; m 1993 *Kylie Loudon

            3e +David Peter; b 1961; m 1983 *Helen Maree Cassidy and has:

                1f +Meghann Emily; b 1988

                2f +Nadine Alexandra; b 1991

            4e +Paul Gerard; b 1963; m 1988 *Gail Barbara Darling and has:

                1f +Maxwell John; b 1994

                1f +Samantha Cara; b 1989

                2f +Kristy Lea; b 1990

                3f +Nicole Mary; b 1992

            5e +Kevin Patrick; b 1964; m 1986 *Sherree Michele Coleman and has:

                1f +Benjamin William; b 1989

                1f +Abby Louise; b 1989

            1e +Anne Therese; b 1962; has issue

            2e +Carmel Elizabeth; b 1962; m 1985 *Peter David Button and has:

                1f +Stephanie Brianna; b 1991

            3e +Claire Louise; b 1966; m 1991 *Malcolm McGlashan

            4e +Maureen Patricia; b 1973

         2d +Denise Margaret [Mrs Leon Grealy, 1 Bessie St, Dover Gdns, S Australia 5048, Australia]; b 1932; m 1956 *Leon Thomas Grealy and has:

            1e +Stephen Matthew; b 1958; m 1979 *Heather Joy Rana and has:

                1f +Patrick Matthew; b 1985

                2f +Peter John; b 1987

                1f +Christine Anne; b 1982

            1e +Bernadette Anne; b 1957

            2e +Leonie Therese; b 1962; m 1988 *Martin Denis Welsh

        3d +Noeline Carmel [Mrs James Carr, 3 Short St, Glen Waverley, Victoria 3150, Australia]; b 1934; m 1957 *James Carr and has had:

            1e +Michael Joseph; b 1957; m 1981 *Jennifer Iris Robson and has:

                1f +Reuben James; b 19–

                1f +Jemima Rose; b 1982

                2f +Hayley Grace; b 1983

            2e +Damian Peter; b 1962; has issue

            3e +Bernard James; b 1965

            4e +Christopher Patrick; b 1970

            1e +Debra Mary; b 1959; m 1993 *Ian Anthony Neil

2e +Geraldine Frances; *b* 1960; *m* 1990 *Geoffrey John Hanson and has:

 1f +Merrily Esther; *b* 1991

 2f +Ginger Bride; *b* 1991 (twin)

3e +Paula Maree; *b* 1963; *m* 1988 *Daniel John Wain and has:

 1f +Patrick James; *b* 1993

 2f +Lewis Peter; *b* 1993 (twin)

4e +Marita Louise; *b* 1967; *m* 1988 (*divorce* 1993) Robert La Greca

5e +Natalie Ann; *b* 1968

6e Melissa Jane; *b* and *d* 1973

4d +Frances Josephine [Mrs John Dickins, 6 Pinkwood Dve, Belle-vue Pk, Southport, Qld 4215, Australia]; *b* 1944; *m* 1st 1968 Leon Jospeh Pasquarelli (*d* 1979) and has:

 1e +Sergio; *b* 1975

 1e +Maria; *b* 1969

 2e +Sophia; *b* 1971

4d (cont.) Mrs Leon Pasquarelli *m* 2nd 1991 *John Arthur Dickins

5b Allayne Josceline; *b* 1852; *d* 5 July 1886

6b Edward Galbraith Henry; *b* 1853; *d* 17 June 1913

7b Josceline Hugh; *b* July 1856; *m* 12 Oct 1892 Grace Anne (*d* 14 March 1960), dau of Edward Percy Thompson, and *d* 23 Oct 1910, leaving:

1c Henry Edward; *b* 6 Aug 1893; memb HAC, WW I; *ka* 25 Feb 1915

2c Josceline Richard; *b* 1894; *m* 30 Dec 1929 Mary (*d* 23 Dec 1964), dau of Harold Nicholson, of Oak House, Farnworth, Bolton, and *d* 1971, having had:

1d +Hugh Edward [Hugh Percy Esq, 33 Regent St, Lancaster]; *b* 24 Sept 1938; *educ* Gonville and Caius Coll Cambridge (BA) and Manchester Coll of Commerce; ALA; *m* 25 Oct 1969 *Barbara, only dau of — Mulholland, of Lancaster

1d +Eleanor Mary [Mrs James Adams, 1170 Keeler Ave, Berkeley, CA, USA]; *b* 12 Feb 1940; *educ* Trin Coll Dublin; *m* 3 March 1962 *James Rolf Adams, only s of Elmo W Adams, of Burlingame, Calif., and has:

 1e +Katharine Charlotte; *b* 2 May 1963

 2e +Ruth Susannah; *b* 20 March 1965

1c Margaret

2c Constance; *d* unm 30 Jan 1928

1b Elizabeth Mary; *m* 25 May 1871 Rev John Adams, of Bournemouth, Vicar Offchurch, Warwicks, and *d* 11 Jan 1928, leaving issue

2b Charlotte Florentia Frances; *d* unm 12 Jan 1908

3b Emma Annie Isabel; *m* 16 April 1884 Herbert Cranstoun Adams, of Exmouth, and *d* 1943, leaving issue

3a Hugh Josceline, of Eskrigg, Wigton, Cumberland, JP, DL; *b* 9 Dec 1817; *m* 24 Oct 1859 Anne (*d* 25 March 1904), dau of Joseph Story, and *d* 9 Feb 1882, leaving:

1b Edward Josceline, of Eskrigg; *b* 30 Nov 1864; Lt 3rd Bn York and Lancaster Regt; *m* 23 Jan 1907 Helen Elizabeth (*d* 11 April 1954), dau of John Jarvie, and *d* 15 June 1931

1b Mary; *m* Jan 1886 George Browne and *d* 1889

2b Agnes Ellen Josceline; *m* 6 Sept 1888 Frederick George Mather and had issue

1a Gertrude; *m* 12 July 1834 2nd Earl Amherst (*see* 1970 edn, also AMHERST OF HACKNEY, B, preliminary remarks) and *d* 27 April 1890, having had issue

(3) (cont.) The Rt Rev Hugh Percy *m* 2nd 3 Feb 1840 Mary (*dsp* 22 Nov 1851), dau of Countess of Annandale and Hartfell (*qv*) in her own right, and *d* 5 Feb 1856

(4) Josceline, CB (1831); *b* 29 Jan 1784; joined RN 1797, Actg Lt Aug 1803, Lt April 1804, Cdr Jan 1806, Capt Sept 1806, R-Adml 1841, V-Adml 1851, MP Beeralston, Devon, 1806–20; *m* 9 Dec 1820 Sophia Elizabeth (*d* 13 Dec 1875), 3rd dau of Moreton Walhouse (*see* HATHERTON, B), and *d* 19 Oct 1856, having had:

1a Alan; *b* 7 Jan 1825; *d* 25 June 1845

1a Sophia Louisa; *m* 7 July 1846 Col Charles Bagot and *d* 7 Nov 1908, leaving issue (*see* BAGOT, B)

2a Emily; *m* 17 July 1852 Gen Sir Charles Lawrence d'Aguilar, GCB (*d* 2 Nov 1912), and *d* 17 Dec 1919, leaving issue

3a Charlotte Alice; *m* 13 April 1858 Edward Percy Thompson (*d* Oct 1879) and *d* 26 May 1916, leaving issue

(5) Henry, CB; *b* 14 Sept 1785; Lt-Col, ADC to Sir John Moore at Corunna and Duke of Wellington (*qv*) at Waterloo; *d* 1825

(6) William Henry; *b* 24 March 1788; joined RN 1801, Cdr 1810, Capt 1812, R-Adml 1846, MP Stamford, Commr of Excise; *d* unm 5 Oct 1855

(7) Francis John; *b* 1790; Capt 23rd Regt; *d* 23 Aug 1812

(8) Charles PERCY later GREATHEED BERTIE PERCY (sign manual 1826 with arms); *b* 4 March 1794; *m* 20 March 1822 Anne Caroline Greatheed (*d* 8 June 1882 aged 77), gdau and heiress of Bertie Bertie Greatheed, of Guys Cliffe, Warwicks; granted with his sole surv sis by roy licence 16 March 1865 rank of duke's dau/yr s; *d* 11 Oct 1870, leaving:

1a Anne Barbara Isabel; *b* 31 March 1834; *d* 15 Feb 1891

(1) Charlotte; *m* 25 July 1795 3rd Earl of Ashburnham (*d* 27 Oct 1830; *see* ASHBURNHAM, Bt) and *d* 26 Nov 1862, leaving issue

(2) Emily Charlotte; *m* 25 July 1808 Andrew Mortimer Drummond (*see* PERTH, E), of Charing Cross and Denham, Middx, and *d* 22 May 1877, having had issue

The 1st EARL OF BEVERLEY's est s,

GEORGE PERCY, 5th Duke of Northumberland, PC (1842); *b* 22 June 1778; *educ* Eton and St John's Coll Cambridge (MA 1799, LLD 1842); MP (Tory) Beeralston 1799–1830, a Ld Treasury 1804–06, Commr Indian Affrs 1807–12, volunteer soldier against French 1808, Ld Bedchamber to GEORGE IV 1821 and WILLIAM IV July–Dec 1830, Capt Yeoman Gd 1842–46, Tstee Br Museum

1861–67; *m* 22 June 1801 Louisa Harcourt (*d* 30 June 1848), 3rd dau of Hon James Archibald Stuart-Wortley-Mackenzie (*see* WHARNCLIFFE, E), and *d* 21 Aug 1867, having had:

1 ALGERNON GEORGE, **6th Duke**

2 Josceline William; *b* 17 July 1811; *m* 8 Aug 1848 Margaret (*d* 19 June 1885), only dau of Sir David Davidson, of Cantray, Nairn, and widow of Sir Robert Grant, MP, and *d* 25 July 1881, leaving:

 (1) George Algernon; *b* 17 May 1849; Lt-Col Gren Gds; *d* unm 17 July 1931

3 Henry Hugh Manvers, VC (1857 for outstanding bravery at Inkerman), KCB (1873); *b* 22 Aug 1817; *educ* Eton; Ensign Gren Gds 1836, Capt and Lt-Col (and briefly T/Brig-Gen cmdg Br-Italian Legion) Crimean War (wounded at Balaclava and Inkerman, also present Siege Sebastopol), ADC to HM QUEEN VICTORIA 1855–65, Maj 1860, ret 1862, MP (C) N Northumberland 1865–68, Col 89th Regt 1874, Gen 1877, Chev Legn Hon and Kt Medjidie; *d* unm 3 Dec 1877

1 Louisa; *d* unm 23 Dec 1883 aged 81

2 Margaret; *m* 23 Sept 1841 2nd Baron Hatherton (*qv*) and *d* 16 May 1897, having had issue

The 5th DUKE's est s,

ALGERNON GEORGE PERCY, 6th Duke of Northumberland, KG (1885), PC (1859), JP, DL (both Surrey); *b* 20 May 1810; *educ* Eton and St John's Coll Cambridge (LLD 1870); Army 1829–37 (ret as Capt Gren Gds), MP (C) Beeralston 1831–32 and N Northumberland 1852–65; a Ld Admlty 1858–59, V-Pres BOT March-June 1859 and Ld Privy Seal 1878–80, Ld Lt and custos rotulorum Northumberland 1877–99, Hon Col: 5th Bn Northumberland Fus and 1st and 2nd (Percy) Artillery Vols of Northumberland (Vol Offrs decoration), Provincial Grand Master Northumberland Freemasons 1869–86, Pres: Roy Archaeological Inst 1883–92 and RNLI; DCL Durham 1882, FSA 1883; *m* 26 May 1845 Louisa (*d* 18 Dec 1890), dau and coheir of Henry Drummond, MP (*see* PERTH, E), of Albury Park, Surrey, through whom the Albury property came to the Dukes of Northumberland, and *d* 2 Jan 1899, having had:

1 HENRY GEORGE, **7th Duke**

2 Algernon Malcolm Arthur, of Guys Cliffe, Warwicks, JP (Surrey); *b* 2 Oct 1851; *educ* Eton and Ch Ch Oxford (MA); Lt Gren Gds 1872–80, Maj 3rd Bn: Roy Berks Regt 1881–86 and Northumberland Fus 1886–95 (Lt-Col latter 1895–1910, then Col cmdg), MP (C) Westminster 1882–85 and St George's Hanover Sq 1885–87, Warwicks: CA, Chm CC, High Sheriff 1910 and V-Lt, ADC to TM EDWARD VII and GEORGE V 1902–20; *m* 3 Aug 1880 Lady Victoria Frederica Caroline Edgcumbe (*d* 20 Feb 1920), dau of 4th Earl of Mount Edgcumbe (*qv*), and *d* 28 Dec 1933, having had:

 (1) William William, JP; *b* 29 Nov 1884; Lt 3rd Bn Northumberland Fus, CCllr Warwicks, Sub-Lt RNR; *ka* unm aboard HMS *Queen Mary* Battle of Jutland 31 May 1916

 (1) Katharine Louisa Victoria; *b* 22 March 1882; *m* 15 Sept 1904 her cousin Josceline Reginald Heber-Percy and *d* 10 Jan 1964, leaving issue (*see above*)

The 6th DUKE's er s,

HENRY GEORGE PERCY, 7th Duke of Northumberland, KG (1899), PC (1874), JP (Surrey); *b* 29 May 1846; *educ* Ch Ch Oxford; MP (C) N Northumberland 1868–85 (Treas Household 1874–75), called up to Ho Lds 22 July 1887 *vp* as LORD LOVAINE, BARON OF ALNWICK, Militia ADC to TM QUEEN VICTORIA 1892, EDWARD VII 1901 and GEORGE V, Pres Roy Institution 1899, Tstee Br Museum 1900, Ld Lt and custos rotulorum Northumberland 1904, Hon Col 3rd and 7th Bns Northumberland Fus and 1st Northumbrian Bde RFA, Pres Northumberland TFA 1909–18, Chm Northumberland CC, Durham U: memb Senate 1909–12 and Chllr 1913–18, Ld High Steward 1911 Coronation, memb Cncl Roy Soc 1911, LLD, DCL, FRS 1900; *m* 28 Dec 1868 Lady Edith Campbell (*d* 6 July 1913), dau of 8th Duke of Argyll (*qv*), and *d* 14 May 1918, having had:

 1 Henry Algernon George, *Earl Percy*, DL (Northumberland); *b* 21 Jan 1871; *educ* Eton and Ch Ch Oxford (BA, Newdigate Prize for English Verse 1892); MP (C) S Kensington 1895–1909 (fought Berwick-on-Tweed unsuccessfully earlier in 1895 against the future Lib For Sec Sir Edward Grey, later 1st Viscount Grey of Fallodon (*see* GREY, Bt, of Fallodon): Parly U-Sec: India 1902–03 and For Affrs 1903–05, traveller Middle East and Asia Minor with among others his cousin Algernon Heber-Percy (*see above*), Tstee Nat Portrait Gallery 1901, Hon DCL Durham 1907, author: *Notes of a Diary in Asiatic Turkey* (1898) and *The Highlands of Asiatic Turkey* (1901); *d* unm 30 Dec 1909

2 Josceline; *b* 26 Jan 1872; BA; *d* unm 31 Jan 1898

3 Ralph William; *b* 9 March 1877; *d* 28 March 1889

4 ALAN IAN, **8th Duke**

5 William Richard, CBE (1919), DSO (1917); *b* 17 May 1882; *educ* Eton and Ch Ch Oxford (BA 1904); barrister Inner Temple 1906, WW I: Col Gren Gds, GSO(1), Assist Dir Mil Intell Imp Gen Staff 1919 (despatches twice, wounded), Serbian Order White Eagle 4th Cl with swords, Cdr Order King George I Greece; *m* 25 July 1922 Mary (*d* 1984), dau of Capt George Sitwell Campbell Swinton, and *d* 8 Feb 1963, leaving:

 (1) Henry Edward; *b* 30 Oct 1925; *m* 20 Sept 1952 *Eileen Ruth Morley [Mrs Henry Percy, The Pitchmarket, Cerne Abbas, Dorset DT2 7JQ], er dau of Lt-Col Wilmot Smyth Caulfeild (*see* CHARLEMONT, V), and *d* 1985, leaving:

 1a +George Robert; *b* 29 June 1953

 2a +James Edward Caulfeild; *b* 31 May 1958; *m* 1986 (*divorce* 1989) Gay P Lovell-Badge, dau of Mrs John Cator, of Woodbastwick, Norfolk; *m* 2nd 1993 *Hon Zara Jane Digby, only dau of 12th Baron Digby (*qv*)

 1a +Lavinia Mary; *b* 22 Oct 1955

 2a +Susan Clare; *b* 13 April 1961; *m* 1990 *George M Woodruff, 2nd s of James Woodruff, DFC, of Belcombe Court, Bradford-on-Avon, Wilts

 (2) +Gerald [Gerald Percy Esq, The Granary, Nunnery Place, Thetford, Norfolk IP24 2PZ]; *b* 26 April 1928; *educ* Eton and Ch Ch Oxford (MA 1950); *m* 1st 10 Aug 1950; *m* 1st 10 Aug 1950 (*divorce* 1953) Alison Jannice, er dau of Sir Herbert Ribton Meredith, of Nairobi; *m* 2nd 30 Oct 1954 (*divorce* 1975) Jennifer, dau of John Brougham Home-Rigg, of E Transvaal, and has:

 1a +Richard John [Richard Percy Esq, 2 Cottesmore Gdns, London W8 5PR]; *b* 28 Sept 1957; *educ* Eton; *m* 1987 *Deborah Patricia, yr dau of Guy Norman, of Brockham, Surrey, and has:

 1b +Natasha Elizabeth; *b* 25 Jan 1988

 2b +Sabrina Catherine; *b* 11 Feb 1990

2a +Andrew Alan; *b* 22 July 1963; *m* 1988 *LaNora Lynn, yr dau of J R Scott, of Scottsdale, Ariz., and has:

1b +Ayden Jay; *b* 10 Jan 1992

2b +Callum Zane; *b* 22 March 1994

1a +Katherine Susan; *b* 18 Nov 1955; *m* 1982 (*divorce* 1986) John Bentley

2a +Diana Mary; *b* 18 Dec 1965

(2) (cont.) Gerald Percy *m* 3rd 24 Jan 1983 *Victoria, dau of Dr Roger Handerson

6 James; *b* 6 Jan 1885; *d* unm 20 May 1903

7 EUSTACE SUTHERLAND CAMPBELL PERCY, 1st and last BARON PERCY OF NEWCASTLE, of Etchingham, Co Sussex (UK), so *cr* 12 Feb 1953, PC (1924); *b* 21 March 1887; *educ* Eton and Ch Ch Oxford (BA 1907, MA 1913); 3rd Sec Dip Serv 1911–19, MP (U) Hastings 1921–37: Parly Sec: Bd Educn March-May 1923 and Min Health 1923–24, Pres Bd Educn 1924–29, Min without Portfolio 1935–36, ed *The Yearbook of Education* 1932–35, Rector King's Coll Newcastle (subsequently part of Durham U), Pres Roy Institution 1941, Chm Roy Commn on Mental Patients 1954, Hon DCL Durham, Hon LLD: Edinburgh, St Andrews, Columbia (New York) and Durban Us, author: *The Responsibilities of the League* (1920), *Education at the Crossroads* (1930), *Maritime Trade in War* (1930), *Democracy on Trial* (1931), *Government in Transition* (1934), *John Knox* (1937), *The Heresy of Democracy* (1954) and *Some Memories* (1958); *m* 4 Dec 1918 Stella Katherine (*d* 21 Feb 1982 aged 86), dau of Maj-Gen Lawrence Drummond, CB, CBE, MVO (*see* PERTH, E), and *dspm* 3 April 1958, when the Barony expired, leaving:

(1) +Mary Edith; *b* 24 Oct 1919; *educ* Bristol U; *d* unm 27 Nov 1998

(2) +Dorothy Anne [The Hon Mrs Eustace, Glebe House, Boughton Aluph, Ashford, Kent]; *b* 21 Sept 1926; *educ* Durham U (MB and BS 1949); *m* 23 March 1957 *Maj Thomas Robert Hales Eustace, Roy Irish Fus, only s of Louis Charles Moss Eustace, of The Cliff, Mousehole, Penzance, Cornwall, and has:

1a +James Maurice Percy; *b* 26 March 1960; *m* 1986 *Gay Rosemary, dau of Alan Oughton, of the Vale, Findon, W Sussex, and has:

1b +Henry Alan; *b* 1988

2b +David James; *b* 1991

1a +Alicia Mary; *b* 30 April 1958

2a +Katharine (Katrina) Anne, *b* 17 March 1965; *m* 1988 *Andrew J McGladdery, only s of Dr John Arthur McGladdery, and has:

1b +Charles; *b* 1992

1 Louisa Elizabeth; *b* 7 Nov 1869; *d* unm 29 Nov 1893

2 Edith Eleanor; twin with Louisa Elizabeth; *d* unm 2 April 1937

3 Margaret; *b* 30 Aug 1873; *d* unm 29 Jan 1934

4 Victoria Alexandrina; *b* 12 Feb 1875; *d* unm 18 Jan 1958

5 Mary; *b* 30 Aug 1878; *m* 20 Oct 1909 Lt-Col Aymer Edward Maxwell, JP, DL (*see* MAXWELL, Bt), and *d* 18 March 1965, leaving issue

6 Muriel Evelyn Nora; *b* 14 July 1890; *d* unm 23 Nov 1956

The 7th DUKE's 4th but est surv s,

ALAN IAN PERCY, **8th Duke of Northumberland**, KG (1925), CBE (1919), MVO (1919), TD, JP (W R Yorks); *b* 17 April 1880; *educ* Eton and Ch Ch Oxford; Gren Gds 1900–12: Boer War 1901–02 (medal, four clasps), with Egyptian Army 1907–10 (Sudan 1908 (medal with clasp)), ret as Maj 1912, and WW I (official observer 1914–16, GSO(1) and T/Lt-Col 1916–18, Brevet Lt-Col 1918 (despatches), 4th Cl Medjidie, 5th Cl Legn Hon, 3rd Cl St Anne Russia), Hon Col: Tyne Electrical Engrs (TA), 3rd Bn Queen's Roy W Surrey Regt (Reserve) and 6th and 7th Bns Northumberland Fus (TA), Maj Reserve Offrs, Pres Northumberland TAA, ADC to Govr-Gen Canada 1910–11, Ld Lt Northumberland, LLD Cambridge, DCL and Chllr Durham U 1929–30, CA Northumberland, Pres Roy Institution, author: *The Shadow on the Moor* (1931) and *La Salamandre, the Story of a Vivandière* (1934); *m* 18 Oct 1911 Lady Helen Magdalen Gordon-Lennox (*d* 13 June 1965), dau of 7th Duke of Richmond and Gordon (*qv*), and *d* 23 Aug 1930, leaving:

1 HENRY GEORGE ALAN PERCY, **9th Duke of Northumberland**, JP; *b* 15 July 1912 (HM GEORGE V stood sponsor); *educ* Eton; Lt Gren Guards, PPS to Ld Privy Seal June 1935 and Sec State Air Dec 1936; *dsp* (*ka* Tournai) 21 May 1940

2 HUGH ALGERNON, **10th Duke**

3 Richard Charles, DL (Northumberland 1968); *b* 11 Feb 1921 (HM QUEEN MARY stood sponsor); *educ* Eton, Ch Ch Oxford and Durham U; Page to HRH PRINCE ARTHUR OF CONNAUGHT at 1937 Coronation, Capt Gren Gds 1941–45, zoology lecturer Newcastle U, Lt-Col cmdg Northumberland Hus (TA) 1959–61; *m* 1st 10 Sept 1966 Sarah Jane Elizabeth (*d* 1978), dau of Petre Norton, of The Manor House, Whalton, Northumberland, and had:

(1) +Algernon Alan [Algernon Percy Esq, Friar's Well Farmhouse, Hulne Park, Northumberland NE66 2LJ]; *b* 17 March 1969; *educ* Eton and Ch Ch Oxford

(2) +Josceline Richard; *b* 1971; *educ* Eton and St Andrews

3 (cont.) Lord Richard Percy *m* 2nd 1979 *Hon Clayre Campbell [The Lady Richard Percy, 212 Lambeth Rd, London SE1 7JY], 2nd dau of 4th Baron Stratheden and Campbell (*qv*) and formerly w of Hon Nicholas Ridley, MP (*see* RIDLEY, V), and *d* 20 Dec 1989

4 Geoffrey William; *b* 8 July 1925; *educ* Eton; Page to his mother, Mistress Robes, at 1937 Coronation, 2nd Lt Gren Gds 1943–44; *m* 27 May 1955 *Mary Elizabeth [The Lady Geoffrey Percy, Barton House, Monleigh, N Devon EX39 5JX], only dau of Ralph Lea, of Teddington, Middx, and *d* 1984, leaving:

(1) +Diana Ruth; *b* 22 Nov 1956

1 +Elizabeth Ivy, OBE [Her Grace The Dowager Duchess of Hamilton and Brandon OBE, North Port, Lennoxlove, Haddington, E Lothian]; *b* 25 May 1916; one of HM QUEEN ELIZABETH (now HM QUEEN ELIZABETH THE QUEEN MOTHER)'s train bearers at the Coronation 1937; *m* 2 Dec 1937 14th Duke of Hamilton and Brandon (*qv*) and has issue

2 Diana Evelyn; *b* 23 Nov 1917; *m* 29 April 1939, as his 1st w, *6th Duke of Sutherland (*qv*) and *dsp* 1978

The 9th DUKE's next bro,

HUGH (HUGHIE) ALGERNON PERCY, **10th Duke of Northumberland**, KG (1959), TD (1961), PC, JP (Northumberland 1946); *b* 6 April 1914; *educ* Eton and Ch Ch Oxford; Gold Stick-in-Waiting Coronation 1937, Ld-in-Waiting to HM GEORGE VI May-July 1945, Ld Lt Northumberland 1956, Ld Steward Household 1973–88, Hon Col 7th Bn Roy Northumberland Fus TARO 1949, chm Northumberland T&AFA 1949–56 (pres 1956–68), pres TAVR Assoc for North of England 1968, Capt Northumberland Hus Yeo, Pres Roy Ag Soc England 1956 and 1962, Chm Ag Research Cncl 1958–68, Chm Court Durham U 1956–64, Chllr Newcastle U 1964–88, pres: Northumberland Assoc of Boys' Clubs 1942–88, Northumberland Boy Scouts' Assoc 1946–88, Br Horse Soc 1950, Hunters' Improvement and Light Horse Breeding Soc 1954, Br Show Jumping Assoc 1959, N of England Shipowners' Assoc 1952–88, Northern Area Br Legion and Wildfowl Tst 1968–88, memb Roy Commn Historical MSS. 1973–88, chm: Border Forest Pk Ctee 1956–68, Deptl Ctee Slaughter Horses 1952, Deptl Ctee for Recruitment of Veterinary Surgs 1964, Independent Ctee Inquiry Foot-and-Mouth Disease 1968–69, MRC 1969–88, memb: Ag Improvement Cncl 1953–62, Nat Forestry Ctee England and Wales 1954–60 and Hill Farming Advsy Ctee England and Wales 1946–60, Hon Assoc RCVS 1967, KStJ 1957, FRS, Hon DCL Durham 1958; *m* 12 June 1946 *Lady Elizabeth Diana Montagu-Douglas-Scott [Her Grace Elizabeth Duchess of Northumberland, Friar's Well, Alnwick, Northumberland NE66 2LJ; Clive Lodge, Albury, Surrey GU5 9AF], er dau of 8th Duke of Buccleuch (*qv*), and *d* 1988, having had:

1 HENRY ALAN WALTER RICHARD PERCY, **11th Duke of Northumberland**; *b* 1 July 1953 (HM THE QUEEN stood sponsor); *educ* Eton and Ch Ch Oxford; Jt MFH Percy 1989–95, pres: Alnwick & District Ctee for Disabled 1981–95, Alnwick Working Men's Club and Inst, Northumbria Club, Northumbrian Anglers' Fedn, Natl History Soc Northumbria, Northumberland Assoc Boys' Clubs, Northumberland Co Victims' Support Scheme, N of England Community Rels Cncl, Craster Branch RNLI, Surrey Farming and Wildlife Advsy Gp, Roy Northumberland Yacht Club, Tyne Mariners' Benevolent Institution, V-Pres: Ancient Monuments Soc and Internat Sheep Dog Soc, patron: Assoc Northumberland Local History Socs, Berwick-upon-Tweed Preservation Tst, Internat Centre for Child Studies, NE Br Mental Health Fndn, Northumberland Bldgs Preservation Tst, Hounslow and Feltham Victim Support Scheme, Hounslow and Twickenham Br Arthritis Care, Northern Counties Sch for the Deaf, Roy Northumberland Fus Aid Soc and Regimental Assoc, Theatre W4 and Tyneside Cinema, FRSA 1989, film producer (Hotspur Productions); *d* unm 31 Oct 1995

2 RALPH GEORGE ALGERNON PERCY, **12th and present Duke of Northumberland**

3 +James William Eustace [The Lord James Percy, Linhope Lodge, Powburn, Northumberland NE66 4LY]; *b* 18 June 1965; *educ* Eton and Bristol U

1 +Caroline Mary Percy [The Lady Caroline de Cabarrús, Finca del Alamo, Nijar, Almeria, Spain]; *b* 3 May 1947; *m* 12 Jan 1974 *Count Pierre de Cabarrsús, s of Count Jean de Cabarrsús, of Seville, and has:

(1) +Chiara Thérèse Cecilia; *b* 22 Nov 1974

(2) +Diana Marie; *b* 1977

2 +Victoria Lucy Diana Percy [The Lady Victoria Cuthbert, Abbeylands, Alnwick, Northumberland NE66 2JY]; *b* 19 April 1949; *m* 1975 *(John) Aidan Cuthbert, s of Harold Cuthbert by his w Bridget, dau of Sir Edward Milnes Coates, 2nd Bt (*qv*), and has:

(1) +David Hugh; *b* 1987

(1) +Alice Rose; *b* 1978

(2) +Lucy Caroline; *b* 1982

(3) +Mary Belinda; *b* 1984

3 +Julia Helen Percy [The Lady Julia Craig-Harvey, The Lainston Dairy, Sparsholt, Hants SO21 2LR]; *b* 12 Nov 1950; *m* 11 June 1983 *Nicholas Robert Craig-Harvey, s of Andrew John Craig-Harvey, of Sparsholt, Hants, by Mary, dau of Capt Robert Sitwell, CBE, RN, and Barbara (dau of Walter Septimus Fisher by Frances Mercy, dau of Rev Henry Cocks, ggs of 1st Baron Somers, *qv*), and has:

(1) +Christopher Hugh; *b* 4 Oct 1988

(1) +Georgina Elizabeth; *b* 29 May 1986

(2) +Laura Mary; *b* 7 Sept 1992

4 Louise; *b* 25 May, *d* 27 May 1962

Seats: Alnwick Castle, Northumberland; Syon House, Isleworth, Greater London.

Alnwick is of Norman origin and dates from the early 12th century, when the motte and two baileys of earlier times were strengthened with stone in place of wood. About the time of its acquisition by the PERCYs just after EDWARD I's death the keep was augmented by circular towers and the gatehouse further fortified. Such features seem to have been in emulation of EDWARD's Welsh castles. The place was little altered until the 18th century, and after the end of the 16th the Percys ceased to live there at all for several generations. (Details of the subsequent remodelling and improvement are given above against the **1st** and **4th Dukes**.)

Syon lies on the River Thames, the site of a Bridgettine monastery founded by HENRY V as a guilt offering for his father HENRY IV's turning a blind eye to the murder of RICHARD II. Although originally situated upstream at Twickenham it moved to Sion in 1431. At the Dissolution the lands came into the possession of the then Duke of Somerset, who built a new house but did not live to see it finished. Syon's proximity to London made it a convenient prison for high-ranking enemies of the state. It was the residence under house arrest of CATHERINE HOWARD, HENRY VIII's fifth wife, in the period leading up to her execution, and later of LADY JANE GREY. Parliament confined CHARLES I's children there for a time. It was leased by ELIZABETH I to the 'Wizard' **3rd Earl of Northumberland** in 1594 but not till the second half of the 17th century did its history take a pleasanter turn. It was in the 18th century that the present facade of Bath stone was superimposed, although the bulk of the Tudor structure remains underneath this dressing.

Robert Adam, who had already worked on Alnwick, designed much of Syon's interior as well. His work at the latter is said to have established his reputation (probably because it was more easily viewed by London-based leaders of fashion than a fortress in remote Northumberland). He was nevertheless under almost as much constraint, albeit aesthetic, as the noble and royal inmates physically of previous ages. He was obliged to retain the original layout of rooms and was forbidden to roof over the central courtyard, which he had wanted to do. Indeed he only completed a little over half the sequence of public apartments which open off each other round the huge quadrilateral.

The entrance hall is celebrated for its superb bronze copy of the Dying Gaul (which cost the 1st Duke £300 in 1773, or just under £13,750 in late–1990s terms). It also contains marble statues of Ceres, Cicero, Scipio Africanus and a Vestal Virgin. From there one steps up into the Ante-Room, as opulent and almost joyous in the strong colours and sense of triumph it imparts as its predecessor is gelid and austere. The Ante-Room's strong Classical Roman theme, with as its chief decorative feature some verd-antique columns taken from the bed of the Tiber, is highly apposite since Syon appears to be the point on the Thames at which Caesar crossed during his brief incursion into Britain in 54 BC. Indeed a wooden stake stuck in the river bed for defence of the northern shore by Ancient Britons has been preserved and is displayed in Syon's north-west corridor.

Along the next flank of the building lies the dining-room, a serious room for degustation, potation and politicking. The Red Drawing Room comes next, though now its silk wall linings are faded to almost rose tints. Its massive raised ceiling is supported on inward curving plasterwork above a thick gilded cornice and spotted by Cipriani as with a series of gigantic peacock's tail eyes by decorative circles inside eight-sided golden surrounds. The carpet is of exquisite delicacy, with key maeander surround and predominantly rectilinear motifs in the three panels. Rectilinear too are the door supports and pediments; the chimney piece likewise.

The long gallery has a more contemplative atmosphere, and not just because of its soothing eau de Nil colour scheme but through its tapestry of book spines. These face the windows but are broken into manageable masses by slender pilasters painted by Michelangelo Pergolesi and topped with Corinthian capitals separating roundel wall portraits of various Earls and Countesses of Northumberland and their ancestors. There are also at the same level some fine Zuccarelli landscapes. The ceiling here is almost a magnified version of that in the Red Drawing Room, but with a single huge rose inside an octagon occupying the entire width of the ceiling (only 14 feet) for every 14 feet or so of length along a gallery totalling 136 feet. The room is not as drawn out as the West Gallery at Blenheim, but before being decorated would have seemed a great deal narrower and lower, hence giving more the impression of a mere passage unless expanded by the kind of optical illusion of which Adam was master.

NORTON

Arms: Arg. on a bend az. three mascles of the field. **Crest:** On a chapeau az., doubled erm., a stork arg. **Supporters:** On either side a stork arg., gorged with a chain or, suspended therefrom an escutcheon az. charged with a mascle also arg. **Motto:** *Addere legi justitiam decus* ('It is an honour to add justice to law').
Creation: B. (UK) 16 April 1878.

THE 8TH BARON NORTON, of Norton-on-the-Moors, Co Stafford (James Nigel Arden Adderley) [The Rt Hon The Lord Norton, 11 Picaterre, Alderney, Channel Islands] *b* 2 June 1947; *s f* 1993; *educ* Downside; *m* 1st 31 July 1971 (*divorce* 1989) Jacqueline Julie Willett, and has:

1 +EDWARD JAMES ARDEN; *b* 19 Oct 1982

1 *Olivia Fleur Elizabeth; *b* 1979

The 8th BARON *m* 2nd 23 April 1997 *Frances Elizabeth Prioleau, yr dau of George Frederick Rothwell

Lineage: THOMAS ADDERLEY, of Blakehall, Staffs; *m* Joan, dau of John Thirkill, of Smallwood, and *d* between 3 June 1538 and 15 Jan 1538/9, having had, with three daus:

1 Thomas, of Blakehall; *m* Joan, dau of Robert Warner, of Dillhorn, and *d* by 21 Dec 1597; ancestor of the extinct ADDERLEYs of Blakehall

2 John; *d* between 25 May 1583 and 18 Jan 1583/4

3 RALPH

4 Humphrey, of Weddington, Warwicks; Master Wardrobe to HENRY VIII, EDWARD VI, MARY and ELIZABETH, *m* 1st Anne North, of Northants, and had:

(1) Anne; *b* 20 May 1578; *m* William Wightman, of Wyken, Leics

4 (cont.) Humphrey Adderley *m* 2nd 7 March 1581 Elizabeth, dau of Richard Capel, was by her ancestor of the extinct ADDERLEYs of Weddington, and *d* 20 July 1598 aged 86

The 3rd son,

RALPH ADDERLEY, of Coton, Staffs, which he bought from Lord Mountjoy 1558; custos rotulorum and High Sheriff Staffs 1575, lawyer; *m* 1st 10 April 1554 Margaret, dau of Thomas Bagot, of Blithfield (*see* BAGOT, B), and had:

1 Richard, of Coton; *m* Ellen, dau of James Abney, of Willesley, Derbys, and *d* 1641, leaving issue

RALPH ADDERLEY *m* 2nd Felicia (*bur* 9 June 1607), dau of Henry Milward, of Doveridge, Derbys, and *d* 20 April 1598, having by her had, with three daus:

2 William, of St Alban Wood St, London; merchant; *m* 10 Sept 1599 Mary, dau of Thomas Henshaw, of St Mary Magdalen, Milk Street, and *d* 1615

3 Thomas; moved to Ireland; *m* Mary, dau of Sir John Dalzell, of Dromertie, Munster

4 RALPH

5 John, of Chancery Lane and S Mimms, Middx; *m* Winifred, dau of Thomas Oxborough, of King's Lynn, Norfolk, and *dspms* *bur* 28 Jan 1651/2

6 George, of St Alban Wood St, London; *dsp* 1599

The 4th son,

RALPH ADDERLEY, of Alreswas, Staffs; *m* 3 Aug 1609 Elizabeth (*m* 2nd Ralph Floyer, of Hints, Staffs, and *d* 1 May 1661 aged 82), dau of J Noel, of Welsborough, Leics, and was *bur* 15 Feb 1612/13, leaving:

1 Charles (Sir), JP, of Hams Hall, Warwicks, which he bought from Sir J Ferrers; Equerry to CHARLES I, Master of Horse; *bapt* 6 Sept 1610, *m* 1st 17 Nov 1636 Anne, dau and in her issue coheir of Sir Henry Arden, of Park Hall, Warwicks, and had:

(1) ARDEN

(2) Charles; *bapt* 3 April 1640; *m* 3 March 1684/5 Felicia, dau of John Milward, of Snitterton, Derbys, and *dsp* between 14 March 1710/1 and 24 April 1713

(1) Anne; *m* 5 May 1683 Charnock Heron, of Godmanchester, Hunts

1 (cont.) Sir Charles *m* 2nd 9 Feb 1641 Constance, widow of Robert Wilmer, of Sywell, Northants, and dau of James Enlon, of Flore, Northants, and by her had:

(3) James; Turkey merchant; *bapt* 11 April 1643; *dsp* Smyrna between 2 Sept 1671 and Sept 1672

(2) Dorothy; *bapt* 19 Oct 1644; *bur* 8 Nov 1691

1 (cont.) Sir Charles *m* 3rd Felicia (*d* 21 Jan 1645/5), widow of Sir Edward Fitton, 2nd Bt, of Gawsworth, Cheshire, and dau of Ralph Sneyd, of Keele, Staffs; *m* 4th 1662 Frances, widow of William Jesson, of Coventry, and dau and coheir of Richard Cresheld, Serjeant-at-law, of Evesham, Worcs, and was *bur* 30 Aug 1682

His er s by his 1st w,

ARDEN ADDERLEY, of Hams Hall, JP; *bapt* 5 Oct 1637; *m c* 28 May 1664 Mary (*d* 6 Feb 1707/8), dau of William Draper, of May Place, Kent, and *d* 6 April 1727, having had:

1 CHARLES

2 Arden, of Fryan Hall, Essex; *bapt* 9 Nov 1669; had issue

3 William; *b* 26 Feb 1672/3; *d* in or after 1710

4 Robert (Rev); DD, Fell All Souls Oxford, Proctor 1709; *b* 13 June 1674; *bur* 5 July 1717

5 Ralph; *bapt* 28 March 1680

1 Mary; *bapt* 26 Oct 1671; living unm 1710

2 Anne; *bapt* 7 May 1682; *m* 1st 8 Sept 1715, as his 3rd w, Samuel Adderley, of Blake Hall (*dsp* 3 June 1716); *m* 2nd Caesar Colclough, of Delphouse, Staffs (*d* 11 March 1740/1)

The est s,

CHARLES ADDERLEY, of Hams Hall; *bapt* 28 Sept 1667; *m* 1st 8 April 1703 Mary (*bur* 31 Oct 1723), est dau and coheir of Sir William Bowyer, 2nd Bt (*see* DENHAM, B), and had:

1 BOWYER

2 Arden; *b* 1708; *d* young

1 Mary; *bapt* 21 Jan 1705/6; *m* 1st 22 Dec 1726 Thomas Edwards, of Astbury, Cheshire; *m* 2nd *c* 7 Sept 1737, as his 2nd w, Pudsey Jesson, of Langley Hall, Warwicks, and *d* 11 Nov 1747. He *d* 4 May 1748

2 Anne; *bapt* 20 July 1717; *m* 30 Dec 1736 William Arnett, of Tofthouse, Cheshire, and *d* 30 Nov 1777. He *d* 21 May 1784

CHARLES ADDERLEY *m* 2nd Frances, widow of Sir John Chester, 4th Bt, and dau of Sir William Noel, 2nd Bt, and *d* 2 Feb 1746/7

His er s by his 1st w,

BOWYER ADDERLEY, of Hams Hall; *bapt* 2 Feb 1704/5; *m* 1st 22 Aug 1726 Elizabeth (*bur* 3 Sept 1740), er dau of Walter Horton, of Catton, Derbys, and had, with a yst s (Arden, *b* 23 April 1747, *bur* 24 June 1767):

1 Arden; *d* an infant

1 Mary; *b* 1727; *d* unm 23 July 1774

2 Frances; *b* 1729; *d* unm 27 June 1781

BOWYER ADDERLEY *m* 2nd 14 July 1741 his cousin Lettice (*d* 18 July 1784), dau and coheir of Ralph Adderley, of Coton Hall, and *d* 3 Nov 1747, having by her had:

2 Charles Bowyer, of Hams Hall; *b* 27 April 1743; *m c* 21 May 1777 Mary (*d* 24 July 1808), only dau of Robert Hotchkin, of Uppingham, Rutland, and *dsp* 12 April 1826

3 Ralph, of Coton; *b* 12 June 1744; *m* 4 Aug 1778 Dorothy (*d* 10 June 1797), widow of Thomas Birchie Savage, of Elmley Castle, Worcs, and dau and heir of Thomas Kynnersley, of Loxley Park, and *d* 10 Sept 1819, having had:

(1) CHARLES

(2) Ralph, of Coton Hall and Barlaston Hall, Staffs; *b* 15 June 1781; *m* 4 July 1816 Rosamond (*d* 21 Feb 1856), est dau and coheir of William Mills, of Barlaston, and *d* 31 Jan 1851, having had issue

(3) Arden; Adml RN; *b* 14 Aug 1784; *m* 21 Oct 1823 Anne (*d* 6 Dec 1851), only dau of W R Bishton, of Shakerley House, Salop, and *dsp*

(4) George William Bowyer, of Fillongley Hall, Warwicks; *b* 9 Jan 1787; *m* 11 Dec 1823 Caroline (*d* 30 July 1855), yst dau of John Taylor, of Moseley Hall, Worcs, and *dsp* 4 Aug 1872

(1) Letitia Penelope; *b* 3 May 1779; *m* 1st 4 Jan 1798 Andrew Hacket, of Moxhull; *m* 2nd 22 June 1820 Hon Berkeley Noel and *d* 18 Jan 1860, leaving issue (*see* GAINSBOROUGH, E)

The est son,
   CHARLES CLEMENT ADDERLEY; *b* 25 June 1780; *m* 6 June 1811 Anna Maria (*d* 30 April 1827), est dau of Sir Edmund Cradock Hartopp, 1st Bt (*qv*), and *dvp* 30 June 1818, having had, with two daus:

1 CHARLES BOWYER, **1st Baron**

2 Edmund James ADDERLEY later CRADOCK (roy licence 14 May 1886), of Knighton, Leics, DL and JP; *b* 17 Jan 1816; *m* 22 April 1848 Marian Elizabeth (*d* 16 Oct 1882), dau of Sir Joseph Edward Leeds, 2nd Bt (*qv*), and *d* 14 May 1903, leaving issue

The er son,
   CHARLES BOWYER ADDERLEY, **1st Baron Norton**, of Norton-on-the-Moors, Co Stafford (UK), so *cr* 16 April 1878, KCMG (1869), PC (1858), JP, DL Staffs and Warwicks; *b* 2 Aug 1814; BA Oxon, CA Warwicks, MP (C) N Staffs 1841–78, Pres Bd Health March–Sept 1858, V-Pres Ctee Cncl Educn 1858–59, Parly U-Sec Colonies 1866–68, Pres BOT 1874–78; *m* 28 July 1842 Hon Julia Anne Eliza (*d* 8 May 1887), est dau of 1st Baron Leigh (*qv*), and *d* 28 March 1905, having had, with other issue:

1 CHARLES LEIGH ADDERLEY, **2nd Baron Norton**, JP, DL, Rutland and Warwicks; *b* 10 March 1846; BA Oxon; Assist Local Govt Bd Inspr 1870, Priv Sec to Pres BOT 1874–78; *m* 15 Dec 1870 Caroline Ellen (*d* 6 Aug 1922), 3rd dau of Sir Alexander Beaumont Churchill Dixie, 10th Bt, of Bosworth Park, Leics (*see* 1970 edn), and *d* 4 Dec 1926, having had:

   (1) RALPH BOWYER ADDERLEY, **3rd Baron Norton**; *b* 9 Oct 1872; *m* 1899 Mary Louisa (*d* 30 July 1939), widow of Rupert George Inglis Brady and dau of Robert Watson, of Ballydarton, Co Carlow, and *dsp* 17 Oct 1933

   (2) Charles Arthur Reginald Kenelm; *b* 17 May 1881; *d* unm 10 May 1905

   (3) Humphry James Arden; Rifleman London Regt; *b* 16 Oct 1882; *d* 17 June 1917 of wounds recd in action

   (4) Randolph; *b* 16 April 1884; *d* 23 Oct 1928

   (5) RONALD WOOLSTAN FLEETWOOD ADDERLEY, **4th Baron Norton**; *b* 15 Oct 1885; Lt Worcs Regt; *m* 20 Aug 1931 Hylda (*d* Feb 1952), widow of Hilary George Dunbar, of Glasgow, and dau of Robert William Tovey, of Cheltenham, and *dsp* 4 Jan 1944

   (1) Sybil Maud; *m* 2 Aug 1894 Maj John Charles Digby Pinney, Centl India Horse, 4th s of Rev John Charles Pinney, Vicar Coleshill, Warwicks, and *d* 6 April 1960, leaving issue. He *d* 1 Oct 1944

   (2) Rosamond Caroline; *d* young 30 April 1875

   (3) Julia Caroline Margaret; *m* 1st 16 July 1902 (*divorce*) Maj Charles Edward Etches, OBE, Roy Warwicks Regt, s of Edward Etches, of Derby, and had issue; *m* 2nd 1917 John Thomas Parkins, of Charleville Rd, W Kensington, and *d* 7 Dec 1940

   (4) Gwendoline Mary; *d* young 2 June 1886

   (5) Dorothy Evelyn; *m* 10 Oct 1911 Maj William Stuart, IA, and *d* 9 Feb 1974, having had issue. He *d* 1952

   (6) Gladys Isabel Annette; *m* 13 March 1915 Capt George Augustus Carteret Thynne, Roy N Devon Hus, and *d* 16 Oct 1960, leaving issue (*see* BATH, M)

2 HENRY ARDEN, **5th Baron**

3 Reginald Edmund (Rev); MA Oxford, Rector Compton Abbas, Devon; *b* 10 Sept 1857; *d* unm 1 Aug 1934

5 James Granville (Rev); MA Oxon, Preb St Paul's 1935; *b* 1 July 1861; *d* unm 1 June 1942

1 Anna Maria Margarette; *d* unm 21 Sept 1936

2 Frances Georgina Mary; *d* unm 28 Dec 1942

3 Isabel; *m* 20 April 1876 Sir Vaucey Harpur Crewe, 10th and last Bt, of Calke Abbey, Derbys (*see* 1924 edn), and *d* 19 June 1932, leaving issue. He *dspms* 13 Dec 1924

The 4th BARON's uncle,
   HENRY ARDEN ADDERLEY, **5th Baron Norton**, JP, DL; *b* 26 Sept 1854; BA Oxon, CA, barrister, Capt Warwicks Yeo Cav; *m* 30 Aug 1881 Grace (*d* 16 Feb 1944), yst dau of William Bruce Stopford Sackville (*see* COURTOWN, E), and had:

1 HUBERT BOWYER ARDEN, **6th Baron**

1 Muriel Grace; *b* 20 June 1882; *m* 14 June 1906 Sir Edmund Waller, 6th Bt, of Braywick Lodge (*see* 1970 edn), and *d* 11 Nov 1974. He *d* 7 Aug 1954

2 Ruth Margaret; *m* 3 Sept 1907 Rev Elliott Kenworthy Kenworthy-Browne, Hon CF, er s of Rev Elliott Kenworthy-Browne, Rector N Stoneham, Hants, and *d* 19 March 1957, leaving issue. He *d* 9 May 1950

3 Isabel Julia; *m* 1st 30 April 1914 Capt Frederic Augustus Drake, Warwicks Yeo (drowned on a transport 26 May 1918), er s of A F Drake, of Winterbourne Lodge, Lewes, and had issue; *m* 2nd 8 July 1925 Maj Francis Gerald Scott, MC, RA, s of Francis O Scott, of York, and *d* 22 Feb 1933, leaving issue

4 Joan; *m* 15 Jan 1913 Maj-Gen Sir Alan John Hunter, KCVO, CB, CMG, DSO, MC, KRRC, s of John Turner Hunter, and had issue. He *d* 5 March 1942

5 Lettice Mary; *m* 10 Jan 1918 Charles Phillimore Lewton Firth, DL, Capt Worcs Regt, S/Ldr RAF, 2nd s of Bernard Alexander Firth, of Norton Hall, Sheffield, and Coates Manor, Cirencester, Glos. He *d* 25 Aug 1955

The 5th BARON *d* 1 Jan 1945; his only son,
   HUBERT BOWYER ARDEN, **6th Baron Norton**, JP Warwicks; *b* 21 Feb 1886; *educ* Eton and RMC Sandhurst; Lt Scots Gds and Res Offrs, WW I: T/Maj MGC, Hon Maj 1918, Lt-Col 1st Suffolk HG WW II, Pres Church Union 1947–50, Lay Guardian Sanctuary Our Lady of Walsingham, Fell Woodard Schs Midland Area; *m* 9 Jan 1912 Elizabeth (*d* 5 May 1952), dau of William John Birkbeck, of Stratton-Strawless, Norfolk, and had:

1 JOHN ARDEN, **7th Baron**

2 Michael Charles, OBE (1960), DFC, AFC and bar (1948); *b* 8 April 1917; *educ* Radley and Sidney Sussex Coll Cambridge; W/Cdr RAF WW II, Malaya 1950, Korea 1951–52 (ret 1972), King's Commendn for valuable services in the air, Bronze Star Medal and Air Medal of USA; *m* 5 Dec 1953 Margrethe Ann, MRCVS (*d* 1986), only dau of Karl Gerhadt Ornbo, of Hull, and *d* 1992, leaving:

   (1) +Charles Henry; *b* 10 Sept 1954; *m* 2 Oct 1982 *Elizabeth Jane, dau of Sydney Atherton, of Ilkley

   (2) +Anthony John; *b* 22 Dec 1955; *educ* Radley

   (3) +David Michael; *b* 9 June 1962

   (1) *Jane Margrethe [Mrs Kenneth Blackburn, Glen Haven, Long Moss Lane, Whitestake, Preston, Lancs PR4 4XN]; *b* 22 July 1957; *m* 1982 *Kenneth Blackburn and has:

     1a *Emma Margrethe; *b* 1986

     1a *Sara Elisabeth (twin); *b* 1986

1 *Rosemary Etheldreda [The Hon Mrs Drake, 3 The Cloisters, Welwyn Garden City, Herts AL8 6DU]; *b* 17 Oct 1913; *m* 29 Sept 1949 *Rev John Paul Drake, only s of Canon Frederick William Drake, of Isle of Sheppey, and has:

   (1) *Simon Francis; *b* 3 Sept 1956; *educ* St Edward's Sch Oxford; *m* 1981 *Vanessa, dau of Robert Sewell, of Norwich

   (2) *Catherine Elisabeth; *b* 14 Sept 1950; *educ* Oxford High Sch for Girls and Bristol U; *m* 1974 *John William Grace

2 *Elisabeth Joan [The Hon Mrs Campbell, The Priory House, Ascott-under-Wychwood, Oxon OX7 6AW]; *b* 12 June 1919; *m* 5 Jan 1943 Prof (Alexander) Colin Patton Campbell, MB, ChB Edin, MSc Manc, FRCP Edin, FRCPath, Prof Pathology U of Manchester (*d* 19 Nov 1996), late W/Cdr RAFVR, s of Alexander Callander Campbell, of Edinburgh, and has:

   (1) Andrew Colin; *b* 23 Nov 1943; *educ* Radley, Trin Coll Oxford (MA) and Manchester U (BM, BCh, D Phil, MRCPath); *m* 18 Sept 1972 *Gillian Susan Stanley, MB, BCh, and *d* 1990

   (2) *Richard Hubert Alexander [Richard Campbell Esq, 189 Hale Rd, Hale, Cheshire]; *b* 3 May 1946; *educ* Radley and Edin U (MB, ChB, FRCP, FRCP Lond); *m* 18 Sept 1976 *Candace M, dau of Clifford W Richardson, of Stratford St Andrew, Suffolk

   (1) *Rosamund Elizabeth; *b* 11 May 1950; *educ* Withington Girls' Sch and LMH Oxford (MA)

3 *Mary [The Hon Mrs Montgomery-Campbell, 16 Ashworth Rd, London W9 1JY]; *b* 8 Sept 1922; *educ* Radley and Edin U (MB, ChB, FRCP, FRCP Lond); *m* 7 July 1950 Hugh Montgomery-Campbell (*d* 1980), Capt RA WW II, only s of Rt Rev and Rt Hon Henry Colville Montgomery-Campbell, KCVO, MC, PC, DD, Bp London 1956–61, and has:

   (1) *Philip Henry; *b* 19 April 1951; *educ* Shrewsbury, Bristol U (PhD, MSc), Queen Mary Coll London and Leicester U; FRAS, CPhy, FInstP; *m* 1980 Judith Margaret MB, ChB (*d* 1992), dau of Joseph William Yelton, of Earls Colne, Essex

   (1) *Elisabeth Mary; *b* 22 July 1954

   (2) *Veronica; *b* 14 March 1958; *m* 1987 *Jeffrey Mark Berman, est s of Dolph L Berman, of Cincinnati, Ohio

The 6th BARON *d* following a fall from his horse 17 Feb 1961; his er son,
   JOHN ARDEN ADDERLEY, **7th Baron Norton**, OBE (1964); *b* 24 Nov 1915; *educ* Radley and Magdalen Coll Oxford (BA 1938); Maj RE WW II (despatches); *m* 23 July 1946 *Betty Margaret , JP (Warwicks 1965) [The Rt Hon The Dowager Lady Norton JP, Fillongley Hall, Coventry,Warwicks], only dau of James McKee Hannah, of Domaine de Fontvieille, Aix-en-Provence, France, and *d* 1993, leaving:

1 JAMES NIGEL ARDEN ADDERLEY, **8th and present Baron Norton**

2 +Nigel John; *b* 30 March 1950; *educ* Downside and RMA Sandhurst; Maj Life Gds 1971; *m* 1991 *Teresa; dau of Maj John Mills, of Vyse House, Winkfield, Berks, and has:

   (1) *Fleur Charlotte Alice; *b* 1992

NORTON-GRIFFITHS

Arms: Quarterly, 1st and 4th, sa. a flaming sword erect between two gryphons combatant or (for GRIFFITHS); 2nd and 3rd, arg. on a fess raguly between two fleurs-de-lys az. a fleur-de-lys between two crescents or (for NORTON). **Crests:** 1 A demi-lion rampant gu., grasping in the paws a flaming sword erect as in the arms (for GRIFFITHS), 2 A dexter gauntlet closed sa. between two ostrich feathers arg. (for NORTON). **Supporters:** Dexter, a colonial soldier in the uniform of a trooper of the Second Regiment King Edward's Horse, resting the exterior hand upon a terrestrial globe environed with a meridian; sinister, a labourer holding in the exterior hand a jack-hammer drill, all ppr. **Motto:** *Pro Rege et imperio* ('For King and Empire'). **Creation:** Bt. (UK) 14 June 1922.

SIR JOHN NORTON-GRIFFITHS, 3RD BT, of Wonham, Co Surrey [Sir John Norton-Griffiths Bt, PO Box 396, Rutland, VT 05702, USA]; *b* 4 Oct 1938; *s f* 1983; *educ* Eton; FCA, late Sub-Lt RN; *m* 17 Oct 1964 *Marilyn Margaret, er dau of Norman Grimley, of S Blundellsands, Liverpool

Lineage: GRIFFITH REES, of Llanspythid, Breconshire; *m* Mary, dau of John Griffiths, and *d* March 1752, leaving:

JOHN GRIFFITH, of Llanspythid; *b* 1742; *m* 17 March 1766 Joan Brown and had, with other issue:

JOHN GRIFFITHS, of Llanspythid; *b* 1770; *m* 27 Dec 1789 Elizabeth Williams, of St David's, Breconshire, and had:

THOMAS GRIFFITHS, of the Watton, Brecon; *b* 1793; *m* 20 May 1824 Mary (*d* 6 Aug 1839), dau of John Powell, of Alexanderstone, Breconshire, and *d* 28 Jan 1867, leaving:

JOHN GRIFFITHS, of the Watton; *b* 8 March 1825; *m* 1st 12 May 1852 Mary Davies (*d* 26 Oct 1858), dau of Evan Winstone, of Brecon, and had issue; *m* 2nd 28 Feb 1863 Juliet (*d* 4 Dec 1926), dau of Richard William Avery, of London, and *d* 13 Feb 1891, having by her had an only surv s:

Sir JOHN GRIFFITHS later NORTON-GRIFFITHS (deed poll 1917), **1st Bt** (UK), so *cr* 14 June 1922, KCB, DSO; *b* 13 July 1871; Lt-Col 2nd Regt King Edward's Horse; cmded Scouts Matebele War 1896–97 (despatches three times), S/Ldr Brabant's 2nd Colonial Div SA Field Force 1899–1901, Capt and Adj Lord Roberts's Bodyguard, HQ Staff, Boer War 1900–02, MP (C) Wednesbury 1910–18 and Wandsworth Centl 1918–24, raised 2nd King Edward's Horse WW I (despatches three times), T/Lt-Col 1916 attd staff Engr-in-Ch GHQ to organise, initiate and direct tunnelling companies, RE GSO(1) 1916, special mission to Romania for destruction oil wells and corn stores 1916; Grand Star Romania, St Vladimir of Russia 3rd Cl, Offr Legn Hon; *m* 14 Sept 1901 Gwladys (*d* 1 June 1974 aged 101), dau of Thomas Wood, and had:

1 PETER (Sir), **2nd Bt**

2 Michael ; *b* 30 Sept 1908; Capt RE WW II (despatches); *m* 6 March 1936 Elizabeth Gertrude (*m* 3rd 2 Nov 1946 (*divorce* 1954) George Paul Minchin Woodward, s of Herbert Minchin Sadler Paul Woodward, of NJ, USA; *m* 4th 14 Sept 1954 Ralph Arthur Hubbard (*d* 1983) , est s of Capt Gerald Napier Hubbard (*see* ADDINGTON, B), and *d* 1 Dec 1969), formerly w of Henry Reginald Gambier Colclough and yr dau of Stephen Cozens, of Mackney Manor, Wallingford, Berks, and was *ka* Dunkirk 29 May 1940, leaving:

  (1) *Johanna [Mrs Johanna Butt, Culvers Close, Swinbrook, Oxon OX18 4ED]; *b* 23 Oct 1936; *m* 19 Aug 1969 (*divorce* 1996) Keith Martin Butt, MA, Vet MB (Cantab), MRCVS, and has:

    1a *Jason Martin; *b* 7 Aug 1972

    2a *Ben Michael; *b* 14 May 1979

    1a *Martha; *b* 1 Sept 1971; *m* 28 June 1997 *Amaury Thierion de Monclin

1 Ursula, JP (1955); *b* 27 Feb 1903; memb Surrey CC 1949–61; *m* 19 Dec 1922 John Henry Thorpe, OBE, JP, KC, MP Rusholme 1919–24, barrister, Recorder Blackburn, Dep Chm Middx QS, est s of Ven John Henry Thorpe, Archdeacon of Macclesfield, and *d* 8 Aug 1992, having had, with another dau:

  (1) *(John) Jeremy, PC (1967) [The Rt Hon Jeremy Thorpe, 2 Orme Square, London W4 4RS]; *b* 29 April 1929; *educ* Eton and Trin Coll Oxford (Hon Fell

1972); barrister Inner Temple 1954, MP (Lib) Devon N 1959–79, Leader Lib Party 1967–76, FRSA, Hon LLD Exeter 1974; *m* 1st 1968 Caroline (*d* 1970), dau of Warwick Allpass, of Kingswood, Surrey; *m* 2nd 14 March 1973 *Marion, formerly w of 7th Earl of Harewood (*qv*) and dau of Erwin Stein, and has:

    1a *A son

  (1) Camilla; *b c* 1926; *m* Enrique Ellinger (*d* 31 Oct 1944), of Buenos Aires, and *d* by her own hand 16 May 1974, leaving a s and dau

2 Phoebe; *b* 16 Nov 1906; *m* 7 Aug 1947 Edward Bromilow Joynson, MBE, of Longwood House, Churt, Surrey

Sir JOHN *d* 27 Sept 1930; his er son,

Sir Peter Norton-Griffiths, 2nd Bt; *b* 3 May 1905; *educ* Eton and Magdalen Coll Oxford; barrister Inner Temple 1931, Maj Intell Corps and Assist Mil Attaché Madrid WW II, Offr: Order Crown Belgium and Oaken Crown Luxembourg; *m* 15 Oct 1935 Kathryn (*d* 1980), dau of George F Schrafft, of Newton, Mass., and *d* 13 Oct 1983, leaving:

1 Sir JOHN NORTON-GRIFFITHS, **3rd and present Bt**

2 +MICHAEL [Michael Norton-Griffiths Esq, Box 24532, Nairobi, Kenya]; *b* 11 Jan 1941; heir presumptive; *educ* Eton and Keble Coll Oxford (BA, DPhil Zoology); ecologist Serengeti Research Inst 1969–73, md EcoSystems Nairobi 1977–87, head Eastern Sahel Unit World Conservation Union 1988, consultant to Global Environment Monitoring Programme of UN Environment Programme 1989–; *m* 9 Jan 1965 *Ann, only child of G/Capt Blair Alexander Fraser, RAF (*see* DUNDONALD, E), and has:

  (1) +Alastair; *b* 23 Feb 1976

1 *Anne [Mrs Richard Morgan, 10 Multon Rd, London SW18 5LH; Box 24532, Nairobi, Kenya]; *b* 3 Sept 1936; *m* 20 Oct 1956 *Richard Hathaway Morgan, only s of Charles Davis Morgan, and has:

  (1) *Kathryn; *b* 15 Sept 1957

  (2) *Christina; *b* 25 Dec 1958

  (3) *Pascale; *b* 5 April 1960

NORWICH

Arms: Or three lions rampant gu., on a chief az. a portcullis chained between two fleurs-de-lys or. **Crest:** On the battlements of a tower arg. a bull passant sa., armed and unguled or. **Supporters:** On either side a unicorn arg., gorged with a collar, with chain reflexed over the back or, pendant from the collar of the dexter a portcullis chained, and from that of the sinister a fleur-de-lys, both gold. **Motto:** *Odi et amo* ('I hate and I love'). **Creation:** V. (UK) 5 July 1952.

THE 2ND VISCOUNT NORWICH, of Aldwick, Co Sussex (John Julius Cooper, CVO (1993)) [The Rt Hon The Viscount Norwich CVO, 24 Blomfield Rd, London W9 1AD]; *b* 15 Sept 1929; *s f* 1954; *educ* Upper Canada Coll Toronto, Eton, New Coll Oxford (BA 1952) and U of Strasbourg; RN 1947–49, For Serv 1952–64: 3rd Sec Belgrade 1955–57, 2nd Sec Beirut 1957–60, 1st Sec FO 1961–64, chm: Br Theatre Museum 1966–71, Venice in Peril Fund 1970–, Colnaghi 1992–, FRSL, FRGS, FSA, Commendatore Order Merit Italy 1996, author (as John Julius Norwich): *Mount Athos* (with Reresby Sitwell, 1966), *The Normans in the South* (1967), *Sahara* (1968), *The Kingdom in the Sun* (1970), *A History of Venice*: vol I *The Rise to Empire* (1977) and vol II *The Greatness and the Fall* (1981), *Christmas Crackers 1970–79* (1980), *Fifty Years of Glyndebourne* (1985), *A Taste for Travel* (1985), *Great Architecture of the World* (gen ed 1975), *More Christmas Crackers* (1990), *Byzantium: the apogee* (1991), *Byzantium: decline and fall* (1995); *m* 1st 5 Aug 1952 (*divorce* 1985) Anne Frances May, artist, est dau of Hon Sir Bede Edmund Hugh Clifford, GCMG, GCB, MVO (*see* CLIFFORD OF CHUDLEIGH, B), and has:

1 +JASON CHARLES DUFF BEDE [The Hon Jason Cooper, 14 Alexander St, London W2 5NT]; *b* 27 Oct 1959

1 *Alice Clare Antonia (Artemis) Opportune [The Hon Artemis Cooper, 54 St Maur Rd, London SW6]; *b* 22 April 1953; writer, prefers to be known as Cooper; *m* 1986 *Antony James Beevor, s of John Grosvenor Beevor, OBE, of Fulham, and has:

  (1) *Adam John Cosmo; *b* 1993

  (1) *Nella; *b* 1990

The 2nd VISCOUNT *m* 2nd 1989 *Hon Mary (Mollie) Makins, er dau of 1st Baron Sherfield (*qv*) and formerly w of Hon Hugo John Laurence Philipps (later 3rd Baron Milford; *qv*).

Norwich, other creations under title of: In the 12th century the Bigod Earl of Norfolk of the day was sometimes referred to as Earl of Norwich at a time when the distinction between the name of a county and that of the county town was less distinct than today (*c.f.* WINCHESTER, M). But a creation proper under the title Norwich did not take place till the mid-14th century, when a Barony by writ of summons was held by Sir John de Norwich and his grandson, another Sir John, between 1360 and 1373.

In the first year of CHARLES I's reign Edward Denny was created Earl of Norwich but it expired with him some ten years later. His sister's son George Goring was ennobled under the same title during the Civil War (*see* GORING, Bt). This Lord Norwich is less well known than his son, the celebrated royalist cavalry commander Lord Goring, who however died before his father. Shortly after the 2nd and last Goring Earl's death, when the title had again become extinct, it was revived in 1672 for a younger brother of the then Duke of Norfolk (*qv*), passing down with the Dukedom subsequently for just over a century. A descendant in the female line of the Howard grantee of 1672, the then Duke of Gordon, was created Earl of Norwich in 1784, but after only one more generation this creation expired too (*see* HUNTLY, M).

Lineage: CHARLES COOPER, Norwich merchant; had, with a yr s (Samuel, horticulturist):

CHARLES COOPER; Cncllr Norwich, barrister Lincoln's Inn, slr; *b* 1742; *m* 1st — Yarrington and had:

1 Charles Henry; barrister; *m* — Palmer and had three children (*d* infants); had issue by — Durrant:
(1) Charles; slr
(2) Erskine; in Woods and Forests
2 Alfred; served 14th Inf Regt Waterloo; went to Calcutta, where accidentally shot
1 Harriet; *m* Dr Leathe

CHARLES COOPER *m* 2nd Rose White and by her had:
3 WILLIAM
4 Carlos; *d* unm
5 Henry; company agent, auctioneer Northampton; *m* Mary Palmer
1 Rosa; *d* unm
2 Selina; *m* George Palmer, of Bolitree, nr Ross, and had issue
3 Caroline; *d* unm
4 Emma; *m* — Dod, of Diss, Norfolk. He *d* 1836

CHARLES COOPER's 3rd son,
WILLIAM COOPER; BA Oxon, Recorder Ipswich, barrister Lincoln's Inn, author and dramatist; *m* Anna (*d* 1900), dau of Rev — Marsh, Perpetual Curate Calthorpe, Norfolk, and had, with a dau (Agnes, *b* 1836, *m* John Peter Grain and had issue):

1 William Marsh; *b* 1833; *m* Mary, dau of Col Tickel, of Cheltenham, and had:
(1) Philip; Maj RA; *m* Evelyn Close and had two daus
(2) Henry; Sikh Regt; shot himself
(3) Alan Leslie, DSO; FZS, Maj RE, manager Ferreia Mining Co S Africa; *m* Sarah, dau of Gen Russell, of Southampton, and *d* S Rhodesia 1956, having had a s (*d* young) and dau
2 Charles Philip; *b* 1834; barrister, Ch Magistrate Bombay; *m* Beatrice Maud, dau of Surgn-Gen William Paton Partridge, IA, and *d* 1922, leaving issue:
(1) Alfred Cecil (Rt Rev), CBE (1956); *b* 1882; *educ* Bradfield, Christ's Coll Cambridge (BA 1904, MA 1908) and Cuddesdon Theol Coll; Bp Korea 1931–55, Curate St Oswald's, W Hartlepool, 1904–08, Korean Church Mission 1908–55, Assist Bp Bath and Wells 1942–45, POW Korea 1950–53, Chaplain to SLG Sisters 1956–61; *d* unm 17 Oct 1964
(2) Frank Hugh; fruit and bee farmer S Africa; *m* Violet Taylor and *dsp c* 1934
(1) Rose Maud; RRC; *b* 1880
3 Alfred (Sir), of Whiting Bay, Isle of Arran; *b* 1838; *educ* Merchant Taylors'; FRCS (Eng and Edin), Consulting Surgn W London Hosp, V-Pres RCS, Surgn to Roy Soc Musicians, Surgn-Col Duke of York's Loyal Suffolk Hus, Surgn-in-Ordinary to HRH THE DUKE OF EDINBURGH, Chev Order St Stanislas; *m* 4 July 1882 Lady Agnes Cecil Emmeline Duff (*d* 11 Jan 1925), sis of 1st Duke of Fife (*qv*), and *d* 3 March 1908, leaving:
(1) (ALFRED) DUFF, **1st Viscount**
(1) Stephanie Agnes; *b* 1883; *m* 1903 Arthur Francis Levita and *d* 1918, leaving issue. He *d* 1910
(2) Hermione Mary Louise; *b* 1885; *m* 1904, Neil Arnott and *d* 1923, leaving issue
(3) Sybil Mary; *b* 1886; *m* 1905 Richard Vaughan Hart-Davis, yr s of Henry Vaughan Hart-Davis, JP, DL, of Crofton, Kent, and *d* 3 Jan 1927, leaving issue. He *d* 26 Aug 1964

The only son,
(ALFRED) DUFF COOPER, **1st Viscount Norwich** (UK), of Aldwick, Co Sussex, so *cr* 5 July 1952, GCMG (1948), DSO (1918), PC (1935); *b* 22 Feb 1890; Lt Gren Gds WW I (despatches), Priv Sec to Parly U-Sec For Affrs 1922, MP (C) Oldham 1924–29 and St George's Westminster 1931–45, Fin Sec War Office 1928–29 and 1931–34 and Treasury 1934–35, Sec State War 1935–37, First Ld Admlty 1937–38, Min Info 1940–41, Chllr Duchy Lancaster 1941–43, UK Rep French Ctee Nat Libn N Africa 1943–44, Amb France 1944–47, author: *Talleyrand*, *Haig*, *The Second World War*, *David*, *Sergeant Shakespeare*, *Translations and Verses*, *Operation Heartbreak* and *Old Men Forget*; *m* 2 June 1919 Lady Diana Olivia Winifred Maud Manners (*d* 1986), nominally dau of 8th Duke of Rutland (*qv*), and *d* 1 Jan 1954, leaving:

JOHN JULIUS COOPER, **2nd and present Viscount Norwich**

NUGENT of Ballinlough

Arms: Erm. two bars gu. **Crest:** A cockatrice vert. **Motto:** *Decrevi* ('I have decreed'). **Creation:** Bt. (I) 23 July 1795.

SIR JOHN EDWIN LAVALLIN NUGENT, **7TH BT**, of Ballinlough Castle, Co Westmeath, **4th Count of The Austrian Empire**, JP (Berks 1962) [Sir John Nugent Bt JP, Ballinlough Castle, Clonmellon, Navan, Co Meath, Ireland]; *b* 16 March 1933; *s* f 1983; *educ* Eton; High Sheriff of Berks 1981, late Lt Irish Gds; *m* 2 April 1959 *Penelope Anne, er dau of Brig Richard Nigel Hanbury, CBE, TD, DL, of Hay Lodge, Braughling, Herts, and has:
1 +NICHOLAS MYLES JOHN; *b* 17 Feb 1967; *educ* Eton
1 *Grania Clare; *b* 11 Jan 1969

Lineage: HUGH O'REILLY, of Ballinlough Castle; *m* Katherine, dau of Christopher Plunkett, of Clonabrany, Co Meath, and had:

JAMES O'REILLY, of Ballinlough Castle; *m* Elizabeth, dau of Walter White, of Pitchfordstown, Co Kildare, by Mabel, dau of George Aylmer, of Lyons, Co Kildare, and had:

HUGH O'REILLY, of Ballinlough Castle; *m* 1st 1712 Emilia Butler (*dsp*), dau of 6th Viscount Mountgarret (*qv*); *m* 2nd Eleanor, dau of Sir Daniel O'Neill, 3rd Bt, of Killelagh, and had:

JAMES O'REILLY, of Ballinlough Castle; *m* Barbara, dau of Andrew Nugent, of Dysart, Co Westmeath, by Lady Katherine Nugent, dau and coheir of 4th Earl of Westmeath (*qv*), and had:
1 HUGH (Sir), **1st Bt**
2 Andrew; entered Austrian service 1763, FM Austrian Army, fighting at Marengo, Austerlitz and Caldiero, Govr Vienna 1809, Count HRE 1797, Kt Cdr Order Maria Theresa 30 Sept 1805; *m* 1784 Maria Barbara (*dsp*), Countess of Sweerts Spork, of Bohemia
3 James; also entered Austrian military service
1 MARGARET O'Reilly, *cr* BARONESS TALBOT DE MALAHIDE (*qv*)
2 Barbara; *m* 21 May 1777 Thomas Everard, of Randalstown, Co Meath, and was *bur* 24 March 1806, having had issue (*see* EVERARD, Bt)

JAMES O'REILLY's est son,
Sir HUGH O'REILLY later NUGENT (roy licence 11 Sept 1812 on death of his maternal unc John Nugent, of Tulloughan), **1st Bt** (I), so *cr* 23 July 1795, of Ballinlough Castle; *b* 1741; Lt-Col Westmeath Militia; *m* 2 June 1781 Catharine Mary Anne (*d* 1827), only dau and heiress of Charles Mathew, of Thurles, Co Tipperary, uncle of 1st Earl of Llandaff, and *d* 18 Oct 1821, having had:
1 Sir JAMES O'REILLY later NUGENT, **2nd Bt**; *m* 8 Jan 1811 Susan Victoria Regina Mary (*d* Paris 1862), only dau of Baron C P D'Arabet (HRE), and *d* 26 April 1843
2 JOHN (Sir), **3rd Bt**
3 Lavalin; RN; *d* young in the West Indies
1 Eliza; *m* William Connolly, of Elm Park, Co Dublin, and had two sons and a dau
2 Barbara; *m* Col John Everard, of Randalstown, Co Meath (*see* EVERARD, Bt)
3 Isabella; *m* Walter Blackney, of Bally Ellen, MP, and had two sons and three daus

The 2nd Bt's bro,
Sir JOHN O'REILLY later NUGENT, **3rd Bt**; *b* April 1800; Count Austrian Empire, Chamberlain to Emperor Austria, Maj Austrian service; *m* 18 Oct 1842 Letitia Maria (*d* 20 March 1895 aged 79), est dau of Charles Whyte Roche, of Ballygran, Co Limerick, and *d* 16 Feb 1859, leaving:
1 **Sir Hugh Joseph Nugent, 4th Bt**; Count Austrian Empire; *b* 29 Dec 1845; accidentally *k* 23 Oct 1863 while shooting near Stoke-by-Nayland, Suffolk
2 CHARLES (Sir), **5th Bt**
3 John Nicholas; *b* 6 March 1848; Lt RN; *m* 27 Feb 1899 Augusta Constance (*m* 2nd 16 Dec 1902 Attewell Richard Bourne, of Mallow, Co Cork), dau of Col John Henry Ellis Ridley, of Torquay (*see* RIDLEY, V), and *dsp* 12 Sept 1901
4 James, of Wallington House, Fareham; *b* 26 June 1849; *m* 27 Jan 1874 Florence Marion (*d* 23 Feb 1932), est dau of Rev George Hulme, of Shinfield Lodge, Berks, and *d* 26 June 1904, having had:

(1) John Barnewall; b 31 July 1876; d 20 Feb 1928
(2) Andrew George; b 1879; Lt 2nd Bn E Yorks Regt; d unm 22 Nov 1906
(3) Charles James; b 1881; m 1907 Anne (d 17 March 1961), dau of William King, of Napier, NZ, and d 10 Jan 1961, leaving:
  1a James Andrew William; b 14 Oct 1909; m 8 Feb 1936 Dardanella, dau of David Webber, of Wairoa, Hawkes Bay, NZ, and had:
    1b Rodney James; b 10 May 1938; d 31 Jan 1957
    2b +Trevor Charles; b 12 Jan 1941; m 15 Jan 1966 *Barbara June, dau of Edward Bernard Bays of Mastleston, NZ, and has:
      1c +James Bernard; b 6 Sept 1968
      1c *Cassandra; b 7 Nov 1966
    3b +Brian David; b 2 June 1942
    1b *Rayna Joy; b 17 Jan 1941
  2a +Patrick Hulme; b 3 March 1912; m 1940 Mary McFalls Quin (d 198–), of Glasgow, and has:
    1b +Barry Hulme Joseph; b 27 July 1946
    2b +Darryl Charles; b 16 July 1952
    1b *Lynette Ann; b 16 Oct 1940
    2b *Janice Patricia; b 25 April 1944
  3a Frederick; b 25 April 1914; m 1939 Rita Kara, dau of T Carrol, of Wairoa, Hawkes Bay, NZ, and d 1983, leaving:
    1b +Mark; b 11 March 1950
    2b +Valentine; b 13 Feb 1952
    1b *Pearl; b 2 Jan 1940; m 30 Oct 1961 *Gavin James Douglas Heenan and has:
      1c *Raymond James O'Reilly; b 10 Dec 1965
      1c *Sharon Faith Raina; b 23 May 1962
    2b *Brenda; b 20 April 1941
    3b *Diana; b 22 Feb 1954
    4b *Dixie; b 1957
  4a Charles Joseph; b 27 June 1918; m 19– *Kathleen, dau of Edgar Jenkinson, of Gisborne, NZ, and d 1980, leaving:
    1b +Peter James; b 26 July 1947
    2b +Graham; b 13 Oct 1953
    3b +Kenneth John; b 8 Feb 1955
    1b *Margaret Anne; b 20 Nov 1950
    2b *Raewyn Gay; b 1961
  5a Richard King; b 19 Oct 1923; m 1947 *Doreen Mabel, dau of Townsend May, of New Plymouth, NZ, and d 1993 leaving:
    1b *Sandra May; b 6 Oct 1947
    2b *Karen Louise; b 26 Nov 1952
    3b *Anne Marie Eva; b 8 Dec 1954
  6a +Hubert Thomas Michael; b 29 Sept 1925; m 19– *Ngaire, dau of George Able, of Wairoa, Hawkes Bay, NZ, and has:
    1b +Alan Grant; b 24 Nov 1949
    1b *Glenis Joy; b 13 Nov 1950
  1a Kathleen Mary [Mrs Rupert Gower, Opoutama, Hawkes Bay, NZ]; b 29 Dec 1907; m 26 Oct 1927 Rupert Gower, s of Benjamin Gower, of Opoutama, NZ, and has:
    1b *Jocelyn; b 1929
    2b *Rupert; b 1934
    1b *Judith; b 1935
  2a *Florence Maud [Mrs Norman Jones, Fraserton Road, Wairoa, Hawkes Bay, NZ]; b 6 Sept 1916; m 19– *Norman Jones, s of Gilbert Jones, of Wales, and has:
    1b *Howard Gilbert; b 23 Jan 1939; m 1963 *Kathleen Elizabeth Sheridan
    2b *Warren Charles; b 24 March 1942
    3b *Michael O'Reilly; b 31 Oct 1947
  3a *Marie Tephea Diana [Mrs Moat Hoggard, 3/10 Geddis Ave, Maraenui, Napier, New Zealand]; b 26 Aug 1921; m 13 April 1938 Moat Mervyn Hoggard (d 1982) and has:
    1b *Shona Faye; b 24 Aug 1939; m 1960 (divorce 197–) Colin Thomas William Bailey and has:
      1c *Grant Colin; b 7 April 1962; m 1991 *Lynda Gwenith O'Brien and has:
        2d *Laura Jayne; b 1993
      1c *Andrea Jane; b 1 Nov 1960; m 1991 *David Paul Burton and has:
        1d *Rea Louise; b 1993
      2c *Lisa Marie; b 21 Aug 1969
  4a *Anne Barbara; b 24 Aug 1927; m 3 Aug 1951 *Roy Alexander Ross and has:
    1b *Judith Ann [Mrs Robert Smith, c/o Lakeland Marine Ltd, Rauhato, Taupo, PO Box 827, New Zealand]; b 23 July 1953; m 1976 *Robert Chadwick Smith and has:
      1c *Haylee Ann; b 1980
      2c *Renee Adrienne; b 1982
    2b *Deborah Irene; b 16 Aug 1956; m 19– — and has issue
    3b *Sharon Barbara; b 1959; m 19– — and has issue
    4b *Angela Leslie; b 1961; m 19– — and has issue
(4) Hubert Joseph; b 1882; d 1886
(5) Walter Lonergan O'Reilly; b 1884; m 1911 Amelia Bateup (d 1966) and d 31 Jan 1949, leaving:
  1a *Joan Florence [Mrs Donald Fenner, 24 The Boulevard, Pevensey Bay, E Sussex BN24 6SB]; b 1917; m 1940 *Donald Evelyn Fenner and has:
    1b *Janet [Mrs Michael Cansdale, 84 Capelands, New Ash Green, Kent DA3 8LQ]; b 28 Dec 1946; m 1971 *Michael Cansdale and has:
      1c *Andrew Richard; b 27 Nov 1976
      1c *Penelope Alice; b 11 Nov 1972

2a *Marion Kathleen [Mrs Raymond Wicker, Windy Ridge, Punnetts Town, Heathfield, Sussex]; b 1920; m 1944 *Raymond Weedon Wicker and has issue
3a *Gwynneth Eileen Mary [Mrs Alfred Stokes, 25 Victoria Rd, Mayfield, Sussex]; b 1928; m 1949 *Alfred Stokes and has:
  1b *Patrick John; b 1954; m 1979 *Jenny Garsad and has:
    1c *William Conrad; b 1980
  2b *Sally Anne; b 1950; m 1970 *Graham White and has:
    1c *Sarah Jayne; b 1974
  3b *Jennifer Mary; b 1952; m 1972 *Malcolm Palmer and has:
    1c *Aaron James; b 1975
    2c *Paul Malcolm; b 1978
    1c *Michelle Louise; b 1982
    2c *Teresa Jill; b 1962
(6) Wilfrid Basil O'Reilly; b 3 Oct 1885; educ Prior Park Bath; NZ Mounted Rifles WW I, Auckland Infantry WW II; m 8 June 1916 Alice, dau of Theodore Manson West, and has:
  1a *Denise Florence Nobel; b 27 April 1917
  2a *Diana Mary Hampshire; b 19 Dec 1918
(7) Mark Lavallan; b 1891; Assist Paymaster RNR; ka 16 June 1916
(8) Bernard; b 30 Oct 1892; educ St Edmund's Coll Ware; Lt Roy Sussex Regt 1917–21
(1) Florence Marie; b 1 March 1876; m 22 July 1902 Adml William Rawdon Napier, CB, CMG, DSO, and d 13 Dec 1965, leaving issue (see NAPIER and ETTRICK, L)
(2) Kathleen Hilda Mary; m 6 Oct 1903 Capt Patrick Ronald Napier, ASC, yst s of Cdr Lenox Napier, RN, and d 1 April 1948, leaving issue (see NAPIER and ETTRICK, L)
(3) Maude Letitia Mary ; b 10 Jan 1888; d unm 19 Aug 1961
(4) Cora Angela Mary; b 2 Oct 1889
5 Andrew Greville; b 18 June 1852; d 1884
1 Letitia Mary; m 1st 22 Aug 1865 Maj Richard Conolly, of Green Park, Co Westmeath (d 7 Feb 1871); m 2nd 17 Feb 1873 Thomas Thierri Sherlock, est s of David Sherlock, QC, MP, and d 25 Feb 1918, having had issue
2 Kathleen Mary Georgina; m 16 Dec 1875 Thomas Gordon Stoker and d 20 May 1911, leaving issue. He d 1890
3 Helena Mary; m 20 Jan 1876 Richard Charles Lynch, of Petersburg Castle, Co Galway, and d 10 Jan 1946, leaving issue

The 4th Bt's bro,
Sir Charles Nugent, 5th Bt, Count Austrian Empire; b 7 Feb 1847; Lt 17th Lancers; m 15 Nov 1871 Emily Ruth Eades (d 31 Aug 1929), est dau of Thomas Walker, of Berkswell Hall, Warwicks, and Mayfair, and d 22 May 1927, having had:

1 Charles Hugh; b 18 May 1878; m 2 April 1902 Anna Maria (m 2nd 9 Dec 1929 Edwin John King (d 4 Jan 1940) and d 20 March 1964), yst dau of Edwin Adams, and dvp 1 Sept 1903, leaving:
  (1) **Sir Hugh Charles Nugent, 6th Bt**, Count Austrian Empire; b posthumously 26 May 1904; educ Stonyhurst; FO RAFVR WW II (despatches), Capt Irish Free State Army 1941, Kt SMO Malta; m 28 Sept 1931 *Margaret Mary Lavallin [Margaret Lady Nugent, Cronk Ghennie House, Bowring Rd, Ramsey, IoM], er dau of Rev Herbert Lavallin Puxley, of The White House, Chaddleworth, Berks, and d 30 Oct 1983, leaving:
    1a Sir JOHN EDWIN LAVALLIN NUGENT, **7th and present Baronet**
    2a +David Hugh Lavallin [David Nugent Esq, Clobemon Hall, Ferns, Enniscorthy, Co Wexford, Ireland], Count Austrian Empire; b 22 April 1935; educ Eton and RAC Cirencester; late Lt Irish Gds, Kt SMO Malta 1965, Kt Cdr Order Holy Sepulchre Jerusalem with Star; m 1st 28 Sept 1960 (divorce 1990) Lady Elizabeth Maria Guinness, sis of 3rd Earl of Iveagh (qv), and has:
      1b +Charles Rupert; b 24 Jan 1962; m 1989 *Louise V, yr dau of Timothy Nixon, of The Old Vicarage, Pampisford, Cambridge, and has:
        1c +Hugh; b 19–
        2c +James Timothy; b 25 Nov 1996
      2b +Hugo John; b 11 Dec 1963; m 1989 *Louise, yr dau of Thomas Elliot Rutherford, of Park Daill, Hawick, Scotland, and has:
        1c +Isaac Sean; b 1992
      3b +Rory David Neeld Lavallin; b 2 Aug 1971
      1b Sheelin Rose; b 18 May 1967; m 13 July 1996 *Dominic Scriven, s of Tim Scriven and Mrs Valerie Scriven, both of London, and d 30 Oct 1998
    2a (cont.) David Nugent m 2nd 1991 (divorce 19–) Djong-Zha, only dau of In-Suk Hyun, of Seoul, Korea, and formerly w of Sir Richard Heygate, 6th Bt (qv)

Seat: Ballinlough Castle, Clonmellon, Co Westmeath, Ireland. Though they abandoned the old O'Reilly name the Nugents did not abandon their old castle. Instead they remodelled it to conform with the spirit of an age, the 18th century, in which fortifications could be decorative. The first major work was carried out in 1730, although the windows remained narrow, as if harking back to their original purpose of defence. A new roof was put on around 1780, less steeply pitched than the original, though flanked by crenellations. Inside there is some gothic plasterwork but also purely classical decoration, chiefly the extremely fine hall.

NUGENT of Donore

Arms: Erm. two bars gu., in dexter chief a martlet az. for difference. **Crest:** A cockatrice vert, wings elevated, tail nowed, combed and wattled gu. **Supporters:** Dexter, a cockatrice; sinister, a swan, both statant, wings addorsed and gorged with a collar. **Motto:** *Decrevi* ('I have decreed'). **Creation:** Bt. (UK) 30 Sept 1831.

SIR PETER WALTER JAMES NUGENT, 5TH BT, of Donore, Co Westmeath [Sir Peter Nugent Bt, Bay Bush, Straffan, Co Kildare, Ireland]; *b* 26 Jan 1920; *s f* 1955; *educ* Downside; WW II: 2nd Lt Hampshire Regt 1941, Maj 1945 and with 10th Baluch Regt, Tattersalls Irish Agent 1973–83, dir Tattersalls Newmarket and Tattersalls (Ireland) (ret 1989); *m* 1947 *Anne Judith, only dau of Maj Robert Smyth, South Irish Horse, of Gaybrook, Mullingar, Co Westmeath, and has:

1 +(WALTER) RICHARD MIDDLETON [Richard Nugent Esq, 61–66 Yaguchi-dai, Naka-ku, Yokohama 231, Japan]; *b* 15 Nov 1947; *educ* Downside; fin dir (Keiri Torishimariyaku) IMS Japan Kabushiki Kaisha, FCA 1970; *m* 1985 *Okabe Kayoko

2 +Andrew Robert [Andrew Nugent Esq, 7 Liffey Ct, Clare, Co Kildare, Ireland]; *b* 21 Sept 1951

1 *Fiona Aileen [Mrs John Bellingham, Glencara, Ballynacargy, Co Westmeath, Ireland; The Cliffs, Bailyg, Co Dublin, Ireland; Flat 5, 87 Harcourt Terrace, London SW10 9JP; 5 rue Paul-Louis Courier, 75007, Paris, France]; *b* 24 April 1949; *m* 14 Feb 1989 *John Stuart Bellingham (*see* BELLINGHAM, Bt)

2 *Laura Anne [Miss Laura Nugent, 46 Sisters Ave, London SW11 5SN]; *b* 24 April 1954

Lineage: WALTER NUGENT, of Donore (*see* WESTMEATH, E); *m* Mary, dau of Sir James Dillon, of Drumrany, and had:

JAMES NUGENT, of Donore; *m* Elizabeth, dau of Christopher Nugent, er s of 1st Baron Delvin (*see* WESTMEATH, E), and *d* 21 Feb 1580, leaving:

RICHARD NUGENT, of Donore; *m* 1580 Maud, dau of Sir Christopher Barnewall, of Crickstown (*see* BARNEWALL, Bt), and *d* 31 Oct 1616, leaving an er s:

ANDREW NUGENT, of Donore; Capt Confedn of Kilkenny Army 1641, cmdg 100 men at Kilsoglin against the English; *m* Lady Elinor Plunkett, dau of 1st Earl of Fingall (*see* 1970 edn), and had:

WALTER NUGENT, of Donore; indicted with his f for rebelling against the English; *m* Bridget, dau of Christopher Nugent, of Moyrath, and had:

1 Robert, of Donore; *m* Alice Dungan, sis of 1st and 2nd Earls of Limerick of the Jan 1685/6 *cr* (*see* LIMERICK, E, preliminary remarks), and had:
  (1) John, of Donore; *dsp*
  (2) Andrew; had:
    1a James; *dsp* 1690
2 THOMAS
1 Frances; *m* William Bermingham or Birmingham, of Corballis, Co Meath, and had:
  (1) Mary; *m* Peter Delamer, of Balnefield, and had:
    1a Peter Delamer; offr of horse in French service

The 2nd son,
THOMAS NUGENT, of Donore; *m* Catherine Ashe, of Moyvally, and *d* 1699, having had:
1 EDWARD
2 John, of Corballis; MP Fore 1689
3 Andrew, of Dublin; MD; *m* Mary Purcell, of Cromlin, and had, with other issue:
  (1) Thomas; offr in French service

The est s,
EDWARD NUGENT, of Donore; *m* 1st 1703 Mary (*d* 1721), dau of Edward Nugent, of Carlandstown, and had:
1 THOMAS
1 Clare; *m* 1731 John Bryan
2 Mary; *m* Aug 1733 George Browne, MD, and *d* 1736, leaving issue
3 Catharine; *m* 1738 Rev Henry Dunkin

EDWARD NUGENT *m* 2nd 1724 Eleanor (*m* 2nd Oliver Nugent), dau of Charles Dowde, and *d* 1733, leaving by her four sons

His est s,
THOMAS NUGENT, of Donore; *m* 1724 Mary, dau of James Daly, of Carrownekelly (later Dunsandle), Co Galway, and had:
1 Sir JAMES NUGENT, 1st Bt, of Donore (I), so *cr* 18 July 1768, with remainder to his bro; *m* 1st Feb 1761 Catharine, er dau and coheir of Robert King, of Drewstown, Co Westmeath; *m* 2nd —, sis of Lawrence Coyne Nugent, but *dsp*
2 Sir PETER NUGENT, 2nd and last Bt; *m* Mrs Mary Rogers (*d* March 1831) and *dsp* 1797, when the btcy expired
2 John; *dsp*
1 Christina; *m* Pierce Fitzgerald, of Baltinoran, and had, with two other sons:
  (1) Richard; *dsp*
  (2) THOMAS; inherited Donore
  (3) Lattin, of Soho, Co Westmeath

The 2nd Bt's nephew,
THOMAS FITZGERALD later NUGENT; Cdr RN; *m* Mary, dau of Christopher Dardis, of Giggenstown, Co Westmeath, and was drowned 1810 in the *Monkey*, a gun-brig, cruising off the coast of France, having had, with other issue:

Sir PERCY FITZGERALD later NUGENT (roy licence), **1st Bt** (UK), so *cr* 30 Sept 1831; *b* 29 Sept 1797; MP Co Westmeath; *m* 1 May 1823 Elizabeth Maria Eleanor (*d* 1856), only dau of Walter Sweetman, of Dublin, and had, with other issue (*d* young):
1 WALTER GEORGE (Sir), **2nd Bt**
2 Percy; *b* 26 May 1828; CE; *m* 20 Nov 1884 Mary (*d* 18 April 1925), dau of Michael Errington and sis of Sir George Errington, Bt (*see* 1970 edn), and *dsp* 30 April 1900
3 James; *b* 3 Jan 1833; *m* 2 March 1886 Julia Margaret (*d* 30 April 1917), dau of John C Chaplin, and *d* 1922
1 Margaret Louisa; *m* 1882 Peter Nugent FitzGerald, of Soho, Co Westmeath, and *dsp* July 1905. He *d* 1893
2 Anna Maria; *m* 9 Sept 1865 Philip O'Reilly, DL, of Colamber, Co Westmeath, and *d* 23 Nov 1930, leaving issue. He *d* 24 Sept 1912

Sir PERCY *d* 25 June 1874; his son,
Sir Walter George Nugent, 2nd Bt; *b* 23 Jan 1827; Capt 33rd Regt Crimea: fought Alma, Inkerman and Balaclava (Crimean medal and three clasps, Turkish medal and Medjidie); *m* 19 July 1860 Maria More (*d* 21 May 1910), only dau of Richard More O'Ferrall, PC, DL, JP, of Malyna, Co Kildare, and *d* 26 Feb 1893, having had:
1 Sir PERCY THOMAS Nugent, **3rd Bt**; *b* 11 June 1861; *d* unm 5 Feb 1896
2 Laval Arthur, *b* 13 Sept 1863; *d* 19 May 1895
3 WALTER RICHARD (Sir), **4th Bt**
4 George Edward; monk; *b* 11 Jan 1867; *d* 1896
5 Edward John; *b* and *d* 1877
6 Cecil Charles; *b* 7 March 1897; Lt 6th Bn Rifle Bde; *d* unm 1 June 1914
1 Matilda Mary Elizabeth; *b* 26 July 1862; *d* 1871
2 Ellen; *b* 4 Feb 1868; *d* 1949
3 Mabel; *b* 9 Sept 1869; nun; *d* 1945
4 Evelyn Jessie Mary; *b* 15 Aug 1872; *d* unm 17 Sept 1936

The 3rd Bt's yr bro,
Sir Walter Richard Nugent, 4th Bt, DL Co Westmeath (High Sheriff 1922 and 1923); *b* 12 Dec 1865; *educ* Downside and Univ Coll Dublin; MP S Westmeath 1907–18, memb and hon offr Dublin Chamber Commerce, dir and chm Dublin Bd Northern Assur, dir Bank of Ireland 1920, Dep Govr Bank of Ireland 1924, Peace Commr Irish Free State 1924, Steward Turf Club and Nat Hunt Ireland 1923, v-chm Gt Southern Rlwy 1924, chm Gt Southern Amalgamated Rlwys 1925 and Irish Rlwy Clearing House 1926, dep chm Rosslare and Fishguard Rlwy and Harbour Bd 1926, Senator Irish Free State 1928, Pres Dublin Chamber Commerce 1929, memb Roy Commn Paper Imports and Govt War Savings Ctee Ireland 1916 and Daylight Saving Extension Bill Ctee 1916; *m* 15 June 1916 Gladys Aileen (*d* 10 Nov 1957), yr dau of Middleton Moore O'Malley, JP, of Ross House, Westport, Co Mayo, by Letitia Josephine, only dau of David Keyes, of Furry Park, Co Mayo, and *d* 12 Nov 1955, leaving:
1 Sir PETER WALTER JAMES, **5th and present Bt**
1 *Heather Vivian Mary [Heather Lady Prichard-Jones, 30 Claylands Rd, London SW8 1NZ; Moyvore, Mullingar, Co Westmeath, Ireland]; *m* 31 July 1937 (*divorce* 1950) Sir John Prichard-Jones, 2nd Bt (*qv*), and has issue
2 *Gloria Aileen [Mrs Jack McGowran, 33 Villiers St, London WC2]; *m* 1st 28 Nov 1946 (*divorce*) Michael Meade Carvill, Capt Irish Gds, est s of Joseph Aloysius Carvill, of Glengarriff, and has issue; *m* 2nd 19– Jack McGowran (*d* 1973) and has by him:
  (1) *Tara Maria; *b* 6 Nov 1964

NUGENT of Waddesdon

Arms: Erm. two bars within a bordure engrailed gu., on a canton of the last a dagger erect ppr., pommel and hilt or. **Crest:** A cockatrice vert gorged with a plain collar or, pendant therefrom an escutcheon gu., charged with a dagger erect, as in the arms. **Supporters:** Two cockatrices vert, wings addorsed, collared or, pendant therefrom a shield gu., charged with a dagger as in the arms. **Motto:** *Decrevi* ('I have decreed'). **Creation:** Bt. (UK) 28 Nov 1806.

SIR ROBIN GEORGE COLBORNE NUGENT, 5TH BT, of Waddesdon, Co Berks [Sir Robin Nugent Bt, Bannerdown House, Bannerdown Rd, Bath BA1 7LA]; *b* 11 July 1925; *s f* 1970; *educ* Eton and RWA Sch of Architecture; ARIBA 1959, Lt Gren Gds WW II Italy 1944–45 and to 1948; *m* 1st 17 April 1947 (*divorce* 1967) Ursula Mary, er dau of Lt-Gen Sir Herbert Fothergill Cooke, KCB, KBE, CSI, DSO, and has:

1 +CHRISTOPHER GEORGE RIDLEY; *b* 5 Oct 1949; *educ* Eton and UEA; *m* 1985 *Jacqueline Vagba and has:

  (1) +Terence; *b* 1 March 1986

  (2) +Rufus; *b* 1987

  (3) +Benjamin; *b* 1991

2 +Patrick Guy; *b* 10 Nov 1959

1 *Philippa Mary; *b* 4 July 1951

Sir ROBIN *m* 2nd 1967 *Victoria Anna Irmgard, dau of Dr Peter Cartellieri

Lineage: Sir George Nugent, 1st Bt (UK), so *cr* 28 Nov 1806 for mil servs, of Waddesdon, Berks, GCB; *b* 10 June 1757; Col 6th Foot, Govr St Mawes, FM, DCL; *m* 16 Nov 1797 Maria (*d* 24 Oct 1834), 7th dau of Cortlandt Skinner, Attorney-Gen New Jersey, and had:

1 GEORGE EDMUND (Sir), **2nd Bt**

2 Charles Edmund; *b* 15 June 1811; *m* 28 Nov 1837 Louisa Douglas (*d* 18 Dec 1881), dau of Sir Rose Price, 1st Bt, of Trengwainton (*qv*), and *d* 3 March 1890

1 Louisa Elizabeth; *m* 24 Nov 1824 1st Baron Cottesloe (*qv*) and *d* 17 Aug 1875

2 Maria Amelia; *m* 31 July 1832 Rice Richard Clayton, 4th s of Sir William Clayton, 4th Bt (*qv*), and *d* 1880

Sir GEORGE *d* 11 March 1849; his er s,

Sir George Edmund Nugent, 2nd Bt, DL; *b* 12 Oct 1802; Capt and Lt-Col Gren Gds; *m* 13 July 1830 Hon Maria Charlotte Ridley-Colborne (*d* 31 Aug 1883), 2nd dau and coheir of 1st and last Baron Colborne of West Harling (*see* RIDLEY, V), and had:

1 George Grenville; *b* 19 June 1837; *d* 16 March 1838

2 EDMUND CHARLES (Sir), **3rd Bt**

1 Lucy Henrietta; *m* 2 Aug 1860 Sir Francis George Manningham Boileau, 2nd Bt (*qv*), and *d* 19 Nov 1925, leaving issue

2 Margaret Louisa; *d* young 1844

3 Mary Wilhelmina; *m* 26 Oct 1881 Capt Jocelyn Henry Watkin Thomas, Scots Gds, of Belmont, Co Carlow, s of Lt-Gen Henry Thomas, CB, and *d* 24 Jan 1910. He *d* 21 Oct 1932

4 Emily Julia; *m* 3 Sept 1878 Russell Henry Monro, of Somerby Hall, Melton Mowbray, and *d* 4 Feb 1938. He *d* 19 Oct 1922

Sir GEORGE *d* 3 May 1892; his only surv s,

Sir Edmund Charles Nugent, 3rd Bt, JP, DL Norfolk; *b* 12 March 1839; Capt Gren Gds, High Sheriff Norfolk 1900; *m* 30 April 1863 Evelyn Henrietta (*d* 19 Jan 1922), yst dau of Gen Ernest Frederick Gascoigne, Gren Gds, of Raby Hall, nr Liverpool, and had:

1 George Colborne, MVO, JP Norfolk; *b* 22 Feb 1864; Col and T/Brig-Gen formerly Gren Gds, Boer War 1899–1900, cmded Irish Gds Regt and Regtl Dist 1909–13, Cmdt Duke of York's Roy Mil Sch Dover 1913–14, cmdg 5th London Bde 1914, served WW I; *m* 8 Dec 1891 Isabel Mary (*d* 13 Oct 1941), dau of Gen Sir Edward Gascoigne Bulwer, GCB, and was *ka* France 31 May 1915, leaving:

  (1) GEORGE GUY BULWER (Sir), **4th Bt**

  (2) TERENCE EDMUND GASCOIGNE, 1st and last BARON NUGENT, of West Harling, Co Norfolk (UK), so *cr* 22 Aug 1960, GCVO (1952, KCVO 1945, CVO 1937, MVO 1927), MC (1918); *b* 11 Aug 1895; *educ* Eton and RMC Sand-

hurst; Maj Irish Gds WW I (wounded, despatches), Bde Maj Bde Gds 1929–33, Lt-Col 1936, Equerry 1927 to HRH THE DUKE OF YORK (later HM GEORGE VI, to whom Extra Equerry 1937–52, also to HM THE QUEEN 1952–73), Comptroller Ld Chamberlain's Office 1936–60, Perm Ld-in-Waiting 1960–73, Pres Actors' and Actresses' Pension Fund 1953–73 and MCC 1962–63, Grand Offr Legn Hon 1960; *m* 25 April 1935 Rosalie (*d* July 1994), only dau of Brig-Gen Hon Charles Strathavon Heathcote-Drummond-Willoughby, CB, CMG (*see* WILLOUGHBY DE ERESBY, B), and *dsp* 1973, when the Barony expired

2 Edmund Frederick (Rev); *b* 4 Feb 1866; *educ* Ch Ch Oxford (BA 1890, MA 1893); C of E Vicar St Martin's Brighton, Domestic Chaplain to Bp Truro, BRC WW I, ordained RC Priest 1919 (received 1917), Rector SS Simon and Jude RC Ch Streatham Hill 1931–50; *d* 13 May 1950

3 Charles Henry; *b* 4 Feb 1866; Lt Scots Gds; *d* unm 30 April 1887

4 Claud; *b* 10 May 1867; BA Oxon; *d* unm 2 April 1901

1 Evelyn Lilla; *d* unm 3 Nov 1949

2 Violet; *d* unm 2 July 1943

Sir EDMUND *d* 4 Dec 1928; his gs,

Sir (George) Guy Bulwer Nugent, 4th Bt; *b* 5 Nov 1892; *educ* Eton and RMC Sandhurst; Capt and Adj 3rd Bn Gren Gds WW I; *m* 24 Oct 1921 May Esther (*d* 1992), yst dau of Jesse Arthur Bigsby, of S Kensington, and *d* 17 Aug 1970, leaving:

1 Sir ROBIN GEORGE COLBORNE NUGENT, **5th and present Bt**

2 +Jeremy Charles Clare [Jeremy Nugent Esq, Weathervane Cottage, Bigfrith Lane, Cookham Dean, Berks]; *b* 15 April 1936; *educ* Malvern and Worcester Coll Oxford; *m* 18 April 1960 *Joy Jennifer, only dau of Arthur Howard Waterson, of Bathwick, Bath, and has:

  (1) +Nigel Howard Clare; *b* 30 Aug 1963

  (2) +Julian Guy Bulwer; *b* 9 May 1965

  (1) *Fiona Clare; *b* 27 Nov 1967

1 *Dinah [Mrs John Bennett, Farleigh Plain, Hinton Charterhouse, nr Bath, Somerset]; *b* 1922; WRNS WW II; *m* 17 June 1950 *Capt John William Huyshe Bennett, DSC, RN, only s of Maj William Pyt Bennett, RA, and has:

  (1) *Timothy Nugent Huyshe; *b* 27 Aug 1951; *educ* Marlborough

  (2) *Nicholas John William; *b* 14 April 1957

NUNBURNHOLME

Arms: Or a lymphad, sails furled sa., on a chief az. three ducal coronets of the field. **Crest:** Between two coronets as in the arms a demi-wolf sa. holding between the paws a like coronet. **Supporters:** On either side a Benedictine nun holding in the exterior hand a rosary, all ppr. **Motto:** *Pro legibus ac regibus* ('For laws and kings'). **Creation:** B. (UK) 16 Jan 1906.

THE 4TH BARON NUNBURNHOLME, of the City of Kingston upon Hull (Ben Charles Wilson) [The Rt Hon The Lord Nunburnholme, House of Lords, London SW1A 0PW]; *b* 16 July 1928; *s f* 1974; *educ* Eton and RMA Woolwich; Capt 1953, Maj 1962 RHG, ret 1969; *m* 8 April 1958 (*divorce* 19–) Ines Dolores Jeanne, only dau of Gerard Walravens, of Brussels, formerly Belgian Amb Turkey, and has:

1 *Lorraine Mary Charmiane Nicole; *b* 28 Feb 1959

2 *Tatiana Ines Alexandra [The Hon Mrs Dent, Lake Cottage, Shillinglee Park, Chiddingfold, Sussex]; *b* 17 Sept 1960; *m* 1988 *Nigel L Dent, 2nd s of Robin Dent, of Painswick, Glos, and has:

  (1) *Frederick; *b* 1989

  (2) *Harry Barnaby Nigel; *b* 1991

3 *Ines Monica; *b* 13 Feb 1963; *m* 1988 *Anthony Richard Leslie Garton, yst s of Anthony Charles Garton, and has:

  (1) *Tristan John Leslie; *b* 1990

4 *Ysabel; *b* 13 Feb 1963

Lineage: THOMAS WILSON, of Hull and Cottingham, Yorks; *b* 12 Feb 1792; *m* 1 Sept 1814 Susannah (*d* 25 Nov 1879), dau of John West, and *d* 21 June 1869, having had, with other issue:

CHARLES HENRY WILSON, **1st Baron Nunburnholme**, of the City of Kingston-upon-Hull (UK), so *cr* 16 Jan 1906, JP, DL E R Yorks; *b* 22 April 1833; Sheriff Hull 1870, MP (Lib) Kingston-upon-Hull 1874–85 and Kingston-upon-Hull W 1885–1905; *m* 5 Oct 1871 Florence Jane Helen, OBE (1918) (*d* 8 Dec 1932), est dau of Col William Henry Charles Wellesley (*see* WELLINGTON, D), and had:

1 CHARLES HENRY WELLESLEY, **2nd Baron**

2 Guy Greville, CMG (1919), DSO (1902), JP, DL E R Yorks and Kingston-upon-Hull; *b* 19 May 1877; *educ* Eton; Hon Col E R Yorks Yeo, formerly 11th Hus, Boer War 1901–02 (despatches) and WW I (despatches), MP Hull W 1907–18; *m* 1st 23 June 1904 Lady Isabel Innes-Ker (*dsp* 12 Oct 1905), dau of 7th Duke of Roxburghe (*qv*); *m* 2nd 22 May 1911 Avery (*d* 1982), 3rd dau of Geoffrey Fowell Buxton, CB (*see* BUXTON, Bt), and *d* 1 Feb 1943, having had:

  (1) +Jeremy Charles, DFC [Jeremy Wilson Esq DFC, Fulmer Cottage, Fulmer, Bucks]; *b* 21 May 1923; *educ* Eton; F/Lt RAF WW II; *m* 21 July 1944 *June Patricia, dau of Thomas Townsend Bucknill, and has:

    1a +Peter Richard [Peter Wilson Esq, The Red House, Hougham, Lincs NG32 2JD]; *b* 19 April 1945; *educ* Eton; *m* 11 May 1972 *Penelope Ann Verney, only dau of Robert Edwart Gabbett, MBE, MC, RE, of Ballaghtobia, Collan, Co Kilkenny, and has:

      1b *Suzanna; *b* 16 March 1974

      2b *Philippa; *b* 16 March 1974

    2a +Thomas Charles [Thomas Wilson Esq, The Old Rectory, Upper Clatford, Hants SP11 7QP]; *b* 2 June 1946; *educ* Eton; *m* 3 Dec 1980 *(Elizabeth) Jane, dau of Lt-Gen Sir Napier Crookenden, KCB (*see* KINDERSLEY, B) and has:

      1b *James Thomas; *b* 14 March 1984

      1b *Tobina Kate; *b* 23 June 1981

  (1) Oriel Susannah; *b* 21 July 1912; *m* 8 Feb 1933 Robert Hoare, s of Christopher Hoare, of Tyburnia, and *d* 25 Aug 1937, leaving issue. He *d* 26 Jan 1977

  (2) Malise Joy, JP (Rutland 1952); *b* 14 Sept 1913; *m* 23 April 1942 Lt-Col Archibald William Antony Smith, DSO (*d* 1989), s of Archibald Smith, of Market Overton, Rutland, and *d* 1994, leaving:

    1a *Antony Luke [Maj Antony Smith, 28 Beveridge St, Barrow-on-Soar, Loughborough, Leics LE12 8PL]; *b* 12 March 1943; *educ* Eton; CA, Lt Leics and Derbyshire PAO Yeo, Maj TAVR; *m* 1985 *Penny, dau of Maj David R W R Watts-Russell, of Biggin Hall, Benefield, Northants

    2a *Rupert Malise [Rupert Smith Esq, 273 Trinity Rd, London SW18 3SH]; *b* 25 Nov 1944; *educ* Eton; Lt 2nd Bn Coldstream Gds (ret); *m* 1976 *Angela, yr dau of Dr R M Castillo, and has:

      1b *Rowena Jane; *b* 1978

      2b *Jessica Malise; *b* 1980

  (3) *Alison Ann [Mrs Edmund Swetenham, Green Kirtles, Sinnington, N Yorks YO6 6SJ]; *b* 10 Dec 1914; *m* 11 Jan 1938 Brig (John) Edmund Swetenham (*d* 1982), DSO, late 5th Roy Inniskilling Dragoon Gds and RSG, est s of Maj Foster Swetenham, Roy Scots Greys, and has:

    1a *(John) Foster [Foster Swetenham Esq, Pound Farmhouse, Rayne, Essex CM7 5DJ]; *b* 16 Jan 1939; *educ* Eton and RMA Sandhurst; Capt RSG (ret); *m* 4 May 1964 *Marion Sylvia, yr dau of George Alfred Parker, of Gt Bookham, Surrey, and has:

      1b *Jeremy Edmund; *b* 1967; Maj Roy Scots Dragoon Gds (ret); *m* 1993 *Sandrine, dau of Dr Jean-Pierre Martin, of Montgeron, France

      1b *Charlotte; *b* 1966; *m* 1992 *Richard Hamilton Fleetwood Fuller, only s of Edward Hamilton Fleetwood Fuller, of Weybridge, Surrey, and has issue

3 Gerald Valerian; *b* 1885; *d* unm 27 Sept 1908

1 Millicent Florence Eleanor; *m* 1st 10 June 1895 (*divorce* 1905) Sir Charles Edward Cradock-Hartopp, 5th Bt (*qv*); *m* 2nd 14 Dec 1905 (*divorce* 1913) 3rd Earl Cowley (*qv*) and had issue; *m* 3rd 25 July 1914 Maj Grey William Duberley, Gren Gds, of Gaynes Hall, St Neots, Hunts, and *d* 29 Nov 1952. He was *ka* 13 March 1915

2 Enid Edith; *m* 15 Feb 1900 10th Earl of Chesterfield and (4th Earl of) Stanhope (*see* 1967 edn) and *d* 30 Nov 1957

3 Joan Evelyn Jane; *m* 6 July 1899 Guy Thomas Fairfax, of Bilborough, Yorks, and *d* 11 Dec 1960, leaving issue. He *d* 2 Feb 1934

4 Gwladys Alice Gertrude; *m* 3 Aug 1905 2nd Viscount Chaplin (*see* 1970 edn) and *d* 17 Oct 1971, leaving issue

The 1st BARON *d* 28 Oct 1907; his est son,

CHARLES HENRY WELLESLEY WILSON, **2nd Baron Nunburnholme**, CB, DSO; *b* 24 Jan 1875; Pres TFA, City of Lond Imp Vols Boer War 1899–1900 (despatches), Sheriff Hull 1900, MP Hull W 1906–07, Capt RGA WW I, Ld Lt E R Yorks; *m* 12 Feb 1901 Lady Marjorie Cecilia Wynn-Carrington, DGStJ (*d* 17 June 1968), est dau of 1st and last Marquess of Lincolnshire (*see* CARRINGTON, B), and had:

1 CHARLES JOHN, **3rd Baron**

2 (Robert) David; *b* 3 Feb 1916; P/O RAFVR WW II; *ka* 23 March 1941

1 (Cecilia) Monica; *b* 6 June 1902; *m* 28 Feb 1924 6th Earl Winterton (*qv*) and *d* 9 Nov 1974

The 2nd BARON *d* 15 Aug 1924; his er son,

CHARLES JOHN WILSON, **3rd Baron Nunburnholme**; *b* 25 April 1904; *educ* Eton and RMC Sandhurst; Hon Capt QOYD WW II (wounded); *m* 1st 24 Nov 1927 (*divorce* 1947) Lady Mary Thynne (*d* 11 Dec 1974), yst dau of 5th Marquess of Bath (*qv*), and had:

1 BEN CHARLES WILSON, **4th and present Baron Nunburnholme**

2 +CHARLES THOMAS [The Hon Charles Wilson, Banco Fonseca y Burnay, Portimao, Portugal]; *b* 27 May 1935; heir presumptive; *educ* Eton; Page of Honour to HM GEORGE VI 1950–52, memb London Stock Exchange 1956–66; *m* 2 July 1969 (*divorce* 19–) Linda Kay, only dau of Cyril James Stephens, of Challock Lees, Kent, and has:

  (1) +Stephen Charles; *b* 1973

  (1) *Nathalia Ellen; *b* 1971

1 *Charmaine Elizabeth Violet Cecilia [The Hon Mrs Bissill, The Stables, Dawns Lane, Aslockton, Notts]; *b* 4 Aug 1930; *m* 19 Jan 1957 William Rippon Bissill (*d* 1983), er s of William Norman Bissill, and has had:

  (1) John James Rippon; *b* 7 Aug 1957; *d* 1980

  (2) William Henry; *b* 14 March 1960; *d* 1994

  (1) *Kathleen Mary Florence; *b* 14 June 1966; *m* 1991 *Mark Adair Hodson (*see* HODSON, Bt)

The 3rd Baron *m* 2nd 31 Oct 1953 *Alex (*m* 2nd 23 Oct 1975 Harry O J C Jonas), only dau of Capt Douglas Hockly, of Tenterden, Kent, and *d* 1 Jan 1974, leaving by her:

3 +(David) Mark; *b* 5 Aug 1954; *educ* Eton; *m* 1983 *Amanda C, dau of Roger Hayward, of Gardiners Hall, Stoke Ash, nr Eye, Suffolk

NUTTALL

Arms: Or on a pile sa. between in base two roses gu. barbed and seeded ppr. a shacklebolt of the field. **Crest:** A Dalmatian hound sejant ppr., collared and chained and resting the dexter forefoot on a shacklebolt sa. **Motto:** *Aut nunquam tentes aut perfice* ('Either do not attempt, or perfect'). **Creation:** Bt. (UK) 22 June 1922.

SIR NICHOLAS KEITH LILLINGTON NUTTALL, 3RD BT, of Chasefield, Parish of Bowdon, Co Chester [Sir Nicholas Nuttall Bt, PO Box N7776, Nassau, Bahamas]; *b* 21 Sept 1933; *s f* 1941; *educ* Eton and RMA Sandhurst; Capt 1959, Maj 1966 RHG (ret 1968); *m* 1st 20 Dec 1960 (*divorce* 1971) (Rosemary) Caroline, est dau of Christopher York, DL, of Long Marston Manor, Long Marston, Yorks, gs of Sir Frederick Milner, 7th Bt (*qv*), and has:

1 +HARRY; *b* 2 Jan 1963; *m* 27 April 1996 *Kelly Marie, only dau of Anthony E Allen, of Raleigh, NC, and Mrs Susanne Allen Haley

1 *Tamara; *b* 26 April 1967; *m* 19– *Lorenzo Cardi and *d* Aug 1997

Sir NICHOLAS *m* 2nd 1971 (*divorce* 1975) Julia Jill Beresford, dau of Col Thomas Cromwell Williamson, DSO, of Beaumont Hall, Thorpe-le-Soken, Essex, and formerly w of Darel Sausmarez Carey; *m* 3rd 1975 (*divorce* 1983) Miranda Elizabeth Louise (*m* 2nd 23 Dec 1995 2nd Earl of Stockton, *qv*), formerly w of Peter Richard Henry Sellers, CBE, the actor, and dau of Richard St John Quarry and Diana Elizabeth (*m* 3rd 1951 2nd Baron Mancroft, *qv*), and by her had:

2 *Gytha Miranda; *b* 1975

3 *Amber Louise; *b* 1976

4 *Olympia Jubliee; *b* 1977

Sir NICHOLAS *m* 4th 1983 *Eugenie Marie Alicia, est dau of William Thomas McWeeney, and has:

2 +Nicholas Alexander David; *b* 1985

Lineage: EDMUND NUTTALL, of Bury, Lancs; had:

JAMES NUTTALL, of Elmfield, Ashton-on-Mersey, Cheshire; *b* 26 July 1843; *m* 1865 Alice Mary (*d* 5 July 1922), dau of John Grimshaw, and had:

1 EDMUND (Sir), **1st Bt**

2 James; *b* 14 Aug 1877; *educ* Uppingham and Manchester U; *m* 11 June 1902 Beatrice, 4th dau of William Goulden Thompson, and had, with three daus:

  (1) Norman; *b* 12 March 1907; Rifle Bde WW II; *m* 29 Dec 1945 *Monica, dau of Henry Paulyn Gillow, of Bowden, Cheshire, and had:

    1a James Anthony; *b* 10 Oct 1946; *k* in a car crash 196–

    2a *Simon Dominic; *b* 7 May 1958

    1a *Rosemary; *b* 28 July 1948

  (2) *George Geoffrey; *b* 14 June 1908; *m* 15 June 1933 *Mary Browne and has issue

The est son,

Sir Edmund Nuttall, 1st Bt (UK), so *cr* 22 June 1922; *b* 29 May 1870; AMInstCE, head Nuttall & Co, civil engrs and contractors, of Manchester; *m* 8 Jan 1895 Ethel Christine (*d* 30 March 1958), 2nd dau of Rev Frederick Lillington, and had:

1 James Frederick; *b* 30 Sept 1895; *d* 25 Oct 1897

2 EDMUND KEITH (Sir), **2nd Bt**

3 Clive; *b* 5 Oct 1906; *m* 3 Dec 1931 *Eileen Daphne Elizabeth, only dau of Lt-Col Horatio Douglas Russell, DSO, of Woodlands, Wootton Bridge, IoW, and *d* 31 March 1936, leaving:

(1) +Clive Patrick; *b* 5 Sept 1933

Sir EDMUND *d* 11 Oct 1923; his er surv son,

Sir Edmund Keith Nuttall, 2nd Bt; *b* 27 March 1901; Lt-Col RE WW II (despatches); *m* 30 Sept 1925 Gytha Primrose Harrison (*m* 2nd 21 May 1942 Lt-Col (Alexander William) Edward Kirkpatrick, RE, yr s of Sir Cyril Reginald Sutton Kirkpatrick, TD; *d* 6 Sept 1967), est dau of Sydney Harrison Burgess, of Bowden, and *das* 31 Aug 1941, leaving:

Sir NICHOLAS KEITH LILLINGTON NUTTALL, **3rd and present Bt**

NUTTING

Arms: Chevronny of six gu. and vert three gryphons segreant or, on a chief of the last as many nut branches slipped ppr. **Crest:** A demi-gryphon segreant, enclosed between two nut branches ppr. **Motto:** *Mors potior macula* ('Death rather than a blot [on the family escutcheon]'). **Creation:** Bt. (UK) 12 Jan 1903.

SIR (HAROLD) ANTHONY NUTTING, 3RD BT, of St Helen's, Co Dublin, PC (1954) [The Rt Hon Sir Anthony Nutting Bt, 7 Ashchurch Park Villas, London W12]; *b* 11 Jan 1920; *s f* 1972; *educ* Eton and Trin Coll Cambridge; Leics Yeo WW II (invalided out 1940), For Serv France, Spain and Italy 1941–45, MP (C) Melton July 1945–Nov 1956, Jt Parly U-Sec For Affrs Oct 1951–Oct 1954, Min State For Affrs Oct 1954–Oct 1956, Leader UK Delegn UN and UN Disarmament Commn 1954–56, chm: YC and U Movement 1946, Nat Union of C Assocs 1949–1950, Exec Ctee Nat Union 1951, C Overseas Bureau and Nat Exec Ctee C Party 1951–52, special writer *New York Herald Tribune* 1957–58, author: *I Saw For Myself* (1958), *Disarmament* (1959), *Europe Will Not Wait* (1960), *Lawrence of Arabia* (1961), *The Arabs* (1964), *Gordon, Martyr and Misfit* (1966), *No End of a Lesson, The Story of Suez* (1967), *Scramble for Africa* (1970), *Nasser* (1972); *m* 1st 6 Aug 1941 (*divorce* 1959) Gillian Leonora, dau of Edward Joliffe Strutt (*see* RAYLEIGH, B), and has:

1 +JOHN GRENFELL [John Nutting Esq QC, Chicheley Hall, Newport Pagnell, Bucks MK16 9JJ; K3 Albany, Piccadilly, London W1V 9RQ]; *b* 28 Aug 1942; *educ* Eton and McGill U Canada (BA 1964); barrister Middle Temple 1968; Bencher 1991, memb Senate Inns of Court and Bar 1976–80 and 1986–87; V-Chm Criminal Bar Assoc 1995–97; memb Ld Chllr's Advsy Ctee Legal Educn and Conduct 1997, 1st Sr Treasury Counsel 1993–95, Judge Cts of Appeal Jersey and Guernsey 1995–, chm Young Bar 1978–79, Jr and Sr Treasury Counsel Central Criminal Ct 1981–93, Recorder Crown Ct 1986; *m* 4 Dec 1973 *Diane, widow of 2nd Earl Beatty (*qv*) and dau of John Blundell, of Hayling Island, Hants, and step-dau of Capt Duncan Kirk, of Sheaves Farm, Coxwood, Sussex, and has:

(1) +James Edward Sebastian; *b* 12 Jan 1977

(2) *Victoria Emily; *b* 27 Jan 1975

2 +David Anthony, DL (Essex) [David Nutting Esq DL, Newhouse, Terling, Chelmsford, Essex CM3 2QS]; *b* 13 Sept 1944; *educ* Eton and Trin Coll Cambridge (BA 1966); *m* 25 April 1974 *Tessa Anne, only dau of Sir Nigel John Mordaunt, 13th Bt (*qv*), and has:

(1) *Belinda; *b* 18 Aug 1975

(2) *Serena; *b* 24 Nov 1977

(3) *Alexandra; *b* 27 Dec 1978

3 *Zara Nina; *b* 4 Feb 1947; *m* 20 April 1966 (*divorce* 1970) Martin Guy Stephenson, 2nd s of Augustus William Stephenson, of Saxbys Mead, Cowden, Kent, and Mrs (Mary) Gloria Congreve, only child of Maj William La Touche Congreve, VC, DSO, MC, Rifle Bde (*see* HAWARDEN, V), and has:

(1) *Katya; *b* 14 Jan 1967

Sir ANTHONY *m* 2nd 27 May 1961 Anne Gunning (*d* 1990), dau of Arnold Barthrop Parker, of Cuckfield, Sussex, and Mrs Tudor Fitzjohn; *m* 3rd 1991 *Margarita, dau of Carlos Sanchez, of Havana

Lineage: EDWARD NUTTING, of Colchester, Essex; had:

JOHN NUTTING, of Bellevue, Redland, Bristol; *b* 21 Aug 1815; *m* 29 Dec 1846 Eliza, yst dau of Peter Bull, and *d* 3 April 1864, having had:

1 Henry Edward; *b* 12 March 1848; *m* 21 Jan 1874 Frances Elizabeth (*d* 15 May 1937), est dau of John Stedman, of Hampton Lodge, Clifton, and *d* 10 April 1933

2 JOHN GARDINER (Sir), **1st Bt**

3 Frederick George; *b* 21 May 1858

1 Eliza Jane; *m* 1st 5 Dec 1867 Edward Frederick Burke (*dsp* April 1887); *m* 2nd May 1888 Capt Henry Wyatt

JOHN NUTTING's 2nd s,

Sir John Gardiner Nutting, 1st Bt (UK), so *cr* 12 Jan 1903, of St Helen's, Booterstown, Co Dublin, JP, DL Co Dublin; High Sheriff 1895–96; *b* 24 July 1852; *m* 2 Jan 1879 Mary Stansmore (*d* 7 Feb 1929), dau of Restel Ratsey Bevis, of Manor Hill, Claughton, Cheshire, and had:

1 HAROLD STANSMORE (Sir), **2nd Bt**

2 John Godfrey Stansmore; *b* 13 April 1884; *d* 7 March 1925

3 Arthur Ronald Stansmore, OBE (1942), MC; *b* 3 March 1888; *educ* Eton and Trin Hall Cambridge (BA 1910); Capt Irish Gds WW I (despatches); *m* 1st 18 Sept 1912 (*divorce* 1932) Edith Allen (*d* 1953), dau of Walter Brooks, of New York; *m* 2nd 8 Nov 1932 *Patricia Elizabeth [Mrs Arthur Nutting, Stable Cottage, North Breache, Ewhurst, Surrey GU6 7SN], dau of Henry R Jameson, of Drumleck, Bally, Co Dublin, and *d* 23 March 1964, leaving:

(1) +Peter Robert, JP (Inner Lond) [Peter Nutting Esq JP, North Breache Manor, Ewhurst, Surrey GU6 7SN; 103 More Close, St Paul's Close, London W14]; *b* 22 Oct 1935; *educ* Eton; late Lt Irish Gds, past chm Edward & John Burke Ltd, merchant banker, chm N Bentley Gp and N Bentley Securities 1977; *m* 31 March 1965 *Cecilia Hester Marie-Louise Constance, est dau of Maj Cosmo Rex Ivor Russell (*see* AMPTHILL, B), and has:

1a +William Frederick; *b* 19 June 1968

2a +Rupert Edward; *b* 1971

1a *Amanda Charlotte; *b* 25 May 1966; *m* 1991 *James Edward Thornton, est s of Michael Thornton, of Ringwood, Hants

(2) +Nicholas Ronald [Nicholas Nutting Esq, Yard Farm, Ewhurst, Surrey GU6 7SN]; *b* 8 July 1937; *educ* Eton; late Lt Irish Gds, Jt MFH Seavington 1964–75, Jt MFH Chiddingfold, Leconfield and Cowdray 1991–, racehorse trainer under Nat Hunt rules 1968–; *m* 1st 29 March 1962 Caroline Elsie Houghton, only dau of Brig F W Houghton-Beckford, RA, of Vancouver, and has:

1a *(Ann) Olivia; *b* 20 Aug 1963; *m* 1991 *Rupert Hew Williams Barrington (*see* BARRINGTON, Bt)

2a *Sarah Caroline; *b* 24 Jan 1965; *m* 1991 *Sean Eugene John Martin McDonald, er s of John McDonald, of Newry, Co Down

(2) (cont.) Nicholas Nutting *m* 2nd 4 Jan 1977 *Annette Moira, dau of Percy Charles Briscoe by Mrs M E St J Barne, of Sotterley Hall, Beccles, Suffolk

1 Dorothy Stansmore; *m* 10 Dec 1910 Lt-Col Arthur Seymour Toogood, Roy Warwicks Regt, only s of Col — Toogood, RA, and *d* 11 May 1953, leaving issue

2 Mary Stansmore; *d* unm 1 June 1963

Sir JOHN *d* 18 Feb 1918; his est s,

Sir Harold Stansmore Nutting, 2nd Bt, DL (Leics 1931); High Sheriff 1929; *b* 14 Aug 1882; *educ* Eton and Trin Coll Cambridge; ADC to Govr-Gen Australia 1911–13, Capt 17th Lancers WW I (wounded), Quorn: Jt MFH 1930 and MFH 1932, MFH Meynell, Lt-Col cmdg 6th Leics Bn HG WW II; *m* 6 Aug 1913 Enid Hester Nina (*d* 7 July 1961), yr dau of Francis Berry Homan-Mulock, of Bellair, King's Co, Ireland, and *d* 1 May 1972, having had:

1 John Victor Francis; *b* 10 June 1914 (HRH PRINCESS HELENA VICTORIA stood sponsor); *educ* Eton and RMC Sandhurst; Capt Roy Scots Greys WW II; *ka* 19 Nov 1940

2 Edward Christian Frederick; *b* 9 Sept 1917 (HRH PRINCESS CHRISTIAN stood sponsor); *educ* Eton and RMC Sandhurst; Capt RHG WW II; *m* 2 Sept 1939, as her 1st w, Lady Rosemary Alexandra Eliot (*d* 20 April 1963), er dau of 6th Earl of Saint Germans (*qv*), and was *ka* Middle East Jan 1943, leaving:

(1) Davina Rosemary Enid; *b* 8 Aug 1940; *m* 29 May 1960 (*divorce*) John Martin Brenthall Cope, LLB, yst s of G V Cope, of Palmerston N, NZ, and *d* in a car crash 6 Aug 1976, having had:

1a Jonathon Edric; *b* 1961; *d* with his mother 6 Aug 1976

1a *Samantha Mary; *b* 23 Sept 1963

3 Sir (HAROLD) ANTHONY NUTTING, **3rd and present Bt**

OAKELEY

Arms: Arg. on a fess between three crescents gu. as many fleur-de-lys or. **Crest:** A dexter arm embowed in armour ppr., charged with two fleur-de-lys or., each in a crescent gu., in the hand a scimitar also ppr., pommel and hilt gold. **Motto:** *Non timeo, sed caveo* ('I fear not, but am cautious'). **Creation:** Bt. (GB) 5 June 1790.

SIR JOHN DIGBY ATHOLL OAKELEY, 8TH BT, of Shrewsbury [Sir John Oakeley Bt, 10 Bursledon Heights, Long Lane, Bursledon, Hants SO31 8DB]; *b* 27 Nov 1932; *s* f 1987; *educ* privately; md Miller and Whitworth 1972–81, Freedom Yachts 1981–88, manager Dehler Yachts UK 1988–, twice represented UK yachting Olympic Games, author: *Winning* (1968), *Sailing Manual* (1980), *Downwind Sailing* (1981); *m* 16 March 1958 *Maureen Frances, dau of John Cox, of Hamble, Hants, and has:

1 +ROBERT JOHN ATHOLL; *b* 13 Aug 1963; *m* 8 July 1989 *Catherine Amanda, dau of William Knowles, FRCS, and has:

   (1) +William Robert Atholl; *b* 13 Oct 1995

   (1) *Olivia Kate; *b* 15 April 1993

1 *Marina Anne; *b* 28 Jan 1961; *educ* Southampton U (LLM, BA); *m* 14 Oct 1994 *Capt Robert E Gordon, s of Frank Gordon and Mrs Pamela Davies, of Vancouver, and has:

   (1) *Conrad James; *b* 8 March 1991

   (1) *Rebecca Elise; *b* 14 Dec 1993

Lineage: ROGER OCKLEY, of Ockley, Salop, had:

WILLIAM; had:

JENKIN de OKELEY; living 1430; had:

ROGER; had:

JOHN OKELEY; *m* Johan, dau and coheir of William ap Reynald ap Griffith Vachan, of Colbach, and had an est s:

WILLIAM OKELEY, of Okeley; *m* Ellen, dau of Mason of the Castell, and had:

ROWLAND OKELEY, of Okeley; *m* — Hotchkiss, of Lydbury North, Salop, and had:

JOHN OKELEY, of Okeley; *m* the widow of Humphrey Baker and dau of Raff Marston, of Wolston, and had an est s:

ROWLAND OAKELEY, of Okeley; *b c* 1550; *m* Mary (*d* 14 Feb 1629), dau of John Crowther, of Bedstone, and *d* 28 Oct 1622, leaving an est s:

RICHARD OAKELEY, of Okeley; MP Bishop's Castle 1623, royalist Civil War; *m* 1st Mary Combes and *d* 1658, leaving:

WILLIAM OAKELEY, of Okeley; MP Bishop's Castle, High Sheriff Salop 1660; *m* 1st Mary (*dsp*), dau of Walter Waring; *m* 2nd Barbara, dau of John Walcot, of Walcot, Salop, and had, with two er sons (Richard, of Oakeley, ancestor of the OAKELEYs of Oakeley; John, of the Middle Temple, *d* unm):

WILLIAM OAKELEY; *b* 22 Aug 1684; *m* Catherine (*d* 28 Sept 1777), dau of Walter Moseley, of the Mere, Staffs, and *d* 1750, having:

1 William (Rev); Rector Forton, Staffs, Vicar Holy Cross, Salop; *m* 13 April 1749 Christian (*d* 1790), dau and coheir of Sir Patrick Strachan, of Glenkindle Castle, Aberdeenshire, and *d* 1803, leaving, with a dau:

   (1) William; *b* 1750; *m* Margaret, dau and heiress of Evan Gryffydd, of Plas Tan-y-Bwlch, Merioneths, and *d* 1811, leaving an only s:

      1a William Gryffydd, of Plas Tan-y-Bwlch

   (2) **Sir Charles Oakeley, 1st Bt** (GB), so *cr* 5 June 1790 for servs in India; *b* 27 Feb 1751; Hon DCL Oxon, Govr Madras 1790; *m* 19 Oct 1777 Helena (*d* 19 Feb 1839), only dau of Robert Beatson, of Kilrie, Fife, and *d* 7 Sept 1826, having had, with a dau (*d* unm):

      1a **Sir Charles Oakeley, 2nd Bt**; *b* Sept 1778; Dip Serv: Sec Legn Bavaria, Sweden and USA; *m* 20 March 1820 Charlotte Françoise Augusta Gisberte Ramadier, Baroness de Lormet (*d* 2 Oct 1850), only child of Baron Ramadier de Lormet, Col 32nd Regt of Chasseurs and n of the Marquis de la Tour Maubourg, French Amb UK 1819, and *dspm* 30 June 1829, leaving:

1b Helena Sarah Charlotte; *m* 30 Aug 1838 her 1st cousin William Herbert Wodehouse, DL, of Woolmers Park, Herts, and *d* 3 April 1919, leaving issue. He *d* 10 Aug 1903

2b Augusta; *m* 1st 19 March 1846 Henry Hugh O'Donel Clayton, 2nd s of Sir William Clayton, 5th Bt (*qv*), and had issue; *m* 2nd 20 Oct 1863 Maj Robert George Manley, 6th Dragoon Gds, and *d* 15 Nov 1879

3b Georgina; *m* 10 Nov 1852 Alexander Dennistoun, of Glasgow, and *d* 16 June 1914, leaving issue. He *d* 29 Aug 1893

2a Henry; *b* 6 Dec 1787; Judge Moorsheadabad, Bengal; *m* Laura, dau of Col — Ravier, Govr Chandernagore, and *dsp* 3 May 1826

3a HERBERT (Sir), **3rd Bt**

4a Edward; *b* 9 Nov 1796; *d* 8 Dec 1870

5a William, of Glanwilliam, Merionethshire; *b* 12 May 1798; *m* 25 Oct 1827 Mary Maria, only dau of Col Sir Edward Miles, CB, and *d* 11 Dec 1834, leaving:

   1b William Edward, of Plas Tan-y-Bwlch and Cliffe House, Atherstone, Warwicks, JP, DL Merioneths; *b* 1 Aug 1828; *m* 10 April 1860 Hon Mary Russell (*d* 13 Sept 1914), yr dau of Sophia, Baroness De Clifford in her own right (*qv*), and *d* 1 Feb 1912, leaving:

      1c Edward De Clifford William; *b* Nov 1864; Lt Leics Yeo Cav; *d* 30 March 1919

      1c Mary Caroline; *b* 14 Nov 1865; DJStJ; *m* 29 April 1893 William Frederick Inge, of Thorpe Constantine, Staffs, and *d* 20 Nov 1961, leaving issue. He *d* 4 Feb 1903

6a Frederick; *b* 5 Sept 1802; Fell Balliol Coll Oxford, RC Canon St George's Westminster; *d* 29 Jan 1880

1a Henrietta; *m* 9 May 1814 J Mott, of The Close, Lichfield, and *d* 25 Oct 1868, having had issue

2a Georgina; *m* 1804 R Kynaston and had issue

3a Louisa; *m* 1806 George Reid and had issue

4a Amelia; *m* 3 Feb 1812 Chappel Wodehouse, of Eastville, Lincs, only s of Very Rev Chappel Wodehouse, DD, Dean Lichfield, and *d* 5 Sept 1878, leaving issue. He *d* Feb 1815

The 2nd Bt's bro,

Rev Sir Herbert Oakeley, 3rd Bt; *b* 10 Feb 1791; Co-Dean Bocking, Archdeacon Colchester, Preb St Paul's; *m* 5 June 1826 Atholl Keturah (*d* 26 Jan 1844), 2nd dau of Rev Lord Charles Murray-Aynsley (*see* ATHOLL, D), and had, with two daus (*d* unm):

1 CHARLES WILLIAM ATHOLL (Sir), **4th Bt**

2 Herbert Stanley (Sir); *b* 22 July 1830; MA, MusD Oxon, Dublin, St Andrews, Edin and Adelaide, DCL, LLD Aberdeen, Edin and Glasgow, hon memb Musical Acads Rome and Philharmonic Bologna, V-Pres Trin Coll, memb Philharmonic London, Prof Music Edin U, Hon Composer to HM in Scotland; *d* unm 26 Oct 1903

3 (Henry) Evelyn (Sir); *b* 23 Nov 1833; MA, Fell and sr maths lecturer Jesus Coll Cambridge, Ch Inspr training colls 1885–99; *m* 6 Sept 1862 Caroline Howley Turner (*d* 21 Jan 1925), dau of William Hallows Belli, Bengal CS, and *d* 21 Dec 1915, having had, with a s (*d* young):

   (1) Alice Keturah; *b* 27 Sept 1864; *m* 22 May 1890 Arthur Godfrey Roby, KC, barrister, s of Henry John Roby, LLD, of Lancrigg, Grasmere, and *dsp* 11 Feb 1934. He *d* 15 April 1944

   (2) Hilda Diana; *b* 12 Oct 1867; MA Oxon and McGill, DLitt Lond; Reader Philosophy Lond, Warden King's Coll for Women London, Passmore Edwards Settlement and Roy Victoria Coll (McGill U) Montreal, writer; *d* unm 7 Oct 1950

   (3) Caroline Atholl; *b* 6 Jan 1872; *m* 10 Aug 1898 David Arthur Fitzgerald Vesey, OBE, barrister, Assist Legal Advsr Bd Educn, s of Ven Archdeacon F G Vesey, of Huntingdon, and *d* 17 Dec 1928, leaving issue

   (4) Marion Adela; *b* 4 June 1875; *m* 16 Jan 1907 George Murray Wilson, JP, of Dale End, Grasmere, and had issue. He *d* 29 May 1924

4 Edward Murray; *b* 16 May 1840; *educ* Trin Coll Cambridge (BA); house master Clifton, composer for organ; *m* 22 Jan 1884 Emily Frances (*d* 29 May 1911), yst dau of Richard Trotter, JP, DL, 10th of Mortonhall, Midlothian, and *d* 8 Nov 1927, leaving:

   (1) Edward Richard; *b* 18 Nov 1887; *d* 15 Sept 1919

   (1) Charlotte Mary; *b* 15 Dec 1889; *d* unm 8 Aug 1973

1 Charlotte Mary Atholl; *m* 8 Feb 1849 Hon Francis Charles Drummond, 4th s of 8th Viscount Strathallan (*see* PERTH, E), and *d* 13 June 1918

Sir HERBERT *d* 27 March 1845; his est s,

Sir Charles William Atholl Oakeley, 4th Bt; *b* 25 Oct 1828; Capt Bengal Cav; *m* 1st 16 May 1860 Ellen (*d* 20 June 1895), only child of John Meeson Parsons, of Angley Park, Kent, and had issue; *m* 2nd 16 Sept 1896 Elizabeth (*d* 26 Nov 1942), widow of Hamilton Goodall and dau of Henry W Tuson, and *d* 2 Nov 1915, leaving by his 1st w:

1 **Sir Charles John Oakeley, 5th Bt**, JP Kent; *b* 6 May 1862; *educ* Winchester; Capt 4th Bn Queen's Own (Roy W Kent Regt); *m* 1st 13 Aug 1889 Emily (*d* 21 Oct 1932), yr dau of Col Andrew Green, Rifle Bde, and had:

   (1) **Sir Charles Richard Andrew Oakeley, 6th Bt**, JP Kent; *b* 14 Aug 1900; *educ* Eton and Trin Coll Cambridge; proprietor Oakeley, Vaughan & Co, of Lloyd's; *m* 1st 10 Sept 1924 (*divorce* 1932) Audrey Fairless Dampier, est dau of Capt Vivian Trestrail Dampier Palmer, OBE, of Heronden Hall, Tenterden, Kent; *m* 2nd 29 June 1948 (*divorce* 1952) Marina, er dau of Basil Bessel; *m* 3rd 25 Oct 1957 Anne Marie, formerly w of Jack Drummond Rudd, previously widow of Terence McKenna, of Etretat, France, and *dsp* 22 Nov 1959

   (1) Ellen Beatrice; *b* 16 Jan 1891; *m* 1st 12 Feb 1915 Capt Guy William Hopton, Berks Regt (*ka* 28 July 1915), er s of Lt-Gen. Sir Edward Hopton, KCB; *m* 2nd 15 June 1922 Maj Loraine Macgregor Kerr, MC, s of Col John Macgregor Kerr, Madras Cav, and *d* 1967, leaving issue. He *d* 1957

   (2) Emily Charlotte Eileen, MBE (1962); *b* 28 Jan 1896; *m* 31 Dec 1921 Wilfrid Haig Loyd (*d* 17 Sept 1971), yst s of Archie Kirkman Loyd, KC, DL, and had:

1a *Peter Haig [Peter Lloyd Esq, 12 Meadway, London NW11 7JS]; *b* 9 Oct 1922; *educ* Eton; Capt RM; *m* 1st 1950 (*divorce* 1957) Suzanne, only child of Eric McLeod Duncan, and has had:

  1b *William Haig; *b* 6 June 1955

  1b *Julie Caroline; *b* 1952

  2b Penelope; *b* and *d* 8 May 1954

1a (cont.) Peter Loyd *m* 2nd 1961 *Rosemary Joan, er dau of Dr John Moir, and by her has:

  2b *Anthony Simon Haig; *b* 1963

2a *Geoffrey Haig MBE [Geoffrey Loyd Esq MBE, Remenham House, Ocle Pychard, Herefs HR1 3RB]; *b* 17 June 1926; *educ* Eton; *m* 1st 1948 (*divorce* 1967) Patricia Mary, dau of John Eric Maclean, and has:

  1b *Martin Andrew Haig; *b* 1949

  2b *Jeremy Charles Haig; *b* 1954

2a (cont.) Geoffrey Loyd *m* 2nd 1 March 1968 *Dawn, only child of Maj Robert Douglas Baird, MC (*see* BAIRD, Bt, of Newbyth)

3a *Andrew Haig; *b* 12 Aug 1934

1a *Denise Eileen Charlotte [The Rt Hon The Lady Saint Oswald, Nostell Priory, Wakefield, Yorks WJ4 1QE]; *b* 15 Nov 1928; *m* 10 July 1954 *5th Baron Saint Oswald (*qv*) and has issue

1 (cont.) **Sir Charles** *m* 2nd 20 Jan 1934 Ida Margaret Elena, yr dau of Col John Macgregor Kerr, Madras Cav, and *d* 20 July 1938

2 Edward Francis; *b* 29 May 1870; *educ* Clifton and RMC Sandhurst; Maj S Lancs Regt Boer War 1899–1902 (despatches) and WW I (despatches); *m* 26 May 1899 Everilde Anne (*d* 20 April 1968 aged 90), dau of Henry Beaumont, of Grantham (*see* ALLENDALE, V), and *d* 18 Feb 1954, leaving:

  (1) (EDWARD) ATHOLL (Sir), **7th Bt**

  (2) +Rowland Henry [Rowland Oakeley Esq, Gowerbank, Chipping Campden, Glos GL55 6BB]; *b* 28 Jan 1909; *educ* Clifton and New Coll Oxford (BA 1930); CRO 1959–65, Dip Serv 1966–69, Malayan CS 1931–58; *m* 28 Aug 1940 *Diana Margaret, dau of John Arthur Hayward, MD, FRCS, LRCP, and has:

    1a +Christopher Rowland [Christopher Oakeley Esq, 925 Short Street, Mt Helena, WA 6082, Australia]; *b* 22 July 1941; *educ* Winchester, Trin Coll Dublin (BA 1963) and U of W Australia (MBA); FRGS; *m* 19 Feb 1973 *Margaret, yr dau of Gilbert Carson, of Merredin, W Australia, and has:

      1b +Andrew Gilbert; *b* 1 Nov 1974

      2b +Timothy Christopher; *b* 30 Jan 1976

      3b +Paul David; *b* 25 Sept 1978

      1b *Caroline Rachel; *b* 1981

    2a +Henry Francis [Henry Oakeley Esq, 77 Copers Cope Rd, Beckenham, Kent BR3 1NR]; *b* 22 July 1941; *educ* Clifton and St Thomas's (MB, BS Lond 1965); FRCP Lond 1969, MRCPsych, FLS, late consultant psychiatrist St Thomas's Hosp; *m* 20 Jan 1968 (*divorce* 1988) Penelope Susan, BSc, MB, LRCP, MRCS, dau of Wilfred Barlow, BM, BCh, and has:

      1b +Matthew Thomas; *b* 15 Dec 1968; *educ* Dulwich and Trin Coll Oxford (MA); *m* 1993 *Maureen, dau of Joseph O'Hara

      2b +Edward James; *b* 29 March 1970; *educ* Dulwich and Bristol U (PhD); *m* 1991 *Sara, dau of Ryder Dines

      1b *Rachel Mary; *b* 1973; *educ* Sydenham GPDST and Aberystwyth U (MA)

    1a *Rosamond Margaret [Mrs Henry Warriner, Broadmoor Farm, Little Wolford, Warwicks CV36 5LZ]; *b* 4 Aug 1946; *educ* Walthamstow Hall and Sheffield U (BA Econ 1967); *m* 1 Feb 1969 *Henry David Warriner, s of Michael Warriner, of Weston Park, Warwicks, and has:

      1b *Michael Francis; *b* 23 Jan 1970

      2b *Timothy David; *b* 2 June 1974

      1b *Sarah Caroline; *b* 1971

  2a *Auriol Mary [Mrs Nicolas Chisholm, Headmaster's House, Yehudi Menuhin School, Cobham, Surrey KT11 3QQ]; *b* 4 Nov 1947; *educ* Walthamstow Hall, Elmhurst Ballet Sch, Roy Ballet Sch and Bishop Otter Coll; *m* 1977 *(Peter) Nicolas Chisholm

(1) *Rosemary [Mrs Mervyn Sheppard, Linden House, W Wittering, Sussex PO20 8QF]; *b* 1 Oct 1903; *educ* Headington Sch Oxford and Evendine Court Colwall; *m* 27 Jan 1940 Mervyn Cecil ffranck Sheppard, CMG, MBE, Malayan CS, est s of Canon James William ffrank Sheppard, MA, MRSL, and has:

  1a *Lavender Frances [Mrs John Buckland, Tandlaw Steading, Hawick, Roxburghshire TD9 7NY]; *b* 17 Oct 1941; *m* 1st 24 April 1962 (*divorce* 1981) Lt Richard Giles Saker, RN, er s of Maj Richard Kenneth Maitland Saker, CBE, and has:

    1b *Iain Richard Mark; *b* 1962; *educ* Radley; 1st Queen's Dragoon Gds; *m* 1992 *Kate, dau of Ian Macdonald, of Butleigh, Somerset, and has:

      1c *Harry Richard Mervyn; *b* 12 March 1995

      2c *Charley Arthur George; *b* 18 Oct 1997

    2b *Robin David Mervyn; *b* 1963; *educ* Radley

    1b *Emma-Rose Everilde; *b* 1960; *educ* Wychwood Sch Oxford and Eastbourne Coll; *m* 1988 (*divorce* 1994) Joseph Jasiewicz and has:

      1c *Charles Alexander Francis Beaumont; *b* 1992

    2b *Zoë Arabella Helena; *b* 1970; *educ* Oxford High Sch and Durham U (BA)

  1a (cont.) Mrs Lavender Saker *m* 2nd 1987 *(Francis) John Buckland (*see* LICHFIELD, E)

(2) *Mary; *b* 2 April 1913; *educ* St John's Bexhill-on-Sea, St Hilda's Coll Oxford (BA 1935, MA 1939); Headmistress Craighead Diocesan Sch Timaru NZ 1940–55, St Felix's Southwold 1958–78; *d* 18 Dec 1997

3 Herbert William; *b* 13 Oct 1874; *m* 16 July 1896 (*divorce* 1900) Cissy Lillian Emily, yr dau of Joseph William Moore, and *d* 15 May 1931, leaving:

  (1) Clifford Charles William Morland; *b* 25 July 1897

The 6th Bt's cousin,

Sir (Edward) Atholl Oakeley, 7th Bt, of Shrewsbury; *b* 31 May 1900; *educ* Clifton and RMC Sandhurst; Lt Oxford and Bucks LI, heavyweight wrestling champion GB 1930–35, Europe 1932–33; *m* 1st 5 May 1922 (*divorce* 1929) Ethyl

Felice, dau of Timothy O'Coffey; *m* 2nd 17 April 1930 (*divorce* 1951) Patricia Mabel Mary, dau of Lionel Henry Birtchnell, and had:

  1 Sir JOHN DIGBY ATHOLL OAKELEY, **8th and present Bt**

Sir Atholl *m* 3rd 3 April 1952 (*divorce* 1959) Doreen, dau of Stanley Frederick Wells; *m* 4th 9 Nov 1960 *Shirley [Shirley Lady Oakeley, Nomad, Lynton, Devon], only dau of Herbert W Church, and *d* 1987, having by her had:

  1 *Lorna Olivia Athole [Mrs Julian Roe, 6 Birbeck Way, Frettenham NR12 7LG]; *b* 1961; RGN; *m* 1987 *Julian Roe and has a s and dau

Sir Atholl also adopted (1958):

  *Michael; *b* 1945

OAKES

Arms: Or on a fess sa. between in chief an acorn slipped and leaved and in base a maple leaf ppr. three maple leaves of the field.
Crest: Issuant from a chaplet of roses gu. a demi-lion rampant or, grasping in the dexter paw an acorn slipped and leaved and leaved ppr.
Motto: *Per ardua* ('Through difficulties').
Creation: Bt. (UK) 17 July 1939.

SIR CHRISTOPHER OAKES, 3RD BT, of Nassau, in the Bahama Islands [Sir Christopher Oakes Bt, Site 15, Comp 18 RR7, Vernon, BC C1T 7Z3, Canada]; *b* 10 July 1949; *s* f 1966; *educ* Bredon, Tewkesbury and Georgia Mil Acad USA; *m* 1978 *Julie Dawn, dau of Donovan Franklin Cowan, of Regina, Canada, and has:

  1 +VICTOR; *b* 6 March 1983

  1 *Greta Anna Eunice; *b* 1979

Lineage: WILLIAM PITT OAKES, of Sangerville, Maine, USA; *m* Edith Nancy Lewis and had:

  1 Louis; *m* and *d* Nov 1964, leaving issue

  2 HARRY (Sir), **1st Bt**

  1 Jessie; *b* 30 Dec 1877; *m* 1st 10 May 1900 George Jay Babson (*d* 13 June 1921) and had issue; *m* 2nd 10 Feb 1925 Lincoln Paul Ellis, of Leesburg, Va., 2nd s of G R de Ellis y de Moncada, and *d* 20 Aug 1959

  2 Myrtice; *d* unm April 1957

  3 Gertrude; *d* unm 1936

The yr son,

  Sir Harry Oakes, 1st Bt (UK), so *cr* 27 July 1939; *b* 23 Dec 1874; *educ* Dover-Foxcroft Acad and Bowdoin Coll USA (BA 1896); Bahamas: JP and MLC, FRGS, Pres Lake Shore Gold Mine Ontario; *m* 30 June 1923 Eunice Myrtle, dau of Thomas McIntyre, of Sydney, NSW, and was found in bed murdered 12 July 1943; had:

  1 **Sir Sydney Oakes, 2nd Bt**; *b* 9 June 1927; *educ* St Andrew's Coll Aurora, Ontario; Gren Gds WW II 1944–45, Lt Roy Berks Regt 1945–48, Pres Sydeta Securities Ltd; *m* 22 June 1948 Greta, Hon Danish Consul Bahamas 1967–77 (*d* 14 Nov 1977), yr dau of Gunnar Victor Hartmann, and *d* following a car crash 8 Aug 1966, leaving:

    (1) Sir CHRISTOPHER OAKES, **3rd and present Bt**

    (1) *Felicity; *b* 21 July 1952; *m* 1987 *Steven Stuart Simpson

    (2) *Virginia Viveca [Mrs Gavin McKinney, PO Box 556330, Nassau, Bahamas]; *b* 24 March 1954; *m* 1982 *Gavin Andrew McKinney, s of J Andrew McKinney, and has:

      1a *Morgan Gavin; *b* 1983

      1a *Sydney Analia; *b* 1987

  2 William Pitt; *b* 11 Sept 1930; *m* 1952 Eunice Joyce (*m* 2nd March 1961 Robert David Gardiner), only dau of Alfred Bailey, and *dsp* 26 April 1958

  3 +Harry Philip [Harry Oakes Esq, PO Box N222, Nassau, Bahamas]; *b* 30 Aug 1932; *m* 3 March 1958 *Christine, only dau of Rudolf Botsch, of Hamburg, and has:

    (1) +Harry Newell; *b* 14 Dec 1958

    (2) +Philip Gale; *b* 23 Sept 1961

    (3) +Michael Lewis; *b* 7 July 1966

    (1) *Bianca Eunice; *b* 17 Nov 1963

  1 *Nancy [Mrs Patrick Tritton, Marsella 44, Mexico 6, DF Mexico]; *b* 17 May 1925; *m* 1st 1942 (*annulled* 1949) Marie-Alfred Fouquerreaux de Marigny, of

Mauritius; *m* 2nd 29 Dec 1952 (*divorce* 1956, resumed by Bahamian deed poll 1975 2nd husb's surname) Baron Ernst-Lyssardt von Hoyningen-Huene, 2nd s of Baron Hermann von Hoyningen-Huene, of Munich, and by him has:

    (1) *Alexander George Lyssardt; *b* 17 Feb 1955

1 (cont.) Baroness Nancy von Hoyningen-Huene *m* 3rd 1 March 1962 Patrick Claude Henry Tritton (*see* TRITTON, Bt)

2 Shirley Lewis; *b* 10 April 1929; *educ* Vassar (AB 1951) and Yale (LLB 1954); *m* 8 April 1961 Allan Churchill Butler, only s of Dr Allan Macy Butler, of Boston and Martha's Vineyard

OAKSEY, TREVETHIN and

Arms: Per chevron arg. and gu. two crosses raguly in chief of the last and a lamb in base holding with the dexter forefoot a banner and staff all of the first, the banner charged with a cross couped az. **Crest:** A dragon's head erased sa. between two bugle horns counter embowed or. **Supporters:** Dexter, a Guernsey bull; sinister, a hart, both ppr. **Motto:** *Pur fel dur* ('Pure as steel'). **Creations:** B. (UK) (Trevethin) 24 Aug 1921 and (Oaksey) 13 Jan 1947.

THE 2ND BARON OAKSEY, of Oaksey, Co Wilts, and **4th Baron Trevethin**, of Blaengawney, Co Monmouth (John Geoffrey Tristram Lawrence, OBE (1985), JP (Wilts 1978)) [The Rt Hon The Lord Oaksey OBE JP, Hill Farm, Oaksey, Wilts SN16 9HS]; *b* 21 March 1929; *s f* 1971; *educ* Eton, New Coll Oxford (BA) and Yale U; P/O RAFVR, late Lt 9th Lancers, champion amateur Jockey under Nat Hunt Rules 1970–71 (ret 1975), racing correspondent *Sunday Telegraph* (1960–88), also as 'Marlborough' for *Daily Telegraph* (1957–94) and as 'Audax' for *Horse and Hound* (1959–88), TV commentator, dir HTV 1980–91; author: *The Mill Reef Story* (1974), co-author: *A History of Steeplechasing* (1967), *Oaksey on Racing* (1991); *m* 1st 21 May 1959 (*divorce* 1987) Victoria Mary, er dau of Maj John Dennistoun, MBE, of Antwick Stud Ho, Letcombe Regis, Berks; *m* 2nd 1988 *Mrs Rachel Frances Crocker, dau of Alan Hunter, and by his 1st w has:

1 +PATRICK JOHN TRISTRAM; *b* 29 June 1960; *m* 1987 *Lucinda H, est dau of Demetri Marchessini, of Belgravia, and Mrs Nicholas Peto, of Dean Manor, Charlbury, Oxon, and has:

    (1) +Oliver John Tristram; *b* 17 May 1990
    (1) *Calypso Helen; *b* 1987

1 *Sara Victoria [The Hon Mrs Bradstock, Mabberleys, E Garston, nr Newbury, Berks]; *b* 26 July 1961; *m* 1987 *Mark FitzHerbert Bradstock, est s of David Fitz-Herbert Bradstock, MC, of Clanville Lodge, Andover, Hants

Lineage: DAVID LAWRENCE, of Pontypool, Mon; surgn; had:

ALFRED TRISTRAM LAWRENCE, **1st Baron Trevethin**, of Blaengawney, Co Monmouth (UK), so cr 24 Aug 1921, PC (1921), JP, DL Mon; *b* 24 Nov 1843; ktd, High Court Judge 1904, Ld Ch Justice 1921–22; *m* 25 Aug 1875 Jessie Elizabeth (*d* 15 July 1931), dau of George Lawrence, JP, and *d* 3 Aug 1936, having had:

1 Alfred Clive, CBE (1918); *b* Oct 1878; barrister Middle Temple 1902, Slr Min Labour 1907–23, Procurator-Gen and Slr Treasury 1923, Order St Maurice and St Lazarus Italy; *m* 28 July 1924 Mildred Margaret (*m* 2nd 3 Jan 1929 1st Viscount Hailsham (*see* HAILSHAM OF ST MARYLEBONE, B) and *d* 9 Oct 1964), yr dau of Rev Edward Parker Dew, of Breamore, Hants, and *d* 13 March 1926, leaving:

    (1) *Domini Margaret [Mrs Arnold Morgan, Teddards, Filching, E Sussex BN26 5QA]; *b* 8 May 1925; *m* 1979 *Arnold Frank Morgan

2 CHARLES TREVOR LAWRENCE, **2nd Baron Trevethin**, DSO (1918), DL (Breconshire 1949); *b* 29 May 1879; *educ* Haileybury and New Coll Oxford; Lt-Col Roy Horse and Field Artillery WW I (despatches thrice, Order St Anne Russia 2nd Cl), formed LDV Breconshire 1940, Zone Cdr HG, WW II, Scout Commr Wales 1935–47, Commr Radnorshire 1947; *d* unm 25 June 1959

3 GEOFFREY LAWRENCE, **3rd Baron Trevethin** and **1st Baron Oaksey**, of Oaksey, Co Wilts (UK), so cr 13 Jan 1947, DSO (1918), PC (1944), JP (Wilts 1924); *b* 2 Dec 1880; *educ* Haileybury (Pres Cncl 1948) and New Coll Oxford (BA 1901), MA 1906, Hon Fell 1944, Hon DCL 1947); barrister Inner Temple 1906 (Bencher 1932), served WW I (despatches twice), cmded Herts Yeo Bde 1920–26, Counsel Jockey Club 1922–32, Recorder Oxford 1924–28, KC 1925, Attorney-Gen to HRH THE PRINCE OF WALES and memb Cncl Duchy Corn-

wall 1928–32, Commr Assize Oxford Circuit 1931, Col RA (TA), chm Wilts QS and Appeals Ctee to 1955, High Court Judge King's Bench 1932–44, ktd 1932, Ld Justice Appeal 1944–47, Ld Appeal in Ordinary 1947–57, Wilts: V-Lt 1949 (DL 1945–49), Br Memb and Pres Nuremberg Tbnl 1945–46, Pres English Guernsey Cattle Soc; *m* 22 Dec 1921 Marjorie Frances Alice, OBE (1941), TD, JP (Wilts 1946), Controller ATS (*d* 1984), yst dau of Cdr Charles Napier Robinson, RN, and *d* 28 Aug 1971, having had:

    (1) JOHN GEOFFREY TRISTRAM LAWRENCE, **2nd and present Baron Oaksey and 4th present Baron Trevethin**

    (1) *(Mary) Elizabeth [The Hon Lady Adams, 54 Sussex Sq, London W2; The Malt House, Ditchley, Oxon]; *b* 20 Nov 1922; Jr Cdr ATS 1940–46; *m* 29 May 1954 *Sir Philip George Doyne Adams, KCMG, s of George Basil Doyne Adams, MD, of The Warren Ho, Wotton-under-Edge, Glos, and has:

        1a *Geoffrey Doyne; *b* 11 June 1957; *m* 1985 *Anne Louise, yr dau of John Jennings, of Jersey
        2a *Justin Alexander; *b* 22 July 1961
        1a *Lucy Victoria; *b* 8 Sept 1955
        2a *Harriet Mary; *b* 4 July 1959

    (2) *(Enid) Rosamond [The Hon Lady Dundas, 55 Iverna Ct, London W8 6TS]; *b* 19 June 1924; Jr Cdr ATS 1943–46; *m* 28 Jan 1950 G/Capt Sir Hugh Spencer Lisle Dundas, CBE, DSO, DFC, RAF, and has issue (*see* ZETLAND, M)

    (3) (Anne) Jennifer; *b* 24 May 1926; ATS 1944–47; *m* 13 Oct 1951 *Lt-Col Frederick John Burnaby-Atkins, Black Watch [Lt-Col Frederick Burnaby-Atkins, 3 The Street, Oaksey, Wilts SN16 9TG], er s of John Burnaby-Atkins, of Halstead, Kent, and *d* 5 Feb 1995, leaving:

        1a *John Charles Graham; *b* 1961; *m* 1993 *Emma Elisabeth, dau of James Smith, of Forfar, and has:
           1b *Adam Frederick John; *b* 1996
        1a *Charlotte Elisabeth Cecily; *b* 1952; *m* 1980 *J Patrick Crawford, s of Sir (Robert) Stewart Crawford, GCMG, CVO, and has:
           1b *Mark Andrew Frederick; *b* 1990
           1b *Anna Mary Alice; *b* 1982
           2b *Jessie Susan Charlotte; *b* 1985
           3b *Harriet Rosamond; *b* 1988
        2a *Catherine; *b* 1954
        3a *Rosamond Louise; *b* 1957; *m* 1981 *Marc L J-M Weemaels, of Brussels, and has:
           1b *Anthony; *b* 1983
           2b *John; *b* 1985
           3b *David; *b* 1989

1 Enid Lilian; *b* 4 June 1904 Sir George Lewis Barstow, KCB, 2nd s of Henry Clements Barstow, of Hazelbush, York, and *d* 2 July 1970, leaving issue. He *d* 29 Jan 1966

OAKSHOTT

Arms: Per chevron az. and gu. in chief two arrows in saltire between as many branches of oak slipped and fructed or and in base a bear passant arg. **Crest:** In front of a mount vert thereon an oak tree ppr. fructed gold, the main stem transfixed by two arrows in fess, points to the dexter, also ppr., a bow fesswise or. **Motto:** *In quercu robur* ('In oak is strength'). **Creation:** Bt. (UK) 10 July 1959.

SIR ANTHONY HENDRIE OAKSHOTT, 2ND BT, of Bebington, Co Palatine of Chester [The Hon Sir Anthony Oakshott Bt, 1 High St, Fifield, Oxon OX7 6HL]; *b* 10 Oct 1929; *s f* 1975; *educ* Rugby; *m* 6 Aug 1965 (*divorce* 1981) Valerie Anne Doreen (*d* 1988), dau of Jack Vlasto, previously widow of Donald John Ross and formerly w of Michael de Pret-Roose

Lineage: THOMAS WILLIAM OAKSHOTT, of Derby House, Bebington, Cheshire, and Liverpool, JP; Mayor Liverpool; *m* 19 Aug 1858 Alice Eleanor (*d* 3 Nov 1913), dau of Thomas Hunter, and *d* 15 June 1910, leaving:

ARTHUR JOHN OAKSHOTT, of Merle Dene, Bidston, Cheshire, JP Liverpool; *b* 26 Dec 1861; *m* 18 Sept 1895 Elizabeth Strathearn (*d* 1963), dau of Matthew Leggat, of Ontario, and *d* 3 Nov 1917, leaving:

1 Thomas Arthur; *b* 4 Oct 1896; Lt-Col; *m* 2 Jan 1924 Barbara Kathleen, formerly *w* of Renie Patrick Monckton Hoffe-Miles and dau of Herbert Henry Hylton, and *dsp* 29 April 1968

2 **Sir Hendrie Dudley Oakshott, 1st Bt**, so *cr* 10 July 1959 and BARON OAKSHOTT, of Bebington, Co Palatine of Chester (LP), so *cr* 21 Aug 1964 (both UK), MBE (1943); *b* 8 Nov 1904; *educ* Rugby and Trin Coll Cambridge (BA 1926); Lt-Col WW II Middle East and Italy (despatches, invalided 1945), MP (C) Bebington 1950–64, PPS to: Min Supply and Assist Whip 1951–52, For Sec 1959–60 and Chllr Exchequer 1960–62, a Ld Commr Treasury 1952–55, Comptroller Household 1955–57 and Treasurer Household 1957–59 (Govt Whip); *m* 4 Jan 1928 Joan (*d* 1986), dau of Marsden Withington, of London and Buenos Aires, and *d* 1 Feb 1975, when the life Barony expired, leaving:

(1) Sir ANTHONY HENDRIE OAKSHOTT, **2nd and present Bt**

(2) +MICHAEL ARTHUR JOHN [The Hon Michael Oakshott, Kennels Cottage, Blackwood, Auldgirth, Dumfries DG2 0UA]; *b* 12 April 1932; heir presumptive; *educ* Rugby, *m* 1st 27 April 1957 Christina Rose Methuen (*d* 1985), dau of Thomas Banks, of Kenya, and has:

  1a +Thomas Hendrie; *b* 12 June 1959

  2a +Charles Michael [Charles Oakshott Esq, Fares Stables Ltd, Newsells Park, Barkway, Herts]; *b* 21 May 1961; *m* 1989 *Anne C, dau of William Stapleton, and has:

    1b +Patrick Charles; *b* 5 Oct 1997

    1b *Roseanne; *b* 25 March 1990

    2b *Alice; *b* 16 April 1993

  3a +Angus Withington [Angus Oakshott Esq, Flat 9, 21 Eccleston Sq, London SW1V 1NF]; *b* 25 Dec 1965; *m* 28 Feb 1997 *Sarah McKelwie

(2) (cont.) The Hon Michael Oakshott *m* 2nd 1988 *Mrs Helen Clare Jones, dau of Edward Ravell, of Woodhall Spa, Lincs

1 Catharine Macfarlane; *b* 3 Dec 1898; *m* 18 Sept 1929 Cyril Herbert Yeoward, of Overton Lodge, Ludlow, Salop, s of Lewis Herbert Yeoward, of Cheshire, and *d* 30 Aug 1967, leaving issue

2 Elizabeth Strathearn; *b* 9 May 1902; *d* 1934

3 Norah Alice; *b* 24 Dec 1906; *m* — Morland, of Kirkbean, Dumfriesshire

O'BRIEN

Arms: Arg. three lions passant-guardant per pale gu. and az. armed or, all within a bordure vert. **Crest:** From a castle arg. in flames a naked arm embowed, the hand grasping a sword all ppr. **Motto:** *Lamh laidir an nachtar* ('The strong hand uppermost'). **Creation:** Bt. (UK) 25 Sept 1849.

SIR TIMOTHY JOHN O'BRIEN, 7TH BT, of Merrion Square, Dublin, and Borris-in-Ossory, Queen's County; *b* 6 July 1958; *s gf* 1982; *educ* Millfield

Lineage: TIMOTHY O'BRIEN, of Co Tipperary; *m* —, dau of Timothy Madden, of Co Galway, and had:

Sir Timothy O'Brien, 1st Bt (UK), so *cr* 25 Sept 1849 on occasion of HM QUEEN VICTORIA's first visit to Ireland, JP, DL; *b* 1787; MP Cashel 1846–59, merchant Dublin, Ld Mayor Dublin 1844 and 1849; *m* Aug 1821 Catherine, 4th dau of Edward Murphy, of Flemingstown, Co Dublin, and *d* 3 Dec 1862, having had, with a dau (*d* unm):

1 **Sir Patrick O'Brien, 2nd Bt**, JP, DL; *b* 1823; barrister; MA; MP King's Co 1852–85; *m* 29 Aug 1866 Ida Sophia (*d* 12 May 1910), widow of Lt-Gen James Perry and dau of Cdr James Parlby, RN, and *dsp* 25 April 1895

2 Timothy; *m* 3 Sept 1860 Mary (*d* 10 Feb 1922), only dau of Andrew Carew O'Dwyer, of Orlagh, Templeogue, Co Dublin, and *d* 25 April 1869, leaving:

(1) **Sir Timothy Carew O'Brien, 3rd Bt**, JP, DL Co Cork; *b* 5 Nov 1861; *educ* Downside and New Inn Hall Oxford; Lt Derbys Yeo Cav, Hon Maj, Capt 5th Bn Roy Irish Fus, T/Maj Remount Service WW I (despatches); *m* 22 Sept 1885 Gundrede Annette Teresa (*d* 17 Dec 1952), dau of Sir Humphrey de Trafford, 2nd Bt (*qv*), and *d* 9 Dec 1948, having had:

  1a Timothy John Aloysius; *b* 21 June 1892; Lt RFA WW I (despatches); *ka* 7 Aug 1916

  2a **Sir Robert Rollo Gillespie O'Brien, 4th Bt**; *b* 9 June 1901; *educ* Oratory Sch; F/Lt RAFVR WW II; *m* 13 May 1925 Esther Ethel (Tessa), 2nd dau of

---

Norman Alfred Coghill, of Almington Hall, Market Drayton, and *dspm* 18 April 1952, leaving:

  1b *Patricia Mary Gabrielle [Mrs Patricia Chalwin, 45 Burntwood Grange Rd, London SW18 3JY]; *m* 1 Feb 1956 (*divorce* 1961) Walter William Burgoyne Chalwin, only s of W H Chalwin, and has:

    1c *Simon William Burgoyne [Simon Chalwin Esq, 77 Hendham Rd, London SW17 7DH]; *b* 1956; *m* 1983 *Teresa Mary Young

    1c *Nicola Clare [Mrs Richard Jones, 37 Lower Camden, Chislehurst, Kent]; *b* 1957; *m* 1st 1978 (*divorce* 1981) Nicholas George Mark Seymour (see HERTFORD, M); *m* 2nd 1981 *Richard Eric Champion Jones

  2b *Sheelagh Tessa Ursula; *m* 21 Nov 1954 *Caird Wentworth Gordon Wilson, yr s of Lt-Gen Sir Gordon Wilson, KCSI, CB, CBE, MC, and has:

    1c *Robert Caird; *b* 24 Sept 1955; *m* 1993 *Diana Rosemary, dau of David Lethbridge, of Hawkes Bay, NZ, and has:

      1d *Rebecca Frances; *b* 1994

      2d *Chloe Shaunagh; *b* 1996

    2c *Alexander Hugh Gordon [Alexander Wilson Esq, Ramsden Farm, Bethersden, Kent TN26 3JR]; *b* 18 Feb 1957; *m* 1982 *Susan Katharine, dau of Capt H R C Young, RN (ret), and has:

      1d *Philip Hugh Caird; *b* 1984

      2d *Angus Robert Gordon; *b* 1992

      1d *Miranda Frances Katharine; *b* 1986

  3b *Shaunagh Gundrede [Mrs John Addinsell, The Old Hall, Brilley, Whitney-on-Wye, Hereford]; *m* 1972 John Nares Addinsell (*d* 1991)

1a Sicele Julia Mary Annette; *d* 18 June 1931 following an air crash

2a Gundrede Mary Gwendoline; *m* 1 Sept 1947 Richard Forbes Russell and *dsp* 14 March 1971. He *d* 30 May 1960

3a Mariquita Winefride Aloysia; *m* 20 Oct 1915 Capt James Thirkell Price, MC, RFA (*ka* 21 April 1916), s of Edward Allen Price, and had:

  1b James Timothy Noel; *b* posthumously 24 Oct 1916; *educ* Ampleforth, RMA Woolwich and Coll of Ag; Capt RA WW II; *m* 13 March 1943 Hon Anne Margaret Younger, yr dau of 2nd Viscount Younger of Leckie (*qv*), and had issue

4a Ursula Mary Annette; *d* unm 12 March 1919

5a Eileen Mary Frances; *m* 3 Jan 1923 Brig Edward Thomas Arthur George Boylan, CBE, DSO, MC, RHA, of Hilltown, Co Meath, and had issue. He *d* 24 Sept 1959

6a Hilda Moira Clare; *d* unm 6 Sept 1916

7a Doreen Moira

8a Kathleen Moyra Teresa

(2) John George; *b* 10 Jan 1866; T/Capt RFA, Capt Roy Mon Engr Militia, Capt 4th KSLI; *m* 6 Jan 1891 Marion Dora (*d* 19 May 1917), only child of Judge William Henry Cooke, QC, Recorder Oxford, and *dsp* 15 Aug 1920

(3) Edmond Lyons; *b* 27 Nov 1868; *m* 26 April 1897 Audrey Townsend (*d* Jan 1957), dau of David Crawford, of New York, and *d* Aug 1948, leaving:

  1a **Sir John Edmond Noel O'Brien, 5th Bt**, MC (1940); *b* 23 Dec 1899; *educ* Oratory Sch and Pembroke Coll Oxford; Capt Gen List WW II HQ Staff 46 Div; *m* 1st 27 July 1928 (*divorce* 1940) Moira Violet (*d* 10 Jan 1970), est dau of Capt Robert Bingham Brassey (see BRASSEY OF APETHORPE, B); *m* 2nd 11 Sept 1940 Rosemary Brent, formerly *w* of Maj Eric Arthur Staniland, 8th King's Roy Irish Hus, and est dau of Edgar Grotrian (see GROTRIAN, Bt), and by her had:

    1b *Mary Clare [Mrs Frederick Pearson, 43 Finstock Rd, London W10 6LU]; *b* 31 July 1943; *m* 1st 27 Sept 1961 (*divorce* 1976) John Peter James Hare, only s of Henry John Goodson Hare, and has:

      1c +David John Brent [David Hare Esq, Iskeroon, Caherdaniel, Co Kerry, Ireland]; *b* 11 June 1963

      1c *Kerry-Jane [Mrs Stephen Martin, Bell House, Guiting Power, Glos GL54 5UP]; *b* 23 April 1966; *m* 1989 *Stephen Henry Martin, s of René Martin, and has:

        1d *Guy Henry; *b* 1997

        1d *Venetia Rose; *b* 1994

    1b (cont.) Mrs Mary Clare Hare *m* 2nd 1990 *Frederick Edward Pearson

  2a DAVID EDMOND (Sir), **6th Bt**

  3a Edmond Robert Richard; *b* 23 July 1904; RNVR WW II; *m* April 1938 Geraldine Ida (*d* following an accident 11 Oct 1940), formerly *w* of Hon Robert Power Trench, later 4th Baron Ashtown (*qv*), and dau of Sir Henry Foley Grey, 7th Bt (see LAMBERT, Bt), and *das* July 1940

  1a Audrey Mary Elizabeth; *m* 25 June 1925 Thomas Henderson Murray, MC, 7th Dragoon Gds, yr s of Sir John Murray, KCB, of Edinburgh, and *d* 25 Sept 1925

(1) Mariquita Justa; *d* unm 15 June 1950

3 John; Capt 30th Regt and 5th Fus; *d* Jan 1869

1 Kate; *m* 1860 Alexander Morphy, of Dundrum, Co Dublin, and *d* 5 Jan 1894. He *d* 1889

2 Ellen; *m* 19 Jan 1864 John V Cassidy, JP, of Parsonstown, and *d* 20 Dec 1899. He *d* 1898

Sir JOHN *d* 28 Sept 1969; his bro,

Sir David Edmond O'Brien, 6th Bt; *b* 19 Feb 1902; *m* 25 Aug 1927 Mary Alice, yst dau of Sir Henry Foley Grey, 7th Bt (see LAMBERT, Bt), and *d* 1982, having had:

1 John David; *b* 9 June 1928; *m* 5 July 1957 *Sheila Winifred, only child of Sir Charles Arland Maitland Freake, 4th and last Bt (see 1949 edn), and *d* 1980, leaving:

(1) Sir TIMOTHY JOHN O'BRIEN, **7th and present Bt**

(2) +JAMES PATRICK; *b* 22 Dec 1964; heir presumptive; *educ* Millfield

(1) *Doon Veronica; *b* 17 July 1959

(2) *Melanie Frances Ann; *b* 31 Oct 1961

2 Gerald Patrick; *b* 23 April 1930; *educ* Ampleforth; *m* 19 April 1960 *Frances Huband de Savoie [Mrs Gerald O'Brien, 30 Applegarth Rd, London W14], yst dau of Col William Thornton Huband Gregg, DSO, OBE, of Ballyknockane House, Clonmel, Co Tipperary, and *d* 1979, leaving:

(1) *Lyndall Jane; b 10 July 1961
(2) *Lucy Frances; b 9 June 1964
(3) *Rachel Shirin; b 11 Sept 1965
(4) *Deborah Susan; b 30 June 1969
1 *Audrey Mary [Mrs Andrew Dobrzynski, Brand Hall, Norton in Hales, Salop TF9 3PT]; b 21 Aug 1935; m 6 July 1963 *(Conrad) Andrew Roman Dobrzynski, s of Wenceslas Thaddeus Dobrzynski, and has:
(1) *Sophia Catherine; b 14 June 1966; m 11 Oct 1997 *Allan Hepworth, s of Robert Hepworth, of Macclesfield, Cheshire
(2) *Emma Natasha; b 1972

O'CATHAIN

Creation: B. (LP, UK) 1991.

THE BARONESS O'CATHAIN, of The Barbican in the City of London (Detta O'Cathain, OBE (1983)) [The Rt Hon The Baroness O'Cathain OBE, 121 Shakespeare Tower, Barbican, London EC2Y 8DR; Eglantine, Tower House Gdns, Arundel, W Sussex BN18 9RU]; b 3 Feb 1938; educ Laurel Hill, Limerick, and U Coll Dublin (BA); with Aer Lingus Dublin 1961–66; gp economist Tarmac 1966–69; ec advsr Rootes Motors 1969–62; Sr Economist Carrington Vyella 1972–73; ec advsr BL 1973–74; dir market planning Leyland Cars 1974–76; corporate planning exec Unigate 1976–81; Head Strategic Planning Milk Marketing Bd 1981–83 (dir and gen man 1984); md Milk Marketing 1985–88; Advsr on Ag Marketing MAFF 1979–83; dir: Midland Bank 1984–93, Channel 4 1985–86, Tesco 1985–, Sears 1987–94, BA 1993–, BET 1994–96, Thistle Hotels plc 1996–, Saur UK plc 1997–, SE Water 1997–, Mid Sussex Water 1997–; memb Cncl Industrial Soc 1987–92; md Barbican Centre 1990–95; FCIM 1987; FRSA 1986; m 1968 *William Ernest John Bishop

Lineage: CAOIMHGHIN O'CATHAIN; m Margaret — and had:

DETTA; cr a Baroness

O'CONNELL

Arms: Per fess arg. and vert a stag trippant ppr., between three trefoils slipped counterchanged. Crest: A stag's head erased arg. charged with a trefoil, slipped, vert. Motto: Cia'll agus neart ('Reason and strength'). Creation: Bt. (UK) 29 Oct 1869.

SIR MAURICE JAMES DONAGH MacCARTHY O'CONNELL, 7TH BT, of Lakeview, Killarney, Co Kerry, and of Ballybeggan, Tralee, Co Kerry [Sir Maurice O'Connell Bt, Lakeview House, Killarney, Co Kerry, Ireland]; b 10 June 1958; s f 1989; educ Ampleforth; m 1993 *Frances Susan, only dau of Clive Raleigh, of Hong Kong

Lineage: DANIEL O'CONNELL, of Darrynane Abbey, Co Kerry; m Mary O'Donoghue, dau of O'Donoghue Duff, of Anwys, Co Kerry, and had, with 19 other children:

1 Maurice ('Old Hunting Cap'), of Darrynane; educated his n Daniel at his own expense and eventually bequeathed him his estate, worth £1,000 p.a. in 1825 (some £30,000 p.a. in late-1990s terms); dsp

2 Daniel Charles, cr a Count by LOUIS XVI; b c 21 May 1745; Cadet Royal Suédois Inf Regt 1760, Assist-Adj c 1763, Adj Clare Regt Irish Bde c 1764, Brevet Lt-Col, Cross St Louis, Col Salm-Salm German Regt (in French Army), fought with French émigrés as Pte in Berchini's Hus 1792, Col 4th Regt of Irish Bde in British Army c 1794, Lt-Gen French Army c 1816; m 1796 Martha Gouraud, widow of Count de Bellevue and née Drouillard de Lamarre, and dsp 9 July 1833, leaving much of his estate to his n Daniel (see below)

3 Morgan, of Carhen House, Cahirciveen, Co Kerry; m Catherine, dau of John O'Mullane, of Whitechurch, Co Cork, and had, with another intermediate s:

(1) Daniel ('The Liberator'), of Darrinane; b 6 Aug 1775; educ English Coll St Omer and Douai, QC, MP Co Clare 1828 (forbidden to take seat in Parl),

1829–30, Waterford 1830–36, Dublin 1836 (unseated on petition), Kilkenny 1836, Cork 1841, Ld Mayor Dublin 1841; barrister Lincoln's Inn and Gray's Inn, called Irish Bar 1798; m 23 June 1802 his cousin Mary (d 31 Oct 1836), dau of Dr O'Connell, of Tralee, and d 15 May 1847, leaving four sons and three daus

(2) Maurice; educ English Coll St Omer and Douai

(3) Sir James O'Connell, 1st Bt (UK), so cr 29 Oct 1869; b 10 Jan 1786; m 31 March 1818 Jane (d 15 April 1867), dau of The (Charles) O'Donoghue of the Glens, and had:

1a MAURICE JAMES (Sir), 2nd Bt
2a Daniel James, of Grenagh, Kerry, JP; b 5 Oct 1823; High Sheriff 1868, barrister; m 25 June 1863 Frances Mary (d 16 June 1894), yst dau of Denis Shine Lawlor, JP, of Castlelough and Grenagh House, Co Kerry, and d 26 Feb 1888, having had:
  1b James Donal; b 8 Aug 1864; Lt Roy Irish Regt; m 27 Feb 1900 Mary Seraph Messner and dsp 21 Dec 1909
  2b Donal, JP Kerry; b 1 Sept 1867; m 18 Nov 1902 Frances Beatrice Wyndham (d 14 June 1934) and dsp 18 April 1950
  3b Maurice (Rev) (Brother Patrick of Grande Chartreuse); b 1 Sept 1875; d 19 Sept 1957
  4b Morgan Henry; b 28 Jan 1880; S African Constabulary; ka Boer War 3 Feb 1902
  5b (Conail) Geoffrey; b 31 Jan 1882; BL; m 1st 4 Sept 1913 Eleanor Vallely (d 8 Jan 1919); m 2nd 4 Aug 1922 Mary Dean, yst dau of J Irving Crowell, of Van Nuys, Calif, and d 28 July 1955
  6b Edward; b 11 Feb 1884; d 13 Feb 1887
  1b Isabel Maud, OBE; b 11 April 1866; m 23 April 1891 Capt Edmond O'Conor, JP, DL, of Charleville, Co Louth, and d 13 June 1926, leaving issue. He d 31 Aug 1932
  2b Eva; b 17 Oct 1871; d unm 25 Sept 1949
  3b Clare; b 16 Oct 1873; d unm 3 Aug 1918
  4b Mary Bernadette; b 21 Nov 1876; nun Sacred Heart; d 20 Jan 1958
  5b Dorothy; b 8 March 1888; nun; d 3 Dec 1931
3a Charles James; b 15 July 1828; d unm 27 Oct 1893
4a James; b 18 July 1832; d unm 1 Oct 1855
5a Morgan James; b 11 Oct 1833; Maj 1st Royals Crimea (medal and clasp, Sebastopol, Turkish medal, Medjidie 5th Cl) and China 1860 (medal and two clasps); d unm 2 Oct 1870

Sir JAMES d 28 July 1872; his est s,
Sir Maurice James O'Connell, 2nd Bt, JP, DL; b 31 Oct 1821; High Sheriff Co Kerry 1850; m 6 Jan 1855 Emily Clunes (d 23 Jan 1907), dau and coheir of R-Adml Sir Richard O'Conor, KCH, and d 15 Jan 1896, having had:
1 Maurice; b 24 July 1858; Lt 60th Foot S Africa 1880 (medal); ka S Africa 9 Feb 1881
2 Sir Daniel Ross O'Connell, 3rd Bt, JP, DL Co Kerry; High Sheriff 1891; b 18 Jan 1861; d unm 14 May 1905
3 MORGAN ROSS (Sir), 4th Bt
4 James Ross; b 28 Aug 1863; Maj KSLI, Govr Kordofan, Dongola Expdn 1896 (medal and five clasps), Sudan campaign 1898 (medal, 4th Cl Medjidie, 3rd Cl Osmanieh); d 25 Feb 1925
1 Ellen Mary; b 25 Nov 1855; m 19 April 1902 Lt-Gen Sir Charles Tucker, GCB, GCVO, and dsp 27 Dec 1945. He d 22 Dec 1935

The 3rd Bt's yr bro,
Sir Morgan Ross O'Connell, 4th Bt, JP Co Clare, JP, DL Co Kerry; High Sheriff 1907; b 20 July 1862; m 15 Sept 1884 Mary Pauline (d 19 Sept 1934), est dau of Lt-Col James Francis Hickie, JP, of Slevoir, Co Tipperary, and had, with a dau (d unm 1895):
1 MAURICE JAMES ARTHUR (Sir), 5th Bt
2 Donal Bernard, CBE (1943); b 3 June 1893; Capt RN, WWs I and II (cmded HMS Resource Feb 1940–Feb 1946), Kt SMO Malta, Br Museum 1951–58, MRIA, FRSAI, V-Pres Cork Hist and Arch Soc
3 Basil Morgan, JP (Penang 1938), (Singapore 1948); b 15 June 1900; Lt RN, Commr Kedah State Police 1936–38, Dir CID Malayan Union 1946–47, Dep Commr Singapore 1948, CID and Special Branch Malay 1949, KPM 1948, Cross Merit 1st Cl Order Malta 1958, Kt SMO Malta, FRSAI; m 1st 19 April 1935 Lucila Concha (d 15 June 1953), yr dau of Maj Henry Hugh Peter Deasy, 16th Lancers, of Cnoc na Faire, Carrigahorig, Ireland, and had (with two other children, d young):
  (1) +Maurice Hugh Ricardo Ross [Maurice O'Connell Esq, 12 Rostrevor Rd, Dublin 6, Ireland]; b 20 Oct 1936; educ Ampleforth, Peterhouse Cambridge (BA 1958, MA 1962) and Trin Coll Dublin (MEd, HDip Ed.), NUI (Dip Cat); memb Dublin City Cncl 1967–74, Seanad Eireann 1981–83, Nat Exec Fine Gael Party, Replacement Candidate European Parly Elections Dublin 1984; m 22 June 1961 *Ann Marie, est dau of Hugh Gillespie, of The Old Rectory, Kiltegan, Baltinglass, Co Wicklow, Supt Garda Siochana (ret), and has:
    1a +Carlos Donal John; b 21 July 1963; Irish Junior Decathlon Champion
    2a +Morgan Basil Peter; b 13 Aug 1965
    3a +Maurice William Hugh Rickard; b 24 Oct 1966
    4a +Ross Paul Francis; b 23 May 1968
    1a *Lucila Marie Valdemara Georgia; b 1962
    2a *Sarah Emily; b 1973
  (2) +Seamus Morgan Basil Ross; b 22 Nov 1941; educ Ampleforth and Trin Coll Dublin (BA 1963)
3 (cont.) Basil O'Connell m 2nd 7 May 1962 *Georgia Bard, widow of Mortimer Haldeman O'Connor, of Harrisburg, Pa., and dau of Dr Christopher Shearer, FACS, and d 1971
1 Lucila Emily; b 19 Aug 1885; LLA St Andrews, nun Sacred Heart; d 9 Feb 1970

Sir MORGAN d 27 April 1919; his est s,
Sir Maurice James Arthur O'Connell, 5th Bt, MC; b 24 Dec 1889; educ Trin Coll Dublin; Capt Roy Fus (City London Regt) WW I (despatches), Adj 5th Bn

1920, Kt SMO Malta; *m* 1 June 1920 Margaret Mary (*d* 27 Dec 1963), 2nd dau and coheir of Matthew John Purcell, of Burton Park, Buttevant, Co Cork, and had:
1 MORGAN DONAL CONAIL (Sir), **6th Bt**
2 *Joan Mary Lucilla Margaret [Mrs John Hickley, Birchdale, RD10, Waimate, S Canterbury, New Zealand]; *b* 1926; 2nd Offr WRNS 1947–53; *m* 12 Sept 1953 *Lt-Cdr John Allen Victor Hickley, RN, only s of Victor Allen Hickley, and has:
  (1) *Martin Maurice Victor; *b* 12 June 1957; *m* 1984 *Robyn Myrie, est dau of Douglas Williams Jenkins, of NZ, and has:
    1a *Cameron Douglas Victor; *b* 1988
    2a *Patrick Joseph Victor; *b* 1991
    1a *Joanna Louise; *b* 1985
  (1) *Grania Margaret Leslie; *b* 13 March 1959

Sir MAURICE *d* 15 Sept 1949; his only son,
  Sir Morgan Donal Conail O'Connell, 6th Bt; *b* 29 Jan 1923; *educ* Abbey Sch Fort Augustus; Roy Signals WW II; *m* 26 Sept 1953 *Elizabeth [Elizabeth Lady O'Connell, Lakeview House, Killarney, Co Kerry, Ireland], only child of Maj John MacCarthy-O'Leary, 2nd S Lancs Regt (BWV), of Coomlagane, Millstreet, Co Cork, and Lavenders, West Malling, Kent, and *d* 1989, leaving:
1 Sir MAURICE JAMES DONAGH MacCARTHY O'CONNELL, **7th and present Bt**
2 +JOHN MORGAN ROSS MacCARTHY; *b* 17 April 1960; heir presumptive; *educ* Ampleforth, Regent's Park Coll, Oxford (MA) and Guildhall Sch of Music (AGSM)
1 *Frances Mary Margaret MacCarthy [Mrs Roy Telling, Turnpike Cottage, London Rd, Blewbury, Oxon]; *b* 3 Oct 1954; *m* 1986 *Roy W Telling, only s of W Telling, of Wolverhampton, and has:
  (1) *Ross Morgan William; *b* 1989
2 *Susan Jane Anne MacCarthy; *b* 27 Oct 1956; *m* 1993 *Julian R Glasgow, yr s of Dr James Glasgow, of Rockland St Mary, Norwich
3 *Katherine Lucila Jean MacCarthy; *b* 5 May 1964
4 *Claire Helen Pauline MacCarthy; *b* 19 Feb 1969

OGILVY

Arms: Quarterly, 1st and 4th, argent a lion passant-guardant gules, gorged with an open crown and crowned with a close imperial one or (for OGILVY); 2nd and 3rd, argent an eagle displayed sable, beaked and membered gules (for RAMSAY of Auchterhouse). **Crest:** A demi-lion rampant gules, armed azure. **Supporters:** Two wild men, wreathed about the temples and waist with leaves, trampling on serpents and holding branches in their exterior hands, all proper. **Mottoes:** 1 (over the crest) Forward, 2 (under the shield) *Terrena pericula sperno* ('I despise earthly dangers'). **Badge:** A sprig of hawthorn. **Creation:** Bt. (NS) 29 Sept 1626.

SIR FRANCIS GILBERT ARTHUR OGILVY, 14TH BT, of Inverquharity, Forfarshire [Sir Francis Ogilvy Bt, Winton House, Pencaitland, E Lothian EH34 5AT]; *b* 22 April 1969; *s f* 1992; *educ* Edinburgh Acad, Trin Coll Glenalmond and RAC Cirencester (BSc Hons); ARICS; *m* 12 October 1996 *Dorothy Margaret, est dau of Rev Jock Stein and Rev Dorothy Stein, of Carberry Tower, Midlothian

Lineage: Sir WALTER OGILVY, of Auchterhouse; *d* 1391 (*see* AIRLIE, E); had:
Sir JOHN OGILVY; obtained 1420 from his bro Sir Walter, of Lintrathen, Treasurer of Scotland, the lands and territorial Barony of Inverquharity, in Kirriemuir, Forfarshire; had:
1 Alexander, 2nd of Inverquharity; obtained charters from: Alexander Seton, feudal Ld of Gordon, of the lands of Newton, Herdhill and Kinnordie Balbredie, in the (territorial) Barony of Kirriemuir (15 June 1434), Nichol Borthwick of the lands of Ladinch (15 March 1438) and William Gifford of Balnagarroch of the lands of Little Migry (1 April 1439), all confirmed by charter under the Great Seal; had 1444 licence to fortify his house and add an iron gate; *m* Janet, dau and heiress of William Towers, of Barnton, and was *k* Arbroath 23 Jan 1445 in a fight against the Lindsays, leaving:
  (1) Alexander, 3rd of Inverquharity; *d* young *c* 1454
2 WALTER

3 Thomas, of Clova; his descendants carried on a feud with their cousins of Inverquharity for at least a couple more generations

The 2nd s,
  WALTER OGILVY, 4th of Inverquharity; *d* 1481, leaving:
JOHN OGILVY, 5th of Inverquharity; got crown charter of the lands of Middleton and Handwich to him and his w 23 Aug 1487; *m* Margaret, dau of John Rattray of Rattray, and had:
DAVID OGILVY, 6th of Inverquharity; *m* — Norie, of Dunbartonshire, and had:
JOHN OGILVY; *m* Elizabeth, dau of Sir Alexander Guthrie (*k* Battle of Flodden 1513), and *dvp*, leaving:
Sir JOHN OGILVY of Inverquharity; MP (S Parl) 1560; *m* Elizabeth, dau of Thomas Fothringham of Powrie, and had, with a dau (Marian, *m* James Maule of Melgum, s of Henry Maule of Innerpeffer, s of Robert Maule of Panmure; *see* DALHOUSIE, E):
Sir JOHN OGILVY of Inverquharity; *m* 1559 Helen, sis of 5th Lord Ogilvy of Airlie (*see* AIRLIE, E) and had:
1 John (Sir), of Inverquharity; *m* 1580 Elizabeth Ogilvie and *dsp*
2 James; had:
  (1) JOHN
1 Janet; *m* Donald Farquaharson and had seven sons; ancestors of the FARQUHARSONs of Finzean
2 Catherine; *m* David Sibbald of Letham

The gs,
  Sir JOHN OGILVY; ktd 1600; *m* 1588 his cousin Matilda, dau of Thomas Fothringham of Powrie, and *d c* 1624, having had, with four daus:
1 **Sir John Ogilvy, 1st Bt** (NS), so *cr* 29 Sept 1626, with remainder to his heirs male whatsoever, of Inverquharity; *m* 16 Sept 1622 Anne, dau of Sir Alexander Irvine of Drum, by Lady Marion Douglas, dau of 4th Earl of Buchan (*qv*), and *d* by 1663, having had:
  (1) Alexander; royalist Civil War, fought Battles of Brechin, Kilsyth and Philiphaugh, at last of which captured then executed 23 Oct 1646
  (2) DAVID (Sir), **2nd Bt**
  (3) George, of Lunan
  (1) Helen; *m* Sir William Ogilvy, Bt, of Barras
  (2) Anna; *m* her cousin David Ogilvy of Clova
  (3) Margaret; *m* Peter Lyon, 6th of Cossins (*see* STRATHMORE AND KINGHORNE, E)

Sir JOHN's est surv son,
  Sir David Ogilvy, 2nd Bt; MP Co Angus 1665 and 1678; *m* 1662 Margaret, dau of Sir John Erskine of Dun, and *d c* 1679, having had, with three yr sons and three daus:
Sir John Ogilvy, 3rd Bt; *m* 1697 Margaret, est dau of James Ogilvy of Cluny, and *d c* 1735, leaving an est s:
Sir John Ogilvy, 4th Bt; *m* 1st 1720 Helen, dau and coheir of Sir Laurence Mercer of Aldie, and had:
1 JOHN (Sir), **5th Bt**
2 David; Brig-Gen, fought Culloden 1746; *d* 30 May 1781 while Govr St Eustatia, WI
3 Thomas; fought Culloden as Jacobite; later joined the French service

Sir John *m* 2nd Anne (*d* 1 Dec 1750), dau and coheir of James Carnegie of Finhaven, and *d* Feb 1748, having by her had, with another dau:
4 Charles
1 Anne; *m* Rev Charles Roberts

The 4th Bt's est son,
  Sir John Ogilvy, 5th Bt; *m* 1754 Charlotte, est dau and coheir of Walter Tulliedeph of Tulliedeph (later called Baldovan), Forfarshire; sold the lands of Inverquharity and *d* 15 March 1802, having had:
1 **Sir Walter Ogilvy, 6th Bt**; *d* unm 21 Aug 1808
2 **Sir John Ogilvy, 7th Bt**; *d* unm 1819
3 David; Lt-Col; *ka* Egypt 21 March 1801
4 WILLIAM (Sir), **8th Bt**
5 James; *d* in the East Indies
6 Alexander; *b* 17 Sept 1770; *m* 2 Jan 1804 Marcia Anne (*d* 1 April 1861), dau of Maj-Gen Hon Mark Napier (*see* NAPIER and ETTRICK, L), and *d* 2 Nov 1846, leaving, with a dau:
  (1) David; *b* 9 Feb 1813; barrister; *m* 6 July 1843 Eliza Ann Harris, dau of Abercromby Dick, Bengal CS, and *d* 13 Oct 1879, having had:
    1a Alexander William; *b* 9 Sept 1848; Lt RN, Naval Kt of Windsor 1881; *dsp* 28 Aug 1887
    2a Walter Tulliedeph, of Pitfoar House, by Dollar, Clackmannanshire; *b* 9 Aug 1852; *m* 1st 1 June 1878 Eleanor May Edith Lumley (*d* 20 April 1902), dau of Edward Lumley Haworth, and had:
      1b Angus Edward; *b* 9 March 1880; *m* 29 March 1910 Margaret Alice (*d* 20 Sept 1956), 2nd dau of Lt-Col Sir James Frederick Stuart-Menteth, 4th Bt (*qv*), and *d* 15 June 1928, having had:
        1c Walter Tulliedeph; *b* 21 Feb 1911; *m* 1st 11 Dec 1947 Christina Alexandrine Sutherland (*d* 10 Nov 1949), er dau of Alexander Polson, of Larachen, Spinningdale, Sutherland; *m* 2nd 30 Dec 1950 *Audrey Kingsley [Mrs Walter Ogilvy, Rosemary Cottage, Buxted, Sussex], 2nd dau of Arthur George Weeks, of Limpsfield, Surrey, and *d* 1987, having by her had:
          1d *Fiona Audrey; *b* 19 Aug 1952; *m* 1974 (*divorce* 1980) Christopher Cook and has:
            1e *Nicola Jane; *b* 1975
            2e *Claire Annabel; *b* 1977
          2d *Susan Margaret; *b* 10 March 1955; *m* 1974 (*divorce* 1978) John Pelly
        2c Angus Duncan; *b* 24 Oct 1920; *d* 19–

1c Margaret Alyson; *b* 19 April 1914; *d* 5 Oct 1914

2b David, CIE (1935), DSO (1918), OBE (1925); *b* 14 July 1881; *educ* Trin Coll Glenalmond; Col RE (Hon Brig 1934), served Boer War 1901–02 (medal and 5 clasps), E Africa 1903–04 (medal with clasp), WW I (despatches), Afghan War 1919 (medal and clasp) and Waziristan 1923–24 (clasp); *m* 10 July 1906 Vere Grace (*d* 16 Jan 1966), yr dau of Sir Henry Fawcett, KCMG, and *d* 2 June 1949, leaving:

1c *Vere Edith Ogilvy (resumed maiden name by deed poll 1955); *b* 8 May 1912; *m* 17 May 1932 Maj Charles Herbert Harberton Eales, MC, The Guides PFF (Queen's Own Corps of Guides) (*kas* 1941), s of Herbert Lovely Eales, CSI, MA, of Harberton Ho, Headington Hill, Oxford, and has:

1d *(John) David Harberton Eales OGILVY (deed poll 1955) [Lt-Cdr David Ogilvy RN, Witherdon Manor, Beaworthy, Devon EX21 5BS]; *b* 22 Feb 1934; *educ* Dragon Sch and Wellington; *m* 5 July 1958 *Felicity Neilson, dau of Maj Hugh Jack Melville, of Wendover, Bucks, and has:

1e *(David) Guy Francis Melville [Guy Ogilvy Esq, Witherdon Manor, Beaworthy, Devon EX21 5BS]; *b* 2 Oct 1960; *educ* Dragon Sch, Wellington and Exeter U (BA)

2e *Alasdair James Eales [Alasdair Ogilvy Esq, Battlehurst, Kirdford, W Sussex]; *b* 10 Nov 1961; *educ* Dragon Sch and Wellington; served Queen's Own Highrs; *m* 15 July 1989 *Fleur S C, dau of Ian Vergin Brooke, of The Quell, Blackdown, W Sussex, and has:

1f *Flora Alexandra Claire; *b* 23 May 1992

2f *Tara Clementine Alice; *b* 10 Oct 1994

2d Charles Michael; *b* 14 Nov 1941; *educ* Wellington and RMA Sandhurst; served Black Watch; *d* 1977

1d *Mary Ann Vere [Mrs David Makgill-Crichton-Maitland, Daluaine, Rhynie, Aberdeenshire AB54 4HL]; *b* 13 Aug 1935; *m* 1st 27 April 1957 (*divorce* 1973) Maj Charles Pepler Norton, TD, yr s of David G Norton, of Birtles Hall, Chelford, Cheshire; *m* 2nd 1980 Capt James Quintin Penn Curzon (*see* HOWE, E); *m* 3rd 1987, as his 2nd w, *Maj (John) David Makgill-Crichton-Maitland (*see* LAUDERDALE, E) and has by her 1st husb:

1e *Anthony Charles Pepler; *b* 6 April 1958; *m* 19– *S C Jane, only dau of Dr Keith Haward Bywater, of Ruddington, Notts, and has:

1f *Edward James Pepler; *b* 1987

2e *Julian Alexander Pepler; *b* 11 June 1959

1e *Marina Caroline Vere [Mrs James Campbell, c/o Crossways House, Bartlow, Cambridge]; *b* 6 May 1961; *m* 1985 *Capt James Farquhar Robin Campbell, late QOH (*see* CAWDOR, E)

2e *Josephine Sarah Vere; *b* 8 May 1964

3b Walter Tulliedeph; *b* 6 Jan 1883; *m* 8 March 1910 Nora (*d* 11 Aug 1958), dau of Rev Canon Thomas Hewan Archdale, JP, Vicar Tanfield, Tantobie, Co Durham, and 24 Jan 1912, leaving:

1c Walter Tulliedeph (Rev); *b* 16 Jan 1912; *educ* Harrow and BNC Oxford (MA); CF WW II (despatches, POW); *ka* 25 March 1945

1c *Mary Archdale; *b* 20 Dec 1910; *m* 30 Sept 1933 *Col Bryan Stuart Potter, RE, s of Frank Stuart Potter, of Selsey, Sussex, and has:

1d *David Stuart; *b* 20 Dec 1934; *educ* Gordonstoun and Witwatersrand U, S Africa (BSc Eng); *m* 13 May 1961 *Dorothy Ann, est dau of H Longden, and has:

1e *Andrew Tulliedeph; *b* 1963

2e *James Henry Stuart; *b* 1964

3e *Charles David Ogilvy; *b* 1967

1e *Helen Ruth; *b* 1969

2d *Timothy Stuart; *b* 27 April 1938; *m* 1963 *Joan Louise, dau of F St Leger Wills, and has:

1e *Julian Fredercik Stuart; *b* 1964

2e *Thomas George Stuart; *b* 1969

1e *Sophie Elizabeth; *b* 1966

3d *Tulliedeph Ogilvy Stuart; *b* 15 Oct 1942; *m* 1st 19– —; *m* 2nd 19– *Jill, dau of F Muddiman, and has:

1e *Rachel Margaret; *b* 1976

2e *Miriam Nora Louise; *b* 1978

4d *Charles Stuart; *b* 7 Jan 1946; *m* 1970 *Maeve Elfrida, dau of D Band, and has:

1e *Douglas Luke Charles; *b* 1978

1e *Josephine Isabelle; *b* 1981

5d *Roderick Alexander Stuart; *b* 12 Feb 1953; *m* 1976 *Rosemary Jane, dau of P Mallett, and has:

1e *Randolph Bryan Stuart; *b* 1976

2e *Christopher Paul Stuart; *b* 1981

1d *Valerie Stuart; *b* 20 Aug 1936; *m* *Anthony Greville Drew

4b Gilbert Mark Haworth; *b* 1887; Lt-Col KOSB WW I (wounded, despatches), WW II; *m* 11 Jan 1915 Mildred Scott (*d* 13 Jan 1925) and *d* as result of war service 10 June 1945, leaving:

1c *Mildred Cecil; *b* 1916; *m* 3 May 1944 *Thomas Duerdin-Dutton, late Lt RNVR, s of Thomas Duerdin-Dutton, of Springhall, Sawbridgeworth, Herts

1b Marcia Napier; *d* 19–

2b Hilda Edith; *d* 19–

2a (cont.) Walter Ogilvy *m* 2nd 1903 Winnefred (*d* 3 March 1909), dau of Rev Henry Edward Maskew, Rector St James's Ch, Dollar; *m* 3rd 1910 Christina (*d* 23 Dec 1955), dau of Col Bannatyne McLeod, Bombay Artillery, and *d* 13 Nov 1927, having had:

3b A dau; *b* 1909; *d* 19–

4b *Earna; *b* 1909 (twin); *m* 1931 W J Forrester (*d* 1975) and has:

1c *David Alton [David Forrester Esq, 18 Shasta Rd, Lesmurdie, W Australia 6076]; *b* 1932; *educ* Cambridge (MA, LLM, ACIS); barrister; *m* 1959 Fay Garner (*d* 1979) and has:

1d *Richard Alton; *b* 1961

1d *Susan May; *b* 1965

1c *Thelma [Mrs Neil Pearson, Postbag 3795, Marondera, Zimbabwe]; *b* 1934; *m* 1960 Neil Pearson and has:

1d *Lesley Dawn; *b* 1961

2d *Janette Nancy; *b* 1962

3a Angus; *b* 25 Jan 1855; *m* 15 Nov 1886 Rosa Serena (*d* 24 Jan 1923), dau of Abercromby Dick, WS and barrister, and *d* 8 Feb 1928, leaving, with a dau (*d* unm):

1b Abercromby Graham; *b* 1 Oct 1889; *educ* Marlborough; Lt-Col IA, served Mohmand Expdn 1915, Afghanistan 1919 and Waziristan 1920; *m* 17 Jan 1923 Sibyl Mary, dau of Daniel Abbot Green, of East Donyland Hall, nr Colchester, and *d* 19–, having had:

1c Bruce John; *b* 2 Nov 1923; *d* 1947

1c Barbara Elizabeth Graham; *b* 19 April 1928; *d* 1951

1a Marcia Napier; *m* 24 Sept 1874 Horace Bell, Bombay Civ Serv, and had issue

2a Violet Isabel; *m* 8 Dec 1879 Herbert Collingridge (*d* 1931), of Edenholme, Dunbar, and *d* 6 Sept 1954, leaving issue

(1) Charlotte; *m* 1st 3 Jan 1833 William Macfarlane (*d* 1838), of Donavourd, Perthshire; *m* 2nd 29 Dec 1842 Mark Napier (*d* 22 Nov 1869), Sheriff Dumfries, and *d* 14 April 1883, having had issue (*see* NAPIER and ETTRICK, L)

7 Thomas; *d* in India

8 Ramsay; Lt 44th Regt; *ka* taking of St Lucia, WI

9 Adam; Army Offr; *d* WI

The 7th Bt's bro,

Sir William Ogilvy, 8th Bt; R-Adml; *m* 1802 Sarah (*d* 26 May 1854), dau of James Morley, Bombay CS, of Kempshot, Hants, and *d* 1823, having had, with a dau (*d* unm):

1 JOHN (Sir), **9th Bt**

2 Walter; *b* 1804; Maj 69th Regt; *m* 26 Sept 1861 Caroline (*d* 14 Oct 1894), est surv dau of Rev George Tomline Pretyman, Chllr Lincoln Cathedral and Canon Winchester, and *dsp* 21 May 1879

3 William; Bengal CS; *d* 1837

4 James Balfour; Bengal CS; *m* 1833 Anne, only dau of John Kinloch, of Kilrie, Forfar, and *d* 14 July 1848, leaving, with a dau (*d* unm):

(1) Arthur James, of Inverquharity, Richmond, Tasmania; *b* 15 April 1834; *m* 8 Aug 1861 Mary Camilla Letitia (*d* 1891), est dau of William Needham, of Lenton Ho, Notts, and *d* 30 June 1914, leaving, with a dau (*d* unm):

1a Kenneth Arthur; *b* 17 Aug 1863; *d* unm 15 Aug 1943

1a Mary Louisa; *d* unm 17 June 1945

2a Bertha Florence; *b* 18 July 1867; *m* Jan 1891 William Mosey (*d* 13 Nov 1926), slr, of Launceston, Tasmania, and *d* 29 March 1947, leaving issue

(2) William Lewis Kinloch, CB; *b* 30 April 1840; Col KRRC; *m* 22 Oct 1889 Lucy, JP (Hants) (*d* 15 Nov 1946), er dau of William Wickham, DL, MP, of Binsted Wyck, Alton, Hants, and *d* 3 Feb 1900, leaving:

1a William Wickham; *b* 31 Jan 1896; Lt 20th Hus; *d* 23 March 1918 of wounds recd in action

1a Charlotte Helen; *m* 27 April 1926 Sir Edgar Bonham-Carter, KCMG, CIE (*d* 24 April 1956), 5th s of Henry Bonham-Carter, and *d* 198–

5 David; *b* 22 Sept 1809; Capt Bengal Army; *m* 17 March 1835 Caroline Helena (*d* 7 Jan 1911), dau of Lt-Col Carter, 16th Regt, and *dsp* 8 Oct 1876

6 George Keith; Cdr RN; *d* 20 Sept 1846

7 Thomas; *b* 7 Nov 1810; Bombay CS; *m* 16 April 1846 Georgina (*d* May 1884), 3rd dau of Samuel Bosanquet, of Dingestow Court, Mon, and *d* 16 June 1871

8 Alexander Charles; *d* 18–

The 8th Bt's est son,

Sir John Ogilvy, 9th Bt, JP, DL; *b* 17 March 1803; MP Dundee 1857–74, Convenor Forfarshire, Hon Col 1st Vol Bn Black Watch, Maj-Gen Roy Co Archers; *m* 1st 7 July 1831 Juliana Barbara (*d* 27 Dec 1833), yst dau of Lord Henry Howard-Molyneux-Howard, bro of 12th Duke of Norfolk (*qv*), and had:

1 REGINALD HOWARD ALEXANDER (Sir), **10th Bt**

1 Juliana; *m* 27 July 1858 Sir Nelson Rycroft, 4th Bt (*qv*), and *d* 6 Jan 1917, leaving issue

Sir John *m* 2nd 5 April 1836 Lady Jane Elizabeth Howard (*d* 28 July), 3rd dau of 16th Earl of Suffolk and (9th Earl of) Berkshire (*qv*), and *d* 29 March 1890, having by her had, with four daus (*d* unm):

2 Henry Thomas OGILVY later NISBET HAMILTON OGILVY, JP (Lincs), JP and DL (Haddington), of Biel, Prestonkirk, Archerfield, Dirleton, Winton Castle, Pencaitland, and Wellvale, Alford, Lincs; *b* 3 May 1837; barrister; *m* 11 Sept 1888 Mary Georgina Constance (*d* 25 June 1920), only dau of Rt Hon Robert and Lady Mary Christopher Nisbet Hamilton, of Belhaven and Dirleton (*see* ELGIN and KINCARDINE, E), and *dsp* 5 Dec 1909

3 Charles William Norman (Rev); *b* 6 Oct 1839; MA Oxon; Vicar Oswestry, Salop, Rector Hanbury, Worcs; *m* 2 June 1870 Hon Emily Priscilla Maria Ponsonby (*d* 12 May 1926), dau of 2nd Baron De Mauley (*qv*), and *d* 7 June 1903, leaving:

(1) Alice Jane Marion; *d* unm 13 May 1926

(2) Diana Maria Elizabeth, MBE (1918), JP; Mayor Worcester 1931–32, Alderman Worcester 1942; *d* unm 26 March 1955

The 9th Bt's est son,

Sir Reginald Howard Alexander Ogilvy, 10th Bt, JP (Perth and Forfarshire), DL (Forfarshire and Dundee); *b* 29 May 1832; *educ* Oriel Coll Oxford (BA); Hon Col Forfar and Kincardine RF Res Artillery, ADC to HM QUEEN VICTORIA; *m* 27 July 1859 Olivia Barbara (*d* 6 May 1871), only dau of 9th Lord Kinnaird (*see* 1970 edn), and *d* 12 March 1910, having had:

1 Angus Howard Reginald, DSO; *b* 12 Aug 1860; Maj 13th Hus, cavalry instructor to Sultan of Morocco, Boer War 1899–1900; *m* 15 Oct 1890 Isabel Louisa (*d* 21 Dec 1963 aged 99), dau of Hon Ralph Nevill (*see* ABERGAVENNY, M), and *d* 4 July 1906, leaving:

(1) **Sir Gilchrist Nevill Ogilvy, 11th Bt**; *b* 6 Sept 1892; Lt Scots Gds; *ka* 29 Oct 1914

(1) Olivia Frances Isabel; *b* 6 Oct 1891; *m* 21 Jan 1914 Gerald Robert Foster (*d* 9 April 1962), est s of Robert John Foster, DL, of Stockeld Park, Wetherby, Yorks, and *d* 30 Sept 1955, leaving issue

2 **Sir Herbert Kinnaird Ogilvy, 12th Bt**, JP (Dundee and Angus), DL (Angus); *b* 29 June 1865; WS; *m* 15 Dec 1904 Lady Christian Augusta Bruce (*see* ELGIN and KINCARDINE, E) and *d* 1 March 1956, having adopted 1919:

Henry Iain; *b* 23 Aug 1919; *d* following a climbing accident 22 Sept 1940

3 Frederick Charles Ashley, of Baldovan Ho, by Dundee; *b* 9 Aug 1866; Capt RN, Boer War and China 1900; *m* 1 June 1904 Gertrude Lilian (*d* 13 Feb 1971), yst dau of Capt William Sherbrooke, JP, RN, of Oxton Hall, Notts; *m* 2nd 19 Nov 1913 9th Earl of Elgin and (13th Earl of) Kincardine (*qv*); *m* 3rd 30 Aug 1923 Lt-Col John Alexander Stirling, DSO, MC, of Kippendavie, Perthshire, and *d* 28 Nov 1957), and *d* 18 Dec 1909, leaving:

(1) *Ann Howard [Mrs John Gurney, Walsingham Abbey, Norfolk]; *b* 2 May 1905; *m* 2 June 1932 John Gurney, JP (*d* 20 Aug 1997), est s of Sir Eustace Gurney, and has had:

1a *Priscilla Ann; *b* 8 May 1937; *m* 31 May 1958 *(William) Gregory Francis Meath Baker, only s of Francis Ralph Meath Baker, JP, of Hasfield Court, Glos, and has:

1b *(William John) Clovis; *b* 11 May 1959; *educ* Eton and Oxford; *m* 1985 *Elizabeth Diana, est dau of Charles Woodham-Smith, of Earls Court, London, and has:

1c *Boadicea Louisa Ann; *b* 1988

2c *Agnes Charlotte Gertrude; *b* 1990

3c *Constance Daffodil Bohemia; *b* 1992

2b *(Samuel) Justin Francis; *b* 4 Nov 1961; *educ* Eton and Edinburgh Sch of Art; *m* 1989 *Eliza Rose Robertson, yst dau of AVM Geoffrey Cairns CBE, AFC, of Powells, Kenn, Devon, and has had:

1c Samuel Romulus; *b* and *d* 1992

2c *Hannibal Eustace Pilate; 1993

3b *(Hugh) Lysander Luke; *b* 11 Feb 1964; *educ* Eton

4b *Joshua Ralph; *b* 1 Dec 1965; *educ* Eton and Courtauld Inst

2a *Jean Elizabeth, OBE (1977) [The Rt Hon The Lady Mayhew of Twysden OBE, Twysden, Kilndown, nr Cranbrook, Kent TN17 2SG]; *b* 2 Sept 1939; *educ* Downe House, Berks, New Hall Cambridge (BA 1961) and King's Coll London (BD 1984); *m* 15 April 1963 *Baron Mayhew of Twysden (*qv*) and has issue

3a *(Elizabeth) Olivia; *b* 13 Oct 1943; *m* 7 Sept 1968 *Timothy Arnold Neil Bristol, s of Arnold Bristol, of Wootton, Surrey, and has:

1b *Benjamin Timothy Fitzroy; *b* 1972

2b *Samuel Frederick John; *b* 1983

1b *Arabella Fredericka Ann; *b* 1970

4a Elizabeth Rachel; *b* 10 June 1946; *d* 1982

5a *(Ruth) Christian [Mrs George Forestier-Walker, Plum Tree Cottage, North Heath, Chievely, Berks RG16 8UD]; *b* 16 Nov 1948; *m* 8 April 1970 *Maj George Clive Forestier-Walker (*see* FORESTIER-WALKER, Bt)

4 Gilbert Francis Molyneux, JP (E Lothian); *b* 9 April 1868; *educ* Glenalmond and Univ Coll Oxford (BA 1892); *m* 11 June 1912 Marjory Katharine (*d* 28 Dec 1961), dau of Charles Meysey Bolton Clive, JP, of Whitfield, Herefs, and *d* 17 June 1953, leaving:

(1) DAVID JOHN WILFRID (Sir), **13th Bt**

(2) John Augustine; *b* 28 Aug 1915; Lt-Cdr RN WW II (despatches); *m* 31 Jan 1942 *Margaret Vivienne Lyndall [Mrs John Ogilvy, Old North Manse, East Linton, E Lothian], est dau of Col William Thornton Huband Gregg, DSO, OBE, Roy Irish Fus, of Ballyknockane Ho, Co Tipperary, and *d* 1993, having had:

1a Angus William; *b* 6 March 1945; *educ* Eton and Stirling U (BA Hons); *m* 1st 7 June 1968 (*divorce* 1980) Sally Margaret, dau of Michael Long, of Moffat, Dumfriesshire, and had:

1b *ANDREW JOHN; *b* 23 April 1972; heir presumptive

2b +Robert Iain Michael; *b* 1974

1a (cont.) Angus Ogilvy *m* 2nd 1980 *Helen [Mrs Angus Ogilvy, 6 Queen's Rd, King Park, Stirling FK8 2QY], dau of John Dudley Massingham, CMG, of Pershore, Worcs, and *d* 1989, leaving by her:

3b +James Angus John; *b* 1982

4b +Thomas Alasdair William; *b* 1984

1a *Diana Lyndall; *b* 2 Dec 1946

(1) *Katharine Olivia Mary [Mrs William Packe, Low Wood, Winthorpe, Newark, Notts]; *b* 18 Dec 1916; *m* 26 Sept 1947 *William Packe, FRICS, FLAS, only surv s of Charles James Melville Packe, of Rothley, Leics, and has:

1a *Thomas Gilbert [Thomas Packe Esq, East Philipstoun Farmhouse, Linlithgow, W Lothian EH49 7RY]; *b* 22 Aug 1948; *educ* Gordonstoun and RAC Cirencester; *m* 1994 *Sally Margaret, yr dau of Maj John Basil Ready

2a *Andrew James; *b* 11 Jan 1951; *educ* Radley and RAC Cirencester; *m* 1981 *Aloÿse Anne, only dau of Christopher James Morrell Blackie, and has:

1b *Frederick Christopher William; *b* 1987

1b *Olivia Aloÿse Hester; *b* 1984

(2) Margaret Clare; *b* 27 March 1919; *m* 29 June 1950 *(Hugh) Glencairn Balfour-Paul, CMG [Glencairn Balfour-Paul Esq CMG, Uppincott Barton, Shobrooke, Crediton, Devon EX17 1BE], yst s of Lt-Col John William Balfour-Paul, DSO, Marchmont Herald, and *d* 1971, having had:

1a *James Ogilvy; *b* 20 June 1961

1a *Ann; *b* 13 April 1951; *educ* St Andrews

2a *Alison Muriel; *b* 5 May 1954

3a *Catherine Angela; *b* 22 March 1959

(3) *Hester Mary [Mrs David Scott, Glenaros, Aros, Isle of Mull, PA72 6JP]; *b* 9 June 1921; *educ* St Hugh's Coll Oxford (BA) and Edinburgh U (MA); *m* 21 Dec 1951 *David Scott of Glenaros, MA, Clerk H of C, er s of Sir Basil Scott, Ch Justice Bombay, and has:

1a *Colum Basil; *b* 9 June 1954; *educ* Stowe and RAC Cirencester; *m* 1992 *Sarah Louise, yr dau of Michael Charles Watson Credland, and has:

1b *Angus Michael David; *b* 1993

1a *Margaret Isobel; *b* 30 Sept 1952; *educ* Sherborne Sch for Girls; *m* 1991 *Brian Simons and has:

1b *Jamie Mark; *b* 1987

2b *Samuel Isaac Michael; *b* 1992

2a *Christian Mary Gertrude; *b* 5 Sept 1955; *educ* Sherborne Sch for Girls; *m* 1984 *Anthony Latham, s of Leslie Latham, and has:

1b *Andrew David; *b* 1987

2b *Brendan Michael; *b* 1994

1b *Helen; *b* 1986

2b *Mairi Isobel; *b* 1992

3a *Helen Olivia Katharine; *b* 6 Jan 1958; *m* 19– *Alistair Danter, s of John Danter, and has:

1b *Fiona Marie Josée; *b* 1993

1 Violet Olivia Juliana; *b* 22 March 1864; *d* unm 14 Oct 1941

The 12th Bt's n,

Sir David John Wilfrid Ogilvy, 13th Bt, JP (E Lothian 1957), DL (1971); *b* 3 Feb 1914; *educ* Eton and Trin Coll Oxford (BA 1935, MA 1956); CA Edin, RNVR WW II; *m* 31 Dec 1966 *Penelope Mary Ursula [Penelope Lady Ogilvy, Winton Cottage, Pencaitland, E Lothian EH34 5AT], only dau of Capt Arthur Lafone Frank Hills, OBE, of White Court, Penshurst Station, Kent, by Moira Emelina, est dau of Henry Seymour Guinness (*see* GUINNESS, Bt), and *d* 1992, leaving:

Sir FRANCIS GILBERT ARTHUR OGILVY, **14th and present Bt**

OGILVY-WEDDERBURN

Creation: Bt. (UK) 10 Aug 1803.

SIR ANDREW JOHN ALEXANDER OGILVY-WEDDERBURN, 7TH BT, of Ballindean, Perthshire [Sir Andrew Ogilvy-Wedderburn Bt, Silvie, Alyth, Perthshire PH11 8NA]; *b* 4 Aug 1952; *s* † 1977; *educ* Gordonstoun; Lt-Col Black Watch; *m* 1984 *Gillian Meade, yr dau of Richard Boyle Adderley, OBE, of Shepherds Hill, Pickering, N Yorks, and has had:

1 +PETER ROBERT ALEXANDER; *b* 20 April 1987

2 +Geordie Richard Andrew (twin); *b* 20 April 1987

3 Sam; *b* 1990; *d* 1992

1 *Katherine; *b* 1985

Lineage: ROBERT WEDDERBURN; *m* Janet, dau of David Froster in Methven, and *d c* 1518, leaving:

1 James; MP Dundee S Parl 1540; *d* 1544, leaving two sons

2 ROBERT

3 David; had a s (William, settled Aberdeenshire)

4 Alexander; *m* Isabel Anderson and had two sons (Richard; Patrick) and three daus

5 George; *m* Eufame Fowlair and *dsp*

1 Elizabeth; *m* 1st Alexander Lovell; *m* 2nd Alexander Ogilvy, Provost Dundee; *m* 3rd Archibald Campbell; *m* 4th Patrick Lyon, of Dundee, and *d* 1571/72

The 2nd s,

ROBERT WEDDERBURN; *m* Janet Kyd and *d* 1575, leaving, with two yr sons (Peter, of Dundee, *m* Margaret Kinloch and had three daus; Robert, *b* 1546, *m* Margaret, dau of Robert Myln, and *d* 1611, leaving four sons (*dsp* & *vp*)):

ALEXANDER WEDDERBURN; Clerk of Dundee 1557–82; *m* Janet (*d* 19 June 1588), dau of James Myln, and *d* 28 June 1585, having had, with three other sons and two daus:

1 ALEXANDER

2 David; *m* Matild, dau of James Betoun, and *d* 1631, having had four sons (*dsp*) and several daus

3 Robert; *m* Elspet Lovell and *d* 30 Nov 1593, leaving issue

The est son,

ALEXANDER WEDDERBURN, of Kingennie, Forfarshire; *b* 1561; accompanied JAMES VI to England 1603; *m* 1582 Helen, dau of Alexander Ramsay, and *d* 1626, leaving:

1 Alexander, of Kingennie; Clerk of Dundee 1627–33; a male descendant obtained a Crown Charter 1708 erecting the lands of Easter Powrie into a (territorial) Barony of Wedderburn but that branch became *extinct* in the male line on the death of David Wedderburn of Wedderburn 1761, when the ancestor of the present Bt became male representative but the estates were inherited by the SCRYMGEOURs later SCRYMGEOUR-WEDDERBURNs Earls of Dundee (*qv*)

2 JAMES

3 Peter; *m* Helen Lovell and *dsp* 1629

4 William; *m* Jean Pearson and *dsp* 1630

5 John (Sir); Physician-in-Ordinary to CHARLESes I and II; *d* unm 1677

1 Elizabeth; *m* 1st Colin Campbell (*dsp*); *m* 2nd Dr Peter Bruce, of St Andrews, and had issue

2 Magdalene; *m* 1st Rev William Wedderburn, s of Alexander Wedderburn of Pittormie (*see* above); *m* 2nd Sir George Haliburton, Ld of Session as Lord Fodderance

3 Margaret; *m* Thomas Haliburton

4 Marjory; *m* Robert Carnegy of Leuchland

5 Jean; *m* Thomas Boytter

6 Elspeth; *m* Alexander Fothringham

The 2nd son,

JAMES WEDDERBURN; *b* 1589; Clerk of Dundee 1626–27; *m* 1608 Margaret, dau of James Goodman, of St Fort, Fifeshire, and *d* 1627, leaving with two yr sons (William, *d* unm; Sir Peter, of Gosford, Haddingtonshire, had issue; *see* ROSSLYN, E):

Sir ALEXANDER WEDDERBURN, of Blackness, Forfarshire; *b* 22 March 1610; Clerk of Dundee 1633–75, Commr to sign Treaty of Ripon 1641, a deputy to CHARLES I at Newcastle 1646, ktd 1646, Commr from S Parl to London 1653 to negotiate union; *m* Matilda, dau of James Fletcher, Provost Dundee, and *d* 18 Nov 1675, leaving, with other issue:

1 Sir JOHN WEDDERBURN, 1st Bt (GB), so *cr* 9 Aug 1704, of Blackness; *b* 12 Feb 1641; advocate, Clerk of the Bills; *m* 9 April 1667 Rachel, dau of David Dunsmuir, advocate, and *d* 1706, having had, with other issue:

(1) Sir ALEXANDER WEDDERBURN, 2nd Bt; *b* 7 April 1672; Clerk of the Bills; *m* 1 June 1693 Elizabeth, dau of Sir Alexander Seton, 1st Bt, of Pitmedden (*qv*), and *d* Feb 1710, leaving, with other issue:

1a Sir JOHN WEDDERBURN, 3rd Bt; *b* 2 Dec 1700; joined Army; sold Blackness to his cousin and next heir Alexander; *d* unm 1723

(2) David; Maj; *dsp* Siege of Douai 1710

2 James; *b* 1649; Clerk of Dundee 1675–96; *m* 1673 Elizabeth, dau of Robert Davidson, of Balgay, and *d* 1696, leaving, with other issue:

(1) ALEXANDER (Sir), 4th Bt

3 Peter; *b* 1652; *m* Catharine Mann and had two sons (male line died out)

4 Alexander; *b* 1658; *m* Christian Kinloch and had three daus

1 Grizell; *m* her cousin Alexander Wedderburn of Easter Powrie

The 3rd Bt's cousin,

Sir ALEXANDER WEDDERBURN, 4th Bt; *b* 4 Nov 1675; Clerk of Dundee 1696–1717 (dismissed for Jacobitism); *m* 15 Nov 1697 Katharine, dau of John Scott, of Dundee, and *d* 21 Sept 1744, leaving:

1 JOHN (Sir), 5th Bt

2 Robert; *b* 1708; *m* 1738 Isobel Edward, heiress of Pearsie, Forfar, and *d* 1786, leaving:

(1) John; *b* 1744; Lt-Col HEICS; *d* unm 1787

(2) Charles, of Pearsie; *b* 1748; *m* 1st 1787 Anne, dau of John Read; *m* 2nd 1797 Eliza, dau of Dr David Rattray, and *dsp* 1829, having entailed Pearsie on his sis Elizabeth's issue (*see* below)

(3) David WEDDERBURN later WEBSTER-WEDDERBURN; *b* 1766; *m* 1785 Elizabeth (*m* 2nd 24 June 1802 Robert Douglas, of Brigton, Forfar, and *d* 1857), dau of Alexander Read, of Logie, Angus, and *d* 1801, leaving:

1a James (Sir); *b* 1789; Dragoons Offr, ktd 1822; *m* 10 Oct 1810 Lady Frances Caroline Annesley (*d* 22 Jan 1837), dau of 1st Earl of Mountnorris (*see* VALENTIA, V), and *d* 13 Aug 1840, having had, with another s (*d* an infant):

1b Charles Francis Webster; *b* 1 July 1820; Army Offr; *m* 1st 9 Oct 1849 Anne (*d* 2 Nov 1883), dau of William Helyar, of Coker Court, Somerset; *m* 2nd 28 May 1885 Emily Honoria (*dsp* 1892), dau of Rev Hugh Welman Helyar, Rector Sutton Bingham, Somerset, and *d* 28 Feb 1886, having by his 1st w had:

1c Arthur Augustus Helyar; *b* 2 Oct 1853; Dep-Inspr Constabulary Jamaica; *m* 1st 25 April 1888 Katharine Elspeth Maude (*d* 5 June 1907), dau of Henry Charles Hamilton, CSI (*see* HAMILTON, Bt, of Silvertonhill); *m* 2nd 9 April 1913 Henrietta Caroline Bradley (*d* 1 Oct 1946), 3rd surv dau of Thomas Henry Haddan, BCL, barrister, and *d* 11 April 1919, having by his 1st w had:

1d Dorothy Hamilton; *b* 2 March 1901; *m* 1st 17 Sept 1921 Capt Richard P Hewetson, RFA; *m* 2nd 8 Dec 1934 Maj-Gen Allan Cholmondeley Arnold, CIE, CBE, MC, Roy Fus (*d* 29 Jan 1962), s of Lt-Col Arthur S Arnold, of Hartley Wintney, and by her 1st husb had:

1e *Richard Tatton Wedderburn; *b* 26 Jan 1924; P/O RAF

2c Charles Edward; *b* 16 Sept 1855; *m* 5 Sept 1885 Louisa Adele (*d* 12 March 1932), dau of John Kimber, and *d* 5 Dec 1936

3c Albert Annesley; *b* 9 June 1864; *m* 1st 1892 Adelaide (*dsp* 1903), dau of J S Scott; *m* 2nd 1905 Mary McCabe, of Sydney, NSW, and *d* 8 Dec 1929

1c Gertrude Violet; *m* 1st 26 April 1877 Horace Augustus Helyar, DL (*d* 1893), of Coker, Somerset, and had issue; *m* 2nd 3 Nov 1894 2nd Baron Savile (*qv*) and *d* 16 Oct 1912

2b Augustus George; *dsp* 1845

3b George; *b* 1827; Maj 7th Roy Fus; *m* at Corfu 3 March 1853 Caroline (*d* 3 May 1899), dau of Capt William Dixon, RA, and *d* 20 Aug 1875, having had, with other daus (*d* unm):

1c Frances Caroline Valentia; *m* 11 Dec 1895 Paul Frederick Straube and *d* 10 Sept 1932

2c Annie Edith Webster; *m* 21 Feb 1903 Edward Howard Wakefield (*d* 6 April 1930), s of Edward Wakefield, of NZ, and *d* July 1943

3c Maude Gertrude Annesley; *m* 1st 24 Sept 1892 Henry Alexander Hadden and had issue; *m* 2nd 14 Oct 1902 William Henry Rider (*d* 27 Sept 1914); *m* 3rd 2 Oct 1915 Maj Harry Blaikie Brownlow, RA (*d* 19 Sept 1932), and *d* 6 Nov 1930

1b Lucy Sarah Anne; *m* 24 Aug 1834 Rev Alfred Cæser Bisshop, Rector Martyr Worthy, Hants, and *d* 24 April 1864, leaving issue

2a Charles, of Harnish, Wilts; *b* 1799; *m* 11 Dec 1822 Rebecca (*d* 22 June 1858), dau of Sir James Chatterton, Bt (*see* 1874 edn), and *d* 16 Dec 1863, having had:

1b Charles Adrian; *b* 1824; *m* 1851 Frances Mary, dau of Henry Edwin Huntly, and *d* 1885, leaving:

1c Charles George; *b* 1861; *m* 1885 Eliza Marian, dau of John Brown, and *d* 1903, having had three sons (*d* young) and three daus (Mabel Florence; Katherine; Jane)

1c Frances Mary; *m* 1st 1880 Charles Corps (*d* 1881); *m* 2nd 1883 E J D Wigginton and by him had issue

1b Rebecca Georgiana; *m* 1st M Dufour; *m* 2nd M Leon Jean Consigné, of Paris, and *dsp* 1890

1a Anne; *m* 1814 Capt Archibald Murray Douglas, 52nd Foot (*d* 1822), and *d* 1814, leaving issue

2a Mary; *m* 25 March 1815 George Hawkins (*see* HAWKINS, Bt) and *dsp*

(1) Elizabeth; *b* 1746; *m* James Graham, of Meathie, and *d* 1825, having had:

1a David GRAHAM later WEDDERBURN (on inheriting Pearsie); *dsp*

2a John GRAHAM later WEDDERBURN; *dsp* 1870

(2) Katharine; *b* 1750; *m* Robert Stewart and *d* 1795, having had issue, who eventually inherited Pearsie

(3) Isabella; *b* 1753; *m* Rev James Stormonth and *d* 1795, having had issue

3 Thomas; *b* 2 April 1710; *m* 20 Sept 1740 Katharine, dau of Robert Dunbar of Grangehill, and *d* Jan 1771, leaving, with five daus (four of whom *unm*):

(1) Alexander; *b* 1741; *d* unm Jamaica 1770

(2) John, of Clapham; *b* 19 Aug 1743; *m* 27 May 1782 Mary Wisdom (*d* 1835), dau of George Bedward, of Jamaica, and *d* 1820, having had:

1a James; *b* 2 June 1788; *m* 5 July 1817 Isabella (*m* 2nd 8 Oct 1836 Adml Sir C H Fremantle, GCB), dau of David Lyon, and *d* 23 April 1831, having had:

1b John Kellermann; *b* 13 Feb 1818; *m* 23 Feb 1843 Charlotte (*d* 4 April 1894), dau of Gen Sir Thomas McMahon, 2nd Bt, and *d* 4 June 1891, having had:

1c Emily Frederica; *m* 2 July 1863 Sir Carey John Knyvet, KCB (*d* 16 Aug 1903), and *d* 12 May 1916, leaving issue

2c Isabella Lottie; *m* 30 April 1874 Capt Henry Blackburne Hamilton, 6th Dragoon Gds (Carabiniers), later Col cmdg 14th (King's) Hus, and *d* 6 Dec 1881, leaving a s

2a John; *b* 8 Jan 1798; *m* 30 April 1823 Lady Helen Ogilvy, yst dau of 3rd Earl of Airlie (*qv*), and *d* 2 April 1839, leaving:

1b John Walter; *b* 20 July 1824; Capt 42nd Regt; *m* 27 April 1854 Margaret Anne (*d* 1926), dau of Thomas Whaite, Lt 94th Regt, and *d* 20 July 1879, leaving:

1c John Walter Maurice (Rev); *b* 17 March 1855; Rector St Bride's, Onich, Nether Lochabar, Canon Cumbrae Cathedral, Chaplain to Bp Argyll; *d* unm 1934

2c Charles David St Clair, OBE (1918); *b* 7 Feb 1864; Ch Mech Engr E Indian Rlwy; *m* 31 Aug 1898 Louisa Mary (*d* 2 Nov 1931), dau of Maj J E Whaite, and *d* 3 Feb 1931, leaving:

1d David Walter; *b* 8 Aug 1899; Maj RE; *m* 1925 Elizabeth (*d* Nov 1950), dau of J Robertson, of Perth, and *d* 22 Dec 1960, leaving:

1e *Patricia Helen Marjorie; *b* 1927; *m* Sept 1950 *Colin Henry du Plessis, 4th s of Nicholas du Plessis, of Barberton, Transvaal, and has:

1f *Robin St Clair; *b* 1951

2f *Richard Geoffrey; *b* 1952

2e *Averil Elizabeth Vernon; *b* 18 May 1932

1d *Patricia Eileen Margaret; *m* 14 Oct 1931 Maj George Waugh, RE

1c Helen Margaret Ogilvy; *d* unm 1932

2b James Alexander; *b* 1 Aug 1825; Madras CS; *m* 28 March 1848 Marion (*d* 17 Sept 1914), dau of Sir James Cosmo Melvill, KCB, and *d* 19 May 1854, having had, with other issue:

1c Alexander Dundas Ogilvy, CBE (1920), KC, JP Sussex; *b* 7 Aug 1854; *educ* Balliol Coll Oxford (BA); Bencher Inner Temple, Recorder Gravesend 1897–1922; *m* 13 April 1887 Mathilde (*d* 27 Nov 1898), dau of Henry William Segelcke, and *d* 17 July 1931, leaving:

1d Alexander Henry Melvill, CBE (1956), JP Berks; *b* 1 July 1892; *educ* Eton and Balliol Coll Oxford (BA 1917, MA 1922); Capt Black Watch (Roy Highrs) WW I (wounded, despatches); barrister Inner Temple 1917, chm Exec Queen's Inst Dist Nursing 1946–61; *m* 20 April 1921 Cynthia Margaret (*d* 1986), est dau of Cecil Lubbock (*see* AVEBURY, B), and *d* 23 Dec 1968, leaving:

1e David Michael Alexander; *b* 6 Feb 1922; *educ* Eton and Balliol Coll Oxford (BA); Maj, 2 ic 1st Bn Singapore Inf Regt, Gren Gds, WW II; *m* 23 March 1946 *Marigold Diana Sneyd (*m* 2nd 15 Oct 1960 Maj Harold Warren Freeman-Attwood, Gren Gds, er s of Maj-Gen Harold Augustus Freeman-Attwood, DSO, OBE, MC), yr dau of Edward Philips, OBE, of Alsop-en-le-Dale Hall, Derbys, and *d* on duty Singapore 26 Feb 1960, leaving:

1f +Robert David Alexander [Robert Wedderburn Esq, 13 Rothesay Ave, Richmond, Surrey TW10 5EB]; *b* 30 March 1948; *educ* Eton and RAM (MA, GRSM); *m* 1985 *Hazel Eloisa, ARCM, dau of Rev John Ifor-Jones, and has:

1g +Alister Humphrey; *b* 1987

1g *Susannah Kate; *b* 1990

2f +Henry Edward Alexander; *b* 14 May 1954; *educ* Eton and RMA Sandhurst; Lt Gren Gds; *m* 1984 *Sarah Juliet, dau of Anthony John Round, of Layer Marney, Essex, and has:

1g *Polly Alexandra Round; *b* 1986

2g *Louisa Catherine Round; *b* 1990

1f *Sarah Catherine; *b* 18 Dec 1952; *educ* Somerville Coll Oxford; *m* 1979 *Ian Caughlin and has:

1g *Edward David; *b* 1980

1g *Hannah Delia; *b* 1982

1e *(Catherine) Clarissa [Mrs James Robinson, The Chantry, Gt Barford, Beds MK44 3JH]; *b* 21 Jan 1925; *m* 3 Dec 1955 James Francis Robinson, TD, JP, DL, FRICS, Capt 5th Bn Beds and Herts Regt (*d* 1980), s of James Charles Evitt Robinson, CBE, and has had:

1f *Adam James Nicholas [Adam Robinson Esq, 34 Dordrecht Rd, London W3 7TF]; *b* 13 May 1959; *m* 1990 *Katherine Adelaide Harben and has:

1g *Adelaide Harriet; *b* 1991

2g *Rebecca Harben; *b* 1996

2f *David Thomas [David Robinson Esq, 19 Belton Rd, London E7 9PF]; *b* 16 May 1962; *m* 1996 *Debra Jane Ross and has:

  1g *Thomas Isaac; *b* 1995

  2g *Oliver; *b* 1996

1f *Harriet Clarissa [Mrs Richard Bacon, 127 John Ruskin St, London SE5]; *b* 26 Jan 1957; *m* 1985 *Richard Piers Bacon, s of Edward George Hedley Bacon

2e *Elizabeth Jane; *b* 29 Dec 1926; *m* 18 Aug 1949 *Nicolas Ralph Dolignon Furse, yr s of Maj Sir Ralph Dolignon Furse, KCMG, DSO, and has:

  1f *Mark Nicolas Ralph Dolignon; *b* 27 May 1957; *m* 1981 *Heather Campbell and has:

    1g *Samuel Robert; *b* 1982

    2g *Thomas Henry; *b* 1992

    1g *Alice Jane; *b* 1984

  1f *Vanessa Jane; *b* 28 June 1950; *m* 1987 *Dr Robert S Jackson

  2f *Miranda Jill; *b* 10 Aug 1951; *m* 1976 *Carl Johnson and has:

    1g *Jack Nicolas Drummond; *b* 1981

    1g *Tess Jane Dolignon; *b* 1986

  3f *Corinna Margaret Dolignon; *b* 29 June 1954

3e *Olivia Joan [Mrs Rodney Douglas-Pennant, Little White House, Church Lane, Longworth, Oxon OX13 5DX]; *b* 2 June 1934; *m* 1st 7 Sept 1957 (*divorce* 1972) Richard Weston Herbert, s of Preb Joseph Herbert, MA; *m* 2nd 1985, as his 3rd w, Rodney Archibald Douglas-Pennant (*d* 1993; *see* PENRHYN, B) and by her 1st husb has had:

  1f A son; *b* and *d* 30 Aug 1960

  1f *Catherine Alexandra [Mrs Richard Spencer, 6480 North Little Falls Rd, Arlington, VA 22213, USA]; *b* 12 Oct 1963; *m* 1988 *Richard J Spencer, s of Geoffrey Spencer, of Lectoure, France, and has:

    1g *Henry Frederick; *b* 1993

1d Margaret Griselda; *b* 29 April 1888; *m* 1st 9 July 1912 Stuart Andros De la Rue (*d* 26 Oct 1927), yst s of Sir Thomas Andros De la Rue, 1st Bt (*qv*), and had issue; *m* 2nd 17 March 1928 Air Marshal Sir Bertine Entwistle Sutton, KBE, CB, DSO, MC (*d* 28 Sept 1946), and *d* 1987, having had further issue

1c Marion Hester; *m* 1881 Maj Stephen Blyth Moore, Roy Scots (*d* S Africa 4 June 1901), and *d* 11 Feb 1934, leaving issue

3b David Ogilvy; *b* 18 July 1826; *d* unm 2 Sept 1853

1b Helen Georgina Elizabeth; *m* 4 July 1871 Andrew Webster (*dsp* 1876), of Rutherford, Peebles, and *d* 2 Dec 1904

3a James; *b* 1751; *d* unm 1797

1a Elizabeth Susannah; *m* Andrew WEDDERBURN later COLVILE (*see* below) and *dsp* 1803

2a Mary; *m* 1817 Rev John Wellings and *d* 1858, leaving issue

3a Catherine Georgiana; *m* 1810 Patrick Stirling of Kippendavie and *d* 1863, leaving issue

4 Alexander; *b* 1718; *d* unm 1788

1 Elizabeth; *m* Alexander Read of Torbeg and had issue

2 Grizel; *m* James Graham of Meathie and *dsp*

3 Katharine; *m* David Scrymgeour of Birkhill

The 4th Bt's est son,

Sir JOHN WEDDERBURN, 5th Bt; *b* 4 Aug 1704; *m* 22 Oct 1724 Jean, dau of John Fullarton of that Ilk, and having fought as a Jacobite at Culloden 1746 and been taken prisoner was attainted and executed at Kennington Common 28 Nov 1746, when the btcy was forfeited, leaving, with other issue:

1 Alexander; *b* 1727; *dvp* unm

2 John; *b* 21 Feb 1729; Cornet in Lord Ogilvy's (Jacobite) Regt at Culloden; after his f's death lived some years in Jamaica; became head of family on extinction of male line of er branch 1761; *m* 1st 25 Nov 1769 Margaret (*d* 23 March 1775), est dau of David, self-styled 5th Earl of Airlie (*qv*), by his 1st w, and *d* 13 June 1803, having had:

(1) John; *b* 1771; *d* 22 June 1783

(2) **Sir David Wedderburn, 1st Bt** (UK), so *cr* 10 Aug 1803, with remainder, failing heirs male of his own body, to the heirs male of the body of Sir ALEXANDER, 4th Bt (his ggf), of Balindean; *b* 30 March 1775; MP Perth Burghs, PMG Scotland; *m* 2 Sept 1800 Margaret (*d* 14 Feb 1845), 2nd dau of George Brown, of Eillistoun, Roxburghshire, by Dorothea, est dau of Col James Dundas, 24th of Dundas, and *dsps* 7 April 1858, having had two sons (*d* young)

(1) Margaret; *b* 1772; *m* 5 May 1803 Philip Dundas, MP Galton, and *d* 1807, leaving issue

(2) Jean; *b* 31 July 1773; *m* 1805 John Hope Oliphant, HEICS, of Penang, Prince Edward's Island, and *d* 24 Jan 1861, having had issue (*see* 1970 edn RAMSAY, Bt, of Bamff)

2 (cont.) John Wedderburn *m* 2nd 27 Dec 1780 Alicia/Alice (*d* 24 June 1831), 2nd dau of Col James Dundas, 24th of Dundas, and by her had, with other issue:

(3) **Sir John Wedderburn, 2nd Bt**; *b* 1 May 1789; HEICS; *m* 7 Sept 1822 Henrietta Louisa (*d* 7 April 1881), dau of William Milburn, HEICS, and *d* 2 July 1862, having had, with two daus (*d* unm):

  1a John; *b* 9 May 1825; Bengal CS; *m* 29 Jan 1856 Alice, dau of Dandison Coates Bell, Bombay Med Serv, and was murdered with his w and s (John James; *b* 15 Nov 1856) by mutineers at Hissar, Upper India, 29 May 1857

  2a **Sir David Wedderburn, 3rd Bt**; *b* 20 Dec 1835; *educ* Cambridge (BA); Capt 3rd Bn Glos Regt; advocate, MP S Ayrshire 1868–74 and Haddington Burghs; *d* unm 18 Sept 1882

  3a **Sir William Wedderburn, 4th Bt**, of Balindean, JP, DL Glos; *b* 25 March 1838; MP (Lib) Banffshire 1893–1900; Bombay CS 1859–87; *m* 12 Sept 1878 Mary Blanche (*d* 7 Oct 1933), only dau of Henry William Hoskyns, of Somerset, and *d* 25 Jan 1918, having had:

1b Dorothy Hope; *b* 24 June 1879; *m* 11 Feb 1904 Maj Hugh Courtenay Fownes Luttrell, MP (*d* 14 Jan 1918), 2nd s of George Fownes Luttrell, of Dunster Castle, Somerset, and *d* 16 Feb 1960, leaving issue

2b Margaret Griselda; *b* 3 Aug 1884; *m* 19 April 1906 Capt Charles Albert Fremantle, DSO, RN, and *d* 21 March 1918, leaving issue (*see* COTTESLOE, B)

1a Alicia Henrietta; *m* 22 Jan 1862 Gen Sir William Hope, 14th Bt, KCB (*qv*), and *d* 19 June 1901

2a Louisa Jane; *m* 7 Jan 1869 Edward Hope Percival, Bombay CS (*d* 11 May 1904), and *d* 27 April 1895, leaving issue

(4) Alexander, of Inveresk; *b* 18 June 1791; Col Coldstream Gds; *m* 28 Jan 1836 Elizabeth Julia (*m* 2nd 8 Aug 1843 Thomas Tyrwhitt-Drake, JP, DL, of St Donat's Castle, Glam (*d* 24 July 1888), and *d* 4 July 1885, leaving issue), dau of John Stratton, and *dsp* 30 July 1839

(3) Louisa Dorothea; *b* 8 June 1786; *m* 9 Feb 1803 4th Earl of Hopetoun and *d* 16 July 1836, leaving issue (*see* LINLITHGOW, M)

(4) Anne; *b* 14 Feb 1788; *m* 17 June 1805 Sir John Hope, 11th Bt (*qv*), and *d* 17 March 1867, leaving issue

3 James WEDDERBURN later WEDDERBURN-COLVILE of Inveresk; *b* 28 Aug 1730; *m* March 1774 Isabella (*d* 14 Jan 1821), dau of Andrew Blackburn and great-great-niece of 3rd and last Lord Colvill of Ochiltree, and *d* 14 Dec 1807, leaving:

(1) Andrew WEDDERBURN-COLVILE later COLVILE (roy licence 22 June 1814); *b* 6 Nov 1779; *m* 1st 27 Dec 1802 Elizabeth Susannah (*dsp* 22 Dec 1803), dau of John Wedderburn, of Clapham; *m* 2nd 26 June 1806 Hon Mary Louisa Eden (*d* 2 Dec 1858), 5th dau of 1st Baron Auckland (*qv*), and *d* 3 Feb 1856, having by her had, with other issue:

  1a James William (Sir), PC, of Craigflower and Ochiltree, Fife; *b* 12 Jan 1810; Advocate-Gen Bengal Ct 1845, Judge Bengal Supreme Ct 1848 , ktd 1848, Ch Justice 1855, ret 1859; memb Judicial Ctee PC 1871; *m* 13 April 1857 Frances Elinor, dau of John Peter Grant, memb Supreme Cncl Calcutta, and *d* 6 Dec 1880, having had:

    1b Andrew John Wedderburn; *b* 30 Jan 1859; *d* 5 Nov 1876

  2a Eden, of Craigflower; *b* 12 Feb 1819; *m* 4 Dec 1845 Anne (*d* 27 Aug 1891), dau of Col John Maxwell, 15th Foot, and *dsp* 2 April 1893

  1a Isabella; *m* 13 March 1834 Rev Samuel Marindin (*d* 3 Jan 1852), of Chesterton, Salop, and had issue

  2a Georgiana Mary; *m* 29 Sept 1947 1st and last Baron Blachford of Wisdome (*dsp* 21 Nov 1889) and *d* 13 July 1900

  3a Margaret Agnes; *m* 12 Dec 1856 Rev Charles Kegan Paul and *d* 30 March 1905, leaving issue

(2) Peter WEDDERBURN-COLVILE later WEDDERBURN OGILVY (1826 on death of his f-in-law); *b* 23 Sept 1781; *m* 20 April 1811 Anna (*d* May 1853), dau and heiress of James Ogilvy of Ruthven, Forfar, and *d* 30 March 1873, having had, with another s (*d* young) and three daus (*d* unm):

  1a Thomas, of Ruthven, Forfar; *b* 8 Sept 1814; Col 2nd Life Gds; *m* 7 Aug 1856 Lady Henrietta Louisa Fermor (*d* 20 Aug 1888), dau of 4th Earl of Pomfret (*see* HESKETH, B), and *dsp* 12 Oct 1899

  2a Peter; *b* 15 Nov 1815; Madras NI; *dsp* 1847

  3a John Andrew, of Ruthven, Forfar; *b* 2 July 1818; Maj Perthshire Mil (25th KO Borderers); *m* 26 June 1860 Janet Stuart Gray (*d* 7 May 1912), dau of Maj James Coutts Crawford Gray, HEICS, and *d* 17 Sept 1906, having had:

    1b Peter; *b* 8 April 1861; *d* unm 24 March 1883

    2b Charles James; *b* 21 Nov 1862; *d* unm 6 March 1900

    3b JOHN ANDREW (Sir), **5th Bt**

    4b Thomas; *b* 1 Oct 1870; Lt Scottish Horse Yeo; *m* 18 Dec 1899 Marion Agnes (*d* 1940), 2nd dau of Stephen Lancelot Koe, of Brighton, and *d* 25 Jan 1905, leaving:

      1c Donald Stephen; *b* 23 Oct 1900; Sub-Lt RNVR WW II; *m* 1st 11 June 1924 Mona Alys (*d* 12 Dec 1925), 2nd dau of William Moss Eustace, and had:

        1d +Caryl Eustace [Caryl Wedderburn-Ogilvy Esq, Pucklepeggies, 21 South Glassford St, Milngavie, Glasgow]; *b* 10 Dec 1925; ARIBA, DArch Dundee; *m* 16 Feb 1953 *Katharine Mary, DA (Dundee), only dau of William Steele, and has:

          1e +Niall; *b* 5 Aug 1955; *m* 1977 *Elaine Isobel Margaret, er dau of John Coutts Meekison, and has:

            1f *Sarah Victoria; *b* 1983

          1e *Penelope; *b* 12 Sept 1959

          2e *Verity; *b* 9 March 1965

      1c (cont.) Donald Wedderburn-Ogilvy *m* 2nd 7 Feb 1929 Myra Caroline Henrietta (*d* 1990), only dau of Lt-Col Henry Montague Eustace, DSO, Middx Regt, and was *ka* 8 May 1941, having by her had:

        2d +Peter [Lt-Cdr Peter Wedderburn-Ogilvy RN, Oak House, Froxfield, Petersfield GU32 1EE]; *b* 20 March 1931; *educ* RNC Dartmouth; Lt-Cdr RN (ret 1969); *m* 15 Aug 1959 *Philippa Sabine Burt, only child of Col Frederick Arthur Woods, MA, RAPC, and has:

          1e *Finella Sabine Clare; *b* 8 Feb 1962

          2e *Helen Augusta Sophia [Mrs Angus Lawson, The Hay Barn, Upper Harlestone, Northants NN7 4EL]; *b* 14 June 1964; *m* 13 June 1992 *Angus James Lawson, s of Capt John Lawson, of Newton Ferrers, Devon, and has:

            1f *Max Peter Fergusson; *b* 23 Aug 1996

          3e *Andrea Henrietta Louise; *b* 1 Nov 1968

        1d *Alys; *b* 2 April 1930; MCSP; *m* 13 May 1961 John Curtis Wernher Eustace, CIE (*d* 1972), s of Maj-Gen Alexander Henry Eustace, CB, CBE, DSO, and has:

          1e *Catherine Helena; *b* 30 May 1962

          2e *Cassandra Mary; *b* 20 Nov 1963

          3e *Margaret Alison; *b* 20 Nov 1963

          4e *Emily Anne; *b* 31 July 1967

      1c Isla May; *b* 27 Feb 1904; *d* 22 May 1906

5b Donald Stuart; *b* 20 Sept 1874; Lt Scottish Horse Yeo; *d* unm 4 June 1905

6b Walter Gray; *b* 7 July 1880; Capt Scottish Horse Yeo (TF); *m* 23 Feb 1916 Norah Kathleen (*d* 28 Oct 1966), yst dau of C Temple Layton, JP, and *d* following an accident 10 Oct 1944

1b Annie Ethel; *d* unm 22 Oct 1945

2b Isabella; *d* unm 25 March 1949

3b Catherine Lilias; *m* 26 Oct 1909 Robert Henry Bullen, est s of Francis Denis Bullen, MD, of Cork, and *d* 12 Sept 1953

4a James; *b* 4 Aug 1820; Lt-Col Perths Vols, Capt 25th Regt; *m* 24 Jan 1856 Catherine Lilias Harriet (*d* 22 Dec 1909), only child of William Ramsay (*see* 1970 edn RAMSAY, Bt, of Bamff), and *dsp* 28 Jan 1893

(3) James WEDDERBURN-COLVILE later WEDDERBURN; *b* 12 Nov 1782; Slr-Gen Scotland 1816; *m* 28 Oct 1813 Isabella (*d* 2 Nov 1865), sis of Sir George Clerk, 6th Bt (*qv*), and *d* 7 Nov 1822, leaving:

1a James, MD; *b* 23 Sept 1814; *d* unm 1863

2a George, WS, of Edinburgh; *b* 25 March 1817; *d* unm 1865

3a John; *b* 5 July 1820; Maj-Gen Bengal Army; *m* 1846 Matilda (*d* 19 Jan 1874), dau of Don Costello, and *dsp* 4 Jan 1879

4a Andrew WEDDERBURN-COLVILE later WEDDERBURN-MAXWELL (1879), of Middlebie, Dumfriesshire, and Glenlair, Dalbeattie, Kirkcudbrightshire, JP; *b* 16 Dec 1821; Madras CS 1841–78; *m* 14 Sept 1847 Joanna, dau of James Keir, MD, and *d* 12 May 1896, leaving, with a dau (*d* unm):

1b James Andrew Colvile, of Middlebie and Glenlair, JP Kirkcudbrightshire; *b* 5 Feb 1849; Maj Bengal SC, served Jandola Expdn 1880, Burma Campaign 1886–87 (medal with clasp); *m* 29 Oct 1891 Helen Mary Godfrey (*d* 20 July 1946), dau of Rev Henry Godfrey Godfrey-Faussett-Osborne, of Sittingbourne, and *d* 28 Dec 1917, leaving:

1c John, DSO (1943), MC (1918); *b* 20 July 1894; *educ* Charterhouse and RMA Woolwich; Col, T/Brig RA, WWs I and II (wounded); *m* 27 April 1922 Hon Ann Madeline Cunliffe, 2nd dau of 1st Baron Cunliffe (*qv*), and *d* 1990, leaving:

1d +Keir; *b* 27 Oct 1924; *educ* Charterhouse; *m* 1st 2 June 1951 Anne, est dau of Jan Brink, of Johannesburg and Copenhagen, and has:

1e +John; *b* 8 Aug 1952; *m* 1973 *Barbara, only dau of G G Bruwer, of Bulawayo, and has:

1f +James; *b* 1978

2f +A son; *b* 1984

2e +Philip; *b* 11 May 1954; *m* 1978 *Lynda Hopkins

1d (cont.) Keir Wedderburn-Maxwell *m* 2nd 1962 *Janet, dau of Oliver Hodgkin, of Rivonia, Johannesburg, and by her has:

3f +Andrew; *b* 13 Sept 1963

4f +Adrian Keir; *b* 20 Aug 1965

1f *Eloise; *b* 1967

2d +John Anthony [John Wedderburn-Maxwell Esq, Brewer's Farm, W Tisted, Hants SO24 0HQ]; *b* 3 June 1941; *educ* Harrow and Seale Hayne Ag Coll (NDA, CDA); *m* 6 Dec 1969 *Priscilla Aileen Ann, dau of Maj H C Mooney, of Pietermaritzburg, S Africa, and has:

1e +Andrew Franklyn; *b* 1975

2e +Matthew Charles; *b* 1981

1e *Clare Louise; *b* 1971

1d *Gillian; *b* 2 Jan 1928; LRAM, LGSM, AGSM; *m* 1 Nov 1954 *Robert Beaumont Shepherd, s of Percy Beaumont Shepheard, of Ewell, Surrey, and has had, with a dau (*d* an infant Oct 1960):

1e *Simon Beaumont; *b* 18 March 1957

1e *Janet Robina; *b* 13 Sept 1955

2e *Anne Catherine; *b* 13 Jan 1963

3e *Emma Gillian; *b* 6 Dec 1964

2d *Robina [Mrs Douglas Turner, Huntsman's Cott, Whistley Green, Hurst, Reading, Berks]; *b* 9 Sept 1932; *m* 21 Oct 1960 *Capt Douglas John Turner, AFRAeS, BEA, s of John Henry Turner, of Ruislip, Middx, and has:

1e *Amanda Jane; *b* 25 Oct 1961

2c Henry Godfrey, MBE (1930); *b* 31 July 1897; *educ* Charterhouse and RMA Woolwich; Capt Res of Offrs RA WW I, 4th Cl Order Nile; Sudan Pol Serv 1921–46; *m* 1949 Breeda O'Connor and *d* 1970, leaving:

1d +Andrew Patrick; *b* 12 Nov 1949; *educ* Portora Roy Sch

2d +Harry; *b* 16 Oct 1958

1d *Dorothy Breeda; *b* 25 March 1952

3c James; *b* 22 March 1899; 2nd Lt KOSB; *ka* 1 Oct 1918

1c Dorothy Helen; *b* 20 Aug 1892; *d* umn 1 Dec 1870

2c Maud; *b* 11 Oct 1895; WW I as VAD, Women's Legn MT, attd RASC 1918–20; *d* unm 4 Dec 1961

2b Harry George WEDDERBURN-MAXWELL later WEDDERBURN, JP Fife; *b* 18 Nov 1850; *educ* Balliol Coll Oxford (MA); barrister, Administrator-Gen High Ct Madras; *m* 29 Dec 1881 Jane Trevelvan (*d* 29 Dec 1940), dau of David Fremantle Carmichael, Madras CS, and *d* 5 July 1933, leaving:

1c Charles Carmichael; *b* 31 Dec 1882; *m* 21 Dec 1918 Jessie Mary (*d* 10 Nov 1955), only dau of Walter Edwin Fairlie, of Bishopstone, Northwood, and *d* 5 Dec 1951, having had:

1d David Walter Fairlie; *b* 18 Jan 1923; LAC RAFVR WW II; *das* Nov 1941

2d +Michael Charles Fairlie; *b* 27 June 1924; *educ* Woodbridge GS; *m* Sept 1955 *Mary Catherine, dau of Sidney George Esbester, of Duffield, Derbys, and has:

1e +John Michael Champion; *b* 24 April 1957

1e *Katherine Jane; *b* 15 Dec 1958

2e *Claire Mary; *b* 3 Jan 1962

1d *Maisie Jane Fairlie; *b* 15 Nov 1919; *m* 1 Dec 1951 *Francis Charles Wade, s of Charles Cecil Wade, and has:

1e *Nicholas Charles; *b* 22 Aug 1953

2e *David Francis; *b* 22 Aug 1953

2c Harry Francis Keir; *b* 5 April 1899; Lt-Col Black Watch WWs I and II; *m* 5 Oct 1929 *Mary Sharp [Mrs Harry Wedderburn, Mountquhanie, Cupar, Fife KY15 4QJ], dau of Lt-Col Henry Alexander Bethune (*see* 1970 edn BETHUNE, Bt), and *das* 5 Feb 1943, leaving:

1d +Andrew Harry WEDDERBURN later WEDDERBURN-BETHUNE (March 1960 under terms of gf's will) [Andrew Wedderburn-Bethune Esq, Mountquhanie, Cupar, Fife]; *b* 4 Dec 1933; *educ* Trin Coll Glenalmond and RMC Sandhurst; Capt Black Watch (ret 1964); *m* 23 April 1960 *Mary Felicity Lovat, yr dau of Dr Robert Bruce Frazer, and has:

1e +(Alexander) Guy; *b* 19 April 1965; *m* *Lucy, yst dau of D S Rhodes, of Blairgowrie, Perthshire, and has:

1f *Laura Rose; *b* 1993

2f *Anna Jasmine (twin); *b* 1993

2e +Patrick Keir; *b* 6 April 1967

3e +Andrew Michael Stewart; *b* 15 July 1969

4e +Charles Dominic; *b* 26 Sept 1973

1e *Gabrielle Mary; *b* 20 Feb 1962

2e *Frances Catriona; *b* 22 Feb 1964; *m* 1991 *Richard Thurlow

1d *Penelope Mary Bethune [Mrs John Piggott, Newholme, Spalding Rd, Weston Hills, Spalding, Lincs]; *b* 28 Sept 1930; *m* 27 July 1949 *John Piggott, only s of Erastus Piggott, of Lymington, Hants, and has:

1e *John Wedderburn; *b* 1950

2e *Robin Andrew Keir Wedderburn; *b* 1957

1c Margaret; *m* 30 March 1916 her sister's bro-in-law Capt William Henry MacAllan, Cameronians (Scots Rifles) (*d* 2 Aug 1928), s of Allan MacAllan, of Edinburgh, and *d* 19 Sept 1966, leaving issue

2c Beatrix Aytoun; *m* 11 April 1912 Col Allan Ronald MacAllan, Cameronians (Scots Rifles) (*das* 26 Sept 1943), s of Allan MacAllan, of Edinburgh, and *d* 26 Sept 1966, leaving issue

3c *Katharine Anne; *m* 21 Sept 1911 (*divorce* 1945) Capt John Pelham Champion, CBE, DSO, RN (*d* 13 Feb 1955), s of Rev Francis Beresford Champion, Rector Great Bealings, Suffolk

3b Francis Edward Keir; *b* 11 March 1857; ICS; *d* unm 1 Feb 1893

4b Charles Alexander; *b* 1858; Lt 18th Roy Irish Regt; *d* unm 13 Nov 1882

1b Mary; *m* 25 Dec 1891 Charles Cannan (*d* 15 Dec 1919), Fell Trin Coll Oxford, s of David Alexander Cannan, of Kirkcudbrightshire, and *d* St Jean-Cap Ferrat 7 April 1943, leaving issue

1a Janet Isabella; *m* 1838 James Hay Mackenzie (*d* 16 Feb 1852) and *d* 1852, leaving issue

2a Jean; *m* 1838 Peter Blackburn, MP (*d* 20 May 1870), of Killearn, and *d* 1879, leaving issue

3a Jemima; *m* 12 June 1849 Prof Hugh Blackburn, of Roshven, Lochailort, bro of Baron Blackburn of Killearn (LP, *see* 1896 edn), and had issue

(1) Jean; *m* 1807 5th Earl of Selkirk (*qv*)

1 Margaret; *m* Richard Dundas of Blair and had issue

The 4th Bt's cousin,

Sir JOHN ANDREW WEDDERBURN-OGILVY later OGILVY-WEDDERBURN, **5th Bt**, JP Forfar; *b* 16 Sept 1866; *educ* Bath Coll; Maj TFR Scottish Horse WW I; *m* 4 Oct 1909 Meta Aileen Odette (*d* 23 Sept 1952), er dau of Brig-Gen Edward George Grogan, CB, CBE, JP, and *d* 10 March 1956, leaving:

1 (JOHN) PETER (Sir), **6th Bt**

1 *Janet Meta; Jr Cdr ATS WW II; *m* 9 July 1940 Francis William Alfred Fairfax-Cholmeley, CBE (*d* 1983), er s of Hugh Charles Fairfax-Cholmeley, of Swathgill, Hovingham, York, and has had:

(1) Hugh Thomas Andrew; *b* 28 May 1946; *d* in skiing accident 12 April 1968

(1) *Caroline Ann [Mrs Michael Hippisley, Tarrie Bank House, by Arbroath, Angus]; *b* 15 Sept 1941; *m* 29 July 1961 *Michael John Hippisley, er s of John Preston Hippisley, of Stoneaston, nr Bath, and has:

1a *David John; *b* 1971

1a *Fiona Jane; *b* 25 April 1964

2a *Catherine Ann; *b* 21 Sept 1965

3a *Lucinda Mary; *b* 9 May 1969

(2) *Mary Meta; *b* 16 Jan 1948; *m* 1971 *Lt Mohamed Ali Dorgham Methoui and has:

1a *Halim; *b* 1973

2a *Ghazi; *b* 1976

2 *Elspeth Mary; *b* 1913

3 *Katharine Andrea, JP [Mrs George Sisson JP, Planetrees, Wall, Hexham, Northumberland NE46 4EQ]; *m* 1 June 1940 *George Macfarlan Sisson, OBE, s of George Sisson, of Newcastle, and has:

(1) *John Edward [John Sisson, 1120 Blossom Trail, New Castle, CA 95658, USA]; *b* 12 Sept 1943; *educ* Charterhouse and Ch Ch Oxford; *m* 1981 *Dr Judy Pino, of California

(2) *David George [David Sisson Esq, pPovidence House, Blackford, Wedmore, Somerset BS28 4NA]; *b* 6 April 1945; *educ* Rossall and RAC Cirencester; *m* 1st 21 March 1970 (*divorce* 1993) Gillian, dau of Dr Dennis Barnes, of Carlisle and has:

1a *Katherine Rachel; *b* 1971; *m* 20 Sept 1997 *Joseph Francis Horgan, s of Joseph Horgan, of Birmingham

2a *Rosemary Ann; *b* 1973

3a *Suzannah Clare; *b* 1975

(2) (cont.) David Sisson *m* 2nd 1993 *Deirdre Sally Angela, only dau of Colin Page, of Aylesbury, and by her has:

1a *Charles David Page; *b* 25 Feb 1995

(3) *Alexander William [Alexander Sisson Esq, 3 High St, Harrogate HG2 7HX]; *b* 9 March 1949; *educ* Rossall; *m* 1973 (*divorce* 1993) Penelope, 2nd dau of Cdr Harold Turner, of Tacolneston, Norwich, and has:

1a *William George; *b* 1976
1a *Alice Mary; *b* 1978
2a *Emily Rose; *b* 1981
(1) *Julia Andrea; *b* 28 April 1952; *m* 1972 (*divorce* 1987) Timothy Dallas Cairns

The 5th Bt's only son,
    Sir (John) Peter Ogilvy-Wedderburn, 6th Bt; *b* 29 Sept 1917; *educ* Nautical Coll Pangbourne; Cdr RN; *m* 16 March 1946 *Elizabeth Katharine [Dowager Lady Ogilvy-Wedderburn, Wester Strathgarry, Killiecrankie, Perthshire PH16 5LJ], dau of John Arthur Cox, of Drumkilbo, Meigle, Perthshire, and *d* 13 Aug 1977, leaving:

1 Sir ANDREW JOHN ALEXANDER OGILVY-WEDDERBURN, **7th and present Bt**
   1 *Henrietta Katharine [Mrs Sebastian Thewes, Strathgarry House, Killiecrankie, Perthshire PH16 5LJ]; *b* 2 Jan 1947; *m* 5 Aug 1972 *Sebastian P Thewes, only s of John Thewes, of St Thomas Bay, Malta, and has:

    (1) *Robert John Peter; *b* 1974
    (2) *James Andrew; *b* 1976
    (1) *Arabella Katherine; *b* 1979
    (2) *Jemima Caroline; *b* 1981

2 *Jean Aileen [Mrs Sam Chesterton, Buen Vino, Los Marines 21293, Prov de Huelva, Spain]; *b* 18 June 1948; *m* 1983 *Sam Henry Chesterton, yr s of Sir Oliver Sidney Chesterton, MC, and has:

    (1) *Peter-Patrick Santiago (Jago); *b* 1984
    (2) *Charles Ernest Alfonso; *b* 1988
    (1) *Grania Laura; *b* 1986

3 *Elizabeth Helen; *b* 24 Sept 1950

Agga Maha Thray Sithu Burma 1956, Panglima Mangku Negara Fedn Malaya 1959; *m* 30 July 1930 (Alice Alexandra) Constance, JP (Croydon 1954); *d* 30 Nov 1998, er dau of Alderman Walter Robert Wills, Ld Mayor Cardiff 1945–46, and *d* 30 Aug 1976, leaving:

1 GWILYM REES REES-WILLIAMS, **2nd Baron Ogmore**
2 +MORGAN REES [The Hon Morgan Rees-Williams, 50 Novello St, London SW6 4JB]; *b* 19 Dec 1937; heir presumptive; *educ* Mill Hill; Lt Welch Regt (TA); *m* 1st 30 May 1964 (*divorce* 1970) Patricia, only dau of C Paris Jones; *m* 2nd 1972 (*divorce* 1976) Roberta, dau of Capt Alec Stratford Cunningham-Reid, DFC; *m* 3rd 1990 *Beata, dau of Zdislaw Solski, and by her has:
    (1) +Tudor David; *b* 11 Dec 1991
    (2) +Dylan; *b* 1994
1 *(Joan) Elizabeth Rees [The Hon Mrs Elizabeth Harris, 7 Grove Court, Drayton Gdns, London SW10]; *b* 1 May 1936; *educ* Croham Hurst Sch Croydon, Mount Olivet Lausanne and RADA; author *Love, Honour and Dismay*; *m* 1st 9 Feb 1957 (*divorce* 1970) Richard St John Harris, the actor, yr s of Ivan Harris, of Limerick, and has:
    (1) *Damian David; *b* 2 Aug 1958; *m* 1981 *Annabel Joan, only dau of Robert Noel Brand Brooks (*see* CRAWSHAW, B), and has:
       1a *Ella; *b* 1989
    (2) *Jared Francis; *b* 24 Aug 1961; *m* 1989 *Jacqueline, yst dau of Ralph I Goldenberg, of Chicago
    (3) *Jamie St John; *b* 15 May 1963; *m* 1994 *Soumaya —, actress, of Morocco
1 (cont.) The Hon Mrs Elizabeth Harris *m* 2nd 26 Aug 1971 (*divorce* 1975), as his 5th w, Rex Carey Harrison (later Sir Rex Harrison; *d* 1990), the actor, s of William Reginald Harrison, of Liverpool, and brother of Lady Kilmuir (*qv*); *m* 3rd 1981 (*divorce* 1985, resumed name HARRIS by deed poll 1986) Peter Michael Aitken (*see* BEAVERBROOK, B)

OGMORE

Arms: Az. two bars wavy arg., on a chief arched of the second between as many hurts, each charged with a quatrefoil or, a hurt thereon a sun in splendour of the third. **Crest:** A tiger's head couped ppr., charged on the neck with three chevronels couped gu. **Supporters:** Dexter, a tiger ppr., charged on the shoulder with three chevronels couped gu.; sinister, a horse arg. **Motto:** *Ffyddlon hyd angau* ('Faithful unto death'). **Creation:** B. (UK) 5 July 1950.

THE 2ND BARON OGMORE, of Bridgend, Co Glamorgan (Gwilym Rees Rees-Williams) [The Rt Hon The Lord Ogmore, House of Lords, London SW1A 0PW]; *b* 5 May 1931; *s* f 1976; *educ* Mill Hill and St Luke's Coll Exeter; *m* 10 June 1967 *Gillian Mavis, dau of Maurice Keith Slack, of Hindley, Lancs, and has:

1 *Christine Ann; *b* 19 Aug 1968
2 *Jennet Elizabeth; *b* 2 Sept 1970

Lineage: ISAAC WILLIAMS, whose family held a property called Sker, nr Porthcawl, W Glam, was the last to occupy it; *d* 29 Dec 1766, leaving a dau (Elizabeth, known as 'The Maid of Sker' in Welsh ballads, *m* Sept 1766 Thomas Kirkhouse, lawyer, and *d* 3 Jan 1776)

ISAAC's descendant,
   GEORGE WILLIAMS; *b* 1849; engr; *m* 1870 Elvira, dau of John Rees, of Garth Farm, Dowlais, Glam, contractor Dowlais Ironworks, and *d* 1930, leaving:

WILLIAM REES WILLIAMS, of Garth-celyn, Bridgend; *b* 17 Sept 1875; *educ* Bridgend GS, Brighton House Sch Clifton and RVC London (MRCVS 1898); FRCVS, Capt RAVC (TF); *m* June 1902 Jennet (*d* 18 May 1946), dau of Morgan David, of Bridgend, and *d* 14 Dec 1949, leaving:

DAVID REES WILLIAMS, **1st Baron Ogmore**, of Bridgend, Co Glamorgan (UK), so *cr* 5 July 1950, PC (1951), TD; *b* 22 Nov 1903; *educ* Mill Hill and U of Wales; slr 1929, advocate and slr Straits Settlements, MP (Lab) S Croydon 1945–50, pres first Gen Mil Court Berlin 1945, memb UK Mission Sarawak 1946, Chm Burma Frontier Areas Ctee Enquiry 1947, Parly U-Sec Colonies 1947, Cwlth Rels 1950, UK Del to UN 1950, Min Civil Aviation 1951, memb Nigerian Bar 1956, Advsr Malayan Delegn Constitutional Conf Fedn 1956, Lt-Col RA WW II, Mil Govt Germany, dir Leo Laboratories, Property Owners' Buildg Soc, Pres Bridgend YMCA, memb Investiture Ctee Investiture HRH THE PRINCE OF WALES 1969, Order

O'HAGAN

Arms: Quarterly, 1st and 4th, erm. a bend az., on a chief or the last a fleur-de-lys or (for O'HAGAN); 2nd and 3rd, arg. a fess sa., in chief three mullets of the second (for TOWNELEY). **Crests:** 1 On a Roman fasces lying fesswise ppr. a cubit arm vested gu., cuffed erm., the hand holding a dagger erect, both ppr. (for O'HAGAN), 2 On a perch or a hawk close ppr., beaked and belled gold, jessed gu. (for TOWNELEY). **Supporters:** Two lions or, collared gemel sa., pendant therefrom an escutcheon arg. charged with a dexter hand couped gu. **Mottoes:** 1 *Mihi res non me rebus* ('Possessions exist for me, not me for them'), 2 *Buas no bar* ('Victory or death'), 3 *Tenez le vraye* ('Keep the truth'). **Creation:** B. (UK) 14 June 1870.

THE 4TH BARON O'HAGAN OF TULLAHOGUE, Co Tyrone (Charles Towneley Strachey) [The Rt Hon The Lord O'Hagan, The Old Rectory, Weare Gifford, Devon EX39 4QP]; *b* 6 Sept 1945; *s* gf 1961; *educ* Eton and New Coll Oxford (BA 1969, MA); Page Honour to HM THE QUEEN 1959–62, MEP (Ind) 1973–75, memb C working pty reform Ho Lds 1977, Jr Oppn Whip 1977–79, MEP (C) Devon 1979–94; *m* 1st 13 July 1967 (*divorce* 1984) HSH Princess Tamara, est dau of S/Ldr HSH Prince Michael Imeretinsky, RAFVR, of Menton (*see* 1970 edn KINNAIRD, L), and formerly w of Lt-Cdr Thomas Mervyn Smith-Dorrien-Smith, of Tresco Abbey, Scilly Isles, and Menton, and has:

1 *Nina Natalia O'Hagan; *b* 16 July 1968; *educ* N Foreland Lodge and Queen's Coll Oxford

The 4th BARON *m* 2nd 1985 (*divorce* 1995) Mrs Mary Claire Parsons, only dau of Rev Leslie Roose-Francis, of Bodmin, Cornwall; *m* 3rd 1995 *Mrs Elizabeth Lesley Eve Macnamara (*née* Smith) and by his 2nd w has:

2 *Antonia Philippa Mary; *b* 1986

Lineage (of O'Hagan): EDWARD O'HAGAN, of Belfast; *m* Mary, dau of Capt Thomas Bell, and had:

Sir THOMAS O'HAGAN, **1st Baron O'Hagan of Tullahogue**, Co Tyrone (UK), so *cr* 14 June 1870, KP (1882), PC (1861), QC (1849); *b* 29 May 1812; *educ* Belfast Academical Instn; barrister Dublin 1836, Ireland: Commr Nat Educn 1857–85, Bencher King's Inns 1859, Third Serjeant 1859–60, Slr-Gen 1860–61, Attorney-

Gen 1861–65, MP (Lib) Tralee 1863–65, Justice Common Pleas 1865–68, Ld Chllr (1st RC in post since JAMES II's time) 1868–74 and 1880–81, V-Chllr Roy U 1881–85, memb Senate Queen's U; m 1st 5 Feb 1836 Mary (d 1868), dau of Charles Hamilton Teeling, of Belfast, and had, with three other daus (d unm):

1 Charles; b 1838; d 1840

1 Madeleine; m 2 July 1870 Col John MacDonnell, DL, of Kilmore, Co Antrim, and dsp 14 Oct 1875. He d 13 Sept 1905

2 Frances Mary; m 2 Dec 1865 Mr Justice John O'Hagan, Ch Commr Land Court Ireland, and dsp 1910. He d Nov 1890

The **1st Baron** m 2nd 2 Aug 1871 Alice Mary (d 20 Nov 1921), yst dau and coheir of Col Charles Towneley (see below **Lineage (of Towneley)**), and d 1 Feb 1885, having by her had, with a dau (d an infant):

2 THOMAS TOWNELEY O'HAGAN, **2nd Baron O'Hagan of Tullahogue**; b 5 Dec 1878; Lt Gren. Gds; d unm 13 Dec 1900 S Africa

3 MAURICE HERBERT TOWNELEY, **3rd Baron**.

3 Kathleen Mary, Commr Girl Guides Cambs 1915–45; b 13 May 1876; m 20 May 1897 Louis Leopold Martial Baynard de Beaumont (d 6 April 1934) and d 25 March 1974 aged 97, leaving:

  (1) Charles-Louis Leopold Alfred, OBE (1959); b 5 May 1902; educ Trin Coll Cambridge (MA); W/Cdr RAuxAF, Pres Br Empire and Cwlth Fencing Fedn 1950 and Amateur Fencing Assoc 1956; m 1926 Guinevere Madi (d 1 Nov 1969), dau of James Grove-Crofts, and d 1972, leaving:

    1a *Robert Henri Louis Charles [Robin de Beaumont Esq, 25 Park Walk, Chelsea, London SW10 0AJ]; b 27 Sept 1926; educ Trin Coll Cambridge (MA); antiquarian book seller, AADipl; m Jan 1952 (divorce 1969) Joy Daphne Pettigrew and has:

      1b *Dominic Robert Charles Bell [Dominic de Beaumont Esq, 44 First Ave, London SW14 8SR]; b 20 Dec 1959; m 1987 *Gillian Mary-Louise McLaren and has:

        1c *Louis Alexander; b 1995

      1b *Lys Camilla Louise [Ms Lys de Beaumont, 77 Duke's Ave, London N10 2PY]; b 10 Aug 1956; has by *Nicholas Mahoney:

        1c *Fabian William Aimery Mahoney De BEAUMONT

        1c *Nuala Bernice Kathleen Mahoney De BEAUMONT

  (1) Elizabeth Vera Catherine Alice; b 6 March 1898; m 19 July 1932 Maj Hon Richard Coke, 3rd s of 2nd Earl of Leicester (qv), and d 1988, leaving issue

  (2) Marguerite Julia Caroline Jeanne; b 13 May 1899; d 1989

4 Mary Caroline, DBE (1919); b 25 Nov 1879; m 1 Oct 1912 Gen Sir Charles Carmichael Monro, 1st and last Bt, GCB, GCSI, GCMG, and dsp 28 August 1972. He d 7 Dec 1929

The 2nd BARON's bro,

  MAURICE HERBERT TOWNELEY O'HAGAN later TOWNELEY-O'HAGAN (roy licence 23 Nov 1909), **3rd Baron O'Hagan of Tullahogue**, JP Essex, Suffolk, Hants; b 20 Feb 1882; educ Marlborough and Trin Coll Cambridge (BA 1903, MA 1907); Assist Priv Sec to 1st Ld Admlty 1906–07, Ld-in-Waiting (Govt Whip) 1907–10, Capt RHA WW I, Hon Col 4th (Cadet) and 6th Bns Essex Regt (TA), Dir and Controller BRCS Suffolk, Chm Local Employment Ctee Min Labour Holloway, mil memb Essex TAA, Dep Speaker and Dep Chm Ctees Ho Lds 1950–58, County Pres Br Dairy Farmers' Assoc 1912–14, Chm Centl Chamber Ag 1929, memb King's Roll Nat Cncl, Grand Cross Queen Isabella Spain and Polar Star Sweden; m 1st 27 April 1911 Hon Frances Constance Maddalena (d 1 Aug 1931), only dau of 1st Baron Strachie (see 1965 edn), and d 18 Dec 1961, having had:

1 (Thomas) Anthony Edward TOWNELEY-O'HAGAN later Towneley STRACHEY (deed poll 13 Sept 1938); b 13 Sept 1917, educ Eton and Trin Coll Cambridge (BA 1939, MA 1941); WW II: Capt Somerset LI attd 6th/12th Frontier Force Regt (IA) 1941–43, Maj attd Special Forces Middle East and Balkans 1943–44 (despatches), GSO(2) War Office 1945, Sec CLA for Somerset 1946–49, assist ag economist U of Bristol 1949–50, resident land agent to Earl of Selborne 1951–53; m 11 Nov 1944 *Lady Mary Sophia Palmer (m 22nd 1981, as his 2nd w, (Francis) St John Gore, CBE; see GORE, Bt) [The Lady Mary Gore, Grove Farm, Stoke-by-Nayland, Essex CO6 4SL], Ldy-in-Waiting to HRH PRINCESS ELIZABETH 1944–47 (Extra Lady-in-Waiting 1947–49), yst dau of 3rd Earl of Selborne (qv), and d 1955, leaving:

  (1) CHARLES TOWNELEY STRACHEY, **4th and present Baron O'Hagan**

  (2) +RICHARD TOWNELEY; b 29 Dec 1950; heir presumptive; educ Eton and Bath Acad of Art; granted 3 Aug 1963 with sisters rank of baron's dau/yr s; m 1983 *Sally Anne, yr dau of Frederick Cecil Cross

  (1) *Frances Towneley [The Hon Mrs Gibson, The Fold, Parwich, Ashbourne, Derbys]; b 5 March 1948; m 31 March 1967 *Hugh Marcus Thornley Gibson (see GIBSON, B, and COWDRAY, V)

  (2) *Jane Towneley [The Hon Jane Strachey, 24 Kylestrome House, Cundy St, London SW1]; b 10 March 1953; m 1972 (divorce 1977, resumed maiden name) William Stone

1 *Helen Frances Alice [The Hon Mrs Curry-Towneley-O'Hagan, 24 Burgh St, London N1]; b 3 March 1912; VAD WW II; m 23 May 1940 Capt Ian Desmond CURRY later CURRY-TOWNELEY-O'HAGAN (deed poll 1942; d 1969), RA , 2nd s of Thomas David Curry, and has:

  (1) *Padraic Desmond [Padraic O'Hagan Esq, 29 Barons Court Rd, London W14]; sometime dir Rocky Horror Show; m 27 Nov 1971 *Judith Patricia, BA, only dau of Robin Sandbach Borwick (see BORWICK, B), and has:

    1a *Fiann James; b 31 Oct 1974; educ Oundle and London U (BSc)

    2a *Dickon Padraic; b 24 May 1977; educ Oundle

The **3rd Baron** m 2nd 30 July 1937 Evelyn Violet (d 26 Nov 1965), widow of Lt-Col Henry Osbert Samuel Cadogan, Roy Welch Fus, and dau of Harry Thornton Ross, and d 23 Dec 1955

Lineage (of Towneley): RICHARD; inherited c 1235 lands in Tunleia, nr Burnley, Lancs; had:

CECILIA; m John de la Legh (living 1340) and d by 1323, leaving, with an er s (Gilbert, m Alice, dau of Robert Vernon, of Warforth, Cheshire, and dsp):

RICHARD de TOWNELEY; MP Lancs 1361 and 1371, High Sheriff 1375–77, Receiver Duchy Lancaster 1353; m by 1345 Ellen — and d 1381, leaving, with

---

two yr sons (Robert; Henry) and a dau (Alice, m 1356 Edmund Dacre, est s of Sir Thomas Dacre):

JOHN TOWNELEY, of Towneley; b 1350; m 1382 Elizabeth, dau and heir of William de Rixton, and d 1399, leaving, with a dau (Matilda, m Sir William Fleming):

RICHARD TOWNELEY, of Towneley; b 1387; fought Agincourt 1415; m Alice — (living 1454) and d 1454, leaving:

JOHN TOWNELEY, of Towneley, for a chapel at which he had license from the Bp of Lichfield 1446; b c 1414; m 1445 Elizabeth, dau of Richard Sherburne, of Stonyhurst, and d c 1473, leaving, with four yr sons (Lawrence; Nicholas, m 1st Lettice (dsp), dau of William Talbot, m 2nd Elizabeth, widow of William Tempest, of Broughton (see LONDONDERRY, M), and dau of Richard Catterall, and by her was ancestor of the TOWNELEYs of Fulborne; Henry; Barnard) and a dau (Grace, m 1463 Roger Nowell, s of Alexander Nowell, of Read):

Sir RICHARD TOWNELEY, of Towneley; ktd at the Battle of Hutton Field in Wars of Roses 1481; m 1472 Jane, dau of Richard Southworth, of Salmesbury, and d 1482, leaving, with a yr s (Charles) and two daus (Isabel, m 1st Sir John Talbot and 2nd John Hopwood, of Hopwood; Grace, m 1492 Thomas Hesketh, of Rufford; see HESKETH, B):

Sir JOHN TOWNELEY, of Towneley; b 1473; High Sheriff Lancs 1531–40; m 1st Isabel (d 1522), dau and heir of Sir Charles Pilkington, of Gateford, Notts, and had:

1 RICHARD

2 Charles; m Elizabeth, widow of John Nowell, of Read, and dau of — Kay, and had:

  (1) John; m (by dispensation 1556) his 1st cousin once-removed Mary, dau and heir of Sir Richard Towneley, of Towneley (see below)

1 Helen; m Robert Nevile

2 Grace; m 1st Sir Robert Hesketh, of Rufford (see HESKETH, B); m 2nd Lawrence Halbergham

3 Jane; m 1st Thomas Sherburne; m 2nd Ralph Shuttleworth, of Hacking

Sir JOHN m 2nd Ann, dau of Ralph Catterall, and d 1541

The er son,

  RICHARD TOWNELEY, of Towneley; b c 1500; m 1511 Elizabeth, dau and heir of Henry Foljambe, of Walton, Derbys, and d c 1555, having had, with a yr s (John) and two daus (Bennett, m Thomas Nowell, of Read; Grace, m Hugh Halstead):

Sir RICHARD TOWNELEY; ktd at Siege of Leith 1547; m 1536 Frances, dau and heir of Christopher Wymbush, of Nocton, Lincs, and heir of her uncle Sir John Byron, and dvp 1554, leaving surv issue:

MARY Towneley, of Towneley; b 1542; m (by dispensation 1556) her 1st cousin once-removed John TOWNELEY (imprisoned as recusant 1581–1608, when he d) and had, with six yr sons (John, d 1632; Charles; b 1569; Christopher, b 1570, d 1623; Charles, b 1572, d c 1646; Thomas; Nicholas) and seven daus (Jennett; Frances; Mary; Anne, m 1st William Middleton and 2nd Edward Oxborne; Margaret; Elizabeth; Frances):

RICHARD TOWNELEY, of Towneley; b 29 April 1566; m Jane (d 1634), dau of Ralph Assheton, of Great Leaver, Lancs (see CLITHEROE, B), and d 29 Nov 1628, having had, with three er sons (John, d an infant; Richard, compounded for both the Towneley and Nocton estates with the Northern commrs for recusancy 20 Sept 1632, b 16 April 1598, d unm 1635; Thomas, b 1599), three yst sons (John, d an infant; John, d an infant; Christopher, attorney and antiquary, called 'The Transcriber' for having made transcriptions towards a history of Lancs, b 9 Jan 1603/4, m Alice, dau of John Braddyll, and d Aug 1674) and two daus (Frances, nun at St Omer; Anne, b 29 May 1611, m John Plumpton, est s of Sir Edward Plumpton, of Spofforth, Yorks, and d 1643):

CHARLES TOWNELEY, of Towneley; b 22 April 1600; royalist; m 1627 Mary (d May 1690 aged 91), dau of Sir Francis G Trappes-Byrnand, of Nidd, Yorks, and was ka Marston Moor 2 July 1644, his estates being sequestrated and Nocton sold to pay fines, but the Lancs property was preserved through the good offices of his cousin Sir Ralph Assheton, 2nd Bt, leaving, with three yr sons (John, d 1678; Charles; Francis) and three daus (Mary, m Sir Philip Constable, of Houghton, Yorks; Anne, d 1650; Catharine):

RICHARD TOWNELEY, of Towneley; b 1628; FRS; m Margaret (d 20 Jan 1672), dau of Clement Paston, of Birmingham, Norfolk, and d 22 Jan 1706/7, having had, with two est sons (Clement, b 1654, d 14 July 1666; Richard, b 1655, d an infant), four yst sons (John, b and d 1659; John (Rev), RC priest; Richard (Rev), RC priest, b 1664; Thomas, b 1669) and six daus (Mary; Anne; Dorothy, b 1660, m Francis Howard, of Corby, Cumberland, and had issue (see NORFOLK, D); Frances, m Cuthbert Kennet, of Cuxhow; Margaret, nun at St Victoire, Paris, b 1667; Cecily, nun at St Victoire):

CHARLES TOWNELEY, of Towneley; b 19 April 1658; m 1685 Ursula, dau of Richard Fermor, of Tusmore, Oxon, and d 1 March 1712, having had, with four yr sons (Charles, b 1690, d 1713; John, entered French serv and fought in Jacobite Uprising, Chev Order St Louis 1746, translated Hudibras into French verse 1757, b 1697, d unm 1782; George, b 1706, m Mary, dau and coheir of Albert Hodgson, who brought him Leighton Hall, Lancs, and d 1786; Francis, Col in French serv, raised and cmded Jacobite Manchester Regt 1745, b 1709, taken at Carlisle and executed London 30 July 1746) and six daus (Mary, b 1686, d 1716; Ursula, b 1687, d an infant; Charlotte, b 1692, d 1699; Margaret, d an infant; Ursula, nun at Louvain; Theresa, m Sir George Mostyn, 4th Bt (qv), and d 27 March 1766, leaving issue):

RICHARD TOWNELEY, of Towneley; b 1687; m Hon Mary Widdrington (d July 1731), er dau of 3rd Baron Widdrington of Blankney, and d 14 Aug 1735, having had, with four other sons (d in infancy):

1 William, of Towneley; b 1714; m Cecilia, dau and heir of Ralph Standish, of Standish (see NORFOLK, D), and d 2 Feb 1741, leaving:

  (1) Charles; built up the collection of classical antiquities known as 'The Towneley Marbles' (bought after his death by the Br Museum); b 1 Oct 1737; educ Douai; d unm 1805

(2) Ralph TOWNELEY later STANDISH (on inheriting the Standish estate); *b* 18 June 1739; *m* Henrietta, 9th dau of Roger Strickland, of Catterick, Yorks, and *dsp*

(3) Edward TOWNELEY later TOWNELEY-STANDISH, of Towneley and Standish (in which *s* bro); *m* Anne, dau of Basil Thomas Eccleston, of Eccleston, and *dsp* 28 March 1807

(1) Cecilia; *b* 20 July 1741; *m* 1762 Charles Strickland, of Sizergh, and had, with other issue:

　　1a Thomas; inherited the Standish estate from his uncle Edward

2 John, of Towneley, formerly of Cronsay House, Chiswick; *b* 15 June 1731; *s n* Edward in the Towneley estate and his cousin Henry Francis Widdrington in the Stella and Stanley estates, Co Durham; *m* Barbara (*d* 25 Dec 1797), 4th dau of Edward Dicconson, of Wrightington, Lancs, and *d* 13 May 1813, leaving:

(1) PEREGRINE EDWARD

(1) Barbara; *b* 14 April 1758; *m* 1785 Sir William Stanley, 5th Bt, of Hooton, Cheshire (*see* 1893 edn ERRINGTON, Bt, of Hooton), and *dsp* 5 Aug 1836. He *d* 1792

1 Mary Catharine; *b* 1721; *m* 18 June 1748 Thomas Hornyold, of Blackmore Park, Worcs, and *d* 1762, leaving issue. He *d* 25 Feb 1799

JOHN TOWNELEY's only s,

PEREGRINE EDWARD TOWNELEY, of Towneley, JP, DL Lancs; High Sheriff 1831; *b* 10 Oct 1762; *m* 22 April 1794 Charlotte Theresa, dau of Robert Drummond (*see* PERTH, E), and *d* 31 Dec 1846, leaving, with another dau (*d* unm):

1 Charles, JP, DL Lancs; *b* Jan 1803; Lt-Col cmdg 5th Royal Lancs Militia, FRS, FSA; *m* 19 Nov 1836 Lady Caroline Harriet Molyneux (*d* 8 Feb 1866), dau of 2nd Earl of Sefton (*see* 1970 edn), and *d* 5 Nov 1876, having had:

(1) Caroline Theresa; *b* 8 Jan 1838; *m* 10 July 1858 7th Earl of Abingdon (*see* LINDSEY and ABINGDON, E) and *d* 4 Sept 1873, leaving issue

(2) Emily Frances; *m* 6 Aug 1863 Lord Alexander Francis Charles Gordon-Lennox (*see* RICHMOND and GORDON, D) and had issue

(3) Alice Mary; coheir with her sisters to the Towneley estates; *m* 2 Aug 1871 **1st Baron O'Hagan** and *d* 20 Nov 1921, leaving issue (*see above*)

2 John, of Towneley; *b* 16 Feb 1806; Lt-Col 5th Loyal Lancs Militia, MP Beverley 1841–52; *m* 28 Oct 1840 Lucy Ellen (*d* 8 April 1900), dau of Sir Henry Joseph Tichborne, 8th Bt (*see* 1967 edn DOUGHTY-TICHBORNE, Bt), and *d* 21 Feb 1878, having had:

(1) Richard Henry; *b* 5 Feb 1849; *d* unm *vp* 1877

(1) Theresa Harriet; coheir with sisters to the Towneley estates; *m* John Delacour, JP Lancs, 11th Hus, and *dsp* 1923

(2) Lucy Evelyn; *m* 10 Jan 1877 Col John Murray, Gren Gds, of Touchadam and Polmaise, Stirlingshire, and *dsp* 15 June 1928. He *d* 11 Aug 1903

(3) Mary Elizabeth; *b* 16 Nov 1846; Provincial of the English Province Notre Dame Nuns 1886–1922; *d* 31 March 1922

(4) Mabel Anne; *m* 23 Jan 1890 9th Baron Clifford of Chudleigh (*qv*) and *dsp* 24 Jan 1921

1 Frances; *m* 25 July 1821 3rd Baron Camoys (*qv*) and *d* 5 April 1880, leaving issue

OHLSON

Arms: Arg. on waves of the sea a steamship ppr., on a chief az. three fir trees eradicated, also ppr. **Crest:** In front of a sun in splendour ppr. a motor wheel sa. **Motto:** *Alteri si tibi* ('Do as you would be done by'). **Creation:** Bt. (UK) 24 Jan 1920.

SIR BRIAN ERIC CHRISTOPHER OHLSON, 3RD BT, of Scarborough, N Riding, Co York [Sir Brian Ohlson Bt, 1 Courtfield Gdns, London SW5 0PA]; *b* 27 July 1936; *s f* 1983; *educ* Harrow and RMA Sandhurst; late Lt Coldstream Gds, ret money broker

Lineage: ANDERS OHLSON, of Fellingsbro, Sweden; had:

Sir Erik Olof Ohlson, 1st Bt (UK), so *cr* 24 Jan 1920; *b* 19 July 1873; Sheriff Hull 1913–15, chm Hessle UDC 1915–16, Romanian and Venezuelan Consul Hull 1924, Chev Star Romania, ktd 1915; *m* 27 Sept 1906 Jennie (*d* 17 May 1952), dau of Joseph Blakeley, of Whitby, Yorks, and *d* 20 March 1934, leaving:

1 **Sir Eric James Ohlson, 2nd Bt**; *b* 16 March 1911; *educ* Harrow and Trin Coll Cambridge; Romanian and Venezuelan Consul 1936–83; *m* 8 May 1935 *Marjorie Joan [Lady Ohlson, Halfpenny House, 287 Petersham Rd, Richmond, Surrey], 2nd dau of Charles Henry Roosmale-Cocq, of Dorking, Surrey, and *d* 5 March 1983, leaving:

(1) Sir BRIAN ERIC CHRISTOPHER OHLSON, **3rd and present Bt**

(2) +PETER MICHAEL [Peter Ohlson Esq, 33 The Avenue, Kew, Surrey TW9 2AL]; *b* 18 May 1939; heir presumptive; *educ* Harrow and Trin Coll Cambridge (BA 1962); with Express Dairy Co 1974–85 (md Foods Div 1976–80, md 1981–85), Snr Ptnr Tyzack & Ptnrs 1995; *m* 18 Oct 1968 *Sarah, only dau of Maj-Gen Thomas Brodie, CB, CBE, DSO, and has:

　　1a *Gemma; *b* 1971

　　2a *Emily Jane; *b* 1974

(1) *Christine Rose [Mrs Christopher Clancey, 71 Marshalls Drive, St Albans, Herts AL1 4RD]; *b* 10 Dec 1950; *m* 1st 23 Sept 1978 (divorce 19–) Timothy Agnew, er s of M H Agnew, of Slough; *m* 2nd 1985 *Christopher Clancey

2 Gerald Thomas; *b* 3 Aug 1917; *educ* Harrow; *m* 25 Sept 1943 Marjorie Beryl, dau of Trevor Davies, and *d* 31 Aug 1971, leaving:

(1) +Christopher Mark; *b* 3 June 1944; *educ* Harrow

1 Olga Gerda Erica; *b* 6 July 1907; *m* April 1935 Capt Frank Weyer-Brown, RM and F/Lt RAF, 2nd s of Maj EW Brown, and *dsp* 18 Sept 1937

OLIVER OF AYLMERTON

Arms: Per chevron gules and vert in chief two crosses moline or and in base a chaplet of olive also or, a bordure ermine. **Crest:** Within a crown palisado or a grassy mount, thereon a representation of the tower of the church of St John the Baptist at Aylmerton proper, issuing therefrom a cubit arm proper holding a crescent ermine.

Supporters: Dexter, a lion purpure, the dexter paw in a mail gauntlet argent; sinister, an American bald-headed eagle, holding in the dexter claw a quill pen, all proper. **Motto:** *Trwy weithred y dysgir* ('We learn through experience'). **Creation:** B. (LP, UK) 1986.

THE BARON OLIVER OF AYLMERTON, of Aylmerton, Co Norfolk (Sir Peter Raymond Oliver, PC 1980) [The Rt Hon The Lord Oliver of Aylmerton PC, The Canadas, Sandy Lane, Aylmerton, Norfolk NR27 9ND]; *b* 7 March 1921; *educ* The Leys and Trin Hall Cambridge (Hon Fell 1980); 12th Bn RTR 1941–45 WW II (despatches); barrister Lincoln's Inn 1948, QC 1965, Bencher 1973, ktd 1974, High Court Judge Chancery Div 1974–80 (chm Review Body 1979–81), Ld Justice Appeal 1980–86, Ld Appeal in Ordinary 1980–92, memb Restrictive Practices Court 1976–80, Hon LLD: City London Poly 1989, UEA 1991; *m* 1st 1945 Mary Chichester (*d* 1985), dau of Sir Eric Keightley Rideal, MBE, FRS, and has:

1 *David Keightley Rideal [The Hon David Oliver, 13 Old Sq, Lincoln's Inn, London WC2A 3UA]; *b* 1949; *educ* Westminster and Trin Hall Cambridge; barrister Lincoln's Inn 1972, Bencher 1994, Jr Counsel to Dir-Gen Fair Trading; *m* 1st 1972 (*divorce* 1987) Maria Luisa, dau of Juan Mirasierras, of Madrid, and has:

(1) *Daniel; *b* 1974

(2) *Thomas; *b* 1976

1 (cont.) The Hon David Oliver *m* 2nd 1988 *Judith Britannia Caroline, dau of David Henry John Griffiths Powell, and has:

(3) *Rhodri; *b* 1990

(4) *Alexander; *b* 1993

1 *Sarah Chichester; *b* 1951; *m* 1974 (*divorce* 1983, resumed maiden name) James Robert Goldsack and has:

(1) *Katie Louise; *b* 1980

(2) *Rebecca; *b* 1983

BARON OLIVER OF AYLMERTON *m* 2nd 1987 *Wendy Anne, widow of Ivon Lewis Lloyd Jones

Lineage: DAVID THOMAS OLIVER; Fell Trin Hall Cambridge; *m* Alice Maud, dau of George Kirby, and had:

PETER RAYMOND, *cr* a **Baron**

O'LOGHLEN

ANCHORA · SALUTIS

Arms: Gu. a man in armour facing the sinister and shooting an arrow from a longbow, ppr. **Crest:** On a ducal coronet or an anchor erect entwined with a cable ppr. **Motto:** *Anchora salutis* ('The anchor of safety'). **Creation:** Bt. (UK) 16 July 1838.

SIR COLMAN MICHAEL O'LOGHLEN, 6TH BT, of Drumconora, Ennis, Co Clare [Sir Colman O'Loghlen Bt, Ellengrove, Queensland 4077, Australia]; *b* 6 April 1916; *s* unc 1951; *educ* Xavier Coll Melbourne and Melbourne U (LLB, ARA); Capt AIF 1945, Stipendiary Magistrate Lae, Territory New Guinea, Actg Judge Supreme Court Territory of Papua and New Guinea May-Aug 1957; *m* 20 Oct 1939 *Margaret, dau of Francis O'Halloran, of Toorak, Melbourne, and has:

1 +MICHAEL, QC [Michael O'Loghlen QC, Owen Dixon Chambers, 205 William St, Melbourne, VIC 3000, Australia]; *b* 21 May 1945; *educ* Xavier Coll and U of Melbourne (LLB); barrister; *m* 1st 18 March 1967 (*divorce* 1988) Elizabeth Mary, dau of Dr D M Clarke; *m* 2nd 16 Sept 1989 *Elizabeth Margaret, dau of A J Heslop, and by his 1st w has:
  (1) +Hugh; *b* 6 Dec 1968
  (2) +David; *b* 10 Aug 1972
  (3) +Rory; *b* 7 July 1975
2 +Bryan; *b* 30 Aug 1946
3 +Ross; *b* 26 April 1948
4 +Hugh; *b* 29 May 1952
5 +Colman; *b* 21 Nov 1955
6 +Brendan; *b* 18 Sept 1959
1 *Margaret; *b* 1940
2 *Janet; *b* 1942

Lineage: COLMAN O'LOGHLEN, of Gort, Co Clare, JP; *b* 1745; *m* 1st — (*dsp*), sis of Daniel O'Connell, of Kilgory; *m* 2nd Aug 1783 Susannah (*d* 1822), dau of Michael Finucane, MD, of Ennis, and *d* May 1810, having by her had, with two other sons:

1 Hugh, of Gort; *b* 1 Oct 1784; High Sheriff Co Clare 1841; *m* 2 Feb 1815 Barbara (*d* 1820), dau of John Flanagan, of Clogher, Co Roscommon, and *d* 9 May 1849, having had two sons and two daus (*d* unm)
2 Colman; *d* unm 1826
3 **Sir Michael O'Loghlen, 1st Bt** (UK), so *cr* 16 July 1838, KC (1830); *b* 6 Oct 1789; *educ* Erasmus Smith Sch Ennis and Trin Coll Dblin (BA 1809); barrister 1811, frequently jr counsel to Daniel O'Connell (*see* O'CONNELL, Bt), to whose practice he later largely *s*, Third Serjeant 1831, Bencher King's Inns 1832, Slr-Gen Ireland 1834 and 1835, MP Dungarvan 1835 (fought Dublin unsuccessfully 1832), Attorney-Gen 1835, Baron Exchequer Ireland 1836 (1st RC law offr of Crown or judge in Br Isles since JAMES II's time), Master Rolls 1837; *m* 3 Sept 1817 Bidelia, dau of Daniel Kelly, of Dublin, and *d* 28 Sept 1842, having had, with three other daus (*d* unm):
  (1) **Sir Colman Michael O'Loghlen, 2nd Bt**, PC (1868), QC (1852); *b* 20 Sept 1819; *educ* Trin Coll Dublin; barrister 1840, chm QS Carlow 1856–59 and Mayo 1859–61, MP Co Clare 1863–77, Third Serjeant Ireland 1865, Second Serjeant 1866, Judge-Advocate-Gen 1868–70; *d* unm 22 July 1877
  (2) Hugh Ross; *b* 10 May 1827; *d* unm 19 Nov 1850
  (3) BRYAN (Sir), **3rd Bt**
  (4) Michael; *b* 27 Nov 1829; barrister; *d* unm April 1896
  (1) Susan; *m* 14 Sept 1848 John Woulfe Flanagan, DL, of Drumdoe, Boyle, Co Roscommon, and *d* Nov 1880. He *dsp* 28 Sept 1869

The 2nd Bt's bro,

Sir Bryan O'Loghlen, 3rd Bt, KC; *b* 27 June 1828; *educ* Trin Coll Dublin (BA); MP Co Clare 1877–79, practised Melbourne, Australia, where Crown Prosecutor, Attorney-Gen Victoria 1878–81 and 1893–94, Premier 1881–83; *m* 17 Sept 1863 Ella (*d* 6 June 1919), 3rd dau of James Mackey Seward, of Somerset Park, Melbourne, and *d* 31 Oct 1905, leaving:

1 **Sir Michael O'Loghlen, 4th Bt**, JP; *b* 16 Oct 1866; Ld Lt Co Clare, High Sheriff 1910; *m* 16 Jan 1918 Beatrice Mary (*d* 5 Feb 1953), only dau of Sir Michael Murphy, 1st Bt, of Wyckham, Co Dublin (*see* 1963 edn), and *dsp* 23 March 1934

2 Colman Seward; *b* 16 Dec 1869; *d* unm 29 Oct 1909
3 Hugh Ross; *b* 18 Feb, *d* 21 Sept 1872
4 Bryan James; *b* 20 Jan 1875; *m* 2 June 1909 Violet Elizabeth Amelia (*d* 1951), 3rd dau of Daniel Grant, of Bendigo, Australia, and *d* 26 June 1920, leaving:
  (1) *Elizabeth; *m* 19 April 1944 *F/Lt Clifford Ian Cutler, RAAF, and has:
    1a *Elizabeth Ann; *b* 1945
    2a *Felicity Margaret; *b* 1948
5 **Sir Charles Hugh Ross O'Loghlen, 5th Bt**; *b* 6 July 1881; *d* unm 23 July 1951
6 Henry Ross; *b* 29 Nov 1886; *m* Jan 1912 Doris Irene, dau of Maj Percival Horne, RA, and *d* 22 July 1944, leaving:
  (1) Ross Bryan; *b* 15 March 1914; F/O RAAF WW II; *m* 20 Aug 1941 *Phyllis, dau of George Nason, of Horsham, Victoria, Australia, and *d* 14 Jan 1944 a Japanese POW, leaving:
    1a *Susan Ann; *b* 24 Aug 1943
  (2) Sir COLMAN MICHAEL O'LOGHLEN, **6th and present Bt**
  (1) *Ella Allison; *m* 27 April 1944 *John Cardiff O'Connell, F/O RAAF, and has:
    1a *Ross John; *b* 1945
  (2) *Doreen Sinclair
1 Annie Bidelia Margaret; *b* 28 Dec 1864; *m* 11 June 1910 Leo Michael Hernandez de Mulardo, er s of Hernandez de Mulardo, of Rangoon, Burma, and Malaga, Spain, and *dsp* 6 Aug 1952. He *d* 3 Feb 1950
2 Lucy Susan Mary; *b* 11 July 1868; *d* unm 30 July 1942
3 Ella Maude; *b* 7 May 1874; *m* 1922 George Herbert Williams (*d* 1957), s of Hon Sir Hartley Williams, Sr Judge Victoria Supreme Court, and *d* 5 Nov 1960
4 Frances Mary; *b* 20 April 1876; nun; *d* 23 July 1972
5 Clare Mary; *b* 10 Feb 1889; *d* unm 25 Sept 1968
6 Aimee Margaret Julia; *b* 26 May 1891; *d* unm 28 July 1954

O'NEILL

INVITUM·SEQUITUR·HONOS

LAMH   DEARG   EIRIN

Arms: Quarterly, 1st and 4th, per fess wavy, the chief arg. and the base representing waves of the sea, in chief a dexter hand couped at the wrist gu., in base a salmon naiant ppr. (for O'NEILL); 2nd and 3rd, chequy or and gu., a chief vair (for CHICHESTER). **Crests:** 1 An arm embowed in armour, the hand grasping a sword, all ppr. (for O'NEILL), 2 A stork rising with a snake in its beak all ppr. (for CHICHESTER). **Supporters:** On either side a lion gu., gorged with an eastern crown arg., pendant therefrom by a gold chain an escutcheon, that on the dexter charged with the arms of O'NEILL and that on the sinister with those of CHICHESTER. **Mottoes:** 1 (beneath the arms) *Lamh dearg Eirin* ('The Red Hand of Ireland'), 2 (over the crests) *Invitum sequitur honos* ('Honour follows unsought'). **Creation:** B. (UK) 18 April 1868.

THE 4TH BARON O'NEILL OF SHANE'S CASTLE (Raymond Arthur Clanaboy O'Neill, TD (1970)) [The Rt Hon The Lord O'Neill TD, Shane's Castle, Antrim BT41 4NE]; *b* 1 Sept 1933; *s* f 1944; *educ* Eton and RAC Cirencester; late 2nd Lt 11th Hus (Prince Albert's Own), Maj NI Horse TAVR II, Lt-Col RARO, Hon Col NI Horse Sqdn RYR 1986–91, 69 Signal Sqdn NI Horse 1988–93, Chm Ulster Countryside Ctee 1971–75, V-Chm Ulster Folk and Tport Museum 1987–90 (Tstee 1969–90), memb: NI Tourist Bd 1973–80 (chm 1975–80), NI Nat Tst Ctee 1980–91 (chm 1981–91), Museum and Galleries Commn 1987–94; Pres: NI Assoc Youth Clubs 1965–, Roy Ulster Ag Soc 1984–86; Ld Lt Co Antrim 1994– (DL 1967–94); *m* 10 June 1963 *Georgina Mary, er dau of Lord George Francis John Montagu-Douglas-Scott (*see* BUCCLEUCH and QUEENSBERRY, D), and has:

1 +SHANE SEBASTIAN CLANABOY; *b* 25 July 1965; *m* 4 Oct 1997 *Celia, est dau of Peter Hickman, of Kensington

2 +Tyrone Alexander; *b* 24 June 1966

3 +Rory St John; *b* 20 Dec 1968

Lineage: (N.B. The descent of the Portuguese O'NEILLs from the historic Irish family has been called in question following recent research, the details of which had not been assembled at time of going to press.) EOCHU, called *Mugmedon*

('Lord of [many] Slaves') from his slave raids on late-Roman Britain, in one of whch he carried off and married a princess of the Ancient Britons called Carina; KING OF TARA *c* 360; had:

NIALL *Noigiallach* ('of the Nine Hostages'); HIGH KING OF IRELAND (possibly the one who campaigned against the Roman general Flavius Stilicho, f-in-law of the EMPEROR HONORIUS, in whose reign the legions withdrew from Britain); living 400; *k* either by a thunder-bolt or by a hostage KING OF LEINSTER while waging war overseas; although he himself was pagan nearly 300 of his descendants were canonised; *m* Ine, dau of Dubtach, *s* of MOINDACH, KING OF ULSTER, and had, with other issue:

1 LOEGAIRE, HIGH KING IRELAND 428–58; captured by the Leinstermen at Battle of Ath-dara 457; ancestor of the sept O'COINDEALBHAIN, later KINDELLAN or QUINLAN, who held territory in north Meath till 1690

2 CONAL CREMHTHOINN, KING OF MEATH; *d* 480; ancestor of the Kings of Brega and of Uisnech, who formed the pncpl branch of the southern UI NEILL and alternated with the northern UI NEILL in the High Kingship of Ireland, together with 17 other Kings in Ireland, including MAELSECHLAINN THE GREAT (*d* 1022), whose line were Kings of Meath till 1173 and were known as the CLANN COLMAIN, their Chieftains being known as O'MAELSECHLAINN or O'MELAGHLIN

3 Maine; *d* 440; ancestor of a sept in Teffia, Meath, called O'CATHARNAIGH, of whom Tadg (*d* 1084) was called *Sionnach* ('The Fox'), the Chieftains descended from him being styled 'The Fox' from 1522

4 EOGAN, for whom *see* further below

5 CONALL *Gulban*, KING OF TIR CONAILL ('Land of Conall', or Tyrconnell, Donegal), which was his share of the family's conquests in northwest Ulster after 425; his descendants, called CENEL CONAILL, formed one of the main branches of the northern UI NEILL; as 'kindred of St Columba' members of this branch were also Abbots of Iona 563–891 and Dunkeld, Scotland, in the 9th–12th centuries, also KINGS OF SCOTS from DUNCAN I (1034–40) to ALEXANDER III (1249–85/6); *k* by the Firbolgs by 465, leaving, with other issue:

(1) Doi; ancestor of the CENEL DUACH; had:

1a Ninnid; had:

1b BAETAN, HIGH KING IRELAND 572–86; *k* Battle at Leimaneich, leaving issue

(2) Fergus *Cennfada* ('Long-Head'); *m* Eirc, dau of LOARN *Mor* ('The Great'), a King of the Scots who settled in Argyll (whence the name of the district of Lorn), and had, with other issue:

1a Setna; a prince in Ulster; had, with other issue:

1b AINMIRE, HIGH KING IRELAND 566–69; *k* by Fergus mac Nelline, leaving:

1c AEDH, HIGH KING IRELAND 592–98; invaded Leinster both to avenge his f's death and to exact *borama* (cattle tribute), which the Leinstermen never paid without a fight, but *k* by BRAN *Dubh* ('The Black'), KING OF LEINSTER; ancestor of seven other High Kings of Ireland up to 734 and the Chieftains O'GALLACHUBAIR (O'GALLAGHER), O'CANANNAN and O'MAELDORAIDH (O'MULDORY), of Lough Erne

2b Colum; ancestor of St Adamnan, Abbot Iona 679–704

3b Lugald; ancestor of the O'DOMHNAILL, KINGS OF TIR CONAILL till the 17th century and Earls of Tyrconnel 1603–07, the Dukes of Tetuan in Spain, the Counts O'Donell von Tirconell in Austria, and:

1c John O'Donel, The O'Donel of Tirconnell, of Monkstown, Dublin; *b* 23 May 1894; *m* 1937 Eileen, dau of Alfred Reidlinger, and had:

1d *Aodh; *b* 3 Feb 1940

2a Feidhlimidh; *m* Eithne, dau of a cadet of the royal house of Leinster, and had:

1b St Columba; apostle of the northern Picts; *b* 7 Dec 521; founded various Irish monastic churches, Durrow Monastery 553 and the Abbey of Iona 563; converted BRUIDE, KING OF THE PICTS, and inaugurated 574 his own cousin AIDAN as King of the Scots of Dalriada; *d* 9 June 597

2b Eogan; ancestor of the O'FIRGHILs or O'FREELs, hereditary guardians of the rock sanctuary at Kilmacrenan where the Kings of Tir Conaill were inaugurated

(3) Eatach; *m* Didhnat, dau of Meather, and had:

1a St Barrfhionn; Bp Drumcallen, after whom the Hebridean island of Barra may be named

The 4th son,

EOGAN, KING OF AILECH; joined three of his bros in wresting *c* 425 the entire northwest corner of Ireland from the Ulidians who had hitherto held it; established his kingdom in the Peninsula of Innishowen (*i.e.*, Innis Eoghain or 'Eogan's Isle') converted to Christianity *c* 442; *m* Indorb *Finn* ('The White'), a foreign princess, and with her was ancestor of the CENEL EOGHAIN, the pncpl branch of the northern UI NEILL; *d* 465, having had, with other issue, including two yr sons (Eochaid *Binnigh* ('the tuneful'), ancestor of St Maelrubha (642–722), fndr 673 Applecross Abbey in Pictland; Fergus, had, with other issue, Fiachra, Bp Cenel Eoghain *c* 500):

MUIREDACH, KING OF AILECH; eloped with Eirc (*m* 3rd her husb's cousin Fergus *Cennfada*; *see* above), w of a British King called SARAN and dau of LOARN *Mor* (*see* above), and *d c* 480, leaving, with other issue:

1 MUIRCHEARTACH *mac Earca* ('Eirc's son'), HIGH KING IRELAND 512–34; defeated the HIGH KING AILILL *Molt* at Battle of Ocha 482, thus establishing the UI NEILLs alone in the high-kingship; also defeated and *k* OENGUS, KING OF MUNSTER, 489 and DUACH, KING OF CONNAUGHT, 504, adding to his Kingdom of Ailech by conquests in Derry at the expense of the men of Oriel; also defeated the Leinstermen 524 and *k* Sighe mac Dian, whose dau Sin became his concubine and to avenge her f brought about his death by burning down his house while he lay there in a drunken stupor on Hallowe'en 534; *m* Duaibhsech, dau of his enemy DUACH *Teangumha* ('Brazen-tongued'), KING OF CONNAUGHT, and had, with other issue:

(1) FERGUS, Jt HIGH KING IRELAND 563–66 with his (twin?) bro DOMNALL; *d* 566

(2) DOMNALL *Ilcealgach* ('The Deceitful'), Jt HIGH KING IRELAND 563–66 with his bro FERGUS; defeated EOGAN, KING OF CONNAUGHT, on the River Sligo 538, AILILL, KING OF CONNAUGHT, 549, DIARMAID, HIGH KING IRELAND (head of the southern UI NEILL) at Battle of Cul-Dreimhe 561, the Irish Picts 562, the Leinstermen 563; *d* 566, leaving:

1a EOCHAID, Jt HIGH KING IRELAND 569–72 with his uncle BAETAN (*see* above); *k* by CRONAN, KING OF KEENAGHT, 572, being ancestor of the sept whose Chieftains were styled O'DONNGHAILE (O'DONNELLY), and were hereditary marshals of the O'NEILLs till the 17th century

2a COLGU, KING OF AILECH 572–80; *k* 580 in battle by his kinsman AEDH Mac AINMIRE, KING OF TIR CONAILL

3a AEDH *Uairidhnach* ('Of the Ague'), HIGH KING IRELAND 604–12; defeated the Leinstermen and exacted cattle tribute; *d* 612, leaving:

1b MAELFITHRIG, KING OF AILECH 628–30, as which *s* his cousin SUIBHNE (*see* below); *k* in battle by SUIBHNE's bro ERNAINE (*see* below), leaving:

1c MAELDUIN, for whom *see* further below

(3) BAETAN ('Of the Yellow Hair'), Jt HIGH KING IRELAND 569–72 with his n EOCHAID (*see* above); *k* 572 together with latter by CRONAN, KING OF KEENAGHT, leaving:

1a COLMAN *Rimidh* ('The Celebrated'), Jt HIGH KING IRELAND 598–604 with AEDH Slaine ('The Healthy'), head of the southern UI NEILL; broke with the tradition that the royal heir should try to kill his predecessor; *k* by his own bro Lochan 604, leaving:

1b Fina; allegedly mistress of OSWIU, KING OF NORTHUMBRIA 643–670, by whom she supposedly had:

1c ALDFRITH, KING OF NORTHUMBRIA

2a Lochan *Diolmana*

2 Moen; ancestor of the CENEL MOEN, including DOMNALL O'GAIRMLEADHAIGH, KING OF CENEL EOGHAIN 1143–45

3 Feradach; had, with other issue:

(1) Fiachna; Chief of the CENEL FEARADHAIGH; had:

1a SUIBHNE *Menn* ('The Little'), also called 'The Valorous Sage', HIGH KING IRELAND 615–28; *k* and replaced his kinsman MAELCOBHA, HIGH KING IRELAND and Chief of the CENEL CONAILL, 615, after which the two clans were rivals for the northern UI NEILLs' turn in the high-kingship (it alternated with the southern UI NEILL in successive reigns); *k* 628 nr Lough Swilly by Congal Claen; his descendants alternated with the CENEL-Mic-EARCA in the succession to the local Kingdom of Ailech till 700

2a ERNAINE, KING OF AILECH 630–36; *k* by having his own throat cut

4 Eogan; had:

(1) Ronan; had:

1a Feradach; had:

1b St Mura; Abbot Fahan (west of Innishowen); *d c* 645, revered as the particular patron saint of the O'NEILLs

KING MAELFITHRIG's son,

MAELDUIN, KING OF AILECH 671–81; *k* DUNCHAD, KING OF ORIEL, 677, burnt Dun-Ceithirn and in it DUNGHAL, KING of the Irish Picts, also CENNDAELADH, KING OF KEENAGHT, but was himself *k* at Battle at Leathairbhe against his kinsman CONGAL, KING OF TIR CONAILL (later HIGH KING IRELAND); *m* Cacht, dau of MAELCOBHA, KING OF TIR CONAILL, and had:

FERGAL, HIGH KING IRELAND 710–22; defeated the southern UI NEILL of Meath in Armagh 710; *k* leading 21,000 men against the Leinstermen at Allen in Kildare 722; *m* 1st secretly a dau of CONGAL, HIGH KING IRELAND, and had:

1 AEDH *Alainn* ('The Handsome'), HIGH KING IRELAND 734–43; defeated by the CENEL CONAILL 725; campaigned 732–34 once more against them under their Chief FLAITHBERTACH, HIGH KING IRELAND (abdicated 734, after which the CENEL EOGHAIN alone represented the northern UI NEILL in the high-kingship); defeated and *k* in single combat 737 AEDH, KING OF UI CENNSEALAIGH, in revenge for his f's death; himself *k* in battle in Meath against his own successor DOMNALL, KING OF MEATH (head of the southern UI NEILL, hence his heir), leaving:

(1) MAELDUIN, KING OF THE NORTH (*Ri in Fochla*) 787–88; won Battle of Urker over the CENEL CONAILL; had:

1a MURCHAD, KING OF THE NORTH (*Ri in Tuaiscert*) 819–23; *k* MAELBREASAIL, KING OF TIR CONAILL, in battle 819; deposed by his own CENEL EOGHAIN under his cousin NIALL *Caille* (*see* below) 823; ancestor of the Tyrone sept whose Chieftain was styled O'Fhlaithbertaigh (O'Laverty)

KING FERGAL *m* 2nd Athiocht, dau of CIAN, KING OF KEENAGHT, and by her had, with other issue:

2 NIALL, of whom later

3 Conchobhar, whose descendants held Leim-an-Mhadaidh (Limavady); ancestor of the sept whose Chieftain was styled O'Cathain/O'Cahan/O'Cane and became from the 12th century the most powerful *ur-ri* or under-king among the CENEL EOGHAIN

KING FERGAL's 2nd son,

NIALL *Frasach* ('Of the Showers'), HIGH KING IRELAND 763–70 (abdicated following a series of natural disasters such that his reign was deemed inauspicious and became a monk at Iona, where *d* 778; *m* Eithne (*d* 768), dau of Breasal of Brega, and had:

AEDH *Oirdnidhe* ('The Dignified'), HIGH KING IRELAND 797–819; sent ambassadors to CHARLEMAGNE; defeated the CENEL CONAILL 815; *m* Maedhbh, dau of Inreachtach, Ch of Durlas, Antrim, and *d* 819, having had, with other issue:

1 NIALL, of whom later

2 MAELDUIN, KING OF AILECH after 846; became a monk; *d* 867, leaving:

(1) Fachtna; heir to the Northern Kingdom (*Rigdomna in Fochla*); *k* fighting for his cousin KING AEDH *Finnlaith* (*see* below) in his victory over the Meath men and Dublin Norsemen at Killaderry 868

(2) Oengus; heir to the Northern Kingdom (*Rigdomna in Tuaiscert*); beheaded by the Dal Araidhe 883

(3) MURCHAD, KING OF AILECH; heir to the Northern Kingdom; *k* by FLANNAGAN, KING OF FARNEY, 887, leaving:

1a FLAITHBERTACH, KING OF AILECH; *k* by O'Breasail *c* 896; ancestor of RUAIDHRI O'FLAITHBERTAIGH, KING OF CENEL EOGHAIN 1186–87

KING AEDH's son,

NIALL *Caille*, HIGH KING IRELAND 833–46, having deposed his cousin MURCHAD and taken the Northern Kingdom 823; routed the Vikings nr Lough Foyle 823, Norse invaders twice 835, FEIDHLIMIDH, KING OF MUNSTER 840, the Vikings again 843 and the Norsemen again but in pursuing them was drowned in the River Callain; *m* Gormflaith (*d* 860), dau of Dunchad mac Domhnaill, and had:

1 AEDH, of whom later

2 Oengus; ancestor of the CENEL nOENGUSA

3 Flaithbertach; had:

(1) Ualgharg; heir to the Northern Kingdom; *d* 879; ancestor of AEDH O'UALGHAIRG, KING OF CENEL EOHAINN 1065–67

1 A dau; composed a poem on the Battle of Cilluaindaighri, where her s Fiann was *k*; *m* CONAING, KING OF BREGA

KING NIALL's son,

AEDH *Finnliath* ('White-Hair'), HIGH KING IRELAND 862–79; defeated the Norsemen nr Lough Foyle 866 and the Meath- and Leinstermen 868 at Killaderry; *m* Maelmuire, dau of KENNETH Mac ALPIN, KING of the Picts and Scots, and probably widow of RUN, KING of the Britons of Strathclyde, and *d* 879, having had:

1 DOMNALL, KING OF AILECH (which by now included Derry, Donegal and Tyrone, with suzerainty over Armagh, Fermanagh and Monaghan) 887–915; later shared kingship with his bro NIALL; *d* 915, possibly having become a monk or pilgrim; some of his descendants were heirs to the Northern Kingdom or Kings of Ailech down to DONNCHADH, KING OF AILECH 1083, and Ardgar, heir to Ailech (*k* 1124)

2 NIALL, of whom later

1 A dau; *m* OLAF THE YOUNG, KING of the Norse of Dublin 853–72 (*k* in battle in Scotland 874)

KING AEDH's 2nd son,

NIALL *Glundubh* ('Black-Knee'), HIGH KING IRELAND 916–19; mortally wounded 15 Sept 919 in battle nr Dublin against the Norseman SIGTRYG, KING OF DUBLIN and later OF YORK; *m* Gormflaith (*d* 947 after accidentally falling on the sharp-pointed post of her bed), widow of (a) CORMAC, KING OF MUNSTER, and (b) CEARBHALL, KING OF LEINSTER, and dau of his predecessor FLANN *Sionna* ('The Fox'), HIGH KING IRELAND 876–916, and had:

1 Conaing; heir to the high kingship; *k* 1,200 Ulidians in battle near Lough Erne; *d* 937, leaving:

(1) Domnall; had:

1a FERGAL, KING OF AILECH 980–89; *d* 1001; ancestor of the local Kings of Tulach *Og* (Tullahogue) (reigned till 1068)

2 MUIRCHEARTACH, of whom later

3 Maelciarain

KING NIALL's 2nd son,

MUIRCHEARTACH *na Cochall Craicenn* ('of the Leather Cloaks'), KING OF AILECH 938–43; frequently defeated the Norsemen based on Dublin, also carried war into the Norse-occupied Hebrides 941; had established ascendancy over all Ireland on behalf of his f-in-law the HIGH KING by 941; *m* 1st Flann (*d* 940), dau of DONNCHADH, HIGH KING IRELAND 919–44, Chief of the southern UI NEILL, and had, with other issue:

1 FLAITHBERTACH, KING OF AILECH; *k* defending his territory against a raid by the CENAL CONAIL 949

2 DOMNALL, of whom later

1 Donnfhlaith; *m* 1st DOMNALL, KING OF MEATH 951–54, Chief of the southern UI NEILL; *m* 2nd OLAF *Cuaran* ('Hairy-brogues'), KING OF NORTHUMBERLAND 941–44 and 948–52, also KING OF DUBLIN 945–48 and 953–81, who abdicated and *d* as a pilgrim in Iona 981

MUICHEARTACH *m* 2nd 941 Dubhdara, dau of CEALLACH, KING OF OSSORY, and was *k* in battle at Ardee against BLACAR, KING OF DUBLIN, March 943

His 2nd son,

DOMNALL O'NEILL (*i.e.*, *Ua Neill* or 'grandson of Niall'; first of his family so styled, perhaps establishing this later surname as a quasi-title in the period 944–56 when to be gs of NIALL *Glundubh* meant to be heir to the high-kingship despite the usurpation of CONGALACH, KING OF BREGA), *Ardmacha* ('of Armagh'), HIGH KING IRELAND 956–80; *m* Mor, probably dau of TADHG 'of the Three Towers', KING OF CONNAUGHT, and *d* 980, having had:

1 MUIRCHEARTACH *Midheach* ('of Meath', probably from being fostered in Meath, since the Gael kings' and chiefs' sons were always fostered out); heir to the high-kingship; *k* in battle against his uncle OLAF, KING OF DUBLIN, 977, leaving:

(1) FLAITHBERTACH, of whom later

2 Muiredach; had:

(1) Muircheartach; *k* by Conchobhar O'Domhnallain, Ld of Ui Tuirtre, 1015

(2) Lochlann, whose descendants called themselves Mac LOCHLAIBNN; had:

1a ARDGAR, KING OF AILECH 1061–64, having previously held the local Kingship of Tulach *Og* 1051 and 1054–61; *bur* 1064, leaving, with other issue:

1b DOMNALL, HIGH KING IRELAND, 1119–21; ancestor of the Mac LOCHLAINN Kings of the CENEL EOGHAINN (the last of whom, DOMNALL, was *k* at the hands of Brian O'Neill (*see* below) 1241, together with ten of his immediate family and all the other CENEL EOGHAIN Chieftains who opposed O'Neill)

3 AEDH *Craoibhe Tulcha*, KING OF AILECH 989–1004; defeated Ulidians but was *k* in the moment of victory aged 28, leaving issue

4 Aedh II; heir to the Northern Kingdom; *k* 1021

KING DOMNALL O'NEILL's gs,

FLAITHBERTACH *an Trostáin* ('of the pilgrim's staff'), KING OF AILECH 1004–30 and 1033–36, in whose time the capital was probably moved from Ailech to Tulach *Og*; constantly warred with KING BRIAN BORAMA (*see* INCHIQUIN, B); supported restoration of MAELSECHLAINN THE GREAT as HIGH KING (last such of the southern UI NEILL) 1014; abdicated and went on pilgrimage to Rome 1030; resumed crown after son's death 1033; *d* 1036, having had:

1 AEDH, of whom later

2 Domnall; *d* 1027

3 Muircheartach; local King of Tulach *Og*; *k* 1046

4 Muiredach; *k* by the O'LAVERTYs 1039

5 Muiredach; heir to Kingdom of Ailech; *d* in a house fire ignited by Cu-Uladh, local King of Uachtar thire, 1046

KING FLAITHBERTACH's est son,

AEDH *Athlamhan* ('The Handy'), KING OF AILECH 1030–33; heir to high-kingship; *dvp* Nov 1033, having had, with a yr s (Anrothan; allegedly *m* —, dau of the 'King of Scots' (probably the local King of Argyll) and through her acquired perhaps Cowal and Knapdale (Chiefs of the later clans there claimed descent from him); alleged ancestor of the MACLACHLANs of Strathlachlan, the LAMONTs of that Ilk (of whom the LYONs of Glamis (*see* STRATHMORE AND KINGHORNE, E) are possibly cadets), the MacSORLEYs of Monydrain, the McEWENs of Otter, the MACNEILs of Barra and McNEILLs of Gigha and Colonsay, the MacSWINs of Castle Swin and MacSWEENEYs in Donegal):

DOMNALL *an tOgdhamh* ('The Young Ox'), styled KING OF ULSTER 'against opposition'; pretender to the northern throne five years; *k* by Mac LOCHLAINN, the effective king, though the O'NEILLs still held the local kingdom of Tulach *Og*; had:

FLAITHBERTACH *Locha Feadhaidh*, styled KING OF ULSTER 'against opposition'; pretender to the northern throne on coming of age for three years but *k* by Mac LOCHLAINN, leaving:

CONCHOBAR *na Fiodhbhuidhi* ('of the woods'), styled KING OF ULSTER 'against opposition'; pretender to the northern throne ten years after coming of age; *k* by Mac LOCHLAINN, leaving:

TADHG *Glinne* ('of the glens'), styled KING OF ULSTER 'against opposition'; pretender to the northern throne seven years before being *k* by Mac LOCHLAINN, leaving:

MUIRCHEARTACH *Muighe Line* ('of Moylinny'), styled KING OF ULSTER 'against opposition'; pretender to northern throne five years but *k* by Lochlann Mac LOCHLAINN 1160 with four of his sons after winning the Battle of Magh-Luadhat, leaving:

AEDH *Macaemh Tóinleasg* ('The Lazy-arsed Youth'), KING OF CENEL EOGHAIN 1176–77, heir to high-kingship of Ireland; *k* f's killer 1160, restored O'NEILL power and became supreme in the North of Ireland 1176; *k* in battle against his successor MAELSECHLAINN Mac LOCHLAINN 1177, leaving:

1 AEDH *Meth* ('The Fat'), for whom *see* further below

2 Muircheartach; *k* by Mac LOCHLAINN 1202

3 NIALL *Ruadh* ('The Red'), KING OF ULSTER 1230; reigned a month; *m* —, dau of CATHAL *Crobhdearg* ('Red Hand') O'CONOR, KING OF CONNAUGHT 1201–24, and had, with other issue:

(1) BRIAN *Cathan an Duin* ('of the Battle of Down'), last HIGH KING IRELAND 1258–60; became KING OF ULSTER 1241, formed Irish confederacy to expel the English 1256; *m* Jill of Argyll, probably dau of DUNCAN Mac DUGALL, King in the Hebrides and Lord of Lorn, and was *k* 1260 by the English at the Battle of Downpatrick, his head being sent to London, leaving, with other issue:

1a DOMNALL, KING OF ULSTER 1283–86 and 1295–1325; heir to high-kingship; sent aid to ROBERT I (THE BRUCE) KING OF SCOTS against the English; renounced 1316 his right to the Irish high-kingship in favour of EDWARD BRUCE, for whom he fought at Battle of Dundalk 1318; had, with other issue:

1b AEDH *Reamhar* ('The Stout'), KING OF ULSTER 1344–64; deposed his kinsman KING HENRY O'NEILL (of the sr CLANNABOY branch) 1344; was defeated 1345; *m* Gormflaith (*d* 1353), probably dau of AEDH O'DONELL, KING OF TIR CONAILL, and had, with other issue:

1c NIALL *Mor* ('The Elder'), KING OF ULSTER 1364–94; *m* Beanmidhe (*d* 1386), dau of BRIAN MacMAHON, KING OF ORIEL 1365–72, and had, with other issue:

1d Henry *Aimhreidh* ('The Confused'), heir of CENEL EOGHAIN; *m* Affric (*d* 1389), dau of Aedh O'Neill, and *d* 1392, leaving, with other issue:

1e DOMNALL, KING OF ULSTER 1404–32; taken at Battle of Dundalk by English, sent to Tower London 1399, ransomed 1401, struggled long with his eventual successor EOGHAN O'NEILL, who held him prisoner 1410–14; *k* in a skirmish 1432, leaving issue

2d NIALL *Og* ('The Younger'), KING OF ULSTER 1394–1403, also styled *Ua Neill Mor* ('The Great O'Neill'), a sobriquet used by the heads of this branch to distinguish them from their rivals of the senior or Clannaboy branch, whose Chief was styled *Ua Neill Buidhe*; ktd at Dublin by RICHARD II OF ENGLAND 1394; *m* Una (*d* 1417), dau of Domnall O'Neill, and *d* 1403, leaving, with other issue:

1e EOGHAN, KING OF ULSTER 1432–55; abdicated in favour of his s 1455; *m* Catherine (*d* 1427), dau of ARDGAL MacMAHON, KING OF ORIEL 1402–16, and *d* 1456, leaving, with other issue:

1f HENRY, KING OF ULSTER 1455–83; assisted Yorkists in England during Wars of Roses 1460; extended suzerainty over the West of Ireland by 1463; abdicated in favour of his son 1483; *m* Gormflaith (*d* 1465), dau of Domnall McMurrough Kavanagh, styled King of Leinster, and *d* 1489, leaving, with two yr sons

(HENRY, KING OF ULSTER 1493–98; DOMNALL, KING OF ULSTER 1498–1509):

1g CON *Mor* ('The Great'), KING OF ULSTER 1483–93; *m* 1st — and had, with other issue:

1h ART *Og* ('The Younger'), KING OF ULSTER 1514–19; defeated the O'DONELLs of Tyrconnell and secured recognition of his suzerainty over Innishowen and Fermanagh; *d* 1519, leaving:

1i Niall *Conallach*, Tanist (designated heir) to Tir Eoghain or Tyrone; *m* Rose, dau of MANUS O'DONELL, KING OF TIR CONAILL, and *d* 1545, leaving:

1j Terence/Turlough *Lynagh* (Toirdelbach Luineach) (Sir), Dynast of Tyrone 1567–93, 'The Great O'Neill'; after a long struggle against the English resigned Chiefship to his cousin Aedh O'Neill, Earl of Tyrone, and *d* 1595, leaving, with other issue:

1k Sara; *m* her cousin Sir Turlough O'Neill, Lord (Chieftain) of the Fews (*see below*)

1g (cont.) CON, KING OF ULSTER, *m* 2nd by 1479–80 Lady Eleanor FitzGerald, dau of 7th Earl of Kildare (*see* LEINSTER, D), and *d* 1493, having by her had:

2h Sean/Shane, Tanist of Tyrone; *d* 1517, leaving:

1i Henry, of Kinnaird; *d c* 1579, leaving, with other issue:

1j Henry (Sir), of Kinnaird; *k* fighting Sir Cahir O'Dogherty, Ld of Innishowen, 1608, having had, with other issue:

1k Turlough; *d* 1608, leaving:

1l Phelim *Ruadh* ('The Red') (Sir), styled 'The Great O'Neill'; recognised by the POPE as Prince of Ulster; Lt Gen Catholic Army 1641 Uprising; *m* 1st —; *m* 2nd —; *m* 3rd after 1641, as her 2nd husb, Lady Jean, widow of 2nd Lord Hamilton, Baron of Strabane (*see* ABERCORN, D), and dau of 1st Marquess of Huntly (*qv*), and was executed 10 March 1653, leaving:

1m Gordon; Ld Lt Co Tyrone, MP 1689, raised O'Neill's Regt for JAMES II, present Siege Derry, Battle of the Boyne 1690 and Battle of Aughrim 1691, entered French Service 1691, cmdg his Regt against Austrians, and *k* at 1704, leaving issue

3h CON *Bacach* ('The Lame') O'NEILL, KING OF ULSTER 1519–42 and 1st EARL OF TYRONE (I), so *cr* 1 Oct 1542, with remainder to his illegitimate s FERDORAGH/MATTHEW in tail male, after fighting long against the English to maintain his status as an independent sovereign, PC (I 1543); *b c* 1484; ktd 1520–21; allegedly *m* 1st his cousin Lady Alice FitzGerald, dau of 8th Earl of Kildare (*see* LEINSTER, D) by his 1st w; *m* 2nd by 1530 another cousin Mary, dau of Aedh *Buie* O'Neill, Chief of Clannaboy (*see below*), and by her had:

1i Shane *an Diomais* ('The Proud'), also called 'The Great O'Neill'; *b c* 1530; Dynast of Tyrone 1559–1567; after years of resistance to the English submitted to ELIZABETH I in London in person 1562; defeated the Scots of Antrim, capturing their Chief (and his future f-in-law; *see below*), James McDonnell of Islay, and the latter's bro (and his [Shane's] future bro-in-law) Sorley *Buie* (*see* ANTRIM, E) 1565; *m* 1st (*divorce*) Catherine, dau of James McDonnell of Islay, and had:

1j Shane *Og* ('The Younger'); *k* in battle 1581

2j Henry; imprisoned Dublin Castle but escaped 1592

1i (cont.) Shane *an Diomais m* 2nd Catherine, dau of Lachlan Maclean of Dowart (*see* MACLEAN, Bt, of Dowart) and widow (3rd w) of (a) 4th Earl of Argyll (*see* ARGYLL, D) and (b) Calvagh, The O'Donell of Tir Conaill, and was murdered by the McDONNELLs at a peace conference 2 June 1567, having by her had:

3j Art; imprisoned Dublin Castle but escaped, only to freeze to death in the Wicklow Mountains 1592

4j Aedh *Giemhleach* ('of the fetters'); hanged 1590 by his cousin 2nd EARL OF TYRONE (*see below*)

1i Mary; *m* Sorley *Buie* McDonnell (*d* 1589) and *d* 1590, leaving issue (*see* ANTRIM, E)

3h (cont.) The 1st EARL OF TYRONE of the 1542 *cr m* 3rd Mary, dau of Sir Alexander Mac Randal *Buie* McDonnell, of Dunluce, and *d* by 16 July 1559 while seeking refuge in the Pale from his s Shane *an Diomais*; by Alison Kelly, w of a Dundalk blacksmith, he had (and acknowledged as such aged 16):

2i FERDORAGH/MATTHEW O'NEILL, 1st BARON OF DUNGANNON (I), so *cr* 1 Oct 1542; fought incessantly against his half-bro Shane *an Diomais* (who ordered his death 1558), hence often sided with the English; *m* Joan (*m* 2nd Henry O'Neill of the Fews; *m* 3rd by 11 Aug 1589 Sir Owen Mactoole O'Gallagher, of Ballyshannon Castle, and *d* 22 June 1600), dau of Constantine/Cuconnacht *Coarb* Maguire, Dynast of Fermanagh, and had, with other issue:

1j BRIEN O'NEILL, 2nd BARON OF DUNGANNON, as which *s* f 1558, and *de jure* 2nd EARL OF TYRONE, as which must have in effect *s* gf 1559 (but apparently was never so recognised); *d* unm 12 April 1562, murdered by his cousin and rival Turlough Lynagh O'Neill, Tanist to Shane *an Diomais*

2j AEDH/HUGH O'NEILL, last KING OF ULSTER 1598–1603, 3rd and last EARL OF TYRONE, as latter of which only recognised 1585 (and as KING not at all, at any rate by the English) and The O'Neill 1593–1603 from

resignation of Chiefship by his cousin Turlough to his own renunciation of it when making submission to JAMES I on latter's accession; *b* 1550; rose against the English 1598–1602 (his defeat at Battle of Kinsale 24 Dec 1601 ending his resistance); fearing imminent arrest for further disaffection towards the English he left Ireland 14 Sept 1607, initially intending to go to Spain but because of bad weather landing in France then making for Louvain, in the Spanish Netherlands, with nearly 100 compatriots, including his w and three of his sons, and Ruari O'Donell, 1st Earl of Tyrconell, in the episode known as The Flight of the Earls; attainted for high treason and stripped of his titles by 5 Aug 1608; *m* 1st — (*divorce*), dau of Sir Brian MacPhelim O'Neill, Captain or Lord of Clannaboy (*see below*), and had at least one s; *m* 2nd by 14 June 1574 Joan (*d* just prior to 31 Jan 1590/1), half-sis of 1st Earl of Tyrconell and dau of Aedh/Hugh, 23rd Chief of Tir Conaill, by his 1st w, and by her had:

1k HUGH O'NEILL, 4th BARON OF DUNGANNON, as which recognised by a confirmation of his and his f's titles 10 May 1587; *b* just prior to Dec 1585; accompanied his f in resistance to English and the migration from Ireland, hence also attainted 1608; *d* Rome unm & *vp* 23 Sept 1609

2k Henry, self-styled (4th) Earl of Tyrone despite his attainder 1608; *b c* 1586; *educ* Spain; Col of the Irish Regt in service in Flanders under Archduke Albert 1605–17/21, Kt of Santiago; seems to have *m* after July 1615 —, dau of Juan de Mancididor, Sec State to Archduke Albert, but *dsp* seemingly prior to Sept 1617 and certainly by 1621

1k Margaret; *m* 1596 3rd Viscount Mountgarret (*qv*) and *d* 16 Dec 1655, leaving issue

2k Alice; a celebrated beauty; *m* 1604 1st Earl of Antrim (*qv*) of the 1620 *cr* and *d* in or after 1663 aged 80, leaving issue

2j (cont.) The 3rd and last EARL *m* 3rd (elopement) 3 Aug 1591 Mabel (*d* Dec 1595), dau of Sir Nicholas Bagenal, Marshal English Army in Ireland, and sis of his enemy Sir Henry Bagenal, whom he later *k* at his victory over the English of the Yellow Ford on the River Blackwater, nr Armagh, 14 Aug 1598; *m* 4th by 6 June 1597 Catherine (*d* 15 March 1618), sis of Arthur, 1st Viscount Magennis of Iveagh (*see* GUINNESS, Bt, remarks beneath blazon), and *d* Rome 20 July 1616, leaving by her:

3k John/Sean/Shane, self-styled (5th) Earl of Tyrone; *b* 18 Oct 1599; Col Irish Regt of Tyrone in Spanish serv first in Flanders then in Spain, Kt of Calatrava 1632, fought against French at Fuenterrabia 1638, Major Domo Madrid by late May 1639, memb Spanish Supreme Cncl of War 1640; *dspl* 27 Jan 1640/1 (when even had the attainder been lifted the Earldom of Tyrone and Barony of Dungannon would thus have expired) of wounds recd in an unsuccessful attack on Catalan insurgents at Barcelona the previous day, leaving by Isabel O'Donell (cousin of 1st Earl of Tyrconnell):

1l Hugh/Hugo; *b c* 1631; legitimized by PHILIP IV; *dsp* just prior to 27 Oct 1660

4k Con *na Creige* ('of the rock'); *b* 1601; accidentally left behind in the Flight of the Earls; *educ* Eton; *d* unm a prisoner Tower of London 1622

5k Brian; *b* 1604; Page to Archduke Albert *c* 1613; murdered in Brussels by an English agent 16 Aug 1617

2i (cont.) The 1st BARON OF DUNGANNON was *k vp* 1558, leaving illegitimate issue:

3j Art *McBaron* ('son of [the] Baron'); *d* 28 Nov 1618, leaving, with other issue:

1k Art *Og* ('The Younger'); had:

1l Aedh/Hugh *Dubh* ('The Black'), self-styled 6th Earl of Tyrone (Con O'Neill, a presumed memb of the O'NEILL clan having styled himself Earl of Tyrone at some point before 27 Oct 1660); Maj-Gen Confederate Irish forces 1646 (having been a sr cdr of them from 1642 under his unc Owen Roe; *see below*); Govr Clonmel 1650 and Limerick, as which he was obliged to capitulate to Ireton 29 Oct 1651; imprisoned Tower of London Jan 1651/2–April 1653, after which went back to Spain; *dsp* by 1667, *k* fighting in Spanish serv against Portugal

2k Owen Roe/Eoghan *Ruadh* ('The Red'); offr in Spanish serv; held Arras against the French till obliged to capitulate 1640, Gen Irish Confederate Army 1642 on, defeating Scots in Ireland at Benburb 1646; *d* 6 Nov 1649, leaving:

1l Henry Roe or *Ruadh* ('The Red'); *m* Eleanor, dau of Sir Luke FitzGerald, of Tecroghan, Co Meath, and was beheaded at Derry July 1650 after his capture by the English the previous month, leaving:

1m Hugh/Hugo, self-styled (7th) Earl of Tyrone; *b* after 1644; Kt of Calatrava 1667; *dsp* Spain

3k Con Roe or *Ruadh* ('The Red'); had:

1l Bernardo/Brian Roe or *Ruadh* ('The Red'); had:

1m Eugenio/Owen, self-styled (8th) Earl of Tyrone; *educ* Rome; Spanish Offr, raised his own Regt 1663, Col Irish Regt of Tyrone 1673; *dsp* after 1689

4k Brian; had a dau (*m* her cousin Aedh/Hugh O'Neill; *see* below)

2f Aedh; Tanist of Cenel Eoghain; *d* 1475, leaving:

1g ART O'NEILL, KING OF ULSTER 1509–14; had, with a yr s (Niall *Mor*, *d* 1538, leaving Aedh, Lord [Chieftain] of the Fews):

1h Feidhlimidh *Ruadh* ('The Red'), Lord of the Fews, supported Niall *Conallach* O'Neill as Tanist of Tyrone 1531; defeated by his cousin Shane *an Diomais* (*see* above) 1554, leaving:

1i Henry, Lord of the Fews; fought incessantly against Shane *an Diomais*; living 1563; *m* Joan (*m* 3rd Sir Owen O'Gallagher, of Ballyshannon, and *d* 22 June 1600), widow of 1st BARON OF DUNGANNON (*see* above), and had:

1j Turlough (Sir), Lord of the Fews; *m* Sara, dau of Sir Terence/Turlough *Lynagh* O'Neill (*see* above), and *d* 23 Feb 1639, leaving:

1k Henry, Lord of the Fews; *m* Mary, dau of Sir John O'Reilly, and had, with a yr s (John/Shane, f of Thomas Macshane; *see* JOHNSON, Bt, of New York):

1l Turlough, Lord of the Fews; royalist Col Civil War; transplanted by CROMWELL to Co Mayo; *d* 1676, leaving:

1m Con; transplanted to Newcastle, Co Mayo; had, with a dau (Sara, *m* Henry O'Neill (*see* below) and had issue):

1n Henry, of Foxford, Co Mayo; Capt in JAMES II's Irish army 1689; had:

1o Niall, of Cloon, Co Leitrim; living 1717; had:

1p Henry *Ruadh* ('The Red'), of Carrowny, Co Mayo; studied law in France; had, with a dau (Isabel, *m* Don Tadeo O'Sullivan, Count de Berehaven, Kt of Santiago):

1q Niall/Nicolas; won Ltcy 1759 under Capt Don Joseph O'Donnell (ancestor of the Dukes of Tetuan; *see* above) as a prize for Ensigns who had distinguished themselves in mathematics; Lt-Col Spanish serv in Portugal; *dspm*

2q Arturo, 1st Marqués del Norte (Spain), so *cr* 1805; *b* 1736; soldier in Spanish serv in S America and W Indies, Govr Pensacola, Florida, 1781, Capt-Gen Yucatan and Govr Merida 1792, memb Spanish Supreme Cncl of War 1803, served Peninsular War; *d* 9 Dec 1814

3q Turlough; *m* Catherine O'Keeff and had:

1r Arturo, 2nd Marqués del Norte

2r Tulio/Turlough; Lt-Gen Spanish Cavalry, Col Regt of La Princesa; decorated for gallantry Peninsular War at Sieges of Salamanca, Pamplona and Bayonne and Battle of Albuera; *b* 1784; *m* Doña Manuela de Castilla y Quevedo, Marquesa de la Granja, and *d* 1855, leaving:

1s Juan Antonio Luis, 8th Marqués de la Granja, as which s mother 1847; *b* 1821; Caballero de la Real Maestranza, Seville; *m* Doña Luisa Salamanca y Negrete, dau of Count Campo-Alange, Grandee of Spain, and *d* 1877, leaving:

1t Tulio, 9th Marqués de la Granja; *b* 1866; Caballero de la Real Maestranza, Seville; *m* Doña Carmen Larios y Zabala, dau of Marqués de Valleumbroso, and *d* 1914, leaving:

1u Tulio, 10th Marqués de la Granja, Caballero de la Real Maestranza, Seville; *b* 25 March 1888; *m* Doña Maria Angeles Castrillo y Sanjuan, Marquesa de Villaverde de San Isidro (*d* 1988), dau of Marqués de Benamejí de las Cuevas de Becerro, Vizconde de Benaojan, and *d* 24 Oct 1938, leaving:

1v Marcos, 11th Marqués de la Granja, Caballero de la Real Maestranza, Seville; *b* 22 May 1922; *d* Aug 1974

2v *Carlos, 12th Marqués de la Granja, 5th Marqués del Norte, Marqués de Villa Verde and Conde de Benagiar [The Marqués de la Granja, c/A Cortés Llado 1, 41004 Sevilla, Spain]; *b* 2 Oct 1927; Caballero Real Maestranza Caballería de Sevilla, head of Spanish O'NEILLs; *m* 12 Aug 1960 *María de Orueta y Gaytan de Ayala, and has:

2w *Carlos, 5th Marqués de Norte; *b* 3 Jan 1970; economist

2k Aedh/Hugh; *m* —, dau of Brian O'Neill (*see* above), and had:

1l Arturo; Kt of Calatrava, cmded Irish Regt of Tyrone in Spanish serv 1660–63; *m* Leonor, dau of Rory O'More, the brains behind the 1641 Irish Uprising (*see* also LUCAN, E, preliminary remarks), and *d* 1663, leaving:

1m Daniel; Kt of Calatrava, briefly Col Irish Regt of Tyrone aged 7

2m Aedh/Hugh *Buie*, of Creggan; *m* Catherine Magennis and had:

1n Terencio; Lt-Col Regt of Hibernia in Spanish serv, served War of Austrian Succession in Italy, covering retreat at Camposanto but losing half his battalion in casualties 1743, also present Velletri 1744; *k* by Algerian corsairs boarding his troopship 16 Aug 1748

1n Catalina; *m* Enrique/Henry O'Neill, s of Phelim O'Neill, also of the Fews branch of the family, and had:

1o Felix; Kt Mil Order Charles III of Spain, Gen in Spanish serv, fought Camposanto 1743, wounded and captured Velletri 1744, again captured fighting for Prince Charles Edward at Culloden 1746 (released as Spanish subject 1747), Col Regt of Hibernia 1763, Capt-Gen Galicia, Inspr-Gen Spanish Inf, Govr and Capt-Gen Aragon, Pres High Court Aragon, memb Supreme Cncl of War; *m* 1755 Doña Jacoba Varcia, dau of Don Francisco Varcia Sarmiento, and *d* 1796, leaving:

1p Terencio; Kt of Santiago, Col Regt of Hibernia

2p Felix; Kt of Santiago, Adml Spanish Navy 1809; *d* 2 Oct 1812

3p Juan; Col Regt of Navarra, Gen, 2ic defence of Zaragoza against French in Peninsular War; *d* 24 Feb 1809, leaving:

1q Felix; *m* Maria Antonia Rosinol and *d* 1862, leaving issue

4 Domnall; *k* by Mac LOCHLAINN 1239

KING AEDH's est son,

AEDH *Meth* ('The Fat'), KING OF ULSTER 1196–1230, also styled KING OF CENEL EOGHAIN or TIR EOGHAIN (whence derives modern Tyrone); heir to high-kingship; defeated Anglo-Normans 1199, 1200, 1207 and 1211 but was himself defeated by CATHÁN *Carrach* ('The Scabby') O'CONNOR, KING OF CONNAUGHT, and by the Normans 1201 and temporarily deposed (resumed crown when his successor CONOR Mac LOCHLAINN was *k* 1201); *m* Beanmidhe (*d* 1215), dau of UA hEIGNIGH (O'HEGNY OF FERMANAGH), KING OF ORIEL (*k* 1201), and had:

DOMNALL *Og* ('The Younger'), KING OF ULSTER 1231–34, more generally styled KING OF CENEL EOGHAIN or TIR EOGHAIN (his immediate realm where he ruled personally as opposed to the looser northern kingdom over which he reigned as suzerain), heir to high-kingship of Ireland; deposed his predecessor KING DOMNALL Mac LOCHLAINN 1231 but was *k* by him 1234; *m* Cicely (*d* 1250), dau of Mac LOCHLAINN, KING OF CENEL EOGHAIN, and sis or cousin of his slayer, and had, with a yr s (NIALL *Culanach* ('comer-from-behind'), KING OF CENEL EOGHAIN, of which seized the throne 1261, deposed by his bro AEDH 1263, reinstated with Norman help 1286, deposed 1290, reinstated, again with Norman help, 1291 and murdered by supporters of his cousin DOMNALL (who he had deposed 1286), allegedly leaving a dau, who *m* Giollaiosa *Ruadh* ('The Red') O'Reilly, Dynast of East Breffny (*d* 1330)):

AEDH *Buie* ('The Yellow'), from whom derives the *Clann Aedh Buidhe* or Clannaboy, KING OF AILEACH 1260–83, also styled KING OF CENEL EOGHAIN, though his people were weakened by losses against the English at the Battle of Down (*see* above) 1260; deposed in favour of his bro NIALL 1261, restored 1263; sent envoys 1263 to KING HAAKON OF NORWAY offering him the crown of Ireland if he would expel the Anglo-Normans, whom he (AEDH) nevertheless managed to defeat 1275; he also defeated and *k* KING DOMNALL *Og* O'DONELL nr Dungannon 1281; *m* —, dau of Mac Oisdealbhaigh (Mac Costello, probably the Hibernicised Norman Baron Philip de Nangle), and was himself *k* 1283 by BRIAN MacMAHON, KING OF ORIEL and *Giollaiosa* ('The Red') O'Reilly, Dynast of E Breffny, leaving:

BRIAN, KING OF CENEL EOGHAIN, 1291–95; sought Norman help against his cousin KING DOMNALL O'NEILL, who nevertheless defeated and *k* him 1295; it is from just before his time that the English Kings extended the benefit of English law to the 'Five Bloods' of Ireland (the old royal houses of O'Neill of Ulster, O'Melaghlin of Meath, McMurrough of Leinster, O'Brien of Munster and O'Conor of Connaught) so that unlike the other native Irish they had the right to sue in English courts; had, with two yr sons (Aedh, living 1359; Domnall *Donn* ('The Brown'), ancestor of the Clann Domhnuill Donn, Lords [Chieftains] of Ui Tuirtre (Toome in Antrim and Loughinsholin in Derry)):

HENRY, KING OF ULSTER 1325–44; Chief or Prince of Clannaboy, to which territory he was towards the end of his life restricted as ruler, having previously taken advantage of EDWARD BRUCE's attack on the English in Ireland 1318 and the murder of the Red Earl of Ulster's successor 1333 to expand his territory, becoming for a time also KING OF CENEL EOGHAIN and thus over-king of northern Ireland 1325; deposed by the late KING DOMNAII's s Aedh O'Neill with Anglo-Norman help 1344; *d* 1347, leaving, with an er s (Brian, Chief or Prince of Clannaboy 1347–69; taken prisoner while Tanist of Clannaboy by the English 1327; defeated an invasion of Clannaboy by his kinsman and nominal suzerain AEDH O'NEILL, KING OF ULSTER, 1354; *d* 1369):

MUIRCHEARTACH *Cennfhada* ('Long-Head'), Chief or Prince of Clannaboy 1369–95; *m* Agnes, widow of Angus Macdonald, Lord of the Isles 1308–30, and dau of Cumach O'Cathan, under-king of Glengiven, and *d* 1395, having had:

BRIAN *Ballach* ('The Freckled'), Chief or Prince of Clannaboy 1395–1425; murdered by the townsfolk of Carrickfergus 1425, leaving:

1 Henry *Caech* ('The Blind') (probably s by a 1st w); blinded by his bros 1426; *d* 1465; ancestor of the Silocht Henry Caech

2 AEDH

3 Muircheartach *Ruadh* ('The Red'), Ch or Prince of Clannaboy 1444–71; had:

 (1) Feidhlimidh; *k* by his cousin Domnall O'Neill 1497

4 Brian *Gallda* ('The Foreigner')

5 Cu-Uladh *Ballach* ('The Freckled'); ancestor of the O'NEILLs of Killeiter

6 Niall *Gallda*; ancestor of the O'NEILLs of Killultagh

BRIAN's 2nd son,

 AEDH *Buidhe* ('The Yellow'), Chief or Prince of Clannaboy 1426–44; heir to high-kingship of Ireland; *m* Fionnguala (became a nun at Killeigh 1447), widow of NIALL *Garbh* ('The Rough'), KING OF TIR CONAILL 1422–39, and dau of Calvagh O'Connor Faly, Dynast of Offaly, and *d* 25 July 1493, leaving, with three yr sons (Aedh *Og* ('The Younger'), Chief or Prince of Clannaboy 1482–85, *k* by the English 1485, leaving issue; Eoghan, ancestor of Silocht Eoghain in Clannaboy; Brian, *d* 1488, leaving issue:

CON, Chief or Prince of Clannaboy 1471–82; heir to Kingdom of Ulster; *m* Mary (*d* 1488), dau of Sir Donald *Ballach* ('The Freckled') McDonnell (*see* ANTRIM, E), and *d* 1482, leaving, with two yr sons (Eoghan *Ruadh* ('The Red'), *d* 1509, leaving issue; Art, living 1489):

NIALL *Mor* ('The Great'), Chief or Prince of Clannaboy 1485–1512; *m* Ingean-dubh (*d* 1494), dau of AEDH *Ruadh* ('The Red') O'DONELL, KING OF TIR CON-AILL 1461–97, and *d* 11 Aug 1512, leaving:

1 Aedh *Buie*, Chief or Prince of Clannaboy 1512–24; *m* Gormfhlaith (*d* 1524), dau of AEDH *Dubh* ('The Black') O'DONELL, KING OF TIR CONAILL 1497–1537, and was *k* by a body of rival O'Neills and FitzGeralds when returning home from a raiding party 6 Oct 1524, leaving:

 (1) Eoghan; *k* by a party of Scots 1534

 (2) Niall; *k* by the Scots 1537

 (3) Conn; *k* in a raid on his territory 1541

 (4) Domnall; *k* in the same raid 1541

 (1) Mary; *m* 1st by 1530, as his 2nd w, 1st EARL OF TYRONE (*see above*) and had issue

2 Brian *Ballach* ('The Freckled'), Chief or Prince of Clannaboy 1524–29; *m* 1st Sarah, dau of THE O'NEILL, KING OF TYRONE (though whether CON *Mor*, KING OF ULSTER 1483–93, ART *Og*, KING OF ULSTER 1514–19 or even the 1st EARL OF TYRONE (for all of whom *see above*) prior to the conversion of his kingdom into an earldom is unclear; *m* 2nd Sibyl, dau of The Maguire, Lord (Chief) of Fermanagh, and was *k* by Cormac MacQuillan 1529, leaving by his 1st w:

 (1) Murtough *Devlinagh*/Muircheartach *Doibhlenach* (probably so named from being fostered by O'Devlin), Ch or Prince of Clannaboy 1548–52 (last Chief inaugurated according to the old Irish laws); opposed by his cousin (who was also his precedecessor's bro) Aedh, the latter hiring 7,000 Scots and overrunning S Clannaboy; *m* Margaret, dau of The O'Byrne, Dynast of S Wicklow, and was *k* 1552, having had, with other issue:

  1a Domnall; defeated by his f's enemy Aedh O'Neill 1554; *d* by 1567, leaving:

   1b Con *Buidhe* ('The Yellow'); granted by JAMES I several thousand acres in Cos Armagh and Tyrone forfeited by the 3rd and last EARL OF TYRONE following the 'Flight of the Earls' 1607, but forfeited them in turn after taking part in a plot *c* 1615 to capture the Fort of Charlemont; *d* *c* 1630, leaving:

    1c Feidhlimidh/Phelim *Dubh* ('The Black'); took part in the 1641 Uprising, holding Maryborough (modern Portlaoise) until forced to surrender through treachery in his garrison; later held rank of Col under his cousin Owen Roe O'Neill (*see above*) 1649 and fought against CROMWELL 1650; *m* —, dau of Phelim *Dubh* O'Neill, of Kullultagh, by Mary, dau of Con O'Neill, of Castlereagh, and had:

     1d Eimher/Ever; Capt Irish Catholic army in 1641 Uprising; *m* *c* 1670 Catherine, dau of Ever O'Neill, of Killitragh, and had:

      1e Felix/Fiedhlimidh/Phelim; Ensign in Col Gordon O'Neill's Regt under JAMES II Siege of Derry 1689 and Battles of the Boyne 1690 and Aughrim 1691, also defence of Limerick; later went to France with his Regt and entered French Serv 1691, fighting against the Austrians 1692–97, Lt 1698, fought at Luzarra Italy 1702, present Battle of Spier and taking of Brisach and Landau 1703; was in Italy at Sieges of Vercelli, Ivrea and Verrua 1704, at Battles of Cassano 1705 and Calcinato 1706, campaigned Germany 1707 and was *k* with the Irish Brigade fighting for the French at Battle of Malplaquet 1709; *m* 1st Catherine Keating and had issue; *m* 2nd Joan O'Dempsey (*d* 17 April 1722), dau of 1st Viscount Clanmalier, and by her had issue; his s by his 1st w:

       1f Con(stantine), of Dublin; *m* Cecilia, dau of Captain Felix O'Hanlon (s of Col Edmund O'Hanlon, of Killevy, descended from a sis of 3rd EARL OF TYRONE; *see above*), and had, with other issue:

        1g João/Shane; *b* Kilmore, Co Tyrone; settled Portugal 1740, where bought an estate nr Almada on the Tagus; *m* 2 Sept 1750 Valentina, dau of José Ferreira, and had, with two daus (Cecilia; Anna, successive Prioresses Convent of Irish Sisters of Bone Successo, nr Lisbon):

         1h Carlos, of Quintas das Machadas; Professed Kt Order of Christ; *b* 11 June 1760; *educ* St Omer; *m* 17 Sept 1784 Ana-João, dau and eventual heir of Jacob Torlade, Hanseatic Consul at Setubal (s of Heinrich Torlade, Hamburg judge and banker), and *d* 24 June 1835, leaving, with two yr sons (Joaquim; Henry) and several daus:

          1i José-Maria; Cdr Orders of Christ and Our Lady of the Conception of Villa Vicosa, Danish Consul-Gen Lisbon; *b* 14 June 1788; *m* 11 Dec 1814 Dona Ludovina Alves Solano, dau of Antonio Alves, and had, with a dau (Dona Annica, *m* Antonio, 1st Marqués de Vinent):

1j José-Carlos; *b* 28 July 1816; *dsp* 3 Aug 1889

2j Jorge Torlades; Kt of Rose of Brazil, Cdr Dannebrog 1st Cl Denmark, Offr: Order Leopold Belgium, Redeemer Greece, Christ and Our Lady of the Conception Portugal, Greek Consul-Gen and Belgian Hon Consul Lisbon; *b* 15 Dec 1817; *m* 20 July 1846 his cousin Dona Carolina-Teresa (*d* 11 Nov 1893 aged 71), dau of Joaquim O'Neill, and *d* 18 Nov 1890, having had, with a yr s (Arthur, *b* 15 Dec 1852, *m* Dona Maria da Gloria Brito de Carvalho Gorjão, dau of Francisco Gorjão, and *dsp* 9 Nov 1880):

1k Jorge, The O'Neill of Clannaboy; peer of Portugal, Kt SMO Malta, Grand Cross St Gregory the Great, Grand Cross Isabella the Catholic of Spain, Offr Legn Hon, Grand Offr Roy Household to KING OF PORTUGAL; styled Count of Tyrone from 1901 by a family pact on the extinction of the French branch claiming seniority; *b* 15 Feb 1848; *m* 14 July 1872 Dona Maria-Isabel Mazziotti, dau and eventual heir of José-Gregorio Fernandez, Kt Order of Christ, industrialist, and *d* 11 Feb 1925, having had, with a dau (Dona Maria-Teresa, *b* 9 July 1879, *m* 27 Jan 1898 Dom Antonio de Avilez Lobo de Almeida Melo de Castro, cadet of the Counts of Galvelas):

1l Hugo Joseph Jorge Ever, styled The O'Neill of Clannaboy; Lt Portuguese Royal Navy; *b* 7 June 1874; *m* 14 Jan 1906 Dona Julia (*d* 28 Feb 1934), dau of R-Adml Dom Fernando de Serpa Pimentel (yr s of 2nd Visconde de Gouveia and bro of 1st Marqués) by Dona Maria-Ana-Vitoria de Sousa Coutinho, dau of Dom Rodrigo, 3rd Count of Linhares, by Dona Ana-Carlota de Mendoça (dau of Nuno, 1st Duke of Loulé, PM Portugal, by Infanta Ana, dau of JOHN VI, KING OF PORTUGAL 1816–1826 and EMPEROR OF BRAZIL 1816–1822), and *d* 30 March 1940, leaving:

 1m Jorge, recognised as The O'Neill of Clannaboy by Ch Herald of Ireland; *b* 7 Nov 1908; *m* Dona Josefina-Luisa Roquette, dau of Luis-Rafael-Feliciano-da-Conceição Ricciardi (of a Neapolitan noble family from Aversa) by Dona Julieta Roquette (gdau and eventual heir of the 1st Visconde de Alvalade), and had:

  1n *Hugo; *b* 7 March 1939; *m* *Rosa-Maria, dau of Raoul-Jules Empis by Dona Luisa de Sousa Coutinho (dau of 5th Marqués of Valença, Premier Marquis of Portugal, and 17th Count of Redondo), and has:

   1o *Luiza; *b* 27 Jan 1964

   2o *Catarina; *b* 17 Jan 1965

   3o *Maria-Ana Empis; *b* 13 Jan 1966

  1n *Maria-Madalana; *b* 13 Sept 1940; *m* 7 Sept 1961 *Gonçalo Diniz Pinheiro de Melo, gs of 1st Count of Arnoso, and has:

   1o *Gonzalo; *b* 1 Dec 1965

   2o *Nuno; *b* 6 Nov 1966

   1o *Maria Madalena; *b* 30 Aug 1962

   2o *Ana João; *b* 24 March 1964

  2n *Teresa [Sra de Luis Felipe de Camara Pina, rua das Chagos, 20–30 Eo, Lisboa, Portugal]; *b* 26 March 1942; *m* 16 Sept 1966 *Luis Felipe da Camara Pina, s of Gen Luis Maria da Camara Pina by Martha Lima Mayer, and has:

   1o *Marta; *b* 27 Aug 1967

   2o *Maria; *b* 19 July 1969

  3n *Margarida; *b* 18 Jan 1944

  4n *Maria Isabel; *b* 23 March 1947

 2m Fernando; *b* 13 Oct 1914; *m* 6 Oct 1947 *Dona Maria Livia Paes do Amaral Franco, dau of Dr Frederico Franco de Castelo-Branco, s of João Franco, Peer of Portugal (PM and Dictator Portugal 1906–08), and *d* 17 Oct 1974, leaving:

  1n *João Hugo [Dom João O'Neill, Rua Presidente Arriaga 84–1º, 1200 Lisboa, Portugal]; *b* 1951; *m* 29 Sept 1975 *Maria da Graca de Castelo Branco Schedel and has:

   1o *Duarte; *b* 7 May 1979

   1o *Vera; *b* 21 March 1976

  2n *José Maria; *b* 1954; *m* 3 March 1990 *Cecília de Bragança Mendes and has:

   1o *Rodrigo; *b* 17 Feb 1993

   1o *Rita; *b* 5 Jan 1996

  1n Rita Maria; *b* 9 Jan 1950; *m* *Dom Sebastião Maria Sa Coutinho de Lancastre and *d* 9 Oct 1977

  2n *Maria Ana; *b* 26 June 1952; *m* 19– *Manuel Gouveia Portela de Herédia and has:

   1o *Miguel; *b* 30 Nov 1979

   1o *Sofia; *b* 31 May 1975

   2o *Joana; *b* 17 July 1978

 1m *Maria-Ana [Marquesa of Sabugosa, 11 rua Ribeiro Sanches, Lisbon 3; Quinta de Santo Amaro, Azeitao, Portugal]; *b* 30 July 1907; *m* 3 Jan 1929 *Dom João-Jose de Melo, yr s of 12th Count of Sao Lourenço and bro of 4th Marqués of Sabugosa

 2m *Maria-Isabel [Marquesa of Sabugosa, 120 rua 1 de Maio, Lisbon 3; Quinta de Marinha, Cascais,

Portugal]; *b* 27 May 1910; *m* 11 April 1929 *Dom Antonio Vasco Jose de Melo, 4th Marqués of Sabugosa and 13th Count of São Lourenço

2l Jorge-Albert; *b* 6 Dec 1874; *dsp* 8 Dec 1900

3l José-Carlos-Maria-Felix-Bernardo; *b* 8 Jan 1894; *m* 22 Jan 1931 Annie, dau of Jacob Werner, and *d* 2 Feb 1965, leaving:

  1m *Jorge-Bernardo [Dom Jorge O'Neill, rua S Joaquim 6–2 Do, Lisboa, Portugal]; *b* 22 Feb 1937; *m* *Dona Maria da Assunção

  1m *Isabel (Dona); *b* 29 Jan 1939

3j Carlos; *m* Adelaide, dau of Thomas Parsons Custance, and had issue (extinct in male line)

4j Joaquim; *m* Caroline, dau of Patrick John Caffery, and by her had issue (extinct in male line); he also left illegitimate issue, apparently continuing in the male line

5j Henry, 1st and last Visconde de Santa Monica (Portugal), so *cr* 28 Dec 1876; Grand Cordon of Our Lady of the Conception of Villa Vicosa, Grand Cross Rose of Brazil, Grand Cross Crown Italy, Kt Cdr Legn Hon, Grand Offr Roy Household Portugal, Portuguese Min Justice; *b* 3 May 1821; *d* unm 6 Nov 1889, when his title expired

3 FEIDHLIMIDH/PHELIM, of whom later

4 Nial *Og* ('The Younger'), Chief or Prince of Clannaboy 1533–37; *m* —, dau of Macarthan, Dynast of Cenel Faghartach, and had:

(1) Brian *Faghartach*, Chief or Prince of Clannaboy 1537–48; *k* 1548 resisting attack by Shane *an Diomais* (see above), leaving, with other issue:

1a Nial, Chieftain of Clannaboy, as which installed by the English 1575 and again 1602 on failure of Tyrone's Rising; *m* his cousin *d c* 1600, leaving, with other issue:

1b Con, of Castlereagh; imprisoned 1605 but escaped to Scotland; *m* —, sis of Owen Roe O'Neill (see above), and *d* 1619, leaving:

1c Daniel/Domnall; imprisoned as royalist in Tower of London by Parliamentarians on eve of English Civil War but escaped in women's clothing 1642, fought Battles of Marston Moor and Naseby; held rank of Maj-Gen; held Trim against CROMWELL 1649; Groom Bedchamber to the exiled CHARLES II; visited England secretly and was arrested but escaped 1655; Capt King's Own Troop Horse Gds at Restoration, MP St Ives, PMG 1663; *m* Catherine, dau of 2nd and last Baron Wotton of Marley, but *dsp* 24 Oct 1664

2c Con; Col in Irish Catholic Army in 1641 Uprising; murdered 1643 while a prisoner by a Presbyterian minister after surrendering at Clones on promise of quarter

(2) Aedh, Chief or Prince of Clannaboy 1552–55, a position he had claimed previously against his cousin Murtough *Devlinagh* (see above); after intermittent warfare against the English made peace with them and won recognition as Chief; *k* by a bullet in a skirmish with the Antrim Scots 1555, leaving:

1a Eoghain/Owen; *k* in the family feud 1601

(3) Con, Chief or Prince of S Clannaboy 1555 on; *d* 7 April 1589, having had, with other issue:

1a Domnall; *k* by the English 1584

5 Domnall; had issue

6 Murtough/Muircheartach; had issue

NIALL THE GREAT's son,

FEIDHLIMIDH/PHELIM *Bacach* ('The Lame'), Captain or Lord of Clannaboy 1529–33; *d* 1533, leaving:

1 Aedh; joined with the English in raiding territory of Sorley *Buie* McDonnell (see ANTRIM, E) but was *k* by Sorley 1583, leaving, with other issue (who held Clannaboy north of Kellswater):

(1) Niall; *k c* 1600 fighting in Ulster in English service, leaving, with other issue:

1a Niall *Og* ('The Younger'); *m* Alice O'Donell and *d* 1628, leaving:

1b Sir HENRY O'NEILL, 1st Bt (I), so *cr* 23 Feb 1665/6, of Killelagh, Co Antrim; *b* 1625; *m* probably *c* 1655 Eleanor (*m* 2nd James Netterville, 4th s of 2nd Viscount Netterville of Dowth), sis of 1st and last Duke of Tyrconnell (see TALBOT OF MALAHIDE, B), and *d* 1671, having had:

1c Sir NIALL O'NEILL, 2nd Bt, of Killelagh; *b c* 1658; Capt Dragoons in JAMES II's Army 1687, Ld Lt Co Antrim 1689; present Siege of Derry; *m* Jan 1677 Frances Molyneux, dau of 3rd Viscount Molyneux of Maryborough, and *dspm* 8 July 1690 from wounds recd at Battle of the Boyne, being posthumously attainted 1691 and leaving, with four yr daus:

1d Rose; *m* Col Nicholas Wogan, of Rathcoffey, and had:

1e Frances; *m* John Talbot (see TALBOT OF MALAHIDE, B)

2c Sir DANIEL O'NEILL, 3rd and last Bt, as which *s* bro 1690 but was stripped of it by the attainder 1691; MP (I Parl) Lisburne 1689; *m* probably *c* 1690 Mary, est dau of Sir Gregory Byrne, 1st Bt, of Timogue, Queen's Co, but *dspm*, when the btcy expired, leaving:

1d Elinor; *m* Hugh O'Reilly, of Ballinlough, Co Westmeath, and had issue (see NUGENT, Bt, of Ballinlough)

1c Rose; *m* Capt Con O'Neill, of the Fews

2 Brian (Sir), Captain or Lord of Clannaboy, as which initially recognised by the English, also ktd, though later was obliged to repulse an invasion by the English Govr Ulster (see HEREFORD, V), who crossed the Ford of Belfast 1573 and though welcomed by Sir Brian as a guest arranged the massacre of 200 of Sir Brian's people and took Sir Brian and his w in chains to Carrickfergus 1574, where they were put to death 1575; had, with a dau (*m* 1st (*divorce*) 3rd and last EARL OF TYRONE (see above) and 2nd her cousin Nial O'Neill, Chieftain of Clannaboy (*d* 1601), s of Brian *Faghartach*; see above):

(1) SHANE, of whom later

(2) Niall; living 1594

(3) Con; *k* 1585, leaving:

1a Aedh *Og* ('The Younger'); supported his cousin 3rd EARL OF TYRONE against the English but pardoned 1606; had:

1b Brian, of the Feevagh; named heir to the Shane's Castle estates by his cousin Sir Henry O'Neill 1637; ancestor of the O'NEILLs of Carlyan-in-the-Feeva

Sir BRIAN's est son,

SHANE Mac Brian O'NEILL, last Captain or Lord of Clannaboy, as which recognised (and installed) by the English April 1583, MP (I Parl) Co Antrim 1585; rival claimants to the Chieftainry prevented him retaining his original land holdings; joined his cousin 3rd EARL OF TYRONE's Rising 1598–1602 but was pardoned; at the Plantation of Ulster 1603–10 the Clannaboy O'NEILLs were stripped of over 600,000 acres, but the Chief was allowed to keep *c* 120,000 acres and Shane's Castle; *m* 1st Rose, sis of 1st Viscount Magennis of Iveagh (see GUINNESS, Bt, remarks beneath blazon), and had:

1 Henry (Sir), of Shane's Castle; entailed his estates 13 Sept 1637; *m* Martha, dau of Sir Francis Stafford, Govr Ulster, and *d* 8 April 1638, having had, with four other (idiot) daus:

(1) Rose; *m* 1st Marquess of Antrim (see ANTRIM, E) but *dsp* after 1689, when the estates passed to her cousin and heir male

SHANE Mac Brian O'NEILL *m* 2nd Anne, dau of Brian *Carrach* ('The Scabby') O'Neill, Lord of Loughinsholin and Chieftain of Clann Domhnuill Donn (see above), and *d* 23 April 1616, having by her had, with other issue:

2 Art(hur); *m* Grace, dau of Cathal O'Hara, of Crebilly (cadet of the Dynasts of Leyny, Co Sligo), and had:

(1) Cormac, of Shane's Castle; Col in serv of CHARLES II; *dsp*

(2) John; Col in serv of CHARLES II; *m* Rose — and had, with two yr sons:

1a Charles, of Shane's Castle; *m* Lady Mary Paulet, dau of 7th Marquess of Winchester (qv), but *dsp* 1716

3 Phelim *Dubh* ('The Black'); Capt in serv of CHARES II; *m* his er bro's sis-in-law Shelagh (*d* 1690), dau of Cathal O'Hara, and *d* 1677, having had, with four daus:

(1) Brian; *m* Eleanor, dau of Edmond Magennis, of Kilwarlin, and *dvp* 1669, leaving, with other issue:

1a JOHN; *s* to Shane's Castle (see below)

2a Henry; *m* Sara, dau of Con O'Neill, of the Fews, later Newcastle, Co Mayo (see above), and had:

1b Henrietta; *m* Henry O'Beirne, Col Spanish Army, and had:

1c Maria Theresa; *m* 6th Baron Wharton (qv)

(2) Arthur, of Neillsbrook; *m* his cousin Eleanor, dau of Henry O'Neill, of Ballylisnelarney, and was ancestor of the O'NEILLs of Bracart

4 Shane *Og* ('The Younger'), of Ballylisnelarney; *m* Anne — and *d* 1620, being with her ancestor of the O'NEILLs of Ballymoney

SHANE Mac Brian O'NEILL's ggs by his 3rd s Phelim *Dubh*,

JOHN *Sean an Franca* ('French John', since lived Paris before succeeding to the estates) O'NEILL, of Shane's Castle; *m* Charity, dau of Sir Richard Dixon, of Colverstown, and *d* 1739, having had, with a 3rd s (Clotworthy, *dsp*):

1 Henry; *m* Mary, widow of Capt John Bickerstaffe, of Rosegift, in the Largy, and *dvp* 1721, leaving:

(1) Mary; *m* Rev Arthur Chichester, s of Rev William Chichester (by Lydia, dau of Henry Arvse, of Drogheda), s of John Chichester, yr bro of 2nd Earl of Belfast (see DONEGALL, M), and had, with other issue (including a dau Catherine, *m* Samuel Ball, of Grouse Hall, Co Donegal, Capt 6th Dragoon Gds):

1a William (Rev); LLD; Rector Broughshane, Co Antrim, and Clonmany, Co Donegal; *m* 1st Mary Anne, dau of George Harvey, of Malin Hall, and had:

1b Sir ARTHUR CHICHESTER, 1st and last Bt (UK), so *cr* 13 Sept 1821, of Greencastle; MP; *d* unm 25 May 1847, when the btcy expired

1a (cont.) The Rev William Chichester *m* 2nd Mary Anne, dau of Rev Edward Hart, of Kilderry, and *d* 31 Aug 1815, having by her had, with a dau (*d* unm):

2b Edward (Rev); Rector Kilmore, Co Armagh; *m* 23 April 1812 Catherine (*d* 15 April 1875), dau of Robert Young, of Culdaff House, Co Donegal, and *d* June 1840, having had:

1c WILLIAM, **1st Baron**

2c Robert (Rev); *b* 6 April 1814; *m* 1st 5 March 1840 Frances Alicia Anne (*dsp* 31 July 1867), dau of Gen George Vaughan Hart, of Kilderry; *m* 2nd 18 Nov 1869 Harriette Anne (*d* 13 Nov 1928), dau of Ven Townley Blackwood Price, Archdeacon Down, and *d* 2 June 1878, leaving:

1d Anne Henrietta; *d* 1 April 1927

2d Evelyn Maria Catherine; *d* unm 7 June 1958

3c George Vaughan (Rev); Rector Wotton, Surrey; *b* 26 Dec 1819; *educ* Trin Coll Dublin (BA); *m* 26 Aug 1847 Harriet Eleanor (*d* 28 May 1885), dau of Hugh Lyle, of Knocktarna, Co Antrim, and *d* 1898, leaving, with another s (*d* young) and dau (*d* unm):

1d Edward Arthur (Rev); *b* 23 Feb 1849; *educ* St John's Coll Cambridge (MA); RD and Hon Canon Winchester, Vicar Dorking 1885–1921; *m* 23 April 1884 Mary Agnes (*d* 6 Feb 1944), dau of 1st Baron Ashcombe (qv), and *d* 30 Sept 1925, leaving:

1e Arthur O'Neill Cubitt, OBE (1941), MC (1918); *b* 14 July 1889; *educ* Wellington and Trin Coll Cambridge; Lt-Col RA (TA), Capt Surrey Yeo, WW I and WW II 1939–41; *m* 31 July 1924 *Hilda Grace, only child of William Robert Young, PC (see ST HELENS, B), and *d* 9 March 1972, leaving:

1f *Rosemary Hilda [The Rt Hon Rosemary Viscountess Brookeborough, Ashbrooke, Brookeborough, Co Fermanagh]; *b* 12 Feb 1926; *m* 4 March 1949 2nd Viscount Brookeborough (qv) and has issue

2f *Deirdre Wills [Mrs Rodney Windsor, Gracehill House, Stranocum, Co Antrim]; *b* 9 March 1928; *m* 26 April 1951 *Capt Rodney Francis Maurice Windsor, Queen's Bays, s of Maurice Windsor, OBE, and has:

1g *Antony Maurice; *b* 10 Nov 1955; *educ* Harrow

2g *Nicholas Guy; *b* 30 June 1961

1g *Patricia Deirdre; *b* 14 Dec 1953

3f *Finnola Margaret [Mrs D Herbison, Ardvernis Farm, Cullybackey, Ballymena, Co Antrim]; *b* 23 May 1932; *m* 1st 1959 William McWilliams (*d* 11 July 1963) and has:

1g *Grace Mildred; *b* 1 March 1960

2g *Tracey; *b* 18 Sept 1961

3f (cont.) Mrs William McWilliams *m* 2nd 1964 *D Herbison and by him has:

1g *John Patrick Arthur; *b* 5 Sept 1971

3g *Virginia Maria; *b* 3 June 1965

4g *Cathleen Laura; *b* 11 May 1967

2e William George Cubitt; *b* 20 July 1892; Capt City London Bn London Regt; *ka* Somme 15 Sept 1916

1e Harriet Laura; *b* 12 Feb 1887; *m* 8 June 1915 Brig Alexander Henry Delap West (*d* 10 March 1959), DSO, RA, s of Rev H M West, of Folly Court, Wokingham, Berks

2e Mildred Mary; *b* 17 Dec 1890; *d unm* 3 Jan 1965

2d Henry Hugh Lyle; *b* 30 Nov 1855; *d* 4 Sept 1917

3d Arthur George Vaughan; *b* 3 Jan 1865; Maj 26th Serv Bn Numberland Fus, Maj Connaught Rangers; *m* 1st 21 Aug 1902 Marion Frances (*dsp* 9 March 1903), er dau of John Smyth, of Masonbrook, Co Galway; *m* 2nd 28 Sept 1909 Madeline (*d* 22 Oct 1923), widow of Cdr Arthur Charles Middlemass, RN, Inspr-Gen Egyptian Coastgds, and dau of Maj George Augustus Frederick Quentin, 10th Hus, and *d* 30 Dec 1920

4d Alfred Godfrey de Vaud; *b* 7 Nov 1866; Lt-Col IA WW I (wounded twice); *m* 20 May 1901 Agnes Donaldson (*d* 26 Jan 1945), dau of Col John Anderson, and *d* 26 July 1933, leaving:

1e Adelaide Kathleen; *b* 30 July 1903; *m* 1st 1920 (*divorce* 1932) Brig John le Clerc Fowle, IA, er s of Col Sir Henry Walter Hamilton Fowle, KBE; *m* 2nd 1936 Maj J J Clune (drowned at sea WW II), IA, and *d* 25 June 1947

2e *Maureen Agnes [Mrs George Bain, Sandy Lodge, Chagford, Devon]; *b* 21 May 1909; *m* 24 Aug 1929 *Brig George Alexander Bain, OBE, 2nd KEO Gurkha Rifles, IA, yst s of William Bain, of Edinburgh, and has:

1f *Mary Anne Chichester [Lady Campbell, Kilbryde Castle, Dunblane, Perthshire FK15 9NF]; *b* 8 May 1930; *m* 21 May 1952 Sir Colin Moffat Campbell, 8th Bt, MC, of Aberuchill (*qv*), and has had issue

2f Maureen Veronica; *b* 21 June 1931; *m* 18 Aug 1956 *Charles Riou Mosse [Charles Mosse Esq, Chilveny Farm, Throwleigh, Devon EX20 2QG], s of Lt-Col Charles Oliver Mosse, MC, Rajputana Rifles, IA, and *d* 13 Sept 1987, leaving:

1g *Charles David Fairless; *b* 6 March 1959; *m* *Julia Cleves and has:

1h *Jacob Sebastian Fairless; *b* 7 Sept 1986

2h *Oliver Benjamin; *b* 16 July 1989

1g *Rosalind Mary; *b* 10 June 1957; *m* *Richard Nevard and has:

1h *David; *b* 25 Dec 1984

2h *William; *b* 16 Oct 1986

2g *Anne Veronica; *b* 21 May 1962; *m* *Mark Ainsley Tankard and has:

1h *Joshua; *b* 14 Sept 1991

1h *Hannah; *b* 15 May 1989

2h *Kate; *b* 5 July 1993

1d Frances Harriet; *m* 28 Oct 1873 William John Evelyn (*d* 26 June 1908), of Wotton House, Surrey, and *d* 25 July 1897, leaving issue

2d Ada Catherine; *m* 22 June 1876 Reginald Braithwaite (*d* April 1885) and *d* 22 May 1919

3d Mary Georgina; *d unm* 4 Dec 1944

2 Charles, of Shane's Castle; *m* 1736 Catherine, dau of Rt Hon St John Brodrick, MP (*see* MIDLETON, V), and *d* Aug 1769, having had:

(1) JOHN O'NEILL, 1st VISCOUNT O'NEILL, so *cr* 3 Oct 1795, as also earlier 25 Oct 1793 BARON O'NEILL OF SHANE'S CASTLE, Co Antrim (both I), PC (I 1780); *b* 16 Jan 1740; *educ* Trin Coll Dublin and Ch Ch Oxford (MA); MP (I Parl) Randalstown 1761–83 and Co Antrim 1783–93, Ulster delegate to Irish Nat Convention of Reform 1783; Govr Antrim at outbreak of 1798 Uprising, shot an assailant and *d* 17 June 1798 of wounds recd from insurgent pikemen 7 June previously; *m* 18 Oct 1777 Henrietta (*d* 3 Sept 1793 aged 37), only dau and heiress of Charles, Viscount Dungarvan, est s of 5th Earl of Cork and Orrery (*qv*), and had:

1a CHARLES HENRY ST JOHN O'NEILL, 2nd VISCOUNT O'NEILL and 1st and last EARL O'NEILL, so *cr* Aug 1800, as also VISCOUNT RAYMOND (both I), KP (1809), PC (I 1809); *b* 22 Jan 1779; *educ* Eton and Ch Ch Oxford; rep I peer 1801–41, Jt PMG Ireland 1807–31, Ld Lt Co Antrim 1831–41, Col Antrim Militia, V-Adml coast of Ulster, Grand Master Orangemen Ireland; *d unm* 25 March 1841, when the Earldom and 1800 Viscountcy expired

2a JOHN BRUCE RICHARD O'NEILL, 3rd and last VISCOUNT O'NEILL; *b* 30 Dec 1780; *educ* Eton; Ensign Coldstream Gds 1799, Capt 1800, Capt 18th Light Dragoons 1804, Maj 19th Light Dragoons 1807, Lt-Col: Chasseurs Britanniques 1808, 19th Light Dragoons 1810 and Coldstream Gds 1816, Col 1814, Maj-Gen 1825, Lt-Gen 1838, Gen 1854, MP (Tory) Co Antrim 1802–41, Constable Dublin Castle 1811–55, rep I peer 1843–55, V-Adml coast Ulster; *d unm* 12 Feb 1855, when both his titles expired

(2) St John; *b* 6 May 1741; *m* Frances, dau of Robert Borrowes, of Ballybrittas, Queen's Co, and *d* 1790, leaving an only dau (*d unm*)

(1) Anne; *m* Richard Jackson, PC, and had issue

1 Catherine; *m* 19 Oct 1711 7th Viscount Mountgarret (*qv*) and *d* 15 April 1739

The last VISCOUNT O'NEILL's 2nd cousin twice-removed,

Rev WILLIAM CHICHESTER later O'NEILL (roy licence 1855 under terms of will of EARL O'NEILL), **1st Baron O'Neill of Shane's Castle**, Co Antrim (UK), so *cr* 18 April 1868; *b* 4 March 1813; *educ* Foyle Sch Londonderry, Shrewsbury and Trin Coll Dublin; ordained 1837, Preb Ch Ch Dublin 1848–59; *m* 1st 3 Jan 1839 Henrietta (*d* 17 Jan 1857), dau of Robert Torrens, Judge Court Common Pleas Ireland, and had:

1 EDWARD, **2nd Baron**

2 Arthur; *b* 13 Sept 1843; *d* 12 Jan 1870

3 Robert Torrens, JP, DL; *b* 10 Jan 1845; Maj 4th Bn Royal Inniskilling Fus, High Sheriff Co Antrim 1871, MP Mid-Antrim 1885–1910; *d unm* 25 July 1910

1 Anne; *b* 1848; *d unm* 23 Feb 1934

The **1st Baron** *m* 2nd 8 April 1858 Elizabeth Grace (*d* 22 Jan 1905), dau of Ven John Torrens, DD, Archdeacon Dublin, and *d* 18 April 1883

His est s,

EDWARD CHICHESTER later O'NEILL (1855), **2nd Baron O'Neill of Shane's Castle**, JP, DL; *b* 31 Dec 1839; *educ* Trin Coll Cambridge; MP (C) Co Antrim 1863–80; *m* 30 June 1873 Lady Louisa Katherine Emma Cochrane, DGStJ (*d* 10 Aug 1942), est dau of 11th Earl of Dundonald (*qv*), and had:

1 William Thomas Cochrane; *b* 16 Nov 1874; *d* 24 July 1882

2 Arthur Edward Bruce, JP, DL Co Antrim; *b* 19 Sept 1876; *educ* Eton; joined Army 1897, Lt Life Gds 1898, served Boer War 1899–1900 (Queen's Medal, three clasps), Capt 1902–10, Adj 1902, MP Mid-Antrim 1910–14; *m* 21 Jan 1902 Lady Annabel Hungerford Crewe-Milnes (*m* 2nd 9 Feb 1922 Maj James Hugh Hamilton DODDS later CREWE (deed poll 1945), CMG, TD, Consul-Gen at Nice (*d* 28 July 1956), and *d* 14 June 1948, leaving further issue), est dau of 1st and last Marquess of Crewe (*see* 1940 edn) by Sybil Marcia, 4th dau of Sir Frederick Graham, 3rd Bt, of Netherby (*qv*), and was *ka* 6 Nov 1914 (first MP *k* WW I), leaving:

(1) SHANE EDWARD ROBERT, **3rd Baron**

(2) Brian Arthur; *b* 31 March 1911; granted 6 Dec 1929 with siblings rank of baron's dau/yr s, Capt and Adj Irish Gds WW II; *ka* Norway 15 May 1940

(3) TERENCE MARNE O'NEILL, BARON O'NEILL OF THE MAINE, of Ahoghill, Co Antrim (LP, UK), so *cr* 23 Jan 1970, PC (NI 1956), DL (Co Antrim 1948); *b* 10 Sept 1914; *educ* Eton; Capt Irish Gds WW II (wounded), High Sheriff Co Antrim 1953, MP NI Parl 1946–70, Parly Sec Min Health 1948–53, Dep Speaker 1953–56, Min Home Affrs 1956–57 and Fin 1957–63, PM 1963–69; *m* 4 Feb 1944 *Katherine Jean [The Rt Hon Lady O'Neill of the Maine, Lisle Court, Lymington, Hants], dau of William Ingham Whitaker, DL, of Pylewell Park, Lymington, Hants, and *d* 1990, leaving:

1a +Patrick Arthur Ingham [The Hon Patrick O'Neill, 48 Forbes St, Newtown, NSW 2042, Australia]; *b* 18 Jan 1945 (HRH late PRINCESS MARIE LOUISE stood sponsor); *educ* Eton; Lt QRI Hussars; reporter ABC TV, producer Channel 10 Current Affairs, cncllr Nat Tst Australia NSW 1986–87; *m* 1st March 1975 (*divorce* 1984) Anne, dau of Douglas Lillecrapp, of Adelaide; *m* 2nd 1984 *Stella Mary, dau of Sir Alexander Russell Downer, KBE, of Williamstown, S Australia, and by his 1st w has:

1b *Sophie Katherine; *b* 22 March 1976

2b *Elizabeth Mary; *b* 1981

1a *Penelope Anne [The Hon Mrs Crutchley, Mappercombe Manor, Powerstock, Bridport, Dorset]; *b* 15 April 1947; *m* 1st 9 May 1970 (*divorce* 1983) Christopher William Kerr Devas (*see* LOTHIAN, M) and has:

1b *William Thomas; *b* 4 Nov 1975

1a (cont.) The Hon Mrs Penelope Devas *m* 2nd 23 Nov 1984 *Lt-Cdr William Victor Crutchley, RN (ret), s of Adml Sir Victor Crutchley, VC, KCB, DSC (*see* PARKER, Bt, of Shenstone), and by him has:

2b *Arthur Percy; *b* 30 Oct 1987

1b *Daisy Alice; *b* 17 May 1986

(1) Sibyl; *b* 15 Dec 1902; *m* 6 June 1924, as his 1st w, Lt-Col Edward N Buxton, MC (*see* BUXTON, Bt), and *d* 26 July 1946, leaving issue

(2) Mary ('Midi') Louisa Hermione; *b* 19 Aug 1905; *m* 3 April 1934 Lt-Col Derick Ernest Frederick Orby Gascoigne (*d* 11 Aug 1972), 2nd s of Brig-Gen. Sir (Ernest) Frederick Orby Gascoigne, KCVO, CMG, DSO, JP, DL, Gren Gds, and had:

1a *(Arthur) Bamber [Bamber Gascoigne Esq, 1 St Helena Terrace, Richmond, Surrey TW9 1NR]; *b* 24 Jan 1935; *educ* Eton and Magdalene Coll Cambridge (Hon Fell 1996); late 2nd Lt Gren Gds, drama critic *Spectator* 1961–63 and *Observer* 1963–64, TV presenter, notably of *University Challenge* 1962–87, chm: Ackermann Publishing 1981–85 and Friends of Covent Gdn 1991–95, Tstee Nat Gallery 1988–95 and Tate Gallery 1993–95, Dir ROH Covent Gdn 1988–95, memb Cncl Nat Tst 1989–94, author: *Twentieth Century Drama* (1962), *World Theatre* (1968), *The Great Moghuls* (1971), *Murgatreud's Empire* (1972), *The Heyday* (1973), *The Treasures and Dynasties of China* (1973), *Ticker Khan* (1974), *The Christians* (1977), *Images of Richmond* (1978), *Images of Twickenham* (1981), *Why the Rope Went Tight* (1981), *Fearless Freddy's Magic Wish* (1982), *Fearless Freddy's Sunken Treasure* (1982), *Quest for the Golden Hare* (1983), *Cod Streuth* (1986), *How to Identify Prints* (1986), *Amazing Facts* (1988), *Encyclopedia of Britain* (1993); *m* 10 May 1965 *Christina Mary, only dau of Alfred Henry Ditchburn, CBE

2a *Brian Alvary; *b* 16 June 1943; *educ* Eton and King's Coll Cambridge

1a *Veronica Mary [The Hon Mrs William Plowden, 49 Stockwell Park Rd, London SW9]; *b* 7 April 1938; *educ* St Hugh's Coll Oxford (BA); *m* 16 Sept 1960 *Hon William Julius Lowthian Plowden, er s of Baron Plowden (*qv*), and has issue

3 (ROBERT WILLIAM) HUGH O'NEILL, *cr* BARON RATHCAVAN (*qv*)

1 Louisa Henrietta Valdivia; ARRC WW I; *m* 22 July 1907 Charles Edward Norman Leith-Hay of Rannes (*d* 25 May 1939), DL, of Leith Hall, Aberdeenshire, and *d* 14 Jan 1965, having had issue

2 Rose Anne Mary; *m* 15 Jan 1920 V-Adml John William Leopold McClintock (*d* 23 March 1929), CB, DSO, s of Adml Sir Francis Leopold McClintock, and *d* Sept 1976, leaving issue

3 Alice Esmaralda; *m* 29 Nov 1909 John Randal Parsons (*see* ROSSE, E)

The 2nd BARON *d* 19 Nov 1928; his gs,

SHANE EDWARD ROBERT O'NEILL, **3rd Baron O'Neill of Shane's Castle**, DL; *b* 6 Feb 1907; *educ* Eton and RMC Sandhurst; Lt 8th Hus WW II, Ld Lt Co Antrim, Lt-Col NI Horse; *m* 6 Oct 1932, as her 1st husb, Ann Geraldine Mary, est dau of Hon Guy Lawrence Charteris (*see* WEMYSS, E), and was *ka* Italy Oct 1944, leaving:

  1 RAYMOND ARTHUR CLANABOY O'NEILL, **4th and present Baron O'Neill of Shane's Castle**

  1 *Fionn Frances Bride [The Hon Mrs Fionn Morgan, 10 Octavia St, London SW11 3DN]; *b* 9 March 1936; *educ* Heathfield and St Anne's Coll Oxford; *m* 26 July 1961 (*divorce* 1975) John Albert Leigh Morgan, CMG (later Sir John Morgan, KCMG), Amb Mexico 1989, and has:

    (1) *John Edward Rustand; *b* 20 Sept 1964; *m* 25 May 1996 *Natasha, dau of Randal MacDonnell, and has:

      1a *John Arthur Randal; *b* 18 Oct 1996

      1a *Scarlett Louisa; *b* 9 Feb 1998

    (1) *Mary Ann Frances; *b* 11 Oct 1962; *m* 29 July 1989 *Charles Anthony Warneford Gibson, only s of G/Capt Phillip G Gibson, of Manor Farm House, Sawtry, Cambs, and has:

      1a *Alexander Shane Warneford; *b* 8 Feb 1991

      2a *Frederick John Philip; *b* 1993

    (2) *Catherine Martha Annabel; *b* 9 April 1966

Seat: Shane's Castle, Randalstown, Co Antrim. Con, the late–15th-century Chief of Clannaboy, had as his principal residence the Tower of Edenduffcarrick which later came to be called Shane's Castle. It appears to have been added to, still very much as a fortification, in the 17th century. By the 18th century it was turning into more of a fortified house than a castle, with windows of normal size on three storeys over a basement, semi-circular bows at either end and only a low wall separating it from the shores of Antrim Bay. Despite its crenellated parapet at roof-level and similarly shaped top to the curtain wall it was not by now a seriously defensible building. Indeed by the mid–1780s an orangery had been added at one end of the building, as also a terrace along the water's edge for the *bon ton* to promenade up and down and admire the prodigious view.

At the end of the Napoleonic Wars the 1st and last Earl O'Neill brought in John Nash to extend the place. In 1816, the year after the project had commenced, fire, supposedly called up by the O'Neill ancestral banshee, destroyed the house almost completely. (Nash's conservatory on the very shore of Lough Neagh survives, however.) The family moved into the stable block, which was suitably embellished. In the 1860s a new castle was built, the architects being Sir Charles Lanyon and William Henry Lynn, the duo responsible for Castle Leslie (*see* LESLIE, Bt). Their work fell victim to IRA torches in May 1922 and the O'Neills once again retreated to the stable block. A neo-Georgian edifice was erected in the 1960s on the far side of the stables to the former castle.

ONSLOW, Earl

Arms: Arg. a fess gu. between six Cornish choughs ppr. **Crest:** An eagle, *reguard*, preying on a partridge ppr. **Supporters:** Two falcons close ppr., belled or. **Mottoes:** 1 *Festina lente* ('Be quick without impetuosity'), 2 *Semper fidelis* ('Ever faithful'). **Creations:** Bt. (E) 8 May 1674, with precedence of 21 Nov 1660; B. (GB) (Onslow) 19 June 1716, (GB) (Cranley) 20 May 1776; E. And V. (UK) 19 June 1801.

THE 7TH EARL OF ONSLOW, of Onslow, Co Salop, **Viscount Cranley of Cranley**, Co Surrey, **Baron Onslow**, of Onslow, Co Salop, and of West Clandon, Co Surrey, **Baron Cranley of Imbercourt**, Co Surrey, and a **Baronet** (Sir Michael William Coplestone Dillon Onslow, Bt) [The Rt Hon The Earl of Onslow, Temple Court, Clandon Park, Guildford, Surrey GU4 7RQ]; *b* 28 Feb 1938; *s* f 1971; *educ* Eton and Sorbonne; Lt Life Gds 1956–60, chm E+ Trading to 1996, memb governing body Manorial Soc 1989–95, govr Guildford Roy GS, High Steward Guildford; *m* 17 July 1964 *Robin Lindsay, only dau of Maj Robert Lee Bullard III, US Army, by Ann, dau of Alexander Lindsay Aymer (*see* ABERCONWAY, B), and has:

  1 +RUPERT CHARLES WILLIAM BULLARD, *Viscount Cranley*; *b* 16 June 1967

  1 *Arabella; *b* 9 April 1970

  2 *Charlotte Emma Dorothy; *b* 15 Oct 1977

Lineage: ADAM de ANDRESLAWA; living 1174; had:

JOHN de ONDESLOWE, of Ondeslowe, Salop; living 1203; had:

ROGER de ONDESLOWE; *m* 1261 Cecilia, widow of Roger de la More, and *d c* 1283, leaving a 2nd s:

WILLIAM; had:

THOMAS; *d* 1317; ggf of:

THOMAS; *d* 1392, leaving:

JOHN; *m* Margaret, dau of Madoc Kynaston, of Gesnocks, Salop, and *d* 1430, leaving:

ROBERT de ONSLOWE; *m* Katherine, dau of Sir Robert Corbet, of Moreton Corbet (*see* 1970 edn CORBET, Bt), and *d* 1442, leaving:

EDWARD ONSLOW, of Onslow; *m* 1470 Anne, dau and heiress of Richard Houghton, of Houghton, and had, with other issue:

ROGER ONSLOW; *m* 12 April 1509 Margaret, dau of Thomas Poyner, of Beslow, Salop, and had, with an er s (Fulk, Clerk of Parl *temp* ELIZABETH I, *m* Mary, widow of Richard Scott, of Scot's Hall, Brabourne, Kent, and dau of George Whetenall, of Hextal's Place, E Peckham, Kent, and *d* 8 Aug 1602 aged 88):

RICHARD ONSLOW, of Blackfriars, London, and Shrewsbury; barrister, MP Steyning, Recorder London 1563, Attorney-Gen Duchy Lancaster, Slr-Gen 1566, Speaker H of C 1566–71, Attorney-Gen Court of Wards 1567; *m* Catharine, dau and heiress of William Harding, London mercer, of Knoll, Cranley, Surrey, and *d* 1571, leaving, with an er s (Robert, *d unm* 21 July 1574):

Sir EDWARD ONSLOW, of Knoll; *m* Isabel, dau of Sir Thomas Shirley, of Preston Place, Sussex, and *d* 2 April 1615, leaving, with an er s (Thomas, *dsp* 14 Dec 1616):

Sir RICHARD ONSLOW, of Loseley and W Clandon, Surrey; *b c* 1601; Parly Col Civil War, MP Surrey, memb CROMWELL's 'Upper House' 10 Dec 1657; *m* Elizabeth (*d* 29 Aug 1679), dau and heiress of Arthur Strangeways, of Co Durham, and *d* 19 May 1664, having had, with other issue, including two yr sons (Sir Henry, of Drungwick, Sussex, MP Arundel 1656, *m* Jane, widow of Henry Yates, of Warnham, and dau of Sir Francis Stodolp, of Mickleham, and was ancestor of the ONSLOWs of Stoughton, Hunts; Denzil, of Pyrford, Surrey, MP Guildford and Surrey, *m* his er bro's sis-in-law Sarah, widow of Sir John Lewis, 1st and last Bt, of Lidstone, Yorks, and dau of Sir Thomas Foote, 1st and last Bt (*see* below), and *dsp* June 1721):

Sir Arthur Onslow, 1st/2nd Bt (E), so *cr* 8 May 1674 in reversion following his f-in-law's death, with precedence of latter's btcy, of W Clandon, Surrey; *bapt* 22 May 1624; *educ* Queen's Coll Oxford and Lincoln's Inn; MP Bramber 1640 (nullified) and Jan 1640/1–48 and Surrey 1654–55, 1656–58, 1659 and 1679–81 and Guildford 1660 and 1661–79; *m* 1st Rose (*dsp* 11 March 1647/8), only surv dau and heiress of Nicolas Stoughton, of Stoughton, Surrey; *m* 2nd by 1654 Mary, 2nd dau and coheir of Alderman Sir Thomas Foot, 1st and last Bt (E), so *cr* 21 Nov 1660, Ld Mayor London 1649–50 (*dspm* 12 Oct 1687), and *d* 21 July 1688, having by her had, with two other sons (*d unm*):

  1 RICHARD ONSLOW, **1st Baron Onslow**, of Onslow, Co Salop, and of Clandon, Co Surrey, so *cr* 19 June 1716, with remainder in default of male issue to his uncle Denzil and the latter's issue and afterwards to the heirs male of his (RICHARD's) f, PC (1710 and 1714), DL Middx; *b* 23 June 1654; *educ* St Edmund Hall Oxford; MP Guildford 1678/9–81 and 1685–87, Surrey 1688/9–1710 and 1713–15 and St Mawes 1710–13, Lt-Col 1st Marine Regt 1690, Commr for Ld High Adml 1690–93, Speaker H of C 1708–10, a Ld Treasury and Chllr and U-Treas Exchequer 1714–15, Teller Exchequer 1715–17, High Steward Guildford, Ld Lt and custos rotulorum Surrey 1716–17; *m* 31 Aug 1676 Elizabeth (drowned herself in a pond in the Archbishop of London's palace at Croydon 25 Nov 1718 while suffering an excess of melancholia), dau of Sir Henry Tulse, Ld Mayor London 1683–84, and *d* 5 Dec 1717, leaving:

    (1) THOMAS ONSLOW, **2nd Baron Onslow**, DL Westminster; *bapt* 27 Oct 1679; MP (Whig) Gatton 1702–05, Chichester 1705–08, Bletchingley 1708–15 and Surrey 1715–17, Out Ranger Windsor Gt Park 1715–17, LLD Cantab 1717, High Steward Guildford, also Ld Lt and custos rotulorum Surrey 1717–40, Teller Exchequer March 1717/8–40; *m* 17 Dec 1708 Elizabeth (*d* 19 April 1731), only dau and heiress of John Knight, Jamaica merchant, and *d* 5 June 1740, having had, with five daus:

      1a RICHARD ONSLOW, **3rd Baron Onslow**, KB (1752); *b* 1713; *educ* Eton and Sidney Sussex Coll Cambridge (LLD 1749); MP (Whig) Guildford 1734–40, High Steward Guildford and Ld Lt and custos rotulorum Surrey 1740–76; *m* 16 May 1741 Mary (*d* 20 April 1812), dau of Sir Edmund Ellwill, 3rd Bt, of Exeter, and *dsp* 8 Oct 1776

  2 Foot; 1st Commr Excise, MP Guildford 1688; *b* 2 June 1655; *m* Susanna (*d* 10 June 1715), widow of Arnold Colwell and dau and heiress of Thomas Anlaby, of Etton, Yorks, and *d* 10 May 1710, having had, with five daus:

    (1) Arthur, PC (1728); *b c* 1692; barrister, Bencher Inner Temple, Recorder Guildford 1719, MP Guildford 1720–27 and Surrey 1727–61, Speaker H of C 1728–61, Chllr to GEORGE I's w CAROLINE 1729, Treasurer Navy 1734–43, Tstee Br Museum; *m* Anne, dau and coheir of John Bridges, of Thames Ditton, and *d* 17 Feb 1768, leaving:

      1a GEORGE, **1st Earl**

    (2) Richard; Lt-Gen, Govr Fort William and Plymouth; *m* 1st 9 Dec 1726 Rose (*dsp* 8 Feb 1727/8), dau and coheir of John Bridges; *m* 2nd Pooley, dau of Charles Walton, of Little Bursted, Essex, and *d* 16 March 1760, having had:

      1a George; MP Guildford, Lt-Col Gren Gds; *b* 23 April 1731; *m* 29 July 1752 Jane, dau of Rev Thomas Thorp, and *d* 14 Nov 1792, leaving:

        1b George Walton (Rev), of Dunsborough, Surrey; *b* 25 June 1768; *m* 8 July 1800 Elizabeth (*d* 26 July 1846), est dau of William Campbell, and *d* 13 Feb 1844, leaving, with five daus:

1c George Walton; Maj Madras Artillery; *b* 18 Aug 1804; *m* Mary Murray (*d* 18 June 1839), dau of Capt A R Hughes, HEICS, and *d* 30 April 1849, having had, with a dau (*d* unm):

1d George Walton; Lt Madras Artillery; *b* 13 March 1831; *d* 8 March 1854

2d Adolphus Byam; Lt Madras Serv; *b* 13 July 1832; *d* 27 May 1858

3d Alexander Lee (Rev); BA Cantab, Vicar Kingsbury, Warwicks, Chaplain Bombay Presidency; *b* 29 Dec 1835; *m* 11 July 1864 Ellen Elmira (*d* 31 May 1911), 3rd dau of John Warden, memb Cncl Bombay, and *d* 31 March 1912, leaving:

   1e Diana Furneaux; *b* 9 Sept 1865; *d* unm 26 March 1950

   2e Ethel Maud; *b* 18 July 1868; *m* 11 July 1891 George Bridgeford Proctor, MRCS, LRCP, and *d* 17 Dec 1934, leaving issue

1d Rosalie Jane; *m* 1st 22 Sept 1859 Henry Lee Pennell (*d* 1 May 1860); *m* 2nd 5 Nov 1861 Lt-Col Thomas Elliott Hughes, Bengal Artillery, and *d* July 1872

2c Robert Thorp; *b* 25 May 1810; *dsp*

3c Denzil; *b* 21 Jan 1812; *d* unm 25 Dec 1855

4c Pitcairn; Maj RM; *b* 29 May 1813; *m* 16 Aug 1843 Adelaide (*d* 27 Dec 1895), only dau of Capt Saltren Willett, and *d* 6 Feb 1894, leaving, with three daus (*d* unm):

1d Arthur Foot; *b* 2 Oct 1846; *d* 10 Sept 1919

2d William Cleveland; *b* 17 Aug 1848; *m* July 1881 Mary Louisa (*d* 18 May 1933), dau of Rev Thomas Burningham, Rector Charlwood, Surrey, and *d* 29 May 1890, leaving, with another s (*d* an infant):

   1e Guy Cleveland; T/Capt RE; *b* 9 Jan 1884; *m* 27 April 1916 Angela Mary (*d* 7 March 1974), only dau of Robert Pearce, of Ripley Court, Surrey, and *d* 30 Nov 1952, leaving:

      1f +Guildford Arthur Richard [Guildford Onslow Esq, 7 New Rd, Croxley Green, Rickmansworth, Herts]; *b* 28 May 1921; *educ* Cambridge (BA); *m* 27 June 1945 *Ilse, only dau of Julius Sahm, of Munich

      1f *Rose Saltern [Miss Rose Onslow, 9 Rose Lane, Ripley, Woking, Surrey]; *b* 9 Nov 1918

      2f Juliana Mary; *b* 3 Dec 1922; *educ* London U (BA); *m* 19 April 1952 *Andrew Spalding Mackintosh, er s of Rev Robert Smith Mackintosh, of Keld House, Fordingbridge, Hants, and had:

         1g *Robert Andrew Nicholas; *b* 3 Aug 1954

         2g *James Athole Guy; *b* 14 May 1958

         1g *Fiona Margaret; *b* 21 June 1956

         2g *Ruth Alison; *b* 4 Dec 1960

   3d George Thorp, CB; Maj-Gen RMLI, Sudan, Boer War, WW I; *b* 17 July 1858; *m* 3 Sept 1887 Ethel Paul (*d* 28 June 1934), dau of Rev David Kitcat, Rector Westonbirt, Glos, and *d* 14 June 1921, leaving:

      1e Frances Mary; *b* 12 June 1888; *d* unm 25 Jan 1960

      2e Adelaide Ethel Saltren; nun Congregation Presentation of Our Blessed Lady; *b* 17 Jan 1896

1d Edith Rose; *m* 24 May 1877 Maj-Gen Thomas Elliott Hughes, RA (*d* 1886), and *d* 16 Aug 1915, leaving issue

5c Edmund; *b* 12 March 1815; *m* 28 July 1851 Louisa Margaret, dau of C G Strettell, and *d* 26 Aug 1875, leaving:

1d Annette Campbell; *b* 11 Dec 1852; *m* 3 June 1871 Leycester Hudson Greaves

6c Arthur Foot; *b* 5 Feb 1821; *d* 1835

2b Arthur (Rev); Rector Crayford, Kent; *b* 30 Dec 1773; *m* 1st 25 Aug 1803 Marianna (*d* 9 March 1810), 2nd dau of William Campbell, and had:

1c Arthur Pooley, of Send Grove, Send, Surrey; Madras CS; *b* 24 May 1804; *m* 17 July 1832 Rosa Roberta (*d* 4 Jan 1854), dau of Alexander MacLeay, FRS, Speaker 1st Legislative Cncl Australia, and *d* 24 Dec 1889, leaving, with another s (*d* an infant) and five daus (*d* unm):

1d Arthur Alexander Walton, of NSW; Capt RN, MLC; *b* 2 Aug 1833; *m* 31 Jan 1867 Elizabeth (took name MACARTHUR 1892 and *d* 2 Aug 1911), dau of Hon James Macarthur, MLC, of Camden Park, nr Sydney, NSW, and *d* 30 Jan 1882, leaving:

   1e James William ONSLOW later MACARTHUR-ONSLOW; *b* 7 Nov 1867; BA, LLB Cantab, MLC NSW, Maj-Gen Australian Mil Forces, Jubilee and Coronation Medals; *m* 1897 (Enid) Emma (*d* 13 June 1952), dau of Arthur H Macarthur, and *d* Nov 1946, leaving:

      1f James Arthur; *b* 13 Oct 1898; *educ* Armidale Sch, Armidale, NSW, and RMC; Capt 17th Australian Light Horse, Lt 16th Lancers, WW I 1917–18 and WW II, grazier; *m* 1923 Constance Faith (*d* 1962), dau of George Herbert, of Sydney, and *d* 1959, leaving:

         1g +James William MacLeay [James MacArthur-Onslow Esq, Glen Ripple, Bonell's Rd, M/S 2131 Toowoomba, Qld 4352, Australia]; *b* 1 July 1932; *educ* Knox GS Sydney; *m* 1964 *Margaret Alice, dau of Colin Basil Peter Bell, of Brisbane, and has had:

            1h James Stuart Macleay; *b* 17 March 1966; *d* unm March 1996

            1h *Julienne Elizabeth; *b* 1969

         1g *Susan Helen [Mrs Ian Hayman, 57 Epping Rd, Double Bay, NSW 2028, Australia]; *b* 7 June 1935; *m* 1962 *Brig Ian Henry Hayman (ret), Australian Staff Corps, and has:

            1h *Rosemary Susan [Ms Rosemary Hayman, 41 Lamrock Ave, Bondi, NSW 2026, Australia]; *b* 28 Nov 1963

            2h *Charlotte Elizabeth [Mrs Andrew Lennox, 57 Epping Rd, Double Bay, NSW 2028, Australia]; *b* 8 Sept 1966; *m* 1995 *Andrew Ferris Lennox, FRACS, and has:

               1i *William Thomas Onslow; *b* 13 Sept 1997

         2g *Sandra Ruth [Miss Sandra MacArthur-Onslow, Old Boree, Gundaroo, NSW 2620, Australia]; *b* 4 Dec 1936

1f Helen Maud; *b* 9 Nov 1899; *m* 26 July 1919 Maj-Gen Sir Reginald George Stanham (*d* 8 Oct 1957), KCB, The Buffs, and *d* 13 June 1967, leaving issue

2f Elizabeth Enid; *b* 28 Nov 1903; *m* 1935 *S/Ldr Fredrik Ludwig Rothe, RAAF [S/Ldr Fredrik Rothe, 15 Wyuna Rd, Point Piper, Sydney, NSW, Australia], s of Waldemar Henrik Rothe, of Sydney, and *d* 1989, having had:

   1g Anthony Waldemar Frederick; *b* 2 Nov 1938; *d* unm 24 Sept 1959

2e Arthur John ONSLOW later MACARTHUR-ONSLOW; *b* 29 April 1873; *educ* Rugby and Trin Coll Cambridge; Capt NSW Mounted Rifles Boer War 1900 (wounded); *m* 1902 Christian Leslie (*d* 8 Aug 1946), dau of R L Bell, of Mount Mercer, Victoria, and *d* 20 April 1953, leaving:

   1f Richard Walton; *b* 26 Sept 1904; Lt-Col Australian Light Horse WW II; *m* 1 June 1928 Lois Ruth (*d* 1976), dau of Herbert Bowring Greene, of Sydney, and *d* 1981, leaving:

      1g +Richard Bowring [Richard MacArthur-Onslow Esq, Cannabri, Walcha 2354, NSW, Australia]; *b* 16 July 1934; *educ* Geelong GS; *m* 18 Feb 1960 *Christina Helen Huntly Gordon, er dau of Ronald Arthur McWilliam, of Vaucluse, NSW, and has:

         1h +Richard Matthew; *b* 1 May 1962

         2h +Rohan James; *b* 22 Dec 1964

         3h +Lachlan Robert Hugh; *b* 1972

      2g +John Walton; *b* 16 Feb 1943

      3g +William Robert [William MacArthur-Onslow Esq, 140 Stock Rd, Gunnedah, NSW, Australia]; *b* 3 June 1945; *m* 1977 *Sarah, dau of L B Bettington, of Rylstone, NSW, and has:

         1h *Felicity Georgina; *b* 1979

         2h *Jane Belinda; *b* 1982

2f Robert Carstairs; *b* 13 Jan 1908; Australian Mil Forces WW II; *d* unm 16 Aug 1968

1f Robina Elizabeth; *b* 11 May 1910; *m* 15 June 1931 Arthur Roberts,and had issue

2f Rosalind Sibella; *b* 12 Aug 1917; *m* 10 May 1944 John Carter (*d* 1987), s of James Carter, of Kikiamah, and *d* 1997, leaving:

   1g *Charles John; *b* 15 Jan 1950; *m* 1974 *Jane Evelyn, dau of Dr Ian Barrie, of Kempsey, and has:

      1h *Charles Ian Onslow; *b* 1977

      2h *Edward Jack Onslow; *b* 1978

      3h *Thomas James Onslow; *b* 1983

      1h *Phoebe Elizabeth Onslow; *b* 1981

   1g *Prudence Mary Lesley [Mrs Hugh O'Neil, Kikiamah, Young, NSW, Australia]; *b* 13 Feb 1945; *m* 1970 *Hugh Geoffrey O'Neil and has:

      1h *Sophie Christobel Robina; *b* 1973

      2h *Alice Rosanna; *b* 1977

3e George MacLeay ONSLOW later MACARTHUR-ONSLOW, CMG, DSO; *b* 2 May 1875; *educ* Rugby; Brig-Gen AIF WW I, cmdg 1st Cav Div 1927, Order Nile 3rd Cl; *m* 16 Oct 1907 Violet Marguerite (*d* 1981), dau of W F Gordon, of NSW, and *d* 12 Sept 1931, leaving:

   1f *Faith MacLeay [Mrs Ivan Phillips, Cranmer Cottage, Dorchester-on-Thames, Oxon OX10 7HP]; *b* 1910; *m* 11 Jan 1941 Ivan Lloyd Phillips, CBE (*d* 1984), Malayan CS, er s of Rev A Lloyd Phillips, and has:

      1g *Hugh Gerard Lloyd [Hugh Phillips Esq, 18 Stephen St, Paddington, NSW 2021, Australia]; *b* 31 March 1946; *educ* Millfield; *m* 7 Oct 1972 Rosalind (*d* 1995), dau of H B Mackenzie-Wood, of NSW, and has:

         1h *Hugh Edward Paul; *b* 1976

         2h *Julian Thomas; *b* 1979

         1h *Clare Elizabeth; *b* 1974

4e Arthur William ONSLOW later MACARTHUR-ONSLOW; *b* 27 May 1877; Capt 16th Lancers; *m* 20 June 1911 Cristabel Emily Sarah (*m* 2nd 24 June 1916 Capt Hugh Evelyn Allen (*d* 3 Feb 1933), JP, DL, Welsh Gds, and *d* 11 Feb 1943), dau of Col Rowland John Beech, of Brandon Hall, Warwicks, and was *ka* Ypres 5 Nov 1914

5e Francis Arthur ONSLOW later MACARTHUR-ONSLOW; *b* 7 June 1879; *m* 1903 Sylvia Raymond (*d* 1950), dau of Andrew Chisholm, of Goulburn, NSW, and *d* 3 March 1938, leaving:

   1f Denzil (Sir), CBE (1951), DSO (1941), ED (1942); *b* 1904; GOC 2 Div Australian Mil Forces WW II 1939–43 (despatches three times), Maj-Gen 1954, ktd 1964; *m* 1st 5 July 1927 (*divorce* 1950) Elinor Margaret, yr dau of Gordon Caldwell, of S Kensington, and had:

      1g +(Denzil) Ion [Ion MacArthur-Onslow Esq, 2a Holt St, Double Bay, Sydney, NSW, Australia]; *b* 25 Aug 1928; *educ* Rugby; Lt (ret) RNSW Lancers; *m* 2 Feb 1957 *Jenifer Marie, er dau of James Crooks, CVO, FRCS, of Harley St, London, and has:

         1h +Rupert Gordon; *b* 10 Oct 1962; *m* 1989 *Lucienne Mary, yr dau of Neville George Green and has:

            1i +Benjamin George; *b* 7 April 1995

            1i *Lucy Marie; *b* 11 March 1997

         1h *Sophie Rose; *b* 24 Nov 1957; *m* 1st 1987 Julian Henry Nettlefold, yr s of Edward Michael Nettlefold, of Milton Lilbourne, Wilts, and has:

            1i *Harry Michael Frederick; *b* 1989

         1h (cont.) Mrs Nettlefold *m* 2nd 1993 *Peter D Stork and by him has:

            1i *James Kenneth Macarthur; *b* 1993

2h *Verena Marie; b 2 Sept 1960; m 1995 *James Ashley Woodford Craven, s of Cdr James Henry Woodford Craven, DSC, RN (ret), of Bundannoon, NSW, and has:

    1i *Edward James Macarthur; b 17 July 1995

2g +Neil Gordon, ED [Lt-Col Neil MacArthur-Onslow ED, 27 Kemmis St, Randwick, NSW 2031, Australia]; b 21 March 1930; Lt-Col cmdg 1st/15th Armd Regt RNSW; m 1964 *Regina de Tessier, dau of Reginald de Tessier Prevost, of Bellevue Hill, NSW, and has:

    1h +Duncan Reginald; b 1966

    1h *Airlie; b 1969; m 1993 *Peter Albert Hawley, of Vaucluse, Sydney, and has:

        1i *Charles Duncan; b 7 Jan 1997

        1i *Phoebe Regina; b 28 Sept 1994

3g +Euan [Euan MacArthur-Onslow Esq, East Tinwald, Lochmaben, Dumfriesshire]; b 26 Sept 1934

    1g *Diana Florence [Mrs Diana Kewley, East Tinwald, Lochmaben, Dumfriesshire]; b 18 Nov 1931; m 29 Aug 1952 (divorce 1968) Geoffrey Brian Kewley, yr s of R W Kewley, of Johannesburg, and has:

        1h *Robin Geoffrey; b 29 Sept 1953

        2h *Martin William; b 21 Aug 1959

1f (cont.) Sir Denzil Onslow m 2nd 25 Sept 1950 *Dorothy Wolseley, MB, BS [Lady MacArthur-Onslow, Mount Gilead, Campbelltown, NSW, Australia], only child of William Wolseley Scott, of Bellevue Hill, NSW, and d 1984, having by her had:

    4g +Lee; b 11 May 1952; Capt Sydney URRO

    2g *Katrina [Lady Hobhouse, The Manor, Monkton Farleigh, Bradford-on-Avon, Wilts]; b 8 Nov 1953; m 1993 *Sir Charles John Spinney Hobhouse, 7th Bt (qv)

2f Edward, DSO (1943), ED (1945); b 1909; Lt-Col Res of Offrs Australian Light Horse WW II (despatches); m 1932 Winifred Hall (d 1987), dau of William Hall Owen, of Wollongong, NSW, and d 1980, having had:

    1g *Annette Rosemary [Miss Annette Macarthur-Onslow, PO Box 2, Camden, NSW 2570, Australia]; b 21 March 1933

    2g *Pamela Jane [Mrs Arthur Harrison, Box 200 PO, Camden, NSW 2570, Australia]; b 5 Jan 1936; m 1st 24 Oct 1958 (divorce 1968) Paterson James Saunders and has:

        1h *Kirkland Robert Macarthur; b 28 Jan 1961

        2h *Christopher Philip; b 25 Dec 1962

    2g (cont.) Mrs Pamela Saunders m 2nd 1971 *Arthur Leslie Harrison, of S Shields, Co Durham

    3g *Phoebe [Mrs Phoebe Atkinson, Macquarie Grove, PO Box 2, Camden NSW 2570, Australia]; b 29 Aug 1939; m 2 March 1963 (divorce 1981) Hugh Geddes Atkinson, s of Clarence Atkinson, of Seaforth, NSW, and has:

        1h *Jason Hugh; b 30 Jan 1959

        1h *Rachel Ann; b 26 Aug 1963

3f Andrew William; b 1917; S/Ldr RAAF WW II; das Jan 1943

1f Margaret Elizabeth; b 1905; m 1st 17 May 1930 (divorce 1955) Lt-Col Reginald George Michael King, Roy Deccan Horse; m 2nd 10 June 1960 John Sidney Davenport and by her 1st husb had:

    1g *Peter Michael; b 29 July 1934; m 1960 *Diana, dau of Alister Alexander, of Toogooloowah, Qld, and has:

        1h *Alister Andrew; b 1962

        1h *Georgina Susan; b 1964

    1g *Susan Patricia [Mrs Susan Russell, Wayside, Shake Valley, Victoria 3351, Australia]; b 11 June 1931; m 24 Oct 1953 (divorce 1971) James Russell and has issue

1e Rosa Sibella, CBE (1930); d unm 14 July 1943

2e Emily Susan; d unm

2d Guildford MacLeay; Lt 83rd Regt; b 3 June 1836; d unm June 1878

3d Alexander Campbell (Sir); b 17 July 1842, BA Cantab; Attorney-Gen Br Honduras 1878–80 and W Australia 1880–83 (Ch Justice 1883–1901); m 4 Feb 1878 Madeleine Emma (d 5 Oct 1926), dau of Rev Robert Loftus Tottenham (see ELY, M), and d 20 Oct 1908, leaving:

    1e Rosa Sandra Dorothea; m 25 Oct 1905 Sir Jocelyn Bray (d 12 Feb 1964), DL, 3rd s of Sir Reginald More Bray, of Shere, High Court Judge, and d 26 Aug 1966, leaving issue

    2e Lucy Elizabeth Madeleine; b 19 July 1880; m 12 May 1903 Gerard Hamilton Smith (d 16 Oct 1962), est s of Sir Gerard Smith, KCMG, and d 6 Nov 1925, leaving issue

4d Francis Montgomery; b 9 Nov 1843; Lt-Col Madras Cav; m 1 June 1881 Mary Charlotte (d 17 Sept 1938), widow of Brig-Gen Frederick W Jebb and dau of Rev John Girardot, and d 30 Jan 1932

2c William Campbell; b 17 Feb 1806; Lt-Col Madras Army; m 22 Sept 1836 Anne Moriarty (d 6 Jan 1892), est dau of V-Adml P J Douglas, and d 1 Nov 1880, leaving, with a dau (d unm):

    1d Douglas Arthur, JP Carmarths; b 10 Nov 1835; CE; m 10 Nov 1863 Caroline Isabella (d 20 Feb 1929), 2nd dau of Rev Robert Loftus Tottenham (see ELY, M), and d 17 Jan 1921, leaving:

        1e Arthur Loftus, JP Montgomeryshire; High Sheriff 1936–37, T/Lt 1st Bn Montgomeryshire Vol Regt, WW II as Maj HG; b 16 July 1874; educ Harrow and Selwyn Coll Cambridge (BA 1895); m 3 Feb 1900 Mabel (d 24 Nov 1953), er dau of George Blundell Longstaff, JP, MD, of Putney Heath, and Mortehoe, N Devon, and d 11 Aug 1957, having had:

            1f Douglas Arthur George; b 3 Aug 1901; educ Harrow and New Coll Oxford; m Oct 1925 Margaret F Kilgour (d 1985), dau of Maj John Merrick Rayner, AMIME, of Kenya, and d 1966, leaving:

1g +Richard Douglas Loftus [Richard Onslow Esq, 8 Bridgwater Park, Marais St, PO Box 230, Somerset West 7130, S Africa]; b 11 Jan 1928; educ Michaelhouse S Africa and Natal U; KAR in emergency 1952–53, Dist Offr (Kikuyu Gd) 1954; m 1st 4 Nov 1964 (divorce 1968) Elizabeth Frances, formerly w of — Bateman and dau of J Gordon Elworthy, of Dorking, Surrey; m 2nd 16 April 1968 *Ethel Elisabeth Olga Mary von Rietberg (see BRUNNER, Bt), formerly w of Klaus von Brehm, and adopted:

    *Merith Margaret Andrea; b 1972

2g Desmond Merrick; b 14 May 1929; educ Michaelhouse and Natal U (BSc); m 1954 *Sylvia Patricia Melody Wiggins [Mrs Desmond Onslow, PO Box 45, Fourways 2055, S Africa], and d 1983, leaving:

    1h +Roger; b 1965

    1h *Debra Susan; b 1955; m 1977 *David Alan Brokenshire and has:

        1i *Rhett David; b 1982

    2h *Vanessa Mary; b 1960

1g *Patricia Margaret Daisy [Mrs Edmond Fellowes, Seend Green House, Devizes, Wilts]; b 23 May 1941; m 1st 1960 (divorce 1972) Christopher Mackenzie Kennedy; m 2nd 1972 *Edmond Francis Dorset Fellowes (see 1937 edn TWISDEN, Bt) and by her 1st husb has:

    1h *Mark Edward Lucian; b 1966

2g *Prudence Katharine Barbara [Mrs Robin Keigwin, 36 Cargate Ave, Aldershot, Hants GU11 3EW]; b 5 Sept 1946; m 3 Nov 1970 *Lt-Col Robin Keigwin and has:

    1h *Richard Skarratt; b 14 Oct 1973

    2h *Michael Douglas; b 13 May 1975

2f Ralph Denzil; b 11 May 1903; k in a train crash in Wales 26 Jan 1921

3f Guildford Denys; b 18 Aug 1904; k in the same train crash 26 Jan 1921

2e Francis Robert Douglas; b 29 March 1878; educ Exeter Coll Oxford (BA); Lt Gen List; m 29 Aug 1925 Mabel (d 17 Aug 1974), dau of William Strachan, of Edinburgh, and d 29 Aug 1938, leaving:

    1f +CRANLEY GORDON DOUGLAS ONSLOW, BARON ONSLOW OF WOKING (qv)

2f +Ian Denzil [Ian Onslow Esq, 3 Jubilee Cottages, 43 Middle Rd, Lymington, Hants SO41 9HE]; b 14 April 1929; educ Harrow and Grenoble U; late 2nd Lt 24 HAA Regt RA; m 7 Aug 1954 *Marjorie, yr dau of Albert Domville, of Stockton Heath, and has:

    1g +Christopher Denzil; b 14 March 1956; educ Harrow; m 1st 1984 (divorce 1990) Veronica Jane, yst dau of Capt John Stanley Mitcalfe, OBE, VRD, RNR; m 2nd 1993 *Paula Louise Howell, only dau of John Jenkins, MICE, of Inkberrow, Worcs, and by her has:

        1h +Edward John Denzil; b 1991

    2g +Mark Loftus Domville; b 3 Aug 1958; educ Pangbourne; m 1983 *Judith Heather, dau of Peter Smith, of E Grinstead, Sussex

    3g +Michael Piers David; b 3 March 1963; educ Harrow and Stirling U; Capt Roy Scots; m 1993 *Lesley Alison, est dau of Kenneth Jolly, of Gt Baddow, Essex

    4g +Robert Douglas; b 19 Feb 1965; educ King's Sch Bruton

    1g *Victoria Penelope Diana; b 19 Feb 1965; m 1993 Jolyon Robert Lydall Savill (d March 1993)

1e Caroline Annette Tidy; b 15 Aug 1864; m 12 March 1903 John Charles Potter, of Putney, and d 25 July 1919, leaving issue

2e Catharine Isabella Maude; b 12 Sept 1872; m 8 Aug 1901 William Robert Coleridge Beadon, of Oorgaum, S India, and d 25 Nov 1903, leaving issue

2d Harrington Campbell; Capt RN; b 11 Aug 1837; m 1st 8 Dec 1864 Helen (d 20 July 1871), est dau of W P Allardice; m 2nd 5 April 1873 Elizabeth Steer (dsp 31 Oct 1904), dau of Roger Riding, MD, and d 15 Sept 1881, having by his 1st w had, with two sons (d in infancy):

    1e Alexandrina Maria; b 27 Jan 1868

3d George Manners; Col 20th Hus; b 7 Dec 1843; m 1871 Louisa (d Nov 1930), dau of George Cooke, and d 5 Jan 1911, having had, with a s (d an infant):

    1e Ethel Georgy Udea; b 15 April 1873; d unm 1963

    2e Edith Mary; b 6 Feb 1877; d unm 30 Dec 1965

1d Udea Marianne Moriarty; m 19 Jan 1864 Astley Thompson, of Glyn Abbey, Carmarths, and d 9 Dec 1883, leaving issue

3c Richard; b 24 April 1808; m 26 Nov 1831 Harriet Sophia (d 29 Aug 1873), only dau of Vincent Eyre, and d 9 May 1897, leaving, with two sons (d young) and two daus (d unm):

    1d Richard Arthur; b 4 Oct 1832; dsp 1891

    2d William Pooley; d 28 Jan 1873

    3d Walton Vincent; b 6 Aug 1843; m 24 Sept 1874 Henrietta, dau of Henry L Thompson, of London, Ontario, and had:

        1e Richard; b 1875; m —

        1e Lilian

        2e Caroline

4d Albert George; b 30 May 1850; m 13 May 1873 Constance Marie (d 1927), dau of Dr Frederick Buhlmann, of Berne, and d 1927, leaving:

    1e Isabelle Maude; b 3 Feb 1874

    2e Mildred Rita; b 10 Feb 1881; m 1901 G Veditz, of Ocean Park, California, and had issue

2b (cont.) The Rev Arthur Onslow *m* 2nd 17 June 1815 Caroline (*m* 2nd 1853 T J Burton), dau of James Mangles, MP, and *d* 29 Nov 1851, having by her had:

4c Henry John ONSLOW later HUGHES-ONSLOW, of Balkissock, Ayrshire; *b* 31 March 1816; *m* 8 Jan 1861 Judith Charlotte (*d* 23 Feb 1920), dau of William Barras, of Laleham, Middx, and *d* 31 July 1870, leaving:

1d Arthur; Maj 10th Hus; *b* 21 Aug 1862; *m* 3 June 1891 Anne Kathleen (*d* 4 Sept 1952), 2nd dau of George Whitehead, of Deighton Grove, Yorks, and *das* France 17 Aug 1914, leaving:

1e Geoffrey Henry (Sir), KBE (1959), DSC, JP (Ayrshire 1924); Ld Lt 1950–71 (DL 1932–50), CC (Chm 1949–55), Cdr RN, served WWs I and II; *b* 28 Oct 1893; *educ* RNCs Osborne and Dartmouth; *m* 23 Sept 1918 Hon Eileen Mabel Lowther Crofton (*d* 1972), dau of 4th Baron Crofton (*qv*), and *d* 27 Nov 1971, having had:

1f *Auriole Kathleen; *b* 6 Dec 1919; *m* 22 Feb 1945 Lt-Col Rev Simon Charles David Fergusson (*d* 1982) and has issue (*see* FERGUSSON, Bt)

2f *Judith Eileen [Mrs John Lorimer, Kirkangus, Barr, Ayshire]; WW II in WRNS; *b* 17 Feb 1923; *m* 20 June 1945 *Lt John Thornton Lorimer, DSO, DL, RNVR, yst s of Surgn-Cdr James Lorimer, VD, RNVR, and has:

1g *Patrick James; *b* 1 Oct 1946; *educ* Wellington; *m* 1976 *Julia Caroline, dau of Alexander Patrick Pringle, DFC, of Gemilston, Kirkmichael, Ayrshire, and has:

1h *James Seth Patrick; *b* 1979

2h *William Reuben John; *b* 1980

1h *Cressida Flora Kate; *b* 1984

1g *Bridget Katherine Eileen [Miss Bridget Lorimer, 22 Birbeck Rd, London W3]; *b* 14 Aug 1948

3f Bridget; *b* 6 Oct 1924; *m* 12 Aug 1944 *Maj Edmond Annesley Forestier-Walker (*see* FORESTIER-WALKER, Bt) and *d* 22 Dec 1961, leaving issue

4f *Mary [Mrs George Wright, Wainsford House, Everton, Lymington, Hants]; *b* 7 July 1929; *m* 19 Feb 1952 *Lt Cdr George Stewart Wright, VRD, RNR, only s of J L Wright, of Kirkhill, Colmonell, Ayrshire, and has:

1g *Nicholas Peter; *b* 1960

2g *Christopher George; *b* 1964

1e Dorothy Kathleen; *m* 4 March 1919 Capt Douglas Plenderleath Lithgow, MBE, Roy Dragoons (*das* 21 March 1944), s of Samuel Lithgow, CBE, of Bayswater, and had:

1f *William Samuel Plenderleath [Lt-Col William Lithgow, South Newington Mill, Banbury, Oxon]; *b* 18 Feb 1920; *educ* Harrow; Lt-Col 10th Roy Hus (PWO); *m* 21 May 1947 *Patricia, dau of Richard Wellington, of Tasmania, and has:

1g *Richard Plenderleath; *b* 17 July 1955

1g *Jane Kathleen Plenderleath; *b* 21 April 1953

2g *Diana Ursula Bridget; *b* 16 Feb 1960

2f Anthony Onslow Lawrence, MC; *b* 21 April 1921; *educ* Harrow; Brig Black Watch (RHR), staff RMA Sandhurst; *m* 6 Oct 1949 *Bridget Mary, er dau of Sir Christopher Robert Lighton, 8th Bt (*qv*), and *d* 1988, leaving issue

2d Denzil, of Balkissock, Ayrshire; *b* 20 Dec 1863; Maj 6th Bn Dorsetshire Regt WW I (wounded, despatches); *m* 18 April 1888 Marion, CBE (1920) (*d* 23 March 1933), dau and heiress of George Oliver, of Laggan, Ayrshire, and was *ka* 10 July 1916, having had, with a dau (*d* young):

1e Oliver, of Laggan, Ayrshire, JP (1935); CC 1937, memb Roy Co Archers, Capt Irish Gds WW I (despatches), barrister Middle Temple 1926; *b* 16 March 1893; *educ* Eton and RMC Sandhurst; *m* 1 June 1916 (Helen) Ruth (*d* 1980), dau of Rev George Dodds, BD, Min Barr, Ayrshire, and *d* 26 Feb 1972, leaving:

1f Andrew George; *b* 8 March 1920; *educ* Eton and Oxford; Capt Black Watch (RHR) WW II (wounded three times), memb Roy Co Archers; *m* 24 Feb 1944 *Betty, WAAF (*m* 2nd 1994, as his 3rd w, David George Crichton, LVO; *see* ERNE, E) [Mrs David Crichton, 28c Thorney Crescent, Morgans Walk, London SW11 3TT], dau of Col Maurice George Lee, RFC, of Christchurch, NZ (*see* ROSSMORE, B), and *d* 1979, leaving:

1g +James Andrew [James Hughes-Onslow Esq, 42 Knatchbull Rd, London SE5 9QY]; *b* 27 Aug 1945; *educ* Eton; jnlst; *m* 6 Nov 1982 *Christina Louise, dau of Peter Hay, of Melbourne, Australia, and has:

1h +Andrew Peter; *b* 1985

1h *Flora Alice; *b* 1988

2h *Marina Constance; *b* 1990

3h *Harriet Christina; *b* 1993

1g *Elizabeth Mary [Mrs John Hustler, Ripsley House, Liphook, Hants GU30 7JH]; *b* 28 May 1949; *m* 1978 *John Randolph Hustler and has:

1h *Charles James; *b* 1982

2h *Frederick Randolph; *b* 1986

1h *Willa Victoria; *b* 1983

2g *Sarah Jane [Mrs Michael Williams, Werrington Park, Launceston, Cornwall PL15 8TR]; *b* 22 Feb 1954; *m* 1975 *Michael Williams and has:

1h *Thomas Edward; *b* 1976

2h *George Michael; *b* 1979

1h *Camilla Ruth; *b* 1984

2f (Timothy) Neil; *b* 10 Jan 1924; *educ* Eton; Capt Rifle Bde WW II 1944–45, memb Roy Co Archers; *m* 10 March 1950 *Susan [Mrs Neil Hughes-Onslow, 112 Swan Court, Chelsea Manor St, London SW3 5RU], er dau of Sir William Francis Stratford Dugdale, 1st Bt (*qv*), and *d* 7 Aug 1995, leaving:

1g +Archibald (Archie) Edward Neil [Archibald Onslow Esq, 82 Mercers Rd, London N19 4PR]; *b* 20 April 1954; *educ* Eton, BNC Oxford and Oxford Poly; townplanner; has by Mary Ryan, slr, dau of Stewart Ryan, of Henley-on-Thames:

1h *Daniel; *b* 1987

2h *Max; *b* 1989

3h *Euan; *b* 1993

2g +Richard Luke [Richard Hughes-Onslow Esq, 42 Agate Rd, London W6 0AH]; *b* 28 June 1958; *educ* Eton; *m* 1988 *Christine S, dau of Charles Doughty, of Denham Bridge, Devon, and has:

1h +George Oliver; *b* 29 March 1995

1h *Iona Margaret; *b* 1992

1g *Henrietta [Mrs David Cole, 17 Heslop Rd, London SW12]; *b* 5 Aug 1951; *m* 1980 *David W A Cole, s of Sir David Cole, KCMG, MC, and has:

1h *Timothy David; *b* 1985

1h *Lucy; *b* 1983

3f Fergus Erskine; *b* 21 Aug 1929; *educ* Eton and RMA Sandhurst; Capt Rifle Bde, md M&G Assur, memb Roy Co Archers; *m* 11 June 1955 *Rose ('Minnie') Ariel [Mrs Fergus Hughes-Onslow, Lower Norsebury, Stoke Charity, Hants SO21 3PR], 2nd dau of Anthony Ewart Ledger Hill, OBE, DL, of Hockley House, Twyford, Hants, and *d* 23 Nov 1994, leaving:

1g +Anthony Charles [Anthony Hughes-Onslow Esq, Madjeston Farmhouse, nr Gillingham, Dorset SP8 5JH]; *b* 16 July 1957; *m* 1991 *Laura A, dau of L W Newton and Mrs M A J Clark, of Bayswater, and has:

1h +Harry Arthur; *b* 6 Dec 1992

2h +Fergus Ambrose; *b* 15 Sept 1996

1h *Serena Alice; *b* 1 Jan 1995

1g *Olivia [Mrs Michael Winterton, West Coombe Farm, Huish Champflower, Taunton TA4 2HG]; *b* 5 Feb 1960; *m* 1985 *Michael J W Winterton, s of Cdr David Winterton, RN, of Vale House, Halstock, Somerset, and has:

1h *Xan John; *b* 21 Jan 1993

1h *Hermione Rose; *b* 16 Aug 1987

2h *Lucy; *b* 6 Oct 1989

2g *Belinda Marion [Mrs Paolo Scaburri, Hope Cottage, Over Wallop, Hants SO20 8JJ]; *b* 20 July 1962; *m* 1996 *Paolo Scaburri and has:

1h *Elsa Rosa; *b* 5 Jan 1996

1f Virginia Ruth Primrose; *b* 19 April 1917; *m* 1st 4 April 1942 (*divorce* 1953) Maj Robert Boothby How (*d* 1990), Black Watch, yst s of Capt William Fitzherbert How, JP, Roy Irish Rifles, of Balnacarran House, St Andrews; *m* 2nd 21 Oct 1969 Maurice Oliver Pease (*d* 1975) and *d* 7 May 1997, leaving by her 1st husb:

1g *Denzil Robert Onslow [Denzil How Esq, 23 Ladbroke Sq, London W11 3NB]; *b* 3 Aug 1944; *educ* Eton and Trin Coll Cambridge (BA 1966); *m* 1st 25 May 1968 (*divorce* 1985) Sarah Elizabeth, only dau of John Ernest Harley Collins, MBE, DSC (*see* BICESTER, B); *m* 2nd 1989, as her 2nd husb, *Hon Catharine Gina Amita, dau of Baron Glenkinglas (*see* NOBLE, Bt of Ardkinglas), and by his 1st w has:

1h *Nicola Jane Audrey; *b* 1970

2h *Antonia Clare; *b* 1975

3h *Francesca Ruth; *b* 1978

4h *Georgina Louise; *b* 1981

1g *Primrose Jean Onslow [Mrs Primrose Muir, 47 Queensdale Rd, London W11 4SD]; *b* 31 May 1947; *m* 3 May 1969 (*divorce* 1993) Andrew Hugh John Muir and has issue (*see* MUIR, Bt)

2g *(Carolyn) Jane Onslow [Ms Jane How, 9 Wiseton Rd, London SW17 7EE]; *b* 21 Dec 1950; actress; *m* 1st 1977 (*divorce* 1992) Mark Burns; *m* 2nd 1996 *Mark Richard Durden-Smith and by her 1st husb has:

1h *Jack Louis; *b* 1981

2e Reginald, of Balkissock, Ballantrae, Ayrshire; *b* 8 Aug 1895; Lt-Cdr RN (Emerg List); *m* 20 Dec 1934 (*divorce* 1946) Daphne Helen Anne (*d* 1992), only dau of Col Robert Hanbury Brudenell-Bruce, DSO (*see* AILESBURY, M), and *d* 6 Oct 1947, leaving:

1f +Denzil [Denzil Hughes-Onslow Esq, The Old Bake House, The Green, Culworth, Oxon OX17 2BB]; *b* 24 June 1939; *educ* Ampleforth; late 2nd Lt RAC; *m* Oct 1973 *Chloé, dau of Mme de Vic, of St Cloud, Paris, and has:

1g *Sophie Anne Rose; *b* 10 Oct 1974

1f Sally Anne; *b* 20 Dec 1935; *m* 24 July 1961 Clive Nigel Brewer and *d* 22 Oct 1964

3e Nigel; *b* 21 April 1902; *educ* Eton; Lt Scots Gds; *m* 1st 7 Aug 1926 (*divorce* 1929) Marjorie Helen Ruth (*d* 31 Dec 1938), formerly w of Capt William Edward Foster, RAF, and only child of Sir Ernest Frederick George Hatch, 1st and last Bt, KBE (*see* 1927 edn); *m* 2nd 21 May 1941 Barbara Birdie, widow of Randal Charlton and dau of Michael Coplans, of Canterbury, and *d* 20 Oct 1974

3d Constantine Henry; *b* 29 March 1867; R-Adml RN, Egyptian Campaign 1882, Boer War 1899–1900; *m* 1920 Evelyn Oxley and *d* 1949

4d Julius Somerset; *b* 28 Dec 1869; *d* unm 12 Sept 1909

5d Henry Douglas, CBE (1919); *b* 3 Jan 1871; Ch Taxing Master Supreme Court; *d* unm 1 April 1932

5c Charles Hamilton; *m* 9 March 1852 Mary Douglas (*d* 21 Dec 1871), yst dau of Rev G W Onslow, and *d* 11 Feb 1866, leaving:

1d Harry Hamilton; *b* 15 July 1858; *dsp* 1899

1d Minnie Hamilton; *m* 9 May 1878 Pasquale Montuori, of Naples
2d Eva Joan Wiblin; Mother Superior Convent, Little Ealing Lane, London; *d* 1 March 1918
3d Elise Anita Mary
1b Pooley; *m* 1st 23 Jan 1788 V-Adml Sir Francis Drake, 1st and last Bt (*dsp* 19 Nov 1789); *m* 2nd Arthur Onslow, Serjeant-at-law, and *d* 10 Dec 1810
2a Sir RICHARD ONSLOW, 1st Bt (*qv*)
3a Arthur (Very Rev); *b* 31 Aug 1746; DD, Dean of Worcester; *m* 4 Nov 1773 Frances, dau of Constantine Phipps, and *d* 15 Oct 1817, leaving, with a dau (*d* unm):
1b Richard Francis (Ven); *b* 16 Jan 1776; Archdeacon Worcester; *m* 7 July 1801 Harriet Mary (*d* 4 May 1860), dau and coheir of Hon Andrew Foley (*see* FOLEY, B), and *d* 23 Oct 1849, having had, with two daus (*d* unm):
1c Richard Foley, of Standens, Glos; *b* 13 Sept 1802; *m* 5 July 1826 Catherine (*d* 13 Aug 1865), dau of Latham Blacker, of Newent, and *d* 12 March 1879, leaving, with two daus (*d* unm):
1d Andrew George, of Oxenhall, Newent, JP, DL; *b* 10 Oct 1830; Capt 97th and 13th Regt; *m* 13 June 1861 Mary (*d* 25 Jan 1892), yst dau of Sir John Owen, 1st Bt (*qv*), and *d* 26 Aug 1894, having had, with another s (*d* young):
1e Andrew Richard; *b* 9 Feb 1871; *m* 14 April 1896 (*divorce* 1909) Margaret Finch (*d* 30 May 1955), dau of Gerard Finch Dawson, and *dsp* 1950
2e John Geoffrey; *b* 16 April 1873; *d* 20 July 1930
3e William; *b* 20 June 1874; *m* 29 Nov 1902 Andrewina Buchanan (*d* 1960), 6th dau of Andrew Buchanan Torrance, of Kensington, and *d* 1 July 1921, leaving:
1f Robert William; *b* 8 April 1904
4e George Arthur; *b* 29 March 1876; Maj Salop Yeo Boer War 1900–01 and WW I; *m* 1st 10 June 1902 Charlotte Riou (*d* 14 Feb 1932), yst dau of Rev Riou George Benson; *m* 2nd 15 Nov 1933 Maud Elliot (*d* 1986), yr dau of George Steel Travers Harris (*see* 1970 edn HARRIS, Bt, of Chepping Wycombe), and *d* 12 April 1956, leaving by his 1st w:
1f Richard George (Sir), KCB (1958, CB 1954), DSO and three bars (1942, 1944), DL (Salop 1962); *b* 15 April 1904; *educ* RNCs Osborne and Dartmouth; RN WW II (despatches twice), Naval Sec to 1st Ld Admlty 1952–54, Flag Offr Flotillas Home Fleet 1955–56 (Flag Offr cmdg Reserve Fleet 1957), C-in-C Plymouth 1958–60, Adml 1959, ret 1960; *m* 30 April 1932 *Kathleen Meriel [Lady Onslow, Little Ryton House, Ryton, Salop SY5 7LW], er dau of Edmund Coston Taylor, of Church Stretton, and *d* 16 Dec 1975, leaving:
1g +Richard Edmund [Cdr Richard Onslow RN, Preston Bagot House, Preston Bagot, Warwicks B95 5DR]; *b* 12 April 1933; *educ* Radley; *m* 12 April 1961 *Mary-Jean, er dau of Brig Kenneth James Garner Garner-Smith, OBE, of Aird House, by Inverness, and has:
1h +Richard James; *b* 28 Dec 1962; *educ* Eton; Capt Blues & Royals; *m* 1992 *Lucinda Caroline, dau of Patrick Alexander Campbell Fraser, of Borthwickshiels, Hawick, Roxburghs, and has:
1i +Charles Patrick; *b* 1 May 1995
2i +Alexander James; *b* 1 Feb 1997
1i *Rose Kalitza; *b* 17 Dec 1998
2h +Robert Denzil; *b* 31 May 1965; *educ* Eton and Magdalen Coll Oxford; barrister; *m* 8 April 1995 *Tamara, yr dau of Robert Trench Fox (*see* ASHTOWN, B), and has:
1i *Sacha Llewellyn; *b* 18 Feb 1997
2i *Georgia Macdonald; *b* 12 Nov 1998
2g +Denzil John [Denzil Onslow Esq, The Bank House, Richards Castle, Salop]; *b* 15 Oct 1939; *educ* Radley; *m* 16 Oct 1967 *Susan Rosamund, dau of Bertram Leach, of Stapeley, Cheshire, and has:
1h +Andrew John; *b* 16 Sept 1968
2h +James Denzil; *b* 1970
1h *Tamsin Sarah; *b* 29 Jan 1976
2f John; *b* 6 Jan 1906; Maj DCLI; *m* 28 April 1956 *Susan [Mrs John Onslow, Oaklea, Vicarage Hill, Loxwood, Sussex], dau of Roland Percival Neville Towle and Mrs Philip Gregson, and *d* 25 Oct 1985, leaving:
1g +Andrew George [Andrew Onslow Esq, Rylstone, Grove Park, London SE5 8LT]; *b* 10 Feb 1957; *m* 7 Sept 1991 *(Elizabeth) Jane, yr dau of Lt-Col James Barratt Owen, of Bengate, Cumbria, and formerly w of Francis Evans, and has:
1h +Harry James Rufus; *b* 3 Feb 1992
2h +James Andrew Quintus; *b* 7 Dec 1995
1h *Frederica Jane; *b* 27 June 1993
2g +Simon John [Simon Onslow Esq, 65 St Margarets Rd, London TW1 2LL]; *b* 30 July 1960; *m* 1993 *Clare, dau of Norman Lonsdale, of Bridlemere Court, Newmarket, Suffolk, and has:
1h +Jack; *b* 6 Jan 1994
1h *Lucy; *b* 17 Jan 1997
1g Jane Elizabeth; *b* 19 June 1958, *k* car crash 20 Nov 1975
2g *Sarah Margaret [Mrs Simon Harrison, Ironstone Cottage, Lower St, Fittleworth, W Sussex]; *b* 25 Jan 1962; *m* 1990 *Simon F Harrison and has:
1h *Rupert; *b* 1995
1h *Emily Jane Elizabeth; *b* 1992
3g *Rachel Evelyn Mary; *b* 6 Aug 1967
3f Charles Edward, MC and bar; *b* 5 April 1912; Maj KAR WW II; *m* July 1955 *Margaret Mary [Mrs Charles Onslow, c/o Mrs P B

Allen, PO Box 41190, Nairobi, Kenya], dau of Rev William Marsh Lee Evans, of Saxby Rectory, Lincs, and *d* 8 May 1969, leaving:
1g +John Edward [John Onslow Esq, Peponi House School, PO Box 23203, Nairobi, Kenya]; *b* 30 Dec 1956; *m* 1986 *Dora Helen, dau of Christopher Wyborn Armstrong, OBE, of Kwetu Farm, Gilgil, Kenya, and has:
1h +Jasper Denzil; *b* 1994
1h *Kate; *b* Aug 1997
4f Thomas Philip Riou; *b* 10 April 1916; 2nd Lt KSLI WW II; *d* of wounds as POW between 19 May and 17 Nov 1940
1f Mary; *b* 24 March 1903; *m* 14 Jan 1930 Very Rev William Cyril Mayne (*d* 20 July 1962), Dean Carlisle, s of Canon Jonathan Mayne, of Christian Malford, Wilts, and *d* 1990
2f Hope; *b* 7 Feb 1907; *m* 9 Oct 1945 *Robert David Symons and *d* 1989, leaving:
1g *Marygold Cecilia Charlote; *b* 5 Dec 1946
3f *Kathleen Theodosia [Mrs Edward Sherwood, 35 Greyfriars Court, Lewes, E Sussex BN7 2RF]; *b* 27 Oct 1914; *m* 10 Jan 1945 *Edward Godfrey Purvis Sherwood, yr s of Rev Edward Charles Sherwood, of Pampisford, Cambs, and has:
1g Edward Patrick Charles; *b* 28 Jan 1946; *m* 1975 *Margaret Anne, dau of John Van Vechten Veeder, and *d* 1991, leaving:
1h *Edward Godfrey DeWitt; *b* 1978
2h *Peter David Onslow; *b* 1980
1h *Claire Margaret Letham; *b* 1987
2g *Andrew Godfrey Purvis [Andrew Sherwood Esq, 2 Pelham Terr, Lewes, E Sussex BN7 1TY]; *b* 12 April 1950; *m* 1974 *Mary Helen, dau of Hon Francis Michael Hepburne-Scott (*see* POLWARTH, L), and has:
1h *Gideon; *b* 1976
2h *Samuel; *b* 1979
1h *Phoebe; *b* 1983
2h *Lucie; *b* 1987
3g *Thomas James Mulso [Thomas Sherwood Esq, 26 Highclere Rd, New Malden, Surrey KT3 3HJ]; *b* 27 Sept 1951; *m* 1980 *Barbara, dau of Kenneth Walter Emberson, of Copthorne, W Sussex, and has had:
1h David Mathew; *b* and *d* 1986
2h *Nathan John; *b* 1988
1h *Joanna Ruth; *b* 1984
1g *Charlotte Claire; *b* 15 July 1947; *m* 19– *Richard Miller and has:
1h *Lucas; *b* 1987
4f *Denzil Octavia [Rev Sister Denzil Onslow, St Andrew's House, 2 Tavistock Rd, London W11 1BA]; *b* 3 Sept 1919
2d Richard; *b* 18 April 1836; *m* 28 July 1865 Elizabeth Anne, dau of J S Troutbeck, and *dsp* 7 May 1872
3d William Arthur; *b* 15 Dec 1837; *m* 19 Aug 1880 Mary Elizabeth (*d* 30 June 1931), 2nd dau of Rev Theodore Cartwright, of Preston Bagot, and *d* 28 Oct 1903, leaving:
1e Arthur Denzil, MC; *b* 14 Jan 1887; 2nd Lt 4th Bn Roy Warwicks Regt; *ka* 13 Aug 1916
1e Catherine Mary; *b* 15 June 1881; *m* 19 Sept 1905 Frank William Peveril Ryland (*d* 17 March 1944), of Preston Bagot House, Preston Bagot, Warwicks, and *d* 15 Oct 1964
4d George; *b* 30 April 1839; *d* 6 March 1880
1d Anne Theodosia; *m* 2 Oct 1866 Maj William C Hill, of The Cottage, Malvern Wells, and *d* 11 Nov 1907
2d Caroline; *m* 20 Oct 1868 Rev Robert Burroughes (*d* 1890), Rector Pencombe, and *d* 26 April 1918
2c Arthur Andrew (Rev); *b* 27 April 1815; Vicar Newent; *m* May 1843 Harriet Louisa (*d* 9 Jan 1907), 2nd dau of Simon Marshall, and *d* 20 Dec 1864, having had, with two other sons (*d* young or unm):
1d Richard Francis; *b* 6 Aug 1847
2d William Dyson; *b* 6 July 1849; *d* unm 10 April 1903
3d Augustus Paul Lumsden; *b* 25 Aug 1853; *m* 9 Dec 1886 Alice Maud (*d* 1951), dau of William Francis Stevenight, and had, with another s (*d* an infant):
1e Augustus Charles Albert Foley; *b* 14 Feb 1888; *m* 1914 Winifred May (*d* 1975), dau of W R Williams, of Thornton Heath, Surrey, and *d* 1965, leaving:
1f +Winston Hillier Gopal [Winston Onslow Esq, 108 Culvert Rd, London SW11]; *b* 1915; *m* 1939 Kathleen Edis (*d* 1975) and has:
1g *Veronica Vivien [Mrs Alan Wood, 33 Greenways Crescent, Shoreham by Sea, W Sussex BN43 6HR]; *b* 1943; *m* 1969 *Alan Roy Wood, surveyor, and adopted:
*Lucille Ann; *b* 1973
2f Lewis Lumsden William; *b* 1924; jnlst; *d* 1991
1f *Patricia Doreen [Mrs Ronald Coombs, 1 Airey Houses, Scocles Rd, Minster, Isle of Sheppey, Kent]; *b* 1926; *m* 1956 Ronald George Coombs (*d* 1990) and has:
1g *Anne Patricia [Mrs Stephen Smart, 32 Minster Rd, Halfway, Sheerness, Kent]; *b* 1957; *m* 1985 *Stephen David Smart and has:
1h *Sam Kenneth; *b* 1988
2h *Ben; *b* 1990
2e Frederick Hewitt Lumsden; *b* 1 June 1897; *m* 5 April 1939 *Olive Eveline, dau of Ernest Spicer, and *d* 12 March 1969, leaving:
1f +Frederick Winston Lumsden [Frederick Onslow Esq, Red Chimneys, Chalk Lane, E Horsley, Surrey KT24 6TJ]; *b* 29 Jan

1940; *m* 21 March 1964 *Elizabeth Maude, dau of Frank Berenger Benger, of Leatherhead, and has:

1g +Robert Frederick [Robert Onslow Esq, 8 Garden Close, Shamley Green, Surrey]; *b* 25 Feb 1970; *m* 19 April 1997 *Amy, dau of Alan Pryor, of Betchworth, Surrey

1g *Gillian Elizabeth; *b* 12 April 1966

2g *Vivien Gail; *b* 30 June 1967

1e Maude Sarah Louisa; *b* 18 Sept 1894; *m* 1921 Ernest Augustus Tellam and had issue

1d Cecilia Louisa; *m* 12 Feb 1874 Thomas Gervase Finch Dyson and *d* his widow 16 Oct 1893

3c Thomas Phipps; *b* 1818; Capt 67th Foot; *d* 1850

1c Harriott Frances; *m* 12 Dec 1833 Rev Thomas Crommeline (*d* 31 July 1842)

2c Constantina; *m* 16 May 1826 John Freeman (*d* 4 Oct 1870), of Gaines, Herefs, and *d* 8 April 1879

3c Anne Cecilia; *m* 13 July 1836 Rev T J Cartwright and *d* 4 May 1856

2b Arthur Cyril (Rev); *b* 1788; Rector Newington, Surrey; *m* Aug 1812 Elizabeth (*d* 19 Oct 1865), dau of Sir Edward Winnington, 2nd Bt (*qv*), and *d* 6 Feb 1869, having had, with a dau (*d* unm):

1c Cyril Winnington; *b* 17 Dec 1815; *d* 24 July 1866

2c Constantine Phipps; *b* 30 Jan 1817; *d* unm 16 Nov 1887

3c Henry; *b* 5 May 1818; *dsp* 1897

4c Thomas George (Rev); *b* 13 Oct 1826; *m* 1st 22 Sept 1853 Maria Augusta (*d* 27 Feb 1857), 2nd dau of John Hawkins, of Byelands, Herts, and had:

1d Edith Fanny; *m* 31 Jan 1882 Charles Constable Curtis (*d* 13 May 1936), JP, DL, of Langford Hall, Newark, and Swinderby, Lincs, and *d* 19 May 1944, leaving issue

4c (cont.) The Rev Thomas Onslow *m* 2nd 18 Nov 1862 Mary Frances (*d* 25 May 1905), 2nd dau of William Fitzwilliam Burton, of Burton Hall, Co Carlow, and *d* 21 Aug 1911, having by her had:

1d William Henry (Sir), KCMG, CB, JP, DL Dorset; *b* 28 Sept 1863; Boer War 1900 (medal with four clasps), WW I (despatches), Hon Col Dorset Heavy Bde RA 1928, chm TAA , Maj-Gen RA, Order White Eagle Serbia 3rd Cl with swords, Grand Cdr Order Redeemer Greece, Cdr Legn Hon; *m* 15 Dec 1899 Margaret Beatrice (*d* 14 Aug 1954), only dau of Thomas Bates, of Aydon, and *d* 19 June 1929, leaving:

1e Margaret Isobel; *m* 14 July 1923 Cdr Reginald Foster Pitt Maton, OBE, RN (*d* 21 Feb 1965)

3b Phipps Vansittart; *b* 2 Sept 1790; *m* 1st 21 July 1820 Harriet (*d* 5 March 1827), dau of Sir Edward Winnington, 2nd Bt (*qv*), and had:

1c Phipps (Rev); *b* 9 March 1823; BA Oxon; Rector Upper Sapey, Herefs; *m* 23 June 1868 Jane Sophia (*d* 26 Sept 1900), 2nd dau of C W Martin, and *d* 20 July 1903, leaving, with a dau (*d* unm):

1d Henry Phipps; *b* 2 April 1869; *educ* Keble Coll Oxford (BA 1890); *m* 7 Sept 1898 Mabel (*d* 1959), yst dau of T Playford, and *d* 26 Feb 1945, having had, with another s (*d* young):

1e George Francis; *b* 16 Jan 1901; *educ* St Peter's Collegiate Sch Adelaide; *m* 25 April 1929 Una Florence, dau of Charles Rockcliff, of Tasmania

2e Thomas Phipps; *b* 15 April 1907; *m* 12 Jan 1945 Mrs Pauline Calvert (*d* 1970), dau of Kenneth L Shoobridge, of Tasmania, and *d* 1990, leaving:

1f +William Phipps; *b* 14 Oct 1947; *m* 1974 *Victoria, dau of Paul L Abbott, of Calder, Tasmania, and has:

1g *Fiona Louise; *b* 1975

2g *Lucie Jane; *b* 1976

3g *Annabel Rose; *b* 1979

1f *Jane Elizabeth; *b* 11 Dec 1946; *m* 1969 *Christopher Goodwin Morley and has:

1g *Hamish Charles Thomas; *b* 1977

1g *Emma Patricia; *b* 1970

2g *Georgina Joan; *b* 1972

1e Helen May Jane; *b* 19 Oct 1902

2e *Margaret Louise [Mrs Charles Rollins, 12 Burnett St, New Norfolk, Tasmania 7140, Australia]; *b* 11 April 1921; *m* 8 March 1946 Charles Edward Rollins (*d* 1990) and has:

1f *Philip Charles [Philip Rollins Esq, Bombon, nr Richmond, Tasmania, Australia]; *b* 1 Nov 1947; *m* 2 Jan 1970 *Suzanne Mary Martin, of Montrose, Tasmania, and has:

1g *Richard; *b* 1973

1g *Elizabeth; *b* 1976

1f *Susan Louise [Mrs Stephen Jarick, 13 Mt Stuart Rd, Mt Stuart, Tasmania 7000, Australia]; *b* 10 Aug 1951; *m* 1st 8 Jan 1972 (*divorce* 1984) Rodney Sinclair Smith; *m* 2nd 1986 *Stephen Arthur Jarick and by him has:

1g *Michael Stephen; *b* 1985

1g *Sophie May; *b* 1987

3b (cont.) Phipps Onslow *m* 2nd 20 Feb 1834 Lucy (*d* 7 July 1839), yst dau of Walter Michael Moseley, of Winterdine, and *d* 10 May 1867, having by her had, with two daus (*d* unm):

2c Francis Phipps; *b* 18 March 1835; barrister; *m* 28 April 1868 Emily Gertrude (*d* 11 Aug 1912), only surv child of W Digby Seymour, and *d* 27 March 1919, having had, with a s (*d* an infant):

1d Lucy Maud; *d* unm 1945

2d Harriet Katharine, OBE (1919); *d* unm 28 Dec 1926

1c Lucy; *m* 8 Sept 1868 Graves Archer (*d* 1872) and *d* 14 Dec 1913, leaving issue

1b Jane; *m* July 1810 Rev Edward Winnington Ingram (*see* WINNINGTON, Bt) and *d* 10 Dec 1850

1a Elizabeth; *m* Rev Hon George Hamilton (*see* ABERCORN, D) and *d* Jan 1802, leaving issue

The 3rd BARON's cousin,

GEORGE ONSLOW, **3rd Baron Onslow** etc, as which *s* 2nd cousin 1776, and **1st Earl of Onslow**, of Onslow, Co Salop, so *cr* 19 June 1801, as also VISCOUNT CRANLEY OF CRANLEY, Co Surrey (both UK), and earlier 20 May 1776 BARON CRANLEY OF IMBERCOURT, Co Surrey (GB), PC (1767); *b* 13 Sept 1731; *educ* Westminster and Peterhouse Cambridge; Out Ranger Windsor Gt Park 1754–63, MP (Whig) Rye 1754–61 and Surrey 1761–74, a Commr Treasury 1765–77, High Steward Kingston-on-Thames 1768–1814 and Guildford 1776–1814, DCL Oxon, Ld Lt Surrey 1776–1814, Comptroller Household 1777–79, Treasurer Household 1779–80, a Ld Bedchamber 1780–1814, Col Army 1794 and Surrey Fencible Cav 1794–1800; *m* 26 June 1753 Henrietta (*d* May 1802), dau of Sir John Shelley, 4th Bt, of Michelgrove (*qv*), and *d* 17 May 1814, leaving:

1 THOMAS, **2nd Earl**

2 Edward; *b* 9 April 1758; *m* 7 March 1783 Marie Rosalie (*d* 20 Jan 1842), dau of Chevalier Jean de Bourdeille, Seigneur de Constance, and *d* 18 Oct 1829, leaving, with a dau (*d* an infant):

(1) George Louis André; *b* 27 July 1784; Membre de l'Institut de France et du Conservatoire Français, Chev Legn Hon; *m* 23 June 1808 Delphine, dau and heiress of Marquis de Fontanges, and *d* 3 Oct 1852, leaving:

1a Arthur; *b* 3 June 1809; *m* Charlotte, dau of M Costas, and *dsp* 20 Oct 1882

1a Georgine; *b* 16 June 1810; *m* Count d'Hauterive and *d* 1 May 1854, leaving issue

2a Henriette; *b* 13 Aug 1814; *m* Joseph, Marquis de Pierre, and *d* 18 March 1883, leaving issue

(2) Maurice François; *b* 15 Oct 1786; Offr French Army; *m* — Dutreuil and *d* 15 Oct 1834, leaving:

1a George; *b* 30 May 1818; *d* unm 2 July 1898

2a Edward; *b* 29 Oct 1820

1a Gabrielle; *b* 12 Feb 1823; *m* Count d'Auriac and had issue

2a Delphine; *b* 12 Aug 1826; *m* Vicomte de Villepion and had issue

(3) Arthur; *b* 9 May 1788; Capt Garde du Corps du Roi, French Army, Chev Legn Hon; *m* 26 March 1819 Emillia Charlotte (*d* 1 Nov 1843), dau of R Wetherell, of Brighthelmstowe, Essex, and *d* 25 April 1876, leaving:

1a Henry Cranley; *b* 16 Jan 1820; Dep Assist Commissary-Gen; *d* unm 1850

2a Frederick Horace; *b* 3 May 1825; *m* 5 Nov 1867 Alexandrina Ogilvie (*d* 27 Sept 1926), dau of Capt James Vetch, RE, and *d* 27 July 1919, having had:

1b George Shelley; *b* 23 Oct 1868; *d* unm 1 May 1891

2b Arthur; *b* 7 June 1871; *m* 25 Sept 1893 Emily (*d* 29 Oct 1952), dau of W A Howe, ICS, and *d* 9 Dec 1937, having had:

1c George Shelley; *b* 20 April 1897; *d* 11 July 1958

2c Charles Oldfield; *b* 11 Dec 1902; *d* 9 Sept 1922

1c Mary Alexandrina; *b* 16 Sept 1894; *m* 20 July 1935 William Harold Grice (*d* 1959)

2c Valentine Charlotte; *b* 14 Feb 1900; fruit farmer

(4) Auguste Amabel Gabriel; *b* 14 July 1790; *m* 1820 Clotilde, dau of Gen Desaix, and *d* 18 Oct 1859, leaving:

1a Clotilde; *b* 24 July 1829; *m* 1848 Count de Magnac and *d* 15 Feb 1891, leaving issue

The 1st EARL's er s,

THOMAS ONSLOW, **2nd Earl of Onslow**; *b* 15 March 1754; *educ* Westminster and Peterhouse Cambridge (MA 1773); MP (Tory) Rye 1775–84 and Guildford 1784–1806, Out Ranger Windsor Gt Park 1793, Lt-Col Surrey Yeo 1794, Col Army 1794 and Surrey Militia 1797–1812, V-Lt Surrey, High Steward Guildford and Kingston; *m* 1st 20 Dec 1776 Arabella (*d* 11 April 1782), 3rd dau and coheir of Eaton Mainwaring Ellerker, of Risby Park, Yorks; *m* 2nd 13 Feb 1783 Charlotte (*d* 25 April 1819), widow of Thomas Duncombe (*see* FEVERSHAM, B) and dau of William Hale, of King's Walden, Herts, and *d* 22 Feb 1827, leaving by his 1st w, with a dau (*d* unm):

1 ARTHUR GEORGE ONSLOW, **3rd Earl of Onslow**, DL Surrey; *b* 25 Oct 1777; *educ* Harrow and Ch Ch Oxford; *m* 21 July 1818 Mary (*d* 1 March 1830), est dau of George Fludyer, of Ayston, Rutland, by Lady Mary Fane, dau of 9th Earl of Westmorland (*qv*), and had:

(1) Arthur George, *Viscount Cranley*; *b* 16 June 1820; *educ* Ch Ch Oxford (BA); *m* 1 Aug 1850 his cousin Lady Catherine Anne Cust (*d* 18 Oct 1885 aged 62), yst dau of 1st Earl Brownlow (*see* BROWNLOW, B) by his 2nd w Caroline, 2nd dau of George Fludyer, and *dvp* 2 Aug 1856, leaving:

1a Mary Katherine; *b* 14 Aug 1851; *d* unm 23 Jan 1902

2a Katherine Elizabeth; *b* 5 Dec 1853; *d* unm 27 April 1934

3a Emily Marian; *b* Sept 1856; *d* unm 16 Sept 1943

(1) Mary Augusta; *d* unm 30 April 1891 aged 71

2 Thomas Cranley, of Stoke Park, Surrey, and Upton House, Hants; *b* 7 Oct 1778; Col 2nd Surrey Militia, Lt-Col Scots Fus Gds Peninsular War (despatches, medal); *m* 28 May 1812 Susannah Elizabeth (*d* 26 March 1852), 2nd dau and coheir of Nathaniel Hiller, of Stoke Park, Surrey, and *d* 7 July 1861, having had, with two daus (*d* unm):

(1) George Augustus Cranley; *b* 14 May 1813; *educ* Ch Ch Oxford (BA); *m* 11 July 1848 Mary Harriet Anne (*d* 7 Nov 1880), est dau of Lt-Gen William Fraser Bentinck Loftus, of Kilbride, Co Wicklow, and *dvp* 13 April 1855, leaving:

1a WILLIAM HILLIER, **4th Earl**

(2) Guildford James Hiller ONSLOW later MAINWARING-ELLERKER-ONSLOW (roy licence 19 Aug 1861 on inheriting unc's estates), of Risby Park, Yorks, DL; *b* 29 March 1814; MP Guildford, served Scots Fus Gds; *m* 28 April 1838 Rosa Anna (*d* 19 Dec 1889), dau of Gen Denzil Onslow, of Stoughton House, Hunts, and *d* 20 Aug 1882, having had a dau (*d* an infant)

(3) Arthur Edward; *b* 13 Nov 1815; Lt-Col Scots Fus Gds; *m* 30 April 1846 Margaret Anne (*d* 11 April 1892), 2nd dau of Edward Ferrers, of Baddesley Clinton, and *d* 10 July 1897, having had, with another s and dau (both *d* in infancy):

1a Charles Vere Townshend ONSLOW later MAINWARING-ELLERKER-ONSLOW (roy licence 2 March 1898); *b* 31 May 1848; *m* 31 Oct 1876 Amelia Tolson (*d* 5 April 1941), dau of Frederick Roger Carter, and *d* 26 Jan 1927, having had:

  1b Arthur Guildford; *b* 8 July 1888; *educ* Trin Coll Cambridge (BA); F/Lt RAFVR; *m* 12 Jan 1914 Helen Maie, er dau of Reuben Burgess, of Bournemouth, Hants, and *dsp* 8 Dec 1943

  1b Arabella Vere Gwendolen; *b* 21 Oct 1885; nun as Sister Mary Vere; *d* unm 11 Feb 1978

  2b Minnie Margaret Matilda; *b* 23 July 1892; *m* 31 Aug 1914 Sidney Victor Webb Perkins (*d* 25 Jan 1962) and *d* 19 March 1978, leaving:

    1c Barbara Opal Onslow; *b* 25 Oct 1915; *m* 9 Sept 1939 *George Edward Twine, LLB, and had:

      1d *George Nicholas [George Twine Esq, Gridle Ford, Manor Rd, Sherborne St John, Hants]; *b* 13 May 1941; *educ* Hurstpierpoint; *m* 24 June 1967 *Maureen Anne, only dau of Charles Giggs, of Hayling Island, Hants

      2d *Julian Edward; *b* 23 June 1942; *educ* Milton Abbey

2a Arthur Denzil; *b* 25 Jan 1856; *d* 17 Sept 1920

3a Arthur Edward; *b* 1 Sept 1862; *m* 1888 Emma Elizabeth Barnscote and *d* 8 Feb 1927, leaving:

  1b Vivian Isidore; *b* 1888; *m* 1st 3 April 1912 Lily (*d* 1918), er dau of Charles Edward Henson, of Richmond, Surrey; *m* 2nd 8 May 1919 Annie Dorothea Rose (*d* 1972), er dau of Frank Charles Davis, of Evercreech, nr Bath, and *d* 1979, having by her had:

    1c +Arthur Charles Vivian [Arthur Onslow Esq, 21 Sir John Moore Ave, Hythe, Kent CT21 5DE]; *b* 19 Dec 1920; *m* 1951 *Patricia Taylor and has had:

      1d Robert Charles Vivian; *b* 1952; *d* 1990

      2d +Anthony Ernest Edward; *b* 1955

      3d +David Peter; *b* 1959

      1d *Anne Rose; *b* 1957

    2c +Denzil Isidore Charles [Denzil Onslow Esq, 5 Christopher Way, Shepton Mallet, Somerset]; *b* 15 July 1924; *m* 1945 Iris Frances Warren (*d* 1992) and has:

      1d +John M [John Onslow Esq, Little Silvers, Upton Noble, Somerset]; *b* 1948; *m* 1972 *Susan Jane Mary Nicholls and has:

        1e +Stuart John; *b* 1977

      2d +Dennis Raymond [Dennis Onslow Esq, 5 Christopher Way, Shepton Mallet, Somerset]; *b* 1949

      3d +Andrew Martin [Andrew Onslow Esq, 33 Wyville Rd, Frome, Somerset]; *b* 1954; *m* 1981 (*divorce* 1988) Wendy Jacqueline Baker and has:

        1e +Martin Andrew; *b* 1983

        2e +Matthew John; *b* 1984

      4d +Brian S [Brian Onslow Esq, 34 Blenheim Rd, Street, Somerset]; *b* 1957; *m* 1978 *Susan Jane Parsons and has:

        1e +Neil Ian; *b* 1984

        1e *Michelle Claire; *b* 1981

      1d *Daphne Carol [Mrs Derek Jack, Knowberry, Whitstone Rd, Shepton Mallet, Somerset]; *b* 1945; *m* 1st 19- — Howell; *m* 2nd 1991 *Derek Robert Jack and by her 1st husb has:

        1e *Wayne Lee; *b* 1967

        2e *Darren Shaun; *b* 1970

      2d *Sheila Rose [Mrs Raymond Withers, Home, Weymouth Rd, Evercreech, Somerset]; *b* 1946; *m* 1970 *Raymond William Withers and has:

        1e *Paul Neil; *b* 1970

        2e *Mark Andrew; *b* 1973

        3e *Tony Clive; *b* 1980

      3d *Pamela Susan [Mrs Pamela Gregory, 1 Bolters Lane, Downside, Somerset]; *b* 1952; *m* 1969 (*divorce* 19-) Peter John Gregory and has:

        1e *Dean Marcus; *b* 1972

        1e *Mandy Lea; *b* 1969

        2e *Tina Clare Angelina; *b* 1970

      4d *Christine Ann [Mrs Glenn Davies, 34 Wickham Lane, Shepton Mallet, Somerset]; *b* 1953; *m* 1975 *Glenn Robert Davies and has:

        1e *Alan Robert; *b* 1975

        2e *Gary Martin ; *b* 1977

      5d *Linda Dawn [Mrs Linda Whittaker, 16 Westover, Nunney, Somerset]; *b* 1954; *m* 1973 (*divorce* 1984) Laurence Vernon Whittaker and has:

        1e *Steven Raymond; *b* 1974

        2e *Timothy Laurence; *b* 1977

      6d *Sandra Jane [Mrs Philip Farmer, 14 Douglas Dve, Shepton Mallet, Somerset]; *b* 1959; *m* 1977 *Philip Roy Farmer and has:

        1e *Trevor Philip; *b* 1979

        1e *Jennifer Ann; *b* 1980

      7d *Wendy Janice [Mrs Alan Coubrough, 3 Naisholt Rd, Shepton Mallet, Somerset]; *b* 1961; *m* 1987 *Alan William Coubrough and has:

        1e *Craig William; *b* 1990

    1c *Constance Vivienne; *b* 17 Aug 1934; *m* 1st 1960 Stanley W Crabb; *m* 2nd 19- *— Tombs

4a Ferrers Mainwaring; *b* 18 Oct 1863; *m* 28 April 1892 Edith, dau of Alfred Broad, of Plymouth, and *d* 21 Oct 1918

1a Constance Henrietta; *b* 15 Nov 1854; *m* 1885 James Isidore Carter, of Walsingham, Devon

(4) Thomas Frederick; *b* 15 Jan 1821; *dsp* 15 July 1883

---

3 Edward Mainwaring ONSLOW later MAINWARING-ELLERKER-ONSLOW (on inheriting family estates); *b* 2 Oct 1779; Lt-Col Scots Fus Gds Peninsular War and Egypt (medal and two clasps, Egyptian medal); *d* unm 30 July 1861

The 3rd EARL *dspms* 24 Oct 1870; his gn,

WILLIAM HILLIER ONSLOW, **4th Earl of Onslow**, GCMG (1889, KCMG 1887), PC (1903), JP, DL (Surrey); *b* 7 March 1853; *educ* Eton and Exeter Coll Oxford; High Steward Guildford 1875, a Ld-in-Waiting (C) Feb-May 1880 and 1886–87, Del Sugar Bounties Conference 1887, V-Pres Colonial Conference 1887, U-Sec Colonies 1887–88 and 1900–03, Parly Sec BOT Feb-Dec 1888, Govr NZ 1888–92, U-Sec India 1895–1900, CC Surrey, Alderman LCC 1895–99 and City Westminster 1900, Pres Bd Ag 1903–05, Chm Ctees Ho Lds and Dep Speaker 1905–11; *m* 3 Feb 1875 Hon Florence Coulston Gardner (*d* 8 Aug 1934), er dau of 3rd Baron Gardner (*see* 1970 edn) of Uttoxeter, and had:

1 RICHARD WILLIAM ALAN, **5th Earl**

2 Victor Alexander Herbert Hula; *b* 13 Nov 1890 (HM QUEEN VICTORIA stood sponsor); *m* 3 Feb 1919 Muriel (*d* 19 May 1932), Fell and Assoc Newnham Coll and lecturer plant biochemistry Cambridge, only dau of John Wheldale, and *dsp* 27 June 1922

1 Gwendolen Florence Mary, CBE (1920); MP Southend-on-Sea 1927–35; *m* 8 Oct 1903 2nd Earl of Iveagh (*qv*) and *d* 16 Feb 1966, leaving issue

2 Dorothy Evelyn Augusta, CI (1926), DCVO (1953), JP (E R and W R Yorks 1935); Hon LLD Leeds U (1939), Ldy Bedchamber to HM THE QUEEN now QUEEN ELIZABETH THE QUEEN MOTHER) 1937–41 (Extra Lady 1946), DGStJ; *m* 21 Sept 1909 1st Earl of Halifax (*qv*) and had issue

The 4th EARL *d* 23 Oct 1911; his er s,

RICHARD WILLIAM ALAN ONSLOW, **5th Earl of Onslow**, GBE (1938, OBE), PC (1926), JP, DL Surrey; *b* 23 Aug 1876; *educ* Eton and New Coll Oxford (BA 1898, MA 1909); Dip Serv: joined 1901, Attaché Madrid 1902, 3rd Sec Tangier 1903 and St Petersburg 1904, 2nd Sec Berlin 1907, Assist Priv Sec to For Sec 1909–11, Clerk FO 1910, Priv Sec to PUS 1911–13, Assist Clerk 1913–14, a Ld-in-Waiting 1919–20, a Civil Ld Admlty 1920–21, Parly Sec Min Ag 1921, Min Health 1921–23 and Bd Educn 1923–24, U-Sec War and V-Pres Army Cncl 1924–28, Paymaster-Gen 1928–29, Br Del Arms Traffic Conf Geneva 1925, Chm Ctees and Dep Speaker Ho Lds 1931–44, High Steward Guildford, CC Surrey, Col Res Offrs, Hon Lt-Col 3rd Bn Surrey Vol Regt, Hon Col Surrey AA Bn 1927, served WW I (despatches three times), Legn Hon, FSA, PZS, FRHistS, Bailiff Grand Cross OStJ; *m* 22 Feb 1906 Hon Violet Marcia Catherine Warwick Bampfylde, CBE, ARRC, GCStJ (*d* 23 Oct 1954), only dau of 3rd Baron Poltimore (*qv*), and had:

1 WILLIAM ARTHUR BAMPFYLDE, **6th Earl**

1 Mary Florence Violet Margaret; *m* 10 Jan 1933 (*divorce* 1940, resumed maiden name for self and s by deed doll 1940) Capt George Garside, Roy Irish Fus, and *d* 1 May 1970, leaving:

  (1) *Richard Arthur Michael; *b* Nov 1933; *m* 20 Sept 1961 *Barbara Mary, er dau of R H McGrath, of Blackley, Manchester

The 5th EARL *d* 9 June 1945; his only s,

WILLIAM ARTHUR BAMPFYLDE ONSLOW, **6th Earl of Onslow**, KBE (1960), MC (1941), TD, DL (1950–62); *b* 11 June 1913; *educ* Winchester and RMC Sandhurst; Lt Life Gds WW II, Col RAC(TA), Capt Yeomen Gd, Assist C Ch Whip 1951–60, memb Surrey AEC 1951–58, CStJ, CC Surrey 1949–52, LCC 1940–46, High Steward Guildford 1947; *m* 1st 4 Aug 1936 (*divorce* 1962) Hon Pamela Louisa Eleanor Dillon, JP (1951) (*d* 1992), only dau of 19th Viscount Dillon (*qv*), and had:

1 MICHAEL WILLIAM COPLESTONE DILLON, **7th and present Earl of Onslow**

1 *Teresa Lorraine [The Lady Teresa Waugh, Combe Florey House, Somerset TA4 3JD; 7 Phoenix Lodge Mansions, Brook Green, London W6 7BG]; *b* 26 Feb 1940; translator and novelist: *Painting Water* (1983), *Waterloo Waterloo* (1985), *Intolerable Burden* (1987), *Song at Twilight* (1989); *m* 1 July 1961 *Auberon Alexander Waugh (*see* CARNARVON, E) and has:

  (1) *Alexander Evelyn Michael [Alexander Waugh Esq, Stoke Bruerne Park, Towcester, Northants NN1Z 7RZ]; *b* 30 Dec 1963; opera critic; *m* 1990 *Eliza(beth) Beatrice, dau of Alexander Surtees Chancellor (*see* PAGET, Bt, of Cranmore Hall), and has:

    1a *Auberon Augustus Ichabod; *b* 21 April 1998

    1a *Mary Eulalia; *b* 1993

    2a *Sally Alexandra; *b* 1995

  (2) *Nathaniel Thomas Biafra; *b* 12 Dec 1968

  (1) *Margaret Sophia Laura [Mrs Julian Watson, 27 Chesterton Rd, London W10]; *b* 20 June 1962; *m* 1986 *Julian Watson, only s of V-Adml Sir Philip Alexander Watson, KBE, LVO, of The Hermitage, Bodicote, Banbury, Oxon, and has:

    1a *Constance Mary Alabama; *b* 24 July 1990

    2a *Beatrice Teresa Arizona; *b* 1992

  (2) *Daisy Louisa Dominica; *b* 19 Feb 1967; *m* 1995 *Peter de Sales la Terrière and has:

    1a *Panda Sarah; *b* 22 Sept 1997

The **6th Earl** *m* 2nd 30 June 1962 *Nina Edith (Jo) MBE (1953) [The Rt Hon Jo Countess of Onslow MBE, Sturdee's, Freeland, Oxon], dau of Thomas Percival Sturdee, of Basing Close, Thames Ditton, Surrey, and *d* 1971

ONSLOW, Bt

Arms: Arg. a fess gu. between six Cornish choughs ppr. **Crest:** An eagle sa., preying upon a partridge or. **Mottoes:** 1 *Festina lente* ('Make haste but without impetuosity'), 2 *Semper fidelis* ('Always faithful'). **Creation:** Bt. (GB) 30 Oct 1797.

SIR JOHN ROGER WILMOT ONSLOW, 8TH BT, of Althain, Lancashire [Sir John Onslow Bt, c/o Barclays Bank, Fowey, Cornwall PL23 1BA]; *b* 21 July 1932; *s* f 1963; *educ* Cheltenham; *m* 1st 22 Oct 1955 (*divorce* 1973) Catherine Zoia, yr dau of Henry Atherton Greenway, of The Manor, Compton Abdale, Glos, and has:

1 +RICHARD PAUL ATHERTON; *b* 16 Sept 1958

1 *Joanna Elizabeth; *b* 10 Nov 1956

Sir JOHN *m* 2nd 1976 Susan Fay (*d* 10 Feb 1998), 2nd dau of E M Hughes, of Frankston, Victoria, Australia

Lineage: Lt-Gen RICHARD ONSLOW, Govr Plymouth (*see* ONSLOW, E); had a 2nd s:

Sir Richard Onslow, 1st Bt (GB), so *cr* 30 Oct 1797 for his part as 2ic victory of Camperdown, KB; *b* 23 June 1741; V-Adml; *m* 2 June 1773 Anne (*d* 31 Jan 1837), dau of Adml Matthew Michell, of Chitterne, Wilts, and had:

1 Matthew Richard; *m* 30 Nov 1805 Sarah (*m* 2nd S Saunders; *m* 3rd Capt Sir T Carew, RN, est dau of Daniel Seton, Lt-Govr Surat, and *d* 10 Aug 1808, having had:

  (1) Amelia Charlotte; *m* 1st 20 Sept 1828 Robert John Marsham (*dsp* 10 Jan 1838), of Stratton Strawless, Norfolk; *m* 2nd 1842 William H Duff

  (2) Matthewana Sarah; *m* 28 June 1828 Bernard Granville, JP, DL, of Wellesbourne Hall, Warwicks, and *d* 3 Aug 1829, leaving issue. He *d* 6 Jan 1869

2 HENRY (Sir), **2nd Bt**

3 John James; Capt RN, Cdr HM Corvette *Daphne*; *m* 1818 Lavinia (*d* 15 Aug 1871), 2nd dau of Charles Dinning, MD, and *d* 24 Aug 1856, having had:

  (1) William Lake; *b* 1 May 1820; FRAS, Rector Sandringham, Chaplain RN, Naval Instr, Special Instr to HRH PRINCE ALFRED; *d* 30 Aug 1877

  (2) John James; Mate RN, *d* aboard HMS *St Vincent* Lisbon 6 Sept 1847 aged 19

  (3) Charles Thomas Forrest; Lt RM; *d* Hong Kong 12 Aug 1852 aged 26 while serving aboard HMS *Cleopatra*

  (4) Richard Henry; Mate RN; *d* Plymouth 1853 aged 25 while serving aboard HMS *Queen*

  (1) Anne Theresa; *m* 18 Sept 1847 Rev John William Clapcott, BA

  (2) Agnes Mary

1 Frances; *m* 23 Dec 1800, as his 2nd w, Adml Sir Hyde Parker (*see* PARKER, Bt, of Melford Hall) and *d* 1844

2 Anne; *m* 1st 12 Aug 1833, as his 2nd w, 2nd Viscount Lake of Delhi and Laswary (*dsp* 12 May 1836; *see* 1848 edn); *m* 2nd 14 Sept 1837 Lt Henry Gritton, RM, of Greenwich, and *d* 4 April 1853

3 Elizabeth; *m* Robert Lewis, RN, and *d* 21 Nov 1861. He *d* 1840

4 Harriet; *m* Capt J N Creighton and *d* 31 March 1860

Sir RICHARD *d* 27 Dec 1817; his er surv s,

  Sir Henry Onslow, 2nd Bt; *b* 23 April 1784; Capt RA; *m* 7 Feb 1807 Caroline (*d* 6 Jan 1867), dau of John Bond, of Mitcham, Surrey, and *d* 13 Sept 1853, having had, with a dau (*d* unm):

  1 **Sir Henry Onslow, 3rd Bt**, DL; *b* 5 June 1809; Capt 10th Regt; *m* 21 Nov 1848 Ellen (*d* 16 Dec 1877), dau of Samuel Peter, and had with two daus (*d* unm):

    (1) Henry Cranley; *b* Sept 1854; *d* 1861

    (1) Ellen Mary; *m* 8 Feb 1876 Lt-Col William Glencross, JP, Lancs Fus, and *d* 20 Feb 1928, leaving issue. He *d* 5 May 1928

    (2) Ada Ruth; *m* 17 July 1873 Rev John James Glencross Every, Vicar Lanhydrock, Cornwall, and *d* 25 Jan 1926, leaving issue. He *d* 1913

    (3) Augusta Geraldine; *m* 24 Jan 1888 George Hext, yst s of Francis J Hext, of Tredethy, and *d* 9 April 1960 aged 95, leaving issue. He *d* 29 Oct 1920

  2 MATTHEW RICHARD (Sir), **4th Bt**

3 Thomas; *b* 15 March 1812; Madras CS; *m* 1835 Elizabeth Sarah (*d* 9 Oct 1891), dau of Charles Robert, Madras CS, and *d* 2 Aug 1882, leaving:

  (1) Hamilton Cranley; *b* 2 Feb 1836; Madras CS; *m* 30 April 1867 Henrietta Fanny (*m* 2nd 25 May 1875 Col Robert Alexander Gilchrist, IA), dau of Maj-Gen J Forbes Musgrove, IA, and *d* 12 June 1874, leaving, with two daus (*d* unm):

    1a Cranley Charlton, CB (1923), CMG (1915), CBE (1919), DSO (1917); *b* 19 Sept 1869; Col Beds Regt, Isaza Expdn 1892, Chitrai 1895, WW I (wounded twice, despatches, Croix de Guerre), Hon Brig-Gen 1923, Mil Kt Windsor 1930–40; *m* 9 Nov 1904 Sydney Alice Hastings (*d* 22 Jan 1962), yr dau of Surgn-Gen Sir Benjamin Franklin, KCIE, and *d* 17 Dec 1940, having had:

      1b Cranley Cedric Franklin; *b* 8 April, *d* 14 Aug 1906

      2b Denzil Richard Cranley; *b* 27 March 1909; Lt-Cdr RNR WW II (despatches); *m* 7 Sept 1940 Bernardine (*d* 1976), yst dau of David J Blackburn, and *d* 1963, leaving:

        1c *Judith Marilyn [Mrs George Kinnear, 3 Abbots Way, Hartford, Northwich, Cheshire]; *b* 27 March 1946; *m* 1970 *George Sheffield Kinnear and has:

          1d *James Onslow Glyn; *b* 1986

          1d *Amanda Jane; *b* 1971

          2d *Felicity Esther Helen; *b* 1975

      3b Geoffrey Harold; *b* 19 Jan 1912; T/Capt Beds and Herts Regt WW II; *ka* June 1940

      1b Doreen May; *m* 22 Dec 1937 Maj John Reginald Heayns Ellery, s of Reginald Oram Ellery, and *d* 1982

      2b *Margaret Vivien [Mrs Johnston McDowell, The Old Quaker House, Mill Lane, Milverton, Somerset TA4 1LG]; *b* 1918; *m* 19 March 1947 Johnston McDowell (*d* 1990), s of Samuel McDowell, of Belfast, and has:

        1c *Hugh Geoffrey; *b* 18 Sept 1948; *educ* Swansea U; *m* 1976 *Merle Argosino and has:

          1d *Peter Johnson; *b* 1980

        2c *Brian Johnstone [Brian McDowell Esq, Barnsfield, Blundell Rd, Tiverton EX16 4NB]; *b* 6 March 1954; *educ* Haberdashers' Aske's; *m* 19– *Diana Stella Carr and has:

          1d *Harry Cranley Onslow; *b* 1989

          2d *Hugh Donald Johnston; *b* 1992

          1d *Sarah Frances; *b* 1981

          2d *Emily Jane; *b* 1983

        1c *Jane Maureen [Mrs Norman Roberts, 169 Belswaine Lane, Hemel Hemptstead HP3 9XF]; *b* 26 Nov 1945; *m* 16 Sept 1966 *Norman Roberts, s of Benjamin Roberts, of Highbury, and has:

          1d *Jon Michael; *b* 1971

          2d *Andrew David; *b* 1972

        2c *Fiona Margaret; *b* 3 July 1961

      3b *Jocelyn Anne Sydney [Mrs Charles Sheppard, 4 Chapel Close, Castle Cary, Somerset BA7 7AX]; *b* 1922; *m* 13 April 1953 Cdr Charles Sutton Sheppard, OBE, RN (*d* 1992), s of Herbert Charles Sheppard

  (2) Denzil Roberts; *b* 15 June 1839; MP Guildford 1874–85; *m* 2 Aug 1871 Clara Louisa (*d* 28 Nov 1907), yst dau of James Scott, of Tunbridge Wells, and *d* 21 March 1908, leaving two daus (*d* unm)

  (1) Emma Caroline; *m* 25 Nov 1857 Charles Gilbert Master, CSI, and *d* 4 March 1927, leaving issue. He *d* 9 March 1903

  (2) Alice Georgina; *m* 1860 John William Reid, Madras CS, and *d* 1 Jan 1884

  (3) Laura Elizabeth; *m* 24 March 1866 John Child Hanyngton, Madras CS, and had issue. He *d* 1895

  (4) Cecilia Augusta; *m* 1864 Gen Howard Codrington Dowker, CB, s of Lt-Gen Howard Dowker, and had issue. He *d* 4 Dec 1912

  (5) Marion Frances; *m* 1873 Col Evelyn Swinton Skinner, IA, and *d* 3 Feb 1937, leaving issue

  (6) Florence Jane; *b* 27 Oct 1857

4 Arthur Walton; *b* 3 Aug 1818; Lt-Col Bengal Army; *m* 19 Oct 1847 Isabella (*d* 13 Dec 1880), 3rd dau of John Penrice, and *d* 28 May 1895, having had:

  (1) Herbert Arthur Walton; *b* 8 Oct 1851; R-Adml; *d* unm 4 Dec 1906

  (2) Gerald Charles Penrice; *b* 7 Feb 1853; Lt-Col and Brevet-Col RE; *m* 16 Nov 1880 Flora Frances Mary (*d* 2 May 1951), 2nd dau of William Donald, and *d* 16 April 1909, leaving with a dau (*d* April unm):

    1a Arthur Gerald, DSC; *b* 13 May 1885; Lt-Cdr RN Somaliland 1904 (medal with clasp) and WW I; *m* 31 Aug 1912 Elsie Hinde (*m* 2nd 26 June 1918 Adml Sir Henry Daniel Pridham-Wippell, KCB, CVO; *d* 16 Nov 1976), dau of J Hinde Crouch, and *d* 17 June 1918 of wounds recd Battle Jutland, leaving:

      1b *Diana Rosemary [Mrs Patrick Longstaff, Thatchings, Fairwarp, Sussex]; *b* 24 Feb 1915; *m* 15 March 1938 *(Frank) Patrick Harrison Longstaff, Capt 5th Roy Inniskilling Dragoon Gds, 2nd s of Frank Longstaff, and has:

        1c *Nigel Antony Onslow; *b* 6 Nov 1942; *educ* Lancing; *m* 5 July 1966 *Jean Anne, er dau of Samuel McCormick, of Culmullin House, Drumree, Co Meath, and has:

          1d *Julia Rosemary; *b* 28 May 1968

  2a Milo Richard Beaumont; *b* 30 March 1888; Maj 21st Cav IA Mohmand Expdn 1908 (medal with clasp) and Mesopotamia WW I (twice wounded, despatches); *d* 5 Nov 1917 of wounds recd in action

  3a Eric Montague; *b* 16 Oct 1890; *educ* RMC Sandhurst; Maj Roy Warwicks Regt WW I (POW, despatches); *m* 29 Aug 1927 *Nona Osborne, only dau of Ernest Wilshire, of Sydney, NSW

  4a Brian Walton; *b* 24 Aug 1892; Lt KEO Bengal Lancers, IA, ADC to Gen Sir William Birdwood (later FM 1st Baron Birdwood; *qv*) WW I (despatches); *ka* Gallipoli 28 July 1915

  1a Dora Frances; *m* 15 Feb 1904 Col Claud Frederick Pilkington Parry, DSO, RFA, est s of Maj-Gen F W P Parry, and *d* 11 Jan 1957, leaving issue. He was *ka* 20 Aug 1918

2a Violet Isabel; *m* 21 Nov 1901 Maj Alan Goring, 20th Hus, s of Rev John Goring, Rector Weston, and *d* 25 Dec 1945, leaving issue (*see* GORING, Bt)

(3) Richard Cranley; *b* 26 July 1857; Lt-Col and Brevet Col IA, Dep Judge Advocate-Gen India 1907–09; *m* 1883 Edith Margaretta (*d* 18 March 1934), dau of Francis Beer, and *d* 25 Oct 1934, having had, with a dau (*d* unm):

1a Cecil Isabel; *m* 1st 10 Aug 1910 Capt Hyde Gwynne Harrison, Manchester Regt (*ka* Mesopotamia 24 July 1920); *m* 2nd 3 April 1923 Maj Charles Theodore Foster, MC, York and Lancaster Regt

2a Alice Mary; *m* 22 Oct 1914 Maj Francis Richard Savage (*d* 29 April 1960), Cheshire Regt, s of Col J W Savage, RE, and had:

1b *Gerald Onslow; *b* 19 Oct 1916; Maj late Queen's Roy Regt

3a Winifred Ida; *m* 16 July 1919 Lt-Col Alick Gerald Joseph Copeland, Roy Signals (*d* 8 Nov 1964), and had:

1b *Virginia Margaret [Mrs Alfred Anderson, Kublay, Thelma Road, Claremont, Cape Town, S Africa]; *b* 28 Jan 1931; *m* 3 Oct 1959 *Alfred John Anderson

1b *Alison Mary [Mrs Fergus Nugent, PO Ghatsila, District Singhblum, Bihar, India]; *b* 28 Jan 1931; *m* 19 Feb 1955 *Fergus Patrick Nugent and has four sons

(1) Blanche Isabel; *m* 15 July 1870 Sir William Bousfield, LLD, JP, s of W Bousfield, of Streatham, Surrey, and *d* 2 March 1932. He *dsp* 7 April 1910

(2) Florence Maud; *m* 12 Jan 1876 Capt George Burchell Graham, 33rd Regt, s of F Graham, and *d* 15 March 1927. He *d* 1894

(3) Ethel Augusta; *m* 10 June 1880 Charles Loder Gilbert and *d* 1914. He *d* 1914

5 Richard Cranley; Capt 91st Foot; *d* unm

2 Anne Eliza; *m* 25 May 1839 Lt-Gen Henry E Doherty, CB, and *d* 7 Feb 1876. He *d* 15 Sept 1885

3 Frances Anne; *m* 1st 5 July 1838 John Dennistoun, MP (*d* 9 Sept 1870); *m* 2nd Chevalier Frederico Biasini, of Florence, and *d* 7 Dec 1892

The 3rd Bt *d* 20 Nov 1870; his brother,

Sir Matthew Richard Onslow, 4th Bt; *b* 12 Sept 1810; Maj Bengal Cav; *m* 1st 1 May 1837 Eliza Antonia (*d* 15 June 1854), 2nd dau of Brig-Gen Newton Wallace, 53rd NI, and had, with a dau (*d* unm):

1 WILLIAM WALLACE RHODERIC (Sir), **5th Bt**

2 Henry Haworth Newton; *b* 7 June 1852; *m* 1888 Mary (*d* 1926), dau of Rev George Martin, DD, Rector St Breward's, Canon Truro, and *d* 7 Dec 1928, having had a dau (*d* young)

3 John Royds Denistoun; *b* 9 June 1854; Capt Roy Cornwall Rangers Militia; *m* 7 July 1885 Edith Mary (*d* 7 Dec 1930), dau of Thomas Commins, and *d* 3 Nov 1895, leaving:

(1) Cranley Denistoun; *b* 1 July 1886; *d* unm 28 Jan 1905

(2) Humphrey Cedric (Rev); *b* 31 July 1889; *educ* Cheltenham and Corpus Christie Coll Oxford (BA 1913, MA 1916); Rector Plymtree Devon 1929–48, Vicar Crediton; *d* unm 5 Feb 1948

1 Edith Mathewanna; *m* Dec 1870 Henry Mouat Wood, 2nd s of Jacob Wood, of Havre by Marion, 2nd dau of Capt Frederick Campbell, 42nd Highrs (*see* CAMPBELL, Bt, of Aberuchill), and *d* 1926

2 Amelia Francis; *m* 18 May 1871 Col Horace Richard Le Marchant Carey, IA, and had issue

3 Alice Constance Kathleen; *m* 3 July 1873 Harry T Stockton, Lt USN, and *d* 19 Sept 1915, leaving issue. He *d* 6 May 1886

Sir Matthew *m* 2nd 6 Dec 1855 Mary (*d* 1892), dau of J Salter, and by her had:

4 Matthew Richard Septimus (Rev); *b* 27 Nov 1856; *educ* Pembroke Coll Oxford (MA); Rector Stoke Edith Herefs 1905–26, Chaplain RN; *m* 1st 21 Aug 1883 Mary (*dsp* 1884), dau of Rev Edward Jonathan Green, Vicar Leintwardine; *m* 2nd 23 Aug 1894 Fanny Harriet (*d* 13 Dec 1940), 4th dau of Rev Thomas Green, Vicar Aymestry, Herefs, and *d* 30 Nov 1932, having by her had:

(1) Richard Francis John, MVO 4th Cl (1937), DSC (1918); *b* 29 March 1896; Capt RN WW I (despatches) and WW II; *m* 1st 9 Dec 1920 Sylvia Rachel (*d* 15 June 1933), 2nd dau of Rev Alfred Edward Green-Price (*see* GREEN-PRICE, Bt), and by her had:

1a Richard Thomas; *b* 15 Feb 1922; Capt RM WW II (despatches); *m* 30 Aug 1947 *Gillian Doreen [Mrs Richard Onslow, West End House, Hambledon, Hants PO7 6TB]; er dau of Edward Clemson, and *d* 9 Feb 1983, leaving:

1b *(Sylvia) Jane; *b* 17 Nov 1951

2b *Geraldine Victoria [Mrs Nicholas Keith, West End House, Hambledon, Hants PO7 6TB]; *b* 4 Feb 1954; *m* 1987 *Nicholas Mark Keith, s of J R Keith, and has:

1c *William Richard; *b* 1987

1c *Hebe; *b* 1990

1a *Anthea Mary [Mrs Edward Phillips, The Small House, Monnington-on-Wye, Herefs]; *b* 31 Jan 1925; WRNS WW II; *m* 9 Aug 1947 *Maj Edward Courtenay Phillips, MC, JP, DL, 60th Rifles, er s of Gerald Courtenay Phillips, of Street Court, Kingsland, Herefs, and has:

1b *Sarah Angela Josephine [Mrs Robert Corbett, Newchurch Farm, Kinnersley, Herefs]; *b* 2 Dec 1948; *m* 24 Feb 1968 *Robert Anthony Corbett, yr s of Lt-Col Uvedale Shobdon Corbett, DSO, of Shobdon Court, Leominster, Herefs, and has:

1c *Benjamin Edward Thomas; *b* 20 May 1969

2c *Tom; *b* 31 Oct 1971; *m* 1997 *Sarah Moor

1c *Hannah; *b* 21 Sept 1977

2b *Harriet Anne Jennifer [Mrs Peter Cheney, Chase House, Honnington-on-Wye, Herefs]; *b* 7 Aug 1953; *m* 31 July 1977 *Maj Peter Edward Cheney, MBE, Welsh Gds (ret), and has:

1c *Joss Edward; *b* 29 June 1990

1c *Melita Clare; *b* 2 Sept 1982

2c *Theodora May; *b* 5 Nov 1983

3c *Lettice Rose; *b* 23 Oct 1986

(1) (cont.) Capt Richard Onslow *m* 2nd 27 May 1939 Jessie Violet Betty (*m* 2nd 7 July 1951 (*divorce* 1956) Maj Arthur Christopher John Congreve; *d*

1993), dau of Brig-Gen Reynold Alexander Gillam, CMG, DSO, and was *ka* 9 April 1942 cmdg HMS *Hermes*

(2) Thomas; *b* 17 Nov 1897; *educ* Magdalene Coll Cambridge; 2nd Lt KSLI WW I; *ka* 6 Jan 1917

(3) Herbert Frank; *b* 8 May 1899; *educ* Hereford Cathedral Sch and Pembroke Coll Oxford; Lt RM WW I, N Russia 1919; *m* 5 April 1934 Hon Lena Barbara Joan Ogilvie-Grant (*d* 1981), only dau of 4th Baron Strathspey (*qv*), and *d* 26 Feb 1970, leaving:

1a +Roger Cranley Seafield [Roger Onslow Esq, 7 Links View, Baunton Lane, Cirencester, Glos GL7 2NF]; *b* 24 Dec 1934; *educ* Christ's Hosp; *m* 17 Oct 1959 *Eileen Margaret, dau of James Archibald Joseph Barnard, and has:

1b *Susan Helen; *b* 21 March 1965; *m* 1990 *Philip Tattersall

2b *Clare Louise; *b* 18 Feb 1967; *m* 1988 *Alan Robert Smith and has:

1c *Holly Iris; *b* 1988

(1) Mary Camperdown; *b* 11 Oct 1901; *d* 1982

5 Arthur Herbert; *b* 30 June 1862; *m* 21 June 1892 Alice Constance Edith (*d* 1 July 1897), dau of Marmaduke Constable, and *d* 17 Jan 1932, leaving:

(1) Vera Doris

(2) Ethel Muriel; *m* 27 April 1922 Samuel Wilson Lindrea, only s of G W Lindrea. He *d* 1966

Sir MATTHEW *d* 3 Aug 1876; his est son,

Sir William Wallace Rhoderic Onslow, 5th Bt, JP, DL Cornwall and Wilts; *b* 13 Aug 1845; High Sheriff Cornwall 1883, Capt 3rd Bn DCLI, formerly 12th Regt; *m* 11 Feb 1873 Octavia Katherine (*d* 7 June 1931), yst dau of Sir Arthur Knox-Gore, 1st Bt (*see* 1899 edn), and had, with two sons and a dau (*d* young):

1 ROGER WARIN BEACONSFIELD (Sir), **6th Bt**

2 William Gore Alanby; *b* 23 Aug 1887; Paymaster Cdr RN; *d* unm 10 Sept 1954

1 Ethel Nina Amy Onslow; *b* 17 Dec 1873; *m* 7 March 1905 Charles Edward Elwell, s of Edward Elwell, of Neyoddfraith, N Wales, and *d* 12 Aug 1964, leaving issue. He *d* 1946

2 Edith Doreen Onslow; *b* 1 April 1882

3 Gwendolen Muriel Onslow; *b* 26 Oct 1883

Sir WILLIAM *d* 13 Jan 1916; his est surv son,

Sir Roger Warin Beaconsfield Onslow, 6th Bt, JP Cornwall; *b* 29 April 1880; Lt 6th Bn E Kent Regt, Capt 9th Bn DCLI, Lt Suffolk Regt, Boer War 1900–02 and WW I (wounded); *m* 19 Jan 1905 Mildred (*m* 2nd 7 Dec 1932 Capt Utred Arthur Frederick Knox, Roy Irish Rifles (*d* 9 March 1935), s of Utred Augustus Knox, DL, of Mount Falcon, Ballina, Co Mayo, and *d* 28 Aug 1943), est dau of Sir Robert R Wilmot, 6th Bt, and had:

1 RICHARD WILMOT (Sir), **7th Bt**

2 John Vernon; *b* 16 Feb 1919; *educ* Marlborough; AIF WW II; *m* 1 May 1946 *Anne Broun [Mrs John Onslow, Luckington Manor Stables, Luckington, Wilts], dau of Gavin Hutchinson, and *d* 1985, leaving:

(1) *Charlotte Anne Mildred [Mrs Charles Wilkinson, The Coach House, Sutton Benger, Wilts]; *b* 19 Aug 1947; *m* 1974 *Charles E Wilkinson and has:

1a *James Maurice; *b* 1975

2a *John Charles; *b* 1977

1a *Anne Nora; *b* 1980

(2) *Victoria Joy Nora [Mrs Jeffrey Lippiatt, Manor Farm, Alderton, Wilts]; *b* 25 Oct 1950; *m* 1972 *(Lionel) Jeffrey Lippiatt and has:

1a *Miranda Kate; *b* 1978

2a *Emma Suzanna; *b* 1982

1 *(Ursula) Joan; *b* 5 Aug 1916; *m* 8 April 1948 John Archibald Harris, only s of C H Harris, of Salisbury, and has:

(1) *Robert James Onslow; *b* 1952

(2) *Geoffrey Archibald Onslow; *b* 1954

(3) *Richard Charles Onslow; *b* 1958

Sir ROGER *d* 13 Oct 1931; his er son,

Sir Richard Wilmot Onslow, 7th Bt, TD (1943); *b* 30 July 1906; *educ* Cheltenham; Maj 4th/5th Bn DCLI (TA); *m* 1st 21 March 1929 Constance (*d* 10 Dec 1960), only dau of Albert Parker, and:

1 Sir JOHN ROGER WILMOT ONSLOW, **8th and present Bt**

1 *Tessa Elizabeth; *b* 6 Sept 1930; *m* 1st 7 Feb 1953 (*divorce* 1964) John Leonard Hargrave, s of Leonard Oswald Hargrave, and has:

(1) *Belinda Anne Constance; *b* 11 May 1955

(2) *Jane; *b* 9 Oct 1956

1 (cont.) Mrs Tessa Hargrave *m* 2nd Jan 1969 *John Vernon Mossman

2 *Jill Angela [Mrs Patricio Lavin, Casilla 14220, Santiago 15, Chile]; *b* 10 June 1941; *educ* Convent Sacred Heart Malta; *m* 15 Dec 1962 *Patricio Edgar Lavin, er s of Cesar Lavin, of Santiago, and has:

(1) *Sean Paul; *b* 1967

(2) *Christopher Patrick; *b* 1970

(1) *Cecily Ann; *b* 31 Aug 1965

3 *Sally Constance; *b* 12 May 1946

Sir Richard *m* 2nd 14 Sept 1961 Mary (Molly) Nelson, yst dau of Harold Rodney Russell, JP, of Belfast, and *d* 14 July 1963

ONSLOW OF WOKING

Creation: B. (LP, UK) 1997.

THE BARON ONSLOW OF WOKING, of Woking, Co Surrey (Sir Cranley Gordon Douglas Onslow, KCMG (1992), PC (1988)) [The Rt Hon The Lord Onslow of Woking KCMG PC, Highbuilding, Fernhurst, Sussex GU27 3NL]; *b* 8 June 1926; *educ* Harrow, Oriel Coll Oxford (BA 1950) and Geneva U; Lt 7th QOH 1944–48, Capt 3rd/4th Co London Yeo (Sharpshooters) (TA) 1948–52, FO 1951–60: 3rd Sec Rangoon 1953–55, Actg Consul Maymyo, Burma, 1955–56, memb Dartford RDC 1960–62 and Kent CC 1961–64, MP (C) Woking 1964–97, Parly U-Sec DTI (aerospace, shipping) 1972–74, Oppn Spokesman DHSS 1974–75 and Def 1975–76, Min State FCO 1982–83, Chm: Select Ctee Def 1981–82 and 1922 Ctee 1984–92 (memb exec 1968–72, 1981–82 and 1983–92), dir: Argyll Gp 1983–93 and Redifon Ltd 1985– (chm 1988–), MRAeS, Liveryman Fishmongers' Co 1991–; *m* 7 May 1955 *Lady June Ann Hay, yr dau of 14th Earl of Kinnoull (*qv*), and has:

1 *Richard Alan Douglas; *b* 27 June 1956; *educ* Harrow and Oriel Coll Oxford (MA); *m* 1985 *Phyllida K, dau of Michael Moore, of Folly Farm, Lindsey, Suffolk, and has:
  (1) *Thomas Cranley Douglas; *b* 1992
  (1) *Isabella; *b* 1990
1 *Sandra ('Sue') Dorothy; *b* 9 April 1958; *educ* LSE (BSc); *m* 1982 *J Bartlett K Smith, of Dayton, Ohio, and has:
  (1) *Jonathan Christopher; *b* 1990
  (1) *Claerwen Helen; *b* 1988
2 *Caroline Diana; *b* 30 Sept 1959; *educ* Manchester U (BA); *m* 1987 *Joseph V Martino, yr s of J Martino, of New York
3 *Katharine ('Kash') Denise; *b* 22 Feb 1961; *m* 1987 *Nigel P Steer

Lineage: *See* ONSLOW, Earl

OPPENHEIMER

Arms: Az. two swords in saltire ppr., pommelled and hilted or, between two lions passant of the last. **Crest:** A demi-koodoo ppr., resting the sinister hoof on a rose gu., barbed and seeded ppr.
Motto: *In arduis audax* ('Bold even in adversity').
Creation: Bt. (UK) 18 Jan 1921.

SIR MICHAEL BERNARD GRENVILLE OPPENHEIMER, 3RD BT, of Stoke Poges, Co Buckingham [Sir Michael Oppenheimer Bt, L'Aiguillon, Rue des Cotils, Grouville, Jersey, CI JE3 9AP]; *b* 27 May 1924; *s* f 1933; *educ* Charterhouse and Ch Ch Oxford (BLitt 1955, MA 1952); Lt S African Artillery 1943–45; *m* 12 July 1947 *Laetitia Helen, BPhil, MA, DD, er dau of Lt-Col Sir Hugh Vere Huntley Duff Munro-Lucas-Tooth, 1st Bt, MP (*see* LUCAS-TOOTH, Bt), and has:
1 *Henrietta Laetitia Grenville; *b* 24 Dec 1954; *m* 1978 *Adam Lawrence Scott and has:
  (1) *Patrick Aaron; *b* 1986
  (1) *Eleanor Rose; *b* 1989
2 *Matilda Magdalen Grenville; *b* 12 Jan 1956; *m* 1978 *Neil G A King and has:
  (1) *Dorothy Xanthe; *b* 1987
  (2) *Hannah Magdalen; *b* 1988
  (3) *Elsa Mary; *b* 1990
  (4) *Lily Alexandra; *b* 1993
3 *Xanthe Jennifer Grenville [The Hon Mrs Ivo Mosley, Courtyard, Neopardy, Crediton, Devon]; *b* 13 July 1958; *m* 1977 *Hon Ivo Adam Rex Mosley and has issue (*see* RAVENSDALE, B)

Lineage: Sir Bernard Oppenheimer, 1st Bt (UK), so *cr* 18 Jan 1921, of Stoke Poges, Bucks; *b* 13 Feb 1866; chm S African Diamond Corp and New Vaal River Diamond and Exploration Co; inaugurated diamond-cutting factories for Dis-

charged and Disabled Soldiers; *m* 10 Sept 1890 Lena (*d* 15 Nov 1937), dau of Michael Straus, and had:
1 MICHAEL (Sir), **2nd Bt**
1 Elsie Rose; *m* 1st 12 July 1922 (*divorce* 1950) Leonard Lewis Rossiter, slr, barrister Middle Temple, and had issue; *m* 2nd 22 Dec 1952 Col Herbert Louis Mostyn-Owen, late 19th Lancers IA (*d* 17 Feb 1972), 3rd s of Lt-Col Charles Roger Mostyn-Owen, JP
2 *Madeleine Hilda, JP (Wilts 1951) [The Rt Hon The Lady Devlin JP, West Wick House, Pewsey, Wilts]; *m* 12 Feb 1932 Baron Devlin (*d* 1992), PC (LP; *see* 1970 edn), and has:
  (1) *Gilpatrick [The Hon Gilpatrick Devlin, 6 Millfield Lane, London N6 6JD]; *b* 26 Dec 1938; *educ* Winchester and UCL; *m* 25 Feb 1967 *Glenna, er dau of John Parry-Evans, MRCS, of Colwyn Bay, Denbighs, and has:
    1a *Benedict; *b* 23 Nov 1967
  (2) *Dominick; *b* 2 Dec 1942; *educ* Winchester and UCL (LLB); *m* 27 May 1967 *Carla, dau of Lamerto Fulloni, of Rome, and has:
    1a *Daniel; *b* 14 Feb 1968
    2a *Christopher; *b* 22 Aug 1972
    1a *Maddalena; *b* 29 July 1969
  (3) *Timothy; *b* 28 July 1944; *educ* Winchester and Univ Coll Oxford; jnlst; *m* 31 Jan 1967 *Angela, er dau of Albert James Gwynfryn Laramy, of Crosskeys, Mon, and has:
    1a *Sebastian; *b* 31 July 1973
    2a *Fabian; *b* 11 Nov 1975
    1a *Miranda; *b* 13 Dec 1969; *m* 1991 *Neil McPherson and has a dau
    2a *Esmeralda; *b* 23 Sept 1971
  (4) *Matthew; *b* 8 June 1946; *educ* Winchester and New Coll Oxford; *m* 23 July 1969 *Rosemary Joan Boutcher, 3rd dau of Lt-Col Edward Conway van der Kirste, Essex Regt, of Durrington, Wilts, and has:
    1a *William; *b* 17 March 1972
    2a *Edward; *b* 21 April 1975
    1a *Beatrice; *b* 16 May 1970
    2a *Mary; *b* 10 Jan 1977
  (1) *Clare; *b* 2 March 1940; *m* 10 April 1961 (*annulled* 1984) Julian Reginald Desgrand Jermy Gwyn, Prof History Ottawa U, 3rd s of Quintin Jermy Gwyn, CD, Grand Chllr SMO Malta, of Rome and Quebec, and has had:
    1a *Christopher Benedict; *b* 12 Aug 1965
    2a John Joseph; *b* 19 July 1967; *d* 4 Aug 1969
    1a *Frances Deborah; *b* 16 Jan 1962; *m* 19–*Robert and has a s and two daus
    2a *Anya Clare; *b* 28 March 1963; *m* 19–*Jerry Knol and has a dau
    3a *Elin Maria; *b* 23 May 1964; *m* 19– *Robert Vallé and has two sons
  (2) *Virginia [Lady Kennedy, c/o The Rt Hon Lord Justice Kennedy, c/o Royal Courts of Justice, Strand, London WC2A 2LL]; *b* 2 March 1940; *m* 24 April 1965 *Sir Paul Joseph Morrow (Rt Hon Lord Justice) Kennedy, PC, QC, a Ld Justice Appeal 1992–, only s of Dr Joseph Morrow Kennedy, of Sheffield, and has:
    1a *Christopher Laurence Paul; *b* 10 Aug 1966; *educ* Ampleforth; *m* 1992 *Rebecca McCarthy
    2a *John Patrick; *b* 19 Nov 1969
    1a *Joanna Mary; *b* 17 July 1968
    2a *Brigid Madeline; *b* 14 May 1971

Sir BERNARD *d* 13 June 1921; his son,
Sir Michael Oppenheimer, 2nd Bt; *b* 26 Dec 1892; *educ* Cambridge; barrister Inner Temple; *m* 16 Dec 1920 Caroline Magdalen (Ina), CStJ (*m* 2nd 1 June 1935 Sir Ernest Oppenheimer (*d* 25 Nov 1957) and *d* 2 Feb 1971), 3rd dau of Sir Robert Grenville Harvey, 2nd and last Bt, of Langley Park (*see* 1931 edn), and *d* 26 Sept 1933, leaving:
1 Sir MICHAEL BERNARD GRENVILLE OPPENHEIMER, **3rd and present Bt**

OPPENHEIM-BARNES

Creation: B. (LP, UK) 1989.

THE BARONESS OPPENHEIM-BARNES, of Gloucester, Co Gloucester (Sally Viner, PC) [The Rt Hon The Baroness Oppenheim-Barnes PC, 12 Ulster Terrace, London NW1 4PJ]; *b* 26 July 1930; *educ* Sheffield High Sch and Lowther Coll N Wales; social worker with ILEA; MP (C) Glos 1970–87, V-Chm C Parly Prices and Consumer Protection Ctee 1971–73 (Chm 1973–74), Oppn Spokesman Prices and Consumer Protection 1974–79, memb Shadow Cabinet 1975–79, Min State Consumer Affrs DTI 1979–82; Chm: Nat Consumer Cncl 1987–89, Cncl Mgmt Nat Waterways Museum Tst 1988–89; dir: Boots 1982–93, Fleming High Income Investment Tst 1989–97, HFC Bank 1989–; Nat V-Pres NUTG 1973–79 and 1989–90; Pres Glos Dist BRCS 1973–; *m* 1st 1949 Henry Myer Oppenheim (*d* 1980); *m* 2nd 1984 *John Barnes and by her 1st husb has:
1 *Phillip Anthony Charles Lawrence; *b* 1956; *educ* Harrow and Oriel Coll Oxford (MA); MP (C) Amber Valley 1983–97, Parly U-Sec: DOE 1994–95, DTI 1995–97
1 *Carolyn; *b* 1951; *educ* Benenden and London U (BA); *m* 1973 *Martin Robert Selman and has:
  (1) *David Benjamin; *b* 1978
  (1) *Victoria Esther Jeanette; *b* 1977
  (2) *Henrietta Amy Charlotte; *b* 1982
2 *Rosanne [The Hon Mrs Mattick, Pettett's Barn, Hinxton, Cambs CB10 1RF]; *b* 1954; *m* 1st 1984 (*divorce* 1988) David B Williams; *m* 2nd 1993 *Stephen James Mattick and by him has:
  (1) *Olivia Daisy Amelia; *b* 1993

Lineage: MARK VINER; *m* Jeanette — and had:

SALLY, *cr* a **Baroness**

ORAM

Creation: B. (LP, UK) 1975.

THE BARON ORAM, of Brighton, Co E Sussex (Albert Edward Oram) [The Rt Hon The Lord Oram, 19 Ridgeside Ave, Patcham, Sussex BN1 8WD]; *b* 13 Aug 1913; *educ* Brighton GS and LSE (BA Hons); RA WW II 1942–45; research offr Co-op Party 1946–55; MP (Lab and Co-op) E Ham S 1955–74, Parly Sec ODM 1964–69; Co-ordinator Devpt Programmes Internat Co-operative Alliance 1971–73, Devpt Administrator Intermediate Tech Devpt Gp 1974–76; memb Cwlth Devpt Corp 1975–76; Chm Co-op Devpt Agency; a Ld in Waiting 1976–78; author: *Changes in China* (with Nora Stettner, 1987); *m* 1956 *Frances Joan, dau of Arthur Charles and Dorothy Barber, of Lewes, and has:

1 *Mark; *b* 1967
2 *Robin; *b* 1968

Lineage: HENRY ORAM; *m* Ada Edith — and had:

ALBERT EDWARD, *cr* a **Baron**

ORANMORE AND BROWNE

Arms: Argent an eagle displayed with two heads sable langued gules. **Crest:** A griffin's head erased argent langued gules. **Supporters:** Dexter, a knight in chain armour proper belted azure garnished or, holding in his right hand a battle axe chained proper charged on the blade with a cross patée or, on his left arm a pointed shield gules charged with two lioncells or and supported by a band from the right shoulder gules studded and garnished or; sinister, a knight also in chain armour with a surcoat of blue silk, belted gules, leaning his left hand on a two-handled sword, thereon a shield argent charged with an eagle displayed with two heads sable, langued gules. **Motto:** *Fortiter et fideliter* ('Strongly and faithfully').
Creations: B. (I) 4 May 1836 and (UK) 19 Jan 1926.

THE 4TH BARON ORANMORE AND BROWNE OF CARRABROWNE CASTLE in the county of the town of Galway **AND OF CASTLE MacGARRETT** in the Co of Mayo, and **2nd Baron Mereworth**, of Mereworth Castle, Co Kent (Dominick Geoffrey Edward Browne) [The Rt Hon The Lord Oranmore and Browne, 52 Eaton Place, London SW1X 8AL]; *b* 21 Oct 1901; *educ* Eton and Ch Ch Oxford; late 2nd Lt Gren Gds; *m* 1st 5 Feb 1925 (*divorce* 1936) Mildred Helen (*d* 1980), er dau of Hon Thomas Henry Frederick Egerton (*see* SUTHERLAND, D), and has had:

1 +DOMINICK GEOFFREY THOMAS; *b* 1 July 1929; playwright, poet and prose writer; *m* 25 Oct 1957 (*divorce* 1974) Sara Margaret, dau of Dr Herbert Wright, of Dublin

2 +Martin Michael Dominick [The Hon Martin Browne, Berghane Hall, Castle Camps, Cambridge CB1 6TN]; *b* 27 Oct 1931; *educ* Eton; stockbroker; *m* 5 Feb 1958 *Alison Margaret, only dau of John Bradford, of Wormley, Surrey, and has:

(1) +Shaun Dominick; *b* 22 Jan 1964; *educ* Eton; *m* 1990 *Elizabeth Jane, yr dau of Rev Rex Bird, of The Rectory, Monks Eleigh, Suffolk, and has:

1a +Hugo Dominick; *b* 27 June 1997
1a *Ophelia Alexandra; *b* 17 May 1994
2a *Katya Elizabeth; *b* 28 Nov 1995

(1) *Cara Margaret; *b* 14 June 1961; *m* 1988 (*divorce* 1992), as his 1st w, Philip William Howard, er s of Sir John Howard-Lawson, 6th Bt (*qv*)

1 Patricia Helen; *b* 16 Feb 1926; *m* 11 June 1952, as his 1st w, Hon (Michael) Anthony Rathbone Cayzer (*d* 1990), yr s of 1st Baron Rotherwick (*qv*), and *d* 1981, leaving issue

2 Brigid Verena; *b* 25 Dec 1927; *d* 3 Jan 1941

3 *Judith [The Hon Mrs Haslam, The Orangery, Felix Hall, Kelvedon, Essex CO5 9DG]; *b* 23 Sept 1934; *m* 6 June 1958 *(Ralph) Michael Haslam, est s of William Heywood Haslam, OBE, of Whitehall Court, London SW1, and has:

(1) *Christopher William Dominick; *b* 29 June 1960
(2) *David Oliver Myles; *b* 2 March 1962; *m* 1 July 1995 *Clare, 2nd dau of Lt-Col J J B Pope, of Tetbury, Glos
(1) *Carina Judith; *b* 29 Oct 1965; *m* 30 May 1998 *John Gibson

The 4th BARON ORANMORE AND BROWNE *m* 2nd 29 April 1936 (*divorce* 1950) Oonagh (*d* 2 Aug 1995), yst dau of Hon Arthur Ernest Guinness (*see* IVEAGH, E), and formerly w of Hon Philip Leyland Kindersley (*see* KINDERSLEY, B), and by her has had:

3 +Garech Domnagh [The Hon Garech Browne, Luggala, Roundwood, Co Wicklow, Ireland; 13 rue de la Douzaine, Fort George, St Peter Port, Guernsey, CI]; *b* 25 June 1939; *educ* Castle Park Dublin and Le Rosey Switzerland; chm: Claddagh Records, Claddagh Media Ltd and Woodtown Music Publications; *m* 1981 *Princess (Harshad) Purna Devi, *née* Jadeja, dau of HH The Maharaja Mahendra Sinhji of Morvi and HH The Maharani Sri Vijay Kuverba (dau of Khodybha Jhala)

4 A son; *b* 23 Dec, *d* 30 Dec 1943

5 Tara; *b* 4 March 1945; *m* 1963 *Noreen ('Nicky') Anne, dau of Sean MacSherry, of Co Down, and was *k* in a car crash in Chelsea 18 Dec 1966, leaving:

(1) +Dorian Clifford [Dorian Browne Esq, Grange Court, St Peter Port, Guernsey, CI]; *b* 1963; *m* 19 Aug 1989 *Alison, dau of Kenneth Perryman Fry, of Staffs, and has had:

1a Sasha; *b* and *d* 1990
2a +Sebastian; *b* 15 June 1994
3a +Gabriel; *b* 18 March 1997

(2) +Julian Dominick [Julian Browne Esq, Villa Marguerite, St Martins, Guernsey, CI]; *b* 1965; *m* 7 Sept 1990 *Isabella, dau of Cerrajas Jaime Iglesias, of Argentina

The 4th BARON ORANMORE AND BROWNE *m* 3rd 1 Dec 1951 *Constance Vera (Sally Gray, film actress), dau of Charles Edward Stevens

Lineage: STEPHEN BROWNE, of Athenry, Co Galway; *m* Eveline, dau of Geoffrey Lynch, and had, with other issue:

WILLIAM BROWNE, of Athenry; *m* Anastasia (living 1499), dau of Valentine (Vadyn) Blake and great-aunt of Sir Valentine Blake, 1st Bt, of Menlough (*qv*), and had, with two er and three yr sons:

DOMINICK BROWNE, of Barna and Carrabrowne; freedom Galway 1541, Mayor Galway 1575; party to an agreement of 1585 known as the Galway Compositions between ELIZABETH I's Ld Deputy Sir John Perrott and the chieftains and freeholders of Galway, in which his title to extensive estates in Co Galway was thereby confirmed; *m* Bevan, dau of Sir Morogh O'Flaherty, of Iar Connaught, and *d* 1596, leaving, with other issue:

1 GEOFFREY
2 Oliver; Mayor Galway 1609, ancestor of the BROWNEs of Coolarne, Co Galway
3 Edward; *educ* Oxford; Dean Tuam 1607
1 Margery; *m* James Blake, 2nd s of Walter Blake and yr bro of Sir Valentine Blake, 1st Bt (*see* BLAKE, Bt, of Menlough)

DOMINICK BROWNE's est s,

GEOFFREY BROWNE, of Carrowbrowne and Galway; Alderman Galway; bought from the provost and burgesses of Athenry the then dissolved monastery of Mayo, in the Barony of Clanmorris, Co Mayo; *m* Mary, dau and eventually heiress of Edmund McMorrishe (or Prendergast), of Castle Macgarrett (sometimes called Mcgarrett or Mac Garrett), Claremorris, Co Mayo, and *d* 8 April 1608, having had, with twin yr sons (Stephen, SJ, *b* 21 Dec 1595, *d* 1675; Christopher) and two daus (Mary, *m* Sir Peter ffrench (*d* 27 Feb 1631), of Galway, and *d* 1659, having had issue; Juliane, *m* Sir Thomas Blake, 2nd Bt, of Menlough, *qv*):

Sir DOMINICK BROWNE; MP Anthony 1634, Mayor Galway 1634–35, ktd 1635; much of his land confiscated 1654 following CROMWELL's incursion into Ireland; *m* Anastasia, dau of James (Riveagh) Darcy, and *d* 1656, having had, with two est daus (one *m* Walter Blake; another *m* Mathew Martyn):

1 GEOFFREY
2 Nicholas; had two sons (William; Martin)
3 Edward; ancestor of the BROWNEs of Woodstock, Ballindine, Co Mayo
4 Henry, of Kilticolla or Brownehall, Co Mayo; *d* on or after 19 April 1678
1 Mary; *m* 1626 Sir John Browne, 1st Bt, of the Neale, Co Mayo (*see* KILMAINE, B)
2 Gennet; *m* Richard Dillon, of Clonbrock, Co Galway, ancestor of the Barons Clonbrock (*see* 1926 edn)
3 Anne; *m* Patrick French, est s of Sir Oliver French
4 Evelina; *m* 1st Robert French, of Monivea; *m* 2nd, as his 2nd w, Sir Oliver French

Sir DOMINICK BROWNE's est s,

GEOFFREY BROWNE, of Carrabrowne, Co Galway; barrister Middle Temple 1627, MP (I Parl) Athenry 1639 and Tuam 1661, active memb Cncl Irish Confedn set up to oppose English rule 1647 and an envoy sent by them to the Duke of Lorraine 1652; in 1660 was declared rightful owner of 2,000 acres in Co Galway; *m* Mary (*d* 29 July 1671), est dau of Sir Henry Lynch, 1st Bt (*see* LYNCH-BLOSSE, Bt), and *d* 14 Jan 1668, having had, with four yr sons (Martin, James, older than Ignatius; Paul, Henry, yr than Ignatius):

1 DOMINICK
2 Ignatius; *m* (licence 24 Jan 1669) Johanna, dau of Robert Doyne and widow of — Webb, and had:

(1) Mary; *m* Joseph Blake, of Grange (*see* 1920 edn WALLSCOURT, B)
1 Mary; *m* Robert Dillon, of Clonbrock, Co Galway, and had issue (*see* 1926 edn CLONBROCK, B)

GEOFFREY BROWNE's est s,

DOMINICK BROWNE, of Carrabrowne, and Castlemacgarrett; granted 1670 his f's nominated 2,000 acres in Co Galway and 1678 a further 6,500 acres in Co

Mayo, including Castlemacgarrett; Mayor Galway 1688 and 1689; Col Jacobite foot regt; *m* 1st by March 1657 Agnes, dau and heiress of Martyn ffrench, of Galway, s of Jasper ffrench, and by her had three sons (Geoffrey; Martin; Henry) and a dau (Teresa); *m* 2nd Mary, sis of Anthony Lynch, and *d* between 5 Aug 1721 and 17 Jan 1721/2, having by her had a dau (Barbara); his est s by his 1st w:

GEOFFREY BROWNE, of Castlemacgarrett; *b* 1664; barrister Middle Temple 14 May 1685, planted at Castlemacgarrett extensively and built a new house (burned down 1811) to replace the old Prendergast castle there 1694; *m c* 1695 Magdalen (*d* 1705), dau of Peter Blake, of Corbally, Co Galway (see 1920 edn WALLSCOURT, B), and *d* 12 March 1755, having had, with other issue:

1 DOMINICK

2 Henry; *b* 1700; *m* 1748 Mary (*d* Jan 1790), dau of Robert Nugent, of Crossfield, and sis of 1st Earl Nugent (see WESTMEATH, E), and *d* June 1790, leaving, with other issue:

(1) Mary; *m* General Count (of the Holy Roman Empire) O'Donnell

GEOFFREY BROWNE's er s,

DOMINICK BROWNE, of Castle Macgarrett; Col; *m* 1st Elizabeth, dau of Oliver Martyn, of Tulira Castle, Ardrahan, Co Galway (see HEMPHILL, B), and *d* Jan 1776, having had:

1 Margaret; *m* Charles Lambert, of Cregclare, and had issue

2 Alice; *m* Jacob Browne, of Browne Hall, Co Mayo, and had issue

DOMINICK BROWNE *m* 2nd 1754 Henrietta (*d* 1755), dau of Sir Henry Lynch, 5th Bt, of Castlecarra (see LYNCH-BLOSSE, Bt), and by her had:

1 Dominick Geoffrey; *b* 1755; Govr Co Mayo; *m* 20 Aug 1784 Margaret (*d* 29 May 1838), dau and heiress of Hon George Browne (see SLIGO, M), and *d* 8 May 1826, having had, with other issue:

(1) DOMINICK

(2) John Geoffrey (Rev); *b* 1797; Rector Kiddington, Oxford; *m* 1st 1823 Anne (*d* 1855), dau of Thomas Lindsay, of Hollymount, Co Mayo, and had issue; *m* 2nd 1857 Emma, dau of Rev J Hill, Rector Lyme Regis, and widow of Rev G T Spring, incumbent of Hampton Gay, Oxford, and *d* 1877, having by her had:

1a Henrietta; *b* 25 March 1789; *m* 9 Feb 1807 13th Viscount Dillon (*qv*) and *d* 18 March 1862

2a Charlotte Philippa; *m* 21 April 1818 Sir William ffolkes, 2nd Bt (*qv*), and *d* 23 Dec 1882

DOMINICK GEOFFREY BROWNE's est s,

DOMINICK BROWNE, **1st Baron Oranmore and Browne of Carrabrowne Castle** in the county of the town of Galway **and of Castle MacGarrett** in the Co of Mayo (I), so *cr* 4 May 1836, PC (I 7Nov 1834); *b* 28 May 1787; *educ* Eton and St John's Coll Cambridge; MP (Whig) Co Mayo 1814–26 and 1830–36, Ld Lt Co Mayo 1834–42; rebuilt Castle Macgarrett in Tudor Revival style; *m* 5 May 1811 Catherine Anne Isabella (*d* 22 July 1865), est dau and coheir of Henry Monck (see MONCK, V), and *d* 30 Jan 1860, having had:

1 GEOFFREY DOMINICK AUGUSTUS FREDERICK, **2nd Baron**

2 Henry George Monck; *b* 1824; *d* 21 Nov 1843

1 Henrietta Araminta Monck; *m* 17 April 1845 Maj-Gen Charles William Ridley, CB, and *d* 1 March 1869, leaving issue (see RIDLEY, V)

2 Margaret Elizabeth Catharine Augusta; *d* 29 July 1842

The 1st BARON's only surv s,

GEOFFREY DOMINICK AUGUSTUS FREDERICK BROWNE later GUTHRIE (following marriage), **2nd Baron Oranmore and Browne of Carrabrowne Castle and of Castle MacGarrett**, JP (Ayrshire and Co Mayo); *b* 8 June 1819; *educ* Harrow and Trin Coll Cambridge; High Sheriff Co Mayo 1841, rep I peer (C) 1869–1900; *m* 31 Dec 1859 Christina (*d* 1 May 1887), only surv child and heiress of Alexander Guthrie, of The Mount and of Bourtree Hill, Ayrshire, and *d* 15 Nov 1900, having had:

1 GEOFFREY HENRY, **3rd Baron**

1 Mary Christina; *m* 25 Feb 1890 Charles Louis Maurice des Graz, JP, DL (*d* 4 March 1935), er s of César Louis François des Graz, of Toulon, France, and *d* 26 Dec 1948, leaving issue

2 Kathleen Harriett; *d* 6 July 1881

The 2nd BARON's only s,

GEOFFREY HENRY GUTHRIE later BROWNE (resumed 1906), **3rd Baron Oranmore and Browne of Carrabrowne Castle and of Castle MacGarrett** and **1st BARON MEREWORTH**, of Mereworth Castle, Co Kent (UK), so *cr* 19 Jan 1926, KP (1918), PC (I, 1921), JP (Ayrshire and Co Mayo), DL (Co Mayo); *b* 6 Jan 1861; *educ* Trin Coll Cambridge (BA 1883, MA 1886); Lt 4th Bn Roy Scots Fus, High Sheriff Co Mayo 1890, rep I peer (C) 1902–27, KJStJ, memb Irish Convention 1917–18, Commr Congested Districts Bd Ireland 1919, Irish Free State Senator 1921, Grand Offr Order Crown Romania; *m* 2 Jan 1901 Lady Olwen Verena Ponsonby, LGStJ (*k* car crash 7 June 1927), est dau of 8th Earl of Bessborough (*qv*), and *d* 30 June 1927, having had:

1 GEOFFREY EDWARD BROWNE, **4th and present Baron Oranmore and Browne of Carrabrowne Castle and of Castle MacGarrett**

2 Geoffrey Charles Myles; *b* 16 Oct 1912; *educ* Eton, Corpus Christi Coll Cambridge and Trin Coll Dublin; *m* 3 June 1946 (*divorce* 1958) Kathleen Mary, dau of Arland Ussher, of Loughrea, Co Galway, and widow of Capt Joseph Fitzgerald, MC, and *d* 198–

1 Kathleen Marcia; *b* 17 Jan 1903; *m* 24 June 1926 Cotterell Boughton Mordaunt-Smith (*d* 1956), formerly Lt Welsh Gds and Warwicks Yeo, yst s of Mordaunt Kirwan Mordaunt-Smith (see SMITH-GORDON, Bt), and *d* 199–, leaving:

(1) *Michael Cotterell Geoffrey David [Michael Mordaunt-Smith Esq, Wixoe Mill House, Wixoe, Halstead, Essex]; *b* 1927; *educ* Lancing; Lt The Black Watch M East 1945–47 (War Medal and Palestine Stars); *m* 1st 1959 (*divorce* 1971) Diana Katherine, dau of Joseph John Edward Potter, of Cheshunt Great House, Cheshunt, Herts, and has:

1a *Michael Joseph Cotterell Nicholas; *b* 1962

2a *Damian Kirwan Seton Towers; *b* 1968

(1) (cont.) Michael Mordaunt-Smith *m* 2nd 1972 *Alexandra Sarah, dau of Arthur Hugh Alexander Cardew, of Copthorne, Sussex

(1) *Olwen Marcia Blanche [Mrs Hugh Janson, Barn House, Aldbourne, Marlborough, Wilts SN8 2DA]; *b* 1928; *m* 1952 Wayne Ewing Harriss (*d* 1958); *m* 2nd 1960 *Hugh Dearman Janson

2 Christine Louise Beatrix; *b* 7 March 1909; *d* 15 Feb 1910

ORKNEY

Arms: Not matriculated at time of going to press.
Creations: E., V. and B. (S) 3 Jan 1696

THE 9TH EARL OF ORKNEY, Viscount Kirkwall and **Baron Dechmont**, Co Linlithgow (Oliver Peter St John) [The Rt Hon The Earl of Orkney, House of Lords, London SW1A 0PW]; *b* 27 Feb 1938; *s* 3rd cousin 1998; *educ* Woodbridge Sch, U of Br Columbia (BA 1960), LSE (MSc 1963) and London U (PhD 1972); lecturer UCL 1963–64 and U of Manitoba 1964–66, Assist Prof 1966–72, Visiting Prof Carleton U 1981–82, Assoc Prof Political Sci U of Manitoba 1972–, memb RIIA 1962–, Canadian Inst Internat Affrs 1964– (Pres Winnipeg Branch 1971–73), author; *m* 1st 1963 (*divorce* 1985) Mary Juliet, dau of W G Scott Brown, CVO, MD, FRCS, FRCSE, and has had:

1 +OLIVER ROBERT; *b* 19 July 1969

1 *Juliet Elizabeth; *b* 24 Sept 1964

2 *Nicola Jane; *b* 7 March 1966

3 *Lucy Margaret; *b* 1972

The 9TH EARL *m* 2nd 1985 *Mrs Mary Barbara Huck, dau of Dr David B Albertson, of Victoria, BC, and adopted his steps:

*Anthony Cameron ST JOHN; *b* 1969

Orkney, previous creations: For the early history of the Earls of Orkney see CAITHNESS, E. For the Dukedom of Orkney see BUCHAN-HEPBURN, Bt.

In 1581 an illegitimate son of JAMES V by a daughter of the 1st Lord Elphinstone (*qv*) was created Earl of Orkney. Although an early member of the Protestant party in Scotland he had not been wholly hostile to MARY QUEEN OF SCOTS, indeed had been one of her table-companions at dinner the night of Rizzio's murder. He seems in fact to have made friendly gestures to just about every power interested in Scottish affairs, not excluding the English, French and Spanish, let alone factions among Scots. His son, the 2nd and last Earl of this creation, was deprived of his Earldom in 1612 (some two and a half years before his execution for high treason), apparently on account of his tyrannical behaviour towards the Orkney and Shetland islanders. His titles were forfeited at his death in any case.

Lineage: WILLIAM DOUGLAS later DOUGLAS-HAMILTON, DUKE OF HAMILTON (LP); *m* ANNE Hamilton, DUCHESS OF HAMILTON in her own right (see HAMILTON and BRANDON, D), and had a 5th s:

GEORGE HAMILTON, **1st Earl of Orkney**, so *cr* 3 Jan 1696, as also BARON DECHMONT and VISCOUNT KIRKWALL (all S), with eventual remainder to heirs general of his body, KT (1704), PC (March 1710/1–14); *bapt* 9 Feb 1666; Capt 1st (Roy) Scots 1684, having first been commissioned in that rank in his uncle Lord George Hamilton's regt aged five, Col Enniskillen Foot March 1689/90, 7th Foot (Roy Fus) Jan–Aug 1692 and Roy Scots 1692–1737, Brig-Gen 1695, Brig all forces Ireland Sept 1700, Gen Jan 1710/1, FM Jan 1735/6, seeing action at Battles of Boyne 1690, Aughrim 1691, Namur and Steenkirk 1692, Landen 1693 and all four of Marlborough's (*qv*) principal battles, also Sieges of Athlone, Limerick 1691 and Namur 1695; rep S peer 1708–37, Govr Edinburgh Castle 1714–37, Govr Virginia 1714–37, a Ld Bedchamber 1716–27, Lt-Govr Berwick 1733, Ld Lt Lanarks; *m* 25 Nov 1695 Elizabeth (*d* 19 April 1733), a former mistress of WILLIAM III (who after his w's death broke with her but made over to her all JAMES II's Irish estates) and sis of 1st Earl of Jersey (*qv*), and *dspm* 29 Jan 1736/7, having had, with two yr daus (Frances, *m* 27 June 1724 3rd Earl of Scarbrough (*qv*) and *d* 27 Oct 1772, leaving issue; Henrietta, *m* 9 May 1728, as his 1st w, 5th Earl of Cork and Orrery (*qv*) and had issue):

ANNE Hamilton, **Countess of Orkney** in her own right; *m* 29 March 1720 her cousin 9th Baron of Inchiquin (*qv*) and *dspms* 6 Dec 1756, having had, with other issue, including four sons (*d* in infancy):

MARY O'Brien, **Countess of Orkney** in her own right; *b c* 1721; *m* 5 March 1753, as his 1st w, her 1st cousin 10th Baron of Inchiquin (*qv*) and *d* 10 May 1791, leaving:

MARY O'Brien, **Countess of Orkney** in her own right; *b* 4 Sept 1755; *m* 21 Dec 1777 Hon Thomas FitzMAURICE, bro of 1st Marquess of Lansdowne (*qv*), and *d* 30 Dec 1831, having had:

1 John Hamilton, *Viscount Kirkwall*; *b* 9 Oct 1778; *educ* Eton and Corpus Christi Coll Oxford; MP (Tory) Heytesbury 1802–06 and Denbigh Borough 1812–18, FRS 1804; *m* 18 Aug 1802 Hon Anna Maria Blaquiere (*d* 31 Jan 1843), est dau of 1st Baron de Blaquiere of Ardkill (see 1917 edn), and *dvp* 23 Nov 1820, leaving:

(1) THOMAS JOHN HAMILTON, **5th Earl**

(2) William Edward; *b* 21 March 1805; Maj 2nd Life Gds and Denbighs Yeo Cav; MP Bucks 1842–47; *m* 1st 3 Aug 1837 Hester (*d* 24 Aug 1859), dau of Henry Harford, of Down Place, Berks, and had, with other issue:

1a Cecil Henry; *b* 25 Aug 1844; RN; *m* 1870 Elizabeth Maria (*d* 18 April 1902), dau of John Hatton, and *d* 22 April 1917, leaving:

1b Cecil Edward Arthur; *b* 27 July 1871; *m* 11 Sept 1900 Maud Elizabeth Mary (*d* 1970), dau of Thomas George Waller, of Chiswick, and *d* 26 Oct 1964, leaving:

1c Cecil George; *b* 6 Oct 1901; *educ* Bradfield

1c Mildred Lillian; *b* 10 Nov 1902; *m* 8 Feb 1938 Capt John Major Leslie Bostock, 11th King Edward's Own Lancers (Probyn's Horse) (*d* 13 March 1959), s of John Major Leslie Bostock, of Derbys, and had:

1d +Christopher John [Christopher Bostock Esq, 12 Granton Rd, Edinburgh EH5 3QH]; *b* 29 May 1942; *educ* Tonbridge and Edinburgh U (BSc); *m* 6 April 1963 *Yvonne Pauline, dau of William James Kendrick, of Preston, Lancs, and has:

1e +Jason Guy; *b* 1 May 1969

1e +Joanna Clare; b 8 Nov 1963

2e +Camilla Jane; b 26 June 1967

1d +Josephine Mary [Mrs Geoffrey Stonehouse, 7 Parkside Close, E Horsley, Surrey]; b 7 Jan 1939; m 3 Oct 1964 *Geoffrey Francis Stonehouse, s of Geoffrey Francis Stonehouse, of Rishton, Lancs, and has:

1e +Nicholas John; b 2 Nov 1965

1e +Rachel Ann; b 1 March 1967

2e +Stephanie Jane; b 29 Aug 1969

3e +Sarah; b 1972

1c Mildred Esther; d unm 4 Aug 1894

(2) (cont.) Maj The Hon William FitzMaurice m 2nd 3 Oct 1870 Anne Louisa, est dau of John Hatton, of Deal, Kent, and d 18 June 1889

The COUNTESS's gs,

THOMAS JOHN HAMILTON FitzMAURICE, **5th Earl of Orkney**; b 8 Aug 1803; rep S peer 1833–74; m 14 March 1826 Hon Charlotte Isabella Irby (d 7 Sept 1883), dau of 3rd Baron Boston (qv), and d 16 May 1877, having had:

1 GEORGE WILLIAM HAMILTON FitzMAURICE, **6th Earl of Orkney**, KCMG (1875, CMG 1866); b 6 May 1827; joined 92nd Highrs 1845, ADC to Commr Ionian Islands 1851–54, Capt 71st Foot Siege Sebastopol, capture Kertch and Yenikale, Crimean War; Capt Scots Fus Gds 1856–57; rep S peer 1885–89; Grand Cdr Order Redeemer Greece, Kt Medjidie, author (as Viscount Kirkwall): Four Years in the Ionian Islands (1864); m 28 Nov 1872 Amelia (d 11 Nov 1890), widow of Baron de Samuel, Peer of Portugal, and dsp 21 Oct 1889

2 Henry Warrender, of Tregof, Anglesey, DL; b 7 July 1828; High Sheriff Anglesey 1866, Capt 72nd Regt; m 5 Sept 1861 Sarah Jane (d 13 Feb 1880), only child of George Bradley Roose, of Bryntirion, Anglesey, and d 12 Jan 1875, leaving:

(l) Henry George Hamilton; b 6 Sept 1863; Lt 3rd Bn Oxon LI; d unm 27 Jan 1888

(2) EDMOND WALTER FitzMAURICE, **7th Earl of Orkney**, JP, DL (Bucks); b 24 May 1867; educ Cheltenham; Lt-Col 3rd Bn Oxon LI 1898–1903, and WW I; Chm Stewkley DC 1921, MFH Whaddon Chase 1920–23; m 19 July 1892 Constance Macdonald (d 9 May 1946), dau of David Gilchrist, and d 21 Aug 1951, leaving:

1a Mary Constance Hamilton; b 26 Feb 1903; m 29 Oct 1927 Edward Lambert Gosling (d 9 Jan 1960), 3rd s of Francis Gosling, of Welbury, Herts, and dsp 6 Oct 1950

(3) Alexander Edward; b 21 March 1874; granted with sis rank of earl's dau/yr s 23 April 1890; d 26 Aug 1922

(1) Isabella Emily; m 22 Sept 1888 John Burnham Garrett, yst s of W B Garrett, of Wallington, and d 8 April 1928

3 Frederick O'Brien; b 23 April 1830; Cdr RN; m 19 April 1853 Mary Anne Taylor (m 2nd 27 April 1869 Lt-Col Archibal Macintosh and d 26 Jan 1924), est dau of Robert Taylor Spooner Abraham, of Crewkerne, Somerset, and d 26 Oct 1867, leaving:

(l) Frederick John Mangles; b 21 July 1855; d 21 Feb 1869

(2) Douglas Commerell Menzies; b 7 Dec 1861; Lt York and Lancaster Regt, T/Maj Lancs Fus; m 7 Sept 1899 Esther (d 23 May 1933), dau of W G Davis, of Streatley, Berks, and d 13 Jan 1932, having had:

1a Douglas Frederick Harold; b 26 Aug 1890; Capt RNAS; m 17 Feb 1916 Dorothy Jeanette (m 2nd 27 Sept 1939 Cdr Eric Templer Wiggins, DSC, RN), dau of Capt Robert Dickie, RN, and d 29 May 1937, leaving:

1b Douglas Hubert Hamilton; b 29 May 1916; Lt KRRC, WW II; ka 27 Nov 1942

2b CECIL O'BRYEN FitzMAURICE, **8th Earl of Orkney**; b 3 July 1919; RASC 1939, WW II and Korea; m 27 Nov 1953 Rose Katherine Durke (d 27 July 1995), yr dau of Joseph William Durke Silley, of Brixham, Devon, and dsp 5 Feb 1998

2a Archibald Hamilton; b 27 June 1894; Lt RAF, formerly 16th Lancers; ka 12 March 1918

3a Cecil Hamilton Kirkwell; b 24 May 1896; das 1916

(3) Llewellyn Abraham; b 16 Sept 1867; served AIF; m 1890 Alice Ada (d 1947), dau of Robert Gay, of Northumberland, and d 1953, having had:

1a Frederick Maurice; b 1890; d young

2a Llewellyn O'Bryen; b 1892; Capt NZ Forces, WW I

(1) Amicie Mary Hamilton; d unm 1953

4 Alexander Temple; b 23 Jan 1834; Groom Bedchamber to HM EDWARD VII when PRINCE OF WALES; Lt 72nd Regt Crimea and India; m 26 April 1873 Adela Mary (d 2 March 1915), dau of Simon Thomas Scrope, of Danby, Yorks, and widow of Edward Riddell, of Cheesburn Grange, and dsp 19 June 1894

5 (James) Terence, JP Berks; b 26 Feb 1835; Capt RN, Inspr-Gen Prisons Ceylon 1867–71; m 1st 21 March 1861 Frances Rhoda (d 2 June 1907), only dau of Sir William Gore Ouseley, KCB, DCL, and had:

(1) James Campbell Gore Ouseley; b 13 Sept 1866; Lt 74th Highrs, Lt-Col 4th Cameron Highrs, V-Consul Bruges 1905–09; m 1st 13 June 1894 (divorce 1905) Gertrude, only dau of Samuel Bury, of Timperley Hall, Cheshire; m 2nd 25 July 1906 Sibyl Henrietta, CStJ (d 9 May 1949), est dau of Sir Charles Harvey, 2nd Bt (see HARVEY of TASBURGH, B), and dsp 13 April 1934

(l) Harriett Marcia Jane; m 17 June 1890 Hamilton Richard Boyle (see CORK and ORRERY, E) and d 8 Jan 1933

(2) Isabella Annie; m 18 April 1882 Sir Frederic Robert St John, KCMG (d 27 Feb 1923), and d 29 Feb 1948, leaving, with other issue (see BOLINGBROKE and SAINT JOHN, V):

1a (Frederick) Oliver, DSO, MC; had by his 2nd w:

1b OLIVER PETER ST JOHN, **9th and present Earl of Orkney**

(3) Aimée Edith Emily; m 19 June 1889 Maj Gen David George Levinge Shaw (d 26 Jan 1930), 1st Punjab Cav, est son of Maj-Gen David Shaw, MSC, and d 13 April 1890

(4) Mabel Madeline Rhoda; m 1911 Capt Arthur Fletcher, Roy Sussex Regt, and d 25 Sept 1934

5 (cont.) Capt Hon Terence Fitz-Maurice m 2nd 28 Sept 1911 Eleanor (d 5 July 1913), 3rd dau of Capt Septimus H Palairet, 29th Regt, and widow of Henry Hodges, of Bolney Court, Henley on Thames, and d 8 April 1917

l Isabella Emma Elizaeth; m 1st 11 Oct 1858 Samuel Leo Schuster (d 1884), of Leatherhead, Surrey, s of Leo Schuster, of Roehampton, Surrey and had issue; m 2nd 11 Jan 1886 Lt Gen Hon Hussey Fane Keane, CB (see KEANE, Bt), and d 4 Aug 1906

2 Emily Charlotte; d unm 13 Jan 1910

3 Maria Louisa; m 16 Aug 1859 Edmund Robert Spearman, CMG (d 6 Oct 1918), 2nd s of Sir Alexander Young Spearman, 1st Bt (qv), and d 6 Oct 1917, leaving issue

ORME

Creation: B. (LP, UK) 1997.

THE BARON ORME, of Salford, Greater Manchester (Stan(ley) Orme, PC (1974)) [The Rt Hon The Lord Orme PC, House of Lords, London SW1A 0PW]; b 5 April 1923; educ Nat Cncl Labour Colls and WEA; W/O and Navigator RAF Bomber Command 1942–47; memb Sale Borough Cncl 1958–65; MP (Lab) Salford W 1964–83, Salford E 1983–97, Min State: NI 1974–76, DHSS 1976–77, Min Social Security 1977–79, Oppn Spokesman: Health and Social Services 1979–80, Industry 1980–83, Energy 1983–87, Chm PLP 1987–1992; Hon DSc Salford 1985; m 1951 *Irene Mary, dau of Vernon Fletcher Harris, of Worsley, Lancs

Lineage: SHERWOOD ORME, of Sale, Cheshire; had:

STAN(LEY), cr a **Baron**

ORR-EWING, Baron

Arms: Arg. on a chevron, ensigned with a banner between in chief two mullets and in base a representation of the path of two electrons rotating round a nucleus gu., a pair of wings conjoined in lure between two lymphads, sails furled, pennons and flags flying or.
Crest: A demi-lion rampant gu., holding in the dexter paw a mullet az. and resting the sinister paw on a portcullis chained or.
Motto: Audaciter ('Boldly'). **Creation:** Bt. (UK) 27 June 1963, B. (LP, UK) 1971.

THE BARON ORR-EWING, of Little Berkhamsted, Co Hertford, and a **Baronet** (Sir (Charles) Ian Orr-Ewing, Bt, OBE (1945)) [The Rt Hon The Lord Orr-Ewing OBE, House of Lords, London SW1A 0PW]; b 10 Feb 1912; educ Harrow and Trin Coll Oxford (BA 1933, MA 1951), MIEE, MP (C) N Hendon 1950–70, PPS to Min Labour 1951–55, Parly U-Sec Air 1957–59, Parly and Fin Sec Admlty 1959, Civil Ld Admlty 1959–63, V-Chm 1922 Ctee 1966–70, V-Pres Parly and Scientific Ctee 1966, V-Chm (C) Def Ctee 1966–70, late W/Cdr RAFVR, CEng, served WW II N Africa, Italy and NW Europe (despatches), Ch Radar Offr Gen Eisenhower's Staff 1945, with BBC TV 1937–39 and 1946–49; m 2 Sept 1939 *Joan Helen Veronica, only dau of Gordon McMinnies, of Talbot Hotel, Stow-in-the-Wold, Glos, and has:

1 +(ALISTAIR) SIMON [The Hon Simon Orr-Ewing, 29 St James's Gardens, London W11]; b 10 June 1940; heir presumptive to btcy only; educ Harrow, Grenoble U and Trin Coll Oxford (BA 1963); FRICS; m 8 Feb 1968 *Victoria, er dau of Keith Cameron, of Fifield House, Milton-under-Wychwood, Oxon, and has:

(1) +Archie Cameron; b 29 March 1969; educ Harrow

(2) +James Alexander; b 17 Oct 1971; m 10 Jan 1998 *Polly, er dau of Giles Christian Gleadell, of Clapham, and has:

1a *Alma Gillian; b 4 May 1998

(1) *Georgina Victoria; b 1974

2 +(Ian) Colin [The Hon Colin Orr-Ewing, The Old Bakehouse, Shalbourne, Berks SN8 3QD]; b 8 Feb 1942; educ Harrow and Trin Coll Oxford (BA 1964); m 1st 1973 (divorce 1980) Deirdre (Dee) Janet, est dau of Lance K Japhet, of Sandhurst, Johannesburg, and has issue:

(1) +Francis Ian Lance; b 11 June 1975; educ Oxford

(1) *Bridget Joanna; b 19 Jan 1977

(2) (cont.) The Hon Colin Orr-Ewing *m* 2nd 1986 *Fleur, yr dau of Dr Gavin Knight, of Blackwood, Gwent, and by her has:

(2) *Cordelia; *b* 1988

(3) *Daisy Caroline; *b* 1990

3 +Malcolm Archie [The Hon Malcolm Orr-Ewing, The Priory, Syresham, nr Brackley, Northants]; *b* 25 July 1946; *educ* Harrow and Munich U; *m* 1973 *Clare Mary, dau of Brig George Robert Flood, MC, of Cheverell Mill, Little Cheverell, Wilts, and has:

(1) +Edward Archie; *b* 1990

(1) *Harriet Kate; *b* 1975

(2) *Charlotte Rose; *b* 1978

4 +Robert James [The Hon Robert Orr-Ewing, 70 Warwick Gardens, London W14]; *b* 7 Dec 1953; *educ* Harrow; barrister Inner Temple 1976; *m* 16 Oct 1982 *Susannah, dau of Mark Bodley Scott, of Uppfield, Sonning-on-Thames, Berks, and has:

(1) +William Robert; *b* 1985

(2) +Jack Alexander Bodley; *b* 1987

(1) *Alice Josephine; *b* 1989

(2) *Lucy Katharine McMinnies

Lineage: See ORR EWING, Bt

ORR EWING, Bt

Arms: Arg. a chevron gu. ensigned with a banner of the second charged with a canton az., thereon a saltire of the first, all between two mullets in chief and the sun in splendour in base of the second, a bordure indented, also of the second, charged with three martlets of the first. **Crest:** A demi-lion rampant gu. armed and langued az., holding in his dexter paw a mullet also gu. **Motto:** *Audaciter* ('Boldly'). **Creation:** Bt. (UK) 8 March 1886.

SIR RONALD ARCHIBALD ORR EWING, 5TH BT, of Ballikinrain, Co Stirling, JP (Perthshire 1957), DL (1963) [Maj Sir Ronald Orr Ewing Bt JP DL, Cardross, Port of Menteith, Kippen, Stirling FK8 3JY]; *b* 14 May 1912; *s f* 1960; *educ* Eton and RMC Sandhurst, Maj Scots Gds 1932–53, served WW II (POW 1942), memb Roy Co Archers, Grand Master Mason Scotland 1965–69, chm Clayton Dewandre Hldgs 1975–; *m* 6 April 1938 Marion Hester (*d* 31 May 1997), yr dau of Col Sir Donald Walter Cameron of Lochiel, KT, CMG, JP, 25th Chief of Clan Cameron (*see* MONTROSE, D), and has:

1 +ARCHIBALD DONALD [Archibald Orr Ewing Esq, 13 Warriston Crescent, Edinburgh EH3 5LA]; *b* 20 Dec 1938; *educ* Gordonstoun and Trin Coll Dublin (BA); memb Roy Co Archers; *m* 1st 10 Dec 1965 (*divorce* 1972) Venetia Elizabeth, yr dau of Maj Richard Turner, of Co Dublin; *m* 2nd 1972 *Nicola Jean-Anne, only child of Reginald Baron Black (*see* ROXBURGHE, D), and by her has:

(1) +Alastair Frederick Archibald; *b* 26 May 1982

2 +(Ronald) James; *b* 9 Jan 1948; *educ* Gordonstoun and Dundee U (LLB St Andrews 1969)

1 *Janet Elisabeth [Mrs John Wallace, The Furnace, Ashburnham, Sussex]; *b* 9 Nov 1940; *m* 28 March 1969 *John Malcolm Wallace, s of Dr Herbert Kelvin Wallace, of Sussex, and has:

(1) *Jasper Simon; *b* 28 Dec 1973

(2) *Jocelyn James; *b* 1977

(1) *Jemma Louise; *b* 19 Oct 1971

2 *Fiona Marion [Mrs Adrian Drewe, Parsonage Farm House, Ticehurst, E Sussex TN5 7DL]; *b* 3 March 1946; *m* 18 May 1968 *Adrian Peter Drewe, only s of Adrian Francis Drewe, of Ticehurst, and has:

(1) *Jonathan James; *b* 25 June 1971

(2) *Nicholas Robert Patrick; *b* 1982

(3) *Anthony Adrian; *b* 1985

Lineage: ALEXANDER EWING, of Balloch; *b c* 1630; had:

ALEXANDER EWING, of Balloch; *b c* 1660; *m* 1690 Isobel, dau of Donald Ewing of Bernice by Beatrix Campbell of Dunstaffnage, and had:

ALEXANDER EWING; *b c* 1692; *m* 6 June 1719 Jean Allan and had, with an er s (Alexander of Balloch, *b* 29 June 1722, *m* 20 Jan 1758 Janet, dau of John Ewing of Nobleston by Janet Mckinley, and had issue):

ROBERT EWING; *b* 20 May 1724; inherited from his f the lands of Ledrish and Ledrishbeg, parts of the estate of Balloch; *m* 1 Feb 1752 Isobel Buchanan, of the Cameron, and *d* 6 May 1794, leaving a 5th s:

WILLIAM EWING, of Ardvullen, near Dunoon, Argyll; *b* 10 Feb 1772; *m* 7 April 1805 Susan (*d* 29 May 1860), dau of John Orr, Provost Paisley, by Agnes, dau of John Anderson, of Douhill, Glasgow, and had, with three other sons and three daus:

1 William, of Ardvullen; *m* 22 Aug 1867 Edith (*d* 3 Jan 1869), dau of Sir William Jackson, 1st Bt (*see* MATHER-JACKSON, Bt), and *dsp*

2 ARCHIBALD (Sir), **1st Bt**

3 James; *m* 1st a dau of George Robertson, of London, and had:

(1) John; *b* 1854; *m* 1st 1879 Caroline Dora (*d* 1880), dau of — Rogers, and had:

1a Helen Caroline Dora; *b* 1880; *m* Andrew Paterson

(1) (cont.) John Ewing *m* 2nd 1887 Edith Alice (*d* 1941), dau of J Fountain, and by her had:

1a Hugh James, MC; *b* 1891; MD, FRCP; served WW I; *m* 1916 Muriel Isabel (*d* 9 March 1982 aged 89), dau of E E Shaw, and had:

1b *John Eric Hugh, MBE (1962), MC; *b* 1920; *educ* Cambridge (MA); Capt Argyll and Sutherland Highrs WW II, Overseas CS, ret 1966, Registrar Wye Coll Kent; *m* 30 Dec 1950 *Kathleen Rachel, dau of F Cheshire, and has:

1c *Isabel Margaret; *b* 3 May 1954

2c *Alison Kathleen; *b* 22 July 1955

1b *Beatrice Muriel; *b* 2 March 1918; *educ* Bristol U (BA); *m* 28 Aug 1947 *(Kenneth) Rex Hayward, s of Henry Hayward, and has:

1c *Christopher John; *b* 8 Oct 1949

2c *Hugh Graham; *b* 19 Oct 1950

1c *Sheila Rosalind; *b* 23 Sept 1956

2b *Rosemary Joan; *b* 1922

3b *Mary Douglas; *b* 1926; *m* 28 Aug 1956 *Richard David Spear, JP, yr s of George Frederick Spear, and has:

1c *Peter Richard John; *b* 18 Aug 1957

2c *Andrew James Michael; *b* 28 Jan 1960

3c *David Alan Hugh; *b* 11 March 1962

1c *Rosemary Margaret; *b* 22 Dec 1964

2a Edith Wilhelmina (Ina); *b* 1889; *d* unm June 1974

3a Greta; *b* 1892; *m* 1923 Surgn Lt-Cdr O J Michael Kerrigan, RN, s of Dr Kerrigan, of Westmeath, and had two sons and two daus. He *d* Sept 1955

4a Evelyn Margaret; *b* 1893; *m* 1st 1917 William Marshall, RCAF (*ka* 1917), and had a dau; *m* 2nd 1933 W Harvey Williams and *d* 22 Jan 1968

5a Alice; *b* 1895; *m* 1921 Gerald Smith (*d* 1933)

6a Helen Douglas; *b* 1897

(2) Archibald; *b* 1857; *m* 1st 1890 Mary Elizabeth (*d* 1894), dau of Robert Scott, and had:

1a Archibald; *b* 1892; *educ* Pembroke Coll Cambridge (MA) and Bart's Hosp (MB); Surgn-Lt RN WW I; *m* 1919 Gladys (*d* 1965), dau of A Ross, and *d* 14 Feb 1972, leaving:

1b Douglas Archibald; *b* 1920; Capt Argyll and Sutherland Highrs WW II (wounded, POW); *m* 1946 *Nancy C, dau of J M Pringle, and *d* 1996, leaving:

1c *Carolyn Mary; *b* 1947; *m* 1970 Christopher Donald Crabbie (*d* 1992) and has:

1d *Paul Christian; *b* 14 June 1977

2d *Mark William James; *b* 20 Jan 1981

2c *Susan Mary [Mrs Andrew Hamilton, 16 Lyneaoch Place, Edinburgh EH3 7PV]; *b* 23 Aug 1951; *m* 18 Sept 1971 *Andrew Nigel Hamilton, er s of Maj Peter James Sidney Hamilton, MBE, by Alethea Penelope, er dau of Lt-Col Vivian Home Seymer, DSO, MC (*see* THOMSON, Bt, of Old Nunthorpe), and has:

1d *Archie James; *b* 7 Oct 1975

1d *Antonia; *b* 10 Aug 1978

2b *Robin John Alexander [Robin Orr Ewing Esq, 50 Abingdon Court, London W8]; *b* 1921; *educ* Pembroke Coll Cambridge; Capt Argyll and Sutherland Highrs WW II; *m* 1951 *Beryl Maureen, dau of James Bowyer, of IoW, and has:

1c *Archibald Jonathan Bowyer; *b* 19 Sept 1951

2c *Christian James Bowyer; *b* 26 Oct 1954

1c *Alexandra Mary; *b* 25 Feb 1959

1a Helen; *b* 1891; *m* 1915 Hugh F Maclachlan and had issue

2a Mary Alice; *b* 15 Jan 1894; BA Lond; *d* 12 Dec 1950

(2) (cont.) Archibald Orr Ewing *m* 2nd 1897 Alice Kate, dau of Thomas Fox Ferriman, and *d* 1930, having by her had:

2a *James Arthur; *b* 14 March 1903; *educ* Monkton Combe Sch and Pembroke Coll Cambridge; F/Lt RAFVR WW II; *m* 18 June 1932 *Patricia Edna, dau of Daniel J Bell, and has:

1b *Ian Michael; *b* 1935; *educ* King's Sch Canterbury and Pembroke Coll Cambridge (BA); dir Tryst Mouldings & Seals; *m* 15 Sept 1962 *Catherine Margaret, er dau of Sir George Honeyman, CBE, QC, JP, and has:

1c *Duncan Charles; *b* 19 Jan 1964

2c *Andrew John; *b* 22 Dec 1965

1c *Rachel Helen; *b* 5 June 1968

3a Catherine; *b* 1900; MB, BS Lond

(3) Hugh Moody Robertson; *b* 1859; *m* 1883 Helen Margaret (*m* 2nd 1892 Capt William McFarlan, Black Watch; *d* 1912), dau of Archibald Robertson, and *d* 1889, leaving:

1a John, MC; *b* 1884; Maj 16th Lancers WW I (despatches), Assist Ch Constable War Dept Constabulary 1940–47; *m* 23 Nov 1908 Gwendolen Edith (*d* 20 July 1964), dau of Col Charles Herbert Curtis (see CURTIS, Bt), and *d* 8 Jan 1961, leaving:

  1b *(John) Anthony ; *b* 12 March 1914; Capt 16th/5th Lancers WW II (wounded, despatches); *m* 21 Sept 1949 *Audrey Doreen, only child of Lt-Col Charles Edward Tyson, MC, RA, of Rudd Hall, Catterick, Yorks, and has:

    1c *Charles Richard; *b* 20 July 1951

2a Hugh Eric Douglas; *b* 1888; Capt Black Watch WW I; *m* 1st 1912 (*divorce* 1919) Janet, dau of John McKinnon; *m* 2nd 1922 (*divorce* 1943) Esmé Victoria (*d* 5 Dec 1967), dau of Hinton Daniell Stewart (see STEWART, Bt, of Strathgarry), and had:

  1b *(John) Hamish [Hamish Orr Ewing Esq, Fox Mill Farm, Purton, Wilts SN5 9EF]; *b* 17 Aug 1924; late Capt Black Watch, dir Tricentrol plc 1975–86, chm Rank Xerox 1980–86, Pres Inst Manpower Studies 1986–89; *m* 1st 24 Jan 1948 (*divorce* 1954) Morar Margaret, dau of Capt Edward Coverley Kennedy, DSO, RN (see AILSA, M); *m* 2nd 1954 *Ann Mary Teresa, dau of Frederick Terry, of Bexhill, and by his 1st w has had:

    1c *Roderick Coverley Hugh; *b* 15 Nov 1951; *m* 28 April 1984 *Claire, only dau of Torolf Lyth

    1c *Margaret; *b* 27 Dec 1950; *d* 14 April 1961

2a (cont.) Hugh Orr Ewing *m* 3rd 7 April 1948 *Muriel Emma Lucy [Mrs Hugh Orr Ewing, The Grove, Seal, Sevenoaks, Kent], dau of Percy Allen Huntercombe Muschamp, and *d* 18 July 1964

1a Christian Leckie; *b* 1885; *m* 1st 12 July 1905 Maj Eustace Lockhart Maxwell (*ka* 1916), 11th Bengal Lancers, and had issue; *m* 2nd 1918 Capt Arthur Nigel Cahusac, MC, S Wales Borderers

3 (cont.) James Ewing *m* 2nd — Hart and by her had:

  (4) Malcolm Hart; *m* Ida Nicholson and had:

    1a Roy; Lt-Col IA, RA WW I

    2a John; Lt RN; *ka* Battle of Jutland 1916

1 Isabella; *m* Oct 1850 Allan Gilmour, of Eaglesham, and had issue

WILLIAM EWING *d* 11 June 1853; his 5th son,

Sir Archibald Orr Ewing, 1st Bt (UK), so *cr* 8 March 1886, JP Stirling and Inverness-shire, DL Stirling and Dunbartonshire; *b* 4 Jan 1818; MP Dunbartonshire 1868–92, Ensign-Gen Roy Co Archers, Dean Faculties Glasgow U; *m* 27 April 1847 Elizabeth Lindsay (*d* 4 Dec 1915), only dau of James Reid, and *d* 28 Nov 1893, having had, with another dau:

1 **Sir William Orr Ewing, 2nd Bt**, JP Dunbartonshire and Stirling; *b* 14 Feb 1848; Capt and Hon Maj 3rd Bn Argyll and Sutherland Highrs, Memb Roy Co Archers; *m* 18 Nov 1873 Maud (*d* 4 Dec 1930), widow of Wyndham Lewis and dau of William Williams, and *dsp* 20 Aug 1903

2 ARCHIBALD ERNEST (Sir), **3rd Bt**

3 James Alexander; *b* 22 Feb 1857; MA Cantab; Maj Warwicks Yeo Cav, Maj 16th Lancers, ADC to Ld Lt Ireland 1885–90 and C-in-C Ireland 1895; *m* 25 July 1898 Lady Margaret Frances Susan Innes Ker (*d* 15 Dec 1930), est dau of 7th Duke of Roxburghe (qv), and was *ka* Kheis S Africa 28 May 1900, leaving:

  (1) Millicent Lilian Elizabeth; *b* 10 July 1899; *m* 22 Nov 1921 Sir John Francis Roskell Reynolds, 2nd Bt (qv), and *d* 23 Nov 1931, leaving issue

4 John; *b* 29 March 1859; Capt 4th Dragoon Gds; *m* 1st 25 July 1883 Ellen Clarissa (*d* 17 Aug 1914), dau of J Howard Kennard (see KENNARD, Bt), and had:

  (1) Archibald Ian; *b* 7 April 1884; Lt Berks Yeo and F/Lt RAFVR WWs I and II; *m* 24 April 1911 Gertrude Bertha (*d* 10 March 1974), yst dau of Charles Hermann Runge, of Mayfair, and *d* 24 March 1942, leaving:

    1a +Sir (CHARLES) IAN ORR EWING, 1st Bt, and BARON ORR-EWING (LP; qv)

    1a Phoebe Gertrude (Sister Phoebe Gertrude, CSMV); *b* 1 Jan 1915; *d* 17 Jan 1983

  (1) Edith Gwendoline; *m* 11 Aug 1908 Brig-Gen Julian Hasler (*ka* 26 April 1915), E Kent Regt (The Buffs), s of William Wyndham Hasler, and *d* 10 Jan 1959, leaving issue

  (2) Olive, JP (1950); *m* 4 June 1924 Hubert John Bigge, 19th Hus, er s of Edward Ellison Bigge, of Ovingham, Northumberland, and *d* 28 Dec 1952, leaving issue. He *d* 11 May 1952

  (3) Jean; *educ* LMH Oxford (MA, BM, BCh 1924); *d unm* 17 Nov 1944

4 (cont.) Capt John Orr Ewing *m* 2nd 24 Oct 1914 Mary (*d* 15 Dec 1963), dau of Rev A B Coombe, and *d* 21 Feb 1916

5 Charles Lindsay; *b* 8 Sept 1860; MP Ayr Burgh 1895–1903, Capt 3rd Bn Argyll and Sutherland Highrs; *m* 1st 5 Dec 1888 (*divorce* 1894) Hon Beatrice Mary Leslie Ruthven (*d* 24 March 1930), only dau of 9th Lord Ruthven of Freeland (see CARLISLE, E), and had:

  (1) Ian Leslie (Sir); *b* 4 June 1893; *educ* Harrow and Worcester Coll Oxford; Lt Scots Gds, formerly Lt 3rd Bn Roy Scots Fus, ADC, WW I (wounded), MP (C) Weston-super-Mare 1934, PPS to Fin Sec Treasury 1935, Min Ag 1936, Chllr Duchy Lancaster and Min Food 1939, PMG 1940 and Parly Sec Min Food 1942, Memb Rhodesia-Nyasaland Roy Commn 1938–39, ktd 1953, FRSA; *m* 24 Jan 1917 Helen Bridget, MBE (1948) (*d* 1978), dau of Hon Henry Lloyd Gibbs (see ALDENHAM and HUNSDON OF HUNSDON, B), and *d* 27 April 1958, leaving:

    1a *Anthea Helen , JP (Somerset 1952) [Mrs Edward Lowes JP, Thorn Falcon House, Taunton, Somerset]; *b* 16 Nov 1917; *m* 1st 2 Nov 1938 Maj Wilfrid Michael Fox, Coldstream Gds (*d* 1975), only surv s of C L Fox; *m* 2nd 1977 *Edward John Ninien Lowes, er s of Edward Lowes, and by her 1st husb has:

      1b *Charles St Vigor [Charles Fox Esq, Long Hill Farm, Cucklington, Wincanton Somerset]; *b* 14 March 1941; *educ* Eton; *m* 1st 8 Aug 1964 (*divorce* 1992) Charlotte Certhia, yr dau of Dr Mervyn Jeffry Ingram, MB (see INGRAM, Bt); *m* 2nd 1994 *Nicola Louise, dau of Capt Edward de Lerisson Cazenove (see KENNEDY, Bt), and formerly w of Sir Charles Warren, 9th Bt (qv), and by his 1st w has:

        1c *Lawrence St Vigor; *b* 14 Dec 1965

1c *Nina Jane; *b* 1970

1b *(Helen) Mary [Lady Stewart-Wilson, The Old Brewery, N Curry, Somerset TA3 6JS]; *b* 1 Dec 1939; *m* 17 Jan 1962 *Lt-Col Sir Blair Aubyn Stewart-Wilson, KCVO (1994, CVO 1989, LVO 1983), Scots Gds, Master Household and Equerry to HM THE QUEEN 1994–95, yr s of Aubyn Harold Raymond Wilson and Mrs Greville Stewart-Stevens, of Balnakeilly, Perthshire, and has:

  1c *Alice Helen; *b* 14 June 1963; *m* 1985 *Jonathan Cecil Ian Young, only s of Capt H R C Young, RN, of Petersfield, Hants, and has:

    1d *Archibald Blair Cecil; *b* 1991

    1d *India Mary Katherine; *b* 1988

    2d *Minnie Rose; *b* 14 May 1996

  2c *Sophia Mary; *b* 29 March 1966; *m* 1991 *A Bruce McIntosh, est s of Bob McIntosh, and has:

    1d *Lily; *b* 1993

    2d *Kitty; *b* 1994

    3d *Tarn; *b* 21 Dec 1995

  3c *Belinda Anthea; *b* 16 April 1970; *m* 1997 *William Anthony David St Lawrence Gethin (see GETHIN, Bt)

(1) Janet Beatrix; *b* 13 April 1890; *m* 1st 7 Dec 1909 Capt George Culme-Seymour, KRRC (see CULME-SEYMOUR, Bt), and had issue; *m* 2nd 8 July 1918 Rev Geoffrey Harold Woolley, VC, MC, Capt London Regt, Assist Master and Chaplain Harrow 1927, s of Rev G H Woolley, and *d* 14 Feb 1943, leaving issue. He *d* 10 Dec 1968

5 (cont.) Charles Orr Ewing *m* 2nd 28 April 1898 Lady Augusta Helen Elizabeth Boyle (*m* 2nd 30 July 1914 1st Viscount Caldecote (qv); *d* 12 May 1967), est dau of 7th Earl of Glasgow (qv), and *d* 24 Dec 1903, having by her had:

  (2) Edward Lindsay, MC; *b* 11 March 1899; Lt Black Watch WW I (wounded), ADC to Govr-Gen NZ 1927–30; *m* 15 July 1930 Jean Anne, 3rd dau of Adml Sir James Andrew Fergusson, KCB, KCMG (see FERGUSSON, Bt), and *dsp* 25 Nov 1930

  (3) David, DSO (1943), DL (Wigtownshire 1951); *b* 24 March 1900; Capt RN WW I and II; *m* 15 March 1930 Helen Mary Stewart (*d* 1994), dau of Benjamin Noaks, of Bloemfontein, S Africa, and *d* 18 June 1964, leaving:

    1a +Edward Stuart [Maj Edward Orr Ewing Esq, Dunskey, Portpatrick, Stranraer, Wigtownshire DG9 8TJ]; *b* 28 Sept 1931; *educ* Sherborne and RMC Science; Maj Black Watch (ret 1969), Ld Lt Wigtownshire 1989– (DL 1970); *m* 1st 7 June 1958 (*divorce* 1981) Fiona Anne Bowman, yr dau of Anthony Hobart Farquhar; *m* 2nd 1981 *Diana Mary, dau of William Smith Walters, OBE, and by his 1st w has:

      1b +Alastair Lindsay; *b* 28 Nov 1964

      1b *Jane Helen [Mrs Patrick Dear, 83 Albert Bridge Rd, London SW11 4PH]; *b* 31 Jan 1961; *m* 1991 *Patrick (Paddy) Giles Gauntlett Dear, yr s of M A G Dear, of Algarve, Portugal, and has:

        1c *Frederick Edward Gauntlett; *b* 19 Aug 1993

        2c *Maxwell William Gauntlett; *b* 23 April 1997

        1c *Arabella May; *b* 15 March 1995

    2b *Victoria Susan; *b* 28 Sept 1962

    2a +Charles David [Lt-Cdr Charles Orr Ewing RN, Torhousemuir, Wigtown, Newton Stewart DG8 9DJ]; *b* 10 Aug 1936; *educ* Sherborne; Lt Cdr RN (ret 1974); *m* 4 Aug 1962 *Bridget Juliet, only child of Sir Thomas Astley Woollaston White, 5th Bt (see WHITE, Bt, of Wallingswells), and has:

      1b +David Robert; *b* 8 Sept 1964; Black Watch; *m* 1992 *Sally Katrine, er dau of Col R S B Watson, of Edinburgh, and has:

        1c +Andrew Alexander; *b* 12 Sept 1994

        2c +Hamish Thomas; *b* 25 March 1997

      2b +Robert Charles; *b* 23 Feb 1966; *m* 1996 *Amani, yr dau of M L Obeid, of Birmingham

  (2) Barbara Dorothea, JP (Somerset 1947); *b* 25 Aug 1902; *m* 16 May 1931 Lt-Cdr William Edmund Halsey, RN (*d* 1986), 2nd s of Sir Walter Johnston Halsey, 2nd Bt (qv), and *d* 1993, having had issue

1 Janet Edith; *m* 1st 9 Jan 1878 Lt-Col Arthur Grey Hazlerigg, Roy Scots Fus, and had issue (see HAZLERIGG, B); *m* 2nd 25 Feb 1888 Maj Henry Pelham Burn, Rifle Bde, est s of Maj-Gen Henry Pelham Burn, and *d* 15 June 1935, leaving issue. He *d* 9 Nov 1935

The 2nd Bt's bro,

Sir Archibald Ernest Orr Ewing, 3rd Bt, JP, DL (Stirling and Dunbarton); *b* 22 Feb 1853; Memb Roy Co Archers, Capt TFR, formerly 3rd Bn Argyll and Sutherland Highrs; *m* 20 Oct 1879 Hon Mabel Addington (*d* 30 March 1942), dau of 3rd Viscount Sidmouth (qv), and had:

1 NORMAN ARCHIBALD (Sir), **4th Bt**

2 Ernest Pellew; *b* 29 Jan 1882; T/Capt Scots Gds; *ka* 15 Sept 1916

1 Violet Ella; *b* 13 Dec 1881; *m* 12 July 1904 Miles Barne, DSO, of Sotterley Park and Dunwick, Suffolk, and *d* 11 April 1969, leaving issue. He *d* 17 Sept 1917 of wounds recd in action

2 Mabel Ursula; *b* 19 April 1887; *m* 1st 24 July 1913 Brig Gen Gerald Carew Sladen, CB, CMG, DSO, MC, Rifle Bde (*d* 21 April 1930), s of Col Sir Edward Bose Sladen, Madras SC, and had issue; *m* 2nd 1933 Ferdinand SLADEN formerly HIRSCHFELDT

Sir ARCHIBALD *d* 21 April 1919; his only surv son,

Sir Norman Archibald Orr Ewing, 4th Bt, CB (1942), DSO (1914), JP (W Perthshire); *b* 23 Nov 1880; *educ* Eton; Arab Camel Corps Boer War 1899–1901, Egyptian Army 1907–11, Adj 2nd Bn Scots Gds 1911–13, WW I: Col cmdg 2nd Bn Guards 1916–18, T/Brig-Gen and Bde Cdr 45th Inf Bde 1918–19 (wounded twice, despatches five times, Brevet Lt-Col 1919), Hon Brig-Gen 1920, Lt-Col cmdg 7th Bn Argyll and Sutherland Highrs TA 1924–25, 154th Inf Bde TA 1925–29, Hon Col 7th Bn Argyll and Sutherland Highrs 1932–48, Ensign Roy Co Archers, Cdr Stirlingshire and Clackmannanshire HG WW II, V-Lt Stirlingshire, Chm TAA 1931, ADC (additional) to HM GEORGE V 1931, Mil Order Savoy, Croix de Guerre, Legn Honour; *m* 24 July 1911 Laura Louisa (*d* 10 June 1968), 4th dau of Abraham John Robarts, DL, and *d* 26 March 1960, having had:

1 Sir RONALD ARCHIBALD ORR EWING, **5th and present Bt**

2 Alan Lindsay, MC; *b* 13 Jan 1915; *educ* Eton and Edinburgh U (BSc Forestry 1939); 2nd Lt 7th Bn Argyll and Sutherland Highrs (TAR) WW II (twice wounded, despatches, POW), Forest Serv Canada 1948, Master Forestry U California 1951, PhD BC U 1956, forest geneticist; *m* 24 Oct 1945 *Helen Isabelle [Mrs Alan Orr Ewing, 335–3965 Shelbourne, Victoria, BC V8N 6J4, Canada], dau of William Evans, of Toronto, and *d* 26 Feb 1995, having had:

 (1) +Alex(ander) Evans [Alexander Orr Ewing Esq, 3500 Willow St, Vancouver, BC, Canada]; *b* 8 Feb 1947; *m* 1973 *Louise Cantin, of Montreal, and has:

  1a +Simon Alan; *b* 1975

  2a +Etienne Alec; *b* 1979

 (2) William Pellew; *b* 21 June 1950; *d* 23 Feb 1951

 (1) *Isobel Laura; *b* 13 April 1954; *m* 1975 *Robert Wain Reid and has:

  1a *James William; *b* 1986

  1a *Jennifer Laura; *b* 1987

3 Robert Norman, *b* 20 May 1920; 2nd Lt Black Watch WW II; *ka* June 1940

1 *Jean Marjorie [Mrs Alexander Webster, 2a Leigh Court, Avonmore Rd, London W14 8RL]; *b* 6 Jan 1918; *m* 25 Oct 1941 Alexander Robert Webster (*d* 1973) and has:

 (1) *Robert Alexander; *b* 6 Oct 1943; *m* 1968 *Margaret Elizabeth Mary, dau of Gilbert Harrower, and has:

  1a *Andrew Robert; *b* 1970

  1a *Jill Margaret; *b* 1973

 (1) *Yvonne Jean; *b* 31 July 1944; *m* 1st 1965 (*divorce* 1969) Michael Montgomery and has:

  1a *Alan Michael; *b* 1966

  2a *Ian Aston; *b* 1968

 (1) (cont.) Mrs Yvonne Montgomery *m* 2nd 1969 *Leslie Murray, of Killinchy, Co Down, s of Morton Murray, and by him has:

  1a *Laura Kay; *b* 1972

OSBORN

Arms: Arg. a bend between two lions rampant sa. **Crest:** A lion's head erased arg., ducally crowned or. **Motto:** *Quantum in rebus inane* ('How much vanity there is in human affairs').
Creation: Bt. (E) 11 Feb 1661/2.

SIR RICHARD HENRY DANVERS OSBORN, 9TH BT, of Chicksands Priory, Co Bedford [Sir Richard Osborn Bt, 25 Queen's Gdns, London W2 3BD]; *b* 12 Aug 1958; *s f* 1983; *educ* Eton; with Christie's 1979–83, P & D Colnaghi 1984–86, fine art consultant, assoc dir Paul Mitchell Ltd

Lineage: PETER OSBORNE, of Purleigh, Essex; *d* 1442, leaving, with two unm er sons (William; John, a priest) and two daus:

RICHARD OSBORNE; *m* Anne, dau of John Caeston, of Essex, and *d* 1471, leaving, with an er s (John, of Aldern Cross, *m* and had a dau, who *m* William Trafford, of Essex):

RICHARD OSBORNE, of Tyld Hall, Essex; *d* 1544, leaving:

1 John, of Tyld Hall; had, with two yr sons and three daus:

 (1) Richard; *m* 1st — and had four daus (*dsp*); *m* 2nd Elizabeth, sis of Ld Ch Justice Edward Coke (*see* LEICESTER, E), and had three sons (*dsp*)

2 PETER

1 Elizabeth; *m* Sir Richard Bettyson/Betyson, of Chadbury, Kent, and had issue

2 Anne; *m* James Tawke and had three daus

3 Martha O; *m* William Hunt and had a s

The yr son,

 PETER OSBORNE; Treasurer's Remembrancer *temp* HENRY VIII, Keeper Privy Purse to EDWARD VI, imprisoned by MARY, High Commr Ecclesiastical Affrs *temp* ELIZABETH I; MP; bought Chicksands Abbey (later Priory), Beds, 1576; *m* Anne, dau of Dr John Blyth/Blithe, Regius Prof Physic Cambridge, by Alice, sis of Sir John Cheke (tutor to EDWARD VI) and Mary, w of 1st Baron Burleigh (*see* EXETER, M), and had, with nine other sons and daus:

1 JOHN (Sir)

2 Henry; *b* 1559; *m* Margaret — (*d* 1643) and left his South Tonbridge estate to his n Sir John Osborne

1 Elizabeth; *b* 1564; *m* Sir Edward Duncombe, Bt, of Beds (*see* FEVERSHAM, B, for his ancestry)

2 Katharine; *b* 1575; *m* as his 1st w Sir Thomas Cheke, of Pyrgo, Essex, gs of Sir John Cheke (*see above*), and had issue

The est son,

 Sir JOHN OSBORNE, of Chicksands Priory; *b* 1552; Treasurer's Remembrancer *temp* JAMES I, Commr Navy; *m* Dorothy, dau and coheir of Richard Barlee, of Elsenham Hall, Essex, and maternal gdau of 1st Baron Rich (*see* WARWICK, BROOKE and, E), and *d* 4 Nov 1628, leaving, with other issue:

1 PETER (Sir)

2 Christopher; *b* 1586; Capt King's Ships; *d unm*

3 Thomas, of N Fambridge Manor, Essex; *b* 1588; *m* and *d* 1651, leaving:

 (1) Richard; Gentleman Usher to CHARLES I; twice helped him escape from Carisbrooke Castle

 (2) Thomas

4 Robert, *b* 1590; Lt Thirty Years War; served under Count Mansfeld and the Duke of Brunswick; *k* 1623

5 Francis; *b* 26 Sept 1593; Parliamentical Civil War, Master Horse to 3rd Earl of Pembroke, Treasurer's Remembrancer, author: *Advice to a Son* (1656) and *Tradition Memoirs of Reigns of Queen Elizabeth and King James I* (1658); *m* Anna, dau of William Ufflet, and *d* 4 Feb 1658, leaving two sons and three daus

The est son,

 Sir PETER OSBORNE, of Chicksands Priory; Treasurer's Remembrancer, Govr Guernsey under JAMES I and CHARLES I, one of the last royalists to surrender in Civil War; *m* Lady Dorothy Danvers, dau of Sir John Danvers, of Dauntsey, Wilts, by Elizabeth Nevill(e) (dau and coheir of 4th Baron Latymer, *qv*) and sis of 1st and last Earl of Danby of the Feb 1625/6 *cr*, and *d* March 1653, leaving, with three other children:

1 Thomas; *b* 1609; *d* 1637

2 Henry; *b* 1614; Lt-Col Foot; *k* Battle of Naseby 1645

3 JOHN (Sir), **1st Bt**

4 Henry (Sir); *b* 1619; fndr and treasurer Roy Hosp Greenwich; *d* 1675

5 Charles, *b* 1620; royalist Civil War; *kas* 1642

6 Robin (Robert); *b* 1626; *d unm c* 1653

1 Elizabeth; *b* 1610; *m* 1631 Edward Duncombe, of Battlesden, Beds

2 Ann; *b* 1613; *m* Sir Thomas Peyton, of Knowlton, Kent, and had three daus

3 Dorothy; *b* 1627; engaged to Henry, s of OLIVER CROMWELL; *m* Sir William Temple, 1st Bt, of the 1665 *cr* (*see* TEMPLE OF STOWE, E), the letters between husb and w forming one of the great monuments of epistolary literature of the 17th, or indeed any other, century

The 3rd son,

 Sir John Osborne, 1st Bt (E), so *cr* 11 Feb 1661/2, of Chicksands; *b c* 1615; Treasurer's Remembrancer 1674–98; presented with the famous 'warming pan' bed from St James's Palace in which the titular James III, the Old Pretender, was said by his enemies to have been smuggled into the reigning family; *m c* 22 Dec 1647 Eleanor/Elinor (*d* 16 Nov 1677), dau of Sir Charles Danvers, of Baynton, Wilts, and *d* 5 Feb 1698/9, leaving, with two daus:

 Sir John Osborne, 2nd Bt; *b* 1659; *m* 1st Elizabeth (*d* 27 March 1683), dau and coheir of William Strode, of Barrington, Somerset, and had, with a dau (*d* young):

1 John OSBORNE later OSBORN (dropped the 'e' to avoid confusion with the immediate family of his cousin, 1st Duke of Leeds); *bapt* 1 April 1683; *m* 8 Aug 1710 Hon Sarah Byng (*d* Nov 1775), est dau of 1st Viscount Torrington (*qv*), and *dvp* (*bur* 14 Jan 1718/9), leaving, with four other sons and a dau (*d* at birth):

 (1) DANVERS (Sir), **3rd Bt**

 Sir John *m* 2nd 1688 Martha (*bur* 12 Nov 1713), dau of Ld Ch Justice Sir John Keynge, of Southill, Beds, and by her had, with four other sons and four daus:

2 Peter; *bapt* 4 Sept 1690; Capt RN, Capt Roy Hosp Greenwich; *m* 1718 Mary (*d* his widow 1 April 1765), widow of 4th Viscount Molyneux (*see* 1970 edn SEFTON, E), dau of Lt-Gen Bevil Skelton, and *d* 13 Feb 1754, leaving:

 (1) George; *b* 1772; *d* young

 (2) Charles; *b* 1723; Army Offr

 (1) Frances Maria; *b* 1720; nun

3 Robert; *b* June 1696; Commr Navy; *m* and had a s (George) and three daus

4 Henry; *b* 26 June 1797; Adml, MP Bedford, Govr Newfoundland 1729–37, C-in-C Leeward Islands; *m* Mary, dau of Richard Hughes, Commr Navy, and *d* 1771, having had, with other issue:

 (1) Henry; *b* 1743; Page Honour to PRINCESS DOWAGER AUGUSTA OF WALES; *d* 1759

 (2) William; *b* 1752; Lt-Col 7th Light Dragoons; *d* 1814

 (1) Charlotte; *m* 1784 Adml Sir Benjamin Caldwell, GCB, and *d* 1820

 (2) Louisa; *m* Maj-Gen Sir Henry Calder, of Parker Place, Kent, and had issue. He *d* 1789

5 Thomas (Rev); DCL, Rector Campton and Clifton, Beds, Preb Salisbury and Lincoln; *m* 1st Mary, widow of Edward Snagg, of Marston, Beds, and dau of Sir John Willys, 2nd Bt of the 1641 *cr*; *m* 2nd Elizabeth, dau of Dr — Green, Bp Ely, and *d* 1790

Sir JOHN *d* 28 April 1720; his gs,

 Sir Danvers Osborn, 3rd Bt, after whom Danvers, Mass., is called; *b* 17 Nov 1715; MP Beds 1747–53, Col Bedford Regt, which he cmded in the 1745 Uprising, Govr New York; *m* 25 Sept 1740 Lady Mary Montagu (*d* 23 July 1743), 3rd dau of 1st Earl of Halifax of the 1714 *cr* (*see* HALIFAX, E, preliminary remarks), and *d* 27 Dec 1753, leaving, with a yr s (John, *b* 16 July 1743, MP Beds, Col Bedford Regt and Beds Militia, Chargé d'Affaires Naples, Amb Extrdy Dresden, *d unm* 1814):

 Sir George Osborn, 4th Bt; *b* 10 May 1742; Maj-Gen Scots Gds, cmdg Gds N America, Gen and Lt-Col 3rd Foot Gds, Capt 16th Light Dragoons, Maj 18th or Roy Irish Foot, Col 40th/2nd Somerset Foot, Groom Bedchamber to GEORGE III, MP Bedford 1768–84; *m* 1st 1711 Elizabeth (*bur* 16 March 1773), est dau and coheir of John Bannister, of Hill St, Mayfair, and had issue; *m* 2nd 22 Aug 1788 Lady Heneage Finch (*dsp* 4 May 1820), dau of 8th Earl of Winchilsea and (3rd) of Nottingham (*qv*), and *d* 29 June 1818, having by her had a s and dau (*d* young); his only s by his 1st w:

Sir John Osborn, 5th Bt, DL Tower Hamlets; *b* 3 Dec 1772; MA, DCL Oxon, MP Beds 1794–1807 and 1818–20, Cockermouth 1807–09, Queenborough 1812–18, Wigtown Burghs 1821–24, Col Beds Militia, Ld Commr Admlty; *m* 14 Sept 1809 Augusta Frederica Louisa Valentina (*d* 23 July 1870), illegitimate dau of Sir Charles Davers, 6th and last Bt, of Rougham and Rushbrooke, Suffolk, and had, with two other daus (*d* unm):

1 GEORGE ROBERT (Sir), **6th Bt**

2 Charles Davers; *b* 17 April 1819; *m* 2 Jan 1845 Louisa (*d* 30 April 1908), est dau of Rev A Atherley, Vicar Heavitree, and *d* 8 Dec 1846, leaving a s

3 John Brownlow; *b* 6 April 1822

4 Montagu Francis Finch (Rev); *b* 20 May 1824; MA, BD, Hon Canon Newcastle, Vicar Embleton, Northumberland; *m* 5 June 1861 Catherine Barbara (*d* 24 Jan 1907), dau of John Marriott, and *d* 14 Dec 1895, leaving:

  (1) Francis Wilfrid (Rev); *b* 22 April 1862; *educ* Uppingham and Keble Coll Oxford (BA 1884, MA 1892); Vicar Newland, Worcs; *m* 18 Jan 1890 Helen Osborn (*d* 3 April 1953), dau of David Lamb, of New York, and *dsp* 30 Sept 1945

  (2) Montagu John; *b* 19 Feb 1869; *educ* Uppingham, Durnham Sch and Keble Coll Oxford (BA 1891, MA 1896, MusB); FRCO, assist master Malvern; *m* 17 Dec 1918 Dorothy, est dau of Roslin Williams, and *dsp* 19 June 1954

  (1) Margaret; *d* unm 15 May 1942

  (2) Catharine Louisa; *d* unm 20 Jan 1950

  (3) Hilda; *m* 19 Jan 1897 Thomas William Craster, of Craster Tower, Northumberland, and *d* 15 Aug 1938, leaving issue

5 Danvers Henry; *b* 25 Aug 1827; Lt-Col HEICS and IA; *m* 17 March 1862 Annette (*d* 29 March 1928), dau of Thomas Watkins Wilson, MD, Surgn-Maj IMS, of Calcutta, and *d* 5 Feb 1898, leaving:

  (1) Arthur; *b* 19 Aug 1863; Col IA; *m* 8 Dec 1905 Elizabeth Mary (*d* 27 Feb 1947), widow of Arthur Lane, and *d* 25 Oct 1934, leaving:

    1a Sybil Gwendoline; *b* 4 May 1906; *m* 20 April 1935 Col Henry Ironside Davidson, MBE, Kt Grand Cross Order George I Hellenes, s of George Davidson, CBE, and had:

      1b *Ainslie Danvers; *b* 25 Feb 1941; *m* 31 May 1969 *David Philip Johnston, s of Oswald Philip Johnston

  (2) Danvers, JP BC; *b* 14 Nov 1864; with Pacific Cable Bd, Roy Canadian Regt 19th Bde Boer War 1899–1900 (medal with four clasps); *m* 14 Jan 1906 Inez (*d* 1953), 2nd dau of Henry Smith, of Victoria, BC, and *d* May 1929, leaving:

    1a +GEORGE SCHOMBERG later WILLIAM DANVERS (took new forenames by deed poll, registered BC Supreme Court 20 Aug 1936) [William Osborn Esq, 2676 Seaview Rd, Victoria, BC, Canada]; *b* 4 June 1909; heir presumptive; *m* June 1939 *Jean Burns, dau of R B Hutchinson, of Vancouver, and has:

      1b *Cheryl Elizabeth; *b* 9 Aug 1945; *educ* Us of Victoria (BA 1967) and BC (BLS 1969)

    1a Dorothy Annette; *m* 1941 Gordon D MacEachern and had issue

  (1) Laura Constance; *m* April 1894 Lt-Col Henry Dowsley Stacpoole, E Yorks Regt, s of Thomas Stacpoole, and *d* 24 Jan 1949, leaving issue. He *d* Aug 1913

  (2) Annette Frederica Kathleen; *d* unm 1948

Sir JOHN *d* 28 Aug 1848; his est son,

Sir George Robert Osborn, 6th Bt, JP, DL Beds; High Sheriff 1857; *b* 29 Oct 1813; *m* 1st 22 Aug 1835 Lady Charlotte Elizabeth Kerr (*see* LOTHIAN, M) and had:

1 Henry John Robert, JP, DL Beds; *b* 12 Sept 1839; *educ* Harrow; Lt 1st Life Gds; *m* 23 April 1866 Emily (*d* 6 May 1920), 3rd and twin dau of Thomas St Quintin, of Hatley Park, Cambs, and was lost in a collision in the English Channel 29 March 1889, leaving:

  (1) ALGERNON KERR BUTLER (Sir), **7th Bt**

  (1) Laura Helen Charlotte; *b* 18 June 1868; *m* 19 Nov 1901 her 1st cousin Capt Ernest Snowden St Quintin, 19th Hus, and *dsp* 1922. He *d* 8 Nov 1927

2 Francis Mark Seymour; *b* 12 Sept 1841; Capt RN; *d* unm 6 April 1908

3 George Montagu (Rev); *b* 5 May 1843; *educ* Trin Coll Cambridge (MA); Rector Campton, Beds; *m* 13 Jan 1876 Hon Charlotte Jane Kenyon (*d* 27 April 1893), yst dau of 3rd Baron Kenyon (*qv*), and *d* 21 Nov 1910, leaving:

  (1) Muriel; *b* 17 March 1881; *m* 20 Aug 1932 Walter Key Parbury, MRCS, LRCP, Maj RAMC (TF), and *d* 19 Oct 1936. He *d* 8 May 1959 aged 93

4 Mark Charles Danvers; *b* 22 March 1845; Lt RN; *m* 1st 1 Feb 1872 Mary Courtenay (*d* 15 Oct 1884), dau of William Pratt, of Hobart, Tasmania, and had:

  (1) Edith Courtenay Kerr; *d* unm 28 Oct 1931

  (2) Charlotte Eleanor Danvers

  (3) Valentina Frances Laura; *m* 1 Feb 1910 Henry Young, only s of Henry Young, and *d* 25 Oct 1954, leaving issue. He *d* 8 Sept 1939

4 (cont.) Lt Mark Osborn *m* 2nd 31 Dec 1885 Mary Anne Bell (*dsp* 2 Feb 1903), dau of W B Fulton, of Hobart, and *m* 3rd 12 Oct 1904 Clare Harriet (*d* 1920), widow of Rev Henry Gordon Cranmer, Rector Little Staughton, Beds, and *d* 31 July 1928

5 Arthur Edward Danvers (Rev); *b* 6 April 1849; Vicar Haynes, Beds; *d* unm 2 March 1888

1 Charlotte Frederica Caroline; *m* 4 Aug 1869, as his 3rd w, Gen Sir Edward Harris Greathed, KCB, and *d* 22 Oct 1908, leaving issue. He *d* 19 Nov 1881

2 Laura Elizabeth; *b* 19 Feb 1838; *d* unm 30 July 1858

3 Mary Louisa; *b* 11 Jan 1847; *d* unm 31 March 1920

4 Emily Fanny Dorothy; *b* 9 Jan 1851; *m* 19 Aug 1892 her first cousin Hon Mark Henry Horace McDonnell, 2nd s of 5th Earl of Antrim (*qv*), and *dsp* 12 July 1929

5 Harriet Jane; *b* 2 Dec 1852; *m* 22 Dec 1881 Francis Basil Pulteney, of Hargrave, Essex, and *d* 3 Oct 1872, leaving issue. He *d* 1896

6 Edith Caroline Agnes; *b* 6 Oct 1854; *d* unm 20 May 1914

Sir George *m* 2nd 20 May 1871 Mary Elizabeth Anne (*dsp* 20 Feb 1909), 2nd dau of Sir George Sitwell, 2nd Bt (*qv*), and *d* 11 Jan 1892

His gs,

Sir Algernon Kerr Butler Osborn, 7th Bt, JP Beds; High Sheriff 1909; *b* 8 Aug 1870; *educ* Harrow and Trin Hall Cambridge; Capt and Hon Maj 3rd Bn Beds Regt; *m* 3 June 1903 Beatrice Elliot Kennard (*d* 30 Aug 1963), dau of William Bunce Greenfield, DL, JP, formerly of Haynes Park, Bedford, and 35 Gloucester Sq, London W, by Mary Jane, est dau of Robert William Kennard (*see* KENNARD, Bt), and *d* 19 July 1948, having had:

1 Peter Stanley Howard; *b* 20 Aug 1912; *educ* Eton and RMC; Capt Roy Fus, 2nd Lt 4th Hus WW II, author: *Never Again* and *Smash Military Germany For Ever*; *ka* Anzio 4 Feb 1944

2 **Sir Danvers Lionel Rouse Osborn, 8th Bt**; *b* 31 Jan 1916; Intell Dept War Office WW II; *m* 4 Sept 1943 Constance Violette, JP (Surrey 1966), SSStJ, Co-V-Pres St John Amb Nursing Cadets Surrey, Chm Ladies Guild King Edward VII Hosp Offrs (*d* 1988), est dau of Maj Leonard Frank Rooke, KOSB, and *d* 1983, having had:

  (1) Peter Robin Danvers; *b* 23 Aug, *d* 26 Dec 1954

  (2) Sir RICHARD HENRY DANVERS OSBORN, **9th and present Bt**

  (1) Jennifer Anne; *b* 16, *d* 17 March 1945

  (2) *Sarah [Mrs Christopher Saunders-Davies, The Mill House, Greatbridge, Romsey SO51 0HP]; *b* 8 March 1950; *m* 1989 *Christopher Gwyn Saunders-Davies, s of A O Saunders-Davies

1 Dorothy; *b* 8 May 1905; *m* 29 April 1933, as his 2nd w, Gordon Chapman, s of Alfred Chapman, MinstCE (*d* 11 March 1969), and *d* 6 Oct 1986

OSBORNE

Arms: Gu. on a fess or cotised arg. two fountains ppr., over all a bend of the last. **Crest:** A sea lion sejant ppr., holding in the dexter paw a trident sa., headed or. **Motto:** *Pax in bello* ('Peace in war'). **Creation:** Bt. (I) 15 Oct. 1629.

SIR PETER GEORGE OSBORNE, 17TH BT, of Ballintaylor, Co Tipperary [Sir Peter Osborne Bt, 21 St Petersburg Place, London W2 4LA]; *b* 29 June 1943; *s f* 1960; *educ* Wellington and Ch Ch Oxford; *m* 16 Oct 1968 *Felicity Alexandra, only dau of Grantley Herbert Loxton-Peacock, of Belgravia, and has:

1 +GIDEON later GEORGE GIDEON OLIVER; *b* 23 May 1971; *m* 4 April 1998 *Hon Frances Victoria Howell, er dau of Baron Howell of Guildford (*qv*)

2 +Benedict George; *b* 25 July 1973

3 +Adam Peter; *b* 25 March 1976

4 +Theo Grantley; *b* 28 March 1985

Lineage: Sir Richard Osborne, 1st Bt (I), so cr 15 Oct 1629, of Ballintaylor and Ballylemon, Co Waterford; Jt Clerk King's Court Ireland 1616–29, MP Co Waterford 1639–49 and 1661–66; *m* —, dau of Roger Dalton, of Knockmoane, and *d* by 1667, having had, with another s (*dvp*):

1 Sir Richard Osborne, **2nd Bt**; admitted Gray's Inn 1628, MP Dungarvan 1639–49, High Sheriff Co Waterford 1671; *m* Elizabeth — and *d* 2 March 1685, leaving:

  (1) **Sir John Osborne, 3rd Bt**; *m* 1699 Elizabeth (*d* 22 Feb 1733), 4th dau of Col Thomas Walsingham, of Scadbury, Kent (and gdau, maternally, of 2nd Earl of Suffolk; *qv*), and *dsp* 4 April 1713

  (2) **Sir Richard Osborne, 4th Bt**; *d* Oct 1713

  (1) Grace; *m* Beverley Ussher, of Kilmeadon, Co Waterford

  (2) Elizabeth; *m* Very Rev Arthur Pomeroy, Dean of Cork (*see* HARBERTON, V)

  (3) Ann; *m* 1678 Charles Odell, of Castleton, Co Limerick

2 Nicholas, of Cappagh; Clerk of the Crown; *d* between 18 April 1695 and 1696, leaving, with another s:

  (1) THOMAS (Sir), **5th Bt**

  (1) Grace; *m* 1st 1656 John Stout, of Youghal, Co Cork (*dsp*); *m* 2nd Pierce Power, of Knockalare, Co Waterford

3 John; *b c* 1622; *educ* Trin Coll Dublin; *dvp*

4 Roger; *b c* 1623; *educ* Trin Coll Dublin; *m* Mabel, widow of Sir Henry Tynte and est dau of Sir Percy Smyth, of Ballynstray, but *dsp* between 17 Feb 1679 and 1680

The 4th Bt's cousin,

Sir Thomas Osborne, 5th Bt, of Tickenor, Co Waterford; High Sheriff 1672; ktd 1679; *m* 1st Katherine — and had:

1 Nicholas; *m c* 3 July 1684 Anne, est dau of Sir Laurence Parsons, 1st Bt, of Birr (*see* ROSSE, E), and *dvp* 25 Dec 1714, leaving:

  (1) **Sir Nicholas Osborne, 6th Bt**; *m* 1709 Mary (*m* 2nd Col John Ramsay and *d* 9 Feb 1762), dau of Rt Rev Thomas Smyth, DD, Bp Limerick, and *dspm* 13 Jan 1718, having had:

    1a Anne; *m* Henry Vereker, of Roxborough, and had issue (*see* GORT, V)

    2a Dorothy; *m* William Taylor, of Moyallow

  (2) JOHN (Sir), **7th Bt**

  (1) Frances; *m* John Jephson, of Carrick-on-Suir, Co Tipperary

  (2) Arabella; *m* Robert Marshall, Judge Common Pleas 1753

  (3) Mary; *m* 22 Dec 1716 William Moore (*d* 18 March 1735) and had issue

Sir Thomas *m* 2nd 9 Oct 1703 Anne (*m* 2nd Aug 1717 Francis Skiddy, of Dublin), yst dau of Beverley Ussher, and *d* 10 Oct 1715

The 6th Bt's bro,

Sir John Osborne, 7th Bt; barrister, MP Lismore 1719–27 and Co Waterford 1727–43; *m* Editha (*d* 19 Jan 1745), only dau of William Proby, Govr Fort St George, India, and *d* 11 April 1743, having had, with other issue:

Sir William Osborne, 8th Bt, PC (1770); High Sheriff Co Waterford 1750, MP Carysfort 1761–8 and 1783 and Dungarvan 1768–83; *m* (licence 20 March 1749) Elizabeth, est dau of Thomas Christmas, of Whitfield, Co Waterford, and *d* Nov 1783, having had, with a dau (*d* unm):

1 **Sir Thomas Osborne, 9th Bt**; *b* 1757; MP Carysfort 1776–97, Sheriff Waterford 1795; *m* 6 April 1816 Catherine Rebecca (*d* 10 Oct 1856), est dau of Maj Robert Smith, RM, and *d* 3 June 1821, leaving:

  (1) **Sir William Osborne, 10th Bt**; *b* 1817; *d* 23 May 1824, when the estates passed to his sis

  (1) Catherine Isabella; *m* 20 Aug 1844 Ralph BERNAL later BERNAL-OSBORNE (roy licence 12 Aug 1844; *d* Jan 1882), MP, and *d* 20 June 1880, leaving issue (*see* SAINT ALBANS, D)

2 John Proby; barrister, MP Carysfort 1783–88; *d* unm

3 William (Rev); *d* unm

4 HENRY (Sir), **11th Bt**

5 Charles (Rt Hon); MP Carysfort 1790–1800, Judge King's Bench Ireland 1802–17; *m* 14 Aug 1793 his cousin Alicia (*d* 16 May 1847), dau of Thomas Christmas, MP Whitfield, and *d* 5 Sept 1817, leaving:

  (1) William; *b* May 1794; Maj 71st Regt; *m* 7 July 1831 Helen, dau of John Hamilton Colt, of Gartsherrie, and *dsp* 13 July 1867

  (1) Elizabeth; *m* 1 Jan 1823 Gen Sir Michael Creagh, KH (*d* 14 Sept 1860), and *d* 7 Feb 1833, leaving issue

1 Elizabeth; *m* 18 March 1774 1st Earl of Carysfort (*d* 7 April 1828) and *d* 1783, leaving issue (*see* PROBY, Bt)

2 Ada; *m* her cousin Thomas Christmas

The 10th Bt's uncle,

Sir Henry Osborne, 11th Bt; MP Carysfort 1798–98 and Enniskillen 1800; *m* 1st Harriet, dau and coheir of Daniel Toler, MP Beechwood, and niece of 1st Earl of Norbury (*qv*), and had, with other issue:

1 **Sir Daniel Toler Osborne, 12th Bt**; *b* 10 Dec 1783; *m* Jan 1805 Lady Harriette Le Poer Trench (*d* 17 Nov 1855), dau of 1st Earl of Clancarty (*qv*), and *d* 25 March 1853, leaving, with other issue:

  (1) **Sir William Osborne, 13th Bt**, JP, DL; *b* 16 Oct 1805; *m* 22 July 1842 Maria (*d* 25 Oct 1875), only dau of William Thompson, of Clonfin, Co Longford, and *dsp* 2 July 1875

  (2) Thomas Frederic; Maj Madras Army; *m* 25 July 1842 Anne Letitia, only dau of Ven Hon Charles Le Poer Trench, Archdeacon of Ardagh, and both *d* the same day of Asiatic cholera 18 Feb 1846, leaving a s (*d* unm 16 Oct 1862)

  (3) **Sir Charles Stanley Osborne, 14th Bt**, of Beechwood Park, Co Tipperary; *b* 30 June 1825; *m* 1st 13 July 1846 Emilie (*d* 20 Dec 1869), dau of Geantz de Reuilly, of Ardennes, France; *m* 2nd 8 July 1873 Emma (*d* 17 May 1909), dau of Charles Webb, of Clapham Common, Surrey, and *dsp* 16 July 1879

  (1) Anne; *m* 16 Dec 1834 Gen George Wynne (*d* 27 June 1890), Col Cmdt RE, and *d* 29 May 1864, leaving issue

  (2) Harriette; *m* 27 Dec 1836 John Scott Russell (*d* 1 June 1882) and had issue

  (3) Frances; *m* 5 Feb 1829 Rev Joseph Forde Leathley and *d* Feb 1840, leaving issue

  (4) Emily; *m* 1 July 1851 Philip Jocelyn Newton (*d* 20 April 1895), of Dunleckney, Co Carlow, and *d* 31 Dec 1886, leaving issue

1 Eliza; *m* 1804 Thomas G FitzGibbon, of Ballysheida, Co Limerick, and *d* 3 Aug 1853, leaving issue

2 Harriet; *m* M Costy, of Luc, nr Caen, France, and *d* there 10 Dec 1865

Sir Henry *m* 2nd 12 June 1813 Elizabeth (*d* 9 Jan 1864), dau of William Harding, of Ballyduff, Co Tipperary, and *d* 27 Oct 1837, having by her had:

2 Charles; *b* 13 July 1816; *m* 26 Aug 1852 Ann (*d* 30 Nov 1923 aged 91), yst dau of Stephen Geary, of Euston Place, London, and *d* 15 June 1871, having had:

  (1) FRANCIS (Sir), **15th Bt**

  (2) Edward, Mayor Hythe 1922–24, JP; *b* 21 Jan 1861; MLC Hong Kong, WW I in France 1916–18; *m* 21 Feb 1895 Phyllis Eliza (*d* 23 Feb 1966), dau of George Whitley, of Weybridge, and *d* 21 Jan 1939, having had:

    1a Edward; *d* an infant 17 Dec 1902

    2a Stanley Patrick; *b* 7 July 1904; *educ* Felsted and U of Wales (BSc); AFRAeS, Sr Explosives Offr Min Supply; *m* 1st 11 Sept 1931 Muriel Harvey, BA, FRHS (*d* 4 July 1968), dau of Llewellyn Harvey Matthews, of Shrewsbury; *m* 2nd April 1969 *Mary Enid, BA [Mrs Stanley Osborne, Ordesa, Harpswood Lane, Saltwood, Hythe, Kent], dau of Horace Lyon, of Goole, Yorks, and *d* 19 Dec 1989, leaving by his 1st w:

     1b +Anthony Trevor [Anthony Osborne Esq, 22 St Peter's Way, Edgmond, Salop]; *b* 2 Nov 1934; *educ* Felsted and Emmanuel Coll Cambridge (MA); CEng, MICE; *m* 20 Dec 1958 *Beryl Anne, dau of Donald George Shadbolt, of Welwyn Garden City, and has:

      1c +Marcus Duncan Fitzwilliam; *b* 20 Feb 1967

      1c *Catherine Frances; *b* 15 Sept 1961

      2c *Nicola Clare; *b* 13 Dec 1963

     2b +Edward Peter [Edward Osborne Esq, Fairview Cottage, West Down, Ilfracombe, Devon]; *b* 20 Feb 1938; *educ* Felsted and Peterhouse Cambridge (BA); *m* 3 April 1961 *Marjorie, dau of William Newton, of Fleetwood, Lancs, and has:

      1c +John Philip; *b* 20 Feb 1963

      1c *Judith Carol; *b* 4 March 1962

      2c *Janet Elizabeth; *b* 29 March 1964

    1a Sybil Margaret; *b* 28 Nov 1895; *m* 14 June 1927 Hilary Cope Barry, of Nut Trees Cottage, Reydon, Suffolk, and *d* 23 Feb 1973, leaving:

     1b *Michael Ransome; *b* 31 July 1931; *educ* privately; artist craftsman; *m* 1964 *Evelyn Winifred Oxford, of Devon

     1b *Joan Mavis Osborne; *b* 26 June 1934; *m* 18 May 1957 *Martyn Oliver Rudkin and has:

      1c *Catherine Ann; *b* 9 Feb 1960

      2c *Deborah Louise; *b* 19 March 1962

      3c *Sally Maria Joan; *b* 22 June 1965

    2a *Nora Gladys [Miss Nora Osborne, Fieldend, 22 Harpswood Lane, Hythe, Kent]; *b* 31 Aug 1906

    3a Aline Grace; *b* 2 Aug 1909; *d* 22 April 1970

  (1) Isabella Henrietta; *b* 13 July 1853; *m* 1st 25 May 1880 Samuel Alfred Probart, JP (*d* 20 June 1881), of Graaff Relnett, Cape Colony; *m* 2nd 15 Jan 1887 Weeden Dawes (*d* March 1946) and *d* 8 Jan 1939, having had issue

  (2) Elizabeth Emily; *b* 9 Feb 1855; *d* unm 17 Jan 1933

  (3) Catherine Alice; *m* 13 Sept 1890 Charles Edward Commin (*d* 3 May 1947) and *d* 18 Jan 1941, leaving issue

  (4) Constance; *b* 9 Aug 1859; *d* unm 30 Sept 1938

  (5) Eleanor; *m* 2 April 1890 Eugene Sully (*d* 7 June 1938) and *d* 15 March 1960, leaving issue

The 14th Bt's cousin,

Sir Francis Osborne, 15th Bt, JP Sussex; *b* 1 Nov 1856; memb Exec Ctee Standing Cncl Btage; *m* 1 July 1890 Kathleen Eliza (*d* 22 Jan 1953), dau of George Whitfield, JP, of S Kensington and Modreeny, Co Tipperary, and had:

1 GEORGE FRANCIS (Sir), **16th Bt**

2 Derrick; *b* 9 Dec 1897; Lt Durham LI; *ka* France 21 March 1918

1 Dorothy Eileen, of Littlebourne House, Littlebourne, Kent; *b* 3 May 1891

2 Kathleen Muriel; *b* 9 March 1893; *m* 17 Oct 1922 Jack Chambers, of Minnesota, er s of W Chambers, of Winnipeg, and had issue

3 Rosemary Estelle; *b* 23 July 1907; *m* 7 Nov 1935 *Donald McEwen McIntyre, s of William McIntyre, of Comrie, Perthshire, and *d* 8 June 1968, leaving issue

Sir FRANCIS *d* 23 Oct 1948; his only surv s,

Sir George Francis Osborne, 16th Bt, MC; *b* 27 July 1894; *educ* Repton and RMC Sandhurst; Lt-Col Roy Sussex Regt, WW I (wounded twice, despatches twice) and WW II; *m* 27 Feb 1938 Mary Grace (*d* 1987), formerly w of Dr Robert Stavali Aspinall and dau of Clement Samuel Horn, of Goring-on-Sea, Sussex, and *d* 21 July 1960, leaving:

1 Sir PETER GEORGE OSBORNE, **17th and present Bt**

2 +James Francis [James Osborne Esq, Elbridge House, nr Canterbury, Kent CT3 4AU]; *b* 18 Feb 1946; *educ* Seaford Coll and Sorbonne; *m* 9 Oct 1971 *Felicity Jane, only dau of Peter Boutwood, of W Wittering, Sussex, and has:

  (1) +Harry Lucas; *b* 1988

2 (cont.) Mr and Mrs James Osborne also adopted:

  *Toby James Robert; *b* 1977

  *George Dominic Peter (twin); *b* 1977

1 *Jennifer Jane [Mrs Antony Little, 55 Drayton Gdns, London SW10 9RG]; *b* 29 March 1939; *m* 20 May 1966 *Antony Rufus Little

2 *Caroline Mary [Mrs Michael Dodd, 32 Farley Ave, Gorton, Manchester]; *b* 12 Nov 1941; *m* *Michael Dodd

OUTRAM

Arms: Or on a chevron embattled between three crosses flory gu. five escallops of the first. **Crest:** Out of an eastern crown a demi-lion or, gorged with a wreath of laurel ppr., holding between the paws a cross flory gu. **Supporters:** On either side a royal Bengal tiger guardant ppr., gorged with a wreath of laurel vert and on the head an eastern crown or. **Motto:** *Mutare fidem nescio* ('I know not how to change my faith'). **Creation:** Bt. (UK) 10 Nov 1858.

SIR ALAN JAMES OUTRAM, 5TH BT, of Bengal, India [Sir Alan Outram Bt, Harrow School, Harrow on the Hill, Middx HA1 3HW]; *b* 15 May 1937; *s* great-uncle 1945; *educ* Marlborough and St Edmund Hall Oxford (BA 1961, MA 1965); sr master Harrow, Lt-Col TAVR; *m* 24 July 1976 *Victoria Jean, dau of George Dickson Paton, of Bexhill-on-Sea, and has:

1 +DOUGLAS BENJAMIN JAMES; *b* 15 March 1979

1 *Alison Catharine; *b* 14 June 1977

Lineage: EDMUND OUTRAM; designed and laid out the grounds of Alfreton Hall (seat of the MOREWOODS), of Alfreton, Derbys, in which town his family had lived some generations; *m* Millicent — and *d* Dec 1774, leaving, with two yr sons (Edmund, *b* 1735; Benjamin, *b* 1738, *m* and had issue):

JOSEPH OUTRAM, of Alfreton; *bapt* 5 March 1732; civ engr, fndr the Butterley Co, proprietor the King's Head Inn, Alfreton; *m* 1st 2 Aug 1757 Jane Armfield, of Alfreton, and had a s (Edmund, *b* 1759, *d* young); *m* 2nd 25 May 1763 Elizabeth, dau of Edmund Hodgkinson, of Ashover, Derbys, and by her had, with a yst s (John, *bapt* 14 Sept 1772, *d* 1811) and four daus (Sarah, *bapt* 10 Feb 1768; Sally, *bapt* 10 Dec 1769; Anne, *bapt* 22 Feb 1770; Elizabeth, *bapt* 12 Jan 1774):

1 BENJAMIN

2 Edmund (Ven); *b* 15 Sept 1765; DD, Archdeacon Derby, Preb Lichfield, Public Orator Cambridge U; *m* 14 May 1801 Beatrix (*d* 6 Aug 1810), est dau of Richard Postlethwaite, of Lancs, and n of Thomas Postlethwaite, DD, Master Trin Coll Cambridge, and *d* 7 Feb 1821, leaving, with a yr s (Edmund Henry, *d* unm 1832):

  (1) Thomas (Rev); *b* 1802; *m* Ann, dau of Thomas Hodgkinson, of Notts, and *d* 1853, leaving, with a yst s (William, *b* 1839, *d* unm 1869):

    1a Edmund, of Sydney, NSW; *b* 1828; *m* Victoria Clarke, of Sydney, and had three sons (Edmund, *b* 1859; Francis, *b* 1863; Mark, *b* 1864)

    2a George Sandford (Rev); *b* 1829; *m* Diana, dau of Rev John Healy, and had four sons (Edmund; Lancelot; John Francis; Augustus Frederick) and six daus

    1a Adelaide; *m* Rev John Cartmell, Rector Asfordby, Leics, and *d* 1875

    2a Beatrice Elizabeth; *m* Rev Augustus Dobrée Crey

3 Joseph, of Clyde, nr Glasgow; *b* 4 Dec 1771; civil engr; *m* 13 Dec 1802 Elizabeth (*d* 25 May 1866), dau of George Knox, of Craigleigh, and *d* 4 Dec 1830, leaving:

  (1) Joseph, of Halifax, Nova Scotia; *b* 1803; *m* Catherine, dau of Henry Darden, of Baltimore, Md., and had, with three est sons (Joseph, *b* 1833, *m* Mary, dau of Leonard Geldart, of Whitby, Yorks, and *dsp*; Henry Darden, *b* 1834; George Knox, *b* 1835, *jnlst* in USA, *dsp* 1866), two yst sons (Frederick, *b* 1849; Robertson Rogers, *b* 1851) and three daus (Elizabeth, *m* Dr Henry Atkins and had issue; Catherine; Christina, *m* Arthur Mackenzie Edwards, s of Henry Edwards, of Monmouth, and had issue):

    1a Edmund David; *b* 1844; *m* Margaret, dau of William Nicholson, of Kenmare, Co Kerry, and had two sons (William Talbot, *b* 1873; Edmund Darden, *b* 1876) and a dau (Margaret)

  (2) George, of Edinburgh; *b* 1805; advocate, ed *Glasgow Herald*, Scots dialect poet; *m* Frances, dau of William McRobbie, of Kingston, Jamaica, and *d* 1856, leaving four sons and a dau

  (3) David Edmund; *b* 1818; *m* Ann, dau of John Semple, of Rothesay, Bute, and had two sons (James, *b* 1859; John David, *b* 1866)

  (1) Christina; *m* Alexander Gilkisson and *d* 1832

  (2) Sally; *m* 1st her cousin Sir Benjamin Outram, KCB, RN, FRCP, surgn HM's roy yacht, s of Capt Edmund Outram; *m* 2nd Sir George Deas, Slr-Gen Scotland

JOSEPH OUTRAM *m* 3rd 4 Jan 1776 Anne Micklethwaite, of Alfreton, and was *bur* 8 July 1810, having by her had further issue

His est s,

BENJAMIN OUTRAM, of Butterley Hall, Derbys; *b* 1 April 1764; civ engr; *m* 4 June 1800 Margaret (*d* 7 Jan 1863), dau of James Anderson, LLD, and gdau of Sir William Seton, a Scottish Ld of Session as Lord Pitmeddon, and had:

1 Francis; *b* 7 March 1801; 2nd Lt Bombay Engrs; *d* unm by his own hand 18 Sept 1829

2 JAMES (Sir), **1st Bt**

1 Anna Seton; *m* 4 June 1822 George Sligo (*d* Feb 1845), leaving issue

2 Margaret; *bapt* Jan 1804; *m* 24 Dec 1829 Lt-Gen Francis Farquharson, Bombay Army, and *d* 3 March 1831, leaving issue

3 Elizabeth; *d* unm 7 June 1824

BENJAMIN OUTRAM *dvp* 22 May 1805; his yr s,

Sir James Outram, 1st Bt (UK), so *cr* 10 Nov 1858 with annuity of £1,000 (£43,000 in late-990s terms) p.a. to him and his immediate successor, GCB (1857, KCB 1856, CB 1843), KSI (1861), known as 'the Bayard of India'; *b* 29 Jan 1803; *educ* Marischal Coll; Indian cadet 1819, Ensign 4th Native Inf Bombay May 1819, Lt 1st Gren Native Inf Aug 1819, Actg Adj 1820, Adj 44th Native Inf 1824 but exchanged back into 23rd as Adj, agent cmdg Bhil Corps 1825, Capt 1832, political agent Mahi Kanta 1835, Brevet Maj 1839, political agent: Lower Sind 1839, Upper Sind 1841, Brevet Lt-Col 1843, Resident: Satara 1845, Baroda 1847–52 and 1853–54, Maj 1848, Lt-Col 1853, Hon ADC to Govr-Gen 1853, political agent and Commandant Aden June–Nov 1854, Resident Oudh Dec 1854, Maj-Gen 1854, Cdr Br forces Persian War 1856–57 with local rank of Lt-Gen Nov 1856, Ch Commr Oudh 1857–58 and helped suppress Indian Mutiny 1857, Lt-Gen 1858, Freedom City London 1858, Hon DCL Oxon 1862, memb Cncl Govr Gen India, fndr Outram Inst (soldiers' club) Dum Dum; *m* 18 Dec 1835 his cousin Margaret Clementina (*d* 12 July 1911), dau of James Anderson, JP, and *d* 11 March 1863, leaving:

Sir Francis Boyd Outram, 2nd Bt; *b* 23 Sept 1836; BCS, U-Sec Govt NW Provinces 1858–62, served Indian Mutiny (wounded, medal and Queen's thanks); *m* 20 Oct 1860 Jane Anne (*d* 13 Dec 1903), est dau of Patrick Davidson, and *d* 24 Sept 1912, having had:

1 **Sir James Outram, 3rd Bt**; *b* 13 Oct 1864; *educ* Pembroke Coll Cambridge (MA); Maj Res Militia Canada 1916–18; *m* 17 May 1921 Lilian Mary (*d* 9 Dec 1946), dau of Joseph Balfour, and *dsp* 12 March 1925

2 **Sir Francis Davidson Outram, 4th Bt**, OBE (1919); *b* 4 Aug 1867; Capt and Brevet Maj RE, Staff Capt War Office 1914–17, Dep Assist Dir Fortifcn and Works 1917–19; *m* 1st 18 Jan 1893 Maud Charlotte (*d* 3 Feb 1913), yst dau of James Pope Kitchin, and had:

  (1) Marjorie Isabella; *educ* Aberdeen U (MB and ChB 1923); DPH, MOH Potters Bar

2 (cont.) **Sir Francis** *m* 2nd 11 May 1915 Isabel Mary (*d* 11 Nov 1960), er dau of Henry Charles Berry, and *dspm* 30 June 1945

3 Arthur (Rev); *b* 27 Sept 1871; *educ* Corpus Christi Coll Cambridge (MA); CMS Missionary India 1897–1905 (Kaisar-i-Hind medal), Vicar Little Heath Herts 1905–12, Rector: Lillingstone Dayrell Bucks 1912–23, Gt Braxted Essex 1923–28, CF 1917, Hon Chaplain 1919; *m* 27 Sept 1899 Gertrude Ellen (*d* 9 Dec 1962 aged 90), yr dau of Henry P Withers, and *d* 18 March 1937, leaving:

  (1) James Ian; *b* 26 Jan 1902; Admin Serv Nigeria; *m* 28 Dec 1932 Evelyn Mary (*d* 25 Nov 1977), er dau of Rev Charles Gough Littlehales, and *d* 29 July 1937, leaving:

    1a Sir ALAN JAMES OUTRAM, **5th and present Bt**

    1a *Margaret [Mrs Peter Gilbert, 47 Hollis Way, Southwick, Trowbridge, Wilts BA14 9PH]; *b* 22 March 1935; *m* 1st 18 Aug 1956 Richard Coverley Champion, only s of Lt-Col Charles Coverley Champion, DSO, and has:

      1b *Anthony Richard Coverley; *b* 1 Sept 1964

      1b *Jean Margaret; *b* 25 Dec 1958; *m* 1989 *Martin Galloway Booth and has:

        1c *Christopher Albert Galloway; *b* 1990

        2c *Edward Martin Galloway; *b* 1992

      2b *Jennifer Fleur; *b* 29 July 1960; *m* 1983 *David Reginald Higgins and has:

        1c *Stephen Richard; *b* 1988

        1c *Katherine Joanna; *b* 1990

        2c *Rebecca Fleur; *b* 1994

      3b Joanna Esmé; *b* 2 Feb 1963; *m* 1984 *Michael William Gooden and *d* 1986

      1a (cont.) Mrs Champion *m* 2nd 1985 *Peter Denby Gilbert

  (2) Keith Davidson; *b* 9 Nov 1903; Lt Col 5th Roy Gurkha Rifles FF, IA, WW II; *ka* Imphal 30 May 1944

  (1) Jean Marion; *b* 29 April 1906; *d* 1991

4 Henry Lawrence; *b* 16 Oct 1872; *d* 6 April 1876

5 William (Rev); *b* 31 March 1874; *educ* Haileybury and Pembroke Coll Cambridge (BA 1896, MA 1900); Rector Church Knowle Dorset 1947–53; *m* 9 June 1904 Haidée Maria, MBE (1918) (*d* 27 Feb 1934), yst dau of Henry Frederick Beaumont, of Whitley Beaumont, Huddersfield, and *d* 9 March 1958, leaving:

  (1) Francis Henry (Very Rev); *b* 2 Aug 1907; *educ* Marlborough and Pembroke Coll Cambridge (BA 1928, MA 1933); Chaplain RNVR 1940–46, Vicar Sandle Magna with Newmillerdam, Wakefield 1950–60, Dean and Vicar Battle Sussex 1960; *m* 24 April 1946 *Eileen Grace [Mrs Francis Outram, The Annexe, Haining House, Taylor's Lane, Bosham, Sussex], est dau of Rev Lionel Archibald McClintock Newbery, and *d* 1972, leaving:

    1a +John Douglas [John Outram Esq, Haining House, Taylor's Lane, Bosham, Sussex]; *educ* Marlborough, Liverpool U (BEng) and Birmingham U (MSc); md Outram Research Ltd; *m* 1970 *Valerie Ann, dau of Geoffrey Wilson, and has:

      1b +Nicholas Francis; *b* 1973

      2b +Philip Maxwell; *b* 1976

      1b *Rachel Helen; *b* 1978

2b *Katy Ann; *b* 1981

1a *Margaret Eleanor [Mrs Peter Charters, Withybed, Duck St, W Lavington, Wilts SN10 4LG]; *b* 20 March 1949; *m* 1975 *Peter Francis Charters
and has:

    1b *Richard Francis; *b* 1977

    2b *Simon James; *b* 1979

    3b *Robin Andrew; *b* 1982

(2) James Richard; *b* 14 June 1911; *educ* Marlborough and Pembroke Coll
Cambridge (BA 1932); Admin Serv Sarawak; *m* 26 Dec 1939 *Lucy Dora [Mrs
James Outram, Richardson House, Englefield Green, Surrey TW20 0JY], yst
dau of Jacob Andreas Frerichs, of Johannesburg, and *d* 1986, leaving:

    1a +(Francis) William [William Outram Esq, 70 Wroughton Rd, London
    SW11 6BG]; *b* 10 Sept 1946; *educ* Scarborough Coll; *m* 20 July 1996
    *Johanna Catherine, est dau of Michael Royle

    2a +Richard Graham [Richard Outram Esq, 43 Richmond Place, Bath BA1
    4QA]; *b* 10 Sept 1946; *educ* Marlborough

    3a +Keith Alastair; *b* 26 Dec 1947; *educ* Scarborough Coll

    1a *Nicola Elspeth [Mrs David Cooper, 55 Southford Rd, Dartmouth,
    Devon TQ6 9QT]; *b* 19 Sept 1940; *m* 16 June 1962 David Alistair Kingsley
    Cooper (*d* 1988), s of Thomas Esmond Kingsley Cooper, and has:

        1b *James Alexander [James Cooper Esq, 181 Leathwaite Rd, London
        SW11 6RW]; *b* 22 Feb 1969; *educ* King's Sch Worcester and Exeter U

        1b *Jennifer Mary [Mrs Malcolm Yallop, Russets, Weston, Honiton,
        Devon EX14 0PQ]; *b* 10 March 1967; *m* 1994 *Malcolm Bernard Yallop,
        and has:

            1c *Alexander Malcolm; *b* 26 June 1996

(1) *Eleanor Mary; *b* 12 June 1905

1 Mary Frances; *d* unm 31 May 1935

2 Margaret Caroline; *d* unm 15 Aug 1942

3 Jane Anne Eleanor; *d* 25 Feb 1876

4 Ida Mabel; *m* 20 Sept 1905 Capt Vernon Eliott Russell, 28th Glos Regt, and *d* 8
March 1947, leaving issue. He *d* 22 June 1946

OWEN, Baron

Creation: B. (LP, UK) 1992.

THE BARON OWEN, of the City of Plymouth (David Anthony Llewellyn Owen,
CH (1994), PC (1976)) [The Rt Hon The Lord Owen CH PC, 78 Narrow St, London
E14 8BP; The Old Rectory, Buttermere, Wilts]; *b* 2 July 1938; *educ* Bradfield, Sid-
ney Sussex Coll Cambridge (Hon Fell 1977) and St Thomas's Hosp (BA 1959,
MB, BChir 1962, MA 1963); St Thomas's Hosp: Neurological and Psychiatric
Registrar 1964–66, Research Fell Med Unit 1966–68; MP (Lab) Plymouth Sutton
1966–74, (Lab 1974–81, SDP 1981–92) Plymouth Devonport, PPS to MOD
(Admin) 1967, Parly U-Sec: MOD (RN) 1968–70, DHSS 1974, Oppn Spokesman:
Def 1970–72, Energy 1979–80; Min State: DHSS 1974–76, FCO 1976–77; For Sec
1977–79, co-fndr SDP 1981, Chm SDP Parly Ctee 1981–82, Leader SDP 1983–87
and 1988–92 (Dep Leader 1982–83); Chm: Decision Technology Internat
1970–72, Middlesex Holdings plc 1995–, Humanitas 1990–; Co-Chm EC Internat
Conf on former Yugoslavia 1992–95; dir Coats Viyella 1994–, Abbott Lab (USA)
1996–; Chllr Liverpool U 1996–; memb Ind Commns Disarmament and Security
Issues 1980–89, Internat Humanitarian Issues 1983–88; Govr Charing Cross
Hosp 1966–68; Patron Disablement Income Group 1968–; author: *A Unified
Health Service* (1968), *The Politics of Defence* (1972), *In Sickness and in Health*
(1976), *Human Rights* (1978), *Face the Future* (1981), *A Future That Will Work*
(1984), *A United Kingdom* (1986), *Personally Speaking to Kenneth Harris* (1987),
Our NHS (1988), *Time to Declare* (1991), *Seven Ages* (ed, 1992); *m* 1968 *Deborah, dau of Kyrill Schabert, of Long Island, NY, and has issue (none of whom use
their courtesy titles):

1 *Tristan Llewellyn; *b* 1970

2 *Gareth Schabert; *b* 1972

1 *Lucy Mary; *b* 1979

Lineage: Dr JOHN WILLIAM MORRIS OWEN; *m* Mary Llewellyn and had:

DAVID ANTHONY LLEWELLYN, *cr* a **Baron**

OWEN, Bt

Arms: Gules a chevron between three lions rampant or. **Crest:** A
lion rampant or. **Motto:** *Honestas optima politia* ('Honesty is the best
policy'). **Creation:** Bt. (UK) 12 Jan 1813.

SIR HUGH BERNARD PILKINGTON OWEN, 5TH BT, of Orielton, Pembrokeshire [Sir Hugh Owen Bt, 63 Dudsbury Rd, Ferndown, Dorset BH22 8RD]; *b* 28
March 1915; *s f* 1973; *educ* Chillon Coll Switzerland

Lineage: Sir HUGH OWEN, 1st Bt (E), so *cr* 11 Aug 1641, of Orielton, Pembs; MP
Pembroke 1626–60; *m* 1st Frances, dau of Sir John Philips, 1st Bt, of Picton (*see*
ST DAVIDS, V); *m* 2nd Catharine, dau of Evan Lloyd, of Yale, Denbighs, and
widow of John Lewis, of Prescoed, and *d* 1670, having by her had:

Sir HUGH OWEN, 2nd Bt; MP Pembroke 1676–95; *m* 1st his cousin Anne, dau of
Henry Owen, of Bedowen; *m* 2nd Catharine (*dsp*), dau of William Griffith, of Len,
and *d* 1698, having had by his 1st w (with a dau, Catherine, *m* on or after 27 May
1693 John Williams; *see* WILLIAMS-WYNN, Bt):

Sir ARTHUR OWEN, 3rd Bt; MP Pembroke 1695–1727 (riding from Wales
reached Westminster in time to vote for the Act of Settlement 1701 securing the
Hanoverian succession, which passed by one vote only), Ld Lt Pembs; *m* Emma,
dau of Sir William Williams, 1st Bt (*see* WILLIAMS-WYNN, Bt), and *d* 6 June
1753, having had, with other issue:

1 Sir WILLIAM OWEN, 4th Bt; Pembs: MP 1722–74, Ld Lt; *m* 1st Elizabeth
(*dsp*), dau and sole heiress of Thomas Lloyd, of Grove, Pembs; *m* 2nd Elizabeth,
dau of John Williams (*see* WILLIAMS-WYNN, Bt), and *d* 7 May 1781, having by
her had:

    (1) Sir HUGH OWEN, 5th Bt; Pembs: MP 1770–86, Ld Lt; *m* 1775 Anne, dau
    of John Colby, and *d* 16 Jan 1786, leaving:

        1a Sir HUGH OWEN, 6th Bt; MP Pembroke 1809; *b* 12 Sept 1782; *d* unm 8
        Aug 1809

2 John; Lt-Gen, MP W Looe; *m* his cousin Anne, dau of Charles Owen, of Nash,
and *d* Jan 1776, leaving:

    (1) Sir ARTHUR OWEN, 7th Bt; *d* unm 4 Jan 1817

    (2) William; Col 61st Regt, Brig-Gen; *m* 20 Jun 1771 Anne (*d* 20 Sept 1809),
    dau of John Tripp, of Huntspill, and *d* 1795, leaving:

        1a Sir WILLIAM OWEN later OWEN-BARLOW (roy licence 5 Aug 1844),
        8th and last Bt; Attorney Gen Carmarthen circuit, Bencher Middle Temple;
        d unm 25 Feb 1851, when the btcy expired

        1a Emma Anne; *m* 3 Feb 1821 Thomas Jones (*d* 10 May 1871), of Esgair
        Evan, and *dsp* 30 Sept 1861

        2a Frances; *m* 15 June 1815 Rev Charles Tripp, JP, DD (*d* 9 April 1865), Rec-
        tor Silverton, and *d* 27 March 1866, leaving issue

        (1) Emma; *m* Hugh OWEN later OWEN-BARLOW, of Lawrenny

        (2) Corbetta; *m* Joseph Lord and had:

            1a Sir JOHN LORD later OWEN (on inheriting estates of Sir HUGH OWEN,
            6th Bt), **1st Bt** (UK), so *cr* 12 Jan 1813; *b* 1776; Pembs: Ld Lt and MP to 1838
            (Pembroke Dist 1838–61), Govr Milford Haven; *m* 1st 1800 Charlotte (*d* 1
            Sept 1829), dau of Rev John L Phillips, and had:

                1b HUGH (Sir), **2nd Bt**

                1b Charlotte; *m* 2 Aug 1819 John Meares, of Eastington, Pembs, and *d* 20
                Jul 1852

                2b Maria; *m* 20 May 1830 Edward Marcus Whyte, of Hotham, Yorks, and
                d 1836

                3b Ellen; *m* Aug 1831 G B J Jordan, of Pigeonsford, Cards, and Ashdale,
                Pembs, and *d* 1857

                4b Eliza; *m* 29 Oct 1831 Charles Porcher Lang, of Sand Rock, Surrey, and
                d 16 July 1862

            1a (cont.) Sir JOHN LORD later OWEN, **1st Bt**, *m* 2nd 21 Oct 1830 Mary
            Frances (*d* 13 Jan 1874), dau of Edward Stephenson, of Farley Hill, Berks,
            and *d* 6 Feb 1861, having by her had, with other issue:

                2b William; *b* 4 Sept 1834; Lt 23rd R W Fus; *ka* before Sebastopol 29 June
                1855

5b Mary; *m* 13 June 1861 Capt A G Onslow, 13th Regt (*see* ONSLOW, E), and *d* 25 Jan 1892, leaving issue

The 1st Bt's est s,

Sir Hugh Owen, 2nd Bt, DL; *b* 1803; MP Pembroke 1826–38 and 1861–68, Hon Col Pembs Artillery, ADC to HM QUEEN VICTORIA; *m* 1st 12 April 1825 Angelina Maria Cecilia (*d* 4 Sept 1844), sis of 1st Baron Tredegar (*see* 1963 edn), and had, with other issue:

1 HUGH CHARLES (Sir), **3rd Bt**

2 John, JP; *b* 1828; Col cmdg 4th Bde Welsh Div RA; *m* 22 April 1879 Hon Margaret (*d* 11 June 1899), dau of 1st Baron Denman (*qv*) and widow of Edward Cropper, of Swaylands, Kent, and *dsp* 1 or 2 Dec 1890

3 Arthur Rodney; *b* 1829; Cdr RN; *m* Victoria Holmes and *d* 1876, leaving:

  (1) Victoria Angelina; *d* 2 June 1887

4 William, JP, DL; *b* 1832; Lt 52nd Regt; *m* 31 Oct 1861 Bessie, dau of Walter Reynolds, and *d* 30 Nov 1889

Sir Hugh *m* 2nd 28 Oct 1845 Henrietta Fraser (*d* 17 July 1894), dau of Capt Hon Edward Rodney, RN (*see* RODNEY, B), and *d* 5 Sept 1891, having by her had, with two other daus (*d* young):

5 George Rodney; *b* 1859; *m* 1870 Georgina Metcalfe, dau of Capt C G King, and *d* 6 Nov 1886, having had:

  (1) Arthur Edward Rodney; *b* 1877; *m* 1905 Elizabeth, dau of George Edwin Love, and had:

    1a Hugh; *b* 7 Jan 1907

    2a George; *b* 25 Nov 1907

    1a Katherine; *d* 19–

  (1) Alice Georgina

  (2) Kathleen Inez

  (3) Margaret Edith; *m* 3 Nov 1900 Cdr Robert Burton Rodney, USN (*d* 1918)

  (4) Maud Ellen; *d* young

  (5) Georgiana Marian; *m* 1912 Sydney Stuart Gear

1 Alice Henrietta Rodney; *m* 27 Nov 1879 Henry Bowes Scott (*d* 1894), s of Maj-Gen H Y D Scott, CB, and *d* 11 Dec 1925, having had issue

The 2nd Bt's est s,

Sir Hugh Charles Owen, 3rd Bt, JP, DL (Pembs); *b* 1826; Lt 73rd Regt, served Siege of Montevideo 1845–46 and Kaffir War 1846–47 (medal); *m* 27 Nov 1890 Martha Robert Lewis (*d* 16 Feb 1937) and *d* 4 April 1909, having had:

1 JOHN ARTHUR (Sir), **4th Bt**

2 William; *b* 1894; *d* young

3 Augustus; *b* 15 Aug 1895; Lt 8th Bn Somerset LI WW I; *ka* 6 Aug 1918

1 Margaret Catherine Gwenllian; *m* 1912 T George Bennett, of Fishguard, Pembs, and *d* 14 April 1976, having had:

  (1) Joan; *b* 1915; *d* 27 Aug 1973

The 3rd Bt's est s,

Sir John Arthur Owen, 4th Bt; *b* 5 Feb 1892; *educ* Llandovery Coll and St John's Coll Oxford; Capt 11th Bn Somerset LI; *m* 29 Dec 1914 Lucy Fletcher (*d* 9 Aug 1985), est dau of Fred William Pilkington, of Kencott Ho, Lechlade, Glos, and *d* 20 Sept 1973, having had:

1 Sir HUGH BERNARD PILKINGTON OWEN, **5th and present Bt**

2 John William; *b* 7 June 1917; *educ* Charterhouse and RMC Sandhurst; Capt 4th/7th Roy Dragoon Gds; *m* 17 July 1963 *Gwenllian Mary, MBE [Mrs John Owen MBE, 12 Elizabeth Avenue, St Brelade, Jersey, CI JE3 8GR], Wing Offr WRAF, er dau of Ernest Bingley Philips, of Barry, Glam, and *d* 11 June 1995

OXFORD AND ASQUITH

Arms: Sa. on a fess between three cross-crosslets arg. a portcullis of the field. **Crest:** Issuant out of clouds ppr. a mascle gu. **Supporters:** On either side a lion purpure, charged on the shoulder with an open book arg., edged or. **Motto:** *Sine macula macla* ('Spotless'). **Creation:** E. and V. (UK) 9 Feb 1925.

THE 2ND EARL OF OXFORD AND ASQUITH and **Viscount Asquith**, of Morley, Co York (Sir Julian Edward George Asquith, KCMG (1964, CMG 1961)) [The Rt Hon The Earl of Oxford and Asquith KCMG, The Manor House, Mells, Somerset BA11 3PN]; *b* 22 April 1916; *s* gf 1928; *educ* Ampleforth and Balliol Coll Oxford (scholar, MA); Lt RE 1941, Assist DC Palestine 1942–48, Dep Ch Sec Br Admin Tripolitania 1949–50, Dir Interior Tripolitania 1951, Advsr to PM Libya 1952, Admin Sec Zanzibar 1955, Adminr St Lucia 1958–62, Govr and C-in-C Seychelles 1962–67, Commr Br Indian Ocean Territory 1965–67, Constitutional Commr Cayman Islands 1971 and Turks and Caicos Islands 1973–74, KStJ 1962; *m* 28 Aug 1947 Anne Mary Celestine, CStJ, (*d* 19 Aug 1998) only dau of Sir (Charles) Michael Palairet, KCMG, Amb Greece, and has:

1 +RAYMOND BENEDICT BARTHOLOMEW MICHAEL, *Viscount Asquith*, OBE (1992) [Viscount Asquith OBE, Branch Farm, Mells, Somerset]; *b* 24 Aug 1952; *educ* Ampleforth and Balliol Coll Oxford; Dip Serv: FCO 1980–83, 1st Sec Moscow 1983–85, Cabinet Off and FCO 1985–92, Cnsllr Kiev 1992–; *m* 2 Aug 1978 *Clare, er dau of Francis Anthony Baring Pollen (*see* POLLEN, Bt), and has:

  (1) +Mark Julian; *b* 13 May 1979

  (1) *Magdalen Katharine; *b* 30 Dec 1981

  (2) *Frances Sophia; *b* 1984

  (3) *Celia Rose; *b* 1989

  (4) *Isabel Anne; *b* 1991

2 +Dominic Antony Gerard; *b* 7 Feb 1957; *m* 1988 *Louise E, only dau of John E Cotton, of Wollaton, Notts, and has:

  (1) *Gabriela Elizabeth Louise; *b* 1989

1 *(Mary) Annunziata [The Lady Annunziata Asquith, 75 Ladbroke Grove, London W11 2PD]; *b* 28 July 1948; *educ* Mayfield Sussex and Somerville Coll Oxford

2 *Katharine Rose Celestine [The Lady Katharine Page, Upper Leigh Farm, East Knoyle, Wilts SP3 6AP]; *b* 16 Oct 1949; *educ* Mayfield Sussex and King's Coll Lond; *m* 1st 18 July 1970 (*divorce* 1976) Sir Adam Nicholas Ridley (*see* RIDLEY, V); *m* 2nd 16 Feb 1985 *(John) Nathaniel Micklem Page, 2nd s of Sir (Arthur) John Page, MP

3 *Clare Perpetua Frances; *b* 28 March 1955; dep lit ed *Spectator*

Oxford, Earldom of: This title, held originally by the de Veres from 1142 to 1702/3 (*see* SAINT ALBANS, D), was not the earliest post-Conquest earldom creation. But by CHARLES I's reign it had been held in unbroken male succession for so long, and the Wars of the Roses together with the Tudors' use of attainder to cut down overmighty subjects had so depleted the other great medieval families, that Chief Justice Crew could in 1626 deliver his famous rhetorical question (*see* essay by Thomas Woodcock at front of this book) with some cogency.

Aubrey de Vere's choice of Oxford as the name of his title in 1142 was somewhat arbitrary, however. The EMPRESS MAUD had conferred on him an Earldom of Cambridgeshire, together with the third penny of certain revenues from the county for the upkeep of the dignity which at that time was a necessary concomitant of earldoms (*see* NORTHUMBERLAND, D, for discussion of this point). But if Cambridgeshire were in the hands of the King of Scots, which ultimately proved to be the case, and the Empress could not effect an exchange, Aubrey was to take his pick of title from the Earldoms of Berkshire, Dorsetshire or Wiltshire, besides Oxford (or Oxfordshire — there was little distinction between a county name and county town name at this period where earldoms were concerned; *see* WINCHESTER, M, preliminary remarks). Aubrey only seems to have chosen Oxford(shire) because it was the least remote from his own principal land holdings in Essex — which is to say, not close at all, particularly given 12th-century communications.

The 3rd de Vere Earl was one of the barons opposed to KING JOHN at Runnymede in 1215 at the time of the granting of Magna Carta. His position on that occasion is a good example of the different meaning the term baron had at that time (*i.e.*, magnate or tenant in chief of the Crown) from what it does today, *viz.*, holder of a specific degree of lordship of Parliament. De Vere's title of Earl was a real one but it was not a lordship of parliament, for Parliament did not yet exist. Nor did de Vere have a subsidiary barony or viscountcy title in the way that earls now tend to.

The 7th Earl played an important part in the early stages of the Hundred Years War, being a joint commander of the 1st division at both Crécy (1346) and Poitiers (1356). At the latter it was his adroit management of the archers that helped secure victory. The 9th Earl was a great favourite of RICHARD II, who created him Marquess of Dublin (the first marquessate ever conferred in England) and Duke of Ireland, both for life only. The Duke, who was to have gone over to Ireland armed with more than viceregal powers so as to settle its turbulent affairs, in the end never embarked from Wales. Having fallen foul of the Lords Appellant (the clique of nobles opposed to RICHARD II's highhandedness), he was with his hastily assembled army cut off from London by two much stronger forces and obliged to abandon his men and swim the Thames near Radcot Bridge then slink into London disguised as a groom. After an emotional but ineffectual interview with the King he fled to the Low Countries, where some years later he was fatally wounded by a boar during a hunting foray. The de Vere family badge might be a blue boar, but was evidently no help on this occasion. (A boar crops up again in de Vere family history: during a lull in HENRY VIII's 1544 campaign in northern France the 16th Earl astounded French onlookers by coming to a hunt in his nightgown and killing the quarry with a weapon referred to as a 'dancing rapier'.)

The 11th Earl continued the family military tradition by playing an important part at Agincourt (1415), where he was a joint commander of the central block of troops. The 13th Earl was a supporter of Warwick 'the Kingmaker' (and Oxford's brother-in-law) during the Wars of the Roses (*see* ABERGAVENNY, M) but contributed inadvertently to the latter's death at the Battle of Barnet in 1471. This took place in thick fog and at one point the de Vere heraldic device of a star was mistaken by others on his side for their opponent EDWARD IV's sun in its splendour. The resulting confusion led to Warwick and Oxford's defeat. Oxford lived on to fight on the winning side at Bosworth, 14 years later. He also played a leading part in HENRY VII's minor victories over resurgent rebels afterwards, namely Stoke and Blackheath (both 1487).

The 17th Earl was the celebrated courtier of ELIZABETH I's time, also a skilful jouster and a literary man of note, but a reckless spendthrift. His son, the 18th Earl, was as a result obliged to live abroad for some years to economise. The latter signed a remonstrance protesting against the institution of the new order of baronets. He was the last Earl of Oxford to possess Castle Hedingham, the *caput baroniae*, or chief manor of the original Vere land holdings in Essex, also the hereditary Lord Great Chamberlainship. Both these had passed down in the direct male line for over half a millennium. It was on the 18th Earl's death that the dispute arose between the heir general, the 14th Lord (Baron) Willoughby de Eresby (*qv*; *see also* LINDSEY and ABINGDON, E) and the heir male, a second cousin and eventual successor as 19th Earl, which gave rise to Chief Justice Crew's flight of oratory mentioned already.

Crew wished in vain. The de Vere name died out, and with it the Earldom. There was also an answer to that query of his as to where Mortimer was: namely, among the ultimate aspirations of Robert Harley, albeit a generation and more in the future. Harley, the celebrated Lord High Treasurer and Chancellor of the Exchequer of ANNE's reign, took the title 'Earl of Oxford and Earl Mortimer' when ennobled in 1711. It was not then clear that the de Vere Earldom of Oxford was absolutely and incontrovertibly extinct, so that he did so with some apprehension, in particular lest the then Lord Lindsey should object. On the other hand, as Harley put it, if he didn't take it he was sure someone else would. His only connection with the de Veres was that his father's mother had an aunt who married Horatio Vere, Lord Vere of Tilbury, the 15th Earl of Oxford's grandson.

Edward Harley claimed that his brother tacked the 'Mortimer' appellation onto 'Oxford' so as to avoid making the latter title too starkly and unadulteratedly his own. He also alleged a Harley-Mortimer blood link. What that link was is unknown, though Robert Harley's ancestor, another Robert, took as wife an heiress called Margaret Brampton at some point prior to 1309, and the Bramptons were tenants in Herefordshire and Shropshire of the great medieval house of Mortimer. Moreover Brampton Castle, which remained a Harley property for centuries afterwards, lay near Wigmore Castle, the Mortimer *caput baroniae*. Therein perhaps lies the connection. The Harley Earldom of Oxford and Mortimer died out in the mid-19th century. Then in the mid-1920s, some 70 years later, the former Prime Minister Asquith contemplated taking Oxford as his title. GEORGE V expressed himself perfectly satisfied, provided the College of Arms concurred. Asquith was at least a product of the University of Oxford, and a very distinguished one, the most distinguished then living. He had also lived just outside Oxford for over a decade. But his choice brought reproaches from existing members of the Harley family. The reaction of those with de Vere connections appears unrecorded. Eventually Asquith followed Harley's precedent and in the final version of the Earldom coupled the name of Oxford with his own. To some that was perhaps just as presumptuous, particularly as it was under his premiership that the Parliament Act was passed, a measure EDWARD VII called 'the destruction of the House of Lords.'

Lineage: JOSEPH ASQUITH, of Morley, Yorks; *d* 1855; had:

JOSEPH DIXON ASQUITH, of Croft House, Morley; *b* 10 Feb 1825; *m* 1850 Emily (*d* Dec 1888), dau of William Willans, JP, of Huddersfield, and *d* June 1860, having had, with an er s (William Willans, *b* 23 June 1851, *d* 7 Nov 1918) and a dau (Emily Evelyn, *m* 1878 Rev W Wooding and *d* his widow 16 Dec 1937):

HERBERT HENRY ASQUITH, **1st Earl of Oxford and Asquith**, so *cr* 9 Feb 1925, as also VISCOUNT ASQUITH, of Morley, Co York (both UK), KG (1925), PC (1892, I 1916), QC (1890); *b* 12 Sept 1852; *educ* City London Sch and Balliol Coll Oxford (BA and Fell 1874, Hon DCL 1904, Hon Fell 1908); barrister Lincoln's Inn 1876, Bencher 1894, Treasurer 1920, MP (Lib) E Fife 1886–1918 and Paisley 1920–24, Home Sec 1892–95, Chllr Exchequer 1905–98, PM 1908–16, Sec State War and Pres Army Cncl 1914 and 1916, Rector Glasgow U 1905 and Aberdeen U 1908, Er Bro Trin House 1909, FRS, memb Judicial Ctee PC 1925, High Steward City Oxford 1927, hon memb Inns of Court OTC, Ecclesiastical Commr 1892–95, Hon LLD Edin and Glas 1907, Camb 1909, Leeds 1910, St Andrews 1911, Bristol 1912, McGill 1921, Hon DCL Durham 1913, Freeman Cities Leeds and London 1925, author: *Occasional Addresses* (1918), *The Genesis of the War* (1923), *Studies and Sketches* (1924), *Fifty Years of Parliament* (1926), *Memories and Reflections* (1928), *Letters to a Friend* (ed Desmond MacCarthy 1933–34); *m* 1st 23 Aug 1877 Helen Kelsall (*d* 1891), est dau of Frederick Melland, of Manchester, and had:

1 Raymond; *b* 6 Nov 1878; *educ* Winchester and Balliol Coll Oxford; barrister Inner Temple 1904, prospective Parly candidate (Lib) Derby 1914, Lt Gren Gds WW I; *m* 25 July 1907 Katharine Frances (*d* 9 July 1976), dau of Sir John Horner, KCVO, of Mells, Somerset, and was *ka* Somme 15 Sept 1916, leaving:

(1) JULIAN EDWARD GEORGE ASQUITH, **2nd and present Earl of Oxford and Asquith**

  (1) *Helen Frances, OBE (1965) [The Lady Helen Asquith OBE, Tynts Hill, Mells, Somerset]; *b* 1908; *educ* St Paul's and Somerville Coll Oxford (BA 1930); granted with her sis rank of earl's dau 30 April 1928, Schs Inspr

  (1) Perdita Rose Mary; *b* 1910; *m* 14 Jan 1931 4th Baron Hylton (*qv*) and *d* 17 May 1996, leaving issue

2 Herbert ('Beb'); *b* 11 March 1881; *educ* Winchester and Balliol Coll Oxford (Pres Union 1901); barrister Lincoln's Inn 1907, author, Capt RFA WW I; *m* 28 July 1910 Lady Cynthia Charteris (*d* 31 March 1960), dau of 11th Earl of Wemyss (*qv*), and *d* 5 Aug 1947, having had:

  (1) John Michael; *b* 9 May 1911; *d* May 1937

  (2) +Michael Henry [Michael Asquith Esq, 149 Rusthall Ave, London W4 1BL]; *b* 25 July 1914; *educ* Winchester and Balliol Coll Oxford (BA 1937, MA); Friends Ambulance Unit WW II; *m* 1st 17 Feb 1938 (*divorce* 1952) Diana Eveline Montagu, dau of Lt-Col Perceval Lawrence Montagu Battye, MC, and has:

    1a +Stephen Andrew Romily Michael [Stephen Asquith Esq, Hinchwick Manor, Stow-on-the-Wold, Glos]; *b* 17 Jan 1944; *educ* Nautical Coll Pangbourne; *m* 1st 1963 (*divorce* 1975) Nicola, dau of Lt-Cdr Sir Peter Markham Scott, CBE, DSC, of Slimbridge, Glos, and the novelist Elizabeth Jane Howard (later Mrs Kingsley Amis), and has:

     1b +Daniel; *b* 1964

     1b *Emily Rachel; *b* 1965; *m* 1988 *Mark Charles Francis Derrington Bailey (*see* ST CLAIR-FORD, Bt)

     2b *Lucy Kate; *b* 1967

    1a (cont.) Stephen Asquith *m* 2nd 19– *Clare Frances, est dau of Lt-Col John Richard Guy Stanton, MBE, DL, of Snelston Hall, Ashbourne, Derbys

---

(*see* CASTLEMAINE, B), and formerly w of Henry Denis Ernest Boyt, and by her has:

  2b +Thomas Ivo; *b* 1980

  3b *Portia; *b* 1978

  2a +Peter Edward; *b* 22 June 1947; *educ* privately

  1a Annabel Laura Marguerite; *b* 25 March 1939; *educ* Hatherop Castle and Somerville Coll Oxford (BA 1960); *m* 7 Oct 1961 *Jasper R Ungoed-Thomas [Jasper Ungoed-Thomas Esq, 13 Westbourne Park Rd, London W2 5PX], er s of Sir (Arwyn) Lynn Ungoed-Thomas, QC, High Court Judge, and *d* 1971, leaving:

    1b *David Stephen Jerome; *b* 9 Nov 1962

    2b *Michael Fergus Jonathan; *b* 9 April 1965

    3b *Harry Owen Nathaniel; *b* 17 June 1969

(2) (cont.) Michael Asquith *m* 2nd 8 Oct 1953 Helga Birgitta Ebba Elisabeth (*d* 30 March 1998), dau of Dr Walther Sigmund Casimir Ritter, of Stockholm, formerly of Carlsbad

(3) Simon Roland Anthony; *b* 20 Aug 1919; *educ* Westminster; *m* 1 Oct 1942 *Vivien Lawrence [Mrs Simon Asquith, 44 Gilpin Ave, London SW14 8QY], 3rd dau of Maj Sir Lawrence Evelyn Jones, 5th Bt (*see* LAWRENCE-JONES, Bt), and *d* 18 Dec 1973, leaving:

  1a +Conrad Robin [Conrad Asquith Esq, 69c Nightingale Lane, London SW12]; *b* 10 Feb 1945; *educ* Westminster and Ch Ch Oxford; *m* 1977 *Patricia, dau of L E Sproston, of Stoke-on-Trent, and has:

    1b *Daisy; *b* 16 June 1976

    2b *Lily; *b* 12 April 1978

  2a +Ivon Shaun [Ivon Asquith Esq, 21 Minster Rd, Oxford OX4 1LY]; *b* 26 Dec 1946; *educ* Westminster and Ch Ch Oxford; *m* 26 Feb 1982 (*divorce* 1985) Pauline R, dau of Lt-Cdr Paul Murray-Jones, RN, and formerly w of Hon (Maurice) Sebastian Balliol Brett (*see* ESHER, V), and has:

    1b +Thomas; *b* 12 Dec 1982

  2a (cont.) Ivon Asquith has further issue by Katherine Tanya Jury:

    2b *William; *b* 1985

    1b *Rosamund Eloise, *b* 1991

  1a *Rosalind Lucy [Miss Rosalind Asquith, 88 Petherton Rd, London N5 2RG]; *b* 2 May 1948; has issue by John Fordham:

    1b *Frederick Simon Asquith Fordham; *b* 1985

    2b *Leo Robin Asquith Fordham; *b* 1989

3 Arthur ('Oc') Melland, DSO and two bars (1917, 1918); *b* 24 April 1883; *educ* Winchester and New Coll Oxford; Sudan CS 1906–11, Cdr RNVR 1914 and RND WW I, Hon Brig-Gen 1918 (wounded, despatches, Croix de Guerre), Controller Appointments Dept and memb Cncl Min Labour 1918–20, chm Kassala Cotton Co, dir Westminster Bank, Sudan Plantation Syndicate; *m* 30 April 1918 Hon Betty Constance Manners (*d* 12 Sept 1962), 2nd dau of 3rd Baron Manners (*qv*), and *d* 25 Aug 1939, having had:

  (1) *April Mary; *b* 14 April 1919; *m* 19 July 1943, as his 2nd w, 5th Earl of Stradbroke (*qv*) and has issue

  (2) *Jean Constance [Mrs Lawrence Toynbee, Chapel Cottage, Ganthorpe, Terrington, Yorks]; *b* 6 Nov 1921; *m* 20 April 1945 *Lawrence Leif Toynbee, yr s of Professor Arnold Joseph Toynbee, CH, and has:

    1a *Rosalind Catherine [Mrs John Watson, Ganthorpe Hall, Terrington, Yorks YO6 4QU]; *b* 1946; *m* 1st 1972 Joe Pennybacker (*d* 1994); *m* 2nd 1997 *John Philips Watson and by her 1st husb has:

     1b *Thomas Rupert Blaise; *b* 1975

     1b *Kitty Shushanik; *b* 1983

    2a *Celia Jane [Mrs Jeremy Caulton, 19 Berriman Rd, London N7]; *b* 1948; *m* 1966 *Jeremy George Marshall Caulton and has:

     1b *Elisabeth Amy; *b* 1967

    3a *Clare Anne [Mrs Andrew Huxley, 48 Gillespie Rd, London N5]; *b* 1949; *m* 1980 *Andrew David Huxley and has:

     1b *Coral Susan Toynbee; *b* 1984

    4a *Rachel Mary Agnes [Mrs Richard Fletcher, Low Pasture House, Nunnington, York YO6 5XQ]; *b* 1950; *m* 1976 *Richard Alexander Fletcher and has:

     1b *Humphrey Alexander; *b* 1981

     1b *Eleanor Constance; *b* 1978

     2b *Alice Catherine; *b* 1983

    5a *Sarah Alice [Mrs Robert Towler, 14 Lisgar Terrace, London W14 8SJ]; *b* 1953; *m* 1990 *Dr Robert Towler and has:

     1b *Frederick James Edward; *b* 1991

     1b *Madeline; *b* 1993

    6a *Frances Veronica [Mrs Frances Wilson, 8 Miranda Rd, London N19 3RB]; *b* 1958; *m* 1987 (*divorce* 19–) John Samuel Wilson

  (3) *Susan Penelope [Mrs Basil Boothby, 23 Holland Park Ave, London W11 3RW]; *b* 12 July 1922; *m* 18 Sept 1946 (Evelyn) Basil Boothby, CMG (*d* 1990), only s of Basil Tanfield Beridge Boothby (*see* BOOTHBY, Bt), and has issue

  (4) *Christine [Mrs John Clark, Old Laundry Cottage, Clovelly, N Devon]; *b* 23 March 1926; *m* 29 Nov 1952 *John Hatch Clark, only s of Sydney Hatch Clark, and has:

    1a *John Jasper; *b* 15 Jan 1958

    1a *Lucy Caroline; *b* 5 Sept 1953; *m* 1980 *William Francis Sebastian Rickett, s of Sir Denis Hubert Fletcher Rickett, KCMG, CB, and has:

     1b *Oliver Patrick Oscar; *b* 1983

     1b *Rosanna Madeleine; *b* 1986

    2a *Emma Victoria; *b* 18 June 1955

4 CYRIL ASQUITH, BARON ASQUITH OF BISHOPSTONE (LP), of Bishopstone, Co Sussex (UK), so *cr* April 1951, PC (1946), KC 1936; *b* 5 Feb 1890; *educ* Winchester and Balliol Coll Oxford (Hon Fell 1947); barrister Inner Temple 1920, Bencher 1939, Assist Reader Common Law Cncl Legal Educn 1925–28 (memb Cncl 1938–54), Recorder Salisbury 1937–38, memb Gen Claims Tbnl 1939–43, Judge King's Bench 1938–46, Ld Justice Appeal 1946–51, Ld Appeal in Ordinary 1951–54, Chm Commn Higher Educn Colonies 1942–44, Roy Commn Equal Pay Men and Women 1944–46, Capt 16th Bn London Regt WW

I, ktd 1938; *m* 12 Feb 1918 Anne Stephanie (*d* 19 Feb 1964), er dau of Sir Adrian Donald Wilde Pollock, KCMG (*see* POLLOCK, Bt, of Hatton), and *d* 24 Aug 1954, leaving:

(1) Luke; *b* 18 Nov 1919; *educ* Winchester; Capt 60th Rifles WW II, with Kleinwort Benson 1947–79; *m* 2 July 1954 *(Ethel) Meriel [The Hon Mrs Luke Asquith, 31 Trossacks Rd, London SE22 8PY], ballet dancer, er dau of Maurice Cann Evans, and *d* 1994, leaving:

1a *Lucy; *b* 29 June 1962; *m* 1988 *Nicholas John Troop, yr s of Robert Troop, and has:

1b *Vanessa Charlotte; *b* 1990

2b *Laura Alexandra; *b* 1993

2a *Anne; *b* 10 Nov 1965; *m* 1989 *Hon Roderick Alexander Cavendish, only s of 7th Baron Waterpark (*qv*), and has issue

(2) Paul; *b* 4 Jan 1927; *educ* Eton; Coldstream Gds 1945–48; *m* 1st 18 July 1953 (*divorce* 1963) Helena Mary, er dau of Hon Geoffrey John Orlando Bridgeman, MC (*see* BRIDGEMAN, V), and had:

1a +Jonathan Paul [Jonathan Asquith Esq, 8 Colinette Rd, London SW15 6QQ]; *b* 28 Sept 1956; *m* 1984 *Sarah Ann, yst dau of Peter Noel Negretti (*see* EDEN OF WINTON, B), and has:

1b +(Paul) William; *b* 13 June 1988

2b *Matthew Henry George; *b* 3 Oct 1994

1b *Harriet Mary Rose; *b* 26 Sept 1991

1a *(Mary) Clare [Mrs Rory Macnamara, 8 Castello Ave, London SW15 6EA]; *b* 28 July 1954; *m* 1986 *Rory Patrick Macnamara, er s of Carroll Macnamara, and has:

1b *(Charles) Frederick; *b* 1988

1b *Katharine Rose; *b* 1990

2b *Flora Mary; *b* 1993

(2) (cont.) The Hon Paul Asquith *m* 2nd 16 July 1963 *Caroline Anne [The Hon Mrs Paul Asquith, 41 Quarrendon St, London SW6 3ST], yr dau of Sir John Gawen Carew Pole, 12th Bt (*see* POLE, Bt, of Shute House), and *d* 1984, having by her had:

2a +Rupert; *b* 27 May 1965; *m* 17 July 1996 *Alexandra, dau of Morton Neal

2a *Emily Anne; *b* 7 May 1964; *m* 31 Oct 1998 *Christopher Daly, yr s of Lt-Col Denis Daly, of the Roy Hosp Chelsea

(1) Jane; *b* 3 July 1922; *d* 1978

(2) *(Frances) Rose [The Hon Lady Stephenson, 26 Doneraile St, London SW6 6EN]; *b* 4 Oct 1925; *m* 8 Dec 1951 *Sir John Frederick Eustace Stephenson, PC, late Ld Justice of Appeal, 2nd s of Sir Guy Stephenson, CB, by Gwendolen, 5th dau of John Gilbert Talbot, PC, JP, DL (*see* SHREWSBURY and WATERFORD, E), and has:

1a *David Guy; *b* 27 Oct 1954; *educ* Winchester

2a *Daniel Paul; *b* 25 Jan 1960

1a *Mary; *b* 24 Nov 1952; *m* 8 Jan 1972 (*divorce* 1995) Philippe G Wines, only s of E G Wines, and has:

1b *Daniel Philippe Glyn; *b* 1983

1b *Katharine Valerie Rose; *b* 1972

2b *Polly Victoria Jane; *b* 1976

3b *Lucy Helen Mary; *b* 1979

2a *Laura Jane; *b* 16 Jan 1958; *m* 1st 1980 D J Nicholas Bodington, s of Maj W J Bodington, DFC; *m* 2nd 1987 *Andrew F Sykes, yr s of Sir Richard Adam Sykes, KCMG, MC, and has:

1b *Matthew John; *b* 3 June 1991

2b *Sam Richard; *b* 16 March 1995

1b *Amelia Anne; *b* 28 May 1989

1 (HELEN) VIOLET Aquith, BARONESS ASQUITH OF YARNBURY (LP), of Yarnbury, Co Wilts (UK), so *cr* 21 Dec 1964, DBE (1953); *b* 15 April 1887; Pres: Women's Lib Fedn 1923–25 and 1939–45, Lib Pty Orgn 1947–66, RIIA1964, Govr BBC 1941–46, Old Vic 1945, V-Chm Utd Europe Movement 1947, memb Roy Commn Press 1947–49, Patron UN Assoc, Tstee Glyndebourne Arts Tst 1955, Hon LLD Sussex 1963, author: *Winston Churchill as I Knew Him* (1965); *m* 30 Nov 1915 Sir Maurice BONHAM CARTER, KCB, KCVO (*d* 7 June 1960), yst s of Henry Bonham Carter, and *d* 19 Feb 1969, leaving:

(1) MARK RAYMOND BONHAM CARTER, BARON BONHAM-CARTER, of Yarnbury, Co Wilts (LP, UK), so *cr* 1986; *b* 11 Feb 1922; *educ* Winchester, Balliol Coll Oxford (Scholar) and U of Chicago (Cwlth Fell); Capt Gren Gds WW II (despatches, POW 1943, escaped 1943), MP (Lib) Torrington 1958–59, UK Del Cncl Europe 1958–59; dir Wm Collins 1955–58, ROH Covent Gdn 1958; Govr Roy Ballet Sch, Chm Race Rels Bd 1966–71 and Community Rels Commn 1971–77, V-Chm and Govr BBC 1975–81, ed *The Autobiography of Margot Asquith* (1962); *m* 30 June 1955 *Leslie, formerly w of 2nd Baron St Just (*see* 1970 edn) and dau of Condé Nast, of New York, and *d* 4 Sept 1994, leaving:

1a *Jane Mary; *b* 20 Oct 1957; formerly TV jnlst with Channel 4's *A Week in Politics*, press offr Lib Dems 1996–

2a *Virginia Leslie [The Hon Mrs Brand, 1 Kingswood Ave, London NW6 6LA]; *b* 27 Aug 1959; ed at 4th Estate Ltd; *m* 1992, as his 2nd w, *Charles David William Brand and has issue (*see* DACRE, B)

3a *Elizabeth Cressida; *b* 1 March 1961

(2) *Raymond Henry [The Hon Raymond Bonham Carter, 7 West Heath Ave, London NW11 7QS]; *b* 19 June 1929; *educ* Winchester, Magdalen Coll Oxford (BA 1952) and Harvard Business Sch (MBA 1954); 2nd Lt Irish Gds 1947–49, with J Henry Schroder & Co 1954–58, actg advsr Bank of England 1958–63, alternate exec dir UK IMF and memb UK Treasury and Supply Delegn Washington 1961–63, with S G Warburg 1964–79 (exec dir 1967–77), dir: Tport Devpt Gp 1969–77, Banque de Paris et des Pays Bas NV 1973–77, Mercury Securities 1974–77, seconded as Dir Industl Devpt DOI 1977–79, memb Cncl ISS (Hon Treas 1974–84); *m* 26 July 1958 *Elena, dau of Eduardo Propper de Callejon, Spanish Amb Norway, and has:

1a *Edward Henry; *b* 24 May 1960; dep investment offr Jupiter Asset Management 1998–; *m* 1994 *Victoria Studd, TV presenter, and has:

1b *Harry Raymond; *b* 22 Aug 1996

2a *Thomas David; *b* 8 Dec 1961; dir Barclay Tst Personal Investments; *m* 1990 *Virginia Catherine Elizabeth, 2nd dau of Nigel Sharp, and has:

1b *Freddy; *b* 1990

1b *Rose Violet; *b* 1992

1a *Helena [Helena Bonham Carter, c/o Jeremy Conway, Conway van Gelder Ltd, 18/21 Jermyn St, London SW1Y 6HB]; *b* 26 May 1966; *educ* Hampstead High Sch for Girls, Westminster; actress: *Lady Jane* (1985), *A Room with a View* (1986), *A Hazard of Hearts* (1988), *The Mask* (1988), *St Francis of Assisi* (1989), *Getting it Right* (1989), *Hamlet* (1990), *Where Angels Fear to Tread* (1992), *Howard's End* (1992), *Fatal Deception* (1993), *Mary Shelley's Frankenstein* (1994), *The Glace Bay Miner's Museum* (1994), *Margaret's Museum* (in Canada, 1996), *Keep the Aspidistra Flying, Wings of the Dove* (National Board of Review, Los Angeles Film Critics Assoc, Broadcast Film Critics Assoc, Boston Soc of Film Critics Best Actress Awards 1997, Golden Globe, Screen Actors Guild and Oscar Best Actress nominee 1998), *Chinese Portraits* (1997), (films); *Miami Vice* (1987), *The Vision* (1988), *Arms and the Man* (1988), *Beatrix Potter*(1989), *Dancing Queen* (1993), *A Dark Adapted Eye* (1994) (TV); *A Woman in White* (1988), *The Chalk Garden* (1989), *House of Bernarda Alba* (1991), *The Barber of Seville* (1992), *Trelawney of the Wells* (1992) (theatre); *The Reluctant Debutante, Marie Antoinette, The Seagull* (radio)

(1) (Helen Laura) Cressida; *b* 22 April 1917; DipArch Lond; *m* 8 June 1939 Jasper Alexander Maurice Ridley and *d* 10 June 1998, leaving issue (*see* RIDLEY V)

(2) Laura Miranda; *b* 13 Oct 1918; *m* 31 May 1938 Baron (Jo(seph)) Grimond (LP, *cr* 1983), PC, TD, LLD Edin, MP (Lib) Orkney and Shetland 1950–83, Leader Lib Pty 1956–67 (*d* 24 Oct 1993), s of Joseph Bowman Grimond, of St Andrews, and *d* 14 Feb 1994, having had (with another s, *d* young):

1a *John(ny) Jasper; *b* 1946; *educ* Eton, Balliol Coll Oxford and Harvard; for ed *Economist* 1989– (assist ed 1975, Br ed 1976–79, American ed 1979–88); *m* 1973 *Kate, dau of Lt-Col Peter Fleming, OBE, and has:

1b *Mary Jessie; *b* 1976

2b *Rose Clementine; *b* 1979

3b *Georgia Celia; *b* 1983

2a *Thomas Magnus; *b* 1959; *educ* Stromness Acad and Edinburgh U

1a *Grizelda Jane; *b* 1942; *educ* St Paul's Girls' Sch and St Hugh's Coll Oxford

The **1st Earl** *m* 2nd 10 May 1894 (Emma Alice) Margaret ('Margot') (*d* 28 July 1945), 6th dau of Sir Charles Tennant, 1st Bt (*see* GLENCONNER, B), and *d* 15 Feb 1928, having by her had:

5 Anthony ('Puffin'); *b* 9 Nov 1902; *educ* Winchester and Balliol Coll Oxford (BA); film dir (including *The Winslow Boy, The Browning Version, The Millionairess, The Yellow Rolls-Royce*), Govr BFI, Pres ACTT, FBFA , FRSA, Cdr Order Merit Italy; *d* unm 21 Feb 1968

2 Elizabeth Charlotte Lucy; *m* 30 April 1919 Prince Antoine Bibesco, Romanian Min Madrid, s of Prince Alexandre Bibesco, and *d* 7 April 1945, leaving issue. He *d* 2 Sept 1951

OXFUIRD

Arms: Gules three martlets argent. **Crest:** A phoenix in flames proper. **Supporters:** Dexter, a horse at liberty argent, gorged with a viscount's coronet and thereto affixed a chain, maned and hooved or; sinister, a bull sable, horned, unguled, collared and chained or. **Motto:** *Sine fine* ('Without limit'). **Creations:** Bt. (NS) 19 July 1627, L. and V. (S) 19 April 1651.

THE 13TH VISCOUNT (OF) OXFUIRD, **Lord Makgill of Cousland** and a **Baronet** (Sir George Hubbard Makgill, Bt, CBE (1997)) [The Rt Hon The Viscount Oxfuird CBE, Hill House, St Mary Bourne, Hants SP11 6BG]; *b* 7 Jan 1934; *s unc* 1986; *educ* St Peter's Sch Cambridge, NZ, and Wanganui Coll Sch, NZ; commd RAF (GD Branch) 1955–58, Dep Speaker Ho Lds 1990–; *m* 1st 11 Feb 1967 (*divorce* 1977) Alison Campbell, er dau of Neils Max Jensen, of Randers, Denmark, and has had:

1 John Richard James; *b* 15 Dec, *d* 17 Dec 1967

2 +IAN ARTHUR ALEXANDER, *Master of Oxfuird*; *b* 14 Oct 1969

3 +Robert Edward George; *b* 14 Oct 1969

4 +Hamish Max Alistair; *b* 1972

The 13th VISCOUNT *m* 2nd 1980 *Venetia Cunitia Mary, only dau of Maj Charles Anthony Steward, of The Platt, Crondall, Surrey, and by her has:

5 +Edward Anthony Donald; *b* 1983

Lineage: MALCOLM MACGIL, probably s of GILBERT, (feudal) Ld of Galloway (*d* 1185), was ancestor of the MAKGILLs of that Ilk and other MAKGILLs holding lands in Galloway, Ayrshire, Fifeshire, Lanarks, the Lothians, Perths and Roxburghs.

JAMES MAKGILL, a cadet, held the lands of Glenguiken, Kirkcudbrightshire, *temp* JAMES III and IV; *m* Elizabeth, dau of Cunningham of Caprington, and had:

Sir JAMES MAKGILL; Provost Edinburgh *temp* JAMES V; allegedly an early supporter of the Reformation; sold his lands in Galloway and the lands of Park of Stibbery, Lanarks, 1526–36; acquired by charter 7 Sept 1538 lands of Liberton Burn and Senis, nr Edinburgh; *m c* 7 March 1536 Helen, dau of Sir Henry Wardlaw of Torrie, and *d* 1553, having had:

1 John; *m* Margaret, er dau of James Preston, of Valleyfield, and *dvp c* 1552, leaving two daus and coheirs (resigned their f's estate to their unc James 1552):

(1) Margaret; *m* 1553 William Redpath of that Ilk

(2) Alison; *m* Stephen Brounfield of Grenelawdene

2 James (Sir), of Rankeillour, Fifeshire, PC (1561); acquired lands in Fifeshire, Forfarshire, Galloway and Lothian; advocate 1539, Ld of Session and Clerk Registrar 1554 (as latter of which temporarily dismissed for implication in murder of Rizzio), joined Reformers 1559, a Parly Commr, fought against MARY QUEEN OF SCOTS Battle of Langside 1568, Amb England 1570/1 and 1572, Ld Provost Edinburgh Oct 1570; *m c* 1540 Janet, dau of William Adamsoun of Craigcrook, and *d* by 15 Aug 1579, having had:

(1) James, of Rankeillour; *m* (contract 18 April 1578) Jean, dau of Sir David Wemyss of Wemyss (*see* WEMYSS, E), and *d* 6 Nov 1602, leaving, with other issue:

1a James, of Rankeillour; *b* 1576; *m* (contract 20 Sept 1598) Katherine (*d* 1662), dau of George Clephane of Carslogie, and *d* 20 April 1661, having had:

1b David (Sir), of Rankeillour; *m c* 19 Dec 1629 Elizabeth, sis of 1st Lord Ruthven of Freeland (*see* CARLISLE, E), and had, with a yr s (Patrick, *d* unm 5 Nov 1669) and a dau (Margaret, *m* John Skene of Halyairds):

1c James (Sir), of Rankeillour; *m* 1st 24 Aug 1665 Janet, dau of James Crichton, 1st Viscount of Frendraught (*see* ERNE, E, for earlier ancestry); *m* 2nd Isabel, dau of Sir George Preston of Valley Field, and *d c* 3 May 1699, leaving by his 1st w:

1d DAVID MAKGILL, *de jure* 3rd Bt and *de jure* 3rd VISCOUNT OF OXFUIRD; *m* (contract 10 Feb 1693) Janet, est dau and heiress of John Craig of Ramorney, advocate, and *d* Sept 1717, having had, with three other sons:

1e JAMES MAKGILL, *de jure* 4th Bt and *de jure* 4th VISCOUNT OF OXFUIRD; *m* (contract 20 Jan 1720) Jean, dau of Sir Robert Anstruther, 1st Bt, of Balcaskie (*qv*), and *dsp* 26 Sept 1747

1e Katherine; served heiress to er bro 4 July 1765; *m* Alexander Christie (*d* 4 July 1765), writer (legal practitioner) in Edinburgh, and *d* Feb 1774, leaving:

1f Janet; *m* June 1748 Robert Maitland (*see* below) and *dsp* 1 July 1758

2e Isabel; served heiress to her sis 11 April 1776; *m* Rev William Dick (*d c* 2 Feb 1738), Min Cupar 1738, and *d* Jan 1787, leaving:

1f James, of Colluthie; had:

1g Margaret; *m* 1767 Capt Frederick Lewis Maitland (*see* LAUDERDALE, E) and had issue

2b James, of Flasshill, Fife; *m* Jean, dau of Rev Sir Alexander Balfour, Bt, Min Abdie, and *d* Oct 1695, leaving:

1c Ann; *m* John Imbrie, of Flass, Fife, and *d c* 26 Feb 1695

2c Margaret; *m* John Makgill, of Edinburgh, and *d c* 26 Feb 1695

3b John (Rev), of Kemback, Fife, MD; Min Dunbog and Cupar; *m* 1st 25 April 1647 Helen (*d* 20 July 1665), dau of James Forbes of Kilmany by Katharine, dau of James Bethune of Creich, and had, with other issue:

1c Arthur, of Kemback; *b* 15 Dec 1652; Parly Commr Fife; *m* 1st 6 April 1675 Janet (*d* 8 April 1687), dau and heiress of John Ramsay of Brackmont, advocate, by Margaret, dau of Capt James Bruce of Newburn, and had, with other issue:

1d JOHN MAKGILL, *de jure* 5th Bt and *de jure* 5th VISCOUNT OF OXFUIRD, of Kemback and Fingask; *b* 13 June 1676; served heir to his cousin 24 July 1751; *m* 13 June 1706 Agnes, only dau of John Lindsay of Wormiston (*see* LINDSAY, E), and *d* 19 April 1762, having had, with three daus:

1e ARTHUR MAKGILL, *de jure* 6th Bt and *de jure* 6th VISCOUNT OF OXFUIRD, of Kemback and Fingask; *b* 18 May 1709; Capt Cmdt a Scottish Regt in Dutch serv; matriculated arms as heir male of Rankeillour 1771; *d* unm (*bur* 15 Dec 1777)

2e John, of Jamaica; *b* 21 Sept 1715; *dsp* Nov 1741

3e GEORGE MAKGILL, *de jure* 7th Bt and *de jure* 7th VISCOUNT OF OXFUIRD, of Kemback and Fingask; *b* 6 Sept 1723; joined Jacobite army Battle of Preston, served rest of the campaign, wounded Culloden and narrowly escaped capture; went to France; eventually pardoned; Capt 12th Foot Br Army; *m* his cousin Agnes Law (*see* below) and *d* 26 Aug 1797, leaving:

1f JOHN MAKGILL, *de jure* 8th Bt and *de jure* 8th VISCOUNT OF OXFUIRD, of Kemback and Fingask; *bapt* 16 Nov 1790; *m* 13 Nov 1811 Eliza (*d* 11 Aug 1860), er dau of William Dalgleish, of Scotscraig, Fife, and *d* 3 May 1817, leaving:

1g GEORGE MAKGILL, *de jure* 9th Bt and *de jure* 9th VISCOUNT OF OXFUIRD, of Kemback and Fingask; *b* 23 Dec 1812; *m* 20 Nov 1833 Harriet (*d* 7 Nov 1890), dau of Amos Strettell, of Benderton House, Sussex, by Harriet Eliza, dau of John Utterson, of Milland Place, Surrey, and *d* 21 Sept 1878, leaving, with two daus (*d* unm):

1h JOHN, *de jure* (and self-styled?) 10th Bt

2h George Edward; Bengal CS; *m* 1 Sept 1868 Henrietta Julia (*d* 25 Feb 1919), 2nd surv dau of Arthur Littledale, HEICS; *dsp* 3 Aug 1877

3h Arthur; *educ* Univ Coll Oxford (MA); advocate; *d* unm 5 Sept 1899

1g Jane; *m* 20 July 1841 Robert Haldane of Cloanden, Perths, WS, and *d* 24 Feb 1851, leaving issue

2g Agnes; *s* with her sis Jane to the estate of Dura, Fife; *d* unm 15 Nov 1899

3g John (dau); *d* unm 7 Feb 1879

1f Janet; *m* Thomas Horsburgh, Sheriff Clerk of Fife

2f Agnes; *d* unm

3f Catherine; *m* George Greenlaw, WS, and *dsp* Nov 1883

4f Margaret; *m* Alexander Murray Guthrie of Craigie and *d* 1838, leaving issue

2d James; *b* 6 Nov 1680; Capt Spanish Army; *dsp*

3d Thomas; *b* 15 March 1682; MD; *d* unm at Eton

4d David, of Md., USA; *b* 20 April 1686; surgn

1d Margaret; *m* James Martine of Clearmont

1c (cont.) Arthur Makgill *m* 2nd 4 July 1695 Jean, er dau of Sir John Bruce, Bt, of Airth and Stenhouse (*see* 1850 edn), and widow of John Law, of Edinburgh, and *d* 21 Jan 1725, having by her had:

2d Isobel; *m* Mungo Law of Pittillock, Falkland, and had:

1e Mungo, of Pittillock; Maj Scots Greys; *m* Janet, dau of John Pilmroe, and had:

1f Agnes; *m de jure* 7th VISCOUNT (*see* above) and was *bur* 24 Nov 1799, leaving issue

3d Jean; *dsp* 1710

1c Helen; *b* 18 July 1659; *m* 1678 Thomas Nairne of Baldovan

3b (cont.) The Rev John Makgill *m* 2nd 22 Jan 1668 Eupheme Paterson (*dsp*), widow of Gavin Wemyss, of Unthank, and *d* 24 April 1673

1b Jean; *m* John Scrymgeour of Kirkton and had issue (*see* DUNDEE, E)

2b Katherine; *m* Robert Clayhills of Innergowrie

3b Lilias; *m* Henry Pitcairn of Pitlour and had issue

2a Robert; Ld of Session as Lord Foord 1649; *m* Margaret Purves (*d* 1651) and *d* Nov 1651, having had:

1b James, of Fingask; *bapt* 9 Dec 1623; *m* 1655 Margaret Ramsay of Idingtoun and *d c* 22 Feb 1670, leaving:

1c Robert, of Fingask; *d* unm May 1708

1c Jean; *d* unm *c* 18 July 1743

2b Robert; *bapt* 10 July 1627

1b Margaret

3a Alexander; living 30 Nov 1620

4a John; Min Flisk; *m* Eupham Inglis and was ancestor of the MACGILLs of Rumgally

5a David; Prof Montpellier, France; *d* unm

6a Henry (Rev); Min Dunfermline; *m* Catherine Wardlaw and had issue

7a William; MD, a fndr Edinburgh Coll Physicians 1620

8a Hew, of West Grange; *m c* 24 Dec 1652 Margaret, dau of John Cornwall of Bonhard; his line failed with his gs Hew, of Grange (*d* 4 Aug 1720, when his dau Janet was served heir)

9a George; Lt-Col; *d* unm Sept 1648

10a Patrick (Rev); Min Monikie; *m* Joan Irwine; his line failed *c* 1747 with his gs Alexander

1a Jean; *m* 1st William Gourlay of Kincraig; *m* 2nd — Brown of Finmouth

2a Cecilia; *m* Sir John Learmonth of Balcomie

3a Lilias; *m* — Brown, Yr. of Finmouth

(2) John; advocate, Archpresbyter Dunbar; *m* Elizabeth, dau of William Home of Ayton, and *dsp* 2 July 1607

(3) Samuel; burgess Glasgow; granted lands in Ulster 1609; probably ancestor in the female line of Sir John JOHNSTON later MAKGILL, 1st and last Bt (I), so *cr* 10 Nov 1680, of Gill Hall, Co Down (*dsp* 18 Jan 1699/1700)

(4) David; advocate; Preb Fowngarth, Canon Dunkeld 1584/5

(5) Zachary; *m* Bessie Hamilton and had issue

(1) Rachel; *m* 1st 10 May 1576 George Stewart, Yr. of Rosyth; *m* 2nd *c* 1592 Archibald Wauchope of Niddrie

(2) Elspeth; *m c* 3 Oct 1566 David Wode of Dunone

3 David, of Nesbit and Cranston Riddell, Co Edinburgh; a Ld of Session, King's Advocate 27 June 1582; *m* (contract 11 May 1557) Elizabeth (*d* 16 March 1578/9), dau of James Forester of Corstorphine, Edinburgh, and *d* 13 Feb 1595/6, having had, with two other sons:

(1) David, of Cranston Riddell; a Ld of Session 25 May 1597; had charter of his lands 1585; *m* (contract 10 Sept 1583) Mary (*d* 6 Feb 1606), er dau of Sir William Sinclair of Herdmanstoun, and *d* 10 May 1607, having had, with other issue:

1a Sir **James Makgill, 1st Bt** (NS), so *cr* 19 July 1627, with remainder to his heirs male whomsoever, of Makgill, and **1st Viscount of Oxfurd** [*sic*], so *cr* 19 April 1651, as also LORD MAKGILL OF COUSLAND (both S), with remainder to his heirs male and of tailzie and provision whomsoever; Edinburgh; Sheriff 1626, Sheriff Pncpl 1628, Ld of Session 3 Nov 1629 and Feb 1660/1, MP (S Parl) Co Edinburgh 1630, a Commr Exchequer 1644, Feb 1644/5 and Feb 1660/1 and War 1647 and 1648; *m* 1st *c* 20 Dec 1621 Catherine, dau of Sir John Cockburn of Ormiston, and had, with another s (*d* young):

1b James; *dsp*; *bur* 24 Jan 1662

2b Andrew; *b* 26 July 1630; *d c* 1656

3b Patrick; *d* unm 1651

1b Elizabeth; *m* Patrick Hamilton of Preston and had:

1c Thomas, of Preston and Fala; Col; had:

1d Thomas HAMILTON later HAMILTON-MAKGILL, of Fala; *s* to the Oxfuird estates 1758; *m* Elizabeth, dau of Sir John Dalrymple, 3rd Bt, of Cousland, and *d* 1779, leaving:

    1e Elizabeth; *m* 7 March 1760 her cousin Sir John DALRYMPLE later DALRYMPLE-HAMILTON-MAKGILL, 4th Bt, of Cousland and Oxenfoord and had a 4th but est surv s:

        1f JOHN HAMILTON DALRYMPLE-HAMILTON-MAKGILL later DALRYMPLE, 5th Bt, and 8th EARL OF STAIR (*qv*), as which *s* 3rd cousin once-removed 1840; *cr* 16 Aug 1841 BARON OXENFOORD OF COUSLAND; *dsp* 1853

2b Anne; *m* Sir James Richardson of Smeaton

1a (cont.) The **1st Viscount** *m* 2nd *c* 8 July 1646 Christian (*d* March 1664), dau of Sir William Livingston of Kilsyth (*see* DALHOUSIE, E), and *d* 5 May 1663, having by her had, with two other sons (*d* in infancy):

    4b David; *b* 15 May 1649; *d* by 1656

    5b ROBERT MAKGILL, **2nd Viscount of Oxford**; *b* 20 May 1651; incarcerated Edinburgh Castle July 1689 and the following month discharged but banned from Edinburgh eight years and eventually placed under house arrest at Cranston Riddell, for conspiring as a Jacobite; *m* 1st July 1666 Lady Henrietta Livingston (*dsp* Nov 1696), only dau of 3rd Earl of Linlithgow (*see* LINLITHGOW, M, preliminary remarks); *m* 2nd *c* 26 Dec 1684 Jean, est dau of 2nd Earl of Dalhousie (*qv*), and widow of George, Lord Ross, and *dspms* Dec 1705, when his peerages became dormant, having had:

        1c George, *Master of Oxfuird*; *bapt* 21 Jan 1676; Ensign Scots Gds 1700; *dsp* unm Flanders Aug or Sept 1701

        1c Christian Makgill, self-styled Viscountess of Oxfurd from 1706; *b* 16 March 1677; *m* as his 1st w William MAITLAND, 6th s of 3rd Earl of Lauderdale (*qv*), and *d* 1707, leaving:

            1d Robert MAITLAND later MAITLAND MAKGILL, self-styled 4th Viscount of Oxfurd (as which voted in election of rep S peers 1733 but not thereafter); *m* 16 June 1748 Janet, only dau of Alexander Christie, WS, by Katherine, dau of *de jure* 3rd Bt and *de jure* 3rd VISCOUNT OXFUIRD (*see* above), and *dsp* 10 Oct 1755

        2c Henrietta Makgill, self-styled Viscountess of Oxfurd from 1755; *b c* 1682; *m* James HAMILTON of Orbistoun and *dsp* 11 Oct 1758

    6b George; *b* 11 March 1655; Col Foot Gds; *m* Elizabeth Hamilton; *dsp* 15 Dec 1704

    3b Christian; *b* 19 Feb 1654; *m* 1st Alexander Crawford, of Carse; *m* 2nd George Ross, of Galstown

2a John; *b* 1595; *m* Marion Menzies, widow of John Douglas of Archland, and *dspms c* 1677

3a Alexander; *b* 20 July 1600; *dspms c* 1677

1a Elizabeth; *m* (contract 10 July 1612) James, Master of Cranstoun, and had issue

(2) Laurence; Advocate and Commr Supply; *m* 1st 21 June 1598 Jean Crichton and had, with six sons (*dspm* by 9 Dec 1625):

    1a Margaret; served heir to her unc John (*see* below); *m* 25 April 1622 David Heriot

(2) (cont.) Laurence Makgill *m* 2nd *c* 9 Dec 1625 Helen, widow of John Ker of Hiltoune, and *d* by 29 April 1646

(3) John; WS; *m* 1st —; *m* 2nd 6 Aug 1606 Maria Sandilands and *dsp c* 29 April 1646

(1) Elizabeth; *m* 1st Robert Logan of Restalrig; *m* 2nd by 28 April 1579 Sir Thomas Kennedy of Culzean and had issue (*see* AILSA, M); *m* 3rd *c* 4 April 1605 William Mewe of Rowallan and *d* Jan 1622

(2) Jean; *m* Ross of Balneil

1 Agnes; *m* John Hill, Edinburgh burgess

2 Helen; *m* 1st Thomas, 2nd s of Wiliam Cranstoun of Cranstoun; *m* 2nd *c* 1563 William Knowis

The *de jure* 9th VISCOUNT's est s,

JOHN MAKGILL, *de jure* 10th Bt (appears to have assumed btcy prior to its official recognition), and *de jure* 10th VISCOUNT OF OXFUIRD, JP; *b* 6 Feb 1836; Capt RE; *s* to Kemback and Fingask but sold them; *m* 18 April 1866 Margaret Isabella (*d* 18 March 1920), dau of Robert Haldane of Cloanden, and *d* 14 Nov 1906, having had:

1 GEORGE (Sir), **11th Bt**

2 Robert Haldane, CBE (1919); *b* 24 May 1870; MD Edin 1899, DPH Cantab 1901; Lt-Col NZMC, Boer War and WWI; *d* unm 3 Oct 1946

3 John Edward; *b* 11 Nov 1874; *m* July 1897 Muriel Ravenscroft (*d* 5 May 1946), dau of Hon Henry de Bohun Devereux (*see* HEREFORD, V), and *d* 28 Nov 1938, leaving:

    (1) Rodney Devereux; *b* 1901; *m* 1923 *Laura [Mrs Rodney Makgill, 14 Marei Rd, Ellerslie, Auckland, New Zealand], dau of Richard Reynolds, of Cambridge, Auckland, NZ, and *d* 1955, leaving:

        1a +Richard John [Richard Makgill Esq, Matahi Rd, Manawehe, RD Matata, nr Rotorua, New Zealand]; *b* 1926; *m* 1954 *Marjorie Ann Jamieson and has:

            1b +Stuart Rodney; *b* 1956

            2b +Roy Malcolm; *b* 1961

            1b *Janet; *b* 1952

            2b *Yvonne; *b* 1954

        1a *Patricia Ruth [Mrs Alfred Bridger, 44 Kiwi Rd, Devonport, Auckland, New Zealand]; *b* 1923; *m* 1946 Alfred Bridger (*d* 1987) and has:

            1b *Peter James; *b* 1949

            1b *Patricia Ellen; *b* 1947; *m* 1967 *Bruce Wallace Nicklin and has:

                1c *David John; *b* 1969

                2c *Jeffrey Bruce; *b* 1971

                1c *Tracey Rochelle; *b* 1973

            2b *Susan; *b* 1957; *m* 1978 *Grant Brendan Nauman and has:

                1c *Megan Louise; *b* 1981

                2c *Laura Marie; *b* 1982

                3c *Raelene Anna; *b* 1984

                4c *Nicola Lee; *b* 1986

        2a *Muriel Ann; *b* 1927; *m* 17 Sept 1955 *Thomas William Tyrwhitt-Drake, only s of Charles William Tyrwhitt-Drake, of Rickmansworth, Herts, and has:

            1b *Richard William; *b* 17 Nov 1957

            2b *Hugh Charles; *b* 9 March 1959

            1b *Penelope Elizabeth; *b* 7 March 1964

        3a *Nancy Margaret [Mrs Edward Smith, 28 Beaumaris Way, Takanani, Auckland, New Zealand]; *b* 1929; *m* 1954 *(Thomas) Edward Smith, s of Herbert Smith, and has:

            1b *Nigel Thomas; *b* 21 Oct 1957; *m* 1984 *Stephanie Littlejohn

            1b *Deborah Ann; *b* 11 March 1954; *m* 1986 *Fred Hickling and has:

                1c *Amy; *b* 1988

            2b *Sandra Lee; *b* 21 Oct 1957; *m* 1981 *Glen Pryor and has:

                1c *Luke; *b* 1983

                1c *Kate; *b* 1986

        4a *Elizabeth; *b* 1933; *m* 1968 *Capt Thomas Chisholm

    (2) Robert John; *b* 1910; *m* 1940 Marjorie Wardell-Johnson (*d* 1981), of Napier, NZ, and *d* 1983, leaving:

        1a +John Wardell [John Makgill Esq, 2 Belloc St, Cambridge, New Zealand]; *b* 1944; *m* 1971 *Valerie Joan Turner and has:

            1b +Braedon; *b* 1973

            1b *Amanda; *b* 1977

         2a +Hugh Haldane; *b* 1948; *m* 1970 *Pamela Ann Jones and has:

            1b *Lisa; *b* 1972

            2b *Claudia; *b* 1974

            3b *Joanna; *b* 1977

         3a *Simon Redding [Simon Makgill Esq, Lamb St, RD3 Cambridge, New Zealand]; *b* 1949; *m* 1970 *Jane Gifford and has:

            1b *Matthew Simon; *b* 1977

            1b *Louise Clare; *b* 1973

            2b *Miriam Jane; *b* 1975

            3b *Emily Ann; *b* 1980

         4a +Robert Cloan; *b* 1950; *m* 1970 *Josephine Mary Uden and has:

            1b +Robert; *b* 1971

            2b +Dylan; *b* 1975

    (3) James Edward; *b* 1913; F/O RAF WW II; missing presumed *ka* 1942

    (4) +Geoffrey Haldane [Geoffrey Makgill Esq, 30 Kensington Place, Fairfield, Hamilton, New Zealand]; *b* 1915; *m* 1945 *Elizabeth McNiven, of Auckland, and has:

        1a *Penelope Anne [Mrs John Scott, Puketawa, Roberts Rd, RD2, Cambridge, New Zealand]; *b* 1947; *m* 1973 *John Bryce Scott and has:

            1b *William Ruediger Makgill; *b* 1975

            2b *Geoffrey Robert; *b* 1977

    (1) Joanna Maud; *b* 1898; *m* 1927 Brian Preston Stevenson, of Auckland, and had:

        1a *Rodney Brian Preston; *b* 1 Feb 1935; *m* 1958 (*divorce* 1966) Susanne Harle, dau of Robert Harle Giles, of Auckland, and has:

            1b *Mark Preston; *b* 1958

            1b *Victoria Anne; *b* 1960

        1a Cynthia Mary; *b* 1 July 1928; *m* 19 May 1962 John Hampden Hyatt, er s of Kenneth Edwin Hyatt, of Chepstow, Mon, and had:

            1b *Michael John Guthrie; *b* 9 June 1963

            1b *Juliet Mary; *b* 21 Aug 1964

            2b *Susan Joanna; *b* 18 Oct 1967

        2a *Miriam Rosemary; *b* 18 Dec 1930

        3a Joanna Muriel; *b* 18 April 1932; *m* 1961 Chalmers Henry Fairweather, CEng, s of James Henry Fairweather, of Surrey, and had:

            1b *Alastair Andrew Chalmers; *b* 30 Nov 1962

            1b *Sarah Joanna; *b* 9 May 1966

    (2) *Miriam Isabella; *b* 1903; *m* 1955 Hensleigh Carthew Marryat Norris (*d* 1980)

    (3) Muriel Barbara; *b* 1907

    (4) *Margaret Philippa [Mrs Margaret Brown, 1/3 Matai Rd, Green Lane, Auckland 5, New Zealand]; *b* 1918; *m* 1946 (*divorce* 1968) Alexander Hamilton Brown

4 David; *b* 2 Jan 1880; *m* 22 Nov 1909 Margaret Elizabeth (*d* 11 July 1948), yst dau of Ven Archdeacon Palmer, and *d* Oct 1934, leaving:

    (1) +John Palmer [John Makgill Esq, 40 King St, Waiuku, New Zealand]; *b* 1910; *m* 15 June 1938 *Lucy Warner and has:

        1a +Alan Richard John; *b* 1941; *m* 1985 *Heather Dawn, yr dau of Norman Douglas, and has:

            1b *Iona Amie; *b* 1987

         1a *Jennifer Ann [Mrs Bruce Hinton, Te Toro, No 4 RMD Waiuku, New Zealand]; *b* 1939; *m* 1959 *Bruce Hinton and has:

            1b *Stuart Bruce; *b* 1963

            1b *Wendy Lucille; *b* 1960

            2b *Barbara Ann; *b* 1961

    (2) +David Comins [David Makgill Esq, Highfields, RD3, Waiuku, New Zealand]; *b* 1918; WW II with NZ Field Artillery; *m* 14 Jan 1949 *Ena Mary Thompson, dau of Lt-Col Samuel Pell Keyworth, of Much Wenlock, Salop, and has:

        1a *Fiona Margaret; *b* 7 Sept 1951; *m* 1979 *Donald John Macdonald and has:

            1b *Scott Donald; *b* 1983

            1b *Jenny Marie; *b* 1981

    (3) Donald Haldane; *b* 1921

(4) +Stephen Stewart [Stephen Makgill, 492 Coldstream Drive, Berwyn, PA 19312, USA]; *b* 11 Dec 1929; *educ* U of Michigan (BA); FCAS; *m* 17 April 1955 *Joan Maria, dau of John T Woods, of Wethersfield, Conn., and has:

1a +Stephen Stewart; *b* 16 Sept 1958; *m* 1986 *Diane Corcoran

1a *Kathleen Palmer ; *b* 26 Jan 1956; *m* 1981 *Gregory Sisk

2a *Heather Woods [Mrs William Lyon, 12 Arrowhead Rd, Convent Station, NJ, USA]; *b* 15 June 1961; *m* *William Lyon

3a *Allison Ashwell; *b* 16 Dec 1963

(1) *Margaret May; *b* 1912; *m* 1933 Geoffrey Hall Dadley and has:

1a *David Frances, *b* 15 Aug 1934; *m* 13 April 1945 (*divorce* 1969) Joan Muriel Proctor and has:

1b *John David; *b* 1954; *m* 1975 *Sharon Joy Ludwig and has:

1c *Steven Ronald David; *b* 1979

1c *Keri Anne; *b* 1976

2c *Jolene Marie; *b* 1978

2b *Geoffrey Harold; *b* 1956; *m* 1981 *Marie Joan Shergold and has:

1c *Adrian Brent; *b* 1983

1b *Raewyn Anne; *b* 1958; *m* 1982 *Lance Noel Worthington and has:

1c *Amber Chanelle; *b* 1984

2b *Barbara Joan; *b* 1959; *m* 1978 *John Kleber Brooks and has:

1c *Chantal Summer; *b* 1982

3b *Lorraine Sandra; *b* 1961

2a *Peter Geoffrey; *b* 22 March 1936; *m* 11 Jan 1964 *Lesley Germaine Wormald and has:

1b *Sandra Elizabeth; *b* 15 Nov 1965

2b *Helen Deborah; *b* 1967

3a Anthony Eric; *b* 19 Oct 1942

1a *Marian Rose; *b* 12 April 1940; *m* 23 April 1962 *Keith John Kingsford Wormald, of Dunedin, NZ, and has:

1b *Geoffrey John; *b* 28 March 1964

1b *Kirsten Anne; *b* 29 April 1965

2a *Robin Margaret; *b* 7 Dec 1943; *m* 1972 *Peter Clarke and has:

1b *Michael Anthony; *b* 1973

2b *Stephen Matthew; *b* 1974

3a *Rosemary Gwendolyn; *b* 9 Dec 1944

4a *Katherine Ruth; *b* 7 May 1949; *m* 1973 *Ian Thornton and has:

1b *Matthew Antony; *b* 1983

(2) *Alice Mary [Mrs Guy Sanders, Meldon, 5 Castor Bay Road, Milford, New Zealand]; *b* 27 June 1913; *m* 1939 *Col Guy Priestley Sanders, DSO, MInstCE, RNZ Engrs, and has:

1a *Guy Makgill; *b* 1 Oct 1940; *educ* Auckland U (BA(Econ)) and Lincoln Coll Canterbury (DipAgSc); *m* 1972 *Jennifer Chave and has:

1b *Timothy Guy; *b* 1982

1b *Stephanie Claire; *b* 1977

2b *Katherine Alice; *b* 1979

2a *David William Priestley; *b* 2 Jan 1955; *m* 1988 *Gael Frances McKitterick and has:

1b *Ben William; *b* 1989

2b *Jonathan Guy; *b* 1992

3b *Thomas Robert; *b* 17 Jan 1996

1a *Philippa Ann; *b* 13 Jan 1944; *educ* Sch of Arts Auckland (Dip Fine Arts); *m* 1966 *Thomas James Finlayson and has:

1b *Nicholas James; *b* 21 Feb 1968

2b *Tobias David; *b* 1977

2a *Penelope Margaret; *b* 11 July 1950; *m* 1975 *Grant Lyndon Christianson and has:

1b *David Grant; *b* 1979

2b *Michael Scott; *b* 1981

1b *Anna Louise; *b* 8 Sept 1984

(3) *Rose Ashwell [Mrs Ansel Smith, 3029 Mary Avenue SE, Grand Rapidis, MI 49506, USA]; *b* 1916; *m* 1944 *Ansel Brooks Smith, LLB, and has:

1a *Haldane Brooks [Haldane B Smith, 17639 Walnut Trail, Chagrin Falls, OH, USA]; *b* 13 Feb 1947

2a *Byron Whitaker [Byron W Smith, 24 Forest Green Drive, Springfield, IL, USA]; *b* 21 Jan 1950; *m* 1st 1972 (*divorce* 1978) Leona La Claire; *m* 2nd 1981 *Mary Kimbo and by his 1st w has:

1b *Byron Whitaker; *b* 1973

2b *Colin Makgill; *b* 1976

3a *Christopher Carlton; *b* 27 May 1952; *m* 1979 *Leslie Gaye Booth

5 Arthur; *b* 21 Sept 1882; *m* 28 Feb 1911 Mable Sophia Elizabeth (*d* 8 May 1932), dau of William Marsh, and *d* 4 April 1954, leaving:

(1) Mungo Ian; *b* 15 Dec 1911; *m* 20 Feb 1935 *Eugenia Louise [Mrs Mungo Makgill, 31a View Rd, Waiuku, New Zealand], 2nd dau of Samuel Massey, of Belfast, and *d* 23 May 1986, leaving:

1a +Ian James [Ian Makgill Esq, 49 Penny Ave, Mount Roskill, New Zealand]; *b* 22 April 1946; *m* 1975 *Marie Louise Howley and has:

1b *Angela Louise; *b* 1979

2b *Philippa Suzanne; *b* 1982

3b *Jennifer Marie; *b* 1986

1a *Margaret May; *b* 15 Dec 1935

2a *Elizabeth Marion; *b* 4 March 1938

3a *Roberta Louise [Mrs James Brambley, 16 Hogan St, Pukekohe, New Zealand]; *b* 22 April 1942; *m* 1961 *James Samuel Brambley and has:

1b *Douglas James; *b* 1965; *m* 1986 *Fiona Thelma McNally and has:

1c *Samuel James; *b* 1988

2c *Eli Sean; *b* 1992

1c *Renée Vivienne; *b* 1989

1b *Marie-Anne; *b* 1962; *m* 1990 (*divorce* 1993) Michael

2b *Louise Anne; *b* 1963; *m* 1987 *Wayne Robert Callander and has:

1c *Amy Louise; *b* 1993

3b *Vanessa Jane; *b* 1972

4a *Colleen Barbara [Mrs Herbert Lovell, 90 Ranfurly Rd, Manurewa, Auckland 1702, New Zealand]; *b* 26 April 1944; *m* 1965 *Herbert James Lovell and has:

1b *Scott James; *b* 18 Oct 1966; *m* 1989 *Monique Adriana van Meygaarden and has:

1c *Brent William; *b* 1991

2c *Shaun Adrian; *b* 1994

1c *Simone Isabella; *b* 19 Dec 1997

1b *Anna Elizabeth; *b* 9 Sept 1968; *m* 1988 *Michael John Cutts

2b *Kirstene Margaret; *b* 1972

(2) +Douglas Malcolm; *b* 23 Jan 1922; *m* 6 Jan 1945 *Myra Louisa, est dau of Osborne John Morton Pine, of Sandringham, NZ, and has:

1a +Ray Malcolm; *b* 6 Oct 1945; *m* 1969 (*divorce* 1985) Linda Anne Elliment and has:

1b +Daniel Ray; *b* 1970

2b +Jamie Douglas; *b* 1972

1b *Donna Marie; *b* 1974

1a *Joy Louisa; *b* 5 April 1953; *m* 1st 1973 (*divorce* 1979) Karl Verdun Morris; *m* 2nd 1981 *Jeffrey John Wills and by him has:

1b *Kyle Philip; *b* 1985

1b *Anne Marie Frances; *b* 1982

2b *Nicola Susan (twin); *b* 1985

2a *Lynette Jane; *b* 2 Feb 1955; *m* 1979 *Peter Leslie Guinibert, of Titirangi, NZ, and has:

1b *Matthew John; *b* 1985

2b *David James; *b* 1987

(1) *Deborah Elizabeth Mary [Mrs John Clarkson, 110 Bruce McLaren Rd, Henderson, Auckland, New Zealand]; *b* 21 Dec 1914; *m* 23 Aug 1939 *Capt John Lawrence Clarkson and has:

1a *David John; *b* 18 June 1940; *m* 1st 1965 (*divorce*) Helen Gable, of Toowoomba, Qld, and has:

1b *Sean; *b* 1969

1b *Fiona; *b* 1968

1a (cont.) David Clarkson *m* 2nd *Catherine de Boer and by her has:

2b *Euan; *b* 1979

2a *Peter Robert; *b* 22 May 1945; *m* 1968 *Patricia Goffin, of Howick, Auckland, and has:

1b *Stephen; *b* 1973

2b *Wayne; *b* 1980

1b *Michelle; *b* 1971

3a *Alan Richard; *b* 28 Aug 1946; *m* 1970 *Susanne Price, of Otahuhu, Auckland, and has:

1b *Jonathan; *b* 1977

1b *Melissa; *b* 1978

1a *Christine Mary; *b* 18 Nov 1947; *m* 1971 *John Fryer, of Paraparauma, Wellington, and has:

1b *Nicholas; *b* 1976

1b *Kirsten; *b* 1974

1 Agnes Rebecca; *m* 10 Nov 1891 Hamilton Vetch Rutherfurd and *d* 14 Jan 1938, leaving issue

2 Margaret; *m* 14 July 1903 Reginald Dillon Kelsey and had issue

3 Ruth; *m* 8 June 1898 Charles Henry Pentreath, MB, BC, BA, and had issue

4 Grace Gladys; *m* 28 Dec 1915 Arthur James Palmer, s of John Palmer, Archdeacon S Melanesia, and *d* 25 Dec 1952, leaving four sons and two daus

The *de jure* 10th VISCOUNT's est s,

Sir George Makgill, 11th Bt, as which recognised May 1907, and *de jure* 11th VISCOUNT OF OXFUIRD; *b* 24 Dec 1868; *m* 1 Dec 1891 Frances Elizabeth (*d* 16 Dec 1947), est dau of Alexander Innes Grant, of Merchiston, Otago, NZ, by Frances Ann, est dau of Lt-Col Henry Rutherfurd, Bengal Artillery, and *d* 17 Oct 1926, having had:

1 **Sir (John) Donald Alexander Arthur Makgill, 12th Bt,** and **12th Viscount of Oxfuird,** as which recognised 1977; *b* 31 Dec 1899; *educ* Eton and RMC Sandhurst; Maj Coldstream Gds, WWs I and II; *m* 1st 5 July 1927 (*divorce* 1943) Ester Lilian (*d* 1 Nov 1996), yr dau of Sir Robert Bromley, 6th Bt (*qv*), and had:

(1) Anne Elizabeth Jean; *b* 8 Aug, *d* 6 Sept 1928

(2) *Diana Mary Robina, CVO (1990, LVO 1983, MVO 1971) [The Hon Diana Makgill CVO, Clouds Lodge, E Knoyle, Wilts SP3 6BE; 2 Iverna Court, London W8]; *b* 4 Jan 1930; Dip Serv 1961–90, Protocol Consultant 1990, Hon Steward Westminster Abbey 1978, Hon V-Pres Raleigh Internat, V-Chm Women of the Year Luncheon, Action on Addiction, Consultant Princess Helena Coll, Freedom City London 1989, Jubilee Medal 1977, Orders: Al Kawkab 5th Cl 1966, White Rose Finland (Kt) 1969, Stor 1971, Sacred Treasure 5th Cl 1971, Independence UAE 1989

1 (cont.) The **12th Viscount** *m* 2nd 6 Oct 1955 *Maureen [The Rt Hon Maureen Viscountess of Oxfuird, c/o Woodland House, Elms Rd, Freckenham, Bury St Edmunds IP28 8JG], yst dau of Lt-Col Arthur Tilson Shaen Magan, CMG, of Killyon Manor, Hill-of-Down, Co Meath, and formerly w of Col John Herbert Gillington, OBE, MC, and *d* 1986

2 Richard James Robert Haldane, AFC; *b* 5 May 1907; F/O RAF, 2nd Lt 18th London Regt, S/Ldr RNZAF; *m* 6 June 1932 *Elizabeth Lyman, dau of Gorham Hubbard, of Boston, USA, and was *k* in a plane crash 9 Aug 1948, leaving:

(1) GEORGE HUBBARD MAKGILL, **13th and present Viscount of Oxfuird**

(1) *Barbara Frances Katherine [Miss Barbara Makgill, 34 Karaka St, Takapuna, Auckland, New Zealand]; *b* 6 July 1939

1 Harriet Frances Janet; *b* 29 Aug 1893

2 Marie Elspeth Agnes; *b* 17 July 1895; *m* 3 Sept 1913 Col Aubrey Brooke Winch, OBE, RSG, s of Thomas Winch, of Rochester, and *d* 23 May 1939, leaving issue

PAGE WOOD

Arms: Quarterly, 1st and 4th, arg. and or an oak tree on a mount vert, fructed ppr.; 2nd and 3rd, a bull's head erased sa., charged on the neck with a bezant; over all in pale the mace of the Lord Mayor of London. **Crest:** Out of a mural crown arg. a demi-wild-man, wreathed about the temples with oak, fructed, in the dexter hand an oak tree eradicated and fructed, and in the sinister a club, all ppr. **Motto:** Defend. **Creation:** Bt. (UK) 16 Dec 1837.

SIR ANTHONY JOHN PAGE WOOD, 8TH BT, of Hatherley House, Co Gloucester [Sir Anthony Page Wood Bt, 77 Dovehouse St, London SW3]; *b* 6 Feb 1951; *s* f 1955; *educ* Harrow

Lineage: WILLIAM WOOD, of Exeter; had an est s:

Sir Matthew Wood, 1st Bt (UK), so *cr* 16 Dec 1837; *b* 2 June 1768; Alderman, twice Ld Mayor London, MP City London; *m* 5 Nov 1795 Maria (*d* 2 July 1848), dau of John Page, MD, of Woodbridge, Suffolk, and had:

1 JOHN PAGE (Sir), **2nd Bt**

2 WILLIAM PAGE WOOD, 1st and last BARON HATHERLEY OF DOWN HATHERLEY, Co Gloucester (UK), so *cr* 9 Dec 1868; *b* 29 Nov 1801; *educ* Winchester, U of Geneva and Trin Coll Cambridge; barrister Lincoln's Inn 1827, QC 1845, MP (Lib) Oxford 1847–53, Slr-Gen 1851, V-Chllr 1853, a Ld Justice of Appeal Feb 1868, Ld Chllr 1868–72, FRS, DCL Oxon, LLD Cantab; *m* 5 Jan 1830 Charlotte (*d* 10 Nov 1878), only dau of Maj Edward Moor, of Great Bealings, Suffolk, and *dsp* 10 July 1881, when the Barony expired

3 Western, of North Cray Place, Kent; *b* 4 Jan 1804; merchant, MP City London; *m* 16 June 1829 Sara Letitia (*d* 24 April 1870), yst dau of John Morris, of Baker St, and *d* 17 May 1863, leaving:

(1) Western; *b* 22 May 1830; MLC Queensland; *m* 9 Jan 1862 Lucy Elizabeth (*m* 2nd 7 May 1878 George Cresswell Crump, of Chorlton Hall, Cheshire, and *d* 17 March 1907), only dau of Frederick Orme Darvall, 41st Foot, and *d* 15 April 1878, having had:

1a George Orme Western; *b* 19 Nov 1868; *m* 20 April 1904 Helen Portia Rosalind (*d* 1963), dau of Adam Davidson, of Clifton, Darling Downs, Qld, and *d* 1926, leaving:

1b Ernest Cresswell Gaden Western, MBE; *b* 22 Nov 1906; MLA Queensland 1966–69, chm Redland Shire Cncl 1961; *m* 22 Sept 1938 *Mary Tudor [Mrs Ernest Wood, Moonie, 35 Douro Rd, Wellington Point, Qld 4160, Australia], dau of James Winnal Hill, of Goorarooman, Thallon, Qld, and *d* 1984, having had:

1c +Richard Orme Western [Richard Wood Esq, Moonie, 35 Douro Rd, Wellington Point, Qld 4160, Australia]; *b* 9 July 1942; *educ* Queensland U (BEng); *m* 10 Feb 1968 *Jenifer Lynne, dau of N W S Johns, of Clayfield, Brisbane, and has:

1d +Matthew Gaden Western; *b* 17 March 1969

2d +Gregory Orme Western; *b* 26 April 1971

3d +Simon James Western; *b* 14 Oct 1975

2c +Bruce James Western [Bruce Wood Esq, Moonie, 35 Douro Rd, Wellington Point, Qld 4160, Australia]; *b* 25 Aug 1951; *educ* Queensland U (BEng, Hons); *m* 1977 *Yolande Marie-Louise, dau of Pierre Le Manach, of Morlaix, France, and has had:

1d *Nina Marie Western; *b* 1978

2d Adeline Marie Western; *b* and *d* 1981

3d *Sophie Yolande Western; *b* 1981

4d *Nicole Alexandrina Western; *b* 1985

5d *Stephanie Adeline Western; *b* 1987

1c *Nina Helen Western; *b* 14 Sept 1939

2c *Rosamond Mary Western; *b* 8 Oct 1944; *educ* Queensland U (Dip Speech Therapy); *m* 21 April 1972 *John Franklin Verity Haselwood, s of J Haselwood, of Maroona, Jandowae, Qld, and has:

1d *Richard Franklin; *b* 8 March 1974

2d *Douglas Holmes; *b* 1976

1d *Louise Mary; *b* 7 May 1975

2b +Bernard Page Western [Bernard Wood Esq, 57 Gregory St, Mackay, Qld, Australia]; *b* 29 Feb 1908; Lt RANVR WW II; *m* 1951 *Phyllis May, dau of William Henry Andrew, of Mackay, Qld

3b +Evelyn Hatherley Davidson Western; *b* 3 Aug 1911; *m* 22 Dec 1937 *Ena Meyer and has:

1c +Ian Hatherley Western [Ian Wood Esq, 1 Croston St, Clontarf Beach, Qld, Australia]; *b* 4 April 1942; *m* 19– *June Margaret Huch, dau of Huch Redcliffe, and has:

1d +Cameron Hatherley; *b* 11 July 1966

2d +Scott Norman; *b* 4 April 1969

1d *Rowena Maree; *b* 1971

2c +David Orme Western; *b* 8 Dec 1946; *educ* Queensland U (MB, BS)

1b *Helen Constance Western; *b* 3 Jan 1905; *m* 1949 *Stanley Gordon

2b *Waveney Patricia Western; *b* 1914; *m* 7 Sept 1943 *Capt Robert Gladstone Deacon, Australian Forces, of Allora, Qld, and has:

1c *Helen Page; *b* 21 Feb 1945; *m* 5 Aug 1967 *Keppel James Coughlan, MSc (Ag), of Paddington, Qld

1a Constance Lucy; *b* 19 Aug 1864; *m* Charles Barrington Philpott (*d* 1927) and had issue

2a Edith Maud; *b* 19 Dec 1866; *d* unm 19 Aug 1954

(2) Frederick John (Rev); *b* 15 June 1834; *educ* Trin Coll Cambridge (MA); Vicar Headingley, Leeds, Hon Canon Ripon, Chaplain to Bp Chester, Proctor in Convocation Archdeaconry of Ripon; *m* 6 June 1883 Rose Lucy (*d* 11 Aug 1934), dau of Maj-Gen Charles Trigance Franklin, CB, RA, and *d* 8 July 1913

(1) Sarah; *m* 22 Aug 1857 William Shadforth Boger and *d* 31 May 1870

(2) Harriet Charlotte; *m* 18 June 1861 Sir Nevile Lubbock, KCMG, and *d* 20 Nov 1878, leaving issue (see AVEBURY, B)

(3) Alice Phelips; *m* 1871 Lt-Col William James Morris, IA, and *d* 1 Dec 1892

1 Maria Elizabeth; *m* 18 July 1827 Edwin Maddy, DCL, of Matson Ho, Glos, and *d* his widow 5 Aug 1878

2 Catharine; *m* 12 July 1830 Charles Stephens, of Earley Court, Berks, and *d* his widow 18 March 1875

Sir MATTHEW *d* 25 Sept 1843; his est son:

Rev Sir John Page Wood, 2nd Bt; *b* 25 Aug 1796; Vicar Cressing, Essex, Rector St Peter's Cornhill; *m* 16 Feb 1820 Emma Caroline (*d* 15 Dec 1879), dau of Sampson Michell, RN, of Croft West, Cornwall, Adml in Portuguese service, and had, with other issue:

1 FRANCIS (Sir), **3rd Bt**

2 Charles Page, of Wakes Hall, Wakes Colne, Essex, JP, DL; *b* 21 May 1836; *m* 21 May 1864 Minna (*d* 29 Aug 1922), dau of Thomas White, of The Manor House, Wethersfield, and Berechurch Hall, Colchester, and *d* 19 Feb 1915, having had:

(1) Hatherley Page; *b* 10 March 1869; *m* 12 Feb 1910 Kathleen (Alla) (*m* 2nd 1915 Col Evelyn FitzGerald Michell Wood, CB (see below), and *d* 23 April 1950), yst dau of Reginald Robert Morton, and *d* 31 Dec 1913

(1) Minna Evangeline, of Wakes Hall, Essex; *m* 24 June 1892 Augustus Maunsell Bradhurst (*d* 25 Dec 1923), s of Henry Maunsell Bradhurst, of Pinehurst, NY, and *d* 6 Feb 1946, leaving issue

3 (Henry) Evelyn (Sir), VC, GCB, GCMG, JP, DL Essex; *b* 9 Feb 1838; severely wounded in scaling-ladder party of Naval Bde before Sebastopol in attack on Redan 18 June 1855, barrister Middle Temple 1874, sometime in 90th Regt, formerly RN, served Indian Mutiny, Ashanti War, Zulu War and in Egypt, cmded E Dist troops Colchester 1886–88 and troops at Aldershot 1888–93, QMG 1893–97, Adj-Gen 1897–1901, cmded 2nd Army Corps Dist 1901–04, FM, Col RHG, Gold Stick 1907–19, Constable Tower London 1911–19, Hon Col 5th Bn Essex Regt and Inns of Ct OTC, Hon DCL Oxon, Chev Legn Hon, Kt Medjidie, Crimean Medal; *m* 19 Sept 1867 Hon Mary Paulina Anne Southwell (*d* 11 May 1901), sis of 4th Viscount Southwell (*qv*), and *d* 2 Dec 1919, leaving:

(1) Evelyn FitzGerald Michell, CB, DSO, OBE, DL Essex; *b* 16 Nov 1869; Maj Roy Dragoons, Lt-Col London Bde RGA, Hon Col, Sec City London TA 1915–37, Lt City London, served Ashanti War 1895–96, Boer War 1899–1900 (despatches) and WW I (despatches twice); *m* 1st 20 March 1893 Lilian (*d* 17 Sept 1910), dau of Charles Edward Hutton, of Bayswater, and had:

1a Sheelagh Maria Southwell, MBE (1944), JP; *b* 27 May 1895; *m* 12 Feb 1917 Capt John Edward Eastley, Somerset LI, of Totnes, S Devon, yr s of Charles Henry Eastley, slr, of Paignton

2a Leslie Violet Lucy Evelyn, DBE (1946), TD; *b* 28 Jan 1899; Ch Controller ATS, Dir ATS 1943–46 and World Assoc Girl Guides and Girl Scouts 1951, Chev Legn Hon, US Legn Merit; *m* 1st 8 July 1922 (*divorce* 1939) William John Balfour, 20th Hus, 3rd s of John Balfour, of Moor Hall, Harlow, Essex, and had issue; *m* 2nd 21 Sept 1939 S/Ldr Harry Raymond Whateley, RAFVR, s of Hubert George Whateley, of Kenilworth

3a Ursula Anna Mary; *b* 4 April 1903; *m* 24 Feb 1936 Capt Frederick Walter Keighley, MC (*d* 4 Sept 1947), 2nd s of Frederick Walter William Keighley, of Leamington Spa

(1) (cont.) Col Evelyn Wood *m* 2nd 1915 Kathleen (Alla) (*d* 23 April 1950), widow of Hatherley Page Wood (see above) and dau of Reginald Robert Morton, and *d* 1 Dec 1943, having had:

1a +Matthew Wakefield Drury Evelyn [Lt-Col Matthew Evelyn-Wood RE, 6 The Orchard, Bishopsteignton, Teignmouth, Devon TQ14 9RB]; *b* 9 July 1917; *educ* Brighton Coll and RMC Sandhurst; Lt-Col RE, late Essex Regt, WW II, Korea 1950–53 and Cyprus 1957–60; *m* 1st 5 Sept 1939 Marjorie (*d* 19 Sept 1963), dau of Henry Thomas Longmire, of Liverpool; *m* 2nd 20 June 1967 *Phyllis Margaret Chavasse, formerly w of (William) Raymond John Evelyn Balfour and yr dau of Alfred Ernest Holder (see HOLDER, Bt), and by his 1st w has:

1b +Mark William Evelyn [Mark Evelyn-Wood Esq, Holly Lodge, Sparrowhawk Close, Ewshot, Farnham, Surrey GU10 5TJ]; *b* 1 Aug 1940; *educ* Gosfield Sch; *m* 10 Feb 1962 *Mary June, dau of George Percy Miller, of Brightlingsea and has:

1c +Martin Evelyn; *b* 14 Jan 1963

1c *Michelle Leslie Evelyn; *b* 25 Dec 1965

4a Wendy Evelyn; *b* 27 April 1919; *m* 19 May 1960 Louis Jane, of Zennor, Cornwall (*d* 1983), s of Edwin Charles Jane, of Cadgwith, Cornwall, and *d* 15 Feb 1984

(2) Charles Michell Aloysius, CMG (1919), DSO (1917); *b* 2 April 1873; served Nile Expdn 1898 (despatches, medal, 4th Cl Medjidie), Crete 1898, Boer War 1899–1900 (despatches, Brev Lt-Col, Chev Legn Hon), Col Northumberland Fus (ret 1927); *m* 19 June 1915 Olive Mary de Bathe, only dau of Maj Herbert Miles, of Bude, Cornwall, and *d* 4 April 1936

(3) Arthur Herbert; *b* 26 April 1877; Page of Honour to HM QUEEN VICTORIA, Lt-Col Cameronians (Scottish Rifles), served Tirah Expdn 1897, Nile Expdn 1898, Boer War 1899–1900 (despatches twice) and WW I; *m* 1st 7 Nov 1900 Ethel Mary (*d* Feb 1922), yst dau of Andrew Duncan, barrister, and had:

1a Evelyn Philip; *b* 9 Feb 1903; *educ* RNCs Osborne and Dartmouth and City and Guilds London U Faculty Engrg during apprenticeship to Vickers Ltd; *m* 1st 4 April 1932 (*divorce* 1943) Maeve Audrey, widow of Emile Jacot, and dau of Arthur Theobald Wolfe, of The Poult Houser Tonbridge, Kent, and had:

1b +Diarmuid Evelyn [Diarmuid Wood Esq, Leachin House, Tarbert, Isle of Harris H53 3AH]; *b* 9 Sept 1933; *educ* Gordonstoun; *m* 1st 8 Oct 1960 Beverly, BSc (*d* 1976), dau of William Richard Pearce, of Tenerife, and has:

1c +Damian Evelyn; *b* 17 Feb 1962; *m* 1991 *Clare Natalie, dau of Richard Dallas Harington, of Hill Farm, Felsham, Suffolk, and has:

1d +Benedict Damian Evelyn; *b* 1993

2d +Barnaby Jonathan Evelyn; *b* 1996

1c *Thalia Evelyn; *b* 18 May 1965

1b (cont.) Diarmuid Wood *m* 2nd 1977 *Linda Rosemary, dau of Leonard Pierpoint Petty, of Wrington, Avon, and has:

2c +Duncan FitzGerald Evelyn; *b* 1981

2c *Eleanor Maeve Evelyn; *b* 1984

1a (cont.) Evelyn Wood *m* 2nd 8 Nov 1943 Kamal Jehangir (*d* 1976), dau of Jehangir Fardunji Dastur, of Bombay, and *d* 1976, having by her had:

1b *Ananda Evelyn; *b* 15 Aug 1947; *m* 19– Meena Dyal, of Bombay

2b *Leela Aditi; *b* 1 Sept 1946; *m* 19– *Nick Dirks, of Santa Monica, USA, and has:

1c *Sandhya Elina; *b* 1978

(3) (cont.) Lt-Col Arthur Wood *m* 2nd 6 Aug 1923 Andrina Hunter (*d* 1985), dau of John Fernie, of Aberfeldy, Perthshire, and *d* 6 Sept 1940, having by her had:

2a +Victor Arthur Evelyn; *b* 8 Oct 1927; *educ* Tonbridge; late IA, FRICS, chartered surveyor; *m* 1st 3 July 1951 Olwen Mary (*d* 29 Aug 1960), only dau of Thomas Davis, of Studley, Warwicks, and has:

1b +David Arthur Evelyn; *b* 4 June 1954

2b +Vaughan Thomas Evelyn; *b* 24 March 1959

1b *Bernice Margaret Andrina; *b* 5 July 1952

2a (cont.) Victor Wood *m* 2nd 14 Aug 1963 *Matilde Francesca Rosanna, dau of Gerolamo Zucchelli, of Brione, Riva di Garda, Italy, and by her has:

3b +Victor Vincent; *b* 29 March 1966

2b *Antonia Matilde Marcella; *b* 11 Dec 1964

1a *Marcella Mary; *b* 28 April 1931; *educ* New Hall Sch Chelmsford and London U (BA DipEd); Sister Mary Frances, nun Headmistress of New Hall Sch, Chelmsford, Essex 1963, Canoness Registrar Holy Sepulchre

(1) Anna Paulina Mary; *m* 25 July 1894 Lt-Gen Sir Hew Dalrymple Fanshawe, KCB, KCMG (*d* 24 March 1957), 2nd Dragoon Gds, of Thame, Oxon, and *d* 18 Nov 1929, leaving issue

(2) Marcella Caroline Mary; *m* 9 July 1902 Col Edward Augustine Blount, CBE, Legn Hon, Croix de Guerre, Hon ARIBA (*d* 28 March 1936), 2nd s of Alfred John Blount, and *d* 23 Aug 1946

(3) Victoria Eugénie Mary; *m* 18 July 1907 John Hubert Balfour (*d* 1957), est s of John Balfour, of Moor Hall, Harlow, Essex, and *d* 27 Feb 1961, leaving issue

1 Maria; *m* 10 June 1847 Lt-Col Joseph Chambers, 21st Bengal NI (*d* 1878), and *d* 12 Aug 1905, leaving issue

2 Emma; *m* 18 Jan 1853 Sir Thomas Barrett-Lennard, 2nd Bt (*qv*), and *d* 8 June 1916, leaving issue

3 Anna Caroline; *m* 27 May 1858, Lt-Col Charles Steele, 17th Lancers, est s of Lt-Gen Sir Scudamore Winde Steele, KCB, and *d* 1920

4 Katharine (Kitty); *m* 1st 24 Jan 1867 (*divorce* 1890) Capt William Henry O'Shea, 18th Hus (*d* 22 April 1905); *m* 2nd 2 July 1891 Charles Stewart Parnell (*dsp* 6 Oct 1891), of Avondale, Co Wicklow, MP Cork (*see* CONGLETON, B), and *d* 5 Feb 1921

Sir JOHN *d* 21 Feb 1866; his est surv son,

Sir Francis Wood, 3rd Bt; *b* 20 Feb 1834; barrister, Lt 17th Foot; *m* 20 Feb 1854 Louisa Mary (*m* 2nd 6 May 1874 Col Lewis Jones), est dau of Robert Hodgson, of Appleshaw, Hants, and *d* 21 April 1868, leaving:

1 **Sir Matthew Wood, 4th Bt**; *b* 21 Sept 1857; *m* 31 July 1894 Maud Mary (*d* 17 April 1947), widow of Francis P Leon and dau of Thomas Raynor Brown, and *dsp* 13 July 1908

2 JOHN PAGE (Sir), **5th Bt**

3 Francis Page; *b* 29 April 1862; *m* 1912 Edith (*d* 11 Nov 1948), dau of Capt Frederic A March, and *d* 23 Dec 1921

1 Caroline Emma; *m* 1st 29 Nov 1880 Maj-Gen Charles Hereford (*d* 1891), 3rd s of Richard Hereford, of Sufton Court, Herefs; *m* 2nd 6 Jan 1903 Rev Glenn Brabazon Dalrymple, Rector Ludgershall, Wilts

2 Edith Constance; *m* 1st 1 July 1887 Thomas John-Elmore, of Barcombe House, nr Lewes, Consul Savannah, Ga.; *m* 2nd 12 May 1897 John Law Adam, MB, of Camberley

The 4th Bt's bro,

Sir John Page Wood, 5th Bt; *b* 14 April 1860; Lt-Col and Brevet Col 2nd Bn Border Regt; *m* 22 Sept 1896 Violet Mary Frances Stuart (*d* 17 March 1956), dau of Henry Stuart Johnson, of Edinburgh, and *d* 20 Oct 1912, leaving:

Sir John Stuart Page Wood, 6th Bt; *b* 28 Jan 1898; Cdr RN, served WWs I (despatches) and II; *m* 8 Nov 1919 Barbara Arundell, 1st Offr WRNS (*d* 14 Jan 1971), er dau of Maj Arundell Clarke, Roy N Devon Hus, of Fremington, N Devon, and had:

1 JOHN HATHERLEY (DAVID) (Sir), **7th Bt**

2 +MATTHEW WOOD later PAGE WOOD (deed poll 1955) [Matthew Page Wood Esq, 31 Halsey St, London SW3 2PT]; *b* 13 Aug 1924; heir presumptive; Capt Coldstream Gds WW II NW Europe; *m* 22 Oct 1947 *Betsann, dau of Lt-Col Francis Christesson Darby Tothill, Rifle Bde, of St Anne's Hill Ho, Midhurst, Sussex, by Lady Cynthia, sis of 5th Earl of Bandon (*see* 1970 edn), and has:

(1) *Belinda Jane [Mrs Charles Hoste, The Craig, Montrose, Angus]; *b* 26 Dec 1952; *m* 1st 1 March 1973 (*divorce* 1977) Richard John Crowder, er s of (Frederick) Petre Crowder, QC, MP, of Lodge Farm, Kenilworth, Herts, by Hon Patricia Winifred Mary, dau of 25th Baron Mowbray, Segrave and Stourton (*qv*); *m* 2nd 1985 *Charles Frederick Rutford Hoste and by him has:

1a *James Matthew William Rutford; *b* 1986

(2) *Miranda Elizabeth [Mrs William Kendall, Millow Hall, Biggleswade, Beds]; *b* 1 Feb 1962; *m* 1993 *William B Kendall, s of Graham Kendall, and has:

1a *Emily Lucy Page; *b* 1994

2a *Sophia Lucy Page; *b* 23 June 1996

Sir JOHN *d* 2 April 1955; his er son:

Sir JOHN HATHERLEY (DAVID) WOOD later PAGE WOOD (deed poll 1956), **7th Bt**; *b* 6 Oct 1921; *educ* Westminster; Lt RNVR WW II (despatches); *m* 13 Dec 1947 *Evelyn Hazel Rosemary [Lady Page Wood, The Old Cottage, Wolverton, Hants], yst dau of Capt George Ernest Bellville, of Fermyn Woods Hall, Brigstock, Northants, and *d* 28 Nov 1955, leaving:

1 Sir ANTHONY JOHN PAGE WOOD, **8th and present Bt**

1 *Rosemary Anne; *b* 17 Nov 1948; *m* 14 July 1977 *Hugh M Teacher (*see* MACNAGHTEN, Bt) and has issue

PAGET of Cranmore Hall

Arms: Sa. on a cross invected arg. between four eagles displayed erm. an eagle displayed between four lions passant of the first. **Crest:** A demi-tiger rampant sa., tufted, maned and gorged with a crown vallary arg., holding in the mouth an eagle's leg erased at the thigh or. **Motto:** *Diciendo y haciendo* ('Saying and doing'). **Creation:** Bt. (UK) 6 March 1886.

SIR RICHARD HERBERT PAGET, 4TH BT, of Cranmore Hall, Co Somerset [Sir Richard Paget Bt, Burridge Heath Farm, Little Bedwyn, Wilts SN8 3JR]; *b* 17 Feb 1957; *s* f 1992; *educ* Eton; ind mktg consultant AES 1983–87, Nixdorf Computers 1987–88, Inforem plc 1989–89, sales manager SAS Inst 1989–95; *m* 1985 *Richenda Rachel, dau of Rev Preb John Theodore Cameron Bucke Collins (*see* HAZLERIGG, B), and has:

1 *Emma Rachel; *b* 1986

2 *(Richenda) Elizabeth; *b* 1988

3 *Camilla Mary; *b* 1991

Lineage: JOHN PAGET, of Rugby; *m* 17 Sept 1632 Joyce Harris (*d* May 1691) and was *bur* 30 Nov 1659, leaving, with two daus:

JOHN PAGET; *bapt* 8 March 1639; *m* 9 Sept 1662 Mary Bishop and had, with three daus:

JOHN PAGET; *educ* Queen's Coll Oxford (MA 1685); sold his estate at Daventry; bought the Manor of Pointington, Somerset; Rector Pointington and Sandford Orcas 1691; *bapt* 13 Oct 1663; *m* 5 Dec 1693 Mary (*bapt* 21 Jan 1668; *d* 27 Nov 1735), dau of John Ruddock, of Almsford, Somerset, and *d* 20 April 1745, leaving, with an er s and and four daus:

THOMAS PAGET; *bapt* 11 Jan 1706; MA, Fell Ch Ch Oxford, Rector St Mewan's Cornwall, Clifton Maubank Dorset 1742, Bradford Abbas Dorset 1743, Pointington 1745, Mells 1751; *m* Elizabeth, dau of Richard Cobb, of Basildon, Berks, and had, with other issue:

1 John (Rev); *b* 1728; Vicar Doulting, Somerset; *m* 1st 27 Aug 1757 Anne (*d* Aug 1758), dau of Rev Benjamin Milward, Rector Mells, and had:

(1) Anna Aletheia Elizabetha; *m* 1781 Rev William Phelips, of Montacute, Somerset, and *d* 7 July 1816, leaving issue. He *d* 1806

1 (cont.) The Rev John Paget *m* 2nd Sarah (*d* 29 April 1793), dau of Samuel Jeffery, and *d* 5 Oct 1782, leaving by her an only surv dau:

(2) Sarah Jeffery; *b* Sept 1766; *m* 24 April 1802 Rev Edward Bradford, BD, Rector Stalbridge, Dorset, and *d* 1810, leaving issue

2 RICHARD

3 William; *b* 5 Nov 1735; *m* 1 July 1765 Sarah Salmon, of Wrington, Somerset, and *d* 2 Sept 1785, leaving:

(1) Sarah Maria; *b* 30 Oct 1770; *m* 7 Oct 1790 Rev John Peploe Mosley (*see* RAVENSDALE, B) and had issue

4 Robert; *b* 1739; DCL, Fell Magdalen Coll Oxford; *d unm* 10 Aug 1793

The Rev THOMAS PAGET *d* 2 Jan 1783; his 3rd s,

RICHARD PAGET, of Newberry House and Cranmore Hall, Somerset; *b* 1 Dec 1730; MA; *m* 1 July 1760 Mary (*b* 1 Dec 1732; *d* 2 Nov 1807), est dau and eventually sole heiress of James Moore, of Chilcompton, Somerset (4th s of John Moore, of Newberry House, Kilmerson, by Mary, n of Benjamin Bradford, of Cranmore Hall), through her inherited the Newberry and E Cranmore estates 1779 and 1791, and had:

1 JOHN

2 Richard; *b* 7 July 1766; Probationer Fell Magdalen Coll Oxford, Curate E Cranmore; *d unm* 9 Dec 1794

3 Thomas; *b* 7 Dec 1767; *m* 4 March 1800 his 2nd cousin Mary (*d* 5 Dec 1810), only dau of Francis Moore, of Eggington House, Beds, and *dsp* 10 April 1813

RICHARD PAGET *d* 8 April 1803; his est son,

JOHN PAGET, of Newberry and Cranmore; *b* 12 Dec 1761; *m* 24 Feb 1784 Jane, est dau and eventually sole heiress of Rev Paul George Snow, of Clipsham Hall, Rutland, and *d* 21 Aug 1825, leaving, with other issue:

1 JOHN MOORE

1 Jane Elizabeth; *m* 29 Aug 1809 John Gough, of Perry Hall and Oldfallings Hall, Staffs (*see* 1970 edn CALTHORPE, B), and *dsp* 29 Feb 1848, leaving Old-fallings to her bro

2 Mary Anne (twin); *m* 25 May 1819 Francis Hutchinson Synge, s of Sir Robert Synge, 1st Bt (*qv*), and *dsp* 5 Nov 1871

The son and heir,

JOHN MOORE PAGET, of Cranmore, JP, DL; *b* 17 June 1791; High Sheriff Rutland 1851; sold Clipsham 1865; bought the Manor of Doulting, Somerset; *m* 4 Oct 1827 Elizabeth Jane (*d* 22 Dec 1881), est dau of Rev John Frederick Doveton, JP, DL, of Everdon Hall, Northants, Rector Mells-cum-Leigh and Burnet, Somerset, and *d* 4 June 1866, having had, with other issue:

1 RICHARD HORNER (Sir), **1st Bt**

1 Jane Blanche Somerville; *m* 23 Aug 1851 Henry William Hoskins, of N Perrott, Somerset, est s of Rev Henry Hoskins, Preb Wells, and *d* 10 April 1896, having had issue. He *d* 22 Feb 1904

2 Margaret Doveton; *m* 7 Oct 1856 Lt Col Douglas William Parish Labalmondière, CB, Assist Commr Met Police, and *d* 16 March 1931, leaving issue. He *d* 8 March 1893

JOHN MOORE PAGET *d* 4 June 1866; his yr s,

Sir Richard Horner Paget, 1st Bt (UK), so *cr* 6 March 1886, PC (1895), of Cranmore Hall, JP, DL; *b* 14 March 1832; 66th Regt, Lt-Col 3rd Bn Somerset Vols, Chm QS and CC Somerset, MP E Somerset 1865–68, mid-Somerset 1868–85 and Wells 1885–95; *m* 13 Nov 1866 Caroline Isabel (*d* 29 July 1946), 2nd dau of Henry Edward Surtees, of Redworth Hall, Co Durham, and Dane End, Herts, and had:

1 RICHARD ARTHUR SURTEES (Sir), **2nd Bt**

2 Freville John Moore; *b* 13 Aug 1870; *d* 17 May 1880

3 Geoffrey Moore; *b* 8 Sept 1881; Lt Col Coldstream Gds, Assist Mil Sec to Govr Gen S Africa 1910–14, served Boer War 1901 (medal with two clasps) and WW I (wounded); *d unm* 15 Feb 1941

1 Aletheia Georgina; *m* 19 Jan 1898 Lt-Col Percy Robert Clifton, CMG, DSO, of Clifton Hall, Notts, and *d* 14 Nov 1904, having had issue (*see* BRUCE, Bt, of Downhill)

2 Hylda Snow; *m* 2 Dec 1909 Archibald Edward Balfour, LLM, slr, of Munden Parva, Herts, s of Archibald Balfour, and 24 Nov 1949, leaving issue. He *d* 22 March 1951

3 Dorothy Mary, DGStJ; *m* 2 Nov 1901 1st and last Viscount Gladstone (*see* GLADSTONE, Bt) and *d* 20 June 1953

The 1st Bt *d* 3 Feb 1908; his est s,

Sir Richard Arthur Surtees Paget, 2nd Bt; *b* 13 Jan 1869; *educ* Eton and Madgdalen Coll Oxford; barrister Inner Temple 1895, Hon ARIBA, FRAI, FIPPS Lond, memb Roy Inst, specialist in speech, vocal acoustics and gesture language for educating congenitally deaf, Hon Assoc Memb Inst Town Planning, Sec Submarine and Electrical Sectn Admlty Bd Inventions 1915–18; *m* 1st 31 May 1897 Lady Muriel Evelyn Vernon Finch-Hatton, CBE, fndr St Petersburg hosp for wounded soldiers WW I (*d* 16 June 1938), only dau of 12th Earl of Winchilsea and (7th Earl of) Nottingham (*qv*), and had:

1 Richard Hatton Harcourt; *b* 6 March 1898; *d* Oct 1898

2 JOHN STARR (Sir), **3rd Bt**

1 Sylvia Mary OBE (1976); *b* 10 July 1901; *educ* Roedean and Newnham Coll Cambridge; fndr Prisoners' Wives Serv; *m* 18 Feb 1926 Sir Christopher John Chancellor, CMG (*d* 1989), gen manager Reuters, er s of Lt Col Sir John Robert Chancellor, GCMG, GCVO, GBE, DSO, and *d* 26 Oct 1996, leaving:

(1) *John Paget [John Chancellor Esq, Crown House, Caxton, Cambs]; *b* 1927; *m* 1959 (*divorce* 1968) Hon (Mary) Alice Jolliffe, dau of 4th Baron Hylton (*qv*), and has:

1a *(John) Edward Horner; *b* 1962

1a *Isabel Rose; *b* 1959; *m* 1982 *John Joseph Boothby (*see* BOOTHBY, Bt)

2a *Katharine Sylvia Anthony; *b* 1961; *m* 1989 *William Woodard Self, s of Prof Peter Self, of Canberra, Australia, and has:

1b *Alexis; *b* 1990

3a *Anna Theodora; *b* 1965; actress (notably *Four Weddings and a Funeral*, 1994); has issue

(2) *Alexander Surtees [Alexander Chancellor Esq, 1 Souldern Rd, London W14]; *b* 1940; *educ* Eton and Trin Hall Cambridge; Reuters 1964–74, ITN 1974–75, ed *Spectator* 1975–84, *Time and Tide* 1984–86, *Sunday Telegraph*: dep ed 1986, assoc ed 1994–, US ed *Independent* 1986–88, ed: *Independent Magazine* 1988–92 and *New Yorker* 'Talk of the Town' 1992–93, columnist *The Times* 1992–93; *m* 1964 *Susanna Elizabeth, only dau of Martin Ridley Debenham (*see* DEBENHAM, Bt), and has:

1a *Elizabeth Beatrice; *b* 1964; *m* 1990 *Alexander Evelyn Michael Waugh, s of Auberon Waugh (*see* CARNARVON, E, and ONSLOW, E), and has issue

2a *Cecilia Jane; *b* 1966

(1) *Teresa [Mrs John Wells, 1a Scarsdale Villas, London W8 6PT; Chapel Farm, East Chiltington, E Sussex BN7 3BA]; *b* 1933; *m* 1st 1953 (*divorce* 1977) Edward Victor Gatacre and has:

1a *Thomas Jerome; *b* 1954; *m* 1990 *Elsebeth, dau of Jorgen Tholstrup, and has:

1b *Jack Victor; *b* 1992

2a *William; *b* 1956; *m* 1994 *Catherine Lucy Emily, dau of Sir Nigel Edward Seely, 5th Bt (*qv*), and has:

1b *Amelia Lettice; *b* 7 April 1997

1a *(Alice) Amelia; *b* 1960

2a *Maria Teresa; *b* 1964

3a *Cecily; *b* 1967

(1) (cont.) Mrs Teresa Gatacre *m* 2nd 1982 John Campbell Wells, the writer and actor (*d* Jan 1998), and by him had:

4a *Dorothy (Dolly) Perpetua; *b* 1971

(2) *Susanna Maria [Mrs Nicholas Johnston, Shellingford House, Faringdon, Oxon SN7 7QA]; *b* 1935; *m* 1958 *Nicholas John Johnston, RIBA, and has:

1a *Clara Mary; *b* 1960; *m* 1987 *(Edward) Percy Keswick Weatherall, er s of Capt Anthony Weatherall, of Cowhill Tower, Dumfries, and has:

1b *Bertram Edward Johnston; *b* 1989

1b *Stella Nony; *b* 1991

2b *Ruby Susanna; *b* 1994

3b *Honor Violet; *b* 1997

2a *Lily Silvia; *b* 1962; *m* 1991 *Daniel Stevens, s of Dr Dominic John Charles Stevens, of Bolton

3a *Rose Pamela Muriel; *b* 1963; *m* 1994 *Adam Gardner, s of Michael Gardner, of Cobham, Surrey, and has:

1b *George Nicholas; *b* 1997

4a *Silvy Margaret; *b* 1968; *m* 1993 *Benjamin Joseph Keswick Weatherall, yr s of Capt Anthony Weatherall, and has:

1b *Ida Winefred; *b* 1995

2b *Barley Rose; *b* 1996

2 Pamela Winefred; *b* 7 Aug 1903; *m* 25 Sept 1925 (*divorce* 1935) 2nd Baron Glenconner (*qv*) and *d* 1989, leaving issue

3 Angela Sibell; *b* 14 Nov 1906; *m* 24 May 1928 Sir Piers Kenrick Debenham, 2nd Bt (*qv*), and *d* 16 June 1965, leaving issue

Sir Richard *m* 2nd 22 July 1939 Grace Harley, only dau of Walter Herbert Glover, of Birkdale and Grasmere, and *d* 23 Oct 1955

His only son,

Sir John Starr Paget, 3rd Bt; *b* 25 Nov 1914; *educ* Oundle and Trin Coll Cambridge (BA 1936, MA 1939); FIMechE, FIPE; *m* 11 Nov 1944 *Nancy Mary , JP (Inner London 1955) [Dowager Lady Paget JP, Haygrass House, Taunton, Somerset TA3 7BS], er dau of Lt-Col Francis Woodbine Parish, DSO, MC, KRRC, and *d* 1992, leaving:

1 Sir RICHARD HERBERT PAGET, **4th and present Bt**

2 +DAVID VERNON JOHN [David Paget Esq, Lodge Cottage, Groton, Boxford, Suffolk CO10 5EJ]; *b* 26 March 1959; heir presumptive; *educ* Eton and Trin Coll Cambridge; *m* 1990 *Cluny Patricia Maxine, dau of Cdr Duncan Macpherson, of Radbroke Hall, Salop, and has:

(1) +(Alexander) Lachlan John; *b* 14 June 1994

(1) *Antonia; *b* 10 June 1992

(2) *Catriona Isabel; *b* 28 Nov 1997

1 *Patricia Mary [Mrs Philip Hawkes, 60 rue de Varenne, 75007 Paris, France; Château De Musseny, 21210 Saulieu, France]; *b* 5 Oct 1945; *m* 7 June 1975 *Philip John Anthony Hawkes, s of Frederic Clare Hawkes, and has:

(1) *Lucy Mary; *b* 22 Aug 1980

2 *Rosemary Muriel [Mrs Christopher Inge, Westmead, Bleadney, Somerset BA5 1PF]; *b* 4 April 1948; *m* 22 July 1971 *Christopher Ralph William Richard Inge, est s of Maj Edward Inge, of Brightwell Manor, Wallingford, Berks, and has:

(1) *Alexia Diana Nancy; *b* 1977

(2) *Olivia Dorothy Jane; *b* 1980

3 *Elizabeth Frances, LVO (1998); *b* 3 Feb 1950; Ldy-in-Waiting to HRH PRINCESS MARGARET, COUNTESS OF SNOWDON 1979–; *m* 1st 1981 (*divorce* 1985) Dr Angus A D Blair; *m* 2nd 1989 *Maj-Gen Charles Gerard Courtenay Vyvyan, CB, CBE (*see* VYVYAN, Bt)

4 *Davina Jane; *b* 29 May 1951; *m* 1 Jan 1972 *Rev (James) Adrian Hunter Pollard, s of Maj Benjamin James Prodbury Pollard, and has:

(1) *(Etienne) James Hunter; *b* 1979

(2) *Benjamin David Hunter; *b* 1981

5 *Susan Glynne [Mrs Simon Thornhill, 55 Larkhill Rise, London SW4]; *b* 4 Dec 1960; *m* 1988 *Maj Simon Thornhill, Scots Gds, yr s of Thomas Thornhill, of Buzzards Bay, Mass., and has:

(1) *Catherine Starr; *b* 1991

(2) *Fiona Surtees; *b* 1993

PAGET of Harewood Place

LABOR·IPSE·VOLUPTAS

Arms: Sa. on a cross engrailed, between in the 1st and 4th quarters an eagle displayed and in the 2nd and 3rd a heraldic tiger passant arg., an escallop of the first. **Crest:** A heraldic tiger passant arg., gorged with a collar and charged with two escallops sa.
Motto: *Labor ipse voluptas* ('Work itself is a pleasure').
Creation: Bt. (UK) 19 Aug 1871.

SIR JULIAN TOLVER PAGET, 4TH BT, of Harewood Place, Middlesex, CVO (1984) [Lt-Col Sir Julian Paget Bt CVO, 4 Trevor St, London SW7 1DU]; *b* 11 July 1921; *s* cousin 1972; *educ* Radley and Ch Ch Oxford (MA); Lt-Col Coldstream Gds WW II (ret 1968), Gentleman Usher to HM THE QUEEN 1971–91, Extra Gentleman Usher 1991–, author: *Counter Insurgency Campaigning* (1967), *Last Post: Aden 1964–67* (1969), *The Story of the Guards* (1976), *The Pageantry of Britian* (1979), *Yeomen of the Guard* (1984), *Discovering London's Ceremonial and Traditions* (1989), *Wellington's Peninsular War* (1990), *Hougoument, The Key to Victory at Waterloo* (1992); *m* 3 Dec 1954 *Diana Frances, dau of Frederick Spencer Herbert Farmer, and has:

  1 +HENRY JAMES [Henry Paget Esq, Summerfield, Lt London, Heathfield, E Sussex TN21 0NU]; *b* 2 Feb 1959; *m* 1993 *Mrs Margarete E Varvill, dau of Halfdan Lynner, and has:

    (1) +Bernard Halfdan; *b* 4 July 1994

    (1) *Daphne Ampuria; *b* 9 Sept 1996

  1 *Olivia Jane; *b* 31 July 1957; *m* 1992 *Nigel J Cox, s of Basil Cox

Lineage: SAMUEL PAGET, of Gt Yarmouth; *m* Anne — and had:

SAMUEL PAGET; *b* 1 Dec 1774; Mayor Gt Yarmouth 1818; *m* 8 Dec 1799 Sarah Elizabeth (*d* 22 Nov 1843), est dau of Thomas Tolver, of Chester, and *d* 6 April 1857, having had, with other issue:

  1 Frederick, of Gt Yarmouth; *b* 15 Dec 1805; *m* 1st 2 Feb 1831 Elizabeth Anne Rogers, of Gt Yarmouth (*dsp* 13 June 1832); *m* 2nd 25 Oct 1834 Hester Maria (*d* 1849), dau of Rev Isaac King, Rector Bradenham, and had issue; *m* 3rd June 1853 Sarah Lucy (*dsp* 1 Feb 1880), dau of James Shoubridge, and *d* 15 Aug 1867

  2 George Edward (Sir), KCB; *b* 22 Dec 1809; MD, FRS, DCL, LLD; *m* 11 Dec 1851 Clara (*d* 7 May 1899), dau of Rev Thomas Fardell, LLD, and *d* 29 Jan 1892, leaving issue

  3 **Sir James Paget, 1st Bt** (UK), so *cr* 19 Aug 1871, of Middlesex; *b* 11 Jan 1814; FRS, LLD, DCL, Serjeant Surgn to HM QUEEN VICTORIA; *m* 23 May 1844 Lydia (*d* 7 Jan 1895), yst child of Rev Henry North, Domestic Chaplain to HRH THE DUKE OF KENT, and *d* 30 Dec 1899, having had:

    (1) **Sir John Rahere Paget, 2nd Bt**, KC (1902); *b* 9 March 1848; *educ* Trin Hall Cambridge (BA, LLB); Bencher Inner Temple 1908; *m* 19 July 1833 Julia Norrie (*d* 31 Oct 1926), dau of George Louis Augustus Moke, of New York (*see* NORRIE, B), and *d* 20 Aug 1938, leaving:

      1a **Sir James Francis Paget, 3rd Bt**; *b* 25 Sept 1890; WW II (despatches three times); *m* 14 May 1943 Frances Alexandra Hamilton (*d* 12 Sept 1975), widow of Frederick David Stewart Sandeman and dau of Sir Hugh Fraser, of Stromeferry, Ross-shire, and *dsp* 5 June 1972

      2a George Norrie; *b* 25 Sept 1890; *educ* Wellington and Trin Coll Cambridge; Maj 1st Bn Norfolk Regt WW I (wounded), Wazirstan 1919–21, Lt-Col Pioneer Corps WW II (despatches); *d* unm 27 Feb 1964

      3a Rupert; *b* 19 Sept 1891; *d* 17 July 1903

      1a Margaret Norrie; *b* 30 May 1889; *m* 31 March 1915 Cdr Kenneth Berkeley Mackenzie Churchill, RN (*d* 26 Feb 1975), s of Rev Cameron Churchill, and *d* 23 May 1970 leaving issue

      2a Winifred Norah; *b* 13 Aug 1896; *m* 7 Feb 1918 her cousin Gen Sir Bernard Charles Tolver Paget, GCB, DSO, MC (*see below*), and *d* 1986, leaving issue

    (2) Francis (Rt Rev); *b* 20 March 1851; DD, Bp Oxford 1901–11; *m* 28 March 1883 Helen Beatrice (*d* 22 Nov 1900), dau of Very Rev Richard William Church, Dean St Paul's, and *d* 2 Aug 1911, leaving:

1a Richard James; *b* 7 March 1884; *educ* Shrewsbury and Ch Ch Oxford; Capt 90th Canadian Rifles WW I, Fell Roy Microscopical Soc; *m* 1st 29 Sept 1915 (*divorce* 1925) Jean Ross, dau of George Pickup Holden, JP, and had issue; *m* 2nd 1925 Eruda Carita (*d* 3 Feb 1961), dau of Carlo Saumier, of Riga, Finland, and *d* 6 Jan 1959

2a Edward Francis (Rt Rev), CBE (1950), MC; *b* 8 July 1886; *educ* Shrewsbury and Ch Ch Oxford (BA 1909, MA 1911); DD, Assist Bp Natal, Bp S Rhodesia 1925–52 and Mashonaland 1952–55, Archbp Centl Africa 1955–57, Chaplain-Gen S Rhodesian Forces 1925, ret 1957, Curate St Frideswide Poplar 1911–14, Vicar Benoni Transvaal 1914–25, served WW I (despatches), Chaplain OStJ, Cdr Phoenix Greece 1950; *m* 20 Oct 1932 Rosemary, only dau of Auriol Sealy Allin, of S Rhodesia, by Rose, 2nd dau of Lt-Col Thomas Goddard, 44th Bengal Native Inf, and *dsp* 21 April 1971

3a Bernard Charles Tolver (Sir), GCB (1946), DSO (1918), MC (1915), DL (Hants 1960); *b* 15 Sept 1887; *educ* Shrewsbury and RMC Sandhurst; MA, Oxon and Bucks LI 1907 (Col 1946–56), WW I (despatches, wounded, Brevet Maj 1917), Brevet Lt-Col 1925, Col 1929, GSO(1) Staff Coll Quetta 1932–34, War Office 1934–37, Maj-Gen 1937, cmdg 4th Quetta Inf Bde 1937–38, Cmdt Staff Coll 1938–39, cmded 18th Div 1939–40, Cdr British Land Forces Norway 1940 (despatches), Lt-Gen 1941, CGS Home Forces 1940–41, GOC-in-C SE Cmd 1941, C-in-C Home Forces 1941, 21st Army Gp 1943, Middle East 1944–46, ADC Gen (extra) to HM GEORGE VI 1944–46, Gen 1943, ret 1946, Col Cmdt Recce Corps 1943, Pncpl Ashbridge Coll 1946–49, Govr Roy Hosp Chelsea 1949–56, hereditary Freeman Cork, Italian Silver Medal Valour 1917, Greek Medal Valour, Ch Cdr US Legn Merit, Grand Cross St Olaf Norway, White Lion Czechoslovakia, Polonia Restituta, Gd Offr George I Greece, Leopold I with palm, Croix de Guerre Belgium; *m* 7 Feb 1918 his cousin Winifred Norah (*d* 1986), dau of **Sir John Paget, 2nd Bt** (*see* above), and *d* 16 Feb 1961, having had:

  1b Sir JULIAN TOLVER PAGET, **4th and present Bt**

  2b Anthony Francis Macleod, DSO; *b* 5 Nov 1924; *educ* Radley, Lt Oxon and Bucks LI WW II (despatches), Croix de Guerre; *das* 5 March 1945

4a Humphrey, MC; *b* 14 Sept 1891; *educ* Radley and Ch Ch Oxford; T/Capt and Adj King's Liverpool Regt WW I (despatches), WW II, Lt-Col RE, US Legn Merit; *m* 21 June 1918 Elizabeth Caroline (*d* 9 March 1970), yr dau of Sir Lewis Tonna Dibdin, and *d* 1985, leaving:

  1b *Elizabeth Frideswade (Frida) [Mrs John Maling, 10 Warbler Grove, Waikanae, New Zealand]; *b* 17 July 1921; ATS WW II; *m* 14 Jan 1950 *Lt Col John Darwin Maling, DSO, MC, RA, yst s of James Maling, and has:

    1c *Thomas Anthony Darwin; *b* 2 Feb 1951

    1c *Sarah Geraldine; *b* 13 Dec 1952

    2c *Elizabeth Anne; *b* 13 Dec 1952

    3c *Joanna Katherine; *b* 28 May 1956

  2b *Jean Marianne; WAAF WW II; *b* 12 Feb 1924; *m* 14 Oct 1966 *Robert Ian Cheyne Macpherson, s of Mrs Tite

  3b *Helen Rosemary [Mrs George Longman, 2 Doatshayne Close, Musbury, Devon EX13 6BQ]; *b* 12 Jan 1929; SRN; *m* 5 Nov 1966 *George Albert Longman, s of W A J Longman

1a Beatrice Mary; *b* 17 March 1885; *m* 20 April 1910 Rev George Herbert Jeudwine, Rector Church Oakley, Hants, s of Canon George Wynee Jeudwine, of Harlaxton Rectory, Grantham, Lincs, and *d* 19 July 1954

2a Edith Frideswide; *b* 5 April 1889; *m* 13 Oct 1908 Rev John Macleod Campbell Crum, Vicar Mentmore, Bucks, 2nd s of William Graham Crum, and *d* 25 Nov 1910, leaving issue. He *d* 19 Dec 1958

(3) Henry Luke (Rt Rev); *b* 18 Oct 1853; *educ* Shrewsbury and Ch Ch Oxford; DD, Bp Suffragan Ipswich 1906–09, Stepney 1909–19, Bp Chester 1919–32; *m* 27 Oct 1892 Elma Katie (*d* 24 April 1958), 3rd dau of Sir Samuel Hoare, 1st Bt (*see* 1959 edn TEMPLEWOOD, V), and *d* 26 April 1937, having had:

  1a Samuel James; *b* 13 Sept 1895; *educ* Winchester; Lt 8th Bn Norfolk Regt WW I; *ka* 26 March 1918

  2a Paul Edward, CVO; *b* 24 Jan 1901; *educ* Winchester and Trin Coll Cambridge; F/Lt RAuxAAF WW II, FSA, memb Court Common Cncl London 1949–55, surveyor Fabric St Paul's 1963–69, sr ptnr Seely and Paget, Chartered Architects, FRIBA 1963–69, architect to St George's Chapel Windsor and Portsmouth Cathedral, memb Redundant Churches Fund 1969, CStJ 1962; *m* 10 Aug 1971 Verity, widow of Capt Donald Clive Anderson, IA, and 2nd dau of Rev Dr Francis Rosslyn Courtenay Bruce (*see* BRUCE, Bt, of Downhill), and *d* 13 Aug 1985

(4) Stephen; *b* 17 July 1855; MA Oxon, FRCS; *m* 17 Sept 1885 Eleanor Mary (*d* 24 Aug 1933), dau of Edward Burd, MD, and *d* 8 May 1926, leaving:

  1a Eleanor Katherine; *m* 28 April 1909 Osbert John Radclyffe Howarth, OBE, s of Osbert Henry Howarth, and *d* 1 April 1965, leaving issue. He *d* 22 June 1954

  2a Dorothea Mary; *m* 10 Oct 1911 Sir Basil Edgar Mayhew, KBE, er s of Thomas Edgar Mayhew, of Ipswich, and *d* 22 April 1931, leaving issue. He *d* 2 Nov 1966

(1) Catharine; *m* 30 June 1877 Rev Henry Lewis Thompson and *d* 13 Feb 1937, leaving issue. He *d* 1 Jan 1905

(2) Mary Maud; *d* unm 23 June 1945

PALMER, Baron

Arms: Per saltire az. and gu. two palmer's staves in saltire between four escallops or. **Crest:** Upon a mount vert in front of a palm tree ppr. three escallops fesswise or. **Supporters:** On each side a palmer supporting with the exterior hand a palmer's staff ppr.
Motto: *Per crucem ad palmam.* ('Through the cross to the palm').
Creations: Bt. (UK) 26 Jan 1916, B. (UK) 24 June 1933.

THE 4TH BARON PALMER, of Reading, Co Berkshire and a **Baronet** (Sir Adrian Bailie Nottage Palmer, Bt) [The Rt Hon The Lord Palmer, Manderston, Duns, Berwickshire TD11 3PP]; *b* 8 Oct 1951; *s* unc 1990; *educ* Eton and Edinburgh U; chm HHA Scotland 1994– (memb exec cncl 1980, v-chm 1993), Scottish Rep European Landowning Orgn 1986–92, memb cncl Scottish Landowners' Fedn 1986–92, memb Roy Co Archers to 1996; *m* 7 May 1977 *Cornelia Dorothy Katharine, 2nd dau of Rohan N Wadham, DFC, of Dog Kennel, Exning, Suffolk, and has:

1 +HUGO BAILIE ROHAN; *b* 5 Dec 1980
2 +George Gordon Nottage; *b* 17 Nov 1985
1 *Edwina Laura Marguerite; *b* 20 Feb 1982

Lineage: WILLIAM PALMER, of Long Sutton, Somerset; yeoman; *b* 1672; *m* Mary — (*d* 1750) and *d* 1755, leaving, with another s:

RICHARD PALMER, of Long Sutton; *b* 1706; *m* Betty (*d* 4 Sept 1786), dau of James Salter, of Podimore, Somerset, and *d* 6 Dec 1788, leaving, with another s:

WILLIAM PALMER, of Long Sutton; *b* 1754; *m* 13 May 1783 Hannah (*d* 3 July 1816), dau of Joseph Clark, of Camely, Somerset, and *d* 11 Sept 1816, having had, with five other sons and three daus:

WILLIAM PALMER, of Litton, Long Sutton; *b* 19 July 1788; *m* 29 April 1812 Mary (*d* 21 Dec 1880), dau of William Isaac, of Sturminster Newton, Dorset, and *d* 18 April 1826, having had, with other issue:

1 George, of Marlston House, Newbury, Berks, and Reading, JP and CA Berks, JP Reading; MP Reading 1878–85, a fndr Huntley & Palmers; *b* 18 Jan 1818; *m* 17 Jan 1850 Elizabeth Sarah (*d* 30 March 1894), dau of Robert Meteyard, and *d* 19 Aug 1897, having had:

(1) George William, PC, of Marlston House, Reading: JP (and Berks), MP 1892–95 and 1898–1904, Mayor 1888–89; dir Huntley & Palmers; *b* 23 May 1851; *m* 6 Feb 1879 Eleanor (*d* 9 Feb 1929), er dau of Henry Barrett, and *dsp* 8 Oct 1913

(2) Alfred, of Wokefield Park, Mortimer, Berks, JP; High Sheriff 1905, DSc, Pres Cncl U Reading, dir Huntley & Palmers; *b* 25 Aug 1852; *m* 4 July 1877 Alice Marie (*d* 25 April 1931), dau of William Exhall, JP, of Reading, and *d* 20 May 1936, leaving:

1a Eustace Exall, of Priors Court, Chieveley, Berks, JP Hants and Berks; High Sheriff 1914, dir Huntley & Palmers; *b* 30 July 1878; *m* 23 April 1902 Madeline Mary (*d* 28 July 1958), only dau of Conrad Goodridge Howell, barrister, and *d* 21 July 1931, leaving:

1b Gerald Eustace Howell; *b* 9 June 1904; *educ* Winchester and New Coll Oxford; Hon DLitt Reading 1957, memb Council U of Reading 1936 (Pres 1966–69), MP Winchester 1935–45, Priv Sec to PM 1935, PPS to Parly U-Sec Home Office 1935, Jt PPS to Ld Privy Seal 1942 and Sec State Colonies 1942, Capt RA WW II (despatches), Forestry Commr 1963–65

2b Rodney Howell, MC (1943), of Peasemore Manor, Chieveley, Berks; *b* 24 Nov 1907; *educ* Harrow and Pembroke Coll Cambridge; High Sheriff Berks 1953, 2nd Lt 12th Lancers 1930, WW II: 12th Lancers and 2nd Derbys Yeo, Lt-Col 1943, MFH Tedworth 1938–39, S Berks 1947–53; *m* 1st 19 Sept 1934 (*divorce* 1949) Frances Pauline, only dau of Capt Lachlan Gordon-Duff, and had:

1c *Andrew Eustace, CMG (1987), CVO (1981) [Andrew Palmer Esq CMG CVO, Town Farm Cottage, Little Missenden, Bucks HP7 0QX]; *b* 30 Sept 1937; *educ* Winchester and Pembroke Coll Cambridge (MA); 2nd Lt Rifle Bde 1956–58, For Serv: joined 1961, Consul-Gen Oslo 1979–82, Amb: Cuba 1986–88, Holy See 1991–95, Extra Equerry to HRH THE DUKE OF KENT 1996–; *m* 28 July 1962 *Davina Cecil, yst dau of Sir Roderick (Edward) Barclay, KCMG, GCVO, and has:

1d *Rodney James Andrew; *b* 25 Feb 1963; *educ* Sussex U (PhD)

2d *Michael George Joseph; *b* 9 May 1977
1d *Juliet Frances Jean; *b* 21 Aug 1965; *m* 19 Dec 1991 *Viscount Garmoyle, est s of 6th Earl Cairns (*qv*) and has issue
2b (cont.) Lt-Col Rodney Palmer *m* 2nd 14 June 1949 Nancy Isobel, yr dau of Francis Cecil Albert Hurt, of Alderwasley, Derbys, and *d* 1987
1b Elizabeth Mary; *b* 6 Jan 1906

(3) Sir WALTER PALMER, 1st and last Bt (UK), so *cr* 25 Aug 1904, JP, DL Berks; *b* 4 Feb 1858; MP Salisbury 1900–06, BSc Lond, Chm Cncl U Coll Reading; *m* 8 Feb 1882 Jean (*d* 13 July 1909), dau of William Young Craig, of Milton House, Alsager, Cheshire, MP N Staffs 1880–85, and *d* 16 April 1910, when the btcy expired, leaving:

1a Gladys Milton; *b* 8 Jan 1884; *m* 28 June 1904 Bertram Willes Davrell Brooke (HH Tuan Mudah of Sarawak), Lt RA, 2nd s of HH The Rajah of Sarawak (Sir Charles Anthony Johnson Brooke, GCMG), and *d* leaving issue. He *d* 15 Sept 1965

(4) Lewis, JP Notts; *b* 9 Nov 1860; MA Cantab; barrister Inner Temple; *m* 1886 Emily (*d* 11 Aug 1921), widow of B Forster, CE, and *d* 15 April 1908, leaving:

1a Kenneth Lewis; *b* 2 Aug 1889

(1) Emily; *m* 31 March 1881 Sir Edward Bagnall Poulton, MA, LLD, DSc, FRS, s of William Ford Poulton, of Reading, and *d* 20 April 1939, having had issue. He *d* 20 Nov 1943

(2) Alice Mary; *m* 6 Jan 1885 Augustus Désiré Waller, MD, FRS, LLD, and *d* 22 Oct 1922, leaving issue. He *d* 11 March 1922

(3) Lucy Elizabeth; *m* 3 Sept 1887 Col Lewis Anstruther Hope, CB, and *d* 21 July 1952, leaving issue (*see* HOPE, Bt)

2 Samuel, of Northcourt, Hampstead; *b* 20 Jan 1820; a fndr Huntley & Palmers; *m* 2 Feb 1856 Mary Jane (*d* 17 March 1910), dau of Joseph Marsh, of Stoke Newington, and *d* 9 April 1903, having had:

(1) SAMUEL ERNEST, **1st Baron**

(2) Charles Herbert, of Bozedown House, Whitchurch, Oxford, JP; *b* 23 Dec 1860; dir Huntley & Palmers; *m* 6 Feb 1883 Ethel (*d* 26 Jan 1950), dau of Henry J Turner, of Stockleigh House, Regent's Pk, and *d* 26 May 1937, leaving:

1a (Charles) Eric (Sir), of Shinfield Grange, nr Reading, JP, DL Berks; *b* 26 Nov 1883; *educ* Harrow and Exeter Coll Oxford; 1st Life Gds WW I 1917–18, High Sheriff Berks 1926, ktd 1946, Pres Assoc Biscuit Mfrs, chm: Huntley & Palmers, Assoc Biscuit Mfrs and Huntley, Boorne & Stevens; *m* 28 April 1910 Gwenllian Salier, OStJ, yr dau of David Jones, of Melbourne, and *d* 16 Sept 1948, leaving:

1b *Charles Alan Salier, CBE (1969), DSO (1945) [Lt-Col Charles Palmer CBE DSO, 17 Bolton St, London W1; Forest Edge, Farley Hill Berks]; *b* 23 Oct 1913; *educ* Harrow and Exeter Coll Oxford; Lt-Col RA WW II, chm Assoc Biscuit Mfrs, Pres Reading C Assoc; *m* 1 June 1939 *Auriol Mary, only dau of Brig-Gen Cyril Rodney Harbord, CB, CMG, DSO

1b *Barbara Mary [Mrs James Welch, 26 Montagu Square, London W1; Sarsens, Shipley, Sussex]; *b* 22 May 1911; *m* 1st 30 Jan 1937 (*divorce* 1947) Godfrey Tearle (*d* 8 June 1953), s of Osmond Tearle; *m* 2nd 19 Sept 1950 James Welch (*d* 22 Dec 1967), s of William Lewis Welch, of Sunderland

2a Geoffrey Herbert; *b* 3 May 1888; *educ* Harrow; Capt Queen's Own Oxon Hus WW I, High Sheriff Berks 1932, chm Huntley & Palmers, dir Assoc Biscuit Mfrs, Huntley & Palmers; *m* 25 May 1921 Oenone Florence Mary (*d* 11 Jan 1977), widow of Capt Francis Buchanan Lefroy, Leinster Regt, and yst dau of Judge Hickman Molesworth (*see* MOLESWORTH, V), and *dsp* 16 Dec 1978

1a Ethel Clare; *b* 24 Dec 1885; *m* 4 Feb 1914 Stanley Weston Tomkins, only s of William H Tomkins, and *d* 24 April 1959, leaving issue

2a Vera Constance; *b* 24 Oct 1891

(3) William Howard, JP Berks; High Sheriff 1903–04, chm Huntley & Palmers; *b* 3 Nov 1865; *m* 12 June 1890 Ada Morgan (*d* 22 Sept 1953), dau of William Reed, and *d* 17 March 1923, leaving:

1a Reginald Howard Reed, MC, DL (Berks 1953); High Sheriff 1935, Lt Res Offrs Gren Gds WW I, Jt MFH Garth 1931–36, chm: Assoc Biscuit Mfrs, Huntley & Palmers, dir Huntley, Boorne & Stevens; *b* 7 April 1898; *educ* Eton; *m* 20 Feb 1924 Lena Florence (*d* 1981), er dau of Alexander Blyth Cobham, and *d* 15 Feb 1970, leaving:

1b *William Alexander, CBE (1983), DL (Berks 1992) [William Palmer Esq CBE DL, Bussock Wood, Snelsmore Common, Berks RG16 3BT]; *b* 21 June 1925; *educ* Eton; Capt Gren Gds WW II and Palestine, dir: Huntley & Palmers 1951 (chm 1980–83), Huntly and Palmers Foods plc 1971–83 and Assoc Biscuits, chm Huntly, Boorne and Stevens to 1983, Govr Malvern Girls' Coll 1965–90, King Edward's Sch Whitley, High Sheriff Berks 1974–75, Treasurer U of Reading 1982–95; *m* 14 July 1949 *Cherry Anne, 2nd dau of Capt Arthur Gibbs, and has:

1c *Howard William Arthur; *b* 24 June 1954; *educ* Eton and Univ Coll Oxford; *m* April 1983 *Catherine Margaret Jackson and has:

1d *Thomas Howard; *b* 15 April 1988
1d *Laura Margaret; *b* 11 March 1984
2d *Emily Rose; *b* 25 Jan 1986
3d *Harriet Bridget; *b* 14 May 1991

2c *John Reginald David; *b* 20 April 1957; *educ* Eton and RAC Cirencester; *m* Feb 1984 *Lady Laura Elliot (*see* MINTO, E) and has:

1d *Samuel William; *b* 14 April 1985
2d *Nicholas John; *b* 28 Feb 1987

1c *Serena Barbara; *b* 17 May 1950; *m* 1st 8 June 1974 Mark Edward Trehearne Davies; *m* 2nd Oct 1992 *(Thomas) Michael Beswick Sissons

2c *Alexandra Cherry; *b* 9 April 1952; *m* Oct 1979 *James John Norman Crockatt and has:

1d *Benedict Arthur; *b* 30 March 1983
1d *Kate Laura; *b* 20 Feb 1980

2b *Richard John, JP (Reading 1960) [Richard Palmer Esq JP, Queen Ann's Mead, Swallowfield, Berks]; *b* 5 Nov 1926; *educ* Eton; High Sheriff

Berks 1979–80, Lt Gren Gds 1944–48, dir Huntley & Palmers, Assoc Biscuits and Huntley, Boorne & Stevens, chm Thames Valley Bdcasting plc, dep chm GWR Gp plc, Jt MFH S Berks Hunts 1964; *m* 17 Dec 1951 *Hon Sarah Faith Georgina Spencer, yst dau of 1st Viscount Churchill (*qv*), and has issue

(4) Albert John, DSO, TD, of Fairford Park, Glos, JP, DL; High Sheriff Glos 1921, Lt-Col and Brevet Col Roy Gloucester Hus WW I (despatches), dir Huntley & Palmers, Serbian Order White Eagle 4th Cl with swords; *b* 4 March 1871; *m* 21 Aug 1895 Catherine (*d* 4 Feb 1946), dau of Col Hugh Chetham Lyle, RA, and *dsp* 29 May 1940

(1) Florence Mary, MBE; *d* unm 12 June 1948

(2) Gertrude Isabel; *m* 1st 29 Jan 1891 Charles Henry Weir (*d* 22 Oct 1899); *m* 2nd 8 Oct 1904 Rev Canon Reginald James Lea, Vicar Henfield, Sussex, and *d* 11 July 1959. He *d* 21 Aug 1945

(3) Ellen Maud; *m* 20 Jan 1885 Henry Nicoll, JP, of Bullington Manor, Sutton Scotney, Hants, and *d* 24 Oct 1963, leaving issue. He *d* 13 Sept 1923

(4) Nora Constance; *d* 3 April 1932

The est son,

Sir (Samuel) Ernest Palmer, 1st Bt, and **1st Baron Palmer**, of Reading, Co Berks (both UK), so *cr* 26 Jan 1916 and 24 June 1933 respectively, JP Co London; *b* 28 March 1858; *educ* Malvern; Lt City London, High Sheriff 1924, dir Huntley & Palmers, dep chm GWR 1906–43, RCM: V-Pres 1929, 1st Fell 1921, fndr Berks Scholarship 1902, Patrons' Fund 1903, Ernest Palmer Fund for Opera Study 1924; fndr two scholarships Guildhall Sch Music, Hon Freeman Musicians' Co; *m* 10 Feb 1881 Amy Christiana (*d* 28 Feb 1947), only dau of George Swan Nottage, Ld Mayor London 1884, and had:

1 ERNEST CECIL NOTTAGE, **2nd Baron**

2 Arnold Nottage; *b* 14 Sept 1886; *educ* Winchester and Univ Coll Oxford (BA 1908); FRCM, Hon RWS, artist, with Nat Gallery, wrote commentaries on drawings for OUP, author: *Moveable Feasts*; *m* 19 June 1911 Marjorie (*d* 5 April 1966), dau of Alexander Freeland, and *d* 27 Nov 1973, leaving:

(1) *Susan Helen [Miss Susan Palmer, Fir Tree Farm, Hampstead Norris, Berks]; *b* 3 April 1912

(2) *Felicity Amy [Miss Felicity Palmer, Coombe Farm House, Frilsham, Hermitage, Newbury, Berks]; *b* 2 June 1913

(3) Rachel Joan; *b* 29 Aug 1916; *m* 26 Oct 1957 Guivi Malville

(4) *(Nancy) Gillian [Mrs David Pilkington, Appledown, Frilsham, Hermitage, Newbury, Berks]; *b* 22 May 1918; *m* 19 Oct 1943 *David Charles Bethune Pilkington, OBE, er s of Col Lionel George Pilkington, MC, by Evelyn Carnegie, 2nd dau of Sir Alexander Sharp Bethune, 9th Bt (*see* 1970 edn), and has:

  1a *Julian Alexander Bethune; *b* 1946; *m* 1974 *Susan Anne West and has:

    1b *Oliver; *b* 1975

    1b *Louise; *b* 1978

    2b *Felicity (twin); *b* 1978

  2a *Susan Elizabeth; *b* 1948; *m* 1st 1969 (*divorce* 1981) John Dallas Scott and has:

    1b *Mungo; *b* 1974

    1b *Mercedes; *b* 1971

  2a (cont.) Mrs Susan Scott *m* 2nd 1984 *T Johnson, of Hobart, Tasmania

The 1st BARON *d* 8 Dec 1948; his er son,

ERNEST CECIL NOTTAGE PALMER, **2nd Baron Palmer**; *b* 9 June 1882; *educ* Winchester and Oriel Coll Oxford (BA 1905); ACA, dep chm Huntley & Palmers, v-chm Assoc Biscuit Mfrs; *m* 9 June 1909 Marguerite (*d* 13 Sept 1959), dau of William McKinley Osborne, of Boston, US Consul-Gen London, and *d* 6 June 1950, leaving:

1 RAYMOND CECIL PALMER, **3rd Baron Palmer**, OBE (1968); *b* 24 June 1916; *educ* Harrow and Univ Coll Oxford; Lt Gren Gds (invalided), chm: Huntley & Palmers, Huntley, Boorne & Stevens, dir Assoc Biscuit Mfrs, SEB, pres Thames Valley TSB; *m* 30 Jan 1941 *Victoria Ellen, only dau of Capt Joseph Arthur Ronald Weston Stevens, and *d* 1990, leaving:

(1) Amanda Victoria; *b* 16 July 1949; *d* 15 Nov 1954

(2) *Carol Lylie [Lady Wodehouse, Kingswood, Medmenham, Bucks SL7 2EU]; *b* 28 Nov 1951; *m* 21 July 1973 *Lord Wodehouse, est s of 4th Earl of Kimberley (*qv*)

(3) *Vanessa Marguerite [The Hon Mrs St John, 20 Sudbroke Rd, London SW12 8TG]; *b* 15 Dec 1954; *m* 16 July 1977 *Robert W St John, 2nd s of Lt-Col Charles St John, of Glebe Manor, Havant, Hants, and has:

  1a *Edward Robert Cecil; *b* 1982

  1a *Camilla Victoria Celia; *b* 1980

  2a *Laura Zoë Lylie; *b* 1985

  3a *Melissa Lucy Amanda; *b* 1986

2 Gordon William Nottage (Sir), KCVO (1988), OBE (1957, MBE 1944), TD, JP (Berks 1956), DL (1960); *b* 18 July 1918; *educ* Eton and Ch Ch Oxford; High Sheriff Berks 1965, Hon Col Berks and Westminster Dragoons, cmdg Berks Yeo 1954–57, Lt-Col RA staff WW II, KStJ; Ld Lt Berks 1978–89, Chm Berks T&AFA, FRCM, Treas Reading U 1955 (V-Pres 1965), memb cncl Bradfield Coll, sales/mktg dir Assoc Biscuit Mfrs, md Huntley & Palmers 1960–65, dir Huntley, Boorne & Stevens, American Bronze Star 1945; *m* 6 May 1950 *Lorna Eveline Hope, DL (Berks 1989) [The Hon Lady Palmer DL, Harris House, Mortimer, Berks RG7 3NT; Edrom Newton, Duns, Berwickshire], er dau of Maj Charles William Hugh Bailie, and *d* 3 July 1989, having had:

(1) ADRIAN BAILIE NOTTAGE PALMER, **4th and present Baron Palmer**

(2) +Mark Hugh Gordon [The Hon Mark Palmer, 68 Endlesham Rd, London SW12]; *b* 16 Sept 1954; *educ* Eton; granted rank of baron's s 1991; jnlst, exec dir *Daily* and *Sunday Express*; *m* 1 July 1982 *Irene, dau of Guillermo Aranda, of Los Angeles, and has:

  1a +Henry Gordon William; *b* 17 March 1987

  1a *Olivia Lorna Aranda; *b* 25 July 1990

1 Marjorie Elizabeth; *b* 24 April 1910; *m* 9 June 1945 Frederick Richard Brown, MBE (*d* 1991), Capt RASC, s of Roger Grounds Brown, of Liverpool, and *d* 2 March 1996, leaving:

(1) *Christopher Frederick; *b* 22 Oct 1946; *educ* Wellington; *m* 1972 (*divorce* 1996) Suzanne Ryder

(2) *Ian Cecil Roger [Ian Brown Esq, 57 Lankin Blvd, Orilla ONT C3V 6T1, Canada]; *b* 6 Dec 1948; *educ* Marlborough and Fitzwilliam Coll Cambridge; *m* 1st 1981 Grace Rasmussen; *m* 2nd 19– (*divorce*) Anne Gowan; *m* 3rd 19– *Susan —

(3) *Richard Philip [Richard Brown Esq, 80 Wandle Rd, London SW17 7DW]; *b* 5 Feb 1952; *educ* Marlborough; *m* 1982 *Alexandra Margaret Aldcroft

(1) *Jennifer Elizabeth [Miss Jenny Brown, Bayfield House, 38 Bathwick Hill, Bath BA2 6LD]; *b* 13 June 1953; *m* 12 June 1975 (*divorce* 1983) Brian Shephard

2 Audrey Vivien; *b* 2 Sept 1912; *d* 29 April 1917

PALMER, Bt, of Carlton

Arms: Sa. a chevron or between three crescents arg.
Crest: A wyvern, wings addorsed or, armed and langued gu.
Motto: *Par sit fortuna labori* ('May the success be equal to the labour'). **Creation:** Bt. (E) 7 June 1660.

SIR GEOFFREY CHRISTOPHER JOHN PALMER, 12TH BT, of Carlton, Co Northampton [Sir Geoffrey Palmer Bt, Carlton Curlieu Hall, Leics LE8 0PH]; *b* 30 June 1936; *s* f 1951; *educ* Eton; *m* 24 July 1957 *Clarissa Mary, er dau of Stephen Francis Villiers-Smith by Olivia Mary, er dau of Lt Col Hon Cuthbert James, CBE, JP, MP (*see* NORTHBOURNE, B), and has had:

1 Geoffrey; *b* and *d* 25 March 1966

1 *Sophia Mary; *b* 11 Dec 1959; *m* 1987 *Michael H W Neal, of Legsheath, Sussex, only s of (Harry) Morton Neal, CBE, of Great Sarratt Hall, Sarratt, Herts, and has:

(1) *Harry Morton Geoffrey; *b* 1988

(1) *Jemima Mary; *b* 1991

2 *Celina Lucinda [Mrs William Francklin, The Oak House, Hinxton, Cambs]; *b* 15 May 1961; *m* 1986 *William Alexander Mavourn Francklin, yr s of Cdr (Mavourn Baldwin) Philip Francklin, DSC, of Gonalston Hall, Notts, and has:

(1) *Henry Alexander John; *b* 1988

(1) *Clementine; *b* 1990

(2) *Daisy; *b* 1993

3 *Isabella Anne; *b* 27 Aug 1962; *m* 1993 *David W R Harrington, s of Ronald Harrington, and has:

(1) *Lavinia Juliet; *b* 1994

4 *Rosanna Jane; *b* 16 Aug 1967; *m* 1993 *Edward J G Peel, s of John Peel

Lineage: WILLIAM PALMER; lawyer, *fl* early 15th century; *m* Amy, dau and heiress of Nicholas Ward, of Carlton, Northants, who brought him half the estate (the other half he bought); ancestor of:

THOMAS PALMER, of Carlton; *m* Catherine, dau of Sir Edward Watson, of Rockingham, and sister of 1st Baron Rockingham (*see* 1970 edn SONDES, E), and had:

Sir Geoffrey Palmer, 1st Bt (E), so *cr* 7 June 1660, of Carlton; *b* 1598; MP Stamford 1649–52, royalist Commr Uxbridge negotiations towards end of Civil War 1645, Attorney-Gen 1660–70, Ch Justice Chester 1661–62, ktd; *m* 1625 Margaret (*d* 16 May 1655), dau of Sir Francis Moore, Serjeant-at-law, of Fawley, Berks, and *d* 5 May 1670, leaving, with other issue:

Sir Lewis Palmer, 2nd Bt; MP Higham Ferrers 1661–97; *m* 1st 1654 Jane (*d* 11 Feb 1700), dau and coheir of Robert Palmer, of Carlton Scroop, Lincs; *m* 2nd Frances — (*d* by 31 Aug 1703) and *d* 1714, having by his 1st w had, with four daus:

1 **Sir Geoffrey Palmer, 3rd Bt**; *b* 12 June 1655; MP Leics 1707–22; *m* Elizabeth, dau and coheir of Thomas Grantham, and *dsp* 29 Dec 1732

2 Robert; *b* 8 Dec 1656; *m* Hester, dau of Sir Francis Lawley, 2nd Bt (*see* 1932 edn WENLOCK, B), and *d* 1724, leaving, with other issue:

(1) **Sir Thomas Palmer, 4th Bt**; MP Leics 1754–65; *m* 1735 Jemima (*d* 22 June 1763), dau of Sir John Harpur, Bt, of Calke Abbey (*see* 1924 edn CREWE, Bt), and *d* 14 June 1765, having had, with another s (*d* young) and two daus:

  1a **Sir John Palmer, 5th Bt**; *b* 1735; MP Leics 1765–80; *m* 23 July 1768 Charlotte (*d* 7 Aug 1783), dau of Sir Henry Gough, 1st Bt, of Edgbaston, Warwicks (*see* 1970 edn CALTHORPE, B), and *d* 11 Feb 1817, having had:

1b Thomas; *b* 1771; *m* Dec 1798 Sophia (*d* 1851), dau of Sir Justinian Isham, 7th Bt, of Lamport (*qv*), and *dvp* 4 June 1810, leaving:

  1c **Sir Thomas Palmer, 6th Bt**; *d* unm 16 April 1817

  1c Caroline Sophia; *m* 21 July 1827 Maj Robert Close and had issue

2b **Sir John Henry Palmer, 7th Bt**; *b* 11 April 1775; BA Oxon, Sheriff Northants 1819; *m* 3 May 1808 Mary Grace (*d* 26 Nov 1853), est dau of 2nd Baron Sondes (*see* 1970 edn SONDES, E), and *d* 26 Aug 1865, having had, with other issue:

  1c **Sir Geoffrey Palmer, 8th Bt**; *b* 9 June 1809; BA Oxon, barrister, High Sheriff Northants 1871, Capt Leics Yeo; *d* unm 10 Feb 1892

  2c **Rev Sir Lewis Henry Palmer, 9th Bt**; *b* 16 Aug 1818; *educ* Ch Ch Oxford (MA); Rector E Carlton 1843–78; *d* unm 28 April 1909

  1c Grace; *m* 30 Sept 1846 Rt Rev Edward Trollope and *d* 21 Oct 1890, leaving issue (*see* TROLLOPE, Bt)

3b Henry (Rev), of Withcote Hall, Leics; *b* 4 Jan 1780; *m* 27 June 1816 Elizabeth (*d* 8 Nov 1860), dau of Rev Samuel Heyrick, and *d* 14 Aug 1856, having had, with other issue:

  1c Frederick, of Withcote, JP, DL (Rutland); High Sheriff 1865, Col cmdg PAO Leics Imp Yeo, Capt 27th Regt; *b* 15 July 1825; *m* 14 Nov 1850 Mary (*d* 25 Jan 1907), only dau of William Henry Harrison and sis of Col William Henry Harrison-Broadley, MP, of Welton House, Yorks, and *d* 27 Jan 1907, leaving:

    1d (EDWARD) GEOFFREY BROADLEY (Sir), **10th Bt**

    1d Mary Sophia; *d* unm 24 Aug 1913

    2d Hester Alice; *m* 8 April 1886 Charles Henry Vane Holder (*d* Jan 1940) and *dsp* May 1940

    3d Emily Heyrick; *d* unm May 1939

  2c Charles Samuel (Rev); *b* 29 May 1830; *educ* Exeter Coll Oxford (MA); Canon Hereford, RD Weobley, Proctor in Convocation Hereford, Rector Eardisley; *m* 16 Nov 1854 Ellen (*d* 23 July 1905), dau of Rev Canon Henry Douglas, of Durham, and *d* 10 March 1921, having had:

    1d Henry William; *b* 18 Sept 1856; *d* 21 July 1858

    1d Mabel Jane; *m* 15 Feb 1881 Richard Crawshay Bailey (*d* 19 July 1916) and *d* 16 Oct 1909, leaving issue (*see* GLANUSK, B)

    2d Margaret Eleanor; *m* 23 April 1891 Charles Henry Fehler Christie (*d* 1 July 1924), of Chipping Ongar, Essex, and *d* 7 March 1943, having had issue

  3c Thomas, JP Herefs; *b* 8 Dec 1832; Hon Maj and Adj E R Vols Hull, Capt 47th Regt Crimea (medal and clasps); *m* 20 Sept 1860 Harriet Elizabeth (*dsp* 24 Jan 1912), dau of Edward Dawson, of Whatton and Launde Abbey, Leics, and *d* 15 April 1929

  4c Herrick Augustus; *b* 28 Sept 1835; Hon Maj Glam Militia, Capt 62nd Regt (Crimean medal and clasp, 5th Cl Medjidie); *m* 21 Nov 1861 Dorothy Susan (*d* 9 Jan 1914), dau of Sir Arthur Grey Hazlerigg, 12th Bt (*see* HAZLERIGG, B), and *d* 17 Dec 1908, having had:

    1d Heyrick Arthur; *b* 23 May 1864; *d* 25 July 1937

    2d Frederick Charles; *b* 21 Nov 1866; Capt 1st Garrison Bn Manchester Regt, Maj 6th Bn Manchester Regt; *m* 15 Sept 1897 Eleanor Annie (*d* 28 Dec 1941), dau of Henry Wilson Sharpin, FRCS, of Brighton, and *d* 16 Dec 1930, leaving:

      1e Dorothy Esther; *b* 1898

      2e Eleanor Joan; *d* unm

    3d Robert Henry, DSO (1917); *b* 19 Feb 1868; Strathcona's Horse Boer War (wounded, medal with clasps), Lt-Col 49th Bn Canadian Inf (Edmonton Regt) BEF WW I (despatches five times, Belgian Croix de Guerre with palms); *m* 2 June 1909 Margaret Finch (*d* 30 May 1955), er dau of Gerard Finch Dawson, and *d* 5 Sept 1947, having had:

      1e Robert Herrick Geoffrey; *b* 22 Feb 1910; *d* 5 Feb 1912

      2e +Robert Henry Charles [Robert Palmer Esq, 3480 Simpson St, Apt 901, Montreal, Quebec H3G 2N7, Canada]; *b* 24 June 1916; *educ* Clifton and Wadham Coll Oxford (MA 1945, BMus 1945); F/Sgt RAF WW II, ARCM, ARCO, music master Westminster Abbey Choir Sch 1957, dir choir U of Victoria BC 1966–70 (conductor 1965–69), organist St Mary the Virgin Oak Bay Victoria 1961–83, organist Royal Chapel Windsor 1938–39

      1e *Mary Margaret Elizabeth; *b* 25 March 1914; *m* 29 May 1944 Genille Hilton Jordayne Cave-Browne-Cave (*see* CAVE-BROWNE-CAVE, Bt)

  4d Charles; *b* 21 June 1869; *d* 7 Dec 1921

  5d Henry Cecil; *b* 7 Nov 1873; *d* 3 July 1891

  6d Francis Hubert, MC (1918); *b* 6 Aug 1877; T/Capt Cheshire Regt WW I (wounded twice, despatches); *m* 1st 23 Jan 1907 (*divorce* 1924) Elsie Edit (*d* 10 Oct 1954), yst dau of Rev Walter Baptist Money, Rector Weybridge, and had:

    1e Pamela Frances; *b* 15 Oct 1911; *m* 1st 26 July 1935 Evan Morgan (*d* 22 Dec 1942), only s of Charles Morgan, OBE; *m* 2nd 27 Sept 1944 Albert Keith Smith, s of John Smith, of Ablington, Glos, and *d* 13 Oct 1952

  6d (cont.) Francis Palmer *m* 2nd 28 Oct 1924 Margery Edith (*d c* 1952), est dau of Robert Garland, of Seaford, Sussex, and *d* 7 Dec 1951

  7d Thomas Martival; *b* 13 May 1880; *m* 21 April 1908 Ellen (*d* 26 Dec 1930), dau of Albert Fleming, MD, of Holbrook, Suffolk, and *d* 6 June 1917

    1d Elizabeth Ethel; *d* unm 6 July 1948

    2d Barbara Gwendoline Mary Isabel; *m* 10 Feb 1904 Fort Greenwood, 5th s of Thomas Greenwood, of Todmorden, and *d c* 1955, leaving issue

    3d Henrietta Dorothy; *m* 21 April 1915 Joseph Skuse, s of William Skuse, and *d* 19 Jan 1955, having had issue. He *d* 28 May 1941

  1c Mary Jemima; *m* 7 Oct 1847 Francis Leslie Pym (*see* PYM, B) and *d* 14 June 1898, leaving issue

The 9th Bt's cousin,

Sir (Edward) Geoffrey Broadley Palmer, 10th Bt, JP, DL Leics; *b* 14 June 1864; *educ* Magdalene Coll Cambridge (MA); High Sheriff Rutland 1910, Maj 3rd and

7th Bns Leics Regt; *m* 8 Jan 1891 Sibyll Caroline (*d* 21 July 1933), dau of Capt William James Smith-Neill, RA, of Barnwell and Swindrige Muir, Ayrshire, and had:

  1 GEOFFREY FREDERICK NEILL (Sir), **11th Bt**

  2 Lewis Henry; *b* 27 Jan 1903; *educ* Lt 15th/19th Hus; *m* 1st 8 June 1935 (*divorce* 1940) Pamela, only child of John Rowland Harries; *m* 2nd 27 July 1940 (*divorce* 1950) Mary Kathleen, dau of William Fletcher, of Arlecdon, Cumberland, and *d* 30 Dec 1974

  1 Sibyll Alice Bridget; *b* 27 Nov 1891; *m* 2 April 1913 Francis Edward Michael Reading, of Withcote Hall, Oakham, Rutland, only surv s of Lt-Col Francis William Reading, Leics Regt, and had issue

Sir GEOFFREY *d* 15 May 1925; his er son,

Sir Geoffrey Frederick Neill Palmer, 11th Bt, JP, DL Leics; *b* 20 Sept 1893; *educ* Repton and Trin Coll Cambridge; Lt-Col Coldstream Gds WW I (wounded, two medals, 1914 star), WW II; *m* 14 Dec 1932 Cicely Kathleen (*m* 2nd 1 Oct 1952 Robert William Banner Newton and *d* 1989 having had further issue), dau of Arthur Clifford Radmall, and *d* 22 Nov 1951, leaving:

  1 Sir GEOFFREY CHRISTOPHER JOHN PALMER, **12th and present Bt**

  2 +JEREMY CHARLES [Jeremy Palmer Esq, 6 Furber St, London W6 0HE; Westwater House, Axminster, Devon EX13 7JD]; *b* 16 May 1939; heir presumptive; *educ* Eton and U of Tours; dir Bulland Taylor; *m* 24 July 1968 *Antonia Rosamund Clare, yst dau of Astley Dutton, and has:

    (1) +Drew Herrick; *b* 18 Dec 1974

    (2) +Tom Jeremy; *b* 3 May 1977

PALMER, Bt, of Grinkle Park

Arms: Sa. on a chevron between three crescents in chief and a lion passant in base arg. two tilting spears chevron-wise ppr. **Crest:** In front of a tilting spear erect ppr. a wyvern or, resting the dexter foot on a crescent arg. **Motto:** *Par sit fortuna labori* ('May the success be equal to the labour'). **Creation:** Bt. (UK) 31 Aug 1886.

SIR (CHARLES) MARK PALMER, 5TH BT, of Grinkle Park, Co York, and of Newcastle-upon-Tyne [Sir Mark Palmer Bt, 15 Bramerton St, London SW3; Mill Hill Farm, Sherborne, Glos GL54 3DU]; *b* posthumously 21 Nov 1941; *s f* 1941; *educ* Eton; Page Honour to HM THE QUEEN 1956–59; *m* 1976 *Hon Catherine Elizabeth Tennant, yr dau of 2nd Baron Glenconner (*qv*), and has:

  1 +ARTHUR MORRIS; *b* 9 March 1981

  1 *Iris Henriette; *b* 1977; *educ* Bedales and St Mary's Wantage; model

Lineage: GEORGE PALMER, of Boston, Lincs, and Monkwearmouth, Co Durham; *m* Eleanor Street and had:

GEORGE PALMER, of Newcastle-upon-Tyne; *b* 31 July 1789; *m* 29 Dec 1813 Maria (*d* 2 Feb 1864), dau of Thomas Taylor, of Hill House, Monkwearmouth, and *d* 10 Dec 1866, leaving, with other issue:

  1 George, of Greenwood, Hants; *b* 24 Nov 1814; *m* 14 Nov 1848 Annie, dau of William Neesham, of Laleham, Middx, and *d* 29 July 1879, having had issue

  2 William Henry, of Port Mulgrave, Hinderwell, Yorks; *b* 8 Oct 1820; *m* 29 May 1855 Lavinia, dau of Richard Brown, of Hinderwell, and *d* 3 June 1857, having had issue

  3 CHARLES MARK (Sir), **1st Bt**

  4 Henry Burton; *b* 8 Sept 1831; *m* 9 Sept 1858 Sarah Elizabeth, dau of Richard Brown, of Hinderwell, and *d* 21 July 1910, leaving issue

  1 Maria; *m* 23 July 1850 William Henry Porter, of Edinburgh, and *d* 23 April 1855, leaving issue

The 3rd son,

Sir Charles Mark Palmer, 1st Bt (UK), so *cr* 31 Aug 1886, VD, JP, DL Co Durham and N R Yorks, of Grinkle Park, Yorks; *b* 3 Nov 1822; MP N Durham 1874–85 and Jarrow 1885–1907, Cdr Order SS. Maurice and Lazarus Italy, Hon Col Cmdt 1st Durham RE Vols and Submarine Mining Vol RE, dir Suez Canal Co, fndr Palmer Shipbuilding, Mayor Jarrow 1875 and 1902–03; *m* 1st 29 July 1846 Jane (*d* 6 April 1865), dau of Ebenezer Robson, of Newcastle, and had, with two other sons:

1 **Sir George Robson Palmer, 2nd Bt**; *b* 5 Jan 1849; *educ* Harrow; *d* unm 23 Aug 1910

2 ALFRED MOLYNEUX (Sir), **3rd Bt**

Sir Charles *m* 2nd 4 July 1867 Augusta Mary (*d* 2 Dec 1875), dau of Alfred Lambert, of Paris and Massa di Carrara, Italy, and *d* 4 June 1907, having by her had:

3 Claude Bowes, CBE (1918), JP, DL Co Durham; *b* 29 March 1868; *educ* Cheltenham and abroad; Hon Lt-Col (formerly cmdg) RAMC (V), Lt Army Motor Res, Cmmr St John's Ambulance Bde, KJStJ, Br and French Red Cross WW I; *m* 20 Oct 1897 Marian, OBE, ARRC, DGStJ, Belgian Order Queen Elisabeth (*d* 9 Sept 1952), formerly w of Edmund Jenkins and dau of Edward Charlton Ramsey, and *d* 7 April 1949

4 Lionel Hugo; *b* 22 Oct 1870; Capt 3rd Bn W Yorks Regt and Roy NW Mounted Police Canada, Boer War 1901–02 (despatches, Queen's medal with four clasps, Hon Lt), Freeman Newcastle 1902; *m* 1st 6 Feb 1893 Ida Brae (*d* 4 June 1905), dau of Wilberforce Wilson, Surveyor-Gen Hong Kong, and had:

  (1) Claudia Augusta Geraldine; *b* 18 Jan 1896; *m* 5 March 1932 Joseph Edgar Brown, Dep Inspr-Gen Indian Police, and *d* 14 Nov 1933, leaving issue. He *d* 24 Sept 1949

  (2) Victoria Louisa; *b* 28 May 1897; *m* 6 June 1923 John James Dickie (*d* 2 Aug 1953), er s of Alexander Perry Dickie, and *d* 1 Jan 1991, having had issue

4 (cont.) Capt Lionel Palmer *m* 2nd 10 May 1906 Blanche (*d* 21 Aug 1965), only dau of Walter Balmford, of York, and *d* 7 Sept 1914, having by her had:

  (1) Charles Lionel; *b* 7 Feb 1909; *educ* Cheltenham and Trent Coll; Capt RCASC; *m* 29 July 1937 Karoline (*d* 3 Jan 1995), LRAM (Eloc), only dau of Maj Karl Gach, of Vienna, and *d* 1987, leaving:

    1a *Diana Lillian [Miss Diana Palmer, 7811 Yonge St, Apt 1110, Thornhill, Ontario L3T 4S3, Canada]; *b* 3 Nov 1939

    2a *Marjorie Tessa [Mrs Dennis Tallevi, 3430 Halstead Rd, Mississauga, Ontario L5L 4H2, Canada]; *b* 30 April 1950; *m* 1978 *Dennis Tallevi

  (3) Marjorie Blanche; *b* 31 Jan 1907; memb Imp Soc Teachers Dancing, Jr Cdr ATS; *m* 9 Sept 1939 Philip Ashford Klitz (*d* 12 June 1942), s of Maj R W Klitz, and *d* 14 June 1996

Sir Charles *m* 3rd 17 Feb 1877 Gertrude (*d* 21 Jan 1918), dau of James Montgomery, JP, DL, of Cranford, Middx, and by her had:

5 Godfrey Mark, JP N R Yorks; *b* 4 Aug 1878; Maj TFR, MP Jarrow 1910–22, PPS to 1st Ld Admlty 1917–18; *m* 17 July 1906 Eleonora Mary (*d* 11 March 1965), dau of Alexander Geddes, and *d* 12 June 1933, leaving:

  (1) Mark, TD; *b* 4 Feb 1917; *educ* Eton and abroad; Hon Maj WW II, Maj 2nd Bn Princess Louise's Regt, Middx Regt (TA), US Bronze Star; *m* 12 July 1939 *Rosemary Aileen, er dau of Edward Welton, and *d* 21 Feb 1995, having had:

    1a Adrian Mark; *b* 27 May 1944; *educ* Eton; *k* car crash 2 Nov 1967

    1a *Ferelith Alison; *b* 9 Dec 1946; *m* 1st 21 April 1971 (*divorce* 1984) Ashley Gordon Down, only s of John Down, of Sydney, NSW, and has:

      1b *John Mark Palmer; *b* 1979

      1b *Selina Eleanor; *b* 1975

    1a (cont.) Mrs Ferelith Down *m* 2nd 1988 *Hon James Reginald Drummond (*see* PERTH, E)

  (1) Brenda Eleonora Mary; *b* 11 July 1907; *m* 18 Sept 1929 Col Cuthbert Vaux, MC, TD, Northumberland Hus Yeo (*d* 27 April 1960), est s of Major Cuthbert Vaux, of Dryburn Hall, Co Durham, and *d* 19 Dec 1955, leaving issue

  (2) *Myrtle Frances [Mrs Edward Tetley, East Cottage, Oswaldkirk, York YO6 5XZ]; *b* 11 April 1912; *m* 1st 17 Sept 1940 (*annulled* 1944, resumed maiden name by deed poll 1944) F/Lt Guy Robinson, RAF, s of B A Robinson, of Scalby, Yorks; *m* 2nd 24 Jan 1949 (*divorce* 1962) Horace Barker, s of Lancelot Harold Barker, and has:

    1a *Rachel Kay [Mrs Christopher Wilson, 8 Foskett Rd, London SW6]; *b* 27 May 1950; *m* 1974 *Christopher Rodney Wilson and has:

      1b *Mark Christopher; *b* 1984

      1b *Serena Annabel; *b* 1980

  (2) (cont.) Mrs Myrtle Barker *m* 3rd 21 April 1967 *Edward Walsh Tetley, s of Dr Walsh Tetley

1 Hilda Gertrude Montgomerie; *b* 6 July 1884; *d* unm 4 Jan 1946

The 2nd Bt's bro,

Sir Alfred Molyneux Palmer, 3rd Bt, JP Jarrow; *b* 3 June 1853; *educ* Harrow; CA Co Durham, High Sheriff 1915; *m* 31 March 1884 Ellen Edith (*d* 15 Nov 1945), dau of Frederick George Younge, and had:

1 Frederick Charles; *b* 3 Dec 1884; *m* 7 Oct 1913 Mabel Frances (*d* 30 March 1966), est dau of Norton Joseph Hughes-Hallett, OBE, DL, and *d* 29 March 1931, leaving:

  (1) ANTHONY FREDERICK MARK (Sir), **4th Bt**

  (1) *Diana Mabel [Mrs William Huntington, Bonawe House, Taynault, Argyll]; *b* 29 Oct 1917; *m* 4 Nov 1939 S/Ldr William Vivian Huntington, JP, RAFVR (*d* 1989), est s of Maj Arthur William Huntington, DSO, and has:

    1a *Nicholas Charles; *b* 2 Oct 1940; *educ* Eton

    2a *Anthony Patrick; *b* 9 July 1942; *educ* Eton

    3a *Peter William; *b* 20 June 1945; *educ* Tabley House Sch; *m* 1983 (*divorce* 1994) Philippa Carolyn, er dau of Sir Archibald Edmonstone, 7th Bt (*qv*), and has:

      1b *Thomas William; *b* 1988

      1b *Louise Mary; *b* 1986

    4a *Richard Ian; *b* 25 Oct 1946; *educ* Gordonstoun

  (2) *Angela [Mrs John Turnbull, Well Cottage, Lingen, Bucknall, Salop SY7 0DY]; *b* 6 Jan 1921; WRNS WW II; *m* 24 July 1948 Lt-Col John Turnbull (*d* 1986), MC, 11th Hus (PAO), only s of Alfred Turnbull, and has:

    1a *Richard; *b* 21 June 1951; *educ* Eton; *m* 1978 *Sally, dau of Donald McKeen, and has:

      1b *Robert; *b* 1980

      2b *James; *b* 1982

    2a *Michael; *b* 19 Feb 1953; *educ* Eton

    1a *Anna; *b* 21 April 1950

---

1 Phyllis Adela; *b* 4 Jan 1888; *m* 1st 19 Nov 1908 (*divorce* 1935) Philip Durning Holt, JP, barrister, 3rd s of Robert Durning Holt, and had issue; *m* 2nd 5 Sept 1935 Lt-Col Campbell Newll Watson, DSO (*d* 15 Sept 1957)

2 Evelyn May; *m* 16 March 1924 John Robert Rankin Fullerton, est s of John Skipwith Herbert Fullerton, of Thribergh Park, Yorks, and *d* 7 Aug 1960, leaving issue. He *d* 14 Jan 1966

3 Gladys Mary; *b* 30 July 1893

4 Audrey; *b* 6 Oct 1898; ATS WW II

Sir ALFRED *d* 9 Aug 1935; his gs,

Sir Anthony Frederick Mark Palmer, 4th Bt; *b* 29 Aug 1914; *educ* Marlborough and RMC Sandhurst; WW II: 2nd Lt Yorks Dragoons Yeo, Lt Northumberland Fus, Maj RA; *m* 4 Sept 1939 *Henriette Alice, DCVO (1977), JP (*m* 2nd 17 Feb 1953 Brig Sir Alexander Abel Smith, KCVO, JP, TD (*d* 1980)), Ldy-in-Waiting to HRH PRINCESS ELIZABETH 1949, Woman Bedchamber to HM THE QUEEN 1952–53 and 1973–, Extra Woman Bedchamber 1953–73, dau of Cdr Francis Charles Cadogan, RN (*see* CADOGAN, E), and was *ka* Syria 18 May 1941, leaving:

1 Sir (CHARLES) MARK PALMER, **5th and present Bt**

1 *Antonia Mary [The Lady Christopher Thynne, Britmore House, Donhead St Andrew, Dorset SP7 9EB]; *b* 2 Aug 1940; *m* 6 June 1968 *Lord Christopher John Thynne, 2nd surv s of 6th Marquess of Bath (*qv*), and has issue

PALMER, Bt, of Wanlip Hall

Arms: Arg. two bars sa., charged with three trefoils, two and one, slipped of the first; in chief a greyhound courant of the second, collared or. **Crest:** On a mount vert a greyhound sejant sa., gorged with a collar or, rimmed gu. and charged on the shoulder with a trefoil slipped arg. **Creation:** Bt. (GB) 28 July 1791.

SIR JOHN EDWARD SOMERSET PALMER, 8TH BT, of Wanlip Hall, Co Leicester [Sir John Palmer Bt, Court Barton, Feniton, Devon EX14 0BD]; *b* 27 Oct 1926, s f 1963; *educ* Canford, Pembroke Coll Cambridge (BA 1951, MA Ag 1957) and Durham U (MSc Ag Eng 1953); Lt RA 1945–48, N Nigeria Civ Serv 1952–61, with R A Lister & Co 1962–63, Overseas Liaison Unit Nat Inst Ag Engrg 1964–68, consultant dir W S Atkins (Agriculture) 1979–87; *m* 8 Sept 1956 *Dione Catharine, 2nd dau of Charles Duncan Skinner, and has:

1 +ROBERT JOHN HUDSON [Robert Palmer Esq, 31 Wandle Rd, London SW17 7DL]; *b* 20 Dec 1960; *educ* St Edward's Sch Oxford and Durham (BA) and Cambridge Us (BA); *m* 1990 *Lucinda Margaret, dau of Michael Barker, and has:

  (1) +Charles Henry Somerset; *b* 12 Oct 1992

  (1) *Alice Harriet; *b* 28 Oct 1994

1 *Harriet Alyson Ducarel; *b* 21 May 1959; *m* 1987 *Andrew Lorne Campbell Byatt, s of Sir Hugh Campbell Byatt, KCVO, CMG, and has:

  (1) *Douglas Edward Campbell; *b* 23 Feb 1989

  (1) *Emma Alyson Campbell; *b* 14 Feb 1992

Lineage: JOSEPH HUDSON (s of Charles Hudson), of Boutherbeck, nr Keswick, Cumberland; *b c* 1668; Dutch Consul Tunis; *m* Sarah, dau of William Plowman, of Livorno, merchant, and *d* Port Mahon 1754, leaving, with a dau (Jane Catharine, *m* George Keate, of London, and had issue):

Sir Charles Grave Hudson, 1st Bt (GB), so *cr* 28 July 1791; *b* 3 April 1730; dir South Sea Co, High Sheriff Leics 1784; *m* 1st 8 March 1766 Catherine Susannah (*d* 24 Jan 1805), est dau and heiress of Henry Palmer, of Wanlip Hall, Leics (*see* SELBORNE, E), and had surv issue, with three other daus (*d* unm):

1 CHARLES THOMAS (Sir), **2nd Bt**

2 John Samuel; *m* 14 Jan 1822 his cousin Maria, est dau of Ralph Allen, barrister, and *dsp* 17 May 1832

1 Harriett; *m* 1804 Sir John Richardson, Judge Queen's Bench, and *d* 1840, leaving issue

Sir Charles *m* 2nd 13 Jan 1806 Sarah (*dsp* 5 Sept 1811), dau of Peter Holford, and *d* 24 Oct 1813

His est son,

Sir CHARLERS THOMAS HUDSON later PALMER (roy licence 13 Nov 1813 under terms of will of gf Henry Palmer), **2nd Bt**; *b* 20 May 1771; *m* 14 July 1802 Harriot (*d* 22 Jan 1848), 3rd dau of Sir William Pepperell, 1st and last Bt, and *d* 30 April 1827, having had, with two other daus (*d* unm):

1 Sir GEORGE JOSEPH HUDSON later PALMER, **3rd Bt**, High Sheriff Leics; *b* 20 Dec 1811; *m* 26 Feb 1836 Emily Elizabeth (*d* 6 Oct 1871), yst dau of George Peter Holford, of Westonbirt, Glos, and *d* 22 Feb 1866, leaving:

(1) **Sir Archdale Robert Palmer, 4th Bt**, JP; CA Leics, Lt Rifle Bde; *b* 1 Nov 1838; *educ* Eton; *m* 19 Aug 1873 Lady Augusta Amelia Shirley (*d* 10 Feb 1933), only surv dau of 9th Earl Ferrers (*qv*), and *dsp* 26 July 1906

(2) **Sir George Hudson Palmer, 5th Bt**, of Wanlip Hall; *b* 9 Aug 1841; *educ* Eton and Balliol Coll Oxford (BA); barrister Lincoln's Inn; *d* unm 23 Oct 1919

(1) Emily Francis; *m* 12 Dec 1871 James Tomkinson, PC (*d* 10 April 1910), of Willington Hall, Tarporley, Cheshire, MP Crewe, and *d* 10 May 1905, leaving issue

2 Charles Archdale (Rev); *b* 1 Oct 1814; Rector Wanlip; *m* 27 Feb 1838 Elizabeth Julia Finch (*d* 5 Jan 1901), dau of John Finch Simpson, of Launde Abbey, Leics, and *d* 27 March 1860, leaving:

(1) Charles Thomas, JP Glos; *b* 28 May 1842; *m* 21 Feb 1882 Frances Rachel (*d* 11 Dec 1930), widow of Rev Richard Henry Wingfield Digby and dau of Charles Wriothesley Digby (*see* DIGBY, B), and *d* 18 Dec 1916

(2) William Henry (Rev), of The Barton, Martinhoe, N Devon; *b* 30 May 1844; *educ* Trin Coll Cambridge (MA); Rector Wanlip; *d* unm 3 Nov 1907

(3) John Ducarel; *b* 7 May 1852; *dsp* 23 Feb 1887

(4) FREDERICK ARCHDALE (Sir), **6th Bt**

(1) Mary Elizabeth; *d* unm 7 Sept 1931

1 Caroline Harriet; *m* 17 Jan 1850 Rt Rev Charles John Abraham, DD, Bp Wellington, NZ, and *d* 16 June 1877, leaving issue. He *d* 4 Feb 1903

The 5th Bt's cousin,

Sir Frederick Archdale Palmer, 6th Bt; *b* 25 Aug 1857; *m* 29 Dec 1892 Lilian (*d* 22 Jan 1947), dau of Gen Edward Arthur Somerset, CB (*see* BEAUFORT, D), and had:

1 JOHN ARCHDALE (Sir), **7th Bt**

2 Edward Ducarel; *b* 1897; *ka* 30 Oct 1917

3 Philip Somerset, of The Creel, Harbottle, Northumberland; *b* 2 April 1899; *m* 8 June 1939 Elizabeth Alyson Blanche, widow of Capt Edward Clennell Fenwicke-Clennell, MC, of Harbottle Castle, and *dsp* 29 Aug 1984

Sir FREDERICK *d* 17 Nov 1933; his er surv son,

Sir John Archdale Palmer, 7th Bt, DL (Glos 1956); *b* 10 Nov 1894; *educ* Reading Sch; RA WW II, CStJ; *m* 20 Sept 1922 Kathleen, yr dau of Herbert Smith, and *d* 24 June 1963, leaving:

1 Sir JOHN EDWARD SOMERSET PALMER, **8th and present Bt**

2 +Robert Archdale [Robert Palmer Esq, Dorhall Farm, Chaddesley Corbett, Worcs DY10 4QQ]; *b* 21 Nov 1930; *educ* Canford and St Andrews (MA 1951); Assist Registrar Birmingham U, Sr Assist Sec 1962–89, Civ Serv Uganda 1955–62, 2nd Lt RA 1952–54; *m* 26 Jan 1963 *Rosalie Margaret, only dau of Keith Monk Newell, and has:

(1) *Philip David Archdale; *b* 7 Jan 1969; *m* 1996 *Alison, only dau of John Howard Murray, of Stockton-on-Tees

(2) +Jeremy Frederick Mathews; *b* 3 March 1972

(1) *Catherine Ducarel; *b* 30 Oct 1963; *m* 1991 *Stephen William Milgrew Piggin, s of Desmond Piggin, of Auckland, NZ, and has:

1a *Hannah Ducarel; *b* 2 April 1995

(2) *Sarah Rosalie; *b* 17 July 1965; *m* 1992 *Peter Mark Creber, s of David Creber, of Saltash, Cornwall, and has:

1a *Thomas Jack; *b* 1994

2a *David Alexander; *b* 11 June 1996

PALUMBO

Arms: Vert, a pale or, over all an escarbuncle counterchanged. **Crest:** The top of a dovecot or, perched on its conical roof vert a dove, wings elevated and addorsed gold. **Supporters:** Dexter, an alsatian dog; sinister, a fox proper, each resting the exterior foreleg on a rectangular plinth gold, the compartment comprising a circle of paving stones proper. **Motto:** *Loyauté me lie* ('Loyalty binds me'). **Creation :** B. (LP, UK) 1991.

THE BARON PALUMBO, of Walbrook, City of London (Peter Garth Palumbo) [The Rt Hon The Lord Palumbo, Bagnor Manor, Bagnor, Berks RG16 8AG]; *b* 20 July 1935; *educ* Eton and Worcester Coll Oxford (MA); Chm: Arts Cncl 1989–94, Tate Gallery Fndn 1986–87, Painshill Park Tst Appeal 1986–, Serpentine Gallery 1994–; Tstee: Mies van der Rohe Archive 1977–, Tate Gallery 1978–85, Whitechapel Art Gallery Fndn 1981–87, Writers' and Scholars' Educnl Tst 1984– (Hon Treas 1984–), Nat Hist Museum 1994–; memb Cncl Roy Albert Hall 1995–; Govr LSE 1976–94; Chllr Portsmouth U 1992–; Hon FRIBA, Hon DLitt Portsmouth 1993, Hon FFB 1994, Hon FIStructE 1994, Order Southern Cross Brazil 1993; *m* 1st 1959 Denia (*d* 1986), dau of Maj Lionel Wigram, and has:

1 *James Rudolph; *b* 1963; *educ* Eton and Oxford; proprietor Ministry of Sound nightclub, memb Citizens Charter Mark (grant-making body) 1997–; *m*(?) but in any event has by *Atoosa —, formerly of Iran now of Dubai:

(1) *Alessandro; *b* 1991

1 *Annabella Jane; *b* 1961; *m* 1991 *Hugh H C Adams, yr s of Geoffrey Adams, of Chilton Foliot, Wilts

2 *Laura Elizabeth; *b* 27 Dec 1967; *educ* London U; *m* 17 Sept 1994 *Neel Tikkoo and has:

(1) *Lydia Rose; *b* 19 April 1997

BARON PALUMBO *m* 2nd 1986 *Hayat, er dau of Kamel Morowa, and by her has:

2 *Philip Rudolph; *b* 11 July 1992

1 *Petra Louise; *b* 22 July 1989

2 *Lana Rose; *b* 25 March 1991

Lineage: RUDOLPH PALUMBO; *m* Elsie — and had:

PETER GARTH, *cr* a **Baron**

PARK OF MONMOUTH

Creation: B. (LP, UK) 1990.

THE BARONESS PARK OF MONMOUTH, of Broadway, Co Hereford and Worcester (Daphne Margaret Sybil Désirée Park, CMG (1971), OBE (1960)) [The Rt Hon The Baroness Park of Monmouth CMG OBE, House of Lords, London SW1A 0PW]; *b* 1 Sept 1921; *educ* Rosa Bassett Sch, Somerville Coll Oxford (MA) and Newnham Coll Cambridge; Cdr WTS FANY 1943–48, Allied Commn Austria 1946–48, FO and FCO 1948–79; UK Delegn NATO 1952, 2nd Sec Moscow 1954, 1st Sec Leopoldville 1959, Lusaka 1964, Consul-Gen Hanoi 1969–70, Chargé d'Affaires Ulan Bator 1972; Pncpl Somerville Coll Oxford 1980–89; Memb: Cncl VSO 1981–84, Br Library Bd 1981–86 ; Govr BBC 1982–87, Pro-V-Chllr Oxford U 1985–89, Chm Legal Aid Advsy Ctee to Ld Chllr 1986–92, Roy Commn on Historical Monuments 1989–94, Memb Bd Sheffield Devpt Corp 1989–92, Dir Devpt Trust Zoological Soc London 1989–90, Govr Ditchley Fndn 1989–, Memb: Thatcher Fndn 1992–, Cncl GB-Sasakawa Fndn 1994–; Tstee: Jardine Educnl Trust 1991–, Roy Armouries Devpt Trust 1991–92; Fell Chatham House; Hon Res Fell Kent U 1971–72; Hon LLD Bristol 1988, Mount Holyoke Coll 1992; Hon Fell Somerville Coll Oxford 1990; FRSA, MRSA

Lineage: JOHN ALEXANDER PARK; had:

DAPHNE MARGARET SYBIL DESIREE, *cr* a **Baroness**

PARKER of Melford Hall

Arms: Quarterly, 1st and 4th, sa. a buck's head cabossed between two flaunches arg (for PARKER); 2nd and 3rd, az. a chevron between three lozenges or (for HYDE). **Crest:** A dexter arm erect vested az., slashed and cuffed arg., holding in the hand ppr. an attire of a stag gu. **Motto:** *Fideli certa merces* ('To the faithful reward is certain'). **Creation:** Bt (E) 1 July 1681.

SIR RICHARD WILLIAM HYDE PARKER, 12TH BT, of Melford Hall, Co Suffolk, DL (Suffolk 1995) [Sir Richard Parker Bt DL, Melford Hall, Long Melford, Suffolk CO10 9AA]; *b* 5 April 1937; *s f* 1951; *educ* Millfield and RAC Cirencester; High Sheriff Suffolk 1995–96; *m* 10 Nov 1972 *(Elizabeth) Jean, only child of Sir (Henry John) Lindores Leslie, 9th Bt (*qv*), of Wardis, and has:

1 +WILLIAM JOHN HYDE; *b* 10 June 1983
1 *Beata Hyde; *b* 29 Aug 1973
2 *Margaret Hyde; *b* 29 Aug 1973
3 *Lucy Hyde; *b* 8 Sept 1975

Lineage: *See* MORLEY, E, for the earliest generations.

WILLIAM PARKER, of Hoberton, Devon, and Shoreditch, Somerset; *b c* 1550; *m* 1st Elizabeth Lane; *m* 2nd Dorothy Muttlebury and was *bur* 12 Sept 1628, leaving, with other issue by both *ws*:

HUGH PARKER, of Shoreditch; *m* Mary, dau of Thomas Hutchins, of Holway, Somerset, and *dvp* 1627, leaving:

1 **Sir Hugh Parker, 1st Bt** (E), so cr 1 July 1681, with remainder to the *s* of his bro Henry; *b* 1606/7; Alderman City London; *dsp* 1696/7
2 Henry, *m*; had:
   (1) **Sir Henry Parker, 2nd Bt**; *m* Margaret (*d* 6 Jan 1728/9), dau and eventual heiress of Rt Rev Alexander Hyde, LLD, Bp Salisbury, *s* of Sir Lawrence Hyde, of Dinton, Wilts (unc of Edward Hyde, 1st Earl of Clarendon of the 1661 cr; *see* CLARENDON, E, preliminary remarks), and *d* 25 Oct 1713, having had, with other issue:
      1a Hugh; *m* Anne (*m* 2nd 10th Earl of Clanricarde; *see* SLIGO, M), est dau and coheir of John Smith, Commr Excise, and *d* 1712, leaving, with other issue:
         1b **Sir Henry John Parker, 3rd Bt**; *m* 1st Anne (*d* 1733), dau and heiress of Simon Barwell, of Leicester, and had two daus (*d* unm); *m* 2nd Catherine, dau and heiress of John Page, of Putney, and *d* 1771, having by her had a *s* (John, *dvp* 1767) and two daus
         1b Margaret; *m* Thomas Nugent, Count de Valdesoto in Spain
      2a Hyde (Rev); Rector Tredington, Worcs; *m* Mary, dau of John Reeves, and *d* 24 May 1726, leaving, with two daus:
         1b **Rev Sir Henry Parker, 4th Bt**; DD, *d* unm 10 July 1782
         2b **Sir Hyde Parker, 5th Bt**; *b* 1 Feb 1713/4; served merchant navy(?) before entering RN *c* 1738, Lt Jan 1744/5, Capt March 1747/8, R-Adml 1778, Cdr Leeward Islands station 1779, V-Adml 1780, C-in-C Br fleet at drawn Battle of Dogger Bank against Dutch 5 Aug 1781, C-in-C E Indies 1782; *m* 1734 Sarah, dau of Hugh Smithson, of Northumberland, and was last seen leaving Rio de Janeiro aboard his new 60-gun flagship the *Cato* on 12 Dec 1782, hence presumed drowned or possibly murdered by natives on the Malabar Coast, where he is thought to have been shipwrecked, leaving:
            1c **Sir Harry Parker, 6th Bt**; *b* 1735; *m* 1766 Bridget, dau of William Creswell, of Creswell, Northumberland, and *d* 15 Jan 1812, having had, with two daus:
               1d **Sir William Parker, 7th Bt**; *d* unm 1 April 1830
               2d **Sir Hyde Parker, 8th Bt**; *b* 1785; MP W Suffolk; *d* unm 21 March 1856
            2c Hyde (Adml Sir); *b* 1739; ktd 1779; *m* 1st Anne, dau of John Palmer Boteler, and had, with another *s*:
               1d Hyde, CB; V-Adml, Sr Naval Ld Admlty, Kt Isabella Catolica Spain; *m* 16 July 1821 Caroline (*d* 10 Nov 1854), dau of Sir Frederick

Morton Eden, 2nd Bt (*see* EDEN OF WINTON, B), and *d* 26 May 1854, leaving, with other issue:
               1e WILLIAM (Sir), **9th Bt**
               1e Louisa Ann; *m* 3 May 1857 Frederick Morton Eden and *d* 9 March 1868, leaving issue (*see* EDEN OF WINTON, B)
               2e Caroline Maria; *m* 12 April 1849 Col John Home Purves (*d* 2 July 1867), Equerry to HRH THE DUCHESS OF CAMBRIDGE, and *d* 11 Nov 1890, leaving issue (*see* 1970 edn HOME-PURVES-HUME-CAMPBELL, Bt)
               2d John Boteler, CB; *b* 29 May 1786; Maj-Gen; *m* 3 Nov 1814 Mary (*d* 12 June 1844), dau of Adml Sir Home Popham, KCB, and *d* 25 March 1851, having had, with other issue:
                  1e John Home; *b* 2 June 1819; *m* 18 Sept 1862 Anna Jane (*d* 28 March 1903), only dau of William Fraser, Yr. of Culbokie, and *d* 15 Oct 1881, leaving issue
                  2e Harry Richard; *b* 8 May 1821; Lt 1st Bombay Lancers; *m* 22 Dec 1853 Louisa (*d* 1901), dau of Adml John Duff Markland, and *d* 16 Aug 1907, leaving:
                     1f Hyde; *b* 30 Oct 1854; *m* 2 Sept 1902 Constance, dau of Francis Denman Peacock, and *d* 13 April 1936
                     2f Arthur Popham Hyde; *b* 1 May 1857; *m* 1880 Dora May (*d* 3 Nov 1921), dau of Edmund Wilmot (*see* WILMOT, Bt), and *d* 8 May 1942, having had:
                        1g Arthur Charles Hyde; *b* 1880; *d* unm 8 Sept 1966
                        1g Dulcibella Roby Hyde; *m* 1921 Robert Hay and *d* 12 Dec 1931, leaving issue
                     3f Harry Richard Hyde; *b* 20 May 1859; *m* 4 Oct 1893 Fanny Laura (*d* 7 March 1952), dau of John Collis, and *d* 11 Feb 1946, having had:
                        1g Reginald John Hyde; *b* 1895; *m* 1 Oct 1927 Violet, dau of — Jackson, and *d* 17 Nov 1957, leaving:
                           1h +(Reginald Harry) Richard Hyde [Richard Parker Esq, 6 Manor Close, Ickleford, Hitchin, Herts]; *b* 1930; *m* 1st 23 March 1957 (*divorce* 1961) Dorothy Margaret Stanley; *m* 2nd 1962 *Ann Bulmer and by her has had:
                              1i Simon Richard; *b* Aug 1966; *d* 1985
                              1i *Emma Jayne Hyde; *b* 1962
                           1h *Eve Frances Hyde [Mrs William Leavey, 4 Salcombe Dve, Early, Reading, Berks]; *b* 1932; SRN; *m* 1 Aug 1968 *William Leavey
                        2g Edward Hyde; *b* 29 Jan 1899; *m* 28 July 1928 Ethel, dau of Henry Mortimore, and *d* 19–, leaving:
                           1h +Alan Hyde; *b* 27 Feb 1933; *educ* Hertford and Birmingham U (BSc)
                           2h +David Hugh Hyde [David Parker Esq, 16 May Tree Ave, Garden Village, Hull, Yorks]; *b* 23 Oct 1934; *educ* Haileybury; DipEd; *m* 28 March 1959 *Brenda, dau of Henry McIntosh, BEM, and has:
                              1i *Rosemary Hyde; *b* 15 Feb 1960
                              2i *Anne Hyde; *b* 19 Sept 1962
                           2h (cont.) Mr and Mrs David Hyde adopted:
                              *Michael Jong; *b* 12 June 1964
                        3g Richard; *b* 1902; *d* 1935
                        4g Arthur Charles Hyde; *b* 4 April 1911; *m* 2 Dec 1950 *Mabel, widow of — Futter and dau of William Gray, and *dsp* 29 Oct 1966
                        1g Margaret Hyde; *b* 1907; *m* 25 May 1944 Capt Frank Mitchell, RE, *s* of Henry Mitchell
                     1f Mary Louisa Hyde; *d* unm 7 Dec 1943
                  1e Matilda Anne; *m* 19 April 1853 Rev William Walton Herringham, Rector Old Cleeve, and *d* 26 Feb 1904, leaving issue
            2c (cont.) Sir Hyde *m* 2nd 23 Dec 1800 Frances (*d* March 1844), dau of Adml Sir Richard Onslow, Bt (*qv*), and *d* 16 March 1807, having by her had, with two daus:
               3d Richard, Gen, Hon Col 5th Dragoon Gds; *d* unm March 1885 aged 81

The 8th Bt's cousin,
   Sir William Parker, 9th Bt, DL Suffolk; *b* 2 Sept 1826; Capt 44th Regt, MP W Suffolk 1832–34; *m* 22 Nov 1855 Sophia Mary (*d* 16 May 1903), 2nd dau of Nathaniel Clarke Barnardiston, of The Ryes, Sudbury, Suffolk, and had:
1 Hyde; *b* 1 Jan 1861; Lt and Adj 1st Bn King's Liverpool Regt; *d* 10 Dec 1887
2 WILLIAM HYDE (Sir), **10th Bt**
3 Edmond Hyde, CB (1918); *b* 30 Jan 1868; *educ* Stubbington and RNCS; Adml, cmded Trg Sqdn 1912–14, HMS *Superb* Grand Fleet WW I, ADC to HM GEORGE V 1917, Dir Mobilisation Admlty 1918–21, cmded Portsmouth Div Res Fleet 1921–22, Res Fleet 1922–23, Order St Anne Russia; *m* 8 Sept 1908 Helen Margaret (*d* 8 Nov 1959), yr dau of Rev George Raymond Portal (*see* PORTAL, Bt), and *dsp* 19 Aug 1951
4 Hugh Hyde; *b* 18 July 1869; Capt 3rd Suffolk Regt; *d* unm 21 July 1898
5 Laurence Hyde; *b* 23 Oct 1870; *m* 19 April 1906 Ada Laetitia Moor (*d* 2 Feb 1968), est dau of Joseph Alphonsus Horsford, MRCS, of Long Melford, Suffolk, and *d* 16 Dec 1950, having had:
   (1) Laurence Edmond Hyde; *b* 24 Feb 1912; Fl/Lt RAFVR WW II; *m* 1 Jan 1953 *Margaretha Van Thörne, dau of Mrs Ditlef Nielsen, of Gothenburg, Sweden, and *d* 25 Oct 1994, leaving:
      1a +Anthony Laurence Hyde [Anthony Hyde Parker Esq, Smeetham Hall, Bulmer, Suffolk CO10 7EU; *b* 4 Dec 1958; *m* 1986 *Bridget Charlotte, yst dau of Arthur Stearns, of Ranworth House, Harleston, Norfolk, and has:
         1b +Thomas Frederick Laurence Hyde; *b* 1989
         1b *Sophie Antonia Hyde; *b* 1992
      2a +Michael Edmond Hyde; *b* 6 Feb 1961
      1a *Jane Katarina Hyde; *b* 1954; *m* 1977 *J Skybak

(2) Anthony Edington Hyde; *b* 9 Nov 1915; F/O RAF WW II; *ka* 14 Sept 1940

(1) *Mary Hyde [Miss Mary Parker, Smeetham Hall, Bulmer, Suffolk]; *b* 19 March 1908; S/Offr WAAF WW II (despatches)

(2) Dorothy Bridget Hyde; *b* 6 March 1909; *d* 17 Nov 1918

6 Harry Hyde; *b* 2 Aug 1872; *d* 23 Sept 1893

7 John Barnardiston Hyde; *b* 7 April 1879; Capt RE WW I, 4th Cl Medjidie; *m* 31 Jan 1906 Dora Katherine (*d* 22 Oct 1957), dau of Canon — Bromley, of Newcastle-on-Tyne, and *d* 22 June 1972, having had:

(1) Edmond Francis Hyde; *b* 15 April 1912; QALAS, Admlty Surveyor Lands Malta 1942–45; *m* 15 Jan 1946 *Naomi Margaret [Mrs Edmond Parker, Huish Farm, Huish Episcopi, Somerset], only dau of Dr Donald Carmichael Thomas, and *d* 17 Oct 1966, leaving:

1a *Auriol Katherine Hyde [Mrs Meyrick Griffith-Jones, King's Stag House, King's Stag, Sturminster Newton, Dorset]; *b* 29 Jan 1950; *m* 28 Dec 1974 *Meyrick D Griffith-Jones, 13th/18th Roy Hus (Queen Mary's Own), s of Trevor Griffith-Jones, of Prospect House, Rowde, Wilts, and has had:

1b *Edmond Laugharne Hyde; *b* 1979

2b Jocelyn Hyde Laugharne; *b* 1980; *d* 1988

3b *Piers Laugharne Hyde; *b* 1989

1b *Eluned Hyde Laugharne (twin); *b* 1989

2a *Sophia Naomi Lucy Hyde [Mrs Sophia Gray-Read, The Forge, Gotton, Somerset]; *b* 30 May 1952; *m* 1970 (*divorce* 1992) Glynn Mark Alexander Gray-Read and has:

1b *Oliver Mark Forrester; *b* 1980

2b *Julian Frederick Thomas; *b* 1982

3a *Harriet Ann Hyde [Mrs Alexander Maxwell Findlater, The Grammar House, The Hill, Langport, Somerset TA10 9PU]; *b* 8 Aug 1953; *m* 23 April 1983 *Alexander John Maxwell Findlater, only s of Herbert Maxwell Findlater ERD, MA, FRGS, and has:

1b *Frederica Harriet; *b* 24 Oct 1986

2b *Leonora Frances; *b* 19 July 1988

1 Anne Hyde; *b* 4 Oct 1856; *m* 29 April 1886 Col Arthur Staniforth Hext, Suffolk Regt, of Trenarren, Cornwall, and *d* 26 Aug 1947, leaving issue. He *d* 12 Nov 1926

2 Margaret Hyde; *b* 24 Jan 1858; *m* 15 Feb 1881 George Eden Hunt, JP, of Wadenhoe House, Northants, est s of George Ward Hunt, PC, and *d* 5 April 1932, leaving issue. He *d* 28 Feb 1892

3 Sophia Hyde; *b* 25 Oct 1859; *d* unm 27 March 1956

4 Amy Hyde, nun; *b* 27 Dec 1864; *d* 17 Oct 1956

5 Mary Hyde; *b* 4 July 1866; *m* 25 April 1889 Charles Arthur Abraham, s of Canon Abraham, and *d* 26 Sept 1945, leaving issue. He *d* 20 Sept 1937

6 Dorothy Hyde; *b* 11 Nov 1877; *m* 30 Dec 1903 Hugh Wilfrid Sherlock, s of Rev Harry Sherlock, Rector Bildeston, and *d* 27 May 1964, leaving issue. He *d* 22 Sept 1957

Sir WILLIAM *d* 24 May 1891; his est surv son,

Rev Sir William Hyde Parker, 10th Bt, JP Suffolk; *b* 8 April 1863; *educ* Clare Coll Cambridge (MA); CA Suffolk, Chaplain to Bp Barbados; *m* 18 Nov 1890 Ethel (*d* 26 Oct 1941), only dau of John Leech, of Gorse Hall, Cheshire, and had:

1 WILLIAM STEPHEN HYDE (Sir), **11th Bt**

2 Harry Hyde; *b* 17 Feb 1905; *educ* Harrow; *m* 1 June 1935 Elizabeth Alice, dau of Capt Charles Cadwaladr Trevor-Roper (*see* TEYNHAM, B)

1 Mary Stephanie Hyde; *b* 26 Dec 1894; *m* 25 Oct 1919 Capt Kenneth William Gordon Duke, RN, yst s of Col John Duke, and *d* 7 Feb 1953, leaving issue. He *d* 12 April 1966

Sir WILLIAM *d* 16 Feb 1931; his er son,

Sir William Stephen Hyde Parker, 11th Bt; *b* 23 Jan 1892; *educ* Malvern and Magdalene Coll Cambridge; Lt 1st King's Dragoon Gds WW I; *m* 25 Nov 1931 Ulla Ditlef (*m* 2nd 26 April 1954 Frederick William Hammond (*d* 5 Nov 1967)) and *d* 3 Dec 1998, only dau of Prof Christian Ditlef Nielsen, DPh, of Copenhagen, and *d* 29 July 1951, leaving:

1 Sir RICHARD WILLIAM HYDE PARKER, **12th and present Bt**

1 *Elisabeth Mary Hyde [The Rt Hon The Lady Camoys, Stonor Park, Henley on Thames, Oxon]; *b* 3 Sept 1939; *m* 11 June 1966 *7th Baron Camoys (*qv*) and has issue

Seat: Melford Hall, Long Melford, Suffolk. Visitors to the exceptionally handsome town of Long Melford are often surprised by the proximity of two very large mansions, Kentwell Hall and Melford. Their entrances are only a few hundred yards apart. But while Kentwell is up a drive, Melford abuts on the Green, though the other houses around it are few, for despite the church's sitting at the top of the slope on the northern side, the main part of the town is well away to the south. The large number of East Anglian mansions per square mile arises from the fact that by the 16th century there were already many merchant princes in that part of the world who made most of their money in the City of London, in the cloth trade or otherwise, but kept up a squire's way of life in the country. They did not need as large an acreage as their fellow squires elsewhere in England, who often had to maintain their houses from agricultural rents alone.

The 16th-century parts of Melford date from quite early in that era, though it has been suggested that the foundations may be older, part of a building owned by the pre-Reformation Abbots of Bury St Edmunds. The most noticeable Tudor features today are the four narrow turrets with their ogee-shaped caps along the back elevation, the centre two of which flank a typically Tudor gate house (now, however, incorporated into the rest of that front) of the sort that may be seen at St James's Palace, Hampton Court and Eton. Internally the Long Gallery survives from the 16th century too, albeit denuded of its early decorative features such as an intricately plastered ceiling.

The original occupant of the house as we (more or less) see it now was Sir William Cordell, who took up residence by 1554, though he had bought the Manor of Long Melford back in 1545. He had reached the heights of his profession as a lawyer under MARY, becoming Solicitor-General in 1553 and Master of the Rolls in 1557, but although ELIZABETH I stripped him of his Privy Counsellorship she allowed him to remain as Master of the Rolls, and he entertained her at Melford on 4 August 1578. He founded the alms houses which are such an attractive fea-

ture of the entrance to the church across the Green. His sister, a Mrs Allington, inherited the Hall in the first instance but by 1643, well before the creation of the Cordell baronetcy, it had been bought from her married daughter's branch of the family (called Savage) by Robert Cordell, later Sir Robert, 1st Bt, a connection of Sir William Cordell's on the male side.

With the extinction of the Cordell baronetcy in 1704 on the death in a fall from his horse of Sir John Cordell, 3rd Bt, the Melford estate passed to Sir Charles Firebrace, 2nd Bt, who had married Sir John's younger sister Margaret. It is probably during the Firebrace tenancy that the superb rococo chimney piece in the drawing room was inserted. Sir Charles's son Sir Cordell Firebrace, 3rd Bt, died without issue in 1759, leaving the Melford estate to his widow Bridget, one of the Bacons of Shrubland (*see* BACON, Bt). She subsequently married William Campbell, brother of the 4th Duke of Argyll (*qv*). The Parkers only acquired Melford towards the end of the 18th century (William Campbell died in 1787, his wife in 1782). After the Napoleonic Wars the new owner, probably **Sir William Parker, 7th Bt**, who had inherited from his father the year of Borodino, embarked on a remodelling programme. He employed Thomas Hopper, the architect who had added the Gothic conservatory to Carlton House in London and who also worked on Slane (*see* CONYNGHAM, M).

It is presumably during Hopper's time that many of the old mullion windows were replaced by large multi-pane sash types. It is certainly Hopper who added the gateway to the main street running north-south beside Long Melford Green. Internally he is responsible for the library, the lofty entrance hall and the gallery above the staircase. The staircase itself, however, although 18th–century, was installed after fire damaged much of the east wing in the last war. The **11th Bt** made Melford over to the National Trust, but his son and successor still occupies it.

PARKER of Shenstone Lodge

Arms: Gu. a chevron between three leopard's faces or.
Crest: A leopard's head affrontée erased or, ducally gorged gu.
Motto: *Sub libertate quietem* ('Peace under liberty').
Creation: Bt. (UK) 18 Dec 1844.

SIR (WILLIAM) PETER BRIAN PARKER, 5TH BT, of Blackbrook House, Co Southampton, and Shenstone Lodge, Co Stafford [Sir Peter Parker Bt, Apricot Hall, Sutton-cum-Beckingham, Lincs LN5 0RE]; *b* 30 Nov 1950; *s f* 1990; *educ* Eton; FCA, ptnr Stephenson Nuttall & Co Newark, chartered accountant 1988–; *m* 1976 *Patricia Ann, dau of R and Dorothy Evelyn Filtness, of Lea Cottage, Beckingham, Lincs, and has:

1 +JOHN MALCOLM; *b* 14 May 1980

1 *Lucy Emma; *b* 1977

Lineage: THOMAS PARKER, of Bulwell, Notts; *m* Elizabeth, dau and heiress of Adam de Gotham, of Norton Lees, Derbys, and *d* 1400, leaving, with two yr sons (Thomas, of Sprotborough, Yorks, and Little Norton, had a dau and heiress who *m* Thomas Moore, of Greenhill Hall, Norton, and had issue; William, of Shirland) and four daus:

ROBERT PARKER, of Norton Lees; living 1407; *m* Elizabeth, dau and coheir of John Birley, of Bernes, Yorks, and had, with another s and three daus:

JOHN PARKER, of Norton Lees; living 1411; *m* Helen, dau of Roger North (*see* GUILFORD, E), of Walkeringham, Notts, and had, with four yr sons (Thomas, of Norton Lees, *m* his cousin — Parker and was ancestor of the PARKERs of Ecclesfield and Whitley Hall, Yorks; Robert, of Ulley, Yorks; Henry, Groom Bedchamber to HENRY VIII, *dsp*; William, of Luton, Beds, Sewer (superintendent of service at table) to HENRY VIII, *m* Margaret, widow of John Shirley, of Enfield, Middx, and dau of John Wroth, of Durance, and had a dau (Barbara, *m* 1st John Wickham, of Enfield, and 2nd John Taylor)) and four daus:

JOHN PARKER, of Norton Lees; *m* Elizabeth, dau of Ralph Eyre, of Ollerton Hall, Derbys, and had, with two yst sons (Henry; Anthony) and a dau (Margaret, *m* John Selicke, of Hazlebarrow Hall):

1 John, of Norton Lees; *m* Margery (*d* 19 Feb 1579/80), dau of Humphrey Okeover (*see* WALKER-OKEOVER, Bt), and had, with seven other sons (all *dsp*)

and four daus (Elizabeth; Jane, d May 1575; Jocosa; Dorothy, m 1st John Castlyn, of Hemswortyh in Norton, 2nd John Rhodes, and 3rd William Towers):

(1) John, of Norton Lees; m Barbara, dau of Sir William West, of Amerdon, Essex, and Darley Abbey, and d 1 April 1607, having had, with four other children:

1a John, of Norton Lees; bapt 13 Sept 1563; m Mary (m 2nd Humphrey Cardinal, of Hornby, Lincs), dau of William Mason, of Egmanton Hall, Notts, and d 1615, having had, with two daus:

1b John, of Norton Lees; m Anne (m 2nd Thomas Woolhouse, of Shapwell), dau of Gilbert Linacre, of Plumbley Hall, and d 25 Dec 1630, leaving:

1c Anne; bapt 7 May 1629; m Francis Barker, of Dore (d 1685), and was ancestor of Sir Robert Barker, 1st Bt, of Bushbridge, Surrey, so cr 24 March 1781 (extinct 1789)

2 George, of Parwich, Derbys; m Margaret, dau of Humphrey Pole, and had:

(1) William, of Parwich; b 1554; m Elizabeth, dau of Humphrey Wilson, and d 1632, having had, with an er s (Thomas, of Bolsham, Cambs, m Elizabeth, dau of Thomas Hobson, the Cambridge carrier whose take-it-or-leave-it policy when hiring out horses gave rise to the expression 'Hobson's Choice' and had issue):

1a George, of Park Hall, Staffs; b 1592; High Sheriff 1625, Clerk of Assize; m Grace, dau of Hugh Bateman, of Hartington, Derbys, and d 9 May 1675, having had:

1b WILLIAM

2b Thomas, of Leek, Staffs; m Anne Venables and had issue (see MACCLESFIELD, E)

3b Robert; Cup Bearer to CATHERINE OF BRAGANZA, w of CHARLES II

1b Anne; m Richard Leving, of Parwich, Recorder Chester

2b Elizabeth; m John Sleigh, of Bigging Grange, Derbys

The est son,

WILLIAM PARKER, of Park Hall, JP; royalist cdr of foot Civil War; m 1st Bridget, dau of James Carrier, of Helpstone, Northants, by Elizabeth, 2nd dau of Thomas Parker, of Browsholme; m 2nd Helen, widow of John Coyney, of Weston Coyney, and dau and coheir of John Dawes, of Caughley, Salop, and by his 1st w had:

GEORGE PARKER, of Park Hall; m Margaret, dau of Sir John Turton, of Orgreave, Staffs, Judge King's Bench, and was bur 24 April 1716, leaving:

Sir THOMAS PARKER, PC, of Park Hall; b 1695; barrister Middle Temple 1724, King's Serjeant 1736, Baron Exchequer 1738, Judge Common Pleas 1740, Ld Ch Baron Exchequer 1742–72; m 1st 1731 Anne, dau and coheir of James Whitehall, of Pipe Ridwan, Staffs, acquired that estate through her, and had:

1 Thomas, of Park Hall; b 28 Sept 1732; High Sheriff 1786; m 2 May 1764 Mary (d 8 March 1815), dau and heiress of Thomas Hawe, of Walsall, and d 2 Dec 1797, having had, with other issue:

(1) Mary Anne; m 14 April 1810 2nd Viscount Saint Vincent (qv) and d 3 Jan 1855, leaving issue

2 George, of Almington, Staffs; b 1734; m 4 Feb 1760 Elizabeth (d 3 June 1808), dau of John Turton, of Orgreave, and d 9 Jan 1819, leaving, with two er sons:

(1) WILLIAM, (Sir), 1st Bt

Sir THOMAS m 2nd 1 March 1740 Martha, widow of Henry Carrier and dau and coheir of Edward Strong, and d 29 Dec 1784, having by her had two daus

His gs,

Sir William Parker, 1st Bt (UK), so cr 18 Dec 1844, GCB (1843, KCB 1834, CB 1815), DL Staffs; b 1 Dec 1781; RN: joined 1793, Actg Lt 1796, Lt March 1799, Actg Capt 1 May 1799, Cdr 10 Oct 1799, Capt 1801; as Capt HMS Amazon was under Nelson's command in the pursuit of the French Adml Villeneuve to the WI 1805; subsequently ordered on separate patrol from Nelson's fleet, thus missing Trafalgar; captured the French ship Belle Poule March 1806; bought Shenstone Lodge, nr Lichfield, Staffs; Capt HMS Warspite as sr naval offr Greek coast 1828, cdr royal yacht Prince Regent Dec 1828, R-Adml 1830, 2ic Channel Sqdn 1831, a Ld Admlty July–Dec 1834 and April 1835–May 1841, C-in-C China station, where took Amoy, Ningpo, Woosung, Shanghai and Chi-kiang-foo during hostilities, V-Adml 1841, C-in-C Mediterranean 1845, cmded Channel Fleet 1846, Adml 1851, C-in-C Devonport 1854–57, R-Adml UK 1862, Adml of the Fleet 1863, first ADC to HM QUEEN VICTORIA; m 10 June 1810 Frances Anne (d 9 Jan 1871), yst dau of Sir Theophilus Biddulph, 5th Bt (qv), and had, with other issue:

1 WILLIAM BIDDULPH (Sir), 2nd Bt

2 George, of Delamore, Ivybridge, Devon, JP; b 1 Sept 1827; Adml; m 1st 25 April 1857 Anne Elizabeth (d 25 Oct 1895), only child of William Mackworth-Praed, of Delamore, and had:

(1) William Frederic, of Delamore; b 1 Aug 1860; Maj and Brevet-Col Rifle Bde; m 1st 1885 Helinor Katherine (d May 1896), dau of Col Fitzroy Stephen, CB, Rifle Bde, and had:

1a William Mackworth; b 1 Sept 1886; Capt Rifle Bde (Prince Consort's Own), Adj 8th Bn; m 7 Feb 1912 Lilian Ursula, OStJ (m 2nd 4 April 1921 V-Adml Everard John Hardman-Jones, CB, OBE (d 28 June 1962); d 6 Nov 1966), yst dau of Col Sir Arthur Pendarves Vivian, KCB (see SWANSEA, B), and was ka 30 July 1915, leaving:

1b Frederic Anthony Vivian, JP (1964), DL (Devon 1964); b 11 Feb 1913; educ Winchester and RMC Sandhurst; CC Devon 1960–64, Maj Rifle Bde WW II (POW 1940–45); m 1st 20 Jan 1937 (divorce 1946) Pamela Mary, dau of Charles George Edgar Farmer, of Nonsuch Park, Surrey, and had:

1c Mark Anthony Charles; b 25 April 1938; d unm 24 March 1969

1b (cont.) Frederic Parker m 2nd 4 Oct 1947 Diana Mary, formerly w of John Arden Franklyn and only dau of Brig-Gen Bryan James Curling, DSO

1b *Letitia Margaret [Mrs Dennis Dollard, Delamore, Cornwood, Ivybridge, Devon]; b 6 Nov 1914; ATS WW II; m 19 Sept 1942 Maj Dennis Seaver Dollard (d 1983), s of Richard Seaver Dollard, and has:

1c *Anthony Brian Christopher; b 14 Jan 1949; educ Downside; 2nd Lt RGJ 1969

2c *Gavin James Dominic; b 24 July 1950; educ Downside

2a Cyril George; b 10 Nov 1890; educ Wellington and RMC Sandhurst; Lt Roy Fus, Roy NW Mounted Police Canada 1912–19, Canadian Expdny Force 1918; m 1st 4 Sept 1921 Beatrice (d 20 Dec 1928), dau of W Harris, of Dunstable, and had:

1b +Laurence Frederick Cyril; b 16 June 1922; Canadian Forces WW II; m 1952 *Dorothy May, dau of R S Kent, and has:

1c +Allen Kent; b 1954

1c *Beatrice Anne; b 1952

2c *Donna Gail; b 1956

3c *Nancy Kay; b 1958

2a (cont.) Cyril Parker m 2nd 22 Jan 1934 Margaret May, widow of Wallace Bruce Macdougall, of Edmonton, Alberta, and est dau of John Holmes Graham, of Minden, Ontario, and d 15 April 1968

1a Marjorie Helinor; memb Kent CC; m 23 May 1914 Adml Robert Nesham Bax, CB, JP, s of Capt Bonham Bax, RN, and had issue. He d 21 Sept 1969

(1) (cont.) Col William Parker m 2nd 2 Aug 1899 Alice (d 26 April 1929), dau of Gen Reynell Taylor, CB, CSI, and d 17 Oct 1941, having by her had:

3a Robert William, CBE (1954), JP (Somerset 1961); b 15 March 1902; R-Adml, Dep Engr-in-Ch Admlty 1953–56, WWs I and II; m 1st 18 Feb 1928 (divorce 1933) Jean, dau of Henry Mackay; m 2nd 26 Oct 1935 Naomi Vyvian, yr dau of C V Espeut

(2) Mackworth Praed; b 23 Sept 1865; m 25 Jan 1893 Sybil Edith (d 3 Feb 1934), 2nd dau of Lt-Col John Arthur Thomas Garratt, of Bishop's Court, Exeter, and d 4 Nov 1926, leaving:

1a Gerard; b 16 June 1896; educ Malvern and RMC Sandhurst; Capt Devonshire Regt, WW I (wounded twice, despatches twice) and WW II; m 1st 9 June 1921 Dorothy (d 17 March 1956), dau of Lt-Col Francis Marwood Hext, of Redhayes, nr Exeter; m 2nd 2 April 1958 Jill Lettice Mary, er dau of Richard William Kandahar Nott, and d 1976, having by her had:

1b +Gerard Mackworth [Gerard Parker Esq, 127 Wardo Ave, London SW6 6RB]; b 10 Dec 1958, m 3 July 1987 *Michaela Louise, dau of John Frank William Burton, and has:

1c *Christopher Mackworth John; b 8 Nov 1994

1c Alexandra Nichola Mary; b 29 Oct 1990

2b +Julius Praed; b 26 Dec 1959; m 1992 *Doreen, dau of Finbar Murphy, and has issue

1b *Susan Mary; b 19 Aug 1961; m 12 Sept 1987 *David Carroll, son of John Carroll, and has issue

1a Sybil Muriel; b 1895; m 2 Feb 1921 Maj Montagu Irvine Gedoin Jenkins, DSO, Devonshire Regt (d 2 March 1948), s of Col R G Jenkins, and d 1978 leaving:

1b *Vivien Naomi; b 17 Feb 1930

(1) Mary Frances Susan; d unm 22 March 1936

(2) Evelyn Annie; m 16 Feb 1887 William Coryton, JP, DL, of Pentillie Castle, Cornwall, and d 13 May 1948, leaving issue. He d 27 Aug 1919

2 (cont.) Adml George Parker m 2nd 29 June 1903 Rachel Violet, est dau of John Holmes, of Calcutta, and d 31 Aug 1904

1 Frances Jane; m 10 Dec 1861 Francis Abbott, Sec GPO Scotland, and d 7 Nov 1871

2 Charlotte Martha; m 15 July 1850 Adml Hon George Henry Douglas (d 19 June 1905), 2nd s of 18th Earl of Morton (qv), and d 20 Dec 1909, leaving issue

3 Rose Augusta; m 16 Sept 1848 Lt-Col Edward John Vesey Browne (d 19 Sept 1894), of Dromard, Co Limerick, and d 25 Sept 1903

Sir WILLIAM d 13 Nov 1866; his est son,

Sir William Biddulph Parker, 2nd Bt, JP Hants, DL Staffs; b 14 Aug 1824; Lt Scots Gds; m 1st 6 June 1855 Jane Constance (dsp 20 July 1879), only dau of Sir Theophilus Biddulph, 6th Bt (qv); m 2nd 22 Nov 1887 Kathleen Mary (d 8 Jan 1917), dau of Lorenzo Kirkpatrick Hall, and by her had:

1 WILLIAM LORENZO (Sir), 3rd Bt

2 Henry Edward; b 11 Jan 1891; F/Lt RAF, F/Sub-Lt RNAS; m 1928 Beatrice Marie, dau of S A Bartlett

1 Constance Kathleen Rose; b 18 Sept 1894; m 1 June 1916 (divorce 1945) Adml Sir Douglas Blake Fisher, KCB, KBE, only s of Adml William Blake Fisher, CB, and had issue

Sir WILLIAM d 23 Jan 1902; his er son,

Sir William Lorenzo Parker, 3rd Bt, OBE (1919), JP (Breconshire 1932, Hants 1924); b 9 Jan 1889; educ Eton and New Coll Oxford (BA 1910); Breconshire: Ld Lt 1959–64 (V-Lt 1957–59, DL 1948–57 and 1965–71); Capt 9th Bn Hampshire Regt WW I (despatches); m 5 June 1915 Ruth Margaret Sillery (d 10 April 1971), dau of Alan Bertram Hanbury-Sparrow, JP, and had:

1 (WILLIAM) ALAN (Sir), 4th Bt

2 John Douglas; b 22 April 1924; educ Eton and New Coll Oxford (MA 1949); Lt Irish Gds WW II; m 7 June 1958 Iris Anne (d 23 May 1959), yr dau of Cdr George Arthur Titterton, RN, and d 1980, leaving:

(1) +Timothy John; b 17 May 1959

1 *(Ruth Kathleen) Betty [Mrs Richard Cole-Hamilton, Hawthorn Villa, 386 Ferry Rd, Edinburgh EH5 3QG]; b 12 Nov 1920; FANY WW II; m 9 Aug 1947 Richard Arthur Cole-Hamilton (see ENNISKILLEN, E) and has issue

The 3rd Bt d 27 Oct 1971; his er s,

Sir (William) Alan Parker, 4th Bt; b 20 March 1916; educ Eton and New Coll Oxford (BA 1937); Capt RE WW II; m 20 Feb 1946 *Sheelagh Mary [Sheelagh Lady Parker, The Old Rectory Nursing Home, Church Lane, Averham, Notts], only dau of Dr Sinclair Stevenson, and d 1990, leaving:

1 Sir (WILLIAM) PETER BRIAN PARKER, 5th and present Bt

1 *Lindy Ruth [Mrs Robert Moore, Bennachie, Carmel Rd, Holywell, Clwyd CH8 7DD]; b 29 Oct 1947; educ Durham U (BA); m 16 Aug 1969 *Prof Robert Samuel Moore, PhD, s of Douglas Kenneth Moore, and has:

(1) *David Kenneth; b 1974

(1) *Heloise Catherine; b 1976

PARKINSON

PARMOOR

Arms: Quarterly gules and azure, a fret throughout argent, on a chief per pale azure and gules a hart's head cabossed between two lion's heads guardant or, langued argent, all within a bordure ermine. **Crest:** A crown palisado, therein a grassy mount and thereon a crane statant proper holding in its beak a rose gules barbed and seeded, slipped and leaved proper. **Supporters:** Dexter, a crane statant regardant proper; sinister, a hart rampant regardant, also proper, attired or, the compartment comprising a grassy mount proper with on each side and growing therefrom three roses gules barbed and seeded, slipped and leaved all proper. **Creation:** B. (LP, UK) 1992.

THE BARON PARKINSON, of Carnforth, Co Lancaster (Cecil Edward Parkinson, PC (1981)) [The Rt Hon The Lord Parkinson PC, House of Lords, London SW1A 0PW]; *b* 1 Sept 1931; *educ* Roy Lancaster GS and Emmanuel Coll Cambridge (BA 1955, MA 1961); certified accountant 1960; Chm: Hemel Hempstead C Assoc 1966–69, Herts 100 Club 1968–69; MP (C) Enfield W 1970–74, Herts S 1974–83, Hertsmere 1983–92, Sec C Parly Fin Ctee 1971–72, PPS to Min for Aerospace and Shipping DTI 1972–74, Assist Govt Whip 1974, Oppn Whip 1974–76, Oppn Spokesman Trade 1976–79, Min State DTI 1979–81, Chm C Party 1981–83 and 1997–98, Paymaster Gen 1981–83, Chllr Duchy Lancaster 1982–83, Sec State: DTI 1983, Energy 1987–89, Tport 1989–90, Chm Anglo-Swiss Parly Gp 1979–82; Pres Anglo Polish C Soc 1986–; chm: Planet Online, Usborne plc and Eurorail to 1995, dir: Amertrans, Hertfordshire Business Centre, Integrated Technology (Europe), Jarvis Harpenden Hldgs, Midland Expressway, Mobile Phone Super-cover, Odyssey Corp, Resolution Security; Treas Politeia 1995–; author: *Right at the Centre* (1992); *m* 1957 *Ann Mary, dau of F A Jarvis, of Harpenden, Herts, and has:

   1 *Mary; *b* 1959
   2 *Emma; *b* 1961; *m* 1991 *John Owrid
   3 *Joanna; *b* 1963; *m* 1988 *Mark Bamber

BARON PARKINSON also has by *Sarah, dau of Col Hastings Keays:

   4 *Flora; *b* 31 Dec 1983

Lineage: SIDNEY PARKINSON, of Carnforth, Lancs; had:

CECIL EDWARD, *cr* a **Baron**

Arms: Chequy ermines and arg., on a chevron vert five horseshoes or. **Crest:** An ostrich's head couped arg., gorged with a coronet of fleur-de-lys and holding in the beak a horse shoe or. **Supporters:** On either side a sea-horse ppr. supporting a pennon ermines charged with a swan rousant arg., beaked and legged gu., ducally gorged and lined or. **Motto:** *Fronti nulla fides* ('Do not trust in appearances'). **Creation:** B. (UK) 16 Jan 1914.

THE 4TH BARON PARMOOR, of Frieth, Co Buckingham ((Frederick Alfred) Milo Cripps) [The Rt Hon The Lord Parmoor, Dairy, Sutton Veny, Wilts BA12 7AL]; *b* 18 June 1929; *s f* 1977; *educ* Ampleforth and Corpus Christi Coll Oxford

Lineage: RICHARD CRISPE, of Cirencester, Glos, was probably one of the CRISPEs of Copcott, Oxon (originally of Stanlake, Oxon, where William Crispe was living 1207); *m* Alice — and *d c* 1575, leaving:

EDWARD CRIPPS, of Cirencester; *m* Jane — (*d* 1626) and was *bur* 1618, having had:

JOHN CRIPPS, of Cirencester, living 1643; *m* Margery — (*d* 1666) and had:

JOHN CRIPPS, of Cirencester; *b* by 1618; *m* 1648 Mary Brown (*d* 1695) and *d* 1696, having had:

JOHN CRIPPS, of Cirencester, *bapt* 1657; *m* Susanna — (*d* 1750) and was *bur* 1695, having had:

JOHN CRIPPS, of Cirencester; *b* 1691; *m* 21 April 1720 Dorothea (*d* 1757), dau of Rev Joseph Harrison, MA, Vicar Cirencester, Rector Daglingworth, Glos, and *d* 30 Aug 1769, leaving, with an er s John (*b* 1722, issue died out 1830; his n Joseph inherited the estate):

JOSEPH CRIPPS, of Cirencester; *b* 7 Feb 1729; *m* Hester, dau of William Hall, of Arlington, Glos, and *d* 28 May 1792, having had:

JOSEPH CRIPPS, of Cirencester, Glos, JP, DL; Chm QS, MP Cirencester 1806–12 and 1818–41; *b* 10 March 1765; *m* 1st 17 April 1786 Elizabeth (*d* 15 April 1799), er dau of Benjamin Harrison, of Lee, Kent, Govr and Treas Guy's Hosp; *m* 2nd 1801 Dorothea, dau of Benjamin Harrison, and *d* 8 Jan 1847 leaving, with other issue:

Rev HENRY CRIPPS; *b* 1787; *educ* New Coll Oxford (MA); Rector Preston All Saints, Vicar Stonehouse, Glos; *m* 7 July 1812 Judith, sis of Sir William Lawrence, 1st Bt, of Ealing Park (*qv*), and *d* 7 Nov 1861, leaving an est s:

HENRY WILLIAM CRIPPS, of Parmoor, Bucks, QC (1866), JP, DL; *b* 20 March 1815; *educ* New Coll Oxford (MA 1842); barrister Middle Temple 1840, Bencher 1866, Recorder Lichfield 1852, Chllr Diocese Oxford 1883, Chm Bucks QS; *m* 5 March 1845 his cousin Julia (*d* 13 July 1912), dau of Charles Lawrence, and had:

   1 Henry Lawrence, of Shifford, Oxon, and S Kensington; *b* 8 Jan 1846; *educ* New Coll Oxford (BA 1868); *m* Nov 1872 Mary Pennington (*d* 30 Oct 1919), dau of Capt Francis Rivers Freeling, 3rd s of Sir Francis Freeling, 1st Bt (*see* 1940 edn), and *d* 11 Nov 1915, leaving issue
   2 (William) Harrison, of Glendaruel, Argyll, and Marlebone; *b* 15 Jan 1850; FRCS, Consulting Surgn St Bartholomew's Hosp; *m* 1st 26 July 1877 Blanche (*d* 2 June 1905), dau of Richard Potter, of Rusland Hall, and Standish Place, Glos, and had issue; *m* 2nd 3 Feb 1907 Giulia Orfeo, dau of Col Michael Ravogli, of Rome, and *d* 8 Nov 1923
   3 (CHARLES) ALFRED, **1st Baron**
   4 Frederick Edward; *b* 27 April 1855; *d* 24 June 1871
   5 Arthur Devereux; *b* 18 May 1858; *m* 3 Jan 1889 Georgina Amelia (*d* 3 Jan 1922), dau of Rev Frederick Harry Hotham (*see* HOTHAM, B), and *dsp* 29 Dec 1903
   1 Julia Marina; *m* 16 April 1873 Theodore Stretch, er s of Ven Theodore Carlos Benoni Stretch, Archdeacon Melbourne, and had issue
   2 Katharine Alice; *m* 3 Jan 1883 Rev Francis Lochee Nash, Vicar Lane End, Bucks, and *d* Jan 1922, leaving issue
   3 Judith Emily; *m* 20 Aug 1872 Rev Frederick Henry Slocock, Vicar Mottisfont, Hants, and had issue. He *d* 16 Feb 1901

4 Rosa Margaret; *m* 2 Jan 1878 Robert Taunton Raikes, JP (*d* 24 Aug 1919), of Treberfydd, Brecknock, and *d* 29 Aug 1923, leaving issue

5 Edith Eleanor; *m* 3 Jan 1883 her cousin Rev Alfred Herbert Stanton (*d* 5 Dec 1947), Vicar St Peter-in-the-East, Oxford, and *d* 15 Feb 1949, leaving issue

HENRY CRIPPS *d* 14 Aug 1899; his 3rd s,

(CHARLES) ALFRED CRIPPS, **1st Baron Parmoor**, of Frieth, Co Buckingham (UK), so *cr* 16 Jan 1914, KCVO (1908), PC (and memb Judicial Ctee 1914), QC (1890), JP and Chm QS Bucks 1910–25; *b* 3 Oct 1852; *educ* Winchester and New Coll Oxford (BA 1874, BCL 1876, MA 1876, Hon Fell); Sr Studentship Inns of Court 1876, barrister Middle Temple 1877, Bencher 1893, Treas 1917, MP Stroud 1895–1900, Stretford 1901–06 and Wycombe 1910–14, Chllr and Vicar-Gen York 1900–41, Vicar-Gen Canterbury 1902–24, Chm Canterbury Ho Laymen, First Chm Ho Laity Nat Ch Assembly 1920–24, Ld Pres Cncl Jan-Nov 1924 and 1929–31, UK rep Cncl League Nations, Attorney-Gen PRINCEs OF WALES 1895–1901, 1901–10 and 1910–14, Fell St John's Coll Oxford 1875–81; *m* 1st 27 Oct 1881 Theresa (*d* 22 May 1893), dau of Richard Potter, and sis of the socialist writer Beatrice Webb, and had:

1 ALFRED HENRY SEDDON CRIPPS, **2nd Baron Parmoor**; *b* 27 Aug 1882; *educ* Winchester and New Coll Oxford (BA 1907, MA 1929); Capt Lincs Yeo TF, barrister Middle Temple 1907, Bursar Queen's Coll Oxford 1928–45, Fell 1929; *d* 12 March 1977

2 FREDERICK HEYWORTH CRIPPS, **3rd Baron Parmoor**, DSO and bar (1918), TD, DL (Bucks 1929); *b* 4 July 1885; *educ* Winchester; Lt-Col Roy Bucks Hus WW I (wounded, despatches), Lt-Cdr RNVR WW II, Hon Col 13th Lancs Para Bn, Croix de Guerre Belgium; *m* 8 Oct 1927 (*divorce* 1951) Violet Mary Geraldine (*d* 1983), formerly w of 2nd Duke of Westminster (*qv*) and dau of Sir William Nelson, 1st Bt (*qv*), and *d* 5 Oct 1977, leaving:

(1) (FREDERICK ALFRED) MILO CRIPPS, **4th and present Baron Parmoor**

3 Leonard Harrison, CBE (1918); *b* 21 April 1887; *educ* Radley and RMC Sandhurst; Maj 4th Hus WW I (wounded, despatches twice), chm Elder Dempster Lines 1941–46, fndr LHC Corp S Africa, Controller Stores Dept Min Munitions; *m* 5 April 1913 Miriam Barbara (*d* 30 July 1960), dau of Sir Matthew Ingle Joyce, PC, High Court Judge, and *d* 1 Feb 1959, leaving:

(1) (Matthew) Anthony Leonard, CBE, DSO (1943), TD, QC (1958); *b* 30 Dec 1913; *educ* Eton, Ch Ch Oxford and Army and RAF Staff Coll Haifa; barrister Middle Temple 1938 (Master Bench 1965) and Inner Temple 1961, Judge Canterbury Court of Arches 1969–79, Recorder Nottingham 1961–71, memb Senate Four Inns Court 1967–71 and 1982–83, memb Bar Cncl 1967–69 and 1970–74, Recorder Crown Court 1972–87, Maj Leics Regt WW II, chm: Reigate C Assoc 1960–64, Billbrook Finance Ltd, memb Exec Ctee C Nat Union 1964–72, Dep Sr Judge Br Sovereign Bases Area Cyprus 1978–94, v-pres Bonaventure Investments (Canada), dir Caledonian African Investment Tst (S Africa), author: *The Agricultural Holdings Act, 1948*, 9th edn *Cripps on Compulsory Acquisition of Land; Powers, Procedure and Compensation*; *m* 21 June 1941 (Dorothea) Margaret (*d* 1992), CC Surrey (1965–66), only dau of George Johnson Scott, and *d* 25 Jan 1997, leaving:

1a +(MICHAEL LEONARD) SEDDON [His Honour Judge Cripps Esq, Bessemers, Moor Wood, Lane End, High Wycombe, Bucks HP4 3HZ]; *b* 18 June 1942; heir presumptive; *educ* Eton; barrister Middle Temple 1965, Lincoln's Inn 1969 and Inner Temple 1975, Circuit Judge 1998; *m* 12 June 1971 *(Elizabeth) Anne, only dau of Maj William Millward-Shennan, and has:

1b Alexander Matthew Seddon; *d* 20 Feb 1973

2b +Henry William Anthony; *b* 2 Sept 1976

1b *Stephanie Margaret Julia; *b* 4 Oct 1974

2a +Jeremy George Anthony; *b* 2 July 1943; *educ* Eton, Case Western Reserve U Cleveland, Ohio (BA Political Science 1969) and Union Inst Cincinnati (PhD); ACA 1967, FCA, CPA, C parly candidate Hammersmith 1979, European controller Parker Hannifin Corp 1973, Prof Accountancy Heidelberg Coll Tiffin; *m* 26 Aug 1972 *Mary Elizabeth, only dau of Walter Howe, of Golf Manor, Cincinnati, and has:

1b +Scott Anthony Charles; *b* 11 Jan 1978

2b +Clark Robert Leonard; *b* 22 Nov 1980

1b *Lynne Margaret; *b* 4 May 1983

3a +Richard James Nigel [Richard Cripps Esq, 36 Napier Ave, London SW6 3PT]; *b* 15 March 1956; *educ* Eton and St Catharine's Coll Cambridge (MA); slr; *m* 1987 *Margaret Jude, 3rd dau of Sam S Mullin, of Osterville, Mass., and has:

1b +Leonard Samuel Anthony; *b* 23 Feb 1989

2b +John Richard Charles; *b* 29 March 1991

3b +Frederick Alfred Michael; *b* 27 June 1992

1b * Julia Margaret Ruth; *b* 4 July 1994

2b *Theresa Barbara Jude; *b* 22 July 1997

(2) +Charles Thomas Joyce [Charles Cripps Esq, 41 Somerset Rd, London SW19]; *b* 7 Oct 1916; *educ* Eton and Ch Ch Oxford; memb London Stock Exchange, RA (AA), Capt RTR WW II; *m* 5 April 1941 *Noreen, dau of Dr Hugh Pierce, and has:

1a +Charles Hugh [Charles Cripps Esq, 136 Sherborne Court, 180 Cromwell Rd, London SW5 0SU]; *b* 25 Feb 1946; *educ* Eton

2a +Paul Alfred [Paul Cripps Esq, 7 Pont St, London SW1X 9EJ]; *b* 10 Nov 1950; *educ* Eton, Sorbonne and LSE (BSc)

4 (Richard) Stafford (Sir), CH (1951), PC (1941), KC (1927); *b* 24 April 1889; *educ* Winchester and UCL; barrister Middle Temple 1913, Bencher 1930, ktd 1930, MP (Lab) Bristol E 1931–50 and Bristol SE Feb–Oct 1950, Slr-Gen 1930–31, Min Ec Affs 1947, Pres BOT 1945–47, Chllr Exchquer 1947–50, Amb USSR 1940–42, Min Aircraft Prodn 1942–45, Ld Privy Seal and Leader H of C Feb-Nov 1942, Rector Aberdeen U 1942, FRS, Hon DCL Oxon 1949, Hon LLD Liverpool 1949; *m* 12 July 1911 Isobel (*d* 1979), GBE (1946), FRSA, Special Grand Cordon Brilliant Star China, dau of Cdr Harold William Swithinbank, FRS, FRGS, JP, DL, of Denham Court, Bucks, and *d* 21 April 1952, leaving:

(1) John Stafford (Sir), CBE (1968); *b* 10 May 1912; *educ* Winchester and Balliol Coll Oxford; ed *The Countryman* 1947, Chm Witney RDC 1959–62, Rural Ctee Nat Cncl Soc Serv 1962, RDCs Assoc 1967, memb Exec Ctee CPRE 1963, SE Ec Planning Cncl 1966; *m* 1st 29 Dec 1936 (*divorce* 1971) Ursula, er dau of Arthur Cedric Davy, of Whirlow Court, Sheffield, and had:

1a David Stafford; *b* 21 May 1940; *educ* Bryanston and Reading U; *m* 1968 (*divorce* 1981) Bridget Ayerst and *d* 1990, leaving:

1b *Jennifer Bridget; *b* 1969

2b *Nicola Ann; *b* 1971

3b *Angela Claire; *b* 1973

2a +Timothy Francis [Timothy Cripps Esq, 10 High St, Harston, Cambridge]; *b* 4 May 1943; *educ* Eton and Trin Coll Cambridge; *m* 1969 –

3a +Christopher John [Dr Christopher Cripps, 2 Sunhouse, Mitcheldean, Glos GL17 0DY]; *b* 30 Aug 1947; *educ* Bryanston, King's Coll Cambridge and Architectural Assoc, PhD Liverpool 1981; *m* 1976 (*divorce* 1997) Alyson, only dau of Cyril Laverick, and has:

1b +Joe John Allan; *b* 1978

1b *Rosie Helen Zoë; *b* 1985

4a +Richard Andrew [Richard Cripps Esq, 3 Moat Cottages, Filkins, Glos]; *b* 15 Jan 1954; *educ* Bryanston and Southampton U

1a *Judith Ursula [Mrs Sarjit Heyer, 10 Brookside, Headington, Oxford OX3 7PJ]; *b* 2 Nov 1938; *educ* Cheltenham Ladies' Coll and Somerville Coll Oxford; *m* 1964 Sarjit Heyer (*d* 1974) and has:

1b *Jasdev Philip; *b* 29 Oct 1968; *educ* Cheney and Cambridge U; *m* 11 March 1997 *Malaika, dau of Barry Riley

2b *Daleep Andrew; *b* 12 June 1971

1b *Amrik Frances; *b* 7 June 1967

2a *Rachel Theresa [Mrs Bernard Rosedale, Thornsend, Kingsbury Hill, Marlborough, Wilts]; *b* 11 March 1945; *educ* Cranborne Chase and Sussex U; *m* 1969 *(James Oriel) Bernard Rosedale, MB, BS, and has:

1b *Nicholas Oriel Rupert; *b* 1972

2b *Lawrence Andrew; *b* 1974

3b *Benjamin James; *b* 1976

1b *Katherine Jane; *b* 1978

(1) (cont.) Sir John Cripps *m* 2nd 1971 *Ann Elizabeth [Lady Cripps, Fox House, Filkins, Glos], dau of Edwin G K Farwell, and *d* 1993

(1) (Isobel) Diana; *b* 2 Sept 1913; *m* 20 Sept 1938 (*annulled* 1940) Lawrence Purcell Weaver, est s of Sir Lawrence Weaver, KBE, FSA

(2) Anne Theresa, CBE (1983); *b* 12 April 1919; *educ* St Anne's Coll Oxford; WRNS WW II; chm Nat Assoc Citizens' Advice Bureaux 1979–84, memb Direct Servs Standards Bd 1985–92 and Electricity Consumers' Cncl 1978–90; *m* 20 July 1945 *Sir Robert Cornwallis Gerald St Leger Ricketts, 7th Bt (*qv*), and *d* 16 Jan 1998, leaving issue

(3) *Enid Margaret [Mrs Joseph Appiah, PO Box 829, Kumasi, Ashanti, Ghana]; *b* 21 May 1921; *m* 18 July 1953 *Joseph E Appiah, s of J W K Appiah, Ch Sec Ashanti Confederacy, and has:

1a *Kwame Anthony Akroma-Ampim Kusi; *b* 8 May 1954; *educ* Bryanston and Clare Coll Cambridge; Prof Dept African American Studies Harvard; author: *In My Father's House* (1997)

1a *Isobel Takyiwa [Mrs Klaus Endresen, c/o Norsk Hydro, Private Bag 13303, Windhoek, Namibia]; *b* 19 Nov 1955; *educ* Badminton and Sussex U; *m* 1980 *Klaus Endresen and has:

1b *Kristian Gyamfi; *b* 1981

2b *Anthony Finn; *b* 1984

3b *Per Kojo; *b* 1987

2a *Amy Adwoa [Mrs Olawale Edun, 4b Hawksworth Rd, Ikoyi, Lagos, Nigeria]; *b* 3 Aug 1959; *educ* St Louis Secondary Sch Kumasi, Roedean, Sussex U and Leeds U; *m* 1982 *Olawale Edun and has:

1b *Babatunde Adetomiwa Stafford; *b* 1984

2b *Adedeji Olamide; *b* 1986

3b *Adedamola Oluwatobi; *b* 1989

3a *Theresa Jane (Abena); *b* 3 July 1962; *educ* Sidcot Sch and St Godric's Coll

1 Ruth Julia; *m* 11 July 1912 Sir Alfred Charles Glyn Egerton, MA, FRS, s of Sir Alfred Mordaunt Egerton, KCVO, CB, and *d* 27 March 1978 aged 94. He *d* 7 Sept 1959

The **1st Baron** *m* 2nd 14 July 1919 Marian Emily (*d* 6 July 1952), dau of John Edward Ellis, PC, of Scalby, Yorks, and *d* 30 June 1941

PARRY

Creation: B. (LP, UK) 1975.

THE BARON PARRY, of Neyland, Co Dyfed (Gordon Samuel David Parry, DL (Dyfed 1993)) [The Rt Hon The Lord Parry DL, Willowmead, 52 Port Lion, Llangwm, Dyfed SA62 4JT]; *b* 30 Nov 1925; *educ* Trin Coll Carmarthen and Liverpool U; teacher 1945–52; house master Co Secondary Sch Haverfordwest 1952–62 and 63–68; Inst of Educn Liverpool U 1962–63; Warden Pembse Teachers' Centre 1967–76; Chm Wales Tourist Board 1978–84; Memb: BTA 1978–84, Cncl OU (Chm Advsy Ctee Studies in Educn 1978–83); V-Pres Mentally Handicapped Soc Wales, Cwlth Games Appeal Ctee Wales 1979, Year of Disabled People Wales 1979, S Wales Regn Nat Soc for Mentally Handicapped Children, Welsh Nat Cncl YMCA; Pres: Wales Spastics Soc, Pembs Spastics Soc, Pembs Multiple Sclerosis Soc, Keep Wales Tidy Ctee 1979– (Chm 1979–86), British Inst Cleaning Science 1981–91, British Cleaning Cncl (Chm 1983–), Milford Docks Co 1991– (Chm 1984–91), Tidy Britain Gp 1991–; Chm: Clean World Internat, Keep Britain Beautiful Campaign 1986–, Taylorplan Services 1987–, Br Travel Educnl Tst; Fell Tourism Soc 1979; FRSA; Fell Hotel and Catering and Institutional Management Assoc 1980; BICSc 1981; Hon Fell: James Cook U Australia 1989, Inst Wastes Management Trin Coll Carmarthen 1990, Wales Poly 1991, Glamorgan U; Hon Dr Ed Wales; *m* 1948 *Glenys Catherine, dau of Jack Leslie Incledon, and has:

1 *Catherine Anne; *b* 1955

Lineage: Rev THOMAS LEWIS PARRY; *m* Anne Evans and had:

GORDON SAMUEL DAVID, *cr* a **Baron**

PASLEY

PRO·REGE·ET·PATRIA·PUGNANS

Arms: Azure on a chevron argent, between two roses in chief of the last, and in base an anchor or, three thistles slipped proper. **Crest:** Out of a naval coronet gold a sinister arm in armour proper, grasping in the hand a staff, thereon a flag argent, charged with a cross wavy gules and on a canton azure a human leg erect, couped below the knee or. **Motto:** *Pro rege et patria pugnans* ('Fighting for king and country'). **Creation:** Bt. (GB) 1 Sept 1794.

SIR (JOHN) MALCOLM SABINE PASLEY, 5TH BT, of Craig, Co Dumfries [Sir Malcolm Pasley Bt, 25 Lathbury Rd, Oxford OX2 7AT]; *b* 5 April 1926; *s* f 1982; *educ* Sherborne and Trin Coll Oxford; Magdalen Coll Oxford: Emeritus Fell 1958–, Laming Travelling Fell Queen's Coll Oxford 1949–50, lecturer German (also BNC) 1950–58, Fell and Tutor 1958–86, V-Pres 1979–80, Hon DPhil Giessen 1986, FBA 1991; *m* 20 Feb 1965 *Virginia Killigrew, dau of Peter Lothian Killigrew Wait, of Kew, and has:

1 +ROBERT KILLIGREW SABINE; *b* 23 Oct 1965

2 +Humphrey Sabine; *b* 4 Dec 1967

Lineage: JAMES PASLEY, of Craig, nr Langholm, Dumfriesshire; *b c* 1695; *m* Magdalen, dau of Robert Eliott, of Middlemiln, Roxburghs, and *d* 13 April 1773, leaving, with four daus:

1 Robert; *b* 30 Jan 1727; *m* Christian, dau of Alexander Pringle, of Whytbank, and had issue

2 James, *dsp*

3 John of Colney Hatch, Middx; *d* unm 1804

4 Gilbert; Surgn-Gen Madras; *m* Hannah Dashwood and *d* 1781

5 THOMAS (Sir), **1st Bt**

6 Charles; *b* 25 Feb 1740; London merchant; *m* 21 Feb 1780 Jane, dau of John Carlyle, and had issue

The 5th s,

Sir Thomas Pasley, 1st Bt (GB), so *cr* 1 Sept 1794, with remainder to the heirs male of his daus successively; *b* 2 March 1734; RN: joined 1751, Lt 1757, Cdr 1762, C-in-C Medway 1788, R-Adml 12 April 1794, lost a leg but gained a btcy and a pension of £1,000 (over £40,000 in late-1990s terms) p.a. following his distinguished performance under Howe (*qv*) at the 'Glorious' First of June 1794 victory over the French, V-Adml the White 1795, C-in-C The Nore 1798 and Plymouth 1799, Adml 1801; *m* Mary, dau of Thomas Heywood, Deemster (Judge), of The Nunnery, IoM, and *d* 29 Nov 1808, leaving, with a yr dau (Magdalen, *m* 1798 Col Thomas Dowdeswell (*dsp* Nov 1811), of Pull Court, Worcs, and *d* 1841):

MARIA Pasley; *m* 21 Aug 1800 Maj John SABINE, Gren Gds, and had:

Sir THOMAS SABINE later PASLEY (1809 under terms of gf's will), **2nd Bt**, KCB (1873); *b* 26 Dec 1804; *educ* RNC; RN: joined 1818, Lt 1824, Cdr 1828, Capt 1831, Superintendent Pembroke and Devonport Dockyards 1854–56 and 1857–62 respectively, R-Adml 1856, V-Adml 1863, Adml 1866, C-in-C Portsmouth 1866–69; *m* 10 June 1826 Jane Matilda Lily (*d* 15 May 1869), est dau of Rev Montagu John Wynyard, Rector W Runton and St Martins's Micklegate, York, and *d* 13 Feb 1884, having had, with two daus (*d* unm):

1 Thomas Malcom Sabine; *b* 23 July 1829; Capt RN; *m* 13 Feb 1860 Emma Louisa (*d* 4 April 1894), est dau of John Losh, of Trinidad, and *d* 29 Jan 1870, leaving:

(1) **Sir Thomas Edward Sabine Pasley, 3rd Bt**; *b* 12 Nov 1863; *educ* Cavendish Coll Cambridge (BA); Capt Roy Berks Regt, Adj 1st Vol Bn, Boer War 1899–1900 (despatches twice, medal with tree clasps, Brevet Maj), WW I; *m* 17 April 1890 Lady Constance Hastings (*d* 25 Aug 1922), est dau of 13th Earl of Huntingdon (*qv*), and *dspm* 7 April 1947, leaving:

1a Constance Irene Sabine; *b* 30 April 1891; *m* 16 June 1917 Maj Claude Daubuz, OBE, MC, RA (*d* 5 Oct 1939), s of Capt R C Daubuz, RE, and *d* 2 June 1962, leaving issue

2a Norah Margaret Sabine; *b* 26 Jan 1902; *m* 16 Sept 1933 Clifford Jeal, yr s of J F Jeal, and had:

1b *John Julian Timothy [John Jeal Esq, 2 Healey St, London NW1]; *b* 27 Jan 1945; *educ* Westminster and Ch Ch Oxford (BA 1966); *m* 11 Oct 1969 *Joyce, dau of William Timewell

1b *Thomasina Joanna [Mrs Edgar Beck, Coombe Priory, Shaftesbury, Dorset]; *b* 11 Dec 1934; *m* 11 Sept 1957 *Edgar Philip Beck, s of Edgar Charles Beck, and has issue

(2) Malcolm Sabine; *b* 17 April 1870; Capt RN; *m* 16 Jan 1897 Nona Marion (*d* 17 Aug 1949), dau of John Marshall Paine, and *d* 24 Jan 1947, leaving:

1a RODNEY MARSHALL SABINE (Sir), **4th Bt**

(1) Matilda Sabine; *b* 6 April 1861; *m* 15 Oct 1885 Maj-Gen James Hutchinson Swanton, RMLI (*d* 30 March 1928), and *d* 13 Sept 1932, leaving issue

(2) Georgina Sabine; *b* 29 Aug 1862; *d* unm 9 Dec 1944

(3) Ellen Sabine; *b* 17 May 1869; *m* 1 Oct 1902 Maj Francis Edward Glossop, Leics Regt (*d* 11 Dec 1931), s of Rev George Goodwin Pownall Glossop, and *d* 18 Feb 1958

2 Rodney Stewart Lyons Sabine; *b* 27 April 1832; *m* 23 April 1868 Annie (*d* 10 Oct 1923), dau of William McLeod, of Dunedin, NZ, and *d* 2 June 1909, leaving:

(1) Montagu Thomas Sabine; *b* 13 June 1869; *m* 8 Nov 1900 Agnes Jane (*d* 14 Jan 1965), dau of John Innes, of Invercargill, NZ, and *d* 24 July 1947, having had:

1a Rodney Sabine; *b* 13 Oct; *d* 16 Oct 1901

1a *Nancy Sabine [Mrs Robert Paterson-Barr, 1360 Burnaby St, Vancouver, BC, Canada]; *b* 31 Dec 1907; *m* 17 June 1932 Robert Paterson-Barr, s of Robert Byers-Barr, of Dunedin, NZ

(2) William Sabine; *b* 4 Sept 1870; *m* 8 Jan 1900 Florence Annie Heloise (*d* 1959), dau of W H Kinnersley, and *d* 6 Nov 1938, leaving:

1a Eric Kinnersley Sabine; *b* 13 Oct 1900; *m* 1st 8 May 1928 Thelma (*d* 3 April 1948), dau of John Nicholas Power, of Auckland, and *d* 1975, leaving:

1b +Thomas Sabine [Thomas Pasley Esq, 141 Moana Ave, Nelson, New Zealand]; *b* 28 April 1930; memb Real Estate Inst NZ; *m* 15 Nov 1958 *Helen Aroha, er dau of Justin Beauchamp Foster-Barham, of Nelson, NZ, by Phyllis Edith, er dau of Algernon Burton, and has:

1c +Malcolm Sabine; *b* 9 March 1960

2c +Alastair Sabine; *b* 15 Jan 1963; *m* 1993 *Elizabeth, dau of William Rackley, of Nelson

3c Hamish Sabine; *b* 21 Feb 1964; *k* in an accident 1982

2b +Warren Sabine [Warren Pasley Esq, 3 Butler St, Opawa, Christchurch, New Zealand]; *b* 10 Feb 1931; *m* 1955 (*divorce* 1980) Margaret Mae, dau of John Douglas McIntosh, of Dunedin, and has:

1c +Jonathan Douglas Sabine; *b* 1961

1c *Joanna Tui Sabine; *b* 1959

3b +John Clinton Sabine [John Pasley Esq, 116 Queen St, Northcote, Auckland, New Zealand]; *b* 24 July 1936; *m* 1960 *Monica Therese, dau of Patrick Riley, of Christchurch, NZ, and has:

1c +Mathew Patrick; *b* 1961; *m* 1984 *Julie, dau of Roderick Langridge, of Auckland, and has:

1d +Thomas Michael; *b* 1988

2c +Paul Joseph Eric; *b* 1962; *m* 1991 *Amanda, dau of John Fear, of Auckland, and has:

1d *Emma Rose; *b* 1994

3c +John Nicholas; *b* 1963

4c +Thomas Anthony; *b* 1966; *m* 1988 *Jane, dau of Sean Walsh, of Auckland, and has:

1d +Andrew Sean Sabine; *b* 1990

1d *Alexandra Hannah Sabine; *b* 1992

1c *Clare Monica; *b* 1968

1a (cont.) Eric Pasley *m* 2nd 15 June 1950 his 1st cousin Rona Norma Sabine (*d* 1978), only dau of Russell Sabine Pasley (*see below*)

1a *Dorothy Madeleine Sabine; *b* 4 Nov 1906; *m* 3 Dec 1939 Victor Patrick Coghlan (*d* 1986), s of John Coghlan

2a Lily; *b* 28 May 1917; *m* 10 Nov 1937 Harry Douglas Double, er s of Cecil Double, of Invercargill, and had issue

(3) Clinton Heywood Sabine; *b* 4 March 1872; *m* 1905 Jean (*d* 18 Jan 1938), dau of John Brown, of Dunedin, and *d* 24 Aug 1936

(4) Russell Sabine; *b* 26 Sept 1876; *m* 19 Aug 1902 Mabel Wellington (*d* 11 March 1952), dau of G Tracey-Stevens, and *d* 7 Aug 1945, leaving:

1a Maitland Sabine; *b* 30 May 1914; RNZNVR WW II; *m* 22 June 1943 *Nancy Molyneux [Mrs Maitland Pasley, 56 Severn St, Islands Bay, Wellington, New Zealand], dau of John Phillips, and *d* 1972, having had:

1b +Philip Sabine; *b* 6 March 1945; *m* 1969 *Colleen Monica, er dau of Daniel Doyle, and has:

1c +Stuart Sabine; *b* 1974

1c *Andrea Sabine; *b* 1972

2c *Vanessa Sabine; *b* 1977

2b +Russell Sabine; *b* 13 Sept 1947

1b *Christine Sabine; *b* 2 May 1950; *m* 1972 *Robert John Lang

1a Rona Norma Sabine; *b* 24 Feb 1907; *m* 15 June 1950 her 1st cousin Eric Kinnersley Sabine Pasley (*see above*)

(1) Margaret Sabine; *m* 30 March 1910 Thomas Bragg (*d* 22 Jan 1949), of Bragg's Bay, Stewart Island, NZ, and *d* 6 Oct 1954, leaving issue

(2) Jane Matilda Lily Sabine; *m* 7 Dec 1903 Arthur Frederick Bent and *d* 1916

(3) Edith Annie Sabine; *m* 12 April 1909 George Evelyn Adams and had issue

3 Maitland Warren Bouverie Sabine, Maj RA, Adj Sussex Art; *b* 17 July 1834; *m* 20 Oct 1859 Katherine Henson (*m* 2nd 1885 A Halstead; *d* 8 Jan 1905), dau of Maj—Grehan, 78th Highrs, and *d* 6 June 1881, having had, with a dau (*d* unm):

(1) Maitland Stewart Sabine; *b* 14 Aug 1861; *m* 1896 Beryl (*d* 1939), dau of E S Mercer, and had a dau

(2) Montagu Wynyard Sabine; *b* 30 June 1863; Capt RA Burma War 1887–89 (medal, two clasps), Chin-Lushai Expdn 1888–90 (clasp), Kidderzai Expdn 1890, Chitrai Relief Force 1895 (medal, clasp) and Tirah Expdn 1897–98

(despatches, three clasps); m 7 Oct 1891 Grace Lilian (d 13 April 1919), dau of Capt John Henry Herbert St John, 20th Regt, and d 29 Nov 1944, leaving:

1a Joseph Montagu Sabine, CB (1952), CBE (1944), MVO 4th Cl (1936); b 5 Sept 1898; Maj-Gen RA WW I, GOC 1st AA Gp WW II, Commr Surrey St John's Ambulance Bde 1954–59, OStJ 1954; m 1st 22 Sept 1926 (divorce 1948) Christina Joan, yst dau of John Darby, of Hillmorton House, Rugby, and had:

 1b *Anne Sabine [Mrs Guy Rowbotham, Nobles House, 18 Station Rd, Petersfield, Hants GU32 3ES]; b 21 Sept 1929; m 1st 26 Nov 1951 (divorce 1977) Maj John George Melsom, only s of Lt-Col Basil George Melsom, and has:

  1c *Andrew John [Andrew Melsom Esq, South House, Ham, Wilts SN8 3RB]; b 1 Feb 1953; educ Uppingham; m 1980 *Melanie Claire, dau of Maj James Derek Kenyon-Hague (see THOMPSON, Bt, of Hartsbourne Manor), and has had:

   1d *Harry George; b 1984

   2d Andrew Jack; b 1987; d 1988

   1d *Edwina Lily; b 1989

   2d *Cecily Kate; b 1992

 1b (cont.) Mrs Anne Melsom m 2nd 1978 *Brig Guy Reginald Rowbotham, CBE

1a (cont.) Maj-Gen Joseph Pasley m 2nd 1 July 1950 Dorothy Beatrice, widow of F/Lt Clarence William Parsons and yst dau of Wilfred John Fance, and d 1978, having by her had:

 1b +Malcolm Peter Sabine; b 13 Feb 1956; educ Marlborough

1a Margaret Sabine; m 10 Jan 1914 Gerald Stanley Prest (d 23 Feb 1956), est s of Stanley Faber Prest, and d 22 Aug 1967, leaving issue

2a Lillian Katherine Sabine; b 1895; m 9 Sept 1919 Alexander Louis Courtenay Lumsden (d 14 July 1959), s of Charles Arthur Lumsden, and had:

 1b *Alexander Sabine Courtenay [Alexander Lumsden Esq, The White House, Deptford, Wilts]; b 1921; Fl/Lt RAFVR WW II; m 1st 1943 Elisabeth Jean, dau of G/Capt B P H de Roeper, AFC, RAF, and has:

  1c *Julia Frances Sabine; b 1945

 1b (cont.) Alexander Lumsden m 2nd 1951 Elisabeth Vrena, dau of S/Ldr W R Adkins, and by her had:

  1c *Peter Alexander Courtenay; b 1961

  2c *Penelope Elisabeth Courtenay; b 1956

 1b (cont.) Alexander Lumsden m 3rd 1969 *Elizabeth Moncrieff, dau of Lt-Col Alexander Robert Cheale, TD, of Tunbridge Wells, and formerly w of Colin W Morley

(3) Edward Hugh Sabine; b 21 March 1869; Dist Supt Police NWP India; m 10 May 1895 Cara Wemyss (d 5 May 1929), dau of Maj-Gen Thomas James Quinn, ISC, and d 1 April 1929, having had:

 1a Thomas Edward Sabine; b 26 May 1896; 2nd Lt KOSB; missing believed ka 11 April 1918

 1a Madalene Doris Sabine; b 23 Feb 1898

(4) Henry Diggles Sabine; b 5 July 1871; m 1895 Lillian (d 7 Dec 1953), dau of Capt Charles Horteis Rhys, and d June 1925, leaving:

 1a Maitland Henry Sabine; b 1898; d June 1921

 1a Winifred Sabine; m 18 Dec 1953 Alfred Thomas Wright, s of George Wright

(5) Clinton St Clair Sabine; b 31 Jan 1874; m Violet Katherine, widow, dau of Arthur Ellis, and had issue

(1) Mary Lily Sabine; m 2 Aug 1887 Walter Ellis Boucher, 4th s of James George Boucher, JP, and d 5 Dec 1937, leaving issue. He d 5 July 1930

(2) Nancy Adair Sabine; m 1896 John Montgomery Young and dsp 3 Dec 1903

(3) Florence Sabine (twin with Henry Diggles); m 3 April 1893 (divorce) Harrington Mann (d 28 Feb 1937), s of John Mann, CA, and d 1956, leaving issue

4 Montagu John Henry Sabine; b 10 Dec 1835; d 1845

5 Hamilton Sabine; b 28 Jan 1837; educ Trin Coll Oxford (BA); Capt Cape Mounted Rifles; m 1st 27 March 1860 Catherine Anne (d 21 July 1872), est dau of Lt-Col Hon Richard Hare (see LISTOWEL, E), and had, with another s (d an infant):

 (1) Thomas Hamilton Sabine, MVO; b 10 May 1861; Paymaster RN, Sec RYS Cowes; m 23 Dec 1899 Alice Marion Margaret Watson (d 27 April 1930), dau of Thomas Conolly, and d 25 Feb 1927, leaving:

  1a Thomas Wynyard Sabine; b 19 June 1902; Roy Canadian Art and RAOC WW II; m 9 Oct 1946 Mrs Elizabeth Dundensing (d 3 Sept 1956), dau of Edward Howell Jones, of Freeman, W Virginia; m 2nd 19– Charlotte Potter; m 3rd 19– Marguerite Green and d 1981

  1a Violet Gatherine Sabine; b 30 Nov 1900; m 26 Nov 1924 Capt Percy John Warren McClenahan, MC, 5th/8th Punjabis, IA (shot by a Sepoy at Lahore cantonment 9 Dec 1930), 2nd s of Archdeacon McClenaghan, and d 2 Dec 1975, leaving:

   1b *Rosemary [Mrs Theon Wilkinson, 76½ Chartfield Ave, London SW15 6HQ]; b 1 March 1928; m 21 July 1949 *Theon Charles Wilkinson, MBE, FIPM, Gurkha Rifles, Colonial Serv, and has:

    1c *Wynyard Russell Theon; b 2 Nov 1951; m 10 March 1990 (divorce 19–) Juliet Edwards and has:

     1d *Sebastian Russell; b 20 Nov 1990

   2b *Valerie Joan [Mrs Malcolm Syms, Mile Path House, Hook Heath, Woking, Surrey GU22 0DY]; b 17 July 1929; m 20 April 1949 * Capt Malcolm Henry Syms, RM, s of Surgn R-Adml Gilbert Francis Syms, and has:

    1c Jeremy Francis; b 1950; educ Downside; d 10 July 1979

    1c *Charlotte Prudence Elizabeth; b 1954; educ Royal Naval Sch; m 17 Oct 1992 *(David) Michael Ralph Williams (see WILLIAMS, Bt of Bridehead) and has issue

  2a Margaret Rachel Sabine; b 18 Nov 1904; d unm 25 June 1961

 (2) Richard Sydney Sabine; b 18 Sept 1862; Lt RN; m 9 Nov 1897 Mary Victoria (d 24 Oct 1942), yst dau of Sir Henry Dairymple Des Voeux, 5th Bt (see 1940 edn), and d 28 June 1911, leaving:

1a Arthur Dalrymple Sabine; b 14 July 1903; educ Cambridge (BA); m 1st 2 Sept 1943 Doris (d 31 Jan 1950), dau of Herbert Rastell; m 2nd 1 Sept 1950 Hilda Mary, dau of William H Gardner, of Northampton, and d 1980, having by her had:

 1b *Victoria Mary Sabine; b 4 Aug 1952; m 1975 *Fernando Antonio Palacios, of Santiago, Chile

1a Catherine Constance Sabine; b 2 Aug 1900

2a Sybil Mary Sabine; b 21 Oct 1901; m 18 Oct 1930 Donald James Henry Maclennan, s of Donald Maclennan, and had:

 1b *Angela Sybil Joan; b 6 April 1934; m 21 Dec 1961 *John Malcolm Page, s of A Stanley Page, of Acomb, York, and has:

  1c *Christopher David; b 15 May 1963

  2c *Jonathan Richard; b 5 Aug 1965

  3c *Antony Graham; b 11 Dec 1966

3a *Audrey Christina Sabine; b 5 May 1905

(3) Charles Malcolm Sabine; b 25 Jan 1864; m 11 Jan 1903 Berthe Maria Mathilde (d 1964), dau of Count Herluison de Rilly, and d 16 May 1907, leaving:

 1a Sydney Montagu Sabine; b 1 Nov 1903; AIF WW II (invalided), US Army Tport Serv, American Red Cross; m 1 July 1935 May (d 1968), er dau of John Elliot, and dsp 1966

 2a +Charles Hamilton Sabine [Charles Pasley Esq, 55 Ewan St, Margate 4019, Qld, Aust]; b 1906; RAAF WW II (despatches); m 14 Nov 1933 *Marjorie May, er dau of C F Heales, slr, and has:

  1b *Helen Sabine; b 20 Nov 1934

5 (cont.) Capt Hamilton Pasley m 2nd 30 Jan 1877 Maude Eleanor Barlow Scheer, dau of Roger Hawkes, and d 28 Feb 1890

6 Russell Graves Sabine; b 7 April 1838; Capt RN; d 31 Dec 1884

7 Clinton Heywood Sabine; b 30 April 1841; d 20 Nov 1870

1 Jane Matilda; m 16 June 1851 Col Walter-Samuel Stace, RE, and d 28 Sept 1895, leaving issue. He d 25 Sept 1869

2 Madalene Sabine; m 3 April 1877 Sir Henry Jenkyns, KCB, and d 7 Dec 1935. He d 10 Dec 1899

The 3rd Bt's n,

Sir Rodney Marshall Sabine Pasley, 4th Bt; b 22 Feb 1899; educ Sherborne and Univ Coll Oxford (MA); 2nd Lt RA WW I, Headmaster Centl GS Birmingham 1943–59; m 7 April 1922 Aldyth Werge (d 23 Jan 1983 aged 84), dau of Maj Lancelot Cecil Bray Hamber, and d 1982, leaving:

1 Sir (JOHN) MALCOLM SABINE PASLEY, **5th and present Bt**

1 Pepita Sabine; b 23 Jan 1925; m 26 April 1957 Stanford Merrifield, s of Leonard Stanford Merrifield, and had:

 (1) *Giles Stanford; b 16 Feb 1958

 (1) *Hannah Marion; b 5 April 1960

(PASTON-)BEDINGFELD

Arms: Quarterly, 1st and 4th, erm. an eagle displayed gu. (for BEDINGFELD); 2nd and 3rd, arg. six fleurs-de-lys, three, two and one, az., a chief indented or (for PASTON). **Crests:** 1 An eagle displayed or (for BEDINGFELD), 2 A griffin sejant, wings elevated or, gorged with a collar gu., therefrom a line held in the beak and terminating in a ring of the last (for PASTON). **Mottoes:** 1 Despicio terrena, solem contemplor ('I avert my gaze from worldly objects; I look only on the sun'), 2 De mieulx je pense en mieulx ('I do better to think of better things'). **Badge:** A fetterlock (badge of the house of YORK, granted by EDWARD VI). **Creation:** Bt. (E) 2 Jan 1660/1.

SIR EDMUND GEORGE FELIX (PASTON-)BEDINGFELD, 9TH BT, of Oxburgh, Co Norfolk [Sir Edmund Paston-Bedingfeld Bt, The Old Stables, Gt Barton, Suffolk, IP35 2RZ]; b 2 June 1915; s f 1941; educ Oratory Sch and New Coll Oxford; Maj Welsh Gds (Res Offrs), Lt 5th Bn Roy Norfolk Regt, WW II (despatches and wounded), Freeman City London, Liveryman Bowyers' Co, U-Sec Ag Div RICS 1966, md Handley Walker (Europe) 1969–80, Pres Suffolk Heraldry Soc 1993–; m 1st 6 June 1942 (divorce 1953) Joan Lynette (d 22 Jan 1965), dau of Edgar George Rees, of Holmesleigh, Llanelli, and has:

1 +HENRY EDGAR [Henry Bedingfeld Esq, Oxburgh Hall, King's Lynn, Norfolk PE33 9PS]; *b* 7 Dec 1943; *educ* Ampleforth; has dropped PASTON for all but legal and official purposes (as an official of the Coll of Arms); chartered auctioneer 1968, chartered surveyor 1970, Coll Arms: Rouge Croix Pursuivant 1983, York Herald 1993, Sec Standing Cncl Baronetage 1984–88, Kt SMO Malta; Freeman City London, Liveryman Scriveners' and Bowyers' Cos, V-Pres Norfolk Heraldry Soc and Cambridge U Heraldic and Genealogical Soc and Suffolk Family Historical Soc, memb cncl Heraldry Soc 1976–85 and 1990–; author: *Oxburgh Hall, The First 500 Years* (1982), (jtly) *Heraldry* (1993); *m* 7 Sept 1968 *Mary Kathleen, er dau of Brig Robert Denis Ambrose, CIE, OBE, MC, of Malta, and has:

(1) +Richard Edmund Ambrose; *b* 8 Feb 1975; *educ* Ampleforth and Manchester U (BA)

(2) *Thomas Henry; *b* 6 Sept 1976; *educ* Ampleforth

(1) *Katherine Mary; *b* 4 Oct 1969; *educ* St Mary's Cambridge and Bath U (BSc, BArch)

(2) *Charlotte Alexandra; *b* 6 May 1971; *educ* St Mary's Cambridge

1 *Alexandra Winifred Mary; *b* 3 Sept 1947; *m* 16 May 1970 (*divorce* 1977) James Michael Yearsley, er s of J Yearsley, and has:

(1) *Simon; *b* 25 Feb 1973

(1) *Nicola; *b* 1 March 1971

(2) *Jennifer; *b* 1976

1 (cont.) Mrs Alexandra Yearsley *m* 2nd 1978 *Jack Pemberton and by him has:

(2) *Benjamin; *b* 1981

(3) *Joseph; *b* 1983

(3) *Grace; *b* 1985

Sir EDMUND *m* 2nd 31 May 1957 Agnes Kathleen Susan Anne Danos (*d* 5 June 1974), dau of Miklos Gluck, of Budapest; *m* 3rd 20 Nov 1975 Mrs Peggy R Hannaford-Hill (*d* 1991), of Zimbabwe; *m* 4th 1992 *Mrs Sheila Riddell, est dau of John Douglas, of Edinburgh

Lineage: OGERLIS; a Norman; held land at Bedingfield, Suffolk, by 1100, ancestor of:

PETER de BEDINGFELD, whose family held Bedingfield, Suffolk, lived *c* 1156; his descendant:

EDMUND BEDINGFELD; *m* Margaret (*d* 1446), dau of Sir Robert Tuddenham and sis and coheir of Sir Thomas Tuddenham (executed 1462), who brought her husb wide estates, including the Manor of Oxburgh, Norfolk (acquired by the WEYLANDs 1274 and inherited subsequently by the TUDDENHAMs), and *d* 1446, leaving an only s:

THOMAS BEDINGFELD; *m* Anne (*d* 1453), dau and heir of John de Waldegrave, and *d* 1453, leaving:

Sir EDMUND BEDINGFELD, KB; *m* Margaret, dau of Sir John Scott, PC, of Scott's Hall, Kent, Govr Calais and Dover, and *d* 1496, leaving:

Sir EDMUND BEDINGFELD; ktd 1523; custodian of CATHERINE OF ARAGON after her divorce from HENRY VIII when rusticated to Kimbolton; *m* Grace, dau of 1st Baron Marn(e)y by his 2nd w Elizabeth (dau of Alderman Nicholas Wilford/Wyfold, Ld Mayor London 1450–51 and a prosperous grocer), and *d* 1553, leaving:

Sir HENRY BEDINGFELD, PC (1553); *b* Sept 1511; MP Suffolk 1553 and Norfolk 1553, 1554 and 1557; among the first to declare for MARY on the death of EDWARD VI, for which besides his PC-ship he was allegedly granted a pension of £100 p.a.(*c* £25,000 in late-1990s terms) and some of the confiscated estates of the poet-rebel Sir Thomas Wyatt; custodian of PRINCESS (later QUEEN) ELIZABETH May 1554–June 1555; *m* Katherine, dau of Sir Roger Townshend (*see* TOWNSHEND, M), and *d* 1583, leaving an est s:

EDMUND BEDINGFELD; *m* Anne, dau of Sir Robert Southwell, of Hoxne, and *d* 1585, leaving:

THOMAS BEDINGFELD; *m* Frances, dau and coheir of John Jerningham, of Somerleyton, and *d* 1590, leaving:

Sir HENRY BEDINGFELD; *b c* 1587; royalist Civil War, hence imprisoned Tower London by Parliamentarians; *m* 1st Elizabeth, dau of Lord William Howard, of Naworth Castle, Cumberland (*see* CARLISLE, E, and NORFOLK, D), and had a s (Thomas, Col, *dsp* 26 April 1665); *m* 2nd Elizabeth, dau and coheir of Peter Hoghton, of Hoghton Tower, Lancs, probably est s (*dspm* & *vp*) of Sir Gilbert de Hoghton, 2nd Bt (*qv*), and *d* 22 Nov 1657, soon after his release, having by her had an only surv s:

Sir Henry Bedingfeld, 1st Bt (E), so *cr* 2 Jan 1660/1 in recompense for his losses in the royalist cause during the Civil War (when he fought as a Capt in CHARLES I's armies) and Interregnum years (computed at £47,194 18s 8d, or well over £3,150,000 in late-1990s terms); *b* Sept 1614; *m* April 1635 Margaret (*d* 14 Jan 1702), dau and heiress of Edward Paston, of Appleton, Norfolk, and *d* 24 Feb 1684/5, having had an est s:

Sir Henry Bedingfeld, 2nd Bt; *b* 1636; ktd between 1660 and 1682; *m* 1st Lady Anne Howard (*dsp* 19 Sept 1682), only surviving child and heiress of 2nd Earl of Berkshire (*see* SUFFOLK and BERKSHIRE, E); *m* 2nd *c* 1685 Elizabeth (*d* 13 April 1690), yst dau of Sir John Arundell, of Lanherne, Cornwall, by his 1st w Elizabeth, dau of 3rd Baron Teynham (*qv*), and *d* 14 Sept 1704, leaving, with two daus (Margaret, *m* 1704 Sir John Jerningham, 4th Bt (*see* STAFFORD, B), and *dsp* 23 Dec 1756; Frances, *m* Sir Francis Anderton, Bt), an only s:

Sir Henry Arundell Bedingfeld, 3rd Bt; *m* 28 Aug 1719 Lady Elizabeth Boyle (*d* 25 Nov 1751), est dau of 3rd Earl of Cork (*see* CORK and ORRERY, E), and *d* 15 July 1760, having had, with other issue:

Sir Richard Henry Bedingfeld, 4th Bt; *b* 14 Sept 1720; *m* 30 March 1761 Mary Browne (*d* 17 Sept 1767), dau of 6th Viscount Montagu, and *d* 27 March 1795, having had an only s:

Sir Richard Bedingfeld, 5th Bt; *b* 3 Aug 1767; *m* 16 June 1795 Charlotte Georgiana (*d* 29 July 1854), sis of 2nd Baron Stafford (*qv*), and *d* 22 Nov 1829, having had, with other issue:

Sir HENRY RICHARD BEDINGFELD later PASTON-BEDINGFELD (roy licence 16 April 1830), **6th Bt**; *b* 10 May 1800; *m* 30 Aug 1826 Margaret Anne PASTON later BISSHOPP (roy licence 26 March 1841; *d* 31 Jan 1887 aged 79), only child and heir of Edward Paston, last of the Pastons of Paston, formerly Earls of Yarmouth and in the 15th century a family on their way up in the world whose celebrated letters are an invaluable source of social history for that period as seen from the provincial gentry's point of view, and *d* 4 Feb 1862, having had:

1 HENRY GEORGE (Sir), **7th Bt**

2 Raoul Stephen PASTON-BEDINGFELD later BISSHOPP (roy licence 23 Sept 1887) later still PASTON-BEDINGFELD again; *b* 1 April 1835; Lt-Col late POW Own Norfolk Artillery Militia; *m* 26 April 1897 Katherine Gregory (*d* 3 Sept 1939), widow of Henry Alexander Claremont Lyne Stephens, of Grove House, Roehampton, and dau of Edward Walker, of Henbury Manor, Wimborne, Dorset, and *dsp* 4 June 1910

1 Matilda Charlotte; *m* 2 July 1855 Capt George Nevill, 7th Roy Fus (*d* 1906), 2nd s of Charles Nevill, of Nevill Holt, Leics, and *d* 31 Dec 1905, having had issue

2 Mary Geraldine; *m* 8 Oct 1867 Edward Southwell Trafford, JP (*d* 2 Aug 1912), of Honington Hall, Grantham, Lincs, 2nd s of Edward William Trafford, JP, of Brundall House, Norfolk, and *dsp* 10 Aug 1869

3 Mary Gabrielle; *m* 21 June 1880 Ferdinand John Eyre (*d* 1 May 1928), of Moreton Hall, Bury St Edmunds, yst s of V A Eyre, of Lindley Hall, Leics, and *d* 12 Jan 1937

The 6th Bt's er s,

Sir Henry George Paston-Bedingfeld, 7th Bt, DL Norfolk; High Sheriff 1882; *b* 21 June 1830; *m* 17 Oct 1859 Augusta Lucy (*d* 2 March 1929), only child of Edward John Clavering, of Callaly Castle, Northumberland, and *d* 18 Jan 1902, having had:

1 HENRY EDWARD (Sir), **8th Bt**

2 Richard Henry Clavering; *b* 2 Jan 1862; *d* 10 Aug 1931

3 Charles; *b* 25 July 1864; *d* 13 Feb 1936

4 Edward Arthur; *d* young 16 March 1878

5 William Felix; *b* 1873; *d* unm 29 May 1911

6 Francis Augustus; *b* 13 May 1874; *m* 1926 Dorothy Mary Hooker, of Kingston, Surrey, and *d* 20 Jan 1950, leaving:

(1) +Richard Francis [The Rt Rev Richard Paston-Bedingfeld, Padre Pio Mission, PO Harding 4680, Natal, S Africa]; *b* 1930; *educ* Marist Bros Coll Observatory, Johannesburg; missionary, consecrated Bp in irregular orders 1987

(1) *Elizabeth Mary Teresa [Sister Mary Frances, PO Box 117, Eersteriuier 7103, Cape Province, S Africa]; *b* 1928; nun Inst of Blessed Virgin Mary

7 Hubert; *b* 1877

1 Alice Mary; Grand Cordon Turkish Order Shefa Kat; *m* 1st 12 Jan 1891 V-Adml James Lacon Hammet, CVO (*d* 15 Feb 1905), and had a dau (Violet, *d* 17 Feb 1987); *m* 2nd 1 Oct 1906 Cdr Clement La Primaudaye, CVO, RN (*dsp* 31 May 1910), and *d* 22 Sept 1947

2 Mary Maud; nun Order Holy Child; *d* 26 March 1962

3 Edith Mary; nun Order Holy Child

4 Mary Augusta; *d* in infancy

The 7th Bt's est s,

Sir Henry Edward Paston-Bedingfeld, 8th Bt, JP; *b* 29 Aug 1860; Maj 3rd Bn Liverpool Regt; *m* 21 June 1904 Sybil (*d* 13 May 1985), est dau of Henry Alexander Claremont Lyne-Stephens (1st husb of his aunt by marriage), and *d* 18 May 1941, having had:

1 Henry Stephen Augustus; *b* 5 June 1906; *d* 27 Feb 1917

2 Anthony Raoul Ferdinand; *b* 22 Oct 1912; *d* 10 May 1914

3 Sir EDMUND GEORGE FELIX PASTON-BEDINGFELD, **9th and present Bt**

1 Margaret Mary Anastasia; *b* 24 April 1905; *d* 3 Sept 1993

2 Elizabeth Marie Gabrielle; *b* 7, *d* 9 Dec 1910

3 *Frances Mary Teresa [Mrs Philip Greathead, PO Box 14, Kalk Bay 7990, Cape Province, S Africa]; *b* 13 June 1919; *m* 1st 18 Oct 1949 Frank Douglas Playford, MIMechE (*d* 23 Jan 1956), est s of Frank Lumley Playford; *m* 2nd 1957 Maitland Gardner Maitland-Nimmo (*d* 1977), yr s of Sir Adam Nimmo, KBE; *m* 3rd 1978 Philip James Greathead (*d* 1997) and has by her 2nd husb:

(1) *Adam Peter; *b* 1960; *m* 1989 *Sandra Cavalieri and has a s and dau

(1) *Mariella; *b* 1958; *m* 1981 *Rodney Vincent Norman and has:

1a *Natasha Felicity; *b* 1982

2a *Sarah Frances; *b* 1984

Seat: Oxburgh Hall, Swaffham, Norfolk. Licence to crenellate was granted Sir Edmund Bedingfeld in 1482, by which time true castles were becoming obsolete. Indeed Oxburgh is a fortified manor rather than castle. Nonetheless the gate-tower, rising 80 feet, with ornamental brick work to each turret, is very imposing. So too is the moat surrounding the entire mansion, though this ran dry in the summer of 1996. The small porthole-like lights on the flanking turrets to the gate-tower promise more storeys than are delivered. Of the latter there are three internally. One chamber above the arch is called the King's Room, commemorating HENRY VII's stay there in 1487, the room still further above being known as the Queen's Room, named after HENRY's consort ELIZABETH OF YORK, who occupied it on the same occasion. The only other reigning monarch to visit Oxburgh has been HM THE QUEEN in 1993.

In the 17th-century Civil War Parliamentarians destroyed the eastern side of Oxburgh so extensively that it took the best part of a century to put right. The 18th-century restoration work was little in keeping with the original style of architecture, and matters were not helped in this regard by the **4th Baronet's** demolishing the old medieval great hall and kitchens on the southern side. In the 19th century the **6th Baronet** succumbed to the prevailing enthusiasm for things gothic. He undertook a building programme that attempted more closely to recreate the original, giving Pugin one of his earliest commissions and calling in the father-and-son team of John and John Chessell Buckler, though both are better known for their aquatint engravings and drawings than as architects.

The **7th Baronet** carried out further work, constructing a linking south corridor between east and west sections. It was during his time that John Dibblee Crace was employed to fashion the elaborate ceiling in the west wing, with its ornate heraldic design.

Oxburgh the house has become again the Bedingfelds' chief seat in the sense of residence, though made over to the National Trust in 1952 after being repurchased by the **8th Baronet**'s widow following disposal of the estate the year before.

PATTEN

Creation: B. (LP, UK) 1997.

THE BARON PATTEN, of Wincanton, Co Somerset (John Haggitt Charles Patten, PC (1990)) [The Rt Hon The Lord Patten PC, House of Lords, London SW1A 0PW]; *b* 17 July 1945; *educ* Wimbledon Coll and Sidney Sussex Coll Cambridge; University lecturer 1969–79, Fell Hertford Coll Oxford 1972–94, memb Oxford City Cncl 1973–76, MP (C) Oxford 1979–83, Oxford W and Abingdon 1983–97, PPS to Mins State Home Office 1980–81, Parly U-Sec: NI 1981–83, DHSS 1983–85, Min State DOE 1985–87, Home Office 1987–92, Sec State DES 1992–94; advsr Charterhouse plc 1997–; author: *The Conservative Opportunity* (ed, with Lord Blake (*qv*), 1976), *English Towns 1500–1700* (1978), *Pre-Industrial England* (1979), *The Expanding City* (ed, 1983), *The Penguin Guide to the Landscape of England and Wales* (1986), *Things to Come: the Tories in the 21st Century* (1995); *m* 1978 *Louise Alexandra Virginia, 2nd dau of John and Claire Rowe, and has a dau

Lineage: JACK PATTEN; *m* Maria Olga Sikora and has:

JOHN HAGGITT CHARLES, *cr* a **Baron**

PAUL

Arms: Azure, on each of three piles rayonny or, one issuing from the dexter and two from the sinister a pile gules. **Crest:** Issuing from a lotus or, a girl child proper, vested azure holding aloft in the dexter hand a dove, wings elevated argent. **Supporters:** On either side an Indian elephant azure, tusked unguled and grasping with the trunk a torch enflamed or. **Badge:** Five lotuses the slips inwards and surmounted by a tiger's face or striped sable. **Motto:** Truth, freedom and compassion. **Creation:** B. (LP, UK) Aug 1996.

THE BARON PAUL, of Marylebone, City of Westminster (Swraj Paul) [The Rt Hon The Lord Paul, Caparo House, 103 Baker St, London W1M 1FD]; *b* 18 Feb 1931; *educ* Punjab U and MIT; ptnr Apeejay Surrendra Gp India 1953; fndr-chm: Natural Gas Tubes Ltd UK 1966, Caparo Gp 1978–, Caparo Industries 1981–, Indo-Br Assoc 1975–; chm: Caparo Inc USA 1988–, Armstrong Equipment Ltd 1989–, CREMSA (Spain) 1989–, ENSA (Spain) 1989–; FRSA; Padma Bhushan 1983; Hon PhD American Coll Switzerland 1986; Hon DSc Hull 1992; Corporate Leadership Award MIT 1987; author: *Indira Gandhi* (1984, 2nd edn 1985); *m* 1956 *Aruna Vij and has had three sons and a dau and a son deceased

Lineage: PAYARE PAUL; *m* Mongwati — and had:

SWRAJ, *cr* a **Baron**

PAUNCEFORT-DUNCOMBE

Arms: Quarterly, 1st and 4th, per chevron engrailed gu. and arg. three talbot's heads erased counterchanged, in the centre chief a cross-crosslet gold, for distinction (for DUNCOMBE); 2nd and 3rd, gu. three lions rampant arg. (for PAUNCEFORT). **Crests:** 1 Out of a ducal coronet or a horse's hind leg sa., the shoe arg. charged (for distinction) with a cross-crosslet gold (for DUNCOMBE), 2 A lion rampant arg., ducally crowned or, charged on the shoulder with an escallop sa. (for PAUNCEFORT). **Motto:** *Non fecimus ipsi* ('We have not done it ourselves'). **Creation:** Bt. (UK) 25 May 1859.

SIR PHILIP DIGBY PAUNCEFORT-DUNCOMBE, 4TH BT, of Gt Brickhill Manor, Buckinghamshire, DL (Bucks 1971) [Sir Philip Pauncefort-Duncombe Bt DL, Gt Brickhill Manor, Milton Keynes, Bucks MK17 9BE]; *b* 18 May 1927; *s f* 1971; *educ* Stowe; ret as Maj Gren Gds 1960, Co Cmdt Bucks Army Cadet Force 1967–70, High Sheriff Bucks 1987–88, Harbinger Gentlemen at Arms 1993–97 (memb 1979–97), CStJ 1972; *m* 4 April 1951 *Rachel Moyra, CStJ (1975), yr dau of Maj Henry Gerald Aylmer (*see* AYLMER, B), and has:

1 +DAVID PHILIP HENRY [David Pauncefort-Duncombe Esq, Westfield Farm, Gt Brickhill, Bucks MK17 9BG]; *b* 21 May 1956; *educ* Gordonstoun and RAC Cirencester; *m* 1987 *Sarah Ann, er dau of Reginald T G Battrum, and has:

  (1) +Henry Digby; *b* 16 Dec 1988

  (1) *Laura Mary; *b* 1991

1 *Diana [Mrs Jeremy West, The Grange, Gt Horwood, Milton Keynes, Bucks]; *b* 2 Aug 1953; *m* 1974 *Jeremy David Trevor West (*see* GRAVES, B) and has:

  (1) *Edward; *b* 1984

  (1) *Katrina; *b* 1981

2 *Charlotte; *b* 8 Aug 1967

Lineage: GEORGE PAUNCEFORT; had:

RICHARD PAUNCEFORT; acquired the Manor of Hasfield, Glos; had:

Sir RICHARD PAUNCEFORT, of Hasfield; living 1255; *m* Isabel, dau and heir of Robert Grimbald, of Clopton, Northants, by Aumary —, and had:

Sir GRIMBALD PAUNCEFORT, of Hasfield; Keeper Forest of Dean, played a leading part in defence of Gloucester against Prince EDWARD (later EDWARD I) 1264 during the Barons' War 1264–67; *d* 1287, leaving, with another s (Grimbald, of Harfield, *d* 1314):

Sir AUMARY PAUNCEFORT, of Hasfield and Crickhowell, Breconshire; *d* 1332, leaving, with another s (Sir Grimell, *dsp*):

Sir HUGH PAUNCEFORT, of Carrn, Hasfield and Crickhowell; *m* Catherine — (*d* 1382) and *d* 1379, leaving:

Sir JOHN PAUNCEFORT, of Hasfield and Crickhowell; *d* 1369; *m* Alice, dau of Sir Andrew Herie, and had:

Sir THOMAS PAUNCEFORT, of Northall, Glos; *m* Agatha, dau of Sir Henry Owgan by his 1st w, and had:

HENRY PAUNCEFORT; *m* Katherine, dau of John Guise, and had:

JOHN PAUNCEFORT, of Hasfield; *m* 2nd Bridget, dau and at length coheir of Sir John Tate, Ld Mayor London, and *d* 31 March 1516, leaving:

RICHARD PAUNCEFORT, of Hasfield; *m* Dorothy, dau of John Ashfield, of Heythrop, Oxon, and *d* 1594, leaving:

JOHN PAUNCEFORT, of Hasfield; *m* Dorothy, dau of W Hickman, of Woodford, and had:

RICHARD PAUNCEFORT, of Hasfield (sold 1598 to Edward Banter); *m* Anne, dau and heir of Edmund Rudin, of Walhouse, Worcs, and had, with other issue:

GRIMBALD PAUNCEFORT; Receiver Duchy Lancaster; *m* Anne, dau of Samuel Tracy, of the Priory, and Clifford, Herefs, and n of Sir Paul Tracy, 1st Bt, of Stanway, Glos, and *d* Dec 1645, leaving, with other issue:

TRACY PAUNCEFORT, of Gray's Inn; *m* Mary, dau of George Billingsley, of Middx, and had, with another s (Edward, *m* 27 April 1701 Rebecca, dau and coheir of Sir Samuel Moyer, 1st and last Bt, of Pitsey Hall, Essex):

TRACY PAUNCEFORT, of Kingston-upon-Thames, Surrey; *m* Jane, dau of John Partridge, and *d* Aug 1728, leaving:

TRACY PAUNCEFORT, of Witham; *m* Anne, sis of 1st and last Baron Whitworth of Galway, and had, with another s and a dau (both *d* unm):

EDWARD PAUNCEFORT, of Witham; *m* 29 April 1737 Mary, only dau and heir of William Dodd, of Berks, and *d* June 1759, leaving:

GEORGE PAUNCEFORT, of Witham; Maj; *m* 12 Jan 1769 Henrietta, yr dau and coheir of Simon Digby, of N Luffenham (*see* DIGBY, B), and *d* 8 Oct 1786, leaving:

PHILIP DUNCOMBE PAUNCEFORT later PAUNCEFORT-DUNCOMBE (roy licence 29 July 1805), of Gt Brickhill, Bucks, and Witham; *b* 16 July 1784; High Sheriff Bucks 1824; *m* 1st 1813 Lady Alicia Margaretta Hockmore Lambart (*d* 3 April 1818), dau of 7th Earl of Cavan (*qv*), and had, with other issue:

   1 PHILIP DUNCOMBE (Sir), **1st Bt**

   1 Honora Henrietta; *m* 1 Dec 1835 Charles Benet Drake Garrard, JP (*d* 13 June 1884), of Lamer Park, Herts, and *d* 1 Aug 1892

PHILIP PAUNCEFORT-DUNCOMBE *m* 2nd 21 Aug 1823 Sophia Frances, yst dau of Sir William Foulis, Bt, of Ingleby Manor, Yorks, and *d* 15 March 1849, having by her had two daus

His only s,

   Sir Philip Duncombe Pauncefort-Duncombe, 1st Bt (UK), so *cr* 25 May 1859, JP, DL, of Gt Brickhill Manor, Bucks; *b* 8 Jan 1818; *m* 1 May 1844 Sophia Caroline (*d* 30 Dec 1889), yst dau of Col Thomas Philip Maunsell, MP, of Thorpe Malsor, Northants, and had:

   1 PHILIP HENRY (Sir), **2nd Bt**

   1 Caroline Alicia Georgiana; *d* unm 26 Nov 1903

   2 Isabel Margaretta Cockayne; *m* 3 Feb 1873 Arthur Flower (*d* 1 March 1911), bro of 1st and last Baron Battersea (*see* 1907 edn), and *d* 21 June 1936, leaving issue

   3 Evelyn Constance Venetia; *d* unm 27 April 1933

Sir PHILIP *d* 13 June 1890; his only son,

   Sir Philip Henry Pauncefort-Duncombe, 2nd Bt, DL Bucks; *b* 4 June 1849; *m* 4 Dec 1883 Flora (*m* 2nd 10 June 1908 Arthur Lucas (*d* 7 Feb 1926) and *d* 7 Sept 1927), dau of Sir Alexander Matheson, 1st Bt (*qv*), and had:

   1 EVERARD PHILIP DIGBY (Sir), **3rd Bt**

   1 Constance Flora Eleanor; *b* 5 Dec 1884; *m* 17 Nov 1914 Turner Henderson (*d* 10 Dec 1956), 2nd s of John Henderson, of Studley Priory, Oxon, and *dsp* 9 Sept 1975

Sir PHILIP *d* 26 Aug 1895; his only son,

   Sir Everard Philip Digby Pauncefort-Duncombe, 3rd Bt, DSO (1918), JP (Bucks 1914), DL (1934); *b* 6 Dec 1885; *educ* Eton and Trin Coll Cambridge (BA 1907, MA 1911); Hon Attaché Dip Serv 1908–09; Bucks: Chm Standing Jt Ctee 1938–60, CA, High Sheriff 1949; Maj TA, served WW I (despatches three times), WW II in HG (cmdg Bucks Northern Sector), Croix de Guerre; *m* 16 Nov 1922 Evelyn Elvira, dau of Frederick Anthony Denny, of Horwood House, Bucks, by Maude Marion, est dau of Sir Cuthbert Quilter, 1st Bt (*qv*), and *d* 8 Dec 1971, leaving:

   1 Sir PHILIP DIGBY PAUNCEFORT-DUNCOMBE, **4th and present Bt**

   1 *Sophia [Mrs Archibald Yuill, 32 Eresby House, Rutland Gate, London SW7 1BG]; *b* 1 July 1925; *m* 5 Oct 1957 *Archibald Evariste Yuill, JP, and has:

     (1) *William George Henry; *b* 15 Sept 1961; *m* 20 Sept 1997 *Nicola Anne Dowling, of Northwood, Middx

PEARSON

Creation: Bt. (UK) 30 Dec 1964.

SIR (FRANCIS) NICHOLAS FRASER PEARSON, 2ND BT, of Gressingham, Co Palatine of Lancaster [Sir Nicholas Pearson Bt, c/o Nat West Bank, 55 Main St, Kirkby Lonsdale, Cumbria]; *b* 28 Aug 1943; *s f* 1991; *educ* Radley; Capt 3rd Bn Rifle Bde 1961, ADC to Cdr Far East 1967–68 and C-in-C Far East 1968–69, Prospective Parly Candidate (C) Oldham W 1976–79; *m* 14 Oct 1978 *Henrietta Elizabeth, dau of Cdr Henry Pasley-Tayler, of Coton Manor, Guilsborough, Northants

Lineage: FRANCIS FENWICK PEARSON, of Storrs Hall, Arkholme, Carnforth, Lancs; *m* Louisa, dau of — Hutchinson, of Liverpool, and had:

FRANK PEARSON; Capt Loyal N Lancs Regt, slr; *m* Susan Mary (*d* Aug 1962), dau of Robert Palmer, of Kirkby Lonsdale, Westmorland, and *d* Feb 1917, leaving:

   1 FRANCIS FENWICK (Sir), **1st Bt**

   2 Richard Alexander Richmond Bagot; *b* 10 Oct 1914; *educ* Uppingham and Trin Hall Cambridge; Major RA; *m* 4 Feb 1939 *Evelyn Katharine, dau of Col William Dillworth Crewdson, CB, TD, JP, DL, of Helme Lodge, Natland, Kendal, and *d* 19–, leaving:

     (1) *Richard John Crewdson [Richard Pearson Esq, 28 Middleton Rd, Shenfield, Essex]; *b* 4 May 1940; *educ* St Edward's Sch Oxford and St Andrews (MA); ACA; *m* 30 Nov 1968 *Catriona Wallace, dau of Robert Struthers Angus, of Lancs

     (2) *Alexander William Peter Nichols; *b* 17 Feb 1948; *educ* St Edward's Sch Oxford

     (1) *Rachel Evelyn; *b* 8 Jan 1942; MAOT; *m* 16 July 1966 *Andrew Charles John Robertson, s of J A C Robertson, CB, and Mrs G M Thomson

---

1 *Violet Susan [Miss Violet Pearson, The Old Vicarage, Hornby, Lancaster LA2 8JT]; *b* 21 March 1906; lecturer Dept Educn Newcastle U, actress and writer (ret)

2 Mary Louisa; *b* 29 March 1907; *m* 29 March 1934 Philip Tennant Sinker (*d* 1 March 1986), s of Rev Francis Sinker, of Ilkey, Yorks, and *d* 9 Feb 1995, leaving:

   (1) *David Tennant [David Sinker Esq, Tare Close, Bennington, Stevenage, Herts]; *b* 12 May 1938; *educ* Winchester and Trin Coll Cambridge; *m* 6 Aug 1966 *Alice Selina Marjorie, dau of Charles Townley, and has:

     1a *Andrew Tennant; *b* 8 July 1968

   (2) *Nigel Dalcour; *b* 19 April 1946; *educ* Winchester and Jesus Coll Cambridge (Cricket Blue 1966)

   (1) Catherine Ann; *b* 19 May 1936; *m* 15 June 1961 *Christopher Ridsdill Smith, s of Geoffrey Ridsdill Smith, of Cambridge, and *d* April 1992

FRANK PEARSON's est son,

   Sir Francis Fenwick Pearson, 1st Bt (UK), so *cr* 30 Dec 1964, MBE (1945), of Gressingham, Co Palatine of Lancaster, DL (Lancs 1971); *b* 13 June 1911; *educ* Uppingham and Trin Hall Cambridge (MA 1931); 1st Gurkha Rifles 1932–36, ADC to Viceroy India 1934–36, Indian Political Serv 1936–47, Ch Min Jaipur State 1945–47, MP (C) Clitheroe 1959–70, Ld Commr Treasury 1962–63, PPS to PM 1963–64, chm Centl Lancs New Town Devpt Corp 1971; *m* 20 April 1938 *Katharine Mary [Katharine Lady Pearson, The Old Vicarage, Burton in Lonsdale, Carnforth, Lancs], dau of Rev David Denholm Fraser, of Sprouston, Kelso, Roxburghshire, and *d* 1991, leaving:

   1 Sir (FRANCIS) NICHOLAS FRASER PEARSON, **2nd and present Bt**

   1 *Susan Alison Mary [Mrs Peter Sharp, Linden Hall, Borwick, Carnforth, Lancs LA6 1JR]; *b* 12 Jan 1941; *m* 1 July 1961 *(Edward) Peter Sharp, s of Edward Salkeld Sharp, of Grey Walls, Silverdale, Lancs, and has had:

     (1) *James Edward; *b* 1967

     (1) *Harriet Nicola; *b* 1962

     (2) Joanna Katharine Rose; *b* 1963; *d* 1989

PEARSON OF RANNOCH

Creation: B. (LP, UK) 1990.

THE BARON PEARSON OF RANNOCH, of Bridge of Gaur, in the District of Perth and Kinross (Malcolm Everard MacLaren Pearson) [The Rt Hon The Lord Pearson of Rannoch, 52 Minories, London EC3; Rannock Barracks, Rannoch Station, Perthshire PH17 2QE]; *b* 20 July 1942; *educ* Eton; fndr: Pearson Webb Springbett (PWS) Gp 1964 and Rannoch Tst 1984; chm: Rannoch Protection Gp 1979– and PWS Holdings plc 1988–; dir Highland Venison Ltd 1984–89; memb: CNAA 1983–93 (Hon Treas 1986–1993), Ho Lds Select Ctee EC 1992–, Sub Ctee C Environment and Social Affrs 1992–; Hon Pres Nat Soc for Mentally Handicapped People in Residential Care 1994–; *m* 1st 1965 (*divorce* 1970) Francesca, dau of Giuseppe Frua de Angeli, and has:

   1 *Silvia Maria Francesca; *b* 1966; *m* 1995 *Piers Le Marchant and has issue (*see* LE MARCHANT, Bt)

BARON PEARSON OF RANNOCH *m* 2nd 1977 (*divorce* 1996) Hon (Francesca) Mary Charteris, only dau of Baron Charteris of Amisfield (*qv*), and has:

   2 *Marina MacLaren; *b* 1980

   3 *Zara Alexandra Mary; *b* 1984

Lineage: JOHN MacLAREN PEARSON; Col; had:

MALCOLM EVERARD MacLAREN, *cr* a **Baron**

PEASE of Hummersknott

Arms: Per fess az. and gu. a fess nebuly erm. between two lambs passant in chief arg. and in base upon a mount ppr. a dove rising arg., holding in the beak a pea-stalk, the blossom and pods also ppr. **Crest:** Upon the capital of an Ionic column a dove rising, holding in the beak a pea-stalk as in the arms, all ppr. **Motto:** *Pax et spes* ('Peace and hope'). **Creation:** Bt. (UK) 25 June 1920.

SIR RICHARD THORN PEASE, 3RD BT, of Hummersknott, Borough of Darlington, Co Durham, DL (Northumberland 1990) [Sir Richard Pease Bt DL, Hindley House, Stocksfield-on-Tyne, Northumberland NE43 7SA]; *b* 20 May 1922; *s f* 1969; *educ* Eton; late Capt 60th Rifles, v-chm Barclays Bank 1974–, dir Barclays Insur Servs, chm Yorks Bank; *m* 9 March 1956 *Anne, only dau of Lt-Col Reginald Francis Heyworth, Roy Dragoons, and formerly w of F/Lt David Henry Lewis Wigan, RAFVR, and has:

1 +RICHARD PETER; *b* 4 Sept 1958
1 *Carolyn Thorn; *b* 8 June 1957; *m* 1981 *John Silvester Varley, only s of Philip Varley, of Garden House, Barford Hill, Warwicks, and has:
  (1) *George John; *b* 1994
  (1) *Emma Thorn Anne; *b* 1989
2 *Nichola; *b* 3 April 1961; *m* 1991 *R Crispin Odey, only s of Richard Odey, of The Kennels, Hotham, Yorks, and has:
  (1) *Felix Crispin; *b* 1994
  (1) *Sophia Anne; *b* 1997

Lineage: ARTHUR PEASE (*see* PEASE, Bt, of Hutton Lowcross); *b* 12 Sept 1837; MP Whitby 1880–85 and Darlington 1895–98, Mayor Darlington 1873–74; *m* 14 April 1864 Mary Lecky (*d* 14 Dec 1915), dau of Ebenezer Pike, of Besborough, Co Cork, and had:

1 ARTHUR FRANCIS, **1st Bt**
2 HERBERT PIKE PEASE, 1st BARON DARYNGTON, of Witley, Surrey (UK), so *cr* 12 Feb 1923, PC (1917), JP (N R Yorks and Surrey) DL (N R Yorks); *b* 7 May 1866; *educ* Brighton Coll and Trin Hall Cambridge; MP Darlington 1898–Jan 1910 and Dec 1910–23, Assist PMG 1915–22, Pres Church Army, Chm Ho Laity Nat Church Assembly, Ecclesiastical Commr 1923 on, Church Estates Commr 1926; *m* 5 June 1894 Alice Mortimer (*d* 24 Dec 1948), 2nd dau of Very Rev Herbert Mortimer Luckock, Dean Lichfield, and *d* 10 May 1949, having had:
  (1) Ronald Herbert Pike; *b* 3 Oct 1896; Lt Coldstream Gds; *ka* 15 Sept 1916
  (2) JOCELYN ARTHUR PIKE, 2nd and last BARON DARYNGTON; *b* 30 May 1907; *educ* Eton and Trin Coll Cambridge (BA 1928, MA 1931); barrister Inner Temple 1932, assist master Doon House and Stone House prep Schs Thanet; *d* unm 1994, when the Barony expired
  (1) Margaret Alice; *d* unm 20 March 1975 aged 79
  (2) Ruth Evelyn; *m* 30 June 1925 Lt-Cdr Norman Ernest Archer, CMG, OBE, RN, s of Walter Edward Archer, CB, of Chelsea, and had:
    1a *Ronald Walter; *b* 12 Dec 1929; *m* 14 Nov 1959 *Catherine Mary, est dau of Marcus R C Overton, and has:
      1b *James Norman; *b* 10 Aug 1960
      2b *Michael Marcus; *b* 1962
      3b *Edward John Harold; *b* 1964
      1b *Mary Ruth Elizabeth; *b* 27 Feb 1966
    1a *Esther Joy; *b* 24 May 1926; *m* 1 April 1952 *Robert Blackburn and has:
      1b *Kari Ruth; *b* 30 March 1954
      2b *Lucy Patricia; *b* 24 Feb 1956
  (3) Phyllis Helen; *b* 12 Sept 1904; *educ* Newnham Coll Cambridge (BA 1926) and LSE; AMIMSW, Head Almoner St Stephen's Hosp 1942–65
3 Claud Edward, JP N R Yorks; *b* 27 Nov 1874; *educ* Harrow and Trin Coll Cambridge (BA 1896); Army Lt, dir Barclays Bank; *m* 12 Dec 1901 Lucy Victoria, OBE (1918) (*d* 3 Feb 1953), 7th dau of William Clayton Browne-Clayton, JP, DL, of Browne's Hill, Co Carlow, and *d* 22 March 1952, leaving:

  (1) *Diana Vere; *b* 4 Oct 1902
  (2) *Lucy Margaret; *m* 26 July 1939 Maj Claud Cecil O'Hagan, MC, KAR (*ka* 22 July 1943), er s of Capt Claud O'Hagan, of Kenya
  (3) *Olive Mary Caroline; *m* 6 Feb 1929 William Milne Ross-Skinner, s of Sir Harry Ross-Skinner, and has:
    1a *Jean Olive; *b* 14 Nov 1929; *m* 23 March 1963, as his 2nd w, *Baron Gilbert (*qv*)
    2a *Shelagh Milne; *b* 16 July 1933; *m* 20 Nov 1963 *Arthur Cecil Levita, s of Lt-Col Sir Cecil Bingham Levita, KCVO, CBE, JP, DL
  (4) *Julia Victoria; *m* 15 Sept 1934 Maj Peter Stapleton Buxton and has issue (*see* BUXTON, Bt)
1 Alice Mary, *d* unm 1944
2 Rosa Elizabeth; *d* unm
3 Winifred Pike, JP; *m* 25 April 1903 Roger William Bulwer Jenyns (*d* 10 April 1936), of Bottisham Hall, Cambs, and *d* 17 Sept 1957, leaving issue
4 Evelyn Ada, OBE (1918); *d* unm 3 May 1950

ARTHUR PEASE *d* 27 Aug 1898; his est s,
  Sir Arthur Francis Pease, 1st Bt (UK), so *cr* 25 June 1920, JP (Co Durham), DL; *b* 11 March 1866; *educ* Trin Coll Cambridge (MA); CA Co Durham, High Sheriff 1920, 2nd Civil Ld Admlty 1918–19; *m* 1 Oct 1889 Laura Matilda Ethelwyn (*d* 4 Jan 1936), dau of Charles Peter Alix, DL, JP, of Swaffham Prior House, Cambs, and had:

1 RICHARD ARTHUR (Sir), **2nd Bt**
1 Mary Ethelwyn; *b* 18 Feb 1892; *d* 14 Jan 1981
2 Dorothy Laura; *b* 21 April 1893; *m* 6 Dec 1927 Lt-Col John Harold Mousley, DSO, TD, RE (*d* 28 Jan 1959), son of James Alfred Mousley, of Leamington, and *d* 3 Sept 1971, leaving:
  (1) *James Arthur [James Mousley Esq, Saunder Brow, 523 Newchurch Rd, Newchurch-in-Rossendale, Lancs BB4 9HH]; *b* 20 Feb 1931; *educ* Pembroke Coll Cambridge (BA); *m* 21 Oct 1961 *Gro Rieve, only dau of Leif Rieve Kristiansen, of Oslo, and has:
    1a *John Rieve; *b* 5 Aug 1964
    1a *Kristin Ethelwyn; *b* 18 Oct 1962
    2a *Karl Jane; *b* 20 Sept 1966
  (1) *Laura Frances [Miss Laura Mousley, The Rookery, Middleton Tyas, Richmond, Yorks]; *b* 18 March 1929
  (2) *Ethelwyn Ada [Mrs Christopher Dixon, Forge Cottage, Hurst Green, Surrey]; *b* 18 Jan 1933; *m* 8 Oct 1955 *Christopher John Arnold Dixon, s of Hubert John Dixon, MC, and has:
    1a *Anthony John; *b* 16 May 1958
    2a *Timothy James; *b* 28 Jan 1962
    3a *Michael Christopher; *b* 10 Nov 1963
    1a *Phyllida Mary; *b* 2 July 1960
3 Elizabeth Frances; *b* 2 Aug 1894; *m* 25 Nov 1919 Capt Sir Frank O'Brien Wilson, CMG, DSO, RN (*d* 7 April 1962), 4th s of Col John Gerald Wilson, CB, JP, DL, of Cliffe Hall, Yorks, and *d* 2 Sept 1974, leaving:
  (1) *Richard O'Brien; *b* 28 April 1922; Lt RN WW II; *m* 18 Sept 1947 *Anne Florence, yr dau of Maj John Leslie Rowan-Thomson, and has:
    1a *Jeremy James O'Brien; *b* 8 Oct 1949
    2a *Patrick Murrough; *b* 17 March 1951
    3a *Michael Rowan; *b* 18 Aug 1952
    4a *Graeme Richard; *b* 5 Jan 1958
  (2) *Arthur Denis; *b* 1 Sept 1924; Lt RN WW II; *m* 1st 26 June 1946 (*divorce* 1967) Claire, dau of Langton Highton, of Cumberland, and had:
    1a *Christopher Denis Langton; *b* 9 Aug 1949
    1a *Hilary Frances; *b* 4 Aug 1947
  (2) (cont.) Arthur Wilson *m* 2nd 17 Feb 1968 (*divorce* 1982) Mrs Jillian Hoy Brauer, dau of George Thomas Skinner, of Kenya; *m* 3rd 2 Nov 1989 *Judy Maxted and *d* 10 June 1990
  (1) *Elizabeth Theresa [Mrs George Churcher, Primrose Cottage, 4 Humphries Rd, Frankson, Victoria 3199, Australia]; *b* 30 Oct 1920; *m* 12 Aug 1959 Lt-Col George Maurice Churcher, MC, RA (*d* 28 Dec 1979), er s of George Churcher, of Lindfield, Sussex, and has:
    1a *Catherine Elizabeth; *b* 6 April 1962
  (2) *Dorothy Vivien; *b* 22 Jan 1928

Sir ARTHUR *d* 23 Nov 1927; his only son,
  Sir Richard Arthur Pease, 2nd Bt, JP (N R Yorks 1920), DL (1923); *b* 18 Nov 1890; *educ* Eton and Trin Coll Cambridge; Capt Northumberland Hus Yeo WW I; *m* 1st 17 Jan 1917 Jeannette Thorn (*d* 3 Nov 1957), yr dau of Gustave Edward Kissel, of New York, USA, and had:

1 Arthur Peter; *b* 15 Feb 1918; *educ* Eton; F/O RAFVR WW II; *ka* 15 Sept 1940
2 Sir RICHARD THORN PEASE, **3rd and present Bt**
3 +Derrick Alix 'Sandy'; *b* 4 March 1927; *educ* Eton and Trin Coll Cambridge; High Sheriff Gtr London 1972, Lt RA 1948–49, Chm Investment Management Ctee Centl Bd Finance C of E 1974 and Nat Mutual Life Assur Soc 1975; *m* 24 July 1951 *Hon Rosemary Portman, yr dau of 5th Viscount Portman (*qv*), and *d* 28 May 1998, leaving:
  (1) +Jonathan Edward; *b* 8 June 1952; *educ* Eton; *m* 1979 *Mary, dau of Francis Moore Dutton, of Tushingham Hall, Whitchurch, Salop, and has:
    1a *Catherine Annie; *b* 1982
    2a *Victoria Margaret; *b* 1983
    3a *Alice Rosie; *b* 1991
  (2) +Christopher Berkeley; *b* 27 April 1958; *m* 1989 *Mariana, er dau of Robert Steuart Fothringham of Pourie-Fothringham and Murthly (*see* GAINSBOROUGH, E), and has:
    1a +Edward Robert; *b* 1991
    1a *Dorothea Elizabeth; *b* 1992
    2a *Sybilla Mary; *b* 1994
  (3) +Arthur David; *b* 3 March 1961; *m* 1994 *Lucilla K H, dau of T H Regis, of Wheathampstead, Herts

(1) *Rosalind Jeannette; b 10 Oct 1954; m 1st 22 July 1974 (divorce), as his 1st w, Joss Hanbury, er s of Col James Robert Hanbury, of Burley-on-the-Hill, Rutland (see BIRKIN, Bt), and has:

    1a *James Robert; b 7 July 1979

    2a *William Edward; b 1983

    1a *Susanna Rosemary; b 1977

(1) (cont.) Mrs Rosalind Hanbury m 2nd 22 Dec 1997 *Rodney Portman (see PORTMAN, V)

1 *Aline Thorn; b 27 Jan 1919; m 1st 1 May 1940 P/O Patrick Claude Hannay AAF, (ka 24 May 1940), er s of Claude Patrick Hannay, of Villa Solidor, Dinard; m 2nd 12 Feb 1941 (divorce 1954) 3rd Earl of Inchcape (qv) and has issue; m 3rd 4 June 1955 (divorce 1968) Thomas Chambers Windsor Roe, OBE (d 1988), s of John Valentine Roe, and by him has:

    (1) *Patrick Rupert Windsor; b 29 Feb 1960

    (1) *Oriel Melanie Thorn; b 10 July 1956

Sir Richard m 2nd 19 April 1961 Laura Margaret (d 19 Dec 1983), widow of Lt-Col Arnold Ramsay Keppel, KOYLI (see ALBEMARLE, E), and dau of Hughes Martin, formerly of Tullaghreine, Co Cork, and d 13 Nov 1969

PEASE of Hutton Lowcross

Arms: Per fess az. and gu. a fess nebuly erm. between two lambs passant in chief arg. and in base upon a mount ppr. a dove rising arg., holding in the beak a pea-stalk, the blossom and pods also ppr. **Crest:** Upon the capital of an Ionic column a dove rising, holding in the beak a pea-stalk, as in the arms, all ppr. **Motto:** *Pax et spes* ('Peace and hope'). **Creation:** Bt. (UK) 18 May 1882.

SIR (ALFRED) VINCENT PEASE, 4TH BT, of Hutton Lowcross and Pinchinthorpe, Co York [Sir Vincent Pease Bt, 149 Aldenham Rd, Guisborough, Cleveland TS14 8LB]; b 2 April 1926; s half-brother 1963; educ Bootham Sch York and Durham Sch of Ag Houghall

Lineage: JOSEPH PEASE, of Shafton, W R Yorks; b 1665; m 1705 Ann Coldwell, heiress in her issue of her brothers William and Thomas, and d 1719, leaving a 2nd s:

EDWARD PEASE, of Darlington, Co Durham; bapt 26 Sept 1711; m 2 Oct 1735 Elizabeth (d 22 Feb 1783), dau and coheir of Michael Coates, of Langleyford, Co Durham, and d 14 Nov 1785, leaving an est s:

JOSEPH PEASE, of Darlington; b 25 March 1737; m 13 Oct 1763 Mary (d 17 July 1821), dau of Richard Richardson, of Hull, and d 3 April 1808, leaving, with a yr s (Joseph, ancestor of the PEASEs of Pendower and Barons Wardington, qv) and a dau (Elizabeth, m 18 Oct 1798 John Hustler (dsp 18 Jan 1842), of Bradford):

EDWARD PEASE, of Darlington; b 31 May 1767; m 3 Nov 1796 Rachel (d 18 Oct 1833), dau of John Whitwell, and had, with other issue (dsp):

1 John, of Darlington; b 30 Sept 1797; m 26 Nov 1823 Sophia (d 6 Aug 1870), dau of Joseph Jowitt, and d 29 July 1868, leaving two daus

2 JOSEPH

3 Henry, of Pierremont and Stanhope Castle, Co Durham; b 4 May 1807; MP S Durham 1857–65; m 1st 25 Feb 1835 Anna (d 27 Oct 1839), dau of Richard Fell, of Belmont, Uxbridge, and had issue; m 2nd 19 Jan 1859 Mary (d 25 Sept 1909), dau of Samuel Lloyd, of Wednesbury, and d 30 May 1881, having had issue

1 Elizabeth; m 7 May 1829 Francis Gibson (d 19 Dec 1858), of Saffron Walden, and d 31 Jan 1866, leaving issue

EDWARD PEASE d 31 July 1858; his 2nd son,

JOSEPH PEASE, of Southend, Darlington, Cliffe House, Marske-by-the-Sea, Yorks; b 22 June 1799; MP S Durham 1832–41 (first Quaker MP); m 20 March 1826 Emma (d 11 April 1860), yst dau and coheir of Joseph Gurney, of Lakenham Grove, Norwich, and d 2 Feb 1872, leaving, with other issue:

1 JOSEPH WHITWELL (Sir), **1st Bt**

2 Edward; b 24 June 1834; m 26 Feb 1862 Sarah (d 14 June 1877), dau of Charles Sturge, of Bewdley, Worcs, and d 13 June 1880, leaving:

(1) Beatrice Mary; m 17 Feb 1885 6th Earl of Portsmouth (qv) and d 13 Dec 1935

3 Arthur; b 1837; d 1898, leaving issue (see PEASE, Bt, of Hummersknott)

4 Gurney; b 28 Feb 1839; m 22 April 1863 Katherine (d 15 April 1915), dau of John Jowitt Wilson, of Kendal, and d 10 June 1872, leaving issue

5 Charles; b 7 April 1843; m 27 Sept 1871 Sarah Elizabeth (d 19 June 1924), dau of Henry Bewley, of Willow Park, Co Dublin, and d 9 July 1873, having had a s (d young)

1 Rachel; b 15 June 1831; m 1st 6 March 1851 Charles Albert Leatham (d 11 March 1858), of Gunnergate Hall, Cleveland, and had issue; m 2nd 21 Sept 1875 William Fowler (d 16 Sept 1905), MP Cambridge, and d 1912

2 Elizabeth Lucy; b 21 Jan 1833; m 30 July 1857 John Fowler (d 4 Dec 1864), of Ackworth, Yorks, and d 2 Sept 1881, leaving issue

The est son,

Sir Joseph Whitwell Pease, 1st Bt (UK), so cr 18 May 1882, of Hutton Lowcross, and Pinchinthorpe, Yorks, JP, DL Co Durham and N R Yorks; b 23 June 1828; MP S Durham 1865–85 and Barnard Castle 1885–1903; m 23 Aug 1845 Mary (d 3 Aug 1892), dau of Alfred Fox, of Falmouth, and had:

1 ALFRED EDWARD (Sir), **2nd Bt**

2 JOSEPH ALBERT PEASE, cr BARON GAINFORD (qv)

1 Emma Josephine; m 17 Nov 1880 Vincent Walde Calmady Calmady-Hamlyn JP, (d 2 Sept 1897), of Leawood and Paschoe, Devon, and d 23 June 1888, leaving issue

2 Sarah Charlotte; m 17 Feb 1897 Howard Hodgkin (d 11 April 1932), barrister, a Pncpl Clerk Charity Commn, and d 18 April 1929, leaving issue

3 Maud Mary, JP Beds; d unm 28 Feb 1947

4 Helen Blanche, JP Co Durham; m 15 Jan 1890 her cousin Edward Lloyd Pease (d 15 March 1934), of Hurworth Moor, Co Durham, and d 16 March 1951, leaving issue

5 Lucy Ethel, OBE (1918); m 3 Dec 1890 Gerald Buxton and d 24 July 1940, having had issue (see BUXTON, Bt)

6 Agnes Claudia Fox; m 29 Nov 1898 Alfred Wilson (d 25 April 1924), of Woodcroft, Edgbaston, s of John Edward Wilson, of Wyddrington, Edgbaston, and d 24 Jan 1955, leaving issue

Sir JOSEPH d 23 June 1903; his er son,

Sir Alfred Edward Pease, 2nd Bt, JP (N R Yorks), DL (London and N R Yorks); b 29 June 1857; educ Trin Coll Cambridge; Lt City London, MP York 1885–92 and Cleveland 1897–1902, RM Transvaal 1903–05, Army Remount Service 1914–19; m 1st 10 Feb 1880 Helen Ann (d 4 Nov 1910), sis and coheir of Sir Thomas Fowler, 2nd and last Bt, of Gastard House (see 1902 edn), and had:

1 **Sir Edward Pease 3rd Bt**; b 15 Dec 1880; educ Winchester and Trin Coll Cambridge; Sudan Political Service 1903–11, WW I with King Edward's Horse 1915 (severely wounded), Political Service Iraq 1917, E Lancs Regt 1918, HG WW II; m 29 Nov 1919 Ida Mary, yst dau of James Lawrance, of Cambridge, and dsp 14 Jan 1963

2 Christopher York; b 24 June 1886; Capt 21st Yorks Hus attd W Yorks Regt WW I; m 22 Dec 1910 Margaret Philippa (d 10 June 1959), yst dau of Walter Johnson, JP, of Arncliffe Hall, Northallerton (see BELL, Bt), and was ka 9 May 1918, leaving:

(1) Ingram Edward; b 28 Feb 1914; educ Magdalen Coll Oxford (BA); P/O RAFVR; k in a flying accident 18 Feb 1939

(1) *Rachel Hebe Philippa [Mrs Richard Smith, Derwent Waters Residential Club, Cadbury Rd, Claremont, Tasmania 7011, Australia]; b 19 Dec 1911; served QARANS 1939–40; m 3 Aug 1940 *Lt-Cdr Richard Selby Smith, RNVR, MA Oxon, Prof Emeritus Educn Tasmania U, 2nd s of Selby Smith, of Hall Place, Barming, Maidstone, and has:

    1a *Christopher Selby [Prof Christopher Smith, 50 Rotherwood St, Richmond, Victoria 3121, Australia]; b 1942; DPhil Oxon, Prof Monash U; m 1967 *Joy Miriam, dau of Thomas McGeehan, of Myrtleford, Victoria, Australia, and has:

        1b *David Richard Selby; b 1969

        2b *Hugh Thomas Selby; b 1975

    2a *Peter Selby [Peter Smith Esq, 1 Hill St, Blackburn, Victoria 3101, Australia]; b 1948; BCE; m 1971 *—, dau of John Holroyd, of Rosanna, Victoria, and has:

        1b *Andrew Selby; b 1976

        1b *Anne Jane; b 1974

        2b *Robyn Clare; b 1980

1 Lavender Mary; b 24 June 1889; m 5 Oct 1910 Capt Walter Sandfield Medlicott, 21st Northumberland Hus, er surv s of Henry Edmonstone Medlicott, of Sandfield, Potterne, Wilts, and had issue

Sir Alfred m 2nd 28 Sept 1912 Laure Marianne (d 25 Jan 1922), dau of Louis Philippe Sugnet de Montmagny by Lina Henriette, née Jomini; m 3rd 1 Aug 1922 Emily Elizabeth (d 1979), JP N R Yorks, adopted dau of James Smith, of Thornaby in Cleveland, Yorks, and d 27 April 1939, having by her had:

3 Sir ALFRED VINCENT PEASE, **4th and present Bt**

4 +JOSEPH GURNEY [Joseph Pease Esq, Beckses Barn, nr Penruddock, Cumbria CA11 0RX]; b 16 Nov 1927; heir presumptive; educ Bootham Sch York; memb Guisborough UDC 1950–53, Pres NW Regnl Lib Party 1970 and 1971; m 24 June 1953 *Shelagh Munro, dau of Cyril Gounod Bulman, of Great Langdale, Ambleside, Westmorland, and has:

    (1) +Charles Edward Gurney; b 17 July 1955; educ Heversham Sch and Bootham Sch York

    (2) *Jane Elizabeth Gurney; b 15 June 1957; m 1990 *Colin Charles Bright, er s of William C J Bright, of Southsea, Hants, and has issue

2 *Anne Phillida [Mrs Anne Chetwynd-Stapylton, 110 Western Rd, Lewes, E Sussex BN7 1RR]; b 4 May 1923; PO WRNS WW II; m 20 Feb 1946 Maj Edward Mark Chetwynd-Stapylton (see CHETWYND, V) and has issue

3 Judith; b 16 Jan, d 11 April 1925

PEEK

2 Violet Eveline, CBE (1947); b 6 Dec 1886; WW I in Egypt with VAD, CC 1934, pres Berks Branch BRCS 1946–61, CA 1949–61 Berks, Czech Meritorious Service Medal 1st Cl 1945, Order of Mercy and bar; m 10 March 1915 Capt Sir Henry Benyon, 1st and last Bt (d 15 June 1959), and d 3 Feb 1964
3 Gwendolen; b 4 Nov 1890; m 28 Sept 1918 Adml Sir Frederick Hew George Dalrymple-Hamilton, KCB, and d 8 Nov 1974, leaving issue (see STAIR, E)
4 Kathleen Marian, JP (Devon 1951); b 17 April 1900; d unm 14 Dec 1952

PEEL

Arms: Azure an estoile argent, in chief three crescents of the last. **Crest:** Two hazel nuts slipped proper. **Motto:** *Le maitre vient* ('The Master comes'). **Creation:** Bt. (UK) 13 May 1874.

SIR WILLIAM GRENVILLE PEEK, 5TH BT, of Rousdon, Devon, DL (Devon 1966) [Sir William Peek Bt DL, Weekemoor, Loddiswell, Devon TQ7 4DY]; b 15 Dec 1919; s cousin 1996; educ Eton; Capt 9th Lancers WW II (despatches); m 8 July 1950 *Lucy Jane, yst dau of Maj Edward Dorrien Smith, DSO, KSLI, of Weir Point, Restronguet, Falmouth, and has:

  1 +RICHARD GRENVILLE; b 3 Feb 1955; educ Eton; late 2nd Lt 9th/12th Lancers

  1 *Jane Elizabeth; b 27 Nov 1952; m 20 July 1974 *James Robertson, er s of Prof N F Robertson, of Boghall Farm, Biggar Rd, Edinburgh
  2 *Mary Susannah; b 19 May 1957
  3 *Katharine Julia; b 20 July 1960

Lineage: JAMES PEEK, of Watcombe, Torquay, and London (s of John Peek, of Loddiswell, Devon); b 8 June 1800; m 1st 19 Feb 1824 Elizabeth (d 4 Oct 1867), only dau of James Masters, of London, and had, with a dau (d unm):

1 HENRY WILLIAM (Sir), **1st Bt**
2 Edward (Rev); b 26 June 1841; MA; d 31 Dec 1898
1 Julia; b 27 Feb 1831; m 24 April 1856 Thomas Stone, of Blackheath, and d 12 Aug 1861
2 Hannah; b 22 Feb 1835; m 1866 Thomas Ness (d 1878), of Daracombe, Newton Abbot, and dsp 1896

JAMES PEEK m 2nd 13 Oct 1868 Jane (dsp 1 April 1903), dau of Sampson Trehane, of Exeter, and d 23 Jan 1879

His er son,

Sir Henry William Peek, 1st Bt (UK), so cr 13 May 1874, DL Devon; b 26 Feb 1825; MP Mid-Surrey 1808–84; m 20 July 1848 Margaret Maria (d 2 May 1884), 2nd dau of William Edgar, of Eagle House, Clapham Common, and d 26 Aug 1898, leaving an only s:

Sir Cuthbert Edgar Peek, 2nd Bt, JP Devon, Middx and London; b 30 Jan 1855; educ Pembroke Coll Cambridge (MA); FSA, Lt City London; m 3 Jan 1884 Hon Augusta Louisa (d 3 Nov 1934), dau of 8th Viscount Midleton (qv), and d 6 July 1901, having had, with a dau (d an infant):

1 **Sir Wilfrid Peek, 3rd Bt**, DSO, JP Devon; b 9 Oct 1884; High Sheriff Devon 1912, Maj Royal 1st Devon Yeo, WW I in Mesopotamia on Staff 1916–19 (despatches); m 7 May 1913 Edwine Warner (d 5 Sept 1959), yr dau of William Henry Thornburgh, of St Louis, USA, and d 12 Oct 1927, leaving:

  (1) **Sir Francis Henry Grenville Peek, 4th Bt**; b 16 Sept 1915; educ Eton and Trin Coll Cambridge; ADC to Govr of Bahamas 1938–39, Lt Irish Gds WW II (despatches); m 1st 16 Jan 1942 (divorce 1949) Ruby Joy Ann (m 3rd 1951 1st Baron Rootes (qv) and d 28 Dec 1968), widow of Sir Charles Thomas Hewitt Mappin, 4th Bt (see 1970 edn), and only dau of Capt Gordon Duff, RGA; m 2nd 24 Nov 1949 (divorce 1967) Marilyn (m 2nd 1967 Peter Quennell), dau of Dr Norman Kerr, of Eleuthera, Bahamas, and by her had:

    1a Charles Edward Francis; b 5 May 1956; d 20 Nov 1976

  (1) (cont.) **Sir Francis** m 3rd 2 Oct 1967 *Caroline Anne [Caroline Lady Peek], Villa du Parc, 8 Avenue Jean de Noailles, Cannes 06400, France], formerly w of John Wolfgang von Kotze and er dau of Sir Robert Lucien Morrison Kirkwood, KCMG, of Haven House, Sandwich, Kent, and Craigton, Irishtown, Jamaica, and d 19 June 1996

  (2) Roger Grenville; b 6 Sept 1888; Capt 9th Lancers, ADC to GOC-in-C GB, served WW I (POW); m 16 Jan 1919 Hon Joan Penelope Sclater-Booth (d 23 Feb 1976), dau of 2nd Baron Basing (qv), and was k whilst on duty in Ireland 23 March 1921, leaving:

    (1) Sir WILLIAM GRENVILLE PEEK, **5th and present Bt**

    (2) Roger John; b 17 Jan 1921; educ Eton; Lt Roy Dragoons WW II; ka Libya June 1942

1 Margaret; b 18 Dec 1885; m 1 Oct 1908 Sir Philip Francis Cunningham Williams, 2nd Bt (d 6 May 1958), of Bridehead, Dorset (qv), and d 5 Sept 1948, leaving issue

Arms: Argent three sheaves of as many arrows proper, two and one banded gules, on a chief azure a bee volant or, a martlet gules for cadency. **Crest:** A demi-lion rampant argent, gorged with a collar azure charged with three bezants, holding between the paws a shuttle or. **Supporters:** Dexter, a lion regardant argent; sinister, a gryphon regardant or, each gorged with a chain of the last, pendant therefrom an escutcheon azure, charged with a representation of the Speaker's mace erect, also or. **Motto:** *Industria* ('Industry'). **Creations:** Bt. (GB) 29 Nov 1800, V. (UK) 9 May 1895 (Peel of Sandy), V. and E. (UK) 10 July 1929.

THE 3RD EARL PEEL, Viscount Clanfield, of Clanfield, Co Hampshire, **Viscount Peel of Sandy**, Co Bedford, and a **Baronet** (Sir William (Willie) James Robert Peel, Bt) [The Rt Hon The Earl Peel, Kilgram Grange, Jervaulx, N Yorks HG4 4PQ]; b 3 Oct 1947; s f 1969; educ Ampleforth, Tours U and RAC Cirencester; Chm Game Conservancy Tst 1994– (V-Chm 1990–94), memb: Nature Conservancy Cncl England 1991–96 and Cncl Duchy Cornwall 1993– , Ld Warden Stannaries 1994– ; m 1st 28 March 1973 (divorce 1987) Veronica Naomi, dau of Maj (John) Alastair Livingston Timpson, MC (see HOUSTOUN-BOSWALL, Bt), and has:

  1 +ASHTON ROBERT GERARD, *Viscount Clanfield*; b 16 Sept 1976

  1 *Iona Joy Julia; b 18 Sept 1978

The 3rd EARL m 2nd 1989 *Hon Mrs Charlotte Clementine Hambro (see HAMBRO, B), yr dau of Baron Soames (LP; see MARLBOROUGH, D), and by her has:

  2 *Antonia Mary Catherine; b 1991

Lineage: ROBERT PEELE, originally of E Marton-in-Craven; moved to Hole House, Blackburn, Lancs, and d 1608, leaving, with other issue:

WILLIAM PEELE, of Hole House; had:

WILLIAM PEELE, of Hole House; m 1619 Margaret Livesey and d 9 March 1651, leaving:

ROBERT PEELE, of Hole House; had, with a yr s (Rev Nicholas, Curate Blackburn):

ROBERT PEELE, of Peele Fold, Oswaldtwistle, nr Blackburn; m 1681 Anne, dau of James Warde, of Oswaldtwistle, and d 1733, leaving, with a yr s (Nicholas, of Lower Darwen, Lancs; m Elizabeth Shorrock) and four daus:

WILLIAM PEELE, of Peele Fold; b 1682; m 9 Aug 1712 Jane, dau of Lawrence Walmesley, of Upper Darwent, Lancs, and d 1755, having had, with three other sons and six daus:

ROBERT PEEL, of Burton-on-Trent and Ardwick, nr Manchester; b 1723; m 28 Aug 1744 Elizabeth (d March 1796), dau of Edmund Haworth, of Walmesley Fold, Lower Darwen, and d 12 Sept 1795, having had, with two er sons:

Sir Robert Peel, 1st Bt (UK); so cr 29 Nov 1800; b 25 April 1750; Govr Christ's Hosp, V-Pres Lit Fund, MP Tamworth 1790–1818; m 1st 8 July 1783 Ellen, dau of William Yates, of Spring Side, nr Bury, and had:

1 **Sir Robert Peel, 2nd Bt**; b 5 Feb 1788; educ Harrow and Ch Ch Oxford; MP (Tory, later C) Oxford U and Tamworth, Parly U-Sec Colonies 1810, Ch Sec Ireland 1812, Home Sec 1822 and 1828, PM 1834 and 1841–46; m 8 June 1820 Julia (d 27 Oct 1859), yst dau of Gen Sir John Floyd, 1st Bt (qv), and d 2 July 1850 following a fall from his horse, having had:

  (1) **Sir Robert Peel, 3rd Bt**, GCB, PC; b 4 May 1822; MP Tamworth 1850–80, Huntingdon 1884–85 and Blackburn 1885–86, Sec Legn and Chargé d'Affaires Berne 1846–50, a Ld Admlty 1855–57, Attaché 1856 Special Embassy Russia coronation Czar, Ch Sec Ireland 1861–65; m 17 Jan 1856 Lady Emily

Hay (*d* 4 April 1924), dau of 8th Marquess of Tweeddale (*qv*), and *d* 9 May 1895, leaving:

  1a **Sir Robert Peel, 4th Bt**; *b* 12 April 1867; *educ* Harrow and Balliol Coll Oxford; Lt Staffs Yeo Cav 1906–09; *m* 1897 Mercedes, dau of Baron de Graffenried, of Thun, Switzerland, and *d* 12 Feb 1925, leaving:

    1b **Sir Robert Peel, 5th Bt**; *b* 8 April 1898; *m* 5 Jan 1920 Beatrice Gladys, the actress Bea Lillie (*d* 1989 aged 94), dau of John Lillie, of Hillsborough, Co Down, and *d* 6 April 1934, leaving:

      1c **Sir Robert Peel, 6th Bt**; *b* 17 Dec 1920; Ordinary Seaman RN WW II; *ka* in HMS *Tenedos* (bombed in Colombo Harbour) 5 April 1942

  1a Victoria Alexandrina Julia (HM QUEEN VICTORIA stood sponsor); *m* 10 Nov 1887 Daniel F P Barton (*dsp* April 1907) and *d* 16 Dec 1935

  2a Evelyn Emily; *m* 31 Oct 1901 Sir (James William) Ronald Macleay, GCMG, only s of Col A C Macleay, CB (*d* 5 March 1943), and *d* 20 Aug 1960, leaving issue

  3a Agnes Helen; *m* 1st 22 Nov 1894 Daniel van de Heydt (*d* 5 April 1911), of Hochdahl, and had issue; *m* 2nd 25 June 1919 Arthur Gilstrap Soames (*d* 22 July 1934), JP, DL, of Sheffield Park, Uckfield, Sussex, and *d* 6 Feb 1964

  4a Gwendolin Cecilia; *b* 1872 *m* 1896 Capt Victor von Muller (*d* 1959), Prussian Army, and had issue

(2) Frederick (Sir), KCMG, PC; *b* 26 Oct 1823; Ch Rlwy Commr, MP Leominster and Bury, MA Cantab; *m* 1st 12 Aug 1857 Elizabeth Emily (*dsp* 30 July 1865), dau of John Shelley, of Avington; *m* 2nd 3 Sept 1879 Janet (*d* 15 March 1925), 2nd dau of Phillip Pleydell Bouverie (*see* RADNOR, E), and *dsp* 6 June 1906

(3) William (Sir), VC, KCB; *b* 2 Nov 1824; Capt RN, served Crimea and India; *d* unm 27 April 1858

(4) John Floyd; *b* 24 May 1827; Capt Scots Fus Gds; *m* 1851 Annie (*dsp* 31 Jan 1904), est dau of Edward Jenney, of Roscrea, Co Tipperary, and *d* 21 April 1910

(5) ARTHUR WELLESLEY, **1st Viscount**

(1) Julia; *m* 1st 12 July 1841 6th Earl of Jersey (*qv*) and had issue; *m* 2nd 12 Sept 1865 Charles Brandling (*d* 16 Sept 1894), of Middleton Hall, Yorks, and *d* 14 Aug 1893

(2) Eliza; *m* 25 Sept 1855 Hon Francis Stonor and *d* April 1883, leaving issue (*see* CAMOYS, B)

2 William Yates, PC, MP; *b* 3 Aug 1789; *m* 17 June 1819 Lady Jane Elizabeth Moore (*d* 5 Sept 1847), 2nd dau of 2nd Earl Mountcashell (*see* 1915 edn), and *d* 1 June 1858, having had, with six other daus:

(1) Robert Moore; *b* 16 April 1827; Capt Inniskilling Dragoons; *m* 14 Sept 1865 Ann Augusta (*d* 16 Dec 1897), yst dau of Joseph Welch, of Martin's Grove, Carmarths, and *d* 17 Oct 1878, leaving:

  1a Robert; *b* 6 Aug 1866; Capt 3rd Bn Manchester Regt; *m* Mildred — and *d* 7 Dec 1917

  2a William Herbert Gylby; *b* 15 March 1872; *m* 1st 10 June 1896 Ethel Hutchison (*d* 24 Jan 1919), dau of T Wilson Caird, and had:

    1b Robert Herbert Wilson; *b* 24 Aug 1898; *d* 1 March 1914

  2a (cont.) William Peel *m* 2nd 1 Oct 1919 Elizabeth Anne (*d* 1933), dau of Evan Jones, of Edgbaston, Birmingham, and *d* 28 Feb 1928

  3a Lawrence Moore; *b* 8 May 1876; *educ* Malvern and UCL; *m* 10 Aug 1899 Ida Susan Agnes (*d* 15 April 1940), est dau of John Robert Headech, JP, of Johnstown Park, Nenagh, Co Tipperary, and *d* 11 April 1963, having had:

    1b Lionel Victor Moore; *b* 23 Jan 1901; *m* 29 Nov 1924 *Muriel Mildred, dau of M A Murphy, of Cowley, Alberta, and *d* 6 Feb 1937, leaving:

      1c +Robert John; *b* 14 March 1927; *m* 27 Feb 1949 *Mona Jean, yst dau of Capt A A E Batchelor, of Chilliwack, and has:

        1d +Robert Lionel; *b* 5 July 1952; *m* 1972 *Sheila, 6th dau of Austin Byrnes, of Chilliwack

        2d +Rodney Robin; *b* 2 Dec 1955

        3d +Darcy Edward; *b* 29 June 1965

        1d *Susan Holly; *b* 2 Oct 1958

      2c +Lionel Brian [Lionel Peel Esq, 7682, 126A Street, North Surrey, BC, Canada]; *b* 29 March 1931; *m* 20 Dec 1952 *Beverley Ann, only dau of Harvey G Cook, of Cultus Lake, BC, and has:

        1d +Brian Gregory; *b* 18 April 1954; *m* 1973 *Sylvia, dau of Clarence Hala, of Chilliwack, and has:

          1e +James Nathan; *b* 1974

          2e +Jason Randall; *b* 1976

      2c (cont.) Lionel Peel adopted:

        *Kathryn Patricia; *b* 1964

        *Kimberley Ann; *b* 1965

      1c *Iris Patricia; *b* 7 Dec 1929; *m* 7 Sept 1952 *Lorne Albert Gehman, er s of Lorne Robert Gehman, of Cultus Lake, and has:

        1d *Blair Lee; *b* 15 Jan 1957

        2d *Lane Peel; *b* 28 Oct 1958

        3d *Dane Robert; *b* 12 Nov 1959

        4d *Christie Robin; *b* 4 July 1962

        5d *Regan Corey; *b* 24 Oct 1965

        1d *Shannon Dee; *b* 9 April 1954

  1a Linda Augusta Jane; *m* 15 April 1891 Eustace Rhodes St Clair Corbin (*d* 21 Sept 1909), MB, MRCS, and had issue

(2) William Yates; Capt Scots Gds; *m* Alice Emma (*m* 2nd 11 March 1881 St George Dyson Mansergh) and *d* 20 Dec 1879, having had:

  1a Emmie Laura Jane; *d* umn 13 Feb 1926

  2a Edith; *m* 1st 5 Feb 1908 F W Staunton (*d* 18 March 1908); *m* 2nd 30 Jan 1909 G M Strangam (*d* 26 May 1932), of Carrington, Co Waterford

(3) Frederick (Rev); *b* 16 Aug 1833; *educ* Oriel Coll Oxford (MA); Vicar Little Malvern Worcs 1875–05; *m* 17 May 1859 Adelaide Frances Isabella (*d* 18 Dec 1917), 3rd dau of 2nd Baron Sudeley (*qv*), and *d* 31 March 1915, having had issue

  1a Arthur Robert (Sir), KCMG (1917); *b* 15 Aug 1861; *educ* Eton; Envoy Extrdy and Min Plen Bangkok 1900–15, Rio de Janeiro 1915–18, Envoy Extrdy, Min Plen and Consul-Gen Sofia 1920–21, Nat Order Civil Merit Bulgaria; *m* 17 Sept 1921 Grace (Legn Hon; *d* 27 July 1963), est dau of Alberto Landsberg, of Rio de Janeiro, and *dsp* 7 Oct 1952

  2a William Charles; *b* 27 Feb 1863; *m* 1st 1889 Marion Georgiana Frances (*d* 1897), dau of Libert Chandler, of USA, and had:

    1b George; *b* 10 Dec 1896; MD, physician and surgeon; *m* 17 April 1930 Martha Estelle, dau of James Louis Covin, of Mount Carmel, S Carolina

    1b Alfreda Adelaide Marion; *b* 26 Oct 1890; *d* unm 1954

  2a (cont.) William Peel *m* 2nd 1900 Leonie Rose (*d* 16 Oct 1956), dau of Constant Hallu, of France, and *d* 13 May 1930, having by her had:

    2b Frederick de Layney (known as Frederick William); *b* 21 March 1900; engr, granted UK citizenship 1936; *m* 10 Oct 1924 Martha Grace, dau of William B Young, of Memphis, Tenn., and *d* 1978, leaving:

      1c +Frederick William [Lt-Col Frederick Peel USAF (ret), PO Box 292, Paris, TN, USA]; *b* 31 Aug 1925; pilot 8th Bomber Sqdn 1941–52; *m* 1st 27 Dec 1945 (*divorce*) Clarellen, dau of Harold Popham, of Caruthersville, Mo., and has:

        1d +Frederick William; *b* 31 Jan 1947

        1d *Martha Frances; *b* Nov 1949

      1c (cont.) Lt-Col Frederick Peel *m* 2nd 16 June 1954 *Clara Elizabeth, dau of F B Hoover, of Enid, Okla., and by her had:

        2d +John Hoover; *b* 14 Sept 1962; *m* 1985 *Karen Denise, dau of W Sanders, of Paris, Tenn.

        2d *Traci de Layney; *b* 22 Dec 1955

      2c Robert Dudley; *b* 27 Aug 1937; *educ* U of the South, Sewanee, Tenn. (BEcon 1956), and Bethany Coll, Lindsborg, Kans. (BA 1962); Maj USAAF, 81st Security Sqdn, RAF Station, Bentwater, Suffolk; *m* 3 Aug 1963 *Mary Elizabeth [Mrs Robert Peel, 2933 Caballero Drive, Jacksonville, FL 32217, USA], only dau of Lawrence J Macdonald, of Cleveland, Ohio, and *d* 1982, leaving issue:

        1d *Elizabeth Anne; *b* 2 Sept 1964; *m* 1987 *Jeffrey Alan Styerwalt and has:

          1e *Sean William; *b* 1990

          2e *Brian Robert; *b* 1992

        2d *Mary Martha; *b* 1 Nov 1966; *m* 1991 *Christian Simon Bahn

        3d *Katherine Louise; *b* 1970

      3c +Robert de Layney [Lt-Col Robert Peel USAAF (ret), 3908 Leon Drive, Plano, TX 75074, USA]; *b* 31 May 1939; *educ* U of the South; pilot F105 Flighter Bomber, shot down and prisoner N Vietnam 1965, Capt Southwest Airlines; *m* 1976 *Christine Ann, dau of Walter Trimailo, and has:

        1d *Delaney Anne; *b* 1978

        2d *Kathryn Eve; *b* 1985

    3b Charles William; *b* 1904; *m* 17 Nov 1929 *Catherine Veronica, est dau of S A Puskac, of Hamilton, Ohio, and *dsp* 1980

    4b Jack John; *b* 1908; *d* 1916 Ceylon

    5b Lincoln Henry Tracey (Joseph); *b* 1909; changed name from Evelyn Ker Semer; *m* 9 March 1946 *Hazel Pearl, dau of John Geuer, of Victoria Park, W Australia, and *d* 1993, leaving:

      1c +Kevin John [Kevin Peel, 66 Chislehurst Rd, Lesmurdie, WA 6076, Australia]; *b* 6 Dec 1946; *m* 1967 *Cheryl Anne, dau of Albert George Lawrence, of Madora Bay, W Australia, and has:

        1d +Gary John; *b* 1970

        2d +Christopher James; *b* 1973

    6b Laurence Donald Tracey; *b* 1917; *m* 1950 *Corinne Beatrix Crutchley and *d* 1983, leaving:

      1c *Suzanne Caroline; *b* 1951; *m* 1970 *Paul Raymond Martin and has:

        1d *Philip Andrew; *b* 1977

        1d *Joanna Corinne Judith; *b* 1984

    2b Carmen Radegonde

    3b Estelle Frances; *b* 1901; *m* 19– 1st T S Patterson, of Los Angeles; *m* 2nd 19– Christopher Lewis (*d* 1942)

    4b *Dorothy Léonie; *b* 1911; *m* 1938 Donnington Dade (*d* 1976)

    5b Xzavia Sérèna; *b* 1915; *m* — and *dsp* 1989

  3a Alfred Henry; *b* 31 March 1864; *m* 1915 Louisa, dau of Gen — Cookson, and *d* 11 Sept 1931

  4a Henry Tracey; *b* 12 Jan 1867; Lt Coldstream Gds; *d* 16 Oct 1893

  1a Gertrude Emma; *d* unm 20 July 1934

  2a Leila Georgina; *m* 23 July 1894 5th Viscount Gage (*qv*) and *d* 17 March 1916, leaving issue

  3a Constance Madeline; *d* unm 24 Feb 1948

(4) Francis; *b* 1 Feb 1835; Capt 34th Regt; *m* 27 March 1873 Caroline Edith Blanche (*d* 30 Dec 1890), yst dau of Anthony Brown Story, and *d* 3 Sept 1894, leaving:

  1a Robert Francis, CMG (1922); *b* 30 April 1874; Capt Coldstream Gds, served Boer War 1899–1902 and WW I, MP Woodbridge 1910–20, Lt-Col and Brevet Col 4th Bn E Surrey Regt, Govr St Helena 1920, St Helena and Ascension 1922; *m* 8 Nov 1903 Alice Maud (*d* 21 March 1957), 2nd dau of Col Sir Thomas Charlton Meyrick, 1st Bt (*qv*), and *d* 10 Aug 1924, leaving:

    1b Chiverton Robert; *b* 31 March 1908; *educ* Harrow and Trin Coll Cambridge; Maj Coldstream Gds WW II; *m* 26 Aug 1959 Bridget Honoria (*d* 1994), yr dau of Edward Hornby Beckwith by Janet, 2nd dau of R-Adml Sir Edward Chichester, 9th Bt (*qv*), and *d* 19–

    1b *Hermione Mary [Mrs Robert Oliver, Ditton Farm, St Owen's Cross, Ross-on-Wye, Herefs]; *b* 9 Feb 1912; *m* 12 July 1939 Lt Robert Ormsby Oliver, RNVR (*d* 1973), yr s of Godfrey Ryder Oliver, of Devon, and has had:

      1c *Lyon Robert; *b* 2 Nov 1949; *educ* Bromsgrove and Cheltenham Art Coll; artist and designer

      1c Anne Faulkener; *b* 23 April 1942; *d* unm Italy 22 Sept 1968

      2c Violet Ellen Antoinette; *d* unm 16 July 1956

(1) Elizabeth; *m* 14 Sept 1848 Rev Robert Seymour Nash, Canon Bristol, and had issue. He *d* 1904

(2) Flora Jane; m 5 Jan 1860 Capt Francis SIDEBOTTOM later SIDEBOTTOM-VENNER, IA, and d 1876, leaving issue

(3) Matilda Katherine; m Rev Frederick Gooch (see GOOCH, Bt, of Benacre)

3 Edmund; b 8 Aug 1791; MP Newcastle-under-Lyme; m 2 Jan 1812 Emily, 2nd dau of John Swinfen, of Swinfen, Staffs, and d 1 Nov 1850, leaving:

(1) Robert; Capt 8th Hus; d 1851

(2) Edmund Yates; Lt-Col 11th Hus; d 25 March 1885 aged 68

(3) William; b 1818; Maj 1st Bengal Dragoons; m and d 23 June 1882, leaving:

1a Amelia Maria

4 John (Very Rev); b 22 Aug 1798; DD, Dean Worcester; m 6 May 1824 Augusta (d 11 Sept 1861), dau of John Swinfen, of Swinfen, Staffs, and d 20 Feb 1875, having had:

(1) Augustus Robert Lawrence; d 2 June 1870 aged 45

(2) Herbert Richard (Rev); b 8 Feb 1831; MA; m 6 Sept 1853 Georgina Maria (d 11 July 1907), dau of Rev Thomas Baker, and d 2 June 1885, leaving:

1a Herbert; b 9 Jan 1856; m 1898 Muriel Hilda (d 4 Jan 1923), dau of George Miller, and d 28 Jan 1933, leaving:

1b Bertha; b 5 Feb 1900; SSStJ; d unm 14 Jan 1974

1a Alice; b 20 June 1854; m 10 Jan 1884 Col Arthur Howard Heath, TD, MP Leek, bro of Sir James Heath, 1st and last Bt (see 1940 edn), and had issue. He d 21 April 1930

2a Amy; b 4 Jan 1859; m 25 Feb 1886 Rev James Henry Savory and d 23 March 1929, leaving issue. He d 5 Aug 1903

3a Augusta; b 15 March 1862; m 1st 22 Nov 1883 William Wykeham Tyrwhitt Drake, of Shardeloes, and had issue. He d 29 July 1919. She m 2nd 3 July 1929 Frederick P Game, s of George Game, of Poyntington, Dorset, and d 18 Oct 1935. He d 16 Feb 1935

(1) Julia Emily Augusta; m 30 July 1846 3rd Baron Henley (qv) and d 15 Feb 1862, leaving issue

5 Jonathan, PC; b 12 Oct 1799; DCL, Lt-Gen, MP Huntingdon, Sec State War; m 19 March 1824 Lady Alicia Jane Kennedy (d 11 May 1887), dau of 1st Marquess of Ailsa (qv), and d 13 Feb 1879, having had, with a dau (d unm):

(1) Robert Kennedy; b 5 Sept 1825; d 17 April 1863

(2) Edmund Yates; b 24 July 1826; Lt-Col 85th Foot and 12th Regt of Turks; m 6 Oct 1848 Maria Frances Knighton, dau of Richard Chadwick, and d 24 April 1900, leaving:

1a Ernest Hope; b 15 Sept 1853

2a Frederick; b 16 Aug 1855; Brevet Col RE; m 11 Nov 1876 Anne Madeline (d 1 Aug 1916), dau of Maj-Gen Henry Young Darracot Scott, CB, RE, FRS, and d 27 Nov 1912, leaving:

1b Archibald; b 18 Feb 1878; Lt West India Regt; m 1908 Marie, dau of Henry Whiteley, of Wakefield, Yorks, and d 7 June 1932, leaving:

1c +Maurice [Maurice Peel, 31 Seves St, Altona, Melbourne, Australia]; b 4 Jan 1910; m March 1935 *Louisa Myrtle, dau of John Newby Carter, and has:

1d +Maurice Newby; b Dec 1935

2d +Alfred George; b 1940

3d +Stanley Charles; b 1946

4d +Cyril Ronald; b 1952

1d +Ethel Violet [Mrs Kevin Anderson, 59 Bladin Street, Laverton N, Melbourne, Victoria, Australia]; b 19 Dec 1937; m 2 Oct 1959 *Kevin George Anderson, s of Andrew Anderson, of Melbourne, and has:

1e *Kevin John; b 12 Aug 1960

2e *Brett Lewin; b 31 Oct 1961

3e *Steven Maurice; b 21 Feb 1963

1e *Vanessa Lee; b 28 June 1968

2d *Lorraine Ruth; b 1945

2b Laurence; b 11 July 1881; Commr Chinese Maritime Customs; d 4 May 1935

1b Violet Adela; m 16 Nov 1922, as his 2nd w, Col Edward Stockley Sinnot, CMG, TD, JP, DL, of Tuffley Grange, Glos, s of James Sinnott, of Clifton, Bristol, and d 4 Aug 1969 aged 100

2b Ellen Margaret; m 1911 Maj James Allan Beau (d 1923), IA, s of Maj-Gen John W F Beau, and had issue

3a Edmund; b 14 April 1857; Lt RA, Inspr-Gen Jamaica Constabulary; d unm 18 Feb 1907

1a Adelaide Cecillia; b 13 May 1850; d unm 21 Dec 1932

2a Isabel; b 28 Dec 1851; m 2 Aug 1876 Adm Sir Compton Edward Domville, GCB, GCVO (d 19 Nov 1924), and d 10 Jan 1929

3a Charlotte Frances Yates; b 11 March 1859; m 10 Aug 1882 Molyneux Barton (d 4 July 1917), barrister, and d 1931, leaving issue

4a Florence; b 27 Aug 1861; d unm 23 Nov 1941

(3) Archibald, JP, DL Denbighs, JP Herts; b 23 Jan 1828; MA Oxon; m 1st 25 May 1857 Mary Ellen (d 9 Sept 1863), dau of Lt-Gen Sir William Henry Roger Palmer, 4th Bt, of Castle Lackin, Co Mayo (see 1902 edn), and had:

1a William Frederick; b 21 March 1861; Capt 2nd Life Gds and 3rd Dragoon Gds, Midshipman RN; d unm 9 March 1910

1a Mary Adela; m 23 June 1891 Capt George Ralph Capel Curzon Fenwick, Roy Welch Fus (d 28 Oct 1909), and d 10 Dec 1941, leaving issue

2a Ellen, CBE (1918); m 1st 2 Sept 1980 Maj Henry Graham (d 13 Feb 1907), 20th Hus, and had issue (see ROBOROUGH, B); m 2nd 20 Feb 1908 1st and last Baron Askwith (d 2 June 1942) and d 12 Jan 1902, leaving further issue

(3) (cont.) Archibald Peel m 2nd 15 Aug 1867 Lady Georgiana Adelaide Russell, dau of 1st Earl Russell (qv), and d 9 Aug 1910, having by her had:

2a Edward John Russell, CMG (1918), DSO (1915) and bar (1918); b 31 Aug 1869; Hon Brig-Gen RA Boer War 1899–1900 and WW I (wounded, despatches); m 13 June 1901 Mary Louisa (d 3 July 1959), dau of Edgar Atheling Drummond (see PERTH, E), and d 20 March 1939, having had:

1b John; b 11 May 1907; Midshipman RN; d at sea 30 April 1929

2b Peter, MC (1940); b 6 June 1908; Maj Rifle Bde WW II (wounded, POW); m 22 Jan 1936 *Valerie, only dau of Maj Fervys Charles Neville, DSO, of The Manor House, Freckenham, Suffolk

1b *Rosemary [Mrs John Morris, Ingoldisthorpe Hall, King's Lynn Norfolk; 19 Kensington Pk Gdns, London W11]; m 21 Aug 1950 *John V Morris, s of Edward Morris

3a Jonathan John Russell; b 8 Aug 1872; with Min of Labour, Lt Roy Fus; m 20 Oct 1915 Gwyneth (d 6 Sept 1919), dau of Robert William Keate, Govr-in-Ch W Africa, and d 8 Nov 1936

4a Alfred Michael John Russell; b 16 Sept 1873; m 10 Jan 1906 Kathleen (m 2nd 1926 Ernest Charles Pulbrook (d 1940) and d 1968), dau of J J de C Walsh, of Gwelo, Rhodesia, and d 20 June 1907, leaving:

1b Archibald John Russell; b 2 Feb 1907; Maj RA; m 1946 Patricia Virtue (d 1980), only dau of Col Baldwin Salter Millard, TD, of Hampstead, and d 1978, leaving:

1c +Jeremy Robert [Jeremy Peel Esq, Willow Cottage, La Pouquelaye, St Helier, Jersey CI]; b 4 Dec 1946; m 1st 1970 (divorce 1974) Shirley Ann Brett and has:

1d +Mark Jeremy Russell; b 1971

1c (cont.) Jeremy Peel m 2nd 1984 *Angela Betty, only dau of Edward David Neal, of Jersey

2c +Michael John Russell; b 13 March 1952

1c *Caroline Georgiana [Mrs Paul Bancroft, Caroline House, South Rd, Oundle, Peterborough]; b 19 Aug 1948; m 1970 *Paul Fisher Bancroft and has:

1d *Adam Fisher; b 1973

2d *Oliver Robert; b 1976

3d *Jonathan Guy; b 1979

1d *Imogen Georgiana Patricia; b 1984

2c *(Elizabeth) Francesca [Mrs Francesca Peel, 7/46 High St, Kensington 5068, S Australia]; b 5 Jan 1950; m 1972 (divorce 1978) Andrew Swart and has:

1d *Sara Gemma; b 17 July 1980

5a Fergus Lister Grosvenor John Russell; b 17 Oct 1876; Lt 1st Bn Oxon LI Boer War 1900–01; d unm Nov 1946

3a Fanny Agatha Louisa; m 3 June 1897 Capt Hubert Lavie Butler, Roy Scots Fus (d 31 Jan 1937), s of Charles Butler, of Herts and Bayswater, and d 29 July 1915, leaving issue

4a Ethel Adelaide Georgiana; d unm 13 Jan 1945

5a Grace; m 1st 23 April 1908 (divorce 1916) Joseph Wingfield Henry, Northumberland Fus, and had issue; m 2nd 26 Jan 1937 Lt-Col Hon Francis Henry Cecil Weld-Forester, 3rd s of 5th Baron Forester (qv), and d 12 July 1973 aged 95

(4) John; b 11 April 1829; Lt-Gen, Kt Medjidie; d unm 17 Nov 1892

(5) William Augustus; b 27 Nov 1833; Inspr Local Govt Bd; d unm 15 May 1899

(1) Alice; m 26 Sept 1861 Sir Robert Burnett Morier (d 16 Nov 1893), GCB, GCMG, PC, Amb Russia, and d 24 Feb 1903, leaving issue

(2) Adelaide Georgiana; m 9 Aug 1864 1st Baron Biddulph (qv) and d 22 May 1872, leaving issue

6 Laurence; b 1801; m 20 July 1822 Lady Jane Lennox (d 27 March 1861), dau of 4th Duke of Richmond (see RICHMOND and GORDON, D), and d 10 Dec 1888, having had, with a dau (d unm):

(1) Charles Lennox (Sir), GCB; b 19 June 1823; Clerk PC 1875–98; m 27 April 1848 Caroline Georgina (d 26 April 1892), er dau of 1st Baron Templemore (see DONEGALL, M), and d 19 Aug 1899, having had, with a dau (d unm):

1a Charles Augustus; b 6 Oct 1849; d 7 May 1867

2a George Arthur; b 31 Dec 1852; m 31 Aug 1895 Ellen (d 6 Nov 1958), dau of George McDowell, and d 23 May 1910, leaving:

1b Frances Caroline; m 1st 26 Oct 1921 Maurice Whippy Garrard (d 1 Sept 1934), s of B W Garrard, of Wokingham, Berks, and had issue; m 2nd 4 Feb 1935 Harold Gascoyne Glazebrook Brooke Joynson, MFH (d 1969), est s of Harold Mead Joynson, of Wootton Courtenay, Somerset, and Springfields, Banbury, Oxon, and d 14 Feb 1966

2b Vera Jane; d unm Nov 1968

3a Horace; b 8 Sept 1857; m 29 July 1899 Violet (d 23 Oct 1948), dau of Ralph Dalyell, CB, of Lingo, Fife, and d following an accident 20 Oct 1940, leaving:

1b Charles Algernon; b 17 April 1906; educ Eton; Lt-Col 3rd Hus; m 12 Dec 1933 *Katherine Louise, 3rd dau of Ernest George Pretyman, PC, of Orwell Park, and had:

1c Jeremy Charles; b 8 Sept 1934; educ Eton and Ch Ch Oxford (MA); Lt 3rd Hus; m 24 Nov 1960 (divorce 1971) Sheila Mary Rose, only dau of Capt Charles Elphinstone Fordyce, of Bracken Lodge, Churt, Surrey, by Hon Violet Ethel Mary, 2nd dau of 1st Baron Windlesham (qv), and d 1988, leaving:

1d +Robert-Frederick Charles [Robert Peel Esq, 6 Terrick Cottages, Terrick, Aylesbury, Bucks]; b 9 Feb 1962; m 1991 *Elizabeth Mary, yr dau of Geoffrey Green, of Ayr, Ontario, and has:

1e *Katherine Sheila Anne; b 12 Sept 1995

2e *Alice Lucy Elizabeth; b 27 Oct 1998

2d +James Arthur Lennox; b 13 Feb 1964; m 1987 *Belinda Margaret Emma, yr dau of Nicholas Smith, of Charney Bassett, Oxon

1b Pamela Georgina; b 1 May 1900; m 1st 31 Oct 1924 (annulled 1928) Charles Frederick Spencer Chichester (see DONEGALL, M); m 2nd 21 Dec 1934 John Wrench; m 3rd 27 Nov 1952 Maj John Edward Durrant Shaw (d 21 April 1955), TD, JP, er s of James Edward Shaw, of Welburn Hall, Yorks, and d following a car crash 17 Sept 1962

2b Marjorie Violet; b 19 May 1902; m 22 June 1921 Maj Evelyn Ronald Moncrieff Fryer, MC, Gren Gds (d 3 Nov 1967), only s of Frederick Eustace Reade Fryer, of Bury Hill, Woodbridge, Suffolk, and had issue

4a Edward Laurence; b 19 Jan 1860; m 1st 5 Sept 1895 Mary Caroline (d 15 July 1899), only dau of Charles Spencer Scrase Dickins, DL, of Coolhurst, Sussex, and had:

1b Caroline Marian; *d* following a car crash 7 June 1968

2b Joan May Cecilia; *m* 15 March 1923 Capt Richard Bernard St Quintin Wall, Gren Gds, er s of Rev Richard Wall, of Bobbing, Sittingbourne, Kent, and had:

  1c *Michael Edward St Quintin [Cdr Michael Wall RN, 2 Chester House, 231 Kensington Rd, London SE11]; *b* 25 Aug 1926; *educ* RNC Dartmouth; *m* 1st 9 Aug 1952 (*divorce*) Sheila Mary, dau of Victor Coope Ponsonby (*see* DE MAULEY, B), and has:

    1d *Hugo St Quintin [Hugo Wall Esq, 101 Drive Mansions, Fulham Rd, London SW6]; *b* 18 Feb 1954

    1d *(Sarah) Fenella [Miss Fenella Wall, 101 Drive Mansions, Fulham Rd, London SW6]; *b* 4 June 1955

  1c (cont.) Cdr Michael Wall *m* 2nd 27 June 1975 *(Alice) Anne, CVO, Assist Press Sec to HM THE QUEEN, wid of Adml Sir Geoffrey Hawkins, KBE, CB, MVO, DSC, of Grafton Underwood, Kettering, Northants

  2c *Christopher Robin St Quintin [Christopher Wall Esq, The Apple Orchard, Bradenham, Bucks]; *b* 29 March 1929; *educ* Eton and RMA Sandhurst; Capt Gren Gds; *m* 28 June 1961 *Francesca Giovanna Maria, only dau of Giovanni Fummi (*see* CRAWFORD and BALCARRES, E), and has issue

4a (cont.) Edward Peel *m* 2nd 11 May 1905 Constance Madeline Emma (*d* 12 June 1961), 2nd dau of Lt-Col William Mure of Caldwell, DL, MP, Scots Gds, and *d* 9 Oct 1936

5a Algernon Robert, MVO; *b* 20 Jan 1862; Priv Sec to Ld Lt Ireland; *d* 26 June 1920

6a Alfred Lennox; *b* 8 Nov 1863; *d* 17 Feb 1864

1a Florence Caroline, CBE (1920); DJStJ, Order of Mercy; *m* 20 April 1871 Col Charles Seymour Corkran (*d* 22 Nov 1921), Gren Gds, and *d* 19 Dec 1942, having had issue

2a Augusta Jane; *m* 18 June 1878 Montagu Turner (*d* 25 Jan 1908), yst s of Henry Scott Turner, High Bailiff Westminster, and had issue

(2) Arthur Lennox; *b* 30 May 1825; Lt-Col 52nd Regt; *d* unm 14 Jan 1875

(3) Alfred Lennox (Rev); *b* 4 June 1827; Rector St James Dunbrody and Killesk, Co Wexford; *d* unm 4 Nov 1863

(4) Cecil Lennox; *b* 18 April 1830; Lt-Col Scots Gds; *m* 3 Jan 1867 Hon Caroline Susan Mary (*d* 28 Aug 1916), er dau of 2nd Viscount Combermere (*qv*), and *d* 27 April 1910, leaving, with another dau:

  1a Cecil Hester Lennox; *m* 7 Sept 1898 Leicester Morgan Reed (*d* 1944) and *d* 27 Dec 1951, leaving issue

  (1) Constance Augusta Lennox; *m* 8 Aug 1863 Col George Grant Gordon, CVO, CB, and *d* 14 April 1921, leaving issue (*see* HUNTLY, M)

1 Mary; *m* 9 Jan 1816 George Robert Dawson, PC, of Castle Dawson, Co Derry, and *d* Jan 1848, leaving issue

2 Elizabeth; *m* 30 Dec 1805 Very Rev William Cockburn (*d* 30 April 1858), Dean York, and *d* 16 June 1828

3 Harriet Eleonora; *m* 11 March 1824 2nd Baron Henley (*qv*) and *d* 7 May 1869

Sir Robert *m* 2nd 18 Oct 1805 Susanna (*d* 10 Sept 1824), aunt of Sir William Henry Clerke, 10th Bt (*qv*), and *d* 3 May 1830

His 5th s,

ARTHUR WELLESLEY PEEL, **1st Viscount Peel of Sandy**, Co Bedford (UK), so *cr* 9 May 1895, PC (1884), JP, DL Warwicks, JP Beds; *b* 3 Aug 1829; *educ* Eton and Balliol Coll Oxford; MP (Lib) Warwick 1865–86 and Warwick and Leamington 1885–95, Parly Sec Poor Law Bd 1868–71 and BOT 1871–73, Patronage Sec Treasury 1873–74, Parly U-Sec Home Dept 1880, Speaker H of C 1884–95, Chm Tstees Nat Portrait Gallery, Tstee Br Museum, Visitor Balliol Coll and Hon DCL Oxon 1887; *m* 14 Aug 1862 Adelaide (*d* 5 Dec 1890), er surv dau of William Stratford Dugdale (*see* DUGDALE, Bt), and had:

1 WILLIAM ROBERT WELLESLEY, **1st Earl**

2 (Arthur) George Villiers, JP, DL Warwicks; *b* 27 Feb 1868; *educ* Harrow and New Coll Oxford (BA 1891, MA 1894); Maj Beds Yeo, formerly Oxon Imp Yeo, Maj RM, Clerk Treasury, served WW I (despatches twice), MP Spalding 1917–18, Offr Legn Hon; *m* 6 Oct 1906 Lady Agnes Lygon (*d* 15 March 1960), 4th dau of 6th Earl Beauchamp (*see* 1970 edn), and *d* 25 April 1956, leaving:

  (1) George Frederick; *b* 28 Jan 1921; *educ* Harrow and New Coll Oxford; Roy Berks Regt WW II (invalided), Air Ministry (Flying Training Command), PA to Custodian Pusey Memorial Library Oxford 1950–52, Assist Custodian 1952–54, Assist Oxford U Faculty of Theology Library 1953–54, BRCS Hospital Librarian OStJ 1955–67, Archives Assist USPG 1967–69, Assist Educn Library Reading U 1969–79; *m* 26 July 1960 *Elizabeth Mary, only dau of John Vickers Coker, and *d* 24 Oct 1996

  (1) *Juliet Agnes [Mrs George Thorne, 24 Swallowfield Park, Reading, Berks RG7 1TG]; *b* 14 May 1919; *m* 18 April 1942 *Maj George Thorne, MC, ERD, DL, Gren Gds, 2nd (twin) s of Gen Sir (Augustus Francis) Andrew Nicol Thorne, KCB, CMG, DSO and two bars, DL, of Knowl Hill House, Berks, by Margaret, 10th dau of 2nd Baron Penrhyn (*qv*), and has:

    1a *Robert George [Robert Thorne Esq, Ovington House, Ovington, Hants]; *b* 7 Feb 1943; *educ* Eton and RAC Cirencester; with Barclays Bank 1964; *m* 1990 *Sarah Veronica Bond, *née* Priestley

    2a *Ian David Peel [Ian Thorne Esq, Beauchamp Barn, Kneesall, Notts NG22 0AS]; *b* 14 Oct 1944; *educ* Eton, RMA Sandhurst and Trin Coll Oxford (BA 1969, MA 1973); Capt Gren Gds, High Sheriff Notts 1986; *m* 1992 *Paula Nkechi Enwezoh and has:

      1b *Davina Nkechi Rozelle; *b* 29 Nov 1992

    1a *Viola Georgina Juliet [Mrs Nicholas Halsey, The Golden Parsonage, Gt Gaddesden Row, Herts HP2 6HG]; *b* 20 Sept 1948; *m* 1976 *Nicholas Guy Halsey, TD, DL Herts (1998), FRICS (*see* HALSEY, Bt)

3 Sir SIDNEY CORNWALLIS PEEL, 1st and last Bt (UK), so *cr* 14 July 1936, CB (1929), DSO (1917), TD, of Eyworth, Beds, DL; *b* 3 June 1870; *educ* Eton and New Coll Oxford (BA 1894, MA 1896); Fell Trin Coll Oxford, barrister Lincoln's Inn 1898, Lt-Col and Col Beds Yeo, served Boer War 1900 and WW I 1914–17 (despatches), Dep Steward Oxford U, Cdr Hafidian Order Morocco,

MP (C) Uxbridge 1918–22; *m* 18 Feb 1914 Lady Delia (Adelaide Margaret) Spencer, DCVO (1950, CVO 1947), est dau of 6th Earl Spencer (*qv*), and *dsp* 19 Dec 1938, when the btcy expired

4 Maurice Berkeley (Rev), MC (1915) and bar (1917); *b* 23 April 1873; *educ* New Coll Oxford (BA); Rector Wrestlingworth, Vicar Eyworth Beds 1906–09, St Paul Beckenham 1909–15 and Tamworth Staffs 1915–17, T/CF 4th Cl WW I (wounded, despatches); *m* 29 July 1909 Emily (*d* 24 March 1912), yr dau of Julius Alington, JP, of Little Barford Manor House, Beds, and was *ka* 14 May 1917, leaving:

  (1) David Arthur, MC; *b* 4 Oct 1910; Maj Irish Gds WW II; *m* 14 April 1936 *Hon Sara Carola Vanneck [The Hon Mrs Peel, Huntingfield Hall, Halesworth, Suffolk 1P19 0QA], er dau of 5th Baron Huntingfield (*qv*), and was *ka* Sept 1944, leaving:

    1a +Jonathan Sidney, CBE (1994), MC (1957), JP [Jonathan Peel Esq CBE MC JP, Barton Hall, Barton Turf, Norfolk NR12 8AU]; *b* 21 June 1937; *educ* Norwich Sch, Eton and St John's Coll Cambridge (MA), served Malaya 1957, Congo 1960–61, Page of Honour to HM GEORGE VI 1951–52 and HM THE QUEEN 1952–53, dir Norwich Union Insur 1973–, chm Pleasureworld plc, CC and V-Ld Lt Norfolk 1980, High Sheriff 1984, chm: Broads Authority 1985–, Norfolk CC Planning and Tport Ctee 1989–93, Nat Tst E Anglia Regn 1981–90, Nat Tst Properties Ctee 1990–, Norwich Sch and How Hill Tst for Environmental Educn; dep chm Nat Tst 1992–, V-Pres Norfolk Naturalists Tst; *m* 20 Jan 1965 *Jean Fulton, er dau of ACM Sir Denis Hensley Fulton Barnett, GCB, CBE, DFC, and has:

      1b +Robert Denis; *b* 9 Sept 1976

      1b *Ruth Miranda; *b* 29 March 1966

      2b *Emily Sara; *b* 17 Nov 1967; *m* 1990 *Mario de Pina Antunes and has:

        1c *Anibal-Jorge; *b* 10 April 1991

      3b *Anne Louise; *b* 18 June 1970

      4b *Delia Mary; *b* 26 July 1974

    2a +Charles David; *b* 26 Dec 1940; *educ* Eton and Norwich Sch; ARIBA; *m* 26 May 1973 *Catherine Anne, yst dau of Duncan Robert Mackintosh, OBE, of Woodfolds, Oaksey, Wilts, and has:

      1b *Thomas David; *b* 1975

      1b *Elizabeth Alison; *b* 18 May 1977

    3a Robert Alexander; *b* 17 Sept 1943; *educ* Eton and RNC Dartmouth, Lt RN; *d* unm 9 Sept 1969

    1a *Julia Victoria [Mrs Nicholas Longe, Hasketon Manor, Woodbridge, Suffolk IP13 6HZ]; *b* 18 March 1939; *m* 14 March 1970 *Nicholas Longe, High Sheriff Suffolk 1984–85, AInst MSM, er surv s of Lt-Col Roland Bacon Longe, KSLI, of Hasketon Lodge, Woodbridge, and has:

      1b *William Martin Peel; *b* 1972

      2b *David John Hastings; *b* 1975

  (1) Mary Emily; *b* 20 March 1912; *d* unm 19 Sept 1934

1 Julia Beatrice; V-Pres St Mary's Hosp Paddington; *m* 24 April 1895 James Rochfort Maguire (*d* 18 April 1925), CBE, MP W Clare, s of Rev John M Maguire, Rector Kilkeedy, Co Limerick, and *dsp* 25 May 1949

2 Agnes Mary; RRC, DGStJ; *m* 11 Feb 1899 Maj Charles Sydney Goldman (*d* 2 April 1958), RGA, MP Penrhyn and Falmouth, s of B N Goldman, of Cape Colony, and *d* 27 Feb 1959 age 90, leaving issue

3 Ella Frances; *d* unm 21 July 1900

The 1st VISCOUNT *d* 24 Oct 1912; his est son,

WILLIAM ROBERT WELLESLEY PEEL, **1st Earl Peel**, so *cr* 10 July 1929, as also VISCOUNT CLANFIELD, of Clanfield, Co Hampshire (both UK), GCSI (1932), GBE (1919), TD, PC (1919), JP, DL Beds; *b* 7 Jan 1867; *educ* Harrow and Balliol Coll Oxford (BA 1889); barrister Inner Temple 1893, Lt 13th Middx RV, Lt-Col Beds Yeo, MP (U) Manchester S 1900–06 and Taunton 1909–12, memb LCC 1900–19 (Chm 1914), JP, DL Beds; *b* 7 Jan 1867; *educ* Harrow and WW I despatches), Jt Parly Sec Min Nat Serv 1917–19, Parly U-Sec War and Air and V-Pres Army Cncl 1919–21, Min Tport 1921–22, Chllr Duchy Lancaster 1921–22, Sec State India 1922–24 and 1928–29, First Commr Works and Public Bldgs 1924–28, Ld Privy Seal 1931, Hon Col 105th (Beds Yeo) Bde 1922–37, Chm Burma Round Table Conf 1931, Wheat Commn 1932, Roy Commn Despatch Business at Common Law 1934–36, Palestine Roy Commn 1936, memb Roy Commn Port London and Indian Jt Ctee 1933–34, Govr Victoria U Manchester, Offr Legn Hon, US DSM; *m* 11 April 1899 Hon Eleanor (Ella) Williamson (*d* 1949), dau of 1st and last Baron Ashton (*see* 1930 edn), and had:

1 ARTHUR WILLIAM ASHTON, **2nd Earl**

1 Doris, JP (London 1939, Sussex 1948); *b* 25 March 1900; *m* 15 Feb 1927 Lt-Col Latham Valentine Stewart Blacker, OBE, RA (TA), IA (*d* 19 April 1964), of Cold Hayes, Liss, Hants, est s of Maj Latham Blacker, RA, and maternal gs of Marie Leszczinska, ggdau of last Elector of Posen (bro of STANISLAS LESZCZINSKI KING OF POLAND), and had, with other issue:

  (1) *David Stewart Wellesley Blacker, JP, DL; *m* 1960 *Hon Mary Rose, dau of 2nd Baron Rathcavan (*qv*), and has issue

The 1st EARL *d* 28 Sept 1937; his only son,

Sir Arthur William Ashton Peel, 7th Bt, as which *s* cousin 1942, and **2nd Earl Peel**; *b* 29 May 1901; *educ* Eton and Balliol Coll Oxford (BA 1924); v-chm Nairn and Williamson (Hldgs) and Nairn-Williamson Ltd, dir: Lancashire Steel Corp, Sea Insur, Assist Sec Roy Commn Land Drainage 1927, Pres Lancashire Assoc Boys' Clubs 1934–68, dep chm LMSR 1946–48, Ld Lt Lancs 1948–50, KStJ, Upper Bailiff Weavers' Co 1958–59, Hon LLD Lancaster 1967, Hon Freeman Lancaster; *m* 11 March 1946 Catherine Kathleen (*b* 20 June 1913; *d* 27 July 1972), dau of Michael McGrath, of Ballyculane, Co Cork, and *d* 22 Sept 1969, leaving:

1 WILLIAM JAMES ROBERT PEEL, **3rd and present Earl Peel**

2 +Robert Michael Arthur [The Hon Robert Peel, Berryhill Farm, Coedkernew, Newport, Gwent]; *b* 5 Feb 1950; *educ* Eton and Hertford Coll Oxford; *m* 21 July 1973 *Fiona Natalie, dau of Charles Davidson, of Dunhampstead House, Droitwich, Worcs, and has:

  (1) *Kathryn Beatrice; *b* 1978

  (2) *Hermione Juliet; *b* 1979

  (3) *Eleanor Lindsay; *b* 1981

PELLY

DEO · DUCENTE · NIL · NOCET

Arms: Or on a bend engrailed azure, between two trefoils slipped vert, three martlets argent. **Crest:** Issuant from a crown vallary or, charged on the rim with three hurts, an elephant's head argent. **Motto:** *Deo ducente nil nocet* ('God guiding, nothing hurts'). **Creation:** Bt. (UK) 12 Aug 1840.

SIR RICHARD JOHN PELLY, 7TH BT, of Upton, Essex [Sir Richard Pelly Bt, The Manor House, Preshaw, Hants SO32 1HP]; *b* 10 April 1951; *s* unc 1993; *educ* Wellington and Wadham Coll Oxford (BA); *m* 1983 *Clare Gemma, dau of Harry Wilfred Dove, of Winchester, and has:

1 +ANTHONY ALLWYNE; *b* 30 Oct 1984
2 +James Richard; *b* 2 Dec 1986
3 +Harry Philip; *b* 8 Nov 1988

Lineage: JOHN PELLYE, of Okeford Fitzpaine, Dorset; living 1539 and 1569; *m* Emma — and had, with an er s (William, of Okeford Fitzpaine, *m* and had issue):

THOMAS PELLY, of Poole *c* 1582; *b c* 1545; *m* 1st Mary, dau of Robert Nicles, Mayor of Poole 1580, and had four sons and three daus; *m* 2nd Susanna — and by her had two daus; his est s:

WILLIAM PELLY, of Poole, where he owned considerable property; *bapt* 22 Nov 1593; Overseer of the Poor 1622; *m* 1st 25 Aug 1617 Joan Marmer and had nine sons and a dau; *m* 2nd Susanna — and *d* 1659, having by her had two sons and a dau; the 3rd s by his 1st w:

WILLIAM PELLY, of Poole; *bapt* 24 Sept 1620; *m* Alice — and was *bur* 1 May 1691, leaving an est s:

JOHN PELLY, of Poole; *bapt* 8 Sept 1644; a Yr Bro Trin House 1684; *m* 16 Dec 1668 Sarah Smith and had, with two other sons and four daus:

JOHN PELLY, of Upton, Essex, and Goodmansfield, London; *b* 6 Feb 1683; Capt HEICS, Yr Bro 1715 and Er Bro Trinity House 1744; *m* 1st Martha Lapthorne and had two sons and a dau; *m* 2nd Grisel (*dsp*), dau of Capt Thomas Collet, of Barking, and *d* 14 Feb 1762; his er s:

JOHN PELLY, of Upton, and Aveley, Essex; *b* 9 June 1711; Capt HEICS, Yr Bro Trin House 1736; *m* Elizabeth (*d* 6 Nov 1761), dau and heiress of Henry Hinde, of Upton, and *d* 22 Nov 1762, leaving:

1 HENRY HINDE, of whom presently

2 John (Rev); *b* 27 Oct 1754; Rector Weston-under-Edge; *m* Eugenia (*d* 8 Feb 1831), widow of Henry Creswick and dau of — Roberts, of Lisbon, and *d* 17 Nov 1809, leaving:

(1) John Hinde; *b* 19 May 1786; *m* Elizabeth (*d* 11 Sept 1852), dau of Joseph Lewis, of Lypiatt House, Stroud, and *d* 17 March 1852, leaving:

1a John Hinde; *b* 26 Sept 1811; *m* 30 Sept 1835 Selina Ellen, dau of — Richards, of Mount Retford, Exeter, and *d* 1857, leaving issue

2a Augustus; *b* 17 July 1816; *m* 1st Jane Albertina, dau of James Scott; *m* 2nd Elizabeth Charlotte, dau of John Hickmore, and *d* 1875, leaving issue

3a Henry Joseph; *b* 9 Jan 1818; Gen Bombay Staff Corps, served Scinde 1840–47, Adj-Gen Battles of Meanee and Hyderabad; *m* 16 Feb 1850 Deborah Elizabeth, dau of John Morris, and *d* Dec 1891, leaving:

1b Henry Gerald; *b* 24 April 1857; Maj RA, served Afghan War 1879–80, Egyptian Campaign 1882, Boer War 1899–1901; *m* 12 Aug 1886 Edith, dau of Rev G H Turner, of Berkeley Chapel, Mayfair, and had:

1c Lionel Hinde; *b* 20 April 1889; *m* 19– Eileen Turner and *d* 1964, leaving:

1d *Peter Charles Henry; *b* 1915; *m* 19– *Winifred Perry and has:

1e *Christopher Martin Hinde; *b* 1943

4a Saville Marriott; *b* 28 March 1819; CB, *b* 28 March 1819; FRCS, Inspr-Gen Hosps Bombay Army; *m* 9 Nov 1850 Jane Billing, dau of John Morris, of Bengal, and *d* 1895, leaving:

1b Stanley Augustus; *b* Oct 1853; Vicar Swanicke, Alfreton; *m* 1st 11 Feb 1879 Louisa, dau of Lt Ross, and had:

1c Richard Stanley (Rev); *b* 10 March 1881; Rector Yarkhill; *m* 1917 Dorothy Jessie Piper (*d* 27 March 1934), dau of Rev A H Parmenter, and *d* 9 May 1932, leaving:

1d Desmond Aubrey Stanley; *b* 3 March 1919; *m* 20 Aug 1948 *Patricia Anne [Mrs Desmond Pelly, Bishopswood Farm, Sonning Common, Oxon], dau of Col Guy de Pass, DSO, OBE, and *d* 9 Dec 1993, leaving:

1e *Richard Guy Stanley [Richard Pelly Esq, Home Farm, Wakefield Lodge Estate, Potterspury, Northants]; *b* 23 March 1951; *m* 4 Dec 1976 *Elizabeth Wigram, yr dau of Martin Lloyd, of Pitchcombe, Glos, and has:

1f *James Aubrey Stanley; *b* 13 March 1982
1f *Sarah Elizabeth; *b* 22 Nov 1979

2e *John Marriott; *b* 23 Feb 1953; *m* June 1983 *Caroline Mary, dau of Christopher Griffith, of Natal, S Africa and has:

1f *Alice Mary; *b* 12 Oct 1987
2f *Celia Anne; *b* 16 July 1990

3e *Michael Desmond Eliot; *b* 30 Oct 1954; *m* 19– (*divorce* 19–) —

1e *Carolyn Ann; *b* 24 May 1949; *m* 22 May 1971 *Thomas Alexander Fortescue Frost, yr s of T F C Frost and Mrs F E Cleary, both of Mayfair, and has:

1f *Alexander Fortescue; *b* 15 Oct 1975
2f *William; *b* 9 Nov 1978
3f *Edward; *b* 18 Oct 1985

2d *Anthony Edward [Anthony Pelly Esq, Sowells Farm, Kentisbeare, Devon]; *b* 5 March 1923; *educ* St Edmund's Sch Canterbury; S/Ldr RAF 1941–69 (despatches); *m* 22 March 1953 *Miriam Leonora, dau of S/Ldr H A Castaldini, of Bournemouth, and has:

1e *Judy Amanda; *b* 4 Dec 1955
2e *Sarah Georgina; *b* 15 March 1958

3d Michael Richard Parmenter; *b* 27 May 1925; *educ* St Edmund's Sch Canterbury; RAF WW II; *m* 14 Feb 1967 *Angela Mary, dau of R O Peate, of Moat Farm, Tunbridge Wells, Kent, and *d* 1990, leaving:

1e *Rose; *b* 26 Jan 1971

1c Evelyn; *b* 19 April 1883; *d* 28 Nov 1977

1b (cont.) Stanley Pelly *m* 2nd Agnes Henrietta, dau of Rev J E Campbell Colquhoun

2b Saville Herbert; *b* 1861; DCLI; *m* Isabella, dau of Rev J King, of Looe, Cornwall, and *dsp* 1899

5a Stanley; *b* 1820; *dsp* 1841

6a Lewis (Sir), KCB, KCSI; *b* 14 Nov 1824; *m* 1 Aug 1878 Amy, dau of Rev John Lowder, Br Chaplain Shanghai, and *d* 1892

(2) George; *b* 20 Aug 1787; *d* 1788

(3) William; *b* 19 June 1788; *m* Lucy, dau of Thomas Gunston, and *d* 1829, leaving:

1a Augustus Edward; *b* 28 Jan 1823; with Hudson Bay Co; *m* 28 Aug 1849 Anne Rose, dau of Robert Clouston, of Smoogro, Orkney, and *d* 17 May 1907, leaving issue

(4) Robert Parker; *b* 10 Jan 1790; Capt HEICS; had issue

(5) George; *b* 8 April 1791; Capt HEICS; *d* unm 30 Nov 1866

(6) Augustus; *b* 6 March 1792; Lt RN; *d* unm 28 July 1820

(7) Edward; *b* 23 Feb 1794; *dsp*

(8) Charles Francis; *b* 2 April 1797; *dsp* 1875

3 George; *b* 30 Aug 1747; *d* 24 March 1787

1 Elizabeth; *b* 2 Dec 1736; *m* Benjamin Harrison, Treas Guy's Hosp, and *d* 28 Feb 1817, leaving issue

2 Martha; *b* 25 Feb 1750/1; *m* 13 March 1781 Rev John Sibley, of Walcot, Bath, and *d* 3 April 1830, leaving issue

The est son,

HENRY HINDE PELLY; *b* 6 June 1744; High Sheriff Essex 1780, Capt HEICS, a Yr Bro Trin Ho 1771, Er Bro 1786; inherited the Upton and Aveley Estates of the PELLY and HINDE families; *m* 13 July 1776 Sally Hitchen (*d* 15 May 1824), dau and coheir of Capt John Blake, HEICS, of Watcombe, Hants, and *d* 23 Feb 1818, having had:

1 JOHN HENRY (Sir), **1st Bt**

2 Charles; *b* 13 Sept 1779; Capt RN, served under Nelson (wounded 1801), presented with a sword by the Patriotic Fund 1804 after capturing a Dutch brig *Atlanta*; cmded HMS *Mercury* 1805 and HMS *Bucephalus* 1810; *m* 14 June 1804 Mary (*d* 7 April 1830), dau of J Bullock, of Speen, and *d* 16 Nov 1811, leaving issue

3 Francis (Rev); *b* 24 Dec 1780; Rector Siston, Glos; *m* 1st 30 Oct 1806 Mary (*dsp* 11 March 1810), dau of George Anson Nutt, of Wellesbourne, Warwicks; *m* 2nd 16 Feb 1813 Mary Anne (*d* 5 Nov 1857), dau of Theophilus Richards, and *d* 3 July 1844, leaving by her:

(1) Justinian; *b* 20 April 1818; *m* 1 April 1849 Fanny, 4th dau of Rupert Ingleby, of Cheadle, Staffs, and *d* 17 Feb 1893, having had, with other issue:

1a Bernard; *b* 5 June 1860; *m* Feb 1900 Elizabeth Montgomery (*d* 24 Nov 1958), er dau of Dr Thomas Taylor Minor, of Seattle, USA, and *d* 10 Aug 1938, leaving:

1b Bernard Berenger; *b* 19 May 1901; *educ* Yale (BA 1923); *m* 28 June 1930 *Elizabeth, dau of Arthur P Nute, and *d* 14 Nov 1986, leaving:

1c *Bernard Berenger; *b* 6 April 1931; *m* 24 June 1961 *Elizabeth Noland Stone and has:

1d *Bernard Christopher; *b* 1 May 1962; *m* 1997 *Erin Marshall
2d *Caleb Stone; *b* 18 March 1964; *m* 1989 *Kathleen Rogers and has:

1e *Noland Thomas; *b* 13 Nov 1995

1d *Margaret Carter; *b* 26 March 1966; *m* 1996 *Erik Morrow Chorlton

2c *Charles Arthur [Charles Pelly, 12440, NE 24th, Bellerne, WA 98004, USA]; *b* 28 July 1937; *m* 16 July 1968 *Jennifer Paul and has:

1d *Charles Cameron; *b* 16 Oct 1970

3c Peter Ingleby; *b* 28 Sept 1939; *d* 11 May 1941

2b Thomas Minor; *b* 22 Aug 1902; Memb US Ho Reps; *m* 24 May 1927 Mary Virginia Taylor and *d* 1973, leaving:

  1c *Thomas Minor; *b* 7 Sept 1928; *m* 1st 15 June 1950 Margaret McAlpin (*d* 5 March 1957) and has:

    1d *Margaret Mary; *b* Jan 1952

    2d *Elizabeth Mary; *b* 5 Aug 1953

  1c (cont.) Thomas Pelly *m* 2nd 11 April 1958 *Sally Anne Shannon and by her has:

    1d *Thomas Taylor; *b* 7 June 1960

    2d *Richard; *b* 1962

    3d *Michael; *b* 1964

    3d *Shannon Virginia; *b* 26 Feb 1959

  1c *Marion Elizabeth; *b* 27 April 1931

3b Launcelot Ingleby; *b* 22 June 1906; *d* unm 12 Nov 1928

4b *Francis Justinian; *b* 31 March 1913; *m* 26 June 1942 *Nancy Bertha Lane and has:

  1c *Wendy Frances; *b* 20 July 1943

  2c *Nancy Anne; *b* 4 Feb 1953

2a Justinian; *b* 21 May 1864; *m* 11 Sept 1894 Sarah Cecilia, dau of Stephen Kinsey, of Llanidloes, Wales, and *d* 19 Jan 1948, having had:

1b Acton Francis; *b* 16 Aug 1895; *m* 1 Jan 1937 Roberta Isobel Edmondson

2b Rupert Justinian; *b* 24 June 1899; *d* 12 Nov 1902

3b Raymond Stephen Ingleby; *b* 17 Feb 1902; *m* 14 June 1924 *Norma Muir and *d* 1964, leaving:

  1c *Wilfred Raymond Francis; *b* 15 March 1925; *m* 9 Aug 1947 *Patricia Grace Roberts and has:

    1d *Wilfred Douglas; *b* 28 May 1952; *m* 19– *— and has:

      1e *Michael; *b* 1978

      2e *Todd; *b* 1981

    1d *Patricia Marilyn; *b* 14 Aug 1948

    2d *Judith Anne; *b* 20 Sept 1949

  2c *Robert Lyle; *b* 12 April 1926; *m* 22 Feb 1948 *Betty Elizabeth Clarke and has:

    1d *Clifford Raymond; *b* Nov 1948; *m* 19– *— and has:

      1e *Stephen; *b* 1971

    2d *Robert Clarke; *b* 28 Dec 1953; *m* 19– *— and has:

      1e *Robert; *b* 1974

      2e *Jeffrey; *b* 1976

  3c *Jack Donald; *b* 9 March 1928; *m* 5 Sept 1951 *Irene Goldie Julseth and has:

    1d *Joseph Alan; *b* 17 July 1954; *m* 19– *— and has:

      1e *Kristopher; *b* 1977

      2e *Nicholas; *b* 1980

  1c *Mildred Ann; *b* 10 Oct 1934; *m* 24 Sept 1954 *Ronald Leslie Keith

1b *Frances Miriam; *b* 5 April 1905; *m* 19– *J R Donovan

4 Raymond, CB; *b* 9 April 1784; Lt-Col 16th Queen's Lancers; *m* 1818 Louisa Margaret (*d* 1882), dau of Robert Henry French, of Dublin, and *d* 20 Dec 1845, having had issue

1 Mary; *b* 7 April 1778; *m* 1 June 1797 Benjamin Harrison, Jr Treas Guy's Hosp, and had issue

The est son,

Sir John Henry Pelly, 1st Bt (UK), so *cr* 12 Aug 1840; *b* 31 March 1777; Capt HEICS, Govr Hudson Bay 1822–52 (Dep Govr 1812), Yr Bro Trin Ho 1803, Er Bro 1823, Dep Master 1834, memb Court Bank of England 1822–52 (Dep Govr 1839–41, Govr 1841–42); *m* 13 July 1807 Emma (*d* 20 April 1856), 6th dau of Henry Boulton, MP Worcester, of Thorncroft, Surrey, and had:

1 JOHN HENRY (Sir), **2nd Bt**

2 Raymond, of Hollington House, Sussex, JP, DL; *b* 28 April 1810; *m* 10 June 1835 Louisa (*d* 1896), dau of Joseph Fry, of Plashet House, Essex, and *d* 21 June 1886, having had:

(1) Charles Raymond; *b* 19 Feb 1837; *m* 26 July 1864 Louisa Catherine Emma (*d* 12 Nov 1938), dau of Sir Robert North Collie Hamilton, 6th Bt, of Silverton Hill (*qv*), and *d* 12 June 1879, leaving:

1a Charles Hamilton Raymond; *b* 24 April 1867; Lt-Col RA WW I; *m* 1st 8 July 1897 Mary Elizabeth (*d* 24 Jan 1945), widow of Capt Frederick Trevitt, JP, of Haslemere, Surrey; *m* 2nd 14 April 1947 *Alice Margaret, formerly w of G/Capt Ralph Woodcock Gifford Lywood and yr dau of Frederick Smith, and *dsp* 26 Dec 1952

1a Constance Louisa; Medal Queen Elisabeth Belgium and war Victory medals; *m* 1st 21 Sept 1882 (*divorce* 1895) Richard Davis Matthey (*d* 9 Jan 1929) and had issue; *m* 2nd 7 Sept 1895 Lloyd Harry Baxendale, JP (*d* 21 May 1937), of Greenham Lodge, Newbury, Berks, and *d* 7 Jan 1944

2a Ethel Henrietta; *m* 21 Aug 1889 Charles Edward Grey Hatherell (*d* 2 Sept 1937), JP, of Radford House, nr Leamington, and *d* 25 Oct 1952, leaving issue

3a Adelaide; *m* 29 April 1914 Sidney Beckwith (*d* 6 Jan 1924), er s of Thomas Percival Beckwith, and *d* 10 June 1958

(2) Raymond Percy (Rev); *b* 18 March 1841; *educ* Trin Coll Cambridge (MA); Hon Canon Worcester, Vicar Gt Malvern 1896–1910; *m* 4 Feb 1864 Alice Schaffalitzky (*d* 6 Sept 1928), dau of Col George Larkins, Bengal Artillery, and *d* 16 Oct 1911, leaving:

1a Douglas Raymond (Rev), DSO (1918), VD; *b* 20 Feb 1865; *educ* Emmanuel Coll Cambridge (MA); Matabele War 1896–97 (medal and clasp) and WW I (despatches three times); Rector Woolbeding, Midhurst, Hon CF 2nd Cl 1921; *m* 14 May 1898 Verena Noellie (*d* 6 Oct 1952), 5th dau of Rev George W Herbert, and *d* 14 March 1943, having had:

1b Claude Bernard Raymond (Sir), GBE (1958, CBE 1942), KCB (1954, CB 1950), MC (1933); *b* 19 Aug 1902; *educ* Rugby, and Cranwell; RAF: served N Kurdistan 1931–32, WW II (despatches three times), Assist Ch Air Staff (Op Requirements) 1948–51, Directing Staff IDC 1952, C-in-C

Middle East Air Force 1953, Controller Aircraft Min Supply 1956, ACM (ret 1959), memb UKAEA for Weapons R and D 1960–65, Order King George I Greece 1946; *m* 15 Feb 1930 Margaret Ogilvie (*d* 1990), only dau of Edward J Spencer, of Hove, and *d* 12 Aug 1972, having had:

  1c John Douglas Raymond; *b* 22 Jan 1934; *d* 29 June 1937

  2c +Raymond Blake (Rev) [The Rev Dr Raymond Pelly, 12 Kio Crescent, Hataitai, Wellington, NZ]; *b* 25 June 1938; *educ* Rugby and Worcester Coll Oxford; *m* 1st 11 Jan 1964 Joanna Bickmore, yr dau of John Anthony Clark, of Somerset, and has had:

    1d +Aidan John Raymond; *b* 13 Nov 1970

    1d Gail; *b* 26 Feb; *d* 4 June 1965

    2d *Monica; *b* 12 March 1966

    3d Catherine Hilda; *b* 29 Sept 1967; *educ* Dartington; *d* 1984

  2c (cont.) The Rev Raymond Pelly *m* 2nd 1990 *Barbara Helen, er dau of Alan Craig, and has:

    2d +Thomas Douglas Raymond Craig; *b* 15 March 1993

  3c +David Claude Raymond [David Pelly Esq, Dairy Farmhouse, Coltishall, Norfolk NR12 7AH]; *b* 5 July 1941; *educ* Rugby; *jnlst*; *m* 1974 *Philippa, only dau of Peter Bowman, of Hitchin, Herts, and has:

    1d *Tessa Patricia; *b* 1977

    2d *Lorna Jane; *b* 30 May 1979

  1c *Jane Elizabeth [Mrs Jack Guest, 6161 Lacon Rd, Denman Island, BC, V0R1T0, Canada]; *b* 24 July 1931; *m* 1960 *Jack E Guest and has:

    1d *John William; *b* 8 Nov 1961

    1d *Margaret Elizabeth; *b* 30 Dec 1960

    2d *Maire Frances; *b* 18 Sept 1963

2b Peter Douglas Herbert Raymond, CB (1958), DSO (1942); *b* 24 Sept 1904; R-Adml WW II (despatches, Offr Order Orange Nassau Holland), ret 1960; *m* 29 Dec 1932 Gwenllian Violet (*d* 1987), yr dau of Hon George Henry Edwardes (*see* KENSINGTON, B), and *d* 1980, leaving:

  1c *Sara-Ann [Mrs Peter Low, Darsham House, nr Saxmundham, Suffolk IP17 3PZ]; *b* 1 Feb 1937; *m* 1 May 1968 Peter Low (*d* 1997), est s of Peter Low, and has:

    1d *Tobias Blake; *b* 7 Aug 1969

    2d *Nathaniel Peter; *b* 1971

  2c *Richenda [Mrs Douglas Miers, East Farmhouse, Wylye, Wilts]; *b* 27 Jan 1939; *m* 3 April 1959 *Maj Douglas Alexander Nigel Capel Miers, QO Highrs, er s of Col Ronald Douglas Martin Capel Miers, DSO, QO Cameron Highrs, and has:

    1d *Lucian Douglas Ronald Capel; *b* 1962

    1d *Mary Ann Capel; *b* 1961

    2d *Victoria Jane Capel; *b* 1964

    3d *Henrietta Alice Capel; *b* 1966

  3c *Clare Margaret [Mrs Timothy Ireland, Eatons Farm, Ashurst, W Sussex]; *b* 13 Jan 1942; *m* 21 Feb 1963 *Timothy Lawrence Ireland, ACII, AMCIB, only s of Henry Lawrence Ireland, of Rudgwick, Sussex, and has:

    1d *Mark Peter Lawrence; *b* 6 May 1965

    2d *Blake Timothy Lawrence; *b* 1972

    1d *Nicola Gwenllian; *b* 5 May 1966

    2d *Gemma Mary Clare; *b* 18 April 1974

3b Blake Raymond, OBE (1944); *b* 31 May 1907; *educ* Wellington and Emmanuel Coll Cambridge (BA 1928 MA 1950); ADC to Govr NSW 1937–38, G/Capt RAAF WW II (despatches), MLA NSW 1950–57, chm: Rio Tinto Mining, Co of Australia 1956–62, Unity Life Assur 1960, Mary Kathleen Uranium Ltd 1956; v-chm Conzinc Riotinto Australia Ltd 1962–67 (dir 1968); dir: Zinc Corp, Merchant Bills Corp, Hamersley Iron Pty and Langridge Bldg Soc, Hon Treas Australian Jockey Club, V-Pres Equestrian Fedn Australia NSW Branch, Dep-Chm Universities Board NSW 1967–90; *m* 29 Sept 1938 *Mary Pamela Laidley [Mrs Blake Pelly, 3 Vaucluse Rd, Sydney, NSW 2030, Australia], only dau of Vincent Laidley Dowling, of Sydney, and *d* 1990, leaving:

  1c *Andrew Douglas Blake [Andrew Pelly Esq. 8 Johnston Crescent, Lane Cove, Sydney, NSW 2066, Australia]; *b* 4 Sept 1939; *educ* King's Sch Parramatta; exec Television Corp 1964–87; *m* 1st 26 May 1961 (*divorce* 1978) Gaye Delyss, dau of Gordon Clempson Evans, of Chatswood, NSW, and has:

    1d *Fiona Elizabeth; *b* 5 Nov 1964

    2d *Vanessa Pamela; *b* 27 April 1967

  1c (cont.) Andrew Pelly *m* 2nd 1983 *Maria Rita, dau of Frank Van Ierland, of The Netherlands, and by her has:

    1d +Richard Francis Blake; *b* 1984

  2c *Michael Francis Blake [Michael Pelly, 56 Crescent Rd, Hamilton, Brisbane, Qld, Australia]; *b* 17 Sept 1947; *m* 1983 *Nora Danaher and has:

    1d *Martine Pamela; *b* 1984

    2d *Simone Veronica; *b* 1986

  1c *Angela Mary Blake [Mrs John Compton, 248 La Perouse St, Red Hill, ACT]; *b* 22 June 1942; *m* 9 July 1965 *Cdr John Spencer Compton, RAN, and has:

    1d *James Gregory Spencer; *b* 1967

    2d *Blake John Raynorp; *b* 1970

    3d *Henry Charles Grenville; *b* 1977

4b John Raymond; *b* 19 Oct 1912; *d* 29 April 1913

1b Theodora; *b* 27; *d* 31 May 1900

2b *Stella Elizabeth Mary [Mrs William Gowers, 15 The Mint, Wallingford, Oxon]; *b* 3 Dec 1908; *m* 9 Aug 1934 *William Richard Gowers, CBE, Mayor Oxford 1954–55, only s of Sir Ernest Arthur Gowers, GCB, GBE, and has:

  1c *William Patrick; *b* 5 May 1936; *educ* Radley, and Clare Coll Cambridge (MA, MusB, PhD); ARCO; *m* 23 Sept 1961 *Caroline Molesworth, yr dau of Dr Timothy Maurice, of Marlborough, Wilts, and has:

1d *William Timothy; b 20 Nov 1963

1d *Rebecca Mary; b 27 Oct 1965

2d *Katherine; b 1970

1c *Ann Elizabeth Mary [Mrs Roger Scott, 417 Swann Rd, St Lucia, Brisbane 4067, Qld, Australia]; b 25 Oct 1938; BEd, PhD; m 19 Oct 1963 *Prof Roger Dennis Scott, DPhil, s of Leonard Allan Scott, of Westbury, Tasmania, and has:

1d *Richard Andrew; b 1 Sept 1964; Midshipman RAN

2d *Alexander Patrick; b 2 April 1967

2a Claude Raymond; d 8 Dec 1878

3a Raymond Theodore, CB (1919), CMG (1919), DSO, (1916) and bar (1919); b 30 July 1881; educ Haileybury; Boer War 1900–01 (medal with four clasps), WW I (despatches seven times, two brevets, 1914 star, Croce di Guerra, Order St Maurice and St Lazarus Italy): Col and Hon Brig-Gen Loyal N Lancs Regt, T/Lt-Col cmdg Princess Patricia's Canadian LI 1915–16 and 8th Bn Royal Irish Rifles 1916–17, T/Brig-Gen and Bde Cdr 1917; Hon Brig-Gen 1921, Mil Kt Windsor 1942; m 4 April 1910 Moriet Elsie Maxwell (d 6 Feb 1965), yr dau of Major Gen Gethin Creagh, CB, and d 28 June 1952, leaving:

1b *Pamela Moriet; b 30 March 1911; m 1st 14 Aug 1935 Frank Rough (d 28 Sept 1966), s of S M Rough, and has:

1c *Caroline [Mrs John Lawrenson, The Old Rectory, Gt Waldingfield, Suffolk]; b 11 Nov 1940; m 20 July 1963 *John Ralph Lawrenson, s of Col Ralph Lawrenson, DSO, of Stroud, Glos, and has:

1d *Frank Ralph; b 1 April 1967

1d *Sophie Patricia; b 27 Nov 1968

1b (cont.) Mrs Frank Rough m 2nd 24 June 1968 John Moore Lorimer (d 1982); m 3rd 1993 *Donald Pearson Paton, DFC

2b *Patricia Carlota [Mrs Alan Maccoy, The Coach House, Church Rd, Shillingstone, Dorset DT11 0SL]; b 16 Sept 1915; m 29 May 1948 *Lt-Cdr Alan Harold Maccoy, DSC, RNVR, er s of Harold Maccoy, of Casita, Itchenor, and adopted:

*Paul John Raymond; b 3 March 1958; m 1986 (divorce 1996) Leigh Thelma Sessions

*Catherine Richenda; b 8 March 1959; m 1981 *David Peter Pickering, of Bermuda, and has:

1d *Samantha Clare; b 1990

4a Raymond; b 17 July 1887; d unm 7 March 1905

1a Alice Mabel; m 1 Oct 1885 Rev Arthur Durrant, Vicar Leverstock Green, Herts, and d 2 Oct 1927, leaving issue

2a Ellen Geraldine; m 4 April 1899 Henry Knollys Foster, OBE (d 1950), of Mount Skippitt, Kings Thorne, Hereford, s of Rev H Foster, of Malvern, and d Dec 1964, leaving issue

3a Margaret Evelyn; m 21 Oct 1891 Godfrey Lawford (d 1930) and d 27 Aug 1958, leaving issue

4a Dorothy Christabel; m 1st 13 May 1916 Capt Hugh Mortimer Rowland (d 20 Dec 1932), 2nd/1st N Somerset Yeo; m 2nd 16 Sept 1937 3rd Baron Airedale (see 1970 edn), DSO, MC, and d 2 April 1970

5a Ina Marjorie Gwendoline, OBE (1934); m 1st 17 June 1910 (divorce 1921) Maj Hon Christopher William Lowther (see ULLSWATER, V) and had issue; m 2nd 7 Dec 1921 (divorce 1948) Lt Gen George Hugo Cholmondeley (see CHOLMONDELEY, M) and d 9 July 1969

3 Charles; b 31 July 1812; MCS; m 18 April 1839 Julia Henrietta (d 1886), dau of Rev Richard Stewart Dobbs, of Bay Lodge, Co Antrim and d 30 Dec 1885, leaving:

(1) Charles Henry (Rev); b 7 July 1844; MA Dublin; Vicar Barton-Hartshorn with Chetwode, Buckingham, 1910–12, Chaplain Madras; m Sept 1867 Katherine (d 17 Jan 1907), dau of Lt-Col Gardiner Harvey, Madras Army, and d 30 March 1921, having had:

1a Charles Brent Neville; b 25 Feb 1870; Indian Police, Lt Indian Defence Force; m 17 Jan 1901 Annie Harvey (d 13 Jan 1963), dau of Col Alexander Sinclair Grove, DSO, and d 6 May 1933, leaving:

1b Charles Sinclair, JP (Dorset 1952); b 12 Sept 1902; Cdr RN; m 16 Nov 1928 Caroline Mary (d 1992), yst dau of Charles Samuel Facey, MB, of Chickerell, Weymouth, and d 8 Dec 1967, leaving:

1c +Charles Patrick [Charles Pelly Esq, St Mary's Lodge, Chitterne, Wilts BA12 0LH]; b 12 Oct 1935; educ Marlborough; m 24 Sept 1966 *Avis Olga dau of S/Ldr William Henry Tregoning Woon, BEM, of Plympton, Devon, and has:

1d +Nigel William Sinclair; b 5 June 1968

2d +Stephen Grenville; b 28 July 1970

3d +Simon Charles Tregoning; b 10 May 1973

2c +William Rupert Brent [William Pelly Esq, Bell Cliff, 7 Broad St, Lyme Regis, Dorset, DT7 3QD]; b 18 Dec 1943; Nautical Coll Pangbourne; m 21 Oct 1967 *Judith Rowena, yr dau of Prof Norman Henry Gibbs by Joan Frances Ruth, yr dau of Norman Victor Leslie Melville (see LEVEN and MELVILLE, E), and has:

1d +Benjamin Rupert William; b 1972

2d +Joel Peter Sinclair; b 1980

1d *Zinnia Joanne; b 22 March 1970

2d *Tabitha Louise; b 1978

1c *Jane [Mrs Kenneth Mills, The Elms, East St, Chickerell, Weymouth, Dorset]; b 8 March 1931; m 9 March 1957 *Capt Kenneth Howard Mills, RN, s of Capt Ronald George Mills, DSO, DSC, RN, and has:

1d *Charles Richard; b 26 Jan 1958

2d *Patrick George; b 20 Dec 1963

1d *Cecilia Jane; b 15 Jane, 1959

2b Henry Patrick Neville; b 12 Jan 1912; Maj 16th Punjab Regt (IFF) WW II; m 29 April 1939 Marion Veronica (d 1992), er dau of Major Harry Sanderson, of Galashiels, Roxburghs, and was k in a flying accident in Assam 9 Feb 1945, leaving:

1c +George Michael Harvey [George Pelly, Arosa, Hawksdown, Walmer, Deal, Kent CT14 6PN]; b 22 May 1944; educ Wellington and RMA Sandhurst; m 1979 *Diana Montgomery, er dau of Maj D Montgomery, of Wotton, Surrey, and has:

1d +Henry; b 30 July 1983

1d *Grace Catherine; b 1981

2d *Rachel; b 30 July 1983

1c *Sarah Rutherford [Mrs Jonathan Lawley, Forrold Cotttage, Earl Stonham, Suffolk IP14 5EL]; b 21 April 1941; m 29 Aug 1966 *Jonathan Coldstream Lawley, est s of Wilfred Lawley, OBE, of Teheran, and has:

1d *Thomas Henry; b 1973

1d *Juliet Rosemary; b 22 Jan 1969

2d *Katherine Jane; b 8 May 1970

1b *Betty Joan; b 14 Sept 1905; m 1st 25 June 1924 (divorce 1939) George Wallis Newport Clark (d 21 July 1955), of Carnabane, Upperlands, Co Derry, 2nd s of Alexander Wallis Clark, DL, of Ampertaine, Upperlands, and has issue; m 2nd 8 July 1939 Maj Alexander Maitland Stuart (d 1 July 1958), RA, s of James Stuart, of Somerset, Coleraine

2a William Francis Henry; b 9 April 1874; Maj 9th Bn Royal Inniskilling Fus; m 29 April 1901 Rosa Theodora (d 13 March 1940), dau of William Vinicombe Davy, and was ka 1 July 1916, leaving:

1b John Denis Cavendish; b 23 July 1903; WW II RNVR; m 1st 5 July 1929 (divorce 1933) Hon Elizabeth Ponsonby (d 31 July 1940), only dau of 1st Baron Ponsonby of Shulbrede (qv); m 2nd 27 Feb 1935 Constance Cecily (d 31 March 1964), only dau of Maj John Somerled Thorpe, MC, of Coddington, and d 1989

2b Charles Nigel Cavendish, OBE (1944); b 20 July 1908; Capt BOAC; m 2 July 1934 Betty Joan (d 29 Oct 1995), dau of Lt-Col Lionel Webster Cole, OBE, of Cairo, and d Nov 1966, leaving:

1c +Christopher Patrick Cavendish [Christopher Pelly Esq, 57 Corbière Ave, Parkstone, Poole, Dorset BH12 4JJ]; b 30 June 1939; educ Campbell Coll Belfast and Trin Coll Dublin (BA 1962, MA 1966); m 5 April 1969 *Brenda Amy Grosvenor, only dau of Alfred Mutlow Grosvenor Herd by Heather Sybil, yst dau of Cdr Dudley Charles Stuart, RN (see BUTE, M), and has:

1d +Nigel Christoper Grosvenor; b 31 July 1973

1d *Amanda Rachel; b 15 Sept 1970

2c Marcus (Mark) Nigel; b 23 Feb 1941; Hong Kong Police; m 1st 1971 Peggy Jane, dau of Robert A Wright, of Victoria, BC; m 2nd 1978 *Barbara [Mrs Marcus Pelly, 22 Nicholli St, S Duncraig, WA 6023, Australia], dau of S Mason, of Harare, Zimbabwe, and d 25 Dec 1996, having by her had:

1d +Nicholas Julian; b 1982

2d +Andrew Jonathan; b 1984

1c *Sally Joan [Mrs Paul de Rham, The Lawns, 17 Moorlands Rd, West Moors, Wimborne, Dorset]; b 20 July 1944; m 23 Sept 1967 *Paul Edmond Arthur de Rham, er s of Bernard de Rham, of Villars-sur-Ollon, Switzerland, and has:

1d *Marc Edmond; b 8 Aug 1970

1d *Joanna Claire; b 15 Sept 1968

2d *Lucy Caroline; b 1976

3d *Sophie Charlotte; b 1979

3a John Stanley Richard; b 25 April 1875; d unm 28 March 1903

4a Frank le Quesne; b 2 March 1880; educ St Peter's Sch York and Aberdeen U (MB and ChB 1903); served Boer War (Victoria Medal and two clasps), WW I as T/Capt RAMC; m 15 June 1910 Jessie Letitia (d 29 Feb 1944), 2nd dau of Dr Nathaniel Goodchild, of Highgate Road, London

5a George Sinclair; b 12 Dec 1885; Capt Bengal Nagpur Railway Bn, Aux Force India, Supt Tportn (Traffic) Bengal Nagpur Rlwy; m 1912 Honora Isabel, KIH (S) (d 1 June 1946), dau of Rev F C Boyd, and d 28 Oct 1946, leaving:

1b Kathleen Bridget; b 1913; m 12 July 1944 Capt Tom Woods Hilton, s of George Hilton, of Negrelos, Portugal, and had issue

2b Norah Patricia; b 28 Oct 1914; Kaisar-i-Hind Bronze Medal; m 2 Aug 1939 Lt-Col David Leslie Vivian Rowe, CBE, MC, only s of Josiah Arthur Vivian Rowe, MC, of Michaelmas Cottage, Sway, Hants, and had:

1c *Janet Vida [Mrs John Brierley, 19B Raja Santosh Road, Alipore, Calcutta, India]; b 6 Sept 1941; m 6 June 1964 John Frederick Brierley and has issue

2c *Hilary Diana; b 27 Dec 1948

1a Rosetta; b 23 Oct 1868; m 1st 15 May 1889 Charles William Martin, MCS (d Nov 1906); m 2nd 1910 Harry Seymour Mullins (d 1925), ICS, Madras Survey, and dsp 1920

2a Annie Harriet; b 27 Oct 1872; m 14 Nov 1893 Lt-Col John Donaldson (d 1 Oct 1943), RAMC, and d 11 Aug 1960, leaving issue

3a Ethel Mary; b 23 Sept 1876; m 1 Aug 1899 John Folliott Young (d 16 May 1947), s of Robert George Young, of Culdaff, Co Donegal, and d 29 June 1959, leaving issue

(2) Richard Stewart; b 13 June 1846; m 19 May 1875 Frances Anne (d 1911), dau of George Robinson, and d 1928, having had:

1a Henry Conway Dobbs; b 1878; m 1903 Brenda (d 5 Sept 1935), dau of W D Horsley, MCS and d 25 March 1908, leaving:

1b +Stuart Horsley; b 19–

2b +Ralph Horsley [Ralph Pelly, 110, 7052 Linden Ave, South Burnaby, BC, Canada]; b 23 March 1907; BC Civil Service; m 1928 *Jacobina Benson, dau of G N Landscrown, engr, of Aberdeen, and has:

1c +Bruce Conway [Bruce Pelly, 1922 Belle Isle Place, North Vancouver, BC, Canada]; b 19 Sept 1933; RCN 1950–55, served Korean War, Regnl Supervisor-Gen Agencies Zurich Life Insur Canada; m 1962 *Lucille Odette, dau of Rev Ernest Amex, of Quebec, and has:

1d +Scott Bruce; b 2 Nov 1965

1d *Susanne Lucille; b 12 July 1963

2c +Brian George [Brian Pelly, 5451 Canada Way, Burnaby 2, BC, Canada]; b 28 Oct 1938; Dist Manager Hoover Co; m 4 June 1958 *Bernice Lorraine, dau of Sgt E E Cave, RCMP, of Vancouver, and has:

1d +Michael George; b 20 March 1961

2d +Steven Todd; b 20 March 1963

1d *Lisa Lorraine; b 10 Nov 1964

2d *Michele Kim; b 10 Nov 1966

1c *Patricia Landscrown; b 15 Sept 1929; m *George E Belsham and has issue

3b +Conway Horsley; b 19–

2a George Stuart, of Port Dover, Ontario, Canada; b 23 July 1888; m 22 June 1927 Adah Maud, dau of Ward Sovereign

1a Rebecca Julia; m 1894 William Henry Barrett and d 25 Oct 1898, leaving issue

2a Ellie May; m 1902 John Hugh McMullin and d 1932, leaving issue

3a Frances Kathleen; b 24 July 1883; m 26 April 1915 Maj Ralph Stanley Worsley, MC, Canadian Res of Offrs, and d 3 Jan 1966, leaving issue

(3) Edward; b 2 Nov 1848; m 22 March 1876 Ellen (d 1892), dau of John Garrioch, of Manitoba, Canada, and d 18 Feb 1928, having had:

1a Percy Bertram; b 1878; d 21 Nov 1914

2a Edward Raymond; b 1890; bank manager; m 1st 23 Nov 1918 Frances Muriel (d 4 Dec 1943), dau of Rev Alfred Shidrick, Vicar Milton-under-Wychwood, Oxon; m 2nd 18 Dec 1944 *Dorothy Jean Edna [Mrs Edward Pelly, #3–1531 Bernard Ave, Kelowna, V1Y 6R9, Canada], er dau of J M Dadson, of Winnipeg, Manitoba, and d 16 Sept 1963, having by her had:

1b John Edward; b 7 June 1947; m 1975 *Patricia [Mrs John Pelly, 3837 Princess Ave, N Vancouver BC, V7N 2E6, Canada], 2nd dau of Jack F Cogger, of Surrey, and d 10 July 1995, leaving:

1c +Tod Cogger; b 1978

2c +Edward Reid; b 1979

1b *Mary Ann [Mrs Douglas Snowsell, 2545 Eastview, Saskatoon, SK, S7S 3G5, Canada]; b 2 Oct 1945; m 20 May 1967 *Douglas Alva Snowsell, s of James Snowsell, of Kelowna, BC and has:

1c *Brandon James; b May 1969

2c *Colin David; b 1970

1a Ina Rosalie; d young

2a Kathleen; m 7 Oct 1903 Myers A Irish, of Manitoba, and d Jan 1953, leaving issue

3a Emily Olivia; m 15 June 1909 Frederick Temple Cornwall (d 8 May 1961), barrister, and had issue

(4) Francis Raymond; b 21 Dec 1851; R-Adml; m 17 May 1881 Mary (d 20 June 1945), dau of Rev Robert Posnett, Rector Laracor, Co Kildare, and d 15 Nov 1907, leaving:

1a Hutcheson Raymond; b 22 Sept 1887; educ Cheltenham and RMC Sandhurst; Lt-Col IA WW I (despatches); m 1913 Kathleen Mary (d 1984), dau of Edward Clifford-Walsh, of St Aidens, Arklow, and d 1979 having had:

1b Clifford Raymond, DSC; b 1917; Lt RN WW II; ka 22 Nov 1944 when cmdg HM Submarine Stratagem

1b *Dorothy Mary [Miss Dorothy Pelly, 77 Archway St, London SW13 0AN]; b 1 Aug 1921; served WW II Burma and India (despatches)

1a Eily Amy; m 1919 Jerome O'Hanlon, manager Nat Bank

2a Dorothy May Fairfax; m 18 Dec 1916 Brig Moray Martin Milne-Thomson, RA (d 14 Oct 1964), s of Col A Milne-Thomson, CMG, RAMC, of Devon, and had issue

(1) Harriet Emma; m 14 April 1859 Col Charles John Pearse, IA (d 1919), and d 28 Nov 1928, leaving issue

(2) Mary; m 7 April 1864 William D Horsley (d 1899), MCS and d 9 May 1924

(3) Julia; m 9 Oct 1861 Thomas Frederick Andrew Agnew and d 15 April 1934, leaving issue (see AGNEW, Bt, of Lochnaw)

(4) Louisa Jane; m 18 Nov 1865 Sir David Monro of Allan (d 9 Jan 1909), Capt Madras NI, and d 4 May 1929, leaving issue

(5) Emily Macaulay; b 3 Aug 1857; m 6 Jan 1882 Frederick Maitland-Heriot and d 24 Sept 1918, leaving issue (see LAUDERDALE, E)

4 Albert; b 3 Sept 1813; m 4 Oct 1844 Barbara Ellen (d 21 Dec 1898), dau of Rev Thomas Streatfeild, of Chart's Edge, and d 18 Sept 1894, leaving:

(1) Albert Champion; b 8 Aug 1845; m 25 Sept 1878 Alice (d 3 March 1929), dau of Charles Augustus Ferguson, of Lee, Kent, and d 16 March 1915, leaving:

1a Albert Edgar Champion; b 19 Nov 1879; m 6 June 1904 Agnes May, dau of William Hall, of Chesterfield, and d 17 June 1958, leaving:

1b John; b 1 May 1905; m 1st 1 Aug 1931 Bertha (dsp 6 Aug 1935), dau of John William Selwin Taylor, of Alfreton, Derbys; m 2nd 14 Jan 1942 Hilda May (d 1977), er dau of Thomas Brewer Barrow, of Bristol, and d 1981, leaving:

1c +Derek John [Derek Pelly Esq, Jakob-Schmid-Str 19, 85221 Dachau, Germany]; b 19 April 1946; educ Bedminster Down Comprehensive Sch and BAC Tech; IEng, MIMechIE, MIED; m 1985 (divorce 1993) Elvira Maria Lutz

2b Noel Henry; b 25 Dec 1906; m 14 May 1932 *Marjorie, dau of Frank Harold Hinton, of Forest Hill, London SE23, and d 1974, leaving:

1c +Raymond Frank [Raymond Pelly Esq, 27 Harrington Villas, Brighton, Sussex BN1 6RG]; b 17 Oct 1940; LI Biol; m 1st 12 Sept 1964 Janet, dau of Alexander Edward Head, of Walton-on-Thames, Surrey, and has:

1d *Nicole Louise; b 24 March 1966; has issue:

1e *Grace; b 1991

2d *Lisette Suzanne; b 1969

1c (cont.) Raymond Pelly m 2nd 1994 *Pauline Ruth Rowlands, dau of William Dey, of Ripon, N Yorks

3b Edgar Frank; b 16 Jan 1919; m 4 Aug 1941 *Dulcie Vera [Mrs D Smith, 4 Probyn Close, Frenchay, Bristol] (m 2nd 1959 D Smith), dau of Charles Manning, of Bristol, and d 22 Sept 1954, having had:

1c Michael John; b 22 May 1953; d 2 April 1956

1c *Dorinda May; b 6 Feb 1945; m 27 Feb 1965 *John Kenneth Scoltock, BSc (Mech Eng), s of Leslie Scoltock, of Much Wenlock, Salop, and has:

1d *Simon John; b 10 July 1969

1d *Amanda Louise; b 13 April 1968

2c *Julia Ruth [Mrs Terry Gilborson, 89 Gorse Hill, Fishponds, Bristol]; b 4 Aug 1947; m 1966 *Terry Gilborson, s of Ivor Gilborson, of Bristol, and has:

1d *Mark Julian; b 7 Nov 1966

1d *Sarah Lewise; b 14 Dec 1969

1b Kathleen Ruth; b 12 Sept 1908; m 4 Aug 1941 Kennard Hudswell Stallworthy, s of George Hudswell Stallworthy, of Portsmouth, and adopted a dau

2b Winifred Ina; b 7 June 1910; m 26 Sept 1936 Stanley Allison, s of Edward Allison, of Rotherham, Yorks, and had:

1c *John [John Allison Esq, 178 Walton Park, Pannal, Harrogate HG3 1RJ]; b 26 June 1938; ACIB; m 25 Aug 1962 *Margaret, dau of Frank Hartley, of Sheffield, and has:

1d *Paul James; b 2 Feb 1968; m 20 Jan 1996 *Joanne, dau of John Stewart, of St Andrews

1d *Claire Louise; b 22 Feb 1964; m 5 May 1992 *Gary David Poulter, of Mytonon Swale, and has:

1e *Jack David; b 28 Oct 1996

2e *Matthew James; b 3 Dec 1997

2c *Donald [Donald Allison Esq, 312 Hollinsend Rd, Sheffield, Yorks]; b 16 Dec 1941; m 14 Nov 1964 *Annita June, dau of Frederick Meredith, of Sheffield, and has:

1d *Steven John; b 22 April 1965; m 1 June 1996 *Lisa Elsdon and has:

1e *Lauren Dawn Louise; b 16 Nov 1995

1c *Margaret; b 17 July 1945; m 25 April 1975 *Brian Martin

1a Evelyn Alice Champion; b 15 Aug 1881; m 20 Dec 1915 Leslie Tait (d 1950), of Alberta, Canada, and had issue

2a Blanche Marianne Champion; b 10 April 1883; m 15 June 1908 Arthur William Harris and d 20 April 1920, leaving issue

3a Constance Maud Champion; b 14 June 1887; m Nov 1914 (divorce 1957) Henry Austin Stubbington and d 19 Feb 1960, leaving issue

(2) William Henry; b 29 May 1847; m 1st 16 May 1882 Eleanor Lucy (d 10 April 1883), dau of John Sisson Steele, MRCS, of Holmfield, Reigate, and had:

1a Russell George; b 1 April 1883; FRIChem; m 10 Aug 1909 Frances Carruthers (d 28 March 1944), 2nd dau of Sir Francis Carruthers Gould, and d 7 June 1967, having had:

1b Russell; b Aug 1910; educ Mercer's Sch, Edinburgh U (BSc 1931) and Imp Forestry Inst Oxford; with Scottish Woodland Owners Assoc, Conservator Forests Sierra Leone; m 13 Sept 1945 *(Agnes) Mysie [Mrs Russell Pelly, 32 Verena Terrace, Perth PH2 0BZ], er dau of Frank Henry Macpherson, slr, of Ayr, and d 1993, leaving:

1c *Frances Elsie; b 21 July 1947; ARSA

2c *Lindsay Grace; b 24 May 1950; m 1976 *John Warrender Gow and has:

1d *David Russell; b 1979

1d *Hazel Joan; b 1977

2d *Morven Elizabeth; b 1983

3c *Mysie Ann; b 26 Jan 1953; m 1981 *Robert Ferguson and has:

1d *Ruaraidh; b 1989

1d *Shuna Margaret; b 1985

2b Michael Beaumont; b 13 April 1912; educ Maldon GS Essex

3b Ronald John Sisson; b 19 Oct 1913; d 18 April 1914

4b Anthony Roger; b 2 March 1915; educ Maldon GS; Capt RAC WW II; m 1st 24 Jan 1947 (divorce 1965) Joan Olive, er dau of G/Capt Martin William Flack, CBE, MB, RAF, and had:

1c *Sarah Jane; b 1 Oct 1949

4b (cont.) Anthony Pelly m 2nd 13 Jan 1967 *Eileen [Mrs Anthony Pelly, 73 Warrington Crescent, London W9], formerly w of Harold Cleveland and dau of Joseph Prior

(2) (cont.) William Henry m 2nd 19 Sept 1907 Edith Anne (d 3 June 1968), dau of W H Nash, of Reigate, and d 14 Jan 1932, having by her had:

1a Edith Streatfield; b 23 Aug 1908; m 14 March 1940 *Lt Alastair Reginald Scott Cumming, Malay Regt, yst s of Alexander Cumming, OBE, and had:

1b *Alastair Michael; b 22 Dec 1941; educ Bradfield and RMA Sandhurst; Capt Gordon Highrs; m 12 Sept 1964 *Hilary Katherine, only dau of Geoffrey Copland Gray, and has:

1c *Emma Marian; b 27 Jan 1967

2c *Fiona Helen; b 2 Oct 1969

2b *Ian Scott; b 8 Aug 1946

(3) John Henry; b 17 Dec 1848; Capt RN; m 11 June 1885 Mary Rose (d May 1927), dau of James Lyon Thorne, Fleet Paymr RN, of Southsea, Hants, and d July 1920, leaving:

1a John Henry ; b 20 Aug1886; Lt-Col Worcs Regt WW I (star, two medals); m 2 June 1921 Dorothy Gladys, yr dau of James Percy Alwyne Gabb, MD, of Poyle Mount, Guildford, and d 18 July 1969, leaving:

1b Dorothy Joan; b 20 Nov 1922; m 1942 (divorce 1957) W/Cdr William Deane Symes, RAF, and d 19 June 1968, leaving issue

2a Charles Thorne; b 7 Nov 1890; m 20 June 1922 Lilian May (d 1976), dau of Engr R-Adml John Ham, CB, and d 25 Feb 1966, leaving:

lb *Diana May; b 25 Dec 1923; m 11 May 1946 *Anthony Fairey Needell, AMRINA, s of Philip Gregory Needell, of Watford, and has:

1c *Michael Anthony; b 25 Nov 1948; educ Ottershaw

2c *Timothy Richard; b 29 Oct 1951; educ Ottershaw

3c *Christopher Charles; b 8 July 1967

2b *Pauline Elizabeth [Mrs Aveling Pickard, The Coach House, Copsen Lane, Oxshott, Surrey]; b 15 March 1927; m 1st 19 June 1948 (divorce) Peter Anthony Welsford, ACA, only s of E P Welsford, and has:

1c *Paul Simon; b 14 April 1953; educ Reed's, Cobham

2c *Penelope Ann; 15 June 1949; m 1975 *Stuart Hall and has:

1d *Simon Leslie; b 1983

2d *Oliver Charles; b 1986

2b (cont.) Mrs Pauline Welsford m 2nd 1961 *Aveling Jocelyn Pickard

1a Marie Rose; b 18 July 1893

(4) Frederick Streatfield; b 17 Dec 1848 (twin with John Henry); Lt-Cdr RN; m June 1899 Harriot Wren Plaistowe (d 1939) and d 7 Dec 1914, having had:

1a Leonora Wren; b 17 Aug 1900; m 7 June 1948 Capt Charles Percival Cyrus Daniell, Welch Fus (d 1950), and dsp 21 Jan 1963

2a *Freda Sylvia [Mrs Philip Kemp, Highgate, PO 39, Ramsgate, Natal, S Africa]; b 25 Jan 1902; m 1 Jan 1954 *Prof Philip Kemp

(5) Herbert Alexander; b 17 June 1855; m 1st 1882 Florence Hafel; m 2nd 17 June 1899 Ada Roylance and d Jan 1937

(1) Harriet Barbara; b 19 March 1851; m 20 Dec 1878 Herbert Samuel Fenning (d 1911) and had issue

(2) Alice Leonora; b 27 March 1857; d 7 Dec 1944

5 Richard Wilson, DL; b 1 Nov 1814; Capt RN, Yr Bro Trin Ho 1846, Er Bro 1852; m 30 April 1851 Katherine Jane (d 1 Nov 1901), dau of John Gurney Fry, and d 25 May 1890, having had:

(1) John Gurney Richard; b 25 March 1855; m 1st 27 Feb 1878 Jane Gurney (d 10 March 1917), dau of Charles Albert Leatham, and had:

1a Vivian Gurney; b 5 June 1881; m 1st 22 June 1907 (divorce) Dorothy Penrose (d 1972), est dau of William Henry Sewell, of Epping Place, and had:

1b +Douglas Gurney; b 30 April 1910; educ Harrow; Lt RA WW II, High Sheriff Essex 1962; m 14 May 1935 *Monica, only dau of Lt-Col Arthur Wignall Tate (see TATE, Bt), and has:

1c +John Gurney [John Pelly Esq, Spring Hill, E Malling, Kent]; b 3 June 1938; educ Harrow; m 13 Oct 1972 *Vanda, dau of Col Hubert Allfrey, of Clock House, Lintch, Maidstone, Kent, and has:

1d +Sam Gurney; b 2 May 1974

2d +Jamie; b 15 May 1976; educ Harrow

3d +Guy Wignall; b 1982

2c +William Henry [William Pelly Esq, The Old Rectory, Sherrington, Wilts] b 23 Oct 1946; educ Harrow; m 11 Feb 1975 *Anne, yr dau of Francis Byrne, racing jnlst, of Fulham, and has:

1d +Henry Francis; b 6 Sept 1978

2d +Rupert Alexander; b 1980

1c *Claire Rose [Mrs Stuart Murray Threipland, Homington Farm, Homington, Salisbury, Wilts]; b Nov 1943; m 1st 20 Jan 1966 (divorce 1981) 17th Earl of Pembroke and (14th Earl of) Montgomery (qv) and has issue; m 2nd 1984 *Stuart Wyndham Murray Threipland

1a (cont.) Vivian Pelly m 2nd 7 Sept 1946 *Hilda Victoria [Mrs Vivian Pelly, Rosewood Cottage, Birch Close, Haywards Heath, Sussex], dau of Henry John Cole, and d 1 Dec 1949

2a Eustace Gurney; b 3 July 1886; Lt Dragoon Gds; m 1 Dec 1924 Dulcibella, formerly w of Llewellyn Arthur Hughes-Jones and dau of Robert Hillyard Henry Eden (see AUCKLAND, B), and dsp 13 Feb 1954

1a Elaine; b 22 Dec 1878; d unm 8 Aug 1956

2a Kathleen; b 8 Dec 1883; d unm 10 July 1957

(1) (cont.) John Pelly m 2nd 9 April 1918 Clare Emily (d 2 July 1959), 4th dau of Edward North Buxton (see BUXTON, Bt), and d 4 Nov 1940

(2) Richard Arnold (Rev), TD; b 25 Dec 1856; educ Trin Coll Cambridge (BA 1881, MA 1884); Hon Canon Chelmsford, Chaplain to Bp Chelmsford 1923; m 1st 26 April 1882 Margaret Jane (d 28 Nov 1903), dau of Thomas Fowell Buxton (see BUXTON, Bt), and had:

1a Arnold Claude (Rev); b 21 Feb 1883; educ Marlborough and Trin Coll Cambridge (BA 1904, MA 1910); Vicar St Mary's Bury St Edmunds 1935–60, Canon St Edmundsbury and Ipswich 1950, Pncpl St Andrew's Coll Gorakpur India, Kaisar-i-Hind gold medal; m 25 March 1920 Constance Emily (d 22 March 1976), yst dau of Rev Henry Stern, of Gorakpur, and d 1972

2a Donald Geoffrey; b 3 Aug 1884; educ Marlborough; Hon Capt RE, TF; m 30 July 1913 Joan King (d 19 June 1964), dau of John Caldwell Uhthoff, MD, FRCS, of Brighton, and dsp 7 Dec 1961

3a Richard Lawrence (Rev); b 18 July 1886; educ Marlborough and Clare Coll Cambridge (BA 1910, MA 1912); CF 1915–18 (despatches), V-Pncpl Bishop's Coll Calcutta 1918–26, Rector St Paul's Sch Darjeeling 1929–33, Vicar Shoreditch 1934–37, Canon Res St Nicholas's Cathedral Newcastle 1937–45, Rector Trowbridge 1945–54, Canon Salisbury 1952–76, Vicar Farley-cum-Pitton 1954–57; m 20 Aug 1927 (Rosa) Salome (d 10 april 1995), MB, MRCS, LRCP, dau of Rt Rev John Wordsworth, DD, Bp Salisbury, and d 7 April 1976, leaving:

1b +Richard Christopher Wordsworth [Richard Pelly Esq, Stonyroad, Audishaw Lane, Boylestone, Derbys DE6 5AE]; b 5 Feb 1938; educ Marlborough and Clare Coll Cambridge; m 30 June 1962 *Ruth Elinor, twin dau of Philip J Askey, of Weaverham, Cheshire, and has:

1c +Richard Hugh; b 4 Jan 1964

2c +David John; b 1972

1c *Katherine Jane; b 9 July 1966; m 1991 *Jasper John Pleydell-Bouverie (see RADNOR, E)

2b +Hugh John Wordsworth [Hugh Pelly Esq, Wake House, Ebbesbourne Wake, Wilts SP5 5JL]; b 17 Dec 1945; educ Marlborough and Middx Hosp (MB, BS Lond 1969, DCH); m 1972 *Jane Mary Fergusson and has:

1c +Tom Fergus; b 1975

2c +Matthew David; b 1977

3c +Adam; b 1979

4c +Christopher Hugh; 1982

1c *Claire Alexandra; b 1990

1b *Elizabeth Mary [Mrs Wyndham Jordan, 81A Beccles Rd, Bungay, Suffolk NR35 1HU]; b 22 Sept 1929; SRN; m 28 June 1952 Capt Wyndham Mackay Jordan, BM, BCh, DRCOG (d 27 March 1996), s of Rev Arthur Benjamin Jordan, and has:

1c *Christopher Wyndham [Christopher Jordan Esq, Highbury, Love Lane, Shaw, Berks RG14 2DY]; b 27 Aug 1956; educ Norwich Sch and Essex U (BSc); m 11 Aug 1979 *Gillian Smith, BA, PGCEd (Oxon), and adopted:

*Anthony Christopher; b 23 Nov 1989

*Zhala Anne ; b 6 Jan 1987

1c *Rosalind Cicely [Mrs Robert Tatam, 21 Sheredan Rd, London E4 9RW]; b 31 Jan 1955; MA; m 20 Dec 1986 *Robert Tatam and has:

1d *Luke Wyndham Charles; b 1 Aug 1989

2c *Diana Salome [Mrs Timothy Benge-Abbott, 7 Southland Close, Colchester, Essex CO4 4QH]; b 14 March 1959; BA; m 1983 *Timothy Benge-Abbott and has:

1d *Daniel; b 10 Aug 1986

2d *Joel Matthew; b 5 Feb 1989

3c *Alison Faith [Mrs Timothy Clarke, Norfolk House, 1 Grange Rd, Bishops Stortford, Herts CM23 5NG]; b 11 Nov 1961; MB, BS, DRCOG, DCH, MRCGP; m 1983 *Timothy Clarke, BSc, PhD, and has:

1d *Fiona; b 23 May 1994

2b *Rosa Jane [Miss Rosa Pelly, 20 Middle St, Harnham, Salisbury SP2 8LL]; b 14 Feb 1931; educ LMH Oxford (BA 1953); Headmistress Fiwasaye Girls' GS Akure W Nigeria, Fed Govt Coll Benin Nigeria, St Michael's Sch, Limpsfield, Surrrey

3b *Juliet Rachel [Mrs William Webb, 44 Mill Rd, Salisbury SP2 7RS]; b 14 Nov 1933; m 16 May 1964 *William Gibbins Webb, MA, DipEd, s of Thomas Gibbins Webb, of Towcester, Northants, and has:

1c *Rachel Sally; b 7 Feb 1965

2c *Rhoda Jane [Mrs Andrew Agerbak, 8 Orchard Gate, Greenford UB6 0QN]; b 2 Dec 1966; m 1989 *Andrew Thomas Agerbak and has:

1d *Elinor; b 4 Oct 1994

2d *Isobelle; b 10 Jan 1997

4b *Robina Catherine [Mrs Robina Hattersley, 3 Mill Race, Salisbury SP2 7RX]; b 10 Aug 1935; m 4 Jan 1958 (divorce 1986) Timothy Sherwood Hattersley, MB, BCh, yst s of Col S M Hattersley, MC, RAMC, of Overy Staithe, Norfolk, and has:

1c *Andrew [Andrew Hattersley Esq, 9 Elm Grove Rd, Topsham, Exeter EX3 0EQ]; b 22 Dec 1958; MB, BChir, MRCP; m 1986 *Katharine Dick and has:

1d *Mark; b 11 April 1995

1d *Ruth; b 7 Dec 1991

2d *Rosie; b 23 June 1993

2c *William John [William Hattersley Esq, 18 Honey Lane, Hurley, Maidenhead, Berks SL6 6RH]; b 6 Oct 1960; BSc

3c *Richard Wordsworth [Richard Hattersley Esq, 15 Orchard Ave, Lower Parkstone, Dorset BH14 8AH]; b 2 April 1964; MB, BS; m 1991 *Susan Herbert and has:

1d *Emma; b 26 Aug 1997

4a Francis Brian, AFC; b 2 April 1889; educ Sherborne and Trin Coll Cambridge; Lt WW I, Gen Sec Shaftesbury Homes and Arethusa Training Ship 1927–54; m 3 June 1913 Edith Beatrice (d 1984), 2nd dau of Rev William James Packe, Vicar Feering, Kelvedon, and d 1984, leaving:

1b Michael Brian; b 18 June 1915; educ Bryanston; m 29 June 1946 *Mary Margaret [Mrs Michael Pelly, Fairview, 71 High St, Rode, Bath BA3 6PB], er dau of Herbert Southernden Burn, CBE, of Ivy Cottage, Cleeve, nr Bristol, and d 1994, leaving:

1c +Roger Brian; b 17 June 1950; educ Bryanston and Southampton and Birmingham Us (MSc); MIOSH; m 1st 1980 (divorce 1986) Monica Giovanna Deorsola; m 2nd 1987 *Kiki Joyce McFarlane

2c +David Arnold [David Pelly Esq, 56 Honeybrook Rd, London SW12]; b 11 May 1954; educ Bryanston and York and Bradford Us (BTech); m 1989 *Deborah Susan Mattison and has:

1d +Henry Theodore; b 1992

2d +Francis Michael; b 1994

1c *Nicola Susan [Miss Nicola Pelly, 3255 Cedar Ave, Westmount, Montreal, Quebec H3Y 1Z6, Canada]; b 18 Feb 1948; educ Sherborne Sch for Girls and Sidcot Sch; m 1972 (divorce 1977) Peter Charles Jeffery; has issue by Harry Parnass:

1d *Arikshaan Mikael; b 1992

1d *Talia Shane; b 1984

2b +Peter Richard [Peter Pelly Esq, Green Farm, Bovingdon Green, Herts HP3 0LF]; b 17 June 1916; educ Bryanston; CEng; m 25 Aug 1945 *Kathleen Irene, yst dau of S W Moorhouse, of Guildford, and has:

1c *Lynda Ann [Mrs Edward Macalister-Smith, 9 Whittox Lane, Frome, Somerset BA11 3BY]; b 12 Jan 1947; m 1980 *Edward Macalister-Smith, MSc, BSc, and has:

1d *Sam Henry; b 1982

1d *Mathilda Rose; b 1983

2c *Kathleen Georgina [Mrs E Caldwell, Moses Plat Farm, Speen, Bucks HP27 0SD]; b 6 Jan 1951; m 1975 *E V Caldwell, BA

1b *Margaret Beatrice [Mrs Jovan Ulic, Rosebay Cottage, 15 Langham Place, Rode, Somerset BA3 6PL]; b 1921; m 1st 2 Oct 1943 (divorce 1959) Theodore Sanger, s of Dr Frederick Sanger, of Tamworth-in-Arden, Worcs, and has:

1c *Melody; b 16 Dec 1947; m 1970 *Peter Wright and has:

1d *Megan Jenett; b 1973

2d *Alice Rosamund; b 1979

3d *Madalene Rose; b 1980

2c *Katrina Scarlett; *b* 22 Aug 1952; *m* 1977 *Michael Power and has:
  1d *Katherine; *b* 1978
  2d *Molly; *b* 1980
  3d *Ellen; *b* 1983
1b (cont.) Mrs Margaret Sanger *m* 2nd 31 May 1969 *Jovan Ulic, s of Illja Ulic, of Belgrade

5a Arthur Roland; *b* 14 Nov 1895; *educ* Marlborough and Trin Coll Cambridge (BA 1919, MA 1922); Capt 5th Bn Norfolk Regt, Bursar Cheltenham Coll 1938–61; *m* 21 April 1920 Phyllis Elsie (*d* 1974), er dau of Alexander Duff Henderson, of Hampstead, and *d* 2 June 1966, leaving:

1b +John Gordon [John Pelly Esq, Aniceford House, Stockton-on-Teme, Worcs WR6 6UX]; *b* 27 Nov 1923; *educ* Marlborough; Lt RNVR WW II (despatches); *m* 18 Jan 1947 *Patricia, er dau of Major Hugh Clarence Fuller, of Arran Lodge, Crossabeg, Co Wexford, and has:

1c +(John) Henry Patrick Fuller [Henry Pelly Esq, Cleave House, Fordcombe, Kent TN3 0RJ]; *b* 27 Sept 1953; *educ* Marlborough; *m* 1980 *Susan Elizabeth, dau of Michael A Briggs, of Harts, Penhurst, Kent, and has:
  1d +Freddie John Fuller; *b* 3 July 1986
  1d *Clare Elizabeth; *b* 8 June 1984
  2d *Serena Rose; *b* 17 Oct 1989
1c *Priscilla Jane; *b* 19 Feb 1949; *m* 8 April 1972 *David Dalziel Mundell, est s of G M D Mundell, of Elgin, Condamine, Australia, and has issue:
  1d *John Dalziel; *b* 11 May 1977
  2d *Andrew Hugh Dalziel; *b* 30 June 1979
  1d *Sarah Richenda; *b* 11 June 1973
  2d *Lucinda Clare; *b* 10 June 1975
2c *Caroline Anne [Mrs Michael Howard, Green Farm, Sankyns Green, Worcs]; *b* 23 Nov 1950; *m* 8 Sept 1973 *Michael Eliot Howard, er s of (Eliot) (Charles) Stewart Howard, TD, DL, of Duckswich House, Upton-on-Seven, Worcs, and has:
  1d *Nicholas Henry; *b* 22 May 1979
  2d *Harry Eliot; *b* 18 Sept 1982
  1d *Joanna Clare; *b* 9 Aug 1977
2b +Derek Roland [Derek Pelly Esq, Kenbank, St John's Town of Dalry, Kirkcudbrightshire DG7 3TX]; *b* 12 June 1929; *educ* Marlborough and Trin Coll Cambridge (BA 1952, MA 1956); Lt RA 1947–49, formerly JP Essex, chm Barclays Internat, dep-chm Barclays Bank; *m* 20 June 1953 *Susan, er dau of John Malcolm Roberts, FRICS, of Greenwich, and has:
1c +Samuel Roland; *b* 25 March 1960
1c *Rosemary Jane; *b* 10 Jan 1955; *m* 1988 *Mark C Campbell, s of D M Campbell, of Colesbourne, Glos, and has:
  1d *Alexander Leo; *b* 23 Aug 1990
  2d *Euan Henderson; *b* 13 April 1992
2c *Catherine Susan; *b* 24 May 1958; *m* 1982 (*divorce* 1998) Simon A W Osborn, only s of Col M A C Osborn, of Shaftesbury, Dorset, and has:
  1d *George Ashby Arthur; *b* 27 Sept 1990
  1d *Cicely Mai Elsie; *b* 28 May 1986
  2d *Anna Catherine Pelly; *b* 26 Feb 1988
1b *Mary Duff [Mrs George Stevens, Barn Corner, All Cannings, Wilts SN19 3NX]; *b* 25 March 1921; WRNS WW II; *m* 22 June 1945 *Lt George Thomas Bridges Stevens, RNVR, slr, s of Col George Bridges Stevens, of Ceylon, and has:
1c *Charles Bridges; *b* 19 May 1946; *educ* Cheltenham; *m* 1972 *Jeanette MacDonald, dau of Walter Moore, of Barbados, and has:
  1d *Edward George Bridges; *b* 1976
2c *David George; *b* 22 April 1951; *educ* Cheltenham and St Bartholomew's Hosp (BSc, MB, BS); *m* 1976 *Philippa Mary, dau of Charles Richard Pemberton Steer, of Llandevaud, Gwent, and has:
  1d *Hugh Richard; *b* 1979
  2d *Alec Charles; *b* 1982
1c *Lucia Mary; *b* 16 Jan 1956; *m* 1981 *Philip Charles Dinkel, RIBA, s of Prof Michael Dinkel, of Bussage, Glos, and has:
  1d *Henry Michael George; *b* 1988
  2d *(William) Theodore John; *b* 1990
  1d *Charlotte Mary; *b* 1986
2b *Janet Elizabeth [Mrs Janet Fenwick, 83 Bainton Rd, Oxford OX2 7AG]; *b* 30 May 1926; *m* 12 Sept 1953 (*divorce* 1981) Michael Lindsay Fenwick, PhD, s of Lindsay Fenwick, of Salcombe, Devon, and has:
1c *Alison Jane; *b* 8 Aug 1955
2c *Anne Richenda; *b* 2 Aug 1957
3c *Juliet Nicola [Mrs Derwin Nazarino, 4305 SW 100th St, Seattle, WA, USA]; *b* 1 Dec 1959; *m* 1992 *Derwin Nazarino and has:
  1d *Joel; *b* 1994
  1d *Sarah Nicola; *b* 1997

1a Janet Catherine; *b* 16 Aug 1890; *m* 14 Oct 1913 Capt Edward Randall Cubitt (*ka* Gallipoli 12 Aug 1915), 5th Bn Norfolk Regt, er s of Edward George Cubitt, of Honing Hall, Norfolk, and *d* 2 Jan 1970, leaving issue
2a Margaret Richenda; *b* 9 Dec 1892; *d* 16 Jan 1894

(2) (cont.) The Rev Canon Richard Pelly *m* 2nd 7 June 1906 Dora Isobel (*d* 14 May 1915), est dau of Sir Edward Hildred Carlile, 1st Bt, CBE (*see* 1940 edn), and *d* 2 Dec 1949

(3) Edmund Nevill Richard; *b* 12 Dec 1858; *m* 12 July 1887 Emma Mary (*d* Dec 1939), dau of John Fowler, of Leeds, and *d* 1 Oct 1931, having had:

1a John Noel, CBE; *b* 15 June 1888; Capt RN WW II, Yr Bro Trin Ho 1927; *m* 22 Jan 1924 Rosalind (*d* 9 Sept 1957), only dau of R G Gatehouse of Abbot's Grange, Bebington, Cheshire, and *das* 6 June 1945, leaving:

1b +(John) Stewart Gatehouse [Stewart Pelly Esq, Great Wilsey Farm, Haverhill, Suffolk]; *b* 10 Dec 1930; *m* 10 Sept 1960 *(Helen) Josephine, only dau of Denys Heaton Hirst, of Huddersfield, and has had:

1c Sarah Elizabeth; *b* 9 June; *d* 12 June 1963
2c *Jennifer Œnone; *b* 3 Oct 1965
3c *Catherine Allison; *b* 15 Aug 1967
4c *(Rosemary) Helen; *b* 20 Nov 1969
5c *Isobel Serena; *b* 4 March 1973
1b *Rosemary Œnone [Mrs Gordon Nelmes, Gardeners Farm, Hatfield Peverel, Essex CM3 2NS]; *b* 15 May 1927; *m* 18 July 1956 Gordon Nelmes (*d* 1992), yst s of Ernest Nelmes, of Hull, and has:
1c *John Pelly; *b* 21 Oct 1957; *m* 1988 *Fiona Jane, dau of Robert Nalder, of Underriver, Kent, and has:
  1d *Flora Mary; *b* 14 Nov 1991
  2d *Emma Rosemary; *b* 21 Nov 1993
  3d *Elizabeth Margaret; *b* 17 May 1996
2c *Godfrey Edward; *b* 29 Sept 1959
3c *Edmund Gordon; *b* 16 Dec 1965
1c *Rosalind Jane; *b* 21 July 1962; *m* 1986 *Charles Richard Maurice Bishop, s of Brig Richard Bishop, and has:
  1d *Thomas Richard Chilton; *b* 31 March 1993
  1d *Rosanna Emily Margaret; *b* 1 Sept 1990
  2d *Victoria Œnone Jane; *b* 1 Sept 1994

2a Edmund Godfrey, DSO (1918), MC; *b* 19 Oct 1889; Lt-Col ASC (MT) WW I (despatches) and WW II; *m* 24 May 1919 Isabel Amy (*d* 1988), dau of Robert Henry Fowler, of Moor House, Moortown, Leeds, and Park Sq, Regent's Park, and *das* 28 Oct 1939, leaving:

1b +Robert Hubert [Robert Pelly Esq, Victoria House, Pierce Lane, Fulbourn, Cambs CB1 5DL]; *b* 17 Aug 1923; *educ* Shrewsbury and Trin Coll Cambridge (BA); Capt Lothians and Bdr Yeo WW II (despatches); *m* 17 Feb 1951 *Eirolys Elizabeth, er dau of Major Le Gendre George William Horton-Fawkes, OBE, DL, of Farnley Hall, Otley, Yorks, and has:
1c +Richard Fowler; *b* 4 July 1955; *m* 1983 *Michelle Colette, yr dau of Dr Henri Bouteille, of St Etienne, France, and has:
  1d *Isabelle; *b* 1986
  2d *Victoria Sarah; *b* 1988
  3d *Mathilde; *b* 1990
2c +(Robert) Simon Horton [Simon Pelly Esq, 47 Isis St, London SW18 3QL]; *b* 31 March 1960; *m* 1989 *Rachel M, yst dau of Peter Hamilton-Ely, of Fovant, Wilts, and has:
  1d +Hugh; *b* 6 Jan 1995
  2d +Rupert; *b* 21 July 1997
  1d *Camilla; *b* 21 Feb 1993
1c *Serena Louise; *b* 13 Feb 1953; *m* 1974 *Stephen John Richards and has:
  1d *Thomas Linton; *b* 1980
  1d *Clare Lucy; *b* 1979
1b Antoinette Joan; *b* 21 April 1920; VAD WW II; *m* 22 July 1942 Capt Kenneth William Macleod (*d* 1983), London Scottish, s of E D Macleod, of Highgate, and *d* 1997, leaving:
1c *Neil Godfrey; *b* 21 Dec 1947; *educ* Embley Park Sch; *m* 1973 *Sheila Anne, dau of Crawford Tyler, of Ontario, and has:
  1d *Steven Kenneth; *b* 1975
  2d *Jeffrey; *b* 1985
  1d *Amy; *b* 1978
  2d *Diana; *b* 1981
1c *Allison Anne [Mrs Geoffrey Fellows, 27 Mallard Drive, Woodford Halse, Northants NN11 3EJ]; *b* 22 July 1946; *m* 1st 14 Sept 1968 Robert Hellett (*d* 1970), 6th s of Henry Hellett, of Park Lane Farm, Kimbolton, Hunts, and has:
  1d *Robert Henry; *b* 1970
1c (cont.) Mrs Robert Hellett *m* 2nd 1975 *Geoffrey Hugh Fellows
2c *Flora Margaret; *b* 28 Oct 1952; *m* 1976 *Graham Gilbert and has:
  1d *Kris Graham; *b* 1978
  2d *Rory Neil; *b* 1980

3a Hubert Richard; *b* 7 Sept 1895; *educ* Charterhouse; Lt 7th Bn Essex Regt; *ka* Gallipoli 9 Oct 1915

4a Denis Edward; *b* 16 Feb 1898; Cdr RN; *m* 1st 30 Dec 1925 Grace Olympia (*d* 27 Jan 1951), yst dau of P E Laurence, of The Grove, Witham, Essex; *m* 2nd 19 Sept 1951 *Margaret Mary, widow of F T Turnbull, and *dsp* 10 July 1970

1a Cicely Edith, JP Essex; *b* 16 June 1891; *d* unm 7 Jan 1969

(4) Herbert Cecil; *b* 27 Nov 1860; *m* 1st 21 March 1882 Mary Richenda (*d* 11 May 1919), dau of H W Carter, JP, of The Limes, Walthamstow, and had:

1a Humphrey Richard; *b* 31 July 1886; Capt RE (TF); *m* 8 Feb 1916 Barbara Vidal (*d* 17 June 1965), dau of Frederick Scrutton, of Woolpits, Nutfield, and *d* 9 May 1955, leaving:

1b Diana; *b* 8 May 1917; *m* 17 April 1936 *Robert Arthur Byas Sheppard, MC, s of Gerald Arthur Sheppard, of Bembridge, IoW, and had issue
2b *Juliet [Mrs George Bray, Cobblers Cottage, Bishop Monkton, N Yorks]; *b* 28 Jan 1920; *m* 8 Oct 1946 Major George Ian Bray, MBE (*d* 1985), er s of Col George Bray, of Causeway House, Adel, Leeds, and has:
1c *Rose Elizabeth *b* 19 Sept 1950
2c *Annabel Lucy; *b* 19 Sept 1950

2a Gilbert Cecil; *b* 26 July 1892; Capt RN; *m* 15 Jan 1921 Constance Margery (*d* 16 March 1962), est dau of Frederic Edward de Tweenbrook Glazebrook, of Manila, Philippines, and *d* 23 Feb 1961, leaving:

1b +David Cecil [Lt-Cdr David Pelly RN, Westerly, 5 The Marches, Fernhurst, Haslemere GU27 3DT]; *b* 17 March 1922; *educ* RNC Dartmouth; served WW II (despatches, Croix de Guerre), Yr Bro Trin Ho 1951; *m* 29 July 1950 *Angela Mary, only dau of Capt Wilfrid Pearse Gandell, CBE, RN, of Slinfold, Sussex, and has:

1c +Richard Cecil; *b* 31 May 1951; *educ* Marlborough and Selwyn Coll Cambridge (MA, MSc, CEng), MI MechE, FIMarE, MInstD; Capt RN, Yr

Bro Trin Ho 1994; m 1974 *Fleur Veronica, only dau of John Desmond Proctor, of Reigate, Surrey, and has:

  1d +Jonathan Henry; b 1988

  1d *Cécile; b 1977

  2d *Victoria Clare; b 1982

2c +Nicholas John; b 14 April 1953; educ Marlborough, Birmingham U (BSc) and London Business Sch (MSc); m 1st 1977 (divorce 1987) Elaine Margaret, er dau of George G Illingworth, of Cupar, Fife, and has:

  1d +Alistair George; b 1981

  1d *Catriona Marie; b 1983

2c (cont.) Nicholas Pelly m 2nd 1990 *Sally, dau of Jack Odell, of Topeka, Kansas, and by her has:

  2d +James David; b 1992

3c +Patrick David [Patrick Pelly Esq, 18 Badshot Park, Badshot Lea, Farnham, Surrey GU9 9JZ]; b 25 March 1955; educ Marlborough and Manchester U (BSc, MCIT); m 1985 *Margaret Julie, dau of Scott Gray, of Coal Aston, Sheffield, and has:

  1d +Ralph Jonathan; b 1986

  2d +Christopher Scott; b 1988

4c +Gilbert Ralph; b 9 March 1966; educ Marlborough; Capt RM; FRGS; m 1995 *Jane Anna (MA Oxon), dau of John Bagley, of Lanteglos-by-Foey, Cornwall

1c *Alexandra Helen [Mrs Ian Pearson, The Anchor, Anchor Rd, S Moreton, Oxon OX11 9AN]; b 15 Feb 1961; educ Midhurst GS and Birmingham U (BSocSc); m 1988 *Ian Mark McLaren Pearson, est s of Malcolm J S Pearson, and has:

  1d *Hamish James McLaren; b 1993

  1d *Katherine Rose McLaren; b 1995

2b +John Kenneth [John Pelly Esq, Cedar Croft, Rural Route 5, Bolton, Ontario L7E 5S1, Canada]; b 14 Nov 1923; Lt RN (ret); m 8 Oct 1946 *Joan Campbell, only dau of John Campbell Fraser, of Cedar Ridge, Scarborough, Ontario, Canada, and has:

1c +David Fraser; b 19 June 1948; BSc (RMC) Lt-Cdr Canadian Armed Forces (ret), FRGS, FRCGS; m 1st 23 May 1970 (divorce 1974) Sara Lynn, dau of Mrs Alan Nicholson, of Fredericton, New Brunswick; m 2nd 199– *Laurie, dau of Joseph McGinnis, of New Jersey

2c +Brian Gordon [Brian Pelly Esq, 41 Underhill Crescent, Aurora, Ontario L4G 5S3, Canada]; b 16 July 1954; BMath Waterloo U; ASA, ACAS; m 1978 *Lynn Dorothy, er dau of Russell Henry Pearson, of Manitoulin Island, Ontario, and has:

  1d +Kyle Russell John; b 1984

  1d *Heather Kathryn; b 1981

  2d *Colleen Leslie; b 1986

1c *Elizabeth Gail [Mrs John Henry, 127 Parkview Ave, Willowdale, Ontario, Canada M2N 3Y4]; b 1 May 1951; m 1975 *John David Henry and has:

  1d *Kimberly Beth; b 1981

  2d *Robyn Lynn; b 1984

  3d *Laura Louise; b 1986

3b +Peter Jeremy [Peter Pelly Esq, Under Westwood, Upper Swainswick, Bath BA1 8BZ]; b 2 Dec 1930; m 14 Feb 1953 *Dorothy Joan (Joanna), only dau of Capt Thomas William Robert Hill, RA, and adopted dau of Christopher Ransom, and has:

1c +Anthony John; b 18 May 1956; m 1983 *Jane Chisholm, only dau of Noel Hair, of Wylam, Northumberland, and has:

  1d +Stephen Nicholas James; b 1985

  2d +David Samuel Henry; b 1988

  1d *Joanna Elizabeth Chisholm (twin); b 1988

1c *Lyndsay Madeleine; b 29 June 1954; m 1980 *Peter St L Kyrke-Smith, s of B H S Kyrke-Smith, of Penbedw, Nannerch, Clwyd, and has:

  1d *George Henry; b 1991

  1d *Laura Elizabeth; b 1983

  2d *Hannah Sarah; b 1985

  3d *Rebecca Lucy; b 1987

2c *Elizabeth Joanna Clare; b 21 July 1958; m 1990 *Anthony John Fielding, of Slaley, Northumberland, and has:

  1d *Leo Anthony; b 1993

  1d *Molly Alexandra; b 1992

3c *Nicolette Jane; b 12 July 1960

4c *Ann Catherine; b 12 March 1964

3a Kenneth Raymond (Sir), MC; b 9 Nov 1893; educ Charterhouse; Capt RASC WW I, Pres Chamber Shipping 1956–57, Chm Lloyd's Register of Shipping 1957–63, ktd 1961; m 15 Oct 1919 Elspeth Norna (d 6 June 1978), est dau of Robert Campbell Grant, of Hale Edge, S Nutfield, and d 30 Sept 1973, leaving:

1b +(Andrew) Desmond, DFC [Desmond Pelly Esq DFC, Halings, Balcombe, Sussex]; b 28 Aug 1923; F/Lt RAF WW II; m 9 June 1945 *Nancye Jean, dau of Lt-Col Eric Tillyer Tatham, of Haywards Heath, by Hon Lettice Theresa, est dau of 10th Baron Digby (qv), and has:

1c +Ian Raymond; b 29 March 1949; educ Malvern; m 1974 (divorce 1993) Alana Murray, of Brisbane, Australia

1c *Angela Pauline; b 23 Jan 1947; m 25 July 1970 (divorce1987) Douglas F Wentzel, est s of D B Wentzel III, of Quebec, and has:

  1d *Kristian Douglas Andrew; b 1979

  1d *Karla Juli-Anne; b 1973

  2d *Alexandra Korin; b 1975

2c *Christine Mary; b 12 Feb 1952; m 1972 *Timothy Cross, Col RAOC, and has:

  1d *Alexander Leigh; b 1974

  2d *Stephen David; b 1990

  1d *Gemma Charlotte; b 28 Feb 1977

  3c *Fiona Elizabeth; b 15 Dec 1955

1b *Ursula Elspeth [Mrs Robert Brown, New Barn, Colgate, Sussex]; b 31 Dec 1921; WRNS WW II; m 24 Feb 1945 Lt Robert George Malloch Brown, SANF(V) (d 11 May 1967), yst s of Robert W Malloch Brown by Mrs R F Symonds, of Cathcart, S Africa, and has:

1c *George Mark; b 16 Sept 1953; educ Marlborough; m 1989 *Patricia Anne Cronam and has:

  1d *Maddison Jane; b 1991

  2d *Isabel Anne; b 1994

1a Gwynneth Mary; m 29 April 1909 John Keble Guy, of Kitfield Barn, Ardingly, Sussex, and d 18 Feb 1963, leaving issue

(4) (cont.) Herbert Pelly m 2nd 15 Nov 1924 Eileen Boyd Carpenter (d 22 May 1949) and d 4 May 1935

(5) Alfred Digby; b 7 Sept 1862; m 5 April 1899 Evelyn Sophia (d 27 March 1970), 4th dau of Rev Canon Edward John Harford, and d 20 Jan 1940, leaving:

1a +Richard Edward; b 29 May 1905; m 21 April 1941 Diana Marthe Desgrand Mitchell (d 1991) and has:

1b *Louise Sophia [Ms Louise Pelly QC, 310 Lake Promenade, Toronto, Ont, Canada M8W 1B5]; b 27 Oct 1943; educ Concordia U Montreal (BA 1973), McGill (LLB 1976, BCL 1977) and Harvard (LLM 1978); barrister Quebec 1979 and Ont 1990; QC 1991, joined Stikeman, Elliott 1980, ptnr 1985–94, private practice 1994–; m 1967 (divorce 1971, resumed maiden name) Donald John Mactaggart, only s of Norman C W Mactaggart, of Montreal, and has:

  1c *Alexandra Caroline Diana PELLY; b 1985

2b *Harriet Elizabeth Annabel [Mrs Gerald Graham, 70 Third Ave, Ottawa, Ont K1S 2J8, Canada]; b 5 May 1948; educ McGill (BAPsych 1977, MSW 1985); m 1st 1984 (divorce 1988) Francis Roland Stark; m 2nd 1991 *Gerald Graham

1a Violet Evelyn; b 11 June 1900; m Feb 1923 Marquis de Ruvigny (d 10 May 1941), genealogist, and d 1996, leaving:

1b *Michael Francis Wriothesley; b 11 May 1927; m 26 Jan 1956 *Patricia Kirkpatrick, est dau of C Kirkpatrick Pile, of Barbados, and has:

1c *Rupert Francis James Henry; b 19 July 1959; ptnr Price Waterhouse 1992–; m 1987 *Kumudini Nelun, yst dau of Dr C S Ratnatunga, of Woodside Park, London

1c *Rachel Anne [Mrs Philip Rubery, Westcourt Houst, The Chase, Oxshott, Surrey]; b 2 Nov 1959; m 1976 *Philip Alan Rubery and has:

  1d *Henry Philip Michael Nicholas; b 1984

  1d *Georgina Rachel Eugenie; b 1983

(6) Henry Bertram (Sir), KCVO, CB, JP Surrey; b 9 Sept 1867; served WW I (despatches), Order St Maurice and St Lazarus Italy 4th Cl, Order St Vladimir Russia with swords, Order El Nhada 1st Cl, Yr Bro Trin Ho 1894; m 14 Dec 1904 Lillian Katherine Hawkshaw (d 20 Sept 1966), er dau of Sir William Vincent, 12th Bt (see 1940 edn), and d 27 Dec 1942, leaving:

1a +Douglas Charles Vincent [Cdr Douglas Pelly RN, 4 Shapley Hill, Odiham Rd, Winchfield, Hants RG27 8BU]; b 24 June 1908; served WW II (despatches); m 15 Aug 1938 *Catherine Loraine, dau of Edwyn Conran, of Buenos Aires, and has:

1b +(Douglas) Edwyn Vincent [Edwyn Pelly Esq, 10 Freelands Rd, Cobham, Surrey KT11 2ND]; b 23 Sept 1951; educ Marlborough; Surrey CC; m 17 Aug 1974 *Susan Margaret, dau of George Hards, of Cobham, and has:

  1c +Matthew James; b 1984

  1c *Jessica; b 1975

  2c *Samantha; b 1976

1b *Anne Loraine; b 16 July 1939; m 20 Aug 1966 *Lachlan Nicholas Ferrar Forbes, er s of Lachlan Maxwell Forbes, of Milton House, Milton, Cambridge, and has:

  1c *Lachlan Pelly Ferrar; b 24 April 1970

  2c *Angus Maxwell; b 25 June 1971

2b *Gillian Esmé [Mrs Timothy Caffell, 54 Tartar Rd, Cobham, Surrey]; b 26 March 1942; SRN (1964), RMN; m 1983 *Timothy C Caffell, 2nd s of E W Caffell, of Cobham, and has:

  1c *Anna Margaret Juliet; b 1985

3b *Catherine Elizabeth; b 22 July 1948; m 1973 *Simon Maxwell and has:

  1c *Daniel; b 1976

  2c *Oliver; b 1977

  3c *Dominic; b 1981

2a +Adrian Vincent, LVO (1971, MVO 1962), JP [Adrian Pelly Esq LVO JP, Coombeside, E Meon, Hants GU32 1PB]; b 16 Aug 1919; Lt RNVR WW II, HM's Land Steward Roy Farms Windsor 1951–71; m 24 July 1975 Margaret Esterel (d 5 May 1997), dau of Lt-Col Roger Uvedale Lambert, MBE

1a Esterel Alice Muriel, OBE (1953); b 12 Jan 1906; m 7 Nov 1928 Brig Philip Reginald Antrobus (d 1986), CBE, MC, RE, s of Sir Reginald Laurence Antrobus, KCMG, CB, and d 30 April 1997

2a Andrea Evelyn; b 8 Aug 1917; RNVAD WW II; m 17 Jan 1970 *Rev John Algernon Peyton Hoskyns (see HOSKYNS, Bt), and d 23 April 1991

(7) Frederick Raymond; b 11 Aug 1869; m 4 Sept 1906 Beatrice Alice (d 7 Jan 1940), dau of Rev Arthur Henry Delmé Radcliffe, Rector Holwell, and dsp 16 Oct 1940

(1) Emma Maria; m 19 Nov 1874 John Henry Buxton and d 22 Oct 1924, leaving issue (see BUXTON, Bt)

(2) Edith Rachel; m 5 Oct 1887 Rev Canon John Battersby Harford (d 7 Jan 1937), DD, Res Canon Ripon, and d 2 Nov 1925, leaving issue

(3) Alice Maud; m 28 Sept 1897 Rev Henry Theodore Cavell (d 1914), Vicar Woodford Wells, Essex, and d 10 Aug 1958, leaving issue

6 Edmond; b 18 July 1816; m 5 March 1846 Anna Rebecca (d 25 Dec 1907), est dau of Jonathan Chapman, of Wanstead, Essex, and dsp 19 May 1865

7 Alfred; b and d 1820

8 Octavius, JP; b 7 May 1823; Capt 7th Madras Light Cav, Col Edin Artillery Militia; m 7 Jan 1847 Justina (d 18 May 1904), dau of Holwell Fisher, of Plaistow, and dsp 30 April 1904

9 Percy Leonard, of Oakley, Merstham; b 21 March 1826; m 2 June 1852 Eliza Anne (d 17 Feb 1924) dau of John Sanderson Rigge, of Belmont Castle, and d 4 June 1892, leaving, with other issue:

(1) Percy John, JP Glos; b 19 May 1853; m 15 May 1879 Florence Marion (d 10 Feb 1953), dau of Henry Butler, of Elmore, Chipstead, and d 1 Feb 1932, leaving:

1a Florence Irene Clare; b 5 March 1884; d unm 19 June 1954

2a Doris Eileen; b 1 Aug 1890; d unm 7 July 1955

3a Iva Marion; b 14 Jan 1900; Ch Cmdt ATS WW II; d unm 9 Nov 1985

(2) Leonard, JP Essex; b 19 Sept 1856; Maj Essex Imp Yeo; m 28 Oct 1880 Elizabeth (d 23 May 1930), dau of Charles Albert Leatham, of Gunnersgate Hall, Yorks, and d 22 Sept 1913, leaving:

1a Eric Percy Leonard; b 26 Nov 1894; educ Wellington and Trin Coll Cambridge; 2nd Lt TFR WW I (wounded); m 1924 Helen Marjorie (d 16 Jan 1968), dau of Edmund Richmond Wade, of Boston, Mass., and d 14 Feb 1978, leaving:

1b *Rosamund Ann [Mrs Elliott Viney, Cross Farmhouse, Quainton, Bucks HP22 4AR]; b 9 Feb 1927; m 3 June 1950 *Elliott Merriam Viney, DSO, MBE, TD, DL, FSA, est s of Col Oscar Vaughan Viney, TD, DL, of Aylesbury, and has:

1c *Diana Susan [Mrs Hugh Scrimgeour, 1 Teignmouth Rd, London NW2]; b 22 Jan 1952; m 1979 *Hugh Scrimgeour, s of Robin Scrimgeour, of Lockeridge, Marlborough, and has:

1d *Daniel; b 1981

2d *Alexander; b 1984

1d *Sophie Rebecca; b 1988

2c *Amanda Louise [Mrs Tom Deakin, 9 Hazlebury Rd, London SW6]; b 19 Oct 1954; m 1983 *Tom Deakin and has:

1d *Jack Elliott; b 1987

2d *Charley; b 1989

1a Christabel; b 4 Sept 1881; m 1st 27 April 1909 Leigh Udall Kent (d 1919), of Cunnynhame House, St Albans, and had issue; m 2nd 1920 (divorce 1929) S/Ldr William Herbert Mackenzie, AFC, RAF, of Victoria, BC, and had further issue; m 3rd May 1931 Capt Arthur Leslie Moore, 4th Cav IA, of Old Hall, High Hurstwood, Buxted, Sussex, and d 30 April 1952

(1) Ada; m 27 Aug 1890 Rev Honyel Gough Rosedale (d 14 Jan 1928), DD, FSA, Rector Copford, Essex, and d 17 May 1937, leaving issue

(2) Beatrice; m 26 June 1890 Robert Campbell Grant (d 18 Feb 1931), of Hale Edge, South Nutfield, and d 5 Oct 1946

1 Juliana Sally; m 3 Oct 1832, W Stores Fry (d 26 Aug 1844)

2 Emma Eugenia, m 1 May 1833 R Foster Reynolds (d 1845) and d 1 May 1893, aged 81

Sir JOHN d 13 Aug 1852; his est son,

Sir John Henry Pelly, 2nd Bt; b 30 March 1809; m 1st 19 Dec 1840 Johanna Jane (d 2 Feb 1856), dau and coheir of John Carstairs, of Stratford Green, Essex, and had:

1 **Sir Henry Carstairs Pelly, 3rd Bt**, JP, DL; b 23 April 1844; MP Huntingdon, Capt 2nd Life Gds; m 22 Nov 1872 Lady Lilian Harriet Charteris (m 2nd 31 July 1882 Sir Henry Francis Redhead Yorke, KCB (d 12 Jan 1914), and d 11 April 1914; see WEMYSS and MARCH, E), and d 4 June 1877, leaving:

(1) Annie Evelyn; LGStJ, Ldy-in-Waiting to HRH THE DUCHESS OF CONNAUGHT; m 19 April 1913 Capt Thomas Henry Rivers Bulkeley, CMG, MVO, Scots Gds (ka Oct 1914), s of Col Charles Rivers Bulkeley, CB, and d 11 July 1923, leaving issue

(2) Constance Lillian; m 25 Jan 1900 27th Earl of Crawford and (10th Earl of) Balcarres (qv) and d 8 Jan 1947, leaving issue

2 Charles Raymond, RN; b 16 June 1845; d unm 23 July 1866

1 Emma Cecil; m 5 April 1866 Walter Douglas Dumbleton and d 20 July 1885

2 Helen; d 3 Oct 1856

3 Evelyn Juliana; m 27 Aug 1867 James Henry (d 1916), of Lingmell, Putney Heath, and d 13 June 1934, leaving issue

Sir John m 2nd 13 Nov 1860 Blanche Elizabeth (d 16 Feb 1925), dau of Sir Frederick Vincent, 11th Bt (see 1940 edn), and d 20 Dec 1864, having by her had:

3 Alwyne Vincent; b 19 Oct 1861; d 6 March 1876

4 HAROLD (Sir), **4th Bt**

5 Arthur Norris; b 15 May 1864; educ Eton; Lt Roy Sussex Regt; m 9 June 1923 Helen Amy (d 27 Oct 1960), widow of George Atwood and dau of W H Laverton, of Leighton House, Westbury, Wilts, and d 11 Jan 1950

The 3rd Bt's half-brother,

Sir Harold Pelly, 4th Bt, JP Dorset; b 28 Feb 1863; educ Harrow and Ch Ch Oxford (BA 1885); T/Capt 1st Vol Bn Dorset Regt, Lt Roy Wilts Yeo Cav; m 5 March 1889 Anna Maria (d 12 Dec 1939), 2nd dau of Maj Robert Poore (see POORE, Bt), and had:

1 (HAROLD) ALWYNE (Sir), **5th Bt**

2 Phillip Vincent; b 20 Sept 1898; educ Wellington; Lt Household Bn and Gren Gds WW I (despatches); m 19 March 1932 Pamela Mary (d 24 Jan 1970), only child of Sir Frederick Henry Arthur Des Voeux, 7th Bt (see 1940 edn), and d 1991, leaving:

(1) +Brian Raymond [Brian Pelly Esq, 1253 Via Landeta, Palos Verdes Estates, CAL 90274, USA]; b 14 March 1935; educ Lancing; m 7 July 1962 *Dinah, er dau of Rev Gerald Alfred Hutchison, of Littleton Drew Rectory, Chippenham, Wilts, and has:

1a +Ivan Raymond [Ivan Pelly Esq, 2957 Glen Albyn Drive, Santa Barbara, CA 93105, USA]; b 25 Oct 1963; m 4 Oct 1997 *Polly Kimberley Balsillie, dau of Mrs Gail Tyler, of Santa Barbara, Calif.

2a +Oliver Harding [Oliver Pelly, 13355 Tiverton Rd, San Diego, CA 92130, USA]; b 6 June 1966; m 11 Oct 1997 *Kirsten Kailani, dau of Mrs Ann Johnson, of Edwardsburg, Mich.

1a *Annabel Marguerite Pamela [Mrs Orland Estevan, 13402 Heritage Way, #708, Tustin, CA, USA]; b 28 Feb 1970; m 30 Nov 1996 *Orland Estevan, yr s of Eduardo Estevan, of Toronto

(2) +Antony Roger [Antony Pelly Esq, Commongate Farm, Holnest, Dorset]; b 20 Oct 1937; educ Lancing; BSc, FRICS, late Lt RHA; m 7 Sept 1963 *Susan Fiona, yr dau of Maj Denis William Powlett Milbank (see MILBANK, Bt), and has:

1a *Helen Fiona [Mrs Nicholas Chapman, 32a Wingford Rd, London SW2]; b 18 July 1964; m 23 Dec 1989 *Nicholas J Chapman, only s of J A Chapman, of Little Blair, Hill Head, Hants, and has:

1b *Fred(rick) (Freddy) Nicholas Anthony; b 19 Nov 1992

1b *Katie Calypso Fiona; b 24 July 1995

2b *Tatiana Poppy Ruth; b 16 Sept 1996

2a *Anna Maria Alice [Mrs Nicholas Richards, Hill View, Wheatley Rd, Forest Hill, Oxford OX33 1EW]; b 7 Jan 1967; m 1988 *Nicholas Mark Ryman Richards, er s of Nigel Richards, of Richmond, Surrey, and has:

1b *Benita Frances; b 29 Nov 1994

2b *Lottie Mariah; b 16 July 1997

(3) +Roland Des Voeux [Roland Pelly Esq, Limes Court, Stanstead, Essex]; b 13 Feb 1943; educ Cheltenham; slr; m 28 Sept 1968 *Diana, yr dau of Capt James FitzGibbon, RN (ret), of Thames, NZ, and Mrs George Tayler, of New Malden, Surrey, and has:

1a +Richard Philip; b 1971

1a *Claire Mary; b 1982

(4) +Philip Harold [Philip Pelly Esq, Purples Farm, Bardfield Saling, Essex]; b 3 Oct 1948; educ London U; BA, DipEd, slr 1977, Dist Judge 1997–; m 1970 *(Margaret) Helen, dau of Canon Daniel Ernest John Anthony, of Sherston, Wilts, and has:

1a +Thomas Phillip Anthony; b 1980

1a *Katherine Louisa; b 14 Nov 1977

(1) *Pamela Margaret Evelyn [Mrs Maurice Greening, Ladyfield, Acton Turville, Badminton, Glos]; b 22 July 1933; m 10 Jan 1957 *Maurice John Greening, only child of John Greening, of Purton Wilts, and has:

1a *Harold John; b 12 Feb 1958

2a *James Timothy; b 16 Jan 1960

3a *Maurice Vincent; b 16 Jan 1964

1a *Mary Jacqueline; b 12 Jan 1962

(2) Clare Richenda; b 8 May 1940; m 24 Aug 1963 *Henry Hartley [Henry Hartley Esq, Old Rectory Cottage, Grittleton, Wilts], s of Harry Hartley, of Nailsworth, Glos, and d 1987, leaving:

1c *Mark William; b 13 Oct 1964

1c *Madeline Mary; b 8 Sept 1967

1 Benita Blanche; b 31 May 1892; m 1st 16 Sept 1913 Sir Thomas Evans Keith Lees, 2nd Bt (qv); m 2nd 7 Dec 1929 FM 1st Viscount Alanbrooke (qv) and was k in a car crash 4 May 1968, leaving issue

2 Madeline Annie Pamela; b 11 Feb 1895; m 30 Dec 1915 Col Sir John Victor Elliott Lees, 3rd Bt (qv), and d 28 July 1967, leaving issue

3 Mary Evelyn; b 14 Jan 1901; m 9 Nov 1921 Hugh Maurice Hill (d 2 Feb 1934), 2nd s of Gathorne Hill, of Claverton Manor, Bath, and d 1990, leaving issue

Sir HAROLD d 3 Nov 1950; his er son,

Sir (Harold) Alwyne Pelly, 5th Bt, MC (1918); b 27 Aug 1893; educ Wellington and Merton Coll Oxford; T/Capt Household Bn France and 7th QO Hus Mesopotamia WW I, Maj 7th QO Hus, Instr Cavalry Sch Netheravon 1920–22 and Equitation Sch Weedon 1922–24, Adj Leics Yeo 1927–31; m 27 June 1917 Caroline Earle (d 25 Sept 1976), 4th dau of Richard Heywood Heywood-Jones, of Badsworth Hall, Yorks, and d 1981, leaving:

1 **Sir John Alwyne Pelly, 6th Bt**, JP (Hants 1966), DL (1972); b 11 Sept 1918; educ Canford and RMC Sandhurst; Maj Coldstream Gds WW II 1939–42 (POW) and Malaya 1948–49, High Sheriff Hants 1970; m 1st 11 Sept 1943 (divorce 1950) (Ava) Barbara Ann (m 2nd 1951 (divorce 1964) Maj David Michael de Lérisson Cazenove), only dau of Brig Keith Frederick William Dunn, CBE; m 2nd 26 May 1950 Elsie May (d 1987), yr dau of L Thomas Dechow, of S Rhodesia, and by her had:

(1) *Margaret Elizabeth Rosanne; b 30 May 1952

(2) A dau; b and d 1 March 1956

1 (cont.) **Sir John** m 3rd 1990 his 1st w *Barbara [Barbara Lady Pelly, 9 Brook St, Bishop's Waltham, Hants SO3 1AX] and d 1993

2 Richard Heywood; b 25 April 1920; educ Wellington; FLAS, T/Capt RASC WW II; m 24 July 1948 *Mary Elizabeth [Mrs Richard Pelly, Loup House, Lyme Rd, Axminster, Devon], dau of John Luscombe, of North Huish, Devon, and d 1988, leaving:

(1) Sir RICHARD JOHN PELLY, **7th and present Bt**

(1) *Jane Carol; b 18 May 1949; BA; m 1974 *Charles Scott Bowring PhD, s of Frederick Bowring, of Tunbridge Wells, and has:

1a *Thomas Scott; b 1975

1a *Rosemary Carol; b 1977

3 Harold Peter; b 26 Sept 1922; d 30 Jan 1923

4 +Frederick Michael [Frederick Pelly Esq, West Lodge, Preshaw, Upham, Hants]; b 3 March 1926; RN WW II; m 1 Nov 1952 *Jill Elizabeth, est dau of Col William Patrick Stewart Curtis (see CURTIS, Bt), and has:

(1) +Patrick Michael [Patrick Pelly Esq, Wormit House, Wormit, Fife, Scotland]; b 12 June 1954; m 1980 *June, dau of W G Edgar, and has:

1a *Louise Mary; b 1986

2a *Charlotte Elizabeth; b 1991

(2) Alwyne Nicholas; b 12 Sept 1955; BSA Police; d 1987 in Harare, Zimbabwe

(3) +Frederick Peter Douglas [Frederick Pelly Esq, BP 478, Abidjan, Côte d'Ivoire]; b 5 July 1959; m 1987 *Evelyne, yst dau of Maurice Souilhe, of Paris, and has:

1a +Curtis Vincent; *b* 1987
2a +Alwyne Nicolas; *b* 1988
1a *Adderley Charlotte; *b* 1991
1 *Carol Patricia Benita [Mrs Michael Blake, Lippen Wood Farm, W Meon, Hants]; *b* 9 April 1928; *m* 20 June 1947 Lt-Cdr (Thomas) Michael Blake, RN (*d* 1984), RN, only s of Jack Blake, of Sleepers Hill, Winchester, and has:
  (1) *Caroline Patricia; *b* 21 March 1949; *m* 1976 *John Henry Edmund Lushington and has:
    1a *Katherine Elizabeth; *b* 1979
    2a *Philippa Alice; *b* 1981
  (2) *Juliet; *b* 21 Dec 1950; *m* 1972 *Howard Neil Fairman and has:
    1a *Lutia Charlotte; *b* 1974
    2a *Georgina; *b* 1976
  (3) *Annabel; *b* 7 March 1953; *m* 1974 *Richard Huxley Cowen and has:
    1a *Emma; *b* 1976
    2a *Victoria; *b* 1977
    3a *Charlotte Annabel; *b* 1982

PEMBROKE and MONTGOMERY

UNG · JE · SERVIRAY

Arms: Per pale azure and gules, three lions rampant argent. **Crest:** A wyvern wings elevated vert, holding in the mouth a sinister hand couped at the wrist gules. **Supporters:** Dexter, a panther rampant guardant argent, incensed, spotted or, vert, sable, azure and gules alternatively, ducally collared azure; sinister, a lion argent, ducally collared or. **Motto:** *Ung je serviray* ('I will serve but one master').
Creations: E. (E) 11 Oct 1551(Pembroke) and 4 May 1605 (Montgomery), B. (E) 10 Oct 1551 (Herbert) and 4 May 1605 (Herbert of Shurland) and (UK) (Herbert of Lea) 15 Jan 1861.

THE 17TH EARL OF PEMBROKE AND 14TH EARL OF MONTGOMERY, Baron Herbert, of Cardiff, Co Glamorgan, **Baron Herbert of Shurland,** in the Isle of Sheppey, Co Kent, and **Baron Herbert of Lea,** Co Wilts (Henry George Charles Alexander Herbert) [The Rt Hon The Earl of Pembroke and Montgomery, Wilton House, Salisbury, Wilts SP2 0BJ]); *b* 19 May 1939 (HRH THE late DUKE OF KENT stood sponsor); *s f* 1969; *educ* Eton and Ch Ch Oxford; RHG 1958–60, film dir (documentary) and producer (titles include *Emily* (1980)), winner of an award for landscape heritage work for Wilton House 1975, Hereditary Grand Visitor Jesus Coll Oxford; *m* 1st 20 Jan 1966 (*divorce* 1981) Claire Rose, only dau of Douglas Gurney Pelly (*see* PELLY, Bt), and has:

1 +WILLIAM ALEXANDER SIDNEY, *Lord Herbert; b* 18 May 1978
1 *Sophia Elizabeth; *b* 10 Dec 1966
2 *Emma Louise; *b* 12 March 1969
3 *Flora Katinka; *b* 22 Sep 1970

The 17th and 14th EARL *m* 2nd 1988 *Miranda Juliet, dau of Cdr John Somerville Kendal Oram (*see* CAIRNS, E), and by her has:

4 *Jemima Juliet; *b* 4 Oct 1989
5 *Alice Mary; *b* 10 Nov 1991
6 *Katie Ella; *b* 26 Aug 1997

Earldom of Pembroke: Those who were created Earls of Pembroke before the rise of the Herberts from the 15th century on were predominantly close relatives of the reigning monarch. This was not so in the first and historically most important case, however. Gilbert Fitz Gilbert or de Clare was made Earl of Pembroke in 1138 by KING STEPHEN, his elder brother Richard Fitz Gilbert or de Clare being father of the Alice/Adelaide who married William de Percy (*see* NORTHUMBERLAND, D). In the period of unrest and indecisive civil war known as the Anarchy, when followers of STEPHEN, HENRY I's nephew, struggled with the EMPRESS MAUD, HENRY I's daughter, Gilbert Earl of Pembroke sided with each one. He already held Chepstow, on the Welsh-English borders. In 1144 he pushed far into South Wales and established himself at Carmarthen.

His son the 2nd Earl of Pembroke ('Strongbow') was instigator of the Anglo-Norman/Cambro-Norman incursion into Ireland in 1169 or 1170. Pembroke himself managed to subdue Leinster. His daughter and ultimately heiress married William (the) Marshal, who was created Earl of Pembroke in 1199 by KING JOHN, though he may already have had some kind of status as Earl of Pembroke in right of his wife. William Earl of Pembroke supported JOHN in the struggle with the barons leading to Magna Carta and became Regent for HENRY III on JOHN's death. The Earldom of Pembroke was then held by five sons of William in succession, each of whom died either without legitimate issue or without any issue at all. Accordingly, on the death of the fifth and youngest son the Earldom reverted to the Crown. Nevertheless HENRY III's half-brother William de Valence, who married a niece of these last five Earls of Pembroke, is sometimes referred to by contemporary sources as Earl of Pembroke. His aspirations in that direction were promoted by the fact that HENRY III had presented him with Pembroke Castle. In addition de Valence's widow Joan by dint of usage, plus inheritance of the feudal Lordship of Pembroke, came to be known as Countess of Pembroke. And their son, Aymer de Valence, who was no more formally created Earl of Pembroke than his father had been, was nevertheless coming to be generally recognised as Earl of Pembroke by some ten years after his father's death. Aymer's wife founded Pembroke College Cambridge.

On Aymer's death in 1324 his great-nephew Laurence, 3rd Lord (Baron) Hasting(e)s, inherited the Earldom (*see* HASTINGS, B), though by a somewhat shaky legality, and it remained with his heirs till 1389, when Hasting(e)s's direct line died out and it reverted to the Crown.

In 1414 HENRY IV conferred the Earldom of Pembroke on his youngest son Humphrey, but for life only. On Humphrey's death the Earldom was conferred jointly on William de la Pole, 4th Earl of Suffolk, and his wife Alice, a granddaughter of Geoffrey Chaucer, but the title was forfeited just over three years later when William was executed. Jasper Tudor, HENRY VII's uncle, was created Earl of Pembroke by HENRY VI c late 1452 but died without legitimate issue in 1495. The last non-Herbert Earl of Pembroke was EDWARD IV's eldest son and heir, one of the Princes in the Tower, on whom the title was conferred in 1479. On his nominally ascending the throne as EDWARD V in 1483 the title merged with the Crown.

Lineage: For earlier generations *see* POWIS, E, **Lineage (of Herbert)**.

WILLIAM HERBERT, **1st Earl of Pembroke,** so *cr* 11 Oct 1551, as also the previous day 10 Oct 1551 BARON HERBERT of Cardiff, Glamorgan (both E), KG (1549), PC (1553 and again 1558); *b c* 1506; Gentleman Pensioner 1526, Esq of the Body by 12 Jan 1534/5, Jt Attorney-Gen Glamorgan 1534/5; granted a lease of Abergavenny Priory 1537; one of the newly formed body called the Spears 1539; Govr Aberystwyth and Carmarthen Castles 1543; ktd by 3 Jan 1543/4; granted lands formerly belonging to Wilton Abbey Jan 1543/4; Gentleman Privy Chamber by 20 Jan 1543/4 and subsequently Ch Gentleman both to HENRY VIII and EDWARD VI; Steward Duchy of Lancaster lands in Wilts 1545, MP Wilts 1545–51, Keeper Baynard's Castle (London, subsequently the Earls of Pembroke's London residence till the Great Fire of 1666) and Doorward Devizes Castle, also Steward roy lands in the West 1546, a Govr of EDWARD VI Jan 1546/7, Master Horse 1548–52, Ch Commr Mints Feb 1549/50, Pres Cncl of Wales 1550–53 and 1555–58, Ld Lt Wilts 1551–69/70 and Somerset 1559–69/70; Commr to execute penal laws against Catholics and survey exchequer accounts 1552, also Church goods and plate and the state of the Ordnance 1553; a supporter on the death of EDWARD VI of LADY JANE GREY, allegedly through fear of potential material loss to himself should a Catholic come to the throne, but declared sufficiently early for MARY to be made PC by her; cmded roy troops against Sir Thomas Wyatt when the latter headed an uprising Feb 1553/4; Lt-Gen beyond the seas March 1554/5, Lt and Capt-Gen Calais 1556 and 1557, Ld Steward Household 1568–69/70; *m* 1st *c* 1538(?) Anne (under 15 on 20 May 1529; *d* 20 Feb 1551/2), dau of Sir Thomas Parr, of Kendal and sis of HENRY VIII's last w CATHERINE, and had:

1 HENRY, **2nd Earl**
2 Edward (Sir), of Powis Castle (*see* POWIS, E)
1 Anne; *m* 17 Feb 1562/3 Francis, Lord Talbot (*dsp* & *vp* 1582), est s of 6th Earl of Shrewsbury and Waterford (*qv*), and *d* by 11 Jan 1592/3

The **1st Earl** *m* 2nd *c* May 1552 Lady Anne Talbot (*dsp* 18 July 1588), dau of 4th Earl of Shrewsbury and Waterford (*qv*) and widow of Peter Compton (*see* NORTHAMPTON, M), and *d* 17 March 1569/70

His *er* s,
HENRY HERBERT, **2nd Earl of Pembroke,** KG (1574), KB (1553); *b* probably after 1538; Jt Keeper with his f of Clarendon Forest 1553, Gentleman Bedchamber to PHILIP (II of Spain, consort in England of MARY) 1554–58, Commr Musters 1569, Ld Lt: Wilts (1570), Somerset (1585) and N and S Wales, the Welsh Marches and Herefs, Mon, Salop and Worcs (Feb 1586/7), High Steward Salisbury by Dec 1582, Pres Cncl of Wales 1586–1600/1 and V-Adml S Wales, a Commr trial MARY QUEEN OF SCOTS 1586, MA Oxon 1592; *m* 1st 21 May 1553 Lady Katharine Grey, dau of Henry, 1st Duke of Suffolk of the 1551 *cr*, and sis of LADY JANE GREY (the marriage, which was unconsummated, was declared null and void after the fall of the Grey family); *m* 2nd 17 Feb 1562/3 Lady Katharine Talbot (*dsp, bur* 15 May 1576), dau of 6th Earl of Shrewsbury and Waterford (*qv*); *m* 3rd 21 April 1577 Mary (a celebrated patroness of literary men and collaborator with her bro Sir Philip Sydney in translating the Psalms, also on the novel *Arcadia*; *d* 25 Sept 1621), dau of Sir Henry Sydney (*see* DE L'ISLE, V), and *d* 19 Jan 1600/1, having had, with a dau (*d* young):

1 WILLIAM HERBERT, **3rd Earl of Pembroke,** KG (1603), PC (1611, Scottish PC 1617); *b* 8 April 1580 (ELIZABETH I was his godmother); *educ* New Coll Oxford (MA 1605); Gentleman Privy Chamber and Keeper Clarendon Forest 1603, High Steward Duchy Cornwall and Ld Warden Stannaries 1603/4, Ld Lt: Cornwall 1604–30 and Somerset and Wilts 1621–30, Constable St Briavel's Castle and Warden Forest of Dean Jan 1607/8, Cncllr for Colony of Virginia 1609, Capt Tower and Isle of Portsmouth and Constable Porchester Castle 1609, Ld Chamberlain Household 1615–26, Commr for executing office of Earl Marshal 1616–21, Constable Radnor Castle 1616, Chllr Oxford U (Pembroke Coll there was named after him on its refounding 1624) Jan 1616/7–30, Grand Warden and Grand Master Freemasons 1618–30, Jt Commissioner Gt Seal May–July 1621, Warden New Forest 1624, High Steward Honour of Tutbury, Norwich Cathedral, Hereford and Totnes, also Exeter 1625, Memb Cncl of War 1626, Ld Steward Household 1626–30, Ld Commr Admlty 1628, Ch Justice in

Eyre S of Trent 1629–30, V-Adml S Wales; *m* 4 Nov 1604 Lady Mary Talbot (*d* March 1649/50), est dau of 7th Earl of Shrewsbury and Waterford (*qv*), and *dsps* 10 April 1630, having had:

(1) Henry, *Lord Herbert*; *b* by 21 April 1620; *dvp* an infant

1 (cont.) The **3rd Earl** also had a s, either still-born or who *d* shortly after birth, by Mary Fitton, a Maid of Honour to ELIZABETH I and the original, as some (though not Dr Rowse) have supposed, of Shakespeare's 'Dark Lady' of the sonnets; it was for his affair with her that Ld Pembroke was banished the Court and committed to the Fleet Prison 1600/1; he and his bro and successor the **4th Earl** are the dedicatees of Shakespeare's first folio and it has been suggested that the **3rd Earl** is the 'WH' described by Shakespeare as the 'onlie begetter' of his sonnets

2 PHILIP HERBERT, **1st Earl of Montgomery**, so *cr* 4 May 1605 (his cousin Lord Herbert of Chirbury (*see* POWIS, E)'s castle of Montgomery being presented to him by JAMES I on that occasion, though Lord Montgomery subsequently (1613) sold it back to the other branch of the family for £500, or just under £40,000 in late-1990s terms), as also BARON HERBERT OF SHURLAND, in the Isle of Sheppey, Co Kent (both E), and **4th Earl of Pembroke** (on er bro's death), KG (1608), KB (1603), PC (1624, Scottish PC 1641); *b* 16 Oct 1584; *educ* New Coll Oxford (MA 1605); Gentleman Privy Chamber 1603–25, MP Glamorgan 1604–05; Chllr and Chamberlain Anglesey, Caernarvs and Merioneths 1605–49/50, premier Cncllr for Colony of Virginia March 1611/2, High Steward: Oxford U 1615–41, Westminster 1628–49/50, Duchy Cornwall 1630 and Exeter 1635, Keeper Palace of York Place Westminster 1616, Constable Queenborough Castle 1617, Ld Lt: Kent March 1623/4, Bucks 1628–41, Somerset 1630–43, Wilts 1630–49/50 and Cornwall 1630–42, Ld Chamberlain 1626–41, Ld Warden Stannaries 1630, V-Adml S Wales, Constable St Briavel's Castle and Warden Forest of Dean 1631, Capt-Gen of a regt in campaign against Scots 1639–40, Chllr Oxford U 1641–43 and 1647–50, Parliamentarian in Civil War: Ld Lt Hants Feb 1641/2, Mon, Glam and Breconshire 1642, Kent 1642, Somerset 1643 and Cards 1646, Memb Ctee Safety 1642 and Assembly of Divines 1643, Govr IoW 1642–47, Capt-Gen in the West 1642, Commr Admlty 1645, voted a dukedom by Parl 1645, Constable Windsor Castle 1648–49/50, High Steward and Keeper Pk of Greenwich 1648, Memb Cncl State Feb 1648/49–49/50, MP Berks 1649; *m* 1st 27 Dec 1604 Lady Susan de Vere (*b* 26 May 1587; *bur* 1 Feb 1628/9), 3rd dau of 17th Earl of Oxford (*see* SAINT ALBANS, D), and had, with other issue:

(1) James, *Lord Herbert of Shurland*; *b* July 1616 (JAMES I was godfather); *dvp*, *bur* 29 Aug 1617

(2) Henry, *Lord Herbert of Shurland*; *b c* 19 March 1617/8; *dvp*, *bur* 5 April 1618

(3) Charles, *Lord Herbert of Shurland*, KB (Feb 1625/6); *b* by 20 Aug 1619; *educ* Exeter Coll Oxford; *m* 8/18 Jan 1634/5 Lady Mary Villiers (aged then *c* 12; she *m* 2nd Aug 1637 James Stuart, 1st Duke of Richmond of the 1641 *cr* (*see* MORAY, E); *m* 3rd *c* Nov 1664 Thomas Howard, yr bro of 1st Earl of Carlisle (*qv*), and was *bur* 28 Nov 1685), dau of 1st Duke of Buckingham of the 1623 *cr* (*see* JERSEY, E), and *dsp* & *vp* Jan 1635/6

(4) PHILIP, **5th/2nd Earl**

(1) Anna Sophia; *m* 27 Feb 1625 1st Earl of Carnarvon (*see* DORMER, B, also CARNARVON, E, preliminary remarks) and had issue

2 (cont.) The **4th/1st Earl** *m* 2nd 1 June 1630 Anne Clifford, Baroness Clifford in her own right (*see* DE CLIFFORD, B), and *d* 23 Jan 1649/50

His est surv s,

PHILIP HERBERT, **5th Earl of Pembroke** and **2nd Earl of Montgomery**, *bapt* 20 Feb 1620/1; *educ* Exeter Coll Oxford; MP Wilts April-May 1640 and Glamorgan 1640–49, Jt Ld Lt Somerset 1640–42, a Parliamentarian Civil War: Parly nominee for Ld Ltcy of Mon, Breconshire and Glam Feb–July 1642, Visitor Jesus Coll Oxford, Cncllr of State 1651–52 (Pres June–July 1652), Militia Commissioner S Wales 1655, Ld of Trade 1660; it has been sugested he was a Quaker; *m* 1st 28 March 1639 Penelope (*bapt* 2 Oct 1620; *d* by 1647), only dau and heiress of Sir Robert Naunton and widow of 2nd Viscount Bayning of Sudbury, and had:

1 WILLIAM HERBERT, **6th Earl of Pembroke** and **3rd Earl of Montgomery**; *b* 1640; MP Glamorgan 1661–69; *d* unm 8 July 1674

The **5th/2nd Earl** *m* 2nd by 1649 Katherine (*bur* 28 Feb 1677/8), yst dau of Sir William Villiers, 1st Bt (*see* JERSEY, E), and *d* 11 Dec 1669, having by her had, with two other daus (*d* unm):

2 PHILIP HERBERT, **7th Earl of Pembroke** and **4th Earl of Montgomery**, KB (1661); *bapt* 5 Jan 1652/3; Ld Lt Wilts 1675–83, tried twice for two separate murders, the first time being found guilty of manslaughter by a majority vote of his peers but on claiming benefit of Statute (something it was possible to do but once) paid a fine only, the second time being found guilty by an ordinary jury but being pardoned by CHARLES II; *m* 17 Dec 1674, as her 1st husb, Henriette Mauricette (*m* 2nd Timoléon Gouffier, Marquis de Thois, and *d* 1/12 Nov 1728), yr dau of Guillaume de Penancoët, Sieur de Kérouaille (Brittany), and sis of the Duchess of Portsmouth, one of the more notorious of CHARLES II's mistresses, and *d* 29 Aug 1683, leaving:

(1) Charlotte; *m* 1st 17 and 21 July 1688 2nd Baron Jeffreys of Wem (*see* JEFFREYS, B) and had issue; *m* 2nd 28 Aug 1703 1st Viscount Windsor (*see* PLYMOUTH, E) and *d* 13 Nov 1733, having had further issue

3 THOMAS, **8th/5th Earl**

1 Susan; *m* 3rd Baron Poulett (*see* 1970 edn POULETT, E) and had issue

2 Mary; *m* as his 2nd w Sir John Posthumus Sydenham, 2nd Bt, of Brympton, Somerset, and had issue

3 Catherine; *m* Sir John Williams, 2nd Bt (*dsp* Nov 1704), of Llangibby, Mon

The 5th/2nd EARL's 3rd s,

THOMAS HERBERT, **8th Earl of Pembroke** and **5th Earl of Montgomery**, KG (1700), PC (1689); *b c* 1656; *educ* Ch Ch Oxford; MP Wilton 1679–81, Ld Lt: Wilts 1683–87 and 1688/9–1733 and S Wales and Mon 1694–1715, FRS 1685 (Pres 1689–90), Amb to States-Gen (Netherlands) April–Oct 1689 and 1705, Ld of Trade and Plantations 1689, 1st Ld Admlty Jan 1689/90–92 and March 1701–Jan 1701/2, Er Bro Trin House 1691 (Master 1692–94), Ld Privy Seal March 1691/2–99, 1st Plen Congress of Ryswick 1697, Ld Pres Cncl 1699–Jan 1701/2 and 1703–08, Ld High Adml Jan-May 1702 and 1708–09, Ld Lt Ireland 1707–08, High Steward Salisbury 1708; the principal founder of the magnificent art collection which for the most part remains at Wilton today, although his *Wilton Diptych* was sold in 1929; *m* 1st 26 July 1684 Margaret (*d* 17 Nov 1706), only dau and heiress of Sir Robert Sawyer, of Highclere, Hants, Attorney-Gen under CHARLES II, and had, with other issue:

1 HENRY, **9th/6th Earls**

2 William; *m* Catherine Tewes and had issue (*see* CARNARVON, E)

3 Nicholas; *m* 19 July 1737 Anne, dau and heiress of Dudley North, of Glemham Hall, Suffolk (*see* GUILFORD, E), and *d* 1775, leaving an only dau:

(1) Barbara; *b* July 1742; *m* 29 July 1765, as his 1st w, 2nd Earl of Aldborough (*d* 2 Jan 1801; *see* TOLLEMACHE, B) and *dsp* 11 April 1785

1 Catherine; *m* Sir Nicholas Morice, 2nd Bt, MP Newport and *d* 1716, leaving issue (*see* SAINT LEVAN, B)

2 Rebecca; *m* 20 May 1732, as his 2nd w, 14th Lord (Baron) Abergavenny (*d* 21 Sept 1744; *see* ABERGAVENNY, M) and *d* 20 Oct 1758, leaving issue

The **8th/5th Earl** *m* 2nd 21 Sept 1708 Barbara (*d* 1 Aug 1722), dau of Sir Thomas Slingsby, 2nd Bt, of Scriven, York, and widow of (a) Sir Richard Mauliverer, 4th Bt, and (b) 2nd Baron Arundell of Trerice, and by her had:

3 Barbara; *m* Dudley North, of Glemham Hall, Suffolk (*see* GUILFORD, E)

The **8th/5th Earl** *m* 3rd 14 June 1725 Hon Mary Howe (*m* 2nd 9 Oct 1735 Hon John Mordaunt, bro of 4th Earl of Peterborough (*see* MORDAUNT, Bt), and *d* 12 Sept 1749), Maid of Honour to CAROLINE PRINCESS OF WALES 1720–25 and Ldy of the Bechamber to HRH after the latter became Queen as consort to GEORGE II, dau of 1st Viscount Howe (*see* HOWE, E), and *d* 22 Jan 1732/3 without further issue

His est s,

HENRY HERBERT, **9th Earl of Pembroke** and **6th Earl of Montgomery**, PC (Jan 1734/5); *b c* 1689; *educ* Ch Ch Oxford; Ld Bedchamber (Whig) to GEORGE II, Lt-Gen 1742 (Maj-Gen 1735), Lt-Col Coldstream Foot Gds 1717, Col 1st Troop Life Gds 1721–33, Col King's Own Regt of Horse (subsequently 1st Dragoon Gds) 1733–43, Ld Lt Wilts and High Steward Salisbury 1733–49/50, Groom of Stole and 1st Ld Bedchamber 1735–49/50, FRS 1743; as an amateur architect he joined with Colen Campbell and Roger Morris in designing Marble Hill House at Twickenham (*see* SUFFOLK and BERKSHIRE, E); *m* 28 Aug 1733 Hon Mary FitzWilliam (*bapt* 8 Sept 1707; Maid of Honour to QUEEN CAROLINE; *m* 2nd 4 Sept 1751 Maj North Ludlow Bernard; *d* 13 Feb 1769), est dau of 5th Viscount Fitzwilliam of Merrion, and *d* 9 Jan 1749/50, leaving:

HENRY HERBERT, **10th Earl of Pembroke** and **7th Earl of Montgomery**; *b* 16 July 1734; *educ* Eton; High Steward Salisbury 1750, served army: Ensign Bland's Dragoons 1752, Capt 1st Dragoon Gds 1754, Lt-Col 1st Foot Gds 1756, Lt-Col 15th Light Dragoons 1759–62, Adj-Gen 1760–61, Maj-Gen 1761, Commanded Cavalry Bde Germany 1761–63, Col 1st Dragoons 1764–94, Lt-Gen 1770, Gen 1782, Ld Lt Wilts 1756–80 and 1782–94, ADC to GEORGE II 1758–60, Ld of Bedchamber to GEORGE III 1756 (as PRINCE OF WALES), 1760–63 and 1770–80, Govr Portsmouth 1782–94; author of books on horsemanship; he also erected the stables at Wilton; *m* 12 or 13 March 1756 Lady Elizabeth Spencer (*b* 29 Dec 1737; Ldy of the Bechamber to QUEEN CHARLOTTE 1783–1818 and the woman whom GEORGE III supposed in his bouts of insanity to be his w; *d* 30 April 1831), 2nd dau of 3rd Duke of Marlborough (*qv*), and *d* 26 Jan 1794, leaving:

1 GEORGE AUGUSTUS, **11th/8th Earl**

The **10th/7th Earl** had illegitimately by Elizabeth Catherine (Kitty), dau of Thomas Orby Hunter, a Ld of the Admlty:

2 Augustus Retnuh (*i.e.*, 'Hunter' reversed) REEBKOMP (an anagram of 'Pembroke'); *educ* Eton

The 10th/7th EARL's only legitimate s,

GEORGE AUGUSTUS HERBERT, **11th Earl of Pembroke** and **8th Earl of Montgomery**, KG (1805), PC (1784); *b* 10 Sept 1759; *educ* Harrow; served army: Ensign 12th Foot 1775, Capt 75th Foot and 1st Dragoons Jan and Dec 1778 respectively, Maj 22nd Dragoons 1781, Lt-Col 2nd Dragoon Gds 1782, Col 1793, Maj-Gen 1795, Col 6th Dragons 1797–1827, Lt-Gen 1802 and Gen 1812, MP (Whig to 1783, Pittite thereafter) Wilton 1780–85 and 1788–94, V-Chamberlain Household 1784–94, Ld Lt Wilts 1794–1827, Amb (special mission) Vienna 1807, Govr Guernsey 1807–27; *m* 1st 8 April 1787 his 1st cousin Elizabeth (*d* 25 March 1793), yr dau of Topham Beauclerk (the friend of Dr Johnson; *see* SAINT ALBANS, D), and had:

1 George; *b* 26 March 1788; *dvp* 5 July 1793

2 ROBERT HENRY HERBERT, **12th Earl of Pembroke** and **9th Earl of Montgomery**; *b* 19 Sept 1791; *educ* Harrow; High Steward Wilton; *m* 17 Aug 1814 (*annulled* 1818 under pressure from his f) Princess Octavia Spinelli (*b c* 1793; *d* Dec 1857), widow of Prince Butera, of Sicily, and dau of the Duke of Laurino, and *dsp* Paris 25 April 1862

3 Charles; *b* 1793; *d* 1798

1 Diana; *b* 5 Feb 1790; *m* 17 May 1816 2nd Earl of Normanton (*qv*) and *d* 2 Dec 1841, leaving issue

The **11th/8th Earl** *m* 2nd 25 Jan 1808 Catherine (*b* 24 Oct 1783; *d* 27 March 1856), only dau of Simon Romanovitch, 3rd Count Woronzow, GCB, Russian Amb to UK, and *d* 26 Oct 1827, having by her had:

4 SIDNEY HERBERT, **1st Baron Herbert of Lea**, Co Wilts (UK), so *cr* 15 Jan 1861, PC (1845); *b* 16 Sept 1810; *educ* Harrow and Oriel Coll Oxford (Pres Union 1830, BA 1831); MP (Tory, then Peelite, thereafter Liberal) S Wilts 1832–61, Jt Sec Bd Control Jan-April 1835, Sec Admlty 1841–45, Sec for War: 1845–46, 1852–55 (during Crimean War, in which he became friendly with Florence Nightingale so that her passage to the Crimea was facilitated) and 1859–61, Colonial Sec 8–22 Feb 1855, Tstee Nat Portrait Gallery 1856–61, high churchman who built new parish church at Wilton in Byzantine style at a reputed cost of £30,000 (roughly £1,350,000 in late-1990s terms); *m* 12 Aug 1846 Mary Elizabeth (*b* 21 July 1822; turned RC 1862; *d* 30 Oct 1911), only dau of Lt-Gen Charles Ashe à Court-Repington, CB, and n of 1st Baron Heytesbury (*qv*), and *d* 2 Aug 1861, having had:

(1) GEORGE ROBERT CHARLES HERBERT, **2nd Baron Herbert of Lea**, later **13th Earl of Pembroke** and **10th Earl of Montgomery**; *b* 6 July 1850; *educ* Eton; U-Sec for War (Conservative) 1874–75, Tstee Nat Portrait Gallery 1887–95, cmded S Wilts Bn Vols, built and endowed Pembroke Technical Sch nr Dublin, author: *South Sea Bubbles by the Earl and the Doctor* (with Dr George Kingsley, 1872); *m* 19 Aug 1874 Lady Gertrude Frances Talbot, dau of 18th Earl of Shrewsbury and Waterford (*qv*), and *dsp* 3 May 1895

(2) SIDNEY, **14th/11th Earl**

(3) William Reginald; *b* 21 May 1854; RN, granted 30 May 1862 with siblings rank of earl's dau/yr s; lost at sea on board HMS *Captain* 6 Sept 1870

(4) Michael Henry (Sir), KCMG (1902), CB (1896), PC; *b* 25 June 1857; Amb Washington 1902–03; *m* 27 Nov 1888 Lelia ('Belle') (*d* 19 Nov 1923), dau of Richard T Wilson, of Newport, RI, and New York, and *d* 30 Sept 1903, leaving:

    1a Sir SIDNEY HERBERT, 1st and last Bt (UK), so *cr* 18 July 1936, of Boyton, Co Wilts; *b* 29 July 1890; *educ* Eton and Balliol Coll Oxford; Maj Res Offrs Roy Wilts Yeo, Capt RHG WW I (despatches, three medals), Priv Sec to Sec State War 1919–20, MP (U) Scarborough and Whitby 1922–31 and Abbey Div of Westminster 1932–38 (PPS to Pres Bd Educn Nov 1922–Aug 1923 and PM Aug 1923–Jan 1924 and Nov 1924–June 1927); *d* unm 22 March 1939, when the btcy expired

    2a Michael George; *b* 1893; Lt: Roy Wilts Yeo, RHG and Guards MG Regt WW I; *d* unm 26 Sept 1932

(1) Mary Catherine; *m* 27 Nov 1873 Friedrich, Baron von Hügel (*b* May 1852; distinguished biblical commentator; *d* 27 Jan 1925), of Kensington, and *d* 2 Dec 1935, leaving issue

(2) Elizabeth Maud; *m* 25 June 1872 Sir (Charles) Hubert Hastings Parry, 1st Bt, CVO, JP (*b* 27 Feb 1848; the celebrated composer; *d* 7 Oct 1918), of Highnam Court, Glos, and *d* 28 Feb 1933, leaving two daus

(3) Constance Gladys; *m* 1st 6 July 1878 4th Earl of Lonsdale (*qv*) and had issue; *m* 2nd 7 May 1885 2nd Marquess of Ripon (*d* 22 Sept 1923; *see* 1923 edn) and *d* 27 Oct 1917

2 Elizabeth; *b* 31 March 1809; *m* 3 July 1830 3rd Earl of Clanwilliam (*qv*) and *d* 20 Sept 1858, leaving issue

3 Mary Caroline; *b* 22 March 1813; *m* 11 May 1837 2nd Marquess of Ailesbury (*qv*) and *d* 20 Jan 1892

4 Catherine; *b* 31 Oct 1814; *m* 27 Sept 1836 6th Earl of Dunmore (*qv*) and *d* 12 Feb 1886, leaving issue

5 Georgiana; *b* 3 Aug 1817; *m* 18 Aug 1840, as his 1st w, 4th Marquess of Lansdowne (*qv*) and *dsp* 28 Feb 1841

6 Emma; *b* 23 Aug 1819; *m* 16 Sept 1839 3rd Viscount de Vesci (*qv*) and *d* 10 Oct 1884, leaving issue

The 13th/10th EARL's next bro,

    SIDNEY HERBERT, **14th Earl of Pembroke** and **11th Earl of Montgomery**, GCVO (1896), PC (1895); *b* 20 Feb 1853; *educ* Eton and Ch Ch Oxford (BA 1875); Capt Wilts Yeo Cav, MP (C) Wilton 1877–85 and Croydon 1886–95, C Whip 1885–86 and 1886–92, Mayor Wilton 1899, Ld Steward Household 1895–1905; *m* 29 Aug 1877 Lady Beatrix Louisa Lambton (*d* 12 March 1944), est dau of 2nd Earl of Durham (*qv*), and *d* 30 March 1913, leaving:

1 REGINALD, **15th/12th Earl**

2 Sir GEORGE SIDNEY HERBERT, 1st and last Bt (UK), so *cr* 1 March 1927, of Wilton, Co Wilts, TD, JP, DL; *b* 8 Oct 1886; *educ* Eton and Magdalen Coll Oxford; CC Wilts, Hon Attaché Berne 1911, Hon Col 4th Bn Wilts Regt, served WW I, Gentleman Usher to TM GEORGE V 1928–36 and EDWARD VIII 1936, ADC to HM GEORGE VI 1936–42 and Groom-in-Waiting and Gentleman Usher 1937–42; *d* unm 30 Jan 1942, when the btcy expired

1 Beatrix Frances Gertrude; *m* 1st 29 April 1903 Maj Sir Neville Rodwell Wilkinson, KCVO, FSA (*d* 22 Dec 1940), Ulster King of Arms and Res of Offrs Coldstream Gds, and had issue; *m* 2nd 5 March 1942 7th Earl of Wicklow (*see* 1970 edn) and *d* 3 Dec 1957

2 Muriel Katherine; *m* 5 Aug 1920 Arthur John Jex-Blake, MD, FRCP, 2nd s of Very Rev Thomas William Jex-Blake, DD, Dean Wells, and *d* 13 Feb 1951, leaving issue

The 14th/11th EARL's er s,

    REGINALD HERBERT, **15th Earl of Pembroke** and **12th Earl of Montgomery**, MVO (4th Cl 1918, 5th Cl 1901); *b* 8 Sept 1880; *educ* Eton and RMC Sandhurst; Hereditary Visitor Jesus Coll Oxford, Lt-Col RHG, ADC to C-in-C Ireland 1912–13 and Lt-Gen Sir W P Pulteney 1914, served WW I (despatches, Legn Hon, Orders Rising Sun and St Maurice and St Lazarus Italy), Mayor Wilton 1932–46 and 1954 (*d* 8 Feb 1973), sis of 6th Marquess of Anglesey (*qv*), and *d* 13 Jan 1960, leaving:

1 SIDNEY CHARLES, **16th/13th Earl**

2 David Alexander Reginald; *b* 3 Oct 1908; *educ* Eton; author: *Second Son* (1972), *Engaging Eccentrics* (1990) and *Relations and Revelations* (1992), sometime Lt RNVR; *d* unm 3 April 1995

3 Anthony Edward George, DSO (1945), TD (1945); *b* 12 Sept 1911; *educ* Eton; Lt-Col Roy Wilts Yeo WW II (wounded), Lt-Col cmdg 1948–51; *d* unm 22 Aug 1971

1 Patricia, DCVO (1953), JP (1961); *b* 12 Nov 1904; Ldy Bedchamber to HM QUEEN ELIZABETH (subsequently THE QUEEN MOTHER) 1937–94; *m* 26 Sept 1928 3rd Viscount Hambleden (*qv*) and *d* 19 March 1994, leaving issue

The 15th/12th EARL's est s,

    SIDNEY CHARLES HERBERT, **16th Earl of Pembroke** and **13th Earl of Montgomery**, CVO (1945), JP (Wilts 1954); *b* 9 Jan 1906; *educ* Eton and Pembroke Coll Oxford; CC and CA (1942–67) Wilts, Ld Lt Wilts 1954–69, Pres: Wilts T&AFA, St John's Cncl, Boy Scouts' Assoc Wilts and Historic Churches Tst, Hereditary Visitor Jesus Coll Oxford, Equerry to HRH THE late DUKE OF KENT 1935–42, Comptroller and Priv Sec to HRH THE late DUCHESS OF KENT 1942–48, served WW II, Tstee Nat Gallery 1942–49 and 1953–60 and Nat Portrait Gallery 1944–58, memb Roy Commn Historical MSS. 1941–58, KStJ, author: *Henry, Elizabeth and George* (The Pembroke Papers), vol I (1939), vol II (1950) and *A Catalogue of the Collection of Paintings and Drawings at Wilton House* (1968); *m* 27 July 1936 Lady Mary Dorothea Hope, CVO (1947), DL (*d* 16 Jan 1995), Ldy-in-Waiting to HRH THE late DUCHESS OF KENT 1934–49 (Extra Ldy-in-Waiting 1949–68), Hon 1st Offr WRNS, only surv dau of 1st Marquess of Linlithgow (*qv*), and *d* 16 March 1969, leaving:

1 HENRY GEORGE CHARLES ALEXANDER HERBERT, **17th and present Earl of Pembroke** and **14th Earl of Montgomery**

---

1 *Diana Mary [The Lady Diana Herbert, The Old Rectory, Wilton, Salisbury]; *b* 19 April 1937 (HRH THE late DUCHESS OF KENT stood sponsor)

Seat: Wilton House, Wilton, nr Salisbury, Wilts. Long before the present structure was built there was an Abbey at Wilton which dated from Saxon times. The only pre-Reformation part to survive is attached to the stables, most of the abbey buildings being demolished soon after the **1st Earl** acquired the lands, although their replacement — a Tudor mansion similar to the present one in being arranged as a quadrilateral surrounding an inner courtyard — only lasted till 1647, when almost all of it burnt down. A completely new house was finished *c* 1653, to designs which are said to have been enriched by advice from the now aged Inigo Jones but which certainly profited from direct help by Jones's pupil John Webb. It lasted intact until the early 19th century, when alterations in the neo-Gothic taste were carried out by James Wyatt. The hybrid version is what the visitor sees today. Wilton is perhaps best known for an internal feature, the Double Cube room. This measures 60' long by 30' wide and 30' high and is therefore the dimensions of two cubes of 30' along each of their sides, hence the name. It was designed principally to display the Van Dyck portraits of the **4th Earl of Pembroke** and his family.

PENDER

Arms: Quarterly, 1st and 4th, gules on a bend nebuly argent two lion's heads erased of the first (for PENDER); 2nd and 3rd, per bend sable and argent two bendlets between a unicorn's head erased in chief and three cross-crosslets in base, all counterchanged (for DENISON). **Crests**: 1 A demi-lion or, holding in the dexter paw a seax proper, pommel and hilt gold, and resting the sinister paw on a terrestrial globe proper, 2 In front of a sun rising in splendour a dexter arm in bend proper, vested gules, gutté d'eau, cuff erminois, the fore-finger pointing to an estoile or. **Supporters**: On either side a figure of Hermes standing on a cable-grapnel, the dexter holding in the exterior hand a caduceus, the sinister a flash of lightning, all proper. **Motto**: *Persevero* ('I persevere')
Creation: B. (UK) 12 June 1937.

THE 3RD BARON PENDER, of Porthcurnow, Co Cornwall (John Willoughby Denison-Pender) [The Rt Hon The Lord Pender, North Court, Tilmanstone, Kent CT14 0JP]; *b* 6 May 1933; *s* f 1965; *educ* Eton; late Lt 10th Roy Hus, Capt City London Yeo (TA), dir Globe Investment Tst Ltd 1969–70, jt chm Bremar Tst 1977–83, J J L D Frost plc 1983–84, V-Pres Roy Sch for the Deaf 1992–; *m* 19 Nov 1962 *Julia, yr dau of Richard Nevill Cannon, OBE, of Coombe Place, Lewes, Sussex, and has:

    1 +HENRY JOHN RICHARD; *b* 19 March 1968; *educ* Eton; *m* Sept 1994 *Vanessa, dau of John Eley, of NSW

    1 *Emma Charlotte; *b* 1 Feb 1964; *m* 1992 *Matthew Christopher Anthony Brett (*see* ESHER, V)

    2 *Mary Anne Louise; *b* 17 Nov 1965

Lineage: JAMES PENDER, of the Vale of Levan, Dunbartonshire; *m* Marion Mason and had:

Sir JOHN PENDER, GCMG, of Middleton Hall, Linlithgow, Footscray, Kent, and St James's, JP, DL Lancs, Denbighs, Argyllshire, Kent, Linlithgow and Middx; *b* 10 Sept 1816; MP Totnes 1865–66 and Wick 1872–85 and 1892–96, Fell Imp Inst and Roy Socs of England and Scotland and Scottish Antiquarian Soc, chm: Globe Telegraph and Tst and Metropolitan Electric Supply Co, Grand Cordon Medjidie, Kt Cdr St Saviour Greece, Order Conception and Rose, Grand Cross Roy Mil Order Our Saviour Jesus Christ Portugal, Offr Legn Hon; *m* 1st 28 Nov 1840 Marion (*d* 16 Dec 1841), dau of James Cearns, of Glasgow, and had:

    1 Sir JAMES PENDER, 1st and last Bt (UK), so *cr* 3 Sept 1897, of Thornby Hall, Thornby, Northants, JP Northants, Linlithgow and Wilts; *b* 28 Sept 1841; *educ* UCL (BA); MP Mid-Northants 1895–1900, Lt 25th Foot; *m* 7 May 1867 Mary Rose (*d* 2 May 1932), dau of Edward John Gregge-Hopwood, of Hopwood Hall, Lancs, and *dsp* 20 May 1921, when the btcy expired

Sir JOHN *m* 2nd 12 June 1851 Emma (*d* 8 July 1890), only surv child and heiress of Henry Denison, of Daybrook, Arnold, Notts, and by her had:

    2 Henry Denison; *b* 8 Oct 1852; *d* unm 13 Jan 1881

3 John Denison PENDER later DENISON-PENDER (roy licence 8 May 1890) (Sir), GBE, KCMG, JP Argyll; b 10 Oct 1855; chm Eastern Telegraph Co, Kt Cdr Dannebrog, Grand Cross Our Lady of Conception Portugal, Grand Gordon Osmanieh; m 2 Aug 1879 Beatrice Katherine (d 11 Nov 1920), only dau of Cuthbert Ellison, and d 6 March 1929, having had:

(1) JOHN CUTHBERT, **1st Baron**

(2) Henry Denison, DSO (1918), OBE (1942), MC (1915), JP (Dorset 1926); b 2 April 1884; educ Eton; Capt and Brevet Maj RSG, Bde Major 1916, WW I (despatches), High Sheriff Dorset 1935, Dep Ch Censor Centl Telegraph Office 1939–42; m 21 Jan 1913 Doris Louise Sydney (d 2 May 1952), est dau of Sydney Fisher, of Amlington Hall, Tamworth, and d 16 Feb 1967, leaving:

1a Pamela Beatrice Rose; b 20 Dec 1913; m 1 March 1941 *Gen Sir Kenneth (Thomas) Darling, GBE, KCB, DSO, Roy Fus [Gen Sir Kenneth Darling GBE KCB DSO, Vicarage Farmhouse, Chesterton, Oxon OX6 8UQ], est s of George Kenneth Darling, CIE, ICS, of Aldeburgh, Suffolk, and d 1990

2a *Barbara; b 15 Nov 1915; m 1st 16 Feb 1945 Maj Henry Owen Fellowes, Seaforth Highrs, RFC and RAF (d 14 March 1959), s of Jacob Fellowes, ironmaster, of Darlington, and had:

1b *Alexander Henry Owen [Alexander Fellowes Esq, 2 Clough Dve, Birshall, nr Leeds, Yorks]; b 18 Jan 1946; m 19– *May Mahon, of Leeds

2a (cont.) Mrs Henry Fellowes m 2nd 14 May 1960 *Thomas David Gwynn Davies, s of Thomas Davies, of Wandsworth

3a *Cynthia Sydney [Mrs Roger Mortimer, The Millers House, Kintbury, Berks RG17 9UR]; b 28 Feb 1921; m 10 Dec 1947 Maj Roger Francis Mortimer, Coldstream Gds (d 27 Nov 1991), only s of Haliburton Stanley Mortimer, of Knightsbridge, and has:

1b *Charles Roger Henry; b 4 April 1952; educ Eton

1b *Jane Clare [Mrs Paul Torday, Nilston Rigg, Hexham, Northumberland NE4 7S]; b 23 Jan 1949; m 19– *Paul Torday and has:

1c *Piers Francis; b 6 April 1974; educ Eton and Oxford

2c *Nicholas Lazlo; b 12 Dec 1976; educ Eton

2b *Louise Star [Mrs Henry Carey, 4 Gowan Ave, London SW6 6RF]; b 12 Jan 1957; m 2 July 1977 *Henry Carey and has:

1c *Benjamin Charles Carew; b 25 July 1985

1c *Rebecca Louise Carew; b 20 Sept 1978

1 Anne Denison; b 9 Nov 1853; d unm 19 April 1902

2 Marion Denison; b 4 Dec 1856; m 24 July 1875 Sir (George) William des Voeux, GCMG (d 15 Dec 1909; see 1940 edn Des VOEUX Bt), and d 28 July 1955, leaving issue

Sir JOHN d 7 July 1896; his gs,

JOHN CUTHBERT DENISON-PENDER, **1st Baron Pender**, of Porthcurnow, Co Cornwall (UK), so cr 12 June 1937; b 11 May 1882; educ Eton; MP (U) Newmarket 1913–18 and Balham and Tooting 1918–22, memb LCC for S St Pancras 1910–19, Govr and jt md Cable and Wireless Hldgs, jt pres Marconi Internat Marine Communication Co, chm Eastern and Associated Telegraph Cos, dir Cable and Wireless, Globe Telegraph and Tst, Cable Investment Tst, Northern Assur, Nat Provincial Bank, P&O and Br India Steamship Navigation, Kodak and Direct Spanish Telegraph Ltd, Hon Col City London Signals (TA), served WW I, Cdr Order Dannebrog; m 6 Feb 1906 Irene (d 29 May 1943), only dau of Sir Ernest de la Rue KCVO, JP, of Lower Hare Park, Cambs, and had:

1 JOHN JOCELYN, **2nd Baron**

2 Richard Ernest, TD; b 6 Nov 1914; educ Eton; Maj Roy Signals (TARO), ADC to C-in-C Home Forces 1939, served WW II (wounded, despatches, US Bronze Star), memb London Stock Exchange; m 19 Dec 1939 Louise (d 14 April 1973), only dau of Henry Gilbey Riviere, of Chelsea, and d 1984, leaving:

(1) +James Henry; b 16 April 1942; educ Eton; m 1st 10 July 1971 Gillian, yst dau of John Curtis Barnett, of Threepwood Hall, Haydon Bridge, Northumberland, and has:

1a +Jamie Alexander; b 1 June 1973

2a +Nicholas John; b 30 Sept 1974

(1) (cont.) James Denison-Pender m 2nd 1994 *Caroline Anne, dau of Maj Timothy Stuart Lewis (see DAVENTRY, V) and formerly w of Sir (Frederick Douglas) David Thomson, 3rd Bt, of Glendarroch (qv)

(2) +Michael Richard [Michael Denison-Pender Esq, The Hazard, Sandwich Bay, Kent CT13 9PG]; b 16 April 1942; educ Eton; m 14 Oct 1972 *Nadine, yr dau of Henri Villiger, of Aigle, Switzerland, and has:

1a +Dominic Michael; b 12 Jan 1975

(1) *Linda Louise [Mrs John Bayman, Middle Cottage, Sandwich Bay, Kent CT13 9PG]; b 10 June 1948; golfer; m 23 Nov 1973 *John Edward Bayman, s of Lewis A Bayman, of Mickle Hay, Danbury Park, Danbury, Essex, and has:

1a *Alexander Christian Gray; b 29 Dec 1976

1a *Caroline Louise; b 6 March 1975

1 *Gladys Gaynor; m 25 July 1934 Gersholm Stewart, CBE, barrister, only surv s of Sir Gersholm Stewart, KBE, and has:

(1) Gersholm John; b 26 April 1935; educ Eton; m 26 April 1963 *Georgina Christine (m 2nd 19– *Robert Eric Marcus West), dau of Brig George David Renny, CBE, DSO, of Woking, and d 24 July 1985, leaving:

1a *Robert Gersholm; b 1964

2a *Alastair Douglas; b 1966

1a *Katherine Louise; b 1975

The 1st BARON d 4 Dec 1949; his er son,

JOHN JOCELYN DENISON-PENDER, **2nd Baron Pender**, CBE (1946); b 26 Jan 1907; educ Eton and Magdalen Coll Oxford; Govr Cable and Wireless Hldg, dir Commercial Union Assur and Direct Spanish Telegraph Co, Pres Royal Albert Hall 1952–65, V-Chm Bd Govrs Charing Cross Hosp 1960–65; m 22 July 1930 Camilla Lethbridge (d 1988), dau of Willoughby Arthur Pemberton (see LETHBRIDGE, Bt), and d 31 March 1965, leaving:

1 JOHN WILLOUGHBY DENISON-PENDER, **3rd and present Baron Pender**

2 +Robin Charles [The Hon Robin Denison-Pender, Jessups, Mark Beech, Kent TN8 5NR]; b 7 Sept 1935; educ Eton; late Lt 11th Hus, High Sheriff Kent 1993, memb Stock Exchange; m 7 May 1966 *Clare Nell, only dau of Lt-Col James Currie Thomson, MBE, TD, JP, of Stable Court, Walkern, Stevenage, Herts, by

Letitia Blanche, er dau of Hon Malcolm Algernon Borthwick (see BORTHWICK, L), and has:

(1) +Jocelyn Andrew; b 31 July 1967; m 17 June 1995 *Georgina, 2nd dau of Charles Fane (see WESTMORLAND, E), and has:

1a +Maximillian Robin; b 12 Dec 1997

(2) +Peter Robin; b 1 Aug 1972

(1) *Sacha Louise; b 10 May 1969; m 1993 *Jonathan David Forbes (see ROPNER, Bt, of Thorp Perrow)

1 *Ann Camilla [The Hon Lady Dent, 44 Smith St, London SW3]; b 18 June 1931; m 2 Oct 1952 *Sir Robin John Dent, KCVO, s of R-Adml John Dent, CB, OBE, of Sway, Hants, and has:

(1) *Annabel Jane [Mrs James Meade, Pitt Vale Farm House, Pitt, Winchester, Hants SO22 5QW]; b 15 Oct 1954; m 1981 *James John Meade, s of J A Meade, and has:

1a *Thomas Edward; b 1988

1a *Katherine Anne; b 1984

2a *Susanna Clare; b 1986

(2) *Jennifer Ann; b 27 May 1957; m 29 Sept 1982 *Andrew Everard Martin Smith, s of Julian Ronald Martin Smith, of Hunstanton, Norfolk, and has:

1a *David Julian; b 1984

1a *Henrietta Camilla; b 1986

2a *Rosanna Marcia (twin); b 1986

PENRHYN

Arms: Quarterly, 1st and 4th, per bend sinister erm. and ermines a lion rampant or (for PENNANT); 2nd and 3rd, grand quarters, 1st and 4th, arg., a human heart gu., ensigned with an imperial crown or, on a chief az. three mullets of the field; 2nd and 3rd, arg., three piles gu., in chief two mullets of the field (for DOUGLAS). **Crests:** 1 Out of a ducal coronet an antelope's head arg., maned and tufted or (for PENNANT), 2 A sanglier between two clefts of an oak tree fructed, with a lock holding them together, all ppr (for DOUGLAS). **Supporters:** On either side an antelope ppr., collared and chained or, the dexter having suspended from the collar an escutcheon gu. charged with a man's head couped and affrontée ppr. **Mottoes:** 1 (above the sinister crest) *Lock sicker* ('Be secure') and 2 (beneath shield) *Æquo animo* ('With an even mind'). **Creation:** B. (UK) 3 Aug 1866.

THE 6TH BARON PENRHYN OF LLANDEGAI, Co Carnarvon (Malcolm Frank Douglas-Pennant, DSO (1945), MBE (1943)) [The Rt Hon The Lord Penrhyn DSO MBE, Littleton Manor, Littleton, Hants SO22 6QU]; b 11 July 1908; s f 1967; educ Eton and RMC Sandhurst; Col KRRC WW II; m 9 June 1954 *Elizabeth Rosemary, OStJ, only dau of Brig Sir Percy Robert Laurie, KCVO, CBE, DSO, JP, of Wavendon Lodge, Bucks, and has:

1 *Gillian Frances; b 2 Sept 1955; m 22 Nov 1997 *Robin Erksine Greenwood, s of Peter and Pamela Greenwood, of S Cadbury, Somerset

2 *Rosemary; b 26 Oct 1957; m 1984 *Sir Thomas Richard Troubridge, 7th Bt (qv)

Lineage: JOHN DOUGLAS (bro of 17th Earl of Morton; qv); m Lady Frances Lascelles, dau of 1st Earl of Harewood (qv), and had a 3rd s:

EDWARD GORDON DOUGLAS later DOUGLAS PENNANT (roy licence 25 Jan 1841), **1st Baron Penrhyn of Llandegai**, Co Carnarvon (UK), so cr 3 Aug 1866; b 20 June 1800; Col Gren Gds, Caernarvs: Ld Lt, Hon Col Militia, MP 1841–66; m 1st 6 Aug 1833 Juliana Isabella Mary (d 25 April 1842), est dau and coheir (with her sister Emma-Elizabeth Alicia, w of 2nd Baron Sudeley; qv) of George Hay Dawkins-Pennant (see also HAWARDEN, V), of Penrhyn Castle, Caernarvs, who inherited the Penrhyn estates from his great-uncle (bro of his grandmother Elizabeth, w of Henry Dawkins, of Jamaica) Richard Pennant, 1st and last Baron Penrhyn, of Penrhyn, Co Louth (I) (cr 19 Nov 1783 (s of John Pennant, who had bought the half of the Pennant estate not owned by his w Bonella, neé Hodges); m 16 Nov 1765 Anne Susanna, dau of Lt-Gen Hugh Warburton; dsp 1808), and had, with other issue:

1 GEORGE SHOLTO GORDON DOUGLAS-PENNANT, **2nd Baron Penrhyn of Llandegai**, JP, DL Caernarvs; *b* 30 Sept 1836, Caernarvs: CC, Maj cmdg Rifle Vols, MP 1866–68 and 1874–80; Hon Col 4th Bn Roy Welch Fus; *m* 1st 23 Aug 1860 Pamela Blanche (*d* 5 Feb 1870), dau of Sir Charles Rushout Rushout, 2nd Bt (*see* 1931 edn), of Sezincote, Glos, and had:

(1) EDWARD SHOLTO DOUGLAS-PENNANT, **3rd Baron Penrhyn of Llandegai**, JP, DL Caernarvs and Northants; *b* 10 June 1864; CA Northants, Maj 1st Life Gds Res Regt, formerly Lt 1st Life Gds, Lt-Col Bucks Imp Yeo, Hon Col 4th Bn Roy Welch Fus, MP Northants S 1895–1900, Freedom Bangor 1926; *m* 6 Dec 1887 Hon Blanche FitzRoy (*d* 28 Nov 1944), dau of 3rd Baron Southampton (*qv*), and *d* 22 Aug 1927, having had:

1a Alan George Sholto; *b* 11 June 1890; ADC to Govr Bengal 1914, Lt Gren Gds WW I; *ka* 29 Oct 1914

2a HUGH NAPIER DOUGLAS-PENNANT, **4th Baron Penrhyn of Llandegai**, JP, DL Caernarvs; *b* 6 Aug 1894; *educ* Eton and RMC Sandhurst; served WW I (1914–15 star, two medals), Hon Col 6th Bn Roy Welch Fus 1932–46, Ld Lt Caernarvs 1933–41, Pres C Assoc Carnarvon, KStJ; *m* 25 April 1922 (*divorce* 1941) Hon Sybil Mary Hardinge, OStJ, yr dau of 3rd Viscount Harding (*qv*), and *dsp* 26 June 1949

1a Linda Blanche; *b* 25 Jan 1889; *m* 27 March 1915 Maj Charles Henry Geoffrey Mansfield Clarke, MVO (*see* CLARKE, Bt, of Dunham Lodge), and *d* 8 July 1965, having had issue

2a Pamela; *b* 11 May 1896; *m* 3 Sept 1919 6th Earl of Yarborough (*qv*) and *d* 31 Jan 1968, leaving issue

3a Sybil Mary; *b* 19 Jan 1901; *m* 12 April 1926 5th Viscount Portman (*qv*) and *d* 1975, leaving issue

(1) Kathleen; *m* 19 Oct 1886 7th Viscount Falmouth (*qv*) and *d* 29 Dec 1953, leaving issue

(2) Alice; Hon Sister OStJ; *d* unm 16 March 1939

(3) Pamela Georgina, MBE (1920); *m* 20 Sept 1883 Col Hon Henry Richard Howel Lloyd-Mostyn (*see* MOSTYN, B) and *d* 20 July 1949, leaving issue

(4) Hilda; *d* unm 11 Feb 1959 aged 93

(5) Ina, OBE (1918); *m* 15 Jan 1902 Maj-Gen Arthur Edmund Sandbach, CB, DSO, RE (*d* 25 June 1928), of Hafodunos, Abergele, and Bryn Gwyn, Oswestry, and *d* 13 July 1942, leaving issue

(6) Violet Blanche; memb LCC Educn Ctee, Health Insur Commr Wales 1911–18, Cmdt WRAF 1918; *d* unm 12 Oct 1945

1 (cont.) The **2nd Baron** *m* 2nd 21 Oct 1875 Gertrude Jessy (*d* 20 Feb 1940), only surv dau of Rev Henry Glynne, Rector Hawarden, and *d* 10 March 1907, having by her had:

(2) George Henry; *b* 26 Aug 1876, Capt Gren Gds Boer War 1900–02 (despatches) and WW I (despatches); *ka* 11 March 1915

(3) Charles, JP Suffolk; *b* 7 Oct 1877; Lt Coldstream Gds, Boer War 1899–1902 (despatches twice) and WW I; *m* 28 Jan 1905 Lady Edith Anne Dawson (*m* 2nd 14 Nov 1916 Capt Charles Ashe Windham, MC, Norfolk Regt (*d* 9 Sept 1940), and *d* 17 Feb 1974, leaving issue), er dau of 2nd Earl of Dartrey (*see* 1933 edn), and *dsp ka* 29 Oct 1914

(7) Gwynedd; *m* 18 Nov 1899 Sir William Eley Cuthbert Quilter, 2nd Bt (*qv*), and *d* 14 Oct 1960, leaving issue

(8) Lilian; served WW I (star, two medals); *d* unm 23 May 1968

(9) Winifred; *d* unm 9 Dec 1972

(10) Margaret; *m* 29 July 1909 Gen Sir (Augustus Francis) Andrew Nicol Thorne, KCB, CMG, DSO, DL, Gren Gds (*d* 25 Sept 1970), s of Augustus Thorne, JP, DL, of London W1, and *d* 23 Oct 1967, leaving issue

(11) Nesta; *b* 21 March 1888; *m* 16 Feb 1920 Col Sir Edward Courtenay Thomas Warner, 2nd Bt (*qv*), and *d* 4 March 1970, leaving issue

(12) Elin; *m* 14 Oct 1920 2nd Baron Cochrane of Cults (*qv*) and *d* 19 Feb 1934, leaving issue

2 Archibald Charles Henry; *b* 22 Nov 1837; Lt-Col Gren Gds; *m* 5 Jan 1865 Harriet Ella (*d* 12 Feb 1942), 2nd dau of 2nd Baron Gifford (*qv*), and *d* 7 Sept 1884, leaving:

(1) FRANK, **5th Baron**

(2) Claud, JP Essex; *b* 12 Nov 1867; *educ* Eton and New Coll Oxford (BA 1891, MA 1909); barrister Inner Temple 1894, Chllr Diocese of Bangor 1909–41; *m* 8 June 1922 Christian Eleanor Margaret (*d* 10 Feb 1968), dau of Sir Harry William Neville Goschen, 1st Bt (*qv*), and *d* 12 March 1955, leaving:

1a Henry, JP; *b* 13 June 1925; *educ* Eton and Trin Coll Cambridge (BA 1946); *m* 26 Oct 1957 *Pamela (*m* 2nd 1988 Very Rev Patrick Reynold Mitchell, Dean Windsor) [Mrs Patrick Mitchell, The Deanery, Windsor Castle, Berks SL4 1NJ], only dau of Alfred Gaspard Le Marchant (*see* LE MARCHANT, Bt), and *d* 1986, having had:

1b David; *b* 6 Aug 1961; *d* 25 Dec 1974

2b +Rupert Henry; *b* 6 Feb 1963; *m* 16 April 1994 *Caroline, dau of Michael Fass, of Edinburgh

3b Andrew Claud; *b* 8 Aug 1967; *d* 30 June 1993

4b Edward Alfred; *b* 8 Aug 1967; *d* June 1989

1b *Venetia [Mrs Liell Francklin, 62 Brodrick Rd, London SW17 7DY]; *b* 13 March 1960; *m* 1988 *(Charles) Liell Philip Francklin, er s of Cdr (Mavourn Baldwin) Philip Francklin, DSO, JP, of Gonalston Hall, Notts, Ld Lt Notts and has:

1c *Jack; *b* 199–

1c *Flora; *b* 1990

2c *Katharine Josephine; *b* 1992

1a *Margaret [Mrs Patrick Lloyd, Valaford, W Anstey, S Molton, Devon EX36 3PW]; *b* 28 May 1923; *m* 12 Jan 1956 *Patrick John Lloyd, twin s of Edmund Commeline Lloyd, of Pitsworthy, Exford, Somerset, and has:

1b *John Philip; *b* 27 Aug 1960; *m* 11 July 1992 *Kate, yr dau of Hugh O'Neill, of Binfield House, Oxted, Surrey, and has:

1c *Harry Felix; *b* 3 April 1994

2c *Bertie Hugh; *b* 5 May 1997

1b *Phyllida Christian; *b* 17 June 1957

2a Ann; *b* 10 Feb 1930; *m* 4 Aug 1960 Michael Frederick Wilson, only s of Gerald Hammersley Wilson, of Kintbury, Berks, and *d* 19–, leaving:

1b *Fiona Margaret; *b* 4 July 1962; *m* 19– *Robert Wolstenholme and has:

1c *James Michael; *b* 27 March 1994

2c *Patrick John; *b* 2 Oct 1996

2b *Sara Nicola; *b* 20 March 1964

(3) Algernon; *b* 19 Nov 1872; *m* 16 April 1896 Grace Talcott (*d* 25 Sept 1952), dau of Richard Talcott Morgan, and *d* 30 April 1925, leaving:

1a Mariella; *b* 8 May 1901; *m* 20 March 1923 Francis Carlton Bennett, Lt RN, yr s of Sir Albert James Bennett, 1st Bt (*qv*), and had issue

(4) Edric; *b* 19 Feb 1878; *d* 12 Aug 1887

(5) Archibald; *b* 25 May 1881; Lt Herts Yeo, formerly 3rd Bn Roy Scots, S African Constabulary Boer War 1901 (wounded, despatches) and WW I, ADC Personal Staff; *m* 1st 15 Nov 1905 Gwendoline (*d* 14 Aug 1965), dau of Alexander Fraser, JP, of Westerfield, Suffolk (*see* 1970 edn FRASER OF LONSDALE, B), and had:

1a Ian; *b* 21 Aug 1906; *m* 14 April 1931 Mary Florence (*d* 1980), dau of Maj John Williams, DL, of Scorrier House, Cornwall, and *d* 3 March 1941 following a car crash, leaving:

1b *Daphne Mary [Miss Daphne Douglas-Pennant, Hedge Barton, Widecombe-in-the-Moor, Devon TQ13 7TS]; *b* 14 March 1932; *m* 1st 18 Aug 1953 (*divorce* 1964) Capt Maurice Douglas Evans, RM, yr s of C Douglas Evans, of Monkstown, Co Dublin, and has:

1c *Jeremy Douglas; *b* 12 Aug 1958

1c *Claire Douglas; *b* 29 Jan 1954

2c *Rosemary Douglas; *b* 29 Jan 1956

1b (cont.) Mrs Daphne Evans *m* 2nd 20 Jan 1965 (*divorce* 1992, resumed maiden name) Francis Seymour Hurndall Waldron, s of Brig Frank Brereton Hurndall, MC

2a Rodney Archibald; *b* 8 Feb 1913; *educ* Radley; Maj KRRC; *m* 1st 29 March 1945 Rosemary June (*d* 13 June 1946), formerly w of Capt William Frederick Delap, of Kenya, and dau of John Wilfred Munroe and Mrs Guy Hanmer (*see* HANMER, Bt); *m* 2nd 7 Aug 1947 Agnes Nydia (Nancye) (*d* 1984), only child of Arthur Robertson Brailey, FRCS, and by her had:

1b +Hugh Archibald [Hugh Douglas-Pennant Esq, Churchgate House, Stansfield, Suffolk CO10 8LT]; *b* 23 Sept 1951; *educ* Eton; 2nd Lt Roy Yeo; *m* 1st 1976 (*divorce* 1982) Henrietta, dau of Col Oliver Berger, of Pimlico, and has:

1c +Oliver Andrew; *b* 11 Feb 1979; *educ* Radley

1c *Lucy Annabel; *b* 14 Feb 1977; *educ* St Mary Calne and Edinburgh U

1b (cont.) Hugh Douglas-Pennant *m* 2nd 5 Nov 1983 *Sarah Rosamund, yst dau of Lt-Col Jocelyn Eustace Gurney, DSO, MC, DL, of Tacolneston Hall, Norwich, and by her has:

2c *Ian Christopher; *b* 3 June 1986

3c +David Arthur; *b* 4 Aug 1989

1b *Anthea Rose [Mrs Andrew Sutherland, Berachak, RMB 8230, Hamilton, VIC 3300, Australia]; *b* 24 Aug 1948; *m* 12 Feb 1983 *Andrew Lachlan Sutherland and has:

1c *Diana Elisabeth; *b* 28 Dec 1983

2c *Sarah Felicity; *b* 19 March 1985

2a (cont.) Maj Rodney Douglas-Pennant *m* 3rd 1985 *Mrs Olivia Joan Herbert [Mrs Rodney Douglas-Pennant, Little White House, Church Lane, Longworth, Oxon OX13 5DX], yst dau of Alexander Henry Melvill Wedderburn, CBE (*see* WEDDERBURN, Bt), and formerly w of Richard Weston Herbert, and *d* 21 Dec 1993

(5) (cont.) Archibald Douglas-Pennant *m* 2nd 3 Nov 1967 *Jean, dau of Alexander Maclean, of Nairn, and *d* 3 April 1971

(1) MURIEL, *cr* VISCOUNTESS DAVENTRY (*qv*)

(2) Rachel; *b* 12 July 1874; *m* 21 Jan 1897 Hon Gilbert Vanden-Bempde-Johnstone, s of 1st Baron Derwent (*qv*), and *d* 15 July 1968, leaving issue

1 Caroline Elizabeth Emma; *m* 31 Aug 1857 1st Baron Magheramorne, KCB (*d* 27 June 1890), and *d* 1 June 1924, leaving issue (*see* HOGG, Bt)

The **1st Baron** *m* 2nd 26 Jan 1846 Lady Maria Louisa FitzRoy (*d* 10 May 1912), dau of 5th Duke of Grafton (*qv*), and *d* 31 March 1886, having by her had:

2 Louisa Mary; *d* unm 19 June 1911

3 Mary Georgiana; *d* unm 27 March 1926

4 Eva Anna Caroline; *m* 31 Aug 1871 Lord William Frederick Ernest Seymour and *d* 3 Jan 1934, leaving issue (*see* HERTFORD, M)

5 Gertrude Alice Emma; *d* unm 20 July 1944

6 Adela; *d* unm 26 May 1955

The 4th BARON's cousin,

FRANK DOUGLAS-PENNANT, **5th Baron Penrhyn of Llandegai**, JP Northants; *b* 21 Nov 1865; *educ* Eton and RMC Sandhurst; Lt-Col cmdg 1914–15 10th Service Bn KRRC, Boer War 1901–02 and WW I; *m* 1st 25 April 1892 (*divorce* 1903) Maud Eleonora (*d* 12 Dec 1936), er dau of Col John Hardy, 9th Lancers, and had:

1 Cyril Eustace (Sir), KCB (1950, CB 1945), CBE (1943), DSO (1944), DSC; *b* 7 April 1894; *educ* RNCs Osborne and Dartmouth; served WW I (despatches) and WW II (despatches), Ch Naval Staff Offr and Dep Ch Staff to SACSE Asia 1945–46, Cmdt Jt Servs Staff Coll 1947–48, V-Adml 1948, Flag Offr (Air) and 2ic Mediterranean Station 1948–50, Adml Br Jt Servs Mission Washington 1950–52, C-in-C The Nore 1952–53, Legn Hon and Croix de Guerre avec palmes, Cdr US Legn Merit; *m* 1st 6 Jan 1917 (*divorce* 1936) Phyllis Constance, only dau of Col Oswald Mosley Leigh, TD, JP, of Belmont Hall, Cheshire, and had:

(1) *Sheila Florence [Mrs Ronald Cobb, 197 Park West, Marble Arch, London W2]; *b* 11 Jan 1918; *m* 1st 23 May 1946 (*divorce* 1950) Anthony Brine, est s of William Brine, of W Hayes, Hants, and has issue; *m* 2nd 8 March 1951 Ronald Arthur Cobb, s of Rev Arthur Charles Cobb, of Arundel House, E Grinstead, Sussex

1 (cont.) Adml The Hon Sir Cyril Douglas-Pennant *m* 2nd 5 April 1937 *Sheila, 2nd dau of Stanley Brotherhood, JP, of Thornhaugh Hall, Peterborough, by Vera, 4th dau of Charles Durant Kemp-Welch, JP, DL, of Ascot, and *d* 3 April 1961

1 Bridget Violet; *b* 21 Sept 1899; *m* 15 Nov 1923 Maj-Gen Charles Harvey Miller (*d* 23 Dec 1974), CB, CBE, DSO, DL, RAC, Ch Staff to HRH THE late DUKE OF GLOUCESTER in Australia 1946–47, only *s* of Robert Miller, of Dummer Grange, Basingstoke, and *d* 19 March 1978, having had issue

2 Eileen Maud; *b* 22 Jan 1901; Naval VAD WW II; *d* unm 4 May 1998

The **5th Baron** *m* 2nd 18 April 1905 Alice Nellie (*d* 17 Dec 1965), only dau of Sir William Charles Cooper, 3rd Bt, of Woollahra (*qv*), and *d* 3 Feb 1967, having by her had:

2 MALCOLM FRANK DOUGLAS-PENNANT, **6th and present Baron Penrhyn of Llandegai**

3 +NIGEL [The Hon Nigel Douglas-Pennant, The Swallows, 43 Kingsdon, Somerton, Somerset TA11 7JX]; *b* 22 Dec 1909; heir presumptive; *educ* Eton and Clare Coll Cambridge (BA, 1931); Maj RM WW II; *m* 1st 6 Sept 1935 Margaret Dorothy (*d* 2 Oct 1938), yst dau of Thomas George Kirkham, of Westholm, Jordanhill, Glasgow, and has:

  (1) +Simon [Simon Douglas-Pennant Esq, Mulberry House, Old Church Rd, Colwall, Worcs WR13 6HB]; *b* 28 June 1938; *educ* Eton and Clare Coll Cambridge (BA 1961, Cricket Blue); *m* 5 Oct 1963 *Josephine Maxwell, yr dau of Robert Upcott and Mrs David Maurice Annett, of Worcester, and has:

    1a +Edward Sholto; *b* 6 June 1966; *educ* Malvern

    2a +Hugo Charles; *b* 21 April 1969; *educ* Malvern

    1a *Sophie Margaret; *b* 11 Dec 1964; *m* 1989 *Michael Robert Trotter, yst s of John Trotter, of London, and has:

      1b *Hugo William; *b* 1991

      2b *Archie Milo; *b* 1994

      1b *Claudia Rosanna; *b* 13 Dec 1997

    2a *Harriet Josephine *b* 25 May 1972

3 (cont.) The Hon Nigel Douglas-Pennant *m* 2nd 20 July 1940 Eleanor Stewart (*d* 1987), est dau of Very Rev Herbert Newcome Craig, Dean Kildare; *m* 3rd 21 Oct 1993 *Stella, widow of Rev Robert Wingfield Digby (*d* 16 July 1983), and dau of Stanley Bradwell, MC, DCN, of Buxton, Derbys, and by his 2nd w has:

  (2) +Philip Morton [Philip Douglas-Pennant Esq, Tisbury House, Tisbury, Wilts]; *b* 7 Feb 1947; *educ* Eton; *m* 13 Dec 1975 *Sarah Frances Jane, yr dau of Maj-Gen Ronald Edward Coaker, CB, CBE, MC, of Seaton Old Rectory, Uppingham, Rutland, and has:

    1a +John Morton Ronald; *b* 5 May 1987

    1a Anna Susan; *b* 9 July 1979; *d* 1993

    2a *Camilla Faith; *b* 19 Jan 1981

  (1) *Brigid Elizabeth [Mrs Brigid Peat, 8 Magrath Ave, Cambridge CB4 3AH]; *b* 10 May 1943; *m* 27 Jan 1972 (*divorce* 19–) Richard Henry Peat, er s of Sir Henry Peat, KCVO, DFC, FCA, of Victoria, London SW1, and has:

    1a *Harry Mark Richard; *b* 28 May 1974

    1a *Laura Katharine Alice *b* 29 Aug 1976

3 *Susan Victoria [The Hon Susan Douglas-Pennant, Adam's Cottage, Horningsham, Wilts BA12 7LG]; *b* 24 May 1918; *educ* Owlstone Croft Cambridge, St Bartholomew's Hosp London and Wellhouse Hosp Barnet; SRN, SCM

Insur of Canada 1968–, FRSA 1975, Knight Cdr Roy Order of George I of Greece 1963, Cdr Valour of Cameroons 1963, Grand Offr Order Leopold Belgium 1963, Order Homayoun Iran 1959, Grand Cross Merit W Germany 1959; *m* 20 June 1928 (Ethel) Mary (*d* 1991), only dau of Henry Theophilus Johnson, of Putney, and has:

1 +JOHN RAYMOND, TD (1965) [John Perring Esq TD, 21 Somerset Rd, Parkside, London SW19 5JZ]; *b* 7 July 1931; *educ* Stowe; Sheriff City of London 1991–92, Master Merchant Taylors' Co 1988 and 1994, FRSA, OStJ 1992; *m* 21 July 1961 *Ella Christine, dau of Anthony George Pelham (see CHICHESTER, E), and has:

  (1) +John Simon Pelham; *b* 20 July 1962

  (2) +Mark Ralph Pelham; *b* 25 Jan 1965

  (1) *Emma Mary; *b* 7 Oct 1963; *m* 11 June 1994 *Christian Philip Heyman, s of Hans Heyman, of Dorking, Surrey, and has:

    1a *Benjamin Edward; *b* 24 March 1997

  (2) *Anna Margaret; *b* 24 Nov 1968; *m* 5 Sept 1992 *Edward Pery Standish (see BYRON, B)

2 Richard Eric; *b* 25 May 1933; *educ* Stowe; FCA; *m* 10 April 1964 Evelyn Faith Frances (*m* 2nd 1974 (*divorce* 1982, resumed 1st married name by deed poll 1983) William John Stainton Clutterbuck), dau of Sir Peter Arthur Percival Hay Aitken, of Lowlands Hall, Stonham Aspal, Suffolk, and *d* 1971, leaving:

  (1) +Christopher James; *b* 23 Feb 1965

  (2) +Antony William; *b* 18 Nov 1967

  (3) +Graham Michael; *b* 1970

3 +Michael Arthur; *b* 23 April 1937; *educ* Stowe, Trin Coll Cambridge (MA, MB, BChir), St Bartholomew's Hosp and U of Capetown, MB, BChir, FCP (SA); *m* 30 Sept 1961 (*divorce* 1988) Elizabeth, dau of A/Cdre Eric Delano Barnes, CB, AFC, and has:

  (1) +Nicholas David Delano; *b* 10 Oct 1963

  (2) +Michael Charles Delano; *b* 7 April 1965

  (3) +Thomas Edward Delano; *b* 1971

  (4) +Ralph Andrew Delano; *b* 1973

Lineage: HENRY PERRING, of Willesden; *m* Elizabeth — and had:

JOHN ERNEST PERRING (Sir), JP, DL London and Middx; *b* 16 Jan 1870; chm John Perring Ltd and Jackaman Ltd, memb LCC 1922–37, ktd 1934, Hon Col 36th (Middx) AA Searchlight Bn RA (TA), KStJ; *m* 1897 Florence OStJ (*d* 12 June 1960), dau of Charles Higginson, and *d* 23 March 1948, leaving:

1 John William; *b* May 1898; *m* 1921 Marie, dau of J R T Nind, and had issue

2 RALPH EDGAR (Sir), **1st Bt**

1 Marion Florence

2 Doris Inez

PERRY OF SOUTHWARK

PERRING

Arms: Argent on a pile barry wavy of eight azure and of the field between two walnut trees eradicated proper a lion rampant gules. **Crest:** Upon the trunk of a walnut tree fesswise with two branches sprouting or therefrom proper, a sword erect or. **Motto:** Proud to serve. **Creation:** Bt. (UK) 27 Nov 1963.

SIR RALPH EDGAR PERRING, 1ST BT, of Frensham Manor, Co Surrey, JP (Co London 1943) [Sir Ralph Perring Bt JP, 15 Burghley House, Somerset Rd, London SW19 5JB]; *b* 23 March 1905; *educ* U Coll Sch; Lt RA (TA) WW II 1939–40 (invalided), chm and md Perring Furnishings 1948–81 and John Perring Ltd, Common Cnclman Corp of London 1948–51, Alderman (Langbourn Ward) 1951–75, chm Spitalfields Market Ctee 1951–52, memb LCC 1952–55, Sheriff City London 1958–59, Ld Mayor 1962–63, Master Tinplate Workers' Co 1944 and Parish Clerks' Co 1962 and 1963, memb Court Painter-Stainers' Co, Pres City Livery Club 1951–52, Govr Christ's Hosp, St Bartholomew's Hosp 1963– and Imp Coll Science and Technology, V-Pres Roy Bridewell Hosp, V-Chm Ctee for Exports to Canada 1964–67, chm 1967–69, Lt City London, KStJ, ktd 1960, dir Confedn Life

Arms: Sable, in dexter chief a sun in splendour issuant and in base a pear slipped and leaved gold (for PERRY), on an inescutcheon of pretence argent a cross of lozenges, in the first quarter a crescent enclosing a quaver and in the fourth quarter a cinquefoil gules (for WELCH). **Supporters:** Dexter, a marmalade tom cat proper; sinister, upon a pile of three books, the spines visible bound gules, the pages edged gold, a Persian cat sable, the nose, breast and feet argent, each supporting between the forepaws a quill argent penned or. **Motto:** *Ancilla domini* ('The handmaid of the Lord') **Creation:** B. (LP, UK) 1991.

THE BARONESS PERRY OF SOUTHWARK, of Charlbury, Co Oxon (Pauline Welch) [The Rt Hon The Baroness Perry of Southwark, House of Lords, London SW1A 0PW]; *b* 15 Oct 1931; *educ* Girls' High Sch Wolverhampton and Girton Coll Cambridge (MA); teacher UK, USA and Canada 1953–56 and 1959–61; lecturer: philosophy: Manitoba U 1956–59 and Massachusetts U 1961–62; educn Exeter U 1962–66 and Oxford 1966–70; schs inspr 1970–86 (staff inspr 1975–81, ch inspr 1981–86); dir S Bank U 1987–92 (V-Chllr 1992–93); Pres Lucy Cavendish Coll Cambridge 1994–; memb: Governing Body Inst Devpt Studies Sussex U 1987–94, Br Cncl Ctee on Internat Co-opn Higher Educn 1987–, ESRC

1988–91, Bd Govrs S Bank Centre 1992–, PM's Advsy Panel Citizens Charter 1993– (Chm 1997–), Nat Advsy Cncl Educn and Training Targets 1993–, Ho Lds Select Ctee Sci and Tech Overseas Project Bd 1993–, NI Higher Educn Cncl 1993–94; Chm DTI Export Gp for Educn and Trg Sector 1993; Rector's Warden Southwark Cathedral 1990–, Govr ESU 1997–; Freeman City London 1992, Liveryman Bakers' Co 1992; Hon FCP 1987, Hon FRSA 1988, Hon Fell Sunderland Poly 1990; Hon LLD Bath 1991; Hon DLitt Sussex 1992; Hon DEd Wolverhampton 1994, Hon LLD Aberdeen 1994; author: *The Future of Higher Education* (1991), *Women in Education Management* (1992), *Education in the Age of Information* (1993), *What is Quality in Higher Education?* (1993); m 1952 *George Walter Perry and has:

1 *Christopher George; b 1953; educ Abingdon; m 1987 *Elizabeth Mary Edwardes and has a dau

2 *Timothy John Welch; b 1962; educ Beckett's Sch, Chesham, Bucks; m 1984 *Jeannie Ross McKenzie

3 *Simon Jeremy Welch; b 1966; educ Sevenoaks

1 *Hilary Anne Welch; b 1955; m 1st 1975 (divorce 1990) John Hayward and has a dau; m 2nd 1990 *Thomas Charles Winstone and by him has two daus

Lineage: JOHN GEORGE EMBLETON WELCH; m Elizabeth — and had:

PAULINE, cr a **Baroness**

PERRY OF WALTON

Creation: B. 1978

THE BARON PERRY OF WALTON, of Walton, Co Bucks (Sir Walter Laing Macdonald Perry, OBE (1957) [The Rt Hon The Lord Perry of Walton OBE, 2 Cramond Rd South, Edinburgh EH4 6AD]; b 16 June 1921; educ Ayr Acad, Dundee High Sch and St Andrews (MB ChB 1943, MD 1948, DSc 1958); MO: Colonial Med Serv Nigeria 1944–46 and RAF 1946–47; memb: MRC 1947–52, Br Pharmacopoeia Commn 1952–68; Dir Dept Biological Standards Nat Inst Med Research 1952–58; Sec Br Pharmacological Soc 1957–61; Prof Pharmacology Edinburgh U 1958–68 (V-Principal 1967–68); V-Chllr OU 1969–80, ktd 1974; Chm: Community Radio Milton Keynes 1979–82, Research Def Soc 1979–82 (Pres 1993–), Living Tapes 1980, Delegacy of Goldsmith's Coll 1981–84, Standing Ctee Continuing Educn, U Grants Ctee, Videotel Marine Internat 1985–, Nat Advsy Body for Public Sector Higher Educn 1985–89; Dep Leader SDP Ho Lds 1981–83 and 1988–89; Consultant UN U; Fell: OU 1981–, UCL 1981–; Hon DSc Bradford 1974; Hon LLD Dundee 1975; Hon DHL Maryland 1978, State U NY 1982; DU: Athabasca 1979, Stirling 1980, OU 1981; Hon DLitt Deakin U Australia 1981, Andhra Pradesh OU 1992; Hon DEd Victoria U 1992; Wellcome Gold Medal 1994; MRCP Edin 1963, FRCPE 1967, FRCP 1968; FRSE, FRS; author: *Open University* (1976); m 1st 1946 (divorce 1971) Anne Elizabeth Grant and has:

1 *Michael John [The Hon Michael Perry, 9 Queens Ave, Perth, Australia]; b 1948; m 1970 *Kathleen Anne Sutherland Elliott and has:

(1) *Lindsay; b 19-

(1) *Hannah; b 19-

2 *Alan Malcolm [The Hon Alan Perry, 43 Meadway, London NW11 7AX]; b 1950; m 1976 *Naomi Melanie, dau of Dr Abraham Freedman, MD, FRCP, of Hampstead, and has three sons

3 *Niall Fletcher [The Hon Niall Perry, 53 Putnoe Lane, Bedford]; b 1953; m 1978 *Sandra Buchanan and has two daus

BARON PERRY OF WALTON m 2nd 1971 *Catherine Hilda, dau of Ambrose Crawley, and by her has:

4 *Robin Charles Macdonald; b 1973

5 *Colin Stuart Macdonald; b 1979

1 *Jennifer Joan; b 1981

Lineage: FLETCHER S PERRY; m Flora Macdonald and had:

WALTER LAING MACDONALD (Sir), cr a **Baron**

PERTH

Arms: Or, three bars wavy gules. **Crest:** A falcon rising proper. **Supporters:** Two wild men wreathed about the temples and loins with oak-leaves, each holding a club resting on his exterior shoulder, proper. **Mottoes:** 1 (over crest) *Virtutem coronat honos* ('Honour crowns virtue'), 2 (below shield) Gang warily. **Creations:** L. (S) 29 Jan 1487/8 (Drummond) and 31 Jan 1608/9 (Maderty), E. (S) 4 March 1604/5, V. and L. (S) 6 Sept 1686 (Drummond of Cromlix).

THE 8TH EARL OF PERTH, Viscount Strathallan, Lord Drummond, Lord Maderty and Lord Drummond of Cromlix ((John) David Drummond, PC (1957)) [The Rt Hon The Earl of Perth PC, Stobhall, by Perth PH2 6DR; 14 Hyde Park Gdns Mews, London W2 2NU]; b 13 May 1907; s f 1951 and as Territorial Baron of Lennox and Hereditary Steward of Menteith and Strathearn; educ Downside and Trin Coll Cambridge; rep S peer 1952–63; Lt Intell Corps 1940, seconded War Cabinet and Min Production 1942–46, Min State Colonial Affairs 1957–62, First Crown Estate Commr 1962–77; Chm Ditchling Fndn 1963–66, dir RBS, Schroders Ltd, Tate and Lyle Ltd and Dominion-Lincoln Assur, Chm Reviewing Ctee Export Works of Art 1972–76, memb: Court St Andrews U 1967–86, Advsy Cncl V&A 1971–72, Tstee Nat Library Scotland 1968–, Hon FRIBA 1978, Hon FRIAS 1988, Hon ESA 1994, Hon LLD St Andrews 1986, sponsor 'Campaign for Scottish Assembly'; m 4 Aug 1934 Nancy Seymour (d 1996), dau of Reginald Fincke, of New York, and has:

1 +JOHN ERIC, *Viscount Strathallan* [Viscount Strathallan, 46 Tite St, London SW3 4JA; Stobhall, by Perth PH2 6DR]; b 7 July 1935; educ Downside, Trin Coll Cambridge (BA 1956) and Harvard (MBA); m 1st 7 Jan 1963 (divorce 1972) Margaret Anne, only dau of Robin Gordon, and has had:

(1) +James David; b 24 Oct 1965

(2) +Robert Eric; b 7 May 1967

(1) Annabella Margaret; b 18 June, d 21 June 1964

1 (cont.) *Viscount Strathallan* m 2nd 1988 *Mrs Marion Elliot

2 +James Reginald [The Hon James Drummond, Churchill House, Dinder, Somerset BA5 3RW]; b 28 July 1938; educ Downside and Trin Coll Cambridge; m 1st 24 July 1961 (divorce 1985) Marybelle, dau of Capt Charles Gordon, of Petersfield, Hants; m 2nd 1988 *Ferelith Alison, dau of Mark Palmer (see PALMER, Bt, of Grinkle Park) and formerly w of Ashley Gordon Down

Lineage: Sir MALCOLM DRUMMOND, of a family which allegedly migrated from Hungary to Scotland in the 11th century, acquired lands from the Earls of Menteith (see MORAY, E); had:

1 JOHN, his successor

2 Maurice; ancestor of the DRUMMONDs of Concraig and Megginch

1 Margaret; m 1st Sir John Logie; m 2nd April 1363 (divorce 1370) DAVID II

The er son,

JOHN DRUMMOND; Baillie of Dull; m Mary of Montifex, had a charter of her lands Feb 1367 and had:

1 Malcolm (Sir); acquired Cargill, Stobhall, Kinloch and other lands from his aunt QUEEN MARGARET; m as her 1st husb Isabel Douglas, Countess of Mar (qv) in her own right, and was murdered sp prior to 8 Nov 1402 by Highland marauders allegedly under Alexander Stewart, 'The Wolf of Badenoch', who then m Countess Isabel himself

2 JOHN (Sir)

3 William; ancestor of the DRUMMONDs of Carnock

1 Annabella; m 1367 ROBERT III and d 1401

The 2nd son,

Sir JOHN DRUMMOND of Cargill and Stobhall, Perths; Justiciar Scotland; had:

Sir WALTER DRUMMOND; m Margaret, dau of Sir William Ruthven of Ruthven, and had, with two yr sons:

Sir MALCOLM DRUMMOND of Cargill and Stobhall; m 1445 Mariot, dau of Sir David Murray of Tullibardine (see ATHOLL, D), and d 1470, leaving an est s:

JOHN DRUMMOND, **1st Lord Drummond** (S), so *cr* 29 Jan 1487/8, but without any indication of a remainder, although from the fact of its not being assumed or claimed by Jean, dau and heir general of the **1st Earl of Perth** (*see* below) it would subsequently have been (and is here) inferred as being with limitation to heirs male, PC (S 1488); Judiciar Scotland 1488, Constable Stirling Castle, envoy to England 1495 and 1511–12/3; imprisoned in Blackness Castle 1515–16 and temporarily deprived of his peerage for an assault on Sir William Comyn, Lyon King of Arms; *m* Lady Elizabeth Lindsay, dau of 4th Earl of Crawford (*see* CRAWFORD and BALCARRES, E), and had:

1 Malcolm; *dvp* unm

2 William, *Master of Drummond*; helped burn down Monzievaird Church, in which had sought refuge several of the MURRAYs, with whom he had a feud; *m* 1st by 5 March 1478/9 Lady Isabel Campbell, dau of 1st Earl of Argyll (*see* ARGYLL, D); *m* 2nd by 14 June 1493 Mariot/Marjorie (*m* 2nd by Feb 1507/8 Sir James Sandilands, 7th of Calder; *see* TORPHICHEN, L), only dau of Archibald Forrester of Corstorphine, and *dvp* between July 1503 and July 1504, leaving by his 1st w:

  (1) Walter, *Master of Drummond*; *m* Feb 1513/4 his cousin Lady Elizabeth Graham, dau of 1st Earl of Montrose (*see* MONTROSE, D), and *d* 1518, leaving:

    1a DAVID, **2nd Lord**

3 David; tried and executed at Stirling for the incineration of various of the MURRAYs, in which he presumably took a leading part along with his er bro

4 John; ancestor of the DRUMMONDs of Innerpeffray

1 Margaret; privately *m* JAMES IV; poisoned with two of her sisters 1501

2 Elizabeth; *m* George, Master of Angus, and with him was a great-great-grandparent of Henry, Lord Darnley (*see* MORAY, E)

3 Beatrix; allegedly *m* 1st Earl of Arran (*see* ARRAN, E, preliminary remarks) by whom she certainly had issue

4 Annabella; *m* 1st Earl of Montrose (*see* MONTROSE, D)

5 Eupheme; *m* 4th Lord Fleming; poisoned 1501

6 Sybilla; poisoned 1501

The 1st LORD's ggs,

DAVID DRUMMOND, **2nd Lord Drummond**; *m* 1st 1535 Margaret, (conceivably illegitimate) dau of Alexander Stewart, Bp of Moray (*see* MORAY, E), and had:

1 Sybilla; *m* Sir Gilbert Ogilvy

The **2nd Lord** *m* 2nd by 7 Dec 1543 Lilian, dau of 2nd Lord Ruthven (*see* CARLISLE, E), and *d* 1571, having by her had:

1 PATRICK DRUMMOND, **3rd Lord Drummond**; *b* 1550; Protestant; *m* 1st by 21 Oct 1572 Lady Elizabeth Lindsay, dau of 9th Earl of Crawford (*see* CRAWFORD and BALCARRES, E); *m* 2nd 1588 his cousin Agnes (*dsp*), dau and coheir of Sir John Drummond of Innerpeffray and widow of (a) 3rd Earl of Eglinto(u)n (*see* EGLINTON and WINTON, E) and (b) Sir Hugh Campbell, and *d* in or shortly after 1602, having by his 1st w had:

  (1) JAMES DRUMMOND, **1st Earl of Perth** (S), so *cr* 11 Feb 1605, with remainder it is thought to heirs male whatsoever, PC (S Jan 1607/8 and March 1609/10); *b c* 1580; envoy to Spain 1605; *m* 19 April 1608 Lady Isabel Seton, dau of 1st Earl of Winton (*see* EGLINTON and WINTON, E), and *dspm* 18 Dec 1611, leaving:

    1a Jean; *m* 1632 13th Earl of Sutherland (*qv*)

  (2) JOHN DRUMMOND, **2nd Earl of Perth**, PC (S 1616); *b c* 1584; *educ* Dunblane GS and Bordeaux U; Covenanter by 1638 and Parly Commr of War Perths also Col start of Civil War but later appears to have turned royalist and was fined £5,000 (just under £1,700,000 in late-1990s terms) 1654; *m c* Aug 1613 Lady Jean Ker, est dau of 1st Earl of Roxburghe (*see* ROXBURGHE, D), and *d* 11 June 1662, having had:

    1a Henry, *Lord Drummond*; *b* 1 Aug 1614; *dvp* Sept 1622

    2a JAMES DRUMMOND, **3rd Earl of Perth**, PC (S 1662 and 1674); *b c* 1615; Col Inf Regt Scottish Army 1640, Parly Col Foot Perths Civil War 1643, later royalist and captured Battle of Philiphaugh 1645 then royalist Col of Horse Perths 1650; *m* 6 Nov 1639 Lady Anne Gordon (*d* 9 Jan 1656), dau of 2nd Marquess of Huntly (*qv*), and *d* 2 June 1675, having had:

      1b JAMES DRUMMOND, **4th Earl of Perth**, KT (1687), PC (S Jan 1677/8 and E 1685–Feb 1688/9) and titular 1st Duke of Perth, Marquess of Drummond, Earl of Stobhall, Viscount Cargill and Baron Concraig (all nominally S), so *cr* 10 March 1689/90 at Dublin by JAMES II and VII but after his having been deemed to have abandoned the throne of England and Scotland (though not yet *de facto* of Ireland), with remainder to heirs male; *b* 7 July 1648; Justice Gen S and Extrdy Ld of Session 1682–84, High Chllr Scotland 1684–88; openly Catholic and ch minister Scotland under JAMES II, Commr Treasury 1686–89; imprisoned 1688–93 following JAMES II's flight, Govr to titular Prince of Wales (later titular James III) 1696–1706, made KG by titular James III 1706; *m* 1st 10 Jan 1670 Lady Jane Douglas, dau of 1st Marquess of Douglas (*see* HAMILTON and BRANDON, D), and had:

        1c James, titular 2nd Duke of Perth; *b* Jan/Feb 1673/4; cmded Jacobite cavalry Battle of Sheriffmuir 13 Nov 1715 and was attainted 17 Feb 1715/6; *m c* 5 Oct 1706 Lady Jean Gordon (*d* 30 Jan 1773), dau of 1st Duke of Gordon (*see* HUNTLY, M), and *d* at Paris 6 April 1720, having had:

          1d James, titular 3rd Duke of Perth; *b* 11 May 1713; fought in Jacobite army Prestonpans, Carlisle, Stirling and Culloden (wounded), attainted 1746; *d* unm during his passage to France after the failed Uprising aboard the French frigate *La Bellone* 11 or 13 May 1746

          2d John, titular 4th Duke of Perth; *b* 1714; Col regt called 'the Royal Scots' in the French service, for which he recruited in Scotland 1744, fighting with it in the 1745 Uprising at Battles of Falkirk (wounded) and Culloden; attainted 1746; served under Marshal Saxe at Siege of Bergen-op-Zoom 1747 with rank of Maj-Gen; *d* unm 28 Sept 1747

      1b (cont.) The **4th Earl** *m* 2nd *c* 5 Oct 1676 his cousin Lilias, dau of James Drummond of Machany and widow of 2nd Earl of Tullibardine (*see* ATHOLL, D, and by her had:

2c John, titular 5th Duke of Perth; *b* 1679; sent to Scotland by titular James III 1715 to foment Jacobite Uprising; *m* 1st *c* 26 Nov 1707 Marjory, dau of David Fothringham; *m* 2nd *c* May 1722 Lady Mary Stewart (*d* 4 Feb 1773), dau of 4th Earl of Traquair (*see* MORAY, E), and *dsp* 27 Oct 1757

1b (cont.) The **4th Earl** *m* 3rd *c* Jan 1685/6 Lady Mary Gordon (*d* 13 March 1726), dau of 3rd Marquess of Huntly (*qv*) and widow of Adam Urquhart of Meldrum, and *d* at St Germains 11 May 1716, having by her had:

    3c Edward, titular 6th Duke of Perth; *b* 1690; active Jacobite in 1715 Uprising, later cavalry Gen in French Army; *m* 25 Nov 1709 Lady Elizabeth Middleton, dau of 2nd Earl of Middleton, and *dsp* 6 Feb 1760

2b JOHN DRUMMOND, **1st EARL OF MELFORT, VISCOUNT OF FORTH, LORD DRUMMOND OF RICCARTOUN, CASTLEMAINS AND GILSTOUN**, so *cr* 12 Aug 1686, as also earlier 14 April 1685 VISCOUNT OF MELFORT and LORD DRUMMOND OF GILLESTOUN (all S), KT (1687), PC (S 1678, E Jan 1684/5–Feb 1688/9), in addition to JAMES II and VII (with whom he fled abroad on the arrival of WILLIAM III 1688 and who made him KG 1692), after the latter had been deemed to have abandoned the throne, titular Baron of Cleworth (presumably nominally E) 7 Aug 1689 and titular Duke of Melfort, Marquess of Forth, Earl of Isla and Burntizland, Viscount of Rickerton, Lord Castlemains and Galston (nominally S) 17 April 1692, with remainder to his issue by his 2nd w; *b c* 1650; Master Ordnance 1680, Sec of State 1684; outlawed in England and Scotland 1694 and attainted 2 July 1695, when his substantive titles were forfeited, though following JAMES II's death 1701 LOUIS XIV recognised him as Duc de Melfort; *m* 1st 30 Sept 1670 Sophia, dau and eventual heiress of Robert Maitland of Lundin, Fife, by Margaret, dau of John Lundin, and had:

1c John; *d* unm

2c James; *d* unm

3c Robert; *m* 20 Jan 1704 Anne, dau of Sir James Inglis of Cramond, Bt, and *d* 1716, leaving:

    1d John; *d* unm 9 Oct 1735

    2d James LUNDIN later DRUMMOND (1760), self-styled 10th Earl of Perth (to which title he would indeed have been entitled but for the attainder); *b* 6 Nov 1707; *m* Lady Rachel Bruce (*d* 29 June 1769), dau of 7th Earl of Kincardine (*see* ELGIN and KINCARDINE, E), and *d* 18 July 1781, having had, with another s (*dvp* unm):

      1e Thomas LUNDIN later DRUMMOND, styled *Lord Drummond* from 1760; *bapt* 21 July 1742; Offr War of American Independence, captured 1776; *d* unm & *vp* in the Bermudas 1780

      2e JAMES LUNDIN later DRUMMOND, 1st and last LORD PERTH, BARON DRUMMOND of Stobhall, Co Perth (GB), so *cr* 26 Oct 1797; *b* 12 Feb 1744; Capt 42nd Highrs; the Drummond estates were restored to him 1785; *m* 31 March 1785 Clementina (*d* 31 Aug 1832), dau of 10th Lord Elphinstone (*qv*), and *dspms* 2 July 1800, when the Barony expired, having had:

        1f Sarah Clementina; *m* 19 Oct 1807 22nd Lord (Baron) Willoughby de Eresby (*qv*)

1c Mary; *m* 1st Gideon Scott of Highchester (*d* by 1707; *see* POLWARTH, L); *m* 2nd between 1707 and 11 Nov 1718 Sir James Sharp, 2nd Bt, and *d* 4 Oct 1754, leaving issue by him (*see* 1970 edn SHARP BETHUNE, Bt)

2b (cont.) The 1st EARL OF MELFORT *m* 2nd 1680 Euphemia, dau of Sir Thomas Wallace of Craigie, Ld Justice Clerk Scotland, and *d* Paris 25 Jan 1714/5, leaving by her:

4c John, titular 2nd Duke of Melfort; *b* 26 May 1682; Maj-Gen Jacobite forces Scotland 1715; *m* 25 March 1707 Marie Gabrielle, Countess of Lussan in her own right (*d* 15 May 1741), only dau of Jean d'Audebert, Count of Lussan, and widow of Henry FitzJames, titular Duke of Albemarle (to whom John was ADC), and *d* Paris 29 Jan 1754, having had, with a dau (*d* young):

    1d James, titular 3rd Duke of Melfort and COUNT OF LUSSAN through his mother; *b* 16 March 1707/8; *m* 29 Jan 1755 Marie, dau of François de Berenger, and *d* 25 Dec 1766, having had (with two daus):

      1e James Louis, titular 4th Duke of Melfort; *b* 14 Aug 1750 but by his parents subsequnt marriage would have been legitimated under Scottish law, though this would not (even had he lived under Scottish jurisdiction, which he did not) have entitled him to assume his father's French title of Count; Gen French Army; Kt of St Louis; *m* 30 April 1788 Aglae Elizabeth Jacqueline, dau of Marquis d'Oms, and *dspm* Sept 1800, the Languedoc estates of the Counts of Lussan having been sequestrated during the French Revolution 1792

      2e Charles Edouard, titular 5th Duke of Melfort; *b* 1 Jan 1752; took proceedings 1803 in the Court of Session for the recovery of the lands and titles of Lord Drummond and Earl of Perth, but the action dismissed 1808 as he could produce no title to sue and being a Catholic prelate (in the papal household in Rome) could not bring his claim before the Ho Lds; petitioned again for restoration of titles 1823 and (after Catholic Emancipation) 1838, unsuccessfully; *d* 9 April 1840

      3e Henry Benedict; Capt French Navy, Chevalier St Louis; *d* unm 6 April 1779

      4e Léon Maurice; *b* 12 April 1761; petitioned for restoration of Drummond estates on grounds of his own legitimacy in contrast to the status of his er bros; *m* 26 Nov 1794 Marie Elizabeth Lucie de Longuemare (*d* 12 Aug 1824) and *d* 26 April 1826, leaving surv issue:

        1f GEORGE DRUMMOND, **5th Earl of Perth** on reversal of attainder 28 June 1853 and DUKE OF MELFORT, COUNT OF LUSSAN and BARON De VALROSE in France following judgement as to his right to those titles 1841 by the Conseil d'Etat and Tribunal de la Seine; *b* 6 May 1807; Capt 93rd Highrs 1826, Maj Victoria

Rifles 1853–59; *m* 1st 19 May 1831 Baroness Albertine von Rothberg Rheinweiler Coligni (*d* 2 June 1842), widow of Gen Count Rapp, Peer of France, and had:

1g James Maurice Willoughby; *b* 12 Aug 1832; *d* Feb 1833

2g George Henry Charles Francis Malcolm, *Viscount Forth*; *b* Naples 13 May 1834; served 42nd Highrs Crimea (bore the colours at The Alma, also fought Sebastopol); *m* 24 Oct 1855 (separated 1858) Harriet Mary (*m* 2nd 29 Oct 1861 (*divorce* 21 June 1867) Edward Cholmeley Dering and *d* 30 April 1868, est dau of Hon Adolphus Capell and niece of 6th Earl of Essex (*qv*), and poisoned himself 8 Oct 1861, having had:

1h George Essex Montifex, *Lord Drummond*; *b* 3 Sept 1856; *d* unm 4 Aug 1887

1f (cont.) The **5th Earl** *m* 2nd 9 Aug 1847 Susan Henrietta (*d* 11 Sept 1886), dau of Thomas Bermingham Daly Henry Sewell, of Athenry, Co Galway, by Harriet, dau of 1st Baron Sewell (*qv*) and widow of Col William Burrowes, of Dangan Castle, Co Meath, and *dspms* 28 Feb 1902, when the Earldom of Melfort, Viscountcy of Forth and Lordship of Drummond of Riccartoun, Castlemains and Gilstoun became extinct or dormant, the French Dukedom of Melfort expired and the other French titles passed to his yst (but only surv) dau, having by her had, with another dau (*d* young):

1g Marie Auguste Gabrielle Berengere Blanche; *b* 15 Dec 1848; *m* 24 April 1871 Col Mackenzie Fraser, of Castle Fraser and Inveralochy, Aberdeenshire (*d* 19 May 1897), and *dsp* 5 Feb 1874

2g Marie Louise Susan Edith Grace, COUNTESS OF LUSSAN and BARONESS De VALROSE in France; *b* 29 April 1854; *d* unm 22 July 1937

1f Lucy Clementina; granted rank of earl's dau 30 Sept 1853; *m* 8 Sept 1823 Francis Henry Davies (*d* 23 Oct 1863), Registrar Court of Chancery, and *d* 27 April 1879, leaving issue

2d Louis; *b* 16 Feb 1709; Jacobite, 2ic Roy Scots Battle of Culloden; Lt-Gen French Army; Grand Cross St Louis, Govr Normandy; *d* 8 July 1792

3d John; *b* 21 Oct 1711; Maj-Gen in Polish Serv

5c Thomas; *d* unm 1715

6c William; Abbé Prieur of Liège; *d* in Spain 1742

7c Andrew, Count de Melfort; Lt-Gen in French service, Grand Cross of St Louis; *m* Magdalene Silvia de St Hermione and had:

1d Louis, Count de Melfort; Lt-Gen in French service, Inspr-Gen Cav and Grand Cross St Louis; *m* 1759 Jean Elizabeth, dau of Peter John Francis de la Porte, Marquis de Presles, and *d* Nov 1788, leaving:

1e Louis Peter Francis Malcolm, Count de Melfort; Maj-Gen in French service; *m* Lady Caroline Mackenzie, only child of 1st and last Earl of Seaforth of the 1771 *cr* (*see* CROMARTIE, E), and *d* 1833, leaving, with a dau:

1f Louis, Comte de Melfort; *b* 1791; Col French Staff Corps, Kt of St Louis and St Ferdinand in Spain; *m* 1823 Eudoxia Saulnier de Cherriers and *d* 1888, leaving:

1g Marie; *m* 1869 Baron Durand de Fontmagne

2g Alice; *m* 2 April 1852 Charles Muyart de Voulgans

3g Edith; *m* 1853 René de Fleischmann

2f Edward; *b* 1801; Offr of Hus; Page of Honour to Prince Murat; *m* 1827 Marie Naysmith and *d* 1844, leaving:

1g Albina; *m* 1849 Baron van Havre, of Belgium

2g Cécile; *m* 1st 22 Feb 1851 Adml Hon Sir Fleetwood Pellew, KCH, s of 1st Baron Exmouth (*qv*); *m* 2nd 22 Feb 1860 7th Earl of Berkeley (*see* BERKELEY, B) and *d* 1 Nov 1914, leaving issue

1b Anne; *m* 12th Earl of Erroll (*qv*)

3a Robert; *d* unm in France

4a John (Sir), of Logie Almond; ancestor of Rt Hon Sir William Drummond, Amb to the Sublime Porte (*d* 29 March 1828, when this branch became extinct in the male line)

5a WILLIAM DRUMMOND later KER, 2nd EARL OF ROXBURGHE; had issue (*see* ROXBURGHE, D)

1a Jean; *m* 3rd Earl of Wigtoun

2a Lilias; *m* 1643, as his 1st w, 2nd Earl of Tullibardine and had issue (*see* ATHOLL, D)

(1) Katherine; *m* James, Master of Rothes (*see* ROTHES, E)

(2) Lilias; *m c* 1590, as his 1st w, 1st Earl of Dunfermline (*see* EGLINTON and WINTON, E) and *dspm* 8 May 1601

(3) Jean; *m* 1st Earl of Roxburghe (*see* ROXBURGHE, D)

(4) Elizabeth; *m* 5th Lord Elphinstone (*qv*)

(5) Anne; *m* 1st Patrick Barclay of Towie; *m* 2nd 1st Lord Fraser (*see* SALTOUN, L)

2 JAMES, **1st Lord Maderty** (*see below*)

2 Jean; *m* 4th Earl of Montrose (*see* MONTROSE, D)

3 Agnes/Anne; *m* 29 Oct–1 Nov 1580, as his 1st w, 18th/2nd Earl of Mar (*qv*) and had issue

4 Lilias; *m* David, Master of Crawford

5 Catherine; *m* by 15 Nov 1576 1st Earl of Tullibardine of the 1606 *cr* (*see* ATHOLL, D) and had issue

6 Mary; *m* Sir James Stirling of Keir

The 2nd LORD DRUMMOND's 2nd s,

JAMES DRUMMOND, **1st Lord Maderty** (S), so *cr* 31 Jan 1608/9, JP (Perths 1613); MP Perth 1585, 1592, 1593, 1597 and 1600; *m* Jean, dau of Sir James Chisholm of Cromlix, and *d* Sept 1623, having had, with two daus:

1 JOHN DRUMMOND, **2nd Lord Maderty**; royalist Civil War; *m c* 30 April 1609 Margaret Leslie, dau of 1st Lord Lindores (*see* ROTHES, E), and *d* between 1649 and 1651, leaving an est s:

(1) DAVID DRUMMOND, **3rd Lord Maderty**; *m* 1st 6 Feb 1637/8 Alison (*d* March 1639), dau of John Creighton of Haltoun and Luncardie, and had an only child:

1a Margaret; *d* unm 1642

(1) (cont.) The **3rd Lord** *m* 2nd *c* 10 Dec 1641 Lady Beatrix Graham, dau of the 4th Earl of Montrose (*see* MONTROSE, D), and *dspms* 20 Jan 1691/2, leaving by her:

2a Margaret; *m* John Graham, PMG of Scotland

3a Beatrix; *m* 1st Earl of Hyndford

4a Mary; *m* John Haldane of Gleneagles

(2) WILLIAM DRUMMOND, **1st Viscount Strathallan**, so *cr* 16 Aug 1686 as also LORD DRUMMOND OF CROMLIX (both S), with remainder, failing heirs male of the body, to heirs male whatsoever, PC (S Jan 1666/7–May 1674 and Jan 1685/6); *b* 1617/8; *educ* St Andrews; royalist Civil War, served England, Ireland and Scotland, captured by Parly troops Battle of Worcester 1651 and imprisoned Windsor Castle 1651–52; joined Russian army and fought against Poles and Tartars 1655–65, Lt-Gen; Gen forces Scotland 1666–67, MP Perths 1669–74, 1678, 1681–82 and 1685–86, Commr S Treasury March 1685/6 and 1687; *m* 28 Feb 1667/8 Elizabeth, dau of Sir Archibald Johnston of Warriston and widow of Thomas Hepburn of Humbie, and *d* 23 March 1687/8, leaving, with a dau (Margaret, *m* 7th Earl of Kinnoull, *qv*), an only s:

1a WILLIAM DRUMMOND, **2nd Viscount Strathallan** and **4th Lord Maderty** (as which *s* unc); *b* 8 Aug 1670; *m* just before 14 Jan 1687/8 his cousin Elizabeth, dau of 1st EARL OF MELFORT (*see* above), and *d* 7 July 1702, leaving an only s:

1b WILLIAM DRUMMOND, **3rd Viscount Strathallan**; *b* 1694; *dsp* 26 May 1711

2 James (Sir), of Machany; royalist Col Perthshire Foot; *m* Catherine, est dau of Sir John Hamilton of Leitrick and sis of 1st Lord Bargeny, and had, with other issue:

(1) James (Sir), of Machany; fined £500 1654 for royalism; *m* 1st Mary, dau of Sir James Haliburton of Pitcur, and had a s (*d* an infant); *m* 2nd Anne, dau of George Hay, 1st of Kellour, s of 8th Earl of Erroll (*qv*), and widow of William Moray, 10th of Abercairny, and *d* 1675, leaving:

1a John (Sir); Jacobite, forfeited his property 1690; *m* Margaret, dau of Sir William Stewart of Innernytie, and *d* 1707, leaving, with other issue:

1b WILLIAM, **4th Viscount Strathallan**

2b Andrew, of Stanmore, Middx; *b* 1688; fndr Drummond's Bank; bought the sequestrated Drummond property of Machany and Strathallan Castle 1752 from the Crown (*see* below against **5th Viscount**); *m* 7 Nov 1716 Isabella Strahan, of London (*d* 13 Feb 1731), and *d* 2 Feb 1769, leaving, with a dau (Isabel, *m* 1739 Capt Peters):

1c John, of Stanmore; MP Thetford; *b* 27 April 1723; *m* 22 Dec 1744 Charlotte (*d* 7 March 1793), dau of Lord William Beauclerk, 2nd s of 1st Duke of St Albans (*qv*), and *d* 25 July 1774, leaving, with two daus:

1d George, of Stanmore; *b* 1758; *m* 30 Nov 1779 Martha (*d* Aug 1788), est dau and coheir of Hon Thomas Harley, son of 3rd Earl of Oxford and Mortimer (*see* OXFORD AND ASQUITH, E, preliminary remarks), and *d* 6 March 1789, leaving:

1e George Harley, of Stanmore and Drumtochty; *b* 23 Nov 1783; *m* 9 Feb 1801 Margaret (*d* 28 July 1853), dau of Alexander Munro, of Glasgow, and *d* 21 March 1855, leaving:

1f George, of Stanmore; *b* 12 Feb 1802; *m* 14 April 1831 Marianne (*d* 1 Dec 1842), 2nd dau of Edward Berkeley Portman (*see* PORTMAN, V), and *d* 5 Jan 1851, leaving, with four daus:

1g George James; *b* 22 June 1835; *m* 6 July 1876 Elizabeth Cecile Sophia (*d* 4 Aug 1921), dau of Rev Frederick John Norman by Lady Adeliza, dau of 5th Duke of Rutland (*qv*), and *d* 31 Jan 1917, leaving:

1h George Henry; *b* 3 March 1883; Lt W Kent Yeo and Notts RHA WW I (wounded); High Sheriff Northants 1927, memb IOM Ho of Keys 1946–51; *m* 1st 11 Jan 1917 Helena Kathleen (*d* 15 Dec 1933), only dau of T Grattan Holt, of Carberry and Bally Chrystal, Queen's Co, and had:

1i *Eve; *b* 16 Jan 1918; *m* 19 May 1951 Raymond Vincent de Trafford (*d* 14 May 1971), yst s of Sir Humphrey Francis de Trafford, 3rd Bt (*qv*)

2i *Rosemary Lucia; *b* 21 Jan 1919; *m* 16 Jan 1945 Lt-Col (Brevet-Col) Neil Phipps Foster, DL, Life Gds, and Northants Yeo, only s of Maj Phipps Foster, and has:

1j *Alexander Neil; *b* 9 Oct 1945; *educ* Eton; *m* 26 March 1969 *Hon Gillian Rosemary, only dau of 22nd Lord Forbes (*qv*), and has:

1k *Lucia Katharine; *b* 12 Feb 1970

1j *Roseanne Madeline; *b* 16 Sept 1947

3i *Edwina Gillian; *b* 21 April 1920 (HRH THE DUKE OF WINDSOR stood sponsor); *m* 29 July 1952 Cmdt Eric R Miville (*d* 30 March 1967), Legn Hon, Croix de Guerre, Swiss Cavalry and French For Legn, only s of Rodolphe J Miville-Burckhardt, of Switzerland

4i *Diana Kathleen; *b* 11 April 1926; *m* 19 July 1950 Hon John Astor (*see* ASTOR OF HEVER, B) and *d* 1982, leaving issue

1h (cont.) George Drummond *m* 2nd 30 Oct 1940 *Honora Myrtle Gladys, dau of Lt-Col Duncan Wilfred Lambart Spiller, DSO, of St Donaghs, Portmarnock, Co Dublin, and *d* 12 Oct 1963, having by her had:

1i +George Albert Harley [George de Vere Drummond Esq, The Barn, 6 Bannatyne Gdns, Christchurch, Barbados, W Indies]; *b* 9 March 1943 (HM GEORGE VI stood sponsor); *educ* Gordonstoun, Institut D'Schmidt Switzerland and Weylands Acad Wisconsin, USA; *m* 1st Jan 1971 (*divorce*

1974) Rachel, est dau of Michael Marley, of Kingston, Jamaica, and has:

1j +George Manley; b 20 Nov 1971

1i (cont.) George de Vere Drummond m 2nd 1982 *Debra Jane, only dau of R B Hankins, of Hertford, and by her has:

1j *Sarah Georgina Joy; b 1982

2j *Jade Alexandra; b 1984

5i *Annabella Elizabeth Sarah; b 24 Aug 1941

6i *Omega Margaret [Mrs Robert Pouget, 63 Bagley Wood Rd, Kennington, Oxford OX1 5LY]; b 18 March 1944; m 22 Dec 1961 *Robert Armand Yves Pouget, 2nd s of Baron Antoine Pouget, of Paris, and has:

1j *Antoine-Xavier George; b 23 July 1962

2j *Robert Harley; b 20 Sept 1965

3j *Alexandre Drummond; b 14 Dec 1967

4j *William Francis; b 1975

7i *Isobel Camilla (Millie) [Miss Isobel Drummond, PO Box 11, Orgiva, Granada, Spain; c/o 44 Newfield Rd, Liss Forest, Hants GU33 7BW]; b 4 Jan 1946

2h David Robert; b 30 Oct 1884; Lt Scots Gds; m 10 Sept 1907 Hilda Margaret (m 2nd 7 May 1936 Maj John Elgee Gunning, JP, of Co Tyrone (d 26 Dec 1950), and d 1972), dau of Alfred Helyer Harris, of Donnington, Chichester, and was ka 3 Nov 1914, leaving:

1i *Joan Cécile; b 8 Jan 1909; m 1st 17 June 1933 (divorce 1939) Maurice James Newcomb, 2nd surv s of James Henry Newcomb, and has:

1j *Nicholas James [Nicholas Newcomb Esq, 27 Bishops Court Drive, Bishops Court, CP 7700, S Africa]; b 19 Aug 1935; m 1966 *Lorna Faith Maree and has:

1k *Graeme James; b 1970

1k *Angela Jean; b 1973

1i (cont.) Mrs Joan Newcomb m 2nd 14 Jan 1942 (divorce 1949) Maj Charles St John Colthurst, RA (see COLTHURST, Bt); m 3rd 1950 (divorce 1970) Arthur Raywid; m 4th 1971 Alan James Fuller Eberle, MBE, BM, BCh (d 1988), of Crediton, Devon, and has by her 2nd husb:

1j *Joanna [Mrs Martin Butler, 43/299 Burns Rd, Lane Cove, NSW 2066, Australia]; b 31 Jan 1948; m 1975 *Martin Butler

2i *Violet Hilda [Mrs Anthony Swetenham, Highfield House, Mandeville Rd, Saffron Walden, Essex]; b 30 July 1911; m 1st 1 Dec 1933 (divorce 1945) John Peter Pardoe, er s of John Hubert Pardoe, of Barnsley, Yorks; m 2nd 20 Feb 1948 *Anthony C Swetenham, yst s of Maj Foster Swetenham, RSG, and has by her 1st husb:

1j *Julian Hugh [Julian Pardoe Esq, Brinkley House, Brinkley, Suffolk CB8 0RD]; b 1935; educ Eton; m 1960 *Camilla Guendolen, dau of Arthur Gruffyd Tudor-Evans, of Cheshire, and has:

1k *Simon David; b 1962; m 1995 *Fiona D Barrett, of Henley, Oxon, and has:

1l *Isabella Laura; b 1996

1k *Joanna Clare; b 1963

2k *Fiona Mary; b 1965; m 1994 *Nigel M Powell, of Whatton, Notts, and has:

1l *Annabel Alice; b 1994

2l *Poppy Clare; b 1996

3i *Winifred Pansy; b 3 June 1914; m 19 June 1947 Daniel Ferguson Aitken, MA, BLitt, s of Very Rev — Aitken, of New Zealand, and d 1995, leaving:

1j *David James [David Aitken Esq, 42 Leinster Square, London W2]; b 17 March 1948; educ Tonbridge and Balliol Coll Oxford (BA)

1j Elizabeth Ann; b 26 Oct 1949

3h Alexander Victor; b 20 Oct 1888 (HM QUEEN MARY stood sponsor); Capt W Kent Yeo and Lt 2nd Life Gds; m 24 Oct 1914 Ellen Pauline Matthew (Pauline Chase, actress, who d 3 March 1962), dau of Ellis Bliss, of Washington, USA, and d 29 April 1937, leaving:

1i Alexander Peter; b 15 June 1927 (HRH PRINCESS ALICE, COUNTESS OF ATHLONE, stood sponsor); m 2 Nov 1954 *Anne Audrey Ruth, dau of Frank Seamer, of Leigh, Kent, and d 1987, leaving:

1j +Harrie Malcolm; b 11 March 1962

1j *Alexandra Elspeth; b 15 Nov 1957

2j *Marina Jane; b 10 Dec 1959

1i Ann; b 1 July 1919; m 1948 Hendrick Adriaans Schouwenaar (d Dec 1968) and d 1 Dec 1962, leaving issue

2i *Jane; b 5 Aug 1925; m 2 March 1946 (divorce 1968) Irving Howbert, Lt USNR, s of William Irving Howbert, of Colorado Springs, and has:

1j *William Irving; b 22 Nov 1948; educ Emmanuel Coll Cambridge

1j *Anne Noël; b 11 Dec 1950; m — Plunkett-ffrench

2j *Janet Scott; b 27 Oct 1953

1h Cecile Elizabeth; b 7 Aug 1878; m 25 April 1907 3rd Marquess of Aberdeen and Temair (qv) and d 17 Sept 1948, leaving issue

2h Adeliza Beatrix; b 20 June 1879; m 6 June 1905 Lt-Col Albert Henry Royds, OBE, Scots Gds (d 7 May 1952), and d 1 June 1959, leaving issue (see STRAFFORD, E)

3h Ida Mary; b 26 June 1880; m 4 May 1904 Col Hon Sir Maurice Charles Andrew Drummond, KBE, CMG, DSO, Black Watch (d 21 Feb 1957), 3rd s of 10th Viscount Strathallan (see below), and d 11 Dec 1966, leaving issue

4h Euphemia Mabel; b 30 June 1881; m 1st 4 Sept 1907 Capt Alexander Brodie of Lethen, Scots Gds (dsp 9 Jan 1908); m 2nd 22 March 1911 Maj-Gen Sir Arthur Wigram Money, KCB, KBE, CSI (d 25 Oct 1951), s of Gilbert Pocklington Money, and d 13 Sept 1964, leaving issue

2f Henry Dundas; b 17 Dec 1812; m 1 Dec 1838 Sophia Jane, dau of Charles C Mackinnon, and dsp 25 July 1867

2e Andrew Mortimer; b 9 Nov 1786; banker; m 25 July 1808 Lady Emily Charlotte Percy, dau of 1st Earl of Beverley (see NORTHUMBERLAND, D), and d 1 June 1864, having had, with other issue:

1f Mortimer Percy; b 7 Sept 1816; m 1st 8 Oct 1840 Jane (dsp), est dau of James Drummond Nairne; m 2nd 10 Sept 1857 Emmeline Fanny (d 10 May 1915), only dau of Rev Francis G Rawlins, Rector Leaden Roding, Essex, and d 5 Oct 1893, leaving:

1g Mortimer Percy George Douglas; b 27 Nov 1860; T/Capt Remount Service, ADC to GOC 38th Div BEF, WW I (despatches); m 1890 Alice Lydia (d 11 Jan 1938), dau of William C Ward, of Harborne House, Tenterden, and d 8 Dec 1936, leaving:

1h Euphemia Sybilla; b 2 May 1902; m 25 Aug 1925 Montague Arthur Weaver Bridgman (d 1951), s of Arthur Weaver Bridgman, of Victoria, BC, and had:

1i *Hamish Drummond; b 1929; Lt-Cdr RCN; m 1973 *Sheila Gwynneth, dau of J V Boys, of Victoria, BC, and has:

1j *Montague Jefferay; b 25 Feb 1974

1i *Rosemary Maud [Mrs M Penn, Michaelmas House, 4045 Rainbow Road, Victoria, BC, Canada]; b 1926; m 1951 *Michael John William Penn, of Kent, and has:

1j *Andrew Montague; b 1954

2j *Nigel Rupert Drummond; b 1956

3j *Malcolm Michael; b 1965

1j *Caroline Mary; b 1952

2j *Briony Elizabeth Heather; b 1960

2i *Gillian Alice; b 1936; m 1954 *Cdr Keith Murray Young, RCN, of Kelowna, BC, and has:

1j *Jan Murray; b 1958

1j *Nicola Rosemary; b 1955

2j *Catriona Elizabeth; b 1963

3i *Heather Jane; b 1943; m 1968 *John Boyd Robertson, of Barrie, Ontario, and has:

1j *Hamish John Willard; b 1969

2j *Matthew Boyd; b 1972

1j *Catelin; b 1974

1g Mary Frances; b 3 July 1863; d unm 6 April 1904

2g Emmeline Ada Louisa; b 15 Nov 1865; m 4 Aug 1892 Breedon Newland Everard (d 26 July 1939), of Bardon Hall, Leics, and d 17 Nov 1917

1f Eleanor Charlotte; m 20 June 1848 V-Adml George Wodehouse and d 27 March 1888, leaving issue (see KIMBERLEY, E)

2f Cecil Elizabeth; m 8 Jan 1840 Rev Heneage Drummond (d 13 Sept 1881), of Leckhamsted, Bucks, and d 16 March 1897, leaving issue (see below)

3f Agnes Priscilla; m 27 Feb 1851 Rev Berdmore Compton (d 3 Jan 1908), of Atherstone Hall, Warwicks, and d 13 Nov 1902, leaving issue

4f Susan Caroline; m 16 Sept 1844 Harvey Drummond (d 1 Oct 1875) and d 3 Feb 1905, leaving issue (see below)

1e Henrietta Martha; m 19 April 1803 Adml Sir Charles Hamilton, 2nd Bt, KCB (d 14 March 1849), of Trebinshun (see 1970 edn), and d 10 March 1857, leaving issue

2d John; b 1766; London banker; m 1st 11 June 1789 Hester (d 24 Sept 1802), dau of Thomas Cholmondeley, of Vale Royal, sis of 1st Baron Delamere (qv), and had:

1e John of Redenham, Hants; b 10 Jan 1791; banker; m 22 April 1816 Georgina Augusta (d 11 Oct 1878), 4th dau and coheir of Adml Sir Elias Harvey, GCB, of Rolls Park, Essex, by Lady Louise Nugent, dau and coheir of Robert, Earl Nugent, and d 10 Feb 1864, having had:

1f Harvey, JP; b 2 April 1817; London, banker; m 16 April 1844 Susan Caroline, dau of Andrew Mortimer Drummond (see above), and d 1 Oct 1875, having had, with other issue:

1g Allan Harvey; b 7 Feb 1845; BA, SCL Oxford; Maj 3rd Bn Northumberland Fus; banker; m 4 March 1886 Lady Katherine Adine Geraldine Hervey (d 2 Nov 1948), er dau and coheir of 3rd Marquess of Bristol (qv), and d 28 Jan 1913, leaving:

1h Frederick Hervey John, MC; b 24 May 1892; Capt Gren Gds (SR), formerly Warwicks Yeo, WW I (wounded, despatches); m 14 Jan 1928 Elisabeth (d 4 Jan 1962), widow of Col Frank Cogan, and dsp

2h James Andrew John; b 26 Nov 1896; d 27 Aug 1897

1h Margaret Hester; b 8 July 1888; m 7 Feb 1911 Ven James Hamilton Francis Peile, Canon Res Worcester, Archdeacon Worcester 1921–38, er s of Sir James Braithwaite Peile, KCSI, and d 20 Feb 1940, leaving issue

2h Alice Mary; b 16 Aug 1890; d unm 16 Oct 1961

3h Constance Adine Maud; b 15 Jan 1895; m 19 Dec 1922 Griffith Sutton-Nelthorpe (d 23 Nov 1947), s of Maj Robert

Nassau Sutton-Nelthorpe, of Scawby Hall, Lincs, and *d* 10 Dec 1923, leaving issue (*see* SUTTON, Bt)

2g Malcolm Hugh; *b* 1 Nov 1848; Cdr RN, Consul Oporto; *m* 14 Jan 1891 Mabel Jeannie Otway (*d* 18 Sept 1922), 2nd dau of Maj Henry Otway Mayne, Cdr Mayne's Horse, and *d* 2 Aug 1916, leaving:

1h Malcolm David George; *b* 16 Oct 1895; Lt RFC WW I Dardanelles and Salonica (wounded), Bronze Medal Italy; *d* 24 March 1925

1h Susan Iris Harriet; *b* 3 March 1892; *d* unm 15 Jan 1915

3g Archibald Spencer; *b* 9 Oct 1853; FRAS; Maj Scots Gds; *m* 5 Feb 1891 Helen Sherer (*d* 9 March 1951), er dau of John William Burns, of Kilmahew, and *d* 6 Feb 1921, leaving:

1h Hervey Gerald Burns, MC; *b* 10 July 1898; Lt 1st Bn Scots Gds WW I (despatches); *ka* 3 Sept 1918

1h Helen Susan; *b* 21 July 1896; *m* 11 Jan 1921 St John Swan and *d* 7 Feb 1955, leaving issue

1g Susan Horatia; *b* 21 Oct 1851; *m* 6 Feb 1877 Richard Cecil Corbett, RHA (*d* 12 Sept 1931), and *d* 20 May 1929, leaving issue

2g Katherine Georgina; *b* 14 Jan 1859; *m* 20 July 1880 Lt-Col Charles A R Leslie (*d* 18 Nov 1930), of Balquhain, and *d* 1 Dec 1936, leaving issue

3g Isobel Hester; *b* 21 May 1860; *m* 23 Nov 1882 Hon Ernest Bowes-Lyon (*d* 27 Dec 1891), s of 13th Earl of Strathmore and Kinghorne (*qv*), and *d* 15 July 1945, leaving issue

2f Frederick Thomas; *b* 24 June 1818; *m* 25 April 1850 Agnes Caroline, 2nd dau of W P Brigstocke, and *d* 12 Oct 1877

3f John William; *b* 16 Aug 1819; *d* 1851

4f Francis Berkeley; *b* 16 Dec 1825; HEICS; *m* 1855 Ellen (*m* 2nd May 1864 William Molloy Stewart (*see* STEWART, Bt, of Ramelton) and *d* 17 Dec 1917), dau of W H Urquhart, and *d* at sea 27 June 1859, leaving:

1g John William Ainslie; *b* 23 June 1857; Maj Scots Gds; *m* 25 Feb 1886 Florence Charlotte (*d* 1944), dau of John George Blencowe, of Bineham, Sussex, and *d* 2 Aug 1936, having had:

1h Frederick John; *b* 15 June 1891; *ka* E Africa 3 Nov 1914

2h Francis William; *b* 4 Sept 1894; *educ* Eton; WW I as Lt RE, WW II as Capt Gen List; stockbroker; *m* 4 Sept 1946 Jean, dau of Maj-Gen Sir Archibald Buchanan Ritchie, KBE, CB, CMG, of Donnington, Hayes, Newbury, and widow of Lt-Col James Doyle, TD, DL, and *dsp* 9 Feb 1957

1h Agnes Harriet; nun Community of St John the Baptist Windsor; *d* 15 March 1963

2h Hester Katherine; *m* 11 Oct 1917 Rev Canon Richard Edward Parsons and *d* 17 June 1954, leaving issue (*see* ROSSE, E)

1g Alice; *m* 2 April 1881 Lt-Col John James Money Simons, IA, of Londonderry, and *d* 1924

2g Ellen Julia Maud; *m* 5th July 1884 Edward Woodfield Collin, BCS, and had issue

3g Frances Georgina; *m* 2 April 1881 Philip Nolan, BCS (*d* 28 April 1902), and had issue

5f Hugh Fitzhardinge; *b* 30 Jan 1830; Maj Scots Fus Gds; *k* before Sebastopol 13 Aug 1855

6f Edward; *b* 11 March 1883; BCS; *m* 7 Aug 1862 Lucy Marion (*d* 5 April 1922), dau of Rev Charles J Barnard, and *d* 30 Nov 1916, leaving:

1g Edmund Berkeley; *b* 9 Jan 1867; *m* 6 June 1888 Mabel (*dsp* 29 Sept 1888), dau of Rev Francis Edward Tuke, Vicar Borden, and *d* 11 June 1961

2g Eustace Hervey; *b* 13 Aug 1870; *educ* Clifton; Lt RA Boer War; *d* 25 Aug 1954

1g Lilias Caroline; *b* 9 March 1868; *m* 1st 3 Aug 1897 (*annulled* 1905) John Cuthbert Eyre Leslie, yr s of Charles Stephen Leslie; *m* 2nd 31 July 1906 Capt William Edward Murray (*ka* Sept 1914), Gordon Highrs, of The Manor House, Littlehampton, 3rd s and eventual heir of Lt-Col John Murray of Mastrick, and *d* 5 April 1959, having added her maiden name to his by deed poll 1919, leaving, with two daus:

1h Edward John MURRAY later DRUMMOND-MURRAY (roy licence 11 Jan 1919); *b* 17 June 1907; *educ* Beaumont; Capt Roy Sussex Regt WW II, memb Richmond Borough Cncl; *m* 1st 1 Dec 1928 (*divorce* 1936) Eulalia Ildefonsa Wilhelmina (*d* 1988), dau of William Anthony Raymond Heaven, of Ashfield, Queen's Co, and had:

1i *(William Edward) Peter Louis [Peter Drummond-Murray of Mastrick, 67 Dublin St, Edinburgh EH3 6NS]; *b* 24 Nov 1929; *educ* Beaumont; dir Utd and Gen Tst, Slains Pursuivant of Arms to Ld High Constable of Scotland (*see* ERROLL, E), SMO Malta: Kt Honour and Devotion 1971, Grand Cross Obedience 1984, Chllr Br Assoc 1977–89, Scottish Del 1989–; KStJ 1988; *m* 12 July 1954 *Hon Barbara Mary Hope, yst dau of 2nd Baron Rankeillour (*qv*), and has:

1j *Andrew Philip; *b* 3 July 1958; *m* 1981 *Susan Fiona Dorinthea, dau of Prof Donald Michie (*see* ABERCONWAY, B), and has:

1k *John Douglas; *b* 1986

1k *Jessica Catharine; *b* 1983

2k *Laura Catriona; *b* 1988

2j *James; *b* 25 Nov 1959; *m* 1989 *Namkhang, dau of Mak Tonwong, of Thailand

3j *Robert; *b* 4 March 1965

4j *Walter David; *b* 1973

1j *Isabel Mary; *b* 2 June 1966

2i *Ian Malcolm Gerard; *b* 17 Oct 1930; *educ* Beaumont; *m* 1st 25 July 1952 (*divorce* 1960) Marguerite Mary, dau of Dr Robert Robertson MacGibbon, of Huddersfield, and has:

1j *Hamish William Ian Algernon; *b* 14 March 1953

2j *Jasper Robert Ian Douglas; *b* 27 Feb 1954

3j *Ruaraidh Angus Ian Alastair; *b* 7 July 1955

4j *Alexander Sebastian Hugh Ian; *b* 14 June 1956

1h (cont.) Edward Drummond-Murray of Mastrick *m* 2nd 5 March 1936 Auriol Enid, dau of Cyril Broxholm, of Manchester, and *d* 1976, leaving by her:

3i *Anthony John; *b* 9 March 1944

4i *Niall Andrew; *b* 30 June 1947

5i *Richard Mark; *b* 4 Dec 1948

1f Hester Eliza; *b* 16 Oct 1820; *d* unm 1852

2f Georgina Charlotte; *b* 7 Nov 1822; *m* 12 June 1845 Alexander John Talbot EUSTACE MALPAS formerly EUSTACE, only s of Sir William Cornwallis Eustace (*d* 1870), and *d* 1887, leaving issue, who resumed the surname EUSTACE only

3f Henrietta Maria; *b* 14 June 1831; *m* 4 April 1853 Sir Campbell Munro, 3rd Bt, of Lindertis (*qv*), and *d* 28 Aug 1912, leaving issue

1e Charlotte; *b* 10 Nov 1791; *m* 27 Nov 1823 Robert Hibbert (*d* 17 Dec 1829), of Chalfont Lodge, Bucks, and *d* 15 March 1876

2e Harriet Anne; *b* 21 Dec 1795; *d* 6 July 1865

2d (cont) John Drummond *m* 2nd 1 May 1806 Barbara (*d* 9 Aug 1832), dau of Charles Chester, of Chicheley, Bucks, and *d* 28 May 1833, having by her had:

2e Spencer; *b* 12 Oct 1808; with Treasury; *d* 18 April 1869

3e Heneage (Rev); *b* 7 July 1810; Rector Leckhampstead; *m* 8 Jan 1840 Cecil Elizabeth (*d* 16 March 1897), dau of Andrew Mortimer Drummond (*see* above), and *d* 13 Sept 1881, having had:

1f Algernon Heneage; *b* 1 July 1844; Capt Rifle Bde; *m* 2 Oct 1879 Margaret Elizabeth (*d* 3 May 1941), er dau of William Benson, of Langtons, Alresford (*see* 1953 edn CHARNWOOD, B), and *d* 28 Feb 1932, having had:

1g Algernon Cecil Heneage; *b* 20 Aug 1880; *educ* Eton; Sub-Lt RNVR; *m* 15 Feb 1917 Janetta (*d* 7 Jan 1958), yst dau of Col John Ormsby Vandeleur, CB, of Ballincourty, and *d* 3 May 1975, having had:

1h +Spencer Heneage, DSC [Capt Spencer Drummond DSC RN, Keepers Cottage, Petersfield, Hants GU31 5RD]; *b* 2 June 1922; Capt RN, served WW II; MPhil; *m* 17 Dec 1949 Patricia Pauline (*d* 18 March 1998), dau of Lt-Col Michael Keane, OBE, RAMC, and has:

1i +Crispin Heneage [Crispin Drummond Esq, 11 Clifton Rd, Winchester, Hants]; *b* 17 Aug 1955; *m* 1981 (*divorce* 1996) Marta A Tuey, of Boston, Mass., and has:

1j +Lewis Spencer Heneage; *b* 1987

1j *Kate Elinor; *b* 1984

2j *Juliet Vandeleur; *b* 1988

2i +Hereward John Heneage [Hereward Drummond Esq, 3 Sleepers Hill Gdns, Winchester, Hants]; *b* 23 April 1959; *m* 1987 *Felicia, er dau of George A Shepherd, CMG, of Meonstoke, Hants, and has:

1j +Thomas Anthony Heneage; *b* 1988

2j +Frederick Algernon Heneage; *b* 1991

1j *Isabella Mary Heneage; *b* 1989

2j *Lucinda Jane Heneage; *b* 1993

1i *Deirdre Mary; *b* 16 March 1953; *m* 16 April 1977 *Peregrine Tatton Eyre Massy and has issue (*see* MASSY, B)

2i *Ianthe Mary; *b* 29 Dec 1960

3i *Helena Mhairi; *b* 5 Nov 1963; *m* 1990 *Andrew P Johnstone, only s of Rev B Johnstone, of NSW, and has:

1j *William Drummond; *b* 1993

2j *Alistair James; *b* 1996

1j *Stephanie Margaret; *b* 1994

2h +John Vandeleur Heneage [John Drummond Esq, 9 Upper Wheelan St, Newlands, Cape 7700, S Africa]; *b* 31 May 1924; pilot E and S African Rlwys and Harbour servs (ret); *m* 8 Dec 1951 *Annette, yr dau of Dr Alan William Stuart Sichel, MD, LLD, DO, DOMS (Pres BMA 1951–52), of S Africa, and has:

1i +Anthony Christopher Heneage [Anthony Drummond Esq, 6 York Rd, Claremont, CP, S Africa]; *b* 28 Jan 1954; *m* 1990 *Fiona, dau of John Nugent, of Linthorpe, Cleveland, and has:

1j *Charlotte; *b* 1992

2i +Richard Stuart Heneage; *b* 28 June 1962

3i +Hugo Alistair Heneage [Hugo Drummond Esq, 6 Grove Rd, Mowbray, CP, S Africa]; *b* 15 March 1965; *m* 1990 *Karen, dau of Leslie Joubert, of Mowbray

1i *Amanda Elizabeth; *b* 14 March 1956

1h Barbara Jean; *b* 5 April 1919; *d* 10 March 1920

2h *Margaret Frederica [Mrs John Money, Tanglewood, 72 Skinburness Rd, Silloth, Carlisle, Cumbria CA5 4QF]; *b* 10 Sept 1926; *m* 17 Sept 1949 *John Ironside Money, yr s of Col Rowland Money, of Dorset, and has:

1i *Paul Spencer Kyrle [Dr Paul Money, Barnaribbon, Garney PO, Co Sligo, Ireland]; *b* 26 June 1950; *educ* St George's Coll Salisbury, Rhodesia, and Trin Coll Dublin; FRCGP; *m* 1973 *Berta Williams and has:

1j *Brendan; b 20 May 1977
2j *Justin; b 27 Oct 1978
1j *Laura; b 15 Sept 1983
2i *Brian Ironside [Brian Money Esq, The Mount, Camp Rd, Maryport, Cumbria]; b 19 Nov 1953; educ St George's Coll and St Mary's Hosp London; m 1983 *Janet Dickson and has:
2j *Duncan; b 13 March 1988
2j *Michael; b 1 March 1990
1j *Anne (twin); b 1993
2j *Fiona; b 1993
3i *Colin Francis Drummond; b 30 Sept 1956; educ St George's Coll; m 19– *Sharnay Shaw and has:
1j *Kurt; b 1990
2j *Brett; b 1997
1i *Olivia Margaret [Mrs Anton Verwoerd, The Nook, 235 Skinburness Rd, Silloth, Cumbria CA5 4QS]; b 30 Sept 1959; educ Nagle House Zimbabwe; m 1985 *Anton Verwoerd, of Cape Town, and has:
1j *Clare; b 1993

2g Spencer Heneage; b 12 Aug 1884; Capt Rifle Bde; ka 30 July 1915

3g Geoffrey Heneage, VC; b 25 Jan 1886; Lt-Cdr RNVR WW I (wounded, despatches, Legion of Honour), WW II 1939–41, Coronation Medal 1937; m 2 July 1918 Maude Aylmer Tindal (d 27 Sept 1967), yst dau of Lt-Col Bernard Tindal Bosanquet, DL, Rifle Bde, of Middx, and das 21 April 1941, leaving:

1h +(Geoffrey) Mortimer Heneage [Lt-Cdr Mortimer Drummond RN, Faringdon, Hill Head, Hants PO14 3JX]; b 13 Oct 1920; educ Eton; Lt-Cdr RN WW II; m 3 April 1956 *Sarah Madeline, only dau of Richard Walter Spencer, of Yarmouth, IoW, and has:

1i +John Richard Geoffrey; b 4 Feb 1957; educ Eton, Christ's Coll Cambridge (MA) and Lincoln Coll Oxford (MA, PGCE); Cdr RN (ret); m 16 March 1996 *Constance Catherine Laura, only dau of Nickolay Andreyev, of Cambridge, and has:

1j *Laura Tatiana Rowena; b 18 Dec 1996

2i +Charles Mortimer Geoffrey; b 14 Oct 1958; educ Pangbourne; m 19 July 1997 *Caroline, yst dau of Prof Meulemans and Mme Lucienne Wauters

1i *Caroline Jane; b 24 June 1963; educ St Swithun's and Seale Hayne Ag Coll (BSc)

1h *(Aylmer) Merelina [Miss Merelina Drummond, 4 Minto St, Newington, Edinburgh EH9 1RG]; b 26 July 1919; SRN

2h *Iris Mary Elizabeth [Mrs John Fenton, Bar Ewing, Balmaclellan, by Castle Douglas, Kirkcudbrightshire DG7 3PX]; b 10 April 1926; WRNS WW II 1943–45; m 15 Nov 1947 *Lt-Cdr John Munro Crosland Fenton, DSC, RN, s of Capt Eric Crosland Fenton, RN, of Bovey Tracey, Devon, and has:

1i *Jeremy John Crosland [Jeremy Fenton Esq, 2 Royal Crescent, Edinburgh EH3 6PZ]; b 18 Feb 1949; educ Glenalmond and Magdalene Coll Cambridge (MA); Midshipman RN; Master Edinburgh Acad

2i *James Heneage Crosland [James Fenton Esq, Balfour Cottage, Abernyte, Perthshire PH14 9ST]; b 19 March 1952; educ Glenalmond, Durham U (BSc) and London U (PhD); memb Br Antarctic Survey 1973–78; ecologist Nat Tst Scotland; m 1987 *Susan Claire, dau of H J Wrenn, of Harmby, Yorks, and has:

1j *Mairi Alice; b 1989

3i *Geoffrey Eric Crosland [Geoffrey Fenton Esq, Grove Cottage, Blackford, Somerset BS28 4NG]; b 11 April 1954; educ Trin Coll Glenalmond and St John's Coll Oxford (BA, Msc); md UK on Line; m 1980 *Elizabeth Tyrie, yst dau of Prof J K T L Nash, of Bucks, and has:

1j *Rosemary Tyrie; b 1985
2j *Isabel Shield; b 1988
3j *Lucy Crosland; b 1991

4g Josceline Heneage, OBE (1946), DSC; b 4 Aug 1888; educ Eton; Cdr RN WW I (despatches), Assist Sec Forces Help Soc 1937–53; m 15 April 1944 Gwendolen Theresa, yr dau of James Laing, of Kirkcudbrightshire

5g Frederick Boyd Heneage, MC; b 15 Feb 1890; educ Eton; Lt-Col Rifle Bde, WW I (wounded), WW II, Colonial Admin Service, Priv Sec to FM Lord Plumer 1925–28, Sec Imp Inst 1930–35, Dep Comptroller Dominion Students London House 1935–39, Supervisor CS Courses Oxford U 1946–71; d unm 5 May 1971

6g Mortimer Heneage; b 16 Feb 1892; d unm 5 March 1911

7g Maurice John Henage; b 18 Sept 1894; educ Haileybury; Capt 10th Bn Lancs Fus WW I (wounded), chartered accountant 1921–64; m 28 Sept 1922 Celia (d 14 Sept 1964), dau of Canon John Vaughan, of Winchester, and d 30 July 1975, leaving:

1h +Christopher John Vaughan (Rev) [The Rev Canon Christopher Drummond, 77 Markham Rd, Capel, Surrey RH5 5JT]; b 25 Aug 1926; educ Winchester, Magdalen Coll Oxford (MA 1951) and Ridley Hall Cambridge (MA 1956, Tutor 1956–59); Lt Roy Signals WW II, Chaplain Clare Coll, Chaplain to Cambridge U Pastorate 1959–62, Lecturer and V-Pncpl Immanuel Coll Ibadan Nigeria 1963–69, Vicar St John's Walthamstow 1969; m 18 June 1960 *Gwyneth May, only dau of George Timmis, of Clayton, Staffs, and has:

1i +Peter John Vaughan; b 7 Jan 1963; m 19– *Katherine Bryan and has:
1j +Timothy; b 28 July 1994
1j *Lucy Rose; b 18 Sept 1996
1i *Gillian Clare; b 27 April 1961; m 19– *Rowland Howarth and has:
1j *Peter; b 10 Dec 1990
1j *Annabel Clare; b 21 March 1993

2h +Josceline Maurice Vaughan (Rev) [The Rev Josceline Drummond, 3 Fryth Mead, St Albans, Herts AL3 4TN]; b 3 April 1929; educ RNC Dartmouth, London U (Dip Th 1958, BD 1970) and Wycliffe Hall Oxford; Lt RN Korea 1952–53; m 1st 31 March 1962 Christine Mary (d 1987), dau of Alfred George Read, of Derby, and has:

1i +Andrew Paul Graham; b 8 Nov 1970; educ London U (BA)
1i *Lydia Rosalind; b 3 Aug 1964; educ Glasgow U (BSc DPhil 1997); m 1989 *Stephen Keith Pierce, of Hastings

2h (cont) The Rev Josceline Drummond m 2nd 1988 *Susan Helena, dau of William Bolitho Rowe and widow of Rev Canon Andrew Bowman

1h *Rosalind Margaret Vaughan [Dr Rosalind Dépas, 83 Riverside, Cambridge CB5 8HN]; b 9 March 1924; Assoc Prof English City U New York, PhD; m 1st 6 Aug 1947 (divorce 1955) Mark Arthur Monson Roberts, yst s of George Augustus Roberts, CBE, FRCS, of Winchester, Hants, and has:

1i *Julian Francis; b 24 Aug 1950; educ Winchester and Caius Coll Cambridge (MA); m 1990 *Margarethe and has:
1j *Hilary; b 26 April 1990
2j *Alexander; b 4 March 1992

1h (cont.) Mrs Rosalind Roberts m 2nd 23 April 1965 *Spencer Dépas and by him has:

1i *Sophie Margaret; b 26 Aug 1967; m 1993 (divorce 1996) Stuart Dempster and has:
1j *Zeke; b 8 Jan 1990
1j *Maya Lisa; b 26 April 1993

1g Barbara; b 28 Sept 1881; d unm June 1968

2g Isobel; b 16 July 1887; m 18 Jan 1906 Neville Leckonby Phipps (d 23 May 1968), er s of Arthur Leckonby Phipps, and d 18 Dec 1976, leaving issue

1f Alice Emily Barbara; m 24 Jan 1872 Rev Sir Frederick Boyd, 6th and last Bt (d 13 Feb 1889), and dsp 23 Feb 1890

1a Lilias; m 1st 1667, as his 3rd w, 2nd Earl of Tullibardine (see ATHOLL, D); m 2nd her cousin 4th Earl of Perth

1 Catherine; m 1st Lord Rollo (qv) and had issue

The 3rd VISCOUNT STRATHALLAN's cousin,

WILLIAM DRUMMOND, 4th Viscount Strathallan; Jacobite in both 1715 and 1745 Uprisings but was not prosecuted after 1715, though captured at Sheriffmuir; k at Culloden 16 April 1746, thereby avoiding forfeiture under the Act of Attainder against Jacobites passed later that year; m c 1 Nov 1712 Margaret, dau of Lord William Murray, afterwards 2nd Lord Nairne (qv), leaving:

1 JAMES DRUMMOND, 5th Viscount Strathallan; b 10 June 1722; Offr in Ld John Drummond's Jacobite regt in France 1740, took part in 1745 Uprising and fought at Falkirk 17 Jan 1745/6 and Culloden 16 April 1746, after which he fled to France, being attainted (with the Machany estate and Strathallan Castle being forfeited as well as the titles) as of 18 April 1746 when he had not given himself up by 12 July 1746; m seemingly Nov 1750 Euphemia (d 5 July 1796), yst dau of Peter Gordon, 11th of Abergeldie, Aberdeenshire, and d 22 June 1765, having had, with other issue (d young or unm):

(1) James; b 1752; offr RN; d unm 1775

(2) Andrew; b 15 Jan 1758; Ensign 1st Foot Gds (Br Army) 1773, Capt 1777, Maj 1797, Lt-Col 1798, served War American Independence 1776–77, Low Countries 1793–94, Gen 1812, Col 11th Veteran Bn 1807–14, Govr Dumbarton Castle 1810–17; petitioned unsuccessfully to have his titles restored 1787–90; d unm 20 Jan 1817

(1) Margaret; m John Augustus Haldane

2 William; m Anne (d 31 May 1782), 2nd dau of Brig-Gen David Nairn, of the French service, and d 25 May 1772, leaving:

(1) William Henry; b 1765; Col 27th Regt; d unm 1796

(2) JAMES ANDREW JOHN LAURENCE CHARLES, 6th Viscount

3 Robert, of Cadland, Hants, and Charing Cross; London banker; m 1753 Winifred, dau of William Thompson, of Ipsden, Oxon, and d 1804, leaving, with other issue:

(1) Andrew Berkeley, of Cadland; b 11 Sept 1755; banker; m 2 April 1781 Mary (d 18 Sept 1839), dau of 2nd Earl of Egmont (qv), and d 27 Dec 1833, leaving:

1a Andrew Robert, of Cadland; b 28 July 1794; Treas RN Sch Deptford; m 7 March 1822 Lady Elizabeth Frederica Manners (d 20 March 1886), dau of 5th Duke of Rutland (qv), and d 20 June 1865, leaving, with other issue:

1b Andrew John; b 13 May 1823; d unm 29 Sept 1910

2b Edgar Atheling, of Cadland, JP, DL; b 21 Aug 1825; Lt RN; m 25 Nov 1858 Hon Louisa Theodosia Pennington (d 17 June 1886), dau of 3rd Baron Muncaster (see 1917 edn), and d 10 May 1893, leaving:

1c Andrew Cecil, of Cadland, JP, DL; b 28 Jan 1865; d 2 Feb 1913

2c Maldwin, of Cadland, DL Hants; b 9 March 1872; Capt KRRC, Matabeleland 1896 (medal), WW I; High Sheriff Hants 1923; m 3 Sept 1908 Albertine (d 18 Sept 1915), dau of Louis C Huck, of Chicago, and widow of Marshall Field, Jr, of Chicago, and d 12 March 1929

3c Cyril Augustus, of Cadland, JP, DL Hants; b 5 April 1873; Maj Yeo, Boer War, WW I; OStJ; m 1st 13 Dec 1897 Edith Belle (d 27 Oct 1917), dau of L T Wilkins, of Southampton, and had:

1d Sybelle Winifred Louisa, JP; *b* 29 Oct 1898; CC Hants; SSStJ; *m* 1st 12 Oct 1920 Gerald James Pixley, 9th Bn Hants Regt, s of James Aiken Pixley, LLB, and had issue; *m* 2nd 27 Nov 1930 Hon John de Bathe Crossley (*d* 24 June 1935), 2nd son of 1st Baron Somerleyton (*qv*), and *d* 26 June 1963, leaving issue

3c (cont.) Maj Cyril Drummond *m* 2nd 7 Oct 1930 Mildred Joan Harrington (*m* 2nd 15 April 1948 A/Cdre John Charles Quinnell, CB, DFC (*d* 1983), s of John Busted Quinnell, of Edenburn, Richmond and Paris, and *d* 1977), dau of Horace Humphrys, and *d* 7 Feb 1945, having by her had:

1d +Maldwin Andrew Cyril, OBE (1990), JP, DL [Maldwin Drummond Esq OBE JP DL, Cadland House, Calshot Rd, Fawley, Hants SO45 1AA; Wester Kames Castle, Port Bannatyne, Isle of Bute]; *b* 30 April 1932; *educ* Eton and RAC Cirencester; Capt Queen's Roy Rifles (TA); High Sheriff Hants 1980, CC (1967), Verderer New Forest 1961–, memb Br Tport Docks Bd, Southampton, Chm Sail Trg Assoc, Prime Warden Fishmongers' Co 1996–97 (Warden 1995–96), chm New Forest Ctee 1990–, Hon DSc; *m* 1st 17 Sept 1955 (*divorce* 1977) Susan Dorothy Marie Gabrielle, 2nd dau of Sir Kenelm Henry Ernest Cayley, 10th Bt (*qv*), and has:

1e *Frederica Elizabeth; *b* 21 Sept 1957; *m* 11th July 1984 *Lt-Col Miles Templer, 17th/21st Lancers, s of FM Sir Gerald Templer, KG, GCB, GCMG, KBE, DSO, and has:

1f *Gerald; *b* 1986

2f *(Robert) Benjamin; *b* 1987

2e *Annabella Virginia; *b* 5 March 1959; *m* 1980 (*divorce* 1988) Capt Christopher E Robinson, 17th/21st Lancers, er s of Edward Robinson, of Withypool, Somerset, and has:

1f *Edward; *b* 1982

2f *Jeremy; *b* 1984

1d (cont.) Maldwin Drummond *m* 2nd 1978 *Gillian Vera, yr dau of Charles Gavin Clark (*see* ROYDEN, Bt), and formerly w of Alexander Graham Athol Turner Laing, and by her has:

1e +Aldred Robert Alexander; *b* 1978

2d Robert Edgar Atheling; *b* 22 June 1933; *educ* Eton and Ch Ch Oxford; *m* 1958 (*divorce* 1967) Phyllis, dau of Marshall Field, of New York, and formerly w of Hernando Samper, and *d* 1995, leaving:

1e +Maldwin Marshall; *b* 4 Jan 1959

1e *Fiona Mary; *b* 17 April 1960; *m* 1980 *Albemarle John Cator (*see* CAYLEY, Bt) and has:

1f *John; *b* 1983

2f *Robert; *b* 1985

2e *Bettina; *b* 10 April 1963

3d Aldred Strathallan Dundas; *b* 12 Feb 1935; *educ* Eton and Magdalen Coll Oxford; *d* 1975

1d *Annabella Frances Serena; *b* 10 Jan 1938; *m* 1st 5 Oct 1957 (*divorce* 1961) (David) Arthur Talbot Rice (*see* DINEVOR, B); *m* 2nd 15 Aug 1961 (*divorce* 1972) Gerald Hochschild, of Santiago, Chile; *m* 3rd 1973 *John Philip Pochna, of Caherass, Croom, Co Limerick, and has by her 2nd husb:

1e *Maurice Leo Robert; *b* 20 Feb 1962

2e *Fabrizio Gerald Arturo; *b* 18 April 1963

3e *Augustin Emil; *b* 24 Aug 1965

4c Henry Ludovic; *b* 16 Oct 1874; RN; *d* 29 Feb 1896

1c Lilias Elizabeth; *m* 8 Dec 1887 Rev Robert Manners Norman (*d* 1 Feb 1895) and *d* 18 May 1928

2c Edith Mary Frances; *d* unm 17 Jan 1950

3c Winifred Louisa; *m* 28 April 1892 John Allan Maconochie Welwood (*d* 25 May 1934) and *d* 18 March 1941, leaving issue

4c Constance Louisa; *m* 12 June 1897 Francis Algernon Fulford, JP (*d* 5 Nov 1926), of Fulford, Devon, and *d* 3 April 1935, leaving issue

5c Mary Louise; *b* 5 April 1876; *m* 13 June 1901 Brig-Gen Edward John Russell Peel and *d* 3 July 1959, leaving issue (*see* PEEL, E)

6c Jean Cicely; *d* unm 29 March 1904

3b Alfred Manners; *b* 28 Aug 1829; Capt Rifle Bde, Crimea (medal and clasp and Turkish medal); *m* 5 July 1878 Augusta (*dsp* 28 April 1908), 3rd dau of Robert Verschoyle, of Kilberry, and *d* 11 May 1921

4b Victor Arthur Wellington (Sir), KCMG, CB; *b* 4 June 1833; Chargé d'Affaires Bavaria, Res Min Munich and Stuttgart, Grand Cross St Michael Bavaria and Friedrich of Wurttemburg; *m* 1882 Elizabeth, Lady of Honour Roy Order Therese Bavaria (*d* 26 March 1912), dau of Charles Lamson, of New York, and *dsp* 22 March 1907

5b Cecil George Assheton, of Enderby Hall, Leics, JP, DL; *b* 14 April 1839; Capt Rifle Bde and Leics Militia; High Sheriff 1885; *m* 26 Oct 1871 Charlotte Amelia (*d* 24 April 1924), dau of William Leigh Brook, of Meltham Hall, and *d* 6 Dec 1903, having had:

1c Charles Brook Assheton; *d* an infant 4 May 1873

2c Francis Cecil; *d* an infant 24 March 1876

3c Cecil Rowland Brook; *b* 28 Jan 1882; Midshipman RN; *d* 21 July 1897

4c Eric Roderick Brook, JP; *b* 22 May 1884; *educ* Clifton; T/Capt Rifle Bde, Lt 7th Bn, Rifle Bde, CA Leics; *m* Feb 1905 Frederica Lilian (*d* 24 Jan 1964), dau of J Norrey Norris, and *d* 13 April 1954, having had:

1d Geoffrey Brook, JP (1961); *b* 27 Oct 1905; CC Leics 1958; *m* 31 May 1939 *Mary Barbara [Mrs Geoffrey Drummond, 1 Granville Crescent, Leicester], dau of James Arthur Unitt, MRCS, LRCP, of Quorn, Leics, and *d* 1976, having had:

1e +Frederick Brook [Frederick Drummond Esq, Enderby Hall, Enderby, Leics]; *b* 16 March 1946; *educ* Haileybury; *m* 1st 1974 (*divorce* 1979) Gillian Victoria, dau of Donald Leslie Bridges, and has:

1f +Roland Brook; *b* 1975

1e (cont.) Frederick Drummond *m* 2nd 1980 *Mrs Evelyn Clare Ann Jackson, dau of James Allen, and by her has:

2f +Leigh James Brook; *b* 1981

1f *Kimberley Brook; *b* 1985

1e *Cherry Barbara; *b* 6 March 1940; *m* 22 Aug 1959 *Derek Cyril Gibbs, s of Cyril R Gibbs, of Ramsgate, Kent, and has:

1f *Nicholas Cary; *b* 1960

2f *Alistair Corin; *b* 1972

1f *Scarlet Kathryn; *b* 1961

2d Frederic Cecil; *b* 17 Dec 1907; Capt Leics Regt (attd KAR) WW II; *das* 10 July 1940

5c Edward Atheling Brook; *b* 10 May, *d* 28 June 1892

1c Elizabeth Cecil; *m* 17 Feb 1912 Arthur de Winton Snowden, CBE, BCh (*d* 20 May 1950), 2nd s of Preb J H Snowden, and *d* 28 Sept 1941, leaving issue

2c Muriel Constance; *m* 18 Jan 1900 Cecil Henry Haig, of Hereford (*d* 3 March 1947), s of Augustus Haig, of Radnorshire, and *d* 26 Dec 1944, leaving issue

3c Lily; *b* 28 May 1875; *m* 17 March 1909 Maj Beauchamp Kerr-Pearse, CMG, MVO, Rifle Bde (*d* 26 Sept 1934), and *d* 30 Aug 1969, having had issue

4c Grace Janet; *m* 26 Oct 1918 John Cecil Openshaw Bradbury (*d* 13 Jan 1955), s of John Buckley Bradbury, Downing Prof Medicine Cambridge

5c Margaret Annabella; *b* 1879; *d* 9 March 1973

6c Dorothy Charlotte; *m* 14 Jan 1918 Maj Sir David John Montagu-Douglas-Scott, KCMG, OBE (*see* BUCCLEUCH and QUEENSBERRY, D), and *d* 3 Dec 1965, having had issue

7c Violet Emily; *b* 3 Oct 1888; *m* 8 Oct 1912 Capt Miles Bury Selby-Smyth, Rifle Bde (*ka* 15 March 1915), s of Lt-Col E G Selby-Smyth, of Sunbury, and had:

1d Pamela Dorothy Beaujolois; *b* 25 Aug 1913

1b Annabella Mary Elizabeth; *m* 4 Dec 1844 1st Baron Lamington (*d* 15 Feb 1890; *see* 1949 edn) and *d* 17 Feb 1917, leaving issue

2b Frederica Mary Adeliza; *m* 8 Oct 1846 9th Earl of Scarbrough (*qv*) and *d* 2 April 1907, leaving issue

2a William Charles, JP, DL; *b* 14 July 1796; Lt-Col 10th Hus; *d* 4 Jan 1881, leaving:

1b William Charles; *b* 11 Sept 1837; Maj 3rd Bn Hants Regt, Capt 95th Foot; *m* 1st 1 Jan 1870 Rosalind Blanche Vansittart (*d* 28 July 1876), 3rd dau of William Charles Humphrys, of Bursledon, Hants, and had:

1c Angela Nora Edith Humphrys; *m* 1887 John Arthur Levett (*d* 13 June 1942), of Blackheath, and had issue

1b (cont.) Maj William Drummond *m* 2nd 1885 Jessie Maria (*d* 23 Jan 1926), dau of Adml Wigston, of Bitterne Court, Hants, and *d* 14 Jan 1916

1a Mary; *m* 18 Oct 1839 Rt Rev Francis Fulford, DD, JP, Bp Montreal (*d* Oct 1868), 2nd s of Lt-Col Baldwin Fulford, JP, of Great Fulford, Devon, and *d* 21 Oct 1873, leaving issue

2a Catherine Isabella; *m* 27 March 1826 Rev Henry Perceval and *d* 12 Feb 1870, leaving issue (*see* EGMONT, E)

(2) Charles; *b* 24 June 1759; London banker; *m* 26 July 1789 Frances Dorothy (*d* 24 Feb 1831), 2nd dau of Rev E Lockwood, of Dews Hall, Essex, and *d* 2 March 1823, leaving:

1a Charles; *b* 4 Sept 1790; *m* 15 July 1819 Mary Dulcibella (*d* 20 March 1862), dau of 1st Baron Auckland (*qv*), and *d* 28 Aug 1858, leaving:

1b Robert; *b* 26 July 1822; *m* 25 April 1854 Augusta Charlotte (*d* 20 Sept 1911), yst surv dau of Col Charles Mackenzie Fraser of Castle Fraser, nephew of 1st and last Lord Seaforth, Baron Mackenzie of Kintail (*see* CROMARTIE, E), and *d* 29 April 1881, leaving:

1c Charles; *b* 17 Feb 1855; *m* 7 Sept 1892 Lady Caroline Elizabeth Boyle (*d* 4 Dec 1958), sis of 12th Earl of Cork and Orrery (*qv*), and *d* 5 Oct 1932, having had:

1d Robert Charles Crosbie; *b* 5 Oct 1896; 2nd Lt Coldstream Gds; *ka* 28 Nov 1917

2d Angus Julian; *b* 2 Jan 1910; Lt (S) RNVR WW II; *m* 11 Nov 1961 Hon Theodosia Beatrix Catherine Mary Meade (*see* CLANWILLIAM, E) and *d* 31 Dec 1997, having adopted:

*Charles; b 1 Feb 1962; *educ* Westminster; *m* 1991 *Deirdre, dau of Kevin Ford, of Canberra, and has issue

*Mary; *b* 26 May 1954; *m* 11 Nov 1988 David Michael Parker (*d* 13 June 1990) and has issue

*Magdalen; *b* 16 May 1956

1d Angela Cecilia Mary; *b* 7 June 1903; *d* unm 17 Feb 1932

2c Wingfield Fraser; *b* 22 Sept 1861; *d* 11 Jan 1908

3c Kenneth Mackenzie; *b* 9 Sept 1862; Maj 2nd Bn Leinster Regt; *d* 25 May 1932

1c Sybil; *b* 26 Aug 1858; *d* 27 Aug 1919

2c Winifred; *b* 23; *d* 24 April 1864

2b Charles; *b* 23 Jane 1824; *m* 28 April 1857 Charlotte Mary, est dau of Morgan Popkin Traherne, JP, DL, of Coytrahen, Glam, and *dsp* 9 July 1888

3b Maurice, CB; *b* 9 July 1825; *m* 12 Jan 1847 Hon Adelaide Lister (*d* 27 April 1911), est dau of 2nd Baron Ribblesdale (*see* 1925 edn), and *d* 18 May 1891, having had:

1c Lister Maurice; *b* 23 Aug 1856; barrister, Met Police Magistrate 1913–16, Kt Order St Gregory the Great; *d* unm 27 Feb 1916

1c Adelaide Maura; *d* 19 July 1892

2c May Theresa Ella; *b* 3 June 1876 Basil Champneys (*d* 5 April 1935), of Frognal, Hampstead, er surv s of Dean of Lichfield, and *d* 25 Feb 1941, leaving issue

3c Miriam Frances Lilian; *m* 27 April 1886 George John Barry Hayter and *d* 22 March 1931, leaving issue

4c Mary Dulcibella; *d* 28 May 1864

5c Monica Catherine Anne Louise; *b* 27 June 1868; *d* unm 31 May 1957

4b Walter; *b* 5 July 1830; *m* 8 July 1852 Isabella Mary (*d* 21 Nov 1911), dau of Lionel Charles Hervey (*see* HERVEY-BATHURST, Bt), and *d* 23 April 1883, having had:

 1c Lionel Charles; *b* 9 May 1853; *m* 19 Aug 1884 Hon Amy Harriott Gurdon (*m* 2nd 17 April 1895 Capt Alfred Ridley, King's Own Regt (*dsp* 29 March 1898); *m* 3rd 22 Aug 1905 Maj Charles Stirling, RA, er s of Gen Sir William Stirling, KCB, and *d* 13 May 1944), dau of 1st Baron Cranworth (*qv*), and *dsp* 5 March 1891

 2c Ernest Morton; *b* 6 Nov 1855; *d* 11 Nov 1876

 3c Berkeley Walter; *b* 31 March 1866; Lt RN; *d* unm 11 Sept 1903

 4c Henry Walter; *b* 17 June 1867; *m* 24 Oct 1903 Mary Louisa Margaret (*d* 13 Aug 1938), only dau of Theophilus John Levett, JP, DL, MP, of Wychnor Park, and *d* 31 July 1937

 1c Mabel Mary; *m* 9 March 1880 Sir Vesey George Mackenzie Holt, KBE (*d* 6 Dec 1923), of Mount Mascal, Bexley, and *d* 10 Aug 1930, leaving issue

 2c Violet Catherine; *d* unm 1 Nov 1937

 3c Dulcibella Frances; *d* unm 21 Sept 1951

 4c Mary Selina; *m* 25 Jan 1890 Algernon Henry Peter Strickland (*d* 22 Feb 1928), of Tewkesbury, and *d* 13 Dec 1949, leaving issue (*see* STRICKLAND-CONSTABLE, Bt)

5b Morton (Rev); *b* 8 Feb 1832; Rector Wanstead, Essex; *m* 5 Dec 1861 Caroline (*d* 24 Nov 1918), yst dau of Morgan Popkin Traherne, JP, DL, of Coytrahen, Glam, and *d* 23 March 1898, leaving:

 1c Edmund Traherne; *b* 1 Jan 1864; *m* 11 June 1892 Isabel Henrietta (*d* 3 March 1955), dau of William Knights, of Nethercote, Walthamstow, and *d* 30 Dec 1935, leaving:

  1d Edith Charlotte; *b* 5 April 1893; *m* 4 Sept 1915 Rev Edmund Arthur Du Cane (*d* 5 July 1950), Vicar Abbotsham, s of Maj-Gen Sir Edmund Frederick Du Cane, KCB

  2d Isabel Hilda; *b* 3 May 1896; *m* 30 Sept 1922 Maj Christopher Hamer Rawdon, KOYLI (*d* 5 Nov 1956), only s of Canon James Hamer Rawdon, and *d* 23 April 1971, leaving:

   1e *Christina Isabel Drummond; *b* 25 July 1927; *m* 10 Oct 1970 *Graham William Graham

 2c Gerald Morton; *b* 17 April 1866; *m* 27 June 1896 Alice Edith (*d* 10 Oct 1946), dau of Col William Julius Marshall, of Gidea Hall, Essex, and *d* 9 Aug 1941, leaving:

  1d Edward Morton; *b* 11 March 1898; G/Capt RAF, Lt 3rd Bn Black Watch; *m* 10 Nov 1922 Edith Daphne Eunice (*d* 1989), 4th dau of Wilfrid Doneraile Stanhope Taylour (*see* HEADFORT, M), and *d* 1993, leaving:

   1e +David James Morton [David Drummond Esq, Blacklands, Meshaw, Devon EX36 4NG]; *b* 28 Oct 1925; *educ* Reading U (BSc 1951); Lt Black Watch WW II 1943–45; *m* 1st 14 Sept 1949 (*divorce*) Cecily Winifred Jillian, only dau of Cdr Alan Douglas Bruford, VRD, RNVR, of Hailsham, Sussex; *m* 2nd *Diana Mary, only child of Frederick Turner, of Barnstaple, Devon, and by her has had:

    1f James Edward Morton; *b* 4 July 1966; *d* 1992

    1f *Lilias; *b* 29 March 1962

    2f *Amanda; *b* 27 July 1963

   1e *Charmian Eunice [Mrs George Gundry-White, 49 Tooting Bec Gdns, London SW16 1RF]; *b* 3 Oct 1923; WAAF WW II *m* 22 Aug 1951 *George Geoffrey Gundry-White, yr s of Col Gundry-White, Roy Norfolk Regt, and has had:

    1f *Timothy; *b* 16 June 1955

    2f *Patrick; *b* 25 July 1957

    3f Alexander; *b* 25 July 1957; *k* 1989

    4f *Jasper; *b* 39 May 1959

    5f *Henry Simon; *b* 19 Oct 1960

    1f *Katherine Jane Louise; *b* 7 June 1952

    2f *Madelaine Anne; *b* 19 Feb 1954

    3f *Laura; *b* 16 June 1955

   2e *Jean; *b* 11 Sept 1927; *m* 26 April 1948 *Gerald Charles Grenfell Robins, er son of Leonard A C Robins, of Linden House, Hendon, and has:

    1f *Charles David Anthony; *b* 7 July 1953; *educ* Crookham House, Newbury

    1f *Angela Daphne; *b* 13 Nov 1955

    2f *Marion Gertrude; *b* 13 Aug 1960

  2d Charles Morton; *b* 7 Feb 1903; Lt-Col RE, WW II in E African Engrs; *m* 18 March 1937 Violet Emily Agnes, dau of William Andrew Pitcairn, of Edinburgh, and BC, Canada; *d* 1991

  3d Andrew Morton; *b* 1 Sept 1904; Lt Gordon Highrs WW II

 1c Caroline Dulcibella; *b* 22 Feb 1865; *d* unm 12 June 1909

 2c Maud Margaret Frances; *b* 26 June 1870; *d* unm 1944

6b Edward; *b* 23 June 1834; *m* 26 Feb 1878 Jane Mary Anne (*d* 4 Nov 1914), only dau of James George Tayler, and *dsp* 15 July 1882

1b Theresa Charlotte; *m* 2 Sept 1868 Thomas Prendergast (*d* 1886) and *d* 10 April 1890

2b Eleanor Mary; *b c* 1822; *d* 5 April 1887

3b Mary Dulcibella; *m* 17 Oct 1850 Richard Wellesley (*d* 8 May 1861) and *d* 5 Aug 1874

2a Edward; *b* 30 March 1792; Priv Sec to PM (*see* PEEL, E); *d* 25 Jan 1843

3a Berkeley; *b* 27 May 1796; Lt-Gen; Extra Groom-in-Waiting to HM QUEEN VICTORIA; *m* 5 April 1832 Maria (*d* Nov 1872), dau of William Arthur-Crosbie, and *d* 3 May 1860

4a Arthur (Rev); *b* 20 Aug 1797; Rector Charlton; *m* 1st 13 May 1830 Margaretta Maria (*d* 6 Aug 1854), dau of Sir Thomas Maryon Wilson, 7th Bt (*see* 1970 edn), and had, with two other daus (*d* unm):

1b Charles Spencer; *b* 9 Dec 1834; *m* 28 Oct 1862 Mary (*d* 1920), est dau of John Stewart Innes, of Grafton, Canada West, and *d* 14 Dec 1912, leaving:

 1c Lilias Charlotte; *m* 14 Aug 1903 Daniel Dickinson, of Toronto

 2c Catherine Georgina

 3c Gertrude Emily; *m* 1885 Walter Wilson Nation (*d* 1918), manager Dominion Bank, Toronto, and had issue

2b Arthur Hislop (Rev); *b* 5 April 1843; MA Oxon; Vicar All Saints Maidenhead 1876–1917, Hon Canon Ch Ch Oxford, Proctor in Convocation; *m* 1st 28 Oct 1808 Armynel Mary (*d* 31 March 1876), 3rd dau of Rev Charles F R Baylay, and had:

 1c Arthur Berkeley; *b* 27 Nov 1869; Lt-Col IA, Political Dept; *m* 18 Jan 1894 Edith Charlotte (*d* 9 Jan 1919), 2nd dau of Sir Henry Edward Francis Lambert, 6th Bt (*qv*), and *d* 11 Nov 1918, having had:

  1d Nigel Felton; *b* 2 Feb 1895; 2nd Lt (T/Capt) KRRC; *ka* 20 Dec 1916

  2d Eric Arthur; *b* Sept 1900; Capt RN; *m* 1st 6 Sept 1924 (*divorce* 1938) Molly Beryl, yst dau of Hugh William Croft, of Ledbury, Herefs, and had:

   1e Ronald Nigel; *b* 1 Aug 1925; *m* 1st 1948 (*divorce*) Josephine Marie, dau of Jules Pourbaise, Count de Bey, and had:

    1f +Iain Stewart; *b* 1950

   1e (cont.) Ronald Drummond *m* 2nd 1960 *Dinah [Mrs Ronald Drummond, 41 Glanymor, Aberavon, Dyfed], dau of Ralph Adams, and *d* 1978

   2e +John Berwick Lindsay; *b* 25 Nov 1927; Capt RAOC; *m* 21 Nov 1953 *Daphne Mary, er dau of Rev Edward Percy Woollcombe, OBE, of Somerset, and has had:

    1f +Richard John; *b* 10 Dec 1963

    1f *Penelope Anne; *b* 10 Oct 1954

    2f Susan Mary; *b* 16, *d* 29 July 1956

    3f *Sarah Jane; *b* 21 June 1958

    4f *Catriona Caroline; *b* 8 July 1961

   3e +Charles Iain [Charles Drummond Esq, Lochranza, Monument Lane, Chalfont St Peter, Bucks]; *b* 23 March 1932; *educ* St Edmund Hall Oxford (BA 1955); *m* 3 March 1962 *Christine Mary, only dau of Eric Stevenson Browne, of Wallasey, Cheshire, and has:

    1f *Clare Elizabeth; *b* 13 Dec 1967

  2d (cont.) Eric Drummond *m* 2nd 12 Dec 1938 (*divorce* 1947) Elnah Raymond Russell, dau of Henry Russell Wilding, of London, and by her had:

   1e *Fiona Elnah Russell; *b* 13 Nov 1940; *m* 1st 4 April 1963 (*divorce* 1966) Julian Patrick Selby Ormond, yr s of William Patrick Selby Ormond, of Wendens Ambo, Essex; *m* 2nd 19 May 1967 *(Robert) Adrian Cowell, yr s of Frank Richard Cowell, of Kemsing, Kent, and by him has:

    1f *John Maximilian Arthur; *b* 1972

    1f *Sophia Russell Lilian; *b* 4 June 1969

   2e *Deirdre Georgina; *b* 10 Oct 1944; *m* 1969 *Nigel Builder

  2d (cont.) Eric Drummond *m* 3rd 19 Oct 1954 *Barbara, dau of Wilfred Barnard Faraday, barrister, of Leamington Spa, and Recorder Barnstaple and Bideford, and *d* 26 June 1970

2b (cont.) The Rev Canon Arthur Drummond *m* 2nd 17 June 1878 Anna Harriet (*d* 15 Dec 1915), yst dau of Rev William Dodsworth, and *d* 19 Feb 1925, having by her had:

 2c Malcolm Cyril; *b* 24 May 1880; *educ* Ch Ch Oxford (MA); *m* 1st 27 June 1906 Zina Lilias (*d* 15 Sept 1931), dau of George Macartney Ogilvie, ICS, and had:

  1d +(Arthur Malcolm) James [James Drummond Esq, Glengairn, 7 Aberdeen Rd, Tarland, Aberdeenshire AB34 4UA]; *b* 23 April 1911; Capt Roy Berks Regt WW II, chartered accountant Roy Nat Parks of Kenya; *m* 1st 15 Jan 1938 (*divorce* 1952) Moyra Blanche Yseult (*d* 1982), er dau of Frederic Barnard Elliot, CBE, and has:

   1e +Hamish Guy [Hamish Drummond Esq, PO Box 310 Grand Cayman, British West Indies]; *b* 6 March 1939; *m* 1964 *Valerie Louise, dau of Tyril McLaughlin, of Cayman Islands, and has:

    1f +Andrew Simon Hamish; *b* 1970

    1f *Katherine Nicola; *b* 1966

   1e (cont.) Hamish Drummond also adopted:

    *Deborah Ann Eileen; *b* 1961

    *Charmaine Alexandra; *b* 1963

  1d (cont.) James Drummond *m* 2nd 1954 *Patricia, dau of Guy Cave, and by her has:

   2e +David James; *b* 1960; RAF; *m* 1984 *Beverley, dau of John Steward, of Cambridge, and has:

    1f +Matthew Thomas; *b* 1993

    1f *Rebecca Jemma; *b* 1984

    2f *Emily Lisa; *b* 1986

    3f *Francesca Claire; *b* 1989

   1e *Nicola Gesina; *b* 1956

   2e *Alexina Mary; *b* 1957; *m* 1977 *Arthur John Menzies, of Coirmoir, Torphins, Aberdeenshire, and has issue

  1d Elspeth Mary; *b* 15 March 1907; *m* 7 Feb 1935 John Finch MacIntyre, son of John Turnbull MacIntyre, and had:

   1e *John Malcolm Drummond [John MacIntyre Esq, Rowan Tree Cottage, Ridgway Hill Road, Farnham, Surrey]; *b* 9 Dec 1938; *educ* Fort Augustus Abbey Sch and Glasgow U; RAF 1957–60; *m* 8 Feb 1964 *Elisabeth Anne, dau of Douglas James Lionel Routh, MRCS, LRCP, of Torquay, Devon, and has:

    1f *James Amand Routh; *b* 12 Sept 1967

    1f *Catriona Elspeth; *b* 28 Dec 1964

2e *Archibald Duncan Ogilvie; b 5 Aug 1940; educ Fort Augustus Abbey Sch and RMA Sandhurst; Lt RMP; m 20 Oct 1962 *Dilys Mary, dau of Leslie Stuart, and has:

　1f *Duncan James Callum; b 1964

　1f *Fiona Mary Elspeth; b 1963

3e Peter; b and d 5 May 1942

4e *Andrew Turnbull; b 17 July 1943; educ Oban High Sch; RAF 1962–65; m 31 Jan 1970 *Susan, est dau of Brian Blennerhasset

5e Roderick Hugh; b 5 Aug 1945; d 24 Feb 1946

1e *Christian Margaret Lilias; b 2 March 1937; m 3 Jan 1959 *Michael Henry Charles Petre, only surv s of Bernard Francis Petre (see PETRE, B), and has issue

2e *Janet Marian; b 5 Feb 1947; m 1970 *John Donald Roberts

2d *Anna Mary; b 28 April 1909

2c (cont.) Malcolm Drummond m 2nd 16 June 1934 Margaret Triquet (d 1988), 3rd dau of Rev Arthur Browning, Rector Pangbourne, Berks, and d 10 April 1945

1b Frances Emily Cadogan; m 29 Dec 1857 Gen Edmund Henry Cox, RMA (d 1893), and d 7 April 1893, leaving issue

2b Julia; m 20 April 1870 Francis Adams, of Llyfnant, Cheltenham, and d 20 Oct 1907, leaving issue

3b Jane Charlotte; m 1st 26 Nov 1867 Henry Scott Gresley (dsp 27 Jan 1868); m 2nd 29 Oct 1878 Rev Nigel Walsingham Gresley (d 10 Nov 1909; see 1970 edn GRESLEY, Bt) and dsp 9 April 1900

4a (cont.) The Rev Arthur Drummond m 2nd 14 Sept 1857 Caroline Eliza Moring (dsp 7 April 1906), dau of R T M Grey, and d 26 Feb 1862

(3) Henry Roger (Rev); educ Ch Ch Oxford (MA); Rector Fawley, Hants; m Susannah (d 15 Nov 1808), yr dau of William Wells, of Holmewood, Hants, and d 27 July 1806, leaving, with other issue:

1a Andrew; d young

2a Henry Andrew; b 16 Dec 1791; Capt HEICMS; m 7 Oct 1819 Maria (d 14 Jan 1859), only dau of Capt William James Turquand, RN, and d 5 Aug 1869, having had:

　1b Barbara Catherine; b 10 March 1824; d unm

　2b Susan; d unm

　3b Henrietta; b 1 June 1826; m 15 June 1858 Prof F Le Gros Clark, FRS (d 1892), and d 9 June 1903, leaving issue

1a Catherine Elizabeth; b 1789; m 20 Aug 1822 Rev George Randolph, Rector Eastey, Kent, and Coulsdon, Surrey, and d 1873, leaving issue

4 Henry, of The Grange, Hants, and Charing Cross; banker; m 21 March 1761 Elizabeth (d 25 March 1819), dau of Hon Charles Compton (see NORTHAMPTON, M), and d 1795, leaving:

(1) Henry; b 13 Jan 1762; London banker; m 13 Feb 1786 Anne (m 2nd 18 Dec 1798 James Strange and d Jan 1852), dau of 1st Viscount Melville (qv), and d 4 July 1794, leaving:

1a Henry, of Albury Park, Surrey; b 4 Dec 1786; MP, FSA; m 23 June 1807 Lady Henrietta Hay-Drummond (d 7 Oct 1854), dau of 10th Earl of Kinnoull (qv), and d 20 Feb 1860, having had, with other issue:

　1b Louisa; m 26 May 1845 6th Duke of Northumberland (qv) and d 18 Dec 1890, leaving issue

2a Robert; b 24 June 1789; d 17 June 1811

3a Spencer Rodney (Rev); b 17 Dec 1790; m 6 May 1817 Caroline (d 7 April 1858), only dau of Montagu Montagu, and d 7 March 1882, leaving:

　1b Caroline Anne; m 26 April 1849 Rev Henry John Vernon and d 11 July 1883

1a Elizabeth; m 1 Aug 1815 John Portal and d 21 May 1877, leaving issue (see PORTAL, Bt)

The 5th VISCOUNT's n,
JAMES ANDREW JOHN LAURENCE CHARLES DRUMMOND, **6th Viscount Strathallan**; b 24 March 1767; Chief of Br settlement Canton, China; MP (Tory) Perths 1812–24, titles restored by Act of Parl 17 June 1824; rep S peer 1825–51; m 18 Jan 1809 Lady Amelia Sophia Murray (d 19 June 1849), dau of 4th Duke of Atholl (qv), and d 14 May 1851, having had:

1 WILLIAM HENRY, **7th Viscount**

2 James Robert (Sir), GCB; b 15 Sept 1812; Adml; Gentleman Usher Black Rod, a Ld Admlty 1861–66; m 5 Feb 1856 Catherine Frances (d 20 April 1914), dau of Adml Hon Sir George Elliot, KCB (see MINTO, E), and d 7 Oct 1895, leaving:

(1) Laurence George, CB (1907), CBE (1919), MVO (1906), JP, DL (Kent); b 13 March 1861; Maj-Gen cmdg 3rd Bn Scots Gds, Brig-Gen cmdg 7th Inf Bde, Southern Cmd 1908–12, DAQMG 2nd Army Corps and cmdg 19th Inf Bde 1914; Page of Honour to HM QUEEN VICTORIA, Mil Sec to Govr-Gen Canada, served Bechuanaland 1884–85, Ashanti 1895–96, Sudan 1898 (despatches), Boer War (despatches), WW I (despatches), Japanese Order Rising Sun 2nd Cl with Star; m 5 May 1886 Katherine Mary (d 1947), Japanese Order Precious Crown (d 9 Sept 1947), dau of Hugh Lindsay Antrobus (see ANTROBUS, Bt), and d 20 May 1946, having had:

1a Lindsay; b 31 Jan 1891; educ Eton; Lt 2nd Dragoons, RSG WW I, HG WW II; chm and md Lindsay Drummond Ltd; m 23 July 1924 Susan Cynthia Frances (d 1981), only dau of Alick William Cradock-Hartopp (see CRADOCK-HARTOPP, Bt), and d 21 June 1951, leaving:

　1b *Olivia Joan [Mrs James Perry, The Mill House, Winchelsea, E Sussex]; b 14 Feb 1929; educ Westonbirt and Sorbonne; m 1957 *Maj James Stuart Perry, SAS Regt, only s of Col Samuel Thomas James Perry, MC, TD, DL, of Cheshire, and has:

　　1c *Marcus Lindsay; b 30 May 1957

　　2c *Oliver James; b 5 June 1958

2a +James Arthur Laurence [Cdr James Drummond RN, Rectory House, Ogbourne St George, Wilts]; b 21 July 1905; T/F/O RAF WW II; m 15 Dec 1936 Patricia Marie (d 1990), only dau of Col Sir Edward Scott Worthington, KCVO, CB, CMG, CIE

1a Esmé Helen; b 21 Jan 1887; d 28 July 1899

2a Stella Katherine; b 22 May 1895; m 4 Dec 1918 1st Baron Percy of Newcastle (see NORTHUMBERLAND, D) and had issue

　(1) Lilias Anne; d unm 10 Feb 1945

　(2) Kate Gertrude; d unm 21 Feb 1936

　(3) Mary Virginia; d unm 12 Aug 1933

3 Edmund (Sir), KCIE; b 17 Jan 1814; barrister; Auditor-Gen India 1856–62, Lt Govr NW Provinces 1856–62 and memb Council; m 16 Nov 1837 Julia Mary (d 30 Nov 1898), dau of J C C Sutherland, of Calcutta, and d 10 Jan 1895, having had, with other issue:

(1) Edmund Charles; b 4 Aug 1841; Adml; C-in-C E Indies Station 1895–98; m 4 July 1872 Dora (d 20 Dec 1878), est dau of John Naylor, of Leighton Hall, Montgomeryshire, and d 6 May 1911, leaving:

1a John (Ian) Edmund, DL Forfarshire; b 5 July 1873; V-Adml, E Africa 1890, Boer War (despatches), WW I, Silver Medal Italy; m 18 June 1910 Louisa Olive (d 4 Oct 1965), dau of Sir Campbell Munro, 3rd Bt, of Lindertis (qv), and dsp 15 Nov 1926

1a Mary; d unm 11 Dec 1959

2a Constance Dora; m 14 Sept 1912 Adml Edward Francis Bruen, CB (d 22 Nov 1952), 2nd s of Henry Bruen, PC, of Co Carlow, and had issue

(2) Francis Colebrooke DRUMMOND later BERESFORD-DRUMMOND; b 6 Nov 1846; Capt Dorset Regt and 7th Dragoon Gds; m 23 June 1875 Marcia de la Poer (dsp 29 June 1908), only dau of Sir George de la Poer Beresford, 2nd Bt (see BERESFORD-PEIRSE, Bt), and d 9 April 1926

(1) Julia Mary; m 3 March 1863 Horace Abel Cockerell, CSI (d 23 April 1908), s of J Cockerell, and d 1891, leaving issue

4 Francis Charles; b 6 Sept 1815; m 8 Feb 1849 Charlotte Mary Atholl (d 13 June 1918), dau of Very Rev Sir Herbert Oakeley, 3rd Bt (qv), and dsp 26 Oct 1904

5 Robert Andrew John; b 4 Aug 1820; ICS; m 8 Nov 1854 Anna Maria (d 22 April 1871), dau of Compton Reade, and d 29 June 1887, having had:

(1) Frederick; b 22 Dec 1855; d 21 Sept 1856

(2) Malcolm; b 22 March 1857; m 23 Aug 1928 Rosa Elizabeth, dau of A C Hill, and dsp 1 Sept 1947

(3) Henry Murray (Rev); b 1 March 1858; Rector Byford with Mansel Gamage, Herefs, 1908–16; m 16 Oct 1888 Katherine Gamand (d 5 Feb 1950), dau of James Gwillim, and d 8 March 1932, having had:

1a Henry Murray; b 24 Aug 1893; 2nd Lt 8th Bn Roy Highrs; das 26 May 1916

1a Anna Maud; b 7 Dec 1889; d 9 Nov 1946

2a Olivia Margaret Murray; b 3 Oct 1891

(4) Walter John; b 24 June 1861; d unm 26 May 1918

(5) Robert Hugh; b 25 May 1862

(6) Herbert Charles; b 4 May 1864; m 7 Aug 1911 Helen Frances Mitcheson (d 19 April 1935), dau of Stanley Clark Bagg, of Montreal, and widow of Albert Edward Lewis, of Vancouver, and d 14 July 1938

(7) Arthur David; b 13 Oct 1865; m 26 April 1910 Constance Margaret, dau of John Parker, and d 9 Oct 1942

(8) Maurice Frederick; b 22, d 31 Dec 1866

(9) Ernest George (Rev); b 15 Feb 1868; MA Cantab; m 4 Oct 1911 Mabel Louisa (d 1 July 1943), dau of Maj-Gen R Godfrey Jones, ISC, and dsp 5 Nov 1946

(1) Anna Euphemia; b 18 Dec 1859; d unm 14 April 1904

6 Frederick; b 23 April 1822; HEICS; d 15 May 1848

1 Marianne Jane; m 18 Jan 1842 George Drummond Graeme, KH (d 20 Dec 1854), Maj Hanoverian Service, of Inchbackie and Aberuthven, Perthshire (see MONTROSE, D), and d 19 May 1876, leaving issue

2 Emily Anne; d 17 June 1829

The 6th VISCOUNT's est son,
WILLIAM HENRY DRUMMOND, **7th Viscount Strathallan**; b 5 March 1810; rep S peer 1853–86; Ld-in-Waiting; m 25 July 1833 Christina Mary Hersey (d 14 Feb 1867), sis of Sir David Baird of Newbyth, 2nd Bt (qv), and d 23 Jan 1886, having had:

1 JAMES DAVID, **8th Viscount**

2 William Henry; b 1 Aug 1845; ka Zululand July 1879

3 Robert Charles; b 2 Sept 1850; Capt Seaforth Highrs; d 27 June 1921

1 Amelia Anne; m 13 May 1858 Lt-Col Charles Greenhill Gardyne, DL (d 25 Nov 1923), Coldstream Gds, of Finavon, Angus, and d 5 Nov 1912, leaving issue

2 Margaret Alice; d unm 24 Aug 1875

3 Hersey Annabella; b 23 Oct 1846; d unm 23 Feb 1939

4 Frances Mary; b 1 July 1848; Maid of Honour to HM QUEEN VICTORIA 1872–1901; d unm 14 Jan 1947

The 7th VISCOUNT's est son,
JAMES DAVID DRUMMOND, **8th Viscount Strathallan**, JP, DL Perthshire; b 23 Oct 1839; Lt-Col 6th Dragoon Gds, Capt Bucks Yeo Cav; rep S peer 1890–93; m 1st 11 Feb 1868 Ellen (d 5 June 1873), 2nd dau of Cudbert B Thornhill, ICS, and d 5 Dec 1893, having had:

1 WILLIAM HUNTLY DRUMMOND, **9th Viscount Strathallan** and **6th Earl of Perth** (as which s distant cousin 1902); b 5 Aug 1871; Capt 3rd Bn Black Watch; m Jan 1911 Anna (d 3 Oct 1967), dau of Jacob Strauss, of Prague, and dsp 20 Aug 1937

1 Henrietta Alice; b 1869; d Feb 1870

2 Ellen Hersey; b 25 Oct 1872; d 2 Dec 1873

The **8th Viscount** m 2nd 27 Oct 1875 Margaret (d 5 Dec 1920), est dau of William Smythe, of Methven Castle, Perthshire, and by her had:

2 JAMES ERIC, **7th Earl**

3 Maurice Charles Andrew (Sir), KBE (1939), CMG (1919), DSO (1916); b 30 Nov 1877; educ Eton; Col Black Watch, Adj 2nd Bn 1904–07, Staff Capt No 1 Dist Scottish Cmd 1908–12, ADC to GOC Scottish Cmd 1912–13, Staff Capt 1915, DAAG 1915–17, AAG 1917–18, Assist Dir 1918–19, AAG 1920–23, Dep Dir Staff Duties Air Min 1923–27, AQMG E Cmd 1927–31, PA to Commr Met Police 1931, Ch Constable 1932, Dep Assist Commr 1933–35, Assist Commr Jan 1935, Dep Commr 1935–46; Page of Honour to HM QUEEN VICTORIA,

served Boer War (wounded, despatches), WW I (wounded, despatches five times, Legn Hon), OStJ; *m* 4 May 1904 Ida Mary (*d* 11 Dec 1966), 3rd dau of George James Drummond, of Swaylands, Penshurst, Kent (*see* above), and *d* 21 Feb 1957, leaving:

(1) +Maurice James David; *b* 17 Nov 1907; *educ* Eton; barrister Lincoln's Inn 1952; Hon Lt-Col Seaforth Highrs, memb Roy Co Archers

(1) Myra; *b* 15 April 1905; *m* 23 July 1935 Martin Roland Soames, s of Edward Roland Soames, and had issue

(2) *Monica Katharine; *b* 14 Sept 1916; *m* 20 April 1949 (*divorce* 1954) Francis Brian Sylvester Grimston (*see* VERULAM, E); *m* 2nd 21 July 1977 *Marcel Dingli-Attard dei Baroni Inguanez, BPhil, PhD, Heraldic Consultant, Baroncino of Ortigos, Hemsija, and Zabbaria, er s of Joseph Dingli-Attard de Baroni Inguanez, 18th Baron Hemsija and Zabbaria, 17th Baron Ortigos, of Maison Mon Plaisir, Mountbatten Street, Blata-I-Bajda, Malta GC

4 Edmund Rupert, CB (1937), CVO, DL (Ross and Cromarty 1956–60); *b* 8 May 1884; V-Adml, COS and Maintenance Capt to C-in-C Portsmouth 1930–32, COS to C-in-C America and WI Station 1932–33, First Naval memb NZ Naval Bd, cmded NZ Station 1935–38, ADC to HM GEORGE VI 1936, WW I: Battle of Jutland, WW II: Flag Offr i/c Portland Naval Base, Ch Staff Rosyth; *m* 11 May 1910 Lady Evelyn Frances Butler, er dau of 4th Marquess of Ormonde (*qv* 1970 edn), and *d* 9 Sept 1965, having had:

(1) James Ralph, DSO, DSC; *b* 28 March 1918; Lt RN, WW II; *ka* in cmd of HM Submarine *Sickle* 18 June 1944

(1) Anne; *b* 30 June 1911; *m* 1st 15 July 1930 (*divorce* 1941) Charles Michael Stratton, 2nd s of Charles John Stratton, and had issue; *m* 2nd 14 Feb 1941 (*divorce* 1946) Lt-Col Laurence Hyde Neild Bickmore, OBE, Roy Norfolk Regt, s of Harry C Bickmore, JP, and had further issue; *m* 3rd 16 Jan 1947 (*divorce* 1960) Lt-Col Iain Arthur Murray, DSO and bar (*see* DUNMORE, E); *m* 4th 25 Aug 1961 Brig James Charles Windsor Lewis, DSO and bar, MC (*d* 27 Oct 1964), only s of James Windsor Lewis, of Llwydcoed, Glam

(2) Jean Constance; *b* 20 Aug 1914; WW II as Sr Cmdt ATS; *m* 17 July 1947 Lt-Col (Walter) George Finney, TD (*d* 1 Oct 1973), only s of Walter Finney, of Edgbaston, Birmingham, and *d* 4 April 1997, leaving:

1a *Sarah Anne; *b* 11 May 1948; *m* 24 July 1971 *Giles Philip Curtis (*see* CURTIS, Bt) and has issue

2a *(Rachel) Mary; *b* 8 Aug 1950; *m* 24 July 1976 *John Jeremy Windham (*see* BOWYER-SMYTH, Bt) and has issue

3a *Elizabeth Jean; *b* 9 May 1952; *m* 1979 *Andrew William Kennedy Merriam (*see* AILSA, M) and has:

1b *Alexander George Laurence; *b* 1984

1b *Henrietta Jean; *b* 1982

(3) Margaret Cicely; *b* 13 Feb 1880; *m* 17 Dec 1912 Alfred Browning Stanley Tennyson and *d* 9 June 1963, leaving issue (*see* TENNYSON, B)

(4) Sybil Frances; *b* 20 Dec 1881; *d* unm 5 June 1965

The 15th EARL's half-bro,

JAMES ERIC DRUMMOND, **7th Earl of Perth**, GCMG (1934, KCMG 1916), CB (1914), PC (1933), DL (Hants); *b* 17 Aug 1876; *educ* Eton; rep S peer 1941–52; Clerk FO 1900, Priv Sec to: U-Secs For Affairs 1906–12, PM 1912–15 and For Sec 1915–19; Sec-Gen League Nations 1919–33; Amb Rome 1933–39, Ch Advsr For Publicity Min of Info 1939–40; Chm Hants Rivers Catchment Board 1942–47, Hon DCL Oxford and Liverpool; *m* 20 April 1904 Hon Angela Mary Constable Maxwell (*see* HERRIES OF TERREGLES, L) and *d* 15 Dec 1951, leaving:

1 JOHN DAVID DRUMMOND, **8th and present Earl of Perth**

1 Margaret Gwendolen Mary; *b* 5 May 1905; *m* 3 Feb 1937 John Walker, son of Hay Walker, of Pittsburgh, Pa., and had:

(1) *John Anthony Drummond; *b* 30 June 1942

(1) *Gillian Elizabeth Mary; *b* 22 June 1940

2 *Angela Alice Maryel [The Lady Angela De Wichfeld, 41 Lennox Gdns, London SW3; Marciana, Marina-Elba, Italy]; *b* 5 March 1912; *m* 1st 14 June 1937 (*divorce* 1959) Count Alessandro Agosto Giovanni Giacinto Barnabo Manassei di Collestate (*d* 20 Aug 1962), s of Count Manassei di Collestate, and has:

(1) *John Paul James Alessandro Camillo; *b* 16 Dec 1937; *m* 16 Dec 1965 (*divorce* 1975) Hon Susan Addington, 2nd dau of 7th Viscount Sidmouth (*qv*), and has:

1a *Hugo Alexander; *b* 12 Dec 1969

1a *Marina Catherine; *b* 14 Nov 1967

(2) *Michael David; *b* 2 April 1947; *m* 1978 Vanessa Bettine (*d* 1985), only dau of Cdr William Gordon Jack, RN (*see* TOLLEMACHE, B), and has:

1a *Nicholas Jason; *b* 1980

1a *Polly Tessa; *b* 1978

2a *Clare Alexandra; *b* 1981

3a *Miranda Frances Vanessa; *b* 1985

(1) *Alessandra Mary; *b* 27 Feb 1939; *m* 1959 *Franceso Montesi Righetti

2 (cont.) Lady Angela Manassei di Collestate *m* 2nd 26 Sept 1960 *Viggo Dmitri De Wichfeld, yr s of Stamhusbesidder Jorgen Adalbert Wichfeld, of Denmark, by Monica Emily Massy-Beresford (*see* MASSY, B)

3 *Gillian Mary [The Lady Gillian Anderson, Wilderwick House, East Grinstead, W Sussex RH19 3NS]; *b* 17 Feb 1920; *m* 28 Jan 1946 Capt John Murray Anderson, MC and bar (*d* 1991), Seaforth Highrs, memb Roy Co Archers, s of Lt-Col Ian Forest Anderson, OBE, JP, DL, and has:

(1) *James Ian [James Anderson Esq, Roro Lodge, Glenlyon, Perths PH15 2PW]; *b* 1 Nov 1952; *educ* Eton; memb Roy Co Archers; *m* 1st 1981 (*divorce* 1985) Victoria Anne, twin dau of Henry Robert Hildyard, of Sussex, and has:

1a *Alice Mona; *b* 1983

(1) (cont.) James Anderson *m* 2nd 1988 *Hon Emily Mary, dau of 3rd Viscount Astor (*qv*) and formerly w of Alan Gregory, and by her has:

1a *Thomas Alexander; *b* 1990

2a *Rory John; *b* 1991

2a *Liza Kate; *b* 1993

3a *Isobel Nancy (twin); *b* 1993

(1) *Sarah Mary; *b* 17 May 1947

(2) *Elizabeth Jane; *b* 1949

---

(3) *Camilla Gillian; *b* 12 April 1957; *m* 1st 4 Aug 1979 (*divorce* 1992) Matthew Aidan Craig Balfour, s of John Balfour, of Birling, Kent, and has:

1a *Alexander John; *b* 1986

1a *Emily Kate Mary; *b* 1984

(3) (cont.) Mrs Camilla Balfour *m* 2nd 1993 *Mark Ronald Shearring, 3rd s of Ronald George Shearring

PESTON

Creation: B. (LP, UK) 1987

THE BARON PESTON, of Mile End, Greater London (Maurice Harry Peston) [The Rt Hon The Lord Peston, Queen Mary Coll, London U, London E1]; *b* 19 March 1931; *educ* Bellevue, Bradford, Hackney Downs London, LSE (BSc Econ) and Princeton USA; sci offr and sr sci offr Army Ops Research Gp 1954–57; assist lecturer, lecturer and reader economics LSE 1957–65; ec advsr: Treasury 1962–64, MOD 1964–66; memb: Ho Lds Select Ctee Nationalised Industries 1966–70 and 1972–73, CNAA 1967–73, SSRC 1976–79; special advsr to Sec State: DES 1974–75, Prices 1976–79, Cncl Roy Pharmaceutical Soc GB 1986–; Queen Mary Coll London U: Prof Economics 1965–88, Emeritus Prof 1988–, Fell 1992–; Chm: Pools Panel 1991–, NFER 1991–; Fell: Portsmouth Poly 1987, QMW 1992; author: *Elementary Matrices for Economics* (1969); *Public Goods and the Public Sector* (1972), *Theory of Macroeconomic Policy* (1974, 2nd edn 1982), *Whatever Happened to Macroeconomics?* (1980), *The British Economy* (1982, 2nd edn 1984); *m* 1958 *Helen, dau of Joseph Conroy, and has:

1 *Robert James Kenneth; *b* 1960

2 *Edmund Charles Richard; *b* 1964

1 *Juliet Clare Elaine; *b* 1961

Lineage: ABRAHAM PESTON; *m* Yetta — and had:

MAURICE HARRY, *cr* a **Baron**

PETIT

Arms: Azure, on a chevron argent, between three urns of the last, therefrom issuant flames proper, as many bees volant, also proper. **Crest:** A ship under sail at sea, in front thereof an anchor fesswise, all proper. **Motto:** *Consequitur quodcunque petit* ('He obtains whatever he seeks'). **Creation:** Bt. (UK) 1 Sept 1890.

SIR DINSHAW MANOCKJEE PETIT, 4TH BT, of Petit Hall, Island of Bombay [Sir Dinshaw Petit Bt, Ruimzicht 207, 1068 CV Amsterdam, Netherlands]; *b* 13 Aug 1934; *s* f 1983 and changed his name from Naswanji Dinshaw Petit to Dinshaw Manockjee Petit; *educ* Prince of Wales Indian Mil Coll and Malvern; Pres: N M Petit Charities, Sir D M Petit Charities, F D Petit Sanatorium, Petit Girls' Orphanage, D M Petit Gymnasium, J N Petit Inst of Native Gen Dispensary and Persian Zoroastrian Amelioration Fund, tstee Soc for Prevention Cruelty Animals, memb Management Ctee B D Petit Parsi Gen Hosp; *m* 1st 18 April 1964 (*divorce* 1985) Nirmala Mody, dau of Maj-Gen — Nanavati, MC, and has:

1 +JEHANGIR; *b* 21 Jan 1965

2 +Framjee; *b* 5 Dec 1968

Sir DINSHAW *m* 2nd 1986 *Elizabeth Maria Tinkelenberg

Lineage: NUSSERWANJEE COWASJEE; *b* 1770; *m* Bhikhaijee, dau of Framjee Jogajee Pahrana, and *d* 20 Dec 1820, having had:

MANOCKJEE NUSSERWANJEE PETIT; *b* 26 Aug 1803; merchant; *m* Humabal Jejeebhoy Dadabhoy Moogana (*b* 1809; *d* 13 Oct 1851) and *d* 21 May 1859, having had, with a yr s (Nusserwanjee Manockjee, *d* unm Nov 1891):

Sir JEJEEBHOY FRAMJEE PETIT later DINSHAW MANOCKJEE PETIT (under terms of a trust of 25 lakhs of rupees which also imposed the name on his successors), **1st Bt** (UK), so *cr* 1 Sept 1890, with limitation to his 2nd s and the latter's heirs male and in default thereof to the other sons and their heirs male of the body; *b* June 1823; Sheriff Bombay, ktd 1887, cotton mill-owner, memb Parsee Punchayet Bombay, delegate Parsee Ch Matrimonial Court, Pres:Assoc Amelioration of Poor Zoroastrians in Persia and Petit Charity Funds, Petit Inst Parsee Orphanage; Memb Municipal Corp Bombay, MLC Govt Bombay; *m* 27 Feb 1837 Sakerbai Framjee (*d* 5 March 1890), dau of Framjee Bhikhajee Panday, of Bombay, and had:

1 Cowasjee Dinshaw; *b* 6 June 1845; *m* 17 Feb 1859 Awabai Merwanjee Jejeebhoy Moogana (*d* 1909) and *d* 23 Oct 1878, having had:

(1) Manockjee Cowasjee; *b* 18 July 1863; *m* 28 Feb 1872 Humabai Sorabjee Jamsetjee (*d* 22 June 1942) and *d* 30 Nov 1935

(2) Merwanjee Cowasjee; *b* 18 July 1863; *d* 9 June 1879

(3) Pestonjee Cowasjee; *b* 10 Sept 1866; *m* 8 May 1894 Perojbai Cowasjee Parukh (*d* 12 June 1945) and *d* 1932, leaving:

  1a Hirabai; *b* 10 Sept 1896

(4) Hormusjee Cowasjee; *b* 11 Nov 1868; *m* 12 April 1891 Perozbai Sorabjee Patuck and *d* 1939, leaving:

  1a Cowasjee; *b* 14 Dec 1893; *m* 1919 Nawajbai Pherozshaw Dadyburjor and had:

    1b *Sorabjee; *b* 1921; *m* 1946 *Cleta Mathias and has:

      1c *Marius; *b* 1948

      2c *Stephen; *b* 1950

      3c *Sean; *b* 1953

      4c *Gavin; *b* 1960

      1c *Cory Ann; *b* 1951

      2c *Jenne Lou; *b* 1955

    2b *Sheila; *b* 1926; *m* 1953 *Julian Bartlett and has:

      1c *Darius; *b* 1955

      2c *Zarir; *b* 1958

      3c *Pheroza; *b* 1959

  2a *Dinshawjee, BA, LLB, slr Bombay High Court; *b* 14 July 1903; *m* 1940 *Mitha D Pocha, BA, and has:

    1b *Homa Dinshaw [Homa Petit, Ram Mansion, Nepean Sea Road, Bombay 6, India]; *b* 5 Dec 1945; *educ* The Cathedral and John Connor High Sch and Sydenham Coll of Commerce and Economics (BCom Bombay)

    1b *Freny Dinshaw; *b* 10 Sept 1941; *educ* Elphinstone Coll, Bombay U (BA, S K Patel gold medal) and Berkeley U California (MA)

  1a Mithibai; *b* 10 April 1892

(5) Cursetjee Cowasjee; *b* 29 June 1871; *d* 1926

(6) Virbaijee Cowasjee; *b* 23 Dec 1872; *m* 11 Dec 1883 Nusserwanjee Muncherjee Cama and *d* 1934, leaving:

  1a Muncherjee Nusserwanji, JP (Bombay State 1958); *b* 25 June 1895; *educ* Bombay U (BSc); owner *Bombay Chronicle*; *m* 1919 Avabai Dunjibhoy Jeejeebhoy and had:

    1b *Nusserwanji; *b* 4 Feb 1921; *m* 1945 *Banoo M Cassinath and has:

      1c *Virbajee; *b* 14 Oct 1950

      2c *Muncherji; *b* 1 Jan 1957

      3c *Hormusji; *b* 13 Feb 1961

    2b *Rustomji; *b* 22 May 1922. *m* 1951 *Mehroo J Kapadia and has:

      1c *Meherwanji; *b* 9 Aug 1954

      2c *Avabai; *b* 28 June 1957

  1a Perojbai; *b* 13 Dec 1892; *m* Tehmurasp M Cama

  2a Ruttenbai; *b* 14 Sept 1897; *m* Rustom S Ghandi

  3a Sheernaj; *b* 4 July 1902

  4a Tehemina; *b* 19 Dec 1906; *d* 1915

(7) Ardesir Cowasjee; *b* 22 May 1874; *d* 22 Oct 1886

(8) Sorabjee Cowasjee; *b* 9 April 1877; *m* 1896 Jerbal Burjorjee Lam

(9) Furdoonjee Cowasjee; *b* 29 Oct 1878; *m* 4 Jan 1899 Dinbia Bomonkee Petit (*see below*) and *d* 27 Jan 1964

(1) Mithibai Cowasjee; *b* 18 March 1870; *m* 1883 Merwanjee Dhunjebhoy Jejebhoy Moogana and *d* 19–

(2) Soonabai Cowasjee; *b* 15 Aug 1875; *m* 1899 Jehangir Framjee Batliboy and had issue

2 Framjee Dinshaw; *b* 19 Jan 1848; *m* 17 Feb 1859 Awabal Nusserwanjee Manockjee Petit and *dvp* 8 Aug 1895, leaving:

(1) JEJEEBHOY FRAMJEE (DINSHAW MANOCKJEE) (Sir), **2nd Bt**

(1) Humabai Framjee; *b* 12 Aug 1881; *m* J K Mehta and *d* 29 Oct 1955

3 Bomanjee Dinshaw; *b* 27 March 1859; MLC Bombay, chm Bank of Bombay, Tstee Parsee Panchayat, JP, merchant and millowner; *m* 25 Feb 1872 Gulbai Nanabhoy Byramjee Jejeebhoy Moogana, and *d* 17 Dec 1915, having had:

(1) Jehangir Bomonjee; *b* 21 Aug 1879; merchant, millowner, memb Bombay Municipal Corp 1901–30, Parsee Ch Matrimonial Court Delegate 1902–22, Hon Presidency Magistrate 1904–15, Fndr-Pres B D Petit Parsee Gen Hosp 1912–46 and Indian Progressive Fedn 1920, Memb Indian Chamber Commerce 1913–14, Fndr and Hon Sec Imp Indian Citizenship Assoc 1915–32 and Victoria Meml Sch for Blind, Pres Bombay Millowners' Assoc 1915–16 and 1928–29, Tstee Parsee Punchayet Bombay 1916–34, memb: Bombay Improvement Bd 1920–30, Bombay Devpt Bd 1920–34, MLC Bombay 1921–34, Fndr *The Indian Daily Mail* 1923–31, Fell Bombay U 1928–34, pres Bombay SPCA 1933; *m* 7 May 1898 Jaijee Sorabee Patuck, MBE, Kaisar-i-Hind silver medal (*d* 15 June 1954), and *d* 4 Feb 1946, leaving:

  1a Byramjee; *b* 21 Nov 1900; *educ* Cambridge (BA); barrister; *m* 19– Eileen Terry and *d* 28 June 1950

  2a Dinshaw ; *b* 19 July 1905; *educ* Cambridge (BA 1928); barrister 1929, MRCS, LRCP 1943, DPM 1948; *m* 13 Oct 1928 Esme Violet Ingram (*d* Oct 1969) and *dsp* 25 March 1969

  1a Hilla; *b* 20 Jan 1899

(2) Dhunjibhoy Bomanjee, JP Bombay; *b* 12 Sept 1881; merchant, millowner; Hon Presidency Magistrate, Hon Sec and Treas Gokuldees Tejpa Hosp Nursing Assoc, memb Millowners' Assoc Bombay, delegate Parsee Ch Matrimonial Court; *m* 15 Feb 1900 Hamabai (*d* 2 July 1949), est dau of Jaibhoy Ardeshir Sett, and *d* 14 April 1957, leaving:

1a +Manockjee [Manockjee Petit, Sett Minar, Pedder Road, Bombay, India]; *b* 10 Nov 1900; *educ* Bombay U (BA); Pres B D Petit Parsee Gen Hosp 1957; *m* 21 March 1927 *Perin Maneckji Vacha

1a *Rati (became Buddhist 1946, renamed Li Gotami); *b* 22 April 1906; *m* 1st 7 April 1934 (*divorce*) Karl J Khandalawala, barrister; *m* 2nd 23 April 1947 *Lama Anagarika Govinda

2a *Comie [Mrs Rustom Vakharia, Silvan Roche, 21 Carmichael Road, Bombay 26, India]; *b* 3 Nov 1908; *educ* Bombay U (BA, LLB, BT); *m* 1939 *Rustom F Vakharia and has:

  1b *Sylla [Mrs Girish Malvi, Anand, 8th Rd, Khar, Bombay 52, India], MSc; *b* 21 April 1940; *m* 19– *Girish Malvi and has:

    1c *Shona; *b* 11 April 1969

    2c *Roshan, BA; *b* 28 Nov 1943

(1) Dinbai Bomanjee; *b* 27 Sept 1882; *m* 4 Jan 1899 Furdoonjee Cawasjee Petit (*see above*) and *d* 1965

(2) Peroshaw Bomanjee; *b* 13 Nov 1884; *d* unm 1954

(3) Maneckbai Bomanjee; *b* 11 Nov 1887; *m* 1916 Sorab Nanabhoy Moos, CIE, MA, and had:

  1a *Behman Sorab; *b* 18 Nov 1917; MD, MRCP; *m* 1956 *Bhikhu, dau of Meherwanji Batliboy, and has:

    1b *Darius; *b* 13 Dec 1957

  2a *Jamshed Sorab, MD, MRCP; *b* 25 Sept 1925; *m* 1953 *Perin, dau of Kaikobad Junaiwalla, and has:

    1b *Feroze; *b* 30 Oct 1957

    1b *Deena; *b* 3 June 1954

  1a *Silla Sorab [Mrs Navai Ardeshir, Salisbury House, 82 Pali Hill, Bandra, Bombay 50 AS, India]; *b* 21 Dec 1921; *m* 22 Sept 1947 *Navai J Ardeshir and has:

    1b *Jer Navai; *b* 5 March 1949

    2b *Sohrab Navai; *b* 23 April 1962

    1b *Shireen Navai; *b* 7 Dec 1951

    2b *Frainy Navai; *b* 4 May 1955

1 Bhikhaijee Dinshaw; *b* 29 Sept 1844; *m* 11 Feb 1857 Dady Nusserwanjee Dadysett and had issue

2 Navajbai Dinshaw; *b* 6 June 1849; *m* 17 Feb 1859 Peroshaw Merwanjee Jeejeebhoy Moogana

3 Ruttenbai Dinshaw; *b* 19 Nov 1854; *m* 11 May 1867 Framjee Dorabjee Panday and *d* 5 Nov 1885, leaving issue

4 Humabai Dinshaw; *b* 3 May 1856; *m* 11 May 1807 Framjee Rustomjee Cama and had issue

5 Heerabai Dinshaw; *b* 19 Oct 1857; *m* 11 Feb 1870 Jamsetjee Nusserwanjee Petit (*d* 1888)

6 Manockbai Dinshaw; *b* 11 Oct 1860; *m* 28 Aug 1879 Peroshaw Bomonjee Jejeebhoy Moogana and had issue

7 Buchoobai Dinshaw; *b* 11 Oct 1862; *m* 9 Oct 1876 Merwanjee Sorabjee Jamsetjee (*d* 1900)

8 Gulbai Dinshaw; *b* 16 Nov 1865; *m* 5 March 1872 Rostomjee Nanabhoy Beramjee Moogana and *d* 1878

The 1st Bt *d* 5 May 1901; his gs,

Sir Jamsetjee Jejeebhoy Petit, 2nd Bt, JP; *b* 7 June 1873; *m* 3 March 1894 Dinbai, dau of Sir Jamsetjee Jejeebhoy, 3rd Bt (*qv*), and had:

1 FRAMJEE DINSHAW (DINSHAW MANOCKJEE) (Sir), **3rd Bt**

2 Manockjee Dinshaw; *b* 30 April 1904; *d* 10 March 1950

3 Jamsetjee Dinshaw; *b* 14 Dec 1911; *d* 3 Jan 1959

1 Ruttenbai Dinshaw; *b* 20 Feb 1900; *m* Mahomed Ali Jinnah (*d* 11 Sept 1948), barrister, fndr Pakistan, and *d* Feb 1929, leaving issue

The 2nd Bt *d* 29 March 1933; his est s,

Sir Dinshaw Manockjee Petit, 3rd Bt; *b* 24 June 1901; *educ* Trin Hall Cambridge (BA 1924); barrister Inner Temple 1925, Pres J N Petit Tech High Sch for Boys Poona and A F Petit High Sch for Girls, Chm J N Petit Inst, Pres SPCA Bombay and Petit Hosp for Animals, hon life memb RSPCA London, life Govr Royal Hosp for Incurables London, Pres Northbrook Soc London, V-Pres Br Assoc Alpes-Maritimes France; *m* Sylla (*d* 21 June 1963), dau of R D Tata, of Bombay, and *d* 1983, leaving:

1 Sir NASWANI later DINSHAW MANOCKJEE PETIT, **4th and present Bt**

1 *Dina; *b* 13 Sept 1931; *m* 17 April 1961 *Yves Jean Robert Louis Morange and has:

(1) *Shireen Isabelle; *b* 13 Jan 1962

(2) *Ann Dina; *b* 21 April 1965

PETO of Barnstaple

Arms: Barry or and gules per pale indented counterchanged, in chief a boar's head erased proper and in base two annulets counterchanged. **Crest:** On a rock proper a sinister wing or, thereon three annulets gules. **Motto:** *Ad finem fidelis* ('Faithful to the end'). **Creation:** Bt. (UK) 27 Jan 1927.

SIR MICHAEL HENRY BASIL PETO, 4TH BT, of Barnstaple, Co Devon [Sir Michael Peto Bt, Kirknewton House, nr Wooler, Northumberland NE71 6XF]; *b* 6 April 1938; *s f* 1980; *educ* Eton and Ch Ch Oxford (MA 1965); barrister Inner Temple 1960, memb Stock Exchange 1963–98, Canada Life 1998–; *m* 1st 24 Oct 1963 (*divorce* 1971) Sarah Susan, yst dau of Sir Dennis Frederic Bankes Stucley, 5th Bt (*qv*), and has:

1 +HENRY CHRISTOPHER MORTON BAMPFYLDE [Henry Peto Esq, Court Hall, North Molton, Devon EX36 3HP]; *b* 8 April 1967; *educ* Eton; *m* 27 June 1998 *Louise Imogen, dau of Christopher Balck-Foote, of Berks

1 *Emma Rose; *b* 28 May 1965; *m* 1994 *Harry N Matovu, yr s of Leonard Matovu, of Vienna, and has:

   (1) *Joseph Nathaniel Bukenya; *b* 17 Aug 1997

2 *Marina Sarah; *b* 24 Sept 1968

Sir MICHAEL *m* 2nd 1971 *Lucinda Mary, dau of Sir Charles Douglas Blackett, 9th Bt (*qv*), and formerly w of Ewan Iain Macleod Hilleary, and by her has:

2 +Hugh David; *b* 1974

3 +Charles Michael; *b* 1977

Lineage: Sir SAMUEL MORTON PETO, 1st Bt (*see* PETO, Bt, of Somerleyton); had a 7th s:

Sir Basil Edward Peto, 1st Bt (UK), so *cr* 27 Jan 1927, JP Wilts; *b* 13 Aug 1862; MP (C) E Wilts 1910–18 and Barnstaple 1922–23 and 1924–35, Commr for repatriation of Belgian refugees 1918, Cdr Order Leopold Belgium; *m* 30 Aug 1892 Mary Matilda Annie (*d* 3 Nov 1931), dau of Capt Thomas Carpendale Baird (*see* HAWARDEN, V), and *d* 28 Jan 1945, leaving:

1 **Sir (James) Michael Peto, 2nd Bt**, JP (Ross-shire 1952), DL (1951); *b* 8 May 1894; *educ* Harrow and Balliol Coll Oxford; Lt-Col Coldstream Gds, WWs I (despatches) and II, DAQMG Staff HQ London Dist 1939, AQMG 1940, AD Tport War Office (MLO to Min Tport 1942–45); *m* 17 Feb 1920 Frances G (*d* 14 March) 1971), est dau of Rev Canon William Hartley Carnegie, Sub-Dean Westminster Abbey, and *d* 24 March 1971, leaving:

   (1) *Serena Mary Francesca [Serena Lady Matheson of Matheson, Trees Farm, Standerwick, Somerset BA11 2PP; Dalmhor, North Side, Duirinish, Kyle of Lochalsh, Ross-shire IV40 8BE]; *b* 28 Feb 1928; *m* 21 April 1954 Maj Sir Torquhil Alexander Matheson, 6th Bt (*qv*), and has issue

2 CHRISTOPHER HENRY MAXWELL (Sir) **3rd Bt**

3 (Basil Arthur) John; *b* 13 Dec 1900; *educ* Harrow and St John's Coll Cambridge (BA 1922); Maj King's Dragoon Gds, ADC to Govr Bombay 1929–31, MP King's Norton 1941–45, PPS to Chm Oil Control Bd 1941–45; *m* 18 July 1934 *Patricia Geraldine [Mrs Hugh Ryder, 66 Whitelands House, Cheltenham Terr, London SW3] (*m* 2nd 12 June 1955 Lt-Col Hugh Granville Leveson Dudley Ryder, TD; *see* HARROWBY, E), yst dau of Gerald Macleay Browne, OBE, and *d* 3 Feb 1954, leaving:

   (1) +Jonathan Basil Morton [Jonathan Peto Esq, Bealings House, Woodbridge, Suffolk IP13 6NP]; *b* 9 Dec 1942; *educ* Eton; Coldstream Gds 1962–66, ADC to Govr Qld 1963–66; *m* 28 May 1969 *Hon Selina Lilian Hughes-Young, 2nd dau of 1st Baron St Helens (*qv*), and has:

     1a +Amyas John; *b* 22 Dec 1969

     2a +Harold Patrick Basil; *b* 24 Oct 1974

     1a *Daisy Elizabeth; *b* 9 June 1971

     2a *Augusta Mary; *b* 14 Sept 1977

     3a *Violet Selina; *b* 15 Feb 1984

   (1) *Virginia Anne [Mrs George Cox, Raswell Cottage, Loxhill, Surrey GU8 4BG]; *b* 25 June 1935; *m* 27 April 1955 (*divorce* 1981) Gerard Wyndham Morgan-Grenville (*see* KINLOSS, L) and has issue; *m* 2nd 5 Dec 1998 *George A Cox

---

   (2) *Joanna Dava [Mrs Charles Moncrieff, Easter Elcho, Rhynd, Perthshire PH2 8QQ]; *b* 5 Dec 1938; *m* 15 June 1957 *Capt Charles St John Graham Moncrieff, Scots Gds (*see* BOLINGBROKE and SAINT JOHN, V), and has:

     1a *Alexander Charles Graham; *b* 12 Sept 1967

     1a *Charlotte Henrietta; *b* 26 April 1959; *m* 1987 (*divorce* 1993) Benjamin Heath, yr s of William Heath, of Guildford, and has:

       1b *Rory William; *b* 1988

       1b *Pollyanna Rose; *b* 1992

     2a *Miranda Caroline; *b* 1961; *m* 1983 *Hon Mark Francis Robert Baring, est s of 7th Baron Ashburton (*qv*), and has issue

     3a *Rosanna Claire; *b* 23 April 1965; *m* 1995 *David Charles McCraith, er s of Anthony McCraith

   (3) *Sarah Christian Pandora; *b* 6 July 1940; *m* 29 Aug 1959 *Adml of the Fleet Sir (David) Benjamin Bathurst (*see* BATHURST, E) and has issue

The 2nd Bt's bro,

   Sir Christopher Henry Maxwell Peto, 3rd Bt, DSO (1945), DL (Devon 1950–55, Wilts 1956); *b* 19 Feb 1897; *educ* Harrow and RMC Sandhurst; served WW I (wounded, despatches), WW II (wounded, despatches three times), Col 9th Queen's Royal Lancers 1950–60, later Brig cmdg, MP Barnstaple 1945–50 and N Devon 1950–55, CC Wilts 1955, Chm TA&AFA Wilts 1957–61, Legn Hon, Orders Leopold Belgium, White Lion Czechoslovakia, Polonia Restituta, French and Belgian Croix de Guerre, Czech War Cross; *m* 3 Oct 1935 Barbara (*d* 1992), yr dau of Edwyn Thomas Close, of Camberley, Surrey, and *d* 19 May 1980, leaving:

1 Sir MICHAEL HENRY BASIL PETO, **4th and present Bt**

2 +Nicholas John [Nicholas Peto Esq, Grey Walls, Chadlington, Oxon OX7 3NQ]; *b* 4 Oct 1939; *educ* Eton and RMA Sandhurst; Capt 9th/12th Lancers, ADC to GOC 2 Div 1964; *m* 1st 11 April 1969 (*divorce* 1978) Anne Colquhoun, er dau of John Tyson, of New York, and has:

   (1) +Alexander Tyson; *b* 5 July 1973

2 (cont.) Nicholas Peto *m* 2nd 1979 (*divorce* 1989) Lucinda Hilary, dau of Owen George Endicott Roberts and formerly w of Demetri P Marchessini; *m* 3rd 1991 *Zoë, dau of Charles Douglas Neville Walker, of Paris, and formerly w of Anthony Henry (Harry) Westropp

1 *Elizabeth Mary [Mrs Ronald Murphy, Shippool House, Innishannon, Co Cork, Ireland]; *b* 8 July 1936; *m* 28 May 1958 *Ronald Philip Murphy, yr s of Norbert Murphy, of Lauriston, Glanmire, Co Cork, and has:

   (1) *Charles Christopher Ronald; *b* 15 April 1959

   (2) *Richard Norbert; *b* 15 April 1961

PETO of Somerleyton

Arms: Barry of six per pale indented or and gules, two annulets in fess all counterchanged. **Crest:** On a rock proper a sinister wing or, charged with three annulets in chevron gules. **Motto:** *Ad finem fidelis* ('Faithful to the end'). **Creation:** Bt. (UK) 22 Feb 1855.

SIR HENRY GEORGE MORTON PETO, 4TH BT, of Somerleyton, Co Suffolk [Sir Henry Peto Bt, Stream House, Selborne, Alton, Hants GU34 3LE]; *b* 29 April 1920; *s f* 1978; *educ* Sherborne and Corpus Christi Coll Cambridge; late Capt RA; *m* 1947 *Frances Jacqueline, JP (Guildford 1962), dau of Ralph Haldane Evers, of Milan, and has:

1 +FRANCIS MICHAEL MORTON [Francis Peto Esq, Cowdenknowes Mains, Earlston, Berwickshire TD4 6AA]; *b* 11 Jan 1949; *educ* Sherborne and Leeds U; *m* 12 Oct 1974 *Felicity Margaret, er dau of Lt-Col John Alan Burns (*see* HOPE-DUNBAR, Bt), and has:

   (1) +David James Morton; *b* 25 Aug 1978

   (2) +George Francis John; *b* 1980

2 +Robert Henry Haldane [Robert Peto Esq, 117 East Sheen Ave, London SW14 8AX]; *b* 18 Sept 1950; *educ* Sherborne and Corpus Christi Coll Cambridge; *m* 1975 *Susan, only dau of William Judge, of E Sheen, and has:

   (1) +Thomas William Morton; *b* 22 Nov 1977

   (2) +Edward Henry Haldane; *b* 7 Oct 1979

Lineage: JAMES PETO; *m* Mary Bennet and had:

WILLIAM PETO, of Cookham, Berks; *b* 19 July 1768; *m* 29 Oct 1808 Sophia, dau of Ralph Alloway, of Dorking, and *d* 12 Jan 1849, leaving:

1 (SAMUEL) MORTON (Sir), **1st Bt**

2 William, of Cookham; *b* 25 Sept 1811; *m* 3 March 1840 Emma (*d* 15 Aug 1885 aged 75), dau of Joseph Hobbs, of Brockmer, and *d* 25 June 1879, leaving issue

3 James, of Lowestoft, Suffolk, JP; *b* 5 Dec 1815; *m* 30 Jan 1847 Mary (*d* 28 May 1893), dau of John Lawrence, of Bisham, Berks, and *d* 17 June 1898, leaving issue

1 Sophia; *m* 24 Oct 1839 W French, of London

2 Ann; *m* 6 July 1843 Edward Ladd Betts, of Preston Hall, Kent, JP

The est son,

Sir (Samuel) Morton Peto, 1st Bt (UK), so *cr* 22 Feb 1855; *b* 4 Aug 1809; building and rlwy contractor, MP Norwich, Finsbury and Bristol; *m* 1st 18 May 1831 Mary (*d* 20 May 1842), dau of Thomas de la Garde Grissell, of Stockwell, Surrey, and had, with a dau (*d* unm):

1 **Sir Henry Peto, 2nd Bt**, DL Dorset; *b* 10 Aug 1840; *educ* Trin Coll Cambridge (MA, Pres Union) and London U (BA); barrister Inner Temple; Dorset: CC 1886–1913, High Sheriff 1897–98; *m* 16 July 1874 Mary Ann Susan (*d* 9 Aug 1939), yr dau of Rev Thomas Fuller, Vicar St Peter's, Eaton Sq, and *dsp* 6 April 1938

1 Mary; *m* 22 Sept 1852 Penruddocke Wyndham (*d* 29 July 1910) and *d* 1 May 1876, leaving issue

2 Ann; *m* 25 April 1854 James Alexander Campbell (*d* 9 May 1908), PC, of Stracathro, MP Glasgow and Aberdeen U, and *d* 15 Sept 1887, leaving issue

Sir Morton *m* 2nd 12 July 1843 Sarah Ainsworth (*d* 6 Jan 1892), est dau of Henry Kelsall, of Rochdale, and *d* 13 Nov 1889, having by her had:

2 Morton Kelsall; *b* 5 Dec 1845; *m* 12 Nov 1884 Olivia Georgina Elizabeth (*d* 23 July 1945), dau of Capt Hon Francis Maude, RN (*see* HAWARDEN, V), and *d* 13 March 1921, leaving:

(1) HENRY FRANCIS MORTON (Sir), **3rd Bt**

(2) Raymond Harold Kelsall; *b* 16 Nov 1897; *educ* Lond U (BSc); *k* while climbing on the Jungfrau 19 Aug 1931

(1) Ruth Sarah Maude; *b* 16 Nov 1885; Head Mistress St George's Sch San Remo; *d* unm 4 March 1975

(2) Dorothy Olivia Georgiana, OBE (1920), KPM; *b* 15 Dec 1886; Staff Offr Women's Section Met Police 1930–32, Superintendent 1932–46, Staff Offr Surrey Special Constabulary 1951–59; *d* 26 Feb 1974

(3) Katharine Ainsworth; *b* 7 April 1892; *d* unm 29 Dec 1976

(4) Audrey Elizabeth; *b* 21 April 1894; *m* 10 Feb 1923 (*annulled* 1933) Robert Andrew Yates, s of Dr G W Yates, of Dublin, and *dsp* 27 Nov 1958

3 William Herbert; *b* 15 Jan 1849; *m* 30 Dec 1874 Kate (*d* 1 Nov 1922), dau of Sir Robert Palmer Harding, KCB, and *d* 20 Sept 1927, having had:

(1) Ralph Harding; *b* 11 Feb 1877; Lt 10th Roy Hus, Maj RAF, Lt Roy E Kent Yeo, 2nd Sec Dip Serv; *m* 1st 21 July 1909 (*divorce* 1923, she resumed maiden name 1926) Frances Ruby Vera (*d* 27 July 1951), only child of Col Walter James Lindsay (*see* CRAWFORD and BALCARRES, E), and had:

1a Timothy Clement, MC; *b* 23 Jan 1921; Capt Scots Gds WW II; *d* of wounds in Italy 24 April 1945

1a *(Maud) Rosemary [Miss Maud Peto, c/o Coutts Bank, Duncannon Branch, 440 Strand, London WC2]; *b* 29 March 1916 (HM QUEEN MAUD OF NORWAY stood sponsor); *m* 27 July 1934 (*divorce* 1958 resumed maiden surname by deed poll 5 June 1961) Viscount Hinchingbrooke (later 10th Earl of Sandwich; *qv*) and has issue

(1) (cont.) Maj Ralph Peto *m* 2nd 1 Dec 1937 HSH Princess Mechtilde Christiane Lichnowsky (*d* 4 June 1958), widow of HSH Karl Max, 6th Prince Lichnowsky, GCVO, former German Amb to UK, and dau of Count Maximillian von Arco-Zinneberg, and *d* 3 Sept 1945

(2) Geoffrey Kelsall (Sir), KBE (1939, CBE 1919); *b* 8 Sept 1878; *educ* Eton; Capt Roy Wilts Yeo WW I, MP Frome 1924–29 and Wolverhampton Bilston 1931–35, PPS to: Sec for Mines 1926, Parly U-Sec India 1928 and Pres BOT 1931–35, Chm Food Cncl 1936–39, memb Runciman Mission Czechoslovakia 1938, Dir Projectile Contingents Min Munitions, Dep Regnl CD Commr SW Div 1939–40, Regnl Commr 1940, Regnl Controller Min Supply S Region 1941–45; *m* 1 July 1903 Pauline (*d* 30 Nov 1950), widow of Lt-Col Reginald Cockayne-Frith, 15th Hus, and dau of William Quirin, of Boston, USA, and had:

1a Anthony; *b* 1 July 1907; *educ* Eton; *m* 3 Sept 1936 Baroness Barbara Wrangel (*d* 23 Feb 1987), dau of Baron Hermann Wrangel, of Sweden, and *d* 18 July 1994, having had:

1b Derek; *b* 26 April 1940; *d* 27 Jan 1941

1b *Ursula; *b* 30 April 1938; *m* 13 Feb 1960 *Richard Alan Opperman, yr s of Maj Reginald Opperman, of Thedden House, Hants, and has:

1c *Mark Richard Charles; *b* 5 Jan 1963

2c *Nicholas Richard James; *b* 22 Nov 1965

1a Pamela Gladys Berthe; *b* 26 Feb 1910; *m* 1st 1 Nov 1932 Thomas John Henry Vincent Lane (*d* 10 July 1941), er s of John Henry Hervey Vincent Lane, JP, DL, of King's Bromley, Staffs, and had:

1b *Thomas Ronald Henry; *b* 27 March 1934

1b *Jane; *b* 20 June 1935

1a (cont.) Mrs Thomas Lane *m* 2nd 27 Nov 1942 Col William Scurfield Swire Sanguinetti, Roy Hants Regt (*d* 28 Sept 1969), s of Maj William Roger Sanguinetti, OBE, MC, and *d* 16 Jan 1982

(2) (cont.) Sir Geoffrey *m* 2nd 9 Oct 1951 Edna Frances (*d* 21 March 1977), widow of Capt Sir Denzil Cope, 14th Bt (*see* 1970 edn), and yst dau of Edward Banker Hilton, of New York and Paris, and *d* 8 Jan 1956

(3) Richard Ainsworth; *b* 30 Jan 1882; Capt Warwickshire RHA; *d* unm 16 May 1963

(4) Clement Henry; *b* 8 July 1884; Capt 10th Royal Hus; *ka* 17 Nov 1914

(1) Sybil Harding; *b* 4 Oct 1875; *m* 27 April 1897 Henry Dudley Scott (*d* 3 Dec 1943), JP Wilts, s of Robert Herries Dudley Scott, of Grainville Manor, St Helier, Jersey, and Brunswick Sq, Brighton, and *d* 6 June 1963, having had issue

(2) Gladys Marion; *b* 8 May 1880; *m* 26 Jan 1905 Lt-Col William Athol Murray, CMG, DSO, DL, RHA (*d* 13 Nov 1953), of Bembridge, IOW, yst s of Dr William Murray, of The Hall, Armathwaite, and *dsp* 15 July 1948

4 (Samuel) Arthur; *b* 9 Aug 1852; *m* 7 Dec 1875 Ellen Cornelia (*d* 18 Oct 1947), dau of Sir Robert Palmer Harding, and *d* 21 Jan 1942, leaving, with a dau (*d* unm):

(1) Marjory Kathleen; *b* 30 Sept 1876; *m* 27 June 1901 Maj Reginald Charles Coldwell (*d* 18 Dec 1933), s of Maj — Coldwell, 5th Dragoon Gds, and *d* 15 Jan 1943

(2) Joan Ainsworth; *b* 24 Oct 1882; *m* 22 July 1909 Maj James Leslie Cross (*d* 23 Aug 1955), est s of Percy Cross, of Catthorpe, and had issue

(3) Evelyn Molly; *b* 9 Nov 1884; *m* 23 Jan 1908 Brig-Gen Sir (Robert) Harvey Kearsley, KCVO, CMG, DSO (*d* 9 May 1956), Extra Equerry to HM THE QUEEN, est s of Maj Robert Wilson Kearsley, 5th Dragoon Gds, and *d* 24 May 1960, leaving issue

5 Harold Ainsworth; *b* 11 July 1854; *d* 16 April 1933

6 Frank Kelsall; *b* 14 Feb 1858; *m* 28 July 1887 Cecilia (*d* 6 Sept 1935), dau of W H Cane, MD, of Uxbridge, and widow of C H Pawson, of Farnley House, Dursley, and *d* 27 Dec 1935, having had:

(1) Valentine Frank Cane; *b* 14 Feb 1889; Lt 89th Punjabis, IA, RO, Lt 6th Bn Lancs Fus, served WW I; *d* unm 6 April 1960

(2) Walter Samuel; *b* 31 May 1890; architect, RE WW I; accidently *k* on service abroad 26 Dec 1917

(1) Constance Evelyn Cane; *b* 23 Nov 1891; *d* 19–

(2) Marion Ainsworth; *b* 1893; *d* 19–

7 Sir BASIL EDWARD PETO, 1st Bt, of Barnstaple (*qv*)

4 Sarah Maude; *b* 1847; *m* 29 Oct 1874 Clement Crossley (*d* 19 Oct 1882), of Burton Pynsent House, Curry Rivel, Taunton, and *d* 12 Oct 1938, leaving issue

5 Emily Lydia; *d* unm 18 June 1931

6 Ellen Edith; *m* 5 June 1883 William Roland Mitchell, JP (*d* 18 Feb 1925), of Seaborough Court, Crewkerne, and *d* 8 Oct 1941, having had issue

7 Helen Agnes; *b* Aug 1860; *m* 4 Sept 1885 Lawrence Ingham Baker, JP (*d* 2 Sept 1934), of Wayford Manor, Crewkerne, s of Lawrence James Baker, JP, of Brambridge Park, Hants, and *d* 15 April 1957, leaving issue

The 2nd Bt's n,

Sir (Henry) Francis Morton Peto, 3rd Bt, JP Dorset; *b* 18 Nov 1889; *educ* Eton; Cdr RN WW I; *m* 1st 16 July 1919 Edith (*d* 26 Dec 1945), only dau of George Berners Ruck Keene, of Lexden, Colchester, and had:

1 Sir HENRY GEORGE MORTON PETO, **4th and present Bt**

2 +William Neill [William Peto Esq, Lapford Wood House, Lapford, Devon EX17 6QU]; *b* 19 July 1922; *educ* Sherborne; *m* 1st 23 July 1943 (*divorce* 1962) Jacqueline Mary Valentine (*d* 29 July 1971), yst dau of Gurth Edelsten, of S Africa, and has had:

(1) +James Francis Morton [James Peto Esq, Glan Cerrig, Llanfaglan, Gwynedd LL54 5RF]; *b* 7 July 1944; *educ* Milton Abbey; mechanical engr; *m* 1st 26 April 1969 Daphne (*d* 1981), yr dau of Thomas Henry Kennedy, of Blackwood, Auldgirth, Dumfriesshire, and has:

1a +Mark Edward; *b* 20 July 1971

2a +Alexander George; *b* 1979

1a *Rebecca Jane; *b* 23 Jan 1975

(1) (cont.) James Peto *m* 2nd 1987 *Dorothy, yr dau of Maurice Wilson, of Cooper House, Selside, Kendal

(2) +William Gurth [Maj William Peto, Anwoth House, Gatehouse-of-Fleet, Castle Douglas, Kirkcudbrightshire DG7 2EF]; *b* 6 Feb 1949; *educ* Wellington and RMA Sandhurst; late Maj 13th/18th Roy Hus; *m* 1976 *Alice Caroline, dau of Dermot Holdsworth Harling Turner, of Kildalloig, Campbeltown, Argyll, and has:

1a +Roland Harry Morton; *b* 28 Oct 1982

1a *Alice Jane; *b* 16 Jan 1979

(1) Edith Margaret Jane; *b* 8 April; *d* 25 Dec 1947

2 (cont.) William Peto *m* 2nd 11 Aug 1962 Ann Bernal (*d* 26 Nov 1996), only dau of Lt-Col Theodore Thompson Laville, of Devon; *m* 3rd by 24 June 1997 *Rowan Margaret, *née* Cunningham, widow of Lt-Cdr David Dewar Crichton, RN

Sir Francis *m* 2nd 14 Sept 1948 Rosemary Grizel, widow of Maj Thomas Lionel Ashburner Clapton, Durham LI, and 2nd dau of R-Adml Archibald Cochrane, CMG (*see* DUNDONALD, E), and *d* 28 May 1978, having by her had:

3 +Raymond John [Raymond Peto Esq, Ridgeway House, Child Okeford, Dorset DT11 8QY]; *b* 30 March 1950; *educ* Ampleforth and Brunel U; *m* 1986 *Monica Marie, dau of Thomas Barlow, of Chapeltown, Yorks

PETRE

Arms: Gules a bend or between two escallops argent. **Crest:** Two lion's heads, erased and addorsed, the dexter or, collared azure, the sinister azure, collared or. **Supporters:** Dexter, a lion regardant or, collared azure; sinister, a lion regardant azure, collared or.
Motto: *Sans Dieu rien* ('Nothing without God').
Creation: B. (E) 21 July 1603.

Arms of most recent Baroness Furnivall [*see* **Lineage (of Furnival)** below]: Quarterly of ten, 1st, gu. a bend or between two escallops arg. (For PETRE); 2nd, gu. on a bend between six cross-crosslets fitchée arg. an escutcheon or, charged with a demi-lion rampant pierced through the mouth by an arrow, within a double tressure flory counter-flory of the first (for HOWARD); 3rd, gu. a lion rampant arg. (for MOWBRAY); 4th, sa. a lion rampant arg., ducally crowned or (for SEGRAVE); 5th, gu. three lions passant guardant or, a label of three points arg. (for BROTHERTON); 6th, barry of eight or and gu. (for FitzALAN); 7th, gu. a lion rampant or (for d'ALBINI); 8th, gu. a lion rampant within a bordure engrailed or (for TALBOT); 9th, gu. a saltire arg., a martlet sa. for difference (for NEVILL); 10th, arg. a bend between six martlets gu. (for FURNIVALL). **Supporters:** On either side a greyhound arg., the dexter charged on the shoulder with a glove ppr. thereon an escutcheon of the arms of Furnivall; the sinister charged on the shoulder with eight arrows interlaced saltirewise banded gu. **Motto:** *Sans Dieu rien*.

THE 18TH BARON PETRE, of Writtle, Co Essex (John Patrick Lionel Petre, DL (Essex 1991)) [The Rt Hon The Lord Petre DL, Ingatestone Hall, Essex; Writtle Park, Highwood, Essex CM1 3QF]; *b* 4 Aug 1942; *s f* 1989; *educ* Eton and Trin Coll Oxford (BA); Offr Bro OStJ 1994; *m* 16 Sept 1965 *Marcia Gwendolyn, only dau of Alfred Plumpton, of Portsmouth, and has:

1 +DOMINIC WILLIAM; *b* 9 Aug 1966; *educ* Worth Abbey and Exeter U

2 +Mark Julian; *b* 7 Nov 1969; *educ* Worth Abbey and Merton Coll Oxford

1 *Clare Helen; *b* 24 Nov 1973; *educ* New Hall Sch and Roy Holloway Coll London

Lineage (of Petre): JOHN PETRE, of Exeter; *educ* Exeter Coll Oxford; a prosperous tanner; had:

Sir WILLIAM PETRE; LLD; a pncpl Sec of State 1543–66; *m* 1st Gertrude, dau of Sir John Tyrell, of Warley, Essex, and had:

1 John; *dvp & sp*

1 Dorothy; *b* 1535; *m* 1555 Nicholas Wadham (*d* 20 Oct 1609), of Merrifield, Somerset, fndr with his w of Wadham Coll Oxford, and *d* 16 May 1618

2 Elizabeth; *m* John Gostwick, of Willington

Sir WILLIAM *m* 2nd by 1543 Anne, widow of Thomas Tyrell (s of Sir John Tyrell, of Heron Place, Essex) and dau of Sir William Browne, Ld Mayor London 1514, and *d* 13 Jan 1571/2, having by her had:

2 Edward; *dvp & sp*

3 Sir JOHN PETRE, **1st Baron Petre**, of Writtle, Co Essex (E), so *cr* 21 July 1603, of Ingatestone Hall, West Horndon (formally Thorndon) Hall (which he bought from the MORDAUNTs *c* 1573 (*see* MORDAUNT, Bt) and which was destroyed by fire 1878) and Writtle (all Essex); *b* 20 Dec 1549; *educ* Middle Temple; Essex: Sheriff 1575–76, MP 1584–87, Commr Victuals and Musters and Ld Lt; ktd 1576; *m* 17 April 1570 Mary, dau of Sir Edward Waldegrave, (*see* WALDEGRAVE, E), and *d* 11 Oct 1613, having had, with two yr sons:

(1) WILLIAM PETRE, **2nd Baron Petre**; *b* 24 June 1575; *educ* Exeter Coll Oxford; MP Essex 1597–98, ktd 1603; *m* 8 Nov 1596 Lady Katherine Somerset, 2nd dau of 4th Earl of Worcester (*see* BEAUFORT, D), and *d* 5 May 1637, leaving an est surv s:

1a ROBERT PETRE, **3rd Baron Petre**; *b* 22 Sept 1599; *educ* Exeter Coll Oxford; *m* 1620 Mary Browne, dau of 2nd Viscount Montagu, and *d* 23 Oct 1638, leaving an est s:

1b WILLIAM PETRE, **4th Baron Petre**; *b c* 1626; royalist Civil War; accused by Titus Oates 1678 of complicity in 'Popish Plot'; *m* 1st Lady Elizabeth Savage (*dsp* and *bur* 19 July 1665), dau of 2nd Earl Rivers; *m* 2nd by 15 April 1675 Bridget, dau and coheir of John Pincheon, of Writtle, but *dspm* imprisoned in the Tower of London 5 Jan 1683, leaving:

1c Mary; *m* George Heneage, of Hainton

2b JOHN PETRE, **5th Baron Petre**; *bapt* 24 June 1629; *d* unm 22 Jan 1684/5

3b THOMAS PETRE, **6th Baron Petre**; *bapt* 5 Dec 1633; Ld Lt Essex Feb-Oct 1688; *m* Mary, dau of Sir Thomas Clifton, Bt, of Lytham, Lancs, and *d* 5 Jan 1706/7, leaving:

1c ROBERT PETRE, **7th Baron Petre**; *bapt* 17 March 1689/90; *m* 1 March 1711/2 Catherine (*m* 2nd 2 April 1733 15th Baron Stourton; *see* MOWBRAY, SEGRAVE and STOURTON, B), dau of Bartholomew Walmsley, of Dunkenhalgh, Accrington, Lancs, and *d* 22 March 1713, leaving:

1d ROBERT JAMES PETRE, **8th Baron Petre**; *b* posthumously 3 June 1713; *m* 2 May 1732 Lady Anna Maria Barbara Radclyffe (*d* 31 Jan 1760), dau of 3rd Earl of Derwentwater (*see* NEWBURGH, E), and *d* 2 July 1742, having had, with three daus:

1e ROBERT EDWARD, **9th Baron**

1a Mary; *m* 20 Nov 1616 3rd Baron Teynham (*qv*)

3 Catherine; *m* as his 1st w Sir John Talbot and had issue (*see* SHREWSBURY and WATERFORD, E)

The 8th BARON's only son,

ROBERT EDWARD PETRE, **9th Baron Petre**; *b c* Feb 1741/2; *m* 1st 19 April 1762 Anne (*dsp* 5 Jan 1787), dau and coheir of Philip Howard (*see* below **Lineage (of Furnivall)**), and had:

1 ROBERT EDWARD, **10th Baron**

2 George William; *b* 10 Jan 1766; *m* 6 Aug 1786 Maria (*m* 2nd 1802 Henry William Espinasse; *d* 11 June 1837), dau of Philip Howard, of Corby (*see* NORFOLK, D), and *d* 22 Oct 1797, having had:

(1) George; *d* March 1829

(2) Henry William, of Dunkenhalgh; *b* 23 April 1791; *m* 1st 17 July 1818 Elizabeth Anne (*d* 13 Sept 1828), est dau of Edmund John Glynn, of Glynn, Cornwall, and had:

1a Henry, of Dunkenhalgh, JP, DL; *b* 17 Aug 1821; *m* 13 Aug 1846 Mary (*d* 1 Jan 1880), dau of Edmond de la Poer, of Gurteen, Co Waterford, and *dsp* 25 April 1900

2a George Glynn (Sir), KCMG, CB, JP, of Dunkenhalgh; *b* 4 Sept 1822; Attaché Frankfurt 1846, Hanover 1852, Paris 1853 and 1857, The Hague 1855, Naples 1856, Sec Legation Hanover 1859, Copenhagen 1864–65 and Brussels 1866, Sec Embassy Berlin 1868, Min Resident Stuttgart 1872, Envoy Extrdy and Min Plen Argentina 1881, Paraguay 1882 and Portugal 1884–93; *m* 10 April 1858 Emma Katharine Julia (*d* 27 Dec 1916), 5th dau of Major Ralph Henry Sneyd, and *d* 17 May 1905, having had:

1b George Ernest Augustus Henry, of Dunkenhalgh; *b* 5 Aug 1860 (THE KING OF HANOVER stood sponsor); *d* unm

2b Henry Cecil, CMG (1916), OBE (1919); *b* 27 Oct 1861; Col Rifle Bde, served Boer War 1901–02 (Queen's medal with three clasps) and WW I (despatches twice); *m* 10 April 1899 Marjorie Elizabeth (*d* 11 Aug 1928), dau of Richard Arthur Hamilton Seymour (*see* CULME-SEYMOUR, Bt), and *dsp* 17 Sept 1939

3b Algernon Henry Edward; *b* 4 June 1863; Consul-Gen Rio de Janeiro; *d* 21 May 1895

4b Alfred Ralph William George; *b* 13 June 1866; *m* 25 April 1892 Gertrude (*d* 1934), dau of E Briggs, and *d* 1959, having had:

1c Charles; *b* 28 April 1895

2c Alfred Ralph; *b* 4 Dec 1896

3c Algernon; *b* 1898; *d* 1906

4c George Ernest; *b* 28 Oct 1899

1c Florence Gertrude; *b* 20 Feb 1893; *m* 30 April 1918 Sir John Frederick Ellenborough Crowder (*d* 9 July 1961), MP, JP, s of Augustus George Crowder, of London W, and had issue

2c Katherine Violet; *b* 20 Feb 1902

3c Charlotte Grace; *b* Nov 1903; *d* 22 July 1924

4c Dora; *b* June 1907

5b Herbert Arthur; *b* 7 March 1868; *d* 23 Jan 1937

6b Charles Bernard; *b* 3 Jan 1870; *educ* Naval and Mil Coll Gosport; Capt 60th KRRC Boer War 1899–1902 (despatches twice, Queen's medal with four clasps, King's medal with two clasps), attd E Lancs Regt WW I; *m* 2 Feb 1903 Muriel Rosalind (*d* 5 July 1961), dau of William D Anderson, of Cheltenham, and *d* 20 Feb 1949, leaving:

1c Robert (Bobby) Charles; *b* 15 Feb 1912; *educ* Harrow and RMC Sandhurst; Capt Scots Gds, Maj WW II with 1st and 2nd Bns (Norway 1940, Italy 1943–45), won Grand National 1946 on *Lovely Cottage*; *m* 1st 20 Sept 1934 Mary Delphine, er dau of Maj Claud Chichester, of Tunworth Down, Basingstoke, and had:

1d +Charles Henry [Charles Petre Esq, Tunworth Down House, Basingstoke, Hants RG25 2LD]; *b* 23 April 1936; *educ* Downside and Ch Ch Oxford; *m* 10 Jan 1963 *Melanie Beatrix, est dau of (Henry Peregrine) Rennie Hoare by Lady Beatrix Cadogan (*see* CADOGAN, E), and has had:

1e (Robert) Henry; *b* 10 Dec 1968; *educ* Eton; *d* 1992

1e *Fenella Delphine; *b* 8 June 1967; *m* 10 May 1997 *Andrew Gray, est s of Hugh Gray, of Hindhead, Surrey

2d +Robert Bernard [Robert Petre Esq, Down Farm House, Tunworth, Hants]; *b* 3 Jan 1938; *educ* Downside; 2nd Lt (Res) Scots Gds; *m* 1970 *Caroline, dau of Lt-Col Peter Jackson, of Wappenham, Northants, and has:

1e *Edward Robert; *b* 5 Feb 1976

1e *Georgina Sarah; *b* 7 March 1974

1d *Claudia Mary Delphine [Mrs Ambrose Scott-Moncrieff, Ragmore, Tunworth, Hants]; *b* 6 May 1943; *m* 1971 *Ambrose Patrick Eustace Scott-Moncrieff, yr s of David William Hardy Scott-Moncrieff, of Rock Cottage, Basford Hall, Staffs, and has:

1e *Chlöe; *b* 1976

1c (cont.) Maj Robert Petre *m* 2nd Oct 1975 *Mrs Sonia Greenish [Mrs Robert Petre, Little Bignor Farm, Kirdford, W Sussex RH14 0LT], yr dau of Capt William A K Redfern, of S Kensington, and *d* 3 Aug 1996

1c Kate Rosalind Florence; *b* 5 Nov 1903; *m* 14 Jan 1925 Col John Wingfield Renny-Tailyour, DSO, DL, RA (*d* 9 Dec 1969), of Dubton House, Montrose, and *d* 16 Nov 1956, leaving issue

2c Elsie Glynn; *m* 1st 3 July 1926 Capt Alwyne Malcolm Fawcett (*d* 22 Aug 1933), MC, RA, est s of Lt-Col James F M Fawcett, 5th Lancers, and had issue; *m* 2nd 29 Nov 1944 Francis George Hurt (*d* 25 May 1952), est s of Maj Francis Cecil Albert Hurt, of Alderwasley Hall, Derbys, and had issue; *m* 3rd 21 June 1955 (*divorce* 1958) Lt-Col Michael Wallington, MC, Roy Sussex Regt, 2nd s of John Arthur Beach Wallington; *m* 4th 16 March 1959 Alec James Helms, 2nd s of Henry Walter Helms, of Thame, Oxon

3c Christine Marjorie; *b* 1910; BRCS 1938–48; *m* 1st 8 Oct 1931 (*divorce* 1943) Jerrard Ross Williamson, only s of Charles Swinton Williamson, of Aborfield Grange, nr Reading, and has:

  1d *Charles Anthony [Lt-Cdr Charles Williamson RNR, Whitehouse Farm, Crowfield, Suffolk IP6 9TF]; *b* 9 Feb 1933; *educ* RNC Dartmouth; *m* 1 April 1967 *Philippa Marie-Theresa, dau of Lt-Col M R Braithwaite, and has:

    1e *Robert Jerrard; *b* 15 Sept 1969

    1e *Lucy Charlotte; *b* 18 June 1968

  2d Timothy Jerrard; *b* 23 Dec 1936; *educ* Marlborough; *m* 16 April 1970 *Christine, only dau of Sir Robert Mark, Commr Met Police, of Esher, Surrey, and *d* May 1977, leaving:

    1e *Marcus; *b* 1974

    1e *Rachel; *b* 1971

  1d *(Theresa) June [Mrs John Chester, Clarewood Cottage, London Rd, Camberley, Surrey]; *b* 20 June 1934; *m* 2 Oct 1961 *John Chester and has:

    1e *Anthony James; *b* 2 Oct 1965; *educ* Liverpool and Edinburgh Us (PhD)

3c (cont.) Mrs Christine Williamson *m* 2nd 7 April 1943 *Carson Alan Kossatz, Cameron Highrs, of Ottawa, est s of Emile Kossatz, of Pembroke, Ontario, and *d* 26 Aug 1997, having by him had:

  3d Robin Martin; *b* 1949; *educ* St George's Coll Weybridge; *d* 1977

7b Walter Reginald Glynn, DSO; *b* 14 Dec 1873; Capt Port of Constantinople, served WW I (despatches), R-Adml; *m* 22 Jan 1906 Agnes Marie (*d* 21 Sept 1963 aged 83), yst dau of Eugene Cadic, of Rennes, France, and *d* 26 Dec 1942, leaving:

  1c +Walter George Glynn [Walter Petre Esq, La Mouette, Sark, Channel Isles]; *b* 28 Oct 1906; *educ* Oratory Sch; ARAeS, MSLAE, S/Ldr RAF, later with BOAC; *m* 12 April 1939 Myra Millicent (*d* 8 March 1984), only dau of Arthur Willows, of Rushton Manor, nr Kettering, and has:

    1d +Michael Bernard [Michael Petre Esq, Four Winds, Cookham Dean, Berks]; *b* 30 Sept 1946; *educ* St George's Coll Weybridge; *m* 1978 *Pauline Carole McCormack, dau of Lionel Alfred Weston, and has:

      1e +Nicholas Charles Lionel Glynn; *b* 1980

      2e +Simon Robert Glynn; *b* 1983

    1d *Geraldine Marie [Mrs Michael Guest, La Mouette, Sark, CI]; *b* 12 Nov 1944; *m* 1st 23 Sept 1967 (*divorce* 1987) David Robin Mears and has:

      1e *Edward Petre [Edward Petre-Mears Esq, Baytree Cottage, Sark, CI]; *b* 13 Nov 1968

      2e *Justin PETRE-MEARS; *b* 24 Nov 1972

    1d (cont.) Mrs Geraldine Mears *m* 2nd 13 June 1992 *Michael Guest

    2d *Anne Rosalie; *b* 19 Aug 1949

2c Henry Edward; *b* 9 Nov 1907; *educ* Oratory Sch and Nautical Coll Pangbourne; Lt-Cdr RNR WW II; *m* 9 Sept 1939 *Rosemary Sonia [Mrs Henry Petre, 10 Camden Rd, Eastbourne, E Sussex], er dau of Benjamin Gottschalk, of London NW1, and *d* 1994, leaving:

  1d *Cecilia (Cylla) Marie; *b* 28 June 1940; *m* 11 June 1964 *Douglas Milton Wiggins, MBE, yr s of Edward Alfred Wiggins, of Walton-on-the-Naze, Essex, and has had:

    1e A son; *b* and *d* 6 May 1965

    2e A son; *b* and *d* 28 July 1973

    3e *Nicholas James Petre; *b* 3 Sept 1974

    1e *Emma Jane; *b* 28 May 1966; *m* 1988 *David Hamish Easdale, s of Hamish Easdale, of Gerrards Cross, Bucks

    2e *Katherine Blanche; *b* 26 Jan 1968

    3e *Henrietta Clare; *b* 5 May 1969

  2d *Teresa Jane Glynn [Mrs George Hutchinson, 3 Westdean Cottages, Westdean, Seaford, Sussex]; *b* 29 Dec 1944; *m* 16 Dec 1976 *George Andrew Hutchinson, s of John Robert Hutchinson, of Barnstaple, and has:

    1e *Rupert Charles Petre; *b* 1981

    1e *Amanda Jane Petre; *b* 1979

  3d *Sonia Rosemary [Mrs Robert Hancock, 8 Daisy Lane, Hurlingham, London SW6]; *b* 26 March 1946; *m* 2 July 1966 *Dr Robert Peter Dawbney Hancock, RAMC, er s of Francis William Hancock, of Guildford, and has:

    1e *Benjamin Charles Petre; *b* 1971

    2e *Toby Charles Petre; *b* 25 June 1975

    3e *Bertie Petre Oliver; *b* 20 July 1979

    1e *Scarlett; *b* 1981

3c Edward Joseph Algernon; *b* 30 July 1911; *educ* Oratory Sch; Capt Black Watch and Essex Regt WW II (wounded); *m* 1st 11 June 1938 Diana Perry; *m* 2nd 15 Sept 1948 *Helen Beresford, formerly w of Capt Kenyon Goode, of Nassau, and *d* 19–

4c Gerard Malcolm Mary Laurence; *b* 12 Aug 1916; Maj Essex Regt WW II; *m* 21 May 1941 *Pamela Marian (*m* 2nd 2 March 1946 Col Desmond John H Bannister, MBE, MC, Devon and Dorset Regt, yr s of A C Bannister, of Budleigh Salterton), dau of Capt G Brian Pratt, RA, of Edge Grove, Aldernham, Herts, and was *ka* Caen 11 June 1944, leaving:

  1d +Andrew Charles Malcolm Glynn; *b* 20 Feb 1944; *educ* Downside

1c *Mary Katherine Gabrielle [Miss Marie Petre, Kenmare, Main Road, Southbourne, Sussex]; *b* 5 June 1909

2c *Madeline Marie Ethel [Mrs Desmond Clarke, Elm Cottage, Caldbeck, Cumbria CA7 8EA]; *b* 16 June 1913; *m* 15 Jan 1944 Maj-Gen Desmond Alexander Bruce Clarke (*d* 1986), CB, CBE, RA, yr s of Robert Thomas Clarke, LLD, ICS, of Weybridge, and has:

  1d *Desmond Walter Robert [Desmond Clarke Esq, Old Dairy Cottage, Winchester, Hants]; *b* 8 Jan 1945; *educ* Austin Friars Sch Carlisle and RMA Sandhurst; Capt RA; *m* 31 Jan 1970 *Fiona Mary, dau of John Harrison, of Wilmington, Sussex, and has:

    1e *Duncan Robert Petre; *b* 1971

    2e *Sebastian Alexander; *b* 1982

    1e *Philippa Kate; *b* 1975

  2d *Dominic Michael Bernard [Dominic Clarke Esq, 15 Norfolk Mansions, Prince of Wales Dve, London SW11]; *b* 28 Feb 1949; *educ* Austin Friars Sch Carlisle

  3d *Damian Anthony John [Damian Clarke Esq, 4 School Terrace, Reading, Berks]; *b* 2 May 1958; *m* 1986 *Imogen, dau of Rev David Cooke, of The Rectory, Stone, Berks, and has:

    1e *Edward; *b* 1986

    2e *Henry; *b* 1988

    3e *George; *b* 1989

  1d *Antoinette Marie Edwina [Mrs David Ward, The Green, Caldbeck, Cumbria]; *b* 5 March 1947; *m* 1978 *David Ward and has:

    1e *Andrew; *b* 1981

    2e *Robin; *b* 1982

    1e *Rachel; *b* 1979

  2d *Amicie Mary Bernadette; *b* 20 Aug 1950; *m* 8 April 1972 *David Thompson and has:

    1e *Joseph Andrew; *b* 1975

    2e *Toby; *b* 1977

    3e *Benedict; *b* 1985

    1e *Jessica; *b* 1983

3c *Monica Mary [Miss Monica Petre, Kenmare, Main Rd, Southbourne, Hants]; *b* 28 Dec 1919

1b Florence Katharine; *b* 16 July 1859; *d* 19 March 1869

(2) (cont.) Henry Petre *m* 2nd 20 April 1830 Adeliza Maria (*d* 9 Sept 1833), dau of Henry Howard, of Corby (*see* NORFOLK, D), and by her had:

3a Edward Henry, of Whitley Abbey, Warwicks, JP, DL; *b* 21 Feb 1831; High Sheriff Warwicks 1877; *m* 29 Oct 1857 Lady Gwendoline Elizabeth Talbot, sis of 17th Earl of Shrewsbury and Waterford (*qv*), and *d* 21 Nov 1902, leaving:

  1b Oswald Henry Philip PETRE later TURVILLE-PETRE (roy licence 18 May 1907), TD, of Bosworth Hall, Leics, JP Warwicks and Leics, DL Warwicks; *b* 27 May 1862; *educ* Ch Ch Oxford (BA); High Sheriff Leics 1912, Maj and Hon Lt-Col TFR, Northants Yeo, Maj and Hon Lt-Col Warwicks Yeo, Kt SMO Malta; *m* 24 Jan 1899 Margaret Lucy, JP Leics (*d* 20 March 1954), yst dau of Laurence Trent Cave, of Ditcham Park, Petersfield, and Knightsbridge, and *d* 16 June 1941, leaving:

    1c Francis Adrian Joseph; *b* 4 March 1901; *educ* Exeter Coll Oxford (BA); *d* unm 16 Aug 1942

    2c Edward Oswald Gabriel; *b* 25 March 1908; *educ* Ampleforth and Ch Ch Oxford (BA 1931, MA 1936); BLitt, Hon DPhil U of Iceland 1961, Vigfusson Reader Ancient Icelandic Literature and Antiquities Oxford 1941, Prof 1953, Kt Order Falcon Iceland 1956, Cdr 1963; *m* 7 Jan 1943 *Joan Elizabeth [Mrs Edward Turville-Petre, 18 Hungate St, Aylsham, Norfolk], BLitt, er dau of Sam Blomfield, of Colchester, and *d* 1978, leaving:

      1d +Thorlac Francis Samuel [Prof Thorlac Turville-Petre Esq, Dept of English, Nottingham University, Nottingham NG7 2RD]; *b* 6 Jan 1944; *educ* Magdalen Coll Sch Oxford and Jesus Coll Oxford (BA 1966, MA, Blitt); Prof Medieval English Lit; *m* 8 July 1967 *Ingrid Elizabeth, dau of Rudolf Zimmerlund, of Stockholm, and has:

        1e +Francis Gustaf; *b* 18 April 1971

        2e +Crispin Gabriel; *b* 25 Oct 1974

      2d +Merlin Oswald [Merlin Turville-Petre Esq, Hallcroft, Hazles Cross Rd, Kingsley, Stoke-on-Trent ST10 2AY]; *b* 2 July 1946; *educ* Oratory Sch; *m* 1973 (*divorce* 19–) Christine Margaret, dau of Ivor Lee-Smith, of Newbury, Berks; *m* 2nd 1995 *Geraldine Bragg and by his 1st w has:

        1e *Daisy Kate; *b* 1975

        2e *Martha Amanda; *b* 1978

    3d Brendan Arthur Auberon; *b* 16 Sept 1948; *educ* Magdalen Coll Sch; *d* 6 Dec 1992

  1c Gwendoline Mary Etheldreda; *b* 16 Oct 1902; *m* 30 Sept 1938 Lt-Col Roland Greenwood (*d* 22 Dec 1949), Highland LI, and *d* 1994 leaving issue

  2c Alethea Mary Elizabeth Evelyn; *b* 31 Oct 1904; *m* 29 April 1930 Maj David Turville-Constable-Maxwell, TD, RA (*see* HERRIES OF TERREGLES, L), and *d* 29 Sept 1995, leaving issue

  3c Marion Margaret Josephine; *b* 22 March 1906; *m* 28 Aug 1934 Daniel Adrian Francis Cave, est s of Capt Adrian Cave, 10th Roy Hus, and *d* 1992, leaving issue

2b Bertram Edward; *b* 20 April 1873; *m* 5 Oct 1911 Ruth (*d* 23 Aug 1976), dau of Lord Ernest James Seymour (*see* HERTFORD, M), and *d* 8 March 1962, having had:

1c Myles Seymour Edward; *b* 26 April 1913; Maj DCLI WW II; *m* 15 Sept 1938 Audrey Catherine (*d* 15 July 1989), er dau of Col John Nevile Chaworth-Musters, DSO, OBE, TD, JP, of Annesley Park, Notts (*see* WESTMORLAND, E), and was *ka* Libya 5 June 1942, having had:

1d Martin Anthony Chaworth; *b* 23 Jan 1940; *educ* Ampleforth; *m* 17 Feb 1968 *(Selina) Frances Gladstone [Mrs Martin Petre, c/o Cross House, Henstridge, Templecombe, Somerset], yr dau of Brig Philip William Gladstone Pope, DSO, MC, ADC, of Cross House, Henstridge, and *d* 1991, leaving:

1e +Edward Myles Chaworth; *b* 9 Jan 1971

1e *Henrietta Claire Gladstone; *b* 27 May 1969

2e *Isabel Mary Hartsthorne; *b* 27 May 1973

2d +Robin David Oswald [Maj Robin Petre, Flaxbourne, Seddon, New Zealand]; *b* 19 April 1942; *educ* Ampleforth and RMA Sandhurst; Hon Maj 17th/21st Lancers (ret 1974); *m* 27 April 1968 *Cecily Constance, er dau of Simon Scrope, of Flaxbourne House, Great Ouseburn, Yorks, and has:

1e *Diana Audrey Constance; *b* 14 Feb 1969

2e *Nicola Mary Catherine; *b* 2 July 1971

1b Mary Adela; *b* 23 May 1861; *d* 4 June 1938

2b Mary Gwendoline; *b* 9 Sept 1865; *m* 1st 8 Sept 1887 Sir Henry Alfred Joseph Doughty-Tichborne, 12th Bt (*see* 1956 edn), and had issue; *m* 2nd 7 May 1914 Lt-Col Frank de Rittich Mauduit IA, (*d* 4 July 1931), only s of Francis de Mauduit, and *d* 23 March 1950

4a Oswald; *b* 15 Aug 1832; Lt 6th Dragoon Gds; *d* 1855

(2) (cont.) Henry Petre *m* 3rd 4 Nov 1834 Martha Agatha (*m* 2nd 1 Oct 1859 Arthur Houlton), dau of John Hofnell, and *d* 26 Nov 1852

(3) Philip William; *b* 22 Jan 1794; *m* 1833 Mrs Maria Annoot and *d* 22 Aug 1846, leaving:

1a Louis William Henry; *b* 1833; *m* 1 March 1862 Sabine Mathilde Philomène (*d* 10 Feb 1901), dau of Louis Claude de Fontange, and *d* 1903, having had, with two other sons:

1b Edward Philip William; *b* 22 Sept 1869; *m* 20 March 1890 Zoila Rosa del Carmen Larenas (*d* 11 Dec 1953) and *d* 1923, leaving:

1c Alberto Alphonso; *b* 5 Dec 1890

2c Eduardo Louis Ernesto; *b* 23 July 1896; *m* 1921 Annabelle Wilson, of New York, and *d* 1947

3c Luis Enrique; *b* 28 July 1898; *m* 19– Else Newman Etienne and had:

1d *Agnes Petre Newman; *b* 1924; *m* 1945 (*divorce* 1952) Fernando Zilleruedo Vargas, Lt Chilean Air Force, of Quintero, Chile, and has:

1e *Fernando; *b* 1951

1e *Marie-Agnes; *b* 1946

2e *Marie-Luz; *b* 1948

1c Blanca Natalia Gabriela; *b* 21 Aug 1892; *m* 1914 R-Adml Roberto Chappuzeau, Chilean Navy (*d* 1944), and had issue

2c Anna Lucia; *b* 12 Oct 1894; *m* 1923 Col Aquiles Vergara Vicuña, Bolivian Army

1b Anne Martha Rosa; *b* 26 Nov 1877; *m* 27 Aug 1900 Henry Hudson (*d* 16 Dec 1943), ARCA, and *d* 13 July 1959, leaving issue

(4) William Thomas; *b* 5 Oct 1796; *d* 9 Jan 1858

(1) Emily Maria; *m* 27 Dec 1819 Robert Espinasse (*d* 1840) and *d* 1829

1 Anne Catherine; *m* 7 Aug 1796 Gen Denzil Onslow, of Staughton House, Hunts, and *d* 5 Oct 1798

The **9th Baron** *m* 2nd 16 Jan 1788 Juliana (*d* 16 April 1833), dau of Henry Howard, of Glossop (*see* NORFOLK, D), and by her had:

3 Robert Edward, of Stapleton Park, Yorks; *b* 26 Sept 1794; MP; *m* 21 July 1829 Laura Maria (*d* 24 June 1886 aged 75), dau of 2nd Baron Stafford (*qv*) and *dsp* 8 June 1848, aged 53

2 Julia Maria *m* 15 April 1833 Sir Samuel John Brooke-Pechell, 3rd Bt (*see* 1970 edn PECHELL, Bt), and *dsp* 6 Sept 1844

3 Catherine Anne; *d* 13 March 1830

The 9th BARON *d* 2 July 1801; his est son,

ROBERT EDWARD PETRE, **10th Baron Petre**; *b* 2 Sept 1763; *m* 14 Feb 1786 Mary Bridget (*d* 30 May 1843), dau of Henry Howard, of Glossop, and sis of his step-mother and 12th Duke of Norfolk (*qv*), and had, with other issue:

1 WILLIAM HENRY FRANCIS, **11th Baron**

2 Charles Berney, of Shenfield House, Essex; *b* 17 Dec 1794; *m* 31 May 1822 Eliza (*d* 6 Sept 1835), dau of Edward Charles Howard (*see* NORFOLK, D), and *d* 18 June 1854, having had, with another dau:

(1) Charles Edward, Capt 7th Dragoon Gds; *b* 16 July 1823; *m* 23 May 1849 his cousin Charlotte Elizabeth (*d* 31 Oct 1903), dau of **11th Baron Petre**, and *d* 13 June 1899, having had:

1a Augustus William Berney (Rt Rev Monsignor); *b* 9 Nov 1850; *d* 21 March 1897

1a Blanche Mary; *d* unm 1 May 1900

(1) Louisa Frances; *m* 5 Aug 1857 Robert Thomas Eyston (*d* 24 April 1887), yst s of Charles Eyston, JP, DL, of East Hendred, Berks, and *d* May 1884, having had issue

1 Maria Juliana; *m* 30 April 1805 Stephen Phillips and *d* 27 Jan 1824

2 Juliana Anne; *m* 5 July 1812 James Weld (*d* 26 Feb 1855), 7th s of Thomas Weld, of Lulworth Castle, Dorset, and *d* 5 June 1862, having had issue

3 Elizabeth Anne Mary; *m* 15 May 1817 Michael Henry Blount, of Mapledurham, Oxon, and *d* 4 March 1848

4 Anna Maria; *m* 16 Jan 1838 Arthur Hughes (*d* a few months after) and *d* 14 Oct 1864

5 Arabella, nun; *d* 24 June 1886 aged 75

The 10th BARON *d* 29 March 1809; his son,

WILLIAM HENRY FRANCIS PETRE, **11th Baron Petre**; *b* 22 Jan 1793; *m* 1st 2 June 1815 Frances Charlotte (*d* 29 Jan 1822), est dau of Sir Richard Bedingfeld, 5th Bt (*see* PASTON-BEDINGFELD, Bt), and had:

1 WILLIAM BERNARD, **12th Baron**

---

2 Henry William, of Springfield Lawn, Essex, DL; *b* 23 Jan 1820; *m* 1st 6 June 1842 Mary Ann Eleanor (*d* 3 Sept 1885), only dau of Richard Walmesley, of Middleton Hall, Essex, and had, with other issue:

(1) Francis William; *b* 8 Sept 1847; *m* 1 March 1881 Margaret (*d* 21 July 1933), est dau of Edward Bowes Cargill, of Dunedin, NZ, and *d* 10 Dec 1918, leaving:

1a Edward Henry; *b* 2 Dec 1881; Maj Roy Suffolk Regt Boer War 1900–02 and WW I; *d* unm 1942

2a Bernard Francis; *b* 1 Nov 1884; NZ Expdny Force WW I; *m* 20 Nov 1922 Anna Constance (*d* 1975), dau of Capt F J Easther, RN, of Dunedin, NZ, and *d* 10 July 1942, leaving:

1b +Francis John [Francis Petre Esq, 18 Ketton Place, St Albans, Christchurch 5, New Zealand]; *b* 25 Aug 1923; NZ Forces WW II; *m* 23 Aug 1947 Patricia Josphine (*d* 1990), dau of Walter Corcoran, of Dunedin, and has:

1c +John Bernard [John Petre Esq, 540 Tay St, Invercargill, New Zealand]; *b* 14 Oct 1949; *m* 1972 *Kathleen Cullen and has:

1d +Brendan John; *b* 1973

2d +Damian Roy; *b* 1977

3d +Matthew Patrick; *b* 1982

1d +Rebecca Maree; *b* 1980

2c +David Christopher [David Petre Esq, 205 Valley View, RD4 Tiritea, Palmerston North, New Zealand]; *b* 6 Oct 1954; *m* 1st 1978 (*divorce* 19–) Meryl Kemp; *m* 2nd 19– *Glenda Barnaby and by his 1st w has:

1d +Denis Christopher; *b* 1985

2d +Michael Francis; *b* 1987

1d *Amy Elizabeth; *b* 1981

2d *Josephine Mary; *b* 1982

3c +Gerard Michael [Gerard Petre Esq, 307 Lyttelton St, Spreydon, Christchurch, New Zealand]; *b* 28 Jan 1959

1c *Frances Mary [Mrs Michael Pucilowski, 10 Briar Place, Christchurch, New Zealand]; *b* 6 July 1948; *m* 1974 *Michael Pucilowski and has:

1d *Anna Gabrielle; *b* 1976

2d *Jane Frances; *b* 1978

2c *Philippa Josephine [Mrs James Goater, 16 Knowles St, Christchurch, New Zealand]; *b* 21 Sept 1951; *m* 1983 *James Frederick Goater, of Nagoya, Japan, and has:

1d *Oliver James; *b* 1984

1d *Georgina Naomi (twin); *b* 1984

2b +Robert Cargill [Robert Petre Esq, 16 Milburn St, Corstorphine, Dunedin, New Zealand]; *b* 18 June 1925; *m* 27 Nov 1954 *Emily Waiwaha Kohere, of Rotorua, NZ, and has:

1c +Robert Bernard; *b* 15 July 1961; *m* 1994 *Moana Colbert and has:
1d +Rogan James; *b* Oct 1997

2c +Christopher Andrew; *b* 4 Nov 1963; *m* 15 Nov 1997 *Janine Millar

1c *Mary Ellen; *b* 21 Sept 1955; *m* 1977 *Neville James Forrest and has:

1d *James Andrew; *b* 1980

2d *Garth Alan; *b* 1982

2c *Raewyn Kuru; *b* 19 Oct 1957; *m* 1979 *Martin Allen Hay and has:

1d *Larry Dwain; *b* 1981

1d *Kuru Anne; *b* 1984

3c *Jennifer Ann; *b* 25 Sept 1965; *m* 30 Nov 1991 *Wayne David Pitcaithly and has:

1d *Rebekah Emily; *b* 15 July 1996

1b +William Bernard [William Petre Esq, 23A Coughtrey St, Dunedin, New Zealand]; *b* 5 Dec 1927; *m* 1974 *Margaret Doreen —

1b *Constance Elizabeth Mary [Mrs Lambertus Snellaert, 4 Bentley Ave, Glenfield, Auckland 10, New Zealand]; *b* 12 Nov 1931; *m* 5 Jan 1955 *Lambertus Jacobus Snellaert and has:

1c *Peter William; *b* 17 Oct 1957

2c *Michael John; *b* 27 March 1961; *m* 1982 *Bernadette Cleary and has:

1d *Sarah Louise; *b* 1989

2d *Claire Michelle; *b* 1991

3c *Philip Bernard; *b* 27 May 1965

1c *Jacqueline Mary; *b* 6 Sept 1956; *m* 1978 *Daniel Tangata and has:

1d *Nicholas Tobias; *b* 1981

2d *Benjamin Daniel; *b* 1991

1d *Helen Frances; *b* 1983

2d *Anna Elizabeth; *b* 1990

2c *Catherine Elizabeth; *b* 17 Sept 1959

3a William Robert Joseph; *b* 24 Nov 1886; *m* 1918 Alice Carr Robinson, of N Zealand, and *d* 24 April 1954

4a Joseph Austin; *b* 18 Oct 1893; Lt NZ Forces WW I; *m* 1st April 1921 Eleanor (*d* 1935), yst dau of H H Norton, of Auckland, NZ; *m* 2nd 17 Jan 1940 Leonora Agnes (*d* 16 June 1941), dau of Robert M Sunley, of Christchurch, NZ, and *d* 1972, having by her had:

1b +Anthony John [Anthony Petre Esq, 3 Paulus Terrace, Cashmere, Christchurch 2, New Zealand]; *b* 3 April 1941; *educ* St Bede's Coll Christchurch; *m* 4 Feb 1967 *Barbara Anne, 3rd dau of Charles Edwin Armstrong, of Geraldine, NZ, and has:

1c +Robert Joseph; *b* 1973

1c *Ruth Leonora; *b* 1968

2c *Adrienne Joanne; *b* 1970

5a Henry William; *b* 10 June 1899; NZ Forces WW II; *m* 11 Aug 1931 Cicely Beresford (*d* June 1990), 2nd dau of Anthony Francis FitzHerbert (*see* FitzHERBERT, Bt), and *d* 1983

6a Philip Lewis, NZ Forces WW II; *b* 16 April 1903; *d* unm 11 April 1968

1a Rosamond Margaret; *b* 7 Feb 1883; *m* Aug 1922 Armand Sibretti, of Rome, and *d* 15 Feb 1954, leaving issue

2a Gertrude Mary; *b* 23 Aug 1888; *d* unm Feb 1972

3a Constance Mary, Sister of Mercy; *b* 11 Aug 1890; *d* Nov 1967

4a Isobel Mary; *b* Oct 1895; *m* May 1922 Hubert V O'Beirne (*d* 30 May 1959) and had:

  1b *Joseph Francis; *b* 12 Dec 1923; *m* 7 April 1951 *Moana, dau of William H Kent, of Auckland, NZ, and has:

    1c *Derek Francis; *b* 4 Feb 1952

    2c *Roderick William; *b* 17 Feb 1953

    1c *Bridgid Margaret; *b* 19 May 1954

    2c *Catherine Mary; *b* 16 Aug 1960

  2b *Cecil Hugh [Cecil O'Beirne Esq, Lud Valley, RDI, Nelson, New Zealand]; *b* 19 May 1931; *m* 18 April 1964 *Lynda Brynhild, est dau of Mrs M Hawes, of Alawhai, Nelson, NZ, and has:

    1c *Helen Denise; *b* 23 Nov 1969

  1b *Margaret Ellen [Mrs Richard Langbein, 25 Black St, Stoke, Nelson, New Zealand]; *b* 22 June 1925; *m* 3 Feb 1951 *Richard John Langbein, est s of Edward Langbein, of Stoke, Nelson, NZ, and has:

    1c *Brian Richard; *b* 20 May 1954

    2c *Christopher Edward; *b* 27 Sept 1958

    3c *Peter Hugh; *b* 25 Jan 1961

    1c *Janet Helen; *b* 5 Jan 1953

    2c *Patricia Margaret; *b* 24 April 1956

    3c *Susan Mary; *b* 3 Oct 1959

5a Monica Helen Mary; *b* 12 Oct 1897; *m* 16 June 1930 Capt John Niall Fox, MC, RE (*d* 11 Nov 1968), s of Col F J Fox, RHA, of Fox Hall, Co Longford, and *d* 11 July 1983, leaving:

  1b *Francis Bernard Niall [Mr Francis Fox, Flat 3, 17 Brougham St, Wellington, New Zealand]; *b* 17 March 1936; LLB, barrister and slr High Court NZ 1961

  1b Clair; *b* and *d* 16 Dec 1931

  2b Cara; *b* and *d* 12 Aug 1933

  3b Margaret; *b* and *d* 12 Aug 1933

6a Agnes Dorothy Mary; *b* 16 March 1901; *m* 18 April 1933 Frank Parris (*d* 12 Nov 1954) and had:

  1b *David Francis; *b* 6 July 1936

  1b *Helen Mary Jean; *b* 21 Feb 1934

  2b *Catherine Mary; *b* 9 April 1935

  3b *Elinor Mary; *b* 25 Jan 1939

7a Margaret Elizabeth Mary; *b* 16 April 1905

(2) Oswald Arthur; *b* 8 Sept 1848; *m* Isabel, dau of Maj — Leach, and had:

1a Archibald

1a Helen

2a Mabel; *m* George Austin and had issue

3a Patricia; *m* Ernesto de Fernandez Artiga and had issue

4a Dorothy

(3) Sebastian Henry; *b* 21 Oct 1856; slr; *m* 18 June 1881 Elise (*d* 4 Jan 1946), dau of W Edmund Sibeth, of Rowney Abbey, Herts, and *d* 21 Feb 1934, leaving:

  1a Henry Aloysius, DSO (1916), MC; *b* 12 June 1884; slr 1905, Maj RAF WW I (despatches); *m* 6 Aug 1929 Kathleen Coad, widow of Langley Lefroy and dau of Robert L Detires, of Toronto, and *dsp* 24 April 1962

  2a Edward; *b* 27 April 1886; *d* 24 Dec 1912

  3a William; *b* 12 Oct 1888; FLAS, Capt RASC and F/Cdr RAF WW I (despatches); *m* 4 June 1925 Margaret Gwladys (*d* 1 May 1982), dau of Archibald Dacres Bruce, of Acton Burnell Park, Salop, and *d* 3 Aug 1955, leaving:

    1b *Ann Mary Margaret [Mrs John Hales-Tooke, 8 Priory Rd, Cambridge CB5 8HT]; *b* 27 March 1926; *educ* Somerville Coll Oxford (MA); *m* 15 Nov 1955 John Edward Turner Hales-Tooke (*d* 1992), est s of John Baseley Hales-Tooke, MC, of Cathedral Close, Norwich, and has:

      1c *Jonathan Petre Turner Paul; *b* 29 June 1957; *m* 1994 *Breda Flaherty

      2c *Hugh Benedict Milton; *b* 20 April 1959

      3c *Giles Anthony Raphael; *b* 24 Oct 1964

    2b *Mary Elise [Mrs Leonard Pardoe, 7 Hereford Sq, London SW7]; *b* 28 May 1929; *m* July 1951 *Leonard Norman Pardoe, 2nd s of W A L Pardoe, of Otterhampton, Somerset, and has:

      1c *Sebastian William Joseph; *b* 11 Aug 1956; *m* 1980 *Amanda Walley and has:

        1d *Charles Edward Adam; *b* 1990

        2d *Harry; *b* 1993

      2c *Matthew James Wentworth; *b* 1960; barrister Inner Temple 1992

      1c *Louise Mary Anne; *b* 26 Aug 1952; has:

        1d *Claudia Louise Isobel Chapman; *b* 1993

    3b Helen Elizabeth; *b* 25 April 1939; *m* 12 Feb 1967 *Peter Gordon Halsted, only s of C G V Halsted, of Paradise Bay Hotel, Malta, and *d* 1982

  4a Bernard Francis; *b* 5 Dec 1891; Capt MT RASC WW I (despatches); *m* 20 Nov 1926 *Mary Lucy [Mrs Bernard Petre, Ferwood Lea, Oakley, Fife], dau of Archibald Dominic Smith Sligo, of Inzievar, Oakley, Fife, and *d* 4 Jan 1977, having had:

    1b John Leslie Joseph; *b* 25 Dec 1928; *d* Jan 1929

    2b +Michael Henry Charles; *b* Oct 1930; Hon DPh U of Brasilia 1965; *m* 3 Jan 1959 (*divorce* 1980) Christian Margaret Lilias, er dau of John Franc Finch McIntyre by Elspeth Mary, er dau of Malcolm Cyril Drummond (*see* PERTH, E), and has had:

      1c Liam John Joseph; *b* and *d* 27 Aug 1959

      2c +Benedict Francis Joseph; *b* 16 July 1967

      3c +Gavin Ruaraidh Joseph; *b* Nov 1969

      1c *Tanya Mairi; *b* 4 Jan 1961; *m* 1981 *Nicholas Lunn

      2c *Helena Mary Alathea; *b* 1964

3c *Kathryne Maria; *b* 1965

4c *Elspeth Moira; *b* 1972

5a John Joseph, DSC; *b* 11 April 1894; S/Cdr RNAS WW I (despatches, Croix de Guerre); *ka* 13 April 1917

1a Mary Josephine Lawrentia; *b* 10 Aug 1882; *d* unm 18 Jan 1959

2a Sybil Mary; *b* 26 June 1899; *m* 27 Dec 1921 F/Lt William Frederick R Gough, s of Frederick Gough and Lady Bellingham, of Castle Bellingham, and *d* 17 April 1929, leaving issue

(4) Robert George; *b* 17 June 1861; *m* 1 March 1892 Elizabeth Grace (*d* Feb 1937), dau of Robert Ferguson, of Southbridge, Canterbury, and *d* 27 Oct 1922, having had:

  1a Robert John; *b* 1894; NZ Forces WW I; *ka* 1915

  2a +Francis William [Francis Petre Esq, 28 Hautana Square, Lower Hutt, New Zealand]; *b* 1902; *m* 1st 6 April 1932 (*divorce* 1944) Gertrude Fey, dau of Philip Lowry Wright, of Bicton, Napier, NZ, and:

    1b +John Lowry; *b* 18 June 1934; *m* 28 Aug 1962 *Susan Helen, dau of Edwin Thomas Durrant, of Auckland, NZ, and has:

      1c *Michael; *b* 8 Aug 1964

      2c +Daniel; *b* 9 Sept 1966

      1c *Sally; *b* 18 July 1963

  2a (cont.) Francis Petre *m* 2nd 21 Aug 1947 *Athalie Millicent, dau of Albert Henry Eaton, of Raumati S, NZ, and by her has:

    2b +Robert Bruce; *b* 20 Feb 1952

    1b *Ann Mary Elizabeth; *b* 15 Sept 1948; *m* 1972 *Robert Joseph Stella and has:

      1c *Daniel John; *b* 1976

      2c *Nicholas James; *b* 1979

      1c *Lucy Jane; *b* 1982

    2b *Eleanor Jane; *b* 13 Aug 1954; *m* 1976 *John Kane, of Wellington, NZ, and has:

      1c *Alexander John Petre; *b* 1985

      1c *Eleanor Mary Petre; *b* 1989

1a Sybil Mary; *m* 14 Dec 1926 Vincent Aubrey Ward (*d* 9 Feb 1946), CBE, 2nd s of Sir Joseph George Ward, 1st Bt, of Wellington (*qv*)

2a Elizabeth Bertha; *m* 18 Feb 1942 Lloyd Kendall Wilson, only s of Charles Kendall Wilson

(5) John; *b* 11 Oct 1866

(1) Lucy Agnes; *m* 14 June 1871 Philip Wellesley Colley (*d* 19 April 1926), of Mayfair, and *d* 21 Jan 1923, leaving issue

(2) Mary Julia; *m* 9 Jan 1873 Edward Carington Wright, of Kelvedon Hall, Essex, and had issue

(3) Dorothy Mary; *m* 10 May 1881 Theodore Sibeth, yst s of W E Sibeth, of Rowney Abbey, and had issue

(4) Mabel Mary; *m* 28 July 1891 Frank Chadwick

(5) Sybil Mary, nun; *d* 29 April 1937

(6) Florence Mary; *m* 22 July 1893 Surgn Lt-Col Charles Randolph Kilkelly, CMG, MVO, MB, BCh, Gren Gds (*d* 1953), s of Surgn-Gen Charles Edward Kilkelly, JP, FRCS, of Drimcong, Co Galway, and *d* 24 Jan 1956, leaving issue

(7) Helen Mary; *m* 12 April 1887 Sir William Lawrence Young, 8th Bt, of North Dean (*qv*), and *d* 11 June 1921

2 (cont.) The Hon Henry Petre *m* 2nd 12 July 1886 Sara (*d* 11 April 1928), widow of Lt-Col Julian Horne Holme, 3rd Middx Artillery, and dau of Stephen Joseph Cantwell, and *d* 3 Dec 1889

1 Mary Agnes; *m* 29 Oct 1838 James Alexander Douglas (*d* 11 June 1862), of Gray's Inn and Ealing, and *d* 22 Aug 1886

2 Charlotte Elizabeth; *m* 23 May 1849 her cousin Charles Edward Petre (*d* 13 June 1899), only s of Hon Charles Petre, and *d* 31 Oct 1903, having had issue (*see above*)

The **11th Baron** *m* 2nd 14 April 1823 Emma Agnes (*d* 10 Feb 1861), 2nd dau of Henry Howard, of Corby Castle, Cumberland (*see* NORFOLK, D), and by her had:

3 Frederick Charles Edmund, JP Essex; *b* 22 Dec 1824; *m* 29 July 1847 Georgiana (*d* 11 April 1868), est dau and coheir of Sir Christopher John Musgrave, 9th Bt, of Hartley Castle (*qv*), and *d* 18 July 1906, having had, with other issue:

(1) Reginald William; *b* 23 April 1851; *educ* Beaumont; *m* 30 April 1889 Caroline, dau of J Alexander Preston, of Baltimore, USA, and had:

  1a Reginald M; *b* 14 June 1893; *d c* 1915

  2a Alexander Preston; *b* 31 Oct 1894; *m* 20 April 1935 *Stuart, dau of Stuart Olivier, banker, of Baltimore

  1a Constance Achsah Ridgeley; *b* 1 May 1897; *m* April 1921 William Carrington Stettinius, s of Edward R Stettinius, and had issue

(2) Douglas; *b* 8 Nov 1852; *m* 1879 Agnes M (*m* 2nd 17 Aug 1920 Capt Algernon Learmonth, Essex Regt), dau of John C Hunter, and *d* 1912

(3) Alfred; *b* 8 Feb 1854; *educ* Beaumont

(4) Hubert Francis; *b* 1 Oct 1861; *educ* Beaumont

(5) Cuthbert Joseph; *b* 15 March 1864; *educ* Beaumont

(1) Constance; *m* 15 Jan 1873 Brodie Manuel de Zulueta, Count de Torre Diaz (*m* 2nd 1892 Hon Bertha Mary Agnes Clifford, dau of 8th Baron De Clifford (*qv*), and *d* 20 Sept 1918), and *d* Jan 1890

(2) Gertrude; *b* 29 Sept 1855; nun

(3) Agnes Mary; *b* 28 Jan 1863; *d* unm 5 June 1939

4 Arthur Charles Augustus, of Coptfold, Essex; *b* 29 March 1827; *m* 4 July 1855 Lady Katherine Howard (*d* 27 Dec 1882 aged 51), yst dau and coheir of 4th Earl of Wicklow, KP (*see* 1970 edn), and *d* 4 Nov 1882, leaving, with other issue:

(1) Laurence Joseph, of Coptfold; *b* 3 Oct 1864; Lt Roy W Surrey Regt; *m* 10 Oct 1890 Jennie (*d* 1 Sept 1943), dau of A Williams, of Cincinnati, USA, and *d* 3 April 1944, leaving:

  1a Louis John; *b* 24 June 1891; *educ* Beaumont; *d* unm 8 Dec 1942

  2a Roderick Lawrence; *b* 1 Aug 1902; *d* unm 12 July 1964

  1a Mildred Mary; *b* 10 Nov 1895; FRGS, racing motorist, pioneer aviatrix, first solo flight to Japan 1930, Order Million Elephants and White

Umbrella; m 16 Feb 1926 (divorce 1941) Hon Victor Austin Bruce, 4th s of 2nd Baron Aberdare (qv)

(1) Beatrice Mary; m 11 Feb 1879 Henry Ferrers Ferrers (d 23 Sept 1916), of Pentreheylin Hall, Oswestry, est s of Capt Boydell Croxton, and d 20 June 1930, having had issue

(2) Adela Jane; m 28 Oct 1879 John Michael Sweetman Powell (d 8 March 1907), of Lamberton Park, Queen's Co, and dsp 10 March 1947

(3) Emma Agnes; b 28 Feb 1862; Sister of Charity; d 20 May 1954

(4) Maude Dominica Mary; b 4 Aug 1863; d unm 16 Dec 1942

(5) Margaret Mary; b 26 July 1875; m 1 June 1897 Capt Ralph Philip Clutton, RN (d 27 March 1942), s of Henry Clutton, of S Kensington, and d 6 Sept 1969, leaving issue

5 Edmund George; b 23 June 1829; m 3 June 1851 Mary Anne (d 4 Aug 1895), est dau of Loraine M Kerr, and d 1 Sept 1889, leaving:

(1) Francis Loraine, OBE; b 22 Feb 1852; BCS, barrister; m 20 Jan 1887 Maud Ellen (d 22 Oct 1945), yr dau of Rev W C Rawlinson, Rector Chedburgh, Suffolk, and d 9 May 1925, leaving:

1a Roderick Loraine, CB (1940), DSO (1917), MC; b 28 Nov 1887; educ Downside and RMC Sandhurst; cmded Dorsetshire Regt WW I (despatches seven times), Ch Staff and Cdr Sudan 1936–38, Cmdt Sr Offrs Sch 1938–39 (Brig), Maj-Gen S Wales Borderers 1939, served WW II, Cdr 12th Div and 'Petreforce' France, 48th Div and Northumbrian Dist; m 12 July 1922 Katherine Sophia (d 25 June 1973), only dau of Herbert William Bryans, DL, of The Priory, Bradford-on-Avon, Wilts, and Sheerwater Court, Byfleet, Surrey, and d 21 July 1971, leaving:

1b +Francis Herbert Loraine [His Honour Francis Petre, The Ferriers, Bures, Suffolk C08 5DL]; b 9 March 1927; educ Downside and Clare Coll Cambridge (BA); barrister Lincoln's Inn 1952, Dep Chm E Suffolk QS 1970, Circuit Judge 1972–97, Regular Judge Centl Criminal Court 1982–93, Chm Police Complaints Authority 1989–92; m 19 April 1958 *Mary Jane, est dau of Everard Charles Xavier White, of NZ, and has:

1c +Jonathan Charles Loraine [Jonathan Petre Esq, 29 Algarve Rd, London SW8]; b 17 Jan 1959; m 1987 *Emma Victoria, twin dau of Neil Hobson, of London, and has:

1d +Robert Francis; b 1989

1d *Eleanor Mary Rosamond; b 1993

2c +William Francis; b 20 March 1963

3c +Hugh Robert Edward; b 9 Feb 1970

1c *Harriet Mary [Mrs Mark Hinton, 58 Nasmyth St, London W6 0HB]; b 28 Sept 1961; m 1987 *Mark William Hinton, er s of Dr Michael Hinton, of W Burton, Sussex

1b *(Mary) (Coletta) Rosamond; b 11 Oct 1928; m 31 Dec 1960 *David Reginald Whately, only s of Joseph Anthony Davis Whately, of Chiddingly, Sussex, and has:

1c *Roderic Joseph; b 5 July 1962

2c *Francis Richard; b 2 Nov 1966

1c *Alice Katherine Mary; b 21 March 1964

1a Enid Beatrice; b 3 March 1890; d unm 13 Oct 1962

2a Elaine Maud; b 5 May 1894; m 19 Nov 1921 Lt-Cdr Reginald Dudley Rowe, DSC, RN (d 30 April 1966), and had:

1b *Barry Loraine Dudley, DSC and bar; b 2 Sept 1922; educ RNC Dartmouth; m 16 Sept 1948 *Margaret, dau of Robert E Lynch, of Washington, DC, and has:

1c *Philip Barry; b 23 May 1959

1c *Annette Loraine; b 18 Dec 1949

2c *Jacqueline Margaret; b 8 April 1956

(1) Rosamond Catherine, MBE; b 25 Aug 1857; m 1st 18 Feb 1886 4th Earl of Bantry (d 30 Nov 1891; see 1891 edn); m 2nd 7 Dec 1897 2nd Baron Trevor (qv) and d 5 Feb 1942

6 Albert Henry; b 15 March 1832; m 3 April 1883 Katherine Elsie (m 2nd 10 Nov 1919 Sir Charles Hawtrey (d 30 July 1923); d 14 Nov 1930), dau of Rev William Robinson Clark, DCL, and d 5 April 1917, having had a s (d young)

3 Agnes Louisa Catherine; m 30 Sept 1845 8th Baron De Clifford (qv) and d 25 May 1891 aged 65

The 11th BARON d 3 July 1850; his est son,

WILLIAM BERNARD PETRE, 12th Baron Petre, Grand Cross Order of Pius IX; b 20 Dec 1817; m 26 Sept 1843 Mary Theresa (d 31 Dec 1895), est dau of Hon Charles Thomas Clifford (see DE CLIFFORD, B), and d 4 July 1884, leaving:

1 WILLIAM JOSEPH PETRE, 13th Baron Petre; b 26 Feb 1847; RC priest, Domestic Prelate Vatican; d 8 May 1893

2 BERNARD HENRY PHILIP PETRE, 14th Baron Petre; b 31 May 1858; Lt Lincoln Regt; m 6 June 1899 Etheldreda Mary (Audrey) (d 4 Nov 1959), Order of Mercy, dau of Rev William Robinson Clark, DD, DCL, Vicar Taunton and Preb Wells, and d 16 June 1908, leaving:

(1) MARY FRANCES KATHERINE Petre, BARONESS FURNIVALL (19th holder) in her own right (see Lineage (of Furnivall) below), as which recognised on termination of abeyance 3 May 1913; b 27 May 1900; m 1st 20 July 1920 (divorce 1931) Capt Augustine Willington Shelton AGAR, VC, DSO, RN (d 31 Dec 1968), s of John Shelton Agar, of Ceylon and Woolmount, Co Kerry, and had:

1a A son; b and d 1 Jun 1922

(1) (cont.) BARONESS FURNIVALL m 2nd 23 Feb 1932 (divorce 1944) William Herbert Shelley DENT, MC (d 12 May 1981), only s of Herbert Dent, of Canton, China, and d 24 Dec 1968, when the Barony fell into abeyance between her daus, leaving:

1a +ROSAMOND MARY [Sister Ancilla OSB, St Mildred's Abbey, Minster, Kent]; b 3 June 1933; educ Holychild Convent Mayfield

2a +PATRICIA MARY [The Hon Mrs Bence, Trotwood, Gresham Rd, Limpsfield, Surrey RH8 0BS]; b 4 April 1935; m 1st 25 Aug 1956 (divorce 1963) Capt Thomas Hornsby (d 1967), Durham LI, s of Thomas Walton Hornsby, of Blackhill, Co Durham, and has:

1b +Walton Francis Petre; b 21 April 1958

1b +Clare Mary Petre [Mrs Robert Harbord, Grey Gables, High St, Longborough, Glos GL56 0QE]; b 25 Jan 1957; m 1984 *Robert Ralph Harbord (see SUFFIELD, B) and has issue

2a (cont.) The Hon Mrs Patricia Hornsby m 2nd 1970 *Lt Roger Thomas John Bence, Westminster Dragoons, and by him has:

2b +Richard William Petre; b 1976

2b +Katharine Rosamond Petre; b 1971

3 PHILIP BENEDICT JOSEPH, 15th Baron

4 Joseph Lucius Henry; b 22 April 1866; Capt Suffolk Yeo Cav; ka Boer War 24 Jan 1900

1 Frances Mary; m 4 Sept 1873 7th Earl of Granard (qv) and d 25 May 1920, having had issue

2 Isabella Mary; m 14 Sept 1869 Frederick Stapleton-Bretherton (d 13 April 1919), JP, of The Hall, Rainhill, Lancs, and Heathfield House, Fareham, and d 15 July 1919, leaving issue

3 Margaret Mary; nun

4 Katherine Mary Lucy; d unm 21 Oct 1932

5 Theresa Mary Louisa; nun

6 Mary Winifrede; Sister of Charity; d unm 31 July 1947

7 Eleanor Mary; m 25 Aug 1880 Edward Southwell Trafford (d 2 Aug 1912), of Wroxham Hall, Norfolk, and d 17 Nov 1908, leaving issue

8 Monica Mary; m 5 Feb 1879 Lt-Col John Erdeswick Butler-Bowdon, DL (d 2 Jan 1929), of Southgate, Derbys, and Pleasington Hall, Lancs, and d 15 May 1907, having had issue

The 14th BARON's bro,

PHILIP BENEDICT JOSEPH PETRE, 15th Baron Petre; b 21 Aug 1864; Lt 3rd Bn E Lancs Regt; m 19 July 1888 Julia Mary (d 23 Oct 1931), est dau of George Cavendish-Taylor and gdau of Charles Carroll, of Carrolton, Md., and had:

1 LIONEL GEORGE CARROLL 16th Baron

1 Barbara Louisa Mary; b 7 May 1889; m 29 April 1919 Robert Boyne Wallace Crothers (d 22 Feb 1969), est s of Wallace Crothers, of Chew Magna, Somerset

2 Clare Stella Mary; b 24 Feb 1893; m 20 Oct 1920 Col Dennis Malcolm King, DSO, and bar, MC, The King's Regt (d 12 Aug 1960), s of Edward J King, of Calcutta, and d 15 Jan 1960, leaving issue

The 15th BARON d 6 Dec 1908; his only son,

LIONEL GEORGE CARROLL PETRE, 16th Baron Petre; b 3 Nov 1890; Capt Coldstream Gds; m 28 June 1913 Catherine Margaret, JP Essex (m 2nd 21 July 1921 Sir Frederick Carne Rasch, 2nd Bt (qv), and d 1983), only child of Hon John Richard de Clare Boscawen, DL (see FALMOUTH, V), and had:

1 JOSEPH WILLIAM LIONEL, 17th Baron

1 *Elizabeth Mary Lionel Margaret [The Hon Mrs Healing, The Priory, Kemerton, Glos GL20 7JN]; b posthumously 13 Dec 1915; m 27 May 1935 Maj Robert Peter Healing (d 1991), only s of Lt-Col Robert Kingsbury Healing, Duke of Wellington's Regt, of Camberley, Surrey, and has had:

(1) Michael Lionel Kingsbury; b 10 March 1936; educ Eton; Maj Gren Gds; m 14 April 1966 *Amanda Mary, dau of Frank R Rabone, of Gatcombe Park, Minchinhampton, Glos, and d 5 March 1970

(2) *Julian Robert Peter [Julian Healing Esq, Château d'Astis, 64450 Astis, France]; b 23 Oct 1939; educ Eton; m 1970 *Sabine Marie Louise Françoise, dau of Christian de Sorbier de Pougnadoresse, of Magescq, France

(1) *Susan Elisabeth [Mrs Edward Carbutt, Mount Hall, Great Horkesley, Essex CO6 4BZ]; b 15 Sept 1945; m 11 Oct 1966 *Edward Reymond Carbutt and has issue (see DE MONTMORENCY, Bt)

(2) *Carolyn Margaret [Mrs Christopher Clayton, 1 Faucett St, London SW10 9HN]; b 15 Sept 1945; m 25 Sept 1972 *Christopher Sands Clayton, slr, er s of Archibald Sands Clayton, of Lane House, Bracknell, Berks, by Hon Ruth Evelyn, JP, yst dau of Baron Goddard, GCB, PC (see 1970 edn)

The 16th BARON d 30 Sept 1915 of wounds recd in action in France; his only s,

JOSEPH WILLIAM LIONEL PETRE, 17th Baron Petre; b 5 June 1914; educ Eton; Capt 5th Bn Essex Regt, 2nd Lt Coldstream Gds SR WW II; m 25 Oct 1941 *Marguerite Eileen [The Rt Hon The Dowager Lady Petre, 32 The Downs, Rosemary Lane, Gt Dunmow, Essex], dau of Ion Wentworth Hamilton, of Nettlebed, Oxon, and d 1989, leaving:

1 +JOHN PATRICK LIONEL, 18th and present Baron Petre

Lineage (of Furnivall): GERARD de FURNIVALL(E), whose name probably derived from Fourneville, near Honfleur in Normandy, accompanied RICHARD I to the Holy Land and was present at Acre 1191; granted land by KING JOHN 1200; m Andel — and had:

GERARD de FURNIVALL(E); m Maud (d on or after 23 June 1247), dau and heiress of Willian de Luvetot, feudal Ld of Worksop, Notts (d by 1181) by Maud (b c 1161), dau of Walter fitz Robert, and d 1219, having had, with two yr sons (Gerard, living 1265, ancestor of the FURNIVALLs of Munden, Herts; William, of Rotherham, Yorks, m Ada (living 1268), dsp by 1260):

THOMAS de FURNIVALL(E), of Sheffield, Yorks, and Worksop, Notts; feudal Ld of Hallamshire; granted by HENRY III 1237 wardship and marriage of William, s of Roger de Moubray; m Berta (m 2nd Ralph (le) Bigod (d by 28 July 1260), 3rd s of 3rd Earl of Norfolk; see NORFOLK, D, preliminary remarks), and d on or after 13 April 1238, having had:

1 Gerard (Sir); feudal Ld Hallamshire; m Maud (m 2nd c 1270 9th Earl of Warwick (see WARWICK, BROOKE and, E) of the 1088 cr and d April 1301), est dau of Sir John fitz Geoffrey and sis and eventual coheir of Sir Richard fitz John, of Shere and Fambridge, and dsp by 18 Oct 1261

2 THOMAS (Sir)

1 A dau; m William de Moubray (see above)

The yr s,

Sir THOMAS de FURNIVALL(E), of Brassington, Eyam, Stoney Middleton, Derbys, Grassthorpe and Worksop, Notts, and Sheffield, Yorks; feudal Ld Hallamshire; licensed 1270 to build a castle at Sheffield; d 12 May 1291, having had:

Sir THOMAS de FURNIVALL(E), 1st LORD (Baron) FURNIVALL(E) (E), so cr (according to later doctrine) by writ of summons to Parl 24 June 1295; fought at

Battle of Falkirk against Scots 1298; m 1st by Jan 1272/3 Joan, dau of 1st Lord (Baron) le Despenser of the putative 1264 cr (see FALMOUTH, V), and had:

   1 THOMAS, 2nd LORD
   1 Catherine; m 2nd Lord (Baron) Thweng and dsp 1349
   3 Eleanor; m by 1309 2nd Lord (Baron) Mauley

The 1st LORD (Baron) FURNIVALL(E) m 2nd by 8 June 1322 Elizabeth (d Aug 1354), widow of 2nd Lord (Baron) Montagu of the 1299 cr and dau of Sir Piers de Mo(u)ntfort, of Beaudesert, Warwicks, and d just prior to 18 April 1332, having had another s (William), whether by his 1st or 2nd w is unknown

His er s,

   THOMAS de FURNIVALL(E), 2nd LORD (Baron) FURNIVALL(E), as which called to Parl by writ vp from 25 Aug 1318, it being probable that the summons was to him in right of his w's position as a great heiress; b c 1291–1301; m 24 Feb 1317/8 Joan (b 9 or 11 Aug 1303; m 1st 28 April 1317 John de Montagu (dsp & vp by 14 Aug1317), est s of 2nd Lord (Baron) Montagu of the 1299 cr (see above); d 2 Oct 1334), est dau and coheir of Theobald de Verdun, 1st/2nd Lord (Baron) Verdun, who brought him Alton Castle and other estates in Staffs, and d 5, 7 or 14 Oct 1339, having had, with other issue:

   1 THOMAS de FURNIVALL(E), 3rd LORD (Baron) FURNIVALL(E); b 22 June 1322; served in the expedn to France that culminated in the victory of Crécy 1346; m 1st by 1336 Margaret — (d on or after 20 June 1344); m 2nd Joan (d 1395/6), dau and heir of Sir Thomas de Mounteney, of Cowley and Shirecliffe, Yorks, and Bulcote, Notts, and formerly w of Sir John Bret, and dsp 21 April 1365
   2 WILLIAM, 4th LORD
   1 Maud; m 2nd Lord (Baron) Marmion and was living 1348
   2 Margaret; b 1320; allegedly m 3rd Lord (Baron) Montfort (dspmsl 24 Jan 1369/70) and d 29 Oct 1339

The 3rd LORD's yr bro,

   WILLIAM de FURNIVALL(E), 4th LORD (Baron) FURNIVALL(E); b 25 Aug 1326; held the Manor of Farnham Royal, Bucks, by service of providing a glove for the King's right hand on his coronation day and supporting the King's right arm while he held the sceptre; these services were rendered by (a) 4th LORD at RICHARD II's coronation, (b) Thomas Nevill, in right of his w, at HENRY IV's coronation, (c) the 1st Earl of Shrewsbury and Waterford, again in right of his w, at HENRY V's coronation, (d) the 5th Earl of Shrewsbury and Waterford and de jure 10th LORD (Baron) FURNIVALL at EDWARD VI's coronation, (e) the 7th Earl of Shrewsbury and Waterford and de jure 12th LORD (Baron) FURNIVALL at JAMES I's coronation and (f) the 6th Duke of Norfolk and de jure 15th LORD (Baron) FURNIVALL at CHARLES II's coronation, on the the last two occasions by virtue of tenure of the Manor of Worksop, which the 7th Earl of Shrewsbury and Waterford and de jure 12th LORD (Baron) FURNIVALL had exchanged for Farnham Royal; m between 3 Feb 1364/5 and 20 Jan 1365/6 Thomasine, widow of Sir John de Dagworth, of Dagworth, Suffolk, and Bradwell, Essex, and dspm 12 April 1383, leaving an only dau:

JOAN de Furnivall(e), de jure BARONESS FURNIVALL(E) in her own right according to later doctrine; b c 1368; m by 1 July 1379, as his 1st w, Thomas de NEVILL(E) (see ABERGAVENNY, M), regarded as 5th LORD (Baron) FURNIVALL(E) in right of his w, though called to Parl by writ 20 Aug 1383 as NEVILL OF HALUMSHIRE [sic], and had:

MAUD de Nevill(e), de jure BARONESS FURNIVALL(E) in her own right according to later doctrine; b c 1392; m by 12 March 1406/7, as his 1st w, Sir John TALBOT, 1st Earl of Shrewsbury and Waterford (qv), who was called to Parl as LORD (Baron) De FURNYVALL or De HALOMSHIRE [sic] in right of his w 26 Oct 1409, and d c 1423, leaving:

JOHN TALBOT, de jure 7th LORD (Baron) FURNIVALL(E) and 2nd Earl of Shrewsbury and Waterford; had:

JOHN TALBOT, de jure 8th LORD (Baron) FURNIVALL(E) and 3rd Earl of Shrewsbury and Waterford; had:

GEORGE TALBOT, de jure 9th LORD (Baron) FURNIVALL(E) and 4th Earl of Shrewsbury and Waterford; had:

FRANCIS TALBOT, de jure 10th LORD (Baron) FURNIVALL(E) and 5th Earl of Shrewsbury and Waterford; had:

GEORGE TALBOT, de jure 11th LORD (Baron) FURNIVALL(E) and 6th Earl of Shrewsbury and Waterford; had:

GILBERT TALBOT, de jure 12th LORD (Baron) FURNIVALL(E) and 7th Earl of Shrewsbury and Waterford; d 1616, when the Earldoms passed to his bro while the Baronies or right thereto of Furnivall(e), Strange (of Blackmere) and Talbot are deemed by later doctrine to have fallen into abeyance between his daughters, having had, with two sons (dvp unm) and two er daus (see also PEMBROKE and MONTGOMERY, E, and LUCAS OF CRUDWELL, B):

ALATHE(I)A Talbot, who on the death of her siblings inherited sole right to the abeyant Baronies, thus becoming according to later doctrine de jure BARONESS FURNIVALL(E) in her own right; m 1606 Thomas HOWARD, 21st/14th Earl of Arundel, 3rd Earl of Surrey and 1st Earl of Norfolk (see NORFOLK, D), and d 24 May 1654, having had, with other issue:

HENRY FREDERICK HOWARD, 22nd/15th Earl of Arundel, 4th Earl of Surrey and 2nd Earl of Norfolk; dvm 1652, leaving, with other issue:

   1 THOMAS HOWARD, de jure 14th LORD (Baron) FURNIVALL and 5th Duke of Norfolk; d unm 1677
   2 HENRY HOWARD, de jure 15th LORD (Baron) FURNIVALL and 6th Duke of Norfolk; had:
      (1) HENRY HOWARD, de jure 16th LORD (Baron) FURNIVALL and 7th Duke of Norfolk; dsp 1701
      (2) Thomas; d 1689, leaving:
         1a THOMAS HOWARD, de jure 17th LORD (Baron) FURNIVALL and 8th Duke of Norfolk; dsp 1732
         2a EDWARD HOWARD, de jure 18th LORD (Baron) FURNIVALL and 9th Duke of Norfolk; dsp 1777, when the Dukedom passed to his cousin but the Baronies of Furnivall, Strange (of Blackmere) and Talbot, or right thereto, fell into abeyance between the representatives of his deceased yr bro (as

also did the Baronies of Mowbray and Segrave; see MOWBRAY, SEGRAVE and STOURTON, B)

3a Philip, of Buckenham, Norfolk; m 8 Nov 1739, as his 2nd w Henrietta (d 26 March 1782), dau and coheir of Edward Blount, of Blagdon, Devon, and widow of Peter Proll, of Antwerp, and d 23 Jan 1749/50, having by her had, with a s (d young):

   2b ANN Howard; b 29 Aug 1742; m 19 April 1762, as his 1st w, **9th Baron Petre** (see above) and d 5 Jan 1787, leaving:
      1c **10th Baron Petre**; had:
         1d **11th Baron Petre**; had:
            1e **12th Baron Petre**; had:
               1f **13th Baron Petre**
               2f **14th Baron Petre**; had:
                  1g MARY FRANCES KATHERINE Petre, BARONESS FURNIVALL

Seat: Ingatestone Hall, Ingatestone, Essex. Despite the Petres' unswerving Catholicism since the reign of QUEEN MARY, they had acquired the manor of Ingatestone in 1539 as part of the spoils of the suppressed Barking Abbey. Indeed the Sir William Petre who as Secretary of State 1543–66 was one of Thomas Cromwell's chief lieutenants in bringing about the Dissolution of the Monasteries. The house rose remarkably quickly, being finished externally less than ten years after the 1539 Act authorising the complete destruction of all remaining monastic foundations. It took until around 1560 to complete internally, however, but at least Sir William lived to see his new house ready to inhabit. The layout consisted of three courts, which were constructed of brick.

Shortly after Sir William's death the family established their main residence at Thorndon and in the later 18th century part of Ingatestone was pulled down and the rest split into separate dwellings. Proper restoration had to wait till a generation after the fire that destroyed Thorndon (see above), indeed till after World War I, during which period the Petres moved back into one wing while the Essex Records Office occupied the other.

PETRIE

Arms: Azure on a bend, between in chief a stag's head couped and in base three crosses crosslet fitchée argent, as many escallops gules. **Crest:** A demi-eagle displayed proper gazing at a sun or. **Motto:** Fide sed vide ('Trust but observe'). **Creation:** Bt. (UK) 20 June 1918.

SIR PETER CHARLES PETRIE, 5TH BT, of Carrowcarden, Castleconnor, Tireragh, Co Sligo, CMG (1980) [Sir Peter Petrie Bt CMG, 16A Cambridge St, London SW1V 4QH; 40 rue Lauriston, Paris 75116, France; Le Hameau du Jardin, Lestre, 50310 Montebourg, France]; b 7 March 1932; s half-bro 1988; educ Westminster and Ch Ch Oxford (BA Lit Hum, MA); 2nd Lt Gren Gds 1954–56, Dip Serv 1956–89: 2nd Sec UK Del NATO Paris 1958–61, 1st Sec and HC New Delhi 1961–64, Chargé d'Affaires Katmandu 1963, 1st Sec Br Mission UN New York 1969–73, Counsellor Bonn 1973–76, Head European Integration Dept FCO 1976–79, Min Paris 1979–85, Amb Belgium 1985–89, Advsr Govr Bank of England 1989–; m 8 Nov 1958 *Lydwine Marie Fortunata, dau of Count Charles Alphonse van Oberndorff, of The Hague, Paris and Domaine d'Orio, Hendaye, and has:

   1 +CHARLES JAMES; b 16 Sept 1959; educ American Coll Paris (BA) and INSEAD Fontainebleau; 2nd Lt 67th French Inf Regt, ch sr consultant Coopers and Lybrand 1987–90, UN Emergency Unit Sudan 1990–92, UN Operation Somalia 1992–94; m 1981 *France, dau of Count Bernard de Hauteclocque, and has had:
      (1) +Arthur Cecil; b 15 Feb 1987
      (2) +Oliver Bernard; b 12 July 1989
      (3) +Victor François; b 1992
      (1) Cecilia Marie Bernard; b and d 1985
   2 +Wilfrid John; b 18 Oct 1965; educ Ecole St Jean de Passy, Lycée Louis Le Grand and Ecole Polytechnique; m 1989 *Fabienne, dau of Louis Lacaille, of Paris
   1 *Leticia Jacqueline Fortunata Cecilia; b 28 March 1961; m 1989 *Pierre-André de Chalandaer and has:

(1) *François; *b* 1990

(2) *Jacques; *b* 1992

Lineage: PETER PETRIE, of Newburgh, Fife; had:

ALEXANDER PETRIE, of Carrowcarden, Enniscrone, Co Sligo; *b* 14 Aug 1823; *m* 1845 Margaret, dau of Charles Lyell, of Abernethy, Perthshire, and had, with an er s (Peter, of Knoxbarrett, nr Ballina, Co Mayo, *dsp* 1931):

Sir Charles Petrie, 1st Bt (UK), so *cr* 20 June 1918 JP Liverpool, DL Lancs; *b* 23 Feb 1853; Liverpool: Alderman, Ld Mayor 1901–02, memb W Lancs TFA, pres Liverpool Constitutional Assoc, ktd 1903; *m* 30 Sept 1880 Hannah Lindsay, Medal of Queen Elisabeth of Belgians (*d* 27 April 1933), dau of William Hamilton, of Liverpool, and *d* 8 July 1920, leaving:

1 **Sir Edward Lindsay Haddon Petrie, 2nd Bt**; *b* 30 Sept 1881; *educ* Shrewsbury and Pembroke Coll Cambridge; served WW I; *m* 24 April 1912 Blanche (*d* 16 Aug 1968), dau of C J Allen, of Stanbury, Berks, and *dspm* 13 Dec 1927, leaving:

(1) *Violet Haddon [Mrs William Allison, 6 Camus Park, Edinburgh EH10 6RY]; *b* 23 March 1913; *m* 1st 9 Jan 1937 (*divorce*) Charles Edward Wilson Sleigh, yr s of Sir William Lowrie Sleigh, LLD, JP, DL, and has:

1a *Thomas Edward [Thomas Sleigh Esq, The Gardens Cottage, E Saltoun, E Lothian EH34 5DS]; *b* 27 Aug 1939; gen sales dir Rossleigh; *m* 30 Sept 1965 *Daphne Mary Walker, dau of Dr Charles Boness-Jones, of Bengal, and has:

1b *David Edward; *b* 1969

2b *Charles Timothy Fisher; *b* 1971

1b *Patricia Mary; *b* 1967

1a *Rosemary Anne [Mrs George Dobry, 40 Chester Row, London SW1]; *b* 15 Dec 1937; *m* 1st 1956 (*divorce* 1975) Walter Ronald Alexander and has:

1b *Walter; *b* 1957

2b *Charles Edward; *b* 1963

1b *Rosalind; *b* 1959

2b *Caroline; *b* 1961

1a (cont.) Mrs Rosemary Alexander *m* 2nd 1982 His Honour Judge (George Leon Severyn) Dobry, CBE

(1) (cont.) Mrs Violet Sleigh *m* 2nd 21 Dec 1950 William Dalziell Mungall Allison (*d* Dec 1957), only s of William S Allison, JP, DL, of Edinburgh, and by him has:

2a *Robert William Mungall; *b* 20 Dec 1951; *m* 1982 *Pamela Louise, dau of William Dougal Taylor

(2) *Mary Bianca [Miss Mary Petrie, Little Bracken, Lincoln Dve, Pyrford, Surrey]; *b* 15 Nov 1918

2 **Sir Charles Alexander Petrie, 3rd Bt**, CBE (1957); *b* 28 Sept 1895; *educ* privately and Corpus Christi Coll Oxford (BA 1919, MA 1921); historian, FRHistS, corresponding memb Roy Spanish Acad of History and Hispanic Soc of America, Hon Counsellor Institute Fernando Catolico of Zaragoza 1959, Hon DPhil U of Valladolid 1964, Lt RGA WW I, Kt Order Civil Merit Spain, Cdr Order Isabella the Catholic Spain, Commendatore Crown Italy, Order George I Greece; author: *The History of Government* (1929), *George Canning* (1930), *The Jacobite Movement* (1932), *History of Spain* (with Louis Bertrand, 1934), *The Four Georges: a revaluation* (1935), *The Stuarts* (1937), *Life and Letters of Sir Austen Chamberlain* (2 vols, 1939, 1940), *Diplomatic History 1713–1933* (1946), *Earlier Diplomatic History 1492–1713* (1949), *Chapters of Life* (1950), *The Marshal Duke of Berwick* (1953), *The Carlton Club* (1955), *Wellington: a reassessment* (1956), *The Spanish Royal House* (1958), *The Powers Behind the Prime Ministers* (1959), *The Victorians* (1960), *The Modern British Monarchy* (1961), *Philip II of Spain* (1963), *King Alfonso XIII* (1963), *Scenes of Edwardian Life* (1965), *Don John of Austria* (1967), *Great Beginnings* (1967), *The Drift to World War 1900–1914* (1968), *King Charles III of Spain* (1971), *A Historian Looks at His World* (1972); *m* 1st 7 Oct 1920 (*divorce* 1926) Ursula Gabrielle Borthwick (*d* 27 Oct 1962), est dau of Harold Chaloner Dowdall, KC, of Oxford, and had:

(1) **Sir (Charles) Richard Borthwick Petrie, 4th Bt**, TD; *b* 19 Oct 1921; *educ* Radley and New Coll Oxford; Lt-Col REME WW II and TA 1952, memb Oxon T&AFA; *m* 27 Nov 1962 Jessie Ariana Borthwick (*d* 8 July 1995), dau of Cdr Patrick Straton Campbell, JP, RN, of Westleton, Saxmundham, Suffolk, and *dsp* 1988

2 (cont.) **Sir Charles** *m* 2nd 24 Feb 1926 Jessie Cecilia (*d* 1987), Mayor Kensington 1954–56, er dau of Frederick James George Mason, of Cheam, Surrey, and *d* 23 Nov 1977, having by her had:

(2) Sir PETER CHARLES PETRIE, **5th and present Bt**

PEYTON OF YEOVIL

PATIOR·POTIOR

Arms: Sable a cross engrailed, in the first quarter a mullet or. **Crest:** A griffin sejant or. **Supporters:** Dexter, on a mount vert with four oak sprigs growing therefrom fructed or, a bull rampant regardant in trian aspect sable, armed, membered, the tail tuft and muzzle or, unguled gules, holding in the mouth an oak sprig fructed or and a shamrock slipped vert; sinister, on a mount vert growing therefrom four shamrocks slipped proper, a griffin segreant regardant or, grasping in the beak a shamrock slipped proper and an oak sprig fructed gold. **Motto:** *Patior Potior* ('I endure, I obtain'). **Creation:** B. (LP, UK) 1983.

THE BARON PEYTON OF YEOVIL, of Yeovil, Co Somerset (John Wynne William Peyton, PC (1970)) [The Rt Hon The Lord Peyton of Yeovil PC, The Old Malt House, Hinton St George, Somerset TA17 8SE; 6 Temple West Mews, West Sq, London SE11 4TJ]; *b* 13 Feb 1919; *educ* Eton and Trin Coll Oxford; 2nd Lt 15th/19th Hus 1939 (POW 1940–45); barrister Inner Temple 1945; MP (C) Yeovil 1951–83; Parly Sec Min Power 1962–64, Min Tport 1970, Min Tport Industs DoE 1970–74; chm: Texas Instruments 1974–90, Br Aluminium 1987–91; Treas Zoological Soc London 1984–91; author: *Without Benefit of Laundry* (autobiography); *m* 1st 1947 (*divorce* 1966) Diana, dau of Douglas Clinch, of Durban, and has:

1 *Thomas Richard Douglas; *b* 1950; *educ* Eton; *m* 1981 *Vivien, dau of Dr Jack Birks, CBE, and has had:

(1) *Joseph Anthony Charles; *b* 1986

(2) *David Christopher William; *b* 1990

2 Charles Michael Eliot; *b* 1955; *d* 1960

1 *Sarah Grenville; *b* 1948; *m* 1st 1971 Dugald Graham-Campbell and has issue; *m* 2nd 16 Jan 1996 *Rex Chester

BARON PEYTON OF YEOVIL *m* 2nd 1966 *Mary Constance, dau of Col Hon (Everard) Humphrey Wyndham, MC (*see* EGREMONT, LECONFIELD and, B) and formerly w of Ralph Hamilton Cobbold

Lineage: IVOR ELIOT PEYTON; *m* Dorothy Helen — and had:

JOHN WYNNE WILLIAM, *cr* a **Baron**

PHILIPSON-STOW

Arms: 1st and 4th, vert on a cross nebuly between four leopard's faces or a rose gu. (for STOW); 2nd and 3rd, gu. two chevronels between three boar's heads couped erm. (for PHILIPSON).
Crests: 1 Issuant from an antique crown or, charged with a rose gu., a leopard's face gold between two wings vert (for STOW), 2 Issuant from a mural crown or, charged with a rose gu., a plume of five ostrich feathers alternately arg. and gu. (for PHILIPSON).
Motto: *Fide non fraude* ('By faith not trickery').
Creation: Bt. (UK) 26 July 1907.

SIR CHRISTOPHER PHILIPSON-STOW, 5TH BT, of Lodsworth, Sussex, DFC [Sir Christopher Philipson-Stow Bt DFC, 26 Cambridge St, Penetanguishene, Ont L9M 1E6, Canada]; *b* 13 Sept 1920; *s* 1st cousin 1982; *educ* Winchester; F/Lt RCAF (Res), F/Lt RAF WW II; *m* 1952 *Elizabeth Nairn, dau of James Dixon Trees, of Toronto, and widow of Maj Frederic George McLaren, 48th Highrs, of Canada, and has:

1 +ROBERT MATTHEW [Robert Philipson-Stow Esq, 32 John St, Thornhill, Ontario, Canada L3T 1X8]; *b* 29 Aug 1953; *educ* Thornhill Secondary Sch and Waterloo U Ont (BASc, PEng)

2 +Rowland Frederic; *b* 2 Sept 1954; *educ* Thornhill Secondary Sch and Waterloo U (BASc, PEng); *m* 1979 *Mary Susan, dau of William J N Stroud, of Thornhill, and has:

  (1) +Christopher William; *b* 1983

  (1) *Kimberly Susan; *b* 1981

Lineage: THOMAS STOW(E), of N Wheatley, Notts; had:

WILLIAM STOW, of East Stockwith and Morton, Lincs; *b* 1686; *m* Elizabeth, dau and coheir of Robert Hopkins, of Tresswell, Notts, and *d* 1724/5, leaving, with other issue:

WILLIAM STOW, of West Stockwith in Mistertin, Notts; *b* 1715; *m* Elizabeth — and was *bur* 3 Sept 1754, leaving, with an er s:

GEORGE STOW, of Sutton Ashfield, Notts; *bapt* 11 Jan 1740; *m* 23 Aug 1767 Elizabeth (*d* 6 May 1782), only dau and eventual heiress of John Wilberfoss, of Gainsborough (a descendant of the WILBERFORCEs of Wilberforce, Yorks), by Elizabeth, est dau and eventual heiress of Richard Philipson, of Beverley, Yorks, and *d* 1773, having had:

GEORGE STOW, of London; *b* 19 Aug 1768; *m* 22 July 1792 Ann (*m* 2nd William Cradock, of Nuneaton, and *d* Jan 1841), dau and coheir of Humphrey Winter, of Coton Ho, Warwicks; and *d* 21 May 1794, having had, with a dau (*d* young):

GEORGE STOW, of Nuneaton, Warwicks; *b* posthumously 15 Aug 1794; *m* Feb 1820 Sarah, dau of William Bartlett, of Brentford, by Ann Carey, and *d* 24 Oct 1845, leaving:

1 George William, of Orange Free State; *b* 2 Feb 1822; FGS, FRGS; *m* 1st 23 July 1844 Caroline Elizabeth (*dsp* 1866), dau of James Skinner, of Bathurst; *m* 2nd 7 Jan 1868 Frances Sophia (*dsp* 1868), dau of Rev John Heaviside; *m* 3rd 13 Sept 1869 Fanny Louisa Russel (*m* 2nd 17 Feb 1886 Rev Henry James Organ and *d* 1 Dec 1902, leaving issue), dau of Assist Commissary-Gen de Smidt, and *dsp* 17 March 1882

2 FREDERIC

3 John, of Tarkastad, Cape Colony; *b* 23 Sept 1830; *m* 1 Dec 1856 Lydia Hurst (*d* 21 March 1886), dau of William Parke, and *d* 1920, leaving:

  (1) George; *b* 14 Aug 1859; *m* 19 Dec 1907 Alexandria Sinclair, dau of Charles Louis Fanner, of Port Elizabeth, S Africa

  (2) John; *b* 12 Aug 1862; *m* 4 Jan 1894 Margaret, dau of Henry Mann, of London, and had:

    1a William Philipson; *b* 2 Feb 1895

    1a Lydia Philipson, twin; *b* 2 Feb 1895; *d* 15 Jan 1896

    2a Jessie Philipson,

  (3) William Wilberfoss Philipson; *b* 4 May 1870; *ka* Boer War 29 July 1901

  (4) Alfred Heaviside Philipson; *b* 31 Dec 1873; *d unm* 14 Feb 1903

  (1) Sarah Elizabeth

  (2) Charlotte Lydia

  (3) Anne Mary; *d* in infancy, 2 Aug 1865

  (4) Isabella Philipson; *m* 1 Dec 1888 George Norman Price and had issue. He *d* 28 June 1906

  (5) Lydia Philipson

4 Henry Ryder, of Sydney, NSW; *b* 16 Jan 1836; *d unm* 31 Dec 1856

1 Ann; *m* 31 Aug 1845 Rupert Pincott, MRCS, of Geelong, Victoria, and had issue. He *d* 1902

2 Elizabeth Wilberfoss; *m* 1864 Adolphus Constantine Brewer and *dsp* 27 Aug 1876. He *d* April 1870

3 Isabella Sarah; *m* 24 Jan 1856 Lt-Col Robert Thomas Wolfe and *d* 25 Dec 1895, having had issue. He *d* 10 April 1908

4 Mary; *m* 13 Oct 1860 Col Robert Mead, Dep Commissary-Gen Ordnance, and had issue. He *d* 10 March 1902

5 Emma Charlotte; *d unm* 1894

The 2nd son,

FREDERIC STOW, of Steenbokspan, Orange Free State; *b* 15 Feb 1828; *m* 24 June 1848 Fanny (*d* 24 Nov 1888), dau of Samuel Sanders, of Burton-on-Trent, Staffs, and *d* 27 May 1897, having had, with other issue:

Sir FREDERIC SAMUEL STOW later PHILIPSON-STOW (roy licence 28 Feb 1891), **1st Bt** (UK), so *cr* 26 July 1907, of Blackdown House, Lodsworth, Sussex, and Cape Town; *b* 28 Sept 1849; *m* 22 Dec 1874 Florence Henchman (*d* 22 Dec 1930), dau of Henry Hewitt, of Cape Town, and *d* 17 May 1908, having had:

1 **Sir Elliot Philipson Philipson-Stow, 2nd Bt**; *b* 12 July 1876; Lt 14th Hus Boer War 1900–02 and WW I; *m* 5 Oct 1904 Edith Maud Gore (*d* 19 Nov 1943), yst dau of Edmond Henry Cokayne Pery-Knox-Gore (*see* LIMERICK, E), and *d* 23 Sept 1954, leaving:

  (1) **Sir Frederic Lawrence Philipson-Stow, 3rd Bt**; *b* 19 Sept 1905; *educ* Eton; *m* 1st 29 Sept 1932 (*divorce* 1951) Daphne Morris (*d* 4 Nov 1960), er dau of William George Daffarn, of Haslemere; *m* 2nd 30 April 1951 Cynthia Yvette, formerly *w* of Francis Romaine Govett, of Knightsbridge, and only dau of William Robertson Jecks, of Johannesburg, and *dsp* 9 Jan 1976

  (2) **Sir Edmond Cecil Philipson-Stow, 4th Bt**, MBE (1946); *b* 25 Aug 1912; Maj DCLI WW II; *d unm* 14 June 1982

  (1) Dorothy Barbara; *b* 4 Dec 1909; *m* 9 Oct 1936 Lt-Col John Bampfylde Peter-Hoblyn, DCLI, only *s* of Henry Godolphin Peter-Hoblyn, of Colquite, Cornwall, and had issue

  (2) Margaret Aileen; *b* 25 Aug 1912

2 Robert Frederic Philipson; *b* 8 March 1878; *educ* Harrow, Balliol Coll Oxford and Leyden U; barrister Inner Temple 1905; *m* 1st 1906 Fernande (*d* 22 May 1920), dau of Marc Dieuset, of Paris; *m* 2nd 20 April 1922 Hélène Marguerite Dieuset (*d* 22 March 1952) and *dsp* 3 June 1949

3 Henry Matthew Philipson, JP Surrey; *b* 11 Sept 1880; *educ* Winchester, Bergakademie Freiburg and Columbia U USA (Eng Diploma); *m* 31 Aug 1918 Elizabeth Willes, dau of Sir Thomas Willes Chitty, 1st Bt (*qv*), and *d* 15 Sept 1953, leaving:

  (1) Sir CHRISTOPHER PHILIPSON-STOW, **5th and present Bt**

4 Gordon Philipson; *b* 12 Jan 1885; *d* 15 Aug 1898

5 Rowland Miles Philipson; *b* 23 June 1893; Lt Roy Lancaster Regt; *d* 13 Sept 1920

6 Guyon Philipson; *b* 9 Sept 1898; *educ* Winchester and Trin Coll Cambridge; Lt RA WW I 1917–18, Staff Maj WW II, US Bronze Star, memb bd Miles Druce 1922–72; *m* 24 Oct 1925 Alice Mary (*d* 1989), only child of R Hilton Fagge, of Melton Mowbray, and *d* 1983, leaving:

  (1) +Robert Nicholas [Robert Philipson-Stow Esq, Priors Court, Long Green, Glos GL19 4QL]; *b* 2 April 1937; *educ* Winchester; FCA, 2nd Lt RHG 1955–57; *m* 25 Sept 1963 *Nicolette Leila, er dau of Hon Philip Leyland Kindersley (*see* KINDERSLEY, B), and has:

    1a +Robert Rowland; *b* 23 Sept 1970; Capt Blues and Royals

    2a +Edward Miles; *b* 30 April 1972

    1a *Georgina Mary; *b* 26 Oct 1976

  (1) *(Helen) Rosemary; *b* 19 Sept 1934

1 Alice Ellinor Philipson; *d unm* 7 March 1974 aged 91

2 Dorothy Florence Philipson; *m* 7 Sept 1926 Bache Thornhill Heathcote, *s* of T B Heathcote, of Betchworth, Surrey, and *d* 25 Sept 1945, having had issue

3 Audrey Frances Philipson, CBE (1956), JP and CA Lancs; *m* 20 Jan 1914 Lt-Col Sir James Worsley-Taylor, 2nd Bt (*see* 1956 edn), and *d* 2 May 1966, having had issue. He *d* 27 April 1933

PHILLIMORE

FORTEM · POSCE · ANIMUM

Arms: Sable three bars indented erminois, in chief an anchor between two cinquefoils or. **Crest:** In front of a tower argent, thereon a falcon volant proper holding in the beak a lure gold, three cinquefoils fesswise or. **Supporters:** On either side an owl proper, charged with an anchor or. **Motto:** *Fortem posce animum* ('Pray for a brave soul'). **Creations:** Bt. (UK) 28 Dec 1881, B. (UK) 2 July 1918.

THE 5TH BARON PHILLIMORE, of Shiplake, Co Oxford, and a **Baronet** (Sir Francis Stephen Phillimore, Bt) [The Rt Hon The Lord Phillimore, Coppid Hall, Binfield Heath, Oxon RG9 4JR]; *b* 25 Nov 1944; *s f* 1994; *educ* Eton and Trin Coll Cambridge, barrister Middle Temple (1972); *m* 27 March 1971 *Nathalie Berthe Louisa, dau of Michael Anthony Pequin, of Paris, and has:

1 +TRISTAN ANTHONY STEPHEN; *b* 18 Aug 1977
2 +Julian Michael Claud; *b* 3 Nov 1981
1 *Arabella Maroussia Eleanor; *b* 22 Feb 1975

Lineage: WILLIAM FYNIMORE, of Dursley, Glos; *m* Isabel — and *d* 1508, leaving:

JOHN FYNAMORE, of Cam, Glos; *m* Alice Tyndale, and *d c* 1530, leaving:

WILLIAM PHINIMORE, of Cam; *m* Alice — (*d* 1586), and *d* 1590, leaving:

RICHARD PHINIMORE; *m* Margaret Trotman and *d* 1616, leaving:

JOHN PHILLIMORE, of Cam; *b* 1590; *m* Joan Nelme and *d* 1681, leaving:

JOHN PHILLIMORE, of Cam; *b* 1634; *m* Eleanor Atherly and *d* 1711, having had:

JOSEPH PHILLIMORE, of Cam; *b* 1669; *m* Anna D'Oyley and *d* 1704, leaving:

ROBERT PHILLIMORE, of Kensington, Middx; *b* 1699; *m* 1743 Elizabeth Jephson, n of William Jephson, of Kendalls, Herts, and *d* 10 Aug 1779 aged 80, leaving, with an er s (William, of Kendalls, ancestor of William Brough Phillimore, of Kendalls, who *dsp* 5 Feb 1887, leaving his property to his cousin the **1st Baron**):

Rev JOSEPH PHILLIMORE; *b* 1750; Vicar Ortun-on-the-Hill, Leics; *m* 5 Jan 1775 Mary (*d* 2 Feb 1810), dau of John Machin, of Kensington, and had, with three daus:

1 JOSEPH
2 William, of Deacon's Hill, Herts, JP; *b* 6 Feb 1777; barrister; *m* 4 April 1807 Almeria (*d* 22 May 1851), yr dau of Godfrey Thornton, of Mogerhanger, Beds, and *d* 28 Nov 1860, leaving issue
3 John (Sir), CB, of The Ray, Maidenhead, Berks; *b* 18 Jan 1781; Capt RN; *m* 17 Feb 1830 Baroness Catherine Harriet von Raigersfeld (*d* 7 Dec 1841), yr dau of R-Adml Baron von Raigersfeld, s of the Austrian Min to UK, and *d* 20 March 1840, leaving:

(1) Henry Bouchier, CB, of Lansdown, Bath; Adml; *m* Anne Ellen, dau of Edmond Dewar Bourdillon, and *d* July 1893 aged 59, leaving:

1a John Ernest, ICS; *b* 18 Feb 1869; *m* Helen Todd (*d c* 1949) and *d* 29 July 1927

2a Hugh Bouchier; *b* 16 Dec 1873; *m* Lucy Mary Bedford (*d* 1931) and *d* of wounds 15 June 1915, leaving:

1b John Hugh Bouchier; *b* 1911; *educ* Westminster; Maj 9th Lancers WW II (wounded); *m* 1st Marjorie Isabel (*d* 27 Nov 1973), dau of James Summerhill, and had:

1c +John James Jocelyn (Toby) [John Phillimore Esq, Town Court Farm, Bayham Rd, Tunbridge Wells TN2 5HU]; *b* 26 Feb 1942; *educ* Millfield and Bordeaux U

1b (cont.) Maj John Phillimore *m* 2nd 30 June 1955 (*divorce* 1960) Mrs Alison Russell, dau of Sir Nigel Campbell; *m* 3rd 1960 *Nadine Felicite Sydney, Croix de Guerre, widow of Capitaine Paul Mezan, Chev Legn Hon, Companion Order Liberation, Croix de Guerre, MC, and dau of Capt Arthur John Swinton, RE, and *d* 26 May 1973

1b *Mary Jocelyn Bouchier; *b* 1904

3a Reginald Henry, CIE (1944), DSO (1918); *b* 19 June 1879; *educ* Westminster and RMA Woolwich; Col RE WW I (despatches four times), WW II as Capt RE, on Gen Staff, AHQ Simla 1940–42, Survey India 1903–34 and

1942–46, author: *History of Survey of India*; *m* 1910 Eileen Elizabeth (*d* 21 March 1968), dau of Samuel Crosthwait, of Co Carlow, and *dsp* 30 Oct 1964

4a William Raigersfeld, CBE (1940); *b* 24 March 1884; *educ* Cheltenham; Capt RN, served WWs I and II, cmdg Contraband Control, Ramsgate; *m* 15 April 1914 Vera Winifred (*m* 2nd 4 Feb 1961 R-Adml Frank Elliott, OBE (*d* 20 Aug 1970 aged 80), s of Frank Elliott), and *d* 3 May 1950, leaving:

1b *(Hugh) David [David Phillimore Esq, Hill House, Highfield Lane, Thursley, Surrey GU8 6QJ]; *b* 22 March 1922; WW II with RAF; *m* 10 June 1957 *Catherine Lucy, yr dau of Anthony C Barnes, DSO, OBE, of Cobham, Surrey, and has:

1c *Clare Penelope; *b* 1 April 1964

2b *(William Harry) Edmund OBE [Cdr Edmund Phillimore OBE RN, Nunton House, Beckington, Somerset BA3 6SJ]; *b* 3 Sept 1931; *m* 10 June 1961 *Christina Elizabeth, yr dau of Col W D Macrae, MC, TD, of Holmehill, Dunbartonshire, and has:

1c *William Andrew Justin; *b* 3 Nov 1962; *m* 28 Sept 1996 *Joanna Godden

1c Penelope Carolyn Mary; *b* 26 July 1966; *d* 8 June 1989

1b *Pamela Joyce [Miss Pamela Phillimore, 3 Cedar Court, Raveridge Lane, Bishops Waltham, Hants SO32 1DX]; *b* 26 Jan 1917

2b *Margaret Alice [Miss Margaret Phillimore, 3 Cedar Court, Raveridge Lane, Bishops Waltham, Hants SO32 1DX]; *b* 20 Oct 1919

1a Grace; *b* 1867; *d* unm 1945

2a Mary; *b* 1870; *m* Capt William Elwin Napier (*d* 14 Jan 1952), 4th s of Rev Alexander Napier, Vicar Holkham, Norfolk, and *dsp* 15 June 1958

3a Agnes Elizabeth; *d* by 1905

4a Rose Kathleen; *d* by 1905 aged 20

5a Margaret; *b* 1880; *d* May 1926

6a Ruth; *b* 6 July 1882; *d* 1973

7a Eleanor; *b* 2 Sept 1886; *m* 1914 M J E R Orchard, MB (*d* June 1968), and *d* 18 Feb 1964, leaving issue

4 Robert (Rev); *b* 1783; Rector Slapton, Bucks, Vicar Shipton-under-Wychwood, Oxon; *d* unm 25 Sept 1852

5 George; *b* 1784; Lt RN; *d* unm 19 Dec 1807

The Rev JOSEPH PHILLIMORE *d* 29 July 1831; his s,

JOSEPH PHILLIMORE, of Shiplake House, JP; *b* 14 Sept 1775; Advocate Admlty, Regius Prof Civil Law Oxford, Chll dioceses of Oxford, Worcester and Bristol, MP St Mawes and Yarmouth, DCL Oxon; *m* 19 March 1807 Elizabeth (*d* 5 March 1859), dau of Rev Walter Bagot, Rector Blithfield and Leigh, Staffs (bro of 1st Baron Bagot; *qv*), and had, with another s (*d* young) and two daus (*d* unm):

1 John George, of Shiplake, QC; *b* Jan 1808; MA, MP Leominster 1852–57, author; *m* 1 Aug 1839 Rosalind Margaret, yr dau of Sir James Lewis Knight Bruce, PC, V-Chllr, Ld Justice, and *d* 27 April 1865, leaving:

(1) Egerton Grenville Bagot; *b* 20 Dec 1856; *educ* Ch Ch Oxon (MA); *m* twice and *d* 3 June 1937, leaving by his 1st w, with two other daus:

1a John George; *b* 24 Oct 1880; *educ* Berkhamsted GS and Merton Coll Oxford; RAMC WW I; *d* unm 13 Nov 1961

1a Rosalind Margaret; *d* unm 21 Feb 1953 aged 71

2 ROBERT JOSEPH (Sir), **1st Bt**

3 Charles Bagot; *b* 1 Sept 1818; *m* 2 Aug 1860 Caroline Sophia (*d* 7 April 1913), dau of Rev Thomas Randolph, Rector Much Hadham, Herts, Chaplain to HM QUEEN VICTORIA, and *dsp* 21 Dec 1894

4 Greville (Rev); *b* 5 Feb 1821; Rector Ewelme, Oxon; *m* 16 April 1857 Emma Caroline (*d* 24 April 1911), dau of Ambrose Goddard, of The Lawn, Swindon, Wilts, MP, and *dsp* 21 Jan 1884

5 Augustus (Sir), KCB, DL Hants; *b* 24 May 1822; Adml, C-in-C Devonport 1884–87; *m* 29 March 1864 Harriet Eleanor (*d* 4 Sept 1924), dau of Hon George Matthew Fortescue (*see* FORTESCUE, E), and *d* 25 Nov 1897, leaving:

(1) Richard Fortescue (Sir), GCB (1929, KCB 1919, CB 1914), KCMG (1918), MVO (1905), JP Hants; *b* 23 Dec 1864; *educ* Westminster and HMS *Britannia*; WW I: cmded HMS *Inflexible*, Pncpl Beach Master Gallipoli 1915, attd Russian Imp HQ 1915–16 with rank of R-Adml, Cdr 1st Battle Cruiser Sqdn 1916–18, Adml cmdg Aircraft Carriers March 1918, Pres Post-War Questions Ctee 1918–19, V-Adml cmdg Home Fleet 1922, C-in-C Devonport 1923–26, Pncpl Naval ADC to HM GEORGE V 1928–29, Cdr Legn Honour, Order Rising Sun Japan 2nd Cl, Orders SS Vladimir and Stanislaus Russia; *m* 21 Dec 1905 Violet Gore (*d* 31 Jan 1963), yr dau of Henry Hobhouse Turton, and *d* 8 Nov 1940, leaving:

1a Richard Augustus Bagot, DL (Hants 1965); *b* 9 Jan 1907; *educ* RNCs Osborne and Dartmouth; Cdr RN WW II, High Sheriff Hants 1960; *m* 28 June 1948 *Pamela Mary, yr dau of Lt Col Arthur James Darlington, DSO, of Little Meon House, Soberton, Hants, and had:

1b *Peter Richard; *b* 10 Feb 1950; *educ* Marlborough and Edinburgh U

2b *Roger Henry; *b* 30 Aug 1951; *educ* Marlborough

3b *Charles Robert; *b* 28 Jan 1953; *educ* Marlborough

4b *Mark Augustus; *b* 26 April 1956; *educ* Marlborough

2a John Gore, CMG (1946), DL (Kent 1979); *b* 16 April 1908; *educ* Winchester and Ch Ch Oxford (BA 1929, MA 1960); merchant banker, md Baring Bros 1949–72, dir Brascan Ltd, Cwlth Devpt Fin, W H Smith and Tribune Investment Tst, Rhodes Tstee, ptnr Roberts, Meynell and Co Buenos Aires 1936–48, Rep Treasury and Bank of England S America 1940–45, High Sheriff Kent 1975, Liveryman Fishmongers' Co (5th Warden 1973–75, 2nd Warden 1975–76), Order Mavo Argentina 1961; *m* 14 June 1951 *Jill Irene, 2nd dau of Capt Mason Scott, RN (*see* SCOTT, Bt, of Beauclerc), and has:

1b *John Francis; *b* 16 June 1952; *educ* Winchester

2b *Hugh Richard; *b* 28 Dec 1959

1b *Louisa Mary; *b* 6 March 1954; *m* 29 April 1975 *John Charles Rudolph Paravicini, s of Col Vincent Paravicini, of Nutley Manor, nr Basingstoke, Hants

2b *Penelope Jane; *b* 14 Jan 1956

3a Robert Fortescue, MBE (1943), DSC (1944), JP (Hants 1962); *b* 16 May 1912; *educ* Winchester; Capt RN WW II; *m* 8 July 1939 Rachel Louise (*d* 17 Jan 1998), yst dau of George Kidston, CMG, of Hazelbury Manor, Box, Wilts, and had:

    1b *William Dominic; *b* 30 March 1948; *educ* Winchester

    1b *Christine Mary; *b* 10 Feb 1946

    2b *Clare Elizabeth; *b* 30 June 1949; *m* 19– *Andrew Grant and has issue (*see* ARBUTHNOT, Bt, of Edinburgh)

    3b *Prudence Anne; *b* 2 Jan 1953

    4b *Harriet Lucy; *b* 1 Feb 1964

1a *Margaret Caroline [Mrs Richard Wells, Meonwood, Woodend, Wickham, Hants]; *b* 4 Nov 1914; *m* 12 Sept 1942 *Cdr Richard Frederick Wells, OBE, DSC, RN, er s of Capt Norman Ffolliott Wells, OBE, VRD, RNVR, of Mariners Cottage, Felixstowe Ferry, and has:

    1b *Thomas Norman; *b* 22 June 1943; *educ* Radley and McGill U Montreal (BA); ADO N Nigeria Govt 1964–65, with: Standard Bank 1966, Metal Box 1967

    2b *Jonathan Richard; *b* 1 April 1945; *educ* Milton Abbey and Shuttleworth Ag Coll

    3b *Francis William; *b* 30 Aug 1947; *educ* Eton and RNC Dartmouth

    4b *Anthony Stephen; *b* 4 June 1950; *educ* Eton and Exeter U

(2) George Grenville; *b* 28 Oct 1867; *educ* Westminster and Ch Ch Oxford (MA); BCL, barrister 1891, Hon Sec Internat Law Assoc, Assist Charity Commr 1905–12, Dist Registrar Bristol and Winchester 1914–25; *m* 1 Aug 1893 May Melba (*d* 26 Nov 1925), dau of Henry William Franklyn, of Shedfield Lodge, Hants, and *d* 20 Sept 1925, having had:

    1a Henry Augustus Grenville; *b* 31 July 1894; *educ* Westminster and Ch Ch Oxford (BA 1922, MA 1923); assist master Cothill Sch, WW I Punjab and Palestine (wounded), HG WW II; *d* unm 19 Sept 1969

    2a Matthew Arden; *b* 17 March 1896; *educ* Westminster and Ch Ch Oxford; 11th Bn Essex Regt WW I; *ka* 25 June 1916

    1a Hester Mary Melba; *b* 7 Oct 1900; *m* 11 June 1932 Gen Sir Frederick Alfred Pile, 2nd Bt (*qv*), and *dsp* 8 Dec 1949

(3) Charles Augustus; *b* 11 Aug 1871; *educ* Westminster and Ch Ch Oxford (MA); Assist Priv Sec to 1st Earl St Aldwyn (*qv*), ptnr Coutt's Bank 1935, dir Ag Mortgage Corp; *m* 8 Dec 1908 Alice (*d* 25 July 1965), 2nd dau of Col William Henry Campion, CB, of Danny, Sussex, and *d* following a car crash 30 Oct 1950, having had:

    1a (Henry) Josceline (Sir), OBE (1946), PC (1968); *b* 1910; *educ* Eton and Ch Ch Oxford; barrister Middle Temple 1934, RA and Col Staff WW II, QC 1952, Bencher 1959, Recorder Poole 1946–54 and Winchester 1954–59, High Court Judge 1959–68 , ktd 1959, Ld Justice Appeal 1968–74, Dep-Chm Oxfordshire QS 1956–62, Chm 1962, Jr Counsel Nuremberg Trials; *m* 1938 *Katharine Mary, JP (Oxon 1955), dau of Lt-Cdr Leycester Curzon Maude Roxby, RN, and *d* 4 June 1974, leaving:

        1b *Sarah Susan; *b* 1 May 1940; *m* 14 May 1964 *Sir Richard Thomas Williams-Bulkeley, 14th Bt (*qv*), and has issue

        2b *Josceline Mary [Mrs Josceline Morley-Fletcher, 73 Primrose Mansions, Prince of Wales Drive, London SW11]; *b* 7 Jan 1946; *m* 14 Jan 1967 (*divorce* 19–), as his 1st w, Hugo David Montagu Morley-Fletcher and has issue (*see* TWEEDDALE, M)

    2a Walter Augustus; *b* 7 Sept 1915; *educ* RNC Dartmouth; Submarine Service WW II; *kas* 21 June 1942

    1a *Violet Alice Valentine; *b* 1909; *m* 1 Feb 1935 (*divorce* 1941) Maj Clement Walter Rowland Hill and has issue (*see* HILL, V)

    2a *Mary Harriet, MBE (1967) [Miss Mary Phillimore MBE, 19 Daver Court, Chelsea Manor St, London SW3]; *b* 12 April 1912

(4) John Swinnerton; *b* 26 Feb 1873; *educ* Westminster and Ch Ch Oxford (MA); Hon LLD St Andrews, LittD Trin Coll Dublin, Prof Greek and Humanity Glasgow U; *m* 26 July 1900 Margaret Cecily (*d* 6 Aug 1965 aged 90), only dau of Rev Spencer Compton Spencer-Smith (*see* SPENCER-SMITH, Bt), and *d* 16 Nov 1926, leaving:

    1a John Michael Fortescue; *b* 8 Sept 1903; Cdr RN WW II, Managing Govr Marist Fndn Memorial Tst; *m* 8 Oct 1945 *Felicity, only dau of Capt Albert Broughton, RA, and *d* 23 Jan 1971, leaving:

        1b *David Phillimore [David Phillimore Esq, 195 Rivermead Court, Ranelagh Gdns, London SW6]; *b* 22 Sept 1946; *m* 19 Dec 1969 *(Elizabeth) Louise, only dau of H N Murfin, of Johannesburg, and has:

            1c *Robert; *b* 8 Nov 1973

            1c *Kate; *b* 6 Oct 1975

        2b *John Roger Broughton [John Phillimore Esq, 195 Rivermead Court, Ranelagh Gdns, London SW6]; *b* 21 June 1949

        1b *Margaret Violet; *b* 13 April 1954

    1a Cynthia Louise; *b* 1901; *m* 2 Feb 1924 Lt-Cdr Kenneth Cary Helyar, DSO, RN (*d* 18 June 1941), s of Col Charles Helyar, of Poundisford Lodge, Taunton, and has:

        1b *Vincent John [Vincent Helyar Esq, Little Fulwood, Trull, Taunton, Somerset]; *b* 29 Nov 1924; *educ* Radley

        2b *Roger Michael [Roger Helyar Esq, 1 Radnor Cottage, Manor Brook, London SE3]; *b* 6 May 1930; *m* 3 Dec 1957 *June Muriel, only dau of Col John Theodore Milner, OBE, of Tisbury, Wilts, and has:

            1c *William Francis Kenneth; *b* 16 Oct 1962

        1b *Angela Mary; *b* 6 Dec 1932; *educ* London U (BA 1965)

(5) Valentine Egerton Bagot, CBE (1920), DSO (1900); *b* 14 Feb 1875; *educ* HMS *Britannia*; Lt Naval Bde relief Legns Peking (despatches) and WW I, Naval Advsr Br Mil Mission S Russia, Capt, ret 1928; *m* 1st 16 June 1908 Mary Kathleen (*d* 1909), dau of George Robinson, of Overdale, Yorks; *m* 2nd 16 Aug 1910 Ines Sceberras-d'Amico (*d* 21 Oct 1952), dau of Baron di Castel Cicciano, and *d* 24 Oct 1945

(6) Edward Granville (Rev); *b* 7 Sept 1876; *educ* Westminster and Keble Coll Oxford (BA 1899, MA 1929); Deacon 1900, Priest 1902, Chaplain St Catherine's Home Ventnor 1941–53, Vicar W Fordington with St Mary Dorchester;

m 1st 1903 Mabel von Essen (*d* 1911), dau of Henry Moberly, of Bitterne, Hants, and had:

    1a Barbara Louise Agnes; *b* 1905

    2a Audrey Magdalen Dominica Gwladys, BEM (1941); *b* 1907

    3a Audrey Mary Francisca; *b* 1909

    4a Joyce Elizabeth; *b* 1911; *m* 15 Oct 1947 John Christie, s of James Patrick Christie, of Langside, and had:

        1b *John Edward Phillimore; *b* 27 Aug 1948; *educ* St Aloysius Coll Glasgow

        2b *James Patrick Phillimore; *b* 21 Sept 1949; *educ* St Aloysius Coll

        3b *Joseph Adrian Fortescue; *b* 10 Nov 1950; *educ* St Aloysius Coll

        4b *Michael Phillimore; *b* 9 Aug 1952; *educ* St Aloysius Coll

        5b *(Gerard) Richard Grenville; *b* 3 Dec 1953; *educ* St Aloysius Coll

        6b *Henry Augustus Granville (twin); *b* 3 Dec 1953; *educ* Ventnor Co Secondary Sch IoW

        7b *Edmund Campion Phillimore; *b* 5 April 1955; *educ* Roy Russell Sch Croydon

(6) (cont.) The Rev Edward Phillimore *m* 2nd Gertrude May (*d* 1929), dau of Rev Thomas Greenland, Rector Raithby, Lincs, and *d* 21 April 1959

(1) Violet Elizabeth Annie; *b* 28 Dec 1869; *m* 1 June 1893 John Edward Arthur Willis-Fleming, JP, DL (*d* 28 Oct 1949), of Stoneham, Hants, and *d* 7 Feb 1960, leaving issue

Dr PHILLIMORE *d* 24 Feb 1855. His 3rd son,

Sir Robert Joseph Phillimore, 1st Bt (UK), so *cr* 28 Dec 1881, of The Coppice, Shiplake, PC (1867); *b* 5 Nov 1810; *educ* Westminster and Ch Ch Oxford; barrister Middle Temple 1841, MP Tavistock 1853–57, Advocate Admlty, Judge Cinque Ports, Chllr Dioceses of Oxford, Salisbury and Chichester, Queen's Advocate, ktd 1862, Judge High Court Admlty and Arches Court 1875, DCL Oxon; *m* 19 Dec 1844 Charlotte (*d* 19 Jan 1892), dau of John Denison, of Ossington Hall, Notts, and sis of 1st and last Viscount Ossington (*see* 1873 edn), and *d* 4 Feb 1885, having had, with several daus (*d* unm):

Sir Walter George Frank Phillimore, 2nd Bt, and **1st Baron Phillimore**, of Shiplake, Co Oxford (UK), so *cr* 2 July 1918, GBE (1928), PC (1913), JP Oxon; *b* 21 Nov 1845; Fell All Souls, bencher Middle Temple, High Court Judge 1897, official Archdeaconry Colchester, Treas 1908–09, Chllr Lincoln Docese, Ld Justice Appeal 1913, FBA, DCL Oxon, Hon LLD Edin and Birmingham, Cdr Order Crown Belgium; *m* 26 July 1870 Agnes (*d* 25 Jan 1909), est dau of Charles Manners Lushington, MP Canterbury, by Henrietta, sis of 1st Earl of Iddesleigh (*qv*), and had:

1 Robert Charles; *b* 19 Aug 1871; *educ* Ch Ch Oxford (BA); barrister; *m* 12 Dec 1895 Lucy (*d* 30 Oct 1957), est dau of William Fitzpatrick, and *dsp* 12 Sept 1919

2 Evelyn George; *b* 5 Sept; *d* 22 Nov 1873

3 GODFREY WALTER, **2nd Baron**

4 Stephen Henry (Ven), MC (and bar); *b* 14 Dec 1881; *educ* Winchester and Ch Ch Oxford (BA 1904, MA 1909); CF WW I, Rector Stepney 1926–33, Vicar St Thomas Regent St 1934–40, Rector St George's Hanover Sq 1940–54, Archdeacon Middx 1933–53, Archdeacon Emeritus 1953–56, Cdr Order Orange Nassau Netherlands; *d* unm 16 April 1956

1 Eleanor Mary; *m* 17 Sept 1895 Francis John Kynaston Cross (*d* 31 Dec 1950), JP, barrister, of Aston Tirrold Manor, Didcot, Berks, 2nd s of Edward Cross, JP, of Bradford House, Bolton, and *d* 30 May 1949, leaving issue

2 Margaret Blanche; *m* 29 July 1899 Judge Eustace Gilbert Hills, KC (*d* 17 Oct 1934), s of Herbert Hills, Judge Internat Court Appeals, Egypt, and *d* 19 Oct 1904, having had issue

3 Grace Agnes; *m* 1 June 1911 Roland Edmund Lomax Vaughan Williams, KC (*d* 22 Jan 1949), Recorder Cardiff 1930–45, only s of Ld Justice Roland Lomax Bowdler Vaughan Williams, PC, of High Ashes, Abinger, Surrey, and *dsp* 5 Oct 1966

The 1st BARON *d* 13 March 1929; his er surv son,

GODFREY WALTER PHILLIMORE, **2nd Baron Phillimore**, MC, DL Oxon; *b* 29 Dec 1879; *educ* Winchester and Ch Ch Oxford (BA 1902, MA 1909); Capt 3rd Bn Highland LI WW I (wounded, POW), FRSA; *m* 1st 5 July 1905 Dorothy Barbara (*d* 2 Sept 1915), er dau of Lt-Col Arthur Balfour Haig, CVO, CMG, JP, 28th of Bemersyde, Berwickshire (*see* HAIG OF BEMERSYDE, E), and had:

1 Anthony Francis; *b* 2 Feb 1907; Capt 9th Lancers WW II; *m* 18 July 1934 *Anne Julia [The Hon Mrs Anthony Phillimore, Coppid Hall, Henley-on-Thames, Oxon], 2nd dau of Major-Gen Sir Cecil Edward Pereira, KCB, CMG, of Kensington, and was *ka* France *c* 23 May 1940, leaving:

    (1) ROBERT GODFREY PHILLIMORE, **3rd Baron Phillimore**; *b* 24 Sept 1939; *educ* Winchester and RMA Sandhurst; 2nd Lt 9th/12th Lancers; *m* 1st 1974 (*divorce* 1982) Amanda, dau of Carlo Hugo Gonzales-Castillo by Aida Aramburu; *m* 2nd 1983 *Maria [The Rt Hon Maria Lady Phillimore, Crumplehorn Barn, Corks Farm, Dunsden Green, Berks], dau of Ilya Slonim by Tatiana Litvinov, and *d* 1990

    (1) *Frances Phoebe [The Hon Mrs Gibson, Quinta das Madres, Ulgueira, Colras, 2710 Sintra, Portugal]; *b* 24 June 1938; granted rank of baron's dau 24 May 1949; *m* 1st 16 Feb 1961 (*divorce* 1978) Colin John Francis Lindsay-MacDougall of Lunga, only s of Major John Stewart Lindsay-MacDougall of Lunga, DSO, MC, Argyll and Sutherland Highrs, and has issue (*see* CRAWFORD and BALCARRES, E); *m* 2nd 1980 *Joseph Peter Gibson, s of Charles Gibson, of Kelty Hill, Kelty, Fife

2 CLAUD STEPHEN PHILLIMORE, **4th Baron Phillimore**; *b* 15 Jan 1911; *educ* Winchester and Trin Coll Cambridge (BA 1933); architect, Actg Maj 11th City London Yeo Light AA Bde RA (TA) WW II; *m* 17 Feb 1944 Anne Elizabeth (*d* 13 Aug 1995), est dau of Maj Algernon Smith-Dorrien-Smith, DSO, JP, of Tresco Abbey, Isles of Scilly, and *d* 1994, leaving:

    (1) FRANCIS STEPHEN PHILLIMORE, **5th and present Baron**

    (1) *(Marion) Miranda [The Hon Mrs Miranda Montagu Douglas Scott, 65 Cloncurry St, London SW6 6DT]; *b* 9 May 1946; *m* 9 June 1973 (*divorce* 1985) Thomas Walter Montagu Douglas Scott (*see* BUCCLEUCH and QUEENSBERRY, D) and has:

        1a *Alice Amaryllis; *b* 24 Oct 1978

3 Robert George Hugh, OBE (1945); b 23 Sept 1913; educ Winchester, RMA Woolwich and Trin Coll Cambridge (BA 1936); Col RE WW II (despatches), US Bronze Star and Croix de Guerre with palm; m 12 Dec 1944 *Sheila Bruce [The Hon Mrs Robert Phillimore, Brook Cottage, Mill Rd, Shiplake, Oxon], 2nd Offr WRNS, 2nd dau of John Farquhar MacLeod, JP, MB, Ch.B, of Peterculter, Aberdeenshire, and d 1984, leaving:

(1) *Annabel Margaret [Mrs Hugo Gamble, The Mill House, Shiplake, Oxon RG9 3LY]; b 1 April 1947; m 1978 *Hugo Massey Gamble, s of Brig Geoffrey Massey Gamble, CMG, OBE, of The Little White Cottage, Rotherfield Greys, Oxon, and has:

1a *James Hugo Phillimore; b 1979
1a *Lucinda Diana MacLeod; b 1981
2a *Rosemary Leigh Phillimore; b 1984

(2) *Lindsay Mary MacLeod [Mrs Charles Dewhurst, Ellanore House, Ellanore Lane, West Wittering, Sussex PO26 8AN]; b 23 July 1951; m 1977 *Charles F Dewhurst, s of Col F W Dewhurst, of Pound Cottage, Buckland Monachorum, S Devon, and has:

1a *Robert Edward Charles; b 1984
1a *Anna Elizabeth MacLeod; b 1987

(3) *(Sheila) Leigh [Mrs Matthew Thorne, The Mount, Bannerdown Rd, Batheaston, Bath BA1 8EG]; b 6 Aug 1952; m 1978 *Matthew W J Thorne, s of Robin Thorne, CMG, OBE, of The Old Vicarage, Old Heathfield, Sussex, and has:

1a *Robin Lindsey Phillimore; b 1983
2a *Andew Robert Wadman; b 1986
3a *Edward; b 1989
1a *Aelene Elizabeth; b 1981
2a *Marini Annabel; b 1992

(4) *Elizabeth Ann Haig [Mrs Timothy Brutton, Greenmoor Hill Farm, Woodcote, Reading, Berks RG8 0RT]; b 22 March 1955; m 8 April 1978 *Timothy H S Brutton, s of Rev R S Brutton, of Langton Matravers, Dorset, and has:

1a *Emma Penelope Phayre; b 1981
2a *Victoria Anne Haig; b 1983
3a *Clare Elizabeth MacLeod; b 1986

4 Miles Godfrey Walter; b 24 Feb 1915; educ Winchester and Trin Coll Cambridge; served US Forces WW II; m 23 Sept 1946 *Margaret, dau of Gibson Lamb Caldwell, of Kenwood Place, Wheeling, W Virginia, and d 17 Sept 1972, leaving:

(1) *Dorothy Eleanor Barbara; b 11 Dec 1949; m 1st 14 Aug 1973 Robert William Drumm, yr s of Thomas Edward Drumm, of Rockville, Md.; m 2nd 1982 *Wayne Amos Rayfield

1 Mary; b 25 June 1909; d an infant
2 *Phoebe Margaret Dorothy [The Hon Lady Rose, 2 East Lodges, Hardwick, Oxon RG8 7RB]; b 29 Feb 1912; m 3 June 1937 Sir Charles Henry Rose, 3rd Bt, of Hardwick House (qv), and has issue

The 2nd **Baron** m 2nd 16 Nov 1923 Marion (d 22 Feb 1950), formerly w of (a) Reginald Barclay and (b) Capt Charles Bryce, Coldstream Gds, and dau of Maj-Gen Cecil Robert St John Ives, of Moynes Park, Essex, by Susan Ann, est dau of 4th Baron Talbot de Malahide (qv), and d 28 Nov 1947

PHILLIPS

VERITAS · VINCET

Arms: Or on a pile azure between two greyhounds courant in base sable a lion rampant of the first, guttée de poix. **Crest:** A demi-lion azure between two nuggets of gold, charged on the shoulder with two annulets interlaced palewise or. **Motto:** Veritas vincet ('Truth conquers'). **Creation:** Bt. (UK) 10 Feb 1912.

SIR ROBIN FRANCIS PHILLIPS, 3RD BT, of Tylney Hall, Rotherwick, Co Southampton [Sir Robin Phillips Bt, 12 Manson Mews, London SW7]; b 29 July 1940; s f 1944; educ Aiglon Coll Switzerland

Lineage: PHILIP SAUNDERS PHILLIPS, London merchant, had a 3rd surv s:

Sir Lionel Phillips, 1st Bt (UK), so cr 10 Feb 1912, JP, DL Hants; b 6 Aug 1855; High Sheriff Hants 1903; m 22 Aug 1885 Dorothea Sarah Florence Alexandra (d

23 Aug 1940), dau of Albert Frederick Ortlepp, of Colesberg, Cape Colony, S Africa, and had:

1 Harold Lionel, MBE; b 4 June 1886; educ Eton and Balliol Coll Oxford; Capt RAF (SR) WW I (despatches); m 11 June 1913 Hilda Wildman (m 2nd 15 July 1935 John Dewar Lammie), only dau of Frank Hills, JP, of Hamilton, Canada, and d 22 June 1926, leaving:

(1) LIONEL FRANCIS (Sir), **2nd Bt**

(1) Hilda Elizabeth; m 1st 4 Oct 1941 (divorce 1946) Lt-Col Peter Mant MacIntyre Kemp, DSO, yr s of Sir Norman Kemp; m 2nd 3 Aug 1946 Lt-Col George Victor Seymour (see HERTFORD, M) and d 1986, leaving issue
(2) *Mary Pamela [Mrs Arthur Hunt, Moat Manor, Kingston Blount, Oxon OX9 4RZ]; b 1919; m 26 June 1943 *Arthur Owen Hunt, 2nd s of Col Gerald Owen Hunt, and has:

1a *Clive Anthony [Clive Hunt Esq, Glebe House, Antrobus, Cheshire CW9 6JW]; b 29 Aug 1944; educ Eton; m 1980 *Philippa Jane Samuel and has:

1b *William Edward; b 1987
1b *Annabel Carolyn Philippa; b 1984

2a *David Charles [David Hunt Esq, Poplar Cottage, Compton, Surrey GU3 1JF]; b 8 Aug 1947; educ Eton; m 1974 *Julia Vivian Bennett and has:

1b *Peter Lionel; b 1981
1b *Gemma Helen b 1976
2b *Vanessa Caroline; b 1979

1a *Paula Caroline [Miss Paula Hunt, 164 Elsley Rd, London SW11 5LQ]; b 7 May 1950

2 Francis Rudolph, MC; b 11 April 1883; Capt Surrey Yeo; m 4 Feb 1920 Eileen Cecily, OBE (1950) (d c 1963), est dau of Capt John Harold Mander, OBE (see MANDER, Bt), and dsp 24 June 1942

1 Edith; b 15 Dec 1891; m 1st 3 Oct 1912 Lt-Col John Stuart-Wortley (see WHARNCLIFFE, E) and had issue; m 2nd 6 Oct 1919 Sir William Newzam Prior Nicholson (d 16 May 1949), s of William Newzam Nicholson, MP, of Newark-on-Trent, and d 30 Aug 1958, leaving further issue

Sir LIONEL d 2 July 1936; his gs,

Sir Lionel Francis Phillips, 2nd Bt; b 9 March 1914; educ Eton, chartered accountant, Capt RA WW II; m 2 Sept 1939 *Camilla Mary (m 2nd 18 July 1950 John George Pisani (d 1982) [Mrs John Pisani, 21 Chancellor House, 17 Hyde Park Gate, London SW7 5DQ], s of George Constantine Pisani, er dau of Capt Hugh Algernon Parker (see MACCLESFIELD, E), and was ka Italy 6 July 1944, leaving:

Sir ROBIN FRANCIS PHILLIPS, **3rd and present Bt**

PHILLIPS OF ELLESMERE

Creation: B. (LP, UK) 1994.

THE BARON PHILLIPS OF ELLESMERE, of Ellesmere in the County of Shropshire (Sir David Chilton Phillips, KBE (1989)) [The Rt Hon The Lord Phillips of Ellesmere KBE, 35 Addisland Court, Holland Villas Rd, London W14 8DA]; b 7 March 1924; educ Ellesmere C of E Schs, Oswestry Boys' High Sch and U Coll Cardiff; radar offr RNVR 1944–47, postdoctoral fell Nat Research Cncl Canada 1951–53, research offr Nat Research Labs Ottawa 1953–55, research worker Davy Faraday Research Lab Roy Instn London 1955–56 (Visiting Prof Physiology 1979–85), Prof Molecular Bio Physics and Fell Corpus Christi Coll Oxford 1966–90 (Emeritus Prof and Hon Fell 1990–), chm ABRC 1983–93, memb MRC 1974–78; dir Celltech 1982–97, FRS 1967 (V-Pres 1972–73 and 1976–83), FInstP, ktd 1979, V-Pres Fndn for Science and Technology 1995–, Tstee Wolfson Fndn 1988–, Govr De Montfort U 1993–, Hon FRSE 1991, Hon FRCP 1991, Hon DSc: Leicester 1974, U of Wales 1975, Chicago 1978, Exeter 1982, Warwick 1982, Birmingham 1987, Glasgow 1990, Glamorgan 1994 and Bath 1994, Hon PhD Weizmann Inst of Science 1990, DUniv Essex 1983 and Stirling 1995; Chm Finsbury Communications 1992–95; m 1960 *Diana Kathleen Hutchinson and has:

1 *Sarah Anne; b 7 June 1962

Lineage: CHARLES HARRY PHILLIPS; m Edith Harriet Finney and had:

DAVID CHILTON (Sir), cr a **Baron**

PICKTHORN

Creation: Bt. (UK) 31 Jan 1959.

SIR JAMES FRANCIS MANN PICKTHORN, 3RD BT, of Orford, Co Suffolk [Sir James Pickthorn Bt, 45 Ringmer Avenue, London SW6 5LP]; b 18 Feb 1955; s f 1995; educ Eton and Reading U (Bsc); m 17 Jan 1998 *Clare Louise, yr dau of Brian Craig-McFeely, of Sevenoaks

Lineage: WILLIAM HENRY BULLER PICKTHORN; had:

CHARLES WRIGHT PICKTHORN; b 1862; Master Mariner; m 23 Dec 1888 Edith Maud Berkeley (d 1937), dau of Henry Nanton Murray, of Mount Horne, Grenada, and d 1917, leaving:

1 KENNETH WILLIAM MURRAY, **1st Bt**

2 Charles Edward Murray, MC; b 20 Sept 1895; educ Aldenham; RFC WW I; m 2 March 1932 Hilda, dau of George Pyper, of Exeter, and d 3 March 1938, leaving:

(1) *Catherine; b 15 Feb 1936; m 3 April 1965 *Maj Charles John Gun Delamain, 13th/18th Roy Hus (QMO), only s of Col Charles Beevor Harty Delamain, OBE, MC, of Spain, and has:

1a *Charles Edward Murray; b 22 Jan 1966

2a *Alexander John; *b* 14 June 1967

1 Gladys Murray; *b* 24 Feb 1895; *m* 17 May 1928 Charles Bertram Hodgson-Nicoll (*d* 17 July 1950), s of Charles Rice Hodgson-Nicoll, of Copt Hall, Mill Hill, and *d* 6 Dec 1969, leaving issue

2 Catherine Irene Murray; Abbess of Holy Cross, Stapehill, Dorset

CHARLES PICKTHORN's est son,

Sir Kenneth William Murray Pickthorn, 1st Bt (UK), so *cr* 31 Jan 1959, PC (1964); *b* 23 April 1892; *educ* Aldenham and Trin Coll Cambridge (BA 1913, MA 1919, LittD 1936, Fell and lecturer Corpus Christi Coll 1914 (Pres 1937–44)); London Regt, RFC and RAF WW I; MP (C) Cambridge U 1935–50 and Carlton 1950–66, Parly Sec Min Educn 1951–54, memb Roy Comm Historical MSS. 1941–66; *m* 23 July 1924 Nancy Catherine Lewis (*d* 15 July 1982), dau of Lewis Matthew Richards, barrister, of Knightsbridge and S Wales, and had:

1 CHARLES WILLIAM RICHARDS (Sir), **2nd Bt**

2 +HENRY GABRIEL RICHARDS [Henry Pickthorn Esq, 54 Chelsea Park Gdns, London SW3 6AD]; *b* 29 Sept 1928; heir presumptive; *educ* Eton and Trin Coll Cambridge; *m* 9 July 1955 *Mary, only dau of Cecil James Juxon Talbot Barton, CMG, OBE, of The Old Coach House, Rye, Sussex, and has:

(1) +John Edward Juxon; *b* 23 Jan 1957

(2) +Robert Andrew Barnabas; *b* 11 June 1961; *m* 1995 *Katherine, dau of Anthony Garnett, of Gastard, Wilts, and has:

1a +Arthur William Garnett; *b* 22 Nov 1996

(3) +Thomas David Alexander; *b* 16 July 1967; *m* 1993 *Nicola, dau of His Hon Judge (John Declan) Sheerin, of Rougham, Suffolk, and has:

1a *Alice Mary Ella; *b* 22 Feb 1996

2a *Emma Frances Suzanne; *b* 2 Oct 1997

(1) *Henrietta Cicely; *b* 10 April 1959; *m* 1982 *John Ramsay Lloyd-Jones and has issue (see MAITLAND, Bt)

1 *Catherine Ann Monica [Mrs Neil Iliff, 32 Chipstead St, London SW6 3SS]; *b* 4 May 1925; *m* 6 May 1950 Neil Atkinson Iliff, CBE (*d* 5 Jan 1972), only s of Charles Wilkinson Iliff, of Macartney House, Greenwich Park, and has:

(1) *Charles; *b* 24 July 1952; *educ* Eton and Trin Coll Cambridge; *m* 1989 *Monica, dau of Jerome Dessain and has:

1a *Jonathan; *b* 17 Feb 1993

1a *Lucy; *b* 1 May 1991

(1) *Catherine; *b* 21 Nov 1955; *m* 1989 *Andrew Saul and has:

1a *Edmund; *b* 10 Nov 1990

1a *Nancy; *b* 6 Feb 1994

(2) *Elizabeth Anne Julia; *b* 28 March 1957

(3) *Mary; *b* 25 Dec 1958

(4) *Georgina Margaret; *b* 16 April 1963; *m* 1994 *Tobias Farrell and has:

1a *Gabriel; *b* 9 June 1995

Sir KENNETH *d* 12 Nov 1975; his est son,

Sir Charles William Richards Pickthorn, 2nd Bt; *b* 3 March 1927; *educ* Eton and Corpus Christi Coll Cambridge (BA); RNVR 1945–48, barrister Middle Temple 1952; *m* 5 July 1951 *Helen, only dau of Sir James Gow Mann, KCVO, and *d* 20 June 1995, leaving:

1 Sir JAMES FRANCIS MANN PICKTHORN, **3rd and present Bt**

1 *Caroline; *b* 26 Jan 1958

2 *Frances; *b* 9 April 1960 *m* 1982 *Crispin N Kelly, 3rd s of Bernard Kelly (see NORFOLK, D)

PIERCY

Arms: Per fess indented gu. and arg., in chief three pierced mullets arg., in base a lion rampant guardant sa. **Crest:** Issuant from a bezant in front of two spears in saltire, points upwards ppr., a demi-lion guardant sa., charged on the shoulder with a pierced mullet arg. **Motto:** *Spes in Deo* ('Hope in God') **Creation:** B. (UK) 14 Nov 1945.

THE 3RD BARON PIERCY, of Burford, Co Oxford (James William Piercy) [The Rt Hon The Lord Piercy, 13 Arnold Mansions, Queen's Club Gdns, London W14 9RD]; *b* 19 Jan 1946; *s* f 1981; *educ* Shrewsbury and Edinburgh U (BSc 1968); AMIEE, FCCA

Lineage: AUGUSTUS EDWARD PIERCY; had, with three daus (Jane; Rosetta Edith, *d* unm 14 Jan 1970 aged 80; Alma, Dr):

WILLIAM PIERCY, **1st Baron Piercy**, of Burford, Co Oxford (UK), so *cr* 14 Nov 1945, CBE (1919); *b* 7 Feb 1886; *educ* LSE (later lecturer and Govr); memb Allied Provisions Export Commn WW I, Dir Br Min Food USA, Head Br Petroleum Mission Washington, Pncpl Assist Sec Min Supply and Min Production, PA to Dep PM WW II, Dir Bank England, memb Nat Investment Cncl, Pres Nat Inst Industl Psychology and Roy Statistical Soc 1954, chm Industrial and Commercial Fin Corp 1945–64 and Wellcome Tst 1960–65, Order Leopold Belgium; *m* 1st 14 April 1915 Mary Louisa, OBE (*d* 8 Jan 1953), dau of Hon Thomas Henry William Pelham, CB (see CHICHESTER, E), and had:

1 NICHOLAS PELHAM, **2nd Baron**

1 Penelope Katherine , CBE (1968); *b* 15 April 1916; *educ* St Paul's Girls' Sch and Somerville Coll Oxford; U-Sec Min Technology; *d* unm 27 Dec 1997

2 *Joanna Elizabeth [The Hon Mrs Turner, Gable Cottage, 55 Witney St, Burford, Oxon OX18 4RZ]; *b* 10 Jan 1923; *educ* St Paul's Girls' Sch and Somerville Coll Oxford; Headmistress Badminton Sch Bristol; *m* 13 Aug 1968 *James Francis Turner, er s of Rev Percy Reginald Turner, of The Old Rectory, Wem, Salop

3 Priscilla Jane; *b* 7 Oct 1926; *educ* Downe House Sch and LSE; *m* 18 Nov 1950 (*divorce* 1972) Rev Thomas Fish Taylor, only s of Alexander Rattray Taylor, of Hamilton, Lanarks, and *d* 1995, leaving:

(1) *Francis Nicholas; *b* 22 July 1954; *educ* Millfield

(1) *Ann Clemency; *b* 7 Oct 1952

(2) *Helen Mary; *b* 27 Nov 1957

(3) *Bridget Jane; *b* 5 June 1961

The **1st Baron** *m* 2nd 16 July 1964 *Veronica [The Rt Hon Veronica Lady Piercy, Fair View House, Marton, Sinnington, York YO6 6RD], Dipl Social Admin (LSE) 1969, BA OU 1992, 2nd dau of John Hordley Warham, of Wembly Park, Middx, and *d* 7 July 1966

His only son,

NICHOLAS PELHAM PIERCY, **2nd Baron Piercy**; *b* 23 June 1918; *educ* Eton and King's Coll Cambridge (BA 1940, MA 1944); Lt (A) RNVR WW II ; *m* 28 Oct 1944 Oonagh Lavinia, JP (*d* 1990), dau of Maj Edward John Lake Baylay, DSO, and *d* 22 March 1981, leaving:

1 JAMES WILLIAM PIERCY, **3rd and present Baron Piercy**

2 +MARK EDWARD PELHAM [The Hon Mark Piercy, 39 Carson Rd, London SE21 8HT]; *b* 30 June 1953; heir presumptive; *educ* Shrewsbury and New Coll Oxford; barrister Lincoln's Inn; *m* 31 March 1979 *Vivien Angela, dau of His Hon Judge (Evelyn Faithfull) Monier-Williams, and has:

(1) +William Nicholas Pelham; *b* 11 March 1989

(1) *Katherine Henrietta; *b* 1 Aug 1982

(2) *Olivia Charlotte; *b* 19 Aug 1984

(3) *Harriet Lavinia; *b* 17 Jan 1987

1 *Charlotte Mary [The Hon Mrs Ropner, 1 Sunningdale Gdns, Stratford Rd, London W8 6PX]; *b* 24 May 1947; *educ* Badminton Sch; *m* 1st 14 Nov 1966 (*divorce* 1985) Paolo Emilio Taddei, 5th s of Enrico Taddei, of Florence, and has:

(1) *Guido; *b* 4 Dec 1970

(1) *Caroline Rachel; *b* 7 Aug 1967

1 (cont.) The Hon Mrs Charlotte Taddei *m* 2nd 1985, as his 2nd w, *(William Guy) David Ropner and has further issue (see ROPNER, Bt, of Preston Hall)

2 *Lavina Caroline [The Hon Mrs Sealy, Timber Hill, Chobham, Surrey]; *b* 24 May 1947; *educ* Badminton Sch and St Hugh's Coll Oxford (BA 1969); *m* 1 May 1971 *Nicholas John Elliot Sealy (see CHICHESTER, E) and has:

(1) *Edward John Pelham *b* 1975

(1) *Lucinda Clare *b* 17 July 1977

3 *Henrietta Jane [The Hon Mrs Tomba, via Corona 40, Camporformio (UD), Italy]; *b* 17 Feb 1951; *educ* Badminton Sch and St Andrews (MA); *m* 1985 *Tullio Luigi Giuseppe Tomba and has:

(1) *Tommaso Piercy; *b* 1987

(2) *Francesco Piercy; *b* 1989

PIERS

Nobilis · est · ira · leonis

Arms: Azure, three lions passant-guardant in fess between two double cotises argent. **Crest:** An arm embowed vested azure, charged with three plates and cuffed argent, the hand holding a broken flagstaff, the flag azure, on a chief argent three torteaux.
Motto: *Nobilis est ira leonis* ('Noble is the lion's anger').
Creation: Bt. (I) 18 Feb 1660/1.

SIR JAMES DESMOND PIERS, 11TH BT, of Tristernagh Abbey, Co Westmeath [Sir James Piers Bt, 3635 Bluebonnet Rd, N Vancouver, BC VR7 4C9, Canada]; *b* 24 July 1947; *s f* 1996; *educ* Shawnigan Lake Sch, Shawnigan Lake, Vancouver Island, BC, and U of Victoria, BC (BA); barrister and slr 1974, ptnr Russell and DuMoulin; *m* 1975 *Sandra Mae Dixon and has:

   1 +STEPHEN JAMES; *b* 1979

   1 *Christine Sarah; *b* 1976

Lineage: RICHARD PIERS, of Piers Hall, Yorks, had:

WILLIAM PIERS; migrated to Ireland 1566; soldier there; granted much land, including Abbey of Tristernagh, Co Westmeath; Govr Carrickfergus and Seneschal of Co Antrim; given a reward of 1000 marks 1569 for bringing in the head of the Irish chief Shane O'Neill (*see* O'NEILL, B); *d* 1602, leaving an only *s*:

HENRY PIERS, of Tristernagh; travel writer about Germany and Italy; *m* Jane, dau of Thomas Jones, DD, Archbp of Dublin and Ld Chllr of Ireland (and sister of 1st Viscount Ranelagh), and *d* 16 Sept 1623, leaving an est *s*:

Sir WILLIAM PIERS; *m* Martha, dau of Sir James Ware the elder, and *d* 1638, leaving, with yr sons and at least one dau (Mary, *m* 31 Dec 1646, as his 2nd w, Henry Jones, Bp Meath; *see* below):

Sir Henry Piers, 1st Bt (I), so *cr* 18 Feb 1660/1, of Tristernagh; *b c* 1628; ktd 1658, Sheriff Cos Longford and Westmeath 1657 and 1658, MP Cos Longford and Westmeath, King's Co 1659 and St Johnstown Co Longford 1661–66, Sheriff Co Westmeath 1663; *m c* 1653 Mary, dau of Dr Henry Jones, Bp Meath, by his 1st w Jane Cullum, and *d* 19 Sept 1691, having had, with seven other sons and six daus:

Sir William Piers, 2nd Bt; *b c* 1653; *m c* 1678 Honora, sister of 1st Earl of Kerry (*see* LANSDOWNE, M), and *d* 2 June 1693, having had, with other issue, including a yr *s* (William, *m* Elizabeth, dau of Edward Croker, of Rawleighstown, Co Limerick, and had issue):

Sir Henry Piers, 3rd Bt; *b* 1678; *m* 1st Jane, dau of John Pigott, of Kilfinny, Co Limerick, by Gertrude, dau of Sir Thomas Southwell, 1st Bt (*see* SOUTHWELL, V); *m* 2nd 8 Dec 1729 Catherine (*d* 8 June 1737), widow of 3rd Earl of Barrymore and dau of 2nd Baron Barry of Santry, and *d* from overdosing on opium 14 March 1733, having had by his 1st w, with other issue, including an er *s* (Lewis, *m* Cecilia Lynch, of Galway, and *dsp*):

Sir John Piers, 4th Bt; *m* 17 May 1739 his first cousin Cornelia Gertrude (*d* 14 Jan 1777), dau of Southwell Pigott, of Capard, Queen's Co, and *d* 14 Feb 1746/7, having had, with other issue:

Sir Pigott William Piers, 5th Bt; *b c* 1742; *educ* Trin Coll Dublin (BA 1762); Sheriff Co Westmeath 1774; *m* 17 April 1771 Elizabeth, only dau and heiress of John Smythe, of Dublin, and *d* 1798, having had, with two other sons (*dsp*):

   1 **Sir John Bennett Piers, 6th Bt**; *m* 1st Aug 1796 Mary (*dsp* & *vp* 1798), dau of Rev Joseph Pratt, of Cabra Castle, Co Cavan, by Sarah, dau of 1st Viscount Mountmorres of Castlemorres (*see* DE MONTMORENCY, Bt); *m* 2nd 1815 Elizabeth King (*d* 17 Feb 1862) and *dspm* 22 July 1845, having by her had issue (born before their marriage):

     (1) William Stapleton

     (2) John

   1 (cont.) (and after their marriage):

     (1) Louisa Adelaide; Canoness Royal Order of St Anne of Bavaria; *d* unm

     (2) Florence Anna Marie Stapleton Frederica; *m* July 1842 Count Louis Le Coat de Kerveguen (*d* 1892) and *d* 16 Oct 1906, leaving issue

   2 Frederick; *b* 1788; *m* 31 Dec 1807 Phoebe (*d* July 1867), dau of Samuel Hartney, of Pallace, Co Limerick, and *d* 28 Oct 1844, having had:

     (1) HENRY SAMUEL (Sir), **7th Bt**

     (2) Richard; went to America

     (1) Elizabeth; *m* 26 Nov 1845 Richard Young, of Dublin, and had issue

   3 Octavius (Rev); *b* 1788; Vicar Preston, Dorset; *m* 21 Dec 1813 Jane (*d* 20 July 1871), dau of Rev Thomas Tristram, and *d* 23 Feb 1848, having had, with three other sons (*dsp*):

     (1) Henry; *b* 3 June 1818; MRCSE, Dep Inspr-Gen Hosps and Fleets; *m* 28 Nov 1854 Ellen Sarah (*d* 25 Dec 1926), dau of John Colborn, of Cork, and *d* 30 Nov 1901, having had:

       1a Henry Octavius; *b* 1 Jan 1856; Lt-Col and Brevet Col RA; *m* 1886 Lise Agnes (*d* 2 Sept 1937), dau of Dep Surgn-Gen Johnston-Ferguson, and *d* 8 Feb 1945, leaving:

         1b Gwendolen May; *b* 1889

       1a Fanny Ellen

       2a Caroline Mary; *m* 27 May 1896 Lt-Col James Henry Paine, DSO, RGA (*ka* 25 July 1918), 3rd *s* of James Paine, of Springfield, nr Taunton, and *d* 10 July 1924, having had issue

     (2) William Dewé; *b* 6 Aug 1820; *m* 3rd 1 Nov 1871 Letitia Ellen Clayton (*m* 2nd 15 June 1910 Thomas Frederick Jennings Bramley, of Tunbridge Wells, *s* of Frederick Jennings Bramley), dau of Rev James Daubeny, and *d* 4 May 1876

     (3) Thomas Tristram; *b* 7 March 1824; Col HEIC; *m* 2 March 1854 Charlotte Mary (*d* 12 Aug 1906), dau of Rev Henry Baker Tristram, and *d* 29 May 1873, leaving:

       1a William Barrington; *b* 4 April 1859; Lt-Col IA, cmdg Serv Bn Beds Regt and 27th Bn Trg Res; *m* 16 April 1891 Mary Catherine Emily Price (*d* 8 Dec 1942), dau of Price Morris, of Plas Clough, Denbighs, and *d* 27 June 1917, leaving:

         1b William Price Barrington; *b* 30 Nov 1905; *educ* Cheltenham; RA; *m* 18 June 1935 Ursula Mary Bence (*d* 1993), dau of Rev George Alfred Charles Smith-Cranmoor, Rector Baldock, Herts, and *d* 1974, leaving:

           1c +Anthony Tristram Barrington [Anthony Piers Esq, Withy Cottage, Wrantage, Somerset TA3 6DJ]; *b* 6 June 1939; *educ* Plumtree Sch Rhodesia and RMA Sandhurst; Capt 1st Bn Devon and Dorset Regt and N Rhodesia Regt; *m* 1st 6 June 1964 (*divorce* 1981) Susan Jacqueline Dawn, dau of Lt-Col H T Bayldon, MC, of Las Palmas, and has:

              1d +Christopher William Barrington; *b* 1973

              1d *Ann-Marie Barrington; *b* 14 Sept 1965; *m* 1988 *Kevin and has:

                 1e *Connor Sebastian; *b* 1990

                 2e *Rory Leto; *b* 1992

              2d *Bridget Dawn Barrington; *b* 14 Oct 1967; *m* 1993 *Anton Matthews

           1c (cont.) Anthony Piers *m* 2nd 1981 *Mrs Mary Gertrude Eveleen Croft, dau of D H Baker, of Farnham, Surrey

           2c +Brian William Barrington [Brian Piers, 7 Ross St, Toowoomba, Queensland 4350, Australia]; *b* 16 Sept 1941; *educ* Plumtree Sch and Gwebi Ag Coll Rhodesia; *m* 1970 *Stephanie Ellen Elizabeth dau of Capt — Attoe, of London, and has:

              1d +Robert Courtney Barrington; *b* 1973

              1d *Samantha Barrington; *b* 1971

           3c +Charles Barrington [Charles Piers Esq, 95 Belladona Rd, Roodekranz Ext 7, Roodepoort 1725, Transvaal, S Africa]; *b* 8 Oct 1943; *educ* Plumtree Sch Rhodesia and RMA Sandhurst; Capt 1st Bn Rhodesian African Rifles; *m* 1980 *Judy Melanie Pamela, dau of P D Fuller, of Surugwi, Zimbabwe, and has:

              1d +Niall Barrington; *b* 1984

       2a Samuel Octavius (Rev); *b* 23 Feb 1869; *educ* Trin Hall Cambridge (MA); Lt Gordon Highrs, Sr Chaplain Madras, ret 1922; *m* 17 Oct 1901 Mabel Marion (*d* 28 Dec 1951), dau of G Smith, of Ipswich, and *d* 13 Nov 1940, leaving:

         1b Charles Stuart Tristram; *b* 17 Jan 1920; Sub-Lt RN WW II; *d* as a result of enemy action 21 March 1941

         1b *Violet Marion; *m* 1st 1 Sept 1931 Louis Brown (*d* 1934), of Chicago; *m* 2nd 6 June 1939 *George Paul and by him has:

           1c *Jacqueline Evelyn; *b* 1940

        2b *Evelyn Helena [Mrs Robert Fowler, 40 Belle Vue Gardens, Kemp Town, Brighton, Sussex]; *m* 1st 22 Oct 1938 George Damer, Lt RCA (*ka* 27 April 1944), *s* of Timothy Damer, of Toronto, and has:

           1c *George Terence Stuart [George Damer Esq, 14 Beech Rd, Reigate, Surrey RH2 97R]; *b* 29 Sept 1940; *educ* Douai (BSc); dir *Financial Times* (ret); *m* 13 June 1964 *Michèle Mary Godwin, dau of Leonard William Prouten, of Brighton, and has:

              1d *Justin Dawson; *b* 17 March 1967; *educ* Douai (BSc); chartered accountant; *m* 1996 *Samantha Durrant

              1d *Miranda Jane; *b* 2 June 1968; *m* 1994 *Charles Blease and has:

                 1e *Isaac Benjamin; *b* 19–

                 2e *Otis Samuel; *b* 19–

              2d *Annabel Katie Louise; *b* 1974; *m* 1997 *Julian Barfield

         2b (cont.) Mrs George Damer *m* 2nd 1972 *Robert Owen Fowler, AMIEE, of Liverpool, Nova Scotia

         3b *Ruth Pauline [Mrs Thomas Hazeldine, Blueberry Shores, Liverpool, Nova Scotia BOT 1KO, Canada]; *m* 20 April 1946 *Capt Thomas Eric Hazeldine, AMICE, RE, Indian Engrs, er *s* of T F Hazeldine, of Withdean, Sussex, and Natalie Lady Ricketts, and has:

           1c *Keith Trevor; *b* 1947; BEng, MBA; *m* 1970 *Ethel Mae Fraser and has:

              1d *Julia Lee; *b* 1975

              2d *Amy Katherine; *b* 1977

              3d *Laura Mae; *b* 1979

           2c *Piers Martin; *b* 1957; *m* 1st 1984 Iva MacKenzie (*d* 1992) and has:

              1d *Tia Lee-Anne; *b* 1984

              2d *Dana Christine; *b* 1986

           2c (cont.) Piers Hazeldine *m* 2nd 1994 *Wendy Wyer and by her has:

3d *Heidi Lee Grace; b 1974
1c *Carol Anne; b 1948; m 1970 *James E Dewar and has:
   1d *Brydone Michael; b 1980
   1d *Jennifer Laura; b 1975
   2d *Kimberly Margaret; b 1978
2c *Sally Jane; b 1949; m 1971 *Dr Arnie Chestnut and has:
   1d *Matthew Robert; b 1979
   1d *Heidi Anne; b 1974
   2d *Shannon Gail; b 1977
3c *Gail Melisa [Mrs William Moffat, 6620 Jubilee Rd, Halifax, Nova Scotia B3H 2H4, Canada]; b 1955; m 1980 *William Moffat and has:
   1d *Jonathan Eric Douglas; b 1991
   2d *Luke Stuart; b 1994
   1d *Rachel Alexandra Hazeldine; b 1990
1a Helen Louisa; b 30 April 1861; m 21 July 1897 Alfred Cecil Langston, PWD, Madras, and d 18 Dec 1944, leaving issue
(4) Shute Barrington; b 15 Jan 1828; Capt RN; m 5 June 1863 Jane Cunninghame (d April 1925), dau of Peter Handyside, MD, FRCSE, memb Roy Co Archers, and d 14 Aug 1876, leaving:
1a Shute Barrington; b 10 April 1864; OStJ; m 1888 Gertrude (d 1938), 3rd dau of Charles Henry, of Nottingham, and d 1947, leaving:
1b Walter Barrington; b 1890; manager Bank of Montreal, Haney, BC; m 1913 Mary Cecilia Onn and d 10 Sept 1964, leaving:
   1c Grahame Barrington; b 7 July 1913; m 1950 *Shirley O'Brien and d 1980, leaving:
      1d +Richard Barrington; b 1953
   2c Cecil Edwin; b 29 July 1914; S/Sgt RCMP; m 14 March 1941 *Ethel Ruth Sheppard [Mrs Cecil Piers, PO Box 301, Montrose, BC V0G 1PO, Canada] and d 1987, leaving:
      1d +Kenneth Barrington [Kenneth Piers Esq, Schelf Straat No 1, 3295TK S'Gravendeel, Holland]; b 13 April 1943; educ U of British Columbia; equipment manager Sea Train Inc 1969–; m 9 Dec 1966 *Maartje, dau of — Wolf, of Delfzijl, Holland
      1d *Penelope Ann [Mrs Brian Denton, 2134 Graham Ave, Prince Rupert, BC V8J 1C8, Canada]; b 7 July 1946; registered nurse; m 1972 *Brian Denton and has:
         1e *Trevor Piers; b 1975
         1e *Laura Lynn; b 1973
   3c +Harry Gordon; b 1920; W/O RCAF, Inspr Customs and Immigration, ret; m 1st 1946 (divorce 1968) Sally Chisholm and has:
      1d +James Walter; b 1947
   3c (cont.) Harry Piers m 2nd 1970 *Helen Audreychuk, dau of — Street
   1c *Kathleen Margery; b 1916; m 1943 *Winston Eric Dunning, ed/publisher The Gazette, Haney, BC, s of C E Dunning, and has:
      1d *Ross Barrington; b 4 June 1945; educ St George's Sch Vancouver
      2d *Paul Hasley; b 25 Aug 1954
      1d *Janis Kathleen; b 16 Feb 1950; educ Roy Acad Dancing London
2b Grahame Sedway; b 1892; m 1917 Dorothy Mary (d 1971), dau of G D Heather, and d 13 April 1970, leaving:
   1c *Heather; b 1918; m 24 March 1945 *Anthony Tresiddar Freeman, FCA, s of Edmund Freeman, of Bore Place, Chiddingstone, Kent, and has:
      1d *Michael Edmund Piers; b 16 Jan 1946
      2d *Piers Anthony; b 25 March 1956
      1d *Chloe Anne; b 19 Feb 1949
      2d *Amanda Jane; b 24 May 1953
1b Gladys Nottingham; b 1893; m 1920 W Serle (d 1940) and had:
   1c *Patrick Philip Oswald; b 1921; S/Ldr RAF, ret; m 1st 1940 Sheila Foster, of Bexhill-on-Sea, and has:
      1d *Roy Anthony Michael; b 1941; Inspr Met Police; m 1964 *Elizabeth Mary — and has:
         1e *Paul; b 1966
         2e *Keith; b 1968
         1e *Fiona; b 1965
      2d *John Patrick David; b 1944; Capt RAOC
      3d *Peter Norman James; b 1949; RAF
   1c (cont.) Patrick Serle m 2nd 1965 *Nicole Lecoq and by her has:
      3d *Robert Barrington; b 1966
2b Margery Barrington; b 1896; m 1921 Clive Marshall and had issue
2a Henry Handyside Bruce; b 3 Nov 1865; m 2 Sept 1902 Eva Gertrude (d 9 March 1962 aged 87), dau of George Brice Pennell, CE, and d 7 May 1935, leaving:
1b Eustace Pennell, TD; b 11 Oct 1910; educ Ch Ch Oxford (MA); Hon Maj Roy Signals TA; m 22 Feb 1941 *Jean Mavis [Mrs Eustace Piers, 1 Mitre Place, The Park, Castle Cary, Somerset BA7 7EP], dau of John Edward S Ralph, of Streatham Hill, London, and d 17 Aug 1979, leaving:
   1c +William James Shute Barrington [William Piers Esq, 101 Aylesbury Rd, Aston Clinton, Bucks HP22 5AJ]; b 25 July 1948; educ Millfield and Brunel U (BTech, MIMech E); m 14 Oct 1978 *Janet Anne, dau of K A Fream, of Bristol, and has had:
      1d +Adam Ralph Barrington; b 16 June 1980
      2d Oliver Henry; b 28 Oct 1982; d 3 Dec 1984
      3d +Thomas Michael; b 14 March 1985
      1d *Sarah Elizabeth; b 18 May 1987
   1c *Angela Mary [Mrs Peter Watson, 66 Finches Gdns, Lindfield, Sussex RH16 2PB]; b 1 April 1942; m 9 June 1965 *Peter Kiero Watson, s of James Christian Victor Kiero Watson, of Hinstock, Salop, and has had:
      1d *James Kiero; b 14 Oct 1966
      2d *Thomas Piers Kiero; b 31 May 1969; d 1970
      3d *Edward Piers Kiero; b 1970

2c *Clare Rosamund Pennell [Mrs Peter Dodd, 4 Russell Rd, London W14]; b 25 July 1948; m 1984 *Peter William Dodd
2b George Michael Barrington; b 11 Sept 1919; 2nd Lt RE WW II; ka 20 March 1941
1b *Mary Eva Patricia [Mrs Arthur Grundy, The Old Rectory, 10 Old Port Rd, Wenvoe, Cardiff CF5 6AN]; b 16 March 1905; m 1 Aug 1939 Arthur Mather Grundy (d 8 July 1940), s of Albert Walker Grundy, of Prestwich, and has:
   1c *John Martin [Col John Grundy, Highlands, St Lythans, Cardiff CF5 6BQ]; b 30 April 1940; educ Repton and Hertford Coll Oxford; Col Roy Regt Wales, ret; m 8 June 1974 *Sheila Mary Evans and has:
      1d *James David Piers; b 8 March 1976
      1d *Anna Charlotte; b 18 Feb 1980
2b Margaret Marion; b 4 Nov 1906; m 10 Dec 1938 *Rt Rev Leslie Stibbard, Assist Bp Newcastle, NSW, and d 8 Aug 1997, leaving:
   1c *David Piers [David Stibbard Esq, Roughit, via Singleton, Hamilton 2330, NSW, Australia]; b 18 Aug 1943; m 20 Aug 1966 *Janet Pauline, 2nd dau of Henry Arthur Dale Harrison, of Lawrence, NSW, and has:
      1d *Dermot Harrison; b 25 July 1969
      1d *Samantha Marion; b 23 March 1968
      2d *Fenella Joanne; b 30 June 1973
   2c *Stephen Patrick [Stephen Stibbard Esq, 145A Everton St, Hamilton, NSW 2303, Australia]; b 6 June 1947; m 1974 *Jillian Margaret, dau of Bruce Robert McGavin, of New Lambton, NSW, and has:
      1d *Sophie Anne; b 1 April 1989
      2d *Clare Angela; b 23 June 1992
   1c *Ruth [Mrs Noël McFayden, 38 Janet St, Merewether, NSW, Australia]; b 19 Feb 1940; m 5 Jan 1963 *Noël Bernard McFayden, s of Norman Charles McFayden, of Hamilton, NSW, and has:
      1d *David James; b 9 Jan 1964; RAN (ret); m 31 Oct 1993 *Petrina Lee Muxlow and has:
         1e *Jack David; b 23 Oct 1995
         2e *Mitchell James; b 12 Aug 1997
      2d *Michael Stuart; b 13 Aug 1969; m 25 April 1993 *Kim Leanne Rowley and has:
         1e *Emma Ruth; b 2 Oct 1993
      1d *Lisa Jane; b 26 July 1965
   2c *Miriam Anne [Mrs George Swan, 16 Raymond St, Speers Point, NSW, Australia]; b 16 March 1950; m 1969 *George David Swan and has:
      1d *Fiona Louise; b 18 Sept 1969; m 2 May 1992 *Richard Jenkins
      2d *Jennifer Anne; b 27 April 1972
3b *Helen Alice [Mrs John Mortimer, Foxlease, Maiden Bradley, Warminster, Wilts BA12 7JG]; b 1 Aug 1914; m 13 Jan 1944 Rev John Lionel Mortimer (d 1 June 1983), s of Rev John Mortimer, of Dunedin, NZ, and has:
   1c *Lawrence George (Rev) [The Rev Lawrence Mortimer, The Vicarage, Wootton Wawen, Solihull B95 6BD]; b 9 May 1945; educ Lancing, St Edmund Hall Oxford and St Chad's Durham; communications offr Diocese of Coventry; m 1st 1973 Catriona Lane (d 1982) and has:
      1d *John Lawrence; b 25 March 1978
      1d *Rebecca Magdalena Helen; b 4 Aug 1974
      2d *Rosamund Clare; b 1 Nov 1976
   1c (cont.) The Rev Lawrence Mortimer m 2nd 1992 *Rosemary Barralet
   2c *Michael Piers [Michael Mortimer Esq, 5 Bearwood Cottages, The Street, Wrecclesham, Farnham GU10 4PE]; b 22 Sept 1946; educ Grenville Coll; m 1985 *Ann, dau of James Jenkinson, of Aldershot, and has:
      1d *Benjamin; b 24 May 1987
      1d *Emily; b 30 Sept 1985
   3c *Christopher Hugh [Christopher Mortimer Esq, Foxlease, Maiden Bradley, Wilts BA12 7JG]; b 1 Oct 1949; educ Lancing and Bede Coll Durham
3a William Cuningham; b 30 June 1867; d 26 Aug 1886
4a Peter David Handyside; b 6 May 1869; Colonial CS; m 11 June 1910 Rose Sydney FitzMaurice (d 26 Jan 1962), yst dau of **Sir Eustace FitzMaurice Piers, 8th Bt** (see below), and d 1943
5a Edward Cecil; b 30 Jan 1871; d 1930
6a Claude Pigott; b 1 July 1875; RE, joined Br Army in New York, served WW I; d 1927
1a Irene Walsh Shute; b (posthumously) 18 Oct 1876; d March 1932
(1) Eliza Jane; b 2 May 1816; m 21 July 1941 Rev Hastings Hawes Harrington and d Jan 1895, having had issue
(2) Helen Clara; b 9 Nov 1825; m 25 June 1850 Charles Hastings Snow, of Wellington, NZ, and had issue

The 6th Bt's nephew,
Sir Henry Samuel Piers, 7th Bt; b 6 May 1811; m 24 Nov 1838 Alice (d 7 Feb 1906), yst dau of John T Glindon, RN, and had, with another s (d young) and dau (d unm):
1 EUSTACE FitzMAURICE (Sir), **8th Bt**
1 Maude Mary Florence; m 15 Sept 1870 Major-Gen Denzil Hammill (d 2 Dec 1891), CB, Gordon Highrs (75th Regt), and had issue
2 Elizabeth Catherine

Sir HENRY d 15 April 1850; his er son
Sir Eustace FitzMaurice Piers, 8th Bt, JP Herts; b 28 Oct 1840; Maj 4th Bn Manchester Regt; m 20 July 1869 Rose (d 11 Nov 1891), yst dau of Charles Saunders, of Fulwood Park, Liverpool, and had:
1 CHARLES PIGOTT (Sir), **9th Bt**
1 Mary Wilbraham; d unm 16 March 1955
2 Honora FitzMaurice; d unm 25 Dec 1955

3 Rose Sydney FitzMaurice; *m* 11 June 1910 her cousin Peter David Handyside Piers (*see* above) and *dsp* 26 Jan 1962

Sir EUSTACE *d* 10 May 1913; his son,

Sir Charles Pigott Piers, 9th Bt; *b* 27 June 1870; *educ* Eton and Trin Hall Cambridge (BA 1894); served Boer War 1900–01 (Queen's medal, four clasps) and WW I: Maj 29th (Vancouver) Bn Canadian Expdny Force 1915–16, Intell Offr and GSO(3) 1916, Staff Capt Canadian GHQ 1916–19, Hon Maj 4th Bn Sherwood Foresters, author: *Sport and Life in British Columbia*; *m* 27 Aug 1902 Hester Constance Stella (*d* 6 Oct 1936), est dau of Samuel Richard Browis, JP, of Ibstone House, Oxon, and *d* 27 June 1945, leaving:

Sir Charles Robert FitzMaurice Piers, 10th Bt; *b* 30 Aug 1903; *educ* RNCs Osborne and Dartmouth; Lt-Cdr RCNVR WW II, branch manager Doherty Roadhouse & McCuaig Duncan, BC; *m* 19 Sept 1936 Ann Blanche Scott (*d* 1975), only dau of Capt Thomas Ferguson, Roy Highrs, and *d* 1 Jan 1996, having had:

  1 Sir JAMES DESMOND, **11th and present Bt**

  1 Sarah Constance; *b* 27 Jan 1942; *m* 1970 *Michael C Weld and *d* 1988, leaving:

    (1) *Diana Kristen; *b* 1971

    (2) *Andrea Jane; *b* 1974

PIGOT

Arms: Ermine three lozenges conjoined in fess sable. **Crest:** A wolf's head erased argent. **Motto:** *Toutfoys prest* ('Always ready'). **Creation:** Bt. (UK) 5 Dec 1764.

SIR GEORGE HUGH PIGOT, 8TH BT, of Patshull, Staffordshire [Sir George Pigot Bt, Mill House, Mill Lane, Padworth, Berks RG7 4JX]; *b* 28 Nov 1946; *s* f 1986; *educ* Stowe; *m* 1st 2 Dec 1967 (*divorce* 1973) Judith, er dau of Maj John Hele Sandeman-Allen, RA, of Chelsea, and has:

  1 *Melanie Barbara; *b* 4 Dec 1969

Sir GEORGE *m* 2nd 1980 (*divorce* 1993) Lucinda Jane, yr dau of Donald Charles Spandler, of Chiddingfold, Surrey, and by her has:

  1 +GEORGE DOUGLAS HUGH; *b* 17 Sept 1982

  2 +Robert Edward Richard; *b* 1984

Lineage: HUGH PIGOT, of Peploe, Salop; *m* Elizabeth Dicken and *d* 1697, leaving, with six er sons:

RICHARD PIGOT, of Westminster; *bapt* 6 Oct 1679; *m* Frances (*m* 2nd Lt-Col John Wyvell and *d* 29 Dec 1769), dau of Peter Goode, and *d* 31 Dec 1729, leaving:

  1 **Sir George Pigot, 1st Bt** (UK), so *cr* 5 Dec 1764, with remainder, in default of male issue, to his bro Robert, and on failure of the latter's issue to the other brother Hugh and his heirs male) of Patshull, Staffs (an estate he bought for £100,000, or over £5,375,000 in late-1990s terms), also 1st and last BARON PIGOT OF PATSHULL, Co Dublin (I), so *cr* 18 Jan 1766; *b* 4 March 1719; writer to HEIC 1737, Sub-Sec, Clerk of the Peace, Coroner, Co's Slr and Clerk Court Appeals HEIC 1742, Govr Fort St George Madras 1755–63 and 1775–77, MP (Tory) Wallingford 1765–68 and Bridgnorth 1768–77, LLD Cambridge; *dspl* (possibly murdered) 11 May 1777 in the HEIC's Garden House, nr Fort St George, after being illegally detained at HEIC's instigation (having fallen out with them), when the Barony expired, leaving:

    (1) Richard; Col 4th Dragoon Gds, Gen; *d* 22 Nov 1868 aged 94

    (2) Hugh (Sir), KCB; Adml the White; *d* 30 July 1857 aged 82

    (1) Sophia; *m* 14 March 1776 Hon Edward Monckton (*see* GALWAY, V)

  2 Robert (Sir), **2nd Bt**

  3 Hugh; *b* 28 May 1722; Adml; *m* 1st Elizabeth, dau of Peter le Neve, and had with a dau:

    (1) Henry (Sir), GCMG; Gen, captured Malta from the French; *dsp* 7 June 1840 aged 89

  3 (cont.) Adml Hugh Pigot *m* 2nd Frances (*d* 13 April 1811), dau of Sir Richard Wrottesley, 7th Bt (*see* WROTTESLEY, B), and *d* 15 Dec 1792, having by her had, with another dau:

    (1) Caroline; *m* 10 Sept 1800 Rev Lord Henry FitzRoy and *d* 1 Jan 1835, leaving issue (*see* GRAFTON, D)

  1 Margaret; *m* 1755 Thomas Fisher

The 1st Bt's bro,

Sir Robert Pigot, 2nd Bt; *b* 20 Sept 1720; Col 38th Foot, Lt-Gen; *m* 18 Feb 1765 Anne (*d* July 1772), dau of Allen Johnson, of Kilternan, Co Dublin (and sis of Sir Allen Johnson Walsh and Gen Sir Henry Johnson, both *cr* Bts; *see* 1953 edn JOHNSON-WALSH, Bt, and JOHNSON, Bt, of Bath), and had, with a dau (*d* unm):

  1 GEORGE (Sir), **3rd Bt**

  2 Hugh; Capt RN; *d* unm at Lisbon

  3 Robert; Col; *m* 14 June 1801 Mary, dau and coheir of John Williamson, and *d* 1805, leaving:

    (1) Robert; *m* 1st 12 July 1842 Harriet Margaret (*d* 1852), dau of Gen — Cheney, of Badger Hall; *m* 2nd 28 April 1855 Anna Maria (*d* 6 Nov 1880), dau of Gen Sir William Clinton, GCB, of Cockeenhatch, and *dsp* 8 Jan 1873

    (2) Charles Henry; *b* 1806; *m* 10 Dec 1833 Leonora (*d* 24 March 1848), 2nd dau of Sir William Russell, Bt, of Charlton Park (*see* 1850 edn), and *d* 1 May 1840, leaving with a dau (*d* unm):

      1a Henry; *d* unm

      2a Hugh; *b* 26 Jan 1839; barrister; *m* 9 July 1873 Gwendoline (*m* 2nd 29 April 1911 Col Thomas Mayhew, RA), 3rd dau of Capt Richard Beaumont, RN, and *dsp* 21 Oct 1907

      1a Julia; *m* 1st 29 June 1880 Arthur Frederick Astley (*dsp* 29 Dec 1883; *see* 1970 edn ASTLEY, Bt); *m* 2nd 1887 Rev Arthur Castell Wright (*d* 27 Jan 1905), Chaplain RN, and *d* 24 Feb 1906

    (3) George; *d* unm at Corfu 1830

Sir ROBERT *d* 11 Aug 1796; his est son,

Sir George Pigot, 3rd Bt; *b* 19 Oct 1766; Gen; *m* 18 July 1796 Mary Anne (*d* 20 Nov 1833), dau of Hon John Monckton (*see* GALWAY, V), and had, with four other daus:

  1 George; *dsp*

  2 ROBERT (Sir), **4th Bt**

  3 John; *dsp*

  4 Henry Orlando; *d* Nov 1840

  5 Arthur; *d* unm 9 May 1865

  1 Georgiana; *m* Aug 1828 Rev Robert Wrottesley (*d* 30 Jan 1838) and *d* 12 Oct 1872

  2 Fanny Henrietta; *m* 4 April 1839 Rev Charles Grey Cotes, Rector Stanton St Quinton, Wilts, 2nd s of John Cotes, of Woodcote, Salop, and *d* April 1865

  3 Laura Millicent; *m* 29 Oct 1835 George Holyoake, CB (*d* 1879; *see* 1902 edn GOODRICKE, Bt)

  4 Caroline Octavia; *m* 1835 Francis Charles FitzRoy (*see* GRAFTON, D) and *d* 2 Sept 1854

Sir GEORGE *d* 24 June 1841; his 2nd son,

Sir Robert Pigot, 4th Bt, DL Salop; *b* 1801; MP Bridgnorth 1832–37 and 1838–53; *m* 1st 5 Oct 1826 Mary (*dsp* 5 Sept 1847), dau of William Bamford, of Bamford, Lancs; *m* 2nd 22 Jan 1850 Emily Georgiana Elise (*d* 25 Feb 1917), dau of Samuel Yates Benyon, of Ash Hall, Salop, and had:

  1 GEORGE (Sir), **5th Bt**

  2 Arthur John; *b* 23 Feb 1852; *d* unm 12 May 1895

  1 Elinor; *m* 1st 10 July 1880 Charles Herbert Whaley (*d* 1885), of Taplow, Bucks, and had issue; *m* 2nd 19 April 1890 Alfred Jacobson, 6th Dragoon Gds, of Quarndon Hill, Derbys, and *d* 8 March 1916, having had further issue

Sir ROBERT *d* 1 June 1891; his er son,

Sir George Pigot, 5th Bt; *b* 15 Dec 1850; *m* 19 Aug 1879 Alice Louisa Raynsford (*d* 25 June 1934), dau of Sir James Thompson Mackenzie, 1st Bt, of Glen Muick (*qv*), and *d* 25 May 1934, leaving:

  1 **Sir Robert Pigot, 6th Bt**, DSO, MC; *b* 3 May 1882; *educ* Eton; F/O RFC 1913–14, WW I: Col Rifle Bde, Brig-Gen 1918 (despatches, two brevets), W/Cdr RAFVR WW II; *m* 21 Aug 1913 Norah Beatrice Oakeley (*d* 26 Nov 1969), yr dau of Capt Charles Reginald Hargreaves, of Remenham, Wraysbury, Berks, and had:

    (1) *Margaret [Mrs John Dent, Manor Farm, Broughton, Hants]; *b* 21 Sept 1914; *m* 1st 15 May 1940 Maj Donald Ian Molteno, Black Watch (*ka* Feb 1945), only s of Donald Jarvis Molteno, JP, of Glenlyon, Perthshire, and has:

      1a *Susan Ferelith [Mrs Timothy Ashfield, 37 Perrymead St, London SW6]; *b* 27 Feb 1941; *m* 4 April 1961 *Timothy Robert Malden Ashfield, only s of (Claude) Robert Wodley Ashfield, of Podkin Farm House, High Halden, Kent, and has:

        1b *A son; *b* 21 April 1970

      2a *Gillian; *b* 24 Oct 1942; *m* 17 May 1969 *Jeremy James, s of Francis James, of Ashdown Corner, Portishead, Bristol

    (1) (cont.) Mrs Donald Molteno *m* 2nd 15 Feb 1949 *(Edward) John Macdonald Dent, only s of Edward John Dent, of Burley, Hants

    (2) *Jean; *b* 21 Sept 1914; *m* 16 Sept 1944 Capt (Atholl) Murray Robertson, Black Watch (RHR), s of George Dickson Robertson, of Bowdon, Cheshire, and has:

      1a *Alastair John; *b* 22 Jan 1946; *educ* Trin Coll Glenalmond

    (3) *Diana Gillian [Miss Diana Pigot, Yarlington Lodge, Wincanton, Somerset]; *b* 28 May 1918

  2 George Douglas Hugh; *b* 2 Aug 1883; *educ* Eton; *m* 15 Dec 1910 Hersey Elizabeth (*d* 1 Feb 1970), est dau of Gerald Rivers Maltby, MVO, Lt RN, and *d* 26 May 1959, leaving:

    (1) (ROBERT) ANTHONY (Sir), **7th Bt**

    (1) Hersey Alice; *b* 18 Sept 1911

    (2) *Priscilla Anne; *m* 1st 23 May 1942 Havilland Anthony Mackworth Drake (*d* 18 July 1948), s of Aylmer Mackworth Drake, of Guernsey; *m* 2nd 29 Feb 1952 (*divorce* 1966) Alexander Gortschakov, only s of Lt-Gen Alexander Gortschakov, Imp Russian Army

  1 Eileen Marguerite Elinor, JP; *m* 6 Nov 1906 (*divorce* 1938) Lt-Col Reginald Baskerville Jervis Crawfurd, DSO (*d* 5 Aug 1947), Coldstream Gds, only s of Charles William Jervis CRAWFURD formerly SMITH, of Brocksford Hall, Derbys, and *d* 14 Aug 1966 aged 86, leaving issue

  2 Norah Edith; *m* 30 March 1918 Capt Victor Reginald Booth, Gordon Highrs (*d* 29 May 1943), s of Herbert Booth, of New York, and had:

(1) *David Reginald Peter [David Booth Esq, 130 Old Bath Road, Cheltenham, Glos GL53 7DP]; *b* 6 Dec 1921; *educ* Charterhouse; F/Lt RAF WW II; *m* 24 April 1952 *Anne Burgess, dau of Brig-Gen Oscar James Gatchell, of Saunderstown, RI, USA, and has:

  1a *Anthony Robert James [Anthony Booth Esq, 15 Sherwood Drive, Hollis, NH 03049, USA]; *b* 25 June 1953; *educ* Cheltenham and Reading U; *m* 28 June 1986 *Sarah Beth Ellis, and has:

    1b *Allison Margaret; *b* 5 May 1989

    2b *Caroline Anne; *b* 15 July 1991

  1a *Nora Jane [Mrs Timothy Wait, 33 Marlborough Cresc, Old Woodstock, Oxon OX20 1YJ]; *b* 1 May 1957; *educ* Cheltenham Ladies Coll; *m* 25 July 1987 *Timothy Michael Anthony Wait, and has:

    1b *George David; *b* 28 April 1991

    1b *Rosemary Anne; *b* 20 Nov 1988

Sir ROBERT *d* 27 Dec 1977; his nephew,

Sir (Robert) Anthony Pigot 7th Bt, CB (1964), OBE (1959); *b* 6 July 1915; *educ* Stowe; Maj-Gen RM, served WW II (despatches), Directing Staff Staff Coll Camberley 1946–48, Dep Sec NATO Standing Gp Washington 1954–57, Dep Standing Gp Rep N Atlantic Cncl Paris 1957–59, Ch Staff RM 1960–64, ret 1964, md Bone Bros 1964–66, dir: John Brown Plastics Machinery 1965–66, Exec Appointments Ltd 1968–86, V-Pres St John Ambulance Bde IoW, Cncl and Ctee memb Union Jack Servs Clubs, Jt Master IoW Foot Beagles; *m* 1st 7 Oct 1942 Honor (*d* 26 Nov 1966), dau of Capt Wilfred St Martin Gibbon, and had:

1 Sir GEORGE HUGH PIGOT, **8th and present Bt**

1 *Louise [Mrs Peter Mellor, Brinksway House, Shottermill, Surrey]; *b* 21 July 1943; *m* 8 Sept 1966 *Peter Mellor, s of A R Mellor, of Lamb Cottage, Newtown, IoW, and has:

  (1) *Nicola; *b* 1 Oct 1970

  (2) *Suzanna; *b* 1975

  (3) *Katherine; *b* 1979

Sir Anthony *m* 2nd 28 Sept 1968 *Sarah Anne [Sarah Lady Pigot, Garden House, 5 St Luke's Dve, Bembridge, IoW PO35 5XA], est dau of David Richard Colville (*see* COLVILLE OF CULROSS, V), and *d* 1986, having by her had:

2 +Robert James; *b* 6 Sept 1971; *educ* Eton

2 *Sarah Sophia; *b* 29 May 1975

PIGOTT

Arms: Ermine three lozenges (or pikeheads) in fess sable, a crescent for difference. **Crest:** A wolf's head erased proper, collared or. **Motto:** *Hic et alibi* ('Here and elsewhere'). **Creation:** Bt. (UK) 3 Oct 1808.

SIR (BERKELEY) HENRY SEBASTIAN PIGOTT, 5TH BT, of Knapton, Queen's Co [Sir Henry Pigott Bt, Brook Farm, Shobley, Hants BH24 3HT]; *b* 24 June 1925; *s f* 1982; *educ* Ampleforth; WW II 1944–45 with RM, farmer; *m* 4 Sept 1954 *Jean (Olive), only dau of John William Balls, of Holly Lodge, Surlingham, Norfolk, and has:

1 +DAVID JOHN BERKELEY [David Pigott Esq, 91 Bellemoor Rd, Upper Shirley, Hants SO1 2QW]; *b* 16 Aug 1955; *educ* Moor Park Ludlow and Hurn Court Sch Bournemouth; *m* 1st 1981 (*divorce* 1984) Alison Fletcher; *m* 2nd 1986 *Julie, dau of Eric Gordon Wiffen, of Bassett, Hants, and by her has:

  (1) *Christabel Maria; *b* 1989

2 +Antony Charles Philip; *b* 1 June 1960

1 *Sarah Jane Mary; *b* 27 April 1964

Lineage: The senior line of this family settled at Chetwynd Park and Edgmond, Salop; another owned Doddeshall Park, Bucks; the third went to Ireland.

JOHN PIGOTT, of Dysart, Queen's Co, which granted 1562; *m* Johanna Walsh (*m* 2nd John Barnes) and *d* 27 April 1570, leaving:

Sir ROBERT PIGOTT, of Dysart (erected into Manor of Dysart 1639); *m* 1st Anne (*d* 9 Oct 1599), gdau of Sir Anthony St Leger (*see* DONERAILE, V), and had, with three sons:

1 JOHN

2 Alexander, of Innishannon; Col

Sir ROBERT *m* 2nd Thomasine, widow of Peper Baptiste Castillon and dau and coheir of Christopher Peyton, and by her had, with other issue:

3 William, of Kilfinny; ancestor of the PIGOTTs of Capard

1 Thomasine; *m* 1st Argentine Hull, of Leamcon; *m* 2nd Col Prime Iron Rochfort; *m* 3rd George Peyton, of Streamstown, Co Westmeath

Sir ROBERT *d* between 23 May 1641 and 17 April 1644; his est son,

JOHN PIGOTT, of Grangebegg, Queen's Co; MP 1634–46; *m* Martha, dau of Sir Thomas Colclough, of Tintern Abbey, Co Wexford, and had, with five daus:

1 Robert, of Dysart; ancestor of the PIGOTTs of Dysart

2 Thomas, PC, of Long Ashton, Somerset; MP Queen's Co 1661

3 ALEXANDER

4 John, of Kilfanny; *m* 2nd Mary, widow of Pierce Moore and dau of Francis Edgeworth, of Edgeworthstown; by his 1st w he was ancestor of the PIGOTTs of Raheenduff and had:

  (1) Ann *m* Francis Cosby, of Vicarstown, only s of Thomas Cosby, of Vicarstown, and had issue

JOHN PIGOTT was *k* in battle by 10 March 1646; his 3rd son,

ALEXANDER PIGOTT, of Innishannon, Co Cork; MP Maryborough (modern Portlaoise) 1661; *m* Anne, widow of Thomas Adderley and dau of Sir Edward Bolton, of Brazil, Co Dublin, and *d* after 17 Sept 1680, leaving, with a dau:

THOMAS PIGOTT, of Chetwynd, Co Cork; *m* Jane (*d* 1710), dau of Sir Emanuel Moore, Bt, of Ross Carbery, Co Cork (*see* 1926 edn), and had, with four yr sons and three daus:

EMANUEL PIGOTT, of Chetwynd; MP Cork 1735–60; *m* 1st Lucy, dau of George Rogers, of Ashgrove, and had issue; *m* 2nd Judith, dau of Richard Warburton, and *d* 30 June 1762, having by her had a s and three daus; his est s by his 1st w:

GEORGE PIGOTT, of Chetwynd; *m* Jane, dau of Richard Warburton, of Garrahinch, Queen's Co, and *d* 1773, leaving:

THOMAS PIGOTT, of Knapton, Queen's Co; Maj-Gen, Govr Cork, MP Taghmon 1776–83 and Midleton 1783–93; *b* 13 Oct 1734; *m* 13 Sept 1763 Priscilla, dau of William Carden, of Lismore, Queen's Co, and *d* 12 Oct 1793, having had, with three yr sons (including Rev Thomas, *m* 30 July 1813 Mary, est dau of Richard Croasdaile, of Rynn, Queen's Co, and *d* 1834, leaving issue):

Sir George Pigott, 1st Bt (UK), so *cr* 3 Oct 1808; *b* 22 Oct 1766; Capt 17th Dragoons, Lt-Col Roden's Regt of Fencible Cav; *m* 15 Feb 1794 Annabella (*d* 9 Jan 1863), dau of Rt Hon Thomas Kelly, Judge Common Pleas Ireland, and had, with other issue:

1 THOMAS (Sir), **2nd Bt**

2 William, of Dullingham, Cambs, DL; *b* 29 Oct 1804; *m* 1st 23 June 1827 Harriet (*d* 12 March 1838), dau of Lt-Gen Christopher Jeaffreson, of Dullingham House, and had:

  (1) Christopher William PIGOTT later JEAFFRESON (roy licence 21 Jan 1839) and later still ROBINSON (roy licence 24 Aug 1857), of Denston, Suffolk, and Dullingham, Cambs, DL; *b* 23 Jan 1836; *m* 17 Feb 1870 Mary (*d* 30 June 1939), est dau of John Dunn Gardner, of Chatteris, Cambs, and *dsp* 23 June 1889

  (1) Ada; *m* 15 March 1853 John Dunn Gardner (*d* 11 Jan 1908), DL, of Chatteris, MP Bodmin 1841–47, and *d* 4 April 1915, leaving issue

  (2) Harriet; *d* 10 Nov 1916

2 (cont.) William Pigott *m* 2nd 18 Oct 1847 Charlotte Maria (*d* 8 Sept 1884), widow of 1st Baron Keane of Ghuznee and Cappoquin (*see* KEANE, Bt) and dau of Col — Boland, and *d* 23 March 1875

3 Wellesley Pole (Rev); *b* 30 March 1808; MA, Rector Fugglestone-cum-Bemerton and Fovant, Wilts; *m* 1st 3 June 1845 Maria (*dsp* 19 Dec 1851), dau of Adml Lord Henry Paulet, GCB (*see* WINCHESTER M); *m* 2nd 22 April 1858 Fanny (*d* 1 May 1897), 2nd dau of Bernard Granville, of Wellesbourne Hall, Warwicks, and *d* 27 Feb 1890, leaving:

  (1) Wellesley George, OBE (1919), of The Weirs Cottage, Brockenhurst, JP; *b* 20 April 1861; Lt-Col Rifle Bde; *m* 7 July 1891 Helen Louise (*d* 1940), widow of Capt Frederick W Ind, RA, and only dau of Capt Thomas Donaldson, 3rd Hus, and *d* 2 Dec 1935, having had:

    1a Gerald Wellesley; *b* 3rd Sept 1896; 2nd Lt RFA; *d* 14 May 1915 of wounds recd in action

  (2) Henry à Court; *b* 25 Feb 1870; MA Oxon; *m* 3rd May 1899 Violet Margaret (*m* 2nd 12 Sept 1917 Max Georges de Crelier (*d* 15 June 1923) and *d* 9 Nov 1951), dau of Frederick Astell Lushington (*see* LUSHINGTON, Bt), and *dsp* 27 April 1908

  (1) Fanny Ada; *m* 25 May 1886 Lt-Col Charles Berkeley Pigott, CB, DSO, only s of **Sir Charles Pigott, 3rd Bt**, and *d* Jan 1944, leaving issue (*see* below)

1 Salisbury Harriet; *m* 11 October 1838 Count Gustave Sayn-Wittgenstein-Sayn (*d* 1846), of Munich, and *d* 13 April 1904 aged 98, having had issue

Sir GEORGE *d* 28 May 1844; his est son,

Sir Thomas Pigott, 2nd Bt; *b* 12 Oct 1796; Capt RHG; *m* 24 Oct 1831 Georgiana Anne (*m* 2nd 1855 John Frederick Baillie, of Leys Castle, Inverness-shire (*d* 1865)), dau of William Brummell, of Wivenhoe, Essex, and *d* 7 Oct 1847, leaving, with a dau (Mary Elizabeth Sydney; *d* unm 2 May 1913):

Sir Charles Robert Pigott, 3rd Bt, JP, DL Bucks; *b* 13 April 1835; Lt 90th Foot Crimea 1855 (severely wounded, medals and clasp); *m* 1st 30 Oct 1856 Mary Louisa (*d* 11 April 1873), yst dau of Capt Charles Hallowell Carew, RN, of Beddington Park, Surrey, and had:

1 Charles Berkeley, CB, DSO; *b* 13 Jan 1859; Lt-Col 21st Hus; *m* 25 May 1886 his cousin Fanny Ada Pigott (*see* above) and *dvp* 12 Sept 1897, leaving:

  (1) BERKELEY (Sir), **4th Bt**

  (1) Florence Ada Cecile (Yvonne); *m* 1st 28 Dec 1920 Roland William Edward Ruddock, Ceylon Survey Dept (*d* 15 July 1942); *m* 2nd 12 Feb 1946 Maj Leslie Fitzroy Richard, RA, RAF (*d* 5 March 1947), est s of Walter Richard, of Edinburgh

1 Florence Louisa; *d* unm 27 Feb 1877

Sir Charles *m* 2nd 14 July 1880 Margaret Mary Pole (*d* 9 Dec 1924), widow of Capt John Chidley Coote (*see* COOTE, Bt), and er dau of Sydney Cosby, and *d* 6 April 1911

His gs,

    Sir Berkeley Pigott, 4th Bt; *b* 29 May 1894; *educ* Wellington; Maj 17th/21st Lancers WW II, Verderer New Forest 1955–67; *m* 21 April 1919 Christabel Charlotte (*d* 30 April 1974 aged 85), yr dau of Rev Frederick Hermann Bowden-Smith, of Careys, Brockenhurst, and *d* 9 May 1982, leaving:

1 Sir (BERKELEY) HENRY SEBASTIAN PIGOTT, **5th and present Bt**

1 *(Mary) Stephanie [Mrs Walter Higham, 12 Dragon St, Petersfield, Hants]; *b* 29 Oct 1920; *m* 1st 14 May 1951 (*annulled* 1954) Peter Friedrich Sika, s of Ministerialrat Dr Wilhelm Sika, of Vienna; *m* 2nd 21 Dec 1959 *Cdr Walter Ernest Higham, RN, s of Ernest John Higham, of Mayfair, and has had:

  (1) *Stephen Walter; *b* 3 Oct 1960

  (2) Charles Richard; *b* 26 Aug; *d* 18 Oct 1965

2 *(Mary) Veronica [Mrs Stefan Wysogota-Kwasniewski, Martyr's Way, Walsingham, Norfolk]; *b* 5 Aug 1922; *m* 27 Oct 1944 *Stefan Wysogota-Kwasniewski, s of Wladislaw Wysogota-Kwasniewski, of Warsaw, and has:

  (1) *Casimir Stefan; *b* 1946; *m* 1973 *Laura Clements and has:

    1a *Alexandra Christabel; *b* 1980

  (1) *Sabina Orietta; *b* 1945; *m* 1st 1964 Derek Johnstone Brooke and has:

    1a *Gregory Damien Amadeus; *b* 1965

  (1) (cont.) Mrs Brooke *m* 2nd 1968 *Andrew Holt and by him has:

    2a *Trystan; *b* 1969

    3a *Thor; *b* 1973

    4a *Luke; *b* 1977

PIGOTT-BROWN

Arms: Quarterly, 1st and 4th, gu. a chevron or, between two bear's paws erased in chief arg. and four hands conjoined in saltire of the second in base a chief engrailed of the last, thereon an eagle displayed sa. (for distinction), in the honour point a cross-crosslet of the third (for BROWN); 2nd and 3rd, erm. three fusils conjoined in fess sa. (for PIGOTT). **Crest:** A bear's paw erased arg., issuant out of a wreath of oak vert, holding a sinister hand ppr. (for BROWN). **Motto:** *Est concordia fratrum* ('There is unity among brothers'). **Creation:** Bt. (UK) 5 Jan 1903.

SIR WILLIAM BRIAN PIGOTT-BROWN, 3RD BT, of Broome Hall, Holmwood, Surrey [Sir William Pigott-Brown Bt, 47 Eaton Mews North, London SW1X 8LL]; *b* 20 Jan 1941; *s* f 1942; *educ* Eton; champion amateur jockey, night club proprietor

Lineage: Sir WILLIAM BROWN, 1st Bt, of Richmond Hill (*qv*); had an est s:

ALEXANDER BROWN, of Beilby Grange, Yorks; *dvp* 8 Oct 1849, leaving a 3rd s:

Sir Alexander Hargreaves Brown, 1st Bt (UK), so *cr* 5 Jan 1903, JP Lancs and Surrey; *b* 11 April 1844; MP (Lib then Lib U) Wenlock 1868–85 and Wellington 1885–1906, Hon Col Lancs and Cheshire RGA, formerly Cornet 5th Dragoon Gds; *m* 5 Jan 1876 Henrietta Agnes Terrell (*d* 14 May 1921), dau of Charles Ridpath Blandy, of Madeira, and had:

1 Gordon Hargreaves; *b* 31 July 1880; Capt Coldstream Gds, Boer War 1901–02 and WW I (wounded); *m* 18 Oct 1910 Editha Ivy (*d* 8 Feb 1964, having recd by roy warrant 9 June 1922 rank of bt's widow and added by roy licence 6 May 1925 the name and arms of PIGOTT for herself and issue), er dau of Adml William Harvey Pigott, of Doddershall Park, Bucks, and was *ka* 29 Oct 1914, leaving:

  (1) JOHN HARGREAVES (Sir), **2nd Bt**

  (1) *Joan Terrell Hargreaves [Lady Prideaux, Rallywood, Ockley, Surrey]; *b* 18 Dec 1911; *m* 22 Nov 1934 Col Sir John Francis Prideaux, OBE, DL (*d* 1993), 2nd s of Walter Prideaux, of Hamsell Lake, Eridge, and has:

    1a *(Christopher) John [John Prideaux Esq, Doddershall Park, Aylesbury, Bucks]; *b* 12 Nov 1936; *educ* Eton; *m* 16 April 1959 *Celia, only dau of Sir Peter Averell Daniell, TD, DL, of Glebe Ho, Buckland, Surrey, and has:

      1b *David John; *b* 5 Oct 1962; *m* 1989 *Sally M, dau of Ian Liddell, of Sheering, Essex, and has:

        1c *Thomas; *b* 1992

        2c *Charles; *b* 1996

      1b *Lavinia Marion; *b* 3 Feb 1961; *m* 1st 1981 Barry J Cameron, of W Australia; *m* 2nd 1992 *Allan Gilfillan (Sam) Mainds and by him has:

        1c *Polly; *b* 1994

    2a *Michael Charles Terrell [Michael Prideaux Esq, Selehurst, Lower Beeding, Sussex]; *b* 23 Oct 1950; *educ* Eton and Trin Coll Cambridge; *m* 1975 *Mrs Susan H Monsarrat, dau of Peto Bennett, of Jersey, and has:

      1b *John Peto; *b* 1979

      1b *Laura Hargreaves; *b* 1976

    1a *Editha Anne [Mrs Alaster Templeton, The Old Rectory, Whatfield, Suffolk]; *b* 4 Sept 1940; *m* 1968 *Alaster Templeton and has:

      1b *Katherine Elizabeth; *b* 1968

      2b *Jane Celia; *b* 1970

  (2) *Patience Hargreaves, JP; *b* 15 Feb 1915; *m* 15 Feb 1939 F/O Charles Augustus Lee Steere, AAF (presumed *ka* over Dunkirk 27 May 1940), est s of Sir Ernest Augustus Lee Steere, of Perth, W Australia, and has:

    1a *Gordon Ernest; *b* 26 Dec 1939; *educ* Eton and Trin Coll Cambridge; *m* 1966 *Mary Kathrine, dau of Innes Stuart, of Ethie Mains, Arbroath, Angus, and has:

      1b *A dau; *b* 3 March 1971

2 Walter Hargreaves; *b* 6 Sept 1881; *educ* Trin Coll Cambridge (MA); *m* 22 July 1913 Alberta Laura (*m* 2nd 9 Nov 1937 Maj Alexander Innes, MC (*see* INNES, Bt, of Balvenie), and *d* 24 Sept 1975), dau of Capt Guy Mainwaring, RN, and *d* 2 June 1936, leaving:

  (1) Alexander Bruce Hargreaves; *b* 24 April 1918; Lt Scots Gds WW II; *ka* Belgium 4 Oct 1944

  (2) Hugh Gordon Hargreaves; *b* 29 Oct 1920; *d* unm 7 March 1943

  (1) *Susan Henrietta Hargreaves [Mrs Curtis Delmar-Morgan, Eadens Wedge, E Meon, Hants]; *b* 22 Nov 1914; *m* 3 Jan 1935 Curtis Delmar-Morgan, DSC, RNVR (*d* 1987), yr s of John Delmar-Morgan, of Chelsea, and has:

    1a *Michael Walter; *b* 1 March 1936; *educ* Eton; late 2nd Lt Scots Gds; *m* 17 Feb 1962 *Marjorie Rosemary, dau of John Logan, of Masterton, NZ, and has:

      1b *Benjamin John; *b* 29 March 1966

      1b *Katharine Susan; *b* 1968

      2b *Alexandra Jane; *b* 1971

    2a *Jeremy Hugh; *b* 27 May 1941; *educ* Eton; *m* 1966 1st Nicole Jane, dau of Howard Eden Smith, and has:

      1b *Piers Jonathan; *b* 1974

      1b *Frances Jane; *b* 1971

    2a (cont.) Jeremy Delmar-Morgan *m* 2nd 1978 *Mary E, dau of R J Hope, of Cookham Dean, Berks, and by her has:

      2b *Alexander Curtis; *b* 1981

      2b *Alice Clodagh; *b* 1984

    1a *(Dorothy) Sarah; *b* 14 May 1956; *m* 1979 *Peter S Cooper and has:

      1b *Robert James; *b* 1989

      1b *Elizabeth Anne; *b* 1987

  (2) *Margaret Hargreaves [Mrs Alexander Nelson, Muckairn, Taynuilt, Argyllshire; Ardlussa, Isle of Jura, Argyllshire]; *b* 7 Feb 1917; *m* 1st 27 July 1938 Robert Graham (Robin) Fletcher (*d* 23 June 1960), s of Capt Alexander Leslie Fletcher, RN, of Kensington; *m* 2nd 1 Feb 1961, as his 2nd w, *Alexander Ronan Nelson, yr s of Thomas Arthur Nelson, of St Leonard's, Edinburgh, and Achnacloich, Connel, Argyll, and has by her 1st husb:

    1a *Alastair Robert Leslie; *b* 2 March 1941; *educ* Eton; *m* Feb 1964 *Maria Lucia Simões and has:

      1b *Robin Simões; *b* 1972

      1b *Monica Simões; *b* 1966

      2b *Katia Simões; *b* 1967

    2a *Charles Hugh [Charles Fletcher Esq, Ardlussa, Isle of Jura, Argyllshire]; *b* 25 Dec 1946; *educ* Eton; *m* 27 April 1970 *Rose Noreen Nugent, dau of W N Sherlock, and has:

      1b *Andrew Charles; *b* 1972

      1b *Catriona Rose; *b* 1973

      2b *Elizabeth Noreen; *b* 1976

    3a *Ronald James [Ronald Fletcher Esq, Eastern Lennieston, Thornhill FK8 3QP]; *b* 22 Nov 1948; *educ* Eton; *m* 1974 *Damaris Hunneman and has:

      1b *Ewan James; *b* 1978

      2b *Robert Gordon; *b* 1980

    1a *Fiona Margaret; *b* 6 Aug 1939

    2a *Katharine Hargreaves; *b* 29 June 1953; *m* 1977 *Douglas Johnson and has:

      1b *Fiona Mary; *b* 1977

      2b *Helen Margaret; *b* 1979

  (3) Mary Elizabeth Hargreaves; *b* 8 May, *d* 13 Sept 1922

1 Agnes Sara Hargreaves; *m* 15 Dec 1908 Brig-Gen James Bruce Jardine, CMG, DSO, DL (*d* 17 March 1955), of Chesterknowes, by Selkirk, Roxburghshire, 5th Lancers, s of Manfred Leslie Palmes Jardine, of Craigroyston, Midlothian, and *d* 19 March 1961, leaving issue

2 Gladys Emily Hargreaves; *m* 26 June 1907 Maj Geoffrey Edward Huth, JP, Lt Coldstream Gds and Maj E Surrey Regt (*d* 9 Feb 1967), er s of Edward Huth, DL, of Wykehurst Park, Sussex, and *d* 27 June 1968, leaving issue

The 1st Bt *d* 12 March 1922; his gs,

Sir John Hargreaves Pigott-Brown, 2nd Bt; *b* 16 Aug 1913; *educ* Trin Coll Cambridge (BA); Capt Coldstream Gds WW II; *m* 6 April 1940 *Helen Viola Egerton [Mrs Charles Radclyffe, Lew, Oxon] (*m* 2nd 20 April 1948 Capt Charles Raymond Radclyffe, RSG, only s of Raymond Augustus Edward Radclyffe, of Lew, Oxon), only dau of Gilbert Egerton Cotton (*see* COMBERMERE, V), and was *ka* Tunisia 25 Dec 1942, leaving:

1 Sir WILLIAM BRIAN PIGOTT-BROWN, **3rd and present Bt**

PIKE

Arms: Or on a cross gules a churchwarden's staff, headed of a mitre or, on a chief sable a castleford fine stoneware teapot proper.
Supporters: On either side a fox, the dexter gorged with a wreath of ivy, the sinister with a wreath of rosemary proper, each resting the interior hind foot on a portcullis or, the compartment comprising a grassy mount proper. **Motto:** Faithful endeavour.
Creation: B. (LP, UK) 1974.

THE BARONESS PIKE, of Melton, Co Leicester (Dame Irene Mervyn Parnicott Pike, DBE (1981)) [The Rt Hon The Baroness Pike DBE, Hownam, Kelso, Roxburghshire TD5 8AL]; *b* 16 Sept 1918; *educ* Hunmanby Hall E Yorks and Reading U (BA); WAAF 1941–46; Memb WRCC 1955–57; MP (C) Melton 1956–74; Assist PMG 1959–63, Jt Parly U-Sec Home Office 1963–64; Memb Robens Ctee Safety and Health at Work 1970–72; Chm WRVS 1974–81; dir: Watts, Blake and Bearne 1964–, Dunderdale Investments; chm: IBA Gen Advsy Cncl 1974–79, Broadcasting Complaints Commn 1981–85

Lineage: IVAN SAMUEL PIKE; had:

IRENE MERVYN PARNICOTT, *cr* a **Baroness**

PILDITCH

VINCIT QUI SE VINCIT

Arms: Per chevron invected sable and or two ancient galleys in chief, in base an eagle displayed, all counterchanged. **Crest:** A bear sejant proper, muzzled and gorged with a chain or, pendant therefrom an escutcheon sable, charged with an eagle displayed gold. **Motto:** *Vincit qui se vincit* ('He conquers who is in command of himself'). **Creation:** Bt. (UK), 28 June 1929.

SIR RICHARD EDWARD PILDITCH, 4TH BT, of Bartropps, Weybridge, Co Surrey [Sir Richard Pilditch Bt, 4 Fishermans Bank, Mudeford, Dorset BH23 3NP]; *b* 8 Sept 1926; *s* bro 1954; *educ* Charterhouse; RN WW II India and Ceylon; *m* 7 Oct 1950 *Pauline Elizabeth Smith, ward of Miss Marie Michaelis, MBE, MA, of Blunt House, Oxted, Surrey, and has:

1 +JOHN RICHARD; *b* 24 Sept 1955; *educ* privately

1 *Fiona; *b* 13 Nov 1951; *m* 1982 *Patrick John Payne, s of Austin Ralph Payne

Lineage: PHILIP JOHN PILDITCH, of Compton, Plymouth; had an est s:

Sir Philip Edward Pilditch, 1st Bt (UK), so *cr* 28 June 1929, JP (Co London); *b* 12 Aug 1861; *educ* Cheverley Hall Sch Mannamead and King's Coll London; memb LCC 1907–19 (V-Chm 1913–14), MP (U) Spelthorne 1918–31, fndr Pilditch, Chadwick and Co, architects, Capt 1st Sussex Vol Art, fndr and hon treas Bn Funds for London, Middx and Surrey Bns of New Army WW I, ktd 1918, author: *Retrenchment*, *The Eighties and To-day*, *Elizabethan Plymouth*, *Hadrian's Wall*; *m* 11 July 1888 Emily Mary (*d* 15 Jan 1955), est dau of John Lewis, of Richmond, and had:

1 PHILIP HAROLD (Sir), **2nd Bt**

2 Edgar Lewis, TD; *b* 29 June 1901; *educ* Eton and Trin Coll Oxford (MA); Maj RA (TA) WW II (despatches, US Bronze Star), slr 1926; *m* 5 Nov 1936 *Anne Goodchild, 2nd dau of Richard Llewellyn Weeks, of Broomhaugh House, Riding Mill, Northumberland, and formerly w of — Goodchild, and *d* 1986, leaving:

  (1) +Simon Andrew Llewellyn [Simon Pilditch Esq, c/o Nat Westminster Bank Ltd, 64 Bayswater Rd, London W2]; *b* 9 Feb 1938; *educ* Eton, McGill (BA) and RAC Cirencester; co dir, MRAC; *m* 6 Sept 1969 (*divorce* 19–) Ute, yr dau of Siegfried Johannes Mayr, of Kitzbühel, Austria, and has:

    1a *Olivia Margaret; *b* 1970

1 Mabel Emily (May); *m* 8 Jan 1919 Maj Henry Alexander Hammick , OBE, MC (see HAMMICK, Bt), and *d* 1990, leaving issue

Sir PHILIP *d* 17 Dec 1948; his er son,

Sir Philip Harold Pilditch, 2nd Bt; *b* 30 Oct 1890; *educ* Winchester and Pembroke Coll Cambridge; Maj RA (TAR), WW I (despatches) and WW II 1939–41; *m* 1st 23 March 1918 (*divorce* 1936) Frances Isabella, yr dau of John George Weeks, JP, of Bedlington, Northumberland, and had:

1 **Sir Philip John Frederick Pilditch, 3rd Bt**; *b* 11 Aug 1919; *educ* Winchester and Trin Coll Oxford; Lt RA WW II (invalided); *m* 2 June 1948 *(Phyllis) Jean (*m* 2nd 1977 David Smith) [Mrs David Smith, 2 St Mary's Mews, Ludlow, Salop SY8 1DZ], er dau of Maj Dudley Cautley Stewart-Smith, MBE, of Weybridge, Surrey, and *d* 11 May 1954, leaving:

  (1) *Frances Jean; *b* 14 June 1952; *m* 1978 *George Phillips Yeats, s of George Yeats, and has:

    1a *Frederick Xavier; *b* 1983

  (2) *Felicity Mary [Mrs Richard Austin, Buttergate Barn, Sykes' Fold, Leeming, W Yorks BD22 9SH]; *b* posthumously 21 Oct 1954; *m* 1975 *Richard Austin, s of Herbert Wilfred Charles Austin, and has:

    1a *Nicholas Charles; *b* 1982

    1a *Charlotte Susan; *b* 1985

2 Sir RICHARD EDWARD PILDITCH, **4th and present Bt**

Sir Philip *m* 2nd 1936 Patricia (*m* 2nd 22 June 1951 Lt-Col Raymond Francis Lewis Thomas, IA, only s of William Daniel Thomas, and had further issue), only dau of Alexander W Whittet, of Hollybrook House, Broughton Gifford, Wilts, and 19 Dec 1949, having by her had:

1 *Rosalind Phyllis Muriel; *b* 21 May 1946; *m* 20 Dec 1969 *Allan Owen-Taylor, s of Leslie H Owen-Taylor (see ROTHES, E)

PILE

SINE · LABE · NOTA

Arms: Azure three piles argent, on a chief ermine a castle proper between two harps or stringed of the second. **Crest:** On a ducal coronet or, charged with a cross botony azure, a pelican with wings addorsed and inverted proper. **Motto:** *Sine labe nota* ('Notable for being without dishonour'). **Creation:** Bt. (UK) 24 Sept 1900.

SIR FREDERICK DEVEREUX PILE, 3RD BT, of Kenilworth House, Rathgar, Co Dublin, MC (1945) [Col Sir Frederick Pile Bt MC, Beadles, Cowbeech, E Sussex]; *b* 10 Dec 1915; *s* f 1976; *educ* Weymouth Coll and RMC Sandhurst; served WW II, Br Jt Servs Mission Washington 1957–60, Col RTR, Comdt RAC Tank Driving and Maintenance Sch Bovington Dorset 1960–64; *m* 1st 6 March 1940 Pamela (*d* 19 Aug 1983), est dau of Philip Henstock, of Falkland Garth, Newbury, and has had:

1 David Alistair; *b* 20 Feb; *d* 24 July 1948

1 *Fiona Devereux; *b* 6 Oct 1941; *m* 1976 *Mark William Towse

2 *Vanessa Anne [Mrs Rory Mackean, 4 Colyton Rd, London SE22]; *b* 30 Sept 1951; *m* 1972 *Rory Gilchrist Graham Mackean and has:

 (1) *Thomas; *b* 1985

 (1) *Charlotte; *b* 1979

 (2) *Virginia; *b* 1980

Sir FREDERICK *m* 2nd 1984 *Mrs V Josephine A Culverwell, formerly w of Gerald D Culverwell

Lineage: THOMAS PILE, of Brixham, Devon; *b* 26 Sept 1746; *m* 17 June 1776 Elizabeth Phillips and had:

JAMES PHILLIPS PILE, of Brixham; *b* 14 Oct 1787; *m* 12 Oct 1818 Sarah (*d* 31 March 1838), dau of John Hawkins, of Ilfracombe, and *d* 29 May 1835, leaving, with other issue:

THOMAS PILE, of Sandymount, Dublin; *b* 27 July 1819; *m* 4 May 1848 Anne (*d* 27 Oct 1872), dau of George Poole, of Tenby, S Wales, and *d* 26 April 1899, leaving, with other issue:

Sir Thomas Devereux Pile, 1st Bt (UK), so *cr* 24 Sept 1900, DL Co and City of Dublin; *b* 27 Feb 1856; High Sheriff Co Dublin 1898, Ld Mayor Dublin 1900; *m* 3 May 1882 Caroline Maude (*d* 20 May 1948), dau of John Mann Nicholson, JP, of Rathgar, and had:

1 FREDERICK ALFRED (Sir), **2nd Bt**

2 Walter Devereux; *b* 24 Jan 1887; Maj RFA (SR) WW I (despatches), Croix de Guerre and Order Crown Belgium; *m* 14 Sept 1921 Margaret Lucy, MBE (1961) (*d* 1989), est dau of Thomas Irvine Bonner, MB, CM, of Shipley, Yorks, and *d* 1 Nov 1959, leaving:

 (1) *Margaret Patricia Devereux; *b* 5 Jan 1923; *educ* London U (BSc 1946)

 (2) *Anne Devereux [Mrs David Daniel, The White House, 56 Lark Lane, Liverpool L16 8YA]; *b* 2 June 1932; *m* 27 Dec 1961 *David Evan Daniel, s of Herbert McWilliam Daniel, MD, FRCS

3 Cyril John; *b* 27 May 1897; F/Lt RFC; *ka* 29 April 1917

1 Eileen Maud; *b* 23 March 1883; *m* 7 Jan 1919 Capt Ronald Devereux Carty, RASC, s of William Carty, JP, of Dublin, and *d* 8 Nov 1959

Sir THOMAS *d* 17 Jan 1931; his er son,

 Sir Frederick Alfred Pile, 2nd Bt, GCB (1945, KCB 1941, CB 1938), DSO (1918), MC; *b* 14 Sept 1884; *educ* St Andrew's Coll Dublin and RMA Woolwich; served WW I (despatches), Assist Dir Mechanization War Office 1928–32, cmded Canal Bde Egypt 1932–36, Maj-Gen 1937, Cdr 1st AA Div TA 1937–39, GOC-in-C AA Command (TA) 1939–45, Lt-Gen 1939, Gen 1941 Roy Tank Corps, ret 1945, Dir-Gen Housing Min Works April–Oct 1945, Hon LLD Leeds U 1942, Cdr US Legn Merit, Gen Col-Cmdt RA 1945, chm Fothergill and Harvey Ltd Manchester 1956–64 and Cementation Co Ltd 1961–63; *m* 1st 9 Jan 1915 (*divorce* 1929) Vera Millicent, only dau of Brig-Gen Frederick Charles Lloyd, CB, and had:

1 Sir FREDERICK DEVEREUX PILE, **3rd and present Bt**

2 John Devereux (Sir); *b* 5 June 1918; *educ* Weymouth Coll and Trin Coll Cambridge (BA 1939); Maj RA (TA), dir Imperial Tobacco 1973 and Tobacco Securities Tst; *m* 15 Sept 1946 *Katharine Mary [Lady Pile, Munstead, Godalming, Surrey GU8 4AR], er dau of Austin George Shafe, of Henley-on-Thames, and *d* 13 Dec 1982, leaving:

 (1) +ANTHONY JOHN DEVEREUX JP [Anthony Pile Esq JP, The Manor House, Pitsford, Northants NN6 9AZ]; *b* 7 June 1947; heir presumptive; *educ* Durham Sch; *m* 1977 *Jenny Clare, 2nd dau of Peter Youngman, of Westleton, Suffolk, and has:

  1a +Thomas Charles Devereux; *b* 6 April 1978

  2a +Hugh James Devereux; *b* 22 Jan 1980

  1a *Harriet Rose Devereux; *b* 30 March 1983

 (2) +Timothy Simon Devereux [Timothy Pile Esq, 1 Beech Park Dve, Barnt Green, Birmingham B45 8LZ]; *b* 18 Feb 1953; *educ* Haileybury and Durham U (BA); *m* 1977 *Patricia Thomas and has:

  1a +Jonathan Matthew Devereux; *b* 1981

  2a +Christopher James Devereux; *b* 1984

  1a *Victoria Jane Devereux; *b* 1987

  2a *Rebecca Claire Devereux; *b* 1991

 (1) *Jennifer Jane Devereux [Mrs Huw Alban Davies, Troutbeck, Otford, Kent TN14 5PH]; *b* 2 Jan 1950; *m* 1973 *Huw Alban Davies, MA, DM, FRCP, and has:

  1a *Henry Christopher; *b* 1975

  1a *Hester Margaret; *b* 1977

  2a *Katharine Clare (twin); *b* 1977

 (2) *Sarah Katharine Devereux [Mrs David Jones, The School House, Station Rd, Errol, Perthshire PH2 7QB]; *b* 20 July 1960; *m* 1st 1987 C Richard J Bate; *m* 2nd 1994 *David Alan Jones and has:

  1a *Oliver David; *b* 1994

Sir Frederick *m* 2nd 11 June 1932 Hester Mary Melba (*d* 8 Dec 1949), only dau of George Grenville Phillimore (*see* PHILLIMORE, B); *m* 3rd 22 Jan 1951 *Molly Eveline Louise Mary, late Ch Cdr ATS, widow of Brig Francis Wyville Home, of Belgravia, and only child of Ralph Smyth, of Newtown, Drogheda, Co Louth, and *d* 14 Nov 1976

PILKINGTON OF OXENFORD

Creation: B. (LP, UK) Nov 1995.

THE BARON PILKINGTON OF OXENFORD, of West Dowlish, Co Somerset (Rev Canon Peter Pilkington) [The Rt Hon The Lord Pilkington of Oxenford, Oxenford House, nr Ilminster, Somerset TA19 0PP]; *b* 5 Sept 1933; *educ* Dame Allan's Sch Newcastle and Jesus Coll Cambridge (BA (1955, MA 1958); assist master St Joseph's Coll Chidya Tanganyika 1955–57, ordained 1959, Curate Bakewell Derbys 1959–62, assist master Eton 1962–75 (Master in College 1965–75), Headmaster King's Sch Canterbury 1975–86, High Master St Paul's 1986–92; Memb Parole Bd 1990–95; Chm Broadcasting Complaints Commn 1992–96; Hon Canon Canterbury 1975–90 (Canon Emeritus 1990–); C educn and employment Spokesman Ho Lds 1997–98; *m* 1966 Helen (*d* 1997), dau of Charles and Maria Wilson, and has two daus

Lineage: FRANK PILKINGTON; *m* Doris — and had:

PETER, *cr* a **Baron**

PINSENT

Arms: Argent a saltire flory vert between four chaffinches proper.
Crest: Upon a fleur-de-lys couped vert two chaffinches addorsed proper. **Motto:** *Je pense en bien* ('I think well of it').
Creation: Bt. (UK) 3 Feb 1938.

SIR CHRISTOPHER ROY PINSENT, 3RD BT, of Selly Hill, City of Birmingham [Sir Christopher Pinsent Bt, The Chestnuts, Castle Hill, Guildford, Surrey GU1 3SX]; *b* 2 Aug 1922; *s* f 1978; *educ* Winchester; LAC RAF WW II, portrait painter, lecturer and tutor Camberwell Sch Art 1962–86; *m* 27 June 1951 *Susan Mary, dau of John Norton Scorer, of Walcot Lodge, Fotheringhay, Northants, and has:

1 +THOMAS BENJAMIN ROY; *b* 21 July 1967

1 *(Laura) Candace; *b* 15 April 1954; *m* 1978 *Timothy Bartel Smit, s of Jan Adrianus Bartel Smit, of Arnhem, Holland, and has:

 (1) *Jeremy Alexander Bartel; *b* 1980

 (2) *Samuel Christopher; *b* 1984

 (1) *Laura Marian; *b* 1982

2 *Joanna Mary; *b* 25 Feb 1957; *m* 1991 *James David Simpson, s of John Leonard Simpson, of Woodlands Farm, Barwick-in-Elmet, Yorks, and has:

 (1) *Ella Bennett; *b* 1993

Lineage: RICHARD STEELE PINSENT, of Devonport; had:

Sir Richard Alfred Pinsent, 1st Bt (UK); so *cr* 3 Feb 1938; *b* 3 Aug 1852; *educ* Amersham Hall Caversham and Edinburgh Academy; slr 1873, sr memb Cncl of Law Soc and chm Statutory Discipline Ctee, Pres 1918–19, Hon MA Birmingham 1919, Hon LLD Birmingham 1928; *m* 7 Aug 1878 Laura Proctor (*d* 27 Oct 1931), dau of Thomas Ryland, JP, of Erdington, Warwicks, and had:

1 ROY (Sir), **2nd Bt**

2 Clive; *b* 16 June 1886; Cdr RN, WW I and WW II 1939–42 (invalided); *m* 14 July 1921 Kathleen Jane (*d* 1974), dau of George Macpherson, JP, DL, of The Lloyd House, nr Wolverhampton, and Edinglassie Lodge, Huntly, Aberdeenshire, and *d* 18 Aug 1948, leaving:

 (1) Andrew Clive Macpherson; *b* 4 June 1922; Lt-Cdr RN WW II; *m* 27 Jan 1945 Gloria Poppy Marie (*d* 1979), 3rd Offr WRNS, dau of Maj Cecil Herbert Tollemache, and *d* 1982, leaving:

  1a +Antony Andrew Macpherson [Anthony Pinsent Esq, 4 North Pallant, Chichester, W Sussex]; *b* 26 Feb 1946; *educ* Radley; *m* 24 April 1969 *Clare Natalie, yr dau of Victor H Reynolds, of Portugal and London, and has:

   1b +Charles Victor R; *b* 1973

   1b *Amelia Clare; *b* 26 Feb 1976

2a +David Tollemache; *b* 14 June 1948; *educ* Radley *m* 1976 *Susie, dau of Mrs J Chandler, of Mosman, NSW, and has:

  1b *Rollo Tollemache; *b* 1978

1a *Susan Catherine; *b* 9 Oct 1953; *m* 1976 *Kerry John Pfeiffer, 2nd s of Anthony Pfeiffer, of NSW, and has:

  1b *Olivia K; *b* 19–

(2) James Macpherson; *b* 3 May 1925; Lt-Cdr RN WW II; *m* 1st 23 June 1956 (*divorce* 1972) Daphne Miranda, only child of Capt Kenneth Lanyon Harkness, CBE, DSC, RN, of Petersfield, Hants, and has:

1a +Oliver Clive; *b* 3 April 1964; *m* 1989 *Catherine C, dau of R C Bennett, of Putney, and has:

  1b +Benjamin; *b* June 1992

  1b *Hannah; *b* Oct 1994

1a *Camilla Louisa; *b* 21 Jan 1962; *m* 1983 (*divorce* 1996) Capt Mark P Colacicchi, 13th/18th R Hus (QMO), est s of Count Paul Colacicchi, of Fulham, and has:

  1b *James Paul; *b* 1985

  2b *Rory Adam; *b* 1986

  1b *Sophie Antonia; *b* 1989

(2) (cont.) James Pinsent *m* 2nd 1976 *Eleanor Mary Penrose (Audrey) [Mrs James Pinsent, 13 Felden St, London SW6 5AE], dau of Dr Victor Penrose Robinson, MA, BM, BCL, and *d* 1983

(3) +Ewen Macpherson (Rev) [The Rev Ewen Pinsent, The Cross House, Child Okeford, Dorset]; *b* 29 Dec 1930; Lt RN (ret); *m* 26 May 1962 *Jean Grizel, only dau of Maj-Gen Neil McMicking, CB, CBE, DSO, MC, of Eastferry, Dunkeld, Perthshire, and has:

  1a +Thomas Neil; *b* 6 Nov 1964

  2a +Matthew Clive *b* 10 Oct 1970

  1a *Katherine Jane; *b* 20 Feb 1963; *m* 1991 *Thomas W Tyson, twin s of D Tyson, of Dorf House, Widdington, Essex

  2a *Emma Charlotte; *b* 6 Nov 1964

3 John Ryland, CBE (1949), DSO (1918); *b* 12 Aug 1888; *educ* Winchester (assist master 1926–34); Col RE WW I (despatches four times, brevet), re-employed WW II, Alderman Winchester City Cncl, Mayor Winchester 1936–37, Civ Serv Commr (Chm CS Selection Bd) 1945–50, Offr Legn Hon; *m* 16 Sept 1915 Kathleen May (*d* 7 Dec 1969), dau of Col Ernest Joseph George Boyce, RE, and *d* 3 Oct 1957, leaving:

(1) +John Laurence [John Pinsent Esq, Higher Ludbrook, Ermington, S Devon]; *b* 26 June 1916; *educ* Winchester and Trin Coll Cambridge; Maj RA WW II, slr 1946, farmer; *m* 6 Feb 1940 *Margaret Molyneux, est dau of Richard Vernon Favell, of Cornwall, and has:

  1a +John Edward; *b* 1 Feb 1950; *educ* Winchester

  1a *Margaret Anne [Mrs John Simpson, The Vicarage, Curry Rivel, Somerset]; *b* 15 May 1941; *m* 13 June 1964 *Rev John Lawrence Simpson, ARCM, Chaplain Repton Sch, only s of Col Selwyn George Simpson, OBE, of Huntley, Glos, and has:

    1b *Benjamin John Lawrence; *b* 1970

    1b *Joanna Mary; *b* 29 Dec 1965

    2b *Jessamine Anne; *b* 29 March 1968

  2a *Mary [Mrs Denis Archdale, Roseworthy Barton, Camborne, Cornwall]; *b* 17 Jan 1943; *m* 5 Dec 1964 *Denis Theodore Archdale, yst s of Mervyn Henry Dawson Archdale, JP, DL, and has:

    1b *Nicholas Henry; *b* 1966

    2b *Audley Mervyn; *b* 1969

    1b *Rachael Mary; *b* 1968

  3a *Jennifer; *b* 2 Dec 1944; *m* 29 March 1969 *Capt Christopher Louis Wreford-Brown, DSO, RN, and has:

    1b *Paul Christopher; *b* 21 Sept 1972

    1b *Julia Anne; *b* 25 Feb 1970; *m* 16 April 1994 *William Gifford Scott and has:

      1c *George William Gifford; *b* 28 May 1997

    2b *Amanda Jane; *b* 10 May 1976

  4a *Elizabeth Jane; *b* 4 March 1948

(2) +Richard Alan; *b* 26 July 1931; *educ* Winchester and RAC Cirencester; *m* 15 May 1954 *Mary, yst dau of G/Capt John Benjamin Graham, MC, AFC, OBE, and has:

  1a *Dinah Elizabeth; *b* 21 Sept 1955

  2a *Susan Melanie; *b* 10 July 1964

4 Laurence Alfred; *b* 17 Oct 1894; T/Lt N Staffs Regt; *d* of wounds 15 Aug 1915

5 Phillip Ryland; *b* 26 Sept 1897; T/2nd Lt RFC; *d* of wounds 24 Sept 1916

Sir RICHARD *d* 2 Oct 1948; his er surv son,

Sir Roy Pinsent, 2nd Bt; *b* 22 July 1883; *educ* Marlborough and Univ Coll Oxford (BA 1903); slr 1909, Lt RE WW I; *m* 1st 19 June 1913 Marion Jordan (*d* 1914), est dau of George Jordan Lloyd, FRCS, of Edgbaston, Birmingham; *m* 2nd 8 July 1918 Mary Tirzah (*d* 9 April 1951), dau of Dr Edward Geoffrey Walls, of Southfields, Mavis Enderby, Spilsby, Lincs, and *d* 16 Dec 1978, leaving:

1 Sir CHRISTOPHER ROY PINSENT, **3rd and present Bt**

2 +Michael Roy [Michael Pinsent Esq, 61 Wellington Rd, Birmingham]; *b* 4 Feb 1927; *educ* Marlborough; Lt Roy Signals WW II, slr 1952; *m* 1st 26 July 1952 (*divorce* 19–) Stella Marie, er dau of Basil Priestman, of Birmingham, and has:

  (1) +William Ross; *b* 25 May 1955; *educ* Bedales

  (1) *Nicola Jane; *b* 8 Dec 1957

  (2) *Tonya Mary; *b* 22 April 1959; *m* 1986 *William James Wood, yr s of Sir Frank Wood, KBE, CB, and has:

    1a *Richard Foucard; *b* 1989

1 *Rosemary [Mrs Keiden Barrow, Hazelhope, Stalisfield, Kent ME13 0HY]; *b* 22 March 1930; *educ* Edgbaston High Sch; *m* 28 June 1960 *Keiden John Knapp Barrow, est s of John Andrew Robert Knapp Barrow, MI MechE, MINA, FCMS, MIMarE, of Mombasa, Kenya, and has:

(1) *Clive Andrew Knapp; *b* 31 March 1962; *m* 1991 *Lynne Catherine, dau of Roy Thornton Marsden, of Taupo, NZ, and has:

  1a *Daniel James Knapp; *b* 18 Oct 1994

  1a *Alexandra Catherine; *b* 1991

  2a *Georgia Nicol; *b* 24 Sept 1997

(1) *Clare; *b* Sept 1964; *m* 1987 *Alastair Michael Gordon, s of Alexander Nigel Gordon and has:

  1a *Tom Alex; *b* 22 Aug 1995

PITKEATHLEY

Creation: B. (LP, UK) 1997.

THE BARONESS PITKEATHLEY, of Caversham, Roy Co of Berks (Jill Elizabeth Bisson, OBE (1993)) [The Rt Hon The Baroness Pitkeathley OBE, House of Lords, London SW1A 0PW]; *b* 4 Jan 1940; *educ* Ladies' Coll Guernsey and Bristol U; social worker 1961–64; vol serv co-ordinator Manchester and Essex 1970–83; Nat Consumer Cncl 1983–86; Advsr Griffith's Review of Community Care 1986–88; Dir Nat Cncl for Carers 1986–88; Ch Exec Carers Nat Assoc 1988–; V-Pres Community Cncl Berks 1990–; memb: RSA 1992, Health Advsy Service 1993–; author: *When I Went Home* (1978), *Mobilising Voluntary Resources* (1982), *Volunteers in Hospitals* (1984), *Supporting Volunteers* (1985), *It's my duty, isn't it?* (1989), *Only Child* (with David Emerson, 1994), *Age Gap Relationships* (1996); *m* 1961 (*divorce* 1978) W Pitkeathley and has a s and dau

Lineage: RONALD WILFRED BISSON; *m* Edith May Muston and had:

JILL ELIZABETH, *cr* a **Baroness**

PLANT OF HIGHFIELD

Creation: B. (LP, UK) 1992.

THE BARON PLANT OF HIGHFIELD, of Weelsby, Co Humberside (Raymond Plant) [The Rt Hon The Lord Plant, Master's Lodgings, St Catherine's College, Oxford OX1 3UJ]; 6 Woodview Close, Bassett, Southampton SO2 8P2]; *b* 19 March 1945; *educ* Havelock Sch Grimsby, King's Coll London (BA) and Hull U (PhD 1971); sr lecturer philosophy Manchester U 1967–69; Prof Politics Southampton U 1979–; Master St Catherine's Coll Oxford 1994–, Pro-Chllr; Stevenson Lecturer Glasgow U 1981; Agnes Cumming Lecturer UCD 1988; Stanton Lecturer Cambridge 1989–90 and 1990–91; Sarum Lecturer Oxford 1991; Ferguson Lecturer Manchester U 1994; Scott Holland Lecturer 1995; Charles Gore Lecturer 1995; columnist *The Times* 1988–92; Chm Lab Party Commn Electoral Systems 1991–93; Hon DLitt: Guildhall U 1993, Hull 1994; author: *Hegel* (1974, 2nd edn 1984), *Community and Ideology* (1974), *Political Philosophy and Social Welfare* (1981), *Philosophy Politics and Citizenship* (1984), *Conservative Capitalism in Britain and the United States: a critical appraisal* (1988), *Modern Political Thought* (1991); *m* 29 July 1967 *Katherine Sylvia, dau of Jack Dixon, and has:

  1 *Nicholas; *b* 1969

  2 *Matthew; *b* 1971

  3 *Richard; *b* 1976

Lineage: STANLEY PLANT; *m* Marjorie East and had:

RAYMOND, *cr* a **Baron**

PLATT

Arms: Or fretty sa. plate on a pale gu. a rod of Aesculapius gold.
Crest: In front of a demiplate a nightingale in full song ppr.
Motto: *Concordia res parvae crescunt* ('With amity small concerns become great ones'). **Creation:** Bt. (UK) 14 July 1959.

SIR PETER PLATT, 2ND BT, of Grindleford, Co Derby [The Hon Sir Peter Platt Bt, 1 Ellison Place, Pymble, NSW 2073, Australia]; *b* 6 July 1924; *s f* 1978; *educ* Abbotsholme Sch, Magdalen Coll Oxford (BA 1949, BMus 1950, BLitt 1954, MA 1954) and RCM; WW II 1942–45 with RNVR Coastal Forces (despatches), lecturer and sr lecturer music Sydney U 1952–57, Prof Music Otago U NZ 1957–75 and U of Sydney 1975–89, FGSM 1973; *m* 21 Dec 1948 *Jean Halliday, ARCM, dau of Charles Philip Brentnall, MC, MB, ChB, FRCOG, of Manchester, and has:

1 +MARTIN PHILIP [Martin Platt Esq, 9 Glenross St, Dunedin, New Zealand]; *b* 9 March 1952; *m* 1971 *Frances Corinne Moana, dau of Trevor Samuel Conley, and has:
  (1) +Philip Stephen; *b* 17 Oct 1972
  (2) +Timothy Martin; *b* 1980
  (1) *Suzanne; *b* 1971
  (2) *Rachael; *b* 1976
1 *Margaret; *b* 18 Oct 1949; *m* 6 Dec 1969 (*divorce* 1978) Anthony Pratt Kaye, of Dunedin, NZ
2 *Katherine; *b* 5 Sept 1956; *m* 1988 *Alexander Hendrik Vincent Beasley, s of Robert Beasley, of Auckland, NZ

Lineage: JOHN THOMAS PLATT, of Lancs; ran away to sea and returned to London penniless so worked as a Spitalfields weaver; had:

JAMES PLATT; *b c* 1831; fndr James Platt and Co, whole-sale woollen merchants, St Martin's Lane; made a fortune but later went bankrupt; *m c* 1859 Emma Jane (*d* 1911), dau of Samuel Holman, of Long Acre, formerly of Silverton, Devon, by Emma Elizabeth Boden, actress, and *d* 1912, having had:

1 James; *b c* 1860; author, linguist and etymologist, contributed to Murray's OED; *m* 1897 Maria Tupman and *d* 1910, leaving:
  (1) Irene; *b* 1898
2 Charles; *b c* 1862; author
3 WILLIAM
1 Agnes; *b* 1872; authoress and play reader

JAMES PLATT's yst son,
  WILLIAM PLATT; *b* 11 Jan 1867; author; entered f's business in London; schmaster Grindleford, Derbys, 1910; *m* 1897 Susan Jane, LLA St Andrews, schoolmistress and Schs Inspr (*d* 1942), dau of William Willis, of Loughgall, Co Armagh, later of Tayport, Fife, and *d* 1943, leaving:

1 Maurice; *b* 19 Aug 1898; MEng, CEng; had:
  (1) *Derek James; *b* 2 Dec 1918; *m* 1 June 1943 *Joan Evelyn and has:
    1a *Michael Maurice; *b* 10 June 1948
    1a *Denise Veronica; *b* 22 Feb 1944
  (2) *William David (Rev) [The Rev David Platt, 10 Denchworth Rd, Wantage, OX12 9AO]; *b* 18 Jan 1931; *m* 30 Aug 1958 *Gillian Mary, dau of Rev St John Beverley Groser, of Stepney, and has:
    1a *Rachel Mary; *b* 20 June 1959
    2a *Katharine; *b* 22 Oct 1960
  (3) *Charles Michael; *b* 26 April 1945
  (1) *Yvonne Mary; *b* 4 Oct 1923; *m* 20 June 1945 *Peter Melsome Woolley, s of Maj Richard Melsome Woolley, CBE, of Salisbury, and has:
    1a *John Richard; *b* 29 Dec 1949
    1a *Rosemary Anne; *b* 9 June 1947
2 ROBERT (Sir), **1st Bt**

WILLIAM PLATT's yst son,
  Sir Robert Platt, 1st Bt, and BARON PLATT, of Grindleford, Co Derby (LP, both UK), so *cr* 14 July 1959 and 16 Jan 1967 respectively; *b* 16 April 1900; *educ* King Alfred's Sch Hampstead, The Home Sch Grindleford and Sheffield U (MB, ChB 1921, MD 1923); MRCP Lond 1925, FRCP Lond 1935, Hon MSc Manchester 1949, Hon LLD Sheffield and Belfast 1959 and Manchester 1969, Hon MD Bristol

1959, Physician Roy Infirmary Manchester, Prof of Medicine Manchester U 1946–65, pres Roy Coll of Physicians London 1957–62, chm Manchester Chamber Concerts Soc 1952–65, Hon Memb Assoc of American Physicians 1960, Hon Fell American Coll of Physicians 1961, Physician Roy Infirmary Sheffield 1931–46, ed *Quarterly Journal of Medicine* 1948–58, memb MRC 1953–57, Chm Clinical Research Bd 1964, served WW I 1918 Infantry and WW II 1941–45 with RAMC (T/Brig 1945, ret as Col 1945); *m* 1st 18 Aug 1922 (*divorce* 1974) Margaret Irene, MB, ChB (Sheffield), DPM (Manchester) (*d* 1987), dau of Arthur Charles Cannon, schoolmaster, of Sheffield, and had:

1 Sir PETER PLATT, **2nd and present Bt**
1 *Joan Elizabeth [The Hon Mrs Allen, 10 Buckwood Close, Hazel Grove, Stockport, Cheshire]; *b* 6 May 1927; *educ* Slade Sch of Art and Manchester U (BA 1952); *m* 20 Sept 1952 *John Bunting Allen, MSc, s of Edmund Allen, Offr Merchant Marine, of Seaham, and has:
  (1) *Jonathan Robert; *b* 15 Sept 1953
  (2) *Paul Bunting; *b* 4 April 1956
  (3) *Mark Benedict; *b* 28 Jan 1965
2 *Helen Margaret [The Hon Mrs Stowasser, 10 Lantana Lane, Mapleton, Qld 4560, Australia]; *b* 16 March 1933; *educ* Newnham Coll Cambridge (BA 1954); *m* 10 July 1954 *Cecil Henry Stowasser, BA Comm, DipEdPsych, s of Marian Stowasser, of Karlsbad, Czechoslovakia, and has:
  (1) *Peter; *b* 31 Oct 1955
  (2) *Robert; *b* 3 Nov 1956
  (3) *Michael; *b* 28 Feb 1960

Sir Robert *m* 2nd 16 Jan 1974 *Sylvia Jean [Sylvia Lady Platt, 40 Arthurs Bridge Rd, Horsell, Surrey GU21 4NT], formerly w of John Alfred Haggard and dau of Sidney Charles Careley, of Thames Ditton, Surrey, and *d* 30 June 1978

PLATT OF WRITTLE

Arms: Vert four seaxes in cross, their blades outwards proper, hilts, quillons and pommels or, and as many aerofoils in saltire argent, all between four plates. **Supporters:** Dexter, perched upon the stock of an anchor a kingfisher, wings elevated and addorsed proper; sinister, a lion, the wings also elevated and addorsed, supporting a patriarchal cross gules, the compartment comprising a grassy mount, springing therefrom founts of water proper. **Motto:** *Aime Dieu et tous* ('Love God and everyone'). **Creation:** B. (LP, UK) 1981.

THE BARONESS PLATT OF WRITTLE, of Writtle, Co Essex (Beryl Catherine Myatt, CBE (1978), DL (Essex 1983)) [The Rt Hon The Baroness Platt of Writtle CBE DL, House of Lords, London SW1A 0PW]; *b* 18 April 1923; *educ* Westcliffe High Sch for Girls, and Girton Coll Cambridge (MA, Hon Fell 1988); memb Chelmsford RDC 1958–74, Essex CC 1965–68 (Alderman 1969–74, v-chm Educn Ctee 1969–71, chm 1971–80; chm CC 1980-83); memb Cambridge U Appointments Bd 1975–79; Memb Court: Essex U and Brunel U 1985–92, Cranfield U 1989–; Pres: Inst Trg and Devpt 1985–87, Cambridge U Engrs Assoc 1987–; Chm: Equal Opportunities Commn 1983–88, Women's Working Gp Industry Matters 1986–90; memb: CNAA 1973–79, Cncl CGLI 1974–94, Engrg Cncl 1981–90, Advsy Ctee on Women's Employment 1981–90, Ho Lds Select Ctee Sci and Tech 1982–85 and 1990–94, Cncl RSA 1983–88, Careers Research and Advsy Centre 1983–93, Bd British Gas 1988–94, Engrg Trg Auth 1990–92, COPUS 1990–93, Cncl Fndn for Sci and Tech 1991–; V-Pres: UMIST 1985–92, ACC 1992; Trustee Homerton Coll 1970–81; Chllr Middx U 1994–; Pres Pipeline Industries Guild 1994–; Liveryman Engineers' Co, Freeman City London 1988; Hon DSc: City U 1984, Salford 1984, Cranfield 1985, Nottingham Trent 1993; Hon D: OU 1985, Essex U 1985, Middx U1993; Hon DEng Bradford; Hon DTech: Brunel 1986, Loughborough 1993; Hon LLD Cantab 1988; Hon FIMechE 1984, Hon Fell: Wales Poly, UMIST, Women's Engrg Soc 1988; FRSA, Hon FCP 1987, Hon FITD 1994; *m* 1949 *Stewart Sydney Platt and has:

1 *Roland Francis [The Hon Roland Platt, Headley House, 40 Headley Chase, Brentwood, Essex CM14 5BN]; *b* 1951; FCA; *m* 1982 *Louise M, yr dau of Lionel Jackson, of Shenfield, Essex, and has a s and two daus

1 *Victoria Catherine; *b* 1953; MA, FCA, ATII; *m* 1984 *Rhodri Davies, s of His Hon Judge John Davies, QC, and has three daus

Lineage: ERNEST MYATT; *m* Dorothy — and had:

BERYL CATHERINE, *cr* a **Baroness**

PLOWDEN

Arms: Azure a fesse dancettée, the upper points terminating in fleurs-de-lys or. **Crest:** A buck passant sable, attired or. **Creation:** B. (LP, UK) 1959.

THE BARON PLOWDEN, of Plowden, Co Salop (Sir Edwin Noel August Plowden, GBE (1987, KBE 1946), KCB (1951)) [The Rt Hon The Lord Plowden GBE KCB, Martels Manor, Dunmow, Essex CM6 1NB]; *b* 6 Jan 1907; *educ* Switzerland and Pembroke Coll Cambridge (Hon Fell 1958); Min Ec Warfare 1939–40, Min Aircraft Production 1940–46 (ch exec and memb Aircraft Supply Cncl 1945–46), Cabinet Office 1947, Ch Planning Offr and Ch Ec Planning Bd Treasury 1947–53; V-Chm Temporary Cncl Ctee NATO 1951–52; Advsr Atomic Energy Orgn 1953–54; Visiting Fell Nuffield Coll Oxford 1956–64; Chm: UKAEA 1954–59, Ctee Control Public Expenditure 1959–61, Standing Advsy Ctee Pay Higher Civ Servs 1968–70, Equity Capital for Industry Ltd 1976–83, Police Complaints Bd 1976–81, Top Salaries Review Body 1981–89 (memb 1977–81), CBI Companies Ctee 1976–80 and Ctees Enquiry: Organisation Representational Servs Overseas 1963–64, Future UK Aircraft Industry 1964–65, Structure Electricity Supply Industry 1974–75, CBI Aims and Organisation 1974–75; Pres Tube Investments 1976–90 (Chm 1963–76); Dep Chm Ctee Enquiry Police 1977–79; Independent Chm Police Negotiating Bd 1979–82; Pres London Graduate Sch Business Studies 1976–90 (Chm Governing Body 1964–76); dir: C Tennant Sons & Co 1938–49, CU Assur 1946–78, Nat West Bank 1960–77; Memb: Ford European Advsy Cncl 1976–83, Internat Advsy Bd SE Bank NA 1982–87; V-Chm CBI Presidents Ctee 1977–80; Hon DSc: Pennsylvania State U, Aston U; Hon DLitt Loughborough U; *m* 20 June 1933 *Dame Bridget Horatia, DBE (1972), JP (London 1961), Hon LLD Leicester 1968, Hon MA OU 1974, Hon DLitt Loughborough 1976, chm: Tube Investments, IBA 1975, Police Complaints Bd 1976, Centl Advsy Cncl Educn 1963–66, Govrs Philippa Fawcett Coll Educn, Robert Montefiore Comprehensive Sch, Delves House and Woking Ladies Guild, memb Educn Ctee ILEA and V-Chm Schs Sub-Ctee 1967, Pres Professional Classes Aid Cncl, Dep Chm BBC 1975, memb Nat Theature Bd 1976, V-Chm Trust Houses Ltd, dau of Adml Sir Herbert William Richmond, KCB (*see* BELL, Bt), and has:

1 *William Julius Lowthian [The Hon William Plowden, 49 Stockwell Park Rd, London SW9 0DD]; *b* 7 Feb 1935; *educ* Eton, King's Coll Cambridge and California U; staff writer *Economist* 1959–60, with BOT 1960–65, Lecturer in Govt LSE 1965–71 (Visiting Prof in Govt 1982–88, memb Court Govrs 1987–), with CPRS Cabinet Office 1971–77, Hon Prof Dept Politics Warwick U 1977–82, U-Sec DTI 1977–78, Dir-Gen Roy Inst Public Admin 1978–88, Exec Dir UK Harkness Fellowships 1988–91 (Sr Advsr 1991–), Visiting Prof Bath U 1992–, Assoc Dir Atlantic Fellowships 1995–; author: *The Motor Car and Politics in Britain* (1971), *Inside the Think Tank: advising the Cabinet 1971–1983* (with Tessa, now Baroness, Blackstone, 1988), *Mandarins and Ministers* (1994); *m* 16 Sept 1960 *Veronica Mary, only dau of Lt-Col Derek Ernest Frederick Orby Gascoigne (*see* O'NEILL, B), and has:

(1) *Benedict Edmund; *b* 3 May 1963; *educ* Pimlico Comprehensive Sch, Bedales, Ch Ch Oxford, Manchester U, Brighton Poly and Bristol U

(2) *Luke Piers; *b* 11 Nov 1967; *educ* Pimlico Comprehensive

(1) *Frances Helen; *b* 27 March 1965; *educ* Pimlico Comprehensive

(2) *Eleanor Mary; *b* 5 April 1969; *educ* Pimlico Comprehensive

2 *Francis John [The Hon Francis Plowden, 4 Highbury Rd, London SW19 7PR]; *b* 25 June 1945; *educ* Eton and Trin Coll Cambridge; ACA; with Treasury/Cabinet Office 1981–83, ptnr Coopers & Lybrand 1982– (ic Govt Servs 1986–94, managing ptnr internat affrs 1995–, memb exec ctee C & L Internat); Govr Roy Ballet Sch, Tstee Roy Armouries; author: *The State Under Stress* (with Sir C Foster, 1995); *m* 1984 *Mrs Geraldine Miles, er dau of Gerald Wickman, of Orton Longueville, Peterborough, and has:

(1) *George Frederick Wickman; *b* 25 May 1995

1 Anna Bridget, CBE (1997); *b* 18 June 1938; *educ* New Hall Chelmsford and London U Inst Archaeology; archaeological conservator, co-fndr Plowden and Smith (conservators) 1985, Tstee Edward James Fndn 1991–97 and V&A, V-Pres Roy Warrant Holders Assoc; *d* unm 21 Aug 1997

2 *Penelope Christina [The Hon Mrs Martin, 43 Lansdowne Gdns, London SW8]; *b* 29 Oct 1941; *educ* St Mary's Convent Ascot and New Hall Cambridge; *m* 1st 29 Oct 1965 (*divorce* 1975) Christopher Roper (*see* LOVELACE, E); *m* 2nd 25 July 1981 *Rees T Martin, s of Leslie Martin, of Napier, NZ, and by him has:

(1) *Henry; *b* 1984

Lineage: ROGER de PLOWDEN; had:

PHILIP de PLOWDEN, of Plowden, Salop; living *c* 1220; had:

JOHN de PLOWDEN, of Plowden; living *temp* HENRY III; had:

JOHN de PLOWDEN; of age by 11 March 1282/3; MP Plowden 1316; *m* Matilda, dau of Sir Adam de Montgomery, and had:

JOHN de PLOWDEN, of Plowden; *m* Johanna, dau of John Salter, of Salter's Hall, Salop, and had:

  1 JOHN
  2 William; *m* Cecilia, dau and heiress of Thomas Mitton
  1 Rose; *m* Sir Rowland Wedingburg
  2 Elizabeth; *m* Sir Robert Corbett, of Lee, Salop
  3 Joyce; *m* John Gatacre, of Gatacre, Salop
  4 Elinor; *m* Roger Corbett, of Lee, Salop
  5 Katharine; *m* Sir Geoffrey Harley, of Brampton, Salop
  6 Margaret; *m* — Mitton, of Weston, Salop

The er s,
JOHN de PLOWDEN, of Plowden; *m* Matilda, dau of Sir John Burley, and had, with a dau (Katharine; *m* John Higgons, of Stretton, Salop):

EDMUND PLOWDEN, of Plowden and Shrewsbury; living 1434 and May 1451; *m* Jane, dau of Edmund Cleobury, and had:

JOHN PLOWDEN, of Plowden; *m* Margaret, dau of John Blawney/Blayney, and had:

HUMPHREY PLOWDEN, of Plowden and Bishop's Castle; *m* Elizabeth, dau of John Sturry, of Down Rossall, Salop, and widow of William Wollascot, and *d* 10 March 1557, leaving, with an est s (John, *dsp*), two yst sons (Edward, *m* Mary, dau of Thomas Lee, of Langley, and had a s Humphrey (*dsp*) and seven daus (Margaret, *m* Richard Sandford; Jane, *m* 1st Richard Blunden, of Burghfield, Berks, and 2nd Lewis Jones; Elizabeth, *m* Peter Greenway; Anchoret, *m* Rowland Eyton, of Eyton, Salop; Anne, *m* Thomas Higge; Mary, *m* Charles Needham; Joyce, *m* Leonard Meysie):

EDMUND PLOWDEN, of Plowden; *b* 1517; Serjeant-at-law; *m* Katherine, dau of William Sheldon, of Beoley, Worcs, and *d* 1584, leaving a 2nd s:

FRANCIS PLOWDEN, of Plowden; *b* 1562; *m* Mary, dau of Thomas Fermor, of Summertown, Oxford (*see* HESKETH, B), and *d* 11 Dec 1652, leaving with other issue, including a 2nd s (Edmund, of Wanstead, Hants, apparently one of the grantees by CHARLES II of vast tracts of N America known as Lords Palatine, *m* Mabel, dau of Peter Mariner, and *d* on or after 29 July 1665, being with her ancestor of the PLOWDENs of Lasham and Ewhurst):

FRANCIS PLOWDEN, of Plowden; *m* Elizabeth, dau and heiress of Alban Butler, of Aston-le-Walls, Northants, and 1st cousin once-removed of the hagiographer Rev Alban Butler (*see* Section Washington, AMERICAN PRESIDENTIAL FAMILIES, 1994, Morris Genealogical Books SA), and *d* 18 Jan 1661, leaving:

EDMUND PLOWDEN, of Plowden and Aston-le-Walls; *m* Elizabeth, dau of Richard Cotton, of Bedhampton, Sussex, and *d* 20 May 1666, having had, with several other sons (*dsp*):

  1 EDMUND
  2 Francis; Comptroller Household to JAMES II; *m* 1 Oct 1699 Mary (*d* 26 April 1765), sis of 2nd and 4th Earls of Stafford of the 1688 *cr*, and *d* April 1712, leaving issue (*see* STAFFORD, B)
  1 Elizabeth; *m* Walter Blount, of Mapledurham

The er s,
EDMUND PLOWDEN, of Plowden and Aston-le-Walls; *m* Penelope, dau and coheir of Sir Maurice Drummond, and *d* 27 Nov 1677, having had, with four other sons (all Jesuits) and a dau (Dorothy, *m* 1st Philip Draycott and 2nd Sir William Goring, 3rd Bt (*qv*) of the 1622 *cr*):

WILLIAM PLOWDEN, of Plowden and Aston-le-Walls; *b* 1666; Col in JAMES II's Foot Gds, rebuilt the Manor House at Aston; *m* 1st Mary Morley; *m* 2nd Mary, est dau of John Stonor (*see* CAMOYS, B), and by her had two sons and three daus; *m* 3rd Mary, 2nd dau of Sir Charles Lyttelton, 3rd Bt (*see* COBHAM, V), and *d* 5 March 1740/1; his s by his 2nd w:

WILLIAM PLOWDEN, of Plowden and Aston; *m* 1726 Frances, dau of 5th Baron Dormer (*qv*), and *d* 27 Aug 1754, leaving, with three other sons and three daus:

EDMUND PLOWDEN, of Plowden and Aston; *m* 20 July 1755 Lucy (*d* 4 July 1765), dau of William Thompson, of Leicester Sq, London, and gdau and coheir of Sir Berkeley Lucy, 3rd Bt, of Broxbourne, Herts, and *d* 9 Jan 1768, leaving, with an er s (Edmund, of Plowden and Aston-le-Walls, *m* 1776 Anna Maria, dau of Robert Burton, of Longner, Salop, and *d* 4 April 1838, leaving an only child, Anna Maria, *m* Rev John Eyton (*d* 10 Jan 1823), Vicar Wellington and Rector Eyton, and *d* 1825, leaving six sons and three daus):

WILLIAM XAVERIUS PLOWDEN; *m* 13 Nov 1707 Mary, dau of Simon Winter, and *d* Nov 1824, leaving, with a dau (Anna Maria, *d* unm):

  1 William Henry Francis, of Plowden and Aston-le-Walls; *b* 21 Oct 1802; High Sheriff Salop 1848; *m* 23 Jan 1834 Barbara (*d* 26 June 1853), er dau of Francis Cholmeley, of Brandsby Hall, Yorks, and *d* 23 July 1870, leaving, with other issue:

    (1) William Francis, of Plowden and Aston-le-Walls, JP, DL; *b* 3 June 1853; *m* 12 Oct 1874 Lady Mary Dundas (*see* ZETLAND, M) and *d* 8 July 1914, having had, with two er sons and a yst s (all *dsp*):

      1a Roger Edmund Joseph, JP, of Plowden; *b* 5 June 1879; *educ* Beaumont; Lt 7th Roy Welsh Fus and Salop Yeo WW I; *m* 1st 19 Dec 1919 Mary Florence (*d* 11 May 1930), est dau of Capt Harry Cholmondeley, of Redlynch House, Wilts, and had:

        1b *William Francis Godfrey, JP (Salop 1953) [William Plowden Esq JP, The Old Farmhouse, Choulton, Shropshire SY7 8AH]; *b* 4 Dec 1925; *educ* Beaumont and RAC Cirencester; Lt Salop Yeo and Rifle Bde WW II, High Sheriff Salop 1967; *m* 17 July 1951 *Valerie Ann, only dau of Cdr Athelstan Paul Bush, DSO, RN, of Tockington Court, nr Bristol, and has:

1c *Roger Godfrey Paul; b 8 Feb 1953; educ Ampleforth and RAC Cirencester; Lt Welsh Gds 1972–76; m 21 Oct 1995 *Helen Mary Errington, dau of Ralph Gilbey, of Broad Oak Farm, Cucklington, Somerset, and has:

1d *Mary Isabel; b 14 Oct 1997

2c *Francis Richard Piers; b 12 Jan 1957; educ Ampleforth and RAC Cirencester; m 11 Aug 1990 *Emma C, dau of W S Parkinson, and has:

1d *Richard Alexander William; b 1 Oct 1993

2d *Alexander Edward Stuart; b 4 June 1996

3c *Charles Edward Philip; b 31 Dec 1960; educ Ampleforth and Magdalen Coll Oxford; m 13 April 1991 *Ruth M, dau of Andrew Hindhaugh, and has:

1d *Eliza Mary Rose; b 10 May 1994

2d *Grace; b 2 April 1996

1c *Jacqueline Mary Prudence; b 27 Feb 1954

1b *Mary Agnes; b 16 Feb 1921; m 10 Oct 1947 *Edward Bevis Watson-Smyth, s of Edward Watson-Smyth, and has issue

2b Anne Mary; b 26 April 1922; d unm 1 Jan 1970

3b *Gabrielle Marie [Mrs David Benson, Aston Hall, Craven Arms, Salop]; b 10 July 1923; m 4 March 1947 *Maj David Benson, RHA, yst s of Lt-Col John Benson, MC, and has a s and dau

2 Charles Joseph, of Florence and Rome; b 1805; m 1847 Eliza, dau of Capt George Bryan, MP, of Jenkinstown, Co Kilkenny, and d 28 Feb 1884, leaving:

(1) Charles William, of Rome; b 13 Oct 1849; m 1877 Josephine, dau of Joseph Senior, and d 1942, leaving:

1a Edmund Charles Sheldon; b 24 Oct 1879; educ Beaumont; m Cecily — and d 1936, leaving:

1b *Edmund Francis Joseph; b 1915; educ Ampleforth; Maj RE; m *Mary Pinkerton and has had:

1c Ian; b 1941; d 1943

2c *David

1c *Anne

1b *Marion

2b *Lettice

2a Richard Anthony Aston, DSO; b 24 May 1881; educ Beaumont and HMS Britannia; served WW I (despatches), ADC to HM GEORGE V, R-Adml, ret 1933, reemployed WW II as Cdre Ocean Convoys; m 1911 Phyllis Mary (d 1 May 1968), dau of H Pasley Higginson, MICE, of Wellington, NZ and was ka 24 Feb 1941, having had:

1b Richard George Wynyard; b 1919; d 1920

2b *Anthony Ralph; b 14 July 1926; educ Sherborne; m 3 April 1959 *Elizabeth Ann, dau of John Ferguson, of Rednal, Worcs, and has:

1c *Richard Wynyard James Edmund; b 10 Feb 1962

2c *Charles Anthony Agar; b 28 March 1964

3c *Giles Iain Aston; b 30 Sept 1966

1c *Camilla Ann Sheldon; b 6 Sept 1960

2c *Penelope Elizabeth Drummond; b 30 Sept 1966

1b *Pamela Mary; b 20 Oct 1913; m 1940 Lt Peter Gordon Sedgwick, RN (ka 17 Oct 1942) and has:

1c *Nigel Richard Gordon; b 20 Sept 1941; late Lt RN (ret 1967), with Mardon Flexible Packaging; m 25 Nov 1967 *Juliet Mary, dau of Cdr Meyrick Frederick Legge Beebee, of Womaston House, Presteigne, Radnorshire, and Mrs D W Vaughan, of The Old Rectory, Wherwell, Hants, and has:

1d *Anne Frances; b 14 Jan 1969

2d *Katherine Frances; b 27 July 1970

2b *Patience Vera; b 16 Dec 1915; m 6 May 1941 Cdr Anthony Kennett, RN, and has:

1c *Susan Royle; b 10 March 1942; m 3 May 1969 *Richard Henry Persse, s of Brig L Persse, DSO, of Whitefield Farm House, Wiveliscombe, Somerset

2c *Sarah Jane [Mrs John Tricks, Box 216, Nadi Airport, Fiji; St Mary's, Broadstreet, Wrington, nr Bristol]; b 1 Feb 1944; m 20 Dec 1964 *John Edward Tricks, s of Denis Norman Frederick Tricks, and has:

1d *Nigel James; b 9 Oct 1964

2d *Jeremy John Anthony; b 1 March 1970

1d *Juliet Lucy; b 30 Oct 1965

3c *Chantal Mary; b 29 Jan 1956

3a Hugh Vincent Butler; b 26 March 1883; educ Beaumont; m Mabel Hutchinson and d 7 July 1963, leaving:

1b *Dorothea; b 20 Nov 1914; m Lt-Col D Addison, MC, 3rd RTR, and has:

1c *Donald Andrew Plowden; b 16 Feb 1950; educ Cokethorpe and RAC Cirencester

1c *Philippa Jane; b 11 Dec 1953

1a Dorothy Josephine Lucy; b 29 May 1885; m W C Roche, s of Sir George Roche, of Dublin, and d 1 July 1913, leaving issue

(2) Francis High, CB; b 15 Aug 1851; Maj-Gen Oxon LI; m 14 April 1885 Isabel (d 27 Feb 1914), 2nd dau of Maj John Augustus Fane (see WESTMORLAND, E), and d 24 Aug 1911, leaving an est s:

1a Hugh Charles; b March 1886; m 24 Feb 1913 Josephine Evelyn, dau of William O Brooke, of Bournemouth, and had:

1b *Barbara

2b *Judith

2a Geoffrey Francis; b 9 Dec 1888; Maj Oxon and Bucks LI; m 1916 Elizabeth Somervell Lodge and d 7 Nov 1949

1a Sybil Mary Ann; b 1 Sept 1887; m 22 June 1915 Tristram James Pine-Coffin (ka Russia 23 Sept 1919), Devon Regt, yst s of John Richard Pine-Coffin, JP, DL, of Portledge, Devon, and d 10 Dec 1960, leaving issue

(3) Roger Herbert, of Strachur Park, Loch Fyne, Argyllshire, JP; b 14 Oct 1853; educ Downside; m 1st 1888 Minnie (d 4 April 1899), dau of James Jump, and had:

1a Humphrey Roger; b 23 April 1889; educ Oratory Sch and Clare Coll Cambridge; Maj 17th Lancers; m Madeleine Slater, of USA, and das Feb 1942

2a Piers Standish, OBE (1944); b 24 March 1899; educ Eton and RMC Sandhurst; 17th Lancers, served WWs I and II (despatches), ADC to HC Egypt 1925–28, Lt-Col RSG; m 28 June 1928 Ethel Muriel Cynthia, est dau of Maj Edward Ashton Critchley, JP, DL, of Stapleton Tower, Annan, Dumfriesshire, and had:

1b *Giles Roger; b 22 Oct 1929; educ Ampleforth and RMA Sandhurst; Capt late RSG; m 15 Oct 1955 *Violet Florine Sarah, er dau of Brig Hartley Alfred Maconochie, CBE, DSO, of Zealandia, Asheville, NC, USA, and Bagatelle, Bermuda, and has:

1c *Philip Edward Hartley Standish; b 2 March 1961 (HRH THE DUKE OF KENT stood sponsor)

2c *Piers Crispin Harry; b 15 Jan 1964

2b *Julian Piers; b 9 Jan 1931; educ Ampleforth; m Dec 1957 *Judith, dau of Peter Rathvon, of New York and Los Angeles, and has:

1c *Julian Peter; b 27 Jan 1960

2c *Geoffrey Roger; b 21 Jan 1963

3c *Damien Andrew; b 13 Oct 1965

1b *Perdita Remony [Mrs Edward L Burlinghame, 425 E 86th St, New York, NY, USA]; m 18 May 1963 Edward Livermore Burlinghame, only s of Anson Burlinghame, of New York and New Canaan, Conn., and has:

1c *Roger Anson; b 7 Feb 1970

1c *Remony Elizabeth; b 17 May 1964

2c *Phyllida Anne; b 30 June 1965

2b *Phyllida Lovaine [Mrs David Gibbs, Braishfield Manor, Romsey, Hants]; m 6 June 1959 *David Evelyn Gibbs, only s of Brig Lancelot Merivale Gibbs, CVO, DSO, MC (see ALDENHAM and HUNSDON OF HUNSDON, B), and has issue

(3) (cont.) Roger Plowden m 2nd 3 June 1901 Helen (d 6 May 1977 aged 104), dau of William Stanley Haseltine, of USA and Rome, and d 16 May 1921, having by her had:

3a Roger Stanley; b 12 March 1902; Rifle Bde, Capt US Army 1941–45, WW II; m 193– *Mary, dau of George Butler, of New York, and d 26 Sept 1960, leaving:

1b *David; m 20 June 1962 *Pleasance Coggershall, of New York, and has:

1c *John Stanley; b 22 June 1965

2c *Daniel Coggershall; b 3 March 1967

1b *Joan; m 1957 *Gordon B Younce, of California, and has:

1c *Mathew Baldwin; b 13 July 1959

2c *Gregory Stanley; b 15 Dec 1961

4a EDWIN NOEL AUGUST, cr a Baron

5a Francis Herbert Benedict; b 18 Nov 1914; d 22 Jan 1928

1a *Helen Penelope; b 11 March 1909; m 10 Feb 1934 Harry Vaux, Colonial Serv, s of Rev George Bowyer Vaux, of Odiham, Hants, and has:

1b *Nicholas Francis; b 15 April 1936; educ Stonyhurst; Capt RM; m 17 Dec 1966 *Zoya, only dau of Lt-Gen Peter William Cradock Hellings, CB, DSO, MC, and has:

1c *Zoya Frances; b 18 Oct 1967

1b *Helen Camilla Mary; b 9 Dec 1938; m 2 Dec 1961 *Maj Desmond Williamson, RA, s of Lt-Col Frank Williamson, OBE, of Cheltenham, and has:

1c *Claire Anne Helen; b 13 May 1964

2c *Penelope Jane; b 11 Aug 1968

3c *Sarah Frances; b 11 Aug 1968

2b *Caroline Margaret; b 16 July 1942; m 19 Dec 1966 *James Stephen Sollins, only s of Dr I V Sollins, of Rye, NY, and has:

1c *Stephen Nicholas; b 18 Nov 1967

PLUMB

Creation: B. (LP, UK) 1987.

THE BARON PLUMB, of Coleshill, Co Warwicks (Sir (Charles) Henry Plumb, DL (Warwick 1977)) [The Rt Hon The Lord Plumb DL, The Dairy Farm, Maxstoke, Warwicks B46 2QJ]; b 27 March 1925; educ King Edward VI Sch Nuneaton; memb Cncl NFU 1959– (V-Pres 1964–65, Dep Pres 1966–69, Pres 1970–79, ktd 1973; Chm: Br Ag Cncl 1975–79, Internat Ag Trg Programme Tst 1987–, Ag Mortgage Corp 1994–95; Memb: Duke of Northumberland's Ctee Enquiry on Foot and Mouth Disease 1967–68, Cncl CBI, Cncl Animal Health Tst; Pres: Comité des Organisations Professionels Agricoles de la CEE 1975–77, Roy Ag Soc 1977 (Dep Pres 1978), Nat Fedn Young Farmers' Clubs 1976–86, Internat Fed Ag Producers 1979–82; MEP (C) Cotswolds 1979–86 (Chm Ag Ctee 1979–82, Leader European Democratic Gp 1982–87); Pres European Parl 1987– 89; Chllr Coventry U 1995–; Order Merit: Portugal 1987, Luxembourg 1988, Spain (Gd Cross) 1989, W Germany Kt Chllr's Cross 1990, Greece (Gd Cross Order Phoenix) 1996; Patron Warwicks Co Fed YFC 1974–; Hon Pres Ayrshire Cattle Soc; pres Farm Africa; Liveryman Farmers' Soc; Hon DSc Cranfield 1983, Hon LLD Warwick 1990, Hon DSc De Montfort U 1995; FRSA 1970, FRAgS 1974; m 1947 *Marjorie Dorothy, dau of Thomas Victor Dunn, of Bentley, Warwicks, and has:

1 *John Henry [The Hon John Plumb, Southfields, Coleshill, Warwicks B46 3EJ]; b 1951; educ Solihull Sch, Wye Coll and London U (BSc 1973); m 1975 *Beatrix, dau of David Somoza, of Buenos Aires, and has:

(1) *David Henry; b 1979

(1) *Alison Ruth; b 1976

(2) *Liliane; b 1983

1 *Elizabeth Marjorie [The Hon Mrs Holman, 9 Wilderness Mount, Seal Hollow Rd, Sevenoaks, Kent]; *b* 1948; *m* 1971 (*divorce* 19–) Robin Arbuthnot; *m* 2nd 1982 *Maj Anthony Holman and by him has:

  (1) *Thomas Henry; *b* 1984
  (2) *Charles Anthony; *b* 1986

2 *Christine Mary [The Hon Mrs Mayo, The Garth, Kirkby Lane, Great Broughton, N Yorks]; *b* 1950; *m* 1973 *Benjamin John Mayo, FEng, and has:

  (1) *Katherine Elizabeth; *b* 1977
  (2) *Sarah Louise; *b* 1979
  (3) *Stephanie Caroline; *b* 1983

Lineage: CHARLES PLUMB, of Ansley, Warwicks; *m* Louise, dau of Henry Fisher, of Over Whitacre, Warwicks, and had:

(CHARLES) HENRY (Sir), *cr* a **Baron**

PLUMMER OF ST MARYLEBONE

Arms: Barry wavy argent and azure, on a chief vert three stirrups argent. **Crest:** On the battlements of a tower proper two surveyor's ranging rods in saltire company argent and gules, enfiling a stirrup argent. **Supporters:** Two herons proper standing on a grassy mount and extending the inner leg above a portcullis chained gold and set amid madonna lilies growing from each mount proper.
Motto: *Erectus non elatus* ('Exalted but not haughty').
Creation: B. (LP, UK) 1981.

THE BARON PLUMMER OF ST MARYLEBONE, in the City of Westminster (Sir (Arthur) Desmond Herne Plummer, TD, JP (Co London 1958), DL (Gtr London 1970)) [The Rt Hon The Lord Plummer of St Marylebone TD JP DL, 4 The Lane, London NW8 0PN]; *educ* Hurstpierpoint and Coll of Estate Management; T/Lt-Col RE WW II; memb: St Marylebone Borough Cncl 1952–65 (Mayor 1958–59), LCC St Marylebone 1960–65, ILEA 1964–76, ktd 1971; GLC: memb Cities London and Westminster 1964–73 and St Marylebone 1973–76, Oppn Leader 1966–67 and 1973–74, Leader 1967–73; Memb: TA Sports Bd 1953–79, London Electricity Consultative Cncl 1955–66, S Bank Theatre Bd 1967–74, Standing Conf SE Planning 1967–74, Tport co-ordinating Cncl London 1967–69, Local Authority Conditions of Service Advsy Bd 1967–71, Exec Ctee Br Section Internat Union Local Authorities 1967–74, Exec Ctee Nat Union C and U Assocs 1967–76, Ct Lond U 1967–77, St John Cncl London 1974–; Chm St Marylebone C Assoc 1965–66, Nat Employers' Life Assoc 1983–89; Dep Chm Nat Employers' Mutual Gen Insur Assoc 1973–86; memb Lloyd's; Chm: Horserace Betting Levy Bd 1974–82, Epsom and Walton Downs Trg Grounds Mgmt Bd 1974–82, Nat Stud 1975–82; Pres: London Anglers' Assoc 1976–, Thames Angling Preservation Soc 1970–, Metropolitan Assoc Bldg Socs 1983–89, pres Portman Bldg Soc 1990– (Chm 1983–90); Liveryman Tin Plateworkers Co; Hon FFAS 1966, KStJ 1986, FAI 1948, FRICS 1970, FRSA 1974; author: *Time for Change in Greater London* (1966), *Report to London* (1970), *Planning and Participation* (1973); *m* 1941 Ella ('Pat') Margaret (*d* 20 Dec 1998), dau of Albert Holloway, and has:

1 *Sally Jane; *b* 1945; *m* 1991 (retains maiden name) *Richard F Lowe, s of W Lowe, of Danehill, W Sussex

Lineage: ARTHUR HERNE PLUMMER; *m* Janet McCormick and had:

(ARTHUR) DESMOND HERNE (Sir), *cr* a **Baron**

PLUNKET

Arms: Sable a bend between a tower in sinister chief and a portcullis in dexter base, all or. **Crest:** A horse passant argent, charged on the side with a portcullis sable. **Supporters:** Dexter, an antelope or; sinister, a horse argent, each gorged with a plain collar sable, pendant therefrom by a chain a portcullis, also sable.
Motto: *Festina lente* ('Be quick without impetuosity').
Creation: B. (UK) 1 May 1827.

THE 8TH BARON PLUNKET OF NEWTON, of Co Cork (Robin Rathmore Plunket) [The Rt Hon The Lord Plunket, Rathmore, Chimanimani, Zimbabwe; 39 Lansdowne Gdns, London SW1 2EL]; *b* 3 Dec 1925; *s* bro 1975; *educ* Eton; Capt Rifle Bde WW II 1943–47; *m* 8 Nov 1951 *Jennifer, 2nd dau of Bailey Southwell, of Crocodile Leap, Olivenhoutpoort, S Africa, by Erica, dau of Durban Barry, of Umtali, S Rhodesia

Lineage: Rev PATRICK PLUNKET; *b* 1684; *educ* Edinburgh U (MA); *d* 1760, leaving, with other issue:

Rev THOMAS PLUNKET, of Glennan, Co Monaghan; Presbyterian Minister Enniskillen, Co Fermanagh, and N Dublin; *m* Mary, dau of David Conyngham, of Letterkenny, Co Donegal, and had issue (including an er s Patrick, of Dublin, physician, *m* Louisa, 4th dau of Joseph Henry, of Straffan, Co Kildare, MP); his 4th s:

WILLIAM CONYNGHAM PLUNKET, **1st Baron Plunket of Newton**, Co Cork (UK), so *cr* 1 May 1827, PC (I 1805, GB 1827); *b* 1 July 1765; *educ* Trin Coll Dublin and Lincoln's Inn London; barrister Dublin 1787, KC 1795, MP (I Parl) Charlemont 1798–1800 and (UK Parl, Whig) Midhurst Jan–April 1807 then Dublin U 1812–27, Slr Gen Ireland 1803–05, Attorney-Gen Ireland 1805–07 and 1822–27, Ch Justice Common Pleas Ireland 1827–30, Ld Chllr Ireland, 1830–Nov 1834 and April 1835–41; *m* 20 Oct 1790 Katharine (*d* 14 March 1821), only dau of John McCausland, of Strabane, MP Co Donegal, and *d* 5 Jan 1854, having had, with two other daus:

1 THOMAS SPAN PLUNKET, **2nd Baron Plunket of Newton**, PC (I 1846); *b* 1792; *educ* St John's Coll Cambridge; BD, DD, Vicar Bray, Co Wicklow, Dean Down 1831–339, Bp Tuam, Killala and Achonry 1839–66; *m* 26 Oct 1819 Louisa Jane (*d* 14 Jan 1893), dau of John William Foster, of Fanevalley, Co Louth, MP Dunleer, and *dspms* 19 Oct 1866, having had, with other issue:

  (1) Katherine; *b* 22 Nov 1820; *d* unm 14 Oct 1932 aged 111
  (2) Mary Elizabeth Alice; *m* 15 Jan 1862 Col Sir Thomas Oriel Forster, 3rd Bt, CB (*dsp* 28 Dec 1895), and *d* 2 May 1908

2 JOHN, **3rd Baron**

3 David; barrister, Prothonotary Court Common Pleas Ireland; *m* 27 Dec 1837 Louisa (*d* 27 Aug 1895), est dau of Robert Aldridge Busby, and *d* 12 Sept 1868

4 William Conyngham (Rev); Rector Bray, Co Wicklow; *d* unm Sept 1857

5 Patrick; Judge Bankruptcy Ct Ireland; *m* 24 May 1838 Maria Eliza (*m* 2nd 2 Aug 1883 Col Henry Musters, of Brianstown, Co Longford, and *d* 1892), dau of John Atkinson, of Ely Place, Dublin, and *d* July 1859, leaving:

  (1) William Conyngham; *b* 18 Feb 1839; Lt 22nd Regt; *dsp*
  (2) Cedric John Charles; *b* 31 March 1854; *m* 4 Aug 1881 Alice (*d* 6 Oct 1925), 3rd dau of Francis P Cupiss, FRCS, of St Servan, France, and *d* 26 Jan 1898, leaving:

    1a Cedric John; *b* 15 April 1893; Lt RFA; *ka* 6 Aug 1917
    1a Agnes Kathleen Alice; *b* 15 March 1882; *m* 1st 17 March 1904 Thomas Henry Wilson (*d* 31 Jan 1929), of Tucuman, Argentina; *m* 2nd 1929 Stewart Shipton (*d* 6 March 1939) and *d* 29 July 1966
    2a Gladys May; *b* 4 May 1887; *m* 30 Aug 1913 Alban Robert Whiteway (*d* 19–), slr, and *d* 27 Sept 1959
    3a Mabel Cecilia; *b* 20 May 1897; *m* 4 Aug 1925 Rodney Colvill-Jones (*d* 1953) and had issue

  (1) Constance Gertrude Maria; *m* 9 Feb 1866 Richard Mayne Tabuteau, of Dublin, s of Bartholomew Molière Tabuteau, of Simmons Court, Co Dublin

6 Robert (Very Rev); *b* 11 March 1802; Dean Tuam, Rector Headfort; *m* 27 March 1830 Mary (*d* 1886), dau of Sir Robert Lynch-Blosse, 8th Bt (*qv*), and *d* 14 May 1867, leaving, with other issue:

(1) Catherine; *m* 1 Sept 1853 Rev Weldon Ashe (*d* 4 July 1874), Preb Tuam, Rector Annaghdown, and had issue

(2) Isabella; *m* 24 Sept 1856 George St Tyner, FRCSI (*d* 1893), and had issue

(3) Frances Mary Jane; *m* March 1857 Rev George Oliver Brownrigg (*d* 1897), Rector Ballinrobe, Tuam, and *d* 31 Dec 1928, leaving issue

(4) Mary Lynch-Blosse; *m* 19 Dec 1872 Robert Vicars Fletcher, MD, FRCSI, and had issue

1 Elizabeth; *m* 5 April 1824 Rev Sir Francis Lynch-Blosse, 9th Bt (*qv*), and *d* 3 April 1885, leaving issue

2 Isabella; *m* 1846 Henry Quin, of Burleigh, Co Wexford, and *d* 3 Aug 1857

The 2nd BARON's brother,

JOHN PLUNKET, **3rd Baron Plunket of Newton**, QC (1837); *b* 10 July 1793; barrister Dublin 1817, Crown Prosecutor Munster Circuit; *m* 5 April 1824 Charlotte (*d* 11 Sept 1886), dau of Rt Hon Charles Kendal Bushe, Ld Ch Justice King's Bench Ireland, and had, with three other daus (*d* unm):

1 WILLIAM CONYNGHAM, **4th Baron**

2 Charles Bushe, JP; *b* 16 June 1830; Assist Resident Councillor Penang, Registrar Supreme Court and Ch Magistrate Police Hong Kong; *m* 18 Oct 1860 Emmeline Rebecca (*d* 1 April 1914), dau of James Morrell, and *d* 21 Dec 1880, having had:

(1) David Darley; *b* 24 Aug 1869; *m* 26 April 1900 Helen Rosanna (*d* 12 April 1951), yst dau of Thomas Greene, of 49 St Stephen's Green, Dublin, and *d* 8 Aug 1956, leaving:

1a Brian Thomas; *b* 5 June 1903

1a Nancy Emmeline; *b* 17 Sept 1901; *m* 3 Sept 1927 Colin Kingsley Stringer, 2nd *s* of George Ralph Herbert Stringer, of Countess Cross, Earl's Colne, and had:

1b *Hugh Conyngham [Hugh Stringer Esq, 14 Kents Rd, South Chard, Somerset]; *b* 27 Nov 1928; *m* 22 April 1954 *Kathleen Stevens

2b *Richard Darley [Richard Stringer Esq, Riverside, Abbey View, Dutton Hill, Dunmow, Essex]; *b* 2 July 1933; *m* 24 Jan 1958 (*divorce* 1969) Gaye Fellowes and has:

1c *Susan Gail; *b* 25 March 1963

1b *Hermione Ann [Mrs Edward Hubert, Top Cottage, Upper Oddington, Glos]; *b* 8 Nov 1929; *m* 19–*Edward Geoffrey Hubert and has:

1c *Jeremy; *b* 16 Oct 1968

1c *Ann; *b* 26 Oct 1963

2a *Rosamond Sylvia [Mrs Henry Jerrard, Hillside, Newcourt Ave, Bray, Co Wicklow, Ireland]; *b* 5 Sept 1908; *m* 1939 A/Cdre Henry Sam Francis Temple Jerrard, CBE, RAF (*d* 6 Dec 1961), and has:

1b *David Grattan [David Jerrard Esq, Hillside, Newcourt Ave, Bray, Co Wicklow, Ireland]; *b* 21 Jan 1944; *m* 12 May 1969 *Norah Maureen Nolan, dau of Alphonsus Reginald Timothy Nolan, of Bray

1b *Helen Frances; *b* 25 July 1941; *m* 6 Oct 1962 *John Patrick Roe

(1) Charlotte Emmeline; *d* unm 30 Jan 1933

(2) Phoebe Kathleen; *b* 1863; *d* unm 12 June 1960

(3) Flora Louisa; *d* unm 25 Nov 1947

(4) Violet Zoe; *d* unm 17 Oct 1942

3 DAVID ROBERT PLUNKET, 1st and last BARON RATHMORE OF SHANGANAGH, Co Dublin (UK), so *cr* 14 Nov 1895, PC (1880), QC (I 1868); *b* 3 Dec 1838; *educ* Trin Coll Dublin; barrister 1862, legal advsr I Govt 1868–69, MP (C) Dublin U 1870–95, Slr-Gen Ireland 1875–77, Paymaster-Gen 1880, first Commr Works 1885–86 and 1886–92; *d* unm 22 Aug 1919, when the title expired

4 Arthur Cecil Crampton; *b* 11 May 1845; served 8th Foot, Gen Agent for Ireland to Hon The Irish Society; *m* 10 Sept 1870 Louisa Frances (*d* 3 Dec 1929), only child of James Hewitt (*see* LIFFORD, B), and *d* 21 Oct 1884, leaving:

(1) Edward Cecil Lifford; *b* 17 Aug 1871; *m* 23 Nov 1940 *Inez [Mrs Edward Plunket, 132 Holland Rd, London W14], 6th dau of John V de Sousa, of Br Guiana, and *dsp* 25 Nov 1946

(2) Henry Coote Lifford; *b* 6 Jan 1875; *m* March 1912 Emily Evelyn Marjorie (*d* 17 Aug 1968), dau of Severne Rowlands, of Queensland, and *d* 1955, leaving:

1a +Arthur Robert Lifford [Arthur Plunket Esq, 130 Sevenoaks Rd, Orpington, Kent]; *b* May 1914; *m* 3 Sept 1938 *Elsie, dau of Hugo Krieger, of Prague

(3) Archibald John Lifford; *b* 18 Sept 1877; *m* 15 Dec 1909 Mary Calvert (*d* 19 Oct 1937), er dau of Henry Frederick Swan, CB, of Prudhoe Hall, Northumberland, and *d* 4 Feb 1940, having had:

1a *Norah Mary Lifford [Mrs Hugh Baker, 198 Middle Dve, Darras Hall, Ponteland, Northumberland]; *b* 12 June 1912; *m* 1 Sept 1939 *Hugh Honner Sancroft Baker, Capt RE, *s* of Eric Sancroft Baker, of Stoke Fleming, S Devon, and has:

1b *Terence Sancroft [Terence Baker Esq, 72 Woodlands, Fleet, Hants]; *b* 4 June 1941; *educ* Marlborough; Licentiate Inst Metallurgists 1968; *m* 1st 26 Aug 1967 Penelope Frances, dau of Francis Forrest, of Newcastle; *m* 2nd 1980 *Anne Dorothy Hicklin and by her has:

1c *Nicholas Sancroft; *b* 1981

2c *Daniel Sancroft; *b* 1983

2a Audrey Vivian Lifford; *b* 17 Jan 1879; *d* 21 Jan 1914

(4) James Pratt Lifford; *b* 20 May 1880; *d* 23 Aug 1899

(1) Vivien Charlotte Lifford; *b* 11 Jan 1873; *m* 9 Sept 1897 Brig-Gen George Herbert Sanders, CB, CMG, DSO, RA (*d* 23 Oct 1935), bro of 1st and last Baron Bayford (*see* 1940 edn), and *d* July 1944, leaving issue

(2) Louisa Frances Lifford; *b* 13 Feb 1876; Sister Community of Saint Mary the Virgin Convent, Wantage, Berks; *d* 6 July 1965

(3) Eleanor Alice Lifford; *b* 17 Jan 1879; *d* unm 24 Jan 1960

(4) Ruby Isabel Lifford; *b* 7 Dec 1881; *m* 8 Oct 1903 Rev Bernard McNaughton Hawes, Vicar Sutton-on-Trent, Notts, and *d* 29 April 1917, leaving issue

(5) Irene Arthur Lifford; *b* 9 May 1835; *d* unm 11 April 1970

5 Patrick Henry Coghill; *b* 11 May 1845; Supt Police Straits Settlements 1873–80, formerly 70th Foot; *m* 18 June 1878 Anne Agnes (*d* 20 Oct 1936), yst

dau of John Murray, of Marlfield, Clonmel, Co Tipperary, and *d* 5 Feb 1924, leaving:

(1) Charlotte Mabel; *b* 14 Oct 1879

(2) Evelyn Jane Ranger; *b* 8 Nov 1880

(3) Agnes Josephine Bushe; *b* 10 Jan 1882; *d* unm 2 May 1962

(4) Kathleen Sybil; *b* 3 March 1885; *d* 2 Jan 1921

1 Anna; *m* 18 Nov 1851 Rt Rev John R Darley (*d* 20 Jan 1884), DD, Bp Kilmore, and *dsp* 14 April 1900

2 Katherine Frances; *m* 18 Feb 1851 Sir John Joscelyn Coghill, 4th Bt (*qv*), and *d* 25 Aug 1881, leaving issue

3 Charlotte; *m* 6 Jan 1853 Thomas Henry Barton (*d* 19 April 1878) and *d* 30 May 1918, leaving issue

4 Louisa Lilias; *m* 27 July 1852 Richard Jonas Greene, 2nd *s* of Rt Hon Richard Wilson Greene, Baron Exchequer Ireland, and *d* 30 March 1891, leaving issue

5 Selina Maria; *m* 1 Feb 1864 Sir Philip Crampton Smyly (*d* 8 April 1904), MD, and *d* 5 Dec 1921, leaving issue

The 3rd BARON *d* 16 April 1871; his er son,

Most Rev WILLIAM CONYNGHAM PLUNKET, **4th Baron Plunket of Newton**; *b* 26 Aug 1828; DD, LLD, Primate Ireland, Senator Roy U of Ireland, Precentor St Patrick's Catherdral 1869–76, Bp Meath 1876–84, Archbp Dublin 1884–97; *m* 11 June 1863 Anne Lee (*d* 8 Nov 1889), only dau of Sir Benjamin Lee Guinness, 1st Bt (*qv*), and had, with two daus (*d* unm):

1 WILLIAM LEE, **5th Baron**

2 Benjamin John (Most Rev); *b* 1 Aug 1870; *educ* Harrow and Corpus Christi Coll Cambridge (BA 1895, MA 1898, DD 1913); Bp Tuam 1913–19 and Meath 1919–25; *m* 7 July 1904 Dorothea Hester (*d* 8 July 1936), 3rd dau of Sir Thomas Butler, 10th Bt, of Cloughgrenan (*qv*), and *d* 26 Jan 1947, leaving:

(1) David Pierce Conyngham; *b* 21 March 1908; *educ* Harrow; *m* 24 April 1930 Sybil Marjorie (*d* 1982), yr dau of Alfred Archer, of Seaford, Sussex, and *d* 18 Feb 1956, leaving:

1a Simon Patrick Conyngham; *b* 9 Aug 1932; *educ* Haileybury and ISC; Lt 12th Royal Lancers, memb Lloyd's; *m* 12 Oct 1955 *Susan Diana (*m* 2nd 1972 Martin John Faber Morrison; *m* 3rd 1979 Maj Richard Harden) [Mrs Richard Harden, Hunters Hill Farm, Nether Stilton, N Yorks], dau of R V Fairney, of Hartley End House, Hartley Wintney, Hants, and *d* 30 Dec 1968, leaving:

1b +Piers Robert Conyngham [Piers Plunket Esq, 1430 E Mountain St, Pasadena, CAL 91104, USA]; *b* 27 June 1959; *m* 1989 *Cordelia M, dau of Colin Hart, of Charlbury, Oxon, and Hon Mrs Patrick Penny (*see* MARCHWOOD, V), and has:

1c +Simon Tuam Conyngham; *b* 1991

2c +Oliver David Conygham; *b* 1994

1b *Sara Doon [Mrs Luca Cumani, Bedford House, Bury Rd, Newmarket, Suffolk]; *b* 19 Jan 1957; *m* 1979 *Luca Matteo Cumani, trainer, *s* of Sergio Cumani, of Milan, and has:

1c *Matthew Sergio Simon; *b* 1981

1c *Francesca Deepsea; *b* 1983

2a David Archer Lee; *b* 29 Oct 1936; *educ* St Columba's Dublin; *m* 23 May 1964 *Philippa Susan [Mrs David Plunket, Flat 2, 57 Sinclair Rd, London W14 0NR], yr dau of Capt Brian St George Daly, Lancs Fus, of Templeogue House, Co Dublin, and *d* 8 March 1997, leaving:

1b *Emma Elizabeth Lee; *b* 12 April 1966

2b *Arabella Susan; *b* 8 Jan 1969

(2) Benjamin William Alan, MVO (1939); *b* 28 July 1912; *educ* Harrow and Pembroke Coll Cambridge; Hon Attaché Dip Serv 1934–43; *m* 5 Aug 1943 Pamela (*d* 1990), 3rd dau of Charles W Whatley, of Burderop, Swindon, and *d* 1981, leaving:

1a +Charles Patrick Benjamin MBE (1995), DL [Charles Plunket Esq MBE DL, Belle Isle, Lisbellaw, Co Fermanagh, N Ireland]; *b* 2 July 1947; *educ* Harrow; *m* 1990 *Fiona, yr dau of Gerald James, of Aston Rowant, Oxon, and has:

1b *Emily Lee; *b* 1991

2b *Olivia Kate; *b* 1993

1a *Elizabeth Lee [Miss Elizabeth Plunket, 386 Upper Montague St, London W1]; *b* 6 March 1946

(1) Hester Elizabeth Lee; *b* 19 May 1905; *m* 19 Nov 1936 Richard Sinclair Connell, yst *s* of Rev Charles John Connell, and *d* 1982

(2) Olive Dorothea, OStJ; *b* 8 April 1911; *m* 19 April 1933 8th Earl Fitzwilliam (*see* 1970 edn) and *d* 14 Dec 1975, leaving issue

1 Olivia Anne; *b* 5 April 1873; *m* 24 Aug 1895 Sir John Robert Bramston Pretyman Newman (*d* 12 March 1947), of Newberry Manor, Co Cork, est *s* of John Newman, DL, of Dromore, Mallow, Co Cork, and *d* 24 Jan 1896

2 Kathleen Louisa; *b* 22 Feb 1877; *m* 22 Feb 1909 Maj Edward Lycett Lyon (*d* Sept 1916 from wounds recd in action), 18th Hus, *s* of Edward Lyon, of London and New York, and *d* 3 May 1956, leaving issue

The 4th BARON *d* 1 April 1897; his son,

WILLIAM LEE PLUNKET, **5th Baron Plunket of Newton**, GCMG (1910, KCMG 1905), KCVO (1903, CVO 1900), KBE (1918), DL (Co Dublin); *b* 19 Dec 1864; *educ* Harrow and Trin Coll Dublin; Hon Attaché: Rome 1889–92, Constantinople 1892–94; Priv Sec to Lds Lt Ireland 1900–04, Govr and C-in-C NZ 1904–10, KGStJ; *m* 4 June 1894 Lady Victoria Alexandrina Hamilton-Temple-Blackwood (*m* 2nd 1 Oct 1920 Col Francis Powell Braithwaite, CBE, DSO, MC, Northumberland Fus (*d* 23 Dec 1952), 2nd *s* of Rev John Masterman Braithwaite, Vicar Croydon, and *d* 11 Feb 1968 aged 94), dau of 1st Marquess of Dufferin and Ava (*see* DUFFERIN AND CLANEBOYE, B), and had:

1 TERENCE CONYNGHAM, **6th Baron**

2 Brinsley Sheridan Bushe; *b* 28 June 1903; A/F/Lt RAFVR WW II 1939–41; *m* 16 Nov 1927 (*divorce* 1940) Aileen Sibell Mary (*m* 2nd 1956 (*divorce* 1965) Valerian Stux-Rybar), est dau of Hon Arthur Ernest Guinness (*see* IVEAGH, E), and *das* Nov 1941, having had:

(1) Neelia Clotilde; *b* 10 May 1929; *m* 1st 18 Sept 1950 (*divorce* 1955) Capt Bazil Christian de Las Casas (*d* 17 Jan 1960), 8th King's Roy Irish Hus, *s* of

Manuel de Las Casas, of Horwood, Bideford, N Devon, and had issue; *m* 2nd 3 Feb 1956 (*divorce* 1959) Michael Francis Maclean, s of John Francis Maclean, of Bernithan Court, Ross-on-Wye, Herefs; *m* 3rd July 1962 *Maj Stewart Macpherson Reynolds, Welsh Gds, est s of Maj S R Reynolds, and *d* Jan 1995

(2) Doon Aileen; *b* 8 Oct 1931; *m* 9 Oct 1958 5th Earl Granville (*qv*), and had issue

(3) Marcia Lee; *b* 2 March 1933; *d* 25 Dec 1936

3 (Denis) Kiwa; *b* 6 Feb 1909; *educ* Malvern; Capt Queen's Westminsters, KRRC (TA), WW II; *m* 26 Nov 1962 Pamela Mary (*d* 25 Oct 1994), dau of James Watherston, Lt Black Watch, of Christchurch, NZ, and Edinburgh, and *dsp* 8 May 1970

1 Helen Cecil Olive; *b* 15 April 1895; *m* 24 Jan 1916 Maj Arthur Tahu Gravenor Rhodes, MVO, Gren Gds (*d* 11 March 1947), s of Arthur Rhodes, of Christchurch, NZ, and *d* 24 Feb 1968, leaving issue

2 Eileen Hermione; *b* 15 July 1896; *m* 12 Oct 1931 Capt Rowland Lionel Barnard, RE (*d* 23 Oct 1955), s of Col W A M Barnard, Gren Gds, and *d* 1966, leaving a s and dau

3 Moira Violet Maria; *b* 23 Nov 1897; *m* 1st 30 Jan 1923 Lt-Col Herbert Frederick Edgar Smith, DSO, 60th Rifles (*d* 25 June 1940), s of F E Smith, of Oswick Hall, Fakenham, Norfolk, and had issue; *m* 2nd 15 May 1944 (*divorce* 1952) Capt Ian Reddie Hamilton Black, CBE, RN, s of Capt Henry Somes Black, of Dysart, Fife, and *d* 14 June 1987

4 Joyce Laline; *b* 9 Jan 1901; *m* 2 Feb 1921 Capt Charles Stanley Lucas Whidborne, MBE (*d* 6 July 1961), 14th Hus, s of Rev George F Whidborne, of Hammerwood Lodge, Sussex, and *d* 12 July 1973, leaving issue

5 Ethne Victoria Manene; *b* 31 March 1907; *d* 24 May 1919

The 5th BARON *d* 24 Jan 1920; his est son,

TERENCE CONYNGHAM PLUNKET, **6th Baron Plunket of Newton**; *b* 12 July 1899; *educ* Wellington; Lt Rifle Bde WW I 1918 (two medals), ADC personal staff 1919; *m* 4 Dec 1922 Dorothée Mabel, widow of Capt Jack Barnato, RAF, and dau of Joseph Lewis, of Mayfair, and was *k* with his *w* in an air crash California 24 Feb 1938, leaving

1 PATRICK TERENCE WILLIAM SPAN PLUNKET, **7th Baron Plunket of Newton**; KCVO 1974 (CVO 1963, MVO 1955); *b* 8 Sept 1923; *educ* Eton and Magdalene Coll Cambridge; Lt-Col Irish Gds WW II (wounded), Equerry to TM GEORGE VI March 1948–52 and THE QUEEN 1952–75, Dep Master Household 1954–75, Tstee Wallace Collection; *d* unm 28 May 1975

2 ROBIN RATHMORE PLUNKET, **8th and present Baron Plunket of Newton**

3 +SHAUN ALBERT FREDERICK SHERIDAN [The Hon Shaun Plunket, 11 Ennismore Gdns, London SW7]; *b* 5 April 1931; heir presumptive; *educ* Eton and Institut de Touraine; late Lt Irish Gds, ADC to GOC(2) Inf Div, Dist Comdt, Kenya Police (Reserve), Fell IOD; *m* 1st 14 Dec 1961 (*divorce* 1980) Judith Ann, er dau of Gerard Patrick Power, of Lapworth, Warwicks, and has:

(1) +Tyrone Shaun Terence; *b* 5 Feb 1966; *educ* Eton and Buckingham U; Page of Honour to HM THE QUEEN to 1979

(1) +Loelia Dorothée Alexandra; *b* 26 April 1963

3 (cont.) The Hon Shaun Plunket *m* 2nd 25 Sept 1980 Elizabeth (*d* 1986), formerly *w* of Antonio de Sancha and dau of Helge Drangel, of Stockholm; *m* 3rd 1989 *Andrea Barbara, dau of Andre Milos, of Budapest, and formerly *w* of Sheldon Reynolds

PLYMOUTH

Arms: Quarterly, 1st and 4th, arg. on a fess sa. three mullets or (for CLIVE); 2nd and 3rd, gu. a saltire arg. between twelve cross-crosslets or (for WINDSOR). **Crests:** 1 A griffin statant arg., ducally gorged gu., 2 A stag's head affronteé, couped at the neck arg., attired or. **Supporters:** Two unicorns arg., armed, maned, tufted and unguled or. **Motto:** *Je me fie en Dieu* ('I trust in God'). **Creations:** B. (E) soon after 3 Nov 1529, E. (UK) 18 Dec 1905.

THE 3RD EARL OF PLYMOUTH, *Viscount Windsor,* of Saint Fagans, Co Glamorgan, and **Lord** (Baron) **Windsor** (which alone of these titles is heritable by females or their issue, hence the + against members of the family of both sexes) (Other Robert Ivor Windsor-Clive, DL (Salop 1961)) [The Rt Hon The Earl of Ply-

mouth DL, The Stables, Oakly Park, Ludlow, Salop SY8 2JW; 48 Burton Court, London SW3]; *b* 9 Oct 1923; *s f* 1943; *educ* Eton and Trin Coll Cambridge (BA); T/Capt Coldstream Gds WW II 1941–45, Tstee Nat Gallery 1960–67, memb Standing Commn on Museums and Galleries 1972–82, Chm Reviewing Ctee Works of Art 1982–85, FRSA 1953, KStJ; *m* 11 Oct 1950 *Caroline Helen, only dau of Edward Denis Rice, of Dane Court, Eastry, Kent, and has:

1 +IVOR EDWARD OTHER, *Viscount Windsor* [Viscount Windsor, Oakly Park, Ludlow, Salop SY8 2JW]; *b* 19 Nov 1951; *educ* Harrow; co-fndr and dir Centre for the Study of Modern Art 1973–76; *m* 6 July 1979 *Caroline Anne, dau of Frederick Nettlefold (*see* SCARSDALE, V), and has:

(1) +Robert Other Ivor; *b* 25 March 1981

(2) +Frederick John Richard; *b* 21 April 1983

(3) +Edward James Archer; *b* 18 July 1994

(1) +India Harriet; *b* 3 Sept 1988

2 +Simon Percy; *b* 19 Nov 1956; *educ* Harrow

3 +David Justin [The Hon David Windsor-Clive, 29 Cheyne Court, Flood St, London SW3]; *b* 4 Sept 1960; *educ* Harrow and RAC Cirencester; late bill broker with King & Shaxson, currently runs Internet Music Shop; *m* 1986 *Camilla Jane, est dau of John Squire, of Marbella, Spain, and Mrs John Ticehurst, of Chelsea, and has:

(1) +James; *b* 1991

(2) +Alexander; *b* 1993

1 +Emma [The Lady Emma Windsor-Clive, The Granary, Yeabridge, Somerset TA13 5LW]; *b* 13 Feb 1954; *m* 12 April 1975 (*divorce* 1992) Robert Arthur Smith-Dorrien-Smith, er s of Lt-Cdr Thomas Mervyn Smith-Dorrien-Smith, JP, RN, of Tresco Abbey, Isles of Scilly, and has:

(1) +Adam Robert Smith; *b* 13 March 1978

(2) +Michael Horace; *b* 1987

(1) +Frances Marcella; *b* 7 June 1980

Previous creations: A Barony of Wyndesore or Windsor is deemed by later doctrine to have been created in favour of William de Wyndesore, of a possible cadet branch of the Windsors dealt with below, in 1381 when he was called to Parliament by writ. On his death without issue, or perhaps without legitimate issue (for his wife's two daughters, both called Joan, were either not by him or born out of wedlock), the Barony expired. This first and last Lord (Baron) Windsor or Wyndesore served in France during the Hundred Years War and in Ireland. He was also in charge of defences on the English-Scottish border in Cumberland, where his branch of the family (if it was the same family) had been settled since at least the 12th century. He was briefly imprisoned in the Tower of London in 1376 on charges of taking bribes while the King's Lieutenant in Ireland, and the next year Parliament exiled his wife Alice, *neé* Perrers, who had been the late EDWARD III's mistress. Shortly before his ennoblement he was entrusted with suppressing the Peasants' Revolt, and just before that had been in charge of the Castle and town of Cherbourg, in English-occupied France, so that his multifarious activities in the public service, rather than his usefulness in making a married woman of a superannuated royal paramour, should probably be seen as the reason for his elevation to the peerage.

An Earldom of Plymouth was conferred in 1675 on one of CHARLES II's bastard sons. This was Charles FitzCharles, begotten by the King out of Catherine Pegge, a Derbyshire beauty who later married Sir Edward Green, 1st Bt. This Lord Plymouth married a daughter of the 1st Duke of Leeds (*see* 1963 edn) and died without issue at the Siege of Tangier in 1680, when his Earldom expired.

Lineage: WALTER Fitz OTHO of Fitz OTHER; held among other manors that of Stanwell, Middx, at the Domesday Survey 1086; *m* Beatrice — and *d* in or after 1100, leaving, with two yr sons (Gerald, *see* LEINSTER, D; Robert de Windsor, feudal Baron of Eston, Essex):

WILLIAM Fitz WALTER; *s f* as Warden Forests in Berks and Castellan Windsor, accordingly taking the name De WINDSOR; the EMPRESS MAUD confirmed to him all the grants made to his ancestors of the custody of Windsor Castle and lands (including Stanwell) as in the time of her father, HENRY I; had (with possibly another yr s, Alexander de Windsor or Wyndesore, whose gggs William de Wyndesore was *cr* 16 July 1381 LORD (Baron) WYNDESORE or WINDSOR; *see* **Previous creations** above):

1 WILLIAM (Sir)

2 Hugh; Ld of Manor of W Horsley, Surrey, which passed through female heirs to the Barons Berners (*qv*)

The er son,

Sir WILLIAM de WINDSOR; held 20 kts fees 1165, accompanied RICHARD I 1194 in his expdn to Normandy (at that time part of the King of England's domains), where he relieved Verneuil, then being besieged by PHILIP AUGUSTUS OF FRANCE; had:

WALTER de WINDSOR; had, with two daus:

WILLIAM de WINDSOR; living 1212; had:

WILLIAM de WINDSOR; *m* Agnes — and *d c* 1275, leaving:

1 WILLIAM

2 Hugh; had:

(1) Joan; *m* Sir Richard de Dray

The er son,

WILLIAM de WINDSOR; *m* Margaret, sis of Sir John Drokensford, and *d c* 1279, leaving an est s:

Sir RICHARD de WINDSOR; MP Berks and Middx; served in Scottish wars; *m* Julian, dau of Sir Nicholas Stapleton, of Hachilsay, Yorks, and *d c* 1326, leaving, with a yr s (William, Rector of Stanwell):

RICHARD de WINDSOR; MP Berks and Middx; *m* 1st Joane — and had a dau; *m* 2nd Julian, dau and coheir of James Milyns, of Hants, by Margaret, dau and coheir of William de Bintworth, and had issue; *m* 3rd Claricia, widow of John Yorke and dau of John Drokensford, and *d* 1367; his s by his 1st w:

Sir JAMES de WINDSOR; ktd by EDWARD III; *m* Elizabeth, dau and coheir of Sir John Strechie, of Wombro (Wanborough), Wilts, and *d* 2 Oct 1371, leaving an only s:

Sir MILES de WINDSOR; testified in the Scrope and Grosvenor controversy (*see* WESTMINSTER, D); *m* Alice, dau of Adam de Wymondham, of Wymondham, Norfolk, and had:

BRIAN de WINDSOR; *m* Alice, dau of Thomas Drewe, of Segrave, Leics, and had, with an er s (Miles, *d* unm):

RICHARD de WINDSOR; *m* Christian, dau of Richard Falconer, and had an only s:

MILES de WINDSOR; *m* Joan, dau of Walter Green, of Bridgnorth, Salop, and *d* Italy en route to the Holy Land as a pilgrim 30 Sept 1451, leaving:

THOMAS WINDSOR; *b c* 1440; Constable Windsor Castle for life 1484; *m* by 1 Feb 1465/6 Elizabeth (*m* 2nd Sir Robert Litton), er dau and coheir of John Andrews, of Baylham, Suffolk, by Elizabeth, dau and coheir of John Stratton by Elizabeth, dau and heiress of Sir Hugh Luttrell, and *d* 29 Sept 1485, leaving an est surv s:

ANDREW(S) WINDSOR, **1st Lord** (Baron) **Windsor**, so *cr* soon after 3 Nov 1529, KB (1509), PC (*c* Feb 1525/6); *b* 1467; Bencher Middle Temple by 1500, Keeper Gt Wardrobe 1506–43, Steward Windsor 1512, Kt Banneret following HENRY VIII's evanescent victory over the French at the Battle of the Spurs 16 Aug 1513, Sheriff Beds and Bucks 1526, MP Bucks 1529, granted monastic lands neighbouring Stanwell 1539, a circumstance which has been cited to support the theory that the peerage creation was with remainder to heirs male, hence presumably by letters patent, although by 1660 it was viewed as being one by writ, hence heritable by and through females (*see* below against the 1st EARL OF PLYMOUTH of the 1682 *cr*); forced by HENRY VIII 1542 to surrender the Manor of Stanwell, which his family had held since 1086, for property in the west of England, chiefly the lands in Worcs which had previously belonged to Bordesley Abbey (the family's chief seat until after the **2nd Earl**'s death in 1943 being Hewell Grange there) and to a lesser extent that of Minchinhampton, Glos (formerly belonging to Sion Monastery; *see* also ROYAL FAMILY against HRH THE PRINCESS ROYAL); *m* Elizabeth, sis of 2nd Baron Mountjoy, and *d* 30 March 1543, having had, with three other sons and four daus, a 2nd but est surv s:

WILLIAM WINDSOR, **2nd Lord** (Baron) **Windsor**, KB (1533); *b* 1498; Bencher Middle Temple 1533, MP Wycombe 1529–36; *m* 1st by 16 May 1536 Margaret, dau and heiress of William Sambourne, of Fernham, Shrivenham, Berks, and had, with other issue, including an est s (Thomas, *d* young):

1 Thomas (Sir), KB (Feb 1546/7); *m* 29 Nov 1544 Dorothy, dau of 3rd Lord (Baron) Dacre (of Gilsland) (*see* DACRE, B), and *dspm* & *vp* Dec 1552

2 EDWARD, **3rd Lord**

1 Mary; *m* William Scott, Ld of the Manor of Mote, Rye, Sussex (*d* 11 Dec 1637), and had issue

2 Anne; *m* 1st Baron Grey of Groby and *d* 1605, leaving issue (*see* 1970 edn STAMFORD, E)

The **2nd Lord** *m* 2nd by Easter 1554 Elizabeth, widow of Richard Paulet, yr bro of 1st Marquess of Winchester (*qv*), and 2nd dau and coheir of Peter Coudray, of Herriard, Hants, and *d* 20 Aug 1558, having by her had a s and dau (*dsp*)

The est surv son,

EDWARD WINDSOR, **3rd Lord** (Baron) **Windsor**; *b c* 1532; ktd 1553, Bencher Middle Temple 1571; *m* between 1553 and 1558 Lady Katherine de Vere (*d* 17 Jan 1599), er dau of 16th Earl of Oxford (*see* SAINT ALBANS, D), and *d* 24 Jan 1574/5, leaving:

1 FREDERICK WINDSOR, **4th Lord** (Baron) **Windsor**; *b* 2 Feb 1558/9; *d* unm 24 Dec 1585

2 HENRY WINDSOR, **5th Lord** (Baron) **Windsor**; *b* 10 Aug 1562; *m* by 1586 Anne (*d* 27 Nov 1615), yr dau and coheir of Sir Thomas Rivett, of Chippenham, Cambs, and Stoke-by-Nayland, Suffolk by his 2nd w Griselda (*see* ANGLESEY, M), and *d* 6 April 1605, leaving:

(1) THOMAS WINDSOR, **6th Lord** (Baron) **Windsor**, KB 1610; *b* 29 Sept 1591; *m* by 14 Jan 1607/8 Lady Katherine Somerset, dau of 4th Earl of Worcester (*see* BEAUFORT, D), but *dsp* 6 Dec 1642, when the Barony fell into abeyance

(1) Elizabeth; *m* 24 July 1616 Dixie Hickman, of Kew, Surrey, and had:

1a THOMAS WINDSOR HICKMAN later WINDSOR, **7th Lord** (Baron) **Windsor** (as which *s* unc on termination of abeyance in his favour 16 June 1660, having already inherited the unc's estates) and 1st EARL OF PLYMOUTH (E), so *cr* 6 Dec 1682, PC (1685); *b c* 1627; royalist Civil War (fought Battle of Naseby 1645), Ld Lt Worcs 1660–87, Govr Jamaica 1661–Feb 1663/4, Col 3rd Dragoon Gds 1685–87; *m* 1st 12 May 1656 Anne (*d* 22 March 1666), dau of Sir William Saville, 3rd Bt of, Thornhill, Yorks, and sis of 1st Marquess of Halifax of the 1682 *cr* (*see* HALIFAX, E, preliminary remarks), and had, with a dau (*d* an infant):

1b Other, *Lord Windsor*; *b* 12 Sept 1659; *m c* 20 Oct 1673 Elizabeth (*m* 2nd Edward Wyke and was *bur* 29 Jan 1667/8), dau and heiress of Thomas Turvey, of Walcot and Wadborough, Worcs, and *dvp* 11 Nov 1684, having had, with other issue:

1c OTHER WINDSOR, **8th Lord** (Baron) **Windsor** and 2nd EARL OF PLYMOUTH; *b* 27 Aug 1679; *educ* Ch Ch Oxford; Ld Lt Cheshire, Denbighs and Flintshire 1713–14, Recorder Worcester 1720; *m* 27 April 1705 Elizabeth (*d* 10 June 1711), dau and heiress of Thomas Whitley, of Peel, Cheshire, and *d* 26 Dec 1727, having had, with another s (*dsp*):

1d OTHER WINDSOR, **9th Lord** (Baron) **Windsor** and 3rd EARL OF PLYMOUTH; *b* 30 June 1707; *educ* Eton; *m* 7 May 1730 Elizabeth (*d* 9 Nov 1733), only dau and heiress of Thomas Lewis, of Soberton, Hants, and *d* 23 Nov 1732, leaving an only s:

1e OTHER LEWIS WINDSOR, **10th Lord** (Baron) **Windsor** and 4th EARL OF PLYMOUTH; *b* 12 May 1731; *educ* Eton and Queen's Coll Oxford; Ld Lt Glam 1754–71; *m* 11 Aug 1750 Hon Catherine Archer (*d* 12 Aug 1790), dau of 1st Baron Archer of Umberslade, and *d* 21 April 1771, having had:

1f OTHER HICKMAN WINDSOR, **11th Lord** (Baron) **Windsor** and 5th EARL OF PLYMOUTH; *b* 30 May 1751; *educ* Eton; *m* 20 May 1788 his cousin Hon Sarah Archer (*m* 2nd 24 July 1800 1st Earl Amherst (*see* AMHERST OF HACKNEY, B, preliminary

remarks) and *d* 27 May 1838), est dau and coheir of 2nd Baron Archer of Umberslade, and *d* 12 June 1799, leaving:

1g OTHER ARCHER WINDSOR, **12th Lord** (Baron) **Windsor** and 6th EARL OF PLYMOUTH; *b* 2 July 1789; *educ* Harrow and Ch Ch Oxford; *m* 5 Aug 1811 Lady Mary Sackville (*m* 2nd 25 May 1839 1st Earl Amherst (*see* above) and *dsp* 30 July 1864), dau of 3rd Duke of Dorset (*see* SACKVILLE, B), and *d* 20 July 1833, when the Barony of Windsor fell into abeyance between his sisters

1g Maria; *b* 1790; *m* 25 Oct 1811 3rd Marquess of Downshire (*qv*) and *d* 7 April 1855, leaving issue

2g HARRIET, **Baroness Windsor** in her own right, of whom presently

2f Thomas, RN; *b* 19 May 1752; *m* 1793 — dau of John Bagenal, of Berks, and *dsp* 1832

3f Rev ANDREWS WINDSOR, 7th EARL OF PLYMOUTH; *b* 12 May 1764; *educ* Eton, Ch Ch Oxford and Trin Hall Cambridge; Vicar Rhayader, Radnorshire, 1789 and Tardebigg 1791, Rector Draycott-Cerne, Wilts, 1800 and Rochford, Essex, 1814; *d* unm 19 Jan 1837

4f HENRY WINDSOR, 8th and last EARL OF PLYMOUTH; *b* 1 Feb 1768; *educ* Eton; Ensign Coldstream Gds 1788; 111th Foot: Lt and Capt 1792, Maj 1794, Lt-Col 1795; Lt-Col Worcs Provisional Cav 1797; *m* 12 July 1798 Anne (*d* 30 Jan 1850), dau of Thomas Copson, and *dsp* 8 Dec 1843, when the Earldom expired

1f Katherine Sydney; *b* 1755; *m* 26 July 1785 Sir James Tylney-Long, 7th Bt, of Draycot, and *d* 5 Jan 1823, leaving issue

2f Elizabeth; *b* 1757; *m* 30 March 1776 Gore Townsend, of Honington, Warwicks, and *d* 2 April 1821, leaving issue

3f Anne; *b* 1762; *m* 7 June 1787 Rev Sir Thomas Broughton, 6th Bt, of Broughton (*qv*), and *dsp* 9 Aug 1793

4f Sarah; *b* 1763; *m* 4 Aug 1786 Sir William Champion de Crespigny, 2nd Bt (*see* 1949 edn), and *d* 22 Dec 1825, leaving issue. He *d* 28 Dec 1829

1b Mary; *m* 1672 Sir Thomas Cookes, Bt, and *dsp* 3 Jan 1694

1a (cont.) The **7th Lord** *m* 2nd 9 April 1668 Ursula (*d* 22 April 1717), dau and coheir of Sir Thomas Widdrington, of Cheeseburn Grange, Northumberland, Speaker H of C, and *d* 3 Nov 1687, having by her had, with a dau (*d* unm):

2b THOMAS WINDSOR, 1st VISCOUNT WINDSOR OF BLACKCASTLE (I), so *cr* 19 June 1699, as also 1 Jan 1711/2 BARON MOUNTJOY OF THE ISLE OF WIGHT (GB); *b* 1669; MP Droitwich 1685–87, Bramber 1705–08 and Monmouth 1708–12, Lt-Col 3rd Dragoon Gds 1690, Groom Bedchamber to WILLIAM III 1691–1701/2, Brig-Gen March 1701/2, Maj-Gen Jan 1703/4, Col 3rd Dragoon Gds 1712–March 1716/7; *m* 28 Aug 1703 Charlotte (*d* 13 Nov 1733), widow of 2nd Baron Jeffreys of Wem (*see* JEFFREYS, B) and dau of 7th Earl of Pembroke and (4th Earl of) Montgomery (*qv*), and *d* 8 June 1738, leaving, with another dau:

1c HERBERT WINDSOR, 2nd and last VISCOUNT WINDSOR OF BLACKCASTLE; *bapt* 1 May 1707; MP ('Tory) Cardiff 1734–38; *m* 12 Aug 1735 Alice (*d* 24 Nov 1776), sister and coheir of Sir James Clavering, 4th Bt, and *dspms* 25 Jan 1758, when both titles expired, having had:

1d Charlotte Jane; *m* 12 Nov 1766 1st Marquess of Bute (*qv*) and *d* 28 Jan 1800, leaving issue

2d Alice Elizabeth; *m* 4 Feb 1768 2nd Marquess of Hertford (*qv*) and *dsps* 11 Feb 1772

1c Ursula; *m* 20 March 1736 John Wadman, of Imber, Wilts

2c Charlotte; *m* 18 April 1736 John Kent, of Salisbury

3c Catherine; *m* 10 Feb 1740/1 Matthews Estevenon, of Holland

3b Dixey; Fell Trin Coll Cambridge, MP Cambridge U; *m* Dorothy, dau of Sir Richard Stote, but *dsp* 22 Oct 1743

4b Andrews; Brig-Gen, MP Bramber; *d* unm

5b William; *d* an infant, July 1682

2b Ursula; *m* 28 March 1703 Thomas Johnson and *d* 20 Aug 1737

3b Elizabeth; *m* 21 July 1720 Sir Francis Dashwood, 1st Bt (*see* DASHWOOD, Bt, of West Wycombe)

1a Mariana; *m* Sir Henry Hunloke, Bt

2a Catherine; *m* John Columbine

(2) Elizabeth; *m* 1st her cousin Sir Andrews Windsor (*dsp*); *m* 2nd Sir James Ware and had issue

The 12th LORD (Baron) WINDSOR (and 6th Earl of Plymouth)'s yr sister,

HARRIET Windsor later Windsor-Clive (roy licence 8 Nov 1855), **Baroness Windsor** in her own right on termination of abeyance 25 Oct 1855; *b* 30 July 1797; *m* 19 June 1819 Hon Robert Henry Clive (*d* 20 Jan 1854), of Oakly Park, Salop, MP, 2nd s of 1st Earl of Powis (*qv*), and had:

1 Robert CLIVE later WINDSOR-CLIVE; *b* 24 May 1824; *educ* Eton and St John's Coll Cambridge; MP (C) Ludlow 1852–54 and S Salop 1854–59, Lt-Col Worcs Yeo Cav 1854–58; *m* 20 Oct 1852 Lady Mary Selina Louisa Bridgeman (*d* 12 July 1889), dau of 2nd Earl of Bradford (*qv*), and *d* 4 Aug 1859, leaving:

(1) ROBERT GEORGE, **1st Earl**

(1) Georgina Harriet Charlotte; *b* 6 Oct 1853; granted with her sisters rank of baron's daus 1870; *d* unm 8 Nov 1924

(2) Henrietta Lucy; *b* 1 April 1855; *d* 19 April 1922

(3) Mary Agnes; *b* 29 May 1856; *m* 18 July 1892 John Knowsley Thornton (*d* 3 Jan 1904), of Hildersham Hall, Cambs, and *d* 9 Jan 1923, leaving issue

2 George Herbert Windsor CLIVE later WINDSOR-CLIVE, JP, DL Worcs, JP Salop; *b* 12 March 1835; Lt-Col Coldstream Gds, MP Ludlow 1860–85; *m* 17 Oct 1876 Hon Gertrude Albertina Trefusis (*d* 11 Feb 1878), dau of 19th Baron Clinton (*qv*), and *d* 26 April 1918, leaving:

(1) George, CMG (1919), DL (1947); *b* 6 April 1878; *educ* Eton and RMC Sandhurst; MP Ludlow 1923–45, Lt-Col Coldstream Gds, Boer War 1899–1901, WW I and with Inter-Allies Control Commn 1920–22; *m* 19 Nov 1912 Sidney

Guendolen (d 5 July 1935), only dau of Charles Carmichael Lacaita, of Selham House, Petworth, by Mary Annabel, er dau of Sir Francis Hastings Charles Doyle, 2nd Bt (see 1970 edn), and d 25 June 1968, leaving issue (in remainder to Barony of Windsor only):

1a +Robert Charles [Brigadier Robert Windsor-Clive, The Pleck, Ashford Carbonel, Salop SY8 4DB]; b 29 April 1919; educ Eton and RMC Sandhurst; Brig cmdg 3rd Bn Coldstream Gds 1956–59, cmded Regt 1961–64, cmded 159 (WB) Bde TA 1964–66, Ch Staff Lond Dist 1966–69, served WW II (wounded, despatches); m 29 Dec 1949 *Olive Mary, yr dau of Lt-Col Francis Longueville, DSO, MC, of Inwood, All Stretton, Salop, and has:

1b +George Francis [Maj George Windsor-Clive, Balak Farm, Marridge Hill, Ramsbury, Wilts SN8 2HG]; b 26 Jan 1954; educ Eton and RAC Cirencester; Lt Coldstream Gds 1975, Maj (TA) Roy Yeo 1981–92, md Windsor Clive Internat; m 1988 *Anna Georgina, dau of Antony Leaf, of Cleeve House, Ampney St Peter, Glos, and has:

1c +Thomas Robert; b 26 Jan 1992

2c +John Antony; b 30 Oct 1993

1b +Annabel Mary [Mrs Mark Savage, Castlett Farm Cottage, Guiting Power, Glos GL54 5UZ]; b 29 March 1951; m 1979 *Mark Savage, s of G A R Savage, of Cirencester, and has:

1c +Gabriel Frances; b 1984

2c +Victoria Mary; b 1987

2a +Francis Archer [Francis Windsor-Clive Esq, Toneys, Bromsberrow, Herefs HR8 1SF]; b 25 Dec 1922; educ Eton; late Capt Coldstream Gds WW II (wounded, despatches); m 30 Oct 1945 *Anne Gertrude, er dau of Lt-Col Francis Longueville (see above), and has:

1b +Edward Archer [Edward Windsor-Clive Esq, 54 Oxberry Ave, London SW6 5SS]; b 23 Oct 1946; educ Ampleforth and RMA Sandhurst; Maj Coldstream Gds; m 1982 *Grania M S, dau of M E F S FitzGerald, of Hill Place, Haywards Heath, Sussex, and has:

1c +Robert Michael; b 27 Dec 1985

1c +Sophie Anne; b 21 May 1983

2b +Robert Ivor [Robert Windsor-Clive Esq, Cefn Ceist, Michaelchurch, Herefs HR20 0JY]; b 4 May 1950; educ Ampleforth and RAC Cirencester; professional Nat Hunt Jockey, manager Worcester Racecourse 1976–77; m 1 Sept 1981 (divorce 1990) Aricelli Romero and has:

1c +Francisco Alexis; b 22 June 1982

1c +Ana Willow; b 12 Feb 1983

3b +Other John [Maj Other Windsor-Clive, Oaklands, Whiteleaved Oak, Eastnor, Herefs HR8 1SE]; b 14 April 1958; educ Ampleforth and RMA Sandhurst; Maj Coldstream Gds

4b +William Henry [William Windsor-Clive Esq, Bury Court, Redmarley, Glos GL19 3LB]; b 6 Jan 1960; educ Belmont Abbey and RAC Cirencester; m 11 Feb 1989 *Jane, dau of J R Lawther, of Little Arley, Birtsmorton, Worcs, and has:

1c +Harriet Ann; b 25 Sept 1990

2c +Phoebe Jane; b 13 June 1993

1b Frances Anne; b 28 Oct 1948; BEd (Cantab); m 1972 *Maj Andrew Stow, RE, and d 18 Feb 1992, leaving:

1c +Catherine Mary; b 24 June 1974; educ Cambridge (MEng)

2c +Isobel Anne; b 14 July 1976; educ Cambridge (BA)

3c +Elizabeth Rose (twin); b 14 July 1976

3a +Everard Ivor [Col Everard Windsor-Clive, The Leys, Stoke Bliss, Worcs WR15 8QJ]; b 29 July 1925; educ Eton; Col Coldstream Gds, cmded 2nd Bn 1967–69, cmded Regt 1973–75, served WW II

1a Mary Phyllis; b 28 March 1921; d unm 1 Jan 1989

3 William Windsor; b 11 Aug 1837; k in a train crash 24 Sept 1857

1 Henrietta Sarah; watercolourist; m 24 Nov 1853 Edward Hussey (d 3 Sept 1894), of Scotney Castle, Sussex, and d 30 Jan 1899, leaving issue

2 Mary; d 16 June 1873

3 Victoria Alexandrina (HM QUEEN VICTORIA stood sponsor); m 9 April 1874 Rev Edward Farington Clayton (d 24 Nov 1907), Rector Ludlow 1867–1907, and d 18 July 1920, leaving issue

BARONESS WINDSOR d 9 Nov 1869; her gs,

ROBERT GEORGE WINDSOR-CLIVE, **14th Lord** (Baron) **Windsor** (as which s grandmother 1869) and **1st Earl of Plymouth**, Co Devon, so cr 18 Dec 1905, as also VISCOUNT WINDSOR, of St Fagans, Co Glamorgan (both UK), GBE (1918), CB (1905), TD, PC (1891), DL Worcs and Salop; b 27 Aug 1857; educ Eton and St John's Coll Cambridge; Glam: Ld Lt 1890–1923, Pres TFA, Hon Col Yeo and RGA also 2nd and 3rd Bns Worcs and Welch Regts respectively, Paymaster-Gen 1891–92, First Commr Works 1902–05, Hon LLD, High Steward Cambridge U, Tstee Nat Gallery, Mayor Cardiff 1895, Sub-Prior OStJ, Offr Legn Hon; m 11 Aug 1883 Alberta Victoria Sarah Caroline, DJStJ (d 22 Aug 1944), dau of Sir Augustus Berkeley Paget, GCB, PC (see ANGLESEY, M), and had:

1 Other Robert, Viscount Windsor; b 3 Oct 1884; Capt Worcs Yeo, ADC to HC S Africa and Viceroy India; d unm at Agra 23 Dec 1908

2 IVOR MILES, **2nd Earl**

3 Archer; b 6 Nov 1890; Lt Coldstream Gds; ka 25 Aug 1914

1 Phyllis; b 28 Dec 1886; m 9 Oct 1924 Maj Hugh Gordon Benton, 2nd Lancers (Ind Cav) (d 10 Feb 1931), and d 3 March 1971, leaving:

(1) +(Caroline Rose) Melissa Benton; b 1928

The 1st EARL d 6 March 1923; his only surv son,

IVOR MILES WINDSOR-CLIVE, **2nd Earl of Plymouth**, PC (1929), DL Worcs and Salop; b 4 Feb 1889; educ Eton and Trin Coll Cambridge; Capt Worcs Yeo, Hon Col Glamorgan RGA, Ld Lt Glam, MP (C) Ludlow 1922–23, PPS to Home Sec 1922, Capt Gentlemen-at-Arms 1925–29, Parly U-Sec: Dominion Affrs Jan-June 1929, Tport 1931–32, Colonial Office 1932–36 and FO 1936–39, memb Roy Commn on Ancient Monuments in Wales and Monmouthshire 1934 (Chm 1935), Hon Freeman Cardiff 1936, GCStJ; m 14 July 1921 Lady Irene Corona Charteris (d 1989), DGCStJ, Sr Cmdt ATS, 3rd dau of 11th Earl of Wemyss (qv), and d 1 Oct 1943, leaving:

1 OTHER ROBERT IVOR WINDSOR-CLIVE, **3rd and present Earl of Plymouth**

2 +Richard Archer Alan [The Hon Richard Windsor-Clive, Combe, Nettlecombe, Taunton, Somerset TA4 4HS]; b 5 Feb 1928; educ Eton and Trin Coll Cambridge; late Lt RA, chm Bayfine Ltd 1973–85, dir Highgate Optical and Industrial 1976–; m 1st 30 April 1955 (divorce 1968) Joanna Mary, er dau of Edward Corbet Woodall, OBE (see CRAWLEY-BOEVEY, Bt), by Janet Inez, er dau of Rev Canon Arthur Stafford Crawley, MC, Canon St George's Chapel, Windsor Castle, and has:

(1) +Stephen Miles; b 7 June 1956; educ Eton

(1) +Cathryn Harriet; b 8 Nov 1958; m 1983 *Thomas P Macfarlane, s of Craig Macfarlane, and has:

1a +Cosmo; b 1987

2a +Ivo; b 1988

3a +Pascoe; b 1996

1a +Rose; b 1990

2a +Jessie; b 1994

2 (cont.) The Hon Richard Windsor-Clive m 2nd 5 Aug 1968 (divorce 1997) Hon (Mary) Alice, formerly w of John Paget Chancellor and only dau of 4th Baron Hylton (qv), and has:

(2) +Nell; b 28 Oct 1974

3 Rowland David Owain; b 30 Aug 1938; educ Eton; d unm 2 Aug 1965

1 Gillian Mary; m 1st 24 Sept 1941 (divorce 1947) Wilfred Wooller, Lt RA, s of Wilfred Wooller, of Colwyn Bay; m 2nd 10 May 1947 Lt Albertus Jacobus de Haan (d 1991), DFC (Netherlands), Croix de Guerre Belgium, Roy Netherlands Navy s of Jan Cornelius de Haan, of Nieuw Loosdrecht, Holland, and was k in a car crash 10 Dec 1961, leaving:

(1) +Julian Jan Ivor [Julian de Haan Esq, Southfield House, Forthampton, Glos GL19 4RA]; b 5 May 1948; educ Gresham's; FCA, ATII; m 16 Sept 1972 *(Juliet) Clare, only dau of Maj Henry Benjamin van der Gucht, MC, by Pamela Sabina, er dau of Capt Algernon Walter Strickland (see STRICKLAND-CONSTABLE, Bt), and has:

1a +Luke Archer; b 1973; educ Eton, Cheltenham and Reading U

2a +Tom Julian; b 1976; educ Cheltenham

1a +Sophia Gillian; b 1979; educ Malvern Girls' Coll

(2) +Archer Anthony [Archer de Haan Esq, Cookeridge Farm, Bromfield, Salop SY8 2JY]; b 10 June 1950; educ Gresham's; m 1st 1975 (divorce 1987) Amanda Ball and has:

1a +Toby Archer; b 1976

1a +Laura Mary Emma; b 1979

(2) (cont.) Archer de Haan m 2nd 1987 *Vivien Whittall and by her has:

2a +Hugo Julian Archer; b 5 March 1992

2a +Frances Catherine; b 1988

3a +Hannah Gillian (twin); b 1988

(3) +Andrew David [Andrew de Haan Esq, Thameside Cottage, Church Rd, Longworth, Oxon OX13 5DX]; b 12 Feb 1954; educ Northease Manor, Lewes; m 1981 *Emma Katherine, yst dau of Cdr Christopher William Stuart Dreyer, DSO, DSC

(4) +Valentine Nicholas; b 24 March 1956; educ Stanbridge Earls Sch; m 1985 *Virginia Ann, dau of Bruce Balentyne Kerr, and has:

1a +Alexander Bruce; b 19 April 1988

1a +Melissa Gilian; b 17 June 1990

2 +Clarissa [The Lady Clarissa Egleston, 7 Ernest Gdns, London W4]; b 15 Jan 1931; m 24 April 1953 *Maj Keith Maclean Forbes Egleston, Rifle Bde, yr s of Maj Thomas Buchanan Maclean Egleston, MC, of White Hart Lodge, Limpsfield, Surrey, and Mrs Richard Wellesley, of The Old Malt House, Shipton-under-Wychwood, Oxon, and has:

(1) +Hugo Vivyan; b 10 May 1955; educ Eton

(1) +Sarah Caroline; b 13 July 1956

(2) +Harriet Gina; b 9 Oct 1962; m 1988 *Simon Richard Alsop, only s of B G P Alsop, of Ashtead, Surrey

3 +Rosula Caroline [The Lady Rosula Glyn, 17 Cadogan Place, London SW1X 9SA]; b 30 April 1935; OStJ; m 4 Jan 1962 Maj Sir Alan Glyn, ERD, (d 4 May 1998), MP Clapham 1959–64 and Windsor and Maidenhead 1970–92, s of John Paul Glyn, RHG, and has:

(1) +Mary Caroline; b 23 Feb 1963; m 1993 *Capt Adrian John Weale, s of Dr K E Weale, of Chiswick, and has:

1a +Robert Kenneth; b 1994

(2) +Anne Serena; b 2 March 1964

POLE of Shute House

Arms: Azure semée of fleurs-de-lys or a lion rampant argent.
Motto: *Pollet virtus* ('Virtue is powerful').
Creation: Bt. (E) 12 Sept 1628.

SIR (JOHN) RICHARD WALTER REGINALD CAREW POLE, 13TH BT, of Shute House, Devonshire, DL (Cornwall 1988) [Sir Richard Pole Bt DL, Antony House, Torpoint, Cornwall, PL11 2QA]; *b* 2 Dec 1938; *s* f 1993; *educ* Eton and RAC Cirencester; Lt Coldstream Gds 1958–63, Liveryman Fishmongers' Co 1960 (memb Court Assistants 1993), ARICS 1967, CC Cornwall 1973–93, High Sheriff 1979, memb: Devon and Cornwall Ctee Nat Tst 1978–83, MAFF Regnl Advsy Ctee 1970–80, Devon and Cornwall Police Authority 1973–89 (chm 1985–87), SW Regnl Ctee W of England Bldg Soc 1989–91, Govr Seale Hayne Ag Coll 1979–89 and Plymouth Coll 1985–96, dir SWEB 1981–90, dir Theatre Royal Plymouth 1985–97, pres: Roy Cornwall Show 1981, Surf Life Saving Assoc of GB 1975–86, Countryside Commr 1991–96, Tstee Nat Heritage Memorial Fund 1991– and Tate Gallery 1993–; *m* 1st 27 Sept 1966 (*divorce* 1973) Hon Victoria Marion Ann Lever, 2nd dau of 3rd Viscount Leverhulme (*qv*); *m* 2nd 1974 *Mary, MVO (1983), dau of Lt-Col Ronald Dawnay (*see* DOWNE, V), and by her has:

1 +TREMAYNE JOHN CAREW; *b* 22 Feb 1974; *educ* Eton

2 +John Alexander George Carew; *b* 25 July 1975; *educ* Eton; Page Honour to HM QUEEN ELIZABETH THE QUEEN MOTHER 1990–92

Lineage: Sir JOHN POLE, of Pole, Cheshire; had:

Sir JOHN POLE, V-Adml West of England; had:

ARTHUR POLE; *m* Elizabeth, dau and heiress of John Pole, of Devon, and had:

JOHN POLE; *m* Johanna, dau of Richard Code, of Gidleigh, Devon, and had:

JOHN POLE; *m* 1st Johanna, dau and heiress of Robert Count; *m* 2nd Edith, dau of Robert Titerleigh, of Titherleigh, Devon, and by her had:

WILLIAM POLE; *m* 1st 1540 Margaret Waller; *m* 2nd Agnes, dau of John Drake, of Ashe, great great great-aunt of 1st Duke of Marlborough (*qv*), and by her had:

WILLIAM POLE; *m* Katherine (*bur* 9 Nov 1583), dau of John Popham, of Huntworth, and was *bur* 24 Aug 1587, leaving:

Sir WILLIAM POLE, of Colcomb, Devon; *bapt* 27 Aug 1561; antiquary; *m* 1st 30 July 1583 Mary (*bur* 8 May 1606), est dau and coheir of Sir William Periam, Ld Ch Baron Exchequer, and had six sons and five daus; *m* 2nd Jane (*bur* 17 Jan 1623/24), widow of Roger How and dau of William Symes, of Chard, Somerset, and *d* 9 Feb 1635, having by her had no issue; his est s:

Sir John Pole, 1st Bt (E), so cr 12 Sept 1628; MP Devon 1626, High Sheriff 1638–39, Parliamentarian Civil War; *m* 1st 5 Jan 1613/4 his cousin Elizabeth (*d* 16 April 1628), dau of Roger How, London merchant, and had, with a s (*d* young) and dau (*d* unm):

1 William (Sir); *bapt* 6 Dec 1614; MP Honiton 1640–42, ktd 1641; *m* 1st Grace (*dsp* 1639), dau of Sir Thomas Trenchard; *m* 2nd Catharine (*bur* 17 Jan 1642/3), only dau of Henry St Barbe, of Ashington, and was *bur* 20 Jan 1648/9, leaving four daus

2 COURTENAY (Sir), **2nd Bt**

1 Martha; *m* 1 June 1631 William Everitt

2 Jane; *m* 28 Sept 1657 John Croker

Sir John *m* 2nd Mary, widow of William Lockland, of Bromley St Leonard's, Middx, and *d* 16 April 1658

His 2nd but est surv s (presumably by his 1st w),

Sir Courtenay Pole, 2nd Bt; *bapt* 17 Feb 1618/9; *educ* Lincoln's Inn; MP Honiton 1661–79, High Sheriff Devon 1681–82, royalist Civil War; *m* by 1649 Urith, dau of Thomas Shapcote, of Shapcote, and was *bur* 13 April 1695, having had, with another s and three daus (including Jane, *m* 1st Sir Coplestone Bampfylde, 2nd Bt (*see* POLTIMORE, B), *m* 2nd Edward Gibbons):

Sir John Pole, 3rd Bt; *b* 17 June 1649; MP Lyme Regis 1685–87 and 1689–90, Bossiney 1698–1700, Devon 1701–02, E Looe 1702–05 and Newport Cornwall 1705–08; *m* Anne (*bur* 1 March 1713/4), sis of Sir William Mor(r)ice, 1st Bt, and *d* 13 March 1707/8, having had:

1 Sir William Pole, 4th Bt, of Shute; *bapt* 17 April 1678; MP Devon 1712, Master Household to QUEEN ANNE; *m* Elizabeth (*bur* 12 April 1758), dau of Robert Warry, and *d* 31 Dec 1741, leaving:

(1) **Sir John Pole, 5th Bt**; *m* 1st Elizabeth (*d* 13 Aug 1758), dau and coheir of John Mills, of Woodford, and *d* 19 Feb 1766, leaving:

1a Sir JOHN WILLIAM POLE later De La POLE (roy licence 1790, discontinued by his immediate successor), **6th Bt**; *m* 9 Jan 1781 Anne (*d* 12 Feb 1832), only dau of James Templer, of Stover House, Devon, and *d* 30 Nov 1799, leaving:

1b **Sir William Templer Pole, 7th Bt**, DCL; *b* 2 Aug 1782; *m* 1st 24 Aug 1804 Sophia Anne (*d* 17 March 1808), only dau of George Templer, of Shapwick House, Somerset, and had:

1c Sir JOHN GEORGE De La POLE later REEVE De La POLE (roy licence 1838), **8th Bt**; *b* 21 Jan 1808; *m* 1st 26 March 1829 Margaretta (*d* June 1842), 2nd dau of Henry Barton, of Saucethorpe Hall, Lincs, and had:

1d Margaretta Luchesa Jane Maria; *m* 1st 1 Feb 1849 Lt-Col John Templer West, Gren Gds, est s of Adml of the Fleet Sir John West, KCB; *m* 2nd 1860 Henry Vansittart Pennefather, Capt 41st Foot (*d* 9 Aug 1888)

1c (cont.) Sir John *m* 2nd 2 Feb 1843 Josephine Catherine Denise Carré, of France (*m* 2nd 1881 Antoine Pierre Roupe; *dsp* 1 Jan 1907), and *d* 19 May 1874

1b Sir William *m* 2nd 30 Aug 1810 Charlotte (*d* 2 Oct 1877), only dau of John Fraser and n of John Farquhar, of Fonthill Abbey, Wilts, and *d* 1 April 1847, having by her had:

2c **Sir William Edmund Pole, 9th Bt**; *b* July 1816; barrister; *m* 26 April 1841 Margaret Victoriosa (*d* 23 Nov 1886), 2nd dau of Adml Hon Sir John Talbot, GCB (*see* TALBOT DE MALAHIDE, B), and *d* 21 March 1895, leaving:

1d Sir EDMUND REGINALD TALBOT POLE later De La POLE, **10th Bt**; *b* 22 Feb 1844; *m* 1st 25 Sept 1877 Mary Ann Margaret (*d* 10 May 1878), widow of Capt John Ormsby Phipps, 3rd Hus, and only child of Capt Hastings Sands, 3rd Dragoon Gds; *m* 2nd 18 Dec 1884 Elizabeth Marion (*d* 28 May 1912), dau of Charles Rhodes, and *dsp* 26 Aug 1912

2d **Sir Frederick Arundell de la Pole, 11th Bt**, JP; *b* 25 Dec 1850; High Sheriff Devon 1917; *d* unm 12 Feb 1926

3d Arthur Lionel POLE later De La POLE; *b* 10 Jan 1854; Maj 3rd Vol Bn Devonshire Regt; *m* 24 April 1884 Edith Sarah, dau of Thomas Hounsell, of Berbice, Br Guiana, and *dsp* 17 Feb 1904

1d Julia Margaret; *d* young

2d Jane Victoria; *d* young

3d Emily Charlotte Augusta; *m* 22 May 1878 Richard Hake Bush, MD, and *d* 29 Oct 1927. He *d* 14 Feb 1890

4d Georgina (twin with Arthur Lionel); *d* 12 Feb 1854

5d Edrica Blanche; *d* unm *c* 1946

6d Geraldine Eleanor

3c Reginald Frederick; *b* 20 Oct 1818; *d* 6 Oct 1848

1c Charlotte; *b* 13 Sept 1813; *d* unm 1898

2c Jane Maria; *m* 12 Feb 1833 E Wyndham Harrington Schenley, Acting Judge Havanna, and *d* 23 April 1837, leaving issue

1b Marianne; *m* J M West, of New House, Glam

(1) (cont.) **Sir John Pole, 5th Bt**, *m* 2nd Anna Maria Palmer (*m* 2nd George Clavering).

2 John; *d* unm 20 June 1710

3 Carolus (Rev); *bapt* 25 May 1686; Rector St Breock, Cornwall; *m* 23 Aug 1714 Sarah, est dau of Jonathan Rashleigh, of Menabilly, Cornwall, by Jane or Sarah, er dau by his 1st w of Sir John Carew, 3rd Bt, of Anthony, Cornwall, and *d* 1731, leaving:

(1) Reginald, of Stoke Damerel, Devon; *b* 1717; *m* Anne (*d* 25 April 1758), 2nd dau of John Francis Buller, of Morval, Cornwall, and *d* 11 Nov 1769, leaving:

1a Reginald POLE later POLE-CAREW, of Antony, PC; *b* 28 July 1753; U-Sec Home Dept, MP; *m* 1st 18 Nov 1784 Jemima (*d* 16 July 1804), only dau and heiress of Hon John Yorke, 4th s of 1st Earl of Hardwicke (*qv*), and had, with other issue:

1b Joseph, of Anthony; *b* 29 Sept 1787; *m* 1st 10 Sept 1810 Caroline, dau of John Ellis, er bro of 1st Baron Seaford (*see* HOWARD DE WALDEN, B), and had:

1c Jemima; *m* 12 June 1842 Count Paul de Snasin, of Russia, and *d* Sept 1845, leaving issue

1b (cont.) Joseph Pole-Carew *m* 2nd Mrs — Cadogan and *d* 9 March 1852

1b Charlotte Jemima; *m* 1st 1806 Charles Garth Colleton, of Haines Hill, Berks; *m* 2nd Count Alphonse de Morel Champemonte and had issue

2b Harriet; *m* 19 Aug 1819 1st Earl of St Germans (*qv*) and *dsp* 4 March 1877

3b Agneta; *m* 24 Oct 1813 Thomas Somers Cocks (*d* 10 March 1859) and *d* 14 Sept 1836, leaving issue

4b Amabel; *m* 6 March 1821 Francis Glanville (*d* 24 April 1881), of Catchfrench, Cornwall, and *d* 12 April 1871, leaving issue

1a (cont.) Reginald Pole-Carew; *m* 2nd 4 May 1808 Hon Caroline Anne Lyttelton (*see* COBHAM, V) and *d* 3 Jan 1835, having had, with other issue:

2b William Henry, of Antony, JP, DL; *b* 30 July 1811; High Sheriff 1854, MP E Cornwall 1845–52; *m* 28 Aug 1838 Frances Anne (*d* 10 Oct 1902), 2nd dau of John Buller, of Morval, and *d* 20 Jan 1888, having had:

1c Reginald (Sir), KCB, CVO, of Antony, JP, DL Cornwall, JP Co Tipperary; *b* 1 May 1849; Afghan War 1879–80, Egypt 1882, Burma 1886–87, Boer War 1899–1900, MP Bodmin 1910–16, Dep Warden Stannaries Cornwall and Devon 1911–24, Lt-Gen Coldstream Gds, Inspr-Gen TF 1914; *m* 19 Feb 1901 Lady Beatrice Butler (*d* 29 Feb 1952), er dau of 3rd Marquess of Ormonde (*see* 1970 edn), and *d* 19 Sept 1924, leaving:

1d JOHN GAWEN (Sir), **12th Bt**

2d Patrick William Butler; *b* 25 Aug 1913; *educ* Eton and RMC Sandhurst; Lt Coldstream Gds, Maj Irish Gds, WW II; *m* 1st 17 Jan 1939 (*divorce* 1950) Sonia (*d* 1976), yst dau of Sir (William Eley) Cuthbert Quilter, 2nd Bt (*qv*), and had:

1e *Rosemary; *b* 24 June 1940

2d (cont.) Maj Patrick Pole-Carew *m* 2nd 19 April 1950 *Mary Patience [Mrs Patrick Pole-Carew, Clashaphouca, Clogheen, Co Tipperary, Ireland], formerly w of Ronald Ewan Cameron and dau of Maj Richard Ernest Gilchrist Phillips, and *d* 23 June 1971

1d Marye Frances; *b* 19 April 1903

2d Victoria Geraldine; *b* 21 Oct 1904; *m* 8 April 1929 Cdr Peter Du Cane, OBE, RN, er s of Charles Henry Copley Du Cane, formerly of Braxted Park, Essex, and had issue

2c Charles Edward; *b* 26 Dec 1853; *m* 16 Sept 1886 Ellen Henrietta (*d* 17 Oct 1932), est dau of William Ayshford Sanford, of Nynehead Court, Somerset, and *d* 18 May 1938, having had:

1d Gerald Ayshford; *b* 7 Aug 1887; Maj Somerset LI, Capt 3rd/4th Bn DCLI, mining engr; *m* 15 Oct 1915 Eileen Lorna (*d* 1989), yr dau of Surgn-Maj George Henry Kenneth MacDonald O'Callaghan, CMG, RAMC, and *d* 9 Nov 1969, leaving:

1e +Charles Oliver [Charles Pole-Carew Esq, Flat B, 1 Royal Crescent, London W11 4SL]; *b* 27 Sept 1923; *educ* Clayesmore; served Roy Queen's Regt 1941–47, Civil Staff Met Police Offr New Scotland Yd 1948–88

2e +Christopher Gerald [Christopher Pole-Carew Esq, Shute Barton, Shute, Devon EX13 7PT]; *b* 17 May 1931; *educ* RNC Dartmouth; High Sheriff Notts 1979–80; *m* 3 April 1954 *Gillian Elizabeth, dau of Clive Mence Burton, of S Africa, and has:

1f +Gerald Anthony Peregrine [Gerald Pole-Carew Esq, High Waterston Farm, nr Dorchester, Dorset DT2 7SW]; *b* 2 Sept 1957; *educ* Radley and RMA Sandhurst; Coldstream Gds; *m* 1st 1984 Claudia A, only dau of David Wolfers, of Barnes, London; *m* 2nd 1992 *Georgina E M, dau of Charles Harris, of Kenya, and has:

1g *Tatiana Cecily Alice; *b* 1993

2g *Alexandra Cornelia Rose; *b* 199–

1f *Delia Elizabeth; *b* 13 Feb 1955; *m* 1981 *Charles Benedict de Broca Madden, yst s of Dr James George Madden, of the Glebe House, Tollesbury, Essex, and has:

1g *James Antony Grellan; *b* 1982

2g *Edward Christopher Otha; *b* 1984

3g *Thomas Mark Ambrose; *b* 1988

2f *Camilla Janet; *b* 12 May 1961; *m* 10 July 1982 *Dominic John Earle Welby, 2nd s of Sir (Richard) Bruno Gregory Welby, 7th Bt (*qv*)

1e *Geraldine Frances Flora; *b* 24 May 1917

2e *(Eileen) Loveday [Mrs Loveday Miller, 83 Gowan Ave, London SW6 6RQ]; *b* 20 May 1930; *m* 15 Jan 1955 (*divorce* 1964) Brian Arnold Miller, s of W S Miller, of Hove

2d Charles William; *b* 3 July 1893; *d* 16 June 1913

3d Wymond Nicholas Richard; *b* 3 Oct 1896; Lt 1st Bn DCLI; *ka* 6 Nov 1917

1d Frances Ione; *m* 20 Nov 1918 Lt-Col Roy Morell, DSO, OBE, AIF Res Offrs, s of James Harris Morell, of Sydney, NSW, and *d* 11 March 1967, leaving issue

3c William Lyttelton; *b* 29 April 1856; *d* 22 May 1861

4c Gerald (Rev); *b* 18 Feb 1858; *educ* Trin Hall Cambridge (MA); *d* 5 Oct 1922

1c Geraldine Maria; *d* unm 23 Sept 1886

2c Fanny Julia; *d* unm 3 May 1939

3c Caroline Lyttelton; *m* 30 Dec 1896 Francis William Loring (*d* 29 Oct 1905), of Boston, Mass., and *d* 8 Sept 1911

3b Gerald (Rev); *b* 26 Aug 1815; BA Oxon, Vicar Antony; *m* 24 June 1841 Harriet Eliza (*m* 2nd 9 Oct 1849 Rev James Buller Kitson (*d* 13 July 1870) and had issue), est dau of John Buller, of Morval, and *dsp* 14 March 1845

5b Caroline; *m* 15 Aug 1837 Maj-Gen James Bucknall Estcourt (*das* Crimea 24 June 1854), 2nd s of T G B Estcourt, MP Oxford U; raised to rank of a KCB's widow 1856

6b Francis Antonia; *m* 31 Dec 1834 Joseph Yorke (*d* 4 Feb 1889), of Forthampton Court, Tewkesbury, and *d* 27 Feb 1889, leaving issue

7b Juliana; *m* 8 Jan 1839 1st Baron Robartes of Lanhydrock and of Truro (*d* 9 March 1882; *see* 1970 edn CLIFDEN, V) and *d* 12 April 1851, leaving issue

2a Sir CHARLES MORICE POLE, 1st and last Bt (UK), so *cr* 1801, KCB, Adml; *b* 18 Jan 1757; *m* 10 June 1792 Henrietta (*d* 16 Nov 1818), dau of John Goddard, of Woodford Hall, Essex, and *dspm* 31 Aug 1830, when the btcy expired, leaving:

1b Henrietta; *m* Sir William Stuart, of Tempsford Hall, Beds, and *d* July 1853

2b Anna Maria; *d* unm

3a Edward (Rev); *b* 14 April 1758; DD, Rector Barford, Wilts; *m* 1801 Jane (*d* 1854), dau of William Robinson, and *d* 28 Dec 1837, leaving, with other issue:

1b Reginald (Rev); *b* 27 Oct 1801; Rector Yeovilton, Somerset; *m* 29 Sept 1836 Jane (*d* 1896), dau of Alexander Powell, and *d* 1888, leaving:

1c George Henry Law; *b* 12 Sept 1837; *d* 22 Feb 1876

2c Reginald Carew; *b* 6 Aug 1843; Lt RN; *d* 4 May 1877

3c Alexander Edward, JP Somerset; *b* 23 Feb 1848; barrister, Recorder Newcastle-under-Lyme; *m* 23 July 1873 Joanna (*d* 10 Jan 1930), dau of Rev Charles Raikes Davy, of Tracy Park, Glos, and *d* 18 April 1909, leaving:

1d Alexander Charles Reginald; *b* 1878; *educ* Clifton; Lt RASC; *m* 1st 1918 Amy Marion (*d* 21 June 1947), widow of Albert Edwards-Webb and dau of George Treasure; *m* 2nd 1948 Hilda, widow of James Chesterfield, and dau of George Sanderson, and *dsp* 3 Feb 1957

1d Mabel Maria; *m* 11 Sept 1921 Bernard James Edwards Myatt (*d* 15 June 1924) and *dsp* 10 April 1942

2d Ethel Agneta; *m* 17 June 1914 Robert D'Eyncourt Day (*d* 20 Feb 1928), er s of Frank Day, and *d* 19–

4c John Lionel; *b* 30 Dec 1858; barrister; *d* unm 11 Dec 1892

1c Henrietta Maria; *m* 9 April 1865 H F Mutukisna (*dsp* 1873) and *d* 9 July 1904

2c Mary Stuart; *d* 20 Dec 1919

3c Joanna Augusta; *d* unm 11 Sept 1930

4c Agneta Jane; *m* 6 May 1873 Alex J Garrett (*d* 1906) and *d* 3 Aug 1939

5c Anna Maria; *d* unm

6c Louisa Margaretta; *d* unm 14 April 1935

7c Augusta Katherine Antonia; *d* unm 8 June 1940

2b Edward POLE later De La POLE (Rev); *b* 1 Sept 1805; MA Oxon; *m* 21 May 1839 Mary Anne (*d* 1901), dau of Frederick John Chapman, and *d* 1890, leaving:

1c Edward Frederick; *b* 30 March 1840; *d* unm 1866

2c Reginald Carolus; *b* 6 April 1841; Judge Ceylon CS; *m* 22 March 1864 Annie (*d* 1928), dau of Rev Robert Pargiter, Vicar Towersey, Oxon, and *d* 1897, leaving:

1d Reginald Charles Somers; *b* 10 Dec 1864; Assist Surveyor Ceylon; *m* 1891 Gertrude Sarah (*d* 7 Jan 1913), dau of Robert Greason, of Ceylon, and *d* 12 July 1914, leaving:

1e Reginald Edward Morice; *b* 25 Aug 1893; *m* 17 Nov 1924 *Dorothy Ethel Christine, dau of Charles William Searle, JP, and *d* 26 Nov 1948, leaving:

1f *Pauline Marjorie Doreen; *b* 12 Nov 1925; *m* 21 July 1951 *S/Ldr Frederick John Crewe, RAF, s of William Arthur Crewe, and has:

1g *Roderic Guy Pole; *b* 20 May 1952; *educ* Stanborough Park; *m* 1987 *Tina Norris

2g *Alistair Frederick; *b* 12 Aug 1954; *m* 1978 *Elaine Ruth Blackburn and has:

1h *Sam Richard; *b* 1978

2h *Joseph Paul; *b* 1982

1g *Felicity Jane; *b* 19 May 1953; *m* 1978 (*divorce* 1983) Paul Antoni Coleburt

2g *Virginia Rosamarie Pauline; *b* 7 Oct 1955; *m* 1984 *Derek Alan Lawrence

2f *Rosemary Ethel Greason [Mrs Patrick Walsh, 18 Denewood Rd, West Moors, Wimborne, Dorset]; *b* 13 Feb 1927; *m* 1957 *Patrick Eric Edward Walsh, er s of Maj Eric Alfred Walsh, RA, and has:

1g *Guy Patrick [Guy Walsh Esq, 66 North St, Crewkerne, Somerset]; *b* 27 Oct 1957; *m* 1982 *Rachel Gough

1g *Penelope Jane; *b* 6 Oct 1958

2g *Jill Christine; *b* 1 Aug 1960

3g *Kim Elizabeth; *b* 14 Dec 1962

3f *Lucille Dorothy Carew [Mrs Stuart Keir, Brook Cottage, Tanhouse Rd, Oxted, Surrey]; *b* 5 Oct 1938; *m* 18 Oct 1969 *Stuart Malcolm Forbes Keir, yr s of Donald Forbes Keir, and has:

1g *James Alexander; *b* 1976

2e (Lionel) Robert Glanville; *b* 29 Oct 1902; *m* 21 July 1924 (*divorce*) Gertrude Maude, dau of R Gregory, and *d* 10 June 1965, leaving:

1f +Reginald Robert; *b* 19 June 1925; *m* 24 Oct 1953 *Sylvia Patricia Sullivan and has:

1g +A son

1g *Susan Carole; *b* 27 Nov 1954

2g *A dau

3e Percival Arthur Carew; *b* 10 April 1904; *m* 15 Feb 1934 Irene Clare (*d* 1975), dau of Alexander French, of Calcutta, and *d* 16 May 1965, leaving:

1f +Geoffrey Arthur [Geoffrey Pole Esq, 3 Mill Pond Rd, Windlesham, Surrey]; *b* 3 March 1935; *m* 24 Feb 1961 *Patricia, dau of W Sweetman, of Birmingham, and has:

1g *Julia; *b* 1963

2g *Diane (twin); *b* 1963

3g *Susan Caroline; *b* 1964

2f +Roger Charles; *b* 5 Jan 1939; *m* 2 March 1959 (*divorce*) Joyce, dau of W Powell, and has:

1g +Mark Nicholas Charles; *b* May 1961

2g +John Damien; *b* 1967

1g *Carey Thérèse; *b* 1959

2g *Joanne Sarah; *b* 1963

1f *Jennifer Clare [Mrs Dudley Wheeler, 31 Friar's Pardon, Hurworth-on-Tees, Co Durham]; *b* 6 Oct 1937; *m* 30 Sept 1961 *Dudley Hastings Wheeler and has:

1g *Clare Frances; *b* 30 Oct 1963; *m* 20 Oct 1990 *Richard Edward Jones and has:

1h *Thomas Edmund; *b* 28 June 1996

1h *Emma Jennifer Lily; *b* 2 April 1998

2g *Alison Mary; *b* 25 May 1966; *m* 27 Aug 1994 *Robert James Havelock Whittenbury

1e Stephanie Lyttelton Antoinette; *b* 18 Feb 1896; *m* 1st 11 Nov 1918 (*divorce*) Walter Sidney Flindall, s of Albert Flindall, of Leytonstone, and had issue; *m* 2nd 1942 Herbert R Wratten, s of Charles Henry Wratten, of Ceylon

2e Muriel Blanche Trelawney; *b* 11 May 1908; *m* 26 April 1934 Stanley John Campbell, s of Archibald S Campbell, of Sydney, NSW, and had:

1f *John Howard; *b* 19 May 1945

1f *Valdene Rae [Mrs Timothy Herold, 6 Denman Street, Warrawee 2074, Australia]; *b* 26 Sept 1936; *m* 20 Dec 1958 *Timothy James Francis Herold, s of Cecil Leonard James Herold and Mrs Herbert Pritchard-Gordon, of Hove, Sussex, and has:

  1g *Richard Anthony John; *b* 6 Nov 1960

  2g *Alastair James Campbell; *b* 23 June 1967

  1g *Philippa Leslie; *b* 9 Oct 1959

  2g *Suzanne Jayne; *b* 10 March 1964

2f *Doronée Felicia [Mrs Peter Gybbon-Monypenny, Tudor Rose Cottage, Robertsbridge, Sussex]; *b* 21 July 1942; *m* 1st 1964 (*divorce* 1974) Clive Murree Perkins, s of W H R Perkins, of Colchester, Essex, and has:

  1g *Amanda Caryll; *b* 11 Feb 1967

2f (cont.) Mrs Doronée Perkins *m* 2nd 1974 *Maj Peter Gybbon-Monypenny, Queen's Regt, and by him has:

  1g *Duncan Reginald; *b* 1975

2d Percival Edward; *b* 3 Aug 1867; *m* 28 Oct 1905 Margaret Edith (*d* 1941), 2nd dau of John Leith, JP, of Aberdeen, and *d* 10 March 1952, leaving:

  1e +John Edward Carolus [John Pole Esq, Gushetneuk, Bieldside, Aberdeen]; *b* 10 Sept 1906; *m* 1 May 1942 *Joan Alexandrina Lamont, 2nd dau of Robert Mitchell, of Aberdeen

3d Clarence Dyke; *b* 6 Jan 1871

4d Clement John; *b* 30 Dec 1872; *m* Lucy Catherine Stringer (*d* 11 May 1951) and *dsp* 30 April 1951

5d Albert Edward; *b* 20 Nov 1875; *m* 30 July 1907 Sophia Buckingham (*d* 1955), er dau of Edward Alexander Buckingham Hay, of Dunbreck, and *d* 22 Oct 1940, leaving:

  1e +Edward Alexander; *b* 7 March 1911; *m* 7 Dec 1940 *Sheila Ferguson, dau of James Welsh, of Glasgow

  2e Reginald Carew; *b* 2 Dec 1914; Roy Signals WW II; *m* 1939 *Mary MacKinnon, dau of R P Don, of Glasgow, and *d* 19–, leaving:

    1f +Reginald Carew; *b* 2 May 1942

    1f *Isabel Buchanan Colquhoun; *b* 5 July 1947

  1e *Annie Laing Hay; *b* 1908

6d Claude Carew; *b* 3 Aug 1877; *d* in infancy

7d Charles Carew; *b* 1878

8d Courtenay Alexander; *b* 1888; *m* 1917 Janet Watson (*d* 1955), dau of James Deans, of Glasgow, and *d* 1967 leaving:

  1e +Reginald Alexander [Lt-Cdr Reginald Pole VRD RNR, Ardfern, 12b Cawdor St, Nairn]; *b* 1920; Lt (S) RNVR WW II, Clyde Div RNR 1946–65, Lt-Cdr RNR, fndr memb RNVR Club Scotland (S V Carrick) Glasgow; *m* 1959 *Dorothy Betty Wallace, dau of David Green Roddick, of Glasgow

  2e Courtenay Deans Carew; *b* 1925; RN WW II; *m* 1951 Aileen Munro, dau of John M Crawford, and had:

    1f +Alan John Carew; *b* 1958

1d Annie Mabel Pole; *m* 1902 Albert Leonard Coomber

2d Blanche Caroline Edith

3d Marie Stuart

3c Arthur Stuart; *b* 16 March 1844; *d* 19 April 1926

4c Henry Lionel; *b* 8 Oct 1846; *m* 1st 22 Dec 1866 (*divorce*) and had:

  1d Edward Lionel Carew; *b* Sept 1868

  2d John Gaspar; *b* 1 Jan 1870; *d* 1928, leaving a dau

  3d Ernest Frederick; *b* 26 Aug 1871

  1d Edith

4c (cont.) Henry Pole *m* 2nd Mary (*d* 16 April 1939), dau of John Warwick, and *d* 10 April 1930, having by her had:

  2d Agneta Aurelienne Buller

5c John; *b* 11 April 1848; *m* 1877 Charlotte (*d* 1896), dau of Rev Robert Pargiter, and *d* 1913, having had:

  1d John; *d* young

  2d (Herbert) Edward; *b* 22 Oct 1882; *m* 25 Oct 1930 Iris Ena Mary, dau of Dr Marsh, MD, and *d* 28 June 1965, leaving:

    1e *Millicent Rosemary [Mrs Peter Cox, Petamille, 3 Park Way, Great Bookham, Surrey]; *b* 23 July 1933; *m* 6 July 1958 *Peter Cox, s of H R Cox, and has:

      1f *Gawen Peter; *b* 21 Sept 1967

      1f *Emma Louise; *b* 25 July 1964

  1d Charlotte Fanny; *b* 29 Jan 1878

  2d Katherine Dora; *b* 23 June 1880; *d* unm 1905

  3d Edith Eveline; *b* 7 Dec 1884; *m* 1922 J F F Folingsby-Walker, of Vicars Cross, Chester, and *d* 21 March 1957

  4d Caroline Mary; *b* 5 April 1886; *m* — Hutchinson. He *d* 1942

6c Charles Francis; *b* 20 Nov 1863; *d* unm 1907

1c Mary Anne Catherine; *m* 2 April 1865 William Douglas Cox (*d* 1905) and *d c* 1900, leaving issue

2c Caroline Jane; *m* 4 Oct 1877 Rev Daniel Evans (*d* 1915), Rector Llanmaes, Glam, and *d* 1926, leaving issue

3c Stephenie Frederica; *m* 8 June 1876 Edward Hilton Glendower Bradshaw and *d* his widow 20 June 1934, leaving issue

4c Edith Buller; *d* unm 1942

5c Ethel Stuart; *d* unm 1947

1a Anne; *m* 20 May 1772 1st Baron Somers (*qv*) and *d* 1833, leaving issue

2a Sarah; *m* Henry Hippisley Coxe, of Ston Easton

1 Urith; *m* Sir John Trevelyan, 2nd Bt, of Nettlecombe, Somerset (*qv*)

The 11th Bt's 7th cousin,

Sir JOHN GAWEN POLE-CAREW later CAREW POLE (deed poll 28 May 1926), **12th Bt**, DSO (1944), TD (1946); *b* 4 March 1902; *educ* Eton and RMC

Sandhurst; Coldstream Gds 1923–39 (ADC to C-in-C India 1924–25, Comptroller to Govr-Gen Union S Africa 1935–36, Palestine 1936, Col), WW II (despatches): Lt-Col cmdg 5th Bn DCLI 1939–43, cmdg 2nd Bn The Devonshire Regt 1944, Col 2nd Army 1944–45, ret 1945; Cornwall: JP 1939, CC 1946 (Chm 1952–63), CA 1954–66, Ld Lt 1962–77 (V-Lt 1950–1962, DL 1947–50), High Sheriff 1947–48; Hon Col Duke of Cornwall's LI (TA) 1958–67, memb: Gentlemen-at-Arms 1950 (Standard Bearer 1968–72), Duchy Cornwall Cncl 1952–68, Western Area Bd Br Tport Commn 1955–61, Centl Tport Consultative Ctee GB 1948–54, SW Electricity Consultative Cncl 1949–52 (V-Chm 1951–52), Jockey Club 1969, Court Fishmongers's Co 1957 (Warden 1966, Prime Warden 1969), chm Devon and Cornwall Ctee Lloyds Bank 1956, dir Lloyds Bank 1956, Keith Prowse 1969, v-chm Westward TV 1960, Nat Hunt Steward 1953–56, KStJ 1972; *m* 1st 12 June 1928 Cynthia Mary, OBE (1959) (*d* 14 March 1977), only dau of Walter Spencer Morgan Burns, of North Mymms Park, Herts, and had:

1 Sir (JOHN) RICHARD WALTER REGINALD CAREW POLE, **13th and present Bt**

1 *Elizabeth Mary [Mrs David Tudway Quilter, Milton Lodge, Wells, Somerset BA5 3AQ]; *b* 14 April 1929; *m* 30 Oct 1953 *David Cuthbert Tudway Quilter, DL, only s of Percy Cuthbert Quilter (*see* QUILTER, Bt), and has issue

2 *Caroline Anne [The Hon Mrs Paul Asquith, 41 Quarrendon St, London SW6 3ST]; *b* 11 Jan 1933; *m* 16 July 1963, as his 2nd w, Hon Paul Asquith (*see* OXFORD AND ASQUITH, E) and has issue

Sir John *m* 2nd 1979 *Joan Shirley [Joan Lady Carew Pole, Horson House, Torpoint, Cornwall PL11 2PE], widow of (a) Maj Jocelyn Arthur Persse, Rifle Bde (*kas* El Alamein 1942), and (b) Lt-Col Francis Edgar Fulford (*d* 1969), of Dunsford, Devon, and *d* 1993

POLE of Wolverton

Arms: Argent a chevron between three crescents gules, a mullet azure for difference. **Crest:** A falcon rising proper, differenced as in the arms. **Supporters:** On either side a lion regardant proper, each debruised by a pale of three colours, the first half per pale gules and argent, the second half azure. **Motto:** *Pollet virtus* ('Virtue excels').
        Creation: Bt. (GB) 28 July 1791.

SIR PETER VAN NOTTEN POLE, 5TH BT, of Wolverton, Co Southampton [Sir Peter Van Notten Pole Bt, 130/60 Kalinda Drive, City Beach, WA 6015, Australia]; *b* 6 Nov 1921; *s* cousin 1948; *educ* Guildford GS and Perth Tech Coll; F/Sgt RAAF WW II 1941–45, company manager (ret), FASA, ACIS; *m* 30 April 1949 *Jean Emily, dau of Charles Douglas Stone, of Borden, W Australia, and has:

1 +PETER JOHN CHANDOS [Peter Pole Esq, 41 Webster St, Nedlands 6009, W Australia]; *b* 27 April 1952; *m* 1973 *Suzanne Norah, BAppSc (MT), dau of Harold Raymond and Gwendolene Maude Hughes, of Nedlands, W Australia, and has:

  (1) +Michael van Notten; *b* 12 May 1980

  (2) +Andrew van Notten; *b* 4 Feb 1986

  (1) *Naomi Suzanne; *b* 20 May 1983

1 *Anne [Mrs Martin Carr, Bridgetown, WA 6255, Australia]; *b* 11 March 1957; *m* 1982 *Martin Paul Carr

Lineage: — van NOTTEN, of Nijmegen, Low Countries (now The Netherlands); had:

PIETER van NOTTEN; *m* Maria Iante van der Stengh and had:

LAMBERT van NOTTEN, of The Hague; *m* Amelia, dau of Nicholas Arnouds, and had:

ABRAHAM van NOTTEN; of Amsterdam; *m* Sarah Susannah Braine, of Braine-le-Comte, Flanders, and had:

CHARLES van NOTTEN; *b* Amsterdam 21 Oct 1702; settled London 1720; *m* 2 May 1733 Susanna (*d* 2 April 1774), dau of David Bosanquet, of London, and *d* 1 March 1750, having had, with other issue:

1 Sir CHARLES van NOTTEN later POLE (sign manual 7 March 1787), **1st Bt** (GB), so *cr* 28 July 1791, of Wolverton, Hants; *b* 14 Jan 1735; *m* 9 Sept 1769 Millicent (*d* Nov 1818), er dau and eventual coheir of Charles Pole (*d* Oct 1779), of Holtcroft, MP Liverpool, 5th s of Samuel Pole, of Radbourne (*d* Feb 1730), and had, with other issue:

(1) PETER (Sir), **2nd Bt**

(2) Charles POLE later van NOTTEN-POLE (roy licence 19 July 1853), of Wyck Hill House, Glos; *b* 16 Nov 1772; *m* 2 Nov 1795 Felizarda Matilda (*d* 26 Jan 1872), dau of Richard Buller, and *d* 8 Sept 1864, leaving, with two daus:

1a Charles Richard, of Wyck Hill House; *b* 27 Jan 1797; *m* 22 Sept 1824 Anne Eliza (*d* 29 Sept 1879), only dau of Edward Rudge, of Abbey Manor, Worcs, and *d* 10 Aug 1879, leaving, with two daus (*d* unm):

1b Charles, JP Devon; *b* 10 Dec 1828; Maj-Gen Gren Gds; *m* 1st Marie Antoinette (*dsp* 1896), dau of J Penrice; *m* 2nd 13 Jan 1903 Ella Cleather, dau of Rev W E Collinson, Rector Watton, and *dsp* 14 April 1909

2b Edward Clitherow; *b* 15 Aug 1830; *m* 1st Mrs Thomas Powell (*d* 1892); *m* 2nd 14 Nov 1907 Elizabeth Elinor (*dsp* 1 April 1910), 3rd dau of Rev E D Ward, Vicar Overchurch, Birkenhead, and *d* 6 April 1922

2a William; *b* 6 July 1798; barrister; *m* 17 Nov 1852 Harriet, 3rd dau of Hieronimus Burmester, and *dsp*

3a Watson Buller (Rev); *b* 20 July 1803; MA Oxon; Rector Upper Swell and Condicote, Glos; *m* 11 Aug 1846 Matilda, est surv dau of **Sir Peter Pole, 2nd Bt** (*see below*), and *d* 26 Sept 1900

4a Mundy; *b* 8 Nov 1804; Maj 46th Regt; *m* 13 July 1841 Anne Frances Pole, widow of Arthur Salwey and only dau of Adml I G Manley, of Manley Hall, Staffs, and *dsp* 30 Nov 1900

5a Arthur Cunliffe; *b* 3 July 1806; Lt-Gen Col 63rd Foot; *m* 13 May 1845 Philippa Maria (*d* 22 Jan 1881), est dau of Maj W M Carew, and *d* 21 Aug 1873, having had:

1b Arthur Charles, Capt 13th Hus; *b* 4 Dec 1847; *m* 29 Oct 1878 Margaret Louisa (*d* 18 April 1928), dau of Sir John Dick-Lauder, 8th Bt (*qv*), and *d* Lucknow 13 Dec 1879, leaving:

1c Margaret Florence; *m* 28 July 1904 David William Milne-Holme (*d* 27 July 1918), of Wedderburn and Paxton, Berwicks, and *d* 20 April 1951, leaving issue

1b Florence Amy; *b* 16 March 1850; *d* unm

2b Philippa Matilda; *m* 1st 5 April 1870 Henry Soppitt (*d* 1886), s of Gen — Soppitt, and had issue; *m* 2nd 20 Aug 1879 Maj WA Hicks, and *d* 23 March 1908, having had further issue

6a Lambert; *b* 9 April 1808; *m* 8 May 1839 his cousin Ann (*d* 22 Feb 1904), dau of Rev Henry Pole, of Waltham Place, s of Sir Charles Pole, **1st Bt** (*see below*), and *d* 1 Dec 1906, having had:

1b Lambert Henry; *b* 30 April 1842; *d* unm 17 Sept 1884

1b Anna Felizarda; *b* 21 Oct 1840; *m* 8 Sept 1868 Thomas William Wedlake and had issue

2b Agnes Geraldine; *b* 17 March 1844; *d* unm 23 May 1909

3b Frances Harriet; *b* 17 Oct 1845; *d* unm 16 March 1932

4b Phillippa Eliza; *b* 28 Aug 1847; *d* unm 26 Feb 1873

5b Edith Matilda; *b* 25 July 1848; *m* 21 Aug 1877 Edward Shepherd and had issue

(3) Henry (Rev); *b* 29 Oct 1781; *m* 14 July 1814 Anne (*d* 10 Nov 1864), dau of John Blagrave, of Calcot Park, Berks, and *d* 23 May 1865, leaving:

1a Henry, of Watermoor, Glos; *b* 20 Nov 1819; *m* 12 April 1849 Eliza Anne (*d* 1878), dau of Rev Watson William Dickens, Rector Adisham, Kent, and *d* 29 May 1906, leaving:

1b George Henry Thomas, of Watermoor, Glos; *b* 8 Nov 1852; Capt 18th Hus; *d* unm 19 Jan 1910

1b Constance Laura; *b* 18 Feb 1850; *m* 29 July 1882 William Reginald Joseph FitzHerbert HERBERT later HUDDLESTON (roy licence 16 May 1922), of Clytha, Mon (*d* 16 Oct 1929), and had issue

1a Frances; *b* 14 Oct 1815; *m* 21 Sept 1841 Rev John William Routh (*d* 25 Feb 1905), Rector Tilehurst, Berks, and *d* 18 Jan 1904, leaving issue

2a Anne; *b* 3 Jan 1817; *m* 8 May 1839 her cousin Lambert van Notten-Pole (*d* 1 Dec 1906) and *d* 22 Feb 1904, leaving issue (*see above*)

3a Agnes; *b* 25 Oct 1820; *m* 1st 16 Oct 1839 George Smith Thornton (*d* 27 April 1868), of Marden Hill, Herts; *m* 2nd 12 June 1869 John Henry Blagrave, of Calcot Park, Berks, and had issue

Sir CHARLES *d* 18 June 1813; his est son,

Sir Peter Pole, 2nd Bt; *b* 20 Oct 1770; *m* 24 Dec 1798 Anna Guildelmina, est dau of Richard Buller, of Cumberland St, London, and *d* 30 Aug 1850, having had, with other issue:

1 Sir PETER POLE later Van NOTTEN-POLE (roy licence 11 June 1853), **3rd Bt**, JP, DL; *b* 11 Feb 1801; MA; *m* 1st 28 July 1825 Lady Louisa Pery (*d* 6 Aug 1852), dau of 1st Earl of Limerick (*qv*); *m* 2nd 24 Sept 1863 Louisa (*d* 4 Feb 1912), 3rd dau of Samuel Lands, HEICS, of Bombay, and *d* 13 May 1887, leaving by his 1st w:

(1) Cecil Charles; *b* Dec 1829; *m* 23 April 1861 Frances Anna (*d* 5 Jan 1921), est dau of Rev Hon Henry Rice, Rector Gt Rissington, Glos (*see* DINEVOR, B), and *dvp* 17 Sept 1876, leaving:

1a **Sir Cecil Pery Van Notten-Pole, 4th Bt**, JP Warwicks, Glos, and Worcs; *b* 30 March 1863; *educ* Mil Coll Oxford; Maj Roy Def Corps and 23rd London Regt TF, Lt and Hon Capt Glos Imp Yeo; *m* 27 June 1894 Frederica Katherine (*d* 14 Jan 1940), 3rd dau of Sir Thomas Freake, 2nd Bt (*see* 1949 edn), and *dsp* 21 May 1948

2a Gerald Charles; *b* 28 July 1866; *d* unm 15 Dec 1947

3a Chandos Edward; *b* 6 Nov 1872; Lt 2nd Dragoon Gds; *d* unm 12 Nov 1947

1a Annie Louise; *b* 25 Jan 1862; *m* 28 Oct 1886 Sydney Fisher (*d* 16 April 1927), of Amington Hall, Tamworth, 5th s of Charles Fisher, of Tamworth, and *d* 12 March 1950, leaving issue

2a Ethel Margaret; *b* 5 Jan 1865; *d* unm 28 March 1957

3a Florence Maud; *b* 15 Feb 1868; *d* unm 20 Oct 1960

4a Cicely; *b* posthumously 24 March 1877; *m* 19 Aug 1897 Arthur William Previté (*d* 27 March 1948), JP, of The Gables, Turvey, Beds, 3rd s of Joseph Weedon Previté, of Blackheath, and had issue

(1) Alice Louisa Chandos; *m* 21 Oct 1862 Rev Charles T Weatherley (*d* 1894) and *d* 14 April 1901, leaving issue

(2) Margaret Caroline Chandos; *m* 28 April 1864 Thomas Baker, of Herne Bay, Kent, and had issue

2 Richard (Rev), of Wolverton and Ewhurst, Hants; *b* 21 Jan 1802; RD; *m* 26 Nov 1836 Elizabeth Anna (*d* 7 March 1894), dau of Richard Elmhirst, of West Ashby, Lincs, and *d* 29 June 1893

3 Edward; *b* 26 Aug 1805; Col 12th Lancers, Gen; *m* 30 Sept 1841 Fanny (*d* 24 July 1857), dau of Col George Grogan, and *d* 3 Feb 1879, leaving:

(1) Edward Albert; *b* 9 Nov 1843; Capt 12th Lancers; *m* July 1866 Emma Catherine (*d* 17 June 1911), 2nd (twin) dau of Maj-Gen Frank Adams, CB, and *d* 16 Dec 1884, leaving:

1a Edward Alexander Chandos; *b* 7 May 1867; *m* 1st 29 Oct 1910 Gertrude Magdalene (*d* 18 Dec 1933), dau of Herbert Emms, of Worcester, and had:

1b Esmé Katherine; *b* 26 June 1911; *m* 21 Sept 1935 (*divorce*) Raphe Willoughby Humphrey (*d* 8 Nov 1961), only s of Ralph Charles Humphrey, of Hove, Sussex, and *d* 1 June 1996, having had:

1c *Ralph Gordon Chandos; *b* 1936

2c Michael Sacheverell Willoughby; *b* 1939; *d* 1984

1a (cont.) Edward Pole *m* 2nd 21 June 1935 *Mrs Evelyn Catherine Remington, dau of Capt E C Smith, of Clacton, and *d* 23 Dec 1945

2a Reginald Adams Chandos; *b* 20 May 1870; *d* unm 2 June 1903

3a George Sacheverell Chandos; *b* 11 Oct 1871; *m* 27 April 1907 Annie Gertrude (*d* 16 Dec 1933), only dau of Alexander Cowan, of Eileanach, Inverness, and *d* 20 Jan 1937, having had:

1b Reginald Sacheverell Chandos; *b* 10 April 1908; *d* 11 Sept 1926

4a Arthur Chandos; *b* 7 July 1874; *m* 11 Dec 1920 Marjorie, dau of Charles Hargrave, of Glen Forrest, W Australia, and *d* 17 May 1944, leaving:

1b Sir PETER Van NOTTEN POLE, **5th and present Bt**

1b *Marjorie Van Notten [Miss Marjorie Pole, 83/60 Kalinda Drive, City Beach, WA 6015, Australia]; *b* 2 Jan 1923

2b Ellen van Notten; *b* 28 Feb 1929

1a Fanny Chandos; *m* 23 May 1907 Ernest Sydney Martin, of Ebworth Park, Glos, est s of Sir Acquin Martin, and *d* 25 March 1939, leaving issue

(2) Reginald Edward; *b* 18 May 1855; Capt Hants Yeo Cav, Maj 3rd Bn Roy W Surrey Regt, and RAF; *m* 3 Nov 1880 Ethledreda Frances (*d* 9 Dec 1935), dau of Rev Alfred Bowyer Smijth (*see* BOWYER-SMYTH, Bt), and *d* 13 Nov 1926, having had:

1a Edward Francis Reginald; *b* 14 April 1884; *d* unm 24 Oct 1909

(1) Louisa Elizabeth; *m* 23 Oct 1884 John Kincaid (*dsp* 17 Sept 1900), of Shortheath House, Wreccelsham, Farnham, est s of Thomas Kincaid, of Glasgow, and *d* 13 Aug 1919

1 Matilda; *m* 11 Aug 1846 her cousin Rev Watson Buller van Notten-Pole (*see above*) and *d* 25 May 1887 aged 80

2 Maria; *m* 19 Jan 1832 4th Earl Winterton (*qv*) and *d* 25 June 1904, leaving issue

POLLEN

Arms: Azure on a bend cotised or between six lozenges argent, each charged with an escallop sable, five escallops vert. **Crest:** A pelican, wings expanded in her nest, per pale or and azure, vulning herself and feeding her young proper, charged on the wing with a lozenge argent, thereon an escallop sable. **Creation:** Bt. (GB) 15 May 1795.

SIR JOHN MICHAEL HUNGERFORD POLLEN, 7TH BT, of Redenham, Hants [Sir John Pollen Bt, Manor House, Rodbourne, Wilts SN16 0EX; Lochportain, Isle of North Uist, Outer Hebrides]; *b* 6 April 1919; *s* cousin 1959; *educ* Downside and Merton Coll Oxford; Capt RA WW II (despatches); *m* 1st 10 May 1941 (*divorce* 1956) Angela Mary Oriana, er dau of Maj Felix John Russi, MC, 5th Royal Inniskilling Dragoon Gds, of Killochan Cottage, Girvan, Ayrshire, and has:

1 +RICHARD JOHN HUNGERFORD; *b* 3 Nov 1946; *educ* Worth; *m* 1971 *Christianne, dau of Sir Godfrey Agnew, KCVO, CB (*see* TYRWHITT, Bt), and has had:

(1) +William Richard Hungerford; *b* 28 June 1976

(2) +Jonathan Charles; *b* 1979

(3) +Andrew Francis; *b* 1982

(4) +Alexander Christian; *b* 1986

(5) Joseph Anthony; *b* and *d* 1991

(1) *Isabel Mary Ruth; *b* 1975

(2) *Alice Charlotte Mary; *b* 1984

(3) *Beatrice Veronica Mary; *b* 1992

1 *Jane Oriana Mary [Mrs Roger Grafftey-Smith, Monks Farmhouse, Sherborne, Glos GL54 3DR]; *b* 28 Feb 1942; *m* 28 March 1962 *Roger Tilney Grafftey-Smith, er s of Sir Laurence Barton Grafftey-Smith, KCMG, KBE, of Broom Hill House, Loddenham, Suffolk, and has had:

(1) *Simon Laurence [Simon Grafftey-Smith Esq, 29E Warwick Sq, London SW1 V2; The School House, Rodbourne, Wilts]; *b* 22 Jan 1968; *educ* Winchester and Exeter U; with Guiness Mahon 1989–

(2) *Max Anthony; *b* 1974

(1) A dau; *b* and *d* 15 March 1967

(2) *Selina Dora [Mrs Charles Faircloth, Flat C, 57B Fulham High St, London SW6 3JS]; *b* 17 Feb 1971; *m* 22 June 1996 *Charles Hooton Faircloth and has:

1a *Felix Hooton; *b* 1 Oct 1996

Sir JOHN *m* 2nd 8 Jan 1957 Diana Alice Jubb (*d* 24 Sept 1995), dau of Albert Edward Timbrell, slr

Lineage: EDWARD POLLEN, of Lincs; settled London as merchant; *d c* 1636, leaving, with two other sons (*d* unm):

JOHN POLLEN; London merchant, MP Andover; *m* Anne, widow of Nicholas Venables and dau of William Bernard, and had:

JOHN POLLEN; MP Andover; *m* 1st Elizabeth, dau of Philip Jackson, of London, and had:

1 Edward; had:

(1) Edward, of New Inn; *m* Elizabeth Welsh and *d* 1775, leaving, with other issue:

1a George (Rev); Rector Little Bookham, Surrey; had issue

JOHN POLLEN *m* 2nd Frances, dau of Edward Exton, and by her had a s (*d* young); *m* 3rd Mary, dau of Edward Sherwood, and by her had, with other issue:

2 John, of Andover; barrister, Judge in Wales, MP Andover 1734–54; *m* Hester, sister of Sir Paulet St John, 1st Bt, MP (*see* ST JOHN-MILDMAY, Bt), and *d* 24 July 1775, leaving, with other issue:

(1) **Sir John Pollen, 1st Bt** (GB), so cr 15 May 1795, of Andover and Redenham, Hants; *m* 1st 1 Feb 1778 Louisa (*d* 18 July 1798), only dau of Walter Holt, of Redenham; *m* 2nd Charity Anne (*d* 13 July 1830), dau and coheir of Richard Southby, of Bulford, Wilts, and *d* 17 Aug 1814, leaving by his 1st w:

1a **Sir John Walter Pollen, 2nd Bt**; *b* 6 April 1784; Col S Hants Militia; *m* 9 Sept 1819 Charlotte Elizabeth (*d* 7 Oct 1877), only dau of Rev John Craven (*see* CRAVEN, E), and *dsp* 2 May 1863

2a Richard, of Lincoln's Inn and Rodbourne, Wilts; *b* 17 April 1786; *m* 14 Jan 1815 Anne (*d* 28 Dec 1865), dau of Samuel Pepys Cockerell, of Westbourne, and *d* 7 Feb 1838, leaving, with other issue:

1b **Sir Richard Hungerford Pollen, 3rd Bt**; *b* 19 Oct 1815; *m* 1st 5 June 1845 Charlotte Elizabeth (*d* 22 Feb 1860), dau of John Godley (*see* KILBRACKEN, B), and had, with other issue:

1c **Sir Richard Hungerford Pollen, 4th Bt**, JP Wilts; *b* 6 Oct 1846; Lt-Col 4th Bn Glos Regt; *m* 8 June 1875 Frances Anne St Albyn (*d* 6 June 1941), est dau of William Savage Wait, of Woodborough, Somerset, and *d* 5 May 1918, leaving:

1d **Sir Richard Hungerford Pollen, 5th Bt**, JP Wilts; *b* 23 June 1878; Lt 4th Bn Glos Regt; *d* umn 18 Aug 1930

2d **Sir John Lancelot Hungerford Pollen, 6th Bt**; *b* 27 April 1884; *educ* Eton; Lt RFA WW I 1916–19; *m* 14 June 1928 Edith Muriel (*d* 2 Feb 1949), dau of Rev John Augustus Lloyd, and *dsp* 14 March 1959

1d Hester Caroline Jessie; *b* 22 Sept 1885; *d* unm 8 Oct 1940

2c Charles John Hungerford; *b* 22 Jan 1858; *d* 8 April 1922

1c Mary Caroline; *b* 25 Sept 1847; *m* 5 June 1873 Rev Edwin George Wyld, of Salisbury, Vicar Melksham, Wilts, and *d* 30 Aug 1911, leaving issue

2c Laura Susan; *b* 30 March 1851; *d* unm 24 Dec 1937

1b (cont.) **Sir Richard** *m* 2nd 29 Sept 1870 Frances Mary (*dsp* 13 March 1932), yst dau of W B Aird, and *d* 8 April 1881

2b John Hungerford; *b* 19 Nov 1820; Fell Merton Coll Oxford, FSA; *m* 1855 Maria Margaret (*d* 18 Jan 1919), 2nd dau of Rev Charles John Le Primaudaye, and *d* 2 Dec 1902, having had:

1c John Hungerford (Rev), SJ; *b* 21 Sept 1858; *d* 28 April 1925

2c Walter Hungerford; *b* 11 Oct 1859; Lt RE; *d* umn 26 March 1889

3c Anthony Cecil Hungerford (Rev), DSC; *b* 22 Dec 1860; Priest Birmingham Oratory, Chaplain RN WW I (despatches, wounded); *d* 5 Oct 1940

4c Francis Gabriel Hungerford, CBE (1919); *b* 25 March 1862; Capt RN, served Sudan 1884–85 (medal with clasp), Burma 1886 (medal) and WW I as Sr Naval Offr Grimsby (despatches); *m* 4 Nov 1890 Flora Mary (*d* 1 Jan 1936), only dau of James Logan Dunolly, and *d* 28 April 1944, leaving:

1d John Francis Hungerford; *b* 8 Aug 1891; Lt-Cdr RN; *m* 19 Dec 1915 Marguerite (Peggy), dau of Sir Frederick Charles Wallis, MB, FRCS, and *d* 15 Dec 1943, leaving:

1e Sir JOHN MICHAEL HUNGERFORD POLLEN, **7th and present Bt**

1e *Susan Mary Nancy [Miss Susan Pollen, By Scarlett's Wood, Hare Hatch, Twyford, Berks]; *b* 7 Feb 1917

2d Walter Michael Hungerford (Sir), MC (1915); JP (Glos 1949); *b* 10 Aug 1894; Capt 2nd Bn Scottish Rifles WW I 1914–17 (wounded twice, despatches), Egyptian Army with Sudan Political Service 1917–26, CC Glos 1946, ktd 1959; *m* 2 Dec 1925 *Rosalind Frances [Lady Pollen, Norton Hall, Mickleton, Glos], 2nd dau of Robert Ben-

---

son, of Buckland Park, Withyham, Sussex, and Mayfair, and *d* 21 June 1968, leaving:

1e +Peregrine Michael Hungerford [Peregrine Pollen Esq, Norton Hall, Mickleton, Glos GL55 6PU]; *b* 24 Jan 1931; *educ* Eton and Ch Ch Oxford; ADC to Govr Kenya 1955–57, with Sotheby's 1957–82 (dir 1961), pres Sotheby Parke Bernet Galleries New York 1965–72, exec dep chm 1975–77, dep chm 1977–82; *m* 26 June 1958 *Patricia Helen, 3rd dau of Lt-Col Gerald Barry, MC (*see* BARRY, Bt), and has:

1f +(Peregrine) Marcus Hungerford; *b* 28 Dec 1963; *educ* Eton

1f *Susannah Hungerford; *b* 5 Sept 1959; *educ* Oxford High Sch and London U; dir Sotheby's; has:

1g *Houghharry; *b* 1996

2f *Arabella Rosalind Hungerford; *b* 22 June 1961; *educ* St Swithun's Winchester and Queen's Coll London; dress designer, novelist (as Bella Pollen): *All About Men* (1996); *m* 1st 1985 Giacomo Dante Algranti, s of Gilberto Algranti, of Milan, and has:

1g *Jesse Gilberto; *b* 1986

2g *Samuel Peregrine; *b* 1989

2f (cont.) Mrs Arabella Algranti *m* 2nd 19– *Hon David Macmillan, bro of 2nd Earl of Stockton (*qv*), and has further issue

1e *Pandora Mary [Mrs Charles Moorhead, Argyll House, Cirencester, Glos]; *b* 11 March 1928; LRCP, LRCPI, late Pncpl Hatherop Castle Sch, Glos; *m* 6 July 1949 Charles Edward Moorhead, OBE, TD, MB, Ch B (*d* following an accident 1 March 1953), s of James Herbert Moorhead, of Bray, Co Wicklow, and has:

1f *Rosalind Mary Catherine [Mrs Dermot Gleeson, c/o M J Gleeson Gp, Haredon House, London Rd, Cheam, Surrey]; *b* 11 May 1950; *m* 1978 *Dermot Gleeson and has:

1g *Patrick Charles Thomas; *b* 1984

1g *Catherine Mary; *b* 1981

2f *Annabel Mai; *b* 1 July 1951; *m* 19– *Hjalmar Schiøtz, of Norway, and has:

1g *Tanja Katrine; *b* 1976

2g *Marianne; *b* 1981

3g *Nina; *b* 1985

1d Mary Margaret; WW II 1940–42 in MTC; *m* 1st 1916 (*divorce* 1928) Maj James Douglas Macindoe, OBE, MC, Scots Gds (*d* 30 Nov 1954), s of James Black Macindoe, of Glasgow, and had issue; *m* 2nd 29 July 1931 Lt-Cdr Keith William Newall, RN (*d* 20 April 1938)

2d Flora Anne; *m* 1st 11 May 1922 (*divorce* 1924) Allan Scott Wilkinson, s of Thomas William Wilkinson; *m* 2nd 20 Dec 1927 Lt-Col Alexander Clarence Harcourt, DSO, MC (*d* 1946), and has issue

5c George Charles Hungerford (Rev); *b* 1 May 1863; SJ; *d* 19 Oct 1930

6c Arthur Joseph Hungerford; *b* 13 Sept 1866; *educ* Trin Coll Oxford (MA); barrister, Coronation Medals 1902 and 1911, Gen Service Medal 1914; *m* 7 Sept 1898 Maud Beatrice (*d* 12 May 1962), dau of Sir Joseph Lawrence, and *d* 28 Jan 1937, having had:

1d Arthur Joseph Lawrence; *b* 13 Oct 1899; *educ* Downside; F/Lt RAFVR, sculptor; *m* 11 Feb 1926 Hon Daphne Baring (*d* 1986), er dau of 3rd Baron Revelstoke (*qv*), and *d* 21 July 1968, leaving:

1e Francis Anthony Baring; *b* 2 Dec 1926; *educ* Downside and Trin Coll Cambridge (BA); Lt Roy Fus, FRIBA; *m* 11 July 1950 *(Marie-)Thérèse (*m* 2nd 1993, as his 2nd w, 7th Viscount Sidmouth, *qv*), 2nd dau of Hon Sir Joseph Alfred Sheridan, LLD, of Nyeri, Kenya, and *d* 1987, leaving:

1f +John Stephen Hungerford; *b* 23 Aug 1959; *m* 1988 *Jacqueline Ann, yr dau of Brian H Caro, of The Old Rectory, Wittersham, Kent, and has:

1g +Francis Arthur Hungerford; *b* 1989

2g +Anthony Oswald Lawrence; *b* 1992

1f *Mary Clare [Viscountess Asquith, The Manor House, Mells, Frome, Somerset]; *b* 2 June 1951; *m* 1978 *Raymond, Viscount Asquith, er s of 2nd Earl of Oxford and Asquith (*qv*), and has issue

2f *Katherine Mary; *b* 25 July 1954; *m* 11 July 1979 *Richard Pflaum, s of George Pflaum and Mrs Robert Elliott, and has:

1g *Dominic Richard; *b* 1985

1g *Julia; *b* 1982

2g *Thea Mary; *b* 1990

3f *Roseanna Mary; *b* 25 Oct 1956; *m* 1984 *Ferdinand Carabott-Tortell and has:

1g *Arthur John Rupert; *b* 1986

1g *Juno Clare Emily; *b* 1989

4f *Mary Louise; *b* 29 June 1969

2e +Patrick Laprimaudaye [Patrick Pollen Esq, Prospect Lodge, Ballyanne, New Ross, Co Wexford, Ireland]; *b* 12 Jan 1928; *educ* Ampleforth and Slade Sch of Fine Art; *m* 26 Feb 1963 *Nell, yst dau of John Murphy, of Sweetmount House, New Ross, Co Wexford, and has:

1f +Patrick Benedict Peter; *b* 12 Jan 1965

2f +Ciaran; *b* 12 Sept 1966

3f +Laurence Joseph; *b* 1968

4f +Christopher; *b* 1972

1f *Patricia; *b* 19 March 1970

1e Cecilia Mary; *b* 2 March 1930; *m* 24 May 1952 *Christopher Robert Hull, yr s of His Hon Sir Hubert Hull, CBE, of Kensington, and *d* 3 July 1991, having had:

1f Maurice Hubert; *b* and *d* 13 Oct 1954

2f *Rupert Teilo David; *b* 16 June 1959

3f *Casper William; *b* 9 Oct 1960

4f *Thomas Richard; *b* 2 March 1964

5f *Simon Paul Timothy; *b* 3 March 1966

1f *Lucy Bridget; *b* 26 Sept 1955

2f *Barbara Margaret; *b* 26 Sept 1957

2e *Lucy Margaret [Mrs Philip Jebb, Beenham Hatch, Bucklebury, Berks RG7 6NR]; *b* 27 March 1932; *m* 10 Dec 1955 Philip Vincent Belloc Jebb (*d* 7 April 1995), est s of Reginald Jebb, of King's Land, Shipley, Horsham, Sussex, and has:

1f *Matthew Hilary; *b* 15 Jan 1958; *m* 1987 *Serena Emma Rose, er dau of Hon Richard Morgan Oliver Stanley, and has issue (*see* STANLEY OF ALDERLEY, SHEFFIELD and, B)

2f *Louis Bernard Alexander; *b* 20 May 1959

1f *Magdalen Marianne Francesca; *b* 9 Oct 1956

2f *Christian Agnes Valentine; *b* 25 Feb 1961; *m* 27 Aug 1993 *Anthony Spence, s of Julian Spence, and has:

1g *George Julian; *b* 12 June 1995

1g *Isabel Alice; *b* 19 June 1994

3e *Mary Rose Catherine [Mrs Hugo Brunner, 26 Norham Rd, Oxford OX2 6SF]; *b* 5 Oct 1940; *m* 7 Jan 1967 *Hugo Laurence Joseph Brunner, yst s of Sir Felix John Morgan Brunner, 3rd Bt (*qv*), and has issue

4e *Margaret Mary Clare [Mrs Patrick Kelly, 23 Charleville Rd, Rathmines, Dublin, Ireland]; *b* 29 Oct 1943; *m* 9 July 1966 *Patrick Hyde Kelly, yr s of Robert Kelly, of Blackrock, Dublin, and has:

1f *Arthur Edmund Campion; *b* 2 March 1971

2f *James Patrick Simeon; *b* 1980

1f *Beatrice Maeve; *b* 4 Jan 1968

2d +John Anthony Lawrence [John Pollen Esq, Lime Tree House, Upper Strand St, Sandwich, Kent]; *b* 12 Sept 1900; *educ* Downside; *m* 8 April 1931 Bridget Gertrude (*d* following a car crash 27 Feb 1956), dau of Maj Cuthbert Leigh Blundell-Hollinshead-Blundell, of Slaugham Place, Haywards Heath, Sussex (*see* 1970 edn ASTLEY, Bt), and has:

1e *Anne Bridget; *b* 12 Nov 1934

1d Margaret Mary; *b* 7 Sept 1901; *d* 4 Aug 1905

7c Stephen Hungerford, CMG; *b* 2 May 1868; ADC to Viceroy India 1890–98, served NWF India 1898 (medal), Staff Boer War 1899–1900 (despatches, medal with six clasps) and WW I (despatches twice), Col Wilts Regt, memb Gentlemen-at-Arms 1919–35, Legn Hon, 2nd Cl Order Nile, Offr Crown Italy; *m* 7 March 1905 Catherine Hetherington (*d* 11 July 1954), yst dau of Sir John Muir, 1st Bt (*qv*), and *d* 25 March 1935, leaving:

1d Stephen Derek Hungerford, MBE (1945); *b* 4 Jan 1908; *educ* Downside and Trin Coll Oxford (BA 1930, MA 1955); Lt-Col RA WW II (despatches); *m* 11 Aug 1944 Marion Kendal (*d* 1990), dau of Thomas Storie Dixson, and *d* 25 Dec 1969, leaving:

1e Anthony Stephen Hungerford; *b* 22 July 1945; *educ* Eton and RMA Sandhurst; murdered by IRA 14 April 1974

1e *Helen Leigh; *b* 29 Dec 1948

2e *Margaret Anne; *b* 5 March 1952

1d *Margaret Edyth Pamela; *b* 24 June 1906; *m* 26 July 1929 (*divorce* 1940) S/Ldr Peter Eustace Burrell, RAF, yr s of Sir Merrik Raymond Burrell, 7th Bt, CBE (*qv*), and has issue

2d *Barbara Heather; *b* 6 Dec 1911

8c Clement Hungerford; *b* 25 May 1869; Lt-Col 1st Bn Kootenay Regt, Canadian Force, WW I; *m* 10 July 1912 Mabel Brenda (*d* 17 June 1964), dau of Alan Southey Dumbleton, of Victoria, BC, and *d* 4 Aug 1934, leaving:

1d +Hubert Clement Hungerford [Maj Hubert Pollen, Green Gates, 3 Dinorben Ave, Fleet, Hants GU13 9SG]; *b* 17 April 1913; *educ* Downside; Maj RAPC, formerly Capt IA; *m* 27 Nov 1954 *Quita, est dau of Alfred Edward Baker, of Salop and Sydney, NSW

1d *Cynthia Brenda [Mrs Ronald Marshall, 7 Mount Terrace, Taunton, Somerset TA1 3QG]; *b* 17 Oct 1914; *m* 14 Jan 1943 Lt Ronald Malcolm Marshall, RN (*d* 1981), s of Malcolm Marshall, of Beccles, Suffolk, and Mrs Montagu Lyons, of Wavendon Fields, Bletchley, Bucks, and has:

1e *(Robin) Michael Hungerford; *b* 24 Oct 1943; *educ* Beaumont

2e *Bernard Mark Sebastian; *b* 8 July 1945; *educ* Beaumont

3e *John Henry Hubert; *b* 3 Sept 1948; *educ* Beaumont

4e *Clement Wilfrid Ronald Pollen; *b* 30 Dec 1951; *educ* St John's, Beaumont

1e *Rosemary Winefride Brenda; *b* 27 Aug 1950

1c Anne Gertrude Mary; nun; *d* 27 Nov 1934

2c Margaret Winifred; *d* 10 May 1937

1b Laura Susan; *m* 15 June 1840 Charles Griffiths Wynne-Finch and *d* 7 March 1851, leaving issue (*see* AYLESFORD, E)

POLLOCK

Arms: Quarterly, 1st and 4th, azure three fleurs-de-lys within a bordure engrailed or, in dexter chief point on a canton ermine a portcullis of the 2nd (for POLLOCK of Balgray); 2nd and 3rd, vert a saltire or between three bugles in fess and in base argent garnished gules within a bordure engrailed, dexter chequy of the 2nd; the whole within a bordure ermine (for POLLOCK of that Ilk). **Crest:** A boar passant quartered or and vert, pierced through the sinister shoulder with an arrow proper. **Supporters:** Two talbots sable, each gorged with a collar or, pendant therefrom a portcullis of the last. **Motto:** *Audacter et strenue* ('Boldly and earnestly'). **Creation:** Bt. (UK) 2 Aug 1866.

SIR GEORGE FREDERICK POLLOCK, 5TH BT, of Hatton, Middlesex [Sir George Pollock Bt, 83 Minster Way, Bath BA2 6RL]; *b* 13 Aug 1928; *s* f 1963; *educ* Eton and Trin Coll Cambridge (BA 1953, MA 1957); 2nd Lt 17th/21st Lancers 1948–49, slr 1956, Hon Fell Roy Photographic Soc (Pres 1978), FBIPP, FRSA, memb London Salon of Photography, late chm London Salon of Photography and Photenrop (UK) Ctee, artist photographer; *m* 7 Dec 1951 *Doreen Mumford, only dau of Norman Ernest Keown Nash, CMG, of Westcott, Surrey, and has:

1 +DAVID FREDERICK [David Pollock Esq, 21 Meare Close, Tadworth, Surrey KT20 5RZ]; *b* 13 April 1959; *m* 1985 *Helena R, only dau of L J Tompsett, OBE, of Tadworth, Surrey, and has:

(1) *Anna-Lisa Frances; *b* 1989

1 *Charlotte Anne; *b* 21 May 1952

2 *Catherine Frances Jill; *b* 2 May 1955

Lineage: DAVID POLLOK of that Ilk; *m* Marion, dau of William Stewart, of Castlemilk, and *d* 1545, leaving, with an er s (John, had issue):

CHARLES POLLOK of Greenhill, Dumfriesshire; *m* Janet Stirling and had, with an er s (John, of Greenhill):

DAVID POLLOK of Lee and Balgray, Dumfriesshire; *m* Jonet Pollok and *d* 1631, leaving, with an er s (Charles):

JOHN POLLOK of Balgray; *m* his cousin Jeane, dau of Robert Pollok of that Ilk, and *d* 1650, leaving, with two er sons (David, of Balgray, *b c* 1631, had issue; John):

DAVID POLLOCK, of Spittal, Co Durham; yeoman; *b c* 1662; *m* 1st Elizabeth Tait and *d* 16 Oct 1743, leaving, with other issue, including an er s (John, Burgess Berwick, *b c* 1705, *d* 9 April 1750, leaving issue):

DAVID POLLOCK; *b* 30 Oct 1740; saddler to GEORGE III; *m* 12 Dec 1779 Sarah Homeria (*d* 7 Feb 1817), dau of Richard Parsons, Dept Comptroller Excise, and *d* 1 Sept 1815, leaving, with other issue:

1 David (Sir); *b* 2 Sept 1780; Ch Justice Bombay, Bencher and Treas Middle Temple; *m* 10 Dec 1807 Elizabeth Gore (*d* 16 April 1941), dau of John Atkinson, of Islington, and *d* 22 May 1847, leaving issue

2 William; *b* 13 Jan 1782; *m* 19 July 1810 Elizabeth (*d* 20 Oct 1810), dau of Doves Egg, and *d* 30 Dec 1816

3 FREDERICK (Sir), **1st Bt**

4 Sir GEORGE POLLOCK, 1st Bt, so *cr* 26 March 1872 (*see* MONTAGU-POLLOCK, Bt)

5 John Henry, of Overndale, Downend, near Bristol; *b* 7 July 1792; *m* 18 June 1833 Frances (*d* 1883), dau of John Worrall, and *d* 9 Nov 1873

The 3rd s,

Sir Frederick Pollock, 1st Bt (UK), so *cr* 2 Aug 1866, PC; *b* 23 Sept 1873; *educ* St Paul's and Trin Coll Cambridge (BA 1806, MA 1809, Fell 1807); barrister Middle Temple 1807, Northern Circuit, KC 1827, Commissary Cambridge U 1824–35, Attorney-Gen 1834–35 and 1841–44, ktd 1834, Lord Ch Baron Exchequer 1844; *m* 1st 25 May 1813 Frances (*d* 25 Jan 1827), dau of F Rivers, of Spring Gdns, and had, with a s (*d* an infant) and dau (*d* unm):

1 (WILLIAM) FREDERICK (Sir), **2nd Bt**

2 Robert John; *b* 4 Aug 1816; 8th Madras Cav, barrister; *m* 1st 6 Feb 1940 Ellen Forrest (*d* 2 Nov 1846), dau of Adml Peter Douglas, and had two daus (*d* unm);

m 2nd 2 May 1848 Julia (*d* 15 June 1914), 5th dau of Rev James Clements, of Haverfield, Yorks, and *d* 7 May 1853, having by her had, with a dau (*d* unm):

(1) Robert Erskine, KC, JP Glos; *b* 29 June 1849; LLB Cantab, Bencher Middle Temple, Dep Chm Glos QS; *m* 11 Sept 1884 Mary Viner (*d* 23 April 1910), only dau and heiress of Capt Frederick Carl Playne, Rifle Bde, of Avening Court, Glos, and *d* 4 Jan 1915, having had:

1a Frederick Robert; *b* 24 Oct 1885; Lt Coldstream Gds; *ka* 23 Oct 1914

2a Martin Viner, of Avening Court; *b* 15 May 1888; *educ* Trin Coll Cambridge (LLB); barrister Middle Temple, Lt 3rd Bn S Wales Borderers; *ka* 9 May 1915

(2) Archibald Gordon; *b* 17 Nov 1851; *m* 17 April 1884 Marian (*d* 22 May 1937), est dau of George Hamilton Fletcher, JP, of Surrey, and *d* 21 April 1937, having had:

1a Hamilton Rivers, JP Wilts; *b* 24 Dec 1884; *educ* Trin Coll Cambridge (MA); barrister Middle Temple, Capt Liverpool Regt, attd RAF, 2nd Chm Wilts QS; *m* 1 Feb 1912 Eveline Morton (*d* 1940), yst dau of Thomas Bell, JP, of Newcastle, and *d* 11 June 1940, leaving:

1b +Martin Rivers; *b* 10 Dec 1914; *educ* Winchester and Trin Coll Cambridge (BA, Sr Scholar 1936, MB, ChB 1940, MA 1951); MRC 1945–65, FRS 1962, Prof Biology Edinburgh U 1965; *m* 12 March 1941 *Jean Ilsley, er dau of Frank Ilsley Paradise, and has:

1c +Julian Rivers; *b* 4 Dec 1942; *educ* William Ellis Sch and Edinburgh U (MA 1967); *m* 6 Sept 1969 *Patricia Diana, yr dau of A/Cdre John Downey

2c +Jonathan Ilsley; *b* 11 Dec 1948; *educ* William Ellis Sch and Edinburgh U; *m* 1980 *Susan, dau of Dr Tom Pollock

1c *Jessamy; *b* 20 Oct 1941

2c *Lisa Jane [Mrs Richard Robinson, 12 Scovesdale, 13 Beulah Hill, London SE19]; *b* 20 Feb 1944; *m* 29 March 1968 *Richard Robinson and has:

1d *Sara Miranda; *b* 18 Feb 1969

1b *Marian Eveline; *b* 22 March 1918; *m* 30 July 1956 *Thomas Edgar Foulkes, s of S H Foulkes, of Upper Wimpole St, London W1, and has issue

2b *Margaret Gordon [Mrs Paul Lendvai, 7/10 Wohllebengasse, Vienna, Austria]; *b* 7 March 1921; *m* 1st 31 March 1943 (*divorce* 1961) Boris Kidel, only s of George Kidel, and has:

1c *Andrey [Andrey Kidel, 2713 O St, NW, Washington, BC, USA]; *b* 20 Nov 1943

2c *Mark Rivers; *b* 6 July 1947

2b (cont.) Mrs Margaret Kidel *m* 2nd 17 July 1962 *Paul Lendvai, only s of Dr Andor Lendvai, of Budapest

2a Reginald Gordon; *b* 9 Nov 1888; *d* umn 11 Oct 1913

1a Venetia Sophie; *b* 14 April 1887

(1) Florence Julia; *m* 5 Aug 1880 Sir Robert Garnet Head, 3rd Bt (*qv*), and *d* 30 Aug 1931, leaving issue

3 George Frederick; *b* 1 June 1821; barrister, Sr Master Supreme Court 1851–1901, Queen's and King's Remembrancer 1886–1902; *m* 18 Dec 1851 Frances Diana (*d* 30 Dec 1891), est dau of Rev Henry Herbert, Rector Rathdowney, Queen's Co, and *d* 19 May 1915, having had, with a s (*d* young) and dau (*d* unm):

(1) Henry Frederick; *b* 9 Feb 1855; MP Spalding 1895–1900; *m* 30 Dec 1879 Phyllis Julia (*d* 1950), only dau of Maj-Gen Arthur Broome, CSI, RA, and *dvp* 2 May 1901, having had:

1a Ralph Charles Geoffrey; *b* 16 Aug 1881; *educ* Wellington and Trin Coll Cambridge; Col 2nd/12th FF Regt IA (joined 1901; ret 1935), WW I (wounded), 51st Sikh FF and QVO Corps of Guides 1916–25, Cmdt 2nd/12th FF Regt 1926–30, AQMC Eastern Cmd 1930–35, reemployed WW II, AAQMG 18th Div Sept 1938–Feb 1940, cmded Mil Mission Norway 1940 (despatches), Head Mil Mission to Czech Ind Bde 1940–43, Order White Lion Czechoslovakia, Cdr St Olaf Norway; *m* 15 Nov 1911 Ruby Weld-Forester (*d* 31 May 1962), dau of Lt-Col Harry Hammersley St George, and *d* 11 April 1945, having had:

1b Harry Guy St George; *b* 30 Aug 1918; *educ* Wellington and RMA Woolwich; Maj RA WW II (wounded, despatches); *d* of wounds 26 Oct 1944

2b (Ralph) John Hamilton; *b* 15 July 1921; *educ* Wellington and Trin Coll Cambridge (BA 1943); Maj RA WW II (wounded, despatches), Liveryman Stationers Co; *m* 1st 4 June 1948 (*divorce* 1955) Patricia Clarice Marion, dau of Capt Arthur Thomas Thompson, Northants Regt, and had:

1c Robert; *b* and *d* 4 Feb 1951

1c *Sally Anne St George; *b* 17 April 1952

2b (cont.) Maj (Ralph) John Pollock *m* 2nd 30 July 1957 (*divorce* 1968) Elizabeth Ormond, formerly w of Robert Martin and dau of Charles Mills Maclean, of Savannah, Ga.; *m* 3rd 1 Feb 1968, as her 4th husb, Lady Zinnia Rosemary (*d* 13 July 1997), only child of 4th Earl of Londesborough (*qv*) and *d* 1980

2a Arthur Jocelyn Coleman, CBE (1941); *b* 14 July 1891; *educ* Wellington and RMA Woolwich; served WW I (despatches thrice, star, two medals), WW II 1939–44 (despatches thrice), Staff Capt Mil Inter-Allied Missions Berlin 1920–26, Brevet Lt-Col 1930, CI Sch AA Defence, Biggin Hill, cmded: RA Treaty Port Irish Free State 1934, 6 AA Regt RA 1936, (as Brig) 41st Anti-Aircraft Group (TA) 1938 and Anti-Aircraft Group E Mediterranean (also Advsr to C-in-C Middle East) 1942, Dir Middle East Div Min Info 1944, Head Middle East Info Dept FO 1946, Maj-Gen, ret 1950, memb Worthing RDC 1950, County Ch Warden CD W Sussex 1954; *m* 25 Jan 1936 *Angela [Mrs Arthur Pollock, Timber Cottage, Warningcamp, Arundel, Sussex], only dau of Patrick Kirwan, of Galway, and *dsp* 19 Feb 1968

1a Nina Phyllis; *m* 17 Jan 1906 Brig-Gen Clennell William Collingwood, CMG, DSO, RA (*d* 5 April 1960), 2nd s of Maj-Gen Clennell Collingwood, RA, and *d* 25 June 1962, leaving issue

(2) Charles Edward; *b* 5 May 1857; Lt, BCS; *d* 8 Aug 1881

(3) William Rivers; *b* 2 Feb 1859; MD Cantab, FRCP; *m* 27 Feb 1889 Annie Athol (*m* 2nd 1 March 1921 Cecil Hugh Myddleton Hughes, OBE, MB (*d* 2

May 1960), and *d* 5 Feb 1958), est dau of James Horne Stewart, of Bathurst, NSW, and *d* 5 Oct 1909, leaving:

1a Humphrey Rivers; *b* 25 Nov 1889; *educ* Wellington and Trin Coll Cambridge (BA 1911, MA, MB, BCh 1920); MRCS, LRCP 1914, Capt RAMC 1915–19; *m* 24 April 1920 Eleanor Violet (*d* 1973), dau of Willoughby Aston Littledale, and *d* 7 Nov 1964, leaving:

1b *Mary Rivers [Mrs Philip Coad, 129 Swan Court, Chelsea Manor St, London SW3 5RY]; *b* 7 Feb 1921; MCSP; *m* 1st 13 Feb 1960 Charles Tristan D'Oyly, MBE (*d* 1981), er s of Arthur Frederick D'Oyly, of Pimlico; *m* 2nd 1990 Philip R R Coad, MC (*d* 1993)

2b *Joan Littledale [Mrs Francis de Hamel, 25 Howard St, Macandrew Bay, Dunedin, NZ]; *b* 31 March 1924; *educ* LMH Oxford (BA 1945, MA 1951); *m* 24 April 1948 *Francis Alexander de Hamel, MD (Otago), MRCS, LRCP, DPH (Lond), DIH (Otago), only s of Maj E A de Hamel, of Salisbury, Wilts, and has:

1c *Michael Alexander; *b* 30 April 1949; *educ* Otago U (MA), MRSP; *m* 1982 *Alison Patricia Holcroft, of Nelson, NZ, and adopted:

*Stephen Wai Lam; *b* 1984

2c *Christopher Francis Rivers; *b* 20 Nov 1950; *educ* Otago U (BA) and New Coll Oxford (D Phil); FSA; dir Sotheby's; *m* 1st 1978 (*divorce* 1989) Christine Leslie Carmody, of Nelson, NZ, and has:

1d *Alexander John Pudsay; *b* 1981

2d *Edwin Willoughby Rivers; *b* 1984

2c (cont.) Christopher de Hamel *m* 2nd 1993 *Mette Tang, dau of Axel Tang Svendsen, of Copenhagen, and formerly w of David Melville Bromby Simpson

3c *Geoffrey William; *b* 12 June 1953; *m* 1981 *Philippa Sarah, dau of Dr Max Nash, of Remuera, NZ, and has:

1d *Adam Culyer Nash; *b* 1983

1d *Jane Sarah Nash; *b* 1985

4c *Richard John Bruno; *b* 10 Aug 1960; *educ* Canterbury U (MSc); *m* 1987 *Philippa Lynne White, MD, of Blenheim, NZ, and has:

1d *Roy William; *b* 1991

2d *James Michael; *b* 1993

3d *Thomas Richard; *b* 2 Jan 1997

5c *Quentin David Humphrey; *b* 11 Oct 1963; *educ* Otago U (LLB); *m* 1991 *Judith Anne Clark, of Christchurch, NZ, and has:

1d *Stephanie Jane Littledale; *b* 1992

2d *Kathryn Anne Taylor; *b* 18 Sept 1995

1a Katharin Diana Rivers

(4) ERNEST MURRAY POLLOCK, 1st VISCOUNT HANWORTH (*qv*)

(5) Bertram (Rt Rev), KCVO (1921); *b* 6 Dec 1863; DD Cantab, Bp Norwich 1910–42, Master of Wellington Coll 1893–1910, Chaplain-in-Ordinary to HM EDWARD VII; *m* 11 Oct 1928 Joan Florence Helena (*d* 1986), 4th dau of Rev Algernon Charles Dudley Ryder (*see* HARROWBY, E), and *d* 17 Oct 1943, leaving:

1a *(Mary) Rosalind Francis Felicia [Miss Rosalind Pollock, Bickers End, Wenhaston, Suffolk IP19 9BU]; *b* 24 April 1931 (HM QUEEN MARY stood sponsor)

(1) Harriet Sophia; *b* 10 Dec 1853; *d* unm Jan 1948

4 Charles Edward (Sir); *b* 31 Oct 1823; Baron Court of Exchequer, High Court Judge; *m* 1st 31 Aug 1848 Nicola Sophia (*d* 15 Nov 1855), 2nd dau of Rev Henry Herbert, and had:

(1) Herbert Charles (Rev); *b* 1 May 1852; MA Cantab, barrister, Canon Rochester, Rector W Hackney; *m* 18 Oct 1883 Flora Grace (*d* 2 March 1942), 3rd dau of John Turner, of Oaklands, Wimbledon Park, and *d* 10 Sept 1910, leaving:

1a Nora; *b* 30 Oct 1884; *d* unm 9 Aug 1968

2a Gladys Nicola; *b* 28 Oct 1888; *d* unm 17 April 1969

(1) Fanny; *m* 2 Feb 1869 Thomas William Bischoff and *d* 9 Jan 1878, leaving issue

4 (cont.) Sir Charles Pollock *m* 2nd 25 Aug 1858 Georgina (*d* 24 April 1864), 3rd dau of Samuel George William Archibald, Master Rolls Nova Scotia, and by her had:

(2) Charles Stewart; *b* 4 April 1864; MA Cantab; *d* 14 March 1890

(2) Joanna de Morlot; *d* unm 14 March 1949

4 (cont.) Sir Charles Pollock *m* 3rd 23 Dec 1865 Amy Menella (*d* 23 Jan 1922), dau of Hassard Hume Dodgson, and *d* 21 Nov 1897, having by her had:

(3) George Hume; *b* 25 April 1870; *m* 25 Sept 1900 Margaret Agnata, dau of Sir Richard Harington, 11th Bt (*qv*), and *d* 12 March 1924, leaving:

1a Charles Harington, DSC (1944); *b* 1 Sept 1906; Cdr RN WW II (despatches); *m* 18 June 1938 Patricia Aileen Domville (*d* 26 June 1957), widow of Capt Leicester Leverin, RCE, and dau of Herbert Payne Heming, of Victoria, BC, and *d* 1983, leaving:

1b *Ann Patricia [Mrs Richard Wallace, Kemps Hill Green, Clavering, Essex]; *b* 15 Nov 1939; *m* 25 March 1961 *Maj Richard Cecil Wallace, RASC, 2nd s of Thomas Wallace, MB, BCh, BChem, BSc, of Cardiff, and has had:

1c *Charles Pollock; *b* 21 Nov 1963

2c *Oliver James Shannon; *b* 1970; *d* 1976

1a *(Agnata) Cecilia [Miss Cecilia Pollock, Quendon Cottage, Quendon, Essex]; *b* 15 Oct 1907

2a *Margaret Georgina [Mrs Richard Gabb, Beverley House, 55 Chapel St, Stansted Mountfitchet, Essex CM24 8AE]; *b* 1 Dec 1913; *m* 3 April 1948 Richard Tresillian Gabb (*d* 1986), MB, BCh, MRCS, LRCP, 2nd s of Harry Secretan Gabb, MB, BCh, of Hastings

(4) Robert; *b* 15 Oct 1874; *educ* Charterhouse and Trin Coll Cambridge (BA 1896); slr 1900; *m* 12 Jan 1914 Ethel Mary Purefoy (*d* 1970), only dau of James Crofts Powell, of Belgravia, and *d* 12 Feb 1957, having had:

1a +Martin James [Martin Pollock Esq, West Crosside, Knowstone, S Molton, N Devon]; *b* 6 Dec 1914; *educ* Charterhouse and Trin Coll Cambridge

(BA 1936); Lt RNVR WW II, slr 1946; m 17 Oct 1942 Pamela Valentine (d 19 Oct 1997), only child of Valentine Leslie Douglas Uzielli, and has:

  1b +Robert Valentine; b 6 Jan 1957;

  1b *Carolyn Alice [Mrs Anthony Henson, Elm Tree House, Tillers Green, Glos]; b 11 Dec 1944; m 1st 19 April 1967 (divorce 1971) (Michael) Bernard Thorold (see THOROLD, Bt) and has issue; m 2nd 1976 *Anthony Edward Henson

  2b *Rosalind Janet; b 30 Aug 1948; SEN; m 8 Feb 1975 *John E Fawkes, er s of Dr M A Fawkes, of Merrow, Guilford, and has:

    1c *Mark Alexander; b 25 April 1977

    1c *Juliette Elizabeth; b 1982

2a Robert Michael; b 21 Dec 1919; Lt Queen's Bays (Dragoons) WW II; d of wounds recd in action 4 Aug 1942

3a +John Charles (Rev) [The Rev John Pollock, Rose Ash House, S Molton, Devon EX36 4RB]; b 9 Oct 1923; educ Charterhouse and Trin Coll Cambridge (BA 1946, MA 1948); Capt Coldstream Gds WW II, assist master Wellington 1947–49, Deacon 1951, Priest 1952, Rector Horsington 1953–58, Chaplain to High Sheriff Devon 1990–91, author: Earth's Remotest End, Hudson Taylor and Maria, Way to Glory, Billy Graham, The Christians From Siberia, Moody Without Sankey, The Apostle, The Master, Wilberforce, Gordon, Fear No Foe, Kitchener: The Road to Omdurman (1998) and other books; m 4 May 1949 *Anne, only child of Sir Thomas Richard Fiennes Barrett-Lennard, 5th Bt (qv)

  1a *Honor Purefoy [Mrs James Priestley, Cottage D, Headbourne Worthy, Hants SO23 7JG]; b 29 Aug 1916; m 9 Sept 1939 *Maj James Frederick Priestley, MC, Coldstream Gds, 2nd s of Hugh William Priestley, and has had:

    1b *Hugh Michael [Hugh Priestley Esq, 52 Stanford Rd, London W8 5PZ]; b 22 Aug 1942; educ Winchester and Worcester Coll Oxford (MA 1964); m 9 July 1968 *Caroline Clarissa Duncan, only dau of Brig John Hume Prendergast, DSO, MC and bar, of Fieldways, Trowbridge, Wilts, and has:

      1c *Alexandra Mary Duncan; b 3 Feb 1971

      2c *Susannah Caroline Louise; b 14 Aug 1974

    2b *Richard James; b 11 May 1947; educ Winchester; m 1980 *Iona Rosalind, dau of Maj Ion Melville Calvocoressi, MBE, MC (see AILSA, M), and has:

      1c *Laura Katherine; b 1982

      2c *Rosanna Victoria; b 1985

      3c *Isabel Louise; b 1988

  1b *Sarah Veronica [Mrs Robert Thorne, Ovington House, Alresford, Hants SO24 0RB]; b 23 Sept 1944; m 1st 19 Jan 1967 Brian David Bond (d 1981), s of Stanley Shaw Bond and Mrs David Willis, of Norton Manor, Sutton Scotney, Hants, and has:

    1c *Michael Alan Shaw; b 5 Oct 1968

    2c *Edward Brian Shaw; b 23 Feb 1970

    1c *Annabel Clare; b 28 Feb 1971; m 1997 *Michael Smyth-Osborn

    2c *Marina Alice; b 1976

  1b (cont.) Mrs Sarah Bond m 2nd 1990 *Robert George Thorne (see PEEL, E)

  2b Julia Elizabeth; b 5 Feb 1952; d 1977

(5) Hassard Hume, MC; b 16 March 1876; educ Charterhouse and Trin Coll Cambridge, Maj RFA (TF) WW I (despatches twice); d unm 26 Feb 1949

(3) Isabel Amy; d March 1936

(4) Helen; b 5 June 1868; d unm 5 Dec 1957

(5) Kate; m 10 June 1893 Samuel Bostock, JP (d 9 May 1938), of Sparshott Manor, Hants, yr s of Samuel Bostock, of Walton Heath, Epsom, and d 9 Nov 1954, leaving issue

(6) Ethel Caroline; b 1877; m 28 June 1905 Lt Ernest SCHWANN later BAGEHOT (deed poll 1917), Scottish Horse (d 20 Nov 1961), s of F S Schwann, of Wimbledon, and d 1974, leaving:

  1a Christopher Pollock; b 5 Feb 1909; m 12 May 1939 *Joan Marjorie [Mrs Christopher Bagehot, 40 Greenford Rd, Harrow, Middx], dau of Alexander Davis, of Nairobi, and d 12 June 1964, leaving:

    1b *Richard Sidney [Richard Bagehot Esq, Beverley, London Rd East Amersham, Bucks HP7 9DT]; b 27 Feb 1941; educ St Mary's Coll Nairobi; slr 1967; m 1 April 1967 *Diana Joyce, dau of Allan Ker, of Nairobi, and has:

      1c *Alexander Scott; b 23 Oct 1975

      1c *Claire Fiona; b 6 June 1972

    1b *Ann Carol [Miss Ann Bagehot, 33 Stanley Ave, Greenford, Middx UB6 8NW]; b 14 Oct 1944

  1a *Mary Pollock; b 10 May 1906

(7) Margaret Homera; b 7 July 1879; d unm 18 April 1940

(8) Gertrude Menella; b 27 Dec 1882 d unm 23 Jan 1972

5 Henry; b 17 Feb 1826; Master Supreme Court; m 2 Feb 1860 Amelia (d 13 April 1919), 3rd dau of Charles Bailey, of Lee, Lynton, Devon, and d 15 May 1889, leaving:

(1) Marion Amelia; m 1st 15 Dec 1892 (divorce 1910) Charles Vernon Boys, FRS (later Sir Charles Boys; d 30 March 1944), s of Rev Charles Boys, and had issue; m 2nd 8 Dec 1910 Andrew Russell Forsyth (d 2 June 1942), LLD, DSc, DMath, FRS, Prof Mathematics Imp Coll of Sci and Tech, s of John Forsyth, and d 1920

6 Frederick Richard (Sir), KCSI; b 12 Jan 1827; Maj-Gen Col BSC, Commr Punjab; m 26 Nov 1856 Adriana (d 12 Dec 1917), yst dau of Sir Nicholas Harris Nicolas, GCMG, and d 24 Dec 1899, leaving, with other issue:

(1) Dighton Nicholas; b 5 March 1864; educ King's Coll Cambridge (BA); barrister, memb Bar Cncl 1926; m 22 Dec 1921 Hon Margaret Anna, er dau of 1st Viscount Buckmaster (qv), and d 9 March 1927, leaving:

  1a +Richard Stanley [Richard Pollock Esq, 20 Porchester Terrace, London W2]; b 26 Nov 1922

  2a +John Dighton; b 9 May 1924

(2) Adrian Donald Wilde (Sir), KCMG (1938); b 24 Sept 1867; Lt City London, City Remembrancer 1903–12, City Chamberlain 1912–43, ktd 1921; m 17 March 1894 Hon Mary Honorah Rhoda Gully (d 21 Aug 1961), 3rd dau of 1st Viscount Selby (qv), and d 21 Aug 1943, leaving:

  1a Anne Stephanie; b 27 April 1896; m 12 Feb 1918 Baron Asquith of Bishopstone (see OXFORD AND ASQUITH, E) and d 19 Feb 1964, leaving issue

  2a Elizabeth Mary; b 3 Aug 1898; m 26 Feb 1926 (divorce 1943) James Cecil Irving McConnel, Res Offrs Scots Gds, est s of James Irving McConnel, of Compton, Surrey, and d 6 Jan 1970, leaving issue

(3) Percy Napier; b 8 March 1875; Army Lt; d unm 10 Oct 1895

(1) Grace Mary Nicholas; m 10 Oct 1876 Edward Child Haynes and d 5 June 1907, leaving issue

(2) Mabel Homera; m 14 April 1894 Maj Lincoln Sandwich (d 12 Sept 1927), 8th Hus, s of Humphrey Sandwich, CB

1 Frances Homera; m 28 Aug 1838 Rt Hon Sir Samuel Martin (d 1883), LLD, Baron Court Exchequer, and d 19 April 1874, leaving issue

2 Louisa Dorothea; m 2 March 1854 Charles Creed (d 1868) and d 11 May 1883, leaving issue

3 Emma; m 25 Oct 1851 Alexander Hamilton (d 25 June 1904), JP, of Inistioge, Co Kilkenny, and had issue

4 Grace Anne; m 21 Dec 1850 Henry Arthur Herbert (d 16 April 1910), s of Rev Henry Herbert, Rector Rathdowney, and d 25 Nov 1914, leaving issue

Sir Frederick m 2nd 7 Jan 1834 Sarah Anne Amowah (d 1 April 1895), 2nd dau of Capt Richard Langslow, of Hatton, Middx, and by her had, with two other sons (d in infancy) and four other daus (d unm):

7 Arthur Julius; b 7 Feb 1835; MD, FRCP; m 21 Feb 1861 Ellen (d 25 Oct 1895), 4th dau of Charles Bailey, of Lee, Lynton, N Devon, and d 11 May 1890, leaving:

(1) Arthur Julius, Capt RA; b 21 Aug 1863; d 28 May 1914

(2) Henry Edward (Sir), KC; b 16 Dec 1864; educ Charterhouse; barrister Inner Temple 1887, Hong Kong 1900, MLC and MEC Hong Kong, ktd 1924; m 5 March 1906 Pauline, OBE (1941) (d 16 July 1960), dau of Henry Oakley, and dsp 2 Feb 1953

(3) Charles Frederick, OBE (1918), AFC; b 17 July 1866; slr, Lt-Col RAF; d 17 July 1919

(1) Caroline; b 4 Aug 1862; m 22 Nov 1893 Thomas William Waller and d 10 Oct 1941, leaving issue

8 Edward James (Sir); b 1 Feb 1841; barrister, Official Referee Supreme Court 1897–1927, FRCS, ktd 1922; m 25 April 1871 Alice Georgiana (d 23 April 1929), only dau of Warren de la Rue, DCL, FRS, and d 14 April 1930, having had:

(1) Cecil Warren; b 28 March 1872; d 21 July 1891

(2) Harold Warren; b 18 July 1877; educ Haileybury and Trin Coll Cambridge (BA 1899); barrister Inner Temple 1901, Lt RAF; m 19 July 1906 Hilda (d 7 June 1952), dau of Henry Warlters Horne, barrister, and d 31 May 1957, leaving:

  1a Warren Dennis Michael; b 11 May 1909; educ Marlborough and Trin Coll Cambridge (BA 1931, MA 1942); m 15 Dec 1938 Elspeth Olive (d 19 Jan 1992), 2nd dau of Ven Harry Sydney Radcliffe, BD, Archdeacon Lynn, of Gaywood Rectory, Norfolk, and d 21 Oct 1986

(3) Douglas Warren, MBE (1919); b 31 Oct 1878; educ Winchester and New Coll Oxford (BA 1901, MA 1911); Lt RE; m 2 Oct 1907 Helene Charlotte (d 3 July 1975), dau of Paul Gadban, of Fairholme, Southborough, and d 23 Nov 1958, leaving:

  1a Jack Warren; b 17 May 1913; educ Winchester and New Coll Oxford (BA 1935, MA 1947); Maj RA WW II; m 23 April 1949 *Hazel [Mrs Jack Pollock, The Bridge House, Shoreham, Kent TN14 7SJ], widow of Maj Howard Bourne, HAC, and est dau of Henry Arthur Hinton, of Shrewsbury, and d 19 June 1981, leaving:

    1b +Nicholas Charles Valentine [Nicholas Pollock Esq, 22 Oaklands Dve, London W12 0JA]; b 18 Sept 1950; educ Winchester, New Coll Oxford (MA) and Southampton U (MSc)

    2b +Christopher James Douglas [Christopher Pollock Esq, 30 London St, Whitchurch, Hants RG28 7LQ]; b 26 April 1956; educ Winchester and Worcester Coll Oxford; m 1984 *Sarah, dau of David Geddes Mitchell, of Iffley, Oxford, and has:

      1c +Felix Alexander; b 1989

      2c +Tobias Frederick; b 1992

      1c *Eliza Madeline; b 28 Jan 1995

    1b *Miranda Penelope Gillian [Mrs Nicholas O'Brien, Hawthorn Cottage, Moushill Lane, Milford, Godalming, Surrey GU8 5BH]; b 4 April 1952; m 1992 *(Brian Edward) Nicholas O'Brien (see INCHIQUIN, B)

  1a Joan Pauline; b 26 Sept 1909; m 8 Jan 1935 Edward Hugh Heath (d 19 Aug 1945), s of Richard Heath, of Yoke Farm, Strood, Kent, and d 11 Aug 1978, leaving:

    1b *Jane Elizabeth [Mrs Bryan Horne, Kenilworth, 138 Stout St, Gisborne, New Zealand]; b 5 Nov 1939; m 3 March 1962 *Bryan Ballantyne Horne and has:

      1c *Fiona Ballantyne; b 22 Sept 1966

      2c *Tiffany Anne; b 8 Sept 1969; m 1992 *Peter Kenneth Jefferies and has:

        1d *Christopher Ballantyne; b 8 Dec 1992

        2d *Joel Bryan Heath; b 11 Jan 1994

      3c *Melanie Hélène; b 27 June 1973

(1) Muriel Agnes; d 4 Dec 1937

(2) Ella Helen; d 3 June 1924

(3) Hilda Mary; d unm 1941

(4) Constance Emily; m 27 June 1906 Arthur Henry Pollock Horne (d 6 Sept 1958), only s of Henry Walters Horne, of Wimbledon, and d 26 Aug 1961, leaving issue

5 Clara Jessie; m 7 Sept 1858 Rt Hon Sir Joseph William Chitty (d 15 Feb 1899), Ld Justice Appeal, and d 6 Jan 1922, leaving issue

6 Anna; *m* 6 April 1874 Maj Charles Richard Cock (*d* 23 Nov 1879) and *d* 24 June 1926, leaving issue

7 Frederica Julia; *m* 20 March 1866 Maj Charles Edward Macaulay, Bengal Army, Assist Commr Punjab, 2nd s of Rev John Macaulay, Rector Aldingham, and *d* 11 Nov 1874

8 Laura Frances; *m* 1st 20 March 1866 Col Charles H Tilson Marshall, Bengal Army, and had issue; *m* 2nd 8 Nov 1878 Col Edward Merry Larminie, RE (*d* 1905), and *d* 4 Nov 1912, leaving further issue

Sir FREDERICK *d* 22 Aug 1870; his est surv son,

Sir (William) Frederick Pollock, 2nd Bt; *b* 3 April 1815; *educ* Trin Coll Cambridge (scholar 1835, MA 1840); barrister 1838, Queen's Remembrancer and Sr Master Supreme Court; *m* 30 April 1844 Juliet (*d* 28 June 1899), dau of Rev Henry Creed, Vicar Corse, and had:

1 FREDERICK (Sir), **3rd Bt**

2 Walter Herries; *b* 21 Feb 1850; *educ* Trin Coll Cambridge (MA); barrister Inner Temple, ed: *Saturday Review*; *m* 11 Jan 1876 Emma Jane (*d* 26 April 1922), dau of Col James Kennard Pipon, Seigneur de Noirmont, Jersey, and *d* 21 Feb 1926, leaving:

(1) Guy Cameron; *b* 6 Nov 1876; *educ* Eton; Lt RNVR and RGA WW I, author and jnlst, managing ed *Morning Post*; *m* 7 Aug 1901 Edith (*d* 21 June 1965), dau of Gen William Lenox Ingall, CB, and *dsp* 1 Feb 1957

3 Maurice Emilius; *b* 28 March 1857; *m* 1st 28 June 1880 Lydia Helen Roberts (*dsp* 1884); *m* 2nd 1889 Mabel (*d* 1937), dau of John Macpherson, of Victoria, and *d* 23 April 1932

Sir FREDERICK *d* 24 Dec 1888; his est son,

Sir Frederick Pollock, 3rd Bt, PC, KC; *b* 10 Dec 1845; *educ* Eton and Trin Coll Cambridge (MA 1870, Fell 1868, Hon Fell); barrister and Bencher Lincoln's Inn, Correspondent Institut de France, Associate Memb Roy Belgian Acad, Prof Jurisprudence Oxford 1883–1903, Prof Common Law Inns of Court 1884–89, ed Law Reports 1895–1935, Judge Admlty Court Cinque Ports 1914; DCL Oxon, Hon Fell Corpus Christi Coll Cambridge, Hon LLD Paris, Cantab, Edin, Dublin, Harvard, Columbia and Oslo, FBA, FSA; *m* 13 Aug 1873 Georgina Harriet (*d* 30 March 1935), yr dau of John Deffell, of Calcutta, and had:

1 FREDERICK JOHN (Sir), **4th Bt**

1 Alice Isabella; *b* 15 June 1876; *m* 1st 10 Nov 1902 (*annulled* 1912) Sydney Philip Perigal Waterlow (later Sir Sydney Waterlow, KCMG, CBE) (*see* WATERLOW, Bt); *m* 2nd 15 June 1912 Orlando Cyprian Williams, CB, MC, DCL (*d* 10 March 1967), s of T Cyprian Williams, of Bayswater, and *d* 28 June 1953, leaving issue

Sir FREDERICK *d* 18 Jan 1937; his only s,

Sir Frederick John Pollock, 4th Bt; *b* 26 Dec 1878; *educ* Eton and Trin Coll Cambridge (BA 1900, Fell 1902, MA 1904); barrister Lincoln's Inn 1907, author and jnlst, served Russia under Russian Red Cross 1915–18, Offr Legn Hon 1947, Order St Anne Russia with Swords; *m* 1st Lydia (*d* 3 Sept 1921), formerly w of Prince Vladimir Vladimirovitch Bariatinsky and dau of General Boris de Hubbenet; *m* 2nd 28 April 1925 Alix (*d* 14 April 1968), dau of Jean Julien l'Estom Soubiran, of Bordeaux, and *d* 22 July 1963, leaving:

Sir GEORGE FREDERICK POLLOCK, **5th and present Bt**

POLTIMORE

DELECTARE · IN · DOMINO

Arms: Or on a bend gu. three mullets arg. **Crest:** A lion's head erased sa., ducally crowned or. **Supporters:** On either side a lion regardant sa., ducally crowned gu. and gorged with a collar gemelle or, therefrom pendant an escutcheon of the arms. **Motto:** *Delectare in Domino* ('Rejoicing in the Lord'). **Creation:** Bt. (E) 14 July 1641; B. (UK) 10 Sept 1831.

THE 7TH BARON POLTIMORE, of Poltimore, Co Devon, and a **Baronet** (Sir Mark Coplestone Bampfylde, Bt) [The Rt Hon The Lord Poltimore, c/o Christie's, 8 King St, London SW1Y 6QT]; *b* 8 June 1957; *s gf* 1978; *educ* Radley; dir Christie's 1987– (Assoc dir 1984–87); *m* 12 June 1982 *Sally Anne, dau of Dr Norman Miles, of The Old House, Caythorpe, Lincs, and has:

1 +HENRY ANTHONY WARWICK; *b* 3 June 1985

2 +Oliver Hugh Coplestone; *b* 1987

1 *Lara Fiona Brita; *b* 1990

Lineage: JOHN BAMPFYLDE; presumably of the family of the same name who held the manors of Poltimore, Devon, *temp* JOHN and EDWARD I; certainly held the manor of Weston Bampfylde, Somerset; *m* Eleanor, dau of Humphrey Beauchamp, and was ancestor in the 10th generation of:

Sir AMIAS BAMPFYLDE; *m* Elizabeth, dau of Sir John Clifton, of Barrington, Somerset, and had an est surv s:

JOHN BAMPFYLDE, of Poltimore; MP Devon 1628–29; *m* Elizabeth, dau of Thomas Drake, of Buckland, and had a 3rd but est surv s:

Sir John Bampfylde, 1st Bt (E), so *cr* 14 July 1641, of Poltimore; MP Penryn; *m* Gertrude, dau of Amias Coplestone and coheir of her brother, John Coplestone, of Coplestone and Warleigh, Devon, and had, with other issue:

Sir Coplestone Bampfylde, 2nd Bt; *m* 1st Margaret, dau of F Bulkeley, of Burgate, Hants; *m* 2nd Jane, dau of Sir Courtenay Pole, 2nd Bt (*see* CAREW POLE, Bt), and *d* 1691, having by his 1st w had, with other issue:

1 Hugh; *m* Mary, dau of Hugh Clifford (last of the CLIFFORDs of Boscombe and King's Teighton), and was *k vp* by a fall from his horse, leaving:

(1) COPLESTONE WARWICK (Sir), **3rd Bt**

(2) John; *b* 1691; MP Devon; *m* 1st Elizabeth (*dsp*), dau of — Bassett, of Heanton Court, Devon; *m* 2nd Margaret, dau and heiress of Sir Francis Warre, Bt, of Hestercombe, and *d* 1750, having by her had, with other issue:

1a Coplestone Warre; *dsp* 1791

1a Margaretta; *m* George Tyndale, of Bathford, Somerset, and had issue

The gs,

Sir Coplestone Warwick Bampfylde, 3rd Bt; MP Exeter 1711 and Devon 1714; *m* Gertrude, widow of Sir Godfrey Copley, Bt, and dau of Sir John Carew, 3rd Bt, of Antony, Cornwall (*see also* POLE, Bt, of Shute), and *d* 1727, leaving, with a dau (Mary, *m* 1st her cousin Sir Coventry Carew, 6th Bt, of Antony, and 2nd William Buller, MP W Looe):

Sir Richard Warwick Bampfylde, 4th Bt; MP Devon; *m* 1 Aug 1742 Jane (*d* 5 Feb 1789), dau and sole heiress of Col John Codrington, of Wraxall, Somerset, and *d* 5 Aug 1776, leaving, with other issue:

Sir Charles Warwick Bampfylde, 5th Bt; *b* 23 Jan 1753; DCL, MP Exeter; *m* 1776 Catherine, est dau of Adml Sir John Moore, Bt, KB, gs of Charles, Viscount Moore (*see* DROGHEDA, E), and was shot dead April 1823 by an ex-servant, Morland, who immediately afterwards committed suicide, leaving:

Sir George Warwick Bampfylde, 6th Bt, and **1st Baron Poltimore**, of Poltimore, Co Devon (UK), so *cr* 10 Sept 1831; *b* 23 March 1786; *educ* BNC Oxford; Col N Devon Militia, Ld-in-Waiting (Lib) 1840–41; *m* 1st 2 May 1807 his cousin Emma Penelope (*d* 24 Dec 1835), only dau of Rev Ralph Sneyd, Precentor St Asaph and Chaplain to GEORGE IV, by Penelope, 2nd dau of Adml Sir John Moore, Bt (*see* above), and had a dau (Emma Catherine, *b* 22 June 1810, *d* 25 March 1835); *m* 2nd 16 March 1836 Caroline (*d* 29 May 1863), est dau of Lt-Gen Frederick Buller, of Pelynt and Lanreath, Cornwall, and *d* 19 Dec 1858, having by her had:

AUGUSTUS FREDERICK GEORGE WARWICK BAMPFYLDE, **2nd Baron Poltimore**, PC (1872), JP, DL Devon; *b* 12 April 1837; *educ* Harrow and Ch Ch Oxford; CA Devon, High Steward S Molton, Maj Devon Yeo Cav, Treas Household 1872–74; *m* 27 July 1858 Florence Sara Wilhelmine (*d* 24 Feb 1909), 2nd dau of Richard Brinsley Sheridan, MP, of Frampton Court, Dorset (himself gs of the playwright), and had, with two daus:

1 COPLESTONE RICHARD GEORGE WARWICK, **3rd Baron**

2 Charles Warwick; *b* 22 Dec 1867; *m* 2 June 1891 Edith Annie (*d* 1959), yst dau of Edward Browne, and *d* 26 Aug 1931, leaving:

(1) Richard Warwick; *b* 30 Dec 1903; *m* 22 Oct 1932 Ethe (*m* 2nd Joseph Sweeney), dau of — Mauris, and *d* 26 March 1942, leaving:

1a *Sonya [Mrs Ronald Lyttle, 1070A Avenue Rd, Toronto 12 Ontario, Canada]; *b* 8 March 1937; *m* 17 Oct 1959 *Ronald Patrick Trevor Lyttle, s of Frank Lyttle, of Lymac House, Letterkenny, Co Donegal

(1) Marcia Warwick; *b* 26 Feb 1893; *m* 22 Sept 1917 Dugald McFarian McCaul (*d* 1961), s of Gilbert J McCaul, of Chislehurst, Kent, and had issue

(2) Edith Warwick; *b* 15 July 1895

(3) Barbara Warwick; *b* 22 Nov 1898; *m* 20 March 1921 George Priddey-Smith and had:

1a *Nigel Derek; *b* 14 Dec 1922

1a *(Ylga) Philippa; *b* 4 June 1924

2a *June Denzilla Haidee; *b* 3 June 1927; *m* 1953 *David Thomas

3 Francis Warwick; *b* 1 Feb 1885; Lt 4th Bn Devonshire Regt, Dist Offr Tanganyika 1920–40; *m* 30 June 1911 Margaret Harriet (*d* 13 May 1968), only dau of Robert Martin, of Belfast, and *d* 22 Dec 1940, leaving:

(1) John Augustus Frederick Warwick; *b* 15 May 1912; Maj 2nd Bn Devonshire Regt (6th Airborne Div) WW II; *ka* Normandy 12 June 1944

(1) *Caroline Warwick [Mrs Caroline James, Springfield House, West Clandon, Guildford, Surrey]; *b* 1 Feb 1920; WW II in WAAF; *m* 1st 3 June 1942 (*divorce* 1951) W/Cdr Dean Lenthal Swifte, RAAF, yr s of Alan Henry Swifte, of Melbourne, Australia; *m* 2nd (*divorce* 1984) 4 Aug 1951 Edward Foster James, CMG, OBE, of the FO, only s of Foster James, of Croxley Green, Herts, and has:

1a *David Peter [David James Esq, 18 Girdlers Rd, London W14]; *b* 1954

1a *Susan Alexandra Caroline; *b* 1952; with FCO; *m* 1979 (*divorce* 1982, resumed maiden name) Timothy Ison

2a *Penelope Sarah (twin) [Mrs Christopher Stewart-Moore, 71 Milson Rd, London W14 0LH]; *b* 1954; *m* 1981 *Christopher Wyndham Hume Stewart-Moore (*see* LLEWELLYN, Bt)

The 2nd BARON *d* 3 May 1908; his est son,

COPLESTONE RICHARD GEORGE WARWICK BAMPFYLDE, **3rd Baron Poltimore**, JP, DL Devon; *b* 29 Nov 1859; Lt 1st Life Gds and Capt Roy N Devon Yeo; *m* 19 May 1881 Hon Margaret Harriet Beaumont (*see* ALLENDALE, V) and *d* 2 Nov 1918, leaving:

1 GEORGE WENTWORTH WARWICK BAMPFYLDE, **4th Baron Poltimore**, JP Devon; *b* 23 Sept 1882; *educ* Eton; Lt Gren Gds, Personal and QMG's staff and

Lincoln Yeo WW I (despatches twice), Maj Roy N Devon Yeo, High Steward S Molton, MFH Dulverton 1920–63 and West Dulverton 1940–65; *m* 1st 10 March 1910 Cynthia Rachel (*d* 6 Sept 1961), only dau of Hon Gerald William Lascelles, CB (*see* HAREWOOD, E), and had:

(1) Coplestone John de Grey Warwick; *b* 24 March 1914; 2nd Lt RHG; *d* 3 Oct 1936

(1) Sheila Margaret Warwick; *b* 26 Oct 1912; *m* 5 Jan 1932 Maj Sir Dennis Frederic Bankes Stucley, 5th Bt (*qv*), and *d* July 1996, leaving issue

1 (cont.) The **4th Baron** *m* 2nd March 1962 Barbara Pitcairn (*d* May 1969), widow of James David Walker and dau of Peter Nicol, of Kirkintilloch, Dunbartonshire, and *d* 13 July 1965

2 ARTHUR BLACKETT WARWICK BAMPFYLDE, **5th Baron Poltimore**; *b* 29 Nov 1883; *educ* Eton; *m* 1st 28 Nov 1916 Catherine Frances Graham (*d* 9 April 1938), dau of Gen Hon Sir David Macdowall Fraser, GCB (*see* SALTOUN, L); *m* 2nd 4 May 1939 (*divorce* 1948) Mabel Violet Blanche (*d* 12 Jan 1957), formerly w of Walter Thomas Meyrick (*see* MEYRICK, Bt), and est dau of Col Arthur Hill Sandys Montgomery, Rifle Bde, of Grey Abbey, Co Down, and *dsp* 10 June 1967

3 HUGH DE BURGH WARWICK, **6th Baron**

1 Violet Marcia Catherine Warwick, CBE (1920); ARRC 1919, DGStJ; *m* 22 Feb 1906 5th Earl of Onslow (*qv*) and *d* 23 Oct 1954, leaving issue

The 5th BARON's brother,

HUGH DE BURGH WARWICK BAMPFYLDE, **6th Baron Poltimore**; *b* 25 March 1888; *educ* New Coll Oxford (BA 1910, MA 1918); Maj KAR WW I, CC Wilts 1937–45; *m* 12 Aug 1918 Margaret Mary (*d* 29 Dec 1981 aged 97), 3rd dau of 4th Marquis de la Pasture, of France, and *d* 26 March 1978, having had:

1 Anthony Gerard Hugh; *b* 2 Jan 1920; *educ* Winchester and RMC Sandhurst; Capt Rifle Bde WW II 1939–40 (POW); *m* 25 Oct 1947 *Brita Yvonne (*m* 2nd 9 Oct 1975 (Albert Norman) Guy Elmes) [Mrs Guy Elmes, Stable Cottage, Donnington Grove, Newbury, Berks], only dau of Baron Rolfe Cederstrom by Hon Hermione Frances Caroline, 3rd dau of 2nd Baron De Ramsey (*qv*), and *d* 2 Jan 1969, having had:

(1) MARK COPLESTONE BAMPFYLDE, **7th and present Baron Poltimore**

(1) *Christine Margaret Hermione [Mrs Joseph Scott Plummer, Mainhouse, Kelso, Roxburghshire]; *b* 19 Oct 1948; *m* 1st 1970 (*divorce* 1977) Peter William Denby Roberts (*see* ROBERTS, Bt, of Milner Field); *m* 2nd 1977 *(Patrick) Joseph Scott Plummer (*see* KINROSS, B)

(2) Fiona Cecilia; *b* 13 July 1959; *d* 4 Oct 1965

2 +David Cecil Warwick [The Hon David Bampfylde, Coombe Lea, Malmesbury, Wilts SN16 9NF]; *b* 3 March 1924; *educ* Eton; Capt KRRC WW II 1942–45 (wounded); *m* 15 April 1950 *Jean Margaret, er dau of Lt-Col Patrick Kinloch Campbell, Black Watch, and has:

(1) +Michael Hugh Warwick [Michael Bampfylde Esq, Tower Farm Cottage, Towerhead Rd, Banwell, Avon BS24 6PQ]; *b* 5 Sept 1951; *educ* Milton Abbey and RMA Sandhurst; late Capt QOH; *m* 24 April 1981 *Sarah Fenella, only dau of Cdr Michael Edward St Quintin Wall, RN (*see* DE MAULEY, B), and has:

1a +Edward David Warwick; *b* 1986

1a *Laura Margaret; *b* 1989

(2) +Richard Ian David [Richard Bampfylde Esq, 31 Fernhurst Rd, London SW6 7JN]; *b* 3 July 1953; *educ* Milton Abbey and RMA Sandhurst; late Capt 15th/19th Roy Hus; *m* 1st 1980 (*divorce* 1989) Sara Elizabeth Spicer, only dau of Maj Kenneth Spicer Few, of Cambridge; *m* 2nd 1990 *Charlotte Mary, yr dau of Lt-Col John Monsell Christian, MC, and formerly w of John Angus Harcourt Gold (*see* 1956 edn TRENT, B), and by her has:

1a *Camilla; *b* 1994

(3) +John Spencer Warwick [John Bampfylde Esq, 56 Ames St, Paekakariki, Wellington, New Zealand]; *b* 3 Nov 1960; *educ* Radley and Bristol U; MBA Cranfield; *m* 1990 *Mrs Nicola Duffain, yr dau of Sir Charles Henry McLeod, 3rd Bt (*qv*)

POLWARTH

FIDES·PROBATA·CORONAT

Arms: Quarterly, 1st and 4th grand quarters quartered, 1st, vert a lion rampant argent (for HUME); 2nd, argent three papingoes vert (for PEPDIE); 3rd, gules three piles engrailed argent (for POLWARTH); 4th, argent a cross engrailed azure (for ST CLAIR of Herdmanston); over all on an escutcheon azure an orange with the stalk erect, slipped proper, and over it an Imperial Crown; 2nd grand quarter, or two mullets and a crescent in base azure (for SCOTT OF HARDEN); 3rd grand quarter quartered, 1st and 4th, gules on a chevron argent a rose between two lioncels combatant of the first (for HEPBURNE of Humbie); 2nd and 3rd, argent three dock leaves vert (for FOULIS). **Crests:** 1 A lady richly attired, holding in her dexter hand the sun and in her sinister a half-moon, all proper (for SCOTT of Harden), 2 Issuing out of a man's heart or an arm from the elbow proper brandishing a scimitar of steel, with cross and pommel of gold (for POLWARTH), 3 An oak tree proper and a horse passant argent, saddled and bridled gules (for HEPBURNE of Humbie). **Supporters:** Dexter, a lion rampant regardant argent, langued gules; sinister, a mermaid, holding in her sinister hand and resting on her shoulder a mirror, all proper. **Mottoes:** 1 *Reparabit cornua Phoebe* ('The moon will replenish her horns'), 2 *Fides probata coronat* ('Approved faith crowns') (for POLWARTH), 3 Keep tryst (for HUMBIE). **Creation:** L. (S) 26 Dec 1690.

THE 10TH LORD POLWARTH (Henry Alexander Hepburne-Scott, TD, DL (Devon)) [The Rt Hon The Lord Polwarth TD DL, Wellfield Parva, Hawkchurch, Axminster, Devon EX13 5UT]; *b* 17 Nov 1916; *s* gf 1944; *educ* Eton and King's Coll Cambridge (BA 1938, MA 1950); WW II as Capt Lothians and Border Yeo; memb Roy Co Archers, rep S peer 1945–63, chartered accountant, ptnr Chiene and Tait, CA Edin 1950–68, Govr Bank Scotland 1966–72 (Dir 1950–72 and 1974–87), chm Gen Accident Fire and Life Assur Corp 1968–72, dir: ICI Ltd 1969–72 and 1974–81, Halliburton Co (USA) 1974–87, Canadian Pacific 1975–86, Sun Life Assur Co Canada 1975–84, Total Oil GB 1975–; Min State Scottish Office 1972–74, Pres Scottish Cncl (Devpt and Industry) 1955–72, V-Ld Lt Borders Regn 1975– (DL Roxburghs 1962–75), memb Franco-Br Cncl 1981–90, Ho Lds Select Ctee Trade 1984–85, Chm: Scottish Nat Orchestra Soc 1975–79, Scottish Forestry Tst 1987–90, Murrayfield Hosp 1982–90; Chllr Aberdeen U 1966–86, Hon LLD St Andrews, Aberdeen 1962, Hon DLitt Heriot Watt, Stirling, FRSE, FRSA, Hon FRIAS; *m* 1st 4 June 1943 (*divorce* 1969) Caroline Margaret (*d* 1982), 2nd dau of Capt Robert Athole Hay (*see* HAY, Bt, of Smithfield), and has:

1 +ANDREW WALTER, *Master of Polwarth* [The Master of Polwarth, 72 Cloncurry St, London SW6; Harden, Hawick, Roxburghshire TD9 7LP]; *b* 30 Nov 1947; *educ* Eton and Trin Hall Cambridge; with Baring Bros Merchant Bankers; *m* 20 March 1971 *Isabel Anna, er dau of Maj John Feville Henry Surtees, OBE, MC, late Lt Rifle Brigade, and has:

(1) +William Henry; *b* 21 March 1973

(2) +Robert Mungo; *b* 16 July 1974

(1) +Georgina May; *b* 11 March 1979

(2) +Caroline Rose; *b* 5 May 1983

1 +Sarah Margaret [The Hon Mrs Macnab of Barravorich, 16 Cupar Rd, London SW11]; *b* 7 Oct 1944; *m* 23 April 1977 *Hamish Macnab of Barravorich, s of Brig J F Macnab, and has:

(1) +Lucy Margaret; *b* 23 Dec 1978

(2) +Clare Sarah; *b* 1980

2 +Diana Mary [The Hon Mrs Bradshaw, 397 Wellesley St East, Toronto, Ontario, Canada M4X 1H5]; *b* 30 June 1946; *m* 30 June 1977 *Richard James Bradshaw, s of A J Bradshaw, of Rushden, Northants, and has:

(1) +James Edward Merton; *b* 5 Oct 1983

(1) +Jenny Alexandra; *b* 1 Feb 1979

3 +Mary Jane [The Hon Mrs James Wilson, 65 Upland Rd, Brookline, MA 02146, USA]; *b* 16 Feb 1955; *m* 7 June 1980 *Hon James McMoran Wilson, er s of 2nd Baron Moran (*qv*), and has issue

The 10th LORD *m* 2nd 8 Aug 1969 *Jean, only dau of Adml Sir Angus Edward Malise Bontine Cunninghame Graham of Gartmore, KBE, CB, and formerly w of Baron Jauncey of Tullichettle (*qv*)

Lineage (of Hume, later Hepburne-Scott): Sir PATRICK HOME of Polwarth, Berwicks (descended from Sir Patrick Home of Wedderburn; *see* HOME, Bt); *m* Julian (*m* 2nd 1613, as his 3rd w, 1st Earl of Haddington, *qv*), 2nd dau of Sir Thomas Kerr of Ferniehirst (*see* LOTHIAN, M), and *d* 10 June 1609, leaving:

Sir PATRICK HOME/HUME, 1st Bt (NS), so *cr* 28 Dec 1625, of Polwarth; MP Berwicks 1630; *m* by 1640 Christian (*m* 2nd by 1656 4th Lord Jedburgh; *see* LOTHIAN, M), dau of Sir Alexander Hamilton of Innerwick, and *d* April 1648, leaving an est s:

Sir PATRICK HUME, 2nd Bt, and **1st Lord Polwarth** (S), so *cr* 26 Dec 1690, with remainder to the heirs male of his body and to the heirs of those heirs (which latter part of the remainder clause was construed as including female issue and heirs thereof by the Ho Lds 1835 ruling; *see* below), as also 23 April 1697 1st EARL OF MARCHMONT, VISCOUNT BLASONBERRIE, LORD POLWARTH OF POLWARTH, REBRAES AND GREENLAW (S), with in the latter case remainder to his heirs male whatsoever, PC (S 1690); *b* 13 Jan 1641; MP Berwicks 1669–74 and 1689–90, Ld Chllr Scotland 1696–1702; held in custody twice 1675–79 by reason of his hostility to the Govt and would have been taken a third time for suspected involvement in the Rye House Plot 1683 but that he went into hiding and ultimately fled to the Low Countries; returned and again was obliged to go into hiding for his part in Argyll's rising on behalf of the Duke of Monmouth and a Protestant succession 1685, hence his titles forfeited, though they were restored him 1690 on his having returned to British shores again in the train of WILLIAM III after having spent the time since his being wanted in Ireland, France, Geneva and Holland; *m* 29 Jan 1660 Grizel (*d* 11 Oct 1703), dau of Sir Thomas Ker of Cavers, and *d* 2 Aug 1724, having had, with other issue:

> 1 Patrick, *Lord Polwarth*, PC (S 1698); *b* 11 Nov 1664; Ld High Treasurer S 1698, Col Scots Dragoons 1707; *m* 1st 2 Dec 1697 Elizabeth, dau of Sir John Hume, Bt, of Hume Castle, Ireland; *m* 2nd april 1703 Jean, dau of 6th Earl of Home (*qv*), and *dsp* & *vp* 25 Nov 1709
>
> 2 ALEXANDER, **2nd Lord**
>
> 3 Andrew, of Kimminghame, Berwicks; *b* 19 July 1676; Ld of Session; *m* 1700 Elizabeth, dau of John Douglas, and *d* 16 March 1730, leaving:
>
>> (1) John; *b* 1711; Army Offr; *m* 1734 Margaret (*d* 17 Aug 1781), dau of William Drummond of Grange, and *dsp* 28 Sept 1738
>>
>> (1) Elizabeth; *m* Charles St Clair of Herdmanston; *de jure* 2nd/11th Lord Sinclair (*qv*) and *d* 12 March 1784, leaving issue
>>
>> (2) Helen; *m* June 1735 Andrew Wauchope of Niddrie and had issue
>
> 1 Grizel; *b* 1665; *m* 17 Sept 1692 George Baillie and had issue (*see* HADDINGTON, E)
>
> 2 Anne; *b* 4 Nov 1677; *m* 1698 Sir James Hall, 2nd Bt, of Dunglass (*qv*), and *dsp* 24 Jan 1699, leaving issue
>
> 3 Jean; *b* 22 March 1682/3; *m* 1703 7th Lord Torphichen (*qv*) and *d* 10 Dec 1751, leaving issue

The 1st LORD's est surv son,

ALEXANDER HUME later HUME-CAMPBELL (following marriage), **2nd Lord Polwarth** and 2nd EARL OF MARCHMONT, KT (Feb 1724/5), PC (S and GB 1726); *b* 1 Jan 1675; *educ* Utrecht U; advocate 1696, ktd 1696, MP (Whig) Kirkwall 1698–1702 and Berwicks 1706–07, Ld of Session as Lord Cessnock 1704–14, Sheriff Berwicks 1714–25, raised troops against Jacobites 1715, Envoy Denmark 1716–21, Ld Clerk Register Scotland 1716–33, Jt Amb Congress at Cambrai 1722–25, rep S peer 1727–34, Govr Bank Scotland 1728–Feb 1739/40; *m* 29 July 1697 Margaret (*d* March 1722), dau and heiress of Sir George Campbell of Cessnock, Ayrshire, and *d* 27 Feb 1739/40, leaving, with other issue (*d* unm):

> 1 HUGH, **3rd Lord**
>
> 2 Alexander; *b* 15 Feb 1708; MP Berwick 1734–60; *m* 16 July 1737 Elizabeth Pettis (*d* 6 Sept 1770) and *dsp* 19 July 1760
>
> 1 Anne; *m* Sir William Purvis, Bt (*d* 18 June 1762), and *d* 2 April 1784, leaving issue (*see* 1970 edn HOME-PURVES-HUME-CAMPBELL, Bt)
>
> 2 Jean; *m* Jan 1743 James Nimmo and *dsp* 10 Oct 1770

The 2nd LORD's er surv son,

HUGH HUME-CAMPBELL, **3rd Lord Polwarth** and 3rd EARL OF MARCHMONT, PC (1762); *b* 15 Feb 1708; MP (anti-Walpole Whig) Berwick 1734–40, rep S peer 1750–84, Govr Bank Scotland 1763–90, Keeper Gt Seal Scotland 1764–94; *m* 1st 1 May 1731 Anne (*d* 9 May 1747), dau and coheir of Robert Western, of London, and had:

> 1 Patrick; *d* young
>
> 1 Anne Hume-Campbell; *b c* 1734; *m* 23 Oct 1755 Sir John PATERSON, 3rd Bt (*d* 14 Jan 1782), of Eccles, Berwicks, and *dvp* 27 July 1790, having had:
>
>> (1) ANNE Paterson, *de jure* LADY POLWARTH in her own right; claimed title 1818; *m* 19 Feb 1778 Sir Philip ANSTRUTHER later ANSTRUTHER-PATERSON, 3rd Bt, MP (*see* ANSTRUTHER, Bt), and *dsp* 11 March 1822
>
> 2 Margaret; *m* 20 Sept 1763 Maj-Gen James Stuart and *dsp* & *vp* 7 Jan 1765
>
> 3 DIANA Hume-Campbell, *de jure* LADY POLWARTH in her own right; *b* 4 June 1735; *m* 18 April 1754 Walter SCOTT of Harden (*d* 25 Jan 1793) (*see* below) and *d* 20 July 1827, having had, with other issue:
>
>> (1) HUGH, **6th Lord**
>>
>> (1) Anne; *b* 10 June 1755; *d* unm 15 Mar 1819

The **3rd Lord** *m* 2nd 30 Jan 1747/8 Elizabeth (*d* 12 Feb 1797), dau of Windmill Crompton, of Hatton Gdn, London, a bankrupt linen draper, and *dspms* 10 Jan 1794, when all his titles bar the Ldship of Parl of Polwarth became dormant, having by her had:

> 2 ALEXANDER HUME later HUME-CAMPBELL, styled *Lord Polwarth* 1750–76; *b* 30 July 1750; *cr vp* 20 May 1776 BARON HUME OF BERWICK (GB); *m* 16 July 1772 Amabell, Countess de Grey of Wrest and Baroness Lucas of Crudwell (*qv*) in her own right, and *dsp* & *vp* 9 March 1781, when his GB Barony expired

The 3rd LORD's gs,

HUGH SCOTT later HEPBURNE-SCOTT (added on inheriting Dec 1820 his cousin James Hepburn of Humbie's estates), **6th Lord Polwarth**, as which rec-

ognised 25 June 1835; *b* 10 April 1758; MP Berwicks 1781–84 (his election for the same constituency 1780 having been declared void; though unseated then, he lost much more than the right to put 'MP' after his name, since his rival for nomination as candidate had been his uncle Sir John PATERSON, 3rd Bt, the last EARL OF MARCHMONT's own favoured aspirant; the EARL accordingly disinherited his gs as regards the family property); *m* 29 Sept 1795 Harriet (*d* 19 Aug 1853), Maid-of-Honour to HRH THE PRINCESS OF WALES at latter's marriage, dau of Hans Moritz, Count von Brühl, Saxon Amb to UK, by Hon Alicia Maria, *née* Carpenter, widow of 2nd Earl of Egremont (*see* EGREMONT, LECONFIELD and, B), and *d* 29 Dec 1841, having had, with other issue:

> 1 HENRY FRANCIS, **7th Lord**
>
> 2 William Hugh (Rev); *b* 11 May 1801; Rector Maiden Newton, Dorset, Preb Sarum; *m* July 1833 Eleanor Sophia (*d* 4 Sept 1853), est dau of Ven Charles Baillie-Hamilton (*see* HADDINGTON, E), and *d* 11 April 1868, having had, with three daus (*d* unm):
>
>> (1) William George; *b* 11 Feb 1841; Cdr RN; *d* 21 July 1881
>>
>> (1) Diana Alicia; *m* 13 June 18– Lt-Col John Almarus Digby (*see* DIGBY, B) and *d* 6 May 1878, leaving issue
>>
>> (2) Charlotte Elizabeth Sophia; *m* 8 Dec 1863 Sir George Hugh Wyndham, KCMG, CB (*d* 10 Feb 1916), of Petersfield, and *d* 18 June 1920, leaving issue
>
> 3 Francis; *b* 31 Jan 1806; barrister; MP Roxburghs 1841–47 and Berwicks 1847–63; *m* 22 July 1835 Julia Frances Laura (*d* 7 Feb 1868), only surv child of Rev Charles Boultbee by Laura, sis and sole heiress of 4th and last Earl of Egremont, and *d* 9 March 1884, having had, with a dau (*d* unm):
>
>> (1) Frances Margaret Julia; *m* 23 June 1874 Joseph William Baxendale, DL (*d* 23 June 1915), and *d* 8 July 1925, leaving issue
>
> 1 Elizabeth Anne; *m* 3 Oct 1835 Col Charles Wyndham (*see* EGREMONT, LECONFIELD and, B) and *d* 21 Aug 1873, having had issue
>
> 2 Ann; *m* 27 Dec 1831 Hon Charles Baillie, Ld of Session as Lord Jerviswood, and *d* 16 Aug 1880, having had issue (*see* HADDINGTON, E)

The 6th LORD's est son,

HENRY FRANCIS HEPBURNE-SCOTT, **7th Lord Polwarth**; *b* 1 Jan 1800; MP (Tory) Roxburghs 1826–32; rep S peer 1843–67, Ld Lt and Sheriff Pncpl Selkirk 1846–67, a Ld-in-Waiting Feb-Dec 1852, 1858–59 and 1866–67; *m* 11 Nov 1835 Georgina (*d* 2 April 1859), sis of 10th Earl of Haddington (*qv*), and *d* 16 Aug 1867, having had, with two daus (*d* unm):

> 1 WALTER HUGH, **8th Lord**
>
> 2 Henry Robert; *b* 6 Jan 1847; *educ* Oxford (MA); Capt E Lothian Yeo Cav; barrister; *m* 10 April 1880 Lady Ada Home (*d* 1 June 1932), 2nd dau of 11th Earl of Home (*qv*), and *d* 4 March 1914, leaving:
>
>> (1) James Cospatrick; *b* 24 May 1882; *m* 28 Oct 1907 Lady Isobel Alice Adelaide Kerr, dau of 9th Marquess of Lothian (*qv*), and was *k* in a car crash 20 July 1942, leaving:
>>
>>> 1a +Michael Henry [Michael Hepburne-Scott Esq, Througham Slad Manor, Bisley, Glos GL6 7AW]; *b* 4 Jan 1909; *educ* Radley; Maj 16th/15th Lancers; Dep Assist Dir Army Legal Servs War Office WW II; *m* 1st 28 Oct 1931 (*divorce* 1949) Frances Elizabeth (*d* 1984), dau of Rev George Victor Collier, of Kingston Blount, Oxon, and has had:
>>>
>>>> 1b David Michael Cospatrick; *b* 4 Dec 1935; *educ* Eton and King's Coll Cambridge (MA); assist master Westminster; *d* 4 June 1992
>>>>
>>>> 2b +Walter Francis [Walter Hepburne-Scott Esq, Pantiles, Beeches Rd, Farnham Common, Bucks SL2 3PS]; *b* 2 Jan 1944; *educ* Eton and St Thomas's Hosp Med Sch (MB, BS 1968, LLB) MRCGP, DObst R COG; *m* 1st 22 June 1968 (*divorce* 1977) Fiona Mary, only dau of Frey Richard Ellis, MD, MCPath, of Epsom; *m* 2nd 1983 *Teresa Gail, dau of Frederick John Major, and by his 1st w has:
>>>>
>>>>> 1c +Henry Walter; *b* 2 Feb 1970; *educ* Reading U; *m* 7 Dec 1996 *Rebecca Ann, dau of Robert Crawford, and has:
>>>>>
>>>>>> 1d *Charlotte Ann; *b* 9 May 1998
>>>>>
>>>>> 2c +George Walter; *b* 13 Nov 1971
>>>>>
>>>>> 3c +Edward Walter; *b* 26 Feb 1974; *m* 8 Oct 1995 *Tania, dau of Harold Pisa
>>>
>>> 1a (cont.) Michael Hepburne-Scott *m* 2nd 24 Nov 1949 *Rohilla Ada May, dau of Herbert A Smith and formerly w of Otto Pelz, of Vienna, and by her has:
>>>
>>>> 1b +Angela Susan [Mrs John Davies, Througham Slad Manor, Bisley, Glos GL6 7AW]; *b* 24 March 1949; *m* 1st 1973 Othmar Schimek (*d* 4 Sept 1991); *m* 2nd 10 Dec 1992 *John Llewelyn Davies, barrister and by her 1st husb has:
>>>>
>>>>> 1c +Othmar Michael; *b* 12 March 1974
>>>>>
>>>>> 1c +Isabelle Alice; *b* 19 Dec 1983
>>>
>>> 2a Walter Schomberg; *b* 14 Sept 1910; *educ* Radley; ARIBA; Capt RE WW II; *m* 15 Feb 1945 Deborah (*d* 1993), only child of 2nd Lt Tudor Ralph Castle, Queen's Roy Regt, and *d* 11 Feb 1998, leaving:
>>>
>>>> 1b +James Ralph Schomberg; *b* 12 May 1947; *educ* Nautical Coll Pangbourne
>>>>
>>>> 2b (Lyulph) Mark Esme; *b* 15 March 1949; *m* 1980 *Jane Anne, er dau of Peter Telford, of Southam, Leamington Spa, and *d* 19–
>>>
>>> 3a Francis William; *b* 8 Dec 1915; *educ* Eton; Maj RASC WW II; *d* 28 May 1992
>>
>> (2) Francis William; *b* 19 Aug 1886; Canadian Engrs, Lt RN; *das* 4 May 1915
>>
>> (1) Lucy Georgina; *b* 11 Feb 1881; *d* unm 24 Sept 1960
>>
>> (2) Mary Helen Charlotte; *b* 21 Jan 1885; *m* 11 Nov 1909 Reginald George Chetwynd-Talbot, CBE, and *d* 29 Sept 1922, leaving issue (*see* SHREWSBURY and WATERFORD, E)
>
> 1 Harriet Frances; *m* 17 Oct 1872 Hon Henry Baillie-Hamilton and *d* 18 March 1925, having had issue (*see* HADDINGTON, E)

The 7th LORD's est son,

WALTER HUGH HEPBURNE-SCOTT, **8th Lord Polwarth**, JP and DL (Roxburghs), JP (Berwicks); *b* 30 Nov 1838; *educ* Harrow; Capt Roy Co Archers, Ld Lt Selkirkshire 1878–1920, rep S peer 1882–1900; *m* 1st 30 Jan 1863 Mary (*d* 13 Feb 1914), est dau of 5th Earl of Aberdeen (*see* ABERDEEN AND TEMAIR, M), and had:

1 WALTER GEORGE, **9th Lord**

2 Henry James; *b* 9 April 1866; *m* 8 June 1893 Elizabeth (*d* 2 April 1940), 3rd dau of T C Booth, of Warlaby, Northallerton, and *d* 4 June 1926

3 George; *b* 15 May 1871; *educ* Cambridge (MA, MD); *m* 10 April 1895 Annie Mary (*d* 9 Jan 1938), yr dau of J C Smith, of Newport-on-Tay, and *dsp* 10 Feb 1942

4 Robert; *b* 1 May 1873; *educ* Trin Coll Cambridge; *m* 28 Sept 1915 Elsa Margaret Berry (*d* 2 May 1961), dau of David Berry Hart, MD, of Edinburgh, and *d* 11 Oct 1950

5 Charles Francis; *b* 18 Aug 1874; *educ* Trin Coll Cambridge; Hon Maj Scottish Horse Boer War 1902–03 and WW I; *m* 12 Jan 1905 Elma, dau of Johnson Driver, of Maryton, Forfarshire, and *d* 30 Oct 1956, leaving:

  (1) Elma Katherine

1 Georgina Mary; *b* 31 Dec 1868; *d* unm 15 April 1947

2 Lillian; *b* 23 Dec 1875; *d* unm 17 Feb 1953

3 Mary Harriet, MBE (1952); *b* 21 May 1877; Deaconess Church of Scotland, missionary India 1905 on, Pncpl Instn for Blind Kalimpong (ret 1952), Hon DD St Andrews 1937, Kaisar-I-Hind medal 1st Cl; *d* unm 15 June 1964

4 Grisell Katherine; *b* 25 April 1879; *m* 25 April 1924 Arthur Thomas Sutton (*d* 15 Dec 1932), s of J Sutton, of Manchester, and *dsp* 17 March 1945

5 Katherine Grace; *b* 19 Oct 1885; *d* unm 27 Jan 1928

The **8th Lord** *m* 2nd 14 Jan 1915 Katherine Grisell (*d* 14 Aug 1938), n of 10th Earl of Haddington (*qv*), and *d* 13 July 1920

His est s,

  WALTER GEORGE HEPBURNE-SCOTT, **9th Lord Polwarth**, CBE (1919), JP (Roxburghs), DL (Berwicks and Selkirks); *b* 7 Feb 1864; *educ* Eton and Trin Coll Cambridge (BA 1885); Chm Gen Bd Commrs Lunacy Scotland 1897–1909 and Prison Commn Scotland 1909–29, Lt-Col and Hon Col cmdg 8th Roy Scots Lothian Regt, Chm E Lothian TAA 1910–20, rep S peer 1929–44, Ld Lt E Lothian 1937–44, Hon LLD Edinburgh 1937; *m* 23 Nov 1888 Edith Frances (*d* 25 March 1930), est dau of Sir Thomas Fowell Buxton, 3rd Bt (*qv*), and *d* 24 Aug 1944, having had:

1 Walter Thomas, *Master of Polwarth*, JP and DL (Roxburghs), DL (Selkirks); *b* 22 April 1890; *educ* Trin Coll Cambridge (BA 1912); Capt TAR Offrs, Lothian and Border Horse Yeo; Ordinary Dir Bank Scotland and Life Assoc Scotland; *m* 3 Nov 1914 Elspeth Glencairn, JP (*d* 5 Aug 1964), 2nd dau of Rt Rev Archibald Euan Campbell, DD, DCL, Bp Glasgow and Galloway, by Helen Anna, dau of 8th Viscount Midleton (*qv*), and *d* 7 Sept 1942, leaving:

  (1) HENRY ALEXANDER HEPBURNE-SCOTT, **10th and present Lord Polwarth**

  (2) +Francis Michael, MC (1945) [The Hon Francis Hepburne-Scott MC, Newhouse, Lilliesleaf, Melrose, Roxburghshire]; *b* 29 Sept 1920; *educ* Eton and King's Coll Cambridge; granted July 1945 rank of Ld of Parl's yr s; Maj Lothians and Border Horse WW II; FRICS, FLAS, consultant ptnr Smiths Gore, chartered surveyors; *m* 8 Feb 1946 *Marjorie Hamilton, only dau of Horatio John Ross, of Biggar Park, Biggar, and has:

    1a +James Patrick [James Hepburne-Scott Esq, Larkhill, Lauder, Berwickshire TD2 6RS]; *b* 21 July 1947; *educ* Eton and RMA Sandhurst; Lt Black Watch (RHR); *m* 1972 *Christian Diana, dau of Maj John Freville Henry Surtees, OBE, MC, of Wylye, Wilts, and has:

      1b +Walter Robert; *b* 1974

      2b +George James; *b* 1983

      1b +Emily May; *b* 1977

    2a +Michael Francis [Michael Hepburne-Scott Esq, Wester Newhouse, Lilliesleaf, Melrose, Roxburghshire]; *b* 4 June 1959; *m* 1984 *Viola Susan, dau of Christopher Heywood, and has:

      1b +Francis Hedley; *b* 1987

      2b +Malcolm Ross; *b* 1988

    1a +Mary Helen; *b* 16 Nov 1949; *m* 1974 *Andrew Godfrey Purvis Sherwood (see ONSLOW, E)

2 Alexander Noel; *b* 14 Oct 1892; 2nd Lt Scots Gds; *ka* 16 May 1915

3 Patrick John; *b* 25 April 1899; *educ* Merchiston and Trin Coll Cambridge (BA 1921, MA 1925); Assist Chaplain St Mary's Cathedral Edinburgh 1930–31, Priest Cambridge Mission Delhi 1931–34, Curate All Saints S Acton 1934–37, Rector St Paul's Wokingham 1937–46, Chaplain to Benedictines of Malling Abbey 1946–48, Rector Kirkley 1948, turned RC 1955; *m* 1st 20 Aug 1925 Cona (*d* 12 Nov 1961), dau of Cyril Fielding-Smith, and had:

  (1) Patricia Mary; *b* 20 Nov 1926; *m* 1 June 1966 Peter Rudolph Ramm, of Lowestoft, and *d* 27 Sept 1995, leaving issue

  (2) +Ann Harriet [Mrs Colin Baxter, Red Tiles, Deanfoot Rd, West Linton, Peebleshire EH46 7DX]; *b* 25 July 1929; *m* 11 May 1963 *Colin Andrew Baxter, WS, er s of Andrew Paterson Baxter, of Edinburgh, and has:

    1a +Patrick Ian [Patrick Baxter Esq, Girwoodend Farm, Auchengray, Lanarks]; *b* 25 April 1968

3 (cont.) The Hon Patrick Hepburne-Scott *m* 2nd 17 April 1963 Margaret Mary (*d* 1982), est dau of Arthur George Riddle, of Harrow, and *d* 1982

1 Helen Victoria; *b* 7 May 1891; *m* 3 Jan 1919 George Freeland Barbour (*d* 18 Nov 1946), DPhil, of Perthshire, s of Rev R W Barbour, of Bonskeid, and had issue (see FERGUSSON, Bt)

2 Margaret Mary; *b* 1 June 1895; *m* 7 Jan 1928 Douglas Benzies (*d* 12 July 1948), 2nd s of Peter Benzies, of Edinburgh

3 Edith Christian; *b* 20 Aug 1901; *m* 30 Dec 1926 Lt-Col George Theodore Herbert Capron, RE, est s of George Herbert Capron, of Southwick Hall, and had issue

4 Grizel Francis Catherine; *b* 28 Nov 1903; *educ* Girton Coll Cambridge; *d* unm 25 Jan 1955

Lineage (of Scott): WALTER SCOTT, of Synton, Selkirkshire; *m* 1st Marjorie, dau of William Cockburn of Henderland, and had a s (Walter, of Synton, *dsp*); *m* 2nd Margaret, dau of James Riddell of that Ilk, and by her had, with three yr sons (William, of Huntly; James, of Satchels, ancestor of the SCOTTs of Satchels; Thomas, of Whitehaughbrae) and eight daus, an est s (2nd in all):

ROBERT SCOTT of Stirches; had charter of the lands of Harden 3 Jan 1501; had, with an est s (Walter, of Synton; ancestor of the SCOTTs of Synton (extinct 1720)) and a yst s (David, living 9 May 1526):

WILLIAM SCOTT of Harden, of which had charter from his bro Walter (confirmed by Lord Home 25 May 1535); *m* —, dau of Ker of Fernielee, and *d* Feb 1561, leaving:

WALTER SCOTT of Harden, of which had charter from Lord Home 18 Aug 1559; *d c* 1563, leaving, with a yr s:

WALTER SCOTT of Harden, called 'Auld Wat'; prominent in border warfare; *m* 1st (contract 21 March 1567) Mary, called 'the Flower of Yarrow', dau of John Scott of Dryhope, and had:

1 WILLIAM (Sir)

2 Hugh, of Greenhead; *m* (contract 17 March 1621) Jean, dau and heiress of Sir James Pringle of Galashiels, and was ancestor of the SCOTTs of Gala

3 Walter, of Essinside; *m* (contract 22 April 1614) Elspeth, dau of John Hay of Haystoun, and *d c* 18 Feb 1641

4 Francis, of Howfuird; *m* 1624 Isobel, sis of Sir Walter Scott of Whitslaid, and was ancestor of the CORSE-SCOTTs of Synton

1 Margaret; *m* Gilbert Ellot (*sic*) of Stobs and had issue (see ELIOTT, Bt)

2 Esther; *m* 1st Elliot of Falnash (for whose early ancestry see ELIOTT, Bt); *m* 2nd George Langlands of that Ilk

3 Janet; *m* (contract 23 Oct 1613) Thomas Scott, s of Walter Scott of Whitslaid

WALTER SCOTT of Harden *m* 2nd (contract 9 April 1598) Margaret, dau of John Edgar of Wedderlie and widow of William Spottiswood of that Ilk, and by her had:

4 Margaret; *m* 1st (contract 12 Sept 1621) David Pringle, Yr. of Galashiels; *m* 2nd *c* 1625 Sir William Macdougall of Mackerstoun (*d* 1629)

The est s,

Sir WILLIAM SCOTT of Harden; MP Selkirk 1641–46; had grants of the lands of Tarras 29 May 1606 and of other lands at various dates; Lt Border Garrison 1617, ktd 1618, Sheriff Selkirk 1625 and 1645; *m* 1st (contract 14 July 1611) Agnes, dau of Sir Gideon Murray of Elibank (see ELIBANK, L); *m* 2nd (contract 15 April 1633) Margaret, dau of William Kerr of Linton (for whose early ancestry see LOTHIAN, M), and by his 1st w had:

1 William (Sir), of Harden; ktd 1660; *m* (contract 26 Oct 1641) Christian, dau of 7th Lord Boyd (of Kilmarnock) (see KILMARNOCK, B), and *d* 2 Feb 1699, leaving:

  (1) William (Sir), of Harden; MP Selkirk 1689–93; *m* 16 March 1673 Jean (*m* 2nd (contract 30 June 1710) Sir William Scott of Thirlestane), only dau of Sir John Nisbet of Dirleton, and *d* 12 Aug 1707

  (2) Robert, of Harden; *m* Jean (*d* April 1718), dau of Sir Thomas Ker of Fernielee, and *dsp* 2 March 1710

  (1) Christian; *m* (contract 24 July 1673) William Ker of Chatto (for whose early ancestry see LOTHIAN, M)

  (2) Margaret; *m* (contract 24 Nov 1680) Sir Patrick Scott, Bt, of Ancrum (*d* 1734; see 1902 edn)

2 GIDEON (Sir), for whom see below

3 Walter, of Raeburn, called 'Wat Wudspurs'; *m* Anne Isabel, dau of William Macdougall of Makerstoun, and was ancestor of the SCOTTs of Raeburn and the author Sir Walter Scott, 1st Bt, of Abbotsford (see 1850 edn)

4 James; *m* (contract 8 Feb 1659) Agnes, 2nd dau of Sir Walter Riddell of that Ilk, and was ancestor of the SCOTTs (later SCOTT-KERRs) of Thirlestane

5 John, of Woll; MP Roxburghs 1693–1702; *m* Agnes, dau of Robert Scott of Harwood and was ancestor of the SCOTTs (later SCOTT-PLUMMERs) of Woll

1 Elizabeth; *m* (contract 18 April 1634), as his 1st w, Sir Andrew Kerr, 1st Bt, of Greenhead (for whose early ancestry see LOTHIAN, M)

2 Margaret; *m* (contract 10 Oct 1638) Thomas Ker of Mersington

3 Janet; *m* (contract 22 Jan 1659) John Murray, s of Sir John Murray of Philiphaugh (*d* 1655)

The 2nd son,

Sir GIDEON SCOTT, of Highchester, Roxburghs; MP Roxburghs 1650; ktd 1660, Sheriff Pncpl 1657; *m* (contract 26 Jan 1643) Margaret, dau of Sir Patrick Hamilton of Preston, and *d* shortly after 5 Aug 1673, having had, with other issue:

1 WALTER SCOTT, EARL OF TARRAS, LORD ALEMOOR AND CAMPCASTELL (all S), so *cr* 4 Sept 1660 in consequence of his marriage, but for life only (a not uncommon means in the 17th century of giving the husb of a peeress of Scotland in her own right a commensurate dignity); *b* 23 Dec 1644; a Commr for the Border 1672, 1674 and 1684; remanded in custody Edinburgh Castle Sept 1684 on suspicion of involvement in plot of Duke of Monmouth (his bro-in-law), tried and found guilty 6 Jan 1684/5, hence deprived of his honours and lands (sentence annulled 22 July 1690); supported Glorious Revolution 1688; Commr of Supply 1690; *m* 1st 9 Feb 1658/9 Mary, Countess of Buccleuch in her own right (see BUCCLEUCH and QUEENSBERRY, D); *m* 2nd 31 Dec 1677 Helen, dau of Thomas Hepburn(e) of Humbie, E Lothian, and *d* 9 April 1693, leaving by her:

  (1) Gideon, of Highchester; *b* 18 Oct 1678; *m* 1st (contract 5 Nov 1697) Anne (*dsp*), dau of Sir Francis Kinloch, 1st Bt, of Gilmerton (*qv*); *m* 2nd 28 Feb 1700 Lady Mary Drummond (*m* 2nd Sir James Sharp, 2nd Bt (see 1970 edn SHARP BETHUNE, Bt); *d* 11 Oct 1754), dau of 1st Earl of Melfort (see PERTH, E), and *d* 1707, having by her had, with a dau (*d* unm):

    1a Walter, of Harden; *s* his cousin Robert 1710 (see above) and *dsp* 13 Nov 1719

    2a John, of Harden; *m* 1719 Lady Jean Erskine (*d* 17 July 1735), dau of 4th Earl of Kellie (see MAR and KELLIE, E), and *d* June 1734, having by her had two daus

  (2) Walter, of Harden; *b* 6 Jan 1682; *m* 1st (contract 7 April 1709) Agnes (*dsp*), dau of John Nisbet of Nisbetfield; *m* 2nd 10 July 1719 Agnes, dau of William Scott of Thirlestane, and by her had:

    1a Christian; *b* 4 July 1721

  (2) (cont.) Walter Scott of Harden *m* 3rd (contract 13 Feb 1724) Ann, dau of John Scott of Gorranberry, and by her had, with other issue:

1a Walter, of Harden; *b* 31 Dec 1724; MP Roxburghs 1747–65, Receiver-Gen Customs 1765; *m* 18 April 1754 Diana, 3rd dau of **3rd Lord Polwarth** (*see* above)

2a Francis, of Beechwood; *b* 7 Feb 1732; *m* 28 March 1776 Mary (*d* 8 April 1819), dau of Sir Alexander Don, Bt, of Newton, and *d* 4 Aug 1803, leaving issue

(2) (cont.) Walter Scott of Harden *m* 4th (contract 5 Oct 1736) Christian (*dsp*), dau of Henry Ker of Frogdean, and *d* Jan 1746

(1) Margaret; *b* 19 Oct 1690; *m* 1708 Thomas Gordon, 3rd s of William Gordon, Lt in Col Wood's Regt of Foot

1 Agnes; *m* (contract 17 Dec 1659) John Riddell, Yr. of Riddell

2 Margaret; *m* 11 Feb 1679 James Corbet, Yr. of Tolcorse

3 Agnes; *m* 1st 8 April 1687 Sir James Grant, 1st Bt, of Dalvey (*qv*); *m* 2nd Dr William Rutherford, of Barnhills

PONSONBY

Arms: Gules a chevron between three combs argent. **Crest:** Out of a ducal coronet or three arrows, points downwards, one in pale and two in saltire, entwined at the intersection by a snake proper.
Motto: *Pro rege, lege, grege* ('For king, law and common people').
Creation: Bt. (UK) 27 Jan 1956.

SIR ASHLEY CHARLES GIBBS PONSONBY, 2ND BT, KCVO (1993), MC (1945), of Wootton, Co Oxford [Sir Ashley Ponsonby Bt KCVO MC, Woodleys, Woodstock, Oxon OX20 1HJ]; *b* 21 Feb 1921; *s f* 1976; *educ* Eton and Balliol Coll Oxford; Capt Coldstream Gds 1943 WW II (wounded), on Staff Bermuda Garrison 1945–46, md J Henry Schroder Wagg, Church Commr 1963, Ld Lt Oxon 1980–96 (DL 1974–80), KStJ 1989; *m* 14 Sept 1950 *Lady Martha Butler, yr dau of 6th Marquess of Ormonde (*see* 1970 edn), and has:

1 +CHARLES ASHLEY [Charles Ponsonby Esq, Grims Dyke Farm, Woodstock, Oxon OX20 1HJ]; *b* 10 June 1951; *educ* Eton and Ch Ch Oxford (MA); *m* 1983 *Mary Priscilla, yr dau of A R Bromley Davenport, of Over Peover, Knutsford, Cheshire, and has:

(1) +Arthur Ashley; *b* 15 Sept 1984

(2) +Frederick Edward; *b* 1986

(1) *Alice Elizabeth; *b* 1988

2 +Rupert Spencer; *b* 8 Feb 1953; *educ* Eton and Reading U; *m* 1985 *Amanda, MBE, er dau of Michael Keith Beale Colvin, MP (*see* CAYZER, B), and has:

(1) +George Edward Michael; *b* 1996

(1) *Emily Mary; *b* 1990

(2) *Eleanor Rose; *b* 1993

3 +Luke Arthur; *b* 15 July 1957; *educ* Eton; *m* 1985 *Nicola J, yr dau of Gen Sir Roland Kelvin Guy, KCB, CBE, DSO, of Stourpaine, Dorset, and has:

(1) +Edmund (Ned) Brabazon; *b* 1989

(2) +William Roland Ashley; *b* 10 Sept 1995

(1) *Lucy India Clare; *b* 1991

4 +John Piers; *b* 26 June 1962; *educ* Eton and Gonville and Caius Coll, Cambridge; *m* 1994 *Serena N, dau of Robert Marshall, of Nairobi, and has:

(1) +James Robert Edwin; *b* 20 Jan 1997

(2) +Henry (Harry) Alexander; *b* 1 Feb 1998

Lineage: The Hon EDWIN PONSONBY (*see* DE MAULEY, B); had an est s:

Sir Charles Edward Ponsonby, 1st Bt (UK), so *cr* 27 Jan 1956, TD, DL (Oxon 1944); *b* 2 Sept 1879; *educ* Eton and Balliol Coll Oxford (BA 1901); served WW I (wounded), Col and Brevet-Col 97th (Kent Yeo) Field Bde RA 1930–36, MP (C) Sevenoaks 1935–50, Hon Col 297th (Kent Yeo) Light AA Regt 1942–49, Croix de Guerre, PPS to Sec State War 1940 and For Sec 1941–45; *m* 23 July 1912 Hon Winifred Gibbs, JP (*d* 1984), est dau of 1st Baron Hunsdon of Hunsdon (*see* ALDENHAM and HUNSDON OF HUNSDON, B), and *d* 1976, leaving:

1 Sir ASHLEY CHARLES GIBBS PONSONBY, **2nd and present Bt**

1 *Pricilla Dora [Priscilla Lady Bacon, Orchards, Raveningham, Norwich NR14 6NS]; *b* 1913; *m* 15 Jan 1936 Sir Edward Castell Bacon, 14th Bt (*qv*), and has issue

2 *Diana Mary [Mrs Mark Meynell, 2 Double St, Framlingham, Suffolk IP13 9BN]; *b* 1916; *m* 4 July 1940 *Rev Canon Mark Meynell (*see* HALIFAX, E) and has issue

3 *Lavinia Rosalind [Lady Hamilton, Lordington House, Chichester, W Sussex PO18 9DX]; *b* 1919; *m* 16 May 1947 *Sir Michael Aubrey Hamilton, MP, er s of Bp Eric Knightly Chetwode Hamilton, KCVO, and has:

(1) *John Ashley; *b* 5 Feb 1948; *educ* Eton and Univ Coll Oxford; *m* 1975 *Audrey Carola, only dau of Capt Nigel William Ivo Naper (*see* VALENTIA, V), and has:

1a *Mark Emmanuel Naper; *b* 1979

2a *Robin Michael Elijah; *b* 1982

3a *Oliver Salvador John; *b* 1984

1a *Meg Rosaleen Gabriel; *b* 1977

(1) *Caroline Mary; *b* 8 May 1950; *m* 1980 *Stephen M Codner, s of John Codner, of Breadstone House, Glos, and has:

1a *Jesse Anne; *b* 1981

2a *Rose Elizabeth; *b* 1983

3a *Alice Mary; *b* 1989

(2) *Susanna; *b* 16 May 1954; *m* 1982 *Rufus Anthony Reade and has:

1a *Benedict; *b* 1984

1a *Hannah; *b* 1988

(3) *Jane Lavinia; *b* 24 April 1958; *m* 1984 *Garth K P Watkins and has:

1a *Jonathan Michael; *b* 1986

2a *Simon Alexander; *b* 1988

4 *Juliet Barbara Anna [Mrs James Ramsden, Old Sleningford Hall, Ripon, N Yorks HG4 3SD]; *b* 1923; *m* 25 June 1949 *James Edward Ramsden, PC, MP, only s of Capt Edward Ramsden, MC, JP, of Breckamore Hall, Ripon, and has:

(1) *Thomas James Ponsonby; *b* 20 Dec 1950; *educ* Eton; *m* 1983 *Jane Ann, yr dau of John Eustice, of Omaha, Neb., and has:

1a *James Thomas Eustice; *b* 1985

2a *Matthew John; *b* 1987

3a *William Joseph; *b* 1990

1a *Mary Juliet Eustice; *b* 1984

(2) *George Edward [George Ramsden Esq, The Old Rectory, Settrington, N Yorks]; *b* 12 June 1953; *educ* Eton; *m* 1986 *Jane Slane Sloan, er dau of Rev William Thompson, of Oxnam Manse, Jedburgh, Roxburghs, and formerly w of Anthony Charles Vaughan Wynn (*see* NEWBOROUGH, B), and has:

1a *Edward William; *b* 1989

1a *Laura Vida; *b* 1988

2a *Juliet Charlotte Rose; *b* 1992

(3) *Richard Ashley [Richard Ramsden Esq, 10 Michael Fields, Forest Row, E Sussex RH18 5BH]; *b* 14 June 1954; *educ* Eton; *m* 1978 *Kristin Maria, only dau of John Waldroup, of Carmel, Calif., and has:

1a *Thalia; *b* 1985

2a *Marika; *b* 1986

3a *Kaelyn; *b* 1988

(1) *Emma Juliet Geraldine [Mrs John Oliver, Spindrift, Otters Creek, Zeeköevleï, Cape Town 7945, S Africa]; *b* 5 June 1957; *m* 1981 *Rev John G W Oliver, only s of G F Oliver, MBE, and has:

1a *Sarah; *b* 1993

(2) Charlotte Mary Rose; *b* 16 Jan 1960; *m* 1982 Mark Lawrence Cheverton, yr s of Rev David Cheverton, of Cruachan Cottage, Preston-under-Scar, Yorks, and was *k* with her husband in a car crash 1991

PONSONBY OF SHULBREDE

Arms: Gules a chevron between three combs argent. **Crest:** Out of a ducal coronet azure three arrows, one in pale and two in saltire, points downwards, entwined by a snake proper.
Motto: *Pro rege, lege, grege* ('For king, law and common people').
Creation: B. (UK) 17 Jan 1930.

THE 4TH BARON PONSONBY OF SHULBREDE, of Shulbrede, Co Sussex (Frederick Matthew Thomas Ponsonby) [The Rt Hon The Lord Ponsonby of Shulbrede, House of Lords, London SW1A 0PW]; *b* 27 Oct 1958; *s f* 1990; *educ* Holland Pk Comprehensive, Cardiff U and Imperial Coll London; Cncllr (Lab) Wandsworth 1990–94; Oppn Frontbench Spokesman Educn Ho Lds 1992–97, deleg Cncl Europe and WEU 1997–; FIMM 1996, CEng 1997

Lineage: ARTHUR AUGUSTUS WILLIAM HARRY PONSONBY, **1st Baron Ponsonby of Shulbrede**, of Shulbrede, Co Sussex (UK), so *cr* 17 Jan 1930, JP (W Sussex); *b* 16 Feb 1871 (yst s of Gen Sir Henry Frederick Ponsonby, GCB, PC; *see* BESSBOROUGH, E); *educ* Eton and Balliol Coll Oxford; Page of Honour to HM QUEEN VICTORIA 1882–87, Dip Serv 1894–1903 (Constantinople 1894–97, Copenhagen 1899–99, FO 1900–02), Priv Sec to PM 1905–07, MP (Lib) Stirling Burghs 1908–18 and (Lab) Sheffield Brightside 1922–30 (fought Taunton 1906 and Dunfermline Burghs 1918, both as Lib), Parly U-Sec: For Affrs Jan–Nov 1924 and Dominion Affairs July-Dec 1929, Parly Sec Min Tport 1929–31, Chllr Duchy Lancaster March-Aug 1931, Ldr Oppn Ho Lds 1931–35, memb cncl RCM, author: *The Camel and the Needle's Eye* (1909), *The Decline of Aristocracy* (1912), *Democracy and Diplomacy* (1915), *Wars and Treaties (1815–1914)* (1917), *Rebels and Reformers* (with his w, 1917), *Religion in Politics* (1921), *English Diaries* (1923), *Now Is The Time* (1925), *More English Diaries, Scottish and Irish Diaries* (1927), *Samuel Pepys* (1928), *Casual Observations* (1929), *Queen Victoria* (1933), *John Evelyn* (1934), *Life Here and Now* (1936) and *Henry Ponsonby (his life from his letters)* (1942); *m* 12 April 1898 Dorothea (*d* 11 July 1963), dau of Sir Charles Hubert Hastings Parry, 1st and last Bt, CVO (*see* 1918 edn, also PEMBROKE and MONTGOMERY, E), and *d* 24 March 1946, leaving:

  1 MATTHEW HENRY HUBERT, **2nd Baron**

  1 Elizabeth; *b* 28 Dec 1900; one of the brightest of the 'Bright Young Things' whose careless hedonism enlivened the 'Twenties; *m* 5 July 1929 (*divorce* 1933) John Denis Cavendish Pelly (*see* PELLY, Bt) and *d* 31 July 1940

The 1st BARON's only s,

  MATTHEW HENRY HUBERT PONSONBY, **2nd Baron Ponsonby of Shulbrede**, JP (W Sussex, 1955); *b* 26 July 1904; *educ* Leighton Pk and Balliol Coll Oxford; FRCM, memb cncl RCM; *m* 5 Dec 1929 Hon Elizabeth Mary Bigham (*d* 1985), only dau of 2nd Viscount Mersey (*qv*), and *d* 1976, having had:

  1 THOMAS ARTHUR, **3rd Baron**

  2 William Nicholas; *b* 21 June 1933; *d* 11 Jan 1942

  1 *Laura Mary [The Hon Laura Ponsonby, 17 South End, Kensington Sq, London W8 5BU]; *b* 31 Oct 1935; *educ* Langford Grove and Guildhall Sch of Music (AGSM); guide lecturer and Educn Offr 1965–94 Kew Botanic Gdns, pres Haslemere Natural History Soc 1983–92, v-pres Haslemere Recorded Music Soc 1986–, hon botanist Haslemere Educnl Museum, author: *A List of Flowering Plants and Ferns of Haslemere and District* (1978) and *Marianne North at Kew Gardens* (1990)

  2 *Rose Magdalen [The Hon Mrs Owen-Smith, 48 Westgate, Chichester, W Sussex PO19 3EU]; *b* 19 Nov 1940; *m* 24 Sept 1966 *Brian David Owen-Smith, MB, BCh, FRCP, yr s of Col Cyril Robert Smith, OBE, of W Wickham, Kent, and has:

    (1) *Timothy Clive; *b* 25 April 1968

    (1) *Emma Elizabeth Jane; *b* 22 Aug 1971

  3 *Catherine Virginia [The Hon Mrs Russell, Shulbrede Priory, Lynchmere, Haslemere, Surrey]; *b* 21 July 1944; *m* 1972 *Ian Macdonald Affleck Russell and has:

    (1) *Harriet Mary; *b* 1977

    (2) *Joanna Elizabeth; *b* 1979

The 2nd BARON's er s,

  THOMAS ARTHUR PONSONBY, **3rd Baron Ponsonby of Shulbrede**; *b* 23 Oct 1930; *educ* Bryanston and Hertford Coll Oxford; Lt RARO, Kensington and Chelsea: Cncllr 1956–65, Alderman 1964–74, Ldr Lab Gp 1968–73, Lab candidate Heston and Isleworth 1959 gen election, GLC: Alderman 1970–77 and chm: Centl Area Bd (Tport Planning Ctees) 1973–76, Covent Gdn Ctee 1973–75 and Cncl 1976–77, Ho Lds: Oppn Whip 1979–81, Dep Ch Oppn Whip 1981–82 and Ch Whip 1982–90, Gen Sec Fabian Soc 1964–76 (Assist Gen Sec 1961–64), Govr LSE 1970–90, chm: Charity Law Reform Ctee 1974–90, London Tourist Bd 1976–80, Age Concern (Gtr London) 1977–78, Gtr London Citizens Advice Bureaux Service Ltd 1977–79, London Convention Bureau 1977–85, Bd Tstees Community Projects Fndn 1978–82, Local Govt Training Bd 1981–90, Ld Chllr's Advsy Ctee Appointment Magistrates Inner London 1987–90, Football Pools Panel 1987–90, Tourism Soc 1980–83 (pres 1984–90), Galleon Tst 1981–90 (pres Galleon World Travel Assoc 1977–90), Rona-Naive Artists Ltd 1978–83, Freeman City London 1977, Liveryman Wheelrights' Co 1980; *m* 1st 21 July 1956 (*divorce* 1973) Ursula Mary (*m* 2nd 1974, as his 2nd w, John Ingham Brooke; *see* HEWETT, Bt), yr dau of Cdr Thomas Stanley Lane Fox-Pitt, OBE, RN (ret) (*see* LOWTHER, Bt), and had:

  1 FREDERICK MATTHEW THOMAS PONSONBY, **4th and present Baron Ponsonby of Shulbrede**

  1 *Julia Mary; *b* 8 May 1960; *educ* Holland Pk Comprehensive and UEA

  2 Charlotte; *b* 22 July 1961; *d* unm 2 Dec 1980

  3 *Rachel Elizabeth Emma; *b* 25 June 1964

The **3rd Baron** *m* 2nd 18 May 1973 *Maureen Estelle [The Rt Hon The Lady Ponsonby of Shulbrede, 261 Kennington Rd, London SE11 6BY], dau of Alfred William Windsor, of Reigate, Surrey, and formerly w of Dr Paul Campbell-Tiech, of Geneva, and *d* 1990

POOLE

Arms: Per saltire or and barry undy argent and azure in chief and in base a portcullis chained, also azure. **Crest:** A lion's gamb erased or enfiled by a crown composed of four trident heads set upon a rim azure. **Supporters:** On either side a crane proper, about the neck a purse azure garnished gold. **Motto:** Strive for the right. **Creation:** B. (UK) 11 July 1958.

THE 2ND BARON POOLE, of Aldgate in the City of London (David Charles Poole) [The Rt Hon The Lord Poole, 53 The Chase, London SW4 0NY]; *b* 6 Jan 1945; *s f* 1993; *educ* Gordonstoun, Ch Ch Oxford and INSEAD Fontainebleau (MBA); memb Stock Exchange; *m* 1st 21 Sept 1967 (*divorce* 1975) Fiona, dau of John Donald, of Fulham, and has:

  1 +OLIVER JOHN; *b* 30 May 1972; *educ* Eton and St Anne's Coll Oxford

The 2nd BARON *m* 2nd 20 June 1975 Philippa, dau of Mark Reeve of Lower Brook House, Kings Somborne, Hants; *m* 3rd 1995 *Mrs Lucinda Edsell

Lineage: HENRY POOLE; regularly did business at Lloyd's Coffee House (forerunner of the modern Lloyd's); *d c* 1793, leaving:

ZACHARIAH POOLE; memb Lloyd's; *m* Elizabeth Sanderson and had, with a dau (Elizabeth):

JOHN POOLE; *b* 1797; fndr John Poole & Sons; *m* Maria Kenny and had, with a yr s (Edward John, memb Lloyd's) and three daus (Frances, *m* Henry King; Bertha, *m* Dr J Hale; Clara, *m* George Long):

HENRY SANDERSON POOLE; memb Lloyd's; *m* Edith Gorton and had, with three daus:

  1 Arnold Henry; *b* 1861; memb Lloyd's; *m* Beatrice Frodsham and *d* 1934, having had, with another s (*d* young) and four daus:

    (1) John Sanderson; Maj, memb Lloyd's; *d* 1966

    (2) Alick Hugh; memb Lloyd's; *ka* 1944, leaving issue

  2 Alick Sanderson; *b* 1868; *d* 1893

  3 Donald Louis; *b* 1868; memb Lloyd's; *m* 1899 Therese Lillian Frodsham (*m* 2nd 1924 George Downing Perry (*d* 1932); *m* 3rd 1935 Col T H Minshall, DSO, and *d* 25 Sept 1969), and *d* 1921, leaving:

    (1) OLIVER BRIAN SANDERSON POOLE, **1st Baron Poole** (UK), of Aldgate, in the City of London, so *cr* 11 July 1958, CBE (1945, OBE 1943, MBE 1942), TD (1945), PC (1963); *b* 11 Aug 1911; *educ* Eton and Ch Ch Oxford (BA 1932); memb LLoyd's 1933, Life Gds 1932–33, Warwicks Yeo 1934–45, Lt-Col (Hon Col) TA, WW II Middle East, N Africa and NW Europe (HQ 8th Army Long Range Desert Gp and HQ 21 Army Group; despatches three times), US Legn Merit 1945, MP (C) Oswestry 1945–50, Jt Hon Treas C Party 1952–55, Chm C Party 1955–57, Dep-Chm 1957–59, Jt Chm May–Oct 1963, V-Chm 1963–64, dir S Pearson and Sons, Whitehall Securities Corp, Lazard Bros, a Govr Old Vic 1948–63, Tstee Nat Gallery 1963, Hon DSc City U 1970, Kt Cdr Order Orange Nassau with swords (Netherlands) 1945; *m* 1st 6 Sept 1933 (*divorce* 1950) Betty Margaret (*d* 1988), dau of Capt Dugald Stewart Gilkison, The Cameronians, and had:

    1a DAVID CHARLES POOLE, **2nd and present Baron Poole**

    1a *Caroline [The Hon Lady Lucas-Tooth, Parsonage Farm, East Hagbourne, Didcot, Oxon OX11 9LN]; *b* 2 Sept 1934; *m* 29 June 1955 *Sir (Hugh) John Lucas-Tooth, 2nd Bt (*qv*), and has issue

    2a *Alison Victoria; *b* 15 Dec 1936; *m* 2 Feb 1961 *Dr Fritz Zankel, only s of Joseph Zankel, of Vienna, and has:

      1b *Michael Rudolph; *b* 6 Oct 1962

      2b *Thomas Joseph; *b* 3 Dec 1964

      1b *Olivia; *b* 1977

    3a *Sheila Marian [The Hon Mrs Ireland, 74 Clancarty Rd, London SW6]; *b* 1 March 1940; *m* 1st 16 Sept 1966 (*divorce* 19–) (Anthony William Paul) Cob Stenham, only s of Bernard Basil Stenham, of Montreux, Switzerland; *m* 2nd 1980 *George Ian Kenneth Ireland

    (1) (cont.) The **1st Baron** *m* 2nd 9 May 1952 (*divorce* 1965) Daphne Wilma Kenyon (*d* 12 Sept 1995), formerly w of Brig Algernon George William Heber-Percy (*see* NORTHUMBERLAND, D) and only dau of Eustace Bowles

(formerly Parker), JP (*see* MACCLESFIELD, E); *m* 3rd 4 April 1966 *Barbara Ann [The Rt Hon Barbara Lady Poole, 24 Campden Hill Gate, Duchess of Bedford Walk, London W8 7QH], dau of Eric Albert Taylor, of Kinsbourne Green, Herts, and *d* 1993

POORE

Arms: Argent a fess azure between three mullets gules.
Crest: A cubit arm erect vested sable, slashed argent, cuffed ermine, charged with two mullets in fess or, grasping in the hand an arrow proper. **Motto:** *Pauper non in spe* ('Not poor in hope').
Creation: Bt. (GB) 8 July 1795.

SIR HERBERT EDWARD POORE, 6TH BT, of Rushall, Wilts [Sir Herbert Poore Bt, Curuzu Ciatia, Corrientes, Argentina]; *b* April 1930; *s* f 1938

Lineage: PHILIP POORE, of Amesbury, Wilts; *d* 1571 aged 75 and had:

PHILIP POORE, of Durrington, Wilts; had:

EDWARD POORE, of Durrington; barrister Inner Temple; *m* Margaret, dau of Rev Abraham Conham, Canon Salisbury, and had, with other issue:

1 Philip, of Durrington; *d* 1661, leaving:

(1) Philip, of Durrington; *m* Elizabeth, dau of John Codrington, of Didmarton, Glos, and *d* 1693, having had issue

2 Abraham; royalist Civil War, when lost much of his property by confiscation; *m* 2 Aug 1647 Alice, dau of Thomas Moore, of Durrington, and *d* 10 May 1698, leaving an only surv s:

(1) Edward; bought the manor of Figheldean, Wilts; *m* 18 May 1675 Anne, dau of William Smart, of Alton, Hants, and had:

1a Edward, of Andover

2a Smart; *s* his f at Figheldean

3a ABRAHAM

1a Anne; *m* Thomas Lydiard, of Rookley, Wilts

EDWARD POORE's yst s,

ABRAHAM POORE, of Enford, Wilts; bought the Manor of Combe, Wilts; *m* 17 May 1711 Anne, only dau of John Herne, of Netheravon, Wilts, and had, with a yr s (John; *s* his f at Enford; *d* unm 1797) and two daus (Hester, *m* her cousin Smart Poore, of Alton; the other dau *d* unm):

EDWARD POORE; *b* 22 May 1715; bought Manors of Rushall and Charlton, Wilts, establishing his seat at Rushall; High Sheriff Wilts 1773; *m* 15 May 1737 Barbara (*d* 8 June 1745), dau of Paul Methuen, of Bradford, Wilts, and *d* 10 April 1788, leaving:

1 Edward; *b* 22 Nov 1742; *m* 12 Sept 1771 Anna Maria (*d* 18 May 1812), dau of James Montagu, of Lackham, Wilts, and *d* 30 Dec 1795, leaving:

(1) Edward; *b* 10 Feb 1773; *m* 1st 11 Dec 1794 Martha Anne (*d* 16 Feb 1801), 2nd dau of George Wolff, Danish Consul London, and had:

1a EDWARD (Sir), **2nd Bt**

1a Matty Wolff; *m* 19 June 1823 George Chilton, of the Inner Temple, and *d* 11 May 1828

(1) (cont.) Edward Poore *m* 2nd 3 July 1802 Elizabeth, 2nd dau of Rev Edward Gibson (s of Edmund Gibson, Bp London), and *d* 17 July 1814, having by her had:

2a Richard Francis Gibson; *b* 1804; Capt 15th Hus; *m* 30 April 1828 Margaret Henrietta Cottnam (*d* 20 May 1870), dau of Lt-Col Lauchlan Maclean, Resident Govr Tower London, and *d* 4 Sept 1852, leaving:

1b Ernest Herbert; *b* 13 June 1831; *m* 11 Nov 1856 Sarah, dau of William Light, and *d* 25 Feb 1898

1b Annette Henriette Wolff; *m* 18 June 1850 Rev George Richard Bigge (*d* 17 Jan 1886; *see* 1970 edn SELBY-BIGGE, Bt) and *d* 28 Aug 1913, leaving issue

2a Annette Gibson; *m* 8 Aug 1822 Rev Joseph Haythorne (*d* 5 Feb 1867), Vicar Congresbury, Somerset, and *d* 27 Nov 1866

3a Eleanora Charlotte Montagu; *m* 20 Oct 1830 William Long (*d* 28 Jan 1875), of Hurts Hall, Suffolk, and *d* 12 Jan 1900, leaving issue

(2) John Montagu; *b* 18 Dec 1782; *m* 21 July 1803 Elizabeth (*d* 29 Aug 1846), dau of Rev Charles Chauncy, and *d* 5 Dec 1808, leaving:

1a Robert Montagu; *b* 6 May 1804; *m* 16 May 1833 Anna Maria (*m* 2nd 9 Dec 1839 Mark Anthony Saurin and *d* 15 May 1865), dau of J H Massy-Dawson, MP (*see* MASSY, B), and *d* 9 April 1837, having had, with a dau (*d* young):

1b Robert, JP, of Old Lodge, Salisbury, Wilts; *b* 5 May 1834; Maj 8th Hus Crimean War and Indian Mutiny 1857–58; *m* 5 May 1863 Juliana Benita (*d* 8 Sept 1926), dau of R-Adml Armar Lowry-Corry (whose widow was granted the title and precedence of a widow of a KCB 1856), and *d* 22 June 1918, leaving:

1c Robert Montagu, CIE (1918), DSO (1900), JP, DL (Dorset); *b* 20 March 1866; Col 7th Hus, served Matabele and Mashonaland Campaigns 1896–97 (despatches, Brevet), Boer War 1899–1902 (despatches three times, two medals, eight clasps) and WW I (despatches, Brig-Gen 1915); *m* 29 Sept 1898 Lady Flora Maria Ida Douglas-Hamilton (*see* HAMILTON and BRANDON, D) and *d* 14 July 1938

2c Mark Saurin; *b* 26 May 1869; Capt 3rd Bn Liverpool Regt; *m* 9 Aug 1900 Irene (*m* 2nd 3 Oct 1933 Maj Harry Grant Thorold (*d* 15 April 1946), of Cranford Hall, Northants, and *d* 15 June 1943), only child of Edward Hanslope Watts, of Hanslope Park, Bucks, and *d* 11 Jan 1931, having had:

1d Edward; *b* 19 June 1901; *d* 30 May 1916

2d Robert POORE later POORE-SAURIN-WATTS (roy licence 14 Oct 1932), JP (Bucks); *b* 8 Jan 1904; *educ* Harrow and St John's Coll Cambridge; Ld Manors of Hanslope and Castlethorpe; *m* 1 Sept 1945 *Rosemary Philippa [Mrs James Richardson, Brown Edge, W Malvern, Worcs WR14 4BJ] (*m* 2nd 1974 James Richardson), 2nd dau of Maj Richard Norman Winstanley, of Rownhams House, Hants, and *d* 13 Sept 1973, having had:

1e Robert Mark; *b* 25 April 1946; *d* 23 April 1953

2e Edward Richard POORE-SAURIN-WATTS later POORE (1983); *b* 22 March 1948; *educ* Harrow and Lausanne U; *d* 30 June 1991

3e +Andrew Philip [Andrew Poore-Saurin-Watts Esq, 22 Vanneck Sq, London SW15 5DY]; *b* 5 July 1951; *educ* Milton Abbey and Lausanne U

1d *(Louisa) Florentia [Mrs Leslie Haslett, Apt 404, 1460 Docteur Penfield, Montreal, PQ, Canada]; *b* 6 Jan 1905; *m* 2 March 1932 Leslie Woods Haslett (*d* 1992), yr s of R W Haslett, of Budleigh Salterton, Devon, and has:

1e *(Leslie) Mark; *b* 1933; *m* 1959 *Jane Aikins, dau of Robert David Mulholland, of Montreal, and has:

1f *Andrew Mark; *b* 1961

2f *Thomas Leslie; *b* 1962

3f *Peter Aikins; *b* 1964

1f *Jennifer Anne; *b* 1968

2e *Richard Stuart; *b* 1940; *m* 1965 *Katharine, dau of Ernest Boyne, of St John, New Brunswick, and has:

1f *Christopher Leslie; *b* 1967

2f *Michael; *b* 1970

3f *Robert; *b* 1970

1e *Christian Florentia; *b* 1935; *m* 1956 *David Gladwin Turnbull, of Rothesay, New Brunswick, and has:

1f *Douglas Alasdair Stuart; *b* 1958

2f *Charles Laughlin; *b* 1960

3f *Douglas David; *b* 1963

1f *Christian Benita; *b* 1957

2e *Benita Jane; *b* 1938

2d Sybil Madeleine; *b* 14 March 1906; *m* 20 July 1935 her distant cousin Maj Charles Gilbert DAVIES-GILBERT formerly HARDING (deed poll 30 June 1926), MBE, est s of Maj Charles Henry Harding, JP, of Birling Manor, East Dean, Sussex, by Patience (dau of Crew Davies Gilbert and Grace Catherine Rose, *née* Massy-Dawson; *see* MASSY, B) and *d* 3 Aug 1981, leaving issue

3c Roger Alvin, DSO; *b* 8 July 1870; Lt-Col Roy Wilts Yeo and T/Maj Roy Welch Fus Boer War 1899–1902 (despatches, Queen's Medal, seven clasps) and WW I; *m* 9 Dec 1913 Lorne Margery (*d* 198–), dau of Maj Richard James William Dennistoun, N Staffs Regt, and was *ka* 26 Sept 1917, having had:

1d (Roger) Dennistoun; *b* 19 Aug 1916; *educ* Eton and King's Coll Cambridge (MA); W/Cdr RAF WW II; *m* 24 March 1949 *Peta [Mrs Dennistoun Poore, 5A Pembroke Gdns, London W8 6HS], dau of William George Coast, of Finchley, and widow of W/Cdr Walter Ronald Farley, DFC, and *d* 1987, leaving:

1e *Victoria Lorne Peta; *b* 26 April 1956; *m* 1981 *(Geoffrey Robert) James Borwick (*see* BORWICK, B) and has issue

1d Lorne Heather Dennistoun; *b* 23 Dec 1914; *d* 22 Feb 1915

4c Philip; *b* 4 June 1874; mining engr; *m* 16 Oct 1918 Cicely Eleanor (*d* 1978), est dau of Sir Edward Arthur Barry, 2nd Bt (*qv*), and *d* 27 July 1937, having had:

1d +Philip Barry, MC (1944) [Maj Philip Poore MC, Pakaraka, RD2 Kaikohe 0400, Bay of Islands, New Zealand]; *b* 7 Nov 1919; Maj Wilts Regt WW II; *m* 6 Feb 1954 *Jennifer, yst dau of Lt-Col Stanley Charles Harwood Worseldine, IMS, of Redcliffs, Christchurch, NZ, and has:

1e +Philip William; *b* 21 Aug 1956

1e *Anna Cicely; *b* 3 Dec 1954

2e *Sara Eleanor; *b* 1958

3e *Helen Jennifer; *b* 1960

2d John; *b* and *d* 3 Jan 1921

3d +Robert Roger [Robert Poore Esq, 21B Kelvin Rd, Remuera, Auckland, New Zealand]; *b* 21 June 1924; AMNZIE 1961, BSc 1949; *m* 25 Oct 1952 Diana Marion (*d* 13 Nov 1996), er dau of John Davis Canning, of Oakbourne, Waipukurau, NZ, and has:

1e *Marion Rosalind; *b* 15 Nov 1953

2e *Caroline Louise; *b* 31 March 1955

3e *Elizabeth Julia; *b* 16 March 1957

4e *Judith Rosamund; *b* 5 Dec 1958

1d *Anne Benita [Mrs Thomas Lindesay, PO Box 164, Kerikeri, Bay of Islands, New Zealand]; *b* 4 Feb 1922; *m* 27 July 1946 Thomas Campbell Lindesay (*d* 29 Dec 1989), yr s of Reginald Frederick Brydges Lindesay, of Paihia, Bay of Islands, NZ, and has:

1e *Philip Edward [Philip Lindesay Esq, 9 St Benedict's St, Auckland, New Zealand]; *b* 22 Aug 1947; *m* 1971 *Barbara Lesley Hargrave

2e *Thomas Reginald; *b* 23 Oct 1953

1e *Clare [Mrs Michael Gadsby, Flat 1, Marchwood Crescent, London W5]; *b* 20 Dec 1950; *m* 1st 1972 (*divorce* 19–) Rodney Burke; *m* 2nd *Michael Gadsby

2e *Erica Anne; *b* 11 May 1955

2d Eleanor; *b* 10 Oct 1928; *m* 8 Dec 1956 Nigel Malcolm Kennedy (*d* 1974), yr s of Col M W Kennedy, of Richmond, Natal, S Africa, and *d* 20 March 1988, leaving:

1e *Malcolm Alistair Robert; *b* 12 Sept 1957

2e *Hamish Alexander Nigel; *b* 28 Feb 1959

3e *Christopher William; *b* 2 May 1966

1e *Sally Anne; *b* 7 Jan 1963

2e *Katherine Fiona; *b* 8 Feb 1964

1c Louisa Benita; *m* 28 Nov 1896 Sir Alexander Wilson (*d* 6 Sept 1907), Sheriff Calcutta, Pres Bengal Chamber Commerce, and *d* 22 March 1946

2c Anna Maria; *m* 5 March 1889 Sir Harold Pelly, 4th Bt (*qv*), and *d* 12 Dec 1939, leaving issue

3c Nina Mary Benita; DGStJ, chm exec cncl Animal Def Soc, held HM QUEEN MARY's canopy at Coronation 1911; *m* 4 Dec 1901 13th Duke of Hamilton and (10th Duke of) Brandon (*qv*) and *d* 12 Jan 1951, leaving issue

2b John Charles Montagu; *b* 23 June 1809; *d* unm 12 Nov 1873

2 **Sir John Methuen Poore, 1st Bt** (GB), so *cr* 8 July 1795, with special remainder, failing heirs male of his body, to his er bro Edward and the latter's male issue; *b* 8 June 1745; High Sheriff Wilts 1797; *d* unm 1 June 1820

His great-nephew,

Sir Edward Poore, 2nd Bt; *b* 4 Dec 1795; *educ* Magdalen Coll Oxford; *m* 6 Jan 1818 Agnes (*d* 13 Oct 1868), 3rd dau of Sir John Marjoribanks, 1st Bt (*see* 1888 edn), and *d* 13 Oct 1838, having had:

1 EDWARD (Sir), **3rd Bt**

1 Alicia Charlotte; *m* 16 Nov 1843 Rev F M Cunningham, Rector Brightwell, Oxon, s of Rev J W Cunningham, Vicar Harrow, and *d* 12 July 1894

2 Eleanor; *m* William Baillie Money and *dsp* 2 July 1873

3 Agnes Georgina; *m* 17 Aug 1847 Henry John Standly and *d* 23 Jan 1867

4 Anna Maria Barbara; *m* 1st 30 Nov 1848 Stuart E MacKechnie (*d* May 1853); *m* 2nd 15 July 1872 John Shephard Maskew, MD (*d* 1892), and *d* 21 Dec 1899, leaving issue

5 Grace Stuart; *m* 15 May 1855 Walter Williams (*d* 1880), of Worthy Park, Winchester, and had issue

Sir EDWARD's only s,

Sir Edward Poore, 3rd Bt; *b* 6 March 1826; Lt Scots Fus Gds 1844–48; *m* 18 Sept 1951 Frances Elizabeth (*d* 21 April 1926), dau of Rev Henry Riddell Moody, Rector Chartham, Kent, Hon Canon Canterbury, and *d* 23 Nov 1893, leaving:

1 **Sir Richard Poore, 4th Bt**, KCB, CVO, JP, DL (Wilts); *b* 7 July 1853; served RN: Naval Bde Malay Peninsula 1875–76 (Perak Medal with clasp, despatches, promoted Lt), Alexandria Bombardment 1882 (medal with clasp, bronze star, despatches, 4th Class Medjidie), Nile Expedn 1885 (despatches, clasp, promoted Cdr), ADC to HM EDWARD VII 1901–08, R-Adml Mediterranenan and Channel Fleets 1904–05, C-in-C Australia Station 1908–11 and The Nore 1911–15, Grand Offr Legn Hon and Grand Cross Crown Italy 1917; *m* 14 Sept 1885 Ida Margaret (*d* 5 Feb 1941), dau of Rt Rev Charles Graves, DD, DCL, FRS, Bp Limerick, and aunt of the poet Robert Graves, and *d* 8 Dec 1930, having had:

(1) Roger; *b* 27 June 1886; Sub-Lt RN then Lt RFA; *ka* 19 Sept 1915

2 Herbert; *b* 26 Jan 1863; *m* 1891 Josefina (*d* 13 Sept 1947), dau of Maximo Pujol, and *d* 30 May 1905, leaving:

(1) **Sir Edward Poore, 5th Bt**; *b* 1894; *m* 1922 *Amelia, dau of Santiago Guliemone, of Estancia La Blanca, Estacion Acuna, Corrientes, Argentina, and *d* Feb 1938, leaving:

1a Sir HERBERT EDWARD POORE, **6th and present Bt**

1a *Elsie Nelly; *b* 1923; *m* 26 Feb 1947 Jorge Ball, s of Alberto Carlos Ball, of Buenos Aires, and has:

1b *Jorge Eduard; *b* 18 May 1948

2b *Alberto Carlos; *b* 14 June 1949

3b *Roberto; *b* 5 Dec 1954

1b *Susana Beatriz; *b* 17 June 1952

2a *Betty Gladys; *b* 1926

(2) Philip; *b* 1896; *d* unm 23 March 1917

(3) +NASIONCENO; *b* 1900; heir presumptive; *m* 19– Juana Borda (*d* 7 Oct 1943) and has:

1a *Roger Ricardo; *b* 21 Oct 1930

2a +Roberto [Roberto Poore, Beazley 3818, Pto C, Buenos Aires, Argentina]; *b* 18 Dec 1932; *m* 1964 *Norma Onhaso

3a +Percy Nasionceno [Percy Poore, Belgrano 912, Curuzu Cuatia, Corrienves, Argentina]; *b* 11 Sept 1941

1a *Argentina [Argentina Poore, Moliere 834, Pto 2, Buenos Aires, Argentina]; *b* 10 Oct 1927

2a *Gloria [Gloria Poore, Moliere 834, Pto 2, Buenos Aires, Argentina]; *b* 22 Oct 1928

3a *Tady Esterlina [Tady Poore, Belgrano 912, Curuzu Cuatia, Corrientes, Argentina]; *b* 19 Jan 1938

(4) Diego; *b* 1903; *d* unm 1921

(1) Dolores; *b* 1892; *d* unm 4 Aug 1951

(2) Francesca; *b* 1898

(3) *Rosalie; *b* 1905; *m* 1930 Juan F Garmedia

1 Elsie; *d* unm 3 April 1937

2 Katharine; *d* unm 13 March 1947

PORRITT

Arms: Or a serpent in bend vert between two lion's heads erased gules, on a chief of the last two swords points upwards in saltire of the first, between as many roses argent both surmounted by another rose gules barbed and seeded proper. **Crest:** On a wreath or and gules a demi-heraldic antelope gules, armed azure, collared or, holding a torch of the last inflamed proper between two fern fronds vert. **Motto:** *Sapienter et fortiter ferre* ('Bearing oneself wisely and with fortitude'). **Creation:** Bt. (UK) 25 Jan 1963.

Jonathon Espie Porritt [Jonathon Porritt, 9 Lypiatt Terrace, Cheltenham, Glos GL50 2SX]; *b* 6 July 1950; *s f* 1994 but does not use title; *educ* Eton and Magdalen Coll Oxford; teacher ILEA 1975–84, Dir Friends of the Earth 1984–90, Ecology Party: parly candidate 1979 and 1983 gen elections, candidate European elections 1976 and 1984, memb cncl 1978–80 and 1982–84, chm 1979–80 and 1982–84, presented BBC TV's *Where On Earth Are We Going?* 1990 (book version under same title 1991), author: *Seeing Green — the Politics of Ecology* (1984), *Friends of the Earth Handbook* (1987), *The Coming of the Greens* (1988), *Save the Earth* (ed, 1991) and *Captain Eco* (children's book, 1991); *m* 1986 *Sarah, dau of Malcolm Staniforth, of Malvern, Worcs, and has:

1 *Eleanor Mary; *b* 1988

2 *Rebecca Elizabeth; *b* 1991

Lineage: Rev THOMAS PORRITT; migrated from England to Wellington, NZ; *m* Elizabeth Dunlop (*d* 1919) and *d* 3 Dec 1924, leaving:

1 Edmund W; *b* 29 Aug 1865; had:

(1) Eric A, MC; *b* 27 Oct 1895

(2) Athol E A; *b* 23 July 1901; *d* 1919

2 Oswald Henry; *b* 10 Jan 1868; *educ* Wellington Coll NZ; *m* 13 April 1898 Florence Mary (*d* 12 Oct 1945), dau of H S McKellar, of Wellington, NZ, and *d* 25 July 1958, having had:

(1) Arnaud Leslie; *b* 19 Feb 1900; *educ* Wanganui Collegiate Sch; *d* 4 March 1919

(2) Basil Ainslie; *b* 29 June 1903; *educ* Wanganui Collegiate Sch; *d* 17 May 1956

(1) *Margaret Russell [Miss Margaret Porritt, 89a Winchester St, Merivale, Christchurch, New Zealand]; *b* 1 Feb 1913

3 ERNEST EDWARD

4 Harold Elliott; *b* 1874; *educ* Wanganui Collegiate Sch

5 Oscar A

The Rev THOMAS PORRITT's 3rd s,

ERNEST EDWARD PORRITT, VD, JP; *b* 19 March 1870; *educ* Wanganui Collegiate Sch; MD, FRCS, served Samoan Expdny Force 1914, Offr i/c NZ Hosp Ship *Maheno* 1916–17 with rank of Col; *m* 22 May 1899 Ivy Elizabeth (*d* 20 May 1914), dau of Alexander John Mackenzie, of Abingdon, Lanarks, and *d* 30 April 1950, leaving:

1 **Sir Arthur Espie Porritt, 1st Bt**, and BARON PORRITT, of Wanganui, New Zealand, and of Hampstead, Greater London (both UK), so *cr* 25 Jan 1963 and (LP) 1973 respectively, GCMG (1967, KCMG 1950), KCVO (1957), CBE (1945, OBE 1943); *b* 10 Aug 1900; *educ* Wanganui Collegiate Sch, Otago U, Magdalen Coll Oxford (BA 1925, MB, MA, Hon DSc 1963) and St Mary's Hosp London (BCh 1928, MCh 1932); Surgn-in-Ordinary to HRH THE DUKE OF YORK 1936, Surgn to HM Household 1937–46 and HM GEORGE VI 1946–52, Serjeant-Surgn to HM THE QUEEN 1952–67, Consulting Surgn Army 1954–67 and Brig RAMC 21 Army Gp, Govr-Gen NZ 1967–72, dir Sterling Winthrop 1973–94, chm: Medical Advsy Ctee Min Overseas Devpt and Medical Servs Review Ctee 1958, MRCS Eng, LRCP London 1928, FRCS 1930, Hon LLD St Andrews, Otago and New Zealand Us, Hon FRCS Edinburgh, Glasgow, Ireland, Canada, Hon FRACS Australia, Hon Fell S African Coll, Hon Fell American Coll Surgns, Hon MD Bristol, Hon FRCP, Hon FRCOG, PRCS 1960–63,

PBMA 1960–61, PRSM 1966–67, Master Apothecaries' Soc 1964–66, memb Internat Olympic Ctee 1935–94, V-Pres Br Empire and Cwlth Games Fedn, Olympic Bronze Medallist 100 metres 1924, V-Pres AAA, US Legn Merit, author: *Athletics* (with D G A Lowe, 1929) and *Essentials of Modern Surgery* (with R M Handfield-Jones, 1938); *m* 1st 1926 Mary Frances Wynne, dau of William Bond; *m* 2nd 20 Dec 1946 Kathleen ('Kay') Mary (*d* 13 July 1998), 2nd dau of Alfred Sydney Peck, of Spalding, Lincs, and *d* 1 Jan 1994, when the Barony expired, leaving:

(1) (Sir) JONATHON ESPIE PORRITT, **2nd and present Bt**

(2) +JEREMY CHARLES [The Hon Jeremy Porritt, Château de la Chevalerie, 27680 Saint-Samson-de-la-Roque, France]; *b* 19 Jan 1953; heir presumptive; *educ* Eton; *m* 1980 *Penny, dau of J H Moore, of London, Ontario, and has:

  1a +Andrew Sebastian Alexander; *b* 1982

  2a +Hugo James; *b* 1986

(1) *Joanna Mary [The Hon Mrs Meredith-Hardy, 23 Baronsmead Rd, London SW13]; *b* 19 July 1948; *m* 26 July 1969 *Simon Patrick Meredith-Hardy, er s of Patrick Talbot Meredith-Hardy, TD, of Grovehurst, Horsmonden, Kent, and has:

  1a *Henry Patrick; *b* 1975

  2a *George Peter; *b* 1978

2 Charles Howard; *b* 25 March 1902; *educ* Wanganui Collegiate Sch; *m* 7 March 1928 *Alice [Mrs Charles Porritt, 5 Midway Ave, Castor Bay, Auckland, New Zealand], dau of F Creighton, and *d* 5 April 1985, leaving:

(1) *Alice Elizabeth [Mrs Murray Francis, 5 Midway Ave, Castor Bay, Auckland 1309, New Zealand]; *b* 23 March 1936; *m* 7 June 1958 *Murray Bowler Francis, s of Maurice Francis, of N Auckland, NZ, and has:

  1a *Rodney Brett; *b* 25 Oct 1965; *m* 20 Dec 1992 *Shanly, dau of David Shirreffs, of Milford, Auckland, and has:

    1b *Tobias David Rodney; *b* 8 April 1996

    1b *Devon Alice Shanly; *b* 1 Dec 1993

    2b *Imogen Amy Marea; *b* 17 April 1998

  1a *Victoria Leigh; *b* 10 Oct 1967; *m* 22 Dec 1996 *Andrew Mason Parker, s of Graham Parker, of Christchurch, NZ

PORTAL

Arms: Per saltire azure and gules, a castellated portal flanked by two towers argent; on a chief ermine a crescent of the first between two mullets of the second. **Crest:** A portal as in the arms, each tower charged with a fleur-de-lys in chief azure, and a wreath of laurel in base vert. **Motto:** *Constanter* ('Constantly'). **Creation:** Bt. (UK) 11 March 1901.

SIR JONATHAN FRANCIS PORTAL, 6TH BT, of Malshanger, Church Oakley, Co Southampton [Sir Jonathan Portal Bt, Burley Wood, Ashe, Hants RG25 3AG]; *b* 13 Jan 1953; *s* f 1984; *educ* Marlborough and Edinburgh U (BCom); gp fin controller Henderson Admin 1989–91, fin dir Grosvenor Ventures Ltd 1992–93, FCA (ACA 1977), memb Clothworkers' Co, Fin Consultant (JP Assocs) 1993–; *m* 9 Oct 1982 *Louisa Caroline, est dau of Sir (Frederick) John Charles Gordon Hervey-Bathurst, 7th Bt (*qv*), and has:

  1 +WILLIAM JONATHAN FRANCIS; *b* 1 Jan 1987

  2 +Robert Jonathan; *b* 5 Feb 1989

  3 +John Arthur Jonathan; *b* 7 April 1993

Lineage: LOUIS PORTAL; living 1456; had:

JEAN PORTAL, of Bagnois, near Orange, Provence, France, and of Cadignac, near Sabran; *m* Andrève Lansagne (*m* 2nd Louis Cordier) and *d c* 1495, leaving:

JEAN PORTAL, of Bagnois and Cadignac; Mayor Bagnois; *m* Agnès Pérusin and *d* 1534, leaving, with three yr sons and four daus:

FRANCOIS PORTAL, of Bagnois and Cadignac; infantry Lt; *m* (contract 19 April 1530) Madeleine (a Huguenot; *d* 1588), dau of Jacques des Mares, Bachellor-ès-Droits, Lieutenant de Viguier, Juge de Roquemaure, by Honorate Granier, and *d c* 1571, leaving, with two er sons, two yr sons and five daus:

GUILLAUME PORTAL, of Bagnois, *bapt* there 14 July 1551; *m* (contract 2 April 1588) Marie, dau of Moreir de Mirman by Catherine Suisse, and *d c* 1600, leaving, with three yr sons:

ETIENNE PORTAL, of Bagnois; ecuyer, one of the Anciens du Consistoire de Bagnois; *m* (contract 28 April 1632) Lucrèce, dau of Jean de Perrotet, of Orange, by his w Isabeau de Sameria, and *d c* 1671, leaving, with a yr s and two daus:

JEAN FRANCOIS PORTAL, of Poitiers; *b* 3 Nov 1642; ecuyer, Conseiller du Roi, Seigneur de la Vau-Guiot, forced 1699 to emigrate to escape from religious persecution, settling in London; *m* 1st (contract at Poitiers 10 Feb 1682) Françoise Grimaudet, dau of Benjamin Grimaudet, Seigneur des Giraudières, by Jeanne Pain; *m* 2nd 28 April 1700 Marie, dau of Jacques Gousset, sometime minister of the reformed church at Poitiers, and *d* 1705, having had by his 1st w, with an est s, two yst sons and seven daus:

1 Peter William (Pierre Guillaume) (Rev); *bapt* 25 Dec 1685 at Poitiers; Rector Clowne, Derbys, Vicar South Fambridge, Essex; *m* 2 Jan 1724 Mary Magdalen (*d* 1754), dau of Andrew Meure, of Leatherhead, and *d* 1768, having had:

(1) Andrew (Rev); *b* 1725; *educ* Oxford (MA); Vicar St Helen's Abingdon, trans *The Orations of Eschines against Ctesiphon* (1755); *m* Frances Nethersole (*d* May 1772) and *d* July 1775, having had issue

(2) Abraham, of London; *b* 1726; goldsmith and author; *m* 1st 21 Aug 1748 Elizabeth Nethersole (*d* 25 Feb 1758); *m* 2nd 19 Aug 1758 Elizabeth, dau of Bernard Bedwell, of Abingdon, and *d* 1809, having by his 2nd w had, with other issue (*d* young):

  1a William Nash; *b* 16 Dec 1770; *m* Elizabeth Sarah Street and *d* at sea 1807, leaving:

    1b Emma; *m* 1831 William Turner, banker, of Naples, and had:

      1c Frederick Torquato TURNER later PORTAL-TURNER (added 1898)

  2a Richard Brinsley, of Daventry, Northants; *b* 30 Nov 1784; *m* 31 May 1807 Mary (*d* 19 March 1858), dau of Thomas Woolston, and *d* 1 Oct 1859, having had:

    1b Richard Brinsley, of Tonge House, W Norwood; *b* 15 May 1808; *m* 28 June 1837 Sarah Hariott (*d* 22 Dec 1881), dau of Thomas Robinson, and *d* 3 Jan 1900, having had:

      1c William Richard, of Tonge House; *b* 29 June 1838; *educ* Pembroke Coll Oxford (MA)

      2c Charles Edward; *b* 1 Aug 1843; *d* umn 1 Oct 1872

      3c Horace John; *b* 9 April 1845; *m* 18 April 1878 Mary Louisa (*d* 15 March 1931), dau of William Lanphier Anderson, and *d* 26 Dec 1910, leaving:

        1d Daisy Melita; *b* 23 Feb 1879; *m* 5 Dec 1908 William Alexander Rhind and *d* S Africa 2 Oct 1964, leaving issue. He *d* 27 April 1955

        2d Amy Irena; *b* 10 March 1880; AA, LLA; *d* umn 29 Oct 1919

        3d Gwladys Anderson Madelein; *b* 18 Feb 1882; *m* 18 Jan 1910 Alan Tatham Shores, s of John Wallis Shores, CMG, and *d* 2 Nov 1961, leaving issue

        4d Irma Horace Lanphier; *b* 5 Feb 1885; *m* 20 April 1912 Brig Norman Macdonald McLeod, DSO, MC, RA, s of Lt-Gen Sir John C McLeod, GCB, and had:

          1e *Norman Portal; *b* 10 Oct 1916; *educ* RMA Woolwich; Maj RA WW II; *m* 1st June 1940 Priscilla Anne Lushington and has:

            1f *David Norman Kelty [David McLeod Esq, c/o Bank of Scotland, 8 Morningside Rd, Edinburgh 10]; *b* 12 Oct 1941; *educ* RMA Sandhurst; Capt RA, seconded AAC Malaysia, served Borneo 1965; *m* 18 March 1967 *Sandra Claire Ford and has:

              1g *Angus Edward Kelty; *b* 29 Dec 1969

            2f *Richard Arthur Kelty; *b* 16 June 1943; *educ* RNC Dartmouth; Lt RN

          1e (cont.) Maj Norman MacLeod *m* 2nd 11 Dec 1965 *Mrs Kathleen Margaret Blackstone

          2e *John Chetham [John McLeod Esq, Little Carvedras, Constantine, nr Falmouth, Cornwall]; *b* 20 March 1918; *educ* RMA Woolwich; Capt RA; *m* 28 Nov 1959 *Ann Patrica, er dau of Lt-Col James Douie Glegg, Dublin Fus, by Marjorie Mibah Charmand, and has:

            1f *Hamish John Macdonald; *b* 21 Oct 1960

          1e *Irma Patricia Macdonald; *b* 3 Jan 1926

      1c Sarah Henrietta; *m* 10 April 1860 William Augustus Sabonadiere and *d* 11 Dec 1885, leaving issue. He *d* 29 Aug 1896

      2c Mary; *m* 8 April 1869 Charles Burrell and had issue. He *d* 8 Jan 1895

      3c Amy; *m* 25 June 1868 Robert Russell Hyatt, yst s of Rev Charles James Hyatt, and had issue. He *d* 19 Sept 1888

      4c Julia Elizabeth; *d* 13 Feb 1913

      5c Bertha Mary

    2b Bernard Bedwell; *b* 29 Nov 1811; *m* 9 May 1837 Lucy (*d* 8 Aug 1884), dau of Thomas Welch, and *d* 28 July 1889, having had:

      1c Bernard Bedwell; *b* 23 April 1844; *m* 24 June 1884 Ethel Leach and *d* 17 Aug 1903, leaving:

        1d Lucy Welch; *d* umn 6 Feb 1915

      2c Frederich Welch; *b* 22 Feb 1847; *m* 30 Aug 1883 Marion Caroline, dau of Rev John Wallace, and *d* 30 Dec 1925, leaving:

        1d *Andrew Wallace; *b* 12 June 1892; Lt 3rd Bn Roy W Surrey Regt WW I (wounded); *m* Evelyn Marshall and had:

          1e *Julian Robert Andrew; *b* 29 Feb 1924

          2e *Richard Wallace [Dr Richard Portal, The Briars, Beech Road Hill, Swanland, E Yorks]; *b* 26 May 1925; *educ* Bryanston, Peterhouse Cambridge (MA, LLB) and Middx Hosp Med Sch (MB, BS Lond 1956); MRCP Lond 1959, MD Lond 1966, Consultant Cardiologist Hull Hosps, RN WW II 1943–46; *m* 2 July 1966 *Pamela, MB, BS Lond 1963, only dau of J W Burrill, of Bromley, Kent, and has:

            1f *Robert John; *b* 13 April 1967

            1f *Janet Caroline; *b* 21 Aug 1969

          3e *Burnaby Mark [Barnaby Portal Esq, South Farm, S Petherton, Somerset TA13 5AE]; *b* 11 Oct 1935

        1d Olive; *b* 10 July 1884; *d* umn 1960

2d Freda Marion; *b* 13 March 1886; *m* 17 Aug 1911 Canon William Alexander Dunn, Vicar Kingswood, Surrey, 1931, Hon Canon Southwark Cathedral, and had:

  1e *Andrew Hunter; *b* Oct 1916

  1e *Ursula Mary; *m* 27 Sept 1939 Rt Rev Oliver Stratford Tomkins, DD, Bp Bristol, s of Rev Leopold Charles Fellows Tomkins, and has issue

3d Katherine; *b* 29 Aug 1887; *m* 11 June 1918 Lt-Col Horace Cyril Benjamin Hickling, CBE, DSO, MC, s of Horace Hickling, of Woking, and has issue. He *d* 13 Sept 1948

4d Agnes Joan; *m* 1925 Col Guy Hamilton Russell, CIE, DSO, MC, s of Lt-Col Charles Russell, RA, and had issue. He *d* 21 Oct 1958

5d Maude Elsie; *b* 8 Dec 1890; *m* Arthur George Bailey and *d* 20 May 1964, leaving issue. He *d* 5 Nov 1964

1c Laura; *m* 12 April 1863 Frederick Everitt and had issue

2c Lucy Welch

3c Emily; *m* 25 June 1891 Gottfried Friederich Ebeling (*d* 16 April 1912)

3b William Thomas, of Springfield, Northants; *b* 25 Oct 1816; *m* 1st 9 Aug 1849 Betsey (*d* 10 Jan 1856), dau of George Attenborough, of Braybrooke, Northants, and had:

1c Edward Robert, of Eddington House, Hungerford, later Sulham House, Pangbourne, Berks, JP, DL; *b* 22 April 1854; *educ* Ch Ch Oxford (MA); barrister Inner Temple 1880, Maj Berks Imp Yeo; *m* 1st 17 Jan 1878 Rose Leslie, dau of John Moore Napier (*see* NAPIER and ETTRICK, L), and had:

  1d William Robert Napier; *b* 10 May, *d* 23 July 1881

  2d John Leslie, DSO; *b* 13 April 1886; *educ* Eton; Maj Oxon and Bucks LI WW I and Waziristan 1922–23, NDC 1939, 8th Somerset LI, RAF Regt WW II; *m* 2 April 1921 Violet Eleanor, dau of Maj-Gen Thomas Stanford Baldock, CB

  3d Gervas Edward; *b* 18 Jan 1890; Lt-Col IA, WWs I and II; *m* 6 Jan 1927 Iris Mary, er dau of Sir Montagu Sherard Dawes Butler, KCSI, CB, CVO, CIE, CBE, and *d* 3 Dec 1961, leaving:

    1e *Jane Gillian; *b* 11 Dec 1929; *m* 23 April 1955 (*divorce* 1959) Gavin Bramhall Bernard Welby, only s of Bramhall James Welby, of S Africa, and has:

      1f *Justin Portal; *b* 6 Jan 1956; *educ* Eton

    2e *Susan Mary Geraldine; *b* 28 Oct 1931; *m* 31 July 1954 *James Macdonald Batten, barrister, only s of Gordon James Batten, MBE, of Guildford, and has:

      1f *Charles James; *b* 18 Sept 1958

      1f *Amanda Rose; *b* 25 Dec 1956

1c (cont.) Edward Portal *m* 2nd 10 Aug 1892 Ellinor Kate (*d* 25 Nov 1946), dau of Capt Charles West Hill, 69th Regt, and *d* 26 March 1953, having by her had:

4d CHARLES FREDERICK ALGERNON PORTAL, VISCOUNT PORTAL OF HUNGERFORD, of Hungerford, Co Berks, so *cr* 28 Jan 1946, with remainder to heirs male of his body, as also previously 17 Sept 1945 BARON PORTAL OF HUNGERFORD, of Hungerford, Co Berks (both UK), with remainder in default of heirs male of his body to his est dau and the heirs male of her body, in default of which to every other dau by primogeniture and the heirs male of their bodies, KG (1946), OM (1945), GCB (1942, KCB 1940, CB 1939), DSO (1917) and bar (1918), MC (1917), DL (W Sussex 1951); *b* 21 May 1893; *educ* Winchester and Ch Ch Oxford (Hon Student 1941), joined RFC 1915 and RAF 1918, served WW I (despatches), staff Dir Ops and Intell Air Ministry 1930–34, OC Br Forces Aden 1934–35, RAF Instr IDC 1935–37, AVM 1937, Dir Orgn Air Min 1937–38, Air Memb Personnel Air Cncl 1939–40, Air Marshal 1939, AOC-in-C Bomber Cmd March-Oct 1940, Ch Air Staff 1940–45, Air Ch Marshal 1940, Marshal of the RAF 1944, Controller Atomic Energy Min Supply 1946–51, chm: Br Aluminium 1953–59, Br Match Corp 1959–64, BAC 1960–68, Dominion Students Hall Trust 1952–65, Govt Tstees Nuffield Tst for Forces of Crown, King Edward VII Hosp Midhurst 1950–68, dir Whitbread Investment Co, Pres MCC 1958–59, V-Patron Offrs' Assoc, Dep Chm RAF Benevolent Fund, Pres RAF Escaping Soc, Freedom City London 1946, Grand Cross: Legn Hon, St Olaf Norway, George I Greece, Netherlands Lion, Crown Belgium; Order White Lion Czechoslavakia, 1st Cl Order Polonia Restituta, US DSM, Hon DCL Birmingham, Bristol, Belfast, Durham, Hon DSc Reading; *m* 22 July 1919 Joan Margaret (*d* 19 June 1996), yst dau of late Sir Charles Glynne Earle Welby, 5th Bt (*qv*), and *d* 22 April 1971, when the Viscountcy expired, having had:

  1e Richard; *b* and *d* 12 Sep 1921

  1e ROSEMARY ANN PORTAL, BARONESS PORTAL OF HUNGERFORD; *b* 12 May 1923; Section Offr WAAF WW II 1942–46; *d* unm 1990, when the Barony expired

  2e Mavis Elizabeth Aloutte; *b* 13 June 1926

5d Reginald Henry (Sir), KCB (1946, CB 1946), DSC (1916); *b* 6 Sept 1894; *educ* RNC Dartmouth; served RN and RNAS WWs I and II, cmded HMS *York* 1939–41 (despatches) and HMS *Royal Sovereign* 1941–42, Assist Ch Naval Staff (Air) 1943–44, Flag Offr Naval Air Stations Australia 1944–46, Jt Ch Staff Australia 1946–47, Flag Offr (Air) Home 1947–51, ret as Adml 1951, ADC to HM GEORGE VI 1943; *m* 16 Sept 1926 Helen Sophia (*d* 3 April 1983), dau of Frederick Anderson, of Standen, Hungerford, and *d* 18 June 1983, leaving:

  1e *Christopher [Christopher Portal Esq, Monkhouse Farm, Merriott, Somerset TA16 5PQ]; *b* 8 July 1927; *educ* Nautical Coll Pangbourne and Balliol Coll Oxford (MA); *m* 29 July 1951 *Julia Jean, only dau of Lt-Col Richard George Reginald Oxley, KRRC, of Somerset, and has:

    1f *Matthew; *b* 9 Sept 1952; *educ* Maidstone GS; *m* and has issue

    2f *Robert Martin; *b* 1 Sept 1956; *educ* Cranbrook; *m* and has issue

---

1f *Margaret Jane; *b* 29 Jan 1954

2f *Katharine Mary; *b* 26 Feb 1958

2e *Anthony [Lt-Cdr Anthony Portal RN, South Leith Cottage, Eastleigh Rd, Havant, Hants PO9 2NY]; *b* 19 June 1932; Fell Inst Linguists (French); *m* 20 May 1956 *Chantal Marie-Françoise, yst dau of Baron Gabriel Marie-François Guerrier de Dumast, of Château de Rozet, St Vit Doubs, France, and has:

  1f *Frederick [Frederick Portal Esq, 24 Rue Roosevelt, L-8344 Olm, Luxembourg]; *b* 27 Sept 1958; *educ* Marlborough and Birmingham U (BSc, BComm); MBA 1997; *m* 19– *Isabelle (PhD, MD), est dau of Jacques Rolland, of Fontaine les Dijon, France and has:

    1g *Jacques-Antoine Charles; *b* 27 April 1997

    1g *Helen Marie-Claire; *b* 7 Feb 1994

    2g *Caroline Marie Ségolène; *b* 8 March 1996

  2f *William [William Portal Esq, 77 Duncan Rd, Southsea, Hants PO5 2QU]; *b* 10 Sept 1961; *educ* St John's Coll Southsea and Birmingham U (BSc Econ)

  3f *Philip Jeremy [Philip Portal Esq, 48 Main Rd, Emsworth, Hants PO10 8AU]; *b* 16 Sept 1963; *educ* St John's Coll Southsea; proprietor Portal, Dingwall & Norris, wine shippers; *m* 1st 1986 (*divorce* 1992) Carole Mary Esmonde, dau of Cdr E Bowerman, RN, of Eastleigh House, Havant; *m* 2nd *Teresa Joanna, dau of Lt Cdr David P Lown, RN, of Hayling Island, and has:

    1g *Edward Anthony Reginald; *b* 30 July 1993

    1g *Emma Elizabeth; *b* 6 Dec 1994

    2g *Katherine Anne; *b* 18 March 1996

1e *Helen Morar [Mrs John Lucas, Lambrook House, East Lambrook, Somerset TA13 5HW]; *b* 30 May 1929; *m* 17 June 1961 *John Randolph Lucas, FBA, er s of Ven Egbert de Grey Lucas, Archdeacon Durham, and has:

  1f *Edward de Grey; *b* 3 May 1962; *educ* Winchester; *m* 1992 *Claudia Sinnig, of Gotha, Germany, and has:

    1g *John Maximilian Sinnig; *b* 19 May 1993

    2g *Hugo Darius; *b* 19 Aug 1995

  2f *Richard Henry; *b* 22 April 1966; *educ* Winchester; *m* 1993 *Ania Motylewska, of Cracow, Poland, and has:

    1g *Helena Alicja; *b* 13 Dec 1996

  1f *Helen Mary; *b* 3 Nov 1964

  2f *Deborah Joan; *b* 21 July 1967

2e *Mary Elizabeth [Mrs John Graham, Broomie Knowe, Claygate by Canonbie, Dumfriesshire DE14 0SA]; *b* 15 Aug 1937; *m* 16 Dec 1969 *John B Graham, only s of Frederick Lawson Graham, and has:

  1f *Jonathan Birkett Andrew; *b* 30 Nov 1977; *educ* St Andrews

6d Hubert Victor Evelyn; *b* 24 Dec 1895; *m* 1945 Nora (*d* 30 July 1968), yr dau of Norman B Stewart, MB, of Edinburgh, and *d* 20 Nov 1955

7d Mervyn Robert; *b* 24 May 1902; *d* 3 March 1909

8d Nigel Hugh; *b* 24 May 1902; Sub-Lt RN; *d* unm 30 April 1926

1c Esther; *b* 5 July 1850; *d* 25 July 1861

2c Alice Mary; *b* 8 Nov 1852; *d* 12 April 1865

3b (cont.) William Portal *m* 2nd 26 Aug 1860 Frances, widow of Arthur Morgan and dau of John Marshall, and *d* 12 Oct 1889

1a Elizabeth; *b* 13 Oct 1759; *m* John Thompson and had issue

2a Mary; *b* 17 April 1762; *m* John Woodin and had issue

3a Anne Cracroft; *b* 29 Dec 1766; *m* Moreton Walhouse Littleton and *d* 17 March 1843, having had issue (*see* HATHERTON, B)

4a Martha; *b* 2 Feb 1768; *m* 1st William Burton; *m* 2nd James Rondeau, of The Manor House, Bull's Cross, Enfield, Middx, and *dsp* Feb 1855

(3) William; *b* 1735; *m* twice and *d* 6 March 1815, having by his 1st w Elizabeth Yates had, with other issue (*d* unm):

1a William Benjamin (Rev); *b* 1767; *educ* St John's Coll Oxford (scholar, MA); Rector Wasing, Berks, Vicar Sandford, Oxon, Select Preacher to Oxford U 1804; *d* unm 1882

(1) Mary; *b* 1728; *m* William Nethersole and had issue

2 Henri/Henry, of S Stoneham and later of Freefolk, Hants; *b* Poitiers 1690; naturalised at Winchester 1711; entered paper-making trade and acquired the contract 1724 for manufacturing notes for the Bank of England; *m* 26 Dec 1715 Dorothy Hasker (*d* 29 Oct 1784), of Norrington, Overton, and *d* 30 Sept 1747, having had:

(1) JOSEPH

(1) Priscilla; *m* William Bridges

(2) Elizabeth; *m* William Peachy and *d* 9 Oct 1774, leaving issue

(3) Dorothy; *m* Charles Simkins, of Avebury, Wilts, and had issue

(4) Charlotte; *m* 16 Aug 1755 John Slade and had issue (*see* SLADE, Bt)

HENRY PORTAL's only s,

  JOSEPH PORTAL, of Laverstoke, Hants, JP; *b* 14 Aug 1720; High Sheriff Hants 1763; *m* 3 Nov 1748 Sarah (*d* 27 Dec 1802), dau of Gen John Peachy, of Alverstoke, Hants, and *d* 14 Dec 1793, having had:

1 Harry, of Laverstoke; *b* 1752; Capt 10th Hus; *d* unm 19 March 1801

2 William, of Ashe Park and later Laverstoke; *b* 12 Feb 1755; *m* 1789 his cousin Sophia (*d* 19 Jan 1837), sis of Sir John Slade, 1st Bt (*qv*), and *d* 12 Feb 1846, leaving a dau (*d* unm 1875)

3 JOHN

1 Charlotte; *m* 12 Feb 1795 Rev Sir John Filmer, 7th Bt (*see* 1916 edn), and *dsp* Aug 1813

2 Elizabeth; *m* Rev Stiverd Jenkings, of Locking, Somerset

JOSEPH PORTAL's yst s,

  JOHN PORTAL, of Freefolk Priory and Laverstoke, JP, DL; *b* 29 April 1764; *m* 1st 6 Oct 1794 Mary (*d* 1813), dau of John Corrie, of Hoddesdon, Herts, and had, with three sons and two other daus (all *d* young):

1 Caroline; *m* Rev William Knight, Rector Steventon, Hants, and nephew of Jane Austen, and *d* 20 March 1837, leaving issue

2 Charlotte; *m* 22 June 1831 Maurice Cely Trevilian, JP (*d* 26 Feb 1861), of Mildelney, Somerset, and *d* 27 Sept 1874, leaving issue

3 Frances; *m* 4 Dec 1828 Rev David Rodney Murray (*see* ELIBANK, L) and *d* 1892, leaving issue

JOHN PORTAL *m* 2nd 1 Aug 1815 Elizabeth (*d* 21 May 1877), only dau of Henry Drummond, of The Grange, Hants (*see* PERTH, E), and *d* 7 May 1848, having by her had, with another s (*d* young):

1 Melville, of Laverstoke, JP, DL; *b* 31 July 1819; MA, barrister, chm QS, MP N Hants 1849–57, High Sheriff Hants 1863; *m* 9 Oct 1855 Lady Charlotte Mary Elliot-Murray-Kynynmound (*d* 3 June 1899), dau of 2nd Earl of Minto (*qv*), and *d* 24 Jan 1904, having had, with a dau (*d* unm):

(1) Melville Raymond; *b* 9 Oct 1856; Capt Roy Lancs Regt; *das* Uganda 27 May 1893

(2) Gerald Herbert (Sir), KCMG (1892), CB (1888); *b* 13 March 1858; *educ* Eton; attd Agency and Consulate Gen Egypt; after bombardment of Alexandria 1882 was awarded medal with clasp and bronze star; Sec to Br Agency Cairo 1885–91, Actg Agent and Consul Gen Egypt 1886–88 and 1890, special mission to KING JOHN of Abyssinia 1887 (Offr St Maurice and St Lazarus Italy, Abyssinian Order Solomon), Actg Consul-Gen Zanzibar 1889–91, Consul-Gen Zanzibar (also Commissioner there) and for German E Africa 1891–94; *m* 1 Dec 1890 Lady Alice Josephine Bertie, JP (*d* 7 May 1950), 2nd dau of 7th Earl of Abingdon (*see* LINDSEY and ABINGDON, E), and *dsp* 25 Jan 1894

(3) Alaric William John; *b* 24 June 1861; Cdr RN; *d* unm 11 March 1906

(1) Adela Harriet, CBE (1920); *m* 20 May 1885 Lt-Gen Sir Alfred Edward Codrington, KCB, KCVO, CB, and *d* 14 Feb 1935, leaving issue (*see* CODRINGTON, Bt, of Dodington (1876))

(2) Katharine Charlotte; *m* 16 April 1896 Francis Walter Montagu-Douglas-Scott (*see* BUCCLEUCH and QUEENSBERRY, D) and *d* 12 Nov 1917

2 Robert, of Ashe Park, JP (Hants); *b* 7 Nov 1820; Capt 4th Light Dragoons (participated Charge Light Bde Crimean War), Lt-Col 5th Lancers; *m* Feb 1856 Eliza Charlotte (*d* 19 July 1902), dau of Maj-Gen Taylor, CB, of Ogwell, Devon, Lt-Govr Sandhurst, and *d* 24 Dec 1888, leaving:

(1) Evelyn Adela

3 WYNDHAM SPENCER PORTAL (Sir), **1st Bt**

4 George Raymond (Rev); *b* 28 Feb 1827; Rector Burghclere, Hants, Hon Canon Winchester; *m* 26 Dec 1860 Helen Mary Charlotte (*d* 9 May 1904), dau of — Solesby and widow of W Daubuz, of Killiow, Cornwall, and *d* 3 April 1889, having had, with other issue:

(1) Henry Raymond; *b* 4 Oct 1863; Lt 81st Regt; *d* unm 1885

(2) Maurice Raymond, DSO (1918); *b* 29 March 1870; Maj Remount Serv WW I; *m* 12 Oct 1897 Clara Ethel (*d* 11 June 1960), dau of George Jardine Kidston, of Finlaystone, Renfrew, and *dsp* 30 Dec 1955

(1) Helen Violet; *m* 31 Aug 1897 Richard Francis Nicholson (*see* NICHOLSON OF WINTERBOURNE, B) and *d* 2 Oct 1927, leaving issue

(2) Helen Margaret; *m* 17 Sept 1908 Adml Edmund Hyde Parker, CB (*see* PARKER, Bt, of Melford Hall), and *d* 8 Nov 1959

4 Adela; *m* 3 March 1840, as his 2nd w, Edward Knight (*d* 5 Nov 1879), of Chawton House, Hants, and Godmersham Park, Kent, est bro of her est sister's husb, and *d* 28 June 1870, leaving issue

5 Jane Eliza; *m* Sept 1863 Maj Thomas Dundas, 12th Regt (*d* 20 July 1902), and *d* 14 Nov 1900, leaving issue (*see* 1970 edn DUNDAS, Bt, of Arniston)

JOHN PORTAL's 3rd surv s,

Sir Wyndham Spencer Portal, 1st Bt (UK), so *cr* 11 March 1901, JP, DL (Hants); *b* 22 July 1822; *educ* Harrow and RMC Sandhurst; Ld Manor and patron livings Laverstoke and Freefolk, Capt Hants Yeo Cav 1842–65, v-chm and chm LSWR 1875–1900; *m* 19 April 1849 Mary Jane (*d* 4 Nov 1903), dau of William Hicks-Beach (*see* SAINT ALDWYN, E), and *d* 14 Sept 1905, leaving:

1 **Sir William Wyndham Portal, 2nd Bt**, JP; *b* 12 April 1850; *educ* Eton and Ch Ch Oxford (BA 1874, MA 1876); Ld Manor and patron livings Laverstoke and Freefolk; Hants: Chm QS, High Sheriff 1886, CC 1889–1931 (Alderman and V-Chm 1897–1920),V-Lt (previously DL) and Capt Artillery Militia, KJStJ, Order Mercy, Hon Freeman Winchester, dir and dep chm LSWR, chm Portals Ltd, Jr Bro Trin House, FSA; *m* 23 June 1880 Florence Elizabeth Mary, CBE, DGStJ (*d* 30 Dec 1931), dau of Hon St Leger Richard Glyn (*see* WOLVERTON, B), and *d* 30 Sept 1931, having had:

(1) **Sir Wyndham Raymond Portal, 3rd Bt**, and 1st and last VISCOUNT PORTAL, of Laverstoke, Co Southampton, so *cr* 1 Feb 1945, as also earlier 26 Jan 1935 BARON PORTAL, of Laverstoke, Co Southampton (both UK), GCMG, DSO (1917), MVO (1917), JP, PC (1942); *b* 9 April 1885; *educ* Eton and Ch Ch Oxford; Lt Hants Carabiniers, joined 9th Lancers 1905 and 1st Life Gds 1908, resigned as Lt 1911, served WW I (Lt-Col cmdg Household Bn and MG Bn, despatches, Brevet-Maj), Ld Lt Hants 1947–49, chm: Portals Ltd, Wiggins Teape & Co 1919, Compass Investment Tst, GWR 1944–47 (dir GWR 1927–40), Disabled Persons Corp, Nat Camps, 14th Olympic Games, Bacon Development Bd, Coal Production Ctee Wales and Treasury Fund Special Areas Reconstruction Ltd, V-Chm King George V Jubilee Tst, Ch Industl Advsr to Govt for four special areas, dir Commercial Union Assur, Regnl Commr Wales (Civ Def) 1939, Addnl Parly Sec to Minr of Supply 1940–42, Minr Works and Planning, 1st Commr Works and Public Bldgs 1942–44, Freeman Cardiff and Merthyr Tydfil, Hon LLD Wales 1937; *m* 20 April 1909 Lady (Louise) Rosemary Kathleen Virginia Cairns, MBE (1919), JP, and CA Hants (*d* 17 May 1962), only child of 2nd Earl Cairns (*qv*), and *dsp* 6 May 1949, when his peerages expired

(2) Robert St Leger; *b* 20 Nov 1892; Lt Rifle Bde, formerly T/Lt RHG; *m* 24 Nov 1920 (*annulled* 1922) Gwendoline, dau of Maj Eustace Scott Williams, DL, and *d* 20 July 1926

(1) Margery; *m* 1st 24 July 1907 Maj Thomas Geoffrey Rawstorne (*d* 31 July 1917 of wounds recd in action), Lancs Hus, of Dolwen, Newbridge-on-Wye, s of Lawrence Rawstorne, DL, of Hutton Hall, Preston, Herefs; *m* 2nd 27 Nov 1918 Charles Henry Evan-Thomas, JP (*d* 13 Sept 1943), of Caerwnon, Radnorshire, s of Charles Evan-Thomas, of Gnoll, Glam, and *dsp* 12 Dec 1962

(2) Mary Florence; *m* 16 Feb 1904 Capt Hon Charles Henry Stanley Monck, Coldstream Gds, er s of 5th Viscount Monck (*qv*), and *d* 12 Feb 1918, leaving issue

2 **Sir Spencer John Portal, 4th Bt**, JP; *b* 14 May 1864; *educ* Winchester and Ch Ch Oxford; Lt Hants Yeo, first chm (later pres) TSB Assoc and chm Nat Provincial Insur, v-chm Internat Thrift Inst 1930–31, dir Roy Exchange Assur, ktd 1928; *m* 4 Dec 1890 Mary Laura Florence (*d* 4 April 1932), dau of Col William Mure, MP, of Caldwell, and *d* 25 Nov 1955, having had:

(1) Oldric Spencer; *b* 12 Oct 1893; Capt Household Cav WW I; *ka* 3 May 1917

(2) Raymond Spencer; *b* 28 Jan 1897; Sub-Lt RN WW I; *ka* off Jutland 31 May 1916

(3) FRANCIS SPENCER (Sir), **5th Bt**

(1) Constance Spencer; *m* 3 Dec 1929 Rev Mellis Stuart Douglas (*d* 6 March 1963), s of Justyn George Durham Douglas, MC, of Bournemouth

3 Bertram Percy (Sir), KCB (1937), DSO (1902), JP, DL (Hants); *b* 10 Jan 1866; *educ* Wellington and RMC Sandhurst; joined 17th Lancers 1885 (commanded as Lt-Col and Brevet-Col 1903–07), ADC to Govr Madras 1896–98, Boer War 1899–1902 (despatches, S African Medal with three clasps, King's Medal with two clasps) and WW I (despatches, cmded Reserve Cav Regt 1914–16 and Cav Bde France 1916–18), Hon Brig-Gen 1919, Chm Hants and IoW TAA 1925–38, CC Hants and V-Lt 1932–42, CA Hants 1943, Govr Wellington Coll 1934–44; *m* 12 April 1899 Hon Margaret Louisa Littleton (*d* following a car crash 7 Feb 1945), dau of 3rd Baron Hatherton (*qv*), and *d* 7 Feb 1949, leaving:

(1) Melville Edward Bertram, MBE (1946); *b* 1 June 1900; *educ* Eton and RMC Sandhurst; Maj Coldstream Gds 1927, commnd 17th Lancers 1921, ADC to his f-in-law when Govr Madras 1924–27 and Viceroy and Actg Govr-Gen India 1929, seconded to Malay Regt 1935–45 (prisoner at Changi 1942–45), Queen's Messenger 1951–61; *m* 27 Nov 1926 Hon Cicely Winifred Goschen (*d* 1980), yr dau of 2nd Viscount Goschen (*qv*), and *d* 1971, leaving:

1a +Simon George Melville [Simon Portal Esq, 9 Kelso Place, London W8 5QD]; *b* 18 Sept 1927; *educ* Radley; late Capt 17th/21st Lancers (Palestine 1948, Korea 1950–51 attd 8th Hus and Trucial Oman Levies 1955–56), ADC to C-in-C Far East Land Forces 1958–59, memb London Stock Exchange 1960–65; *m* 13 June 1962 (*divorce* 1971) Gillian, yst dau of Maj James Cyril Aubrey George Dance, MP, of Moreton House, Moreton Morrell, Warwicks, and has:

1b +Robert Melville; *b* 3 July 1967; actor

(1) *Charlotte Mary [Mrs Richard Longfield, Lower Silton, Gillingham, Dorset]; *b* 1903; *m* 27 April 1929 Col Richard James Longfield, JP (held HAAKON VII OF NORWAY's Liberty Cross and *d* 1987), 2nd s of Maj Lewis Longfield, of Longueville, Mallow, Co Cork, and has had:

1a *Desmond Richard Henry [Brigadier Desmond Longfield, Paccombe Farm House, Downton, Salisbury, Wilts SP5 3PP]; *b* 24 Feb 1931; *educ* Wellington; Brig RA; *m* 8 Aug 1959 *Jennifer, yr dau of Clement William Robert Spencer Thomas, of Upper Honeydon, nr Bedford, and has:

1b *James Desmond Spencer; *b* 2 March 1964; *m* 1993 *Rosalind S G, 2nd dau of Michael Pulvertaft, of Sunshine Beach, Qld, and has:

1c *Mathilda Sarah Graham; *b* 1996

1b *Melanie Louisa; *b* 29 May 1961; *m* 1986 *Simon Jonathan and has:

1c *Oliver George David; *b* 1990

2c *Robert Patrick James; *b* 1992

1c *Sophie Charlotte; *b* 1995

2b *Harriet Sarah; *b* 9 Aug 1965; *m* 12 Oct 1996 *Jeremy Richard Skeet and has:

1c *Eloise Kate Longfield; *b* 1995

3b *Charlotte Jane; *b* 1970

1a Susan Mary; *b* 24 Feb 1935; *educ* St George's Sch Ascot and Guildhall Sch of Music and Drama (Silver Medal and Singing Prize 1957); singer as Susan Longfield (particularly oratorio), LRAM, AGSM, commemorated in the Susan Longfield Memorial Award at Guildhall; *m* 16 Feb 1963 David Ralph Bastin (*k* Addis Ababa air disaster 18 April 1972), only s of Maj-Gen George Edward Restalic Bastin, CB, OBE, of Dunmoorland, Dunmow Hill, Fleet, Hants, and *d* 27 Aug 1970, leaving:

1b *Peter George; *b* 8 May 1964

(2) *Hyacinthe Eveline [Mrs Malcolm Mackintosh, Orchard Plot, East Chaldon, Dorset]; *b* 1904; *m* 15 Nov 1929 Malcolm Arthur Aeneas Mackintosh (*d* 1966), 2nd s of Duncan Houston Mackintosh, of Drumallin, Inverness, and has:

1a *Angus Malcolm [Angus Mackintosh Esq, St Algar's Farm, West Woodlands, Frome, Somerset]; *b* 23 Nov 1930; *educ* Marlborough; *m* 27 Sept 1958 *Brenda Joyce, er dau of Clement William Robert Spencer Thomas and sis of his cousin's w, and has had:

1b Ewan Angus; *b* 9 June 1960; *d* 1977

2b *Robert Malcolm; *b* 20 June 1962

3b *Alexander William; *b* 25 Dec 1964

4b *William Aeneas; *b* 1973

1a *Anne Evelyn [Mrs John Harrison, Ashford House, Madley, Herefs HR2 9NJ]; *b* 21 Jan 1936; *m* 1986 *John Bennett Harrison

(3) *Margaret Cecilia [Mrs John Litchfield, Snowfield, Bearsted, Kent]; *b* 19 July 1908; *m* 23 Sept 1939 Capt John Shirley Sandys LITCHFIELD-SPEER later LITCHFIELD (deed poll 29 Dec 1949), OBE, RN, MP (C) Chelsea 1959–66 (*d* 1993), est s of R-Adml Frederick Shirley Litchfield-Speer, CMG, DSO, of Wateringbury Place, Kent, and has:

1a *Mark Shirley Portal [Mark Litchfield Esq, The Hermitage, Boxley, Maidstone, Kent]; *b* 1 Nov 1940; *educ* Eton and RNC Dartmouth; late Lt RN; *m* 1974 (*divorce* 1978) Marcia Osorio and has:

1b *Vasco; *b* 1974

1b *Larissa; *b* 1975

1a Sophie Mary Cecilia; *b* 8 Dec 1942; *m* 1970 *John Irvin [John Irvin Esq, 6 Lower Common South, London SW15] and *d* 1992, leaving:

1b *Luke Litchfield; *b* 1973

1b *Emilie Jane; *b* 1970

2b *Amy Hyacinthe; *b* 1978

2a *Virginia Margaret; b 14 Oct 1945

(4) *Sophie, MBE (Mily, 1947), TD (1953) [Miss Sophie Portal MBE TD, Southington House, Overton, Basingstoke, Hants]; b 1 July 1910; Jr Cdr ATS WW II

(5) *Cecilia Violet [Mrs Nigel Hoare, Southington House, Overton, Hants]; b 1911; m 20 Sept 1937 Lt-Col Nigel Walter Hoare, OBE, TD, RA (d 1988), 3rd s of Walter Robertson Hoare, of Daneshill, Basingstoke, and has had:

1a *Hyacinthe Cecilia; b 15 Oct 1938; m 22 July 1961 (divorce 1972) Piers Scandrett Harford, yr s of Sir Arthur Harford, 2nd Bt (qv), and has issue

2a *Joanna Bridget [Mrs Jeremy Durham-Matthews, Southington House, Overton, Hants RG25 3DA]; b 31 Aug 1940; m 28 Oct 1961 *Jeremy Francis Patrick Durham-Matthews, late Irish Gds, only s of Capt J R Durham-Matthews, Irish Gds, and Mrs J D Moore, of Loxwood, W Sussex, and has:

1b *John Patrick Nigel; b 24 Feb 1967; educ Eton; m 1995 *Helen Jane, est dau of Peter Smith, of Taverham, Norfolk

1b *Miranda Elizabeth [Mrs Simon Collins, The Elms, Tilshead, Salisbury, Wilts]; b 29 Aug 1962; m 1988 *Simon Hitchman Collins and has:

1c *Timothy Walter Hitchman; b 1988

1c *Isabel Cecilia; b 1990

2c *Frances Joanna; b 1994

3c *Millicent Jane; b 1997

2b *Lucy Mary [Mrs Richard Bamford, Axmansford Cottage, Axmansford, Hants RG26 5SB]; b 30 July 1965; m 1989 *Richard John Bamford and has:

1c *Constance Amelia; b 1991

2c *Elizabeth Maria; b 1993

3c *Henrietta Mary; b 1996

3b *Catherine Ann; b 1972

3a *Louisa Margaret [Mrs Trevor Newman, The Holt, Ashford Hill, Berks]; b 6 Feb 1945; m 3 Aug 1968 *Trevor John Bisset Newman, 2nd s of William Newman, of London SE, and has:

1b *Zachary John Bisset; b 1972

1b *Henrietta Louisa; b 1975

2b *Veronica Margaret; b 1977

4a Henrietta Maria; b 19 Dec 1947; k in a car crash 21 June 1969

1 Constance Mary; m 1st 26 April 1871 William Howley Kingsmill, JP, DL (d 25 April 1894), of Sydmonton Court, Hants, and had issue; m 2nd 2 Feb 1910 George Herbert Pember (d 22 March 1921), of Fair Oak Park, Hants, and d 26 Feb 1947

2 Eleanor Jane; m 6 April 1875 Chaloner William Chute, DL (d 30 May 1892), of The Vyne, Basingstoke (see 1956 edn CHUTE, Bt), and d 26 March 1944, leaving issue

3 Mary Adelaide; m 3 June 1880 2nd Baron Addington (qv) and d 3 Dec 1933, leaving issue

4 Eveline Maude; m 25 Aug 1881 Hon Evelyn Hubbard and d 29 Oct 1945, leaving issue (see ADDINGTON, B)

Sir SPENCER's only surv s,

Sir Francis Spencer Portal, 5th Bt, DL (Hants 1967); b 27 June 1903; educ Winchester, Ch Ch Oxford and McGill U Montreal; Capt Welsh Gds (Gds' Armoured Div), High Sheriff Hants 1963, pres Portals Holdings Ltd, dir Roy Exchange Assur Co Ltd, pres and chm YMCA S Regn, memb YMCA Nat Cncl, chm YMCA Nat Commn 1969, FRSA, Belgian Croix de Guerre 2nd Class; m 1st 9 Dec 1930 Rowena (d 14 Aug 1948), only dau of Paul Selby, of Johannesburg, and had:

1 *(Rowena) Jeanne [Mrs Richard Altham, Crunnells Green House, Preston, Hitchin, Herts SG4 7UF]; b 16 Nov 1931; m 28 Sept 1957 Richard James Livingstone Altham, only s of Harry Surtees Altham, CBE, DSO, MC, of Winchester, and has:

(1) *David Richard Spencer [David Altham Esq, The Old Rectory, Southery, Norfolk PE38 0MD]; b 19 Jan 1959; m 12 June 1993 *Sandra Louise Bunn, of Arizona

(2) *Robert Patrick James [Robert Altham Esq, 2 Willow Walk, Cambridge CB1 1LA]; b 25 July 1960

(3) *Alastair John Livingstone [Alastair Altham Esq, 1 Devereux Rd, London SW11 6JF]; b 7 Aug 1963; m 21 May 1994 *Carolina Wilhelmina Koopman and has:

1a *Harry Willem Livingstone; b 19 Sept 1995

2a *Angus John Learmouth; b 10 Oct 1997

2 Coralie Mary; b 4 May 1937; m 12 Dec 1966 *Brian Harry Wright, RD [Brian Wright Esq RD, 56 Brompton Sq, London SW3], er s of Harry Wright, of Ashtead, Surrey, and d 198–, leaving:

(1) *Alexander Francis; b 6 March 1968

(1) *Rowena Sarah; b 26 Feb 1970

Sir Francis m 2nd 7 Oct 1950 *Jane Mary [Jane Lady Portal DL, Priors Barton Cottage, Kingsgate Rd, Winchester, Hants SO23 9QF], dau of Albert Henry Williams, OBE, of The Flint House, Langstone, Hants, and d 11 Nov 1984, leaving by her:

1 Sir JONATHAN FRANCIS PORTAL, **6th and present Bt**

2 +Philip Francis; b 6 July 1957; educ Radley and Durham U; m 1989 *Catherine Decker and has:

(1) +Simon Joe; b 1988

(2) +Louis Philip; b 1991

(3) +Daniel Sandy Philip; b 1995

(1) *Mary Jane; b 13 Oct 1955

PORTARLINGTON

Arms: Quarterly, 1st and 4th, barry nebuly of six argent and gules, over all a bend engrailed azure (for DAMER); 2nd and 3rd, azure a chevron ermine between three arrows points downwards or; on a chief argent three martlets sable, and on a canton gules a mullet or (for DAWSON). **Crests:** 1 Out of a mural crown or a talbot's head azure, eared gold (for DAMER); 2 A cat's head, full faced, erased near the shoulders, of a tabby colour, holding in the mouth a rat sable (for DAWSON). **Supporters:** Two heraldic tigers, proper.
Motto: Vitæ via virtus ('Virtue is my way of life').
Creations: B. (I) 29 May 1770, V. (I) 24 July 1776, E. (I) 21 June 1785.

THE 7TH EARL OF PORTARLINGTON, in Queen's County, **Viscount Carlow**, Co Carlow, and **Lord Dawson, Baron Dawson of Dawson's Court**, Queen's Co (George Lionel Yuill Seymour Dawson-Damer) [The Rt Hon The Earl of Portarlington, 118 Wolseley Rd, Point Piper, NSW 2027, Australia; Gledswood, Melrose, Roxburghshire TD6 9DN]; b 10 Aug 1938 (HRH THE late DUKE OF KENT stood sponsor); s gf 1959; educ Eton; Page of Honour to HM THE QUEEN April 1953–Feb 1955; 2nd Lt Irish Gds 1956–58; dir: G S Yuill and Co Sydney 1964, Clyde Agriculture Ltd (Sydney) 1994–, Scottish Mortgage & Tst plc (Edinburgh) 1997–, pres Australian-Malaysia-Singapore Assoc 1965–; m 26 July 1961 *Davina, est dau of Sir Edward Henry Windley, KCMG, KCVO, by Patience Ann, née Sergison-Brooke (see BROOKEBOROUGH, V), and has:

1 +CHARLES GEORGE YUILL SEYMOUR, Viscount Carlow [Viscount Carlow, c/o John Swire & Sons, GPO Box 1, Hong Kong]; b 6 Oct 1965; educ Eton and Edinburgh U (MA); Page of Honour to HM THE QUEEN 1979–81

2 +Edward Lionel Seymour, MVO (1994) [The Hon Edward Dawson-Damer, Gledswood, Melrose, Roxburghshire TD6 9DN]; b 10 Nov 1967; Equerry to HM QUEEN ELIZABETH THE QUEEN MOTHER 1992–94, Capt

3 +Henry Lionel Seymour [The Hon Henry Dawson-Damer, 118 Wolseley Rd, Point Piper, NSW 2027, Australia]; b 5 Aug 1971; educ Eton and Edinburgh U (MA)

1 *Marina Davina [The Lady Marina Dawson-Damer, 76 Burton Court, Franklins Row, London SW3 4SX]; b 8 Aug 1969

Other Portarlington creation: The Earl of Galway (see GALWAY, V, preliminary remarks) had conferred on him as a subsidiary title a Barony of Portarlington in 1692.

Lineage (of Damer): JOSEPH DAMER, of Chapel, Devon; m Jane, dau of William St Lo, of Dorset, and had, with a yr s (Ambrose, b 1572):

ROBERT DAMER, of Chapel; b 1571; m 1600 Mary, dau of Edward Colmer, and had, with a dau (Elizabeth):

1 John, of Godmanston; b 1602; m 1628 Elizabeth, dau of Rev William Maber, and had, with other issue (dsp):

(1) Joseph; Parly Army offr Civil War; sold his lands in Somerset and Dorset and bought others in Ireland, where he settled 1661/2; d unm 6 July 1720 and bequeathed his estates to his nephew John

(2) George; m 1644; m Sarah, dau of Richard Fowler, and d 1730, having had:

1a John, of Shronehill, Co Tipperary; bought 1722 for £22,000 (just under £1,500,000 in late-1990s terms) from Robert Curtis (who in turn had bought the same property from the Duke of Ormonde (see 1970 edn ORMONDE, M) in 1703) the town and lordship of Roscrea, Co Tipperary, where a mansion called Damer House still occupies the premier site within the walls of the castle and commemorates the family's ascendancy, though it seems they never lived there; m 1724 Margaret, est dau of Andrew Roe, of Roesborough, Co Tipperary, and dsp 1768, when the estates passed to his bro

2a JOSEPH

1a Elizabeth; m 1717 Edward Clavell, of Smedmore

GEORGE DAMER's yr s,

JOSEPH DAMER, of Winterbourne-Came, Dorset; b 1676; MP 1722–27, described by the writer Horace Walpole (a cousin of Anne Damer (the w of the est s of the 1st Earl of Dorchester; see below) as a miser and usurer; m 6 Dec 1714

Mary, dau of John Churchill, of Henbury, Dorset, and *d* 1 March 1736/7, having had:

1 JOSEPH DAMER, 1st EARL OF DORCHESTER, so *cr* 18 May 1792, as also VISCOUNT MILTON OF MILTON ABBEY, Co Dorset (both GB), and earlier 3 July 1753 BARON MILTON OF SHRONEHILL, Co Tipperary (I), also 10 or 11 May 1762 BARON MILTON OF MILTON ABBEY, Co Dorset (GB), PC (I 1753); *b* 12 March 1717/8; MP (Whig) Weymouth 1741–47, Bramber 1747–54 and Dorchester 1754–62; High Steward Dorchester, built the model village of Milton Abbas, Dorset, to the designs of Sir William Chambers on a sloping site selected by 'Capability' Brown as replacement for a market town he had had demolished (flooding the valley, in particular the home of a local lawyer called Harrison who had opposed the land clearance) on the grounds that it ruined his view; *m* 21 July 1742 Lady Caroline Sackville (*b* 6 March 1718; *d* 24 March 1775), only surv dau of 1st Duke of Dorset (*see* SACKVILLE, B), and *d* 12 Jan 1798, having had

(1) John; *b* 25 June 1744; *m* 14 June 1767 Anne (*b* 1749; a distinguished sculptor, who among other commissions executed a bust of Charles James Fox for the EMPEROR NAPOLEON and one of Nelson for HRH THE DUKE OF CLARENCE and was left Strawberry Hill by her cousin Horace Walpole (*see* above); she *d* 28 May 1828), only child of FM Henry Seymour Conway, bro of 1st Marquess of Hertford (*qv*), and shot himself dead 15 Aug 1776

(2) GEORGE DAMER, 2nd and last EARL OF DORCHESTER, PC (GB 1794, I 1795); *b* 28 March 1746; *educ* Eton and Trin Coll Cambridge (MA 1769); MP (Whig) Cricklade 1768–74, Crail 1778–80, Dorchester 1780–91, Malton 1792–98 and (I Parl) Naas 1795–97, Maj 87th Foot 1779, Lt-Col W Indies 1782, Ch Sec to Ld Lt Ireland 1794–95, Ld Lt Dorset 1803–08; *d* unm at Dorchester House, Park Lane (site of the modern hotel of that name), 7 March 1808, when his titles expired

(3) Lionel; *b* 16 Sept 1748; *m* 16 April 1778 Williamsa, dau of William Janssen, s of Sir Stephen Janssen and niece of Sir Stephen Theodore Janssen, 4th and last Bt, and *dsp* 28 May 1807

(1) Caroline; *b* 4 May 1752; *d* unm 1829, when the Damer estates, which included Milton Abbey, passed to her cousin **1st Earl of Portarlington** (*see* below)

2 John, of Winterbourne-Came; *b* 27 Oct 1720; LLD, MP Dorchester; *m* Martha, dau of Samuel Rush, of Benhall, Suffolk, and *d* 26 Dec 1783

3 George; MP Dorset 1750–51; *d* unm 1752

1 Mary; *m* 8 Dec 1737 **1st Viscount Carlow** (*see* below) and had:

(1) JOHN DAWSON, **1st Earl**

2 Martha; *b* 23 April 1719; *m* 1st 17 June 1741 Sir Edward Crofton, 4th Bt (*dsp* 26 March 1745), of The Mote, Co Roscommon; *m* 2nd Ezekiel Nesbitt, MD, and *d* July 1777

Lineage (of Dawson): WILLIAM DAWSON, the first member of the family known to have settled in Ireland; Collector Revenue Cos Down and Antrim and Carrickfergus *temp* CHARLES II; *m* Elizabeth, dau of Alexander Jardine, one of the JARDINEs of Applegirth (*see* JARDINE, Bt, of Applegirth), and had:

EPHRAIM DAWSON; MP Queen's Co; bought Portarlington and other estates; *m* Anne, dau and heiress of Samuel Preston, of Emo, Queen's Co, 2nd s of John Preston, of Ardsallagh, Co Meath, and *d* 27 Aug 1746, leaving a 2nd but est surv s:

WILLIAM HENRY DAWSON, **1st Viscount Carlow**, Co Carlow (I), so *cr* 24 July 1776, as also earlier 29 May 1770 LORD DAWSON, BARON DAWSON OF DAWSON'S COURT, in the Queen's County (both I); MP Portarlington 1733–60 and 1769–90 and Queen's Co 1761–68, Govr Queen's Co 1750 on; *m* 8 Dec 1737 Mary (*d* 2 June 1769), est dau of Joseph Damer, of Winterbourne-Came, Dorset (*see* above) and *d* 22 Aug 1779, having had, with four yr sons and three daus:

JOHN DAWSON, **1st Earl of Portarlington**, Queen's Co (I), so *cr* 21 June 1785, PC (Ireland, 1795); *b* 23 Aug 1744; *educ* Eton and Trin Coll Cambridge; MP Portarlington 1766–68 and Queen's Co 1768–71 and 1776–79, Govr Queen's Co 1779–98, commissioned Emo Court, nr Portlaoise, Co Laois, from James Gandon *c* 1790 (house completed 1834–36 in the 2nd Earl's time by Lewis Vulliamy), commanded Queen's Co Militia in suppressing the 1798 Uprising; *m* 1 Jan 1778 Lady Caroline Stuart (*b* May 1750; *d* 20 Jan 1813), 5th dau of 3rd Earl of Bute (*see* BUTE, M), and *d* 30 Nov 1798, having had:

1 JOHN DAWSON, **2nd Earl of Portarlington**; *b* 26 Feb 1781; *educ* Eton; Army: Lt 20th (E Devon) Foot 1798, Capt 23rd Light Dragoons 1800 and 16th (Queen's) Light Dragoons 1804, Maj 4th Garrison Bn 1806 and 3rd (E Kent) Foot 1807, Lt-Col 10th (N Lincs) Foot 1808 and 23rd Light Dragoons 1809–15 (served Peninsula, where present Talavera 1809, and Waterloo Campaign, where present at Quatre Bras and Waterloo (the latter so late in the day — 1900 hrs), though from negligence or physical indisposition rather than pusillanimity, that he was retired), Col 1814; *d* unm 28 Dec 1845

2 Henry DAWSON later DAWSON-DAMER (roy licence 14 March 1829 on inheriting part of the Damer estates), of Milton Abbey, Dorset; *b* 19 July 1786; Capt RN; *m* 20 May 1813 Eliza (*d* 12 June 1857), dau of Capt Edmund Joshua Moriarty, RN, by Lady Lucy Luttrell, dau of 1st Earl of Carhampton, and *d* 27 May 1841, leaving:

(1) HENRY JOHN REUBEN DAWSON-DAMER, **3rd Earl of Portarlington**, KP (1879), DL; *b* 5 Sept 1822; rep I peer (C) 1855–89; *m* 2 Sept 1847 Lady Alexandrina Octavia Vane, dau of 3rd Marquess of Londonderry (*qv*), and *dsp* 1 March 1889

(1) Jane; granted with her sisters 13 Feb 1846 rank of earl's daus; *d* 26 Aug 1853

(2) Caroline Maryr; *m* 16 Dec 1847 Adml Sir George St Vincent Duckworth-King, 4th Bt, KCB (*d* 18 Aug 1891; *see* 1970 edn), and *d* 5 Dec 1851, leaving issue

(3) Elizabeth Williamsa Anne; *m* 20 Dec 1847 her cousin Col Hardress Luttrell Saunderson (*b* 1822; Capt 66th Regt, Col Cavan Militia; *d* 21 June 1881), est s of Col Hardress Robert Saunderson, of Northbrook House, Hants, by Lady Maria Anne Luttrell-Olmius, dau of 3rd and last Earl of Carhampton, and *dsp* 13 Feb 1897

(4) Louisa Georgiana; *m* 3 March 1853 Capt John Chichester Knox, 2nd Dragoon Gds, s of Rt Hon George Knox (*see* RANFURLY, E), and *dsp* 25 April 1904

3 George Lionel DAWSON later DAWSON-DAMER (roy licence 14 March 1829 on inheriting part of the Damer estates), CB, PC; *b* 28 Oct 1788; *m* 1825 Mary Georgiana Emma (*d* 30 Oct 1848), dau of Lord Hugh Seymour (*see* HERTFORD, M), and *d* 14 April 1856, having had:

(1) LIONEL SEYMOUR WILLIAM, **4th Earl**

(1) Georgiana Augusta Charlotte Caroline; *m* 11 March 1847 3rd Earl Fortescue (*qv*) and *d* 8 Dec 1866, leaving issue

(2) Cecilia Blanche Horatio Seymour; granted with her surv sisters rank of earl's daus; *m* 26 April 1859 Lt-Col Francis Haygarth, Scots Fus Gds (*d* 18 April 1911), and *dsp* 30 July 1922

(3) Alice Henrietta; *d* young

(4) Evelyn Mary Stuart; *m* 19 April 1855 Capt Francis Sutton, RHG, 3rd s of Sir Richard Sutton, 2nd Bt (*qv*), and *d* 27 Oct 1899, leaving issue

(5) Constance Wilhelmina Frances; *m* 26 Aug 1856 Sir John Leslie, 1st Bt (*qv*), and *d* 25 June 1925, leaving issue

4 Lionel Charles; *b* 7 May 1790; *m* 15 Sept 1820 Lady Elizabeth Emily Nugent (*d* 6 Sept 1863), 2nd dau of 7th Earl of Westmeath (*qv*), and *d* 25 Feb 1842, leaving, with other issue:

(1) George Frederick; *b* 1 June 1827; Capt RE; *m* 31 Aug 1854 Elizabeth (*m* 2nd 10 Jan 1859 John Roddam Spencer Stanhope, yst dau of John James King, of Preston Candover, Hants, and was *ka* Sebastopol 6 June 1855, leaving:

1a Georgina Frederica; *b* posthumously 6 Oct 1855; *m* Feb 1875 Arthur Henry Mure (*d* 12 Feb 1931), of S Kensington, and *d* 12 April 1944, having had issue

(1) Caroline Margaret; Maid-of-Honour to HM QUEEN VICTORIA; *m* 10 March 1851 her cousin 3rd Baron Congleton (*qv*) and *d* 17 Jan 1912, leaving issue

(2) Frances Catherine; *m* 4 Jan 1858 Lt-Col Henry Torrens d'Aguilar, Gren Gds (*d* 1895), est s of Sir George d'Aguilar, KCB, and *d* 25 Feb 1899, leaving issue

5 William Mackenzie; *b* 1793; *m* 1st 1820 Patience (*d* 1821), yst dau of Gen Scott; *m* 2nd 1827 Louisa Frances (*d* 24 June 1847), dau of S T Wright, and by her had, with two sons (*d* young):

(1) Lionel Digby William (Rev); *b* 9 Nov 1832; Vicar Canford, Dorset, Hon Canon Salisbury; *m* 26 Oct 1871 Edith Sophia Harriet (*d* 24 Jan 1905), dau of Raikes Currie, of Minley Manor, Hants, and *dsp* 3 July 1888

(2) John William George; *b* 11 Oct 1834; Lt RN; *d* unm 14 March 1869

(1) Louisa Mary Anne; *m* 4 April 1854 Richard Cane (*d* 2 March 1891) and *d* 6 May 1855

5 (cont.) The Hon William Dawson-Damer *m* 3rd 20 May 1856 Julia, yst dau of Capt Hopkinson, RN, and *d* 16 Feb 1859

1 Caroline Elizabeth; *m* 4 Feb 1801 1st Baron Congleton (*qv*) and *d* Paris 16 Feb 1861

2 Louisa Mary; *m* 2 Feb 1829, as his 2nd w, Rev Walter Davenport Bromley, of Baginton, and *d* 18 Aug 1845

3 Harriet; *m* 4 May 1813 Very Rev and Hon David Erskine (*see* BUCHAN, E) and *d* 16 Dec 1827, leaving issue

4 Anna Maria; *d* 12 Dec 1866

The 3rd EARL's cousin,

LIONEL SEYMOUR WILLIAM DAWSON-DAMER, **4th Earl of Portarlington**, DL; *b* 7 April 1832; *educ* Eton; Scots Fus Gds 1849–56 (Capt Crimean War, present Battles of the Alma and Inkerman), MP (C) Portarlington 1857–65 and 1868–80; *m* 19 April 1855 Hon Harriet Lydia Montagu (*b* 23 July 1829; *d* 23 Nov 1894), 2nd dau of Gen 6th and last Baron Rokeby of Armagh, GCB (*see* 1883 edn), and *d* 17 Dec 1892, leaving:

1 LIONEL GEORGE HENRY SEYMOUR, **5th Earl**

2 Montagu Francis Beauchamp Seymour; *b* 1 Oct 1864; *m* 5 Feb 1896 Margaret Stirling (*d* 18 June 1951), dau of Thomas MacLeod, of Brisbane, and *d* 24 March 1898, leaving:

(1) Mary Lydia Seymour; *d* unm 4 May 1969

1 Mary Frances Seymour; *b* 26 July 1860; *m* 21 July 1880 Hon Algernon Henry Mills, 2nd s of 1st Baron Hillingdon (*d* 21 Oct 1922; *see* 1970 edn), and *d* 24 Feb 1895, leaving issue

The 4th EARL's er s,

LIONEL GEORGE HENRY SEYMOUR DAWSON-DAMER, **5th Earl of Portarlington**, JP (Dorset and Queen's Co), DL; *b* 19 Aug 1858; *educ* Eton; Lt 2nd Bn Scots Gds 1878–86, Hon Col 4th Bn Leinster Regt, Capt and Hon Maj Dorset Yeo Cav, rep I peer (C) 1896–1900; *m* 25 Oct 1881 Emma Andalusia Frere (*m* 2nd 25 Sept 1901 3rd Viscount Portman (*qv*) and *d* 13 May 1929), only child of Lord Nigel Kennedy (*see* AILSA, M), and *d* 31 Aug 1900, leaving:

1 LIONEL ARTHUR HENRY SEYMOUR, **6th Earl**

2 George Seymour; *b* 30 July 1892; Lt 10th Hus and Dorset Yeo; *d* 12 April 1917 of wounds recd in action

1 Aline Mary Seymour, MBE (1946); *b* 18 Oct 1884; *m* 15 Oct 1904 Lt-Col Valentine Vivian, CMG, DSO, MVO, Gren Gds (*d* 1 Feb 1948), er s of William Vivian, of 185 Queen's Gate, London SW, and *d* 12 Sept 1953, leaving issue

2 Christian Norah; *b* 7 Aug 1890; Coronation Medal 1937; *m* 1st 17 Sept 1914 Capt Hon Fergus Bowes-Lyon (*ka* 1915, *see* STRATHMORE AND KINGHORNE, E) and had issue; *m* 2nd 4 June 1919 Capt William Frederick Martin, JP, Indian Police, 3rd s of Charles William Wall Martin, LLD (*d* 6 Oct 1947), of Killeshandra, Co Cavan, and *d* 29 March 1959, leaving further issue

3 Moyra Marjorie; *b* 23 March 1897; *m* 3 June 1924 Capt James Brinsley Peter FitzGerald (*see* FitzGERALD, Bt, of Valencia) and had issue; they both *d* following a car crash 17 April 1962

The 5th EARL's er s,

LIONEL ARTHUR HENRY SEYMOUR DAWSON-DAMER, **6th Earl of Portarlington**; *b* 26 Aug 1883; *educ* Eton; 2nd Lt Irish Gds 1903–05, Lt 4th Bn Leinster Regt WW I; *m* 2 Feb 1907 Winnafreda, only child of George Skelton Yuill, of Knightsbridge, and *d* 4 July 1959, having had:

George Lionel Seymour, *Viscount Carlow*; *b* 20 Dec 1907; *educ* Eton; Lt Res of Offrs Gren Gds WW I, A/Cdre AAF 1938; *m* 7 Jan 1937 Peggy (*m* 2nd 14 Nov 1945 (*divorce* 1956) Peter George Hodges Nugent, s of Col George Hodges Nugent, RA, of Churt, Surrey (*see* 1970 edn NUGENT OF GUILDFORD, B), and *d* 1 Nov 1963), yr dau of Charles Cambie, of Toronto, and was *kas* 17 April 1944, leaving:

1 GEORGE LIONEL YUILL SEYMOUR DAWSON-DAMER, **7th and present Earl of Portarlington**

2 +Lionel John Charles Seymour [The Hon Lionel Dawson-Damer, 1 Rose Bay Ave, Bellevue Hill, NSW 2023, Australia]; *b* 12 Oct 1940 (HRH PRINCESS MARINA DUCHESS OF KENT stood sponsor); *educ* Eton; *m* 1st 10 Dec 1965 (*divorce* 1975) Rosemary (Rosie) Ashley Morrett (*m* 2nd 1977 (*divorce* 1983), as his 3rd w, 7th Marquess of Northampton, *qv*), only dau of P G M Hancock, of Nottingham, and Mrs Magin Hancock, of Tinkers Castle, Zelah, Cornwall; *m* 2nd 1982 *Ashley, dau of W/Cdr W Mann, of Australia

PORTER OF LUDDENHAM

Creation: B. (LP, UK) 1990.

THE BARON PORTER OF LUDDENHAM, of Luddenham, Co Kent (Sir George Porter, OM (1989)) [The Rt Hon The Lord Porter of Luddenham OM, The Old Rectory, Luddenham, Kent ME13 OTE; 53 Prince's Gdns, Exhibition Rd, London SW7]; *b* 6 Dec 1920; *educ* Thorne GS, Leeds U (BSc) and Emmanuel Coll Cambridge (MA, PhD, ScD, Fell 1952–54, Hon Fell 1967); RNVR Radar Offr WW II; Demonstrator Physical Chemistry Cambridge 1949–52, Assist Dir Research Physical Chemistry 1952–54; Assist Dir Br Rayon Research Assoc 1954–55; Sheffield U: Prof Physical Chemistry 1955–63, Firth Prof 1963–66, Head Chemistry Dept 1955–66; memb: ARC 1964–66, Advsy Scientific Ctee Nat Gallery 1966–68, BBC Sci Consultative Gp 1967–75, Cncl OU 1969–75, Sci Museum Advsy Cncl 1970–73, SRG Cncl and Science Bd 1976–80, ACOST 1987–91, Academia Europaea 1987; ktd 1972; Dir and Resident Prof Roy Inst 1966–85; Tstee: BM 1972–74; Pres: Chemical Soc 1970–72, Comité Internat de photobiologie 1968–72, Nat Assoc for Gifted Children 1975–80, R and D Soc 1977–82, Roy Soc 1985–90, Assoc for Sci Ed 1985, BAAS 1985–86; Counsellor Inst Molecular Science Okasaki Japan 1980–83; Research Prof Imperial Coll 1987–; Chm Centre for Molecular Sciences 1990–; Chllr Leicester U 1986–; Hon DSc Oxford, Hon LLD Cambridge, Jt Nobel Prize Chemistry 1967, Faraday Medal Roy Soc Chemistry 1981, Davy Medal 1971, Rumford Medal 1978, Copley Medal Royal Soc 1990, FRS 1960, Hon Fell: QMC, Imperial Coll; Hon FRSE 1983, Hon FRSC 1991, Hon Memb Roy Inst 1988, For Assoc American Acad Arts and Sciences; Master Salters' Co 1993–1994 (Liveryman 1981–); author: *Chemistry for the Modern World* (1962), TV Series: *Laws of Disorder* (1965–66), *Young Scientist of the Year* (1966–81); *Time Machines* (1969–70), *Controversy* (1971–75), *Natural History of a Sunbeam* (1976–77); *m* 1949 *Stella Jean, dau of Col George Arthur Brooke, of Leeds, Kent, and has:

1 *John Brooke [The Hon John Porter, 18 St Paul's Place, Islington, N1 2QF]; *b* 1952; *educ* Oundle, Emmanuel Coll Cambridge (BCh 1977, MB 1978) and U Coll Hosp London; MRCP (UK) 1980, MRCPath 1988; *m* 1989 *Suzanne Margaret, dau of David William Church, of Beaconsfield, Bucks, and has:

(1) *William John; *b* 1991

2 *Andrew Christopher George [Dr The Hon Andrew Porter, 64 Grafton Rd, London W3 6PF]; *b* 1955; *educ* Oundle, Westminster, Bristol U and Linacre Coll Oxford (DPhil); *m* 1997 *Margaret Jane, dau of James Philip Dallman, of Hayes, Kent

Lineage: JOHN SMITH PORTER; had:

GEORGE (Sir), *cr* a **Baron**

PORTLAND

Arms: Azure, a cross moline argent. **Crest:** Out of a ducal coronet proper two arms counter-embowed vested gules, on the hands gloves or, each holding an ostrich feather argent. **Supporters:** Two lions double-queued, the dexter or, the sinister sable. **Motto:** *Craignez honte* ('Fear shame'). **Creations:** E., V and B. (E) 9 April 1689, Count (HRE) 1732.

THE 12TH EARL OF PORTLAND, Co Dorset, **Viscount Woodstock**, Co Oxford, **Baron of Cirencester**, Co Gloucester, and a **Count of the Holy Roman Empire** (Timothy Charles Bentinck) [The Rt Hon The Earl of Portland, 3 Stock Orchard Crescent, London N7 9SL]; *b* 1 June 1953; *s* 1997; *educ* Harrow and UEA (BA); actor as Timothy Bentinck: roles include David Archer in BBC Radio's *The Archers*; also computer programmer, writer and composer; *m* 1979 *Judith Ann, dau of John Robert Emerson, of Cheadle, Staffs, and has:

1 +WILLIAM JACK HENRY, *Viscount Woodstock*; *b* 19 May 1984

2 +Jasper James Mellowes; *b* 12 June 1988

Earldom of Portland: There have been two other creations with this name. The first, on 17 Feb 1632/3, was in favour of Sir Richard Weston, KG, PC. Sir Richard's grandfather, another Richard Weston, is said to have founded the family's fortunes at that stage in English history by amassing wealth in the law as a judge in the Court of Common Pleas during ELIZABETH's reign. Sir Richard's father, Sir Jerome or Hierome Weston, was High Sheriff of Essex at the end of the 16th century. However, some sources speak of the 16th–17th-century Westons as descending from a knightly family who enjoyed some local prominence first in Staffordshire and later in Essex as far back as the 12th century. And the mid-17th-century historical writer Lord Clarendon, who was far from prejudiced in Weston's favour, calls his family a good one and ancient.

Sir Richard Weston was an MP for much of JAMES I's reign and was also frequently occupied in high offices of state maintaining the navy. He was sent abroad on diplomatic missions and became Chancellor of the Exchequer in 1621, remaining in office till 1628, by which time CHARLES I had come to the throne. In that year he was created Baron Weston of Neyland, with remainder to heirs of his body by his 2nd wife rather than the more usual heirs by either of his two wives. The reason for this, it is thought, was the madness of his son by his first wife. That son died shortly before his father, however. Lord and Lady Portland were accused by contemporaries of being crypto-Catholics, whereas the Bentinck Earls of Portland were among the chief supporters of that Protestant Succession in the late 17th and early 18th centuries out of which they did so conspicuously well.

The 2nd Earl of Portland of the 1632/3 creation followed in his father's footsteps as MP and diplomat. He was a royalist in the Civil War. The 3rd Earl, son of the 2nd Earl and grandson of the 1st, was killed in a sea battle off Lowestoft in the 2nd Dutch War of 1665, so that it was ironic when a Dutch family became possessed of the title of Earl of Portland a quarter of a century later. The 4th and last Earl of Portland of this earliest creation died in poverty in 1688.

JAMES II created the 1st Earl of Torrington (*see* POWIS, E, subsection HERBERT OF CHIRBURY) Earl of Portland in the Jacobite peerage after going into exile, but the Lord Portland in question died unmarried in 1698.

Lineage: The BENTINCKs are of the ancient nobility of the duchy of Guelder in The Netherlands, where at the beginning of the 14th century a castle of Benting or Bentinck, near Gorsel, between Deventer and Zutphen, was in the possession of a knight who seems to have taken his name from that place. The extinct Dukes of Portland were, and the extant Earls of Portland are, of a junior line. The senior line have been styled Barons in the Netherlands from the 16th century and as descendants of an ancient noble family who had been knights of their province hundreds of years earlier were nominated into the knighthood in 1814 and officially recognised as noble in 1819 following the establishment of the House of Orange as a reigning dynasty at the close of the Napoleonic Wars.

WICHERUS BENTING; witnessed signature of Bp Willibold of Utrecht at foundation of Zwolle 1233; had, with an er s (Henrik, Surety ('Borge') of the town of Zutphen 1312):

WILLEM BENTING; had:

HELMICH BENTING; ktd 1340, sold his estates at Doornick to Willem van der Horst; *m* Mechtildis — and had, with an er s (Goswin, *d* March 1380, leaving a widow Aleydis, who gave a sum of money to the chapter of Deventer for the benefit of her husband's soul and her own):

JOHAN BENTING; inherited Olst 1392 and had, with three er sons, a yst s and two daus:

GERRIT/GERARD BENTING/BENTINCK; memb of knighthood of the duchy of Guelder; had:

HENDRICK BENTING; endowed 1400 by the Bp of Cleves with a fief (Borgleen) at Huessen; endowed the Chapter at Walsberg 1411; *m* Elizabeth — and had, with an est s and two yst sons:

HENRICH BENTINCK; as esquire ('Knape') represented , together with two of his two bros, the district of Veluwe at the Diet of Nymegen 1436; joined army of Duke of Guelder at the request of the town of Elburg; taken prisoner at Battle of St Hubert 1444 by the Duke of Berg and a ransom paid by Elburg for his release; *m* Gertruid or Gertrude, dau of John van Huls, and *d* 1477, leaving, with two er sons (Gerrit, sold the Castle of Bentinck, *dsp*; John, *m* but *dsp*):

HENDRIK BENTINCK, of Het ('The') Loo (now the royal Netherlands summer residence), Berenkamp, etc; also owned Oostenhof, the estate of Manen, in Epe, and a house at Hattem; *m* Margaret van Dam (*d* 1500), divided his estates among his children 1501 and *d* 1502, leaving, with an est s and two yst ones:

HENDRICK BENTINCK, called 'The Best'; inherited estate of Manen 1501; *m* Catherine, dau and heiress of William Lering, of Velde, Zutphen, who inherited Velde 1516, and *d* 1548, leaving, with three yr sons and two daus:

WILLIAM, BARON BENTINCK, of Velde, which he inherited from his mother 1535; *m* Margaret, dau of Hendrik, Count van Erckelens, by his w Gertruid van Deest, and had, with an est s and three yr sons:

EUSEBIUS, BARON BENTINCK, of Velde; *m* 1563 Sophia (*d* 1624), 2nd dau and coheir of John, Baron d'Ittersum, of Werkern, and *d* 1584, leaving, with an er s and two daus:

HENDRIK, BARON BENTINCK, of Werkeren, Seneschal ('Drost') of Ysselmuiden and Salland; *m* 1st 1591 Elsabe, dau of Wolf, Baron d'Ittersum, of Garner; *m* 2nd 27 Aug 1615 Anne Beninga, of Grimmersum, widow of Nicholas, Baron d'Echten, and *d* 1 Sept 1639, leaving by his 1st w, with four er sons, a yst s and two daus:

BERNARD, BARON BENTINCK; Lord of Diepenheim, Schoonheten, etc, in the Province of Overyssel, Seneschal or Provost of Deventer; *m* 21 Dec 1638 Anne or Anna (*d* 30 March 1685), dau of Hans Hendrik van Bloemendaal, Seneschal of Vianen, and *d* 29 July 1668, having had, with other issue:

1 Henry, Baron Bentinck, of Diepenheim; *b* 7 Oct 1640; Seneschal of Twenthe; Cavalry Col; *m* 21 Oct 1680 Baroness Ida Magdalen D'Ittersum (*d* 18 Nov 1728) and *d* 9 Feb 1691, having had, with other issue:

(1) Anne Agnes, heiress of Diepenheim; *b* 15 Sept 1681; *m* 26 Jan 1699 her cousin Willem, Baron Bentinck, of Schoonheten, and *d* 3 Sept 1717, leaving issue (*see* below)

(2) Mechtild Anne; *b* 2 April 1683; *m* Lambert Joost de Hambroeck, of Arendshorst

(3) Johanna Isabella; *b* 2 April 1683; *m* John Zeger van Walvelde

2 Eusebius Borchard, Baron Bentinck, of Schoonheten; *b* 14 May 1643; Upper Burgomaster of Maastricht and Hasselt; *m* 1st 4 Nov 1670 Elizabeth, dau of Diderik, Baron de Brakell, and had, with other issue:

(1) Willem, Baron Bentinck, of Schoonheten; *b* 23 Nov 1673; *m* his 1st cousin Anna Agnes (*d* 3 Sept 1717), est dau of Henry, Baron Bentinck (*see* above), and *d* 1747, leaving:

1a Bernhard Hendrik, Baron Bentinck, of Schoonheten and Diepenheim; Kt of Overyssel 1723, Coadjutor of the Teutonic Order; *m* Bona Elizabeth Jurrianne, dau of Ambrosius du Tertre, and *d* 1773, having had, with other issue:

1b Volkier Rudolf, Baron Bentinck; *b* 19 June 1738; Land Commandeur Teutonic Order, Balye (magistrate) Utrecht, Lt-Col Br Army, Govr Guernsey, Maj-Gen in a Scottish Regt, QMG Netherlands Army under WILLIAM, PRINCE OF ORANGE; *m* Henrietta, heiress of Baron van Haersolte, and *d* 25 Dec 1820, leaving a dau (*d* unm)

2b Derk, of Diepenheim; *b* 1741; *m* Elizabeth, dau of Baron Arend Sloat, of Warmelo, and *d* 1813, having had:

1c Berend Hendrik Wolter Jan, Baron Bentinck, of Diepenheim; *b* 1781; Auditor Gen, Memb: Court of Justice and Cncl Cape of Good Hope, Comthur Teutonic Order, Balye Utrecht; *m* 1839 Adelaide Eliza (*d* 1857), dau of Sir Josias Henry Stracey, 4th Bt (*qv*), and *d* 10 April 1849, leaving:

1d Walter Theodore Edward, 13th Baron Bentinck; *b* 20 March 1840; Lt 15th Hus; *m* 26 Feb 1862 Henrietta Jane Christina (*d* 9 May 1924), dau of William Hinton, of The Til, Maderia, and *d* 22 June 1901, having had:

1e Walter Guy, 14th Baron Bentinck, CMG (1912), CBE (1919), DSO (1902), JP (1913), DL (Kincardineshire 1930); *b* 5 Nov 1864; *educ* Marlborough and RMC Sandhurst; Maj Rifle Bde Boer War 1899–1902 (wounded, despatches, Queen's medal with six clasps, King's Medal with two clasps), DC Vereeniging, Transvaal, RM Wakkerstrom, Transvaal, Assist Imp Sec to HC S Africa, Union Medal S Africa 1910, by roy licence 12 Sept 1911 he and his heirs male in succession were permitted to use the Netherlands title of Baron in the UK, served WW I (Offr i/c records 1915–20, GSO War Office 1916, Lt-Col Reserve of Offrs 1919, despatches); *m* 1 March 1904 Anne Elizabeth (*d* 19 Jan 1934), 3rd dau of Lt-Col William Burnett-Ramsay of Banchory (*see* RAMSAY, Bt, of Balmain), and *d* 7 July 1957, leaving:

1f Wolter Thomas Bernhard Ramsay, 15th Baron Bentinck; *b* 30 Sept 1905; *educ* Eton and RMC Sandhurst; Lt 5/7th Bn Gordon Highrs TAR, ADC to Govr Falkland Islands; *m* 1 April 1935 (*divorce* 1948) Mildred Russell (*d* 28 April 1972) and had:

1g *(Wolter) Guy Ian Ramsay [Baron Bentinck, 60 Airyhall Drive, Aberdeen, AB15 7QB]; *b* 15 June 1939; *educ* Prince Edward Sch Zimbabwe; *m* 15 June 1963 *June Anne, dau of William Wood, of Aberdeen, and has:

1h *Gary Ramsay [Gary Bentinck Esq, 6 Berryhill Place, Newtonhill, Kincardineshire AB3 2QZ]; *b* 23 July 1964; BA, DPA, MIPD; *m* 25 July 1992 *Lorna Lennox Sheed, BEd (CNAA), DPM, Grad IPD

2h *Guy Ian [Guy Bentinck Esq, 164 Craighurst Ave, Toronto, ONT M4R 1K2, Canada]; *b* 6 June 1966; MA, CA; *m* 24 July 1993 *Kathryn Ann Jenkins, BComm, CA

3h *Raymond William Maurice [Raymond Bentinck Esq, 10 Dorset Place, Merchiston, Edinburgh EH11 1JE]; *b* 3 March 1971; BSc

1f (cont.) Wolter, 15th Baron Bentinck, *m* 2nd 12 Jan 1949 Agnes (*d* 1977), dau of Alexander Fowlie, of Banchory, and *d* 28 June 1959

2e Reginald Joseph; *b* 5 Sept 1869; Lt-Col 7th Bn Northants Regt, Capt 30th Lancers, IA, Boer War 1899–1902 (Queen's medal with three clasps); *m* 14 Nov 1912 Florence Federika de Vere, dau of William Nelthorpe Beauclerk, JP, DL (*see* SAINT ALBANS, D), and *d* 21 May 1937, leaving:

1f George Walter Zeno; *b* 2 Nov 1913; *educ* Cheltenham; *d* 199–

1f Gwynella de Vere; *b* 1915; *d* 199–

2f Moyra de Vere; *b* 1917; OM (Malta); *m* 28 Nov 1947 *Dom(inic) Mintoff, PM Malta 1971–84, s of Laurence Mintoff, and *d* 16 Dec 1997, leaving:

1g *Anne [Mrs Bernard McKenna, Flat 2, Plaza Court, Bahar ic-Caghaq, Malta]; *b* 4 May 1949; *m* Aug 1971 *Bernard McKenna and has:

1h *Emma; *b* 7 June 1984

2g *Joan [Mrs David Bland, 111 Wildcat Hollow, Kyle, TX 78640, USA]; *b* 21 Aug 1951; *m* 7 March 1991 *David P Bland and has:

1h *Danny Xandru; *b* 2 Aug 1984

1h *Cetta Sian; *b* 10 Oct 1982

3f *Primrose de Vere; *b* 1920; *m* 1951 *Surgn Lt-Cdr Richard Howard Cowling, RN, and has:

1g *Charles Richard Bentinck; *b* 23 March 1952; *educ* Haileybury

2g *Peter John; *b* 3 Jan 1954; *educ* Haileybury

3e (Baron) Sir Rudolf Walter, KCB (1926, CB 1916), KCMG (1919); *b* 20 March 1868; *educ* HMS *Britannia*; RN: joined 1882, served E Sudan 1891 (Khedive's Bronze Star), Flag Cdr to C-in-C China 1904–06, commanded RNC Osborne 1913, Ch of Staff to V-Adml Beatty (*see* BEATTY, E) Jutland 1916 (despatches), ADC to HM GEORGE V 1918–19, Naval Sec to 1st Ld Admlty 1918–21, R-Adml 1st Battle Sqdn Atlantic Fleet 1921, C-in-C Africa Station 1922–24, V-Adml 1924, cmdg Res Fleet 1926, C-in-C Plymouth 1926–29, Adml 1928, Orders Sacred Treasure 3rd Class and Rising Sun Japan, Crown Italy and St Vladimir Russia 3rd Class with swords, Cdr Legn Hon; *m* 13 April 1898 Mabel (*d* 14 Feb 1948), only dau of Timothy Fetherstonhaugh, JP, DL, of Kirkoswald, Cumberland, and Hon Maria Carleton, dau of 3rd Baron Dorchester (*see* 1898 edn), and *d* 31 March 1947, leaving:

1f (Baron) Wolf Wolter Rudolf; *b* 28 Nov 1903; Capt RN WW II, Ch Staff Offr to Sr Br Naval Offr and Flag Offr (Liaison) Middle East 1949; *m* 19 April 1940 Yvonne (*d* 16 July 1986), dau of Col Harold Street, DSO, of Castlemead, Hythe, Kent, and *d* 6 Dec 1992, having had:

1g *Guy Rudolf [Baron Guy Bentinck, Erth Barton, Elmgate, Saltash, Cornwall PL12 4QY]; *b* 11 Feb 1941; *educ* Eton; *m* 19 Nov 1970 *Phoebe Georgina, only dau of Christopher Money Harris, JP (*see* HARRIS, B), and has:

1h *Caspar William [Baron Caspar Bentinck, 34b Wandsworth Common W Side, London SW18 2EF]; *b* 30 May 1974; *educ* Eton

2h *Chloe; *b* 1978

2g A son; *b* and *d* 2 April 1942

3g *Vivian Mark; *b* 10 Feb 1945 (HH THE late PRINCESS HELENA VICTORIA stood sponsor); *educ* Eton; Maj RM; *m* 8 Jan 1983 *Dr Miranda Whitehead and has:

1h *George William Brian; *b* 24 Nov 1983

1h *Alice Yvonne; *b* 23 July 1986

1f Renira; *m* 10 Oct 1931 Lt-Col Walter John Stopford, MC (*see* COURTOWN, E), and *d* 1983

4e Arthur Harold Walter, CIE (1926); *b* 29 Dec 1875; *educ* Harrow and Balliol Coll Oxford (BA and MA 1901); ICS (Commr Assam); *m* 1st 2 June 1903 Emma Elizabeth Kemble (*d* 20 Aug 1932), dau of George Sydney Hayes, and had:

1f Dirk Walter; *b* 1 Sept 1909; *educ* Harrow and Cambridge (MA, MB, BCh); MRCS, LRCP (London 1936), MRCOG 1949, Maj RAMC; *m* 2 Aug 1938 *Amelia, dau of Alfred Watkin, and *d* 30 Dec 1962

1f *Antoinette Waltera [Mrs Denis Pirrie, Windover, Underhill Lane, Westmeston, Hassocks, Sussex]; *b* 29 April 1906; *m* 31 July 1931 Denis Pirrie, s of Dr Pirrie, of Eastbourne, and has:

1g *Robert Jan; *b* 10 Dec 1937

2g *Michael Gerrit; *b* 29 Sept 1939

3g *Timothy Martin; *b* 24 May 1943

1g *Jennifer Clare; *b* 31 March 1933; *m* 21 Aug 1954 *James Cleland McVeigh, MA, MSc, CEng, s of James Cleland McVeigh, of Saintfield, Co Down, and has:

1h *Patrick Cleland; *b* 24 April 1956

2h *Robert Shaun; *b* 6 Sept 1959

1h *Virginia Clare; *b* 23 Sept 1961

2g *Antonia Mary; *b* 30 Oct 1948

4e (cont.) Arthur Bentinck *m* 2nd 15 May 1933 Edith White (*d* 31 Oct 1933), dau of Capt Philip Winchester, of Bamburgh, Northumberland; *m* 3rd 29 Sept 1937 Eunice (*d* 27 Dec 1945), dau of Capt H Gosset, RE, and *d* 7 June 1964

5e Bernard Walter; *b* 16 July 1877; MA Oxon, Capt 13th Bn Rifle Bde, barrister Middle Temple; *d* unm 27 June 1931

1e Millicent Annemie; *d* unm 10 May 1931

2e Adelaide; *m* 30 April 1902 Charles Read Seymour (*d* 6 Nov 1934), barrister, of Crowood, Wilts, and Bereweeke House, Winchester, er s of Rev Charles Frederick Seymour, Rector Winchfield, and *d* 10 Oct 1941, leaving issue

2c Arend William; *d* young

3c Rudolf Florenz Carl, of Schooneten; *b* 8 Oct 1785; Comthur Teutonic Order, Balye Utrecht; *m* Wilhelmina Henrietta van Marle and *d* 26 May 1857, leaving issue; ancestor of:

1d Rudolf; *m* Sigrid van Karnebeek and had:

1e Adolph Willem Carel; *b* 3 Sept 1905; *educ* Nederlands Lyceum The Hague and Utrecht U; with Netherlands Trading Soc and Min Finance, Min For Affrs: joined 1937, Chargé d'Affaires: Budapest (*ad interim*) 1939–40 and Cairo 1940–45, Min-Counsellor London 1945–50, Min Berne 1951–56, Netherlands Memb European Commission Saar Referendum, Dep-Sec-Gen NATO 1956–58, Amb to: UK and Iceland 1958–63 and France 1963, Cdr Order of Orange Nassau, Chev Netherlands Lion; *m* 1938 *Baroness Gabrielle Thyssen-Bornemisza de Kaszony and *d* 19–, leaving:

1f *Steven-Carel Johannes [Baron Steven-Carel Bentinck van Schoonheten, Chalet Eugenia, Talstrasse, 7250 Klosters, Switzerland; Moyns Park, Steeple Bumpstead, Essex]; *b* 1 March 1957; *educ* American Sch Paris, Valley Forge Mil Acad USA and Brunel Sch of Economics UK; chm: Applied Power Technology International and Scientia Ltd; *m* 19–(*divorce* 1996) Nora, dau of Fernand de Picciotto and formerly w of Prince Adam Czartorysky; *m* 2nd 1998 *Lisa, dau of Arlene Hogan by her late husb Maurice, of Ballsbridge, Dublin, and has:

1g *Elizabeth Mary Wilhelmina; *b* 22 Oct 1998

1f *Henriette Luisa; m 13 June 1967 (divorce 1973), as his 1st w, 7th Marquess of Northampton (qv) and has issue

3b Wolter Jan Gerrit; b 1747; Adml Netherlands Navy; d of wounds naval battle of Dogger Bank 1781

4b Carl; b 1751; Lt-Gen Netherlands Army, Chamberlain to PRINCE WILLIAM OF ORANGE; d 1825

2 (cont.) Eusebius Borchard, Baron Bentinck, m 2nd 1687 Baroness Hendrina Schimmelpenninck van der Oye, widow of Vincent Adolphus van Baer Brandsenburg, and d 25 Oct 1710

3 HANS WILLIAM, 1st Earl

BERNARD, BARON BENTINCK's 3rd s,

Baron HANS WILLIAM BENTINCK, **1st Earl of Portland**, Co Dorset, so cr 9 April 1689, as also BARON OF CIRENCESTER, Co Gloucester, and VISCOUNT WOODSTOCK, Co Oxford (all E), KG (March 1696/7), PC (Feb 1688/9–March 1701/2); b 20 July 1649; Page of Honour c 1664, Nobleman of the Chamber 1672 and subsequently confidential advsr to PRINCE WILLIAM OF ORANGE (later WILLIAM III of England), accompanied WILLIAM to England 1670 on a visit and 1688 to settle in England on the latter's being offered the English crown; Groom Stole, 1st Gentleman Bedchamber and Keeper Privy Purse Feb 1688/9–1700; served PRINCE/KING WILLIAM's armies: Cornet 1668, Capt 1672, Col Dutch Regt of Horse Gds 1675 (brought the regt to England 1688 but resigned command when it returned to The Netherlands 1699), Lt-Gen Battle of the Boyne 1690, also saw action at Steinkirk 1692, Landen 1693 and Siege of Namur 1695, Gen of Horse 1697, Amb to Paris 1698, Ranger Windsor Gt Pk 1697, impeachment voted against him by H of C 1 April 1701 but dismissed by Ho Lds 24 June 1701, DCL Oxford 1670; m 1st 1 Feb 1677/8 Anne (d 20 Nov 1688), Maid of Honour to MARY PRINCESS OF ORANGE (later QUEEN MARY), sis of 1st Earl of Jersey (qv), and had, with other issue:

1 Willem; b just prior to 3 March 1681; d 26 May 1688

2 (WILLIAM?) HENRY BENTINCK, **2nd Earl of Portland** and 1st DUKE OF PORTLAND, so cr 6 July 1716, as also MARQUESS OF TITCHFIELD, Co Southampton (both GB); b 17 March 1682; MP (Whig) Southampton 1705–08 and Hants 1708–09, Capt and Col 1st Troop Life Gds 1710–13, Ld Bedchamber 1717–26, Govr and V-Adml Jamaica 1721–26 (a post of relatively small prestige but accepted by him after he had lost huge sums in the South Sea Bubble); m 9 June 1704 Lady Elizabeth Noel (b c 1688; d 19 March 1736/7), er dau and coheir of 2nd Earl of Gainsborough (qv), and d en poste in Jamaica 4 July 1726, leaving:

(1) WILLIAM BENTINCK, **3rd Earl of Portland** and 2nd DUKE OF PORTLAND, KG (1740/1); b 1 March 1708/9; educ Eton; FRS 1739, DCL Oxford 1755; m 11 July 1734 Lady Margaret Cavendish Harley (b 11 Feb 1714/5; celebrated by the poet-diplomat Matthew Prior, who had accompanied the 1st Earl of Portland on one of his most important missions, as 'My noble, lovely little Peggy'; d 17 July 1785), only dau and heiress of 2nd Earl of Oxford and Earl Mortimer by his w Lady Henrietta Cavendish Holles (only dau of 1st and last Duke of Newcastle-upon-Tyne of the 1694 cr; through Lady Margaret Welbeck Abbey, Notts, came to the Dukes of Portland, as also, according to modern doctrine, did a right of representation as coheir to the Barony of Ogle (E, confirmation 1628 of a cr by writ of summons 1461) as a result of its falling into abeyance on the death of the 2nd and last Duke of Newcastle-upon-Tyne of the March 1664/5 cr, he being f-in-law of the Duke of Newcastle of the 1694 cr mentioned above), and d 1 May 1762, having had, with two other daus:

1a WILLIAM HENRY CAVENDISH BENTINCK later CAVENDISH-BENTINCK (roy licence 5 Oct 1801), **4th Earl of Portland** and 3rd DUKE OF PORTLAND, KG (1794), PC (1765); b 14 April 1738; educ Westminster and Ch Ch Oxford (MA 1757, DCL 1792); MP (Whig) Weobley 1761–62 (Pittite in Ho Lds from 1793–94), PM April–Dec 1783 and 1807–09, Home Sec 1794–1801 and Ld Pres Cncl 1801–05, Ld Chamberlain 1765, Ld Lt Ireland April–Aug 1782, High Steward Bristol 1786, Chllr Oxford U 1792–1809, Recorder Nottingham 1794, Ld Lt Notts 1795–1809, Er Bro Trin House 1797–1809 (Master 1807–09), FRS 1766, FSA 1775; m 8 Nov 1766 Lady Dorothy Cavendish (b 27 Aug 1750; d 8 June 1794), only dau of 4th Duke of Devonshire (qv), and d 30 Oct 1809, having had:

1b WILLIAM HENRY BENTINCK later SCOTT-BENTINCK (roy licence 19 Sept 1795) later still CAVENDISH-SCOTT-BENTINCK, **5th Earl of Portland** and 4th DUKE OF PORTLAND, PC (1827); b 24 June 1768; educ Westminster and Ch Ch Oxford (DCL 1793); MP (Whig to 1793–94, thereafter Pittite then Tory) Petersfield 1790–91 and Bucks 1791–1809, a Ld Treasury March–Sept 1807, Ld Privy Seal April–July 1827, Ld Pres Cncl 1827–28, Ld Lt Middx 1794–1842, FRS, FSA; m 4 Aug 1795 Henrietta (d 28 April 1844), est dau and coheir of Gen John Scott, of Balcomie, nr Crail, Fife (and sis of Mrs George Canning, with whose celebrated statesman husb (see GARVAGH, B) Ld Titchfield (as he then still was) became close friends, thus infecting his f the 3rd Duke with Canning's pro-Pitt sympathies), and d 27 March 1854, having had, with two daus (d unm):

1c William Henry Cavendish, Marquess of Titchfield; b 21 Aug 1796; d unm 4 or 5 March 1824

2c WILLIAM JOHN CAVENDISH CAVENDISH-SCOTT-BENTINCK, **6th Earl of Portland** and 5th DUKE OF PORTLAND; b 17 Sept 1800; Ensign and Lt Gren Gds July 1818, Cornet 10th Hussars Nov 1818, Capt: 7th Hussars 1821, 2nd Life Gds 1823 and Roy W India Rangers 1824–30, Lt and Capt Gren Gds 1830, MP (Canningite Tory) King's Lynn 1824–26, Lib-Conservative as a peer, became a recluse in later life and occupied himself constructing a vast system of underground chambers at Welbeck Abbey, the family seat; d unm 6 Dec 1879, when the coheirship to the Barony of Ogle held by his family devolved on his two surv sisters (and ultimately on Lucy, Dowager Baroness Howard de Walden, since her yr sis Mary dsp)

3c (William) George Frederick; b 27 Feb 1802; educ Eton(?) and Ch Ch Oxford(?); Cornet 10th Hussars 1819, exchanged into 41st Regt 1822, Maj 2nd Life Gds 1825, Priv Sec to his unc George Canning (For Sec and Ldr Ho of Commons) 1822–25, MP (Whig to 1828, Canningite to 1834, Tory or Conservative (Anti-Peelite from 1845) thereafter) King's Lynn 1828–48, nominal ldr Protectionist Tories 1846–47 and promoter of the young Disraeli; gentleman rider 1824–45 (won first public match Goodwood 1824), celebrated stud-owner (won Thousand Gns 1837,

1840 and 1842, Two Thousand Gns 1838 and 1840, Oaks 1840) and reformer of laxity on the turf; d unm 21 Sept 1848

4c Henry William; b 9 June 1804; Tstee Br Museum, MP N Notts; d 31 Dec 1870

1c Charlotte; m 14 July 1827 1st and last Viscount Ossington (see 1873 edn), assumed 26 June 1882 by roy licence the surname of SCOTT in lieu of DENISON and the arms of Scott quarterly with those of Bentinck and Cavendish, and d 30 Sept 1889

2c Lucy; m 8 Nov 1828 6th Baron Howard de Walden (qv) and d 29 July 1899, leaving issue

3c Mary; m 5 Oct 1854 Lt-Col Sir William Topham (d 7 June 1895), Lt Gentlemen-at-Arms, and d 20 July 1874

2b William Henry BENTINCK later CAVENDISH-BENTINCK, GCB (1815, KB 1813), GCH (1817); b 14 Sept 1774; Ensign Coldstream Gds 1791, Capt 2nd Light Dragoons 1792, Lt-Col 24th Light Dragoons 1794, attd Gen Suvarov's army and Austrian forces N Italy 1799–1801, Maj-Gen c 1805, C-in-C Br Forces Sicily 1811, Col 11th Dragoons, MP: Camelford March-May 1796, Notts 1796–1803, 1812–14 and 1816–26, King's Lynn 1826–27 and Glasgow 1836–39, Govr Madras 1803–07, Govr-Gen Bengal 1827–33 (as which abolished suttee) and 1st Govr-Gen India 1833–35; m 19 Feb 1803 Lady Mary Acheson (d 1 May 1843), 2nd dau of 1st Earl of Gosford (qv), and dsp Paris 17 June 1839

3b William Charles Augustus BENTINCK later CAVENDISH-BENTINCK; b 1780; Lt-Col; m 1st 21 Sept 1808 Georgiana Augusta Frederica Seymour (d 10 Dec 1813) and had a dau (d unm); m 2nd 23 July 1816 Anne Wellesley (d 19 March 1875), illegitimate dau of 1st Marquess Wellesley (see WELLINGTON, D) presumably by his 1st w Hyacinthe Roland, and formerly w (divorce 1816) of Sir William Abdy, 7th Bt (qv) of the 1641 cr, and d 28 April 1826, having by her had:

1c Charles William Frederick (Rev); b 8 Nov 1817; m 1st 26 Sept 1839 Sinetta (dsps 19 Feb 1850), dau of James Lambourne; m 2nd 13 Dec 1859 Caroline Louise (m 2nd 30 Nov 1870 Harry Warren Scott (dsp 23 Aug 1889), 3rd s of Sir William Scott, 6th Bt, of Ancrum; see 1902 edn), est dau of Edwyn Burnaby, of Baggrave Hall, Leics, and d 17 Aug 1865, having by her had:

1d Nina Cecilia, GCVO; b 11 Sept 1862; m 16 July 1881 12th Earl of Strathmore (see STRATHMORE AND KINGHORNE, E) and d 23 June 1938, leaving issue

2d Anne Violet; b 1864; d unm 15 May 1932

3d Hyacinth (twin with Anne Violet); m 1901 Augustus Edward Jessup, of Philadelphia, and d 9 Dec 1916, leaving issue

2c Arthur; b 10 May 1819; Lt-Gen, Col 7th Dragoon Gds; m 1st 18 Feb 1857 Elizabeth Sophie (d 4 Jan 1858), est dau of Sir St Vincent Hawkins-Whitshed, 2nd Bt (see 1871 edn), and had:

1d WILLIAM JOHN ARTHUR CHARLES JAMES, **7th Earl of Portland** and 6th DUKE OF PORTLAND, KG (1900), GCVO (1896), TD, DL (Ayrshire), PC (1886); b 28 Dec 1857; s step-mother as 2nd BARON BOLSOVER 7 Aug 1893; educ Eton; Lt Coldstream Gds 1877–80, Pres Notts TAA, Lt-Col HAC 1881–89 and Hon Col 4th Bn Sherwood Foresters from 1889, Master of the Horse (C) 1886–92 and 1895–1905, Ld Lt: Caithness 1889–1919 and Notts 1898–1939, CA Notts, Provincial Gnd Master Freemasons Notts 1898–1933, Chllr Order Garter 1937–43, Tstee Br Museum, Chm 1st Roy Commn Horsebreeding, Roy Victorian Chain 1932, GCStJ, Gnd Cross Charles III of Spain and 1st Class Order St Sava Serbia, Gnd Cordon Crown Belgium; author: Men, Women and Things, Fifty Years and more of Sport in Scotland, Memories of Racing and Hunting and The Red Deer of Longwell and Braemore; m 11 June 1889 Winifred Anna, DBE (1935), JP (Notts) (b 7 Sept 1863; Mistress of the Robes to HM QUEEN ALEXANDRA 1913–25, DJStJ; d 30 July 1954), only dau of Thomas Yorke Dallas-Yorke, JP, DL, of Walmsgate Lincs, and d 26 April 1943, leaving:

1e WILLIAM ARTHUR HENRY CAVENDISH-BENTINCK, **8th Earl of Portland** and 7th DUKE OF PORTLAND, KG (1948), JP (Caithness 1926), DL (1927); b 16 March 1893; educ Eton; Capt RHG and ADC Personal Staff WW I 1914–16, Lt-Col Notts Yeo (TAR) 1933–36, Pres Notts TAA 1939, Hon A/Cdre No 616 (S Yorks) Aux Sqdn RAF 1939, Hon Col RA (TA) 1943, MP (U) Newark Nov 1922–April 1943, Assist Whip 1927, Jr Ld of Treasury 1928–29 and Aug-Nov 1931, Jt MFH Rufford 1930, CC Notts 1932, Ld Lt 1939–62, Chllr Nottingham U 1955, Hon LLD Nottingham 1955, KStJ; m 12 Aug 1915 Ivy Gordon-Lennox, DBE (1958) (Maid of Honour to HM QUEEN ALEXANDRA 1912–15; d 3 March 1982), only child of Lord Algernon Charles Gordon-Lennox (see RICHMOND and GORDON, D), and d 21 March 1977, having had:

1f *(Alexandra Margaret) Anne [The Lady Anne Cavendish-Bentinck, Welbeck Woodhouse, Worksop, Notts S80 3BJ]; b 6 Sept 1916; CStJ

2f (Victoria) Margaret; b 9 Oct 1918; granted rank of duke's dau Coronation 1937 when one of HM THE QUEEN's (now HM QUEEN ELIZABETH THE QUEEN MOTHER's) trainbearers; m 12 April 1950 *Gaetano Parente, Prince of Castel Viscardo, est s of Marchese Enrico Parente and Marchesa Maria Parente dei Principi Imperiali di Francavilla, and d 29 Aug 1955, leaving:

1g *William Henry Marcello; b 18 Feb 1951

2e (Francis) Morven Dallas; b 27 July 1900; educ Eton and Ch Ch Oxford; RAFVR, Lt Notts Yeo (TA), chm Nottingham branch Alliance Assur, pres Mansfield and Dist Music Club; d unm 22 Aug 1950

1e Victoria Alexandrina Violet, CVO (1953); b 27 Feb 1890 (HM QUEEN VICTORIA stood sponsor in person); Extra Woman of the Bedchamber to HM QUEEN ELIZABETH later HM QUEEN ELIZABETH THE QUEEN MOTHER 1937; m 25 Nov 1918 Capt Michael John Erskine Wemyss of That Ilk (d 1982; see WEMYSS and MARCH, E) and d May 1994, leaving issue

2c (cont.) Gen Arthur Cavendish-Bentinck, *m* 2nd 10 June 1862 Augusta Mary Elizabeth, yr dau of Very Rev and Hon Henry Montague Browne (*see* KILMAINE, B; she was *b* 8 Nov 1834 and *d* 7 Aug 1893, having been *cr* 23 April 1880 BARONESS BOLSOVER of Bolsover Castle, Co Derby (UK); the *cr* was with remainder not primarily to the heirs male of the body of Gen Cavendish-Bentinck — who had died two and a half years previously — *by* Augusta, but to heirs male of the body of the dead General *tout court*; this had the effect of eventually merging the Barony with the Dukedom of Portland, since the General had already had a s by his 1st w who had inherited the Dukedom from a cousin a few months before his step-mother Baroness Bolsover was ennobled and who inherited the latter's Barony some 13 years later when she died), and *d* 11 Dec 1877, having by her had:

2d Henry, of Underley Hall, Kirkby Lonsdale, Westmorland, JP (Westmorland); *b* 28 May 1863; *educ* Eton and Ch Ch Oxford; granted with siblings 23 Feb 1880 rank of duke's dau/yr s, MP (C) Norfolk NW 1886–92 (fought seat unsuccessfully 1885), Nottingham S 1895–1906 and 1910–29, Memb LCC 1907–10, Lt-Col Derbys Yeo (TD) Boer War 1899–1900 and WW I (Dardanelles 1915), Westmorland: Ld Lt 1927 and CA, Hon Col: 4th Bn Border Regt and 24th (Derby Yeo) Armoured Car Corps RTC; *m* 21 Jan 1892 Lady Olivia Caroline Amelia Taylour, DGStJ (*d* 26 Nov 1939), only surv child of Thomas, Earl of Bective (*see* HEADFORT, M), and *dsp* 6 Oct 1931

3d William Augustus, DSO; *b* 31 Jan 1865; Maj 10th Hus Boer War 1899–1900; *d* unm 4 Nov 1903

4d Charles, DSO (1916), JP, DL (both Notts); *b* 7 Oct 1868; *educ* Eton; 9th Lancers Boer War 1899–1900 (wounded, despatches, brevet and Queen's medal with three clasps), Lt-Col WW I (AAG BEF 1915, wounded, despatches three times); *m* 27 Feb 1897 Cecily Mary, DGStJ (*d* 30 Jan 1936), dau of Charles Seymour Grenfell (*see* GRENFELL, B), and *d* 19 June 1956, leaving:

1e Elizabeth; *b* 27 Sept 1901; *m* 29 April 1925 (*divorce* 1954) Roger Henry Wethered, s of Henry Wethered, of Worplesdon, Surrey, and *dsp* 13 Aug 1977

2e Alice; *b* 10 Oct 1904; *m* 23 April 1930 Maj Terence Andrew Alfred Watt, Life Gds (*kas* flying 17 July 1942), only s of Capt Samuel Alexander Watt, of Belton, Uppingham, Rutland, and had:

1f *Michael Andrew [Michael Watt Esq, Greens Park, Blakesley, Northants NN12 8SD]; *b* 14 April 1933; *educ* Eton; 2nd Lt Life Gds; *m* 7 Nov 1959 *Susan Myrtle, only dau of Maj Leigh Ingham Tomkins Whitaker, of Land of Nod, Headley, Hants, and has:

1g *Charles Andrew [Charles Watt Esq, 7 Castletown Rd, London W14 9HE]; *b* 6 March 1964; *educ* Eton

2g *David Alexander [David Watt Esq, 52 Danes Rd, London SW6 7EN]; *b* 10 April 1968; *educ* Eton

1g *Sarah Alice; *b* 5 March 1962

2g *Pollyanna; *b* 19 Jan 1971

1d Ottoline Violet Anne; *b* 16 June 1873; *m* 8 Feb 1902 Philip Edward Morrell (*d* 5 Feb 1943), of Bloomsbury and Garsington Manor, Oxford, MP Oxford S 1906–10 and Burnley 1910–18, only surv s of Frederick Morrell, of Black Hall, Oxon, and *d* 21 April 1938, having had issue

1c Anne; *d* unm 7 June 1888

2c Emily; *m* 8 Nov 1845 Rev Henry Hopwood (*d* 25 Feb 1859), Rector Bothal, Northumberland, and *d* 6 Jan 1850, leaving issue

4b Frederick, CB; *b* 2 Nov 1781; Maj-Gen, MP; *m* 16 Sept 1820 Lady Mary Lowther (*d* 21 Oct 1862), dau of 1st Earl of Lonsdale (*qv*), and *d* 11 Feb 1828, leaving:

1c George Augustus Frederick, PC; *b* 9 July 1821; MA, MP, Parly Sec BOT 1874–75, JAG 1875–80; *m* 14 Aug 1850 Prudence Penelope (*d* 22 June 1896), dau of Col Charles Powell Leslie (*see* LESLIE, Bt), and *d* 9 April 1891, leaving:

1d William George, JP (Dorset); *b* 6 March 1854; *educ* Cambridge (MA); MP Penryn and Falmouth 1886–95, Tstee Br Museum; *m* 12 Aug 1880 Elizabeth (*d* 4 Nov 1943), dau of Maturin Livingston, of Staatsburgh, NY, and *d* 22 Aug 1909, leaving:

1e Mary Augusta; *b* 10 June 1881; *m* 3 Nov 1906 John Gorman Ford, 1st Sec US Legation Rome, and *d* 9 May 1913

2e Ruth Evelyn; *b* 5 March 1883; *m* 9 Feb 1907 Walter Spencer Morgan Burns (*d* 24 Dec 1929), of North Mymms Park, Herts, s of Walter Hayes Burns, of New York, and had issue

2d (William George) Frederick, JP (Dorset); *b* 26 Aug 1856; *educ* Westminster and Trin Coll Cambridge (BA 1878); barrister Lincoln's Inn 1879, Sec Roy Commn Educn 1886–88, FSA, Tstee Br Museum, Lt Sherwood Rangers Yeo Cav; *m* 8 Aug 1887 Ruth Mary St Maur (*d* 28 Jan 1953), dau of Edward Earl St Maur (presumably illegitimate, since Lord St Maur *dspl*), er s and heir of 12th Duke of Somerset (*qv*), and *d* 13 Nov 1948, leaving:

1e FERDINAND WILLIAM CAVENDISH-BENTINCK, **9th Earl of Portland** and 8th DUKE OF PORTLAND, KBE (1956), CMG (1941), MC; *b* 4 July 1888; *educ* Eton and RMC Sandhurst; Maj KRRC WW I cmdg a Co of Cadets RMC 1917 (wounded, despatches), unofficial memb Exec Cncl Kenya 1938–60, Min Ag and Natural Resources Kenya 1945–55, Speaker Legislative Cncl Kenya 1955–60, Chm E African Inter-territorial Ag, Forestry and Fisheries Research Cncl 1955–61, Chm and Fndr Kenya Assoc, Timber Controller E Africa 1940–45, Chm Settlement and Production Bd Kenya and Tanganyika League and Africa Def Fedn, Offr Order Crown Belgium; *m* 1st 9 May 1912 (*divorce* 1950) Wentworth Frances (*d* 25 June 1964), yr dau of William James Hope-Johnstone (*see* LINLITHGOW, M); *m* 2nd 21 Sept 1950 Gwyneth Ethel, MBE (*d* 7 March 1996), dau of John Wesley Edwards, of Shettlewood Estate and Montpelier, Jamaica, and widow of Col David Alexander Jefferson Bowie, RA, and *d* 13 Nov 1980

2e George Augustus Frederick; *b* 30 May 1891; *d* 7 June 1892

3e (VICTOR FREDERICK) WILLIAM CAVENDISH-BENTINCK, **10th Earl of Portland** and 9th and last DUKE OF PORTLAND, CMG (1942), DL (Caithness 1927); *b* 18 June 1897; *educ* Wellington; 2nd Lt Gren Gds 1918, Attaché HM Legation Oslo 1915, 3rd Sec Warsaw 1919, 2nd Sec 1920, to FO 1922 again 1925 and again 1937, 2nd Sec Paris 1923 and The Hague 1924, 1st Sec Paris 1928, Athens 1932, Santiago 1934, Counsellor 1942, Assist U-Sec 1944, Chm JIC Chs Staff 1939–45, FO Advsr to Dirs Plans 1942–45, Amb Poland 1945–47, chm Bayer UK 1968–86, dir: Philip Hill Investment Tst and Berger (UK) Ltd; *m* 1st 16 Feb 1924 (*divorce* 1948) Clothilde Bruce, dau of James Bruce Quigley, of Dallas, Texas, and had:

1f William James; *b* 6 July 1925; *educ* Eton; P/O RAF; *m* 1st Aug 1949 (*divorce* 1954) Patricia Constance Margaretta Collins; *m* 2nd 14 Dec 1954 (*divorce* 1960) Mrs Inger Maria Sandra von Strelov, dau of J P Grantzau-Christensen, of Copenhagen; *m* 3rd 20 Dec 1960 (*divorce* 1965) (Eleanor) Barbara Muriel, yst dau of Lt-Col Reginald Arthur Lygon (*see* 1970 edn BEAUCHAMP, E), and *dsp* 4 Sept 1966

1f *Mary Jane [The Lady Mary Graubard, 8 Maple Ave, Cambridge, MA 02139, USA]; *b* 16 Dec 1929; *m* 1st 20 April 1963 (*divorce* 1978) Alexander Constantine Georgiades, of Pilton, Oundle, yr s of Constantine Georgiades, and has:

1g *William James; *b* 18 March 1967

2g *David Constantine; *b* 9 Jan 1969

1f (cont.) Lady Mary Georgiades *m* 2nd 5 Aug 1978 *Prof Stephen Richards Graubard, s of Harry Graubard, of New York

3e (cont.) The **10th Earl**/9TH DUKE OF PORTLAND *m* 2nd 27 July 1948 *Kathleen Elsie [Her Grace The Duchess of Portland, 21 Carlyle Sq, London SW3], yr dau of Arthur Barry, of Montreal, and former w of Arthur Ritchie Tillotson, and *d* 1990, when the Dukedom, Marquessate and Barony of Bolsover expired

1e Lucy Joan; *m* 9 Nov 1922 Sir Reginald Hervey Hoare, KCMG, Envoy Extrdy and Min Plen Persia 1931–34 and Romania 1934–41 (*d* 12 Aug 1954), yst s of Charles Hoare, of 37 Fleet St, London, by Katherine, dau of Rt Rev Lord Arthur Hervey (*see* BRISTOL, M), and *d* 29 June 1971, leaving:

1f *Joseph Andrew Christopher [Joseph Hoare Esq, Hartridge Manor Farm, Cranbrook, Kent TN17 2NA]; *b* 23 March 1925; *educ* Le Rosey, Eton, Southampton U and Balliol Coll Oxford (MA); F/O RAF Regt BAOR 1946–47 and Pilot 604 Sqdn RAuxAF 1951–57, memb London Stock Exchange 1957–77, dir Canadian Overseas Packaging Industs 1962–, chm Assoc of Chartered and Tech Analysts 1970–73, farmer 1972–, underwriting memb Lloyd's 1985–, property developer 1986–; *m* 23 Jan 1963 Lady Christina McDonnell (*d* 1991), only dau of 8th Earl of Antrim (*qv*), and has, with other issue:

1g *Jane; *b* 23 Dec 1963; *m* 15 Dec 1990 *Patrick William Cromeck Warrington, s of Maj Anthony John Cromeck Warrington, and has issue

2e (Venetia) Barbara; *b* 1902; granted rank of duke's dau 1977; *d* unm 198–

1d Christina Anne Jessica; *m* 3 Aug 1874 Sir Tatton Sykes, 5th Bt (*see* SYKES, Bt, of Sledmere), and *d* 2 June 1912, leaving issue

2d Mary Venetia; *m* 7 Dec 1885 John Arthur James, MVO (*dsp* 30 April 1917), of Coton House, Rugby, Warwicks, and *d* 2 May 1948

1b Charlotte; *m* 31 March 1793 Charles Greville, s of Fulke Greville, of Wilberry, Wilts, and *d* 28 July 1862, leaving issue (*see* WARWICK, BROOKE and, E), the est s being Charles Greville the diarist

2a Edward Charles; *b* 3 March 1743/4; *m* 28 Dec 1782 Elizabeth (*d* 1837), est dau of Richard Cumberland, the dramatist and essayist, and *d* 8 Oct 1819, having had:

1b William Harry Edward (Rev); *b* 2 Feb 1784; RD, Rector Sigglesthorne, Hull, Canon and Archdeacon Westminster; *m* 19 July 1814 Frances (*dsp* 13 March 1862), dau of Rev Thomas Constable, and *d* 29 Sept 1868

2b Cavendish Charles; *b* 1785; *d* 1889

1b Harriet Elizabeth; *m* 1809, as his 2nd w, Sir William Mordaunt Sturt Milner, 4th Bt (*qv*), and *d* 31 Dec 1862, having had issue

2b Charlotte Georgiana Sophia; *m* 1814 Lt-Gen Sir Robert Garrett, KCB, of Ellington, Isle of Thanet, and *d* 6 Nov 1819

1a Elizabeth; *b* 27 July 1735; *m* 22 March 1759 1st Marquess of Bath (*qv*) and *d* 12 Dec 1825, leaving issue

2a Henrietta; *b* 8 Feb 1737; *m* 28 May 1763 5th Earl of Stamford (*d* 28 May 1819; *see* 1970 edn) and *d* 4 June 1827, having had issue

(2) George; *b* Dec 1715; Col of Foot; *m* 29 June 1753 Mary Davies (*m* 2nd June 1759 Cdre Walter Griffith) and *d* 1 March 1759

(1) Anne; *m* Col Daniel Paul and *d* July 1749

(2) Isabella; *m* 8 Nov 1739 Henry Monck, of Charleville, Co Wicklow, and *d* 1783, leaving issue (*see* WATERFORD, M)

(3) Amelia; *m* Jacob Arend, Baron de Wassenaer, and *d* 1756

1 Mary; *b* 1679; *m* 1st 28 Feb 1698 2nd Earl of Essex (*qv*); *m* 2nd Aug 1714 Sir Conyers D'Arcy, KB (*dsp* 1 Dec 1758), and *d* 20 Aug 1726

2 Anne Margaretta; *b* 1683; *m* 1701 Arend, Baron de Wassenaer Duvenvoirde, States Gen Amb Extrdy to GB, and *d* 3 May 1763

3 Frances Wilhelmina; *b* 18 Feb 1684; *m* 19 Dec 1706 4th Baron Byron (*qv*) and *d* 31 March 1712, leaving issue

4 Isabella ('Belle'); *b* 4 May 1688; *m* 2 Aug 1714 1st Duke of Kingston-upon-Hull (*d* 1726) and *d* 23 Feb 1728, leaving issue

The **1st Earl** *m* 2nd 12 May 1700 Jane Martha (*b* 1672; Maid of Honour and Governess to daus of GEORGE II; *d* 26 May 1751), 6th dau of Sir John Temple, of East Sheen (*see* TEMPLE OF STOWE, E), and widow of 3rd Baron Berkeley of Stratton (*see* BERKELEY, B), and *d* 23 Nov 1709, having by her had:

3 William, of Rhoon and Pendrecht (Holland) and Terrington St Clements, Norfolk, 1st Count Bentinck (HRE), so *cr* 1732 for himself and all his descendants by the EMPEROR CHARLES VI; *b* 6 Nov 1704; *m* 1 June 1733 Countess Charlotte Sophie (*b* 4 Aug 1715; *d* 5 Feb 1800), only dau and heiress of Anthony II, Count of Aldenburg, Sovereign Lord of Kniphausen, Varel, etc, by his w Princess Wilhelmina Maria of Hesse-Homburg, and *d* 13 Oct 1774, leaving:

(1) Christian Frederick Anthony, Count Bentinck de Varel; *b* 15 Aug 1734; *s* mother as Sovereign Lord of Kniphausen and Varel in virtue of a family agreement 1754; *m* 5 Oct 1760 Mary Catherine (*d* 23 Oct 1793), est dau of John, Baron de Tuyll de Serooskerken, by Lady Ursula Christine de Reede-Ginkel, dau of 2nd Earl of Athlone, and *d* 1 April 1768, leaving:

1a William Gustavus Frederic, 2nd Count Bentinck, Sovereign Lord of Kniphausen and Varel; *b* 1762; *m* 1st 1791 Baroness Ottoline Frederica Louisa (*d* 1799), dau of Baron Arend de Reede-Lynden, and had:

1b William Anthony; *b* 6 Oct 1799; *d* 26 March 1813

1b Maria Antonietta Charlotte, of Voorst; *b* 24 July 1792; *m* 1st 28 Oct 1813 Baron de Nyvenheim (*d* 1820); *m* 2nd 21 June 1822 Count de Rechteren and *d* 29 July 1832

2b Ottoline Frederica Louisa, of Nederhemert; *b* 7 Aug 1793; *m* 1815 Charles, Baron de Nagell, and *d* 15 Nov 1868

1a (cont.) William, 2nd Count Bentinck, *m* 2nd 1816 Sarah Margaret Gerdes and *dspml* 22 Oct 1835, whereupon a lawsuit ensued for the Sovereign Lordship of Kniphausen and Varel, which was finally annexed 1854 to the Grand Duchy of Oldenburg

2a John Charles; *b* 2 July 1763; Maj-Gen Br Army; *m* 20 March 1785 Lady Jemima Helena de Reede-Ginkel (*d* 6 Sept 1839), dau of 5th Earl of Athlone, and *d* 23 Nov 1833, leaving:

1b William Christian Frederick, 3rd Count Bentinck; *b* 15 Nov 1787; Chamberlain to King of The Netherlands; Kt Cdr Teutonic Order; by a decree of 1845 the German Diet recognised the right of the Counts Bentinck to the dignities and privileges of the mediatised Houses of Germany with the style *Erlaucht* ('Most Illustrious'); *m* 16 April 1841 Countess Pauline Albertine (*d* Wildenfels 12 Oct 1898), 2nd dau of Count Münnich, a Count of the Empire, and *d* The Hague 8 June 1855, leaving:

1c Jacqueline Christine Anne Adelaide; *b* 4 Jan 1855; *m* 5 Nov 1874 Frederick Magnus, Count Solms-Wildenfels (*d* 25 Nov 1910), and *d* 12 Dec 1933, leaving issue

2b Charles Anthony Ferdinand, 4th Count Bentinck, of Middachten Castle, The Netherlands; *b* 4 March 1792; Lt-Gen, Col 12th Foot, served Peninsular War with 1st Bn Coldstream Gds (wounded Barossa 1812), Staff Waterloo 1815, Kt Cdr Teutonic Order, granted 1888 by HM QUEEN VICTORIA permission for all his descendants to bear the Countly title; *m* 30 Jan 1846 Countess Caroline Mechtild Emma Charlotte Christina Louisa (*d* 28 Feb 1899), est dau of Charles, reigning Count of Waldeck and Pyrmont, and *d* Bergheim, Waldeck, 28 Oct 1864, having had:

1c Henry Charles Adolphus Frederick William, 5th Count Bentinck to 1874, when renounced that title; *b* 30 Oct 1846; Kt Cdr Teutonic Order, Lt-Col Coldstream Gds; *m* 8 Dec 1874 Henrietta Eliza Cathcart (*d* 10 Feb 1934), est dau of Robert McKerrell by Emily, dau of Lt-Gen William Staveley, CB, and *d* 18 June 1903, leaving:

1d Robert Charles; *b* 5 Dec 1875; Derbys Yeo, Capt Remount Serv WW I; *m* 8 Sept 1915 Lady Norah Ida Emily Noel (*d* 23 May 1939), dau of 3rd Earl of Gainsborough, and *d* 12 March 1932, leaving:

1e HENRY NOEL BENTINCK, **11th Earl of Portland**; *b* 2 Oct 1919; *educ* Harrow and RMC Sandhurst; cowboy in California, Lt Coldstream Gds WW II (wounded twice, POW), talks producer BBC, jackaroo sheep station Tasmania 1952–55, author: *Anyone Can Understand the Atom* (1965), *The Avenue of Flutes* (children's fiction, 1966), *Isoworg* (thriller, 1971) and *Life is a Sum Humanity is Doing Wrong* (unpublished by his death), TV playwright: *Countdown at Woomera* (1961), ad exec J Walter Thompson 1959; *m* 1st 13 Oct 1940 Pauline Ursula (*d* 11 Jan 1967), yst dau of Frederick William Mellowes, of Hampstead, and had:

1f TIMOTHY CHARLES ROBERT NOEL BENTINCK, **12th and present Earl of Portland**

1f *Sorrel Deirdre [The Lady Sorrel Bentinck, 18 Rankeillor St, Edinburgh EH8 9HZ]; *b* 22 Feb 1942; *m* 24 June 1972 (*divorce* 1988, resumed maiden name 1990) Sir John Philip Lister Lister-Kaye, 8th Bt (*qv*), and has issue

2f *Anna Cecilia [The Lady Anna Bentinck, 64 Croftdown Rd, London NW5 1EN]; *b* 18 May 1947; *m* 1st 24 July 1965 (*divorce* 1974) Jasper Hamilton Holmes, only s of Cdr Cecil Holmes, of Little Basing, Hants; *m* 2nd 1975 (*divorce* 1977) Nicholas George Spafford Vester; resumed maiden name and has issue by Arnold George Francis Cragg, s of Rt Rev Kenneth Cragg, Assist Bp Oxford Diocese:

1g *Gulliver Jack Bentinck CRAGG; *b* 1 July 1978

2g *George Finn Gareth Bentinck CRAGG; *b* 4 Oct 1980

1g *Charlotte Sophie Campden Bentinck CRAGG; *b* 23 March 1988

1e (cont.) The **11th Earl** *m* 2nd 23 Feb 1974 *Jenifer [The Rt Hon Jenifer Countess of Portland, Little Cudworthy, Dolton, N Devon, EX19 8PU], only dau of Reginald Hopkins, of London N2, and Mrs Nancy McLaren, of Betweenways, Guernsey Rd, Ferring-by-Sea, Sussex, and *d* 30 Jan 1997

1e *Brydgytte Blanche [The Lady Brydgytte van der Wyck Bentinck, Rykstraatweg, 242 9752 CK Haren, Groningen, The Netherlands]; *b* 11 Nov 1916; *m* 2 Feb 1937 Jonkheer Adriaan Hendrik Sibble van der Wyck (*d* 1973), Attorney to HM JULIANA QUEEN OF THE NETHERLANDS and Capt Roy Netherlands Horse Artillery, yst s of Jonkheer E R Van der Wyck, Chamberlain to HM WILHELMINA QUEEN OF THE NETHERLANDS, and has:

1f *Evert Rein Robert Henry; *b* 12 Aug 1945

2f *Douglas Roderick Arthur Duncan; *b* 9 Aug 1955

1f *Caroline Norah Frédérique Adrienne [Baroness Collot d'Escury, Hoer and Bosch, Kloosterzande, Zeeuws Vlaanderen, The Netherlands]; *b* 1 June 1938; *m* May 1961 *K- J- A-, Baron Collot d'Escury, Estate Agent for the Crown Property in the Province of Zeeland, and has:

1g *Guyon Adolf André; *b* 25 April 1962

2g *Robert Willem Frederick; *b* 1970

1g *Juliette Brydgytte Blanche; *b* 17 Aug 1963

2g *Marina Caroline Norah; *b* 30 March 1965

2f *Brydgytte Agnes Dawn [Mevrouw Brydgytte Vermeer, 1 Gaast, Friesland, The Netherlands]; *b* 6 Jan 1940; *m* 2 March 1968 (*divorce* 1990) Paul Heinz Maria Dirk Vermeer and has:

1g *Robert Paul Adriaan Henry Simon; *b* 14 Oct 1968

1g *Fiona Victoria Regina Brydgytte; *b* 1970

2g *Nadia Norah Noel; *b* 1971

3f *Reina Jeanne Woltera [Mevrouw H W van Harrenveld, De Buitenhof, Brummen, Geldersland, The Netherlands]; *b* 2 Dec 1942; nurse; *m* 1973 *H W van Harrenveld, judge, and has:

1g *Hugo Johannes Hendrik; *b* 1974

2g *Diederik Godard Adriaan Roelant; *b* 1980

3g *Wendela Blanche Catherine; *b* 1977

2d Charles Henry (Rev Sir), KCMG (1937, CMG 1923); *b* 23 April 1879; *educ* Trin Coll Cambridge and Wycliffe Hall Oxford; Dip Serv 1904–41 (Envoy Extrdy and Min Plen: Addis Ababa 1925–28, Peru and Ecuador 1929–33, Sofia 1933 and Prague 1936, Amb to Chile 1937–40), Count HRE, Deacon June 1941, Priest Dec 1941, Vicar W Farleigh Kent 1941–46, Chaplain Ch Ch Brussels, Hon Chaplain Br Embassy Brussels 1946, Officiating Chaplain: RAF 1946 and 1947 and to HM Forces Belgium 1947–48; *m* 9 May 1922 Lucy Victoria, only dau of Sir Thomas Fowell Victor Buxton, 4th Bt (*qv*), and *dsp* 26 March 1955

3d Henry Duncan, *b* 24 June 1881; *educ* Harrow and Trin Coll Cambridge (BA 1902); Count HRE, Maj Coldstream Gds; *d* unm 20 Oct 1916 from wounds recd Battle of the Somme 15 Sept 1916 (despatches)

4d Arthur William Douglas, DSO (1941); *b* 24 July 1887; *educ* Eton and Trin Coll Cambridge (BA 1909); Count HRE, Lt-Col Coldstream Gds, served WWs I and II (KAR (Br E Africa) 1913–14 (wounded), BEF 1914 (wounded), Egyptian Army 1916–17, Abyssinia under FO 1917–20, Ethiopia 1940–41 (despatches, Haile Selassie Mil Medal with Palm 1941), Burma and China 1941–42, Br Mil Mission to Egyptian Army 1942–45), also Iraq 1922–23 and 1926–27, served Internat Police Saar Plebiscite 1934–35, Br Ambulance Serv Red Cross Abyssinia 1936, observer Sudetenland 1938, Br Mil Admin Somalia 1946–48, Kenya Police Reserve Mau Mau Emergency 1952–54; *d* unm 26 Nov 1962

1d Renira Christine; *b* 6 Nov 1877; *m* 6 Dec 1898 Baron Alexander de Heeckeren de Kell, CBE (*d* 4 June 1945), Col Reserve Offrs and Chamberlain Extrdy to HM WILHELMINA QUEEN OF THE NETHERLANDS, and *d* 22 April 1953, leaving issue

2d Ursula Victoria Henrietta; *b* 18 Nov 1884; VAD France WW I, London Aux Amb Serv WW II and BRC Relief Europe 1945

3d Naomi Mechtild Henrietta, twin with her brother Arthur; served Physiotherapy Unit WW I, London Aux Amb Serv WW II and BRC relief in Europe 1945; *d* unm 17 July 1959

2c William Charles Philip Otto ALDENBURG-BENTINCK, 6th Count Bentinck; *b* 28 Nov 1848; *s* 1874 as Count Bentinck on the resignation of his er bro as such and obtained roy licence to bear title Count HRE as a Br subject in England; assumed by patent 1889 the title of Count of Waldeck-Limburg and was hereditary member of the Upper House of Parliament in Württemberg; Grand Cross of the Order of the Red Eagle of Prussia, Kt Cdr Teutonic Order, KJStJ, 3rd Sec Diplomatic Serv; *m* 8 March 1877 Baroness Mary Cornelia (*d* 15 Sept 1912), dau and coheir of Charles, Baron de Heeckeren de Wassenaer, of Twickel, Grand Master of the Horse to WILLEM III OF THE NETHERLANDS, and *d* 2 Nov 1912, leaving:

1d William Frederick Charles Henry, 7th Count Bentinck; *b* 22 June 1880; Coadjutor and 73rd elective Land Cdr Teutonic Order, KJStJ, formerly hereditary memb of Upper Chamber of Württemberg, Attaché Imp German Embassy London, Balye Utrecht 1958; *m* 27 Aug 1923 Adrienne, dau of Jonkheer Philip Ernst Vegelinvan Claerbergen, of The Hague, and formerly w of René Labouchère, and *d* 29 Dec 1958, leaving:

1e *Sophie Mechtild Marie [Countess Enrico Gaetani dell'Aquila d'Aragona, Pizzofalcone 43, Naples, Italy]; *b* 10 June 1924; *m* 29 Nov 1950 *Count Enrico Gaetani dell'Aquila d'Aragona, PhD, s of Count Paolo Gaetani, and has:

1f *Benedetta Rita Maria; *b* 3 April 1953

2f *Jacobella Immacolata Scolastica; *b* 12 May 1956

3f *Giovanella Maria; *b* 2 July 1961

2e *Isabelle Adrienne [Countess Aurel zu Ortenburg, 8601 Schloss Birkenfeld, Hassfurt, Uterfranken, Germany; Kasteel Middachten, De Steeg, The Netherlands]; *b* 3 July 1925; *m* 20 Dec 1951 *Count Aurel Ladislaus Franz Heinrich Ernst zu Ortenburg, s of Franz Carl Julius Albrecht, Count zu Ortenburg, Seigneur of Tambach, and has:

1f *Franz Wilhelm Friedrich Ladislaus; *b* 12 June 1953

2f *Philipp Wilhelm; *b* 9 April 1955

1f *Nadine Marie Elisabeth Johanna; *b* 1 May 1957; *m* 1981 *Count Albrecht von Brandenstein-Zeppelin

2d Frederick George Unico Williams, Kt Teutonic Order; *b* 21 June 1888; *d* unm 18 April 1942

1d Mechtild Corisande Renira Mary; *b* 20 Dec 1877; *m* 1 Sept 1905 Casimir, 2nd Prince Castell-Rudenhausen (*d* 25 April 1933), and *d* 13 Dec 1940, leaving issue

2d Isabella Antoinette Mary Clementina; *b* 15 Nov 1889; *m* 6 Aug 1914 Count Wilhelm zu Solms Sonnenwalde and had:

1e *Alfred [Count Alfred zu Solms Sonnenwalde, Weldam, 7475 MJ Markelo, The Netherlands]; *b* 4 July 1932; *m* 17 Oct 1992 *Christine Hüsmert, MD, and has:

1f *Mary Charlotte Sophie; *b* 24 July 1993

2f *Caroline Anne Amalia; *b* 13 Aug 1994

3f *Isabelle Rosa Catherine; *b* 29 Aug 1996

1e Marie Helen Luise Clementine; *b* 15 April 1917; *m* 6 Sept 1951 *Günther von Bunau and *d* 10 Aug 1996, leaving:

1f *Rudolf; *b* 30 April 1953

3c Charles Renaud Adalbert; *b* 9 Feb 1853; Capt *à la suite* Prussian Army, Kt Cdr Teutonic Order; *m* 28 Sept 1878 (*divorce* 1885), as her 1st husb, Countess Helena Agnes Alexandrina Amelia Caroline (*d* Berlin 5 March 1942), only dau of Adalbert, Count of Waldeck and Pyrmont, and *d* 19 Oct 1934, leaving:

1d Mary Amelia Mechtild Agnes; *b* 16 Sept 1879; *m* 7 June 1922 Baron Rudolf Frederik de Heeckeren de Wassenaer (*d* 26 July 1936)

4c Godard John George Charles, of Amerongen Castle, The Netherlands, Seigneur of Amerongen, Ginkel, Elst, Zuylestein, Lievendaal, Eck and Wiel, etc; *b* 3 Aug 1857; Coadjutor Teutonic Order, KJStJ; *m* 12 June 1884 Countess Augustine Wilhelmine Louise Adrienne de Bylandt (*d* 27 Jan 1916), dau of Count Auguste de Bylandt, and *d* 4 Jan 1940, having had:

1d Charles Arthur Renaud William Godard Augustus; *b* 16 Aug 1885; Kt Cdr Teutonic Order, Netherlands Envoy Extrdy and Min Plen Budapest; *d* unm 24 March 1964

2d Godard Adrian Henry Jules, 9th Count Bentinck and Baron Aldenburg; *b* 21 Feb 1887; Kt Cdr Teutonic Order, electro-technical engr and entomologist; *m* 1st 11 Jan 1921 Jacoba (*d* 12 Jul 1949), dau of Jacobus Johannes van den Heuvel, and had:

1e *Louise Adrienne Jacoba [Vrouwe George de Brauwere, Zuylestein, Leersum, Utrecht, The Netherlands]; *b* 27 April 1923; *m* 8 Dec 1954 George Léon Alex de Brauwere dit de Steelant (*d* 1992) and has:

1f *Alain George François [Alain de Brauwere dit de Steelant, 25 Kazernestraat, The Hague, The Netherlands]; *b* 15 Oct 1961; attorney practising in the Netherlands Supreme Court; *m* 1994 *Gemma Anna Maria Wilhelmina Bakx

1f *Jemima Sophie Adrienne; *b* 6 June 1958; architect; *m* 1980 *G R Scherpbier, engr, of Delft

2d (cont.) The 9th Count Bentinck *m* 2nd 1961 *Alida [Countess Bentinck, 22 Saxen Weimarlaan, Amsterdam, The Netherlands], dau of Frits Vlieger, and *d* 5 Aug 1968

3d John Victor Richard Rodolphe; *b* 5 Feb 1895; Kt Cdr Teutonic Order, Lt-Cdr German Navy, psychologist; *m* 17 March 1952 *Anna Margot Agnes [Countess John Aldenburg-Bentinck, Amerongen Castle, The Netherlands], dau of Ferdinand Fehrer, and *dsp* 26 Feb 1963

4d Alfred Louis Henry Godard; *b* 27 Dec 1897; *d* 30 Jan 1905

5d William Henry Ferdinand Godard; *b* 20 Dec 1900; *m* 27 Feb 1941 *Mathilde Marie Elisabeth Caroline [Countess William Aldenburg-Bentinck, Wassenaarse weg 365, The Hague, The Netherlands], dau of Prof R Stutzer and formerly w of F Meyeringh, and *d* in a car crash 16 July 1956

1d Elizabeth Mechtild Marie Sophie Louise; *b* 31 May 1892; *m* 7 Oct 1920 Sigurd von Ilsemann, Capt Prussian Army (*d* 6 June 1952), and *d* 15 Feb 1971, leaving issue

1c Victoria Mary Frederica Mechtild; *b* 6 Sept 1863; *d* unm 5 Feb 1949

3b Henry John William (Sir), KCB; *b* 8 Sept 1796; Gen Coldstream Gds, cmded Gds Bde Crimea 1854, Cdr Legn Hon, Col 28th Regt, Groom-in-Waiting to HM QUEEN VICTORIA; *m* 10 March 1829 his distant cousin Renira Antoinette (*d* 23 Sept 1889), dau of Adml Sir James Hawkins-Whitshed, 1st Bt, GCB (*see* 1871 edn, also below), and *d* 29 Sept 1878

1b Antoinette Wilhelmina Jane; *b* 18 Dec 1785; *d* 30 Jan 1870

(2) John Albert, of Terrington St Clements, Norfolk; *b* 29 Dec 1737; Capt RN; *m* 17 July 1763 Renira (*d* 1792), 2nd dau of John, Baron de Tuyll de Serooskerken, and *d* 23 Sept 1775, leaving:

1a William; *b* 17 June 1764; V-Adml; *m* 20 Oct 1802 Lady Frances Augusta Eliza Pierrepont (*m* 2nd 30 July 1821 Henry William Stephens and *d* 10 Feb 1847), only dau of 1st Earl Manvers (*see* 1953 edn), and *d* 21 Feb 1813, leaving:

1b George William Pierrepont, JP, DL, of Terrington St Clements; *b* 17 July 1803; MP W Norfolk; *d* unm 20 Feb 1886

2b Henry Paget Aldenburg; *b* 2 Nov 1805; *d* 26 Jan 1840

3b Charles Aldenburg, of Indio, Devon, and Terrington St Clements; *b* 22 March 1810; *m* 1st 10 May 1849 Harriet (*d* 15 March 1853), 3rd dau of Baldwin Fulford, of Fulford, Devon, and had:

1c William Fulford; *b* 13 May 1850; *d* 9 March 1862

2c Henry Aldenburg, JP (Devon); *b* 7 Jan 1852; *educ* Oxford (BA); barrister, High Sheriff Devon 1918; *m* 9 July 1890 Alma Martha (*d* 7 March 1947), est dau of Adml Lord Clarence Paget, GCB (*see* ANGLESEY, M), and *dsp* 28 April 1938

3b (cont.) Charles Aldenburg Bentinck *m* 2nd 20 Jan 1858 Frances (*d* 25 Jan 1904), 2nd dau of Martin Williams, of Bryn-Gwyn, Montgomeryshire, and *d* 7 Feb 1891

1b Renira Henrietta Aldenburg; *m* 21 July 1842, as his 2nd w, Rev George Martin (*d* 27 Aug 1860), Canon Residentiary Exeter, and *d* 16 Jan 1868, having had issue

2a John (Rev); *b* 1769; *d* unm 1804

1a Sophia Henrietta; *m* 11 Dec 1791 Adml Sir James Hawkins-Whitshed, 1st Bt, GCB (*d* 29 Oct 1849), and *d* 20 Jan 1852, leaving issue a s, who *s* his f in the btcy, and a dau:

1b Renira Antoinette; *m* her cousin Col Henry Bentinck (*see above*)

2a Charlotte Frances; *m* 12 Nov 1785 Sir Robert Shore Milnes, 1st Bt (*d* 1837), and *d* 1850

3a Henrietta Elizabeth; *m* 3 April 1804 Adml Sir George Martin, GCB, and *d* 1806

4 Charles John; *b* 2 June 1708; *m* 11 Jan 1739 Lady Margaret Cadogan, dau and coheir of 1st Earl Cadogan (*qv*), and *d* 18 March 1779

5 Sophia; *m* 24 March 1728 Henry de Grey, Duke of Kent, KG (*see* GREY, B, and LUCAS OF CRUDWELL, B), and *d* 5 June 1741, leaving issue

6 Elizabeth Adriana; *m* 18 Dec 1720 Hon Henry Egerton, Bp Hereford (*d* 1 April 1746), 5th s of 3rd Earl of Ellesmere (*see* GREY EGERTON, Bt), and *d* 1765

7 Harriet; *m* 15 Oct 1728 1st Earl of Clanbrassil (*d* 12 March 1758) of the 1756 *cr*, and *d* 10 June 1792, leaving issue (*see* DUFFERIN AND CLANEBOYE, B)

8 Barbara; *m* 18 Feb 1733/4 2nd Baron Godolphin (*dsp* 25 May 1785) and *d* 1 April 1736

PORTMAN

Arms: Quarterly, 1st and 4th, or a fleur-de-lys azure (for PORTMAN); 2nd and 3rd, gules a chevron erminois between ten crosses patée argent, six in chief and four in base (for BERKELEY). **Crests:** 1 A talbot sejant or (for PORTMAN), 2 A unicorn passant gules, armed and crined or (for BERKELEY). **Supporters:** Dexter, A savage, wreathed about the head and waist with ivy, in his dexter hand a club resting on the shoulder, proper; sinister, a talbot or. **Motto:** A clean heart and a cheerful spirit. **Creations:** V. (UK) 28 March 1873, B. (UK) 27 Jan 1837.

THE 9TH VISCOUNT PORTMAN OF BRYANSTON, Co Dorset, and **Baron Portman of Orchard Portman**, Co Somerset (Edward Henry Berkeley Portman) [The Rt Hon The Viscount Portman, Clock Mill, Clifford, Herefs HR3 5HB; 46 Pont St Mews, London SW1X 0AF]; *b* 22 April 1934; *s* unc 1967; *educ* Canford and RAC Cirencester; late RN, farmer, Jt MFH Golden Valley (Herefs) 1995–; *m* 1st 26 Sept 1956 (*divorce* 1966) Rosemary Joy, er dau of Charles Farris, of Coombe Bissett, Wilts, and has:

1 +CHRISTOPHER EDWARD BERKELEY [The Hon Christopher Portman, 38 Seymour St, London W1H 6BP]; *b* 30 July 1958; *m* 1st 30 July 1983 Caroline, dau of Terence Ivan Steenson, of Caversham, Berks, and has:

(1) +Luke Oliver Berkeley; *b* 31 Aug 1984

1 (cont.) The Hon CHRISTOPHER PORTMAN *m* 2nd 7 Dec 1987 *Patricia Martins, dau of Bernardino Pim, of Rio de Janeiro, and has:

(2) +Matthew Bernardo Berkeley; *b* 24 Sept 1990

(3) +Daniel Edward Berkeley; *b* 27 July 1995

1 *Claire Elizabeth [The Hon Mrs Robinson, Boxford House, Boxford, Berks RG16 8DP]; *b* 1 Oct 1959; *educ* St Mary's Wantage, Winkfield Place and Marlborough Secretarial Coll Oxford; *m* 8 Jan 1983 *(Anthony) Henry Robinson, only s of Anthony Leonard à Court Robinson, of Butcombe, Avon, and has:

(1) *Anthony; *b* 1984

(2) *James; *b* 1985

(3) *Patrick; *b* 1987

The 9th VISCOUNT PORTMAN *m* 2nd 31 March 1966 *Penelope Anne Hassard, yr dau of Trevor Robert William Allin, of The Barn House, North Moreton, Berks, and by her has had:

2 +Alex(ander) Michael Berkeley; *b* 19 Aug 1967; *educ* Harrow; racing driver; *m* 1992 *Emma Esma, dau of Christopher Morgan, of Ste Saturnin-les-Apt, Vaucluse, France, and has:

(1) +Maximilian Edward Berkeley; *b* 2 Jan 1996

3 +Justin Trevor Berkeley; *b* 23 Feb 1969; *educ* Harrow; artist

4 +Piers Richard Berkeley; *b* 30 May 1971; *m* 17 June 1995 *Alexandra, only dau of Sir Christopher Thompson, 6th Bt (*qv*)

5 Matthew Gerald Berkeley; *b* 12 Aug 1973; *d* 1990

Lineage: THOMAS PORTMAN, whose gf had borne the family arms which are still in use today, lived *temp* EDWARD I; ancestor of:

JOHN PORTMAN; *m* Alice, dau of William Knoell, of Samford Orcas, Dorset; *bur* 5 June 1521, having had:

Sir WILLIAM PORTMAN, JP Somerset; lawyer, granted a wardship by HENRY VIII 1533, administrator of CATHERINE OF ARAGON's will, judge 1547, ktd 1547, Ld Ch Justice 1554; *m* Elizabeth, dau and heiress of John Gilbert, and *d* by 10 Feb 1556/7, leaving, with a dau (Mary, *m* John Stowell):

Sir HENRY PORTMAN; *m* Jane, dau of Thomas Michell, and *d* 1590, leaving:

Sir JOHN PORTMAN, 1st Bt, of Orchard Portman (E), so *cr* 25 Nov 1612; ktd 3 Feb 1604/5, Sheriff Somerset 1606–07; *m c* 1600 Anne (*m* 2nd Thomas Nevill and *d* 1651/2), dau of Sir Henry Gifford, and *d* 4 Dec 1612, having had, with a dau (*m* Sir Edward Seymour, 3rd Bt; *see* SOMERSET, D):

1 Sir HENRY PORTMAN, 2nd Bt; *b c* 1595; MP Somerset 1621–22; *m* 20 July 1615 Lady Anne Stanley (*m* 2nd 1st Earl of Ancram (*see* LOTHIAN, M) and *d* Dec 1654), dau of 6th Earl of Derby (*qv*), and *dsp* Feb 1623/4

2 Sir JOHN PORTMAN, 3rd Bt; *b c* 1605; *educ* Wadham Coll Oxford; *d* unm there 12 Dec 1624

3 Sir HUGH PORTMAN, 4th Bt; *b c* 1608; *educ* Exeter Coll Oxford; MP Taunton 1625 and 1628–29; *d* unm by 14 May 1632

4 Sir WILLIAM PORTMAN, 5th Bt; *b c* 1610; *educ* Wadham Coll Oxford and Middle Temple; Sheriff Somerset 1637–38, MP Taunton April–May 1640 and 1640–Feb 1642/3 (taken prisoner after Battle of Naseby 1645, his estate being sequestrated by Parliamentarians for £20,000 (*c* £1,350,000 in late-1990s terms); *m* by 1644 Elizabeth, dau and coheir of John Colles, of Barton, by Elizabeth, dau and sole heiress of Humphrey Wyndham, of Wiveliscombe, and *d* Sept 1645 or 1648 while imprisoned in the Tower of London, leaving:

(1) Sir WILLIAM PORTMAN, 6th and last Bt, KB (1661); *b c* 1641 or 1644; *educ* All Souls Coll Oxford; FRS 1664, MP Taunton 1661–79 and 1685–90, with Lord Lumley (*see* SCARBROUGH, E) captured Duke of Monmouth 8 July 1685 following latter's failed uprising, suppressed at the Battle of Sedgmoor 6 July 1685; *m* 1st Elizabeth, dau and heiress of Sir John Cutler, 1st Bt; *m* 2nd Elizabeth, dau of Sir Thomas Southcote, of Buckland All Saints, Devon; *m* 3rd Mary, dau and heiress of Sir John Holman, but *dsp* 20 March 1689/90, when the btcy expired, leaving Orchard Portman and other estates worth £8,000 (*c* £600,000 in late-1990s terms) p.a. to his cousin Henry SEYMOUR later PORTMAN

1 Joan; *m* George Speke, of Whitelackington, Somerset, and had:

(1) Philippa; *m* Edward BERKELEY (*see* BERKELEY, B), of Pylle, Somerset, s of Sir Edward Berkeley, of Pylle (*d* 1654, s of Sir Henry Berkeley, of Bruton (ancestor of the extinct Viscounts Fitzhardinge and Earls of Falmouth) and gs of Sir Maurice Berkeley, of Burton, descended from the 1st/2nd Lord (Baron) Berkeley of the 1295/1308 *cr*; *see* BERKELEY, B), by Margaret, dau of John Holland, of Steyning, Sussex, and *d* 1699, leaving:

1a Edward, of Pylle; *m* Elizabeth, dau of John Ryves, of Ranston, Dorset, and *d* 1707, having had:

1b Edward; *d* an infant

2b Maurice; of Pylle; *dsp* 1717

3b William BERKELEY later PORTMAN (Act of Parl 9 GEORGE II), of Pylle; *m* 8 Jan 1708 Anne (*d* 10 May 1752), dau of Sir Edward Seymour, 4th Bt (*see* SOMERSET, D), and *d* 1737, leaving:

1c Henry William Berkeley, of Orchard Portman and Bryanston; *m* Anne, dau of William Fitch, and *d* 1761, leaving:

1d Henry William, of Orchard Portman and Bryanston; *m* Anne, dau of William Wyndham, of Dinton, and had, with three daus:

1e Henry Berkeley; *m* 1793 Hon Lucy Elizabeth Dormer, dau of 8th Baron Dormer (*qv*), and *d* 1804, leaving:

1f Charlotte Fanny; *m* 5th Earl Poulett (*b* 5 July 1783; *dsps* 20 June 1864; *see* 1970 edn) and *d* 27 March 1877, having had issue

2e Edward Berkeley, of Orchard Portman and Bryanston; *b* 1771; *m* 1st 28 Aug 1798 Lucy (*d* 25 March 1812), dau of Rev Thomas Whitby, of Cresswell Hall, Staffs, and had:

1f EDWARD BERKELEY, **1st Viscount**

2f Henry William Berkeley, of Dean's Court, Dorset, JP; *b* 8 May 1801; *m* 8 May 1832 Harriet Emily (*d* 23 Aug 1890), dau of T L Napier Sturt, and *d* 31 March 1879, having had issue

3f Wyndham Berkeley; *b* 4 June 1804; Capt RN; *m* 28 Sept 1829 Sarah (*d* 16 May 1880), dau of Thomas Thornhill, of Riddlesworth, Norfolk, and *d* 7 July 1883, leaving issue

4f Henry FitzHardinge Berkeley (Rev); *b* 23 Jan 1811; *educ* Oxford (MA); Rector Staple Fitzpaine and Orchard Portman; *m* 24 Aug 1840 Frances Anne (*d* 19 May 1889), est dau of Rev W N Darnell, BD, Rector Stanhope, Co Durham, and *d* 6 March 1893, leaving issue

1f Lucy Mabella; *m* 26 May 1824 George Digby Wingfield Digby, JP, DL (*d* 7 May 1883), of Sherborne Castle, Dorset, and *dsp*

2f Maryanne; *m* 14 April 1831 George Drummond (*see* PERTH, E) and *d* 1 Dec 1842

3f Harriet Ella; *m* 4 March 1827 William Stratford Dugdale (*see* DUGDALE, Bt) and *d* 17 April 1903, leaving issue

2e (cont.) Edward Berkeley Portman *m* 2nd 22 March 1816 Mary (*dsp* 31 Oct 1852), est dau of Sir Edward Hulse, 3rd Bt (*qv*), and *d* Rome 19 Jan 1823

2 Anne; *m c* 1630 Sir Edward Seymour, 3rd Bt (*d* 7 Dec 1688), of Berry Pomeroy, and *d* 1695, having had, with other issue (*see* SOMERSET, D):

(1) Henry SEYMOUR later PORTMAN (on inheriting his cousin the 6th and last Bt's estates); *m* 1st Penelope, dau of Sir William Haslewood, of Maidwell; *m* 2nd Meliora, dau of William Fitch, of High Hall, Dorset, and *dsp* Feb 1727/8, when his estates passed by entail to his cousin William BERKELEY later PORTMAN (*see* above)

3 Elizabeth; *m* John Bluet, of Holcombe

EDWARD BERKELEY PORTMAN's est s,

EDWARD BERKELEY PORTMAN, **1st Viscount Portman of Bryanston**, Co Dorset, so *cr* 28 March 1873, as also earlier 27 Jan 1837 BARON PORTMAN OF ORCHARD PORTMAN, Co Somerset (both UK); *b* 9 July 1799; *educ* Eton and Ch Ch Oxford (BA 1821, MA 1826); MP (Whig) Dorset 1823–32 and Marylebone 1832–33, Ld Lt Somerset 1839–64, Memb Cncl: Duchies Cornwall 1840 and Lancaster 1847, PRAS 1846, 1856 and 1862, Ld Warden Stannaries 1865–88; *m* 16 June 1827 Lady Emma Lascelles, Ldy Bedchamber to HM QUEEN VICTORIA 1837–51 and Extra Ldy thereafter, 3rd dau of 2nd Earl of Harewood (*qv*), and *d* 19 Nov 1888, having had, with two daus (*d* unm):

1 WILLIAM HENRY BERKELEY, **2nd Viscount**

2 Edwin Berkeley; *b* 3 Aug 1830; Fell All Souls, BA, BCL, barrister, MP (Lib) N Dorset 1885–92; *m* 14 May 1887 Caroline Ella (*d* 8 Jan 1938), dau of David Ward Chapman, and *d* 27 April 1921, leaving:

(1) Violet Guendolen; *b* 9 May 1889; *m* 2 Jan 1909 Frank Charles Lindo (*d* 22 Jan 1938), only s of Charles Lindo, of Bayswater, and *d* 18 April 1951, leaving issue

3 Maurice Berkeley; *b* 18 Jan 1833; *m* 1st 4 June 1856 Helen Vidal (*d* 30 March 1860), dau of John Harris, of Eldon House, London, Canada West, and had:

(1) Berkeley, of King's Barrow, Wareham, Dorset; *b* 8 April 1857; *m* 6 Feb 1883 Jessie Campbell (*d* 5 Nov 1946), dau of Gen Sir Robert Percy Douglas, 4th Bt, of Carr (*see* 1940 edn), and *d* 7 Aug 1918, leaving:

1a Maurice Percy Berkeley; *b* 7 Aug 1884; Cdr RN; *m* 2 Feb 1918 Joan Wycliffe (*d* 4 April 1971), est dau of Maj-Gen Charles William Thompson, CB, DSO, and *d* 17 Aug 1928, leaving:

1b +Berkeley Charles Berkeley [Berkeley Portman Esq, Danley Hill, Lynchmere, Surrey]; *b* 15 June 1919; *educ* Wellington; Lt RN (ret), underwriting memb Lloyd's, dir Hudson and Vernon 1973–; *m* 24 Oct 1944 *(Sheila Margaret) Penelope, WRNS, dau of Capt Francis Douglas Mowat, RN, and has:

1c +Rodney John Berkeley [Rodney Portman Esq, 3 Harley Gdns, London SW10]; *b* 15 Dec 1947; *educ* Wellington and Trin Coll Cambridge (MA); land agent 1970–73, fndr: Mander Portman Woodward Ind Sixth Form Coll 1973 and Berkeley Reafforestation Tst 1973, Freeman City London, Liveryman Gunmakers' Co, ARICS; *m* 1st 9 March 1976 (*divorce* 1992) Angela Theresa, only dau of Maj Jack Pringle, MC, of Tisbury, Wilts, and has:

1d +Guy Seymour Berkeley; *b* 12 Sept 1977; *educ* Stowe

2d +John Berkeley; *b* 21 Aug 1982

1d *Olivia Joan; *b* 1 Nov 1979

1c (cont.) Rodney Portman *m* 2nd 22 Dec 1997 *Rosalind, dau of Derrick Pease (*see* PEASE, Bt of Hammersknott) and formerly w of Joss Hanbury (*see* BIRKIN, Bt)

1c *Celia Rose Berkeley [Mrs Anthony Edwards, Salterton House, nr Salisbury, Wilts SP4 6AN]; *b* 30 Jan 1946; *m* 15 April 1972 *Anthony William Charlton Edwards, slr, yst s of William Edwards, of Walnut Tree House, Clent, nr Stourbridge, Worcs, and has:

1d *Berkeley Humfrey Charlton; *b* 8 Oct 1978

1d *Marcella Louise Charlton; *b* 24 May 1973

2d *Imogen Patricia Charlton Cartwright; *b* 13 Sept 1975

3d *Hermione Celia Charlton; *b* 6 March 1982

2c *Lucy Joan Berkeley [Mrs Ian Parsons, Newmains, Stenton, E Lothian EH42 1TQ]; *b* 15 Jan 1953; *m* 1983 *Ian Parsons, est s of Edward Victor Parsons, of Harlow, Essex, and has:

1d *Hugh Stanley; *b* 1988

1d *Jessie Catherine; *b* 1986

2d *Elspeth Caroline; *b* 1990

3c *Edwina Penelope Berkeley; *b* 10 Oct 1956; *m* 1986 *Timothy J Hicks, yst s of William Hicks, of Leckhampton, Glos, and has:

1d *James; *b* 1988

2d *Frederick; *b* 1991

1d *Camilla; *b* 1986

2d *Chloë; *b* 1989

4c *Rachel Mary Berkeley [Mrs Pasolini, 14 Ladbroke Gdns, London W11 2PT]; *b* 11 Dec 1961; *educ* Charterhouse; *m* 19– *— Pasolini

2b John Maurice Berkeley; *b* 28 April 1921; Lt RN WW II; *kas* in HM Submarine *Vandal* 24 Feb 1943

(2) Maurice William; *b* 10 Oct 1858; Cdr RN; *m* 12 Sept 1889 Mary (*d* 23 Dec 1929), dau of Capt Thomas Hudson, RN, of Flixton, Suffolk, and widow of Herbert Wybault Colvin, and *d* 15 May 1915, leaving:

1a Guy Maurice Berkeley, CB (1952), TD, DL (London); *b* 4 Aug 1890; *educ* Winchester and New Coll Oxford; barrister Inner Temple 1914, served WWs I and II, Brig (TA), ADC to HM KING GEORGE VI 1940–52, Chm Co London TA&AFA 1948–54, Hon Col The Rangers (Rifle Bde) TA 1946, md Allen Harvey and Ross Ltd (bankers); *m* 18 Oct 1922 Miriam Katherine (*d* 1 July 1975), 2nd dau of Capt George William Taylor, of Orchards, Godalming, Surrey, and *d* 16 July 1961, having had:

1b +Anthony Seymour Berkeley [Anthony Portman Esq, Rushmore Farm, Upton, Hants SP11 0JN]; *b* 23 March 1928; *educ* Eton; Lt Dorset Regt, High Sheriff Hants 1992; *m* 7 April 1961 (*divorce* 1995) Penelope Helen Kathleen, dau of Capt Derrick Warner John Candy, of Kingston Warren, Wantage, Berks, and has:

1c +Michael Henry Berkeley [Michael Portman Esq, The New House, Farmington, Glos GL54 3ND]; *b* 21 Feb 1962; *m* 13 June 1992 *Al(ison) G S, only dau of R A Bench, of Minchinhampton, Glos, and has:

1d +Guy Ralph Berkeley; *b* 2 Aug 1996

2d +Henry Edmund Berkeley; *b* 21 July 1997

2c +Jonathan Guy Berkeley; *b* 18 June 1965

1b Diana Fany; *b* 10 Aug 1923; SOE FANY WW II; *m* 4 Feb 1945 F/O Raymond Guy Manning, RAF, er s of J J Manning, AMICE, of Brighton, and was *k* with him in a flying accident in Italy 19 Feb 1945

2b *Lusia Edwina [Mrs Christopher Howard, Ryton Corner, Ryton, Salop SY5 7LW]; *b* 6 June 1931; *m* 29 May 1952 Christopher David Howard (*d*

13 July 1991), only s of Dr Richard Christopher Howard, of Hurst Green, Surrey, and has:

1c *Davina Elizabeth [Mrs James Vernon, The Hall, Lygan-y-Wern, Clwyd CH8 8BD]; b 8 July 1953; m 30 May 1981 *James William Vernon, er s of Sir Nigel Vernon, 4th Bt (qv), and has issue

2c *Belinda Jane [Mrs Timothy Evans, Little Mapp Farm, Kenley, Salop SY5 6NR]; b 6 Oct 1956; m 5 Sept 1981 *Timothy Michael Evans, er s of Geoffrey Evans, of Church Stretton, Salop, and has:

1d *Alice Valerie Katherine; b 3 Dec 1983

2d *Camilla Rose Lusia; b 11 Feb 1986

3d *Florence Diana Elizabeth; b 4 Aug 1991

(3) Maurice Vidal; b 21 March 1860; RIM 1876–79, Assist Supt Andaman and Nicobar Islands, Offr ic the Andamanese 1879–1900, Fell Calcutta U; d 14 Feb 1935

3 (cont.) The Hon Maurice Portman m 2nd 3 Oct 1867 his cousin Evelyn Harriet Lavinia (d 27 Jan 1927), dau of Maj Henry William Berkeley Portman (see above), and d 12 Jan 1888, having by her had:

(4) Cecil Berkeley; b 12 Sept 1869; m 6 Dec 1902 Florence Wyndham (d 22 April 1967 aged 89), dau of Maj Lachlan Forbes, 31st Regt, and d 10 March 1915, leaving:

1a *Marigold Florence Lavinia [Mrs Raymond Patterson, 2685 Queenswood Dve, Victoria, BC V8N 1X6, Canada]; b 5 Oct 1903; m 4 July 1929 Raymond Patterson (d 1984) and has:

1b *Alan Noel [Alan Patterson Esq, c/o 2685 Queenswood Dve, Victoria, BC V8N 1X6, Canada]; b 15 Oct 1936; m 28 Dec 1965 (divorce 1975) Mary Elizabeth Ann, er dau of Jeffrey Vincent Boys, of Vancouver, and has:

1c *Jeremy Patrick Murray; b 25 July 1967

1c *Samantha Jeanne; b 12 March 1969

2c *Jennifer Anne; b 1970

2b *Robert George [Robert Patterson Esq, 745 Greenlea Dve, Victoria, BC, Canada]; b 15 May 1944; m 23 March 1974 *Susan Veronica Mary, only dau of Henry Kenneth Graham Martyn, of Falmouth, Cornwall, and has:

1c *Mark Richard Murray; b 1978

1c *Claire Elizabeth Olive; b 1980

1b *Janet Murray [Mrs David Blanchet, 1230 Gladwin Dve, North Vancouver, BC, Canada]; b 21 May 1930; m 1 April 1949 David John Hilary Blanchet (d 1981), s of Geoffrey Orme Blanchet, of Vancouver Island, and has:

1c *Julia Claire Janet; b 18 Oct 1949; educ Simon Fraser U, Burnaby, BC

(5) Montague Berkeley; b 6 July 1872; Lt Somerset LI; m 13 Dec 1899 Jessie Elizabeth (d 3 Jan 1953), dau of George Edwin Lance, BCS, and d 9 Feb 1937, leaving:

1a Gerald Berkeley; b 11 Feb 1903; educ Haileybury; Lt-Col RA WW II; m 1st 15 July 1928 (divorce 1945) Joan, dau of Lt-Col George Turner, S Wales Borderers; m 2nd 28 Aug 1945 (divorce 1950) Cicely Faulkner, dau of Godfrey Ryder Oliver, and by her had:

1b +Michael Berkeley [Lt-Col Michael Portman, Port Hill, Northam, Devon]; b 28 Feb 1947; educ Wellington and RMA Sandhurst; Lt 15th/19th King's Roy Hus, Lt-Col Light Dragoons; m 1979 *Penelope Jane, er dau of Brig Harry Wilkinson Bishop, FRCVS, of W Malvern, Worcs, and has:

1c +Edward Berkeley; b 1983

1c *Lucy Serena; b 1985

1a (cont.) Lt-Col Gerald Portman m 3rd 17 July 1950 Maj Elisabet (d 1979), dau of Samuel Wohlin, of Lidingo, Brevik, Sweden, and d 7 Aug 1954

(1) Gertrude Emma; b 15 May 1871; m 30 July 1902 William Hunter Gandy, FCS, FRGS (d 27 Jan 1916), and d 13 Dec 1959, leaving issue

4 Walter Berkeley (Rev); b 1 Dec 1836; educ Oxford (BA); Rector Corton Denham, Sherborne; m 5 Oct 1864 Alice (d 25 July 1917), yr dau of Sir John Mordaunt, 9th Bt (qv), and d 22 March 1903, leaving:

(1) Alan Berkeley (Rev); b 17 Feb 1872; educ Wellington and Univ Coll Oxford (MA); Preb Wells, Rector Corton Denham; m 12 July 1913 Eva Cecil Violet (d 6 Oct 1969 aged 92), dau of David Alfred Ker, of Montalto and Portavo, Co Down, by Hon Eva Bateson, er dau of 1st Baron Deramore (qv), and dsp 3 Nov 1953

(2) Lionel; b 26 Dec 1873; author; m 24 Oct 1905 Isabel Edith (d 4 Feb 1959), only dau of Hon Alfred Erskine Gathorne-Hardy (see CRANBROOK, E), and dsp 12 Oct 1940

(3) Francis John; b 24 March 1878; educ Oxford (BA); d unm 2 May 1905

(1) Ethel; b Oct 1866; d unm 26 May 1961

The 1st VISCOUNT's est s,

WILLIAM HENRY BERKELEY PORTMAN, 2nd Viscount Portman of Bryanston, GCVO (1918), JP (Somerset and Dorset), DL; b 12 July 1829; educ Eton and Merton Coll Oxford; chm Dorset CC, MP (Lib) Shaftesbury 1852–57 and Dorset 1857–85 but after 1886 a Liberal Unionist, Col W Somerset Yeo Cav 1854, Commr City London Police 1918; m 1st 21 June 1855 Hon Mary Selina Charlotte Fitzwilliam (d 4 Jan 1899), posthumous dau, sole child and heiress of William Charles Fitzwilliam, Viscount Milton (b 18 Jan 1812; dvp 8 Nov 1835; see 1970 edn FITZWILLIAM, E, also JENKINSON, Bt), and had, with two daus (d an infant and unm respectively):

1 Edward William Berkeley, JP (Dorset), DL (Somerset); b 30 July 1856; educ Eton and Ch Ch Oxford; High Sheriff Somerset 1898, Maj Dorset Yeo; m 7 July 1892 Hon Constance Mary Lawley (d 4 May 1951), dau of 2nd Baron Wenlock (see 1932 edn) and widow of Capt Hon Eustace Vesey (see DE VESCI, V), and dsp 27 April 1911

2 Walter George Berkeley; b 2 June 1858; d 14 Dec 1865

3 HENRY BERKELEY PORTMAN, 3rd Viscount Portman of Bryanston, JP (Sussex); b 16 Feb 1860; educ Eton and Ch Ch Oxford; Capt and Hon Maj Dorset Yeo; m 25 Sept 1901 Emma Andalusia Frere (d 13 May 1929), only dau of Lord Nigel Kennedy (see AILSA, M) and widow of 5th Earl of Portarlington (qv), and d 18 Jan 1923, leaving:

(1) Selina Luisa; b 11 Sept 1903; d unm 17 July 1945

4 CLAUD BERKELEY PORTMAN, 4th Viscount Portman of Bryanston, JP (Dorset and Warwicks); b 1 Nov 1864; educ Eton; Capt Dorset Yeo Cav; m 1st 9 Feb 1888 (divorce 1897), as her 1st husb, Mary Ada (d 13 May 1900), only dau of Maj Francis Gordon-Cumming (see GORDON-CUMMING, Bt), and had:

(1) Guinevere; b 5 Jan 1889; d 5 July 1975

(2) Joan; b 24 Aug, d 12 Sept 1890

4 (cont.) The 4th Viscount m 2nd 12 March 1898 Harriette Mary (d 22 Dec 1939), 2nd dau of William Stevenson, of Boquhan, Stirling; Kensington Cottage, Newmarket, Cambs; and 4 Princes Gate, London SW7, and d 6 June 1929, having by her had:

(1) EDWARD CLAUD BERKELEY PORTMAN, 5th Viscount Portman of Bryanston, JP (Warwicks); b 8 July 1898; educ Eton and RMC Sandhurst; Capt Life Gds and Guards MG Regt 1914–19, sometime Jt-MFH Warwickshire and MFH Taunton Vale; m 12 April 1926 Hon Sybil Mary Douglas-Pennant (d 5 July 1975), yst dau of 3rd Baron Penrhyn (qv), and d 14 July 1942, leaving:

1a *Sheila Constance; b 25 June 1927; m 8 May 1951 *6th Viscount Knutsford (qv) of Knutsford and has issue

2a *Rosemary [The Hon Mrs Pease, 2 Britten St, London SW3 3TU; Folly Farm, Ashill, Somerset TA19 9NW]; b 3 March 1931; m 24 July 1951 Derrick Allix Pease (see PEASE, Bt, of Hummersknott) and has issue

(3) Sylvia Grace; b 19 March 1900; m 25 April 1932 Maj Thomas Gerard Du Buisson, MBE, MC, RA, yr s of Thomas Du Buisson, of Snower Hill, Betchworth, Surrey, and d 198–

(4) Jocelyn; b 27 May 1903; m 27 Nov 1923 Capt James Albert Garland Emmet, 1st Life Gds, est surv s of Maj Robert Emmet, DSO, and had issue

5 SEYMOUR BERKELEY PORTMAN, 6th Viscount Portman of Bryanston; b 19 Feb 1868; d unm 2 Nov 1946

6 GERALD BERKELEY, 7th Viscount

1 Emma Selina; b 5 April 1863; m 7 May 1885 11th Earl of Leven and Melville (qv) and d 1 March 1941, having had issue

2 Susan Alice; b 30 March 1866; m 8 Aug 1893 Alan William Heber-Percy and d 21 Aug 1933, leaving issue (see NORTHUMBERLAND, D)

The 2nd Viscount Portman of Bryanston m 2nd 2 June 1908 Frances Maxwell Buchanan (d 13 Nov 1939), dau of Boyd Alexander Cuningham, RN, and widow of Andrew James Livingstone Learmonth, and d 16 Oct 1919

The 6th Viscount's bro,

GERALD BERKELEY PORTMAN, 7th Viscount Portman of Bryanston; b 23 Jan 1875; educ Eton and RMC Sandhurst; Capt 10th Hus 1901 (joined 1895), ADC to Viceroy India 1901–02, Boer War 1899–1900 and WW I, dir Alliance Assur 1923–26, MFH Portman 1932–40; m 16 July 1902 Dorothy Marie Isolde (d 21 May 1964), dau of Sir Robert Sheffield, 5th Bt (qv), and d 3 Sept 1948, leaving:

1 GERALD WILLIAM BERKELEY PORTMAN, 8th Viscount Portman of Bryanston; b 20 Aug 1903; educ Eton and RMC Sandhurst; Capt RASC 1940–45, dir Alliance Assur; m 1st 27 Jan 1926 (divorce 1946) Marjorie Josephine Bentley, only dau of George Bentley Gerrard, of Montreal; m 2nd 11 April 1946 *Nancy Maureen [The Rt Hon Nancy Viscountess Portman, Sutton Waldron House, Blandford, Dorset], 4th dau of Capt Percy Herbert Franklin, RN, of Ropley, Hants, and dsp 3 Nov 1967

2 Michael Berkeley; b 20 Jan 1906; educ Charterhouse; served FAA, minesweepers, ATA and small vessels pool 1940–45; m 1st 1 Sept 1930 (divorce 1938) (Madelene) June (d 16 Sept 1947), 2nd dau of David Charles, and had:

(1) EDWARD HENRY BERKELEY PORTMAN, 9th and present Viscount Portman of Bryanston

(1) Davina Isolde; b 10 Jan 1932; m 1st 29 June 1954 (divorce 1965) Peter John Francis West, only s of A/Cdre Ferdinand Maurice Felix West, VC, CBE, MC, of Archways, Sunningdale, Berks; m 2nd T M Smyth and d 8 Nov 1971

2 (cont.) The Hon Michael Portman m 2nd 11 Oct 1938 Marjorie Kerr, dau of Frederick William Harris and Mrs Hans Blehr, of Bergen, Norway, and d 25 Oct 1959, having by her had:

(2) Michael William Berkeley; b 15 Oct 1943; educ Winchester; d unm 15 Nov 1983

(2) *Synöve Isobel ('Suna') [The Hon Suna Portman, Portman Lodge, Durweston, Dorset DT11 0QA]; b 10 Nov 1939; m 1st 1968 (annulled 1970) Martin Wilkinson and has:

1a *Heron Berkeley; b 25 Sept 1968

(2) (cont.) The Hon Suna Portman m 2nd 4 March 1970 (divorce 1981) Simon Boyle; m 3rd 20 Sept 1997 *Patric Morrissey and by her 2nd husb has:

2a *Kestrel Berkeley; b 6 Oct 1970

3a *Storm Simon; b 4 March 1979

1 Penelope Isobel; b 21 July 1913; m 1st 8 Feb 1934 (divorce 1949) Brig Archer Francis Laurence Clive, DSO and bar, MC, Gren Gds (see BUXTON, Bt), est s of Lt-Gen Sir George Sidney Clive, GCVO, KCB, CMG, DSO, of Perrystone Court, Herefs, and had issue; m 2nd 1 March 1949 David Arthur Salvin Bowlby, 2nd s of Arthur Salvin Bowlby, of Gilston Park, Harlow, Essex, and d 198–

PORTSMOUTH

EN SUIVANT LA VÉRITÉ

Arms: Argent a bend wavy sable. **Crest:** A mermaid, holding in the dexter hand a comb, in the other a mirror, a handle or, all proper. **Supporters:** Two chamois or wild goats sable. **Motto:** *En suivant la vérité* ('In following the truth'). **Creations:** B. and V. (GB) 11 June 1720, E. (GB) 11 April 1743.

THE 10TH EARL OF PORTSMOUTH, Co Southampton, **Viscount Lymington** and **Baron Wallop**, of Farley Wallop, Co Southampton (Quentin Gerard Carew Wallop) [The Rt Hon The Earl of Portsmouth, Farleigh House, Farleigh Wallop, Hants RG25 2HT]; *b* 25 July 1954; *s gf* 1984; *educ* Eton and Millfield; Hereditary Bailiff Burley (New Forest), Pres Basingstoke C Assoc, Patron Hants branch BRCS, Dir Grainger Tst, Liveryman Fishmongers Co 1997; *m* 1st 10 Feb 1981 (*divorce* 1984) Candia Frances Juliet (Candia McWilliam the novelist: *A Case of Knives* etc; *m* 2nd Fram Dinshaw, Fell St Catherine's Coll Oxford), only dau of Colin McWilliam and adopted dau of 4th Baron Strathcona and Mount Royal (*qv*), and has:

1 +OLIVER HENRY RUFUS WALLOP, *Viscount Lymington*; *b* 22 Dec 1981

1 *Clementine Violet Rohais; *b* 20 Nov 1983

The 10th EARL *m* 2nd 16 March 1990 *Annabel, est dau of Ian Fergusson, of Tudor Place, Richmond Green, Surrey, and has:

2 *Rose Hermione Annabel; *b* 23 Oct 1990

Lineage: MATTHEW de WALLOP; *fl temp* KING JOHN; gf of:

Sir RICHARD WALLOP; had an only dau and heiress:

ALICE Wallop; *m* Peter de BARTON, feudal Ld of West Barton, Hants; their gs and heir:

RICHARD; took name WALLOP, inherited as RICHARD de WALLOP; MP Hants *c* 1329; *m* Alice, dau of Sir John Husee, of Betchworth Castle, Surrey, and had an est s:

THOMAS WALLOP; *m c* 1343 Margaret Wellington and had:

JOHN WALLOP; MP Salisbury *temp* HENRY IV; *m* Avice, dau of John Buck, and *d c* 1438, having had:

THOMAS WALLOP; *m* Margaret, dau and heiress of Nicholas Valoynes, feudal Ld of Farley and Clydesden, Hants, and *dvp*, leaving, with three yr sons:

JOHN WALLOP; inherited the estates of the VALOYNEs through his mother and made his chief residence the manor house of Farley Mortimer (so called from the manor's owners earlier in the century; the name was subsequently changed to Farley Wallop and by the 19th century was spelled Farleigh); Farley remained the chief residence of JOHN WALLOP's descendants until destroyed by fire in 1667 (it was rebuilt 1733 by the **1st Earl**); Sheriff Hants *c* 1455 and 1461, MP Hants *c* 1473; *d* 1486, having had:

1 Richard; Sheriff Hants 1502; *m* Elizabeth, dau and coheir of — Hampton, of Old Stoke, Hants, and *dsp c* 1503

2 Robert (Sir); *dsp* 1535

3 Stephen; *m* —, dau of Hugh Ashley, of Wimborne St Giles, Dorset, and had an est s:

(1) John (Sir), KG (1544); said to have been among the 1,500 men under Sir Edward Poynings sent by HENRY VIII in 1511 to help the Regent of the Netherlands put down an uprising in the Low Countries province of Guelderland; ktd by 1513, Gentleman Privy Chamber to HENRY VIII; participated in operations against the French as Capt of at least two ships of war 1513 and 1514; Envoy to Regent of the Netherlands 1515 and 1526; fought on behalf of KING EMMANUEL OF PORTUGAL against the Moors in N Africa 1516–18, Kt Order of Christ Portugal by 1518; mil serv in Ireland and France 1518–23; Constable Trim, Ireland, 1522–23; High Marshal Calais 1524 and Lt of Calais 1529; Envoy France 1527/8 and as Amb 1532–41; granted former monastic lands at Barlinch, Somerset, and several manors in Somerset and Devon 1538; Capt of Guisnes (then still part of English possessions around Calais) 1541, memb Cncl of Deputy of Calais, cmded English mil ops Picardy against French 1543, commr for settling Anglo-French border northern France 1550; *m* 1st Elizabeth, dau of Sir Oliver St John (*see* BOLINGBROKE and ST JOHN,

V) and widow of 8th Earl of Kildare (*see* LEINSTER, D); *m* 2nd Elizabeth, dau of Sir Clement Harleston, of Ockenden, Essex, and *dsp* 13 July 1551

(2) Oliver (Sir); ktd at Battle of Musselburgh 1547 against Scots; *m* 1st Bridget, dau of — Pigot, of Beechampton, Bucks, and had, with three sons:

1a Rose; *m* Walter Lambert (*see* CAVAN, E)

(2) (cont.) Sir Oliver *m* 2nd Anne, dau of Robert Martin, of Athelhampton, Dorset, and widow of Thomas Tregonwell, and *d* 1566, having by her had, with an intermediate s and two daus:

1a HENRY (Sir)

2a Richard, of Bugbrooke, Northants; *m* Mary, sis and coheiress of William Spencer, of Everton, Northants, and had:

1b Richard; *bapt* 10 June 1616; *educ* Pembroke Coll Oxford (BA 1635); barrister Middle Temple 1646 (Bencher 1666, Treasurer 1673), defended Titus Oates in latter's trial for perjury 1685, Cursitor Baron of the Exchequer 1696; *m* Marie — and *d* 22 Aug 1697, leaving a dau, who herself had issue

Sir OLIVER WALLOP's est s by his 2nd w,

Sir HENRY WALLOP, JP (Hants 1569); *b c* 1540; ktd 1569, MP Southampton 1572, V-Treasurer Ireland 1579, Ld Justice Ireland 1582–99, where acquired considerable estates, including the lands of Enniscorthy Abbey, Co Wexford (*c* 12,500 acres) and Adare Abbey, Co Limerick, both on lease 1586 and then outright, together with those of Enniscorthy Castle 1595; entertained ELIZABETH I at Farley Wallop 1591; *m* Katherine (*d* 16 July 1599), dau of Richard Gifford, of Somborne, Hants, and *d* 14 April 1599, having had, with a 2nd s (Oliver, shot by native Irish in the woods at Enniscorthy June 1598) and a 3rd s (*das* overseas):

Sir HENRY WALLOP; *b* 1568; often deputised for his f in Dublin, ktd 1599, MP between 1601 and 1642, Sheriff Hants 1602 and 1603 and Salop 1605, Memb Cncl Marches of Wales 1617; *m* Elizabeth (*d* 1624), only dau and heiress of Robert Corbet, of Morton Corbet, Salop, through whom he acquired the manor and seat of Red Castle, with other lordships and manors in Salop, and *d* 5 Nov 1642, having had, with five daus:

ROBERT WALLOP; *b* 20 July 1601; *educ* Hart Hall Oxford; MP: Andover 1621–22, 1623–24 and 1627–53, Hants 1625, 1625–26 and 1658–59 and Whitchurch 1660; opposed CHARLES I in Civil War; one of the King's judges at his trial in Whitehall but did not sign the warrant for execution, Memb: 1st Cncl of State 1649, 2nd Cncl of State 1650–51, 4th Cncl of State 1651–52 and 5th Cncl of State 1652–53 and Rump Parl Cncls of State 1659 and 1660; at the Restoration he was subject to a resolution of Parliament disbarring him from the enjoyment of his estate, degrading him from his gentility and imprisoning him for life, also sentencing him on each succeeding anniversary of CHARLES I's execution in January to be drawn upon a sledge to and under the gallows of Tyburn with a halter round his neck; *m* 1st, presumably as her 1st husb, Lady Anne Wriothesley (*m* 2nd(?), as his 1st w, 1st Earl of Gainsborough (*qv*) of the 1682 *cr* and *d* by 6 March 1662), dau of 3rd Earl of Southampton (*see* SOUTHAMPTON, B, preliminary remarks); *m* 2nd 166–, as her 1st husb, Elizabeth, dau of — (*m* 2nd by May 1669 — Needham), and *d* in The Tower of London 19 Nov 1667, having had:

HENRY WALLOP; MP Whitchurch in the 1st Parliament of CHARLES II; *m* Dorothy (*d* 1704), yst dau and coheir of John Bluet, of Holcombe Regis, Devon, and *d* 25 Jan 1673, having had:

1 Henry

2 JOHN; *m* Alicia (*d* 20 Oct 1744), dau and coheir of William Borlase, of Gt Marlow, Bucks, and *d* 29 Jan 1693/4, having had, with another s (er than the **1st Earl**):

(1) Bluet; said to have had an income of £4,000 p.a. (*c* £155,000 p.a. in late-1990s terms); *d unm* 30 Oct 1707

(2) JOHN, **1st Earl**

(1) Mary; first Ldy of Bedchamber to PRINCESS ANNE, est dau of GEORGE II; *m* 12 Dec 1709 2nd and last Baron Herbert of Chirbury of the 1694 *cr* (*see* POWIS, E)

The yr surv s,

JOHN WALLOP, **1st Earl of Portsmouth**, Co of Southampton, so *cr* 11 April 1743, as also earlier 11 June 1720 BARON WALLOP, of Farley Wallop, Co of Southampton, and VISCOUNT LYMINGTON, Co of Southampton (all GB); *b* 15 April 1690; *educ* Eton and at Geneva; fought Battle of Oudenarde 1708, Hereditary Bailiff Burley, New Forest, MP (Whig) Hants 1715–20 and a Ld Treasury 1717–20, Ch Justice in Eyre North of Trent 1732–34, Ld Lt and custos rotulorum Hants 1733–42, V-Adml Hants and Ld Warden New Forest 1733–42, Govr IoW 1734–42, V-Adml IoW 1734 and Govr and V-Adml IoW 1745/6–62, Govr Foundling Hosp 1739–62, DCL Oxford 1755; *m* 1st 20 May 1716 Lady Bridget Bennet (*d* 12 Oct 1738), est dau of 1st Earl of Tankerville (*qv*), and had, with five other sons and four daus (all *d* in infancy):

1 John, *Viscount Lymington*; *b* 3 Aug 1718; *educ* Ch Ch Oxford; Page of Honour 1739, MP (Whig) Andover 1741–49; *m* 12 July 1740 Catherine (*d* 15 April 1750), dau and heiress to the tune of £60,000 (just over £3,100,000 in late-1990s terms) of John Conduitt, Master of the Mint, by Catherine, dau of Robert Barton and his w Hannah, herself half-sis of Sir Isaac Newton, whose papers and scientific collections thus came into the possession of the WALLOPs, while as will be seen the forename Newton appears regularly among successive members of the family; *dvp* 19 Nov 1749, leaving, with another s and a dau:

(1) JOHN, **2nd Earl**

(2) Henry; Groom Bedchamber to GEORGE III, MP Whitchurch; *d unm* Aug 1794

(3) Barton (Rev); *b* 3 Jan 1744; Master Magdalene Coll Cambridge; *m* 14 May 1771 his cousin Camilla Powlett (*d* 29 Sept 1820), sis and coheir of William Powlett SMYTH later POWLETT, of Samborne, Hants, and er dau of Rev Richard Smyth, of Itchen and Crux Easton, Hants, Rector Myddle, Salop, by Annabella, dau of William Powlett (er s of Lord William Powlett, 2nd s of 1st Duke of Bolton; *see* WINCHESTER, M), and *d* 1 Sept 1781, leaving, with a dau (Urania, *m* Rev Henry Wake):

1a William Barton; *b* posthumously 24 Dec 1781; Maj; *m* 21 Sept 1807 Elizabeth (*d* Nov 1812), dau of Maj Ward, and *d* Dec 1824, leaving:

1b William Barton Powlett WALLOP later WILLIAM-POWLETT (presumably added to commemorate his paternal gf's mother-in-law's f and gf), of Northolme Wainfleet, Lincs; *b* 6 Sept 1808; Capt 60th Rifles; *m* 10 Nov 1870 Ellinor (*d* 1881), dau of John Willis Fleming, of Chilworth, Hants, and *d* 7 Dec 1886, leaving:

    1c Barton Newton Wallop; *b* 8 Dec 1871; Maj Roy Fus WW I; *m* 4 Sept 1895 Emily Charlotte Tyndall (*d* 17 March 1954), dau of James Reibey, and *d* 19 April 1953, leaving:

        1d Newton James Wallop, DSC, JP (Devon 1950); *b* 26 June 1896; *educ* RNCs Osborne and Dartmouth; Capt RN WWs I and II; *m* 24 April 1929 Barbara Patience (*m* 2nd her deceased husb's yr bro V-Adm Sir Peveril William-Powlett; *see* below), 2nd dau of Sir Bernard Eyre Greenwell, 2nd Bt (*qv*), and *d* 10 Nov 1963, leaving:

           1e +Oliver Newton Wallop, JP, DL (Devon) [Oliver William-Powlett Esq JP DL, Cadhay House, Cadhay, Devon EX11 1QT]; *b* 28 Jan 1933; *educ* Eton; Lt RNR, High Sheriff Devon 1989

           1e *Ann Patience Wallop [Mrs Thomas Thistlethwayte, Summerhayes, Throwleigh, Devon EX20 2HX]; *b* 12 Feb 1930; *m* 10 Oct 1953 *Lt-Col Thomas Noel Thistlethwayte, 2nd Greenjackets, KRRC, est s of Arthur Donald Claud Thomas Thistlethwayte, of Bursledon Lodge, Bursledon, Hants, and has:

              1f *Rupert Thomas Newton [Rupert Thistlethwayte Esq, Donns Farm, Homersfield, Norfolk IP20 0NS]; *b* 19 Jan 1955; *educ* Eton; *m* 1982 *Elisabeth Anne, only dau of Francis Cator (*see* STOREY, Bt), and has:

                1g *Emma; *b* 1983

                2g *Katharine; *b* 1985

              1f *Jane Camilla [Mrs Timothy Dodd, 56 Chancellor's Rd, London W6 9RS]; *b* 2 June 1957; *m* 1991 *Timothy L S Dodd, only s of Lewis Dodd, of Newport, Dyfed, and has:

                1g *Peter Alexander; *b* 1992

                2g *Jeremy Aran; *b* 1994

                3g *Mathew Ralph; *b* 1997

           2e *Sara Elizabeth Wallop; *b* 23 June 1936; *m* 1st 30 April 1960 (*divorce* 19–) Hon (Edward) David Bruce, yst s of 10th Earl of Elgin and (14th Earl of) Kincardine (*qv*), and has issue; *m* 2nd 6 March 1998 *G Alastair Lean

        2d Peveril Barton Reibey Wallop (Sir), KCB (1953, CB 1949), KCMG (1959), CBE (1945), DSO (1942), DL (Devon 1973); *b* 5 March 1898; *educ* RNCs Osborne and Dartmouth; served RN (Midshipman 1914, Lt 1918, Cdr 1931, Capt 1938, R-Adml 1948, V-Adml 1950) WWs I (Gallipoli and Jutland) and II (Dir Manning 1939–40, Ch Staff Force H 1941–42, Capt Home Fleet 1944–45), ADC to HM GEORGE VI 1947–52, Naval Sec to 1st Ld Admlty 1948–50, Flag Offr Destroyers Mediterranean 1950–51, C-in-C S Atlantic 1952–54, Govr S Rhodesia 1954–59, v-chm (chm 1962–74) Appledore Shipbuilders Ltd, 3rd Cl Order Polonia Restituta, KStJ, High Sheriff Devon 1972, played rugby for England 1922; *m* 1st 27 Oct 1923 Helen Constance Forbes, CStJ (*d* 20 April 1965), dau of James Forbes Crombie, of Aberdeen, and had:

           1e *Olivia Pansy Wallop [Mrs John Wood, Coombe Down, Beaminster, Dorset]; *b* 27 April 1925; *m* 23 March 1950 *Lt-Col John Clairmont Wood, only s of John Clairmont Wood, of Coombe Down, and has:

              1f *Giles Powlett Clairmont [Giles Wood Esq, Millground, Beaminster, Dorset DT6 3LY]; *b* 3 Nov 1954; *educ* Eton; *m* 1988 *Frances Mary Catherine Stewart and has:

                1g *Robert; *b* 1991

                2g *Rollo; *b* 1992

              1f *Charlotte Knollys Olivia; *b* 16 March 1953; *m* 1977 *Philip Gilbert Herbert Bradley and has:

                1g *William; *b* 1980

                2g *Piers; *b* 1982

                3g *Timothy; *b* 1985

              2f *Louisa Ella Delamotte; *b* 22 July 1959; *m* 1987 Richard Charles Hawker (*d* 1992) and has:

                1g *John Henry Gore; *b* 1988

                1g *Constance Rose Knollys; *b* 1990

            2e *Helen Vernon Wallop; *b* 16 Dec 1927; *m* 17 May 1951 *Lt-Cdr Henry Victor Bruce of Salloch, RN, est s of Capt Hon John Bernard Bruce, RN (*see* ELGIN and KINCARDINE, E), and has issue

           3e *Judith Jean Wallop; *b* 7 Feb 1936; *m* 29 Oct 1955 *Sir Michael Jeremiah Colman, 3rd Bt (*qv*), and has issue

        2d (cont.) V-Adml Sir Peveril William-Powlett *m* 2nd 22 Jan 1966 his er bro's widow Barbara (*d* 11 Oct 1997; *see* also above) and *d* 1985

        3d Oliver Richard Ferdinand; *b* 1900; 2nd Lt 7th Hus; *d* unm 30 April 1921

        4d Peter de Barton Vernon, MC (1941); *b* 22 Oct 1903; *educ* Winchester and RMC Sandhurst; Lt 7th Hus, Maj 3rd Hus (Res) 1939–44 (POW), memb London Stock Exchange; *m* 30 July 1935 Hon Katherine Elizabeth Keyes (*d* 5 Nov 1996) (*see* KEYES, B) and *d* 1988, leaving:

           1e +Barton Roger Wallop [Barton William-Powlett Esq, Piercewebbs, Clavering, Essex]; *b* 14 Jan 1938; *educ* Winchester and Trin Coll Oxford; *m* 29 Aug 1962 *Judith, er dau of Colin Silk, of Lewes, E Sussex, and has:

              1f +Patrick Henry Wallop; *b* 13 March 1964

              2f +Thomas Wallop; *b* 28 May 1968

              1f *Katherine Wallop [Mrs Joshua Danziger, 17 Neard St, London W1V 3HQ]; *b* 28 Sept 1965; *m* 1990 *Dr D Joshua Danziger, s of Dr Arnold M Danziger, of Wilmslow, Cheshire, and has:

              1g *Samson Peter; *b* 24 Aug 1995

    1e *Mary Wallop [Mrs Jonathan Janson, 6 Edwardes Square, London W8 6HE]; *b* 24 June 1936; *m* 30 July 1957 *Jonathan Janson, er s of Capt Rex Janson, VRD, RNVR, of Sea Bank, Hayling Island, Hants, and has:

        1f *Nicola Claire Wallop; *b* 29 May 1959; *m* 1985 *Richard Henry Alexander Southby (*see* SOUTHBY, Bt, and LINLITHGOW, M) and has issue

        2f *Lucinda Katrina [Mrs Andrew Watt, 33 Chaldon Rd, London SW6 7NH]; *b* 7 May 1961; *m* 1991 *Andrew Peter Watt, s of Cdr Alexander Strachan Watt, of Ditcheatt, Somerset, and has:

            1g *Georgiana Louisa Janson; *b* 1993

        3f *Sara Arabella; *b* 28 March 1965

    1c Camilla Henrietta Maria Wallop; *b* 16 Jan 1873; *m* 6 June 1901 Alexander Popham, s of Rev V W Popham, and *d* Nov 1914, leaving issue

    2c Dorothea Ellinor Mary Wallop; *b* 20 April 1874; *d* unm 21 June 1954

    3c Katherine Gertrude Wallop; *b* 28 March 1876; *m* 9 Sept 1902 Henry Mostyn-Walker (*d* 1925), only s of Henry Walker, of Perdiswell, Worcs, and *d* 7 Feb 1958, leaving issue

    4c Rose Maria Wallop; *b* 1884; *m* 14 Dec 1910 Herbert Thomas Parnell Mayne, s of John Parnell Mayne, and *d* June 1924, leaving issue

  2b Newton Ward; *b* July 1810; *m* 25 Oct 1847 Elizabeth, dau of Dr McBride, and *d* 10 April 1880, leaving:

    1c Ellinor Gourdin; *d* unm 24 Jan 1880

  1b Henrietta; *m* 3 Dec 1851 Alexander Atherton Park (*d* 21 Nov 1871) and *d* 22 July 1888 aged 77, leaving issue

(4) Bennet; *b* 29 Jan 1745; *d* 12 Feb 1815, leaving a son

(1) Catherine; *m* 3 Oct 1770 Hon Lockhart Gordon and *d* May 1812, leaving issue (*see* HUNTLY, M)

The **1st Earl** *m* 2nd 9 June 1741 Hon Elizabeth Griffin (*bapt* 30 Nov 1691; *dsp* 13 Aug 1762), sis of 3rd and last Baron Griffin of Braybrooke and widow of Henry Grey, of Billingbear, Berks, MP Reading, and *d* 22 Nov 1762

His gs,

JOHN WALLOP, **2nd Earl of Portsmouth**; *b* 29 June 1742; Hereditary Bailiff Burley; rebuilt family property of Hurstbourne Park, Hants (the manor of Hurstbourne Priors in which it lay having been acquired by Sir Henry Wallop 1636 from Sir Robert Oxenbridge for £1,747. 12s. 4d, or *c* £85,000 in late-1990s terms), employing James Wyatt; *m* 27 Aug 1763 Urania (*b* 18 Jan 1742/3; *d* 29 Jan 1812), 4th dau of Coulson Fellowes (*see* DE RAMSEY, B), and *d* 16 May 1797, having had, with an est s (*d* young):

  1 JOHN CHARLES WALLOP, **3rd Earl of Portsmouth**; *b* 18 Dec 1767; Hereditary Bailiff Burley; *m* 1st 19 Nov 1799 Hon Grace Norton (*dsp* 15 Nov 1813), dau of 1st Baron Grantley (*qv*) of Markenfield; *m* 2nd 7 March 1814 (*dissolved* by a Chancery decree 1823 on the grounds of Lord Portsmouth's unsoundness of mind, which was held to have existed from 1 Jan 1809), as her 1st husb, (Mary) Anne, est dau of his (Ld Portsmouth's) pncpl tstee John Hanson, of Bloomsbury Sq, London (*m* 2nd 10 Oct 1828 William Rowland Alder, of Horncliffe Hall, by whom she is thought to have been the mother of the dau Henrietta *b* — nominally to the Portsmouths — in Edinburgh 7 Aug 18(?)19(?); Lady Portsmouth used to keep a whip under her pillow to subdue her 1st husb); *dsp* 14 July 1853

  2 NEWTON, **4th Earl**

  3 Coulson; *m* 2 April 1802 Catherine Townley, only dau of Maurice Keatinge, and *d* 31 Aug 1807

  1 Urania Annabella; *d* 17 Dec 1844

  2 Henrietta Dorothea; *m* 19 Jan 1816 Rev John Comyns Churchill and *d* 10 June 1862

The 3rd EARL's next bro,

NEWTON WALLOP later FELLOWES (roy licence 7 Aug 1794 on inheriting estates of his maternal unc Henry Arthur Fellowes), **4th Earl of Portsmouth**; *b* 26 June 1772; *educ* Eton, Middle Temple and Trin Coll Cambridge (MA 1792); Hereditary Bailiff Burley, Capt 1st Co S Devon Militia 1795 and 1st (E) Devon Regt of Militia 1820, MP (Whig) Andover 1802–20 and N Devon 1832–37; *m* 1st 30 Jan 1795 Frances (*d* 15 March 1819), 4th dau of Rev Castell Sherard, of Glatton, Hunts, and had:

  1 Henry Arthur Wallop; *b* 1799; MP Andover 1831–35; *dvp* unm 15 Feb 1847

  2 Newton John Alexander; *b* 27 March, *d* Sept 1801

  1 Henrietta Caroline; *m* 14 Dec 1826 Joseph Chichester Nagle, of Calverleigh, Devon, and *d* 2 Jan 1808

The **4th Earl** *m* 2nd 24 June 1820 Lady Catherine Fortescue (*d* 17 April 1854), 2nd dau of 1st Earl Fortescue (*qv*), and *d* 9 Jan 1854, leaving by her:

  3 ISAAC NEWTON, **5th Earl**

  2 Catherine Henrietta; *m* 29 July 1843 Seymour Phillips Allen (*d* 13 March 1861), of Cresselly, Pembs, and *d* 9 Sept 1900, leaving issue

  3 Hester Urania; *m* 26 Oct 1847 Ralph Merrik Leeke (*d* 26 Nov 1882), of Longford Hall, Salop, and *d* 30 July 1887, having had issue

  4 Camilla Eleanor; *m* 8 June 1852 her 1st cousin Hon Dudley Francis Fortescue (*see* FORTESCUE, E) and *d* 5 Aug 1920

The 4th EARL's only surv s,

ISAAC NEWTON FELLOWES later WALLOP (resumed on inheriting Earldom, change confirmed by roy licence 1995), **5th Earl of Portsmouth**; *b* 11 Jan 1825; *educ* Rugby and Trin Coll Cambridge; Hereditary Bailiff Burley; *m* 15 Feb 1855 Lady Eveline Alicia Juliana Herbert (*d* 30 Sept 1906), dau of 3rd Earl of Carnarvon (*qv*), and *d* 4 Oct 1891, leaving:

  1 NEWTON WALLOP, **6th Earl of Portsmouth**, JP (Devon and Hants), DL (Co Wexford); *b* 19 Jan 1856; *educ* Eton and Balliol Coll Oxford (Pres Union 1877, BA 1879, MA 1881); Hereditary Bailiff Burley, FSA 1878, FZS, CA Hants, Commr for Inverness-shire and Eccleslastical Commr England 1909, MP (Lib to 1886, thereafter U to 1905, when joined a Lib govt committed to Home Rule for Ireland) Barnstaple 1880–85 and N Devon 1885–91, U-Sec War and Civilian Memb Army Cncl 1905–08; *m* 17 Feb 1885 Beatrice Mary, only child of Edward Pease (*see* PEASE, Bt, of Hutton Lowcross), and *dsp* 4 Dec 1917

2 JOHN FELLOWES WALLOP, **7th Earl of Portsmouth**, JP (Devon); *b* 27 Dec 1859; *educ* Eton and Trin Coll Cambridge (BA); Hereditary Bailiff Burley, V-Lt Devon, Priv Sec to Govr Tasmania; *d* unm 7 Sept 1925

3 OLIVER HENRY, **8th Earl**

4 Robert Gerard Valoynes, JP (London); *b* 6 July 1864; Priv Sec to Govr Straits Settlements 1885–87 and Govr Queensland 1891–94; *d* unm 22 Aug 1940

5 Arthur George Edward (Rev); *b* 12 Oct 1867; BA Oxon; *d* unm 22 Dec 1898

6 Frederick Henry Arthur; *b* 16 Feb 1870; *educ* Ch Ch Oxford; Assist Priv Sec to Pres Bd Ag, Tstee Nat Portrait Gallery 1918–48; *d* unm 9 Aug 1953

1 Catherine Henrietta, JP (Salop); DJStJ, author: *Old Shropshire Life*; *m* 7 Dec 1876 Charles George Milnes(-)Gaskell, PC, JP, DL, MP (Lib) Morley, W R Yorks, 1885–92 (*d* 9 Jan 1919), of Wenlock Abbey, Salop (which he left to his w), s of James Milnes-Gaskell, the great friend of Gladstone's youth, and *d* 21 Aug 1935, leaving issue

2 Eveline Camilla; *m* 20 Sept 1888 Sir William Brampton Gurdon, KCMG, CB, PC, MP (*d* 31 May 1910; *see* CRANWORTH, B), and *dsp* 14 Sept 1894

3 Rosamond Alicia; *m* 9 Feb 1882 Augustus Langham Christie (*d* 7 April 1930), of Tapeley Park, Instow, Devon, and *d* 19 Nov 1935, leaving issue

4 Dorothea Hester Bluet; *m* 11 Feb 1886 Sir Richard Nelson Rycroft, 5th Bt (*qv*), and *d* 29 Dec 1906, having had issue

5 Gwendolen Margaret; *m* 3 Feb 1891 Vernon James Watney (*d* 27 Aug 1928), of Cornbury Park, Charlbury, Oxon, est s of James Watney, MP Surrey, and *d* 14 Feb 1943, leaving issue

6 Henrietta Anna; *m* 14 Oct 1890 John Carbery Evans (*d* 30 Sept 1954), barrister, of Townsend Manor, Middle Wallop, Hants, and *d* 28 Feb 1932, leaving issue

The 7th EARL's bro,

OLIVER HENRY WALLOP, **8th Earl of Portsmouth**; *b* 13 Jan 1861; *educ* Eton and Balliol Coll Oxford; Hereditary Bailiff Burley; *m* April 1897 Marguerite (*d* 9 May 1938), dau of Samuel Johnson Walker, of Ky., USA, and *d* 10 Feb 1943, having had:

1 GERARD VERNON, **9th Earl**

2 Oliver Malcolm; *b* 1905; *educ* Yale; rancher, served USAAF WW II; *m* 1st 1 June 1929 Jean (*d* 7 April 1943), er dau of Edward Small Moore, of New York, and had:

(1) +Edward John; *b* 26 June 1930; *m* 1st 1952 (*divorce* 1959) Carrol Robertson and has:

1a +John Michael; *b* 6 Feb 1955

(1) (cont.) Edward J Wallop *m* 2nd 7 June 1962 *Victoria Nelson, only dau of H Lyman Stebbins, of New York, and Mrs Angus Mackinnon, of Hunton Manor, Sutton Scotney, Hants, and by her has:

2a +Andrew Gerard; *b* 13 March 1965

3a +Sam Huntington; *b* 1972

1a *Alexandra Marcina; *b* 14 April 1969

(1) (cont.) Mr and Mrs Edward J Wallop adopted:

*Harriet Walker; *b* 3 Sept 1968

(2) +Malcolm [Malcolm Wallop, Canyon Ranch, Big Horn, WY 82833, USA]; *b* 27 Feb 1933; *educ* Yale; US Army 1955–57, memb Wyoming Ho of Reps 1969–73, Wyoming Senate 1973–77, US Senator (R) from Wyoming 1976–94, Senate Observer Arms Control Negotiations, Memb CSCE, proprietor Canyon Ranch, chm and ceo Frontiers of Freedom Inst, Bd of Dirs Hubbell Incorp and El Paso Energy Co Inc, author: *A Changing America* and *The Arms Control Delusion*; *m* 1st 1955 (*divorce* 1966) Josephine Vail Stebbins and has:

1a +Malcolm Moncreiffe (Henry); *b* 31 Dec 1957

2a +(Oliver) Matthew; *b* 30 April 1960

3a +Paul Stebbins; *b* 26 Aug 1963

1a *Amy Vail; *b* 17 Aug 1962

(2) (cont.) Senator Malcolm Wallop *m* 2nd 27 March 1967 (*divorce* 1982) Judith Warren; *m* 3rd 26 May 1984 *French Carter Gamble, formerly w of Wilfred L Goodwin III

(1) *Jean Margaret; *b* 29 April 1934; *m* 7 Jan 1956 *7th Earl of Carnarvon (*qv*) and has issue

(2) *Carolyn Walker [Mrs Irving N Alderson Jr, Bones Brothers Ranch, Burney, MT, USA]; *b* 6 July 1939; *m* 5 Jan 1963 *Irving Newman Alderson, Jr, s of Irving Newman Alderson, and has:

1a *Natalie Moore; *b* 12 Dec 1963

2a *Jean; *b* 1965

3a *Mary Roberts; *b* 1968

2 The Hon Oliver M Wallop *m* 2nd 26 Sept 1944 (*divorce* 1954) Mrs Alberta Jannapola Hines; *m* 3rd 25 Sept 1954 Carolyn (*d* 1973), dau of Harvey Parker Towle, MD, and formerly w of Henry Sturgis Russell, of Glenbrook, Nevada, and *d* 1980

The 8th EARL's er s,

GERARD VERNON WALLOP, **9th Earl of Portsmouth**; *b* 16 May 1898; *educ* Winchester and Balliol Coll Oxford; Lt 2nd Life Gds and Gds MG Regt 1916–19, MP (U) Basingstoke May 1929–Feb 1934, memb Milk Mktg Bd 1933–34, V-Chm Hants War Ag Ctee 1939–47, V-Pres and Chm CLA 1947–49, Pres Kenya Electors' Union 1953–55, Chm Forest Advsy Ctee for Kenya Govt 1955–61, corporate memb for Ag Kenya Legislative Cncl 1957–61, V-Chm E African Natl Resources Research Cncl 1963–84, Hereditary Bailiff Burley, author: *Git le Coeur* (1928), *Ich Dien*; *The Tory Path* (1931), *Horn, Hoof and Corn* (1932), *Famine in England* (1938), *Alternative to Death* (1943), *British Farm Stock* (1950), *A Knot of Roots* (autobiography, 1965); *m* 1st 31 July 1920 (*divorce* 1936) Mary Lawrence (*d* 6 Aug 1964), dau of Waldron Kintzing Post, of Bayport, Long Island, NY, and had:

1 Oliver Kintzing, *Viscount Lymington*; *b* 14 Jan 1923; *educ* Eton; Lt RNVR WW II; *m* 1st 26 June 1952 (*divorce* 1954) Maureen, only dau of Lt-Col Kenneth Bridges Stanley, MBE, of S Kensington; *m* 2nd 31 May 1954 (*divorce* 1974) Ruth Violet (*d* 2 Jan 1978), yst dau of Brig-Gen Gerald Carew Sladen, CB, CMG, DSO, MC, and formerly w of Richard Desborough Malcolm Mason, of Mau Narok, Kenya, and by her had:

(1) QUENTIN GERARD CAREW WALLOP, **10th and present Earl of Portsmouth**

(1) *Lucinda Ruth [The Hon Mrs Bellville, Manor Farm House, Cliddesden, Hants]; *b* 9 Feb 1956; *m* 1984, as his 2nd w, *Patrick Anthony Ewen Bellville, only surv s of Anthony Seymour Bellville, of Bembridge, IoW, and has:

1a *Blaise Anthony Valentine; *b* 1985

2a *Oscar Rupert Kintzing; *b* 1986

3a *Archie Seymour; *b* 1988

(2) *Emma Geraldine Anne [The Hon Mrs Cordingley, Cheesecombe Farm, Hawkley, Hants]; *b* 5 Oct 1958; *m* 27 June 1981 *Gerald Thomas Cordingley, s of Thomas Cordingley, of Bridlington, Yorks, and has:

1a *Katie Madeleine; *b* 1983

2a *Venetia Ruth; *b* 1985

3a *Jennifer Rose; *b* 1991

1 (cont.) Viscount Lymington *m* 3rd 26 March 1974 *Julia [Viscountess Lymington, 5 Venner House, 47 Bourne St, London SW1W 8UR], dau of Cdr (William) Graeme Ogden, DSC, and formerly w of Peter Robin Kirwan-Taylor, and *dvp* 5 June 1984

1 *(Anne) Camilla Eveline [The Lady Rupert Nevill, 35 Upper Addison Gdns, London W14 8AJ; Old Hove Farm, Glynde, E Sussex]; *educ* Longstowe Hall; served WRNS WW II, Pres: Regnl Arts Assoc Kent, Surrey and Sussex (Chm 1972–89) and E Sussex and W Kent branch NSPCC, dir Southern TV, Tstee: Glyndebourne Arts Tst and Roy Pavilion Brighton, Chm Regnl Ctee Kent and E Sussex Nat Tst 1986–96, V-Pres Brighton Festival, memb Reviewing Ctee Export of Works of Art 1982–86, Tstee Charities Aid Fndn; *m* 22 April 1944 Lord Rupert Charles Montacute Nevill (*d* 1982), yr s of 4th Marquess of Abergavenny (*qv*), and has had issue

The **9th Earl** *m* 2nd 14 Aug 1936 Bridget Cory, CStJ (*d* 15 Dec 1979), only dau of Capt Patrick Bermingham Crohan, RN, of Owlpen Old Manor, Uley, Glos, and *d* 28 Sept 1984, having by her had:

2 +Nicholas Valoynes Bermingham [The Hon Nicholas Wallop, 15 Tregunter Road, London SW10 9LS]; *b* 14 July 1946; *educ* Stowe; art dealer; *m* 1 Oct 1969 *Lavinia, only dau of David Karmel, CBE, QC, JP, of Gt Rissington Hill, Glos, and Belgravia, and has:

(1) +Henry Robert Newton; *b* 22 Nov 1974

(1) *Victoria Urania Sophia; *b* 1 Feb 1972

2 Philippa Dorothy Bluet; *b* 21 Aug 1937; *m* 6 June 1963, as his 1st w, *8th Earl Cadogan (*qv*) and *d* 1984, having had issue

3 *Jane Alianora Borlase [The Lady Jane Wallop, 1 Broadmere, Farleigh Wallop, Basingstoke, Hants]; *b* 24 Feb 1939

POUND

Arms: Argent a sword erect proper surmounted of a fess gules, thereon three mullets argent, in chief two boar's heads erased sable. **Crest:** A castle of two towers proper, thereon an escutcheon argent charged with a sword erect proper. **Motto:** *Fide et vigilantia* ('By faith and watchfulness'). **Creation:** Bt. (UK) 3 Aug 1905.

SIR JOHN DAVID POUND, 5TH BT, of Stanmore, Middx [Sir John Pound Bt, Brookland, 32 Yarnborough Hill, Oldswinford, Worcs; 42 Purbeck Drive, Lostock, Lancs BL6 4JF]; *b* 1 Nov 1946; *s* f 1980; *educ* Burebank Sch, Aylsham, Norfolk; Liveryman Leather Sellers' Co; *m* 1st 20 July 1968 (*divorce* 1978) Heather Frances O'Brien, only dau of Harry Jackson Dean, of Redcote, The Park, Mansfield, Notts, and has:

1 +ROBERT JOHN; *b* 12 Feb 1973

Sir JOHN *m* 2nd 1978 *Penelope Ann, er dau of Grahame Arthur Rayden, of Bramhall, Cheshire, and has:

2 +Christopher; *b* 1982

3 +Nicholas Edward; *b* 1986

Lineage: HENRY POUND, of Leadenhall Street, London; had:

Sir John Pound, 1st Bt (UK), so cr 3 Aug 1905, of Stanmore; *b* 27 June 1829; Lt City London, Common Cllr 1869, Alderman Aldgate Ward 1892–1915, Sr Sheriff 1895–96, Ld Mayor London 1904–05, Master: Leathersellers', Fruiterers' and Fanmakers' (Livery) Cos, Chm LGO Co, head firm of John Pound and Co (portmanteau mfrs), Grand Offr: Portuguese Order of Christ and Spanish Order of Isabella the Catholic, Cdr: Japanese Order of the Rising Sun and Legion of Honour of France; *m* 3 Dec 1856 Harriet (*d* 2 Jan 1918), est dau of Thomas Lulham, of Harley Place, Bow, London, and *d* 18 Sept 1915, having had:

1 John Lulham; *b* 28 Sept 1858; *d* 25 Feb 1859

2 (JOHN) LULHAM (Sir), **2nd Bt**

3 Percy Herbert; *b* 11 Aug 1870; Lt City London; *m* 1st 8 Oct 1895 (*divorce* 1930) Maud, dau of Frederick Wood, of Lordship Park, London, and had:

  (1) Sybil Gwendolen; *b* 12 Dec 1896; *m* 25 Nov 1916 Alexander Harvey (*d* 1 May 1952), s of Charles Harvey

3 (cont.) Percy Pound *m* 2nd 4 July 1930 *Doris Girling, only dau of Edward Herbert Mathew, and *d* 11 Jan 1951

1 Harriet Lizzie; *b* 23 March 1860; *d* unm 20 Feb 1947

2 Annie; *b* 15 Jan 1864; *d* unm 17 Oct 1943

3 Jessie; *b* 29 Sept 1866; *m* 7 March 1891 Alfred Victor Allen (*d* 26 March 1941), of Sydenham, and *d* 14 Jan 1943, leaving issue

Sir JOHN's 2nd s,

Sir (John) Lulham Pound, 2nd Bt, JP; *b* 2 March 1862; Lt City London, CC City of London Div 1919–28, Master Leatherseller's Co 1928–29, Alderman Aldgate Ward 1915–21; *m* 16 June 1886 Julia Isabella (*d* 4 June 1938), dau of Alfred Allen, of Highbury New Pk, London, and *d* 7 Sept 1937, having had:

1 John Russell; *b* 7 June 1887; *educ* St John's Coll Oxford (MA); assist master Shrewsbury, Capt 3rd Bn Shropshire LI WW I; *m* 31 March 1914 Elsie Irene (*m* 2nd 1 June 1918 Richard Gladstone Warner (*d* 30 July 1941), s of Weston Warner, of Whiston Priory, Ford, Salop; *m* 3rd 12 July 1955 Ven Richard Mervyn Cole-Hamilton; *see* ENNISKILLEN, E), yr dau of William Henry Pendlebury, of Canonbury, Kingsland, Salop, and was *ka* 27 April 1915

2 ALLEN LESLIE (Sir), **3rd Bt**

3 Graham Trevor, OBE (1949); *b* 23 Jan 1890; *educ* Merchant Taylors'; BSc, MInstCE, Maj RE 1915–19 (wounded); *d* unm 23 Feb 1964

4 Murray Stuart; *b* 18 April 1891; *educ* Pembroke Coll Cambridge (BA); 2nd Lt (SR) Roy W Surrey Regt; *d* 7 Nov 1914 of wounds recd in action

1 Muriel Irene; *b* 13 Sept 1893

2 Olive Winifred; *b* 7 Aug 1895; *educ* Newnham Coll Cambridge (MA)

Sir LULHAM's 2nd s,

Sir Allen Leslie Pound, 3rd Bt; *b* 31 Oct 1888; *educ* Merchant Taylors' and London U (LLB); slr 1911, Lt Roy Fus 1915–18, sole memb law firm of Pound and Pound, of Egham and Bracknell; *m* 1st 15 Feb 1916 (*divorce* 1925) Margery, 2nd dau of Stephen G Hayworth, of Clapton, and had:

1 DEREK ALLEN (Sir), **4th Bt**

1 Eileen Margery; *b* 18 Dec 1916

Sir Allen *m* 2nd 21 Nov 1925 Leonie May (*d* 31 July 1950), dau of Leon Mozin and widow of F/Lt Stephen James Chapman, RAF, and *d* 15 Nov 1952

The 3rd Bt's only s,

Sir Derek Allen Pound, 4th Bt; *b* 7 April 1920; *educ* Shrewsbury; Lt RA and Essex Regt 1941–46, co dir; *m* 28 Oct 1942 *Joan Amy [Joan Lady Pound, 9 Anmer, Sandringham, Norfolk], dau of James Woodthorpe, of Boston, Lincs, and *d* 1980, having had:

1 Sir JOHN DAVID POUND, **5th and present Bt**

1 *Diana Marilyn [Mrs Keble Paterson, Hadley House, Beche Rd, Cambridge]; *b* 17 Oct 1944; *m* 7 May 1966 *Keble Stuart Paterson, only s of George Ronald Irvine Paterson, of Ravenys, Stratford St Mary, Suffolk, and has:

  (1) *Timothy Keble; *b* 13 Aug 1968

  (1) *Caroline Elizabeth; *b* 1971

POWELL

ANIMA · IN · AMICIS · UNA

Arms: Gules, a lion rampant within a bordure engrailed or, in the dexter chief a mullet argent within an annulet of the second for cadency. **Crest:** A lion's head erased argent, gorged with a collar flory counterflory gules. **Motto:** *Anima in amicis una* ('One spirit among friends'). **Creation:** Bt. (UK) 5 March 1897.

SIR NICHOLAS FOLLIOTT DOUGLAS POWELL, 4TH BT, of Wimpole Street, London [Sir Nicholas Powell Bt, Hillside Estate, Box 17, Bromley, Zimbabwe]; *b* 17 July 1935; *s* f 1980; *educ* Gordonstoun; Lt Welsh Gds 1953–57, co dir; *m* 1st 26 May 1960 (*divorce* 1987) Daphne Jean, yr dau of Maj George Henry Errington, MC, of Chadwell Hall, Essex, and Monkton Ranch, Figtree, Zimbabwe, and has:

1 +JAMES RICHARD DOUGLAS; *b* 17 Oct 1962; *educ* Peterhouse Zimbabwe and RAC Cirencester; *m* 1991 *Susanna Frances, er dau of David Murray Threipland, and has:

  (1) +Douglas James Folliott; *b* 22 Oct 1992

  (1) +Cordelia Catherine; *b* 16 March 1995

1 *Catherine Mary; *b* 6 June 1961; *m* 1991 *Walter Ruprecht, est s of Joseph Ruprecht, and has:

  (1) *Nicholas Joseph Laurence; *b* 6 June 1996

  (2) *Alexander Dominic; *b* 24 Jan 1998

  (1) *Anastasia Laura; *b* 1993

Sir NICHOLAS *m* 2nd 10 July 1987 *Davina Hyacinth Berners, 3rd dau of Michael Edward Ranulph Allsopp (*see* HINDLIP, B), and by her has:

2 +Benjamin Ranulph Berners; *b* 5 Jan 1989

3 +Oliver Michael Folliott; *b* 4 Nov 1990

2 *Mamie Josephine Berners; *b* 21 April 1992

Lineage: WALTER POWELL, of Bucknell, Salop, who claimed descent from RHYS Ap TEWDWR MAWR, a pre-English Conquest ruler of Dehenbarth (S Wales) and was allowed armorial bearings attributed by tradition to RHYS at the Heralds' Visitation 1633; *m* Margery, dau and coheir of Richard Skull, of Much Cowarne, Herefs, and *d* 1567, leaving, with another s:

THOMAS POWELL, of Bucknell; *m* 27 April 1574 Maria, dau of John Walcot, of Walcot, Salop, by Mary, dau of Sir Peter Newton, Chllr to HENRY VII, and *d* 1611/2, having had, with a yr s and dau:

JOHN POWELL; High Sheriff Radnorshire 1641, bought the Stanedge or Stanage Park estate in that county 1632; *m* 1st 1623 Jane (*d* 1624), dau of Thomas Docwra, of Puttridge, Hitchin, Herts; *m* 2nd Elizabeth (*d* 1636), dau of Richard Walmesley, and had two sons (William, *d* 1632; James, Rector Brangwyn 1668–96) and a dau (Rachel); his only s by his 1st w:

SAMUEL POWELL, of Stanedge; *b* 1624 at Hamburg; naturalised in England 1628; *m* Elizabeth — (*d* by 1698) and *d* 1686, leaving an est s:

SAMUEL POWELL, of Stanedge; High Sheriff Radnorshire 1685; *m* Elizabeth Folliott (*m* 2nd Rev Thomas Jones, of Cwm, Flints, and Goodrich, Herefs, and *d* 12 May 1725), sis and coheir of 3rd and last Baron Folliott, and *d* Sept 1700, having had, with other issue:

1 Folliott, of Stanedge; *bapt* 31 July 1691; High Sheriff Radnorshire 1725; *m* 1714 Constance, dau of Thomas Cutler, of Street Court, Herefs, and *d* 7 June 1737, having had, with three sons (*d* young):

  (1) Constance; *m* Edmund Cox, Capt Queen's Dragoon Gds, and *dsp*

  (2) Anne; *b c* 1717; *m* Richard Ward and *d* 1809, leaving issue

  (3) Sarah; *m* Thomas Cooke, Surgn Queen's Dragoon Gds, and *dsp*

2 SAMUEL

1 Elizabeth; *m* 1717 Richard Knight, of Croft Castle, and had issue

The yr s,

SAMUEL POWELL, of Liverpool and later Stanedge Park; *bapt* 5 Jan 1694; *m* 1720 Elizabeth (*d* 18 Dec 1781), dau of Rev Richard Richmond, Rector Walton and Sefton, nr Liverpool, and *d* 17 April 1745, having had, with three other sons (*dsp*):

1 RICHARD

1 Elizabeth; *m* Matthew Stronge and had issue (*see* STRONGE, Bt)

2 Mary; *b c* 1724; *m* William Higginson, of Whitechurch and Liverpool, and *dsp* 1808

3 Sarah; *m* Ralph Robinson, of Liverpool, and *dsp* 1783

4 Rebecca; *m* Capt Alexander Duff, of Mayer, Banffshire, and *d* 1775, leaving issue

SAMUEL POWELL's est s,

RICHARD POWELL; *b* 1732; sold Stanedge Park to his unc Richard Knight; *m* Elizabeth (*d* 1822), only surv dau of John Cottrell, of Scarborough, and *d* 24 July 1794, having had:

1 Samuel, of Hammerton Hall, nr Boroughbridge, Yorks, and Brandlesome Hall, Lancs; *b* 28 Jan 1760; *m* 24 Feb 1796 Frances (*d* 1850), er dau of Henry Richmond, MD, of Liverpool and Bath, and *d* 16 June 1834, having had seven sons and three daus; ancestor of the POWELLs of Sharow (*see* below against **2nd Bt**)

2 John; *b* 1763; *d* unm 1788

3 JOHN FOLLIOTT

1 Harriott; *m* 1794 Holland Watson, of Stockport, and *d* 1819, leaving issue

RICHARD POWELL's 3rd s,

JOHN FOLLIOTT POWELL, sometime of Sandy Brook, Derbys, later of Leamington, Warwicks; *b* 27 Dec 1771; *m* Feb 1801 Frances (*d* 1859), est dau of Charles Armett, and niece of Sir Joseph Scott, 1st Bt, of Great Barr, Staffs (*see* 1970 edn), and *d* 9 Nov 1839, having had, with other issue (*d* unm):

1 William, of Tickford Abbey, Bucks; *b* 8 Aug 1805; *m* 1833 Eliza, dau of Thomas Miller, and *d* 1880, having had, with two other sons and four daus:

  (1) Thomas Folliott, of Tickford Abbey; *b* 1834; Capt 6th Foot; *m* 1868 Amy Winter (*d* 1934) and *d* 1899, leaving, with other issue:

    1a Edward Henry; *m* Margaret Winter (*d* 1918) and *d* 1914, leaving:

      1b *Edward (Rev); *b* 27 Nov 1909; MA 1952; Ld Manor Belcham St Paul, Essex, and Vicar there 1942, RD 1948, Rector Ovington and Tilbury, Essex, 1943, memb Halstead RDC 1946 (chm Public Heath Ctee 1949–59), surrogate 1951, Chaplain Regular Army Res; *m* 2 Oct 1940 *Anne Woodhouse, er dau of Percy C Newton, of Downham, Essex, and has:

        1c *Richard Folliott; *b* 3 Dec 1942; *educ* Lancing; Capt Welsh Gds, Assist Adj RMA Sandhurst 1969; *m* 20 July 1968 *Lindsay, only dau of Richard Coombe, of Prathall, Cutthorpe, Chesterfield, Derbys

2c *Charles Edward; *b* 5 March 1944; *educ* Lancing

3c *William Rhys; *b* 3 Aug 1948; *educ* Lancing and Emmanuel Coll Cambridge

1c *Rosalind Mary; *b* 16 Sept 1945

2c *Christina Anne; *b* 15 Nov 1950

(2) Charles William, of Stony Stratford, Bucks; *b* 1836; *m* 18– Fanny Isabella (*d* 1915), 2nd dau of Rev Charles William Selby-Lowndes, Rector N Crawley, Bucks, and had:

1a Greville Angus Montacute Charles William; *b* 1867; *m* 6 April 1904 Julia Margaret Arabella (*d* 16 March 1955), yr dau of Col James Henry Gordon, CB, DSO, IA, and *d* 23 Sept 1936, leaving:

1b *Adam Gordon [Adam Powell Esq, West View Farm, St George's Rd, Salfords, Surrey]; *b* 1912; *m* 1st 1939 (*divorce* 1956) Mary Isobel, dau of B E Stroud, of The Priory, Stone, Staffs; *m* 2nd 1956 *Violet, dau of Alfred Swaine Methold, of Thorne Court, Bury St Edmunds, Suffolk

2 SCOTT

3 Harrison; *b* Oct 1820; *m* twice and left issue in Australia

1 Frances; *b* 14 Oct 1802; *m* Aug 1825 Rev Peyton Blakiston, MD, FRS, s of Sir Matthew Blakiston, 2nd Bt (*qv*), and *d* 23 Feb 1858, leaving issue

2 Elizabeth Anne; *b* 29 Nov 1812; *m* 1837 Rev Thelwall Salusbury, Vicar Offley, Herts (*see* 1868 edn SALUSBURY, Bt), and *d* Oct 1882, leaving issue

JOHN FOLLIOTT POWELL's 2nd s,

SCOTT POWELL; *b* 13 Nov 1809; Capt 23rd Regt Roy Welch Fus; *m* 25 Sept 1840 Eliza (*d* 15 Aug 1888), dau of Richard Meeke, and *d* 14 April 1855, having had:

1 Lillwall Scott; *b* 7 July 1841; served 19th Foot; *d* 25 April 1861

2 (RICHARD) DOUGLAS (Sir), **1st Bt**

3 Charles Folliott; Lt 96th Foot, Maj 5th Gurkhas and Indian SC; *ka* Afghan War 1878

1 Emily Mary Armett; *m* Rev Henry Arnott, FRCS (*d* 14 April 1855), Rector Beckenham, Kent, Hon Canon Rochester

SCOTT POWELL's 2nd s,

Sir (Richard) Douglas Powell, 1st Bt (UK), so *cr* 5 March 1897, KCVO; *b* 25 Sept 1842; *educ* Streatham, U Coll Hosp; MD (London), FRCP (Pres 1905–10), Hon MD (Dublin), Hon FRCP (I), Hon LLD (Aberdeen 1906 and Birmingham 1909), Hon DSc (Oxford) 1907, Hon FRSM, KGStJ, Physician Extrdy to HM QUEEN VICTORIA 1887–99 and Physician-in-Ordinary 1899–1901, Physician Extrdy to HM EDWARD VII 1901–07 and Physician-in-Ordinary 1907–10, Physician-in-Ordinary to HM GEORGE V 1910–25, Consultant Physician: Middx Hosp, Hosp for Consumption at Brompton, and at Ventnor, and Dental Hosp, dep chm Clerical, Medical and Gen Life Assoc, author: *On Diseases of the Lungs and Heart*, Harveian Oration (1914), *On Advances in Knowledge regarding the Circulation and Attributes of the Blood since Harvey's Time*; *m* 1st 30 Oct 1873 Juliet (*d* 18 March 1909), 2nd dau of Sir John Bennett, FRAS, Sheriff London 1871–72, and had:

1 DOUGLAS (Sir), **2nd Bt**

2 Charles Folliott Borradaile; *b* 19 Dec 1879; Lt 1st Bn KOYLI; *ka* Boer War 13 July 1901

3 Scott; *b* 10 April 1885; *educ* Ch Ch Oxford (BA); Capt 8th Bn Roy Welch Fus; *d* of wounds recd in action Mesopotamia 4 April 1916

1 Dorothy Juliet; *m* 22 Feb 1900 Edward Arthur Leadam (*d* 2 June 1928), of Austin Friars, only s of William Ward Leadam, MD, of London, and *d* 14 Aug 1946, leaving issue

2 Evelyn Sydney; *m* 8 Oct 1900 Sir R Malcolm McIlwraith, KCMG, KC (*d* 18 March 1941), of S Kensington, only s of Robert McIlwraith, of Chelsea, and *d* 20 April 1921, leaving issue

Sir Douglas *m* 2nd 16 Oct 1917 Edith Mary Burke (*d* 18 Aug 1834), yr dau of Henry Wood, of Bayswater, and *d* 15 Dec 1925

The 1st Bt's only surv s,

Sir Douglas Powell, 2nd Bt, CBE; *b* 8 July 1874; *educ* Magdalen Coll Oxford (BA); Maj and Brevet Lt-Col Roy Welch Fus Boer War and WW I; *m* 10 Feb 1904 his distant cousin Albinia Mariel (*d* 17 May 1959), est dau of William Folliott Powell, of Sharow Hall, Ripon, Yorks, and *d* 28 Feb 1932, having had:

1 RICHARD GEORGE DOUGLAS (Sir), **3rd Bt**

1 Elizabeth Juliet; *b* 24 March 1905; *m* 1st 16 April 1931 Percy John Harratt, er s of John Harratt, and had issue; *m* 2nd Oliver D Wood and *d* April 1956

2 Pamela Mary; *b* 31 July 1911; *m* 5 April 1933 George Clark Tozer (*d* 1973), only s of George Tozer, of Mallards, Beaulieu, Hants, and had:

(1) *Simon George Douglas [Simon Tozer Esq, Staplefords Farm, Bures, Sussex]; *b* 24 Dec 1933; *educ* Winchester and Trin Coll Cambridge; late Welsh Gds, mktg exec Total Oil Products; *m* 28 Jan 1958 *Elizabeth Ann St John, dau of Cyril William St John Turner, of Thames Ditton, Surrey, and has:

1a *Rupert Charles; *b* 19 April 1966

1a *Melanie Frances; *b* 1 Nov 1958

(2) *Richard Edward; *b* 25 Jan 1945; *educ* Winchester and Trin Coll Cambridge; *m* 21 June 1969 *Caroline Anne Kitchener, yr dau of Lt-Col Richard Harlachenden Carwardine Probert, OBE, of Little Bevills, Bures, Suffolk

(1) *Pamela Dorothy Susan; *b* 30 Nov 1937; *m* 6 Aug 1966 *Cdr (Edward) Murray Grahame Johnstone, RN, and has:

1a *Andrew Thomas Grahame; *b* 8 July 1967

1a *Jemima Elizabeth; *b* 14 Feb 1969

2a *A dau; *b* 21 Feb 1971

Sir DOUGLAS's only s,

Sir Richard George Douglas Powell, 3rd Bt, MC (1944) and bar (1945); *b* 14 Nov 1909; *educ* Eton; Maj Welsh Gds WW II (Belgian Croix Militaire 1st Cl 1947), Assist Mil Attaché Brussels 1946–48, dir: Bovis Hldgs Ltd and Bovis Ltd, Heldring & Pierson (UK), F English Gp, BUPA Medical Centre, The TH Inc Gp (UK), Russell Garratt 1974–80, Dir-Gen IOD 1954–74, Pres British Houses Export TB Soc 1974–80, Dep Chm Ctee on Invisible Exports 1968–76; *m* 1st 23 Feb 1933 Elizabeth Josephine (*d* 1979), only dau of Lt-Col Osmond Robert McMullen, CMG, of Presdales Hall, Ware, Herts, and had:

---

1 Sir NICHOLAS FOLLIOTT DOUGLAS POWELL, **4th and present Bt**

1 *Bryony Josephine Anne [Mrs Bryony Thomasson, 19 Ackmar Rd, London SW6 4UP]; *b* 30 Dec 1933; *m* 11 Jan 1955 (*divorce* 1968) Christopher Lucas Thomasson, s of Franklin Thomasson, of The Old Manor, Ellisfield, Hants, and has:

(1) *Samuel Charles; *b* 27 July 1956

(1) *Mary Elizabeth; *b* 10 Oct 1958

2 *Julia Mary [Mrs Jeremy Twynam, Merestones, Woolstone, Oxon SN7 7QL]; *b* 27 Dec 1943; *m* 10 Feb 1973 *Jeremy John Twynam, s of James Twynam, of Kitemore House, Faringdon, Oxon, and has:

(1) *Henry Thomas Alexander; *b* 1977

(1) *Leonora Mary Alexandra; *b* 1975

Sir Richard *m* 2nd 1980, as her 1st husb, *Alice Maria (*m* 2nd Lt-Col Donald John Arthur Grant), er dau of Wilhelmus den Bode, of Utrecht, and *d* 16 July 1980

POWER

Arms: Or on a bend gules between two fox's heads erased proper, three crescents of the first, on a chief of the second as many escallops argent. **Crest:** A stag's head erased proper, gorged with an antique crown and between the attires a cross patée or. **Motto:** *Pro patria semper* ('Ever patriotic'). **Creation:** Bt. (UK) 1 Feb 1924.

SIR ALASTAIR JOHN CECIL POWER, 4TH BT, of Newlands Manor, Parish of Milford, Co Southampton [Sir Alastair Power Bt, c/o 3 Burnett Rd, Christchurch, Dorset BH23 2DL]; *b* 15 Aug 1958; *s f* 1984

Lineage: JOHN POWER, of Eldon, Co Down, Ireland; *d* 1873, leaving:

WILLIAM TAYLOR POWER, of Eldon House, Co Down; *m* Cecilia (*d* 1874), dau of Col John Burgoyne, and *d* 29 Nov 1916, leaving:

1 Frederick Joseph; *b* 21 April 1869; *d* 24 July 1936

2 **Sir John Cecil Power, 1st Bt** (UK), so *cr* 1 Feb 1924; *b* 21 Dec 1870; MP (C) Wimbledon Oct 1924–June 1945; *m* 14 Oct 1902 Mabel Katherine Louisa (*d* 31 March 1945), est dau of John Hartley Perks, JP, of S Kensington and Slade Hill, Wolverhampton, and *d* 5 June 1950, having had:

(1) IVAN McLANNAHAN CECIL (Sir), **2nd Bt**

(2) +George Frederick Cecil McLannahan [George Power Esq, 3 Burnett Rd, Christchurch, Dorset BH23 2DL]; *b* 28 June 1919; *educ* Eton and in Switzerland; Actg Maj Welch Regt WW II, sometime Capt War Dept Fleet (explosives salvage), borough cncllr Lymington 1948–65, memb Hants CC Adoption Ctee 1950–65, Harbour Commissioner 1960–65, fndr Sea Rescue Service (subsequently inshore rescue RNLI), govr: Wessex Hosp Gp and Hants CC Schs, memb Territorial Ctee, undwriting memb Lloyd's 1977–87; *m* 1st 20 July 1940 (*divorce* 1948) Joy Mervyn, dau of Geoffrey Noott, JP, MRCS, MRCP, of Ferndown, Dorset, and has:

1a +David George Cecil [David Power Esq, Islands, Acedia, Casares, Malaga, Costa del Sol, Spain]; *b* 21 Sept 1941; *educ* Repton; *m* 1968 *Jennifer Anne, dau of Cdr Thompson, of Jersey, and has:

1b *January Georgina; *b* 1979

2a +Mervyn Peter; *b* 21 March 1944; *educ* Repton; *m* 1976 *Diana Louise, dau of Graham Alexander Michael, of Wigston, Leics, and has:

1b +Henry George Alexander; *b* 1978

1b *Camilla Joy Cynthia; *b* 1976

(2) (cont.) George Power *m* 2nd 30 July 1948 (Monica) Angela Mary (*d* 1990), 2nd dau of Cdr Henry Guy Stanton, RN, of Cornwall (*see* CASTLEMAINE, B), and by her has :

1a *Bridie Maureen McLannahan [Mrs Joseph Bonello, Riverside, Westover Lane, Ringwood, Hants]; *b* 10 June 1951; *m* 1972 *Joseph Gavin Michael Bonello, of Purley, Surrey, and adopted:

*Michael Gavin James Stuart; *b* 1976

*George Gavin Richard Matthew; *b* 1977

2a *Sheena Patricia McLannahan; *b* 18 Feb 1954; *m* 1975 *Capt Peter Jeremy Walton Ledger, RM (ret), of Tarrant Hinton, Dorset, and has:

1b *Araminta Elizabeth Walton; *b* 1984

3a *Louisa Roxane McLannahan [Mrs Louisa Barrell, 83 High Town Rd, Ringwood, Hants BH21 1NS]; *b* 18 May 1957; *m* 1st 1976 Robert Derek Philip (*k* 1983), met policeman, and has:

  1b *Niesha Roxane McLannahan; *b* 1983

3a (cont.) Mrs Robert Philip *m* 2nd 1987 (*divorce* 1991) Jeremy David Barrell, BSc, and by him has:

  2b *Susanna Louise Roxane; *b* 1988

(2) (cont.) George Power *m* 3rd 24 May 1995 *Elizabeth, dau of Dr and Mrs Rawlins, of Garn Dolbenmaen, Gwynedd

1 Mary Lois Cecil; *m* 19 Dec 1930 (*divorce* 1961) Col Richard William Spraggett, CMG, CVO, CBE, MC, RM, er s of G W Spraggett, and had:

(1) *Ian Richard [Ian Spraggett Esq, 5 Lara St, Malvern, Victoria 3144, Australia; Regent House, 89 Kingsway, London WC2]; *b* 15 May 1934; *educ* Geelong GS Australia; Liveryman Clothworkers' Co

(1) *Elizabeth Anne [Mrs Clive Coogan, 15 Irilbarra Rd, Canterbury, Melbourne, Australia]; *b* 28 Sept 1937; *m* 23 March 1957 *Dr Clive Keith Coogan, only s of Rupert Coogan, of Sydney, Australia, and has:

  1a *Nicholas Brian Clive; *b* 30 March 1960

  2a *Justin John; *b* 5 Nov 1966

  1a *Karina Elizabeth; *b* 23 July 1962

2 Cynthia Mabel Cecil; *d* 11 Oct 1974

3 *Lilian Hartley Cecil [Mrs Paul Kingston, 400 N Flagler Dve, Apt 1105, W Palm Beach, FL 33401, USA]; *m* 30 Dec 1939 Paul Van Kleek Kingston, MD (*d* 1988), er s of Dr Charles Kingston, of W Vancouver, BC, and has:

(1) *Peter Charles; *b* 6 March 1945; *m* 1983 *Nancy Allison, dau of Oscar Clark, and has:

  1a *Alexander; *b* 1984

  2a *Christopher; *b* 1984 (twin)

  3a *Philip; *b* 1988

(2) *Timothy Paul; *b* 27 July 1949; *m* 1st 1983 (*divorce* 1987) Kathleen Procopio; *m* 2nd 1992 *Tani Bowman

(1) *Katharine Martha; *b* 14 July 1943; *m* 1968 (*divorce* 1993) Jack Calvin Hartje, PhD, of Florida, and has:

  1a *Neil; *b* 1978

  1a *Naomi; *b* 1974

Sir JOHN's er s,

Sir Ivan McLannahan Cecil Power, 2nd Bt; *b* 29 Nov 1903; *educ* Charterhouse and New Coll Oxford (MA); chm Stepney Tst 1934–41, Memb LCC 1937–41, served RAF WW II; *m* 1st 1 June 1927 (*divorce* 1935) Nancy Hilary, dau of Rev John William Griffiths, of Virginia Water, Surrey, and *d* 13 Feb 1954, having had:

1 JOHN PATRICK McLANNAHAN (Sir), **3rd Bt**

1 *Hilary Diana Cecil [The Rt Hon The Countess of Buchan, Newnham House, Newnham, Hants]; *b* 10 Oct 1930; *m* 21 Feb 1957 *17th Earl of Buchan (*qv*) and has issue

Sir Ivan *m* 2nd 18 Jan 1935 Margaret Mari (*d* 24 June 1936), only dau of William Henry Stevenson; *m* 3rd 10 Aug 1937 Kathleen Edyth (*d* 197–), yr dau of John Clerke Gloster, ICS, and *d* 13 Feb 1954.

Sir IVAN's only s,

Sir John Patrick McLannahan Power, 3rd Bt; *b* 16 March 1928; *educ* Pangbourne; RN 1946–48, rep with Cunard Steamship Co 1945–58, md Arthur Beale Ltd, London and Chichester, dir Kingsway Offices Co and assoc cos; *m* 1st 19 Oct 1957 (*divorce* 1967) Melanie, adopted dau of Hon Richard Alastair Erskine, of Reynolds House, Bordon, Hants (*see* BUCHAN, E), and had:

1 Sir ALASTAIR JOHN CECIL POWER, **4th and present Bt**

2 +ADAM PATRICK CECIL; *b* 22 March 1963; heir presumptive

1 *Belinda Jane; *b* 10 May 1960

Sir John *m* 2nd 19 May 1970 (*divorce* 1974) (Alison) Tracey, assist ed *Horse World*, only dau of George Cooper, of Amberley Place, Amberley, W Sussex, and *d* 24 May 1984

POWERSCOURT

Arms: Arg. on a bend gu. three pairs of wings conjoined in lure of the field. **Crest:** A demi-eagle, wings expanded arg., looking at the sun in its glory. **Supporters:** Two pegasi arg., winged, maned, hoofed and wings addorsed or. **Motto:** *Fidelité est de Dieu* ('Faithfulness is from God'). **Creations:** V. (I) 4 Feb 1743, B. (I) 4 Feb 1743 and (UK) 27 June 1885.

THE 10TH VISCOUNT POWERSCOURT, of Powerscourt, Co Wicklow, **Baron Wingfield**, of Wingfield, Co Wexford, and **Baron Powerscourt**, of Powerscourt, Co Wicklow (Mervyn Niall Wingfield) [The Rt Hon The Viscount Powerscourt, Tarabeg, Dunsany, Co Meath, Ireland]; *b* 3 Sept 1935; *s f* 1973; *educ* Stowe and Trin Coll Cambridge; late 2nd Lt Irish Gds; *m* 1st 15 Sept 1962 (*divorce* 1974) Wendy Anne Pauline, er dau of Ralph Chivas Golly Slazenger, of Powerscourt, Enniskerry, Co Wicklow, and has:

1 +(MERVYN) ANTHONY; *b* 21 Aug 1963; *educ* Sibford Sch, nr Banbury, Oxon

1 *Julia Margaret; *b* 5 Aug 1965

The 10th VISCOUNT *m* 2nd 15 March 1978 *Pauline, dau of W P Van, of San Francisco

Lineage: The WINGFIELDs, like many families of medieval origin, take their name from a place, in this case one in Suffolk. Subsequently the most successful branch of the family migrated from that most easterly of English counties west to Ireland, and accumulated estates and titles there. They are not the only family of Suffolk origin who made substantial territorial acquisitions in Ireland. Both the Pakenham Earls of Longford and the Cavendish Dukes of Devonshire did so; moreover both the latter families still possess magnificent Irish seats. But the Wingfields have been more closely involved with their adoptive country at an institutional level since it became independent of Britain. True, the 5th Earl of Longford made a speech at the Oxford Union when an undergraduate defending the 1922 assassination by Sinn Feiners in London of Field Marshal Sir Henry Wilson, Bt. And he nobly supported the Gate Theatre in Dublin for many years after the founding of the Irish Free State. In contrast the CAVENDISHes had been almost over-represented among the high officials of the old regime. But the **8th Viscount Powerscourt** actually served as a Free State Senator for many years.

Powerscourt, the eponymous family seat in the mountains of Co Wicklow above Dublin, has been described by the architectural historian Mark Bence-Jones as probably the most celebrated Irish country house in existence. Its proximity to the capital and its spectacular situation looking out towards the peak known as the Sugarloaf have surely helped make it so. The same writer adds that the ballroom there was the grandest country house interior in Ireland, this time without any qualification. Sadly the operative word is 'was' (although in summer 1997 the house was reopened to the public as a shopping mall and plans to restore such gems as the ball-room could not entirely be ruled out). Powerscourt's central portion was reduced to a shell by fire in 1974. By then it had been sold to the Slazengers, whose daughter was the present Lord Powerscourt's first wife. It is nevertheless well worth visiting, both for its splendid gardens and its pets' cemetery, said to be the largest in a private garden anywhere.

The senior branch of the WINGFIELDs, that of Letheringham, in Suffolk, are extinct. A junior branch were the WINGFIELDs of Crowfield, Suffolk. Harbottle Wingfield, of Crowfield, went in 1669 to Port Royal, Jamaica, and may have left descendants in Jamaica who if extant would be the senior surviving branch.

ROBERT de WINGFIELD, of Wingfield, Suffolk; *m* Joan, dau of John Falstaff, Falstolf or Fastolf, and had:

THOMAS de WINGFIELD, of Wingfield; *m* Alice, dau of Nicholas de Weyland, and had:

Sir JOHN de WINGFIELD, of Wingfield; *m* Anne, dau of Sir John Peche, and had, with two er sons:

1 JOHN (Sir)

2 Richard; feudal Ld of Denington, Suffolk, 1342; had:

(1) William (Sir), of Denington; *d* 1 July 1398, leaving:

  1a William; *dsp c* 1418

Sir JOHN's 3rd–born but est s dealt with here,

Sir JOHN de WINGFIELD; *m* the dau and heiress of — Honeypot and had, with another s:

1 John (Sir), feudal Ld Wingfield 1330–58; *m* Alianore, dau of Sir Gilbert de Glanville, and had:

(1) Katharine; *m* Michael de la Pole, 1st Earl of Suffolk of the 1385 *cr*, by whom she was great-grandmother of John de la Pole, 2nd Duke of Suffolk, who *m* Elizabeth Plantagenet, sis of EDWARD IV and RICHARD III

2 Thomas (Sir), of Letheringham; *m* by 1365/6 Margaret, dau and heiress of William Bovile, also of Letheringham, and widow of Sir William Carbonell, of Badingham, Suffolk, and *d* between 17 July and 27 Sept 1378, having had, with a dau (Margaret, *m* Sir Thomas Hardell):

(1) John (Sir), of Letheringham; MP Suffolk 1384, ktd 1389; *m* Margaret, dau of Sir Hugh Hastings, of Elsing, Norfolk, and had:

1a Robert (Sir), of Letheringham; *m* Elizabeth, dau of Sir John Russell, of Strensham, Worcs, and *d* 3 May 1409, having had an er s:

1b Robert (Sir), of Letheringham; ktd 1426, MP Suffolk 1428/9; *m* Elizabeth (*m* 2nd 1431 William de Hardwicke, of Hardwicke Hall, Derbys), dau and coheir of Sir Robert Goushill, of Heveringham, Notts, by Lady Elizabeth FitzAlan, dau of 11th/4th Earl of Arundel (*see* NORFOLK, D) and widow of Thomas Mowbray, 1st Duke of Norfolk of the 1397 *cr* (*see* MOWBRAY, STOURTON and SEGRAVE, B), and *d* 1431, having had by her, with three daus (including Elizabeth, *m* Sir William Brandon and was grandmother of Charles Brandon, 1st Duke of Suffolk of the 1513/4 *cr* and bro-in-law of HENRY VIII; also Katharine, *m* John Bonvyle) and two other sons:

1c JOHN (Sir)

2c Robert (Sir); MP Herts 1450/1, ktd 3 May 1471; *m* Anne, dau and heiress of Sir Robert de Hanling and widow of Sir William Chamberlayne, KG, and *dsp*

3c Thomas (Sir); ktd 1471; *m* 1st Mary, dau of Sir Roger Clifford; *m* 2nd Philippa (*m* 3rd 26 Aug 1471, as his 3rd w, Edward Grimston; *see* VERULAM, E), sis of 1st Earl of Worcester of the 1449 *cr* (*see* BEAUFORT, D, preliminary remarks) and widow of 9th Lord (Baron) de Ros (*qv*) of Helmsley, and *dsp*

4c Henry (Sir), of Orford, Suffolk; ancestor of the WINGFIELDs of Tickencote and WINGFIELDs of Virginia and Georgia, USA, also of S Africa, and the PARRY-WINGFIELDs

5c Anthony, of Glossop, Derbys, ancestor of the WINGFIELDs of Onslow

Sir ROBERT's est s,

Sir JOHN WINGFIELD, KB (1461), PC, of Letheringham; Sheriff Norfolk and Suffolk 1443–44 and 1461, Commr to negotiate with French ambassadors at Amiens 1477; *m* Elizabeth (*d* between 14 July 1497 and 22 Dec 1500), dau of Sir John FitzLewis, of West Horndon, Essex, by Elizabeth, dau and heiress of Robert Nevill, and *d* 10 May 1481, having by her had, with four daus and by some other person at least one illegitimate s (Richard Urry):

1 John (Sir); Sheriff Norfolk and Suffolk 1483 and 1497, attainted 1483, restored in blood after the Battle of Bosworth 1485; *m* Anne Tuchet, dau of 6th Lord (Baron) Audley (*see* 1970 edn), and had:

(1) Anthony (Sir), KG (1541), PC (1539), JP (Suffolk 1510); *b c* 1485; fought in France 1513 and 1523, ktd 1513, Sheriff Norfolk and Suffolk 1515–16, MP Suffolk 1529–35 and 1547–52 and Horsham 1544, Commr for Dissolution Monasteries Suffolk (granted 1537 land previously belonging to Campsie Priory and 1539 Woodbridge and Letheringham Priories entire), V-Chamberlain 1539, Capt Gd 1539–52 (was the offr who arrested Thomas Cromwell 1540 and Protector Somerset 1549), Comptroller Household 1549/50–52, Jt Ld Lt Suffolk 1551–52; *m* Elizabeth, dau of 14th Earl of Oxford (*see* SAINT ALBANS, D), and *d* 15 Aug 1552, having had, with other issue:

1a Robert (Sir), of Letheringham; MP Suffolk; *m* 1st Cecily, 2nd dau of 2nd Lord (Baron) Wentworth (*see* LYTTON, E); *m* 2nd — and *d* 1597, leaving by his 1st w, with other issue:

1b Anthony (Sir); *dsp* 1605

2b Thomas (Sir), of Letheringham; *m* 1st —; *m* 2nd Elizabeth, sis of Sir Dru Drury (*see* WAKE, Bt), and *d* 22 Jan 1609, having had:

1c Sir ANTHONY WINGFIELD, 1st Bt (E), so *cr* 17 May 1627, of Godwyns, Suffolk; *b c* 1585; Sheriff Suffolk 1637–38; *m* Anne (*d* by May 1642), dau of Sir John Deane, of Deane's Hall, Gt Maplestead, Essex, and *d* 30 July 1638, having had:

1d Sir RICHARD WINGFIELD, 2nd Bt, of Letheringham; *m* 1st 11 June 1649 Susanna, dau of Sir John Jacob, 1st Bt, by his 1st w Elizabeth, dau of John Halliday, and had:

1e Sir ROBERT WINGFIELD, 3rd Bt, of Letheringham; *b c* 1652; *d* unm 1671

1d (cont.) Sir RICHARD *m* 2nd Mary, dau of Sir John Wintour, of Lydney, Glos, by Mary (*d* by 1657), dau of Lord William Howard (*see* NORFOLK, D), and *d c* 1656, having had:

2e Sir HENRY WINGFIELD, 4th Bt, of Easton, Suffolk, and Letheringham; *b c* 1655; *m* Lady Mary Tuchet (*d* 15 Oct 1675), dau of 4th Earl of Castlehaven (*see* 1970 edn AUDLEY, B), and *d* 1677, having had:

1f Sir HENRY WINGFIELD, 5th Bt, of Letheringham; *b c* 1673; sold the Letheringham estate and followed JAMES II into exile in France; *m* — Guarigues, of Toulouse, and *dsp* 1712

2f Sir MERVYN WINGFIELD, 6th and last Bt; *b c* 1675; *m* Mary, dau of Theobald Dalton, of Greenan, Co Westmeath, and *dspm* shortly after 1727, when the btcy expired, leaving:

1g Mary; *m* Francis Dillon, of Proudstown, Co Meath, *cr* a Baron of the Holy Roman Empire by JOSEPH II 2 Aug 1767, and had:

1h John Talbot, Baron Dillon

2h Francis; Lt-Gen in Austrian service, *cr* a Baron of the Holy Roman Empire; had issue

3h William Mervyn; *m* Sophia, dau of Chevalier Austin Parke Goddard, of Brampton, Kent, and had:

1i John Joseph

1i Henrietta Sophia

2a Richard, of Wantisden, Suffolk; *m* Mary, yr dau of John Hardwick and sis of 'Bess of Hardwick' (*see* DEVONSHIRE, D, and SHREWSBURY and WATERFORD, E), and had issue (not necessarily in the order given), with an est s:

1b Anthony; *b c* 1550; *educ* Trin Coll Cambridge (scholar 1573, BA 1573/4, Fell 1576, MA 1577) and Gray's Inn; Reader in Greek to ELIZABETH I, Public Orator Cambridge 1580/1–89, Proctor 1582, MP Ripon 1592/3, tutor to 2nd Earl of Devonshire when still William Cavendish and the 2nd Earl's yr bro Charles (later Sir Charles; *see* DEVONSHIRE, D); *d c* 1615

2b John (Sir); Capt of Foot in Low Countries against Spaniards 1585 (wounded Battle of Zutphen 1586 and ktd then), Govr Gertruydenberg 1587–89, Master Ordnance English forces Brittany 1589–91; *m c* 1582, as her 2nd husb, Susan, dau of Baroness Willoughby de Eresby (*qv*) in her own right by her 2nd husb Richard Bertie and widow of 4th Earl of Kent (*see* GREY, B), and was *ka* in Earl of Essex's (*see* HEREFORD, V) raid on Cadiz 1596, in which enterprise he had the rank of Col, leaving:

1c Peregrine

3a Anthony; Gentleman Usher to ELIZABETH I; *d* 1593

2 Edward (Sir); ktd in Granada 1485; *dsp*

3 Henry, Rector Beaconsthorpe, Norfolk, 1480

4 John (Sir); ancestor of the extinct WINGFIELDs of Dunham Magna, Norfolk

5 William; Sewer (official with responsibility for service at table) to HENRY VII; *dsp* 1491

6 Thomas (Sir); allegedly *ka* Battle Bosworth 1485

7 Robert (Sir), PC (by Dec 1521); *b c* 1464; helped suppress Cornish rebels 1497, envoy to HOLY ROMAN EMPEROR MAXIMILIAN by Jan 1508 and again Feb 1511, ktd and granted manor of Orford, Suffolk, by 2 July 1509, Cncllr and Kt Body by 10 Feb 1511, Amb to Lateran Council Aug 1511, Marshal Calais (still then an English possession) jtly with bro Sir Richard July 1513–20 and later Lt of Calais and Dep 1526–31, Mayor Calais 1534, memb Lincoln's Inn 1520, Amb to HOLY ROMAN EMPEROR CHARLES V 1521, Kt Holy Sepulchre, Amb to MARGARET OF SAVOY 1522; *m* after 4 July 1519, as her 2nd husb, Joan (*d* after 7 Nov 1535), illegitimate dau of Sir Edward Poynings, KG, and widow of 8th Lord (Baron) Clinton (*qv*), and *dsp* 16 March 1539

8 Walter (Sir); *dsp*

9 LEWIS/LODOVIC

10 Edward; *m* Margaret Wentworth and had issue

11 Richard (Sir), KG (1523), JP; *b c* 1469; *educ* Cambridge, Ferrara U Italy and Gray's Inn; cdr with er bro against Cornish rebels 1497, Esq Body to HENRY VII 1500, ktd by 14 Nov 1511, Marshal Calais singly 1511 then jtly with er bro 1513 on, envoy to arrange Holy League between Castile and Aragon, England, the Holy Roman Empire, the Papacy and Savoy against France 1512–13, Kt-Marshal Calais April 1513, Jt-Dep Calais Aug 1513–May 1519, granted reversion 1519 of Manors of Clopton Halle, Cretyngham, Donyngton and Ilkettyshall, all in Suffolk, on death of Countess of Oxford; Inspr Ordnance 1519; Amb to: France 1520 and HOLY ROMAN EMPEROR CHARLES V in promoting English attempts to mediate between him and France 1521, granted Castle and Manor of Kimbolton, Hunts, 1522 and Manors of Swyneshede and Hardewyke together with sundry adjoining land (part of the recently attainted Duke of Buckingham's estates) 1523, Chllr Duchy Lancaster and High Steward Cambridge U 1524; *m* 1st, as her 3rd husb, Lady Katherine Woodville (*d* by 1513), 5th dau of 1st Earl Rivers and widow of (a) 2nd Duke of Buckingham of the 1444 *cr* (whence her 3rd husb's being granted former Stafford lands; *see* STAFFORD, B) and (b) Jasper Tudor, 1st and last Duke of Bedford of the 1485 *cr* (*see* BEDFORD, D, preliminary remarks), also sis of ELIZABETH, w of EDWARD IV, but had no issue by her; *m* 2nd, as her 1st husb, Bridget (*m* 2nd Sir Nicholas Hervey; *see* BRISTOL, M), dau and heiress of Sir John Wiltshire, Comptroller Calais, and *d en poste* Toledo, Spain, 22 July 1525, having had, with two other sons and four daus:

(1) Charles; *b c* 1513

(2) Thomas Maria; godson of Cardinal Pole and QUEEN MARY, hence his second forename; *m* — Kerrye, of Yorkshire, and had:

1a Edward Maria; *b c* 1560; granted with others a patent to colonise Virginia 1606, sailed there with first group of colonists 1607 (the only original patentee to do so), Pres Cncl Virginia May–Sept 1607 and after being overthrown (due to his self-regard and inability to get along with social inferiors) returned to England, where was living unm at Stoneley, Hunts, 1613

12 Humphrey (Sir), JP (Essex and Suffolk 1509), of Brantham Hall, Suffolk; *educ* Gray's Inn; Chamberlain to MARY QUEEN OF FRANCE and Duchess of Suffolk, HENRY VIII's sis, 1515; Speaker H of C 1533/4, ancestor of the WINGFIELDs of Brantham, Wakefield, and Norton, also of the WINGFIELD-DIGBYs and DIGBY-WINGFIELDs

Sir JOHN's 9th s,

LEWIS/LODOVIC WINGFIELD, of Southampton; *m* —, dau of Henry Noon, and had, with a dau:

1 John; living 1538; *dsp*

2 Richard (Sir); Govr Portsmouth *temp* ELIZABETH I; *m* Christian(a), only dau of Sir William FitzWilliam, of Milton, and sis of Sir William FitzWilliam, Ld Dep Ireland 1572–75 and 1588–94, and had, with a yr s (John, Dean Kilmacduagh 1621–24, *dsp* 1624):

(1) Sir RICHARD WINGFIELD, 1st and last VISCOUNT POWERSCOURT, Co Wicklow (I), so *cr* 19 Feb 1617/8, PC (1600); *b c* 1550; began mil career under unc, Ld Dep Sir William Fitzwilliam, in the long-drawn out attempt by ELIZABETH I to reduce Ireland, Deputy also to Sir Henry Wallop (*see* PORTSMOUTH, E), V-Treasurer Ireland, 1580–c 1586; later undertook mil serv Low Countries against Spain, also Portugal 1589 and Brittany 1591, but returned to Ireland 1595, ktd 9 Nov 1595 and made Marshal of Ireland and the army there 1600 (confirmed in the post by JAMES I and granted lands 1603 (regrant 1609) at Fercullen, Co Wicklow, which totalled just under

12,500 acres and which in 1611 were erected into a manor, that of Powerscourt); participated in plantation of Ulster, being granted 2,000 acres around Dungannon, Co Tyrone, known as the manor of Benburb; MP (I Parl) Downpatrick 1613–15; granted lands around Arklow, Co Wexford, which were later erected into the manor of Wingfield, Ld Justice Ireland March 1613/4 and 1622–25, Memb Cncl to Pres Munster 1615; *m* Frances (*d* by 30 Nov 1631), dau of William Rugge or Repps, of Felmingham, Norfolk, and widow of Edward, 3rd Baron Cromwell of the 1540 *cr* (*see* CROMWELL, B, preliminary remarks), and *dsp* 9 Sept 1634, when the Viscountcy expired, while the estates passed to his 1st cousin Richard's s Sir Edward, of Carnew

3 Thomas; *dsp*

4 George; *m* Ratcliffe, dau of Sir Gilbert Gerrard, Master Rolls *temp* ELIZABETH I, and had:

(1) Richard, of Robertstown, Co Limerick; *m* Honora, dau and coheir of Teige O'Brien, of Smithstown, 2nd s of 1st Baron Inchiquin (*qv*), and had:

1a Edward (Sir), of Carnew, Co Wicklow; soldier in Ireland late 1590s; *m* Anne (*d* 11 July 1636), dau of 3rd Baron Cromwell of the 1540 *cr*, and *d* 22 April 1638, having had, with three other sons and a dau:

1b Richard, of Powerscourt; MP (I Parl) Boyle 1639; *m* 7 May 1640 Elizabeth (*m* 2nd 12 April 1646 Edward Trevor, bro of 1st Viscount Dungannon of the 1662 *cr*; *m* 3rd Sir John Ponsonby; *see* BESSBOROUGH, E), est dau of Sir Henry Folliott, 1st Baron Folliott of Ballyshannon, and *d* 1644/5, having had, with a dau Anne (*d* unm):

1c FOLLIOTT WINGFIELD, 1st and last VISCOUNT POWERSCOURT (I), so *cr* 22 Feb 1664/5; *bapt* 2 Nov 1642; MP (I Parl) Co Wicklow 1661–66, custos rotulorum Co Wicklow 1671; *m* Sept 1660 Lady Elizabeth Boyle (*d* 17 Oct 1709), est dau of his guardian, 1st Earl of Orrery (*see* CORK and ORRERY, E), and *dsp c* 5 Feb 1717/8, when the Viscountcy expired

2b Francis; *dsp*

3b Lewis, of Scurmore, Co Sligo; *m* Sidney, dau of Sir Paul Gore, 1st Bt (*qv*), and *d* after 1 Sept 1653, having had, with two yr sons (Thomas, *dsp*; Richard, *dsp*) and three daus:

1c Edward; heir to estates of his cousin Folliott, 1st and last Viscount Powerscourt of the 2nd (1665) *cr*; barrister, MP (I Parl) Wicklow; *m* 1st Eleanor, 2nd dau of Sir Arthur Gore, 1st Bt, of Newtown Gore, Co Mayo (*see* ARRAN, E), and had:

1d RICHARD, **1st Viscount**

1d Isabella; *m* April 1722 Sir Henry King, 3rd Bt, and had issue (*see* KINGSTON, E)

2d Sidney; *m* 17 April 1723 Acheson Moore, MP, of Aghnecloy, Co Tyrone, and *d* 10 Dec 1727, leaving issue

1c (cont.) Edward Wingfield *m* 2nd — (*d* 12 Jan 1728), dau of William Lloyd, Bp Killala, and *d* 7 Jan 1728

1a Honora; *m* Donogh McConnor O'Brien, of Lemeneagh

2a Eleanor; *m* Murrough O'Brien (*see* INCHIQUIN, B)

EDWARD WINGFIELD's only s,

RICHARD WINGFIELD, **1st Viscount Powerscourt**, of Powerscourt, Co Wicklow, so *cr* 4 Feb 1734/4, as also BARON WINGFIELD, of Wingfield, Co Wexford (both I), PC (I 1746); *bapt* 19 Aug 1697; *educ* Trin Coll Dublin; MP (I Parl) Boyle 1727–43/4, commissioned Richard Castle to design Powerscourt (constructed 1731–40); *m* 1st 30 Aug 1721 Anne (*dsp*), dau of Christopher Usher, of Usher's Quay, Dublin; *m* 2nd 13 April 1727 Dorothy (*d* 21 July 1785), dau of Hercules Rowley, of Summerhill, Co Meath, and *d* 21 Oct 1751, having had:

1 EDWARD WINGFIELD, **2nd Viscount Powerscourt**; *b* 23 Oct 1729; *educ* Trin Coll Dublin and Middle Temple; MP Stockbridge, Hants, 1756–61; *d* unm 6 May 1764

2 RICHARD, **3rd Viscount**

1 Frances; *m* 26 Nov 1747 1st Baron Annaly (*qv*) and was *bur* 16 Aug 1794

2 Isabella; *m* 7 March 1770 Sir Charles Style, 5th Bt (*qv*), and *d* 4 Sept 1808, leaving issue

The 2nd VISCOUNT's yr bro,

RICHARD WINGFIELD, **3rd Viscount Powerscourt**; *bapt* 24 Dec 1730; *educ* Trin Coll Dublin and Middle Temple; MP (I Parl) Co Wicklow 1761–64; *m* 7 Sept 1760 Lady Amelia Stratford (*d* 11 Oct 1831), dau of 1st Earl of Aldborough, and *d* 8 Aug 1788, having had, with two other daus (*d* unm):

1 RICHARD, **4th Viscount**

2 John WINGFIELD later WINGFIELD-STRATFORD (added 1802); *b* 2 Aug 1772; Lt-Col; *m* 1st 25 April 1797 Frances (*d* 13 July 1827), only child of Leonard Bartholomew, of Addington Place, Kent, and had:

(1) John, JP, DL, of Addington Park, Kent; *b* 10 Dec 1810; High Sheriff Kent 1873; *m* 10 Dec 1844 Jane Elizabeth (*d* 20 Feb 1897), dau of Gen Sir John Guise, 3rd Bt (*qv*), and *d* 8 May 1881, having:

1a Edward John, JP, of Addington Park; *b* 26 Feb 1849; Lt Scots Gds; *d* unm 21 April 1903

2a Henry Verner, of Delbury Hall, Craven Arms, Salop; *b* 9 Sept 1851; Capt Rifle Bde; *m* 8 Aug 1893 Grace (*d* 10 Feb 1932), widow of Maj James Atkinson, of Elm Court, Kent, and *d* 21 Nov 1923

3a Cecil Vernon, CB (1918), CMG; *b* 7 Oct 1853; Col RE, Brig-Gen WW I (despatches four times), Ch Engr Irish Command 1907–10; *m* 12 Oct 1881 Rosalind Isabel, MBE (1920) (*d* 18 March 1953), dau of Rev and Hon Edward Vesey Bligh (*see* DARNLEY, E), and *d* 5 Feb 1939, leaving:

1b Esmé Cecil; *b* 20 Sept 1882; *educ* Eton and King's Coll Cambridge (BA 1904, MA and Fell 1907, DSc (Econ) London 1913); Capt 4th Bn Roy W Kent Regt WW I, author; *m* 30 Dec 1915 Barbara Elizabeth (*d* 1 Sept 1976), only dau of Lt-Col Francis Lancelot Henry Errington by Hon Louisa Anna Maria Parnell, dau of 3rd Baron Congleton (*qv*), and *d* 20 Feb 1971, leaving:

1c *Roshnara Barbara [Mrs Wingfield-Stratford-Orr, Lakeview House, Station Lane, Kirby Bellars, Melton Mowbray, Leics LE14 2ED]; *b* 9 Nov 1916; jnlst; *m* 1st 25 Jan 1941 (*divorce* 1949) 5th Baron Wrottesley (*qv*) and has issue; *m* 2nd 11 March 1950 (added WINGFIELD-STRATFORD for herself and issue (deed poll 1970)) *Lt-Col

Norman David Melville Johnstone, MBE, Gren Gds, s of Maj Charles Melville Johnstone, of Croy, Dunbartonshire; *m* 3rd 9 May 1998 (assumed by deed poll ORR instead of JOHNSTONE) *Ronald Henry Davidson Orr; and by her 2nd husb has:

1d *Esmé Edward Melville [Esmé Wingfield-Stratford-Johnstone Esq, Château de Sours, 33750 St Quentin de Baron, France]; *b* 1950; *m* 1972 *Sara, dau of Maj Richard Francis Birch Reynardson (s of Lt-Col Henry Thomas Birch-Reynardson, CMG; *see* DE MAULEY, B), and has:

1e *Rupert Leo Esmé; *b* 1975

2e *Dickon; *b* 1978

3e *Harry Crocker; *b* 1983

1d *Victoria Rose Charlotte; *b* 1954; *m* 1982 *William John Corby, only s of R A Corby, of Berkhamsted, Herts, and has:

1e *Roshnara; *b* 1983

2e *Diana; *b* 1986

3e *Christina; *b* 1988

2b Geoffrey Edward, CBE (1944), MC (1918); *b* 18 Jan 1887; *educ* Eton; Col 1st Bn Roy W Kent Regt WW I (despatches, Croix de Guerre with palms), AAG

1b Rosalind Frances Cecily; *b* 28 Aug 1893; *m* 1st 25 Feb 1915 (*divorce* 1929) Cecil Ireland Blackburne (*d* 14 Dec 1963, having dropped MAZE by roy licence 5 Aug 1914), er s of William Peter Blackburne-Maze, and had issue; *m* 2nd 2 Aug 1929 Lt-Col Lawrence Francis Garrett, DSO, MC, RA (*d* 5 June 1967), only s of Lewis Edward Garrett, and *d* 197–

4a Leonard Guise; *b* 26 Sept 1856; JP Natal; *m* 13 Dec 1880 Alethe Sylva (*d* 15 March 1911), dau of Capt Alexander Nixon Montgomery, 7th Roy Fus, and *d* 28 June 1941, having had:

1b Mervyn Edward John; *b* 7 Sept 1883; T/Capt and Adj 12th Bn Worcester Regt; *m* 7 April 1914 Doris Amie (*m* 2nd 30 July 1925 Jannion Steele Elliott, of Dowles Manor, Bewdley, Worcs (*d* 31 March 1942)), dau of John Eccleston Sheldon, of Barnt Green, Worcs, and *d* 22 July 1922, leaving:

1c Avriel Ann; *b* 15 Aug 1915; *m* 13 Sept 1939 Sir Antony Guy Acland, 5th Bt, of Oxford (*qv*), and *d* 7 July 1943, leaving issue

1b Maud Frances Jane; *m* 20 June 1912 Col Bernard Bowles Colbeck, DSO, s of Thomas William Colbeck, MRCS, of St Leonards, and *dsp* 10 May 1947

2b Agnes Mary; *m* 26 May 1908 Col John Hugh Morris, DSO, OBE, RASC (*d* 28 Jan 1963), s of Edmund Leigh Morris, of Brighton, and had:

1c *Sylvia Marie Heather [Mrs Andrew Usher, Old Coastguard House, Shingle Street, nr Woodbridge, Suffolk]; *b* 12 Oct 1909; *m* 25 April 1942 Cdr Andrew Balmer Usher, RN, s of Thomas Leslie Usher, of Edinburgh, and has:

1d *Heather Mary Lynn; *b* 7 Aug 1943; *m* 4 June 1966 *Richard Michael Davies, s of Col R A Davies, of Foxhanger, Burwash, E Sussex, and has:

1e *Michael Richard; *b* 21 Jan 1969

2d *Valerie Clare; *b* 9 Feb 1948

2c *Valerie Murielle [Mrs Peter Howorth, Hill House, Kingsthorne, Birch, Herefs]; *b* 25 March 1916; *m* 21 April 1951 *Col Peter John Howorth, RA, s of Col Henry Godfrey Howorth

3b Murielle Alethe Victoria; *m* 30 June 1912 Col Richard Osbaldeston Spencer-Smith and *d* 12 July 1931, leaving issue (*see* SPENCER-SMITH, Bt)

4b Hermione; *m* 18 Nov 1915 Brig Gilbert John Victor Shepherd, CBE, DSO, RE, only s of Rev T C Shepherd, Govt of India Chaplain, and *d* 25 Aug 1966, leaving issue

5a Howard; *b* 13 Nov 1859; Capt: Roy Welch Fus, W Yorks Regt, Bechuanaland Expdn 1883, Boer War 1900–01 and WW I; *m* 22 Oct 1902 Christian Margaret (*d* 2 Nov 1931), dau of David Scot Duncan, of Monkton House, Mussleburgh, and widow of W Roland

6a Richard Nevill; *b* 8 June 1861; Boer War 1900–01; *m* 16 Dec 1891 Grace Dorothea (*d* 2 March 1956), dau of Capt Alexander Nixon Montgomery, 7th Roy Fus, and *d* 18 Oct 1942, having had:

1b Esmé John Richard; *b* 12 Feb 1897; Sub-Lt RN; *ka* 15 March 1918

1b Georgina Grace Ida; *b* 20 June 1899; *m* 1st 23 June 1926 William Jannion Elliott (*d* 22 Feb 1929), only s of Jannion Elliott, of Dowles Manor House, Bewdley; *m* 2nd 30 March 1933 Wilfrid Cole, MBE, s of William Henry Cole, of Penzance, and *d* 199–

7a Francis Mervyn; *b* 27 Aug 1864; Lt 3rd Bn Roy W Kent Regt; *m* 16 Jan 1906 Nora (*d* 9 May 1953), dau of George Matthey, FRS, of Cheyne House, Chelsea, and *d* 18 Dec 1932, having had:

1b Mervyn Verner; *b* 5 Sept 1907; *educ* Cheltenham; Lt Res Offrs Scots Gds WW II, Freeman City London; *m* 26 June 1935 (*divorce* 1951) Ann Helen, dau of Douglas Charles Stewart-Sandeman (*see* 1940 edn STEWART-SANDEMAN, Bt), and *d* 7 May 1982, leaving:

1c +(Mervyn) Peter Douglas [Peter Wingfield-Stratford Esq, 28 Lansdowne Rd, London W11]; *b* 14 June 1936; *educ* Cheltenham; *m* 12 April 1969 *Jane, yst dau of Dr Edward Worsley Burstal, of Lutterworth, Leics, and has:

1d +James Richard Mervyn; *b* 1973

1d *Annabel Jane; *b* 9 Aug 1971

1c *Georgina Isabel; *b* 6 Sept 1939; *m* 28 July 1962 *Lt John Leonard M Modley, RE, of Cherry Cottage, Corfe Castle, Dorset, er s of W/Cdr Leonard William Waldron Modley, OBE, GM, and has:

1d *Drummond; *b* 1963

2d *Alexander John; *b* 8 Aug 1965

1b Georgina Frances; *b* 13 Sept 1910; *d* 25 April 1924

1a Isabella Margaret; *m* 14 Jan 1868 Rev James Newton Heale, Vicar St Thomas, Bethnal Green, and *d* his widow 23 Dec 1933, leaving issue

2a Frances Charlotte; *m* 24 Nov 1875 Sir Henry Michael Hawley, 5th Bt (*qv*), and *d* 10 Sept 1926, leaving issue

3a Emily Rose; *m* 9 Sept 1875 Lt-Col Henry Waugh Renny Tailyour, RE (*d* 15 June 1920), of Borrowfield, Forfar, and *d* 22 July 1904, leaving issue

4a Florence Mary; *m* 10 April 1883 Capt Henry Lawrence Daly, 15th Hus, and *d* 1947, leaving issue

5a Georgiana Maud; *m* 2 June 1891 Maj Howard Guise and *d* 14 Nov 1945, leaving issue (*see* GUISE, Bt)

6a Violet Alice Ethel; *m* 25 Jan 1893 Cdr Bertie Angelo Cator, RN (*d* 30 Oct 1933), and *d* 16 March 1916, leaving issue

(1) Frances Amelia; *m* 21 July 1832 Ven John Cecil Hall, Archdeacon of Man (*d* 8 Feb 1844)

(2) Isabella Harriet; *m* 21 July 1832 John Malcolm, JP, DL, 14th of Poltalloch, Argyllshire (*d* 30 May 1863), and *d* 30 Sept 1858, leaving issue

2 (cont.) Col John Wingfield-Stratford *m* 2nd 1 Aug 1833 Harriette (*d* 28 March 1863), dau of Henry Grant, and *d* 9 Aug 1850

3 Edward of Cork Abbey, Dublin; *b* 2 Aug 1772; Col; *m* 17 April 1797 Harriet Esther Westenra (*d* 16 Dec 1858), sis of 2nd Baron Rossmore (*qv*), and *d* 24 Aug 1859, having had:

(1) Harriet; *m* 1819 Sir William Verner, 1st Bt, MP (*d* 20 Jan 1871; *see* 1970 edn), and *d* 6 Sept 1877, leaving issue

1 Emilia; *m* 1817 Robert Deane Spread, Capt 15th Foot (*d* 5 Feb 1840), and *d* 6 June 1840

The 3rd VISCOUNT's est s,

RICHARD WINGFIELD, **4th Viscount Powerscourt**; *b* 29 Oct 1762; one of only five Irish peers who voted against the Act of Union (of the I Parl with the Br Parl) of 1800; *m* 1st 30 June 1789 Lady Catherine Meade (*d* 1793), 2nd dau of 1st Earl of Clanwilliam (*qv*), and had:

1 RICHARD, **5th Viscount**

2 John; *b* 4 Sept 1791; served Peninsular War; *d* Coimbra, Portugal, 18 May 1811

3 Edward (Rev); *b* 20 Nov 1792; Vicar Bagenalstown, Co Kilkenny; *m* 12 April 1819 Louisa Joan (*m* 2nd 2 Aug 1833 Robert Richard Tighe; *d* 17 June 1874), 3rd dau of Hon George Jocelyn (*see* RODEN, E), and *d* 6 Sept 1825, leaving, with a dau (*d* unm):

(1) Richard Robert, JP; *b* 20 Aug 1820; Dip Serv, DCL; *m* 21 June 1845 Fanny (*d* 28 Oct 1904), dau of Michael Hinton Castle, of Stapleton, Glos, and *d* 21 March 1896, having had, with three daus (*d* unm):

1a Edward John; *b* 23 Aug 1846; Cdr RN; *d* unm 10 March 1888

2a Richard William, of S Rhodesia; *b* 18 Dec 1849; *m* 26 Dec 1889 Jessie Emily (*m* 2nd 24 July 1920 Thomas Edward Broster (*d* 1942); *d* 27 Jan 1937), dau of Benjamin Mitchell Kennedy, and *d* 9 Aug 1918, leaving:

1b Richard Mervyn, MC; *b* 1894; Lt RFA WW I (S African Rebellion 1914, German SW Africa 1914–15, Flanders 1915–19 (wounded)); *m* 11 Feb 1918 Lynette Agnes (*d* 22 Jan 1968), yst dau of Maj Sydney Cowper, CMG, JP, of Wynberg, S Africa, and *d* 1951, having had:

1c Richard Sydney Mervyn; *b* 5 March 1923; 2nd Lt SAAF WW II; *ka* Italy 1945

1c Lynette Clare; *b* 7 March 1919; *m* 1st 1940 (*divorce* 1943) Colin Youart Tose; *m* 2nd 1943 Col Jan Andries Beyers Sandenbergh, OBE, SAAF, and had:

1d *Peter Wingfield; *b* 23 March 1955

1d *Lynette Catherine Wingfield; *b* 15 April 1945; *m* 1967 *Ian Chisholm Bell, s of John Chisholm Bell, of Highlands, Rhodesia

2d *Mervyn Wingfield [Mrs Phillip Jourdan, 74 Second Ave, Melville, Johannesburg, S Africa]; *b* 15 March 1949; *m* 19– *Dr Phillip Montgomery Jourdan

2c *Elizabeth Sonia; *b* 2 Jan 1925; *m* 1st 1944 (*divorce* 1945) Basil Wilson and has:

1d *Sandra Lynn Wingfield; *b* 1945

2c (cont.) Mrs Elizabeth Wilson *m* 2nd 194– *F/Lt M J Dunne and by him has:

1d *Richard Matthew Wingfield; *b* 1948

2d *Lesley Clare Wingfield; *b* 1952

3d *Robin Elizabeth Wingfield; *b* 1954

2b Edward George; *b* 1896; *m* 1932 Geraldine (*d* 22 Feb 1949), dau of — Bird, and *d* 16 May 1941

3b Noel Sparks; *b* 1907; *educ* Prince Edward Sch, Salisbury (S Rhodesia); Commr Oaths, sometime MP Marandellas, S Rhodesia Parl (first elected 1954); *m* Dec 1933 Mary Joan Wood (*d* Sept 1992) and *d* Feb 1992, leaving:

1c +Patrick Noel [Patrick Wingfield Esq, Belvedere North, PO, Goromonzi, Zimbabwe]; *b* 1934; *m* 1st 1960 (*divorce* 1971) Jean, dau of David Morris Williams, of Blantyre, Nyasaland (now Malawi), and has had:

1d +Richard David Noel; *b* 31 Aug 1966

1d Sandra Joan; *b* 29 Nov 1963; *d* 1976

1c (cont.) Patrick N Wingfield *m* 2nd 1973 *Margaret, dau of J H McKenzie Finch, of Canterbury, Kent, and has:

2d +Jeremy James; *b* 1974

2d *Clare Muriel; *b* 1975

1c *Jenepher Cynthia [Mrs Guy Hensman, 9 Palma Vista, 39 Oxford Rd, Avondale, Harare, Zimbabwe]; *b* 9 March 1937; *m* 21 Oct 1961 Guy Colin Hensman (*d* 1993), s of Colin Hensman, of Zimbabwe, and has:

1d *David Guy; *b* 22 March 1965

1d *Bridget Ann; *b* 17 Sept 1963

1b Muriel Emily; *b* 1892; *m* 1st 1914 Alfred Julius Bradshaw (*d* 12 Jan 1936) and had issue; *m* 2nd March 1939 Charles Edward Smith (*d* Jan 1949)

2b Eveline Jocelyn; *b* 1898; *m* 1919 Robert Binnie Dryborough and had issue

3b *Clare Mary Sophia; *b* 1904; *m* 1926 Sydney William Hall Kennard (*d* 1970) and has:

1c *David George [David Kennard Esq, Private Bag 1549, Grahamstown 6140, S Africa]; *b* 4 July 1929; *educ* Hilton Coll Natal; *m* 30 June 1956 *Isabella, dau of Maurice Henry de Vere Pennefather, of Fort Victoria, Rhodesia (now Zimbabwe), and has:

1d *Roland Derek; *b* 10 April 1958

2d *Nigel Hugh; *b* 12 April 1961

1d *Kate Ellen; *b* 1971

2c *Desmond Richard [Desmond Kennard Esq, 2 Wharncliffe Gdns, Beacon Bay, S Africa]; *b* 23 July 1935; *educ* Hilton Coll, Natal; *m* 1956 *Cynthia Norma, dau of Dr William Beck, of Potchefstroom, and has:

1d *Mark William; *b* 1959

2d *Grant Richard; *b* 1961

3d *Brett Wingfield; *b* 1964

1d *Leigh Mary; *b* 1954

3a George Henry; *b* 2 June 1852; *d* 5 Feb 1884

4a John Leslie; *b* 26 Sept 1853; *m* 1880 Laura Louisa Josepha, dau of William Frederick Elsner, and *d* 10 July 1931, leaving:

1b Gladys Vivian Laura; *b* 1884; *m* 22 July 1918 William Henry St Vincent Booth, RAF (*d* 8 Oct 1958), and had:

1c *Robert Henry St Vincent [Robert Booth Esq, 1050 Belvedere Dve, Capilano, N Vancouver, BC, Canada; 320 E 3rd St, N Vancouver, BC, Canada]; *b* 8 Sept 1919; *m* 8 Oct 1946 *Cora E B Cumming and has:

1d *Greg Wingfield; *b* 20 Aug 1950

1d *Leanne Gordon [Ms Leanne Booth, Apt 5, 812 Chesterfield N, Vancouver, BC, Canada]; *b* 27 Aug 1947

2d *Carol Jean; *b* 8 July 1956

5a Robert Hinton; *b* 12 Dec 1855; *d* 15 Dec 1937

6a Maurice de Vesci; *b* 8 April 1866; *m* 11 Nov 1908 Ethel Grey, dau of George Sharpe, of Lima, Peru, and *d* 14 June 1940, leaving issue:

1b Robert George; *b* 3 March 1910; Lt: 5th Bn Somerset LI 1929–38 and RAOC 1938–42, Lt-Col REME WW II, CREME Gibraltar 1948–51 and 21 (Northern) Corps Troops (TA) 1951–54; *m* 7 Jan 1947 *Mary Maud, dau of Sydney Rolfe, of Poole, Dorset, and *dsp* 23 Nov 1976

1a Fanny Catherine; *m* 1st 2 June 1880 6th Earl of Wicklow (*d* 1891; *see* 1970 edn) and had issue; *m* 2nd 10 April 1894 Marcus Francis Beresford (*see* WATERFORD, M) and *d* 3 Feb 1914

2a Mary; *m* 24 March 1886 Henry Alan Bulwer and *d* 1908

3a Isabella; *m* 21 Sept 1886 Maj Cornwallis Robert Ducarel Gun-Cuninghame, JP, DL (*d* 6 Sept 1928), and *d* 30 June 1902, leaving issue

(2) George John; *b* 11 Jan 1822; *m* 13 March 1851 Sophia (*d* 29 Dec 1899), sis of Sir Philip Duncombe Pauncefort-Duncombe, 1st Bt (*qv*), and *d* 8 April 1860, leaving, with two daus (*d* unm):

1a Anthony Henry (Sir), JP, DL, of Ampthill House, Beds; *b* 8 Sept 1857; *educ* Harrow and Ch Ch Oxford; Chm QS to 1936, High Sheriff Beds 1903, ktd 1937, memb Cncl RZS, owned private zoo; *m* 9 Feb 1888 Julia (*d* 17 Sept 1905), yst dau of Richard Benyon, of Englefield House, Berks, and *d* 20 Sept 1952, having had:

1b Anthony Edward Foulis, of Gransden Hall, nr Sandy, Beds, JP; *b* 12 Sept 1892; Capt RCOS (TAR), 3rd Bn Beds Regt; *m* 11 July 1927 Margaret Brinsmade (*d* 25 March 1995), dau of Prof John Douglas Adam, DD, of New York, and *d* 19 May 1946, leaving:

1c Gervase Christopher Brinsmade; *b* 17 Aug 1931; Lt RN; *m* 2 Aug 1958 *Mary Margaret [Mrs Dennis Neal, Hackney Lodge, Melton, nr Woodbridge, Suffolk IP12 1NL], er dau of Dennis McGuinn, of Haverford, Pa. (*m* 2nd 14 Aug 1973 Dennis Henry Bagshaw Neal), and *d* 26 April 1964, leaving:

1d +Andrew Nicholas Brinsmade, ED; *b* 30 July 1959; *educ* Worth and Bristol U; Maj Roy Hong Kong Regt (Vols) and Roy Yeo, slr; *m* 1989 *Caroline Jane Victoria, yst dau of John Francis Felix Porter, of Martock, Somerset, and has:

1e +Edward Nicholas Anthony; *b* 1991

2d +Henry John Gervase; *b* 1964

1d *Nicola Caroline McGuinn [Mrs Mark Jerram, Van Cottage, Compton Chamberlayne, Salisbury, Wilts SP3 5DB]; *b* 14 Feb 1961; *m* 1986 *Mark Godfrey Jerram, only s of Maj Geoffrey Forster Jenner Jerram by Anne, dau of Capt John Haggas Brigg (*see* PRINCE-SMITH, Bt), and has:

1e *Alexander Geoffrey Wingfield; *b* 1989

2e *Dominic Alistair; *b* 1990

2d *Philippa Susan [The Hon Mrs Anthony Monckton, c/o FCO, King Charles St, London SW1A 2AH]; *b* 6 April 1962; *m* 1985 *Capt Hon Anthony Leopold Colyer Monckton, yst s of 2nd Viscount Monckton of Brenchley (*qv*), and has issue

1c (Eileen) Patricia Brinsmade; *b* 18 Nov 1928; *m* 24 Jan 1966 *Prince Dmitri Galitzine, only s of Prince Nicholas Emanuelovich Galitzine, Marshal Nobility Odoevsk (Govt Tula Province), Russia, and *d* 198–, leaving:

1d *Marina Dmitrievna; *b* 9 Aug 1968

2b Cecil Andrew Foulis; *b* 30 Nov 1895; *educ* Eton and RMC Sandhurst; Lt 13th Hus, Maj 5th Bn Beds and Herts Regt, TAR, Hon Attaché Brussels; *m* 11 Jan 1927 Elizabeth Jocelyn Rhys, dau of Maj William Jocelyn Rhys Wingfield (*see below*), and *dsp* 20 Feb 1966

2a Granville Foulis; *b* 18 April 1859; Capt 7th Hus, ADC to Govr Madras; *d* unm 10 April 1891

(3) Edward Ffolliott; *b* 6 Aug 1823; Capt 2nd Life Gds; *m* 1 May 1848 Hon Frances Emily Rhys (*d* 26 Nov 1863), est dau and coheir of 4th Baron Dinevor (*qv*), and *d* 26 Sept 1865, having had, with other issue:

1a Edward Rhys, JP, DL, of Barrington Park, Burford, Oxon; *b* 9 March 1849; served 60th Rifles, Maj 4th Bn Gloucestershire Regt; *m* 2 May 1871 Edith Caroline (*d* 21 Dec 1935), dau of Rev Peter Almeric Wood, Canon Middleham, and *d* 14 March 1901, leaving:

1b Mervyn Edward George Rhys, JP, DL, of Barrington Park; *b* 24 May 1872; *educ* Eton; 2nd Life Gds, Lt-Col cmdg 3rd Bn Glos Regt, Boer War

1900–01 and WW I, High Sheriff Oxon 1934; *m* 12 Nov 1919 Florence Marguerite Erle (*d* 1990), dau of Lt-Col Richard Erle Benson, and *d* 2 Jan 1952, having had:

  1c Mervyn Richard Edward Anthony Rhys; *b* 25 May 1922; *educ* Eton and Ch Ch Oxford; served LAC, RAFVR WW II; *k* Canada 25 July 1942

  2c +Charles Talbot Rhys, DL (Glos, 1963) [Charles Wingfield Esq DL, Barrington Park, Great Barrington, Burford, Oxon OX18 4TA]; *b* 13 Feb 1924; *educ* Eton and Ch Ch Oxford; Lt Coldstream Gds WW II (wounded), High Sheriff Glos 1962; *m* 9 Oct 1954 *Hon (Cynthia) Meriel Hill, yr dau of 6th Baron Sandys (*qv*), and has:

    1d +Richard Mervyn Rhys; *b* 28 March 1967; *educ* Eton

    1d *Venetia Blanche; *b* 13 May 1956; *m* 21 Oct 1978 *Richard Crosbie Dawson, 3rd s of Maj Robert Clarkson Crosbie Dawson, by Gillian, *née* Sutton, ggdau of Sir Richard Sutton, 4th Bt (*qv*), and has:

      1e *Anthony Charles; *b* 1983

      2e *George Robert; *b* 1985

      1e *Charlotte Rose; *b* 1990

    2d *Olivia Patricia; *b* 1 May 1958

    3d *Diana Mary; *b* 20 Jan 1961; *m* 1986 *Robert Anthony Copley (*see* LOUDOUN, E) and has issue

  3c +David de Cardonnel Ffolliott Rhys [David Wingfield Esq, 134 Finborough Road, London SW10]; *b* 6 April 1933; *educ* Bradfield; *m* 1982 *Mrs Mary Ann E I Harrison

  4c +Jonathan Fitz Uryan Rhys; *b* 10 March 1935; *educ* Eton; *m* 1970 *Judith, dau of Albert George James Gibbons and widow of Hon Philip Inman, only s of 1st and last Baron Inman (*see* 1970 edn), and has:

    1d *Annabel Lucy; *b* 1973

    2d *Felicity Jane; *b* 1975

  1c *Mary Florence Eleanor [Mrs Neville Cole, Windrush Lodge, Nazeing, Essex]; *b* 14 Sept 1920; *m* 4 Oct 1945 *Neville Thomas Cole, S/Ldr RAF, only s of Frederick Cole, and has:

    1d *Michael Duncan Mervyn; *b* 1946

    2d *Edward Charles Ffolliott George; *b* 27 March 1954

    1d *Rachel Elizabeth Rosemary; *b* 1948

  2c *Elizabeth Marguerite [Miss Elizabeth Wingfield, Fayre Court, Fairford, Glos]; *b* 27 Feb 1926

2b William Jocelyn Rhys; *b* 25 March 1873; Maj 19th Hus, Staff Capt 1915, DAAG 1916, T/Lt-Col 1918; *m* 16 Oct 1902 Sybil Annesley Giana (June) (*d* 2 April 1959), yst dau of Col William Thomas Markham, of Becca Hall, Yorks, and *d* 10 July 1942, leaving:

  1c William Thomas Rhys; *b* 21 Feb 1907; *educ* Bedford Sch; Maj RAC (Capt Northamptonshire Yeo, TA) WW II; *m* 5 June 1936 *Patricia [Mrs William Wingfield, Angel House, Elton, Peterborough, Cambs], only child of Maj-Gen Sir William James Norman Cooke-Collis, KBE, CB, CMG, DSO, of Castle Cooke, Co Cork, and *d* 18 Sept 1976, leaving:

    1d +Jocelyn James Rhys [Jocelyn Wingfield Esq, 18 Chiddingstone St, London SW6 3TG]; *b* 15 Dec 1937; *educ* Eton; Capt KOYLI, 1st Bn Cyprus, BAOR, Malaya, Brunei, Sarawak and Thailand, Assist Instr Jungle Warfare Sch Malaya 1962–63, Sarawak Rangers 1964–66, ret, divnl dir overseas Save the Children Fund; *m* 25 May 1968 *Sara Elizabeth, only child of Sir (Edward John) Patrick Boschetti Ffolkes, 6th Bt (*qv*), and has:

      1e *Serena Geraldine Rhys; *b* 24 June 1969

      2e *Camilla Patricia Rhys; *b* 15 Oct 1971

    2d +Robert Talbot Rhys [Dr Robert Wingfield, The Spring House, Grimston, Leics LE14 3BZ]; *b* 12 April 1940; *educ* Stowe and Trin Coll Dublin (BA 1964, PhD (Geology) 1968); with Br Geological Survey; *m* 18 Oct 1969 *Anne Mary, er dau of Lt-Col Toby W Hamilton, of Nunholm House, Dumfries, and has:

      1e +James Hamilton Rhys; *b* 6 June 1971

      2e +Charles Timothy; *b* 9 Feb 1974

    3d +George Anthony Rhys [George Wingfield Esq, Hearne House, N Wootton, Shepton Mallet, Somerset BA4 4HW; 14a Sussex Mansions, Brompton Rd, London SW7]; *b* 21 July 1942; *educ* Eton and Trin Coll Dublin (BA); with IBM; *m* 8 June 1968 *Gloria, only dau of Bernard Bolingbroke-Kent, of Cerne Easter, Westerham, Kent, and has:

      1e +Rupert Bolingbroke Rhys, *b* 1972; *educ* Eton

      2e +Michael Somerset Rhys; *b* 4 March 1975; *educ* Blundell's

  1c Elizabeth Jocelyn Rhys; *b* 20 Aug 1903; *m* 11 Jan 1927 her cousin Maj Cecil Andrew Foulis Wingfield, s of Sir Anthony Henry Wingfield (*see* above)

  2c Susan Averil Rhys; *b* 1 April 1914; *m* 27 Dec 1951 *John Anthony Sabini [John A Sabini, c/o Trans Arabian Pipe Line Co, PO Box 1348, Beirut, Lebanon], late US For Serv, s of Gen D J Sabini, US Army, of Honolulu, and *d* 1 June 1963, leaving:

    1d *A dau; *b* 19–

3b Charles John Fitzroy Rhys (Sir), KCMG (1933); *b* 18 Feb 1877; *educ* Charterhouse; Capt 7th Bn Roy Fus, Dip Serv: Counsellor Madrid 1919, Brussels 1922–26, Rome 1926–28, Envoy Extrdy and Min Plen Bangkok 1928–29, Oslo 1929–34, Holy See 1934–35, Amb Extrdy and Plen Lisbon 1935–37; *m* 7 March 1905 Lucy Evelyn (*d* 1977), est dau of Sir Edmund Douglas Veitch Fane, KCMG, and *d* 26 March 1960, leaving:

  1c Diana Evelyn; *b* 12 Dec 1907; *m* 29 Aug 1935 Baron Alessandro Corsi (*d* 1987), Capt Roy Italian Navy, s of Baron Corsi di Turri, of Rome, and *d* 19–, leaving:

    1d *Raimondo Tristano [Baron Raimondo Corsi, via Rovani 6, 20052 Monza, Italy]; *b* 21 Dec 1937; Kt Honour and Devotion SMO Malta, Kt Justice Sacred Mily Constantinian Order St George; *m* 18 April 1964 *Donna Maria Francesca di Lorenzo and has:

      1e *Carlo Alessandro; *b* 31 July 1965

      1e *Diana Lucrezia; *b* 1970

    2d *Antonio Giuliano [Baron Antonio Corsi, via Massimi 27, 00136 Rome, Italy]; *b* 26 April 1941; *m* 1st 1967 (*divorce* 1978) Maria Grazia Barbiani and has:

      1e *Flavio Alessandro; *b* 1968

    2d (cont.) Baron Antonio Corsi *m* 2nd 1979 *Giovanna Attanasio and has:

      1e *Benedetta Lucy; *b* 1983

4b Maurice ffolliott Rhys; *b* 8 Sept 1879; *educ* Charterhouse and Magdalen Coll Oxford; Capt Oxfordshire LI WW I (wounded); *m* 1st 1 Jan 1904 (*divorce* 1911) Lydia Agnes (*d* 26 Aug 1963), 4th dau of Henry Rudge, and had:

  1c Muriel Violet; *b* 20 Feb 1905; *m* 5 Dec 1933 Lt-Col Alister Maynard, MBE, Seaforth Highrs, s of Fleming Maynard, and *d* 198–, leaving:

    1d *Venetia Caroline; *b* 22 March 1936; *m* 1st 21 June 1957 (*divorce* 1971), as his 2nd w, John Howard Cordle, MP (C) Bournemouth E and Christchurch 1959–74 and Bournemouth E 1974–77, s of Ernest William Cordle, of Worthing, Sussex, and has:

      1e *Rupert Alister Peter John; *b* 14 May 1959

      1e *Sophie Jane; *b* 9 Feb 1958

      2e *Marina Rose; *b* 6 May 1960; *m* 1 July 1987, as his 2nd w, *4th Viscount Cowdray (*qv*) and has issue

      3e *Rachel Venetia; *b* 3 Aug 1963

    1d (cont.) Mrs Venetia Cordle *m* 2nd 19– *Ross Skinner

    2d *Sandra Elizabeth [Mrs Sandra Mackinlay MacLeod, Elm Tree Farm, Durley, Hants SO32 2AA]; *b* 19 Jan 1939; *m* 17 May 1958 (*divorce* 1966) Michael John Mackinlay MacLeod, s of John Mackinlay MacLeod, and has:

      1e *Torquil John [Torquil Mackinlay MacLeod Esq, Elm Tree Farm, Durley, Hants SO32 2AA]; *b* 7 Jan 1959; *educ* Eton and Durham U (BA 1981); barrister

      2e *Jocelyn Maurice Edward [Jocelyn Mackinlay MacLeod Esq, 17 Granard Ave, London SW15 6HH]; *b* 10 Feb 1961; *educ* Eton

      3e *Caspar Charles [Caspar Mackinlay MacLeod Esq, Elm Tree Farm, Durley, Hants SO32 2AA]; *b* 21 Jan 1963; *educ* Eton

4b (cont.) Capt Maurice Wingfield *m* 2nd 10 Oct 1916, as her 2nd husb, Stephanie Agnes (*d* 9 Dec 1918), widow of Arthur Francis Levita and dau of Sir Alfred Cooper (*see* FIFE, D and NORWICH, V); *m* 3rd 9 March 1928, as her 2nd husb, Muriel Jessie (*m* 3rd 1944 Maj Frederick Graham St Clair-Keith; *d* 23 Oct 1959), formerly w of Edward Molyneux, of Paris, and dau of Hon James Dunsmuir, of Hatley, Park, BC, ex-Premier BC, and *d* 9 April 1941

5b Cecil John Talbot Rhys; *b* 25 July 1881; Capt KRRC; *m* 6 Dec 1904 Lady Violet Nita Poulett (*d* 10 March 1966), yr dau of 6th Earl Poulett (*see* 1970 edn), and *d* 29 April 1915 of wounds recd in action, leaving:

  1c Edward William Rhys; *b* 26 Aug 1905; *educ* Eton and RMC Sandhurst; Maj KRRC WW II; *m* 30 March 1935 *Lady Norah Beryl Cayzer Jellicoe, 4th dau of 1st Earl Jellicoe (*qv*), and *d* 20 Jan 1984, having had:

    1d +Philip John [Philip Wingfield Esq, Salterdridge, Cappoquin, Co Waterford, Ireland]; *b* 8 April 1938; *educ* Eton; *m* 11 Jan 1971 *Susan Johanna, er dau of Maj-Gen Ronald Edward Coaker, CB, CBE, MC, by Johanna, dau of Francis Curzon Curzon, of Lockington Hall, Derbys, and has:

      1e +Edward Mervyn; *b* 1973; *educ* Eton and Trinity Coll Dublin (scholar)

      1e *Venetia Sophie; *b* 3 March 1975

      2e *Sarah Jane; *b* 9 Feb 1978

    2d Jeremy Roger; *b* 26 May 1945; *educ* Switzerland; *d* 22 Feb 1970

    1d *Jacqueline [Mrs Anthony Vivian, 22 Henning St, London SW11 3DR]; *b* 22 March 1936; *m* 14 June 1967 *Brig Anthony Chester Vivian, CBE, ADC, RWF, s of Maj G L Vivian and Mrs Ian McEwan

    2d *(Elizabeth) Jane; *b* 24 Jan 1941

1b Muriel Frances Caroline; *b* 3 Jan 1878; *m* 5 Oct 1909 Hon Piers Edwin Dutton (*d* 21 Jan 1929), bro of 6th Baron Sherborne (*see* 1970 edn)

2b Gwenllian Edith Emily; *b* 23 Aug 1882; *m* 30 June 1908 Lt-Col Samuel James Chatterton Prittie Perry, FRCS, RAMC (*d* 3 May 1943), and had issue

2a Charles George Lewis; *b* 2 May 1850; Maj 2nd Bn Dorsetshire Regt; *m* 18 April 1888 Beatrice Marion (*d* 18 Jan 1895), dau of Edward Lysaght Griffin, of Bray, Co Wicklow, and *d* 26 March 1890, leaving:

  1b Charles Trevor; *b* 2 March 1889; T/Lt Roy Dublin Fus; *m* 22 Jan 1914 Liliane Laure Agnes (*d* 1979), only child of Vladimir Czerny, of Petrograd, by Angele, *née* Comtesse Cassini de Merindol, and *d* 17 April 1924, leaving:

    1c *Tatiana (Tania) Elianore Lucile Beatrice [Mrs Alan Drake-Brockman, The Splatts, Spaxton, Bridgwater, Somerset]; *m* 31 Jan 1947 Brig Alan Godfrey Drake-Brockman, OBE, RE (*d* 14 Nov 1976), s of Lt-Col Vivian Godfrey Drake-Brockman, MRCS, LRCP, IMS, and has:

      1d *Trevor Vivian; *b* 1950

    2c *Yvonne Angéle Primrose Czerny [Miss Yvonne Wingfield, 61 Rue Prevost Martin, Geneva, Switzerland]

3a George Talbot; *b* 26 March 1853; Capt RN, Supt Ind Store Dept; *m* 12 April 1882 Maud (*d* 11 Feb 1945), dau of R-Adml Joseph Edward Maitland Wilson, RN, and *d* 19 July 1936, leaving:

  1b Ela Mary; *b* 7 Aug 1883; *d* 19 May 1967

  2b Joan ffolliott; *b* 26 Jan 1885; *d* 10 April 1962

  3b Rhona Frances; *b* 26 Feb 1886

  4b Elianore Maud Rhys; *b* 8 March 1887; *d* 6 Jan 1978

4a Henry Jocelyn; *b* 26 Nov 1863; *m* 12 June 1889 Sybil Mary Kerr (*d* 22 Dec 1954), 2nd dau of V-Adml Mark Pechell (*see* PECHELL, Bt), and *d* 5 Sept 1919, having had:

  1b Granville Harry; *b* 1892; 2nd Lt 5th Bn KRRC; *ka* 12 July 1916

2b Bryan ffolliott; *b* 1894; Cdr RN; *m* 9 June 1934, as her 1st of three husbs, Aline Monica, only dau of Lt-Col Frederick Fenn Elwes, IMS (ret), and *d* 28 Sept 1935

1b Dorothy Maud; *b* 8 May 1890; *d* 26 Jan 1922

2b Jocelyn Sybil; *b* 12 July 1891; *d* 27 May 1975

1a Maud Isabella; *d* 12 April 1949

The **4th Viscount** *m* 2nd 9 Feb 1796 Isabella (*d* 5 April 1848), 2nd dau of Rt Hon William Brownlow, and *d* 19 July 1809, having by her had:

4 William (Rev); *b* 21 May 1799; Vicar Abbeyleix, Queen's Co (now Co Laois); *m* 14 Sept 1830 Elizabeth (*d* March 1856), dau of Rev Thomas Kelly, of Kellyville, Queen's Co, and *d* 13 March 1880, having had, with other issue:

(1) Richard Thomas; *b* 19 Oct 1835; Capt 52nd Regt; *m* 13 April 1864 Isabella (*d* 23 Feb 1927), dau of Rev Edward Guille, of Jersey, and *d* 26 July 1870, leaving, with an unm dau:

1a William Edward (Rev), DSO (1917); *b* 14 Feb 1867; Rector Broome and Thwaite St Mary, Norfolk, Lt-Col RFA, T/Lt-Col cmdg Artillery Bde WW I (wounded, despatches three times); *m* 24 March 1896 Elizabeth Mary (*d* 25 Nov 1939), dau of George Frederic Trench (*see* ASHTOWN, B), and *d* 25 Jan 1927, leaving:

1b Richard James Trench; *b* 28 Dec 1896; T/Lt RFA WW I (despatches); *ka* 27 April 1916

2b John Anthony David; *b* 2 July 1905; *educ* Marlborough; MIMM, SAInstMM, mining engr; *m* 22 Dec 1934 Eileen Earle (*d* 1982), dau of Hugh Melville, of Johannesburg, and *d* 1983, leaving:

1c Anthony Richard Melville; *b* 20 Jan 1941; *educ* St Andrew's, Grahamstown; *d* 1993

2c +John Mervyn [John Wingfield Esq, 4 Lewis Crescent, Gt Abingdon, Cambs CB16 AG]; *b* 21 Dec 1944; *educ* St Andrew's Grahamstown, Witwatersrand U (BSc 1967) and Trin Coll Cambridge; 2nd Lt SAAF (Active Citizen Force); *m* 1970 *Diana Kay, dau of F C Harris, of Newlands, Cape Town, and has:

1d +Richard John; *b* 1972

2d +David Mervyn; *b* 1975

3d +Christopher Robert; *b* 1978

3c +Robert Edward Melville [Robert Wingfield, 9918–27th Place SW, Edmonds, WA 98020, USA]; *b* 8 Dec 1950; *educ* St Andrew's Grahamstown and Rand U (BSc); civil engr; *m* 1979 *Carol, dau of P Jansen, of Seattle, and has:

1d +Jeremy; *b* 1981

1d *Joanna Ruth; *b* 1980

1c *Elizabeth Melville [Mrs Hugh Williams, 04 Glen Street, Kenmare, S Africa 1739]; *b* 7 May 1936; *educ* Rand U (BSc 1957) and London U (MSc 1961); geologist; *m* 9 Feb 1963 *Hugh Vincent Williams, MSc, and has:

1d *Katharine Elizabeth; *b* 10 May 1965

2d *Julia Margaret Frances; *b* 29 April 1969

3d *Susan Eileen Isabella; *b* 5 Dec 1970

2c Rosemary Patricia; *b* 4 July 1938; *d* 1986

3b +Mervyn Robert George, DSO (1942), DSC and bar [Capt Mervyn Wingfield DSO DSC RN, Fairwinds, Highfield Crescent, Hindhead, Surrey]; *b* 16 Jan 1911; Capt RN (Naval Attaché Athens, Dir Underwater Weapons Admlty) WW II (despatches), ADC to HM THE QUEEN 1962–67; *m* 25 July 1936 *Sheila Mary, only dau of Maj John Henry Pige Leschallas, and has:

1c +Richard Mervyn [Richard Wingfield Esq, Chiltern House, Hardwick Rd, Whitchurch-on-Thames, Oxon RG8 7HW]; *b* 30 Dec 1942; *educ* Wellington, Pembroke Coll Cambridge (BA 1964, MA 1968) and Southampton U (MSc); MICE, MCIWEM, CEng, with Sir Alexander Gibb & Ptnrs; *m* 26 July 1969 *Diana, dau of Peter Michael Longhurst, of Haslemere, Surrey and has:

1d +James Richard; *b* 24 Oct 1973

1d *Caroline Sarah; *b* 9 Aug 1976

2c +(William) Peter [Peter Wingfield Esq, 47 Combemartin Rd, London SW18 5PP]; *b* 7 May 1948; *educ* Wellington and Sussex U (BA); musician; *m* 24 May 1975 *Patricia Jane, dau of G A Slatter

1c *Cicely [Mrs David Knowles, 2 Spencer Rd, S Croydon CR2 7EH]; *b* 20 Sept 1940; *m* 18 Jan 1964 Lt-Cdr David Barry Knowles, RN (*k* naval air crash 4 Dec 1967), s of Peter Sandiford Knowles, of Combe, Oxford, and has:

1d *Alastair David; *b* 15 Nov 1964; *m* 6 Sept 1997 *Sarah, dau of Philip Harris, of Farnham, Surrey

1d *Melanie Kathleen; *b* 10 Oct 1966

1b Charlotte Elfreda; *b* 5 Sept 1898; *m* 5 July 1923 Capt Hugh M S Mundy, DSC, RN (*d* 11 Jan 1947), 2nd s of George William Mundy, of Douglas, IoM, and *d* 198–, leaving:

1c *Timothy Richard Wingfield [Lt-Cdr Timothy Mundy RN, 57A Croham Rd, S Croydon CR2 7HE]; *b* 1 Sept 1930; *m* 28 Oct 1967 *Jill, est dau of Joseph W Dagleish, of Greenock, and has:

1d *Annabelle Rosemary Wingfield; *b* 10 Nov 1968

2d *Nicola Jill Wingfield; *b* 22 Aug 1970

1c *Pauline Elizabeth [Mrs Thomas Daly, 4 Montgomery Court, Birdhurst Rd, S Croydon, Surrey CR2 7EF]; *b* 24 Oct 1927; *educ* LMH Oxford (BA 1948); *m* 20 Dec 1958 Thomas Alfred Daly (*d* 1979), s of Thomas A Daly, of Cork, and has:

1d *Hugh Thomas Patrick; *b* 29 April 1968; *m* 7 July 1990 *Clare, dau of Jeffrey Matthews, of Winchester

1d *Deirdre May Elizabeth; *b* 30 Nov 1959; *m* 30 Jan 1993 *Edward Conway, s of John Joseph Conway, of London, and has:

1e *Luke Edward Thomas; *b* 8 June 1995

2d *Joanna Charlotte Alice; *b* 11 March 1963; *m* 25 April 1987 *Dr Alexandros Trompetas, s of Gerasimos Trompetas, of Athens, and has:

1e *Anna May; *b* 3 March 1992

2e *Isabella Jane; *b* 18 Dec 1994

2b Eveline Isabella; *b* 5 July 1903; *d* 4 July 1918

3b Rosalie Emma Ruth; *b* 26 Sept 1908; *m* 29 July 1933 Ronald Holms Proctor, yr s of Rev William Proctor, of Barnet, Herts, and *d* 1985, having had:

1c Patrick Wingfield; *b* 26 March 1935; *d* 1 May 1966

(1) Elizabeth Isabella; *m* 12 Aug 1858 Henry FitzGeorge Colley (*d* 24 Nov 1886) and *d* 18 Nov 1903, leaving issue

(2) Isabella Frances; *m* 28 July 1871 Maj Robert Tankerville Webber, 2nd Bn Roy Welch Fus (*d* 4 May 1909), 4th s of Charles Tankerville Webber, QC, and *d* 4 Oct 1930, leaving issue

1 Catherine; *m* 8 July 1833 Rev Arthur Newcombe, of Abbeyleix, Queen's Co, and *d* 1835, leaving issue

2 Emily; *m* 4 June 1827 16th Baron Saye and Sele (*qv*) and *d* 20 June 1837, leaving issue

The 4th VISCOUNT's est s,

RICHARD WINGFIELD, **5th Viscount Powerscourt**; *b* 11 Sept 1790; rep I peer 1821–23; *m* 1st 6 Feb 1813 Lady Frances Theodosia Jocelyn (*d* 10 May 1820), est dau of 2nd Earl of Roden (*qv*), and had:

1 RICHARD, **6th Viscount**

1 Catherine Anne; *m* 21 Dec 1835, as his 1st w, Rev and Hon Andrew Godfrey Stuart, 3rd s of 2nd Earl Castle Stewart (*qv*), and *d* 25 Dec 1845, leaving issue

The **5th Viscount** *m* 2nd 29 June 1822 Theodosia (*d* 31 Dec 1836), n of 2nd and 3rd Earls of Wicklow (*see* 1970 edn), and *d* 9 Aug 1823

The 5th VISCOUNT's only s,

RICHARD WINGFIELD, **6th Viscount Powerscourt**; *b* 18 Jan 1815; *educ* Ch Ch Oxford; MP (Tory) Bath 1837–41, had the gardens at Powerscourt laid out in the Italian manner by Daniel Robertson, of Kilkenny, from 1842; *m* 20 Jan 1836, as her 1st husb, his cousin Lady Elizabeth Frances Charlotte Jocelyn (*m* 2nd 30 April 1846 4th Marquess of Londonderry (*qv*); *d* 2 Sept 1884), est dau of 3rd Earl of Roden (*qv*), and *d* 11 Aug 1844, leaving:

1 MERVYN, **7th Viscount**

2 Maurice Richard; *b* 13 Jan 1839; 1st Life Gds; *m* 11 July 1865 Mary Agnes (*d* 6 April 1875), yst dau and coheir of James Block, of Charlton, Wilts, and sis of 2nd w of 3rd Baron Sherborne (*see* 1970 edn), and *dsp* 14 Feb 1866

3 Lewis Strange; *b* 25 Feb 1842; *educ* Eton and Bonn, Germany; actor in burlesque and straight theatre (for example Roderigo in *Othello* at the Haymarket Theatre Aug 1865), a male nurse in lunatic asylum, warder in a prison, surgn to wounded during Siege of Paris in Franco-Prussian War 1870, pioneer traveller to the remoter provinces of China, painter (memb Roy Hibernian Acad), theatrical costume designer (including one for Lily Langtry as Cleopatra in *Antony and Cleopatra* 1880), theatre critic for the *Globe* under the *nom de plume* Whyte Tyghe, lecturer for the Internat Health Exhibition 1884 on 'Her English Dress', war correspondent, served Sudan Expdn 1884, author: *Under the Palms in Algeria and Tunis* (1868), *Slippery Ground* (novel, 1876), *Lady Grizzle: an Impression of a momentous Epoch* (1878), *My Lords of Strogue: a Chronicle of Ireland from the Convention to the Union* (1879), *In Her Majesty's Keeping* (1880), *Gehenna, or Havens of Unrest* (1882), *Abigail Rowe: a Chronicle of the Regency* (1883), *Notes on Civil Costume in England* (1884), *Barbara Philpot: a Study of Manners* (1886), *Lovely Wang: a Bit of China* (1887), *The Curse of Koshin: a Romance* (1888), *Wanderings of a Globetrotter in the Far East* (1889) and *The Maid of Honour: a Tale of the Dark Days of France* (1891); *m* 16 June 1868 Hon Cecilia Emily Emma FitzPatrick (*d* 3 Nov 1918), 4th dau of 1st Baron Castletown (*see* 1937 edn), and *dsp* 12 Nov 1891

The 6th VISCOUNT's est s,

MERVYN WINGFIELD, **7th Viscount Powerscourt**, PC (I 1897), JP (Co Dublin and Co Wicklow), DL (Co Wicklow); *b* 13 Oct 1836; *educ* Eton; Lt 1st Life Gds 1854–62, rep I peer 1865–1904 (Lib till 1886, U thereafter), finished the remodelling of the gardens at Powerscourt initiated by his f (bought in 1872 from PRINCE NAPOLEON the two 17th-century bronze statues of Aeolus, God of the Winds, which abut the lake below the house) and greatly added to the splendour of the house's interior by adding Italian Baroque furniture, chandeliers and a chimney piece, *cr* 27 June 1885 BARON POWERSCOURT, of Powerscourt, Co Wicklow (UK), Pres Roy Dublin Soc 1892–97, a Ld Justice Ireland 1902, author: *The Wingfield Memoirs* and *History of Powerscourt*; *m* 26 April 1864 Lady Julia Coke (*d* 7 Aug 1931), est dau of 2nd Earl of Leicester (*qv*), and *d* 5 June 1904, leaving:

1 MERVYN RICHARD, **8th Viscount**

2 Maurice Anthony, CMG (1918), CVO (1953), DSO (1916); *b* 21 June 1883; *educ* Charterhouse and RMC Sandhurst; served WWs I (despatches, two brevets) and II (Dir Quartering War Office 1939–41), Maj-Gen Rifle Bde, Croix de Guerre, Legn Honour, Order Rising Sun Japan 3rd Cl, Offr Crown Belgium, Crown Italy, memb Gentlemen-at-Arms 1928 (Harbinger 1950, Standard Bearer 1952–53), chm A W Bain and Sons, pres Corps Insur Brokers 1952–55; *m* 10 Oct 1906 Sybil Frances (*d* 20 Dec 1967), only dau of Frederick Dawson Leyland, of The Vyne, Basingstoke, Hants, and *d* 14 April 1956, leaving:

(1) Anthony ('Tony') Desmond Rex, DSO (1943), MC; *b* 20 Feb 1908; *educ* Eton and RMC Sandhurst; Hon Brig 10th Hus, WW II (cmded 2nd Armoured Bde Normandy 1944 and Germany 1945, wounded, Order Leopold Belgium, Belgian Croix de Guerre), Assist Racing and Stud Manager to HM THE QUEEN 1957–63, sec Meath Foxhounds, memb Irish Turf Club and Irish Nat Hunt Ctee (sr steward 1964); *m* 16 May 1935 Juliet ('Judy') Constance (*d* 1980), only dau of William Burroughs Stanley, JP, DL, of Coolamber Manor, Co Westmeath, and *d* 1 Nov 1995, leaving:

1a *Deirdre Jocelyn [Mrs Basil Pegg, The Old Rectory, Ovington, Hants SO24 0RF]; *b* 11 July 1936; *m* 23 Oct 1969 *Basil Tierney Pegg, only s of Col A C Pegg, and has:

1b *Jonathan Mark; *b* 1973; *educ* Eton

1b *Camilla Louise; *b* 1971

(1) Jocelyn Sybil Julia; *b* 7 Sept 1913; *m* 1st 18 June 1940, as his 2nd w, Lt-Col Clifford Willoughby (Peter) Hordern (*d* 26 Aug 1966), yst s of Peter Hordern, of Alverstoke, Hants, and had:

1a Peter Anthony; *b* 19 Dec 1941; *d* 20 May 1953 following a cricket accident

(1) (cont.) Mrs Peter Hordern *m* 2nd 4 Feb 1970 Ralph Hamilton Cobbold (*d* 1987), s of Col Ralph Pattison Cobbold, DSO, and *d* 18 Feb 1995

1 Olive Elizabeth; *b* 6 Nov 1884; *m* 17 Dec 1908 Maj William John Bates van de Weyer, MVO (*d* 1 April 1946), est s of Victor William Bates van de Weyer, JP, of New Lodge, Berks, and had issue

2 Clare Meriel; *b* 5 June 1886; *m* 10 Jan 1917 4th Baron Templemore (*see* DONEGALL, M) and *d* 23 July 1969, leaving issue

3 Lilah Katherine Julia; *b* 13 Jan 1888; *m* 21 Nov 1912 Maj Sir (Arthur) Clive Morrison-Bell, 1st and last Bt of the 1923 *cr* (*see* MORRISON-BELL, Bt), and had issue

The 7th VISCOUNT's er s,
MERVYN RICHARD WINGFIELD, **8th Viscount Powerscourt**, KP (1916), MVO (1902), JP (Co Dublin); *b* 16 July 1880; Ld Lt Co Wicklow, Comptroller Household to Ld Lt Ireland 1906–07, Capt Special Res Irish Gds WW I (Belgian Croix de Guerre), Ch Commr Boy Scouts Assoc Irish Free State, Memb Irish Senate; *m* 9 June 1903 Sybil, DGStJ (*d* 6 Dec 1946), 2nd dau of Walter Pleydell-Bouverie (*see* RADNOR, E), and *d* 21 March 1947, having had:

1 (MERVYN) PAT(RICK), **9th Viscount**

2 Bryan Edward; *b* 12 Aug 1908; *d* 4 Dec 1925

1 Doreen Julia; *b* 29 March 1904; *m* 10 Jan 1928 FitzHerbert Wright, er s of Capt Henry FitzHerbert Wright, of Yeldersley Hall, Derbys, and *d* 199–, leaving:

(1) *Bryan Henry FitzHerbert [Maj Bryan Wright, The Dower House, Doddington Park, Chipping Sodbury, Bristol BS17 6SF]; *b* 1934; *educ* Eton; Maj Blues and Royals

(1) *Brigid Louise [Mrs Julian Salmond, The Old Manor Farmhouse, The Street, Didmarton, Avon GL9 1DT]; *b* Nov 1928; *m* 1950 *Julian John William Salmond, s of Marshal of the RAF Sir John Maitland Salmond, GCB, GCVO, DSO (*see* GRENFELL, B), and has:

1a *David John Julian

(2) *Davina Julia [The Rt Hon The Lady Loch, c/o Vern Leaze, Calne, Wilts SN11 0NB; Lochluichart, by Garve, Ross-shire]; *b* 1931; *m* 1st 1950 (*divorce* 1975) Sir Richard Boughey, 10th Bt (*d* 1978), and has issue; *m* 2nd 1979 4th and last Baron Loch, MC (*d* 1991; *see* 1970 edn)

(3) *Susan Mary; *b* 1937; *m* 1st 1956 (*divorce* 1974) Maj Ronald Ivor Ferguson (*see* ROYAL FAMILY, also DACRE, B) and has issue; *m* 2nd 1975 Hector Barrantes (*d* 19–), polo player, of Argentina, and *d* in a car crash 19 Sept 1998

The 8th VISCOUNT's only surv s,
(MERVYN) PAT(RICK) WINGFIELD, **9th Viscount Powerscourt**; *b* 22 Aug 1905; Maj Roy Irish Fus, Lt 8th Arab Force WW II (prisoner), Ch Scout Commr Republic Ireland 1947; *m* 16 Dec 1932 Sheila Claude (*d* 1992), author: *A Kite's Dinner* (poems, Poetry Society choice 1954), *Real People* (1952) and *Sun Too Fast* (1974), only dau of Col Claude Beddington, of Mayfair, by Frances Ethel, er dau of Francis Berry Homan-Mulock, JP, of Ballycumber House, King's Co (now Co Offaly), and *d* 3 April 1973, leaving:

1 MERVYN NIALL WINGFIELD, **10th and present Viscount Powerscourt**

2 *Guy Claude Patrick [The Hon Guy Wingfield, PO Box 186, Applegate, CA 95703–0186, USA]; *b* 5 Oct 1940; *educ* Millfield, Culver-Stockton Coll (Canton, Mo.), Lincoln Coll (Lincoln, Ill.) and Washington U, St Louis, Mo.

1*Grania Sybil Enid [The Hon Lady Langrishe, Arlonstown, Dunsany, Co Meath, Ireland]; *b* 25 April 1934; *m* 21 April 1955 *Sir Hercules Ralph Hume Langrishe, 7th Bt (*qv*), and has issue

POWIS

Arms: Per pale azure and gules three lions rampant argent. **Crest:** A wyvern vert, holding in the mouth a sinister hand couped at the wrist gules. **Supporters:** Dexter, an elephant; sinister, a griffin, wings expanded, both argent, the latter gorged with a ducal coronet gules and charged with five mullets in saltire sable. **Motto:** *Ung je serviray* ('I will serve but one master'). **Creations:** B. (I) 15 March 1762 (Clive of Plassey), (GB) 13 Aug 1794 (Clive of Walcot) and (UK) 14 May 1804 (Powis of Powis Castle and Herbert of Chirbury), E. and V. (UK) 14 May 1804.

THE 8TH EARL OF POWIS, Co Montgomery, **Viscount Clive of Ludlow**, Co Salop, **Baron Clive of Plassey**, Co Limerick, **Baron Clive of Walcot**, Co Salop, **Baron Powis of Powis Castle**, Co Montgomery, and **Baron Herbert of Chirbury**, Co Salop (John George Herbert) [The Rt Hon The Earl of Powis, Powis Castle Estate Office, Welshpool, Powys SY21 8RG]; *b* 19 May 1952; *s f* 1993; *educ* Wellington and McMaster U, Ontario, Canada (MA, PhD 1994); sometime lecturer McMaster U, Assist Prof Redeemer Coll Ontario 1990–92; *m* 1977 *Marijke, dau of Martin Guther, of Hamilton, Ontario, and has:

1 +JONATHAN NICHOLAS WILLIAM, *Viscount Clive*; *b* 5 Dec 1979

2 *Stephanie Moira Christina; *b* 1982

3 *Samantha Julie Esther; *b* 1988

Powis, other so-called creation: For the claim by Henry Vernon to be Lord Powis, *see* VERNON, B

Lineage (of Clive): The CLIVEs are first known to have settled in Shropshire *temp* HENRY II.

RICHARD CLIVE, of Huxley, Cheshire, and Styche, nr Market Drayton, Salop, was 12th in descent from Henry de Clive, of Clive, a village some eight miles north of Shrewsbury; *m* Margaret, dau of Sir Richard Corbet, of Moreton Corbet (*see* 1970 edn CORBET, Bt), by Elizabeth, dau of 1st Lord (Baron) Ferrers (of Chartley) (*see* HEREFORD, V), and had, with three daus and two yr sons:

RICHARD CLIVE, of Huxley and Styche; living *temp* HENRY VII; *m* Jane, sis of Sir William Brereton, of Brereton, Cheshire, and *d* 22 April 1572, leaving, with five daus:

Sir GEORGE CLIVE, of Huxley and Styche; Chllr Exchequer Ireland; *m* Susannah, dau of Henry Copinger, of Buxhall, Suffolk, and had, with an er s (Joshua, of Huxley, *m* Mary, dau of Andrew Charlton, of Apley Castle, and left an only surv dau Rachel, *m* 1619 Thomas Wilbraham; *see* SKELMERSDALE, B):

AMBROSE CLIVE, of Styche; *m* Alice, dau of T Townshend, of Brackenack, Norfolk, and had:

ROBERT CLIVE, of Styche; MP Long Parliament (1640–60); *m* Mary, dau of Sir E Abyn, and had:

GEORGE CLIVE; *m* Mary, dau and heiress of Martin Husbands, of Wormbridge, Herefs, and *dvp*, leaving:

1 ROBERT

2 George; Cursitor Baron Exchequer; *d* unm

3 Edward, of Wormbridge; *m* Sarah, dau of — Key, Bristol merchant, and had an est s:

(1) Edward (Sir), of Wormbridge; *b* 1704; barrister Lincoln's Inn 1725, MP St Michael's, Cornwall, 1741, Serjeant-at-Law and Baron Exchequer 1745, Judge Court Common Pleas 1753, ktd 1753, ret 1770; *m* 1st Elizabeth, dau of Richard Symons, of Mynde Park, Herefs; *m* 2nd Judith, yst dau of his cousin Rev Benjamin Clive, and *dsp* 16 April 1771

The est s,
ROBERT CLIVE, of Styche; *m* Elizabeth, dau of R Amphlett, of the Four Ashes, Worcs, and had:

1 RICHARD

2 Benjamin (Rev); Vicar Duffield, Derbys; ancestor of the CLIVEs of Whittfield and CLIVEs of Perrystone Court; had:

(1) Robert (Rev); Rector Moreton, Preb Westminster; *m* 26 Nov 1759 his cousin Rebecca Clive (*see* below)

(1) Judith; *m* her cousin Sir Edward Clive (*see* above)

ROBERT CLIVE's er s,
RICHARD CLIVE, of Styche; MP Montgomeryshire; *m* Rebecca, dau and coheir with her sis Sarah, w of 12th Lord Sempill (*qv*), of Nathaniel Gaskell, of Manchester, and *d* May 1771, having had, with six other children:

1 ROBERT, **1st Baron**

2 William; *b* 29 Aug 1745; *m* 25 Aug 1790 his 2nd cousin Elizabeth Clive, dau of John Rotton, and *d* 23 June 1825, leaving, with a dau and six other sons:

(1) William (Rev); *b* 14 March 1795; Vicar Welshpool, Archdeacon Montgomery; *m* 28 Oct 1829 Marianne (*d* 16 Feb 1841), 4th dau of George Tollet, of Betley Hall, Staffs, and had an only surv dau:

1a Marianne Caroline; *m* 5 June 1862 Rev Hon John Bridgeman, s of 2nd Earl of Bradford (*qv*; *see* also BRIDGEMAN, V)

1 Rebecca; *m* 26 Nov 1759 her cousin Rev Robert Clive (*see* above) and *d* 1825

2 Sarah; *b* 20 April 1737; *m* 29 Aug 1753 Sir (James) John Markham, 4th and last Bt (*d* 1779), and *dsp* 2 Feb 1828

3 Judith; *m* 29 Jan 1757 Thomas Wolley, of Shrewsbury

4 Frances; *m* 7 July 1758 Mathew Wilson and had issue (*see* WILSON, Bt, of Eshton Hall)

5 Anne; *m* Hon George Sempill, s of 12th Lord Sempill (*qv*)

RICHARD CLIVE's est s,
ROBERT CLIVE ('Clive of India'), **1st Baron Clive of Plassey**, Co Clare (I), so cr 15 March 1762, KB (1764); *b* Styche 29 Sept 1725; *educ* Merchant Taylors'; architect of Britain's early ascendancy in India: joined HEICS 1744; tfd to HEIC mil serv as Ensign 1747; won personal distinction at unsuccessful Siege of Pondicherry 1748; Lt at taking of Devikota 1749 (cmdg forces that stormed the breach); Capt 1751; took Arcot 1751 and held it 11 weeks with 200 men against over 7,000 besiegers; won Battles of Arni and Kaveripak; Lt-Col and Lt-Govr Fort St David 1756; began process of avenging Black Hole of Calcutta on its perpetrator, the Surajah Dowlah, Subah of Bengal, first by recapturing Calcutta and bringing the Surajah to immediate terms, also capturing the French settlement of Chandernagore, then by deposing the Surajah, which he achieved at Plassey (23 June 1757), where with 3,200 men he routed 50,000 foot and 18,000 horse; Govr Calcutta 1758–60; defeated Dutch near Chinsura and negotiated a treaty highly beneficial to HEIC 1758; returned to Britain 1760 but revisited Calcutta 1765 (promoted Maj-Gen 1764), where Govr and C-in-C till 1767; MP (Whig) St Michael's 1754–55 (unseated on petition) and Shrewsbury 1761–74, though subject to an inquiry by a Parly select ctee 1763–64; DCL Oxon 1760, FRS 1768, Ld Lt Salop and Montgomeryshire 1772–74; *m* Madras 15 March 1752/3 Margaret (*d* 21 Feb 1817), dau of Edmund Maskelyne, himself 3rd s of Nevil Maskelyne, of Purton,

Wilts, and sis of Nevil Maskelyne, FRS, Astronomer Royal 1765–1811, also of Edmund Maskelyne (Jr), an early friend and companion in adversity of Clive's, and *d* 22 Nov 1774, it was previously thought by his own hand, either deliberately or inadvertently, but a recent biography suggests he was murdered, quite possibly by his w, having had:

1 EDWARD, **1st Earl**

2 Robert; *b* 30 Aug 1769; Lt-Col; *d* 28 July 1833

1 Rebecca; *m* 14 March 1780 Lt-Gen John Robinson (*k* Dec 1798 in the uprising in Ireland of that year) and *d* Dec 1795, leaving issue (*see* SAINT GERMANS, E)

2 Charlotte; *d* unm

3 Margaret; *m* 11 April 1788 Lt-Col Lambert Theodore Walpole (*see* WALPOLE, B) and *d* June 1814

The 1st BARON's er s,

EDWARD CLIVE, **1st Earl of Powis**, in Co Montgomery, so *cr* 14 May 1804, as also BARON POWIS, of Powis Castle, Co Montgomery, BARON HERBERT OF CHIRBURY, Co Salop, VISCOUNT CLIVE OF LUDLOW (all UK), and earlier 13 Aug 1794 BARON CLIVE OF WALCOT, Co Salop (GB), PC (1805); *b* 7 March 1754; *educ* Eton and Ch Ch Oxford; MP (Tory, but voted with Whigs 1783–94) Ludlow 1774–94, Recorder Shrewsbury 1775 and Ludlow 1801, Ld Lt: Salop 1775–98 and 1804–39 and Montgomeryshire 1804–30, Col 1779, memb Bd Ag 1793, Govr Madras 1798–1803, named Ld Lt Ireland 1805 but did not visit that country; *m* 7 May 1784 Lady Henrietta Antonia Herbert (*d* 3 June 1830), sis and heiress of 2nd and last Earl of Powis of that *cr* (*see* below, **Lineage (of Herbert)**), and *d* 16 May 1839, having had:

1 EDWARD, **2nd Earl**

2 Robert Henry, of Oakley Park; *b* 15 Jan 1789; MP S Salop; *m* 19 June 1819 Lady Harriet Hickman, Baroness Windsor (*see* PLYMOUTH, E), and *d* 20 Jan 1854, leaving issue

1 Henrietta Antonia; *m* 4 Feb 1817 Sir Watkin Williams-Wynn, 5th Bt (*qv*), and *d* 22 Dec 1835, leaving issue

2 Charlotte Florentia; Governess to PRINCESS (later HM QUEEN) VICTORIA; *m* 29 April 1817 3rd Duke of Northumberland (*qv*) and *dsp* 27 July 1866

The 1st EARL's er s,

EDWARD CLIVE later HERBERT (roy licence 9 March 1807 under terms of will of unc, 2nd and last Earl of Powis of the 1748 *cr*), **2nd Earl of Powis**, KG (1844); *b* 22 March 1785; *educ* Eton and St John's Coll Cambridge (MA 1806, LLD 1835); MP (Tory) Ludlow 1806–39, Ld Lt Montgomeryshire 1830–48, Col cmdg Montgomeryshire Militia 1846, memb Roy Cmmn English and Welsh Bishoprics 1847, DCL Oxon 1844; *m* 9 Feb 1818 Lady Lucy Graham (*d* 16 Sept 1875), 3rd dau of 3rd Duke of Montrose (*qv*), and *d* 17 Jan 1848 of gunshot wounds sustained at the hands (inadvertently) of one of his yr sons while shooting pheasant, having had, with a dau (*d* unm):

1 EDWARD JAMES HERBERT, **3rd Earl of Powis**; *b* 5 Nov 1818; *educ* Eton and St John's Coll Cambridge (BA 1840, LLD 1842); MP (C) N Salop 1843–48, Lt-Col S Salop Yeo 1848, DCL Oxford 1857, High Steward Cambridge U 1863–91, Ld Lt Montgomeryshire 1877–91; *d* unm 7 May 1891

2 Percy Egerton (Sir), KCB (1869, CB 1856), PC (1867); *b* 15 April 1822; *educ* Eton and RMC Sandhurst; Ensign 43rd LI 1840, Lt 1841, Capt 1846, Maj 1853, served S Africa 1851–53, Lt-Col 1853, AAG 2nd Div Crimean War (severely wounded Alma, wounded Sebastopol, Brevet Col, Crimean Medal and three clasps), QMG evacuation Crimea, Lt-Col 82nd Foot 1858 suppression Indian Mutiny, Dep QMG Horse Gds 1860–65, AQMG Aldershot 1865–67, Maj-Gen 1868, Lt-Gen 1875, Col 74th Highlanders 1876, ADC to HM QUEEN VICTORIA, Treas Household 1867–68, MP (C) Ludlow 1854–60 and S Salop 1865–76, Offr Legn Honour, Kt 3rd Cl Medjidie, Cdr 2nd Cl SS. Maurice and Lazarus Sardinia, Hon Col Salop Rifle Vols 1870; *m* 4 Oct 1860 Lady Mary Caroline Louisa Petty-FitzMaurice, gdau of 3rd Marquess of Lansdowne (*qv*), and *d* 7 Oct 1876, having had:

(1) Henry Edward; *b* 28 June 1861; *d* 8 Aug 1865

(2) GEORGE CHARLES HERBERT, **4th Earl of Powis**, JP (Salop), JP and DL (Montgomeryshire); *b* 24 June 1862; *educ* Eton and St John's Coll Cambridge (BA 1885, MA 1905); Salop: Ld Lt 1896, Pres TAA, CA 1897–1946, KStJ (and Prior Wales); *m* 21 Aug 1890 Hon Violet Ida Evelyn Lane-Fox, Baroness Darcy de Knayth (*qv*) in her own right, and *d* 9 Nov 1952, having had:

1a Percy Robert, *Viscount Clive*; *b* 2 Dec 1892; Scots Gds 1914, Lt Welsh Gds 1915, Capt 1916; *d* unm 13 Oct 1916 of wounds recd in action Somme Sept 1916

2a MERVYN HORATIO HERBERT, *Viscount Clive* and 17th LORD (Baron) DARCY DE KNAYTH, as which *s* mother 1929; *b* 7 May 1904; *educ* Eton and Trin Coll Camb (BA); barrister Inner Temple 1929, S/Ldr RAFVR WW II; *m* 18 Oct 1934 *Vida, OStJ (*m* 2nd 24 Oct 1945 Brig Derek Shuldham Schreiber, MVO (*see* MARLESFORD, B) [Mrs Derek Schreiber, Fir Hill, High St, Droxford, Hants SO32 3QL; 59 Cadogan Place, London SW1X 9RS], only dau of Capt James Harold Cuthbert, DSO, of Beaufront Castle, Hexham, Northumberland, and was *kas* March 1943, leaving:

1b *DAVINA MARCIA INGRAMS, *née* Herbert, BARONESS DARCY DE KNAYTH (*qv*)

1a Hermione Gwladys; *b* 17 Sept 1900; *m* 6 Nov 1924 Count Roberto Lucchesi Palli, 11th Duke della Grazia and 13th Prince di Campofranco, Bailiff Grand Cross SMO Malta, est s of 12th Prince di Campofranco, and *d* 25 May 1995, leaving:

1b *Violet Lucchesi Palli

(1) Magdalen Lucy; *b* 26 July 1864; granted 17 Oct 1891 with her sis rank of earl's dau; *d* unm 27 Oct 1957

(2) Margaret Augusta; *m* 16 Feb 1897 Thomas Richard Cholmondeley (*d* 7 Feb 1922), est s of Rev Richard Hugh Cholmondeley, of Condover Hall, Salop, and *d* 7 July 1952, leaving issue

3 George (Very Rev); *b* 25 Nov 1825; MA; Dean Hereford; *m* 15 Oct 1863 Elizabeth Beatrice (*d* 4 July 1883), 4th dau of Sir Tatton Sykes, 4th Bt, of Sledmere (*qv*), and *d* 15 March 1894, leaving:

(1) Mary Anne; *m* 25 Oct 1898 Maj William Clive Hussey, CVO (*d* 20 June 1929), 2nd s of Edward Hussey, JP, DL, of Scotney Castle, Kent, and *d* 10 July 1942, leaving issue

(2) Winifred Lucy Elizabeth; *d* unm 28 Dec 1948

4 Robert Charles, JP, DL (Salop); *b* 24 June 1827; *educ* Eton and St John's Coll Cambridge (MA 1848); barrister, CA Salop, High Sheriff 1878, Chllr Lichfield Diocese 1875–99; *m* 22 June 1854 Anna Maria (*d* 13 March 1906), dau and heiress of Edward Cludde, of Orleton, and *d* 31 Oct 1902, leaving, with two daus (*d* unm):

(1) Edward William, CB, JP (Salop); *b* 22 March 1855; Col KRRC, Zululand 1879, Sudan 1884, Boer War 1902, ADC to Govr Fiji Islands 1880–83; *m* 12 Jan 1887 Beatrice Anne (*d* 8 June 1928), dau of Sir Hedworth Williamson, 8th Bt (*qv*), and *d* 28 Dec 1924, leaving:

1a EDWARD ROBERT HENRY HERBERT, **5th Earl of Powis**, CBE (1945), TD, DL (Salop 1953); *b* 19 May 1889; *educ* Eton and Ch Ch Oxford (MA); CC Salop 1947–58, Maj (Hon Col) KRRC, WWs I (wounded) and II (Lt-Col cmdg 5th Bn KSLI 1939–40 and Lt-Col KSLI (TA) 1939–45, AAG War Office 1940–45), Iraq 1920, CStJ; *m* 12 March 1932 Ella Mary (*d* 198–), 5th dau of Col William Hans Rathborne, RE, of Kilcogy, Co Cavan, and widow of Capt Peter Douglas Colin Eliot, IA, also formerly w of Col Frank Alan George Macartney, OBE, MC, DL, IA, and *dsp* 15 Jan 1974

2a CHRISTIAN VICTOR CHARLES HERBERT, **6th Earl of Powis**; *b* 28 May 1904; *educ* Oundle, Trin Coll Cambridge (BA) and UCL; barrister Inner Temple 1932, Maj (1943) RAOC India and UK WW II, FRAS, Priv Sec to Govrs Br Honduras 1947–55 and Br Guiana 1955–64; *dsp* 1988

1a Dorothy Marguerite Elizabeth, OBE (1919); granted 31 March 1953 with siblings rank of earl's yr s/dau; *m* 5 Aug 1914 Hon Robert Henry Trefusis (*d* 1 July 1958), yst s of 20th Baron Clinton (*qv*), and *d* 25 Dec 1956, leaving issue

2a Phyllis Hedworth Camilla; *m* 1 June 1918 Martin Drummond Vesey Holt (*d* 2 Nov 1956), s of Sir Vesey George Mackenzie Holt, KBE, and *d* 8 Oct 1972, leaving:

1b *Vesey Martin Edward, DL (Salop 1986), of Orleton Hall (made over to him by his unc, **5th Earl of Powis**) [Vesey Holt Esq DL, Orleton Hall, Wellington, Salop TF6 5AA]; *b* 28 March 1927; *educ* Radley and RAC Cirencester; CC Salop 1968–74 and 1977–98, Govr Wrekin Coll 1970–97, memb Salop Valuation Panel 1970– (dep chm 1984–90, chm 1990–95, dep Pres 1995–), Pres: Shropshire County Cricket Club 1973–, Minor Counties Cricket Assoc 1983–96 and Wrekin C Assoc 1983–92, memb Ag Land Tbnl 1975–97, High Sheriff Salop 1981; *m* 12 March 1955 *Elizabeth Jane DL (Salop 1995), dau of John Geoffrey Sanger, of Herons Farm, Kirdford, W Sussex, and has:

1c *Peter John Vesey [Peter Holt Esq, Burcott Manor, Wrockwardine, Telford, Shropshire TF6 5DW]; *b* 21 Jan 1956; *educ* Eton; jnlst, author: *Clive's Footsteps* (1990), *The Big Muddy* (1991), *Stars of India* (1998); *m* 14 June 1997 *Sarah Elizabeth, formerly w of Michael Theodoron and dau of Eric Gantlett, of Castle Eaton, Wilts, and has:

1d *Dorothy Elizabeth Vesey; *b* 22 Dec 1997

1c *Amanda Phyllis Vesey [Mrs Charles Bathurst, 42 Stanford Rd, London W8 5PZ]; *b* 2 April 1958; *m* 28 Aug 1988 *Charles Colin Addington Bathurst (*see* BLEDISLOE, V) and has:

1d *Theophilus Christopher Vesey; *b* 17 Aug 1992

1d *Ianthe Elizabeth Sophie; *b* 22 April 1997

(2) Graham Cludde; *b* 19 Nov 1856; FRGS, Lt-Col Roy Fus, Afghan campaign 1879–80; *d* unm 24 Sept 1917

(3) Arthur Frederick; *b* 10 Dec 1866; FRGS, King's Messenger, Lt HAC, Boer War 1900; *d* unm 21 Feb 1907

(1) Beatrice Mary; *m* 11 July 1883 George Henry Vaughan Jenkins (*d* 1910), of Herbert Park, Armidale, NSW, Australia, and *d* 27 Aug 1931, leaving issue

5 William Henry, JP (Salop and Northants); *b* 8 Feb 1834; Maj-Gen 4th W India Regt Crimea 1855, Mayor Shrewsbury 1889; *m* 30 Nov 1871 Sybella Augusta (*d* 28 Oct 1926), n of Sir Frederick Milbank, 1st Bt (*qv*), and *d* 29 Jan 1909, leaving, with two daus (*d* unm):

(1) Henry James; *b* 10 March 1882; *d* unm 14 Nov 1911

(2) Percy Mark (Rt Rev), KCVO (1954); *b* 24 April 1885; *educ* Rugby and Trin Coll Cambridge (BA 1907, MA 1911, DD 1922); Deacon 1908, Priest 1909, Curate Rugby 1908–15, Vicar St George's Camberwell and Warden Trin Coll Cambridge Mission 1916–22, RD Camberwell 1918–22, Chaplain to HM GEORGE V 1921–22, Archdeacon Southwark 1922–26 (Canon 1924–26), Bp Suffragan Kingston-upon-Thames 1922–26, 1st Bp Blackburn 1926–42, Chaplain and Sub-Prelate OStJ 1939, Clerk Closet to TM GEORGE VI 1942–52 and THE QUEEN 1952–63, Bp Norwich 1942–59, Hereditary Freeman Shrewsbury; *m* 19 Sept 1922 Hon Elaine Letitia Algitha Orde-Powlett (*d* 198–), only dau of 5th Baron Bolton (*qv*), and *d* 22 Jan 1968, leaving:

1a GEORGE WILLIAM, **7th Earl**

2a David Mark; *b* 2 Jan 1927; *educ* Rugby and Trin Coll Cambridge (BA 1949, MA 1953); granted 1991 with siblings rank of earl's dau/yr s; publisher: chm and md Herbert Press 1976–95, md Paul Elek Publishing 1977, consultant Benn Bros 1980–84, md Rainbird Publishing Gp 1974–77, publishing dir and ch exec Studio Vista 1966–74 and editorial dir 1963–66, ed: *The Penguin Book of Narrative Verse* (1960), *Comic Verse* (1962), *Keats* (1963), *George Herbert* (1963), *Romeo and Juliet* (1965), author: *The Operas of Benjamin Britten* (1979), *The Everyman Book of Evergreen Verse* (1981), *The Gallery of World Photography: The Human Figure* (1982) and *The Everyman Book of Narrative Verse* (1990), schoolmaster Eton 1954 and Christ's Hosp 1955–61; *m* 1 Jan 1955 *(Monica) Brenda [The Hon Mrs David Herbert, 46 Northchurch Rd, London N1 4EJ; Grove Lodge, Church Path, Faringdon, Oxon], only dau of Laurence Edmund Swann, of The Cottage, Bilting Lane, Ashford, Kent, and *d* 18 Nov 1996, having adopted:

*Charles (Charlie) Clive; *b* 28 Oct 1959; *educ* Bryanston and William Ellis Sch

*Emma Katherine Elaine; *b* 1 June 1961; *m* 1985 (*divorce* 1996) Julian Smyth Hore, of Grenfell, Australia

3a +Andrew Clive [The Hon Andrew Herbert, 39 Queensdale Road, London W11]; *b* 15 April 1933; *educ* Repton; late Capt Roy Norfolk Regt, film dir, ed and producer; *m* 12 Jan 1963 (*divorce* 1971) Carol Mae, yst dau of John Charlton and Mrs M A Charlton, and has had:

1b +Nicholas Mark; *b* 21 Oct 1963

2b Hugo Clive; *b* 1 July 1965; *d* 1985

3a (cont.) The Hon Andrew Herbert *m* 2nd 1983 *Edith Ann, yr dau of Alexander Dominguez, of Glendale, Calif., and has:

   3b +Timothy James; *b* 1987

   1b *Amanda Colleen; *b* 1983

1a *Elizabeth Barbarina [The Lady Elizabeth Holden, Meadows End Cottage, Long Meadow End, Craven Arms, Salop SY7 9AQ]; *b* 30 April 1928; *m* 15 May 1948 Maj Hubert Robert Holden, MC, JP (*d* 1987), Roy Norfolk Regt, only surv s of Robert Millington Holden, of Sibdon Castle, and has:

   1b *Robert David [Robert Holden Esq, 94 Frithville Gdns, London W12 7JW; Sibdon Castle, Craven Arms, Salop]; *b* 14 Jan 1956; *educ* Eton; chm Robert Holden Ltd 1978– and dir Fine Arts Courses Ltd 1985–; *m* 18 June 1988 *Susan Emily Frances, dau of Sir Joshua Rowley, 7th Bt (*qv*), and has:

     1c *Hubert Joshua Robert; *b* 10 March 1997

     1c *Lucia Hermione Sophia; *b* 10 March 1997

   1b *Caroline Elizabeth Mary-Anne [Mrs Caroline Pieckielon-Slowik, Holmleigh Cottage, Chirbury, Powys]; *b* 23 Jan 1950; *m* 1971 (*divorce* 1981) Richard Matthew Pieckielon-Slowik and has:

     1c *Daniel George Robert; *b* 1973

     1c *Amy Elizabeth; *b* 1976

  2b *Sarah Barbarina [Mrs Alan Hodgson, 8 Ashburnham Grove, Bradford 9, W Yorks]; *b* 19 March 1953; *m* 1974 *Alan Hodgson and has:

     1c *Matthew William; *b* 1976

     2c *Thomas Edward; *b* 1983

     1c *Emily Barbarina; *b* 1979

  3b *Jane Amanda [Mrs Robert Jones, Garthmyl House, Garthmyl, nr Beriew, Powys]; *b* 20 June 1954; *m* 1978 *Robert Glyn Jones, s of Robert Jones, of Johannesburg, and has:

     1c *William Edward Robert; *b* 1981

     2c *Samuel Bruno; *b* 1982

     1c *Flora Nancy Sarah; *b* 1990

1 Lucy Caroline; *m* 14 Sept 1865 Frederick Calvert, QC (*d* 6 June 1891), and *d* 3 May 1884

2 Charlotte Elizabeth; *m* 20 Oct 1846 Hugh Montgomery, JP, DL (*d* 29 May 1894), of Grey Abbey, Co Down, and *d* 15 May 1906, having had issue

The 6th EARL's second cousin,

GEORGE WILLIAM HERBERT, **7th Earl of Powis**; *b* 4 June 1925; *educ* Eton and Trin Coll Cambridge (BA 1949); FLAS, ARICS; *m* 26 July 1949 *Hon Katharine Odeyne de Grey [The Rt Hon The Dowager Countess of Powis, Marrington Hall, Chirbury, Montgomery, Powys], yst dau of 8th Baron Walsingham (*qv*), and *d* 13 Aug 1993, having had:

  1 JOHN GEORGE HERBERT, **8th and present Earl of Powis**

  2 +Michael Clive [The Hon Michael Herbert, Wicken Hall, Wicken, Cambs CB7 5XT]; *b* 22 Aug 1954; *educ* Wellington, Christ's Coll Cambridge (MA) and London Business Sch (MSc); *m* 19 Aug 1978 *Susan Mary, only dau of Guy Baker (*d* 1982), of Welshpool, Powys, and has:

    (1) +Thomas Guy Clive; *b* 1981

    (2) +Mark Philip Clive; *b* 1983

    (1) *Joanna Frances Clare; *b* 1987

  3 +Peter James [The Hon Peter Herbert, 9 Turnberry Court, Iona Way, Haywards Heath, W Sussex R16 3TD]; *b* 26 Dec 1955; *educ* Wellington; *m* 1978 *Terri, yr dau of Sean McBride, of Callan, Co Kilkenny, and has:

    (1) +Oliver George Laurie; *b* 1983

    (1) *Sophie Louise Mary; *b* 1980

    (2) *Lucy Alison Julia; *b* 1988

  4 +Edward David; *b* 1 July 1958; *educ* Bryanston, Lancaster U (BSc) and Spurgeon's Coll (BA); ACMA; *m* 1985 *Diana Christine, er dau of Cedric Shore, and has:

    (1) +David Andrew; *b* 1988

    (1) *Joy Sarah; *b* 1986

The **7th Earl** also adopted:

  *Lorraine Elizabeth; *b* 3 April 1961; *m* 1981 *Roger Samuel Jones and has issue

  *Nicola Wendy; *b* 9 May 1962; *m* 1985 *Robert Thomas Buxton and has issue

Lineage (of Herbert): GODWIN; *d* 1199, leaving:

HERBERT Ap GODWIN, of Cilleculum; living 1207; had:

CYNHAETHWY Ap HERBERT; living between 1183 and 1198; had:

ADAM Ap CYNHAETHWY; *m* Cristin, dau of Gwarin Ddu, and had:

JENKIN Ab ADAM, of Gwern-ddu, Llandeilo Bertholau, Abergavenny; *m* Lowri, dau of Philip ab Adam Fychan, and had:

GWILYM Ap JENKIN; Master Sgt Abergavenny 1340; *m* Gwenllian, dau of Hywel Fychan ap Hywel and *d c* 1377, leaving, with numerous other issue:

THOMAS Ap GWILYM, of Perth-hir, Rickfield, Mon; *m* Mawd, dau of Sir John Morley, of Llansanffraid, nr Abergavenny, and *d* 1438, having had, with four er sons:

Sir WILLIAM THOMAS, called *Y Marchog Glas o Went* ('The Blue Knight of Gwent'), of Raglan, Mon, the (feudal) lordship of which he bought from 1st Lord (Baron) Berkeley (*qv*); ktd 1415; *m* 1st his former employer Elizabeth (to whom he had been steward), dau and heiress of Sir John Bluet, of Raglan, and widow of Sir James Berkeley (by whom she was mother of the 1st Lord (Baron) Berkeley; *see* above); *m* 2nd, as her 2nd husb, Gwladus (*d* 1454), dau of Dafydd Gam (*ka* Agincourt) and widow of Sir Roger Vaughan, of Tretower (also *ka* Agincourt), and *d* 1446, having by her had:

  1 WILLIAM, took surname HERBERT, 1st EARL OF PEMBROKE, so *cr* 8 Sept 1468, as also earlier 26 July 1461 BARON HERBERT/HERBERD (both E) by writ, KG (1461/2); *b c* 1423; ktd 1449, served Hundred Years War (captured by French 1450 at Formigny), Yorkist Wars of Roses, Sheriff Glamorgan and Morgannoc and Constable Usk Castle 1459, MP Herefs 1460–61, Ch Justice and Chamberlain S Wales 1461, granted 3 Feb 1461/2 castle, town and lordship of Pembroke, with other castles, following surrender of Pembroke Castle to him

by Lancastrians five months previously, Ch Justice N Wales 1467; *m c* 1455 Anne (living 1486), dau of Sir Walter Devereux (*see* HEREFORD, V), and was beheaded 27 July 1469 following his capture by a pro-Earl of Warwick faction among EDWARD IV's nominal supporters at Battle of Edgcot, nr Banbury, Oxon, one or three days earlier, having had, with eight daus (including Catherine, *m* by 1 Oct 1490, as his 2nd w, 3rd Lord (Baron) Grey (of Ruthin); *see* GREY, B):

  (1) WILLIAM HERBERT, 2nd EARL OF PEMBROKE (resigned title 1479 since EDWARD IV wished to confer on his own s and heir, later EDWARD V, doing so in July of that year) later (and instead) 1st and last EARL OF HUNTINGDON (E), so *cr* 4 July 1479 with initially remainder to the heirs of the body of his f and in a confirmation of 1484 and 1488 with remainder to his f's heirs male of the body; *b c* 1455; ktd 1465, Commr Array S Wales and Marches 1471 and again jtly 1483, Ch Justice and Chamberlain S Wales 1471 and Ch Justice again 1483, Chamberlain to PRINCE OF WALES (later EDWARD V); *m* 1st Sept 1466 Lady Mary Woodville, dau of 1st Earl Rivers of the 1466 *cr* and sis of ELIZABETH, QUEEN CONSORT of EDWARD IV, and had:

    1a ELIZABETH Herbert, deemed by later doctrine BARONESS HERBERT in her own right; *m* 1st Earl of Worcester (*see* BEAUFORT, D), for whom *see* also below

  (1) (cont.) The 1st and last EARL OF HUNTINGDON of the 1479 *cr m* 2nd between 3 March and 29 Sept 1483/4 Katharine, illegitimate dau of RICHARD III, and *dspm* 16 July 1491, when the Earldom expired

  (2) Walter (Sir), of Caldicot; ktd 1475; *m* Lady Anne Stafford, dau of 1st Duke of Buckingham of the 1444 *cr* (*see* STAFFORD, B), but *dspl* 1507

  (3) George (Sir), of St Julians, Mon; ktd 1487; *d* 1504; gggf of:

    1a Mary Herbert; *m* 1st BARON HERBERT OF CHIRBURY of the 1629 *cr* (*see* below)

1 (cont.) The 1st EARL OF PEMBROKE of the 1468 *cr* also had two or more illegitimate sons; one of them, by Mawd, dau of Adam (Turberville) ap William ap Howell Graunt, was:

  (4) Richard, of Ewias, Herefs; Gentleman Usher to HENRY VII, Constable and Porter Abergavenny Castle 1509; *m* Margaret, dau and coheir of Sir Mathew Cradock, of Swansea, and widow of John Malefant, and *d* by 23 Sept 1510, having had:

    1a George (Sir), of Swansea; ancestor of the HERBERTs of Swansea

    2a WILLIAM HERBERT, 1st EARL OF PEMBROKE of the 1551 *cr* (*see* PEMBROKE and MONTGOMERY, E); had, with other issue:

      1b Edward (Sir), of Red Castle (also called Pool Castle, *Castell Coch* ('Red Castle', from the colour of the stone it was built with), Poole or Pole Castle), ultimately known as Powis Castle, which he bought 1587, together with the district roundabout known as Powisland, from Edward Grey, an illegitimate s of Edward Grey, 4th and last holder of the putative Barony of Grey (of Powis), sometimes also referred to as Baron Powis (E, (?)*cr* by writ of summons *c* 1455; (?)*extinct* 1551); *m* Mary, dau and heiress of Thomas Stanley, Master of the Mint 1570, of Standon, Herts, and *d* 23 March 1594/5, having had, with three other sons and two daus:

        1c Sir WILLIAM HERBERT, 1st BARON POWIS, of Powis, Co Montgomery (E), so *cr* 2 April 1629, KB (1603); *b* 1573 or 1574; MP Montgomery 1597–98, 1604–11, 1614, 1621–22 and 1624–29, Memb Cncl for Wales 1608 and 1633, Sheriff Montgomeryshire 1613, Constable Radnor Castle and Steward Radnor 1631; held Powis Castle for CHARLES I till it fell to Parliament Civil War 1644; *m* by 1600 Lady Eleanor Percy (*d* 24 Dec 1650), dau of 2nd Earl of Northumberland of the 1557 *cr* (*see* NORTHUMBERLAND, D), and *d* 7 March 1655/6, having had, with a yr s and four daus (two of whom *d* in infancy):

          1d Sir PERCY HERBERT, 1st Bt (E), so *cr* 16 Nov 1622, and 2nd BARON POWIS; *b* by 1600; MP Shaftesbury 1620/1–22 and Wilton 1624–25, ktd 1622, Memb Cncl Wales 1633, royalist Civil War; *m* 19 Nov 1622 Elizabeth (*d* 8 Oct 1662), sis of 1st Earl of Craven (*qv*) of the March 1664/5 *cr*, and *d* 19 Jan 1666/7, having had, with a dau:

            1e Sir WILLIAM HERBERT, 2nd Bt, and 3rd BARON POWIS; *b c* 1626; *cr* 4 April 1674 EARL OF POWIS, Co Montgomery, and 24 March 1686/7 VISCOUNT MONTGOMERY, of the town of Montgomery, and MARQUESS OF POWIS (all E), Col 4th Foot 1687–88, Ld Lt Co and City of Chester Feb 1687/8, Steward roy manors Carmarths, Radnor and Denbigh April 1688; suspected of involvement in Popish Plots and incarcerated Tower London 1678–84; after Glorious Revolution 1688 accompanied JAMES II to France and Ireland and was by him *cr* 12 Jan 1688/9 titular Duke of Powis and Marquess of Montgomery, also titular JAMES PC (I), Ld Chamberlain Household and KG (1692); outlawed in Britain for high treason Feb 1689/90; *m* 2 Aug 1654 his distant cousin Lady Elizabeth Somerset (*d* 11 March 1690/1), Ldy Bedchamber to CATHERINE, QUEEN CONSORT of CHARLES II, and Governess to the children of JAMES II 1688–90, er dau of 2nd Marquess of Worcester (*see* BEAUFORT, D) and 6th in descent from the marriage of Charles Somerset, 1st Earl of Worcester, who before his elevation to the Earldom seems to have sat in Parliament as Baron Herbert in right of his w, with the only dau of WILLIAM HERBERT, 1st and last EARL OF HUNTINGDON of the 1479 *cr* (*see* above), and *d* 2 June 1696, leaving:

              1f Sir WILLIAM HERBERT, 3rd Bt, etc and 2nd MARQUESS OF POWIS (outlawry reversed 1722), DL (Merionethshire, Pembs, Cards, Carnarvs, Mon and Anglesey 1688); *b c* 1665; Page Honour to JAMES II at his coronation 1685, Col Foot Regt 1687–88; outlawed for suspected Jacobitism 1696 and imprisoned 1689, 1696–97 and 1715; *m c* 1695 Mary (*d* 8 Jan 1723/4), dau and coheir of Sir Thomas Preston, 3rd Bt, of Furness, and *d* 22 Oct 1745, leaving:

                1g Sir WILLIAM HERBERT, 4th and last Bt, etc and 3rd and last MARQUESS OF POWIS; *b c* 1698; *educ* Clare Coll Cambridge; *d unm* 8 March 1747/8, when all his titles expired

                2g Edward; *m* 7 July 1734 Henrietta, dau of 1st Earl Waldegrave (*qv*), and *d* Nov 1734, leaving:

1h Barbara; *b* posthumously 24 June 1735; *m* 30 March 1751 her distant cousin 1st EARL OF POWIS of the 1748 cr (for whom *see* further below) and *d* 12 March 1786

1g Mary; *m*, as his 2nd(?) w, Joseph, Count Gage (*see* GAGE, V)

2g Anne; *m c* 18 Jan 1728/9, as his 2nd w, 6th Baron Arundell of Wardour (*d* 30 June 1746; *see* 1940 edn) and *dsp* 2 Oct 1757

3g Charlotte; *m* 1st Edward Morris; *m* 2nd Edward Williams

4g Theresa; *m* as his 1st w Sir Robert Throckmorton, 4th Bt (*d* 8 Dec 1791; *see* 1970 edn), and had issue

1f Mary; *m* 1st Hon Richard Molyneux (*dsp*), est s of 3rd Viscount Molyneux of Maryborough (*see* 1970 edn SEFTON, E); *m* 2nd by 1690 Francis Browne, 4th Viscount Montagu (*cr* 1554; *extinct*(?) 1797; he *dsp* 1708); *m* 3rd by 22 Aug 1716 Sir George Maxwell, 3rd Bt (*dsp* 1719), and *d* 30 Oct 1744

2f Frances; *m* 4th Earl of Seaforth (*see* CROMARTIE, E)

3f Anne; *m c* 23 May 1687 Francis Smith, 2nd Viscount Carrington (*cr* 1643; *extinct* 1706)

4f Lucy; *b* 1669; professed in the English Augustine convent at Bruges 1693, Prioress 1707, devotional writer (*see The Devotions of the Lady Lucy Herbert of Powis*, ed Rev John Morris, SJ, 1873); *d* 19 Jan 1743/4

5f Winifred; *b c* 1679; *m* 1699 5th Earl of Nithsdale (*see* HERRIES OF TERREGLES, L) and *d* 1749, having had issue

2 Richard (Sir), of Coldbrooke, Abergavenny; also took surname HERBERT; *m* Margaret, dau of Thomas ap Gruffudd ap Nicolas, of Dinefwr (*see* DINEVOR, B), and *d* July 1469, being beheaded with his bro just after the Battle of Edgecot (*see* above), having had, with illegitimate issue:

(1) William (Sir); ktd 1497; *d* 1534 or 1535; ancestor of the HERBERTs of Coldbrooke

(2) RICHARD (Sir), for whom *see* further below

(3) John, of Laugharne, Carmarths; *dspm*

Sir RICHARD's 2nd s,

Sir RICHARD HERBERT, of Montgomery; *b* 1468; ktd 1513, Gentleman-Usher Privy Chamber to HENRY VIII; *m* 1st Marged, dau of Gwilym ap Rhys, of Llwyn-hywel, Llandovery, Carmarths; *m* 2nd by 1513 Ann, dau of David ap Ieuan ap Llywelyn Fychan, and had issue by both ws; his s by his 2nd w:

Sir EDWARD HERBERT, of Montgomery Castle and Blackhall, Montgomeryshire; *b* 1513; Dep-Constable Aberystwyth Castle March 1543/4, MP Montgomeryshire 1553 and 1556–57, Sheriff Montgomeryshire 1557 and 1568, served Battle of St Quentin 1557, Esq Body to ELIZABETH I; *m* Elizabeth, dau of Mathew *Goch* ('The Red') Price, of Newtown, Montgomeryshire, and *d* by 20 May 1593, having had, with six daus:

1 Richard, of Llyssin or Llysmawr, Montgomeryshire; Sheriff Montgomeryshire 1576 and 1584, (?)MP Montgomeryshire 1585–86; *m* as her 1st husb Magdalen (*b c* 1568; a close friend and inspiration to the poet John Donne; *m* 2nd Sir John Danvers, yr bro of 1st and last Earl of Danby; *d* June 1627), dau of Sir Richard Newport (*d* 1570) by Margaret, dau and heiress of Sir Thomas Bromley, and had:

(1) EDWARD HERBERT, 1st BARON HERBERT OF CHIRBURY (E), so *cr* 7 May 1629, as also earlier 13 Dec 1624 BARON HERBERT OF CASTLE ISLAND alias OF THE CASTLE OF THE ISLAND OF KERREY (I), KB (1603), PC; *b* 3 March 1582/3; *educ* Univ Coll Oxford; MP Montgomeryshire 1601 and Merionethshire 1604–11, Amb France 1619–24, tepid royalist (some sources say actually neutral) in Civil War, Warden Stannaries 1646, best-known as a philosopher and historical and religious writer (considered the earliest deist): *De Veritate* (1624), *De Religione Gentilium* (1645), *Life and Raigne of King Henry VIII* (1649), *Expeditio Buckinghami Ducis* (1656), *Autobiography* (not published till 1764, and then in an edition for private circulation by Horace Walpole), *Poems* (1665); *m* 28 Feb 1598/9 Mary (*d* 29 Oct 1634), dau and heiress (notably of the Co Kerry estate commemorated in her husb's title in the Irish peerage) of Sir William Herbert, himself ggs of Sir George Herbert, 3rd s of 1st Earl of Pembroke of the 1463 *cr* (*see* above), and *d* 5 Aug 1648, having had, with at least two other sons and two daus:

1a RICHARD HERBERT, 2nd BARON HERBERT OF CHIRBURY; MP Montgomeryshire April–May 1640 and Montgomery borough 1640–42, unlike his f a staunch royalist in Civil War, raising a regt of 12,000 foot and acting as Govr Bridgnorth and Aberystwyth for CHARLES I; *m* 19 Nov 1627 Lady Mary Egerton (*d* 1659), dau of 1st Earl of Bridgwater (*see* GREY EGERTON, Bt), and *d* 13 May 1655, having had, with two other sons and two er daus:

1b EDWARD HERBERT, 3rd BARON HERBERT OF CHIRBURY, PC (I 1669); *b c* 1633; royalist, joined abortive uprising by Gen Booth 1659 on behalf of CHARLES II, custos rotulorum Montgomeryshire and Denbighs 1660–78 and 1666–78 respectively; *m* 1st by 1660 Anne (*dsp* after 1660), dau of Sir Thomas Middleton, of Chirk Castle, Denbighs; *m* 2nd 20 Aug 1673, as her 1st w, Elizabeth Brydges (*bapt* 25 March 1651; *m* 2nd in or after 1684, as his 2nd w, 2nd Earl of Inchiquin (*d* Jan 1691/2) (*see* INCHIQUIN, B); *m* 3rd by Aug 1694 (*divorce* in or after 1697 on the grounds of her husb's bigamy, though a judgment to that effect is thought to have been overturned on appeal) 4th Baron Howard of Escrick (*dspl* 29 April 1715) (*see* SUFFOLK and BERKSHIRE, E); *m* 4th 1712 — George, said to have been a French Protestant, and *dsp* 3 Feb 1717/8), dau of 6th Baron Chandos of Sudeley (*see* TEMPLE OF STOWE, E), and *dsp* 9 Dec 1678

2b HENRY HERBERT, 4th and last BARON HERBERT OF CHIRBURY; *b c* 1640; also joined Gen Booth's uprising (*see* above), served under Duke of Monmouth (*see* BUCCLEUCH and QUEENSBERRY, D) in mil ops France 1672 till succeeding his bro; custos rotulorum Montgomeryshire 1679, Cofferer Household to WILLIAM III 1689–91 (having been among those who took up arms for WILLIAM when still Prince of Orange 1688), Col 23rd Foot (Welsh Fus) March–April 1689; *m c* Dec 1681 Katherine, dau of 1st Earl of Bradford (*qv*) of the 1694 *cr*, and *dsp* 21 April 1691, when all his titles expired

1b Magdalen; *m* Sir Charles Morley, of Droxford, Hants, and had issue (*see* WINCHESTER, M)

2b Florentia; *m* her cousin Richard Herbert (*see below*)

(2) Richard; soldier Low Countries; *bur* Bergen-op-Zoom *c* 1622

(3) William; soldier Denmark and Low Countries; *d* young

(4) George; *b* 3 April 1593; *educ* Westminster and Trin Coll Cambridge (Fell 1614, Public Orator 1618/9–27); the celebrated clergyman (ordained 1630, thereafter incumbent of Fugglestone with Bemerton, nr Salisbury) and poet (*The Temple* (1633), *Remains* (1652), *Works in Prose and Verse*), also prose-writer, notably of *A Priest in the Temple*; *m* 5 March 1628/9, as her 1st husb, Jane (*m* 2nd Sir Robert Cook, of Highnam House, Glos, and was *bur* 1656), a relative of the 1st Earl of Danby (*cr* 1626; *extinct* 1643), and *dsp* (*bur* 3 March 1632/3)

(5) Charles; *b* 1592; *educ* Winchester and New Coll Oxford (Fell 1613); *d* 1617

(6) Henry (Sir); *b* 1595; *educ* at home and in France; ktd Aug 1623, Master Revels to JAMES I and CHARLES I *c* 1623–42 and CHARLES II 1660–63, Gentleman Privy Chamber, High Sheriff Worcs 1648, MP Bewdley 1661–73; *m* 1st — and had:

1a William; *b* 1 May 1626; *d* young

1a Vere; *b* 29 Aug 1627; *m* Sir Henry Every, 2nd Bt (*qv*)

2a Frances; *b* 29 Dec 1628; *d* young

(6) (cont.) Sir Henry *m* 2nd *c* 1650 Elizabeth (*d* 7 July 1698), dau of Sir Robert Offley, of Dalby, Leics, and *d* 27 April 1673, having by her had, with two daus:

2a HENRY HERBERT, 1st BARON HERBERT OF CHIRBURY, Co Salop (E), so *cr* 28 April 1694; *b* 24 July 1654; MP (Whig) Bewdley 1677–79 and 1689–94 and Worcester 1681, Ld of Trade 1707–08/9; *m* 12 Feb 1677/8 Anne, dau and coheir of John Ramsey, London Alderman, and *d* 22 Jan 1708/9, leaving:

1b HENRY HERBERT, 2nd and last BARON HERBERT OF CHIRBURY of the 1694 *cr*; *educ* Westminster; MP (Whig) Bewdley 1708–09 (unsuccessful contestant same seat 1705); *m* 12 Dec 1709 Mary, sis of 1st Earl of Portsmouth (*qv*), and *dsp* by suicide, due allegedly to money problems, 19 April 1738

(7) Thomas; *b* posthumously 15 May 1597; page to Sir Edward Cecil in Germany, where also saw mil action, later became a sea captain, also miscellaneous writer; *d c* 1642

2 MATHEW

3 Charles; had:

(1) Edward (Sir); Attorney-Gen *temp* CHARLES I, Ld Keeper Gt Seal 1653–54 to the exiled CHARLES II; *m* Margaret, dau of Sir Thomas Smith, Master Requests, of Parson's Green, Middx, and widow of Thomas Carey (2nd s of 1st Earl of Monmouth; *see* FALKLAND, V), and had:

1a Charles; *d unm, ka* Battle of Aughrim 12 July 1691 fighting for WILLIAM III

2a Edward (Sir), PC (1685), KC (1677); *b c* 1645–48; *educ* Winchester and New Coll Oxford (Fell 1665, BA 1669); barrister Inner Temple 1675, Bencher 1682, Chllr Regalities and Temporalities Co Tipperary by Feb 1681/2, Ch Justice Chester and Flint 1683, ktd Feb 1683/4, MP Ludlow 1685–87, Serjeant-at-law 1685, Ch Justice King's Bench 1685 and Common Pleas 1687–88; with JAMES II in France Dec 1688 and Ireland 1689–90 (hence back in England outlawed for high treason Feb 1689/90), being *cr* by him by 20 Feb 1692/3 Earl of Portland; *d unm* 8 Nov 1698

3a ARTHUR HERBERT, 1st and last EARL OF TORRINGTON, Co Devon, so *cr* 29 May 1689, as also BARON HERBERT OF TORBAY, Co Devon (both E), with special remainder to his bro Charles and the latter's heirs male of the body in default of such of his own, PC (*b* Feb 1688/9–92); *b* 1647–49; joined Navy 1663, Lt 1666, Capt *Pembroke* Nov 1666, served against Algiers pirates in Med 1669–72, cmded *Dreadnought* Battle of Solebay 1672 in 3rd Dutch War, V-Adml Feb 1677/, Adml and C-in-C against Algiers pirates 1680–83, a Commr Admlty 1683 and 1684, R-Adml of England Jan 1683/4–March 1686/7, Master Robes March 1684/5–March 1686/7; MP (Whig) Dover 1685–87 and Plymouth 1689, Col 15th Foot 1686–March 1686/7 (relieved of all posts for declining to vote for repealing Test Act); Lt-Gen-Adml of fleet bringing WILLIAM III from Holland to England 1688, First Commr Admlty March 1688/9–92, b 1689/90, Er Bro Trin Ho 1689–1716 (Master 1689–90), Adml and C-in-C Channel and coast of Ireland, as which closed with a larger French naval force in Bantry Bay 1 May 1689 (thanks of Parl 21 May), V-Adml and Lt of Admlty of England 1689–90, Adml and C-in-C combined Anglo-Dutch fleet at French victory of Beachy Head 30 June 1690, for which imprisoned Tower London and court martialled 10 Dec 1690 (acquitted but never again given a command); *m* 1st *c* 2 Nov 1672 Anne (separated by 6 March 1684/5), dau of George Hadley, of Southgate, Middx, London grocer, and widow of Walter Phe(a)sant, of Upwood, Hunts; *m* 2nd *c* 1 Aug 1704 Anne, dau of Sir William Armine, 2nd Bt, and widow of (a) Sir Thomas Wodehouse (*see* KIMBERLEY, E) and (b) 2nd Baron Crew of Stene, and *dsp* 14 April 1716, when his titles expired

1a Margaret; *m* — Agar

4 George, of New Coll Oxford

Sir EDWARD HERBERT's 2nd s,

MATHEW HERBERT, of Dolguog, Montgomeryshire; MP 1586–87, did mil service Low Countries; *m* Anne, dau of Sir Charles Fox, of Bromfield, Salop, and had:

1 Francis, of Dolguog, whose estates were sequestrated for his loyalty to CHARLES I in the Civil War; *m* 1st Abigail, dau of William Garton; *m* 2nd by 25 June 1619 Mary (*dsp*), dau of Dr Richard Parry, Bp St Asaph, and by his 1st w had:

(1) Sir MATHEW HERBERT, 1st and last Bt (E), so *cr* 18 Dec 1660, of Bromfield, Salop; *m* Mary (*d* 14 Feb 1669/70), 4th and yst dau of Sir Thomas Lucy, of Charlecote, Warwicks (*see* RAMSAY-FAIRFAX-LUCY, Bt), *dsp* and was *bur* 30 Oct 1668 or 1669, when the btcy expired

(2) Richard, of Dolguog and Oakley Park, Ludlow, Salop; *b c* 1629; *m* his cousin Florentia (*d c* 1694), sis of 4th and last Baron Herbert of Chirbury of the 1629 *cr* (*see* above), and *d* 1676, having had:

1a Francis, of Dolguog and Oakley Park; *b* 1667; was bequeathed entire property of his maternal unc 4th and last BARON HERBERT OF CHIRBURY of the 1629 *cr*; *m* Dorothy (*d* 1717), dau of John Oldbury, London merchant, and *d* Feb 1719, leaving, with two other sons and three daus:

1b HENRY ARTHUR HERBERT, 1st EARL OF POWIS, Co Montgomery, so *cr* 27 May 1748, as also VISCOUNT LUDLOW, of Co Salop, and BARON POWIS OF POWIS CASTLE, Co Montgomery (all GB), also earlier 21 Dec 1743 BARON HERBERT OF CHIRBURY, Co Salop (GB), and (later) 16 Oct 1749 BARON HERBERT OF CHIRBURY AND OF LUDLOW, Co Salop (GB), with in the case of the last title special remainder, failing heirs male of his body, to his bros Richard and Francis, of Powis Castle, Montgomeryshire (altered by William Baker 1748), and Oakley Park, Montgomeryshire (altered and enlarged by William Baker 1748–58); *b c* 1703; MP (Whig) Bletchingley 1724–27 and Ludlow 1727–43, Ld Lt: Salop 1734–61 and 1764–72 and Montgomeryshire 1761–72, Recorder Ludlow 1747, Treasurer to FREDERICK PRINCE OF WALES 1737–38, Comptroller Household May–Nov 1761, Treasurer 1761–65, Col 1745, Maj-Gen 1755, Lt-Gen 1759, Gen 1772; *m* 30 March 1751 Barbara, dau of Lord Edward Herbert and n of 3rd and last MARQUESS OF POWIS (*see* above), and *d* 10 Sept 1772, leaving, with three other daus:

1c GEORGE EDWARD HENRY ARTHUR HERBERT, 2nd and last EARL OF POWIS of the 1748 *cr*; *b* 7 July 1755; *educ* Eton; Recorder Ludlow 1776, Ld Lt Montgomeryshire 1776–1801 and Salop 1798–1801; *d* unm 16 Jan 1801, when his titles expired, leaving his estates to his n Edward, s of his only sis:

1c Henrietta Antonia Herbert; *m* 7 May 1784 **1st Earl of Powis** of the 1804 *cr* (*see* above)

2b Richard; MP Ludlow
3b Francis, of Ludlow; *d* 1719
4b Herbert; *d* 1719
5b John; *d* 1719
2a George; had issue
1a Mary

PRENTICE

Creation: B. (LP, UK) 1992.

THE BARON PRENTICE, of Daventry, Co Northants (Sir Reg(inald) Ernest Prentice, PC (1966), JP (Croydon 1961)) [The Rt Hon The Lord Prentice PC JP, Wansdyke, Church Lane, Mildenhall, Wilts SN8 2LU]; *b* 16 July 1923; *educ* Whitgift Sch and LSE (BSc); RA 1942–46, 2nd Lt 1943; staff memb TGWU 1950–57, MP (Lab) E Ham N 1957–74, (Lab to 1977, C 1977–79) Newham NE 1974–77, (C) Daventry 1979–87, Min State DES 1964–66, Min: Public Building and Works 1966–67, Overseas Devpt 1967–69, Alderman GLC 1970–71, Lab Spokesman Employment 1972–74, Sec State DES 1974–75, Min: (Lab) Overseas Dept 1975–76, (C) Social Security 1979–81; Memb Exec Ctee Nat Union C Assocs 1988–90; Pres Assoc Business Execs 1983–, ktd 1987; author: *Social Welfare and the Citizen* (jt author, 1957), *Right Turn* (1978); *m* 1948 *(Vera May) Joan, dau of Mrs Rosa Godwin, of Hatfield Heath, Herts, and has:

1 *Christine Ann; *b* 1951

Lineage: ERNEST GEORGE PRENTICE, of Thornton Heath, Surrey; *m* Elizabeth — and had:

REGINALD ERNEST, *cr* a **Baron**

PRESCOTT

Arms: Per chevron pean and erminois on a chief or a rose gules, barbed and seeded proper, between two leopards's faces sable. **Crest:** Upon the battlements of a tower proper a leopard statant sable. **Motto:** *Vincit qui patitur* ('He conquers who endures').
Creation: Bt. (UK) 30 June 1938.

SIR MARK PRESCOTT, 3RD BT, of Godmanchester, Co Huntingdon [Sir Mark Prescott Bt, Heath House, Moulton Rd, Newmarket, Suffolk, CB8 8DU]; *b* 3 March 1948; *s* unc 1965; *educ* Harrow; racehorse trainer

Lineage: JOHN PRESCOTT, of Blackburn; had:

Sir William Henry Prescott, 1st Bt (UK), so *cr* 30 June 1938, CBE (1929), JP, DL Middx; *b* 26 March 1874; barrister Gray's Inn 1909, WW I: attd 1st Army France, Maj RE cmdg 222nd Field Co (despatches), MP (C U) N Tottenham 1918–22; Middx: High Sheriff 1929, CA, Chm CC 1936–37, Chm Edmonton Petty Sessions, E Middx Drainage Ctee, Met Water Bd 1928–45, Lee Conservancy Bd and Lee Conservancy Catchment Bd, memb Middx TA&AFA, Hon Col 1st AA Div Signals, memb Hunts CC, High Sheriff Cambs and Hunts 1938, Hon Fell and Pres Inst of Sanitary Engrs, memb Govt Advsy Ctees Water and Roads, Pres Br Waterworks Assoc, Hon memb Instn of County and Municipal Engrs, Master Paviors' Co, Liveryman Glazier's Co, V-Pres Roy Hosp and Home for Incurables Putney and UDCs Assoc, Govr Prince of Wales Gen Hosp Tottenham, Tstee Alexandra Palace, Medaille du Roi Albert Belgium, ktd 1922, MInstCE, MIMechE, FRSA; *m* 27 Dec 1897 Bessie (*d* 12 Sept 1940), dau of Mark Stanley, of Ambleside, and *d* 15 June 1945, leaving:

1 **Sir Richard Stanley Prescott, 2nd Bt**; *b* 26 Jan 1899; artist, civil engr, WW I with 5th Bn Beds Regt, WW II with RCAF (invalided); *d* unm 21 Jan 1965

2 (William Robert) Stanley; *b* 25 April 1912; *educ* Boardman's and St John's Coll Cambridge (BA 1934); barrister Gray's Inn 1935, MP Darwen (Lancs) 1943–51, Freeman City London, memb Court Common Cncl 1945–50, Hon Capt Roy Signals (TA), served WW II (invalided 1943), V-Pres Nat Chamber Trade; *m* 1st 29 Sept 1939 (*divorce* 1951) Gwendolen (*m* 2nd Daniel Orme (*d* 1972) and *d* 1992), only child of Leonard Aldridge, CBE, of S Kensington, and had:

(1) Sir MARK PRESCOTT, **3rd and present Bt**

2 (cont.) Stanley Prescott *m* 2nd 22 June 1951 Sheila Kathleen Walker, er dau of Surgn R-Adml David Walker Hewitt, CB, CMG, MB, BCh, FRCS, of Alverstoke, Hants, and *d* 6 June 1962

1 *Bernice Louise, MBE (1978) [Mrs Reginald Gray MBE, 24 St Katherine's Mews, Totnes, Devon]; *b* 1903; Mayor Godmanchester 1937–39; *m* 6 July 1928 *Reginald Edgar Gray and has:

(1) *David Stanley; *b* 1931

2 Grace Geraldine, JP; barrister Gray's Inn 1930, Mayor Godmanchester 1932

PRESTON

Arms: Erm. on a chief sa. three crescents or. **Crest:** A crescent or.
Motto: *Lucem spero clariorem* ('I hope for a brighter light').
Creation: Bt. (UK) 30 May 1815.

SIR RONALD DOUGLAS HILDEBRAND PRESTON, 7TH BT, of Beeston St Lawrence, Norfolk [Sir Ronald Preston Bt, 68 Saxmundham Rd, Aldeburgh, Suffolk IP15 5PA]; *b* 9 Oct 1916; *s* f 1976; *educ* Westminster, Trin Coll Cambridge (MA Hons) and Ecole des Sciences Politiques Paris; Maj Intell Corps WW II, correspondent: Reuter's Belgrade 1948–53, *The Times* Vienna 1953–60, Tokyo 1960–63, Dip Serv 1963–76; *m* 1st 12 Jan 1954 (*divorce* 1971) Smilya, dau of Mihailo Stefanovic, advocate, of Belgrade, Yugoslavia; *m* 2nd 1972 *Pauleen Jane, dau of Paul Lurcott, of Albany Cottage, Fairwarp, Sussex

Lineage: HENRY HULTON, of Andover, Hants; 1st Commr Customs Boston, Mass.; *m* 20 Sept 1766 Elizabeth (*d* 15 April 1805), est dau of Isaac Preston, of Beeston St Lawrence, and *d* Feb 1790, leaving, with two other sons:

1 THOMAS (Sir), **1st Bt**

2 Henry, barrister Lincoln's Inn, Recorder King's Lynn; *b* 18 May 1769; *m* 28 May 1797 Sophia (*d* 14 Jan 1840), dau of Rev Whitley Heald, and *d* 3 May 1820, leaving:

3 Edward; *b* Oct 1771; DD, Rector Gaywood; *m* 10 Dec 1801 Pleasance (*d* 11 Feb 1830), dau of Thomas Bagge (*see* BAGGE, Bt), and *d* 15 Feb 1817, leaving issue

The est son,
Sir THOMAS HULTON later PRESTON, **1st Bt** (UK), so *cr* 30 May 1815; *b* 29 Aug 1767; *m* 1st 26 Nov 1792 Elizabeth (*dsp*), dau of George Adams, of Lichfield; *m* 2nd 21 March 1799 his yr bro's future sis-in-law Jane (*d* 22 Aug 1846), yst dau of Thomas Bagge, and by her had, with five other daus (*d* unm):

1 JACOB HENRY (Sir), **2nd Bt**

2 Thomas Edward, MA; *b* 17 Nov 1816; *m* 7 Aug 1845 Caroline (*d* 8 Feb 1857), 2nd dau of William Willoughby Prescott, of Hendon, and *d* 23 Feb 1890, leaving, with two other sons and two daus (all *d* unm):

(1) Henry Edward; *b* 15 May 1847; Lt-Col RA; *m* 22 Jan 1878 Mary Row (*d* 28 Feb 1928), widow of Lt Robert Turing Bruce, RA, and dau of William Henry Mare, and *d* 7 Aug 1905, having had:

1a Philip Henry Hulton; *b* 30 Dec 1879; *educ* Cheltenham; Lt-Col RA WW I (despatches); *m* 23 Feb 1914 Dorothy May, only dau of Brig-Gen Herbert Alexander Kaye Jennings, CIE, RA, and *d* 1963, leaving:

1b Philip Henry Herbert Hulton, OBE (1945); *b* 11 Dec 1914; *educ* Wellington; Lt-Col S Lancs Regt, formerly 2nd KEO, Gurkha Rifles, IA, WW II (despatches); *m* 1st 9 Nov 1940 Katherine Janet (*d* 14 Nov 1968), 2nd dau of Dr Benjamin Charles Broomhall, of Little Mount, Redlynch, Salisbury, and *d* 1973, leaving:

1c +PHILIP CHARLES [Philip Preston Esq, 3 Place Gilbert Gaffet, Crécy-en-Ponthieu, 80150 Somme, France]; *b* 31 Aug 1946; heir presumptive; *educ* Nautical Coll Pangbourne; *m* 1980 *Kirsi Sylvi Annikki, dau of Eino Yrjö Pullinen, of Finland, and has:

1d +Philip Thomas Henry Hulton; *b* 1990

1d *Katherine Louise Tuula; *b* 1982

2d *Emily Jean Charlotte; *b* 1985

1c *Caroline Elizabeth [Mrs Paul de la Praudiere, 128 Palewell Park, London SW14 8JH]; *b* 24 Jan 1943; *m* 1974 *Paul Louis Edelin de la Praudiere and has:

1d *Philip Louis; *b* 1975

2d *William Francis Paul; *b* 1977

1b (cont.) Lt-Col Philip Preston *m* 2nd 19– *Jean Mary, dau of Harold Neale Turner

1b *Marjorie [Mrs Miles Cheales, Willow Cottage, Broad St, Guildford, Surrey]; *b* 1917; *m* 4 Nov 1939 *Miles Pacey Cheales, yr s of Alan Edgar Cheales, of Ingleborough, Lincs, and has:

1c *Justina Victoria; *b* 1945

2c *Briony Margaret; *b* 1948

3c *Mary Henrietta Miles; *b* 1951; *m* 1971 *Philip Alastair Barter and has:

1d *Oliver Philip Tom; *b* 1975

2d *Alexander John; *b* 1975

4c *Alexandra Marjorie; *b* 1952; *m* 1976 *Charles Thornton Hardy

1a Mary Louisa; *b* 16 Oct 1878; *m* 25 Aug 1910 Lt-Col Rowley Richard Hill, DSO, RA (*d* 20 Jan 1955), yst s of Col F C Hill, Essex Regt, and *d* 23 Jan 1947, having had issue

2a Edith Caroline; *b* 6 March 1881; *m* 14 Jan 1925 Harry Wakefield Story (*d* Jan 1947), of Oakwood, Burwash Common, Sussex, 2nd s of Col Philip Story, Scottish Rifles, and *d* 11 April 1933

3a Constance Ester Sophia; *b* 13 Nov 1882; *m* 21 Nov 1911 Capt William Gabbett Ashton Shuttleworth, RN (*d* 19 May 1968), yst s of Col Ashton John Shuttleworth, RA, of Hathersage Hall, Derbys, and *d* 6 Sept 1953, leaving issue

4a Dorothy; *b* 11 April 1886; *d* unm 30 Jan 1958

(2) Francis William; *b* 30 Aug 1851; barrister; *m* 14 Jan 1892 Georgina Charlotte (*d* 31 Oct 1936), dau of James Fellowes (*see* DE RAMSEY, B), and *d* 7 Nov 1898, leaving:

1a Violet Gertrude Alice; *b* 27 June 1894; *m* 19 April 1922 Capt Geoffrey Meredyth Keble-White, RN (*d* 2 June 1961), s of Arthur Keble-White, of Chevington, Suffolk, and *d* 23 Jan 1963, leaving issue

(3) Frederick George; *b* 18 Nov 1855; Lt-Col IA; *m* 14 April 1879 Marie Louise (*d* 4 Feb 1915), dau of Louis Mamo, of Malta, and *d* 20 Sept 1927, having had, with two sons (*d* young):

1a Alice Maud; *b* 11 Jan 1880; *d* unm June 1961

2a Ethel Frances; *b* 21 July 1882; *m* 21 July 1925 Edwin William Bool, only s of E Walter Bool, of Croydon

1 Eliza; *m* 9 Dec 1834 William Webber, s of Joseph Webber, of Freston, Suffolk, and *d* 16 June 1884, leaving issue

2 Pleasance; *m* 31 July 1828 Rev J Burroughes (*d* 19 May 1872), of Lingwood Lodge, Norfolk, and *d* 4 Jan 1870

3 Frances; *m* 11 July 1833 her cousin Sir William Bagge, 1st Bt, MP (*qv*), and *d* 27 May 1887, leaving issue

4 Emilia; *m* 13 Feb 1848 Rev Vincent Edward Eyre (*d* 27 Aug 1855), Rector Cranwich, Norfolk

5 Octavia Thomazine; *m* 29 Nov 1838 Rev Edward Eyre (*d* 1863), Rector Larling, Norfolk, and *d* 8 Jan 1904, leaving issue

Sir THOMAS *d* 21 April 1823; his est son,

Sir Jacob Henry Preston, 2nd Bt, DL Norfolk; *b* 25 Jan 1812; High Sheriff Norfolk 1847; *m* 4 Nov 1846 Amelia (*d* 2 July 1872), dau of William Willoughby Prescott, of Hendon, and *d* 19 Oct 1891, having had, with four daus (*d* unm):

1 **Sir Henry Jacob Preston, 3rd Bt**, JP; *b* 15 Sept 1851; Capt E Div RA; *m* 16 Dec 1885 Mary Hope (*d* 23 Jan 1925), dau of Edmund Lewis Clutterbuck, of Hardenhuish Park, Wilts, and *d* 9 Jan 1897, having had:

(1) **Sir Jacob Preston, 4th Bt**; *b* 6 May 1887; *educ* Trin Coll Cambridge (BA, LLB); *d* unm 12 Feb 1918

(2) **Sir Edward Hulton Preston, 5th Bt**, DSO (1918), MC, JP (Norfolk 1920), DL (1950); *b* 17 Sept 1888; *educ* Charterhouse; Capt and Brevet-Maj Roy Sussex Regt, AA and QMG and T/Lt-Col 1918 WW I, CC Norfolk, High Sheriff 1956; *m* Sept 1920 Margaret, est dau of Benjamin Bond-Cabbell, JP, DL, of Cromer Hall, Norfolk, and *d* 7 Dec 1963, leaving:

1a *Juliet Mary [The Hon Mrs Richard Manners, Cromer Hall, Norfolk]; *b* 10 Nov 1921; *m* 14 July 1945 *Hon Richard Neville Manners, 2nd son of 4th Baron Manners (*qv*), and has issue

2a *Patricia Evelyn [Mrs John Todhunter, Home Farm House, Cromer, Norfolk NR27 9JG]; *b* 25 Feb 1923; *m* 14 March 1962 John Louis Benedict Todhunter, CMG, OBE (*d* 1980), s of Col Herbert William Todhunter, CMG, KOSB

(3) Thomas Frederick; *b* 1889; Lt Norfolk Yeo and FFC; *ka* 24 Jan 1917

(1) Netty Louisa; *b* 14 Nov, *d* 13 Dec 1892

(2) Hope Amy Constance; *b* 27 May 1894; *m* 26 Nov 1918 René Hugo Esencourt (*d* 9 June 1958) and *d* 12 June 1956, leaving issue

2 William Thomas; *b* 19 Jan 1858; Lt Gordon Highrs; *m* 23 Jan 1879 Alice Mary (*d* 3 Aug 1947 aged 90), 2nd dau of Capt Frederick Hildebrand Stevens, RN, and *d* 29 Dec 1903, leaving, with a dau (*d* unm):

(1) THOMAS HILDEBRAND (Sir), **6th Bt**

(1) Gertrude Frances Crofts; *m* 9 Dec 1909 Bertie Bowman Barton (*ka* 30 Nov 1917), of the Inner Temple, s of Bowman Barton, of Botcherby Grange, Cumberland

(2) Violet Madge; *m* 12 April 1928 Capt Cyril Gascoigne Lloyd (*d* 13 Jan 1965), E R Yorks Yeo, s of Maj Henry John Greame Lloyd, DCLI, and had issue

3 George Edward, of Keys Hill, Wroxham, JP Norfolk; *b* 12 June 1861; *d* unm 30 Jan 1909

1 Frances Amelia; *m* 17 April 1884 Frederick Scott Hohler, JP (*d* 18 Jan 1920), s of Henry Booth Hohler, DL, of Fawkham Manor, Kent, and *d* 24 May 1920, leaving issue

The 5th Bt's cousin,

Sir Thomas Hildebrand Preston, 6th Bt, OBE (1934); *b* 2 June 1886; *educ* Westminster and Trin Hall Cambridge; Chargé d'Affaires Lithuania 1930–40, Min Lithuania 1940–41, Counsellor Embassy Cairo 1941–48, author: *Before the Curtain*; *m* 3 Oct 1913 Ella Henrietta (*d* 1989), dau of Friedrich von Shickandantz, and *d* 1976, leaving:

1 Sir RONALD DOUGLAS HILDEBRAND PRESTON, **7th and present Bt**

1 *Tatiana Stella Gertrude [Mrs Eugene Hartzell, Pfarrhofgasse 13/21, Vienna 111, Austria]; *b* Vladivostok 13 July 1920; formerly leading soprano of D'Oyly Carte Opera Co; *m* 12 May 1962 *(Ralph) Eugene Hartzell, MusM Yale, er s of Prof R E Hartzell, of Kent, Ohio, and has:

(1) *Eugenie Belinda Tamara; *b* 20 Feb 1963

(2) *Melanie-Anne Sonya; *b* 24 Aug 1964

PREVOST

Arms: Azure a dexter arm in fess issuing from a cloud in the sinister fess point, the hand grasping a sword, erect proper, pommel and hilt or, in chief two mullets argent. **Crest:** A demi-lion rampant azure, charged on the shoulder with a mural crown or, the sinister paw grasping a sword erect, as in the arms. **Supporters:** Two grenadiers of the 16th (or Bedfordshire) Regt of Infantry, each supporting with the exterior hand a flag flying gules, that on the dexter flowing towards the sinister, inscribed 'West Indies', that on the sinister flowing towards the dexter, inscribed 'Canada'. **Motto:** *Servatum cineri* ('Kept for the dead'). (The Supporters and Motto were granted Oct 1816 to the 2nd Bt by royal warrant. An older motto (*J'ai bien servi* ('I have served well')) is used by the rest of the family.) **Creation:** Bt. (UK) 6 Dec 1805.

SIR CHRISTOPHER GERALD PREVOST, 6TH BT, of Belmont, Hampshire [Sir Christopher Prevost Bt, 1 Crispian Close, London NW10]; *b* 25 July 1935; *s* f 1985; *educ* Cranleigh Sch; late 60th Regt, Kenya Serv Medal 1955; *m* 6 Jan 1964 *Dolores Nelly, only dau of Dezo Hoffmann, of Neasden, and has:

1 +NICHOLAS MARC; *b* 13 March 1971

1 *Ruth Annette [Mrs Steven Wrench, 61 Walton Rd, Clacton-on-Sea, Essex CO15 6EB]; *b* 11 June 1964; *m* 1986 *Steven Walter Wrench and has:

(1) *Laura Annette; *b* 1988

Lineage: AYME PREVOST, of Bossy, Gex, France; presumably a Huguenot (of a family allegedly originating in Poitou); moved to Geneva 1572; had:

PIERRE JEAN LOUIS PREVOST; *b c* 1550; citizen of Geneva 1578; *d* 1617, leaving:

MARC PREVOST; *b* 1589; *d* 1648, leaving, with numerous other issue, including a yr s (Jacques, ancestor of Sir Augustus Prevost, Bt; *see* 1913 edn):

JEAN LOUIS PREVOST; *b* 1617; *d* 1707, having had:

JEAN LOUIS PREVOST; *b* 1659; *dvp* 1702, leaving:

AUGUSTIN PREVOST, of Geneva; *b* 14 June 1695; *m* Louise (*d* 1743), dau of Gideon Martine, 1st Syndic (Mayor) Geneva, and *d* 24 Jan 1740, leaving, with five daus:

  1 Jean Louis; *d* young

  2 AUGUSTIN(E)

  3 Jacques PREVOST later MACKAY (roy licence 1 Sept 1775); *b* Dec 1736; Lt-Gen Br Forces, Col 60th Regt; *m* March 1751 Anne Louisa, dau and heiress of Hugh Mackay of Scowrey, and had issue; their descendants settled in Holland

  4 Jacques Marc; Lt-Col 60th Rifles Siege of Savannah, Ga., 1779 in War of American Independence; *m* Theodosia (*m* 2nd 1782 Aaron Burr, V-Pres USA, and *d* 1794, leaving further issue), dau of Theodosius Bartow, of Shrewsbury, NJ, and *d* 1779, having had issue

The 2nd son,

AUGUSTINE PREVOST; settled in England; served Earl of Albermarle's Regt of Horse Gds and 60th Royal America Regt at Battles of Fontenoy 1745 and Quebec 1759, Gen cmdg Br forces in beating off the French at Siege of Savannah 1779; bought the Greenhill Grove estate, Herts; *b* 22 Aug 1723; *m* 29 Aug 1765 Anne Margaret (*d* 17 Oct 1809), dau of the Chevalier George Grand, of Amsterdam, and *d* 4 May 1786, leaving, with another dau (*d* young):

  1 GEORGE (Sir), **1st Bt**

  2 James; *b* 29 Dec 1771; Adml; *m* 1st 1 Jan 1799 Frances Sophia (*d* 1 Feb 1813), dau of Rev Francis Haultain, of Weybridge, Surrey, and had issue; *m* 2nd 22 Feb 1814 Mary d'Yranda (*d* 28 Aug 1831), dau of Lewis de Teissier, of Woodcote Park, Surrey, and *d* 25 Oct 1855, leaving further issue

  3 William Augustus, CB; *b* 9 Aug 1777; Maj-Gen The Buffs and 67th Regt; gold medal for gallantry Anglo-Spanish defeat of French at Barossa 1811 in Peninsular War; *m* Henrietta, dau of Charles Hamilton, of Hamwood, and *dsp* 8 Aug 1824

  1 Anne; *m* E Hyde Clarke, of Swanswick

The est son,

Sir George Prevost, 1st Bt (UK), so *cr* 6 Dec 1805; *b* 19 May 1767; Col 16th Regt, Govr-Gen and Cdr forces Br N America; Lt-Gen 60th Regt; *m* 19 May 1789 Catherine Anne, dau of Maj-Gen — Phipps, RE, by Jane, sister of Lt-Gen Sir John Macleod, GCH, and *d* 5 Jan 1816, having had, with two daus (*d* unm):

Ven Sir George Prevost, 2nd Bt; *b* 20 Aug 1804; MA, Canon Gloucester, Vicar Stinchcombe, Glos; Archdeacon Gloucester 1865–81; *m* 18 March 1828 Jane (*d* 17 Jan 1853), only dau of Isaac Lloyd Williams, of Lincoln's Inn, and Cymcynfelin, Cards, and *d* 18 March 1893, having had, with a dau (*d* unm):

  1 George Phipps; *b* 10 Nov 1830; Lt-Col 23rd Roy Welch Fus, AAQMG Home Dist, served Crimea (wounded), medal and clasp and Turkish medal, Relief Lucknow (wounded, medal and clasp); *m* 26 April 1862 Charlotte Arabella (*d* 8 Oct 1910), est dau of Sir Charles Henry John Anderson, 9th Bt, and *dsp* & *vp* 27 March 1885

  2 **Sir Charles Prevost, 3rd Bt**, JP Glos; *b* 15 Dec 1831; Lt-Col 31st Regt, served Crimea (wounded, medal and clasp and Turkish medal); *m* 22 Jan 1856 Sarah Margaret (*d* 18 Sept 1919), 2nd dau of Rev Thomas Keble, Vicar Bisley, Glos, and *d* 24 Nov 1902, having had, with two other daus (*d* young):

    (1) CHARLES THOMAS KEBLE (Sir), **4th Bt**

    (2) George Herbert; *b* 12 April 1868; Lt-Col IA, formerly 60th Rifles, Manipur Expdn 1891 (medal and clasp), WW I (despatches, two medals and star), CD WW II; *m* 21 Dec 1901 Katharine Alice (*d* 31 Jan 1911), dau of William Rickards Glennie, of Chilbolton, Hants, and *d* 3 March 1951, leaving:

      1a Katharine Alice Glennie; *b* 4 March 1905; *m* 17 Sept 1929 Rev Hugh Gethin Hanmer Griffith (*d* 14 Oct 1966), 4th s of Rev Gethin Williams Griffith, and had:

        1b *Glyn Kebie Gethin (Rev) [The Rev Glyn Griffith, 71 Livingstone Rd, Derby]; *b* 15 Feb 1937; *educ* St John's Sch Leatherhead and St David's Coll Lampeter (BA); ordained 1969; *m* 3 July 1969 *Hermanna Gerada, yst dau of Carel Limburg, of Baarn, Holland

        1b Nesta Katharine; *b* 21 May 1931; *d* unm 8 April 1962

        2b *Barbara Ann; *b* 26 July 1933; *educ* Bristol U (BA); ALA

      2a Annette Dora; *b* 29 Jan 1911

      3a *Constance Charlotte [Miss Constance Prevost, 14 Lancaster Ave, Farnham, Surrey]; *b* 29 Jan 1911 (twin)

    (1) Elizabeth Jane; *d* unm 14 Feb 1927

    (2) Constance Margaret; *d* unm 7 May 1957 aged 98

    (3) Mary Eleanor; *d* unm 18 June 1942

    (4) Dora Katherine, Deaconess; *d* unm 10 April 1956 aged 94

    (5) Lucy Harriet; *d* unm 18 Sept 1957 aged 88

    (6) Alice Maud; *d* unm 6 April 1944

Sir CHARLES's er son,

Sir Charles Thomas Keble Prevost, 4th Bt, JP Glos; *b* 19 July 1866; *educ* Keble Coll Oxford (BA); *m* 6 Feb 1907 Beatrice Mary, only dau of Rev James Atkinson Burrow, of Tunstall, Kirkby Lonsdale, and had:

  1 Sir GEORGE JAMES AUGUSTINE (Sir), **5th Bt**

  1 Margaret Elizabeth; *b* 15 Jan 1908; *m* 30 Aug 1939 John Reginald Wood, s of John Wood, of The Gables, Gresford, nr Wrexham, and had issue

Sir CHARLES *d* 6 April 1939; his only son,

Sir George James Augustine Prevost, 5th Bt; *b* 16 Jan 1910; *educ* Repton; Staff Capt HQ N Command India and Duke of Wellington's Regt WW II; *m* 1st 1935 Muriel Emily (*d* 12 July 1939), dau of Lewis William Oram, of Kensington, and had:

  1 Sir CHRISTOPHER GERALD PREVOST, **6th and present Bt**

  1 *Felicity Jane [Mrs Hisham Pilus, 192 Jalan Terasek, Bangsar, Kuala Lumpur 59100, Malaysia]; *b* 10 Dec 1936; *m* 1970 *Hisham Pilus and has:

    (1) *Muhammad Yusuf; *b* 1977

    (1) *Sofia Jane; *b* 1972

    (2) *Sarah Louise; *b* 1974

Sir George *m* 2nd March 1940 (*divorce* 1940) Phyllis Mary Catherine Mattock; *m* 3rd 1952 *Patricia Betty [Patricia Lady Prevost, 45 Carneton Close, Quantock, Newquay, Cornwall], dau of William Porter, of Kilburn, and *d* 1985, having by her had:

  2 +James William; *b* 1952; *educ* Aldenham

  3 +Edward Charles; *b* 1953; *educ* Aldenham

PRICE

ARR · DWRR · Y · GYD

Arms: Sable a chevron erminois between three spear's heads argent, embrued at the points proper. **Crest:** A dragon's head vert, erased gules, holding in the mouth a sinister hand erect, couped at the wrist, dropping blood, all proper. **Motto:** *Arr dwrr y Gyd* ('All depends on God'). **Creation:** Bt. (UK) 30 May 1815.

SIR FRANCIS CARADOC ROSE PRICE, 7TH BT, of Trengwainton, Cornwall, QC (1991) [Sir Francis Price Bt QC, 9626–95 Ave, Edmonton, Alberta, Canada T6C 2A4]; *b* 9 Sept 1950; *s* f 1979; *educ* Eton, Melbourne U (LLB) and Alberta U (LLM); *m* 1975 *(Hon Madam Justice) Marguerite Jean, dau of Roy Samuel Trussler, of Victoria, BC, and has:

  1 *Adrienne Calantha Rose; *b* 26 July 1976

  2 *Megan Kathleen Rose; *b* 29 Sept 1977

  3 *Glynis Nicola Rose; *b* 3 Jan 1982

Lineage: FRANCIS ROSE, of Wales; Army Capt at capture Jamaica 1655, subsequently settling there; *m* Elizabeth Booth, widow of Col William Rose, and had, with other issue, including a dau (Elizabeth, *m* Francis Rose, of Rose Hall, Jamaica):

CHARLES PRICE, of Worthy Park; Col; adoptive heir of his maternal halfbrother, Thomas (s of the above-mentioned Col William Rose), inherited Rose Hall, St Thomas's-in-the-Vale and other Jamaican estates; *m* Sarah, dau of Philip Edmunds, of Jamaica, and *d* 20 May 1730, leaving:

  1 Sir CHARLES ROSE, 1st Bt (GB), so *cr* 13 Aug 1768, of Rose Hall, Jamaica; called 'The Patriot' for his public benefactions; memb Jamaican House of Assembly 1732–63, Speaker 1746–63; *b* 20 Aug 1708; *m c* 1733 Mary Sharpe and *d* 26 July 1772, leaving:

    (1) Sir CHARLES ROSE, 2nd and last Bt; memb Jamaican House of Assembly 1753–75, Speaker 1763–75; *m* Elizabeth Hanmer (*d* 1771), widow of John Woodcock and dau of John Hudson Guy, formerly of Donnington Castle, Newbury, Ch Justice Jamaica, and *dsp* 18 Oct 1788, when the btcy expired

  2 Thomas; *m* Anne Moor, but *dsp*

  3 John; *m* 1736 Margaret, 2nd dau of John Badcock by Perthesia, dau of John Keigwin, of Penzance, and *d* 4 Feb 1739, leaving:

    (1) John, of Worthy Park; *b* 25 June 1738; *m* 1764 Elizabeth Williams, dau of John Brammer, of St John's, Jamaica, and *d* Jan 1797, leaving, with other issue:

      1a ROSE, (Sir), **1st Bt**

JOHN PRICE's only surv son,

Sir Rose Price, 1st Bt (UK), so *cr* 30 May 1815; *b* 21 Nov 1768; *educ* Harrow; *m* 1795 Elizabeth (*d* 2 Dec 1826), yst dau of Charles Lambart (*see* 1970 edn LAMBART, Bt, of Beau Parc), and *d* 24 Sept 1834, having had, with four other daus (*d* unm):

  1 Rose Lambart; *b* 4 July 1799; *educ* Eton; *m* 26 Jan 1824 Catherine (*d* 13 Feb 1874), widow of 2nd Earl of Desart and dau of Maurice N O'Connor, of Mount Pleasant, King's Co, and *dvp* 15 Jan 1826, leaving:

    (1) Maria; *m* 16 May 1843 John La Touche, DL (*d* 17 Sept 1904), of Harristown, Co Kildare, and *d* 21 Nov 1906, leaving issue

  2 Sir Charles Dutton Price, 2nd Bt; *b* 7 Dec 1800; *d* unm 18 May 1872

  3 Francis; *b* 11 March 1804; *educ* Eton; Capt 19th Foot and 78th Highrs; *m* 1st 16 June 1835 Catherine Henrietta (*d* 20 May 1839), 3rd dau of Henry Hewitt, of Cork, and had:

    (1) ROSE LAMBART (Sir), **3rd Bt**

    (2) Henry Talbot; *b* 20 March 1839; Capt RN, Govr Liverpool Prison, served China War 1857 (medal with two clasps); *m* 22 Oct 1870 Elizabeth Charlotte (*d* 20 July 1915), 2nd dau of Charles Hewitt, MD, and *d* 25 March 1915, having had:

1a Francis Henry Talbot; *b* 28 May 1872; Capt 6th Bn DCLI, served Matabele campaign 1895–96 and WW I; *m* 11 April 1899 Florence May (*d* 21 July 1970), only dau of Frederick Hurdle, of Amersham Hill Lodge, High Wycombe, and *d* 1 May 1930, leaving:

  1b Leslie Frederick Talbot; *b* 25 Sept 1903; F/O RAF; *m* 27 Sept 1924 (*divorce* 1953) Hon Diana Frederica Gifford (*d* 1979), sis of 5th Baron Gifford (*qv*), and *d* 1972, leaving:

    1c +Maurice Rose Talbot [Maurice Talbot Price Esq, 32 Clearview St, Bowral, NSW, Australia]; *b* 12 June 1929; *m* 13 June 1959 *Elaine, only dau of C J Burford, of Kuala Lumpur and Sydney, NSW, and has:

      1d +Martin Paul; *b* 8 Nov 1961

      2d +Michael John; *b* 19 Oct 1964

    2c +Michael Henry Charles [Michael Talbot Price, 558 Greenhill Rd, Burnside, S Aust, Australia]; *b* 12 April 1932; *m* 10 March 1962 *Lyndsay June, dau of C L Messner, of Harpenden, Herts, and has:

      1d +Nicholas Frederick; *b* 26 March 1964; *m* 15 Aug 1992 *Caroline Anne, dau of Keith Platts of Harpenden, Herts, and has:

        1e *Charlotte Anne; *b* 30 April 1994

        2e *Isabelle Caroline; *b* 19 Aug 1997

      2d +David Aldrich; *b* 7 July 1966

    1c *Pamela; *b* 26 Sept 1925; *m* 23 Sept 1944 John William Reid, DFC, only s of G G H Reid, of Grassington, Rotherham, NZ, and has:

      1d *Martin James; *b* 30 Dec 1945; *m* 1970 *Elizabeth, dau of H H Harvey Renwick, of Marlborough, NZ, and has:

        1e *Timothy Edward; *b* 1974

        2e *David Charles; *b* 1976

        3e *Nicholas Martin; *b* 1977

      2d *William John; *b* 15 Aug 1951; *m* 19– *Robyn, dau of L McNeill, of Nelson and has:

        1e *Toby John; *b* 1984

        1e *Amelia Jane; *b* 1986

      1d *Julia; *b* 30 Aug 1948; *m* 1978 *Philip de Weck

      2d *Diana; *b* 5 Oct 1949; *m* 1972 *Peter Vernon Arnott Anderson and has:

        1e *George Peter; *b* 1979

        1e *Caroline; *b* 1977

      3d *Isabella Patricia; *b* 1957; *m* 1983 (*divorce* 1996) Gerrit Vlaming

  1b *Olive May Talbot; *b* 7 May 1900; *m* 3 March 1924 Count St John Vivian Beaumont de Beaufort Molyneux (*d* 1962), HRE *cr* 1710, s of Edward Elcock Molyneux, LLD, barrister

2a Lewis; *b* 21 Aug 1874; *d* unm 11 April 1909

3a Ralph Moreton Aldworth; *b* 28 April 1878; *d* unm 1911

4a Rose Percy Caradoc; *b* 21 Dec 1883; Capt RIN, Naval Adviser to Govt of Burma, Yr Bro Trin House, served off Somali Coast 1908–09, Persian Gulf 1911 and WW I (despatches); *m* 1st 5 Nov 1914 Ann Nicol (*d* 22 Sept 1930), er dau of William C Aikman, of Liverpool; *m* 2nd 24 Sept 1948 *Helen Mary, dau of Richard Bosustow, of Manor Farm, Ruan Major, Cornwall, and *d* 28 Dec 1959

5a Arthur Vreichvras Rose; *b* 18 Dec 1885; *d* unm 4 Dec 1944

1a Rose Lizzie; *b* 12 July 1873; *m* 3 Sept 1898 Sidney Reginald Dyer (*d* 14 March 1934), JP, MD, MRCS, barrister Middle Temple, Commr Prisons, s of Joseph Dyer, of Chiswick, and *d* 26 Dec 1969, having had issue

2a Gertrude Louisa; *m* 5 Dec 1911 Thomas Graham Hungerford, RMLI, only s of Col Hungerford, RMLI, and *d* 1 March 1924

3a Kathleen; *m* 9 July 1902 Joseph Mason (*d* 5 Nov 1935), of Thorleby House, Skipton in Craven, Yorks, and *d* 1941, leaving issue

4a Sybille Dorothy; *m* 11 Jan 1919 Brig Sidney Arthur Hodder Hungerford, MC, IA (*d* 5 May 1959), s of George Bentinck Hungerford, of Co Cork

3 (cont.) Capt Francis Price *m* 2nd 1859 Mary, widow of John Cozens, and *d* 14 Sept 1863

4 John; *b* 21 Oct 1808; Ch Magistrate Hobart, Van Diemens Land, 1838–46, Civil Govr Norfolk Island 1846–54, Inspr-Gen Penal Establishments Australia 1854–57; *m* 12 June 1838 May (*d* 2 Oct 1894 aged 80), est dau of Maj James Franklin and n of R-Adml Sir John Franklin, explorer and Govr Van Diemen's Land, and *d* 27 March 1857, having had:

  (1) John Frederick (Sir), KCSI; *b* 3 Oct 1839; Madras CS 1862–97; *m* 28 April 1863 Alice (*d* 29 Aug 1931), yr dau of Hon H D Phillips, Madras CS, Memb Cncl, and *d* 12 June 1927, having had:

    1a Frederick William Clarence; *b* 24 May 1865; *d* unm 12 Dec 1915

    2a George Dominic, CMG (1918); *b* 10 Nov 1867; Col W Yorks Regt, Hon Brig-Gen 1924, served W Coast Africa 1893–94 and WW I (despatches, brevet), Legn Hon, Orders White Eagle Serbia 3rd Cl, St Stanislas 1st Cl, St Vladimir Russia 2nd Cl; *m* 7 Dec 1918 Alice Frances (*d* 27 Feb 1930), widow of V-Adml F C B Robinson and dau of Col Cyril Blackburne Tew, 15th Regt, and *d* as a result of enemy action 27 Feb 1943

    3a Thomas Herbert Francis, CMG (1918), DSO (1917); *b* 29 June 1869; Col 1st Bn DCLI, Hon Brig-Gen 1921, Tirah campaign, Boer War and WW I (despatches six times); *m* 14 Jan 1919 Lurline May (*d* 19 Aug 1959), widow of Maj John Arthur Higgon, Royal Welch Fus, of Scolton, Pembs, and dau of Hon Henry Moses, MLC, of Sydney, NSW, and *dsp* 14 Feb 1945

    1a Charlotte Mary Emily; *m* 1885 Maj Frederic Philip Smyly, S Wales Borderers, 2nd s of Philip Smyly, of Drayton Lodge, Monkstown, Dublin

    2a Harriet Alice Franklin; *m* 1892 Maj L McClintock, RHA, and *d* 16 Aug 1963, leaving issue

    3a Lindley Winifred Ruby; *m* 1893 Henry Percival Hodgson and had issue

  (2) James Franklin, RIN; *b* 20 March 1841; *d* 27 July 1878

  (3) Thomas Caradoc Rose, CB; *b* 21 Oct 1841; Lt-Col 103rd (later Roy Dublin Fus) and Madras SC, served Boer War 1899–1900, Comdt Cwlth Forces Victoria April 1902 and Qld July 1902–03; *m* 1st 5 Aug 1874 Mary Dennistoun (*d* 22 March 1899), est dau of Thomas Baillie (*see* BAILLIE, Bt), and had, with another s (*d* an infant):

1a Thomas Rose Caradoc, CMG (1919), DSO (1917); *b* 2 Aug 1875; *educ* Melbourne and RMC Sandhurst; psc, Hon Brig-Gen 1931 Probyn's Horse and cmdg Welsh Gds, served NW Frontier 1897–98, Seistan Boundary Commn 1903, Tibet 1904, WW I (despatches four times, Legn Hon, Brevet Lt-Col, GOC 11th Bde), cmded 142 Bde 1924–28, Cmdt Hythe Wing Small Arms Sch 1928–31, Brig cmdg N London sub-area 1939–41, CD WW II; *m* 29 Aug 1911 Dorothy Patience (*d* 11 Nov 1969), only dau of Sir Henry William Verey, JP, of Bridge House, Twyford, Berks, Official Referee Supreme Court, and *d* 20 Oct 1949, leaving:

  1b Robert Caradoc Rose, DSO (1943), OBE (1951); *b* 31 May 1912; *educ* Wellington and RMC Sandhurst; Lt-Col Welsh Gds WW II (despatches), High Sheriff Berks 1975; *m* 6 April 1946 *Hon Maureen Maude Tower Butler, 2nd dau of 17th/27th Baron Dunboyne (*qv*), and *d* 28 May 1988, leaving:

    1c +(Thomas Geoffrey) Timothy Rose [Timothy Rose Price Esq, The Wadfield, Winchcombe, Glos GL54 5AL]; *b* 16 Sept 1948; *educ* Eton; *m* 17 May 1975 *Leila Anne Katherine, only dau of Maj Sir Richard Guy Carne Rasch, 3rd Bt (*qv*), and has:

      1d +Dominic Charles; *b* 4 March 1978

      2d +Patrick David Caradoc; *b* 24 Jan 1980

      1d *Katherine Leila Sarah; *b* 6 April 1985

    1c *Sarah Maureen Rose [Mrs Michael Burrell, 6 St Peter's Sq, London, W6 9AB]; *b* 5 Jan 1947; *m* 7 Sept 1968 *Michael John Burrell, barrister, yr s of Roy Herbert Adams Burrell, OBE, of The Grange, Tadcaster, Yorks, and has:

      1d *James Michael; *b* 28 May 1976

      1d *Amanda Caroline; *b* 26 Aug 1971

      2d *Nicola Sarah; *b* 22 June 1973

  2b Dennistoun John Franklin Rose; *b* 23 June 1915; *educ* Radley and Worcester Coll Oxford; actor as Dennis Price; studied at Embassy Theatre Sch, stage debut *Behind Your Back*, Croydon Rep Theatre 1937, appeared with Noel Coward in *This Happy Breed* and *Present Laughter*, Arts Theatre, films: *Kind Hearts and Coronets, The Bad Lord Byron, Private's Progress, Caravan, The Millionairess, Bell, Book and Candle, Tunes of Glory*; *m* 29 June 1939 (*divorce* 1950) Joan Schofield, yr dau of Maj-Gen Arthur Cecil Temperley, CB, CMG, DSO, and *d* 1973, leaving:

    1c *Susan Joan Rose [Mrs Thomas Mapp, 85 Langham Rd, Teddington, Middx TW11 9HG]; *b* 7 July 1940; *m* 22 Sept 1967 *Thomas Henry Mapp, jnlst, UN Medal, Commendation Medal, US Army Korea 1952, s of Charles Harold Mapp, MBE, of Taverham, Norfolk, and has:

      1d *Joel Dennis; *b* 1979

      1d *Kate Miranda; *b* 1972

    2c *Tessa Alexandra Rose [Mrs Hugh Burnett, 36 Wilbury Villas, Hove, E Sussex BN3 6GD]; *b* 30 Oct 1943; *m* 16 Jan 1965 *Hugh Thomas Burnett, FCA, er s of Brian Noel Burnett, of Le Jonquet, Toulon, France, and has:

      1d *Rupert Thomas; *b* 1971

      1d *Lucy Eleanor; *b* 28 Feb 1966; *m* 1990 *Roger Bracken and has:

        1e *Sophie Madeleine; *b* 1992

        2e *Lily Matilda; *b* 6 Feb 1997

      2d *Emily Tamelayne; *b* 7 July 1968; *m* 23 July 1994 *Gavin McWhirter and has:

        1e *Felix George; *b* Sept 1997

  1b *Mary Dorothy Rose [Mrs John Wiseman, Hornbeam House, Waltham St Lawrence, Berks RG10 0JJ]; *b* 25 May 1918; *m* 4 Sept 1948 *John Dugdale Holt Wiseman, PhD, late Dep Keeper Mineralogy Natural History Museum, yst s of Robert Holt Wiseman, and has:

    1c *John Paul Holt [John Wiseman Esq, Coarsewell Farm, Ugborough, Devon]; *b* 16 Nov 1949; *educ* Shrewsbury; *m* 1989 *Jane Trant and has:

      1d *Catherine Jane; *b* 1990

      2d *Alice Mary; *b* 1995

2a Vivian Franklin Lyon Rose; *b* 4 May 1881; Lt-Cdr RN, Lt RIM, served Somaliland 1903 (medal), Persian Gulf 1909–14 (medal) and WW I; *m* 1912 Jean Purvis Mills (*d* 14 July 1939) and *das* 5 Nov 1915, leaving:

  1b *Vivian Judith Elizabeth Rose; *b* 15 Aug 1915; *m* 1937 Col George Francis Taylor, CBE (*d* 1979), s of George Arthur Taylor, of Melbourne, Australia, and has:

    1c *Jeremy Vivian George; *b* 1940; *m* 1967 *Sally, dau of John Parnell, and has:

      1d *Gemma Vivian; *b* 1971

    1c *Sarah Jane Elizabeth; *b* 1943; *m* 1968 *Thomas Peart, and has:

      1d *Rachel; *b* 1969

      2d *Scarlett; *b* 1971

    2c *Anna-Lisa; *b* 1949

3a Franklin Alexander Dennistoun Rose; *b* 16 May 1885; *m* 1st 1913 Isobel (*d* 1960), dau of — Donaldson, of Berwick on-Tweed, and had:

  1b Tom; *d* 1941

3a (cont.) Franklin Price *m* 2nd 1960 *Isabel Elsie Kuhn and *d* 13 Feb 1964

1a Lorna Mary Elizabeth Rose; *b* 2 Aug 1876; *m* 27 Nov 1901 Ainsle Mills (*d* 8 Aug 1908), of Uardry, Hay, NSW, and *d* Feb 1925, leaving issue

(3) (cont.) Col Thomas Rose *m* 2nd 30 April 1902 Emeline Shadforth (*d* 192–), est dau of Hon Robert Dyce Reid, of Kilbryde, Armadale, Melbourne, and *d* 3 July 1911

(1) Emily Mary

(2) Anna Clara; *m* 1866 Rev Rowland Hayward (*d* 1910), of Victoria

(3) Jane de Winton; *m* 1876 George Knox (*d* 1888), est s of Hon Edward Knox, of Fiona, Sydney, and *d* 4 Feb 1937, leaving issue

5 George, of Worthy Park, Jamaica; *b* 10 April 1812; *m* 1st 17 Oct 1839 Hon Emily Valentine Plunkett (*d* 20 Sept 1864), dau of 14th Baron Dunsany (*qv*), and had, with a dau (*d* unm):

(1) George Edward; *b* 1842; Cdr RN, MP Devonport 1874–92; *m* 6 Feb 1873 Gertrude Laurence (*d* 10 Aug 1939), adopted dau of Phoebe Locke (widow of Joseph Locke, MP), and *d* 29 June 1926, leaving:

  1a Gertrude Emily Rose; *m* 28 Nov 1899 V-Adml James Rose Price Hawksley, CB, CVO (*d* 7 April 1955), s of James Taylor Hawksley, of Caldy Island, Tenby, and *d* 2 Jan 1949

  2a Gwendolen Rose; *m* 23 Oct 1906 Rev Edward Septimus King (*d* 28 Nov 1925), Rector Glemham, Suffolk, s of Rev Richard Henry King, of Little Glemham Rectory, Suffolk, and *d* 19 June 1955, leaving issue

  3a Elma Rose; *b* 14 April 1886; *m* 29 Oct 1907 Henry Wolley Leigh-Bennett (*d* 17 June 1951), of Thorpe Place, Chertsey, and Donnington Grove, Newbury, and *d* 31 July 1969, having had issue

(1) Emily Julia; *m* 7 Oct 1869 James Taylor Hawksley (*d* 2 Aug 1891), only s of J Wilson Hawksley, of Caldy Island, and *d* 15 March 1906, leaving issue

(2) Charlotte Eliza; *m* 8 Jan 1879 Rev Reginald Henry Dyke Acland-Troyte (*see* ACLAND, Bt, of Columb St John) and *dsp* 24 July 1917

5 (cont.) George Price *m* 2nd 15 Jan 1874 Isabel Ellen Hills (*d* 1 May 1904), widow of Lt John James MacDonald, 71st Highrs, and dau of George Harrison, of Stanground Manor, Northants, and *d* 29 Sept 1890, having by her had:

(2) Cyril Oliver Rose, MBE (1920); *b* 10 April 1880; *m* 10 Sept 1910 Edith Muriel (*d* 1 Dec 1956), yr dau of Donald Campbell Ridout, of Toronto, and *d* 17 Dec 1961, leaving:

  1a +George Donald Rose [George Price Esq, 26 Utkinton Rd, Tarporley, Cheshire CW6 0HS]; *b* 2 Aug 1911; *educ* Emmanuel Coll Cambridge (sr scholar 1932, BA 1933, MA 1938); *m* 25 Oct 1947 *Dorothy Christine, dau of Maj Eric Fairclough, DSO, of The Cliff, Acton Bridge, Cheshire

6 Thomas; *b* 3 Nov 1817; 60th Rifles, Lt-Govr Dominica; *m* 26 May 1845 Anne (*d* Virgin Islands 1858), dau of F H Macnamara, 62nd Regt, and *d* 1865, leaving, with another s and dau (*d* unm):

(1) Arthur Henry, of Quinta Illapal, Valparaiso, Chile; *b* 11 Jan 1850; *m* 21 Aug 1872 Minna (*d* 8 Nov 1938), dau of Samuel Percy Oxley, of Valparaiso, and *d* 28 July 1916, leaving:

  1a Arthur Douglas; *b* 8 May 1873; *m* 1st 14 Feb 1901 (*divorce* 1922) Wilhelmine Marion (*d* 26 Oct 1955), dau of Robert Adolphe Claude, of Valparaiso, and had:

    1b Violet Marion Rose; *b* 15 Feb 1902; *m* 27 Feb 1926 Joaquín Santiago Andrés Munoz Arlegui (*d* 29 Nov 1939), s of Adml Joaquin Munoz Hurtado, Chilean Navy, of Valparaiso, and *d* 7 July 1969, leaving:

      1c *Joaquin Santiago Federico; *b* 4 Aug 1930; *m* 3 Dec 1964 *Maria Eugenia Bravo Aguirre and has:

        1d *Joaquin; *b* 20 Jan 1970

        1d *Caroline Vivian Rose; *b* 10 Oct 1965

      1c *Veronica Marion; *b* 11 June 1927; *m* 1st 10 March 1951 Alexander Edmund Gough Gubbins Browne (*d* 1 Oct 1952) and has issue; *m* 2nd 3 Oct 1960 *Alfonso Necochea Beauchemin and has further issue

    2b *Beatrice Mary Rose; *b* 4 Nov 1904; *m* 19–– (*d* 19–)

    3b *Olivia Margaret Rose; *b* 27 Aug 1910; *m* 9 April 1932 *José-Maria Souviron, of Malaga, Spain, and has:

      1c *Alvaro Souviron Price; *b* 15 Feb 1933; *m* 14 Sept 1958 *Ximena Grebe, of La Serena, Chile, and has:

        1d *Pilar Souviron; *b* 27 June 1959

        2d *Beatrice Souviron; *b* 13 May 1960

      2c *Jacqueline Souviron Price; *b* 15 Jan 1936; *m* 30 Sept 1958 *Luis Urrejola Dittborn, of Santiago, and has:

        1d *Daniel Urrejola; *b* 30 Sept 1959

        2d *Sebastian Urrejola; *b* 25 Nov 1961

        1d *Caroline Urrejola; *b* 23 May 1962

    4b *Eveleen Mina Rose; *b* 16 May 1913; *m* 19– (*divorce* 19–) —

  1a (cont.) Arthur Price *m* 2nd 6 April 1922 Augustine Laetitia, only dau of Jacques Benoit, of Foix, Ariage, France, and *d* 23 Nov 1951

  2a Thomas Rose (Rev); *b* 13 May 1874; *educ* Trin Coll Cambridge (BA, LLM); Vicar All Saints Halifax 1907–36; *m* 23 April 1901 Frances Louisa Salisbury (*d* Dec 1944), dau of Frederick Churchill, MD, FRCS, of S Kensington, and *d* 1940, having had, with another s and dau (*d* young):

    1b Thomas Neville Churchill Rose (Rev); *b* 17 April 1911; *educ* St Andrews and Ridley Hall Cambridge (MA 1935); Vicar Gt Longstone 1950–55, All Saints' Matlock Derbys 1955–65 and St Matthias's Ilsham Torquay 1965–70; *m* 11 Sept 1939 Edna Mary (*d* 1979), dau of Howard Nume Edge, of Torquay, and *d* 1970, leaving:

      1c +Robin Francis Neville Rose [Robin Price Esq, Trouts Holiday Flats, South Hallsands, nr Kingsbridge, Devon]; *b* 28 Feb 1945; *m* 1970 *Alison Margaret, dau of Denis Rogers, of Torcross, Devon, and has:

        1d +Andrew Rose; *b* 1975

        1d *Sarah Rose; *b* 1973

      1c *Heather Mary Rose [Mrs Harry Barron, Denysholme, Chilworth Old Village, Hants]; *b* 22 Nov 1942; *m* 1st 3 April 1965 (*divorce* 1976) Richard James Biddle, slr, s of George William Biddle, of Tewkesbury, Glos, and has:

        1d *Marc Jonathan Seymour; *b* 7 Oct 1967; *m* 1st 1993 (*divorce* 1997) Payang Tingan; *m* 2nd *Ines Marylou Nicholas and has:

          1e *Jakob Sol Nicholas; *b* 2 May 1997

        2d *Roy Lindley Stirling; *b* 24 March 1969

        3d *Paul Ashley Sheridan; *b* 27 Feb 1974

        1d *Tiffany Lynn; *b* 1 July 1970

      1c (cont.) Mrs Heather Biddle *m* 2nd 21 Oct 1978 *Harry Denys Barron

    1b Madeleine Rose; *b* 1 July 1903; *m* Nov 1931 *John Ernest Simpson and *d* 31 March 1936

    2b Rosalind Maud Rose; *b* 2 April 1906; *m* 31 July 1951 Alfred Sidney Charles Overton, s of Edwin Charles Overton, of Salisbury

    3b Geraldine Minna Violet Rose; *b* 16 Dec 1908; *educ* St Andrews (MA 1933); *m* 11 May 1938 Herbert Goldberg, MB, ChB, FACS, of Bethesda, Md., s of David Goldberg, and had issue

  4b *Joy Gerradine Salisbury Rose [Mrs Rupert Pearce, Hoon Hay Valley, Christchurch 3, New Zealand]; *b* 4 Feb 1918; *m* 6 March 1939 *Rupert Pearce, s of Rupert Pearce, of Christchurch, and has:

    1c *Peter Wayne; *b* 1947; *m* 1969 *Kay Teresa Harris and has:

      1d *Jeremy Robert; *b* 1974

      1d *Lisa Kelly; *b* 1972

      2d *Anna; *b* 1977

    1c *Wendy Lynne; *b* 1941; *m* 1964 *William Harper Ritchie and has:

      1d *Peter Graham; *b* 1966

      2d *Grant Phillip; *b* 1970

      1d *Kathryn Margaret; *b* 1968

    2c *Pauline Frances; *b* 1944; *m* 1968 *Donald George Foster and has:

      1d *Daniel Richard; *b* 1970

      1d *Emily Victoria; *b* 1971

      2d *Faye Louise; *b* 1974

    3c *Faye Fiona; *b* 1949; *m* 1970 *Wayne Allan Parkhill and has:

      1d *Jesse Andrew; *b* 1981

      1d *Charlotte Faye; *b* 1979

    4c *Estelle Suzanne; *b* 1951; *m* 1972 *Christopher John Alleyne and has:

      1d *Timothy Francis; *b* 1984

      1d *Melissa Gerrardine; *b* 1975

      2d *Holly Felicity; *b* 1979

  3a Samuel Percy; *b* 11 Dec 1878; *m* 1st 17 April 1906 Margaret Elinor (*d* 12 Oct 1906), dau of James Grant, of Dunheanish, Oban; *m* 2nd 26 Oct 1912 Anita, dau of TA Mackay, of Concepcion, Chile, and by her had:

    1b Arthur Thomas Rose; *b* 28 April 1916; F/O RAF WW II; *ka* Battle of Britain 2 Sept 1940

    2b +John Samuel Rose [John Price Esq, Cerro Verde, Concepcion, Chile]; *b* 3 Feb 1921; P/O Chilean Air Force (Res); *m* 27 March 1943 Joan Margaret (*d* 25 Oct 1954), dau of Frank Williams, of Cochabamba, Bolivia, and has:

      1c +Samuel John Rose; *b* 18 March 1950

      2c +Peter Rose; *b* Oct 1954

      1c *Anita Margaret Rose; *b* 5 Aug 1944

      2c *Sandra Joan Rose; *b* 3 June 1947

      3c *Jennifer; *b* 1953

    3b +Michael Patrick Rose; *b* 10 Aug 1922; P/O Chilean Air Force (Res); *m* 12 May 1945 *Evelyn Mabel, dau of Eric Saffery, of Talcahuano, Chile, and has:

      1c +Anthony Samuel Patrick Rose; *b* 1953

      2c +Thomas Eric Rose; *b* 22 Oct 1954

      1c *Heather Evelyn Rose; *b* 22 Oct 1946

      2c *Marilyn Joan Rose; *b* 11 Aug 1949

      3c *Gillian Rose; *b* 7 Nov 1951

  1b Anita Margaret Rose; *b* 3 April 1914; *d* unm 18 April 1937

  2b *Carmen Rose; *m* 1st 15 July 1935 Lt Oswald Marcus Cheeke, DSC, RN (*ka* 5 March 1941), s of Maj — Cheeke, of London, and has:

    1c *Marcus Oswald; *b* 1936

    2c *Francis Patrick; *b* 1940

  2b (cont.) Mrs Carmen Cheeke *m* 2nd 2 April 1942 (*divorce* 1951) James Byrne, s of John Byrne, of Vina del Mar, Chile, and by him has:

    1c *Jacqueline; *b* 1945

    2c *Rosanna Amber; *b* 1949

  2b (cont.) Mrs Carmen Byrne *m* 3rd March 1953 *Manuel Hidalgo and by him has:

    3c *Ana Manuela; *b* 19–

    4c *Maria Victoria (twin); *b* 19–

  3b *Pearl Rose [Mrs Edward Yriberry, 462 Casilla, Valparaiso, Chile]; *m* 1st 10 Dec 1938 (*annulled* 1945) Rudolf Seyler and has:

    1c *Christopher Louis; *b* 1939

  3b (cont.) Mrs Pearl Seyler *m* 2nd 15 Aug 1947 *Edward George Yriberry, s of Peter Yriberry, of Vina Del Mar, and by him has:

    1c *Pearl Anita; *b* 1954

  4a Frederick Talbot; *b* 19 Oct 1880; *d* unm 1909

  5a Lilford Neville Rose; *b* 8 Oct 1886; *m* 4 Oct 1911 Eveleen Pender, dau of Alexander Finn, FRGS, Consul-Gen Valparaiso, and *dsp* 1 Feb 1961

  1a Minna Violet; *m* 26 March 1907 (*annulled* 1914) John George Maxwell Brownjohn, 3rd s of Rev S D Brownjohn, and *d* 1949

  2a Pearl Isabel Alice; *m* 12 Sept 1908 (*divorce* 1935) Archibald Rosburgh Balfour, MC (*d* 21 Aug 1958), Capt Lothian and Border Horse Yeo, merchant, of Valparaiso, and *d* 11 March 1950, leaving issue

1 Elizabeth Mary; *m* 26 June 1830 John Basset, DL (*d* 4 July 1843), of Theidy Park, Cornwall, and had issue

2 Charlotte; *m* July 1838 Thomas Charles Higgins, of Turvey House, Beds, and *d* his widow 25 Oct 1868

3 Louisa Douglas; *m* 1837 Charles Edmund Nugent (*d* 3 March 1890), 2nd s of Sir George Nugent, 1st Bt, GCB, of Waddesdon (*qv*), and *d* 18 Dec 1881

4 Jane Frances; *m* 28 April 1846 Hon Percy Moreton, s of 1st Earl of Ducie (*qv*), and *d* 19 Aug 1903, having had issue

The 2nd Bt's nephew,

Sir Rose Lambart Price, 3rd Bt; *b* 28 July 1837; Maj RMLI; *m* 3 Jan 1877 Isabella (added FOTHERGILL by roy licence 1895; *d* 30 Nov 1918), yst dau of John William Tarleton, of Killeigh, King's Co, and *d* 17 April 1899, leaving:

1 **Sir Rose Price, 4th Bt**; *b* 28 July 1878; Lt KRRC; *ka* S Africa 9 June 1901

2 FRANCIS CARADOC ROSE (Sir), **5th Bt**

3 William Vreichvras Rose; *b* 30 May 1882; Lt 9th Lancers S Africa 1900–01; *d* unm 20 Jan 1907

The 4th Bt's bro,

Sir Francis Caradoc Rose Price, 5th Bt, JP Glam; *b* 29 June 1880; *educ* Wellington; High Sheriff Glam 1922, Hon Col 53rd (Welsh) Divl Signals (TA) 1923–28,

Maj Glam Yeo, Lt Roy Welch Fus Boer War 1900–01; *m* 1 June 1909 Marjorie Isabel (*d* 11 Dec 1955), dau of Capt Sir William Russell, of Hawkes Bay, NZ, and had:

1 ROSE FRANCIS (Sir), **6th Bt**

2 William Russell Rose; *b* 6 July 1916; Maj 5th Roy Gurkha Rifles (FF) WW II; *m* 1st 3 Feb 1945 (*divorce* 1953) Joan Ross-Hurst, of Calcutta; *m* 2nd 2 July 1954 *Aline Flora, dau of David Silverman, and *d* 1985, having by her had:

  (1) *Gillian Isobel; *b* 31 July 1959

  (2) *Julia Jane; *b* 17 June 1962

3 Michael Rose; *b* 26 Jan 1922; *d* unm 7 Oct 1966

1 Diana Harriette; *b* 14 May 1912

2 *Helen Jocelyn [Mrs Logan Scott-Bowden, Prospect Farm, Cottesmore Lane, Ewelme, Oxon]; *b* 2 July 1920; *m* 16 Sept 1950 Brig Logan Scott-Bowden, DSO, OBE, MC, RE, only s of Lt-Col Jonathan Scott-Bowden, CBE, TD, JP, of Colwall, Herefs, and has:

  (1) *Robert Logan, MBE (1992); *b* 1955; Lt-Col Roy Scots, served NI; *m* 1980 *Nicola Frances, yr dau of Maj H T K Phillips, of Longcot, Oxon, and has:

    1a *Christopher William; *b* 1987

    1a *Camilla Frances; *b* 1984

  (2) *James Russell; *b* 1958; Maj Welsh Gds; *m* 1988 *Nicola Jane, yr dau of Anthony J V Shepherd, of Park Farm, Alderley, Glos, and has:

    1a *Harry Russell; *b* 1989

    2a *Edward Jonathan; *b* 1991

    3a *Arthur James; *b* 1993

  (3) *Peter William; *b* 1962

  (1) *Claire Anne; *b* 1951

  (2) *Fiona Susan [Mrs Charles Wilmoth, 2 Bould Farm Cottages, Chipping Norton, Oxon OX7 6RT]; *b* 1952; *m* 1978 *Charles John Maitland Wilmoth, yr s of Victor J Wilmoth, of Jordans, Bucks and has:

    1a *George James; *b* 1980

    1a *Harriette Jocelyn; *b* 1984

  (3) *Alexandra Marjorie; *b* 1960; *m* 1990 *Andrew H C Ballingall, only s of H Campbell Ballingall, of Simonstown, S Africa

3 *Anne Charlotte [Miss Anne Price, 14 rue du Pont aux Choux, Paris, France]; *b* 2 Oct 1927

Sir FRANCIS *d* 24 Feb 1949; his est son,

Sir Rose Francis Price, 6th Bt; *b* 15 March 1910; *educ* Wellington and Trin Coll Cambridge (BA 1931); Capt 4th/11th Sikh Regt IA WW II (POW); *m* 7 March 1949 *(Kathleen) June [June Lady Price, Dormer Cottage, Park Rd, Stoke Poges, Bucks SL2 4PG], yr dau of Norman William Hutchinson, of Toorak, Melbourne, and *d* 21 Sept 1979, leaving:

1 Sir FRANCIS CARADOC ROSE PRICE, **7th and present Bt**

2 +NORMAN WILLIAM ROSE [Norman Price Esq, 73 Fawnbrake Ave, London SE24 0BE]; *b* 17 March 1953; heir presumptive; *educ* Eton and Gordonstoun; *m* 1987 *Charlotte Louise, dau of Randolph Rex Bivar Baker, of Yelverton, Devon, and has:

  (1) +Benjamin William Rose; *b* 16 Sept 1989

  (2) +Timothy Charles Rose; *b* 27 Oct 1991

PRICHARD-JONES

Arms: Gu. a lymphad with sail hoisted and pennons flying to the dexter or, on a chief of the last two escutcheons of the field. **Crest:** A demi-lion rampant gu., resting the sinister paw on a boar's head erased or. **Motto:** *Ventus secundet* ('May a favourable wind follow').
Creation: Bt. (UK) 15 July 1910.

SIR JOHN PRICHARD-JONES, 2ND BT, of Bron Menai, Co Anglesey [Sir John Prichard-Jones Bt, Allenswood House, Lucan, Co Dublin, Ireland]; *b* 20 Jan 1913; s f 1917; *educ* Eton and Ch Ch Oxford (MA 1934); barrister Gray's Inn 1936, Capt The Bays (SRO); *m* 1st 31 July 1937 (*divorce* 1950) Heather Vivian, er dau of Sir Walter Richard Nugent, 4th Bt, of Donore (*qv*), and has:

1 +DAVID JOHN WALTER; *b* 14 March 1943; *educ* Ampleforth and Ch Ch Oxford (BA 1964)

Sir JOHN *m* 2nd 2 Feb 1959 *Helen Marie Therese, est dau of Joseph Francis Frederick Liddy, dentist, of Drogheda, and by her has:

1 *Susan Marie; *b* 7 Nov 1959

Lineage: RICHARD JONES, of Tyn-y-coed, Newborough, Anglesey; had a 3rd s:

Sir JOHN PRICHARD JONES later PRICHARD-JONES (deed poll 1917), **1st Bt** (UK), so cr 15 July 1910, of Bron Menai, Dwyran, Llangeinwen, Anglesey, JP, DL (Anglesey); *b* 31 May 1845; High Sheriff Anglesey 1905, memb cncl U Coll N Wales, Treas Nat Museum Wales, built Gt Hall of U Coll Bangor and fndr Prichard Jones Institute and Cottage Homes Newborough, Anglesey; Freedom Caernarvon 1910 and Bangor 1911, LLD; *m* 1st 28 Feb 1878 Mary Coggan (*d* 1 Oct 1901), dau of Vincent Coates, of Muchelney, Somerset; *m* 2nd 21 Jan 1911 Marie (*m* 2nd 12 March 1926 14th Baron Louth (*qv*) and *d* 21 April 1941), yst dau of Charles Read, slr, of Hampstead, and *d* 17 Oct 1917, leaving by her:

1 Sir JOHN PRICHARD-JONES, **2nd and present Bt**

2 Richard William; *b* 28 Oct 1914; *educ* Eton and BNC Oxford; Capt RA WW II; *m* 27 Feb 1943 *Margaret Woodburn (Sally) [Mrs Richard Prichard-Jones, The Forge, Whittlesford, Cambs], yr dau of S/Ldr Ronald Herbert Wingfield Davidson, and *d* 1986, leaving:

  (1) +Richard Stephen; *b* 23 Nov 1952; *educ* Bryanston

  (1) *Marie Anne; *b* 14 June 1948; *m* 2 June 1970 *Edward Pearce-Serocold, only s of Lt-Col Walter Pearce-Serocold, DSO, TD (*see also* ALDENHAM and HUNSDON OF HUNSDON, B), of Ashe House, Overton, Hants, by his 1st w Ann

PRIMROSE

Arms: Per fess argent and ermines on a fess vert between a millrind accompanied by two cross crosslets fitchée in chief gules and a salmon on its back in base of the first, ringed or, three primroses stalked and leaved proper. **Crest:** A hand holding a primrose proper.
Motto: *Fide et fiducia* ('Fidelity and confidence').
Creation: Bt. (UK) 7 July 1903.

SIR JOHN URE PRIMROSE, 5TH BT, of Redholme, Dumbreck, Govan, Co of City of Glasgow [Sir John Primrose Bt, Puerto Victoria, Alto Parana Misiones, Argentina]; *b* 28 May 1960; s f 1986; *educ* St Peter's Sch and Mil Acad Buenos Aires; *m* 1983 (*divorce* 1987) Marion Cecilia, dau of Hans Otto Altgelt, of Buenos Aires, and has:

1 *Christine Anne; *b* 1984

2 *Jennifer Diana; *b* 1986

Lineage: WILLIAM PRIMROSE, of Glasgow; *b* 11 Aug 1779; *m* 12 Nov 1804 Christina Brown (*d* 6 Feb 1850), and *d* 8 Dec 1850, leaving a 4th s:

WILLIAM PRIMROSE; *b* 23 May 1820; Glasgow merchant; *m* 1st 1844 Margaret Fennie (*dsp* 1845), of Kilmarnock; *m* 2nd 10 Nov 1846 Anne (*d* 9 May 1903), dau of John Ure, of Glasgow, and *d* 12 Jan 1891, leaving by her an est s:

Sir John Ure Primrose, 1st Bt (UK), so cr 7 July 1903 on the occasion of the visit of TM EDWARD VII and QUEEN ALEXANDRA to Glasgow, JP, DL Glasgow, JP Lanarks; *b* 16 Oct 1847; *educ* Collegiate Sch Glasgow; memb Glasgow City Cncl 1886 (Ld Provost 1903–05), Chm Clyde Navigation Tstees 1892–97, LLD Glasgow; *m* 1st 6 Dec 1877 Margaret Jane (*d* 13 Sept 1896), dau of James Adam, of Glasgow, and had issue; *m* 2nd 21 Dec 1897 Anna (*dsp* 13 May 1913), dau of Alexander Spence Wylie, of Glasgow; *m* 3rd 8 Sept 1915 Muriel (*d* July 1945), widow of James Donald, and dau of Edwin Pilling, of Liverpool and Rochdale, and *d* 29 June 1924; his s by his 1st w:

Sir William Louis Primrose, 2nd Bt, JP Lanarks; *b* 1 June 1880; *m* 25 June 1907 (*divorce* Scotland 1944) Elizabeth Caroline (*d* 12 April 1951), dau of Hugh Dunsmuir, of Glasgow, and had:

1 JOHN URE (Sir), **3rd Bt**

2 Hugh Dunsmuir; *b* 9 Oct 1909; *educ* Uppingham; F/O RAF; *m* 21 Dec 1935 *Kathleen, dau of Samuel Tyler, of Long Sutton, Lincs, and *d* 1979, leaving:

  (1) +Ian Dunsmuir [Ian Primrose Esq, Lymburghs Farm, Marnhull, Dorset DT10 1HN]; *b* 1 Feb 1941; *educ* King's Coll Taunton; *m* 1971 *Roberta Jeanette, dau of Frederick Clapp, of Bristol, and has:

    1a +James Robert; *b* 1973

1a *Fiona Joanne; *b* 1971
2a *Nicola Kathryn; *b* 1976
Sir WILLIAM *d* 23 Dec 1953; his er son,
   Sir John Ure Primrose, 3rd Bt; *b* 15 April 1908; *educ* Rugby and RMC Sandhurst; Lt QO Cameron Highrs 1928–33, Mil Intell WW II; *m* 12 April 1933 Enid, dau of James Evans Sladen, of BC, Canada, and had:
Sir Alasdair Neil Primrose, 4th Bt; *b* 11 Dec 1935; *m* 24 Oct 1958 *Elaine Noreen [Elaine Lady Primrose, Ada Elflein 3155, 1642 San Isidro, Provincia de Buenos Aires, Argentina], only dau of Edward Cecil Lowndes, of Buenos Aires, and *d* 1966, leaving:

1 Sir JOHN URE PRIMROSE, **5th and present Bt**
2 +ANDREW RICHARD; *b* 19 Jan 1966; heir presumptive
1 *Doris Sofia; *b* 6 June 1962
2 *Deborah Marina; *b* 1964

PRINCE-SMITH

Arms: Per chevron nebuly or guttée de sang and gu. two stag's heads cabossed in chief of the last and a rose in base arg., barbed and seeded ppr. **Crest:** A dragon's head erased gu., charged with a rose as in the arms, between a stag's attires or. **Motto:** *Firmior quo paratior* ('The more prepared, the more powerful').
Creation: Bt. (UK) 11 Feb 1911.

SIR (WILLIAM) RICHARD PRINCE-SMITH, 4TH BT, of Hillbrook, Keighley, W R Yorks [Sir Richard Prince-Smith Bt, 40–735 Paxton Dve, Rancho Mirage, CA 92270–3519, USA]; *b* 27 Dec 1928; *s* f 1964; *educ* Charterhouse and Clare Coll Cambridge (MA); *m* 1st 11 Oct 1955 Margaret Ann, only dau of Dr John Carter, of Essex; *m* 2nd 1975 *Ann Christina, dau of Andrew Faulds, OBE, of Lee Wick Farm, St Osyth, Clacton-on-Sea, Essex, and by his 1st w has:

1 +JAMES WILLIAM [James Prince-Smith Esq, Morton Hall, Norwich, Norfolk NR9 5JS; 2 Grosvenor Ave, Richmond TW10 6PO]; *b* 2 July 1959; *educ* Gresham's, Buckingham U and RMA Sandhurst; late Capt 13th/18th Hus (QMO), Yorks Sqdn QOY
1 *Elizabeth Ann; *b* 8 May 1957; *m* 1987 *Colin Earl

Lineage: HUGH SMYTHE, of Kildwick-in-Craven, Yorks; *b c* 1520; *d* Feb 1589, leaving:

THOMAS SMITH, of Colling in Kildwick; *m* Alice — (*d* Sept 1591) and *d* Nov 1620, leaving:

HUGH SMITH, of Colling; *b* 1577; *m* Katherine — (*d* Aug 1637) and *d* Nov 1623, leaving:

PETER SMITH, of Colling; *m* 1 Dec 1623 Agnes Jackson (*d* April 1639) and had:

HUGH SMITH, of Kildwick; *b* 1627; *m* 20 April 1653 Jennett Scarborough and had:

GEORGE SMITH, of Kildwick; *b* 1657; *m* 12 May 1678 Deborah Ellis (*d* 1690) and had:

JAMES SMITH, of Colling and later Carlton-in-Craven, Yorks; *b* 1684; *m* 21 Jan 1704 Ann Tillotson and *d* May 1730, leaving:

JAMES SMITH, of Stockbridge in Bingley, Yorks; *b* 1726; *m* 1st 30 June 1752 Elizabeth Mounding (*d* 31 Dec 1767) and had issue; *m* 2nd 13 April 1769 Mary (*d* 12 Jan 1796), widow of Samuel Oddy, of Keighley, W R Yorks, and dau of John Parker, of Bingley, and by her had, with other issue:

WILLIAM SMITH, of Keighley; *bapt* 14 Dec 1774; *m* 15 May 1794 Elizabeth (*d* 1 July 1845), dau of Joseph Thompson, of Keighley, and *d* 7 Sept 1850, having had, with seven other sons and two daus:

PRINCE SMITH, of Holly House, Keighley; *b* 17 Jan 1804; *m* 29 Aug 1830 Martha (*d* 28 Aug 1859), dau of John Edmondson, of Keighley, and *d* 23 March 1890, having had, with an er s (Edmundson; *d* 7 March 1835 aged 3) and several daus:

Sir Prince Smith, 1st Bt (UK), so *cr* 11 Feb 1911, JP E and W R Yorks; *b* 3 Sept 1840; *m* 20 Dec 1864 Martha Ann (*d* 1 Dec 1913), dau of John Greenwood, of Skipton-in-Craven, Yorks, and had:

1 PRINCE (Sir), **2nd Bt**
1 Lucy; *b* 27 Dec 1865; *d* unm 15 May 1928
2 Helen; *b* 26 Oct 1867; *d* 5 June 1878
3 Martha; *b* 4 Feb 1872; *d* unm 22 March 1923
Sir PRINCE *d* 20 Oct 1922; his only s,
   Sir PRINCE SMITH later PRINCE-SMITH (deed poll 28 Oct 1922), **2nd Bt**; *b* 15 Oct 1869; High Sheriff Yorks 1934; *m* 14 Nov 1894 Maud Mary (*d* 25 May 1939), dau of Henry Wright, slr, of Mayfield, Keighley, and had:
1 WILLIAM (Sir), **3rd Bt**
1 Doris Evelyn; *b* 2 Dec 1895; *m* 3 Sept 1919 Capt John Haggas Brigg, FLAS, est s of Thomas Brigg, JP, of High House, Addingham, and *d* 8 Jan 1970, leaving issue (*see* POWERSCOURT, V)
2 Joan Mary; *b* 6 June 1903; *m* 2 June 1926 David Allan Hield, 2nd s of David Hield, of Wingfield, Bingley, and *d* 3 April 1967, leaving issue
Sir PRINCE *d* 2 July 1940; his only s,
   Sir William Prince-Smith, 3rd Bt, OBE (1944), MC; *b* 10 Aug 1898; *educ* Charterhouse; Lt RFA WW I (despatches), Chm E R Yorks Ag Exec Ctee 1948–50, Pres Yorks Ag Soc 1956; *m* 30 Jan 1923 Marian Marjorie (*d* 1 Feb 1970), er dau of Thomas Nickell Lean, of Liverpool and Cornwall, and *d* 10 July 1964, leaving:
1 Sir WILLIAM RICHARD PRINCE-SMITH, **4th and present Bt**
1 *Eileen Marjorie Clare [Mrs Stephen Smith, Eastlands, 91 Pool Rd, Otley, W Yorks LS21 1DY]; *b* 25 Feb 1932; *m* 19 Sept 1959 *Stephen Hattersley Smith, er twin s of Richard Hattersley Smith, of Shoebridge Ho, Eastburn, Yorks, and has:
(1) *Christopher Stephen Hattersley; *b* 11 March 1963; *m* 1988 *Tanya Gwynne Hutchinson
(1) *Jane Clare Hattersley; *b* 21 April 1961; *m* 1985 *Michael John Clark
(2) *Vanessa Jill Hattersley; *b* 3 April 1965; *m* 1990 *Daniel James Martin

PRINGLE

Arms: Az. three escallops or. **Crests:** 1 An escallop or, 2 A saltire az. within a garland of bay-leaves ppr. **Motto:** *Coronat fides* ('Faith crowns [endeavour]'). **Creation:** Bt. (NS) 5 Jan 1682/3.

SIR STEUART ROBERT PRINGLE, 10TH BT, KCB (1982), of Stichill, Roxburghshire [Lt-Gen Sir Steuart Pringle Bt KCB, c/o 35 Stroud Green, Newbury, Berks]; *b* 21 July 1928; *s* f 1961; *educ* Sherborne; RM: 2nd Lt 1946, 42 Commando 1950–52, Adj Commando Sch 1952–54, HQ 3 Commando Bde 1956–57, 40 Commando 1957–59, Ch Instr Signal Trg Wing 1959–61, Bde Sign Offr 3 Commando 1961–63, Def Planning Staff 1964–67, Ch Signal Offr 1967–69, 40 Commando 1969–71, CO 45 Commando Gp 1971–74, HQ Commando Forces 1974–76, RCDS 1977, Maj-Gen Commando Forces 1978–79, Ch Staff to Cmdt Gen 1979–81, Cmdt-Gen 1981–84, Col Cmdt 1989–90, Rep Col Comdt 1991–92; chm and ch exec Chatham Historic Dockyard Tst 1984–91, pres St Loye's Fndn 1984–, Liveryman Plaisterers' Co 1984, Hon DSc City U 1982, Hon LLD Exeter 1994, Hon Adml Texas Navy; author: *Peace and the Bomb* (contributor, 1982), *The Future of British Sea Power* (1984); *m* 5 Sept 1953 *Jacqueline Marie, only dau of Wilfrid Hubert Gladwell, of La Rocque, Jersey, and has:

1 +SIMON ROBERT [Simon Pringle Esq, 5 Hyde Vale, London SE10 8QQ]; *b* 6 Jan 1959; *educ* Worth Abbey and Trin Coll Oxford (BA); *m* 1992 *Pamela Margaret, dau of George Hunter, of Belfast, and has:
(1) *Siena Evangeline; *b* 13 Jan 1994
2 +Julian Andrew James; *b* 4 March 1961
1 *Shelagh Mary Frances [Mrs Gary Newton, 35 Stroud Green, Newbury, Berks]; *b* 11 Oct 1954; *m* 1st 6 Sept 1975 Jasper J H Dale, only s of Cdr J H Dale, RN, and Mrs L C Letts; *m* 2nd 19– *Gary Nicholas Newton and by him has:
(1) *Jessica Anne; *b* 12 June 1978
(2) *Katherine Frances; *b* 9 Jan 1980
(3) *Alexa Mary Elizabeth; *b* 23 Oct 1983
2 *Nicola Ann; *b* 16 Jan 1956; *m* 1981 *Clive Gordon Harris and has:
(1) *Robert Keith; *b* 26 Jan 1985
(2) *Callum Charles; *b* 22 Jan 1994
(1) *Geraldine Marie; *b* 9 Oct 1982

Lineage: The PRINGLES of Stichill are the heirs male and representatives of the PRINGLES or HOPPRINGILLS of Craigleith (also called Craiglatch and Newhall), in Ettrick Forest, Selkirkshire

WILLIAM PRINGLE, s of David of Smailholm, first ranger of the Ward of Tweed, Constable of Cessford Castle, *fl* between 1467 and 1494; *d* in or after 1499, having had:

ALEXANDER PRINGLE; *fl* between 1468 and 1490; apparently *dvp*, leaving:

ROBERT PRINGLE; *d* 1539, leaving, with three yr sons (George; John; James):

ALEXANDER PRINGLE of Newhall, later of Whittoun; *d* by 1569, leaving, with a yr s (Robert) :

GEORGE PRINGLE of Craigleith; *d* 1602, leaving:

1 George, of Craigleith; *m* Margaret Ker and *d* by 1631, having had, with two daus :

  (1) James, of Craigleith; *d* 1635, leaving:

    1a Robert; settled his lands 1667 on his heirs male, then heirs male of his unc Robert, then on the heirs male of Robert Pringle of Stichill; *dsp*

    (2) Robert, in Carberton and later of Newhall; *dsp* 1672

2 Robert, 1st of Stichill which he bought 1628, together with other lands 1629, 1632 and 1636; *b c* 1581; Treas Depute Scotland 1613; MP Roxburghs 1639–41; *m* Catherine Hamilton, of the HAMILTONs, Bts, of Silverton Hill (*qv*), and *d* 1649, having had, with four daus (of whom the 2nd *m* Ker of Graden (a property which passed to the HOMEs (*see* HOME, E) via Andrew Ker of Cessford (*see* LOTHIAN, M) by his dau Margaret's marriage with Sir John Home of Cowdenknows or Ersiltoun) and had issue; Anna, *m* Sir James Home of Eccles (for whose earlier ancestry *see* HOME, E) and had issue; Christina, *m* Hugh Wallace, Yr. of Craigie, Ayrshire):

  (1) John; *m* Margaret Scott, illegitimate dau of 1st Earl of Buccleuch (*see* BUCCLEUCH and QUEENSBERRY, D), and *dvp*, having had, with other issue:

    1a **Sir Robert Pringle, 1st Bt** (NS), so *cr* 5 Jan 1682/3, of Stichill and from 1667 of Newhall; MP Roxburghs 1678 and 1682; *m* 1660 Margaret, dau of Sir John Hope, 2nd Bt (*qv*), and had, with other issue:

      1b JOHN (Sir), **2nd Bt**

      2b Walter (Sir), of Lochton; advocate, Ld of Session as Lord Newhall; *m* —, dau of Johnston of Hilton, and had issue (his male descendants failed in the 3rd generation)

      3b Robert, PC; Sec-at-War; *m* — Law and had:

        1c Robert; *educ* Middle Temple; *d* unm 1771

      4b Thomas; WS; ancestor of the PRINGLEs of Edgefield and PRINGLEs of Weens

      1b Katherine; *m* Sir John Home of Blackadder (for whose early ancestry *see* HOME, Bt) and had issue

      2b Mary; *m* Henry Borthwick of Pilmuir, *de jure* 12th Lord Borthwick (*qv*)

      3b Bethia; *m* 1st — Deans of Woodhouselee; *m* 2nd — Stewart of Stewartfield; *m* 3rd — Kerr of Littledean and by her 1st husb had issue

    2a Walter, of Graycrook; advocate; *m* Jean, dau of James Deans, of Edinburgh, and *d* in or after 1679

  (2) Walter, of Greenknowe, Berwicks; Covenanter; *m* Janet, 2nd dau of James Pringle of Torwoodlee, and had issue

Sir ROBERT's est son,

Sir John Pringle, 2nd Bt, of Stichill; *bapt* 2 July 1662; *m* (contract 19 July 1688) Magdalen (*d* Dec 1739), dau of Sir Gilbert Eliott, 1st Bt (*qv*), and *d* April 1721, having had:

1 ROBERT (Sir), **3rd Bt**

2 Gilbert; Dragoons Offr; *m* Margaret, only dau and heiress of John Pringle of Torsonce, and *dsp*

3 Walter, of Torsonce; advocate, Sheriff Roxburghs; *d* unm

4 Sir JOHN PRINGLE, 1st and last Bt (GB), so *cr* 5 June 1766; *b* 10 April 1707; MD Leyden 1730, Prof Moral Philosophy Edinburgh 1733–44; Physician to: Forces in Flanders 1744 and GEORGE III 1774; Pres Roy Soc 1772–78; *m* 14 April 1752 Charlotte (*d* 29 Dec 1753), dau of Dr Oliver, MD, of Bath (commemorated in the eponymous biscuit), and *dsp* 18 Jan 1782, when the btcy expired

1 Margaret; *m* as his 2nd w Sir James Hall, 2nd Bt, of Dunglass (*qv*) and had issue

2 Katherine; *m* William Hamilton of Bangour and had issue

Sir JOHN's est son,

Sir Robert Pringle, 3rd Bt, of Stichill; *bapt* 6 Oct 1690; *m* 1723 Katherine (*d* 28 May 1745), est dau of James Pringle of Torwoodlee, and *d* 14 Dec 1779, having had, with two daus (*d* unm):

1 John; *dvp* young 1740 at Edinburgh Castle

2 JAMES (Sir), **4th Bt**

3 Francis; WS; *d* unm

1 Magdalen; *m* 1759 her cousin Sir John Hall, 3rd Bt, of Dunglass (*qv*) and had issue

Sir ROBERT's 2nd son,

Sir James Pringle, 4th Bt, of Stichill; *bapt* 6 Nov 1726; served Fusiliers, Col 59th Regt, Lt-Col Southern Fencibles, cmded Roxburghs Yeo Cav; HM's Master of Works Scotland, MP Berwicks 1761–79; *m* 11 Sept 1767 Elizabeth (*d* 9 Oct 1826), 2nd dau of Norman Macleod of Macleod, 22nd Chief, and *d* 7 April 1809, having had, with two daus (*d* unm):

1 Robert, Yr. of Stichill; *m* 22 April 1806 Sarah (*d* June 1806), dau of Maj-Gen Norman Macleod of Macleod, 23rd Chief, and *dvp* 1806

2 **Sir John Pringle, 5th Bt**; *b* 20 Jan 1784; *m* 1st 2 June 1809 his er bro's sis-in-law Emilia Anne (*d* 22 Feb 1830), dau of Maj-Gen Norman Macleod of Macleod, and *d* 15 June 1869, having had, with three daus (*dsp* or unm):

  (1) James, yr of Stichill; *d* unm 21 Aug 1865

  (2) Norman; RE cadet Woolwich; drowned in Thames

  (3) John Robert; Madras CS; *m* 21 Aug 1844 Hester Helen, dau of Gen Malcolm McNeill, Madras Army, bro of Alexander McNeill of Colonsay, gf of 1st

and last Baron Colonsay of Colonsay and Oronsay (*see* 1874 edn), and *d* 5 Sept 1847, leaving:

    1a Emily Eliza Steel; *m* 1st 19 Dec 1865 John Gordon of Cluny, Aberdeenshire (*dsp* 3 March 1878; for his family's early ancestry *see* HUNTLY, M); *m* 2nd 5 Dec 1880 Sir Reginald Archibald Edward Cathcart, 6th and last Bt (*dsp* 14 May 1916; *see* 1916 edn), and *d* 6 Aug 1932

    (1) Katherine; *m* 29 July 1845 Archibald SWINTON later CAMPBELL-SWINTON, of Kimmerghame (*d* 27 Nov 1890) and *d* 24 May 1846, leaving issue

    (2) Anne Crawfurd; *m* 1 July 1854 Cdr Hon Charles St Clair, RN (*d* 8 Feb 1863), 2nd s of 4th/13th Lord Sinclair (*qv*), and *d* 15 Dec 1899, leaving issue

2 (cont.) **Sir John** *m* 2nd 10 Oct 1831 Elizabeth Maitland, er dau of 4th Earl of Breadalbane and Holland (*qv*), and by her had:

  (3) Mary Gavin; *m* 18 July 1861 Hon Robert Baillie-Hamilton, s of 10th Earl of Haddington (*qv*), and *dsp* 11 April 1911

  (4) Magdalen Breadalbane; *m* 1st 9 July 1863 Alexander Anderson, of Newstead, Australia (*d* 1871); *m* 2nd 21 Jan 1874 Sir Robert Bateson Harvey, 1st Bt (*d* 23 March 1887), and *d* 28 April 1913

3 NORMAN (Sir), **6th Bt**

1 Eliza; *m* Archibald Todd of Drygrange and *d* his widow Oct 1865

2 Mary; *m* George Baillie, of Jerviswoode and Mellerstain, and had issue (*see* HADDINGTON, E)

The 5th Bt's bro,

Sir Norman Pringle, 6th Bt; *b* 22 July 1787; Maj 21st Regt Northern Br Fus, Consul Stockholm and Dunkirk; *m* 17 Jan 1826 Anne (*d* 4 Aug 1883), est dau of Robert Steuart of Alderston, and *d* 18 April 1870, having had, with two daus (*d* unm):

1 NORMAN WILLIAM DRUMMOND (Sir), **7th Bt**

2 Francis John; *b* 1839; Army Lt; *d* unm

3 Walter Louis; *b* 1846; sr clerk PC office; *d* 3 Aug 1884

Sir NORMAN's est son,

Sir Norman William Drummond, 7th Bt, JP Selkirk; *b* 16 April 1836; Col cmdg 1st Bn S Staffs Regt, memb Roy Co Archers; *m* 10 Jan 1871 Louisa Clementina (*d* 29 July 1922), yst dau of Robert Steuart of Alderston, MP, and *d* 21 July 1897, leaving:

1 NORMAN ROBERT (Sir), **8th Bt**

1 Magdalen Valerie; *d* 15 Feb 1925

2 Violet Louisa Maria; *m* 4 Oct 1927 Arthur Worsley (*d* 28 Nov 1937) and *d c* March 1961

Sir NORMAN's only son,

Sir Norman Robert Pringle, 8th Bt; *b* 18 Oct 1871; Lt Army Pay Dept, T/Capt Inland Water Tport; *m* 1902 Florence Madge (*m* 2nd Archibald MacGregor), only child of J Vaughan, of Rochester, and *das* 8 April 1919, following which the Newhall estate was sold 1920, leaving:

1 **Sir Norman Hamilton Pringle, 9th Bt**; *b* 13 May 1903; *educ* Stonyhurst, F/O RAFVR WW II; *m* 15 Sept 1927 Winifred Olive (*d* 1975), dau of Joseph Curran, of Folkestone, and *d* 8 Feb 1961, leaving:

  (1) Sir STEUART ROBERT PRINGLE, **10th and present Bt**

2 Ronald Steuart; *b* 26 April 1905; *m* 31 Dec 1938 Janet Patricia (*d* 1983), dau of Capt George Todd Pickford, RNR, of Nairobi, and *d* 24 July 1968, leaving:

  (1) +Norman Murray; *b* 27 April 1941; FCIS, FCMA; *m* 1st 11 Sept 1966 Lysbet Watkins-Pitchford; *m* 2nd 1993 *Patricia Nadine Millem and has by his 1st w:

    1a +Alastair Steuart Ronald; *b* 1972

    1a *Sian Amanda; *b* 1972

  (2) +James Bruce [James Pringle Esq, 5 St Mary's Place, Newbury, Berks RG14 1EG]; *b* 1943; *m* 11 Sept 1965 *Rosemary Jean Collis and has:

    1a +Andrew James Edward; *b* 5 Dec 1975

    1a *Jean Frances [Mrs David Paddick, 7 Sagecroft Rd, Thatcham, Berks RG18 3FF]; *b* 20 Nov 1967; *m* 28 Sept 1996 *David Anthony Paddick

    2a *Marion Clare; *b* 17 Dec 1970

    3a *Angela Mary; *b* 8 Dec 1971

  (1) *Priscilla Frances [Mrs Priscilla Dorman, 89 Craven Rd, Newbury, Berks RG14 5NL]; *b* 6 Nov 1944; *m* 1st 8 Aug 1964 (*divorce* 1972) Antony Mark Dorman, of Kenya; *m* 2nd 21 May 1976 (*divorce* 24 Sept 1991) Derek John McIntosh and by her 1st husb has:

    1a *Louise Margaret; *b* 13 Aug 1965; *m* 198– (divorce 8 May 1996) Paul John Preston and has:

      1b *Leigh Mark; *b* 4 July 1985

      2b *Christopher James; *b* 16 Nov 1988

      3b *Robert Steven; *b* 18 June 1990

      4b *Steven Jonathon; *b* 8 Nov 1992

      1b *Lisa Clare; *b* 30 Dec 1987

3 James Drummond; *b* 12 April 1906; *m* 1st 1932 (*divorce* 1946) Nina Beryl (*d* 1988), dau of P W Trutwein, Sessions Judge Burma, and had:

  (1) +Norman Alastair [Norman Pringle Esq, 27 Lynton Green, Maidenhead, Berks]; *b* 1933; *educ* Stonyhurst; *m* 1955 (*divorce* 1979) Diana Joan, dau of Victor Clarke, and has:

    1a +Robin Alistair; *b* 1961; *m* 1984 *Anne Samuel

    1a *Susan Jane; *b* 1960; *m* 1st 1977 (*divorce* 1980) Alan Watkins; *m* 2nd 1980 *Tony Bennett and by him has:

      1b *Nadia; *b* 1980

    2a *Dawn Anne; *b* 1965; *m* 1982 *Terry Spracklen, and has:

      1b *Kayleigh Louise; *b* 1985

      2b *Beth Kelcei; *b* 1991

      3b *Lydia Kimberley; *b* 1993

3 (cont.) James Drummond *m* 2nd July 1947 *Mrs Pauline Cunliffe and *d* 1960, having by her had:

  (2) +John; *b* 1948

  (1) *Melanie Ann; *b* 14 April 1955

1 Mary Elizabeth; *b* 14 Nov 1916; *m* 1st 6 Oct 1938 (*divorce* 1963) Maj George Wallace Anderson, MC, only s of George Wallace Anderson, of Brazil; *m* 2nd 1963 *Richard Anthony Mann Roberts, only s of Capt R M Roberts, of Leighton Buzzard, and *d* 31 May 1996, leaving by her 1st husb:

    (1) Veronica Bethia; *b* 1939; *m* 19– — and *d* 1976, leaving issue

1 (cont.) Maj and Mrs Anderson also adopted:

    *John Louis Wallace [John Anderson Esq, 1 St John's Rd, Newbury, Berks RG14 7PY]; *b* 6 Feb 1950

PRIOR

Creation: B. (LP, UK) 1987.

THE BARON PRIOR, of Brampton, Co Suffolk (James (Jim) Michael Leathes Prior, PC (1970)) [The Rt Hon The Lord Prior PC, House of Lords, London SW1A 0PW]; *b* 11 Oct 1927; *educ* Charterhouse and Pembroke Coll Cambridge (Hon Fell 1992); 2nd Lt Roy Norfolk Regt 1946; MP (C) Lowestoft 1959–83, Waveney 1983–87, PPS to: Pres BOT 1963, Min Power 1963–64 and Leader Oppn 1965–70, Min MAFF 1970–72, Ld Pres Cncl and Leader H of C 1972–74, Oppn Spokesman Employment 1974–79, Sec State: Employment 1979–81, NI 1981–84, Dep Chm C Party 1972–74 (V-Chm 1965); dir: United Biscuits 1984–, Barclays Bank 1984–89, Barclays International 1984–89, J Sainsbury 1984–92, chm: GEC 1984–98, Gt Ormond St Wishing Well Appeal 1985–89, Cncl on Industry and Higher Educn 1986–91, Archbishops Commn on Rural Areas 1988–1991, Special Tstees Gt Ormond St 1989–, Alldes 1989–94, Industry and Parl Tst 1990–94, Rural Housing Tst 1990–, Roy Veterinary Coll 1990, E Anglian Radio 1992–; Memb Advsy Cncl: Tenneco European 1986–, American Internat Gp 1988–; Tstee Internat Centre Child Studies 1987–91; Chllr Anglia Poly U (Hon PhD) 1992–96; author: *The Right Approach to the Economy* (jt author, 1977), *A Balance of Power* (1986); *m* 1954 *Jane Primrose Gifford, 2nd dau of AVM Oswyn George William Gifford Lywood, CB, CBE, and has:

1 *David Gifford Leathes [The Hon David Prior MP, Swannington Manor, Norwich, Norfolk NR9 5NR]; *b* 1954; MP (C) N-Norfolk 1997–; *m* 1987 *Caroline, dau of Peter Holmes, of The Old Rectory, Shotesham, Norwich, and has:

    (1) *Nicholas James Peter; *b* 1988

    (1) *Helena Caitlin Elizabeth (twin); *b* 1988

2 *Simon Gilman Leathes [The Hon Simon Prior, Church Farm, Shadingfield, Suffolk NR34 8DF]; *b* 1956; *m* 1985 *Vivien Ann, dau of Peter George Keely, of Beccles, and has:

    (1) *Alice Rebecca; *b* 1986

3 *Jeremy James Leathes [The Hon Jeremy Prior, The Moat House, Old Hall, Brampton, Suffolk NR34 8EE]; *b* 1962; *m* 1988 *Camilla Sarah, er dau of Julian Riou Benson, of The Old Rectory, Abbots Ann, Hants, and has:

    (1) *Oliver James Leathes; *b* 1991

    (2) *Edward Thomas Leathes; *b* 1993

1 *Sarah-Jane Leathes [The Hon Mrs Roper, Widbrook House, Cookham, Berks SL6 9RD]; *b* 1959; *m* 1982 *David Alexander Roper, s of Thomas Alexander Roper, of Niagara, Canada and has:

    (1) *Lucy Victoria; *b* 1987

    (2) *Alexandra Florence (twin); *b* 1987

    (3) *Rosanna Jane; *b* 1989

Lineage: CHARLES BOLINGBROKE LEATHES PRIOR, of Norwich; *m* A S M — and had a 2nd s:

JAMES (JIM) MICHAEL LEATHES, *cr* a **Baron**

PROBY

Arms: Quarterly, 1st and 4th, ermine on a fess gules a lion passant or (for PROBY); 2nd and 3rd, argent two bars wavy azure, on a chief azure an estoile between two escallops or (for ALLEN). **Crest:** An ostrich's head erased proper, ducally gorged and holding in the beak a key or. **Motto:** *Manus hæc inimica tyrannis* ('This hand is unfriendly to tyrants'). **Creation:** Bt. (UK) 30 Jan 1952.

SIR PETER PROBY, 2ND BT, of Elton Hall, Co Huntingdon [Sir Peter Proby Bt, Pottle Green, Elton, Peterborough PE8 6SG]; *b* 4 Dec 1911; *s f* 1979; *educ* Eton and Trin Coll Oxford (BA 1934); Capt Irish Gds WW II, FLAS, Bursar Eton 1953–71, Ld Lt Cambs 1981–84 (previously DL), FRICS; *m* 15 Jan 1944 *Blanche Harrison, only dau of Col Henry Harrison Cripps, DSO, of Bath Lodge, Ballycastle, Co Antrim, and has had:

1 John Granville; *b* 7 Sept 1946; *educ* Eton and Trin Coll Oxford; *d* 17 Dec 1971

2 +WILLIAM HENRY [William Proby Esq, Elton Hall, Elton, Peterborough, PE8 6SH]; *b* 13 June 1949; *educ* Eton, Lincoln Coll Oxford (MA) and Brooksby Coll of Ag; FCA, chm HHA Taxation Comm 1986–94, pres HHA 1993– (dep pres 1988–93), farmer; *m* 1974 *Meredyth Anne, dau of Dr Timothy David Brentnall, of Corner Cottage, Preston, nr Uppingham, Leics, and has:

    (1) *Alexandra Meredyth Anne; *b* 1980

    (2) *Alice Katherine; *b* 1982

    (3) *Frances Rose Gwyneth; *b* 1986

    (4) *Isabella Victoria Hamilton; *b* 1991

1 *Sarah Blanche [Mrs Peter Mills, 158 Tachbrook St, London SW1]; *b* 9 May 1945; *educ* LMH Oxford (MA, BM, BCh); *m* 6 July 1968 *Peter George Mills, MA, BCh, FRCP, est s of Dr George William Mills, MBE, of Dundee, and has:

    (1) *James Douglas George; *b* 4 Dec 1972

    (2) *Robert Peter; *b* 15 May 1975

    (1) *Elizabeth Sarah Jane; *b* 1980

2 *Charlotte Mary; *b* 27 May 1957; *educ* LMH Oxford (MA, MB, BS), MRCP; *m* 1984 *Stephen John Hay, son of Maj John Hay, of Cheltenham, and has:

    (1) *Matthew John Claud; *b* 1990

    (1) *Matilda Blanche; *b* 1989

    (2) *Flora Millie Rose; *b* 1994

3 *Christine Elisabeth; *b* 27 May 1957; *m* 10 Dec 1983 *Christopher T C Dobbs, yst s of J A Dobbs, of Charlton Musgrave, Somerset, and has:

    (1) *Rachel Alice; *b* 1992

    (2) *Lucy Harriet; *b* 25 July 1995

Lineage: RANDOLPH PROBY, of Chester, later of Brampton, Hunts, *temp* EDWARD VI; *m* — Bernard and had, with an er s (Ralph, of Brampton, *dsp* 1605):

Sir PETER PROBY, of Brampton and Elton, Hunts, and Rans, Amersham, Bucks; Ld Mayor London 1622–23; *m* Elizabeth, widow of Edward Henson, of London, and dau of John Thorowgood, of Temple Cheston, Herts, and Chivers, Essex, and *d* 1624, having had, with two daus:

1 Heneage (Sir), of Elton and Rans; *b* 1600; Sheriff Bucks, MP Agmondesham (Amersham); *m* Ellen, dau of Edward Allen, of Finchly, Middx, and *d* 10 Feb 1662/3, leaving, with two daus:

    (1) Sir THOMAS PROBY, 1st Bt (E), so *cr* 7 March 1661/2, of Elton and Rans; *b c* 1634; MP Agmondesham 1660 and 1666–79 and Hunts 1679–81; *m c* 1673 Frances, dau of Sir Thomas Cotton, 2nd Bt, of Conington, and *dspms* 1689, when the btcy expired, leaving:

        1a Alice; *m* 1689 Hon Thomas Watson Wentworth (*d* 1723), 3rd s of 2nd Baron Rockingham (*see* 1970 edn SONDES, E), and had issue

    (2) John, of Elton; barrister, MP Hunts 1693–95, 1698–1702 and 1708–10; *m* Jane, dau of Sir Richard Cust, 1st Bt, of Pinchbeck (*see* BROWNLOW, B), and *d* 1710, leaving:

        1a Frances; *d* unm 1711

    (3) Heneage; *d* unm 7 May 1699

2 Henry, of The Middle Temple; Common Serjeant City London; *m* Ellen, dau of William Benham, London merchant, and *d* 1660, leaving, with three other daus:

    (1) Henry; *d* unm

    (2) Edward; *d* unm

    (1) —; *m* Sir Francis Clarke

3 Edmund; DD, Rector Broughton Gifford, Wilts; *dsp* by 1684

4 Emanuel, of St Gregory, London; *m* Mary, dau of John Bland, of London, merchant, and *d* by 28 April 1646, leaving, with other issue:

    (1) Peter, of Putney, Surrey, and London; merchant; *m* Grace, dau of Sir Richard Ford, and *dsp* by 21 Nov 1684

    (2) Charles; *m* — (*m* 2nd Thomas Lucas, of Fort St George, Madras), sis of George Torriano, of London, and had, with other issue:

        1a William, of Elton and Rans; HEICS, Govr Fort St George, Madras; *m* Henrietta, dau of Robert Cornwall, of Berrington, and *d* Jan 1739, leaving, with a dau (Edith, *m* Sir John Osborne, 7th Bt (*qv*), and *d* 19 Jan 1745, leaving issue):

            1b John, of Elton; MP Hunts 1722–27 and Stamford 1734–47; *m* 5 Jan 1719/20 Jane Leveson-Gower (*d* 10 June 1726), est dau of 1st Baron Gower of Stittenham (*see* SUTHERLAND, D), and *d* 16 March 1762, leaving:

                1c JOHN

                2c William; *d* unm 1741

                3c Thomas; *b* 1723; *k* at the attack on Ticonderoga July 1758

                4c Charles; *b* 1725; Capt RN, Commr Chatham Dockyard; *m* 1758 Sarah, dau of Philemon Pownell, of Plymouth, and *d* 1799, having had issue

                5c Baptist (Very Rev); *b* 1726; DD, Dean Lichfield 1776–1807, Rector Doddington, Isle of Ely, 1752–1807 and Thornhaugh, Northants; *m* Mary, dau of Rev John Russell, Preb Peterborough and Lincoln, and *d* Jan 1807, having had, with three other daus:

                    1d Baptist John (Rev); *b* 1761; Vicar St Mary's, Lichfield; *m* Mary Susannah, yst dau of Sir Nigel Bowyer Gresley, 6th Bt, of Knypersley (*see* 1970 edn), and *d* 1829, leaving, with two daus:

                      1e William Henry Baptist; *b* 15 Oct 1794; Cdr RN; *m* 23 April 1831 Louisa Mary, only dau and heir of Rev Samuel How, of Strickland, Dorset, and Southleigh, Devon, and *d* 26 Nov 1839, having had, with other issue:

                        1f William Henry Baptist (Rev); *b* 20 Feb 1832; *educ* Trin Coll Cambridge (MA); Curate St Augustine, Haggerston, 1867–68; *m* Blanche, dau of George Arnald

2e John Carysfort (Rev); *b* 20 Aug 1798; *educ* Trin Coll Cambridge (MA); Mil Chaplain HEICS, Rector St Peter Chesil, Winchester; *m* 18 July 1826 Lydia Martyn (*d* 19 Feb 1883), 4th dau of Rev David Brown, Sr Mil Chaplain HEICS, Provost Coll of Fort William, Calcutta, and *d* 18 May 1868, having had, with two daus:

  1f Martyn Carysfort (Rev); *b* 15 Aug 1843; *educ* Trin Coll Dublin (MA); Vicar Chaceley, Worcs; *m* 3 April 1869 Ellinor Charlotte, dau of Rev John Christopher Lloyd, of Dublin, and *dsp*

  2f David-Granville; *b* 26 April 1845; served RN, Dist Supt Police Centl Province India; *m* 2 March 1872 Fanny Augusta Maria, dau of Frederick Augustus Oakes, Capt and Brevet-Maj Madras Horse Artillery, and had:

    1g Granville Lovell Carysfort; *b* 9 May 1873; *d* 7 Oct 1876

    2g William Carysfort; *b* 26 Nov 1881; RCMP, served Imp Yeo Boer War 1899–1902; *d* unm July 1957

    3g John Joshua; *b* 14 June 1884

    4g Francis Henry; *b* 16 Jan 1886

    1g Mary Augusta; *m* May 1897 Henry Lloyd Young, of Agricola, N Alberta, Canada

2d Charles James (Rev); *b* 23 Jan 1771; Canon Windsor, Vicar Twickenham; *m* 30 June 1814 Frances (*d* 6 March 1843), dau of Rev John Sharrer, Vicar Canwick, Lincs, and *d* 2 Feb 1859, leaving:

  1e Charles John; *b* 17 Sept 1815; Br Consul Florence; *m* 14 July 1853 Elizabeth, only child of R-Adml Edward Chappell, and *d* 4 Jan 1868, leaving:

    1f Granville Noel Anstruther; *b* Oct 1858; Capt and Dep-Assist Commissary-Gen Ordnance, Lt Roy Dublin Fus

    1f Florence Angelica Sophia; *m* 3 April 1873 Montagu Fullerton Armstrong (*d* 9 Feb 1926), 5th s of Sir Andrew Armstrong, 1st Bt, of Gallen Priory (*qv*), and *d* 10 July 1936, having had issue

  2e Churchill; *b* 1817; *d* unm Aug 1851

  1e Frances Susan; *d* 15 April 1899

  2e Gertrude Mary; *m* 27 Aug 1844 Edward Nathaniel Conant (*d* 17 Sept 1901), of Lyndon Hall, Rutland, and *d* 27 March 1866, leaving issue

  3e Agnes Mary; *m* 6 Sept 1859 Rev Seymour Neville, Vicar Wraysbury, Bucks, and *d* 12 Oct 1860

3d Joshua John; Judge HEICS

1d Mary; *m* 22 April 1782 1st and last Lord Seaforth, Baron Mackenzie of Kintail (*see* CROMARTIE, E) and *dspms* 27 Feb 1829, having had issue

2d Caroline; *m* 5 July 1792, as his 1st w, Edward Grove, DCL, of Shenstone Park, Staffs, s of William Grove, DCL, of Honiley, Warwicks, and *d* 2 Feb 1800, having had issue

The est son,

Sir JOHN PROBY, 1st BARON CARYSFORT, of Carysfort, Co Wicklow (I), so *cr* 23 Jan 1752, KB (1761), PC (I 1758); *b* 25 Nov 1720; *educ* Jesus Coll Cambridge (MA 1742); MP (Whig) Stamford 1747–54 and Hunts 1754–68, a Ld Admlty 1757 and 1763–65; *m* 27 Aug 1750 Hon Elizabeth Allen (*d* 18 March 1783), dau of 2nd Viscount Allen (*see* 1939 edn), and *d* 18 Oct 1772, leaving, with a dau (Elizabeth, *b* 1752, *m* 1774 Thomas James Storer (*d* 1792) and *d* 1808, leaving issue):

JOHN JOSHUA PROBY, 2nd BARON CARYSFORT and 1st EARL OF CARYSFORT (I), so *cr* 20 Aug 1789, as also 21 Jan 1801 BARON CARYSFORT of the Hundred OF NORMAN CROSS (UK), KP (1784), PC (I 1789); *b* 12 Aug 1751; *educ* Westminster and Trin Coll Cambridge (MA 1770, LLD 1811); FRS 1779, FSA 1804, DCL Oxford 1810, Jt Master Rolls Ireland 1789–1801; *m* 1st 18 March 1774 his cousin Elizabeth (*d* Nov 1783), dau of Rt Hon Sir William Osborne, 8th Bt, of Newtown, Co Tipperary (*qv*), and had:

(1) William Allen, *Lord Proby*; *b* 19 June 1779; *educ* Rugby; Capt RN 1798, MP Buckingham 1802–04; *dvp* unm of yellow fever while in cmd of HMS *Amelia* off Surinam 6 Aug 1804

(2) JOHN PROBY, 2nd EARL OF CARYSFORT; *b* 1780; *educ* Rugby; Gen, served Germany, Egypt, the Peninsula and The Netherlands, MP Buckingham 1805–06 and Hunts 1806–07 and 1814–18; *d* unm 11 June 1855

(3) GRANVILLE LEVESON PROBY, 3rd EARL OF CARYSFORT; *b* 1782; *educ* Rugby; Adml RN, served Battles of the Nile 1798 and Trafalgar 1805, MP Co Wicklow 1816–29, High Sheriff 1831; *m* 5 April 1818 Isabella (*d* 22 Jan 1836), dau of Hon Hugh Howard, MP (*see* 1970 edn WICKLOW, E), and *d* 3 Nov 1868, having had:

  (1) John Joshua, *Lord Proby*; *b* 3 April 1823; *educ* Balliol Coll Oxford (BA 1844), *dvp* unm 19 Nov 1858

  (2) GRANVILLE LEVESON PROBY, 4th EARL OF CARYSFORT, KP (1869), PC (1859); *b* 14 Sept 1824; Capt 79th Highrs, Comptroller Household 1859–66, MP Co Wicklow 1858–68; *m* 19 July 1853 Lady Augusta Maria Hare (*d* 24 March 1881), dau of 2nd Earl of Listowel (*qv*), and *dsp* 18 May 1872

  (3) Hugh; *d* in Australia 1852

  (4) WILLIAM PROBY, 5th and last EARL OF CARYSFORT, KP (1874), JP, DL Hunts, JP Northants; *b* 18 Jan 1836; *educ* Eton and Trin Coll Cambridge (BA 1858); High Sheriff 1865 and HM's Lt and custos rotulorum Co Wicklow 1890–1909; *m* 11 April 1860 Charlotte Mary (*d* 13 Jan 1918), est dau of Rev Robert Boothby Heathcote (*see* HEATHCOTE, Bt, of London), and *dsp* 4 Sept 1909, when all his titles expired

  (1) Frances; *d* unm 15 May 1863

  (2) Elizabeth Emma; *m* 7 Aug 1844 Lord Claud Hamilton (*see* ABERCORN, D) and *d* 24 June 1900, leaving, with other issue:

    1a DOUGLAS JAMES

  (3) Isabella; *d* 10 Jan 1866

  (4) Theodosia Gertrude; *m* 10 Sept 1859 William Montague Baillie (*d* 11 Sept 1902) and *d* 21 Oct 1902, leaving issue

1 Gertrude; *b* 14 March 1782; *d* 1835

The 1st EARL *m* 2nd 13 May 1787 Elizabeth (*d* 2 Dec 1842), sis of 1st Marquess of Buckingham (*see* TEMPLE OF STOWE, E), and *d* 7 April 1828, having by her had:

4 George; *b* 24 Nov 1790; *d* 19 April 1791

2 Charlotte; *b* 10 Feb 1788; *d* unm 23 Jan 1860

3 Frances; *b* 13 March 1789; *d* unm 24 March 1855

4 Elizabeth; *b* 19 April 1792; *m* 2 Feb 1816 Capt William Wells, RN (*d* 13 Aug 1826), of Holme Wood House, Hunts, and *d* 17 Oct 1869, leaving issue

The 5th and last EARL's nephew,

DOUGLAS JAMES HAMILTON later PROBY (roy licence 1904), of Elton, JP (Hunts 1912, Northants 1923), DL (Hunts 1925, Northants 1918, Co Wicklow 1918); *b* 23 Sept 1856; *educ* Eton and Ch Ch Oxford (MA 1912); High Sheriff Cambs and Hunts 1923, Lt-Col and Brevet-Col Irish Gds, MP Saffron Walden Jan-Dec 1910; *m* 6 July 1882 Lady Margaret Frances Hely-Hutchinson (*d* 2 March 1937), 2nd dau of 4th Earl of Donoughmore (*qv*), and *d* 18 Nov 1931, having had:

1 Granville, CB, JP (1911), DL (1936), of Elton Hall and Glenart, Arklow, Co Wicklow; *b* 13 Sept 1883; *educ* Eton and Trin Coll Oxford (MA 1912); Capt Beds Yeo WW I (wounded), barrister Inner Temple 1920, CC Hunts 1931, High Sheriff Cambs and Hunts 1935, Ld Lt Hunts 1946, Clerk Ho Lds, FSA, FRHistS; *d* unm 9 March 1947

2 Claud Richard; *b* 26 April 1885; *educ* HMS *Britannia*; Cadet RN; *d* 18 Feb 1901

3 RICHARD GEORGE (Sir), **1st Bt**

4 Jocelyn Campbell Patrick; *b* 3 March 1900; *educ* Eton and Magdalen Coll Oxford (MA 1926, BLitt 1924); barrister Inner Temple 1923, lecturer history U of Toronto 1926–29, graduate of Kirksville Coll of Osteopathy and Surgery, Mo., 1934; *m* 1st 16 Aug 1930 Elisabeth Angelique (*d* 26 Jan 1962), est dau of William Archibald Hastings Kerr, of Toronto, and adopted:

  *Allen Patrick; *b* 30 Oct 1942; *educ* Lancing; *m* 21 July 1969 *Gloria Florence, er dau of William Hughes, of Fortchester, Inch, Co Wexford

  *Miranda Ruth [Mrs Roger Brown, 31 Portman Ave, London SW14]; *b* 20 May 1937; *m* 3 April 1967 *Roger Arthur Martin Brown, only s of Hugh Brown, of Buenos Aires, and has:

    1a *Peter Martin; *b* 7 April 1969

4 (cont.) Jocelyn Proby *m* 2nd 3 Jan 1969 *Katherine, widow of Brig John Henry Edward, 6th Baron de Robeck, CBE, RA, and er dau of Lt-Col Hugh Simpson, RA, of Hutton House, Hutton-in-the-Forest, Penrith, Cumberland

1 Betty Alice Adeline; *b* 17 May 1889; *m* 27 April 1920 Lt-Col Sir Henry Charles Lowry-Corry, MC, and had issue (*see* BELMORE, E)

The 3rd son,

Sir Richard George Proby, 1st Bt (UK), so *cr* 30 Jan 1952, MC, JP (Hunts 1932, Suffolk 1923); *b* 21 July 1886; *educ* Eton and RMA Woolwich; Lt RFA 1906–10, Capt Essex Yeo 1913, served WW I, Maj 1919, Priv Sec to 1st Chm Ag Wages Bd 1918, Chm Hunts War Ag Ctee 1939, Liaison Offr to Min Ag 1941–44 and 1952–55, CC Hunts 1947, High Sheriff Cambs, Hunts and Isle of Ely 1953, V-Lt Hunts 1957–79 (DL 1952–57), Pres: CLA 1947, Roy Forestry Soc 1956–58, Hunts C Assoc, Nat Union of C and U Assocs 1958, Timber Growers Organisation 1961, memb Wilson Ag Reorganisation Ctee 1955, Forestry Ctee GB, V-Pres Land Agents' Soc and Roy Smithfield Club, memb Cncl Roy Ag Soc England; *m* 1st 7 Feb 1911 Betty Monica (*d* 19 Feb 1967), est dau of Alexander Henry Hallan Murray, of Sandling, Hythe, Kent, and had:

1 Sir PETER PROBY, **2nd and present Bt**

2 Claud, Capt Irish Gds WW II; *b* 5 Feb 1917; *educ* Eton and Magdalene Coll Cambridge (BA 1938); *m* 12 Sept 1942 *Patricia Amelia [Mrs Claud Proby, 1 Chestnut Close, Gt Waldingfield, Suffolk], dau of Lt-Cdr Vyvyan Whitmore Pearce, RN, and *d* 1987, leaving:

  (1) +Patrick James [Patrick Proby Esq, 21 Greenacres, Gt Waldingfield, Suffolk]; *b* 8 Dec 1944; *educ* Eton

  (1) *Caroline Fiona; *b* 4 Aug 1943; *m* 1st 27 Sept 1969 (*divorce* 1988) 6th Viscount Hampden (*qv*) and has issue; *m* 2nd 1990 *Christopher K St J Bird

  (2) *Joanna Margaret [Dr Joanna Woods, c/o Ministry for Foreign Affairs, Parliament Bldgs, Wellington, New Zealand]; *b* 22 Nov 1946; *m* 3 Oct 1970 *Edward Richard Woods, NZ Amb France, est s of Archdeacon Samuel Woods, of The Vicarage, Mayfield, NZ, and has:

    1a *James Christopher; *b* 28 Jan 1972; *educ* Winchester and Trin Coll Cambridge

    2a *Samuel Richard; *b* 7 May 1973; *educ* Winchester and Magdalen Coll Oxford

  (3) *Jocelyn Elizabeth; *b* 1 Oct 1950; *m* 1993 *Donald Retson, of Edmonton, Alberta, and has:

    1a *Serena Christine; *b* 1992

3 Richard; *b* 27 July 1923; *educ* Eton and Trin Coll Oxford (MA); Sub-Lt (A) RNVR WW II; *k* car crash 14 March 1958

1 Mary, JP (1960); *b* 6 Oct 1913; Sr Cdr ATS WW II (despatches), CC 1949–51 London and 1961 Cumberland; *m* 28 July 1949 1st Baron Inglewood (*qv*) and had issue

2 *Margaret, JP (Dorset 1965) [Mrs Jack Cripps JP, Bramble Cottage, 10 French Mill Lane, Shaftesbury, Dorset]; *b* 21 July 1920; *m* 17 July 1948 *Jack Harry Harrison Cripps, only s of Col Henry Harrison Cripps, DSO, of Bath Lodge, Ballycastle, Co Antrim, and has:

  (1) *Harry Richard; *b* 26 Sept 1949; *educ* Marlborough and Clare Coll Cambridge; *m* 1974 *Vivien Barbara, dau of Roy North, and has:

    1a *Elizabeth Blanche; *b* 1977

    2a *Sarah Margaret; *b* 1979

  (2) *Peter John; *b* 10 April 1954; *educ* Marlborough; *m* 1983 *Hazel Anne, dau of Jack Fox

  (3) *Thomas Philip; *b* 10 April 1954; *educ* Marlborough; *m* 1979 *Elizabeth Margaret, dau of Oliver Sugden, and has:

    1a *Margaret Jane; *b* 1981

  (1) *Barbara Mary; *b* 31 May 1952; *educ* Marlborough; *m* 1973 *Giles T R Droop and has:

    1a *Alastair Philip; *b* 1980

1a *Alison Jane; b 1978
3 *Patience [Lady Moberly, 35 Pymers' Mead, Croxted Rd, London SE21 8NH]; b 27 July 1923; educ LMH Oxford (BA 1945, BM and B Ch); MRCP Lond 1950; m 18 April 1959 Sir John Campbell Moberly, KBE, CMG, Counsellor For Serv, 2nd s of Sir Walter Hamilton Moberly, GBE, KCB, DSO, of Oxford, and has:

(1) *Richard John; b 4 June 1962; m 1992 *Catharine J F, dau of Noel Baker
(2) *Nicholas Hamilton; b 11 May 1963; m 1991 *Margaret Fiona Clare, dau of J H Callan, of Horley, Surrey, and has:

1a *Emma Lucy Victoria; b 1993
(1) *Clare Elizabeth; b 27 June 1967

Sir Richard m 2nd 31 May 1972 *Mrs Yvonne Harris (m 3rd 1991 Eric Holman Stirk) [Mrs Eric Stirk, Abbey Lodge, Bewerley, W R Yorks], dau of Walter Edwin Ambrose Helps, of Trevarth Manor, Gwennap, Cornwall, and widow of F/Lt Reginald Kenneth Harris, RAF, and d 15 Jan 1979

Seat: Elton Hall, Peterborough, Cambs. The PROBYs only came into possession of Elton in the 17th century, although it had been built as far back as the 15th, when the SAPCOTEs owned it. The tower, which with the chapel forms the core of the late medieval structure, still displays the Sapcote arms. The chief building programme since the 15th century took place from the late 18th onwards, though the north wing was slightly extended in Sir Thomas Proby's time around the mid-17th century. This major new extension and remodelling seems to have been almost exactly contemporaneous in its final stages with the Napoleonic Wars. Inevitably a degree of gothicisation took place, although that to the western elevation was soon removed. (Internally, however, there is a splendid room still as it was when Strawbery Hill was the height of fashion: the upper octagon chamber.) Over half a century later the 4th Earl of Carysfort put up the main tower. He also installed a billards room. The library has an exceptional book collection.

PROCTOR-BEAUCHAMP

Arms: Quarterly, 1st and 4th, arg. a chevron sa. between three martlets gu. (for PROCTOR); 2nd and 3rd, gu. a fess between six billets, three and three, barways, or, a canton erm. (for BEAUCHAMP). **Crest:** On a mount vert a pied greyhound sejant ppr., collared or. **Motto:** Toujours fidèle ('Always faithful'). **Creation:** Bt. (GB) 20 Feb 1744/5.

SIR CHRISTOPHER RADSTOCK PROCTOR-BEAUCHAMP, 9TH BT, of Langley Park, Norfolk, and White Hall, Tottenham, Middlesex [Sir Christopher Proctor-Beauchamp Bt, The Coach House, Balfour Mews, Sidmouth, Devon EX10 8XL]; b 30 Jan 1935; s f 1971; educ Rugby and Trin Coll Cambridge (BA 1958, MA 1961); slr with Gilbert Stephens, Exeter (ret); m 27 Nov 1965 *Rosalind Emily Margot, 3rd dau of Gerald Percival Wainwright, of St Leonards-on-Sea, Sussex, and has:

1 +CHARLES BARCLAY; b 7 July 1969; m 22 June 1996 *Harriet, er dau of Anthony Meacock, of W Hoathly

2 +Robert Ivor; b 1971

1 *Rosalind Caroline; b 2 March 1967

Lineage: EDWARD BEAUCHAMP; had:

EPHRAIM BEAUCHAMP, of Boreham, Herts; m 2nd Letitia, dau of John Coppen, of Pulox Hill, Beds, and d 16 Sept 1728, having had:

THOMAS BEAUCHAMP; m Anne, dau of William Proctor, of Epsom, Surrey, and dvp 15 June 1724, leaving an only s:

Sir WILLIAM BEAUCHAMP later BEAUCHAMP-PROCTOR (Act of Parl 1745 under terms of will of his uncle George Proctor, of Langley Park, Norfolk), **1st Bt** (GB), so cr 20 Feb 1744/5, KCB, of Langley and White Hall, Tottenham, Middlesex; bapt 11 May 1722; MA Oxon, MP Middx 1747–68, Col E Middx Militia; m 1st 1746 Jane (d 10 May 1761), dau of Christopher Tower, JP, of Huntsmoor Park, Bucks, and had, with other issue:

1 THOMAS (Sir), **2nd Bt**

Sir WILLIAM m 2nd 13 May 1762 Letitia (d 12 Jan 1798), est dau and coheir of Henry Johnson, of Gt Berkhamsted, Herts, and had, with three other sons and two daus (all d unm):

2 William Henry, of Forthampton, Glos; b 9 April 1769; m June 1790 Frances Mary (d 30 July 1844), dau and coheir of Rev William Davie (see FERGUSON-DAVIE, Bt), and d 9 May 1806, leaving:

(1) Henry William Johnson BEAUCHAMP-PROCTOR later BEAUCHAMP (Rev); b 28 July 1793; Rector Monks Risborough, Bucks; m 16 Oct 1821 Catharine (d 31 Aug 1868), only dau of Rev Robert Vernon, Rector Himbleton, Worcs, and d 25 Jan 1863, leaving:

1a William; b 17 Dec 1824; d 29 May 1858
2a George Christopher Proctor (Rev), of The Vine, Chilton, Berks; b 17 Dec 1824; m 24 Jan 1866 Alice Maria (d 1880), dau and coheir of Edward Legh, of The Lyones, Lewisham, and d 20 Nov 1889, having had:

1b Charles Legh Proctor; b 18 July 1868; m 4 Oct 1896 Aurelia Mary, only dau of Henry A Kletzka, of Oakland, Calif.
1b Alice Ethel; m 6 Jan 1903 Rev William McCarthy, BCL, Rector Collyweston, Stamford, s of Patrick McCarthy, and d 14 May 1910, leaving issue

3a Charles Davie; b 14 Oct 1826; dsp
4a Willoughby James; b 25 Feb 1828; m 30 July 1862 Elizabeth Maria (m 2nd 1886 Charles Giles Douglas, BCS, Indian Forest Dept, and d 10 Sept 1918), er dau of Rev Isaac King, Rector Bradenham, Bucks, and d 6 March 1874, having had:

1b Willoughby George; b 1 Aug 1864; Capt Royal Indian Marines; m 1st 1888 Mary (d 8 July 1910), dau of Rev Joshua Greaves, and had:

1c Willoughby Greaves, CBE (1946), VD; b 5 April 1890; Capt Ceylon RNVR; m 8 April 1912 Kathleen Alice (d 1983), 2nd dau of Dr William Bedell Benison, of King's Heath, Worcs, and d 24 Feb 1960, having had:

1d *Kathleen Patricia [Mrs Alfred Morant, Rooftops, 19 Church St, Wiveliscombe, Somerset TA4 2LR]; b 17 March 1913; Jr Cdr ATS WW II; m 7 April 1947 Alfred Thomas Morant (d 1987), s of Thomas Henry Morant, and has:

1e *Willoughby Vivian Paul [Willoughby Morant Esq, 520 Rue le Bouvier, 76160 St Martin du Vivier, France]; b 23 May 1950; educ King's Coll Taunton; m 1st 1975 (divorce 1996) Monica Oates; m 2nd 1997 *Marie Roda and has:

1f *Marc Alfred Roger; b 1996

2e *Julian Philip; b 26 Sept 1953; educ King's Coll Taunton; m 1977 *Jane Peppard and has:

1f *Timothy Charles; b 1982
1f *Donna Kathleen; b 1979

1e *Auriol Ann Melicent [Sga Ottavio Croze, 592B Dorsoduro, 30123 Venice, Italy]; b 17 July 1948; m 1975 Ottavio Croze (d 1993) and has:

1f *Ottavio Alfred; b 1976
1f *Cristina; b 1979

2d Elaine Joyce; b 15 Jan 1916; m 1st April 1936 (divorce 1954) Edward Gordon Windus and had:

1e *Michael Edward Beauchamp; b 12 Sept 1937; m 1st 1965 (divorce 1971) Evelyn Vera Pugh; m 2nd 1990 *Paola Elaine Ozkizil and by his 1st w has:

1f *Dirk Edward Beauchamp; b 1966; m 1993 *Isobel Mary Chisholm
1f *Fiona Elaine Beauchamp; b 1968; m 1992 *James David McAllister and has:

1g *Hamish James; b 1994

1e *Stefanie Gail [Mrs Robin Outram, PO Box 797, Kilifi, Kenya]; b 24 July 1940; m 1959 *Robin Outram and has:

1f *Steven Jeremy; b 27 March 1960; m 1992 *Colleen Carr-Hartley and has:

1g *Ryan Stephen; b 1993
2g *Oliver; b 21 Feb 1996

2f *Christopher James; b 6 Sept 1961; m 1989 *Helen Lewis and has:

1g *Joshua Martin; b 1990
2g *Anthony James; b 1992
3g *Sam; b 11 Dec 1997

1f *Suzanne Nicola Gail; b 1963; m 1988 *Gordon Russell St Amond Millar and has:

1g *Craig Russell St Amond; b 1990
1g *Kaila Gail Belinda; b 1991

2d (cont.) Mrs Elaine Windus m 2nd 14 May 1955 Anthony Edward Davy Windus (d 25 Oct 1989) and d 6 March 1996

3d A dau; b 2 Jan, d 3 Jan 1922

4d *Barbara Meredith [Mrs Ronald Lushington, Box 1091, Fourways 2055, Transvaal, S Africa]; b 14 Oct 1923; m 15 Sept 1943 Ronald Arthur Lushington, Maj IA (d 9 March 1996), and has:

1e *Christopher Saxton; b 24 Jan 1947; m 1982 *Maria Gabriella Quatrocchi and has:

1f *Shaun Robert; b 1983
1f *Kaley Nicola; b 1986
2f *Daniella Ashley; b 14 June 1991

1e *Madeleine Dawn; b 10 July 1945; m 1972 *Raynes Lloyd Sherwell and has:

1f *Francis Lloyd; b 1975
1f *Isla Madeleine; b 1977

2c Harold Charles; b 25 Oct 1891; Cdr RIN; m 4 April 1918 Olive (d 1983), dau of Maurice Smelt Duke, MRCS, and d 28 Sept 1942, having had:

1d Harold Gordon Willoughby; b 18 Jan 1919; d 8 Oct 1933
2d +Peter Clare [Peter Beauchamp Esq, 31 Langham Gdns, London W13 8PY]; b 27 Nov 1928; educ Cheltenham; late RAFVR and HAC, life FRSA 1958

1d *Elisabeth Proctor [Mrs James Cooper, 18 Clarence Hill, Dartmouth, Devon]; b 27 May 1922; m 4 May 1946 *Maj James Paten Cooper, CPM, RAC, s of H Douglas Cooper, and has:

1e *Charles James Beauchamp Douglas; b 4 March 1954; m 1985 *Anne Nicholson

1e *Caroline Elizabeth Beauchamp Paten; b 22 Aug 1949; m 1977 *Richard Barton and has:

1f *Ashley Douglas; b 1982

1f *Hannah Olive; b 1979

2e *Rosemary Deborah Beauchamp; b 4 Dec 1951; m 1991 *Philip Ashbourn and has:

1f *Rose Emily; b 1992

3c Lawrence King; b 23 June 1900; Cdr RN; m 9 April 1924 Helen Mary Victoria, dau of Robert Edward Stuart, of Stroud, and d 4 June 1966, leaving:

1d +Julian Lawrence Stuart [Cdr Julian Beauchamp RN, Springfield House, Nunney, Somerset BA11 4LG]; b 3 April 1928; educ Kelly Coll Tavistock; MNI, Assoc RINA; m 1st 1951 (divorce 1966) Jennifer, only dau of Harry George Parkes, of Wolverhampton, and has:

1e +Timothy Christopher Julian; b 11 Jan 1952; educ Kelly Coll, Birmingham U and London U; BSocS, MA; m 1977 *Anna Maria Magdalena, dau of Henryk Zukowski, of Warsaw, and has:

1f +John Christopher Michael; b 1981

1e *Caroline Susan [Mrs Stephen Woods, Greystones, Le Mont de Rozel, St Martin, Jersey, CI]; b 10 Dec 1954; m 1st 1977 Graeme Stanley Thomson Gibson (d 1978); m 2nd 1979 *G Stephen W Woods and has:

1f *(Gerald) Alexander William; b 1981

1f *Georgina Rozelle; b 1982

1d (cont.) Cdr Julian Beauchamp m 2nd 24 Aug 1968 Isobel Mary (d 1992), dau of Thomas Layfield, of Beckenham, and widow of Lt-Cdr Peter Fickling RN, and by her has:

2e *Fenella Jane Isobel; b 1 Jan 1970; educ St Mary's Wantage, Dauntsey's Sch and Kingston U (BA Fine Arts); m 16 May 1998 *Joshua Fitch, s of Colin Fitch, of Royston, Herts

1d (cont.) Cdr Julian Beauchamp m 3rd 10 Sept 1994 *Felicity Daphne Dorina, dau of Maj-Gen Robin Cotton Money, CB, MC, and widow of Gerrard Riddick

1d Sheila Frances; m 24 Aug 1946 Jack Eric Jones (d 4 Feb 1955), s of Albert John Jones, of Hillside Cottage, Blockley, Glos, and d 1988, having had:

1e Roger Beauchamp Spencer; b 10 April 1947; educ Christ's Hosp, St Paul's and Pembroke Coll Oxford; d 1987

2e *Andrew Julian Stuart; b 3 Oct 1950; educ Reed's Sch Cobham and St John's Coll Oxford

1d (cont.) Mrs Jack Jones m 2nd 22 June 1963 *Douglas George Horace Frank, QC, est s of George Maurice Frank, and by him had:

1e *Joanna Helen Louise; b 11 June 1965; m June 1995 *William Scott-Kerr

2e *Amelia Phoebe; b 21 May 1967

2d *Daphne Helen; b 1932

1c *Evelyn Frances Joyce; b 27 April 1903; m 10 Nov 1928 *Richard Feltrim Fagan, MB, BS, DPH, yr s of Lt-Col Christopher George Forbes Fagan, and has issue

1b (cont.) Capt Willoughby Beauchamp m 2nd 5 April 1911 Emily Elizabeth (d 5 March 1929), est dau of William Henry Herbert, of Gt Missenden, Bucks, and d 28 Oct 1922

2b Henry King, CIE; b 12 Dec 1866; MRAS, FRHS, Fell Madras U; m 23 Oct 1897 Mabel (d 5 April 1948), 2nd dau of Harry Hammond-Spencer, of Teignmouth, S Devon, and d 19 Feb 1907, having had:

1c Hampden Yorke; b 27 March 1900; d 18 Oct 1903

2c Henry Rex, OBE (1968); b 23 June 1906; educ Uppingham and RMC Sandhurst; Capt Roy Leics Regt WW II, Brig RAPC; m 1st 22 May 1937 (divorce 1947) Moira Helen, yst dau of G H Normand, of Edinburgh, and had:

1d +David FitzGerald; b 26 June 1940; educ Uppingham and Trin Coll Oxford; m 1971 *Victoria-Mary, dau of James Clark, of Connecticut, and has:

1e *Gillian Alexandra; b 1973

2e *Catriona Clare; b 1974

3e *Tanya Catherine; b 1976

2c (cont.) Brig Henry Beauchamp m 2nd 24 Dec 1954 *Mrs Elisabeth Margaret Dobson [Mrs Henry Beauchamp, Oakfields, 20 Buckstone Close, Everton, Hants], dau of A H Ford-Moore, of Salisbury, and d 1991

3b Vernon Francis; b 26 Nov 1869; m 1897 Amy (d 1948), dau of William Henry Herbert, of Gt Missenden, Bucks, and d 1949, leaving:

1c Francis William Herbert; b 30 Nov 1898; m 1927 Anne, dau of William H Pearson-Lamprecht, of Cleveland, Ohio, and had:

1d *Patricia [Mrs James Ralston Scobie, 49 S Circle Drive, Pasatiempo, Santa Cruz, CA, USA]; b May 1930; m 1 Nov 1957 *James Ralston Scobie, PhD, and has issue

2c Alan Charles Douglas; b 31 July 1901; m 1944 Olga, dau of W Rhodes, and d 1976, leaving:

1d +Hugh Alan Vernon; b 1945

3c +Lucien Willoughby [Lucien Beauchamp, 9 Sunset Dve, S Easton, MA 12375, USA]; b 16 May 1903; m 13 Nov 1937 *Nancy Knight, dau of Bradley Richards, of Boston, and has:

1d +Peter Willoughby; b 1943; m 1970 *Stacy Ann, dau of Joseph Maurice Scanlon, of Middleborough, Mass.

1d *Sandra; b 1945

1c *Leucha Elizabeth Vivian, twin with her bro; m 1931 Raymond Cooper Hewett, only s of F J Hewett, of Nova Scotia, and has issue

1b Edith Elizabeth; m 1885 Hugh Edward Clerk, CIE, and d 4 March 1933, having had issue (see CLERK, Bt)

2b Katherine; m 19 Nov 1885 Leighton Greaves, s of Rev Joshua Greaves, of Gt Missenden, and d 25 March 1944, leaving issue. He d 3 Nov 1938

3b Ellen Mary; m 27 Dec 1889 Cdr Edward Jackson Beaumont, RIN, s of Thomas Beaumont, of Bombay, and had issue. He d 15 Feb 1933

1a Laetitia Mary; d unm 30 May 1911

2a Katherine Agneta Penelope; m 28 July 1853 Lt-Col Trevor Cotton Bird, HEICS. He dsp 8 Sept 1871

3a Frances Margaret; m 25 Sept 1861 Rev George Sketchley Ffinden, Vicar Downe, Kent, and had issue. He d June 1911

4a Sophia Elizabeth; m 6 Nov 1861 Rev Edward Duncan Hall, Rector Coln St Denis, Glos, and d 8 Oct 1899, leaving issue. He d 5 June 1874

5a Julia Isabella; d 11 Dec 1921

6a Georgiana Mary; d 20 March 1922

(2) Joseph Sidney BEAUCHAMP-PROCTOR later BEAUCHAMP, of Hurst, Berks; b 2 Oct 1797; m 20 May 1847 his cousin Louisa (d 1885), dau of G E Beauchamp-Proctor, of Beech Hill (see below), and d 18 March 1871, having had:

1a Sydney Charles (Rev); b 14 March 1848; MA Oxon; Rector Little Laver, Essex, 1888–1915; m 1885 Annie Evelyn (d 28 Oct 1913), 5th dau of Rev John Alexander Blackett-Ord, of Whitfield, Northumberland, and dsp 2 April 1917

2a Robert; b 13 Aug 1850; m 10 Oct 1891 Elizabeth (d 7 July 1915), dau of William Hazledine Austin, and d 19 April 1914

3a Edward Barnard (Rev); b 21 Nov 1851; m 6 Oct 1891 Fanny Esther (d 7 March 1934), dau of Rev Stewart Dixon Stubbs, and dsp 14 Dec 1902

1a Louisa Mary; d unm 23 June 1930

2a Ellen Frances; m 13 Sept 1881 Thomas Bertram Udall, barrister, and had issue. He d 1909

3a Georgiana Agneta Geraldine; m 1885 John Houchen and had issue. He d 1920

4a Agneta Harriet; m 2 June 1886 Alexander Edward Hurford, of Looe, Cornwall

(3) Charles Eustace BEAUCHAMP-PROCTOR later BEAUCHAMP; b 20 Dec 1799; RA; m 3 June 1846 Charlotte (d 10 Dec 1878 aged 60), dau of George Tomlinson, of Claines, and d 26 Jan 1861, leaving:

1a Arthur James; b 20 Aug 1852; m 20 Aug 1879 Jane (d 22 Dec 1885), dau of James Francis, and d 16 Sept 1912, leaving:

1b Arthur William Brograve Proctor; b 4 Sept 1883

1b Agneta Frances, OBE (1919); MA, OStJ, Official Fell, Sec and Treasurer Somerville Coll Oxford 1925–43

1a Mary Charlotte; m 1877 Alfred Lyne Bradby and d 1935, having had issue

(4) Willoughby; b 1800; d unm

(5) Maurice BEAUCHAMP-PROCTOR later BEAUCHAMP; b 27 July 1801; Capt IA; m 1836 Elizabeth Pitcher (d 1837) and d 1863, leaving:

1a Fitzmaurice; b 15 March 1837; Maj-Gen 7th Fus; m 1st 10 Oct 1866 Lisa (dsp 1884), yst dau of R C Kingsford; m 2nd 21 Jan 1891 Gertrude, dau of Rev N E Lightfoot, Rector Islip, Northants, and dsp 9 April 1911

(6) James BEAUCHAMP-PROCTOR later BEAUCHAMP (Rev); b 1 July 1804; Rector Crowell, Vicar Sherborne; m 2 Oct 1833 his cousin Margaret Sophia (d 1879), sis of Sir George Beaumont, 8th Bt (qv), and d 1891, leaving:

1a Frances Bridget; d unm 22 Aug 1906

2a Mary Lætitia; m 1881 Frederick Palliser de Costabadie

3a Margaret Agneta; m 1869 William Cawood Sheen

(1) Letitia Ann; m Rev Charles Dunne, Rector Earl's Croome, Worcs, and dsp

The 1st Bt d 13 Sept 1773; his est son

Sir Thomas Beauchamp-Proctor, 2nd Bt; b 29 Sept 1756; educ Christ's Coll Cambridge (MA); High Sheriff Norfolk 1780–81; m 5 March 1778 Mary (d 25 Dec 1847), 2nd dau of Robert Palmer, of Sonning, Berks, and had, with other issue:

1 WILLIAM (Sir), **3rd Bt**

2 George Edward BEAUCHAMP-PROCTOR later BEAUCHAMP, of Thetford; b 23 July 1785; m 1st 23 July 1808 Helen Louisa (d 18 May 1849), dau of Robert W Halhed, of The Priory, Beech Hill, Reading, and had, with other issue:

(1) George Thomas; b 28 Sept 1812; HEICS; m 2 May 1833 Hester Maria Fredericka (d 22 Nov 1893), dau of Thomas Daniel, MCS, and d 2 Jan 1894, leaving, with other issue:

1a George Edward Henry; b 21 March 1834; Maj-Gen Madras Army; m 15 Nov 1866 Emily Charlotte (d 26 March 1940), dau of Henry Wood, HEICS, and d 19 July 1894, leaving:

1b Louisa Mary Catherine; m 28 Sept 1909 Henry Hope Joseph (d 31 Dec 1931) and d 29 Sept 1955

2b Alice Kaye; m 16 Nov 1895 Alan Hicks, of The Stone Ho, Bolney, Sussex, s of Henry Hicks, of Heath Ho, Weybridge, and d 28 Feb 1948, having had issue. He d 22 Nov 1950

3b Bertha Josephine; d unm 31 March 1957

4b Ruth; b 27 Aug 1887; d unm 23 Aug 1903

2a Halhed Scott; b 31 Oct 1848; m 15 Jan 1872 Florence (d 10 May 1935), dau of Rev James Richard Rumsey, and d 7 April 1921, leaving:

1b George James Douglas; b 10 Nov 1879; m 9 April 1914 Eveline (d 25 July 1953), only dau of J Bush, of Elham, Kent, and dsp 14 July 1953

1b Florence Annie Frederica; d unm 14 Jan 1901

2b Lilian Lucy Stephenson; m 27 April 1920 Timothy Conroy, s of Daniel Conroy, of Co Cork, and d 7 March 1938

3b Mercy Mary Beatrice; m 1st 11 March 1903 William Arthur Johnson (d 1917), only s of W Johnson, of Belfast, and had issue; m 2nd 1918 Thomas Cuthbert Henderson (d 1935)

(2) Robert William (Rev); b 28 Nov 1813; Rector Wickmere with Wolterton, Norfolk; m 28 Sept 1839 Alicia (d 1892), dau of Capt Pearson

(3) Edward Halhed; b 23 May 1815; Capt RN; m 28 March 1848 Anna Maria Louisa (d 22 Nov 1910), dau of Nathaniel John Halhed, HEICS, and d 18 July 1885, leaving:

  1a Edward Hayes; b 19 Oct 1852; m 19 Oct 1881 Elinor (d 1927), dau of Col T M Haultain, of Auckland, NZ, and d 1897, leaving:

    1b Edward Guy; b 1885; m Sept 1918 Louise Frances Caroline, dau of A T Haultain, of Napier, NZ, and had:

      1c +Trevor Haultain; b 1919; Capt Res Offrs NZ Forces WW II; m 17 May 1952 *Beryl Irene, er dau of Herbert Maxwell, of Otorohango, Wakaito, NZ, and has:

        1d +Robin Max; b 25 April 1953

        1d *Christine; b 21 Sept 1960

  2b Herbert Rolf Haultain, DCM; b 1890; Lt NZEF; m 1st 14 Nov 1918 Ida (d 1952), only dau of John Stevenson, of Naumai, Wanganui, NZ, and had:

    1c +John Proctor [John Beauchamp Esq, 91 Deep Creek Rd, Torbay, Auckland 10, New Zealand]; b 1923; NZ Forces WW II; m 14 April 1947 *Barbara Allison, est dau of Oliver Coupland, of Wanganui, and has had:

      1d John Haultain; b and d 1948

      2d +Warwick Rolf; b Jan 1952; m 1974 *Jan, dau of Lester Wintere, of Parr Terr, Milford, NZ

      3d +Michael Douglas; b Dec 1957; m 1978 *Laura Ann, dau of Rev Campbell Nicol, of Milton, S Otago, NZ, and has:

        1e +Christopher David; b 1979

        2e +Robin Anthony Nicol; b 1985

      4d +Bruce Proctor; b 1963

      1d *Margaret Anne; b 1947; m 1st 1966 Colin Daniel Mayes; m 2nd 1974 *Stewart Rankin and by him has:

        1e *Douglas John; b 1978

      2d *Jane Allison; b Feb 1949; m 1974 *Alan Stewart Davis

      3d *Elizabeth Claire; b Feb 1956; m 1974 *Peter David Anderson

    1c *Jill [Mrs Ronald Parkin, 2 Webster St, Westown, New Plymouth, New Zealand]; b April 1926; m 1949 *Ronald Parkin and has:

      1d *Carolyn; b 31 March 1950

      2d *Jan; b 23 Jan 1952

      3d *Andrew; b 28 Jan 1954

  2b (cont.) Herbert Beauchamp m 2nd 1955 Mary Joyce (d 1979), dau of Capt James Stevenson Hempton, of Dunedin, NZ, and d 1968

  3b Philip Kay Halhed; b 1897; d Oct 1913

  1b Esmé Constance; m 5 Dec 1912 George Herbert Usher, MD, FRCS, and had issue

  2a Herbert Lloyd; b 10 Sept 1854; m 1886 Rose Katherine (d 1941), dau of Maj Henry Grimston Hale, and d 1888, leaving:

    1b Hugh Edward; b 1886; m 1st 10 Dec 1907 Grace Ethel, dau of F Quistorf, of Santa Cruz, Calif., and had:

      1c *Dorothy Margaret; b 1909; m 1931 *Harry Eugene Lennon, of King's City, Calif.

    1b (cont.) Hugh Beauchamp m 2nd Tekla (d 19–), dau of Carl Viborg, of Stockholm, Sweden, and d 1962

    2b Herbert Cecil; b 1888; m 13 Dec 1913 Dora (d 1968), dau of H Dohrmann, of Reinbeck, Iowa, and d 1969, leaving:

      1c +David Dohrmann [David Beauchamp, 830 Overhill Dve, Redding, CA 96001, USA]; b 1916; educ U of Calif (AB 1938); 1st Lt USAF WW II; m 30 May 1941 *Jean Anita, dau of Wade Greening Moores, of Redding, and has:

        1d +Mark David; b 1 Oct 1952; m 1st 1980 (divorce 1987) Carla Jenoyce Norton, of Redding; m 2nd 1988 *Ellen Paris, of Santa Monica

        1d *Sarah Caroline; b 14 June 1954; m 1988 *Harry Holverson, of Arcata, Calif., and has:

          1e *Elizabeth Jean; b 1989

      2c John Herbert; b 1919; US Army; d 1954

    1b Gladys Mary; d unm 2 Nov 1910

  3a Francis Arthur; b 16 Nov 1857; m 4 Feb 1892 Beatrice Frances (d 4 Jan 1948), dau of Gen Sir Richard Kelly, KCB, and d 1 June 1926, leaving:

    1b Marjorie Ellie Frances; b 27 Jan 1893; d unm 27 June 1967

  1a Annie Louise; b 11 Jan 1849; d unm 3 June 1950

  2a Alice Emily; d unm 8 Sept 1929

  3a Constance Isabella; d unm 11 May 1896

(4) Henry Champion; b 8 Aug 1827; m 2 April 1857 Maria Louisa (d 24 July 1875), dau of Thomas Carter, and d 12 April 1904, having had:

  1a Henry Herman Edward; b 16 April 1861; d 24 July 1879

  2a James Lloyd Hobart; b 21 Sept 1862; m 5 Sept 1891 Maria Radford Knight, dau of Augustus George Stead, and d 12 Aug 1927, leaving:

    1b Marie Georgiana; b 1892; m 14 July 1928 Robert Desmond Carruthers, only s of George J Carruthers, of New Barn, Kent, and had:

      1c *Marie Lucy Beauchamp; b 1930

2 (cont.) George Beauchamp m 2nd 1855 Elizabeth (d 28 Jan 1918), dau of Frederick Chapman, of Mavis Enderby, Lincs, and d 21 Dec 1868

Sir THOMAS d 29 March 1827; his er son,

Sir William Beauchamp-Proctor, 3rd Bt; b 14 Oct 1781; Adml RN; m 20 May 1812 Anne (d 6 Feb 1859), dau of Thomas Gregory, of Springfield, Essex, and had, with other issue:

1 THOMAS WILLIAM BROGRAVE (Sir), **4th Bt**

2 William Henry BEAUCHAMP-PROCTOR later BEAUCHAMP (Rev); b 16 March 1818; Rector Chedgrave, Incumbent Langley, Norfolk; m 31 Dec 1845 Augusta (d 21 March 1887), dau of Dr T Arnold, of Stamford, and d 19 March 1853, having had, with other issue:

---

(1) Arthur Henry Selby; b 3 Jan 1848; d 20 Nov 1867

(2) Sir EDWARD BEAUCHAMP, 1st Bt, so cr 1911 (see 1970 edn BEAUCHAMP, Bt, of Grosvenor Place)

(3) Henry Woodrooffe (Rev); b 25 Dec 1851; MA Cantab; Rector Copdock, Ipswich; m 29 Aug 1876 Katherine Mary (d 22 July 1950), only child of Rev Charles Snell, Rector Oulton, Suffolk, and d 16 July 1915, leaving:

  1a Ronald Charles William, FRPS; b 23 July 1877; educ Winchester and Trin Coll Cambridge (BA 1898); m 1st 19 July 1905 Helen (divorce 1929; he remarried her 1945) (d 25 March 1966), dau of Edward Jerram Herbert, of Oulton, Suffolk, and had:

    1b William Dashwood Proctor; b 9 April 1913; with Min of Info; ka off Singapore 11 Feb 1942

    1b Barbara Proctor; b 25 Jan 1909; WW II as Sr Cdr ATS, author

    2b Anne Proctor; b 9 April 1913; d unm 16 June 1934

  1a (cont.) Ronald Beauchamp m 2nd 22 Feb 1930 (divorce 1945) Mary Eleanor (d 16 Dec 1952), widow of Lt-Col Alfred Edward FitzGerald, E Surrey Regt, and 2nd dau of Col Thomas Angelo Irwin, JP, DL, of Lynehow, Carlisle, and Solport, Cumberland, and d 26 March 1961

  2a Maurice Henry (Rev); b 18 Sept 1886; educ Uppingham and Exeter Coll Oxford (BA 1911, MA 1912); Assist Priest Cowley, Oxford (Vicar 1928–39); d unm 5 May 1966

  1a Sybil Katherine; m 20 March 1920 Brig Frederick Cromie de Butts, CB, DSO, MC, IA, only s of Capt Frederick Robert McCrea de Butts, MA

3 Robert; b 16 Oct 1819; served RN; m 14 June 1854 Elizabeth Beatrice, dau of Henry Symons, MD, and d 12 Oct 1889, leaving:

  (1) William Penn; b 5 Feb 1857

  (2) George Fox; b 4 Sept 1859; d 1955

  (3) Walter Mannering; b 20 Sept 1861

  (4) Robert Ephraim; b 4 April 1865

  (5) Cecil Brograve; b 30 Aug 1867; d May 1934

  (6) Frank Skipwith; b 6 Sept 1871

  (7) Reginald Percy; b 19 May 1873; m 14 June 1904 Malvina Blanche Natalie (d 7 Feb 1969), dau of Jonathan Purdy Plummer, and d 1944, leaving:

    1a Percy Tremayne, JP; b 1908; m 1935 Eileen Alice (d 10 May 1964), dau of Arthur Edward Croft, and d 18 Aug 1959, leaving:

      1b +Anthony Tremayne; b 1937; m 9 Dec 1961 *Nancy Anne, dau of Mark Vincent Jones, of Muddy Creek, Tasmania, and has:

        1c +Christopher Tremayne; b 1 Jan 1964

        2c +Mark Andrew; b 1972

        1c *Wendy Anne; b 8 July 1965; m 1984 *Allan Gregory Mason

      1b *Suzanne Elizabeth; b 1946

    2a +Geoffrey Frank [Mr Geoffrey Beauchamp, El-Retiro, Roseveare, W Tamar, Tasmania, Australia]; b 1914; m 27 Dec 1950 Dorothy Vernon (d 1970), dau of Thomas Vernon Lewis, of Hawthorne, Victoria, and has:

      1b *Pamela Nerida; b 13 Feb 1952

    1a Vonda Laura; m 15 May 1933 Ronsley Miles Ponsonby, of Hampstead. He d 17 May 1964

    2a Nerida Nadine; b 1916; m 1935 (divorce 1943) Ronald Breadalbane Postle

  (1) Leila Merino; m 1st 1881 Frank Swift (d 1884); m 2nd Herbert Piper, of Bendigo, Australia

  (2) Laura Gertrude

Sir WILLIAM d 14 March 1861; his est son,

Sir THOMAS WILLIAM BEAUCHAMP-PROCTOR later PROCTOR-BEAUCHAMP (roy licence 9 July 1852), **4th Bt**, DL Norfolk; b 2 July 1815; Lt RHG, High Sheriff Norfolk 1869; m 15 June 1852 Hon Caroline Esther Waldegrave (d 3 July 1898), yst dau of 2nd Baron Radstock (see WALDEGRAVE, E), and d 7 Oct 1874, leaving:

1 **Sir Reginald William Proctor-Beauchamp, 5th Bt**, JP, DL Norfolk; b 23 April 1853; Maj 2nd Bde E Div Norfolk Artillery; m 7 June 1880 (divorce 1901) Lady Violet Julia Charlotte Maria Jocelyn (d 22 Oct 1925), only child of 5th Earl of Roden (qv), and d 10 Nov 1912, leaving:

  (1) Sheila Ginevra Hilda Mary; m 22 June 1909 Hermon Barker-Hahlo, of Foxlease Park, Lyndhurst, only s of George Hahlo, of Manchester, took by roy licence 18 Oct 1934 the name BEAUCHAMP and d 20 Jan 1953, Langley Park passing to her only s:

    1a Jocelyn George Reginald BARKER-HAHLO later BEAUCHAMP (roy licence 1931); b 15 Feb 1910; educ Eton; Lt-Cdr RNVR WW II; d unm 13 March 1958

  (2) Nadine Sophia Charlotte; m 1st 23 April 1910 (divorce 1914) Edward Graves Brinkley, 2nd s of John Lloyd Brinkley DL, of Fortland, Co Sligo; m 2nd 15 Sept 1915 (divorce 1921) Sir George Bettesworth Piggott, KBE (d 14 March 1952); m 3rd 10 Sept 1923 (divorce 1927) Maj Nigel D Stewart, s of Capt Neil P Stewart, of Plas Lodwie, Bangor; m 4th 11 May 1928 Capt Ralph Holme Woodcock, est s of Edward Holme Woodcock, of Wigan, Lancs, and d 20 Sept 1949

2 Granville Pelham; b 20 Aug 1855; d 9 Dec 1889

3 **Sir Horace George Proctor-Beauchamp, 6th Bt**, CB; b 3 Nov 1856; Lt-Col cmdg 15th Bn Norfolk Regt, Brevet Col cmdg 20th Hus, served Suakin 1885, Sudan 1888, Boer War 1901–02 and WW I; m 15 Nov 1892 (divorce 1915) Florence, dau of H M Leavitt, of New York, and was ka Suvla Bay 12 Aug 1915

4 MONTAGU HARRY (Sir), **7th Bt**

5 Algernon; b 2 April 1867; d 6 March 1879

1 Ida Caroline; m 6 Oct 1891 Col Robert Henry Curzon Drury-Lowe, Gren Gds, 3rd s of William Drury Holden Lowe, JP, DL, of Denby and Locko, and d 12 Dec 1951. He d 4 Jan 1907

2 Hilda; m 10 Dec 1884 Sir John Edward Kynaston Studd, 1st Bt, OBE (qv), and d 22 April 1921, leaving issue

3 Constance, twin with Hilda; m 1st 30 July 1889 William Douglas Robinson-Douglas, of Orchardton, Castle Douglas, Scotland (d 3 Oct 1921); m 2nd 13 May 1926 William Jardine Herries Maxwell, OBE, of Munches, and d 4 June 1941. He d 31 July 1933

4 Maud; m 1889 Rev William Thomas Baring Hayter, Master of Old Charterhouse, London, EC, 1927–35, Chaplain OStJ, Dean Gibraltar, 3rd s of Harrison Hayter, Pres ICE, and d 18 Feb 1956, leaving issue. He d 21 Aug 1935

The 6th Bt's bro,

Rev Sir Montagu Harry Proctor-Beauchamp, 7th Bt; b 19 April 1860; educ Trin Coll Cambridge (MA); missionary W China, Vicar Monkton Combe 1914–18, Pncpl Chaplain Mediterranean Expdny Force 1916 (despatches), CF N Russian Expdny Force 1919, Hon CF 1921, FRGS, FRES; m 20 April 1892 Florence (d 2 May 1955), dau of Robert Barclay, of Reigate, and had:

1 Montagu Barclay Granville; b 4 Aug 1893; Lt 1st/5th Bn Norfolk Regt; ka Suvla Bay 12 Aug 1915

2 Victor Cuthbert; b 7 June 1898; d 27 July 1899

3 IVOR CUTHBERT (Sir), **8th Bt**

4 +Basil Ralph [Basil Proctor-Beauchamp Esq, Penhwyr, Dinas Cross, Newport, Dyfed SA42 0UQ]; b 17 June 1906; educ Marlborough and Toronto U (DipAg); m 1st 1932 (divorce 1957) Joan, dau of Tom Storey, and has:

(1) +Nicholas [Nicholas Proctor-Beauchamp Esq, 26 Howard St, Thatto Heath, St Helens, Lancs SA10 3RG]; b 8 Nov 1935; FRHS, FPWI; m 1964 *Pauline, dau of Jacob de Mos, of Hook of Holland, and has:

1a *Alison de Mos; b 12 March 1965

2a *Sarah Jane; b 17 Aug 1966

3a *Victoria Isobel; b 20 July 1967

(1) *Carol Margot [Mrs Claude Swain, 29 Springhead, Tunbridge Wells, Kent TN2 3NY]; b 5 May 1933; m 4 Oct 1958 *F/Lt Claude de Pina Downs Swain, RAF, yr s of Capt Claude de Pina Downs Swain, of Southsea, and Mrs Alan Beard, of Kisumu, Kenya, and has:

1a *Charles de Pina Beauchamp; b 17 Aug 1959; m 1984 *Caroline Kerr, dau of Alexander Alfred Stuart, of Gerrards Cross, and has:

1b *Charles Douglas Stuart; b 1988

1b *Victoria Caroline; b 1989

2b *Alexandra Philida; b 1997

1a *Claudia Fenella; b 3 Nov 1961; m 1983 *Richard William Pettifer, s of W/Cdr John Kenyon Pettifer, RAF, of Little London, Bucks, and has:

1b *Julian Richard; b 1987

2b *William Gregory; b 1989

3b *Felix George; b 1991

1b *Miranda Imogen Hilary; b 1995

(2) *Elisabeth Waldegrave [Miss Elizabeth Proctor-Beauchamp, Flat 3, Croft Rd, Willesborough, Kent TN24 8AZ]; b 1934

4 (cont.) Basil Proctor-Beauchamp m 2nd 8 June 1957 *Diana, formerly w of Arno Rohde and dau of Lt-Col Bernard H Elliott, RA, of Goring Ho, N Woodchester, Glos, and by her has:

(3) *Sophie Joy [Miss Sophie Proctor-Beauchamp, 43 Richmond Ave, London N1 0MB]; b 16 March 1958

1 (Muriel) Esther Dornie; b 23 Jan 1897; d unm 23 June 1967

Sir MONTAGU d 26 Oct 1939; his er surv son,

Rev Sir Ivor Cuthbert Proctor-Beauchamp, 8th Bt; b 19 Aug 1900; educ King's Coll Cambridge (MA); Police Surgn Essex Constabulary, Medical Missionary China Inland Mission, Medical Advsr Centl Asian Mission, MB, BCh, MRCS, LRCP; Memb Cncl China Inland Mission, ordained 1964; m 30 Sept 1933 Caroline Muriel (d 1987), dau of Frank Densham (see HAZLERIGG, B), and had:

1 Sir CHRISTOPHER RADSTOCK PROCTOR-BEAUCHAMP, **9th and present Bt**

2 +Anthony Hazlerigg (Rev) [The Rev Anthony Proctor-Beauchamp, The Rectory, 18 Thorpe Rd, Kirby Cross, Essex CO13 0LT]; b 25 Feb 1940; educ Monkton Combe Sch and Trin Coll Cambridge (BA 1961, MA 1966); MICE (1968), ordained 1975; m 30 May 1965 *Anne Elise, er dau of Rev Thomas Hewitt, MTh, of Worthing, and has:

(1) +Guy James [Guy Proctor-Beauchamp Esq, 97 Avenue Rd, Portswood, Hants SO14 6BD]; b 23 Feb 1967; m 1992 *Hilda Catherine, dau of R H Craig, of Campbeltown, Argyll

(2) +Julian Thomas; b 11 Oct 1968

(1) *Claire Alexandra; b 1970

1 *Rosemary Jean; b 2 Dec 1936; m 4 April 1964 *Thomas Henry Geake, AMI-MechE, only s of Frank Henry Geake, of Caversham, Berks, and has:

(1) *William Beauchamp; b 11 Nov 1968

(1) *Elisabeth Marjorie; b 17 May 1965

(2) *Helen Mary; b 23 July 1967

PRYKE

Arms: Per pale or and argent, on a cross invected azure two fasces erect in pale and as many mascles in fess all of the first. **Crest:** Two arms embowed vested azure, cuffs argent, the hands proper, supporting a fasces erect or, each arm charged with a mascle of the last. **Creation:** Bt. (UK) 3 Nov 1926.

SIR DAVID DUDLEY PRYKE, 3RD BT, of Wanstead, Essex [Sir David Pryke Bt, 27 Wantz Haven, Princes Rd, Maldon, Essex CM9 7HA]; b 16 July 1912; s f 1959; educ St Lawrence Coll Ramsgate; memb Court Common Cncl City London 1960, Liveryman Turners' Co 1961, Master 1985–86; m 10 Oct 1945 *Doreen Winifred, er dau of Ralph Bernard Wilkins, of Winchmore Hill, London N, and has:

1 *Madge [Mrs Keith Pettit, 21 Wards Rd, Newbury Park, Ilford, Essex IG2 7BA]; b 22 Nov 1946; m 4 Sept 1971 *Keith Robert Pettit, Dip Arch (Hons) RIBA, s of Harry Walter Pettit, and has:

(1) *Stephen Robert; b 26 July 1975

(1) *Christine Yvonne; b 21 Feb 1978

2 *Anita; b 6 May 1949; m 6 May 1969 *Edwin Mark Lightstone, s of Harris Lightstone, and has:

(1) *Alexander James Mark; b 6 Dec 1976

(2) *Peter David Edward; b 18 Feb 1982

(1) *Tamsin Anna Frances; b 6 March 1980

Lineage: RICHARD REEVE PRYKE, of Bury St Edmunds, had:

Sir William Robert Pryke, 1st Bt (UK), so cr 3 Nov 1926, JP (1921); b 15 March 1847; sr ptnr Pryke and Palmer, of London EC, Lt and Alderman City London (Sheriff 1921), Ld Mayor 1925–26, memb: Lee Conservancy and Wanstead UDC, Govr Body Irish Soc, Court Common Cncl 1887–1920, ktd 1921; m 12 Dec 1878 Marguerite Harriot (d 27 Nov 1925), dau of Robert Stiles, of St John's Wood, and had:

1 WILLIAM ROBERT DUDLEY, (Sir), **2nd Bt**

2 Richard Frederick Norman; b 26 Oct 1886; served WW I; m 1927 *Doris Kathleen, dau of John Russell Kingston, of Wanstead, and dsp 29 Nov 1958

3 Hamer Forest Stanley; b 12 March 1889; educ Forest Sch; underwriting memb Lloyd's, Capt HAC Res, Lt City London, WW I (1914–15 star, two medals); d unm 20 Jan 1950

1 Mabel Marguerite; m 12 Oct 1907 Arthur Edmund Howard (d 22 July 1929), s of James Howard, of Wanstead, and had issue

2 Ethel Annie; m 6 Nov 1926 Cyril Turner, slr, of London E11, s of James Turner, of Wanstead

Sir WILLIAM d 30 March 1932; his est son,

Sir (William Robert) Dudley Pryke, 2nd Bt; b 5 March 1882; educ City of London Sch; chm and md Pryke and Palmer Ltd, memb Common Cncl City London; m 15 July 1911 Marjorie (d 7 Feb 1936), dau of Henry Greenwood Brown, and d 23 March 1959, leaving:

1 Sir DAVID DUDLEY PRYKE, **3rd and present Bt**

2 William Dudley; b 18 Nov 1914; educ Highgate Sch; Capt DCLI WW II, Liveryman Plumbers' Co (Master 1969–70); m 2 March 1940 Lucy Irene (Peggy) (d 1984), dau of Frank Madgett, of Whetstone, London N, and d 1994, leaving:

(1) +CHRISTOPHER DUDLEY [Christopher Pryke Esq, 69 Wendell Rd, Stamford Brook, London W12 9SB]; b 17 April 1946; heir presumptive; educ Hurstpierpoint; m 1973 (divorce 1986) Angela Gay, dau of Harold Noel Meek, of Holly Cottage, Crowell, Oxon, and has:

1a +James Dudley; b 29 Dec 1977

(1) *Rosemary Susan [Miss Rosemary Pryke, 21 Eastern Rd, Fortis Green, London N2]; b 13 Nov 1949

3 Peter Stanley, MBE; b 31 July 1916; educ Charterhouse and King's Coll Cambridge (MA 1938); Lt-Col IA WW II (despatches twice), GSO(1) 5th EI Div SEAC; k plane crash India 9 Feb 1945

1 *Patricia Margaret [Miss Patricia Pryke, 40 Temple Ave, Whetstone, London N20]; b 19 Jan 1919

PRYS-DAVIES

Creation: B. (LP, UK) 1982.

THE BARON PRYS-DAVIES, of Llanegryn, Co Gwynedd (Gwilym Prys Prys-Davies) [The Rt Hon The Lord Prys-Davies, Lluest, 78 Church Rd, Tonteg, Pontypridd, Mid Glam CF38 1EN]; *b* 8 Dec 1923; *educ* Towyn Sch and UCW Aberystwyth (LLB 1949, LLM 1952); RN 1942–46; Law Faculty UCW Aberystwyth 1946–52; slr 1956, ptnr Morgan, Bruce & Nicholas 1957–1987, consultant 1987–; Memb: Welsh Advsy Ctee ITA 1966–69, Welsh Cncl 1966–69, Advsy Gp Use Foetuses and Foetal Material for Research 1972, Working Party 4th TV Serv Wales 1975, EEC Ec and Social Ctee 1978–82; Chm Welsh Hosps Bd 1968–74; Special Advsr Sec State Wales 1974–78, Oppn Spokesman: Health 1983–89, NI 1982–93, Wales 1987–97, memb Ho Lds Select Ctee: Parochial Charities Bill and Small Charities Bill 1983–84, Murder and Life Imprisonment 1988–89; memb Br-Irish Inter-Parly Body 1990; V-Pres Coleg Harlech 1989–; OStJ; author: *A Central Welsh Council* (1963), *Y Ffermwr a'r Gyfraith* (1967); *m* 1951 *Llinos, dau of Abram Richard Evans, and has:

1 *Catrin Prys; *b* 1957; *m* 1980 *Andrew Peter Waugh and has:
  (1) *Matthew Prys; *b* 1989
  (2) *Owen Prys; *b* 1992
2 *Ann Prys; *b* 1959
3 *Elin Prys; *b* 1963

Lineage: WILLIAM DAVIES; *m* Mary Matilda — and had:

GWILYM PRYS later PRYS-DAVIES (1982), *cr* a **Baron**

PUTTNAM

Arms: Or within an orle of roses a gateway composed of a central arch between two lesser arches and surmounted by a segmental pediment gules. **Crest:** A harp or standing on a closed book fesswise proper bound gules. **Supporters:** Dexter, a curlew proper gorged with a plain collar argent charged with square billets sable; sinister, a stork proper gorged with a plain collar argent charged with square billets sable. **Motto:** *Servio ut vivam* ('I Serve that I may live'). **Creation:** B. (LP, UK) 1992.

THE BARON PUTTNAM, of Queensgate, Roy Borough of Kensington and Chelsea (Sir David Terence Puttnam, CBE (1983)) [The Rt Hon The Lord Puttnam CBE, 13 Queen's Gate Place Mews, London SW7 5BG]; *b* 25 Feb 1941; *educ* Michenden GS London; advertising exec 1958–66, photographer's agent 1966–68, film producer 1968–: *Bugsy Malone* (1976), *Midnight Express* (1978), *Chariots of Fire* (1981), *Local Hero* (1982), *Cal* (1984), *The Killing Fields* (1985), *The Mission* (1986), *Memphis Belle* (1990), *Meeting Venus* (1991), *Being Human* (1993), *War of the Buttons* (1994); chm: Enigma Productions 1978–96, Nat Film and Television Sch 1988– (Govr 1974–), Internat Television Enterprises 1988–, NESTA (National Endowment for Science, Technology and the Arts) 1998–; Chm and CEO Columbia Pictures 1986–88; Visiting Industrial Prof Bristol U Drama Dept 1986–; Dir: Nat Film Finance Corp 1980–85, Anglia TV Gp 1982–, Village Roadshow Corp 1989–, Survival Anglia 1989–, Chrysalis Gp 1993–96; V-Pres BAFTA 1993; memb Br Screen Advsy Cncl 1988; Pres CPRE 1985–92; Tstee Tate Gallery 1986–93; First Chllr Sunderland U 1997–; FRGS; FRSA; FRPS; Hon Fell Manchester Polytechnic 1990; Hon FCSD 1990; Hon FLI; Hon LLD Bristol 1983; Hon DLitt Leicester 1986, Bradford 1993; Hon LittD Leeds 1992, Humberside 1992, Westminster 1997, Sunderland 1992; Michael Balcon Award BAFTA 1982; Officier de l'Ordre des Arts et des Lettres 1992, ktd 1995; *m* 22 Sept 1961 *Patricia Mary Jones and has
1 *Alexander David; *b* 1966
1 *Deborah Jane; *b* 1962; *m* 1985 *Loyd Grossman and has:
  (1) *Florence Grace; *b* 1989
  (2) *Constance Catherine; *b* 1991

Lineage: LEONARD ARTHUR PUTTNAM; *m* Marie Beatrix Goldman and has:

DAVID TERENCE, *cr* a **Baron**

PYM

UBI·SERITUR·IBI·FLOREAT

Arms: Quarterly, 1st and 4th, sable on a fess engrailed between three owls or, a trefoil slipped vert between two cross crosslets of the first, all within a bordure of the second (for PYM); 2nd, vert on a cross engrailed ermine a lion rampant regardant sable, in the dexter canton a mullet or (for KINGSLEY); 3rd, sable three salmon haurient per pale argent and or (for ORDE). **Crest:** Upon a mount vert a hind's head erased or, gorged with a collar nebuly azure and holding in the mouth a trefoil slipped vert. **Supporters:** Dexter, rampant upon a sandy mount with tussocks of grass proper a warhorse in trian aspect sable, mane, tail and hooves or, on its head a chanfron and on the neck a crinet, both argent, gorged with a double chain, pendant therefrom a portcullis gold; sinister, rampant upon a like mount a bull in trian aspect sable, armed and unguled or, gorged with a double chain, pendant therefrom a portcullis gold. **Motto:** *Ubi seritur ibi floreat* ('Bloom where you are planted'). **Creation:** B. (LP, UK) 1987.

THE BARON PYM, of Sandy, Co Beds (Francis Leslie Pym, MC (1945), PC (1970), DL (Cambs 1973)) [The Rt Hon The Lord Pym MC PC DL, Everton Park, Sandy, Beds SG19 2DE]; *b* 13 Feb 1922; *educ* Eton and Magdalene Coll Cambridge (Hon Fell 1979); Capt 9th Queen's Roy Lancers WW II (despatches); C candidate Rhondda W 1959 gen election, MP (C) Cambs 1961–83, Cambs SE 1983–87, Assist Govt Whip 1962–64, Oppn Whip 1964–67, Oppn Dep Ch Whip 1967–70, Parly U-Sec Treasury and Govt Ch Whip 1970–73, Sec State NI 1973–74, Oppn Spokesman: Ag 1974–76, H of C Affrs and Devolution 1976–78, For and Cwlth Affrs 1978–79, Sec State Def 1979–81, Chllr Duchy Lancaster, Paymaster Gen and Leader H of C 1981, Ld Pres Cncl and Leader H of C 1981–82, For Sec 1982–83; Pres Atlantic Treaty Assoc 1985–88; Chm: ESU 1987–92 and Political Honours Scrutiny Ctee; dir Christie Brockbank Shipton Ltd 1994–; author: *The Politics of Consent* (1984), *Sentimental Journey* (1998); *m* 1949 *Valerie Fortune, er dau of Francis John Heaton Daglish, and has:

1 *(Francis) Jonathan [Jonathan Pym Esq, 53 Ridgway Place, London SW19 4SP]; *b* 21 Sept 1952; *educ* Eton and Magdalene Coll Cambridge; ptnr Travers Smith Braithwaite, slrs, 1984–; does not use courtesy title; *m* 1981 *Laura Elizabeth Camille, yr dau of Robin Alfred Wellesley, and has:
  (1) *(Francis) Matthew; *b* 1984
  (2) *Oliver Quintin; *b* 1988
  (1) *Katie Camille; *b* 1985
2 *Andrew Leslie [The Hon Andrew Pym, The Elms, Everton, Sandy, Beds SG19 2JU]; *b* 30 Nov 1954; *educ* Eton and RAC Cirencester; FRICS; *m* 1976 *Ruth Alison, dau of Benjamin Peter Skelton, and has:
  (1) *Benjamin Ruthven; *b* 1979
  (1) *Jessica Mary; *b* 1982
1 *Charlotte Hazell [The Hon Mrs Lightbody, 2 Greenbank Drive, Sefton Park, Liverpool L19 1AW]; *b* 2 July 1950; *m* 1984 *Ian Nye Lightbody and has:
  (1) *Thomas Hugh; *b* 1986
  (1) *Helena Rosamund; *b* 1988
2 *Sarah Lucy [The Hon Mrs Walton, Thockrington, Colwell, Northumberland NE48 4DH]; *b* 18 Dec 1958; *m* 1985 *Peter Walton and has:
  (1) *James Peter; *b* 1986
  (1) *Victoria Lucy; *b* 1988

Lineage: WILLIAM PYM, of St Martin-in-the-Fields, London, and Heath and Reach, Leighton Buzzard, Beds; *b* 1619; *m* Margaret Harris and *d* 1672, leaving, with two yr sons and daus:

WILLIAM PYM, of Norton Bury, Herts; *b* 1645; *m* 1679 Elizabeth, yst dau of Henry Crosse, and *d* 1716, leaving, with two yr sons and daus:

WILLIAM PYM, of Radwell and Norton; *b* 1680; *m* 1719 Catherine, dau of Rev William Wollaston, and *d* 1729, leaving, with three yr sons:

WILLIAM PYM, of Radwell; *b* 1723; *m* 18 Oct 1748 Elizabeth, dau and heir of Heylock Kingsley, of Hazells Hall, Beds, which he thus acquired (it was sold by Lord Pym in the 1980s), and *d* July 1788, leaving, with a yr s and dau:

FRANCIS PYM, of Hazells Hall; *b* 1756; MP Beds; *m* May 1784 Anne, dau of Robert Palmer, of Holme Park, Berks, and *d* 1833, having had, with other issue:

1 FRANCIS

2 William Wollaston (Rev); *b* 1792; Rector Willian, Herts; *m* 1st 1822 Sophia Rose, 6th dau of Adml Samuel Gambier (bro of 1st and last Baron Gambier of Iver), and had, with two er sons:

(1) William Mills Parry (Rev); *b* 1839; Rector Corsham, Wilts; *m* 21 Oct 1863 Maria Georgina, 3rd dau of Henry Every (*see* EVERY, Bt), and *d* 19 July 1872, leaving issue

(2) Charles Guy, of Caesar's Camp, Sandy, Beds, and S Kensington, JP, DL; *b* Feb 1841; MP Bedford 1895–1906, High Sheriff London 1911; *m* 1885 Emily Mildred, dau of Henry Sykes Thornton, of Battersea Rise, and *d* 10 Nov 1918, leaving, with an er dau:

1a Marjorie Florence; *b* 14 May 1891; *m* 1st 3 Feb 1910 (*divorce* 1921) Herbert Walter Acland-Troyte, MC (*see* ACLAND, Bt, of Columb John) and had issue; *m* 2nd 19 June 1922 André Cluysendar, of Brussels

2 (cont.) The Rev William Pym *m* 2nd 1843 Edith Elizabeth, dau of V-Adml Noble, and *d* 1852, having by her had:

(3) Horatio Noble; *b* 2 July 1844; *educ* Bedford Sch; *m* 1st 12 Sept 1876 Sarah Juliet, dau of Edmund Backhouse (*see* BACKHOUSE, Bt), and had, with an er s (*d* young):

1a Charles Evelyn (Sir), CBE (1939, OBE 1919), JP (1913), DL (Kent 1938); *b* 11 Jan 1879; *educ* Eton and Magdalen Coll Oxford; Capt 5th Lancers, Maj Suffolk Yeo, Boer War 1901–02 and WW I (despatches twice); Kent: CA, V-Chm CC 1936–49, Chm 1949–52, ktd 1959, CStJ; *m* 7 June 1905 Violet Catherine, dau of Frederic Lubbock (*see* AVEBURY, B), and *d* 1971, leaving:

1b John; *b* 12 May 1908; *educ* Eton and Trin Coll Cambridge; Lt-Col RE WW II (despatches), FRIBA, AMPTI; *m* 17 Dec 1930 *Diana, only dau of Brig-Gen Sir John Gough, VC, KCB, CMG, and *d* 22 Nov 1993, leaving:

1c *John Nicholas; *b* 6 April 1947; *educ* Bryanston and Harvard; *m* 17 Sept 1976 *Hope Brook, only dau of Prof Joseph Auerbach, and has:

1d *William; *b* 5 Sept 1980

1d *Celia Evans; *b* 25 May 1978

2d *Martha Elizabeth; *b* 14 July 1983

1c *Jill; *b* 15 Oct 1933; *m* 13 Jan 1962 *Prof Charles Antony Richard Hoare, FRS, est s of Henry Samuel Malortie Hoare, and has had:

1d *Thomas Edward; *b* 25 May 1964; *m* 5 Sept 1993 *Kalwinder Sandhu and has:

1e *Jhansi; *b* 6 May 1996

2d Matthew John; *b* 30 Dec 1967; *d* 6 April 1981

1d *Joanna Francis; *b* 9 Dec 1965; *m* 28 Jan 1996 *Gavin Colthart

2c *Carol; *b* 19 April 1936; *m* 19– *Edwin St Clair Taylor, yr s of Frederick John Taylor, of Johannesburg, and has:

1d *Alexis Paul; *b* 1 Jan 1962; *m* 14 May 1993 *Andrea Bottomley and has:

1e *Innes Primrose; *b* 8 Sept 1993

2e *Freya May; *b* 28 May 1995

1d *Chloe Emma; *b* 26 June 1964; has:

1e *Lily Grace; *b* 18 Oct 1994

2e *Fern Maude; *b* 12 April 1996

2b *Roland; *b* 14 June 1910; *educ* Eton and Slade Sch Art; RA WW II

3b Martin Jeremy; *b* 23 May 1919; *educ* Eton and Trin Coll Cambridge; Capt The Buffs WW II (wounded), md Hambros Bank; *m* 16 March 1947 *Jean, yr dau of Maj Douglas Duff Maxwell, and *d* 14 Nov 1981, leaving:

1c *Simon Charles; *b* 4 Oct 1947

2c *Richard Anthony; *b* 2 May 1949

1c *Daphne Lucinda; *b* 28 Nov 1956

1b *Mary Elizabeth; *b* 8 Oct 1914; *educ* Downe House Sch and Paris; *m* 8 March 1941 Lt Henry Patrick Cobb, DSC, RNVR (*ka* 20 July 1942)

(3) (cont.) Horatio Pym *m* 2nd 2 May 1881 Jane Hannah Backhouse, dau of Robert Barclay Fox, of Penjerrick, Cornwall, and *d* 5 May 1896, having had:

1a Juliet Caroline Fox; *b* 26 March 1882; *d* 1 Aug 1905

2a Yolande Nina Sylvia Noble; *b* 17 May 1883; *m* 29 June 1909 Arnold Harding Ball (*ka* 1918), 3rd s of W E Ball, and *d* Sept 1928, having had issue

FRANCIS PYM's est s,

FRANCIS PYM, of Hazells Hall and Radwell House, Herts; *b* 22 June 1790; *m* 13 Oct 1816 Jane Elizabeth, dau of 7th Earl of Leven and (6th Earl of) Melville (*qv*), and *d* 23 Feb 1860, leaving, with other issue:

1 Francis Leslie, of Hazells Hall and Radwell House, JP, DL; *b* 14 Sept 1818; *educ* Rugby and Trin Coll Cambridge; *m* 7 Oct 1847 Mary Jemima, yst dau of Rev Henry Palmer (*see* PALMER, Bt, of Carlton), and was *k* in a train crash 23 April 1860, having had, with other issue:

(1) Francis, of Hazells Hall, JP, DL Beds; *b* 6 Dec 1849; *educ* Eton and Ch Ch Oxford; 1st Life Gds, High Sheriff Beds 1903, Ld Manor of Sandy and Girtford; *m* 16 July 1891 Alice Conway, dau of Sir George Colthurst, 5th Bt (*qv*), and *dsp* 7 June 1927

(2) Frederick William, of Hazells Hall, JP (Beds 1904); *b* 27 Jan 1859; *educ* Radley and BNC Oxford; Capt 3rd Militia Bn Beds Regt, Ld Manor of Sandy and Girtford, Patron living of Sandy; *d* unm 9 July 1941

2 Alexander, of Brickhill House, Beds, JP; *b* 8 Jan 1820; *m* 21 Dec 1847 Eliza Elizabeth, 2nd dau of Sir Albert Pell (*see* SAINT JOHN OF BLETSO, B), and *d* 13 Aug 1889, having had, with other issue:

(1) Walter Ruthven (Rt Rev); *b* 22 June 1856; Vicar Rotherham, Yorks; Bp: Mauritius 1898–1904, Bombay 1904–08; *m* 8 Aug 1883 Lucy Anne, dau of Thomas Threlfall, of Lytham, Lancs, and *d* 2 March 1908, leaving, with other issue:

1a Leslie Ruthven, JP, DL Mon; *b* 24 May 1884; *educ* Bedford Sch and Magdalene Coll Cambridge; Pres Land Agents' Soc 1936, MP Monmouth 1939–45, Ld Commr Treasury 1942, a Sr Ld Treasury 1945; *m* 1 Jan 1914 Iris Rosalind, dau of Charles Somerville Orde, of Hopton, and *d* 17 July 1945, leaving:

1b FRANCIS LESLIE, *cr* a **Baron**

1b *Rosalind Ann; *b* 19 Feb 1915

2b *Bridget Clare; *b* 19 May 1916

3b *Catherine Lucy; *b* 9 March 1920; *m* 27 Feb 1943 *Peter Cresswell Jones, only s of Lt-Col Walter Thomas Cresswell Jones, CB, DSO, RMLI, and has:

1c *Timothy Cresswell; *b* 1 April 1944; *educ* King's Sch Worcester and Magdalene Coll Cambridge; *m* 10 Jan 1970 *Peta Mary Mcnab and has issue

2c *Richard Leslie; *b* 18 Aug 1946; *educ* King's Sch Worcester and Exeter Sch; *m* 16 Feb 1985 *Sarah Catherine Pickles and has issue

3c *Stephen Buxton; *b* 12 July 1950; *educ* Exeter Sch

4c *John Robert; *b* 14 Oct 1952; *educ* Exeter Sch and Durham U; *m* 21 April 1990 *Susan Jackson and has issue

2a Francis Guy; *b* 4 Nov 1893; *educ* Rossall; *m* 4 April 1922 Octavia Florence, dau of Archibald Weyland Ruggles-Brise (*see* RUGGLES-BRISE, Bt), and *d* 1987, leaving issue

1a Lucy Barbara, MBE (1957); *b* 31 July 1895; *m* 14 March 1939 Sir Edward Ruggles-Brise, 1st Bt (*qv*), and *d* 1979

(2) Claude George Melville, JP (Lincs, Parts of Kesteven 1912); *b* 10 Aug 1860; *m* 13 Nov 1890 his cousin Lucy Victoria, dau of Alexander Samuel Leslie Melville (*see* LEVEN and MELVILLE, E), and *d* 2 Sept 1944, having had, with two other sons (*das* and *ka* WW I):

1a Alexander Ruthven, JP (Kent 1964), DL (1963); *b* 7 Oct 1891; *educ* Winchester; Maj Irish Gds, WWs I (despatches) and II; Kent: CC 1947 on (V-Chm 1963–64, Chm 1964), CA 1957 on; *m* 4 Aug 1921 Violet Helen Marie, dau of V-Adml Sir George Warrender, 7th Bt (*see* BRUNTISFIELD, B), and *d* 13 Aug 1971, having had, with an est s (*ka* WW II) and a dau (*d* in a riding accident):

1b *The Rev Victor Francis; *b* 22 Aug 1924; *educ* Nautical Coll Pangbourne and Architectural Assoc; served WW II, AADipl, ARIBA 1952; St John's Coll Durham 1974; Curate St Andrew's Keighley 1976, Chaplain Bethany Fellowship 1979; *m* 6 Dec 1963 *Marigold Ishbel Geraldine Mary Jessamine, est dau of Michael Harmsworth (*see* ROTHERMERE, V), and has:

1c Alexander Michael Francis; *b* 3 June 1970; Lt RN; *d* in an accident 1995

2c *John Andrew Dudley; *b* 15 Dec 1971

1c *Rebekah Mary Jane; *b* 1 April 1975

2c *Victoria Naomi Jessamine; *b* 2 May 1978

2b *Martin Hugh, JP (Kent 1964); *b* 28 Feb 1927; *educ* Sutton Valence and RAC Cirencester; late Lt Irish Gds, Chm W Ashford RDC; *m* 3 Dec 1960 *Phillada Hilary, yr dau of Robin Michael Charles Nunneley, of Chelsea, and has:

1c *William Alexander Charles; *b* 17 April 1968; *educ* Eton; late Lt Irish Gds

1c *Lucy Jane; *b* 24 Sept 1961; *m* 1st 4 April 1987 Anthony Granville Brooking (*d* 11 March 1988) only s of Lt-Col Granville Reginald Arthur Brooking, 4th/7th Dragoon Gds; *m* 2nd 17 Feb 1990 *William George Cubitt, Coldstream Gds, 2nd s of Thomas Randall Cubitt, of Honing, Norfolk, and by him has:

1d *James William; *b* 25 July 1992

2d *Edward George; *b* 1 March 1994

1d *Charlotte Mary; *b* 28 Jan 1991

2c *Emma Mary; *b* 25 June 1963; *m* 20 April 1991 *James Killingworth Hedges, 2nd s of Richard Hedges, of Charlton, Dorset, and has:

1d *Robert Killingworth; *b* 2 Feb 1997

1d *Harriet Fiona; *b* 25 Jan 1994

2d *Emily Phillada; *b* 14 July 1995

3c *Serena Lindesay; *b* 26 Feb 1965

1 Jane Anne; *m* 23 Jan 1845 Rt Rev Hon Samuel Waldegrave, Bp Carlisle (*see* WALDEGRAVE, E), and had issue

QUEENSBERRY

FORWARD

Arms: Quarterly, 1st and 4th, arg. a King's heart crowned gu., on a chief az. three stars of the first (for DOUGLAS); 2nd and 3rd, az. a bend between six cross-crosslets fitchée or (for MAR); all within a bordure or, charged with a double tressure flory counter-flory gules (honourable augmentation 20 April 1682). **Crest:** A heart gu., crowned and winged or. **Supporters:** Two flying horses arg., winged or. **Motto:** Forward. **Creations:** L. (Douglas of Hawick and Tibberis) and V. (Drumlanrig) (S) 1 April 1628; E. (Queensberry) (S) 13 June 1633; Bt. (NS) 26 Feb 1667/8; M., E. (Drumlanrig and Sanchar), V. (Nith, Torthorwald and Ross) and L. (Douglas of Kinmonth, Midlebie and Dornock) (S) 11 Feb 1681/2.

THE 12TH MARQUESS OF QUEENSBERRY, Earl of Queensberry, Earl of Drumlanrig, Viscount of Drumlanrig, Viscount of Nith, Torthorwald and Ross, Lord Douglas of Hawick and Tibberis, Lord Douglas of Kinmonth, Midlebie and Dornock and a Baronet (Sir David Harrington Angus Douglas, Bt) [The Most Hon The Marquess of Queensberry, House of Lords, London SW1A 0PW]; *b* 19 Dec 1929; *s f* 1954; *educ* Eton; Lt RHG (Blues), Prof Ceramics RCA 1959–, Pres Design and Industries Assoc 1976–78, FCSD, sr FRCA 1990, Hon DDes Staffs 1993; *m* 1st 18 July 1956 (*divorce* 1969) Anne, dau of Maurice Sinnett Jones and formerly w of George Arthur Radford, and has:

  1 *Emma Cathleen; *b* 13 Sept 1956

  2 *Alice; *b* 23 July 1965; co-fndr with husb of Escape Artists (organisation providing work for ex-prisoners); *m* 28 July 1995 *Simon Melia

The 12th MARQUESS *m* 2nd 10 July 1969 (*divorce* 1986) Alexandra Mary Clare Wyndham, dau of Guy Wyndham Sich, of Chiswick, and by her has:

  1 +SHOLTO FRANCIS GUY DOUGLAS, *Viscount Drumlanrig*; *b* 1 June 1967

  2 +Milo Luke Dickon; *b* 6 April 1975

  3 +Torquil Oberon Tobias; *b* 2 Nov 1978

  3 *Kate Cordelia Sasha; *b* 21 Nov 1969

Lineage: WILLIAM DOUGLAS, 1st of Douglas; *b* 1174; *d* 1213, leaving:

ARCHIBALD DOUGLAS, 2nd of Douglas; had, with a yr s (Andrew; *see* MORTON, E):

Sir ARCHIBALD DOUGLAS, 3rd of Douglas; *b* 1240; *d* 1274, leaving, with an er s (Hugh, *dsp* by 1289) and a dau (Willelma, *m* 1st William, Stn Chief of the GALBRAITHs (*see* STRATHCLYDE, B); *m* 2nd Gilbert of Butternock (in right of his w) and with him was probably ancestor of the Dukes of Abercorn, *qv*):

Sir WILLIAM, 5th of Douglas, called *Le Hardi* ('The Bold'); *d* a prisoner of the English in London 1298, leaving:

  1 James (Sir), called 'The Good Sir James', 6th of Douglas; *k* in Spain 1330, leaving:

    (1) William, 7th of Douglas; *d* unm 19 July 1333

  1 (cont.) 'The Good Sir James' also had illegitimate issue:

    (2) ARCHIBALD DOUGLAS, 3rd EARL OF DOUGLAS, called 'The Grim'; *b c* 1325; fought alongside his cousin 2nd EARL (*see* below) at Battle of Poitiers against the English 19 Sept 1356; Ld Warden Marches 1368–1400; *m c* 23 July 1362 Lady Joan, only child of Maurice Moray, 1st Earl of Stratheran of the Feb 1343/4 *cr*, and widow of Sir Thomas Moray, feudal Ld of Bothwell, and *d* between 24 Dec 1400 and 9 Feb 1400/1, leaving:

      1a ARCHIBALD DOUGLAS, 4th EARL OF DOUGLAS; *b c* 1370; Ld Warden Marches 1400; led a Scottish expedn into England 1401; captured by Harry Hotspur (*see* NORTHUMBERLAND, D) Battle of Homildon Hill (in which the 4th EARL lost an eye) against English 14 Sept 1402; joined Hotspur in rebellion against HENRY IV and was captured Battle of Shrewsbury 1403, following which held prisoner by English till 1408; feudal Ld Annadale 1409; Lt Gen in French serv and *cr* 19 April 1424 DUKE OF TOURAINE (France), with remainder to heirs male of his body; *m* by 1390 Lady Margaret Stewart, est dau of ROBERT III (then Earl of Carrick), and was *ka* 17 Aug 1424 at defeat of French and their Scottish allies by the English at Verneuil, leaving an only surv s:

        1b ARCHIBALD DOUGLAS, 5th EARL OF DOUGLAS and 2nd DUKE OF TOURAINE, also *cr vp* COUNT OF LONGUEVILL, Normandy, by CHAR-

LES VII OF FRANCE; a Scottish Amb to English 1424 to negotiate ransom of JAMES I; Co-Regent Scotland 1437, Lt Gen of the Kingdom (of Scotland) 1438; *m* (papal dispensation 24 Feb 1422/3) Eupheme (*m* 2nd *c* 25 Feb 1440/1, as his 1st w, 1st Lord Hamilton; *see* ABERCORN, D), est dau of Eupheme, Countess of Stratheran in her own right (2nd holder of the 1371 *cr*), and *d* 26 June 1439, leaving:

          1c WILLIAM DOUGLAS, 6th EARL OF DOUGLAS, 3rd and last DUKE OF TOURAINE and 2nd and last COUNT OF LONGUEVILL; *b c* 1424; rebelled with his yr bro, hence executed by beheading for high treason 24 Nov 1440, having *m* Janet, dau of 2nd Earl of Crawford (*see* CRAWFORD and BALCARRES, E); *dsp*, when the Dukedom and Countship expired and the Ldships of Annandale and Bothwell ultimately passed to the Crown, though the Ldship of Galloway passed to his sis

          2c David; *dsp*

          1c Margaret, called 'The Fair Maid of Galloway'; *m* 1st her cousin 8th EARL OF DOUGLAS (*see* below); *m* 2nd (*divorce* following his attainder) her cousin 9th EARL OF DOUGLAS (*see* below); *m* 3rd 1459/60, as his 1st w, 1st Earl of Atholl of the 1457 *cr* (*see* MORAY, E), and *d* by 1475

      2a JAMES DOUGLAS, 7th EARL OF DOUGLAS and 1st EARL OF AVONDALE (S), as which *cr c* 1437, of Balveny, Banffshire, called 'The Great'; Warden W Marches; *m*(?) 1st(?) Lady Beatrice Stewart (*dsp c* 1424), dau of Robert, Duke of Albany ; *m* 2nd(?) by 7 March 1425/6 Lady Beatrice Sinclair (attainted with her three est surv sons June 1455; *d* apparently in England by 8 Feb 1462/3), dau of 2nd Earl of Orkney of the 1379 *cr* (*see* CAITHNESS, E), and *d* 22 March 1442/3 or 28 March 1443, leaving, with other issue (all of whom died out in the male line by *c* 1506):

        1b WILLIAM DOUGLAS, 8th EARL OF DOUGLAS and 2nd EARL OF AVONDALE; *b c* 1425; ktd 1430, Lt Gen of the Kingdom (of Scotland) 1443–49, Warden Marches 1450; *m* (papal dispensation for consanguinity 24 July 1444) Lady Margaret Douglas (*see* above) but was stabbed 22 Feb 1451/2 by JAMES II in person at Stirling Castle after attempting to mount opposition to the body of men about the King's person who made up what may be called the 'Court' party; *dsp*

        2b JAMES DOUGLAS, 9th and last EARL OF DOUGLAS and 3rd and last EARL OF AVONDALE, KG (*c* 1463), called 'Heriot-Muir'; twin with next yr bro; tried to take revenge for his er bro's death at the hands of JAMES II but initially made his peace with that King 1452 only to turn on him two years later and at the head of 40,000 followers publicly accuse him of murder, having meanwhile become involved in the Wars of the Roses in England, where he sided with the DUKE OF YORK against HENRY VI; back in Scotland his 40,000 followers melted away following the abandoning of his cause by his principal supporters, notably Lord Hamilton (*see* ABERCORN, D), and he was attainted 10 and 12 June 1455 and stripped of his titles; fled to England, where received graciously by both EDWARD IV and HENRY VI, despite their representing contending factions in the Wars of the Roses; the Scottish Parl issued a proclamation 1484 granting a reward for his apprehension and death, whereupon he marched into Scotland at the head of an army under himself and the Duke of Albany; JAMES II beat him and Albany 22 July 1484 at the Battle of Kirtle (between Lochmaben and Carlisle) and held him captive at Lindores Abbey; *m* 1st *c* 26 Feb 1452/3 his cousin Lady Margaret Douglas (*see* above); *m* 2nd Anne, dau of John Holand, Duke of Exeter, widow of (a) Sir John Nevill(e) (s of 2nd Earl of Westmorland of the 1397 *cr*; *see* ABERGAVENNY, M), and (b) 1st Lord (Baron) Neville of the 1459 *cr* (also *see* ABERGAVENNY, M), and *dsp* shortly after 22 May 1491

        3b ARCHIBALD DOUGLAS, regarded as EARL OF MORAY from 3 July 1445, when took seat in Parl, by virtue of his marriage and the power of the DOUGLASes (*see* MORAY, E, preliminary remarks); rebelled against JAMES II alongside his er bro 9th EARL OF DOUGLAS in revenge for the murder of his est bro 8th EARL (*see* above), following which JAMES took the Earldom into the possession of the Crown; rose in rebellion a second time and was defeated and *k* Arkinholm 1 May 1455, being posthumously attainted and formally stripped of his title 12 June 1455; *m* between Aug 1434 and 26 April 1442 Elizabeth (*m* 2nd (*divorce* by 10 March 1459/60) 2nd Earl of Huntly (*see* HUNTLY, M); *m* 3rd, as his 2nd w, Sir John Colquhoun of Luss; *see* COLQUHOUN, Bt), yr dau of 4th Earl of Moray of the March 1371/2 *cr* (*see* DUNBAR, Bt, of Mochrum), and *dsp*

        4b HUGH DOUGLAS, 1st and last EARL OF ORMOND (S), so *cr* by 3 July 1445; won victory over English of Sark 23 or 24 Oct 1449; joined er bros in rebellion against JAMES II 1452; Sheriff Lanarks 1454; *dsp*, being captured after defeat by JAMES II at Arkinholm 1 May 1455, stripped of his title, attainted and executed

        5b John (Sir), feudal Ld of Balveny, of which stripped 1455 for rebellion; fled to England but returned and was executed Edinburgh *c* July 1463; *dsp*

        6b Henry; priest

        7b George; *d* unm aged *c* 14

  2 Hugh; feudal Ld of Douglas, which renounced 1342 in favour of his n 1st EARL OF DOUGLAS (*see* below); *d* unm

  3 Archibald (Sir); Regent Scotland April-July 1333; *m* Beatrix, dau of Sir Alexander de Lindsay (*see* CRAWFORD and BALCARRES, E), and was *k* 19 July 1333, leaving a 2nd but only surv s:

    (1) WILLIAM DOUGLAS, 1st EARL OF DOUGLAS (S), as which *cr* 26 Jan 1357/8; of age by 1348; present Battle of Poitiers 1356, where wounded fighting alongside the French against the English; *m* probably just prior to 13 Nov 1357 Margaret, Countess of Mar (*qv*) in her own right, and adopted her Earldom as his own by 21 June 1374; *d* May 1384, having had, with other issue (*see* MAR, E):

      1a JAMES DOUGLAS, 2nd EARL OF DOUGLAS and by sources writing long after his death referred to from time to time as Earl of Mar in right of his mother; *b c* 1358; ktd 1378; *m c* 23 Sept 1371 Isabel, dau of ROBERT II by his 2nd w Eupheme, and *dspsl*, being *k* Battle of Otterburn (*see* NORTHUMBERLAND, D) *c* 19 Aug 1388, leaving illegitimate issue:

        1b William (Sir); granted (territorial) Barony of Drumlanrig, Dumfries; cdr in wars with England, envoy to England to negotiate release of

JAMES I 1412; granted confirmatory charter 1412 of (territorial) Baronies of Drumlanrig (in Durisdeer, Upper Nithsdale, Dumfriesshire), Hawick and Selkirk; *m* Elizabeth, dau of Sir Robert Stewart of Durrisdeer, and was *k* France 1427, leaving:

  1c William (Sir), 2nd of Drumlanrig; *m* Jean, dau of Sir Herbert Maxwell of Carlaverock, and *d* 1458, leaving:

    1d William, 3rd of Drumlanrig; present Siege of Roxburgh 1460 and Battle of Alnwick 1462; *m* Margaret, dau of Sir William Carlyle of Torthorwald, and *d* 1464, leaving:

      1e William (Sir), 4th of Drumlanrig; *ka* 22 July 1484 Battle of Kirtle, fighting for the Crown against his cousin 9th EARL OF DOUGLAS (*see above*), who had invaded from England, leaving:

        1f James, 5th of Drumlanrig; *m* 1470 Janet, dau of David Scott of Buccleuch (*see* BUCCLEUCH and QUEENSBERRY, D), and *d* 1498, leaving:

          1g William (Sir), 6th of Drumlanrig, of which, with Drumlanrig Castle, granted charter 1492, also charters of land in Dalgarnock 1500 and the (territorial) Baronies of Tibberis 1509 and Hawick 1511; *m* Elizabeth, dau of Sir John Gordon of Lochinvar (for whose earlier ancestry *see* HUNTLY, M), and was *ka* Flodden 9 Sept 1513, leaving:

            1h JAMES (Sir)

            2h Robert; Provost Lincluden; ancestor of the DOUGLASes of Burford

            1h Janet; *m* after 4 July 1509, as his 1st w, 4th Lord Maxwell (*see* MAXWELL, Bt)

            2h Agnes; *m* Andrew Cunningham of Kirkshaw

          1g Janet; *m* Roger Grierson (*see* GRIERSON, Bt) and had issue

  2b Archibald; ancestor of the DOUGLASes of Cavers, Hereditary Sheriffs of Teviotdale

(1) The 1st EARL also had illegitimate issue by Margaret Stewart, Countess of Angus in her own right (*see* MORAY, E, and HAMILTON and BRANDON, D)

(1) Eleanor; *m* 1st Alexander Bruce, 3rd and last Earl of Carrick (*dspm* 19 July 1333) of the *c* 1330 *cr*; *m* 2nd by 1349 James Sandilands, 1st of Calder (*see* TORPHICHEN, L), and by him had issue; *m* 3rd by 1364 (indeed probably by 1361) William Towers of Dalry; *m* 4th by 1368 Sir Duncan Wallace of Sundrum; *m* 5th *c* 18 March 1376, as his 2nd w, Sir Patrick Hepburn of Ha(i)les (*see* BUCHAN-HEPBURN, Bt)

The er son,

Sir JAMES DOUGLAS, 7th of Drumlanrig; joined his cousin Sir Walter Scott of Buccleuch June 1526 in trying to rescue JAMES V from the Earl of Angus; ktd 1553, Warden W March 1553–54; *m* 1st 1513 (*divorce*) Margaret Douglas, sis of 6th Earl of Angus (*see* BUCCLEUCH and QUEENSBERRY, D), and had:

  1 Janet; *m* 1st Sir William Douglas of Cashogle; *m* 2nd John Charteris of Amisfield (*see* WEMYSS and MARCH, E)

  2 Margaret; *m* John Jardine of Applegirth

  3 Nicola; *m* as his 2nd w John Johnstone of Johnstone and had issue (*see* ANNANDALE AND HARTFELL, E)

Sir JAMES *m* 2nd Christian, sis of 2nd Earl of Eglinto(u)n (*see* EGLINTON and WINTON, E), and *d* 1578, having by her had:

  1 William (Sir), of Hawick; fought Battle of Langside 1568; *m* Margaret, dau of Sir John Gordon of Lochinvar, and *dvp*, leaving:

    (1) JAMES (Sir)

    (1) Margaret; *m* Sir Robert Montgomery, Bt, of Skelmorley

    (2) Janet; *m* Sir James Murray of Cockpool

  4 Margaret; *m* 1st *c* 4 June 1561 7th Ld Crichton of Sanquhar (*see* BUTE, M) and had issue; *m* 2nd *c* 16 May 1571 5th Earl of Menteith (*see* MONTROSE, D); *m* 3rd Wauchope of Niddry

  5 Helen; *m* Roger Grierson of Lag and had issue (*see* GRIERSON, Bt)

  6 Janet; *m* 1st James Tweedy of Drumelzier; *m* 2nd Sir William Ker of Cessford and had issue (*see* ROXBURGHE, D)

  7 Christian; *m* Sir Alexander Stewart of Garlies

Sir JAMES DOUGLAS's gs,

Sir JAMES DOUGLAS, 8th of Drumlanrig; *m* Mary, dau of John, 5th Lord Fleming, and *d* 15 Oct 1616, having had:

  1 WILLIAM (Sir)

  2 James, of Mouswald

  3 David, of Airdoch

  4 George, of Penziere; priest in Dumfriesshire; hanged drawn and quartered in England 9 Sept 1587 for professing his faith and saying mass

  1 Janet; *m* William Livingston of Jerviswood

  2 Helen; *m* John Menzies of Castlehill

The est s,

Sir WILLIAM DOUGLAS, 9th of Drumlanrig and **1st Earl of Queensberry** (S), so *cr* 13 June 1633 (as EARL OF QUEENSBERRIE [*sic*], VISCOUNT OF DRUMLANRIG, LORD DOUGLAS OF HAWICK AND TIBBERIS), as also 1 April 1628 LORD DOUGLAS OF HAWICK AND TIBBERIS and VISCOUNT OF DRUMLANRIG, LORD DOUGLAS OF HAWICK AND TIBBERIS, all with remainder to his heirs male bearing the surname and arms of Douglas, JP (Dumfries 1623); ktd *c* 1612, Provost Lincluden *c* 1616, Sheriff Dumfries 1620; *m c* 20 July 1603 Isobel, 4th dau of 1st Earl of Lothian (*see* LOTHIAN, M), and *d* 8 March 1639/40, having had, with another s (*d* unm):

  1 JAMES DOUGLAS, **2nd Earl of Queensberry**; *b* 8 Jan 1621/2; royalist Civil War, hence imprisoned Carlisle 1645; by the Restoration he had been fined or otherwise lost £234,879 Scots (well over £6,300,000 in late–1990s terms); *m* 1st (contract 4 June 1630) Mary (*dsp* 29 Oct 1633), yst dau of 2nd Marquess of Hamilton (*see* HAMILTON and BRANDON, D); *m* 2nd (contract 26 March 1635) Margaret, dau of 1st Earl of Traquair (*see* MORAY, E), and *d* 1671, having by her had:

    (1) WILLIAM DOUGLAS, **1st Marquess of Queensberry**, so *cr* (as QUEENSBERRIE [*sic*]) 11 Feb 1681/2, as also EARL OF DRUMLANRIG AND SANCHAR, VISCOUNT OF NITH, TORTHORWALD AND ROSS AND LORD

DOUGLAS OF KINMONTH, MIDLEBIE, AND DORNOCK (all S), with remainder to his heirs male whatsoever, and 3 Nov 1684 DUKE OF QUEENSBERRIE [sic], MARQUESS OF DUMFRIESSHYRE [*sic*], EARL OF DRUMLANRIG AND SANQUHAR, VISCOUNT OF NITH, TORTHORWALD AND ROSS, LORD DOUGLAS OF KINMONT, MIDLEBIE AND DORNOCK (all S), with remainder to heirs male of his body, PC (S Jan 1666/7–74, E 1685–Feb 1688/9), JP (1663); *b* 1637; Commr Excise 1661, Sheriff and Coroner Dumfriesshire 1663 and 1669, Cdr Dumfriesshire Horse Militia 1668, Ld Justice-Gen Scotland 1680–82, Extrdy Ld Session 1681–86 and 1693–95, Ld High Treasurer Scotland 1682–86, Constable and Govr Edinburgh Castle 1682–86, Ld HC to S Parl 1685, Commr Treasury 1695; *m* 1657 Isabel, dau of 1st Marquess of Douglas (*see* HAMILTON and BRANDON, D), and *d* 28 March 1695, having had, with a yr s (George, *d* unm):

  1a JAMES DOUGLAS, **2nd Marquess of Queensberry**, 2nd DUKE OF QUEENSBERRY etc and 1st DUKE OF DOVER, as which *cr* 26 May 1708, as also BARON RIPON, Co York, and MARQUESS OF BEVERLEY, Co York (all GB), with remainder to his 3rd s Charles and the latter's yr bros in tail male, KG (1701) PC (S 1684 and 1689, GB 1707); *b* 18 Dec 1672; Provost Dumfries 1683, a Ld Exchequer 1685 and 1690, Lt-Col Dundee Horse 1684, Col 6th Scots Horse Gds, Gentleman Bedchamber 1689–1702, a Commr Treasury Scotland March 1691/2–1704 and 1705–07, Actg Ld High Treasurer Scotland 1694, Ld Privy Seal Scotland 1696–1702 and 1705, Extrdy Ld of Session 1696–1711, Ld High Commr S Parl 1700, 1702, 1703 and 1706, a Ld Treasury Scotland 1705, rep S peer 1707–08, Jt Keeper Privy Seal July 1709, 3rd Pncpl Sec State with responsibility for Scotland Feb 1708/9–11; was regranted 17 June 1706 all his 1684 titles to him and his heirs of entail succeeding to the Queensberry estates and descended from the **1st Earl** and he settled them on his 3rd s, bypassing his 2nd and then est surv s; *m* 1 Dec 1685 Mary, sis of 2nd Earl of Cork (*see* CORK and ORRERY, E), and *d* 6 July 1711, having had:

    1b William, *Earl of Drumlanrig*; *b* 18 May, *dvp* 21 Oct 1696

    2b JAMES DOUGLAS, **3rd Marquess of Queensberry**; *b* 2 Nov 1697; homicidal maniac, probably congenital, but certainly by 17 June 1706 when he was bypassed in entail of the estates and the 1684 titles (*see above*); known as 'The Cannibalistic Idiot' from his slaughtering, then spitting and roasting a young scullion in the Holyrood kitchens after being left unattended in his cell there by his keepers, they having gone to enjoy the Edinburgh riots over the Act of Union 1707; *bur* 17 Feb 1714/5

    3b CHARLES DOUGLAS, **4th Marquess of Queensberry**, also 3rd DUKE OF QUEENSBERRY etc and 2nd and last DUKE OF DOVER etc, PC (1726); *b* 24 Nov 1698; *cr vp* 17 June 1706 EARL OF SALLWAY ([sic], *i.e.*, Solway), VISCOUNT OF TIBBERIS and LORD DOUGLAS OF LOCKERBIE, DALVEEN AND THORNHILL (all S), with remainder to his yr bros; a Ld Bedchamber 1720–27, Ld Lt Dumfriesshire and Kirkcudbrightshire 1721, V-Adml Scotland 1722–29, Capt-Gen Roy Co Archers 1758–78, Keeper Gt Seal of Scotland 1761–63; *m* 10 March 1720 Catherine (Kitty), dau of 4th Earl of Clarendon (*qv*, preliminary remarks) of the 1661 *cr*, and *d* 22 Oct 1778, when all his titles *cr* 1706 and 1708 expired, having had:

      1c Henry, *Earl of Drumlanrig*; *b* 30 Oct 1722; *educ* Winchester and Ch Ch Oxford; soldiered in Italy *c* 1741; *m* 24 July 1754 Elizabeth (*dsp* 7 April 1756), dau of 2nd Earl of Hopetoun (*see* LINLITHGOW, M), and accidentally shot himself dead with one of his own pistols 19 Oct 1754

      2c Charles, *Earl of Drumlanrig*; *b* 17 July 1726; *educ* Winchester and Ch Ch Oxford; MP (Tory) Dumfriesshire 1747–54; *d* unm 24 Oct 1756

      4b George; *b* 20 Feb 1701; *d* unm Paris 1725

    1b Isabel; *b* 4 Dec 1688; *d* 7 July 1694

    2b Elizabeth; *b* 11 Aug 1691; *d* 17 July 1695

    3b Mary; *b* 4 Feb 1699; *d* 16 Nov 1703

    4b Jean; *m* as his 1st w 2nd Duke of Buccleuch and had issue (*see* BUCCLEUCH and QUEENSBERRY, D)

    5b Anne; *m* 23 Jan 1733, as his 1st w, Hon William Finch (*see* WINCHILSEA and NOTTINGHAM, E) and *dsp* 26 Oct 1741

  2a WILLIAM DOUGLAS, 1st EARL OF MARCH, so *cr* 20 April 1697, as also BARON DOUGLAS OF NEIDPATH, LYNE AND MUNARD and VISCOUNT OF PEEBLES (all S), with remainder to heirs male of his body; in default of which to the other heirs male and of entail contained in his enfeoffments of the lands and Lordship of Neidpath (referring to Neidpath Castle and large Peeblesshire estates conferred on him by his f at the time of his marriage); Lt-Col of Horse *temp* JAMES II, Govr Edinburgh Castle 1702–04; *m c* 12 Oct 1693 Lady Jean Hay, 2nd dau of 1st Marquess of Tweeddale (*qv*), and *d* 9 Sept 1705, leaving:

  1b WILLIAM DOUGLAS, 2nd EARL OF MARCH; *b c* 1696; *m* Lady Anne Hamilton (*b* 5 April 1698; *s* f 3 Dec 1744 as Countess of Ruglen in her own right; *m* 2nd 2 Jan 1747 Anthony Sawyer and *d* 21 April 1748), est dau of 1st Earl of Ruglen (so *cr* 25 April 1697, as also Viscount of Riccartoun and Lord Hillinghouse (all S)) and 3rd Earl of Selkirk (*qv*; *see* also HAMILTON and BRANDON, D), and *d* 7 March 1730/1, leaving:

    1c WILLIAM DOUGLAS, **5th Marquess of Queensberry** and 4th DUKE OF QUEENSBERRY etc, as which *s* cousin 1778, also 3rd EARL OF MARCH, as which *s* f, and 3rd EARL OF RUGLEN, as which *s* mother, KT (1763); known as 'Old Q'; *b* 16 Dec 1725; *educ* Winchester; a Ld Bedchamber 1760–89, rep S peer 1761–86, V-Adml Scotland 1767–76, last first Ld of Police in Scotland 1776–82; *cr* 21 Aug 1786 BARON DOUGLAS OF AMESBURY, Co Wilts (GB); *dspl*(?; but *see* HERTFORD, M, against w of 3rd Marquess for discussion of this point) unm 23 Dec 1810, when the Earldom of Ruglen and its associated titles together with the 1786 Barony expired, the Dukedom and other titles *cr* 1684 passed under the terms of the regrant of 1706 to the 3rd Duke of Buccleuch (*see* BUCCLEUCH and QUEENSBERRY, D), and the Earldom of March, Viscountcy of Peebles and Lordship of Parl of Douglas of Neidpath, Lyne and Munard passed to his cousin (*see* WEMYSS and MARCH, E)

  1a Anne; *m c* 13 Aug 1697, as his 1st w, 4th Earl of Wemyss (*see* WEMYSS and MARCH, E) and *d* 23 Feb 1699/1700 after her clothing had caught fire while she was saying her prayers, leaving issue

(2) James; Lt-Gen; *m* Anna Hamilton and *d* 1691, leaving:

1a William; *dsp* 4 April 1712

(3) John; *k* Siege of Treves after 8 Aug 1675

(4) Robert; *k* Siege of Maastricht 1676

(1) Margaret; *m* Sir Alexander Jardine, 1st Bt, of Applegirth (*qv*)

(2) Catherine; *m* her cousin **Sir James Douglas, 1st Bt** (*see* below)

2 William (Sir), of Kelhead, Dumfriesshire; Army Offr, Govr Carlisle 1647; *m* 1st Agnes, dau of the heiress of George Fawside of Fawside; *m* 2nd 1649 Jean, dau of Sir Robert Stuart and widow of Andrew Riddell, of Hayning, and *d* 1673, leaving by his 1st w an est surv s:

(1) **Sir James Douglas, 1st Bt** (NS), so *cr vp* 26 Feb 1667/8, of Kelhead; *b* 19 Feb 1639; *m c* 28 Oct 1667 his cousin Catherine, 2nd dau of **2nd Earl of Queensberry**, and *d* by April 1708, leaving:

1a **Sir William Douglas, 2nd Bt**; *b* probably *c* 1675; *m c* 8 Sept 1705 Helen (*d* 20 July 1754), dau of Col John Erskine (*see* ROSSLYN, E), and *d* 10 Oct 1733, leaving, with other issue:

1b **Sir John Douglas, 3rd Bt**; *b* probably *c* 1708; MP Dumfries burghs 1734–36 (unseated) and Dumfriesshire 1741–47; imprisoned Tower London 1746–48 for suspected Jacobitism; *m c* 1730 Christian (*d* Nov 1741), dau of Sir William Cunningham, 2nd Bt, of Caprington, and *d* 13 Nov 1778, having had, with two other sons and two other daus:

1c **Sir William Douglas, 4th Bt**; *b* probably *c* 1730; MP Dumfries burghs 1768–80; *m* 21 May 1772 Grace (*d* 25 March 1836), est dau and coheir of William Johnston of Lockerbie, Dumfriesshire, and *d* 16 May 1783, leaving, with three other daus (*d* unm):

1d **Sir Charles Douglas, 5th Bt**, of Kelhead, and **6th Marquess of Queensberry** etc, as which *s* cousin 1810, KT (1821); *b* March 1777; rep S peer 1812–32, a Ld Bedchamber 1831–35, Ld Lt and Sheriff Pncpl Dumfriesshire 1819–37, Col Dumfries Militia, a Ld in Waiting; *cr* 7 June 1833 BARON SOLWAY OF KINMOUNT, Co Dumfries (UK); *m* 13 Aug 1803 Caroline, 3rd dau of 3rd Duke of Buccleuch and Queensberry (*qv*), and *dspm* 3 Dec 1837, when the UK Barony expired, having had, with two other daus:

1e Louisa Anne; *m* 11 April 1833 Thomas Charlton Whitmore, MP (*d* 13 March 1865), of Apley Pk, Salop, and *d* 31 Aug 1871

2e Mary Elizabeth; *b c* 1808; *m* 17 Feb 1831 Rev Thomas Wentworth Gage (*see* GAGE, V) and *d* 16 May 1888

3e Harriet Christian; *m* 13 May 1841 Very Rev Hon Augustus Duncombe (*see* FEVERSHAM, B) and *d* 26 July 1902, leaving issue

4e Jane Margaret Mary; *m* 27 Jan 1841 her cousin Robert Johnstone Douglas of Lockerbie (*d* 12 Oct 1866) and *d* 15 April 1881, leaving issue

5e Elizabeth Katinka; *m* 7 Nov 1861 Henry St George Foote and *d* 26 April 1874

6e Anne Georgina; *m* 11 Dec 1845 Charles Stirling Home Drummond Moray, JP, DL (*d* 24 Sept 1891), 19th of Abercairny, and of Blair Drummond, Ardoch, Millearne and Douglas House, Petersham, and *d* 28 Nov 1899, having had issue

2d JOHN, **7th Marquess**

3d Henry Alexander; *b* 7 Oct 1781; *m* 31 Aug 1812 Elizabeth (*d* 1837), 2nd dau of Robert Dalzell (*see* 1940 edn CARNWATH, E), and *d* 16 March 1837, having had, with other issue:

1e Robert DOUGLAS later JOHNSTONE-DOUGLAS, of Lockerbie; *b* 6 Oct 1814; *m* 27 Jan 1841 his cousin Jane Mary Margaret, dau of **6th Marquess of Queensberry**, and *d* 12 Nov 1866, leaving, with other issue:

1f Arthur Henry, of Lockerbie, JP and DL (Dumfriesshire); *b* 23 June 1846; 42nd Highrs; *m* 14 July 1869 Jane Maitland (*d* 26 May 1930), dau of Stair Hathorn Stewart, of Physgill and Glasserton, Wigtownshire, and *d* 26 March 1923, leaving:

1g Robert Sholto; *b* 3 Dec 1871; *m* 19 April 1913 Bettina (*d* 20 April 1961), 2nd dau of Harman Grisewood, of Daylesford, Worcs, and *d* 10 March 1958, leaving:

1h +Robert Arthur Sholto; *b* 4 Feb 1914

1h *Elizabeth Gwendolen Teresa; *b* 2 June 1916; *m* 1st 25 Sept 1954, as his 2nd w, 6th Earl of Craven (*qv*), and has issue; *m* 2nd 27 July 1966 *Kenneth Harmood Banner

2g Walter Henry George; *b* 22 Dec 1886; Capt Lanarks Yeo WW I; fndr and dir Webber-Douglas Sch of Singing and Dramatic Art; *d* unm 11 Aug 1972

1g Sibyl; *b* 26 Aug 1870; *d* unm 3 April 1953

2g Margaret Jean; *b* 21 Dec 1872; *m* 26 April 1894 Lt-Col Hon Douglas George Carnegie and *d* 31 July 1960, leaving issue (*see* NORTHESK, E)

3g Muriel Grace; *b* 4 June 1874; *m* 19 Aug 1908 Charles Henry Scott-Plummer (*d* 26 June 1940), of Sunderland Hall, Selkirk, and *d* 3 March 1961, leaving issue

4g Bridget Helen; *b* 28 Nov 1875; *d* unm 23 Dec 1967

5g Olive Christian; *b* 21 May 1878; *m* 20 Dec 1905 Lt-Col Francis John Carruthers, CB (*d* 22 May 1945), of Dormont, and *d* 11 Jan 1977, leaving issue

6g Caroline Elsie; *b* 26 Oct 1879; *m* 18 Aug 1903 2nd Baron Kinross (*qv*) and *d* 18 Feb 1969, leaving issue

7g Octavia; *b* 24 Aug 1881; *m* 8 Aug 1908 Maj Carleton Salkeld, JP, DL, 10th Hus (*d* 30 March 1959), and *d* 4 Jan 1968, leaving issue

8g Nina, OBE (1919); *b* 24 Aug 1881; Div Dir WRNS WW I; *m* 10 April 1919 Stair Agnew Gillon (*d* 11 Aug 1954), 5th s of Andrew Gillon, JP, DL, of Wallhouse, and *d* 14 July 1964, having had issue

2f Cecil Francis; *b* 19 Oct 1847; Lt-Col 5th Lancers; *d* unm 10 Aug 1894

1f Grace Elizabeth; *m* 19 Sept 1867 4th Baron Kensington (*qv*) and *d* 19 Jan 1910, leaving issue

2f Alice Louisa; *m* 23 Feb 1874 Charles Stewart, of Achara, Duror of Appin, Argyll (*d* 2 Aug 1916), 4th s of Duncan John Stewart, and *d* 25 Feb 1933

2e Henry Alexander (Rt Rev); *b* 22 Feb 1821; DD, Bp Bombay; *m* 20 Nov 1849 Eliza (*d* 1 Oct 1892), est dau of James Hoskins, of Alverstoke, and *d* 13 Dec 1875, having had, with another s (*d* young) and a dau (*d* unm):

1f Archibald Charles; *b* 2 Jan 1861; *m* 16 Dec 1896 Betty (*d* 29 Feb 1960), dau of Andrew Simpson McClelland, CA, of Glasgow, and *d* 6 Oct 1939, leaving:

1g Archibald Andrew Henry; *b* 4 Jan 1902; *educ* Clifton and Glasgow U (BSc), MI Mech E, LRAM; *m* 19 June 1935 (*divorce* 1980) Majorie Gordon (*d* 1992), er dau of Henry Brown, MB, of Rannoch, and *d* 24 May 1997, leaving:

1h +Archibald Sholto Gordon [Archibald Douglas Esq, 10 Coleford Rd, London SW18]; *b* 22 March 1937; *educ* Loretto; *m* 1984 *Mrs Victoria Ann Adam, only dau of James Bonnyman, of Florida

2h +Ian Andrew McCelland [W/Cdr Ian Douglas, 6 Ansley Rd, Houghton, Cambs PE17 2DQ]; *b* 7 Jan 1939; *educ* Loretto; *m* Nov 1967 *Jennifer Merrett, of Plymouth, and has:

1i +Andrew James Sholto; *b* 1973

1i *Kristen Lucy; *b* 22 Nov 1969

1h *Katherine Veronica [Mrs Richard Clegg, Ford Farm, Wootton Courtenay, Somerset TA24 8RW]; *b* 2 April 1943; *educ* Moreton Hall and King's Coll U Durham (BA); *m* 31 Aug 1963 *Richard Ninian Barwick Clegg, QC, only s of Sir Cuthbert Barwick Clegg, TD, of Westmorland, and has:

1i *Aidan Charles Barwick; *b* 8 Oct 1966

2i *Sebastian James Barwick; *b* 30 Aug 1969

1i *Flavia Mary Rosabel; *b* 3 Aug 1968

2h *Ursula Rosemary [Mrs William Righter, 10 Quick St, London N1]; *b* 2 April 1943; *educ* Moreton Hall and Girton Coll Cambridge (BA); *m* 30 March 1968 William Harvey Righter (*d* 14 April 1997), Reader English and Comparative Lit Warwick U, s of Richard Righter, of Kansas City

2g +James Sholto, TD, of Rhodesia; *b* 22 July 1905; *educ* Repton; Lt-Col 51st (Westmorland and Cumberland) Field Regt RA (TA) WW II (wounded)

1g Marjorie Charlotte; *b* 20 Aug 1900; *m* 28 July 1927 *David Gordon Cochran, LLB, est surv s of Francis James Cochran, of Balfour, and had:

1h *Hugh Douglas; *b* 26 April 1932; *educ* Loretto and Trin Coll Oxford; *m* 1st 12 April 1958 Joan (*d* 2 March 1961), 2nd dau of John Fleming, of Colthill, Aberdeenshire, and has:

1i *David Alexander; *b* 1958

1i *Joanna Mary Isabella; *b* 1960

1h (cont.) Hugh Cochran *m* 2nd 4 Aug 1962 *Maria-Luisa, dau of Marco Minio-Palvello, of Venice, and by her has:

2i *Marco Gordon; *b* 1963

3i *Adam Michelangelo; *b* 1967

2h *Francis Gordon; *b* 7 April 1934; *educ* Loretto, Trin Coll Oxford (BA) and Aberdeen U (LLB); slr 1960; *m* 14 Sept 1963 *Ann Jill, dau of William Leslie John Starr Reynolds, of Dorset, and has:

1i *Neil Reynolds; *b* 12 April 1965

2i *Jeremy Douglas; *b* 7 April 1969

1i *Nichola Vivien; *b* 9 April 1967

2h *Diana Marjorie; *b* 18 July 1928; *m* 23 Dec 1950 (*divorce* 1965) Rev Alan Robson, s of Frederick Edwin Robson, of Southsea, Hants, and has:

1i *Mark Bennet; *b* 5 July 1956

2i *Simon Patrick; *b* 14 Aug 1961

1i *Lucy Diana; *b* 2 March 1954

2g *Lucy Elizabeth; *b* 15 May 1907

1f Margaret; *b c* 1854; *d* unm 1 Sept 1943

2f Catherine Mary Grey; *m* 1894 Rev Francis Ainger (*d* 30 Oct 1905), Rector Jedburgh, and *d* 31 Dec 1942, having had issue

3f Katherine Helen; *b c* 1864; *d* unm 9 Feb 1953

3e John, CMG; *b* 6 March 1828; Premier Qld, Special Commr Br New Guinea; *m* 1st 1861 Mary (*d* 23 Nov 1876), dau of Rev J Simpson and widow of William Howe, of Glenile, NSW; *m* 2nd 1877 Sarah, dau of Michael Hickey, of Ballimorris, Co Clare, and *d* 23 July 1904, having by her had:

1f Edward Archibald; *b* 2 Nov 1877; *educ* Ipswich GS and St Benedict's Coll Fort Augustus; barrister Qld 1901, Puisne Judge Supreme Court Qld 1929; *m* 1907 Annette Eileen (*d* 13 July 1966), dau of Virgil Power, Judge Supreme Court Qld, and *d* 27 Aug 1947, having had:

1g John Power; *b* 4 Nov 1907; *d* 13 Sept 1931

2g +Edward Sholto (Sir) [Maj Sir Edward Douglas, 81 Markwell St, Hamilton, Queensland, Australia]; *b* 23 Dec 1909; *educ* St Ignatius Coll, Sydney; Maj AIF, slr 1934, ktd 1977; *m* 1939 *Mary Constance, dau of C M Curr, of NSW

3g Robert Alexander; *b* 12 Jan 1913; *d* 1923

4g +Robert High (Rev); *b* 7 Aug 1914; *educ* St Ignatius Coll Sydney

5g David Alistair; *b* 17 May 1917; *d* 1921

6g +Kenneth Maxwell (Rev); *b* 16 Jan 1921; *educ* Downlands Coll, Toowoomba, Qld; slr 1945, ordained 1956

7g +Gavin James; *b* 30 April 1926; *educ* Downlands Coll and Qld U (MB, BS 1948); FRACS (1955); *m* 1951 *Clare, dau of J H McHugh, of Townsville, and has:

1h +Edward John; *b* 23 Jan 1952

2h +Andrew Benedict; *b* 27 Jan 1957

3h +Gavin Gerard; *b* 24 Nov 1958

4h +Christopher; *b* 6 Sept 1962

1h *Margot Anne; *b* 29 May 1953

2h *Helen Penny; *b* 14 Aug 1955

3h *Annette Josepha; *b* 19 March 1960

4h *Mary Patrice; *b* 15 Sept 1964

8g +Andrew Brice [Andrew Douglas Esq, 17 Sutherland Ave, Ascot, Queensland 4007, Australia]; *b* 30 July 1931; *educ* Downlands Coll; *m* 1957 *Lorraine, dau of R J Lawson, of Brisbane, and has:

1h +Sholto Francis (Rev); *b* 1958; *educ* Downlands Coll, Qld U (BA), Monash U (Dip Ed) and Melbourne U (B Theol); ordained 1988

2h +David James; *b* 1960; *educ* Downlands Coll and Qld U (B Comm), ASA 1989; *m* 1991 *Karen, dau of B Emerson, of Dover, Kent, and has:

1i *Alexandra Helen; *b* 1993

3h +Maxwell Richard; *b* 18 March 1966; *educ* St Joseph's Coll Brisbane and Qld U (BSc 1986)

4h +Andrew Brice Christopher; *b* 1968; *educ* St Joseph's Coll Brisbane and Qld U (BA, LLB 1991)

1g *Evelyn Clare Mary; *b* 28 Aug 1911

2g Helen Cecilia; *b* 15 July 1924; *m* 1960 *Llewelyn David Hughes, MC, and *d* 7 June 1965, leaving two daus

3g Clare Catherine; *b* 30 April 1929; *d* 6 Sept 1932

2f Henry Alexander Cecil; *b* 8 April 1879; MLA Qld 1908–15, Min 1915; *m* 1st 1910 Flora Isabel (*d* 1910), dau of Charles Hugh Macdonald, of Kikcoy, Qld; *m* 2nd 1914 Catherine Cecilia (*d* 1977), dau of Hon T C Beirne, MLC, of Brisbane, and *d* 30 Aug 1952, having by her had:

1g Henry Beirne; *b* 10 March 1921; RAAF; *kas* Canada 30 April 1941

2g +Alexander Michael [Mr Alexander Douglas, 17 Palm Ave, Ascot, Queensland, Australia]; *b* 11 Nov 1926; *educ* Downlands Coll Qld; AIF 1944–45; *m* 15 Sept 1954 *Morna Therese, dau of Michael Patrick O'Rourke, of Brisbane, and has:

1h +Henry Alexander Michael; *b* 25 July 1955; *educ* St Joseph's Coll and Qld U (MB, BS); *m* 1984 *Frances Michelle, dau of Eric Donnelly, of Brisbane, and has:

1i +Eric Michael; *b* 1987

2i +Joseph Henry; *b* 1988

1i *Alexandra Kate; *b* 1991

2h +Richard John; *b* 6 Sept 1957; *educ* St Joseph's Coll and Qld U (BCom, LLB); barrister 1980; *m* 1981 *Rosemary Nerida, dau of R Wylie, of Brisbane

3h +Alexander Rodney; *b* 24 Nov 1958; *educ* St Joseph's Coll and Qld U (MB, BS 1981); *m* 1983 *Susan Kim, dau of C Primmer, of Rockhampton, Qld

4h +Andrew Beirne; *b* 12 May 1960; *educ* St Joseph's Coll and Qld U (BCom 1982)

5h +James Patrick; *b* 1965; *educ* St Joseph's Coll Brisbane

1g Mary Beirne; *b* 15 Dec 1915; *m* 14 Sept 1938 *John Peter Fihelly and had:

1h *John Douglas; *b* 16 April 1948

1h *Mary Carolyn; *b* 29 Aug 1939

2h *Sue Catherine; *b* 16 Oct 1944

2g *Sybil Catherine [Mrs Alan Bryan, 14 Inverness St, Ascot, Queensland 4007, Australia]; *b* 22 July 1918; *m* 31 May 1943 *Lt-Cdr Alan B Bryan, RAN, and has:

1h *Alan Douglas; *b* 12 June 1944; MB, BS, FRACP; *m* 1972 *Margaret Suzanne van Rompaey and has:

1i *Thomas Charles; *b* 1975

1i *Sophie Elizabeth; *b* 1973

2i *Olivia Catherine; *b* 1977

3i *Chloe Margaret; *b* 1979

2h *Henry Beirne; *b* 11 June 1947; MB, BS; *m* 1982 *Patricia Mary Johnson and has:

1i *Henry William; *b* 1986

2i *Michael Charles; *b* 1987

1i *Brigid Catherine Cecilia; *b* 1984

3h *Edward Alan; *b* 8 Nov 1954; BComm; *m* 1st 1982 (*divorce* 1990) Heather Joy Killen; *m* 2nd 1990 *Felicity York Sharples and by her has:

1i *Isobel Rose; *b* 1992

4h *Neil Beirne; *b* 15 Dec 1959; BBus; *m* 1983 *Lisa Marie Walsh and has:

1i *Edward George Peter; *b* 1986

2i *George Bernard Joseph; *b* 1990

1i *Lucy Cecilia; *b* 1985

2i *Harriet Catherine (twin); *b* 1986

3i *Annie Beatrice; *b* 1992

4i *Charlotte Mary (twin); *b* 1992

1h *Mary Christine; *b* 28 Feb 1949; *m* 1973 *David Walter Drake, BComm, FCA, and has:

1i *Alexander Bryan; *b* 1974

2i *Nicholas Thomas; *b* 1977

3i *Douglas Romeo; *b* 1983

1i *Elizabeth Sybil; *b* 1980

3f Hugh Maxwell, JP Qld; *b* 21 May 1881; Lt 47th Bn AIF; *m* 21 Dec 1904 Hannah Elizabeth (*d* 24 July 1950), 2nd dau of E L Thornton, of Warwick, Qld, and *das* 8 April 1918, having had, with another s (*d* an infant):

1g +Henry Alexander [Henry Douglas Esq, 37 Ormond St, Ascot, Queensland, Australia]; *b* 12 June 1908; *m* 1938 *Ethel Audrey, dau of Dr A E Malaher, and has:

1h +Henry John [Henry Douglas Esq, 91 Ashworth Ave, Frenche's Forest, NSW, Australia]; *b* 1942; *m* 8 Jan 1966 *Susan Marguerite Eileen, dau of Edwin William Clark, of Sydney, and has:

1i +Geoffrey Peter; *b* 1970

2i +Ian Andrew; *b* 1971

1i *Elizabeth Jane; *b* 7 Oct 1967; *m* 1989 *Conrad Cholakos

2i *Kathryn Ann; *b* 1973

1h *Katherine; *b* 1938; *m* 5 April 1961 (*divorce* 1982) John Francis Douglas, s of Archibald Douglas, of Springfield, W Qld, and has:

1i *Andrew Francis; *b* 4 Oct 1963

2i *Graham John; *b* 14 May 1965

3i *James Scott; *b* 24 Oct 1968

2g +Edward Octavius; *b* 2 Aug 1913

1g Margaret; *b* 4 Nov 1909; *d* unm 29 May 1939

4f Robert Johnstone; *b* 13 April 1883; *educ* Sydney U (BA 1904); barrister 1906, Puisne Judge Supreme Court N Qld 1923; *m* 15 Jan 1912 Alice May (*d* 21 Nov 1954), dau of Andrew Ball, of Townsville, Qld, and *d* 1972, leaving:

1g +Robert Andrew, AM (1984) [Maj Robert Douglas AM, 18 Lawson St, Hermit Park, Townsville, Qld 4812, Australia]; *b* 26 March 1915; *educ* St Joseph's Coll Nudgee and Melbourne U (MB, BS 1939); FRACP 1967, FRCP (Lond) 1952; Maj AAMC WW II; physician Townsville Hosp; *m* 1949 *Barbara, dau of Rev John Shaw, of Adelaide, and widow of Henry Buzolich, of Melbourne, and has:

1h +Robert John [Robert Douglas Esq, 13 Drewett St, Surrey Hills, Melbourne, Victoria 3127, Australia]; *b* 9 Nov 1950; *educ* James Cook U (BA) and Melbourne U (MBA); *m* 1983 *Lynne, dau of Capt James Erskine Muirhead, of Melbourne, and has:

1i +James Robert; *b* 1986

1i *Sarah Jane; *b* 1984

2h +Sholto James Shaw; *b* 12 Feb 1962

1h *Catriona; *b* 14 April 1952; *m* 1983 *Geoffrey Charles Beams, MB, BS, FRANZCP, and has:

1i *Alexander Thomas; *b* 1986

2i *Michael Robert Charles; *b* 1988

1i *Catherine Alice; *b* 1990

2h *Barbara Selina; *b* 8 Aug 1953; BSW JCU 1997; *m* 1974 *Philip William Hale, BA JCU 1979, Dip Psych Flinders U 1981, and has:

1i *Nathan Alexander; *b* 1974

1i *Emily Angela; *b* 1975

3h *Sarah; *b* 1955

2g James Archibald; *b* 14 Aug 1917; *educ* St Joseph's Coll Nudgee; Maj AIF WW II, barrister 1946, Puisne Judge Supreme Court Qld 1965; *m* 2 Feb 1943 *Marjorie Mary, dau of James Campbell Ramsay, of Brisbane, and *d* 1984, leaving:

1h +Robert Ramsay, QC (1982) [W/Cdr Robert Douglas QC, 18 Towers St, Albion Heights, Brisbane, Queensland, Australia]; *b* 25 Nov 1944; *educ* Villanova Coll Coorparoo and Qld U (LLB); W/Cdr RAAF (Res), RFD; barrister 1968, Judge Advocate Australian Def Forces, Kt Honour and Devotion SMO Malta; *m* 1970 *Jennifer Farmar, dau of Frank Wilmot Horton, of Blenheim, NZ, and has:

1i +Robert Horton; *b* 1970

2i +William John Archibald; *b* 1975

1i *Charlotte Mary; *b* 1972

2h +Francis Maxwell, QC (1988) [Francis Douglas Esq QC, 4 Wiston Gdns, Double Bay, Sydney, NSW 2028, Australia]; *b* 23 Aug 1946; *educ* Villanova Coll, Qld U (BA, LLB) and Cambridge (LLB); barrister Qld 1969, NSW 1975; *m* 1st 1972 (*divorce* 1995) Sigrun Baldvinsdottir, dau of Baldvin Einarsson, of Reykjavik, and has:

1i +James Baldvin; *b* 1974

1i *Helga Sigrun; *b* 1979

2i *Sara Kristin; *b* 1989

2h (cont.) Francis Douglas *m* 2nd 15 Dec 1995 *Lisa Anne, dau of Remo Laurence Contamessa, and by her has:

2i +Sholto Francis Alexandre; *b* 22 Feb 1996

3h +James Sholto, QC (1989) [James Douglas Esq QC, 9 Lucinda St, Taringa, Queensland, Australia]; *b* 8 Feb 1950; *educ* Villanova Coll, Qld U (BA, LLB) and Cambridge (LLB); barrister 1973; *m* 1980 *Margaret Anne, dau of Francis Xavier Kennedy, of Brisbane, and has:

1i +Francis Sholto; *b* 1983

1i *Hannah Mary; *b* 1986

1h *Catherine Alice Mary [Mrs William McCourt, 9 Glostermin, Whyenbah St, Hamilton, Queensland, Australia]; *b* 10 April 1948; BA, LTCL, ASDA 1969; *m* 1st 1974 (*divorce* 1977)

Roger John Stredwick; *m* 2nd 1981 *William Charles Edward McCourt, of Brisbane

3g +Hugh Maxwell; *b* 27 Nov 1920; *educ* St Joseph's Coll Nudgee; Capt AIF WW II; *m* 1947 *Jean Duncan, only dau of E L Love, of Adelaide, and has:

1h John Duncan; *b* 18 Dec 1949; *d* 1985

1g *Beatrice Rose Mary [Mrs Cornelius Howard, 984 Burke Rd, Deepdene, Melbourne, Australia]; *b* 17 Feb 1919; *m* 1947 Cornelius James Howard (*d* 1980) and has:

1h *Catherine Mary; *b* 25 Sept 1952; *m* 1977 *Peter Capell Dobson, MB, BS, MRCOG, FRCS Ed, FRACOG, and has:

1i *Michael Howard; *b* 1980

1i *Elizabeth Mary; *b* 1978

2i *Sarah Catherine; *b* 1982

3i *Alice Jane; *b* 1985

2h *Elizabeth Anne [Mrs Christopher Dawson, 33 Dorking Rd, Box Hill, Victoria, Australia]; *b* 29 Sept 1953; *m* 1978 *Christopher John Dawson and has:

1i *Emma Catherine; *b* 1984

2i *Juliet Beatrice; *b* 1986

3i *Maria Irene; *b* 1988

4i *Tess Elizabeth; *b* 1992

2g *Alice Mary; *b* 13 Sept 1922; *m* 1949 *Thomas William Capell, MB, BS, FRACS, MRCOG, and has:

1h *William Douglas; *b* 13 July 1951

2h *Andrew Thomas; *b* 23 Sept 1954

1h *Jane Marie; *b* 16 March 1950

4e Edward Octavius, of Killichassie, Perthshire; *b* 19 Sept 1830; *m* 3 Nov 1859 Hannah Charlotte (*d* 27 April 1921), dau of Sir John James Scott-Douglas, 3rd Bt, and *dsp* 9 March 1890

1e Eliza; *m* 23 June 1853 John Campbell Shairp (*d* 18 Aug 1886) and *d* 25 May 1903, leaving issue

4d William Robert Keith, of Grangemuir, Fife; *b* 1783; MP Dumfriesshire 1812–32; granted with surv er and junior siblings 16 May 1837 rank of marquess's dau/yr s; *m* 24 Nov 1821 Elizabeth (*d* 25 April 1864), est dau of Walter Irvine, of Tobago, and Luddington Ho, Surrey, and *d* 5 Dec 1859, having had, with three daus (*d* unm):

1e William DOUGLAS later DOUGLAS-IRVINE, of Grangemuir, Fife; *b* 1824; Sec Legation Vienna; *d* unm 5 Aug 1868

2e Walter DOUGLAS later DOUGLAS-IRVINE, of Grangemuir, Fife, JP, DL; *b* 7 July 1825; MA Oxon; *m* 13 Jan 1870 Anne Frances (*d* 19 Feb 1917), only dau of Robert Jones Lloyd, MD, physician County Hosp Roscommon, and *d* 7 March 1901, having had, with a dau (Elizabeth, *d* unm):

1f William Keith; *b* 10 Feb 1876; *d* unm 3 April 1957

2f Walter Francis; *b* 26 Aug 1878; T/Capt RFA WW I (wounded); *m* 23 Jan 1925 Mrs Gladys Norgrave Jones, 2nd dau of Maurice Mills, and *dsp* 16 July 1950

3f Henry Archibald DOUGLAS-IRVINE later DOUGLAS (1919) (Rev); *b* 18 March 1883; *educ* Edinburgh U (MA 1905) and Ch Ch Oxford (BA 1944, MA 1947); Rifleman WW I, Vicar Salton Yorks 1932–37; *m* 6 May 1913 Beatrice Alice Mabel (*d* 1976), dau of Thomas William Gratix, of Liverpool, and *d* 27 Dec 1962, leaving:

1g +Walter Francis Edward [Walter Douglas Esq, 32 St Leonards St, Stamford, Lincs PE9 2HL]; *b* 31 Jan 1917; *educ* Exeter Coll Oxford (MA 1950); *m* 30 Dec 1944 Eugenie Nellie (*d* 1988), 2nd dau of Gustave Chaudoir, of Highgate, and has:

1h +Francis Gustave [Francis Douglas Esq, 12 Woodlands, Kerry Pike, Co Cork, Ireland]; *b* 4 Feb 1946; *educ* New U of Ulster (BSc, MA1976), Hull U (PhD 1993); *m* 1976 Hilary Agnes (*d* 1996), dau of G A Deane, of Armoy, Co Antrim, and has:

1i +Niall Edward; *b* 1978

1i +Aoife Lucy; *b* 1983

2h +Mark Gavin [Mark Douglas Esq, 60 Church St, Market Deeping, Peterborough PE6 2HL]; *b* 13 Dec 1958; *m* 1981 *Sally Knew

1h *Ruth Mary [Mrs William Wright, 10a Tower Ave, Chelmsford, Essex CM1 2PW]; *b* 20 Oct 1947; *educ* St Martin's Coll of Art (Dip AD 1969) and Goldsmith's Coll (PGCE, MA 1992); *m* 1971 *William Francis Wright, only s of Canon Edgar and Dr Marie Wright, of Stamford, and has:

1i *Henry Joseph [Henry Wright Esq, 57 South Primrose Hill, Chelmsford, Essex]; *b* 1967

2i *Francis Reuben [Francis Wright Esq, Flat 4, 56–57 Ainger Rd, London NW1]; *b* 1973

3i *Barnabas Mark; *b* 1981

1i *Rebecca Elizabeth [Mrs Caswell Coggins, 63a Upper Clapton Rd, London]; *b* 1976; *m* 1995 *Caswell Andrew Coggins and has:

1j *Jack Andrew; *b* 1996

2h *Josephine Eugenie; *b* 30 Oct 1950; *m* 1st 1973 (*divorce* 1981) Alan Michael Locker; *m* 2nd 1984 *Peter John JAKINS formerly JARMAKOWIECZ and by her 1st husb has had:

1i *Benjamin Harvey [Benjamin Locker Esq, 30 Havelock Rd, Norwich NR2 3HG]; *b* 9 Aug 1974; *educ* St Andrews U (MA 1997)

2i *Joseph Charles; *b* 24 Sept 1978

3i Samuel William; *b* and *d* 1980

3h *Rachel Margaret [Mrs Richard Palmer, 43 Lime Grove, Newark NG24 4AQ]; *b* 20 Sept 1954; *m* 1974 *Richard David Palmer and has:

1i *George Richard; *b* 1982

2i *Thomas Jonathan; *b* 1983

3i *John Henry; *b* 1987

1i *Lucy Rebecca; *b* 8 Aug 1991

4f Charles Gordon; *b* 14 April 1885; *d* unm 17 Feb 1946

5f Edward Percy DOUGLAS-IRVINE later DOUGLAS (1919), MC; *b* 26 Nov 1886; T/Capt RFA WWI (despatches), Capt Gen Serv and Pioneer Corps WW II; *m* 1st 11 Oct 1918 his cousin Alice Margaret, dau of Sir John Douglas, KCMG (see below); *m* 2nd (*divorce* 1949) Alice Audrey Sharman; *m* 3rd April 1949 *Hester Vivian, dau of Frederick Claude, of Valparaiso, Chile, and widow of F/Lt J G Madden-Simpson, RAF

1f Lucy Christina; *d* unm 29 Aug 1940

2f Helen Florence DOUGLAS-IRVINE later DOUGLAS; *educ* St Andrews (MA); historian and fiction-writer; *d* unm 22 May 1947

3f Elizabeth

3e Charles Irvine DOUGLAS-IRVINE later DOUGLAS; *b* 29 July 1837; *m* 4 March 1862 Margaret Elizabeth, MBE (*d* 17 Aug 1920), dau of Arthur Holmested, of Osgood Hall, Toronto, and *d* 19 Feb 1918, leaving, with another s and a dau (*d* in infancy):

1f Archibald Charles; *b* 3 July 1864; *m* 9 April 1890 Katie Sieveright (*d* 21 Oct 1954), dau of Thomas Lee, and *d* 17 Nov 1937, having had:

1g John Sholto; *b* 4 Sept 1895; BEF WW I; *das* 30 Nov 1918

2g Archibald Frank; *b* 26 Oct 1901; *m* 4 July 1927 Marion E, yst dau of A L Hall, of Manitoba, and *dsp* 31 Oct 1952

1g Edith Rosalind; *b* 29 Oct 1891; *m* 28 Dec 1946 Claude Bulling (*d* 30 Aug 1950) and *d* 23 Aug 1960

2g Helen Catherine; *b* 14 Jan 1899; *m* 14 July 1923 Stephen John Billings and *d* 26 March 1969, leaving a s

2f Henry Sholto; *b* 1 April 1868; *m* 19 Aug 1919 Barbara Margaret, dau of John Hay, of Barbarafield, Temuka, NZ, and *d* 28 April 1930

3f Frank; *b* 23 May 1870; *ka* Boer War 18 Feb 1901

4f Robert Keith; *b* 15 Aug 1874; *m* 23 April 1902 Louisa Mary (*m* 2nd 20 Aug 1924 Maj Hugh Fraser, MC, 13th Bn Rifle Bde, and *d* 1954), yst dau of Rev Horace Charles Ripley, Vicar Minster Lovell, Oxford, and *d* at sea 10 Oct 1917, leaving:

1g Archibald William; *b* 15 June 1907; *educ* Malvern and BNC Oxford (MA); Maj Intell Corps WW II; *m* 2 June 1934 Barbara Middlemost (*d* 29 May 1970), yr dau of Herbert Pratt Bairstow, and *d* 27 March 1998, leaving:

1h *Janet Valerie; *b* 2 Aug 1937; *m* 8 Aug 1959 *Judge John Percival Harris, DSC, of Cobham, Surrey, and has:

1i *Steven Oliver; *b* 4 March 1965; *educ* Wellington and Bristol U (BSc); *m* 1993 *Diana Elizabeth Jonas

1i *Juliet Caroline [Mrs Alistair Timms, Heath End, Bowhead Green, Surrey GU6 6NW]; *b* 2 May 1961; *m* 19– *Alistair Charles Timms and has:

1j *Charles Benjamin Alistair; *b* 1991

1j *Amelia Charlotte; *b* 1993

2i *Charlotte Beatrice [Mrs Charlotte Fuller, 12 Ruvigny Gdns, London SW15 1JR]; *b* 10 Nov 1963; *m* 19– (*divorce* 19–) Nicholas Michael Frederick Fuller

2h *Alison Rosemary [Mrs Brian Woodcock, La Cohue, Hérupe, St John, Jersey, CI JE3 4FN]; *b* 24 June 1939; *m* 19 May 1967 *Brian Woodcock and has:

1i *James William; *b* 29 Nov 1970; *educ* Uppingham and Buckingham U (BA)

1i *Sara Jane; *b* 13 June 1969; *m* 21 Feb 1998 *Alasdair Gordon Patrick Crosby

1g Catherine Grace; *b* 19 Nov 1903; *m* Feb 1929 Lt-Col Jack Walter Hallowes, MC, KSLI (*d* 14 July 1967), and *d* 7 Feb 1959, leaving issue

5f John Campbell; *b* 17 Sept 1876; *m* 7 Feb 1910 Violet Douglas (*d* 1972), yst dau of C J Daniell, of Argentina and of Cheltenham, and *d* 1960, leaving:

1g +(Charles) Sholto [Maj Sholto Douglas, Old School House, Little Ballinluig, Grandtully, Perthshire]; *b* 28 Oct 1915; Maj KOSB WW II; *m* 29 Aug 1941 Christian Frances (*d* 1990), dau of Maj-Gen Francis James Marshall, CB, CMG, DSO, and has:

1h *Helen Frances [Mrs Clive Walker, 37 Hans Schoeman St, Malanshof, Randberg 2194, S Africa]; *b* 9 Aug 1942; *m* 1971 *Clive Eden Walker and has:

1i *Alice Megan; *b* 1973

2i *Mary Louise; *b* 1976

2h *Katharine Ann [Mrs Robert Price, Urlar Farm, Aberfeldy, Perthshire]; *b* 13 July 1943; *m* 1st 18 Jan 1969 (*divorce* 1983) Timothy MacDermot-Roe and has:

1i *Charles Alexander; *b* 1974

1i *Katherine Emma; *b* 1972

2h (cont.) Mrs Katharine MacDermot-Roe *m* 2nd 1984 *Robert Athelston Price, and has:

2i *Robert John Crossley; *b* 1984

2i *Sarah Margaret; *b* 1986

3h *Margaret Jean [Mrs David Short, PO Box 880, Harrismith 9880, S Africa]; *b* 24 March 1945; *m* 1976 *David Eric Short and has:

1i *Alan Douglas; *b* 1977

2i *Brian Eric; *b* 1979

1g *Violet Katherine [Mrs F W Sandars, La Guarida, Jesus Pobre, Gata de Gorgos, Alicante, Spain; Drumcrowie, Malin, Co Donegal, Ireland]; *b* 13 Nov 1910; *m* 1st 27 March 1935 John

Griffith O'Donoghue (*d* 1976), s of Digby O'Donoghue; *m* 2nd 1982 *Brig F W Sandars, DSO, and by her 1st husb has:

1h *Katherine Susan [Mrs Alan Liddle, Knockanboy House, Dervock, Co Antrim BT53 8AA]; *b* 22 March 1936; *m* 1956 *Alan Louis Kestell Liddle, Colonial Serv, Kenya, and has:

1i *Nicholas John Kestell; *b* 1958

2i *Alan Digby Simon; *b* 1959

1i *Juliet Susan; *b* 1965

2h *Margaret Ann (Peggy) [Mrs Christopher Waller, Groves Farm, Erbistock, Clwyd]; *b* 18 Dec 1938; *m* 1960 *Maj Christopher James Waller, QRIH, and has:

1i *Sarah Louise; *b* 1961

2i *Celia Katherine; *b* 1963

2g Winifred Evelyn; *b* 13 June 1912; *m* 15 Feb 1935 William Blackmore Storey, s of Harley Storey, and *d* Oct 1968, leaving issue

3g *Margaret Elizabeth [Mrs John Cooper, Cherryhill Farm, RRI, Freelton, Ontario, Canada]; *b* 25 Jan 1918; *m* 13 March 1945 *John Craigmyle Cooper and has:

1h *Ian Alexander Douglas; *b* 25 July 1947

2h *Peter Craigmyle; *b* 28 May 1952

1h *Margaret Jane; *b* 7 Oct 1948

1f Agnes Mary (twin); *m* 11 June 1908 her cousin Rev Stair Douglas (*see* below) and *d* 7 Aug 1956

2f Margaret Amy; *b* 6 Oct 1872; *m* 16 Aug 1899 W Mullock Boultbee (*d* 1912), of Toronto, and *d* 1952, leaving issue

1d Mary; *m* 20 March 1817 Maj-Gen Sir Thomas Sidney Beckwith, KCB (*d* 15 Jan 1831), and *d* 15 Jan 1841

2c Charles James Sholto; Collector Customs Jamaica; *m* 1st Basilla, dau of James Dawes, of Rockspring, Jamaica, and widow of Richard Quarrell, and had:

1d James Sholto; *b* 3 July 1757; Maj; *m* 13 March 1784 Sarah (*d* Aug 1829), dau of James Dawes, of Rockspring, and *d* 12 Jan 1830, having had, with other issue:

1e James Dawes (Sir), GCB; *b* 14 Jan 1785; Col 42nd Regt, Lt-Govr Guernsey, Col 8th Regt Peninsular War, cmded a Bde at Busaco, Salamanca, Pyrenees, Nivelle, Nive, Orthes and Toulouse; *m* 7 Sept 1815 Marianne (*d* 1 June 1861), yst dau of William Bullock, and *d* 6 March 1862, having had, with four daus (*d* unm):

1f James; *b* 6 Nov 1817; Maj 60th Rifles; *m* 15 Nov 1853 Georgina Agnes (*m* 2nd 17 May 1866 Rev Thomas Rawson Birks), only surv child of Col William Beresford, of Stapleford Hall, Notts, and *dsp* 23 April 1858

2f Sholto James; *b* 14 June 1820; barrister; *m* 17 May 1853 Ann Harriet (*d* 26 May 1877), dau of William Mills, of Saxham Hall, Suffolk, and *d* 10 June 1868, leaving:

1g Sholto James; *b* 20 March 1854; Bengal CS; *m* 4 March 1882 Lucy Anne, dau of Col A E Campbell, ISC, and *d* 18 Dec 1930

2g Herries Sholto; *b* 5 May 1855; RN; *d* 22 Aug 1878

3g Archibald John Sholto; *b* 2 Oct 1856; *d* 29 Aug 1888

1g Edith Clara; *m* 20 June 1882 Sholto George Douglas Skrine (*d* 27 June 1927) and *d* 28 Sept 1931, leaving issue

3f Stair; *b* 28 Nov 1827; CS Mauritius; *m* 6 May 1858 Janet Mary, dau of John Marshall, of Headingley, Yorks, and *d* 12 July 1861, having had a dau (*d* 6 Nov 1859)

4f Edward; *b* 10 April 1831; Assist Colonial Sec Mauritius; *m* 21 May 1861 Anne (*d* 27 Jan 1937), dau of Hon James Arbuthnot, of Mauritius (*see* ARBUTHNOT, Bt, of Edinburgh), and *d* 21 June 1867, having had:

1g Montagu William, CSI (1919), CIE (1903); *b* 23 Nov 1863; Lt-Col IA, Ch Commr and Supt The Andamans, Dep Commr Delhi 1898–1903, memb Exec Coronation Durbar Ctee 1903; *m* 14 Feb 1891 Helen Mary Isabelle, OBE (*d* 23 Feb 1943), dau of Ven Archdeacon G W Downer, of Kingston, Jamaica, and *d* 24 Feb 1957, leaving:

1h Edward Montagu; *b* 31 Oct 1891; LDS, RCS Eng (1928); Capt Welch Regt WW I (POW), Roy Army Dental Corps WW II; *m* 30 Oct 1937 *Lavinia Rosa, dau of John Wood

2h Archibald Stair Montagu, MM; *b* 15 July 1897; served WW I 1915–16 (wounded), Maj RAMC WW II (Special Malariologist Instr N African and Italian Campaigns) 1943–45; MRCS Eng and LRCP Lond 1925; *m* 25 Feb 1926 *Barbara Assheton, dau of George Assheton Watson, and *dsp* 10 Feb 1971

1h Helen Elizabeth; *b* 25 June 1893; FRGS, LLCM (Music); Kaisar-i-Hind silver medal; author; *m* 15 April 1920 Geoffrey Bernard Douglas-Pulleyne (*d* 1956), Indian Police, 7th s of Benjamin Collett, of Leeds, and had issue

5f William (Rev); *b* 22 Sept 1833; *m* 11 Sept 1861 Emily (*d* 12 Feb 1909), dau of John Wilson, and *d* 25 May 1879, leaving:

1g Stair (Rev); *b* 23 May 1867; *educ* Oriel Coll Oxford (MA); Examining Chaplain to Bp Moray, Ross and Caithness, Canon St Andrew's Cathedral Inverness, Priest in charge St Ninian's Church Invergordon 1926–40; *m* 11 June 1908 his cousin Agnes Mary Douglas (*see* above) and *dsp* 6 April 1940

6f Charles; *b* 21 Dec 1835; Capt 15th Regt BNI; *m* 21 Jan 1862 Charlotte, est dau of Capt J H Armstrong, and *dsp* 29 March 1886

7f John (Sir), KCMG; *b* 5 Dec 1836; Colonial Sec Ceylon; *m* 6 Sept 1871 Alice Ann (*d* 22 Nov 1929), dau of Rt Rev Piers Calverley Claughton, Bp Colombo 1862–75, and *d* 23 Aug 1885, leaving:

1g Francis William; *b* 31 Dec 1874; Br Resident Labuan, Sec to Sultan Selangor, Malayan CS, Maj RAC (MT) WW I; *m* 7 July 1908 Violet Eleanor Jane (*d* 19 Oct 1956), dau of John More O'Ferrall, of Kildare, and *d* 21 Dec 1953, leaving:

1h Joan Margaret; *m* 25 Sept 1928 Peter Maurice Jacques Koch de Gooreynd (*d* 8 Dec 1973), yst s of William Julien Maurice Koch de Gooreynd, of Belgium and Belgravia (*see* also LINDSEY and ABINGDON, E), and had:

1i Timothy William Jacques Leopold; *b* 15 Aug 1930; *educ* Eton; Lt Scots Gds; *m* 17 Sept 1953 *Maunagh Jean Hennessy, MBE (*see* WINDLESHAM, B), and *d* 1987, leaving issue

2i *Simon Philip Julian Guy; *b* 14 Nov 1936; *educ* Millfield; Lt Irish Gds

1i *Enriqueta Mary Jeanne; *b* 12 Jan 1933; *m* 1 Jan 1953 (*divorce* 1976) Hon John Martin Lindesay-Bethune, yr s of 14th Earl of Lindsay (*qv*), and has issue

2h Helen Sholto; *b* 1910; *m* 1st 28 April 1932 Capt Edward William Eric Mann (*ka* 13 Dec 1942), only surv s of Eric William Mann, of Peasmarsh, Sussex; *m* 2nd 1950 Wilfred Harry Levita, s of Claud E Levita by Esmé Grace Virginia, JP (later w of 2nd Baron Savile; *qv*)

2g Reginald Stair; *b* 20 March 1877; Sarawak CS; *m* 21 Jan 1914 Helen, 2nd dau of John Rowland Swaine, of Camberley, and *d* 3 Sept 1933, having had:

1h Peter Rowland Stair; *b* 11 Nov 1914; *d* 1927

2h John Sholto; *b* 5 June 1916; *d* 1918

1g Ethel Mary; *m* 1 Oct 1904 Maj-Gen Sir Horace de Courcy Martelli, KBE, CB, DSO, RA, Lt-Govr Jersey (*d* 11 March 1959), s of Col Thomas Challenor Martelli, RA, and *dsp* 25 April 1961

2g Alice Margaret; *m* 11 Oct 1918 her cousin Capt Edward Percy Douglas, MC (*see* above), and *d* 1 Jan 1931

3g Helen; *m* 24 May 1915 Cecil Huntley Wilkinson, of Ceylon, and *d* 21 June 1937, leaving issue

2e Sholto; Maj 63rd Regt; *m* 25 March 1830 Henrietta Patricia (*m* 2nd 13 June 1844 Lt-Col Ferdinand White, CB, 40th Regt, and *d* 27 Dec 1859), dau of John Burnett, and *d* 24 Dec 1838, leaving:

1f Edward Sholto; RN; *d* unm 20 Feb 1853

1e Sarah; *m* 16 July 1817 her cousin **7th Marquess of Queensberry** (*see* below) and *d* 13 Nov 1864

2d John Graham; *dsp* 1807

3d Stair; *b* 27 Oct 1764; R-Adml the Blue; *m* 24 July 1802 Anne (*d* 4 June 1865), dau of John Payne, and *d* 22 Nov 1826, leaving, with four other daus:

1e Stair (Rev); *b* 22 Sept 1804; Canon Chichester; *m* 15 Feb 1831 Mary Edith (*d* 12 July 1886), yst dau of Woodbine Parish, of Bawburgh Old Hall, Norfolk, and *dsp* 8 May 1874

1e Elizabeth Louisa; *m* 5 May 1830 Rev Henry J Legge (*see* DARTMOUTH, E) and *d* 28 Oct 1840, leaving issue

2c (cont.) Charles Douglas *m* 2nd Mary, dau of Rev Richard Bullock, DD, and by her had:

4d Charles; *dsp* 1806

5d Edward Bullock; *b* 28 June 1774; *m* 14 Feb 1811 Harriet (*d* 2 Nov 1850), dau of Rev Richard Bullock, DD, and *d* 7 July 1830, leaving:

1e Edward (Rev); *b* 1 Dec 1819; RC priest; *d* 23 March 1898

1d Lucy Maria; *m* Rev T Newton and *d* 1811

1c Janet; *m* 13 Nov 1767 William Irving, of Bonshaw, and had issue

2c Catherine; *m* 13 Nov 1767 William Butler, MD, of London, and *dsp*

2b Charles, of Breconwhat, Dumfriesshire; HEICS; *m* Mrs Young and *dsp* 13 Dec 1770

3b James, MD; *m* Mary, dau of Sir Patrick Maxwell, Bt, and had two sons (*d* unm) and five daus

4b Stewart; Lt-Gen, Col 99th Foot; *d* unm 30 June 1795

5b Erskine, of Hexham, Northumberland; *m* Eleanor, widow of Thomas Witter, and *d* 10 Feb 1791, having had:

1c William Erskine; *b* 15 Aug 1766; *d* 17 Sept 1771

1c Helen Frances Catherine; *m* 11 Oct 1790 Rt Rev Daniel Sandford, DD, Bp Edinburgh (*d* 14 Jan 1830), and *d* 11 Jan 1837, leaving issue

6b Francis Edward; *m* Mrs Hunter and *dsp* 21 July 1793

7b David; *m* —, dau of William Thompson, and had, with 13 other children:

1c William, of Greencroft, Annan, Dumfries; *b* 26 May 1754; Lt-Col 85th Foot (ret 1802); *m* 1st 27 Oct 1795 Catherine (*d* 1823), dau and coheir of William Johnstone, of Lockerbie, Dumfriesshire, and had:

1d David William Archibald, of Camp de Cesar, Pouzac, France; *b* 13 Sept 1798; Capt 20th Foot (ret 1839); *m* 1st 1829 Catherine (*d* 15 May 1832), dau of François Cledou, of Pouzac, and had:

1e Gavin James Saturn, of Victoria, Australia; *b* 29 Nov 1830; *educ* L'Ecole d'Evangelique and Lille U (BA 1847); emigrated to Port Philip Colony Australia 1848, JP and CC Lowan, Victoria, 1876–95; *m* 22 Jan 1851 Margaret Ethelda (*d* 1895), dau of Edward Moore, of Dublin, and *d* 29 Nov 1917, having had:

1f David Edward; *b* 1855; *d* young

2f Gavin Moore, of Lillimur, Victoria; *b* 1860; *m* 1903 Mary McSweyn and *d* 1943, leaving:

1g Gavin William; *b* 1906; State Riveria and Water Supply Co, Victoria; *m* 1928 Agnes Salkeld and had:

1h +Basil Clive; *b* 23 Dec 1929; *m* 19 Dec 1959 *Lillian, dau of Henry Callender, and has:

1i +Philip Basil; *b* 19–

1i *Debra Janette; *b* 6 Feb 1961

2i *Wendy Helen; *b* 1 Oct 1962

2h +William Alfred; *b* 29 Jan 1931; *m* 1959 *Shirley, dau of John Martin, and has:

1i +Stephen John; *b* 24 Dec 1959

1i *Susan; *b* 25 July 1962

3h +Robert Graeme; *b* 3 Oct 1937; has:

  1i +Graeme Kenneth; *b* 19–

1h *Barbara Dawn; *b* 1933

2h *Margaret Agnes; *b* 1934; *m* *Keith Cartwright

3h *Janice Wendy; *b* 1936; *m* 19– *Geoffrey Rickard and has:

  1i *Craig Geoffrey; *b* 19–

4h *Strella Fay; *b* 1941

2g +Ronald David Edward; *b* 1910; *m* 1930 *Iris Stokes and has:

1h +Arthur James; *b* 1931

2h +Ronald William [Ronald Douglas Esq, Kings Rd, Emerald, Victoria, Australia]; *b* 1935; *m* 1961 *Gwen Hall and has:

  1i +Stephen John; *b* 1962

3h +Clive Reginald [Clive Douglas Esq, 63 Shaftesbury St, Coburg, VIC 3058, Australia]; *b* 30 June 1937

4h +Kenneth Gavin [Kenneth Douglas Esq, 98 The Fairway, Kingsbury, Victoria, Australia]; *b* 1939

5h +Allan David [Allan Douglas Esq, 28 Rubicon St, Broadmeadows, Victoria, Australia]; *b* 1943

1g Delphine Margaret; *b* 1904; *m* William Dale, and had issue

3f William Robert; *b* 1863 (twin with Elizabeth); *d* unm 1933

4f Rolland Edward Ellerman; *b* 3 July 1874; Victoria Mounted Constabulary; *m* 22 Oct 1902 Anne Amelia (*d* 8 March 1958), dau of Thomas Martin, of Ballarat, Victoria, and *d* 27 Oct 1906, leaving:

1g Clive Martin; *b* 27 July 1903; *educ* Melbourne U; DMus Melbourne, FIAL, orchestral conductor ABC 1936–66, composer; *m* 15 Aug 1936 Marjorie Eloise, dau of William John Joseph Ellis, of Bendigo, Victoria, and had:

  1h +Lynne Gavin; *b* 23 Nov 1944; Dip Art (RMIT), artist and designer

1f Ellen Louisa; *b* 1851; *m* James Munn and had issue

2f Margaret Catherine; *b* 1853; *m* William Scott and had issue

3f Mary Jane Wilhelmina; *b* 1859; *d* unm

4f Emily Gavina; *b* 1859; *d* unm

5f Elizabeth (twin with William Robert); *b* 1863; *m* James McKay and had issue

6f Louisa Gabriella; *b* 1865; *m* James Hopkins and had issue

7f Agnes Blanche; *b* 1867; *m* James Chaston and had issue

8f Delphine May; *b* 1869; *m* Samuel Martin and had issue

9f Ethelda Jessie; *b* 1872; *m* John Hill and had issue

10f Victoria Rose; *b* 1876; *m* Claude Yelland and had issue

2e Aristide; *b* 11 May 1832; *d* unm

1d (cont.) Capt David Douglas *m* 2nd 1834 Marguerite (*d* at sea with dau 1840), dau of Charles Suzan, of Pau, France, and *d* New York 1841, having by her had:

1e Catherine; *b* 23 Jan 1835; *d* unm *c* 1910

2e Mary; *b* 17 Jan 1836; *d* at sea with mother 1840

3e Jeanne Hélène; *b* 20 May 1838; *d* unm *c* 1920

4e Chrétienne Louisa; *b* 20 May 1838; *d* unm *c* 1892

1d Mary; *b* 1796; *m* 5 April 1821 Lt-Gen Sir Charles William Maxwell, CB, KCH (*d* 1848), Govr St Christopher, WI, and *d* 9 Jan 1823

1c (cont.) Lt-Col William Douglas *m* 2nd 29 Nov 1824 his cousin Wilhelmina Douglas and *d* May 1831

2c John Erskine; *b* 29 Oct 1757; Adml; *m* 1818 Catherine Anne (*d* 1885), dau of John Griffith and widow of Maj White, and *d* 25 July 1847, leaving, with another dau (*d* unm):

1d Helen Catharine; *b* 1819; authoress; *m* 21 Nov 1843 Lt-Gen Colin Mackenzie, CB, Madras Serv (*d* 1881), and *d* 31 March 1910

2d Louisa; *b* 1821; *d* unm 1890

1b Catherine; *m* 11 Oct 1725 Sir William Maxwell, 2nd Bt, of Springkell (*see* HERON-MAXWELL, Bt) and *d* 29 Sept 1761, leaving issue

2b Jean; *m* 30 April 1727 Hugh Maxwell, of Dalswinton, Dumfriesshire

3 Archibald, of Dornoch, Dumfriesshire, which he had from his f; had:

(1) William, of Dornoch; had:

1a William, of Dornoch; had:

1b James, of Dornoch; had:

1c James, of Dornoch; *b* 1720; *m* Philadelphia, dau of Sir John Johnstone, of Westerhall, 1st Bt (*qv*), and had:

1d Archibald; *dsp*

1d Clementine; *m* Robert Fergusson of Craigdarroch (their gdau Ludivina Loughnan *m* Sir Charles Stuart- Menteth, 1st Bt; *qv*)

2d Philadelphia; *m* Robert McMurdo of Dumgans

2c William, of Bodsbeck; *dsp*

1 Margaret; *m* (contract 29 Nov 1622) 1st Earl of Hartfell (*see* ANNANDALE AND HARTFELL, E) and had issue

2 Janet; *m* (contract 28 July 1640) Thomas Maclellan, 2nd Lord Kirkcudbright (*see* 1832 edn), and *dsp*

The 6th MARQUESS's bro,

JOHN JOHNSTONE-DOUGLAS (on inheriting the Lockerbie estate from his mother) later DOUGLAS, **7th Marquess of Queensberry**; *b* 1779; Ld Lt and Sheriff Pncpl Dumfriesshire 1837–56; *m* 16 July 1817 his cousin Sarah, dau of Maj James Sholto Douglas, and *d* 19 Dec 1856, leaving, with a dau (Georgina, *b* 25 July 1819):

ARCHIBALD WILLIAM DOUGLAS, **8th Marquess of Queensberry**, PC (1853); *b* 18 April 1818; *educ* Eton; Offr 2nd Life Gds (ret 1844), MP (Peelite) Dumfriesshire 1847–56, Ld Lt and Sheriff Pcpl Dumfriesshire 1850–56, Comptroller Household 1853–56; *m* 28 May 1840 in Scotland and again 2 June 1840 Caroline Margaret (*d* 14 Feb 1904), yr dau of Gen Sir William Robert Clayton, 5th Bt, MP,

and shot himself dead (whether accidentally or not is unclear) with his own gun 6 Aug 1858 while out after rabbits, leaving:

1 JOHN SHOLTO, **9th Marquess**

2 Francis William Bouverie; *b* 8 Feb 1847; *k* climbing on the Matterhorn 14 July 1865

3 Archibald Edward (Very Rev); *b* 17 June 1850; RC priest, Hon Canon Galloway; *d* 13 Feb 1938

4 James Edward Sholto; *b* 25 May 1855; Lt W Kent Militia; *m* 4 Sept 1888 Martha Lucy (*d* 31 Jan 1941), dau of Frederick Hennessy and widow of Richard Hennessy (*see* WINDLESHAM, B), and *dsp* 5 May 1891

1 Gertrude Georgiana; *m* Nov 1882 Thomas Stock and *d* 25 Nov 1893

2 Florence Caroline; *b* 25 May 1855; *m* 3 April 1875 Sir Alexander Beaumont Churchill Dixie, 11th Bt (*d* 21 Aug 1924; *see* 1970 edn), and *d* 7 Nov 1905, leaving issue

The 8th MARQUESS's est son,

JOHN SHOLTO DOUGLAS, **9th Marquess of Queensberry**, DL (Dumfriesshire); *b* 20 July 1844; *educ* Magdalene Coll Cambridge; served RN 1859–64 (ret as Lt), rep S peer 1872–80, Lt-Col 1st Dumfriesshire Rifle Vols; originated the 'Queensberry Rules' for boxing, of which sport he himself was allegedly the best amateur practitioner of his day; author *The Spirit of the Matterhorn* (blank verse 'meditation', 1881); *m* 1st 26 Feb 1866 (*divorce* 1887) Sibyl (*d* 31 Oct 1935), yr dau of Alfred Montgomery, and gdau of Sir Henry Conyngham Montgomery, 1st Bt; *m* 2nd 7 Nov 1893 (*annulled* 1894) Ethel, dau of Edward Charles Weeden, of Eastbourne, and *d* 31 Jan 1900, having by his 1st w had:

1 FRANCIS ARCHIBALD DOUGLAS, 1st and last BARON KELHEAD, of Kelhead, Co Dumfries (UK), so *cr* 22 June 1893; *b* 3 Feb 1867; *educ* Harrow and Sandhurst; Lt 2nd Bn Coldstream Gds 1887–93, Assist Priv Sec to For Sec (Lord Rosebery, who as PM rewarded him with his peerage) 1892–94, Ld-in-Waiting 1893–94; *d* unm *vp* in a shooting accident 18 Oct 1894, when the Barony expired

2 PERCY SHOLTO, **10th Marquess**

3 Alfred Bruce; *b* 22 Oct 1870; *educ* Winchester and Magdalen Coll Oxford; ed *The Academy* 1907–10; author: *The City of the Soul* (1899), *Sonnets* (1909), *Oscar Wilde and Myself* (1914), *Sonnets — In Excelsis* (1924), *The Autobiography of Douglas* (1929), *Sonnets and Lyrics* (1935), *Oscar Wilde: A Summing Up* (1940); *m* 4 March 1902 Olive Eleanor (*d* 12 Feb 1944), dau and heiress of Col Frederic Hambledon Custance, CB, Gren Gds, and *d* 20 March 1945, leaving:

(1) Raymond Wilfrid Sholto; *b* 17 Nov 1902; Scots Gds; *d* unm 10 Oct 1964

4 Sholto George; *b* 7 June 1872; Lt 4th Bn Northants Regt; *m* 1st 1895 (*divorce* 1920) Loretta Mooney and had:

(1) Bruce Francis Sholto; *b* 1 April 1897; Lt 4th Bn S Staffs Regt; *ka* 14 April 1915

(2) Sholto Augustus; *b* 5 Nov 1900; took French nationality 1938; *m* 29 Dec 1925 Isabelle (*d* 1993), dau of François Raymon, and *d* 11 June 1950, leaving:

1a +Douglas Bruce Georges; *b* 29 Jan 1926

2a Alfred; *b* 29 Oct 1928; *d* 1985

3a +Robert; *b* 1 Jan 1933; *m* 1963 *Nicole Bourgeois and has:

  1b *Marie Cristine; *b* 6 May 1965

4a Francis; *b* 6 July 1936; *d* 20 June 1950

5a Georges; *b* 30 July 1938; *d* 28 July 1978

6a +Noel; *b* 27 Dec 1939

1a *Elisabeth Georgette; *b* 4 Sept 1927; *m* Aug 1952 Jean Masoin (*d* 1990), artist, and has:

  1b *Sybil Elisabeth Marie Louise; *b* 31 May 1953; *m* 1985 *Daniel Rohemer and has:

    1c *Alexandre; *b* 1988

    2c *Louis Adrien; *b* 1990

    1c *Aurélia; *b* 1986

2a Dorothy; *b* 27 Dec 1929; *d* 19 July 1936

3a *Sybil; *b* 30 July 1931; *m* 10 Dec 1966 *Nigel Paul Mitchell-Carruthers, only s of Col Nigel Laurie Mitchell-Carruthers, and has:

  1b *Bruce Nigel Lawrence [Bruce Mitchell-Carruthers Esq, Enbelis, Massaguel, 81110 Tarn, France]; *b* 10 Jan 1968; *m* 1988 *Cecile, dau of Alain Badaroux, and has:

    1c *Pauline; *b* 1991

    2c *Laurie Marianne; *b* 1994

    3c *Eve; *b* 1997

  1b *Cecilia Elisabeth; *b* 1973

4a *Marguerite Jeanette; *b* 30 July 1941; *m* 1st 25 Aug 1969 (*divorce* 1973) Jean Demol and has:

  1b *Ysabelle; *b* 22 May 1965

4a (cont.) Mrs Marguerite Demol *m* 2nd 1974 *Count Xavier de Chagny and has:

  1b *Godefroy; *b* 1975

5a *(Marie) Jeanne [Mrs Wesley Christie, 44 Howard Rd, Wokingham, Berks RG11 2BX]; *b* 20 May 1944; *m* 1st 1970 Horace Warren Hastings-Hodgkins (*d* 1972) and has:

  1b *Warren Sholto Olivier; *b* 1966; MA Cantab; *m* 1992 *Pamela, dau of Kuldip Khosla, and has:

    1c *James Oliver Douglas; *b* 5 April 1995

    2c *Thomas Paul; *b* 26 Dec 1998

  2b *Julian Percy Herbert; *b* 1967

  3b *Alistair John Hughes; *b* 1970

5a (cont.) Mrs Horace Hastings-Hodgkins *m* 2nd 1978 *Wesley Alan Christie and has:

  4b *Michael Ian Jerôme; *b* 1974

  1b *Jasmine Elisabeth Céline; *b* 1976

4 (cont.) Lord Sholto Douglas *m* 2nd 23 April 1921 (*divorce* 1925) Georgina Leonora Barnard (*d* 30 April 1969), dau of Richard Frederick Hendrick Mosselmans; *m* 3rd 11 Oct 1926 Lily Louise (*d* 22 Aug 1945), dau of Charles Edmunds and widow of Mendelssohn Pickles, and *d* 6 April 1942

1 Edith Gertrude; *b* 31 March 1874; *m* 25 March 1899 St George William Lane Fox-Pitt (*d* 6 April 1932), s of Gen Augustus Henry Lane Fox-Pitt-Rivers, of Rushmore, Wilts, and *d* 20 July 1963

The 9th MARQUESS's est surv son,

PERCY SHOLTO DOUGLAS, **10th Marquess of Queensberry**; *b* 13 Oct 1868; Midshipman RN, Lt 3rd Militia Bn KOSB, roadhouse manager Canada, gold prospector Australia, jnlst in Chicago and New York 1911; *m* 1st 11 Sept 1893 Anna Maria (*d* 25 April 1917), yst dau of Rev Thomas Walters, Vicar Boyton, Cornwall; *m* 2nd 4 Dec 1918 Marie Louisa (*d* 4 April 1956), dau of Richard Bickel, of Cardiff, and widow of Ernest Morgan, and *d* 1 Aug 1920, having by his 1st w had:

1 FRANCIS ARCHIBALD KELHEAD, **11th Marquess**

2 Cecil Charles; *b* 27 Dec 1898; *educ* Lancing and RMC Sandhurst; Lt KOSB and RFC WW I (wounded); *m* 20 July 1927 Ruby (*d* 9 May 1981), 2nd dau of George de Vere Fenn and formerly w of St Bede Kirkley, and *d* 26 Feb 1981, leaving:

  (1) *Susan Jean [Baroness Botho von Bose, Apt 1203, 1166 Bay St, Toronto, Ont M5S 2X8, Canada]; *b* 6 Feb 1939; *m* 23 June 1965 *Baron (Joachim) Botho Carl Waldemar Georg Hasso von Bose, est s of Baron Carl Georg Thilo Hasso von Bose, of Cologne-Marienburg, by Baroness Juliane von Koch, of Wuppertal

1 Dorothy Madeline; *b* 5 July 1894; *educ* St Paul's Girl's Sch; WWs I and II with BRCS; *m* 4 Oct 1924 Capt Esmond Brasnell Palmer, Roy Scots (*d* 5 Aug 1953), 3rd s of William Clayton Palmer

The 10th MARQUESS's er son,

FRANCIS ARCHIBALD KELHEAD DOUGLAS, **11th Marquess of Queensberry**; *b* 17 Jan 1896; *educ* Harrow and RMC Sandhurst; Capt Black Watch (Roy Highrs) WW I (wounded twice), rep S peer 1922–29, memb London Stock Exchange; *m* 1st 4 Dec 1917 (*divorce* 1925) Irene Clarice, musical comedy actress (*d* 24 Oct 1977), only dau of Henry William Richards, of Salcombe, Devon, and had:

1 Patricia Sybil; *b* 24 Dec 1918; *m* 1st 27 Jan 1938 (*divorce* 1950) Count John Gerard de Bendern, Br amateur golf champion 1931, 2nd s of Maurice Arnold, Count de Bendern (formerly Baron de Forest) (*see* GERARD, B), and had:

  (1) *Simon

  (1) *Emma; *m* 1st 1971 (*divorce* 1974) Nigel Richard Patton Dempster, gossip columnist (*m* 2nd 1977, as her 2nd husb, Camilla, only child of 11th and last Duke of Leeds (*see* 1963 edn) and formerly w of Robert Julian Brownlow Harris; *see* HARRIS, B); *m* 2nd Aug 1975 (*divorce* 19–), as his 2nd w of three, Giles Trentham, and has by him:

    1a *Amber; *b* c 1976; *educ* Oxford

  (1) (cont.) Mrs Emma Trentham *m* 3rd 19– (*divorce* 19–) Prince George Galitzine and by him has:

    1a *Dmitri; *b* c 1987

  (1) (cont.) Mrs Emma Galitzine *m* 4th June 1998 her 2nd husb *Giles Trentham

  (2) *Caroline; *m* 19– *Barney Wilen, jazz saxophonist

1 (cont.) Countess de Bendern *m* 2nd 1952 (*divorce* 1960) Hermann Hornak and had issue

The **11th Marquess** *m* 2nd 18 March 1926 (*divorce* 1946) Cathleen Sabine (*d* 9 Sept 1959), memb Roy Soc Portrait Painters, dau of Harrington Mann, and by her had:

1 DAVID HARRINGTON ANGUS DOUGLAS, **12th and present Marquess of Queensberry**

2 *Jane Katherine [The Lady Jane Cory-Wright, 11 Stowe Rd, London W12 8BQ]; *b* 18 Dec 1926; *m* 25 Aug 1949 (*divorce* 1985) David Arthur Cory-Wright, 3rd s of Capt Sir Geoffrey Cory-Wright, 3rd Bt (*qv*), and has issue

The **11th Marquess** *m* 3rd 23 April 1947 Muriel Beatrice Margaret (Mimi) (*d* 1992), dau of Arthur John Rowe Thornett and formerly w of Albert Sydney Gore Chunn, and *d* 27 April 1954, leaving by her:

2 +Gawain Archibald Francis [The Lord Gawain Douglas, 2 Archery Sq, Walmer, Kent CT14 7HP]; *b* 23 May 1948; *educ* Downside and RAM (LRAM); *m* 30 April 1971 *Nicolette, yr dau of Col F A Eustace, OBE, RM, of Hong Kong, and has:

  (1) +Jamie Sholto; *b* 1975

  (1) *Dalziel Frances; *b* 1971; *m* 1995 *Michael O'Halloran, TV cameraman

  (2) *Elizabeth Meriel; *b* 1974

  (3) *Natasha Rose; *b* 1976

  (4) *Margarita Consuela; *b* 1978

  (5) *Mary Anne; *b* 1981

QUILTER

Arms: Argent on a bend invected gules between three Cornish choughs bendwise proper two cross-crosslets of the field. **Crest:** In front of a dexter arm embowed in armour proper, garnished or, the hand in a gauntlet also proper, grasping a battle-axe, handle sable, headed argent, around the arm a scarf of the last, a Cornish chough proper. **Motto:** *Plutôt mourir que changer* ('Better to die than change'). **Creation:** Bt. (UK) 13 Sept 1897.

SIR ANTHONY RAYMOND LEOPOLD CUTHBERT QUILTER, **4TH BT**, of Bawdsey Manor, Bawdsey, Suffolk [Sir Anthony Quilter Bt, Sutton Hall, Sutton, Woodbridge, Suffolk]; *b* 25 March 1937; s f 7 Feb 1959; *educ* Harrow; *m* 13 June 1964 *Mary Elise, er dau of Col Brian Sherlock Gooch, DSO, TD, JP, DL (*see* GOOCH, Bt, of Benacre), and has:

1 +GUY RAYMOND CUTHBERT; *b* 13 April 1967; *m* 1992 *Jennifer J, only dau of John Redvers-Cox, of Melton, Suffolk, and has:

  (1) +William Raymond Cuthbert; *b* 29 Nov 1995

  (2) +Henry Guy Cuthbert; *b* 13 Aug 1997

1 *Juliet Elise; *b* 10 July 1965

Lineage: SAMUEL SACKER QUILTER, of Walton, Suffolk; *b* 1779; *m* Sarah Chapman (*d* 1861) and *d* 1833, having had, with other issue:

WILLIAM QUILTER, of Norfolk St, Mayfair; *b* 7 Aug 1808; *m* 15 March 1834 Elizabeth Hariot (*d* 29 June 1874), dau of Thomas Cuthbert, and *d* 12 Nov 1888, leaving:

1 (WILLIAM) CUTHBERT (Sir), **1st Bt**

2 Edward Frederick, of Hill House, Belstead, Suffolk, and Mayfair; *b* 8 Feb 1848; *d* unm 20 July 1905

3 Harry; *b* 24 Jan 1851; *m* Mary Constance Hall and *d* 10 July 1907, leaving issue

1 Elizabeth; *m* 10 Feb 1869 Charles Eley (*d* 10 June 1902), of Highland Lodge, E Bergholt, Suffolk, and *dsp* 17 Oct 1899

2 Sarah Ellen; *m* 26 Sept 1895 Capt Alexander Allen Muter, of Erewhon, Dovercourt, Essex, and *d* 30 Nov 1923

WILLIAM QUILTER's est s,

Sir (William) Cuthbert Quilter, 1st Bt (UK), so *cr* 13 Sept 1897, of Bawdsey Manor, Suffolk, JP, DL; *b* 29 Jan 1841; CA Suffolk, MP Sudbury 1885–1906; *m* 7 May 1867 Mary Ann (*d* 12 Sept 1927), dau of John Wheeley Bevington, and *d* 18 Nov 1911, having had:

1 WILLIAM ELEY CUTHBERT (Sir), **2nd Bt**

2 John Arnold Cuthbert; *b* 24 Jan 1875; Lt-Col cmdg Hood Bn RND, Maj Gren Gds, Mil Sec to Govr-Gen Australia; *ka* Dardanelles 6 May 1915

3 Roger Cuthbert; *b* 1 Nov 1877; *educ* Eton; composer: *Love at the Inn*, *The Blue Boar* light opera and incidental music for *As You Like It*, *Where the Rainbow Ends*, *Children's Overture*, *Serenade*, *Three English Dances*, *Song Cycle*, *To Julia*, also songs, part-songs, choruses; *d* unm 21 Sept 1953

4 Percy Cuthbert; *b* 5 Feb 1879; *m* 12 Jan 1909 (Gladys) Clare Alice (*d* 1973), 2nd dau of Charles Clement Tudway, DL, of The Cedars, Wells, and *d* 10 June 1947, leaving:

  (1) +David Cuthbert QUILTER later TUDWAY QUILTER (deed poll Nov 1962), JP (Somerset 1959 and 1963) [David Tudway Quilter JP Esq, Milton Lodge, Wells, Somerset BA5 3AQ]; *b* 26 March 1921; *educ* Eton; Coldstream Gds 1940–46, High Sheriff Somerset 1974, V-Ld Lt Somerset 1978–95 (DL 1970–78), local dir Barclays Bank; *m* 30 Oct 1953 *Elizabeth Mary, est dau of Col Sir John Gawen Carew Pole, 12th Bt (*qv*), and has had:

    1a +Simon John Cuthbert; *b* 26 March 1955; *educ* Eton

    1a *Susan Clare Evelyn [Mrs Charles Dingwall, The Manor House, West Hendred, Oxon]; *b* 9 July 1957; *m* 1st 7 Oct 1978 James (Jamie) Henderson (*d* 1991), yr s of Robert Henderson, of Welwyn, Herts, and has:

      1b *Sophie; *b* 23 July 1979

      2b *Emily; *b* 2 Aug 1981

      3b *Alice; *b* 10 May 1985

    1a (cont.) Mrs Jamie Henderson *m* 2nd 19– *Charles Dingwall and has:

1b *A son; *b* 1993
2a Melanie; *b* 14 Feb, *d* 1 May 1959
3a *Lucy Anne; *b* 6 May 1961; *m* 1984 *Dr Christopher D B Daniel, yr s of Ian Daniel, of Fressingfield, Suffolk, and has:
    1b *Jonathan David; *b* 1985
    1b *Katie; *b* 1987
(1) Beryl Joan; *b* 3 Nov 1909; *m* 19 July 1933 2nd and last Baron Charnwood (*see* 1953 edn)
(2) Ann; *b* 18 May 1913; *m* 1 Oct 1936 6th Baron Skelmersdale (*qv*) and *d* 1974, leaving issue
(3) *Diana Primrose [Mrs Archibald Tennant, 12 Victoria Sq, London SW1]; *b* 4 Jan 1916; *m* 1st 25 Feb 1942 (*annulled* 1945) Brig Lancelot Merivale Gibbs, CVO, DSO, MC (*see* ALDENHAM and HUNSDON OF HUNSDON, B); *m* 2nd 16 Sept 1947 Archibald Tennant (*see* GLENCONNER, B) and has issue
5 Eustace Cuthbert, OBE; *b* 15 Feb 1881; Maj 4th Bn Suffolk Regt WW I; *m* 29 May 1906 Cecil Bligh (*d* 12 July 1950), only dau of Phillip Nutting, of Stanmore, Middx, and *d* 21 Jan 1934, leaving:
(1) Ronald Eustace Cuthbert; *b* 9 April 1907; *educ* Eton; *m* 9 Oct 1934 Doreen Mary (*d* 1988), er dau of Charles Sandbach Parker, CBE, of Fairlie Ho, Fairlie, Ayrshire, and *d* 4 Feb 1972, leaving:
    1a William Ronald Cuthbert, of Onehouse Lodge, Stowmarket, Suffolk; *b* 25 Jan 1937; *educ* Eton and Magdalene Coll Cambridge (BA 1960); *m* 2 June 1962 *Jennifer Ann [Mrs Reginald Hill, Holfield Grange, Coggeshall, Essex] (*m* 2nd 1985 Reginald J T Hill), dau of Cdr Evelyn John Tamlyn, RD, RNR, of Yew Tree Farm, Pleshey, Essex, and *d* 1981, leaving:
        1b +Benjamin William Cuthbert [Benjamin Quilter Esq, Titirangi, Auckland, New Zealand; *b* 3 Nov 1963; *m* 1992 *Helen Lidwina, dau of Hendrik Akerboom, of NZ, and has:
            1c +Samuel William John; *b* 1993
        1b *Melissa Jane [Mrs Dennis Embleton, London House, Charsfield, Suffolk]; *b* 7 Feb 1966; *m* 1992 *Dennis Embleton, s of Dr Philip Embleton, of Aldeburgh, and has:
            1c *(Dennis) Harry Faraday; *b* 1993
    2a +Thomas Eustace Cuthbert [Thomas Quilter Esq, 8 Grosvenor Crescent Mews, London SW1]; *b* 7 Oct 1940; *educ* Eton and RCM; *m* 1st 25 Jan 1966 (*divorce* 1969) Joy Winifred Therese (*m* 2nd 14 Sept 1974 John William Hume), dau of W/Cdr G F Roedel-Duffy, AFC, of Kencot, Oxon; *m* 2nd 1992 *Mary T Griffiths
(2) John Cuthbert; *b* 24 June 1910; *educ* Eton; Coldstream Gds 1940–1946; *d* unm 16 Aug 1983
1 Maude Marion; *m* 10 May 1888 Frederick Anthony Denny (*d* 18 Jan 1941), of Horwood Ho, Winslow, Bucks, and Mayfair, er s of Edward Maynard Denny, of London, and *d* 19 Oct 1949, leaving issue
2 Norah Blanche; *m* 1st 3 March 1898 Capt William George Percival Miller, 3rd Bn Loyal N Lancs Regt (*d* 1 Sept 1906), of Thistleton, Lancs, and had issue; *m* 2nd 10 July 1913 Maj Guy Noel Vivian, OBE, JP, Gren Gds (R) (*d* 13 Nov 1930), and *d* 10 Dec 1947, having had further issue
Sir CUTHBERT's est s,
   Sir (William Eley) Cuthbert Quilter, 2nd Bt, JP; *b* 17 July 1873; *educ* Harrow and Trin Coll Cambridge (BA 1896); Capt TFR and Rlwy Tport Offr, Maj Suffolk Yeo, MP Sudbury 1910–18; *m* 18 Nov 1899 Hon Gwynedd Douglas-Pennant (*d* 14 Oct 1960), dau of 2nd Baron Penrhyn (*qv*) and *d* 18 Sept 1952, having had:
1 George Eley Cuthbert; *b* 23 Nov 1900; *d* 18 March 1919
   2 **Sir (John) Raymond Cuthbert Quilter, 3rd Bt**; *b* 25 Feb 1902; *educ* Eton; Lt Gren Gds; *m* 3 July 1935 *Margery Marianne [Margery Lady Quilter, Pettistree Hall, Sutton, Woodbridge, Suffolk], dau of Maj Sir (James) Douglas Cooke, of S Kensington, and *d* 7 Feb 1959, leaving:
      (1) Sir ANTHONY RAYMOND LEOPOLD CUTHBERT QUILTER, **4th and present Bt**
1 Inez; *b* 22 Jan 1904; *m* 19 April 1955 Brig Raleigh Charles Joseph Chichester-Constable, CBE, DSO, JP, DL (*d* 26 May 1963), est s of Lt-Col Walter George Raleigh Chichester-Constable, JP, DL, of Burton Constable and Wood Hall, Hull
2 Zoe Gwynedd; *b* 22 Jan 1912; *m* 5 Jan 1939 Lt-Col Brian Morton Forster Franks, DSO, MC, only s of Lt-Col George Despard Franks, CMG, DSO, 19th Hus, and *d* 1 July 1979, leaving issue
3 *Sonia [Mrs William Luddington, Walnut Tree House, Turweston, Northants]; *b* 27 July 1917; *m* 17 Jan 1939 (*divorce* 1950) Capt Patrick William Butler Pole-Carew (*see* POLE, Bt, of Shute House) and had issue; *m* 2nd 8 Dec 1958 Maj William Henry Cropley Luddington, MC, JP (*d* 5 April 1965), 9th Lancers, er s of Lt-Col W J C Luddington and Mrs D E Vinning, of Green's Norton, Northants

QUINTON

Arms: Argent a tilting spear in bend sable, grip, butt and coronal or, between two bends also sable, in chief three roses gules, barbed and seeded proper, and in base as many martlets also gules. **Crest:** A quintain proper. **Supporters:** Dexter, a fox rampant proper; sinister, a griffin segreant per fess azure and or, both gorged with a coronet flory gold. **Motto:** *Il ose aussi douter* ('He dares also to doubt') **Creation:** B. (LP, UK) 1982.

THE BARON QUINTON, of Holywell, City of Oxford and Co Oxon (Anthony Meredith Quinton) [The Rt Hon The Lord Quinton, A11 Albany, Piccadilly, London W1V 9RD; Mill House, Turville, Oxon RG9 6QL]; *b* 25 March 1925; *educ* Stowe (Govr 1963–84, Chm Govrs 1969–75) and Ch Ch Oxford (BA 1948); RAF WW II, Fell: All Souls 1949–55, New Coll Oxford 1955–78 and Winchester Coll 1970–85, Pres Trin Coll Oxford 1978–87; Delegate OUP 1970–76, Memb Arts Cncl 1979–82, Chm Bd Br Library 1985–90, FBA 1977 (V-Pres 1985–86); author: *Political Philosophy* (ed, 1967), *The Nature of Things* (1973), *Utilitarian Ethics* (1973), *The Politics of Imperfection* (1978), *Francis Bacon* (1980), *Thoughts and Thinkers* (1982); *m* 1952 *Marcelle, dau of Maurice Wegier, of New York, and has:
1 *Edward Frith [The Hon Edward Quinton, 1A 29 Earls Court Sq, London SW5 9DB]; *b* 1957; *educ* Winchester and Imp Coll London; *m* 1987 (*divorce* 1998) Sarah Eve, dau of A W Travis, of the Seychelles
1 *Joanna; *b* 1955; *m* 1st 1974 (*divorce* 1981) Francis Joseph Fitzherbert-Brockholes, est s of Michael John Fitzherbert-Brockholes (2nd but est surv s of Maj John William Fitzherbert-Brockholes, CBE, MC, JP, DL, by Hon Eileen French (*see* DE FREYNE, B); *m* 2nd 1981 *Jonathan Nelson, of New York

Lineage: RICHARD FRITH QUINTON; Surgn-Capt RN; *m* Gwenllyan Letitia (*d* 1978) and *d* 1935, leaving:

ANTHONY MEREDITH, *cr* a **Baron**

QUIRK

Creation: B. (LP, UK) 1994.

THE BARON QUIRK, of Bloomsbury, London Borough of Camden ((Charles) Randolph Quirk) [The Rt Hon The Lord Quirk, House of Lords, London SW1A 0PW]; *b* 12 July 1920; *educ* Douglas High Sch IOM, UCL (MA, PhD, DLit, Lecturer English 1947–54, Quain Prof Eng Lang and Lit 1968–81, Fell); RAF WW II, Cwlth Fund Fell Yale and Michigan U 1951–52, Durham: Reader Eng Lang and Lit 1954–58, Prof Eng Lang 1958–60; V-Chllr London U 1981–85, Dir Survey English Usage 1959–81, memb: Senate London U 1970–85, Bd Br Cncl 1983–91, RADA Cncl 1985–; Pres: Inst Linguistics 1982–85, Br Acad 1985–89, Coll Speech Therapists 1987–91; V-Pres Fndn Sci and Tech 1986–90, Govr: ESU 1980–85 (V-Chm Eng Lang Ctee 1985–), Richmond Coll London 1981–, City Tech Colls 1986–; Chm Br Library Advsy Ctee 1984–; Tstee Wolfson Fndn 1987–; memb Academia Europaea 1988, For Fell: Roy Belgian Acad Sciences 1975, Roy Swedish Acad 1987, Finnish Acad Scis 1991, American Acad Arts and Scis 1994; Hon FCST, Hon FIL, Hon Fell: Imp Coll 1985, QMC 1986, Goldsmiths' Coll 1987, King's Coll London 1990; Hon Bencher Gray's Inn 1982, Hon DU Essex and Brunel, DUniv OU, Hon DLitt Reading, Newcastle, Durham, Bath, Salford, California, Sheffield, Glasgow, Poznan, Nijmegen, Richmond Coll; Hon DCL Westminster; Hon LLD Leicester and London, Hon DSc Aston, Jubilee Medal Inst Linguistics 1973; author: *The Concessive Relation in Old English Poetry* (1954), *Studies in Communications* (contributor, 1955), *An Old English Grammar* (coauthor 1955), *Charles Dickens and Appropriate Language* (1959), *The Teaching of English* (coauthor 1959), *The Study of the Mother-Tongue* (1991), *The Use of English* (1962), *Prosodic and Paralinguistic Features in English* (coauthor 1964), *A Common Language* (coauthor 1964), *Investigating Linguistic Acceptability* (coauthor 1966), *Essays on the English Language — Mediaeval and Modern* (1968), *Elicitation Experiments in English* (coauthor 1970), *A Grammar of Contemporary English* (coauthor 1972), *The English Language and Images of Matter* (1972), *A University Grammar* *of English* (1973), *The Linguist and the English Language* (1974), *Old English Literature: a practical introduction* (coauthor 1975), *A Corpus of English Conversation* (coauthor 1980), *Style and Communication in the English Language* (1982), *A Comprehensive Grammar of the English Language* (coauthor 1985), *English in the World* (coauthor 1985), *Words at Work: lectures on textual structure* (1986), *English in Use* (coauthor 1990), *A Student's Grammar of the English Language* (coauthor 1990), *An Introduction to Standard English* (coauthor 1993), *Grammatical and Lexical Variances in English* (1995); *m* 1st 1946 (*divorce* 1979) Jean (*d* 1995), dau of Ellis Gauntlett Williams; *m* 2nd 1984 *Gabriele, dau of Judge Helmut Stein, and has by his 1st w two sons

Lineage: THOMAS QUIRK, of IOM; *m* Amy Randolph — and had:

(CHARLES) RANDOLPH, *cr* a **Baron**

RADCLIFFE

Arms: Argent a bend engrailed sable, charged with a crescent of the field for difference. **Crest:** A bull's head erased sable, horns argent, tipped or, gorged with a ducal coronet of the second. **Motto:** *Virtus propter se* ('Virtue for its own sake'). **Creation:** Bt. (UK) 2 Nov 1813.

SIR SEBASTIAN EVERARD RADCLIFFE, 7TH BT, of Milnesbridge House, Yorks [Sir Sebastian Radcliffe Bt, Château de Cheseaux, 1033 Vaud, Switzerland]; *b* 8 June 1972; *s f* 1975

Lineage: The RADCLIFFEs allegedly descend from James (de) Radclyffe, of Langley, Lancs, who was yr s of James de Radclyffe and gs of Richard de Radclyffe, High Sheriff 1421–24 and MP Lancs 1424, and one of those who had fought in the English army at the Battle of Agincourt in 1415. Richard's yr bro Sir John de Radclyffe was ancestor of the extinct Radcliffes or Ratclyffes Earls of Sussex (*see* FITZWALTER, B). Their second cousin Thomas *m* Margaret Parr, aunt of HENRY VIII's last w KATHERINE, and was ancestor of the extinct Earls of Derwentwater (*see* NEWBURGH, E). The DE RADCLYFFEs descended from a knight who was a follower of WILLIAM I (THE CONQUEROR) and who was granted the manor of Radeclive (*i.e.*, of the red cliff), Lancs, after the Conquest.

JAMES (de) RADCLYFFE; *m* 14– Joan — and *d* 1486, leaving, with another s and two daus:

ROBERT LANGLEY (so called, in an age when surnames as understood in the 20th century had still to evolve, from the family's purchase of the manor of Langley, Lancs), of Agecroft Hall, Pendlebury, Lancs (dismantled 1925 and re-erected in Virginia); *m* his distant cousin Eleanor, 3rd dau of William de Radclyffe (*d* 15 May 1497), of Ordsall, Notts, by Jane, dau of Sir Edmond Trafford (possibly identical with one of the persons of the same name in the article DE TRAFFORD, Bt; *qv*), and was supposedly ancestor of:

WILLIAM RADCLIFFE, of Milnsbridge, Yorks; acquired property there through his w Elizabeth, whose 1st husb John Dawson had lived there; *d* 20 May 1748, leaving:

1 William, of Milnsbridge House; Lt-Col W Yorks Militia; *d* unm 26 Sept 1795, leaving his estates to his n the **1st Bt**

2 Charles, of York; *m* Francina, dau and coheir of Richard Town, MD, and had three daus

1 MARY Radcliffe; *m* Joseph PICKFORD, of Alt Hill, Lancs, descended from a Macclesfield family, and had:

(1) Sir JOSEPH PICKFORD later RADCLIFFE (roy licence 19 Dec 1795 under terms of unc's will), **1st Bt** (UK), so *cr* 2 Nov 1813 (with the unusual waiver of a patent fee, for his energy as a magistrate in suppressing unrest in 1812); *b* 8 May 1744; *m* 1st 3 March 1763 Katherine (*d* 15 May 1765), dau and heiress of Thomas Percival, of Royton Hall, Lancs, and had a s (William, *dsp* 18 Dec 1763); *m* 2nd 16 Nov 1765 Elizabeth (*d* 26 March 1796), dau and sole heir of Richard Sunderland, of High Sunderland, Yorks, and by her had:

2a Joseph (Rev); *b* 31 Aug 1766; *m* 19 Sept 1796 Mary, only dau of Sir Archibald Grant, 3rd Bt, of Monymusk and Cullen (*qv*), and *d* 17 May 1804, leaving, with three daus (*d* unm):

1b JOSEPH PICKFORD (Sir), **2nd Bt**

3a Charles; *b* 21 July 1769; Cdr RN; *m* Mary Emily, dau of C V Mackinnon, and had:

1b Francis Pickford (Rev); *b* 10 June 1801; Rector Hagworthingham, Lincs; *m* Dec 1831 Sophia (*d* 1888), dau of Mathew Bancroft Lister, of Burwell, Lincs, and *d* 1883, leaving, with two other daus (*d* unm):

1c Georgiana Mary Radcliffe; *m* 13 Sept 1860 her cousin Arthur Reginald St Clair Radcliffe (*d* 8 Aug 1913) and *d* 1869, leaving issue (*see below*)

2c Katharine Elizabeth Edith; *m* 1863 Francis Worsley, s of Rev W Worsley, Rector Bratoft, Lincs, and *d* 1884, leaving issue

1a Mary; *m* 1st Joseph Starkie, of Redvales; *m* 2nd J D Macbride, DCL, FSA, Pncpl Magdalen Hall, Oxford

2a Harriet; *m* Dr William Alexander (*d* 1808)

3a Hannah; *m* William Wilcock, of Halifax

(1) (cont.) The **1st Bt** *m* 3rd 8 April 1807 Elizabeth (*dsp* 22 Nov 1855), yst dau of Richard Creswick, of Sheffield, and *d* 19 Feb 1819

His gs,

Sir Joseph Pickford Radcliffe, 2nd Bt; *b* 5 June 1799; *m* 29 Oct 1819 Jacobina Maria (*d* 10 May 1868), yst dau of Capt John Macdonell, and *d* 29 Nov 1872, having had, with another s (*d* young) and four daus (*d* unm):

1 JOSEPH PERCIVAL PICKFORD (Sir), **3rd Bt**

2 Charles John; *b* 23 Sept 1829; *m* 2 Aug 1860 Clementina Maria (*d* 27 April 1906), 2nd dau of Anthony George Wright Biddulph, of Burton Park, Sussex, and Brambletye House, Sussex, and *d* 15 May 1908, having had:

(1) Joseph Anthony, of Ordsall, Tywford, Berks; *b* 30 July 1861; *d* unm 16 Nov 1916

(2) Charles James Forbes; *b* 8 July 1864; *m* 20 March 1901 Caroline Emily Ann, dau of John Octavius Weston, of Picton, NZ

(3) Arthur Ranald Macdonell; *b* 1 June 1867; *d* unm 27 Jan 1907

(4) George Gilbert Biddulph; *b* 1 Oct 1869; *d* 11 May 1879

(1) Gwendaline Amelia Mary; *d* unm 5 March 1954 aged 91

3 Arthur Reginald St Clair; *b* 9 Nov 1830; *m* 13 Sept 1860 his cousin Georgiana Mary (*see above*) and *d* 8 Aug 1913, having had, with a dau (*d* unm):

(1) Charles Arthur Forbes; *b* 30 June 1861; *d* 15 Dec 1937

(2) Francis Joseph; *b* 19 Feb 1863; *d* 7 March 1912

4 Godfrey Edward Alister; *b* 27 June 1832; Capt 5th W Yorks Regt; *m* 14 April 1863 his sis-in-law Geraldine Mary (*d* 13 Feb 1917), 3rd dau of Anthony George Wright Biddulph, of Burton Park, and *d* 1923, having had:

(1) Francis Joseph; *b* 13 Sept 1865; Maj 5th Bn Lancs Fus Boer War 1899–1902; *d* unm 3 May 1905

(2) Alister Joseph; *b* 12 June 1867

(1) Mary Frances; *b* 28 March 1864

1 Jacobina Maria Sophia; *m* 1 June 1841 Samuel James Brown (*d* 22 Sept 1891), of Loftus Hill, Yorks, and *d* 23 July 1910, leaving issue

2 Eliza Matilda Mary; *m* 1 June 1841 Sir George Armytage, 5th Bt (*qv*), and *d* 2 March 1898, leaving issue

3 Amelia Frances; *m* 5 Nov 1846 David Arthur Leahy (*d* 1892), est s of David Leahy, of Shanakill House, Co Cork, and *d* 15 Sept 1906

4 Flora Macdonell; *m* 21 Nov 1848 Joseph Weld (*d* 13 July 1889), 3rd s of Joseph Weld, of Lulworth Castle, Dorset, and *d* 8 Jan 1882, having had issue

The 2nd Bt's est s,

Sir Joseph Percival Pickford Radcliffe, 3rd Bt, JP (Staffs and W R Yorks); *b* 4 Oct 1824; *m* 20 Oct 1854 Katharine Mary Elizabeth (*d* 8 Dec 1906), only surv child of Sir Edward Doughty, 9th Bt (*see* 1967 edn DOUGHTY-TICHBORNE, Bt), and *d* 27 April 1908, having had, with three other daus (*d* young):

1 JOSEPH EDWARD (Sir), **4th Bt**

2 Henry Joseph Francis; *b* 14 June 1862; Capt 2nd Bn QO Cameron Highrs WW I; *m* 15 Jan 1896 Gertrude Mary Philomena (*d* 15 March 1955), dau of John Coventry (*see* COVENTRY, E), and *d* 25 Oct 1928, leaving:

(1) +Henry Edward Joseph [Henry Radcliffe Esq, Manor Cottage, Lympsham, Weston-super-Mare, Somerset]; *b* 18 March 1904; *educ* Beaumont; *m* 19 April 1939 *Ursula Mary Skeet, yr dau of Frederick Dickinson Workman, of Hyde, Fordingbridge, Hants, and has:

1a *Sally Anne Ursula [Mrs Geoffrey Taylor, Willow Cottage, Strawberry Lane, Dundry, Bristol]; *b* 2 March 1940; *m* 3 Sept 1966 *Geoffrey Peter Montgomery Taylor, s of Maj M C Taylor, MBE, of Bithams Girth, Chew Magna, Somerset, and has:

1b *Justin Peter; *b* 18 Sept 1968

1b *Juliet Clare; *b* 1970

2b *Lucinda Jane; *b* 1971

3b *Kirsty Anna; *b* 1974

(1) *Gertrude Mary Catherine [Mrs Gertrude Bower, 20 The Bungalows, Old Vicarage, Stockland, Bridgwater, Somerset]; *b* 8 Jan 1903; *m* 24 Feb 1925 (*divorce* 19–) Philip George Bower, 60th Rifles (*d* 1939), only s of George Bower, of Temple Lodge, Lyndhurst, Hants

3 Philip John Joseph, CMG (1918); *b* 1 Nov 1863; Col RE WW I; *m* 1 Feb 1893 Maud (*d* 24 May 1944), dau of Sir Frederick Aloysius Weld, GCMG, of Chideock Manor, Dorset, and *d* 17 Feb 1943, having had:

(1) Arthur Philip Joseph, MC; *b* 14 Jan 1896; Capt, Actg Maj RFA WW I (despatches); *d* 18 Aug 1917 from wounds recd in action

(1) Mary; *b* 26 Jan 1894; *m* 2 June 1919 Capt Bernard Percy Turnbull Lees, MC (*see* LEES, Bt, of South Lytchett Manor) and had issue

4 Bernard Percival Joseph; *b* 12 Dec 1869; *educ* Stonyhurst; *m* 24 June 1896 Georgina Mary (*d* 26 Dec 1941), dau of Maurice Murray, DL, of Beech Hill, Co Cork, and *d* 29 Sept 1948, having had:

(1) Percival Victor Alban; *b* 2 June 1897; *educ* Stonyhurst; Lt 5th Bn Yorks Regt and MGC; *ka* 25 Nov 1917

(2) Cyril William Joseph, JP (Worcs 1956); *b* 13 April 1902; *educ* Stonyhurst; Kt of Grace and Devotion SMO Malta 1949; *m* 1 June 1940 *Joan, dau of Frederick J Nesbitt, and *d* 19–

5 Roger Chideock Joseph; *b* 1872; *educ* Stonyhurst; Lt Durham Artillery Militia, Capt RASC WW I; *d* unm 8 Feb 1955

1 Mary Agnes Katharine; *d* unm 10 Feb 1952 aged 94

2 Mary Filumena; *m* 7 Jan 1899 William Joseph Manley (*d* 3 Dec 1914), of Crimple House, Harrogate, est surv s of George Manley, of Spofforth Hall, Yorks, and *d* 29 April 1941, leaving issue

3 Mary Katharine Theresa; nun as Mother Mary Aloysius; *d* 6 April 1950

The 3rd Bt's est s,

Sir Joseph Edward Radcliffe, 4th Bt, JP (W R Yorks); *b* 1 Aug 1858; *educ* Oscott Coll; Capt 3rd Bn Princess of Wales's Own Yorks Regt, Maj Vol Bn W Yorks Regt; *m* 1 Feb 1881 Mary Katherine (*d* 3 Jan 1943), 2nd dau of John Reginald Talbot (*see* TALBOT DE MALAHIDE, B), and *d* 29 Sept 1949, having had:

1 EVERARD JOSEPH (Sir), **5th Bt**

2 Joseph Francis Edward; *b* 15 March 1891; Lt Northumberland Fus WW I 1914–15 (wounded), Irish Govt Delegate on Perm Ctee Int Inst Ag, Gentleman-in-Waiting to HH THE POPE; *m* 26 July 1922 Marjorie Sophia (*d* 24 Oct 1973), est surv dau of Sir Francis Charles Edward Denys-Burton, 3rd Bt (*see* 1959 edn DENYS, Bt), and *d* 13 March 1940, having had:

(1) *(Elizabeth) Denyse Mary; *b* 24 July 1923; WAAF WW II 1942–45; *m* 10 May 1952 *Yves Michel Bonapace, MSc (Ag), and has:

  1a *Charles David; *b* 8 Jan 1954

  2a *(Ian) Marc; *b* 12 Aug 1956

  3a *William; *b* 25 Sept 1958

  1a *Caroline Elizabeth; *b* 10 Feb 1955

  2a *Jane Mary; *b* 1961

  3a *Isabelle; *b* 1964

(2) Marie Gabrielle Winefride; *b* 9 April 1926; *d* 6 Jan 1928

(3) *Louise Marie Antoinette [Mrs Alec Carn, Highbury, Thornford, Sherborne, Dorset DT9 6QD]; *b* 21 Oct 1928; *m* 27 Oct 1956 *Alec Pearson Carn, only s of Lt-Col A T Carn, and has:

  1a *Nicholas Denys Pearson [Nicholas Carn Esq, 4 Park Village East, London NW1 7PX; The Old Manse, Stansfield, Suffolk]; *b* 6 Sept 1957; *educ* Bradfield and Oxford (MA 1987); *m* 1987 *Eveline, dau of Louk Ochtmann, of Brussels, and has:

    1b *Alexander Radcliffe; *b* 6 Dec 1993

    1b *Gabrielle Emily Johanna; *b* 19 Dec 1996

  2a *Jonathan Patrick Joseph; *b* 17 March 1960; *educ* Bradfield and Reading U (BSc)

  1a *Vanessa Mary; *b* 22 Jan 1963; MRCVS Bristol 1987, PhD 1994

  2a *Francesca Georgina; *b* 22 May 1969; *educ* Exeter U (BSc 1992)

  3a *Alexandra Sophia; *b* 10 Feb 1972; *educ* Bradfield and UCL (BA 1993)

3 Reginald Joseph Charles; *b* 1893; *d* 10 Feb 1900

4 Robert John Peter Joseph; *b* 29 June 1898; Lt 14th (King's) Hus, Res of Offrs; *m* 27 Nov 1929 Ursula Evelyn Mary (*d* in a domestic fire 1977), est dau of Lt-Col Miles John Stapylton, OBE, of Myton Hall, York, and *d* 1974, leaving:

(1) John Charles Joseph; *b* 31 July 1934; *d* 22 March 1989

(2) +Peter Martin Joseph [Peter Radcliffe Esq, Sandylands, Sutton-on-Forest, York]; *b* 29 Aug 1941; *educ* Blackfriars Sch, Northants; *m* 30 Nov 1963 *Pamela Ann, 2nd dau of George C Johnson, of Husthwaite, Yorks

(3) +Thomas Joseph Henry; *b* 30 April 1943

(1) *Rosemary Anne Ursula Katherine; *b* 7 Sept 1930; *m* 12 April 1950 Louis Bertram Hawkswell (*d* 1987), s of Frederick William Hawkswell, of Stamford, Lincs, and has:

  1a *Frederick Andrew Joseph; *b* 4 Feb 1951; *educ* Belmont Abbey Herefs; *m* 1974 *Linda Anne Todd and has:

    1b *Michael Andrew William; *b* 1976

    2b *Benjamin James; *b* 1977

  2a *Martin Louis; *b* 19 April 1955; *educ* Belmont; *m* 1976 *Elsa Catherine Hall and has:

    1b *Oliver Alan Louis; *b* 1979

    2b *Nicholas Martin; *b* 1983

  3a *Anthony Robert; *b* 30 June 1956; *educ* Belmont; *m* 1979 *Linda Middleton

  4a *Philip William; *b* 16 Aug 1958; *educ* Belmont; *m* 1981 *Jill Patricia Dorrington and has:

    1b *Jon William Robert; *b* 1984

    1b *Rebecca Eleanor Ann; *b* 1981

  5a *Simon; *b* 1968

  1a *Elizabeth Ann; *b* 27 Feb 1960; *m* 1980 *Anthony George and has:

    1b *Daniel George Louis; *b* 1980

    1b *Bronwen Ann; *b* 1982

(2) Janet Cecilia Bridget Mary; *b* 30 Sept 1931; *d* 27 July 1933

(3) *Mary Elizabeth Jane [Mrs Philip Abbott, The Colt House, Oulston Rd, Easingwold, Yorks]; *b* 26 Jan 1939; *m* 1st 15 Aug 1957 John William Courtney (*d* 1969), 3rd s of George F Courtney, of Buckland, Devon, and has:

  1a *Miles Stewart John; *b* 6 Feb 1965; *m* 1989 *Tracy Anne Clarke

  1a *Rosemary Elizabeth [Mrs David Kuba, 99 Bad Dargain Lane, York]; *b* 6 April 1967; *m* 26 Oct 1995 *David Patrick Kuba and has:

    1b *Claire Laura; *b* 18 May 1996

(3) (cont.) Mrs John Courtney *m* 2nd 1985 Philip Leslie Abbott (*d* 19 Dec 1991)

5 (Charles Joseph) Basil; *b* 9 Oct 1900; *educ* Downside and Faraday House; FIEE; *m* 4 Jan 1939 (Kathleen) Norah Anne (*d* 1994), only dau of Norman Percy, of Ceylon, and *d* 13 July 1983, leaving:

(1) +Francis Charles Joseph [Francis Radcliffe Esq, 11 King's Bench Walk, Temple, London EC4 7EQ]; *b* 23 Oct 1939; *educ* Ampleforth and Gonville and Caius Coll Cambridge (BA 1960, MA 1965); barrister Gray's Inn 1962, Recorder 1979–83, memb Assoc Lawyers for Defence of Unborn, fought York 1979 gen election as Christian: stop abortion candidate, fndr York Christian Pty 1981; *m* 17 Aug 1968 (*divorce* 1982) Nicolette Helene, est dau of Eugene Randag, of Lodge Hill Farm, Butler's Cross, Bucks, and has:

  1a +Edward Eugene Joseph; *b* 1969

  1a *Colette Anne; *b* 1971

2a *Alexandra Mary; *b* 1972

(2) +(Bryan) Anthony Joseph [Anthony Radcliffe Esq, 24 Abbotsbury Close, London W14]; *b* 4 Feb 1941; *educ* Ampleforth; slr 1963; *m* 4 Sept 1965 *Pisana, yr dau of Count Giuseppe Petrobelli Anselmi, of Prato della Valle, Padua, and has:

  1a +Mark Anthony Joseph; *b* 23 June 1967

  2a +Harry Joseph; *b* 1972

  1a *Isabella Carolina; *b* 11 June 1974

(1) *(Kathryn) Anne; *b* 9 Sept 1943; *m* 14 Aug 1965 *Anthony John Tulk-Hart Bigland, of Bigland Hall, Ulverston, and has:

  1a *Benedict James; *b* 1967

  1a *Emma Lucy; *b* 23 May 1967

  2a *Sophie Kathryn; *b* 1970

1 Mary Winefride Teresa; *m* 1st 7 Sept 1914 Capt Thomas Cecil de Trafford, Roy Fus (*see* DE TRAFFORD, Bt); *m* 2nd 5 June 1924 7th Baron Vaux of Harrowden (*qv*) and *d* 14 Dec 1944

The 4th Bt's est s,

Sir Everard Joseph Radcliffe, 5th Bt, JP (N R Yorks); *b* 27 Jan 1884; *educ* Downside and Ch Ch Oxford (BA 1906); Capt Yorks Hus Yeo WW I attd Intell Corps, Kt Cdr Order St Gregory; *m* 27 Jan 1909 Marguerite Magdalen Ashton (*d* 20 June 1943), 3rd dau of Capt Henry Ashton Case, of Beckford Hall, Glos, and *d* 23 Nov 1969, having had:

1 (JOSEPH BENEDICT) EVERARD HENRY (Sir), **6th Bt**

2 Hugh John Reginald Joseph, MBE (1944); *b* 3 March 1911; *educ* Downside; Lt-Col (Hon) London Scottish WW II, dep chm London Stock Exchange 1967–70, chm Dun and Bradstreet 1974–76, Kt Cdr Papal Order St Sylvester 1965, Kt of St Gregory 1984; *m* 1937 *Marie-Therese (Mariquita) [Mrs Hugh Radcliffe, The White House, Stoke, Hants SP11 0LU], yst dau of Maj-Gen Sir Cecil Pereira, KCB, CMG, and *d* 1993, leaving:

(1) +MARK HUGH JOSEPH RADCLIFFE, DL Hants (1997) [Mark Radcliffe Esq DL, The Malt House, Upton, Hants SP11 0JS]; *b* 22 April 1938; heir presumptive; *educ* Downside; 2nd Lt Coldstream Gds; dir TI Group plc 1978–91; dep dir-gen CBI 1991–94; chm: Upton Management Services Ltd 1992–, Metsec plc 1993–, SEC plc 1997; dir: London Stock Exchange 1994–, Securities and Futures Authority Ltd 1993–, William Jacks plc 1994– and Reliance Security Gp plc 1995–; memb AIM Market Advsy Ctee 1995–, Cabinet Office Civ Serv Private Sector Interchange Panel 1996–; High Sheriff Hants 1996–97; *m* 20 Feb 1963 *Anne, twin dau of Maj-Gen Arthur Evers Brocklehurst, CB, DSO, of Woodborough Manor, Pewsey, Wilts, and has:

  1a *Lucinda Mary; *b* 20 May 1964

  2a *Emily Marie Louise; *b* 24 Aug 1968; *m* June 1996 *Alex Rogers

  3a *Camilla Mary; *b* 1971

(2) +Anthony Joseph [Anthony Radcliffe Esq, The Old Vicarage, Langford, Glos GL7 3LF]; *b* 17 Jan 1942; *educ* Downside; *m* 11 June 1964 *Rachel Mary, est dau of Joseph Russell Goddard, of Harmony Hall, Barbados, and has:

  1a +James Russell Joseph; *b* 13 April 1965; *m* 1992 *A Louisa, yst dau of Mrs Elizabeth Poyser, of South Place, Moor Pk, Middx, and has:

    1b *Polly Anna; *b* 1992

    2b *Helena; *b* 1994

  2a +Julian Everard Joseph; *b* 14 Oct 1967; *m* 19– *Deborah, dau of T Key, of Compton, Berks, and has:

    1b +Matthew Joseph; *b* 12 Jan 1997

  1a *Philippa; *b* 14 May 1975

(3) +Timothy Peter Joseph (Most Rev) [The Most Reverend Father Radcliffe OP, Convento San Sabina, Piazza P d'Illiria 1, Aventino, 00153 Rome, Italy]; *b* 22 Aug 1945; *educ* Downside and St John's Coll Oxford (MA, Hon Fell 1993); joined Dominican Order 1965, Chaplain Imperial Coll 1976–78, Prior Blackfriars Oxford 1982–88 (theology teacher there 1978–88), memb Theology Faculty Oxford U 1985–88, Prior Provincial English Province Dominicans 1988–92, Master 1992–, Grand Chllr Pontifical U of St Thomas (Angelicum) Rome and U of Santo Tomas, Manila, Philippines, Grand Chllr Theological Faculty Fribourg U Switzerland, Pres Conference Major Religious Superiors 1991–92, chm edtl bd New Blackfriars 1983–88, Hon Dr Providence Coll, RI, USA

(4) +Paul John Joseph [Paul Radcliffe Esq, Rudges Hill, Ramsden, Oxon OX7 3AT]; *b* 23 June 1949; *educ* Downside; *m* 1978 *Norah H, yr dau of Sigmund Hjornevik, and has:

  1a +Alexander Hugh Joseph; *b* 1982

  1a *Emma Marie Clare; *b* 1980

(5) +Richard Joseph [Richard Radcliffe Esq, 50 Burlington Lane, London W4 2RR]; *b* 5 April 1954; *educ* Downside; *m* 1981 *Gillian, dau of Maj D W Mart, of Felixstowe, Suffolk, and has:

  1a +Harry Hugh Joseph; *b* 1985

  1a *Lucy Elizabeth; *b* 1983

(1) *(Teresa) Jane [Miss Jane Radcliffe, 97 Altenburg Gdns, London SW11 1JQ]; *b* 14 Sept 1939; Inst Blessed Virgin Mary Ascot 1957–84

3 Harry Peter Joseph; *b* 4 April 1914; P/O RAF WW II; *kas* 24 March 1949

4 Michael Anthony Joseph; *b* 30 Oct 1917; *educ* Downside; Maj Yorks Dragoons WW II 1939–44 (POW); *m* 14 March 1947 *Mary, yr dau of A Brook Edwards by Marion (later *m* 8th Earl of Carrick and 4th Baron Chesham, *qqv*), and *d* 19–

5 David Edward Joseph; *b* 1 May 1922; *educ* Downside; Capt Irish Gds; *m* 5 April 1946 *Rita Dorcas, only dau of Maj Thomas Johnson and Mrs Margarita Bourne, of Montreal, and *d* 198–

The 5th Bt's est s,

Sir (Joseph Benedict) Everard Henry Radcliffe, 6th Bt, of Milnesbridge House, MC, JP (W R Yorks 1960); *b* 10 March 1910; *educ* Downside and RMC Sandhurst; Capt KRRC, ADC to Govr and C-in-C Bermuda 1936–39, POW WW II; *m* 1st 10 April 1937 (*divorce* 1968) Elizabeth, est dau of Gilbert Butler, of Utica, NY, and had:

1 Charles Everard Christopher Joseph; *b* 20 June 1946; *educ* Stonyhurst; *d* unm 24 July 1969

1*Susan Elizabeth Mary; *b* 13 Nov 1940

Sir Everard *m* 2nd 27 Nov 1968, as her 1st husb, *Marcia Anne Helen [Mrs Howard Tanner, Château de Cheseaux, 1033 Vaud, Switzerland] (*m* 2nd 1988 Howard Montagu Stuart Tanner), yst dau of Maj David Turville-Constable-Maxwell (*see* HERRIES OF TERREGLES, L), and *d* Switzerland 7 Feb 1975, having by her had:

 2 Sir SEBASTIAN EVERARD RADCLIFFE, **7th and present Bt**

RADNOR

Arms: Quarterly, 1st and 4th, per fess or and arg. an eagle displayed with two heads sa., on the breast an escutcheon gu., charged with a bend vair (for BOUVERIE); 2nd and 3rd, arg. a bend gu., guttée d'eau, between two ravens sa., a chief chequy or and of the last (for PLEYDELL). **Crest:** A demi-eagle with two heads displayed sa., ducally gorged or; on the breast a cross-crosslet arg. **Supporters:** On either side an eagle regardant, wings elevated sa., gorged with a ducal coronet or, charged on the breast with a cross-crosslet arg. **Motto:** *Patria cara, carior libertas* ('My country is dear; liberty is dearer'). **Creations:** E. (GB) 31 Oct 1765, V. (GB) 29 June 1747, B. (GB) 29 June 1747 (Longford) and 31 Oct 1765 (Pleydell-Bouverie), Bt. (GB) 19 Feb 1713/4.

THE 8TH EARL OF RADNOR, *Viscount Folkestone*, of Folkestone, Co Kent, **Lord Longford, Baron of Longford**, Co Wilts, **Baron Pleydell-Bouverie of Coleshill**, Co Berks, and a **Baronet** (Sir Jacob Pleydell-Bouverie, Bt) [The Rt Hon The Earl of Radnor, Longford Castle, Salisbury, Wilts SP5 4EF]; *b* 10 Nov 1927; *s* f 1968; *educ* Harrow and Trin Coll Cambridge (BA 1950); *m* 1st 8 July 1953 (*divorce* 1962) Anne Garden Farquharson (*m* 2nd 1962 V-Adml Sir John Cox, KCB), only dau of Donald Farquharson Seth-Smith, MC, of Njoro, Kenya, and Whitsbury Cross, nr Fordingbridge, Hants, and has:

 1 +WILLIAM, *Viscount Folkestone* [Viscount Folkestone, Alward House, Alderbury, Wilts SP5 3DJ]; *b* 5 Jan 1955; *educ* Harrow and RAC Cirencester; *m* 11 May 1996 *Melissa, dau of James Stanford, and has:

  (1) *Hope; *b* 4 Nov 1997

 2 +Peter John [The Hon Peter Pleydell-Bouverie, Newcourt Farmhouse, Downton, Wilts; 38 Queensdale Rd, London W11 4SA]; *b* 14 Jan 1958; *educ* Harrow and Trin Coll Cambridge; *m* 1986 *Hon Jane Victoria Gilmour, only dau of Baron Gilmour of Craigmillar (*qv*), and has:

  (1) +Timothy; *b* 1987

  (2) *Jamie; *b* 1989

  (1) *Lara Caroline; *b* 1993

  (2) *Clare Anne (twin); *b* 1993

The 8th EARL *m* 2nd 29 June 1963 (*divorce* 1985) Margaret, dau of Robin Fleming, of Catter Ho, Drymen, Stirlingshire, and by her has:

 1 *Lucy; *b* 6 May 1964

 2 *Martha; *b* 6 May 1964

 3 *Belinda; *b* 9 Nov 1966

 4 *Frances; *b* 24 Oct 1973

The 8th EARL *m* 3rd 1986 *Mrs Mary Jillean Gwenellan Pettit, previously w of Anthony Pettit

Previous creation: The 2nd Baron Robartes of Truro, who was both son-in-law and brother-in-law of the 2nd Earl of Warwick (*see* WARWICK, BROOKE and, E) of the 1618 creation, having married as his 1st wife the Earl's daughter and as his 2nd wife the Earl's sister, was created Earl of Radnor in 1679. This Lord Radnor was Lord Privy Seal 1661–73, Lord Lieutenant of Ireland and Speaker of the House of Lords. The title expired on the death of his grandson the 4th Earl in 1757 (*see* 1970 edn CLIFDEN, E).

Lineage: The surname of the present Earls of Radnor occurs as De BOUVERIE, De La BOUVERIE and Des BOUVERIE(S). The 1st Earl adopted the form BOUVERIE by Act of Parliament 1737 and his yr bro's descendants seem to have dropped the particule de at some subsequent date. The family originated in the Low Countries, but its first member to live in England was:

LAURENCE des BOUVERIES; *b* 1542, yr s of the Sieur des Bouveries, of Château des Bouveries, nr Lille; *m* Barbara van den Hove, n of a rich silk mfr at Frankfurt, and settled at Canterbury 1568; his gs:

Sir EDWARD des BOUVERIES, of London; Turkey merchant (i.e. trading with the Ottoman Empire); *d* 1694, leaving an est s:

Sir William des Bouverie, 1st Bt (GB), so *cr* 19 Feb 1713/4; Turkey merchant; *m* 1st Mary, dau of James Edwards of London, by whom he had no surv issue; *m* 2nd Anne, dau and sole heiress of David Urry, of London, and *d* 19 May 1717, leaving, with a yst s and two daus:

 1 **Sir Edward de Bouverie, 2nd Bt**; *m* Mary, yst dau and coheir of John Smith, of London, and *dsp* 1736

 2 Sir JACOB DE BOUVERIE, **1st Viscount Folkestone**, of Folkestone, Co Kent, so *cr* 29 June 1747, as also LORD LONGFORD, BARON OF LONGFORD, Co Wilts (both GB); *bapt* 14 Oct 1694; *educ* Ch Ch Oxford; MP (Tory) Salisbury 1741–47; *m* 1st 31 Jan 1723 Mary (*d* 24 Nov 1739), dau and sole heiress of Bartholomew Clarke, of Hardingstone, Northants, and had:

  (1) WILLIAM, **1st Earl**

  (2) Edward DE BOUVERIE later BOUVERIE, of Delapré Abbey, Northants; MP New Sarum and Northampton; *m* 30 June 1764 Harriot (*m* 2nd 1811 Lord Robert Spencer, *see* MARLBOROUGH, D), only dau of Sir Everard Fawkener, Amb Constantinople, and *d* 3 Sept 1810, having had, with a dau (*d* unm):

   1a Edward, JP, DL, of Delapré Abbey; *b* 25 Oct 1767; *m* 10 March 1788 Catherine (*d* 29 April 1846), only dau and heiress of William Castle, and *d* 14 April 1858, leaving, with three daus:

    1b Everard William, JP, of Delapré Abbey; *b* 13 Oct 1789; Gen, Col 5th Hus; *m* 3 April 1816 Charlotte (*d* 38 Sept 1874), dau of Col Hugh O'Donel, of Newport Pratt, Co Mayo, and *dsp* 18 Nov 1871

    2b Charles; *d* unm 1817

    3b Francis Kenelm; *b* 7 Aug 1797; Capt 62nd Foot; *m* 2 Nov 1826 Elizabeth, only dau of Henry Sheil, of Castle Dawson, Co Derry, and *d* 19 Sept 1837, leaving:

     1c John Augustus Sheil, JP, of Delapré Abbey; *b* 12 July 1836; High Sheriff Northants 1877, Maj 5th Sherwood Foresters; *m* 9 April 1860 Jane (*d* 19 Oct 1903), dau of S Grey, and *d* 5 Dec 1894, having had:

      1d Francis Kenelm; *b* 24 Jan 1861; *m* 5 Sept 1882 (*divorce* 1884) Caroline, dau of Abraham Hoffnung, and *dsp* 27 April 1891

      2d John Augustus Sheil, of Delapré Abbey; *b* 8 Dec 1866; *educ* Harrow; Capt 3rd Bn Northants Regt; *d* unm 3 May 1905

      1d Caroline Elizabeth; *b* 26 Jan 1863; *m* 5 Dec 1882 Walter Henry Bullock (*d* 23 March 1924), of Faulkbourn Hall, Essex, and *d* Feb 1929, leaving issue

      2d Mary Helen, OBE (1937), JP (Northants), of Delapré Abbey; *b* 20 Sept 1865; *d* unm 20 Jan 1943

      3d Alice Maud; *b* 8 Nov 1868; *m* 4 Feb 1891 William C N Chapman, of Heppington, Canterbury, and *d* 9 Jan 1931, leaving issue

      4d Catherine Jane; *b* 21 Dec 1871; *m* 1st 12 Jan 1898 (*divorce* 1913) William Francis Edolph Andrewes Uthwatt (*d* 5 July 1921), s of Edolph Uthwatt, of Stroud, Glos, and had issue (*see* 1949 edn UTHWATT, B); *m* 2nd 1914 Astley Paston Friend (*d* 22 Jan 1944)

      5d Frederica Gertrude; *b* 16 Jan 1875; *m* 21 June 1905 her er sis's bro-in-law Gerard Thomas Andrewes Chapman Uthwatt (*d* 12 July 1950), of Gt Linford Manor, Newport Pagnell, Bucks, and *d* 30 Oct 1962, leaving issue

    4b James; *b* 21 April 1801; Lt-Col; *m* 11 July 1826 Elizabeth Alston (*m* 2nd 13 Dec 1854 Maj-Gen Edward Matson, RE (*d* 3 Sept 1873), and *d* 21 Jan 1874), dau of Maj James Alston Stewart, of Urrard Ho, Perthshire, and *dsp* March 1845

    2a John (Rev); *b* 13 Jan 1779; Preb Lincoln, Rector Woolbeding, Sussex; *d* 9 June 1855

    3a Henry Frederick (Sir), GCB, GCMG; *b* 11 July 1783; Lt-Gen, Col 97th Regt, Govr Malta; *m* 8 July 1826 Julia (*d* 23 June 1836), dau of Lewis Montolieu and widow of Capt Wilbraham, RN, and *d* 14 Nov 1852, leaving:

     1b Henry Montolieu; *b* 17 Nov 1830; Capt Coldstream Gds; *d* unm *ka* Battle of Inkerman 5 Nov 1854

     1b Henrietta; *m* 1 July 1851 Hugh Montolieu Hammersley (*d* 1896) and *d* 16 March 1929, leaving issue

    1a Harriet Elizabeth; *m* 1790 2nd Earl of Rosslyn (*qv*) and *d* 8 Aug 1810, leaving issue

    2a Mary Charlotte; *m* 21 March 1799 William Maxwell (*d* 7 Sept 1833), of Carriden, and *d* 19 Sept 1816, leaving issue

    3a Jane; *m* Jan 1802 Sir Francis Vincent, 9th Bt (*see* 1970 edn D'ABERNON, V), and *d* 13 April 1805, leaving issue

    4a Diana Juliana; *m* 1812 Hon George Ponsonby (*d* 5 June 1863), 4th s of 1st Baron Ponsonby of Imokilly (*see* BESSBOROUGH, E), and had issue

   (1) Anne; *m* Rev Hon George Talbot (*see* SHREWSBURY and WATERFORD, E)

   (2) Mary; *m* 20 March 1775 4th Earl of Shaftesbury (*qv*) and *d* 12 Nov 1804, leaving issue

   (3) Charlotte; *m* John Grant, of White Waltham, Berks

   (4) Harriet; *b* 17 Oct 1736; *m* 10 July 1775, as his 1st w, Sir James LONG later TYLNEY-LONG, 7th Bt, and *dsp* 12 Nov 1777

 2 (cont.) The **1st Viscount** *m* 2nd 21 April 1741 Elizabeth (*d* 25 Sept 1782), est dau of 1st Baron Romney (*see* ROMNEY, E), and *d* 17 Feb 1761, having by her had:

  (3) Philip BOUVERIE later BOUVERIE-PUSEY; *b* 8 Oct 1746; *m* 20 Aug 1798 Lucy (*d* 27 March 1858), dau of 4th Earl of Harborough (*see* 1859 edn) and widow of Sir Thomas Cave, 7th Bt (*see* CAVE-BROWNE-CAVE, Bt), and *d* 14 April 1828, having had:

   1a Philip, of Pusey House, Faringdon, Berks; *b* 25 June 1799; MP; *m* 4 Oct 1822 Emily Frances Theresa (*d* 16 Nov 1854), dau of 2nd Earl of Carnarvon (*qv*), and *d* 9 July 1855, having had, with a dau (*d* unm):

    1b Sidney Edward, JP, of Pusey House; *b* 15 Sept 1839; *educ* Oxford (BA); *m* 1st 29 April 1871 Wilhelmina Maria (*d* 16 Nov 1885), dau of Lord William Hervey (see BRISTOL, M); m 2nd 5 July 1890 Helen Henrietta (d 4 April 1933), dau of Patrick Grant, of Ballifeary, Inverness-shire, and widow of Rt Hon W N Massey, MP, and dsp 9 Oct 1911

1b Clara; m 30 Oct 1862 Capt Francis Charteris Fletcher (d 25 Jan 1891), 60th Rifles, and d 3 Feb 1911, leaving:

　1c Philip Francis FLETCHER later BOUVERIE-PUSEY (roy licence 1911 on inheriting Pusey estate)

　1c Constance FLETCHER later BOUVERIE-PUSEY; d unm 8 May 1953 aged 83

2a Edward (Rev); b 22 Aug 1800; DD, Canon Ch Ch, Regius Prof of Hebrew, Oxford; m 12 June 1828 Maria Catherine (d 26 May 1839), dau of John Raymond Barker, of Fairford Pk, Glos, and d 16 Sept 1882, leaving, with another dau (d unm):

　1b Philip Edward; b 14 June 1830; d unm 15 Jan 1880

　1b Mary Amelia; m 13 July 1854 Rev James G Brine (d 12 March 1901), DD, and d 12 Oct 1910, leaving issue

3a William (Rev); b 14 May 1810; MA, Rector Langley, Kent; m 7 June 1836 Catherine (d Nov 1873), dau of Thomas Freeman, and d 19 April 1888, leaving, with a dau (d unm):

　1b Henry; b 12 June 1838; 76th Foot; d unm 1869

　2b Edward; b 12 June 1838; Capt RN; m 25 June 1870 Esther Elliot, only dau of Rev Richard Cox Hales, Rector Woodmancote, Sussex, and d 13 Feb 1921, leaving:

　　1c Edward Bouverie; b 19 March 1873; inherited the Pusey estate from his cousin 1933; Capt Labour Corps; m 1st 1914 Lilyan Evelyn (d 9 Nov 1957), dau of W Q Ryan, of Melbourne, Australia; m 2nd 2 April 1958 *Ursula Winchester, dau of George Martin Lind, and dsp 21 Aug 1958

　　1c Catherine Louisa; m 4 Aug 1892 John Bowyer Buchanan Nichols (d 2 June 1939), of Lawford Hall, Essex, and d 2 March 1942, leaving issue

　　2c Ethel Mary; m 28 Aug 1900 6th Baron Braye (qv) and d 7 July 1955, leaving issue

　　3c Lucy; m 18 Dec 1920 Capt Henry Maclean Fothergill, RN, er s of Lt-Col Charles Fothergill, RMA, and had:

　　　1d *Christopher Henry; b 15 Oct 1921; Cdr RN

　3b William; dsp

1a Elizabeth; m 14 Oct 1827 Rev James H Montagu Luxmore (d 1860), s of Bp of St Asaph, and d 23 March 1883

2a Charlotte Bouverie; m 25 June 1839 Rev R L Cotton (d 8 Dec 1880), DD, Provost Worcester Coll Oxford (see COMBERMERE, V), and d 2 July 1833

The 1st VISCOUNT's est s,

WILLIAM BOUVERIE, **1st Earl of** the county of **Radnor**, so cr 31 Oct 1765, with remainder, in default of male issue, to the male descendants of his f, as also BARON PLEYDELL-BOUVERIE OF COLESHILL, Co Berks (both GB), with ordinary remainder to heirs male of his body; b 26 Feb 1725; educ Winchester and Univ Coll Oxford; MP Salisbury 1747–61, Govr: Levant (Turkey) Co 1771–76 and Hosp for French Protestants; m 1st 18 Jan 1747/8 Harriet (dvp 29 May 1750), only dau of Sir Mark Stuart Pleydell, 1st and last Bt, of Coleshill, Berks (who entailed his estates on his gs, the **2nd Earl of Radnor**, and other BOUVERIEs on condition that each heir should add the name PLEYDELL), and had an only s:

1 JACOB, **2nd Earl**

The **1st Earl** m 2nd 5 Sept 1751 Rebecca (d 4 May 1764), 2nd dau of John Alleyne, of Barbados, and sis of Sir John Alleyne, 1st Bt (qv), and by her had:

2 William Henry; b 30 Oct 1752; MP; m 16 Aug 1777 Lady Bridget Douglas (d 26 Feb 1842), dau of 15th Earl of Morton (qv), and d 1806, leaving:

　(1) Charles Henry; b 1782; d 27 May 1836

　(1) Elizabeth; m 4 May 1814, as his 2nd w, George Hay Dawkins-Pennant (d 17 Dec 1840; see PENRHYN, B, and SUDELEY, B) and dsp 7 July 1859

　(2) Maria Rebecca; m 30 Oct 1808 1st Baron Heytesbury (qv) and d 6 Oct 1844, leaving issue

3 Bartholomew; b 29 Oct 1753; MP; m 9 March 1779 Mary Wyndham (d 22 Feb 1832), sis of 9th Baron Arundell of Wardour (see 1940 edn), and d 31 May 1835, having had:

　(1) Henry James; b 1781; Commr of Customs; d 1832

　(2) Edward (Rev); b 15 Aug 1783; educ Oxford (MA 1806); Preb Salisbury, Vicar Coleshill, Chaplain-in-Ordinary to HM QUEEN VICTORIA; m 20 Nov 1811 Lady Frances Charlotte Courtenay (d 29 March 1854), sis of 10th Earl of Devon (qv), and d 22 July 1874, leaving:

　　1a Fanny; d unm 19 Feb 1893

　(3) William Arundell (Ven); b 6 Feb 1797; educ Oxford (MA 1820, DD 1829); Rector Denton Norfolk, Archdeacon Norfolk; m 8 Feb 1831 Hon Fanny (Frances) Sneyd (d 5 March 1884), Maid of Honour to QUEEN ADELAIDE, 3rd dau of Walter Sneyd, of Keele, and dsp 23 Aug 1877

　(1) Charlotte; b 2 Dec 1788; m 7 Aug 1809 Sir Henry St John-Mildmay, 4th Bt, MP (see 1970 edn), and d 5 Aug 1810, leaving issue

　(2) Harriet; m 1st 20 May 1808 (divorce 1815) 4th Earl of Rosebery (qv); m 2nd 1815 her former bro-in-law Sir Henry St John-Mildmay, 4th Bt, and d 9 Dec 1834, leaving issue

　(3) Anna Maria Wyndham; m 12 March 1813 Paulet St John-Mildmay (d 19 May 1845), MP, of Hazelgrove, Somerset, and d 11 Dec 1864, leaving issue (see 1970 edn ST JOHN-MILDMAY, Bt)

4 Edward; b 20 Sept 1760; MP Downton; m 1st 24 May 1782 Lady Catherine Murray (dsp 7 July 1783), est dau of 4th Earl of Dunmore (qv); m 2nd 20 Dec 1785 Arabella (m 2nd 7 Oct 1828 Hon Robert Talbot (see TALBOT DE MALAHIDE, B) and d 29 Oct 1855), dau of Adml Sir Chaloner Ogle, 1st Bt (see 1940 edn), and dsps 30 Dec 1824, having by her had a s (dvp)

The **1st Earl** m 3rd 22 July 1765 Anne (d 18 June 1795), dau of Sir Thomas Hales, 3rd Bt (see ROMNEY, E), and widow of 1st and last Lord Feversham, Baron of Downton (see FEVERSHAM, B), and d 28 Jan 1776, having by her had two daus (both d in infancy)

His est s,

JACOB BOUVERIE later PLEYDELL-BOUVERIE, **2nd Earl of Radnor**; b 4 March 1750; educ Harrow and Univ Coll Oxford; MP Salisbury 1771–76, FSA

1779, Ld Lt Berks 1791–1819; m 24 Jan 1777 his stepmother's dau Hon Anne Duncombe (d 14 Oct 1829), dau and heiress of 1st and last Lord Feversham, Baron of Downton (see FEVERSHAM, B), by his 3rd w Anne, dau and coheir of Sir Thomas Hales, 3rd Bt, the rep of the family of Pym, Bt, of Brymore, Somerset, and d 27 Jan 1828, having had:

1 WILLIAM, **3rd Earl**

2 Duncombe Pleydell; b 28 June 1780; Col RM, V-Adml the Blue; m 27 Dec 1809 Louisa (d 6 June 1852), 2nd dau of Joseph May, of Hale House, Hants, and d 5 Nov 1850, leaving:

　(1) Louisa; m 2 April 1832 Hon Samuel Hay (see ERROLL, E) and d 18 April 1898

3 Lawrence; b 6 Aug 1781; educ Harrow and Oriel and Merton Colls Oxford (MA 1804); barrister Lincoln's Inn 1805; d unm 23 Nov 1811

4 Frederick Pleydell (Rev); b 16 Nov 1785; Canon Salisbury; m 1 Feb 1814 Elizabeth (d 2 July 1846), dau of Sir Richard Joseph Sullivan, 1st Bt (qv), and d 6 June 1857, having had, with three other daus (d unm):

　(1) Frederick William Pleydell; b 18 April 1816; Adml; m 2 Sept 1845 Madeline (d 28 Jan 1914), dau of Josias Du Pré Alexander, and d 17 July 1898, having had, with two daus (d unm):

　　1a Samuel Hay; b 5 March 1855; d 10 March 1931

　　2a Wilfred; b 17 Oct 1856; m 14 Aug 1888 Rachel (d 22 Jan 1922), 3rd dau of George Murray Perry, and d 21 Nov 1922, having had:

　　　1b Samuel Willfred; b 1896; 2nd Lt 19th Bn London Rifle Bde; ka 15 Sept 1916

　　　2b Hugh Wyndham; b Feb 1900; m 1926 Viola Elizabeth, dau of Walter Holloway Usher, and d 1979, having had:

　　　　1c Keith Seymour; b 1929; d 1936

　　　　2c +Robin Wyndham [Robin Pleydell-Bouverie Esq, Longford Manor, PO Box 140, Harding, Natal 4680, S Africa]; b 11 March 1935; m 20 Aug 1960 *Jean Elizabeth Vermaak and has:

　　　　　1d +Kim Wyndham [Kim Pleydell-Bouverie Esq, Sheepwalk Ridge, PO Box 301, Harding, Natal, S Africa]; b 29 Aug 1965; m 1989 *Janine von Falkenhausen and has:

　　　　　　1e +Scott Wyndham; b 1993

　　　　　　1e *Bianca Lee; b 1991

　　　　　1d *Penelope Ann [Mrs James Blaker, PO Box 1987, Estcourt, Natal 3310, S Africa]; b 9 July 1961; m 1985 *James Craig Blaker and has:

　　　　　　1e *Byron Lance; b 1993

　　　　　　1e *Cayley Ann; b 1989

　　　　　2d *Carolyn [Mrs Johnson, Longford Manor, Harding, Natal 4680, S Africa]; b 11 March 1963; m 1988 — Johnson (d 1996) and has:

　　　　　　1e *Jarryd Lee; b 1989

　　　　　　1e *Sarah Jane; b 1991

　　　　　　2e *Jenna Carrie; b 1995

　　　　　3d *Lynn Michelle [Mrs Lance Rorich, Balmoral, PO Box 135, Swartberg 4710, Natal, S Africa]; b 9 Nov 1968; m 1994 *Lance Craig Rorich

　　　　　4d *Rozanne [Miss Rozanne Pleydell-Bouverie, Longford Manor, Harding, Natal, S Africa]; b 1977

　　　　3c +Peter Hugh; b 1943

　　　1c *Joy [Mrs Neville Barrett, 15 Pepworth Rd, Scottsville, Pietermaritzburg 3201, S Africa]; b 1927; m 1950 *Neville Ramsay Barrett and has:

　　　　1d *Roger Hugh [Roger Barrett Esq, 8 Dan Pienaar Rd, Port Shepstone 4240, S Africa]; b 9 Nov 1950; m 1974 *Sally Taylor and has:

　　　　　1e *Mark Hugh; b 1975

　　　　　1e *Leigh; b 1977

　　　　1d *Maureen [Mrs Neil Maxwell, c/o PO Box 1, Winterton 3340 S Africa]; b 6 Aug 1953; m 1978 *Neil Maxwell and has:

　　　　　1e *Greg; b 1985

　　　　　1e *Kirsty; b 1983

　　　　2d *Judy [Mrs Wadham Hull, 39 Fir Tree Ave, Cleland, Pietermaritzburg 3201, S Africa]; b 8 March 1959; m 1981 *Wadham Hewstone Hull and has:

　　　　　1e *Lindsay; b 1984

　　　　　2e *Tarryn; b 1986

　　　2c *Monica Viola [Mrs Norman Herring, Chertsey, Cedarville, Natal 4720, S Africa]; b 1937; m 1960 *Norman Alexander John Herring and has:

　　　　1d *Kerry [Mrs Gavan Gray, 17 Cowan Rd, Hilton, Natal 3245, S Africa]; b 1961; m 1986 *Gavan Gray and has:

　　　　　1e *Darren Alexander; b 1993

　　　　　1e *Hayley; b 1991

　　　　2d *Deborah [Mrs Graeme Holloway, 61 Dennis Rd, Hayfields, Pietermaritzburg, Natal 3201, S Africa]; b 1963; m 1984 *Graeme Holloway and has:

　　　　　1e *Christy; b 1988

　　　　　2e *Tatum; b 1991

　　　1b Agnes Margaret; m 3 April 1913 Francis Reginald Lark, BSA Police, est s of Francis Bothamley Lark, and had issue

　　　2b Ellen Georgiana Kathleen Pleydell-Bouverie; m 18 April 1915 William Barclay Leslie Lowth and had issue

　　3a Josias; b 28 Sept 1858; m Rosina Snell (d 18 July 1934) and d 31 May 1941, leaving:

　　　1b William; b 28 Nov 1887; d unm 29 Nov 1942

　　　2b Nathanial; b 19 July 1893; m 1920 Maud Alice Cross and d 3 March 1955, leaving:

　　　　1c +Leonard [Leonard Bouverie Esq, 20 Clydesbank Cres, Glen Alpine, NSW 2560, Australia]; b 14 Feb 1928; m 1952 *Doreen Vetter and has:

　　　　　1d +Erwin [Erwin Bouverie Esq, 106 Abington Cres, Glen Alpine, NSW 2560, Australia]; b 23 July 1953; m 1st 1974 (divorce 1979) Jacqueline Duffy and has:

1e +Shane; b 16 March 1975

1e *Michele; b 1 May 1978

1d (cont.) Erwin Bouverie m 2nd 1980 *Merilyn Van Rooyen and by her has:

2e +Nathan; b 8 July 1984

2e *Chantal; b 16 Oct 1985

1d *Charmaine [Mrs George Jabbour, 21 Sopwith Ave, Ruby, NSW 2566, Australia]; b 15 Oct 1958; m 1987 *George Jabbour and has:

1e *Daniel; b 6 May 1989

2d *Belinda [Miss Belinda Bouverie, Flat 3, Todd St, Merrylands, NSW 2160, Australia]; b 6 Feb 1966

2c +Peter [Peter Pleydell-Bouverie Esq, 50 Bellevue Rd, Durban, S Africa]; b 5 Oct 1933

1c *Joyce [Mrs Marius Tritsch, 101 Handsworth, Durban, S Africa]; b 11 July 1921; m 1949 *Marius Tritsch

1b Elizabeth; b 30 Oct 1883; d unm Feb 1962

2b Cornelia; b 11 Aug 1885; m 1930 Peter Harley (d 21 June 1941) and d June 1965

(2) Laurence; b 5 Aug 1817; Lt-Col 78th Regt; m 20 Oct 1847 Harriet (d 7 June 1893), dau of Rev Sir Henry Rivers, 9th Bt (see 1970 edn), and d 14 March 1887, having had:

1a Laurence Henry; b 14 Sept 1848; m 1877 Annie Hume (d 10 April 1904), dau of A Gibson and widow of J Edwards, and d 11 Aug 1920, leaving:

1b Annie Marian; m 1898 Harold Whitehead

2a Frederick Arthur; b 17 Oct 1849; d 6 Feb 1893

3a Charles William; b 29 Dec 1850; Capt RN; m 2 April 1879 Isabella Jane (d 20 Aug 1941), est dau of Thomas Robertson, and d 1921

4a Henry Rivers; b 15 Sept 1854; d 9 April 1930

5a Cecil Edward; b 20 March 1856; d 22 March 1877

1a Harriet Isabella; m 6 June 1872 John Lloyd Pierce (d 5 Sept 1891) and had issue

(3) Henry; b 8 Sept 1818; m 1858 Sarah Mary Avons (d 17 Feb 1859), widow of Capt William Hobart Seymour, 99th Regt (see CULME-SEYMOUR, Bt), and dsp 18 Feb 1861

(4) Philip Arthur PLEYDELL-BOUVERIE later PLEYDELL-BOUVERIE-CAMPBELL (1868) later still PLEYDELL-BOUVERIE-CAMPBELL-WYNDHAM (1890), of Dunoon, Argyll, JP, DL; b 8 Aug 1821; Lt-Col Bengal Army; m 7 Aug 1861 Caroline Mary (d 8 Sept 1908), only child of Richard Hetley, of The Close, Salisbury, and d 23 Dec 1900, leaving:

1a Richard Arthur, of Dunoon, Argyll, and Corhampton, Bishop's Waltham, JP (Hants and Argyll); b 6 July 1862; m 20 Oct 1891 Isobel Maude (d 12 May 1936), dau of Laurence Cumberbatch and widow of Arthur S Williams, and dsp 8 Sept 1909

2a Ernest; b 17 June 1866; Lt KRRC; d unm 2 Oct 1888

1a Mary Lilian; b 24 March 1868; m 25 April 1894 Walter Vansittart LONG later CAMPBELL-WYNDHAM-LONG, of Corhampton, Bishop's Waltham, and Glengarr, Dunoon, Argyll

(5) Charles; b 26 Nov 1826; d 26 Jan 1860

(6) Duncombe; b 27 March 1828; Capt 55th Foot; d 10 June 1857

(1) Elizabeth; m 30 June 1859 Rev William Wyld (dsp 18 March 1873), Rector Woodborough, Wilts, and d 19 April 1906

(2) Charlotte Lydia; m 2 Sept 1847 Sir Henry Roper and d 16 Feb 1892, leaving issue (see TEYNHAM, B)

(3) Barbara Emma; m 28 Jan 1874 Lt-Gen J C Haughton, CSI (dsp 1887), Bengal SC, and d 22 Jan 1913

(4) Susan Louisa; m 29 Jan 1850 Rev H B G Astley and d 7 June 1854

5 Philip Pleydell; banker in Westminster, MP; m 7 Nov 1811 Maria (d 27 Nov 1862), 3rd dau of Sir William Pierce Ashe A'Court, 1st Bt (see HEYTESBURY, B), and d 27 May 1872, having had, with a dau (d unm):

(1) Philip, of Heymore Bridgewater, DL (Somerset); b 21 April 1821; MA, High Sheriff Somerset 1878; m 21 Aug 1847 Jane (d Sept 1892), dau of Henry Seymour (see SOMERSET, D), and d 10 March 1890, having had, with a dau (d unm):

1a Henry Hales, of Brymore, Bridgwater, Somerset, JP, DL; b 22 Aug 1848; educ Cambridge (MA); High Sheriff Somerset 1904, Maj W Somerset Yeo; d unm 12 Dec 1925

2a Seymour; b 26 May 1856; High Sheriff Rutland 1913, Capt W Somerset Yeo; m 28 April 1880 Alice Mary (d 11 Sept 1948), dau of Lt-Col Hon Henry Walter Campbell (see CAWDOR, E), and d 22 March 1927, leaving:

1b Philip Hales; b 3 Aug 1900; educ Harrow; Lt-Cdr (A) RNVR, WW II; m 1st 29 Aug 1923 (divorce 1927) Alice Margaret, only child of William Alfred Ingram, of Highbury Grove, London N5, and had:

1c *Patricia [Mrs John Marshall, Hill House, Andover Rd, Newbury, Berks]; b 1924; m 19 March 1949 John Marshall, slr, only s of Angus Marshall, of Newbury, and has:

1d *Roland; b 8 June 1950; educ Bloxham

2d *Richard James; b 28 Aug 1954; educ Radley; has:

1e *Angus; b 1982

2e *Hamish; b 1984

1d *Sheila Ann; b 8 April 1953

1b (cont.) Lt-Cdr Philip Pleydell-Bouverie m 2nd 30 Nov 1927 (divorce 1945) Beth Olivia (d 14 Jan 1948), adopted dau of Brig-Gen Ronald Maclachlan, Rifle Bde, and formerly w of John Fitzhardinge Berkeley Gage (see GAGE, V), and by her had:

2c *Lois [Mrs George Wolff, 528 Morand St, Windsor, Ontario N9G 1H8, Canada]; b 15 Jan 1928; m 4 April 1951 George Gunther Wolff (d 1996), s of Bernard Wolff, of Karlsruhe/Rintheim, and has:

1d *Adrian; b 1957; m 1982 *Mary Anne Schuetter and has:

1e *Adam David; b 1986

1e *Kirsten Marie; b 1988

3c *Xenia [Mrs Alec Ayliffe, 71 Ingram Rd, RD3 Drury, New Zealand]; b 10 Jan 1929; m 1963 *Alec Ronald Ayliffe and has:

1d *Gillian Xenia; b 8 Jan 1966

1b (cont.) Lt-Cdr Philip Pleydell-Bouverie m 3rd 27 Sept 1945 *Kathleen [Mrs Philip Pleydell-Bouverie, 2 Redland Hill, Bristol 6], Sqdn/Offr WAAF, only dau of John Thomas Fell, of Bristol, and d 30 April 1951

1b Joan; b 10 April 1881; m 14 Aug 1902 Charles Prideaux Ogle Selby-Bigge and d 9 July 1949, leaving issue

2b Winifred; b 22 Nov 1883; d unm 15 Feb 1972

3a George; b 18 Oct 1857; Col Coldstream Gds; d 5 Feb 1924

1a Ellen; m 26 Sept 1883 Townsend Molloy Kirkwood (d 1921), of Gore Court, Kent, and S Kensington, and d Nov 1912

2a Janet; m 3 Sept 1879 Sir Frederick Peel, KCMG (see PEEL, E), and d 15 March 1925

3a Constance; m 3 Sept 1879 Hon Alexander Francis Henry Campbell, yst s of 2nd Earl Cawdor (qv), and d 24 Jan 1887, leaving issue

4a Alys; m 2 Feb 1898 Rev Arundell Glastonbury St John-Mildmay (see 1970 edn ST JOHN-MILDMAY, Bt), and d 19 Feb 1947, leaving issue

(1) Letitia Anne; m 29 Nov 1843 Rev Charles Deedes (see DEEDES, B) and d 1887

(2) Caroline; m 23 Oct 1849 Rev Hyde Wyndham Beadon, Vicar Latton, Wilts, and d 8 Feb 1867

(3) Maria; m 1 June 1852 Rev William Pitt Trevelyan and d 9 Oct 1903, leaving issue (see TREVELYAN, Bt, of Nettlecombe)

The 2nd EARL's est s,

WILLIAM PLEYDELL-BOUVERIE, **3rd Earl of Radnor**, DL Wilts; b 11 May 1779; educ Edinburgh, in France and BNC Oxford; MP (Radical Whig) Downton 1801–02 and 1818–19 and Salisbury 1802–18 and 1820–28; m 1st 2 Oct 1801 Catherine (d 17 May 1804), only dau of Henry, Earl of Lincoln (qv), and had an only surv dau:

1 Catherine; m 13 May 1828 Gen Edward Pery Buckley (d May 1873), of New Hall, Col 83rd Foot, and d 21 Feb 1875, leaving issue

The **3rd Earl** m 2nd 24 May 1814 Anne Judith (d 27 April 1851), 3rd dau of Sir Henry St John-Mildmay, 3rd Bt, MP (see ST JOHN-MILDMAY, Bt), and d 9 April 1869, having by her had, with a dau (d young):

1 JACOB, **4th Earl**

2 Edward, PC, of E Lavington Manor, Wilts; b 26 April 1818; educ Trin Coll Cambridge (MA); barrister, MP Kilmarnock 1844–74, U-Sec Home Dept 1850–52, V-Pres BOT 1853–55, Pres Poor Law Bd 1855–58, 2nd Ch Estates Commr 1860–65, Wilts: High Sheriff 1882, Chm QS, CA; FRS; m 1 Nov 1842 Elizabeth Anne (d 10 Aug 1889), yst dau of Gen Robert Balfour, of Balbirnie, and d 16 Dec 1889, having had:

(1) Walter, JP Wilts; b 5 July 1848; Maj 2nd Vol Bn Wilts Regt, CC Wilts; m 1st 22 Feb 1876 Mary (d 18 Jan 1880), dau of Rev William Bridgeman-Simpson (see BRADFORD, E), and had, with a s (d an infant):

1a Mildred Alice; b 10 Feb 1877; m 6 Jan 1903 Charles Hingston, DL (d 18 Jan 1959), s of George Hingston, of Crownhill, S Devon, and had issue

2a Sybil, DGSt J; b 13 Dec 1878; m 9 June 1903 8th Viscount Powerscourt (qv) and d 6 Dec 1946, leaving issue

(1) (cont.) Maj Walter Pleydell-Bouverie m 2nd 31 Oct 1882 Edith Katherine (d 23 Aug 1902), dau of Rev Hon James Walter Lascelles (see HAREWOOD, E), and d 20 May 1893, having by her had:

1a Humphrey, MBE (1919); b 10 Sept 1883; Maj 5/6th Dragoon Gds WW I 1914–16; m 27 June 1922 Margaret Elfrida (d 1976), dau of R A Holden, of Talton House, Stratford-on-Avon, and d 10 Feb 1958, having had:

1b *Ann, of Chorley, Lancs; b 1923; m 1st 1 May 1943 (divorce 1953) Lt-Col Eric Charles Twelves Wilson, VC, 1st Bn NRR, late Surrey Regt, only s of Rev Cyril Charles Clissold Wilson, of Broxbourne, Herts, and has:

1c *Michael Charles Bouverie; b 1947

2c *Anthony; b 1949

1b (cont.) Mrs Ann Wilson m 2nd 1953 John Kennett Walker (d 1954), s of John Walker, of Chorley, Lancs, and by him has:

1c *Diana; b 1954

3a Nancy; b 10 June 1885; d unm 30 Oct 1972

4a Mary; b 13 Dec 1887; d unm 12 April 1945

5a Elizabeth; b 3 Dec 1888; m 13 Feb 1922 Sidney Buchanan, of Artro House, Harlech, and d 28 Dec 1936, leaving issue

(2) Edward Oliver, JP (Wilts); b 12 Sept 1856; educ Trin Coll Cambridge (BA); barrister, FSA; d 13 May 1938

(1) Anne; d unm 12 March 1940

(2) Eglantine; m 5 Dec 1864 Sir Augustus Frederick William Keppel Stephenson, KCB (d 26 Sept 1904), gs maternally of 4th Earl of Albemarle (qv), and d 13 Nov 1925, leaving issue

(3) Ruth; m 27 March 1882 William Rolle Malcolm (d 3 Feb 1923), of Walton Manor, Epsom, and S Kensington, yst bro of 1st Baron Malcolm of Poltalloch (see 1902 edn), and d 19 Nov 1944

1 Jane Harriet; m 8 July 1847 William Ellice (d 1892) and dsp 7 June 1903

2 Mary; b 22 Dec 1825; m 20 Feb 1860 James Plaisted Wilde, 1st and last Baron Penzance, PC (see 1899 edn), and d 24 Oct 1900

The 3rd EARL's er s,

JACOB PLEYDELL-BOUVERIE, **4th Earl of Radnor**, JP, DL Berks; b 18 Sept 1815; educ Harrow and Ch Ch Oxford; Wilts: High Sheriff 1846, Ld Lt 1878–89; m 3 Oct 1840 Mary Augusta Frederica (d 5 April 1879), 3rd dau of 1st Earl of Verulam (qv), and d 11 March 1889, leaving:

1 WILLIAM, **5th Earl**

2 Duncombe, JP (Berks), DL; b 10 Oct 1842; Lt 55th Foot; m 11 July 1883 Maria Eleanor (d 25 Nov 1936), dau of Sir Edward Hulse, 5th Bt (qv), and d 25 Jan 1909, leaving:

(1) (Jacob) Edward; b 12 July 1887; Lt KRRC; d 1 Nov 1914 of wounds recd in action

(1) Mary Eleanor; b 18 June 1885; d unm 18 Aug 1965

(2) Katharine Harriot Duncombe, of Kilmington Manor, Warminster, Wilts; b 7 June 1895

3 Bertrand (Rev); *b* 23 April 1845; *educ* Cambridge (MA); Rector Pewsey, Preb Salisbury; *m* 21 April 1870 Lady Constance Jane (*d* 27 Jan 1922), 2nd dau of 3rd Earl Nelson (*qv*), and *d* 7 Nov 1926

4 John; *b* 18 July 1846; Lt-Col 17th Lancers Zulu War 1879 (medal with clasp); *m* 10 Oct 1882 Grace Harriet (*d* 4 Jan 1953, aged 92), dau of Lt-Gen Robert Malaby, Bombay SC, and *d* 29 March 1925, leaving:

(1) Eveline Maude; *b* 8 Nov 1883; *m* 25 March 1909 Col John Leader (*d* 8 March 1967), er s of Surgn-Maj John Leader, JP, of Keale, Co Cork, and *d* 14 Sept 1974, leaving issue

5 Mark; *b* 27 Sept 1851; barrister; *d* unm 17 Feb 1895

6 Kenelm, of Freelands, Wherwell, Hants; *b* 29 Nov 1852; *m* 1 June 1905 Evelyn Bertie Charlotte (*d* 24 March 1936), 2nd dau of David Maitland-Makgill-Crichton (*see* LAUDERDALE, E), and *d* 11 July 1921, leaving:

(1) +Ralph Kenelm [Ralph Pleydell-Bouverie Esq, 44 Bloomfield Terrace, London SW1]; *b* 12 Dec 1910; *educ* Harrow

(2) +Bertrand Eric [Bertrand Pleydell-Bouverie Esq, Middle Leaze, Coleshill, Swindon, Wilts]; *b* 4 Feb 1914; *educ* RNC Dartmouth and Trin Coll Cambridge (BA 1939); Lt RNVR WW II (despatches); *m* 7 Jan 1950 *Pamela Winifred Mary, only dau of Lt-Col Roderick William Macdonald, CIE, DSO, of Gt Braxted, Essex, and has:

1a +Rupert William [Rupert Pleydell-Bouverie Esq, Waverley House, Monkwood, Hants SO24 0HB]; *b* 23 Dec 1950; *educ* Harrow; FCA; *m* 8 July 1978 *Evelyn Marie, dau of Capt J A Conlon, of Manor Croft, W Ayton, Yorks, and has:

1b +Matthew Alexander; *b* 1979

2b +Edward Richard; *b* 1984

2a +Nigel Justin [Nigel Pleydell-Bouverie Esq, Middle Leaze, Coleshill, Wilts; *b* 3 March 1955; *educ* Harrow, U of BC, Canada, and U of Wales

1a *Prunella Evelyn [Mrs Thomas Miller, 44 Bloomfield Terrace, London SW1; Lyemarsh Farmhouse, Mere, Wilts]; *b* 14 April 1952; *m* 1976 *Thomas Paul Miller and has:

1b *Thomas Bertrand; *b* 1984

1b *Jessica Frances; *b* 1984 (twin)

(1) *Doris, JP (W Suffolk 1952) [Miss Doris Pleydell-Bouverie JP, Pump Lane House, Pump Lane, Bury St Edmunds, Suffolk]; *b* 6 April 1909; *educ* Malvern Girls' Coll and Somerville Coll Oxford; FRSA, CC W Suffolk 1949–63, CA 1963

7 Christopher; *b* 30 Dec 1856; *d* 22 March 1892

8 Frank; *b* 19 April 1858 (twin with Gertrude); *d* unm 15 July 1909

1 Anne; *m* 3 Sept 1867 Archibald Alexander Speirs, DL (*d* 30 Dec 1868), MP, of Elderslie, Renfrewshire, and *d* 18 Sept 1915, leaving issue

2 Margaret; *m* 29 Oct 1873 Maj-Gen David Makgill Crichton-Maitland and *d* 5 Jan 1924, leaving issue (*see* LAUDERDALE, E)

3 Edith; *m* 19 Sept 1876 Charles Cotes (*dsp* 22 Nov 1903), of Burcott, Leighton Buzzard, and *d* 28 Dec 1922

4 Gertrude; *m* 28 April 1896 Arthur Monckton and *d* 11 Jan 1940, leaving issue (*see* GALWAY, V)

The 4th EARL's est s,
WILLIAM PLEYDELL-BOUVERIE, **5th Earl of Radnor**, JP (Wilts and Berks), DL, PC (1885); *b* 19 June 1841; *educ* Harrow and Trin Coll Cambridge; MP (C) S Wilts 1874–85 and Enfield Middx 1885–89, Treasurer Household 1885–Feb 1886 and Aug 1886–91; *m* 19 June 1866 Helen Matilda (*d* 11 Sept 1929), only surv dau of Rev Henry Chaplin, Vicar Ryhall, Rutland (*see* 1970 edn CHAPLIN, V), and *d* 3 June 1900, having had, with another dau (*d* young):

1 JACOB, **6th Earl**

2 Stuart, DSO (1917), OBE (1926), TD; *b* 14 Nov 1877; *educ* Harrow; Col TA, cmdg 52nd (Lond) AA Bde RA and 27th Div Ammunition, WW I (despatches thrice), Mil Memb Kent TAA; *m* 20 Feb 1900 Edith Dorothy (*d* 14 Nov 1949), dau of Albert Vickers, of Knightsbridge, and *d* 6 April 1947, leaving:

(1) Christopher; *b* 4 Nov 1901; *educ* RNCs Osborne and Dartmouth; Lt 16th Bn Lond Regt TA and RN; *m* 30 April 1930 (*divorce* 1939) Kathleen Adele (*d* 1981), only dau of William Henry Carpenter Gelshenen, of NY and Knightsbridge, and *d* 26 June 1949, leaving:

1a *Anne Patricia [Mrs Anne Grant, Standon House, Standon, Herts]; *b* 2 July 1933; *m* 25 April 1953 (*divorce* 1964) Peter James Grant, Lt QO Cameron Highrs (TA), yr s of Lt-Col Patrick Charles Henry Grant, Scots Gds, of Glenrossal, Invershin, Sutherland, and has:

1b *Charles Ludovic; *b* 19 April 1953; *educ* Eton

1b *Laura Marguerite; *b* 22 Jan 1959

(2) Albert Laurence; *b* 8 March 1904; *educ* Charterhouse and Cambridge; F/O RAF; *d* unm 2 Jan 1959

(3) Michael; *b* 24 Nov 1907; *educ* Charterhouse; Maj 6th Airborne Div WW II (wounded); *m* 17 Jan 1935 *Millicent Frances [Mrs Michael Pleydell-Bouverie, 5 Admirals Wharf, Cowes, IoW], dau of Albert Guyton Bristow, of Watersmeet, Uxbridge, and *dsp* 31 Dec 1963

(4) David; *b* 20 April 1911; *educ* Charterhouse; *m* 12 May 1946 (*divorce* 1952) Ava Alice Muriel (*d* 19 July 1956), dau of Col John Jacob Astor by Ava (dau of Edward Willing, of Philadelphia; she *m* 2nd 1919, as his 2nd w, 4th and last Baron Ribblesdale; *see* 1925 edn, also GLENCONNER, B, LOVAT, L, and WESTMORLAND, E), and formerly w of (a) Prince Serge Obolensky, (b) Raimund von Hofmannsthal and (c) Philip John Ryves Harding, and *d* 5 Dec 1994

1 Wilma, CBE (1920); *m* 1st 15 Aug 1889 2nd Earl of Lathom (*see* 1970 edn) and had issue; *m* 2nd 16 Nov 1912 Lt-Gen Sir Henry Merrick Lawson, KCB (*d* 2 Nov 1933), and *d* 10 Feb 1931

The 5th EARL's er s,
JACOB PLEYDELL-BOUVERIE, **6th Earl of Radnor**, CIE (1918), CBE (1919), JP; *b* 8 July 1868; MP (C) S Wilts 1892–1900, Wilts: CA, Ld Lt 1925, served Boer War 1900 and WW I (Legn Hon), Hon Col 4th Bn Wilts Regt (TA), Col and Hon Brig-Gen TFR, T/Brig-Gen Dehra Dun Bde India 1915–17, T/Brig-Gen and Dir Ag Production 1918–19; *m* 20 Jan 1891 Julian Eleanor Adelaide, JP (*d* 5 Jan 1946), CA Wilts, only dau of Charles Balfour (*see* BALFOUR, E), and *d* 26 June 1930, having had:

1 WILLIAM, **7th Earl**

2 Edward, MVO (1939), DL Hants; *b* 10 Sept 1899; Capt RN, served WWs I and II (despatches), Verderer New Forest 1945–51, Chm: New Forest Advisory Ctee 1947–51, New Forest and Christchurch C Assoc 1947–51, New Forest and Dist RDC 1948–51; *m* 2 May 1936 (Alice) Pearl, er dau of Maj Edward Barrington Crake, Rifle Bde, by his 2nd w Clara Alice, er dau of George William Plunkenet Woodroffe, RHG, and widow of 2nd Baron Montagu of Beaulieu (*qv*), and *d* 5 May 1951, leaving:

(1) +Robin [Robin Pleydell-Bouverie Esq, 20 Manson Mews, London SW7 5AF; Curles Close, Bucklers Hard, Hants SO42 7XA]; *b* 16 June 1937; *educ* Harrow; *m* 1st 2 June 1960 (*divorce* 1975) (Anne) Louise (*d* 3 Jan 1996 aged 55), dau of Bruce Durham; *m* 2nd 21 Dec 1978 *Felicity Ruth, yr dau of David Towers Downer, DFC, of Holland Pk, London W11, and has:

1a +Nicholas Edward; *b* 6 Jan 1983

1a *Camilla; *b* 8 Feb 1981

3 Bartholomew, OBE (1945); *b* 6 April 1902; *educ* Harrow and Magdalen Coll Oxford (BA 1924); T/Maj Gren Gds WW II; *m* 1st 11 July 1927 Lady Doreen Clare Hely-Hutchinson (*d* 2 Aug 1942), only dau of 6th Earl of Donoughmore (*qv*); *m* 2nd 22 Jan 1949 Katharine (*d* 12 Oct 1977), dau of Robert E Tod and formerly w of Henry Bradley Martin, of Park Ave, New York, and *d* 31 Oct 1965, having by his 1st w had:

(1) +Simon [Simon Pleydell-Bouverie Esq, The Castle House, Deddington, Oxon OX15 0TT]; *b* 24 April 1928; *educ* Harrow and Trin Coll Cambridge (BA); FCA, late 2nd Lt Life Gds, formerly dir Kasenit; *m* 24 Oct 1961 *Vivien Eleanor, only dau of Sir Richard Michael Keane, 6th Bt (*qv*), and has:

1a +David Archie; *b* 23 July 1964

1a *Grania Clare; *b* 27 May 1962; *m* 1991 *Niels David Scott, s of Wolf Scott, of Geneva, and Fredensborg, Denmark, and has:

1b *Finn; *b* 1992

2a *Juliet Rose; *b* 2 May 1968

3a *Alice Susan; *b* 11 Nov 1970; *m* 1996 *Christian Brotherton, s of Archdeacon Michael Brotherton, of Chichester, Sussex

(1) *Penelope Jane, OBE (1995), JP [Mrs Michael Meredith-Hardy OBE JP, Radwell Mill, Baldock, Herts SG7 5ET]; *b* 4 Nov 1932; *m* 26 July 1955 *Michael Francis Meredith-Hardy, yr s of Howard Meredith-Hardy, and has:

1a *Richard [Richard Meredith-Hardy Esq, Radwell Lodge, Radwell, Herts SG7 5ET]; *b* 23 Aug 1957; *educ* Eton and Birmingham Poly; *m* 1987 *Nicola Louise, est dau of Hugh Morgan Lindsay Smith, of Bank Farm, Brandon Creek, Norfolk, and has:

1b *Hugo; *b* 1994

1b *Alexandra; *b* 1990

2b *Isobel; *b* 1992

2a *Luke; *b* 27 June 1959; *m* 1987 *Clare M, yst dau of William T Minogue, of Kew, Melbourne, Australia, and has:

1b *William Michael; *b* 1992

1b *Katherine Jane; *b* 1988

2b *Georgina Ann; *b* 1990

3a *John Octavian; *b* 21 Dec 1962

4a *Paul Bartholomew; *b* 18 Jan 1966

4 Anthony, DSC (1945); *b* 26 March 1905; Cdr RN WW II (despatches four times), US Legn Merit, CC Berks 1954; *m* 5 Dec 1931 (*divorce* 1942) Anita Estelle Henrietta, dau of Col T Costiander, of Helsingfors, Finland, and *dsp* 25 June 1961

5 Peter, of Landford Lodge, Salisbury, Wilts; *b* 19 Oct 1909; *educ* Harrow and Trin Coll Cambridge; 2nd Lt Roy Wilts Yeo, Maj KRRC, chm Calor Gas Holding Co and Western Gazette Co, dir Bristol Evening Post Ltd; *m* 1st 25 Nov 1938 (*divorce* 1946) Audrey Evelyn (*d* 14 Feb 1968), dau of William Dodge James, CVO, JP, DL, of W Dean Pk, Sussex (*see* FORBES, Bt, of Newe), formerly w of Marshall Field; *m* 2nd 30 Oct 1947 Audrey (*d* 15 Sept 1997), yst dau of Capt Archibald Glen Kidston, JP, of Tyrcelyn, Builth Wells, Radnorshire, and Gwenyfed, Three Cocks, Breconshire, and formerly w of Anthony Seymour Bellville, and *d* 1981, leaving by her:

(1) +James; *b* 24 Feb 1950; *educ* Harrow; *m* 19– *Ann —, and has:

1a +Jeremy; *b* 6 Sept 1998

1 Jeane; *b* 23 March 1892; Ch Cmdt ATS 1938–42; *m* 21 Nov 1914 Capt George Gerald Petherick, Roy 1st Devon Yeo (*d* 1 Nov 1946), est s of George Tallack Petherick, of Porthpean Ho, St Austell, Cornwall, and *d* 16 Aug 1976, leaving issue

2 Katharine; *b* 16 May 1894; *m* 20 Jan 1927 John Henry McNeile, Lt Coldstream Gds, of Nonsuch, Bromham, Wilts, and *d* 1 Nov 1961, leaving issue

3 Elizabeth; *b* 27 June 1897; Co Assist ATS 1940–41; *d* 7 July 1982

4 *Margaret; *b* 26 June 1903; *m* 28 Feb 1923 Lt-Col Gerald Barry and has issue (*see* BARRY, Bt)

5 *Helen, OBE (1946), DL (Berks) [The Lady Helen Smith OBE DL, King's Copse House, Bucklebury, Berks]; *b* 2 Jan 1908; *m* 22 July 1931 *Lt-Col Hon David John Smith, CBE, JP, RA (TA), 3rd s of 2nd Viscount Hambleden (*qv*), and has issue

The 6th EARL's est s,
WILLIAM PLEYDELL-BOUVERIE, **7th Earl of Radnor**, KG (1960), KCVO (1946), JP (Wilts), DL; *b* 18 Dec 1895; *educ* Harrow and Trin Coll Cambridge; Capt 4th Bn Wilts Regt, Maj RA, served WWs I and II, memb Cncl Duchy Cornwall 1923, Keeper Privy Seal 1933, Ld Warden Stannaries Cornwall and Devon 1933–65, chm Lawes Ag Trust Ctee (Rothamsted) 1938–64, forestry commr 1942–68 (chm Forestry Commn 1952–63), Verderer New Forest 1964–68, Pres CLA, Hon V-Pres Land Agents' Soc, Tstee Roy Ag Soc England; *m* 1st 11 Oct 1922 (*divorce* 1942) Helena Olivia (*m* 2nd 1943 Brig Montacute William Worrell Selby-Lowndes, DSO (*d* 1972) and *d* 1985), yst dau of Charles Robert Whorwood Adeane, CB, of Babraham Hall, Cambridge, and

1 JACOB PLEYDELL-BOUVERIE, **8th and present Earl of Radnor**

2 +Reuben [The Hon Reuben Pleydell-Bouverie, Bleak House, Slindon, W Sussex BN18 0RP]; *b* 30 Dec 1930; *educ* Harrow; Lt Roy Wilts Yeo (TA), formerly 2nd Lt RSG; *m* 28 Jan 1956 *Bridget Jane, er dau of Maj John Fowell Buxton (*see* BUXTON, Bt), and has:

(1) +Edward [Edward Pleydell-Bouverie Esq, 29 Malcolm St, Fremantle, Western Australia]; *b* 5 Jan 1957; *m* 1984 *Nichola, dau of Dr John Wood, of Blackheath, and has:

  1a +Nathan John; *b* 1987

  2a +Joshua Edward; *b* 1989

  1a *Monica Alice; *b* 1990

  2a *Jessica Anne; *b* 1994

(2) +Jasper John [Jasper Pleydell-Bouverie Esq, 29 Clapham Common Southside, London SW4]; *b* 18 March 1964; jnlst; *m* 1991 *Katherine Jane, only dau of Richard Christopher Wordsworth Pelly (*see* PELLY, Bt), and has:

  1a +Josiah Edwin; *b* 16 Nov 1997

  2a +Rufus Noah; *b* 16 Nov 1997

(1) *Rosalind Mary [Mrs Jonathan Higham, 30 Princes St, Dunstable, Beds]; *b* 17 May 1960; *m* 1988 *Dr Jonathan Hugh G Higham, est s of J A E Higham, of New York and Chichester, Sussex

1*Jane [The Lady Jane Bethell, Manor Farm House, Long Riston, Hull]; *b* 14 Sept 1923; *m* 27 Sept 1945 (Richard An)T(h)ony Bethell (*d* July 1996), Ld Lt Humberside 1983–96, est s of Capt (William) Adrian Vincent Bethell, of Rise Pk, Hull (*see* COTTERELL, Bt), and has:

  (1) *Hugh Adrian [Hugh Bethell Esq, Rise Pk, Hull]; *b* 23 April 1952; *educ* Eton and Exeter U; *m* 1983 *Sarah Elizabeth, est dau of Maj Thomas Edward St Aubyn, CVO (*see* SAINT LEVAN, B), and has:

    1a *Oliver Anthony; *b* 1985

    2a *Edward; *b* 1987

    3a *Nicholas; *b* 1990

  (2) *William Anthony [William Bethell Esq, Arnold Manor, Long Riston, nr Hull]; *b* 18 May 1957; *educ* Eton; *m* 1983 *Elizabeth Anne, yr dau of Lt Col Charles Samuel Madden, of Co Dublin, and has:

    1a *Christopher Frederick; *b* 1988

    1a *Harriet Primrose; *b* 1986

  (1) *Camilla; *b* 27 June 1946; *m* 17 Dec 1966 *Peter Charles Freeman Gregory-Hood (*see* HOOD, V) and has issue

  (2) *Sarah [Mrs David Brotherton, Whitwell-on-the-Hill, York YO6 7JL]; *b* 13 Aug 1948; *m* 31 May 1969 *David Ratcliffe Brotherton, only s of Charles Frederick Ratcliffe Brotherton, of Kirkham Abbey, York, and has:

    1a *Toby Ratcliffe; *b* 1972

    1a *Serena; *b* 1970

2 Belinda; *b* 15 Jan 1925; *m* 13 Dec 1952 *Sir William Stratford Dugdale, 2nd Bt (*qv*), and *d* 29 July 1961, leaving issue

3 Phoebe; *b* 25 Jan 1932; *m* 8 Jan 1955 (*divorce* 1963) Herbert Beaumont Phipps, 2nd s of John Shafer Phipps, of Westbury Ho, Westbury, Long Island, NY, and *d* 1995, leaving:

  (1) *Hubert Grace; *b* 1 Nov 1957

  (1) *Melissa Adeane; *b* 13 Dec 1955

4 *Harriot [The Lady Harriot Tennant, 30 Abbey Gdns, London NW8 9AT; Balfluig Castle, by Alford, Aberdeenshire AB33 8EJ]; *b* 18 Dec 1935; *m* 11 Dec 1965 *Mark Iain Tennant (*see* GLENCONNER, B) and has issue

The **7th Earl** *m* 2nd 9 Oct 1943 (Anne) Isobel, OBE (1961), DL (Wilts 1987) (*d* 27 July 1998), est dau of Lt-Col Richard Oakley, DSO, JP, Cameronians (Scottish Rifles), of Lawrence End, Beds, and widow of Richard Thomas Reynolds Sowerby, of Lilley Manor, Luton, and *d* 23 Nov 1968, leaving by her:

3 +Richard Oakley, DL (Herts 1992) [The Hon Richard Pleydell-Bouverie DL, Lawrence End, Peters Green, Beds LU2 8PF]; *b* 25 June 1947; *educ* Harrow and RAC Cirencester (NDA 1969); High Sheriff Herts 1998–99; *m* 11 Feb 1978 *Victoria, yr dau of Frank Waldron, of Pond Ho, Kidmore End, Berks, and has:

  (1) +David Oakley; *b* 1979

  (2) +Bartholomew Richard; *b* 1981

  (1) *Harriot Isobel; *b* 1984

RAEBURN

Arms: Or, on a piece of ground in base vert a roebuck statant proper, drinking out of a burn or brook undy argent and azure running bendways, in chief an anchor sable between two roses gules, barbed and seeded of the second. **Crest:** A stag's head proper. **Motto:** *Tutis si fortis* ('Safe if strong'). **Creation:** Bt. (UK) 25 July 1923.

Michael Edward Norman Raeburn [Michael Norman Esq, 1 Spring Cottages, Fletching St, Mayfield, East Sussex TN20 6TN]; *b* 12 Nov 1954; s f 1977 but does not use title; *educ* Halliford Sch Shepperton; *m* 1979 *Penelope Henrietta Theodora, dau of Alfred Louis Penn, of London, and has:

1 +CHRISTOPHER EDWARD ALFRED; *b* 4 Dec 1981

2 +Martin Philip; *b* 13 Jan 1989

1 *Gwendoline Mary Joan; *b* 1983

2 *Janet Maria; *b* 1986

3 *Victoria Beatrix Sarah Gabrielle; *b* 1992

Lineage: WILLIAM RAEBURN; *b* Kilmarnock 1813; *m* Grace (*d* Sept 1877), dau of William Hannay, and *d* 1875, leaving:

1 WILLIAM HANNAY (Sir), **1st Bt**

2 Anthony Hannay; *b* 1853; *m* 19 Oct 1886 Fanny Stuart, dau of Kenneth Bruce Stuart Robertson, of Glasgow and Singapore, and *d* 6 Nov 1924, leaving issue

1 Douglas Jane; *d* 1949 aged 97

The er s,

Sir William Hannay Raeburn, 1st Bt (UK), so *cr* 25 July 1923, JP (Glasgow and Dunbartonshire), DL; *b* 11 Aug 1850; ktd 1918, head of Raeburn and Vérel Ltd, Glasgow, shipowners, Pres UK Chamber of Shipping 1916–18, MP (U) Dunbartonshire 1918–23, Tstee Nat Galleries Scotland 1922–28; *m* 1st 28 Sept 1876 Sarah (*d* 18 Jan 1882), est dau of John Thorburrow Manifold, CE, of Demerara and had, with a dau (*d* unm):

1 (WILLIAM) NORMAN (Sir), **2nd Bt**

2 Ernest Manifold (Sir), KBE (1920, CBE 1919); *b* 13 Dec 1878; Dir-Gen Min of Shipping NY 1919–20; *m* 6 June 1910 Greta Mary Alison (*d* 1975), dau of Engr Capt James Herbert Watson, RN, and *d* 1 June 1922, leaving:

  (1) +(William) Digby Manifold (Sir), KCVO (1979), CB (1966), DSO (1945), MBE (1941) [Maj-Gen Sir Digby Raeburn KCVO CB DSO MBE, 25 St Ann's Terrace, London NW8 6PH]; *b* 6 Aug 1915; *educ* Winchester and Magdalene Coll Cambridge (BA 1936, MA 1940); Maj-Gen Scots Gds, served WW II (despatches), cmded 2nd Bn 1953–55, Lt Col 1956–59, cmded 1st Gds Bde Group 1960–61, Dir Combat Devpt (Army) 1963–65, Ch Staff Allied Forces N Europe 1965–68, Ch Army Instr IDC 1968–70, Keeper Jewel Ho and Govr Tower London 1971–79; *m* 23 April 1960 *Adeline Margaret, yst dau of Thomas Selwyn Pryor, MC (*see* HALSEY, Bt)

  (1) Patricia Manifold; *d* unm 14 Jan 1968

1 Edith Mary; *m* 25 June 1903 Reginald Oliver Elderton (*d* 15 March 1950), s of Frederick Fairlie Elderton, of Tunbridge Wells, and *d* 14 July 1956, leaving issue

Sir William *m* 2nd 8 Feb 1888 Ellinor Martha (*d* 1 Feb 1915), only dau of Rev Archibald Weir, DCL, Vicar Fortyhill, Enfield, and by her had, with a dau (*d* unm):

3 Alfred Anthony Douglas; *b* 23 July 1893; 2nd Lt HLI; *ka* Somme 15 July 1916

2 *Ellinor Eileen; *m* 29 July 1930 Lt-Col Eugene Gonzague Riviere, MBE, MC, The Loyal Regt, s of Henry Gilbey Riviere, of Castle Cary, Somerset, and has:

  (1) *Peter Gerard [Peter Riviere Esq, Little Manor, Bledington, Glos]; *b* 17 Jan 1934; *educ* Stowe, Magdalene Coll Cambridge (BA 1957, MA 1960) and Magdalen Coll Oxford (BLitt 1963, DPhil 1965); *m* 26 May 1962 *Sarah, est dau of Maj-Gen George Douglas Gordon Heyman, CB, CBE, of Mead Ho, Appleshaw, Hants, and has had:

    1a Polly; *b* 14, *d* 15 Sept 1963

    2a *Amelia Sophie; *b* 26 April 1965

    3a *Arabella Rose; *b* 30 Dec 1966

  (1) *Ellinor Ann [Mrs John Cheale, Blackham Court, Withyham, Sussex]; *b* 11 Sept 1931; *m* 23 Oct 1952 *Maj John Michael Cheale, s of Alexander Cheale, and has issue

Sir William m 3rd 5 June 1917 Olga Lucia, dau of Walter Peel Yates, MRCS, of Jersey, and widow of Capt Edward Allan Smeathman Hatton, RMLI, and d 12 Feb 1934

His est s,

Sir (William) Norman Raeburn, 2nd Bt, CBE, KC (1919), JP (Surrey); b 16 Aug 1877; educ Glasgow U (MA, LLB); barrister Middle Temple 1903; m 30 March 1912 Mary Irene (d 4 April 1927), er dau of Frederick Lennard, of Hove, Sussex, and d 5 Feb 1947, having had:

1 **Sir Edward Alfred Raeburn, 3rd Bt**; b 18 May 1919; educ Uppingham and Ch Ch Oxford; Capt RA WW II; m 25 Aug 1950 *Joan [Lady Raeburn, Fourways, Turners Green, E Sussex], er dau of Frederick Hill, of Boston, Mass., and Dartford, Kent, and d 21 April 1977, leaving:

(1) **Sir MICHAEL EDWARD NORMAN RAEBURN, 4th and present Bt**

1 *Sheila Saisie [Miss Raeburn, Denecourt, Cuckmere Rd, Seaford, E Sussex]; b 1913

2 *Irene Muriel [Miss Irene Raeburn, Denecourt, Cuckmere Rd, Seaford, E Sussex]; b 1914

3 Nancy Lennard; d 2 July 1938

RAGLAN

MUTARE · VEL · TIMERE · SPERNO

Arms: Quarterly, France and England within a bordure compony arg. and az. **Crest:** A portcullis or, nailed az., with chains pendant therefrom gold. **Supporters:** Dexter, a panther arg., spotted of various colours, fire issuant from the mouth and ears ppr., gorged with a plain collar and chained or; sinister, a wyvern, wings addorsed vert, holding in the mouth a sinister hand couped at the wrist gu. **Motto:** *Mutare vel timere sperno* ('I scorn to change or fear'). **Creation:** B. (UK) 11 Oct 1852.

THE 5TH BARON RAGLAN OF RAGLAN, Co Monmouth (FitzRoy John Somerset, JP (Mon 1968)) [The Rt Hon The Lord Raglan JP, Cefntilla Court, Usk, Gwent]; b 8 Nov 1927; s f 1964; educ Westminster, Magdalen Coll Oxford and RAC Cirencester; Capt Welsh Gds Res of Offrs, Chm Cwmbran New Town Devpt Corp, Crown Estate Commr 1970–; m 1973 (divorce 19–) Alice, yr dau of Peter Baily, of Gt Whittington, Northumberland

Lineage: The 6th DUKE OF BEAUFORT (qv) had a yst s:

FitzROY JAMES HENRY SOMERSET, **1st Baron Raglan of Raglan**, Co Monmouth (UK), so cr 11 Oct 1852, GCB (1847, KCB 1815), PC (1852); b 30 Sept 1788; educ Westminster; Cornet 4th Light Dragoons 1804, Lt 1805, Attaché Constantinople 1807, Capt 43rd Foot 1808, Brevet Maj 1811, ADC and Mil Sec to 1st Duke of Wellington (qv) 1811 in Peninsular War (present Orthes and Toulouse, gold medal and two clasps for Salamanca and Badajoz, Peninsula medal and five clasps for Ciudad Rodrigo, Busaco, Talavera, Vimiera), Brevet Lt-Col 1812, Capt and Lt-Col 1st Foot Gds 1814, Sec Embassy Paris 1814–15 and 1815–18 (Chargé d'Affaires Jan-March 1815), present Waterloo 1815 (where he lost an arm), Col and ADC to PRINCE REGENT (later GEORGE IV) 1815–22, MP (Tory) Truro 1818–20 and 1826–29, Sec to Master-Gen Ordnance 1819–27, Maj-Gen 1825, Mil Sec to C-in-C 1827–52, Lt Gen 1838, Master-Gen Ordnance 1852–55, Gen 1854, FM 5 Nov 1854 following Battle of Inkerman (which he won against Russians 5 Nov 1854, along with The Alma 20 Sept 1854, as C-in-C UK Forces Crimea), Kt: Maria Theresa Austria, St George Russia 4th Cl, Maximilian Joseph Bavaria, Tower and Sword Portugal and Medjidie 1st Cl; m 6 Aug 1814 Lady Emily Harriet Wellesley-Pole (d 6 March 1881), 2nd dau of 3rd Earl of Mornington (see WELLINGTON, D), and d of cholera 28 June 1855 while on campaign, having had, with two daus (d unm):

1 Arthur William FitzRoy; b 6 May 1816; Page of Honour to GEORGE IV, Brevet Maj Gren Gds; m 8 July 1845 Emilie Marie Louise Wilhelmina (m 3rd 19 March 1850 Henry Boddington Webster, gs of Sir Godfrey Webster, 4th Bt (see 1923 edn), and d 26 Dec 1865), widow of Capt Mellish and dau of Baron von Baumbach, of Hesse, and dsp 24 Dec 1845 of wounds recd at Battle of Ferozeshah 21 Dec 1845

2 RICHARD HENRY FitzROY, **2nd Baron Raglan of Raglan**; b 24 May 1817; educ Ch Ch Oxford; Ceylon Civ Serv 1841–49, Priv Sec to KING OF HANOVER 1849–55, Ld-in-Waiting 1858–59 and 1866–69, Capt Glos Yeo Hus; m 1st 25

Sept 1856 Lady Georgina Lygon (d 30 Sept 1865), 3rd dau of 4th Earl Beauchamp (see 1970 edn), and had:

(1) GEORGE FitzROY HENRY, **3rd Baron**

(2) Arthur Charles Edward; b 11 Dec 1859; educ Eton and RMC Sandhurst; Capt and Adj Rifle Bde; m 27 Nov 1893 Louisa Eliza (d 18 June 1940), dau of John Grant Hodgson, and d 24 March 1948, having had:

1a Nonnan Arthur Henry; b 8 Sept 1894; Lt Gren Gds; ka 23 Oct 1914

1a Victoria Mary Blanche, JP (Berks 1960); b 28 Oct 1906 (HM QUEEN MARY stood sponsor); m 16 Feb 1926 Capt Thomas Leopold McClintock Lonsdale, Gren Gds, only surv s of Thomas Lonsdale, of Temple Grafton Court, Alcester, Warwicks, and had:

1b *Norman John McClintock [Norman Lonsdale Esq, 41 Chelsea Sq, London SW3]; b 3 Dec 1926; m 13 Feb 1967 *Fiona, dau of George Herbert Bentley, of Kenya, and has:

1c *James Leopold Somerset; b 23 Oct 1968; m 18 July 1984 *Laura Monica Greig (see MOWBRAY, SEGRAVE and STOURTON, B) and has had:

1d Thomas Louis James; b and d 1992

2d +Arthur Leopold Greig; b 29 April 1995

1d *Leonora Diana Fiona; b 1986

2d *Rosanna Monica; b 1988

3d *Esme Laura; b 29 April 1995

1c *Joanna Mary; b 6 Oct 1957

2c *Emma Jane Blanche; b 12 May 1962

(3) Granville William Richard; b 9 Sept 1862; Maj, Hon Lt-Col Roy Mon RE (Militia), Lt RN; m 11 June 1892 Malvina Charlotte (d 4 Dec 1924), dau of R-Adml Sir Malcolm Mac Gregor of Mac Gregor, 4th Bt (qv), and d 26 Nov 1901, leaving:

1a Richard Granville, MC (1919); b 15 Aug 1894; Capt RFA WW I (wounded twice); m 18 Jan 1929 Vera May (d 16 July 1931), dau of Louis Gustave Schwabe, and d 20 May 1930

(4) Wellesley Henry; b 6 April, d 16 Aug 1864

(5) Richard FltzRoy; b 9 Aug 1866; Capt Gren Gds; dsp 2 March 1899

2 (cont.) The **2nd Baron** m 2nd 11 Oct 1871 Mary Blanche (d 15 June 1916), est dau of Sir Walter Farquhar, 3rd Bt (qv), and by her had:

(1) Violet Elizabeth Katharine; b 10 Nov 1874; m 8 Dec 1900 Lt-Col Wilfrid Robert Abel Smith, CMG, Gren Gds (d 19 May 1915 of wounds recd in action), of Upton Lea, Slough, and d 29 April 1935, leaving issue

The 2nd BARON d 38 May 1884; his est s,

GEORGE FitzROY HENRY SOMERSET, **3rd Baron Raglan of Raglan**, GBE (1919); b 18 Sept 1857 (KING GEORGE OF HANOVER stood sponsor); educ Eton and RMC Sandhurst; Page of Honour to HM QUEEN VICTORIA 1868–74, Capt Gren Gds 1886–87 (served Afghan War 1879–80, medal and clasp), Lt-Col and Hon Col Roy Mon RE (Militia) 1901–08, U-Sec War 1900–03, Lt-Govr IoM 1902–19; m 28 Feb 1883 Lady Ethel Jemima Ponsonby (d 22 June 1940), dau of 7th Earl of Bessborough (qv), and had:

1 FitzROY RICHARD, **4th Baron**

2 Wellesley FitzRoy; b 13 June 1887; educ Eton; S/Ldr RAFVR, Maj Welch Regt, WWs I (wounded) and II; m 3 April 1917 Lesley (d 1 Dec 1969), yr dau of Frederick George Vivian, of St Fagans, Glam, and d 26 Feb 1969, having had:

(1) Anne Vivian; b 4 May 1919; m 7 March 1942 Lt Andrew John Hugh Payne Cook, RA, s of Rev Gerald Payne Cook, of Clewer Rectory, Windsor, and d 19 July 1946, leaving issue

(2) Mary Felicia; b 26 Dec 1923; m 10 Dec 1945 S/Ldr Thomas Copland Studdert, MD, FRCP, yr s of Thomas George Studdert, and d 10 Nov 1993, leaving:

1a *Christopher John; b 21 Jan 1947; educ Sedbergh

2a *Peter Wellesley; b 12 Jan 1949; educ Sedbergh

3a *Mark Jeremy; b 17 Nov 1953; educ Sedbergh

3 Nigel FitzRoy, CBE (1945), DSO (1919), MC (1918); b 27 July 1893; educ King William's Coll IoM and RMC Sandhurst; Col (T/Brig) Glos Regt, WW I (wounded twice, despatches thrice, Brevet Maj), Afghanistan 1919, WW II (POW, despatches), ADC to Govr S Australia 1920–22, Assist Mil Sec S Cmd India 1926–30, ret 1949; m 16 March 1922 Phyllis Marion Offley (d 25 June 1979), dau of Dr Henry Offley Irwin, of Boulder, W Australia, and d 7 Feb 1990, leaving:

(1) +David Henry FitzRoy [David Somerset Esq, White Wickets, Boar's Head, Sussex TN6 3HE]; b 19 June 1930; educ Wellington and Peterhouse Cambridge (BA 1952, MA 1956), financial advsr and Fell Peterhouse Cambridge 1988–97, Emeritus Fell 1997–; Ch Cashier Bank of England 1980–88; m 16 April 1955 *Ruth Ivy, dau of Wilfred Robert Wildbur, of King's Lynn, Norfolk, and has:

1a +Henry Robert FitzRoy [Henry Somerset Esq, Paul's Farm, Leigh, Kent TN11 8RX]; b 13 Feb 1961; educ Wellington and Trin Hall Cambridge; m 1992 *Jane Laird, dau of Dr Peter Gordon, of Edinburgh, and has:

1b *Alice Caroline Laird; b 23 Oct 1993

2b *Claire Sophie Westwood; b 23 Aug 1995

1a *Louise Charlotte [Mrs John Beach, Coppice Cottage, Ashton-under-Hill, Worcs WR11 6SS]; b 28 Aug 1956; educ Girton Coll Cambridge; m 1981 *John Roberts Beach, s of Gen Sir Hugh Beach, GBE, KCB, MC, and has:

1b *Charles Thomas FitzRoy; b 6 Jan 1993

1b *Georgiana Emily Estelle; b 10 July 1989

(1) Susan Mary; b 19 Feb 1923; m 29 Oct 1953 (divorce 1977) Patrick William Mackenzie Dean (d 10 July 1995), s of Richard Ellis Dean, of Mere Hall, Lincs, and d 6 Jan 1996, leaving:

1a *James FitzRoy; b 4 Aug 1954; m 1987 *Charlotte Janet Rose Unwin and has issue

1a *Julia Mary Mackenzie; b 25 Nov 1956; m 1986 Alexander Archibald Scott (d 30 Sept 1994) and has issue

2a *Veronica Jane Somerset; b 12 Sept 1958; m 1984 *Peter Francis Howard Stephens and has issue

3a *Rosemary Elizabeth; b 3 Jan 1964

1 Ethel Georgiana Frances; *b* 4 June 1889; *m* 26 Nov 1914 Hon William Sholto Douglas, s of 19th Earl of Morton (*qv*), and *d* 10 Oct 1981, leaving issue

2 Frederica Susan Katherine; *b* 31 Aug 1891; *m* 1 July 1922 Cdr Bertram Hughes Hallett, RIN (*d* 21 Feb 1942), s of Col Wyndham Hughes Hallett, and *d* 16 June 1967, leaving issue

3 Ivy Felicia; *b* 30 March 1897; *m* 27 Aug 1947, as his 2nd w, Raymond Marwood-Elton Carey, FRIBA, s of Adolphus Carey, of Bath and Guernsey, and *d* March 1986

The 3rd BARON *d* 24 Oct 1921; his est s,

FitzROY RICHARD SOMERSET, **4th Baron Raglan of Raglan**, JP Mon; *b* 10 June 1885; *educ* Eton and RMC Sandhurst; ADC to Govr and C-in-C Hong Kong 1912–13, served Egyptian Army 1913–19, Assist Political Offr Egyptian Expdny Force 1919–21, Lt-Col cmdg 13th Bn Lond Regt 1924–27, Lt-Col and Brevet Col Roy Mon RE (Militia) 1930–35, Hon Col Roy Mon RE, Maj Gren Gds, Mon: CC 1928–49, Ld Lt 1942–64, Pres Roy Anthropological Inst 1955–57 and Nat Museum Wales 1957–62, OStJ, Order Nile 4th Cl, FSA; *m* 9 April 1923 Hon Julia Hamilton, est dau of 11th Lord Belhaven and Stenton (*qv*), and *d* 14 Sept 1964, having had:

1 FitzRoy; *b* 9 Jan, *d* 13 Jan 1924

2 FitzROY JOHN SOMERSET, **5th and present Baron Raglan of Raglan**

3 +GEOFFREY [The Hon Geoffrey Somerset, Manor Farm, Stanford-in-the-Vale, Oxon SN7 8NN]; *b* 29 Aug 1932; heir presumptive; *educ* Westminster and RAC Cirencester; CC Berks 1966–75, memb Newbury DC 1978–83, Co-Cncllr Oxon 1988–93, Lt Gren Gds Res Offrs; *m* 6 Oct 1956 *Caroline Rachel, only dau of Col (Edward) Roderick Hill, DSO, JP, DL (*see* SAINT ALDWYN, E), and has:

(1) +Arthur Geoffrey; *b* 27 April 1960

(1) *Belinda Caroline; *b* 9 Feb 1958; *m* 1989 *Nicholas Grant Boyd, est s of Cdr Christopher Dennis Boyd, DSC, RN

(2) *Lucy Ann; *b* 8 Feb 1963

1 Janetta; *b* 8 June 1925; *educ* St Hugh's Coll Oxford (MA 1951); *m* 27 July 1956 *Joseph Vincent Ridgely, PhD, est s of Raymond G Ridgely, of St Petersburg, Fla., and *d* 1986, leaving:

(1) *Julia Frances; *b* 14 Aug 1963

2 *Cecily; *b* 10 Aug 1938; *m* 17 June 1961 *Jonkheer Jan Tewdyr Patrick Steengracht van Moyland, Capt Irish Gds (ret), yr s of Baron Steengracht van Moyland, of Pant-y-Goitre, Abergavenny, Mon, and has:

(1) *Henry Jan Berrington; *b* 18 Dec 1963

(1) *Susanna Cecily; *b* 3 Nov 1968

RALLI

Arms: Az. a lion rampant arg. semée of lozenges of the first, in chief a crescent between two crosses couped of the second. **Crest:** A lion as in the arms holding between the paws a cross couped az. **Motto:** βαδιζε την ευηθειαν ('Walk the straight way'). **Creation:** Bt. (UK) 8 Feb 1912.

SIR GODFREY VICTOR RALLI, 3RD BT, of Park Street, Westminster, TD [Sir Godfrey Ralli Bt TD, Great Walton, Sandwich Rd, Eastry, Kent CT13 ODN]; *b* 9 Sept 1915; *s* f 1964; *educ* Eton; Capt Berks Yeo RA WW II (despatches), dir and v-chm Ralli Bros 1946–62 (joined 1936), chm: G & L Ralli Investment and Tstee Co 1962–75 and Gtr London Fund for the Blind 1962–82, dir Guardian; *m* 1st 24 June 1937 (*divorce* 1947) Nora Margaret (*m* 2nd Philip Titterton, MB, ChB), only child of Charles Forman, of Loddon Court, Spencers Wood, Berks, and formerly of Beaurepaire Pk, Hants (which he sold to **Sir Strati Ralli, 2nd Bt**), and has:

1 +DAVID CHARLES [David Ralli Esq, The Old Hall, Hardingham, Norfolk NR9 4EW]; *b* 5 April 1946; *educ* Eton and Harper Adams Ag Coll; farmer, chm Dereham Farm Services 1985–87, dir Mid-Norfolk Farmers 1985–; *m* 15 Feb 1975 *Jacqueline Cecilia, dau of David R Smith, and has:

(1) +Philip Neil David; *b* 31 March 1983

(1) *Marina Louise; *b* 15 May 1980

1 *Louise [Mrs Ewen Cameron, The Old Vicarage, Harringworth, Northants NN17 3AF]; *b* 4 March 1942; *m* 11 Sept 1964 *Ewen James Fassiefern Cameron, of Terrington House, Terrington, Yorks, only s of Lt-Col Bruce Allan Fassiefern Cameron, JP, DL, of Foston Lodge, Yorks, and has:

(1) *James Allan Godfrey; *b* 8 Aug 1965

(2) *Alistair Ewen David; *b* 19 Aug 1968

2 *Tessa RALLI later TITTERTON; *b* 18 Feb 1945; adopted by her mother and stepf, whose surname she took 1952

Sir GODFREY *m* 2nd 24 March 1949 Jean (*d* 10 Feb 1998), dau of Keith Barlow, of Kensington

Lineage: It is not possible to establish a connected descent for the RALLIs until the early 18th century. But it has been alleged that they stem from a family called Raoul or Ralli, of Constantinople, who in turn descended from Raoul Peau-de-Loup ('Wolfskin'), presumably one of the Normans who in the mid-11th century had invaded Southern Italy and Sicily. ROBERT GUISCARD, sovereign DUKE OF APULIA AND CALABRIA, PRINCE OF SALERNO and SUZERAIN OF SICILY, sent Raoul Peau-de-Loup in 1081 to the Byzantine EMPEROR NICEPHORUS III to enquire why he had put in a nunnery ROBERT's dau Helena, who had been betrothed to NICEPHORUS's son. The RAOULs or RALLIs settled in the eastern Aegean island of Chios in the 15th century and in 1511 Michael Ralli, representing the nobility and people of that island, signed a petition to the Republic of Genoa concerning the property of the monastery of Nea Moni.

STEPHEN RALLI, of Chios; *m* Marietta, dau of Pandeli Mavrogordato, and had:

1 JOHN

2 Ambrose; *b* 1731; *m* Despina, dau of Dimitrios Maximo by Vierou Vlasto, of Chios, and *d* 1820, leaving, with other issue:

(1) Stephen; *b* 1763; merchant and banker first at Smyrna then at Constantinople; *m* 1797 Despina (*d* 7 May 1819), dau of John Omiro, and *d* Constantinople 20 Sept 1829, leaving:

1a Ambrose; *b* Smyrna 20 July 1798; *cr* 15 April 1874 Baron Ralli by EMPEROR FRANZ-JOSEF I OF AUSTRIA-HUNGARY; *m* 1st Trieste 17 Sept 1821 Anastasia (*d* 30 April 1834), dau of Stephen Mavrogordato by Maria Courmouti, and had:

1b Despina; *b* 10 Sept 1823; *m* 1847 Pandia Ralli, s of Theodore Ralli, and *d* London 20 April 1855

2b Mary; *b* 29 Sept 1830; *m* 23 Feb 1851 Paul Rodoconachi (*d* 23 Nov 1891), of Liverpool, s of John Rodoconachi, and *d* 9 July 1872, leaving issue

1a (cont.) Ambrose Ralli *m* 2nd 10 Oct 1835 Penelope (*d* 30 Jan 1900), dau of Paul Petrocochino, and *d* Trieste 8 Feb 1886, having by her had:

1b Paul; *b* 15 Nov 1845; *m* 29 April 1875 Caterina (*d* 13 March 1931), dau of Eustratio Stephen Ralli (*see* below), and *d* 8 May 1907, leaving:

1c Ambrose; *b* 1 May 1876; *m* in Venice 17 June 1922 Nora (*d* 4 Aug 1929), dau of Augustus Cavaller, and *d* Trieste 22 May 1938, leaving issue

1c Marie; *b* 7 July 1877; *m* in Trieste 10 Oct 1901 Baron Alexander von Warsberg-Dorth (*d* 15 Sept 1920), s of Baron Oscar von Warsberg-Dorth, and *d* Salzburg 26 June 1938

2c Penelope; *b* 24 April 1883; *m* 16 March 1907 Nicholas Sevastopoulos (*d* Villach 15 Sept 1921), s of Emmanuel Sevastopoulos, and *d* Trieste 6 Oct 1952

2b Stephen; *b* 11 May 1859; *m* 25 April 1889 Argentine (*d* 4 June 1935), dau of Peter Scaramanga, and *d* Trieste 30 Jan 1933, leaving, with other issue:

1c Peter; *b* 10 Sept 1891; *m* Vienna 29 Dec 1915 Valerie, dau of Maximilian Winterritz, and had issue

1a Alexandra; *b* Chios 1801; *m* 1820 Manoli Petrocochino (*d* 2 Dec 1860), s of Dimitrios Petrocochino by Viera Rodocanachi, and *d* Smyrna 1874

2a Sozonga; *b* 19 Nov 1804; *m* Trieste 27 July 1825 Augustus Stephen Ralli (*d* 18 April 1878), s of Stephen Ralli (*see* below), and *d* Marseilles 1 Feb 1878

3a Calliope; *b* 1811; *m* 4 July 1830 Anthony Vlasto, s of Alexander Vlasto, and *d* Marseilles 16 Feb 1895

(2) Costi; *b* Chios 1765; *m* 1793 Alexandra, dau of Zorzis Petrocochino, and was taken prisoner and hanged by the Turks during the Massacre of Chios 6 May 1822, leaving, with other issue:

1a John; *b* Chios 7 Dec 1804; *m* in Vienna 25 Nov 1840 Mary (*d* Monte Carlo 11 Feb 1901), dau of Ambrose Scaramanga by Smaragda Rodoconachi, and *d* Paris 23 Jan 1876, leaving, with other issue:

1b Ambrose; *b* Marseilles 28 Jan 1851; *m* Nice 28 April 1886 Christine (*m* 2nd 16 Jan 1899 Hon Edward Alexander Stonor (*see* CAMOYS, B) and *d* 9 Dec 1958), dau of Richard Ralli (*see* below), and *d* London 21 Nov 1896, leaving issue:

1c John Richard, of Pamphill Manor, Wimborne, Dorset; *b* 26 June 1890; *m* 21 July 1921 Audrey Violet Hatfeild (*d* 24 Sept 1939), only dau of James Francis Hatfeild Harter, JP, DL, of Cranfield Court, Beds, and formerly w of Capt Esmé Francis Wigsell Arkwright, MC, of Lavendon Grange, Turvey, Beds, formerly of Sanderstead Court, Surrey, and *d* 9 April 1942, leaving issue

1c Menda; *b* 24 March 1887; *m* 1st 27 May 1911 Lord Arthur Vincent Hay (*ka* 14 Sept 1914), 2nd s of 10th Marquess of Tweeddale (*qv*), and had issue; *m* 2nd 3 Jan 1916 Col Robert Edward Kennard Leatham, DSO (*d* 11 May 1948), and *d* 5 Jan 1959, leaving further issue

1b Alexandra; *b* Odessa 23 Oct 1841; *m* 15 Feb 1860 Peter Ralli (*d* 30 Jan 1868), s of Pandia Ralli (*see* below), and *d* 31 May 1903, leaving issue

2a George; *b* 1806; *m* 1830 Adèle, dau of Richard Wilkinson, and *d* 1874, leaving:

1b Richard; *b* 6 Dec 1835; *m* Eugenie (*d* Florence 28 Oct 1914), dau of John Wood, and *d* Paris 4 July 1903, leaving:

1c Helen; *b* 1863; *m* 1st Paris 20 Sept 1883 Alexander Ralli, s of Stephen Ralli by Argiro Petrocochino, and had:

1d Marguerite Christine; *m* 7 Dec 1912 11th Marquess of Tweeddale (*qv*) and *d* 15 Oct 1944, having had issue

1c (cont.) Helen Ralli *m* 2nd 29 June 1885 Alfred Joseph Charles Edwards, s of Charles Edwards; *m* 3rd 1907 Lewis Einstein (*d* 4 Dec 1967 aged 91), s of David L Einstein

2c Christine Alexandra; b 19 Jan 1867; m 1st Nice 28 April 1886 Ambrose Ralli (d 21 Nov 1896), s of John Ralli, and had issue (see above); m 2nd 16 Jan 1899 Hon Edward Alexander Stonor, bro of 4th Baron Camoys (qv), and d 9 Dec 1958, leaving further issue

1b Adelina; m John Psiachi

3a Pandeli; b 9 Aug 1814; m 16 May 1850 Harriet (d 30 Jan 1919), dau of Eustratios Stephen Ralli (see below), and d 31 Jan 1873, leaving, with other issue:

1b Constantine RALLI later SCARAMANGA-RALLI (roy licence 8 Aug 1910); b 17 July 1854; m 4 Oct 1890 Marion Gascoigne (d 13 Dec 1896), dau of Samuel Gasgoigne Haines, and had issue

2b John; b 24 July 1869; m 3 Nov 1893 Helen, dau of Col Wemyss Muir, and d 21 June 1899, leaving issue

1b Marie; b 23 Sept 1852; m 4 Jan 1879 Rev John Robertson

2b Harriet; b 6 Jan 1859; m 17 July 1883 Lt-Col Arthur Thomas Rigby Neave (see NEAVE, Bt) and dsp 25 Jan 1947

3 George; b 1733; m 1760 Marietta, dau of Dimitrios Schilizzi, MD, and had issue

4 Strati; b 1741; m 1768 Zambelou, dau of Stephen Mavrogordato, and had issue

1 Helen; b Chios 18 Feb 1722; m 10 Aug 1740 Pandeli Argenti (d 9 Dec 1793), s of Leon Argenti, and d Chios 11 Sept 1800, leaving issue

2 Marietta; b Chios 1735; m Matthew Mavrogordato, s of Nicholas Mavrogordato, and had issue

STEPHEN RALLI's est s,

JOHN RALLI; b 1724; m 1754 Ploumou, dau of Peter Scaramanga, and had:

1 STEPHEN JOHN

2 Peter; b 1757; m Despina (d 1848), dau of Dimitrios Roidi by Catherine Mavrogordato, and dsp

3 Dimitri; b Chios 1758; m Catherine, dau of Pericles Negroponte, and d 14 Feb 1812, leaving, with other issue:

(1) Lucas; b Chios 1794; memb exec ctee which attempted the liberation of Chios 1827, Mayor Piraeus, Grand Offr Order Redeemer Greece; m 1 Sept 1827 Despina (d 10 Oct 1880), dau of Paul Rodocanachi by Arghiro Franghiedi, and d Piraeus 29 Dec 1874, leaving issue

4 Lucas; dsp Livorno 31 May 1792

5 Pandia; b 1773; m Margarita (d 3 March 1871), dau of Augustus Galati, and d 20 April 1859, leaving issue

1 Arghiro; b 1762; m Peter Vouro, s of Zorzis Vouro

2 Julia; b Chios 1767; m 1787 Leoni Condostavlo (k by the Turks during the Massacre of Chios April 1822), s of Leonard Condostavlo by Mina Pitsipis, and d 1804

3 Mary; b 1768; m 1788 Leoni Argenti, s of John Argenti by Loula Caratheodori, and d Livorno 17 Jan 1831

JOHN RALLI's est s,

STEPHEN JOHN RALLI; b Chios 1755; settled Marseilles after Massacre of Chios 1822; m 1784 Julia (d Constantinople 4 Oct 1848), dau of Augustus Sechiari, of Chios, by Virginia Ralli, and d Marseilles 24 Jan 1827, leaving:

1 John; b Chios 3 Nov 1785; settled England 1819 and founded Ralli Bros with his brother Eustratio, later ran firm's business in Odessa; m 1797 Lucia (d Livorno 24 Dec 1873), dau of Giuseppe Storni, and d Paris 8 Oct 1859, leaving:

(1) Stephen; b 1 Aug 1821; merchant banker Odessa, Actual Counsellor of State to TSAR OF RUSSIA; m 1st 1842 Helen Glanopoulo and had two sons (dsp); m 2nd 30 April 1850 Mary (d Cannes 28 Oct 1903), dau of Peter Epites by Helen Serafino, and d Odessa 28 Aug 1901, having by her:

1a Paul; b 2 March 1851; m 2 Sept 1895 Catherine (d April 1929), dau of George Timachenko, and d St Petersburg 16 Feb 1911, leaving:

1b Madeline; dsp Bavaria 1921

2a Peter; b 2 March 1851; Capt Imperial Russian Guard; m St Petersburg 16 April 1889 Mary, dau of Miroslav Kourovsky, and dsp Pau 4 March 1896

1a Helen; b 7 July 1852; m Odessa 30 July 1873 Julius Andreyev (d 1923), s of Ardalion Andreyev, and d Odessa 23 April 1923

2a Lucy; b 26 Dec 1854; m 14 April 1875 Achilles Koumbary (d 1911), s of Stamati Koumbary, and d Odessa 24 Jan 1892

3a Mary; b 11 Jan 1856; m 2 April 1879 Nicolas Iazykov (d 1912), s of Gen Alexander Iazykov by Baroness Constance von Stackelberg, and d Pau 7 Feb 1927

4a Juliet; b 18 May 1859; m 12 Nov 1896 Liddell Morton, s of Fraser Morton by Anna Liddell

5a Elizabeth; b 26 Dec 1871; m Warsaw 2 Feb 1897 Prince Alexis Lobanov-Rostovsky (d Geneva 21 Jan 1921), s of Prince Nicolas Lobanov-Rostovsky by Anna Schablizkin, and had issue

2 Pandia, of Connaught Place, London; b Chios 1793; ran Ralli Bros in London when his bro John went to Odessa; Greek Consul-Gen London, Kt Order Redeemer Greece; m 25 Sept 1831 Marietta (d Marseilles 16 Nov 1860), dau of Peter Scaramanga by Mina Ralli, and d London 9 July 1865, leaving:

(1) Peter, of London; b 16 Nov 1837; m Marseilles 15 Feb 1860 Alexandra (d 31 May 1903), dau of John Ralli (see above), and d 30 Jan 1868, leaving:

1a Pandia, of Ashstead Park, Epsom, Surrey; b 27 Aug 1862; m 3 Aug 1889 Arghiro, dau of John Sechiari, of Braïla, Romania, by Clementine Scaramanga, and dsp 5 Feb 1924

2a Peter, of Bayswater; b 13 June 1868; m 20 July 1895 Mary (d 24 Dec 1961), est dau of **Sir Lucas Eustratio Ralli, 1st Bt** (see below), and d 28 July 1935, having had:

1b Lionel Peter; b 21 Aug 1897; d of wounds recd in action 14 Nov 1918

1b Alexandra; b 20 April 1896; m 21 Oct 1924 Lt-Col Neil Graham Stewart-Richardson, DSO, NI Horse (d 23 Feb 1934), yst s of Sir James Thomas Stewart-Richardson, 14th Bt (qv), and d 2 Aug 1972, leaving issue

1a Marietta; b 11 Dec 1860; m 2 Feb 1882 John Scaramanga (d 20 Sept 1907), s of Pandia Scaramanga by Arghiro Argenti, and d 20 Jan 1927

2a Mary; b 2 Sept 1864; m 5 June 1883 Emmanuel Rodoconachi (d Paris 8 Jan 1934), s of Peter Rodocanachi by Mary, dau of Augustus Ralli (see below), and d Paris 5 Jan 1934

3a Alexandra; b 7 March 1866; m 19 Oct 1889 Theodore Zarifi (d 9 March 1910), s of Michael Zarifi, and d Monte Carlo 29 March 1832

(1) Julia; b 24 June 1832; m 25 Aug 1853 Charles James Monk, JP, DL, MP (Lib U) Gloucester (d 10 Nov 1900), s of Rt Rev James Henry Monk, DD, Bp Gloucester, and d 26 Dec 1870

3 Augustus Stephen; b Chios 10 Jan 1797; ran Ralli Bros in Marseilles; m Trieste 27 July 1825 Sozonga (d Marseilles 1 Feb 1878), dau of Stephen Ralli (see above), and d Marseilles 18 April 1878, leaving:

(1) Stephen, of Marseilles; b 30 Jan 1829; ptnr Ralli Bros; m 27 Oct 1855 Marietta (d 2 March 1922), dau of Anthony Ralli by Catherine Mavrogordato, and d Monte Carlo 2 April 1902, leaving:

1a Anthony Stephen, of Stanhoe Hall, Norfolk; b May 1861; Maj 12th Lancers; m 8 July 1893 Mina (d 20 March 1950), dau of Andrew Scaramanga by Julia Zygomala, and d S Africa, leaving:

1b Stephen Andrew; b 13 Aug 1897; m 1 June 1923 Diana (m 2nd Henry Mardon), dau of Edward Underwood by Louisa St Aubyn Angrove, and d 31 July 1966, leaving:

1c Roderick Stephen Charles; b 20 April 1929; QALAS; m 21 July 1958 *Amanda Jane Hoare [Mrs Roderick Ralli, Barwick House, Stanhoe, King's Lynn, Norfolk PE31 8PZ], and d 8 Jan 1992, leaving:

1d *Andrew Christopher Stephen; b 21 Dec 1959; m 3 March 1987 *Suzy Payne

2d *Luke Robert Charles; b 8 July 1969; m 16 Sept 1995 *Alice Walker, and has:

1e *Charles Roderick; b 30 July 1998

1d *Susan Harriet; b 13 Jan 1963; m 16 Nov 1985 *Robert Barclay

2c *George Anthony; b 3 Oct 1932

1c *Clare Evelyn [Mrs Philip Anley, Sculthorpe House, nr Fakenham, Norfolk]; b 21 Dec 1925; m 15 Sept 1948 Lt-Col Philip Maitland Gore Anley (d 20 Oct 1968), s of Brig-Gen Frederick Gore Anley, CB, of Ryecroft Ho, Bolney, Sussex, and has issue

1b Mary Primrose; b 9 April 1894; m 16 July 1914 Richard Gurney Buxton and d 1972, leaving issue (see BUXTON, Bt)

2a Stephen, of Hassocks, Sussex; b 5 March 1863; m 15 Jan 1907 Ida Cecil, dau of Col Charles Beck by Ida Charlton, and d 25 March 1941, leaving:

1b Charles Stephen; b 5 Nov 1907; m 30 July 1936 *Sidney Agatha Annette, dau of Maj-Gen Charles John Bruce Hay, CB, CMG, CBE, DSO, and Agatha Mangin, and d 13 Aug 1983, leaving:

1c *(John) Stephen [Maj Stephen Ralli, 4 Penzance Place, London W11]; b Karachi 12 Jan 1938; Maj (ret) Rifle Bde; m 4 Oct 1966 (divorce 8 June 1978) Carol Margaret, only child of Hon Douglas Wilkie Westwood (see WESTWOOD, B), and has:

1d *Charles Douglas Stephen; b 15 March 1968

2c *Hugo Charles; b Calcutta 18 Sept 1941; m 16 Nov 1974 *Heidi, only dau of Gerd Luder, of Munich, and has:

1d *Mark-Oliver Luder; b 15 Jan 1979

1d *Tania Vanessa; b 5 March 1976

1c *Prudence Margaret [Mrs Georges Allonsius, 117 Lascelles Blvd, Toronto, Ontario, Canada]; b 19 Oct 1939; m 30 Nov 1973 *Georges Adeleu August Edward Allonsius, er s of Henri Allonsius, of Belgium

2b *Edward John; b 20 Jan 1909; m 16 Oct 1964 *Marianne, dau of Paul Marszbek by Anna Bonczak and formerly w of Ivor Poland

3b Alexander Frederick; b 30 March 1913; d 29 Aug 1981

1a Sozonga; b 28 Dec 1857; m 7 Nov 1876 Georges Philippe Marie, Count Gilbert de Voisins (d 14 Nov 1897), s of Jean Pierre Victor Albert, Count Gilbert de Voisins, of Munich, and d Paris 25 April 1900

2a Caterina; b 5 Feb 1859; m 11 Feb 1879 Alexander Ralli (d 23 Oct 1927), s of Pandia Ralli by Sophia Rodocanachi, and d 12 May 1943, leaving issue

3a Marietta; b 5 March 1863; m 24 Nov 1881 Ambrose Ralli (d 13 March 1898), s of Pandia Ralli

4a Julia; b 2 Aug 1869; m 27 Feb 1902 Henry William Lance, s of Lt-Gen Sir Frederick Lance, KCB

(1) Julia; b Marseilles 22 July 1830; m 8 May 1851 Leonidas Argenti (d 23 Oct 1882), of Marseilles, s of Pandeli Argenti, and d Paris 6 Oct 1922, leaving issue

(2) Marigo; b 15 Sept 1832; m 29 Aug 1853 Peter Rodoconachi (d 18 May 1898), s of Emmanuel Rodoconachi by Franga Mavrogordato, and d Paris 29 Feb 1884, leaving issue

4 Thomas Stephen; b Chios 1799; ran Constantinople firm of Ralli Bros; m 12 May 1833 Marouko (d 20 Dec 1880), dau of Pandely Argenti, and d London 20 Oct 1858, leaving:

(1) Pandeli, JP Surrey, DL Dorset; b Marseilles 22 May 1845; educ King's Coll London (BA); MP (Lib) Bridport 1875–80 and Wallingford 1880–85; d unm Brighton 22 Aug 1928

(1) Janie; b Constantinople 18 Nov 1846; Hon Ldy-in-Waiting to HRH THE DUCHESS OF ALBANY; m 15 July 1868 Hon Sir Richard Charles Moreton, KCVO (see DUCIE, E), and d 25 July 1929, leaving issue

5 EUSTRATIO STEPHEN

1 Ploumou; b 1790; m 1807 Alexander Ralli (captured by the Turks and hanged during Massacre of Chios 6 May 1822), s of Anthony Ralli by his w Julia, and d Marseilles 10 May 1867

2 Vierou; b Chios 30 Dec 1801; m 22 May 1819 Cozi Agelasto (d Constantinople 13 Oct 1865), s of Augustus Agelasto by Angeliki Negroponte, and d London 17 Sept 1885

3 Arghiro; b 1803; m 1820 Emmanuel Psiachi and d 1881

4 Marigo; b in Chios 20 Oct 1806; m 9 Sept 1822 Peter Schilizzi (d 3 April 1877), s of Emmanuel Schilizzi, and d Marseilles 23 March 1891, leaving issue

STEPHEN RALLI's yst s,

EUSTRATIO STEPHEN RALLI, of Scio House, Putney (subsequently a hospital for army offrs), and Bayswater; *b* Chios 22 April 1800; with his bro John established Ralli Bros in London 1819, the family having built up a business mainly in silk, grain and cotton which eventually spread all over Br India and into Armenia; Offr Order Redeemer Greece; *m* London 22 May 1825 Mary (*d* 20 April 1892), er dau of John Mavrogordato, of Chios, by Oriettou Vlasto, and *d* 1 Sept 1884, having had:

1 Stephen; *b* 1 March 1828; *d* 19 March 1844

2 John Eustratio; *b* 7 Feb 1830; *m* 1 Feb 1860 Mimina (*d* 16 Feb 1900), dau of Eustratios Scaramanga by Despina Psycha, and *dsp* 13 July 1879

3 Eustratio; *b* 2 Aug 1844; *d* 22 Dec 1865

4 LUCAS EUSTRATIO (Sir), **1st Bt**

1 Julia; *b* 15 April 1826; *m* 14 May 1846 Demetrius Peter Scaramanga (*d* 17 Dec 1867), s of Peter Scaramanga by Mina Ralli, and *d* 20 May 1910

2 Harriet; *b* 7 Dec 1831; *m* 16 May 1850 Pandeli Constantine Ralli (*d* 31 Jan 1873), of Notting Hill, s of Costi Ralli, and *d* 30 Jan 1919, leaving issue (*see* above)

3 Despina; *b* 27 Aug 1835; *m* 1 March 1855 Emmanuel Mavrogordato (*d* 13 Aug 1909), s of Anthony Mavrogordato by Loula Tamvoco, and *d* 10 Oct 1885, leaving issue

4 Calliope; *b* 25 Oct 1836; *m* 7 March 1861 Alexander Vlasto (*d* 6 June 1899), s of Anthony Vlasto by Calliope, dau of Stephen Ralli, of Constantinople (*see* above), and *d* 15 Sept 1907, leaving issue

5 Caterina; *b* 13 Sept 1851; *m* 29 April 1875 Baron (Paul Ambrose) Ralli (*d* 8 May 1907), of Trieste, and *d* 13 March 1931, leaving issue (*see* above)

EUSTRATIO RALLI's yst s,

Sir Lucas Eustratio Ralli, 1st Bt (UK), so *cr* 8 Feb 1912, of Mayfair and Scio House, Putney; *b* 30 March 1846; *educ* Harrow and Trin Coll Cambridge; head of Ralli Bros, fndr Chios Tst with his bro-in-law Pandeli Leonidas Argenti, Cdr Order Redeemer Greece, Offr Order Holy Sepulchre; *m* 4 Dec 1873 Eugenie (Janie) (*d* 7 April 1935), est dau of Leonidas Pandeli Argenti, of Marseilles, and *d* 5 May 1931, having had:

1 STRATI (Sir), **2nd Bt**

2 Leonidas Lucas; *b* London 31 May 1884; T/Capt RASC WW I; *das* 20 April 1917

1 Mary; *b* New York 12 Aug 1875; *m* 20 July 1895 Peter Ralli (*d* 28 July 1935), of Bayswater, and *d* 24 Dec 1961, leaving issue (*see* above)

2 Julia; *b* Cannes 15 Nov 1877; *m* 11 Jan 1896 Stephen Schilizzi (*d* 18 July 1961) and *d* 13 Oct 1952, leaving issue

3 Janie; *b* London 1 Nov 1881; *m* 21 Jan 1905 Baron Dimitri Jean Economo di San Serff (*d* 31 Oct 1951) and *d* 28 Sept 1959, having had issue

The 1st Bt's er s,

Sir EUSTRATIO LUCAS RALLI later Sir STRATI RALLI (deed poll 19 May 1931), **2nd Bt**, MC; *b* New York 14 July 1876; *educ* Eton and New Coll Oxford (BA 1898); Middx Imp Yeo (medal, four clasps) Boer War 1900–01, Capt RFA WW I, High Sheriff Hants 1943, pres Ralli Bros, dep chm Guardian Assur, chm Orion Insur, dir Maritime Shipping & Trading, Cdr Order George I of Greece; *m* 25 Jan 1915 Louise Warington, of S Kensington, dau of Bernard James Williams, and *d* 12 Nov 1964, having had:

1 Sir GODFREY VICTOR RALLI, **3rd and present Bt**

2 +Lucas John [Maj Lucas Ralli, 14 Oxford Sq, London W2 2PB]; *b* 10 Jan 1920; *educ* Eton; Maj Roy Signals WW II (despatches), dir Ralli Bros to 1962, chm Orion Insur, dir: G and L Ralli Investment and Tstee Co, Life Assoc of Scotland; *m* 1st 7 Sept 1950 (*divorce* 1989) Katia, dau of Constantine Droulia, of Athens, and Mrs Robert N Lauder, of Portman Sq, and has:

  (1) +John Strati [John Ralli Esq, 32 Alma Sq, London NW8 9PY]; *b* 15 July 1956; *educ* Eton; *m* 1986 (*divorce* 1995) Kathryn Martin and has:

    1a *Helen Elizabeth; *b* 1987

    2a *Stephanie Catherine; *b* 1990

  (1) *Dora Louise [Mrs Nicolas Rakic, 18 Bury Walk, London SW3 6QB]; *b* 13 Nov 1953; *m* 1984 *Nicolas Rakic and has:

    1a *Peter Lucas Gradimir; *b* 1988

    2a *Alexander Minas Cedomi; *b* 1988 (twin)

    1a *Anna Katharina Lila; *b* 1985

2 (cont.) Maj Lucas Ralli *m* 2nd 1989 *Mrs Jean Patricia Barrett, dau of Capt Edward Morden Bennett, RN, of Wolfeton Manor, Charminster, Dorset

1 *Diana Myrtle [Mrs Jack Walford, Arlington Lodge, Bibury, Glos]; *b* 13 Feb 1918; *m* 10 Oct 1939 Lt Col John Herbert (Jack) Walford, DSO, Seaforth Highrs (*d* 7 Feb 1976), er s of Hugh Selwyn Walford, and has:

  (1) *Michael Carr [Michael Walford Esq, The Old House, Wolverton, Hants]; *b* 11 March 1943; *educ* Harrow and RAC Cirencester

  (2) *(Ewan) John [Dr John Walford, 203 West Prairie, Wheaton, IL 60187, USA]; *b* 16 Feb 1945; *educ* Harrow, Law School (London and Guildford) and Free U Amsterdam; Speelman Fell Wolfson Coll Cambridge 1976, PhD, Prof Art History Wheaton Coll 1981–; *m* 1972 *Maria, only dau of Pietro Angelo Eligio Dellù, of Milan, and has:

    1a *Samuel Michael; *b* 1973

    2a *David John; *b* 1980

    1a *Deborah Maria; *b* 1978

  (1) *Belinda Mary [Mrs Colin McCorquodale, 8 St Mary Abbots Terrace, London W14 8NX]; *b* 21 April 1941; *m* 1st 23 Sept 1961 (*divorce* 1968) John William Hayter, s of C H Hayter, of Pudlicote Ho, Chilson, Oxon, and has:

    1a *Sarah Miranda; *b* 1964; *m* 1989 *Angus Sladen, s of Toby Sladen, and has:

      1b *Olivia Henrietta Malvina; *b* 1992

      2b *Georgina Ann Diana; *b* 1994

  (1) (cont.) Mrs Belinda Hayter *m* 2nd 1986 *Colin Norman McCorquodale, only s of Maj Angus McCorquodale (*see* 1970 edn McCORQUODALE OF NEWTON, B)

2 *Patience Louise [Mrs William Dunn, Awliscombe House, Honiton, Devon EX14 0NP]; *b* 31 Jan 1922; *m* 5 Feb 1944 *Lt-Cdr William Edward Michael de Sivrac Dunn, RNVR, s of Cecil Dunn, and has:

(1) *Mark de Sivrac; *b* 25 Nov 1947; *educ* Millfield

(1) *Karen Louise [Mrs Alan Grieve, Stoke Lodge, Clee Downton, Ludlow, Salop SY8 3EG]; *b* 30 Oct 1945; *m* 1971 *Alan Grieve and has:

  1a *Thomas de Sivrac; *b* 1973

  1a *Lara Louise; *b* 1974

RAMSAY

Arms: Argent an eagle displayed sable, beaked and membered gules, charged on the breast with a rose of the field. **Crest:** A demi-eagle displayed sable. **Motto:** *Aspiro* ('I aspire'). **Creation:** Bt. (UK) 13 May 1806.

SIR ALEXANDER WILLIAM BURNETT RAMSAY, 7TH BT, of Balmain [Sir Alexander Ramsay Bt, Banchory, PO Box 274, Warren, NSW 2824, Australia]; *b* 4 Aug 1938; *s f* 1965; may well also be heir to the btcy of Burnett of Leys, *cr* 1626 but *dormant* since 1959 (*see* 1956 edn); *m* 16 April 1963 *Neryl Eileen, dau of J C Smith Thornton, of Trangie, NSW, and has:

1 +ALEXANDER DAVID; *b* 20 Aug 1966; *m* 1990 *Annette Plummer and has:

  (1) *Kate Victoria; *b* 27 Dec 1995

  (2) *Skye Elizabeth; *b* 21 Aug 1997

2 +Ian John; *b* 28 Feb 1968; *m* 1993 *Kerry Calvert

3 +David Burnett; *b* 1971

Lineage: JOHN RAMSAY, of Corstoun, Fifeshire; *m* Janet Napier and may have been f of:

Sir JOHN RAMSAY, 1st and last LORD BOTHWELL (S), as which *cr* by 16 Feb 1482/3, of Balmain and Fasque, Kincardineshire; Amb England 1486 and 1488; after JAMES III's murder he was prosecuted and his title forfeited 8 Oct 1488; pardoned 18 April 1497 but not restored to his peerage and only got back part of his lands; other lands in Kincardineshire were granted him and his heirs and erected 13 May 1510 into the free (territorial) Barony of Balmain; *m* 1st just before 6 Nov 15– (*divorce* soon after) Janet Kennedy, a former mistress of JAMES IV; *m* 2nd by 15 Feb 1507/8 Isobel Livingston and was *ka* Flodden 9 Sept 1513, leaving by her:

WILLIAM RAMSAY; *d* by 1510; ancestor of:

DAVID RAMSAY of Balmain; MP (S Parl) Kincardineshire 1612, 1625 and 1630; *m* Margaret, dau of Sir Gilbert Ogilvie of Ogilvie, and *d* 1636, leaving:

Sir GILBERT RAMSAY, 1st Bt (NS), so *cr* 3 Sept 1625, with remainder to heirs male whatsoever, of Balmain; joined Covenanters (Presbyterians opposed to CHARLES I's anglicanising tendencies in church matters) 1636, MP (S Parl) Kincardineshire 1639–41, 1645–46 and 1661–63, Commr Excise 1646; *m*(?) 1st (or even at all?) Elizabeth, dau of George Auchinleck of Balmanno; *m* (2nd?) 1630, as her 2nd husb, Grizel (*m* 3rd, as his 1st w of two, 1st Earl of Middleton of the 1660 *cr* (forfeited 1695) and *d* 1666), dau of James Durham of Pitkerrow and widow of Sir Alexander Fotheringham, and *d c* 1663, leaving by her an only s:

Sir DAVID RAMSAY, 2nd Bt, of Balmain; regranted by charter his lands and barony 1670, MP (S Parl) Kincardineshire 1672–73; *m*(?) (1st?) Margaret, dau of Sir James Carnegie of Balnamoon; *m* 2nd(?) Elizabeth, *née* Coutts, widow of Sir Alexander Burnett, 2nd Bt of Leys, and was *k* Sept 1673 in a fall from his horse, leaving by his 1st w an only s:

Sir CHARLES RAMSAY, 3rd Bt, of Balmain; *m* 1st *c* 1673 Margaret (*dsp*), dau of John Carnegie of Boysack (*see* NORTHESK, E); *m* 2nd Elizabeth, dau of Sir Alexander Burnett, dau of Sir Alexander Falconer of Glenfarquhar, and *d* 1695, having had:

1 Sir DAVID RAMSAY, 4th Bt, of Balmain; MP (S Parl) Kincardineshire 1705–07 and (GB Parl) 1707–08 and 1708–10; *dsp* probably unm Sept 1710

2 Sir ALEXANDER RAMSAY, 5th Bt, of Balmain; advocate 1705, MP (GB Parl) Kincardineshire 1710–13; *d* unm 27 Jan 1754

3 Charles; *m* Catherine, dau of James Mill, of Balweylo, Provost Montrose, and *d* 1727, leaving:

(1) ALEXANDER RAMSAY later RAMSAY-IRVINE, 6th Bt; MP Kincardineshire; *d* unm 11 Feb 1806, when the btcy expired or became dormant (though it was assumed by two bros in succession, of whom the parentage is unknown, *viz.*, (Sir) James Ramsay 1806–07 and (Sir) Thomas Ramsay 1807–30), leaving his estates to his n

(1) Catherine; *m* by 1755 Sir Thomas Burnett, 6th Bt, of Leys, and *d* 10 Dec 1798, leaving, with an er s who *s* to the btcy of Burnett, of Leys:

1a Sir ALEXANDER BURNETT later RAMSAY (roy licence 1806), **1st Bt** (UK), so *cr* 13 May 1806; *b* 1757; *m* 14 Oct 1782 Elizabeth (*d* 11 Dec 1844), dau and coheir of Sir Alexander Bannerman, 4th Bt (*qv*), and *d* 17 May 1810, having had, with five other daus:

  1b ALEXANDER (Sir), **2nd Bt**

  2b Thomas; *b* 24 Feb 1786; Capt 47th Foot; *m* 1st 9 Nov 1816 Jane (*d* Nov 1823), 2nd dau of Patrick Cruikshank of Stracathro, and had:

    1c William RAMSAY later BURNETT-RAMSAY, of Banchory Lodge and Arbeadie; *b* 11 April 1821; Capt Rifle Bde and Lt-Col Forfar and Kincardine Militia Artillery; *m* 26 July 1854 Anne (*d* 13 Oct 1880), dau of Duncan Davidson of Inchmarlo, and *d* 6 Nov 1865, leaving, with two daus (*d* unm):

      1d Thomas, JP, DL (Kincardineshire), of Banchory Lodge; *b* 29 March 1862; Capt Rifle Bde 1892, FRGS; *d* unm S Africa 20 Dec 1901

      1d Frances Mary; *m* 20 Aug 1879 W D Robinson Douglas (*d* 3 Oct 1921), of Orchardton, Kirkcudbrightshire, and *d* 13 June 1881, leaving issue

      2d Annie Elizabeth; *m* 1 March 1904 Walter Guy, 14th Baron Bentinck, and *d* 19 Jan 1934, leaving issue (*see* PORTLAND, E)

    1c Elizabeth Marjorie; *m* 28 May 1858 Rev Alexander J Murray (*d* 1881), of St George's, Croydon, and *d* 3 May 1907, having had issue

    2c Catherine Forbes; *k* in an accident 1943

    3c Jane; *m* 1852 Dr Thom (*d* 1888) and had issue

  2b (cont.) Capt Thomas Ramsay *m* 2nd 28 April 1826 his 1st cousin Margaret (*d* 17 Jan 1836), dau of Sir Robert Burnett, 7th Bt, of Leys, and *d* 17 Dec 1857, having by her had:

    2c Thomas; *b* 1828; *d* 1856

  3b Robert; *b* 27 Feb 1787; Capt 14th Foot; *m* May 1817 Margaret (*d* 8 Jan 1880), 3rd dau of Patrick Cruikshank of Stracathro, and *d* 20 Dec 1846, leaving, with a dau (*d* unm):

    1c Robert, of Howletts, Canterbury; *b* 19 March 1818; *m* 18 April 1855 Susan (*d* 17 Feb 1906), dau of William Fullarton Lindsay Carnegie of Spynie and Boysack (for whose early ancestry *see* CRAWFORD and BALCARRES, E, also NORTHESK, E), and *d* 5 July 1910, having had, with a dau (*d* unm):

      1d Marmaduke Francis, JP (Kent); *b* 8 Dec 1860; *educ* Harrow and Trin Hall Cambridge; *m* 6 July 1895 Alice Katherine Angelique (*d* 10 Feb 1951), dau of Ottiwell Charles Waterfield, JP, of Nackington, Canterbury, and *d* 31 Dec 1947, having had:

        1e John Marmaduke; *b* 5 Sept 1897; Lt Rifle Bde; *d* 13 April 1917 of wounds recd in action

        2e +Robert Ottiwell [Robert Ramsay Esq, Kinblethmont, Arbroath, Angus]; *b* 1 June 1900; *educ* Harrow and Pembroke Coll Cambridge; *m* 24 Feb 1937 *Constance Aileen, only dau of Maj Hugh Bernard German, MC, RAMC, Surgn RN, and has:

          1f +Robert David [Robert Ramsay Esq, West Mains of Kinblethmont, by Arbroath, Angus DD11 4RW]; *b* 8 April 1942; *educ* Harrow and Glasgow U (BSc CEng 1965); *m* 24 Sept 1966 *Penelope Anne, only dau of Michael Gladstone, of Great Shelford, Cambs, and has:

            1g +Robert Nicholas; *b* 12 May 1968; *educ* Harrow and Reading U; *m* 1993 *Jessica McLaren

            2g +Alexander John; *b* 10 July 1969; *educ* Harrow and BNC Oxford

            3g +Jonathan Charles; *b* 1973; *educ* Harrow

          2f +John Lauderdale; *b* 17 April 1945; *educ* Harrow

          1f *Sarah Margaret; *b* 30 Dec 1937; *m* 1st 24 Feb 1962 (*divorce* 1973) Capt David John Wemyss Anstice, 10th Roy Hus, yr s of V-Adml Sir Edmund Walter Anstice, KCB, and has:

            1g *Robert Christian Edmund; *b* 2 Feb 1963

            2g *David Henry; *b* 21 Jan 1964

            3g *James Richard; *b* 10 April 1965

          1f (cont.) Mrs Sarah Anstice *m* 2nd 1976, as his 2nd w, Michael John Eadon Campbell of Dunstaffnage, 21st hereditary Capt of Dunstaffnage (*d* 1981), of Dunstaffnage Castle, Connel, Argyllshire

          2f *Lavinia Jane [Mrs Patrick Chalmers, The White House, Pyrton, Watlington, Oxon]; *b* 27 Dec 1938; *m* 6 June 1959 Patrick Robert Chalmers (*d* 1982), only s of Robert Arthur Chalmers, OBE, AFC, of Aldbar Castle, Brechin, Angus, and has:

            1g *Patrick Robert Graham; *b* 24 May 1960

            1g *Virginia Jane; *b* 20 May 1961

            2g *Lindsay; *b* 10 Oct 1962

            3g *Nicola Katherine; *b* 6 Jan 1964

          3f *Aileen Susanna [Mrs Colin Gibb, Inshewan, Forfar, Tayside]; *b* 26 March 1941; *m* 23 July 1964 *Colin Roderick Alexander Gibb, yr s of John Gibb, of Glen Isla Ho, by Alyth, Perthshire, and has:

            1g *John Alexander Ogilvy; *b* 24 June 1968

            1g *Shanestra Margaret; *b* 26 April 1966

        1e Dorothy Christian; *b* 15 July 1896

        2e Edith Margaret; *b* 16 June 1901; *m* 25 Feb 1926 Maj-Gen Sir Charles Hamilton Boucher, KBE, CB, DSO and bar, IA (*d* 15 Nov 1951), est s of Lt-Col B H Boucher, DSO, of Guernsey, and had:

          1f *William Scott Hamilton [Maj William Boucher, c/o Lloyds Bank, 6 Pall Mall, London SW1]; *b* 19 March 1932; Maj Roy Dragoons; *m* 8 Aug 1962 *Jane, est dau of R-Adml Bryan Cecil Durant, CB, DSO, DSC (*see* HERTFORD, M), and has:

            1g *Henry Francis; *b* 13 Sept 1963

            1g *Alice Sophia; *b* 5 Sept 1965

          1f *Helen Margaret; *b* 7 Aug 1928; *m* 24 Feb 1950 (*divorce* 1962) Maj Kenneth Mahaffy Hutchison, 6th Gurkha Rifles, and has:

            1g *Charles Kenneth; *b* 28 Feb 1951; *educ* Bredon Sch

            2g *Michael Hugh Mahaffy; *b* 1 Dec 1952; *educ* Wellington

            1g *Caroline Susan; *b* 1 March 1957

         3e Frances Marion; *m* 1st 9 Aug 1927 Noel Urquhart Vidal Scrutton, s of Frederick Scrutton, and had issue; *m* 2nd 1948 Frederic de Havas and *d* 26 June 1952

        4e Helen Prudence; *m* 5 Jan 1927 (*divorce* 1933) Maj Henry Eric Southey Harben, er s of Henry Devenish Harben, of Bayswater, and had:

          1f *Henry Peter Bostock [Henry Harben Esq, Tilham Farm, Baltonsborough, Somerset]; *b* 20 Nov 1927; underwriting memb Lloyd's; *m* 1st 11 April 1953 (*divorce* 1964) Adelaide Anne Elizabeth, dau of Surgn R-Adml Sir Henry Ellis Yeo White, KCVO, and has:

            1g *Henry Jonathan; *b* 3 July 1955

            2g *Edward Ramsay; *b* 10 Feb 1970

            1g *Katherine Adelaide; *b* 11 Jan 1957

            2g *Pandora Jane; *b* 10 March 1959

          1f (cont.) Henry Harben *m* 2nd 23 Feb 1965 *Gillian, dau of Brig John Richard Burne, of Grove Cottage, Chiddingfold, Surrey, and formerly w of — Kernick

          1f *Joanna [Mrs Joanna De La Fuente, Loma de Las Vacas, Frigiliana, Malaga, Spain]; *b* 28 June 1931; took De La FUENTE by deed poll for herself and issue; *m* 29 Aug 1952 George Philip Griggs (*d* 12 Sept 1965), s of John William Griggs, and has:

            1g *Adam John; *b* 8 July 1954

            1g *Philippa Mary; *b* 15 Sept 1956

            2g *Hermione; *b* 22 July 1960

            3g *Caroline Frances; *b* 6 Jan 1962

    2d Robert Christian; *b* 1861; *educ* Harrow and Cambridge; *m* Oct 1907 Olive Zillah (*d* 24 Dec 1957), dau of W W Voss, of Penrice, Qld, and *d* 25 June 1957, having had:

      1e +Alexander Robert, DSC and bar [Cdr Alexander Ramsay DSC and bar, 15 Gault Rd, Belair, SA 5052, Australia]; *b* 12 May 1910; *educ* Harrow; Cdr RNVR WW II; *m* 15 March 1944 *Helen Macgregor, dau of J M Shaw, of Lisburn, Co Antrim, and has:

        1f +Colin Robert [Colin Ramsay Esq, 7 Edwards Bay Rd, Mosman, Sydney, Australia]; *b* 13 March 1945; *m* 1968 *Lyndall Clare Sundstrom, of Gatton, Qld, and has:

          1g +Robert Andrew; *b* 1974

          1g *Susan Belinda; *b* 1976

          2g *Sandra Leigh; *b* 1977

        1f *Celia Grace [Mrs Geoffrey Burnett-Smith, 13 Gloucester Ave, Belair, S Australia]; *b* 7 Aug 1947; *m* 1st 19 Feb 1966 (*divorce* 1974) 10th Viscount Chetwynd (*qv*) and has issue; *m* 2nd 1974 *Geoffrey Burnett-Smith and by him has:

          1g *Angus; *b* 1977

         2f *Alexandra Helen Fleur [Mrs Terrence Tarlinton, 40/10 Lower River Terrace, S Brisbane, Qld 4101, Australia]; *b* 7 Aug 1955; *m* 1st 1977 Iain Lovat Fraser (*ka* 1978); *m* 2nd 1986 *Terrence John Tarlinton

      2e Norman Ian; *b* 10 July 1915; *d* 2 Sept 1934

      3e David Malcolm; *b* 16 July 1924; *educ* Harrow; F/O RAF; *m* 6 Jan 1948 *Joan Esme, dau of Cornelius James Murphy, of S Kensington, and had:

        1f +Alan David; *b* 21 Feb 1951; *educ* Harrow

        2f +James Anthony; *b* 14 Sept 1952; *educ* Harrow

        3f +Oliver Dermot; *b* 14 July 1954; *educ* Harrow

        4f +Malcolm Robert; *b* 19 Nov 1956

      1e Susan Mabel Christian; *m* 1st 2 Aug 1933 G/Capt John Wood Homer, RAF, s of G J W Homer, of Seathwaite, Sheringham, and had a s (*kas* 1944); *m* 2nd 1950 John Patrick Wells (*d* 1 Aug 1964) and *d* 1 Aug 1964

      2e Nora Honor; *m* 20 April 1932 Kenneth Arthur William Johnston, Capt Welsh Gds, yr s of Col William James Johnston, CBE, of Lesmurdie, Elgin, and had:

        1f *Alistair Jevon (Jonathan) [Jonathan Johnston Esq, Wood End, Worplesdon, Surrey]; *b* 14 March 1933; *educ* Marlborough and Trin Coll Cambridge (MB, BChir); *m* 24 Jan 1964 *Alexandra Berdoe, dau of Capt David Walter Groos, DSC, RCN, of Victoria, BC, and Lady Mullens, and has:

          1g *Robert Alasdair Berdoe; *b* 21 May 1965

          2g *Rory William Ramsay; *b* 12 March 1969

          1g *Emma Alexandra; *b* 7 Oct 1966

        2f *Raymond Ian; *b* 1 April 1935; *educ* Marlborough; *m* 12 Sept 1964 *Elizabeth Margaret, er dau of Walter Henry Whigham, of Cobham Court, Bekesbourne, Kent, and has:

          1g *A son; *b* 8 June 1971

          1g *Marietta; *b* 13 Nov 1966

          2g *Katrina Elizabeth; *b* 21 Nov 1968

        3f *Duncan Rodney; *b* 6 May 1939; *educ* Harrow; *m* 3 Aug 1963 *Valerie Ann Everell Softly and has:

          1g *Robert Erle; *b* 14 Jan 1965

          2g *A son; *b* 13 Oct 1966

          1g *Honor Katherine Everell

      3e *Olive Joan [Mrs Eric Boucher, The Hollies, Bredgar, Kent]; *b* 1916; *m* 1948 W/Cdr Eric Comyn Boucher, RAF (*d* 19–), and has:

        1f *Angus Comyn; *b* 15 May 1949

        1f *Esther Dawn; *b* 22 May 1951

2f *Vanessa Jane; b 27 Sept 1954

4e Diana Patricia; d unm 6 June 1952

3d Edward Lauderdale; b 1865; d unm 6 Dec 1941

4d Arthur Douglas, OBE (1919); b 1868; educ Harrow; m 9 July 1914 Winifred (d 1979), dau of W H Turner, of Geraldton, W Australia, and d 1 June 1952, leaving:

1e Michael Douglas; b 9 May 1918; educ Harrow and Peterhouse Cambridge; Maj Seaforth Highrs; m 1949 *Eleanor Kinsell [Mrs Michael Ramsay, Lyford Cay, PO Box N7776, Nassau, Bahamas], of Florida, and d 1983, leaving:

1f +Jonathan Chandler Burnett [Jonathan Ramsay Esq, Aerie, PO Box N52, Nassau, Bahamas]; b 23 April 1950; m 1979 *Keren Jane Livingstone-Leonard and has:

1g +Alexander Douglas Burnett; b 1984

1g *Kia Nikisha Burnett; b 1982

1e *Susan Patricia [Mrs Susan Shaw, 18 Cristowe Rd, London SW6 3QE]; b 21 Oct 1926; m 1st 11 Feb 1950 (divorce 1965) Sir Francis David Somerville Head, 5th Bt (qv), and has issue; m 2nd 10 March 1967 (divorce 1988) Henry Jagoe Shaw, MA, FRCS, s of Dr Benjamin Henry Shaw, of St Mawes, Cornwall

5d Norman; b 1869; 2nd Lt 16th Rifle Bde; ka 3 Sept 1916

6d Wilfred Alexander Bannerman; b 1875; d 7 Jan 1880

1d Nina Mary; d unm 25 Dec 1948

2d Edith Patricia; m 8 Sept 1904 William John Knox, of Kintrockat, Brechin, only s of Maj F B Knox, RA, and d 21 Nov 1943, having had issue

3d Mabel; d unm 1932

2c Alexander; b 3 Dec 1823; drowned at sea 20 Oct 1857

3c Marmaduke; b 3 Oct 1834; drowned in Australia 1865

1c Elizabeth Patricia; m 28 June 1877 Maj Francis Fenwick Laye, KOSB (d 1881), and d 23 Jan 1932

4b Rev Edward Bannerman, LLD; Dean Edinburgh; m 1829 Isabella (d 1858), dau of Robert Cochrane, of Halifax, Nova Scotia, and dsp 26 Dec 1872

5b Marmaduke; Fell and Tutor Jesus Coll Cambridge; dsp

6b William (Sir), KCB; b 27 May 1793; R-Adml; d unm 3 Dec 1871

7b Edwin Hewgill

1b Elizabeth; m 7 April 1808 Alexander Renny Tailyour, of Borrowfield

2b Lauderdale; m 1st 10 July 1832 David Duncan, of Rosemont, Forfarshire; m 2nd 12 July 1837 Sir James Horn Burnett, 10th Bt, of Leys, and d 4 Nov 1888, leaving issue

The 1st Bt's est s,

Sir Alexander Ramsay, 2nd Bt; b 14 Feb 1785; MP Kincardineshire; m 1st 1 Aug 1811 Jane (d Aug 1819), est dau and coheir of Francis Russell, of Blackhall, and had:

1 ALEXANDER (Sir), **3rd Bt**

2 William; b 1814; d 1840

3 Francis; b 20 Nov 1815; Capt RA; m 10 Feb 1848 Georgina Hay (d 10 Jan 1876), 3rd dau of William Foreman Home of Wedderburn (for whose early ancestry see HOME, Bt), and d 25 Dec 1867, leaving, with a dau (d unm):

(1) William Alexander; b 5 Dec 1848; Brig-Gen, Col cmdg 9th Regtl Dist 1st Provisional Regt of Hus and formerly 4th Hus; m 2 Sept 1873 Susan Newcombe (d 18 Dec 1916), dau of William Minchener, of Clontarf, Co Dublin, and d 17 March 1933, leaving:

1a Frank William, CB (1919), CMG (1917), DSO (1916), JP Dorset; b 10 Dec 1875; ADC to Govr Madras 1898–1900, Boer War 1901–02 (medal with five clasps) and WW I (despatches seven times, wounded twice, two brevets), Bde Cdr 1916–18, Div Cdr 1918–19, Cdr 6th Inf Bde Aldershot 1919–23, 20th Ind Inf Bde 1925–26 and 5th Quetta Inf Bde 1926–29, Hon Maj-Gen, Middlesex Regt, Order St Maurice and St Lazarus Italy and Croix de Guerre France; m 5 Dec 1929 Amy Frances (m 3rd 5 Feb 1955 Noel John Dawson, s of Horace Spurling Dawson, and d 8 April 1958), dau of Frederick Scott Hohler, JP, and widow of Lt-Col Arthur St Leger Glyn (see WOLVERTON, B), and dsp 1 Oct 1954

2a Alexander Fitzgerald; b 29 Nov 1880; Maj 22nd Cav, IA, Boer War 1900–02 and WW I (wounded); m 1946 Margaret Jenny (d 1980), dau of William Crichton Slagg, barrister, and d May 1962

3a Bertram Home (Sir), KCB (1940), KBE (1943), MVO (1918), DL (Berwicks); b 20 Jan 1883; served Somaliland 1904 and WW I (despatches twice); cmded: HMS M25 1915–17, HMS Broke 1917–19, HMS Weymouth 1924–25, HMS Danae 1925–27, HMS Kent (Flag Capt and Ch Staff FE Station) 1929–31, HMS Royal Sovereign 1933–35, R-Adml and Ch Staff Home Fleet 1935; WW II: V-Adml Dover 1939–42, Dep Naval C-in-C Expdy Force (invasion N Africa) 1942, Cdr Br Naval Task Force (invasion Sicily) 1943, C-in-C Allied Naval Expdny Force (NW Europe) 1943–45; Ch Cdr US Legn Merit, Chev Legn Hon and Croix de Guerre avec palme France, Order Ushakov 1st Cl USSR, Croix de Guerre Belgium, Offr Crown Italy; m 26 Feb 1929 Helen Margaret (d 17 June 1993), of Bughtrig, Coldstream, Berwickshire, dau of Col Charles Thomson Menzies, JP, of Kames, Berwickshire, and was kas France 2 Jan 1945, leaving:

1b +David Francis [David Ramsay Esq, 74857 South Cove Drive, Indian Wells, CA 92210, USA]; b 1 Oct 1933; educ Eton and Trin Coll Cambridge (BA); m 1st 29 Aug 1963 (divorce 1973) Stacey, dau of G S Rogers and Mrs A E Alleston, and has:

1c +Michael Stuart [Michael Ramsay Esq, 17 Royal Crescent, Bath BA1 2LT]; b 21 June 1964; educ Stanbridge Earls; m 16 Oct 1993 *Beatriz Gonzales Pacho, dau of Jesus Paris Gonzales Trapiello, of Aviles, Asturias, Spain, and has:

1d +William Bertram Alexander; b 26 Jan 1997

2c +James Alexander [James Ramsay Esq, 24 Pembridge Villas, London W11 3EL]; b 1 Nov 1967; educ Eton and London Business School (MBA)

1b (cont.) David Ramsay m 2nd 9 Feb 1989 *Pamela Davidson, of Palm Springs, California

2b +Charles Alexander, CB (1989), OBE (1979) [Maj-Gen Charles Ramsay CB OBE, Bughtrig, Coldstream, Berwicks TD12 4JP]; b 12 Oct 1936; educ Eton and RMA Sandhurst; commnd RSG 1956, Maj Roy Dragoon Gds (formerly Scots Greys), Adj Ayrshire Yeo (TA) 1961–63, Cmd and Staff Coll Canada 1967–68, Gen Staff, HQ Army Strategic Cmd 1968–70, Mil Assist to V-Ch Def Staff 1974–77, cmded Roy Scots Dragoon Gds 1977–79 (Col 1992–), Col Gen Staff MOD 1979–80, Cdr 12th Armoured Bde BAOR 1980–82, Dep Dir Mil Ops MOD 1983–84, GOC E Dist 1984–87, Dir Gen Army Orgn and TA 1987–89, dir: John Menzies 1990– and Potomac Hldgs Inc, USA, chm Eagle Enterprises, Bermuda, 1991– and Cockburns of Leith 1992–, ch exec Caledonian Eagle 1992–, memb Roy Co Archers; m 1 Aug 1967 *Hon Mary Margaret Hastings MacAndrew, yr dau of 1st Baron MacAndrew (qv), and has:

1c +William Bertram; b 22 Feb 1969; educ Eton, Newcastle U (BA) and RMA Sandhurst; commnd Roy Scots Dragoon Gds 1992; m 5 July 1997 *Natasha Alexandra, dau of Lt-Col Dudley de Chair, of Tulloch, Inverness-shire, and Mrs Edward Harding-Newman, of Arabella, Ross-shire

2c +Charles Burnett; b 10 Sept 1981; educ Eton

1c *Rowena Cecilia; b 22 Nov 1973; educ North Foreland Lodge and Edinburgh U (BA)

2c *Camilla Georgina; b 22 Jan 1976; educ North Foreland Lodge and U of Northumbria

1a Georgina Frances; m 6 Dec 1900 Col Henry Edward Garstin, DSO (d 10 Jan 1950), RA , and d 12 Dec 1961, leaving issue

2a Elizabeth Grace; m 1st 1 Oct 1912 Capt Meyricke Entwisle Lloyd, Roy Welch Fus (d of wounds when POW Germany 24 Oct 1914), of Dolobran, Isaf, Montgomeryshire, and had issue; m 2nd 8 Jan 1919 Maj Edward Reginald Kearsley, DSO, JP, DL, Roy Welsh Fus, of Stapeley, Overton-on-Dee, Denbighs, s of Maj Robert Wilson Kearsley, 5th Dragoon Gds, of Belgravia, and d 27 May 1966, leaving further issue

(2) Francis Farquharson; b 28 July 1855; Capt Gordon Highrs; m 15 March 1895 Marianne Louisa (d 11 Oct 1903), dau of Maj Philip J Stapleton Barry, RE, and dsp 7 April 1898

1 Mary; m 1st 10 Aug 1837 Rev Bruges Lambert (d May 1843), of Misterton, Somerset; m 2nd 25 Feb 1845 John Sparkes, of Crewkerne, Somerset, and d 5 Jan 1890 aged 77

2 Elizabeth; m 1st 6 June 1843 John Carr (d 24 Aug 1856), 2nd s of John Carr, JP, DL, of Dunston Hill, Co Durham, and Hedgeley, Northumberland; m 2nd 13 June 1860 Charles Murray Barstow (d 1885) and d 14 Feb 1887

Sir Alexander m 2nd 26 Dec 1822 Elizabeth (d 12 Sept 1852), 2nd dau of 1st Baron Panmure of Brechin and Navar (see DALHOUSIE, E), and d 26 April 1852, leaving:

4 Fox Maule; b 24 March 1824; Capt 56th Regt; d 15 March 1860

5 Edward Bannerman; b 12 Oct 1826; joined Madras Army 1844 (Capt 1856, Maj 1862, Lt-Col 1879, Col 1875, Maj-Gen 1876), served Turkish Contingent 1865; d unm 26 Dec 1883

6 George Dalhousie (Sir), CB (1882); b 23 May 1828; War Office 1846–93, ktd 1900, author: The Panmure Papers; m 23 April 1864 Eleanor Julia Charteris (d 15 March 1918), dau of John Crawfurd, FRS, Govr Singapore, and d 16 Jan 1920, having had:

(1) Alexander Panmure Oswald; b 15 April 1867; barrister; d 15 Feb 1897

(1) Elizabeth Edith; m 11 Jan 1894 Rev Barton Reginald Vaughan Mills (d 21 Jan 1932), Vicar Bude Haven, and d 12 Dec 1945, leaving issue

7 Marmaduke; b 10 March 1837; Col Bengal Army; m 14 April 1858 Anna Maria (d 9 May 1905), dau of Lt-Gen James Charles Innes, BSc, and d 23 Jan 1893, leaving, with a dau (d unm):

(1) Marmaduke; b 18 Feb 1859; dsp

(2) Fox Maule; b 3 April 1860; dsp

(3) Alexander Charles Marquis; b 27 July 1866; T/Lt ASC; m 10 Jan 1893 Mary Amelia (m 2nd 19 Oct 1916 Maj Charles Bertram Templer), dau of Alfred John Elkington, of Chelsea, and d 15 Dec 1914

3 Patricia; m 14 May 1872, as his 3rd w, Capt John de Courcy Andrew Agnew, RN (see AGNEW, Bt, of Lochnaw), and dsp 15 July 1910

4 Christina; m 14 Feb 1859 Col Charles Elliot, CB, Madras Army, yst s of James Elliot, of Wolfelee, and d 13 March 1873

5 Georgina Harvey; m 20 April 1861 Lt-Gen Sir Robert John Hay, KCB, and d 3 Jan 1917, leaving issue (see TWEEDDALE, M)

The 2nd Bt's est s,

Sir Alexander Ramsay, 3rd Bt; b 26 May 1813; MP Rochdale; m 29 Dec 1835 Ellen Matilda (d 6 May 1880), est dau of John Smith Entwisle, of Foxholes, Lancs, and d 3 March 1875, having had:

1 ALEXANDER ENTWISLE (Sir), **4th Bt**

2 Hugh Francis; b 23 Nov 1838; m 24 Feb 1868 Jane Maria (d 22 June 1935), dau of Gen Frederick Harvey Sandys, Bengal Army, and d 22 May 1890, leaving:

(1) Hugh Entwisle; b 13 Jan 1871; educ Cheltenham; m 10 Dec 1901 Elsie Lavater (d 9 March 1960), dau of William Cox, and d 20 Dec 1960, having had:

1a Alexander Hugh; b 27 March 1905; educ Cheltenham; m 30 Jan 1937 Ethel Charlotte (d 1993), of Hamilton, NZ, dau of Albert Upton, of Waimai, NZ, and d 5 Nov 1962, leaving:

1b *Patricia Marion [Mrs Carl Watson-Gandy, 3 South Lodge, Stanton Fitzwarren, Wilts SN6 7 SF]; b 26 April 1945; m 22 July 1976 *Carl Donald Tyndale Watson-Gandy, PhD, and has:

1c *Hugh James Ramsay; b 18 Jan 1981

1c *(Jane) Vere; b 4 Aug 1979

2b *Eleanor Margaret [Mrs Serge Artemiev, 12 Stansell St, Shannon, Levin, New Zealand]; b 26 Nov 1949; m 8 Jan 1994 *Serge Artemiev

2a John Entwisle; b 24 Jan 1908; m 11 Jan 1937 Elizabeth Frances (m 2nd N H King and d 19–), dau of A H Crichton, of BC, Canada, and was kas 16 Dec 1941, leaving:

1b +Ian Alexander [Ian Ramsay Esq, 62 Lemington Rd, Westmere, Auckland, New Zealand]; b 21 Feb 1939; LLB (NZ), BCL Oxford; m 1st 29 June 1963 (divorce 1988) Rosalind Sheila, only dau of Frederick Ernest Tolliss, of Hildenborough, Kent, and adopted:

    *Norman Francis; b 1967

    *Nicholas John; b 1968

1b (cont.) Ian Ramsay m 2nd 1988 *Lorraine Gillian Kelly and by her has:

    1c *Alexandra Grace; b 1988

1a *Irene Beatrice; b 7 Dec 1902; m 21 Sept 1929 Ivor George Sullivan (d 28 Sept 1955), s of Arthur George Sullivan, and has:

    1b *Ramsay Wakeford [Ramsay Sullivan Esq, 4460 Cotton Wood Drive, Burlington, Ontario, Canada]; b 9 July 1933; educ Millfield and Loughborough; m 1957 *Eleanor Mary, dau of William Henry Edward Thorpe, of Heanor, Derbys, and has:

        1c *Richard Andrew Ramsay; b 1960

        1c *Fiona Clare; b 1962

        2c *Jennifer Mary; b 1965

    1b *Patricia Berenice [Mrs Michael Mallett, 2 Lansdowne Circus, Leamington Spa, Warwicks]; b 7 Nov 1934; ARCA; m 3 June 1961 *Prof Michael Edward Mallett, DPhil, s of Edward Campbell Mallett, of Gamblesby, Cumberland, and has:

        1c *Lucien Christian Ramsay; b 1976

        2c *Cyprian Casper Alexander; b 1978

(2) Noel Bannerman; b 25 Dec 1875; m 16 Oct 1905 Edith Katharine (d 1962), dau of Francis Johnson, MD, and d 1958, having had:

    1a Noel Entwisle Burnett; b 13 March 1907; Lt RNVR WW II 1939–42 (despatches); m 18 June 1932 *Phyllis Agnes [Mrs Ronald Fielder, 7 Carlton Court, Carlton Rd, Harpenden, Herts AL5 4SY] (m 2nd 1949 Lt-Col Eric T Cuthbert, E Lancs Regt (d 1974); m 3rd 1982 Ronald George Fielder, FICS (d 1997)), dau of Arthur H Kilner, and was ka 19 Aug 1942, leaving:

        1b +Alan Burnett (Rev) [The Rev Canon Alan Ramsay, St Marks Vicarage, Locks Lane, Mitcham, Surrey CR4 2JX]; b 25 May 1934; educ Christ's Hosp and King's Coll London (AKC); Deacon 1963, Priest 1964; m 11 Feb 1967 *Elizabeth, dau of Norman Marsh, and has:

            1c +Christopher; b 27 May 1968

            2c +Matthew John; b 16 Dec 1971

            3c +Francis; b 16 April 1973

            1c *Rachel; b 16 Oct 1969

        2b Duncan Soutter Burnett; b 9 April 1937; m 2 June 1967 *Carole Anne [Mrs Duncan Ramsay, 17 Lambourn Gdns, Harpenden, Herts AL5 4DQ], dau of Dennis H Briars, and d 1988, leaving:

            1c +Benjamin Noel; b 17 April 1969

            2c +Daniel Bruce; b 1971

            1c *Helen Jayne; b 1973

    2a Francis Alexander Burnett; b 30 March 1921; P/O RAF WW II; ka 21 April 1940

    1a *Edith Rosemary Patricia Burnett [Mrs James Gilbert, Rigden's Farm, Leigh, nr Reigate, Surrey; 2969 Kalakaua Ave, Honolulu, Hawaii 96815, USA]; b 7 July 1915; m 1st 20 Jan 1937 Thomas Martin Homfray Pardoe (ka Dec 1941), only s of Col Pardoe, of Buxted, Sussex, and has:

        1b *Hermione Ann Felicity; b 31 Dec 1938; m 4 July 1968 *Robert Kyle Pattinson

    1a (cont.) Mrs Thomas Pardoe m 2nd 14 April 1943 Maj Thomas Brian Carey, RA (d 1970), and by him has:

        1b *Shane Peter; b 18 May 1944; educ Sherborne

        2b *Peter Brian Ramsay; b 30 April 1948; educ Winchester and Trin Coll Oxford

    1a (cont.) Mrs Thomas Carey m 3rd 1975 *Prof James Carl Gilbert, of Hawaii U

(1) Rhoda Beatrice; m 1901 Harold John Craig and had issue

(2) Sybil; m 28 Jan 1896 Frank Cook, s of Arthur Crozier Cook, and had issue

(3) Olive; m 10 Dec 1896 Harry Geary Gardner, OBE, s of Henry J Gardner, of HM's Customs, and had issue

3 John, JP (Hants); b 30 June 1843; Capt RE; m 5 Sept 1876 Florence Mary, JP (d 19 March 1936), only child of Richard J Hilton, of Preston Ho, Faversham, and d 25 Feb 1913, leaving:

    (1) Hilton Alexander, DSO (1916); b 20 Dec 1878; Lt-Col RGA WW I (despatches); d unm 19 Sept 1946

    (2) Norman; b 25 April 1880; Lt 4th Dragoon Gds, formerly RFA, Boer War 1901–02 (despatches) and WW I; ka 4 Nov 1914

    (3) John Richard; b 15 Nov 1883; Maj RFA WW I; ka 6 Jan 1917

    (1) Ethel, MBE (1918); b 1882; m 21 Sept 1906 Maj William Thompson Armitage, RA, s of Rev Arthur Armitage

    (2) Hilda; b 1885; m 1 Jan 1912 Gordon Eugene Spinney, only s of Frank Spinney, of Leamington Spa, and had:

        1a *David John; b Oct 1912

        2a *Martin Giles; b 1916

        1a *Juliet Ethel; b 1914

    (3) Evelyn; b 1887; m 16 Sept 1909 Cuthbert Radcliffe (d 18 April 1924), yst s of Alfred Radcliffe, of Ramsgate, and had:

        1a *Richard; b 1912

        2a *Norman; b 1914

        3a *Michael; b 1918

4 Bertin; b 13 Oct 1850; m 30 June 1881 Kate Graveraet (d 1918), dau of Dr Daniel Webster King, of Green Bay, Wisconsin, and d 23 June 1907, having had:

    (1) Hallie Ellen; m 1st 17 Oct 1907 Rolla Barnum Watson (d 1922), of New York, and had issue; m 2nd March 1929 Gordon N Shaver, KC

    (2) Ethel Katherine; m 18 July 1912 Hugh Park, of Cobalt, Ontario, Canada, and had issue

1 Ellen Augusta; m 2 Dec 1885 Ernest de S Hamilton Browne, s of Maj George Browne, DL, of Comber Ho, Co Londonderry

---

The 3rd Bt's est s,

Sir Alexander Entwisle Ramsay, 4th Bt, JP, DL; b 14 Jan 1837; m 1st 22 Jan 1863 Octavia (d 1 Oct 1877), yst dau of Thomas Haigh, of Elm Hall, nr Liverpool, and had:

    1 Alexander Haigh; b 1 Jan 1866; d 30 Dec 1870

    2 HERBERT (Sir), **5th Bt**

    3 Arthur; b 9 Jan 1871; m 16 Aug 1899 Marion, yst dau of Van Dyke Hoskinson, of Centralia, USA; drowned Grand Rapids, USA, 6 April 1904

    1 Ellen Georgina; m 6 Sept 1893 Maj Arthur Patrick Bateman-Champain, MVO 3rd Gurkha Rifles, (dsp 7 Oct 1907), est s of Col Sir John Bateman-Champain, KCMG, and d 18 Aug 1940

    2 Nora Mabel; d unm 7 July 1953

    3 Florence Augusta; m 29 April 1919 John Bertie Norreys Entwisle (d 20 April 1945), of Kilworth Ho, Rugby, and d 17 Jan 1953

Sir Alexander m 2nd 10 Aug 1880 Caroline Charlotte (d 10 July 1913), yst dau of Thomas James Ireland, of Owsden Hall, Suffolk, and d 1 Oct 1902, having by her had:

    4 Gilbert Ireland; b 31 May 1881; 2nd Lt RGA; drowned Milford Haven 15 Dec 1900

The 4th Bt's est surv s,

Sir Herbert Ramsay, 5th Bt; b 6 Feb 1868; m 3 Jan 1902 Mabel (d 7 July 1939), est dau of William Joseph Hutchinson, of Aldingham, Winton, Australia, and d 22 May 1924, leaving:

    1 ALEXANDER BURNETT (Sir), **6th Bt**

    2 Herbert William Alexander; b 26 May 1907; m 28 March 1936 *Bessie Billingsley [Mrs Herbert Ramsay, 29 Brae St, Inverell, NSW, Australia], yst dau of Dr Wilfred Billingsley Dight, of Sydney, NSW, and d 1987, leaving:

        (1) +William Macalister; b Sept 1939; m 1967 *Susan Thornton, dau of R T Parkinson, of Camla, Wellington, and has:

            1a +Timothy William; b 1969

            2a +William Ross; b 1971

            1a *Jennifer Susan; b 1962

        (1) *Elizabeth Barton [Mrs Peter Gough, 8 Crane Place, Moree, NSW, Australia]; b Feb 1945; m 1966 *Peter Angus Gough and has:

            1a *Simon John; b 1972

            1a *Phillipa Anne [Mrs Stephen Smith, 7 Myall Place, Moree, NSW, Australia]; b 1968; m 1989 *Stephen John Smith and has:

                1b *Nicola Elizabeth Winter; b 1994

            2a *Sandra Elizabeth; b 1969

        (2) *Roslyn Nora; b June 1946; m 1st 1967 Geoffrey Robert Burcham; m 2nd 1987 *Keith Donald Glasson and by her 1st husb has:

            1a *David William; b 1969

            1a *Jacqueline Judith; b 1971

            2a *Georgina Elizabeth; b 1979

    1 Nora Marjorie; m 5 Sept 1928 Brig Adrian Bazely Barltrop, OBE, MC, 3rd Queen Alexandra's Own Gurkha Rifles, 3rd s of Rev Arthur Henry Barltrop, and had issue

    2 *Constance Agnes; b 1 Oct 1912; m 25 June 1938 Arthur Thomas Baldwin (d 1977), s of Arthur Baldwin, and has:

        (1) *Ross Ramsay; b 1943; m 1971 *Susan Joan, dau of S R Oldham, of Matta Mia, Wagga Wagga, NSW, and has:

            1a *Angus Oldham; b 1972

            2a *Richard Arthur; b 1973

        (2) *Malcolm Ramsay [Malcolm Baldwin, Brisendon Ave, Collaroy, NSW, Australia]; b 1946

        (1) *Janet Mabel [Mrs John Francis,Tara, Mumbil, NSW 2820, Australia]; b 1941; m 1962 *John Lyle Francis, s of G H Francis, and has:

            1a *Hubert Thomas Lyle; b 1967

            1a *Regina Constance; b 1965

The 5th Bt's er s,

Sir Alexander Burnett Ramsay, 6th Bt; b 26 March 1903; m 5 Sept 1935 Isabel Ellice, est dau of Arthur William Whitney, of Waugoolla, Woodstock, NSW, Australia, and d 25 Sept 1965, leaving:

    1 Sir ALEXANDER WILLIAM BURNETT RAMSAY, **7th and present Bt**

    1*Enid Ellice [Mrs Reginald Capel, Calool, Manilla, NSW, Australia]; b 30 March 1937; m 26 Sept 1961 *Reginald Geoffrey Capel, s of R Capel, of Tamworth, NSW, and has:

        (1) *Peter Geoffrey; b 10 April 1963; m 1992 *Louise Johnston

        (1) *Diana Enid; b 9 March 1965; m 1994 *Alexander William Campbell Martin, of Jamestown, S Australia

    2 *Patricia Thirza [Mrs Anthony McAlary, Milawa, Warren, NSW, Australia]; b 15 Feb 1940; m 26 April 1965 *Anthony Osborne McAlary, s of Victor McAlary, and has:

        (1) *Anthony Alexander; b 1970

        (1) *Anna; b 29 Nov 1968

RAMSAY OF CARTVALE

Creation: B. (LP, UK) Aug 1996.

THE BARONESS RAMSAY OF CARTVALE, of Langside, City of Glasgow (Margaret (Meta) Mildred Ramsay) [The Rt Hon The Baroness Ramsay of Cartvale, House of Lords, London SW1A 0PW]; *b* 12 July 1936; *educ* Hutchesons' Girls' GS, Glasgow U (Pres Students' Rep Cncl 1958–59) and Inst Internat Studies Geneva; Pres Scottish Union of Students 1959–60, Assoc Sec Europe Co-ordinating Secretariat Nat Unions Students Netherlands 1960–63, manager Fund for Internat Student Co-opn 1963–67, FCO 1969–91: Cnsllr 1987–91, For Policy Advsr Ldr Oppn 1992–94, Special Advsr Shadow Industry Sec 1994–95, Baroness-in-Waiting (Govt Whip) 1998–, Chm Atlantic Cncl to 1998

Lineage: ALEXANDER RAMSAY; *m* Sheila Jackson and had:

MARGARET MILDRED, *cr* a **Baroness**

RAMSAY-FAIRFAX-LUCY

Arms: Quarterly, 1st and 4th, gu. semée of cross-crosslets, three lucies hauriant arg., a canton of the last (for LUCY); 2nd, grand quarter counterquartered, 1st and 4th, arg. three bars gemel sa., surmounted of a lion rampant gu., armed and langued az. (for FAIRFAX); 2nd, party per pale arg. and or an eagle displayed sa., armed, beaked and membered gu. (for RAMSAY); 3rd, counterquartered, 1st and 4th, az. a branch of palm between three fleurs-de-lys or; 2nd and 3rd, gu. three annulets or, stoned ppr.; in the centre of these quarters a crescent or (for MONTGOMERIE); 3rd, gu. three bars or, on a bend ermine a sphinx between the badge of the Royal Portugese Order of the Tower and Sword and the Gold medal presented to Col John Cameron of Fassifern by the Sultan of Turkey for his service in Egypt, on a chief embattled a representation of the town of Aire in France, all ppr. (for CAMERON of Fassifern). **Crests:** 1 Dexter, issuing from a ducal coronet gu. a boar's head arg., gutté-de-poix, between two wings sa. billetté or, the neck charged with a cross-crosslet also sa. (for LUCY); 2 sinister, a lion passant guardant ppr. (for FAIRFAX). **Mottoes:** 1 (dexter) By truth and diligence, 2 (sinister) *Fare fac* ('Deal fairly').
Creation: Bt. (UK) 14 March 1836.

SIR EDMUND JOHN WILLIAM HUGH RAMSAY-FAIRFAX-LUCY, 6TH BT, of The Holmes, Co Roxburgh [Sir Edmund Ramsay-Fairfax-Lucy Bt, Charlecote Park, Warwicks CV35 9ER]; *b* 4 May 1945; *s f* 1974; *educ* Eton, City and Guilds of London Art Sch, Roy Academy Schs of Art; painter; *m* 1st 11 Sept 1974 (*divorce* 19–) Sylvia, dau of W Graeme Ogden, of The Old Manor, Rudge, Somerset; *m* 2nd 1986 (*divorce* 1989), as her 1st husb, Lady Lucinda Lambton (*see* DURHAM, E; she *m* subsequently Sir Peregrine Worsthorne, *see* LINDSEY and ABINGDON, E); *m* 3rd 1994 *Erica, dau of Warren Loane, of Enniskillen, Co Fermanagh, and by her has:

1 +PATRICK SAMUEL THOMAS FULKE; *b* 3 April 1995

Lineage (of Fairfax): V-Adml Sir WILLIAM GEORGE FAIRFAX of the Red (s of Joseph Fairfax, of Windlesham, Surrey, gs of Joseph Fairfax, of Saxton, Yorks, allegedly kin to the Lords Fairfax; *see* FAIRFAX OF CAMERON, L); *b* 1738; served RN 63 years (present taking of Quebec 1759, cmded HMS *Alert* 1778 when took *Le Coureur*, Flag Capt to Lord Duncan aboard HMS *Venerable* at Battle of Camperdown 11 Oct 1797, for which KB and Col RM); *m* 1st 1767 Hannah (*dsp* 1770), dau of Rev Robert Spears; *m* 2nd 1772 —, dau of Samuel Charters, Slr Customs Scotland, and *d* 7 Nov 1813, having by her had, with other issue, including a dau (Mary, *m* 1st 28 June 1804 Samuel Greig, Capt and Commr Russian Navy, s of Sir Samuel Greig, High Adml Russia, *m* 2nd William Somerville):

Sir Henry Fairfax, 1st Bt (UK), so *cr* 14 March 1836 in consideration of his f's naval services; *b* 3 Feb 1790; served Army 1808–44 (with 95th (Rifle Bde) Peninsula War 1812–13, promoted to a Co 85th LI, Col 1841); *m* 1st Jan 1830 Archibald Montgomerie (*d* 13 July 1844), 3rd dau and eventually heiress of Thomas WILLIAMSON later WILLIAMSON RAMSAY, of Lixmount, Co Edinburgh, and Maxton, Roxburghshire, by Elizabeth, dau and eventual coheir of Robert Ramsay of Camno and Arthurstown, Forfarshire, by Jean, only dau and eventual heiress of William Montgomerie, descended from 1st Earl of Eglinto(u)n (*see* EGLINTON and WINTON, E); *m* 2nd 19 Dec 1851 Sarah (*dsp* 23 June 1879), est dau of William Astell, MP Beds, and by his 1st w had:

1 WILLIAM GEORGE HERBERT TAYLOR (Sir), **2nd Bt**

2 Thomas Edward; *b* 1832; barrister, Bengal CS; *d* 5 Oct 1882

3 Henry (Sir), Adml, KCB, JP Roxburghshire, DL; C-in-C Australian Station 1887–89, 2nd Naval Ld Admlty 1889–92, V-Adml cmdg Channel Sqdn 1892–94, C-in-C Devonport 1899–1900, Naval ADC to HM QUEEN VICTORIA; *m* 25 April 1872 Harriet (*d* 17 Sept 1925), yst dau of Sir David Kinloch, 9th Bt, of Gilmerton (*qv*), and *dsp* 20 March 1900

1 Elizabeth Mary Somerville; *m* 1st 17 Sept 1861 James Liebig Gregory (*d* 5 May 1863); *m* 2nd 14 Aug 1884 Col William Marshall Cochrane (*see* DUNDONALD, E) and *d* 6 Nov 1917

Sir HENRY *d* 3 Feb 1860; his est s,

Sir WILLIAM GEORGE HERBERT TAYLOR FAIRFAX later RAMSAY-FAIRFAX (on inheriting 1876 estate of his aunt, Miss Williamson-Ramsay of Maxton), **2nd Bt**, JP, DL Roxburghs; *b* 15 March 1831; Col Crimea, present Sebastopol (medal and clasp and Turkish medal); *m* 17 Sept 1868 Mary Ann Pawson Hargrave (*d* 1 Sept 1924), only dau of William John Pawson, of Shawdon Hall, Northumberland, and had:

1 HENRY WILLIAM (Sir), **3rd Bt**

2 Archibald Montgomerie; *b* 16 Dec 1874; *d* 26 Feb 1878

3 William George Astell, CMG (1918), DSO (1916); *b* 29 July 1876; Cdr RN (Emergency List), Lt-Col, fndr Divorce Law Reform Assoc 1906, Capt 30th Bn Imp Yeo Boer War 1902 (medal with clasps), with Abyssinian Army Somaliland 1903–04 (medal with clasps), WW I at sea RN Div and Tank Corps (T/Brig-Gen and Bde Cdr 1918, despatches four times), Bronze Medal of Roy Humane Soc; *m* 12 Jan 1909 Lilian Kate (*d* 13 June 1957), est dau of Henry Rich, of Malmesbury, Wilts, and *d* 20 Nov 1946, leaving:

(1) John William; *b* 14 Nov 1909; *educ* Gonville and Caius Coll Cambridge (BA 1931); Lt-Col Army Catering Corps WW II, Sec Aylesford Priory 1957–58, House Manager Roy Cwlth Soc's HQ London 1958–61; *m* 1st 22 Nov 1947 (*annulled* 1956) Mrs Audrey Scott-Gibson, yr dau of Rev Lewis Richardson, of Belmont, Axminster, Devon; *m* 2nd 3 June 1964 Mary Dolores (*d* 27 Oct 1978), only dau of Daniel Carroll, of Dublin, by Elizabeth, sis of Sir Pierce Lacy, 1st Bt (*qv*)

(2) +Victor George Hargrave, DSC [Lt-Cdr Victor Ramsay-Fairfax DSC RN, 73 High St, Lavenham, Suffolk CO10 9PT]; *b* 13 June 1912; Lt-Cdr RN WW II (despatches); *m* 14 Sept 1939 Christian Geraldine Mary (*d* 28 April 1967), only child of Lt-Col Frederick Arthur Irby (*see* BOSTON, B), and has:

1a +Victor Ferdinand Desmond; *b* 1 Aug 1944; *educ* Eton

1a *Pepita Christian; *b* 3 Aug 1942; *m* 29 Oct 1976 *Thom Noble

(1) Joan; *b* 15 March 1906; *m* 1st 16 Feb 1935 (*divorce* 1956, resumed maiden name) Maj Norman Ramsay, OBE, IA; *m* 2nd 1 April 1959 A/Cdre Cyril Douglas Adams, CB, OBE, s of L L Adams, of Penn Hall, Parkstone, Dorset, and by her 1st husb had:

1a *Simon John Fairfax [Simon Ramsay Esq, Red House Farm, East Green, Suffolk]; *b* 4 Jan 1938; *educ* Stowe; *m* 11 June 1960 *Dawn, 2nd dau of Eric Burrell, slr, of Danbury, Essex, and has:

1b *Julia Diana; *b* 28 March 1962

2b *Lesley Fiona; *b* 10 Jan 1964

2a *Hamish Francis; *b* 16 July 1942; *educ* Stowe

1 Frances Mary Somerville; *d* unm 14 Sept 1952

2 Elizabeth Jane; *d* unm 5 June 1899

Sir WILLIAM *d* 19 Jan 1902; his est s,

Sir HENRY WILLIAM FAIRFAX later RAMSAY-FAIRFAX later still RAMSAY-FAIRFAX-LUCY (roy licence 26 Aug 1892) later still CAMERON-RAMSAY-FAIRFAX-LUCY (roy licence 25 Feb 1921), **3rd Bt**, CB, JP and DL Roxburghshire and Warwicks; *b* 25 Sept 1870; CA Warwicks, memb Roxburghs CC, Chm Warwicks TA&AFA, Maj 2nd Life Gds, Hon Col 48th Div Train RASC (T), Assist Priv Sec to Fin Sec Treasury 1895–97, Priv Sec to Slr-Gen Ireland 1898–1900, served Boer War 1900 (medal with two clasps), Staff Lt War Office 1901, barrister Middle Temple 1902, Inspr QMG's servs HQ Scottish Cmd 1915–18, Pres Civilian Advsy Bd 4th Army 1919; *m* 1st 26 July 1892 Ada Christina (*d* 17 Dec 1943), dau and heiress of Henry Spencer Lucy, of Charlecote, Warwicks (*see* **Lineage (of Lucy)** below); *m* 2nd 5 Aug 1944 Norah, yst dau of John Hugh Munro Mackenzie, OBE, of Mornish, Isle of Mull, and *d* 20 Aug 1944, having by his 1st w had:

1 William George Thomas Spencer; *b* 7 April 1895; *d* 20 May 1910

2 **Sir Henry Montgomerie Cameron-Ramsay-Fairfax-Lucy, 4th Bt**, MC, DL Warwicks; *b* 20 Oct 1896; *educ* Wellington and RMC Sandhurst; Capt Argyll and Sutherland Highrs, Capt Rifle Bde, WW I (despatches thrice), Iraq 1920–21 and WW II 1940–45 Intell Dept, E Africa Forces and Kenya Def Force; *d* unm 22 Dec 1965

3 BRIAN FULKE (Sir), **5th Bt**

4 Ewen Aylmer Robert; *b* 31 Dec 1899; *educ* Eton, RMC Sandhurst and Trin Coll Cambridge (MA); barrister Middle Temple 1935, Cert Christian Theology Cambridge U 1952, Clerk Merchant Taylors' Co 1937–48, Capt 5th City London Regt TA, Lt Rifle Bde, WW I in Mesopotamia 1919, Malabar 1921 and WW II 1939–40 as GSO (invalided), ADC to GOC Madras Dist 1920–22, author: *Nature of Man*, *Judge Not* (1953) and *Forbidden Freedom* (1959); *m* 4 March 1930 Margaret Westall (*d* 1994), only dau of Sir John Westall King, 2nd Bt, of Campsie (*qv*), and *d* 12 July 1969, leaving:

(1) +Duncan [Duncan Cameron-Ramsay-Fairfax-Lucy Esq, The Malt House, Charlecote, Warwicks CV35 9EW]; *b* 18 Sept 1932; *educ* Eton; FCA; *m* 26 Sept 1964 *Janet Barclay, only dau of Patrick Angus Barclay Niven, of Malt Cottage, Charlecote, and has:

1a +Spencer Angus James; *b* 9 May 1966

1a *Anna Margaret Barclay; *b* 1 Feb 1969

(2) +Robin Spencer; *b* 19 April 1937; *educ* Eton

(1) *Jennifer Frances; *b* 22 Dec 1935; *m* 20 Oct 1962 (Ronald) Ian Talbot Cromartie, CMG (*d* 1987), only s of Ronald Duncan Cromartie, of Peveril Ho, Swanage, Dorset, and has:

   1a *Alan Duncan Talbot; *b* 5 Dec 1964

   2a *David Francis Ian; *b* 7 May 1970

   1a *Selina Margaret Lucy; *b* 27 July 1967

(2) *Christina Alison; *b* 10 Jan 1943; *m* 5 Dec 1964 *John Anthony Chandley Pugh, FCA, yr s of Prof Leslie Penrhys Pugh, CBE, of Magdalene Coll Cambridge, and has:

   1a *Jonathan Chandley; *b* 26 Sept 1966

   1a *Rosanna Lucy; *b* 15 July 1968

   2a *Martha Elizabeth; *b* 1971

1 Alianore Mary Christina; MRCS and LRCP 1943

2 Sybil Radegunde Joyce (twin with Spencer); *d* unm 4 Jan 1957

3 Cecily Alys; *b* 14 Dec 1901; *d* 24 Feb 1902

The 4th Bt's bro,

Sir Brian Fulke Cameron-Ramsay-Fairfax-Lucy, 5th Bt; *b* 18 Dec 1898; *educ* Eton; Maj Cameron Highrs (Adj 1928–31) WW I (wounded), WW II F/Lt ATC 1940–42, ADC to GOC Madras Dist 1922–25 and Ld HC Ch Scotland 1931–34, Steward Nat Greyhound Racing Club 1928–33, children's author: *Horses in the Valley* and *The Children of the House*; *m* 29 July 1933 Alice Caroline Helen Buchan (*d* 1993), only dau of 1st Baron Tweedsmuir (*qv*), and *d* 21 Jan 1974, leaving:

1 Sir EDMUND JOHN WILLIAM HUGH RAMSAY-FAIRFAX-LUCY, **6th and present Bt**

   1 *(Mary Caroline Alys) Emma; *b* 9 Sept 1946; *m* 1st 16 Dec 1967 James Empson Scott, MA, MB, BCh, FRCS, s of James Christopher Scott, FRCS, of The Court House, Kidlington, Oxon; *m* 2nd, as his 2nd w, James Louis Lambe (*see* 1970 edn CORBET, Bt) and by her 1st husb has:

     (1) *Sophie Katherina Rosie; *b* 1970

     (2) *Charlotte Christina Bianca; *b* 1974

Lineage (of Lucy): THURSTANE de CHARLECOTE, allegedly yr s of Thurstane de Montfort, of Beldesert, Warwicks, *temp* RICHARD I; had:

Sir WALTER de CHARLECOTE; granted by Henry de Montfort the Manor of Charlecote (confirmed by RICHARD I); had:

Sir WILLIAM de LUCY; built and endowed Thelsford Priory, Warwicks; *m* Cecilia de Lucy, dau of the feudal Baron of Cockermouth, Cumberland, and *d c* 1247; ancestor of:

Sir THOMAS LUCY, of Charlecote; MP Warwicks 1405; retainer to JOHN OF GAUNT, s of EDWARD III; had:

WILLIAM LUCY, of Charlecote; had:

Sir WILLIAM LUCY, of Charlecote; *d* 1492, leaving:

EDMUND LUCY, of Charlecote; *b* 1464; cmd troops for HENRY VII Battle of Stoke 1487; *m* 1st Elizabeth (*dsp*), dau and heir of Walter Tramsington; *m* 2nd Jane, dau of Richard Ludlow, and *d* by 19 May 1498, leaving an est s:

Sir THOMAS LUCY, of Charlecote; Server to HENRY VIII; *m* Elizabeth, dau of Richard Empson and widow of George Catesby, of Ashby St Ledgers, Northants, and *d* 1525, leaving, with three daus (including Barbara, *m* Richard Tracy; *see* SUDELEY, B) and two sons (Thomas, on whom his f settled the Manor of Cleybrooke, Lincs; Edmund, inherited Manors of Beckering and Sharpenhoe):

WILLIAM LUCY, of Charlecote; *m* Anne, dau of Richard Fermor (*see* HESKETH, B), and *d* 1551, leaving an est s:

Sir THOMAS LUCY; MP Warwicks 1584; rebuilt *c* 1558 Charlecote (it was subsequently almost entirely remodelled in the 19th century and made over to the National Trust 1946); prosecuted Shakespeare for poaching deer in his park at Fulbroke and was lampooned as Justice Shallow in revenge; *m* Joyce, dau and heir of Thomas Acton, of Sutton, Worcs, and *d* 1600, having had, with a dau (Anne, *m* Sir Edward Aston, of Tixhall) an only s:

Sir THOMAS LUCY, of Charlecote; *m* 1st Dorothy, dau of Nicholas Arnold, and had a surv child (Joyce, *m* Sir William Cooke, of Highnam, Glos); *m* 2nd Constance, dau and heir of Richard Kingsmill, of Highclere, Hants, and by her had, with further daus:

1 THOMAS

2 Sir RICHARD LUCY, 1st Bt (E), so *cr* 11 March 1617/8; *b c* 1592; *educ* Magdalen Coll Oxford and Lincoln's Inn; ktd Jan 1617/8, MP Old Sarum 1647–53 and Herts 1654–55 and 1656–58; *m* 1st Elizabeth, widow of (a) Robert West, yr s of 3rd Baron Delaware (*see* DE LA WARR, E) and (b) Sir Robert Oxenbridge and dau and coheir of Sir Henry Cock, of Broxbourne, Herts, through whom Sir RICHARD enjoyed that estate for his life only; *m* 2nd Rebecca (*m* 3rd by 1662, as his 2nd w, Sir Rowland Lytton; *see* LYTTON, E), dau and coheir of Thomas Chapman, of Wormley, Herts, and widow of Sir Thomas Playters, 3rd Bt (*see* 1832 edn), and *d* 6 April 1667, leaving by his 1st w:

   (1) Sir KINGSMILL LUCY, 2nd Bt, of Facombe and Netley, Hants; *b c* 1649; DCL Oxon 1667, admitted Lincoln's Inn 1667, MP Brecknock 1661 (election declared void 17 May 1661) and Andover 1673–78, FRS; *m* 14 May 1668 Lady Theophila Berkeley (*m* 2nd 23 Nov 1682 Robert Nelson, author of *Festivals and Fasts of the Church*, of London), dau of 9th Lord (Baron) Berkeley (*qv*), and was *bur* 20 Sept 1678, leaving an only surv s:

     1a Sir BERKELEY LUCY, 3rd and last Bt, of Facombe and Netley; *b c* 1672; FRS; *m* Catharine, 2nd dau of Charles Cotton, of Beresford, Staffs, and *dspm* 19 Nov 1759, when the btcy expired, having had:

       1b Mary; *bapt* 9 Nov 1709; *m* 14 Aug 1727 Hon Charles Compton and had issue (*see* NORTHAMPTON, M)

       2b Elizabeth; *m* 20 July 1765 Edward Plowden, of Plowden, Staffs

(1) Constantia/Theodocia; *m* by 1667, as his 1st w, Henry Hare, 2nd Baron Coleraine of Coleraine, and had issue

3 George; *k* in France

4 William (Rt Rev), DD; Bp St David's 1660–77; *m* Martha, dau of William Angell, and *d* 4 Oct 1677, leaving issue

5 Robert; *dvp* France 1615

6 Francis, living 1682

Sir THOMAS LUCY *d* 1605; his est s,

Sir THOMAS LUCY, of Charlecote; MP Warwicks; *m* Alice, dau and heir of Thomas Spencer, of Claverden, Warwicks, and *d* Dec 1640, having had:

1 Spencer, of Charlecote; MD Oxford 1643; royalist Col Civil War; *m* Mary, dau of Henry Brett, of Down Hatherly, Glos, and *dsp* 1648

2 Robert, of Charlecote; *m* Margaret (*m* 2nd 4th Baron Arundell of Wardour (*see* 1940 edn) and *d* 23 Dec 1704), dau of Thomas Spencer, of Upton, Warwicks, and had an only dau:

   (1) Bridget; *m c* 1675 4th Viscount Molyneux of Maryborough (*see* 1970 edn SEFTON, E) and *d* 23 April 1713, leaving issue

3 Richard, of Charlecote; *m* Elizabeth, dau of John Urry, of Thorley, IoW, and *d* 1677, having had, with a dau (Constance, *m* 1677 Sir John Burgoyne, 3rd Bt, of Sutton, and *d* 1711, leaving issue), a surv s:

   (1) Thomas, of Charlecote; *m* Catherine, dau of Robert Wheatly, of Brecknol, Bucks, and had an only dau (Elizabeth, *m* Clement Throgmorton, of Haseley, Oxon, and *dspm* 1684)

4 Fulke (Sir); *m* Isabella, dau and sole heir of John Davenport, of Henbury, Cheshire, and had, with other issue:

   (1) Davenport; s to Charlecote; *d* unm 1690

   (2) George; s to Charlecote; *m* 1st Mary, dau and heir of John Brown, of Finham; *m* 2nd Jane, dau and coheir of George Brown, of Coundon, and *dsp* 1721

   (3) William (Rev), DD; s to Charlecote; Rector Hampton Lucy, Preb Wells; *m* Frances, est dau of Henry Balguy, of Hope, Derbys, and *dsp* Feb 1723/4

   (4) Fulke; *m* Elizabeth Mason, of London, and had:

     1a Thomas, s to Charlecote; *d* unm 26 Dec 1744

     2a George; s to Charlecote; High Sheriff Warwicks 1769; *d* unm 1 Dec 1786

   (1) Lucy; *m* Rev John Hammond and was grandmother of:

     1a John HAMMOND later LUCY (roy licence 9 Feb 1788) (Rev); s to Charlecote; *m* Maria, dau of John Lane, of Bentley Hall, Staffs, and *d* 12 Jan 1823, leaving:

       1b GEORGE

       2b John (Rev), JP Warwicks; *b* 1790; *educ* Winchester and Trin Coll Cambridge (MA); Rector Hampton Lucy 1815, Vicar Charlecote 1823; *d* Oct 1874

1 Constance; *m* 1st Sir William Spencer, 2nd Bt, of Yarnton; *m* 2nd Sir Edward Smith, of Whitchurch, Bucks, Ch Justice Common Pleas Ireland 1665–69

2 Bridget; *m* Sir Bryan Broughton

3 Alice; *m* Sir William Underhill

4 Mary; *m* Sir Matthew Herbert

5 Elizabeth; *m* as his 1st w John Walcot (*d* 1702), of Walcot, and *d* 1654, leaving issue

JOHN HAMMOND later LUCY's er s,

GEORGE LUCY, of Charlecote; *b* 8 June 1789; *educ* Harrow and Ch Ch Oxford; MP Fowey 1820–30, High Sheriff Warwicks 1831; *m* 2 Dec 1823 Mary Elizabeth (*d* 15 March 1890), dau of Sir John Williams, 1st Bt, of Bodelwyddan (*qv*), and *d* 30 June 1845, having had:

1 William Fulke, of Charlecote; *b* 10 Sept 1824; *educ* Eton; *d* unm 1 July 1848

2 HENRY SPENCER

3 Herbert Almeric; *d* 3 Aug 1840

4 Reginald Aymer; *d* 11 Feb 1857

5 Edmund Berkeley, of Holly Lodge, Wellesbourne, Warwicks; *b* 1842; *educ* Eton; *m* 1869 Laura Margaret Mulgrave (*d* 9 Sept 1916), dau and coheir of William Standish, of Duxbury Park, Lancs, and *d* 11 June 1909, leaving, with other issue:

   (1) Reginald Standish; *b* 10 May 1880; *educ* Wellington; Lt-Col RA; *m* 17 Feb 1921 Mary (*d* 28 Dec 1969), yr dau of Henry Shaw, of Whitehall, nr Buxton, and widow of Capt A L de C Stretton, MC, and *dsp* 11 Oct 1969

   (2) Edmund Standish; *b* 15 Aug 1881; *educ* Wellington; Maj RGA, Lt Devon Artillery Militia, V-Pres Bath Heritage Soc 1950–55; *m* 28 July 1920 Mildred, only dau of A J Fox, and *dsp* 19 Jan 1966

   (1) Blanche Susan; *b* 30 Nov 1874; *m* 1 June 1908 Col Sandford Raymond Alers Hankey, DSO, JP, 3rd Dragoon Gds, yr son of John Alers Hankey, of Meadfoot Ho, Torquay, Devon, and *d* 26 Jan 1965, leaving a s

   (2) Marguerite Constance; *b* 8 Nov 1882; *d* unm 21 Jan 1961

1 Mary Emily; *m* 21 Oct 1847 Thomas Lloyd Fitz-Hugh, JP, DL, of Plas Power, Denbighs, and *dsp* 15 June 1892

2 Caroline; *m* 2 Sept 1857 Maj-Gen Charles Powlett Lane, 21st Hus, of Badgemore, Oxon, and *d* 5 March 1864, leaving issue

The 2nd s,

HENRY SPENCER LUCY, of Charlecote Park, JP, DL Warwicks; *b* 28 Nov 1830; *educ* Ch Ch Oxford (BA); High Sheriff Warwicks 1857; *m* 5 July 1865 Christina (took name CAMERON-LUCY 1898) (*d* 8 Oct 1919), est dau of Alexander Campbell of Monzie, Perthshire, by Christina, dau and sole heir of Sir Duncan Cameron of Fassifern, Inverness-shire, 2nd and last Bt (*see* 1861 edn), and *d* 6 Nov 1890, having had:

1 Ada Christina; s to Charlecote, also of Mamore and Glenevis, Inverness-shire (in which s her mother); *b* 23 April 1866; *m* 26 July 1892 **Sir Henry William Cameron-Ramsay-Fairfax-Lucy, 3rd Bt** (*see* **Lineage (of Fairfax)** above), and *d* 17 Dec 1943, leaving issue

2 Constance Linda, of Callart, Inverness-shire; coheir with her sis Joyce Alianore; *m* 25 Nov 1902 Maj John St John Secker, 1st Lovat Scouts Yeo (*d* 21 Feb 1956), er s of John Herbert Secker, and *d* 7 March 1955

3 Sibyl Mary; *d* 26 June 1886

4 Joyce Alianore, of Callart; *d* unm 8 March 1948

RAMSDEN

Arms: Argent on a chevron between three fleurs-de-lys sable as many ram's heads couped at the neck argent. **Crest:** A cubit arm in armour proper, the gauntlet holding a fleur-de-lys sable. **Creation:** Bt. (E) 30 Nov 1689.

SIR JOHN CHARLES JOSSLYN RAMSDEN, 9th Bt, of Byram, Co York [Sir John Ramsden Bt, c/o FCO, King Charles St, London SW1A 2AH]; *b* 19 Aug 1950; *s f* 1987; *educ* Eton and Trin Coll Cambridge (MA); Dawnay, Day & Co, merchant bankers, 1972–74, FCO: joined 1975, 2nd Sec Dakar 1976, 1st Sec MBFR Vienna 1978, Head Chancery and Consul Hanoi 1980, FCO London 1982–90, Cnsllr E Berlin 1990, Cnsllr and Dep Head Mission Berlin 1991–93, Head Info Dept 1993–96, UK Dep Perm Rep UN Geneva 1996–; *m* 1985 *(Jennifer) Jane, yr dau of R-Adml Christopher Martin Bevan, CB, of Cranborne, Dorset, and has:

  1 *Isobel Lucy; *b* 1987

  2 *Stella Evelyn; *b* 1989

Lineage: ROBERT RAMSDEN, of Longley Hall, Yorks; had:

JOHN RAMSDEN, of Longley Hall; had an est s:

WILLIAM RAMSDEN, of Longley Hall; recorded his pedigree at Visitation of York 1612; *m* 1st 29 April 1589 Rosamund, dau of Thomas Pilkington, of Bradley, Yorks; *m* 2nd Mary, widow of Henry Batty, of Bershall, Yorks, and *d* 7 June 1623, having by her had no issue and by his 1st w an est surv s:

Sir JOHN RAMSDEN, of Byram and Longley Hall; *b* 13 Oct 1594; MP Pontefract 1627, High Sheriff Yorks 1636; royalist offr Civil War; *m* 1st 1624 Margaret, sis of John Frescheville, 1st and last Baron Frescheville of Staveley (*see also* WINCHESTER, M), and had two sons; *m* 2nd 7 June 1634 Anne, dau and heiress of Lawrence Overton, of London, and widow of (a) George Chamberlayne and (b) John Poole, London Alderman, and *d* 1646, having had no issue by her; his er s:

WILLIAM RAMSDEN, of Longley Hall and Byram; *bapt* 10 April 1625; *m* by 1648 Elizabeth, dau and heiress of George Palmes, of Lindley, Yorks, and *d* 26 Sept 1679, having had, with three other sons:

  1 John (Sir), **1st Bt**

  1 Browne; *m* 1st Sir George Dalston; *m* 2nd Edward Andrews; *m* 3rd Sir Richard Fisher, Bt, and *d* 15 March 1740

  2 Margaret; *m* Sir John Dalston, 2nd Bt, of Dalston

  3 Frances; *m* 2nd Duke of Bolton (*see* WINCHESTER, M)

  4 Mary; *m* Thomas Wilkinson, of Kirkeaton, Yorks

  5 Elizabeth; *m* John Anderson

The only surv s,

  Sir John Ramsden, 1st Bt (E), so *cr* 30 Nov 1689, of Longley Hall and Byram; *b* April 1648; *m* 7 March 1670 Sarah (*d* 14 Jan 1683), only dau and heiress of Charles Butler, of Coates, Lincs, and had, with six yr sons (*d* unm):

  Sir William Ramsden, 2nd Bt; *b* 1672; *m* 6 Aug 1695 Elizabeth (*d* 1764), 2nd dau of 1st Viscount Lonsdale (*see* LONSDALE, E) of the 1696 *cr*, and had, with five other daus (*d* unm):

    1 **Sir John Ramsden, 3rd Bt**; *d* 10 April 1769, leaving:

      (1) JOHN (Sir), **4th Bt**

    2 William, of York; *d* unm 16 Nov 1770

    3 James; Commr wine licence office; *d* unm 7 Oct 1770

    4 Robert, of Osberton, Notts; *b* 1708; Army Offr, present Dettingen and Fontenoy; *m* 13 Jan 1753 Elizabeth, est dau and eventually sole heiress of John Smyth, of Heath Hall, Yorks, and *d* 9 Feb 1769, leaving, with two daus:

      (1) Robert, of Carlton Hall; *bapt* 22 Nov 1753; *m* 1783 Elizabeth (*d* 21 Nov 1807), est dau of Charles Uppleby, of Wootton, Lincs, and widow of Abel Smith, MP, of Wilford, Notts, and *d* 27 April 1830, leaving an er s:

        1a Robert, of Carlton Hall, Notts, JP; *b* 29 March 1784; High Sheriff 1837; *m* 29 July 1816 Frances Matilda (*d* 22 April 1837), dau of John Plumptre, and sis of John Plumptre, of Fredville, MP (E Kent), and *d* 15 Sept 1865, having had surv issue, with three daus (*d* young or unm):

          1b Robert John, of Carlton Hall, JP; *b* 12 June 1817; *educ* Cambridge (MA); *m* 10 Dec 1844 his cousin Mary Matilda (*d* 4 July 1875), est surv dau of Rev Henry Gipps, of Elmley, Kent, Vicar St Peter's, Hereford, by

Emma Maria, 2nd dau of John Plumptre, of Fredville, and *d* 20 March 1892, leaving, with two daus (*d* unm):

           1c Robert Henry, of Carlton Hall; *b* 10 Sept 1845; *m* 31 May 1871 Francesca Romana Maria (*d* 3 Aug 1909), est dau of Charles William Jebb (*see* GLADWYN, B), and *d* 19 May 1874, leaving:

             1d Robert Charles Plumptre, JP (Notts); *b* 9 Feb 1874; *educ* Harrow and Trin Coll Cambridge (BA and LLB 1895); barrister Inner Temple 1901, chm Notts QS 1939–43; *m* 7 Dec 1934 *Mary Isiline [Mrs David Smith, Wigthorpe Hill, Wigthorpe, Notts S81 8BT] (*m* 2nd 29 Sept 1964 David William Smith, s of Richard Smith, of Bolton, Lancs), only dau of Lt-Col William Albert Wetwan, of Ashley Grove, Worksop, and *d* 20 April 1964, leaving:

               1e *Mary [Mrs William Butroid, Wigthorpe Farm, Wigthorpe, Notts S81 8BT]; *b* 19 Sept 1938; *m* 2 April 1960 William Arthur Butroid, s of Herbert Butroid, of Wigthorpe Farm, and has had:

                  1f *Christine Joanna; *b* 14 June 1961; *m* 24 Sept 1994 *Andrew Jonathan Walker, s of George Geoffrey Walker, of Whitwell, and has:

                     1g *William George Butroid; *b* 28 Oct 1996

                  2f Sarah Isiline; *b* 9 Sept 1963; *d* 16 Oct 1984

                  3f *Janet Elizabeth; *b* 16 July 1965; *m* 29 July 1995 *Iain Turley, s of William Turley, of Lesmahagow

           1d Frances Alice Mary; *b* 10 May 1872; *m* 16 April 1896 Rev John Alfred James (*d* 21 Jan 1910), Rector Dodington, Glos, and *d* 21 Oct 1925, leaving issue

          2c Edward Plumptre; *b* 21 March 1848; *m* 3 Sept 1875 Frances Elizabeth (*d* 1941), dau of William Kelly, of Blackheath, and *d* 5 April 1916, having had, with five daus:

           1d John Edward Cecil; *b* 5 July 1881

           2d William Eustace; *b* 4 July 1882; Lt and Adj W Yorks Regt; had a s and six daus

         3c Charles Arthur; *b* 4 April 1849; *m* 15 Sept 1875 Elizabeth Mary (*d* 14 Sept 1939), dau of John Leckenby, JP, FRS, FGS, and *d* 3 Jan 1902, having had:

           1d John Arthur; *b* 6 Nov 1881; *d* unm 10 Jan 1902

           2d Francis Samuel Kennedy; *b* 1885; *d* unm 3 Jan 1902

           1d Edith Elizabeth Mary; *m* 14 April 1897 Walter Henry Fossey (*d* 11 Aug 1938), of Melbourne, and had issue

           2d Emily Gertrude; *m* 21 Dec 1899 Albert W Chartres and had issue

           3d Maud; *m* 11 Sept 1922 William Henry Magnus Munster (*d* 9 April 1936), of Holywood, Co Down, 3rd s of Edward Frederick Munster, of Belfast, and *d* 1954

         4c Algernon Feilden; *b* 11 Sept 1850; *m* 4 May 1892 Mary Smith (*d* 12 Dec 1932), dau of Thomas Purdom, of Hawick, and *d* 16 Feb 1922, leaving:

           1d Edward Feilden; *b* 29 May 1893; *m* 10 March 1928 Rhoda Helen (*d* 1971), dau of Ashmore Mitchell, of Edinburgh, and *d* 1973, leaving:

             1e +Geoffrey Ashmore [Geoffrey Ramsden Esq, 9 Blackford Rd, Edinburgh 9]; *b* 1 Sept 1930

             1e *Marjorie Neish; *b* 27 April 1929; *m* 16 Oct 1954 *Paul Hastings Tennent, 2nd s of Bertram Greig Tennent, of Sheringham, Norfolk, and has:

               1f *Timothy Feilden; *b* 1955

               2f *Stephen John; *b* 1958

               3f *Adrian Paul; *b* 1961

               1f *Mary Frances; *b* 1963

          5c John Pemberton; *b* 28 Jan 1854; *educ* Trin Coll Cambridge (BA); *m* 23 Aug 1883 Alice Louisa (*d* 13 July 1924), dau of Arthur Malet (*see* MALET, Bt), and *d* 27 Jan 1911, leaving:

           1d Arthur Amherst; *b* 11 Feb 1889; served in ranks WW I; *ka* 3 Sept 1916

           2d Ralph Western; *b* 10 Oct 1890; Capt RGA WW I 1915–16; *d* unm 9 Nov 1948

           1d Alice Frida; *m* 10 Sept 1921 Bertram Greig Tennent, only s of Maj T H Tennent, RE, and had issue

           2d Guendolen Ebba; *m* 1928 William Lorymer Cossham, ChB (*d* 4 June 1954), s of William Raymond Cossham, MD, and had:

             1e *Christopher Hugh [Christopher Cossham Esq, Wellesley Ho, Harrietsham, Kent]; *b* 12 April 1929; *m* 1 Feb 1958 *Joanna, dau of Capt M H Howard Smith, of The White Ho, Houghton Regis, Beds

             1e *Jessica May; *b* 25 Sept 1931; *m* 3 April 1954 her cousin *Derek Ramsden Tennent, s of Bertram Greig Tennent, and has:

               1f *Jeremy Pemberton; *b* 26 Feb 1955

             2e *Guendolen Rose; *b* 5 Oct 1934

           3d Frances Teresa; *m* 25 Sept 1928 James Tisdall Davidson, s of William A G Davisdon

           4d Monica Hilda; *m* 25 March 1922 Arthur Morris Penson (*d* 27 April 1954) and had issue

         1c Mary Emma Frances; *m* 16 Nov 1916 Thomas Eadie Purdom, MD, of Croydon, and *d* 14 Feb 1931, leaving issue

        2b Charles Henry (Rev); *b* 6 June 1818; Vicar Chilham, Kent; *m* 24 May 1846 Mary Hamilton (*d* 14 Aug 1902), 2nd dau of Rev Henry Hamilton Beamish, and *d* 18 March 1893, leaving:

         1c Charles Hamilton; *b* 27 March 1847; *m* 1873 Caroline Augusta (*d* 1922), dau of James McEwen, of San Francisco, and *d* 1935, leaving:

           1d Charles Harold Lowther; *b* 29 April 1883; *educ* U of California (BSc 1908); *m* 1st 2 Oct 1912 Cecile Wheeler (*d* 1933), dau of Wendell S Childs, and had:

             1e Charles Dean; *b* 31 Oct 1915; *educ* U of California (BSc 1937); *m* 8 June 1940 Katherine F (*d* 1979), dau of Homer F Lightfoot, and *d* 1981, leaving:

1f +Charles Anthony [Charles A Ramsden, 178 Patricia Dve, Atherton, CA 94027, USA]; *b* 23 Jan 1943; *educ* Stanford U (BSc 1965, MBA 1970); late Lt USNR; *m* 30 Aug 1969 *Naomi, dau of Dr Robert F Robinson, of Corona del Mar, Calif., and has:

  1g *Abigail Leah; *b* 23 July 1976

1f *Katherine Cecile [Mrs Katherine Gannon, 859 Acalanes Rd, Lafayette, CA 94549, USA]; *b* 25 June 1945; *m* 1st 1967 (*divorce* 1971) Grant A Mitchell; *m* 2nd (*divorce* 1996) Michael James Gannon and has:

  1g *Geoffrey Michael; *b* 4 April 1974

  1g *Victoria Cecile; *b* 16 Oct 1976

2e +Scott Carlton [Scott C Ramsden Esq, 226 Hall Dve, Orinda, CA, USA]; *b* 24 Feb 1923; *educ* U of California (BSc); late Lt USNR; *m* 1952 *Mary Alice, dau of Walter Garms, and has:

  1f *Linda Alice; *b* 1954

1e *Dorothy Childs [Mrs Paul Coombs, 4720 W Continental Dve, Glendale, AZ 85308, USA]; *b* 9 Nov 1913; *educ* U of California (BA 1935); *m* 18 Oct 1947 Paul R Coombs (*d* 1992), s of Walter Coombs, and has:

  1f *Walter Ramsden [Walter R Coombs Esq, 3916 W Yucca Dve, Phoenix, AZ 85029, USA]; *b* 21 March 1950; *m* 1972 *Joan Vivian, dau of Robert Grant Comstock, and has:

    1g *Paul Charles; *b* 1986

    1g *Michele Ramsden; *b* 1979

  2f *David Paul [David P Coombs Esq, 215 Northway, Baltimore MD 21218, USA]; *b* 21 July 1952; *m* 1974 *Vivien Gale, dau of Karnig Paternayan, and has:

    1g *Christopher Paternayan; *b* 1983

    1g *Carolyn Paternayan; *b* 1985

  1f *Marjorie Cecile [Mrs David Wellman, 4342 Davenport St NW, Washington, DC 20016, USA]; *b* 1 Feb 1954; *m* 1996 *David Wellman, s of Jerome Wellman

2e *Helen Caroline [Mrs Fred Wagner, 2405 Wedgewood Way, Livermore, CA 94550, USA]; *b* 24 Feb 1923; *m* 1947 *Fred A Wagner, Jr, and has:

  1f *Fred Albert, III; *b* 14 March 1950; *m* 1997 *—

  2f *Jay Thomas; *b* 15 June 1952; *m* 19–

  1f *Caroline Cecile [Mrs William Constable, 8 Memory Lane, Clearlake Highlands, CA 95422, USA]; *b* 24 July 1948; *m* 1974 *William Wesley Constable and has:

    1g *Remington Peter; *b* 1983

    1g *Wendy Erin; *b* 1979

  2f *June Marseillette; *b* 13 Aug 1955; *m* 1978 *David Robert Bedford and has:

    1g *Ryan David; *b* 1981

    1g *Lauren Anne; *b* 1982

1d (cont.) Charles Ramsden *m* 2nd 28 March 1936 Alice (*d* 1963), dau of Lewis D Voice and widow of William Reddick Henderson, and *d* 11 July 1965

2d Percival Scott Webber; *b* 4 Jan 1886; *m* 1 Sept 1910 Abigail E (*d* 1979), dau of F E Philbrick, of Oakland, Calif., and *d* 17 Sept 1958, leaving:

  1e Elizabeth Sarah; *b* 29 April 1912; *m* 1946 Norton A Williams, and *d* 2 Aug 1987, having had:

    1f +Russell A; *b* 28 July 1952

    1f Carolyn Judith; *b* 11 Sept 1948; *d* April 1974

  2e *Shirley Carolyn [Mrs Shirley Peek, Box 515, Albion, CA 95410, USA]; *b* 27 March 1916; *m* 16 Aug 1942 (*divorce* 1946) Leslie A Peek and has had:

    1f Lynne; *b* 17 May 1943; *d* 1993

  3e *Marjorie [Miss Marjorie Ramsden, c/o Box 515, Albion, CA 95410, USA]; *b* 13 July 1917

  4e Patricia; *b* 18 April 1920; *educ* San Francisco State Coll California (BA 1941); *d* 1 Feb 1993

2c Henry Plumptre (Rev); *b* 7 April 1848; *educ* Oxford (BA); Rector Cottingham, Yorks; *m* 26 July 1887 Ethel Frances Alice (*d* 25 Oct 1950), dau of William Henry Havelock, Bombay CS, and gdau of Lt-Col William Havelock, KH (*see* HAVELOCK-ALLAN, Bt) and *d* 6 Dec 1901, leaving, with a dau (*d* young):

  1d William Havelock Chaplin, CB (1943), CBE (1940), DSO (1939), MC (1918); *b* 3 Oct 1888; *educ* Bath Coll; Maj-Gen Hants Regt, WW I, NWFP 1935–37, Palestine 1939 (despatches) and WW II (despatches three times), GOC Sudan and Eritrea 1944–45; *m* 1st 22 Jan 1918 (*divorce* 1946) Christine Adelaide, dau of James Yescombe Baldwin, of Mount Pleasant, Co Cork, and had:

    1e John Yescombe; *b* 13 Oct 1919; Maj RA WW II; with Shell; *m* *Joanna Hamilton and was *k* in Comet air disaster 10 Jan 1954

  1d (cont) Maj-Gen William Ramsden *m* 2nd 21 Sept 1946 *Eugenia Isabella Amy [Mrs William Ramsden, Green Banks, W Chiltington, Sussex], dau of John Francis Whale-Ure, BCL, of Chertsey, Surrey, and formerly w of Maurice Willoughby Wathen, and *d* 16 Dec 1969

  1d Rosamund Mary Lowther; *b* 9 Sept 1892; *d* 14 Oct 1901

  2d Elaine Margaret Frescheville; *b* 11 July 1894; *m* 15 July 1922 Capt John O'Bryen Steward, ICS, s of H F Steward

3c Francis Edward; *b* 24 July 1849; Cdr RN; *m* 7 June 1879 Emma Elizabeth (*m* 2nd Dr Joseph Lyman Prentiss (*d* 1909), of Canon City, Colo., and *d* Sept 1925), dau of Col F W Birch, IA, and *d* 2 April 1882, leaving:

  1d Francis Charles Home; *b* 3 Dec 1880; *m* 1927 *Lilla Marguerita, dau of Charles Mackenzie, and had:

    1e +Francis Birch; *b* 1928

    1e *June Elizabeth; *b* 9 Dec 1929; *m* 25 Oct 1952 *Gordon Floyd Brox and has:

1f *Gary Allan; *b* 26 Sept 1954

2f *Wayne Dale; *b* 14 Aug 1959

3f *Dean Ross; *b* 10 Sept 1962

4c Herbert Frescheville Smyth, CBE (1919), JP Sussex; *b* 6 March 1856; Col IA, Mil Accountant-Gen India, Afghan War 1879–80, Suakin Expdn 1885, Burma Campaign 1886–87 (despatches) and WW I (despatches); *m* 20 Aug 1889 Hon Edwyna Susan Elizabeth, dau of 11th Baron Saye and Sele (*qv*), and *d* 19 Aug 1931, leaving:

  1d Geoffrey Charles Frescheville (Sir), KBE (1948), CIE (1942); *b* 21 April 1893; *educ* Haileybury and Sidney Sussex Coll Cambridge (BA 1919, MA 1925); Capt 1st Bn Roy Sussex Regt WW I 1914–19, Indian CS 1920–48, CP Devpt Advsr to Govr 1945, Fin Commr 1944–47, ret 1948; *m* 25 Oct 1930 Margaret Lovell (*d* 2 Feb 1976) dau of Rev John Robinson, Vicar Downton, Wilts, and *d* 199–

  1d Mary Edwyna; VAD WW I; *d* unm 24 Nov 1961

5c Ernest Western; *b* 27 Jan 1863; *d* 12 Feb 1918

1c Frances Matilda Anne; *m* 19 April 1876 Stafford O'Brien Hoare, DL (*d* 9 Sept 1906), of Turville Pk, Bucks, and *d* 31 Dec 1909, leaving issue

2c Gertrude Mary; *m* 1887 Rev Arthur Johnson Rogers (*d* 15 April 1908), Rector Yarlington, Somerset, and *d* 10 April 1920, leaving issue

3b Edward Stewart (Rev); *b* 14 Jan 1827; *d* unm 28 Nov 1852

4b Henry Stewart; *dsp*

5b Frederick Selwyn (Rev); *b* 12 July 1830; *educ* Cambridge (MA); *m* 23 April 1862 Mary Jane (*d* 1905), dau of Rev Joseph Parker, Rector Wyton, Hunts, and *d* 17 Jan 1865, leaving:

  1c Frederick Plumptre; *b* 8 March 1863; *educ* Oxford (BA); *m* March 1906 Norah Grogan White

6b John Plumptre, of North Ho, Carlton, Notts; *b* 8 March 1832; *d* unm 29 Jan 1906

7b Samuel; *b* 11 April 1837; *d* 20 Aug 1851

8b Pemberton; *b* 11 April, *d* 13 April 1837

1b Emma Louisa; *m* 29 Sept 1853 Rev Henry Gladwin Jebb and *d* 8 Oct 1901, leaving issue (*see* GLADWYN, B)

(2) John (Rev); Rector Crofton, Vicar Arksey, Yorks; *m* 8 Oct 1790 Frances Elizabeth (*d* 13 Dec 1843), est dau of Sir George Cooke, 7th Bt (*qv*), and *d* 12 Oct 1807, having had:

  1a John; *b* 3 Jan 1793; *m* 28 Oct 1829 Maria Jackman (*d* July 1859) and *d* 19 March 1861, leaving:

    1b William John Plantagenet; *b* 30 Sept 1837; *m* 2 July 1861 Emma Mary (*dsp* 9 Sept 1878), dau of Thomas Fairland

  2a George; *b* 13 Jan 1796; *m* 16 Jan 1825 Anna (*d* 3 Jan 1837), dau of John Fullerton, of Thribergh, and had:

    1b Frederick John (Rev); *b* 5 Aug 1836; *educ* Ch Ch Oxford (MA); Rector Uffington; *m* 22 Aug 1865 Anna Cassandra (*d* 5 May 1906), dau of R-Adml Hon Maj Jacob Henniker (*see* HENNIKER, B), and *d* 26 Nov 1903, leaving, with two other daus (*d* unm):

      1c Frederick Frank; *b* 8 Dec 1867; Maj ASC; *m* 27 Sept 1893 Selina Lucinda (*d* 23 Nov 1940), dau of Capt Edmund Mackinnon, 2nd Life Gds, of Binfield, Berks, and *d* 2 April 1937

      1c Cassandra; *m* 14 April 1898 Rev George William Staunton, DCM (*d* 15 Feb 1965 aged 93), Capt RGA, s of Rev Francis Staunton, of Staunton Hall, and *d* 3 Dec 1950, leaving issue

      2c Frances Georgina; *m* 23 Oct 1919 Charles Allan Cooke (*d* 1 Nov 1959), s of James Allan Cooke, of Semer, Suffolk, and *d* 2 Nov 1970

  3a Frank; *b* 28 March 1797; Capt RN; *m* 27 Aug 1835 Elizabeth (*d* 1891), dau of Rev Samuel Smith, DD, Dean Ch Ch Oxford, and *d* 25 Nov 1872, leaving, with another s (*d* an infant):

    1b Frank, of Hexthorpe, Yorks, JP (W R Yorks), DL; *b* 1 Jan 1840; *educ* Ch Ch Oxford (MA); barrister Inner Temple 1866; *m* 7 Nov 1894 Norah Sybell (*d* 24 Feb 1957), 3rd dau of Maj-Gen Hon Edward Archibald Brabazon Acheson (*see* GOSFORD, E), and *dsp* 24 May 1903

    2b Charles; *b* 1843; *d* 1874

5 Thomas; *bapt* 22 July 1709; *m* 14 July 1743 Anne (*d* 1761), dau of Sir Philip Medows, and *dsp* by 1791

6 Frescheville; *bapt* 11 April 1715; Army Offr, present Fontenoy and Dettingen, Lt-Govr Carlisle, Equerry to GEORGE III; *m* 17 March 1761 Isabella, sis of Charles Ingram, 9th and last Viscount of Irvine, and *d* 24 Dec 1804, leaving:

  (1) George; *b* 1761; Capt 15th Hus; *m* Lucy (*d* 17 April 1842), est dau and coheir of Gen Benjamin Carpenter, and *d* 1793, leaving:

    1a George; Lt-Col 1st Foot Gds; *d* 9 Oct 1820

    2a William (Rev); *b* 1787; Rector Ashurst, Kent, and Linwood, Lincs; *m* 5 April 1815 Elizabeth Jane (*d* 1888), dau of Richard Bell, and *d* 4 Nov 1860, having had, with two er sons (*d* young) and a dau (*d* unm):

      1b Arthur Charles, of Stone Ness, Ashurst, Kent, JP; *b* 1 April 1825; Hon Col 2nd Vol Bn The Buffs; *m* Jan 1853 Frances Elizabeth (*d* 24 Oct 1892), dau of John Deacon, of Mabledon, Kent, and *d* 11 Dec 1891, leaving:

        1c Arthur John, JP (Devon); *b* 10 June 1855; Maj 1st Vol Bn RWK Regt; *m* 26 April 1883 Elizabeth Alice (*d* 1943), dau of H W Hawkins, and *d* 15 Nov 1918, leaving:

          1d Arthur Geoffrey Francis, DSO (1918); *b* 13 Aug 1887; Lt Cornwall and Devon Miners RGA, Maj RA, WWs I (despatches, Legn Hon) and II (invalided); *m* 23 Feb 1918 Winifred (*d* 1958), dau of S B Cowan, LLD, and Id 27 March 1945, leaving:

            1e +Geoffrey Anthony Frescheville [Geoffrey Ramsden Esq, Tillies Farm, Forest Green, Surrey]; *b* 24 July 1919; Capt Hants Regt WW II (despatches), LDS; *m* 26 Jan 1952 *Pamela Barnes

            2e Peter Derek Frescheville, of Johannesburg; *b* 27 April 1922; md Thos Aplin Co Lagos; Lt (A) RNVR; *m* 16 June 1958 Barbara (*d* 1992), only dau of W S Alexander, of Durban, and *d* 1993, leaving:

              1f +Gordon Benjamin Frescheville; *b* 1961

              1f *Elizabeth Lee; *b* 1959

              2f *Beverley Anne; *b* 1962

3e +Justin John Frescheville [Justin Ramsden Esq, 8 St Margaret's Rd, Hillcrest, Natal 3610, S Africa]; *b* 27 May 1927; Group Accountant-Sec Tozer, Kemsley & Millbourn (S Africa) (Pty) Ltd, Johannesburg; *m* 1960 *Brigit Joy Barry, dau of F Barry Smith, of Hillcrest, and has:

 1f +John Henry Frescheville; *b* 1963

 2f +Timothy Geoffrey Frescheville; *b* 1965

 1f *Paula Francis Barry; *b* 1967

4e +David Bruce Frescheville [David Ramsden Esq, 51 14th St, Parkmore 2196, S Africa]; *b* 1 March 1929; late Capt RA; *m* 14 July 1958 *Deirdre Mary, yr dau of C E Bouchier, of Pretoria, and has:

 1f +Bruce Frescheville; *b* 1959

 2f +Paul David Frescheville; *b* 1961

 1f *Debra Gail; *b* 1960

 2f *Penelope Ray; *b* 1963

1e *Myra Patricia; *b* 20 April 1921; *m* 1953 *Alan Rowland Lingard Escombe

2e *Arminel Jill [Mrs Richard Leggott, 56 Edwin St, Boston, Lincs]; *b* 31 Aug 1925; *m* 2 April 1952 Lt Cdr Richard Thomas Leggott, MBE, RN, s of Maj John Leggott, and has:

 1f *Arminel Ruth; *b* 1953

 2f *Susan Elizabeth; *b* 1955

 3f *Jenifer Leigh; *b* 1958

2d John Hope Frescheville; *b* 26 July 1896; *educ* Repton; Lt Wilts Regt; *m* 5 June 1930 *Hilda Marguerite Lonnen, dau of E J Simmons, and *d* 1955, leaving:

 1e *Margaret Elizabeth Anne [Mrs T Browne, 10 Church St, Tintinhull, Somerset]; *b* 3 Dec 1932; *m* 1966 *Capt T L Browne, Intell Corps, s of Lt-Col G Browne, and has issue

1d Elizabeth Joan; *m* 12 Oct 1910 Julian Baring-Gould (*d* 7 Oct 1929), s of Rev Sabine Baring-Gould (author *Onward Christian Soldiers* and other hymns), of Lew Trenchard, Devon, and *d* 22 Aug 1969, leaving issue

2d Frances Honor; *d* unm 2 March 1939

2c William Frescheville (Rev); *b* 16 July 1857; *educ* Oxford (MA); Vicar St Saviour's Scarborough

3c George (Rev); *b* 8 March 1862; Rector Muckton with Burwell and Walmsgate; *m* 27 Sept 1886 Elizabeth Jane (*d* 8 Aug 1905), dau of John Wykes, of Daventry, and *dsp*

3a Thomas, of Harcourt Lodge; *b* 1790; *dsp* 1860

1 Catherine; *m* 17 Aug 1736, as his 2nd w, Sir William Lowther, 2nd and last Bt of the Jan 1714/5 *cr* (see LONSDALE, E)

2 Elizabeth; *m* 1771 William Weddell, MP, of Newby

3 Margaret; *m* 1774 2nd Baron Ducie of Tortworth (see DUCIE, E)

The 3rd Bt's only s,

Sir John Ramsden, 4th Bt; *bapt* 1 Dec 1755; MP Grampound 1780–84, High Sheriff Yorks 1797; *m* 7 July 1787 Hon Louisa Susan Ingram-Shepherd (*d* 22 Nov 1857 aged 91), yst dau and coheir of Charles Ingram, 10th and last Viscount of Irvine, *d* 15 July 1839, having had:

1 John Charles, of Buckden and Newby Pk, Yorks; *b* 30 April 1788; MP Malton; *m* 4 May 1814 Isabella (*d* 6 Dec 1887 aged 97), yst dau of 1st Baron Dundas of Aske (see ZETLAND, M), and *dvp* 29 Dec 1836, having had, with another s and two other daus (all *d* young):

 (1) **Sir John William Ramsden, 5th Bt**, VD, JP Yorks, DL Inverness; *b* 14 Sept 1831; *educ* Cambridge (MA); U-Sec War 1857–58, Hon Col 1st W R Bde RFA, High Sheriff Yorks 1868; MP Taunton 1853–57, Hythe 1857–59, W R Yorks 1859–65, Monmouth 1868–74, E Div W R Yorks 1880–85 and Osgoldcross 1885–86; *m* 2 Aug 1865 Lady Helen Guendolen (*d* 14 Aug 1910), yst dau and coheir of 12th Duke of Somerset (*qv*), and *d* 15 April 1914, having had:

  1a **Sir John Frescheville Ramsden, 6th Bt**, DL W R Yorks; *b* 7 Jan 1877; *educ* Eton and Trin Coll Cambridge; High Sheriff Bucks 1920, Capt Norfolk Yeo; *m* 15 May 1901 Joan (*d* 14 Aug 1974), dau of Geoffrey Fowell Buxton, CB (see BUXTON, Bt), and *d* 6 Oct 1958, having had:

   1b John St Maur; *b* 26 April 1902; *educ* Eton and Clare Coll Cambridge; Lt RNVR WW II; *m* 20 Feb 1935 (*divorce* 1947) Lady Catherine Heathcote-Drummond-Willoughby, er dau of 2nd Earl of Ancaster (see WILLOUGHBY DE ERESBY, B), and was *kas* Malaya 7 June 1948, leaving:

    1c *Carola Eloise; *b* 26 Oct 1938; *m* 1st 5 April 1961 George Fillmore Miller III, s of George Fillmore Miller, Jr, of Princetown, Mass., and has:

     1d *Sebastian St Maur; *b* 1965; Capt Blues and Royals; *m* 1991 *Emma Caroline, dau of John Harries, of Esher, Surrey

    1c (cont.) Mrs Miller *m* 2nd 4 July 1974 *Robert E J Philippi, s of Col George Philippi, of Madrid, and by him has:

     2d *James Jeremy George; *b* 1975

   2b Sir (GEOFFREY) WILLIAM RAMSDEN later PENNINGTON (deed poll 1925 under terms of will of his paternal gf's first cousin 5th and last Baron Muncaster; see 1917 edn) later still PENNINGTON-RAMSDEN (deed poll 18 Nov 1958), **7th Bt**; *b* 28 Aug 1904; *educ* Eton and Jesus Coll Cambridge (BA 1925); High Sheriff Cumberland 1962, Maj Life Gds 9th Armoured Div and 14th Army Burma WW II, Silver Jubilee Medal 1935; *m* 6 Oct 1927 Veronica Prudence Betty (*d* 1987), only dau of Frederick William Morley, of Biddestone Manor, Chippenham, Wilts, and *d* 1987, having had:

    1c *Phyllida Rosemary; *b* 11 Feb 1929; *m* 21 June 1955 *Patrick Thomas GORDON-DUFF later GORDON-DUFF-PENNINGTON (deed poll 1955), OBE, DL, er s of G/Capt George Edward Gordon-Duff, CBE, of Hurdle Ho, Amersham, Bucks, and has:

     1d *Prunella Melissa Phyllida [Mrs Donald Gordon, 9 East Rd, N Berwick, E Lothian]; *b* 20 June 1956; *m* 1980 *Donald Gordon

     2d *Anthea [Mrs Timothy Osborn-Jones, 3 Norman Ave, Henley-on-Thames, Oxon]; *b* 8 March 1958; *m* 1982 *Timothy Charles Osborn-Jones, s of Rev Arthur Osborn-Jones, of Brighton, and has:

      1e *Rupert Alexander; *b* 1987

    1e *Katharine Louisa; *b* 1986

   3d *Iona Arabel; *b* 9 April 1961; *m* 1988 *Peter Edward FROST later FROST PENNINGTON (deed poll 1988), s of Robert C Frost, of Ballock, Inverness-shire, and has:

    1e *Ewan Patrick; *b* 1990

    2e *Fraser Robert; *b* 1991

    1e *Isla Rose; *b* 1993

   4d *Rowena [Mrs Robert Morris-Eyton, Hallbeck, Whicham, Cumbria LA18 5LU]; *b* 1 Oct 1963; *m* 1987 *(Martin) Robert Morris-Eyton, only s of John Reginald Morris-Eyton, of Beckside, Whicham, and has:

    1e *Patrick Geordie; *b* 4 Feb 1993

    1e *Isobel Rosemary; *b* 24 Nov 1989

    2e *Rebecca Melissa; *b* 21 June 1991

  2c *Penelope Lucinda [Mrs Peter Laing, Turweston Manor, Brackley, Northants]; *b* 20 Nov 1930; *m* 18 July 1958 *Peter Anthony Neville Pennethorne Laing, Gren Gds, only s of Lt-Col Neville Ogilvie Laing, DSO, 4th Hus, of Fleet Farm Ho, Fleet, Hants, and has:

   1d *Arabella Charlotte Lucinda; *b* 9 March 1960; *m* 1988 *Toby James Foster, er s of David Foster, of Lea Farm, Stopham, Sussex, and has:

    1e *Alexandra Constance Harriet; *b* 1990

    2e *Prudence Charlotte Victoria; *b* 1993

   2d *Venetia Alexandra Veronica Cayetana; *b* 14 April 1961; *m* 1987 *James Anthony Findlay, est s of John Findlay, of Carnell, Kilmarnock, and has:

    1e *Christopher Anthony Genghus; *b* 1991

    2e *Oliver Angus Rhuraidh; *b* 1996

  3c *Annabel [Mrs Edward Smyth-Osbourne, Versions Farm, Brackley, Northants NN13 5JY]; *b* 16 Dec 1931; *m* 6 Feb 1958 Col Edward Timothy Smyth-Osbourne, Coldstream Gds (*d* 1987), only s of Maj John Grenville Smyth-Osbourne, of Blackford Ho, Highclere, Berks, and has:

   1d *Charles William; *b* 7 March 1959; *m* 1986 *Joanna Mary, er dau of Sir Hugh Guy Cubitt, CBE (see ASHCOMBE, B), and has:

    1e *Edward John; *b* 1988

    2e *William Hugh; *b* 1991

    3e *Archie Alexander; *b* 1994

   2d *Julian George [Julian Smyth-Osbourne Esq, Spencer House, Canon's Ashby Court, Daventry, Northants]; *b* 17 Dec 1964; *m* 1990 *Claudia A, yr dau of C N R Proctor, of Brearton, Yorks, and has:

    1e *Luke John; *b* 1996

    1e *Sophie Charlotte; *b* 1997

   3d *Michael Alexander; *b* 24 Jan 1967; *m* 1997 *Annabel Claire, er dau of Brian Bond, of Ovington House, Alresford, Hants

   1d *Rachel Rosa; *b* 31 May 1961; *m* 1989 (*divorce* 1996) Robert Drysdale, yst s of W A Drysdale, and has:

    1e *Francis William; *b* 21 Dec 1992

    1e *Veronica Mary; *b* 12 March 1991

  4c Rachel Melissa Marie Gabrielle; *b* 6 July 1940; *d* 23 Jan 1946

  1b *Mary Joyce [Lady Feilden, Cot Farm, Minster Lovell, Oxford OX8 5RS; Aberarder Lodge, nr Newtonmore, Inverness-shire PH20 1BX]; *b* 12 Nov 1907; *m* 22 Oct 1929 Maj-Gen Sir Randle Guy Feilden, KCVO, CB, CBE (see DACRE, B), and has issue

  1a Guendolen Isabella Jane; *d* an infant 12 Aug 1866

  2a Hermione Charlotte; *b* 17 June 1867; *d* unm 4 June 1951

  3a Rosamund Isabel; *b* 12 Dec 1872; *m* 2 April 1907 Capt Richard Ford, Rifle Bde, est s of Sir Francis Clare Ford, GCB, GCMG, PC, and *d* 5 Nov 1911

 (1) Charlotte Louisa; *m* 18 Nov 1841 Edward Horsman, PC, MP, and *d* 26 Aug 1895

2 William, of Oxton Hall, Yorks; *b* 15 Aug 1789; R-Adml; *m* 6 Aug 1827 Annabella (*d* 1855), est dau of 13th Marquess of Winchester (*qv*), and *d* 30 Dec 1852

3 Henry James, of Oxton Hall, JP, DL; *b* 22 Oct 1799; Capt 9th Lancers; *m* 8 Aug 1829 Frederica Selina (*d* 16 April 1879), 4th dau of 1st Baron Ellenborough (*qv*), and *d* 19 Oct 1871, having had, with two other daus (*d* unm):

 (1) Frederick Henry; *b* 9 June 1830; Capt Coldstream Gds; *ka* Inkerman 5 Nov 1854

 (2) John Charles Francis, of Willinghurst, Surrey, JP (W R Yorks and Surrey), DL; *b* 13 Dec 1835; Capt RA Crimea 1855 and Indian Mutiny 1857; *m* 14 April 1863 Emma Susan (*d* 1897), dau of Rev Edward Duncombe and widow of Ellis Gosling, of Busbridge Hall, Godalming, and *d* 7 Sept 1910, having had, with a dau (*d* unm):

  1a Frederick William; *b* 17 Feb 1864; Capt Coldstream Gds; *m* 30 July 1887 Lady Elizabeth Maud (*d* 27 May 1949), dau of 3rd Marquess Conyngham (*qv*), and *d* 26 Dec 1928, leaving:

   1b Charles Frederick Ingram; *b* 4 May 1888; Sec Dip Serv, Overseas Dir Fedn Br Industs; *m* 12 Jan 1922 Nathalia (*d* 24 Jan 1945), dau of John Pykatcheff, and *d* 2 April 1958

   1b Cynthia Maud; *m* 25 Sept 1917 Sir Roland Thomas Nugent, 1st and last Bt, PC, JP (*d* 18 Aug 1962), of Portaferry (see 1959 edn), and had issue

   2b Moyra Gwendolen; *m* 2 June 1931 Alan Daubeny Russell-Clarke, only s of E Russell-Clarke

   3b Enid Florence Beatrice; *m* 16 July 1929 Capt Phillip Laidlay, KRRC, yr s of John Ernest Laidlay, of Sunningdale, Berks, and had issue

  2a Richard Henry; *b* 10 Nov 1866; *m* 18 Oct 1898 Diana Mostyn (*m* 2nd 18 July 1919 Adml Cecil Spencer Hickley, CB, MVO (*d* 1 May 1941), s of Adml Victor Grant Hickley, and *d* 12 Jan 1947), dau of Charles Mostyn Owen, of Woodhouse, Oxon, and *d* 2 Dec 1916

  3a Caryl John; *b* 18 Dec 1868; Capt and Brevet Maj Seaforth Highrs, Lt-Col RM, RN Div; *m* 8 Jan 1919 Madge Adell (*d* 22 May 1954), dau of William Addison Scott, of Lexington, Ky., and *dsp* 26 Oct 1941

4a Henry RAMSDEN later RAMSDEN-JODRELL (roy licence 15 March 1920), CMG (1917), DL Cheshire; *b* 14 March 1871; *educ* Eton; Lt-Col RA and Dir Min Munitions WW I; *m* 3 June 1902 Dorothy, CBE (1920), JP (Derbys) (*d* 24 April 1958), dau of Col Sir Edward Thomas Davenant Cotton-Jodrell, KCB (*see* COMBERMERE, V), and *d* 3 Sept 1950, leaving:

1b Susan Dorothy; *b* 28 April 1903; *m* 8 Nov 1933 (*divorce* 1952, took name RAMSDEN-JODRELL for self and issue by deed poll 1956) Col Herbert Louis Mostyn-Owen, 19th King George's Own Lancers, IA (*d* 17 Feb 1972), 3rd s of Charles Mostyn-Owen, of Erway, Ellesmere, Salop, and *d* 9 July 1965, leaving a s and dau

2b Frances Barbara; *b* 7 April 1905; *m* 22 Dec 1939 *Maj John Powys Dewhurst, JP, RA, est s of Capt Gerard Powys Dewhurst, of Bodidris, Llandegia, Denbighs and *d* 1980

3b *Mary Angela [Lady Fielden, Park Thatch, Sutton Manor, Sutton Scotney, Hants SO21 3JX]; *b* 2 Aug 1916; *m* 5 Oct 1940 AVM Sir Edward Hedley Fielden, KCVO, CB, DFC, AFC, RAF (*d* 8 Nov 1976), est s of Dr Edward Fielden, of Bracknell, Berks, and has:

1c Mark Edward George; *b* 16 May 1942; *educ* Eton; *k* in accident at Silverstone 1963

1c *Fiona [Mrs Christopher Hart, Eastcourt Farm, Crudwell, Wilts]; *b* 3 Dec 1944; *m* 30 Sept 1966 *Christopher Norman Hart, s of Norman Dudley Hart, of Crowcombe, Somerset

5a Josslyn Vere, CMG (1919), DSO (1915); *b* 1 Dec 1876; *educ* Eton and New Coll Oxford (BA 1899, MA 1902); Lt-Col RFA, Assist Dir War Office WW I (despatches twice); *m* 25 Aug 1909 Olive Clotilde Bouhier (*d* 13 Feb 1977 aged 101), only dau of Frederick William Imbert-Terry (*see* IMBERT-TERRY, Bt), and *d* 20 July 1952, leaving:

1b **Sir Caryl Oliver Imbert Ramsden, 8th Bt**, CMG (1965), CVO (1966); *b* 4 April 1915; *educ* Eton and New Coll Oxford (MA); Maj RA WW II, Assist Mil Attaché Bucharest 1947–49, Dip Serv 1949–67; Priv Sec to PM 1957, Min 1957, Consul Gen Hanover 1957–59, Cnsllr Rio 1959 (Chargé d'Affaires 1960) and Brussels 1962, Pro-Pncpl U Coll Buckingham 1975–79, Cdr Star Ethiopia 1954 and Order Leopold 1966; *m* 6 Oct 1945 *Anne [Anne Lady Ramsden, Vallance Cottage, Upper Chute, Hants SP11 9EH], er dau of Lt-Col Sir Charles George Wickham, KCMG, KBE, DSO, of Ashdene, Comber, Belfast, and *d* 1987, leaving:

1c Sir JOHN CHARLES JOSSLYN RAMSDEN, **9th and present Bt**

(3) Henry James (Rev); *b* 1 Feb 1837; *d* unm 8 Dec 1862

(4) William John Fresheville, of Rogerthorpe Manor, Yorks, JP; *b* 22 May 1845; Hon Maj 3rd Vol Bn Yorks LI, Lt-Col Coldstream Gds, Capt Yorks Dragoons; *m* 15 Feb 1877 Mabel (*d* 12 June 1928), 2nd dau of Gen Hon Sir James Lindsay, KCMG (*see* CRAWFORD and BALCARRES, E), and *d* 8 Jan 1927

(1) Isabella Anne; *m* 26 Oct 1858 Richard Silver Oliver (*d* Feb 1889), of Bolton Lodge, Bolton Percy, and *d* 13 June 1908

(2) Florence Mary Annabella; *m* 1st 30 April 1872 John Hope Barton (*d* 20 March 1876), of Stapleton Pk, and had issue; *m* 2nd 26 Oct 1887 Frank Summer Hatchard (*d* 28 Jan 1920) and *d* 24 Aug 1924

4 Charles, of Newbold Revel, Warwicks; *b* 25 Feb 1801; Army Capt; *m* 14 June 1828 Harriet Frances, dau of 1st Earl of Strafford (*qv*), and *d* 11 Feb 1891

1 Louisa Mary Isabella; *m* 9 Dec 1847 Lord George Quin (*see* HEADFORT, M) and *dsp* 24 Aug 1872

2 Elizabeth Frances; *m* 1 Aug 1821 4th Baron Hawke (*qv*) and *dsp* 26 Aug 1824

3 Caroline Margaret Ramsden; *m* 18 Aug 1831 Rev Lord Charles Paulet, 2nd s of 13th Marquess of Winchester (*qv*), and *d* 6 Oct 1847, leaving issue

4 Frances Catherine; *m* 15 Dec 1828 3rd Baron Muncaster (*see* 1917 edn) and *d* 29 July 1853, leaving issue

RANCHHODLAL

Arms: Azure in base on water a lotus flower leaved proper issuant from the dexter chief a sun in splendour or. **Crest:** An elephant proper resting the dexter forefoot on an escutcheon argent charged with a lotus flower proper. **Creation:** Bt. (UK) 6 Feb 1913.

SIR CHINUBHAI MADHOWLAL RANCHHODLAL, 3RD BT, of Shahpur, Ahmedabad, India; *b* 25 July 1929; *m* 1953 *Muneera Khodad, dau of Khodad Macherjee Fozdar, of Bombay, and has:

1 +PRASHANT; *b* 15 Dec 1955; *m* 1977 *Swati Hrishikesh, dau of Hrishikesh Janakray Mehta, and has:

(1) *Abha; *b* 1980

(2) *Gayatri; *b* 1981

(3) *Roshni; *b* 1988

1 *Radhika; *b* 1954

2 *Prasann [Mrs Arvind Somany, Soma House, Ellis Bridge, Ahmedabad, India]; *b* 1960; *m* 1982 *Arvind Surendra Kumar Somany

3 *Aradhana; *b* 1963

Lineage: — RANCHHODLAL, of Shahpur House, Ahmedabad; had:

MADHOWLAL RANCHHODLAL, of Shahpur House; *b* 12 July 1842; *m* Revabai (*d* 2 July 1897), dau of Jasbhai Hiralal, of Ahmedabad, and *d* 4 April 1901, leaving:

Sir Chinubhai Madhowlal Ranchhodlal, 1st Bt (UK), so *cr* 6 Feb 1913, CIE (1907), of Shahpur; *b* 26 May 1864; ktd 1910, first Hindu *cr* a Bt; cotton mfr; educnl philanthropist; *m* 1st 17 Feb 1876 Devalaxmi (*dsp* 7 Sept 1890), dau of Surajram Sarabhai, of Ahmedabad; *m* 2nd 22 Jan 1891 Sulochana, OBE, dau of Chunilal Khushalrai, and *d* 3 March 1916, having had:

1 **Sir Girijaprasad Chinubhai Madhowlal Ranchhodlal, 2nd Bt**; *b* 19 April 1906; *educ* Gujarat Coll Ahmedabad and U of Bombay; MLA Bombay; *m* 30 Nov 1924 Tanumati Jhaverilal (*d* 1970), dau of Javerilal Mehta, of Ahmedabad, and *d* 1990, having had:

(1) Sir UDAYAN CHINUBHAI later CHINUBHAI MADHOWLAL RANCHHODLAL, **3rd and present Bt**

(2) +Kirtidev CHINUBHAI [Kirtidev Chinubhai, Cinunath Mahader, nr Police Station, Shahibaug, Ahmedabad 380004, India]; *b* 15 March 1932; *m* 1967 *Meera Ratilal, dau of Ratilal Tribhovandas Nanavati, of Surat

(3) +Achyut CHINUBHAI [Achyut Chinubhai, Balantyne Haveli, Three Gates, Ahmedabad 380004, India]; *b* 1941; *m* 1967 *Uttara Vilochan, dau of Vilochan Keshavlal Druva, of Bombay, and has:

1a +Aneesh; *b* 1969

(1) A dau; *b* 1926; *d* 1927

1 Jivantika; *b* 21 March 1895; *m* 25 May 1907 Arat al Laxmilal Mehta (*d* 20 Dec 1908), of Sutar Wada St, Khadia, and had issue

2 Manorama; *b* 29 Oct 1898; *m* 20 Feb 1912 Narsinhrao Vrijlal Munshi (*d* 1917) and had issue

3 Indumati; *b* 17 June 1901; *m* 23 Feb 1916 Chaitanyaprasad Motilal, of Ahmedabad, and had issue

4 Sumati; *b* 14 Feb 1904; *d* 19–

5 *Vasumati; *b* 25 Aug 1913; *m* 4 March 1937 Yashodbar Narmadashanker Mehta, barrister and Gujerati writer, s of Diwan Bahadur Narmadashanker D Mehta, of Shanibaug, Ahmedabad, and has issue

6 Saudamini; *b* 28 Dec 1914

RANDALL OF ST BUDEAUX

Creation: B. (LP, UK) 1997.

THE BARON RANDALL OF ST BUDEAUX, of Co Devon (Stuart Randall) [The Rt Hon The Lord Randall of St Budeaux, House of Lords, London SW1A 0PW]; *b* 22 June 1938; *educ* U Coll Cardiff; with: English Computers and Radio Corp of America 1963–66, Marconi Automation 1966–68, Inter-Bank Research Org 1968–71, BSC 1971–76, BL 1976–80, Nexos Office Systems 1980–81, Plessey Communications Systems 1981–83; MP (Lab) Kingston-upon-Hull W 1983–97, PPS to Shadow Chllr 1984–85, Oppn Spokesman: Ag Food and Fisheries Affairs 1985–87, Home Affrs 1987–92; *m* 1963 *Gillian Michael and has three daus

RANFURLY

MOVEO ET PROFICIOR

Arms: Gu. a falcon volant or within an orle, wavy on the outer and engrailed on the inner edge, arg. **Crest:** A falcon close standing on a perch ppr. **Supporters:** Two falcons, wings inverted ppr., ducally gorged, lined, beaked, membered and belled or. **Motto:** *Moveo et proficior* ('I move and prosper'). **Creations:** B. (I) 8 Jan 1781 (Welles of Dungannon) and (UK) 6 July 1826 (Ranfurly of Ramphorlie), V. (I) 5 July 1791, E. (I) 14 Sept 1831.

THE 7TH EARL OF RANFURLY, Viscount Northland of Dungannon, Co Tyrone, **Baron Welles of Dungannon,** Co Tyrone, and **Baron Ranfurly of Ramphorlie,** Co Renfrew (Gerald Francoys Needham Knox) [The Rt Hon The Earl of Ranfurly, Maltings Chase, Nayland, Essex CO6 4LZ]; *b* 4 Jan 1929; *s* fourth cousin 1988; *educ* Wellington; Lt-Cdr RN (ret), stockbroker, sr ptnr Brewin Dolphin & Co 1982; *m* 22 Jan 1955 *Rosemary Beatrice Vesey, only dau of AVM Felton Vesey Holt, CMG, DSO, RAF, and has:

1 +EDWARD JOHN, *Viscount Northland* [Viscount Northland, 62 Crooms Hill, London SE10]; *b* 21 May 1957; *educ* Leys Sch and Loughborough U (BA); *m* 1st 1980 (*divorce* 1984) Rachel Sarah, dau of Frank Hilton Lee; *m* 2nd 1994 *Johannah Humphrey, dau of S/Ldr Harry Richard Walton, and by her has:
  (1) +Adam Harry; *b* 7 Dec 1994
  (1) *Helen Catherine; *b* 16 Aug 1996
2 +Rupert Stephen; *b* 5 Nov 1963; *educ* Ipswich Sch
1 *Elizabeth Marianne; *b* 24 Feb 1959; *m* 1986 *Simon Empson and has:
  (1) *Lucy; *b* 1987
  (2) *Victoria; *b* 1989
  (3) *Alice; *b* 1993
2 *Frances Christina; *b* 13 Feb 1961; *m* *Henry Gordon-Jones and has:
  (1) *Alexandra; *b* 1983
  (2) *Susannah; *b* 1985
  (3) *Louise; *b* 1988

Lineage: MARK or MARCUS KNOX, of Glasgow; merchant; *m* 1st shortly after 16 Nov 1584/5 Margaret Greenlees (*d* 22 July 1604) and had:
1 William, of Glasgow; merchant; *d* by 1664, leaving:
  (1) John; Mayor Dublin 1685; *d* by 10 Nov 1687
  (2) William, of Castlereagh, Co Mayo; *d* 1707

MARK/MARCUS KNOX *m* 2nd Helen Wilson and by her had:
2 Robert; *b* 5 Aug 1613
3 James; *b* 10 May 1618
4 Thomas; Glasgow merchant; *m* 11 June 1640 Elizabeth, dau of Andrew Spang, of Glasgow, and *d* May 1685, having had, with three other sons and seven daus:
  (1) Thomas, PC; MP Dungannon, Co Tyrone, where he bought land 1692; offered a peerage at the accession of GEORGE I but declined; matriculated arms in Scotland 15 July 1693 as male representative of the KNOXes of Ranfurly (these arms also recorded in Ireland 16 Aug 1707); *m* Mary, dau of Robert Brice, of Co Antrim, and *d* 1728, having had:
    1a Mary; *m* 1701 Oliver St George, PC (*dsp* 1729), bro of 1st and last Baron Saint George of Hatley Saint George
    2a Anne; *m* 1709 Charles Echlin (*d* 10 April 1754), of Ardquin, Co Down, and had issue
  (2) John, of Ballycruly, Co Down; *b* 18 June 1659; settled in Ireland; *m* Elizabeth, dau and heir of Hugh Keith by Elizabeth Ross, of Ballycruly, Co Down, descended from a yr branch of the Earl Marischal's family (*see* KINTORE, E), and *d* 1722, leaving, with other issue:
    1a THOMAS
    1a Margery; *m* by 1725 — de la Hay, of Dellamont, Co Down
    2a Grace; *m* 1st by 1725 — Montgomery; *m* 2nd — Wallace, of Belfast, and had issue

JOHN KNOX's s,
  THOMAS KNOX, of Ballycruly, Co Down, and later of Dungannon, Co Tyrone; MP Dungannon, Dep-Govr Co Tyrone, pedigree attested by Lyon King of Arms 4

May 1757 and continued by a pedigree recorded in the Heralds' Coll London 25 May 1810; *m* 29 June 1722 Hester (*d c* 1766), dau of John Echlin, of Ardquin, Co Down, and *d* 25 March 1769, having had, with five other daus (*d* unm):
1 William; *b* Sept 1735; *d* young
2 THOMAS
3 John, of Waringsfort, Co Down, and Dublin; *b* Feb 1740; *m* 21 March 1766 Anne Phyllis, dau and heir of Henry Waring, of Waringstown, Co Down, and *d c* 1791, leaving issue
1 Hester; *b* 26 April 1723; *m* James Moutray, MP, of Favour Royal, Co Tyrone, and *dsp*
2 Elizabeth; *b* July 1724; *m* 15 Aug 1750 Mathew Forde, of Seaforde, Co Down, and Coolgreany, Co Wexford, and had issue

The surv s,
  THOMAS KNOX, **1st Viscount Northland of Dungannon**, Co Tyrone, so *cr* 5 July 1791, as also earlier 8 Jan 1781 BARON WELLES OF DUNGANNON, Co Tyrone (both I); *b* 20 April 1729; MP Dungannon 1755–81, Govr Co Tyrone; rep I peer (Tory) 1800–18; *m* 23 Aug 1753 Anne (*d* 14 Oct 1803), sis of 1st Viscount de Vesci (*qv*), and *d* 5 Nov 1818, having had:
1 THOMAS, **1st Earl**
2 John; *b* 9 Dec 1758; MP Dungannon, Col 9th Foot, Maj-Gen, Govr Jamaica; *d* unm, lost on passage to Jamaica Oct or Nov 1800
3 Vesey, of Bernagh, nr Dungannon; *b* 29 Feb 1760; Capt 32nd Regt; *m* 8 Oct 1792 Catherine Anne (*d* 7 Oct 1860), dau of Gen James Gisborne, and *d* 2 Feb 1830, leaving:
  (1) Thomas Gisborne; *b* May 1799; *d* Feb 1853
  (2) Edmond Francis (Rev); *b* 2 Jan 1802; *m* April 1831 Mary Anne (*d* 31 March 1883), dau of Rev Bernard John Ward, and *d* 18 Nov 1850, having had, with two other daus:
    1a Vesey Edmund, of Shimnah, Newcastle, Co Down; *b* 24 Jan 1841; 52nd Foot; *m* 1 Oct 1862 Margaret Clarissa (*d* 4 April 1915), dau of Rev James P Garrett, of Kilgarron, Co Carlow, and *d* 3 April 1879, having had:
      1b Edmund Francis Vesey, KC (1906), of Shimnah; *b* 23 Jan 1865; *educ* Keble Coll Oxford (MA); barrister Gray's Inn and Middle Temple, Bencher Gray's Inn 1906, Treasurer 1913, Fell All Souls 1886, MP W Cavan 1890–95 and Londonderry 1895–99; *m* 1st 21 Dec 1891 Annie Elizabeth (*d* 9 Aug 1907), only dau of William Lloyd, of Llanmaes, Glam, and had:
        1c John Vesey; *b* 17 Oct 1892; Lt London Irish Rifles and RFC, Lt Northants Regt; *d* 4 Jan 1918 from injuries recd in flying accident
        2c Columb Thomas; *b* 13 March 1897; *educ* Rugby and RMC Sandhurst; Capt Res of Offrs Queen's Roy Regt and Bimbashi (Maj) Sudan Defence Force, ADC to Govrs Bombay and Uganda, Govr-Gen Sudan and Sirdar of Egypt, Pilot RFC WW I (wounded), WW II dir PR, ENSA, Drury Lane Theatre 1943–55 and Special Duties, author, jnlst and broadcaster (as 'Collie Knox'), FZS; *m* 27 April 1944 (*divorce*1948) Gwendoline Frances Mary, yr dau of E Davidson Mitchell, of Otford, Kent, and *dsp* 3 May 1977
        3c Noel Lloyd; *b* 18 Dec 1906; *educ* St Columba's Coll, Dublin; Lt Roy Tank Corps, King's Messenger 1946–50, Kenya Police Res 1954–55, Roy Ulster Special Constabulary; *m* 1929 (*divorce* 1942) Georgina Gladys, dau of George Oakes, of Gt Missenden, Bucks, and *d* 25 Sept 1962
        1c Dilys Myfanwy; *b* 29 March 1899; *m* 1st 5 Dec 1923 (*divorce* 1933) Lt-Col David Charles Gilbert Dickinson, Queen's Roy Regt (*d* 1943), est s of Rev G L Dickinson, of St Peter Port, Guernsey; *m* 2nd 25 Sept 1934 Lt-Col Arthur Joseph Sullivan, OBE, The Queen's Roy Regt, Offr Br Cncl, s of P J Sullivan, of Bombay, and had:
          1d Christopher; *b* 22 June 1935; *educ* Charterhouse and Balliol Coll Oxford; *d* unm 12 Feb 1958
      1b (cont.) Edmund Knox *m* 2nd 8 April 1917 Agnes Mary (*d* 4 April 1949), dau of Julius Beerbohm and widow of K Nevill, and *d* 15 May 1921
      2b Charles Thomas Gisborne; *b* 31 March 1868; *educ* Rossall; *m* 1st 4 May 1893 Ethel Flora (*d* 1935), yst dau of Surgn-Gen Archibald Henry-Fraser, Army Medical Staff, and had:
        1c Ethel Eileen, of Vancouver; *b* 1894; *m* June 1941 Benjamin Joseph Redding, marine engr
        2c Cecile Grahame; *d* unm 1938
      2b (cont.) Charles Knox *m* 2nd Dec 1936 *Matilda Gertrude, widow of Leland Dundas, and *d* 1957
      3b Alfred William Fortescue (Sir), KCB (1919), CMG (1919); *b* 30 Oct 1870; *educ* St Columba's Coll Dublin and RMC Sandhurst; Lt-Col and Brevet Col 58th Vaughan's Rifles IA, T/Brig-Gen 1917, T/Maj-Gen 1918, Hon Maj-Gen 1920, served NWF India 1901–02 (despatches, medal with clasp), ADC to Viceroy India 1899–1900 and 1902–03, Mil Attaché St Petersburg 1911, served WW I, Ch Br Mil Mission Siberia 1918–20, MP Wycombe 1924–45, Grand Offr Crown Italy, Orders St Vladimir 3rd Cl, St Stanislas 1st Cl, St Anne Russia 2nd Cl, Crown Italy, Sacred Treasure Japan, Legn Hon, Croix de Guerre France and Czechoslovakia with palms, author *With the Russian Army 1914–17*; *m* 21 Dec 1915 Edith Mary (*d* 31 May 1959), dau of Col F J Colin Halkett and widow of Richard Boyle, and *d* 9 March 1964
      4b Harry Hugh Sidney (Sir), KCB (1935), DSO (1917); *b* 5 Nov 1873; *educ* St Columba's Coll Dublin; Northants Regt 1893–1919; NWF 1897–98 (medal with three clasps) and WW I (despatches seven times, brevet), GSO(2) Simla, GSO(1) 15th Div BEF 1915, Brig-Gen Gen Staff 1917–20, Col Staff Coll Camberley 1921, Bde-Cdr and T/Col Cmdt 1923, ADC to HM GEORGE V 1925–26, Maj-Gen 1926, Dir Mil Training War Office 1926–30, Cdr 3rd Div 1930–32, Col of the Regt 1931–43, Lt-Gen 1932, Lt Tower London 1933–35, Gen 1936, Adj-Gen Forces and 2nd Mil Memb Army Cncl 1935–37, Govr Roy Hosp Chelsea 1938–43, Legn Hon, Order Crown Belgium, Croix de Guerre with Gold Star; *m* 24 Oct 1904 Grace Una (*d* 12 June 1954), only dau of Rev Robert Augustine Storrs, Rector Shanklin, and *d* 10 June 1971, leaving:
        1c Una Sheila Colleen; *b* 10 Aug 1905; Kaisar-i-hind Gold Medal (1948); *m* 1st 17 Sept 1924 (*divorce* 1939) Lt-Col Noel David Stevenson,

Black Watch (*d* 15 Oct 1969), 3rd *s* of G C Stevenson, of Cairo, and had issue; *m* 2nd 2 May 1939 Lt-Gen Sir Archibald Edward Nye, GCSI, GCMG, GCIE, KCB, KBE, MC (*d* 13 Nov 1967), HC Canada, *s* of Charles Edward Nye, and had further issue

1b Frances Cecilia Caroline; *m* 7 July 1892 Brig-Gen Robert James Ross, CB, CMG (*d* 25 Dec 1943), *s* of Lt-Col R H Ross, and *d* 1953, leaving issue

2b Elsie Flora Maud; *m* 5 Oct 1904 Maj Clarence Craig, RE (*d* 19 June 1938), 3rd *s* of James Craig, JP, of Craigavon, Belfast, and Tyrella, Clough, Co Down, and *d* 28 Oct 1965 aged 87, leaving issue

2a Henry Bernard; *b* 26 May 1847; Dist Inspr RIC; *m* 1st 14 April 1877 Maria Kathleen (*d* 14 Aug 1888), dau of Archibald Collum, and had:

  1b Mabel Eileen Beatrice; *b* 14 Feb, *d* 14 Dec 1878

  2b Ida Florence Kathleen Knox; *b* 28 Aug 1880; *m* Nov 1905 William J Shanley (*m* 2nd May, dau of Samuel Higgins Borrowes, of Monkstown, Dublin, and *d* 1918), of Rathmines, Dublin, and *d* 18 May 1912

3a Thomas Fortescue; *b* 3 April 1850; *m* 1882 Anna Wenzel and *d* 1 Jan 1889, leaving:

  1b Richard Fortescue; *b* 1883; *d* Feb 1903

  1b Fanny Louisa; *m* 1912 Henry Taylor, of Dublin, slr

1a Catherine Sophia; *m* 30 July 1857 Richard Ross, MD (*d* 1895), and *d* 1911, leaving issue

2a Elizabeth Caroline; *m* 31 May 1894 Maj Anthony Richard Hutchinson, RM (*d* 1911), Roy Welch Fus, of Kiltorkan, Kilkenny, and *d* 1912

(1) Marian Diana; *b* 30 April 1797; *m* Rev Richard Nugent Horner (*d* 1837) and *d* 1884

4 William (Rt Rev); *b* 14 June 1762; DD, Bp Derry; *m* 10 Sept 1785 Anne (*d* 13 Nov 1834), dau of James Spencer, of Rathangan, Co Kildare, and *d* 9 July 1831, leaving, with other issue:

(1) James Spencer (Rev); *b* 26 April 1789; DD, Rector Maghera, Co Derry; *m* 10 Sept 1813 Clara Barbara (*d* 4 April 1862), dau of Rt Hon John Beresford (*see* WATERFORD, M), and *d* 1 March 1862, having had:

  1a Thomas George (Sir), KCMG; *b* Jan 1824; 65th Regt and 98th Regt, served India and China, Agent and Consul-Gen Siam; *m* 1854 Prang (*d* 1888), dau of the Phwia and Mâa Yen, of Somok and Bangkok, and *d* 29 July 1887, leaving:

    1b Thomas; *b* 11 Sept 1859; *d* 1923

    1b Fanny; *m* 11 March 1879 Sum Aang Maude, Pra Preecha, Kon la-Karn (*d* 24 Nov 1879), and had issue

    2b Caroline; *m* Lewis F Leonowens

  2a Charles Beresford (Rev); *b* 22 April 1825; Vicar Lower Beeding, Horsham; *m* 23 April 1857 Christina (*d* 28 July 1916), dau of Rev Edward Leslie (*see* LESLIE, Bt), and *d* Feb 1910, having had:

    1b Charles Edward Leslie Beresford (Rev); *b* 14 Aug 1864; Rector Greinton, Somerset, RD Pawlett; *m* 4 Nov 1903 Ethel Margaret (*d* 13 June 1952), dau of Rev Francis John Dickson, of Ribchester, Lancs, and *d* 12 Feb 1956, leaving:

      1c +Charles Francis BERESFORD-KNOX [Charles Beresford-Knox Esq, 5 Dukes Meadow, Stapleford, Cambs CB2 5BH]; *b* 22 Aug 1917; *educ* Tonbridge and Keble Coll Oxford (BA 1939 MA 1985); Capt RA; *m* 1941 *Margaret Eugenie, dau of Charles Morgan, and has:

        1d +Richard Charles [Richard Beresford-Knox Esq, 8 Finches Close, Stapleford, Cambs CB2 5BL]; *b* 2 Oct 1944; *educ* U Coll Sch and Cambridge Coll of Arts and Technology; *m* 1967 *Doris, dau of Josef Frey, of Bad Wimpfen, Germany, and has:

          1e +Christopher David; *b* 1982

          2e +Nicholas James; *b* 1984

        2d +John Edward [John Beresford-Knox Esq, 14 Park Rd, Limpsfield, Surrey RH8 0AW]; *b* 8 June 1949; *educ* Cambridge High Sch, Keble Coll Oxford (BA 1971) and Nottingham U (MA 1973); *m* 1979 *Jacqueline Rosalind Wildash and has:

          1e *Anna Louise; *b* 1983

          2e *Lucy Elizabeth; *b* 1985

      1c *Margaret Leslie [Miss Margaret Beresford-Knox, 2 Quarry Close, Hansford Sq, Bath, Somerset BA2 5LP]; *b* 1904; *educ* Newnham Coll Cambridge (MA)

    2c Christina Kathleen Mary; *b* 1910; *educ* Somerville Coll Oxford (BA 1931, MA 1938); *d* unm 13 Oct 1996

    2b Francis Spencer; *b* 20 May 1875; *d* 1891

    1b Clara Margaret Isabella; *d* unm 1950

    2b Christina Catherina; *d* unm 31 Dec 1955

    3b Blanche Alberta Alexandra; sister of St Margaret's, E Grinstead; *d* 25 Nov 1961

  3a George Beresford; *b* Jan 1830; Hon Col Londonderry Militia; *d* April 1921

  1a Barbara Anne; *m* 2 Dec 1845 John Stevenson (*d* 2 Nov 1856) and *d* 1899, having had issue

  2a Clara Elizabeth; *m* 1 Jan 1847 John Madden (*d* 4 Feb 1903), of Roslea Manor, Co Fermanagh, and *d* 1 April 1860, leaving issue

  3a Isabella Louisa Georgina; *m* July 1870 her bro-in-law John Madden and *d* 15 Jan 1911

  4a Frances Harriet; *d* unm 25 Nov 1879

(2) William (Rev); *b* 14 May 1790; *m* 1st 24 June 1811 Sarah, dau of Sir A Ferguson, Bt, and had:

  1a William; *b* 1813; Madras CS; *m* 1st 1853 Gertrude (*d* 16 May 1860), dau of Thomas Dabine, RN, and had:

    1b William, of Clonleigh, Co Donegal, JP, DL; *b* 17 Sept 1858; Capt 21st Hus and 4th Bn E Surrey Regt; *d* 15 May 1922

    1b Frances Emma, of Clonleigh; *m* 6 Nov 1878 Lt-Col Robert Hawkes Ellis, JP (*d* 24 Nov 1917), of Rash Ho, Tyrone, and *d* 2 Nov 1926, leaving issue

2b Emily Annie; *m* 15 Feb 1885 Lt-Col Benjamin Geale Humfrey, Leicester Regt (*d* 5 May 1912), of Cavanacor, Co Donegal, and *d* 13 March 1933, leaving issue

1a (cont.) William Knox *m* 2nd 11 July 1862 Mary Isabella (*d* Feb 1914), dau of Benjamin Frend (*see* GOUGH, V), and *d* 27 Oct 1867

2a Andrew Ferguson, of Urney Pk; *b* 1816; *m* 8 Sept 1860 Katherine Georgiana Elizabeth (*d* 1895), 2nd dau of Latham Blacker, of Glenkean, Co Londonderry, and *d* 7 Oct 1870, leaving:

  1b William Ferguson (Rev); *b* 8 Sept 1861; *educ* Hertford Coll Oxford (MA); Priest in Charge St Mark's Mission, Kinning Pk, Glasgow, Rector Ballynascreen, Belfast; *d* 10 Jan 1925

  2b Latham Blacker; *b* 5 Dec 1862; *dsp*

  3b Robert Ferguson; *b* 1 April 1868; Lt-Col RE NWF 1897–98 and Boer War 1900; *m* 1896 Edith Mary (*d* 25 Feb 1960), dau of T W D Humphreys, and *d* 23 Oct 1935, leaving:

    1c William Humphreys; *b* 1897; *educ* Haileybury; Lt-Col RE WW I 1916–18, NWF India 1919, Iraq 1920 and Waziristan 1937; *m* 4 June 1929 *Nell Barbara, dau of T Hope Jones, of Mount Salem, Stillorgan

    2c George Lathum; *b* 1900; *educ* Rugby and Oriel Coll Oxford (MA); *d* 1 Jan 1956

  1b Katherine Eliza; *m* Thomas Perry, of Money Pk, Strabane, Co Tyrone, and had issue

  2b Anne Louisa; *d* umm 13 April 1934

3a Thomas John; *b* 1819; *m* 1849 Emma Augusta (*d* 1909), dau of James Carey, of Guernsey, and *d* Oct 1877, leaving:

  1b Thomas Carey (Rev); *b* 10 Aug 1862; *educ* Exeter Coll Oxford (MA); Curate St John, Broadstone, Rector St Serf, Comrie, Perthshire; *m* 4 June 1891 Georgiana Emily (*d* 8 May 1924), dau of Richard Waller, of Troy, Co Londonderry, and *dsp*

(2) (cont.) The Rev William Knox *m* 2nd 20 Dec 1821 Louisa (*d* 24 Dec 1849), dau of Rev Sir J Robinson, Bt, and *d* 26 Feb 1860, having by her had:

  1a Mary Louisa; *m* 6 Aug 1851 John Boyd, of Ballymaccol, and *dsp* 1 Sept 1878

  2a Anne Eliza; *m* 25 Sept 1856 Ven James Gaspard-le-Marchant Carey (*d* 1885), Archdeacon Essex, and had issue

  3a Charlotte Esther

  4a Frances Emily; *m* 7 Nov 1858 Robert Vesey Truell (*d* 27 Feb 1867) and *d* 26 May 1863, leaving issue

(1) Isabella Charlotte; *m* 24 March 1824 Octavius Wigram (*see* WIGRAM, Bt) and *d* 1 Oct 1863, leaving issue

(2) Selina Elizabeth; *m* 8 Aug 1816 William Ponsonby Barker (*d* 9 Jan 1877), of Kilcooly Abbey, and *d* 28 June 1878

(3) Frances Letitia; *m* 20 Dec 1837 Rev Hon Arthur William Pomeroy and *d* 7 Sept 1889, leaving issue (*see* HARBERTON, V)

(4) Henrietta Mary Octavia; *m* 23 Dec 1845 Adolphe Auguste de Sturler (*d* 1875) and *d* 1879

(5) Emily Lavinia; *m* 11 Aug 1842 Maj-Gen John William Ormsby (*d* 17 March 1869), RA, Govr RMA Woolwich, and *d* 31 May 1880, leaving issue

(6) Helen Adelaide; *m* 19 Sept 1850 Rev W A Ormsby (*d* 1881), Rector Smallburgh, Norfolk, and *d* 27 April 1906, having had issue

5 George, PC; *b* 14 Jan 1765; MP, DCL; *m* 1st 27 Jan 1805 Anne (*d* 1 May 1811), dau of Sir Robert Staples, 7th Bt (*qv*), and had:

(1) Thomas Perry; *b* 15 Oct 1805; *m* 26 Oct 1836 Frances Elizabeth (*d* 9 Oct 1900), dau of Capt Burdett, RN, and *d* 12 Jan 1893, having had:

  1a George Uchter; *b* 10 Oct 1837; Lt-Col RA; *d* unm 4 Dec 1881

  1a Catherine Isabella Florence; *d* unm 15 Nov 1928

(2) Henry Barry (Very Rev); *b* 7 Oct 1807; Co-Dean Bocking, Rector Hadleigh, Suffolk; *m* 1st 30 Sept 1841 Jane (*d* 13 Nov 1846), dau of Rev Hon Arthur Vesey (*see* DE VESCI, V), and had:

  1a Anne Louisa; *m* 11 Jan 1872 John Francis William Walker (*d* 17 Feb 1910), of Rathcarrick, Co Sligo, and *d* 1923, leaving issue

(2) (cont.) The Very Rev Henry Knox *m* 2nd 8 April 1850 Elizabeth Jane (*d* 4 March 1855), dau of Adml Hon Edmond Sexton Pery Knox (*see* below), and *d* 24 Aug 1869, having by her had:

  2a Emily Jane; *d* unm 15 April 1939

(3) George James; *b* 4 March 1810; *d* 11 June 1897

5 (cont.) The Rt Hon George Knox *m* 2nd 1812 Harriet (*d* 20 Jan 1816), dau of Thomas Fortescue, and *d* 13 June 1827, having by her had:

(4) John Chichester; *b* 5 April 1815; Capt 2nd Dragoon Gds; *m* 3 March 1853 Lady Louisa Dawson-Damer (*d* 25 April 1904), sis of 3rd Earl of Portarlington (*qv*), and *dsp* 22 March 1884

(1) Isabella; *m* 3 Oct 1837 John Tisdall, JP, DL (*d* 7 March 1892), of Charlesfort, Co Meath, and had issue

6 Charles (Ven); *b* 10 Feb 1770; Archdeacon Armagh; *m* 20 Dec 1804 Hannah (*d* 1852), dau of Robert Bent, MP, and widow of James Fletcher, and *d* 30 Jan 1825, leaving:

(1) Thomas (Rev); *b* 22 July 1807; Rector Lurgan; *m* 1st 1 Sept 1840 Eliza Winckworth (*d* 3 June 1850), dau of Ellis Bent, and had:

  1a Charles Jeffrey; *b* 7 July 1841; Madras CS; *m* 11 Aug 1864 Elizabeth Georgina (*d* 19 Sept 1874), 3rd dau of Rev Thomas Dawson Logan, Rector Charlestown, Co Louth, and *d* 28 Oct 1881, leaving:

    1b Thomas Vesey Melville; *b* 17 Aug 1865; *educ* Charterhouse

    2b Charles Arthur Northland; *b* 15 Jan 1867

  2a Ellis Henry; *b* 21 Nov 1842

  3a Robert Uchtred; *b* 9 April 1844

  4a Dawson Thomas; *b* 4 May 1845

  5a Vesey; *b* 25 March 1847; Cdr RN; *m* 23 Dec 1885 Helen, 2nd dau of Benjamin Leigh, of Manchester and Valparaiso, and had:

    1b Albert Vesey Bent; *b* 18 Feb 1887

  6a Cheney John Maunsell; *b* 6 Aug 1848

(1) (cont.) The Rev Thomas Knox *m* 2nd 21 Nov 1861 Emily Jane, dau of Rev T D Logan, and *d* 23 May 1871, having by her had:

7a William Arthur Logan; *b* 8 May 1864

8a Thomas George Keith; *b* 15 Jan 1869

1a Frances Mary Winifred

2a Emily Elizabeth

(2) Robert (Most Rev); *b* 25 Sept 1808; DD, Bp Down, Connor and Dromore 1848; Archbp Armagh and Primate All Ireland 1886; *m* 5 Oct 1842 Catherine Delia (*d* 1897), dau of Thomas Gibbon Fitzgibbon, of Ballyseeda, Co Limerick, and *d* 23 Oct 1893, having had:

  1a Charles Edmond (Sir), KCB; *b* 29 Sept 1846; *educ* Eton; served Bechuanaland 1884–85 and Boer War 1899–1902 cmdg Bde as Maj-Gen (severely wounded), Lt-Gen, cmded 4th Div Southern Command 1902–06, Col Salop LI 1907–1921; *d* 1 Nov 1938

  2a Thomas John; *b* 6 July 1848; *m* 8 Aug 1871 Edith Maud (*m* 2nd 10 Feb 1880 Capt John Lewis Vaughan Henry, 2nd Dragoons, est s of Mitchell Henry, of Kylemore Castle, Co Galway, and *d* 9 July 1928), est dau of William Anketell, of Ardtulla, Co Down, and *d* 5 Dec 1875, leaving:

    1b Lilian Aileen Rose; *m* 15 Aug 1900 Aubrey Waithman Long and *d* 25 Aug 1931

  3a Robert John Skeffington; *b* 1851; *d* 5 May 1874

  1a Edith Katherine Mary; *d* 18 May 1923

  2a Evelyn Katherine Isabel; *m* 8 Oct 1903 Maj-Gen Sir Robert Fanshawe, KCB, DSO, DL (*d* 24 Aug 1946), Oxon and Bucks LI, and *d* 1943

(3) Charles George; *b* 6 Sept 1811; LLD, barrister; *m* 1 Sept 1840 Isabella Hannah, dau of Ellis Bent, and *d* 4 June 1878, leaving:

  1a Ada Eliza

  2a Isabel Maud; *d* unm 20 Nov 1881

  3a Kathleen

  4a Mary Gisborne

(4) George John; *b* 18 Oct 1815; *d* unm 1888

7 Edmund (Rt Rev); *b* 6 Jan 1773; DD, Bp Limerick; *m* 22 Feb 1796 Anne Charlotte (*d* 2 Oct 1837), sis of Sir Thomas Hesketh, 3rd Bt (*see* HESKETH, B), and *d* 5 May 1849, leaving:

  (1) Edmund Dalrymple Hesketh (Ven); *b* 10 April 1801; Archdeacon Killaloe; *m* 27 Dec 1825 Agnes Mary (*d* 29 Oct 1890), dau of Lt-Col Hay, and *d* 6 Oct 1884, leaving:

    1a Charlotte; *m* 6 July 1852 Thomas Batt (*d* 1897), of Rathmullan, and *d* 31 Jan 1905, leaving issue

    2a Anne Georgina; *m* 24 Nov 1864 William Dunville (*dsp* 18 May 1874), of Richmond Lodge, Co Down, and *d* 8 Jan 1886

    3a Agnes Isabella; *m* 14 Feb 1850 Gen Henry Harpur Greer, CB (*d* 26 March 1886), of The Grange, Moy, Tyrone, and *d* 4 Aug 1912, leaving issue

  (2) Charles; *b* 27 Jan 1811; *m* 5 July 1838 Mary Anne, est dau of George Hardacre, and *dsp*

  (1) Jesse Diana; *m* 1827 Rev J T O'Neill

  (2) Harriet Anne; *m* 21 Oct 1819 D R Ross (*d* 27 July 1852) and *d* 4 Feb 1864

  (3) Fanny; *m* 24 Aug 1832 Rev Marcus MacCausland (*d* 1881), Rector Birr, and *d* 31 Dec 1894, having had issue

  (4) Anne; *m* 24 Aug 1832 Col Henry Smith, 68th LI (*ka* Inkerman 5 Nov 1854), and *d* 28 April 1859

The 1st VISCOUNT NORTHLAND's est s,

THOMAS KNOX, **1st Earl of Ranfurly** (I), so *cr* 14 Sept 1831, as also earlier 6 July 1826 BARON RANFURLY OF RAMPHORLIE, Co Renfrew (UK); *b* 5 Aug 1754; MP Co Tyrone; *m* 2 June 1785 Hon Diana Jane Pery (*d* 24 Nov 1839), er dau and coheir of 1st and last Viscount Pery of Newtown-Pery (*see* LIMERICK, E), and *d* 26 April 1840 having had, with other issue:

1 THOMAS KNOX, **2nd Earl of Ranfurly**; *b* 19 April 1786; *m* 28 Feb 1815 Mary Juliana (*d* 11 July 1866), dau of Most Rev Hon William Stuart (*see* BUTE, M), and had, with another s and two other daus:

  (1) THOMAS KNOX, **3rd Earl of Ranfurly**; *b* 13 Nov 1816; *m* 10 Oct 1848 Harriet (*d* 16 March 1891), dau of James Rimington, of Broomhead Hall, Yorks, and *d* 20 May 1858, leaving:

    1a THOMAS GRANVILLE HENRY STUART KNOX, **4th Earl of Ranfurly**; *b* 28 July 1849; Capt Gren Gds; *d* Abyssinia 10 May 1875 on a shooting expedition

    2a UCHTER JOHN MARK KNOX, **5th Earl of Ranfurly**, GCMG, PC (I 23 Aug 1905, NI 27 Nov 1923); *b* 14 Aug 1856; Ld-in-Waiting 1895–97, Govr NZ 1897–1904, Dir Ambulance Dept 1915–19, Offr Legn Hon, GCStJ 1927; *m* 10 Feb 1880 Hon Constance Elizabeth Caulfeild (*d* 25 July 1932), only child of 7th Viscount Charlemont (*qv*), and *d* 1 Oct 1933, having had:

      1b Thomas Uchter Caulfeild, *Viscount Northland*; *b* 13 June 1882; Capt Coldstream Gds and ADC to Govr NZ 1903–04, Boer War 1902 (medal with two clasps) and WW I 1914–15, KGStJ; *m* 12 June 1912 Ellen (*m* 2nd 26 Feb 1917 Cdr Hon Geoffrey Edward Mills, RNVR (*see* HILLINGDON, B); *m* 3rd 30 April 1918 (*divorce* 1929) Brig John Michael Stewart Wardell, 10th Hus; *m* 4th 24 April 1929 Julien Joseph Lezard, barrister (*d* 31 Aug 1958), est s of Louis Flavien Lezard, of Kimberley, S Africa, and *d* 2 Jan 1977), yr dau of Sir Daniel Cooper, 2nd Bt, of Woollahra (*qv*), and was *ka* 1 Feb 1915, leaving:

        1c (THOMAS) DAN(IEL) KNOX, **6th Earl of Ranfurly**, KCMG (1955); *b* 29 May 1913; *educ* Eton and Trin Coll Cambridge (BA); 2nd Lt Notts Sherwood Rangers Yeo WW II, ADC to Govr-Gen Australia 1936–38, Govr and C-in-C Bahamas 1953–56, chm: Inchcape Insur Hldgs, Colonial Mutual Life Assur Soc, Madame Tussaud's, The London Clinic and Ranfurly Library Service Ltd, dir Inchcape and Co, memb Lloyd's 1947, chm London Scout Cncl 1957–65, Ch Scouts Commr Greater London 1965–79, pres Shaftesbury Homes and *Arethusa* 1959, Steward Jockey Club 1973–75, KStJ; *m* 17 Jan 1939 *Hermione, OBE (1970), served SOE M East WW II, author *To War with Whitaker* (1994) [The Rt Hon Hermione Countess of Ranfurly, OBE, Gt Pednor, Chesham, Bucks], CStJ, est dau of Griffith Robert Poyntz Llewellyn (*see* LLEWELLYN, Bt), and *d* 1988, leaving:

          1d *Caroline; *b* 11 Dec 1948; *m* 15 April 1975 *John Edward Simmonds, s of John Colin Simmonds, of Croydon, and has:

            1e *Lucy; *b* 1976

            2e *Zara; *b* 1980

            3e *Rose; *b* 1987

        2c Edward Paul Uchter; *b* 23 May 1914; *d* unm 11 Dec 1935

      1b Annette Agnes; *b* 21 Nov 1880; *d* July 1886

      2b Constance Harriet Stuart, DCVO (1960); *b* 21 April 1885; Woman of the Bedchamber to HM QUEEN MARY 1937–53, Ldy-in-Waiting to HRH PRINCESS MARINA, DUCHESS OF KENT 1953–60, DJStJ; *m* 7 Nov 1905 Maj Evelyn Milnes Gaskell, JP, DL, Queen's Own Yorks Dragoons (*d* 14 Sept 1931), s of Rt Hon Charles George Milnes Gaskell, of Thornes Ho, Yorks, and *d* 29 April 1964, having had issue

      3b Eileen Maud Juliana; *b* 3 May 1891; one of HM QUEEN MARY's trainbearers 1911 Coronation (medal); *m* 1st 24 Nov 1914 (*divorce* 1935) Maj Charles Loraine Carlos Clarke, Roy Bucks Hus (*d* 19 Oct 1970), s of Charles Carlos Clarke, and had issue; *m* 2nd 3 Aug 1935 Peter Stanley Chappell, only s of Thomas Stanley Chappell, of Moreton Ho, Moreton Morrell, Warwicks, and *d* March 1972

    1a Agnes Henrietta Sarah; *m* 1870 Nugent Murray Whitmore Daniell (*d* 8 Aug 1908), BCS, and *d* 29 Dec 1921

  (2) William Stuart, JP (Co Tyrone), DL; *b* 11 March 1826; Maj 51st Foot, Hon Col Mid Ulster Artillery, MP Dungannon 1851–74; *m* 26 Aug 1856 Georgiana (*d* 4 Nov 1926), yst dau of John Bonfoy Rooper, of Abbot's Ripton, Hunts, and *d* 15 Feb 1900, leaving:

    1a Thomas Granville, JP (Co Tyrone), DL; *b* 22 Dec 1868; Capt 3rd Bn Roy W Surrey Regt; *m* 24 Feb 1897 Hon Harriet Georgiana Lucia Agar-Ellis (*d* 4 July 1928), dau of 5th Viscount Clifden (*see* 1970 edn), and *d* 15 Jan 1947, leaving:

      1b Constance Georgiana; *m* 6 Oct 1919 Henry Braund (*d* 11 April 1954), MRCS

    1a Violet Mary; *d* unm 23 Dec 1928

    2a Florence May; *m* 14 Nov 1889 Col Albert George Shaw, Queen's Roy W Surrey Regt, and *d* 11 Feb 1943, leaving issue

  (1) Mary Stuart; *m* 20 Sept 1854 John Page Reade, DL (*d* 28 Sept 1880), of Stutton, Suffolk, and *d* 14 May 1903, having had issue

  (2) Louise Juliana; *m* 14 Aug 1839 Henry Alexander and *d* 31 March 1896, having had issue (*see* CALEDON, E)

  (3) Juliana Caroline Frances; *b* 9 Feb 1820; *m* 15 Oct 1862 Gen Sir Edward Walter Forestier Walker, KCB, and *d* 11 Dec 1906, having had issue (*see* FORESTIER-WALKER, Bt)

  (4) Adelaide Henrietta Louisa Hortense; *m* 26 Sept 1850 Joseph Goff (*d* 26 Dec 1872), of Hale Pk, Hants, and *d* 28 Aug 1911, leaving issue

2 Edmond Sexton Pery; *b* 21 July 1787; Adml; *m* 3 July 1813 Jane (*d* 11 June 1875), dau of William Hope-Vere (*see* LINLITHGOW, M), and *d* 24 March 1867, having had, with other issue:

  (1) Thomas Edmond, CB; *b* 16 March 1820; Col Norfolk Regt, Gen; *m* 22 Oct 1846 Lucy Diana (*d* 1 March 1888), dau of Ven William W Maunsell, Archdeacon Limerick, and *d* 27 May 1898, leaving:

    1a Thomas Francis Edmond; *b* 20 Oct 1847; Capt 18th Hus; *m* 13 July 1878 Caroline Woodburn, only dau of J Evelyn K Morley, of Brighton, and *dsp* 8 Feb 1885

    2a William George (Sir), KCB; *b* 20 Oct 1847; Col Cmdt RA, cmded 8th Div 1905–06, served Abyssinia, Ashanti and Russo-Turkish Wars, Afghanistan, Zululand and S Africa, Maj-Gen; *m* 3 July 1889 Alice, MBE (*d* 5 Aug 1929), dau of Sir Robert Dundas, 1st Bt, of Arniston (*see* 1970 edn), and *d* 14 Dec 1916

    3a Frederick Charles Northland; *b* 8 Nov 1857; Lt 85th Regt; *d* unm 30 May 1901

    1a Alice Elizabeth; *m* 15 Jan 1878 Rev Warrenne James Blake (*d* 1927), of Bramerton Hall, Norwich, Vicar Easton, Norfolk, and *d* 20 Nov 1921

  (1) Elizabeth Jane; *m* 8 April 1850 Very Rev Henry B Knox (*d* 24 Aug 1869) and *d* 4 March 1855, leaving issue (*see above*)

3 John Henry; *b* 26 July 1788; *m* 1 Feb 1822 Lady Mabella Josephine Needham, dau of 1st Earl of Kilmorey (*qv*), and *d* 27 Aug 1872, leaving, with two other sons and three other daus:

  (1) Henry Needham; *b* 14 May 1831; Capt RN, nautical assessor BOT and Court of Appeal; *m* 1 March 1859 Alexandrina Henriette Wilhelmina (*d* 5 Dec 1875), dau of Jean Jacques Lavit, and *d* 18 June 1916, having had:

    1a Edward, OBE (1933), JP (Glam and Somerset); *b* 23 Sept 1860; *educ* Eton and Trin Coll Cambridge; Agent to Lord Hylton (*qv*), Capt 2nd Vol Bn Welsh Regt, chm Frome RDC 1916; *m* 28 April 1887 Mabel (*d* 24 July 1943), dau of John Edward Wade, of Brantingham Thorpe, Yorks, and *d* 13 July 1950, leaving:

      1b John Needham; *b* 10 Oct 1890; Capt RN, served Persian Gulf 1911–13 (medal), WW I (despatches, Croix de Guerre with palm) and WW II (Offr US Legn Merit), T/CS FO 1936–40 and Treasury 1947–50; *m* 20 Oct 1926 Monica (*d* 1975), only dau of Maj-Gen Sir Gerald Kitson, KCVO, CB, CMG, of Wendlebury Ho, Bicester, and *d* 5 April 1967, leaving:

        1c GERALD FRANCOYS NEEDHAM KNOX, **7th and present Earl of Ranfurly**

        2c +(Thomas) Anthony (Rev) [The Rev Anthony Knox, Croft Cottage, Little Blenheim, Yarnton, Oxon OX5 1LX]; *b* 5 Aug 1931; *educ* Wellington and St Chad's Coll Durham U (BA 1954); *m* 6 June 1959 *Susan Phoebe, BA, Chm Consumer in Europe Gp, dau of Arthur Pollard Matthews, of Mount Creek Manor, Chattanooga, Tenn., and has:

          1d +James Michael [James Knox Esq, Focus Windsurfing, Magharees, Castlegregory, Co Kerry, Ireland]; *b* 7 Dec 1962; *m* 1997 *Mary O'Shea and has:

            1e *Tom Arthur James; *b* 1992

            2e *Duncan; *b* 1996

          2d +David Andrew [David Knox Esq, c/o FCO (Peking), King Charles St, London SW1A 2AH]; *b* 16 Sept 1965; *m* 1995 *Neeta Bains and has:

            1e +Luke Anand; *b* 1996

1d *Anne Margaret [Mrs Herbert Musisi, PO Box 23363, Kampala, Uganda]; *b* June 1960; *m* 1991 *Herbert Musisi and has:
    1e *Anthony Kiwanuka; *b* 1991
    1e *Susan Mirembe; *b* 1992
2b Thomas Edward Needham; *b* 30 June 1900; Lt RN; *d* unm 28 Sept 1929
1b Mabella Ellinor; *b* 8 May 1889; *d* unm 6 July 1939
1a Lucy; *b* 14 May 1862; sis Community of Holy Family; *d* 2 Feb 1955 aged 92
2a Alice Charlotte; *d* unm 21 July 1912
3a Agnes Mabella; *d* umm
(2) Octavius Newry; *b* 8 April 1836; *m* 23 Aug 1866 Lucy (*d* 10 May 1884), 4th dau of Hon Stephen Edmond Spring Rice (*see* MONTEAGLE OF BRANDON, B), and *d* 13 June 1923, having had, with other issue:
1a Leonard Needham; *b* 20 April 1879; *educ* Haileybury; Capt RASC WW I 1915–20 (Medaille d'Honneur, with swords); *m* 1924 Berthe Helene (*d* 1982), of Lille, dau of Henri Joseph Brel, and *d* 22 Aug 1956, leaving:
    1b +John Leonard (Sir) [Sir John Knox, Tollwood House, South Chailey, E Sussex BN8 4BS]; *b* 6 April 1925; *educ* Radley, Worcester Coll Oxford (BA 1951 MA 1960) and Paris U; Lt RA 1943–47, barrister Lincoln's Inn 1953, Bencher 1977, Attorney-Gen Duchy Lancaster 1984–85, High Court Judge (Chancery) 1985–96, Dep Chm Parly Boundary Commn England 1987–95, Judge Employment Appeal Tbnl 1989–96, ktd 1985; *m* 1st 29 Aug 1953 Anne Jacqueline (*d* 1991), dau of Herbert Mackintosh, of Frensham, Surrey, and has:
        1c +Thomas Francis Needham [Thomas Knox Esq, 4 Alwyne Rd, London N1]; *b* 8 Oct 1964
        1c *Diana Jane [Mrs John Barclay, 18 King Edward Rd, Jordanhill, Glasgow G13 1QW]; *b* 23 June 1957; *m* 1981 *John Martyn Gurney Barclay, yst s of Oliver Rainsford Barclay, of Leicester, and has:
           1d *Robert James; *b* 14 July 1986
           2d *David Timothy; *b* 3 Sept 1988
           1d *Frances Elizabeth; *b* 14 May 1991
        2c *Catherine Mary [Mrs David Robinson, 11 Parkway Gdns, Chandlers Ford, Hants]; *b* 21 June 1959; *m* 1983 *David Alan Robinson and has:
           1d *Edward John; *b* 10 Jan 1989
           2d *Thomas George; *b* 9 Sept 1991
           3d *Alistair David; *b* 12 July 1993
        3c *Margaret Lucy [Mrs Philip Budden, 43 Hook Rd, Ampfield, Romsey, Hants]; *b* 3 Aug 1960; *m* 1986 *Philip Stack Hanson Budden and has:
           1d *Peter James; *b* 21 Dec 1993
           1d *Lucy Anne; *b* 16 March 1992
           2d *Jennifer Helen; *b* 16 June 1996
    1b (cont.) Sir John *m* 2nd 1993 *Benedicta Eugenie, dau of Léon Jean Goossens, CBE, FRCM, the oboist, and widow of Robin Philip Cooksey
    1b *Lucy Mary [Mrs Peter Denholm, Lot 5, Phillips Rd, Byford, W Australia 6122]; *b* 16 Dec 1927; *m* 10 Sept 1960 *Peter James Denholm, yr s of William Herald Denholm, MB, BS, of Co Durham, and has:
        1c *William Leonard; *b* 15 Aug 1962
        2c *John Peter; *b* 22 June 1964
        1c *Eva Mary; *b* 29 Dec 1969
1a Hester; *b* 19 July 1867; *m* 28 Nov 1905 Lt-Col Casimir Arthur Bourne (*d* 1918) and *d* 5 March 1950
2a Dorothea; *b* 5 Feb 1869; *d* unm 18 Nov 1933
3a Evangeline; *b* 10 Dec 1871; *m* 9 Nov 1903 2nd Baron Farrer (*see* 1963 edn) and *d* 30 May 1968, leaving issue
(1) Mabella Frances; *m* 26 Jan 1858 Count Wilhelm von Zeppelin (*d* 30 March 1910) and *d* 11 Sept 1887
(2) Anna Maria Georgiana; *d* unm 8 June 1944 aged 104
(3) Emily Josephine; *m* 15 March 1875 Henry Fox (*d* 10 Jan 1926), of Down View, Banstead, yst s of Sir Charles Fox, and *d* 23 Feb 1938, leaving issue
4 John James; *b* 3 April 1790; Lt-Col; *m* 25 Sept 1824 Mary Louisa (*d* 20 Oct 1868), dau of Edward Taylor, of Bifrons, Kent, and *d* July 1856, leaving:
(1) Emily Louisa Diana; *m* 25 Sept 1845 Sir Robert Dundas, 1st Bt, of Arniston (*see* 1970 edn), and *d* 24 Oct 1881, leaving issue

RANKEILLOUR

Arms: Azure on a chevron or between three bezants a bay leaf slipped vert, a bordure ermine. **Crest:** A broken globe surmounted by a rainbow proper. **Motto:** *At spes infracta* ('But hope is unbroken'). **Creation:** B. (UK) 28 June 1932.

THE 4TH BARON RANKEILLOUR, of Buxted, Co Sussex (Peter St Thomas More Henry Hope) [The Rt Hon The Lord Rankeillour, Achaderry House, Roy Bridge, W Inverness-shire]; *b* 29 May 1935; *s* f 1967; *educ* Ampleforth and privately; farmer, Dep Chm Br Sailors Soc Highlands Scotland

Lineage: JAMES ROBERT HOPE later HOPE-SCOTT (*see* LINLITHGOW, M); *m* 2nd Victoria Alexandrina, est dau of 14th Duke of Norfolk (*qv*), and by her had a 3rd s:

JAMES FITZALAN HOPE-SCOTT later HOPE, **1st Baron Rankeillour**, of Buxted, Co Sussex (UK), so *cr* 28 June 1932, PC (1922); *b* 11 Dec 1870; *educ* Oratory Sch and Ch Ch Oxford; MP (C) Sheffield Brightside 1900–06 and Sheffield Centl 1908–29, PPS to PMG 1896–1901, Pres BOT 1901 and Colonial Sec 1904–05; Treas Household 1915–16, Jr Ld Treasury 1916–19, Fin Sec Min Munitions 1919–21, Chm Ctees and Dep Speaker H of C 1921–Feb 1924 and Nov 1924–29; *m* 1st 15 Nov 1892 Mabel Helen, OBE (*d* 24 April 1938), yr dau of Francis Henry Riddell, of Cheeseburn Grange, Northumberland, and had:

1 ARTHUR OSWALD JAMES HOPE, **2nd Baron Rankeillour**, GCIE (1939), MC; *b* 7 May 1897; *educ* Oratory Sch and RMC Sandhurst; Capt Coldstream Gds, MP (C) Nuneaton 1924–29 and Aston 1931–39, PPS to Min Mines 1924–26, Assist Govt Whip 1935, a Ld Commr Treasury 1935–37, V-Chamberlain Household 1937, Treas Household 1937–39, served WW I (wounded, despatches, Croix de Guerre), Govr Madras March 1940–46, KStJ; *m* 2 June 1919 Grizel (*d* 6 May 1975), Kaisar-i-Hind Gold Medal, yst dau of Brig-Gen Sir Robert Gordon Gilmour, 1st Bt (*see* GILMOUR OF CRAIGMILLAR, B), and *d* 26 May 1958, having had:
(1) *Bridget Mary Hope [The Hon Mrs Coles, 25 Kings Court North, 189 Kings Rd, London SW3 5EQ]; *b* 17 Oct 1920; *m* 25 Jan 1942 Lt-Col George Henry Hugh Coles, E Yorks Regt (*d* 1992), s of Lt-Col James Hugh Coles, DSO, E Yorks Regt, and has:
    1a *Caroline Mary [Mrs Rodney Cotton, The Old Parsonage, Yarlington, Somerset BA9 8DJ]; *b* 3 Dec 1942; *m* 3 April 1965 *Lt-Col Rodney Gilbert Stapleton Cotton, RA, s of Gilbert Henry Cotton, ARIBA, of Crowthorne, Berks, and has:
        1b *Nicholas Henry Stapleton; *b* 3 Sept 1968; Capt Queen's Roy Lancers (ret)
        1b *Martha Louise; *b* 27 Sept 1966; *m* 24 Sept 1994 *Damien John Byrne-Hill, s of Graham John Byrne-Hill, of Kew, Surrey, and has:
           1c *Cosmo George Nicholas; *b* 10 Sept 1995
           2c *William Francis Stapleton; *b* 9 March 1997
    2a *Elisabeth Helena Anne [Mrs Hugh Gillespie, The Old Rectory, Kirby Wiske, Thirsk, Yorks YO7 4ER]; *b* 3 Dec 1944; *m* 2 Sept 1967 *Maj Hugh Rollo Gillespie, Queen's Roy Irish Hus, s of Lt-Col Rollo Franklin Freeth Gillespie, of Sydney, NSW, and has:
        1b *Simon Rollo; *b* 9 Aug 1970
        2b *James Hugh; *b* 8 March 1973
        1b *Alice Catherine Mary; *b* 20 April 1976
    3a *Mary-Jane [Mrs Timothy Gibson, 149 Blythe Rd, London W14 0HL]; *b* 3 Dec 1948; *m* 1987 *Timothy C Gibson, s of Henry L Gibson, of The Old Vicarage, Little Missenden, Bucks, and has:
        1b *Benjamin Henry; *b* 1987
        1b *Kate Louise; *b* 1989
(2) *Jean Margaret [The Hon Lady Wilson, 151 Rivermead Court, Ranelagh Gdns, London SW6 3SF]; *b* 7 Jan 1923; *m* 1st 21 Dec 1942 (*divorce* 1955) Capt Anthony Paul, Oxon and Bucks LI, adopted s of F O Paul, and has:
    1a *(Anthony) Hugh [Hugh Paul Esq, 23 Ludlow, Birch Hill, Bracknell, Berks RG12 7BZ]; *b* 3 March 1951; *educ* Stonyhurst; *m* 1973 *Jacqueline Anne, dau of Richard Francis Winstone, and has:
        1b *Nicholas Anthony; *b* 1975
        2b *Richard James; *b* 1980

1a *Sarah Margaret [Mrs Peter Tait, 15 Westfields Ave, London SW13]; b 25 Dec 1943; m 1st 18 Dec 1965 (divorce 1980) Nigel John Kington-Blair-Oliphant, er s of AVM David Nigel Kington-Blair-Oliphant, CB, OBE, RAF, of Goring-on-Thames, and has:

  1b *Richard Mark; b 28 May 1967

  2b *David Iain; b 18 Feb 1969

1a (cont.) Mrs Sarah Kington-Blair-Oliphant m 2nd 1981 *Peter Tait, s of Lt Col W E Tait, of Bromsgrove, Worcs

2a Susan Caroline; b 24 Jan 1949; d 1986

(2) (cont.) The Hon Mrs Jean Paul m 2nd 3 Oct 1958 *Lt-Gen Sir Alexander James Wilson, KBE, MC (see STARKEY, Bt), and by him has:

  2a *William Robert Bevil [William Wilson Esq, 6 Roundmead Ave, Loughton, Essex]; b 15 Aug 1959; m 1994 *Lisa, only dau of Colin Roby, of Cleveleys, Lancs

  3a *Rupert James [Rupert Wilson Esq, 18 Ansdell Terrace, London W8 5BY]; b 4 Jan 1961

(3) Alison Mary; b 21 Jan 1927; m 29 Jan 1945 (divorce 1959) Maj Bruce Gardiner Merivale-Austin, Black Watch, est s of William Merivale-Austin, of Waterford, Barbados, and d 1992, leaving:

  1a *Griselda Mary [Mrs Ali Jazayeri, 177 Fletchers Way, Hemel Hempstead, Herts]; b 15 Nov 1946; m April 1972 *Ali Jazayeri and has two daus

  2a *Deborah Deirdre Anne [Mrs Paul Calvert, 42 Sterndale Rd, London W14 0HU]; b 12 Jan 1948; m 20 July 1972 *Paul Calvert and has a s and dau

(3) (cont.) The Hon Mrs Alison Merivale-Austin m 2nd 4 June 1960 (annulled 1963) Maj Cyril Ernest Stearns, OBE, KRRC (d 9 Jan 1968), 2nd s of Ernest Fuller Stearns, of Teddington, Middx, and d 1992

(4) *Barbara Mary Hope [The Hon Mrs Drummond-Murray of Mastrick, 67 Dublin St, Edinburgh EH3 6NS]; b 21 Feb 1930; m 12 June 1954 *(William Edward) Peter Louis Drummond-Murray of Mastrick (see PERTH, E) and has issue

2 HENRY JOHN, 3rd Baron

3 Richard Frederick, OBE (1963); b 5 Dec 1901; educ Oratory Sch and Ch Ch Oxford (BA 1923, MA 1934); Headmaster Oratory Sch 1934–38, Section Dir Min Info WW II, CRO 1946–63; m 7 April 1938 Helen Sybil Mary (d 1971), yr dau of Alfred Charlemagne Lambart (see CAVAN, E), and d 9 May 1964, leaving:

  (1) +MICHAEL RICHARD [Michael Hope Esq, The Hollies, Thurton, Norfolk]; b 21 Oct 1940; heir presumptive; educ Downside; m 31 March 1964 *Elizabeth Rosemary, est dau of Col Francis Henry Fuller, Rajputana Rifles, of Genesis Green, Suffolk, and has:

    1a +James Francis Richard; b 1 Aug 1968

    1a *Henrietta Mary; b 8 Jan 1965

    2a *Louisa Evelyn; b 8 Dec 1966

  (2) +Simon James [Simon Hope Esq, 103 Frescade Crescent, Basingstoke, Hants]; b 16 Dec 1941; educ Downside

  (1) *Margaret Mary [Mrs Neil Slater, Marshborough House, Woodnesborough, Kent]; b 17 July 1945; m 10 Sept 1966 *Neil Arnold Slater, s of Arnold Slater, of Enfield, Middx, and has:

    1a *Richard Benjamin Arnold; b 17 March 1968

    1a *Katherine Helen; b 11 Jan 1970

1 Joan Mary; b 12 Aug 1900; served WW II (CD); d unm 7 May 1974

The **1st Baron** m 2nd 15 Sept 1941 Lady Beatrice Minnie (d 25 May 1966), only dau of 9th Earl of Drogheda (qv) and widow of Capt Struan Robertson Kerr-Clark (see 1949 edn INVERCHAPEL, B), and d 14 Feb 1949

The 2nd BARON's bro,

HENRY JOHN HOPE, **3rd Baron Rankeillour**; b 20 Jan 1899; educ Oratory Sch and Ch Ch Oxford; barrister Middle Temple 1925, Lt-Col Scots Gds, WWs I (wounded, despatches) and II, Kt SMO, Kt Cdr Order St Gregory, author; m 19 Dec 1933 *Mary Sibyl [The Rt Hon Lady Rankeillour, Papplewick Lodge, Papplewick, Notts], yr dau of Col Wilfred Ricardo, DSO, of Hook Hall, Surrey, and Bayswater, and d 2 Dec 1967, leaving:

1 PETER ST THOMAS MORE HENRY HOPE, **4th and present Baron Rankeillour**

1 *Anne Mary Elizabeth [The Hon Mrs Dobson, Papplewick Lodge, Notts NG15 8FE]; b 20 Dec 1936; m 5 July 1958 *John Stephen Dobson, JP, er s of John Dobson, of The Old Vicarage, Farnsfield, Notts, and has:

  (1) *Dominic Stephen Christopher Charles; b 15 April 1959; educ Ampleforth and RMA Sandhurst; Maj Scots Gds (ret)

  (1) *Philippa Mary; b 6 June 1961

  (2) *Catherine Teresa; b 19 Oct 1962; m 1988 *Hamish Lindsay McNair, only s of Archibald Alister Jourdan McNair, of Fulham and Spain, and has:

    1a *Mungo Alexander; b 1 May 1992

    1a *Matilda Rose; b 23 Oct 1994

RANKIN

Arms: Or a cinquefoil gules, in chief a battle axe erect between two boar's heads couped, and in base a boar's head couped between two battle axes erect sable. **Crest:** In front of a cubit arm holding a battle axe proper three cinquefoils gules. **Motto:** Prudentia et virtute ('By prudence and strength'). **Creation:** Bt. (UK) 20 June 1898.

SIR IAN NIALL RANKIN, 4TH BT, of Bryngwyn, Co Hereford [Sir Ian Rankin Bt, 97 Elgin Ave, London W9 2DA]; b 19 Dec 1932; s unc 1988; educ Eton and Ch Ch Oxford (BA 1957, MA); Lt (ret) Scots Gds, FRGS; m 1st 2 July 1959 (divorce 1967) Alexandra (Sasha) (m 2nd George Asseily), only dau of Adml Sir Lawrence George Durlacher, KCB, OBE, DSC (see 1970 edn HANSON, Bt, of Bryanston Square), and has:

1 +GAVIN NIALL; b 19 May 1962; educ Eton and Buckingham U; Page of Hon to HM THE QUEEN 1977–79; m 4 Feb 1995 *Alexandra, dau of Yurgen von Knierem and Monica von Pott

1 *Zara Sophia; b 2 July 1960; m 20 Sept 1997 *Hon Humphrey Drummond, 2nd s of Baroness Strange (qv)

Sir IAN m 2nd 1980 *June, er dau of Capt Thomas Marsham-Townshend (see ROMNEY, E) and formerly w of Bryan Montagu Norman, and by her has:

2 +Lachlan John; b 1980; educ Eton

Lineage: JAMES RANKIN, of Mains Ho, Mearns, Renfrewshire; m 1786 Helen Ferguson, of Auchentiber, Ayrshire, and d 1815, having had, with at least two er sons:

ROBERT RANKIN, of Bromborough Hall, Cheshire; b at Mains House; m 17 March 1829 Ann (d 1875), dau of John Strang, of St Andrew's, Canada, and had, with other issue:

Sir James Rankin, 1st Bt (UK), so cr 20 June 1898, of Bryngwyn, Herefs, JP (Herefs), DL; b 26 Dec 1842; educ Trin Coll Cambridge (MA); High Sheriff 1873, Maj 1st Bn Herefs Rifle Vol, MP (C) Leominster 1880–85 and N Herefs 1886–1906 and 1910–12; m 12 Jan 1865 Annie Laura (d 22 June 1920), dau of Christopher Bushell, of Hinterton, Cheshire, and d 17 April 1915, having had:

1 (JAMES) REGINALD LEA (Sir), **2nd Bt**

2 Charles Herbert, CB (1923), CMG (1916), DSO (1900); b 26 May 1873; joined 7th Hus 1893, Col, Hon Brig-Gen 1927, Lt-Col cmdg 4th Hus 1915–16, cmded 105th Inf Bde, Ambala Cav Bde and 4th Cav Bde 1916–19, Sialkot Cav Bde 1920–24, T/Col Cmdt 1921, served Matabeleland 1896, Boer War 1899–1902 (despatches, Queen's Medal, eight clasps, King's medal, two clasps) and WWI (despatches three times, two brevets); m 25 April 1908 Enid Maud (d 13 Aug 1938), only dau of Judge Gwylim Williams (see RHYS WILLIAMS, Bt), and d 8 July 1946, leaving:

  (1) William, OBE (1952); b 13 Feb 1909; educ Eton, Brig 15th/19th Hus, served WW II, cmdg Co of London Yeo (despatches), cmdg 7th QO Hus, Mil Attaché Warsaw, cmdg Gulf of Aden Bde, Order Orange-Nassau Netherlands and Haile Selassie Mil Medal; m 23 May 1939 *Pauline Sinclair, est dau of Oswald Sinclair Haggie, and d 16 March 1968, leaving:

    1a +Mark [Mark Rankin Esq, 5 Albany Mews, Albany Rd, London SE5 0DQ]; b 27 July 1941; educ Felsted and Grenoble U; FRGS, probation offr, Capt 15th/19th King's Roy Hus

    2a +Christopher John [Christopher Rankin Esq, Cefn-y-Bettws, Clyro, Herefs; 535 E 86th St, Apt 19A, NY 10028, USA]; b 12 June 1946; educ Nautical Coll Pangbourne; m 1st 8 June 1968 (divorce 1974) Lucinda Jane, est dau of Lt-Cdr Christopher Godfrey de Lisle Bush, RN, of Frampton Lodge, Frampton-on-Severn, and has:

      1b +Peter William; b 24 Oct 1969

      2b +James Christopher; b 1972

    2a (cont.) Christopher Rankin m 2nd 1975 (divorce 1989) Penelope Jane, dau of Nicholas Robin Benson, of Aycote Ho, Rendcombe, Cirencester, and by her has:

      1b *Clare Louise; b 1978

      2b *Katherine Emily; b 1981

1a *Carolyn [Mrs Brooke Alexander, 59 Wooster St, NY 10012, USA]; *b* 27 April 1943; *m* 16 Dec 1967 *(Edmund) Brooke Alexander, s of R H Alexander, of Los Angeles, and has:

  1b *Emily Sinclair; *b* 1971; *m* 26 May 1997 *Robert Karron

  2b *Jessica Brooke; *b* 1973

2a *Jean Mary [Mrs Charles Letts, The Hendom Barn, Llowes, Herefs HR3 5JX; 9 Stanley Gdns, London W11 2ND]; *b* 10 March 1952; *m* 1977 *Charles Anthony Letts and has had:

  1b *Charles Alexander Frazer; *b* 1980

  2b Benjamin James Mark; *b* and *d* 1982

  3b *Jeremy Finan; *b* 1984

(1) Rhondda; *b* 5 July 1910; *m* 8 March 1945 Maj John Anthony Cobham Shaw, MC and bar, RA, only s of Capt John Leslie Morton Shaw, and *d* 11 Dec 1964, leaving a s and a dau

3 Edwyn Christopher; *b* 3 Jan 1879; *educ* Eton; Lt Yeo; *m* 18 April 1914 Helena Mabel, yr dau of Charles John Galloway, JP, of Thorneyholme, Knutsford, and formerly w of Capt Holmes Chippendall Higgin, and *d* 17 April 1925, leaving:

(1) John Galloway; *b* 9 April 1915; *educ* Eton; Capt Gren Gds WWII; *m* 8 April 1937 *Olivia Mary Beatrice (*m* 2nd 3 Oct 1950 Brig Archer Francis Lawrence Clive, DSO, MC, JP, DL, Gren Gds), er dau of Lt-Col Hon Frederick William Stanley, DSO (*see* DERBY, E), and *dsp* 31 March 1949

4 Robert; *b* 16 Oct 1883; barrister Inner Temple, Capt Irish Gds; *d* 10 Dec 1945

1 Annie Beatrice; *m* 12 Jan 1887 Claude Arthur Cuthbert (*d* 26 Dec 1912), 4th s of William Cuthbert, of Beaufront Castle, Northumberland, and *d* 30 Jan 1943, leaving issue

2 Margaret Ethel; *m* 4 April 1888 Capt Thomas Raymond Symons, JP, DL (*d* 26 July 1922), of Mynde Pk, Herefs, and *d* 3 April 1949, leaving issue

3 Mary Sybil, OBE (1918); *m* 16 July 1903 Maj Charles Francis Kynaston Mainwaring (*d* 30 Jan 1949), DL, of Seven Sisters, Ellesmere, Salop, s of Salusbury Kynaston Mainwaring, JP, DL, of Oteley Pk, Salop and *d* 13 Oct 1956, leaving issue

4 Veronica; *m* 20 April 1909 John Ellison Otto (*d* 9 Nov 1952), barrister Inner Temple, and *d* 29 Oct 1960, leaving issue

The 1st Bt's est s,

Sir (James) Reginald Lea Rankin, 2nd Bt, TD, JP (Herefs), JP (Glos), DL; *b* 31 Aug 1871; *educ* Corpus Christi Coll Oxford (MA); barrister Inner Temple 1899, trooper and Lt Rimington's Guides 1900 Boer War (medal with three clasps, promoted on the field), Priv Sec to Sec State Colonies 1903–04, war correspondent *The Times* Morocco 1908, with Bulgarian Forces 1912 and WW I, Lt-Col cmdg 1st Bn Herefs Regt and Maj 2ic W Kent Yeo 1915, Coronation Medal 1911 and Silver Badge 1915, FRHistS, FRGS, author: *A Subaltern's Letters to his Wife*, *With General d'Amade in Morocco*, *The Inner History of the Balkan War* and other works; *m* 25 July 1896 Hon Nest Rice (*d* 21 June 1943), 2nd dau of 6th Baron Dynevor (*qv*), and *d* 10 Sept 1931, having had:

1 Sir HUBERT CHARLES RHYS RANKIN later HUBERT CHARLES RHYS STEWART RANKIN (deed poll 8 April 1932) later still HUGH CHARLES RHYS RANKIN (Scottish licence Aug 1946), **3rd Bt**; *b* 8 Aug 1899; *educ* Harrow; trooper 1st Roy Dragoons Ireland 1920–22 (invalided), Capt RIASC WW II, V-Pres Scottish Nat Lib Assoc 1928, cncllr Blairgowrie 1948, CC 1949 Perthshire, a sheep judge, Pres Clun Forest Sheep Breeders' Assoc, Rep to Nat Sheep Breeders' Assoc 1928, a Muslim of the Kadaria Sch of Thought, Sr V-Pres Western Islamic Assoc, sometime Pres Br Muslim Soc, tstee London Muslim Mosque, 1st Br Delegate to 1st Pan-European Muslim Conf Geneva 1935, Mahayana Buddhist 1944, V-Pres World Buddhist Assoc (Mahabodhi) 1946, memb Standing Cncl Baronetage 1979–88, FSA Scot; *m* 1st 9 April 1932 Helen Margaret (*d* 22 Sept 1945), dau of Sir Charles John Stewart, KBE, and widow of Capt Colin Frederick Fitzroy Campbell, Scots Gds; *m* 2nd 23 Dec 1946 *Robina Kelly [Robina Lady Rankin, Bracken Cottage, Kindallachan, Pitlochry, Perthshire], FSA Scot, and *d* 1988

2 Arthur Niall Talbot; *b* 6 Aug 1904; *educ* Eton and Ch Ch Oxford (MA); Lt-Col Scots Gds (Emergency Reserve), memb Roy Co Archers, FRGS, FRPS, author: *Haunts of British Divers*, *Antarctic Isle* and other ornithological treatises; *m* 10 Oct 1931 *Lady Jean Margaret Florence Dalrymple, DCVO (1969, CVO 1957) [The Lady Jean Rankin DCVO, House of Treshnish, Calgary, Isle of Mull, Argyll; 3 Catherine Wheel Yard, St James's St, London SW1A 1DR], Woman Bedchamber to HM QUEEN ELIZABETH THE QUEEN MOTHER, er dau of 12th Earl of Stair (*qv*), and *d* 7 April 1965, leaving:

(1) Sir IAN NIALL RANKIN, **4th and present Bt**

(2) +Alick Michael (Sir) [Sir Alick Rankin, 3 Saxe Coburg Place, Edinburgh EH3 5BR]; *b* 23 Jan 1935; *educ* Eton; Lt Scots Gds (Res), ktd 1992; *m* 1st 14 June 1958 (*divorce* 1976) Susan Margaret, er dau of Lt-Col Hugh Littleton Dewhurst (*see* FORTEVIOT, B), and has:

  1a +Rupert Mark; *b* 15 Aug 1962

  1a *Clare Joanna; *b* 27 Feb 1961

  2a *Annabel Louise; *b* 12 March 1964

  3a *Juliet Rachel; *b* 22 April 1970

(2) (cont.) Sir Alick Rankin *m* 2nd 10 Nov 1976 *Mrs Suzetta Barber

RASCH

Arms: Quarterly, azure and gules, a cross parted and fretted or between (1st quarter) a lion rampant per bend sinister ermine and erminois, (2nd quarter) a pelican in her piety argent, (3rd quarter) a gryphon segreant of the third and (4th quarter) a lion rampant of the last. **Crest:** Upon a rock proper a gryphon's head azure collared gemel or, in front thereof a leopard's face, between two fleurs-de-lys of the last. **Motto:** *Fas ducit* ('Right leads the way'). **Creation:** Bt. (UK) 29 Aug 1903.

SIR SIMON ANTHONY CARNE RASCH, 4TH BT, of Woodhill, Danbury, Essex [Sir Simon Rasch Bt, The White House, Manningford Bruce, Wilts SN9 6JW]; *b* 26 Feb 1948; *s f* 1996; *educ* Eton and RAC Cirencester; Page of Honour to HM THE QUEEN 1962–64; *m* 1987 *Julia, er dau of Maj Michael Godwin Plantagenet Stourton (*see* MOWBRAY, SEGRAVE and STOURTON, B), and has:

1 +TOBY RICHARD CARNE; *b* 28 Sept 1994

1 *Molly Clare Anne; *b* 1990

Lineage: FREDERICK RASCH had:

JOHN PETER RASCH, of Merton, Surrey; *m* Louisa Mary (*d* 1836), dau of Rev J Leroux, of Long Melford, Suffolk, and *d* 1842, leaving:

FREDERICK CARNE RASCH, of Woodhill, Danbury, Essex, JP, DL; *b* 13 June 1808; barrister; *m* 10 May 1842 Catherine Jane (*d* 9 April 1881) dau of James Edwards, of The Grove, Harrow and *d* 22 Feb 1876, leaving:

Sir Frederick Carne Rasch, 1st Bt (UK), so *cr* 29 Aug 1903, of Woodhill, Danbury, Essex, JP, DL; *b* 9 Nov 1847; *educ* Trin Coll Cambridge (BA); MP SE Essex 1886–1900 and Mid-Essex 1900–08, Lt 6th Dragoon Gds, Capt and Hon Maj 4th Bn Essex Regt; *m* 16 Dec 1879 Katherine Anne (*d* 16 Jan 1944) dau of Henry Lysons Griffinhoofe, of Arkesden, Essex, and *d* 27 Sept 1914, leaving:

1 **Sir (Frederick) Carne Rasch, 2nd Bt**, JP (Essex), DL; *b* 27 Sept 1880; *educ* Eton; Lt-Col Carabiniers, Boer War 1901–02, WW I (despatches) and II (River Emergency Services 1939–40, cmded 2nd Bn Essex HG 1940–43, Admlty Ferry Crews 1943–45), Lt-Col cmdg 5th Bn Essex Regt (TA) 1922–28, High Sheriff Essex 1924–25, Brevet-Col 1926, Col cmdg 161st (Essex) Inf Bde 1928–32, memb Gentlemen-at-Arms 1929–38, ADC to HM GEORGE V 1931–41; *m* 21 July 1921 Catherine Margaret, JP (Essex) 1920 (*d* 25 July 1983 aged 92), only child of Hon John Richard de Clare Boscawen (*see* FALMOUTH, V) and widow of 16th Baron Petre (*qv*), and *dsp* 12 June 1963

2 Guy Elland Carne, CVO (1936), DSO (1915), DL Wilts; *b* 15 Aug 1885; *educ* Eton; Col Gren Gds, Regtl Dist 1932–37, Gentleman Usher to HM GEORGE VI 1938, Extra Equerry to HRH THE DUKE OF CONNAUGHT 1938–42, served WWs I (despatches, Croix de Guerre) and II (despatches), Brig, High Sheriff Wilts 1952; *m* 19 Oct 1916 Phyllis Dorothy Lindsay (*d* 25 March 1977), dau of Col Hon Alwyne Henry Fulke Greville, CVO (*see* WARWICK, BROOKE and E), and *d* 3 Sept 1955, leaving:

(1) **Sir Richard Guy Carne Rasch, 3rd Bt**; *b* 10 Oct 1918; *educ* Eton and RMC Sandhurst; Maj Gren Gds WW II, memb Gentlemen-at-Arms 1968–88; *m* 1st 14 Jan 1947 (*divorce* 1959) Anne Mary (*d* 1989), est dau of Maj John Henry Dent-Brocklehurst, OBE, of Sudeley Castle, Winchcombe, Glos, and had:

  1a Sir SIMON ANTHONY CARNE RASCH, **4th and present Bt**

  1a *Leila Anne Katherine [Mrs Timothy Price, The Wadfield, Winchcombe, Glos GL54 5AL]; *b* 19 May 1952; *m* 17 May 1975 *(Thomas Geoffrey) Timothy Rose Price (*see* PRICE, Bt) and has issue

(1) (cont.) **Sir Richard** *m* 2nd 14 Jan 1961 *Fiona Mary [Fiona Lady Rasch, The Manor House, Lower Woodford, Wilts; 30 Ovington Sq, London SW3], est dau of Robert Douglas Shaw, of St Leonards-on-Sea, Sussex, and formerly w of Humphrey John Rodham Balliol Salmon, and *d* 24 June 1996

(2) +David Alwyne Carne, DL (Wilts) [Maj David Rasch DL, Heale Stables, Middle Woodford, Wilts SP4 6NT]; *b* 16 Sept 1922; *educ* Eton; Maj Gren Gds WW II (despatches), High Sheriff Wilts 1960; *m* 10 Nov 1953 (Elizabeth) Anne (*d* 1995), only dau of Capt Henry Robert Somers FitzRoy de Vere Somerset, DSO (*see* BEAUFORT, D), and has:

  1a +Guy Martin Carne; *b* 22 Aug 1959; *m* Nov 1996 *Frances, dau of Richard Hulse, of Le Chapel, Netton, Salisbury

1a *Jane Catherine; *b* 3 Dec 1955; *m* 1976 (*divorce* 1980, resumed maiden name) Michael Smedley

2a *Emma Caroline; *b* 3 March 1962; *m* Aug 1996 *Robert Jackson, s of Harry Jackson, of Dorney, Chorleywood, Herts

RASHLEIGH

Arms: Sable a cross or, between in the 1st quarter a Cornish chough argent, beaked and legged gules, and in the 2nd a text T; in the 3rd and 4th a crescent, all argent. **Creation:** Bt. (UK) 30 Sept 1831.

SIR RICHARD HARRY RASHLEIGH 6TH BT, of Prideaux, Cornwall [Sir Richard Rashleigh Bt, Menabilly, Par, Cornwall PL24 2TN]; *b* 8 July 1958; *s* f 1984; *educ* All Hallows' Sch Dorset; *m* 3 Feb 1996 *Emma, est dau of John McGougan and Lady Acland (*see* ACLAND, Bt, of Oxford), and has:

1 +DAVID WILLIAM AUGUSTINE; *b* 1 April 1997

Lineage: JOHN RASHLEIGH, a yr branch of the RASHLEIGHs of Rashleigh, Devon; merchant at Fowey mid-16th century; *m* Alice, dau of William Lanyon, and *d* 10 Aug 1582, leaving, with six daus:

JOHN RASHLEIGH; built a mansion at Menabilly; MP Fowey *c* 1589 and 1597; *d* 1624; ancestor of:

JONATHAN RASHLEIGH, of Menabilly; MP Fowey; *m* 11 June 1728 Mary, dau of Sir William Clayton, 1st Bt (*qv*), and *d* 24 Nov 1764, leaving, with three daus:

1 Philip, of Menabilly; *b* 28 Dec 1729; MP Fowey; *m* Jane (*d* 25 May 1795), dau of Rev Carolus Pole (*see* POLE, Bt), and *dsp* 26 June 1811

2 Jonathan (Rev); *b* 17 Oct 1740; Fell All Souls, Rector Silverton, Devon; *m* 1st 5 March 1771 Catherine (*d* 10 July 1788), dau of Rev William Stackhouse, DD, of Trehane, and had issue; *m* 2nd Jane Cumming, sis of Sir Alexander P Cumming Gordon, Bt, and *d* Sept 1795, having by her had issue

3 JOHN

4 Peter (Rev); *b* 31 Aug 1946; *educ* Oxford (MA), Fell All Souls; Vicar Barking, Essex; Rector Southfleet; *m* 13 Nov 1781 Frances (*d* 14 May 1825), dau and coheir of Rev George Burvill, of Leyborne, and *d* 8 Feb 1836, leaving issue

5 Charles, of St Austell Cornwall; *b* 17 Nov 1747; *m* 1 July 1776 Grace (*d* 17 May 1820), dau of John Tremayne, and *d* 23 March 1823, leaving issue

6 Thomas; *b* 27 June 1749; *m* 22 Dec 1772 Frances Elizabeth Anne, dau of Rev John Lawry, Preb Rochester, and had issue

The 3rd s,

JOHN RASHLEIGH, of Penquite, Cornwall; *b* 20 June 1742; 1st Commr and Receiver Greenwich Hosp; *m* 6 April 1771 Katherine (*d* 1800), dau and coheir of William Battie, MD, of Court Gardens, nr Marlow, Bucks, and *d* 17 May 1803, having had:

1 JOHN COLMAN (Sir), **1st Bt**

2 Jonathan Hawkins, of Chichester; *b* March 1775

3 Charles Watson; *b* 14 July 1784; *d* unm 1805

1 Anne; *m* 30 Nov 1797 William Williams (*see* WILLIAMS, Bt, of Bridehead) and *d* 18 April 1855

2 Louisa; *m* 22 Dec 1801 Thomas Holt White, of Chase Lodge, nr Enfield

The est s,

Sir John Colman Rashleigh, 1st Bt (UK), so *cr* 30 Sept 1831; *b* 23 Nov 1772; *m* 1st 24 May 1808 Harriet (*d* 7 July 1831), 2nd dau of Robert Williams, MP (*see* WILLIAMS, Bt, of Bridehead), and had issue; *m* 2nd 17 Oct 1833 Martha (*d* 9 June 1879), dau of John Gould, MA, and *d* 4 Aug 1847; his 2nd s by his 1st w:

Sir Colman Rashleigh, 2nd Bt, CB, JP, DL; *b* 4 May 1819; High Sheriff Cornwall 1852, MP Cornwall 1874–80, Dep-Warden Stannaries, Hon Col Cornwall and Devon Miners' Artillery; *m* 1 May 1845 Mary Anne (*d* 6 Aug 1893), dau of Nicholas Kendall, MP, of Pelyn, Cornwall, and *d* 27 Oct 1896, having had, with another s (*d* young) and dau (*d* unm):

1 COLMAN BATTIE (Sir), **3rd Bt**

2 John Kendall (Rev); *b* 12 March 1847; *educ* Cambridge (MA); Rector St Mabyn, Cornwall, Hon Canon Truro; *m* 1st 11 July 1871 Charlotte Jane (*d* 25 Dec 1872), only dau of Charles Edward Rashleigh, of Farningham, Kent, and had:

(1) John Kendall; *b* 16 Dec 1872; Lt Cornwall and Devon Miners' Artillery Militia and 5th Bn Roy Irish Fus, Boer War 1900–02 on special service (two medals and six clasps), attd S African Constabulary 1902–04, Special Constable BC Police 1912–13, T/Maj RASC WW I (3 medals, despatches), with Br forces Egypt, Iraq and NW Persia 1919–21 (medal) and WW II Intell Serv, FRGS; *m* 1st 27 May 1903 (*divorce* 1925) Evelyn Anne (*d* 1942), 2nd dau of William Henry Philips Jenkins (*see* JERSEY, E); *m* 2nd 5 April 1932 *Jeffreys McEwen, only dau of Jefferson Martin, of San Francisco, and *dsp* 25 March 1960

2 (cont.) The Rev John Rashleigh *m* 2nd 20 April 1876 Charlotte Maria (*d* 22 Oct 1919), yst dau of Sir Arthur Hodgson, KCMG, of Clopton, Warwicks, and *d* 14 Oct 1933, having by her had:

(2) Edward Colman; *b* 14 Jan 1877; *d* 30 July 1936

(1) Emily; *b* 25 Dec 1879; *m* 1st 8 June 1904 Maj Thomas Langdon Trethewy, DCLI (*d* 16 March 1910), 4th s of Henry Trethewy, of Silsoe, Beds, and had issue; *m* 2nd 4 Jan 1913 Lt-Col Thomas Richard Stokoe, DSO, DCLI, er s of Col Richard Stokoe, ISC, and *d* 28 April 1942, having had further issue

1 Mary; *m* 13 Feb 1878 Henry James Young Jamieson, JP, Lt-Col cmdg Cornwall and Devon Miners' Artillery, only s of James Young Jamieson, of Gainford House, Co Durham, and *d* 8 Feb 1900, leaving issue

The 2nd Bt's est s,

Sir Colman Battie Rashleigh, 3rd Bt, JP, DL; *b* 11 March 1846; Hon Col Cornwall and Devon Miners' Artillery, W Div RA, Dep-Warden Stannaries, Mayor Lostwithiel 1891–94; *m* 1st 10 Oct 1872 Geraldine Frances (*d* 24 Dec 1876), est dau of Lt-Gen Sir Robert Walpole, KCB (*see* WALPOLE, B), and had:

1 **Sir Colman Battie Walpole Rashleigh, 4th Bt**; *b* 17 Nov 1873; *d* unm 22 Feb 1951

2 Spencer Robert; *b* 18 Feb 1876; 2nd Bn Somerset LI Boer War 1901 (two medals with seven clasps); *d* 24 June 1925

Sir Colman *m* 2nd 21 Sept 1878 his sis's sis-in-law Amy Young (*d* 27 Aug 1930), dau of James Young Jamieson, and *d* 28 Oct 1907, having by her had:

3 Harry, JP (Cornwall); *b* 22 May 1880; Lt RASC, Capt Intell Corps, WW I (despatches) and II; *m* 8 Aug 1914 Jane Henrietta (*d* 21 Oct 1969 aged 82), only dau of Evelyn William Rashleigh, of Stoketon, Saltash, Cornwall, and *d* 26 April 1950, leaving:

(1) HARRY EVELYN BATTIE (Sir), **5th Bt**

(2) Peter; *b* 21 Sept 1924; Merchant Navy; *m* 4 Oct 1949 *Lola dau of Thomas Edmonds, of NSW, and *d* 1990, having had:

1a Edward Harry; *b* 28 Nov, *d* Dec 1952

1a *Margaret Anne [Mrs Geoffrey Carruthers, 43 Archdall St, McGregor, Canberra 2615, ACT, Australia]; *b* 16 May 1950; *m* 1970 *Geoffrey Carruthers and has:

1b *Richard; *b* 1976

1b *Keryn; *b* 1973

2a *Bettine Jane; *b* 11 Oct 1954

3a *Jill Vivien [Mrs Max Steiger, 171 Carrington Ave, Hurstville, Sydney, NSW 2220, Australia]; *b* 2 April 1956; *m* 1982 *Max Steiger and has:

1b *Ben; *b* 1988

2b *Todd; *b* 1989

(1) *Elizabeth; *b* 18 May 1915

(2) *Mary Vivien [Mrs Philip Kidd, Lawhyre Lodge, Fowey, Cornwall]; *b* 9 Sept 1917; *m* 25 Jan 1941 Cdr (E) Philip Joseph Kidd, RN, 2nd s of Hugh Kidd, of Weybourne, Holt, Norfolk, and has:

1a Christopher Hugh Rashleigh; *b* 1949; *m* 19– *(Anne) Louise Houblon, only dau of Maj Richard de Warrenne Waller, RA, of Ascot, and *d* 1994, leaving:

1b *George Philip Houblon; *b* 1977

2b *Toby Richard Rashleigh; *b* 1979

1b *Emily Louisa Vivien; *b* 1980

1a *Judith Anne [Mrs Robin Stables, Mill House, Rilla Mill, Cornwall PL17 7NT]; *b* 1941; *m* 1966 *Robin Alec Stables and has:

1b *Timothy Hugh; *b* 1969

1b *Susanna Vivien; *b* 1967

2a *Sarah Vivien; *b* 1943; *m* 1st 1967 (*divorce* 1981) Angus Dormer Crichton and has:

1b *Thomas; *b* 1975

1b *Camilla; *b* 1969

2b *Anne; *b* 1970

2a (cont.) Mrs Sarah Crighton *m* 2nd 1982 *Desmond George Uniacke Bain

3a *Elizabeth; *b* 1946; *m* 1st 1967 (*divorce* 1970) John Ronald Hoskins; *m* 2nd 1979 (*divorce* 1987) Robin Kemp; *m* 3rd 1988 *Christopher Stuart Conwy Morgan and by her 1st husb has:

1b *Charles Frederick; *b* 1972

2b *Henry Selby; *b* 1977

4 Philip, DSO (1919); *b* 7 Sept 1881; Maj RA WW I (wounded, despatches); *d* unm 21 Sept 1949

5 Herbert Battie; *b* 1887; *d* 11 Sept 1890

The 4th Bt's n,

Sir Harry Evelyn Battie Rashleigh, 5th Bt; *b* 17 May 1923; *educ* Wellington Sch Somerset; RAC WW II 1941–46, mechanical engr: Tanganyika 1948–51, John Mowlem and Co London 1952–54, with English Clays Ltd, Cornwall, 1951–52; *m* 8 June 1954 *Honora Elizabeth, only dau of George Stuart Sneyd, of The Watch House, Downderry, Cornwall, and *d* 1984, leaving:

1 Sir RICHARD HARRY RASHLEIGH, **6th and present Bt**

1 *Susanna Jane [Mrs Timothy Emerson, Coleraine, Yelverton, Devon PL20 6 BN]; *b* 19 April 1955; *m* 1984 *Timothy John Peter Emerson, s of Col John Emerson, OBE, TD, DL, of Yelverton, and has:

(1) *Thomas Alexander; *b* 1987

(1) *Charlotte Jane; *b* 1985

2 *Frances Elizabeth (Bess) [Mrs Jonathan Haward, 5 Stratton Terrace, Truro, Cornwall TR1 3EW]; *b* 12 Sept 1956; *m* 1982 *Jonathan Ayton Haward and has:

(1) *Harry Thomas; *b* 1986
(1) *Emma Elizabeth; *b* 1988
3 *Anne Henrietta [Mrs Peter Argles, Green Lane Gardens, Buckland Monachorum, Devon PL20 7 NP]; *b* 21 Nov 1959; *m* 1989 *Peter B R Argles, s of Guy Kingston Argles, of Sutton Valence, Kent, and has:
  (1) *Edward Hugh Rashleigh; *b* 1992
  (2) *Arthur Peter Kingston; *b* 1994
  (3) *Christopher Jonathan Sneyd; *b* 1995
  (1) *Isobel Lydia Anne; *b* 1997

RATHCAVAN

Arms: Quarterly, 1st and 4th, per fess wavy, the chief argent and the base representing waves of the sea, in chief a dexter hand couped at the wrist gules, in base a salmon naiant proper (for O'NEILL); 2nd and 3rd, chequy or and gules, a chief vair; a mullet for difference (for CHICHESTER). **Crests:** 1 An arm embowed in armour, the hand grasping a sword, all proper, 2 A stork rising with a snake in its beak all proper. **Supporters:** On either side a heron proper standing on a billet fesswise wavy argent, charged with a bar wavy azure. **Mottoes:** 1 *Invitum sequitur honos* ('Honour follows him who does not seek it') 2 *Lamh dearg Eirin* ('The red hand of Ireland'). **Creations:** B. (UK) 11 Feb 1953, Bt. (UK) 17 June 1929.

THE 3RD BARON RATHCAVAN, of The Braid, Co Antrim, and a Baronet (Sir Hugh Detmar Torrens O'Neill, Bt) [The Rt Hon The Lord Rathcavan, Cleggan Lodge, Ballymena, Co Antrim, BT43 7JW; 14 Thurloe Place, London SW7 2RZ]; *b* 14 June 1939; *s* f 1994; *educ* Eton; Capt Irish Gds, sometime jnlst with *Financial Times*, *Irish Times* and *Observer*, dir: Lamont Hldgs, Northern Bank 1991–, Berkeley Hotel 1995–97, Old Bushmills Distillery 1988–, St Quentin Ltd 1980–94, The Spectator 1982–84, Savoy Management 1989–94, chm: NI Airports 1986–92, NI Tourist Bd, FRX International; *m* 28 March 1983 *Sylvie Marie-Thérèse, dau of Georges Wichard, of Provence, and formerly w of — Chittenden, and has:
  1 +FRANCOIS HUGH NIAL; *b* 26 June 1984

Lineage: The 2nd BARON O'NEILL (*qv*) had a 3rd s:

Sir Robert William Hugh O'Neill, 1st Bt, and **1st Baron Rathcavan**, of The Braid, Co Antrim (both UK), so *cr* 17 June 1929 and 11 Feb 1953 respectively, PC (I 1921, NI 1922, GB 1937); *b* 8 June 1883; *educ* Eton and New Coll Oxford (BA 1905); fought Stockport 1906, MP (UU) Mid Antrim 1915–22, Co Antrim 1922–50 and N Antrim 1950–52, 1st Speaker NI Parl 1922–29, Chm Conservative Private Membs Ctee 1935–39, Parly U-Sec India and Burma 1939–40, barrister Inner Temple 1909, Lt NI Imperial Yeo, Maj Roy Irish Rifles WW I 1915–18, DJAG Palestine, Pro-Chllr Queen's U Belfast 1922 (Hon LLD 1923), HM's Lt Co Antrim 1949–59; *m* 11 Feb 1909 Sylvia Irene (*d* 19 July 1972), yr dau of Walter Albert Sandeman, of Morden House, Royston, Herts, and *d* 28 Nov 1982, having had:

1 PHELIM ROBERT HUGH O'NEILL, **2nd Baron Rathcavan**, PC (NI, 1969); *b* 2 Nov 1909; *educ* Eton; Maj RA, MP (UU) N Antrim 1952–59 and NI Parl (U then Alliance) 1959–72, NI Govt: Min Educn 1969 and Ag 1969–71; *m* 1st 12 Feb 1934 (*divorce* 1944) Clare Désirée (*d* 3 March 1956), dau of Detmar Jellings Blow (*see* TOLLEMACHE, B), and had:
  (1) HUGH DETMAR TORRENS O'NEILL, **3rd and present Baron Rathcavan**
  (1) *Mary Rose; *b* 26 Aug 1935; *m* 25 April 1960 *David Stewart Wellesley Blacker (*see* PEEL, E) and has:
    1a *Barnaby Stewart Hugh; *b* 3 Feb 1961; *educ* Eton; *m* 1988 *Colleen M—, est dau of Alexander McConnell, of Palmerston North, NZ, and has:
      1b *Julia Adelaide; *b* 1989
    2a *William O'Neill; *b* 29 July 1962; *educ* Eton
    3a *Rohan David Peel; *b* 15 July 1966; *educ* Eton
1 (cont.) The **2nd Baron** *m* 2nd 3 June 1953 *Bridget Doreen, yst dau of Maj Hon Richard Coke (*see* LEICESTER, E) and formerly w of Thomas Richard Edwards-Moss (*see* EDWARDS-MOSS, Bt), and *d* 20 Dec 1994, having by her had:
  (2) *Rosetta Anne [The Hon Mrs Paxman, Ballylina Ho, Borissokane, Co Tipperary, Ireland]; *b* 14 Sept 1954; *m* 16 July 1977 *Capt John Michael Anthony

Paxman, Coldstream Gds, s of Maj Walter John Paxman, of Kingston Hill, Surrey, and has:
    1a *Truscote Phelim; *b* 1985
    1a *Musidora Anne; *b* 1980
    2a *Zena Binny Lavinia; *b* 1982
  (3) Kathleen; *b* 14 Jan, *d* 14 April 1957
  (4) *Moira Louisa; *b* 14 April 1961
  (5) *Grania Elizabeth; *b* 5 Dec 1963
2 Con Douglas Walter (Sir), GCMG (1972, KCMG 1962, CMG 1953); *b* 3 June 1912; *educ* Eton and Balliol Coll Oxford (BA 1934, MA 1937); Fell All Souls 1935–46, barrister Inner Temple 1936, Dip Serv/FO 1936–39, 1943–46 and 1947–68: 3rd Sec Berlin 1938, FO 1943–46, Frankfurt and Bonn 1948–53, Cncllr 1951, IDC 1953, Head FO News Dept 1954–55, Chargé d'Affaires Peking 1955–57, Assist U-Sec FO 1957–60, Amb: Finland 1961–63 and EC Brussels 1963–65, Dep U-Sec FO 1965–68, led Br Delegation to negotiate entry to EEC with rank of Dep U-Sec FCO Sept 1969–72, Intell Corps 1940–43, leader writer *The Times* 1946–47, dir: Hill, Samuel 1968–69, Britain in Europe Campaign 1974–75 and Unigate 1974–88, chm Intervention Bd for Ag Produce 1972–74, author: *Our European Future* (1972); *m* 1st 22 June 1940 (*divorce* 1954) Rosemary Margaret, only dau of Harold Pritchard, FRCP, and had:
  (1) +Rowan Peter Hugh [Maj Rowan O'Neill, Jerome Ho, Front St, Churchill, Bristol BS25 5NG]; *b* 7 Oct 1944; *educ* Eton and Worcester Coll Oxford (BA 1966); Maj Para Regt; *m* 1990 *Mrs Elizabeth A Wilson, dau of Edgar Goad, of Oxshott, Surrey
  (1) *Onora Sylvia CBE, FBA [Dr Onora O'Neill, The Principal, The Principal's Lodge, Newnham College, Cambridge CB3 9DF]; *b* 23 Aug 1941; *educ* St Paul's Girls Sch, Somerville Coll Oxford (BA, MA, Hon Fell 1993), Harvard U (PhD). Asst, then Assoc Prof Barnard Coll, Columbia U 1970–77; U of Essex: Lect 1977–78, Sen Lect 1978–83, Rdr 1983–87, Prof of Philosophy 1987–92; Memb Animal Procedures Cttee 1990–94, Nuffield Cncl on Bioethics 1991– (chm 1996–), Human Genetic Advsy Commn 1996–, Tstee Nuffield Fndn, 1997– (chm 1998–), Fellow Wissenschaftskolleg Berlin 1989–90, Pres Aristotelian Soc 1988–89, Foreign Hon Memb AAAS 1993; *m* 1963 (*divorce* 1976, later resumed maiden name) Edward John Nell, s of Edward John Nell of Riverside, Ill, and has:
    1a *Adam Edward O'Neill; *b* 3 April 1967; *educ* Magdalen Coll, Oxford (BA 1990), barrister, Gray's Inn 1995
    2a *Jacob Rowan; *b* 8 Dec 1969; *educ* Balliol Coll, Oxford (BA 1992), Ludwig Maximilian U Munich, U of London (MSc 1997), Private Secty HM Treasury 1998–
2 (cont.) The Hon Sir Con O'Neill *m* 2nd 30 June 1954 Baroness Carola ('Mady') Hertha Adolfine Emma Harriet Luise (*d* 19 July 1960), est dau of Baron Max Reinhard August von Holzing-Berstett and widow of Baron Wilhelm Pleikart Adolf Ludwig Arthur Marschall von Bieberstein; *m* 3rd 21 Oct 1961 *Anne-Marie [The Hon Lady O'Neill, 45 Godfrey St, London SW3], dau of Bertil Ljungström, of Stockholm, and formerly w of M Lindberg, of Helsinki, and *d* 1988
3 Nial Arthur Ramleh; *b* 5 July 1918; *educ* Eton; Maj Irish Gds; *m* 21 June 1966 *Virginia Lois [The Hon Mrs Nial O'Neill, Crowfield Ho, Crowfield, Suffolk IP6 9TP], only dau of John Douglas Legge (*see* DARTMOUTH, E), and *dsp* 20 April 1980

RATHCREEDAN

Arms: Per fess or and azure, in chief a lion passant sable and in base a maunch ermine. **Crest:** A tiger's head couped at the neck, holding in the mouth a broken spear in bend proper. **Supporters:** On either side a tiger regardant proper, collared and chained argent, the collar of the dexter charged with three roses gules, that of the sinister with three trefoils vert. **Motto:** *Frangas non flectes* ('You may break but shall not bend me'). **Creation:** B. (UK) 27 Jan 1916.

THE 3RD BARON RATHCREEDAN, of Bellehatch Park, Co Oxford (Christopher John Norton) [The Rt Hon The Lord Rathcreedan, Stoke Common House, Purton Stoke, Wilts SN5 9LL]; *b* 3 June 1949; *s* f 1990; *educ* Wellington and RAC; *m* 27 May 1978 *Lavinia Anne Ross, dau of Alan George Ross Ormiston (*see* HAREWOOD, E), and has:

1 *Jessica Charlotte; *b* 13 Nov 1983

2 *Serena Clare; *b* 12 Aug 1987

Lineage: JOHN NORTON; accompanied OLIVER CROMWELL to Ireland and acquired land at Carletown, Co Wexford; *m* Alice — (*bur* 1649) and had an est s:

EPHRAIM NORTON, of Carletown; *m* —, dau of Thomas Tayler, and *d* between 3 Dec 1698 and 16 May 1700, having had, with five other children, an est s:

JOHN NORTON, of Carletown; had:

WILLIAM NORTON; *m* —, dau of James Butler, of Castlecomer, Co Kilkenny, and had an only surv s:

WILLIAM NORTON, JP (Dublin and Meath), of Rathcreedan, Wainsford Ho, Lower Baggot St, Dublin, and Bettystown, Co Meath; *b* 1758; *m* Margaret, dau of J Ryan, LLD, of Dublin and Owney, Co Tipperary, and *d* 12 Feb 1830, leaving an only surv s:

THEOPHILUS NORTON, of Rathcreedan, Wainsford Ho and Lower Baggot St; *b* 1790; Capt Battle Axe Gds and ADC to Ld Lt Ireland; *m* Eliza (*d* 1 Oct 1841), dau of Edward Kent, of St Stephen's Green, Dublin, and had, with other issue, including a yr s (Rev Reuben, BA Dublin 1836, Rector Ballynure in Leighlin, *m* Elizabeth, dau of John Wolffe, LLB, of Lower Fitzwilliam St, Dublin, and *dsp*):

Rev WILLIAM NORTON, of Rathcreedan, Wainsford Ho and Lower Baggot St; *b* 2 Sept 1815; *educ* Dublin (MA 1842); Rector Baltinglass, Co Wicklow; *m* 2 March 1842 Caroline Theresa (*d* 22 June 1893), dau of George Riddock, of Triton Lodge, Co Louth, and *d* 4 July 1881, having had:

1 CECIL WILLIAM, **1st Baron**

2 Reuben, JP Montgomeryshire; *b* 19 April 1853; Capt Durham LI, Col 3rd Bn Suffolk Regt, High Sheriff Montgomeryshire 1915; *m* 1 Sept 1881 Evelyn (*d* 18 Jan 1927), dau of Sir Thomas Gibbons Frost, of Redcliffe, Cheshire, and *d* 30 Aug 1931, leaving:

(1) William Reuben; *b* 20 June 1884; Maj RE WW I

(2) Leopold Grantley; *b* 23 July 1890; Lt 2nd Bn Durham LI; reported wounded and missing 20 Oct 1914

(1) Evelyn Mary; *d* unm 1949

1 Alice Georgina; *m* 1st Thomas Shirley Ball, of Abbeylara, Co Leitrim, Lt 10th Hus; *m* 2nd 11 Sept 1869 Arthur Basil Brooke, RN, and *d* 1 Feb 1915, leaving issue (*see* BROOKEBOROUGH, V)

2 Caroline; *m* 2 June 1870 James Blackwell, of Kinderton, Cheshire, and had issue

3 Roselie Helen; *m* 27 April 1872 Col Hugh Powell Williams, JP, of Dolgerddon, Rhyader, Radnorshire

The Rev WILLIAM NORTON's er s,

CECIL WILLIAM NORTON, **1st Baron Rathcreedan**, of Bellehatch Park, Co Oxford (UK), so *cr* 27 Jan 1916; *b* 23 June 1850; *educ* Trin Coll Dublin, RMC Sandhurst and Staff Coll Camberley; Capt 5th Lancers and Bde-Maj Cavalry Aldershot 1881–82, MP W Newington 1892–1916, Jr Ld Treasury 1905–10, Assist PMG 1910–16, Parly Sec Min Munitions 1919–22; *m* 1st 18 Aug 1880 Cecilia Layfayette (*d* 11 Jan 1898), dau of James Kennedy, of The Limes, Co Down, and widow of William Thomas Cavendish (*see* WATERPARK, B), and had:

1 Felicie; *d* unm 31 Oct 1951

The **1st Baron** *m* 2nd 21 July 1903 Marguerite Cecil (*d* 26 May 1955), yst dau of Sir Charles Philip Huntington, 1st Bt (*see* 1928 edn), and *d* 7 Dec 1930, leaving by her:

1 CHARLES PATRICK, **2nd Baron**

2 Michael Adrian; *b* 6 Aug 1907; *educ* Wellington and Trin Coll Cambridge (BA 1929); *d* 21 March 1991

2 Sylvia Beatrice; *educ* Somerville Coll Oxford (BA 1929); *m* 22 April 1933 W/Cdr Rowland David George, DSO, OBE, RAuxAF (*d* 9 Sept 1997), yst s of John Ellis George, of Combe Pk, Bath, and had issue

The 1st BARON's er s,

CHARLES PATRICK NORTON, **2nd Baron Rathcreedan**, TD; *b* 26 Nov 1905; *educ* Wellington and Lincoln Coll Oxford (BA 1928, MA 1935); barrister Inner Temple 1931, slr 1936, Maj Oxon and Bucks LI (TA) WW II (POW), Master Founders' Co 1970; *m* 7 Aug 1946 *Ann Pauline [The Rt Hon The Dowager Lady Rathcreedan, 8 Pearces Orchard, Henley-on-Thames, Oxon RG9 2LF], er dau of Surgn-Capt William Bastian, RN, and *d* 1990, leaving:

1 CHRISTOPHER JOHN NORTON, **3rd and present Baron Rathcreedan**

2 +ADAM GREGORY [The Hon Adam Norton, 60 Marmora Rd, London SE22]; *b* 2 April 1952; heir presumptive; *educ* Wellington; actor; *m* 19 April 1980 *Hilary, only dau of Edmon Ryan, of Anchorage, Ky., and Mrs Paul McGrath, of New York, and has:

(1) *Emily Beatrice; *b* 1984

(2) *Georgina Christine Ryan; *b* 1988

1 *Elizabeth Ann [The Hon Mrs Scott, 35 Lancaster Rd, London W14]; *b* 17 July 1954; *m* Sept 1988 *Alistair Scott, er s of Prof James S Scott

RATHDONNELL

Arms: Quarterly, 1st and 4th, argent on a bend sable three chess rooks of the field (for BUNBURY); 2nd and 3rd, per pale gules and azure a chevron ermine between three escallops argent (for McCLINTOCK). **Crests:** 1 Two swords in saltire argent, hilted or, pierced through a leopard's face or (for BUNBURY), 2 A lion passant proper (for McCLINTOCK). **Supporters:** Dexter, a lion; sinister, a leopard, both proper, each gorged with a collar ermine and each charged on the shoulder with an escallop argent. **Mottoes:** 1 *Vis unita fortior* ('Power is the stronger for unity') (for BUNBURY), 2 *Virtute et labore* ('By strength and hard work') (for McCLINTOCK). **Creation:** B. (I) 21 Dec 1868.

THE **5TH BARON RATHDONNELL**, of Rathdonnell, Co Donegal (Thomas Benjamin McClintock-Bunbury [The Rt Hon The Lord Rathdonnell, Lisnavagh, Rathvilly, Co Carlow, Ireland]; *b* 17 Sept 1938; *s f* 1959; *educ* Charterhouse and RNC Dartmouth; Lt RN; *m* 2 Oct 1965 *Jessica Harriet, only dau of George Gilbert Butler (*see* DUNBOYNE, B), and has:

1 +WILLIAM LEOPOLD; *b* 6 July 1966; *educ* Charterhouse

2 +George Andrew Kane; *b* 26 July 1968

3 +James Alexander Hugh; *b* 21 Feb 1972

1 *Sasha Anne; *b* 6 Feb 1976

Lineage: ALEXANDER McCLINTOCK, a Scot who settled in Ireland, bought 1597 the Rathdonnell estates, Co Donegal, and had an only s:

ALEXANDER McCLINTOCK, of Trinta, Co Donegal; *m* 1648 Agnes Stenson (*d* 6 Dec 1696), dau of Donald Maclean, and *d* 6 Sept 1670, having had, with a yr s (William, *b* 1657, *m* 1685 Elizabeth, dau of David Harvey, of Dunmore, Co Donegal, and *d* 1724, having had issue):

JOHN McCLINTOCK, of Trinta; *b* 1649; *m* 11 Aug 1687 Janet, 4th dau of John Lowry, of Ahenis, Co Tyrone (*see* BELMORE, E), and *d* 3 Sept 1707, having had, with another s (*d* young):

1 Alexander, of Drumcar, Co Louth; *b* 30 Sept 1692; *m* Rebecca, dau of William Sampson, and *dsp* 25 May 1775, leaving his estates to his n JOHN (*see* below)

2 John, of Trinta; *b* 27 March 1698; *m* Susannah Maria, 2nd dau of William Chambers, of Rock Hall, Co Donegal, and had, with three other daus:

(1) William; *m* Francelina, 3rd dau of James Nesbitt, of Green Hills, and had:

1a John; *m* Grace, dau of Rev Ralph Ralph Mansfield, AM, of Castle Wray, Co Donegal

(2) James, of Trinta; *b* 17 Aug 1739; *m* 1762 Dora Beresford, only dau and heiress of Henry McCullagh, of Ballyarten, Co Derry, and had issue

(3) JOHN

(4) Alexander, of Newtown, Co Louth; *b* 30 March 1746; *m* Dec 1781 Mary, only dau of Samuel Perry, of Perrymount and Seskinore, Co Tyrone, and had issue

(1) Anne; *m* April 1766 Rev John Young (*see* YOUNG, Bt, of Bailieborough) and had issue

3 Robert; *b* 27 Oct 1702; *m* Helen, dau of William Harvey, and had issue

ALEXANDER McCLINTOCK's n,

JOHN McCLINTOCK, of Drumcar; *b* 1 Jan 1742; MP (I) Enniskillen 1783–90 and Belturbet 1790–97; *m* 11 May 1766 Patience, dau of John William Foster (*see* MASSEREEENE and FERRARD, V), and *d* Feb 1799, having had, with three other daus:

1 JOHN

2 Alexander (Rev); *b* 6 Jan 1775; Rector Newtown Barry and Clonegal, Diocese of Ferns; *m* 1790 Anne, dau of Mervyn Pratt, and *d* 6 Aug 1836, leaving issue, now extinct in the male line

3 William Foster; *b* 18 Oct 1777; *m* 1803 Mary, dau of Maj-Gen Helden, and *d* 1838, having had issue

4 Henry; *b* 28 Sept 1783; 3rd Dragoon Gds; *m* Dec 1809 Elizabeth Melesina (*d* 29 Jan 1853), dau of Ven George Fleury, DD, Archdeacon Waterford, and *d* 27 Feb 1843, having had issue

1 Fanny; *m* 6 June 1798 Theophilus Clive, cousin of 1st Baron Clive of Plassey (*see* POWIS, E), and had issue

2 Mary-Anne; *m* Matthew Fortescue, of Stephenstown, Co Louth, and had issue

The est s,

JOHN McCLINTOCK, of Drumcar; *b* 14 Aug 1770; High Sheriff Co Louth 1798, MP Athlone 1823 and Co Louth 1831; *m* 1st 11 July 1797 Jane (*d* 28 April 1801), only dau of William Bunbury, MP, of Moyle, Co Carlow, and *d* 5 July 1855, having had, with a dau:

1 JOHN McCLINTOCK, **1st Baron Rathdonnell**, of Rathdonnell, Co Donegal (I), so *cr* 21 Dec 1868, with limitation to his heirs male, which failing, to the heirs male of his bro William, DL (Co Fermanagh); *b* 26 Aug 1798; *educ* Sandhurst; Offr 74th Foot, Col Louth Regt Rifle Militia, High Sheriff Co Louth 1840, MP (C) Co Louth 1857–59; *m* 1829 Anne (*d* 22 Dec 1889), est dau of Rev John Henry George Lefroy, AM, of Ewsholt House, Hants, and *dsp* 17 May 1879

2 William Bunbury McCLINTOCK later McCLINTOCK-BUNBURY (roy licence 1846 under terms of will of unc Thomas Bunbury), of Lisnavagh; *b* 1800; Capt RN, MP Co Carlow 1846–62; *m* 3 Nov 1842 Pauline Caroline Diana Mary (*d* 1 Jan 1876), 2nd dau of Sir James Mathew Stronge, 2nd Bt (*qv*), and *d* 2 June 1866, leaving, with two daus (*d* unm):

(1) THOMAS KANE, **2nd Baron**

(2) John William, of Moyle, Co Carlow, JP; *b* 1 Sept 1851; High Sheriff Co Carlow 1880, served Scots Greys; *m* 11 Sept 1878 Elizabeth Myra (*m* 2nd 1 June 1896 Baron Maximilian de Tuyll (*d* 7 Nov 1911)), 2nd dau of Robert Watson, of Ballydarton, Co Carlow, and *d* 14 Oct 1893, having had:

1a Geoffrey; *b* 10 Oct 1882; *d* 2 Oct 1892

JOHN McCLINTOCK *m* 2nd 15 April 1805 Lady Elizabeth Trench (*d* 30 May 1877 aged 97), 3rd dau of 1st Earl of Clancarty (*qv*), and by her had:

3 Frederick William Pitt; MA, barrister; *d* unm 1834

4 Charles Alexander; Capt 74th Regt; *d* unm 9 Dec 1833

5 Robert Le Poer (Rev); *b* 10 Aug 1810; Rector Castle Bellingham, Co Louth; *m* 29 July 1856 Maria Susan (*m* 2nd 1 Feb 1883 Francis Burton Owen Cole, DL, of Llys Merichion, Denbighs (*d* 13 Jan 1912), and *d* 14 Jan 1925), only dau of Charles Alexander Heyland by Maria, sis of Sir Robert Montgomery, KCB, and *dsp* 30 June 1879

6 Henry Stanley, of Kilwarlin House, Co Down, JP Cos Antrim, Down and Kildare; *b* 1812; Maj RHA and Antrim Artillery; *m* 1839 Gertrude (*d* 22 March 1864), only dau of Robert La Touche, MP, of Harristown, Co Kildare, and *d* 9 Sept 1898, leaving issue

7 George Augustus Jocelyn, of Fellows Hall, Co Armagh, JP; *b* 22 May 1822; Capt 52nd LI, Lt-Col Sligo Rifles; *m* April 1850 Catherine Caroline Brownlow, dau of Sir James Matthew Stronge, 2nd Bt (*qv*), and *d* 24 Dec 1873, leaving issue

1 Anne Florence; *m* 21 April 1828 Very Rev Hugh Usher Tighe, DD, Dean Derry, and had issue

2 Harriette Elizabeth; *m* 1832 Richard Longfield, MP, of Longueville, Co Cork, and *d* 27 April 1834, leaving issue

3 Emily Selina Frances; *m* 16 Nov 1841 John Butler-Clarke-Southwell-Wandesforde (*see* MOUNTGARRET, V) and *d* 29 Jan 1909

The 1st BARON's n,

THOMAS KANE McCLINTOCK-BUNBURY, **2nd Baron Rathdonnell**, DL (Co Louth); *b* 29 Nov 1848; *educ* Eton; Lt Scots Greys, Capt Leics Yeo Cav, Hon Col 6th Bn Roy Irish Rifles 1896–1929, Co Carlow: Ld Lt, High Sheriff 1876, rep I peer 1889; *m* 26 Feb 1874 Katharine Anne (*d* 13 April 1925), est dau of Rt Hon Henry Bruen, of Oak Park, Co Carlow, and *d* 22 May 1929, having had:

1 William; *b* 15 Sept 1878; *educ* Eton; 2nd Lt Scots Greys Boer War; *d* 17 Feb 1900 of wounds recd in action

2 THOMAS LEOPOLD, **3rd Baron**

1 Isabella Katherine; *b* 28 Dec 1874; *m* 26 July 1894 Lt-Col Forrester Farnell Colvin, CBE, 9th Lancers (*d* 16 Feb 1936), of Shermanbury Grange, Horsham, Sussex, 3rd s of Beale Blackwell Colvin, of Monkhams Hall, Essex, and *d* 30 March 1963, having had issue

2 Mary Emily; *b* 21 April 1876; *m* 3 Nov 1898 Lt-Col Henry Duncombe Bramwell, 15th Hus (*d* 9 Sept 1921), s of Henry Bramwell, of Crown East Court, Worcs, and *d* 26 Dec 1962, leaving issue

3 Pauline Caroline; *b* 11 May 1877; *m* 10 June 1897 Maj Frederick John Dalgety, 15th Hus (*d* 23 May 1926), of Lockerley Hall, Hants, and *d* 25 July 1935, leaving issue

The 2nd BARON's only surv s,

THOMAS LEOPOLD McCLINTOCK-BUNBURY, **3rd Baron Rathdonnell**, MBE; *b* 3 Feb 1881; *educ* Charterhouse and Trin Coll Cambridge (MA); High Sheriff Co Carlow 1909, Capt WW I (despatches, Order Crown Italy, Croce di Guerra); *m* 26 Nov 1912 Ethel Synge (*d* 4 March 1922), 2nd dau of Robert Wilson Ievers, CMG, Ceylon CS, and *d* 28 Sept 1937, leaving:

1 WILLIAM ROBERT McCLINTOCK-BUNBURY, **4th Baron Rathdonnell**, MC (1945); *b* 23 Nov 1914; *educ* Charterhouse and Trin Coll Cambridge (BA 1936); Capt (Hon Maj) 15th/19th Hus, RARO, WW II; *m* 25 Nov 1937 Pamela, artist, Actg 3rd Offr WRNS (*d* 1989, having *m* 2nd 27 May 1961 Maj Hugh Caruthers Massy, *see* MASSY, B), est dau of John Malcolm Drew, of Westmorland, and *d* 13 Oct 1959, having had:

(1) THOMAS BENJAMIN McCLINTOCK-BUNBURY, **5th and present Baron Rathdonnell**

(1) *Katharine Alexandra [The Hon Mrs Doyle, Coole Stables, Rathvilly, Co Carlow, Ireland]; *b* 19 Feb 1940; *m* 1960 James Joseph Doyle (*d* 1993), s of Timothy Doyle, of Tobinstown, Co Carlow, and has issue

(2) *Hermione Jane [The Hon Mrs Macleod, 34 Newell St, Pt Chevalier, Auckland, New Zealand]; *b* 11 Aug 1943; *m* 1988 *Callum Macleod

(3) A dau; *b* 23, *d* 24 May 1946

(4) *Pamela Rosemary [The Hon Pamela McClintock-Bunbury, The Middle Lodge, Kilruddery, Bray, Co Wicklow, Ireland]; *b* 30 July 1948; *educ* Millfield

Seat: Lisnavagh, Rathvilly, Co Carlow, Ireland. This house was actually designed for the **1st Baron's** brother, William, rather than the holder of the title himself. The architect, John McCurdy, stuck to an unpretentious neo-Tudor

style. In the early 1950s the **4th Baron** tore down the part of the house containing the main rooms for the family and transformed the old servants' wing to suit the less lavish way of life demanded by the times. This worked well because the two parts of the original house had not formed an organic whole, and a few bits of ornamentation from the family part of the house were recycled in remodelling the new.

RAVENSDALE

Arms: Quarterly: 1st and 4th sable a chevron between three pickaxes argent (for MOSLEY); 2nd and 3rd argent on a bend sable three popinjays or, collared gules (for CURZON). **Crest:** An eagle displayed ermine. **Supporters:** 1 Dexter, a raven proper (for MOSLEY); 2 sinister, a popinjay proper, collared gules (for CURZON). **Motto:** *Mos legem regit* ('Custom rules the law'). **Creation:** Bt. (GB) 1781, B. (UK) 2 Nov 1911.

THE 3RD BARON RAVENSDALE, of Ravensdale, Co Derby, and a **Baronet** (Sir Nicholas Mosley, Bt, MC (1944) [The Rt Hon The Lord Ravensdale MC, 2 Gloucester Crescent, London NW1 7DS]; *b* 25 June 1923; *s* aunt 1966 in Barony and f 1980 in btcy; *educ* Eton and Balliol Coll Oxford; Capt Rifle Bde WW II 1942–46, author (as Nicholas Mosley): *Spaces of the Dark* (1951), *The Rainbearers* (1955), *Corruption* (1957), *African Switchback* (1958), *The Life of Raymond Raynes* (1961), *Meeting Place* (1962), *Accident* (1964), *Experience and Religion* (1964), *Assassins* (1966), *Impossible Object* (1968), *Natalie Natalia* (1971), *The Assassination of Trotsky* (1972), *Julian Grenfell: His Life and the Times of his Death, 1888–1915* (1976), *Catastrophe Practice* (1979), *Imago Bird* (1980), *Serpent* (1981), *The Rules of the Game: Sir Oswald and Lady Cynthia Mosley 1896–1933* (1982), *Beyond the Pale: Sir Oswald Mosley 1933–1980* (1983), *Judith* (1986), *Efforts at Truth* (autobiography, 1995), *Hopeful Monsters* (1990, Whitbread Prize), *Children of Darkness and Light* (1996); *m* 1st 14 Nov 1947 (*divorce* 1974) Rosemary Laura (*d* 1991), dau of Marshal of the RAF Sir John Maitland Salmond, GCB, CMG, CVO, DSO (*see* LUCAS OF CRUDWELL, B), and has:

1 +SHAUN NICHOLAS [The Hon Shaun Mosley, Sunnybank, Albert Rd, Alexandra Park, Nottingham]; *b* 5 Aug 1949; *educ* Bryanston and Hertford Coll Oxford; *m* 1978 *Theresa Clifford and has:

(1) +Daniel Nicholas; *b* 10 Oct 1982

(2) +Matthew; *b* 6 March 1985

(3) +Francis; *b* 5 July 1988

(4) +Aidan; *b* 1991

(5) +Thomas; *b* 23 Dec 1993

(1) *Monica; *b* 5 June 1996

2 +Ivo Adam Rex [The Hon Ivo Mosley, The Mill House, Upton Hellions, Crediton, Devon EX17 4AE]; *b* 14 April 1951; *educ* Bryanston and New Coll Oxford; ed *The Green Book of Poetry*; *m* 10 Sept 1977 *Xanthe Jennifer Grenville, yst dau of Sir Michael Bernard Oppenheimer, 3rd Bt (*qv*), and has:

(1) +Nathaniel Inigo; *b* 15 July 1982

(2) +Felix Harry; *b* 16 Nov 1985

(3) +Scipio Louis; *b* 7 June 1988

(4) +Noah Billy; *b* 10 Oct 1990

3 +Robert; *b* 24 Dec 1955; *educ* Bedales; *m* 1980 *Victoria McBain, and has:

(1) +Gregory; *b* 9 May 1981

(2) +Orson; *b* 6 June 1994

(1) *Vija; *b* 19 July 1985

1 *Clare Imogen ; *b* 11 Nov 1959; has:

(1) *Rosie; *b* 29 Feb 1992

The 3rd BARON *m* 2nd 19 July 1974 *Verity Elizabeth, 2nd dau of N John (Jack) B Raymond, of Winslade Down House, Basingstoke, Hants, and formerly w of (John) Adrian Bailey, and by her has:

4 +Marius; *b* 28 May 1976

Lineage (of Mosley): The **2nd Bt** of the 1781 and present *cr* states in his *Family Memoirs* that ERNALD de MOSELEY, of Mosley, Staffs; probably of Saxon origin; living before the reign of KING JOHN; had:

1 William; had, with two other daus:

(1) Juliana; *m* John De BILSTON later MOSELEY (took w's name on inheriting her f's lands through her) and had issue, who held the Moseley lands in Staffs till they passed via an heiress to the HORTONs *c* mid-18th century; ancestor also of the MOSELEYs of Norfolk and Salop

2 Osbert/Oswald; had several children; ancestor of:

(1) Jenkyn Moseley, of Hough End, Didsbury, nr Manchester; living 1465; had:

1a James, of Hough End; had:

1b Edward; *m* Margaret (*d c* 1589), dau of Alexander Elcock, of Hillgate, nr Stockport, Cheshire, and *d* 1571, having had:

1c Oswald, of Garret(t) Hall, nr Manchester, which he bought 1593 from Sir John Gerrard, his 1st w's unc; inherited from his f lands in Moston, nr Manchester; *m* 1st —, est dau of Rev Richard Gerrard, DD, Rector Stockport; *m* 2nd Cicely, dau of Richard Tipping, of Manchester, and *d* 1622, having had, with other yr sons:

1d Oswald; *dvp*, leaving:

1e Oswald; *d* young

2d Rowland; *dvp*

3d Samuel; sold the estates inherited from his f by 1631 and settled in Ireland; allegedly f of:

1e John; Clerk of the Crown Ireland *c* 1650; had:

1f Benjamin, of the Inner Temple, London; *b c* 1651; *d* 8 Sept 1734, leaving, with other issue:

1g Edward, of London; *b c* 1706; *d* 3 Dec 1779, leaving a 2nd s:

1h Benjamin, JP Middx 1814; *b* 1 March 1746; Surgn-Gen Jamaica 1775, memb American Philosophical Soc 1775, Magistrate and Assist Judge St Andrew's Parish Jamaica, Ensign 79th Regt, LRCP 1787, Physician to: THE DUKEs of YORK 1788 and CLARENCE 1789 and Roy Hosp Chelsea 1789, MD Leyden 1791, author: *Treatise upon Coffee* (1785), *Tropical Diseases, Military Operations, and the Climate of the West Indies* (1788), *Treatise on Sugar* (1799) and an attack upon cow pox (the vaccination system promoted by Dr Edward Jenner) (1805); *m* 9 Jan 1768 Martha Clare, of Merton, Surrey, and had:

1i William Henry, of Yeoman's Row, London SW; *educ* Eton and Edinburgh and Oxford (MD 1805) Us; Physician to the Forces 1805; *d unm* 1823

2i Henry Crewe; *d* aged 16

1i Martha Elizabeth; *b c* 1775; *d unm* 1847

1h (cont.) Dr Moseley *d* 25 Sept 1819, leaving also an illegitimate dau

2e Benjamin; QMG Parly Army Civil War; *ka* Battle of Worcester 3 Sept 1651

4d Francis; had an only s:

1e Francis; *m* 1643 Ellen, dau of James Lancashire, and had:

1f Thomas; Ld Mayor York 1687

2f Rowland; Sheriff York 1702; *m* Jane, dau and coheir of Charles Rickard, of Heck, and had, with nine daus and seven er sons:

1g Edward; Mayor Newcastle; *m* Hannah, dau of Henry Compleashon, and had issue

1d Margaret; *m* John Vaudrey, of Rydding, Cheshire

2c Nicholas MOSELEY later MOSLEY (Sir); *b c* 1527; London: Alderman Aldersgate Ward *c* 1589, Sheriff 1590, Ld Mayor 1599–1600, ktd *c* 1600; acquired 1596 for £3,500 (over £76,000 in late-1990s terms) in settlement of a debt the Manor of Manchester, which remained in the family till acquired by Manchester Corporation 1846; High Sheriff Lancs 1604; *m* 1st Margaret, dau of Hugh Whitbroke, of Bridgnorth, Salop; *m* 2nd 19 Oct 1592 Elizabeth, dau of John Rookes and widow of — Hendley, of London, and *d* 12 Dec 1612, leaving by his 1st w:

1d Rowland, of The Hough, Staffs; High Sheriff Lancs 1615–16; *m* 1st Anne, dau of Humphrey Houghton, of Manchester, and had, with a s (*d* an infant):

1e Margaret; *m* William Whitmore (*see* WHITMORE, Bt)

1d (cont.) Rowland Mosley *m* 2nd Anne, dau and ultimate heir of Francis Sutton, of Sutton, Cheshire, and *d* 23 Feb 1616/7, leaving by her, with a dau (Ann, *d unm*):

1e Sir EDWARD MOSLEY, 1st Bt (E), so *cr* 20 July 1640, of Manchester and Rolleston; *bapt* Sept 1616; High Sheriff Staffs 1642–43; royalist Civil War (captured by Parly forces Middlewich, Cheshire, March 1642/3 and subsequently fined £4,200 (just under £170,000 in late-1990s terms) plus an annual payment of £64 (over £2,500 in late-1990s terms) plus a further fine of £4,874 (some £205,000 in late-1990s terms) in 1647 to get repossession of his estates); acquitted of rape Jan 1647/8; *m* 15 Nov 1636 Mary, dau of Sir Gervase Cutler, of Stainborough Hall, Yorks, and Breadsall Priory, Derbys, by Elizabeth (dau and heiress of Sir John Bentley, of Breadsall), and was *bur* 4 Dec 1657, leaving:

1f Sir EDWARD MOSLEY, 2nd and last Bt, of Breadsall Priory; *b c* 1639; *educ* BNC Oxford; High Sheriff Lancs 1660, MP St Michael's 1661–65; bought the Hulme estate 1661; *m* April 1665 Catharine (*m* 2nd *c* 6 April 1667 5th Lord (Baron) North and 1st Lord (Baron) Grey (of Rolleston) (*see* GUILFORD, E) and had issue; *m* 3rd (licence 30 April 1691) Col Francis Russell; *see* BEDFORD, D), dau of 1st Baron Grey of Warke (*see* GREY, E), and *dsp* 14 Oct 1655, when the btcy expired

1f Mary; *m* Joseph Maynard, only s of Sir John Maynard, Serjeant-at-law and Commr Gt Seal *temp* WILLIAM III, and had:

1g Elizabeth; *m* Sir Henry Hobart, 4th Bt, and had issue (*see* BUCKINGHAMSHIRE, E)

2g Mary; *b c* 1671; *m* just prior to 12 March 1690/1, as his 2nd w, 2nd Earl of Stamford (*see* 1970 edn), and *dsps* 9 Nov 1722

2f Anne; *d unm*

2d Anthony; *m* a sis of Sir Edward Hewett and *dspl*, leaving illegitimate issue:

1e Anthony

3d Edward (Sir); *b c* 1569; bought Manor of Rolleston, Staffs; barrister Gray's Inn, ktd 1614, Attorney-Gen Duchy Lancaster; *d unm* 1 July 1638

3c Anthony, of Ancoats, which he bought from 1st Baron Byron (*qv*) of Rochdale; *b c* 1537; clothier; *m* Alice, dau of Richard Webster, of Manchester, and *d* 25 March 1607, leaving, with four yr sons and a dau:

1d Oswald; *b c* 1583; *m* Anne, dau and coheir of Ralph Lowe, of Mile End, Cheshire, and *d* 9 Nov 1630, having had:

1e Nicholas, of Ancoats, JP Lancs 1660; *bapt* 26 Dec 1611; royalist Civil War, hence his estates confiscated 1643–46 (he redeemed them for a large fine), Boroughreeve Manchester 1661–62, author *Psychosophia, or Natural and Divine Contemplations of the Passions and Faculties of the Soul of Man* (1653); *m* Jane, dau of John Lever, of Alkrington, and was *bur* 28 Oct 1672, having had, with another s (*d unm*) and four daus:

1f Oswald, of Rolleston, which he inherited from his cousin the 2nd and last Bt of the 1640 *cr*; *bapt* 1 Sept 1639; High Sheriff Staffs 1699–1700; *m* Mary, dau of William Yates, barrister, of Stanley House, Lancs, and was *bur* 2 Sept 1726, having had, with three yr sons (*dspm* or *unm*) and a dau:

1g Sir OSWALD MOSLEY, 1st Bt (GB), so *cr* 18 June 1720, of Rolleston, Staffs; *bapt* 11 Aug 1674; *educ* Oriel Coll Oxford and Gray's Inn; High Sheriff Staffs 1714–15; inherited the Hulme and Manchester estates from his cousin Anne Lady Bland; built Manchester's first Exchange building; as a Jacobite sympathiser seems to have secretly harboured Prince Charles Edward the year before the 1745 Rising; *m* 4 Feb 1702/3 Elizabeth, dau of John Thornhaugh, of Fenton, Staffs, by Elizabeth (dau of Sir Richard Earle, 1st Bt), and *d* 10 June 1751, having had, with two yr sons (*d unm* or *vp*):

1h Sir OSWALD MOSLEY, 2nd Bt, of Ancoats, Hulme and Rolleston; *b* 21 April 1705; Ld Manor of Manchester; *d unm* 26 Feb 1757

2h Rev Sir JOHN MOSLEY, 3rd and last Bt, of Ancoats, Hulme and Rolleston; *educ* Lincoln's Inn and Trin Coll Cambridge; Ld Manor of Manchester, Rector Rolleston 1777–79, also Fenton; *d unm* 22 May or Sept 1779, when the btcy expired

1h Elizabeth; *m* Humphrey Trafford (*see* DE TRAFFORD, Bt) and *dsp*

2f Nicholas, of Manchester and later Shadwell, London; apothecary; *m* Elizabeth Cooke and *d* Nov 1697, having had, with three other sons:

1g Nicholas; *b c* 1693; Manchester wool draper; *m* Elizabeth, dau of William Parker, of Derby, cousin to 1st Earl of Macclesfield (*qv*), and was *bur* March 1734/5, leaving, with three er sons:

1h **Sir John Parker Mosley, 1st Bt** (GB), so *cr* 8 June 1781; *b* 1732; failed hatter in Manchester but underwent a spiritual conversion and in any case inherited estates of his cousin, Rev Sir JOHN MOSLEY, 3rd and last Bt (*see* above); High Sheriff Lancs 1786; *m* 7 April 1760 Elizabeth (*d* 15 Oct 1797), dau of James Bayley, of Withington, Lancs, by Anne, dau of Samuel Peploe, DD, Bp Chester, and had:

1i Oswald, of Bolesworth Castle, Cheshire, which he bought 1785; *b* 17 March 1761; *educ* Manchester and Macclesfield GScs; *m* 3 Feb 1784 Elizabeth, dau and heiress of Rev Thomas Tonman, Rector Little Budworth, Cheshire, and *dvp* 27 July 1789, leaving, with a yr s (*d* young):

1j OSWALD (Sir), **2nd Bt**

1j Elizabeth; *m* 1806, as his 1st w, William Henry Ashurst, of Waterstock, Oxon, Chm Oxon QS, MP Oxon, and *d* 1828, leaving issue

2j Frances; *m* 17 Aug 1807 Sir James Whalley Smyth Gardiner, 3rd Bt (*d* 22 Oct 1851; *see* 1868 edn), and *d* 13 Dec 1855, leaving issue

2i John Peploe (Rev); *b* 13 Dec 1766; Rector Rolleston; *m* 1st 7 Oct 1790 Sarah Maria, dau of William Paget (*see* PAGET, Bt, of Cranmore Hall); *m* 2nd Aug 1827 Frances, widow of Rev Edward Pole, and *d* 3 Feb 1833, leaving by his 1st w:

1j Peploe Paget (Rev); *b* 22 Dec 1793; Rector Rolleston; *m* 5 July 1836 Elizabeth (*d* 18 Sept 1888), dau of Francis Bradshaw, of Barton Blount, Derbys, and *d* 7 April 1868, having had:

1k Paget Peploe, JP Derbys; *b* 12 Aug 1837; Hon Col Derbys Yeo Cav, Capt 11th Hus; *m* 1st 16 May 1861 Caroline Veronica (*d* 3 Nov 1878), dau of William Gerard Walmesley, of Westwood House, Wigan, Lancs; *m* 2nd 12 Aug 1905 Annie Adelaide Flynn (*m* 2nd 15 Nov 1915 Capt Henry Baker-Cresswell, 15th Hus; *dsp* 1 Dec 1928), and *d* Oct 1940), dau of William Jackson, of Melbourne, Australia, and *dsp* 21 Feb 1915

2j John Edward; *b* 31 May 1795; *m* 20 May 1824 Sophia Anne (*d* 1853), dau of William Paget, of Newbury House, Somerset, and *d* 2 June 1862, having had:

1k Caroline Mary Jane; *d unm* 27 Sept 1860

2k Marianne Sophia; *m* 9 April 1861 Rev Robert Wood (*d* 1883) and had issue

3j William Bayley; *b* 19 Aug 1806; 10th Bengal Cav, HEICS; *m* 5 Jan 1836 Maria Sarah (*d* 21 Oct 1878), dau of Samuel Lowe, of The Abbey, Burton-on-Trent, Staffs, and *d* 12 Aug 1848, having had:

1k William Feilden; *b* 1 April 1838; Lt IA; *ka* 18 Nov 1863

2k John Edward Paget; *b* 15 Feb 1841; Lt-Col BSC; *m* 26 Oct 1871 Anna Katharine (*d* 20 May 1934), dau of Thomas Crooke Ainsworth, of Blackburn, Lancs, and *d* 14 Feb 1917, leaving:

  1l John Paget; *b* 9 Oct 1872; barrister, City of London Imp Vols Boer War 1900, Capt RFA (T) WW I, Civ Liabilities Commn 1919; *m* 1st 6 April 1904 Adela Constance Mary (*d* 21 Dec 1915), est dau of George Herbert Strutt, DL, JP, of Makeney House, Derbys, and had:

    1m William George; *b* 14 April 1905

    2m John Herbert; *b* 14 March 1912; *educ* HMS *Conway*; Lt RNR, Merchant Navy WW II (wounded); *m* 1st 21 Dec 1935 (*divorce* 1947) Ethel Marcia, dau of Joseph Hancock, of Derbys, and had:

      1n *Christine Ann [Mrs Clive Dearden, 76 Hillsway, Littleover, Derbys]; *b* 1941; *m* 18 July 1964 *Clive Dearden and has:

        1o *Rosemary Ann; *b* 5 Feb 1969

        2o *Heather Jane; *b* 1971

    2m (cont.) John Mosley *m* 2nd 25 March 1949 (*divorce* 1950) Mrs Elaine Verna Savory, dau of — Buchanan-Muir, of Pietermaritzburg, Natal; *m* 3rd 7 July 1951 (*divorce* 1955) Elizabeth Anna Maria, dau of William Stefak, of Chezen, Poland; *m* 4th 19 July 1962 (*divorce* 1973) Lyla Fay, dau of Robert Hemus, of Auckland, NZ, and *d* 1986

    1m Ann Adela Katharine; *b* 9 April 1907; *m* 14 Oct 1939 Robert de Brath Ashworth, PhD, s of Maj Robert Frederick Weir Ashworth, of Christchurch, NZ, and had issue

  1l (cont.) John W Mosley *m* 2nd 5 May 1937 Mary Euphrasia, MBE (*d* 17 Feb 1952), dau of Godfrey Wedgwood (*see* WEDGWOOD, B), and *d* 16 July 1938

  1l Florence Katharine; *b* 6 Jan 1874; *m* 1st 6 Dec 1892 Capt Frederic Marriner Aston, 6th Bn DCLI (*ka* 7 July 1915), of Washaway, Cornwall, and had issue; *m* 2nd 26 April 1921 Lt-Col Charles Frederick Miller, DSO, DCLI (*d* 23 Feb 1963)

3k Alfred; *b* 26 March 1845; *d* 13 May 1846

4k Oswald Henry (Rev); *b* 27 Sept 1846; Rector Wentworth, Cambs; *m* 9 Nov 1875 Isabel Hutchinson (*d* 6 Oct 1941), 3rd dau of A Campbell, of Culross, and *d* 7 Feb 1899, leaving:

  1l Oswald Feilden; *b* 2 Feb 1880; *m* 5 June 1912 Elizabeth (Ida) (*d* 18 Sept 1959), er dau of William H Palmer, of Torquay, and *d* 31 Dec 1947, leaving:

    1m Oswald Henry Feilden; *b* 4 Feb 1913; *educ* Wellingborough and Swinton Conservative Coll; Lt RAC WW II, C Agent Brighouse and Spenborough 1949–50, St Pancras 1950–52; *m* 1st 23 June 1941 (*divorce* 1952) Mary Angela, dau of Louis de Las Casas, of Elliscombe House, Wincanton; *m* 2nd 23 Feb 1952 *Olga Marie Noelle [Mrs Oswald Mosley, The Gatehouse, Purley Lodge, Purley, Berks], dau of George Ackroyd, and *d* 4 Aug 1995, leaving by his 1st w:

      1n *Sheila Dorothy [Mrs Paul Minet, 3 Apsley Court, Pickforde Lane, Tilehurst, E Sussex TN5 7BJ]; *b* 5 April 1942; *m* 1970 *Paul Brissault Minet and has:

        1o *Isobel Louise [Mrs Timothy Arthur, 60 Claremont Rd, Tunbridge Wells, Kent]; *b* 1971; *m* 1993 *Timothy Gwion Arthur and has:

          1p *Caitlan Moon Minet; *b* 1995

        2o *Anthea [Mrs Sean Mellor, 21 Thames St, Poole, Dorset BH15 1JN]; *b* 1973; *m* 1997 *Sean Mellor

    1m +Robert Anthony [S/Ldr Robert Mosley, 15 Dolvin Rd, Tavistock, S Devon PL19 9EA]; *b* 14 May 1920; late S/Ldr RAF, dir Kennet Assemblies Ltd, Minleys (Cornwall) Ltd and Vieux Temps of Monte Carlo; *m* 26 Feb 1944 (*divorce* 1954) Renée Carmen Cecily, dau of Elias Assouad, of Azzizia, Aleppo, Syria, and has:

      1n +Anthony Noel; *b* 10 Dec 1949; *educ* Kelly Coll; dir Kennet Assemblies Ltd and Minleys (Cornwall) Ltd

      1n Bertha Mary Isobel; *b* 31 March 1945; *m* 24 Feb 1968 *Alistair Maciver, s of Finlay MacFarlane Maciver, of Edinburgh, and *d* 1988, leaving:

        1o *Neil Anthony; *b* 1970

        1o *Katherine Anne Mary; *b* 17 March 1969

  1l Anna Maria; *b* 18 Jan 1877; *m* 19 May 1904 Herbert Henry Thomas, DSc, FRS (*d* 12 May 1935), and *d* 1957, leaving issue

  2l Alice Isabel Etheldreda; *b* 24 Nov 1878; *m* 21 April 1903 Henry Edward Walker (*d* 1922), of Ceylon, s of Rev E R Walker, and *d* Dec 1968, leaving issue

  3l Mary Primrose; *b* 7 July 1882; *m* 18 Sept 1907 Arthur Curtois Howard (*d* 18 Jan 1945), s of Fitzalan Howard, of Holyrood House, Spalding, and had issue

  4l Dora Elizabeth; *b* 20 March 1884; *m* 7 July 1908 Edouard Dunant, s of Charles Albert Dunant, of Geneva, and *d* 21 Dec 1969, leaving issue

1k Maria; *b* 24 Jan 1840; *d* unm 1917

2k Alice Elizabeth; *b* 10 Jan 1849; *m* 13 April 1871 Rev Oswald Master (*d* 15 Nov 1901), Rector Croston, Lancs, and *d* May 1914

1j Mary; *m* Rev Edward Law, of Horsted, Sussex, n of 1st Baron Ellenborough (*qv*), and had issue

2j Anna Maria; *m* Rev Oswald Feilden, of Didsbury, Lancs, and had issue

3j Frances; *m* 26 April 1832 Francis Wedgwood and had issue (*see* WEDGWOOD, B)

3i Ashton Nicholas, of Park Hill, Derbys; *b* 31 March 1768; *m* 10 March 1790 Mary (*d* 9 March 1826), widow of (a) William Elliot, of Derby, (b) Joseph Bird, of Loughborough, and (c) Sir Edward Every, 3rd Bt (*qv*), and dau of Edward Morley, and *d* 2 April 1830, leaving:

  1j Ashton Nicholas Every, of Burnaston House, JP, DL Derbys; *b* 21 Nov 1792; High Sheriff Derbys 1835; *m* 14 Feb 1820 Mary Theresa (*d* 21 June 1869), only dau and heiress of William Stables, of Hemsworth, Yorks, and *d* 4 Oct 1875, having had, with other issue:

    1k Ashton, of Burnaston House, JP, DL Derbyshire, JP Staffs; *b* 5 Feb 1821; Capt 60th Rifles, Col cmdg 5th Bn Derbyshire Regt; *d* unm 15 May 1887

    2k Rowland (Rev), of Burnaston House; *b* 19 March 1830; Rector Egginton, Derbys; *m* 23 Nov 1858 Jane Charlotte Rose (*d* 5 July 1874), 2nd dau of Henry Every (*see* EVERY, Bt), and *d* 24 July 1888, leaving:

      1l Arthur Rowland, of Burnaston House, JP Derbys; *b* 8 May 1862; Maj 6th Inniskilling Dragoons; *m* 16 Oct 1899 Henrietta (*d* 21 July 1939), dau of Henry Bolden, and *d* 20 March 1923

      2l Godfrey, TD, JP Derbys; *b* 15 June 1863; *educ* Corpus Christi Coll Oxford (BA); Lt-Col cmdg 5th Bn Sherwood Foresters, slr (ptnr Taylor, Simpson and Mosley, of Derby), memb Ch Assembly, High Sheriff Derbys 1931; *m* 4 Feb 1918 Hilda Ethelfreda Harpur (took by deed poll 9 Dec 1921 surname FYNDERNE, dropped it by deed poll 2 Feb 1923; *d* 5 June 1949), est dau of Sir Vauncey Harpur Crewe, 10th Bt (*see* 1924 edn), and *dsp* 24 March 1945

      3l Ashton Edward; *b* 24 Oct 1866; *d* 17 July 1911

      4l Wilfrid Rowland; *b* 26 April 1872; *d* unm 25 Dec 1948

      1l Theresa Jane; *d* unm 9 Jan 1936

      2l Helena Rose; *d* 15 July 1874

      3l Mildred Isabel; *d* unm 1 June 1938

      4l Jane Charlotte; *d* 23 Dec 1867

      5l Sibyl Georgiana Rose; *m* 22 Sept 1915 Harry HOFFMEISTER later AUBREY (Dec 1915) (*d* 10 Sept 1938), 4th s of Sir William Hoffmeister, MD, and *d* 28 Sept 1942

      6l Adeline; *d* 1885

      7l Jane Agnes Muriel; *d* unm 13 Sept 1952

  1j Emma Penelope; *m* 21 Dec 1824 Rev Francis Ward Spilsbury (*d* 1864), of Willington, Derbys, and had issue

1i Anne; *b* March 1777; *m* Robert Feilden and *d* 1810, leaving issue

2i Elizabeth; *m* 26 Aug 1790 Rev Streynsham Master (*d* 18 Jan 1864), DD, Rector Croston, Lancs, and *d* 7 March 1853, leaving issue

3i Frances Mary; *m* 12 May 1792 George Smith (*d* 26 Dec 1836), of Selsdon, Surrey, and *d* 5 July 1844, leaving issue

4i Penelope; *m* 22 Dec 1798 Sir Henry Every, 9th Bt (*qv*), and *d* 30 Aug 1812, leaving issue

2e Edward (Sir), of Hulme, Lancs, and Breadsall Priory, which he inherited from his cousin the 2nd and last Bt of the 1640 *cr*; *b c* 1616; *ktd* 1689; *m* Jane Meriel/Muriel, dau of Richard Saltonstall, of Huntwick, Yorks, and *dspm* 1695, leaving:

  1f Anne; *b c* 1662; *m* 31 March 1685 Sir John Bland, 4th Bt, of Kippax Park, Yorks, and *d* 26 July 1734, having had, with other issue:

    1g Sir JOHN BLAND, 5th Bt; MP Lancs 1714; *m* Lady Frances Finch, dau of 1st Earl of Aylesford (*qv*), and had issue

3e Oswald; *m* 1st Ann, dau of William Lever, of Kersall, and had two daus; *m* 2nd Elizabeth, dau of John Lightbourne, and *dspms* 1653

4e Samuel; living in Ireland 1664; *m* but *dsp* 1673

5e Francis (Rev); Rector Wilmslow, Cheshire, 1674–99; *m* Catherine, dau of John Davenport, of Davenport, Cheshire, and was *bur* 14 Aug 1699, leaving, with three other sons (*d* unm) and another dau:

  1f Francis (Rev); Rector Rolleston, Staffs; *m* Jane, dau of William Ellis, of Kiddall, Yorks, and *d* 1738, leaving, with an est s (Francis, *d* unm 1748) and three other sons, also eight daus:

    1g Thomas; Liverpool merchant had a s (Francis, *m* his cousin Margaret, dau of John Cook, of Doncaster, and *dsp* 1781)

    2g John; had, with a dau:

      1h John

    3g William; had, with several other sons and daus:

      1h Charles

      2h William

1h Sarah Mary or Anne Sarah Bennet; *m* 20 Sept 1765 Sir Walter Abington Compton, 5th and last Bt, and *dsp* Nov 1776

1f Anne; *m c* 15 Dec 1674 Richard Whitworth, of Batchacre Park, Aldbaston, Staffs, apparently yr s of John Whitworth, of Blore Pipe, Staffs, by Jane (dau of George Wright, of Shrewsbury), and had, with four yr sons:

1g CHARLES WHITWORTH, 1st and last BARON WHITWORTH OF GALWAY, Co Galway (I), so *cr* 9 Jan 1720/1; *bapt* 14 Oct 1675; *educ* Westminster and Trin Coll Cambridge (Fell 1700); Dip Serv: served Berlin 1699, Ratisbon 1701 (Resident at Imp Diet 1702–04), Chargé d'Affaires Vienna Nov 1703–March 1703/4 and Sept–Nov 1704, Russia: Envoy 1704–09, Amb Extrdy 1709–11 and Amb Extrdy and Plen 1711–12, Min Plen Imp Diet Augsburg and Ratisbon 1714–16, Envoy Extrdy and Plen Berlin 1716–17, Envoy Extrdy April and Min Plen The Hague May 1717–21, Min Plen Berlin 1719–22, Jt Amb and Plen Congress Cambrai 1725; MP Newport IoW 1722–25; *m* June 1720 Madeleine Jacqueline, dau of Albert Henri de Sallengre, Seigneur de Grifoort, and *dsp* 23 Oct 1725, when the title expired

2g Francis, of Leybourne, Kent; MP; *d* 6 March 1741/2, leaving:

1h Charles (Sir), of Leybourne; MP; *m* Martha (*d* 18 March 1786), dau of Richard Shelley, Commr Stamp Office (*see* SHELLEY, Bt), and *d* 22 Aug 1778, leaving:

1i CHARLES WHITWORTH, 1st and last EARL WHITWORTH, so *cr* 25 Nov 1815, as also BARON ADBASTON, Co Stafford, as also earlier 14 June 1813 VISCOUNT WHITWORTH OF ADBASTON, Co Stafford (all UK), as also earlier still 4 April 1800 BARON WHITWORTH OF NEWPORT PRATT, Co Galway (I), GCB (1815, KB 1793), PC (1800); *b* 29 May 1752; *educ* Tonbridge; Ensign 1st Foot Gds 1772, Lt and Capt 1776, served War American Independence, Capt and Lt-Col 1781, exchanged into 104th Foot 1783 (ret 1783); Dip Serv: Min Plen Poland 1786–88, Envoy Extrdy and Plen Russia 1788–1800, Amb Extrdy and Plen Paris 1802–03; memb BOT 1807–25, a Ld Bedchamber March–July 1813, Ld Lt Ireland 1813–17; *m* 7 April 1801 Arabella Diana, est dau and coheir of Sir Charles Cope, 2nd Bt, and widow of 3rd Duke of Dorset (*see* SACKVILLE, B), and *dsp* 13 May 1825, when his titles expired

1i Anna Barbara; *m* 23 July 1782, as his 2nd w, Sir Henry Russell, 1st Bt, of Swallowfield (*qv*), and *d* 1 Aug 1814, having had issue

2f Catherine; *m* Joseph Hooper, of Manchester, and had issue

1e Mary; *m* John Crowther, London merchant, and had issue

2e Margaret; *m* Rev John Ainger [*sic*]

3e Anne; *m* 1st Humphrey Booth, of Salford, Lancs; *m* 2nd Rev Thomas Case (*dsp* by her) and had by her 1st husb:

1f Robert (Sir); Ld Ch Justice Common Pleas Ireland; *m* twice and by his 2nd w had three daus

2f Humphrey, of Dublin; had by his 1st w an er s:

1g Humphrey; had a dau (Lettice, *m* Nathaniel Gore and had issue; *see* GORE-BOOTH, Bt)

Sir JOHN *d* 29 Sept 1798; his gs,

Sir Oswald Mosley, 2nd Bt; *b* 27 March 1785; *educ* Rugby and BNC Oxford; MP Portarlington 1807, Winchelsea 1808, Midhurst 1816 and N Staffs 1832, High Sheriff Staffs 1814, Ch Staffs QS, DCL, FGS and LS, MRI, author *Family Memoirs* (1849); *m* 31 Jan 1804 Sophia Anne (*d* 8 June 1859), 2nd dau of Sir Edward Every, 8th Bt (*qv*), and *d* 24 May 1871, having had, with other issue, including a dau (Octavia, *m* 9 June 1857 Very Rev Edward Spooner (*d* 26 Jan 1899), Co-Dean Bocking, Rector Hadleigh, Suffolk, 3rd s of Ven William Spooner, Archdeacon Coventry, and *d* 18 June 1883):

Sir Tonman Mosley, 3rd Bt, DL; *b* 9 July 1813; served Inniskilling Dragoons; *m* 4 Feb 1847 Catherine (*d* 22 April 1891), dau of Rev John Wood, of Swanwick, Derbys, and had:

1 OSWALD (Sir), **4th Bt**

2 TONMAN MOSLEY, 1st and last BARON ANSLOW, of Iver, Co Buckingham (UK), so *cr* 28 June 1916, CB (1911), JP (Bucks, Derbys), DL (Bucks, Staffs); *b* 16 Jan 1850; *educ* Repton and Corpus Christi Coll Oxford (BA 1872); barrister Inner Temple 1874, C Parly candidate Lichfield 1885 gen election, Lib Parly candidate S Bucks 1914, Chm: Derbys QS 1897–1902, Bucks CC 1904–21, Bucks TFA 1908–19 and N Staffs Rlwy Co 1904–23, KGStJ; *m* 22 Feb 1881 Lady Hilda Rose Montgomerie (*d* 18 June 1928), yst dau of 13th Earl of Eglinton (*see* EGLINTON and WINTON, E), and *dspms* 20 Aug 1933, when the Barony expired, having had:

(1) Nicholas; *b* 28 July 1882; Boer War 1900–02 (Queen's medal, three clasps, King's medal, two clasps), Capt N Staffs Regt 1914, Adj 5th Bn Sherwood Forresters, WW I; *d* unm 1 Aug 1915 of wounds recd in action

(2) Edward Hugh; *b* 16 July 1884; *d* unm 16 July 1910

(1) Hildred; *m* 20 Nov 1918 (*annulled* 1924, resumed maiden name) Capt Gerald Goddard Jackson and *d* 1 Jan 1963

(2) Sybil Hildegarde; *m* 14 Nov 1934 Alastair Turner Wyllie, MIES, AMIMechE, of Ceylon, and *d* 7 July 1962

3 Ernald, of Monksgate House, Nuthurst, Sussex, JP Middx; *b* 29 Oct 1851; *d* 3 Sept 1933

Sir TONMAN *d* 28 April 1890; his est son,

Sir Oswald Mosley, 4th Bt, JP, DL Staffs; *b* 25 Sept 1848; High Sheriff Staffs 1894; *m* 22 Jan 1873 Elizabeth Constance (*d* 13 Nov 1938), 2nd dau of Sir William White, and had:

1 OSWALD (Sir), **5th Bt**

1 Violet; *m* 20 April 1910 Lt-Col John McKie, CBE, DSO, DL (*d* 19 Aug 1934), of Bargaly, Kirkcudbrightshire, and *d* 10 June 1950

2 Geraldine; *m* 28 April 1903 (*divorce* 1926) Frank Outram Ellison (*d* 3 March 1937) and *d* 6 Dec 1954, leaving issue

3 Constance; *m* 11 March 1907 Charles FitzRoy Ponsonby McNeill (*d* 22 Nov 1955), OBE, 3rd s of Capt Duncan McNeill, Scots Greys, and *d* 19 Aug 1963, leaving issue

Sir OSWALD *d* 10 Oct 1915; his only s,

Sir Oswald Mosley, 5th Bt; *b* 29 Dec 1873; Capt 2nd Derbys Yeo WW I 1914–16; *m* 12 Dec 1895 Katharine Maud (*d* 20 June 1948), dau of Capt Justinian Edwards-Heathcote, of Apedale Hall, Staffs, and had:

1 OSWALD ERNALD (Sir), **6th Bt**

2 Edward Heathcote; *b* 25 April 1899; *educ* Rugby and RMC Sandhurst; Maj Roy Dragoons; *m* 1st 2 Aug 1923 (*divorce* 1932) Sylvia Alexandra (*d* 1977), only dau of Col Herbert Alfred Johnston, of Allestree Hall, Derbys; *m* 2nd 9 March 1943 Edith Victoria (*d* 1990), dau of Thomas Leach, of Malvern, and *d* 1980, leaving by his 1st w:

(1) +John Ronald [John Mosley Esq, Flat 31 Chestnut House, East St, Blandford Forum, Dorset DT11 7DU]; *b* 13 Aug 1926; *educ* Stowe; *m* 1st 5 May 1956 (*divorce* 1970) Primrose Antoinette, 2nd dau of F G Hadwen, of Wadebridge, Cornwall; *m* 2nd 26 Feb 1972 *Caroline Rosalind, 2nd dau of H H S Hillier, of Sloane St, London SW1, and by his 1st w has:

1a *Clare [Mrs Mark Bicknell, 66 Camberwell Grove, London SE5]; *b* 11 Aug 1958; *m* 1985 *Mark Bicknell and has:

1b *Augustus Ivo Guy; *b* 1990

1b *Cecilia Elizabeth Rose; *b* 1994

2a *Charlotte Louise; *b* 2 July 1960

(1) Veronica; *b* 24 Nov 1924; *m* 12 Nov 1954 *Peter Hawker [Peter Hawker Esq, Coln House, Coln Rogers, Glos] and *d* 1996, leaving:

1a *Annabel [The Hon Mrs Richard Buxton, Stretchney, Diptford, S Devon]; *b* 1957; *m* 1988 *Hon Richard Christopher Buxton, s of 2nd Baron Noel-Buxton (*qv*), and has issue

3 John Arthur Noel; *b* 12 Dec 1901; *educ* Eton; with Hedderwick & Borthwick, stockbrokers; *m* 1st 23 April 1925 (*divorce* 1936) Caroline Edith Sutton, er dau of Lt-Col George D Timmis, of Matson House, Glos; *m* 2nd 29 Aug 1936 *Anne Marie Vaudescal-Vartejanu [Mrs John Mosley, 92 rue Raynonard, Paris XVI, France] and *d* 14 March 1973, leaving by his 1st w has:

(1) Timothy John Oswald; *b* 6 April 1926; *educ* Eton; Lt Coldstream Gds; *m* 1st 26 March 1955 Pamela, est dau of R Kirk Askew, of Park Ave, New York; *m* 2nd 23 Jan 1958 Brighid Sarah (*d* 1985), only dau of Lt-Col Hon Michael Thomas Henderson (*see* FARINGDON, B), and *d* 1993

(2) +Simon James [Simon Mosley Esq, Flat 4, 59 Onslow Gdns, London SW7 3QF]; *b* 8 April 1927; *educ* Eton and Ch Ch Oxford (MA); late Lt Coldsteam Gds, slr 1956; *m* 15 Dec 1957 *Maria, only dau of Iraklis Zeri, of Athens, and has:

1a +George Christopher [George Mosley Esq, 23 The Little Boltons, London SW10 9LJ]; *b* 28 April 1959; *m* 1992 *Ana-Maria, dau of Miguel Rincon, of Jerez, Spain, by Mrs V Anderson, of London, and has:

1b +Oliver Simon; *b* 5 March 1994

2b +Max Alexander; *b* 24 Nov 1996

1a *Claire Amalia; *b* 23 April 1964; *m* 22 March 1997 *Fabian Bachrach, of New York

Sir OSWALD *d* 21 Sept 1928; his est s,

Sir Oswald Ernald Mosley, 6th Bt; *b* 16 Nov 1896; *educ* Winchester and RMC Sandhurst; Lt 16th Lancers WW I 1915–19 (wounded), MP (CU) Harrow 1918–22, (Ind) 1922–24 and (Lab) 1924 and (Lab) Smethwick 1926–31, Chllr Duchy Lancaster 1929–30, fndr New Pty 1931 and Br Union Fascists 1932, Union Movement parly candidate N Kensington 1959 gen election, author: *The Greater Britain* (1932), *My Answer* (1946), *The Alternative* (1947), *Europe: Faith and Plan* (1958), *300 Questions Answered* (1961), *My Life* (1968); *m* 1st 11 May 1920 Lady Cynthia Blanche Curzon (*d* 16 May 1933), dau of 1st and last Marquess Curzon of Kedleston, and had issue (*see below* **Lineage (of Curzon)**); *m* 2nd in Germany 6 Oct 1936 *Hon Diana [The Hon Lady Mosley, 1 rue des Lacs, 91400 Orsay, France], formerly w of Hon Bryan Walter Guinness (later 2nd Baron Moyne; *qv*) and 3rd dau of 2nd Baron Redesdale (*qv*), and *d* 3 Dec 1980, having by her had (in remainder to btcy only):

3 +(Oswald) Alexander [Alexander Mosley Esq, 31 rue de l'Université, Paris 75007, France]; *b* 26 Nov 1938; *educ* St Martin de France, Pontoise, and Ohio State U; *m* 10 May 1975 *Charlotte Diana, ed *The Letters of Nancy Mitford and Evelyn Waugh* (1996), 2nd dau of Lt-Cdr George Hosselin Marten, MVO, DSC, RN, of Crichel, Wimborne, Dorset, and has:

(1) +Louis; *b* 1983

4 +Max Rufus; *b* 13 April 1940; *educ* Stein an der Traun, Germany, and Ch Ch Oxford; barrister Gray's Inn 1964, md March Engineering, Pres Internat Motor Sports Fedn 1991– and Fedn Internationale de l'Automobile 1993–; *m* 9 July 1960 *Jean Marjorie, er dau of James Taylor, of Chelsea, and has:

(1) +Alexander James; *b* 5 April 1970

(2) +Patrick Max; *b* 18 Feb 1972

Lineage (of Curzon): The 1st MARQUESS CURZON OF KEDLESTON (*see* SCARSDALE, V) and **1st Baron Ravensdale**, of Ravensdale, Co Derby (UK), so *cr* (among other titles) 2 Nov 1911, with remainder in default of male issue to his est dau and the heirs male of her body, failing whom with remainder to his other daus by primogeniture and the heirs male of their bodies; *dspm* 20 March 1925, when the Marquessate expired, leaving by his 1st w:

1 MARY IRENE CURZON, **Baroness Ravensdale** in her own right; *b* 20 Jan 1896; Treas Musicians Benevolent Fund, Chm and Treas World Congress Faiths, V-Pres Nat Assoc Girls Clubs, Chm Highways Clubs of E London, Industl Christian Fellowship cncl memb, V-Chm Roy India, Pakistan and Ceylon Soc, Cdr Roy Order George I Greece; *cr* 6 Oct 1958 a Life Peeress as BARONESS RAVENSDALE OF KEDLESTON, of Kedleston, Co Derby (UK); *d* unm 9 Feb 1966

2 Cynthia Blanche; *b* 23 Aug 1898; MP (Lab) Stoke 1929–31; *m* 11 May 1920 **Sir Oswald Ernald Mosley, 6th Bt** (*see above*), and *d* 16 May 1933, leaving:

(1) **Sir Nicholas Mosley, 7th Bt**, and **3rd and present Baron Ravensdale**

(2) +Michael [The Hon Michael Mosley, Durham Cottage, 4 Christchurch St, London SW3]; *b* 25 April 1932; *educ* Eton and LSE; granted with his sis 1967 rank of baron's dau/yr s

(1) *Vivien Elisabeth [The Hon Mrs Forbes Adam, 11 Mulberry Walk, London SW3 6DZ]; *b* 25 Feb 1921; *m* 15 Jan 1949 Desmond Francis Forbes Adam (*see* FORBES ADAM, Bt) and has issue

3 Alexandra ('Baba') Naldera; *b* 20 March 1904 (HM QUEEN ALEXANDRA stood sponsor); Chm Save the Children Fund 1968–73 (Foreign Relief), CStJ, OM Italian Republic 4th Cl, Cross of Merit SMO Malta 1st Cl; *m* 21 July 1925 (*divorce* 1955) Maj Edward ('Fruity') Dudley Metcalfe, MVO, MC, BA (*d* 18 Nov 1957), Skinner's Horse, ADC to HRH THE PRINCE OF WALES 1921–25, only s of Edward Metcalfe, of Rathfarnham, Co Dublin, and *d* 7 Aug 1995, leaving (in remainder to Barony only):

(1) +David Patrick [David Metcalfe Esq, 15 Wilton St, London SW1]; *b* 8 July 1927; *educ* Eton; Irish Gds, dir Stewart, Smith and Co; *m* 1st 8 Jan 1957 (*divorce* 1964) Alexandria Irene (*d* 28 Dec 1966), dau of Michael Boycun, of Canada, and widow of Sir Alexander Korda, and has:

1a +Julian Edward; *b* 14 Dec 1959

2a +Charles Michael; *b* 8 Oct 1962

1a *Zara Naldera [Mrs Jonathan Colchester, New Place, Ickham, Kent]; *b* 15 Sept 1957; *m* 1989 *Jonathan Halsey Luke Colchester, s of Rev Halsey Sparrowe Colchester, CMG, OBE, of Oxford

(1) (cont.) David Metcalfe *m* 2nd 26 Sept 1968 (*divorce* 1973) Comtesse de Chauvigny de Blot and by her has:

3a +Edward George Anthony; *b* 28 March 1970

(1) (cont.) David Metcalfe *m* 3rd *Sally Howe, dau of Edward E Cullen, of Philadelphia

(1) *Davina Naldera [Mrs Hugo Eastwood, 12 Passmore St, London SW1W 8HP]; *b* 14 Nov 1930; *m* 8 Feb 1966 *(John) Hugo Eastwood, only s of John Francis Eastwood, OBE, KC, and has:

1a *Philip Hugo; *b* 17 Sept 1966

1a *Emma Alexandra; *b* 12 Feb 1969

(2) *Linda Mary [Mrs Henry Mortimer, 14 Elvaston Place, London SW7 5QF; 239 Tangier Ave, Palm Beach, FL 33480, USA]; *b* 14 Nov 1930; *m* 25 Nov 1965 Henry Tilford Mortimer (*d* 1993), s of Stanley Grafton Mortimer, of Tuxedo Park, NY, and has:

1a *John Metcalfe; *b* 7 Oct 1966

2a *Alexander Dudley; *b* 4 Jan 1969

RAVENSWORTH

Arms: Argent fretty gules, on a chief of the last three leopard's faces or. **Crest:** A lion rampant sable, billettée and crowned with an eastern crown or. **Supporters:** Two leopards or, semée of golps, each gorged with a mural crown purpure. **Mottoes:** 1 *Fama semper vivit* ('A good reputation lives for ever'), 2 *Unus et idem* ('One and the same'). **Creations:** B. (UK) 17 July 1821, Bt. (E) 2 Nov 1642.

THE 8TH BARON RAVENSWORTH, of Ravensworth Castle, Co Durham, and a **Baronet** (Sir Arthur Waller Liddell, Bt, JP (Northumberland 1959)) [The Rt Hon The Lord Ravensworth JP, Eslington Park, Whittingham, Northumberland NE66 4UR]; *b* 25 July 1924; *s* cousin 1950; *educ* Harrow; BBC radio engr 1944–50; *m* 1950 *Wendy, adopted dau of J Stuart Bell, of Studio Ho, Cookham, Berks, and has:

1 +THOMAS ARTHUR HAMISH [The Hon Thomas Liddell, Mountain, Whittingham, Northumberland]; *b* 27 Oct 1954; *educ* Gordonstoun and RAC Cirencester; chm Northumberland NFU 1989–90, ctee memb CLA 1990–; *m* 1983 *Linda, dau of Henry Thompson, of Hawthorn Farm, Gosforth, Northumberland, and has:

(1) +Henry Arthur Thomas; *b* 27 Nov 1987

(1) *Alice Lorina; *b* 1986

1 *Jane Alice [The Hon Mrs Rubie, Red Briars, 35 Drax Ave, London SW20 0EQ]; *b* 1952; *m* 1984 *Michael James Crowhurst Rubie, only s of Henry Edward Rubie, of Rustington, W Sussex, and has:

(1) *Sophia Amy Elizabeth; *b* 1 Aug 1986

(2) *Isabel Emma Mary; *b* 15 July 1988

---

(3) *Francesca Louise; *b* 21 Jan 1991

Lineage: THOMAS de LIDDEL/LYDDALE; *m* Margaret, dau of John de Layburne, and had an est s:

THOMAS LIDDELL; Alderman Newcastle; bought Ravensworth Castle 1607 and other estates in Co Durham; *m* Barbara, dau and heir of Richard Strangeways, and had, with three yr sons and two daus:

THOMAS LIDDELL, of Ravensworth Castle; *m* Margaret, dau of John Watson, and *d* 1615, leaving an est s:

Sir Thomas Liddell, 1st Bt (E), so *cr* 2 Nov 1642 for defending Newcastle against the Scots, of Ravensworth Castle; admitted Gray's Inn March 1619/20, royalist Civil War, hence fined £4,000 (just under £250,000 in late-1990s terms) as delinquent; *m* Isabel, dau of Henry Anderson, and *d* 1650, having had, with another dau:

1 Thomas (Sir); *m* Bridget, Maid-of-Hon to ELIZABETH, QUEEN OF BOHEMIA (dau of JAMES I), dau of Edward Woodward, of Lee, Bucks (*m* 2nd Thomas Heneage, of Battersea, Surrey), and *dvp* 1627, leaving:

(1) **Sir Thomas, 2nd Bt**

2 Francis; *m* Elizabeth, dau of Sir George Tonge, of Denton, Co Durham

1 Mary; *m* Sir Nicholas Cole, 1st Bt, of Brancepeth, Co Durham

2 Frances; *m* 1st Thomas Vane, of Raby, Co Durham; *m* 2nd, as his 3rd w of four, Sir John Bright, 1st and last Bt, of Carbrook, Derbys (*see* also below)

The 1st Bt's gs,

Sir Thomas Liddell, 2nd Bt; *m* Anne, dau of Sir Henry Vane the Elder (*see* BARNARD, B), and *d* 1697, having had, with other issue:

1 **Sir Henry, 3rd Bt**

2 Robert; *m* Priscilla (*d* 15 March 1679), dau of William Kiffin, London merchant, and had:

(1) Thomas; *m* Mary Nelthorpe and *d* 14 May 1718, leaving:

1a Henry

The 2nd Bt's er s,

Sir Henry Liddell, 3rd Bt; MP Durham 1689–98 and Newcastle 1700–05 and 1706–10, High Sheriff Co Durham; *m* by 1670 Catharine (*bur* 24 Feb 1703), dau and heiress of Sir John Bright, 1st and last Bt (*see* above), by his 1st w Catharine, dau of Sir Richard Hawksworth, and *d* 1 Sept 1723, having had, with other issue:

1 Thomas; *b c* 1681; *m* 12 Oct 1707 Jane (*d* 1774), dau of James Clavering, of Greencroft, Co Durham, and *dvp* 3 June 1715, leaving:

(1) **Sir Henry Liddell, 4th Bt**, and 1st and last LORD RAVENSWORTH, BARON OF RAVENSWORTH, Co Durham (GB), so *cr* 29 June 1747; *b* 1708; MP (Whig) Morpeth 1734–47; *m* 27 April 1735 Anne (*b* 5 June 1712; *d* 12 June 1794), only dau of Sir Peter Delmé, Ld Mayor London 1723–24, and *dspm* 30 Jan 1784, when the Barony expired, leaving:

1a Anne; close friend of Horace Walpole; *m* 1st 29 Jan 1756 (*divorce* 23 March 1769) 3rd Duke of Grafton (*qv*) and had issue; *m* 2nd 26 March 1769 2nd and last Earl of Upper Ossory (*b* 2 May 1745; *dspml* 1 Feb 1818; *see* 1937 edn CASTLETOWN, B) and *d* 24 Feb 1804, having had a s (*b* 23 Aug 1768) by him before their marriage and while still married to her first husb and by him three daus (*d* young or unm) apparently after their marriage

(2) Thomas; *m* Margaret, dau of Sir William Bowes, of Gibside, Co Durham (*see* STRATHMORE AND KINGHORNE, E), and had:

1a Thomas; *d* unm

2a HENRY GEORGE (Sir), **5th Bt**

2 John LIDDELL later BRIGHT (taken with arms on inheriting most of his maternal gf's estates), of Badsworth, Yorks; *m* Cordelia Clutterbuck and *d* 6 Oct 1737, leaving:

(1) Thomas, of Badsworth; Ld Manor Ecclesall, S R Yorks; *m* Margaret (*m* 2nd 1748 Sir John Ramsden, 3rd Bt (*qv*), and had further issue), dau and heir of William Norton, of Sawley, N R Yorks, and had:

1a Mary; *m* 26 Feb 1752 2nd and last Marquess of Rockingham of the 1746 *cr*, PM 1765–66 and March-July 1782 (*dsp* 1 July 1782; *see* 1970 edn SONDES, E), and *d* 19 Dec 1804

(1) Cordelia; *m* Clifton Wintringham, MD, of York

The 4th Bt's n,

Sir Henry George Liddell, 5th Bt; *b* 25 Nov 1749; *m* April 1773 Elizabeth, dau of Thomas Steele, of Hampsnett, Sussex, and *d* 26 Nov 1791, having had, with three daus:

1 THOMAS HENRY, **1st Baron**

2 Henry George (Rev); *b* 1787; Rector Easington; *m* 11 Nov 1809 Charlotte, 4th dau of Hon Thomas Lyon (*see* STRATHMORE AND KINGHORNE, E), and *d* 9 March 1872, having had, with other issue (in remainder to btcy only):

(1) Henry George (Very Rev); *b* 6 Feb 1811; *educ* Charterhouse and Ch Ch Oxford (BA 1833, MA 1835, BD and DD 1855, DCL 1893); Tutor Ch Ch 1836, Censor Ch Ch 1845, White's Prof Moral Philosophy 1845, Domestic Chaplain to HRH THE PRINCE CONSORT 1846–61, Headmaster Westminster 1846–55, Dean Ch Ch 1855–91, Hon Chaplain to HM QUEEN VICTORIA 1862, V-Chllr Oxford U 1870–74, LLD Edinburgh 1884, author: *Greek-English Lexicon* (ed, with Robert Scott, 1843, 1845, 1849, 1855, 1861, 1869, 1883 (revised edn by Liddell only), 1897 etc) and *A History of Ancient Rome* (1855); *m* 2 July 1846 Lorina (*d* 25 June 1910), dau of James Reeve, of Lowestoft, and *d* 18 Jan 1898, having had:

1a Edward Henry, JP (Hants); *b* 6 Sept 1847; *m* 1st 13 June 1876 Minnie (*d* 10 Oct 1905), 2nd dau of William Cory, of Devonshire Place Ho, and had:

1b Henry Lyon; *b* 29 March 1877; *d* unm 18 Feb 1901

2b Geoffrey William, DSO (1915); *b* 23 Nov 1884; *educ* Eton and RMC Sandhurst; Lt Col Res Offrs Rifle Bde WW I (wounded, despatches); *m* 7 Sept 1915 his cousin Mary Sophia (*d* 1987), 2nd dau of Charles Lyon Liddell (*see* below), and *d* 29 Jan 1955, leaving:

1c +Charles Henry, MC, JP (Hants 1960); *b* 2 July 1917; *educ* Eton and RMC Sandhurst; Maj Rifle Bde WW II (wounded), High Sheriff Hants 1975; *m* 10 March 1944 *Pamela Mary [Mrs Charles Liddell, Fullerton Grange, Andover, Hants SP11 7LA], yst dau of Maj Antony Hubert

Gibbs (see ALDENHAM and HUNSDON OF HUNSDON, B), and d 9 Sept 1998, leaving:

1d +James Edward Cory [James Liddell Esq, Cottonworth House, Fullerton, Hants]; b 13 July 1947; educ Eton and RAC Cirencester; m 1970 *Rachel Anne, yr dau of Maj George De Pree (see GALLOWAY, E), and has:

 1e +Tom Edward Charles; b 1977; educ Milton Abbey

 2e +Hugh Geoffrey; b 1980; educ Milton Abbey

 1e *Georgie Sophia; b 1975

1d *(Mary) Susan [Mrs Antony Ansell, 10 Durand Gdns, London SW9 0PP]; b 20 Dec 1944; m 31 Oct 1964 *Rev Antony Michael Ansell (see FULLER, Bt), and has:

 1e *Michael James Kirkpatrick; b 30 Dec 1970; educ Harrow and Pembroke Coll Cambridge

 1e +Harriet Mary; b 24 July 1966; m 1994 *Robert Lanyon, s of Brig M C Lanyon, MC

 2e *Alexandra Jane; b 4 Oct 1968; m 1991 *Andrew Dunnett, s of Rev Robert Dunnett

2d *Alice Margaret; b 29 April 1950; m 31 March 1973 *Christopher Nicholas Allen, of Newman Street Farm, Doulting, Somerset, s of Douglas Allen, and has:

 1e *Luke Llewellyn Liddell; b 1985

 2e *Jack Basil Charles Liddell; b 1987

 3e *Gus Douglas Oliver Liddell; b 1989

2c +Thomas Lyon [Thomas Liddell Esq, Dormans Corner, Lingfield, Surrey RH7 6PP]; b 12 March 1920; educ Radley and Worcester Coll Oxford; T/Capt Rifle Bde WW II; m 13 Oct 1951 *Susan Mary, 4th (twin) dau of Charles Ronald Vawdrey Coutts, of The Court Lodge, Chelsfield, Kent, and has:

1d +Edward Henry [Edward Liddell Esq, 97 Narbonne Ave, London SW4 9LQ]; b 20 Jan 1953; educ Eton and Magdalene Coll Cambridge; m 1988 *Hon Anna Kinnaird, 2nd dau of 13th Lord Kinnaird (see 1970 edn), and has:

 1e *Patrick Edward Charles; b 1991

2d +Roderick William [Roderick Liddell Esq, 12 Grand Rue Kriegsheim, 67170 Brumath, France]; b 16 March 1955; educ Eton and Worcester Coll Oxford; m 19– *Marie Françoise, yst dau of Cmdt Michel Dujol, of Calaman, Cahors, France, and has:

 1e +Loic; b 1979

 2e +Theo Antonin Thomas; b 1981

3d +David Lyon [David Liddell Esq, Orchard House, Church Rd, Barcombe, E Sussex BN8 5TW]; b 28 Dec 1959; educ Eton and Trin Coll Cambridge; m 1990 *Chloe Camilla Margot, yst dau of Dennis Percy Bertlin, of Castlefield, Bletchingley, Surrey, and has:

 1e +Rupert; b 19–

 1e *Freya Margot; b 1994

 2e *Phoebe Camilla; b 4 March 1998

1d *Emma Mary [Mrs Charles Mackenzie, 4 Vicarage Rd, London SW14 8RU]; b 16 March 1955; educ Wycombe Abbey and St Hilda's Coll Oxford; m 1981 *Charles William Taaffe Munro Mackenzie, 2nd s of John Hugh Munro Mackenzie of Mornish, and has:

 1e *Charles Alexander Munro; b 1983

 2e *Kenneth Thomas Munro; b 1986

 1e *Charlotte Annabella Jemima; b 1990

3c +(William) Adrian [Adrian Liddell Esq, Westover Farm, Goodworth Clatford, Hants SP11 7LF]; b 25 March 1924; educ Radley and Magdalene Coll Cambridge (MA); Sub-Lt RNVR WW II 1944–45 (despatches), ARICS, QALAS; m 7 July 1956 *Anne Primrose, only child of G/Capt Ralp Woodcock Gifford Lywood, RAF, of Scilly, Kinsale, Co Cork, and has:

1d +William George [Dr William Liddell, Riverside, The Strand, Lympstone, Devon EX8 5EY]; b 7 Sept 1958; educ Eton, Keble Coll Oxford (BA) and St Mary's Hosp London; MSc, MBBS, MRCP, MRCGP; m 16 Aug 1997 *Dr Morag MacDougall, BM, MRCGP, dau of Colin MacDougall, of Greenock

1d *Mary Clare; b 10 July 1960; m 1992 *Ralph Wynne Griffiths and has:

 1e *Robert; b 20 June 1994

2d *Caroline Sophia; b 21 May 1962; m 1988 *Dominic Percival Ian Reyntiens (see BRUCE, Bt, of Stenhouse)

4c +Geoffrey Andrew [Geoffrey Liddell Esq, 12 Frewin Rd, London SW 18]; b 10 Oct 1926; educ Radley and Magdalene Coll Cambridge; RN WW II 1944–45, Lt (TA) London Rifle Bde; m 9 Oct 1958 *Jillian Mary, dau of David Walkinshaw, of Haslemere, Surrey, and formerly w of Edward Geoffrey Clifton-Brown (see BROWN, Bt), and has:

1d +Charles David Andrew [Charles Liddell Esq, Stable House, Winton Hill, Stockbridge, Hants]; b 17 Feb 1960; educ Marlborough; m 1986 *Victoria Elizabeth, dau of Geoffrey Herbert Jolly, of The Old Vicarage, Horwich, Lancs, and has:

 1e +Marcus Andrew; b 1988

 1e *Caitlin Alice; b 1991

 2e *Frances; b 14 Dec 1994

1c Phyllis Audrey; b 25 Sept 1918; m 1st 24 Oct 1942 Lt Richard Arthur Edmunds, RNVR (kas 24 Dec 1942), yst s of C C Edmunds, of Ledburn Manor, Leighton Buzzard; m 2nd 28 April 1945 George Ronald Gaunt, only s of L E Gaunt, of Kensington, and d 197–

1a (cont.) Edward Liddell m 2nd 6 Feb 1907 Ethel Sophia Gresham, 2nd dau of Granville William Gresham Leveson-Gower (see SUTHERLAND, D), and d 14 June 1911

2a Frederick Francis (Sir), KCB (1916), KC (1929); b 7 June 1865; educ Eton and Ch Ch Oxford (BA 1888, MA 1892); Fell All Souls 1891–1906, barrister Lincoln's Inn 1894, 2nd Parly Counsel Treasury 1903–17, 1st Parly Counsel 1917–28, Counsel to Speaker H of C 1929–43, Ecclesiastical Commr

1944–48; m 23 July 1901 Mabel Alice (d 15 May 1959), dau of Arthur Magniac, of The Hermitage, Ascot, and d 19 March 1950, leaving:

1b Henry George Magniac, of Colworth, Addo, CP, S Africa; b 7 July 1902; educ Winchester; Rhodesian Forces WW II; m 31 Jan 1932 Amelia Lydia Mary (d 1981), dau of William Albert Walker, of S Rhodesia, and d 1985, leaving:

1c +Eric Henry George [Eric Liddell Esq, 6 Stirling Rd, PO Box 67555, Bryanston 2021, Transvaal, S Africa]; b 19 Sept 1935; m 29 Nov 1958 *Jane-Anne, dau of Maj Walter John Hoskins, RA, of Elston, Wilts, and has:

 1d *Karen Anne; b 2 Jan 1961

 2d *Jacqueline Toni; b 12 July 1962; m 1987 *Rodney Alan Penaluna

 3d *Bridget Alice; b 1 Dec 1964

2b Julian; b 13 Aug 1904; Cdr RN WW II; m 10 Dec 1930 Evelyn Kathleen (m 2nd 3 Feb 1949 Christopher Le Strange Metcalfe, only s of Lt Col Herbert Charles Metcalfe, DSO, late of Inglethorpe Hall, Norfolk), yr dau of Sir Robert Arthur Johnson, KCVO, KBE, of Belgravia, and was accidentally kas 28 Feb 1946

3b Maurice Arthur, OBE (1969); b 12 Sept 1905; educ Marlborough and Ch Ch Oxford (BA 1927); barrister Lincoln's Inn 1930, ptnr Dyson Bell & Co Parly Agents, F/Lt RAFVR WW II 1939–43 (invalided), memb Centl Cncl RAFA; m 28 July 1937 Alix (d 1981), er dau of Adml Mark Edward Frederic Kerr, CB, MVO (see LOTHIAN, M), and d 16 May 1976, leaving:

1c *Virginia Sarah Alix [Mrs Simon Ashton, 27 Newton Rd, London W2 5JR; Point House, Schull, Co Cork, Ireland]; b 16 Sept 1941; m 3 Dec 1962 Simon Claude Ashton, CBE (1981), MA, FCA (d 1986), yr s of S/Ldr Claude Thesiger Ashton, RAF, and has:

 1d *Guy Julian Claude; b 1964; m 1991 *Claire Chapman

 1d *Melanie Isabel; b 1967; m 1994 *Hugh Giles Keyworth Broughton and has:

  1e *Stanley Simon Keyworth; b 26 Dec 1997

 2d *Jessica Alix; b 1970

2c *Judith Rose [Mrs Mark Jackson, The Old Vicarage, Ashton Keynes, Wilts]; b 2 Oct 1944; m 11 May 1969 *(David) Mark Jackson, BA, BM, BCh, yr s of Dr Lawrence Nelson Jackson, MC, TD, and Dr Margaret Constance Noel Jackson, of Crediton, Devon, and has:

 1d *Luke Hadley; b 15 Oct 1970

 2d *Felix Mark; b 1973

1b Bridget Elvira; b 7 Jan 1908; m 1st 24 April 1931 (divorce 1937) Peter Lockwood Smith-Dorrien (k 22 July 1946 in bomb explosion at King David Hotel, Jerusalem), 2nd s of Gen Sir Horace Lockwood Smith-Dorrien, GCB, GCMG, DSO; m 2nd 26 Jan 1939 Lewis Civval, FCA (d 1973), s of Maurice Civval, of London, and d 14 Nov 1998, leaving:

1c *Martha Bridget Liddell [Mrs E J Ivory, Lyfield House, Ewhurst, Cranleigh, Surrey]; b 7 Aug 1941; m 1st 30 April 1966 George Patrick Francis Ennor, only s of Patrick Ennor, of Ewell, Surrey, and has:

 1d *Julian George; b 1970

 2d *Daniel Lewis; b 1974

 1d *Charlotte Annabella; b 8 July 1968

1c (cont.) Mrs Martha Ennor m 2nd 1988 *E J Ivory

2c *Julia Jane Liddell [Mrs Julia Case, 35 Fabian Rd, London SW6]; b 27 Aug 1942; m 1974 (divorce 1988) Oliver James Malim Case

3c *Camilla Frances Liddell [Mrs Philip Case, Halls Farm, Silchester, Berks]; b 26 June 1946; m 1974 *Philip Lee Malim Case and has had:

 1d *Benjamin James Civval; b 1978

 2d *Thomas Henry Civval; b 1980

 1d *Alice Philippa Liddell; b 1975; d 1983

1b (cont.) Mrs Bridget Smith-Dorrien m 3rd Oct 1979 *John Reeder Blandy, OBE

3a Lionel Charles, MVO; b 22 May 1868; BA Oxon; Br Consul Lyons 1902–07 and Copenhagen 1907–11; m 26 April 1902 his sis-in-law Florence Ella (d 15 Feb 1942), dau of Arthur Magniac, and d 21 March 1942, leaving:

1b Lionel Arthur, OBE (1953), TD, of Sherborne St John, Hants; b 11 Feb 1903; educ Winchester and Ch Ch Oxford; Lt Col RA WW II (despatches); m 30 Nov 1928 Beatrice, er dau of Thomas Standish Hillas-Drake, of Eastbourne, and d 19–

2b Philip, of Meadow Farm, Stretham, Cambs; b 3 Oct 1904; educ Winchester; Headmaster St Andrew's Sch Eastbourne 1946; m 2 Aug 1944 *Elizabeth Jane Boret, yr dau of Colledge Leader, of Fairway, Newmarket, and d 1976, leaving:

1c *Susan Jane [Mrs Anthony Hide, Machell Place, Newmarket, Suffolk]; b 26 Oct 1946; m 1970 *Anthony Gatehouse Hide and has:

 1d *Philip Edward; b 1973

 2d *Timothy David; b 1982

 1d *Lucinda Jane; b 21 July 1971

1b Barbara; b 3 Oct 1904; m 5 Dec 1933 Peter Martineau, yst s of Sir William Martineau, JP, of Kincraig, Ross-shire, and Knightsbridge, and d 2 Dec 1959, leaving issue

1a Lorina Charlotte; m 7 Feb 1874 William Baillie Skene, DL (d 10 June 1911), of Hallyards and Pitlour, Fife, yr s of Patrick George Skene, of Hallyards, Fife, and d 29 Oct 1930, leaving issue

2a Alice Pleasance; b 1852; the Alice who inspired Charles Lutwidge Dodgson (Lewis Caroll); m 15 Sept 1880 Reginald Gervis Hargreaves (d 15 Feb 1926), of Cuffnells, Lyndhurst, Hants, and d 15 Nov 1934, leaving issue

3a Edith Mary; d unm 1876

4a Rhoda Caroline Anne, OBE (1920); d unm 19 May 1949

5a Violet Constance, MBE (1920); d unm 9 Dec 1927

(2) Charles; b 1813; engr (chiefly rlwy, including Metropolitan Line from London to Aylesbury), assist to George Stephenson; m 1861 Marion (d 22 Oct 1910), dau of J Hesketh, and d 10 Aug 1894, leaving:

1a Charles Lyon, JP (Sussex); *b* 1861; BA Oxon; *m* 2 April 1891 Margaret Emily Gresham, dau of Granville William Leveson-Gower (*see* SUTHERLAND, D), and *d* 1 March 1911, leaving:

   1b Audrey Margaret; *m* 21 Nov 1917 Maj Charles William de Roemer, JP (*d* 14 April 1963), RFA and RAF, only s of Maj Charles Henry de Roemer, of Lime Park, Hurstmonceux, Sussex, and *d* 15 Aug 1967, leaving issue

   2b Mary Sophia Liddell; *m* 7 Sept 1915 her cousin Lt Col Geoffrey William Liddell and *d* 1987 (*see above*)

   3b Christabel Etrenne; *m* 25 July 1922 Capt Robert Millington Synge and had issue (*see* SYNGE, Bt)

   4b Joan Elizabeth Liddell; *m* 22 March 1934 Richard Walter Dundonald Cave (*d* 1980), only s of Walter Frederick Cave (*see* CAVE, Bt), and *d* 198–

The er s,

Sir Thomas Henry Liddell, 6th Bt, and **1st Baron Ravensworth**, of Ravensworth Castle, Co Durham (UK), so *cr* 17 July 1821; *b* 8 Feb 1775; *educ* Eton and Trin Coll Cambridge (MA 1795); Sheriff Northumberland 1804, MP (Tory) 1806–07; *m* 27 April 1796 Maria Susannah (*d* 22 Nov 1845), dau of John Simpson, of Bradley (*see* STRATHMORE AND KINGHORNE, E), and *d* 8 March 1855, having had, with other issue:

1 HENRY THOMAS LIDDELL, **2nd Baron Ravensworth** and 1st EARL OF RAVENSWORTH OF RAVENSWORTH CASTLE, so *cr* 2 April 1874, as also BARON ESLINGTON OF ESLINGTON PARK, Co Northumberland (both UK); *b* 10 March 1797; *educ* Eton and St John's Coll Cambridge; MP (Tory) Northumberland June 1826–30 (fought same seat unsuccessfully Feb 1826), N Durham 1837–47 and Liverpool 1853–55 (fought S Shields unsuccessfully 1852), Pres Soc Antiquaries Newcastle-on-Tyne 1861, author: *The Wizard of the North and other Poems* (1833), *The Odes of Horace* (English verse trans 1858), *Carmina* (Latin poems 1865), *The Aeneid* (by Virgil, books vii-xii, trans 1872) and *Poems* (1877); *m* 9 Nov 1820 Isabella Horatia (*b* Feb 1801; *d* 5 Aug 1856), er dau of Lord George Seymour (*see* HERTFORD, M), and *d* 19 March 1878, having had, with other issue:

   (1) HENRY GEORGE, **3rd Baron Ravensworth** and 2nd EARL OF RAVENSWORTH OF RAVENSWORTH CASTLE, JP (Northumberland and Co Durham), DL; *b* 8 Oct 1821; *educ* Eton and Ch Ch Oxford; MP (C) S Northumberland 1852–78, Lt-Col Northumberland Yeo 1877, Pres: N of England Steamship Owners' Assoc 1879, Newcastle Soc Antiquaries 1879, Inst Naval Architects 1880 and Roy Ag Soc 1891, DCL Durham 1882; *m* 1st Dec 1852 Mary Diana (*d* 8 Dec 1890), only child of Capt Orlando Gunning-Sutton, RN, and had:

      1a Mary Maud Diana; *m* 17 Nov 1892 Maj-Gen Sir George Townshend Forestier-Walker, KCB, and *d* 24 April 1958, leaving issue (*see* FORESTIER-WALKER, Bt)

      2a Lilian Mary Harriet Diana, MBE (1918); ARRC; *m* 26 July 1906 Capt Hon Gerald FitzMaurice Digby, RN, 4th s of 9th Baron Digby (*qv*), and *d* 18 March 1962, having had issue

   (1) (cont.) The **3rd Baron** *m* 2nd 7 Sept 1892 Emma Sophia Georgiana (*m* 2nd 30 April 1904 her footman James William Wadsworth and *d* 31 Jan 1939), dau of Hon Richard Denman (*see* DENMAN, B) and widow of Maj Oswin Baker-Cresswell, of Cresswell, Northumberland, and *dspm* 22 July 1903

   (2) ATHOLE CHARLES JOHN, **4th Baron Ravensworth** and 3rd and last EARL OF RAVENSWORTH OF RAVENSWORTH CASTLE, JP (Devon and Northumberland), DL (Co Durham); *b* 6 Aug 1883; Capt 60th Rifles; *m* 19 May 1866 Caroline Cecilia (*m* 2nd 21 April 1906 4th Earl of Mount Edgcumbe (*qv*) and *dsp* 23 Feb 1909), 2nd dau of Hon George Edgcumbe (*see* MOUNT EDGCUMBE, E), and *dsp* 7 Feb 1904, when the Earldom and Barony of Eslington of Eslington Park expired

   (1) Maria; *m* 17 April 1861 Gen Sir David Edward Wood, GCB (*d* 16 Oct 1894), and *d* 24 Aug 1883

   (2) Florentia Emily; *m* 18 April 1853 Hugh Robert Hughes (*d* 29 April 1911), of Kinmel and Dinorben, Denbighs, n of 1st Baron Dinorben of Kinmel Park (*see* 1852 edn), and *d* 5 Dec 1909, leaving issue

   (3) Elizabeth; *m* 3 Feb 1863 Sir Hedworth Williamson, 8th Bt (*qv*), and *d* 1 Jan 1920, leaving issue

   (4) Harriette Emily; *m* 4 Feb 1874 Adml of the Fleet Hon Sir Charles Elliott, KCB (*see* MINTO, E), and *d* 6 Feb 1913, leaving issue

   (5) Victoria Isabella; *b* 6 Aug 1841; *m* 29 July 1874 Edward Rowe Fisher-Rowe (*d* 8 Nov 1909), Capt 4th Dragoon Gds, of Thorncombe, Surrey, and *d* 31 March 1935, leaving issue

2 Thomas; *b* 1800; *m* 28 Feb 1843 Caroline Elizabeth (*d* 4 March 1890), est dau of 5th Viscount Barrington (*see* 1970 edn), and *dsp* 9 March 1856

3 George; Army Offr; *m* 23 May 1842 Louisa (*d* 19 May 1873), 2nd dau of Gen Hon Robert Meade (*see* CLANWILLIAM, E), and *d* 15 April 1886

4 Robert (Rev); *b* 24 Sept 1808; Vicar St Paul's Knightsbridge 1851–81; *m* 26 Jan 1836 Emily Ann Charlotte (*d* 22 Oct 1876), dau of Rev Hon Gerald Valerian Wellesley, DD (*see* WELLINGTON, D), and *d* 29 June 1888, leaving, with a dau (*d* unm):

   (1) ARTHUR THOMAS, **5th Baron**

   (2) Gerald George; *b* 13 April 1839; Capt Welch Fus; *m* 1st 12 July 1870 Agatha Catherine (*d* 21 July 1884), est dau and coheir of Adml John Edward Walcott, MP, of Winkton, Hants; *m* 2nd 1 Aug 1885 Elizabeth Amelia (*d* 10 Jan 1935), dau of Charles Reynolds, and *dsp* 7 Sept 1897

   (3) Charles John; *b* 9 Dec 1843; BA Oxon; Assist Librarian Br Museum; granted 1904 rank of baron's yr s; *d* 19 June 1931

5 George Augustus Frederick; *b* 28 July 1812; Col Scots Gds, Groom-in-Waiting to HM QUEEN VICTORIA and Dep Ranger Windsor Gt Pk; *m* 11 May 1842 Cecil Elizabeth Jane (*d* 12 July 1883), 4th dau of Rev Hon Gerald Valerian Wellesley, DD (*see above*), and *d* 14 Dec 1888, having had:

   (1) Edward Thomas (Rev); *b* 20 April 1845; Hon Canon Durham, Vicar Welton St Martin's Northants 1894–1902; *m* 26 Sept 1871 Christina Catharine (*d* 29 June 1927), 2nd dau of Charles Edward Fraser-Tytler, of Aldourie and Balnain, Inverness-shire, and *d* 22 May 1914

   (2) Francis Charles; *b* 1 Feb 1847; *m* 22 April 1884 Kathleen Mary (*d* 28 Feb 1930), dau of George Lane-Fox, of Bramham Pk, Yorks (*see* 1949 edn), BINGLEY, B), and *d* 13 Dec 1911

(3) Frederick Wellesley; *b* 25 Feb 1849; *d* 1851

(4) Augustus Frederick, CVO (1925); *b* 19 July 1852; memb Gentlemen-at-Arms 1895–1926, Comptroller and Treasurer to TRH PRINCE and PRINCESS CHRISTIAN (QUEEN VICTORIA's 3rd dau) OF SCHLESWIG-HOLSTEIN 1915–23, Capt RHA; *m* 1st 9 Jan 1889 Emily (*d* 17 July 1901), dau of Arthur Shinner, of Cheltenham, and had:

   1a Cecil Frederick Joseph, MC (1918); *b* 12 May 1890; *educ* Eton; barrister Middle Temple 1915, T/Lt (A/Capt) KRRC WW I (despatches), Order Crown Belgium; *d* unm 19 Feb 1952

   2a David Edward, MC; *b* 19 Aug 1891; *educ* Charterhouse; Lt Intell Corps, T/Capt RA, WW I (despatches); *m* 14 Jan 1961 Aileen Mary (*d* 14 March 1963), dau of Charles William Booker, of Witley, Surrey, and *dsp* 4 June 1963

   3a Guy Maynard, CB (1953), CBE (1944), MC (1918); *b* 8 Nov 1892; Civ Assist War Office, T/Lt (Actg Capt) RFA WW I (despatches); *m* 7 April 1926 (*divorce* 1943) Hon Calypso Baring, dau of 3rd Baron Revelstoke (*qv*), and *d* 2 Dec 1958, leaving:

      1b +Peter Lorillard [Peter Liddell Esq, Nym Ho, Oakdale Rd, Tunbridge Wells, Kent]; *b* 9 Feb 1927; *educ* Oxford (MA 1954); *m* 1st 14 Aug 1951 (*divorce* 1965) (Phyllis) Anne, dau of Dr F M Cannon, of San Rafael, Calif., and has:

         1c +Peter Guy; *b* 1952; *educ* Sevenoaks; *m* 1st 1977 (*divorce* 1989) Elaine Patricia, est dau of Harold Mountford Wenzel, of Loughton, Essex, and has:

            1d +Thomas Edward; *b* 1984

         1c (cont.) Peter Guy Liddell *m* 2nd 1993 *Hilary Lazenby and by her has:

            1d *Rose Alice; *b* 1992

         2c +John David; *b* 1954; *educ* Sevenoaks; *m* 1994 *Jana Berg

         3c +Thomas Andrew; *b* 1960

         1c *Alice; *b* 1958; *m* 1987 *Paul Richard Wells, s of F/Cdr Oliver Wells, of Ickwell, Beds, and has:

            1d *Harry Augustus; *b* 1992

            1d *Georgina Charlotte; *b* 1988

      1b (cont.) Peter Lorillard Liddell *m* 2nd 1970 *Joan Frances Hopkinson

      1b *Elizabeth Gay [Mrs Alexander van de Pol, 615 Palos Verdes Drive West, Palos Verdes Estates, CA 90274, USA]; *b* 28 Feb 1928; *m* 1st 1946 (*divorce* 1970) Carl Paulson and has:

         1c *Jay; *b* 1950; *m* 1982 *Diane Plummer and has:

            1d *Kyle; *b* 1983

            2d *Scott; *b* 1985

            3d *Derek; *b* 1987

         2c *Mark; *b* 1957

         1c *Sandra; *b* 1947; *m* 1977 *Harry Reese

      1b (cont.) Mrs Elizabeth Paulson *m* 2nd 1973 *Alexander van de Pol

      2b June; *b* 29 March 1930; *m* 25 April 1957 *John Sebastian Macaulay Booth (*see* BOOTH, Bt) and *d* 13 Nov 1968, leaving issue

      3b *Anne Jennifer; *b* 16 May 1931; *m* 1951 (*divorce* 19–) Joseph Enzensberger and has:

         1c *Joseph; *b* 1952

         1c *Janet; *b* 1957

         2c *Ann; *b* 1959

(4) (cont.) Augustus Liddell *m* 2nd 21 Nov 1925 Eydua Mary Gabriel (*d* 13 Dec 1966 aged 87), dau of Prince Arthur Odescalchi, of Szkickzo, Hungary, and widow of Lewis Alexander Scott-Elliott, and *d* 6 April 1929

(1) Minnie Georgiana; *m* 13 July 1865 Charles Balfour and *d* 23 Nov 1927, leaving issue (*see* BALFOUR, E)

(2) Geraldine Mary; *b* 25 Oct 1855; *d* unm 13 July 1948

6 Adolphus Frederic Octavius (Sir), KCB (1880), QC (1861), DL (Co Durham); *b* 15 Jan 1818; *educ* Eton and Ch Ch Oxford (BA 1838, MA 1848, Fell All Souls); barrister Inner Temple 1844, PUS Home Dept 1867–85; *m* 14 Oct 1845 Frederica Elizabeth (*d* 29 Nov 1867), dau of George Lane-Fox (*see* 1949 edn BINGLEY, B), and *d* 27 June 1885, having had:

   (1) Adolphus George Charles, CB (1906); *b* 29 June 1846; *educ* Eton and Balliol Coll Oxford (MA); barrister Inner Temple 1871, Ch Clerk Crown Office 1886–1920, Assist Sec Ld Chllr's Office 1888–1919, Priv Sec to Ld Chllr 1909–15, author: *Notes from the Life of an Ordinary Mortal* (1911); *d* unm 12 Aug 1920

   (2) Walter Bartram; *b* 1 May 1857; *d* 21 April 1864

   (1) Frederica Maria; *m* 17 June 1878 Hon Frederick Canning Lascelles and *d* 17 March 1891, leaving issue (*see* HAREWOOD, E)

   (2) Gertrude Frances Elizabeth; *m* 16 Aug 1890 her cousin Leonard Sartoris (*d* 5 Aug 1929), 2nd s of Alfred Sartoris, of Abbot's Wood, by Hon Mary Barrington, dau of 6th Viscount Barrington (*see* 1970 edn), and *d* 28 Aug 1916, leaving issue

   (3) Mary Beatrice Caroline; *m* 1 March 1897 her bro-in-law and cousin Lionel Charles George Sartoris (*d* 6 April 1911), 3rd s of Alfred Sartoris (*see above*), and *d* 30 July 1951, leaving issue

   (4) Marcia Kathleen Anne; *m* 7 Sept 1880 Col Hon North de Coigny Dalrymple-Hamilton, 2nd s of 10th Earl of Stair (*qv*), and *d* 1 July 1907, leaving issue

1 Maria; *b* 20 April 1798; Ldy Bedchamber; *m* 12 Aug 1818 1st Marquess of Normanby (*qv*) and *d* 20 Oct 1882, leaving issue

2 Anne Elizabeth; *m* 18 April 1826 Sir Hedworth Williamson, 7th Bt (*qv*), and *d* 4 Nov 1878, leaving issue

3 Jane Elizabeth; *m* 21 April 1823 6th Viscount Barrington (*see* 1970 edn) and *d* 23 March 1883

4 Susan; *b* 11 Jan 1810; *m* 14 Oct 1833 4th Earl of Hardwicke (*qv*) and *d* 22 Nov 1886, leaving issue

5 Georgiana; *b* 13 April 1822; Maid-of-Honour to HM QUEEN VICTORIA 1841–45; *m* 4 Sept 1845 2nd and last Baron Bloomfield of Oakhampton and

Redwood and 1st and last Baron Bloomfield of Ciamhaltha, GCB, PC (*dsp* 17 Aug 1879), and *d* 21 May 1905

The 4th BARON's cousin,

ARTHUR THOMAS LIDDELL, **5th Baron Ravensworth**, JP (Co Durham); *b* 28 Oct 1837; served War Office, Hon DCL Durham; *m* 9 Oct 1866 Sophia Harriet (*d* Sept 1918), 2nd dau of Sir Thomas Wathen Waller, 2nd Bt (*see* 1970 edn), and *d* 12 Nov 1919, having had:

1 GERALD WELLESLEY LIDDELL, **6th Baron Ravensworth**, JP (Northumberland and Durham), DL; *b* 21 March 1869; *educ* Winchester; Capt 7th Bn Northumberland Fus, Hon DCL Durham 1929; *m* 11 Oct 1899 Isolda Blanche (*d* 26 March 1938), dau of Charles Glynn Prideaux-Brune, of Prideaux Place, Padstow, Cornwall, and *d* 15 June 1932, having had:

(1) ROBERT ARTHUR LIDDELL, **7th Baron Ravensworth**, TD (1944), JP (Northumberland), DL; *b* 2 Jan 1902; *educ* Winchester and Ch Ch Oxford (BA); Maj RA, formerly Northumberland Hus Yeo (TA); *d* unm 4 Aug 1950

(1) Ellen (Nell) Isolda; *b* 5 July 1905; *m* 25 April 1933 Bernard Adam Hebeler (*d* 21 Feb 1965), er s of Capt Robert Spencer Hebeler, and *d* 5 May 1973, having had issue

(2) *Beatrice Sophie; *b* 23 Sept 1906; *m* 16 Dec 1931 *Edward Richard Speyer, yst s of Edward Speyer, of Ridgehurst, Shenley, Herts, and has:

1a *Jocelyne Isolda [Mrs Alan Tait, 1430 Avenida Marischal Gomez da Costa, Oporto, Portugal]; *b* 1933; *m* 1958 *Alan Richard Tait and has:

1b *Matthew Edward; *b* 1960

2a *Valentine Antonia [Mrs Nicholas Gaffney, Flat 1, 13 South Hill Park Gdns, London NW3]; *b* 1938; *m* 29 June 1974 *Nicholas John Windsor Gaffney

2 Cyril Arthur, JP (Co Durham), DL; *b* 22 June 1872; High Sheriff Co Durham 1917; *m* 5 June 1923 Dorothy Lindop (*d* 13 July 1956), dau of William Brown, of E Riding, Morpeth, Northumberland, and *d* 4 March 1932, leaving:

(1) ARTHUR WALLER LIDDELL, **8th and present Baron Ravensworth**

(1) *Sophie Harriet [The Rev The Hon Sophie Liddell, 31 Hanover Close, Shaftgate Ave, Shepton Mallet, Somerset BA4 5YQ]; *b* 6 July 1927; *educ* Centl High Sch Newcastle and King's Coll Durham; granted rank of baron's dau Oct 1951, Deaconess 1980, Deacon 1987; *m* 1981 *Leslie Charles William Woodhams

3 Athole Robert Henry; *b* 2 Feb 1881; *educ* Charterhouse and Keble Coll Oxford; *d* unm 3 April 1962

1 Emily Agnes; *b* 1 Aug 1867; *d* unm 17 Sept 1934

2 Katherine Anna; *b* 19 June 1871; *d* unm

RAWLINGS

Arms: Quarterly, barry wavy of six argent and azure on a cross gules between in the second and third quarters an escallop azure a seax fesswise, point to the sinister or, surmounted by an ostrich plume palewise argent between in chief and in base a bee volant proper on a bordure azure twelve mullets or. **Supporters:** Dexter, a lion rampant or gorged with a riband azure, pendant from the knot thereof a rose argent barbed and seeded proper; sinister, an elephant ermine gorged with a chain or, pendant therefrom a portcullis sable. **Motto:** *Perseverantia, integritas et fidelitas* ('Perseverance, integrity and loyalty'). **Creation:** B. (LP, UK) 1994.

THE BARONESS RAWLINGS, of Burnham Westgate, Co Norfolk (Patricia Elizabeth Rawlings) [The Rt Hon The Baroness Rawlings, House of Lords, London SW1A 0PW]; *b* 27 Jan 1939; *educ* Oak Hill Haslemere, Le Manoir Lausanne, Florence U, UCL, LSE; with Children's Care Ctee LCC 1959–61, WNHR Nursing Westminster Hosp 1961–68, MEP (C) Essex SW 1989–94 (EDG Dep Whip), fought (C) Essex W and Herts E Euro parly elections 1994 and Sheffield Centl 1983 and Doncaster Centl 1987 UK gen elections, Chm Cncl King's Coll London 1998–; *m* 1962 (*divorce* 1967) Baron Wolfson of Sunningdale (*qv*)

Lineage: LOUIS RAWLINGS; *m* Mary Boas de Winter and had:

PATRICIA ELIZABETH, *cr* a **Baroness**

RAWLINSON

Arms: Sable three swords palewise, the centre one point downwards, the other two points upwards proper, pommels and hilts gold, a chief embattled or, thereon an eastern crown gules.

Crest: Out of an eastern crown or a cubit arm in armour, the hand in a gauntlet, encircled with a wreath of laurel and grasping a sword in bend sinister, all proper, pommel and hilt gold. **Motto:** *Festina lente* ('Make haste slowly'). **Creation:** Bt. (UK) 7 Feb 1891.

SIR ANTHONY HENRY JOHN RAWLINSON, 5TH BT [Sir Anthony Rawlinson Bt, Heath Farm, Guist, Norfolk NR20 5PG]; *b* 1 May 1936; *s f* 1969; *educ* Millfield; Coldstream Gds 1954–56, inventor, fashion photographer; *m* 1st 2 April 1960 (*divorce* 1967) Penelope Byng, 2nd dau of Capt Gambier John Byng Noel, RN (*see* GAINSBOROUGH, E), and has:

1 +ALEXANDER NOEL; *b* 15 July 1964

1 *Caroline Louise Byng; *b* 3 Sept 1962

Sir ANTHONY *m* 2nd 1967 (*divorce* 1976) Pauline, only dau of John Holt Hardy, of Sydney, NSW, and by her has:

2 +Rupert Seymour; *b* 21 Oct 1970

Sir ANTHONY *m* 3rd 1977 (*separated*) *Helen Leone, dau of Thomas Miller Kennedy, of Glasgow, and by her has:

3 +Christopher Thomas Seymour; *b* 1981

Lineage: HENRY RAWLINSON, of Grassyard Hall, Lancs; *b* 8 April 1743; MP Liverpool 1780–84; *m* 14 Aug 1765 Martha, only dau of Peregrine Tyzack, of Newcastle, and *d* Jan 1786, leaving:

ABRAM TYZACK RAWLINSON; *b* 31 July 1777; racehorse-breeder; sold f's Lancs property and bought a house at Chadlington, Oxon, 1805; *m* 18 Aug 1800 Eliza Eudocia Albinia (*d* June 1863), dau of Henry Martin Creswicke, of Moreton-in-Marsh, Glos, and *d* 1 Sept 1845, having had, with other issue:

1 Abram Lindow; *b* 7 Sept 1805; *m* 9 July 1832 Sarah (*d* 7 Sept 1869), dau of Brooke Smith, of Bristol, and *d* 6 Aug 1875, having had issue

2 HENRY CRESWICKE (Sir), **1st Bt**

3 George (Rev); *b* 23 Nov 1812; Camden Prof Ancient History Oxford 1861–88, Fell Exeter Coll, FRGS, Canon Canterbury, Proctor in Convocation for Dean and Chapter Canterbury 1873–98, author *Herodotus* (1858); *m* 6 July 1846 Louisa Wildman, dau of Sir Robert Alexander Chermside, and *d* 6 Oct 1902, having had issue

4 Edward Augustus; *b* 28 Sept 1815; MRCS; *m* 1841 Susan Jane (*d* 4 April 1891), only child of Sir Cuthbert Sharpe, and *d* 14 March 1859, having had issue

1 Maria; *b* 5 Feb 1804; *m* 1833 Brooke Smith, J P, of Bristol, and *d* 3 March 1897, having had issue

2 Georgiana; *b* 14 Nov 1806; *m* 28 July 1849 Rev Lewis Wison Heath, Vicar Newland, Hull, and *dsp* 28 July 1883

ABRAM RAWLINSON's 2nd s,

Sir Henry Creswicke Rawlinson, 1st Bt (UK), so *cr* 6 Feb 1891, GCB (1889, KCB 1856, CB 1844); *b* 11 April 1810; Mil Cadet HEIC 1827, Paymaster 1st Bombay Grenadiers 1829–34, helped reorganise Shah of Persia's army 1833–39, Political Agent Kandahar 1840–42, HEIC Political Agent 1843 and Consul and Resident Baghdad 1843–55 (Consul-Gen 1851–55) (where as an orientalist he was the first person to decipher Persian cuneiform script, apart perhaps from Dr Edward Hincks, of Killyleagh, Co Down, who did so simultaneously but independently), Hon Lt-Col 1856, Crown Dir HEIC 1856, MP (C) Reigate Feb-Sept 1858 (fought same seat unsuccessfully 1857) and Frome 1865–68, Memb Cncl Sec State India 1858–59 and 1868–95, Envoy Extrdy and Min Plen Persia 1859–60 with rank of Maj-Gen, Life Dir Roy Asiatic Soc 1862–95 (Pres 1878–81), Pres RGS 1871–72 and 1874–75 and London Oriental Congress 1874, Tstee Br Museum 1867–95, FRS, DCL Oxon 1850, Hon LLD Cantab 1862 and Edinburgh, Kt Lion and Sun Persia 1st Cl, Order Durrani Persia 3rd Cl, Chev Order Merit Prussia, author *England and Russia in the East* (1875); *m* 2 Sept 1862 Louisa Caroline Harcourt (*d* 31 Oct 1889), dau of Henry Seymour (*see* SOMERSET, D), and *d* 5 March 1895, leaving:

1 **Sir Henry Seymour Rawlinson, 2nd Bt**, 1st and last BARON RAWLINSON, of Trent, Co Dorset (UK), so *cr* 6 Oct 1919, GCB (1919, KCB 1915, CB 1902), GCSI (1924), GCVO (1917), KCMG (1918); *b* 20 Feb 1864; *educ* Eton and RMC Sandhurst; joined 60th King's Roy Rifles 1884, ADC to C-in-C India 1885–90, served Burma 1886–87 (despatches), Capt 1891, Staff Coll Camberley 1892, tfd to Coldstream Gds 1892, Bde Maj Aldershot 1895–98, DAAG Egypt 1898, Nile Expdn 1897–98 (medals with clasps, despatches, present Battles of Atbara and Khartoum), Maj and Brevet Lt-Col 1899, DAAG Natal 1899, Boer War 1899–1902 (despatches five times, Queen's medal with six clasps, King's medal with two clasps, brevet), Brevet Col 1902, AAG War Office 1903, Cmdt Staff Coll Camberley 1903–06, Cdr 2nd Bde Aldershot Cmd 1907–09, Maj-Gen 1909, cmded 3rd Div S Cmd 1910–14, WW I: cmded 4th Div BEF 1914, 4th Army Corps 1914–15 and 4th Army 1915–Feb 1918 and March 1918–19, Lt-Gen 1916, Gen 1917, Br memb Supreme Cncl Allies Versailles Feb-March 1918, memb Army Cncl 1918–19, GOC-in-C: Forces N Russia 1919, Aldershot 1919–20, ADC Gen to HM GEORGE V 1919–23, C-in-C Army India 1920–25, memb Exec Cncl of Govr-Gen 1920–25, Grand Offr Legn Hon, Orders of Leopold Belgium, St George Russia 1st Cl, Danilo and Obelitch Gold Medal Montenegro, Croix de Guerre France and Belgium, US DSM, Hon LLD Cantab, KGStJ; recd thanks of Parl and grant of £30,000 (just under £490,000 in late-1990s terms) for eminent servs WW I; *m* 6 Nov 1890 Meredith Sophia Frances (*d* 29 Sept 1951), only dau of Coleridge John Kennard (*see* KENNARD, Bt), and *dsp* 28 March 1925, when the Barony expired

2 **Sir Alfred Rawlinson, 3rd Bt**, CMG (1916), CBE (1919), DSO (1919); *b* 17 Jan 1867; Lt 17th Lancers, Lt-Col RGA and Cdr RNVR WW I 1914–16, Special Intell Serv with GHQ Army Black Sea 1919–20, imprisoned Erzerum by Turks 1920–21; *m* 1st 25 June 1890 Margarette Kennard (*d* 18 Sept 1907), 6th dau of William Bunce Greenfield, DL, of Bayswater, and had:

   (1) (ALFRED) FREDERICK (Sir), **4th Bt**

   (1) Honour Louisa; *d* unm 2 Aug 1913

   (2) Irene Margarette; *m* 1st 3 Oct 1917 (*divorce* 1933) Neville Brace Colt (*d* 5 March 1968), only s of George Brace Colt, of S Kensington, and had issue; *m* 2nd 1933 Capt John Usher Hogarth, Gren Gds (*das* Italy 19 July 1944), s of Robert George Hogarth, CBE, JP, DL, FRCS, LRCP, and *d* 5 May 1974, leaving further issue

   (3) Mary; *d* in infancy

2 (cont.) **Sir Alfred** *m* 2nd 13 Dec 1913 (*divorce* 1924) Jean Isabella Griffen Aitken and *d* 1 June 1934

The 3rd Bt's only s,

   Sir (Alfred) Frederick Rawlinson, 4th Bt; *b* 23 Aug 1900; *educ* Eton; RAF WW II 1941–45 (invalided); *m* 20 Jan 1934 Bess(ie) Ford Taylor (*d* 30 March 1996), dau of Frank Raymond Emmatt, of Harrogate, and *d* 15 June 1969, leaving:

1 Sir ANTHONY HENRY JOHN RAWLINSON, **5th and present Bt**

2 +(Marcus) Andrew Frederick [Andrew Rawlinson Esq, Stody Hall, Stody, Melton Constable, Norfolk]; *b* 30 Nov 1940; *educ* Canford; *m* 31 Oct 1964 *Miriam Diana, est dau of Richard Joice, of Mill Farm, Newton by Castle Acre, Norfolk, and has:

   (1) *Joanna Jane; *b* 30 Oct 1965

   (2) *Nicola Abigail; *b* 17 Dec 1967

   (3) *Candida Louise; *b* 25 Feb 1974

1*Sarah Jane [Mrs William Bulwer-Long, Heydon Hall, Norwich, Norfolk NR11 6RE]; *b* 25 July 1939; *m* 26 May 1962 Capt William Hanslip Bulwer LONG later BULWER-LONG (deed poll 1963), DL (Norfolk 1992), 9th/12th Lancers (*d* 25 Feb 1996), est s of Brig Hetherington Long, of Heydon, and has:

   (1) *Edward Hanslip; *b* 27 Nov 1966

   (2) *Benjamin Earle; *b* 22 Feb 1970

   (1) *Daisy Lydia; *b* 1975

RAWLINSON OF EWELL

Arms: Or between three towers sable, each charged with a sword, point upwards argent, a pall reversed sable, thereon in chief a lymphad argent and in chevron a lion head erased or between two roses argent, barbed and seeded proper. **Crest:** On a mount vert within a circlet of acorns and harps or a duck proper, holding in the beak an escallop argent. **Supporters:** Dexter, a pegasus sable, maned, hooved and crowned gold; sinister, a llama or, gorged with a ribbon blue celeste and argent, the ends flottant upwards. **Creation:** B. (LP, UK) 1978.

THE BARON RAWLINSON (Peter Anthony Grayson Rawlinson, PC (1964), QC (1959) (NI 1972)) [The Rt Hon The Lord Rawlinson of Ewell PC QC, East Wing, Wardour Castle, Tisbury, Wilts SP3 6RH]; *b* 26 June 1919; *educ* Downside and Christ's Coll Cambridge (Hon Fell); Maj Irish Gds WW II (despatches), barrister Inner Temple 1946, MP (C) Epsom 1955–74 and Epsom and Ewell 1974–78, Recorder Salisbury 1961–62 and Kingston-upon-Thames 1975–, Slr-Gen 1962–64, ktd 1962, Attorney Gen 1970–74, dir Telegraph Gp 1985–, Chm Senate Four Inns and Bar 1975–76, Pres 1986, Leader W Circuit 1975–82, Treas Inner Temple 1984, Hon Fell Coll America's Trial Lawyers, Hon Memb American Bar Assoc; *m* 1st 1940 (*divorce* 1954) Haidee (*d* 1982), dau of Gerald Kavanagh, and has:

1 *Mikaela; *b* 1941; *m* Feb 1964 (*divorce* 1989) Jonathan Irwin, s of John Irwin, of Chiswick, and has:

   (1) *Charles; *b* 24 Sept 1965

   (2) *Luke; *b* 18 Sept 1967

   (3) *Jago; *b* 1972

   (4) *Samson; *b* 1982

2 *Dariel [The Hon Mrs Garnett, 25 St Peter's Sq, London W4]; *b* 25 Sept 1943; *m* 8 Dec 1965 *Harry John Gerard Garnett, s of Maj Henry Claude Lyon Garnett, RHG, of Chelsea, and has:

   (1) *Sophia; *b* 22 Dec 1967; *m* 1994 *Tim Beddow, s of C M Beddow

   (2) *Natasha; *b* 10 Dec 1970; *educ* Edinburgh U; jnlst

3 Haidee; *b* 1948; *m* 1st 26 Sept 1968 Richard Annesley, yr s of Gerald Francis Annesley, of Castlewellan, Co Down, and had:

   (1) *Peter; *b* 7 July 1970

   (1) *Arabella; *b* 1972

3 (cont.) The Hon Mrs Haidee Annesley *m* 2nd 1985 *Maj Ralph Cowdy and *d* 4 June 1997

BARON RAWLINSON OF EWELL *m* 2nd 1954 his cousin *Elaine Angela, dau of Vincent Luis Dominguez (*see* GRAYSON, Bt), and by her has:

1 *Michael Vincent; *b* 24 Jan 1957; *m* 20 Dec 1982 (*divorce* 1990) Maria Alexandra Hilda Madeline de Lourdes, only dau of Anthony Charles Garton, of Kensington

2 *Anthony Richard; *b* 28 Dec 1963; *m* 13 April 1996 *Una, er dau of John Shannon, of Hong Kong

4 *Angela Lorraine; *b* 3 Sept 1962; *m* 1st 1991 Mathew Steinmann; *m* 2nd 24 Feb 1996 *5th Baron Swaythling (*qv*) and by him has issue

Lineage: *See* GRAYSON, Bt

RAYLEIGH

Arms: Azure on a chevron argent between three cross-crosslets fitchée or as many leopard's faces proper. **Crest:** A demi-lion azure, gorged with a mural crown or, holding in the dexter paw a cross-crosslet fitchée or and resting the sinister on a shield sable, charged with a chevron argent, between three cross-crosslets fitchée, also or. **Supporters:** Dexter, a reindeer or, collared and attired sable; sinister, a monkey proper, banded about the middle, and chained, chain reflexed over the back or. **Motto:** *Tenax propositi* ('Tenacious of purpose'). **Creation:** B. (UK) 18 July 1821.

THE 6TH BARON RAYLEIGH OF TERLING PLACE, Co Essex (John Gerald Strutt) [The Rt Hon The Lord Rayleigh, Terling Place, Chelmsford, Essex CM3 2PJ]; *b* 4 June 1960; *s* unc 1988; *educ* Eton, RMA Sandhurst and RAC Cirencester; Lt Welsh Gds; *m* 1991 *Annabel Kate, yst dau of Maj (William) Gary Patterson (*see* MONSON, B), and has:

1 +(JOHN) FREDERICK (FREDDIE); *b* 29 March 1993

2 +William Hedley Charles; *b* 11 Nov 1994

3 +Hugo Richard; *b* 12 Feb 1998

Lineage: JOHN STRUTT, of Moulsham and Springfield, Essex; miller; *m* Jane (*d* 1704), dau of Jonathan Barnard, of Chelmsford, and *d* 1694, leaving, with a yr s (Thomas, of Springfield, *m* Elizabeth Young, of Halstead, and *d* 1729, leaving issue, including the antiquary Joseph Strutt (1749–1802)):

JOHN STRUTT, of Moulsham and Newhouse, Terling; *b* 1666; *m* Anne, dau of William Surrah, of Felsted, and *d* 1736, leaving, with other issue:

JOSEPH STRUTT, of Moulsham; *b* 1702; miller; *m* Mary, dau of Robert Young, of Little Dunmow, and *d* 1772, leaving, with other issue:

JOHN STRUTT, of Terling Place, Witham, Essex (which he bought 1761 from Sir Matthew Featherstonhaugh, 1st Bt); *b* 1727; miller, MP Maldon; *m* 1756 Anne (*d* 3 July 1732), dau of Rev William Goodday, of Strelley, Notts, and Maldon, and *d* 1816, having had, with an est s (John, *d* 1781) and a yst s (William Goodday, bapt 26 Feb 1762, joined 61st Regt, Capt 91st Regt, joined 97th Regt 1782, Maj 60th Regt, Lt-Col 54th Regt, Brig-Gen *c* 1796, Dep-Govr Stirling Castle 1796, Maj-Gen 1798, Govr Quebec 1800, *d* 5 Feb 1848):

JOSEPH HOLDEN STRUTT, DL (Essex), of Terling Place; *b* 21 Nov 1758; *educ* Winchester and BNC Oxford (BA 1782, MA 1785); Lt-Col different regts Essex militia 1782–1823, Col W Essex Militia 1821, MP (Tory) Maldon 1790–1826 and Okehampton 1826–30; *m* 23 Feb 1789 Lady CHARLOTTE MARY GERTRUDE FitzGERALD (*b* 29 May 1758; *cr* 18 July 1821 **Baroness Rayleigh of Terling Place**, Co Essex (UK), as reward for her husb's mil servs (he having refused all personal honours), with remainder to heirs male of her body by her then husb; *d* 13 Sept 1836), dau of 1st Duke of Leinster (*qv*), and *d* 18 Feb 1845, having had:

1 JOHN JAMES, **2nd Baron**

2 William Henry; *b* 1800; *d* 1805

1 Emily Anne; *b* 1790; *d* 14 Dec 1864

2 Charlotte Olivia, of St Catharine's Court, nr Bath; *m* 19 Jan 1841 Rev Robert Drummond (*d* 1883), s of V-Adml Sir Adam Drummond, and *d* 31 Jan 1897 aged 99

The BARONESS's er s,

JOHN JAMES STRUTT, **2nd Baron Rayleigh of Terling Place**; *b* 30 Jan 1796; *educ* Winchester and Oriel Coll Oxford (BA 1818, MA 1821); Maj Eastern Bn Essex Militia to 1823; *m* 3 Feb 1842 Clara Elizabeth La Touche (*d* 4 March 1900), dau of Capt Richard Vicars, RE, of Langford Grove, nr Maldon, and *d* 14 June 1873, having had:

1 JOHN WILLIAM, **3rd Baron**

2 Joseph Henry; *b* 1844; *d* 1845

3 Richard; *b* 19 Feb 1848; *educ* Winchester and Magdalen Coll Oxford (MA); *m* 24 April 1879 Hon Augusta Neville (*d* 22 Jan 1903), only child of 5th Baron Braybrooke (*qv*), and *d* 14 Oct 1927, having had:

(1) Richard Neville; *b* 22 July 1886; *educ* Winchester and Trin Coll Oxford; Lt 2nd Bn Roy Scots; *m* (*divorce* 1915) Vera, dau of Lt A Gordon, RASC, and *d* 18 Oct 1915 of wounds recd in action, leaving:

1a Richard Francis; *b* 1910; *d* unm 21 Sept 1942

(2) Geoffrey St John, CBE (1920), JP (Somerset 1949); *b* 28 March 1888; *educ* Winchester and Magdalen Coll Oxford (BA 1911); Capt 5th Bn Essex Regt WW I 1914–17 (wounded); *m* 25 April 1912 Sybil Eyre (*d* 9 Feb 1975), yst dau of Sir Walpole Lloyd Greenwell, 1st Bt (*qv*), and *d* 2 Oct 1971, having had:

1a +Antony Geoffrey, OBE (1952); *b* 15 Jan 1913; *educ* Winchester; FRAS, FBIS, W/Cdr RAF WW II; *m* 1st 12 Dec 1939 (*divorce* 1951) Ebba, dau of Lief Lunderbye, of Oslo, and has:

1b *Vivienne Ebba [Mrs Richard Sands, Hill Farm Ho, Thorpe Morieux, Suffolk]; *b* 27 Aug 1940; *m* 5 Aug 1968 *Richard Maitland Sands, s of Kenneth Oswald Tatham Sands, of Kenya, and has:

1c *Richard Jonathan Neville; *b* 1974

1a (cont.) Anthony Strutt *m* 2nd 12 July 1951 *Millicent ('Molly') Edith, dau of Aubrey Stephen Waters, of London, and by her has:

1b +Peter Anthony [Peter Strutt Esq, 37 Bearwood Rd, Wokingham, Berks RG11 4TB]; *b* 1949

2b +Stephen Nigel; *b* 5 Aug 1952

3b +Michael Geoffrey; *b* 13 Dec 1958; *m* 1992 *Barbara —

4b +Ian David; *b* 2 March 1965

2b *Denise Olivia [Mrs Denise Lyndale, 14 East St, Ashburton, Devon]; *b* 29 July 1955; *m* 1975 (*divorce* 1990) Richard Lyndale

3b *Pamela Jane; *b* Sept 1957; *m* 1980 (*divorce* 1994) Ian Fielding

2a Ivan Cornwallis, DFC; *b* 7 Feb 1916; *educ* Trin Coll Cambridge (BA); S/Ldr RAFVR WW II; *ka* N Africa 6 Feb 1943

3a Stephen Alistair; *b* 26 July 1918; *educ* Peterhouse Cambridge; Lt RNVR WW II; *m* 17 June 1941 *Felicity Anne (*m* 2nd 28 Oct 1959 Brig David Campbell Mullen, CBE, Highland LI (*d* 13 Sept 1968), s of Edward Mullen, of Glasgow), yst dau of Mervyn Sorley MacDonnell, OBE (High Commr Free City of Danzig 1923–26), and *d* 27 Jan 1949, leaving:

1b +Paul Alistair [Maj Paul Strutt, Flaxmans, W Tytherley, Hants SP5 1NR]; *b* 6 Sept 1944; *educ* Ampleforth; *m* 1977 *Charlotte Yvonne, dau of Brig Mortimer Cecil Lanyon, MBE, MC (*see* AMHERST OF HACKNEY, B), and has:

1c +Richard Alistair Robert; *b* 1986

1c *Louisa Anne; *b* 1982

2b *Stephen Mark Alistair [Maj Stephen Strutt, St Catherine's, Bath, Somerset BA1 8HQ]; *b* 18 July 1948; *educ* Ampleforth and RAC Cirencester; Maj Gren Gds; *m* 1980 *Christina Mary Amoroso, dau of Dr Eric Amoroso Centeno, and has:

1c +Edward Alistair James; *b* 1985

1c *Catherine Mary Felicity Erica; *b* 1983

1b Lucinda Alistaire; *b* 24 July 1942; *m* 1976 *Lt Col Angus Ian Ramsay and *dsp* 1986

(1) Olivia Maude; *b* 11 Sept 1890; *m* 17 July 1913 Granville Edward Bromley Martin (*d* 31 May 1941), yr s of George Edward Martin, DL, of Ham Court, Worcs, and *d* 30 Aug 1953, leaving issue

4 Charles Hedley, JP; *b* 18 April 1849; *educ* Winchester and Trin Coll Cambridge (BA); CA Essex 1888–1925, Chm Essex QS 1904–21, MP (C) E Essex 1883–85 and Maldon 1896–1906, chm Anglo-Dutch Plantations; *m* 5 Nov 1919 Evangeline (*d* 17 Feb 1950), dau of Henry Hoare, of Staplehurst, Kent, and widow of Percy Broderick Bernard (*see* 1970 edn BANDON, E), of Castle Hacket, Ireland, and *d* 19 Dec 1926

5 Edward Gerald, CH (1917); *b* 10 April 1854; *educ* Winchester and Trin Coll Cambridge (BA); Pres Surveyors' Inst 1912, CA Essex, advsr Bd of Ag WW I, dir Yorks Insur; *m* 29 Oct 1878 Maria Louisa (*d* 10 May 1938), dau of John Jolliffe Tufnell, of Langleys, Essex, and *d* 8 March 1930, having had, with other issue:

(1) Gerald Murray, DL (Essex), of New Home, Terling; *b* 9 Oct 1880; *educ* Winchester; Capt Essex Yeo, Lt Suffolk Imp Yeo, High Sheriff 1936; *m* 14 July 1910 Rhoda (*d* 1968), 2nd dau of Collingwood Hope, CBE, KC, Recorder Bolton, of Crix, Hatfield Peverel, and *d* 1955, leaving:

1a James Hedley, MC; *b* 20 April 1913; *educ* Stowe and Trin Coll Cambridge (BA 1935); Maj 104th Essex Yeo Field Bde RA (TA) WW II (wounded, despatches); *d* unm 25 July 1965

1a *Pamela [Mrs Richard Gatty, Pepper Arden, Northallerton, N Yorks DL7 0JF]; *b* 29 Nov 1911; *m* 17 Oct 1935 Richard Gatty, JP (*d* 7 Sept 1975), yr s of Sir Stephen Herbert Gatty, KC, and has:

1b Jonathan; *b* 13 Jan 1937; *m* 1st 1962 (*divorce* 1984) Valerie Cynthia, dau of Alfred H Adcock, of Milford-on-Sea, Hants, and had:

1c *Fiona Katherine Adelaide [Mrs Torquil MacLeod, Mains of Murie Farm House, Errol, Perth]; *b* 16 April 1963; *m* 1992 *Maj Torquil MacLeod, Black Watch (RHR), and has:

1d *Alexander Jonathan Hardine; *b* 23 Jan 1994

2d *Hector John; *b* 7 Dec 1996

1d *Sophie; *b* 19–

2d *Eleanor Katherine; *b* 18 July 1995

2c *Philippa Margaret [Mrs John Lanteri-Laura, 49 Wolfington Rd, London SE27 0RH]; *b* 7 April 1965; *m* 1988 *John Lanteri-Laura and has:

1d *Guido Titus; *b* 14 Oct 1991

1d *Giulietta; *b* 3 Aug 1989

1b (cont.) Jonathan Gatty *m* 2nd 1984 *Cheryll [Mrs Jonathan Gatty, Pepper Arden, Northallerton, N Yorks], dau of George Mansfield, of Risca, Gwent, and *d* 11 Nov 1991, leaving by her:

1c *Richard George; *b* 13 June 1984

1b *Jessica Margaret; *b* 24 May 1938; nun

2b *Rhoda Pamela [Mrs John Bucknill, The Grange, Grateley, Hants SP11 8JR]; *b* 19 June 1943; *m* 1964 *John David Bucknill and has:

1c *Stephen [Stephen Bucknill Esq, Sleepy Cottage, Turville, Oxon]; *b* 3 Nov 1965; *m* 1993 *Amanda Jane Cotton and has:

1d *Benjamin George; *b* 15 May 1997

1d *Rosanne; *b* 25 Sept 1995

1c *Gemma Martha [Mrs Michael Hughes, The Haven, Barkers Hill, Barford St Andrew, Dorset SP7 9EB]; *b* 15 June 1967; *m* 1990 *Michael Anthony Hughes

2c *Charlotte [Miss Charlotte Bucknill, 16 St Albans Grove, London W8 5BP]; *b* 4 June 1969

2a *Ursula Joyce [Mrs James Harden, Hendy, Nanhoron, Pwllheli, Gwynedd]; *b* 17 April 1917; WRNS WW II 1943–45; *m* 27 July 1948 *Maj James Richard Edwards Harden, OBE, DSO, MC, DL, only s of Maj James Edwards Harden, and has:

1b *David James [David Harden Esq, Nanhoron, Pwllheli, Gwynedd]; *b* 29 July 1954; *educ* Westminster; *m* 1983 *Bettina Clare Lascelles, only dau of Col Brian C L Tayleur, OBE, of Nairobi, and has:

1c *Edward James; *b* 1986

1c *Matilda Claire; *b* 1984

1b *Thérèse Annabella; *b* 14 Sept 1949; *m* 1st 1972 (*divorce* 1979) Charles Herbert Pelham (*see* CHICHESTER, E); *m* 2nd 1980 *Lt-Cdr Nigel John Pearson, RN, and has:

1c *James Nicholas; *b* 1985

1c *Lucinda Christine; *b* 1987

2b *Carolyn Emily; *b* 25 Oct 1952; *m* 1986 *Colin Ransford Galloway and has:

1c *Miles Malcolm Ransford; *b* 1989

1c *Tanya; *b* 199–

2c *Zoe; *b* 1992

(2) John James; *b* 26 Oct 1881; *educ* Winchester; *m* 24 Feb 1914 Hon Agnes Dewar, est dau of 1st Baron Forteviot (*qv*), and *d* 12 Nov 1968, leaving:

1a Edward Alexander, DL (Wigtownshire 1966); *b* 29 Nov 1914; *educ* Harrow and BNC Oxford; RAF WW II; *m* 22 April 1975 Janet (*d* 1988), dau of P F Phillips-Higgins, of Wraysbury, Berks, and formerly w of (Jeremy) Mark Roper-Caldbeck, and *dsp* 199–

1a *Joan Eleanor [Miss Joan Strutt, 173 Cranmore Court, London SW3]; *b* 13 Oct 1916

(3) Edward Jolliffe; *b* 4 Jan 1884; *educ* Winchester; Capt 5th Bn Essex Regt; *m* 7 Nov 1912 Amelie (*d* 9 Nov 1954), dau of Frederic Devas, and *d* 24 May 1964, leaving:

1a Mark Frederic, MC, TD, DL (Essex 1954); *b* 24 Sept 1913; *educ* Winchester; Lt-Col RA WW II, chartered surveyor and land agent, FRICS, FAI, High Sheriff Essex 1970; *m* 7 Nov 1946 *Estelle Elaine [Mrs Mark Strutt, Crix, Hatfield Peverel, Essex], est dau of Maj Sir Thomas Reedham Berney, 10th Bt (*qv*), and widow of Maj Kenneth William Bols, IA (*see* STRICKLAND-CONSTABLE, Bt), and *d* 16 June 1982, leaving:

1b *Charlotte Olivia [Mrs Bruce Ryder, Crix, Hatfield Peverel, Essex CM3 2EU]; *b* 12 July 1947; *m* 6 Sept 1969 *Bruce Dudley Ryder (*see* HARROWBY, E) and has issue

2a +Nigel Edward (Sir), TD, DL (Essex 1954) [Sir Nigel Strutt TD DL, Sparrows, Terling, Essex]; *b* 18 Jan 1916; *educ* Winchester and Wye Ag Coll (Fell 1970); memb Braintree RDC 1936 (V-Chm 1955), Chm Terling and Fairshead Parish Cncl 1952–95, Maj Essex Yeo 1937–56 (wounded WW II, POW), part-time memb E Electricity Bd 1964–76, High Sheriff Essex 1966, Pres: CLA 1967–69, Br Friesian Cattle Soc 1974–75 and RASE 1982–83 (Hon FRASE 1971), chm: Ag Advsy Cncl 1969–73 (memb 1963–), Advsy Cncl Ag and Horticulture 1973–80 and Strutt & Parker (Farms) Ltd (also md), late md Lord Rayleigh's Farms Inc, V-Chm NEDC for Ag 1967–82, ktd 1972, Hon DSc Cranfield 1979, Hon PhD Anglia Poly U 1993, Hon Dr Essex U, awarded von Thünen Gold Medal Award by FVS Fndn, Amburgh, 1974, Massey Ferguson Award 1976, Master Farmers' Co 1976–77 (Jr Warden 1974)

1a *Gillian Leonora [Mrs Oliver Brooke, The Manor House, Gt Cheverell, Devizes, Wilts]; *b* 11 June 1918; *m* 1st 6 Aug 1941 (*divorce* 1959) Sir (Harold) Anthony Nutting, 3rd Bt (*qv*), and has issue; *m* 2nd 22 July 1961 Brig Oliver George Brooke CBE, DSO (*see* BROOKEBOROUGH, V)

(1) Emily Norah; *b* 10 Sept 1879; *d* unm 13 Oct 1966

(2) Evelyn Mary; *b* 6 Feb 1883; *m* 17 July 1906 Maj Claude Henry Tritton, OBE, DL (*see* TRITTON, Bt), and *d* 10 Dec 1965, leaving issue

(3) Clara Helena; *b* 25 March 1888; *m* 23 Nov 1915 Lt-Col William Frederick Parsons, DSO, and had issue (*see* ROSSE, E)

6 Hedley Vicars; *b* 17 July 1864; Lt Prince of Wales's Leinster Regt; *m* 30 Sept 1885 Elizabeth (*d* 15 March 1888), dau of John Knight, and *d* 22 Jan 1891, leaving:

(1) Hilda Elizabeth; *b* 28 Oct 1886; *m* 17 July 1912 Francis Deverell, MC (*d* 7 March 1941), Capt and Brevet Maj Lond Regt, yr s of Wykeham Travel Deverell, and had issue

1 Clara Emily Charlotte; *m* 12 Sept 1871 John Paley (*d* 4 Oct 1894), of Ampton Hall, Suffolk, est surv s of Rev George Paley, of Langcliffe, Yorks, and *d* 23 Dec 1912, leaving issue

The 2nd BARON's est s,

JOHN WILLIAM STRUTT, **3rd Baron Rayleigh of Terling Place**, OM (1902), PC (1905); *b* 12 Nov 1842; *educ* Eton, Harrow and Trin Coll Cambridge (BA, Sr Wrangler and 1st Smith's Prizeman 1865, Fell 1866–71, MA 1868); mathematician and scientist, Cavendish Prof Experimental Physics 1879–84, Pres: Br Assoc 1884, Roy Soc 1905–08 (Sec 1885–96, FRS 1873) and Soc Psychical Research 1919, Prof Natural Philosophy Roy Inst 1887–1905, Ld Lt Essex 1892–1901, sat as C Ho Lds, discoverer of the inert gas argon 1894, chm Treasury ctee on founding of Nat Physical Lab 1898, Nobel Prize Physics 1904, Chllr Cambridge U 1908–19, pres special govt advsy ctee aeronautics 1909, Hon DCL: Oxford 1883 and Durham 1913, Hon LLD: Glasgow 1884, McGill 1884, Dublin 1885, Edinburgh 1888 and Birmingham 1909, Hon DSc: Cambridge 1888, Dublin 1892 and Leeds 1910, Hon PhD Heidelberg 1886, foreign memb Acad Sciences Paris, Prussian Order Merit, Offr Legn Hon France, author *Treatise on the Theory of Sound* (1877); *m* 19 July 1871 Evelyn Georgiana Mary (*d* 7 April 1934), 2nd dau of James Maitland Balfour (*see* BALFOUR, E), and *d* 30 June 1919, having had:

1 ROBERT JOHN, **4th Baron**

2 Arthur Charles, CBE (1928); *b* 2 Oct 1878; *educ* HMS *Britannia*; RN: Lt 1900, Cdr 1913, Master Fleet under 1st Earl Beatty (*qv*) 1916–18, Capt 1917, Dir Navi-

gation Admlty 1923–25, R-Adml 1929, ret 1929, V-Adml 1933, re-employed as Cdre Convoys 1940–43 and Naval Offr-in-Command Dartmouth 1943–45 WW II, ADC to HM GEORGE V 1928–29, Order St Stanislas Russia; *m* 6 Dec 1934 Irene (*d* 21 April 1974 aged 90), dau of Baron de Brienen and widow of Capt Hon Cyril Augustus Ward, MVO, RN (*see* DUDLEY, E), and *dsp* 10 Feb 1973

3 Julian Balfour; *b* 16 Aug 1880; *d* 4 Sept 1886

4 William Maitland; *b* 20 July 1886; *d* unm 22 Nov 1912

The 3rd BARON's est s,

ROBERT JOHN STRUTT, **4th Baron Rayleigh of Terling Place**, JP, DL; *b* 28 Aug 1875; *educ* Eton and Trin Coll Cambridge (BA 1897, Fell 1900, MA 1901); FRS 1902 (Rumford Medal 1920, For Sec 1929–34), Prof Physics Coll of Science S Kensington, Emeritus Prof Physics Imperial Coll Science 1908–20, Tstee Beit Memorial Fellowship 1928, Jt Pres Internat Congress Physics 1934, Chm Govrs Imp Coll Sci and Tech 1936–47, Pres Br Assoc 1938, Pres Roy Inst 1945, Hon ScD Dublin, Hon DSc Durham, Hon LLD Edinburgh; *m* 1st 6 July 1905 Lady Mary Hilda Clements (*d* 7 April 1919), 2nd dau of 4th Earl of Leitrim (*see* 1953 edn), and had:

1 JOHN ARTHUR STRUTT, **5th Baron Rayleigh of Terling Place**; *b* 12 April 1908; *educ* Eton and Trin Coll Cambridge (BA 1929, MA 1935); prospective C parly candidate S Bucks 1938 (withdrew before polling day) and Manchester Gorton 1940; *m* 1 Dec 1934 Ursula Mary (*d* 1982), dau of Lt-Col Richard Hugh Royds Brocklebank, DSO, DL, by Charlotte Carissima, dau of Gen Sir Bindon Blood, GCB, GCVO, and *dsp* 7 Feb 1988

2 Charles Richard; *b* 25 May 1910; *educ* Eton and Trin Coll Cambridge (BA 1931, MA 1934); Govr Felsted Sch 1936, Capt RA, dir Australian Estates 1949, Hon Treas Soc Psychical Research 1954, chm Lord Rayleigh's Farms Ltd 1957, V-Pres Ch Army 1963 (memb bd 1950), King Christian IX Liberation Order Denmark; *m* 17 Dec 1952 *Hon Jean Elizabeth Davidson [The Hon Mrs Charles Strutt, Berwick Place, Hatfield Peverel, Essex CM3 2EY], yr dau of 1st Viscount Davidson (*qv*), and *d* 11 Dec 1981, leaving:

(1) JOHN GERALD STRUTT, **6th and present Baron Rayleigh of Terling Place**

(1) *Anne Caroline; *b* 8 Dec; *m* 1988 *Hon Bernard Christison Jenkin, MP, yr s of Baron Jenkin of Roding (LP, *qv*)

(2) *Mary Jean [Mrs Roderick Fraser, Berwicks Farm House, Hatfield Peverel, Essex]; *b* 30 July 1957; *m* 1981 *Roderick Joseph Fraser and has issue (*see* LOVAT, L)

3 +Hedley Vicars [The Hon Hedley Strutt, Mulroy, Carrigart, Letterkenny, Co Donegal, Ireland]; *b* 19 Feb 1915; *educ* Eton and Trin Coll Cambridge; Capt Scots Gds WW II; chm Anglo-Indonesian Plantations Ltd 1964–72

1 Violet Blanche; *b* 21 July 1906; *d* 11 May 1910

2 *Daphne [The Rt Hon The Dowager Lady Acton, 46 Clarence Rd, Moseley, Birmingham B13 9UH]; *b* 5 Nov 1911; *m* 25 Nov 1931 3rd Baron Acton (*qv*) and has issue

The **4th Baron** *m* 2nd 8 July 1920 Kathleen Alice, OBE (1918) (*d* 1980), est dau of John Coppin-Straker, of Stagshaw Ho, Northumberland, and widow of Capt James Harold Cuthbert, DSO, Scots Gds, of Beaufront Castle, Hexham, Northumberland, and *d* 13 Dec 1947, leaving by her:

4 +Guy Robert [The Hon Guy Strutt, The Old Rectory, Terling, Essex CM3 2QE]; *b* 16 April 1921; *educ* Eton and Trin Coll Cambridge (BA 1943)

Seat: Terling Place, Terling, Essex. The original part of the house, a three storeyed block (though the top-floor windows are much smaller than those below), was built in the 1770s. The architect, John Johnson, was particularly prolific in Essex, although himself a native of Leicestershire, and as well as Terling he was responsible for the County Gaol and House of Correction at Chelmsford. One would not guess from its comfortable patrician pediment enclosing the three central bays on each floor in ionic pilasters and low wings stretching out each side, terminating in classical porticos, that it was home to some of the most important scientific experiments of the 19th century, carried out there by the **3rd** and **4th Barons**.

The wings are later than the central portion, being by Thomas Hopper (*see* also CONYNGHAM, M, and PARKER, Bt, of Melford Hall) and dating from the late Regency. Hopper too worked much in Essex. Internally there are more ionic pillars, part of the adornment of the central hall, with its low-pitched dome, balustraded gallery and frieze by John Henning. The latter is by some authorities credited with reproducing friezes from the Parthenon (not just at Terling but in his models), though by others he is stated to have invented designs of his own.

RAYNE

REA

Arms: Per fess dancetty azure and gules a caduceus between in chief two roses or. **Crest:** Upon a wreath or and azure issuant from a circlet or a mount vert, thereon a lion passant gold, murally crowned azure, holding in the dexter forepaw a key erect, wards outwards or. **Supporters:** Dexter, a lion or crowned and gorged with a chain, pendant therefrom two triangles interlaced azure; sinister, a lion azure, crowned and gorged, with a like chain, pendant therefrom a fleur-de-lys gold. **Motto:** Integrity. Enterprise. **Creation:** B. (LP, UK) 1976.

THE BARON RAYNE, of Prince's Meadow, Greater London (Max Rayne) [The Rt Hon The Lord Rayne, 33 Robert Adam St, London W1M 5AH]; *b* 8 Feb 1918; *educ* Centl Fndn Sch and UCL (Hon LLD, Hon Fell 1966); RAF WW II; chm First Leisure Corp 1992–, dir Housing Corp (1974) Ltd 1974–78, Govr: St Thomas's Hosp 1962–74 (Special Tstee 1974–92), Roy Ballet Sch 1966–79, Centre Environmental Studies 1967–73; Memb Gen Cncl King Edward VII's Hosp Fund for London 1966–; Tstee Henry Moore Fndn 1988–, Hon V-Pres Jewish Care 1966–, V-Pres Yehudi Menuhin Sch 1987– (Govr 1966–87), Chm Roy Nat Theatre 1971–88, Fndr Patron Rayne Fndn 1962–, Hon Fell Darwin Coll Cambridge 1966, UCL 1966, LSE 1974, Roy Coll Psychiatrists 1977, King's Coll Hosp Med Sch 1980, Univ Coll Oxford 1982, King's Coll London 1983, Westminster Sch 1989, Roy Coll Physicians 1992, UMDS, Guy's and St Thomas's 1992; Off Legn Hon 1987 (Chevalier 1973); ktd 1969; *m* 1st 1941 (*divorce* 1960) Margaret, dau of Louis Marco, of London, and has:

  1 *Robert Anthony; *b* 1949; *m* 1973 *Jane, dau of Robert Blackburn, and has issue

    1 *Madeleine Barbara; *b* 1943; *m* 1964 *Alan Rayner

    2 *Susan Ann; *b* 1945; *m* 1965 (*divorce* 1974) John Rubin

BARON RAYNE *m* 2nd 1965 *Lady Jane Antonia Frances Vane-Tempest-Stewart, dau of 8th Marquess of Londonderry (*qv*), and by her has:

  2 *Nicholas Alexander; *b* 1969

  3 *Alexander Philip; *b* 1973

  3 *Natasha Deborah; *b* 1966; *m* 1992 *Nicholas J Capstick-Dale, s of J R Capstick-Dale

  4 *Tamara Annabel; *b* 1970

Lineage: PHILIP RAYNE; had an er s:

MAX, *cr* a **Baron**

RAZZALL

Creation: B. (LP, UK) 1997.

THE BARON RAZZALL, of Mortlake, London Borough of Richmond ((Edward) Timothy Razzall, CBE (1993)) [The Rt Hon The Lord Razzall CBE, 4 Carpenter St, London EC4Y 0NM]; *b* 12 June 1943; *educ* St Paul's and Worcester Coll Oxford; Teaching Associate Northwestern U Chicago 1965–66; Frere Cholmeley Bischoff 1966–96 (ptnr 1973–96); memb (Lib) Richmond Cncl 1974– (Dep Leader 1983–); Treas: Lib Party 1986–87, Lib Dem Party 1987–; Pres Assoc Lib Dem Cncllrs 1990–; chm Abaco Investments 1974–90; dir: Cala plc 1973, Star Mining Corp NL 1993–, Speciality Shops plc 1994–; ptnr Argonaut Assocs 1996–; European Lawyer of the Year 1992; *m* 1982 *Deirdre Bourke and has two sons and two daus

Lineage: HORACE RAZZALL, of Scarborough; *m* Sarah Thompson and had:

*LEONARD HUMPHREY RAZZALL; *b* 13 Nov 1913; Master Supreme Court (Taxing) 1954–81; *m* 1936 Muriel (*d* 1968), yr dau of Pearson Knowles, and has:

(EDWARD) TIMOTHY, *cr* a **Baron**

Arms: Or on a fess wavy azure between three stags courant gules a lymphad sails furled of the field. **Crest:** A stag at gaze gules, resting the dexter fore-leg on an anchor or. **Supporters:** On either side a stag gules, each charged on the shoulder with a bezant, thereon an anchor azure. **Motto:** *In omnia promptus* ('Ready for everything'). **Creation:** B. (UK) 3 June 1937, Bt. (UK) 8 July 1935.

THE 3RD BARON REA, of Eskdale, Co Cumberland, and a **Baronet** (Sir (John) Nicolas Rea, Bt) [The Rt Hon The Lord Rea, 11 Anson Rd, London N7 0RB]; *b* 6 June 1928; *s* unc 1981; *educ* Dauntsey's Sch, Christ's Coll Cambridge (MA 1969, MD 1969) and U Coll Hosp (DPH Lond 1966); MRCGP 1971, FRCGP 1989; *m* 1st 24 March 1951 (*divorce* 1991) Elizabeth Anne, est dau of William Hensman Robinson, of Woking; *m* 2nd 1991 *Judith Mary, dau of Norman Powell, of Lytham St Anne's, Lancs, and has by his 1st w:

  1 +MATTHEW JAMES [The Hon Matthew Rea, 12 St Leonard's Bank, Edinburgh EH8 9SQ]; *b* 28 March 1956; *educ* William Ellis Sch and Sheffield U; *m* 19 Nov 1992 *Jenny Haslam and has:

    (1) *Ivan; *b* 26 Nov 1991

    (1) *Ellis Kelsey Haslam; *b* 2 Feb 1989

  2 +Daniel William [The Hon Daniel Rea, 7 Serpentine Rd, Birmingham B29 7HU]; *b* 30 Dec 1958; *educ* William Ellis Sch, Bristol U and UCH Medical Sch; *m* 24 June 1981 *Hon Rebecca Llewelyn-Davies, yst dau of Baron Llewelyn-Davies (*see* 1970 edn), and has:

    (1) +William Alexander; *b* 8 Oct 1991

    (2) +Edward Inigo; *b* 27 Jan 1994

    (3) +Sean Iago; *b* 4 March 1996

  3 +Quentin Thomas; *b* 8 March 1961; *educ* William Ellis Sch and Manchester U; has:

    (1) *Peggy; *b* 9 March 1995

  4 +John Silas Nathaniel; *b* 16 Oct 1965; *educ* William Ellis Sch; *m* Sept 1993 *Andrea, 4th dau of Roy Ross, of Barrington, RI

The 3rd BARON has by *Jane Fawcett, formerly Conniff, née Hardy:

  1 *Bess CONNIFF; *b* 22 July 1975

The 3rd BARON has by *Katya Elizabeth Benjamin:

  2 *Ella ('Rosy') Amy BENJAMIN; *b* 16 Oct 1978

Lineage: DANIEL KEY REA, of Eskdale, Cumberland; *m* 2nd Elizabeth (*d* 1884), 2nd dau of Joseph Russell, of Liverpool, and *d* 1884, leaving an est s:

RUSSELL REA, PC, of Tanhurst, Dorking; *b* 11 Dec 1846; MP, fndr and sr ptnr R and J H Rea, shipowners and merchants; *m* 1872 Jane Philip (*d* 1930), dau of Peter Laurie Mactaggart, of Liverpool, and *d* 5 Feb 1916, leaving, with a yr s (Alec Lionel, CBE (1945), JP, *b* 1878, High Sheriff Westmorland 1917, merchant banker, fndr with Basil Dean of Reandean, producers of plays by John Galsworthy and Clemence Dane, chm Reandco, Master Pattenmakers' Co 1929 and 1939, Overseas League 1930–33 and RADA 1938–39, Chev Legn Hon, *m* 1st 18 April 1900 Ethel Marguerite (*d* 17 Dec 1946), only child of Charles H Requa, of Brooklyn, NY, *m* 2nd 17 July 1947 *Elizabeth Collins and *dsp* 11 Feb 1953):

Sir Walter Russell Rea, 1st Bt, and **1st Baron Rea**, of Eskdale, Co Cumberland (both UK), so *cr* 8 July 1935 and 3 June 1937 respectively; *b* 18 May 1873; *educ* U Coll Sch London; chm Rea, Warren and McLennan, merchant bankers, Pres Free Trade Union, MP (Lib) Scarborough 1906–18, Bradford N 1923–24 and Dewsbury 1931–35 (fought Oldham Dec 1918, Nelson and Colne 1920, Bradford N 1922 and 1924 and Taunton 1929), Jr Ld Treasury 1915–16, Lib Whip 1923–24, Comptroller Household 1931–32, Ch Lib Whip 1931–35; *m* 1st 25 Jan 1896 Evelyn (*d* 28 Sept 1930), dau of John James Muirhead, JP, of Edinburgh, and had:

  1 PHILIP RUSSELL REA, **2nd Baron Rea**, OBE (1946), PC (1962), JP (Cumberland 1949 Gtr London 1961), JP (1966), DL (1955, 1961–76); *b* 7 Feb 1900; *educ* Westminster, Ch Ch Oxford (MA) and U of Grenoble; 2nd Lt Gren Gds WW I 1918 and Lt-Col KRRC attd Special Forces WW II (despatches), Offr Order Crown Belgium 1947, Chev Legn Hon 1949, Croix de Guerre avec Palme 1949, Grand Cdr Ordre de Merite 1969, merchant banker and co dir, prospective Lib candidate Devon 1938–42, with FO 1946–50, Ch Lib Whip Ho Lds 1950–55, Dep Speaker Ho Lds 1950, V-Chm Lib Party Exec Ctte 1950–54, Dep Chm

Ctees 1950–55, Pres Lib Pty 1955–56 (V-Pres 1970–81), memb Political Hons Scrutiny Ctee 1962 and BBC Advsy Cncl 1958–63, underwriting memb Lloyd's, Govr Westminster Sch; *m* 7 April 1922 Lorna (*d* 11 Dec 1978), novelist, yst dau of Lewis Osborne Smith, of Glasgow, and *d* 1981, having had:

(1) Piers Russell; *b* 9 Nov 1925; *d* 2 Sept 1934

(1) Ann Felicity; *b* 15 Jan 1923; 3rd Offr WRNS WW II; *m* 22 June 1945 Maj Malcolm Grane Ludovic Martin Munthe, MC, Gordon Highrs, author, s of Dr Axel Munthe, CVO, of San Michele, Capri, and *d* 1990, having had:

  1a *Adam John [Adam Munthe Esq, 5 Earls Walk, London W8 6 EP]; *b* 10 May 1946; *educ* St Paul's and Ch Ch Oxford; *m* 1975 *Nelly Cécile Rothschild (*see* ROTHSCHILD, B) and has two children

  2a Guy Sebastian; *b* 10 May 1948; *educ* Hurstpierpoint; *d* 12 Sept 1992

  1a *Katriona Periwinkle Philippa Pennington; *b* 13 Jan 1955; *m* 24 June 1995 *Orley Lindgren

2 James Russell; *b* 11 Oct 1902; *educ* Westminster, Grenoble U and Christ's Coll Cambridge (BA 1923, MA 1938); barrister Middle Temple 1927, Lt KRRC and Maj HG; *m* 1st 13 April 1926 (*divorce* 1942) Betty Marion (*d* 2 April 1965), er dau of Arthur Bevan, MD, and had:

(1) (JOHN) NICOLAS REA, **3rd and present Baron Rea**

(2) +Charles Julian [The Hon Charles Rea, 62 Dukes Ave, London N10]; *b* 7 June 1931; *educ* Bryanston and Downing Coll Cambridge (MA, DipEd); granted rank of baron's yr s 1989; *m* 1st 17 Sept 1951 (*divorce* 1964) Bridget, dau of Charles Montagu Slater, of Highgate, and has:

  1a +Steven; *b* 27 June 1956

  1a *Julia; *b* 31 May 1952

(2) (cont.) The Hon Charles Rea *m* 2nd 15 June 1964 *Anne Bernadette, dau of William Robson, of W Chiltington, Sussex, and by her has:

  2a +William; *b* 26 Feb 1965

  3a +James; *b* 26 Feb 1968

  2a *Lucy; *b* 19 May 1966

  3a *Kate; *b* 1972

2 (cont.) The Hon James Rea *m* 2nd 30 Oct 1942 Isobel Mary (*d* 21 Oct 1965), yr dau of Robert William Pringle, of Edinburgh, and formerly w of Michael Shepley, and *d* 15 Aug 1954

3 Findlay Russell; *b* 25 Sept 1907; *educ* Westminster and New Coll Oxford; Lt Intell Corps; *m* 1st 21 May 1932 (*divorce* 1946) Margaret Hermione, est dau of Lt-Col Kenneth Hope Bruce, DSO, Gordon Highrs, and had:

(1) +Benjamin Russell [Benjamin Rea Esq, 84 Doods Park Rd, Reigate, Surrey RH2 0PU]; *b* 24 June 1936; *educ* Bryanston and Trin Coll Oxford; TV dir; *m* 1st 4 April 1964 (*divorce* 1972) Angela, only dau of Arthur Jackson Bradley, of Woodcote, Oxon, and has:

  1a *Susannah Rachel; *b* 15 June 1968

(1) (cont.) Benjamin Rea *m* 2nd 23 Aug 1973 (*divorce* 1995) Dorinda Anne, dau of Stanley Cutting, of Bath Avon, and by her has:

  1a +James Russell; *b* 20 June 1973

  2a +Thomas Russell; *b* 20 Oct 1975

(1) *Joanna, JP (Ormskirk) [Mrs Peter Bartram JP, Foxgloves, Wood Lane, Parbold, Lancs WN8 7TH]; *b* 1 July 1934; *m* 1st 20 July 1957 (*divorce* 1982) Robert Cecil Seeckts, yr s of George Seeckts, and has:

  1a *Richard Philip; *b* 1 Jan 1966

  1a *Rosemary Anne; *b* 26 July 1958

  2a *Sarah Elizabeth; *b* 24 Oct 1960

  3a *Katherine Mary; *b* 25 April 1963

(1) (cont.) Mrs Joanna Seeckts *m* 2nd 1984 *Peter John Bartram, er s of George Hylton Bartram, of Sunderland

3 (cont.) The Hon Findlay Rea *m* 2nd 24 Jan 1947 (*divorce* 1959) Eileen Maude, dau of Lt-Col Isaac Wardle, IA, and formerly w of John Lionel Clemence; *m* 3rd 27 June 1959 *Helen Margaret [The Hon Mrs Findlay Rea, Weald Cottage, Weald, Kent TN14 6PY], dau of Bernard Herman Richardson, of Edinburgh, and formerly w of Donald Crawford Reid, and *d* 1984

1 Isabella; *b* 22 Aug 1897; *educ* Newnham Coll Cambridge; *m* 24 Nov 1922 His Honour Jesse Basil Herbert, MC, QC, County Court Judge (*d* 19 Sept 1972), 2nd s of Sir Jesse Herbert, and had:

(1) *Carola; *b* 17 July 1930; *educ* St Hugh's Coll Oxford (MA); *m* 22 Feb 1966 (*divorce* 1975) Sir Thomas Agnew Beevor, 7th Bt (*qv*)

(2) *Phoebe Herbert, JP (Birmingham 1966) [Mrs Richard Van Oss JP, Arbury House, Aqueduct Rd, Alvechurch, Herefs]; *b* 4 May 1932; *educ* Somerville Coll Oxford (BA); *m* 16 July 1955 *Richard Mark Van Oss, est s of Thomas Van Oss, and has:

  1a *Thomas Richard; *b* 4 April 1957

  1a *Celia Catherine; *b* 10 June 1959

2 Elisabeth, JP (London); *b* 2 May 1911; *educ* Newnham Coll Cambridge (MA); *m* 18 May 1935 *Sir Michael John Sinclair Clapham, KBE (1973) [Sir Michael Clapham KBE, 26 Hill St, London W1X 7 FU], only s of Sir John Harold Clapham, CBE, LittD, FBA, V-Provost King's Coll Cambridge, and *d* 1994, having had:

(1) *Adam John [Adam Clapham Esq, 254 Alexandra Pk Rd, London N22]; *b* 8 April 1940; *educ* Bryanston and Grenoble U

(2) *Charles Marcus [Charles Clapham Esq, 27 Jeffreys St, London NW1]; *b* 28 Oct 1942; *educ* Marlborough and King's Coll Cambridge (BA 1964); FRMetS; *m* 1971 (*divorce* 1980) Margaret Golledge and has:

  1a *Nicolas; *b* 1972

(3) Giles Sinclair; *b* 30 April 1946; *educ* privately; *d* 1990

(1) *Antonia [Mrs Barry Till, 44 Canonbury Sq, London N1]; *b* 27 May 1938; *educ* Cranborne Chase and Newnham Coll Cambridge (BA); *m* 7 July 1966 *Rev Barry Dorn Till, Pncpl Morley Coll, s of John Johnson Till, of Keynsham Ho, nr Bristol, and has:

  1a *Lucy Rose Victoria; *b* 29 March 1969

  2a *Emily Caroline Rose; *b* 4 Sept 1971

The **1st Baron** *m* 2nd 28 April 1931 Jemima (*d* 19 June 1964), dau of Rev Alexander Ewing, and *d* May 1948

READE

CEDANT · ARMA · TOGÆ

Arms: Gules a saltire between four garbs or. **Crest:** On the stump of a tree vert a falcon rising proper, belled and jessed or. **Motto:** *Cedant arma togæ* ('May war give way to the rule of law'). **Creation:** Bt. (E) 4 March 1660/1.

SIR KENNETH RAY READE, 13TH BT, of Barton, Co Berks [Sir Kenneth Reade Bt, 1198 Paddock Place Apt 106, Ann Arbor, MI 48108, USA]; *b* 23 March 1925; *s* cousin 1982; *m* 1944 *Doreen, dau of Edward Vinsant, of Ann Arbor, and has:

1 *Sandra [Mrs Douglas Crawford, 3479 Central, Dexter, MI 48130, USA]; *b* 1945; *m* 1966 *Douglas Crawford and has:

  (1) *Michael; *b* 1966

  (2) *John; *b* 1970

  (1) *Beth; *b* 1975

2 *Karen [Mrs James Lamb, 8531 Jackson, Dexter, MI 48130, USA]; *b* 1948; *m* 1968 *James Lamb and has:

  (1) *Tammy; *b* 1979

  (2) *Jennifer; *b* 1973

3 *Norma [Ms Norma Reade, PO Box 95, Seney, MI 49883, USA]; *b* 1953; has:

  (1) *Richard; *b* 1972

  (2) *William; *b* 1988

  (1) *Sara; *b* 1984

Lineage: THOMAS RE(A)DE, of Abingdon; living 1536; bought Manor of Duns Tew, Oxon, 1545, and Manor of Barton, formerly belonging to Abingdon Abbey, 1550; *m* Anne (*bur* 30 Oct 1575), dau of Thomas Hoo, of the Hoo, Herts, cousin of ELIZABETH I, and was *bur* 27 April 1556, having had, with a dau (*d* unm):

1 THOMAS

1 Katherine; acquired Manor of Ipsden; *m* 5 Sept 1546 Thomas Vachell, MP (*dsps* 3 May 1610), of Coley Park, Berks, and *d* by 1604

2 Elizabeth; *m* by 16 April 1556 Richard Baker, of White Knights, Sonning, Berks, and had issue

3 Marie; *m* 1st Walter Hurst, of Hurst, Berks; *m* 2nd Edward Martyn, of Shinfield, Berks, and *d* 10 Oct 1607, having by him had a dau and heiress

The s,

THOMAS READE, of Barton and Beedon, Berks; *b* 1 July 1545; High Sheriff 1587–88 and 1599, granted arms 1597; *m* by 1568 Mary (*bur* by 14 Sept 1625), sis of Sir William Stonhouse, 1st Bt (*qv*), and had:

1 THOMAS (Sir)

2 John, of Barton Court and Appleford, Berks; *bapt* 13 Oct 1577; *d* unm 10 Jan 1605

3 Richard; *bapt* 16 Aug 1579; lay Rector Culham, Oxon; *m* 1619 Helen (*bur* 25 Feb 1623), dau of Sir Alexander Carr, of Bargrave, Leics, and *d* 1659, having had issue

1 Mary; *m* 14 Sept 1600 Henry Bulstrode (*d* 25 Sept 1604), of Bulstrode, Bucks, and *d* 13 Dec 1614, leaving issue

The est s,

Sir THOMAS READE, of Barton Court, Beedon, Appleford, Ipsden and Duns Tew; *b* 1575; High Sheriff: Berks 1606, Oxon 1615 and Herts 1618; *m* March 1597/8 Mary (*bur* 20 April 1654), dau and coheir of Sir John Brocket, of Brocket Hall, thus acquiring that estate, and was *bur* 20 Dec 1650, having had:

1 William; *bapt* 19 April 1601; *bur* 9 Sept 1625

2 THOMAS

3 Richard; *b* 2 June 1610; allegedly but doubtfully ancestor of the READEs of Rossenara, Co Tipperary

4 Sir JOHN READE, 1st Bt (E), so *cr* 16 March 1641/2 and 25 June 1656 (latterly by OLIVER CROMWELL), of Brocket Hall; *b c* 1616; *educ* Lincoln's Inn; ktd March 1641/2, Sheriff Herts 1655–56 and 1673–74; bought the Calthorp estate, Oxon, 1679; *m* 1st 2 Jan 1640 Susanna (*bur* 18 May 1657) dau of Sir Thomas Style, 1st Bt, and had issue; *m* 2nd 15 Jan 1662/3 Alissimon (desribed as widow of Hon Francis Pierrepont, possibly a yr s of 1st Earl of Kingston-upon-Hull), and was *bur* 6 Feb 1693/4, having had by his 1st w, with three er sons (*d* young):

(1) Sir JAMES READE, 2nd Bt, of Brocket Hall and Duns Tew; *bapt* 10 March 1654/5; *educ* Trin Coll Oxford; Sheriff Herts 1693–94 and Oxon 1700–01; *m* 26 Jan 1689/90 Love, 2nd dau and coheir of Robert Dring, London Alderman, and *d* 16 Oct 1701, leaving, with three other daus (*dsp* or unm):

    1a Sir JOHN READE, 3rd and last Bt, of Brocket Hall and Duns Tew; *b* 1691; *educ* Eton and Wadham Coll Oxford; Jacobite; *d* unm Rome 22 Feb 1711/2, when the btcy expired, though it was assumed from 1810, apparently without foundation, by a READE family of Co Clare and later NSW

    1a Dorothy; inherited the Duns Tew estate; *m* Robert Dashwood and had issue (*see* DASHWOOD, Bt, of Kirtlington Park)

    2a Love; inherited the Brocket Hall estate; *m* 6 Aug 1719 Thomas Winnington (*see* WINNINGTON, Bt), who left Brocket to relatives of his own, who sold it to Matthew Lamb, ancestor of Viscount Melbourne, the PM; Brocket was also owned by another PM, Viscount Palmerston (*see* TEMPLE OF STOWE, E); *see also* BROCKET, B

5 Geoffrey; *d* by 10 Dec 1649

1 Elizabeth; *m* Sir Gilbert Cornewall, (*bur* 5 Oct 1671), of Burford, Salop, and was *bur* 24 Dec 1671, leaving issue

2 Frances; *m* 1 Dec 1624 Sir William Russell, 1st Bt (*d* 30 Nov 1669), of Wytley, Worcs, and had issue

3 Mary; *m* Sir Robert Dormer (*d* 12 May 1689), of Crendon, Bucks

4 Ellen; *dsp* 1669

5 Margaret; allegedly *m* Sir Francis Russell

6 Anne; *m* Richard Winwood (*d* 28 June 1688), of Ditton, Bucks, Serjeant-at-law, and *dsp* 1 March 1693

The 2nd s,

THOMAS READE, of Ipsden and Appleford; *bapt* 22 Feb 1606/7; *m* 8 Sept 1624 Mary, dau of Sir Thomas Cornewall, of Burford, and was *bur* 14 Dec 1634, having had, with other issue (*dvp*):

1 COMPTON (Sir), **1st Bt**

2 Edward, of Ipsden; *bapt* 17 May 1627; *m* 1st *c* 18 Dec 1651 Jane (*d* 14 Aug 1657), dau of Thomas Acton, of Bockleton, Worcs, and had issue; *m* 2nd Elizabeth (*dsp, bur* 28 Nov 1664), dau of John Allen, of Streatley, Berks; *m* 3rd 1665 Ellen (*d* 7 Feb 1685), widow of William Allen, of Goring, Oxon, and was ancestor by her of the READEs of Ipsden; *m* 4th 1697 Susanna — and *d* 12 Jan 1716, having had further issue by her

3 Thomas, of Appleford; *bapt* 10 Aug 1628; *m* 7 March 1657 Anne (*bur* 21 Feb 1704), dau and coheir of Henry Knapp, of Woodcot, Oxon, and *d* 8 March 1701, having had issue

    1 Anne; *m* Maj Thomas Cornewall (*bur* 22 July 1686), of Burford, and was *bur* 15 March 1691, leaving issue

    2 Catherine; *m* Bridstock Harford, MP (*d* 20 April 1683), and *d* 5 March 1665, leaving issue

    3 Mary; *m* John Cornewall (*bur* 6 Aug 1685), of Rochford, and had issue

The est s,

Sir Compton Reade, 1st Bt (E), so *cr* 4 March 1660/1, of Barton Court and Beedon, Denford, Northants, and Shipton Court, Oxon; *bapt* 24 Jan 1625/6; *m* 1650 Mary (*d* 26 April 1703), dau of Sir Gilbert Cornewall, of Burford, and *d* 29 Sept 1679, having had, with an er s (Thomas, *b* 13 Dec 1653; *dvp* 1675) and three daus (Anne, *m* Cornelius Vermuyden and *d* by 7 Oct 1681; Elizabeth, *m* Sir Fairmedow Penyestone, 4th and last Bt (*dsp* 24 Dec 1705); another dau, who *d* unm):

Sir Edward Reade, 2nd Bt; *b* 30 June 1659; *m* Elizabeth (*m* 2nd Henry Farmer and *d* 13 Sept 1730), dau of Francis Harby, of Adston, Northants, and *d* 4 Sept 1691, having by her had, with another s (*d* an infant):

1 **Sir Winwood Reade, 3rd Bt**; *b* 1683; *d* unm 30 June 1692

2 **Sir Thomas Reade, 4th Bt**; *b* 1684; Gentleman Bedchamber to GEORGE I, a Clerk Household to GEORGE II, MP Cricklade; *m* 29 Oct 1719 Jane Mary (*d* 28 June 1721), dau and coheir of Sir Ralph Dutton, 1st Bt (*see* 1970 edn SHERBORNE, B), and *d* 25 Sept 1752, leaving:

    (1) **Sir John Reade, 5th Bt**; *b* 21 June 1721; *m* 1759 Harriet (*d* 23 Dec 1811), dau and heiress of William Barker, of Sonning, and *d* 9 Nov 1773, having had:

        1a JOHN (Sir), **6th Bt**

        2a Thomas (twin with bro); *m* Catherine (*d* 1830), dau of Sir John Hill, and *d* 24 Jan 1837, leaving, with three daus:

            1b John Edmund; *b* 1800; poet; *m* 1 Oct 1847 his cousin Maria Louisa (*d* 24 Nov 1886), er dau of George Compton Reade (*see below*), and *d* 17 Sept 1870, leaving:

                1c Agnes Cornelie; *m* 1 Aug 1881 Arnold HIGHTON later HIGHTON READE (*d* 1914), only s of Gilbert Highton, barrister

            1a Mary; *m* 18 Jan 1768 Sir Elijah Impey (*d* 1 Oct 1809) and *d* 20 Feb 1818, leaving issue

    3 George; *b* 1687; Brig-Gen, MP Tewkesbury; *m* Jane (*d* 1744), dau of Charles Nowes, of Wood Ditton, Cambs, and *dsp* 28 March 1756

The 5th Bt's er s,

Sir John Reade, 6th Bt; *b* 8 March 1762; *educ* Magdalen Coll Oxford (MA); *m* 13 Jan 1784 Jane (*d* 17 Dec 1847), only dau of Sir Chandos Hoskyns, 5th Bt (*qv*), and *d* 18 Nov 1789, having had, with four daus (*d* unm):

1 **Sir John Chandos Reade, 7th Bt**; *b* 3 Jan 1785; *m* 6 Jan 1814 Louise (*d* 6 Feb 1821), n of 7th Lord Elibank (*qv*), and *d* 14 Jan 1868, having had, with two other daus (*d* unm):

    (1) Compton; *b* 17 Oct 1816; *dsp* 31 July 1851

    (1) Clara Louisa; *m* 13 Oct 1846 Hon John Talbot Rice (*see* DINEVOR, B) and *d* 11 Aug 1853

2 George Compton; *b* 8 Jan 1788; *m* 6 March 1809 his cousin Maria Jane (*d* 1837), dau of Sir Hungerford Hoskyns, 6th Bt (*qv*), and *d* 24 Dec 1866, having had:

    (1) George; *b* 1812; Lt Madras Army; *m* 1851 Jane Ann (*d* Sept 1863), dau of J Norton, and *d* 20 Oct 1863, leaving:

        1a **Sir Chandos Stanhope Hoskyns Reade, 8th Bt**, DL; *b* 5 Sept 1851; *m* 11 March 1880 Maria Emma Elizabeth Conway (*d* 11 July 1917), dau and heir-

ess of Richard Trygarn Griffith, of Carreglwyd and Berw, Anglesey, and *dsp* 28 Jan 1890

    1a Louise Jane Elibank; *m* 26 April 1892 Rev Sedborough Mayne Wade (*d* 13 Sept 1933), Rector Bonchurch, IoW, 3rd s of Gustavus Rochfort Wade, of Dublin and Galway, and *d* 18 May 1939

(2) John Stanhope; *m* 1836 Lovica Walton, of Dexter, Mich., and *d* 1883, leaving, with a yr s (Charles Walter) and three daus (Catherine; Christian; Maria Louisa):

    1a GEORGE COMPTON (Sir), **9th Bt**

(3) Chandos; *b* 1817; *d* Sept 1833

(1) Maria Louise; *m* 1 Oct 1847 her cousin John Edmund Reade and *d* 24 Nov 1886, leaving issue (*see above*)

(2) Caroline Jane; *m* — Scur

The 8th Bt's cousin,

Sir George Compton Reade, 9th Bt; *b* 17 Dec 1845; *m* 4 June 1868 Melissa (*d* 16 Oct 1927), dau of Isaac Ray, of Mich., and *d* 7 April 1908 having had:

1 **Sir George Franklin Reade, 10th Bt**; *b* 22 Nov 1869; *m* 19 Dec 1893 Carrie (*d* 17 Feb 1953), dau of Nathan Nixon, of Ann Arbor, Mich., and *d* 30 May 1923, having had:

    (1) **Sir John Stanhope Reade, 11th Bt**; *b* 12 Sept 1896; *m* 7 June 1924 Alice Elizabeth, dau of Lawrence Luke Llewellyn Dubber, of Gayford, Mich., and Berks, UK, and *dsp* 8 Jan 1958

    (2) **Sir Clyde Nixon Reade, 12th Bt**; *b* 8 Sept 1906; *m* 1st 4 Dec 1930 Trilby (*d* 27 May 1958), dau of Charles McCarthy; *m* 2nd 3 Sept 1960 Alice Martha, yst dau of Joseph Asher, of Ohio, and *dsp* 1982

    (1) Florence; *b* Sept 1894; *m* 1912 Lee Hopkins and *d* 21 May 1936, leaving issue

    (2) Hazel; *b* 1899; *m* 9 Aug 1919 John Neil and had:

        1a *Donald George [Donald Neil, 6051 Daft St, Lansing, MI, USA]; *b* 1921

2 Elmer Compton; *b* 1 Nov 1877; *m* 3 July 1902 Leticia Wylie and *d* 1 May 1918, leaving:

    (1) *Laura Leticia; *b* 27 July 1908; *m* 1930 *Gordon Hester

3 Harry Stanhope; *b* 18 April 1884; *m* 3 June 1907 Gertrude Slot (*d* 6 Aug 1934) and *dsp*

4 Emory Isaac; *b* 9 Oct 1887; *m* 13 Nov 1908 Millicent, dau of G Fisk, and *d* 1939, leaving:

    (1) *Irene Nora; *b* 5 Aug 1911; *m* 24 April 1931 *Hugh Peebles and has:

        1a *Robert Bradley; *b* 1932

        2a *David; *b* 1943

        1a *Gloria Ann; *b* 1935

    (2) *Eileen; *b* 16 Nov 1915; *m* 1935 *Ronald Durrett

    (3) *Esther; *b* 11 Aug 1918; *m* 1934 *Lawrence Durrett

5 Leverne Elton; *b* 22 June 1891; *m* 14 Feb 1921 Norma B Ward and *d* 1943, leaving:

    (1) Robert Ward; *b* 11 Oct 1923; *d* 19–

    (2) Sir KENNETH RAY READE, **13th and present Bt**

1 Julia Ann; *b* 25 Dec 1870; *m* 6 April 1893 William C Wylie and *d* 21 Feb 1894, leaving issue

2 Ellen Lovica; *b* 22 March 1874; *m* 1st April 1903 Eli Buck (*d* 1910); *m* 2nd 1914 Jake W Reuter

3 Esther Venelia; *b* 15 Jan 1876; *m* 19 Sept 1900 Dr William C Wyllie, of Dexter, Mich., pres and dir Dexter Savings Bank

4 Edna Estella; *b* 11 Aug 1879; *m* 1910 Cornelius Donehue

5 Sonora Jane; *b* 7 June 1881; *m* 17 Jan 1912 Mark Probert (*d* 6 Aug 1925)

6 Maude; *b* 21 June 1894; *m* 1914 H Stanley Vaughan, of Dexter, and had issue

READING

Arms: Sable a bend between two leopard's faces or, on a chief argent a fasces fesswise proper. **Crest:** In front of a leopard's head couped sable a fasces as in the arms. **Supporters:** On either side a leopard proper, gorged with a collar or, pendant therefrom an escutcheon argent, charged with a human head affrontée proper, erased at the neck, ducally crowned or. **Motto:** *Aut nunquam tentes aut perfice* ('Either complete or do not attempt at all'). **Creations:** B. (UK) 9 Jan 1914, V. (UK) (Reading) 26 June 1916, V. (Erleigh) and E. (UK) 20 Dec 1917, M. (UK) 7 May 1926.

THE 4TH MARQUESS OF READING, Earl of Reading, Viscount Reading, of Erleigh, Co Berks, **Viscount Erleigh**, of Erleigh, Berks, and **Baron Reading**, of Erleigh, Berks (Simon Charles Henry Rufus Isaacs) [The Most Hon The Marquess of Reading, Jaynes Court, Bisley, Glos GL6 7BE]; *b* 18 May 1942; *s f* 1980; *educ* Eton and Tours U France; Lt 1st Queen's Dragoon Gds 1961–64, memb stock exchange 1971–74; *m* 12 May 1979 *Melinda Victoria, yr dau of Richard Dewar, of Shoelands House, Seale, Surrey, and has:

1 +JULIAN MICHAEL, *Viscount Erleigh*; *b* 26 May 1986

l *Sybilla Alice; *b* 3 Nov 1980

2 *Natasha Rose Eleanor; *b* 24 April 1983

Barony of Reading: One of the subsidiary titles along with a projected Earldom of Bunbury and Viscountcy of Wallingford that GEORGE III had intended conferring on his Prime Minister Henry Addington on the latter's leaving office in 1804 (*see* SIDMOUTH, V) was a Barony of Reading. In the event Addington had to be content with a viscountcy only.

Lineage: MICHAEL ISSACS; *b c* 1685; migrated to England from Continental Europe *c* 1700; had:

ISRAEL ISAACS, of Chelmsford, Essex; *b c* 1735; *m c* 1750 Katherine Judah and had, with a yr s (Isaac, *b* 1767):

SAMUEL ISAACS; *b* 1759; *m c* 1795 Sara Levy (*d* aged 103) and *d* 1865, leaving:

MICHAEL ISAACS, of Mitre Street, London; *b c* 1800; *m c* 1829 Sara, dau of Aaron Enrique Mendoza and niece of Daniel Mendoza the boxer (himself ancestor of the comic actor Peter Sellers), and had:

1 Henry Aaron (Sir), JP (London); *b* 15 Aug 1830; memb Corp City London 1862–1909, Alderman Portsoken Ward 1883–91, Sheriff London and Middx 1886–87, ktd 1887, Ld Mayor London 1889–90, Grand Warden Freemasons 1890, Jubilee Medal, author of three books; *m* Sept 1848 Eleanor (*d* 1901), dau of Alexander McDonald Rowland, 9th Holy Boys (9th Regt), and *d* 2 Aug 1909, having had a s (Joseph Alexander) and two daus (Louisa; Sara, deaf and dumb, *d* unm)

2 Joseph Michael, of Finsbury Sq; *b* 1832; merchant; *m* 25 July 1855 Sarah (*d* 12 Sept 1922 aged 87, est of 13 surv children of Daniel Davis, London merchant, by Frances Marks, one of 24 children, and *d* 1908, having had, with two other daus:

(1) Harry Michael; *b* 1858; *m* —

(2) RUFUS DANIEL

(3) Godfrey Charles; md Marconi Wireless Telegraph Co; *m* Lea — and *d* 17 April 1925, leaving:

1a Marcel Godfrey; had:

1b *Richard Marcel; *b* by 1922

2a Dennys Godfrey

(4) Frederick

(5) Albert; *d* as result of accident at school

(1) Frances; *m* Albert Keyzer, stockbroker

(2) (Nelly) Rose; *m* 1st —Aarons (*dsp* by 1833); *m* 2nd Peter Hyams (*d* 1940) and *d* 12 Dec 1942 aged 84, leaving issue

(3) Esther Stella; artist, author *Nicolas Poussin* (1923); *m* 1894 Alfred Sutro, OBE, playwright, translator and novelist, yst s of Sigismund Sutro, FRCP, and *dsp* 1934

The 2nd s,

RUFUS DANIEL ISAACS, **1st Marquess of Reading**, so *cr* 7 May 1926, as also 9 Jan 1914 BARON READING, of Erleigh, Co Berks, 26 June 1916 VISCOUNT READING, of Erleigh, Co Berks, and 20 Dec 1917 EARL OF READING and VISCOUNT ERLEIGH, of Erleigh, Co Berks (all UK), GCB (1915), GCSI (1921), GCIE (1921), GCVO (1922, KCVO 1911), PC (1911), QC (1898); *b* 10 Oct 1860; barrister Middle Temple 1887, Bencher 1904, MP (Lib) Reading 1904–13, ktd 1910, Slr-Gen 1910, Attorney-Gen 1910–13 with seat in Cabinet June 1912–Oct 1913 (first Attorney-Gen so honoured), Ld Ch Justice 20 Oct 1913, Pres Anglo-French Loan Mission to USA 1915, HC and Amb Extrdy and Plen special mission to USA 1918–19, Viceroy India 1921–26, For Sec 1931, Capt Deal Castle 1929–34, Hon Col 5th (Cinque Ports) Bn (T) Roy Sussex Regt, Constable Dover Castle and Ld Warden Cinque Ports 1934, Grand Cordon Order Leopold Belgium, LLD Toronto, Harvard, Yale, Princeton and Columbia, Hon DCL Oxon and Cantab; *m* 1st 8 Dec 1887 Alice Edith, GBE (1920), CI (1921), Kaisar-i-hind Gold Medal (*d* 30 Jan 1930 aged 64), 3rd dau of Albert Cohen, of London; *m* 2nd 6 Aug 1931 STELLA, *cr* BARONESS SWANBOROUGH 1958 (*d* 22 May 1971; *see* 1970 edn), and *d* 30 Dec 1935, leaving by his 1st w:

GERALD RUFUS ISAACS, **2nd Marquess of Reading**, GCMG (1958, KCMG 1957), CBE (1945), MC, TD, PC (1953), KC (1929), DL (London); *b* 10 Jan 1889; *educ* Rugby and Balliol Coll Oxford; barrister Middle Temple 1912, Bencher 1936, Treasurer 1958, Lt-Col Inns of Court OTC 1923–25, Staff Capt 1916, DAAG 1918, WWs I (despatches, Croix de Guerre) and II, Lt-Col cmdg Aux Mily Pioneer Corps Centre 1939–40, Staff Col 1941–43, Brig and Dir Lab HQ 21st Army Gp 1943–45, Hon Col Inns of Court Regt (TA) 1947–59, Chm: Centl Valuation Bd under Coal Mines Act 1938 and Coal Industry Nationalisation Act 1946, Min Labour Appeal Tbnl (Further Educn and Trg Scheme) 1946; Parly U-Sec For Affrs Oct 1951–53, Min State For Affrs 1953–57, Assoc KStK, Grand Cross Order Duarte Dominican Republic 1957; *m* 28 Sept 1914 Hon Eva Violet Mond, CBE (1957), JP (London) (*d* 14 Aug 1973), est dau of 1st Baron Melchett (*qv*), and *d* 19 Sept 1960, having had:

1 MICHAEL ALFRED, 3rd Marquess

1 *Joan Alice Violet, JP (Birmingham 1961) and (Norfolk 1967) [The Rt Hon The Lady Zuckerman, The Shooting Box, Burnham Thorpe, Norfolk]; *b* 19 July 1918; *m* 30 Oct 1939 Baron (Solly) Zuckerman, OM, KCB (LP; *d* 1993), Hon FRCS, FRCP, FRS, MA, Prof Anatomy Birmingham U, Ch Sci Advsr to Govt, Sec to RZS, s of Moses Zuckerman, and has:

(1) *Paul Sebastian; *b* 22 June 1945; *educ* Rugby

(1) *Stella Mary; *b* 26 Sept 1947

2 *Elizabeth Ann Mary [The Lady Elizabeth Hornsby, 29 Warwick Sq, London SW1V 2AD]; *b* 11 Oct 1921; Jr Cdr ATS WW II; *m* 12 Dec 1945 Maj Derek Francis Hornsby, 60th Rifles, KRRC (*d* 23 April 1971), only s of Maj Frank Haultain Hornsby (*see* BELPER, B), and has:

(1) *Richard Gerald [Richard Hornsby Esq, 29 Warwick Sq, London SW1V 2AD]; *b* 24 Dec 1948; *educ* Eton; *m* 1980 (*divorce* 1986) Maria Lara, of San Francisco, and has:

1a *Simon Daniel; *b* 1983

1a *Rachael Sarah; *b* 1982

1a *Annabel Alice; *b* 1991

(2) *David Julian [David Hornsby Esq, 109 Winchester St, London SW1]; *b* 9 Jan 1953; *educ* Eton; *m* 1975 (*divorce* 19–) Julie Ann Witford and has:

1a *Alexander Keith; *b* 1977

2a *Samuel Florian; *b* 1985

3a *Michael David; *b* 1987

The 2nd MARQUESS's only s,

MICHAEL ALFRED RUFUS ISAACS, **3rd Marquess of Reading**, MBE (1945), MC (1940); *b* 8 March 1916; *educ* Eton and Balliol Coll Oxford; Maj Queen's WW II and Staff, memb London Stock Exchange 1953–80; *m* 7 June 1941 *Margot Irene [The Most Hon Margot Marchioness of Reading, Glebe Farm House, Cornwell, Oxon OX7 67X], yr dau of Percival Augustus Duke, OBE, of Walton-on-the-Hill, Surrey (*see* 1970 edn MAPPIN, Bt), and *d* 2 July 1980, leaving:

1 SIMON CHARLES HENRY RUFUS ISAACS, 4th and present Marquess of Reading

2 +Anthony Ian Michael [The Lord Anthony Rufus Isaacs, 9723 Oak Pass Rd, Beverley Hills, CA 90210, USA]; *b* 22 Sept 1943; *educ* Gordonstoun; *m* 1st 1972 (*divorce* 1976) Ann Pugsley; *m* 2nd 1983 *Heide Lund, of Vancouver, BC, and has:

(1) *Tallulah Elke Margot; *b* 1987

(2) *Ruby Jacqueline Kirsten; *b* 1989

3 +Alexander Gerald; *b* 25 April 1957; *educ* St Paul's and Oriel Coll, Oxford (MA); barrister Middle Temple 1982, California Bar 1988; *m* 1993 *Marjorie Frances Bach, dau of Howard Goldbach, of Los Angeles

1 *Jacqueline Rosemary Margot; *b* 10 Nov 1946; *m* 26 June 1976 (*divorce* 1997) Sir Mark William Home Thomson, 3rd Bt, of Old Nunthorpe (*qv*), and has issue

REARDON-SMITH

Arms: Arg. upon a mount vert, in front of an oak-tree fructed ppr. a lion passant gu., in chief three estoiles sa. **Crest:** In front of a mast and sail of a ship ppr., the sail charged with a sphinx couchant sans wings arg., an anchor fesswise sa., entwined with a scroll silver, inscribed 'HMS *Romulus*' in letters also sa. **Motto:** *Quod facio, valde facio* ('What I do I do earnestly'). **Creation:** Bt. (UK) 1 July 1920.

SIR (WILLIAM) ANTONY JOHN REARDON-SMITH, 4TH BT, of Appledore, Co Devon [Sir Antony Reardon-Smith Bt, 26 Merrick Sq, London SE1 4JB]; *b* 20 June 1937; *s* f 1995; *educ* Wycliffe Coll Gloucester; management and charities consultant, tstee and chm Joseph Strong Frazer Tst 1980–, chm N E Rubber Co Ltd 1980–, Nat Serv in RN (Suez) 1956; dir: Sir William Reardon Smith and Sons Ltd, Reardon Smith Line 1959–85, London World Trade Centre 1986–87, Milford Haven Port Authority 1988–, Marine and Port Services 1990–, memb Baltic Exchange 1959–87 (dir 1982–87), Tstee and V-Pres Roy M N Sch Fndn, memb cncl King George's Fund for Sailors; KLJ; Liveryman Shipwrights' and Poulters' Cos; *m* 4 Aug 1962 *Susan Wight, dau of Henry Wight Gibson, of Cardiff, and has:

1 +WILLIAM NICOLAS HENRY; *b* 10 June 1963

2 +Giles Antony James; *b* 12 Feb 1968; *m* 31 Jan 1998 *Janie, 2nd dau of Charles Rowe, of Little Thurlow, Suffolk

3 +Harry Alexander; *b* 1979

1 *Henrietta Nesta; *b* 1965

Lineage: DANIEL REARDON SMITH; *d* 1833, leaving:

THOMAS REARDON SMITH; *b* 1810; *m* 1832 Elizabeth (*d* Jan 1906), dau of Capt Philip Green, and was lost at sea Oct 1859 in cmd of the *Hazard*; his 5th s:

Sir William Reardon Smith, 1st Bt (UK), so *cr* 1 July 1920, JP, DL Glam; *b* 7 Aug 1856; shipowner, Hon Freeman Cardiff 1928 and London 1932; *m* 16 May 1880 Ellen (*d* 9 Aug 1939), dau of Thomas Pickard Hamlyn, and had:

1 WILLIE (Sir), **2nd Bt**

2 Douglas; *b* 10 April 1894; *m* 3 Aug 1916 Gladys May, dau of John Randell, of Cardiff, and *d* 6 June 1961, leaving:

  (1) *Margaret Hamlyn; *b* 12 March 1920; *m* 18 Sept 1945 Denis Maxwell Johnson (*d* 1967) and has:

    1a *Stewart Maxwell; *b* 16 Sept 1949

    2a *Graham Hamlyn; *b* 25 July 1951

  (2) *Jean Reardon; *b* 12 May 1922; *m* 1st 5 Aug 1940 (*divorce* 1957) Morton Fergusson Llewellyn, s of Morton Howell Llewellyn, of Tynewydd, Aberdare, Glam, and has:

    1a *David Morton; *b* 30 April 1942; *educ* Oundle

  (2) (cont.) Mrs Jean Llewellyn *m* 2nd 22 April 1958 *John Douglas Rae, s of Thomas Rae, of Kirkcudbright

1 Lillian Nellie; *m* 16 July 1914 William Gilbert Liley, shipowner (*d* 1955)

2 Gertrude; *m* 16 Dec 1914 Arthur John Popham, shipowner (*d* 17 April 1951)

3 Elizabeth Hamlyn; *m* 25 March 1922 Douglas Aubrey Low (*d* 1955) and had issue

4 Grace Hamlyn

Sir WILLIAM *d* 23 Dec 1935; his er s,

Sir WILLIE REARDON SMITH later REARDON-SMITH (deed poll 20 Dec 1929), **2nd Bt**, JP Glam; *b* 26 May 1887; v-chm Mount Stuart Dry Docks Ltd, dir Ocean Coals and Wilson Ltd, Leeds Shipping Co, Sir William Reardon Smith and Sons, Reardon Smith Line, Devon Mutual Steamship Insur Assoc, UK Mutual Steamship Assur Assoc and Br Corp Registry, Hon Treas Welsh Nat Sch Medicine, OStJ, High Sheriff Glam 1946; *m* 22 June 1910 Elizabeth Ann, dau of John Henry Wakely, of Cardiff, and had:

1 WILLIAM REARDON (Sir), **3rd Bt**

2 Alan John; *b* 28 March 1914; Lt RA WW II (POW); *m* 22 June 1938 Winifred Maud (*d* 1975) dau of Frederick C Williams, and *d* 7 June 1970, leaving:

  (1) +John Philip [John Reardon-Smith Esq, Greenleaves, 301 Marshfield Rd, Castleton, nr Cardiff CF3 8UU]; *b* 12 Jan 1941; *m* 1st 4 April 1964 Josephine

Mireille, dau of Frederick Wilding, of Barry, Glam; *m* 2nd 19– *— and by his 1st w has:

    1a +Charles Alan; *b* 12 March 1965

    2a +Simon John; *b* 28 Aug 1966

    1a *Katharine Lisa; *b* 1971

  (2) +Richard William Alan [Richard Reardon-Smith Esq, The Old Six Bells, Llangattock, Crickhowell, Powys NP8 1PH]; *b* 8 Dec 1946; *m* 1st 1970 (*divorce* 1990) Suzanne Ward, dau of Jonathan Preece Jones, of Coychurch, Glam, and has:

    1a +Dylan Alan John; *b* 1972

    1a *Zahra Elizabeth; *b* 1973

  (2) (cont.) Richard Reardon-Smith *m* 2nd 1990 *Nicola Jane, est dau of Christopher Denis Yapp, of St Mellons, S Glam, and by her has:

    2a +Samuel William; *b* 1990

3 Thomas Hamlyn; *b* 19 Jan 1918; *d* 20 Dec 1921

4 +Douglas Hamlyn [Douglas Reardon-Smith Esq, West Ash Hill, Forches Cross, Newton Abbot, Devon TQ12 6QB]; *b* 26 March 1928; *educ* Marlborough and RAC Cirencester; late 2nd Lt QO 7th Hus; *m* 15 Sept 1949 *Minnie Wanna, dau of John Dawson, of Hankerton, Wilts, and adopted:

  *Hugh David; *b* 1 May 1957

  *Jonathan Owen; *b* 3 Jan 1961; *educ* Marlborough and Cardiff U (BSc); *m* 19 Oct 1991 *Diane Hettie, only dau of Douglas Webb, of Blakeney, Glos, and has:

    1a *Oliver Owen Douglas; *b* 13 March 1993

    1a *Victoria Zoe; *b* 6 Nov 1996

Jane Elizabeth; *b* 15 Feb 1959; *d* 8 June 1977

1 *Mary Ellen [Mrs David Davies, 54 Palace Rd, Llandaff, Cardiff CF5 2AH]; *b* 18 April 1922; *m* 8 May 1947 *Dr David Kenneth Lewis Davies, OBE, RNVR, s of James Lewis Davies, and has:

  (1) *David Christopher [David Davies Esq, 57 Cheriton Dve, Thornhill, Cardiff CF4 9DF]; *b* 16 July 1948; *educ* Bromsgrove; *m* 1st 1974 (*divorce* 1978) Elizabeth Thomas, dau of Dr Anthony Thomas, of Cardiff and has:

    1a *Lucy Alexandra; *b* 1974

  (1) (cont.) David Davies *m* 2nd 1981 *Terry Anne, dau of Colin Smale, CBE, of Cardiff, and has:

    1a *Timothy John; *b* 1984

    2a *James Frederick; *b* 1987

  (2) *Simon James [Simon Davies Esq, 34 Bron Haul, Pentyrch, Cardiff CF4 8TA]; *b* 14 June 1952; *educ* Bromsgrove; *m* 1974 *Carolyn Margaret, dau of William Sutton, of St Fagans, Cardiff, and has:

    1a *Katie Elizabeth; *b* 1976

    2a *Karen Ann; *b* 1979

  (3) *William Peter [William Davies Esq, 19 Cory Crescent, Peterston-super-Ely, Cardiff CF5 6LS]; *b* 27 Dec 1953; *educ* Bromsgrove; *m* 1985 *Heather Roslyn, dau of John Patterson, of Radyr, Cardiff, and has:

    1a *Philip John; *b* 1989

    2a *Robert William; *b* 1992

  (4) *Mark Hamlyn [Mark Davies Esq, 93 Foxbourne Rd, London SW17 8EN]; *b* 13 April 1961; *educ* Clifton Coll

  (1) *Siân Elizabeth [Mrs R Lewis, Brooklyn, Cardiff Rd, Creigian, Cardiff CF4 8NL]; *b* 12 Aug 1956; *educ* Howells Girls Sch, Llandaff; *m* 1979 *Prof R K Lewis, s of Stanley Lewis, of Pontypool, and has:

    1a *Matthew Owain; *b* 1985

    2a *Huw Rhodri; *b* 1993

    1a *Catrin Angharad; *b* 1987

    2a *Ceri Elin; *b* 1990

Sir WILLIE *d* 24 Nov 1950; his est s,

Sir William Reardon Reardon-Smith, 3rd Bt, *b* 1 March 1911; *educ* Blundell's; Maj 34th LAA Regt RA (TA) WW II; *m* 1st 19 Oct 1935 (*divorce* 1954) Nesta Florence (*d* car crash 9 Sept 1959), dau of Frederick J Phillips, of Barry, and had:

1 Sir (WILLIAM) ANTONY JOHN REARDON-SMITH, **4th and present Bt**

2 +Barrie Alan [Barrie Reardon-Smith Esq, Mill House, Ogbourne St George, Marlborough, Wilts SN8 1SV]; *b* 16 Sept 1942; *educ* Wycliffe Coll; *m* 24 June 1965 *Wendy Elizabeth, est dau of George William Bigglestone, of Coventry, and has:

  (1) *Samantha Elizabeth; *b* 6 June 1966

  (2) *Louise Suzanne; *b* 28 Dec 1968

3 +Timothy Henry Neale [Timothy Reardon-Smith Esq, Pentre Cottage, Llanwenarth, Abergavenny, Gwent]; *b* 1 June 1944; *educ* Wycliffe Coll; *m* 14 May 1966 *Lynda Madeleine, est dau of Francis Wallace Preston, of Redditch, Worcs, and has:

  (1) +Philip Timothy Edward; *b* 7 July 1969

  (2) +James Henry Charles; *b* 1971

  (3) +Edward William Neale; *b* 1977

1 *Nesta Suzanne [Mrs Francis Hayes, Llansannor House, nr Cowbridge, Glam CF71 7RW]; *b* 18 May 1939; *m* 26 April 1958 *Francis Edward Sutherland Hayes, DL, yst s of Raymond Stanley Hayes, JP, of Bridgend, Glam, and has:

  (1) *Patrick Neal Sutherland; *b* 5 Nov 1961; *m* 1988 *Jacqueline, dau of John Ford, and has:

    1a *Samuel; *b* 1993

    1a *Aimée; *b* 1990

  (1) *Thira Nesta; *b* 5 April 1960; *m* 1991 *John Rudd

  (2) *Elizabeth Ann; *b* 27 July 1964; *m* 1990 *Ian Mellett

  (3) *Philippa Vera; *b* 21 Sept 1966; *m* 1995 *Vincent Brigode

Sir William *m* 2nd 1 May 1954 *Beryl Frances, dau of William Henry Powell, of Cardiff, and *d* 1995, leaving by her:

4 +David Joseph William; *b* 3 June 1960

2 *Deirdre Ellen; *b* 27 Jan 1955

3 *Amanda Mary; *b* 3 May 1958

4 *Penelope Ann; *b* 22 June 1962

REAY

Arms: Azure on a chevron argent between three bear's heads couped argent muzzled gules a roebuck's head erased between two hands grasping daggers, the point turned towards the buck's head, all proper. **Crest:** A dexter arm erect, couped at the elbow, the hand grasping a dagger, also erect, proper. **Supporters:** Dexter, a pikeman armed at all points; sinister, a musketeer, both proper. **Motto:** *Manu forti* ('With a strong hand'). **Creations:** Bt. (NS) 18 May 1627; L. (S) 20 June 1628; Jonkheer (Netherlands) 20 Feb 1816, B. (Netherlands) 4 June 1822.

THE 14TH LORD REAY, of Reay, Co Caithness, and a **Baronet**, also **Baron Mackay van Ophemert** and Zennewijnen, Netherlands (Sir Hugh William Mackay, Bt) [The Rt Hon The Lord Reay, House of Lords, London SW1A 0PW]; *b* 19 July 1937; *s f* 1963, also as Ch of Clan Mackay (MacAoidh); *educ* Eton and Ch Ch Oxford; MEP (C) 1973–79 (V-Chm C Gp), memb Br Delegn Cncl Europe and WEU 1979–86, Govt Whip 1989–91, U-Sec DTI 1991–92, memb Ho Lds Select Ctee EC 1993–; *m* 1st 14 Sept 1964 (*divorce* 1978), as her 1st husb, Hon (Annabel) Thérèse (Tessa) Fraser, yr dau of 15th Lord (Fraser of) Lovat (*qv*), and has:

1 +ÆNEAS SIMON, *Master of Reay*; *b* 20 March 1965; *educ* Westminster and Brown U, RI

2 +Edward Andrew; *b* 21 Jan 1974

1 *Laura Elizabeth; *b* 25 July 1966

The 14th LORD REAY *m* 2nd 20 June 1980 *Hon Victoria Isabella Warrender, only dau of 1st Baron Bruntisfield (*qv*), and by her has:

2 *Antonia Alexandria; *b* 11 Dec 1981

3 *Isobel Violet Grace; *b* 1985

Lineage: IYE MACETH; first of the Clan Mackay to settle in Strathnaver; Chamberlain to Walter de Baltrode, Bp Caithness 1263, by whose dau he had:

IYE *Mor* ('The Elder'); acquired lands in Durness from his gf the Bp; had:

DONALD; *m* a dau of IYE MACNEIL of Gigha and had:

IYE; murdered with his s in Dingwall Castle 1370 by Nicolas Sutherland of Duffus, bro of 5th Earl of Sutherland (*qv*); had:

DONALD; murdered with his f; had:

ANGUS; had:

ANGUS *Du* ('The Dark'); cmded 4,000 men 1427; *m* by 8 Oct 1415 Elizabeth, sis of Donald, Ld of the Isles, and was *ka* 1433, leaving:

NEIL; living 1437; *m* a dau of George Munro of Foulis (*see* MUNRO, Bt, of Foulis-Obsdale) and had:

ANGUS ROY; *m* a dau of Mackenzie of Kintail (*see* CROMARTIE, E) and was *k c* 1486, leaving:

IYE ROY; granted lands in Caithness and Sutherland 1499, 1504 and 1511; *d* 1517, leaving, with an er s (John, of Strathnaver, *d c* 1529):

DONALD MACKAY of Strathnaver; *m* Helen, dau of Alexander Sinclair of Dunbeath and Stemster, s of 2nd Earl of Caithness (*qv*); present English victory over Scots of Solway Moss 1542, following which JAMES V granted him various lands; *d c* 1550, leaving:

IYE *Du* MACKAY; involved in quarrels with 11th Earl of Sutherland (*qv*), to whom he surrendered 1556, being imprisoned for a while Edinburgh Castle; got back 1571 his f's lands from 5th Earl of Huntly (*see* HUNTLY, M), to whom they had been regranted by the Crown; *m* Christian, dau of William Sinclair of Dun, and *d* 1572, leaving:

HUISTEAN/HUGH *Du* MACKAY of Farr, Tongue, and Strathnaver, Sutherland; *m* 1st Lady Elizabeth/Margaret Sinclair, 2nd dau of 4th Earl of Caithness (*qv*) and widow of William Sutherland of Duffus (*see* DUNBAR, Bt, of Hempriggs), and had an only dau; *m* 2nd 1589 Lady Jane Gordon, er dau of 12th Earl of Sutherland (*qv*), and *d* 11 Sept 1614, having by her had, with a yr s (John, of Dirlet and Strathy) and three daus:

Sir Donald Mackay, 1st Bt (NS), *cr* 18 May 1627, with remainder to heirs male whatsoever, and **1st Lord Reay** (S), so *cr* 20 June 1628, with remainder to his heirs male for ever bearing the name and arms of Mackay (a further patent creating him Earl of Strathnaver was never completed owing to the Civil War), JP (Inverness and Cromarty 1610, Sutherland 1612); *b* March 1590/1; ktd 1616; fought under CHRISTIAN IV OF DENMARK Thirty Years War Germany 1627, such service probably winning him his peerage in that CHRISTIAN's n was CHARLES I, and 1629–30 under GUSTAVUS ADOLPHUS OF SWEDEN; royalist Civil War England and Scotland; *m* 1st Aug 1610 Barbara, sis of 1st Earl of Seaforth (*see* CROMARTIE, E), and had, with an est s (*d* young):

1 JOHN, **2nd Lord**

2 Angus; Lt-Col in Danish Army; *m* (contract 1 May 1659) Catherine, dau of Alexander Gun of Killearnan, and was ancestor of the MACKAYs of Melness

1 Mary; *m* Sir Roderick Macleod of Talisker

The **1st Lord** *m* 2nd by 1631 (*annulled*) Rachel Winterfield or Harrison; *m* 3rd 1631 Elizabeth (*d* shortly after June 1637), dau of Robert Thomson, of Greenwich, Keeper Queen's Wardrobe, and by her had:

2 Ann; *m* Alexander Macdonald, bro of Sir James Macdonald of Sleat (*see* BOSVILLE MACDONALD, Bt)

The **1st Lord** *m* 4th Marjorie, dau of Francis Sinclair of Stirkoke, and by her had, with other issue:

3 William, of Kinloch; *m* Ann, dau of Col Hugh Mackay of Scourie, and had issue

4 Charles, of Sandwood; *m* Elizabeth, dau of Capt William Mackay of Borley, and was ancestor of the MACKAYs of Sandwood

The **1st Lord** *d* Denmark Feb 1649, having also had illegitimate issue by Mary, dau of 11th Earl of Crawford (*see* CRAWFORD and BALCARRES, E):

5 Donald, of Dysart

The est s,

JOHN MACKAY, **2nd Lord Reay**, JP (Sutherland 1663); *b c* 1612; royalist Civil War; *m* 1st 1636 Isabel, allegedly dau of 5th Earl of Caithness (*qv*), and had:

1 George; *dvp* unm in or after 1656

1 Jane; *m* 1st 1665 Robert Gordon, s of 15th Earl of Sutherland (*qv*); *m* 2nd Hugh Mackay of Strathy

The **2nd Lord** *m* 2nd Barbara, dau of Hugh Mackay of Scourie, and *d* in or after late 1680, having by her had, with other issue:

2 Donald, *Master of Reay*; *b c* 1658; *m* (contract 22 Aug 1677) Anne, dau of Gen Sir George Munro of Newmore and Culrain, and *dvp* in an accident (burnt by an exploding barrel of gunpowder while out hunting) 1680, leaving:

(1) GEORGE MACKAY, **3rd Lord Reay**; *b* late 1678; *educ* Holland; FRS 1698; supported Govt in 1715 and 1745 Uprisings; *m* 1st *c* Dec 1702 at Bommel, Netherlands, Margaret, dau of Lt-Gen Hugh Mackay of Scourie, Col 21st Regt of Foot (*ka* Steinkirk 1692), by Clara, 3rd dau of Arnold van Bie, of Wayestein, Netherlands, and had:

1a DONALD MACKAY, **4th Lord Reay**; *m* 1st (contract 23 Aug 1732) Marion (*d* Dec 1740), dau of Sir Robert Dalrymple of Castleton (*see* HAMILTON-DALRYMPLE, Bt), and had:

1b GEORGE MACKAY, **5th Lord Reay**; *b c* 1734; *m* 1st 6 Jan 1758 his cousin Marion (*see* below); *m* 2nd 1 Oct 1760 Elizabeth (*d* Nov 1800), dau of John Fairley/Fairlie, and *dspm* 27 Feb 1768, having by her had three daus

2b HUGH MACKAY, **6th Lord Reay**; *d* unm 26 Jan 1797

1a (cont.) The **4th Lord** *m* 2nd 21 Dec 1741 Christian (*d* 12 July 1790), dau of James Sutherland of Pronsy, and *d* 18 Aug 1761, having by her had:

1b Mary; *m* Maj Thomas Edgar, 25th Foot, and *d* 21 Nov 1813

(1) (cont.) The **3rd Lord** *m* 2nd Janet, dau of John Sinclair of Ulbster (*see* THURSO, V) and widow of Benjamin Dunbar, Yr. of Northfield (*see* DUNBAR, Bt, of Northfield), and by her had:

2a Hugh, of Bighouse; Col; *m* 1st (contract 15 July 1728) Margaret Mackay, coheir of Bighouse (*d* 26 March 1769), and had, with other issue:

1b Janet; *m* Colin Campbell of Glenure (*see* CAMPBELL, Bt, of Barcaldine) and had issue

2b Marion; *m* 6 Jan 1758 **5th Lord Reay** and *dsps* 12 March 1759

2a (cont.) The Hon Hugh Mackay of Bighouse *m* 2nd 14 April 1770 Isabella, dau of Alexander Mackenzie of Lentran, and *d* 12 Nov 1770

1a Anne; *m* (contract 7 Sept 1728) John Watson, of Muir Ho, Edinburgh, and *d* 24 Nov 1780, leaving issue

(1) (cont.) The **3rd Lord** *m* 3rd 11 Aug 1713 Mary, dau of John Doull/Dowell of Thuster, and *d* 21 March 1748, having by her had, with three other daus (*d* unm):

3a George, of Skibo; MP Sutherland 1747 and 1754; Master Scottish Mint; *m* 13 Dec 1766 Anne, 3rd dau of Eric Sutherland, s of 3rd Lord Duffus (*see* DUNBAR, Bt, of Hempriggs), and *d* 25 June 1782, having had:

1b George; *d* unm E Indies 12 Dec 1790

2b ERIC MACKAY, **7th Lord Reay**; *b* Dec 1773; rep S peer 1806–07 and 1835–47; sold family estates to Elizabeth, Countess of Sutherland (*qv*) in her own right, for £300,000 (over £10,500,000 in late-1990s terms); *d* unm 8 July 1847

3b ALEXANDER MACKAY, **8th Lord Reay**; *b* 1775; served Gordon Highrs then Sutherland Highrs, ret as Maj 1817; *m* 8 April 1809 Marion (*d* 2 July 1865), dau of Col Gall, Mil Sec to Warren Hastings when latter Govr India, and widow of David Ross (est s of David Ross, Ld of Session as Lord Ankerville, of Ankerville, Ross-shire), and *d* 18 Feb 1863, having had, with another s (*d* young) and five other daus:

1c ERIC MACKAY, **9th Lord Reay**; *b* 1813; served 60th Rifles; *d* unm 2 June 1875

1c Sophia; *m* Charles Arthur Aylmer

4b Donald Hugh; *b* 31 Dec 1780; granted with surv siblings 18 Aug 1835 rank of Ld of Parl's dau/yr s; V-Adml the Blue 1849; *m* 1848 Helen Martha, dau of William Twinning, Bengal Med Serv, and *dsp* 26 March 1850

1b Elizabeth; *d* unm 10 April 1788

2b Mary; *d* unm 24 Nov 1843

3b Anne; *d* unm 11 Sept 1849

4a Alexander; raised an ind co for Loudoun's Highrs 1745, captured Battle of Prestonpans 21 Sept 1745; MP Sutherland 1761; Lt-Gen, C-in-C forces Scotland 1780; *m* 24 Dec 1770 Margaret (*m* 2nd 4 Oct 1792, as his 2nd w, James Farquharson of Invercauld), dau of Sir William Carr of Ettalf, and *dsp* 31 May 1789

2a Christian; *m* 15 June 1746 Rev John Erskine, DD (*d* 19 Jan 1803), of Carnock, and *d* 20 May 1810, leaving issue

3 Æneas; Brig-Gen and Col-Proprietor Mackay Scottish Regt in serv of Netherlands, where naturalised; *m* 1692 Margaret (*d* 14 Feb 1761), dau of Lt-Col Francis Puchler by Jacoba van Bie, and *d* 1697, leaving:

(1) Donald; *b* 1696; Col in his f's Regt; *m* his cousin Arnolda Margaret van den Steen, and was *k* Siege of Tournai 1745, leaving, with two yr sons (Francis, *dsp* 1817; Daniel, *d* 1782) and a dau (Frances Jacoba, *m* Baron Vygh):

1a Æneas; Col in his f's Regt; *m* Baroness Ursulina Philippina van Haeften van Wadenoyen, and had, with other issue:

1b BARTHOLD JOHAN CHRISTIAAN, BARON MACKAY Van OPHE-MERT (Netherlands), so *cr* 4 June 1822; *m* Jonkvrouwe Anna Magdalena Frederika Henriette van Renesse, of Wilp, and *d* 24 Nov 1854, having had:

1c ÆNEAS MACKAY, **10th Lord Reay**, and BARON MACKAY Van OPHEMERT in the Netherlands; *b* 13 Jan 1807; *educ* Utrecht U; lawyer The Hague, memb Second Chamber States General 1850–62, V-Pres Cncl State 1862–76, Min State 1865–76, Kt Grand Cross Netherland Lion; *m* 27 Oct 1837 Mary Catherine Anne Jacoba (*d* 22 May 1886), dau of Baron James Fagel, memb Dutch Privy Cncl, and *d* 6 March 1876, having had an only surv s:

1d DONALD JAMES MACKAY, **11th Lord Reay**, KT (1911), GCSI (1890), GCIE (1887, CIE 1886), PC (1906); *b* 22 Dec 1839; *educ* The Hague and Leyden U; served Dutch Legation London, memb Dutch Chamber Reps but resigned seat and naturalised UK subject 1877; *cr* 8 Oct 1881 BARON REAY OF DURNESS, Co Sutherland (UK); Rector St Andrews U 1884–86, Govr Bombay 1885–90, Ld Lt Roxburghs 1892–1918, U-Sec State India 1894–95, chm London Sch Bds 1897–1904, first Pres Br Acad 1902–07, LLD Edinburgh 1882 also Glasgow and St Andrews, LittD Oxford 1904, LittD Cambridge 1905, LLD Aberdeen 1905, For Memb French Acad Political Sci; *m* 5 June 1877 Fanny Georgiana Jane, CI (*d* 23 Jan 1917), dau of Richard Hasler, of Aldingbourne, Sussex, and widow of Capt Alexander Mitchell, Gren Gds, MP, of Stow, Midlothian, and *dsp* 1 Aug 1921, when the UK peerage expired

2c John Francis Hendrik Jacob Ernestus; *b* 13 March 1808; *m* 1835 Baroness Margaretha Clara Frances van Lynden (*d* 8 Oct 1869) and *d* 27 July 1846, leaving:

1d Æneas; *b* 29 Nov 1838; Min State, Pres Second Chamber Netherlands Parl, PM Netherlands; *m* 7 July 1869 Baroness Elizabeth Willemina van Lynden (*d* 29 April 1907) and *d* 13 Nov 1909, leaving:

1e ERIC, **12th Lord**

2d Theodoor Philip; *b* 24 April 1840; Pres Chamber of Accounts; *m* 15 July 1868 Baroness Juliana Anna van Lynden (*d* 4 March 1835), dau of Baron Constantijn Willem Ferdinand van Lynden, and *d* 29 Nov 1922, having had:

1e Johan Jacob; *b* 2 Nov 1869; *d* unm 22 Nov 1902

2e Constantyn Willem Ferdinand; *b* 31 Dec 1870; *m* 1st 30 Sept 1898 Jonkvrouwe Petronella Adamina Hœufft (*d* 27 Aug 1933), dau of Jonkheer David Hœufft; *m* 2nd 10 Nov 1937 Dr Cornelia Frida (*d* 30 March 1963), dau of Samuel Katz, and *d* 5 Feb 1955, having by his 1st w had:

1f Jacqueline Jeannette; *b* 14 Dec 1899; *m* 5 June 1946 Jonkheer Dr Johan Fredrik Theodoor van Valkenburg, of Amsterdam, s of Cornelis Constantin van Valkenburg

2f Adelaide Cornelie; *b* 3 July 1902; *m* 30 Nov 1927 Gustaaf Carel Ferdinand Schoch, s of Dr Charles Ferdinand Schoch, of San Francisco

3f Henrietta Margaretha; *b* 16 Sept 1904

4f Margaretha Clara Françoise; *b* 27 Aug 1909; *m* 28 April 1937 Rev Henri Jean Louis André Couvée (*d* 5 Jan 1969), s of Rev Evert Barend Couvée, of Utrecht, and had:

1g *Jean Pierre Henri [Baron Jean Mackay, 61 Joh Bilderstraat, The Hague, Netherlands]; *b* 9 Feb 1939

1g *Petronella Adamina; *b* 12 Jan 1941; *m* *Colin Fisher

2g *Agnès Madeleine Adélaide; *b* 25 Dec 1943; *m* *Antonius van Doorn

3e Æneas; *b* 1 Jan 1872; *m* 2 March 1899 Jonkvrouwe Hermina Clasina (*d* 18 Feb 1945), dau of Lt-Gen Jonkheer Jacobus Catharinus Cornelis den Beer Poortugael, Min of War and Privy Councillor, and *d* 30 July 1932, leaving:

1f Daniel; *b* 16 June 1900; Lt-Col Cavalry R Netherlands Army; *m* 17 March 1927 Henriette Constance Adèle (*d* 1986), dau of Dr Alfred Joan Labouchere, of Zeist, Holland, and *d* 2 Feb 1969, leaving:

1g +Donald [Lt-Col Baron Donald Mackay, 279 Irislaan, 2343 CM Oegstgeest, Netherlands]; *b* 19 April 1928; Lt-Col RNAF (ret); *m* 18 May 1968 (*divorce* 1987) Danielle Christine, dau of Dr Hendrik Gerrit Beins

2g +Alfred Alexander [Baron Alfred Mackay, 248 Parkweg, Voorburg, Netherlands]; *b* 2 April 1930; *m* 18 Sept 1965 *Diana Margaret, dau of Sydney Jesty Elwin, of Strathfield, NSW, and has:

1h +Andrew Robert; *b* 3 Aug 1967

1h *Caroline Jane; *b* 18 April 1969

3g Hugo Carel Æneas; *b* 27 Feb 1936; *m* 1st 4 Dec 1967 Gwendoleen (*d* 1973), dau of Elbert Waller; *m* 2nd 1989 *Hanna, dau of Isaac Samuel Brouwer, and *d* 17 Sept 1995

4g +Eric Joan Maurits [Baron Eric Mackay, Van Calcarlaan 21, Wassenaar, Netherlands]; *b* 26 July 1938; Lt (Res) Roy Netherlands Marine Corps; *m* 4 Oct 1963 *Susan Jane, dau of Francis Loudon McNeill, and has:

1h +Patrick Joan; *b* 21 March 1967

1h *Alexandra; *b* 14 Jan 1966

2h *Helen Danielle; *b* 3 Aug 1969

3h *Madeline; *b* 7 Nov 1971

2f Reinhard Alexander; *b* 28 April 1903; Capt Cav (Res) Roy Netherlands Army WW II, attd Gen Staff, liaison ABDA cmd Java, ADC to Gen Wavell; *m* 11 July 1930 Greta Ernestina (*d* 12 Aug 1995), dau of Jan Adriaan Smits, of The Hague, and *d* 1990, having had:

1g *Sonja Gratia; *b* 19 Sept 1931; *m* 11 July 1953 *Hendrik Willem Balthasar Croiset van Uchelen, s of Dr Gerard Zeger Anthonie Croiset van Uchelen, and has:

1h *Eric Alexander; *b* 1958

1h *Helen Astrid; *b* 1955

3f +Theodoor Philip [Baron Theodoor Mackay, Provinciënlaan 3-53, Heemstede, Netherlands]; *b* 7 April 1911; Burgomaster; *m* 27 Nov 1941 *Zsófia Friderika Emma, dau of Dr Andor Henrik Reusz de Ráthony, of Budapest, and has:

1g +Æneas [Baron Æneas Mackay, Jndustrieweg 10/10A, 1231 KH, Loosdrecht, Netherlands]; *b* 28 Aug 1942; co dir; *m* 1975 *Yvonne Marie-Blanche, dau of Frans Wyers, and has:

1h +Randolph Philip; *b* 1977

2h +Patrick James; *b* 1979

1g *Marguerite Louise [Mme Marguerite Grüninger, La Chaux de Fonds, rue de la Prairie 46, Geneva, Switzerland]; *b* 21 Dec 1943; *m* 31 Oct 1964 *Dr Bernhard Rudolf Grüninger, s of Rudolf Alfred Martin, of Zurzach, Switzerland, and has:

1h *Daniel Robert; *b* 1966

1h *Marie-Anne; *b* 1968

2g *Lilian Mary; *b* 5 Dec 1945; *m* 1970 *Jan William Stuart, of Heemstede, and has:

1h *Wendelien; *b* 1972

2h *Marguérite; *b* 1974

3g *Zsófia Alexandra; *b* 20 Dec 1951; *m* 1979 *Dr Frederik Christiaan Musch, Sec Bank Internat Settlements, Basle, and has:

1h *Willem Heiko; *b* 1980

2h *Onno Frederick Roger; *b* 1984

1h *Clare Alexandra; *b* 1982

1f *Louisa Wilhelmina Elisabeth Amarantha; *b* 21 June 1906

2f *Erica [Baroness Erica Beelaerts van Blokland, Jan Muschlaan 203, 2597TT The Hague, Netherlands]; *b* 23 Aug 1916; *m* 1974 Jonkheer Gerard Beelaerts van Blokland (*d* 30 April 1997), late Dutch Amb USSR

4e Edward; *b* 23 Dec 1873; *m* 18 June 1902 Ina Petronella (*d* 10 Oct 1903), dau of Petrus Lycklama à Nijeholt, and *d* 18 Oct 1950, leaving:

1f *Catharina Margaretha Elisabeth; *b* 4 Oct 1903; *m* 27 Sept 1923 Ernest Johannes Désandré (*d* 1988), s of Georges Henri Julien Désandré, of Amsterdam, and has:

1g *Edward Ernest; *b* 1929

1g *Ina Catherina Elizabeth; *b* 1932

5e Dirk Rijnhard Johan; *b* 19 Dec 1876; *m* 1st 5 July 1906 Johanna Elisabeth (*d* 15 Nov 1920), dau of Abraham Jacob Blaauw, and had:

1f Johan Jacob; *b* 12 Sept 1909; *m* 20 June 1936 *Elizabeth Elder [Mme Johan Mackay, Casilla 116, Talca, Chile], dau of William Chance Holman, of USA, and *d* 27 Jan 1995, leaving:

1g +Derrick Phillipe [Baron Derek Mackay, Casilla 116, Talca, Chile]; *b* 19 April 1937; *m* 30 May 1964 *Juanita Hederra Sepulveda, dau of Augusto Hederra Silva, and has:

1h +Cristian Andrès; *b* 30 May 1965; *m* 1993 *Maria Consuelo Diaz, dau of Patricio Diaz Carrasco, and has:

1i *Maria Consuelo Magdalena; *b* 1994

2i *Sofia Bernardita; *b* 1995

2h +Alezardro Andrès; *b* 13 March 1967

3h *Matias Andrès; *b* 1972

2g +John Hugo [Baron John Mackay, Casilla 116, Talca, Chile]; *b* 15 Oct 1941; *m* 1971 *Sylvia Bravo Perucca, dau of Ladislao Bravo, and has:

1h +John Donald; *b* 1973

1h *Sylvia Francisca; *b* 1972

3g Donald Rynhard William; *b* 17 Sept 1945; *d* unm 27 Jan 1965

1g *Johanna Elizabeth; *b* 10 Jan 1939; *m* 1970 *German del Rio and has:

1h *German Andrès; *b* 1971

2h *Juan Ignacio; *b* 1972

2g *Marie Louise; *b* 25 Jan 1952

2f +Johan Hugo [Cdre Baron Johan Mackay, 29 Ary Schefferstraat, 2597 VN, The Hague, Netherlands]; *b* 26 Nov 1914; Cdre Roy Netherlands Navy (ret); *m* 8 Nov 1945 *Margaret Pearse, dau of Pearse John Herbert, of Perth, W Australia, and has had:

1g +Alexander Rijnhard; *b* 18 Feb 1950; *m* 1st 1972 (*divorce* 1987) Maria Paula Hermanna, dau of Bernardus Petrus Maria Marquering; *m* 2nd 18 Sept 1996 *Tine E Taverne, and by his 1st w has:

1h +Robert Bernard; *b* 1975

2h +Michiel Christiaan; *b* 1978

2g +Donald Johan; *b* 16 June 1964

1g Margaret Elizabeth; *b* 12 Jan 1948; *d* 4 July 1962

2g *Carol Huguette; *b* 2 Dec 1954; *m* 1991 *Dr Eric Paul Jozef Myjer and has:

  1h *Florian Hugo Bob; *b* 1992

  1h *Sandrijn Margaret Maria; *b* 1988

3f +Eric Rynhard Alexander; *b* 21 May 1917; *m* 20 May 1943 *Gertrud, dau of Paul Moritz Robert Ernst Brückmann, and has:

1g +Æneas [Baron Æneas Mackay, 50 Koningin Julianalaan, 5582 JX Waalre, Holland]; *b* 15 Feb 1944; *m* 1971 *Joke, dau of Eduard Strelitski, and has:

  1h +Alexander; *b* 1975

  1h +Fleur; *b* 1977

2g +Paul [Baron Paul Mackay, 83 Hügelweg, Dornach, CH–4143, Switzerland]; *b* 25 May 1946; *m* 1st 1971 (*divorce* 1974) Cornelie Elisabeth, dau of Dr Jan Cornelis Steye Marie Nijenbandring de Boer; *m* 2nd 1982 *Ulrike Borgwardt and by her has:

  1h +Laurens Johannes; *b* 1985

  2h +Ernst Julian; *b* 1987

  3h +Rembert Helias; *b* 1990

3g +Eric [Baron Eric Mackay, 9 Anna Van Burenlaan, 2341 VE Oestgeest, Holland]; *b* 9 Nov 1953; *m* 1982 *Geertje, dau of Dr Boschma and has:

  1h +Bartold; *b* 1987

  2h +Christiaan; *b* 1991

  1h *Charlotte; *b* 1985

1f *Helene Gérardine; *b* 7 June 1907; *m* 23 Dec 1926 Rodney Frederick Jarrett Sterwin (*d* 1981), of Hove, Sussex, s of Philip Jarrett Sterwin, and has:

1g *Peter Philip; *b* 1930

1g *Angela Helen; *b* 1929

2f Anna Maria; *b* 17 March 1913; *m* 1st 3 March 1933 (*divorce* 1948) George Eschauzier, 2nd s of Pierre Eschauzier, of The Hague; *m* 2nd 4 June 1949 Herman Benjamin Baruch (*d* 15 March 1953), late US Amb to Netherlands, s of Simon Baruch; *m* 3rd 8 June 1958 *Rolf Robert [Rolf Robert, 120 Harbour View Lane, Key Largo, FL, USA], s of Karl Robert, and *d* 31 March 1997, leaving by her 1st husb:

1g *Pierre George; *b* 1940

1g *Hilda Susan; *b* 1934

2g *Johanna Elisabeth; *b* 1936

5e (cont.) Dirk R J Mackay *m* 2nd 11 July 1927 (*divorce* 1937) Violet (*d* 9 Sept 1969), dau of Edward Egerts, and by her had:

1f *Patricia; *b* 22 June 1928; *m* 1st 9 June 1951 (*divorce* 1959) Leonard Johannes Mens, s of Leonardus Johannes Mens, and has:

1g *Edward Maarten; *b* 1955

1f (cont.) Patricia Mens *m* 2nd 20 Dec 1962 (*divorce* 1963) Kees Pedro Marlet, s of Petrus Gerardus Marlet; *m* 3rd 7 June 1964 Robert Jan Marie Hoogeweegen, s of Johannes Petrus Marie Hoogeweegen; *m* 4th 21 Oct 1977 *Peter Simonis

5e (cont.) Dirk R J Mackay *m* 3rd 29 Nov 1939 Helena Esmé Egerts (*d* 1990), sis of his 2nd w, and *d* 11 March 1960

6e Daniel; *b* 17 March 1878; Lt Dutch Navy; *m* 1st 14 June 1906 (*divorce* 1921) Helena (*d* 14 Dec 1926), dau of Adolf Friedrich Hommel, of Zurich, and had:

1f Donald Theodoor; *b* 23 Feb 1910; LRCP, LRCS (Edin), LRFP & S (Glasgow) 1951; Lt-Cdr Dutch Navy WW II, with Submarine Serv; *m* 1st 6 Dec 1939 (*divorce* 1945) Jonkvrouwe Alexandra Frederica de Savornin Lohman, dau of Jonkheer Bonifacius Christiaan de Savornin Lohman; *m* 2nd 26 Sept 1945 *Kathleen, dau of Percy Shaw Pearce, of Leicester, and *d* 1 Jan 1992, leaving by her:

1g +Niall; *b* 11 March 1956; *m* 1985 *Jennifer Mary, dau of Hugh Butcher, and has:

  1h +Calum Hugh; *b* 1989

  1h *Georgia Kathleen; *b* 1992

1g *Moira; *b* 9 March 1952

1f Maria Christine Jeannette; *b* 29 April 1907; *d* 21 July 1995

6e (cont.) Daniel Mackay *m* 2nd 5 April 1921 Maria Françoise (*d* 7 April 1959), dau of Hugo Françoise Lamaison, and by her had:

2f *Maria Constantia [Baroness Maria Ridder Van Rosenthal, Voorsterweg 153, Tonden, 6975 AD Tonden, Netherlands]; *b* 10 Sept 1922; *m* 22 May 1947 (*divorce* 1961) Johan Barthold Frans Bosch Ridder Van Rosenthal, s of Dr Ir Edzard Jacob Ridder van Rosenthal, and has:

1g *Lodewijk Henrik Nicolaas; *b* 1948; *m* 1972 *Erica van Hoorn and has:

  1h *Eelco; *b* 1976

  1h *Saskia; *b* 1974

1g *Roelina Gijsbertha Gerardina; *b* 1951; *m* 1978 *Christiaan van Haersma Buma and has:

  1h *Michiel; *b* 1981

  2h *Robert; *b* 1983

2g *Nicolette; *b* 1953; *m* 1975 *Pieter Roodenburg and has:

  1h *Frederiek; *b* 1980

  1h *Roelien Anne; *b* 1978

3f *Juliana Anna [Countess Schimmelpenninck, Houtlaan 50, Leiden, Netherlands]; *b* 7 Nov 1925; *m* 3 June 1950 (*divorce* 1960)

Count Rutger Jan Moritz Albert Schimmelpenninck, s of Count Rutger Schimnelpenninck, and has:

1g *Gerrit Marius; *b* 1951

1g *Marie Danielle; *b* 1952

6e (cont.) Daniel Mackay *m* 3rd 27 Dec 1960 *Anna Minke, dau of Johannes Weyer, and *d* 21 March 1962

7e Norman; *b* 7 March 1882; *d* unm 19 Aug 1963

1e Margaretha Clara Françoise; *b* 16 Jan 1873; *d* unm 5 Oct 1907

2e Maria Jacoba; *b* 1 Aug 1875; *m* 2 June 1910 Dr Pieter Hendrick Willem Gerardus van den Helm (*d* 4 Dec 1954), s of Isaac Jan Jasper van den Helm, and *d* 16 Nov 1964, leaving issue

3d Willem Karel; *b* 17 Aug 1843; *m* 13 Sept 1869 Nicoline (*d* 2 Feb 1905), dau of General Engelvaart, and *d* 1916, having had:

1e Barthold; *b* 14 May 1871; *m* 17 Feb 1898 (*divorce* 1928) Jonkvrouwe Alpheda Louise van der Wyck (*d* 18 March 1935), dau of Jonkheer Cornelis Charles van der Wyck, and *d* 23 Nov 1945, having had:

1f William; *b* 21 July 1901; *d* unm 24 June 1934

1f Justine Cornelia; *b* 17 Nov 1898; *m* 26 May 1925 Marie Jacob Hendrik de Bruyn van Melis-en-Mariekerke (*d* 8 March 1964), Sec High Court of Nobility, s of Willem Hendrik de Bruyn van Mells-en-Mariekerke, and had issue

2f Catharina Wilhelmina Adrienne; *b* 2 May 1905; *m* 1st 22 Sept 1927 (*divorce* 1940) Lambertus Hendrik Slotemaker, s of Dr Albert Willem Slotemaker; *m* 2nd 17 May 1949 (*divorce* 1962) Abraham Antonius Ammerlaan, s of Abraham Ammerlaan, of The Hague

3f *Johanna Elizabeth [Baroness Johanna Baird, Laan van Rijnwijk/Flat 35c, Zeist, Netherlands]; *b* 1 Dec 1907; *m* 1st 1 Dec 1936 Capt Patrick Alexander Agnew (*ka* 12 July 1943, *see* AGNEW of Lochnaw, Bt) and has issue; *m* 2nd 4 Nov 1944 (*divorce* 1965) Lt-Col William Stanley Baird, est surv s of Brig-Gen Edward William David Baird, CBE, of Berwicks

1e Catharina Wilhelmina Adrienne; *b* 21 Aug 1873; *d* unm 1 May 1903

2e Margaretha Johanna; *b* 30 May 1876; *d* 25 Feb 1877

The 11th LORD's cousin,

ERIC MACKAY, **12th Lord Reay**; *b* 2 April 1870; *m* 7 Nov 1901 Baroness Maria Johanna Bertha Christina (*d* 1 April 1932), dau of Baron Alexander van Dedem, and *d* 1 Nov 1921, having had:

1 ÆNEAS ALEXANDER, **13th Lord**

2 +Alexander Willem Rynhard; *b* 7 Dec 1907

3 Eric John William Theodoor; *b* 7 July 1911; *d* unm 27 Feb 1949

1 Maria Christina Elizabeth; *b* 17 Oct 1904

The 12th LORD's est son,

ÆNEAS ALEXANDER MACKAY, **13th Lord Reay**; *b* 25 Dec 1905; *educ* Utrecht U; naturalized Br subject 1938; rep S peer 1955–59; FO 1939–48; *m* 14 April 1936 *Charlotte Mary [The Rt Hon Charlotte Lady Reay, St Johns, 11 High Cross Ave, Melrose, Roxburghs TD6 9SU], only dau of William Younger (*see* YOUNGER OF LECKIE, V), and *d* 10 March 1963, leaving:

1 HUGH WILLIAM MACKAY, **14th and present Lord Reay**

1 *Elizabeth Mary [The Hon Mrs Fairbairn, 38 Moray Place, Edinburgh]; *b* 21 June 1938; *m* 29 Sept 1962, as his 1st w, (*divorce* 1979) Sir Nicholas Hardwick Fairbairn of Fordell, QC, MP (*d* 19 Feb 1995), yr s of Dr William Ronald Dodds Fairbairn, of Edinburgh, and has had:

(1) Edward Nicholas; *b* 7 May, *d* 8 May 1965

(1) *Charlotte Elizabeth; *b* 22 Dec 1963

(2) Micheline Margaret Corinna; *b* 22 Dec 1963; *d* 10 April 1964

(3) *Anna-Karina; *b* 13 May 1966; *m* 29 June 1996 *John Henderson, s of Richard Henderson, of Blairston, Ayr

(4) *Francesca Katherine Nicola; *b* 15 Jan 1969

2 *Margaret Anne [The Hon Mrs Christian, Upper Huntlywood, Earlston, Berwickshire TD4 6BB; # 11 Key Largo Yacht Club, 1501 Ocean Bay Dve, Key Largo, FL 33037, USA]; *b* 13 March 1941; *m* 23 Dec 1976 *Allen Leslie Christian, only s of E L Christian, of Evanston, Ill.

REDESDALE

GOD CARETH FOR US

Arms: Quarterly, 1st and 4th, argent a fess between three moles sable (for MITFORD); 2nd and 3rd, azure three fusils in fess or, a canton ermine (for FREEMAN). **Crests:** 1 Two hands couped at the wrist proper, grasping a sword erect argent, the point and hilt or, the blade enfiled with a boar's head erased sable (for MITFORD), 2 A demi-wolf argent, supporting between the paws a fusil or and gorged with a collar dancetty gules (for FREEMAN). **Supporters:** On either side an eagle rising sable, beaked and legged or, gorged with a wreath of shamrocks proper and charged on the breast with a fusil, also or. **Motto:** God careth for us. **Creation:** B. (UK) 22 July 1902.

THE 6TH BARON REDESDALE, of Redesdale, Northumberland (Rupert Bertram Mitford) [The Rt Hon The Lord Redesdale, 2 St Mark's Square, London NW1 7TP; The School House, Rochester, Tyne and Wear NE19 1RH]; *b* 18 July 1967; *s* f 1991; *educ* Milton Abbey, Highgate and Newcastle U (BA); Lib Dem Spokesman Ho Lds Internat Devpt 1993–; memb Select Ctee Sci and Technology; *m* 10 Oct 1998 *Helen, est dau of David Shipsey

Lineage: Sir JOHN de MITFORD (of Mitford); Northumberland: MP *temp* EDWARD III, RICHARD II and HENRY IV, High Sheriff 1404–05; granted Molesdon 1369 by David de Strathbogie, 12th Earl of Atholl; Keeper Seal to EDWARD, DUKE OF YORK, for Liberty of Tyndale 1386; *d* 16 July 1409, leaving, with a yr s (Anthony, living 1367, ancestor of the MITFORDs of Ponteland) and two daus (Margaret, *m* Sir John Delaval, s of Sir Robert Delaval by Jane, dau of Sir Henry Percy; Alice, *m* 1386 John Whitfield, s of Matthew Whitfield, of Whitfield):

WILLIAM de MITFORD; *b c* 1369; Northumberland: MP 1415 and 1422, High Sheriff 1418 and 1419; *m* Margery, dau of Sir Robert Lisle, of Felton, and *d* by 10 June 1409, leaving:

JOHN de MITFORD; *b* 8 April 1402; High Sheriff Northumberland 1425; *m* Constance, dau of Sir Robert Ogle, and *d* 6 May 1457, leaving:

JOHN MITFORD, of Mitford; *b* 1433; *m* —, dau of Thomas Welteden, and was *k* at Yorkist victory over Lancastrians of Towton 29 March 1461, leaving:

BERTRAM MITFORD, of Mitford; *m* Margaret Lisle, of Felton, and had, with two daus:

GAWEN MITFORD, of Mitford; *m* —, sis of Sir Thomas Foster, of Etherstone, and *d c* 1550, leaving:

CUTHBERT MITFORD, of Mitford; *b c* 1520; granted by John Widdrington 1550 lands in Mitford which had belonged to Newminster Abbey; apptd 1552 with his cousin Anthony Mitford, of Ponteland, Commr for inclosure Middle Marches; *m* 1st Ann Wallis, of Akeld, and had a s and three daus; *m* 2nd Isabel (*dsp*), dau of Martin Fenwick, of East Hedwin and Burroden, and *d* on or after 18 Jan 1593/4, leaving:

ROBERT MITFORD, of Mitford; *b c* 1537; *m* Jane, dau of John Mitford, of Seghill, by his 2nd w Magdalen, dau of John Fenwick, of Kenton, and *d* 1625, having had, with other issue:

CUTHBERT MITFORD; *m* Mary (*d* Nov 1613), dau and heiress of Christopher Wharton, of Offerton, Co Durham, and *dvp* Nov 1613, leaving:

ROBERT MITFORD, of Mitford Castle; *b* 1612; *m* Philadelphia, dau of Humphrey Wharton, of Gillingwood, Yorks, and *d* 1674, having had, with other issue, including two er sons (Humphrey, ancestor of the MITFORDs of Mitford Castle; Rev Cuthbert, Rector Ingram, Fell Caius Coll Cambridge, *d* 1662) and two yr sons (Edward, physician, *d* 1 Jan 1673 aged 26; Rev William, Rector Elsdon, *d* 1715) a 3rd s:

JOHN MITFORD; London merchant; *m* Sarah (*d* between 12 July 1739 and 28 Feb 1739/40), dau and coheir of Henry Powell, of London, and *d* 1720, leaving an est s:

WILLIAM MITFORD, of Newtown and Gilbury House, Hants; *m* Margaret, dau of Robert Edwards, of Wingfield, Berks, and *d* between 7 Jan 1745/6 and Feb 1746/7, having had, with two yr sons:

JOHN MITFORD, of Newton House and Exbury, Hants; barrister Lincoln's Inn; *m* 13 Sept 1740 Philadelphia (*bur* 9 Jan 1797), dau of Willey Reveley, of Newton

Underwood and Throphill, Northumberland, and *d* 16 May 1761, having had, with three daus (*d* unm):

1 William, of Exbury, Hants, Newton Park, Northumberland, and Newby Wisk; *b* 10 Feb 1744; barrister Middle Temple, MP Beeralston 1796–1806 and New Romney 1812–18, Col S Hants Militia, author *The History of Greece* (5 vols 1784–1818); *m* 18 May 1766 Frances (*d* 27 April 1776), dau of James Molloy, of Dublin, and *d* 8 Feb 1827, having had, with other issue:

  (1) Henry; *b* 12 Sept 1769; Capt RN; *m* 1st 1796 Louisa (*d* May 1801), dau of Anthony Wyke, Attorney-Gen Montserrat, and had, with other issue:

    1a Frances; *m* 9 March 1829 her cousin Bertram Mitford (*dsp* 27 Feb 1842), of Mitford Castle

  (1) (cont.) Capt Henry Mitford *m* 2nd 1803 Mary (*m* 2nd 13 April 1809 Farrer Grove Spurgeon-Farrer (*d* 12 Oct 1826, leaving issue), of Brayfield House, Bucks, and *d* 3 April 1860), dau of David Anstruther, s of Alexander, self-styled 4th Lord Newark (see ANSTRUTHER, Bt), and *d* 24 Dec 1803, lost at sea in HMS *York*, leaving:

    1a Henry Reveley, of Exbury House and Newton Park, JP (Hants), DL; *b* posthumously 21 June 1804; *m* 28 Feb 1828 Lady Georgina Jemima (*d* May 1882), 3rd dau of 4th Earl of Ashburnham (see *1924 edn*), and *d* 21 Dec 1883, having had:

      1b Percy; *b* 13 July 1833; barrister, served 43rd and 51st Regts, Scots Gds, Dip Serv 1857–73; *m* 14 April 1863 Hon Emily Marion Tatton Egerton (*d* 5 Dec 1918), dau of 1st Baron Egerton of Tatton (see *1956 edn*), and *dsp* 27 June 1884

      2b Henry; *b* 13 July 1833; *m* 30 May 1871 Johanna Wilhelmine Emillie, dau of Moritz Pauli, of Kronach, Germany, and *d* Feb 1910

      3b ALGERNON BERTRAM, **1st Baron**

  (2) John; *b* 25 May 1772; barrister; *m* 1st 23 Jan 1802 Sarah Woodward (*d* 30 March 1836) and had issue; *m* 2nd 1836 Susan Annette (*m* 2nd 5 Jan 1852 Maj W S R Hodson), dau of Capt Henry, RN, and *d* 20 Jan 1851, having had issue by her

  (3) Bertram; *b* 1 Oct 1774; LLD, barrister Inner Temple, Commr Bankruptcy Ireland; *m* 24 May 1806 Frances (*d* 30 Jan 1867), dau of John Vernon, of Clontarf Castle, Co Dublin, and *d* 16 Dec 1844, leaving issue

2 JOHN MITFORD later FREEMAN-MITFORD (roy licence 28 Jan 1809 on inheriting estates of Thomas Edwards-Freeman, of Batsford Pk, Glos), 1st BARON REDESDALE, of Redesdale, Northumberland (UK), so *cr* 15 Feb 1802, PC (1801), KC (1789); *b* 18 Aug 1748; barrister 1777, MP (Tory) Beeralston 1788–89 and E Looe 1799–1802, ktd 1793, Slr-Gen 1793–99, Attorney-Gen 1799–1801, Speaker H of C 1801–02, Ld Chllr Ireland 1802–06; *m* 6 June 1803 Frances (*d* 22 Aug 1817), dau of 2nd Earl of Egmont (*qv*), and *d* 16 Jan 1830, having had, with three daus:

  (1) JOHN THOMAS FREEMAN-MITFORD, 2nd and last BARON REDESDALE and 1st and last EARL OF REDESDALE, Co Northumberland (UK), so *cr* 3 Jan 1877; *b* 9 Sept 1805; *educ* Eton and New Coll Oxford (MA); Chm Ctees and Speaker Ho of Lds 1851–86, DCL, FSA, author: *Thoughts on English Prosody and Translations from Horace* (1859) and *Further Thoughts on English Prosody*; *d* unm 2 May 1886, when both peerages expired

HENRY REVELEY MITFORD's 3rd s,

ALGERNON BERTRAM MITFORD later FREEMAN-MITFORD (roy licence on inheriting estates of 1st and last EARL OF REDESDALE; *see* above), **1st Baron Redesdale**, of Redesdale, Northumberland (UK), so *cr* 22 July 1902, GCVO (1905), KCB (1906), JP (Glos), DL; *b* 24 Feb 1837; *educ* Eton and Ch Ch Oxford; FO 1858–73; 3rd Sec St Petersburg 1863, Peking 1865 and Japan 1866, Sec Legation 1868, Grand Cordon Rising Sun Japan, Sec Office of Works 1874–86, MP (C) Stratford-on-Avon 1892–95; Tstee Nat Gallery 1908, Govr Wellington Coll 1908, author: *Tales of Old Japan* (trans, 1871), *Memories* (1915) and *Further Memories* (1917); *m* 31 Dec 1874 Lady Clementine Gertrude Helen Ogilvy (*d* 30 April 1932), 2nd dau of 7th Earl of Airlie (*qv*), and *d* 17 Aug 1916, having had:

1 Clement Bertram Ogilvy, DSO; *b* 14 Dec 1876; Maj 10th Hus Boer War 1900–01 (severely wounded) and WW I 1914–15 (wounded, despatches); *m* 25 Nov 1909 Lady Helen Alice Willington Ogilvy (*m* 2nd 11 July 1918 (*divorce* 1931) Lt-Col Henry Courtney Brocklehurst, 10th Hus (*ka* Burma June 1942 (see BROCKLEHURST, Bt); *m* 3rd 21 Feb 1933 Col Harold Bligh Nutting, 15th Bengal Cavalry (*d* 7 July 1954), s of Philip Nutting, of Hazeley Hall, Warwick), 2nd dau of 8th Earl of Airlie (*qv*), and was *ka vp* 13 May 1915, leaving:

  (1) *Rosemary Ann [Mrs Richard Bailey, Mitford Cottage, Westwell, Oxon OX8 4JU]; *b* 19 Sept 1911; *m* 29 Oct 1932 Cdr Richard James Bailey, OBE, RN (*d* 26 Jan 1969), est s of Col Percy James Bailey, of Maugersbury, Glos, and has:

    1a Richard Lee Clement; *b* 7 Sept 1933; *educ* Charterhouse and Trin Coll Cambridge (BA); dir Routledge and Kegan Paul Ltd; *m* 12 Sept 1959 *Barbara Joyce [Mrs Richard Bailey, 49 Lawrence Gdns, London NW7 4JU], er dau of Stanley George Ede, of Fowey, Cornwall, and *d* 26 Jan 1996, leaving:

      1b *Samantha Kate; *b* 25 Sept 1967

    1a (cont.) Mr and Mrs Richard Bailey also adopted:

      *Timothy Richard; *b* 12 Sept 1965

      *Melanie Jane; *b* 11 May 1964

    2a Michael Lee George; *b* 16 Dec 1934; *educ* Charterhouse; *m* 1st 2 May 1964 (*divorce* 1976) Diana, only dau of Maj Laurence Deacon and Mrs Denis Attenborough, of Hatch End, Middx, and had:

      1b *Anthony Michael George; *b* 15 Aug 1966

      1b *Clementine Jane; *b* 21 May 1969

    2a (cont.) Michael Bailey *m* 2nd Diana Maria Theresa (*d* 1986), dau of Bruno Cainero, of Udine, Italy, and *d* 9 Aug 1994, leaving by her:

      2b *Francesca Diana; *b* 1980

    1a *Ann Clementine [Mrs Peter Calver, Whitcliffe Grange Farm, Ripon, N Yorks HG4 3AS]; *b* 31 Oct 1936; *m* 19 June 1964 *Peter Calver, only s of Sir Henry Robert Sherwood Calver, QC

    2a *(Diana) Penelope [Mrs Penelope Leaf, 8 Manor Court, Lawton Ave, Carterton, Oxon OX18 3JY]; *b* 4 May 1940; *m* 6 Aug 1960 (*divorce* 1979) William Henry Gordon Leaf, yst s of Maj James Gordon Leaf, 15th/19th King's Roy Hus, of Ashbourne, Derbys, and has:

      1b *James William Richard Tyrell; *b* 26 June 1963

1b *Jessica Frances Rosemary; *b* 6 Nov 1961

3a *Lavinia Jessica Iris [Mrs Hugh Bailey, Hillcrest, 214 Newmarket Rd, Norwich NR4 7LA]; *b* 3 Sept 1944; *m* 1st 11 Sept 1965 (*divorce* 1974) Anthony Kevin Gunnar Carlson, er s of Dr Kevin Johan Vernon Carlson, of Norwich, and has:

  1b *Sarah Rosemary Iris; *b* 17 Nov 1967; *m* 1992 *Spiros Mouzakitis, of Corfu

  2b *Lucy Christina Dorothy; *b* 17 Feb 1969

3a (cont.) Mrs Lavinia Carlson *m* 2nd 1975 *Hugh Brewis Bailey, MRCS, LRCP, and by him has:

  1b *David Andrew Robert; *b* 1977

4a *Annabel Lee Christine [Mrs Malcolm Valentine, 23 Aspen Way, Cringleford, Norfolk NR4 6UA]; *b* 18 Dec 1945; *m* 1974 *Malcolm Valentine and has:

  1b *Richard William; *b* 1976

  1b *Clare Rosemary; *b* 1978

(2) *Clementine Mabell Kitty [Clementine Lady Beit, Russborough, Blessington, Co Wicklow, Ireland; 137 Beach Rd, Gordon's Bay, CP, S Africa; 2 Little Boltons, London SW10]; *b* posthumously 22 Oct 1915; *m* 20 April 1939 Sir Alfred Lane Beit, 2nd and last Bt (*d* 1994; *see* 1970 edn)

2 DAVID BERTRAM OGILVY FREEMAN-MITFORD, **2nd Baron Redesdale**, JP (Oxon); *b* 13 March 1878; *educ* Radley; Capt Northumberland Fus Boer War 1900–02 (dangerously wounded, Queen's medal, three clasps, King's medal, two clasps), Maj RAF, ADC to GOC 37th Div BEF, WW I 1914–17 (despatches), Memb Ho Lds Select Ctee Peerages in Abeyance 1925; *m* 6 Feb 1904 Sydney (*d* 25 May 1963), er dau of Thomas Gibson Bowles, MP, of Knightsbridge, and *d* 17 March 1958, having had:

(1) Thomas David; *b* 2 Jan 1909; barrister Inner Temple 1932, Maj Queen's Westminster Regt, 2 ic Devonshire Regt WW II; *d* of wounds recd in action Burma 30 March 1945

(1) Nancy, CBE (1972); *b* 28 Nov 1904; author: *Highland Fling* (1931), *Christmas Pudding* (1932), *Wigs on the Green* (1935), *The Ladies of Alderley* (1938), *The Stanleys of of Alderley* (1939), *Pigeon Pie* (1940), *The Pursuit of Love* (1945), *Love in a Cold Climate* (1949), *The Blessing* (1951), *Madame de Pompadour* (1954), *Noblesse Oblige* (ed with Prof A Ross, also contributor, 1956), *Voltaire in Love* (1957), *The Water Beetle* (1962), *The Sun King* (1966), *Frederick the Great* (1970); *m* 4 Dec 1933 (*divorce* 1958) Hon Peter Murray Rennell Rodd, 2nd surv s of 1st Baron Rennell (*qv*), and *dsp* 30 June 1973

(2) Pamela; *b* 25 Nov 1907; *m* 29 Dec 1936 (*divorce* 1951) W/Cdr Derek Ainslie Jackson, OBE, DFC, AFCM, DSc, FRS, MA, RAFVR, s of Sir Charles James Jackson

(3) *Diana [The Hon Lady Mosley, Temple de la Gloire, 91400 Orsay, France]; *b* 17 June 1910; author: *A Life of Contrasts* (1977), *The Duchess of Windsor, Loved Ones, The Writings of Rebecca West*; *m* 1st 30 Jan 1929 (*divorce* 1934) 2nd Baron Moyne (*qv*) and has issue; *m* 2nd in Germany 6 Oct 1936 Sir Oswald Ernald Mosley, 6th Bt (*see* REDESDALE, B), and has further issue

(4) Unity Valkyrie; *b* 8 Aug 1914; *d* unm 28 May 1948 following a 1939 suicide attempt in the English Garden, Berlin

(5) Jessica Lucy; *b* 11 Sept 1917; author *Hons and Rebels* (1960), *The American Way of Death* (1963), *The Trial of Dr Spock* (1969), *Kind and Usual Punishment* (1974), *The American Prison Business* (1975), *A Fine Old Conflict* (1977), *The Making of a Muckraker* (1979), *Faces of Philip: a memoir of Philip Toynbee* (1984), *Grace Had an English Heart: the story of Grace Darling, heroine and Victorian superstar* (1988), *The American Way of Birth* (1992); *m* 1st 18 May 1937 P/O Esmond Marcus David Romilly, RCAF (*ka* Nov 1941), yr s of Col Bertram Henry Samuel Romilly, DSO, and had:

  1a *Anne Constancia [Mrs Edwin Weber, 979 Eden Ave SE, Atlanta, GA 30316, USA]; *b* 1941; *m* 1st 1964 (*divorce* 1975) James Rufus Firman and has:

    1b *James Robert Lumumba; *b* 1967

    2b *Chaka Esmond Fanon; *b* 1970

  1a (cont.) Mrs Anne Firman *m* 2nd 1980 *Edwin Terence Weber

(5) (cont.) The Hon Mrs Romilly *m* 2nd 8 June 1943 *Robert Edward Treuhaft, s of Albin Treuhaft, of New York, and *d* 1996, leaving by him:

  1a [Benjamin Treuhaft, Piano Shop, 2005 Stuart St, Berkeley, CA 94703, USA]; *b* 1947

(6) *Deborah Vivien [Her Grace The Duchess of Devonshire, Chatsworth, Bakewell, Derbyshire DE45 1PP; 4 Chesterfield St, London W1X 7HG]; *b* 31 March 1920; author: *The House: a portrait of Chatsworth* (1982), *The Estate: a view from Chatsworth* (1990), *Farm Animals* (1990), *Treasures of Chatsworth* (1990); *m* 19 April 1941 *11th Duke of Devonshire (*qv*) and has issue

3 BERTRAM THOMAS CARLYLE OGILVY FREEMAN-MITFORD, **3rd Baron Redesdale**, DSO, JP, DL; *b* 2 June 1880; Naval Attaché Copenhagen 1919–22, Capt RN, served WWs I (despatches) and II, cmdg 6th Bn Oxon HG, High Sheriff Oxon 1935, Croix de Guerre, Silver Medal Mil Valour Italy, Roy Humane Soc Bronze Medal; *m* 24 Sept 1925 Mary Margaret Dorothy (*d* 21 June 1967), only child of Thomas Cordes, JP, DL, of Silwood Park, Ascot, and *dsp* 24 Dec 1962

4 JOHN POWER BERTRAM OGILVY FREEMAN-MITFORD, **4th Baron Redesdale**; *b* 31 Jan 1885; Lt 1st Life Gds (Special Res), ADC and Staff Capt WW II 1942–45; *m* 5 Jan 1914 (*annulled* 1914) Marie Anne, only child of Friedrich Viktor von Friedlandler-Fuld, of Berlin, and *dsp* 31 Dec 1963

5 (Ernest) Rupert Bertram Ogilvy; *b* 3 Sept 1895; Sub-Lt RNVR WW I; *m* 1 Aug 1931 Flora (*d* 20 Dec 1981), yr dau of Cdr Gerald Talbot Napier, RN, and widow of Henry Lane Eno, of Bar Harbor, Maine, and *d* 7 Aug 1939, leaving:

(1) CLEMENT NAPIER BERTRAM, **5th Baron**

1 Frances Georgiana; *b* 20 Nov 1875; *m* 30 April 1907 Lt-Col Alexander Horace Cyril Kearsey, DSO, OBE, 10th Hus (*d* 8 Oct 1967), s of Francis Kearsey, of Burstow Hall, Horley, Sussex, and *d* 7 Oct 1951, leaving issue

2 Iris Elizabeth; *b* 28 Feb 1879; *d* unm 11 Sept 1966

3 Joan; *b* 17 Oct 1887; *m* 29 Aug 1907 Denis Herbert Farrer (*d* 8 Feb 1945), of Brayfield, Bucks, T/Capt Northants Regt, yr surv s of Rev Frederick Farrer, of Brayfield, Rector Bourton-on-the-Hill, Glos, and *d* 19 Dec 1976, leaving issue

4 Daphne H M; *b* 3 Sept 1895; *m* 27 Feb 1919 1st Baron Denham (*qv*) and *d* April 1996, leaving issue

The 4th BARON's n,

CLEMENT NAPIER BERTRAM MITFORD, **5th Baron Redesdale**; *b* 28 Oct 1932; *educ* Eton; served Black Watch 1951, KAR Kenya and Uganda 1952, 3rd (K) Bn Malaya 1953, associate dir Erwin Wasey (Advertising) 1960–64, Pres Guild Cleaners and Launderers 1968–70, Roy Soc St George 1975–79 and Br Direct Mail Mktg Assoc 1976–91, V-Pres Chase Manhattan Bank, dir Heron Books; *m* 26 July 1958 *Sarah Georgina Cranstoun [The Rt Hon the Lady Redesdale, 2 St Mark's Sq, London NW1 7TP], yr dau of Brig Alston Cranstoun Todd, OBE, and *d* 1991, having had:

1 RUPERT BERTRAM MITFORD, **6th and present Baron Redesdale**

1 *Emma [The Hon Mrs Wady, Green Batt Ho, The Pinfold, Alnwick, Northumberland]; *b* 27 June 1959; *m* 1985 *George Frederick Wady, yr s of George Wady, of Frinton-on-Sea, Essex, and has:

  (1) *Alexander Bertram; *b* 1989

  (1) *Philippa Bryony; *b* 1992

2 *Tessa [The Hon Mrs Priestman, 19 Pembridge Mews, London W11 3EQ]; *b* 18 Aug 1960; *m* 1990 *Paul Dominic Priestman, yr s of Martin Priestman, of Great Gransden, Cambs

3 (Georgina) Kathryn Mercia; *b* 5 Nov 1961; *d* 1985

4 *Victoria Louise [The Hon Mrs Padgett, 2 St Mark's Sq, London NW1 7TP]; *b* 5 Nov 1962; *m* 1988 *Patrick James Padgett, yr s of James Padgett, of Asheville, NC

5 *Henrietta Jane; *b* 4 Aug 1965

6 *Georgina Clementine; *b* 18 Sept 1968

REDMAYNE

Arms: Gules two chevronels between three cushions ermine, tasselled or, a bordure engrailed argent. **Crest:** In front of a cushion fesswise as in the arms a horse's head argent, maned gules.
Motto: Without blood no victory.
Creation: Bt. (UK) 29 Dec 1964.

SIR NICHOLAS JOHN REDMAYNE, **2ND BT**, of Rushcliffe, Co Nottingham [The Hon Sir Nicholas Redmayne Bt, Walcote Lodge, Walcote, Leics LE17 4JR]; *b* 1 Feb 1938; *s f* 1983; *educ* Radley and RMA Sandhurst; Gren Gds 1958–62, Grieveson Grant and Kleinwort Benson 1963–96; *m* 1st Sept 1963 (*divorce* 1976) Ann (*d* 1985), dau of Frank Saunders, of Kineton, Warwicks, and had:

1 +GILES MARTIN; *b* 1 Dec 1968; *m* 7 July 1994 *Claire O'Halloran

1 *Camilla Jane; *b* 1 Aug 1966; *m* 1st 1989 (*divorce* 1991) Julian Howard Trevor Beach; *m* 2nd 30 March 1996 *Kevin Peacock and by him has:

  (1) *Olivia; *b* 7 Sept 1996

Sir NICHOLAS *m* 2nd 25 May 1978 *Mrs Christine Diane Wood Hewitt, dau of Thomas Wood Fazakerley

Lineage: GEORGE TUNSTAL REDMAYNE, of Great Stoatley, Haslemere, Surrey; *b* Dec 1840; *educ* Tonbridge; architect; *m* 1870 Katharine (*d* 1908), dau of Alfred Waterhouse, of White Knight's Pk, Berks, and sis of Alfred Waterhouse the architect, and *d* 1912, leaving, with an er s (Martin, of California, *b* 1872, *educ* Fettes and Trin Coll Oxford, *d* 1938):

LEONARD REDMAYNE, of Flawborough, Notts; *b* April 1877; *educ* Fettes; civil engr and farmer; *m* June 1903 Mildred (*d* 1955), dau of Edward Jackson, of Charterhouse Sq, London EC, and *d* April 1952, leaving:

1 *Geoffrey Brian [Geoffrey Redmayne Esq, 11 St Thomas Pk, Lymington, Hants SO41 9NF]; *b* Aug 1906; *educ* Marlborough; *m* 1934 *Doreen Ellen, dau of Reginald Dowling, of Newark, Notts, and has:

  (1) *Richard Hugh [Richard Redmayne Esq, Old House, Church Rd, Aylmerton, Norfolk]; *b* 1944; *educ* Marlborough and Trin Hall Cambridge (BA 1967); *m* 3 Sept 1966 *Elsa Harriet, dau of Rev John Bagley, of Ely, Cambs, and has:

    1a *Oliver Stephen Tunstall; *b* 30 April 1968

    2a *Benjamin Hugh; *b* 2 Aug 1969

    1a *Hannah Elizabeth; *b* 14 June 1973

(1) *Diana [Mrs Harold Docherty, Great Hormead Dane, nr Buntingford, Herts SG9 0NT]; *b* 15 July 1935; LRAM; *m* 6 Dec 1958 *Harold Ian Doherty, FCA, and has:

  1a *James Edward; *b* 1 June 1960

  2a *Michael Ian; *b* 10 March 1962

  3a *Richard Peter Harold; *b* 12 April 1970

(2) *Dawn Hilary [Mrs John Thompson, Tichbourne Cottage, 17 Queen's Rd, Lyndhurst, Hants SO43 7BR]; *m* 6 Sept 1958 *John Buckner Thompson, s of Lt-Col B E Thompson, of Andover, and has:

  1a *Timothy John; *b* 5 March 1964

  2a *Patrick Dowling; *b* 5 Jan 1968

  3a *Michael Thomas Redmayne; *b* 24 April 1970

  1a *Claudia Rose; *b* 4 Oct 1962

2 MARTIN (Sir), **1st Bt**

3 *John (Rev), OBE (1945), TD (1946) [The Rev John Redmayne OBE TD, Brackendene, Beechwood Ave, Oatlands, Surrey]; *b* 12 June 1912; *educ* Marlborough and Birmingham U; Deacon 1949, Priest 1950; *m* 16 Sept 1940 *Rosemary Stewart, dau of Col Richard Stephen Murray-White, CBE, DSO, TD, of Johannesburg, and has had:

  (1) *Roderick John; *b* 25 July 1945; *educ* Bloxham, Imp Coll Sci and Tech, and London U (BSc, ACGI); *m* 7 Sept 1968 *Doreen E, dau of Robert Backhouse, of Orpington, Kent

  (1) *Catherine; *b* 5 May 1947

  (2) Joanna; *b* 5 July 1949; *d* 19 April 1955

  (3) *Caroline Mary; *b* 19 April 1954

  (4) *Philippa; *b* 29 Aug 1957

1 *Dorothy; *b* April 1904

2 *Valentine [Mrs William Aylwin, Orchard House, Lamarsh, Suffolk]; *m* 16 Sept 1940 *Brig William Harry Aylwin, s of G/Capt W E Aylwin, of London, and has had a s (deceased) and dau

3 *Katharine; *b* March 1916

The 2nd s,

Sir Martin Redmayne, 1st Bt, and BARON REDMAYNE (LP), of Rushcliffe, Co Nottingham (both UK), so *cr* 29 Dec 1964 and 10 June 1966 respectively, DSO (1944), TD (1952), PC (1959); *b* 16 Nov 1910; *educ* Radley; WW II: cmded 14th Bn Sherwood Foresters Italy 1943, 66th Inf Bde 1944–45, Hon Brig 1945; MP (C) Rushcliffe 1950, Govt Whip 1951, Ld Commr Treasury 1953–59, Dep Govt Ch Whip 1955–9, Parly Sec Treasury and Govt Ch Whip 1959–64, dir: House of Fraser, Harrods and Boots; *m* 6 May 1932 Anne, dau of John Griffiths, of Mountain Ash, S Wales, and *d* 28 April 1983, leaving:

Sir NICHOLAS JOHN REDMAYNE, **2nd and present Bt**

REDWOOD

Arms: Paly of six or and ermine a lion rampant sable, on a chief azure an embattled gateway proper, between two mullets of six points of the first. **Crest:** A rock, therefrom an eagle rising proper, charged on each wing with a mullet of six points, in the beak a staff raguly or. **Motto:** *Lumen sevimus antique* ('We have disseminated knowledge from of old'). **Creation:** Bt. (UK) 24 June 1911.

SIR PETER BOVERTON REDWOOD, 3RD BT, of Avenue Rd, St Marylebone [Col Sir Peter Redwood Bt, c/o Nat West Bank, 80 Market Place, Warminster, Wilts BA12 9AW]; *b* 1 Dec 1937; *s f* 1974; *educ* Gordonstoun; Lt Seaforth Highrs 1956–58, Regular Offr KOSB 1959–78 (ret as Col), consultant SERCO-IAL Ltd (late dir), memb Roy Co Archers, Liveryman Goldsmiths' Co; *m* 22 Aug 1964 *Gillian Waddington, only dau of John Lee Waddington Wood, of Kenya, and has:

  1 *Anna Kathryn; *b* 6 Jan 1967; *m* 1993 *Capt Patrick M Thomson, est s of Brig Michael Thomson, of Trouville, France

  2 *Colina Margaret Charlotte; *b* 8 Feb 1969

  3 *Gaynor Elizabeth; *b* 1972

Lineage: JOHN REDWOOD, of Exeter; baker; *d* 1584, having had, with several daus:

1 Robert; fndr Bristol Library 1615; *m* 1st Anne Farrar (*dsp* 1607), widow of John Carr, fndr Queen Elizabeth's Hosp; *m* 2nd Katheryn James (*d* 1615), widow of Richard Rogers, and *dsp* 1630

2 Richard, of Bristol; *b* 1561; had four sons and three daus

3 Lawrence, of Yeovil; *b* 1566; had issue

4 Hugh, of Exeter; *b* 1568; *d* 1624, having had three sons and two daus

5 Nicholas, of Exeter; *b* 1575; *d* 1619, leaving issue

A yr gs of JOHN REDWOOD by one of his five sons,

  WILLIAM REDWOOD, of Bristol; feltmaker; *m* 1644 Anne Lane and *d* 1668, having had, with an est s (William; *b* 1646, Bristol burgess), two yst sons (Jacob, *b* 1662, *d* 1669; Abraham, ship's master in Jamaica trade; *m* Mehetabel Langford, of Antigua (*d* 1715), and was f of Abraham, fndr Redwood Library, Newport, RI, 1747) and several daus, a 2nd s:

ISAAC REDWOOD; *b* 1652; *m* 1679 Elizabeth Whitwood and had, with other issue, including an er s (James, *b* 1680):

ISAAC REDWOOD, of Bristol and Cowbridge, Glam; *b c* 1690; hatter, bailiff Cowbridge 1748–49; *m* Mary Walters, of Batsleys (*d* 1750), and *d* 1765, having had, with other issue, including two er sons (Rev Charles, *b* 1719, *educ* Jesus Coll Oxford, Curate Cowbridge and Llanbethian 1736; Robert):

ISAAC REDWOOD, of Cowbridge; *b* 1725; *m* 9 April 1752 Jennet Lewis, of Bridgend, Glam (*d* 12 April 1783), and *d* 23 Dec 1775, having had, with an er s (Isaac, *bapt* 1753) and a dau:

THEOPHILUS REDWOOD, of Boverton, Llantwit Major, Glamorgan; *bapt* 23 March 1760; tanner, Quaker, patron of Iolo Morganwg, Bard of Glamorgan; *m* 1st Mary Ann Williams, of Cardiff (*d* 1796), and had, with several daus:

  1 Thomas Lewis; *b* and *d* 1787

  2 John; *b* and *d* 1787

  3 Thomas; *b* 1789; emigrated to America

  4 Isaac, of Neath; *b* 1792; leather mfr, Quaker; *m* 1826 Lydia (*d* 1863), sis of Joseph Tregellis Price, of Neath Abbey, ironmaster, and *dsp* 1873

  5 William, of Neath; *b* 1796; *m* Mary Howell, n of Dr Howell, of Clifton, and had two daus

THEOPHILUS REDWOOD *m* 2nd 6 Aug 1801 Elizabeth (*d* 10 Oct 1846), dau of Thomas Holland, of Penmark, Glam, n and coheir of William Wathen, of Boverton, and widow of Evans Jones, of Boverton and Fonmon, Glam, and *d* 10 Jan 1840, having by her had, with a dau:

  6 Charles; *b* 1802; lawyer, friend of Thomas Carlyle; *d* 1854

  7 THEOPHILUS

  8 Lewis, of The Lawn, Rhymney, Mon; *b* 15 Sept 1808; MRCSE; *m* 26 Oct 1836 Anna Maria, dau of Joseph Hall, and had two sons and two daus

The 7th s,

  THEOPHILUS REDWOOD, of Boverton and Montague St, London; *b* 9 April 1806; Hon PhD U of Geissen, fndr memb Pharmaceutical Soc (Emeritus Prof 1885), Prof Sch Pharmacy 1842, Librarian and Dir Chemical Laboratories to Sch of Pharmacy, ed *Pereira's Selecta e Praescriptus*, published supplement to *Pharmacopoeia* 1847–48–57, ed *British Pharmacopoeia* 1867, Public Analyst 1875–92, Pres Soc Public Analysts, Sec Cavendish Soc, Sec and Treas Chemical Soc; *m* 16 July 1845 Charlotte Elizabeth (*d* 17 Sept 1868), dau of Thomas Newborn Robert Morson, of Queen's Sq, London, and Hornsey, Middx, and *d* 5 March 1892, leaving:

  1 (THOMAS) BOVERTON (Sir), **1st Bt**

  2 Theophilus Horne; *b* 31 July 1849; *m* 18 June 1885 Emily Ann, dau of John Clark, of London, and *d* 31 March 1909, leaving issue

  3 George Herbert; *b* 17 Dec 1852; *m* 2 Oct 1886 Catherine Julia (*d* 21 Oct 1937), dau of Charles Shaw, of Kensington, and *d* 26 Jan 1934, leaving issue

  4 Charles Lewis; *b* 12 Jan 1855; *m* 24 June 1885 Olivia Elizabeth, dau of John Robert Lys, of Jersey, and Pretoria, S Africa, and *d* 24 Sept 1907, leaving issue

  5 Robert; *b* 1 Oct 1856; *m* 4 Oct 1888 Florence (*d* 17 Dec 1922), dau of William Sims Horner, of Fern Hill, Walthamstow, Essex, and had issue

  6 Isaac; *b* 16 Dec 1863; *m* 15 Sept 1892 his er bro's sis-in-law Katherine, dau of William Sims Horner, and *d* 5 April 1910, leaving issue

  1 Mary Ann; *b* 20 Nov 1847; *d* 16 June 1913

  2 Charlotte Elizabeth Morson; *b* 7 Oct 1858; *m* 5 May 1896 Rev William Griffiths Roach, of Llantwit Major, and had issue

The est s,

  Sir (Thomas) Boverton Redwood, 1st Bt (UK), so *cr* 24 June 1911, of Avenue Rd, St Marylebone; *b* 26 April 1846; chemist, engr, advsr on petroleum to Admlty and other Govt Depts, FRS Edin, AInstME, Hon DSc Ohio U, Fell Inst Chemistry and Chemical, Geological and RGS, Pres Soc Chemical Industry 1907–08, Pres Inst Engrs 1913–14 and Inst Petroleum Technologists 1914–15, memb Cncl RSA, author: *Petroleum and its Products* and other works, Chev Order Leopold, ktd 1905; *m* 17 April 1873 Mary Elizabeth (*d* 19 April 1937), er dau of Frederick Letchford, of Walthamstow, Essex, and *d* 4 June 1919, having had:

  1 Bernard Boverton; *b* 21 Nov 1874; *educ* St Peter's Coll Cambridge (BA); *m* 25 March 1905 Gladys Dora (*m* 2nd 25 Dec 1913 William Esmond Peart Robinson, s of William Peart Robinson, of Hyning, Lancs and *d* 25 Feb 1965), dau of William Joseph Pattinson Sherwen of Hensingham, Cumberland, and *dvp* 28 Sept 1911, leaving:

    (1) THOMAS BOVERTON (Sir), **2nd Bt**

    (1) *Patricia Boverton [Mrs Harold Boverton Box, Spring Ducks, Horton Rd, Ashley Heath, Hants BH24 2EU]; *b* 30 March 1910; *m* 1965 Harold Box, s of James Harold Box, of Bognor Regis

  1 Ethel; *b* 5 June 1876; *d* unm 8 Feb 1927

  2 Gwenifryd Gwladys; *b* 8 April 1890

The 1st Bt's gs,

  Sir Thomas Boverton Redwood, 2nd Bt, TD; *b* 15 Oct 1906; *educ* Harrow; served 45th W Country Div, 1st Airborne Div and War Office, Maj RE WW II; *m* 1st 23 Sept 1933 (*divorce* 1943) Ruth Mary, dau of Rev John Henry David Creighton, and had:

  1 Sir PETER BOVERTON REDWOOD, **3rd and present Bt**

Sir Thomas m 2nd 19 Aug 1944 *Ursula, dau of Rev Herbert Percy Hale, and d 11 April 1974, having by her had:

  2 Guy Boverton; b 9, d 12 March 1964

  3 +Robert Boverton; b 24 June 1953; educ Truro Cathedral Sch; m 1978 *Mary Elizabeth Wright and has:

    (1) +James Boverton; b 2 Oct 1985

    (1) *Morwenna Anne Carlisle; b 1982

  4 +Charles Boverton; b 13 March 1956; educ Truro Cathedral Sch

  1 *Anne Boverton; b 28 March 1947; m 21 Dec 1968 *James Embury, yst s of Frederick George Embury, of N Toronto, Canada, and has:

    (1) *Tristan James; b 1971

    (2) *Bartholomew Boverton; b 1972

REES

Arms: Argent two chevrons ermines between three ravens proper. **Crest:** Upon a chapeau doubled ermines a peacock holding in its beak an oak sprig proper. **Supporters:** Two Bengal tigers rampant, the dexter on a grassy mount, growing therefrom two tea-plant flowers, the sinister on a like mount, growing therefrom as many lotus flowers, all proper. **Motto:** *Si fueris felix multos numerabis amicos* ('If you will be happy you will have numerous friends') **Creation:** B. (LP, UK) 1987.

THE BARON REES, of Goytre, Co Gwent (Peter Wynford Innes Rees, PC (1983), QC (1969)) [The Rt Hon The Lord Rees PC QC, Goytre Hall, Abergavenny, Gwent NP7 9DL; 39 Headfort Place, London SW1X 7DE]; b 9 Dec 1926; educ Stowe and Ch Ch Oxford; Scots Gds 1945–48; barrister 1953, Oxford Circuit; MP (C) Dover 1970–74 and 1983-87 and Dover and Deal 1974–83, PPS to Slr-Gen 1972, Min State Treasury 1979–81 and DTI 1981–83, Ch Sec Treasury 1983–85; memb: Court and Cncl Museum of Wales 1987–96, Museums and Galleries Commn 1988–96; dep chm Leopold Joseph plc; m 1969 *Mrs Anthea Peronelle Wendell, dau of Maj Hugh John Maxwell Hyslop, Argyll and Sutherland Highrs, and formerly w of Maj Jack Wendell, Gren Gds

Lineage: This branch of the West Wales REESes was settled latterly at Dolranog, nr Newport, Pembs, and included:

Rev THOMAS MORGAN REES; b 6 Nov 1850; m 18– Mary (d 1923), dau of Owen James, of Dinas, Pembs, and d 1903, leaving, with other issue:

THOMAS WYNFORD REES, CB (1945), CIE (1931), DSO (1919) and bar, MC, DL (Mon 1955), of Goytre Hall; commnd 1916 125th Napier's Rifles IA, served Mesopotamia and Palestine 1917–18, Waziristan 1920, 1922–24 (despatches, Brevet Lt-Col 1926) and 1930–37, WW II in W Desert, Eritrea and Burma (despatches), cmded 10th, 19th and 4th Indian Divs, ret as Maj-Gen 1947; last Br Col Rajputana Rifles; m 1926 Rosalie, dau of Sir Charles Alexander Innes, KCSI, Govr Burma, and had:

  1 PETER WYNFORD INNES, cr a **Baron**

  1 Rosalie Mary; b 23 June 1929; m Richard Charles Brooman-White (d 16 Jan 1964), of Pennymore Furnace, Argyllshire, MP (C) Rutherglen, Parly U-Sec Scottish Office, and d Aug 1976 leaving:

    (1) *Charles James; b April 1959; m 1st (divorce) Caroline, dau of Col E Farr, of Saughton, Cheshire, and has two sons; m 2nd *Gabrielle Sanchez, of Bogotà, Colombia

    (2) *Alexander Richard; b 1962; m *Miranda Lane and has a s and a dau

REES-MOGG

Arms: Quarterly, 1st and 4th, on a fess pean between six ermine spots, the two exterior in chief and the centre spot in base, surmounted by a crescent gules, a cock or (for MOGG); 2nd and 3rd, gules a chevron engrailed erminois between three swans argent, wings elevated or (for REES). **Crests:** 1 Between two spearheads erect sable a cock proper (for MOGG), 2 A swan argent, wings elevated or, holding in the beak a water-lily slipped proper (for REES). **Motto:** *Curae pii Diis sunt* ('The pious are in the care of the Gods'). **Creation:** B. (LP, UK) 1988.

THE BARON REES-MOGG, of Hinton Blewitt, Co Avon (Sir William Rees-Mogg) [The Rt Hon The Lord Rees-Mogg, The Old Rectory, Hinton Blewitt, Avon; 17 Pall Mall, London SW1Y 5NB]; b 14 July 1928; educ Charterhouse and Balliol Coll Oxford (MA, Pres Union 1951); Visiting Fell Nuffield Coll, Oxford, 1968–72, Hon LLD Bath 1977; High Sheriff Somerset 1978; Financial Times; joined 1952, ch leader writer 1955–60, assist ed 1957–60, Sunday Times: city ed 1960–61, political and ec ed 1961–63, dep ed 1964–67, ed The Times 1967–81; Treas IOJ 1960–63, 1966–68 (Pres 1963–64), V-Chm C Party's Nat Advsy Ctee Political Educn 1961–63, Pres English Assoc 1983–84, dir The Times Ltd 1968–81, Times Newspapers Ltd 1978–81, GEC 1981–97 and Private Bank and Tst Co 1993–, V-Chm Govrs BBC 1981–86; chm Pickering & Chatto 1983–, Internat Business Communications plc 1994– and Sidgwick & Jackson 1985–88, jt ed Strategic Investment newsletter, Washington, DC; Chm Arts Cncl 1982–89, Bdcstg Standards Cncl 1988–93, ktd 1981; author: His Majesty Preserved (1954), Sir Anthony Eden (1956), Reigning Error: the crisis of world inflation (1974), An Humbler Heaven (1977), How to Buy Rare Books (1985), Picnics on Vesuvius: steps toward [sic] the millennium (1992); m 1962 *Gillian Shakespeare, yr dau of Thomas Richard Morris, JP, and has:

  1 *Thomas Fletcher; b 1966; educ Downside; m 4 May 1996 *Modwenna Vivien Hornby, dau of Hon Edward Northcote (see IDDESLEIGH, E), and has:

    (1) *William Robert; b 20 Oct 1996

  2 *Jacob William; b 1969; educ Eton and Trin Coll Oxford; C candidate Fife Centl 1997 gen election; fund manager Lloyd George Management

  1 *Emma Beatrice; b 1962; educ St Hugh's Coll Oxford; m 1990 *David William Hilton BROOKS later CRAIGIE (1990), s of Maj Robin Brooks and Mrs Brian Ford, of London, and has had:

    (1) *Wilfred; b 1994

    (2) Stanley; b and d 1994

    (1) *Maud; b 1991

    (2) *Myfanwy; b 1997

  2 *Charlotte Louise; b 1964; educ Heythrop Coll London

  3 *Annunziata Mary; b 1979

Lineage: RICHARD MOGG, of Farrington Gurney Manor, which he built 1635 and which was held by his descendants till 1930; d 1641, leaving, with other issue:

JOHN MOGG; b 1615; m Mary, dau of John Moore, of Kilmerdon, and d 1677, having had, with other issue:

JOHN MOGG, of Farrington Gurney and Ston Easton Minor; b 1650; coal-owner, High Sheriff Somerset 1703; m Dorothy, dau of Edward Hippisley, of Chewton Mendip, and d 1728, leaving:

RICHARD MOGG; b 1690; bought Cholwell House, Somerset (built temp ELIZABETH I) 1726; m Elizabeth, dau of Rev — Turner, of Chewton Mendip, and d 4 Oct 1729, leaving, with three yr sons and a dau:

JOHN MOGG, of Cholwell; b 16 Feb 1722; m Joyce Harris and had, with other issue:

MARY Mogg, of Cholwell; b 24 May 1744; m May 1772 William WOOLDRIDGE, only s of William Wooldridge, of the WOOLDRIDGEs of Dudmaston, Salop, and d 29 Sept 1829, leaving:

MARY Mogg Woolridge, of Cholwell; b 22 Sept 1774; m 12 Aug 1805 Rev John REES later REES-MOGG (roy licence 1805), Preb Tytherington and Chaplain to

DUKE OF CUMBERLAND, s of John Rees, of Wick, Glam, and d 20 March 1846, leaving, with an er s and a dau:

WILLIAM REES-MOGG, of Cholwell, which he demolished 1855 and replaced with a larger house; b 29 April 1815; educ Charterhouse; m 13 July 1847 Ann (d 23 Jan 1892), dau and ultimate heir of William Coxeter James, JP, DL, of Tymsbury, Somerset, and d April 1909, having had, with two yst sons and three daus:

1 William Wooldridge, of Cholwell; b 21 Nov 1848; educ Charterhouse; m 27 Nov 1884 Emily Walcott (d 4 Oct 1938), 3rd dau of Rev Henry Stiles Savory, and d 16 Sept 1913, leaving, with a dau:

(1) Edmund Fletcher, of Cholwell, JP (Somerset 1928); b 11 Nov 1889; educ Charterhouse and Univ Coll Oxford; Lt RASC WW I, Somerset: CC 1937, High Sheriff 1945, CA 1950; m 11 Nov 1920 Beatrice, est dau of Daniel Warren, of Shore Acres, Mamaroneck, NY, and d 12 Dec 1962, leaving:

1a WILLIAM, cr a **Baron**

1a *Elizabeth, JP (Somerset 1963); b 23 Aug 1921; m 17 April 1948 *Peter Breugger, s of Max Wilhelm Breugger, of Mecklenburg, and has:

1b *Anthony; b 20 Jan 1949; educ Bristol GS

2b *Edmund; b 8 May 1951; educ Bristol GS

2 Henry James (Rev); b 31 March 1851; educ Charterhouse and Exeter Coll Oxford; Vicar Midgham, Berks, 1906–26; m 22 Nov 1877 Charlotte Elizabeth Sarah (d 20 Dec 1925), est dau of Henry Newton, of Mount Leinster, Co Carlow, and widow of Capt Thomas John Mitchell, King's Dragoon Gds, and d 30 Sept 1940, having had:

(1) Robert James, DSO; b 4 Sept 1878; Col 18th Roy Irish Regt; m 22 Sept 1913 Evelyn Mary, dau of Sir Arthur Heywood, 3rd Bt (qv), and had issue

(2) Graham Beauchamp Coxeter, OBE (1919); b 10 Sept 1881; educ Haileybury; FRCVS, Vet-Lt-Col RHG, late 1st Life Gds, ret 1936, High Sheriff Warwicks 1941; m 28 June 1922 Kathleen Mary Christina Hamilton, yr sis of 1st Baron Dulverton (qv) and widow of Edward Henry Douty, and d 4 May 1949

REID of Ellon

Arms: Azure a stag's head erased or between two torches inflamed proper, and (honourable augmentation granted 14 June 1911) on a chief gules a lion passant guardant or, armed and langued azure (one of the lions from Roy Arms). **Crest:** A pelican in her nest feeding her young proper. **Supporters:** On either side a royal stag or gorged with a chain proper, suspended therefrom an escutcheon azure charged with the royal crown proper. **Motto:** Nihil amanti durum ('Nothing is hard for one who loves'). **Creation:** Bt. (UK) 28 Aug 1897.

SIR ALEXANDER JAMES REID, 3RD Bt, of Ellon, Aberdeenshire, JP, DL (Cambs) [Sir Alexander Reid Bt JP DL, Lanton Tower, Jedburgh, Roxburghshire TD8 6SU]; b 6 Dec 1932; s f 1972; educ Eton and Magdalene Coll Cambridge; Lt Bn Gordon Highrs 1951–53, served Malaya, Capt 3rd Bn Gordon Highrs (TA) (ret 1964), chm: Ellon Castle Estates 1965–96, Cristina Securities 1970–, Clan Donnachaidh Soc 1994–, Freeman City London 1965, Liveryman Farmers' Co 1965, Chm Govrs Heath Mount Sch Hertford 1976–92; High Sheriff Cambs 1987–88; m 15 Oct 1955 *Michaela Ann, yr dau of Olaf Kier, CBE, of Royston, Herts, and has:

1 +CHARLES EDWARD JAMES [Charles Reid Esq, Larachan House, Spinningdale, Ardgay, Sutherland IV24 3AD]; b 24 June 1956; educ Rannoch and RAC Cirencester

1 *Christina; b 25 April 1958

2 *Jennifer; b 27 Aug 1959; m 1st 1986 (divorce 1991) Stephen J Marsh-Smith, only s of David Marsh-Smith, of Penrhosfeilw, Anglesey; m 2nd 1991 *Nicholas Rory Collins, only s of Bernard Collins, of Bisley, Glos

3 *Alexandra Catherine; b 12 Feb 1965; m 1992 *Charles A Lloyd, only s of John Lloyd, of Tiverton, Devon

Lineage: JOHN REID, of Fortrie, Aberdeenshire; b 26 Jan 1720; m 16 July 1750 Elizabeth Mitchell (d 1786), of Laithers, Aberdeenshire, and d 1775, leaving:

PETER REID, of Muirton, Aberdeenshire; b 6 Jan 1768; m 15 July 1791 Ann (d 21 Dec 1836), 2nd dau of George Lumsden, of Belhelvie, Aberdeenshire, and d 10 May 1795, leaving, with a dau:

JAMES REID, of Muirton; b 6 June 1792; m 28 Dec 1813 Jessie Gray (d 4 April 1866), of Fintray, Aberdeenshire, and d 6 Aug 1862, having had, with an est s, four yst sons and four daus:

JAMES REID, of Ellon, Aberdeenshire; b 18 May 1818; MD; m 28 Dec 1848 Beatrice (d 9 Jan 1912), dau of John Peter, of Canterland, Kincardineshire, and d 26 March 1883, having had, with a yr s (John Peter, of Yokohama, Japan, and Bayswater, b 24 April 1851, m 13 Nov 1881 Mary, est dau of John Peter, of Croyard, Beauly, Inverness-shire, and d 19 Sept 1916, having had issue):

Sir James Reid, 1st Bt (UK), so cr 28 Aug 1897, GCVO, KCB, VD, JP; b 23 Oct 1849; MD Aberdeen U 1875, LLD 1895, FRCO Lond 1892, FRCP I 1900, Physician in Ordinary to TM QUEEN VICTORIA 1889, EDWARD VII 1899–1910 and GEORGE V; m 28 Nov 1899 Hon Susan Baring (d 8 Feb 1961), Maid-of-Honour to HM QUEEN VICTORIA, dau of 1st Baron Revelstoke (qv), and d 28 June 1923, leaving:

1 EDWARD JAMES (Sir), **2nd Bt**

2 (John) Peter Lorne (Sir), GCB (1961, KCB 1957, CB 1946), CVO (1953), DL (E Lothian 1962); b 10 Jan 1903 (HRH PRINCESS LOUISE, DUCHESS OF ARGYLL, stood sponsor); educ RNCs Osborne and Dormount; RN WW II (despatches twice), Ch Staff to C-in-C Portsmouth 1951–53, Flag Offr, 2 ic Mediterranean 1954–55, 3rd Sea Ld, Controller Navy 1956–61, Adml (ret 1961), R-Adml of UK 1962, V-Lt 1964, V-Adml of UK 1966, Pres Br Legion Scotland, dir Richardsons, Westgarth and Co; m 19 April 1933 Jean (d 7 Dec 1971), only dau of Sir Henry Herbert Philip Dundas, 3rd Bt, of Arniston (see 1970 edn), and d 26 Sept 1973, leaving:

(1) +David Lorne Dundas [David Reid Esq, Quinta das Murtas, rua Eduardo Van-Zeller, 2710 Sintra, Portugal]; b 7 Dec 1938; educ Harrow, RMA Sandhurst, Sch of Management, Coll of Aeronautics Cranfield, Berks, and Harvard Business Sch USA (MBA); Lt 15th/19th King's Roy Hus, management consultant Mc Kinsey and Co, Fndr Tstee and Treasurer Shelter 1966–68, Fndr and Chm Dundas Tst; m 1st 20 June 1968 (divorce 1979) Elizabeth, dau of Adam Natt and Mrs Charles Mayne and formerly w of — Wilkinson, and adopted:

*Jacqueline May; b 1956; m 1979 *14th Earl of Northesk (qv) and has issue

*Lorna Victoria; b 1972

(1) (cont.) David Reid m 2nd 1979 *Tedda Ann, dau of Albert Charles Webber, of Litton Cheney, Dorset, and formerly w of James Sholto Arthur Douglas (see MORTON, E), and by her has:

1a +Benjamin James Dundas; b 1983

1a *Leonora Emily Louise; b 1981

(1) *Delia [Lady Montgomery, Kinross House, Kinross]; b 25 July 1935; m 5 April 1956 *Sir Basil Henry David Montgomery, 9th Bt (qv), and has issue

1 Margaret Cecilia; d 8 May 1937

2 Victoria Susan Beatrice; b 1908 (HRH PRINCESS VICTORIA stood sponsor); m 22 April 1935 Leonard St Clair Ingrams, OBE (d 30 Aug 1953), s of Rev William Smith Ingrams, of The Schools, Shrewsbury, and d 23 June 1997, having had:

(1) Peter John; b 1 Feb 1936; educ Shrewsbury and Hertford Coll Oxford (MA, Dip Ed); Lt Coldstream Gds RARO; d 1979

(2) *Richard Reid [Richard Ingrams Esq, Forge House, Aldworth, Reading, Berks]; b 19 Aug 1937; educ Shrewsbury and Univ Coll Oxford; ed Private Eye 1963–86 and The Oldie 1992–; m 24 Nov 1962 (divorce 1993) Mary Joan Morgan and has:

1a *Fred Valentine; b 14 Feb 1964; m 1990 *Sarah Jane Lovett and has:

1b *Otis; b 1990

1a *Margaret (Jubby); b 4 May 1965; m 1990 *David Lionel Ford and has issue (see 1963 edn BRAND, B)

(3) Rupert George; b 16 March 1939; m 1 March 1960 *Baroness Darcy de Knayth (qv) and was k in a car crash 28 Feb 1964, leaving issue

(4) *Leonard Victor, OBE [Leonard Ingrams Esq OBE, Garsington Manor, Oxford]; b 1 Sept 1941; m 19 Sept 1964 *Rosalind Anne, er dau of Antony Ross Moore, CMG, of Brill, Bucks, and has:

1a *Rupert Antony; b 23 Aug 1967

1a *Lucy Sarah; b 3 Dec 1965

2a *Elizabeth; b 9 Feb 1971

3a *Catherine; b 1976

The 1st Bt's er s,

Sir Edward James Reid, 2nd Bt, KBE (1967, OBE 1946); b 20 April 1901 (HM EDWARD VII stood sponsor); Page of Honour to HM GEORGE V 1911–17; educ Eton and King's Coll Cambridge (Browne Medallist 1920, 1921 and 1922, BA 1922, MA 1926); FSA Scot, dir: Bank of Scotland, Baring Bros 1926–66 and Provident Mutual Life Assur Assoc 1938–66 (chm 1963–66), Civil Assist War Office 1940–45, memb London Ctee Hong Kong and Shanghai Banking Corp 1946–66 (dir 1941–46), chm: Br and Chinese Corp Ltd 1946–66, Accepting Houses Ctee 1946–66, Chm Dirs Roy Caledonian Schs Bushey 1947–66 and Br Banking Ctee for German Affrs 1948–65, Pres Inst Bankers 1962–64 and Overseas Bankers' Club 1964–65, Hon Pres Clan Donnachaidh Soc, Hon V-Pres Liverpool Sch Tropical Medicine, Order Rising Sun Japan 2nd Cl; m 18 Jan 1930 *Tatiana [Tatiana Lady Reid, 16 Buckingham Terrace, Edinburgh EH4 3AD], dau of Col Alexandre Fenoult, late Russian Imperial Gd, and d 13 Feb 1972, leaving:

1 Sir ALEXANDER JAMES REID, **3rd and present Bt**

1 Susan Isobel; b 2 Dec 1930; m 27 Nov 1953 Douglas Stanley Charles Weedon (d 1 March 1997), only s of Stanley Weedon, of Winton Croft, Wimborne, Dorset, and d 2 April 1976, leaving:

(1) Patricia Anne; b 24 Oct 1954; d 17 June 1983

(2) *Sarah Jane; b 24 Nov 1958

(3) *Joanna Lesley; b 19 May 1960

(4) *Nicola Mary; b 10 Jan 1962

(5) *Samantha Susan; b 8 Jan 1965

REID of Springburn

Arms: Argent a demi-eagle, wings expanded, in chief an ancient handbell between a mullet in the dexter and a cross moline in the sinister, all sable. **Crest:** A demi-eagle, wings expanded, sable. **Motto:** *Fortitudine et labore* ('By fortitude and labour'). **Creation:** Bt. (UK) 26 Jan 1922.

SIR HUGH REID, 3RD BT, of Springburn, Co Glasgow, and Kilmaurs, Co Ayr [Sir Hugh Reid Bt, Caheronaun Park, Loughrea, Co Galway, Ireland]; *b* 27 Nov 1933; *s* f 1971; *educ* Loretto

Lineage: JOHN REID, of Silverwood, Kilmarnock, Ayrshire; *m* 23 Feb 1748 Elizabeth, dau of William Gilmore, of Kiln, Fenwick, Ayrshire, and had a 5th s:

JAMES REID, of Sanquhar, St Quivox, Ayrshire; *b* 21 Jan 1758; *m* 8 Nov 1793 Susanna (*d* 26 May 1849 aged 79), yr dau of David Brown, of Riccarton, Ayrshire, and *d* 23 Jan 1832, having had, with an est s (David, *b* 1797, *d* 27 Feb 1835), four yst sons (John, *b* 1805, *d* at sea 1825; A son, *b* and *d* 1807; Hugh, *b* 1809, *m* 26 June 1862 Mary Manson and *d* 7 July 1872; Thomas, *b* 1810, *d* 27 May 1829) and three daus (Jane, *b* 1794, *m* 1826 William Crawford and *d* 3 Aug 1833; Margaret, *b* 29 July 1801, *m* 1821 John Wallace and had issue; Ann, *b* 3 Jan 1813, *m* 1833 John Loudon and *d* 21 Sept 1834) a 2nd s:

WILLIAM REID, of Kilmaurs; *b* 1800; *m* 1821 Mary (*d* 27 Feb 1851 aged 54), 3rd dau of Hugh Miller, of Kilmaurs, and *d* 13 Feb 1848, leaving, with two yr sons (Hugh, *b* 31 Aug 1827, *d* Australia 6 Nov 1860; John, *b* 17 Aug 1833, *m* Margaret Bruce and *d* 14 Jan 1901, leaving a s John, *b* 1875) and five daus (Jane, *b* 9 Jan 1822; Susanna, *b* 20 March 1825, *m* Robert Reid and *d* Sydney, NSW, 9 Nov 1916; Mary, *b* 5 Oct 1831, *m* 1st William Miller and had issue, *m* 2nd — Rooke and *d* Sydney 24 Aug 1920, leaving further issue; Margaret, *b* 8 May 1835; Ann, *b* 12 April 1837, *d* Australia 1899):

JAMES REID, JP (Lanarks and Perths), of Auchterarder, Perths; *b* 8 Sept 1823; MInstCE, Pres Inst Engrs and Shipbuilders Scotland 1882–84, Ld Dean of Guild Glasgow 1893–94, Pres Roy Inst Fine Arts Glasgow; *m* 1st 1 Jan 1851 Margaret Ann (*d* 28 Aug 1881), 2nd dau of James Scott, of Greenock, by his 2nd w Elizabeth Thomson, and had, with three s (*d* in infancy):

1 James; *b* 29 Jan 1858; *d* in a shooting accident 10 Nov 1882
2 HUGH (Sir), **1st Bt**
3 John (Sir), KBE (1925), JP (Glasgow and Bute), DL, of Ardencraig, Bute; *b* 28 Oct 1861; Dir: Glasgow Chamber Commerce, Glasgow Roy Infirmary, Scottish Labour Colony Assoc, Pres Glasgow YMCA, V-Pres Scottish Hosp for Limbless Soldiers and Sailors, Deacon Convenor Trades House Glasgow 1921–22, ktd 1918; *m* 12 Oct 1898 Annie Gourlay (*d* 19 April 1934), dau of Henry Shaw Macpherson, JP, and *d* 25 Jan 1933, leaving:
  (1) *Ian Macpherson; *b* 27 June 1902; *educ* Glasgow Acad and Univ Coll Oxford
  (1) *Elizabeth Margaret [Mrs Cecil Salvesen, Saetra Ho, Banchory, Kincardineshire]; *b* 4 June 1900; *m* 8 June 1927 Cecil Gabriel Adolph Salvesen (*d* 3 Nov 1985), 3rd s of George Adolph Stevenson Salvesen, of Edinburgh, and has issue
4 Andrew Thomson, of Auchterarder, VD, JP (Perths and Glasgow), DL Glasgow; *b* 16 July 1863; *educ* Loretto; Lt-Col, MInstCE, memb Roy Co Archers; *d* unm 16 Sept 1940
5 Walter Montgomerie Neilson; *b* 28 Aug 1865; *educ* Loretto; *m* 10 Feb 1906 Maude Ada Mary, dau of Col Joseph Sykes, MD, IMS, and *d* 12 Nov 1933, leaving:
  (1) Walter Joseph; *b* 27 May 1911; *m* 1940 *Patricia Howe and *d* 18 March 1991, leaving:
    1a *James Hugh; *b* 1946
    2a *George Walter; *b* 1948
    3a *Andrew; *b* 1954
  (1) Heather; *b* 16 Nov 1909; *m* 24 Feb 1938 *Noel le Maistre, of Jersey, and *d* 2 June 1988, leaving:
    1a *Ian William; *m* 30 Sept 1967 *Sandra, dau of Maj R G Whitworth
    1a *Janine
6 William; *b* 24 Sept 1867; *d* 31 May 1871

7 Edward Thomas Scott (Rt Rev); *b* 12 Dec 1871; *educ* Fettes and Glasgow U (MA, DD); FSA Scot, Fell Scottish Ecclesiological Soc, Curate Old St Paul's Edinburgh 1897–1900 and St Mary's Cathedral Edinburgh 1900–01, Chaplain 1901–03, Rector St Cuthbert's Hawick 1903–10, CF Stobs 1905–10, Rector St Bride's Glasgow 1910–21, Dean Glasgow and Galloway 1920–21, Bp Glasgow and Galloway 1921–31, Bp St Andrews, Dunkeld and Dunblane 1931–38; *m* 4 Oct 1899 Ethel Shaw (*d* 23 May 1946), dau of Henry Shaw Macpherson, JP, and *d* 27 July 1938, leaving:
  (1) Henry Edward (Rev Canon); *b* 20 Aug 1900; BA; *d* unm 8 Aug 1970
  (2) Eric Charles Scott, OBE; *b* 20 June 1904; BA; *d* unm 28 Aug 1977
  (3) Colin Scott; *b* 11 Sept 1911; *d* unm 4 July 1985
  (1) Ann; *b* 11 Nov 1907; *m* 5 Sept 1933 Ronald Scott-Dempster BL, WS, and *d* 31 Jan 1995, leaving issue
  (2) Nora Margaret; *b* 11 Sept 1911; *d* unm 30 April 1986
1 Elizabeth; *b* 4 May 1856; *d* unm 20 Aug 1912

JAMES REID *m* 2nd 6 June 1886 Charlotte (*d* 16 June 1919), yst dau of John Geddes, of Glass, Aberdeenshire, and sis of Sir William Duguid Geddes, DL, LLD, Pncpl and V-Chllr Aberdeen U, and *d* 23 June 1894

His 2nd s here noticed,

Sir Hugh Reid, 1st Bt (UK), so *cr* 26 Jan 1922, CBE, VD, JP, DL; *b* 9 Feb 1860; Lt-Col, Ld Dean of Guild Glasgow 1916–18, Brig Roy Co Archers, Pres Roy Glasgow Inst Fine Arts 1925–29, memb Bd Tstees Nat Library Scotland, CStJ, MInstCE, LLD Glasgow 1919, Freedom of Glasgow 1917, chm and md N Br Locomotive Co; *m* 8 Aug 1888 Marion Maclune (*d* 7 Dec 1913), yst dau of John Bell, of Craigview, Prestwick, Ayrshire, by his 2nd w Magdalene McAlister Shiels, and *d* 7 July 1935, having had:
1 James; *b* 27 July 1889; *educ* Trin Coll Glenalmond and Trin Coll Cambridge (BA); Capt 10th Bn HLI WW I (despatches); *ka* Battle of Loos 25 Sept 1915
2 DOUGLAS NEILSON (Sir), **2nd Bt**
3 George Hugh Neilson, TD; *b* 30 Dec 1901; *educ* Fettes; Maj 5th/8th Bn The Cameronians (TA) WW II, memb Roy Co Archers; *m* 9 March 1950 Madeleine Graburn (*d* 4 May 1990), 2nd dau of Maurice Wells Bigelow, of Boston, USA, and widow of Capt T Elliott Baird, RA (TA), of Glasgow, and *dsp* 19 April 1961
1 Madeline Constance Maud; *b* 27 July 1892; *m* 10 Feb 1915 Lt Col William Lilburn of Coull, JP, DL, 1st Bn HLI (*d* 31 March 1958), 3rd s of James Lilburn, JP, of Glenora, Renfrewshire, and *d* 27 Nov 1983, having had:
  (1) *Alistair James, of Coull [Alistair Lilburn of Coull, Mains of Coull, Aboyne, Aberdeenshire AB34 4TS]; *b* 15 Dec 1919; *educ* Canford and Faraday Ho; BSc, CEng, MIEE, Lt RNVR WW II (POW 1942–45), Chm NE Regn Roy Scottish Forestry Soc 1961–67, Sec NE Regn Scottish Woodland Owners Assoc, Freeman Berwick-on-Tweed 1947; *m* 10 Aug 1949 *Joan Elizabeth, dau of Kenneth Robert Sutherland, of Wairarapa, NZ, and has:
    1a *James Hugh [James Lilburn Yr. of Coull, Coull House, by Aboyne, Aberdeenshire]; *b* 3 June 1950; *educ* Cokethorpe; Freeman Berwick-on-Tweed; *m* 1st 4 Sept 1973 (*divorce* 1983) Claude Corinne Faure Geors, of Paris; *m* 2nd 23 March 1985 *Irene, dau of George Hanson, and by her has:
      1b *Lewis Alastair James; *b* 18 Feb 1987
      1b *Lucy Alexandra; *b* 3 Oct 1985
      2b *Amy Jane (twin); *b* 1992
      3b *Robyn Kerr (twin); *b* 1992
    1a *Catherine Jane [Mrs Peter Newman, Coryton Manor, Okehampton, Devon]; *b* 18 July 1953; *m* 19 Sept 1981 *Peter Thomas Lydston Newman, s of Thomas Lydston Newman, of Coryton, Devon (*see* NEWMAN, Bt, of Mamhead) and has:
      1b *Rupert Thomas Lydston; *b* 10 April 1984
      2b *William Alastair; *b* 2 Oct 1988
      1b *Harriet Joan; *b* 27 March 1986
  (2) Hugh Neilson, MC; *b* 30 June 1922; *educ* Canford and Pembroke Coll Cambridge; Lt 1st Bn Glasgow Highrs (HLI) WW II; *ka* 19 April 1945
  (3) *Ian Robertson [Ian Lilburn Esq, 13 Ovington Gdns, London SW3 1LE]; *b* 2 June 1927; *educ* Loretto and Pembroke Coll Cambridge; FSA (Scot), FRSA, FRGS, Freeman Berwick-on-Tweed 1949

The 1st Bt's 2nd s,
Sir Douglas Neilson Reid, 2nd Bt, JP (Ross and Cromarty 1934); *b* 12 Feb 1898; *educ* Loretto and Clare Coll Cambridge; Lt HLI, RFC and RAF WW I 1916–18, F/O RAFVR WW II 1939–41, memb Roy Co Archers; *m* 2 June 1926 Margaret Brighton Young (*d* Feb 1992), dau of Robert Young Maxtone, MBE, JP, of Tighnamara, Campbeltown, Argyll, and *d* 31 Aug 1971, leaving:
1 Sir HUGH REID, **3rd and present Bt**
1 *Joan Murray [Mrs John Quinn, Caheronaun, Loughrea, Co Galway, Ireland]; *b* 22 Feb 1929; *m* 6 Aug 1953 *John Francis Quinn, est s of Peter Quinn, of Corragaun, Westport, Co Mayo, and has:
  (1) *John Douglas; *b* 7 April 1954; *m* 30 March 1980 *Carmel Burke and has:
    1a *John David; *b* 1981
    2a *Brian Thomas; *b* 1983
    3a *Niall; *b* 1987
    1a *Siobhan; *b* 1985
  (2) *Peter Francis [Peter Quinn Esq, 77 Lumsden Cres, Almondbank, Perthshire]; *b* 28 Nov 1956; *m* 1983 *Alison Nicol and has:
    1a *Emma Margaret; *b* 1986
    2a *Katy Elizabeth; *b* 1989
  (3) *James Hugh [James Quinn Esq, Caheronaun, Loughrea, Co Galway, Ireland]; *b* 26 Jan 1959; *m* 1987 *Angela Murray and has:
    1a *Peter Daniel; *b* 1991
    2a *Conor Hugh; *b* 1993
    1a *Amy Marie; *b* 1995
  (4) *Michael Joseph; *b* 24 March 1967; *m* 1994 *Nuala Rushe and has:
    1a *Cathal Michael; *b* 1996
  (5) *David Paul; *b* 16 Aug 1968; *m* 1991 *Catherine Daniels and has:
    1a *Daniel Joseph; *b* 1991
    2a *Shane David; *b* 1995

1a *Laura Margaret; *b* 1993

(6) *Kevin; *b* 16 June 1974

(1) *Mary Tereasa [Mrs Martin Dunne, 3 Ferney Grove, Mahon, Black Rock, Co Cork, Ireland]; *b* 26 May 1955; *m* 1991 *Martin Dunne

(2) *Margaret Joan [Mrs Kevin Monahan, Donellan Drive, Loughrea, Co Galway, Ireland]; *b* 28 May 1960; *m* 1991 *Kevin Monahan and has:

1a *Sarah Louise; *b* 1995

(3) *Anne Bernadette; *b* 26 April 1962; *m* 1991 *Hugh Ivory and has:

1a *David Hugh; *b* 1994

1a *Ruth Marie; *b* 1992

2a *Claire Louise; *b* 1992

(4) *Pauline; *b* 13 April 1965; *m* 1989 (*divorce* 19–) — Maher and has:

1a *Caolan Joseph; *b* 1989

1a *Aoife; *b* 1992

REITH

Arms: Or a cross engrailed sable between four mullets gules, on a chief of the last a lion passant of the field. **Crest:** An eagle rising regardant proper. **Supporters:** Two eagles, wings addorsed proper. **Motto:** *Quæcunque* ('Whatsoever'). **Creation:** B. (UK) 21 Oct 1940.

Christopher John Reith [Christopher Reith Esq, Whitebank Farm, Methven, Perthshire PH1 3QU]; *b* 27 May 1928; *s f* as 2nd Baron Reith 16 June 1971 but disclaimed peerage for life 21 April 1972; *educ* Eton and Worcester Coll Oxford (BA 1952, MA 1955); seaman RN 1946–48; *m* 28 May 1969 *(Penelope Margaret) Ann, er dau of Henry Rowland Morris, of Beeston, Notts, and has:

1 +JAMES HARRY JOHN; *b* 2 June 1971

1 *Julie Katharine; *b* 20 Dec 1972

Lineage: ALEXANDER REITH, of Clachanshiels, Stonehaven, Kincardineshire; had:

ALEXANDER REITH, of Powbare, Fetteresso, Kincardineshire, had, with both another s and an est s (John, farmed at Tipperty, Fordoun):

ALEXANDER REITH; *b* 1765; kept toll-houses at Invercairon and Rubislaw; had, with three other sons:

1 John; kept toll-house at Rubislaw; *dspm*

2 GEORGE

3 David; *b* 1814; lawyer Aberdeen and Dundee; *d* 1866

4 Archibald; *b* 1816; medical practitioner; *d* NY, having had, with other issue:

(1) David (Rev Canon); *b* 1842; *educ* Marischal Coll (MA 1862); Curate Brighton, Vicar Greenwich, Canon Rochester 1891, Vicar St Andrew's Watford; *d* 1909, having had, with another s:

1a Roger Archibald; Lt-Col 3rd Buffs Boer War, barrister 1905; *m* 1st Caroline Stuart Radmall and *d* 1964, leaving:

1b *Anthony John; *b* 1908; Col Wilts Regt (Duke of Edinburgh's)

1b *Sylvia Lucy Robertson; *b* 1910

(2) William; *b* 1847; Dist Judge Cyprus 1883–90; *d* 1890

The 2nd s here noticed,

GEORGE REITH, of Aberdeen and Glasgow; *b* 7 April 1811; village wheelwright, lawyer, 1st gen manager: Scottish N Eastern Rlwy, Grand Trunk Rlwys Canada, Clyde Navigation Tst; *m* 21 March 1834 Jane Stuart (*d* 25 Oct 1899), of Glenlivet, and *d* 25 Nov 1889, having had, with four other sons and two daus:

1 Archibald, MB (Aberdeen 1858); *b* 1837; *m* twice and *d* 1894, having had, with seven other children:

(1) George Murray (Rev); *b* 1863; Minister St Cuthbert's Edinburgh; *d* 1948

(2) Charles Edward William, of Edinburgh; *b* 1886; *m* 4 June 1924 Marguerite, er dau of John Wilton Gordon, of Hampstead, and *d* 1957, leaving:

1a Charles Martin (Rev); *b* 1927; *d* 1992

2 George (Very Rev); *b* 6 July 1842; *educ* Aberdeen GS and Marischal Coll, New Coll Edinburgh U and Erlangen U Germany; DD 1892, Moderator Utd Free Church 1914; *m* 9 July 1870 Adah Mary (*d* 15 Dec 1935), 2nd dau of Edward Weston, and *d* 9 Dec 1919, having had:

(1) Archibald (Rev); *educ* Glasgow U (MA 1893); Rector W Halton Lincs 1930; *d* 2 May 1962

(2) Robert Buchanan; *b* 1875; naval architect; *d* Sept 1963

(3) Edmund Ernest; *b* 1876; *d* 1945

(4) George Douglas (Rev); *b* 1880; *educ* Glasgow U (MA, BD 1908), Min Utd Free Church Dumfries, missionary India; *d* 1929

(5) JOHN CHARLES WALSHAM, **1st Baron**

(1) Adah Elizabeth; *b* 1873; *d unm* 1921

(2) Jean Stuart; *b* 1878; *m* 1913 (*annulled* 1923) Douglas Graham, India Forestry Dept, and *d* Dec 1966

GEORGE REITH's gs,

JOHN CHARLES WALSHAM REITH, **1st Baron Reith**, of Stonehaven, Co Kincardine (UK), so *cr* 21 Oct 1940, KT (1969), GCVO (1939), GBE (1934), CB (1945), TD , PC (1940); *b* 20 July 1889; *educ* Glasgow Acad, Gresham's and Roy Tech Coll Glasgow; 5th SR Cameronians WW I 1914, Maj RE (TF) 1915 (wounded), USA 1916–17, Admlty 1917–18, Liquidator Ordnance and Engrg Contracts Min Munitions 1919, 1st Gen Manager and md BBC Ltd 1922–26, Dir-Gen BBC 1927–28, Chm: Imp Airways 1938–39 and BOAC 1939–40, MP Southampton Feb–Oct 1940, Min Info Jan–May 1940, Min Tport May–Oct 1940, Min Works and 1st Commr Works (later Min Works and Planning) Oct 1940–Feb 1942, Lt-Cdr RNVR (Coastal Forces) WW II 1942, Extra Naval Assist to 3rd Sea Ld 1943, Capt RNVR, Dir Combined Ops Material Dept Admlty 1943–45, Dir Cwlth Telecommunications Conf 1945, Cwlth Communications Cncl 1946, Cwlth Telecommunications Bd 1946–50, New Towns Ctee 1946, Hemel Hempstead Devpt Corp 1947–50, Nat Film Finance Corp 1948–50, Colonial Devpt Corp 1950–59, State Building Soc 1960–64, dir Phoenix Assur, V-Chm Br Oxygen 1956–66, Hon LLD Aberdeen and Manchester 1933 and Glasgow 1951, Hon DCL Oxon 1935, Hon Fell Worcester Coll Oxford 1962, Ld Rector Glasgow U 1965–68, Ld High Commr Gen Assembly Ch Scotland 1967–68, memb Roy Co Archers, Hon FRIBA, hon memb Town Planning Inst and Inst Muncpl Engrs, hon memb Inst Chartered Surveyors, MSc Lafayette, USA, 1917, CEng, FICE, Hon Fell Inst Landscape Architects, hon memb Inst Highway Engrs, author: *Into the Wind* and *Wearing Spurs*; ktd 1927; *m* 14 July 1921 Muriel Katharine (*d* 6 July 1977), yr dau of John Lynch Odhams, and *d* 16 June 1971, leaving:

1 CHRISTOPHER JOHN REITH, **briefly 2nd Baron Reith**

1 *Marista Muriel [The Hon Mrs Leishman, 9/23 St Leonards Crag, Edinburgh EH8 9SP]; *b* 10 April 1932; *educ* St George's Ascot and St Andrews (MA 1955); Head Educn Nat Trust Scotland 1976–87, sr ptnr Insite Consultancy 1987–; *m* 3 Dec 1960 *Rev Robert Murray Leishman, only s of Robert H Leishman, of Edinburgh, and has:

(1) *Mark Murray; *b* 4 March 1962

(1) *Iona Marista; *b* 17 July 1963

(2) *Martha Katharine; *b* 22 March 1965

(3) *Kirsty Jane; *b* 17 July 1969

REMNANT

Arms: Sable a bend vair between two sheldrakes proper, all within two flaunches argent and charged with a cinquefoil gules. **Crest:** Between rushes a sheldrake proper, holding in the beak a rose gules, barbed, seeded, leaved and slipped proper. **Supporters:** On either side a dolphin proper charged with a cinquefoil gules. **Motto:** *Palmam qui meruit ferat* ('Let him who has deserved the palm bear it'). **Creations:** Bt. (UK) 14 July 1917, B. (UK) 26 June 1928.

THE 3RD BARON REMNANT, of Wenhaston, Co Suffolk, and a **Baronet** (Sir James Wogan Remnant, Bt, CVO (1979)) [The Rt Hon The Lord Remnant CVO, Bear Ash, Hare Hatch, Reading, Berks, RG10 9XR]; *b* 23 Oct 1930; *s f* 1967; *educ* Eton; Lt Coldstream Gds RARO, FCA 1955, ptnr Touche Ross and Co 1958–70; dir: Australian Mercantile Land and Finance 1957–69 and Australia and NZ Banking Gp 1965–81; chm: Touche Remnant and Co 1980–89 (md 1970–80), TR City of London Tst 1978–90 (dir 1973–90), TR Pacific Investment Tst 1987–94, Nat Provident Inst 1990–95 (dir 1963–95), Learning Through Landscapes Tst 1989– and Assoc Investment Tst Cos 1977–79; dir: Union Discount Co of London 1969–92 (dep chm 1970–86), Ultramar plc 1970–91 (dep chm 1981–91), TR Technology 1988–, Bank of Scotland 1989–96 (chm London Bd 1979–91), London Merchant Securities 1994–; Pres: Nat Cncl YMCAs 1983–96 and Florence Nightingale Fndn; Tstee Roy Jubilee Tsts 1989– (chm 1980–88 and hon treas 1972–80]; Ch Commr 1976–84; Liveryman: Salters' (Master 1995–96) and Chartered Accountants's Cos; Bailiff of Egle, OStJ 1993, GCStJ; *m* 24 June 1953 *Serena Jane, only dau of Cdr Sir Clive Loehnis, KCMG (*see* HARROWBY, E), and has:

1 +PHILIP JOHN [The Hon Philip Remnant, Ham Farm House, Baughurst, Hants RG26 5SA]; *b* 20 Dec 1954; *educ* Eton and New Coll Oxford; FCA 1979; *m* 14 July 1977 *Caroline Elizabeth Clare, yr dau of Godfrey Herbert Richard Cavendish (*see* DEVONSHIRE, D), and has:

  (1) +Edward James; *b* 2 July 1981

  (1) *Eleanor Clare; *b* 9 Aug 1983

  (2) *Sophie Caroline; *b* 19 Jan 1986

2 +Robert James [The Hon Robert Remnant, 20 Jalan Langgak Duta, Taman Duta, Kuala Lumpua SO 480, Malaysia]; *b* 10 Oct 1956; *educ* Eton; *m* 1st 1981 (*divorce* 1991) Sherrie, est dau of Frederick Cronn; *m* 2nd 8 Aug 1996 *Erica Liljenqvist and by his 1st w has:

  (1) +Christopher Michael; *b* 31 Oct 1982

  (2) +Jack Preston; *b* 1989

2 (cont.) The Hon Robert and Mrs Remnant also adopted 1987:

  *Shannon Lynn (male); *b* 1973

3 +Hugo Charles [The Hon Hugo Remnant, West Wing, Capheaton Hall, NE19 2AB]; *b* 28 Nov 1959; *educ* Eton and Newcastle U (BSc); *m* 1993 *Annabelle Rachel, only dau of T R Reynolds, of Tollard Royal, Dorset, and has:

  (1) +Benjamin; *b* 9 July 1998

1 *Melissa Clare JP (Glos) [The Hon Mrs Bradley JP, 1 Thessaly Lodge, Gloucester Rd, Stratton, Glos GL7 2LJ]; *b* 20 May 1963; *educ* Wycombe Abbey and Exeter U; *m* 1990 *David Wilson Bradley, yr s of W A Bradley, of Halls Court, Chesterton, Cambs

Lineage: FREDERICK WILLIAM REMNANT, of Southwold, Suffolk, and Bayswater, JP Suffolk; *b* 18 Dec 1811; *m* 17 Aug 1858 Merrial Julia (*d* 7 Oct 1904), dau of Henry Waterland Mander, and *d* 18 Dec 1885, having had:

1 JAMES FARQUHARSON, **1st Baron**

2 Frederick Mander, of Galley Wood Lodge, Edenbridge, Kent, JP (Suffolk); *b* 25 Nov 1864; *m* 5 Aug 1909 Rhoda Kathleen, dau of David Haughton, of Sutton, E Yorks, and *d* 19 Sept 1945, leaving:

  (1) *Patrick Tyrrell William [Patrick Remnant Esq, Rathburn Cottage, Ballycarnes, Shankill, Co Dublin]; *b* 28 July 1910

  (2) *Henry Frederick; *b* 5 July 1912; F/O RAAF; *m* *Gabrielle Watson and has:

    1a *Benjamin

    2a *Giles

    1a *Judith

    2a *Henrietta

3 Henry Vernon; *b* 1865; *d* 1912

4 Percy Waterland; *b* 22 Aug 1866; memb Inter-Allied Plebiscite Commn; *m* 11 Oct 1900 and *d* 25 Dec 1920

1 Alice Maud; *b* 1 Oct 1861; *m* 26 Feb 1891 Geoffrey Fynes Hollway, s of James Hollway, DL, of Stanhoe Hall, Norfolk, and *d* 22 Dec 1929

The est s,

Sir James Farquharson Remnant, 1st Bt, and **1st Baron Remnant**, of Wenhaston, Co Suffolk (both UK), so *cr* 14 July 1917 and 26 June 1928 respectively, CBE (1919); *b* 13 Feb 1862; *educ* Harrow and Magdalen Coll Oxford (BA 1883); barrister Lincoln's Inn 1886, memb LCC Holborn 1892–1901, MP Holborn 1900–28, memb Roy Commn Canals and Inland Waterways Navigation 1906–10, Lt-Col RASC WW I; *m* 30 Aug 1892 Frances Emily (*d* 23 June 1944), dau of Robert Gosling, DL, of Hassobury, Essex, and *d* 30 Jan 1933, having had:

1 ROBERT JOHN FARQUHARSON, **2nd Baron**

2 Peter Farquharson; *b* 21 Sept 1897; *educ* Eton and Magdalen Coll Oxford; Lt RGA, Lt-Col RA and Staff, WW I 1916–19, WW II, MP Wokingham 1950–59, co dir; *m* 24 Nov 1923 Betty (*d* 10 July 1965), dau of William George Tanner, of Frenchay, Glos, and *d* 14 Jan 1968, having had:

  (1) Bennett James Farquharson; *b* 17 Nov 1924; *educ* Eton; Lt Rifle Bde WW II; *ka* 26 Jan 1945

  (1) *Dawn [Mrs Anthony Hooper, Brook Ho, Doynton, Glos]; *b* 1 Dec 1927; *m* 13 Jan 1951 *Anthony Stewart Hooper, er s of S/Ldr Clifford Alban Hooper, of Nairobi, and has:

    1a *Susan Jane; *b* 1 May 1952

    2a *Mary Sandra; *b* 9 Dec 1953

    3a *Carol Ann; *b* 27 Dec 1956

  (2) *Merrial; *b* 11 Jan 1934; *m* 1st 11 Sept 1954 (*divorce* 1960) Arthur James Wesley-Smith, only s of John Leslie Wesley-Smith, MB, ChB, of Yorks, and has:

    1a *Shane; *b* 25 Dec 1955

    1a *Linda; *b* 6 Oct 1957

  (2) (cont.) Mrs Merrial Wesley-Smith *m* 2nd 5 Sept 1962 Henry James Stockley (*d* 18 Aug 1967), s of Hal Stockley, and by him has:

    2a *Marian Julia; *b* 9 Sept 1963

  (2) (cont.) Mrs Henry Stockley *m* 3rd 31 June 1968 *Ivor John Crosthwaite, DSO, yr s of Capt Henry Tudor Crosthwaite, of Pangbourne, Berks

The 1st BARON's er s,

ROBERT JOHN FARQUARSON REMNANT, **2nd Baron Remnant**, MBE (1945); *b* 29 March 1895; *educ* Eton and Magdalen Coll Oxford; Maj Roy Berks Regt, WW I, WW II, chm: Atlas Electric and Gen Tst, Tst and Agency of Australasia Ltd; *m* 5 June 1924 Norah Susan (*d* 1990), yr dau of Lt-Col Alexander John Wogan-Browne, 33rd Cavalry, and *d* 4 June 1967, leaving:

1 JAMES WOGAN REMNANT, **3rd and present Baron Remnant**

1 *Susan Frances [The Hon Mrs Tyser, West Hanney House, Wantage, Oxon OX12 0LN]; *b* 9 May 1938; *m* 29 March 1967 *Alan Tyser, s of Granville Tyser, of Mayfair, and has:

  (1) *Harry; *b* 17 Nov 1968

RENALS

Arms: Per pale gules and sable, on a fess nebuly argent, between two lozenges in chief and as many fleurs-de-lys in base or, a fasces fesswise, blade downwards proper. **Crest:** Upon a rock a fox sejant regardant proper, charged on the shoulder with a lozenge or and supporting with the dexter foreleg a fasces also proper. **Motto:** *Cavendo tutus* ('Safe by being cautious'). **Creation:** Bt. (UK) 4 Sept 1895.

SIR STANLEY RENALS, 4TH BT [Sir Stanley Renals Bt, 52 North Lane, Portslade, E Sussex BN4 2HG]; *b* 20 May 1923; *s* bro 1961; *educ* City of London Freemen's Sch; late Merchant Navy; *m* 2 Jan 1957 *Maria Dolores Rodriguez Pinto, dau of José Rodriguez Ruiz, and has:

1 +STANLEY MICHAEL [Stanley Renals Esq, 58 Old Shoreham Rd, Brighton, Sussex]; *b* 14 Jan 1958; *educ* Falmer High Sch and Brighton Poly (BSc, CEng, MIMechE, MIMfgE); *m* 1982 *Jacqueline Ann, dau of Roy Dennis Riley, of Hollingdean, Sussex, and has:

  (1) +Lloyd James; *b* 17 May 1985

  (1) *Frances Emma; *b* 1986

Lineage: EDMUND RENALS, of Nottingham; *b* 30 Nov 1773; *m* 10 April 1804 Maria Brotherhood, of Nottingham (*d* 13 Oct 1865), and *d* 10 Sept 1836, having had a 2nd s:

WILLIAM RENALS, of Nottingham; *b* 25 Feb 1810; *m* 2 Jan 1835 Elizabeth (*d* 24 Jan 1890), dau of Rev Joshua Burton, of Sutton-in-Ashfield, Notts, and had, with other issue:

Sir Joseph Renals, 1st Bt (UK), so *cr* 4 Sept 1895; *b* 21 Feb 1843; Memb Aldersgate Ward City of London Corp 1885 (Alderman 1888, Sheriff 1892), ktd 1893, Ld Mayor London 1894–95, Lt City of London, Offr Legn Hon 1895; *m* 1 Jan 1870 Mary (*d* 29 Dec 1908), dau of Alfred Wilson, of The Park, Nottingham, and *d* 1 Nov 1907, having had:

1 JAMES HERBERT (Sir), **2nd Bt**

2 John Burton; *b* 15 Sept 1872; Lt City of London; *m* 5 March 1910 Alice — and *d* 15 March 1934

3 Alfred Wilson; *b* 2 Aug 1877; *d* 21 July 1915

The 1st Bt's est s,

Sir James Herbert Renals, **2nd Bt**; *b* 5 Nov 1870; Lt City of London; *m* 27 April 1918 Susan Emma (*d* 23 Aug 1957), dau of James William Crafter, of Bromley, Kent, and *d* 27 March 1927, having had:

1 Sir Herbert Renals, **3rd Bt**; *b* 29 Sept 1919; *d* 18 Aug 1961

2 Sir STANLEY RENALS, **4th and present Bt**

3 +Charles [Charles Renals Esq, South View, Bird-in-Eye Hill, Uckfield, Sussex]; *b* 5 Oct 1924; *educ* City of London Freemen's Sch; late RAF; *m* 2 Oct 1965 *Sheila Joyce, dau of Aubrey Hugh Berry

1 *Marie

2 Ethel; Freedom City London, Freedom Fruiterers' Co; *m* 1940 Richard Gibson (*d* 13 Dec 1951) and had issue

3 Rieta

4 Constance; *b* 12 Jan 1927; *m* 1st 24 April 1954 (*divorce* 1957) Richard Michael Whittaker, s of Ernest Cecil Wittaker, of S Africa; *m* 2nd 22 Aug 1969 *Lawrence John Taylor, s of Percy William Taylor, of Durban, and *dsp*

RENDELL OF BABERGH

Arms *(depiction not available at time of going to press)*: Gules three interlaced chevronels argent, each ensigned by a brimstone butterfly displayed proper. **Supporters:** On either side a polar bear statant erect proper gorged with a plain collar gobony gules and or fimbriated gules. **Motto:** *Vixi scripsi* ('I have lived, I have written'). **Creation:** B. (LP, UK) 2 Aug 1997.

THE BARONESS RENDELL OF BABERGH, of Aldeburgh, Co Suffolk (Ruth Barbara Grasemann, CBE (1996)) [The Rt Hon The Baroness Rendell of Babergh CBE, 11 Maida Ave, London W2 1SR]; *b* 6 Feb 1930; *educ* Loughton Co High Sch; late jnlst *Chigwell Times*; author: *From Doon with Death* (1964), *To Fear a Painted Devil* (1965), *Vanity Dies Hard* (1966), *A New Lease of Death* (1967), *Wolf to the Slaughter* (1967, televised 1987), *The Secret House of Death* (1968), *The Best Man to Die* (1969), *A Guilty Thing Surprised* (1970), *One Across Two Down* (1971), *No More Dying Then* (1971), *Murder Being Once Done* (1972), *Some Lie and Some Die* (1973), *The Face of Trespass* (1974, TV version *An Affair in Mind* 1988), *Shake Hands for Ever* (1975), *The Fallen Curtain* (1976), *A Demon in my View* (1976, filmed 1991), *A Judgement in Stone* (1977), *A Sleeping Life* (1978), *Means of Evil* (1979), *Make Death Love Me* (1979), *The Lake of Darkness* (1980, TV version *Dead Lucky* 1988), *Put On by Cunning* (1981), *The Fever Tree* (1982), *Master of the Moor* (1982, TV version 1994), *The Speaker of Mandarin* (1983), *The Killing Doll* (1984), *The Tree of Hands* (1984, filmed 1989), *The New Girl Friend* (1985), *An Unkindness of Ravens* (1985), *A Dark-Adapted Eye* (as Barbara Vine, 1986, TV version 1994), *Live Flesh* (1986), *A Fatal Inversion* (as Barbara Vine, 1987, TV version 1992), *Collected Short Stories* (1987), *Heartstones* (1987), *Talking to Strange Men* (1987), *A Warning to the Curious: The Ghost Stories of M R James* (ed, 1987), *The House of Stairs* (as Barbara Vine, 1988), *The Veiled One* (1988, TV version 1989), *The Bridesmaid* (1989), *Ruth Rendell's Suffolk* (1989), *Undermining the Central Line* (with Colin Ward, 1989), *Galloglass* (as Barbara Vine, 1990), *Going Wrong* (1990), *King Solomon's Carpet* (as Barbara Vine, 1991), *The Copper Peacock* (1991), *Kissing the Gunner's Daughter* (1992), *Asta's Book* (as Barbara Vine, 1993), *The Crocodile Bird* (1993), *No Night is Too Long* (as Barbara Vine, 1994), *Simisola* (1994), *Blood Linen* (as Barbara Vine, 1995), *Road Rage* (1997), *The Chimney Sweeper's Boy* (1998); FRSL, Crime Writers' Assoc Diamond Dagger award for lifetime's achievement in crime writing; *m* 1950 (*divorce* 1975, married again 1977) *Donald Rendell and has:

1 *Simon; psychiatric social worker; *m* and has issue

Lineage: ARTHUR GRASEMANN; mathematics and science teacher; *m* Ebba Kruse and *d c* 1973, leaving:

RUTH BARBARA, *cr* a **Baroness**

RENDLESHAM

Arms: Quarterly, wavy, argent and or; 1st and 4th, two demi-vols sa. in pale, points towards the dexter, each charged with a trefoil slipped in fess, the point to the sinister, of the 2nd; 2nd and 3rd, an oak tree eradicated proper, charged with an escutcheon bendways gules, thereon three guttes d'eau. **Crest:** A demi-greyhound salient argent, collared sable, between two wings of the last, each charged with a trefoil slipped or. **Supporters:** Two greyhounds regardant argent, collared sable. **Motto:** *Labore et honore* ('By work and honesty'). **Creation:** B. (I) 1 Feb 1806.

THE 8TH BARON RENDLESHAM OF RENDLESHAM (Charles Anthony Hugh Thellusson) [The Rt Hon The Lord Rendlesham, House of Lords, London SW1A 0PW]; *b* 15 March 1915; *s* unc 1943; *educ* Eton; Capt Roy Signals WW II; *m* 1st 27 April 1940 (*divorce* 1947) Margaret Elizabeth, yr dau of Lt-Col Robin Cowper Rome, MC, RFA, of Woolpit, Suffolk, and has:

1 *Caroline Elizabeth [The Hon Caroline Lady Goring, 25 Queen's Gate Terrace, London SW7]; *b* 2 April 1941; *m* 24 Sept 1960 (*divorce* 1993), as his 1st w, Sir William Burton Nigel Goring, 13th Bt (*qv*)

The 8th BARON *m* 2nd 3 Nov 1947 Clare (*d* 1987), dau of Lt-Col Douglas Howard Gwyn McCririck, of Wiveliscombe, Somerset, and by her has:

1 +CHARLES WILLIAM BROOKE; *b* 10 Jan 1954; *educ* Eton; *m* 1983 *Susan, yst dau of E R Fielding, of Monte Carlo

2 *Sarah Ann; *b* 25 Jan 1949; *m* 1989 *Keir H Helberg, of Washington, DC

3 *Antonia [The Hon Mrs Kirby, 17 Wetherby Gdns, London SW5]; *b* 17 Jan 1956; *m* 1981 *Hugo Giles Stephen Astley Kirby, est s of Giles Kirby, of The Manor Ho, S Harting, Hants, and has:

(1) *Nicholas Charles Astley; *b* 2 May 1983

(1) *Natasha Alexandra; *b* 1985

4 *Jaqumine; *b* 21 Aug 1960; *m* 1987 *Charles Nigel Bromage (*see* CAYZER, B) and has:

(1) *Maximilian Charles; *b* 1993

Lineage: ISAAC de THELLUSSON; Genevan Envoy France *temp* LOUIS XV; had:

PETER THELLUSSON; *b* Paris 27 June 1737; merchant London *c* 1750, naturalised in GB 1762, later bought Ldship of Manor of Brodsworth, Yorks; *m* 6 Jan 1761 Anne, 2nd dau of Matthew Woodford and sis of Sir Ralph Woodford, 1st Bt, of Carleby, Lincs, MP Evesham (*see* 1828 edn), and *d* 21 July 1797, leaving real property bringing in £5,000 (over £180,000 in late-1990s terms) a year and a personal estate of over £600,000 (some £22,000,000 in late-1990s terms), instructing tstees to accumulate profits from this for three generations, excluding his immediate issue (in the subsequent suit Thellusson *v* Woodford 1799 his will was upheld, resulting in the Accumulations Act 1800 to prevent such moves) having had:

1 PETER ISAAC, **1st Baron**

2 George Woodford; *educ* Haileybury; Dir HEIC 1799–1807; *m* 3 April 1791 Mary Anne (*d* 1844), 3rd dau of Philip Fonnereau, and *d* 1811, leaving two daus

3 Charles; MP Evesham; *m* 15 Jan 1795 Sabine, est dau of Abraham Robarts, London banker, and *d* 2 Nov 1815, leaving issue

1 Maria; *m* Hon Augustus Phipps (*see* NORMANBY, M)

2 Anne; *m* 1801 V-Adml William LUKIN later WINDHAM (roy licence 28 April 1824, as heir of William Windham, PC, MP, of Felbrigg, Sec State for War), of Felbrigg Hall, Norfolk

3 Augusta Charlotte; *m* 1st 26 March 1798 Thomas Champion de Crespigny, DCL (*d* 2 Aug 1799), est s of Philip Champion de Crespigny, of Aldborough, Suffolk, 5 Old Palace Yard, Westminster, Burwood Ho, Surrey, Colney Chapel, Herts, Hintlesham Hall, Suffolk, 5 Portland Place, Bath, and Tallyn and Cathodine, Breconshire; *m* 2nd 3 Feb 1827 Sir Joseph Whatley, KCH (*d* 1844), and *d* 24 July 1853

The est s,

PETER ISAAC THELLUSSON, **1st Baron Rendlesham of Rendlesham** (I), so *cr* 1 Feb 1806; *b* 13 Oct 1761; Dir Bank of England 1787–1806, MP (Tory) Midhurst 1795–96, Malmesbury 1796–1802, Castle Rising 1802–06 and Bossiney 1807–08; *m* 14 June 1783 Elizabeth Eleanor, dau of John Cornwall, of Hendon, Middx, and *d* 16 Sept 1808, having had, with other issue:

1 JOHN THELLUSSON, **2nd Baron Rendlesham of Rendlesham**; *b* 12 Sept 1785; *educ* Eton; *m* 1st 30 Nov 1809 Mary Andalusia (*dsp* 15 Aug 1814), 2nd dau of Lt-Gen Samuel Trevor Dickins, RE; *m* 2nd *c* 26 March 1816 Ann Sophia (*d* 31 Aug 1856), 2nd dau and coheir of William Tatnall, of Leiston Old Abbey, Suffolk, and *dspms* 3 July 1832, having by her had:

(1) Frederick Adolphus; *b* 8 July 1821; *dvp* 30 June 1822

(1) Emily Elizabeth Julia; *m* 25 Oct 1847 5th Baron Walsingham (*qv*) and *d* 13 May 1879, leaving issue

(2) Sophia Andalusia Mary; *m* 15 March 1856 Sir William Rose, KCB (*d* 19 Nov 1885), and *d* 13 Nov 1900

2 George; *b* 1791; Lt 11th Dragoons; *k* Batttle of Vittoria 1813

3 Rev WILLIAM THELLUSSON, **3rd Baron Rendlesham of Rendlesham**; *b* 6 Jan 1798; *educ* Eton and Trin Coll Cambridge; Vicar Aldenham, Herts; *m* 10 Jan 1826 Lucy (*m* 2nd 2 Feb 1841, as his 2nd w, Stewart Marjoribanks (*see* 1935 edn TWEEDMOUTH, B) and *d* 12 May 1854), dau of Edward Roger Pratt, of Ryston Hall, Norfolk, and *dsp* 13 Sept 1839

4 FREDERICK THELLUSSON, **4th Baron Rendlesham of Rendlesham**, DL Suffolk; *b* 6 Jan 1798; Army Offr, MP (C) E Suffolk 1843–52; *m* 5 June 1838 Eliza Charlotte (*d* 31 Dec 1840), est dau of Sir George Beeston Prescott, 2nd Bt (*see* 1959 edn), and widow of James Duff, and *d* 6 April 1852, having had:

(1) FREDERICK WILLIAM BROOK, **5th Baron**

(1) Anne Blanche; *d* 26 March 1886

5 Arthur; *b* 10 Dec 1801; *m* 3 Jan 1826 Caroline Anna Maria (*d* 19 June 1877), dau of Christopher Bethell-Codrington (*see* CODRINGTON, Bt, of Dodington (1876)), and *d* 15 June 1858, having had, with three daus (*d* young or unm):

(1) Arthur John Bethell, JP, of Thellusson Lodge, Aldeburgh, Suffolk; *b* 13 Sept 1826; Hon Col Suffolk RV, Maj Coldstream Gds; *m* 1st 8 March 1859 Henrietta Frances Elizabeth (*d* 30 March 1873), yr dau of Frederick William Thomas Vernon-Wentworth, JP, DL, of Wentworth Castle, Yorks, and had:

1a Arthur Wentworth William Augustus; *b* 1 Jan 1863; Capt 1st Bn KOB; *d* unm 25 Jan 1901

1a Augusta Mary Henrietta; *d* young 9 Feb 1863

2a Frederika Charlotte Louisa; *m* 3 Oct 1883 Mortimer Rooke (*d* 16 May 1942), of The Ivy, Chippenham, Wilts, and *d* 27 March 1954, leaving issue

3a Eva Blanche Charlotte; *d* young 30 March 1873

4a Katharine Emily Wilhelmina; *m* 7 Jan 1897 Sir August Fredrich Manns (*dspl* March 1907) and *d* 25 Feb 1921

5a Violet Andalusia; *d* young 31 Dec 1872

6a Selina Mabel Henrietta; *m* 25 April 1902 Herbert Davy Longe, JP (*d* 16 Nov 1949), of Abbot's Hall, Stowmarket, Suffolk, 3rd s of Rev John Longe, of Sternfield, Suffolk, and *d* 31 Dec 1949, leaving issue

(1) (cont.) Maj Arthur Thellusson *m* 2nd 1877 Auguste Mathilde Henriette Louise, dau of George Heine, of Hanover, and *d* 18 Oct 1901

The 4th BARON's only s,

FREDERICK WILLIAM BROOK THELLUSSON, **5th Baron Rendlesham of Rendlesham**, JP, DL Suffolk; *b* 9 Feb 1840; *educ* Eton and Ch Ch Oxford; Suffolk: CA, High Sheriff 1870, Chm CC, MP (C) E Suffolk 1874–85; *m* 4 July 1861 Lady Egidia Montgomerie (*d* 13 Jan 1880), dau of 13th Earl of Eglinto(u)n and (1st Earl of) Winton (*qv*), and *d* 9 Nov 1911, having had:

1 FREDERICK ARCHIBALD CHARLES THELLUSSON, **6th Baron Rendlesham of Rendlesham**; *b* 8 June 1868; *educ* Eton; Capt Suffolk Artillery Militia 1890–93, T/Maj 4th Bn Suffolk Vol Regt, Hon Lt-Col, Gp Cmdt Suffolk Vol Regt, High Sheriff Suffolk 1916; *m* 1st Lilian (*d* 5 April 1931), 4th dau of Joshua Manley, JP, of St Catherine's, Kingston, Jamaica; *m* 2nd 27 Oct 1931 Dolores Olga (*d* 5 Aug 1959), dau of Sir William Lewis Salusbury-Trelawny, 10th Bt (*qv*), and widow of Henry Harcourt Williams, of Pencalenick, Cornwall, and *dsp* 4 July 1938

2 PERCY EDWARD THELLUSSON, **7th Baron Rendlesham of Rendlesham**; *b* 30 Oct 1874; Capt W Kent Yeo, ADC Personal Staff 1918–19; *m* 30 March 1922 Gladys Dunlop, OBE (*d* 6 Nov 1933), only child of Andrew Vans Dunlop Best and formerly w of Hon Alfred Yorke (*see* HARDWICKE, E), and *dsp* 11 Dec 1943

3 Hugh Edmund, DSO; *b* 7 June 1876; Lt-Col Res of Offrs, late RFA, WW I (despatches, Croix de Guerre); *m* 28 April 1914 Gwynnydd Colleton, 5th dau of Brig-Gen Sir Robert Augustus William Colleton, 9th Bt (*see* 1938 edn), and *d* 10 July 1926, leaving:

(1) CHARLES ANTHONY HUGH THELLUSSON, **8th and present Baron Rendlesham of Rendlesham**

(2) +Peter Robert; *b* 25 Jan 1920; *educ* Eton; Capt KRRC WW II, granted with sis rank of baron's dau/yr s 1945; *m* 1st 4 Sept 1947 (*divorce* 1950) Pamela Dione (*d* 7 Dec 1968), dau of Oliver Parker (*see* MACCLESFIELD, E) and formerly w of Maj Timothy Tufnell, MC, Coldstream Gds; *m* 2nd 2 Feb 1952 *Celia, dau of James Walsh, of Loden House, High Wycombe, Bucks, and has:

1a +James Hugh; *b* 7 Jan 1961; *m* 28 Dec 1995 *Jennifer, er dau of Ralph Owers, of Sunningdale, Berks, and has:

1b Abigail; *b* 10 Feb 1998

2a +Peter Richard; *b* 25 Aug 1962

(1) Cynthia Adeline Elizabeth; *b* 20 March 1918

1 Adeline Egidia; *m* 22 April 1891 Maj Lewis Kerrison Jarvis (*d* 16 May 1938), 3rd Co London Yeo, formerly Loyal Suffolk Hus, s of Sir Lewis Jarvis, of Middleton Tower, Norfolk, and *d* 8 Nov 1948, having had issue

2 Miriam Isabel; *m* 26 Feb 1901 (*divorce* 1923) Godfrey Herbert Joseph Williams (*d* 7 April 1956), est s of Morgan Stuart Williams, of Aberpergwm, Neath, Glam, and *d* 11 June 1950, leaving issue

3 Cecilia Blanche; *d* unm 21 Aug 1948

4 Ruby Alexandrina Elizabeth; *m* 29 Nov 1907 Lt-Col Bernard James DUFF later PETRE (roy licence 1882), JP, DL (*d* 1 Feb 1934), of Westwick, Norwich, ISC, est s of James Duff, MP, and *d* 19 Jan 1955, leaving issue

5 Mariota; *m* 28 Aug 1895 5th Earl of Wilton (*qv*) and *d* 19 March 1924, leaving issue

RENFREW OF KAIMSTHORN

Creation: B. (LP, UK) 1991.

THE BARON RENFREW OF KAIMSTHORN, of Hurlet, District of Renfrew ((Andrew) Colin Renfrew) [The Rt Hon The Lord Renfrew of Kaimsthorn, 5 Chaucer Rd, Cambridge CB2 2EB]; *b* 25 July 1937; *educ* St Alban's Sch and St John's Coll Cambridge (BA, PhD, ScD, Pres Union 1961, Research Fell 1965–68, Fell 1981–86); RAF 1956–58; Sheffield U: Lecturer 1965–70, Sr Lecturer 1970–72, Reader 1972 Prehistory & Archaeology, Bulgarian Govt Scholarship 1966, Visiting Lecturer UCLA 1967, Prof Archaeology Southampton U 1972–81, Disney Prof Archaeology Cambridge 1981–, Master Jesus Coll Cambridge 1986–97 and dir McDonald Inst for Archaeological Research; C candidate Sheffield Brightside 1968 by-election (Chm C Assoc 1968–72); Memb Royal Commn Historic Monuments England 1977–87, Historic Buildings and Monuments Commn Advsry Bd 1983– and Sci Panel 1983–89; Chm Nat Curriculum Art Working Gp 1990–91; Freeman City London; Hon DLitt: Sheffield 1987 and Southampton 1988, Hon Dr Athens 1991, FSA 1968, FSAScot 1970, FBA 1980, author: *The Emergence of Civilisation* (1972), *Before Civilisation* (1973), *Investigations in Orkney* (1979), *Problems in European Prehistory* (1979), *Approaches to Social Archaeology* (1984), *The Prehistory of Orkney* (1983), *The Archaeology of Cult* (1985), *Archaeology and Language* (1987), *The Cycladic Spirit* (1991) and other works; *m* 1965 *Jane Margaret, dau of Ven Walter Frederick Ewbank, of Penrith, Cumbria, and has:

1 *Alban; *b* 1970

2 *Magnus; *b* 1975

1 *Helena M; *b* 1968; *m* 6 April 1996 *Jonathan Knight, er s of Philip Knight, of Otford, Kent, and Mrs Hilary Howlett, of Blackheath

Lineage: ARCHIBALD RENFREW, of Giffnock, Glasgow; *m* Helena Douglas Savage and had:

(ANDREW) COLIN, *cr* a **Baron**

RENNELL

Arms: Arg. two trefoils slipped sa., on a chief of the second three crescents of the first. **Crest:** A representation of the Colossus of Rhodes, over the shoulder a bow, in the dexter hand an arrow and in the sinister a cup, all ppr. **Supporters:** On either side a Cornish chough, wings elevated and addorsed ppr., each charged on the breast with a trefoil slipped arg. **Motto:** *Recte omnia duce deo* ('With God for guide, all is right'). **Creation:** B. (UK) 1 March 1933.

THE 3RD BARON RENNELL, of Rodd, Co Hereford ((John Adrian) Tremayne Rodd) [The Rt Hon The Lord Rennell, 3 Briar Walk, London SW15 6UD]; *b* 28 June 1935; *s* unc 1978; *educ* Downside and RNC Dartmouth; Lt RN, served RN 1952–62; former Scottish Rugby internat (capped 14 times), dir Alec Brook Ltd, with Morgan Grenfell 1963–66, freelance jnlst 1966–67, with Marks of Distinction Ltd 1968–79 and Tremayne Ltd 1980–91; *m* 3 May 1977 *Phyllis Caroline, dau of Thomas David Neill, of Co Armagh, and has:

1 +JAMES RODERICK DAVID TREMAYNE; *b* 9 March 1978

2 *Sophie Mary Jane; *b* 3 Feb 1981

3 *Rachel Yvonne Rose; *b* 1987

4 *Lilias Charlotte Allegra Nell; *b* 1989

Lineage: This family is descended from the RODDs, known to have been settled at The Rodd, Herefs, in the 13th century, and is probably connected with the RODEs of Rode Hall, Staffs. Branches of the RODDs settled as early as the 15th century in Cornwall and Devon, intermarrying with the Herefordshire branch. The latter died out in the male line in the 18th century.

FRANCIS RODD; *b* 1683; Capt Coldstream Gds; inherited 1727 the Trebartha estate, Cornwall, from his cousin Mary, dau and heiress of Edmund Spoure, of Trebartha Hall; *m* Alicia (*d* 1770), dau of William Sandford, of Exeter, and *d* 25 Aug 1736, leaving, with other issue:

FRANCIS RODD, of Trebartha Hall, JP; *b* 12 July 1732; Col Roy Cornwall Militia; *m* 1st Jane (*d* 1780), 2nd dau and coheir of John Hearle, of Penryn, Warden Cornish Stannaries; *m* 2nd Anne (*dsp* 1807), dau of William Sanford, of Nynehead Court, Somerset, and *d* 23 Jan 1812, leaving by his 1st w a 3rd s:

Sir JOHN TREMAYNE RODD, KCB; *b* 1769; V-Adml; *m* 5 Oct 1809 Jane, only dau of Maj James Rennell, FRS, Surveyor-Gen Bengal, and *d* 4 Oct 1838, leaving, with two daus (*m* and *dsp*):

JAMES RENNELL RODD; *b* Feb 1812; Maj Roy Cornwall Rangers; *m* Elizabeth Anne (*d* 16 Oct 1915), 3rd dau of Dr Anthony Todd Thomson, and *d* Rome March 1892, having had, with a dau (Frances Emily, *d* unm 22 Feb 1947):

JAMES RENNELL, **1st Baron Rennell**, of Rodd, Co Hereford (UK), so *cr* 1 March 1933, GCB (1920, CB 1897), GCMG (1915, KCMG 1899, CMG 1894), GCVO (1905, CVO 1903), PC (21 Nov 1908); *b* 9 Nov 1858; *educ* Haileybury and Balliol Coll Oxford (Newdigate Prize 1880, BA, Hon Fell 1939); Dip Serv: joined 1884, Sec Legation Cairo 1894–1901, 1st Sec and Counsellor Rome 1901–04, Envoy Extrdy and Min Plen Sweden 1905–08, Amb Italy 1908–19, Chm Cncl Br Sch Rome, actg Agent and Consul Gen Zanzibar, Special Envoy to KING MENELIK of Abyssinia 1897, MP (C) St Marylebone 1928–32; Kt Grand Cross St Maurice and St Lazarus Italy, Grand Offr Crown Italy, Cdr Order Osmanieh, Grand Cross N Star Sweden and Redeemer Greece, Star Ethiopia; *m* 27 Oct 1894 Georgina Lilias (*d* 20 Sept 1951), 5th dau of James Alexander Guthrie, JP, DL, of Craigie, Forfar, by Elinor, 3rd dau of Adml Sir James Stirling, Fndr and 1st Govr W Australia 1829, and *d* 26 July 1941, having had:

1 FRANCIS JAMES, **2nd Baron**

2 Christopher John; *d* 1896

3 Peter Murray Rennell; *b* 16 April 1904; *educ* Wellington and Balliol Coll Oxford; often identified (along with Basil Murray, *see* CARLISLE, E) as the original of Basil Seal in the novels of Evelyn Waugh; Lt-Col Welsh Gds WW II; *m* 4 Dec 1933 (*divorce* 1958) Hon Nancy Mitford, OBE, est dau of 2nd Baron Redesdale (*qv*), and *dsp* 17 July 1968

4 Gustaf Guthrie Rennell, OBE (1945); *b* 13 July 1905; *educ* RNCs Osborne and Dartmouth; Cdr RN (attd RAF 1928), served WW II, Gold Cross Roy Order George I Greece; *m* 1st 6 Dec 1932 (*divorce* 1948) Yvonne Mary (*d* 6 Sept 1982), er dau of Sir Charles Murray Marling, GCMG, CB (*see* MARLING, Bt); *m* 2nd 15

May 1948 (*divorce* 1966) Claude Rosemary, dau of Archibald W D Dove, of Kingston Hill, Surrey, and formerly w of Peter George Calvert, and *d* Florence 26 June 1974, having had by his 1st w:

(1) (David) Saul Rennell; *b* 24 Sept 1933; *educ* Downside and Perugia U, Italy; 2nd Lt RAC; *d* unm 17 Jan 1966

(2) (JOHN ADRIAN) TREMAYNE RODD, **3rd and present Baron Rennell**

1 EVELYN VIOLET ELIZABETH Rodd, BARONESS EMMET OF AMBERLEY (LP, UK), of Amberley, Co Sussex, so *cr* 8 Dec 1964, JP (Sussex), DL (W Sussex); *b* 18 March 1899; *educ* LMH Oxford (MA); memb: LCC 1925–34 and W Sussex CC 1946–67, Alderman 1952–66, MP (C) E Grinstead 1955–64, 1st woman UK rep UN after WW II, Dep Speaker and Dep Chm Ctees Ho Lds 1968–77; *m* 9 June 1923 Thomas Addis EMMET (*d* 3 June 1934), late RN, of Amberley Castle, Sussex, and *d* 10 Oct 1980, having had:

(1) Christopher Anthony Robert, JP (W Sussex); *b* 1925; *educ* Ampleforth and Balliol Coll Oxford (MA); FAA WW II 1943–46, CC W Sussex 1952–62; *m* 1947 *Lady Miranda Mary Fitzalan Howard [The Lady Miranda Emmet, The Stables, Seabeach House, Halnaker, W Sussex PO18 0LX], sis of 17th Duke of Norfolk (*qv*), and *d* 3 March 1996, leaving:

1a *Robert Anthony Bernard [Robert Emmet Esq, Seabeach House, Selhurst Park, Chichester, W Sussex PO18 0LX]; *b* 1958; *m* 1987 *Francesca Lavinia Elizabeth, est dau of Sebastian Snow, and has:

1b *Jules Anthony Christopher; *b* 1990

2b *Marcus Guy Robert; *b* 1992

1b *Cosima Maria; *b* 1996

1a *Teresa Miriam [Mrs Anthony Myers, Hainbury Mill Farm, Ilchester, Somerset BA22 8LB]; *b* 1949; *m* 1969 *Anthony Andrew Myers and has:

1b *Adrian Anthony Geoffrey; *b* 1972; *m* 18 May 1996 *Louise, dau of John Denny, of Wheathampstead

2b *Nicholas Andrew Robert; *b* 1973

2a *Catriona Mary [Mrs Christopher Russell-Pavier, The Old Barn, Clevelode, Worcs WR13 6PD]; *b* 27 June 1951; *m* 1st 1978 (*divorce* 1983) Paul Striberry; *m* 2nd 1984 Christopher Russell-Pavier (*d* 17 March 1994) and by him has:

1b *Charles Adey; *b* 5 Aug 1992

1b *Anna Louise; *b* 12 June 1985

3a *Rowena Mary Gabriel [Mrs Jonathan Malcolm Green, 68 The Drive Mansions, Fulham Rd, London SW6 5JH]; *b* 1954; *m* 1st 1975 (*divorce*) Michael F Hallinan; *m* 2nd 1981 *(Anthony) Jonathan Malcolm Green and by him has:

1b *Thomas Oliver; *b* 1984

2b *James Edward; *b* 1984

1b *Iona Alice; *b* 1989

(2) *David Alastair Rennell [The Hon David Emmet, Casilla de Correo 55174, San Carlos, 20/400 Maldonado, Uruguay]; *b* 1928; *educ* Ampleforth and Worcester Coll Oxford; memb Br Community Cncl Argentina 1964–68, FRGS; *m* 1967 *Sylvia Delia, dau of Willis Knowles, of Buenos Aires, and has:

1a *Thomas Ian David; *b* 1970; *educ* Durham U (BA)

1a *Caroline Ann Gloria; *b* 1968; *educ* Durham U (BA)

(1) *(Gloria) Lavinia Eileen [The Hon Mrs Fleming, Ardath, Shamley Green, Surrey GU5 0SY]; *b* 1924; *m* 1950 *Maj Mark Winton Slane Fleming, OStJ, 10th Roy Hus (PWO), and has:

1a *Andrew Gerard James [Andrew Fleming Esq, Lower Farmhouse, Gt Rissington, Glos GL54 2LH]; *b* 1956; *educ* Leeds U (BSc); FBHI; *m* 1985 *Kathryn Claire Warner and has:

1b *Giles William Slane; *b* 1989

2b *Jack Francis Edmund; *b* 1992

1b *Lucinda Marion Kate; *b* 1987

1a *(Mary) Georgina [Mrs Michael Hardinge, Pintor Gisbert 3, 46006 Valencia, Spain]; *b* 1951; *educ* Edinburgh U (MA); *m* 1972 *Michael David Hardinge and has:

1b *Elizabeth Selene; *b* 1972; *educ* Edinburgh U (BSc)

2a *Sarah Elizabeth Sophia, JP (Glos) [Mrs Jonathan Ward JP, 2 Olive Hill Cottages, Wyck Rissington, Glos GL54 2PW]; *b* 1953; SRN; *m* 1979 *Jonathan Francis Bruce Ward (*see* BRUCE, Bt, of Stenhouse), strategic systems manager OUP, and has issue

3a *Charlotte Ann [Miss Charlotte Fleming, c/o Ardath, Shamley Green, Surrey GU5 0SY]; *b* 1955; wine lecturer and consultant

(2) *(Penelope) Ann Clare [The Hon Mrs Ann Money-Coutts, Flat 4, 43 Onslow Square, London SW7 3LR]; *b* 1932; *m* 1951 (*divorce* 1965), as his 1st w, 8th Baron Latymer (*qv*) and has issue

2 Gloria Elinor; *m* 25 Nov 1926 Simon Edmund Vincent Paul Elwes (*d* 6 Aug 1975), 6th s of Gervase Henry Elwes, JP, DL, of Roxby, Lincs, and *d* 8 Oct 1975, having had:

(1) Giles Gervase; *b* 1927; *d* 1929

(2) *Peter John Gervase [Peter Elwes Esq, 75 Murray Rd, London SW19 4PF]; *b* 1929; *educ* Eton, Miles Aircraft Tech Coll and Kingston and Gateshead Colls Advanced Technology; 2nd Lt Roy Scots Greys BAOR 1950–52, Lt Northumberland Hus 1953–56, with Vickers Armstrong 1948–53, Ransomes & Rapier 1953–56, RTZ 1956–73, md Hamilton Bros Oil and Gas 1973–77, dir: Energy Africa Ltd 1966– and Kleinwort Benson 1977–89, ch exec Enterprise Oil 1983–84, md Renown Energy 1988–89, dep chm and ch exec Hardy Oil and Gas 1989, chm Aminex plc 1966; FlinstPet; *m* 7 May 1960 *Hon Rosalie Ann Hennessy, dau of 2nd Baron Windlesham (*qv*), and has:

1a *Luke Andrew Carey; *b* 26 July 1961; *m* 1987 *Annek du Moulin and has:

1b *Jake Peter; *b* 1993

2b *Tobias Robert; *b* 1995

2a *Benedict James; *b* 4 May 1963; *m* 1991 *Georgina Rapinet and has:

1b *Jasper; *b* 1995

2b *Samuel Joseph; *b* 4 Aug 1997

3a *Marcus David; *b* 27 Nov 1964; *m* 1995 *Sandra Grey

1a *Harriet; *b* 3 Dec 1968

(3) (Bede Evelyn) Dominic; *b* 1931; painter; *m* 27 Jan (Havana) and 1 April (New York) 1958 (*divorce* 1968) Tessa Georgina, interior decorator, dau of Geoffrey Farrer Kennedy, of Tilford, Surrey, and *d* 5 Sept 1975, leaving:

1a *(Steven) Cassian Cary; *b* 1959; Hollywood film producer; *m* *Priscilla Woolworth

2a *Dushaan Damian Cary; *b* 1960

3a *Ivan Simon Cary; *b* 1962

(4) *Timothy Cyprian George Thomas; *b* 1935; *m* 1st 2 Oct 1959 (*divorce* 1969), as her 1st husb, Lorna, sis of Sir Gavin Lyle, 3rd Bt (*qv*), and has:

1a *Ian Antony Archibald de Hoghton Cary; *b* 1961

2a *Gavin Esmond Cary; *b* 1962

1a *Amanda Cary; *b* 1964; actress; *m* 1993 *Matthew Austin, records promoter, and has:

1b *George; *b* 9 Sept 1995

2a *Lydia Cary (twin); *b* 1964; designer

(4) (cont.) Timothy Elwes *m* 2nd 1974 *Leila Frances, dau of Col — Wolsten-Croft and formerly w of John Panton Corbett

The 1st BARON's est s,

FRANCIS JAMES RODD, **2nd Baron Rennell**, KBE (1944), CB (1943), JP (1950), of Rodd, Presteigne, Herefs, which he bought back from his distant cousins the LANEs; *b* 25 Oct 1895; *educ* Eton and Balliol Coll Oxford (MA); served WWs I (despatches, Order St Maurice and St Lazarus Italy) and II (despatches), Maj-Gen Civ Affrs M East, E Africa and Italy; Dip Serv 1919–24 (served Rome, Sofia, where chargé d'affaires, and FO); memb Stock Exchange 1926–29, Bank of England 1929–32, dir Morgan Grenfell 1932, Pres RGS 1945–48, Hon V-Pres and Hon Memb RGS, Visiting Fell Nuffield Coll Oxford 1947–59, dir BOAC 1954–65, Tstee London Museum, memb cncl: Br Assoc, Br Sch Rome and E African Inst History and Archaeology, V-Lt Herefs 1957–73 (DL 1948), Hon LLD Manchester, FSA, author: *People of the Veil, General William Eaton* (1933), *British Military Administration of African Territories, 1940-45* and *Valley on the March* (1958); *m* 3 Aug 1928 Hon Mary Constance Vivian Smith (*d* 31 May 1981), 2nd dau of 1st Baron Bicester (*qv*), and *dspm* 15 March 1978, leaving:

1 *Joanna Phoebe [The Hon Mme Joanna Rodd, Res le Ruscino, 14 quai Antoine Ier, 98000 Monaco; 6 Du Bellay, 9 rue Puget, 061 00 Nice, France]; *b* 4 July 1929; *m* 2 July 1966 (*divorce* Feb 1995) Count Gerard de Renusson d'Hauteville, Chev Legn Hon, Croix de Guerre, yr s of Marquis de Renusson d'Hauteville, of Croissy-sur-Seine, France

2 *Juliet Honor [The Hon Mrs Boobbyer, Little Rodd, Presteigne, Powys LD8 2LL]; *b* 28 Oct 1930; *m* 5 July 1957 *Brian Boobbyer, yr s of Philip Watson Boobbyer, MB, BCh, MRCS, and has:

(1) *Philip Christopher; *b* 8 Sept 1963; *educ* Abingdon, Trin Coll Cambridge, Georgetown U (MA) and LSE (PhD); lecturer Kent U

(2) *Mark Tremayne; *b* 31 March 1967; *educ* Abingdon and Durham U (BA); assist master Wellington; *m* 6 July 1991 *Catherine, er dau of Peter Hannon (*see* MONTROSE, D), and has:

1a *Angus Tremayne; *b* 13 Sept 1992

2a *Luke Francis; *b* 29 July 1994

3 *Mary Elizabeth Jill [The Hon Mrs Daniell, Ashley Farm, Staunton on Arrow, Herefs HR6 9LN]; *b* 5 Feb 1932; *m* 1st 13 Nov 1954 (*divorce* 1983) Michael William Langan Dunne, yst s of Cdr Thomas Bartholomew Dunne, RN (ret), and has:

(1) *(John) Francis Jeremy; *b* 23 Nov 1957

(2) *Stephen Michael Damian; *b* 28 April 1961; *m* 1990 *Anna Louise Garbett and has:

1a *Edward John Francis; *b* 12 Jan 1995

1a *Henrietta Elizabeth Grace; *b* 21 Feb 1992

(1) *Mary Jemima; *b* 27 Nov 1957; *m* 18 Aug 1989 *Philip Julian Lord and has:

1a *Daniel Norsen; *b* 16 Dec 1992

2a *Crispin Hugh; *b* 6 July 1995

1a *Harriet Frances; *b* 29 June 1990

(2) *Teresa Mary Claire; *b* 24 Aug 1962; *m* 6 Nov 1993 *Thomas Calvert and has:

1a *Jack Richard; *b* 20 Feb 1995

1a *Susannah Honor; *b* July 1997

(3) *Miranda Mary ; *b* 28 March 1966; *m* 21 Oct 1995 *Baron William Taxis and has:

1a *Isabella Mary Alice; *b* 16 March 1997

3 (cont.) The Hon Mrs Mary Dunne *m* 2nd 1985 *Christopher Daniell

4 *Rachel Georgiana [The Hon Mrs Rachel Blythe, 14 Lawson Way, Darlington, WA 6070, Australia]; *b* 1 Nov 1935; *educ* St Anne's Coll Oxford (MA) and Bedford Coll London; *m* 30 Oct 1964 (*divorce* 1983) Richard Douglas Gordon Blythe, er s of L Gordon Blythe, of Perth, W Australia, and has:

(1) *Joseph Matthew Gerard; *b* 3 Feb 1968; *educ* U of W Australia (BA)

(2) *Matthew Francis; *b* 9 March 1970

RENSHAW

Arms: Per pale and chevron or and azure, in chief two martlets and in base a bull's head couped, all counterchanged. **Crest:** In front of a griffin's head erased sable a decrescent and an increscent argent.
Motto: *Esse quam videri* ('To be rather than to seem').
Creation: Bt. (UK) 7 Jan 1903.

SIR CHARLES MAURICE BINE RENSHAW, 3RD BT, of Coldharbour, Wivelsfield, Sussex [Sir Charles Renshaw Bt, Tam-na-Margaidh, Balquhidder, Perthshire FK19 8PB; Linwood, Instow, N Devon EX39 4HX]; *b* 7 Oct 1912; *s f* 1976; *educ* Eton; late F/O RAF (invalided); *m* 1st 25 Feb 1942 (*divorce* 1947) Isabel Bassett, dau of Rev John L T Popkin, and has had:

1 Charles Edward Bine; *b* 17 May 1944; *d* 16 Sept 1954

2 +JOHN DAVID; *b* 9 Oct 1945; *educ* AAC Aldershot; *m* 1970 (*divorce* 1988) Jennifer, dau of G/Capt F Murray, RAF, and has:

  (1) +Thomas; *b* 1976

  (1) *Joanna; *b* 1973

  (2) *Catherine; *b* 1978

1 *Margaret Bine; *b* 17 Feb 1943; *m* 5 June 1967 (*divorce* 1988) Dr Lee Coulter Chumbley, s of Dr Charles C Chumbley, of Nashville, Tenn., and has:

  (1) *Roger; *b* 1973

  (2) *Justin; *b* 1977

  (1) *Lucy; *b* 1970

Sir CHARLES *m* 2nd 19– *Winifred May, dau of H F Gliddon, of Ashwater, Devon, and formerly w of James H T Sheldon, and by her has:

3 +Andrew; *b* 1947; S/Ldr RAF; *m* 1977 *Cherry Rose, n of Sir Edward Chichester, 11th Bt (*qv*), and has:

  (1) +Edward Chichester; *b* 1979

  (2) +Rory Andrew; *b* 1980

  (3) +Harry John; *b* 1983

  (1) *Eloise Rose; *b* 1986

4 +Quintus; *b* 1952; *m* 1st 1976 (*divorce* 1979) Heather MacGillivray, of Sydney, NSW; *m* 2nd 1986 *Donna Lee Helmkaump, of Michigan

5 +Edward; *b* 1965

2 *Caroline; *b* 1948; *m* 1987 *Richard Dumbrill, of Epernay, France

3 *Janet; *b* 1950; *m* 1970 (*divorce* 1989) Dr Colin Dodd, PhD, and has:

  (1) *Benjamin; *b* 1976

  (1) *Jennifer; *b* 1971

4 *Helen; *b* 1951; *m* 1st 1976 (*divorce* 19–) Douglas Arthur Coutts, of Lerwick, and has:

  (1) *Andrew; *b* 1977

4 (cont.) Mrs Helen Coutts *m* 2nd 19– *Ian Macdonald, of Dunvegan, Isle of Skye, and has:

  (2) *Calum Ian Berge; *b* 1982

  (3) *Findlay Charles; *b* 1986

  (1) *Eilidh; *b* 1981

  (2) *Fiona May; *b* 1984

Lineage: JOSHUA RENSHAW, of Timperley, Cheshire; *b* 1683; *m* 26 Dec 1712 Sarah Massey (*d* 9 Sept 1729) and *d* 14 June 1730, having had a 2nd s:

THOMAS RENSHAW; *b* 2 May 1716; *m* 1st Ann, dau of Randal Grundy; *m* 2nd Mary Goodwin (*d* 16 Feb 1786), and had a 2nd s by his 1st w:

HENRY GRUNDY RENSHAW; *b* 28 March 1747; *m* 1st 1770 Mary (*d* 26 Oct 1780), dau of William Ivory; *m* 2nd 1785 Ann (*d* 15 Oct 1845), dau of John Wolstenholme, and had an est s:

HENRY GRUNDY RENSHAW; *b* 26 April, 1771; *m* 22 June 1805 Ann (*d* 17 May 1860), dau of William Shaw, and *d* July 1848, leaving, with two yr sons and a dau:

THOMAS CHARLES RENSHAW, QC, of Sandrocks, Sussex; *b* 4 April 1810; Bencher Lincoln's Inn; *m* 8 Oct 1839 Elizabeth (*d* 12 Feb 1893), dau and heiress of George Blaker, of Patcham, Sussex, and *d* 26 May 1886, having had:

1 Walter Charles, KC, of Sandrocks; *b* 24 Sept 1840; *educ* Cambridge (LLM); Bencher Lincoln's Inn; *m* 11 Aug 1870 Elizabeth (*d* 27 Nov 1923), yr dau of John W Wilson, of Elsbroek, Holland, and Villa Christine, Nice, Offr Legn Ho and Kt Order Leopold, and *d* 16 July 1922, leaving issue

2 Alfred George, of Southend Hall, Catford; *b* 8 Sept 1844; *m* 1 July 1891 Emily Jane (*d* 3 Jan 1896), dau of Ashton Case and widow of Maj John Forster, and *dsp* 14 July 1897

3 CHARLES BINE (Sir), **1st Bt**

4 Arthur Henry, of Watlington Pk, Oxon, JP; *b* 18 Feb 1851; *m* 21 Jan 1899 Lady Winifred Edith Clements (*d* 24 Jan 1966 aged 91), dau of 4th Earl of Leitrim (*see* 1953 edn), and *d* 25 Dec 1912, leaving issue

1 Edith Anna; *m* 1st 8 Dec 1875 Thomas Lawford Rolph (*d* 5 Sept 1876); *m* 2nd 28 Oct 1882 James Brown Westray and *d* 4 Jan 1918, leaving issue

2 Mildred Elizabeth; *d* unm 17 Feb 1860

3 Florence Amy; *m* 29 July 1886 Charles Stewart Cox and had issue

The 3rd s,

Sir Charles Bine Renshaw, 1st Bt (UK), so *cr* 7 Jan 1903, JP (Renfrewshire), DL; *b* 9 Dec 1848; CC Renfrewshire, Commr Supply, MP (C) W Renfrewshire 1892–1906; *m* 27 Aug 1872 Mary Home (*d* 13 Feb 1937), 3rd dau of Arthur Francis Stoddard, of Broadfield, of Broadfield, Renfrewshire, and *d* 6 March 1918, leaving:

1 (CHARLES) STEPHEN BINE (Sir), **2nd Bt**

1 Ethel Mary; *b* 10 Aug 1878; *m* 1 March 1905 Rev William Griffith Jones (*d* 28 Oct 1936), Rector Long Marston, Yorks, and *d* 28 Feb 1952, leaving issue

2 Audrey Bine, of Owls Ho, Cowesfield Green, Salisbury, Wilts; *b* 17 Sept 1881; *m* 25 June 1901 Herbert Ogilvie, JP (*d* 10 June 1953), and had:

  (1) Brian Charles Herbert; *b* 12 Feb 1908; *m* May 1952 *Pamela Jane Beekamp, dau of R Buckingham Smith, and *d* 19 Nov 1961

  (2) Patrick Bruce, DSO, DFC; *b* 14 Jan 1910; G/Capt RAF WW II; *m* 1st April 1937 Audrey Mellish (*d* Dec 1938), dau of E Mellish Clark, of Cambridge; *m* 2nd July 1939 *Pamela Lavender (*m* 2nd 4 Sept 1947 Capt Roger Charles Lewis Kennaway; *see* KENNAWAY, Bt), dau of Cdr Tom Claud Mackenzie Bellairs, and *das* 11 Dec 1944, having by her had:

    1a *Audrey [Mrs Elijah Johnson, Mole Cottage, Norton, Yorks]; *b* 31 July 1940; *m* 15 Aug 1961 *Elijah Vivian Johnson, only s of Maj Richard Arthur Johnson, MC, of Chantilly, France, and has:

      1b *Richard Patrick Alan; *b* 26 Oct 1962

    2a *Louisa Patina; *b* 14 Feb 1942; *m* 21 Feb 1970 *Count Alexis Richard Dion Oswold de la Falaise, of Paris

  (1) *Winifred Mary; *b* 6 Jan 1903; *m* 15 Sept 1931 Maj Desbrisay Blundell Mein, DSO, MC (*d* 1937), and has:

    1a *John Desbrisay Blundell; *b* 9 April 1935

    1a *Susan [Mrs Ian Henderson, Longridge, North Chailey, Sussex]; *b* 16 Oct 1932; *m* 10 Oct 1953 *Ian Tudor Henderson and has:

      1b *Julian Tudor; *b* July 1954

      2b *David Tudor; *b* 1956

      1b *Stella Mary; *b* 1961

      2b *Lucinda Jane; *b* 1965

3 Marjory Bine; *b* 26 Nov 1886; *d* unm 21 May 1960

4 Elizabeth Hope Bine; *b* 29 Jan 1892; *m* 1st 4 Sept 1914 Maj Francis William Lindley Gull (*ka* 25 Aug 1918; *see* GULL, Bt); *m* 2nd 16 Dec 1922 Hon Robert William Morgan-Grenville and *d* 19 Feb 1969, leaving issue (*see* KINLOSS, L)

The 1st Bt's only s,

Sir (Charles) Stephen Bine Renshaw, 2nd Bt; *b* 9 Dec 1883; *educ* Charterhouse and Trin Coll Cambridge (BA 1904); Capt Ayrshire Yeo (TA) WW I; *m* 1st 26 Jan 1911 (*divorce* 1939) Edith Mary, 4th dau of R-Adml Sir Edward Chichester, 9th Bt (*qv*), and had:

1 Sir CHARLES MAURICE BINE RENSHAW, **3rd and present Bt**

1 *Julia Noble Bine [Mrs Edward Whitfield, PO Box 3721, Marondera, Zimbabwe]; *b* 21 April 1914; *m* Sept 1940 *Maj Edward William Whitfield, IA, and has:

  (1) *Michael Stephen [Michael Whitfield Esq, Plymtree, Marondera, Zimbabwe]; *b* 28 June 1941; *educ* St George's Coll Salisbury, Rhodesia, and RMA Sandhurst; Capt 3rd Carabiniers (POWDG); *m* 10 Jan 1969 *Lady Fiona Catherine Sinclair, 3rd dau of 19th Earl of Caithness (*qv*), and has:

    1a *Edward James; *b* 21 May 1971

    1a *Christine Louise; *b* 31 Aug 1973

  (2) *Christopher George; *b* 22 Sept 1945; *m* 1976 *Moira Everitt and has:

    1a *Ivan Edward; *b* 1978

    1a *Delia Joy; *b* 1980

  (1) *Wendy Martina; *b* 30 Sept 1942; *m* 1963 *Arthur Guiffre and has:

    1a *Christopher Paul; *b* 1965

    2a *Stephen; *b* 1966

    1a *Karen Elizabeth; *b* 1963

  (2) *Diana Mary; *b* 30 June 1950; *m* 1975 *David Bridge and has:

    1a *Justyn; *b* 1977

    2a *Martin; *b* 1979

2 *(Catherine) Margot [Mrs William Wall, Oakleigh, PO Box 58, Greytown, Natal, S Africa]; *b* 3 Aug 1917; *m* 14 Sept 1945 Lt William Robert Percy Wall, SAAF (*d* 1988), s of Maj PF Wall, 1st Norfolk Regt, of Greytown, and has:

  (1) *Mary Jane; *b* 4 Dec 1948; *m* 20 Dec 1969 *Dr Louis George von Bratt Reynolds, MB, ChB, of Capetown

  (2) *Jessica; *b* 4 March 1950

Sir Stephen *m* 2nd 3 Sept 1939 *Mace Caroline, est dau of Maj George Wynn-Tetley, of Evenley Manor, Brackley, and *d* 1 Nov 1976

RENTON

Arms: Az. a horse forcene, on a chief or a sword, point to the dexter gu., between a portcullis chained and hunting horn stringed az. **Crest:** In front of a horse's head erased or a hunting horn stringed az. **Supporters:** Dexter, a lion guardant purpure, gorged with a fine chain, pendant therefrom a millrind gold; sinister, a stag guardant ppr., gorged with a like chain, pendant therefrom a fetterlock enclosing a heatr gold. **Motto:** *Virtus in actione est* ('Virtue is in action'). **Creation:** B. (LP, UK) 1979.

THE BARON RENTON, of Huntingdon Co Cambs (Sir David Lockhart-Mure Renton, KBE (1964), TD, PC (1962), QC (1954), DL (Hunts 1962, Huntingdon and Peterborough 1964, Cambs 1974)) [The Rt Hon The Lord Renton KBE TD PC QC DL, House of Lords, London SW1A 0PW]; *b* 12 Aug 1908; *educ* Oundle and Univ Coll Oxford; Maj RA WW II, barrister Lincoln's Inn 1933, memb Bar Cncl 1939, Bencher 1962, Treas 1979, memb Senate Inns of Court 1967–71 and 1975–79, MP (C) Hunts 1945–79, Parly Sec Min Fuel and Power 1955–57 and Min Power 1957–58, Jt Parly U-Sec Home Office 1958–61, Min State Home Office 1961–62, Recorder Rochester 1963–68 and Guildford 1968–71, Pres Statute Law Soc 1980–, Dep Speaker Ho Lds 1982–88, Jt-Pres Parly Arts and Heritage Cncl 1992–; *m* 1947 Claire Cicely (*d* 1986), yst dau of Walyer Atholl Duncan, and has:

1 *Caroline Mary [The Hon Mrs Caroline Parr, Port Mary House, Dundrennan, Kirkcudbright DG6 4QU]; *b* 1948; *m* 1st 1970 (*divorce* 1974) Peter Dodds Parker and has issue; *m* 2nd 1977 (*divorce* 1994) Robin Warwick Anthony Parr and has further issue

2 *Clare Olivia [The Hon Mrs Scott, 11 Flodden Rd, London SE5]; *b* 1950; barrister; *m* 1982 *Timothy John Whittaker Scott and has issue

3 *Davina Kathleen; *b* 1954

Lineage: MAURICE WAUGH RENTON; MD, CM, DPH; *m* Eszma Olivia, dau of Allen Walter Borman, of Alexandria, and had:

DAVID LOCKHART-MURE, *cr* a **Baron**

RENTON OF MOUNT HARRY

Creation: B. (LP, UK) 19 April 1997.

THE BARON RENTON OF MOUNT HARRY, of Offham, Co E Sussex ((Ronald) Tim(othy) Renton, PC (1989)) [The Rt Hon The Lord Renton of Mount Harry PC, House of Lords, London SW1A 0PW]; *b* 28 May 1932; *educ* Eton and Magdalen Coll Oxford; joined C Tennant Sons & Co 1954 (dir 1964–73), md Tennant Trading 1964–73, dir: Silvermines Ltd 1964–84, Australia and NZ Banking Gp 1967–76, Fleming Continental European Investment Tst 1992–; MP (C) Mid-Sussex 1974–97, PPS to: Ch Sec Treasury 1979–81, For Sec 1983–84, Parly U-Sec FCO 1985–87, Min State: FCO 1985–87, Home Office 1987–89, Parly Sec Treasury and Ch Whip 1989–90, Min State PC Office 1990–92, memb Select Ctee Nationalised Industries 1974–79, V-Chm C Parly Trade Ctee 1974–79, Chm: C For and Cwlth Cncl 1982–84, Parly Br-Hong Kong All Party Gp 1992–, Pres C Trade Unionists 1980–84 (V-Pres 1978–80); Fell Industry and Parl Tst 1977–79, memb: Advsy Bd Know-How Fund for Centl and E Europe 1992–, Devpt Cncl Parnham Tst 1992–, Criterion Theatre Tst 1992–; APEX memb Cncl Roedean Sch 1982–; Tstee Mental Health Fndn 1985–89; Fndr Pres Nat Music Day 1992–; Chm Outsider Art Archive 1995–; author: *The Dangerous Edge* (1994); *m* 2 April 1960 *Alice Blanche Helen, er dau of Sir James Fergusson, 8th Bt (*qv*), and has:

1 *Alexander James Torr; *b* 5 March 1961

2 *Daniel Charles Antony; *b* 21 Sept 1965

1 *Christian Louise; *b* 9 April 1963; *m* 1993 *Lloyd Michael Gudgeon

2 *Katherine Chelsea; *b* 21 Sept 1965

3 *Penelope Sally Rosita; *b* 1970

Lineage: WILLIAM RENTON, of Parkfoot, Channelkirk, Berwicks; *b* 1705; *m* 27 March 1731 Jean Swinton and *d* 1784, having had:

PATRICK/PETER RENTON, of Edinburgh; *b* 11 March 1743; *m* 19 June 1767 Christina, dau of William Gordon, and *d* 1782, leaving:

WILLIAM RENTON, of Edinburgh; *b* 7 Jan 1774; *m* 7 July 1802 Agnes, dau of Henry Duncan, of Edinburgh, and *d* 9 Feb 1855, leaving:

ALEXANDER RENTON, of Edinburgh; *b* 14 Dec 1819; *m* 21 March 1849 Jane Leishman and *d* 25 Oct 1863, leaving, with an est s, a yst s and two daus:

JAMES HENRY RENTON, of Aspley Guise, Beds, and S Kensington; *b* 4 Sept 1852; *educ* Edinburgh Acad; *m* 1892 Louisa Sophia, dau of Hofprädiger — Brandes, and *d* 22 Nov 1920, having had:

1 Alexander Frederick Gordon, OBE, MC, TD; *b* 9 Jan 1893; Col WW II; *m* 6 Dec 1945 Mharie Hester, yr dau of Sir James Grant, 1st and last Bt, of Househill, Nairn (see 1932 edn), and formerly w of Brig Arthur Darley Bridge, MC, Coldstream Gds

2 Henry Noel Leslie; *b* 18 Dec 1894; *ka* July 1915 WW I

3 Ronald Kenneth Duncan, CBE; *b* 24 Jan 1897; *educ* Harrow and Magdalen Coll Oxford; 11th Hus WW I, barrister Inner Temple 1923, ptnr Dyson, Bell & Co 1930, Intell Corps WW II (despatches, Croix de Guerre); *m* 1st 29 Nov 1923 Hon Margaret Julia Tyrell (*d* 11 Feb 1925), dau of 1st and last Baron Tyrell, GCMG, KCB, KCVO, PC (see 1939 edn); *m* 2nd 23 March 1929 Eileen Doris, MBE, yst dau of Herbert James Torr, of Morton Hall, Lincs, and had:

  (1) *Henry James [Henry Renton Esq, 87 Oakley St, London SW3 5NP]; *b* 25 March 1930; *educ* Eton and Magdalen Coll Oxford; late 2nd Lt Welsh Gds; has:

    1a *H— J—; *b c* 1973; *educ* Eton

  (2) (RONALD) TIM(OTHY), *cr* a **Baron**

RENWICK, Baron

Arms: Argent, a husbandman in the act of sowing, proper, on a chief azure a thunderbolt between two bull's heads cabossed or. **Crest:** A thunderbolt or. **Supporters:** Dexter, a black poodle; sinister, a tabby cat, both proper. **Motto:** *Laborare est orare* ('To work is to pray'). **Creations:** Bt. (UK) 28 June 1927, B. (UK) 23 Dec 1964.

THE 2ND BARON RENWICK, of Coombe, Co Surrey, and a **Baronet** (Sir Harry Andrew Renwick, Bt) [The Rt Hon The Lord Renwick, 47 Cheyne Walk, London SW3]; *b* 10 Oct 1935; *s f* 1973; *educ* Eton; 2nd Lt Gren Gds 1955–56, ptnr W Greenwell & Co stockbrokers, dir Gen Technology Systems, chm EURIM, Save & Prosper and Robert Fleming Inc 1998–; *m* 1st 27 April 1965 (*divorce* 1989) Susan Jane, only child of Capt Kenneth Stephen Bamfylde Lucking and Mrs Moir Patrick Stormonth Darling, of Lednathie, Glen Prosen, Angus, and has:

1 +ROBERT JAMES; *b* 19 Aug 1966; *educ* privately

2 +Michael David; *b* 26 July 1968

The 2nd BARON RENWICK *m* 2nd 1989 *Mrs Homayoun Mazandi, dau of Maj Mahmoud Yazdanparst Pakzad and formerly w of Joe Mazandi, of Los Angeles

Lineage: ANDREW RENWICK, of Windsor; had:

Sir Harry (Benedetto) Renwick, 1st Bt (UK), so *cr* 28 June 1927, KBE (1920); *b* 13 June 1861; AMIEE, dir Feeding Stuffs Min Food 1916–18, chm and md Co of London Electric Supply Co and associated cos; *m* 2 June 1897 Frederica Louisa (*d* 12 July 1927), dau of Robert Laing, of Stirling, and *d* 7 Jan 1932, leaving:

1 ROBERT BURNHAM, **1st Baron**

1 Frederica Selina; *b* 9 July 1899; *d* unm 9 March 1966

2 Agnes Mary; *m* 27 July 1926 Julius Ernest Guthe, of Kepwick Hall, Thirsk, Yorks, and had issue

3 Ella Rosalie; *m* 1st 7 Aug 1925 Cdr Richard Reynell, RN (ret), and had two sons; *m* 2nd 2 Oct 1939 Leslie Wilson Barnett and *d* 26 Nov 1965, leaving by him two daus

The 1st Bt's only s,

  Sir Robert Burnham Renwick, 2nd Bt, and **1st Baron Renwick**, of Coombe, Co Surrey (UK), so *cr* 23 Dec 1964 , KBE (1944); *b* 4 Oct 1904; *educ* Eton and Trin Coll Oxford; chm Co of London Electric Supply Co 1939–48, controller: Communications Air Min and Communication Equipment Min Aircraft Production, memb Aircraft Supply Cncl 1942–45, chm: ATV and IOD, ptnr W Greenwell & Co, dir BICC; *m* 1st 10 June 1929 (*divorce* 1953) Dorothy Mary (*m* 2nd 1953 John Fitzadam Ormiston (*d* 1994)), er dau of Maj Harold Parkes, of The Dial Ho, Alveston, Stratford-on-Avon, and had:

1 HARRY ANDREW RENWICK, **2nd and present Baron Renwick**

1 *Susan Mary, OBE, JP (Hants and SE London) [The Hon Mrs Susan Baring OBE JP, 13 Alexander St, London W2 5NT]; *b* 5 June 1930; *m* 1st 25 Nov 1955 (*divorce* 1984) 7th Baron Ashburton (*qv*) and has issue; *m* 2nd 26 June 1997 *André Newburg but retains first husb's family name

2 Jennifer; *b* 20 March 1932; *m* 1st 18 Nov 1954 (*divorce* 1967) Antony Duncan Rowe, 3rd s of George Duncan Rowe, of Herons Court, Yateley, Hants, and had:

(1) *Giles Timothy Robert [Giles Rowe Esq, Flat 4, 38 Redcliffe Gdns, London SW10]; *b* 26 Aug 1956; *educ* Eton; *m* 1986 (*divorce* 1991) Karma Nabulsi

(1) *Antonia Tanya; *b* 26 July 1959; *m* 1983 *Henry James Stone, of Kingsbridge, S Devon, and has:

1a *Benjamin James; *b* 1986

2a *Liam Henry; *b* 1988

3a *Jacob Antony; *b* 1991

4a *Harry Edward; *b* 1993

1a *Gemma Elizabeth; *b* 1984

2 (cont.) The Hon Mrs Jennifer Rowe *m* 2nd 17 Dec 1973 (*divorce* 1978) Roy Philip Arthur (*d* 1994), s of C Arthur, of Jersey, CI; *m* 3rd 1978 (*divorce* 1989) Robert Ian MacDonald and *d* 1989

3 *Belinda Anne [The Hon Mrs Shephard, The Barn, Elcot, Berks]; *b* 6 March 1934; *m* 19 March 1959 John Horatio Gordon Shephard (*d* 1993), only s of Harold Shephard, and has:

(1) *William; *b* 2 May 1962

(1) *Sarah [Mrs Alexander Scrimgeour, 103 Strathville Rd, London SW18]; *b* 9 Dec 1959; *m* 1st 1988 (*divorce* 1993) Stephen P M Clarke; *m* 2nd 1993 *Alexander J H Scrimgeour

The **1st Baron** *m* 2nd 28 July 1953, as her 2nd husb, (Edith) Joan (*d* 6 Nov 1994), only child of Sir Reginald Clarke, CIE, and widow of Maj John Ogilvie Spencer, Welsh Gds, and *d* 30 Aug 1973

RENWICK, Bt

Arms: Per chevron sable and argent, in chief two lymphads of the second and in base on a mount vert a horse courant of the first. **Crest:** In front of a lion's head erased proper a bugle-horn stringed gules. **Motto:** For true liberty. **Creation:** Bt. (UK) 22 June 1921.

SIR RICHARD EUSTACE RENWICK, 4TH BT, of Newminster Abbey, Northumberland [Sir Richard Renwick Bt, Whalton House, Whalton, Northumberland NE61 3UZ]; *b* 13 Jan 1938; *s* f 1973; *educ* Eton; amateur jockey; *m* 11 June 1966 *Caroline Anne, er dau of Maj Rupert Leonard Milburn (*see* MILBURN, Bt), and has:

1 +CHARLES RICHARD; *b* 10 April 1967; Capt Light Dragoons; *m* 1993 *Mrs Jane ('Yorkie') Ann Lyles, only dau of Stuart Bush, of Holly Farm, Wendling, Norfolk, and has:

(1) +George Charles Eustace; *b* 8 Jan 1995

2 +Harry Timothy; *b* 19 Oct 1968

3 +Rory Eustace Deuchar; *b* 27 March 1975

Lineage: JOHN N RENWICK, of Newcastle; had:

Sir George Renwick, 1st Bt (UK), so *cr* 22 June 1921, JP (Newcastle and Tynemouth), DL (Northumberland); *b* 8 March 1850; shipowner, MP (C) Newcastle 1900–06, 1908–10 and Newcastle Centl 1918–22, chm Manchester Dry Docks, memb Fisher Renwick, shipowners and brokers, of Newcastle, Chev Legn Hon; *m* 1877 Mary Jane (*d* 23 Jan 1933), dau of William John Thompson, of Jubbulpore, India, and *d* 19 June 1931, leaving:

1 JOHN ROBERT (Sir), **2nd Bt**

2 William Henry; *b* 5 March 1880; Maj; *m* 1899 Ethel Maud (*d* 11 June 1944), dau of William Ratcliffe, of Newcastle, and *d* 17 March 1961, leaving:

(1) +Eric Montague; *b* 1904; *m* June 1956 (*divorce* 1960) Marie (Sandra) —

(2) +Aubrey Forster; *b* 1912

(1) *Alexandra Constance; *b* 1902

(2) *Dorothy Forster; *b* 1905

(3) *Pamela Mary; *b* 1920

3 George; *b* 11 Oct 1881; *m* 1906 Nina, dau of John Best Ferrier, of Penarth, S Wales, and *d* 14 Dec 1937, leaving:

(1) +Peter; *b* 1913

(1) *Peggy; *b* 1907; *m* 7 Feb 1931 *Claude Chessher Darling, s of Adam Darling, of Berwick, and has:

1a *David; *b* 12 March 1932

2a *Timothy; *b* 5 Jan 1944

1a *Diana Jane; *b* 17 Nov 1938; *m* 17 Feb 1968 *Peter George Cary Summers and has:

1b *Jonathan Peter; *b* 5 Aug 1969

1b *Caroline Cary; *b* 1971

4 Gustav Adolph; *b* 17 Dec 1883; *educ* Giggleswick; Maj Northumberland Fus WW I (severely wounded, despatches), MP Stretford 1931–35, chm: Road Haulage (Operations) Advsy Ctee Min War Transport 1941, Manchester Dry Docks, Manchester Chamber Commerce, Beresford Atkinson Ltd, chm and govr-dir Fisher-Renwick Ltd, dir Scammell Lorries Ltd; *m* 1907 his er bro's sis-in-law (*see* below) Mabel (*d* 12 Feb 1968), dau of James Deuchar, of Kelso, and *d* 10 Sept 1956, leaving:

(1) Denis Adolph; *b* 1907; *m* 4 July 1934 Phyllis (*d* 1983), only dau of A B Atkinson, and *d* 1983, leaving:

1a +Guy Philip [Guy Renwick Esq, Holystone Grange, Sharperton, Northumberland]; *b* 15 Nov 1936; *educ* Stowe and Christ's Coll Cambridge (MA); late 2nd Lt Roy Scots; *m* 30 June 1966 *(Janet) Melanie, only dau of H James Franklin, FRIBA, AADipl, of West Hepple Farmhouse, Hepple, Northumberland, and has:

1b +Shaun Maurice; *b* 2 April 1970

2b +Maxwell Mark; *b* 1972

5 Septimus, MC (1918); *b* 12 Jan 1886; *educ* privately; 1st Bn Scots Gds WW I, with Fisher Renwick; *m* 1915 Margaret (*d* 1983), dau of James Turnbull, of Durham, and *d* 5 Feb 1966, having had:

(1) +George Lionel [George Renwick Esq, Upend, Newmarket, Suffolk]; *b* 1917

(1) Ann; *b* 1919; *m* 26 June 1948 *Maj Alan Newstead Fradgley, MBE, RE (Kenya), only s of G A Fradgley, and *d* 24 Dec 1958, leaving two sons

(2) *Barbara [Miss Barbara Renwick, Upend, Newmarket, Suffolk]; *b* 1922

The 1st Bt's est s,

Sir John Robert Renwick, 2nd Bt; *b* 13 Nov 1877; *m* 1902 Ethel, dau of James Deuchar, of Kelso, and *d* 20 Nov 1946, leaving:

1 EUSTACE DEUCHAR (Sir), **3rd Bt**

2 +Dudley Cyril Deuchar; *b* 1907

1 *Wendy Deuchar; *b* 19 Sept 1910; served Women's Legn, attd Dutch War Office 1942–45; *m* 23 Aug 1955 *Joseph Alexander Archibald Farrow, est s of Joseph Algernon Farrow, of Peterborough

Sir JOHN's er s,

Sir Eustace Deuchar Renwick, 3rd Bt; *b* 27 Nov 1902; *educ* Uppingham; S/Ldr RAFVR WW II (despatches), shipowner; *m* 15 Sept 1934 *Diana Mary [Diana Lady Renwick, Whalton, Morpeth, Northumberland], est dau of Col Bernard Cruddas, DSO, of Middleton Hall, Morpeth, and *d* following an accident in hunting field 3 Nov 1973, leaving:

1 Sir RICHARD EUSTACE RENWICK, **4th and present Bt**

2 +George Eustace; *b* 26 Nov 1947; *educ* Eton

1 *Julia Diana [Mrs Julia Percy, Greenfields, Wall, Hexham, Northumberland]; *b* 16 Aug 1935; *m* 11 May 1957 (*divorce* 1979) Jervis Joscelyn Percy, er s of Col Joscelyn Edward Seymour Percy, DSO, MC, Durham LI, and Lady Bradford, and has:

(1) *Corinna Josceline; *b* 28 Feb 1964

(2) *Jane Diana; *b* 24 Jan 1966

(3) *Charlotte Elizabeth; *b* 14 Aug 1967

RENWICK OF CLIFTON

Creation: B. (LP, UK) 2 Aug 1997.

THE BARON RENWICK OF CLIFTON, of Chelsea, Roy Borough of Kensington and Chelsea (Sir Robin William Renwick, KCMG (1989, CMG 1980)) [The Rt Hon The Lord Renwick of Clifton KCMG, House of Lords, London SW1A 0PW]; *b* 13 Dec 1937; *educ* St Paul's, Jesus Coll Cambridge (Hon Fell 1992) and Sorbonne; Army 1956–58; Dip Serv: 3rd Sec Dakar 1963–64, FO 1964–66, New Delhi 1966–69, Priv Sec to Min State FCO 1970–72, First Sec Paris 1972–76, Counsellor Cabinet Office 1976–78, Rhodesia Dept FCO 1978–80, Political Advsr to Govr Rhodesia 1980, Visiting Fell Center Internat Affrs Harvard 1980–81, Head Chancery Washington 1981–84, Assist U-Sec FCO 1984–87, Amb: S Africa 1987–91, USA 1991–95, dir Robert Fleming Hldgs, chm Save and Prosper Gp 1996–; FRSA; Hon LLD: Witwatersrand U 1990, American U London 1993; Hon DLitt: William and Mary Coll 1993, Oglethorpe U 1995; author: *Economic Sanctions* (1981), *The Special Relationship: myth or reality?* (1995) and *Fighting with Allies: America and Britain in Peace and War*; *m* 1965 *Annie Colette Giudicelli and has a s and dau

Lineage: RICHARD RENWICK, of Edinburgh; *m* Clarice Henderson and had:

ROBIN WILLIAM, *cr* a **Baron**

REVELSTOKE

Arms: Azure a fess or, charged with a mullet ermine upon a hurt for difference, in chief a bear's head proper, muzzled and ringed or.
Crest: A mullet erminois between two wings argent.
Supporters: Dexter, a bull argent; sinister, a bear proper, muzzled or, each charged on the shoulder with a mullet erminois.
Motto: *Probitate et labore* ('By uprightness and labour').
Creation: B. (UK) 30 June 1885.

THE 5TH BARON REVELSTOKE OF MEMBLAND, of Revelstoke, Co Devon (John Baring) [The Rt Hon The Lord Revelstoke, Lambay Island, Rush, Co Dublin, Ireland]; *b* 2 Dec 1934; *s* f 1994; *educ* Eton

Lineage: Sir FRANCIS BARING, 1st Bt (*see* NORTHBROOK, B), had a 3rd s:

HENRY BARING, of Cromer Hall, Norfolk; had by his 2nd w a 4th s (excluding a s who *dsp*):

EDWARD CHARLES BARING, **1st Baron Revelstoke of Membland**, Co Devon (UK), so *cr* 30 June 1885, of Membland Hall and Revelstoke Manor, Devon; *b* 13 April 1828; *educ* Rugby; Dir Bank of England 1879–91, sr ptnr Baring Bros to 1890, Lt City of London; *m* 30 April 1861 Louisa Emily Charlotte (*b c* 1836; *d* 16 Oct 1892), dau of John Crocker Bulteel, of Flete and Lyneham, Devon, by Lady Elizabeth Grey, dau of 2nd Earl Grey (*qv*), and *d* 17 July 1897, having had, with two other sons (*d* in infancy):

1 JOHN BARING, **2nd Baron Revelstoke of Membland**, GCVO (1911), PC (1902); *b* 7 Sept 1863; *educ* Eton and Trin Coll Cambridge; ptnr Baring Bros 1890, Dir Bank of England 1898–1909, Receiver-Gen Duchy Cornwall 1908, Ld Lt Middx 1926, memb ctee experts Settlement Reparations 1929, Russian Order White Eagle, Grand Cordon Order Rising Sun Japan, Cdr Legion of Honour; *d* unm 19 April 1929

2 CECIL, **3rd Baron**

3 Everard, CVO (1903), CBE (1919); *b* 5 Dec 1865; *educ* Eton and RMC Sandhurst; served Nile Expdn 1897–98 (despatches twice, brevet, two medals with three clasps), Mil Sec Viceroy India 1899–1905, Brig-Gen 10th Hus and Bde Cdr WW I 1916–18, Hon Brig-Gen 1918; *m* 15 Sept 1904 Lady Ulrica Duncombe (*d* 27 April 1935), yst dau of 1st Earl of Feversham (*see* FEVERSHAM, B), and *d* 7 May 1932, leaving:

(1) *Helen [Mrs Gordon Foster, Sleightholmedale, Kirkbymoorside, York YO6 6JG]; *b* 20 Aug 1906; *m* 16 Sept 1939 Maj Gordon Bentley Foster, DL (*d* 1 April 1963), s of Leonard Foster, and has:

1a *Rosanna; *b* 1941; *m* 1965 *Hon Oliver Francis Wintour James, s of Baron James of Rusholme (LP, *see* 1970 edn), and has:

1b *Patrick Esmond; *b* 1967; *m* 26 Oct 1996 *Natasha, dau of Duncan Davidson, of Lilburn Tower, Northumberland, and has:

1c *Arthur Francis; *b* 19 Jan 1998

1b *Helen; *b* 1970

2a *Mary Helen [Mrs John Duncan, The Old Vicarage, York]; *b* 1942; *m* 1981 *John Duncan and has:

1b *Flora; *b* 23 Feb 1983

(2) Audrey; *b* 7 Sept 1909; *m* 1st 29 Nov 1933 (*divorce* 1948) Lt-Col Sir Charles Frederick Richmond Brown, 4th Bt (*qv*), and had issue; *m* 2nd 1947 *Lt-Col Campbell Kirkman Finlay and *d* 1997, having had further issue

(3) Elizabeth; *b* 31 July 1915; *d* unm 1988

4 Maurice, OBE (1918); *b* 27 April 1874; *educ* Eton and Trin Coll Cambridge; Dip Serv 1897–1904: Attaché Paris 1898 and Copenhagen 1900, 3rd Sec 1900, Rome 1902, FO 1903–04, *Morning Post* war correspondent Manchuria 1904 and special correspondent Russia 1905–08 and Constantinople 1909, *Times* special correspondent Balkans 1912, WW I: T/Lt Intell Corps attd RFC BEF 1914, Lt Sept 1915, Capt Oct 1915, Maj 1917, SO2 RAF 1918, Staff Offr Ind Air Force May-Dec 1918 (despatches); Hon W/Cdr RAFO 1925, Offr Legn Honour 1935, FRSL, author: *Hildesheim and Quatre Pastiches* (1899), *The Black Prince* (1902), *Gaston de Foix* (1903), *With the Russians in Manchuria* (1905), *Mahasena* (1905), *Desiderio* (1906), *Sonnets and Short Poems* (1906), *Thoughts on Art and Life of Leonardo Da Vinci* (trans, 1906), *A Year in Russia* (1907), *Proserpine* (1908), *Russian Essays and Stories* (1909), *Orpheus in Mayfair*

(1909), *The Story of Forget Me Not and Lily of the Valley* (1909), *Landmarks in Russian Literature* (1910), *Diminutive Dramas* (1910), *Collected Poems* (1911), *The Russian People* (1911), *The Grey Stocking and Other Plays* (1911), *Letters from the Near East* (1913), *Palamon and Arcite* (1913), *What I Saw in Russia* (1913), *Lost Diaries* (1913), *The Mainsprings of Russia* (1914), *An Outline of Russian Literature* (1914), *Round the World in any Number of Days* (1914), *English Landscape: an anthology* (1916), *Translations by S. C.* (1916), *Poems, 1914–17* (1918), *Translations Ancient and Modern* (1919), *R.F.C.H.Q. 1914–18* (1920), *Poems, 1914–19* (1921), *Passing By* (1921), *The Puppet Show of Memory* (1922), *Overlooked* (1922), *His Majesty's Embassy* (1923), *A Triangle* (1923), *C.* (1924), *Punch and Judy and other Essays* (1924), *Half a Minute's Silence* (1925), *Collected Poems* (1925), *Translations with Originals* (1925), *Cat's Cradle* (1925), *Daphne Adeane* (1926), *Last Days at Tsarskoe Selo* (trans, 1926), *Tinker's Leave* (1927), *Comfortless Memory* (1928), *Algae* (1928), *The Coat without Seam* (1929), *Fantastic* (trans, 1929), *Robert Peckham* (1930), *In the End is my Beginning* (1931), *Lost Lectures* (1932), *Friday's Business* (1932), *Sarah Bernhardt* (1933), *The Lonely Lady of Dulwich* (1934), *Unreliable History* (1935), *Darby and Joan* (1935), *Have you anything to declare?* (1936) and *Russian Lyrics* (1942); *d* unm 16 Dec 1945

5 Hugo, OBE (1919); *b* 6 Oct 1876; *educ* Eton and RMC Sandhurst; Lt 4th Hus, served Tirah Expdn 1897–98 (medal), S Africa (wounded) and T/Capt 10th Hus and GSO Dec 1915 WW I (wounded Ypres), Br Mil Mission Siberia 1918–19, dir Westminster Bank; *m* 1 March 1905 Evelyn Harriet (*d* 22 Jan 1931), 2nd dau of 8th Earl of Shaftesbury (*qv*) and widow of 2nd Baron Magheramorne of Magheramorne (*see* HOGG, Bt), and *d* 20 Aug 1949, having had:

(1) Francis Anthony; *b* 28 Nov 1909; *educ* Eton and Magdalene Coll Cambridge; Lt RA (SRO) WW II; *m* 22 April 1933 Lady Rose Gwendolen Louisa McDonnell, DCVO (1964) (Woman of the Bedchamber to HM THE QUEEN 1953–93; *d* 1993), er dau of 7th Earl of Antrim (*qv*), and *d* of wounds recd in action France three weeks after misreported *ka* June 1940, leaving:

1a +Nicholas Hugo [Nicholas Baring Esq, 43 Sutherland Place, London W2 5BY; The Old Rectory, Ham, Wilts SN8 3QR]; *b* 2 Jan 1934; *educ* Eton and Magdalene Coll Cambridge (BA); 2nd Lt Coldstream Gds 1952–54, ADC to Govr Kenya 1957–58, joined Baring Bros 1958 (*md* Baring Bros & Co 1963–86, dir Barings plc 1985–95 (dep chm 1986–89)), memb City Capital Mkts Ctee 1983–89 (chm 1983–87), pres Liverpool Sch Tropical Medicine 1989–, chm Commercial Union 1990–98 (dir 1968–, dep chm 1983–90), Chm Tstees Nat Gallery 1992– (Tstee 1989–), Nat Tst: memb exec ctee 1965–69 and 1979–, memb cncl 1978–, chm finance ctee 1980–91, memb cncl Baring Fndn 1969– and cncl management Architectural Heritage Fund 1987–; *m* 28 Oct 1972 *Elizabeth Diana, dau of Brig Charles Crawfurd, and has:

1b +Francis Charles; *b* 4 Sept 1973

2b +Tobias Keith Alexander; *b* 10 Feb 1976

3b +Edward Randal; *b* 11 April 1979

2a +Peter; *b* 28 Oct 1935; chm Barings plc 1989–95 and Baring Asset Management 1993–95 (joined Baring Bros 1959, dir 1967), dir Inchcape 1978–96 and British Invisibles 1990–96, dep chm Provident Mutual Life Assur Assoc 1989–96, chm Br Merchant Banking and Securities Houses Assoc 1991–96, Govr London Business Sch 1991–96; *m* 9 Nov 1960 *Teresa Anne, 2nd dau of Hon Sir Maurice Richard Bridgeman (*see* BRIDGEMAN, V), and has:

1b +Guy Francis; *b* 27 Oct 1965; *m* 1995 *Tessa, dau of Andrew Brooks

2b +Max Maurice; *b* 4 Aug 1967

3b +Hugo John; *b* 12 July 1970; *educ* Eton; *m* 19– *Annabel — and has:

1c *Maude Mary; *b* 9 May 1998

1a *Susan Violet [Mrs Joe Rogaly, Old Timbers, Cox's Lane, Shalbourne, Wilts SN8 3PY]; *b* 16 Dec 1938; *m* 29 June 1962 *Henry Joseph (Joe) Rogaly, only s of Nelson Julius Rogaly, of Johannesburg, S Africa, and Mrs W R W Hill, and has:

1b *Benjamin Nelson; *b* 18 May 1963

1b *Sarah Rose; *b* 1 June 1965

2b *Rachel Frances; *b* 3 Sept 1968

3b *Jessica Hilary; *b* 1971

1 Elizabeth; *b* 16 March 1867; *m* 26 April 1887 5th Earl of Kenmare, CVO (*see* 1949 edn), and *d* 21 May 1944, leaving issue

2 Margaret; *b* 14 Dec 1868; *m* 25 July 1887 1st Viscount Althorp (*see* SPENCER, E) and *d* 4 July 1906, leaving issue

3 Susan; *b* 9 Oct 1870; Maid of Hon to HM QUEEN VICTORIA 1898–99; *m* 28 Nov 1899 Sir James Reid, 1st Bt, of Ellon (*qv*), and *d* 8 Feb 1961, leaving issue

The 2nd BARON's bro,

CECIL BARING, **3rd Baron Revelstoke of Membland**; *b* 12 Sept 1864; *educ* Eton and Balliol Coll Oxford (MA); dir Baring Bros; *m* 8 Nov 1902 Maude (*d* 2 April 1922), yst dau of Pierre Lorillard, of Rancocas, NJ, and *d* 26 Jan 1934, leaving:

1 RUPERT BARING, **4th Baron Revelstoke of Membland**; *b* 8 Feb 1911; *educ* Eton and Trin Coll Cambridge; 2nd Lt RAC (TA) WW II, i/c BRC POW food supplies; *m* 1 March 1934 (*divorce* 1944) Hon Florence (Flora) Fermor-Hesketh (*d* 15 Sept 1970), 2nd dau of 1st Baron Hesketh (*qv*), and *d* 18 July 1994, leaving:

(1) JOHN BARING, **5th and present Baron Revelstoke of Membland**

(2) +JAMES CECIL; *b* 16 Aug 1938; heir presumptive; *educ* Eton; *m* 1st 16 Aug 1968 Aneta Laline Dennis, yr dau of Erskine Arthur Hamilton Fisher, and has:

1a +Alexander Rupert; *b* 9 April 1970

2a +Thomas James; *b* 4 Dec 1971

(2) (cont.) The Hon JAMES BARING *m* 2nd 1983 *Sarah, dau of William Edward Stubbs, MBE, and by her has:

1a *Flora Aksinia; *b* 1983

1 Daphne; *b* 15 Feb 1904; *m* 11 Feb 1920 Arthur Joseph Lawrence Pollen and *d* 1986, leaving issue (*see* POLLEN, Bt)

2 Calypso; *b* 15 Oct 1905; *m* 7 April 1926 (*divorce* 1943) Guy Maynard Liddell, CB, CBE, MC (*see* RAVENSWORTH, B), and *d* 25 Oct 1974, leaving issue

REYNOLDS

Arms: Per chevron ermine and or, in chief two lions passant gules and in base three leopard's faces sable. **Crest:** A demi-moorcock displayed proper, charged on each wing with a leopard's face or. **Motto:** *Perseverando* ('By persevering'). **Creation:** Bt. (UK) 6 March 1923.

SIR DAVID JAMES REYNOLDS, 3RD BT, of Woolton, Co Lancaster [Sir David Reynolds Bt, Blanchepierre House, Rue de la Blanchepierre, St Lawrence, Jersey]; *b* 26 Jan 1924; *s f* 1956; *educ* Downside; Capt 15th Hus WW II, memb Lloyd's 1952–; *m* 1966 *Charlotte Baumgartner, of Austria, and has:

1 +JAMES FRANCIS; *b* 10 July 1971

1 *Laura Mary; *b* 1967

2 *Sophie; *b* 1968

Lineage: FRANCIS REYNOLDS, of Mount Vernon, Liverpool; *b* 1749; *d* 1822, leaving:

WILLIAM REYNOLDS, of Oakville, Sandfield Pk, Liverpool; *d* 26 Feb 1857 aged 68, leaving:

FRANCIS WILLIAM REYNOLDS, of Hillside, Woolton, Liverpool; *b* 8 Jan 1825; *m* 15 May 1849 Clare (*d* 14 Feb 1895), dau of George Gibson, of Hornby, Lancs, and *d* 24 March 1899, leaving a 3rd s:

Sir James Philip Reynolds, 1st Bt (UK), so *cr* 6 March 1923, DSO (1917), TD, JP (Lancs), DL; *b* 17 Feb 1865; Lt-Col TFRes FRA, joined Vol Force 1896, Hon Col 3rd W Lancs Bde RA, 2nd Canadian Div and 55th Div BEF WW I 1915–16, High Sheriff Lancs 1927, MP (U) Liverpool Exchange 1929–32, ktd 1920; *m* 13 Jan 1892 Elizabeth Emilia (Leila) (*d* 31 Aug 1961), dau of Nicholas Robert Roskell, and *d* 12 Dec 1932, leaving:

1 JOHN FRANCIS ROSKELL (Sir), **2nd Bt**

2 James Roskell, TD; *b* 9 March 1904; *educ* Downside and Merton Coll Oxford; Maj Duke of Lancaster's Own Yeo WW II, pres Liverpool Cotton Assoc 1953–54, chm Liverpool Savings Bank 1954–55, Freedom City of Padua 1945, Italian Order Merit 1955; *m* 4 July 1931 Helen Mary (*d* 1977), er dau of Charles Richard Gillow, of Leighton Hall, Lancs, and *d* 1982, leaving:

  (1) +Richard James Gillow [Richard Reynolds Esq, Leighton Hall, Carnforth, Lancs]; *b* 16 Jan 1933; *educ* Ampleforth; late Lt Irish Gds; *m* 30 April 1968 *Caroline Susan, dau of Geoffrey Terence Kenyon, of London, and has:

    1a *Katherine Elizabeth Gillow; *b* 14 May 1971

    2a *Lucy Helen Gillow; *b* 1975

  (2) +Simon Anthony [Simon Reynolds Esq, 64 Lonsdale Rd, London SW13 9JS]; *b* 20 Jan 1939; *educ* Ampleforth and Heidelberg U; *m* 31 Jan 1970 *Baroness Beata von Heyl zu Herrnsheim, er dau of Baron Siegfried von Heyl zu Herrnsheim, of Schlosschen, Worms, Germany, and has:

    1a +Stefan Damian; *b* 1970

    2a +Rupert Christian; *b* 1979

    1a *Olivia Helen; *b* 1972

    2a *Leila Barbro; *b* 1976

3 William Francis Roskell; *b* 8 March 1911; *educ* Downside; Maj Irish Gds WW II; *m* 6 Oct 1934 Nancy Blanche, dau of Rupert Bendall, and *d* 1978, leaving:

  (1) +Nicholas Francis Roskell [Nicholas Reynolds Esq, Thornley House, Nether Wallop, Hants SO20 8HA]; *b* 29 July 1938; *educ* Downside and Ch Ch Oxford (MA); ACA, late 2nd Lt Irish Gds; *m* 11 July 1964 *Wendy Helen Broke, twin dau of Lt Nigel Vere Broke Thurston, RN, and has:

    1a +Alexander; *b* 18 Jan 1971

    1a *Lucy Claire Thurston; *b* 27 Jan 1966

    2a *Charlotte Louise; *b* 3 May 1967

  (1) *Juliet Mary Roskell [Mrs Neville Whitbread, Lower Huxley Hall, Cheshire]; *b* 28 June 1936; *m* 24 Feb 1962 *Neville Anthony Leonard Whitbread, ACA, s of Lt-Col Leonard Whitbread, OBE, of Abbotts Ann, Hants, and has:

    1a *James Rupert Sinanian; *b* 1970

    1a *Victoria Mary; *b* 18 Jan 1963

    2a *Alice Mary; *b* 11 July 1964

    3a *Emilia Ann; *b* 1967

1 Monica Bawn; *m* 1st 11 Dec 1919 Edgar Hastings Dowler (*d* 20 Feb 1923) and had issue; *m* 2nd 23 Oct 1924 (*divorce* in France 1932) Capt Charles Francis Onslow Master, only surv s of Charles Onslow Master, of Bourton Grange; *m* 3rd 12 Dec 1933 Frank Christopher Codrington, yr s of Sir William Robert Codrington, 6th Bt, of Dodington (1721) (*qv*), and had further issue

2 Leila Elizabeth Josephine; *m* 1st 17 July 1919 Col George Ferdinand Hay Faithfull, OBE, IA and RAF (*d* 1942), and had issue; *m* 2nd 1944 Cuthbert Worsley

3 Barbara; *m* 3 Oct 1923 Gerald Cyril Russell and had issue (*see* RUSSELL, Bt, of Littleworth Corner)

4 Rhoda Clare

5 Delphine Rose; *m* 1st 31 Jan 1944 Ernst Schwenk Polak, PhD (*d* 1948), s of Emanuel Polak, of Jicin, Czechoslovakia; *m* 2nd 1963 John Trinick

Sir JAMES's est s,

Sir John Francis Roskell Reynolds, 2nd Bt, MBE (1945), JP; *b* 23 June 1899; *educ* Downside and Ch Ch Oxford (BA); High Sheriff Lancs 1952, Lt-Col Irish Gds, WW I and II, dir: Martins Bank Ltd, Sea Insur Co and Harrods, chm Combined Egyptian Mills Ltd, partner Reynolds & Gibson, cotton brokers, of Liverpool; *m* 1st 22 Nov 1921 Millicent Lilian Elizabeth (*d* 23 Nov 1931), dau of James Alexander Orr Ewing (*see* ORR EWING, Bt), and had:

1 Sir DAVID JAMES REYNOLDS, **3rd and present Bt**

1 *Hermione Mary Elizabeth [Mrs Edward Courage, Edgecote, Banbury, Oxon; 31 Abbotsbury Ho, Abbotsbury Rd, London W8]; *b* 30 Aug 1922; *m* 16 Jan 1948 Edward Raymond Courage, CBE (*d* 1982), er s of Raymond Courage, of Edgecote, Banbury, and has:

  (1) *Christopher John; *b* 30 July 1962; *m* 1991 *Alexandra Louise, er dau of John Charles Haynes (*see* VAUX OF HARROWDEN, B), and has:

    1a *Edward Francis; *b* 1992

Sir John *m* 2nd 11 Feb 1933 Eleanor Constance (*d* 28 May 1957), 2nd dau of Lt-Col James Henry Edward Holford, CMG, DSO, and *d* 20 Aug 1956, leaving by her:

2 John Julian; *b* 25 Feb 1942; *educ* Downside; 2nd Lt Irish Gds; *m* 24 Aug 1966 (*divorce* 1970) Carolyne Anne, only dau of Capt Hector Lorenzo Christie, MBE, of Jervaulx Abbey, Ripon, Yorks (*see* ZETLAND, M), and *d* Oct 1995

2 *Merilyn Mary [Ms Merilyn Thorold, Dutch Barge Wiljan, St Mary's Church, Battersea Church Rd, London SW11 3NA]; *b* 16 March 1935; *m* 21 Dec 1954 (*divorce* 1963) Peter Guy Henry Thorold (*see* THOROLD, Bt) and has issue

RHODES

Arms: Azure on a bend between two lozenges or a leopard's face gules between two holly-leaves vert. **Crest:** Two lion's gambs erased gules supporting a lozenge charged with a holly-leaf, both as in the arms. **Motto:** *Per vias bonas* ('By good ways'). **Creation:** Bt. (UK) 29 May 1919.

SIR JOHN CHRISTOPHER DOUGLAS RHODES, 4TH BT, of Hollingworth, Co Chester [Sir John Rhodes Bt, 86 High St, Blakeney, Holt, Norfolk]; *b* 24 May 1946; *s f* 1964; *educ* privately

Lineage: WILLIAM RHODES, of Tintwistle, Cheshire; had:

THOMAS RHODES, of Mersey Bank, Hadfield, Derbys, JP; *m* Amelia Fletcher (*d* 22 Sept 1887) and *d* 14 Aug 1883, leaving an only surv s:

Sir George Wood Rhodes, 1st Bt (UK), so *cr* 29 May 1919, JP (Cheshire); *b* 3 Sept 1860; *m* 1st 13 June 1883 Margaret Catherine (*d* 12 Feb 1915), dau of John Phillips, JP, of Liverpool, and had:

1 JOHN PHILLIPS (Sir), **2nd Bt**

2 Philip Wood; *b* 28 Nov 1894; Cdr RN; *m* 1st 15 May 1919 Judith Beresford (*d* 12 Aug 1942), yr dau of Trevelyan Martin, of London W1, and had:

  (1) *Pamela Beresford [Mrs Peter Coleclough, Longlands Hall, Stonham Aspal, Suffolk]; *b* 28 March 1920; *m* 4 March 1944 *Capt Peter Coleclough, Roy Warwicks Regt, s of Thomas James Coleclough, and has had:

    1a *Jeremy Nigel; *b* 1945

    2a Martin Timothy; *b* 1947; *d* 1985

  (2) *Vivien Patricia [Miss Vivien Rhodes, 1 Dukes Lodge, Holland Park, London W11]; *b* 9 Feb 1927

2 (cont.) Cdr Philip Rhodes *m* 2nd 12 July 1944 *Elspeth [Mrs Philip Rhodes, 181 Cranmer Ct, Sloane Ave, London SW3], dau of Thomas Tod, of Durban, S Africa, and *d* 2 Jan 1956

1 Elizabeth Marjorie (Jill); *m* 1st 24 Sept 1915 1st Baron Strathcarron (*qv*) and had issue; *m* 2nd 22 June 1938 Hedley Ernest Le Bas (*d* 4 Dec 1942), only s of Sir Hedley Francis Le Bas, and *d* 4 Aug 1956

Sir George *m* 2nd 30 Oct 1922 Diana (*d* 13 Dec 1937), dau of Daniel Murphy, of California, and widow of H Morgan Hill, of Washington, DC, and *d* 5 Feb 1924

His er s,

Sir John Phillips Rhodes, 2nd Bt, DSO (1918); *b* 19 July 1884; *educ* Harrow and RMA Woolwich; Lt-Col Res Offrs RE WW I (despatches, Croix de Guerre), MP (C) Stalybridge and Hyde 1922–23, chm Thomas Rhodes, cotton spinners and mfrs, of Hollingworth, Cheshire; *m* 1st 28 July 1913 (*divorce* 1926) Elsie Constance, er dau of Lt-Col George Alexander Maclean Buckley, CBE, DSO, and had:

1 CHRISTOPHER GEORGE (Sir), **3rd Bt**

Sir John *m* 2nd 28 Sept 1926 Doris Mary (*d* 19 May 1982 aged 83), international bridge player, only dau of William Henry Adams, and *d* 14 Nov 1955

His only s,

Sir Christopher George Rhodes, 3rd Bt; *b* 30 April 1914; *educ* Eton and Magdalen Coll Oxford; actor, Lt-Col Essex Regt WW II, Croix de Guerre, US Legn Merit; *m* 1st 30 April 1936 (*divorce* 1942) Mary, only child of Horace Kesteven, of Chelsea; *m* 2nd 18 Jan 1943 *Mary Florence [Mary Lady Rhodes, Purvis Lodge, Cley-next-the-Sea, Norfolk], er dau of Dr Douglas Wardleworth, of Lymington, and *d* 22 June 1964, leaving:

1 Sir JOHN CHRISTOPHER DOUGLAS RHODES, **4th and present Bt**

2 +MICHAEL PHILIP JAMES [Michael Rhodes Esq, Southdown, Blakeney, Norfolk]; *b* 3 April 1948; heir presumptive; *educ* privately; *m* 1973 *Susan Elizabeth, 2nd dau of Richard Patrick Roney-Dougal, of South Lodge, Norton, Salop, and has:

(1) *Louise; *b* 1974

1 *Ursula Catherine [Mrs Peter Roberts, 8 Letheringsett Hill, Holt, Norfolk]; *b* 8 Aug 1944; *m* 18 March 1967 *Capt Peter Herbert Roberts, RA, only s of Maj Herbert Thomas Roberts, of Bexhill-on-Sea, Sussex, and has:

(1) *A dau; *b* 17 May 1970

Rhys Williams

Arms: Per chevron argent and gules, in chief two cocks of the second and in base as many chevronels of the first. **Crest:** Between two fleurs-de-lys argent a goat's head couped sable, with curved horns. **Motto:** *Llafur orfu bobpeth* ('Labour overcame everything').
Creation: Bt. (UK) 25 June 1918.

SIR (ARTHUR) GARETH LUDOVIC EMRYS RHYS WILLIAMS, 3RD BT, of Miskin, Llantrisant, Co Glamorgan [Sir Gareth Rhys Williams Bt, Gadairwen, Groes Faen, Mid Glamorgan CF72 8NU; 9 Matheson Rd, London W14 8SN]; *b* 9 Nov 1961; *s* 1988; *educ* Eton, Durham U (BSc Eng) and INSEAD (MBA); CEng, MIEE, MIMechE, MIOM, MIMgt; dir Centl Europe BPB Gypsum, BPB plc; *m* 14 Sept 1996 *Harriet, dau of Maj Tom Codner, of Glos

Lineage: DAVID WILLIAMS, of Miskin Manor, Llantrisant, and Aberdare, Glam; wrote Welsh poetry under the Bardic name 'Alaw Goch'; *d* 18 Dec 1862, having had an er s:

GWILYM WILLIAMS, of Miskin Manor, JP, DL; *b* 2 May 1839; barrister Inner Temple 1863, Chm QS, Stipendiary Magistrate Pontypridd 1872–84, County Court Judge Mid-Wales 1884–85 and Glam 1885–1906; *m* 7 Dec 1864 Emma Eleanor, LGStJ (*d* 12 Aug 1922), est dau of William Williams, of Neath, Glam, and *d* 25 March 1906, leaving:

1 RHYS (Sir), **1st Bt**

2 Jestyn, JP; Maj Monmouthshire Regt; *m* 18 Sept 1901 Mary Elizabeth Gwyn (*d* 18 Feb 1949), est dau of Joseph Edward Moore-Gwyn, of Dyffryn, and *d* 16 June 1922, leaving issue

3 Arthur Stuart, MVO, OBE; *b* 1870; Capt RHA; Ch Constable W Sussex; *d* 7 Dec 1935

1 Enid Maud; *m* 25 April 1908 Brig-Gen Charles Herbert Rankin, CB, CMG, DSO (*see* RANKIN, Bt), and *d* 13 Aug 1938, leaving issue

The est s,

Sir RHYS WILLIAMS later RHYS RHYS WILLIAMS (deed poll 26 Nov 1938), **1st Bt** (UK), so *cr* 25 June 1918, DSO (1915), KC (1913), JP (Glam); *b* 20 Oct 1865; *educ* Eton and Oriel Coll Oxford (BA 1887); barrister Inner Temple 1890, Chm QS 1906; WW I: Welsh Gds, Capt 1915, T/Maj 1917, Lt-Col 1917, Actg Mil Attaché Tehran 1915–16, Assist Dir-Gen Movements and Rlwys War Office 1917–18, Dep Dir Trg and Staff Duties Admlty Naval Staff 1918 (wounded, despatches twice, Orders St Vladimir Russia with Swords and Lion and Sun Persia), Hon Col 53rd (Welsh) Divl Engrs (TA) 1928; MP (Lib) N Oxon 1918 and Banbury 1918–22, Parly Sec Min Tport Sept-Nov 1919; V-Lt Glam, Recorder Cardiff 1922–30, OStJ; *m* 24 Feb 1921 Juliette Evangeline, DBE, DGStJ, Govr BBC, Assist Section Offr WAAF WW II (*d* 18 Sept 1964), yr dau of Clayton Louis Glyn (*see* GLYN, Bt, of Ewell and Gaunts), and had:

1 Glyn David Rhys; *b* 1 Nov 1921; Capt Welsh Gds WW II (despatches); *ka* N Africa 9 April 1943

2 BRANDON MEREDITH RHYS (Sir), **2nd Bt**

1 *Susan Eleanor [Lady Glyn, Marina Baie des Anges, Ducal Apt U-03, 06270, Villeneuve-Loubet, Alpes Maritimes, France]; *b* 17 May 1923; Jr Cdr ATS WW II, barrister Inner Temple 1950; *m* 2 Oct 1946 Sir Anthony Geoffrey Leo Simon Glyn, 2nd Bt, of Berbice (*d* 20 Jan 1998; *see* DAVSON, Bt), and has issue

2 *(Marion) Elspeth [Mrs George Chowdharay-Best, 27 Walpole St, London SW3]; *b* 30 Dec 1937; *m* 1981 *George Chowdharay-Best

Sir RHYS *d* 20 Jan 1955; his only surv son,

Sir Brandon Meredith Rhys Williams, 2nd Bt; *b* 14 Nov 1927; *educ* Eton; Lt Welsh Gds, with ICI 1948–62, MP (C) Kensington 1968–88, Memb Cncl Europe Consultative Assembly, European League for Ec Co-opn, Br Rep European Parl Strasbourg 1973–84, Assist Dir Spastics Soc 1962–63, Consultant Management Selection Ltd 1963; *m* 14 Feb 1961 *Caroline Susan [Lady Rhys Williams, Gadairwen, Groes Faen, Mid Glamorgan CF72 8NU; 52 Limerston St, London SW10 0HH], est dau of Ludovic Anthony Foster, of Greatham Manor, Pulborough, Sussex, and *d* 18 May 1988, leaving:

(1) Sir (ARTHUR) GARETH LUDOVIC EMRYS RHYS WILLIAMS, **3rd and present Bt**

(1) *Elinor Caroline; *b* 21 Oct 1964

(2) *Miranda Pamela Cariadwen; *b* 5 Nov 1968

Richard

Creation: B. (LP, UK) 1990.

THE BARON RICHARD, of Ammanford, Co Dyfed (Ivor Seward Richard, PC (1993), QC (1971)) [The Rt Hon The Lord Richard PC QC, House of Lords, London SW1A 0PW]; *b* 30 May 1932; *educ* Cheltenham and Pembroke Coll Oxford (BA 1953, MA 1970, Hon Fell 1981); barrister Inner Temple 1955, Bencher 1985; Del Assembly for Cncl Europe 1965–68 and WEU 1965–68; MP (Lab) Barons Court 1964–Feb 1974 (fought S Kensington 1959), PPS to Def Sec 1966–69, Parly U-Sec MOD 1969–70, Oppn Spokesman Bdcstg, Posts and Telecommunications 1970–71, Dep Oppn Spokesman For Affrs 1971–74, UK Perm Rep UN 1974–79, Chm Rhodesia Conf Geneva 1976 and World Trade Centre Wales 1985–, memb Commn EEC 1981–84, Shadow Leader Ho Lds 1992–97, Ld Privy Seal and Leader Lds 1997–98; Memb Fabian Soc and Lab Lawyers; *m* 1st 1956 (*divorce* 1962) Geraldine Maude, dau of Alfred Moore, of Hartlepool, and has:

1 *David Seward; *b* 1959

BARON RICHARD *m* 2nd 1962 (*divorce* 1985) Alison Mary, dau of Joseph Imrie, of Alverstoke, Hants, and by her has:

2 *Alun Seward; *b* 1963

1 *Isobel Margaret Katherine; *b* 1966

BARON RICHARD *m* 3rd 1989 *Janet, dau of John Jones, of Oxford, and by her has:

3 *William John; *b* 1990

Lineage: SEWARD THOMAS RICHARD, of Cardiff; *m* Isabella Irene — and had:

IVOR SEWARD, *cr* a **Baron**

RICHARDSON, Baron

Arms: (granted 6 Dec 1960 to Sir John Samuel Richardson and his descendants and to the other descendants of his father) Sable on a fess engrailed or, between in chief an open book proper, bound gules, edged gold, between two mullets, in base a swan argent, a lion passant guardant also gules. **Crest:** The head of a rhinoceros erased sable, behind the horn a scroll argent inscribed with the words 'Till Time Ceases' in letters gules. **Supporters:** Two horses regardant, the dexter a grey with saddlecloth of the Metropolitan Police Force, the sinister also a grey, with saddlecloth of the RAMC, both saddled, bridled, with headstall, horse-hair plume and breast girth all with silver buckles and bosses proper. **Motto:** By friendship and by service. **Creation:** Bt. (UK) 20 Nov 1963, B. (LP, UK) 1979.

THE BARON RICHARDSON, of Lee, Co Devon, and a **Baronet** (Sir John Samuel Richardson, 1st Bt, LVO (1943)) [The Rt Hon The Lord Richardson LVO, Windcutter, Lee, N Devon EX34 8LW]; *b* 16 June 1910; *educ* Charterhouse, Trin Coll Cambridge (BA 1932, MB, BChir 1936, MA and MD 1940) and St Thomas's Hosp Med Sch; MRCS, LRCP 1935, MRCP Lond 1937, FRCP Lond 1948, FRCPE 1975, Lt-Col RAMC WW II, physician: W Herts Gp Hosps 1946, St Thomas's Hosp 1947–75, King Edward VII's Hosp For Offrs 1964, consulting physician: Met Police 1957–80, London Tport 1964, Hon Consulting Physician Army 1964, Pres: Roy Soc Medicine 1969– and Internat Soc Internal Medicine 1966–, examiner medicine: Cambridge, London, Manchester and Ireland Us, Roy Coll Physicians, Conjoint Board, memb: Bd Govrs St Thomas's Hosp 1953–59 and 1964–74, Cncl Assoc Physicians 1956–59, Roy Coll Physicians 1957–60 and 1967–, Med Soc London (Hon Sec 1959–61), Roy Med Fndn 1960–, Court of Soc Apothecaries London 1960–, GMC 1967–, ktd 1960; *m* 5 June 1933 Sybil Angela Stephanie (*d* 1991), 3rd dau of Arthur Ronald Trist, of Stanmore, Middx, and has:

1 *Elizabeth Anne [The Hon Mrs Stafford, 49 Deodar Rd, London SW15]; *b* 24 July 1937; *m* 1st 22 Nov 1960 (*divorce*) Angus Gavin Lochhead Jack (*see* INGLEFIELD-WATSON, Bt) and has issue; *m* 2nd 1971 *Gregory Edmund Stafford, LLB, and by him has:

  (1) *Samuel; *b* 1975

2 *Susan Clare [The Hon Mrs Wales, 2 Thorne St, London SW13]; *b* 25 March 1940; *m* 1970 *Robert Wales and has:

  (1) *Duncan John Richardson; *b* 1970

Lineage: ROBERT RICHARDSON, of Derbys; *b c* 1610–15; *m* 21 July 1640 Elizabeth Storer and had:

THOMAS RICHARDSON; *bapt* 30 Aug 1645; *m* 1st 14 Feb 1660/1 Dorothy Shooter (*d c* 1667) and had issue; *m* 2nd 24 May 1668 Gertrude Ingman and *d* by 22 March 1681/2, having had by his 1st w:

THOMAS RICHARDSON, of Eckington, Derbys; *bapt* 19 May 1664; had:

BARNABAS/BERNARD RICHARDSON; *bapt* 11 June 1695; had:

JOHN RICHARDSON, of Greenhill, Norton, Derbys; *b c* 1736; apprentice cutler Hallam 1750; *m* 20 Jan 1762 Mary Ouldaker, of Norton (*bur* 13 Dec 1789), and was *bur* 21 Nov 1775, leaving, with an est s (Samuel, *bapt* 25 June 1769, apprentice sickle-smith 1783, Freeman Cutlers' Co Sheffield 1791), a 3rd s (Charles, *bapt* 29 June 1778) and a dau (Sarah, *bapt* 26 Dec 1763):

JOHN RICHARDSON, of Little Norton, Derbys; *bapt* 1 May 1774; scythe mfr; *m c* 1805 Elizabeth — and *d* 10 Sept 1837, leaving, with an est s (William, *bapt* 5 Aug 1805), two yst sons (James; living 29 June 1837; John, living 29 June 1837) and five daus (Elizabeth, *bapt* 18 Dec 1807; Lydia, *bapt* 30 Aug 1810; Eliza, *b c* 1815, living unm 26 Feb 1887; Mary; Sarah), a 2nd s:

SAMUEL RICHARDSON, of Sheffield; *bapt* 29 Nov 1812; die-sinker and cutlery mfr, ptnr with Francis Southen 1847, Freeman Cutlers' Co 1860; *m* 10 Feb 1847 Mary, dau of John Gray, of Radford Place, Sheffield, and *d* 26 Feb 1887, leaving:

1 John Gray (Ven); *b* 2 Sept 1849; *educ* Sheffield Sch and Trin Coll Cambridge (BA 1872, Fell 1874, MA 1875); Deacon 1875, Priest 1877, Curate Holy Trinity Tunbridge Wells 1876–77, Vicar St Michael's Cambridge 1877–78 and Monks Kirby with Withybrook and Copston, Warwicks, 1877–84, Archdeacon Nottingham 1894–1913, RD Southwell Minster and Rector Southwell St Mary

1900–13; *m* 13 Aug 1878 Jane Temple (*d* 3 July 1923), dau of Rev William Henry Perkins, of Tunbridge Wells, and *d* 13 July 1924, leaving:

  (1) Harold Samuel Temple (Rev); *b* 15 July 1882; *educ* Nottingham High Sch and Trin Coll Cambridge (BA 1904, MA 1910); Deacon 1907, Priest 1908, Domestic Chaplain to Bp Durham 1908–11, Rector Hopesay 1921–27 and St Nicholas Hereford 1927–37; *m* 8 Jan 1921 Edith Mary, dau of Rev Richard James Bond, BD, Vicar Ashburton, Devon, and *d* 23 Dec 1937, leaving:

    1a *Brenda Mary [Mrs Anthony Allder, 48 Green End, Gamlingay, Beds SG19 3LF]; *b* April 1922; *m* 24 April 1948 Anthony Harry Allder (*d* Jan 1966), s of Harry William Allder, of Whitby, Cheshire, and has four daus

    2a *Monica Jane Fellowes [Mrs Christopher Ditmas, 7 Heatherfield, Buriton, Hants GU31 5RY]; *b* May 1924; headmistress Lord Digby's Sch Sherborne; *m* March 1946 *Christopher George Hugh Ditmas and has a s and dau

    3a *Dorothy Temple [Mrs Ralph Gardiner, 20 Heatherfield, Buriton, Hants GU31 5RY]; *b* Feb 1926; psychiatric social worker; *m* 1950 *Ralph Stanley Gardiner, s of Albert Gardiner, of Stroud, Glos, and has a s and two daus

    4a *Christine Julia [Mrs John Addison, 111 Elwill Way, Beckenham, Kent BR3 6RX]; *b* 3 June 1929; occupational therapist; *m* 4 April 1951 *John Fox Addison, s of Wilfred Addison, of Thornaby-on-Tees, Yorks, and has two daus

  (1) Agatha Janie Temple; *b* 23 July 1881; *m* 29 April 1909 Edwin Hugh Lewis (*d* 4 Sept 1963), s of James Dawson Lewis, of Brasted, Kent, and *d* 22 March 1967, leaving four sons and three daus

2 Samuel Gray, of Sheffield; *b* 7 Jan 1851; *educ* Sheffield Sch; cutlery mfr, Freeman 1880, Sr Warden 1880, Master Sheffield 1889; *m* 1st 7 May 1877 Eleanor Mary (*d* 16 Dec 1916), dau of John Watson, of Broomhall Pk, Sheffield, stockbroker, and had:

  (1) John Watson; *b* 18 July 1882; *educ* Charterhouse and Trin Coll Cambridge (BA 1903, MA 1907); slr 1907, ptnr Sorby, Hall & Richardson, Sheffield, Maj cmdg 2nd/4th Bn York and Lancaster Regt WW I; *m* 9 July 1908 Elizabeth Blakeney only dau of Sir Samuel Roberts, 1st Bt, PC, JP, DL, of Ecclesall and Queen's Tower, Sheffield (*qv*), and was *ka vp* 3 May 1917, leaving:

    1a Sir JOHN SAMUEL RICHARDSON, **1st and present Bt, and present Baron**

    2a Hugh Blakeney; *b* 13 Nov 1912; *educ* Charterhouse and Trin Coll Cambridge (BA 1934); *d* unm 28 Nov 1972

2 (cont.) Samuel Richardson *m* 2nd 20 Jan 1920 Sophia Margaret Vavasour Waddingham, MD (London) (*d* 22 Jan 1959), er dau of Frederick Richard Vavasour Witts, of Fosse Cottage, Stow-on-Wold, Glos, and *d* 16 May 1934

RICHARDSON, Bt

Arms: Argent an ostrich proper, on a chief sable three lion's heads erased of the field. **Crest:** Upon a rock a lion rampant guardant proper, resting the sinister paw on a mullet gold. **Motto:** *Animo fide et honore* ('By courage, faith and honour'). **Creation:** Bt. (UK) 26 Jan 1924.

SIR ANTHONY LEWIS RICHARDSON 3RD BT, of Yellow Woods, Province of Cape of Good Hope, S Africa [Sir Anthony Richardson Bt, 128 Trafalgar Place, Sandhurst, Sandton 2196, South Africa]; *b* 5 Aug 1950; *s* f 1985; *educ* Diocesan Coll Cape Town; stockbroker Rowe and Pitman, London, later SBC Warburg (dir 1986–), seconded to SBC Warburg Johannesburg 1996–; *m* 1985 *(Honor) Gillian, dau of Robert Anthony Dauney, of Sydney, NSW, and has:

1 +WILLIAM LEWIS; *b* 15 Oct 1992

1 *(Honor) Olivia Phoebe; *b* 1990

Lineage: KAUFMAN RICHARDSON; had:

Sir Lewis Richardson, 1st Bt (UK), so *cr* 26 Jan 1924, CBE (1919); *b* 2 Feb 1873; migrated from UK to S Africa 1882; head L Richardson & Co, of Port Elizabeth, London, NY and Boston, ktd 1921; *m* 7 Aug 1906 Phoebe (*d* 6 April 1953), only dau of Issac Isaacs, and *d* 2 April 1934, leaving:

1 **Sir Leslie Lewis Richardson, 2nd Bt**; *b* 14 Aug 1915; *educ* Harrow; SA Artillery WW II, farmer and co dir, memb L Richardson & Co, of Port Elizabeth and London; *m* 6 March 1946 *Joy Patricia [Joy Lady Richardson, Constantia Village, Cape Town, S Africa], twin dau of Percy J S Rillstone, of Johannesburg, and *d* 1985, leaving:

(1) Sir ANTHONY LEWIS RICHARDSON, **3rd and present Bt**

(2) +Charles John [Charles Richardson Esq, 7 Franconia Rd, London SW4 9NB]; *b* 8 Dec 1955; *educ* Diocesan Coll Cape Town; *m* 1987 *Gigi D M, dau of Lt Col R R Morris, of Huish Farm, Sydling St Nicholas, Dorset, and has:

    1a +George Leslie; *b* 1991

    1a *Jessica Kate; *b* 1988

(1) *Jennifer; *b* 31 Dec 1947; *m* 1984 *Richard Michael Fearon Gold, of Windrush Farm, Stowell, Dorset, est s of Rev Guy Alastair Whitmore Gold, of Bridge Ho, Great Bealings, Suffolk, and has:

    1a *Alexander Leslie Fearon; *b* 1985

    2a *Edward Guy Fearon; *b* 1986

1 Fanny Sarah Ethel; *b* 5 Aug 1907; *d* unm 17 Sep 1955

2 *Audrey Anne; *b* 28 March 1909; *m* 1st 25 Aug 1939 John Henry Muers-Raby (*d* 1973), slr, only s of Rev Andrew Raby, Canon Emeritus Leicester, and has:

    (1) *Nicholas Jonathan [Nicholas Muers-Raby Esq, Townhead House, Stainforth, N Yorks BD24 9PJ]; *b* 18 Aug 1941; *educ* Harrow, RMA Sandhurst and Cranfield Inst Tech (MBA 1973); late Maj Roy Hus (PWO); *m* 1973 *Victoria, dau of Lt-Col Henry Christopher White Bowring, FLAS, of Whelprigg, Casterton, Cumbria, and has:

        1a *Rosanna Louise; *b* 1975

    (2) *Nigel Andrew [Nigel Muers-Raby Esq, Vexford Farm, Higher Vexford, Somerset]; *b* 16 Jan 1949; *educ* Harrow; *m* 1986 *Fiona Jane, dau of Maj Geoffrey Lloyd, and has:

        1a *Thomas Sebastian; *b* 1987

        2a *Oliver Henry; *b* 1991

2 (cont.) Mrs John Muers-Raby *m* 2nd 1983 *Maj-Gen Raymond Cyril Alexander Edge, CB, MBE

RICHARDSON OF DUNTISBOURNE

Arms: Argent a fess wavy bleu celeste between in chief three swords in pale, points upwards fesswise gules, and in base a pair of scales sable, on a bordure also gules eight bezants. **Crest:** A seated female figure representing the Bank of England proper, habited argent, crined and murally crowned or, resting the sinister hand on an oval cartouche carved or, the field argent, thereon a cross gules and holding in the palm of the extended dexter hand a terrestrial globe also proper. **Supporters:** On either side a griffin segreant gules, the wings elevated and bezanty, gorged with a coronet of sword hilts gold. **Motto:** *Usque ad finem* ('Right to the end'). **Creation:** B. (LP, UK) 1983.

THE BARON RICHARDSON OF DUNTISBOURNE, of Duntisbourne, Co Gloucester (Sir Gordon William Humphreys Richardson, KG (1983), MBE (1944), TD (1979), PC (1976), DL (Glos 1983)) [The Rt Hon The Lord Richardson of Duntisbourne KG MBE TD PC DL, House of Lords, London SW1A 0PW]; *b* 25 Nov 1915; *educ* Nottingham High Sch and Gonville and Caius Coll Cambridge (BA, LLB, Hon Fell 1977); Maj S Notts Hus Yeo RHA WW II; barrister Gray's Inn 1946, Memb Bar Cncl 1951–55, Hon Bencher 1973; Chm: J Henry Schroder Wagg & Co 1962–72, Schroders Ltd 1966–73, Schroders Inc (NY) 1968–73, Industl Devpt Advsy Bd 1972–73, Roy Inst Internat Affrs 1984–87, Pilgrim Tst 1984–89, Morgan Stanley Internat Inc 1986–95; Bank of England: a Dir 1967–75, Govr 1973–83; Lt City London 1974–, Dep High Steward Cambridge U 1982–; *m* 1941 *Margaret Alison, er dau of Very Rev Hugh Richard Lawrie Sheppard, Canon and Precentor St Paul's, and has:

    1 *Simon Bruce Sheppard [The Hon Simon Richardson, River House, Bromham Park, Bromham, Beds MK43 8HH]; *b* 1944; *m* 1979 *Miriam Ann, dau of George Harrison Gibson

    1 *Sarah, LVO (1993) [The Hon Lady Riddell LVO, Hepple, Morpeth, Northumberland; 49 Campden Hill Sq, London W8 7JR]; *b* 1942; *m* 1969 *Sir John Charles Buchanan Riddell, 13th Bt, CVO, DL (*qv*), and has issue

Lineage: JOHN ROBERT RICHARDSON; *m* Nellie — and had:

GORDON WILLIAM HUMPHREYS, *cr* a **Baron**

RICHARDSON-BUNBURY

Arms: Quarterly; 1st and 4th, ermine a chess rook between two leopard's faces in bend, between two bendlets sable (for BUNBURY); 2nd and 3rd, azure on a fess argent, between an ancient ship, the sails furled, in chief and a bull's head couped in base, a saltire or (for RICHARDSON). **Crests:** 1 In front of a tree proper on a mount vert a leopard's head, paly of six and sable, transfixed by two arrows in saltire, also proper (for BUNBURY), 2 A lion rampant ermine, in the mouth a trefoil slipped vert, between the fore-paws a torteau, charged with a cross-crosslet or (for RICHARDSON). **Motto:** *Virtus paret robur* ('Virtue appears like an oak'). **Creation:** Bt. (I) 30 Aug 1787.

SIR (RICHARD DAVID) MICHAEL RICHARDSON-BUNBURY, 5TH BT, of Augher, Co Tyrone [Lt-Cdr Sir Michael Richardson-Bunbury Bt RN, Upper House, Crowcombe, Somerset TA4 4AG]; *b* 27 Oct 1927; *s* cousin 1953; *educ* RNC Dartmouth; Lt-Cdr RN (ret 1967); *m* 15 July 1961 *Jane Louise, dau of Col Alfred William Pulverman, IA, and has had:

    1 Roger Michael; *b* 2 Nov 1962; *educ* Sherborne and Manchester U (BA); *dsp* 12 Nov 1994

    2 +THOMAS WILLIAM; *b* 4 Aug 1965; *educ* Millfield and Durham U (BA)

Lineage (of Bunbury): Sir HENRY BUNBURY, of Stanney; ktd 1603 (*see* BUNBURY, Bt); had a yst s:

THOMAS BUNBURY; *b* 1605; *m* 1st Eleanor, dau of Henry Birkenhead, of Backford, and had four sons and six daus; *m* 2nd Margaret, dau of William Wilcox, and *d* 1668, having by her had five sons and two daus; his 3rd s by his 1st w:

BENJAMIN BUNBURY, of Killerig, Co Carlow; settled in Ireland with his yr bro Joseph and two sisters; acquired Killerig and other lands from the Earl of Arran 1669; *m* Elizabeth, widow of Matthew Sheppard, of Owles, Leics, and *d* by 1711, having had, with a dau:

    1 Joseph; ancestor of the BUNBURYs of Johnstown

    2 Benjamin; ancestor of the BUNBURYs of Killerig

    3 Thomas, of Croghna; ancestor of the BUNBURYs of Cranavonane

    4 William; ancestor of the BUNBURYs of Moyle

    5 Mathew, of Kilfeacle, Co Tipperary; *m* Anne Blount and *d* 1733, having had, with other issue:

        (1) BENJAMIN

        (2) Thomas, of Shronell; ancestor of Benjamin Bunbury, of Belmont, Co Waterford

The er s,

BENJAMIN BUNBURY, of Kilfeacle; *m* 1724 Mary, dau of John Kelly, of Clonreher, Queen's Co, and *d* 1765, having had, with three sons (*dsp*):

    1 ELIZABETH Bunbury, of Kilfeacle; *m* St George RICHARDSON, MP Augher 1755–60, and had issue (*see below*)

    2 Diana; *m* May 1772 Sir John Tydd, Bt (*qv*), MP Lamberton, Queen's Co, and *d* 22 Oct 1821

Lineage (of Richardson): ALEXANDER RICHARDSON; held the Drum estate, Kildress, Co Tyrone, by 1618–19; presumably kin to:

WILLIAM RICHARDSON, of Drum, Co Tyrone; High Sheriff Co Tyrone 1662; *m* Mary, dau and coheir of Rev Archibald Erskine, of Augher Castle, Co Tyrone, Rector Errigal Keerogue, s of Sir James Erskine, MP, and gs of Sir Alexander Erskine of Gogar (*see* MAR and KELLIE, E), by whom he acquired Augher, and had, with other issue, including a yr s (Alexander, of Drum, *m* 1st 1682 Margaret (by whom he was ancestor of the RICHARDSONs of Drum), dau of Thomas Goodlatt, of Derrygally, Co Tyrone, *m* 2nd 1695 Margaret, dau of Andrew Baillie of Trinshea and widow of — Hamilton):

ARCHIBALD RICHARDSON, of Castlehill, Augher, and Springtown, Co Tyrone; High Sheriff Co Tyrone 1680, MP Augher 1692–95, attainted by JAMES II's Irish Parl 1689; *m* Jane, dau of James Galbraith, of Rathmoran, Co Fermanagh, and had an est s:

WILLIAM RICHARDSON, JP, of Castlehill and Springtown; High Sheriff Co Tyrone 1716; *m c* May 1709 Lettice, dau of William Wray, of Castle Wray, and Ards, Co Donegal, by Angel, 2nd dau of Col James Galbraith, MP, and had, with other issue:

1 James RICHARDSON later MERVYN, of Castlehill and Springtown; High Sheriff Co Tyrone 1734; *m* 1st 14 Feb 1733 Arabella, dau of Thomas Edwards, of Castlegore, Co Tyrone; *m* 2nd 1739 Anne, widow of Hugh Edwards, of Castle Gore; *m* 3rd —, dau of Audley Mervyn, MP, of Castle Mervyn, Co Tyrone, and *d* 1753, having by her had:

(1) Letitia; *m* 9 June 1764 Lt-Col Hon Richard ROCHFORT later MERVYN (*dsp* 20 Feb 1776), 35th Regt, MP Philipstown, s of 1st Earl of Belvidere

2 St George, of Augher; MP Augher 1755–60, Capt 6th Dragoon Gds (Carabiniers); *m c* May 1749 Elizabeth, 3rd dau of Benjamin Bunbury, of Kilfeacle, Co Tipperary (*see* above), and had:

(1) **Sir William Richardson, 1st Bt** (I), so *cr* 30 Aug 1787, of Augher; MP Augher 1783–90 and Ballyshannon 1798–1800; *m* 1st 21 April 1775 his cousin Eliza, dau of Rev Galbraith Richardson, of Richmond, Co Tyrone, and had, with other issue:

1a JAMES MERVYN (Sir), **2nd Bt**

1a Anne Mervyn; *m* 1798 John Kirke, JP, of Markham Hall, and Retford, Notts, Capt 24th Light Dragoons, Col cmdg Sherwood Rangers, Notts Yeo Cav, and *d* 21 Dec 1815, leaving issue

2a Letitia; *m* 14 Oct 1806 Robert Johnson, QC, of Magheremena Castle, Co Fermanagh, and had issue

(1) (cont.) **Sir William** *m* 2nd Mary, dau and coheir of William Newburgh, of Ballyhaise, Co Cavan, and widow of Carey Hamilton, and *d* 29 Oct 1830 having by her had:

3a Maria Isabella; *m* 27 May 1818 Sir Thomas Charles Yates and had issue

The 1st Bt's s,

Sir James Mervyn RICHARDSON later RICHARDSON-BUNBURY (roy licence 20 April 1822), **2nd Bt**; *b* 1781; *m* 23 June 1810 Margaret (*d* 31 March 1873), dau of John Corry Moutray, of Favor Royal, Co Tyrone, and *d* 4 Nov 1851, having had, with another s and seven daus:

1 **Rev Sir John Richardson-Bunbury, 3rd Bt**; *b* 10 Oct 1813; *m* 5 Dec 1838 Maria (*d* 2 March 1888), dau of William Anketell, of Anketell Grove, Co Monaghan, and *d* 19 Feb 1909, having had:

(1) Mervyn Matthew; *b* June 1841; *m* 6 Dec 1868 Eliza Mary (*d* 30 Aug 1936), 3rd dau of William Thorn, MD, and *dvp* 16 April 1889, leaving, with other issue:

1a Frederick Herbert; *b* 22 Jan 1870; *d* 14 April 1893

2a **Sir Mervyn William Richardson-Bunbury, 4th Bt**; *b* 1 June 1874; *d* unm 21 Oct 1953

1a Irene Matilda; *b* 1 Dec 1871; *m* 1895 Capt Douglas Philip Bayly (*d* 1927), s of Mansel Bayly, and had issue

(1) Matilda Anne; *m* 12 July 1870 George Charles BRACKENRIDGE formerly TRIMBLE (*d* 1879), of Ashfield Pk, Co Tyrone, and *d* 4 Jan 1919, leaving issue

(2) Olivia Emma; *m* 16 April 1891 Col George Atherley William Forrest (*d* April 1904), Hants Regt, and *d* 27 July 1939

2 William; *b* 5 June 1817; *m* 22 July 1857 Amelia Georgiana (*d* 2 Sept 1910), dau of Lt-Col John Molloy, Rifle Bde, and *d* 13 Nov 1877, leaving, with other issue:

(1) Moutray Frederic, of Beachlands, Busselton, W Australia; *b* 6 Jan 1865; AIF WW I; *m* 30 Dec 1896 Mary Capel (*d* 1 April 1949), dau of Frederick Cantell Vines, MD, of Busselton, W Australia, and *das* 19 March 1917, having had:

1a Frederick Moutray; *b* 1896; *d* 28 Nov 1901

2a Richard; *b* 23 May 1899; *m* 25 April 1925 Florence Margaret Gordon, dau of Col Roger Gordon Thomson, CMG, DSO, RA, and *d* 12 July 1951, leaving:

1b Sir (RICHARD DAVID) MICHAEL RICHARDSON-BUNBURY, **5th and present Bt**

2b +Roger Hugh Moutray [Capt Roger Richardon-Bunbury RN, Fonthill Cottages, Lewannick, Launceston, Cornwall PL15 7QE]; *b* 25 Oct 1934; *m* 18 Sept 1965 *Carol Irene, BSc, only dau of F J H Arnold, of Guildford, Surrey, and has:

1c +Robert Moutray; *b* 15 Sept 1968

2c +David; *b* 26 Nov 1972

1c *Judith Mervyn; *b* 7 Feb 1967

2c *Elizabeth; *b* 26 Nov 1972

1b *Margaret Delves [Mrs James Woolliams, Fairview, Pilgrims Way, Boughton Aluph, Kent TN25 0LT]; *b* 27 Sept 1931; SRN; *m* 31 Dec 1966 *James Harvey Woolliams, only s of G/Capt Frank H Woolliams, of Folkestone, Kent, and has:

1c *Richard Frank; *b* 26 Sept 1968

2b *Angela Mervyn; *b* 24 Jan 1946; *educ* Kent U (BA 1968)

3a James; *b* 3 June 1901; *educ* King's Sch Bruton, St John's Coll Oxford (MA) and Paris U (Licencié-ès-Lettres); sometime 2nd master Millfield, Street, Somerset, modern language master Durham Sch 1940–45, Diplome d'études supérieures Paris; *m* 25 July 1938 Betty Winifred (*d* 1984), of Glastonbury, Somerset, dau of Col Roger Gordon Thomson, CMG, DSO, RA (*see* BROUGHTON, Bt), and *d* 4 July 1970, leaving:

1b +Patrick James [Patrick Richardson-Bunbury Esq, PO Box 131, Burswood, W Australia]; *b* 15 July 1939; *educ* Crewkerne Sch and Millfield

2b +William Hedley [William Richardson-Bunbury Esq, Unit 13, 12 Conroy St, Marylands 6051, W Australia]; *b* 7 Oct 1940; *educ* King's Sch Bruton and Durham U (BA); MACE, DipEd; *m* 14 Dec 1964 *Jennifer Anne, only dau of L D Syer, of Folkestone, Kent, and has:

1c *Alison Claire; *b* 1969

2c *Katherine Anne; *b* 1971

3b +Andrew [Andrew Richardson-Bunbury Esq, 104 Hydethorpe Rd, London SW12 0JB]; *b* 15 April 1943; *educ* Millfield and Keble Coll Oxford (MA); DipEd (Makerere U Uganda), CQSW; *m* 28 Feb 1976 *Christine, BA Leeds, CQSW, yr dau of J A Halley, of Workington, Cumberland, and has:

1c +Daniel Christian; *b* 1981

1c *Rebecca; *b* 1980

1a Kathleen; *b* 18 May 1903; *m* 29 April 1926 Guy Waterman Elkington, MB, MRCP (*d* 1967), yr s of Lt-Col H P Elkington, of Hythe, Kent and *d* 1997, leaving:

1b Edward James; *b* 1927; *m* 1958 *Margaret Joan Kent and *d* 1997, leaving:

1c *Timothy Kent; *b* 1962

2c *Christopher John; *b* 1964

3c *David James; *b* 1966

1c *Joanna; *b* 1960

2b *Arthur Guy [Arthur Elkington Esq, Broad-Acres, 12 High St, Wick, Bristol BS15 5QJ]; *b* 1929; *m* 1954 *Rosemary, dau of Seymour Willoughby Anketell-Jones, and has:

1c *Richard Seymour; *b* 1957; *m* 1980 *Alison Goodall and has:

1d *Edwin Guy Goodall; *b* 1987

2d *Rew Seymour Goodall; *b* 1990

1c *Jane; *b* 1955

2c *Margaret; *b* 1959; *m* 1981 *Stephen Govan and has:

1d *Peter Alexander; *b* 1985

2d *Christopher Alan; *b* 1987

3c *Susan; *b* 1962

4c *Elizabeth Anne; *b* 1970

3b *(Christopher) Richard [Richard Elkington Esq, 90 Stafford Rd, Kenwick, W Australia 6107]; *b* 1933; *m* 1967 *Jane Elizabeth, dau of H H Bale, of Kidderminster, and has:

1c *Timothy James; *b* 1970; *m* 1994 *Carolie Ruth, dau of R Burton, of Carlisle, W Australia

2c *Peter Garry; *b* 1971

4b *John Henry [John Elkington Esq, 45 Herreshoff Ramble, Ocean Reef, W Australia 6027]; *b* 1939; *m* 1969 *Norma Joan Darcey and has:

1c *Derek John; *b* 1971

2c *Jeffrey Steven; *b* 1975

1b *Mary Violet [Mrs John Atkinson, 106 Arkana Rd, Balga, W Australia 6061]; *b* 1930; *m* 1961 *John Lawrence Atkinson and has:

1c *Guy Lawrence; *b* 1962

2c *Thomas Geoffrey; *b* 1964; *m* 1996 *Janet Susanne Dow

3c *Garth Peers [Garth Atkinson Esq, 26 Cedric St, Stirling, W Australia 6027]; *b* 1966; *m* 1990 *Maria Dicristofaro and has:

1d *Rebecca; *b* 1993

(2) Archibald Edward; *b* 7 Aug 1868; *m* 1909 Vida Muriel (*d* 1967), dau of Arthur Heppingstone, and *d* 6 Dec 1937, leaving:

1a Archibald Vernon; *b* 1916; *m* 1939 Iris Jensen (*d* 1997) and *d* 1994, leaving:

1b +Edward Vernon; *b* 1941

2b +Richard Archibald; *b* 1943

1b *Dorothy Margaret; *b* 1940

2b *Wendy Muriel; *b* 1944

3b *Patricia Iris; *b* 1946

4b *Doreen Jennifer; *b* 1948

1a Caroline Mervyn; *b* 1910; *m* 7 Feb 1935 John Oliver Coote and *d c* 1991, leaving:

1b *John Edward; *b* 25 Aug 1937

1b *Diana Bunbury; *b* 1 Dec 1935

2a *Dorothy Emilie [Mrs Wilfred Johnston, 49 Clifton St, Nedlands, WA 6009, Australia]; *b* 1911; *m* 1st 8 Nov 1932 Robert Edward Drake-Brockman and has:

1b *Mervyn Molloy [Mervyn Johnston Esq, Chapman Hill, via Busselton, W Australia 6280]; *b* 6 Jan 1934

2a (cont.) Mrs Drake-Brockman *m* 2nd 1940 *Wilfred Gordon Johnston and by him has:

1b *Elizabeth Margaret; *b* 27 April 1941; *m* 19– *Antony Copeland

2b *Judith Bunbury [Mrs Hubert van Helden, 62 Stanley St, Nedlands, W Australia 6009]; *b* 19 May 1942; *m* 1966 *Hubert van Helden and has:

1c *Nicholas; *b* 1966

2c *Vincent; *b* 1971

*Caroline; *b* 1970 (adopted)

3b *Margaret Bunbury [Mrs Peter Shugg, 88 Florence Rd, Nedlands, W Australia 6009]; *b* 3 Feb 1944 ; *m* 1965 *Peter John Shugg, geologist, and has:

1c *Sabina Jane; *b* 19–

2c *Vanessa Amelia; *b* 19–

4b *Vida Bunbury [Mrs Lindsay Hart, Augusta, W Australia 6290]; *b* 6 Jan 1948; *m* 19– *Lindsay Hart

5b *Robin Bunbury; *b* 29 July 1952; *m* 19– *Gregory Kane

3a Marjory Vida; *b* 1918; *m* 1940 Norman William Malcolm (*d* 1972) and *d* 1997, leaving:

1b *Miles William Eric Bunbury [Miles Malcolm Esq, Unit 2, 17 Airlie St, Claremont, W Australia 6010]; *b* 14 Feb 1944; *m* 1972 *Joan Elizabeth Bragg and has:

1c *Marie-Louise Bunbury; *b* 1981

1b (cont.) Miles Malcolm also has issue:

2c *Lisa Joy BROOKES; *b* 1970

2b *Anthony Bunbury [Anthony Malcolm Esq, 93 Stanley St, Nedlands, W Australia 6009]; *b* 12 Feb 1953; *m* 1975 *Sally Bovell and has:

1c *Angus Peter Bunbury; *b* 1983

2c *Dugald Anthony Bunbury; *b* 1987

1c *Daisy Amelia Bunbury; *b* 1979

1b *Sabina Bunbury [Mrs Peter Dempster, Grass Valley, via Northam, W Australia 6401]; *b* 18 March 1947; *m* 1969 *Peter John Dempster and has had:

    1c Anthony Peter; *b* 1973; *d* 1996
    1c Amanda; *b* 1970; *d* 1995
    2c *Amy; *b* 1976
    3c *Amelia; *b* 1981

(1) Isabella Augusta; *m* 1907 William George Pickering, of W Australia, and *d c* 1937

(2) Georgina Kennedy; *m* 1897 Walter A Gale, CMG (*d* 27 July 1927), Clerk Federal Ho of Reps, Melbourne, Australia, and *d c* 1946

(3) Dorothy Flora; *m* 27 Aug 1895 Sir Edward O'Farrell, KCB (*d* 13 Aug 1926), Estate Commr Ireland, s of Michael R O'Farrell, of Park, Youghal, Co Cork, and *d* 17 Dec 1955, leaving issue

(4) Emily Beatrice; *d* unm 22 Jan 1969

(5) Alice Sabine; *d* unm 1963

(6) Olive Mary; *m* 1 Aug 1901 Henry Addison Devereux Capell, JP W Australia, and *d c* 1937, leaving issue (*see* ESSEX, E)

RICHMOND

Arms: Gules on a fess cotised or, between two roses argent, barbed and seeded proper, a lion passant of the field. **Crest:** A demi-stag proper, charged on the shoulder with a rose as in the arms and holding between the fore-legs a rose argent, leaved and slipped, also proper. **Motto:** *Labor vincit* ('Labour conquers'). **Creation:** Bt. (UK) 4 July 1929.

SIR JOHN FREDERICK RICHMOND, 2ND BT, of Hollington, Co Sussex [Sir John Richmond Bt, Shimpling Park Farm, Bury St Edmunds, Suffolk IP29 4HY]; *b* 12 Aug 1924; *s* f 1953; *educ* Eton and Jesus Coll Cambridge (MA); late Lt 10th Roy Hus; *m* 1 Nov 1965 Anne Moreen (*d* 22 Dec 1997), dau of Dr Robert Willan Paylor Hall, MC, and formerly w of R N C Bentley, and has:

    1*Caroline Sarah; *b* 15 July 1966

Lineage: SAMUEL RICHMOND, of Fiskerton; *b* 1746; *m* Anne — and had:

SAMUEL RICHMOND, of Sutton-on-Trent; *m* Elizabeth — and had:

SAMUEL RICHMOND, of Sutton-on-Trent and Marnham; *m* Mary — and had:

HENRY RICHMOND, of Walesby; *b* 1827; *m* 21 Aug 1871 Charlotte (*d* Aug 1921), dau of Owen Page, of Sheffield, and *d* 14 Jan 1887, leaving:

Sir Frederick Henry Richmond, 1st Bt (UK), so *cr* 4 July 1929; *b* 30 Nov 1873; chm: Debenhams Ltd and Harvey Nichols & Co; *m* 1921 Dorothy Agnes, dau of Francis Joseph Sheppard, and *d* 11 Nov 1953, leaving:

    1 Sir JOHN FREDERICK RICHMOND, **2nd and present Bt**

    1 *Anne Elizabeth [Mrs Dudley Reeves, Filgrave House, Newport Pagnell, Bucks]; *b* 5 Oct 1926; *m* 11 April 1958 *Dudley William Reeves, s of C H R Reeves, of Manor Farm, Podington, Beds, and has:

        (1) *Nicholas Mark Renny; *b* 1 Jan 1964

        (1) *Heather Jennifer; *b* 17 Jan 1962; has:

            1a *Myles Edward; *b* 1987

RICHMOND AND GORDON

Arms: Quarterly, 1st and 4th grandquarters, the Royal arms of CHARLES II (quarterly 1st and 4th, France and England quarterly; 2nd, Scotland; 3rd, Ireland) all within a bordure compony argent and gules, charged with eight roses of the 2nd, barbed and seeded proper (for LENNOX), over all an escutcheon gules, charged with three buckles or (for DUKEDOM OF AUBIGNY); 2nd and 3rd grandquarters, quarterly, 1st, azure three boar's heads couped or (for GORDON); 2nd, or three lions, heads erased gules (for BADENOCH); 3rd, or three crescents within a double tressure flory counter-flory gules (for SETON); 4th, azure three cinquefoils argent (for FRASER). **Crests:** 1 A bull's head erased sable, horned or, 2 On a chapeau gules doubled ermine a lion statant-guardant or, ducally crowned gules and gorged with a collar compony of four pieces argent and gules, charged with eight red roses of the last (for RICHMOND) 3 Out of a ducal coronet a stag's head affrontée proper, attired with ten tynes or. **Supporters:** Dexter, a unicorn argent, armed, crined and unguled, or; sinister, an antelope argent, also crined and unguled or, each supporter gorged with a collar compony as the crest. **Mottoes:** 1 *En la rose je fleuris* ('I flourish in the rose'), 2 (over the 2nd crest) *Bydand* ('Remaining'). **Creations:** B. (E) 9 Aug 1675 (Settrington), L. (S) 9 Sept 1675 (Torboultoun), E. (E) 9 Aug 1675 (March), E. (S) 9 Sept 1675 (Darnley), E. (UK) 13 Jan 1876 (Kinrara), D. (E) 9 Aug 1675 (Richmond), D. (S) 9 Sept 1675 (Lennox), D. (UK) 13 Jan 1876 (Gordon), D. (France) Jan 1683/4 (d'Aubigny).

THE 10TH DUKE OF RICHMOND and 5TH DUKE OF GORDON, Duke of Lennox, Earl of March, Earl of Darnley, Earl of Kinrara, Baron of Settrington, Co York, **Lord of Torboultoun**, also **Duke d'Aubigny** in France (Charles Henry Gordon-Lennox) [His Grace The Duke of Richmond and Gordon, Goodwood House, Goodwood, W Sussex PO18 0PX]; *b* 19 Sept 1929; *s* f 1989; *educ* Eton and William Temple Coll Rugby; Hereditary Constable Inverness Castle, Ld Lt W Sussex 1990–94 (DL 1975–90); 2nd Lt KRRC 1949–50; FCA 1956; memb: Ho of Laity Ch Assembly (Diocese of Coventry), Gen Synod C of E (formerly Ch Assembly) 1960–80 (chm Bd for Mission and Unity 1967–77) and Centl Ctee WCC 1969–, chm: Missionary and Ecumenical Cncl Ch Assembly 1967–77, Christian Orgn Res and Advsy Tst 1965–87, Ho of Laity Chichester Diocesan Synod 1976–79, V-Chm Archbp's Commn on Ch and State 1966–70; memb W Midlands Regnl Ec Planning Cncl 1965–68; chm: Rugby Cncl Soc Serv 1961–68, Dunford Coll (YMCA) 1969–82, Goodwood Gp of Cos 1969–, Tstees Sussex Heritage Tst 1978–, Planning for Ec Prosperity Chichester and Arun 1984–89, Chichester Cathedral Devpt Tst 1985–91, Ajax Insur Hldgs 1987–89, Assoc Internat Dressage Event Organisers 1987–94, John Wiley & Sons 1992– (dir 1984–), Chichester City of Culture Ctee 1995–; dir: Industrial Studies Wm Temple Coll 1964–68, HHA (Hon Treas 1975–82, Chm SE Regn 1975–78), CGA 1975– and Radio Victory 1982–87; Pres: Sussex Rural Community Cncl 1973–, Chichester Festivities 1975, Br Horse Soc 1976–78, Br Equestrian Trade Assoc 1980–, S England Ag Soc 1981–82, SE England Tourist Bd 1990– (V-Pres 1974–90), Sussex Co Cricket Club; Sussex CC 1991–, co-proprietor Africa Confidential, Medal of Hon Br Equestrian Fedn 1983, Hon LLD Sussex 1986, Chllr Sussex U 1985– (Treas 1979–82), CIMgt (CBIM 1982); *m* 26 May 1951 *Susan Monica, only dau of Col Cecil Everard Grenville-Grey, CBE (*see* MORRISON-BELL, Bt), and has:

    1 +CHARLES HENRY, *Earl of March and Kinrara* [Earl of March, Goodwood House, Goodwood, W Sussex PO18 0PX]; *b* 8 Jan 1955; *educ* Eton; *m* 1st 3 July 1976 (*divorce* 1989) Sally, dau of Maurice Clayton, and has:

        (1) *Alexandra; *b* 1985

    1 (cont.) The *Earl of March and Kinrara m* 2nd 1991 *Hon Janet Elizabeth Astor, dau of 3rd Viscount Astor (*qv*), and by her has:

        (1) +Charles Henry, *Lord Settrington*; *b* 20 Dec 1994

        (2) +William Rupert Charles; *b* 29 Nov 1996

    1 *Ellinor Caroline; *b* 1952

2 *Louisa Elizabeth; *b* 1967; *m* 1 Nov 1997 *Ben Collings, yr s of Roger Collings, of Thruxton, Herefs

The 10th DUKE also adopted:

*Maria MARCH; *b* 1959

*Naomi ('Nimmy') MARCH; *b* 1962; actress in BBC TV's comedy *Common as Muck*; *m* 19– *Gavin Burke, photographer

Richmond, previous creations: Alan III, a Count of Brittany, whose uncle, another Alan, was probably a companion in arms of WILLIAM I (THE CONQUEROR) at Hastings and was granted vast land holdings in Yorkshire almost immediately after the Conquest, seems to have been recognised as Earl of Richmond by 1136. There is no record of his formal investiture with the dignity, however.

His title derived from Richmond Castle in North Yorkshire, which his uncle Alan had built not long before dying in 1089 and which remained the *caput*, or administrative centre of the honor (agglomeration of knight's fees in a single unit under the feudal system). Richmond Castle was granted to the **1st Duke of Richmond** of the present creation in August 1675, the same month he was first ennobled, but the medieval honor comprised lands throughout eastern England, not just Yorkshire. Earl Alan sided with STEPHEN against the EMPRESS MAUD at the time of the Anarchy. His son Conan IV held the Dukedom of Brittany (right to which he enjoyed through his mother, Alan's wife) as well as the Earldom of Richmond.

Conan IV had an only child, a daughter Constance, who married first Geoffrey, a younger son of HENRY II of England who was thus acknowledged as Earl of Richmond and Duke of Brittany, then Ranulf, Earl of Chester, who styled himself Earl of Richmond and Duke of Brittany too. She divorced Ranulf in 1199 and took a third husband, Guy de Thouars, who ran the Richmond estates but may not necessarily have been recognised as Earl of Richmond. Guy sided with the King of France against KING JOHN of England in 1203, whereupon his English lands were forfeited, after which the question as to whether he enjoyed recognition as Earl hardly arises.

Geoffrey and Constance's son Arthur, better known as the Prince who was probably done away with by KING JOHN, succeeded to the Earldom of Richmond and Dukedom of Brittany. Arthur had a sister Eleanor, who long outlived him, but the next holder of the Earldom of Richmond to be recognised as such was the husband of his niece of the half-blood, Piers de Braine. The latter had married Alice, daughter of Constance by her third husband Guy de Thouars, and had seisin of the Richmond property from January 1218/9, thus becoming its fully fledged Earl, the 1st such of this creation. Not that he enjoyed uninterrupted tenure. He was deprived of his lands (hence the Earldom too according to the system then in force) in 1224, from 1227 to 1229 and again in early 1235.

HENRY III granted the Richmond lands in 1240 to Piers, a younger son of the Count of Savoy, who accordingly became known as Earl of Richmond, though never formally invested as such. On his death the Earldom of Richmond, inasmuch as it had ever been his at all, reverted to the Crown. In 1268 HENRY granted the Earldom of Richmond to Piers de Braine's son John, who forthwith made it over to his own son, another John. (These Johns, who were both known by the surname de Bretagne rather than de Braine, may be regarded respectively as 2nd and 3rd Earls of Richmond of the January 1218/9 creation.) John the younger (*i.e.*, the 3rd Earl), who was temporarily deprived of his estates in England in 1296 for siding with the French, married a daughter of HENRY III. He was killed by a wall falling on him when in Lyons for the coronation of Pope Clement V in 1305. On his death EDWARD I asserted a right to the Earldom of Richmond, together with its castles and territories, but a year later conferred the title on the late Earl's second son John, who thus became 4th Earl of Richmond. Like his predecessors he too suffered temporary confiscation of his estates by the Crown, this time in 1326, though they were given back to him later that year, on 25 December appropriately.

The next Earl of Richmond of this creation (though it has also been asserted that on John the 4th Earl's death the title reverted to the Crown) seems to have been the 4th Earl's nephew John, who had become Duke of Brittany on his father's death twenty years earlier. He was certainly called to Parliament as Earl of Richmond (also as Duke of Brittany, however), the writ of summons being issued in 1335. He died without legitimate issue in 1341.

One of John of Gaunt's subsidiary titles was Earl of Richmond, conferred on him in 1342, but he gave it up in 1372 and it reverted to the Crown. The title was restored by John of Gaunt's father EDWARD III the same year to John de Montfort, Duke of Brittany, nephew of the half-blood of the 5th Earl of Richmond of the January 1218/9 creation, who thus became 6th Earl of Richmond. After the 6th Earl had come to an accommodation with the King of France in 1381 RICHARD II took the Earldom of Richmond away from him. This was in about 1385. Some 14 years later RICHARD restored it. The next year RICHARD was deposed and the 6th Earl of Richmond died. Either the title was looked on by the new regime of HENRY IV as merging in the Crown or HENRY decided not to recognise its restoration in the last year of his predecessor's reign. Either way it was effectively denied to the former holders. Instead HENRY V conferred it on his younger brother John in 1414. The latter held it till his death without legitimate issue in 1435.

The title was next held by the Tudors before they ascended the throne, being conferred on Edmund Tudor, eldest son of Owen Tudor by Katherine, widow of HENRY V, in 1452. The 2nd Earl of Richmond of this 1452 creation became HENRY VII after defeating RICHARD III at Bosworth and the title merged in the Crown. In 1525 HENRY VIII conferred a Dukedom of Richmond on Henry Fitzroy, his illegitimate son by Elizabeth Blount (a Maid of Honour, of all things, to CATHERINE OF ARAGON). The boy, who was only about six at the time, died aged approximately 17, having had no children, when the Dukedom expired also.

For the Dukedom of Richmond that existed between May 1623 and February the following year, also its recreation in favour of the 1623 grantee's nephew in 1641, *see* MORAY, E.

Gordon, previous creations: For the Dukedom of Gordon created in 1684, *see* HUNTLY, M, as also for the Lordship of Parliament of Gordon of Badenoch created in 1599, the Lordship of Parliament of Gordon of Strathavon and Glenlivet created in 1660 and the Barony of Gordon of Huntley [*sic*] created in 1784. For the Viscountcy of Gordon of Aberdeen created in 1814, *see* ABERDEEN, M. A Life Barony of Gordon of Drumearn was conferred in 1876 (the same year as the current Dukedom of Gordon's creation) on Edward Strathearn Gordon, Lord Advocate for Scotland during Disraeli's two premierships.

Lennox, previous creations: A shadowy figure called Alwyn, possibly of Celtic origin, possibly of Saxon origin, possibly of both, may have become Earl of Lennox in the mid-.

12th century. He is also referred to in near-contemporary sources as Mormaer (*see* BUCHAN, E, preliminary remarks) of a territory called Leamhan, from which the Levenax or Lennox is derived. Alwyn's son and grandson, respectively another Alwyn and Maldouen (cognate with Maldwyn), seem to have succeeded to the Earldom, the latter in about 1224. In a list of the seven Earldoms of Scotland which is thought to have represented the old Mormaerships, by now evolved into medieval titles of honour, and which dates from 1237, that of Lennox features. Yet it was missing from a somewhat later list, that of 1244, only to be reinstated in yet a third list, that of 1297. At the time of the earliest of these three lists it was surrendered by Maldouen, the 3rd Earl, to ALEXANDER II for regrant. This was a common Scottish practice.

The Earldom descended to Maldouen's grandson (Malcolm, 4th Earl), then to the latter's son (another Malcolm, 5th Earl) and grandson (Donald, 6th Earl). In about 1364, however, the 6th Earl's daughter Margaret inherited the title as Countess of Lennox in her own right. She married Walter de Fasselane (modern Faslane), who seems to have been recognised as Earl of Lennox in right of his wife since in about 1385 the two of them made the dignity over to their eldest son Duncan. This son, the 8th Earl, who had no legitimate sons, got a regrant of the title from ROBERT III extending the line of descent to his daughter and her husband, though why this was thought necessary, given that the Earldom had already descended in just such a manner only a generation previously, is uncertain. One can only assume that the view of Earldoms in Scotland was changing about this time.

Isabel, the daughter of Duncan, 8th Earl of Lennox, accordingly became Countess of Lennox in her own right, but her husband Murdoch, 2nd Duke of Albany and first cousin of JAMES I, was involved in a plot against the King and executed, along with his father-in-law the 8th Earl of Lennox. It was not till 1473 that an heir to the Earldom emerged, the successful claimant being Sir John Stuart, previously created Lord Darnley. He was the paternal grandson of Elizabeth, youngest sister of Countess Isabel, but inasmuch as right to the Earldom was in dispute between him and a cousin it may be that his taking his seat as Earl in 1488 constitutes a fresh creation.

Thereafter the Earldom descended uninterruptedly from father to son till the time of Matthew Stuart, 4th or 13th Earl of Lennox (depending on one's view of the events of 1488), who was born in 1516 and inherited the title aged 10. A slippery figure who sided now with the pro-French party in Scottish affairs, now with the pro-English one, the 4th/13th Earl actually fought against his own countrymen as part of the English harrying of the Border counties (which included the capture of Edinburgh) in 1544. It was his son who, best known under the title Lord Darnley, married MARY QUEEN OF SCOTS and was father by her of the future JAMES VI and I. Darnley predeceased his father, who became Regent for his grandson in 1570 but held the post only a year, being killed by adherents of MARY (who, however, had already fled to England) in September 1571. The title then merged in the Crown, since its inheritor JAMES VI and I was already King.

The Earldom of Lennox was revived in 1572 for Charles Stuart, a younger son of Earl Matthew, but expired with its holder four years later. It was again revived, this time for Earl Matthew's younger brother Robert, in 1578, but expired once more on the latter's death without legitimate issue in 1586. For the history of the Earldom and Dukedom of Lennox existing between March 1579/80 and 1581 respectively and 1672, *see* MORAY, E. Note that in this last case the Dukedom of Lennox was held with a Dukedom of Richmond, a precedent for the conferring on an illegitimate son of CHARLES II of both Dukedoms in 1675. CHARLES II gave the surname Lennox to his bastard son because he was himself the representative of the Sir John Stuart of Darnley who became in 1488 Earl of Lennox and who claimed to be in his turn the representative of the old medieval house of Lennox. CHARLES II also granted his son the **1st Duke of Lennox** of the present creation the Lennox lands in Scotland, though the latter sold them on in 1702. They eventually ended in the hands of the Duke of Montrose (*qv*).

Lineage: CHARLES II had illegitimately by Louise Renée de Penancöet de Kéroualle, Duchess of Portsmouth (so *cr* (E) for life 19 Aug 1673) and Duchess d'Aubigny (so *cr* (France) Jan 1683/4) (*d* 14 Nov 1734), est dau of Guillaume de Penancöet, Count de Kéroualle, in Britanny:

CHARLES FitzROY later LENNOX, **1st Duke of Richmond**, so *cr* 9 Aug 1675, as also BARON OF SETTRINGTON, Co York, and EARL OF MARCH (all E), and **1st Duke of Lennox**, so *cr* 9 Sept 1675, as also LORD OF TORBOULTOUN and EARL OF DARNLEY (all S), KG (1681), PC (I, 1715); *b* 29 July 1672; granted by his f Oct 1675 £2,000 a year (just under £1,000,000 a year in late-1990s terms) and to him and his heirs 1/- (just under £2.20 in late-1990s terms) commission on every cauldron of coal shipped out of Newcastle; Govr Dumbarton Castle 1681, Master Horse Dec 1681–Feb 1684/5, High Steward York 1683; naturalised in France 1685 and declared himself RC but turned C of E 1692 and took English citizenship; ADC to WILLIAM III 1693–1702, Ld High Adml Scotland 1694, a Ld Bedchamber 1714–23; *m* c 8 Jan 1692/3 Anne (*d* 9 Dec 1722), sis of 3rd Earl of Cardigan (*see* AILESBURY, M) and widow of 2nd and last Baron Belasyse of Worlaby, and *dvm* 27 May 1723, having had, with two daus (Louisa, *m* 3rd Earl of Berkeley; *see* BERKELEY, B; Anne, *m* 2nd Earl of Albemarle; *qv*):

CHARLES LENNOX, **2nd Duke of Richmond** and **2nd Duke of Lennox**, KG (1726), KB (1725), PC (Jan 1734/5); *b* 18 May 1701; RHG: Capt 1722, Col Feb 1749/50–Aug 1750; Brig-Gen 1739, Maj-Gen 1742, Lt-Gen June 1745, Gen Nov 1745 (fought at Dettingen 1743 and in suppression of Jacobite Uprising 1745); MP (Whig) Chichester 1722–23, ADC and Ld Bedchamber to GEORGEs I and II 1724–32 and 1726–35 respectively; Ld High Constable Coronation 1727; Fell Coll Physicians 1728, MFH Charlton 1731, Mayor Chichester 1735, Er Bro Trin Ho 1737–50, Pres FSA 1749–50 and London Hosp 1741; *s* paternal grandmother as **2nd Duke** and Seigneur **d'Aubigny** 1734; Master Horse Jan 1734/5–50, Amb France 1748–49, High Steward Chichester 1749; *m* 4 Dec 1719 Lady Sarah

Cadogan (d 1751), er dau and coheir of 1st Earl Cadogan (qv), and d 8 Aug 1750, having had, with six other children:

1 CHARLES LENNOX, **3rd Duke of Richmond** and **3rd Duke of Lennox**, also **3rd Duke d'Aubigny**, as which recognised by LOUIS XVI 1776, KG (1781), PC (1765); b 22 Feb 1734/5; educ Westminster and Leyden U; Ensign 2nd Foot Gds 1751, Capt 29th Foot 1753, Lt-Col 33rd Foot 1756, Col 72nd Foot 1758 (present attack on Cherbourg 1758 and Battle of Minden 1759), Maj-Gen 1761, Lt-Gen 1770, Gen 1782, FM 1792, Col RHG 1795–1806, V-Pres Soc of Arts, FRS 1755, a Ld Bedchamber Nov-Dec 1760, Ld Lt Sussex 1763–1806, Amb France 1765–66, Sec State Southern Dept May-July 1766, Master Gen Ordnance 1782–83 and Dec 1783–95; surrendered 1800 the 1/- coal duty granted his gf (see above) in return for £19,000 a year (just under £490,000 a year in late-1990s terms); m 1 April 1757 Mary (d 5 Nov 1796), yst dau and coheir of 4th Earl of Elgin (see ELGIN and KINCARDINE, E), and dspl 29 Dec 1806, leaving three illegitimate daus by his housekeeper, to whom he allegedly bequeathed each £50,000 (just under £1,500,000 in late-1990s terms)

2 George Henry; b c 1738; Lt-Gen, MP Sussex; m 25 Dec 1759 Louisa (d 1830), dau of 4th Marquess of Lothian (qv), and d 25 March 1805, leaving:

(1) CHARLES, **4th Duke**

(1) Maria Louisa; d July 1843

(2) Emilia Charlotte; m 1784 Hon Sir George Cranfield Berkeley, GCB, and d 19 Oct 1832, leaving issue (see BERKELEY, B)

(3) Georgina; m 1789 3rd Earl Bathurst (qv) and d 20 Jan 1841, leaving issue

1 GEORGIANA CAROLINA Lennox, LADY HOLLAND, BARONESS OF HOLLAND (GB), so cr 6 May 1762; b 27 March 1723; m 2 May 1744, as his 2nd w, 1st BARON HOLLAND OF FOXLEY (see ILCHESTER, E) and had issue

2 Emilia Mary; m 1st 7 Feb 1747 1st Duke of Leinster (qv) and had issue; m 2nd William Ogilvie, of Ardglass Castle, Co Down, and had further issue (see SAINT ALBANS, D)

3 Louisa Augusta; m 1758 Rt Hon Thomas Conolly, of Castletown, Co Kildare (see STAPLES, Bt)

4 Sarah; m 1st 2 June 1762 (divorce 1776) Sir Thomas Charles Bunbury, 6th Bt (qv); m 2nd 27 Aug 1781, as his 2nd w, Hon George Napier (see NAPIER and ETTRICK, L) and d Aug 1826, leaving issue

The 3rd DUKE's nephew,

CHARLES LENNOX, **4th Duke of Richmond** and **4th Duke of Lennox**, also **4th Duke d'Aubigny**, as which confirmed by LOUIS XVIII 18 March 1818, KG (1812); b 9 Sept 1764; Sec to unc when Master-Gen Ordnance 1784–95, joined Army 1785, ADC to GEORGE III 1795–98, Maj-Gen 1798, Lt-Gen 1805, Gen 1814, Lt-Col 35th Foot 1789 and Col 1803–19 (formerly in Coldstream Gds, but tfd to the other regt after a duel 1789 with GEORGE III's 2nd s FREDERICK, DUKE OF YORK), MP (Tory) Chichester 1790–1806, High Steward Chichester 1807, Ld Lt Ireland 1807–13 and Sussex 1816–19, Govr Hull 1813–14 and Plymouth 1814–19, Govr-Gen Canada 1818–19; m 9 Sept 1789 Charlotte (d 5 May 1842), dau of 7th Marquess of Huntly (qv), who was also 4th Duke of Gordon, and d Canada 28 Aug 1819 of rabies probably brought on after he was bitten by a pet fox, having had:

1 CHARLES, **5th Duke**

2 John George; b 3 Oct 1793; Lt-Col, MP W Sussex; m 29 June 1818 Louisa Frederica (d 12 Jan 1865), 4th dau of Hon John Rodney (see RODNEY, B), and d 10 Nov 1873, having had, with other issue:

(1) Augustus Frederick Francis; b 22 Aug 1824; Maj-Gen; m 1st 3 Nov 1857 Amy de Beauvoir (d 19 Oct 1867), dau of Joshua Priaulx, of Candie, Guernsey, and widow of Thomas Hutchesson, and had:

1a Amyot Maitland Augustus; b 19 Oct 1867; Capt RA; ka Boer War 18 Feb 1900

1a Mabel Elizabeth; m 13 Oct 1881 Rev Canon Frederick Alfred John Hervey, CVO, and d 25 Dec 1939, leaving issue (see BRISTOL, M)

2a Leila Ethel; m 9 Oct 1890 Alexander Donovan (d 30 March 1922), of Carbrooke Hall, Watton, Norfolk, and d 16 April 1920, leaving issue

(1) (cont.) Maj-Gen Augustus Lennox m 2nd 8 Aug 1872 Augusta Emily (d 8 July 1915), 3rd dau of Montagu Wilmot, and d 8 July 1883, having by her had:

2a George Montagu; b 22 Aug 1874; Maj IA; m 13 Dec 1895 Miriam Ellen (Gertrude) (d 26 July 1928), dau of Benjamin Bossingham, and d 9 March 1922

3a Algernon Lionel; b 17 Feb 1876; d 25 Dec 1916

4a Henry de Grey; b 30 Aug 1879; educ Marlborough; m 19 June 1922 Edith Evelyn (d 17 Feb 1932), dau of Sir Arthur Pendarves Vivian, KCB (see SWANSEA, B), and widow of Lt-Col Algernon Bingham Anstruther Stewart, DSO (see GALLOWAY, E), and dsp 26 Nov 1955

3a Sybil; b 19 May 1873; d unm 11 April 1954

(2) Wilbraham Oates (Sir), VC, KCB, JP (Sussex), of E Pallant Ho, Chichester; b 4 May 1830; Gen RE, Dir-Gen Mil Educn, served Crimea 1854–56, Indian Mutiny 1857–58, Franco-Prussian War 1870–71, Turco-Russian War 1876–77; m 1st 16 July 1861 Mary Harriet (d 22 July 1863), dau of Robert Harrison, of Plas Clough, Denbighs, and had:

1a Gerald Wilbraham Stuart; b 29 April 1862; Lt Black Watch, Roy Highrs; m 22 Oct 1907 Agnes Gordon (d 30 March 1950), only child of Lt-Col Francis John Tidy, and dsp 14 June 1937

1a Lilian Emily; d an infant 3 Aug 1863

(2) (cont.) Gen Sir Wilbraham Lennox m 2nd 12 June 1867 Susan Hay (who s to the Sinclair estates on the death of her sis 1910, added by deed poll the name SINCLAIR and d 6 April 1912), sis and coheir of Sir Robert Charles Sinclair, 9th Bt (see SINCLAIR-LOCKHART, Bt), and d 7 Feb 1897, having had:

2a Charles Gordon; b 9 July 1868; d 30 June 1894

3a Cecil George Pelham LENNOX later GORDON-LENNOX-SINCLAIR (on inheriting the Sinclair estates 1912 from his mother) of Murkle, Dounreay and Achvarasdal, Caithness and Stevenson, Haddington; b 28 April 1872; m 30 April 1901 Cordelia Mary Lane (m 2nd 24 July 1924 Fred Day), only child of Titus Walter Brimacombe, of Morwenstow, Cornwall, and d 9 Aug 1922

4a Claud Henry Maitland LENNOX later LENNOX-SINCLAIR (deed poll 21 March 1923); b 20 Oct 1873; educ RMC Sandhurst; Lt 2nd Bn Northumberland Fus; d unm 24 Nov 1947

2a Louisa Edith; b 1 Sept 1869; d 9 March 1870

3a Cecilia Georgina Susan; b 26 Nov 1875

(1) Elizabeth Frederica; Maid of Hon to HM QUEEN VICTORIA; m 12 Nov 1850 Alexander Charles Stuart of Eaglescairnie, Haddington (d 25 Nov 1897), est s of Lt-Gen Hon Sir Patrick Stuart, GCMG (unc of 12th and last Lord Blantyre; see 1900 edn), and d 19 Oct 1890

3 Henry Adam; b Sept 1797; RN; lost overboard from the Blake sailing from Port Mahon 1812

4 William Pitt; b 20 Sept 1799; m 1st 7 May 1824 (divorce 1834) Mary Anne, est dau of George Paton, of the High Sch, Edinburgh, and had a dau (d young); m 2nd 1854 Ellen (d 3 Nov 1859), dau of John Smith, and by her had:

(1) William Robert; b 16 July 1855; d unm 18 April 1907

4 (cont.) Lord William Lennox m 3rd 17 Nov 1863 Maria Jane (d 10 Jan 1916), est dau of Rev Capel Molyneux (see 1940 edn MOLYNEUX, Bt), and dsps 18 Feb 1881

5 Frederick; b 24 Jan 1801; Capt 7th Foot; d 25 Oct 1829

6 Sussex; b 11 June 1802; m 3 April 1828 Hon Mary Margaret Lawless, dau of 2nd Baron Cloncurry (see 1929 edn), and d 12 April 1874, having had:

(1) Berkeley; b 16 July 1828; in the Army; dvp unm 9 June 1857

(2) Sussex William; b 2 Jan 1831; Lt-Gen Madras Inf; m 15 Oct 1867 Eleanor Jane (d 28 Sept 1933), 2nd dau of W H Peters, of Harefield Ho, Devon, and dsp 15 Dec 1898

(3) Charles Edward; b 22 Dec 1834; Capt 102nd Foot, Hon Maj and Staff Paymr; d unm 18 April 1899

7 Arthur; b 2 Oct 1806; Lt-Col, MP, Clerk Ordnance 1844; m 1 July 1835 Adelaide Constance (d 14 Aug 1888), dau of Col John Campbell, of Shawfield, and d 15 Jan 1864, having had:

(1) Arthur Charles Wriothesley; b 1842; d unm 12 Oct 1876

(1) Constance Charlotte Elisa; m 5 March 1867 Sir George Russell, 4th Bt, of Swallowfield (qv), and d 20 June 1925, leaving issue

(2) Ada Fanny Susan; d unm 22 Nov 1881

(3) Ethel

1 Mary; m 11 March 1820 Sir Charles Augustus FitzRoy, KCB (see GRAFTON, D), and d 7 Dec 1847, leaving issue

2 Sarah; m 9 Oct 1815 Gen Sir Peregrine Maitland, GCB (d 1854), C-in-C Madras Army, Govr Cape of Good Hope, s of Thomas Maitland, of New Forest, by Eliza, est dau of Maj-Gen Edward Mathew, and d 8 Sept 1873, leaving issue

3 Georgiana; m 7 June 1824 22nd Lord (Baron) De Ros (qv) of Helmsley and d 15 Dec 1891, leaving issue

4 Jane; m 20 July 1822 Lawrence Peel and d 27 March 1861, leaving issue (see PEEL, E)

5 Louisa Maddelena; m 18 April 1825 William Frederick Fownes Tighe, PC, JP (dsp 11 June 1878), of Woodstock, Co Kilkenny, Ld Lt Kilkenny, and d 2 March 1900

6 Charlotte; m 4 Dec 1823 1st Baron FitzHardinge of Bristol (see BERKELEY, B) and d 20 Aug 1833

7 Sophia Georgiana; m 7 Aug 1838 Lord Thomas Cecil (see EXETER, M) and d 17 Jan 1902

The 4th DUKE's est s,

CHARLES LENNOX later GORDON-LENNOX (roy licence 9 Aug 1836 on inheriting estates of maternal uncle 5th and last Duke of Gordon; see HUNTLY, M), **5th Duke of Richmond** and **5th Duke of Lennox**, also **5th Duke d'Aubigny**, KG (1829); b 3 Aug 1791; educ Westminster and Trin Coll Dublin; Ensign 8th Garrison Bn 1809, Lt 13th Light Dragoons 1810, Capt 92nd Foot 1812 and 52nd Foot 1813, Brevet Maj 1815, Brevet Lt-Col 1816 (served Peninsular War, wounded Battle of Orthez 1814, ADC and Assist Mil Sec to 1st Duke of Wellington (qv) 1810–14, Extra ADC to PRINCE OF ORANGE Waterloo Campaign 1815, Waterloo Slver medal with eight clasps 1816, when ret as Lt-Col); MP (Tory) Chichester 1812–19, Col Sussex Militia 1819–60, PMG 1830–34, V-Adml Sussex 1831, V-Pres Smithfield Club 1832, Steward Jockey Club, High Steward Chichester, Militia ADC to WILIAM IV 1832 and HM QUEEN VICTORIA 1837–41 (Extra) and 1841–60 (Ordinary), Ld Lt Sussex 1835–60; m 10 April 1817 Caroline (d 12 March 1874), est dau of 1st Marquess of Anglesey (qv), and d 21 Oct 1860, having had, with two other daus (d unm):

1 CHARLES HENRY, **6th Duke**

2 FitzRoy George Charles; b 11 June 1820; Offr in the Army; lost in the steamer President 1841

3 Henry Charles George (Rt Hon), PC; b 2 Nov 1821; MA (Oxford); MP (C) Chichester 1846–85, twice a Ld Treasury, Sec Admlty 1868, First Commr Works 1874–76; m 25 Jan 1883 Amelia Susannah (d 6 Feb 1903), widow of John White, of Arddarroch, Dunbartonshire, and dsp 29 Aug 1886

4 Alexander Francis Charles; b 14 June 1825; Capt RHG (Blues); MP Shoreham 1849–59; m 6 Aug 1863 Emily Frances, dau Charles Towneley (see O'HAGAN, B) and d 22 Jan 1892, leaving:

(1) Cosmo Charles; b 17 Aug 1869; m 1898 Marie Susan, DBE (1937) (Marie Tempest, the actress, who m 2nd 1921 W Graham-Browne (d 22 March 1937) and d 14 Oct 1942), est dau of Edward Etherington, and d 31 July 1921

5 George Charles; b 22 Oct 1829; Lt RHG (Blues); MP Lymington; m 3 Aug 1875 Minnie Augusta (d 21 Sept 1913), dau of W H Palmer, of Portland Place, and widow of Maj Edwin Adolphus Cook (see COOK, Bt), and dsp 27 Feb 1877

1 Caroline Amelia; m 4 Oct 1849 5th Earl of Bessborough (qv) and d 30 April 1890

2 Augusta Katherine; m 27 Nov 1851 FM HH PRINCE EDWARD OF SAXE-WEIMAR, Col 1st Life Gds (dsp 16 Nov 1902), and d 3 April 1904

3 Cecilia Catherine; m 17 Nov 1859 4th Earl of Lucan (qv) and d 5 Oct 1910, leaving issue

The 5th DUKE's est s,

CHARLES HENRY GORDON-LENNOX, **6th Duke of Richmond** and **6th Duke of Lennox**, also **6th Duke d'Aubigny**, in addition **1st Duke of Gordon**, so cr 13 Jan 1876, as also EARL OF KINRARA, Co Inverness (both UK), KG (1867), PC (1859), JP (Sussex); b 27 Feb 1818; educ Westminster and Ch Ch Oxford (BA); Offr RHG 1839–44, MP (C) W Sussex 1841–60, ADC to C-in-C 1842–54, Pres Poor Law Bd March–June 1859 and BOT 1867–68 and June-Aug 1885, Leader C Peers Ho Lds

1870–76, Er Bro Trinity Ho 1870–1903, Ld Pres Cncl 1874–80, Ld Lt Banffshire 1879–1903, Pres Ctee Cncl Edcn and Sec Scotland 1885–86, Chllr Aberdeen U 1861–1903, Hon DCL Oxon 1870, Hon LLD Cantab 1894, Chm W Sussex CC; *m* 28 Nov 1843 Frances Harriet (*d* 8 March 1887), est dau of Algernon Frederick Greville (*see* WARWICK, BROOKE and, E), and *d* 27 Sept 1903, having had, with two daus *d* unm):

1 CHARLES HENRY, **7th Duke**

2 Algernon Charles; *b* 19 Sept 1847; Col Gren Gds, Egypt 1882, ADC to HRH THE DUKE OF CAMBRIDGE 1883–95, Boer War 1900–01, Sec Princess Victoria's Rest Clubs for Nurses in France 1918; *m* 31 Aug 1886 Blanche, DBE (1919), DGStJ (*d* 17 Aug 1945), 2nd dau of Col Hon Charles Henry Maynard, only s of 3rd and last Viscount Maynard (*see* 1865 edn), and *d* 3 Oct 1921, leaving:

 (1) Ivy, DBE (1958); *b* 16 June 1887; Maid of Hon to HM QUEEN ALEXANDRA 1912–15; *m* 12 Aug 1915 7th Duke of Portland (*see* PORTLAND, E) and had issue

3 Francis Charles; *b* 30 July 1849; Capt Scots Gds; *d* unm 1 Jan 1886

4 Walter Charles, PC; *b* 29 July 1865; MP Chichester 1888–94, Treasurer Household 1891–92; *m* 6 July 1889 Alice Elizabeth (*d* 7 March 1946), er dau of Hon George Henry Ogilvie-Grant of Grant (*see* SEAFIELD, E), and *d* 21 Oct 1922, leaving:

 (1) Victor Charles Hugh; *b* 10 Sept 1897; *educ* Trin Coll Cambridge; Capt Gren Gds WW I (wounded), jnlst *Daily Mail* 1922–29 (political correspondent 1923–29), *Daily Telegraph* 1930 (dip correspondent 1935); *m* 1st 12 July 1923 (*divorce* 1928) Mrs Anne Dorothy Bridge (*d* 16 March 1963), est dau of Edward Cazalet Browne; *m* 2nd 28 Dec 1932 (*divorce* 1940) Diana Elizabeth Constance (*d* 1982), only dau of Adml Sir Charles Edmund Kingsmill, of Ballybeg, Ottawa, and by her had:

  1a +(Henry) George Charles; *b* 24 Sept 1934; *m* 8 Feb 1958 *Odile, only dau of Raoul Steinmann, of Grenoble, and has:

   1b +Ian Charles; *b* 16 Dec 1958; *m* 1989 *Jeltje, er dau of Owen Aukema, of Holland, Mich., and adopted:

    *Jefferson Charles; *b* 29 March 1995

   2b +Philip George Charles; *b* 13 Sept 1962; *m* 1987 *Junko, dau of Prof Tomio Higuchi, and has:

    1c +Thomas Charles; *b* 1991

    2c +Alec George; *b* 1993

  1b *Geneviève Ann [Frau Rainer Frick, Stutzstrasse 11, 8353 Elgg, Switzerland]; *b* 3 Jan 1961; *m* 1993 *Rainer Frick, s of Wilhelm Frick, of Basel, and has:

   1c *Adrian Bruno; *b* 11 Aug 1996

 (1) (cont.) Capt Victor Gordon-Lennox *m* 3rd 19 May 1958 Norah Julia Wensley, only dau of Edward Guy Schofield, of Leeds, and *d* 25 Jan 1968

The 6th/1st DUKE's est s,

CHARLES HENRY GORDON-LENNOX, **7th Duke of Richmond, 7th Duke of Lennox, 2nd Duke of Gordon** and **7th Duke d'Aubigny**, KG (1905), GCVO (1904), CB (1902), JP, DL Sussex; *b* 27 Dec 1845; *educ* Eton; Gren Gds 1865–69, Col 3rd Roy Sussex Regt Boer War 1901–02 (despatches); MP (C) W Sussex 1869–85 and Chichester 1885–88, CA Sussex; Steward Jockey Club, Ecclesisatical Commr 1885–1903, Militia ADC to TM QUEEN Victoria, EDWARD VII and GEORGE V 1896–1920, Ld Lt and Pres TAA Morayshire and Banffshire, Chllr Aberdeen U 1917, Hon LLD, Lt Roy Co Archers; *m* 1st 10 Nov 1868 Amy Mary (*d* 23 Aug 1879), dau of Percy Ricardo, of Bramley Pk, Surrey, and had:

1 CHARLES HENRY, **8th Duke**

2 Esmé Charles (Sir), KCVO (1939), CMG (1919), DSO (1918), JP, DL Banffshire; *b* 10 Feb 1875; *educ* Eton; Col Scots Gds, Hon Brig-Gen, Boer War 1900–02, S Nigeria 1903–04, WW I (despatches, wounded twice, Brevet), Cdr Order St Maurice and St Lazarus Italy, Yeoman Usher Black Rod, Sec to Ld Great Chamberlain 1929–46; *m* 1st 8 June 1909 (*divorce* 1923) Hon Hermione Frances Caroline Fellowes, 3rd dau of 2nd Baron de Ramsey (*qv*), and had:

 (1) Reginald Arthur Charles; *b* 13 May 1910; *educ* Winchester; Capt Scots Gds WW II; *m* 17 Feb 1942 Pamela Cicely (*d* 11 March 1997), est dau of Capt Christopher Digby Leyland, Life Gds (*see* COTTERELL, Bt), and *d* 30 Aug 1965, leaving:

  1a +James David Charles; *b* 29 Oct 1944; *m* 1973 (*divorce* 1979) Sally Cooper, dau of John Roger Cooper Brain, and has:

   1b +Henry; *b* 1976

  1a *Clare Evelyn; *b* 19 Aug 1946; *m* 1967 *Edmund Clive Lardner-Burke

2 (cont.) Brig-Gen Lord Esmé Gordon-Lennox *m* 2nd 2 Dec 1923 Rosamund Lorys (*d* 6 May 1961), dau of V-Adml Norman Craig Palmer, CVO, of Barnwyke, Chichester, and *d* 4 May 1949, having by her had:

 (2) A son; *b* 11 April, *d* 12 April 1927

 (1) *Sara Carolyn [Lady Fergusson, c/o Coutts & Co, 440 Strand, London WC2R 0QS]; *b* 12 May 1933; *m* 1st 1956 Sir William Andrew Malcolm Martin Oliphant Montgomery Cunninghame, 11th Bt, of Corsehill (*qv*); *m* 2nd 19 Dec 1959 *Sir Ewen Alastair John Fergusson, GCMG, GCVO, er s of Sir Ewen Macgregor Field Fergusson, and by him has:

  1a *Ewen Alexander Nicholas; *b* 30 Nov 1965

  1a *Anna Rosamund Harriot; *b* 15 June 1961

  2a *Iona Frances; *b* 7 May 1967

3 Bernard Charles; *b* 1 May 1878; *educ* Eton and RMC Sandhurst; Maj Gren Gds, Boer War 1899–1900, WW I; *m* 25 July 1907 Hon Evelyn Loch (*k* by enemy action 18 June 1944), 2nd dau of 1st Baron Loch (*see* 1970 edn), and was *ka* 10 Nov 1914, leaving:

 (1) George Charles (Sir), KBE (1964), CB (1959), CVO (1952), DSO (1943); *b* 29 May 1908; *educ* Eton and RMC Sandhurst; Page of Hon to HM GEORGE V 1921–24; Lt-Gen Gren Gds WW II (wounded, despatches); Cmdt RMA Sandhurst 1959–63, Dir-Gen Mil Trg War Office 1963–64, GOC-in-C Scottish Cmd and Govr Edinburgh Castle 1964–66, Col Gordon Highrs 1965–, King of Arms Order Br Empire 1968–88; *m* 16 July 1931 Nancy Brenda (*d* 1993), 2nd dau of Sir Lionel Edward Hamilton Marmaduke Darell, 6th Bt, DSO (*qv*), and *d* 1988, leaving:

1a +Bernard Charles, CB (1986), MBE (1968) [Maj-Gen Bernard Gordon-Lennox CB MBE, Hill House, Eversley, Hants]; *b* 19 Sept 1932; *educ* Eton and RMA Sandhurst; Page of Hon to HM GEORGE VI 1946–49, Gren Gds: cmdg 1st Bn 1974, Lt-Col 1989–95, Maj-Gen, chm Gds Polo Club 1992–; Sr Army memb RCDS 1986–88; *m* 20 Nov 1958 *Sally-Rose, only dau of John Weston Warner, of The Old Rectory, Stanton, Worcs, and has:

 1b +Edward Charles; *b* 30 Jan 1961; *educ* Eton and RMA Sandhurst; Page of Hon to HM THE QUEEN 1974–77; Capt Gren Gds; *m* 1989 *Katharine Elizabeth, est dau of (Robert) Martin Mays-Smith, of Chaddleworth, Berks, and has:

  1c +Alexander Charles; *b* 1990

  1c *Rosie Jennifer; *b* 1992

  2c *Laura Clare; *b* 3 Feb 1995

 2b +Angus Charles; *b* 4 Feb 1964; *m* 1990 *Camilla Douglas, er dau of Ian Alan Douglas Pilkington (*see* FARINGDON, B), and has:

  1c *Geordie Charles; *b* 11 Nov 1998

  1c *Iona Alice; *b* 1993

  2c *Emily Charlotte; *b* 4 July 1995

 3b +Charles Bernard; *b* 18 June 1970

2a +David Henry Charles [Col David Gordon-Lennox, Saxham Hall, Bury St Edmunds, Suffolk IP29 5JW]; *b* 2 Aug 1935; *educ* Eton and RMA Sandhurst; Col Gren Gds; *m* 30 Jan 1982 *Elizabeth C, est dau of Gen Sir William Gurdon Stirling, GCB, CBE, DSO, and has:

 1b *Flora; *b* 3 Nov 1983

(2) Alexander Henry Charles (Sir), KCVO (1972), CB (1961), DSO (1942); *b* 9 April 1911; R-Adml, WW II (despatches); Pres RN Coll Greenwich 1961–62, Sgt at Arms H of C 1961–76, memb Roy Co Archers; *m* 12 Nov 1936 Barbara (*d* 1987), dau of Maj-Gen Julian Steele, and *d* 1987, having had:

 1a +Michael Charles [Capt Michael Gordon-Lennox RN, Fishers Hill, Iping, W Sussex GU29 0PF]; *b* 30 Sept 1938; *educ* Eton and RNC Dartmouth; memb Roy Co Archers; *m* 19 Oct 1974 *Jennifer Susan, dau of Capt Hon Vicary Paul Gibbs, Gren Gds (*see* ALDENHAM and HUNSDON OF HUNSDON, B), and has:

  1b +Hamish Charles; *b* 11 June 1980

  1b *Lucinda Jean; *b* 19 Sept 1975

  2b *Charlotte Louise; *b* 18 Sept 1978

 2a +Andrew Charles [Cdr Andrew Gordon-Lennox RN, Bridge House, Commonside, Westbourne, Hants PO10 8TD]; *b* 16 Jan 1948; *educ* Nautical Coll Pangbourne and RNC Dartmouth; *m* 29 Sept 1973 *Julia Jane Neill, dau of J Morrison, of Minster, Kent, and has:

  1b +Simon Charles; *b* 15 April 1978

  2b +Hugo Charles; *b* 14 May 1980

1 Evelyn Amy; *b* 23 April 1872; *m* 4 Jan 1896 Sir John Richard Geers Cotterell, 4th Bt (*qv*), and *d* 17 Feb 1922, leaving issue

2 Violet Mary; *b* 15 Jan 1874; *m* 30 June 1894 1st Baron Brassey of Apethorpe (*qv*) and *d* 19 Nov 1946, leaving issue

The **7th/2nd Duke** *m* 2nd 3 July 1882 Isabel Sophie (*d* 20 Nov 1887), dau of William George Craven (*see* CRAVEN, E), and *d* 18 Jan 1928, having by her had:

3 Muriel Beatrice; *m* 1st 30 April 1904 (*divorce* 1933) Maj William Malebisse Beckwith, DSO, Coldstream Gds (*d* 24 Dec 1954), only s of Capt Henry John Beckwith, JP, of Millichope Pk, Salop, and had issue; *m* 2nd 2 Aug 1933 Cdr Lewis Derek Jones, RN (*d* 31 Oct 1968), er s of Maj-Gen Lewis Jones, CB, CMG, of Stoke Poges, Bucks, and *d* 4 April 1969

4 Helen Magdalen, GCVO (1938), CBE (1920), JP; Mistress Robes to HM QUEEN ELIZABETH THE QUEEN MOTHER 1937–64, Staff Capt FANY 1939–43, Cdr 1943–46, Patron Surrey BRCS (Pres 1939–53), ADC to HRH PRINCESS ALICE, COUNTESS OF ATHLONE, OC Duchess of Northumberland's Unit 1941–46, Order Mercy, MFH Percy 1930–33 (Jt MFH 1933–47), OStJ; *m* 18 Oct 1911 8th Duke of Northumberland (*qv*) and *d* 13 June 1965, leaving issue

The 7th/2nd DUKE's est son,

CHARLES HENRY GORDON-LENNOX, **8th Duke of Richmond, 8th Duke of Lennox, 3rd Duke of Gordon** and **8th Duke d'Aubigny**, DSO (1900), MVO (1905), JP (Morayshire), DL (Sussex); *b* 30 Dec 1870; *educ* Eton and Ch Ch Oxford; Maj Irish Gds, Lt-Col Sussex Yeo, Gen Res Offrs, ADC to C-in-C Ireland 1895–98 and S Africa Boer War 1899–1900 (despatches); Ld Lt Morayshire; *m* 8 June 1893 Hilda Madeleine, DBE (1946), JP (Sussex and Morayshire), V-Pres SSAFA (*d* 29 Dec 1971 aged 99), est dau of Henry Arthur Brassey (*see* BRASSEY OF APETHORPE, B), and *d* 7 May 1935, having had:

1 Charles Henry; *b* 15 Aug, *d* 5 Sept 1895

2 Charles Henry, *Lord Settrington*; *b* 26 Jan 1899; Lt Irish Gds WW I; *das* Russia 24 Aug 1919

3 FREDERICK CHARLES, **9th/4th Duke**

1 Amy Gwendoline; *b* 5 May 1894; *m* 11 Dec 1917 Sir James Stuart Coats, 3rd Bt (*qv*), and *d* 27 April 1975, leaving issue

2 Doris Hilda; *b* 6 Sept 1896; *m* 10 April 1923 Lt-Cdr Clare George VYNER formerly COMPTON, RN (*see* NORTHAMPTON, M), and had issue

The 8th/3rd DUKE's est surv s,

FREDERICK CHARLES GORDON-LENNOX, **9th Duke of Richmond, 9th Duke of Lennox, 4th Duke of Gordon** and **9th Duke d'Aubigny**; *b* 5 Feb 1904; *educ* Eton and Ch Ch Oxford; Lt RTC and RA (TA), F/Lt RAF WW II, Pres Br Automobile Racing Club, artist; *m* 15 Dec 1927 Elizabeth Grace (*d* 1992), yst dau of Rev Thomas William Hudson, Vicar Wendover, Bucks, and *d* 1989, having had:

1 CHARLES HENRY GORDON-LENNOX, **10th and present Duke of Richmond and Gordon**

2 +Nicholas Charles, KCMG (1986, CMG 1978), KCVO (1988, LVO 1957), CMG (Civil 1978) [The Lord Nicholas Gordon-Lennox KCMG KCVO, South Nore, W Wittering, W Sussex PO20 8AT]; *b* 31 Jan 1931; *educ* Eton and Worcester Coll Oxford; 2nd Lt KRRC; FO: joined 1954, Priv Sec to Amb to USA 1956–60, 2nd Sec (Commercial) Santiago 1961–63 (1st Sec 1962), FO 1963–66, 1st Sec Madrid 1966–71, Head News Dept FCO 1973–74, Counsellor Paris 1975–79, Assist U-Sec FCO 1979–84, Amb Spain 1984–89, Govr BBC 1990–,

dir 1990: Foreign and Colonial Investment Tst; Hon Col 4th Bn RGJ 1990–, Chm Historic Churches Preservn Tst 1997–; Grand Cross Order Isabel la Católica Spain 1986; *m* 14 Jan 1958 *Mary, only dau of Brig Hudleston Noel Hedworth Williamson, DSO, MC (*see* WILLIAMSON, Bt), and has:

(1) +Anthony Charles; *b* 29 April 1969; Ch Bdcstg Offr C Centl Office 1996–

(1) *Sarah Caroline; *b* 20 June 1960; *m* 1988 *Dominic Caldecott, yst s of Andrew Caldecott, of Ramsbury, Wilts, and has:

1a *Frederick Arthur Nicholas; *b* 1989

2a *Thomas Andrew (twin); *b* 1989

3a *Rufus George; *b* 1993

(2) *Henrietta Mary; *b* 8 Jan 1962; *m* 1992 *Michael J Lindsell, of Lymington, Hants, and has:

1a *Albert; *b* 1993

2a *Arthur; *b* 12 Oct 1996

1a *A dau; *b* 25 March 1998

(3) *Lucy Elizabeth; *b* 28 Dec 1965; *m* 7 Dec 1996 *Mark Cornell, s of Brig John Cornell

Seat: Goodwood House, Goodwood, W Sussex. There is some confusion over when the Dukes of Richmond acquired Goodwood. A date in the 1670s, though often put forward, is hardly likely since the **1st Duke** was only born in 1672. The statement that he bought Goodwood from the Compton family in 1720, even though for a while he used it merely as a hunting lodge, seems more plausible. Most of the present building seems to have been begun by Sir William Chambers (who was also responsible for the Kew Pagoda and the remodelling of Somerset House), though again some accounts credit him only with the stable block. That Goodwood, which apparently has Jacobean origins, was added to by Wyatt between 1780 and 1800 seems to be agreed on, however. But even here an original plan for an eight-sided mansion was not adhered to. The reason for the odd obtuse-angled shape to the present house is at least comprehensible when one realises that it is just a portion of a more ambitious polygon.

If the above account suggests a certain hapahazardness, it is not apparent in the present structure. For one thing the setting amid the Downs is too superb. Then again the Sussex flint of the elevations and the unusual turrets at the corners with their shallow-domed roofs lend considerable charm, though at the same time they suggest a much earlier period, being just a little reminiscent of the 11th-century great tower of Colchester Castle. The internal decor was toned down over the last twenty-five years, subordinated to the justly celebrated collection of clocks, furniture, paintings and porcelain, much of which dates from the **3rd Duke**'s time, he being Ambassador to the France of LOUIS XV. The tapestry room, the only surviving interior bearing Wyatt's touch, was an early exception. But in the late 1990s a refurbishment programme under the supervision of Lord March and Kinrara led to the rediscovery of such gems as the yellow scagliola in the Egyptian Dining Room. The **4th Duke** was so extravagant when Lord Lieutenant of Ireland that he had to stop living at Goodwood and take up residence in Brussels. It was there that his Duchess gave the celebrated Ball three nights before Waterloo.

RICKETTS

PREND·MOI·TEL·QUE·JE·SUIS

Arms: Argent on a chevron azure between three roses gules, barbed and seeded proper, two swords in chevron also proper, pommels and hilts or, their points crossing each other in saltire, the dexter surmounted by the sinister, and passing through a wreath of laurel gold, on a chief of the second a naval crown between two anchors erect or. **Crest:** Out of a naval crown or a dexter arm embowed, habited azure and charged on the sleeve with two roses argent, the hand grasping a scimitar; the arm in front of an anchor in bend sinister sable. **Motto:** *Prend moi tel que je suis* ('Take me as I am').
Creation: Bt. (UK) 15 Feb 1828.

SIR ROBERT CORNWALLIS GERALD ST LEGER RICKETTS, 7TH BT, of The Elms Co Gloucester, and Beaumont-Leyes, Co Leicester [Sir Robert Ricketts Bt, Forwood House, Minchinhampton, Glos, GL6 9AB]; *b* 8 Nov 1917; *s* f Nov 1937; *educ* Haileybury and Magdalene Coll Cambridge (BA 1939, MA 1943); Capt Devonshire Regt WW II, PA to Ch Staff Gibraltar 1942–45, ADC to Lt-Govr Jersey

1945–46, slr 1949, ptnr Wellington & Clifford (ret), FRSA; *m* 20 July 1945 Anne Theresa (*d* 16 Jan 1998), 2nd dau of Sir (Richard) Stafford Cripps, CH, PC, QC (*see* PARMOOR, B), and has:

1 +(ROBERT) TRISTRAM [Tristram Ricketts Esq, 47 Lancaster Ave, London SE27 9EL]; *b* 17 April 1946; *educ* Winchester and Magdalene Coll Cambridge (BA 1968); *m* 2 Aug 1969 *Ann, yr dau of Eric William Charles Lewis, and has:

(1) +Stephen Tristram; *b* 1974

(1) *Clare Jessica; *b* 21 Jan 1977

2 +John Stafford [John Ricketts Esq, 92 Thompson Ave, Richmond, Surrey TW9 4JN]; *b* 13 Feb 1956; *educ* Winchester and King's Coll London; *m* 1986 *Jacqueline Zifteh and has:

(1) +Joseph Robert; *b* 1988

1 *Sara Lilian [Mrs Peter Mason, Lane Cottage, Amberley, Glos GL5 5AB]; *b* 6 Nov 1947; *m* 1981 *His Honour (George Frederick) Peter Mason, QC

2 *(Isobel) Theresa; *b* 17 April 1952; *m* 1973 *John Anthony Bird, ed-in-chief *The Big Issue*, and has:

(1) *Patrick Jack; *b* 1975

(1) *Eileen Diana; *b* 1977

Lineage: ROBERT RICKETTS, of Basingstoke, Hants; *m* Sarah — (*bur* 18 Jan 1733) and *d* June 1737, having had, with other issue, including an er s (Robert, *b* 26 Jan, *bur* 29 Jan 1697) and a dau (Sarah, *b* 7 Sept 1698):

ROBERT RICKETTS; *b* 17 March 1702; Mayor Basingstoke 1753–54 and 1762–63; *m* Elizabeth — (*bur* 4 April 1775) and was *bur* 5 Dec 1763, leaving:

WILLIAM RICKETTS; *bapt* 13 Oct 1732; *m* 12 Nov 1767 Ann Brazier (*bur* 2 April 1781) and had, with an er s (William, *bapt* 27 Oct 1768) and a dau (Elizabeth, *bapt* 17 May, *bur* 19 May 1730):

JOHN RICKETTS; *b* 16 March 1737; surgn; Burgess 1770; *m* 24 May 1766 Harriot Grace (*d* 30 April 1807), dau of Rev Robert Roberts, Rector Aldford, Cheshire, and was *bur* 5 April 1788, leaving:

1 John Henry; *b* 17 March 1767; Ensign Bengal Engrs; *k* india 1792, leaving:

(1) John William; *b* 1791; *m* 1816 Sarah Catherine Gardner and *d* 1835, leaving five sons

2 Robert; *b* 18 Aug 1768

3 Gilbert; *bapt* 4 Aug 1770; *m* 23 March 1795 Harriet Worsley, dau of Adml Sir Richard Rodney Bligh, GCB, by Harriet, dau of Sir Edward Worsley, of Gatcombe Pk, IoW, High Sheriff Hants, and *d* 1817, leaving:

(1) Gilbert Tristram (Rev); *b* 2 May 1880; *m* Mary — (*bur* 24 March 1871) and *d* 25 April 1876, having had:

1a Gilbert Wesley Bligh; *bur* 20 March 1871 aged 13

(2) Richard Rodney; *b* 7 Oct 1801; Maj-Gen IA, ret 1860; *m* 1st 1 Sept 1825 Elizabeth Hamilton Montgomery (*d* 1843), dau of Arnold Langley, of Lincoln's Inn and Golding Hall, Salop, and had, with another s and five other daus:

1a Richard Rodney; *b* 1826; Col Madras Inf; *m* 1869 his cousin Matilda Gertrude, dau of Capt A E Langley, 3rd Madras Light Cav, and had, with a s and another dau:

1b Gertrude; *b* 1870

2a George Lancelot William; RN

1a Anna Catherine; *b* 5 May 1830; *m* 2 Jan 1854 Gen Charles Hight, Madras Inf (*d* 26 Dec 1905), s of Rev Thomas Hight, of Deal, Kent, and *d* 11 May 1920, leaving issue

(2) (cont.) Maj-Gen Richard Ricketts *m* 2nd 20 June 1844 Laura, dau of Charles Saunders, and by her had:

3a Gilbert Rodney; *b* 31 March 1847

4a Arthur Rodney; *b* 1854

2a Laura; *b* 1845

3a Rosalie Harriet; *b* 14 Jan 1849; *m* 1st Rev C A Harbord, RN, and had issue; *m* 2nd 14 Dec 1889 James Long Sweetman, Surgn RN

4a Laura Henrietta Rodney; *b* 17 Oct 1850

5a Constance Sophie Rodney; *b* 1852

(3) George Yaldham RICKETTS later WILKINSON (on inheriting the Tapton Hall, Derbys, estate 1831); *b* 1810; *m* 1830 Emily, dau of Joseph Michael Malouck, Prussian consul Liverpool, and had, with other issue:

1a George Lawrence WILKINSON later RICKETTS; *b* 1831; *m* 1865 Clarissa, yr dau of Joseph Harding, of Henbury, Glos

1a Emily; *m* — Dent

2a —; *m* — Johnston

3a —; *m* — Bird

4a Harriet; *b* 2 Aug 1822; *m* — White, s of Gen — White and *d* 17 Sept 1878, leaving issue

4 ROBERT TRISTRAM (Sir), **1st Bt**

1 Eliza Letitia Catherine; *bapt* 24 Oct 1783; *m* John Ogilvie and *d* 1851, leaving issue

The 4th s,

Sir Robert Tristram Ricketts, 1st Bt (UK), so *cr* 15 Feb 1828 for servs in the confrontation at Mobile, Ala., during the War of 1812; *b* 1772; V-Adml the Blue, also served Napoleonic Wars, DCL; *m* May 1802 Rebecca Eliza (*d* 1 May 1859), yr dau of Richard Gumbleton, of Castlerichard, Co Waterford, and *d* 16 Aug 1842, having had:

1 CORNWALLIS (Sir), **2nd Bt**

2 St Vincent William; *b* 24 Nov 1807; Col RSG; *m* 6 April 1842 Georgina Mary (*d* 4 April 1867), dau of Augustus FitzHardinge Berkeley (*see* BERKELEY, B), and *d* 26 March 1866, leaving:

(1) St Vincent FitzHardinge Lennox (Rev); *b* 24 March 1843; *educ* St John's Coll Oxford (MA); *m* 11 Sept 1869 Susan Arabella Henrietta (*d* 2 Feb 1912), only surv dau of V-Adml William Henry Jervis, and *d* 1 March 1915, leaving:

1a Susan Hotham; RRC; *m* 1st 8 May 1894 Capt William Ricketts, RN (*d* 6 Dec 1921) (*see below*); *m* 2nd 1 May 1927 Rev Octavius R Hughes (*d* 23 Dec 1938), Rector Bradenham, Bucks, Chaplain RN 1892–1921, and *dsp* 23 Aug 1944

2a Dorothea Jervis; *d* unm 27 Jan 1944

3a Kathleen Berkeley; *m* 30 June 1908 Edward Reginald Willett (*d* 21 Nov 1941), 2nd s of Louis Edward Willett, of Norwich, and *d* 4 Dec 1957

(2) Frederick Augustus Dashwood; *b* 3 Jan 1846; *d* unm 14 April 1883

(3) Henry Wyndham; *b* 25 June 1849; Capt 2nd Bn Essex Regt (56th); *m* 15 Jan 1880 (*judicial separation* 1885) Georgina Kilderbee (*d* 1924), dau of Sir William Carter Hoffmeister, of Clifton Ho, Cowes, IoW, and *d* 30 May 1930, leaving:

1a Wyndham FitzHardinge Dashwood; *b* 30 Sept 1880; Lt RNVR; *d* unm 20 July 1956

(1) Augusta Georgina; *m* 4 Nov 1869 Rev William Henry Edward Ricketts Jervis (*d* 25 May 1914), Rector Sudborne with Orford, Suffolk, and *d* 1 March 1917, leaving issue

3 William Hamilton; *d* India 1830

4 Simpson Hicks; *b* 26 May 1816; Cdr RN; *m* 14 June 1855 Emma Gertrude (*d* 6 May 1906), yst dau of W G Pigou, 2nd Dragoon Gds, and *d* 12 March 1858, leaving:

(1) Richard Ernest (Rev); *b* 28 May 1856; *educ* Trin Coll Oxford (MA); Vicar Crambe, Yorks 1893–1936, RD Bulmer 1915–28; *m* 25 Oct 1884 Mabel Rose (*d* 1 Nov 1956 aged 100), est dau of Maj Arthur Wellesley Williams (*see* WILLIAMS-BULKELEY, Bt), and *d* 7 July 1941, leaving:

1a Clement Mallory (Rt Rev); *b* 19 Aug 1885; *educ* King's Sch Canterbury, Keble Coll Oxford (BA 1908, MA 1912) and Cuddesdon Coll; Curate St Martin's Salisbury 1910–12, Chaplain Bishop's Coll Cheshunt 1912–14, Incumbent St Michael and All Angels Colombo Ceylon 1914–23, Diocesan and Domestic Chaplain to Bp Wakefield 1923–24, Vicar Holy Trinity Weymouth 1924–37, RD Weymouth 1936–37, Canon Gloucester 1937–45, Examining Chaplain to Bp Gloucester 1937–46, Bp Dunwich and Rector Dennington and Badingham 1945–54, Curate in charge Madehurst W Sussex 1954–61; *m* 17 Feb 1920 Dorothy Frances (*d* 1984), TFNS WW I (despatches 1916), 2nd dau of Rt Rev George Rodney Eden (*see* EDEN OF WINTON, B), and *d* 28 Feb 1961, leaving:

1b +Michael Rodney [Maj Michael Ricketts, Church Farm House, Saxlingham, Norfolk NR25 7JY]; *b* 29 Sept 1923; *educ* Sherborne and Trin Coll Oxford (MA 1951); Maj KRRC WW II (wounded), Housemaster Bradfield, Headmaster Sutton Valence 1967–80; *m* 1 Jan 1958 *Judith Anne Caroline, est dau of Col Thomas Stanley Courtenay-Clack, TD, RA, and widow of Herbert James Corry, and has:

1c +Charles Michael Thomas; *b* 1 Sept 1960; *m* 29 Sept 1990 *Jill Elizabeth Davies and has:

1d +Joseph Charles; *b* 8 June 1992

2d +Thomas Benjamin; *b* 29 Nov 1993

3d +Luke William; *b* 12 Feb 1997

2c +James Rodney Eden; *b* 9 May 1964

1c *Rosemary Courtenay; *b* 19 Nov 1958

2c *Katharine Elizabeth; *b* 31 May 1962

2b +John Eden [John Ricketts Esq, World's End, Reepham, Norfolk NR10 4SA]; *b* 14 March 1926; *educ* Sherborne and Trin Coll Oxford (BA 1950, MA 1952); RM, Housemaster Worksop Coll 1953–83; *m* 31 March 1970 *Isobel Claridge, 2nd dau of Charles Claridge Druce, and has:

1c +Michael Tristram; *b* 20 May 1971

2c +Christopher Eden; *b* 1973

1b *Rosemary Ellison [Mrs Frank Hare, 14 Lee Rd, Aldeburgh, Suffolk IP15 5HG]; *b* 18 April 1928; *educ* Cheltenham Ladies Coll; *m* 8 Oct 1949 *Rev Frank Richard Knight Hare, s of Dr Tom Hare, of St Albans, and has:

1c *Roger John HARE later SHELMERDINE-HARE (deed poll 1989); *b* 19 Jan 1957; *m* 1981 *Caroline Philippa W Shelmerdine and has:

1d *Thomas Shelmerdine HARE; *b* 1985

2d *Rayner Harry HARE; *b* 24 Nov 1990

1d *Alicia Caroline HARE; *b* 1983

2d *Brioni Alexandra HARE; *b* 1988

1c *Elizabeth; *b* 29 Sept 1952; *m* 1972 *Richard Cane and has:

1d *Rachel Simone; *b* 1974

2d *Annabel Louise; *b* 1977

1a Violet Mabel; *b* 1889; *d* 1983

(2) William; *b* 14 Oct 1857; Capt RN, served Egyptian Campaign 1882 (medal with clasp, bronze star); *m* 8 May 1894, as her 1st husb, his cousin Susan Hotham Ricketts (*see* above) and *d* 6 Dec 1921

1 Laetitia Frances Henry; *m* 15 Oct 1828 Augustus Newton (*d* 1862) and *d* 28 Sept 1877, leaving issue

2 Harriet Dorothea; *m* 1st 1844 Rev John Charnock and had issue; *m* 2nd 20 Feb 1868 Edmund Haworth (*d* 1879), of Churchdale, Derbys, and *d* 5 June 1888

3 Lavinia Anne; *d* 20 June 1874

4 Mary; *m* 20 April 1845 Thomas Wright, MD, FRS (*d* 17 Nov 1884), and *d* 30 Sept 1878, having had issue

The 1st Bt's est s,

Sir Cornwallis Ricketts, 2nd Bt; *b* 27 Feb 1803; High Sheriff Leics 1851, Adml; *m* 1st 31 May 1834 Henrietta (*d* 13 Nov 1838), yst dau of Col John TEMPEST previously PLUMBE, of Tong Hall, Yorks, and had:

1 Sir ROBERT TEMPEST RICKETTS later TEMPEST (roy licence 23 April 1884 under terms of proviso in deed of indenture 29 Sept 1852), **3rd Bt**; *b* 7 Dec 1836; *m* 26 July 1861 Amelia Helen (*d* 1869), est surv dau of John Steuart, of Dalguise, Perths (*see* ELIBANK, L), and *d* 4 Feb 1901 leaving:

(1) **Sir Tristram Tempest, 4th Bt**, JP (W R Yorks); *b* 10 Jan 1865; *m* 24 April 1902 Mabel Ethel (*d* 16 April 1906), dau of Maj-Gen Sir George Hall MacGregor, KCB, and *dsp* 23 June 1909

(1) Henrietta Frances May, OBE (1920), of Tong Hall, Yorks, Bradenham, Bucks, and Dalguise, Perthshire; *m* 12 Jan 1886 John Hicks GRAVES later TEMPEST (roy licence 7 Oct 1909; *d* 11 Jan 1915), only s of Rev John Graves, of Bradenham Manor, Bucks, and *dsp* 5 Feb 1948

Sir Cornwallis *m* 2nd 29 Jan 1852 Lady Caroline Augusta Pelham-Clinton (*d* 3 June 1898), 3rd dau of 4th Duke of Newcastle (*see* LINCOLN, E), and *d* 30 Jan 1885, having by her had:

2 FREDERICK WILLIAM RODNEY (Sir), **5th Bt**

1 Augusta Henrietta Mary; *m* 26 April 1876 James Young Stephen, JP (*d* 1909), est s of Oscar Stephen, and *d* 7 April 1910, leaving issue

2 Evelyn Emily Anna Maria; *d* unm 20 Nov 1901

3 Constance Charlotte Rose; *m* 30 July 1887 Rev Charles Edward Stuart Ratcliffe (*d* 12 Oct 1928), Rector Downham, Essex, s of Rev Thomas Ratcliffe, BD, and *d* 14 Nov 1932, leaving issue

4 Gertrude Charlotte Eleanor; *d* unm 11 April 1939

5 Mildred May; *d* unm 1 July 1922

The 4th Bt's half-unc,

Sir Frederick William Rodney Ricketts, 5th Bt; *b* 27 Sept 1857; Lt Scots Gds; *m* 29 May 1879 Alice Eve Grace (*d* 20 June 1931), dau of Charles Fox Webster (*see* 1923 edn WEBSTER, Bt), and *d* 18 Sept 1925, leaving:

1 CLAUDE ALBERT FREDERICK (Sir), **6th Bt**

2 Godfrey Edward Cornwallis; *b* 1886; *m* 1943 *Vivien Olive Guinevere [Mrs Godfrey Ricketts, Flat 2, Abergeldie Marina, Bexhill-on-Sea, Sussex], dau of Vivian Well Hardie

3 Rodney Bernard; *b* 2 Nov 1894; Maj; *m* 16 Sept 1919 Ada, dau of Isaac Sharpe, and had:

(1) Basil Rodney Calder; *b* 23 Aug 1920

1 Kathleen Beatrice Alice; *b* 17 July 1882; *m* 6 Dec 1910 Col Alfred Gerald Meredith Sharpe, DSO, OBE, Roy Berks Regt, s of Alfred Ingram Sharpe, and *d* 1932, leaving issue

The 5th Bt's est s,

Sir Claude Albert Frederick Ricketts, 6th Bt; *b* 27 April 1880; 2nd Lt RGA (TA); *m* 1st 5 Feb 1907 (*divorce* 1936) Lilian Helen Gwendoline (*d* 28 Feb 1955), only dau of Arthur Manley Hill, 5th Fus, and had:

1 Claude Tristram Arthur Nigel; *b* 19 Dec 1908; *d* 20 Jan 1909

2 Sir ROBERT CORNWALLIS GERALD ST LEGER RICKETTS, **7th and present Bt**

1 Alice May Mildred Lilian; *b* 29 Oct 1907; *m* 30 June 1927 Col Richard Rene Dauban, RA (*d* 29 Oct 1968), s of Charles Auguste Dauban, of Paris, and had issue

2 Rosemary Frances Dulcie Geraldine; *b* 22 June 1913; *d* 21 Jan 1915

Sir Claude *m* 2nd 5 Nov 1936 Natalie Patricia, dau of N Howitt and widow of Capt T F Hazeldine, 2nd CM Rifles, and *d* 11 Nov 1937

RIDDELL

Arms: Arg. a chevron gu. between three ears of rye, slipped and bladed vert. **Crest:** A demi-greyhound arg.
Supporters: Two greyhounds arg. **Motto:** I hope to share.
Creation: Bt. (NS) 14 May 1628.

SIR JOHN CHARLES BUCHANAN RIDDELL, 13TH BT, of Riddell, Co Roxburgh, CVO, DL (Northumberland 1990) [Sir John Riddell Bt CVO DL, Hepple, Morpeth, Northumberland NE65 7LN; 49 Campden Hill Sq, London W8 7JR]; *b* 3 Jan 1934, s f 1934; *educ* Eton and Ch Ch Oxford (BA, MA); late Lt Roy Northumberland Fus, 2nd Lt Rifle Bde 1952–54; CA; with IBRD Washington DC 1969–71, Associate First Boston Corp 1972–75, dir First Boston (Europe) Ltd 1975–78, UK Provident Instn 1975–85, Northern Rock Bldg Soc 1981–85, (dep chm 1992–), Northumbrian Water Gp 1992–97, Alpha Bank London Ltd 1995–, chm Govtl Strategic Investment Tst 1995–, dep chm Credit Suisse First Boston Ltd 1990–95 (dir 1978–85) and IBA 1981–85, Priv Sec 1985–90 and Treas 1986–90 to TRH THE PRINCE AND PRINCESS OF WALES, memb Prince's Cncl 1985–90, Extra Equerry to HRH THE PRINCE OF WALES 1990–; fought (C) Durham NW Feb 1974, Sunderland S Oct 1974, memb Bloomsbury DHA 1982–85, Tstee Buttle Tst 1981–87, chm Northumbria Regl Cttee NT 1995–, FRSA 1990; *m* 31 July 1969 *Sarah, LVO, dau of Baron Richardson of Duntisbourne (*qv*), and has:

1 +WALTER JOHN BUCHANAN; *b* 10 June 1974

2 +Hugh Gordon; *b* 29 March 1976

3 +Robert Henry; *b* 5 May 1982

Lineage: ANDREW RIDDELL, of Riddell and Haining, Selkirkshire, to which s 1591; *m* 1st —, dau of Sir James Pringle of Gallowshiels; *m* 2nd Violet, dau of William Douglas of Pompherston, and *d* 1632, having by her had, with other issue, a s (Andrew, ancestor of the RIDDELLs of Haining) and a dau (Margaret, *m* Robert Rutherford of Edgerston); by his 1st w he had, with two yr sons (James; William, ancestor of the RIDDELLs of Muselie):

Sir John Riddell, 1st Bt (NS), so *cr* 14 May 1628 *vp*, with remainder to heirs male whatsoever and with a grant of lands called 'the [territorial] Barony and Regality of New Riddell'; *m* 1st Agnes, sis of Sir Archibald Murray, 1st Bt, of Blackbarony (*qv*), and had, with other issue, including a yr s (Sir William, ktd 1641, Govr Duysburg, Low Countries, *m* 1st a Dutch woman and had issue, *m* 2nd Jean, dau of Sir James Anstruther of Anstruther (*see* ANSTRUTHER, Bt), and had a dau, who *m* David Barclay of Cullerny):

Sir Walter Riddell, 2nd Bt; ktd *vp*; *m* Jane, dau of William Rigg of Aithernie, Fife, and had, with two daus:

1 JOHN (Sir), **3rd Bt**

2 William, of Friershaw, Roxburghs; *m* 1676 Elizabeth, dau of Francis Wauchope, bro of Wauchope of Niddry, and had:

(1) Walter, of Friershaw and Glenriddell, Dumfriesshire; *m* Catherine, dau of Sir Robert Laurie, 1st Bt (*qv*), of Maxwelltown, and *d* Nov 1752, having had:

1a Robert, of Glenriddell; *b* 1700; *m* 29 May 1731 Jean, dau of Alexander Fergusson of Craigdarroch, and *d* 1771, having had, with other issue:

1b Anne; *m* Walter Riddell of Newhouse (*d* 1788) and had issue

2a John, of Grange; *b* 28 Aug 1703; *m* Helen, dau of Sir Michael Balfour, Bt, of Denmiln (*see* 1851 edn), and *d* 19 June 1768, having had:

1b Walter; *dsp* 1762

2b Michael; *m* 1st Margaret, dau of Henry Balfour of Dunbog, and had:

1c Michael; Maj-Gen HEICS; *m* Caroline, dau of Charles F Sheridan, Sec of War Ireland, and *d* 1844, having had, with other issue:

1d Letitia; *b* 1811; *m* Thomas Webster, advocate

2b (cont.) Michael Riddell; *m* 2nd 1801 Janet, est dau of Robert Hunter of Thurston, and *d* Sept 1806, having by her had:

2c John; *b* 1802; *d* unm 1822

3c Robert; *b* 14 March 1804; *m* 6 April 1836 Elizabeth (*d* 8 Aug 1873), dau of V-Adml Henry Vansittart, and *d* 18 Nov 1864, leaving:

1d Robert Vansittart; *b* 12 March 1840; Col RE; *m* 27 April 1870 Louisa Flora Steel (*d* 16 April 1924), est dau of Gen Alexander Dick, and *d* 29 May 1911, leaving:

1e Robert Buchanan, DSO (1918); *b* 1 April 1872; Col RA, Boer War (despatches, brevet, two medals, eight clasps), WW I (despatches); *d* 3 Oct 1923

2e Edward Vansittart Dick, CBE (1919), DSO (1915); *b* 30 March 1873; Col RA, Boer War (brevet, two medals, four clasps), WW I (despatches five times, brevet); *m* 1st 10 Feb 1902 Edith Mary (*d* 4 July 1914), yst dau of Maj-Gen E P Bingham Turner, RA; *m* 2nd 10 Jan 1938 (*divorce* 1942) Vyvyan, yr dau of Rev J J Lewis, MA, and *d* 8 Sept 1942, leaving by his 1st w:

1f Edward Alexander Buchanan; *b* 8 Feb 1903; *educ* Cheltenham; Maj RA; *m* 1st 1 March 1928 Mary, est dau of Stuart Cameron, of Caulfields, Vancouver, BC; *m* 2nd 28 July 1939 Mrs Irene Julia Ballance (*d* 20 June 1961), dau of A W E Bullmore, of Letchworth, Herts; *m* 3rd 15 Feb 1962 *Mrs Mary Kingzett, dau of Lt-Col John Kennington, DSO, MC, JP, DL, of Riby, Lincs, and *d* 1986, leaving by his 1st w:

1g +Stuart Edward, of California; *b* 15 April 1929; *m* 16 Jan 1960 *Emily Spitzer, dau of Whiting N Shepard, of NJ, and has:

1h +Cameron Alexander; *b* 24 March 1962

1h *Romayne Bouvée; *b* 20 March 1964

3e John Balfour, DSO (1915); *b* 2 May 1880; *educ* Cheltenham and RMA Woolwich; Brig; Col RFA, GSO(2) 1916 WW I (wounded, despatches, Belgian Croix de Guerre); *m* 6 Aug 1908 Margaret Alice (*d* 20 Feb 1960), yst dau of J W Smith, JP, of The Rectory, Oundle, and *d* 20 Feb 1960, leaving:

1f John l'Estrange, TD; *b* 30 Sept 1910; *educ* Oundle; Lt-Col RA WW II (despatches), AAG Br Cwlth Forces Korea 1952–53; *m* 4 Sept 1939 *Barbara Agnes, only dau of M McC Fairgrieve, FRSE, and *d* 1984, leaving:

1g +Robert Balfour [Robert Riddell Esq, c/o AIICO Insurance (Nigeria) plc, PO Box 2577, Lagos, Nigeria]; *b* 21 Nov 1940; *educ* Edinburgh Acad, ACII; *m* 1966 (*divorce* 1984) Jean, dau of M Allan, of London

2g +John Gifford [Capt John Riddell, 61 Belle Vue Rd, Salisbury, Wilts SP1 3YE]; *b* 15 Sept 1942; *educ* Edinburgh Acad and HMS *Conway*; Capt Merchant Navy; *m* 17 Sept 1966 *Belinda Irene, only dau of Charles Hensler, of Salisbury, and has:

1h +Benedict Charles John [Benedict Riddell Esq, 7 Castle Hill Place, Castletown, KW14 8UH]; *b* 13 May 1969; *m* 1991 *Karen Anne, dau of Christopher Jones, of Swanfield by Dunnet, Thurso, and has:

1i +Christopher John; *b* 4 Nov 1994

1i *Anna Louise; *b* 28 May 1996

2h +Jonathan David; *b* 25 Jan 1973

3g +Archibald George Vansittart [Archibald Riddell Esq, 31 Marlston Ave, off Lache Lane, Chester]; *b* 20 Oct 1954; *educ* Oundle; *m* 1982 *Patricia Maria, 2nd dau of John B Axon, of Chester, and has:

1h +Andrew John; *b* 1986

2h +Alexander George; *b* (twin) 1986

3g (cont.) Mr and Mrs Archibald Riddell also adopted:

*Kelly Jayne; *b* 1979

1f Editha Margaret; *b* 14 Jan 1913; *d* 30 Nov 1989

2f Elizabeth Charity; *b* 9 March 1917; *m* 30 March 1949 Alan Campbell Sinclair (*d* 1993) and *d* 18 Nov 1996

1e Ethel; *m* 1901 Charles Dingwall Williams and *d* 17 Oct 1932, leaving issue

2d Henry Vansittart; *b* 9 Oct 1841; Col Bengal Inf; *m* 1st 1 Nov 1864 Alice Anne (*d* 1884), dau of Richard Attwood; *m* 2nd 1886 Annie, dau of Stephen Francis Shairp, and *d* 1888, having by his 1st w had:

1e Henry Vansittart; *b* 20 Oct 1869; Lt 50th QO Regt; murdered India 1895

2e Archibald Laurie; *b* 1877

1e Mary Alice; *m* 1st 17 Feb 1885 Capt John Hawley Burke, W Yorks Regt (*d* 24 Oct 1887), and had issue; *m* 2nd 1890 John Burke and *d* 18 April 1951, leaving further issue

2e Clara Edith; *d* unm 1950

3d Walter; *b* 27 April 1845; Lt-Col RA; *m* 27 Sept 1877 Charlotte Margaret, dau of Brig-Gen James George Neill, CB, and *d* 1895, leaving:

1e Florence Agnes Isabel; *b* 26 Oct 1879; *d* unm 8 Aug 1932

1d Mary Clare; *m* 1883 John Broughton (*d* 1906) and *d* 4 Oct 1910

2d Elizabeth Janet

3d Caroline Edith Westby; *m* 2 Sept 1880 Rev John Wynn Werninck and *d* 1881

3 Archibald (Rev); *m* — , dau of Rev — Aikenhead, and *d* 1708, having had, with other issue:

(1) Walter, of Granton; RN; *m* Sarah, sis of Sir John Nisbet, Bt, of Dean (*see* 1839 edn), and *dsp* 1738

(2) John, of Granton, MD; *m* Jane, dau and heiress of William Livingstone, and *d* 1740, leaving:

1a John, of Granton; *m* Christian, dau of Sir John Nisbet, Bt, of Dean, and had issue:

1b John; had issue

2b Henry, of Little Govan; *b* 4 Jan 1745; *m* 1781 Anne (*d* 13 Dec 1827), dau of John Glassford of Dougalstoun, and *d* 4 Sept 1801, having had:

1c John; *b* 4 Oct 1785; antiquary and peerage lawyer; *d* unm 8 Feb 1862

2c Henry (Rev); *b* 23 May 1789; Min of Duns; *m* 1st 2 Oct 1818 Agnes (*d* 1825), dau of Archibald Gilchrist; *m* 2nd 29 Nov 1831 Elizabeth, dau of John Horne, and *d* 15 April 1862, having by her had, with other issue:

1d William; *b* 8 May 1838; *m* 5 Sept 1877 Elizabeth (*d* 3 March 1914), dau of Robert Pringle, and *d* 16 Aug 1900, leaving:

1e William; *b* 1885; *m* 1915 Bertha (*d* 17 Jan 1962), dau of George Spraggon, of Nafferton, Northumberland, and *d* 26 March 1962

2e John; *b* 1895; T/Capt Roy Scots; *m* 1st 1918 (*divorce* 1923) Doris Jones and had:

1f *Irene Yvonne [Mrs Richard Crow, 24 Abbey Walk, Gt Missenden, Bucks HP16 0AY]; *b* 1919; *m* 1943 *Richard Adamson Crow, TD, and has:

1g *Richard Michael; *b* 27 Oct 1944; *educ* Rossall; *m* 1st 1964 (*divorce* 1974) Alexandra Drysdale Love and has:

1h *Simon Richard; *b* 1969

1h *Victoria Caroline; *b* 1965; *m* 1991 *Jason Bacon and has:

1i *Emily Alexandra Mathewson; *b* 1994

1g (cont.) Richard Crow *m* 2nd 1980 *Jean Marie Westbeach and by her has:

2h *Richard James; *b* 1981

3h *William Thomas Adamson; *b* 1984

2h *Caroline Rose; *b* 1987

2g *Michael Anthony; *b* 16 May 1948; *educ* Rossall; *m* 1st 1972 (*divorce* 1984) Penelope Laura Carter; *m* 2nd 1987 *Jill MacKay Ballantyne and by his 1st w has:

1h *Benjamin James; *b* 1976

1h *Rebecca Jane; *b* 1974

2e (cont.) John Riddell *m* 2nd 16 Jan 1924 Alys (*d* 1982), dau of John R Savage, of Edinburgh, and *d* 9 Feb 1959, having by her had:

2f *Audrian [Mrs William Hutchinson, 9 Lorne Ave, Leamington, ONT N8H 2H6, Canada]; *b* 18 April 1926; *m* 2 June 1950 *William Burns Hutchinson, s of William A Hutchinson, of Toronto, and has:

1g *Michael William [Michael Hutchinson Esq, 53 Heathfield Crescent, Waterdown, ONT L0R 2H5, Canada]; *b* 9 June 1961; *m* 1991 *Patricia Eileen Tendam and has:

1h *Matthew Benjamin; *b* 1992

2h *Nicholas William; *b* 4 Aug 1996

2g *Gregory John [Gregory Hutchinson Esq, 28 Pearl St, Leamington, ONT N8H 1J6, Canada]; *b* 1962; *m* 1987 *Rebecca Ann Clark and has:

1h *Andrew John; *b* 1991

2h *Ryan William; *b* 1993

1g *Janet Louise; *b* 7 April 1954

1e Margaret; *m* 12 June 1907 Andrew Stanley Drybrough (*d* 1946), 3rd s of Andrew Drybrough, of Gogar Park, Midlothian, and had issue

2e Elizabeth; *d* 1952

3e Roberta; *m* 18 Nov 1915 Harold Sinclair Coghill, MB (*d* 1919)

4e Henrietta

2d James, of Badulipar, Assam; *b* 28 Dec 1840; *m* 15 Dec 1869 Harriet Anne (*d* 25 March 1921), dau of William Stephen, and *d* 25 June 1903, leaving:

1e Henry James; *b* 21 Oct 1870; Maj 48th Pioneers, IA; *ka* Persian Gulf 22–24 Nov 1915

2e William John; *b* 19 May 1872; India PWD; *d* unm 24 April 1905

3e Walter; *b* 29 Oct 1874; Lt RASC WW I; *m* 25 July 1917 Mary Ellinor (Nora) (*d* 12 Sept 1958), only dau of Dr John Garbutt Hutchinson, of N Lodge, Kineton, and *d* 22 March 1951, leaving:

1f +John Walter Rowland; *b* 3 Jan 1919

1f *Elizabeth Mary Ellinor; b 12 March 1920; m 1st 7 April 1940 Lt-Col Jocelyn Arthur Garnons-Williams, S Wales Borderers (das Italy 14 May 1944), 14th s of Rev Arthur Garnons-Williams, and has:

1g *Elizabeth Dawn; b 24 May 1941; m 1st 1965 (divorce 1971) David Noel Archer Braham; m 2nd 1973 *Clive Anthony John Mitchell and by her 1st husb has:

1h *Felicity Mary Stella; b 1964

1f (cont.) Mrs Jocelyn Garnons-Williams m 2nd 22 March 1945 *Maj James Smith Mirylees, RCS, of Ross-on-Wye, High Sheriff Cards 1968, and by him has had:

1g Andrew Gavin Riddell; b 8 Aug 1951; d an infant

2g *Fiona Nora Margaret; b 6 Dec 1945

3g *Clementina Mary Stewart; b 20 Feb 1953

4g Jacqueline Frances Stewart; b 16 April 1955; d 19–

5g *Jean Sheila Riddell; b 3 June 1956

4e Archibald, DSO; b 2 April 1882; Lt-Col 2nd Punjab Regt IA, Boer War, WW I Mesopotamia and Palestine (despatches), Waziristan 1921 (despatches); m 11 Feb 1907 Edith Mary (d 6 Jan 1947), dau of William M Lawrie, of Seleng, Assam, and d 30 Dec 1970, leaving:

1f +(William) James, MBE (1944) [Maj James Riddell MBE, Foresters, Hightown Hill, Ringwood, Hants BH24 3HQ]; b 27 Dec 1909; educ Harrow and Clare Coll Cambridge; Maj Gen List WW II; m 1st 1 Dec 1959 Jeanette Anne (d 1972), dau of Edward Kessler and formerly w of Ripley Oddie; m 2nd 29 June 1973 *Alison Frances, dau of Arthur Newton Jackson, of Wilmslow, Cheshire, and by her has:

1g *Jemma Jeannette; b 5 Nov 1976

2f Peter John Archibald, CBE (1946); b 20 June 1914; G/Capt RAF WW II (despatches five times), US Legn Merit; m 18 June 1940 (divorce 1968) Cynthia Mary Crompton (d 1993), dau of Brooks Crompton Wood, of Bruern Abbey, Churchill, Oxon, and d 1985, leaving:

1g +Nicholas Peter [Nicholas Riddell Esq, 18 Myddelton Sq, London EC1]; b 24 April 1941; educ Harrow and Magdalene Coll Cambridge (BA); barrister Inner Temple 1964; m 1st 15 Sept 1967 (divorce 1976) Felicity Jane, est dau of D G Rolfe, of Kensington, and has:

1h *Eleanor Mary; b 1972

1g (cont.) Nicholas Riddell m 2nd 1976 *Barbara Helen, est dau of Peter Glucksmann, and by her has:

2h *Juliet Clare; b 1979

3h *Laura Virginia; b 1982

1g *Catherine Mary [Mrs Timothy O'Rorke, 4 Aubrey Walk, London W8 7JG]; b 30 June 1944; m 1976 *Timothy Clare O'Rorke, FRICS, and has:

1h *Mark Henry; b 1978

2h *David Anthony; b 1981

1e Elizabeth Harriet May; b 20 Feb 1879; m 31 Aug 1907 Stanley Allison Hughes, Maj 13th Roy Sussex Regt, and d 25 May 1946

2e Annie Venetia; b 30 Nov 1884; m 17 Feb 1912 William H C Geikie (d 1965), 3rd s of Prof James Geikie, LLD, FRS, of Edinburgh, and d 31 Jan 1970, leaving:

3c James (Rev); b 28 April 1796; Vicar Tutbury; m 15 Jan 1822 Dorothy (d 1886), dau and heiress of John Foster, of Leicester Grange, and d 13 May 1878, having had, with other issue:

1d John; b 7 June 1838; m 1st 15 Nov 1860 Jane (d 1884), dau of William Peppercorn; m 2nd 1885 Gertrude Julia, dau of Rev Richard Smith, and d 1893, leaving by his 1st w:

1e James Foster; b 17 Oct 1861; T/Brig-Gen Northumberland Fus, Hazara Expdn 1888, Boer War, WW I; m 17 April 1912 Margaret Christabel (d 3 March 1938), dau of Henry Hall Scott, of Eilanreach, Inverness-shire, and was ka sp 26 April 1915

1e Alice Dorothy; m 10 Sept 1885 George Edward Bucknill, of Hatfield, and d 21 Dec 1932, leaving issue

2e Catharine Jane; m 1908 Rev Samuel Thomas Boughton, of Kinton, Herefs

1d Anne; m 8 July 1862 Rev Edwin Trevelyan Smith (d 1894) and had issue

2d Henrietta; m 19 Sept 1867 Ven Edwin Palmer and d 20 Jan 1915, leaving issue (see SELBORNE, E)

4c Robert; b 29 May 1797; advocate, Sheriff-Substitute Haddington; m 23 Dec 1834 Susan (d 12 Aug 1847), dau of James Law of Elvingstoun, and d 18 April 1862, leaving:

1d Robert; b 23 March 1840; dsp

2d William Law; b 16 Oct 1843; m Jan 1877 Mary Ann (d 1926), dau of James Frazer, of Taratu, Otago, NZ, and d 1911, leaving:

1e Robert; b 17 June 1879; m 1908 Flora McDonald (d 1961), dau of Charles Samuel George Nicholson, of Duntulm, Isle of Skye, and d 1956, having had:

1f William Law, of Canterbury, NZ; b 31 Jan 1909; m 1940 Jean, dau of Edwin Charles Hocking, of Dunedin, NZ, and had:

1g +Robert James [Robert Riddell Esq, 40 Oriel Ave, Tawa, Wellington, New Zealand]; b 1942; educ Lincoln Coll NZ (BSc Ag); m 1965 *Marion Gwyneth, dau of Kenneth McIntosh, of Rangiora, N Canterbury, NZ, and has:

1h *William Grant; b 1973

1h *Anna Ruth; b 1969

2h *Lynette Judith; b 1970

1g *Eleanor Mary [Mrs Bruce Smart, 7 Kirkdale Place, Ilam, Christchurch, New Zealand]; b 1948; educ Otago U, NZ (BA); m 1st 1964 (divorce 1978) David John Sutherland, of Kurow,

Otago; m 2nd 19– *Bruce Charles Smart and by her 1st husb has:

1h *Elliot David Law; b 1969

1h *Meredith Lawrie; b 1970

2h *Fiona Jean; b 1967

2g *Helen Annette [Mrs Roger Mee, 11 Clark Rd, Ivanhoe, Melbourne, Victoria 3079, Australia]; b 1946; educ Otago U, NZ, (MA); m 1967 *Roger Beach Balfour Mee, MB, ChB, FRACS (NZ), and has:

1h *Jared James Balfour; b 1968

2h *Nicholas Roger Alexander; b 1970

1h *Michaela-Jean Coates; b 1975

2h *Josephine Bridie Mary; b 1982

2f Robert; b 1917; Sgt/Pilot RAF WW II; ka over Germany 1942

3f James; b 6 Jan 1920; WW II with 3rd NZ Tank Corps; m 1950 *Annette Lucy [Mrs J Riddell, The Downs, Geraldine, S Canterbury, New Zealand], dau of Patrick Gilbert Forde, of Christchurch, NZ, and had:

1g +Peter James; b 1958

1g *Judith Mary; b 17 Sept 1952

2g *Sally Anne; b 1954

3g *Annette Joan; b 1956

4f John Buchanan; b 23 June 1924; m 7 Dec 1948 *Barbara Frances, dau of F H Riddenklau, of Rangatata Island, NZ, and d 1969, leaving:

1g +Frank Buchanan; b 19 April 1951

2g +David John; b 1953

3g +Graham Samuel; b 1961

1g *Gail; b 2 Dec 1949

2g *Sandra Ngaire; b 1958

1f *Flora McDonald [Mrs John Wilson, 39 Chapter St, Christchurch, New Zealand]; b 1910; m 1944 John Campbell Wilson (d 1964) and has:

1g *Elizabeth Lyall, MA (NZ); b 1946

2f Kathleen Olga; b 1912; m 1938 Nelson Marshall Aitchison, of Heriot, Otago, NZ, and had:

1g *John Nelson; b 1939; m 1968 *Helen Duff, of Heriot, NZ

1g *Kathleen Margaret; b 1939 (twin); m 1960 *Kenneth Bradshaw and has issue

3f *Charlotte Isabel; b 1913; m 1938 *Ralph Alan Gibson, of Wellington, NZ, and has:

1g *John Hastings ; b 1938; BEng (NZ); m 1964 *Barbara Dawn Shepherd, of Timara, S Canterbury, NZ, and has issue

1g *Margaret Flora; b 1940; m 1961 *Murray Bennett and has issue

4f *Margaret Carlina [Mrs William Kemp Paterson, 2 Kirrimuir St, Dunedin, New Zealand]; b 1914; m 1939 *William Kemp Paterson and has:

1g *Gaynor Margaret; b 1941; m 1969 *John Lyall, of Dunedin

2g *Roberta Joy, BSc (NZ); b 1946; m 1968 *Ian Leslie Stephenson, BSc (NZ), of Hamilton, NZ

3g *Isabel Janice; b 1950; m 1970 *Bruce Ronald Cowan, of Dunedin, NZ

5f *Joan Doreen; b 1921; m 1948 *Herbert Rance Brenton, of Geraldine, Canterbury, NZ, and has:

1g *Mervyn Robert; b 1949

2g *Lyal James; b 1953

3g *Robyn Joan; b 1951

6f *Mary Frazer [Miss Mary Riddell, 165 Weston Rd, Christchurch, New Zealand]; b 1922

2e James Frazer; b 1883; d unm 9 Jan 1902

1e Mary Hepburn; m 14 Nov 1906 Robert Hanning (d 1953) and d April 1958, leaving issue

2e Susan Helen; b 1881; d unm 1961

3e Elizabeth; b 1887; m 1915 Frank Loraine Nicolson (d 1962) and had:

1f *Nancy Loraine; b 9 Sept 1916

2f *Morah Elizabeth; b 18 Oct 1923; m 1947 *Cyril Freemec, of Wanganui, NZ, and has:

1g *Elizabeth Rae; b 1948; m 1966 *Murray James Davis and has:

1h *Timothy Norman; b 1968

1h *Vicky Elizabeth; b 1966

2g *Diane Loraine; b 1951

1d Jane Anna; m 12 April 1860 J C Constable (d 1896) and had issue

2d Susan Mary

1c Christian; m 26 April 1810 Archibald Douglas and d 16 June 1817, leaving issue

2c Jane; d unm Jan 1886

3c Catherine; d unm Oct 1869

4 Thomas; dsp

5 Andrew; had:

(1) Janet; m 1710 George Pringle of Greenknow

Sir WALTER's est son,

Sir John Riddell, 3rd Bt; m 1st Dec 1659 Agnes (dsp), dau of Gideon Scott of Harden; m 2nd 1661 Helen, dau of Sir Alexander Morrison, of Preson Grange, and by her had:

1 WALTER (Sir), **4th Bt**

1 Christian; m Henry, est s of Sir Patrick Nisbet, Bt, of Dean (see 1839 edn), and had issue

Sir John *m* 3rd Margaret, dau of Sir John Swinton of Swinton, and by her had:

2 William; *dsp* 1700

The er son,

Sir Walter Riddell, 4th Bt; *m* 18 April 1692 Mary, dau of John Watt, of Rose-hill, and had, with three daus (of whom Eleanor *m* Robert Carre of Cavers; Sarah *m* John Forrest, gf of Sir James Forrest, Bt; *see* 1928 edn):

1 WALTER (Sir), **5th Bt**

2 Thomas, of Camieston, Roxburghs; *b* 1696; *m* 23 April 1740 Margaret, dau of Rev William Hunter, and *d* 1750, leaving:

(1) William, of Camieston; *b* 1746; *m* 13 Jan 1776 Elizabeth (*d* 1828), only surv dau of John Carre, of Cavers Carre, Roxburghs, and *d* 1829, leaving:

1a Thomas, of Camieston; *b* 23 Aug 1777; *m* 31 Jan 1805 Jane (*d* 11 Jan 1839), dau of Capt Walter Ferrier, of Somerford, Stirling, and *d* 18 April 1826, having had:

1b William, of Camieston, CB; *b* 12 Dec 1805; Maj-Gen; *m* 9 April 1837 Margaret (*d* 1905), dau of Capt John Wilkie, HEIC, and *d* 22 June 1875, having had, with other issue:

1c William Carre, of Camieston; *b* 8 March 1847; Col; Lt-Col Roy Dublin Fus; *m* 20 Oct 1898 Harriet Madeline (*d* 14 April 1939), dau of J J Cousins, of Allerton Park, Leeds, and *d* 26 Sept 1932

1c Margaret Sophia; *m* 15 June 1871 Rev James Robert Chrystal, BD, of The Priory, Hamilton, and had issue

2b Walter RIDDELL later RIDDELL-CARRE, of Cavers Carre, Roxburghs; *b* Aug 1807; *m* 1st 30 Nov 1830 Elizabeth Riddell (*d* 25 Dec 1869), dau of Lt-Col Lachlan Maclachlan, 10th Regt; *m* 2nd 1871 Mary Falconer (*dsp* 12 Nov 1878), dau of William Currie of Linthill, Roxburghs, and *d* 1 Dec 1874, having by his 1st w had:

1c Thomas Alexander, of Cavers Carre, JP; *b* 26 Sept 1831; Lt-Col 3rd Bn Roy Scots Fus; HEICS; *m* 5 Aug 1865 Elizabeth (*d* 28 Feb 1890), dau of Alfred Thomas Fellows, of Beeston House, Notts, and *d* 21 March 1905, leaving:

1d Ralph Gervase, of Cavers Carre; *b* 11 Dec 1868; Maj 3rd Bn Roy Scots Fus; *m* 2 Nov 1905 Kathleen Sadleir Lawe (*d* 28 Jan 1948), dau of Lt-Col Francis Sadleir Stoney, RA, of Co Wicklow, and widow of Lt John Hamilton Elrington Allen, RN, and *d* 25 June 1941, leaving:

1e Gervase Robert; *b* 30 Oct 1906; *educ* Harrow; S/Ldr RAFVR; *m* 4 July 1940 Eileen Inez (*d* 1993), only dau of John Tweedie, of Edradour, N Berwick, and *d* 1989, leaving:

1f +Ralph John [Ralph Riddell-Carre Esq, 31 Hillway, London N6 6QB]; *b* 8 Oct 1941; *educ* Harrow; *m* 24 June 1972 *Valerie Caroline Wells, only dau of W T W Tickler, of Frinton-on-Sea, Essex, and has:

1g +John Timothy; *b* 9 July 1976

2g +Peter Thomas; *b* 25 March 1979

3g +David Alexander; *b* 2 June 1983

2f +Walter Gervase; *b* 10 Jan 1944; *educ* Harrow; CA; *m* 1975 *Carolyn Anne, est dau of Maj A P Ricketts, of The Old Manse, Nigg, Ross-shire, and has:

1g +Andrew Gervase; *b* 1979

2g +James Walter; *b* 1981

1d Elizabeth Olive Geva; *d* unm 1896

2d Grizel Geva; *d* unm 3 Dec 1946

3b John Carre, of Melbourne; *b* 4 June 1809; MLA Victoria 25 years; *m* 22 Oct 1846 Mary Anne Sibella (*d* 1 Jan 1890), dau of Sidney Stephen, Ch Justice NZ, and *d* 22 Dec 1879, having had:

1c Thomas William RIDDELL later CARRE-RIDDELL (1879), VD; *b* 31 Oct 1852; Lt-Col 9th Regt Australian LH; *m* 23 Feb 1886 his cousin Virginia Eleanor Consett (*d* 1898), dau of Montagu Consett Stephen, and *d* 15 Aug 1930, having had:

1d Consett, DSO, VD; *b* 5 Jan 1887; *educ* Melbourne U, BSc, BME, MIE (Aus); Col RAE, WW I (wounded, despatches), WW II; *m* 2 Aug 1923 Thora (*d* 1963), dau of John L Menzies, of Melbourne, and *d* 2 July 1953, leaving:

1e +John Walter Carre [Dr John Riddell, 2/547 Whitehorse Rd, Surrey Hills, VIC 3127, Australia]; *b* 1 May 1925; *educ* Melbourne U (MB, BS); Maj RAAMC WW II; *m* 26 March 1957 Margaret Louise (*d* 1986), only child of R L Krohn, of Kew, Victoria, and has:

1f +Malcolm John Carre; *b* 1 May 1960

2f +David Ronald Carre; *b* 24 Oct 1966; *m* 24 June 1996 *Jaki, dau of John Lagos, of Sydney, and has:

1g *Taylor Lagos; *b* 6 Jan 1997

1f *Fiona; *b* 21 Jan 1958; *m* 1989 *James Posillico, of Bayville, NY, and has issue

2f *Susan Patricia; *b* 6 Dec 1962; *m* 1989 *Michael Underwood Felton

2d Gervase; *b* 27 Aug 1891; Lt Aust Res of Offrs WW I (wounded, two medals); *d* 1978

1d Yolande Sibella; *b* 1889; *d* 1980

2d Geva May; *d* young

3d Eadith Winona; *b* 1895; *m* 18 July 1919 Rev Canon Harry Robert Potter (*d* 28 Oct 1958), Vicar All Saints, Geelong, and *d* 1974, leaving issue

2c John; *b* 19 Sept 1852; *d* 1858

3c Walter John; *b* 19 Oct 1859; chm Melbourne and Metropolitan Bd of Works; *d* 12 March 1930

1c Jane Georgina Vereker; *m* 1 June 1867 Cdr Henry James Stanley, RN (*d* 1887), and *d* 8 Jan 1933, leaving issue

2c Margaret Elizabeth; *d* unm 17 April 1939

3c Annie; *m* 24 Oct 1888 Charles Strachan, Baron de Fegely (*d* 1929), and *d* 6 Aug 1934, leaving issue

4b Thomas; *b* 6 Oct 1810; Capt HEIC; *m* 24 July 1848 Anne Ellen (*m* 2nd Col George Corham Huxham), dau of Capt William Beckett, HEIC, and *d* 1854, leaving:

1c William Henry; *b* 18 Feb 1852; Col Beds Regt; *m* 1st 1881 Julia (*d* 1886), dau of Stephen Francis Shairp, and had:

1d Thomas Henry Stuart; *b* 25 Aug 1882; Lt York and Lancaster Regt; *d* unm 5 Jan 1907

1c (cont.) William Riddell *m* 2nd 1 Jan 1889 Emily Lethbridge (*d* 24 Dec 1950), dau of Col George Rowlandson, IA, and *d* 26 Feb 1907, having by her had:

1d Gladys Lawrie; *b* 11 Nov 1890; *m* 13 July 1915 Brig Alan Bruce McPherson, CBE, MVO, MC, 9th Jat Regt IA, s of Donald William McPherson, of Dunvegan, Isle of Skye, and had issue

5b Robert; *b* 1813; HEIC, RN; *d* unm 1838

1b Lillias Wallace; *m* 1840 Ross Watt and had issue

2b Elizabeth Carre; *d* 1884

3b Georgina Vereker; *m* 1841 Malcolm MacNell Rind, Bengal Med Serv, and had issue

4b Jane Anne; *m* 1843 Surgn-Maj Elijah George Halhed Impey and *d* 1850, leaving issue (*see* BIRDWOOD, B)

2a John Riddell; HEIC Madras; *d* unm 1814

3a Robert RIDDELL later RIDDELL-CARRE, of Cavers Carre; V-Adml; *d* unm 1860

3 William; settled Bermuda; had issue (now extinct)

4 Robert; Min of Lilliesleaf; *m* Esther, dau of John Riddell of Granton, and *dsp*

Sir WALTER's est s,

Sir Walter Riddell, 5th Bt; *b* 1695; *m* 1724 Jane, dau of John Turnbull of Houndwood, and *d* 1765, having had, with other issue:

1 JOHN (Sir), **6th Bt**

2 Thomas, of Besborough, Berwicks; Capt HEICNS; *m* 1767 Elizabeth, dau of Lauchlan Maclauchlan, and *d* 1805, leaving with other issue:

(1) Henry James, KH; Gen, Col 6th Regt, served Peninsular War; *d* 8 March 1861

The 5th Bt's er s,

Sir John Riddell, 6th Bt; *m* 1762 Jane, est dau and eventual heiress of James Buchanan, of Sunden, Beds, and *d* 16 April 1768, having had:

1 **Sir Walter Riddell, 7th Bt**; *b c* 1767; *d* 7 Feb 1784

2 **Sir James Buchanan Riddell, 8th Bt**; *b* 1768; 1st Foot Gds; *d* 4 Sept 1784

3 **Sir John Buchanan Riddell, 9th Bt**; MP Selkirk; *m* 17 Aug 1805 Frances (*d* 30 June 1868), est dau of 1st Earl of Romney (*qv*), and *d* April 1819, having had, with other issue:

(1) **Sir Walter Riddell, 10th Bt**; *b* 8 Aug 1810; Recorder Maidstone 1846–68; Judge Whitechapel County Courts 1863–79; *m* 18 Aug 1859 Alicia (*d* 28 Oct 1912), dau of William Ripley, Lt 52nd LI, and *dsp* 27 Aug 1892

(2) John Charles (Rev); *b* 30 Aug 1814; Rector Harrietsham, Kent, Hon Canon Canterbury; *m* 16 April 1846 Frances Sophia (*d* 23 Dec 1887), dau of George James Cholmondeley (*see* ROMNEY, E), and *d* 2 March 1879, having had:

1a JOHN WALTER BUCHANAN (Sir), **11th Bt**

2a Robert George; *b* 15 Sept 1854; Lt-Col KRRC; *m* 24 April 1895 Agnes Graham (*d* 15 March 1955), dau of Sir William Henry Houldsworth, 1st Bt, MP (*qv*), and was *ka* Boer War 24 Jan 1900, leaving:

1b Margaret Frances; *b* 21 June 1896; *m* 5 Nov 1924 Lt-Col Stafford Hubert Ferrand, DSO, MC, KRRC (*d* 15 March 1975), yst s of William Ferrand, of St Ives, Bingley, Yorks, and had issue

2b Elizabeth Agnes; *b* 14 Feb 1898; *d* unm 7 Dec 1968

3a Charles Sydney (Rev); *b* 30 Aug 1858; *d* 11 June 1886

4a Henry Edward; *b* 25 Jan 1860; Maj KRRC; *m* 5 Nov 1888 Mildred Mary, CBE (*m* 2nd 15 Nov 1902 Lord Robert William Orlando Manners, CMG, DSO, and *d* 19 Jan 1934, leaving issue; *see* RUTLAND, D), dau of Rev Charles Buckworth, of Sherborne St John, Hants, and *das* Boer War 16 March 1900

1a Frances Mary; *d* unm 15 June 1914

2a Mary Amelia; 2nd Mother Superior, Community of Sisters of Christ Kilburn; *d* 27 Nov 1919

3a Sophia Anne; *d* 25 June 1938

4a Margaret Charlotte; *d* 2 June 1871

(3) Charles James, CB; *b* 19 Nov 1817; Maj-Gen RA; *m* 11 Feb 1847 Mary (*d* 29 April 1900), 2nd dau of FM Sir Hew Dalrymple Ross, GCB, and *d* 25 Jan 1903, leaving a dau (*d* unm)

(4) Henry Philip Archibald, CSI; *b* 8 Oct 1819; Post-Office Dir India; *d* unm 20 Jan 1889

(1) Emily; *m* 21 Dec 1843 John Adams (*d* 18 Sept 1848), barrister, est s of John Adams, Serjeant-at-law, and *d* 1881, leaving issue

Sir WALTER's nephew,

Sir John Walter Buchanan Riddell, 11th Bt, JP Northumberland; *b* 14 March 1849; barrister, High Sheriff Noerthumberland 1897; *m* 4 Aug 1874 Sarah Isabella (*d* 4 March 1925), dau of Robert Wharton, barrister, and *d* 31 Oct 1924, having had:

1 WALTER ROBERT BUCHANAN (Sir), **12th Bt**

1 Katharine Margaret; *m* 6 Jan 1904 Col Nigel Keppel Charteris, CMG, DSO, OBE, and *d* 12 Feb 1901, leaving issue (*see* WEMYSS and MARCH, E)

2 Olive Frances; *d* unm 30 May 1958

3 Dorothy Isabel; *d* unm 14 March 1960

Sir JOHN's son,

Sir Walter Robert Buchanan Riddell, 12th Bt, JP Northumberland; *b* 21 April 1879; *educ* Ch Ch Oxford (MA); Capt 1st/9th Hants Regt WW I, chm U Grants Ctee, Pncpl Hertford Coll Oxford 1922–30; *m* 28 Aug 1919 Hon Rachel Beatrice Lyttelton, JP (*d* 26 Aug 1965), yst dau of 8th Viscount Cobham (*qv*), and *d* 5 June 1934, having had:

1 Sir JOHN CHARLES BUCHANAN RIDDELL, **13th and present Bt**

1 *Jean [Lady Pumphrey, Caistron, Thropton, Morpeth, Northumberland NE65 7LG]; *b* 1920; *m* 1 June 1945 *Sir John Laurence Pumphrey, KCMG, and has:

(1) *Matthew James; *b* 1946; *m* 1976 *Pamela Mary Clare, dau of James Wyllie Irving, and has:

1a *John Wyllie Francis; *b* 1979

2a *Maximilian Oscar Edward; *b* 1982

1a *India Victoria; *b* 1988

(2) *Charles Walter Bartholomew; *b* 1948; *m* 1981 *(Cynthia) Penelope Helen, only child of David Bruce (*see* ELGIN and KINCARDINE, E), and has:

1a *Oliver James; *b* 1986

2a *David Laurence; *b* 1989

1a *Katherine Elizabeth; *b* 1983

(3) *Jonathan Henry; *b* 1954; *m* 1982 *Nicola, only dau of J A White, and has:

1a *Jonathan Vivien; *b* 1985

1a *Rebecca Ann; *b* 1986

2a *Olivia Rachel; *b* 1989

(4) *James Laurence; *b* 1964; *m* 1991 *Katherine Lucy, yr dau of David Sanders, of Winchester, and has:

1a *Oliver Thomas; *b* 1996

1a *Camilla Louise; *b* 1993

(1) *Laura Mary Beatrice; *b* 1951; *m* 1983 *Robert James Longair, s of Arthur Longair, of Calgary, and has:

1a *Samuel Christopher; *b* 1985

2a *Alexander Hugh; *b* 1988

1a *Helena Mary; *b* 1990

2 *Mary [Mrs Richard Ollard, Norchard Farmhouse, Morecombelake, Bridport, Dorset DT6 6EP]; *b* 1922; *m* 19 April 1954 *Richard Laurence Ollard, FRSL, FSA, author and ed, yst s of Canon Sidney Leslie Ollard, MA, and has:

(1) *William Richard; *b* 6 Nov 1957

(2) *Edward Christopher; *b* 4 Aug 1959

(1) *Elizabeth Rachel; *b* 22 Oct 1961

3 *Anne; *b* 1924

4 *Hester [Mrs Christopher Pemberton, Place Farmhouse, Bardwell, Suffolk IP31 1AQ]; *b* 1927; *m* 22 Dec 1956 *Christopher Henry Pemberton, est son of Richard Oliver Walpole Pemberton, of Bentons, Bildeston, Suffolk, and has:

(1) *Alexander John; *b* 12 Nov 1957; has:

1a *Jethro Frances; *b* 29 Aug 1987

1a *Sophie Rosamund; *b* 6 Feb 1991

(2) *(Richard) Mark [Mark Pemberton Esq, 17 Melbourne Place, Cambridge]; *b* 25 April 1961; *m* 1993 *Olivia Mary Rokeby Nicolson, dau of Antony Charles Reynardson Fane (*see* WESTMORLAND, E) and formerly w of Adam Nicolson (*see* CARNOCK, B), and has:

1a *Joseph Oliver; *b* 1 June 1995

(3) *Daniel Hugh Vincent; *b* 4 Dec 1962

(4) *Thomas William; *b* 30 Oct 1964

(1) *Isobel Beatrice; *b* 15 May 1959; *m* 1994 *David Goldblatt, 2nd s of Samuel Goldblatt, of Ra'anana, Israel, and has:

1a *Rachel Matilda; *b* 13 Aug 1994

2a *Lily Judith; *b* 5 Jan 1997

RIDLEY

Arms: Gules, on a chevron argent, between three falcons, billed proper, as many pellets. **Crest:** A bull passant, the tail turned over the back gules. **Supporters:** On either side a bull gules, collared gemelle or and charged on the shoulder with three mullets, two and one, pierced argent. **Motto:** *Constans fidei* ('Constant in loyalty'). **Creations:** V. and B. (UK) 19 Dec 1900, Bt. (GB) 6 May 1756.

THE 4TH VISCOUNT RIDLEY and **Baron Wensleydale**, of Blagdon and Blyth, both Co Northumberland, and a **Baronet** (Sir Matthew White Ridley, Bt, KG (1992), GCVO (1994), TD (1960), JP (1957)) [The Rt Hon The Viscount Ridley KG GCVO TD JP, Blagdon, Seaton Burn, Newcastle-upon-Tyne NE13 6DD]; *b* 29 July

1925; *s f* 1964; *educ* Eton and Balliol Coll Oxford; Ld Steward Household 1989–, Northumberland: CA, CC 1958 (chm CC 1967–), Ld Lt 1984– (DL 1968), ADC to Govr Kenya 1952–53, Capt Coldstream Gds, Brevet Col Northumberland Hus (TA), Hon Col Northumberland Hus 1979–, ADC to Pres Cncl TAVR 1984–, Pres: Assoc CCs 1979–, N E Housing Assoc Ltd and Br Beer Soc 1970–73, sometime dir: Northern Rock Bldg Soc, Tyne Tees TV, Barclays Bank (NE), chm: N of England TAVRH 1980– and Northumberland Co Assoc Boys' Clubs 1959–, Chllr Newcastle U 1989– (Hon DCL 1989), KStJ; *m* 3 Jan 1953 *Lady Anne Katharine Gabrielle Lumley, 3rd dau of 11th Earl of Scarborough (*qv*), and has:

1 +MATTHEW WHITE; *b* 7 Feb 1958; *educ* Eton; *m* 1989 *Anya Christine, dau of Dr Robert Hurlbert, of Houston, Tex., and has:

(1) +Matthew White; *b* 27 Sept 1993

(1) *A dau; *b* 16 June 1997

1 *Cecilia Anne; *b* 1 Dec 1953; *m* 14 Oct 1978 *Berkeley Arthur Cole (*see* ENNISKILLEN, E)

2 *Rose Emily [The Hon Mrs Paterson, Shellbrook Hill, Ellesmere, Salop SY12 9EW]; *b* 13 Aug 1956; *m* 26 Jan 1980 *Owen William Paterson, MP, yr s of Alfred Paterson, of Tarporley, Cheshire, and has:

(1) *Felix Charles; *b* 1986

(2) *Edward Owen; *b* 1988

(1) *Evelyn Rose; *b* 1992

3 *Mary Victoria; *b* 30 Nov 1962; *m* 1991 *John James, s of P L James, of Meesden Hall, Herts

Lineage: MATTHEW WHITE, of Blagdon, Northumberland; *m* Elizabeth, dau and heiress of John Johnson, of Bebridge and Newcastle, and had:

1 **Sir Matthew White, 1st Bt** (GB), so *cr* 6 May 1756, with remainder, failing heirs male of his body, to those of his sis Elizabeth, the w of Matthew Ridley, of Heaton and Blagdon, Northumberland; High Sheriff Northumberland 1756–57; *d* unm 21 March 1763

1 ELIZABETH White; *m* 18 Nov 1742 Matthew RIDLEY, of Heaton, Northumberland (*d* 6 April 1778), and *d* 4 May 1764, leaving, with a dau:

(1) MATTHEW WHITE (Sir), **2nd Bt**

(2) Nicholas; *b* 5 March 1748; Master in Chancery; *m* 1790 Letitia, dau of Hugh Atkins, and *dsp* 1 Jan 1804

(3) Henry (Rev); *b* 2 July 1753; DD, Preb Gloucester; *m* Frances (*d* June 1830), dau of Aubone Surtees, of Newcastle, and *d* 11 Oct 1825, leaving, with a dau (Elizabeth, *d* July 1862):

1a Henry John (Rev); *b* 1778; Preb Norwich; *m* 1st 28 Jan 1813 Elizabeth Margaret (*d* 12 Dec 1816), est dau of John Ellis, bro of 1st Baron Seaford (*see* HOWARD DE WALDEN, B), and had:

1b John Henry Ellis; *b* 10 Dec 1816; Col 2nd Dragoon Gds; *m* 25 April 1848 Anna Maria (*d* 1910), only child of Rev J M Brooke, and *d* 1892, leaving:

1c Holt Waring, of Broughton Hall, Rugeley, Staffs; *b* 16 Sept 1850; *m* 1892 Margaret Jane (*d* 27 May 1928), dau of G A Barkley, of Chelsea, and *dsp* 10 Nov 1910

2c Charles Parker, CB (1900); *b* 12 May 1855; Col Manchester Regt, Hon Brig-Gen 1912, served: Egypt, Miranzai Expdn and S Africa; *m* 14 Aug 1879 Edyth Hamilton (*d* 11 July 1928), dau of George Beauchamp Cole, of Heatham Ho, Twickenham, and *d* 9 Feb 1937, leaving:

1d Iris Brooke; *m* 4 Feb 1911 Geoffrey Lowndes Wright, est s of Henry Lowndes Wright, of Burnt Ho, Adlington, Lancs, and had issue

1c Louisa Elizabeth; *m* 10 Feb 1874 V-Adml Sir George Thomas Henry Boyes, KCB (*d* 16 March 1910), and *d* 28 Feb 1923, leaving issue

2c Augusta Constance; *m* 1st 27 Feb 1899 John Nicholas Nugent (*dsp* 12 Sept 1901) (*see* NUGENT, Bt, of Ballinlough); *m* 2nd 16 Dec 1902 Attewell Richard Bourne, of Landscape, Doneraile, and Mallow, Co Cork

1a (cont.) The Rev Henry Ridley *m* 2nd 1823, as her 1st husb, Elizabeth (*m* 2nd 28 Sept 1843 1st Baron Abinger; *qv*), dau of Lee Steere-Steere, and *d* 11 Nov 1834

Sir MATTHEW's n,

Sir Matthew White Ridley, 2nd Bt; *b* 28 Oct 1745; MP Newcastle-upon-Tyne; *m* 12 July 1777 Sarah (*d* 3 Aug 1806), dau and heiress of Benjamin Colborne, of Bath, and *d* 9 April 1813, having had:

1 MATTHEW WHITE (Sir), **3rd Bt**

2 NICHOLAS WILLIAM RIDLEY later RIDLEY-COLBORNE (roy licence 21 June 1803 under terms of will of maternal unc William Colborne), 1st and last BARON COLBORNE OF WEST HARLING, Co Norfolk (UK), so *cr* 15 May 1839; *b* 14 April 1779; *educ* Westminster and Ch Ch Oxford; MP (Whig) Bletchingley 1805–06, Malmesbury 1806–07, Appleby 1807–12, Thetford 1818–26, Horsham 1827–32 and Wells 1834–37, Tstee Nat Gallery 1831–54; *m* 14 June 1808 Charlotte (*d* 17 Feb 1855), dau of Rt Hon Thomas Steele, and *d* 3 May 1854, when the title expired, having had:

(1) William Nicholas; *b* 24 July 1814; *educ* Ch Ch Oxford (BA); MP (Lib) Richmond 1841–46; *d* unm *vp* 23 March 1846

(1) Henrietta Susanna; *m* 12 Aug 1828 Brampton Gurdon, MP (*d* 28 April 1881), of Letton, Norfolk (*see* CRANWORTH, B), and *d* 28 May 1880, leaving issue

(2) Maria Charlotte; *m* 13 July 1830 Sir George Edmund Nugent, 2nd Bt, of Waddesdon (*qv*), and *d* 31 Aug 1883, leaving issue

(3) Emily Frances; *m* 11 April 1833 John Moyer Heathcote (*see* HEATHCOTE, Bt, of London) and *d* 13 Oct 1849, leaving issue

(4) Louisa Harriet; *m* 25 Sept 1840 Harvie Morton Farquhar (*see* FARQUHAR, Bt) and *d* 22 Aug 1870, leaving issue

3 Henry Colborne (Rev); *b* 14 May 1780; Rector Hambleden, Bucks; *m* 21 April 1808 Mary (*d* 13 June 1837), est dau of James Farrer, of Lincoln's Inn Fields (*see* 1963 edn FARRER, B), and *d* 3 Feb 1832, leaving, with a dau (*d* unm):

(1) William Henry (Rev); *b* 2 April 1816; *educ* Oxford (MA); *m* 25 Aug 1841 Sophia Albertina (*d* 1884), dau of Rt Rev Charles Richard Summer, DD, and *d* 17 Feb 1882, leaving, with two daus (*d* unm):

1a Henry Colborne Maunoir; *b* 19 March 1854; *m* 1 June 1886 Florence Myra (*d* 30 Sept 1949), dau of Capt Baldwin Arden Wake, RN (*see* WAKE Bt), and *d* April 1911, leaving:

  1b William Henry Wake, OBE (1949); *b* 23 March 1887; Capt RN, FO 1938–48; *m* 2 Jan 1913 Vera Constance (*d* 19 June 1965), dau of Charles Walker, of Launceston, Tasmania, and widow of Gerald Stuart Eardley-Wilmot (*see* EARDLEY-WILMOT, Bt), and *d* 5 Oct 1957, leaving:

    1c +(William) Terence Colborne, CB (1968), OBE (1954) [Rear-Adml Terence Ridley CB OBE, 4 Hill View Rd, Bath BA1 6NX]; *b* 9 March 1915; R-Adml, WW II (despatches), Adml Supt HM Dockyard Rosyth 1966 (Port Adml 1971–72); *m* 1st 20 Aug 1938 Barbara (*d* 1989), dau of Robert Lea Allen, of Hartford, Cheshire, and has:

      1d +Peter William Wake [Capt Peter Ridley RN, 24 Entry Hill Pk, Bath BA2 5ND]; *b* 27 Nov 1939; *educ* RN Engrg Coll (BSc (Lond) Eng); *m* 14 Aug 1965 *Jenifer Gaye, only dau of Capt William John Macdonald Teale, RN, and has:

        1e +Timothy Jaspar William; *b* 5 Aug 1967; *educ* Marlborough and RAM; assistant master Marlborough; *m* 21 June 1997 *Mrs Judith Taylor

        2e +Nicolas Henry Sumner; *b* 21 June 1971; *educ* Marlborough and City U

    1c (cont.) R-Adml William Ridley *m* 2nd 1993 *Joan Elaine, *née* Dowding, widow of Rev John William Leneve Norman

  2b George Arden; *b* 17 April 1888; Lt 14th Bn W Yorks Regt, Interpreter BEF 1914–17 (wounded); *d* unm 1 July 1962

1a Mary Sophia; *m* 25 Sept 1873 Rev Charles Maunsell Wetherall, Rector Rushton, Kettering, and *d* 29 Nov 1915, leaving issue

(2) Nicholas James (Rev); *b* 7 Jan 1821; *educ* Oxford (MA); *m* 9 Sept 1845 Frances (*d* 18 June 1901), dau of John Touchet, and *d* 1888, leaving:

  1a Edward Nicholas Touchet; *b* 28 June 1849; *d* unm 1 Oct 1879

  2a Henry Matthew; *b* 2 May 1851; *educ* Ch Ch Oxford (MA); Col 7th Hus, High Sheriff Somerset 1920; *m* 5 Sept 1891 Mary Stephanie, OBE (*d* 22 March 1948), dau of William Nicholson (*see* NICHOLSON OF WINTERBOURNE, B), and *d* 24 April 1931

  3a Arthur William; *b* 11 Sept 1852; *educ* Oxford (MA); *m* 9 Feb 1882 Adriana Elizabeth (*d* 21 May 1910), dau of F R Newton, and *d* 10 Aug 1916, leaving:

    1b Mervyn Adrian Touchet, MC; *b* 1886; *educ* Eton; Lt Gren Gds (SR) WW I 1914–19, Extra ADC 1916; *m* 12 May 1920 Sybil Henrietta (*d* 7 Feb 1966), dau of Capt Charles Robert Kennet Fergusson, Cameron Highrs (*see* FERGUSSON, Bt), and widow of Capt Malcolm Cosmo Bonsor (*see* BONSOR, Bt), and *d* 21 Dec 1951, leaving:

      1c *Susan Frances Mary [Mrs Richard Chaplin, Littlefield Farm, E Carlton, Leics]; *b* 22 Feb 1921; *m* 20 Dec 1949 Maj Richard Mark Chaplin, Coldstream Gds (*d* 4 April 1973), only s of Vere Chaplin, of Clipsham Ho, Clipsham, Oakham, Rutland (*see* 1970 edn CHAPLIN, V), and has:

        1d *David Frank; *b* 1951

        2d *Mervyn Henry; *b* 1958

        1d *Serena Jane; *b* 1954

  2b Gerard Arthur; *b* 1894; *educ* Radley; commercial consultant, Lt 3rd Bn E Yorks Regt and 30th Lancers (IA) WW I; *m* 1st 16 Jan 1918 Margaret Frances, dau of Frederick Bale, of Selsey West, Glos; *m* 2nd May Phyllis Barbara, dau of Frederick Watson, of Edinburgh and London, and *d* 1 Dec 1966

  1b Vera Emily, CBE (1945); Pres Fedn Br Insts, Suffolk, Chm Women's Land Army, Suffolk; *m* 18 July 1903 2nd Baron Cranworth (*qv*) and *d* 15 Nov 1966, leaving issue

  2b Marcia Emma; *m* 17 Oct 1911 Maj Philip Pearson Gregory, MC, Gren Gds, only s of Thomas Sherwin Pearson Gregory, of Harlaxton Manor, Grantham, and *d* 6 June 1930

  3b Pamela Frances Ada; *m* 6 April 1920 Col Geoffrey Francis Phillips, CBE, DSO, DCLI (*d* 18 Jan 1968), s of J Hawtin Phillips, and had issue

4a Walter Colborne, JP; *b* 19 Aug 1855; *d* unm 22 Nov 1940

5a James Francis; *b* 12 Jan 1858; *d* unm 3 Jan 1917

6a Alfred Bayley; *b* 14 Sept 1859; Capt 4th King's Own Roy Lancaster Regt; *m* 17 April 1895 Amy Harriott (*m* 3rd 22 Aug 1905 Maj Charles Stirling, RA, (*d* 19 Nov 1914), er s of Gen Sir William Stirling, KCB, and *d* 13 May 1944), dau of 1st Baron Cranworth (*qv*) and widow of Lionel Charles Drummond, and *dsp* 25 March 1898

7a Reginald Oliver, JP; *b* 27 May 1864; *educ* Cambridge (BA); *d* 27 Feb 1936

1a Marian Sarah; *m* 1883 R F Ogilvie Farquharson (*d* 1890), of Haughton, Aberdeenshire, and *d* 20 April 1912

2a Helen Elizabeth; *d* unm 27 Jan 1915

3a Lucy Frances; *d* 9 May 1934

(3) Oliver Matthew (Rev); *b* 12 May 1824; *educ* Oxford (MA); *m* 1st 3 Aug 1852 Louisa Pole (*d* 5 Jan 1858), 3rd dau of William Stuart (*see* BUTE, M), and had:

  1a Stuart Oliver (Rev); *b* 8 June 1853; *educ* Exeter Coll Oxford (MA); Vicar Staverton, Wilts, 1898–1905, St Mark's, Scarisbrick, 1905–11 and Compton Bishop, Somerset, 1911–16; *dsp* 13 April 1935

  2a Henry Nicholas, CMG (1911); *b* 10 Dec 1855; *educ* Haileybury and Exeter Coll Oxford (BA 1878, MA 1881); FRS, FLS, FRHS, assist Botanical Dept Natl History Museum 1880–89, dir Gdns and Forests, Straits Settlements, 1889–1912; *m* 1941 Lily Eliza, dau of Charles Doran, and *dsp* 24 Oct 1956

  3a Charles William (Rev); *b* 28 Dec 1856; *educ* Oxford (MA); Vicar Scarisbrick; *m* 1885 Jessie, dau of Thomas Dowdall, and *dsp* 23 May 1905

  1a Mary Louisa; *m* 14 Feb 1912 Lt-Col John Percy Groves (*d* 13 Feb 1916), Roy Guernsey Artillery and 67th and 27th Regts, and *dsp* 23 March 1935

  2a Fanny Louisa Pole; *d* unm 22 Aug 1935

(3) (cont.) The Rev Oliver Ridley *m* 2nd 17 April 1860 Frances Eliza (*d* 8 Jan 1900), dau of Col H E Keane, and *d* 10 Jan 1907, having by her had:

4a Edward Keane; *b* 5 Nov 1861; Maj Dorset Regt; *m* 24 June 1903 Ethel Janet (*d* 17 March 1962), dau of Alexander Forbes Tweedie, of Rolvenden, and *d* 13 Jan 1947, leaving:

  1b +Edward Alexander Keane, CB (1963); *b* 16 April 1904; *educ* Wellington and Keble Coll Oxford (MA); Assist Treasury Slr 1951–56, Pncpl Assist Treasury Slr 1956–69

  1b Katharine Elizabeth; *b* 25 Sept 1906; *d* unm 18 July 1928

  2b Audrey Janet; *b* 2 Aug 1916; *m* 18 Oct 1941 Robert Ian Sworder (*d* 16 Oct 1980), s of Norman Sworder, of Tawny Hall, Epping, Essex, and *d* 19 Jan 1977, leaving

    1c *Robert Guy [Robert Sworder Esq, 26 Granville Rd, Northchurch, Berkhamsted, Herts HP4 3RN]; *b* 19 July 1953; *m* 1st 18 Oct 1979 (*divorce* March 1991) Nicola Ann, dau of Osbourne Sanders; *m* 2nd 19– *Pauline Joan Catherine Murray, dau of John Mussett, and by his 1st w has:

      1d *Amy Louise; *b* 10 March 1980

      2d *Sarah Joanna; *b* 22 Sept 1982

      3d *Daisy Alexandra; *b* 11 Oct 1985

    1c *Rachel Helen [Mrs Michael Anderson, Quillet, 20 Meadway, Berkhamsted, Herts HP4 2PN]; *b* 10 June 1943; *m* 26 July 1975 *Michael Hugh MacLaren Anderson, s of Lt Cdr James MacLaren Anderson, VRD, and has:

      1d *James Alexander MacLaren; *b* 14 June 1979

      1d *Catriona Sarah Maclaren; *b* 6 May 1977

    2c *Christina Elizabeth [Mrs Antony Thompson, 16 Long Plough, Aston Clinton, Bucks]; *b* 9 Oct 1946; *m* 30 March 1974 *Antony James Aird Thompson, s of Aird Thompson, and has:

      1d *Ian James Aird; *b* 20 March 1975

      1d *Elizabeth Frances; *b* 5 Feb 1977

5a Frank Colborne; *b* 16 Dec 1864; *educ* Oxford (BA); *m* 22 April 1896 Eva Mary (*d* 19 June 1964), dau of Henry Houseman, and *d* 12 June 1940, leaving:

  1b Keith Vivian Colborne; *b* 26 June 1904; CA; *m* 18 Feb 1933 *Joan Madelina Marling [Mrs Keith Ridley, 8 Mill Place, Lisvene, Cardiff CF4 5TF], only dau of Rev Ernest Marling Roberts, and *d* 1977, leaving:

    1c +(Richard) Nicholas [Nicholas Ridley Esq, 53 Pelham St, London SW7 2NJ]; *b* 15 Aug 1939; *educ* Sherborne; *m* 1st 4 June 1963 (*divorce* 1973) Susan Gwynne, dau of R E Hadingham, and has:

      1d *Caroline Lois; *b* 3 March 1964

      2d *Jacqueline Claire; *b* 14 Feb 1966

    1c (cont.) Nicholas Ridley *m* 2nd 1974 (*divorce* 1982) Penelope (Penny) Anne (*m* 2nd 2 Aug 1997 Tony Kench), dau of Roger Melville Brewer, and by her has:

      1d +Michael James; *b* 1976

      2d +Nicholas Mark; *b* 1980

    1c (cont.) Nicholas Ridley *m* 3rd 1984 *Wendy Ann, dau of Denis Hand-Bowman, of Crowborough, E Sussex, and by her has:

      3d *Serena Eloise; *b* 1988

    2c +Henry Colborne [Henry Ridley, 835 W Wolfram, Chicago, IL 60657, USA]; *b* 28 Oct 1944; *educ* Denstone Coll; *m* 22 Dec 1969 *Mary Randall, dau of Alfred Acierto, of Chicago, and has:

      1d *Emily Marling; *b* 1971

      2d *Elisa Acierto; *b* 1975

    1c *Gillian Elizabeth; *b* 30 Sept 1937; *m* 1st 8 Aug 1960 (*divorce* 1980) John Hunt and has:

      1d *Graham [Graham Hunt Esq, 46 Northumberland Ct, 2 Duke St, Banbury, Oxon OX16 8NJ]; *b* 15 Jan 1961; *m* 1986 (*divorce* 1993) Cheryl Haidon, dau of Gordon Taylor, of Stratford-upon-Avon

      2d *Adam Christopher Jonathan; *b* 1974

      3d *Robin Nicholas Andrew; *b* 1976

      1d *Natalie; *b* 15 Nov 1962; *m* 1988 *Simon Halling

    1c (cont.) Mrs Gillian Hunt *m* 2nd 1983 *Peter Dignus Garside

  1b Marjorie Frances; *b* 23 March 1901; *m* 1st 3 Dec 1921 (*divorce* 1931) Capt Leonard Treise Morshead, RE, Res of Offrs (*d* 27 Aug 1931), est s of Leonard Frederick Morshead, ICS, and had:

    1c *Ivo Francis Trelawny (Rev) [The Rev Ivo Morshead, 28 Edge St, London W8 7PN]; *b* 19 May 1927; *educ* Marlborough and Cuddesdon Theol Coll Oxford; FCA, Priest 1964, Priest-in-Charge St John the Baptist, Wimbledon, 1968–73, Vicar: St Mary the Virgin Elham 1973–78 and St Andrew's Whitchurch Devon 1978–91; *m* 8 Feb 1969 *Anne Elisabeth, 2nd dau of Alfred Durham Eric Dunning, of Durban, and has:

      1d *Timothy Francis; *b* 16 Dec 1969

      1d *Elizabeth Trelawny; *b* 14 May 1971

      2d *Sarah Anne; *b* 14 May 1971

    1c *Lavender Evelyn Trelawny [Mrs Cecil Martin, 7 Clock Ho, Mead, Oxshott, Surrey]; *b* 21 Oct 1922; *m* 24 June 1950 *Cecil Philip Creswell Martin, s of J C Martin, of Little Common, Sussex, and has:

      1d *Claire Frances; *b* 4 July 1951

      2d *Virginia Rose; *b* 8 Nov 1953

      3d *Selina Mary; *b* 9 Jan 1957

  1b (cont.) Mrs Marjorie Morshead *m* 2nd 12 Feb 1931 Col Sydney Keith Pembroke (*d* 7 July 1950), The Manchester Regt

6a Clarence Oliver, OBE (1919); *b* 9 Aug 1869; *educ* Harrow; MICE, MIMechE, served Min Munitions WW I; *m* 1st 1896 Anna Arabella (*d* 27 Feb 1898), dau of Gregory William Eccles, and had:

  1b Gerald Horace; *b* 15 Feb 1898; *d* 11 May 1938

6a (cont.) Clarence Ridley *m* 2nd 25 April 1900 Gertrude Henrietta (*d* 13 June 1951), 2nd dau of Henry Houseman, and *d* 24 May 1951, having by her had:

  2b Bernard Keane; *b* 9 Feb; *d* 26 June 1901

1b Olive Christabel; *b* 17 Jan 1903; *m* 13 March 1933 Arthur Robert Lungley Neame (*d* 27 March 1967), yst s of Harry Bayden Neame, and *d* 6 Sept 1963, leaving issue

2b Cicely Joyce; *b* 11 Aug 1904; *d* 27 June 1905

3b *Barbara Frances [Mrs Thomas Bullick, Wolfeton Manor, Charminster, Dorchester DT2 9QH]; *b* 4 Nov 1907; *m* 28 July 1937 Thomas Christopher Selwyn Bullick (*d* 1976), s of Rev Thomas John Bullick, and has:

  1c *Timothy John Ridley [Timothy Bullick Esq, 17 Lime Close, Dorchester, Dorset DT1 2HQ]; *b* 6 Aug 1938; *educ* Bryanston and Worcester Coll Oxford (MA); *m* 24 July 1965 *Teresa Mary, yst dau of Walter Lucian Garstang, of Blackheath, and has:

    1d *David Christopher; *b* 1973

    1d *Claire Elizabeth; *b* 31 Oct 1966

    2d *Judith Catherine; *b* 27 May 1969; *m* 31 Aug 1997 *Graham Alexander Cox, s of Edward Cox, of Chislehurst

  1c *Caroline Bridget [Mrs Anthony Parker, 9 Holton Rd, Buckingham]; *b* 12 May 1941; *m* 29 May 1965 *Anthony Townsend Parker, s of Kenneth George Parker, and has:

    1d *Rachel Sarah; *b* 5 April 1966

    2d *Alison Jane; *b* 10 Feb 1968

    3d *Jessica; *b* 1971

  2c *Sheila Mary [Mrs Geoffrey Clark, 18 Stratton Rd, Prince's Risborough, Bucks HP27 9BH]; *b* 30 May 1945; *m* 16 Aug 1969 *Geoffrey Scott Clark, s of Robert Scott Clark, of Hove, and has:

    1d *Jeremy Scott; *b* 1971

    2d *Jonathan Thomas; *b* 1974

3a Letitia Florence; *d* unm 16 March 1945

4a Alice Catharine; *d* unm 30 Oct 1958

5a Helena Lucy; *d* unm Aug 1945

(1) Mary; *m* 1 July 1834 Rev William M K Bradford and *d* 4 Aug 1894, leaving issue (*see* BRADFORD, Bt)

4 Richard (Rev); *b* 28 Aug 1782; *m* 8 Nov 1810 Catherine Lucy, only dau of Rev Richard Poplewell Johnson, of Ashton-upon-Mersey, Cheshire

5 Charles John (Rev); *b* 5 Sept 1792

1 Henrietta Elizabeth; *m* 1st 22 Aug 1804 Hon John Scott (*see* ELDON, E); *m* 2nd 6 July 1811 James William Farrer (*d* 9 Nov 1863), of Ingleborough, Yorks, and *d* 10 Oct 1853

The 2nd Bt's est s,

Sir Matthew White Ridley, 3rd Bt; *b* 18 April 1778; MP Newcastle-upon-Tyne; *m* 13 Aug 1803 Laura (*d* 22 July 1864), yst dau of George Hawkins, and *d* 14 July 1836, having had:

1 MATTHEW WHITE (Sir), **4th Bt**

2 Charles William, CB; *b* 1812; Maj-Gen, Col 53rd Foot; *m* 17 April 1845 Hon Henrietta Araminta Monck Browne (*d* 1 March 1869), dau of 1st Baron Oranmore and Browne (*qv*), and *d* 1 Feb 1867, leaving:

  (1) Henry Colborne Monck; *b* 1847; 52nd Regt; *m* 1872 Emma, dau of J H Trueman and widow of John Edwards, and *d* 14 June 1919

  (2) Charles Nicholas; *b* 18 Sept 1852; *m* 9 July 1884 Henrietta Agnes (*d* 5 Oct 1932), dau of Edward W H Schenley, of S Kensington, and *d* 7 March 1912, having had:

    1a George Monck; *b* 5 Sept 1891; *d* 8 June 1894

    1a Alberta Mary (HM EDWARD VII stood sponsor); *m* 1st 26 March 1916 (*annulled* 1921) Capt Williamson Wickham; *m* 2nd 22 April 1924 (*divorce* 1934) Col Charles Wesley Weldon McLean, CMG, DSO and 2 bars, RHA (*d* 5 Sept 1962), s of Maj-Gen Hugh H McLean, of Rothesay, New Brunswick, and *d* NZ Aug 1963

  (1) Louisa Katharine; *m* 1st 31 March 1870 (*divorce* 1871) Col Henry Bloomfield Kingscote, RA; *m* 2nd 11 July 1873 Charles Francis Buller; *m* 3rd 28 Aug 1895 Lord Marcus Talbot de la Poer Beresford, KCVO (*see* WATERFORD, M), and *d* 1 Oct 1920

  (2) Alice Henrietta; *m* 7 Jan 1873 Robert Hunt and *dsp* 28 July 1873

3 Henry Richard (Rev); *b* 12 June 1815; *educ* Oxford (MA); Vicar St Cuthbert's, Durham; *m* 23 April 1846 Georgiana Augusta Frederica (*d* 9 Jan 1861), dau of Lt-Gen Sir Thomas Bradford, GCB, GCH, and *d* 16 July 1901, having had:

  (1) Edith Harriet; *m* 2 Dec 1873 Anthony Lax Maynard, JP (*d* Aug 1902), of Skinningrove Hall, Yorks, s of John Charles Maynard, of Harsley Hall, Yorks, and *d* 2 Aug 1940, leaving issue

  (2) Mabel; *d* unm 1 Oct 1914

  (3) Maud

  (4) Ethel Louisa

  (5) Bertha; *m* 21 Oct 1879 Thomas Dundas Bruce (*d* 1893) and had issue

  (6) Mildred; *d* 1868

  (7) Eleanor Dundas

4 William John (Sir), KCMG; *b* 1817; Maj-Gen; *d* unm 27 Nov 1868

5 George, BL; *b* 1818; MP Newcastle 1856–60; *dsp* 1887

1 Sarah; *m* 11 April 1837 John Cookson, JP, DL (*d* 1 March 1892), of Meldon Pk, Northumberland, and *d* 22 July 1864, leaving issue

2 Laura; *m* 2 May 1835 Charles Atticus Monck (*see* MIDDLETON, Bt) and *d* 1873

3 Louisa; *m* 8 July 1831 Martin T Smith (*d* 10 Oct 1880), of Shirley, Surrey, MP, and *d* 1894, leaving issue

4 Marianne; *m* 5 Jan 1839 Rev Andrew Corbett (*d* 1864), Rector S Willingham, Lincs, and *d* 1898

5 Janetta Maria; *m* 23 Feb 1843 Isaac Thomas Cookson, of Swinburne Castle, Northumberland, and *d* 1867

The 3rd Bt's est s,

Sir Matthew White Ridley, 4th Bt; *b* 9 Sept 1807; MP N Northumberland; *m* 21 Sept 1841 Cecilia Anne (*d* 20 April 1845), est dau of 1st and last Baron Wensleydale of Walton (*see* 1868 edn), and *d* 25 Sept 1877, leaving:

1 MATTHEW WHITE, **1st Viscount**

2 Edward (Sir), PC; *b* Aug 1843; *educ* Oxford (MA); barrister Inner Temple 1868, QC 1892, High Court Judge 1897–1917, MP S Northumberland 1878–80, Fell All Souls; *m* 29 July 1882 Alice (*d* 6 June 1945), dau of William Bromley Davenport, MP, of Capesthorne, and *d* 14 Oct 1928, leaving:

  (1) Edward Davenport, MC; *b* 13 June 1883; Col Gren Gds, Ch Instr Small Arms Sch, Hythe, 1925, Ch Inspr Small Arms Enfield 1930, served WW I (wounded); *d* 24 Feb 1934

  (2) Cecil Guy, CBE (1918); *b* 1885; *educ* Harrow and New Coll Oxford (BA 1908); barrister Inner Temple 1911, slr 1923, Assist Master in Lunacy; *m* 26 July 1928 Cicely, dau of Henry Debenham, of Wimbledon, and *dsp* 15 Nov 1947

1 Mary; *m* 14 June 1876 Rev Arthur Octavius Medd (*d* 1894), Rector Rothbury, Northumberland, and *d* 19 July 1902, leaving issue

The 4th Bt's er s,

Sir Matthew White Ridley, 5th Bt, and **1st Viscount Ridley**, so cr 19 Dec 1900, as also BARON WENSLEYDALE, of Blagdon and Blyth, both Co Northumberland (both UK), PC, JP (Northumberland), DL; *b* 25 July 1842; *educ* Oxford (MA); Hon Col Northumberland Hus Imp Yeo, Ecclesiastical Commr England, Chm QS and CC Northumberland, MP N Northumberland 1868–85 and Blackpool 1886–1901, U-Sec Home Dept 1878–80, Fin Sec Treasury 1885–86, Home Sec 1895–1900, Hon LLD Roy U Ireland; *m* 10 Dec 1873 Hon Mary Georgiana Marjoribanks (*d* 14 March 1899), est dau of 1st Baron Tweedmouth (*see* 1935 edn), and *d* 28 Nov 1904, having had:

1 MATTHEW WHITE, **2nd Viscount**

2 Jasper Nicholas (Sir), KCVO (1946), OBE (1919), JP (Suffolk), TD; *b* 6 Jan 1887; *educ* Eton (Fell 1928) and Balliol Coll Oxford (BA 1909, MA 1929); barrister Inner Temple 1912, Maj Northumberland Yeo, DAAG WW I (despatches three times, Legn Hon), Sec Min Labour Trg Grants Ctee 1919–20, chm Coutts and Co, dep chm Nat Provincial Bank, pres London Life Assoc, dir Standard Bank S Africa, Tstee: Nat Gallery 1939–46, Tate Gallery (chm) and Br Museum, memb Roy Commn Equal Pay 1943–45, Hon Sec Contemporary Art Soc; *m* 28 April 1911 Countess Nathalie Benckendorff (*d* 14 March 1968), dau of Count Benckendorff, Russian Amb UK, and *d* 1 Oct 1951, having had:

  (1) Jasper Alexander Maurice; *b* 20 April 1913; *educ* Eton and Balliol Coll Oxford; barrister 1938, Lt KRRC WW II; *m* 8 June 1939 Hon Helen Laura Cressida, er dau of Baroness Asquith of Yarnbury (*see* OXFORD AND ASQUITH, E), and was *k* in a minefield while trying to reach Allied lines in Italy 13 Dec 1943, leaving:

    1a +Adam Nicholas (Sir) [Sir Adam Ridley, 52 Novello St, London SW6 4JB]; *b* 14 May 1942; *educ* Eton, Balliol Coll Oxford (BA 1965) and U of Calif Berkeley; DEA 1965–68, Treasury 1970–71, central policy review stagt 1971–74, Assist Dir CRD 1974–79, special advsr to Chllr Exchequer 1979–84 and Chllr Duchy Lancaster 1985, ktd 1985, dir Hambros 1985–97 and Leopold Joseph Hldgs 1998–, chm Names Advsy Ctee Lloyd's of London 1995–, memb cncl Lloyd's and Lloyd's Regulatory Bd 1997–, Dep Chm Nat Lottery Charities Bd 1995– (memb 1994–95), Chm Tstees Equitas 1996–; *m* 1st 18 July 1970 (*divorce* 1976) his cousin Lady Katharine Asquith (*see* OXFORD AND ASQUITH, E); *m* 2nd 1981 *Margaret Anne (Biddy), yst dau of Frederic L Passmore, and has:

      1b +Jasper; *b* 1987

      2b +Luke (twin); *b* 1987

      3b +Jo; *b* 1988

  (2) Constantine Anthony; *b* 9 March 1916; *educ* Eton and Balliol Coll Oxford; MB, BCh; *d* unm 24 Feb 1970

  (3) Oliver John; *b* 14 Oct 1918; *educ* Eton and Balliol Coll Oxford

  (4) Patrick Conrad Peter; *b* 17 March 1931; *educ* Eton and Ch Ch Oxford; accidentally *k* 11 May 1952

  (1) Katharine Sophy; *b* 19 March 1912; *m* 22 June 1941 Eugene Lampert, DPhil, s of Elias Lampert, and had:

    1a Alexander; *b* 16 Aug 1943; *educ* St Edward's Sch Oxford and New Coll Oxford; *m* 3 April 1965 *Sally [Mrs Alexander Lampert, 20 Diamond Ave, Plymouth, Devon], dau of Lt-Col Anthony William Box, and *d* 15 Oct 1990, leaving:

      1b *Gregory; *b* 14 Aug 1965; *m* 19– *Vanessa — and has:

        1c *Adam; *b* 19–

        1c *Sophie; *b* 19–

      2b *Christopher; *b* 14 Aug 1967

    2a *Nicholas [Nicholas Lampert Esq, 46 Clarence Rd, Moseley, Birmingham B13 9UH]; *b* 25 Aug 1945; *educ* Magdalen Coll Sch Oxford and Balliol Coll Oxford; *m* 1969 *Hon Jill Mary Joan, 4th dau of 3rd Baron Acton (*qv*), and has:

      1b *Katharine; *b* 12 March 1969

      2b *Frances; *b* 12 March 1971; has:

        1c *Jessica Katie HAKIN; *b* 12 July 1996

1 Cecilia Marjorie; *d* unm 16 Aug 1896

2 Stella; *m* 1st 3 May 1905 Rupert Sackville Gwynne, JP (*d* 12 Oct 1924), MP Eastbourne, barrister, of Wootton, Polegate, Sussex, s of James Eglinton Anderson Gwynne, of Folkington Manor, Polegate, Sussex, and had issue; *m* 2nd 19 Oct 1933 Capt John Hamilton (*d* 2 Nov 1952), of Potosi, Bath, Jamaica, Extra ADC to Govr and C-in-C Jamaica, s of John Hamilton, and *d* 8 June 1973

3 Grace; *m* 9 June 1910 3rd Earl of Selborne (*qv*) and *d* 22 Sept 1959, leaving issue

The 1st VISCOUNT's est s,

MATTHEW WHITE RIDLEY, 2nd Viscount Ridley, JP (Northumberland), DL; *b* 6 Dec 1874; *educ* Oxford (BA); Lt-Col Northumberland Hus Yeo, Hon Col 5th Bn Northumberland Fus, MP (C) Stalybridge 1900–04, Priv Sec to: Home Sec 1900–02 and Chllr Exchequer 1903–04; *m* 8 Feb 1899 Hon Rosamond Cornelia Gwladys Guest, DBE (1918) (*d* 2 Dec 1947), 4th dau of 1st Baron Wimborne (*see* WIMBORNE, V), and *d* 14 Feb 1916, leaving:

1 MATTHEW WHITE, **3rd Viscount**

1 (Sally) Gwladys Marjorie; *b* 17 Sept 1900; *m* 24 July 1920 Capt Cecil Maynard Gordon-Ives, Scots Gds (*d* 23 July 1923), s of Col Maynard Gordon-Ives, of Bentworth Hall, Hants, and *d* 28 July 1983, leaving issue

2 Vivien Catherine Evelyn; *b* 15 Dec 1906; resumed Br Nationality 1940; *m* 10 Aug 1934 Baron Hans Karg von Bebenburg, s of Baron Georg Karl von Bebenburg, of Vienna, and had:

(1) *Margaret; *b* 1 June 1937; *m* 1960 *Gerhard Browner

The 2nd VISCOUNT's only s,

MATTHEW WHITE RIDLEY, **3rd Viscount Ridley**, CBE (1938), JP Northumberland, V-Lt; *b* 16 Dec 1902; *educ* Eton and Balliol Coll Oxford; Hon Col Tyne Electrical Engrs, RE (TA) 1935–40, Maj RA (TA), formerly Northumberland Hus Yeo (TA), Hon Col Northumberland Hus 1962, chm: NE Devpt Bd to 1954, Northumberland CC 1941–46 and 1949–52, Rent Control Ctee 1943, Consett Iron Co and Cncl King's Coll Newcastle, dir: Hydrogen Production Air Min 1940–42, Producer Gas Vehicles Min Transport 1942, Yorks Insur, Lloyds Bank and Newcastle and Gateshead Gas Co, Regl Controller N Regn Min Prodn 1942–64; *m* 13 Oct 1924 Ursula, OBE (1953), JP (*d* 28 Dec 1967), 2nd dau of Sir Edwin Landseer Lutyens, OM, KCIE, PRA, LLD, the architect, and *d* 25 Feb 1964, leaving:

1 MATTHEW WHITE RIDLEY, **4th and present Viscount Ridley**
2 NICHOLAS RIDLEY, BARON RIDLEY OF LIDDESDALE (LP, UK), so *cr* 1992; *b* 17 Feb 1929; *educ* Eton and Balliol Coll Oxford; Capt Northumberland Hus (TA), Lt York and Lancaster Regt, AMICE, MP (C) Cirencester and Tewkesbury 1959–92, PPS to Fin Sec Treas 1962–64, Jt Parly Sec Min Technology June-Oct 1970, Parly U-Sec DTI 1970–72, Min State FCO 1979–81, Fin Sec Treasury 1981–83, Sec State Tport 1983–86, Environment 1986–89 and DTI 1989–90, dir Brims & Co 1954–70, Newcastle; *m* 1st 17 Aug 1950 (*divorce* 1974) Hon Clayre Campbell, 2nd dau of 4th Baron Stratheden and Campbell (*qv*), and had:

(1) *Jane; *b* 15 May 1953; *m* 1986 *Stephen Francis Thomas (*see* THOMAS, Bt, of Ynyshir) and has issue
(2) *Susanna; *b* 19 May 1955; *m* 1987 *Charles Christopher Hugh Rickett, s of Christopher Owen Rickett, of Rusper, Sussex, and has:

1a *Benjamin Christopher; *b* 1988
2a *Matthew Charles; *b* 1991
3a *William Oliver Nicholas (twin); *b* 1991

(3) *Jessica Clayre [The Hon Mrs Fletcher, 46 Bolingbroke Rd, London W14]; *b* 5 Sept 1957; *m* 1991 *David M G Fletcher, s of Col Derek Fletcher, and has:

1a *Daisy Columba; *b* 1992

2 (cont.) BARON RIDLEY OF LIDDESDALE *m* 2nd 16 Feb 1979 *Judith (Judy) Mary [The Rt Hon The Lady Ridley of Liddesdale, 33 Carlisle Mansions, London SW1P 1EZ], dau of Dr Ernest Kendall, of Epsom, and *d* 4 March 1993
1 Laura Consuelo; *m* 6 Nov 1954 *Adrian Frederick Mark Carrick, The Queen's Bays, yr s of G P Carrick, of Sanson Seal, Berwick-on-Tweed, and *d* 22 June 1982, leaving:

(1) *Amanda; *b* 24 May 1957
(2) *Emma Clare; *b* 22 Dec 1961
(3) *Kate; *b* 13 Dec 1964

2 +Hugh Macbeth; *b* 18 April 1948; *educ* Rugby; *m* May 1970 *Kathleen Mary, dau of Conrad Salber, of Rochester, NY, and has:

(1) +Zachary John; *b* 1974
(1) *Rachel Mary; *b* 1971

3 +James Erskine; *b* 26 May 1949; *educ* Rugby; *m* 1979 *Victoria Mary, dau of Charles Noel Edmeston, of Alderley Edge, Cheshire, and has:

(1) +Simon Henry Erskine; *b* 1984

4 +Stephen Leacock; *b* 11 April 1952; *educ* Rugby and Capetown U (BA, PGCE); headmaster Westbourne House Sch, Shopwyke, Chichester; *m* 1979 *Sally Anne, dau of H E W (Peter) Kirby, of Felpham, W Sussex, and has:

(1) +William Peter; *b* 1986
(1) *Emily Flora; *b* 1983
(2) *Alice Olivia; *b* 1988
(3) *Melissa Mary; *b* 1989

Lineage: JOHN RIGBY; *b* 1829; *educ* Trin Coll Dublin (MA); *m* Julia (*d* 1903), dau of Thomas Mallinson, and *d* 1 Nov 1916, having had seven sons and a dau; the 3rd s:

Sir Hugh Mallinson Rigby, 1st Bt (UK), so *cr* 24 June 1929, KCVO (1917); *b* 19 May 1870; MS London, FRCS Eng, Col AMS, Serjeant-Surgn to HM GEORGE V 1928–32 and Hon Surgn 1932–36, sometime surgn to HM QUEEN ALEXANDRA, consulting surgn: London Hosp and Poplar Hosp for Accidents, BEF in France 1916 and London Dist 1917–19, FRCSI (Hon), MChRUI (Hon); *m* 12 Oct 1911 Flora (*d* 27 Oct 1970), dau of Norman Macbeth, of Woldingham, and *d* 17 July 1944, leaving:

1 Sir HUGH JOHN MACBETH RIGBY, **2nd and present Bt**
2 +Roger Macbeth [Roger Rigby Esq, Ansty Plum, Ansty, Tisbury, Wilts SP3 5QD]; *b* 7 June 1922; *educ* Winchester and Magdalene Coll Cambridge; Hon Capt RAC; *m* 2 Feb 1957 Patricia Anne (*d* 24 Oct 1996), yr dau of Capt Desmond Nevill Cooper Tufnell, DSC, RN, and has:

(1) *Melissa Terwick; *b* 14 April 1959; *m* 1989 *Christopher Wills and has:

1a *India Macbeth; *b* 1991
2a *Iona Christie; *b* 1993

(2) *Tanya Macbeth; *b* 9 April 1961; *m* 1993 *Mark Anthony Lole and has:

1a *William Thomas; *b* 1996
1a *Amber Macbeth; *b* 1994

1 *Margaret Hamilton [Mrs Richard Briscoe, Maple House, Higher Combe Rd, Haslemere, Surrey GU27 2LQ]; *b* 23 Sept 1919; *m* 12 July 1951 *Richard Kynaston Briscoe, yr s of Sir (John) Charlton Briscoe, 3rd Bt (*qv*)
2 Ann Macbeth; *b* 22 Nov 1925; *d* 4 Feb 1986

RIGBY

Arms: Argent on a cross flory sable a rod of Æsculapius or.
Crest: In front of an antelope's head erased proper, gorged with an antique crown or, two ostrich feathers saltirewise argent.
Motto: *Malo mori quam fœdari* ('I would rather die than be dishonoured'). **Creation:** Bt. (UK) 24 June 1929.

SIR (HUGH) JOHN MACBETH RIGBY, 2ND BT, of Long Durford, in the Parish of Rogate, Co Sussex, ERD [Sir John Rigby Bt ERD, 5 Park St, Macclesfield, Cheshire SK11 6SR]; *b* 1 Sept 1914; *s f* 1944; *educ* Rugby and Magdalene Coll Cambridge (MA); Lt-Col RCT (AER) WW II; *m* 3 Jan 1946 Mary Patricia Erskine (*d* 1988), WRNS, only dau of Edmund Erskine Leacock, of Madeira (s of John Milberne Leacock; *see* ERSKINE, Bt), and has:

1 +ANTHONY JOHN; *b* 3 Oct 1946; *educ* Rugby and Manchester Poly (BA, PGCE); *m* 1978 *Mary, er dau of R G Oliver, of Hope Green, Cheshire, and has:

(1) +Oliver Hugh; *b* 20 Aug 1979
(2) +Rollo Macbeth; *b* 1981
(3) +Tom; *b* 1985
(1) *Flora; *b* 1989

RIPLEY

Arms: Per chevron nebuly or and vert, a cross crosslet between two lions rampant in chief, and a lion rampant between two cross crosslets in base, all counterchanged. **Crest:** A demi-lion regardant vert, gorged with a collar gemel and charged on the body with a cross crosslet or, holding between the paws an escutcheon argent, charged with a cock proper. **Motto:** *Dum spiro spero* ('While I breathe I hope'). **Creation:** Bt. (UK) 8 May 1880.

SIR HUGH RIPLEY, 4TH BT, of Rawdon, Co York, and Bedstone, Co Salop [Sir Hugh Ripley Bt, 20 Abingdon Villas, London W8 6BX; The Oak, Bedstone, Salop]; *b* 26 May 1916; *s f* 1956; *educ* Eton; Maj KSLI WW II (wounded, despatches twice), dir John Walker and Sons Ltd (ret), author *Whisky for Tea*, US Silver Star; *m* 26 March 1946 (*divorce* 1971) Dorothy Mary Dunlop, yr dau of John Cumming Bruce-Jones (*see* DUNLOP, Bt), and has:

1 +WILLIAM HUGH [William Ripley Esq, Dove Cottage, Bedstone, Salop]; *b* 13 April 1950; *educ* Eton and McGill (BA); writer
1 *Caroline (Dorothy) [Mrs Hugh Montgomery-Massingberd, 137 Kennington Pk Rd, London SE11 4JJ]; *b* 26 Jan 1947; *m* 22 Feb 1983, as his 2nd w, *Hugh John MONTGOMERY MASSINGBERD later MASSINGBERD, author, only s of John Michael Montgomery-Massingberd, of Gunby, Lincs

Sir HUGH *m* 2nd 15 June 1972 *(Hilary) Susan, dau of W Parker, of Keythorpe Grange, Leics, and has:

2 *Katherine; *b* 4 March 1974

Lineage: GEORGE RIPLEY, of Bowling, nr Bradford, Yorks; *b* 1759; *m* 29 Jan 1788 Elizabeth Whitaker, of Halifax (*d* 11 Nov 1826), and *d* 3 Dec 1826, leaving, with other issue:

EDWARD RIPLEY, of Bowling; *b* 17 July 1790; *m* 24 Dec 1812 Hannah (*d* 2 Feb 1871), dau of Nathaniel Murgatroyd, of Bradford, and *d* 7 April 1866, leaving:

Sir Henry William Ripley, 1st Bt (UK), so *cr* 8 May 1880, of Acacia, Rawdon, W R Yorks, and Bedstone Ho, Salop, JP, DL; *b* 23 April 1813; MP (Lib) Bradford 1868–69 and 1874–80; *m* 6 Sept 1836 Susan (*d* 5 Dec 1886), dau of John Milligan, of Balmaghie, Kirkcudbrightshire, and *d* 9 Nov 1882, having had, with other issue:

1 EDWARD (Sir), **2nd Bt**

2 George; *b* 31 March 1845; *d* 17 March 1895

3 Sir FREDERICK RIPLEY, 1st Bt (UK), so *cr* 4 Sept 1897, of Acacia, Rawdon, W R Yorks; *b* 28 Nov 1846; *educ* Cheltenham and Ch Ch Oxford; Lt 2nd W Yorks Yeo Cav; *m* 27 June 1876 Katherine (*d* 24 April 1931), dau of David Little, of Mount Royal, Yorks, and *d* 22 Nov 1907, leaving:

  (1) Sir FREDERICK HUGH RIPLEY, 2nd Bt; *b* 7 July 1878; Lt 2nd Life Gds, Capt 3rd Bn Argyll and Sutherland Highrs, served Boer War 1900, WW I (despatches) and WW II; *m* 8 July 1902 Georgina Mary Shute (*d* 28 Oct 1953), yst dau of Francis Adams, and *dsp* 15 July 1945

  (2) Sir GEOFFREY ARNOLD RIPLEY, 3rd and last Bt; *b* 4 Aug 1883; *educ* Eton and Oxford; barrister Inner Temple 1912, Lt 1st Roy Dragoons (SR) WW I (1914–15 star, two medals); *m* 2 Jan 1908 Sybil Augusta (*d* 11 Aug 1954), 2nd dau of Thomas Newman Frederick Bardwell, JP, DL, of Bolton Hall, Yorks, and *dsp* 16 Nov 1954, when the btcy expired

  (3) Charles Roger; *b* 13 Nov 1888; Lt 2nd Bn York and Lancaster Regt; *ka* 22 Oct 1914

  (1) Ethel Margaret Susan; *m* 3 Dec 1902 Brig Charles Russell Terrot, DSO, 6th Inniskilling Dragoons (*d* 1 May 1944), s of Lt-Col C E Terrot, of Nether Newith Hill, Durham, and *d* 24 Sept 1960, leaving issue

  (2) Catherine Alice; *d* unm 10 Feb 1963

4 Henry, JP (W R Yorks); *b* 12 May 1849; *m* 1st 18 July 1876 Emma Alice (*d* 10 Jan 1884), only dau of Col Bruce Seton (*see* SETON, Bt), and had:

  (1) Henry Edward; *b* 6 Jan 1884; Lt RASC; *m* 1st 16 July 1912 (*divorce* 1937) Violet, dau of G Turner Miller, barrister, of Stoneleigh, Cheltenham; *m* 2nd 19 July 1944 Doreen (*d* March 1960), 2nd dau of Daniel Walters, of S Wales, and *d* 29 Dec 1949

  (1) Dorothy Alice Seton; *m* 16 Sept 1914 (*divorce* 1920) Sebastien Gourevitch (*d* 1947), of Smolensk, Russia, and *dsp* 2 April 1959, having taken by deed poll 1920 the name SAYE

  (2) Marian Janet; *m* 14 Jan 1899 Thomas Herbert Littlejohn, FRCS (Edin) (*d* 4 Sept 1905), of Hampstead, s of Sir Henry Littlejohn, of Edinburgh, and *dsp* 19 Oct 1959

4 (cont.) Henry Ripley *m* 2nd 6 Oct 1885 Dorothea Royds (*d* 7 April 1937), 2nd dau of Henry Anthony Grey, of Brent Ho, Salop, and *d* 20 April 1926, having by her had:

  (2) Hugh William Grey; *b* 14 Aug 1886; T/Lt WW I; *d* 24 Dec 1952

5 Hugh, JP (WR Yorks); *b* 4 March 1851; Lt 2nd W York Yeo; *m* 1 Dec 1881 Alice Louisa (*d* 14 Dec 1933), dau of James Robinson Pease, JP, of Westwood, and *d* 9 April 1913

6 Alfred; *b* 8 Nov 1852; Midshipman RN; lost from HMS *Captain* 6 Sept 1870

1 Annie; *m* 9 July 1873 Lt-Col Thomas Joseph Sunderland, of Ravensden Grange, Beds, 3rd Bn Beds Regt, and *d* 6 Nov 1913

2 Phoebe Elizabeth; *m* 30 July 1868 Charles Compton Seton (*d* 18 Nov 1923), Lt RE, and *d* 3 Dec 1873, having had issue

The 1st Bt's est s,

Sir Edward Ripley, 2nd Bt, JP (Salop and W R Yorks), DL; *b* 16 May 1840; *educ* Cheltenham and Ch Ch Oxford BA 1864; barrister Inner Temple 1870, Hon Col, previously Lt-Col 1st Admin Bde W York Art Vol, High Sheriff 1891; *m* 31 July 1877 Eugenie Frederica Fulcher (*d* 8 Dec 1941), dau of Maj-Gen Edward Alfred Green Emmott-Rawdon, of Rawdon, Yorks, and *d* 21 Nov 1903, having had:

1 HENRY WILLIAM ALFRED (Sir), **3rd Bt**

2 Edward Guy, OBE (1919); *b* 6 Oct 1881; Lt Rifle Bde Boer War 1901–02, Capt Motor Tport Army Serv Corps WW I; *d* unm 12 April 1959

3 Hugh Ivor Emmott; *b* 13 Aug 1884; *educ* RMC Sandhurst; Maj Worcs Regt WW I; *d* unm 17 June 1963

1 Annie Winifred (Freda); *m* 27 April 1909 Capt Robert George Geoffrey Harley (*d* 26 Jan 1920), of Brampton Bryan, Herefs, and *d* 3 June 1945

The 2nd Bt's est s,

Sir Henry William Alfred Ripley, 3rd Bt, JP (Salop and Herefs); *b* 3 Jan 1879; *educ* Eton; Capt 1st Roy Dragoons Boer War 1900–02 and WW I, Maj 7th Bn Salop HG WW II 1940–42; *m* 17 Jan 1911 Dorothy (*d* 27 July 1964), est dau of Robert William Daker Harley, of Brampton Bryan, Herefs, by Patience Annie, dau of 6th Baron Rodney (*qv*), and *d* 14 Dec 1956, having had:

1 Edward Robert Guy; *b* 5 Nov 1911; *educ* Stowe; Lt-Col KSLI WW II; *m* 11 March 1944 *Sarah Stella, er dau of Lt-Col Arthur George Pardoe, RE, of Gravel Hill, Kington, Herefs, and was *ka* Normandy June 1944, leaving:

  (1) *Patience Anna [Mrs Richard Morgan, Smithfield House, Llanidloes, Montgomeryshire]; *b* posthumously 1 Dec 1944; *m* 30 Oct 1963 *Richard Michael Tudor Morgan, s of Evan Sylvanus Morgan, of Llanidloes, and has:

    1a *David Paul Edward; *b* 12 Jan 1969
    2a *Timothy Michael Julian; *b* 12 Jan 1969

    1a *Charlotte Sarah; *b* 2 Nov 1965

2 Henry Derek; *b* 28 Jan 1914; *educ* Repton and Oxford (BA 1935); Inspr Sudan Plantation Syndicate, F/Lt RAF (Res) WW II; *ka* nr Agrocastro, Greece, 21 Dec 1940

3 Sir HUGH RIPLEY, **4th and present Bt**

4 Geoffrey Nigel; *b* 18 March 1921; *educ* Stowe; Capt Northants Regt attd IA; *d* 24 May 1989

1 Ruth Patience; *b* 17 Nov 1912; VAD WW II; *d* unm 10 July 1953

2 *Suzan [Mrs Robert de la Garde Savery, The Flat, Manor Farm, Bedstone, Bucknell, Salop]; *b* 31 May 1919; ATS WW II; *m* 6 Jan 1951 *Robert de la Garde Savery, s of Lawrence de la Garde Savery, of Dorridge, Warwicks, and has:

  (1) *Christopher Robert; *b* 7 Jan 1954; *educ* Malvern; *m* 1980 *Margaret, yst dau of Ian Archibald Slater, of Ludlow, Salop, and has:

    1a *Thomas Edward; *b* 1986

    1a *Alice Eugénie de la Garde; *b* 1983
    2a *Annabel Ruth; *b* 1984

  (1) *Chloë Abigail de la Garde; *b* 1955; *m* 1979 *Andrew John Scott Calder and has:

    1a *Guy Leon; *b* 1989
    1a *Poppy Marie; *b* 1981
    2a *Madeleine Clare; *b* 1983

RITCHIE

Arms: Argent an anchor erect sable within a bordure ermine, on a chief of the second three lion's heads erased of the first. **Crest:** Issuant out of an antique crown or a unicorn's head argent, armed gold, charged on the neck with a torteau, thereon an anchor also gold. **Motto:** *Virtute acquiritur honos* ('Honour is acquired by virtue'). **Creation:** Bt. (UK) 23 Jan 1918.

SIR JAMES EDWARD THOMSON RITCHIE, 2ND BT, of Highlands, TD (1943) and two clasps [Sir James Ritchie Bt TD, 3 Farquhar St, Bengeo, Herts SG14 3BN]; *b* 16 June 1902; *s f* 1937; *educ* Rugby and Queen's Coll Oxford; FRSA, FID, Lt-Col Inns of Court Regt (TA), WW II various staff and regimental appointments, CMF 1944–45, co-opted Mil memb Kent T&AFA 1953–67, Pres Br Legion Ashford branch, Patron Ashford and Dist Caledonian Soc, memb Bd Management, chm Finance and Gen Purposes Ctee and Jt Hon Treas Lond Sch Hygiene and Tropical Medicine 1951–61 (co-opted memb Bd Management 1964–67), chm: M W Hardy and Co and associated cos and Chatwood-Milner Ltd, dir: Guardian Assur (Local London Bd), William Ritchie and Son (Textiles) Ltd, memb Court Assistants Merchant Taylors' Co, 1st Upper Warden 1977–; *m* 1st 4 July 1928 (*divorce* 1936) Esme Phyllis (*d* 18 May 1939), only dau of James Montague Oldham; *m* 2nd 9 Dec 1936 Rosemary (*d* 7 Aug 1996), yr dau of Col Henry Sidney John Streatfeild, DSO, TD, of Chiddingstone, Kent, and has:

1 *Louise Katharine; *b* 23 July 1951; *m* 1978 *John Preston

2 *Fiona Ruth; *b* 29 Nov 1952

Lineage: Sir James William Ritchie, 1st Bt (UK), so *cr* 23 Jan 1918, MBE; *b* 7 Aug 1868; Lt City London, Divnl Cmdt Met Special Constabulary; *m* 1st 20 July 1898 (*divorce* 1912) Ada Bevan, dau of Edward Bevan ap Rees Bryant, of Barnet, and *d* 8 May 1937, leaving:

1 Sir JAMES EDWARD THOMSON RITCHIE, **2nd and present Bt**

Sir James *m* 2nd 20 Feb 1913 Edna Muriel (*d* 29 Nov 1951), 3rd dau of James Frederick Emerton, of Cheltenham, and by her had:

2 Patrick John Emerton, DFC (1943); *b* 12 Jan 1914; S/Ldr RAF WW II; *m* 27 Aug 1942 Alison Crawford Porter, MRCS, LRCP, yst dau of Dr Charles Porter, of St John's Wood, London NW, and was *ka* June 1943

3 William Peter Emerton; *b* 15 Sept 1918; *educ* Canford; Queen's Own Roy W Kent Regt WW II, civ serv

4 Michael Alan Emerton; *b* 6 Sept 1920; Lt 13th/18th Roy Hus attd Co of London Yeo WW II; *ka* April 1943

1 *Barbara Anne Lydia Janet [Miss Barbara Ritchie, Crackshill Cottage, Yelverton, Warwicks]; *b* 28 May 1916; ATS WW II 1940–43

2 *Elizabeth Alice Jessie Muriel [Mrs Robert Blake, 5B Grove Hill, Stansted, Essex]; *b* 12 Oct 1922; *m* 1st 16 Dec 1943 (*divorce* 1954) Peter Andrew Soderling, Master-Sgt USAAF, s of Peter Andrew Soderling, of Winslow, Indiana, and has:

  (1) *Mark Andrew Patrick; *b* 2 Oct 1944

2 (cont.) Mrs Elizabeth Soderling *m* 2nd 2 March 1957 *Robert John Ripley Blake, yr s of Robert Ripley Blake, of Hertford

RITCHIE OF DUNDEE

VIRTUTE · ACQUIRITUR · HONOS ·

Arms: Arg. an anchor erect sa., on a chief of the last three lion's heads of the first. **Crest:** Out of an antique crown or a unicorn's head arg., armed gold and charged on the neck with an anchor as in the arms. **Supporters:** On either side a unicorn gu., each gorged with an antique crown and charged on the shoulders, the dexter with a purse and the sinister with a balance, or. **Motto:** *Virtute acquiritur honos* ('Honour is acquired by virtue'). **Creation:** B. (UK) 2 Dec 1905.

THE 5TH BARON RITCHIE OF DUNDEE, of Welders, Chalfont St Giles, Co Buckingham (Harold Malcolm Ritchie) [The Rt Hon The Lord Ritchie of Dundee, The Roundel, Springsteps, Winchelsea, Sussex]; *b* 29 Aug 1919; *s* bro 1978; *educ* Stowe and Trin Coll Oxford (BA 1943, MA 1944); Capt KRRC WW II, headmaster Brickwall Sch, Northiam, Sussex; *m* 23 Aug 1948 *Anne, dau of Col Charles George Johnstone, MC, of Durban, and has:

    1 +(CHARLES) RUPERT RENDALL; *b* 15 March 1958; *educ* Brickwall Northiam; *m* 1984 (*divorce* 1992) Tara, dau of Howard J Koch, Jr, of USA

    1 *Philippa Jane; *b* 14 Aug 1954

Lineage: WILLIAM RITCHIE, of Rockhill, Forfar; *b* 1798; *m* 1st Elizabeth, dau of James Thomson, of Dundee, and had:

    1 Sir JAMES THOMSON RITCHIE, 1st and last Bt (UK), so *cr* 15 Dec 1903, JP (Middx, Surrey and Co and City of London); *b* 21 Sept 1833; Sheriff London 1896–97, ktd 1897, Lt City London, Ld Mayor London 1903–04; *d* 18 Sept 1912, when the btcy expired

    2 John Rait, of Poplar; *b* 2 Aug 1835; *m* 13 July 1854 Lydia Rebecca (*d* 12 Nov 1894), dau of James Lemon, of Loughton, Essex, and *d* 15 Dec 1858

    3 CHARLES THOMSON, **1st Baron**

WILLIAM RITCHIE *m* 2nd Margaret, dau of David Bell, and *d* 1867, having by her had:

    4 Robert Ord, of Battle, Sussex; *b* Feb 1858; *m* 1st 1887 Catherine Anne Gellatly; *m* 2nd 2 June 1894 Ethel Margaret (*d* 1969 aged 103), dau of Christian David Ginsburg, DD, LLD, and *d* 15 Jan 1915

The 3rd s,

    CHARLES THOMSON RITCHIE, **1st Baron Ritchie of Dundee** (UK), so *cr* 22 Dec 1905, PC, JP (Middx, London and Bucks); *b* 19 Nov 1838; Hon Col 1st Vol Bn Queen's Roy W Surrey Regt, formerly Maj 3rd Bn, MP (C) Tower Hamlets 1874–85, St George Div Tower Hamlets 1885–92 and Croydon 1895–1905, Sec Admlty 1885–86, Pres: Local Govt Bd 1886–92 and BOT 1895–1900, Home Sec 1900–02, Chllr Exchequer 1902–03, Ld Rector Aberdeen U 1902–05, Ecclesiastical Commr England 1901, Hon LLD Aberdeen; *m* 7 Dec 1858 Margaret (*d* 10 Feb 1905), dau of Thomas Ower, of Perth, and *d* 9 Jan 1906, having had:

    1 William; *b* 7 June 1862; *d* unm 3 Oct 1879

    2 CHARLES, **2nd Baron**

    3 Harold, DSO and bar; *b* 30 Oct 1876; Lt-Col Cameronians, Actg Lt-Col Queen's Regt; *m* 29 Jan 1907 Ella (*d* 12 Feb 1956, having *m* 2nd 27 Feb 1922 Surgn Lt-Col Evelyn John Hansler Luxmoore, MC, 2nd Life Gds (*d* 28 June 1955)), dau of Robert Chambers Priestley, OBE, JP, of Terrier's Ho, High Wycombe, Bucks, and *d* 28 Oct 1918 of wounds recd in action, leaving:

      (1) Ian Charles; *b* 27 March 1908; Maj RA, WW II with 3rd Bn London Scottish (AA); *m* 1st 29 April 1931 (*divorce* 1946) Ann Dundas, only dau of Gen Sir Robert Dundas Whigham, GCB, KCMG, DSO, and had:

         1a +Harold Bruce [Harold Ritchie Esq, PO Box 431, Eltham, VIC 3095, Australia]; *b* 14 March 1933; *educ* Repton; *m* 1st 25 Nov 1967 (*divorce* 1975) Shirley Anne, dau of Gordon Steele, of Bury St Edmunds, and has:

           1b +Ian Angus Dundas; *b* 1972

         1a (cont.) Harold Ritchie *m* 2nd 1977 *Nancy Leith, dau of Frank Richard Andrewartha, of Maryborough, Victoria, and by her has:

           1b *Fionnah Alice Ellen; *b* 1979

         1a Fiona, of Cuchulainn House, Innishannon, Co Cork; *b* 12 Aug 1934; *m* 24 June 1967 (*divorce* 1975) Kenneth Stewart Donaldson, s of Ernest Donaldson, of Hull, and *d* 1992

      (1) (cont.) Maj Ian Ritchie *m* 2nd 3 Sept 1946 *Mrs Pamela Eveleen Elizabeth White [Mrs Ian Ritchie, Highway House, Hog's Back, Seale, Surrey], only dau of Reginald Henry Vickers, and *d* 1983

      (2) +William Nigel; *b* 1 April 1914; *educ* Harrow; F/Lt RAFVR WW II; *m* 29 Aug 1939 *Baroness Sibylla von Hirschberg, er dau of Baron von Hirschberg, of Murnau, Bavaria, and has:

         1a +James Anthony Gregor [James Ritchie Esq, 108A Dartmouth Rd, London NW2]; *b* 11 Sept 1945; *educ* Harrow and Ch Ch Oxford

         2a +Andrew William [Andrew Ritchie Esq, 53 Egerton Gdns, London SW3]; *b* 15 March 1947; *educ* Harrow and Trin Coll Cambridge

         1a *Caroline Elizabeth [The Hon Mrs Hugh Gathorne-Hardy, Mariners, Bradfield, Berks]; *b* 9 Aug 1943; *m* 4 July 1971 *Hon Hugh Gathorne-Hardy, yr s of 4th Earl of Cranbrook (*qv*), and has issue

      (1) *Jean; *b* 9 May 1910; *m* 22 Oct 1932 Capt John Buller Edward, RN (*ka* 18 May 1940), s of Rev Frederick John Hall, of St Just Northaw, Herts, and has issue

      (2) *Pamela Helen; *b* 26 July 1915; *m* 19 April 1939 *Maj James Dunbar Whatman, MC, Gren Gds, s of Maj Arthur Dunbar Whatman, of Walsham Hall, Walsham-le-Willows, Suffolk, and has issue

    1 Jane Gregor; *b* 19 Nov 1859; *m* 19 July 1888 Thomas Barclay Cockerton (*d* 21 Jan 1917), barrister, and *d* 12 April 1933

    2 Elizabeth Wilhelmina; *b* 1860; *m* 8 July 1891 Sir Mervyn Edmund Macartney (*d* 28 Oct 1932), 4th s of Maxwell Macartney, of Rosebrook, Co Armagh, and *d* 11 March 1950

    3 Margaret Ower; *b* 1864; *m* 14 Dec 1887 George James Young (*d* 17 April 1926), of Bude, Cornwall, s of Gavin David Young, of Adelaide, S Australia, and *d* 11 Jan 1944, leaving issue

    4 Anne Wilmot; *b* 1869; *m* 12 July 1893 Baron Romer, PC (LP; *d* 19 Aug 1944), and *d* 3 March 1948, leaving issue

    5 Mary Emily; *b* 1870; *m* 17 Feb 1900 Baron Russell of Killowen and *d* 10 Nov 1956, leaving issue (see RUSSELL, Bt, of Littleworth Corner)

    6 Maud; *b* 30 Aug 1872; *d* unm 23 Nov 1958

    7 Eleanor; *b* 1874; *d* unm 5 Nov 1955

The 1st BARON's er surv s,

    CHARLES RITCHIE, **2nd Baron Ritchie of Dundee**; *b* 18 Nov 1866; *educ* Westminster (later Govr) and Trin Coll Oxford (BA 1888); Lt City London, Chm PLA 1925–41, Pres: Dock and Harbour Authorities Assoc 1938–41 and Poplar Hosp, Mayor Winchelsea 1924 and 1931; *m* 14 July 1898 Sarah Ruth (*d* 25 Nov 1950), 4th dau of Louis Jennings, MP, and *d* 19 July 1948, having had:

    1 Philip Charles Thomson; *b* 18 May 1899; *educ* Trin Coll Oxford (BA); 2nd Lt Suffolk Regt; *d* unm 13 Sept 1927

    2 JOHN KENNETH RITCHIE, **3rd Baron Ritchie of Dundee**, PC (1965); *b* 22 Sept 1902; *educ* Winchester and Magdalen Coll Oxford; Capt KRRC WW II, memb Cncl London Stock Exchange (dep chm 1954–59, chm 1959–65 and chm supernumerary 1965–72), dir Hutchinsons Ltd, chm English Assoc American Bondholders, Mayor Winchelsea 1934; *m* 17 Feb 1945 Joan Beatrice (*d* 3 Aug 1963), only dau of Rev Henry Charles Lenox Tindall, Rector Iden, Sussex, by Muriel Caroline, est dau of Philip Oxenden Papillon, of Crowhurst Pk and Telham Place, Sussex, and *dsp* 20 Oct 1975

    3 COLIN NEVILLE OWER RITCHIE, **4th Baron Ritchie of Dundee**, of Northiam, Sussex; *b* 9 July 1908; *educ* Down Ho Rottingdean and Trin Coll Oxford (BA 1929); *m* 28 July 1943 Anne Petronill (*d* 1989), dau of Henry Curteis Burra, JP, of Springfield, Rye, Sussex, and formerly w of John Francis Burra Huntley, and *dsp* 16 Nov 1978

    4 (HAROLD) MALCOLM RITCHIE, **5th and present Baron Ritchie of Dundee**

    1 *Margaret Ruth; *b* 13 Nov 1913; *m* 10 Sept 1943 *Maj (William Arthur) Martin Chippindale, Worcs Regt (ret), only child of Edgar John Chippindale, of Flackley Ash, Peasmarsh, and has:

      (1) *Philip John; *b* 5 March 1949; *educ* Aldenham and London Coll of Printing; with Hutchinsons Ltd; *m* 1978 *Sally, dau of Maurice J Ashworth, of Fairlight, Sussex

      (1) *Jean Margaret; *b* 14 July 1945

RIVERDALE

Arms: Per chevron argent and sable, in chief two crosses patée of the second and in base a sun in splendour, per pale or and of the first. **Crest:** In front of a dragon's head sable a sun as in the arms. **Supporters:** Two dragons sable, each charged on the wing, the dexter with a garb and the sinister with a cross patée or. **Motto:** *In arduis fidelis* ('Faithful in difficulties'). **Creation:** Bt. (UK) 26 June 1929, B. (UK) 27 June 1935.

THE 3RD BARON RIVERDALE, of Sheffield, Co York, and a **Baronet** (Sir Anthony Robert Balfour, Bt) [The Rt Hon The Lord Riverdale, House of Lords, London SW1A 0PW]; *b* 23 Nov 1960; *s gf* 1998; *educ* Wellington

Lineage: HERBERT BALFOUR; had, with a yr s (Bertram, *b* 9 Feb 1875, *m* 27 Nov 1901 Minnie Maud Huber (*d* 2 Feb 1949), of Newark, NJ, and *d* June 1944, leaving issue):

Sir Arthur Balfour, 1st Bt, and **1st Baron Riverdale**, of Sheffield, Co York (both UK), so *cr* 26 June 1929 and 27 June 1935 respectively, GBE (1942, KBE 1923), JP; *b* 9 Jan 1873; *educ* Ashville Coll Harrogate; V-Consul Denmark 1899–1947, Consul Belgium 1915–47, Master Cutler Sheffield 1911–12, chm and md Arthur Balfour and Co, steel mfrs, chm: C Meadows and Co, High Speed Steel Alloys, Ctee on Industry and Trade 1924, UK Trade Mission to Egypt 1931, Fire Bdes Ctee 1936, London Advsy Cncl S African Exhibition 1936, Advsy Cncl Sci and Industl Research 1937, RAF Benevolent Fund and Appeals Ctee 1941–, V-Chm Air Cncl Supply Bd, dir: Nat Provincial Bank, Telegraph Construction and Maintenance Co, Halifax Bldg Soc and Sheffield Gas Co, local dir Alliance Assur, memb: Roy Commn Railways 1913, Industl Advsy Ctee to Treasury, Engrg Industs Ctee WW I, Post Office Advsy Cncl 1922, Cotton Arbitration Bd 1929, Imperial Ec Ctee 1930, Chinese Govt Purchasing Commn 1931, Grand Cncl Fedn Br Industs 1935, Advsy Ctee Dept Overseas Trade for NY World's Fair 1938, Mission on Empire Trg Scheme 1940 and Advsy Cncl to Chllr Exchequer 1942, Pres: Sheffield Chamber Commerce 1919 and Assoc Br Chambers Commerce 1923–24, V-Pres Internat Chamber Commerce 1928, Govt Del Ec Conf 1927, leading Br Del Consultative Ctee Ec Conf Geneva 1928, Hon A/Cdre 601 (Co of London) Sqdn, Chev Order Leopold Belgium, Grand Offr Order Crown Belgium, Cdr Order Dannebrog, Offr Legn Hon, memb Order Brilliant Jade China, Hon LLD Sheffield U 1934; *m* 19 Oct 1899 Frances Josephine Keighley, OStJ, Medaille de la Reine Elisabeth (*d* 1 July 1960), dau of Charles Henry Bingham by Josephine, dau of William Keighley, JP, and *d* 7 July 1957, having had:

1 ROBERT ARTHUR BALFOUR, **2nd Baron Riverdale**, JP (Sheffield 1950), DL (S Yorks 1959); *b* 1 Sept 1901; *educ* Oundle; Lt-Cdr RNVR WW II, Consul for Belgium Sheffield Area 1945–98, Master Cutler 1946, Pres: Sheffield Chamber Commerce 1950, Assoc of Br Chambers Commerce 1957–58; memb: Br Nat Ctee Internat Chamber Commerce 1957–58 and IOD; with Balfour Darwins Ltd (pres 1969–75 and chm 1961–69), dir: YTV 1967–73, Nat Prov Bank 1964–69 and Nat West Bank E Regn 1969–71, Belgian Chev Order Crown 1956, Offr Order Leopold II 1971; *m* 1st 1 Sept 1926 Nancy Marguerite (*d* 8 Aug 1928), dau of Engr R-Adml Mark Rundle, DSO, and had:

(1) Mark Robin; *b* 16 July 1927; *educ* Aysgarth Sch and Trin Coll Sch Port Hope Canada; md Balfour Darwins Ltd and Arthur Balfour and Co, dep chm Darwins Ltd, chm Sheffield Rolling Mills Ltd, dep chm Wm Ridgway and Sons, V-Consul Finland 1962; *m* 31 March 1959 Susan Ann (*d* 29 June 1996), est dau of Robert Percival Phillips, of Sheffield, and *d* 30 Sept 1995 leaving:

1a ANTHONY ROBERT BALFOUR, **3rd and present Baron Riverdale**

1a *Nancy Ann; *b* 26 Feb 1963

2a *Kate Frances; *b* 12 Oct 1967

1 (cont.) The **2nd Baron** *m* 2nd 9 Feb 1933 Christian Mary (*d* 1991), er dau of Maj Arthur Rowland Hill (*see* HILL, V), and *d* 26 June 1998, leaving by her:

(2) +DAVID ROWLAND [The Hon David Balfour, Ropes, Grindleford, Sheffield, Yorks]; *b* 15 May 1938; heir presumptive; *educ* Harrow and Queens' Coll Cambridge (BA 1960); *m* 15 Dec 1972 *Mrs Ruth Middleton

(1) *Frances Christian [The Hon Frances Balfour, Ropes, Grindleford, Sheffield, Yorks]; *b* 13 Jan 1946; *educ* Wycombe Abbey and New Hall Cambridge

2 +Hon Francis Henry, TD [Maj The Hon Francis Balfour TD, Garden Cottage, Bathampton, Bath, Somerset]; *b* 25 Aug 1905; *educ* Oundle; Maj RA (TA) WW

II, V-Consul for Denmark 1947–60, Kt Order Dannebrog; *m* 1st 30 March 1932 Muriel Anne (*d* 3 July 1970), er dau of Engr R-Adml Ralph Berry, and has:

(1) +Arthur Michael [Arthur Balfour Esq, Wynthrop, Chorleywood Rd, Herts]; *b* 24 Nov 1938; *educ* Oundle and Bristol U (BSc Eng 1960); GIMechE; *m* 21 April 1962 *Rita Ann, er dau of I C France, and has:

1a +Edward Francis; *b* 5 April 1965

2a +James Henry; *b* 4 Nov 1966

1a *Anna Louise; *b* 1971

(2) +Jeremy Ralph [Jeremy Balfour Esq, 151 Knowle Lane, Brentry, Bristol]; *b* 10 May 1948; *educ* Oundle and Plymouth Poly (BSc); *m* 1974 *Wendy May, dau of W H Seal, of Bath, and has:

1a +Robert Henry; *b* 1980

2a *Rebeccca Anne; *b* 1983

(1) *Bridget Anne [Mrs Peter Graham, 8 Shrimpton Close, Knotty Green, Beaconsfield, Bucks]; *b* 27 March 1933; *m* 26 July 1957 *(Ewan) Peter Graham, only s of Ewan Curwen Graham, of Chelsea, and has:

1a *Philip James; *b* 9 Sept 1959

2a *Stephen Paul; *b* 11 Dec 1960

3a *Adam Timothy; *b* 1 Jan 1964

(2) *Frances Elizabeth [Mrs Charles Plows, Holcombe Cottage, Holcombe Lane, Bathampton, Bath BA2 6UN]; *b* 7 June 1934; *m* 6 Sept 1958 *Charles David Plows, MB, BCh, yr s of Harold Plows, of Leeds, and has:

1a *Ian Julian; *b* 2 Oct 1960

2a *Christopher Mark; *b* 16 May 1962

2 (cont.) Maj The Hon Francis Balfour *m* 2nd 1971 *Daphne Cecelia, dau of A C Moss

1 Mary Josephine; *b* 22 Sept 1900; ARCM; *m* 1st 24 Aug 1931 Ernest Henry Bruce (*d* 21 Sept 1948), Indian Police Serv, s of A C Bruce, of London; *m* 2nd 15 Dec 1954 Sir Raymond Hatherell Fooks, CBE (*d* Feb 1978), yr s of William Henry Fooks, of Leigh-on-Sea, Essex, and *d* 14 April 1978

2 Evelyn Hope; *b* 6 April 1909; *m* 1st 12 April 1930 G/Capt Eustace Jack Linton Hope, AFC, RAF (*ka* over France 6 Aug 1941), s of Maj Linton Hope, of Fernhurst, Sussex, and had issue; *m* 2nd 6 June 1953 Lt-Col John Claude Thurlow Rivett-Carnac, MC (*see* RIVETT-CARNAC, Bt), and *d* 26 April 1967, leaving further issue

3 *Primrose Keighley [The Hon Mrs Minnitt, Whitelocks, Sutton, Sussex]; *b* 19 April 1913; *m* 1st 30 Sept 1933 OLIVER GRAHAME HALL later CLAUDE GRAHAME MUNCASTER (deed poll 1945; *d* 1974), painter, s of Oliver Hall, RA, RWS, of Bay View, Bardsea, Ulverston, Lancs, and has:

(1) *Martin Grahame [Martin Muncaster Esq, Clouds Hill, Lynchmere, Surrey GU27 3NQ]; *b* 17 July 1934; *educ* Stowe; broadcaster; author: *The Wind in the Oak* (1978) and *The Yachtsman's Quiz Book* (1982); *m* 4 April 1959 *Iona MacGeoch, er dau of Donald Gilbert, of Wisborough Green, Sussex, and has:

1a *Timothy Grahame MacGeoch; *b* 28 March 1960

2a *Oliver Martin Keighley; *b* 24 Nov 1964

1a *Miranda Jane [Mrs Gareth Thompson, The Oast Barn, Mount Ephraim Farm, Cranbrook, Kent TN17 3PG]; *b* 27 May 1962; *m* *Gareth John Hunt Thompson, s of Peter Thompson, of Burmiston, Scarborough, Yorks

(2) *Clive [Dr Clive Muncaster, 119 Commonwealth Court, Apt 1, Princeton, NJ 08540, USA]; *b* 24 Jan 1936; *educ* Stowe; composer: *The Happy Hypocrite* and *The Hidden Years*, conductor, fndr Churchill Memorial Concerts Blenheim Palace 1966, fndr and govr Music Therapy Charity Ltd 1969; *m* 31 Oct 1959 *Ursula Mary, er dau of Capt Edward Brotherton-Ratcliffe, and has:

1a *Maximilian Nicholas Clive [Maximillian Muncaster Esq, Low Rigg House, St John's Chapel, Weardale, Co Durham DL13 1QT]; *b* 15 Dec 1960; *m* 4 Feb 1989 *Susannah Mary, yr dau of Timothy Nesbitt-Dufort, of Cherrywood House, Langley, Cheshire, and has:

1b *Patrick Xavier; *b* 29 July 1989

1b *Isabel Beatrix Claire; *b* 4 Feb 1991

2b *Josephine Mary Claire; *b* 12 Sept 1993

3b *Miriam Anna Claire; *b* 8 Feb 1996

2a *Peregrine Luke; *b* 17 Oct 1962; *m* 1986 *Catherine Margaret, dau of Michael Andrew Holford, of Herts, and has:

1b *Dominic Peregrine; *b* 1992

1b *Harriet Mary; *b* 1988

2b *Georgina Margaret; *b* 1990

3a *Crispin Claude [Crispin Muncaster Esq, 2 Cow Lane, Steeple Aston, Oxon OX6 3SG]; *b* 18 Sept 1965; *m* 9 April 1994 *Abigayle Andrea, yr dau of Graham Stuart Caleb, of Hinton Waldrist, Oxon, and has:

1b *Zachary Caleb; *b* 30 Sept 1997

4a *Caspar Amadeus; *b* 15 Feb 1967

5a *Quentin Augustine; *b* 1971

3 (cont.) The Hon Mrs Muncaster *m* 2nd 15 July 1975 *Robert John Minnitt, CMG

RIVETT-CARNAC

Arms: Quarterly: 1st and 4th, arg. and az. two swords in saltire ppr. between three mullets, one in chief and two in fess, and a crescent in base counterchanged (for CARNAC); 2nd and 3rd, per pale arg. and sa. on a chevron between three lozenges as many martlets counterchanged (for RIVETT). **Crests:** 1 A sword erect, pommel and hilt or, issuing from a crescent erm., the internal part gu. (for CARNAC), 2 An arm erect, couped at the elbow, per pale arg. and sa., in the hand ppr. a broken sword of the first, hilt and pommel gold (for RIVETT). **Mottoes:** 1 *Sic itur ad astra* ('Thus does one proceed to Heaven'), 2 Holde faste. **Creation:** Bt. (UK) 12 March 1836.

SIR (THOMAS) NICHOLAS RIVETT-CARNAC, 8TH BT, of Derby and Warborne, Hants [The Rev Canon Sir Nicholas Rivett-Carnac Bt, The Haven, Sandhurst Lane, Little Common, Bexhill-on-Sea, E Sussex TN39 4RH]; *b* 3 June 1927; *s* unc 1972; *educ* Marlborough; Scots Gds 1945–55, ret as Maj, served Malaya 1950 (despatches), Probation Serv 1957–59, ordained 1963, Vicar St Mark's Kennington, London, 1972–89, RD Lambeth 1978–82, Hon Canon Southwark 1980–96, Pastor: Kingdom Faith Ministries Horsham 1989–93, Ashburnham Place 1993– (ret); *m* 1977 *Susan Marigold MacTier, yr dau of C Harold Copeland

Lineage: THOMAS RIVETT, of Derby; blacksmith, later maltster 1653; *m* Barbara — (*bur* 1652) and was *bur* 25 June 1660, having had, with a yr s (John):

1 THOMAS

2 Francis, of Derby; *bur* 25 June 1714, leaving:

(1) Thomas, of Derby; bankrupt Oct 1736; *m* Mary — and had two sons (Thomas, *bapt* 5 Jan 1729/30; William, *bapt* 22 Oct 1733) and two daus (Sarah, *bapt* 14 Dec 1731; Mary, *bapt* 30 Dec 1735)

The er s,

THOMAS RIVETT, of Derby; *bapt* 8 Aug 1658; maltster; *m* 28 Jan 1678/9 Rebecca, dau of William Agard, of Mackworth, Derbys, and was *bur* 17 March 1679, leaving:

THOMAS RIVETT, of Derby and Blore, Staffs, where he bought an estate 1720; *bapt* 22 March 1678/9; maltster; Alderman, Mayor Derby 1715–16; *m* 9 Dec 1708 Elizabeth (*d* 1746), dau of Humphrey Eaton, of Derby, and was *bur* 29 June 1724, having had, with three yr sons (Francis, of Cockpit Hill, Derby, *bapt* 7 Sept 1714, freeman Derby, *bur* unm 6 March 1773; Robert, of Derby, *bapt* 1 Feb 1719/20, merchant, *bur* unm 12 May 1731; Richard, *bapt* 20 Aug 1722, *bur* 12 Feb 1723/4) and four daus (Elizabeth, *bapt* 29 Feb 1711/2, *bur* unm 24 Dec 1746; Catherine, *bapt* 29 Aug 1715; Rebecca, *bapt* 17 Nov 1716; Mary, *bapt* 6 Jan 1718/8, *d* unm; Sarah, *bapt* 7 Aug 1721, *m* 3 April 1743 Sir John Eardley Wilmot (*see* EARDLEY-WILMOT, Bt) and was *bur* 27 July 1772):

THOMAS RIVETT, of Derby, JP, DL (1745), *bapt* 12 May 1713; barrister 1739, Derby; freeman 1738, Mayor 1761–62, MP 1748–54; bought the Calton estate, Staffs, *c* 1750 and Mapleton Manor, Derbys, 1757; co-fndr Cockpit Hill pottery 1750 (it lasted till 1779); High Sheriff Derbys 1757–58 and 1763; *m* April 1749 Anna Maria, dau of Rev Charles Sibley, of Blore, and *d* 6 April 1763, having had, with two other sons (*d* young or unm):

1 Thomas (Rev), of Everton, Hants, and Maresfield, Sussex; *bapt* 31 Dec 1753; *m* Louisa, dau of Sir Culling Smith, Bt, and *dsp*

2 James RIVETT later RIVETT-CARNAC (roy licence 1801 under terms of will of his bro-in-law Gen John Carnac); *bapt* 10 March 1759; HEICS, memb Bombay Govt Cncl; *m* Henrietta, dau of James Fisher ('Beau Fisher'), of Yarmouth, Norfolk, and *d* 16 July 1802, having had, with four daus:

(1) JAMES (Sir), **1st Bt**

(2) Thomas (Rev); *d* 1856.

(3) John; *b* 28 June 1796; Adml; *m* 15 March 1826 Maria Jane (*d* 23 Nov 1882), sis of Sir John Francis Davis, 1st Bt, KCB, of Hollywood, Glos (*see* 1902 edn), and *d* 1 Jan 1869, having had, with other issue:

1a James; *d* 1831

2a John Henry, CIE (1878), VD; *b* 16 Sept 1838; ICS 1858–94, Ld Manor of Stanstead Hall, Suffolk, ADC to HM QUEEN VICTORIA 1891, Hon Col Ghazipur Light Horse and Rifle Vols, Kt Grand Cross North Star Sweden, Grand Cross Order Lion and Sun Persia, FSA, FRAS, Fell Bombay U, Roy Acad Spain, Roy Swedish Acad and Roy Soc Denmark; *m* 28 Dec 1868 Annie Marion (*d* 13 Nov 1935), dau of Maj-Gen Sir Henry Marion Durand, KCSI, CB (*see* DURAND, Bt), and *d* 11 May 1923

3a Edward Stirling; *b* 14 Sept 1841; Col 11th Hus, Mil Sec to Govr Bombay 1877–80; *m* 12 March 1872 Sophia (*d* 15 Dec 1931), dau of John Irving Glennie, and *d* 28 Feb 1888, leaving issue

1 Anna Maria; *bapt* 18 March 1729/30; *m* Edmund Reynolds

2 Elizabeth; *bapt* 8 April 1751; *m* 20 July 1769, as his 2nd w, General John Carnac (*d* 29 Nov 1800), C-in-C Bengal, MP Leominster, and *dsp* 18 Jan 1780

3 Frances; *bapt* 5 March 1755; *m* Edward Ravenscroft

4 Anne Arabella; *bapt* 15 June 1761; *m* 1 Jan 1788 William Richards, of Penglais, Cards

The est s,

Sir James Rivett-Carnac, 1st Bt (UK), so *cr* 12 March 1836; *b* 11 Nov 1784; Chm HEIC, MP Sandwich, Govr Bombay 1838–41; *m* 3 June 1815 Anna Maria (*d* 2 Jan 1859), est dau of William Richardes, of Penglais, Cards, and *d* 28 Jan 1846, having had, with other issue:

1 **Sir John Rivett-Carnac, 2nd Bt**, JP, DL; *b* 10 Aug 1818; MP Lymington 1852–60, Capt 73rd Regt; *m* 19 Dec 1840 Anne Jane (*d* 2 Sept 1876), only child of Samuel Sproule, and *d* 4 Aug 1883, having had:

(1) **Sir James Henry Sproule Rivett-Carnac, 3rd Bt**; *b* 27 June 1846; Lt 73rd Regt; *m* 20 Aug 1872 Mary Jeannie (*d* 5 April 1927), dau of Ambrose Henderson, of Bodmin, Cornwall, and *d* 4 June 1909, having had:

1a **Sir Claud James Rivett-Carnac, 4th Bt**; *b* 21 Dec 1877; Cape Mounted Rifles Boer War 1899–1900 (medal with five clasps); after he had been missing for many years an order of the Chancery Division of 11 March 1924 gave leave to presume his death as on 31 Dec 1909

1a Beatrice Hilda Sproule; *b* 25 Sept 1876; *m* 28 April 1900 (*divorce* 1927) Harry Percival Foulerton, yst s of Capt Alexander Foulerton, Indian Navy, and had issue; *m* 2nd Lt-Cdr J R Allen, RN, and *d* 10 June 1932

2a Muriel Edith Frances; *b* 25 July 1879; *m* 25 April 1908 Francis Charles Montague van Cortlandt (*d* 1953), s of Harry van Cortlandt, and *d* 1 Feb 1959

(2) John Louis; *b* 3 Dec 1851; *d* 28 Dec 1863

(1) Maria Eliza Sproule; *d* 3 June 1862

(2) Frances Henrietta; *m* 18 Jan 1866 Col Henry Stratton Bates (*d* 6 May 1918), 3rd Bn Yorks Regt, est s of Rev J Ellison Bates, and *d* 23 Nov 1925

(3) Caroline Ann Emma; *m* 21 Jan 1875 Maj-Gen John Pennock Campbell (*d* 25 Dec 1903), E Lancs Regt, and *d* 4 July 1921, leaving issue

2 William John; *b* 19 April 1822; HEICS; *m* Sept 1846 Mary Anstruther (*d* 17 Feb 1911), dau of Rev Percival Spearman Wilkinson, and *d* 9 July 1874, having had:

(1) **Sir William Percival Rivett-Carnac, 5th Bt**, of Derby and Warborne, Hants; *b* 1847; *s* first cousin once-removed 1909 but did not assume title till 11 March 1924; *m* 28 April 1885 Frances Maria (*d* 7 Feb 1935), dau of Francis Charles Forbes, Bengal CS, and *d* 21 March 1924, having had:

1a Mary Frances; *d* unm 1 Jan 1951

2a Eleanor Maude; *m* 18 Jan 1912 Claud Robert Nightingale, MC, and had issue (*see* NIGHTINGALE, Bt)

(2) James Frank; Capt Bengal Service; *dsp*

(3) GEORGE CLENNELL (Sir), **6th Bt**

(4) Percy Temple; *b* 12 Jan 1852; Lt-Col and Brevet Col Duke of Wellington's W R Regt, Mashonaland 1897, Boer War 1899–1900 (despatches, medals); *m* 1 Jan 1898 Alice, 2nd dau of Maj Sydney Herbert, of Maritzburg, Natal, and *d* 1932, leaving:

1a +Percival Sydney; *b* 4 Nov 1904; *m* 1950 *Joan, dau of Jeffrey Waddington, and has:

1b +Jeremy Charles Percy [Jeremy Rivett-Carnac Esq, 4400 Telegraph Rd, Cowichan Bay BC, Canada]; *b* 1954; *m* 1981 *Monique Madeleine Marie Faivre and has issue

1a Alice Mary; *b* 28 March 1899; *m* 1924 Capt Scott

(5) Louis Wilfred Guise; *b* 1854; barrister; *m* 22 Oct 1883 Mabel (*d* 26 Sept 1951), dau of Lt-Col William Southey, Madras Staff Corps, and *d* 7 May 1904, leaving:

1a Marguerite Mabel; *b* 23 Feb 1885

2a Sybil Mary; *b* 12 Sept 1886; *m* 8 Nov 1912 Lt-Col Guy Neville Buckland, DSO, RA (*d* 20 Jan 1957), 2nd s of Charles Edward Buckland, CIE, ICS, and had issue

3a Ianthe; *b* 19 Dec 1888; *m* 19 June 1912 Norman Kershaw, s of James Kershaw, of Macclesfield, and had issue

4a Aileen Maud Georgina; *b* 26 July 1892; *m* 21 Oct 1922 Capt Robert Henry Dundas Bolton, OBE (*d* 3 Oct 1964), 2nd Bn Duke of Wellington's Regt, Ch Constable Northants, s of Edward Crawford Bolton, and had issue

(6) Ernest Henry; *b* 30 June 1857; Col IA, Afghan War 1879–80, Egyptian Campaign 1882, 5th Class Medjidie; *d* unm 4 Sept 1940

(7) Wilfrid Theodore; *b* 11 Dec 1864; *d* 4 Feb 1929, having had, with other issue:

1a John, OBE; *b* 11 July 1899; F/O RAF; *d* S Africa May 1931 following an accident

2a Peter; *b* 1900; *m* 1944 Grace Kilgore (*d* 1979), of Traynow, Saskatchewan, and *d* 1948, having had:

1b *Eleanor Grace [Mrs Peter Johnston, RR1 Barrie, Ont L4M 4Y8, Canada]; *b* 1946; *m* 1968 *Peter Johnston and has issue

3 Charles Forbes; *b* 17 Jan 1824; BCS; *m* 1st 7 Aug 1849 Flora Elizabeth (*d* 21 April 1859), dau of J Baker, and had:

(1) Charles James; *b* 18 Feb 1853; ICS 1872–1903, fin advsr Siamese Govt 1898–1906, fin agent 1906–15, Grand Cross Order Crown Siam; *m* 1st 1877 Laura Margaret Marion (*d* 19 June 1905), dau of Col J S Ogilivie, and had:

1a Vernon Charles; *b* 1878; *d* 1953, having had:

1b Nelson Charles; *b* 1906; *m* 1932 Bertha Ella Inez Litt (*d* 1978) and *d* 1979, having had:

1c *Cleone Patricia [Miss Cleone Rivett-Carnac, Finistere, 254 Te Awa Av, Napier, New Zealand]; *b* 1933

2c *Lynette Marion [Mrs Lynette Croft, 66 Glengarry Rd, Glen Eden, Auckland, New Zealand]; *b* 1934; *m* 1956 (*divorce* 1979) John Lathom Croft and has issue

3c *Robyn Genevieve; *b* 1939

2b Maurice Vernon; *b* 1910; *m* 1934 *Merlene Clare Crosby [Mrs Maurice Rivett-Carnac, 24 Churchill St, Whangarei, New Zealand] and *d* 1964, having had:

1c +Paul Charles [Paul Rivett-Carnac Esq, 152 Flower St, Northgate, Brisbane QLD 4013, Australia]; *b* 1945; *m* 1965 *Valerie Kay Anderson and has issue

1c *Marie Anne; *b* 1938; *m* 1957 *Clive Palmer and has issue

2c *Dianne Adele; *b* 1943; *m* 19– *David Lambdin and has issue

(1) (cont.) Charles James Rivett-Carnac *m* 2nd 5 July 1906 Frances Clytie (*d* 1 Jan 1962), dau of Rev Canon Greenstock, and *d* 9 Sept 1935, having by her had:

2a Douglas Charles Mahisra Chula, OBE (1956); *b* 23 Nov 1907; *educ* Exeter Coll Oxford (BA 1930); *m* 23 Nov 1946 *Barbara Joyce [Mrs Douglas Rivett-Carnac, 18 Andrews Way, Salisbury, Wilts SP2 8QR], dau of Arthur R Pratt, and *d* 20 Sept 1989, having had:

1b +Christopher Charles [Christopher Rivett-Carnac Esq, The Old Rectory, Lower Rd, Salisbury, Wilts SP2 9NL]; *b* 24 Dec 1947; *m* 1974 *Sara Catherine, dau of Dr R J C Hutchinson, and has:

1c +Thomas Charles; *b* 1977

2c +Alexander John; *b* 1980

3c +Michael James; *b* 1983

1c *Louise; *b* 1976

2b +John Benedict [John Rivett-Carnac Esq, Lion House, 23 Onslow Rd, Richmond, Surrey TW10 6QH]; *b* 24 Aug 1949; *m* 1975 *Mary Rose, dau of Col K A P Fergusson, and has:

1c +Charles John Fergus; *b* 1991

1c *Sophie Caroline; *b* 1979

2c *Francesca Jane; *b* 1982

3c *Alice Josephine; *b* 1984

3b +Michael Francis [Michael Rivett-Carnac Esq, Mitton House, Round Chimney, St Sampsons, Guernsey, CI]; *b* 27 Nov 1950; *m* 1984 *Roberta Grace, only dau of W/Cdr R O Mearns Jones, and has:

1c *Philippa Jane Mearns; *b* 1988

3a Charles Francis; *b* 28 Feb 1909; *educ* Malvern; Lt-Col IA WW II (wounded); *m* 24 Feb 1936 Lorna (*d* 1993), dau of B Darling, Imperial Bank of India, and *d* 6 July 1958, leaving:

1b Clive John; *b* 9 Feb 1940, *d* 19–

1b *Jacqueline Anne [Mrs David Millar, Bepton Lodge, Bepton, W Sussex]; *b* 19 Nov 1937; *m* 18 Sept 1957 *David Lindsay Millar, OBE, s of D M Millar, of The Chartered Bank, and has:

1c *Guy McIntyre; *b* 21 Feb 1959; *m* 1983 *Kim Lorraine, dau of Philip Birch, and has issue

2c *Mark Charles Forbes; *b* 28 Feb 1961; *m* 1987 *Anna Jo, dau of W/Cdr A MacKinnon, and has issue

3c *Nicholas Lindsay [Nicholas Millar Esq, 35 Tunley Rd, London SW17 7QH]; *b* 29 Dec 1962; *m* 1989 *Karen Elizabeth, dau of Dr Hugh McLean, and has issue

4a Louis Charles Wykeham; *b* 24 May 1912; Capt Sherwood Foresters WW II; *m* 5 July 1939 Alice (*d* 1976), dau of J Docherty, and *d* 1985, having had:

1b +Clive Anthony Charles; *b* 4 May 1940; *m* 1971 *Marilyn, dau of H C Wilkes, and has issue

2b +Louis Charles James [Louis Rivett-Carnac Esq, Anchor Cottage, The Holway, Winterton-on-Sea, Norfolk]; *b* 16 Aug 1942; *m* 1968 (*divorce* 1983) Ann Elsey and has issue

3b +Timothy Charles [Timothy Rivett-Carnac Esq, 1 Julian Rd, Folkestone, Kent]; *b* 4 Oct 1949; *m* 1st 1977 (*divorce* 1983) Virginia Trust and has issue; *m* 2nd 1984 *Michelle Jefferies and has further issue

1b *Nichola Frances; *b* 10 Dec 1947; *m* 1st 1967 (*divorce* 1981) Robin Wentworth Mason; *m* 2nd *Ernest Dare and has issue by her 1st husb

5a Clive Charles; *b* 7 April 1916; Lt Sherwood Foresters; *ka* Palestine 18 Aug 1939

(2) John Thurlow; *b* 26 April 1856; Dep Inspr Gen Indian Police, Burma War 1886–87 (medal with clasp) and Chin-Lushai Expdn 1889–90 (clasp); *m* 15 May 1887 Edith Emily (*d* 16 May 1950), dau of H H Brownlow, and *d* 1948, leaving:

1a John Claude Thurlow, MC (1918), KPM; *b* 14 June 1888, *educ* Eastbourne Coll; Indian Police, 35th Scinde Horse India and 13th Bengal Lancers Mesopotamia WW I, Ch Constable Hunts 1928–57 and Isle of Ely 1931–57, WW II: Lt-Col Mil Govt 1943–45, Ch Public Safety Southern France with US 6th Army 1944; *m* 1st 1923 Ola Jane (*d* 9 Feb 1953), dau of S Wilson, of Maine, USA, and had:

1b *Sheila Veronica Mary; *b* 21 Dec 1927; *m* 1st 22 Jan 1954 (*divorce* 1969) John Coleman Averill; *m* 2nd 1969 Alfred Edwin Valentine (*d* 1981) and has by her 1st husb:

1c *John Miles Rochford; *b* 1 Dec 1958; *m* 1984 *Torill Peele

2c *Andrew Clive Rochford; *b* 9 May 1960

1c *Catherine Veronica; *b* 30 March 1955; *m* 1979 *George Braoudakis and has issue

2c *Elizabeth Jane; *b* 7 June 1957; *m* 1980 *Andrew Barrett and has issue

1a (cont.) Col John Rivett-Carnac *m* 2nd 6 June 1953 Hon Evelyn Hope, widow of G/Capt Eustace Jack Linton Hope, AFC, RAF, and 2nd dau of 1st Baron Riverdale (*qv*), and by her had:

1b +(John Charles) Malcolm [Malcolm Rivett-Carnac Esq, 27 Pilgrim's Lane, Bugbrooke, Northants NN7 3PJ]; *b* 6 June 1955; *m* 1984 *Carol Ann Hedley and has:

1c *Amanda; *b* 17 May 1986

2c *Tamara; *b* 17 March 1989

2a Percy Kenneth; *b* 3 May 1890; Capt IA WW I Egypt, Persian Gulf and E Africa, ret invalided; *d* unm 22 March 1932

3a Herbert Gordon; *b* 15 Feb 1892; *educ* Bradfield; Lt-Col IA (Political Dept), WW I on Gen Staff Mesopotamia, Assist Political Offr Amara, Mesopotamia; *m* 16 June 1925 Cushla Margarette (*d* 1974), dau of Lt-Col Robert Southey Pottinger, Resident Kolhapur, and *d* 6 July 1962, leaving:

1b +Eric Gordon; *b* 7 March 1926

2b +John Southey; *b* 16 April 1929

4a Edward Charles; *b* 31 Aug 1901; *educ* Eastbourne Coll; attd Field Ambulance Unit French Army WW I 1918–19, Commr RCMP; *m* 1st 1932 Mary Dillon (*d* 1970), dau of Lt-Col Francis Bethel Ware, DSO, VD, of London, Ontario; *m* 2nd 1975 *Ora-Lee, dau of Harry Edward Tharsing, of Berkeley, CA, and *d* 1980, having had:

1b *Beverley Ann [Mrs Beverley Griffin, 1746 Garnet Rd, Victoria BC V8P 3E1, Canada]; *b* 29 Nov 1933; *m* 1954 (*divorce* 1968) A F Griffin and has:

1c *Brenda Gayle; *b* 23 Dec 1956; *m* 5 May 1995 *Dr Bruce Taro Yoneda, FRCS (Can), and has:

1d *Taryn Frances Toshie; *b* 8 Dec 1995

2b Mary Frances; *b* 3 March 1940; *m* 1965 (*divorce* 1981, resumed maiden name) Gerald Edward Marshall Beeney and *d* 1985

1a Edith Maud; *b* 15 Jan 1895; *m* 18 June 1917 Maj-Gen Edward Temple, RA (*d* Jan 1961), and had:

1b *Edward Peter [Col Edward Temple, Stablings, Warnock Lane, Lower Willingdon, Sussex]; *b* 9 April 1918; *educ* Malvern; Col RA

2b *John Hugh; *b* 9 Jan 1921; *educ* Bradfield; *m* 5 April 1952 *Audrey Margaret Joan, dau of A W Warr Eaton, of Milford-on-Sea, and has:

1c *Michael Martyn; *b* 26 Jan 1953; *educ* King's Sch Rochester

2c *Andrew William; *b* 28 Oct 1957; *educ* King's Sch Rochester

1c *Jane; *b* 25 July 1955

3b *James David; *b* 5 Feb 1936; *educ* Eastbourne Coll and Queens' Coll Cambridge (BA, Vet MD 1958); *m* 1959 *Nancy Lewis and has:

1c *Sarah; *b* 23 March 1962

2c *Catherine; *b* 18 Aug 1963

3c *Rachel; *b* 6 Feb 1967

(3) Harry Morland; *b* 11 Oct 1857; Bengal CS; *m* Eleanor — (*d* 3 July 1965) and *d* 1948, having had, with another s:

1a Charles Walter; *b* 1893; *m* 1920 Freda Gertrude (*d* 1959), dau of Frederick Hean Roger, of Melbourne, Australia, and *d* 19–, having had:

1b +Gordon Seymour [Gordon Rivett-Carnac Esq, 200 Lawrence Rd, Mt Waverley, VIC 3149, Australia]; *b* 1925; *m* 1949 *Marian Propert, dau of Robert Newman Scott, of Melbourne, and has had issue

2b Roger Arnott James; *b* 1927; *m* 1947 *Lorna Isabel, dau of John Hamilton-Dee, and *d* 1967, having had issue

1a Eleanor Flora; *m* F Cumming

2a Muriel; *m* M. Haywood

3a Holly; *m* Herbert L Bynon

3 (cont.) Charles Rivett-Carnac *m* 2nd 14 June 1865 Isabel Stannus (*d* 2 Jan 1913), dau of Col Alexander Gordon, Madras Army, and *d* 29 Nov 1902, having by her had:

(4) Gordon Forbes; *b* 1866; *d* 19 May 1898

(5) Seymour Gordon; *b* 24 Feb 1868; Col RE; *m* 1st 1893 Martha Ella Maud (*d* 1920), dau of John Latch, and had:

1a Kathleen Maud; *b* 1894; *m* 4 March 1920 Brig John Norman Hildick-Smith, MC, DL, IA (*d* 14 Dec 1973), s of F C Hildick-Smith, of Walsall, and *d* July 1973, leaving:

1b Donald Ryvet, MBE (1944); *b* 3 Dec 1920; *educ* Bedford Sch and RMA Woolwich; Lt-Col RE, Instr Staff Coll Quetta 1956–58, AAQMG Land Forces Persian Gulf, ret 1968; *m* 11 Oct 1947 *Frances Penelope [Mrs Donald Hildick-Smith, Redmarley Orchards, Great Witley, Worcs WR6 6JP], dau of Eric Bache, MC, of Bewdley, Worcs, and *d* 19 Sept 1997, leaving:

1c +Brian Anthony; *b* 15 Sept 1953

1c *Penelope Jane; *b* 20 April 1955

2b Walter John Ryvet; *b* 9 Jan 1927; *educ* Bedford Sch and Pembroke Coll Cambridge (BA 1950, MA 1955); Assist Master King's Sch Canterbury; *m* 4 Sept 1954 *Marion [Mrs Walter Hildick-Smith CBE, 9 The Crescent, Canterbury, Kent CT2 7AQ], CBE, MA, MB, BChir, MRCP, dau of David Cornelius, of Swansea, and *d* 6 June 1987, having had:

1c *David John Ryvet; *b* 30 Aug 1964

1c *Kathleen Wendy Ryvet; *b* 21 June 1958

2c *Philippa Mary; *b* 9 Sept 1960

3c *Bryony Anne; *b* 19 May 1962

4c *Helen Jane; *b* 8 Feb 1968; *d* 19–

1b *Barbara Penelope Ryvet; *b* 22 Sept 1929; *m* 12 Dec 1959 *John R N Butcher and has:

1c *Claudia Virginia; *b* 5 July 1961

2c *Jacqueline Esmé; *b* 9 Aug 1963

3c *Gillian Penelope; *b* 17 Sept 1965

5 (cont.) Col Seymour Rivett-Carnac *m* 2nd 1 Sept 1925 Marian Frances (*d* 1982), est dau of H W Rowland, of The Bryn, Wyesham, Mon, and *d* 22 April 1931, having by her had:

2a Ann; *b* 3 Dec 1928; *educ* Newnham Coll Cambridge (BA 1950, MA 1954); *m* 6 Oct 1956 *Alan Mitchell Burgess [Alan Burgess Esq, 6 Pegman Close, Guisborough, Cleveland TS14 6DL], BA, CEng, MIEE, MInstMC, s of Frank William Burgess, of Bath, and *d* 8 Feb 1991, leaving:

1b *Martin Frank; *b* 4 Feb 1960; *m* 19– *Dr S H M Matthews, MRCPsych

1b *Janet Rachel; *b* 27 Aug 1958

2b *Sarah Kathleen; *b* 29 April 1962; *m* 19– *A M Kay

(6) Ashley Gordon; *b* 1875; *d* 1877

(7) Colin Gordon; *b* 16 Nov 1881; Lt 5th Bn Roy Irish Rifles; *d* unm 25 Dec 1916

(1) Florence Annie Gordon; *b* 1869; *m* 3 Oct 1893 Col Albert Edward Whistler, IA, est s of Gen Whistler, CB, and *d* 5 July 1942, leaving issue

(2) Winifred Gordon; *b* 1871; *d* unm 22 June 1934

(3) Ivy Gordon; *b* 1873; *d* 1874

(4) Muriel Gordon; *b* 15 May 1879; *m* 10 June 1905 Lt-Col Trimnell Martin Ward, IA (*d* 1920), only s of Maj-Gen Ward, of Eastbourne, and *d* 1966, leaving a dau

The 5th Bt's bro,

Rev Sir George Clennell Rivett-Carnac, 6th Bt; *b* 1850; *educ* Trin Coll Cambridge (BA); Rector Woldingham, Surrey; *m* 1st 20 May 1885 Emily Louisa (*d* 22 March 1894), dau of Rev George Crabbe, Rector Merton, Norfolk, and had:

1 **Sir Henry George Crabbe Rivett-Carnac, 7th Bt**; *b* 18 Jan 1889; Indian Police; *d* 1972

2 James William, CB (1945), CBE (1944), DSC, DL (Suffolk 1958); *b* 12 Feb 1891; served WWs I (despatches) and II (despatches twice), Cdre cmdg NZ Sqdn 1939, cmded HMS *Rodney* 1941–43, Flag Offr Br Assault Area Normandy 1944, V-Adml (Q) Br Pacific Fleet 1945, V-Adml, Chm Thingoe RDC 1957–61, Legn Hon and Croix de Guerre; *m* 20 April 1922 Isla Nesta (*d* 1974), yst dau of Harry Officer Blackwood, JP, of Kincurdy, Ross-shire, and *d* 1970, having had:

(1) Rev Sir THOMAS NICHOLAS RIVETT-CARNAC, **8th and present Bt**

(2) +MILES JAMES, DL (Hants 1996) [Cdr Miles Rivett-Carnac DL RN, Martyr Worthy Manor, Winchester, Hants SO21 1DY]; *b* 7 Feb 1933; heir presumptive; *educ* RNC Dartmouth; RN 1950–70 (despatches 1965), Cdr 1965, US Staff Coll 1966, cmded HMS *Dainty* 1967–68, MOD 1968–70; joined Barings 1971, dir: Baring Bros 1976–96 (md 1981), pres Baring Bros Inc 1978, dep chm Barings plc 1988–93, chm: Barings Asset Management 1989–93, Tribune Investment Tst 1985–, dir: London Stock Exchange 1991–94, Allied Lyons plc 1992–, chm Hampshire Boys' Clubs 1982–, memb cncl King George V Fund for Sailors 1989, Er Bro Trinity Ho 1992–, High Sheriff Hants 1995; *m* 11 Oct 1958 *April Sally, dau of Maj Arthur Andrew Sidney Villar, of Knightsbridge, and Mrs Ian N Fyfe-Jamieson, and has:

1a +Jonathan James; *b* 14 June 1962

2a +Simon Miles; *b* 10 Feb 1966; *m* 1994 *Sarah Petrie and has:

1b +Tom Alexander Miles; *b* 5 April 1996

1a *Lucinda Jane; *b* 29 May 1960; *m* 1986 *Hon Valentine Guy Bryan Guinness, 2nd s of 3rd Baron Moyne (*qv*), and has issue

(1) *Isla Carolyn; *b* 20 May 1925; *m* 4 April 1957 *8th Baron Abinger (*qv*) and has issue

1 Evelyn Anna; *b* 20 May 1887; *m* 1915 Benjamin Samuel Wilmot and *d* 6 Feb 1936

Sir George *m* 2nd 11 Sept 1901 Eva Mary Bernard (*d* 8 May 1939), dau of James Orr, and *d* 13 March 1932, having by her had:

3 John Temple; *b* 21 April 1906; Maj Duke of Wellington's Regt WW II; *m* 1st 20 Nov 1941 Sarah Winifred, only dau of Wilfrid Herbert Eglin, of Trimmingham, Halifax; *m* 2nd 1951 Vivienne Mary Fairchild (*d* 1979) and *d* 1991/2, having had by his 1st w:

(1) +(John) Clive; *b* 8 Dec 1944

(1) *Rosemary Jane [Mrs John Gilchrist, 4b Bright St, Western Extension, Benoni, S Africa]; *b* 26 April 1943; *m* 1972 *John Drysdale Gilchrist and has issue

2 *Aileen Mary [Mrs Edward Wakeford, 15a Kensington Mansions, Trebovir Rd, London SW5]; *m* 1945 *Edward F Wakeford

RIX

Arms: Per chevron double-arched, points upwards gules and or, in chief a rose argent between two suns in splendour also or and in base chevronwise a Greek mask of comedy vert and a like mask of tragedy sable. **Crest:** The upper part of a ship's wheel or, standing thereon an avocet, wings elevated proper, gorged with a cronel studded gold, pendant therefrom a cross crosslet fitchy sable. **Supporters:** On either side a labrador dog or, the compartment comprising a grassy mount proper, growing therefrom roses argent barbed and seeded proper, slipped and leaved vert. **Motto:** *Tolerate labores* ('Put up with the workers'). **Creation:** B. (LP, UK) 1992.

THE BARON RIX, of Whitehall, City of Westminster, and Hornsea, Co York (Brian Norman Roger Rix, CBE (1977)) [The Rt Hon The Lord Rix CBE, 8 Ellerton Rd, London SW20 OEP]; *b* 27 Jan 1924; *educ* Bootham Sch York; RAF and Bevin Boy WW II; actor-manager 1948–77 particularly in farces at Whitehall Theatre, also films and TV, radio presenter, dir and theatre controller Cooney-Marsh Gp 1977–80, Sec-Gen MENCAP 1980–87, Chm 1988–98, Pres 1998–; Chm Ind Devpt Cncl for People with Mental Handicap 1981–88; Memb Arts Cncl 1986–93 (Chm Drama Panel to 1993), Memb Barbican Centre Ctee 1993–, Chm Friends of Normansfield 1976–, Libertas 1987–; Hon V-Pres Radio Soc GB, V-Ld Lt Gtr London 1988– (DL 1987–88); ktd 1986, Hon MA Hull 1981, OU 1983, Hon DUniv Essex 1984, Hon LLD Manchester 1986, Hon DSc Nottingham 1987, Hon LLD Dundee 1994; *m* 1949 *Elspet Jeans (actress as Elspet Gray), dau of James MacGregor-Gray, of Surrey, and has:

1 *James MacGregor [The Hon James Rix, 47 Ritherdon Rd, London SW17 8QE]; *b* 1958; *educ* St Paul's and Kent U (BA); *m* 1980 *Helen Middleton Murry and has:

(1) *Benjamin; *b* 1982

(2) *Jack; *b* 1984

2 *Jonathan Robert MacGregor; *b* 1960; does not use courtesy title; *educ* St Paul's and Warwick U (BEd); *m* 1991 *Caroline Cook

1 *(Elspet) Shelley; *b* 3 Dec 1951

2 *Louisa MacGregor [The Hon Mrs Ommanney, 13 Combemartin Rd, London SW18 5PP]; *b* 1955; *educ* Queen's Gate Sch and LAMDA; actress; *m* 1st 1981 (*divorce* 1992) Jonathan Coy, actor, and has:

(1) *Jolyon; *b* 1985

(1) *Charlotte Elizabeth; *b* 1983

2 (cont.) The Hon Mrs Louisa Coy *m* 2nd 199– *Richard Ommanney

Lineage: HERBERT DOBSON RIX, of E Yorks; had:

BRIAN NORMAN ROGER, *cr* a **Baron**

ROBENS OF WOLDINGHAM

Creation: B. (LP, UK) 1961.

THE BARON ROBENS OF WOLDINGHAM, of Woldingham, Co Surrey (Alfred Robens, PC (1951)) [The Rt Hon The Lord Robens of Woldingham PC, Salcombe Court, Cliff Rd, Salcombe, Devon TQ8 8JQ]; *b* 18 Dec 1910; *educ* Manchester Secondary Sch; UDAW Official 1935–45, memb Manchester City Cncl 1942–45, MP (Lab) Wansbeck 1945–50 and Blyth 1950–60, PPS to Min Tport 1945–47, Parly Sec Fuel and Power 1947–51, Min Lab and Nat Serv April–Oct 1951; memb Roy Commn TUs and Employers' Assocs 1965–68, Govr Queen Elizabeth Training Coll for Disabled 1951–80 and LSE 1965–; Chm: NCB 1961–71 (Dep Chm 1960–61), Fndn Automation and Human Devpt 1962–, Cncl Manchester Business Sch 1964–79 , Govrs Guy's Hosp 1965–74, Vickers Ltd 1971–79, MLH Consultants 1971–81, Johnson Matthey 1971–83, St Regis Newspapers, Bolton, 1975–80, St Regis Internat 1976–81, Engrg Industs Cncl 1976– and Alfred Robens Assocs 1984–; Dir: Bank England, Times Newspapers 1967–80, Br Fuel Co 1967–80, AAH 1971–, THF 1971–86, Times Newspapers Hldgs 1980–83, AMI (Europe) 1981–; Pres Advertising Assoc 1963–67 and Snamprogetti 1988– (chm 1980–88); Chllr Surrey U 1966–77; memb NEDC 1962–72, author: *Engineering and Economic Progress* (1965), *Industry and Government* (1970), *Human Engineering* (1970), *Ten Year Stint* (1972), Hon DCL Newcastle, Hon LLD Leicester and Manchester, Hon MIMinE, Fell Manchester Coll Sci and Tech; *m* 1936 *Eva, dau of Frederick Powell, of Manchester, and adopted:

*Alfred; *b* 12 Dec 1935; *educ* Highbury Cross Sch and Croydon Tech; *m* 28 Oct 1967 *Patricia, dau of Frank Bonser, of Skidby House, Epperstone, Notts, and has:

  (1) *Alistair Jack; *b* 20 Dec 1970
  (1) *Emma May; *b* 10 July 1972

Lineage: GEORGE ROBENS, of Manchester; *m* Edith — and had:

ALFRED, *cr* a **Baron**

ROBERTS of Ecclesall and Queen's Tower

Arms: Sable on a chevron couped argent three mullets of the field, a chief dancetté or. **Crest:** Issuant out of a circlet or a demi-lion rampant gules, holding in the paws a mullet gold.
Creation: Bt. (UK) 9 Sept 1919.

SIR SAMUEL ROBERTS, 4TH BT, of Ecclesall and Queen's Tower, City of Sheffield, and West Riding of Yorkshire [Sir Samuel Roberts Bt, Cockley Cley Hall, Swaffham, Norfolk PE37 8AG; 6 Caversham St, London SW3 4AH]; *b* 16 April 1948; *educ* Harrow and Sheffield U (BA); barrister Inner Temple 1972; *m* 23 July 1977 *Georgina Ann, yr dau of David Cory, of S Glamorgan, and has:

  1 +SAMUEL; *b* 12 Aug 1989
  1 *Eleanor Judith; *b* 1979
  2 *Olivia; *b* 1982
  3 *Amelia; *b* 1985

Lineage: SAMUEL ROBERTS, of Stubbin Ho, Ecclesfield, Yorks; *b* 1649; *d* 10 Oct 1715, leaving with other issue:

JACOB ROBERTS, of Bridge Ho, Sheffield; *bapt* 6 Feb 1697; *m* 20 Feb 1723 Mary Hoyland (*d* 19 March 1770), of Lydgate, Sheffield, and had, with other issue:

SAMUEL ROBERTS, of Sheffield; *b* 1732; *m* Mary (*d* 20 May 1802), dau of John Sykes, of Sheffield, and *d* 25 Oct 1799, having had an est surv s:

SAMUEL ROBERTS, of Park Grange, Sheffield; *b* 18 April 1763; *m* 22 Oct 1794 Elizabeth (*d* 15 July 1829), dau of Robert Wright, of N Anston, Sheffield, and *d* 24 July 1848, leaving, with three daus (*d* unm):

SAMUEL ROBERTS, JP (Sheffield and W R Yorks), of Queen's Tower, Sheffield; *b* 13 April 1800; *educ* Cambridge (MA); *m* 1st 7 June 1837 Elizabeth (*d* 1838), dau of Thomas Creswick, of E Hill, Sheffield; *m* 2nd 5 Jan 1841 Sarah Anne (*d* 21 Aug 1897), only dau of Robert Sorby, of Park Grange, and *d* 29 Nov 1887, leaving, with other issue:

Sir Samuel Roberts, 1st Bt (UK), so *cr* 9 Sept 1919, PC (1922), JP (W R Yorks), DL; *b* 30 April 1852; *educ* Repton and Trin Coll Cambridge (MA); barrister Inner Temple 1877, Ld Mayor Sheffield 1899, MP (C) Ecclesall 1902–23, memb Roy Commn King's Bench Div 1913, ktd 1917; *m* 21 Dec 1880 Martha Susan (*d* 25 Feb 1941), only dau of Ven Archdeacon John Edward Blakeney, DD, Vicar Sheffield, Chaplain-in-Ordinary to HM QUEEN VICTORIA, and *d* 19 June 1926, having had:

  1 SAMUEL (Sir), **2nd Bt**
  2 Albert Samuel; *b* 2 Oct 1885; Lt RGA; *m* May — and *d* 10 May 1954
  3 Norman Samuel; *b* 1 April 1888; *m* 18 Dec 1912 Ann Dorothy (*m* 2nd 12 May 1923 Maj Geoffrey Edward Mansfield, MC, RA, of Battersea, and *d* 22 July 1966), dau of Rev Albert Ernest Sorby, Hon Canon Sheffield, and *d* 19 July 1914, leaving:

    (1) Pamela Elizabeth Norma; *m* 8 June 1938 Maj Thomas Egerton Jones, RA (*d* 26 Aug 1948), s of H Egerton Jones, of Groombridge, Sussex, and had:

      1a *David Richard; *b* 3 June 1947
      1a *Margaret; *b* 26 March 1939; *m* 30 March 1968 *Patrick X C Hayes and has:

        1b *Honora Caroline; *b* 11 Jan 1969
      2a *Susan Elizabeth; *b* 31 July 1940
      3a *Diana Mary; *b* 7 Sept 1941; *m* 2 Oct 1965 *Robert Wood, yr s of Arthur Robert Wood, of Rustenburg, S Africa

  4 Alfred Cecil Samuel (Rev); *b* 26 July 1890; *educ* Harrow and Trin Coll Cambridge (BA 1911 MA 1916)
  5 Eric Samuel; *b* 17 May 1893; *educ* Harrow; Lt York and Lancs Regt; *d* unm 6 March 1955
  1 Elizabeth Blakeney; *m* 9 July 1908 Maj John Watson Richardson (*ka* 3 May 1917), Yorks and Lancs Regt, and *d* 25 June 1969, leaving issue

The 1st Bt's est s,
Sir Samuel Roberts, 2nd Bt; *b* 2 Sept 1882; *educ* Harrow and Cambridge (MA LLB); slr 1906, Ld Mayor Sheffield 1919–20, MP (C) Hereford 1921–29 and Ecclesall 1929–35, Master Cutler Sheffield 1935–36; *m* 5 July 1906 Gladys Mary (*d* 11 March 1906), dau of William Ernest Dring, JP, MD, of Tenterden, Kent, and *d* 13 Dec 1955, having had:

  1 Samuel; *b* 28 July 1910; *d* 27 Aug 1928
  2 **Sir Peter Geoffrey Roberts, 3rd Bt**; *b* 23 June 1912; *educ* Harrow and Trin Coll Cambridge (MA); barrister Inner Temple 1936, Maj Coldstream Gds WW II, MP (C) Ecclesall 1945–50 and Heeley 1950–66, Master Cutler Sheffield 1956–57, chm: Newton, Chambers & Co and Wellman, Incandescent (ret 1972), High Sheriff Hallamshire 1970; *m* 5 Dec 1939 Judith Randell (*d* 29 Sept 1998), er dau of Randell George Hempson, of Wallingford, Berks, and *d* 1985, leaving:

    (1) Sir SAMUEL ROBERTS, **4th and present Bt**
    (1) *Jane [Mme Claude Maurin, La Tour Villedon, 18260 Subligny, France; 65 rue de Cévennes, Paris 75015, France]; *b* 27 Oct 1940; *m* 15 Dec 1962 *Claude Henri Jean-Jacques Maurin, yr s of Alexandre Maurin, of Paris XVI, and has:

      1a *Sébastien Alexandre; *b* 6 May 1965; *m* 1994 *Alison, dau of Jonathan Durr, of Cape Town
      2a *Edmond Peter; *b* 1974
      1a *Alicia; *b* 5 July 1967; *m* 1997 *Matthew Suminski, of Milwaukee
      2a *Constance; *b* 1974 (twin)

    (2) *Catherine [Mrs John Longworth, 45 Ranelagh Grove, London SW 1]; *b* 24 Feb 1943; *m* 16 Oct 1965 *John Andrew Longworth, only s of John Lewtas Longworth, of Andwell Mill, Basingstoke, and Mrs Lydia Basilewitch, of Kew, and has:

      1a *Stephanie Lydia; *b* 4 Jan 1968
      2a *Charlotte Gay; *b* 22 June 1970
      3a *Joanna Catherine; *b* 1973

    (3) *Deborah [Mrs Peter Brun, 60 Captain Pipers Rd, Vaucluse, Sydney, NSW 2030, Australia]; *b* 17 June 1946; *m* 5 Aug 1967 *Peter Constantine Brun, 2nd s of Henrik Brun, of Fring Hall, Docking, Norfolk, and has:

      1a *Henry Constantin; *b* 1971
      2a *Peter Maximilian; *b* 1974
      3a *Julian Constantin; *b* 1981
      1a *Rachel; *b* 12 July 1970

    (4) *Rebecca; *b* 24 April 1955; *m* 1978 *Guy Mark Vernon Whitcombe and has:

      1a *Claudia Elizabeth; *b* 1984
      2a *Madeleine Rebecca; *b* 1989

Seat: Cockley Cley Hall, Swaffham, Norfolk. An earlier house dating from the late 17th century was demolished in the early 1870s and replaced by the present structure to designs by R M Phipson. The appearance has been called Italianate but this is something of an exaggeration. The three-storey main block, with dentillated cornice over four-pane sash windows with canted bays on the ground floor, despite superficially Italian features such as tall chimneys, is essentially no different from any High Victorian house in the Little Boltons. A wing to one side may be older. The broken D-shape pediment to the porch looks older too. The property belonged till about half a century before its transformation to a cadet branch of the DASHWOOD Baronets of Kirtlington (*qv*).

ROBERTS of Glassenbury, Kent, Brightfieldstown, Co Cork, and City of Cork

POST·FUNERA·VIRTUS

Arms: Az. on a chevron arg. cotised or three mullets of six points, pierced sa. **Crest:** On a mount vert an eagle displayed erm., wings arg., gorged with a chaplet of ivy ppr. **Motto:** *Post funera virtus* ('Virtue survives death'). **Creation:** Bt. (UK) 20 Sept 1809.

SIR GILBERT HOWLAND ROOKEHURST ROBERTS, 7TH BT, of Glassenbury Kent, of Brightfieldstown, Co Cork, and of the City of Cork [Sir Gilbert Roberts Bt, 3340 Cliff Dve, Santa Barbara, CA 93109–1079, USA]; *b* 31 May 1934; *s* f 1979; *educ* Rugby and Gonville and Caius Coll Cambridge (BA 1957); CEng, MIMechE, with RE Kenya (E African GS Medal); *m* 8 April 1958 *Ines Eleonore, only dau of Alfons Leo Labunski, of Danzig, and has:

1 +HOWLAND LANGDON [Howland Roberts Esq, Dooish, Balleybofey, Co Donegal, Ireland]; *b* 19 Aug 1961; *m* Feb 1991 *Mary Ellen McQuirk

1 *Solveig Margaret [Ms Solveig Roberts, 2327 24th Ave, Oakland, CA 94601, USA]; *b* 27 March 1959; *m* 13 Nov 1994 *Yohay —

Lineage: Rev THOMAS ROBERTS, JP (1663), of Brightfieldstown and Ballyfoyle, Co Cork; *b* 11 Oct 1590; DD, went to Ireland *temp* CHARLES I, Rector St John of Jerusalem and St Nicholas 1639, Chllr Diocese Cork 1661, bought lands in Co Waterford 1662; *m* 1st Elizabeth (by whom he acquired estates in Co Cork), dau of Thomas Nevill, of Cork, and had, with another s:

1 Francis, JP; *bapt* 20 Jan 1644; Lt-Col of Horse; fled to Bristol 8 March 1689, was attainted by JAMES II's Irish Parl May 1689 but returned to Cork 1691; *m* 6 June 1668 Anne Bustead, widow, of Mount Long, Co Cork, and *d* on or after 14 Jan 1696

2 RANDAL

1 Elizabeth; *m* 22 Sept 1666 Capt Thomas Chudleigh, of Kinsale, and had issue

The Rev THOMAS ROBERTS *m* 2nd 1 May 1654 Dorothy, dau of Richard Boyle, DD, Archbishop Tuam, 1st cousin of Earl of Cork (see CORK and ORRERY, E) and widow of Henry Turner, and *d* by 5 May 1664, having by her had, with another dau:

3 John; *b* 1658; *m* 1st May 1696 Elizabeth Fountain (*dsp*), dau of Osborne Edwards, of Ballyhire, and a widow, of Co Wexford; *m* 2nd May 1702 Elizabeth (*dsp* 1702), dau of Arthur Padmore, of Dublin, and *d* on or after 3 Jan 1727

2 Hannah; *m* 14 Aug 1676 Rev George Synge, of Kinsale

3 Margaret; *m* Rev Thomas Cox, Archdeacon Ferns, and had issue

The Rev THOMAS ROBERTS's 2nd s,

RANDAL ROBERTS, of Brightfieldstown; *m* 1st 6 June 1671 Hannah (*d* 1689), dau of Giles Bustead, of Mount Long, Co Cork, and had:

1 THOMAS

2 Francis, of Castlepark, Co Cork; *dsp* on or after 7 Feb 1707

3 John; *b* 1688; *educ* Trin Coll Dublin (BA 1710); *m* 11 Sept 1714 Catherine Chudleigh, widow, and had:

　(1) Michael; *d* young Sept 1731

4 Michael, of Glanworth, Co Cork; *dsp* between 1 April 1741 and 6 May 1742

1 Anne; *m* 18 Jan 1695 John Crowe, of Curraghnahency, Co Cork

2 Hannah; *m* Aug 1701 Ralph Westropp, of Caherdugan, Co Cork, and had issue

RANDAL ROBERTS *m* 2nd 6 July 1691 Martha (*d* 28 May 1719), dau of Francis Hodder, of Hoddersfield, Co Cork, and *d* 20 Oct 1719, having by her had, with a dau (*d* unm):

5 Hodder; ancestor of the ROBERTSes of Kilmoney Abbey

6 Randal (Rev); *b* 7 Oct 1694; *educ* Trin Coll Dublin (BA 1715 MA 1718); Vicar Choral Cork; *dsp* on or after 3 Dec 1753

3 Jane; *m* 12 June 1711 Robert Chudleigh, of Kinsale, and had issue

4 Elizabeth; *m* 10 Sept 1720 Rev George Synge, gs of George Synge, DD, Bp Cloyne (see SYNGE, Bt), and *d* Sept 1766

RANDAL ROBERTS's est s,

THOMAS ROBERTS, of Brightfieldstown; *b* March 1674; *m* 28 Sept 1698 Jane, dau and heiress of William Hodder, of Bridgetown (by Jane his w, dau of Maj John Grove, of Ballyhimock), and had six sons and four daus; the 2nd s:

1 ('Sir') RANDAL ROBERTS, of Brightfieldstown; *b* 16 May 1704; William Hawkins, Ulster King of Arms, allowed him 22 June 1775 the arms above mentioned appearing on the seal of his gf (az. on a chevron arg. three mullets sa.) as lawfully descended in a direct line from Sir Thomas Roberts, of Glassenbury, Kent, Bt; Jane, Duchess of Saint Albans (*qv*), dau and heiress of Sir Walter Roberts, 6th and it was assumed for a time (and may in fact be the case) last Bt, of Glassenbury (*cr* 3 July 1620), accepted this statement of a connection between the ROBERTSes of Brightfieldstown and her own paternal family and in 1776 willed the Glassenbury estate, which for well over 600 years had been held by the same family, originally called Rookehurst and latterly Roobertes, to the ROBERTSes of Brightfieldstown; after a family dispute the Glassenbury estate passed to Thomas Walton Roberts in 1809 as 2nd s, as per the Duchess's will; in this will Sir Thomas's f is styled 'Sir Randal Roberts, Bt' and indeed Randal Roberts styled himself Baronet; *m* 2 Feb 1734 Martha, dau of Ralph Westropp, of Caherdugan, Co Cork, and had, with other issue:

　(1) THOMAS (Sir), **1st Bt**

　(1) Hannah; *m* 20 April 1756 Nicholas Green Evans, of Carker, Co Cork, and had issue

　(2) Jane; *m* 6 Dec 1766 James Norcott, of Springfield, Co Cork

　(3) Anne; *m* 1 Oct 1767 William Anderson, of Aghe Cross, Co Cork

　(4) Frances; *m* 17 Aug 1780 Arthur Norcott, of Park, Co Cork

　(5) Martha; *m c* 22 Oct 1790 Edward Galwey, of Lota, Co Cork

RANDAL ROBERTS's er s,

Sir Thomas Roberts, 1st Bt (UK), so *cr* 20 Sept 1809, of Brightfieldstown; *b* 27 May 1738; *m* 1st 24 Sept 1765 Amy, dau and coheir of William Johnson, of Lizard, Co Limerick, and had, with other issue:

1 WALTER (Sir), **2nd Bt**

1 Martha; *m* 2 Jan 1794 Rev John CRAMER later ROBERTS, of Sally Mount, Co Kildare, and had issue

2 Elizabeth; *m* 21 Aug 1805 William Baker (*d* 27 Nov 1815), of Lismacue

Sir Thomas *m* 2nd 23 Dec 1806 Ann, dau of Thomas Walton, of Walton Court, Co Cork, and *d* 1817, having by her had:

2 Thomas Walton, of Glassenbury, Kent; *bapt* 10 June 1809; Lt-Col and Hon Col Weald of Kent Vols, High Sheriff 1879; *dsp* 4 Oct 1883, having devised his estates to his n, Maj John Roberts Atkin-Roberts

3 Georgina Roberts; *m* 1826 John Drew Atkin, of Merrion Sq, Dublin, and *d* 26 Jan 1873, having had issue

Sir THOMAS's only surv s,

Sir Walter Roberts, 2nd Bt; *b* 13 Nov 1776; High Sheriff Devon 1817; *m* 8 Feb 1800 Catherine Hodgson (*d* 4 Aug 1853), dau of Rev Edmund Gilbert, of Bodmin, descended from Adml Sir Humphry Gilbert *temp* ELIZABETH, half-bro of Sir Walter Raleigh, and *d* 9 Dec 1828, having had, with other issue:

1 THOMAS HOWLAND (Sir), **3rd Bt**

2 Edmund Gilbert (Rev); *b* 8 Dec 1810; BD, Rector Paul's Cray, Kent, and Glanville Wootton, Dorset; *m* 12 July 1836 Elizabeth Anne (*d* 1889), dau of Maj Joyce, of Teignmouth, and *d* March 1856, leaving:

　(1) Thomas Langdon; *b* 17 April 1840; Capt London Irish Rifles; *m* 21 Feb 1862 Emily (*d* 25 Nov 1911), only dau of Thomas Moor, of St Alphege, Canterbury, and *dsp* 29 May 1904

　(2) Herbert; *b* 1847 Dec

1 Anne Gilbert; *m* 4 Jan 1837 Rev J D Perkins, DD, Rector Mamhead, Vicar Dawlish, and *d* 30 Dec 1881

2 Eliza; *m* 1832 Henry W Torrens and *d* 1834

Sir WALTER's er s,

Sir Thomas Howland Roberts, 3rd Bt; *b* 4 Nov 1804; High Sheriff Co Cork 1837; *m* 1st 30 Oct 1834 Eliza Caroline (*d* 3 Oct 1838), 2nd dau of J B Maitland, of Eccles, Dumfriesshire, MP, and *d* 1 March 1864, having had:

1 **Sir Randal Howland Roberts, 4th Bt**; *b* 28 March 1837; Capt 33rd Foot, Maj London Irish Vol Corps; *m* 14 June 1858 Eliza Mary (*d* 8 March 1912), dau of Lt-Col Sidney Turnbull, Bombay Horse Artillery, and *d* 10 Oct 1899, having had:

　(1) Walton Howland; *b* 2 March 1859; *d* 30 Aug 1888

　(1) Anne Sandella; *d* 25 Feb 1864

　(2) Lina Marian; *m* 1 June 1889 Lt-Col Jefferson Serrell Wood, Border Regt (*dsp* 5 March 1907); *m* 2nd 30 July 1912 Maj-Gen Sir William Rice Edwards, KCB, KCIE, CMG (*d* 13 Oct 1923), IMS, and *d* 13 Jan 1919

　(3) Beatrice Sidney Jane Margaret; *m* 8 Nov 1902 John Rigby Murray (*d* 13 Jan 1946), yr s of B Rigby Murray, JP, of Parton Ho, Galloway, and *d* 1957

　(4) Amy Gilbert; *d* an infant 18 Feb 1867

Sir Thomas *m* 2nd 14 June 1842 Anne Elliott (*m* 2nd 20 June 1866 Francis W Lascelles, Madras CS, and *d* 10 Nov 1890), est dau of Cdr William Langdon, RN, of Inwood Lodge, Somerset, and Tasmania, and by her had, with two other daus:

2 HOWLAND (Sir), **5th Bt**

3 Walmorth Howland (Sir), CBE (1920), JP (Staffs); *b* 30 Aug 1855; Lt London Irish Rifles, Judge Marylebone Co Ct, Examiner Ct and Revising Barrister Middx 1918–19, ret 1921, ktd 1921; *m* 12 April 1890 Katherine (*d* 6 Nov 1945), dau of John Gibson Thomson, of Aitechuan, Ardrishaig, Argyll, and *d* 21 Dec 1924, leaving:

　(1) Walter St Clair Howland (Sir), KCMG (1951, CMG 1937), MC, of Leaton Lodge, Bomere Heath, Salop; *b* 14 Dec 1893; *educ* Winchester and BNC Oxford (BA 1916); Lt RFA WW I, Dip Serv 1919–53: 1st Sec 1926, Counsellor 1930, Amb Peru 1945–49, Envoy Extrdy and Min Plen Romania 1949–51 and Holy See 1951–53; *m* 1st 1 May 1924 Helen Cecil Ronayne (*d* 15 April 1951), dau of Col Henry Wilson Weekes, DSO, OBE, RE; *m* 2nd 22 Nov 1952 Cecily

(*d* July 1964), dau of Stanley Grantham Hill, of Qld, and widow of S/Ldr Herbert Edward Ormond, RAFVR, of Merioneths, and *d* 19–

(1) Winifred Elliott; *m* 24 April 1920 Maj Cecil Beckham Harcourt (*d* 1 Sept 1930), IA, s of Charles Knight Harcourt, tea planter, India, and had issue

1 Florence Maria; *m* 13 Oct 1869 Eaton Monins Lascelles (*d* 16 March 1871) and *d* 21 June 1929

Sir RANDAL's half-bro,

Sir Howland Roberts, 5th Bt, VD, JP (Co London), DL; *b* 2 Sept 1845; Lt-Col and Hon Col 3rd (London Irish) Vol Bn Rifle Bde; *m* 21 Oct 1895 Elizabeth Marie (*d* 11 April 1949), 2nd dau of William T La Roche, of Harrington Pk, NJ, and *d* 19 Dec 1917, leaving:

1 THOMAS LANGDON HOWLAND (Sir), **6th Bt**

2 Gilbert Howland, CBE (1944), RD (1964); *b* 11 Oct 1900; Capt RN, CC Devon and Cncllr Torquay Borough, served WW I (three medals) and WW II, 3rd Cl Legn Hon, 3rd Cl Order Polonia Restituta, 2nd Cl Order St Olav Norway, Medal Roy Humane Soc; *m* 1st 15 Oct 1930 (*divorce* 1947) Marjorie, yr dau of John Boultbee Brooks, of Bromsgrove, Worcs; *m* 2nd 23 Aug 1947 *Jean [Mrs Gilbert Roberts, Little Priors, Watcombe, Torquay, Devon], dau of Edward Warren, of Yelverton, Devon, and *d* 1986, leaving by his 1st w:

(1) +Michael Gilbert [Michael Roberts Esq, 502 Queen's Mead, Queen Rd, Rondebosch 7700, S Africa]; *b* 19 June 1932; *educ* Gresham's; late Lt RM; *m* 29 March 1961 (*divorce* 1970) Felicity Roberts, dau of Gordon Charles Sheppard, of Cape Town, and has:

1a +Mark Howland; *b* 28 April 1961

2a +John Langdon; *b* 2 March 1965

1a *Jennifer Leigh; *b* 30 July 1962

(1) *Jill Morna Boultbee; *b* 23 Aug 1933

Sir HOWLAND's er s,

Sir Thomas Langdon Howland Roberts, 6th Bt, CBE (1964), DL (Co London 1962); *b* 18 June 1898; *educ* Westminster and RMA Woolwich; Col RA, served RHA and RFA WW I 1917–1918 (wounded, two medals), KAR and King's Regt, RA WW II (despatches twice), Hon Col 499 (M) HAA Regt (Kensington) RA (TA) and Cdr No 4 Co London HG Sector 1952–56, Col cmdt Co London ACF 1956–1963; *m* 10 Dec 1930 Evelyn Margaret, only dau of Harold Fielding-Hall, Burma Commn, and *d* 8 June 1979, leaving:

1 Sir GILBERT HOWLAND ROOKEHURST ROBERTS, **7th and present Bt**

2 +Walter Rookehurst [Walter Roberts Esq, 72 Eccleston Sq, London SW1V 1PJ]; *b* 1 Aug 1951; *educ* King's Sch Canterbury and Gonville and Caius Coll Cambridge (MA); slr Eng and Wales 1978, Hong Kong 1985, Capt 4th RTR (TA); *m* 1988 *Caroline Heather, dau of Hugh Cocks, of Woodside Green, Essex, and has:

(1) *Charlotte Rosamund; *b* 16 April 1990

(2) *Elizabeth Caroline; *b* 25 Feb 1994

Sir Thomas and Lady Roberts also adopted:

*Rosamund Margaret [Mrs Steven Noel-Hill, 58 Drakefield Rd, London SW17 8RP]; *b* 19 Oct 1951; *educ* Cobham Hall; *m* 1988 *Steven R Noel-Hill

ROBERTS of Milner Field

Arms: Vert on a pile or, between two saltires in base of the last, an angora goat statant proper. **Crest:** Upon two millrinds fesswise or an angora goat as in the arms. **Motto:** *Diligenter et firmiter* ('Justly and firmly'). **Creation:** Bt. (UK) 30 Nov 1909.

SIR WILLIAM JAMES DENBY ROBERTS, 3rd Bt, of Milner Field, Bingley, Co York [Sir William Roberts Bt, Strathallan Castle, Auchterarder, Perthshire PH3 1JZ; Combwell Priory, Flimwell, Wadhurst, Sussex]; *b* 10 Aug 1936; *s* f 1973; *educ* Rugby and RAC Cirencester

Lineage: JOSEPH ROBERTS, of The Marsh, Oxenhope, nr Keighley, Yorks; had:

JAMES ROBERTS, of Haworth, Yorks; *b* 1808; *m* 12 April 1829 Jane (*d* 7 Aug 1878), dau of William Hartley, and *d* 9 Jan 1888, leaving:

Sir James Roberts, 1st Bt (UK), so *cr* 30 Nov 1909, JP; *b* 30 Sept 1848; mill-owner, built model town of Saltaire, Hon LLD Leeds; *m* 14 May 1873 Elizabeth (*d* 27 July 1935), dau of William Foster, of Harden, Yorks, and *d* 31 Dec 1935, having had:

1 Bertram Foster; *b* 4 Jan 1876; *m* 22 April 1903 Eliza Gertrude (*d* April 1953), only dau of Sir Ellis Denby, JP, of Chapel Ho, nr Skipton-in-Craven, Yorks, and *d* 11 Jan 1912, leaving:

(1) JAMES DENBY (Sir), **2nd Bt**

(2) William Denby; *b* 24 July 1909; *educ* Rugby and Univ Coll Oxford (BA); *m* 7 Aug 1935 Helen Fyans (*d* following an accident 26 Oct 1962), yr dau of Herbert Shakespeare Fenwick, of Dunedin, NZ, and *d* 27 April 1966, leaving:

1a +Anthony Fenwick Denby [Anthony Roberts Esq, Mossdale, Conistone-with-Kilnsey, N Yorks BD23 5HS]; *b* 1 July 1938; *educ* Rugby and Univ Coll Oxford (BA); *m* 6 June 1964 *Vanessa Jean Wishart, 2nd dau of Sir (James) Douglas Wishart Thomson, 2nd Bt, of Glendarroch (*qv*), and has:

1b +Jonathan William Denby; *b* 31 Jan 1966

2b +Nicholas David Denby; *b* 4 Dec 1967

3b +James Anthony Denby; *b* 14 Aug 1974

2a +Peter William Denby; *b* 1 Aug 1945; *educ* Rugby and RAC Cirencester; *m* 1st 2 July 1970 (*divorce* 1977) Christine Margaret Hermione Bampfylde (*m* 2nd Joseph Scott-Plummer; *see* KINROSS, B), sis of 7th Baron Poltimore (*qv*), and has:

1b *Emma Louise; *b* 1972

2b *Lucinda Ann; *b* 1973

2a (cont.) Peter Roberts *m* 2nd 1977 (*divorce* 1988) his former w's 2nd husb's former w Grizel Elizabeth-Anne (Lulla), only dau of Col Anthony Gerald Way, MC, of Kincairney, Dunkeld, Perthshire, and formerly w of Joseph Scott-Plummer, and by her has:

1b +William Gerald Denby; *b* 1980

1a *Ann [Mrs Richard Allen, Highfield Lodge, Gt Shefford, Newbury, Berks RG17 7EE]; *b* 24 May 1936; *m* 20 May 1967 *Richard Staines Allen and has:

1b *Adrian James Anthony; *b* 12 Nov 1967

1b *Alison Helen Suzanne; *b* 9 July 1975

2b *Sophie Clare; *b* 18 July 1979

(1) Mary; *b* 15 Jan 1906; *m* 1st 6 Dec 1927 (*divorce* 1933) Charles Vivian Jackson (*d* 30 Dec 1936), er s of Sir Charles Jackson; *m* 2nd 1 June 1933 (*divorce* 1943) Conrad Richard Hinds Howell, est s of Conrad Meredyth Hinds Howell, MD, FRCP, of Harley St, London, and had issue; *m* 3rd 10 May 1944 Dr William Stuart Tegner, s of Frederick May Tegner, of Copenhagen, Denmark, and *d* 28 Aug 1953, leaving further issue

(2) *Catherine Elizabeth; *b* 7 April 1907; *m* 28 March 1928 Robert Hope Donaldson (*d* 1964), er s of R M Donaldson, of Blairvaddick, Rhu, Dunbartonshire, and has:

1a *Robert Bertram; *b* 1929

2a *William James; *b* 1934

2 Joseph Henry Nicholson, JP; *b* 3 Jan 1887; *m* 5 July 1920 Frances Eleanor (*d* 1983), of Jersey, 2nd dau of George Partington, of Tilehurst, Berks, and *d* 21 March 1946, leaving:

(1) +John [John Roberts Esq, L'Etoquet House, St Ouen, Jersey, CI]; *b* 3 May 1921; *m* 1st 9 Aug 1949 (*divorce* 1961) Diana Emily, dau of Lawrence Norris Evans, and has:

1a *Jane; *b* 7 Nov 1953; *m* 1st 1972 (*divorce* 1977) Robin John Kershaw Roberts; *m* 2nd 1978 (*divorce* 1988) Nicholas John Foster Robinson; *m* 3rd 1989 *Robert Walter Armstrong and by her 2nd husb has:

1b *Max Nicholas John; *b* 1984

2a *Sally; *b* 31 May 1955; *m* 1st (*divorce* 1986) Nicholas Albert le Gallais; *m* 2nd 1987 *Hon James David William Bethell, 2nd s of Baron Westbury (*qv*), and has issue

(1) (cont.) John Roberts *m* 2nd 3 March 1962 (*divorce* 1972) Hon Juliana Eveline, 3rd dau of 2nd Viscount Scarsdale (*qv*) and formerly w of (a) George Derek Stanley Smith, (b) Frederick Nettlefold, (c) Sir Dudley Herbert Cunliffe-Owen, 2nd Bt (*qv*); *m* 3rd 1974 *Maryan Gwyneth, dau of Patrick Edward Aston-Talbot, and by his 2nd w has had:

1a John James; *b* 28 Feb 1964; *d* 1986

3a *Lucinda Elizabeth; *b* 14 Feb 1963; *m* 1989 *Pearse Bergin and has:

1b *James Michael; *b* 1993

2b *Sean Alexander; *b* 1997

1b *Laura Alice; *b* 1991

(2) +Henry [Henry Roberts Esq, La Fontaine, Trinity, Jersey, CI]; *b* 16 Dec 1923; *m* 1 Dec 1955 *Anne Dorothy, dau of John Huelin, of Cape Town, and has:

1a *Lesley Anne; *b* 26 Aug 1957

2a *Frances Mary; *b* 17 April 1963

1 Lily May; *b* 16 Feb 1879; *m* 8 April 1902 Sir Frederick Alfred Aykroyd, 1st Bt (*qv*), and *d* 22 March 1964, leaving issue

2 Alice Maud Mary; *b* 27 June 1881; *m* 1st 27 Aug 1902 (*divorce* 1938) Lt-Col Norman Cecil Rutherford, DSO, FRCS, s of J J Rutherford, JP, MD, of Shipley, Yorks, and had issue (who took by deed poll 21 Sept 1927 the name ROBERTS for RUTHERFORD); *m* 2nd 20 Aug 1938 Archibald Stewart Clark, of IOM

The 1st Bt's gs,

Sir James Denby Roberts, 2nd Bt, OBE (1959), JP (Perthshire 1942); *b* 3 June 1904; *educ* Rugby and Univ Coll Oxford; *m* 20 Sept 1927 Irene Charlotte D'Orsey (*d* 4 May 1977), yr dau of William Dunn, MB, JP, of Woodfield Ho, Uppingham, and *d* 10 July 1973, having had:

1 Sir WILLIAM JAMES DENBY ROBERTS, **3rd and present Bt**

2 Andrew Denby; *b* 21 May 1938; *educ* Rugby and Ch Ch Oxford (BA); *d* 19–

3 David Gordon Denby; *b* 5 Jan 1940; *educ* Rugby and Edinburgh U (MA); *m* 17 Nov 1962 *Diana Frances [Mrs Cameron Buchanan, Lawhill House, Auchterarder, Perthshire] (*m* 2nd 1973 Cameron Roy Marchand Buchanan), only dau of Hugh Wilson Jones, of The White Ho, N Lopham, Norfolk, and *d* following a flying accident 24 June 1971, leaving:

(1) +JAMES ELTON DENBY ROBERTS-BUCHANAN; *b* 12 July 1966; heir presumptive

(1) *Gail Antoinette ROBERTS-BUCHANAN; *b* 18 March 1964

4 Ian Michael Denby; *b* 24 May 1944; *d* 31 Oct 1955

1 *Susan Elisabeth [Mrs Douglas Hills, Lynwick House, Rudgwick, Sussex); *b* 4 July 1934; *educ* St Anne's Coll Oxford (MA); *m* 1st 8 Sept 1956 Roger John Edward Liddiard, er s of Aubrey John Liddiard, of Shenstone Ho, Penn Fields, Wolverhampton; *m* 2nd 1974 *Douglas Hills and by her 1st husb has:

(1) *Nicholas Anthony; *b* 19 Dec 1958

(2) *Timothy Mark; *b* 10 Oct 1960

(3) *Jonathan Miles; *b* 27 Sept 1962

(4) *Rupert Alexander; *b* 13 Oct 1966

ROBERTS OF CONWY

Arms: Paly of six argent and vert a cross patonce gules on a chief engrailed of three arches also gules three ancient lamps argent.
Crest: A demi-lion with dragons wings gules, armed argent and grasping with both paws a trumpet palewise, the bell downwards or.
Supporters: On either side a dragon gules armed argent, dimidiating a lion gules armed argent, each supporting with the exterior forefoot a plain carnyx argent, garnished and the bell downwards or.
Motto: *Pleidiol i'm gwlad* ('Loyal to my country').
Creation: B. (LP, UK) 2 Aug 1997.

THE BARON ROBERTS OF CONWY, of Talyfan, Gwynedd (Sir (Ieuan) Wyn Pritchard Roberts, PC (1991)) [The Rt Hon The Lord Roberts of Conwy PC, Tan y Gwalia, Conway, Gwynedd LL32 8TY]; *b* 10 July 1930; *educ* Harrow and Univ Coll Oxford; sub-editor *Liverpool Daily Post* 1952–54, news assist BBC 1954–57, Producer TWW Ltd 1957–59 (Production Controller 1959–60, Exec Producer 1960–68, Welsh Controller 1964–68), Programme Exec Harlech TV 1969; MP (C) Conway 1970–83, Conwy 1983–97, PPS to Sec State Wales 1970–74, Oppn Spokesman Welsh Affrs 1974–79, Welsh Office: Parly U-Sec 1979–87, Min State 1987–94, ktd 1990; V-Pres Assoc DCs 1975–79, memb Gorsedd Roy Nat Eisteddfod 1966 and Court Govrs Nat Library Wales, Nat Museum Wales and U Coll Aberystwyth 1970–91; *m* 1956 *Enid Grace Williams and has three sons

Lineage: Rev E P ROBERTS; *m* Margaret Ann — and had:

(IEUAN) WYN PRITCHARD, *cr* a **Baron**

ROBERTSON OF OAKRIDGE

Arms: Gu. two swords in saltire arg., hilted and pomelled gold, the points downwards, between in chief a sun in splendour, in base a fleur-de-lys or, and in fess two wolf heads erased of the second.
Crest: Issuant from a coronet of fleurs-de-lys or a demi-wolf arg., gorged with an eastern crown gold, supporting with the dexter paw a lance ppr., thereon a pennon per fess gu. and arg. **Supporters:** Dexter, a grey charger in review order; sinister, a springbok proper.
Motto: Fight the good fight. **Creations:** B. (UK) 29 June 1961, Bt. (UK) 4 Oct 1919.

THE 2ND BARON ROBERTSON OF OAKRIDGE, of Oakridge, Co Gloucester, and a **Baronet** (Sir William Ronald Robertson, Bt, of Welbourn, Co Lincoln) [The Rt Hon The Lord Robertson of Oakridge, 30 Grosvenor Rd, Dorchester DT1 2BD]; *b* 8 Dec 1930; *s f* 1974; *educ* Hilton Coll Natal and Charterhouse; Maj Roy Scots Greys (ret 1969), memb London Stock Exchange 1973–95 and Salters' Co (Master 1985); *m* 2 Sept 1972 *Celia Jane, yr dau of William R Elworthy, of The Manor House, Winterborne Monkton, Dorset, and has:

1 +WILLIAM BRIAN ELWORTHY; *b* 15 Nov 1975

Lineage: THOMAS CHARLES ROBERTSON, of Welbourn, Lincs; *m* Ann Dexter Beet and had:

Sir William Robert Robertson, 1st Bt (UK), so *cr* 4 Oct 1919 plus thanks of Parliament and £10,000 (just over £180,000 in late-1990s terms), GCB (1917, KCB 1915, CB 1905), GCMG (1919), GCVO (1931, KCVO 1913, CVO 1910), DSO (1896); *b* 29 Jan 1860; 2nd Lt 3rd Dragoon Gds 1888, Lt 1891, Capt 1895, Maj and Brevet Lt-Col 1900, Col 1903, Maj-Gen 1910, Lt-Gen 1915, Gen 1916, FM 1920; Chitral Relief Force 1895 (despatches, medal and clasp), War Office 1899, DAAG Intell Army HQ S Africa 1900 (despatches, medal and four clasps), Staff Capt Intell Div, AQMG and Assist Dir Intell War Office 1901–07, Brig-Gen Gen Staff Aldershot 1907–10, Cmdt Staff Coll 1910–13, Dir Mil Training War Office 1913–14, QMG BEF 1914–15, CGS BEF 1915, CIGS War Office 1915–18, GOC: Eastern Command 1918, GB 1918–19, Army of the Rhine 1919–20, ADC Gen to HM GEORGE V 1917–20, Col RHG, Hon LLD Cantab 1919, Hon DCL Oxon 1920, Pres Br Legion 1932; *m* 8 Sept 1894 Mildred Adelaide (*d* 18 May 1942), 2nd dau of Lt-Gen Charles Thomas Palin, IA, and *d* 12 Feb 1933, having had, with other issue:

1 BRIAN HUBERT, **1st Baron**

2 Hugh William John; *b* 17 Sept 1909; *d* unm 12 March 1928

1 Rosamund Mildred; *b* 21 Sept 1901; *m* 10 May 1922 Lt-Cdr Walter Lockett Agnew, RN (*d* 12 July 1942), s of Leonard Agnew, of Peover Cottage, Knutsford, Cheshire, and Caradiag, Gairloch (see 1937 edn AGNEW, Bt, of Clendry), and *d* 15 July 1961, leaving issue

2 *Helen Millicent; *b* 17 Dec 1905; *m* 18 Oct 1938 Sir Lacey Eric Vincent, 2nd Bt (*qv*), and has issue

The only surv s,

Sir Brian Hubert Robertson, 2nd Bt, and **1st Baron Robertson of Oakridge**, of Oakridge, Co Gloucester (UK), so *cr* 29 June 1961, GCB (1952, CB 1943), GBE (1949, CBE 1942), KCMG (1947), KCVO (1944), DSO (1919), MC, DL (Glos 1965); *b* 22 July 1896; *educ* Charterhouse and RMA Woolwich; served WW I (despatches), Waziristan 1923–24, ret 1 Jan 1934 as Maj Res of Offrs, re-employed WW II (despatches twice): Ch Admin Offr to Earl Alexander of Tunis Italy 1944–45, restored to Active List 1945 as Maj-Gen, Dep Mil Govr CCG 1945, Lt-Gen 1945, Gen 1946, C-in-C and Br Memb Allied Control Cncl 1945–49, UK HC Germany 1949–50, C-in-C Middle East Land Forces and Col Cmdt RE 1950–53, Col Cmdt REME, ADC Gen to HM GEORGE VI 1949–52, Gen RE, chm: Br Tport Commn 1953–61 and Gen Advsy Cncl ITA, dir Dunlop 1961–69 and Internat Sleeping Car Co, Hon Freeman and Liveryman Salters' Co 1949, Master Salters' Co 1965, CStJ, Legn Hon, US Legn Merit, Hon LLD Cantab 1950; *m* 4 Aug 1926 Edith Christina, OStJ (*d* 3 June 1982), dau of James Black Macindoe, of Glasgow, and *d* 29 April 1974, leaving:

1 WILLIAM RONALD ROBERTSON, 2nd and present Baron Robertson of Oakridge

1 Christine Veronica Helen; *b* 3 Aug 1927; *m* 13 Aug 1949 *Col Robert Hugh Cuming, MBE, JP, DL, RSG [Col Robert Cuming MBE JP DL, Home Farm House, Swanbourne, Bucks MK17 0SW], er s of Hugh Philip Cuming, of Essex, and *d* 21 April 1997, leaving:

(1) *Brian Hugh Douglas, MBE (1998); *b* 27 May 1950; *educ* Oratory Sch; Lt-Cdr RN; *m* 25 March 1977 *M Jane, er dau of Capt R N Heard, RN, of Baughurst, Hants, and has:

   1a *Alexander Hugh Robert; *b* 1983

   2a *Hamish Arthur Brian; *b* 1984

   1a *Victoria Helen; *b* 1980

(2) *Alastair Nicholas; *b* 12 July 1958; Capt Roy Scots Dragoon Gds (ret); *m* 31 May 1997 *Victoria, er dau of Peter Avern, of Kirdford, W Sussex

(1) *Frances Mary Christine; *b* 14 Dec 1952; *m* 1981 *Cdr Francis John Cadman Bradshaw, LVO, RN (*see* CADMAN, B)

2 *(Catherine) Fiona [The Hon Mrs Chapman, 23 Church End, Milton Bryan, Milton Keynes MK17 9HR]; *b* 13 Aug 1939; *m* 21 Jan 1965 *Allan Claude Chapman, DL, er s of Claude Frederick Chapman, of Accrington, Lancs, and has:

(1) *Caroline Fiona; *b* 1968

(2) *Katharine Jean; *b* 1968 (twin); *m* 1993 *David J Cook

ROBINSON of Hawthornden, Wynberg and Dudley House

Arms: Vert three bezants chevronwise between two chevronels, the whole between three demi-stags couped or. **Crest:** A demi-stag or charged with two chevronels vert, supporting with the dexter leg a flagstaff in bend sinister proper, pendant therefrom a banner vert charged with a bezant. **Motto:**   ('I have found').
Creation: Bt. (UK) 27 July 1908.

SIR WILFRED HENRY FREDERICK ROBINSON, 3RD BT, of Hawthornden, Wynberg, in the Province of the Cape of Good Hope in the Union of South Africa, and Dudley House, City of Westminster [Sir Wilfred Robinson Bt, 24 Ennismore Gdns, London SW7 1AB]; *b* 24 Dec 1917; *s* unc 1954; *educ* Diocesan Coll Rondesbosch and St John's Coll Cambridge (BA 1939 MA 1944); Maj Devonshire Regt and Parachute Regt WW II, V-Pncpl Diocesan Coll Sch Rondesbosch, Finance Offr Soc Genealogists 1980–92; *m* 14 March 1946 *Margaret Alison Kathleen, only dau of Frank Mellish, MC, of Cape Town, and has:

1 +PETER FRANK [Peter Robinson Esq, 9 Bingham St, London N1]; *b* 23 June 1949; *m* 1988 *Alison Jane, est dau of D Bradley, of Rochester, Kent, and has three daus

1 *Suzanne Moira [Mrs Steen Rasmussen, Little Marlow Cottage, Wolfe St, Wynberg, CP, S Africa]; *b* 6 June 1947; *m* 23 April 1969 *Steen Flamand Rasmussen, s of H B Rasmussen, of Copenhagen

2 *Clementine Anne Eileen; *b* 31 July 1957; *m* 1981 *Jeffrey Foulser

Lineage: ROBERT JOHN ROBINSON; *m* Martha Emily (*d* 1854), dau of William Henry Strutt, and *d* 1886, having had a yst s:

Sir Joseph Benjamin Robinson, 1st Bt (UK), so *cr* 27 July 1908, of Hawthornden, Wynberg, in the Cape of Good Hope in the Union of S Africa, and Dudley House, City of Westminster, JP Kimberley; *b* 3 Aug 1840; MLA, Mayor Kimberley 1880, cmdt Basuto War, organised and cmded first mounted vol force Griqualand W, chm Robinson's S African Banking Co and gold mines in Transvaal; *m* 3 Oct 1877 Elizabeth Rebecca (*d* 30 March 1930), dau of James Ferguson, of Kimberley, and *d* 30 Oct 1929, having had:

1 Frederick Eustace; *b* 25 Sept 1878; *d* unm 7 May 1917

2 **Sir Joseph Benjamin Robinson, 2nd Bt**; *b* 11 March 1887; *educ* Eton and Trin Coll Cambridge; Rep Union Parl S Africa for Randfontein 1915–19 and Wynberg 1932–38; *m* 5 Sept 1935 Alice Josephine, dau of Daniel Cullen, of Omeath, Co Louth, and *dsp* 16 Nov 1954

3 Wilfred Henry; *b* 18 July 1889; *m* 29 April 1914 Eileen (*d* 30 June 1963), dau of Frederick St Leger, of Claremont, S Africa, and *d* 25 Nov 1922, leaving:

(1) Sir WILFRED HENRY FREDERICK ROBINSON, **3rd and present Bt**

(1) Moira; *b* 24 March 1915; *m* May 1838; *dsp* 8 April 1940

4 Arthur John; *b* 6 April 1891; *d* unm 15 Dec 1922

5 Reginald Charles; *b* 18 Dec 1892; *d* unm 16 Dec 1926

1 Constance Eleanor; *d* 1 April 1935

2 Ida Louise; granted rank and title of Princess by KING OF ITALY for her husb's servs; *m* 21 Sept 1921 Count Natale Labia (*d* 9 Jan 1936), Italian Min Plen in S Africa, and *d* 6 March 1961, leaving issue

3 Maud; *m* 15 Oct 1916 George Young, of London

4 Leonora

5 Elizabeth Rebecca; *d* in infancy

6 Florence Mildred

7 Kathleen Frances; *d* in infancy

8 Josephine; *d* in infancy

ROBINSON of London

Arms: Quarterly: 1st and 4th, quarterly crenellée gules and or, in the 1st quarter, upon the battlements of a tower argent, a lion of England of the second (augmentation granted 20 Aug 1663); 2nd and 3rd, vert a buck trippant within an orle of trefoils slipped or (for ROBINSON). **Crest:** A buck trippant or, collared and lined vert, the collar charged with three trefoils slipped or.
Creation: Bt. (E) 22 June 1660.

SIR JOHN JAMES MICHAEL LAUD ROBINSON, 11TH BT, of London, DL (Northants 1984) [Sir John Robinson Bt DL, Cranford Hall, Cranford, Northants NN14 4AL]; *b* 19 Jan 1943; *s* gf 1975; *educ* Eton and Trin Coll Dublin (BA); chartered fin analyst, pres Northants BRC 1982–90, chm Celebrity Fabrics Ltd, St Andrew's Hosp Northampton 1984–94, Northampton Gen Hosp NHS Tst 1994–; *m* 1968 *(Kathryn) Gayle Elizabeth, only child of Stuart Nelson Keyes, of Orillia, Ontario, and has:

1 +MARK CHRISTOPHER MICHAEL VILLIERS; *b* 23 April 1972

2 +Alexander Frederick Stuart Laud; *b* 1973

1 *Kathryn Anne Elizabeth; *b* 1985

Lineage: Ven WILLIAM ROBINSON (half-bro of Archbp Laud); DD, Archdeacon Nottingham 1635; had a 3rd s:

Sir John Robinson, 1st Bt (E), so *cr* 22 June 1660; *b* 1625; Alderman, Ld Mayor London 1662–63, MP City London 1660 and Rye 1661–79, HEICS, Lt Tower London 1660–79; *m* Dec 1654 Anne (*m* 2nd Sept 1680 William Shenton and *d* Jan 1699), dau of Sir George Whitmore, of Barnes, Surrey, and *d* Feb 1679/80, having by her had:

1 William (Sir); *b* 16 Dec 1655; *d* unm *vp* 14 Feb 1678/9

2 **Sir John Robinson, 2nd Bt**, of Farming Woods, Northants; *b* 1660; *m* 1686 Mary, dau of Sir William Dudley, 1st Bt, and *d* 1693, having had:

(1) Mary; *m* 5 Jan 1708/9, as his 2nd w, 4th Earl of Wemyss (*see* WEMYSS and MARCH, E) and *dsp* between 17 July 1711 and 8 Sept 1712

(2) Anne; *m* July 1718 Richard Fitzpatrick, 1st Baron Gowran, and *d* 24 Nov 1744, leaving issue

3 **Sir James Robinson, 3rd Bt**; *b* 1669; *m* c 1 May 1699 Anne (*d* 1728), 2nd dau and coheir of Sir William Jesson, of Newhouse, Warwicks (*see* JERSEY, E), and *d* 28 Aug 1731, having had an est s:

(1) **Sir John Robinson, 4th Bt**; *b* 1705; Sheriff Northants 1737; *m* 1st 5 May 1726 Mary (*d* 2 Feb 1733/4), only dau and heiress of John Morgan, of Kinsthorpe, Northants, by Triphena, dau and heiress of Robert Sheffield (*see* SHEFFIELD, Bt) and had, with other issue:

  1 GEORGE (Sir), **5th Bt**

(1) (cont.) **Sir John** *m* 2nd 7 June 1736 Elizabeth Perkins, of Marston, Warwicks, and *d* 31 Aug 1765, having by her had a s and dau

The 4th Bt's est s,

Sir George Robinson, 5th Bt; *b* 1730; MP Northampton 1774–80; *m* 2 Dec 1764 Dorothea (*d* 27 Jan 1815), only child of John Chester, of London, by Elizabeth, dau of Sir William Chester, Bt, of Chicheley, by Penelope, dau of George Hewett, of Stretton, Leics, thus acquiring those estates, and *d* 10 Oct 1815, having had, with other issue:

1 **Sir George Robinson, 6th Bt**; *b* 1765; MP Northampton 1820–32; *d* unm 23 Nov 1833

2 William Villiers (Rev); Rector Grafton Underwood and Irchester-cum-Wollaston, Northants; *m* 10 Dec 1795 Anne, dau of Stamp Brooksbank by Anne, dau of Thomas Gataker, and *d* 14 Jan 1829, leaving, with other issue:

  (1) GEORGE STAMP (Sir), **7th Bt**

  (1) Caroline Penelope; *m* 29 Oct 1834 Herman Merivale, CB (*d* 8 Feb 1874), U-Sec India, and had issue

  (2) Emma; *m* 12 Nov 1834 Rev William Duthy (*d* 1889), Rector Sudborough, and had issue

3 Charles; *m* 28 Feb 1805 Charlotte (*m* 2nd 15 June 1814 John George Boss, Capt RN, and *d* 11 Sept 1832), dau of Sir James Pennyman, Bt (*see* 1852 edn), and *d* 8 May 1805

1 Frances Dorothea; *m* 7 May 1790 Charles Hoare (*see* HOARE, Bt, of Barn Elms)

2 Penelope; *m* 12 Oct 1789 Robert Willis Blencowe, of Hayes, Middx, and had issue (*see* below)

The 6th Bt's n,

Rev Sir George Stamp Robinson, 7th Bt; *b* 29 Aug 1797; *educ* Oxford (MA); Rector Cranford, Hon Canon Peterborough; *m* 24 May 1827 his cousin Emma (*d* 20 Jan 1874), 6th dau of Robert Willis Blencowe, and *d* 9 Oct 1873, having had, with other issue:

1 **Sir John Blencowe Robinson, 8th Bt**; *b* 20 May 1830; *m* 5 Dec 1861 Winifred, est dau of Rev Edward Stewart (*see* GALLOWAY, E), and *dsp* 10 Aug 1877

2 FREDERICK LAUD (Sir), **9th Bt**

1 Dorothea Ann Eliza; *m* 27 Oct 1865 Adml Sir Anthony Hiley Hoskins, GCB (*dsp* 21 June 1901), and *d* 7 Oct 1901

The 8th Bt's bro,

Sir Frederick Laud Robinson, 9th Bt, JP; *b* 28 June 1843; Rector Cranford; *m* 14 Dec 1870 Madeleine Caroline (*d* 21 Feb 1909), est dau of Frederick Sartoris, of Rushden Hall, Northants, and *d* 6 Feb 1893, leaving:

1 FREDERICK VILLIERS LAUD (Sir), **10th Bt**

1 Evelyn Dorothy; *b* 4 Aug 1875; *m* 31 Jan 1900 Capt Lindsay Ralph Bagnall, Dep Assist Dir Rlwy Tport, s of Charles Bagnall, MP, and *d* 20 Dec 1963

2 Marjorie Sybil; *b* 11 Jan 1877; *m* 17 Jan 1899 Charles Brooke Whitaker Brook (*d* 19 April 1930), of Geddington, Kettering, s of William Brook, of Healey Ho, Netherton, and *d* 1 March 1967, leaving issue

3 Sylvia Joan; *b* 23 May 1883; *m* 1st 27 April 1903 her sister's bro-in-law Lt-Col Charles Edward Bagnall, 4th Yorks Regt (*d* 1 April 1923), s of Charles Bagnall, MP; *m* 2nd 24 Sept 1925 Maj Archibald Donald Mackinnon, CMG, OBE (*d* 5 Sept 1937), MD, of Isle of Skye, 6th s of Rev Donald Mackinnon, DD, Min Strath, Skye, and *d* 19–

The 9th Bt's only s,

Sir Frederick Villiers Laud Robinson, 10th Bt, MC, JP (Northants); *b* 4 Dec 1880; *educ* Wellington Coll; Capt 2nd Bn Northants Regt, Boer War 1902 (medal with four clasps) and WW I (wounded twice, despatches, Croix de Guerre), Maj 3rd Bn Northants Regt, APM 1915–19; *m* 1st 27 March 1913 (*divorce* 1933) Eileen Minna (*d* 4 Jan 1965), est dau of Harry I Higham, of Mayfair; *m* 2nd 16 Aug 1933 (Frances) Joyce, er dau of Arthur Tyrwhitt-Drake, of Crendle, Sherborne, Dorset, and *d* 19 March 1975, having by his 1st w had:

1 Michael Frederick Laud; *b* 23 Jan 1914; *educ* Eton; Capt Northants Yeo WW II; *m* 1st 23 Dec 1941 (*divorce* 1966) Elizabeth, er dau of Brig Charles Bridge, CMG, DSO, MC, of W Wratting Pk, Cambs; *m* 2nd 3 June 1966 Joan Isabel, dau of Vernon James Reveley, of Upper Warlingham, Surrey, and widow of Hon John Breckinridge Fermor-Hesketh (*see* HESKETH, B), and *d* 16 May 1971, leaving by his 1st w:

  (1) Sir JOHN JAMES MICHAEL LAUD ROBINSON, **11th and present Bt**

  (1) *Anne Elizabeth Villiers; *b* 11 Jan 1950; *m* 1975 *Derek Alan Buckley, and has:

    1a *Samuel Michael; *b* 1978

2 John Ronald Villiers; *b* 8 Sept 1915; Maj KRRC WW II; *ka* Jan 1943

ROBINSON of Toronto

Arms: Or, on a chevron between three stags trippant vert as many cinquefoils of the field. **Crest:** A stag trippant vert bezantée.
Motto: *Propere et provide* ('Quickly and cautiously').
Creation: Bt. (UK) 21 Sept 1854.

SIR CHRISTOPHER PHILIPSE ROBINSON, 8TH BT, of Toronto Canada [Sir Christopher Robinson Bt, Kirks Ferry, 460 RRI, Chelsea, Quebec J0X 1N0, Canada]; *b* 10 Nov 1938; *s* kinsman 1988; *m* 6 Oct 1962 *Judith Barbara, dau of Richard Bishop Duncan, of Ottawa, and has had:

1 Christopher Duncan; *b* 27 Oct 1965; *d* 2 April 1967

2 +PETER DUNCAN; *b* 31 July 1967

3 +Jonathan Richard; *b* 7 Oct 1969

Lineage: JOHN ROBINSON, of Crostwick, Romaldkirk, Yorks; *m* Anne Dent and had a 2nd s:

GEORGE ROBINSON, of Cleasby, Yorks; *m* Frances, dau of Thomas Layton, of Cleasby, and *d* by 1634, having had, with an est s (Thomas, London merchant, royalist Civil War, hence heavily fined, *d* 1648) and an est dau (Clara, *m* 1689 Theophilus Bolton, London merchant, and *d* 1684) a 3rd s:

JOHN ROBINSON, of Cleasby; fined for royalism; *m* Elizabeth (*d* 1688), dau of Christopher Potter, of Cleasby, and *d* 1651, leaving, with other issue:

1 CHRISTOPHER

2 John, PC (1714); *b* Nov 1650; *educ* Oxford (MA 1683, Fell Oriel 1675–86, DD 1710); Chaplain to Swedish Embassy, Envoy Sweden 1683–1708, Vicar Lastington, Yorks, 1694–1709, Dean Windsor 1709, Bp Bristol 1710, Ld Privy Seal 1711, 1st English Plen Utrecht Peace Conf 1712–13, Bp London 1714–23; *m* 1st Mary Langton; *m* 2nd Emma Cornwallis and *dsp* 11 April 1723, when his Manor of Hewick-under-Bridge, nr Ripon, passed to his n Christopher in Virginia but was eventually sold 1778 to 1st Baron Grantley (*qv*)

1 Clara; *m* Sir Edward Wood, Gentleman Usher to CHARLES II's w CATHERINE; Envoy Extrdy Sweden

The est surv s,

CHRISTOPHER ROBINSON, of Rappahannock, Middx Co, Virginia; *b* Cleasby 1645; Sec Virginia *temp* WILLIAM (III) and MARY; *m* 1st Agatha (*d* 25 Jan 1685/6), dau of Bertram Obert, of Rappahannock; *m* 2nd 17 Sept 1687 Catherine (*d* 23 April 1692), dau of Theophilus Hone, of Jamestown, Va., and widow of Robert Beverley, of Beverley, Yorks, and later Virginia, and *d* between 27 Jan and 6 March 1692/3, having had by his 1st w, with other issue:

1 CHRISTOPHER

2 John, of Urbanna, Middx Co, Va.; *b* 1683; Pres Cncl of Virginia; *m* 1st Catharine, dau of Robert Beverley, of Rappahannock; *m* 2nd Mary Welsh, of Essex Co, Va., and *d* 24 Aug 1749, having had:

  (1) Christopher; *b* 1 July 1703; *educ* Oxford (MA 1729); Fell Oriel Coll; *d* unm 20 April 1738

  (2) John; *b* 3 Feb 1704; Treasurer and Speaker Ho Burgesses Virginia; *d* 14 May 1766, leaving issue

  (3) William, of Spotsylvania, Va.; *b* 25 Jan 1709; *m c* 17 Feb 1737 Agatha, dau of Harry Beverley

  (4) Henry; *b* 7 April 1718; *m* Mary Waring and had issue

  (5) Beverley; *b* 11 Jan 1722; Col Guides and Pioneers, in War of American Independence raised King's Loyal American Regt , in which four of his sons served; *m* 7 July 1747 Susanna (*d* 22 Nov 1822), dau of Frederick Philipse, of NY, and *d* 9 April 1792, having had:

    1a Beverley; *b* 10 March 1754; Lt-Col Loyal American Regt; *m* Anna Dorothea Barclay and *d* NY 1815, leaving issue

    2a Morris; *b* 15 Nov 1759; Assist Barrack Master Gen, Lt-Col War American Independence; *m* Margaret Waring and *d* 28 Aug 1815, leaving issue

    3a John; *b* 15 July 1762; Dep Paymaster Gen, memb Cncl and Treasurer Forces of New Brunswick, served War American Independence; *m* Elizabeth (*d* 1828), dau of George Duncan Ludlow, Ch Justice New Brunswick, and *d* 8 Oct 1828

    4a Frederick Philipse (Sir), GCB; *b* 24 Sept 1764; Gen, Govr Tobago; *d* 1 Jan 1852, leaving issue

5a William Henry (Sir), KH; *b* 7 Nov 1765; Gen Forces Canada; *d* 10 Feb 1836, leaving issue

The est s,

CHRISTOPHER ROBINSON, of Urbana; *b* 1682; *m* 12 Oct 1703 Judith (*d* 18 Nov 1720), dau of Christopher Wormley, of Rappahannock, and widow of (a) Corbin Griffin and (b) William Beverley, and *d* 20 Feb 1726, leaving, with other issue:

1 Christopher, of Ch Ch, Middx Co, Va.; *b* 1705; *m* 1st Mary Barclay and had:

(1) Christopher; *b* 9 March 1737/8; *d* unm 1775

1 (cont.) Christopher Robinson *m* 2nd 6 May 1752 Sarah Wormley (*d* 1772) and *d* 1768, having by her had:

(1) Elizabeth; *m* 19 May 1792 William Steptoe

2 Peter, of St John's, King William County, Va.; *b* 5 March 1718; *educ* Oriel Coll Oxford; memb Virginia Ho Burgesses 1758–61; *m* 9 Aug 1750 Sarah Lister and *d* 1765, leaving, with a yr s and three daus:

(1) Christopher, of York (now Toronto) Canada; *b* 1763; Offr Queen's Rangers War American Independence; barrister; *m* May 1784 Esther (*m* 2nd 5 Sept 1802 Elisha Beman and *d* 27 July 1827), dau of Rev John Sayre, of New Brunswick, and *d* 2 Nov 1798, having had three sons and three daus; the 2nd s:

1a **Sir John Beverley Robinson, 1st Bt** (UK), so *cr* 21 Sept 1854, of Beverley Ho, Toronto, CB; *b* 26 July 1791; barrister, Actg Attorney-Gen Upper Canada 1812, Slr Gen 1815, Attorney-Gen 1818, Ch Justice Upper Canada 1829, Pres Ct Appeal and Chllr Trin Coll Upper Canada; *m* 5 June 1817 Emma (*d* 29 May 1865), only surv child of Charles Walker, of Harlesden, Middx, and n of William Merry, Dep Sec War, and *d* 30 Jan 1863, having had:

1b **Sir James Lukin Robinson, 2nd Bt**; *b* 27 March 1818; barrister Middle Temple; *m* 15 May 1845 Elizabeth (*d* 7 March 1896), est dau of John Arnold, late of Halsted, Kent, then of Toronto, and *d* 21 Aug 1894, having had:

1c Henry Grassett; *b* 16 April 1849; *d* unm 8 Dec 1869

2c **Sir Frederick Arnold Robinson, 3rd Bt**; *b* 9 Nov 1855; *m* 15 Nov 1893 Mary Elizabeth (*d* 10 Oct 1942), dau of Issac Hammond Filer, of Quebec, and *dsp* 24 Aug 1901

1c Emma; *d* unm 30 Oct 1864

2c Caroline Longley; *d* young 5 April 1852

3c Marion Louisa; *m* 7 July 1882 Francis Osmond Cayley and *d* 1943, leaving issue (*see* CAYLEY, Bt)

4c Julia Margaret Adelaide

2b John Beverley; *b* 20 Feb 1820; barrister, MP W Toronto, Pres Exec Cncl Canada 1862, Lt-Govr Ontario 1880–87; *m* 30 June 1847 Mary Jane (*d* 18 Jan 1892), 2nd dau of Christopher Alexander Hagerman, Puisne Judge Queen's Bench Upper Canada, and *d* 19 June 1896, leaving:

1c **Sir John Beverley Robinson, 4th Bt**; *b* 2 June 1848; helped suppress Fenian disturbances Canada 1866 (wounded Limeridge); *m* 1st 3 Sept 1873 Margaret (*d* 13 Feb 1875), dau of James MacDonell, of Toronto, and had:

1 Margaret Mary; *m* 21 April 1896 Dalton McCarthy, of Toronto, barrister, and had issue

1c (cont.) **Sir John** *m* 2nd 18 Oct 1892 Eleanor Biggar (*d* 20 April 1947), dau of Charles Henry Cooke, MD, FRCSE, of Toronto, and *d* 11 Nov 1933, having by her had:

1d **Sir John Beverley Robinson, 5th Bt**; *b* 12 Feb 1895; *m* 27 Oct 1934 Maud Eva, 3rd dau of William Charles Coo, of Toronto, Canada, and *dsp* 6 Nov 1948

2c Strachan Napier, of Toronto; *b* 25 Sept 1849

3c Christopher Conway, KC; *b* 17 March 1853; *m* 23 June 1880 Jane (*d* 1915), dau of Norman Torquil McLeod, of Toronto, and *d* 2 March 1907, leaving:

1d **Sir John Beverley Robinson, 6th Bt**; *b* 13 Jan 1885; *m* 5 Nov 1912 Constance Marie, dau of Robert W Pentecost, and *d* 8 June 1954, leaving:

1e **Sir John Beverley Robinson, 7th Bt**, of Toronto; *b* 3 Oct 1913; *d* 1988

1e *Constance Suzette Beverley [Mrs Constance Sutherland, Apt 212, 21 Woodlawn Rd, E Guelph, Ontario, Canada]; *b* 1914; *m* 1939 (*divorce* 1969) Edward William Sutherland and has:

1f *John Warren; *b* 1942; *m* 1962 *Kathleen Croft, of Hamilton, Ontario, and has:

1g *David; *b* 1963

1g *Beth; *b* 1964

2f *Harley Peter; *b* 1948; *m* 1966 *Patricia Carter, of Guelph, Ontario, and has:

1g *Kimberley Deanne; *b* 1967

2g *Joy Patrick; *b* 1969

3f *David Victor; *b* 1948; *m* 1971 *Jacquie Smith, of Hamilton, Ontario, and has:

1g *Tracey; *b* 1973

1f *Wendy Gayle; *b* 1940; *m* 1961 *Anthony Ian Roberts, of London, Ontario, and has:

1g *Paul Douglas; *b* 1968

1g *Nancy Marie; *b* 1962

2g *Patricia; *b* 1964

2f *Suzette Marion; *b* 1944; *m* 1964 (*divorce* 1969) David Teft, of Grimsby, Ontario

2d Norman Macleod Beverley; *b* 8 Sept 1887; *d* 16 Aug 1949

1d Minnie Marguerite (Pearl) Beverley; *b* 13 June 1881

2d Kathleen Augusta Beverley; *b* 1882; *m* 17 Aug 1916 Frank Lee Ingels, of Los Angeles, s of George Ingels, of Kokomo, Ind.

1a Minnie Caroline; *m* 6 Nov 1881 Capt William Forsyth Grant, 82nd Regt (*d* 18 April 1921), and *d* 2 Nov 1923

2c Augusta Louisa; *m* 8 Oct 1898 Fielde Stewart Houston (*d* 7 Feb 1910), of Toronto, barrister, and had issue

3b Christopher, KC (Ontario), of Toronto; *b* 21 Jan 1828; *m* 2 July 1879 Elizabeth Street (*d* 7 April 1927), dau of Josiah Burr Plumb, Speaker Canadian Senate, and *d* 31 Oct 1905, leaving:

1c Christopher Charles, KC; *b* 29 Aug 1883; *m* 31 Dec 1907 Isabel Hodgins (*d* 19 Nov 1962), dau of Charles Robert Webster Biggar, KC, of Toronto, and *d* 28 Feb 1948, leaving:

1d Christopher, QC (Ontario 1950); *b* 22 Jan 1909; *m* 28 Jan 1933 Neville Taylor, dau of R-Adml Walter Rockwell Gherardi, USN, and had:

1e Sir CHRISTOPHER PHILIPSE ROBINSON, **8th and present Bt**

2e +Walter Gherardi, QC [Walter Robinson Esq QC, 69 Douglas Crescent, Toronto M4W 2E6, Canada]; *b* 9 June 1940; *m* 10 Aug 1963 *Alison Jean, est dau of Robert Stewart Fraser, of Vancouver, and has:

1f *Hilary Elizabeth; *b* 15 Nov 1967

2f *Alicia Isabel; *b* 1970

3e +John Mowat; *b* 19 Oct 1942; *m* 1st 24 May 1969 (*divorce* 1982) Joyce, dau of Roy Harrod, of Orsett, Essex; *m* 2nd 1988 *Jane Stewart, dau of Duncan K MacTavish, QC, OBE, of Ottawa and by his 1st w has:

1f +Graeme Harrod; *b* 24 Jan 1970

2f +Christopher Mowat; *b* 1972

1e Neville Gherardi; *b* 25 Sept 1935; *m* 29 Dec 1956 (*divorce* 1967) Georges-Henri Carasso (*d* 1974), of Paris, and had:

1f *Jean Christophe; *b* 16 Feb 1959

2f *Robin; *b* 1979

2d Peter Beverley, of New York; *b* 1915; F/O RAAF (Res); *m* 1st 1938 Elizabeth (*d* 26 Aug 1965), dau of Halsey Frederick, of Mountain Lakes, NJ, and has:

1e *Wendy Bouquet; *b* 1944; *m* 1965 (*divorce* 1975) Martin V Boelitz, of Boston, and has:

1f *Jessica Elizabeth; *b* 1968

2e *Susan Celina; *b* 1946; *m* 1st 1966 (*annulled* 1967) Ira James Sandperl; *m* 2nd Feb 1969 (*divorce* 1981) Pierre Bain, of Pebble Beach, Calif., s of — Bain, of Camps sur Artuby, France; *m* 3rd 19– *David Peterson

2d (cont.) Peter Robinson *m* 2nd 1966 Nancy Carol (*d* 1994), dau of Norris Konheim, of NY, and *d* 1992, leaving by her:

1e +Kenneth Beverley; *b* 1 Nov 1967

3e +Alice Natalie; *b* 24 Aug 1969

3d +Hugh Lukin [Hugh Robinson Esq, 401 Woburn Ave, Toronto, Canada]; *b* 19 June 1916; *m* 1st 1941 (*divorce*1972) Ruth Elizabeth, dau of John Cotter, of Ottawa; *m* 2nd 1973 *Lillian Ruth, dau of Jacob Milton, of Toronto, and by his 1st w has:

1e +John Michael, of Thunder Bay, Ontario; *b* 1946

2e +David Lukin, of Los Angeles; *b* 1951

1e +Elizabeth; *b* 1955; *m* 1976 *Kenneth Quinlan, of Saskatoon, and has:

1f *Andrea; *b* 1984

1d Helen Hilary; *b* 13 Jan 1912; *m* 1936 Douglas Harverson and had:

1e *Philippa Audrey; *b* 17 Nov 1939; *m* 28 April 1971 *Paul Binder Elmhirst, 2nd s of Alfred Octavius Elmhirst, of Houndhill, Worsborough Bridge, Yorks, and has two sons

2e *Celia Margaret; *b* 6 Dec 1942

1d (cont.) Mrs Douglas Harverson also adopted:

*Anthony Paul Timothy; *b* 1 Oct 1962

2d Laura Beverley; *b* 3 May 1913; *m* 1st (*divorce* 1956) Andrew Kalitinsky, of Fort Worth, Tex.; *m* 2nd 1957 *Adolf Kurt Placzek, s of Oswald Placzek, of Vienna, and by her 1st husb has:

1e *Sylvia; *b* 1945; *m* 1966 (*divorce* 1979) Roger Alan Barkley and has:

1f *Ian Andrew; *b* 1970

3d *Wendela Isabel [Mrs Andrew Kalitinsky, 6424 Muirlands Dve, La Jolla, CA, USA]; *b* 4 Nov 1918; *m* 1957 her former bro-in-law *Andrew Kalitinsky

2c (John) Beverley; *b* 19 Oct 1884; 2nd Lt RFC WW I (POW 1915 escaped 1917); *m* 20 Jan 1920 Marion, 2nd dau of Weymouth de Lisle Schreiber, of Toronto, and *d* 24 Jan 1954, leaving:

1d +John Beverley; *b* 20 May 1922; Lt RCNVR WW II; *m* 6 Aug 1948 *Constance Anne, dau of James Bruce MacKinnon, of Toronto, and has:

1e +Bruce Beverley; *b* 11 Aug 1952

2e +Christopher Charles; *b* 13 Dec 1957

1e *Linda de Lisle; *b* 12 Dec 1949

2e *Hilary Anne; *b* 8 Oct 1953

2d +Weymouth Hugh Beverley; *b* 11 June 1927; *m* 7 Sept 1956 *Patricia, dau of Robert James Glendening Innis, of Toronto, and has:

1e *Judith Suzanne; *b* 1957

2e *Jennifer Leslie; *b* 1960

1d *Elizabeth de Lisle; *b* 3 Dec 1924; *m* 1st 29 Dec 1946 Lt John Kingsford Herbert Mason, RCN (*d* 14 April 1952); *m* 2nd 1959 Capt John Litter, RCN, and by her 1st husb has:

1e *David; *b* 1950

1e *Marion Thonia; *b* 1948

2e *Philippa; *b* 1952

3c Duncan Strachan; *b* 4 Dec 1886; *m* 11 March 1916 Emily, er dau of J Gordon Watson, of Brandon, Manitoba, and *d* 1956, leaving:

1d +Gordon Strachan; *b* 1917

2d +John Attrachay, of Toronto; *b* 1920

1d *Mary Emily, of Guelph, Ontario; *b* 1917
2d *Anne, of Phoenix, Ariz.; *b* 1922
3d *Daphne, of Toronto; *b* 1928
1c Mary Adelaide Christobel; *b* 1 May 1882; *d* unm 1951
4b Charles Walker (Sir), KCB (1923, CB 1887); *b* 3 April 1836; *educ* Upper Canada Coll and Trin Coll Toronto; served: Indian Mutiny 1858–59 (medal), Ashanti War 1873–74 (despatches, medal with clasp) and Boer War 1879 (despatches, medal with clasp), Maj-Gen Rifle Bde, AAG Aldershot 1884–89, Assist Mil Sec HQ 1889–92, cmded troops Mauritius 1892–95, Lt-Govr and Sec Roy Hosp Chelsea 1895–98; *m* 16 Oct 1884 Margaret Frances (*d* 9 May 1940), dau of Gen Sir Archibald Alison, 2nd Bt, GCB (*see* 1970 edn), and *d* 20 May 1924, leaving:

1c Charles Archibald Beverley; *b* 5 March 1898; *d* 13 Feb 1966
1c Joan Emma Beverley, of Bideford, Devon; *b* 27 May 1892
2c Dorothy Margaret, of Bideford; *b* 20 Oct 1895
1b Emily Merry; *m* 16 April 1846 Gen Sir John Henry Lefroy, KCMG, CB (*d* 11 April 1890), RA, and *d* 25 Jan 1859, leaving issue
2b Augusta Anne; *m* 31 Oct 1844 James McGill Strachan (*d* 20 Jan 1870), of Toronto, Capt 68th Foot, est s of John Strachan, Bp Toronto, and *dsp* 12 Nov 1900
3b Louisa Matilda; *m* 16 April 1846 George William Allan (*d* 24 July 1902), of Moss Pk, Toronto, barrister, and *dsp* 12 May 1852
4b Mary Amelia; *m* 30 April 1863 Hon Donald Macinnes (*d* 1 Dec 1900), of Hamilton, Ontario, and *d* 16 March 1879, leaving issue

ROBOROUGH

QUOD·TIBI·ID·ALII

Arms: Quarterly: 1st and 4th azure, on a chevron between three eagles rising or as many bars gemels gules, on a chief of the second five lozenges of the first (for LOPES); 2nd and 3rd, in a field a fountain issuant thereout a palm-tree all proper (for FRANCO).
Crests: 1 A lion sejant erminois gorged with a collar gemel as in the arms, reposing the dexter paw on a lozenge azure (for LOPES), 2 A dexter arm couped and embowed, habited purpure, the cuff argent, hand proper, holding therein a palm branch vert (for FRANCO).
Supporters: Dexter, a lion proper gorged with a collar gemel and charged on the shoulder with a lozenge azure; sinister, a bull also proper, charged on the shoulder with a like lozenge.
Motto: *Quod tibi, id alii* ('Do as you would be done by').
Creations: Bt. (UK) 1 Nov 1805, B. (UK) 24 Jan 1938.

THE 3RD BARON ROBOROUGH, of Maristow, Co Devon, and a **Baronet** (Sir Henry Massey Lopes, Bt) [The Rt Hon The Lord Roborough, Bickham House, Roborough, Plymouth, S Devon]; *b* 2 Feb 1940; *s* f 1992; *educ* Eton; late Lt Coldstream Gds, ARICS; *m* 1st 26 Oct 1968 (*divorce* 1986) Robyn Zenda Carol, est dau of John Bromwich, of Stamford Hill, Bacchus Marsh, Victoria, Australia, and has:

1 +MASSEY JOHN HENRY; *b* 22 Dec 1969; *educ* Eton and Durham U; *m* 17 Feb 1996 *Jean, dau of Mr Justice Underwood, of Newtown, Tasmania, by Mrs Sandy Sorell, and has:

(1) +Henry Massey Peter; *b* 30 July 1997

2 +Andrew James; *b* 26 April 1971; *educ* Plymouth Coll; *m* 1993 *Kristina Marie Overbeck
1 *Katie Victoria; *b* 24 March 1976
2 *Melinda Clare; *b* 26 July 1978

The 3rd BARON *m* 2nd 1986 *Sarah Anne Pipon, 2nd dau of Colin Baker, of The Glebe Ho, Peter Tavy, Devon, and by her has:

3 *Emily Jane; *b* 1987
4 *Louisa Constance; *b* 1989

Lineage: MORDECAI RODRIGUEZ LOPES, of Clapham; *m* Rebecca, dau of Manasseh Pereira, of Jamaica, and had:

1 Sir MANASSEH LOPES later MANASSEH MASSEY LOPES (roy licence 1805), **1st Bt** (UK), so *cr* 1 Nov 1805, with remainder to his n, of Maristow House, Devon, JP Devon and Wilts; *b* Jamaica 27 Jan 1755; abjured Judaism for C of E 1802; MP New Romney 1802, Barnstaple 1812 and 1818 (unseated 1819

for bribery at Grampound and sentenced to two years in prison and a £1,000-fine [over £31,000 in late-1990s terms]) and Westbury 1823 and 1826; Recorder Westbury; *m* 1795 Charlotte (*d* 23 March 1833), dau of John Yeates, of Monmouth, and *dspm* 26 March 1831, leaving £800,000 (over £33,250,000 in late-1990s terms), and having had:

(1) Esther; *d* unm 1 July 1819
1 ESTHER Lopes; *m* Abraham FRANCO and had:

(1) Sir RALPH FRANCO later LOPES (roy licence under terms of will of uncle, the **1st Bt**), **2nd Bt**, of Maristow, JP (Wilts and Devon), DL; *b* 10 Sept 1788; MP Westbury and S Devon; *m* 8 May 1817 Susan Gibbs (*d* 26 March 1870), est dau of Abraham Ludlow, of Heywood House, Wilts, by Susan, dau of Gaisford Gibbs by Elizabeth, dau of William Maltravers, of Westbury, and *d* 23 Jan 1854, having had:

1a (LOPES) MASSEY (Sir), **3rd Bt**
2a Ralph Ludlow, JP, DL, of Sandridge Park, Melksham, Wilts; *b* 9 Sept 1820; MA; barrister, High Sheriff Wilts 1869, Recorder Devizes 1877–87; *m* 4 Sept 1851 Elizabeth (*d* 23 Dec 1904), 3rd dau of Samuel Trehawke Kekewich, JP, DL, of Peamore, Devon, MP, and *d* 28 Feb 1898, having had, with a dau (*d* unm):

1b Ralph Kekewich; *b* 4 Dec 1852; barrister; *d* unm 22 March 1895
2b Henry Ludlow; *b* 16 March 1854; Capt 2nd Bn HLI; *d* unm 10 Dec 1882
3b George, JP (Wilts), of Sandridge Park; *b* 28 April 1857; *educ* Jesus Coll Cambridge (BA); MInstCE, Maj Engrg and Rlwy Staff Corps RE; *m* 20 Nov 1897 Hon Ernestine Frances Lopes (*d* 2 Sept 1938), 4th dau of 1st BARON LUDLOW OF HEYWOOD (*see* below), and *dsp* 28 June 1910
3a HENRY CHARLES LOPES, 1st BARON LUDLOW OF HEYWOOD, Wilts (UK), so *cr* 26 July 1897, PC (1885), JP (Wilts and Somerset), DL; *b* 3 Oct 1828; *educ* Winchester and Balliol Coll Oxford (BA); barrister Inner Temple 1852 (Bencher 1870, Treas 1890–91), Recorder Exeter 1867–76, QC 1869, High Court Judge 1876–85, ktd 1876, Ld Justice of Appeal 1885–97, MP (C) Launceston 1868–74 and Frome 1874–76; *m* 20 Sept 1854 Cordelia Lucy (*d* 22 Dec 1891), est dau of Erving Clark, of Efford Manor, nr Plymouth, and *d* 25 Dec 1899, having had:

1b HENRY LUDLOW LOPES, 2nd and last BARON LUDLOW OF HEYWOOD, JP (Wilts and Northants); *b* 30 Sept 1865; *educ* Eton and Balliol Coll Oxford (MA); barrister Inner Temple 1890, Pres and Chm Cancer Hosp, Treas St Bartholomew's Hosp, memb LCC Marylebone 1904–07, Capt Roy Wilts Imp Yeo WW I, MFH Hertford; *m* 1st 25 March 1903 Blanche (*d* 7 April 1911), pres Order League of Mercy, dau and coheir of William Holden, of Palace Ho, Lancs, and widow of 7th Baron Howard de Walden (*qv*); *m* 2nd 25 Sept 1919 Alice Sedgwick, DGStJ, JP (*d* 30 Nov 1945), dau of James Mankiewicz, of Bayswater, and widow of Sir Julius Charles Wernher, 1st Bt (*qv*), and *dsp* 8 Nov 1922, when the title expired
1b Susan Ludlow Cordelia; *m* 1 June 1901 Archibald Bence-Jones (*d* 24 Feb 1937), barrister, s of Henry Bence Jones, FRS (*see* GOSFORD, E), and *d* 20 April 1938, leaving issue
2b Cordella Lucy; *m* 18 July 1896 Sir John Hanham, 9th Bt (*qv*), and *d* 18 April 1945, leaving issue
3b Ethel Maud; *d* unm 11 Dec 1943
4b Ernestine Frances; *m* 20 Nov 1897 her cousin George Lopes (*see* above) and *d* 2 Sept 1938
5b Bertha Susan; *m* 17 Dec 1898 1st Viscount Bledisloe (*qv*) and *d* 6 May 1926
4a Edmund Francis; *b* 19 Oct 1833; *d* 28 Feb 1867
5a George Ludlow, JP (Wilts), DL, of Northleigh, Bradford-on-Avon; *b* 31 July 1836; 16th Lancers; *m* 1 April 1871 Georgina Emma (*d* 17 April 1912), dau of Anselmo de Arroyave, and *d* 3 Oct 1909, leaving:

1b George de Arroyave; *b* 9 Jan 1872; *educ* Eton and Balliol Coll Oxford; *m* 9 June 1913 Maude Mary (*d* 14 Feb 1924), dau of Lawrence Cockburn, of Melbourne, and widow of Capt Granville Forbes, 79th Highrs, and *d* 1 Sept 1929
2b John Ludlow (Rev); *b* 9 April 1882; *educ* Exeter Coll Oxford (BA 1905 MA 1908) and Rome (DD 1918); RC priest; *d* unm 18 Sept 1961

The 2nd Bt's est s,
Sir (Lopes) Massey Lopes, 3rd Bt, PC, JP (Wilts and Devon), DL; *b* 14 June 1818; *educ* Oriel Coll Oxford (MA); MP Westbury 1857–68 and S Devon 1868–85, Civil Ld Admlty 1874–80, Devon: CA, High Sheriff 1857; *m* 1st 11 May 1854 Hon Bertha Yarde-Buller (*d* 13 Jan 1872), only dau of 1st Baron Churston (*qv*); *m* 2nd 25 Aug 1874 Louisa (*dsp* 27 April 1908), dau of Sir Robert Newman, 1st Bt (*qv*), and *d* 20 Jan 1908, succeeded by his 1st w (with two unm daus and Adela Elizabeth, *m* 18 Aug 1883 Henry Prescott Hatch, of Brooklyn, NY, and *dsp* March 1890):

Sir Henry Yarde-Buller Lopes, 4th Bt, and **1st Baron Roborough**, of Maristow, Co Devon, so *cr* 24 Jan 1938, JP (Devon), DL; *b* 24 March 1859; *educ* Eton and Balliol Coll Oxford; barrister Inner Temple 1890, MP (C) Grantham 1892–1900 (fought Totnes 1885 and Torquay 1910), Devon: Lt Roy Yeo Cav, Hon Capt Vol Regt, High Sheriff 1914, chm CC 1916–38, Hon Treas Roy Hosp and Home for Incurables Putney; *m* 10 Oct 1891 Lady Albertha Louisa Florence (*d* 25 March 1941), dau of 4th Earl of Mount Edgcumbe (*qv*), and *d* 14 April 1938, leaving:

1 MASSEY HENRY EDGECUMBE, **2nd Baron**
1 Katharine Frederica Albertha; *b* 25 Sept 1892; *m* 9 Oct 1919 3rd Baron Carnock (*qv*) and *d* 24 Aug 1968, leaving issue
2 Bertha Louisa Victoria; *b* 1895; *m* 29 Dec 1921 V-Adml Sir James Murray Pipon, KBE, CB, CMG, MVO (*d* 14 Jan 1976), est s of Capt John Pakenham Pipon, CB, CMG, RN, and *d* 24 Feb 1971, leaving:

(1) *Michael James; *b* 17 Nov 1933
(1) *Penelope Elizabeth; *b* 11 Dec 1922; *m* 10 Aug 1948 *Colin Harris Baker, s of J R Baker, of Cross Park, Heavitree, Exeter, and has:

1a *Martin; *b* 24 Nov 1959
1a *Ruth; *b* 20 Aug 1949
2a *Sarah; *b* 29 Dec 1951
3a *Fiona; *b* 26 March 1958

(2) *Hermione Alice; *b* 8 May 1928

3 Margaret Beatrice; *m* 26 Jan 1927 Maj Henry Archibald Roger Graham (*d* 25 Feb 1970), er s of Maj Henry Graham, and had:

(1) *Roger Henry William GRAHAM later GRAHAM-PALMER (deed poll 14 Nov 1968) [Roger Graham-Palmer Esq, Cefn Pk, Wrexham LL13 9TT]; *b* 14 Feb 1941; *educ* Radley and Emmanuel Coll Cambridge (MA Ag); *m* 11 June 1969 *Vanessa Audrey, er dau of Walter Neville Drury, TD, of Little Brookstreet, Edenbridge, Kent, and has:

1a *Archibald Roger; *b* 17 July 1970; *educ* Radley and RAC

1a *Annabelle Rae; *b* 29 Sept 1971; *educ* Tudor Hall and Leeds U

2a *Alice Margaret; *b* 26 May 1974; *educ* Ellesmere Sch

3a *Violet Milicent Vanessa; *b* 2 April 1978; *educ* Sherborne and Reading U

(1) *Gillian Mary Millicent [Lady Wagner, 68 Chelsea Sq, London SW3 6LE; Wyndham Cottage, Crespigny Rd, Aldeburgh, Suffolk]; *b* 26 Oct 1927; *educ* Cheltenham Ladies' Coll and Geneva U (Licencée ès Sciences Morales); *m* 26 Feb 1953 Sir Anthony Richard Wagner, KCVO, DLitt, FSA, Garter King of Arms (*d* 5 May 1995), only s of Orlando Henry Wagner, of Chelsea, and has:

1a *Roger Henry Melchior [Roger Wagner, 68 Chelsea Sq, London SW3 6LE]; *b* 28 Feb 1957; *educ* Eton

2a *Mark Anthony; *b* 18 Dec 1958

1a *Lucy Elizabeth Millicent; *b* 22 Oct 1954

(2) *Fiona Margaret [Miss Fiona Graham, 336 Central Pk West, New York 25, NY, USA]; *b* 4 Sept 1929; *educ* Cheltenham Ladies' Coll and London U (MB, BS Lond); MD NY State Bd Certification on Psychiatry USA

(3) *Mavis Ellen [Mrs Anthony Simmonds, 21 Fellbrook, Ham, Surrey]; *b* 8 Dec 1933; *m* March 1960 *Anthony Brian Simmonds, only s of Brian Simmonds and Mrs H A Coysh, and has:

1a *Graham Anthony Scott; *b* July 1961

2a *Keith Richard Scott; *b* July 1961

(4) *Alison Helen Constance, MBE [Mrs Geoffrey Heath MBE, Longacre, Horsleys Green, High Wycombe, Bucks HP14 3UX]; *b* 6 Jan 1937; *educ* Somerville Coll Oxford (MA); *m* 7 Oct 1961 *Geoffrey William Heath, MA, ARCO, only s of W E Heath, and has:

1a *Simon Geoffrey; *b* 1 Aug 1969

1a *Nicola Jane; *b* 14 Nov 1965; *educ* Newnham Coll Cambridge

2a *Miranda Gillian; *b* 24 March 1967; *educ* The Queen's Coll Oxford

4 Constance Elizabeth; *b* 24 Aug 1901; T/Ldy-in-Waiting to HRH THE DUCHESS OF GLOUCESTER 1963; *m* 17 Oct 1939 Sir Marcus John Cheke, KCVO, CMG (*d* 22 June 1960), Min Holy See, 2nd s of Col Edward George Cheke, of The Cockpit, Fair Oak, Hants

The 1st BARON's only s,

MASSEY HENRY EDGECUMBE LOPES, **2nd Baron Roborough**, JP (Devon 1951), DL (1946); *b* 4 Oct 1903; *educ* Eton and Ch Ch Oxford (BA); ADC to Govr-Gen and C-in-C S Africa 1936–37, Maj RSG WW II (wounded), Hon Col 396 LAA Regt RA (TA) 1947–50, Hon Col Devon Army Cadet Force; Devon: V-Lt 1947–58, Ld Lt 1958–92, CA 1958, chm: Dartmoor Nat Pk, Devon Outward Bound Sch, High Steward Barnstaple, memb Cncl of HRH THE PRINCE OF WALES 1958–68, KStJ, Hon LLD Exeter; *m* 15 Oct 1936 *Helen [The Rt Hon Helen Lady Roborough, Bickham Barton, Roborough, S Devon], only dau of Lt-Col Edward Alfred Finch Dawson, JP, Rifle Bde, of Launde Abbey, Leics, and *d* 1992, leaving:

1 HENRY MASSEY LOPES, **3rd and present Baron Roborough**

2 +George Edward [The Hon George Lopes, Gnaton Hall, Yealmpton, Devon PL8 2HU]; *b* 22 Feb 1945; *educ* Eton and RAC Cirencester; *m* 22 Feb 1975 *Hon Sarah Violet Astor, yst dau of 2nd Baron Astor of Hever (*qv*), and has:

(1) +Harry Marcus George; *b* 7 Oct 1977; *educ* Eton

(1) *Lorna Violet; *b* 6 Dec 1979

(2) *Sabrina Helen; *b* 4 Nov 1983

1 Myra Bertha Ernestine; *b* 22 July 1937; *d* 2 Aug 1979

ROBSON OF KIDDINGTON

Arms: Or, a Viking ship, oars in action sable, between two fleurs-de-lys azure. **Supporters:** Dexter, a sea stag argent, attired and finned or; sinister, a sea horse also argent, crined and finned or, the tails proper and each gorged with a baron's coronet also proper. **Creation:** B. (LP, UK) 1974.

THE BARONESS ROBSON OF KIDDINGTON, of Kiddington, Oxfordshire (Inga-Stina Arvidsson, JP (Oxon 1955)) [The Rt Hon The Baroness Robson of Kiddington JP, The Dower House, Kiddington, Oxon OX20 1BU; 1 Whitehall Place, London SW1]; *b* 20 Aug 1919; *educ* Stockholm; Swedish FO 1939–40, UK Min Info 1942–43; Memb Bd Govrs U Coll Hosp 1966–74; Pres: Women's Lib Fedn 1968–70, Lib Party Orgn 1970–71; Chm: Bd Govrs Queen Charlotte's and Chelsea Hosps 1970–84, Lib Party Environment Panel 1971–77; memb Cncl Surrey U 1974; Chm: SW Thames RHA 1974–82, Nat Assoc Leagues Hosp Friends 1985–94, Anglo-Swedish Soc 1983–92; *m* 1940 Sir Lawrence William Robson, FCA, FCMA, JDip, MA (*d* 1982), and has:

1 *(Erik) Maurice William [The Hon Maurice Robson, Kiddington Hall, Woodstock, Oxon; Erchless Castle, Struy, by Beauly, Inverness]; *b* 1943; *educ* Eton and Ch Ch Oxford (MA); FCA, Upper Warden Painter-Stainers' Co 1997–98; *m* 1985 *Chloe Annabel, er dau of Richard Arthur Edwards (*see* HYLTON, B), and has:

(1) *James Patrick; *b* 1990

(1) *Natasha Lilly; *b* 1993

1 *Kristina Elizabeth [The Hon Mrs Mason, 17 Crick Rd, Oxford]; *b* 1946; *m* 1967 *Iain McLaren Mason

2 *Vanessa Jane [The Hon Mrs Potter, Tyler Hall, Tyler Hill, Canterbury, Kent]; *b* 1949; *m* 1973 *Jonathan Martin Potter

Lineage: ERIK R ARVIDSSON; *m* Lilly A Danielson and had:

INGA-STINA, *cr* a **Baroness**

ROCHDALE

Arms: Arg. a chevron engrailed gu. between two estoiles in chief az. and a rose of the second in base barbed and seeded ppr. **Crest:** A cubit arm erect vested az., the hand ppr. grasping a chaplet vert encircling a rose in the arms. **Supporters:** On either side a ram or, charged on the shoulder with a rose gu., slipped and leaved ppr. **Motto:** *Lucem spero* ('I hope for light'). **Creations:** B. (UK) 14 Feb 1913, V. (UK) 20 Jan 1960.

THE 2ND VISCOUNT ROCHDALE, of Rochdale, County Palatine of Lancaster, and **Baron Rochdale**, of Rochdale, County Palatine of Lancaster (St John Durival Kemp) [The Rt Hon The Viscount Rochdale, Rosetrees, Lingholm, Keswick, Cumbria CA12 5TZ]; *b* 15 Jan 1938; *s* f 1993; *educ* Eton; *m* 5 Jan 1960 (*divorce* 1974) Serena Jane, dau of Michael Clark-Hall, of Wissenden, Bethersden, Kent, and Mrs George Trotter, of Brewery Ho, Chirnside, Berwicks; *m* 2nd 16 July 1976 *Elizabeth, dau of Robert Norman Rossiter Boldon, of Cullercoats, Northumberland, and formerly w of James Michael Anderton, and has by his 1st w:

1 +JONATHAN HUGO DURIVAL; *b* 10 June 1961; *educ* Stowe; *m* 1994 *Ming Xian, only dau of Zhu —, of Shanghai

2 +Christopher George; *b* 7 April 1969

1 *Joanna Victoria; *b* 1 Jan 1964

2 *Susanna Jane; *b* 28 Oct 1965

Lineage: JOHN KEMP, of Broomhills, Essex; *m* Susan, dau of Joseph Stonard, of Rochford, Essex, and had a yst s:

GEORGE TAWKE KEMP, JP (Lancs), of Beechwood, Rochdale; *b* 17 March 1810; *m* 2 Aug 1848 Emily Lydia (*d* 2 Dec 1904), 2nd dau of Henry Kelsall, and *d* 20 March 1877, leaving, with five daus (Emily Jessie, *m* 16 July 1883 Thomas Wellesley Pigott, massacred with his w and only child, William Wellesley, in Boxer Rising 9 July 1900; Ellen Constance, *d* 7 May 1922; Susannah Florence, *m* 9 May 1885 Evan Henry Edwards (*d* 1916); Lydia Peto, *d* 5 April 1918; Emily Georgiana, *d* unm 25 Dec 1939):

GEORGE KEMP, **1st Baron Rochdale**, of Rochdale, County Palatine of Lancaster (UK), so *cr* 14 Feb 1913, CB (1937), JP, DL; *b* 9 June 1866; *educ* Shrewsbury, Balliol Coll Oxford and Trin Coll Cambridge (BA); MP (Lib U) Heywood 1895–1906 and (Lib) NW Manchester 1910–12, served Boer War 1900–02, Lt-Col cmdg 32nd Bn Imp Yeo 1902, ktd 1909, WW I: cmded 1st/6th Bn Lancs Fus Gallipoli 1915, T/Brig-Gen 126th and 127th Bdes 42nd Div, Hon Col 6th Bn Lancs Fus, dir Barclays Bank, Ld Lt Middx 1929, Pres TA&AFA Middx, chm Kelsall and Kemp, Rochdale; *m* 5 Aug 1896 Lady Beatrice Mary Egerton, MBE (1920) (*d* 17 Sept

1966 aged 94), 3rd dau of 3rd Earl of Ellesmere (*see* SUTHERLAND, D), and *d* 24 March 1945, having had:

1 JOHN DURIVAL, **1st Viscount**

1 Patience; *b* 24 June 1898; *m* 1st 7 Oct 1920 (*divorce* 1931) Lt-Col (later Brig) Christian George Maude, DSO, OBE, MC, and had issue (*see* HAWARDEN, V); *m* 2nd 16 Jan 1931 Victor Basil John Seely (*see* SHERWOOD, B) and *d* 19 Feb 1935, leaving further issue

2 Diana Helen; *b* 19 July 1904; *m* 27 June 1928 Sir John Denman Barlow, 2nd Bt (*qv*), and *d* 1986, leaving issue

The 1st BARON's only s,

JOHN DURIVAL KEMP, **1st Viscount Rochdale**, of Rochdale, Co Palatine of Lancaster (UK), so *cr* 20 Jan 1960, OBE (1945), TD, DL (Cumberland 1948); *b* 5 June 1906; *educ* Eton and Trin Coll Cambridge (BA 1928); served WW II (despatches), Hon Col 851st (Westmorland and Cumberland Yeo) Ind Battery RA (TA) 1959–67, Col (TA) (Hon Brig), chm: Kelsall and Kemp, Cotton Bd 1957–62 and Nat Ports Cncl 1964–67, v-chm W Riding Worsted and Woollen Mills 1969–93, dir: Consett Iron Co 1956–67 and Williams Deacon's Bank Ltd, dep chm: Williams & Glyn's Bank 1973–93 and Nat and Commercial Banking Gp 1971–93, Companion Memb Textile Inst 1962, Pres: Nat Union Mfrs 1953–56 and Br Legion NW Area 1955–61, memb: Dollar Exports Cncl 1953–60, Western Hemisphere Exports Cncl 1960–64 and Centl Tport Consultative Ctee 1952–57, V-Pres Br Productivity Cncl 1955–56, Govr BBC 1954–59, Chm Ctee Enquiry: Major Ports of GB 1961 and Shipping Industry 1967–70; *m* 18 March 1931 Elinor Dorothea, CBE (1964), JP (Cumberland 1949) (*d* 9 Jan 1997), 2nd surv dau of Ernest Hubert Pease, of Ledge Ho, Bembridge, IoW, and Mowden, Darlington, and *d* 1993, having had:

1 ST JOHN DURIVAL KEMP, **2nd and present Viscount Rochdale**

1 Bryony Joy; *b* 18 June 1947; *d* following a riding accident 19 Sept 1963

ROCHE

Arms: Gu. three roaches naiant within a bordure engrailed arg.
Crest: A rock thereon a stork close, charged on the breast with a torteau and holding in his dexter claw a roach, all ppr.
Motto: *Dieu est ma roche* ('God is my rock').
Creation: Bt. (UK) 8 Aug 1838.

SIR DAVID O'GRADY ROCHE, 5TH BT, of Carass, Co Limerick [Sir David Roche Bt, Norris Castle Farm, Isle of Wight PO32 6AZ; Bridge House, Starbotton, Skipton, N Yorks BD23 5HY; 36 Coniger Rd, London SW6 3TA]; *b* 21 Sept 1947; *s* f 1977; *educ* Wellington and Trin Coll Dublin; Liveryman Sadlers' Co 1970; *m* 24 June 1971 *Hon (Helen) Alexandra Briscoe, er dau of 3rd Viscount Selby (*qv*) and formerly w of Roger Moreton Frewen, and has had:

1 Standish George O'Grady; *b* 28 April 1972; *d* 17 July 1974

2 +DAVID ALEXANDER O'GRADY; *b* 28 Jan 1976; *educ* Durham U (BSc)

1 *Cecilia Evelyn Jonnë; *b* 23 May 1979

Lineage: GEORGE ROCHE; Mayor Limerick 1702 and 1721, MP Limerick 1713 and 1715; *m* 1st Alice, dau of J Vincent, and had a s (Arthur); *m* 2nd Mary Mills, dau of David Bindon, of Clony, and by her had, with a dau (Anne, *m* Major John Carleton Whitelocke, of Priorswood, Co Dublin):

DAVID ROCHE; Mayor Limerick 1749; *m* 1st Mary, dau of G Tierney, and had a s (George); *m* 2nd Bridget, est dau of Stephen Winthrop, of London, and by her had three sons and three daus, of whom the 2nd s:

DAVID ROCHE, JP, of Carass; *m* 1st Frances (*d* April 1818), yst dau of William Maunsell, of Caherdavin, Maryville, and Flag Ho, Limerick, and had:

1 DAVID (Sir), **1st Bt**

1 Bridget; *m* Neptune Blood (*d* 1822), of Brickhill, Co Clare, and had issue

2 Frances; *m* Jeffery Browning, of Carass Court, Co Limerick

DAVID ROCHE *m* 2nd Rebecca (*d* Feb 1836), dau of Capt Long, of Birch Hill, Co Fermanagh, and *d* 27 March 1830, having by her had, with two daus (*d* unm):

2 William, of Dunkip, Co Limerick; *b* April 1821; *m* June 1848 Emily, dau of Robert Borrowes, of Gilltown, Co Kildare, and had issue

---

The er s,

Sir David Roche 1st Bt (UK), so *cr* 8 Aug 1838; *b* 19 Jan 1791; MP Limerick 1832–44; *m* 1st 1 Feb 1825 Frances (*d* Sept 1841), er dau of Lt-Col John Ormsby Vandeleur, of Maddenstown, Co Kildare, and Ballinamona, Co Limerick, and had, with a dau (*d* unm):

1 **Sir David Vandeleur Roche, 2nd Bt**, JP, DL; *b* 24 June 1833; Co Limerick: V-Lt, High Sheriff 1865; *m* 1st 24 Oct 1867 Hon Isabella Susannah Adelaide Massey (*d* 13 Sept 1871), yst dau of 3rd Baron Clarina (*see* 1949 edn); *m* 2nd 4 Dec 1872 Mary Anne (*dsp* 29 Feb 1892), dau of Hugh Massy (*see* MASSY, B), and *d* 19 April 1908, having by his 1st w had:

(1) Isabella Susan Alice; *d* unm 24 April 1948

1 Rosetta; *m* 13 Sept 1846 Richard Steele Fetherstonhaugh (*d* 6 Oct 1896), of Rockview, Co Westmeath, and *d* 14 March 1903, leaving issue

2 Frances Elizabeth; *m* 1st 17 Oct 1848 Sir Philip John William Miles, 2nd Bt (*qv*), and had issue; *m* 2nd 1904 Dr John Nicholls, of St Louis, Mo., and St Ives Cottage, Maidenhead, and *d* 18 Dec 1908

Sir David *m* 2nd 10 June 1844 Cecilia Caroline (*d* 2 June 1877), yst dau of Henry Deane Grady, of Lodge, Co Limerick, and Stillorgan Castle, Co Dublin, and *d* 8 April 1865, having by her had:

2 **Sir David Deane O'Grady Roche, 3rd Bt**, JP (Cos Clare and Carlow); *b* 26 July 1845; *m* 1st 27 Oct 1874 Mary Harriet Frances (*d* 29 Aug 1903), est dau of Colmore Frind Cregoe Colmore, of Moor End, Glos, and had:

(1) David Cecil; *b* 4 Nov 1875; *d* unm 10 Feb 1899

(1) Olive Edith Kathleen; MFH Carlow 1930–65; *m* 16 July 1901 Maj William Charles Hall (accidently *k* Dec 1917), 23rd Roy Welch Fus and Res Bn RI Rifles, 2nd s of Maj William James Hall, of Narrowater Castle, Warrenpoint, Co Down, and *d* 11 March 1965 aged 87, leaving issue

2 (cont.) **Sir Standish** *m* 2nd 20 June 1910 Sybil (*d* 3 Oct 1950), only dau of Col Julius Dyson Dyson Laurie, and *d* 9 Dec 1914, having by her had:

(2) **Sir Standish O'Grady Roche, 4th Bt**, DSO (1942); *b* 13 March 1911; *educ* RNC Dartmouth; ADC to Govr-Gen NZ 1935–37, Lt-Cdr RN WW II (Croix de Guerre), Freeman City London; *m* 9 Feb 1946 *Evelyn Laura [Evelyn Lady Roche, Monte de Cerro, Coroteto, São Bras d'Alportel, Algarve, Portugal], 3rd Offr WRNS, only dau of Maj William Andon, Yorks LI, of Jersey, and *d* 2 April 1977, leaving:

1a Sir DAVID O'GRADY ROCHE, **5th and present Bt**

2a +Timothy O'Grady [Timothy Roche Esq, 40 Redstone Pk, Redhill, Surrey]; *b* 8 Nov 1948; *educ* St Columba's Coll Dublin; Lt (ret) Irish Guards, memb HAC, accountant, Freeman City London; *m* 31 May 1975 *Lorna R A, dau of A T R Nicholson, and has:

1b +Patrick Timothy O'Grady; *b* 1978

2b +Simon James O'Grady; *b* 1980

ROCHESTER

Creation: B. (UK) 23 Jan 1931.

THE 2ND BARON ROCHESTER, of Rochester, Co Kent (Foster Charles Lowry Lamb, DL (Cheshire 1979)) [The Rt Hon The Lord Rochester DL, The Hollies, Hartford, Northwich, Cheshire CW8 1PG]; *b* 7 June 1916; *s* f 1955; *educ* Mill Hill and Jesus Coll Cambridge (BA 1937 MA 1941); Capt 23rd Hus WW II, personnel manager Mond Div ICI 1964–72, Pro Chllr Keele U 1976–86 (D Univ 1986), chm: Cheshire Scout Assoc 1974–81, Chester Coll Govrs 1974–83 and S and Mid Cheshire Dist Manpower Ctee 1980–; *m* 12 Dec 1942 *Mary Carlisle, yr dau of Thomas Benjamin Wheeler, CBE, of Hartford, Cheshire, and has had:

1 +DAVID CHARLES [The Hon David Lamb, The Anchorage, 1 Beresford Ave, Twickenham, Middx TW1 2PY]; *b* 8 Sept 1944; *educ* Shrewsbury and Sussex U; *m* 9 April 1969 *Jacqueline, dau of John Alfred Stamp, of Torquay, and has:

(1) +Daniel; *b* 12 June 1971

(2) +Joe; *b* 18 Oct 1972

2 +Timothy Michael [The Hon Timothy Lamb, 12 Park Ave, St Albans, Herts AL1 4PB]; *b* 24 March 1953; *educ* Shrewsbury and The Queen's Coll Oxford (cricket blue 1973/74); professional cricketer, played for Middx and Northants, Cricket sec Test and Co Cricket Bd 1988–96, ch exec England and Wales Cricket Bd 1997–; *m* 1978 *Denise Ann, dau of John Buckley, of Frinton-on-Sea, Essex, and has:

(1) +Nicholas; *b* 1985

(1) *Sophie; *b* 1983

1 Helen Ruth; *b* 4 Aug 1947; *d* 15 Feb 1952

2 *Elizabeth Mary [The Hon Mrs McIlroy, Diggle, Oldham, Lancs]; *b* 22 Oct 1951; *educ* Howells Sch Denbigh and Hull U; *m* 6 April 1974 *Thomas Meredith McIlroy, s of John McIlroy, of Wollaston, Northants, and has:

(1) *Sam; *b* June 1975

(2) *Duncan; *b* 20 Jan 1977

(3) *John; *b* 17 May 1979

(1) *Catherine, *b* 18 Sept 1989

Rochester, previous creations: In 1652 Henry Wilmot, who had been ennobled as Baron Wilmot nine years previously and succeeded his father as 2nd Viscount Wilmot in the Irish peerage eight years previously, was made Earl of Rochester by CHARLES II. He had been a fairly successful royalist general under CHARLES's father in the Civil War, defeating Waller at Roundway Down in 1643 and Cropredy Bridge the next year, and he was one of the chief counsellors to the new King in exile. He was envoy to various courts in Continental Europe and joined in an attempted royalist rising in England in 1655. His second wife was a daughter of Sir John St John, 1st Bt, of Lydiard Tregoze (*see* BOLINGBROKE and SAINT JOHN, V).

His son the 2nd Earl of Rochester (*see* also MALET, Bt) was the famous poet and rake of Restoration times. (As versifier he influenced Pope.) With the death of his son aged 11 in 1681 the Earldom expired. It was revived the following year for Laurence Hyde, second son of the 1st Earl of Clarendon of the 1661 creation. A man given like his predecessor as Earl of Rochester to too much wine, and intemperate in his speeches as well, so that the opposition speakers in Parliament used to bait him regularly, Hyde headed the Church of England party throughout the reigns of JAMES II, WILLIAM and MARY and QUEEN ANNE. Despite his other failings he was reckoned unusually honest by the standards of the day. With the death of his son the 2nd Earl in 1753 this creation expired too.

Lineage: JOSEPH LAMB; had:

HENRY LAMB, of Fowey, Cornwall; *d* 4 Dec 1890, having had:

BENJAMIN LAMB, of Windlesham, Surrey, and Shorne, Rochester, Kent; *b* 16 Feb 1842; *m* 2 June 1868 Eliza (*d* 28 Oct 1942), only dau of Charles Lowry, of St Mawes, Cornwall, and *d* 22 Aug 1921, leaving:

1 ERNEST HENRY, **1st Baron**

2 Sidney Charles, of Impington, Cambs; *b* 20 March 1878; chm and memb Chesterton RDC, chm Local Appeals Tbnl Mins Labour and Supply, Freeman City London; *m* 1905 Alice Gration (*d* 16 Dec 1924) and *d* 27 July 1970, having had:

(1) Dennis Charles; *b* 18 June 1913; Sgt/Pilot RAFVR WW II; *kas* 18 Oct 1939 while night flying

(1) Constance Alice; *b* 17 Dec 1907; *m* 22 July 1961 *William Henry Frederick Church [William Church Esq, Mount Whistle, Higher Fore St, Marazion, Penzance, Cornwall] and *d* 27 Nov 1983

(2) Doris Mary; *d* 4 Jan 1983

(3) *Irene Kate [Mrs Tom Pattinson, Chymel, Ednovean Lane, Perranuthnoe, Penzance, Cornwall TR20 9LZ]; *b* 26 Jan 1917; *educ* Perse Sch for Girls Cambridge; *m* 30 June 1941 *Tom Pickles Pattinson, MD, BCH, MRCS, LRCP, s of Rev Joseph W Pattinson and Pickles Mrs E Sagar, and has:

1a *Anthony Peter [Anthony Pattinson Esq, Corner House, Killams Close, Taunton, Somerset TA1 3LD]; *b* 28 Dec 1942; *educ* Taunton Sch; *m* 19– (*divorce*) Susan Phippen and has:

1b *Ross Antony; *b* 19 July 1984

2a *Michael Gration [Michael Pattinson Esq, Waterhead Brake, Higher Contour Rd, Kingsmear, Devon TQ6 0AY]; *b* 2 May 1945; *educ* Taunton Sch and Bristol U (BVSc); MRCVS; *m* 13 April 1968 (*divorce* 19–) Frances Elizabeth, LLB, dau of John Buckland Heigham, of Weybridge, Surrey, and Lagos, Nigeria

3 Reginald Percy; *b* 6 June 1879; *m* 25 July 1908 Lilian Winifred Gray (*d* 27 Jan 1950) and *d* 28 Oct 1965, leaving:

(1) *Faith Winifred [Miss Faith Lamb, Cameron, 72 Leckhampton Rd, Cheltenham, Glos]; *b* 2 Sept 1910

4 Gerald Clifford; *b* 25 July 1881; *m* 31 Aug 1922 Alice Ethel Lamb (*d* 9 Nov 1954) and *dsp* 21 July 1955

1 Florence Gertrude; Missionary Ceylon 1892–97; *m* 27 July 1898 James Arthur Duthie (*d* 10 March 1926), Travancore CS, India, and *d* 2 Jan 1962, leaving issue

2 Edith Amy; Missionary Mysore 1897–1902; *d* unm 24 May 1952

3 Ada Louise; *d* unm 15 March 1965

4 Adeline Bertha; *d* unm 15 April 1926

5 Beatrice Maude; *m* 25 April 1895 William Herbert Dean (*d* June 1940) and *d* 12 Jan 1948, leaving issue

6 Mabel Elsie; *d* unm 4 Nov 1928

7 Dora Winifred; *d* unm 17 Jan 1968

BENJAMIN LAMB's est s,

ERNEST HENRY LAMB, **1st Baron Rochester**, of Rochester, Co Kent (UK), so *cr* 23 Jan 1931, CMG (9 Nov 1907), JP (Surrey 1907–); *b* 4 Sept 1876; *educ* Dulwich and Wycliffe Coll, Stonehouse, Glos; tport contractor, chm Foster's Parcels and Goods Express Ltd, memb City London Corp 1903–31, Dep Alderman Candlewick Ward, Lt City London, MP Rochester 1906–Jan 1910 and Dec 1910–18; chm: City London Police Ctee, City London Schs' Ctee, Distress Ctee Centl (Unemployed) Body London 1920–30, Paymaster-Gen 1931–35, Min Labour Spokesman Ho Lds 1931–35, memb PLA and Centl Advsy Water Ctee Min Housing and Local Govt, V-Pres: Methodist Conf 1941–42, Br Cncl Churches 1942–44, Br and For Bible Soc and Nat Children's Home and Orphanage, chm Bridge Ho Estates Tst, Treas Temperance and Social Welfare Dept Wesleyan Methodist Ch 1909–31, ktd 1944; *m* 31 Dec 1913 Rosa Dorothea (*d* 1979), yr dau of William John Hurst, JP, CC, of Drumaness, Co Down, and *d* 13 Jan 1955, leaving:

1 FOSTER CHARLES LOWRY LAMB, **2nd and present Baron Rochester**

2 +Roland Hurst Lowry [The Rev and Hon Roland Lamb, 13 Eversleigh Rise, Darley Bridge, Derbys DE4 2JW]; *b* 27 Oct 1917; *educ* Mill Hill and Jesus Coll Cambridge (BA 1938 MA 1942); RAF Chaplain WW II, Gen Sec Br Evangelical Cncl, Supt Methodist Minister, Travelling Sec Inter-Varsity Fellowship Evangelical Unions; *m* 29 Oct 1943 *Vera Alicia, dau of Arthur Henry Morse, of Walton-on-Naze, Essex, and has:

(1) +Andrew Michael [Andrew Lamb Esq, 5 Flint Lane, S Darley, Derbys]; *b* 4 Jan 1951; *educ* Rydal; *m* 1974 *Helen, dau of Eric Mitchell, of Rugby, and has:

1a +Benjamin James; *b* 1980

1a *Rebecca Mary Alicia; *b* 1982

(1) *Rosemary Elizabeth [Mrs David Pike, 3 Laburnum Rd, Weston-super-Mare, Somerset]; *b* 10 Nov 1947; *m* 29 March 1969 *David Martin John Pike and has:

1a *Martin John; *b* 1973

1a *Sarah Louise; *b* 12 Oct 1971

(2) *Hilary Jennifer [Mrs Howard Jackson, 11 Fox Hill, Selly Oak, Birmingham]; *b* 6 June 1949; *m* 1 April 1972 *Howard Jackson and has:

1a *Nathan Dieter; *b* 1976

1a *Kirsten Renate; *b* 1978

2a *Lydia Ruth; *b* 1985

(3) *Valerie Judith [Mrs Joseph Unsworth, 73 Elwyn Dve, Halewood Village, Liverpool]; *b* 26 Dec 1955; *m* 1978 *Joseph George Unsworth and has:

1a *Joseph Jonathan; *b* 1993

1a *Jodi Ann; *b* 1980

2a *Amy Ruth; *b* 1983

3a *Mia Dawn; *b* 1986

3 Kenneth Henry Lowry, CBE (1985); *b* 23 Dec 1923; *educ* Harrow and Trin Coll Oxford (BA 1946 MA 1951, Pres Union 1944); Instr-Lt RN 1944–46, sr lecturer History and Engrg RNC Greenwich 1947–53, Cwlth Fund Fell Harvard 1953–55, Ch Assist TV Talks BBC 1959–63, Head Religous Bdcstg 1963–66, Sec BBC 1967–68, Dir Public Affairs BBC 1969; *m* 16 April 1952 *Elizabeth Anne Saul [The Hon Mrs Kenneth Lamb, 25 South Terrace, London SW7 2TB], dau of D A Saul and Mrs J B Allan, and *d* 21 June 1995, leaving:

(1) +Stephen Ernest Henry; *b* 16 May 1957; *m* 1993 *Sue M, er dau of W J Turner, of Clevedon, Avon

(1) *Sarah Elizabeth Hurst [Miss Sarah Lamb, 64 Church St, London W7]; *b* 23 Jan 1955

(2) *Caroline Mary Anne [Mrs Paul Knight, 102 Ormeley Rd, London SW12]; *b* 6 June 1966; *m* 1992 *Lt Paul J O Knight, RN, s of Dr Peter Knight, of Austin, Tex.

1 Grace Dorothy Lowry; *m* 20 June 1951 Rev Prof Homer Hasenfflug Dubs (*d* 16 Aug 1969), BD, PhD, only s of Rev Charles Newton Dubs, DD, Supt China Mission Evangelical Ch Hunan, China, and *d* 3 Feb 1953

2 Mary Pleasant Lowry; LRAM; *m* 4 Sept 1941 Rev Desmond William Adair Stride, er s of Cdr Desmond Adair Stride, RN

3 *Muriel Joan Lowry [The Hon Mrs Muriel Collier, 26 George St, Cambridge]; *educ* Oxford (BA 1943 MA 1957); 3rd Sec Br Embassy Oslo, Sr Lecturer Loughborough Coll Educn, PT tutor counsellor OU 1977–84; *m* 29 Aug 1947 (*divorce* 1957) William Oswald Collier and has had issue (*see* MONKSWELL, B)

ROCKLEY

Arms: Barry of ten arg. and az., over all six escutcheons sa., three, two and one, each charged with a lion rampant of the first, and for difference a crescent gu. charged with another crescent or.
Crest: Six arrows in saltire or, barbed and flighted arg., girt together with a belt gu., buckled and garnished gold, over the arrows a morion cap ppr. **Supporters:** On either side a lion erm., gorged with a collar or, pendent therefrom an escutcheon, the dexter sa., a lion rampant arg., and the sinister gu., three tilting spears erect or, headed arg. **Motto:** *Sero sed serio* ('Late but in earnest').
Creation: B. (UK) 11 Jan 1934.

THE 3RD BARON ROCKLEY, of Lytchett Heath, Co Dorset (James Hugh Cecil) [The Rt Hon The Lord Rockley, Lytchett Heath, Poole, Dorset BH16 6AE]; *b* 5 April 1934; *s* f 1976; *educ* Eton and New Coll Oxford; with Wood Gundy Ltd 1957–62, Kleinwort Benson 1962– (dir 1970–, v-chm 1988–93, chm Kleinwort Benson Gp 1994–96), chm: Dartford River Crossing 1988–93, Kleinwort Devpt Fnd 1991–93, Midland Expressway 1992–93, dir: Equity and Law 1980–92, Christies Int 1989–, Cobham plc 1990–, Abbey National 1990–, Foreign & Colonial Investment Tst 1991– and Cadogan Gp Ltd 1996–, memb Design Cncl 1987–93, tstee Nat Portrait Gallery 1981–88, Salters' Co: Upper Warden 1997–98, Master 1998–99; *m* 18 Nov 1958 *Lady Sarah Primrose Beatrix Cadogan, est dau of 7th Earl Cadogan (*qv*), and has:

1 +ANTHONY ROBERT; *b* 29 July 1961; *educ* Eton and Cambridge; *m* 1988 *Katherine (Katie) Jane, dau of G A Whalley, of Chipperfield, Herts, and has:

(1) +William Evelyn; *b* 7 July 1996

(1) *Emily Sarah; *b* 1991

(2) *Lydia Elizabeth; *b* 1994

1 *Caroline Anne; *b* 27 March 1960; *m* 1985 *Mark G Preston, yr s of Simon Preston, of Lowfield Farm, Tetbury, Glos, and has:

(1) *Hugh Simon; *b* 1987

(2) *Edward James; *b* 1989

(1) *Lucy Camilla; *b* 1991

2 *Camilla Sarah; *b* 8 Feb 1965; *m* 3 Oct 1998 *Henry Mountain, s of Nicholas Mountain, of Alresford, Hants

Lineage: Lt-Col Lord EUSTACE BROWNLOW (GASCOYNE-)CECIL (4th s of 2nd Marquess of Salisbury, *qv*); had an est s:

EVELYN CECIL, **1st Baron Rockley**, of Lytchett Heath, Co Dorset (UK), so *cr* 11 Jan 1934, GBE (1922), PC (1917); *b* May 1865; *educ* Eton and New Coll Oxford

(MA); barrister Inner Temple 1889; barrister NSW 1926; Priv Sec to PM 1891–92 and 1895–1902, MP (C) E Herts 1898–1900, Aston Manor 1900–18 and Birmingham Aston 1918–29, Memb: Shipping Subsidies Ctee 1901–02, Public Retrenchment Ctee 1915, Second Chamber Conf 1918 and Roy Commn on Honours 1921–22, Chm Roy Commn on Safety in Coal Mines 1935–38; dir Southern Railway; BGCStJ (Sec-Gen 1915–21); V-Chm Jt War Ctee BRCS and OStJ WW I; author: *Notes of My Journey Round the World* (1889), *Primogeniture* (1895) and *On the Eve of the (South African) War* (1900); m 16 Feb 1898 Hon Alicia Margaret Tyssen Amherst, CBE, DGStJ (d 14 Sept 1941), dau of 1st Baron Amherst of Hackney (qv), and d 1 April 1941, leaving:

1 ROBERT WILLIAM EVELYN, **2nd Baron**

1 Margaret Gertrude, DGStJ; m 7 Feb 1929 Capt Herbert Arthur Cambridge Lane, OBE, RN (d 8 May 1961), s of Frederick George Alexander Lane, of Bloxworth House, Dorset, and d 26 Aug 1962, leaving issue

2 Maud Katharine Alicia; portrait painter; m 17 Nov 1927 (*divorce* 1955) Lt-Col Richard Greville Acton Steel, TD, RA (TA), yr s of Col Richard Acton Steel, CMG, CIE, and d 12 June 1981, leaving:

(1) Juliet Maud; b 21 Sept 1928; d unm 16 April 1982

(2) *Oriel Hermione [Mrs Basil Robinson, 41 Redcliffe Gdns, London SW10 9JH]; b 29 Nov 1930; m 8 Feb 1958 *Basil William Robinson, FSA, FBA, Keeper Emeritus V&A 1972–76, Pres Roy Asiatic Soc 1970–73, only s of William Robinson, and has:

  1a *William James; b 31 May 1959; m 2 Sept 1989 *Elisabeth Maria, only child of Heinrich Goldbach, of Seattle, USA, and has:

    1b *Edward William Henry; b 25 Nov 1993

    1b *Harriet Anne Elisabeth; b 30 Nov 1991

  1a *Alicia Frances; b 24 May 1962; m 5 April 1997 *Dr Ian Martin Cropley, est s of John Cropley, of Culcheth, Cheshire

The 1st BARON's only s,

ROBERT WILLIAM EVELYN CECIL, **2nd Baron Rockley**; b 28 Feb 1901; educ Eton, Ch Ch Oxford and Yale (Davidson Scholar); engr, WW II as Lt-Col RA, Min Supply 1939–43 and Mil Govt (Brig) 1944–45; dir: Foreign and Colonial Tst, Nat Westminster Bank, Clerical, Medical and Gen Life Assur Soc and Kleinwort Benson, dep chm Schweppes; hon co-treasurer Church Army; m 9 May 1933 *Anne Margaret, er dau of Adml Hon Sir Herbert Meade-Featherstonhaugh, GCVO, CB, DSO (see CLANWILLIAM, E), and d 26 Jan 1976, leaving:

1 JAMES HUGH CECIL, **3rd and present Baron Rockley**

2 +Charles Evelyn [The Hon Charles Cecil, Wilcote House, Charlbury, Oxon]; b 15 Nov 1936; educ Eton; m 28 Sept 1965 *Jennifer Anne, only dau of Capt Duncan Mackinnon (see BRASSEY OF APETHORPE, B), and has:

(1) +David; b 14 Jun 1971

(1) *Arabella Elizabeth; b 7 July 1967

(2) *Lucinda Rose; b 4 March 1970

1 *Elizabeth Anne [The Hon Mrs Wills, Gavelacre, Longparish, Andover, Hants SP11 7AL]; b 6 July 1939; m 19 Jan 1961 *Andrew Arnold Lyon Wills (see WILLS, Bt, of Hazelwood)

RODEN

Arms: Az. a circular wreath arg. and sa. with four hawk's bells conjoined thereto in quadrangle or. **Crest:** A falcon's leg erased à la cuisse ppr., belled or. **Supporters:** Two falcons, wings inverted ppr., belled or. **Motto:** *Faire mon devoir* ('Doing my duty').
Creations: Bt. (E) 8 June 1665, B. (I) 29 Nov 1743, V. (I) 6 Dec 1755, E. (I) 1 Dec 1771.

THE 10TH EARL OF RODEN of High Roding, Co Tipperary, **Viscount Jocelyn, Baron Newport of Newport**, Co Tipperary, and a **Baronet** (Sir Robert John Jocelyn, Bt) [The Rt Hon The Earl of Roden, 4 The Boltons, London SW10 9TB; Doon House, Cashel, Co Galway, Ireland]; b 25 Aug 1938; s f 1993; m 1st 10 June 1970 (*divorce* 1982) Sara Cecilia, dau of Brig Andrew Dunlop, DSO, of Que Que, Rhodesia, and has:

1 *Cecilia Rose; b 11 Feb 1976

The 10th EARL m 2nd 1986 *Ann Margareta Maria, dau of Dr Gunnar Albert Philip Henning, of Göteborg, Sweden, and by her has:

1 +SHANE ROBERT HENNING, *Viscount Jocelyn*; b 9 Dec 1989

Lineage: JAMES JOCELYN, of Essex; had:

HENRY JOCELYN; m Jane, dau and heiress of William Chastelyn, and had:

RALPH JOCELYN; living c 1204; m Beatrix — and had:

JOHN JOCELYN; living c 1226; m Katherine, dau and coheir of Thomas Battell, of Ongar, Essex, by Elizabeth, dau and heiress of Sir Richard Enfield, of Enfield, Middx, and had:

THOMAS JOCELYN; living c 1249; m Maud, dau of Sir John Hyde, of Hyde Hall, Herts, thus acquiring that estate; had:

THOMAS JOCELYN; living c 1285; m 1st Alice, dau of William Liston; m 2nd Joan, dau of John le Blount, and by his 1st w had:

RALPH JOCELYN; living c 1309; m 1st Anne, dau of William Sandes; m 2nd Matilda (d 1353), dau of John Sutton, and by her had:

GEOFFREY JOCELYN; living *temp* EDWARD III; m Margaret, dau of Robert Rokell, and had:

RALPH JOCELYN; m Margaret, dau of John de Patmere, and had, with an er s (Thomas, *dsp*):

GEOFFREY JOCELYN; m Katherine, dau of Sir Thomas Braye, and d 1428, having had, with two yr sons (Geoffrey, ancestor of the JOSSELYNs of Horksley, Essex; Sir Ralph, KB, Sheriff London 1458, Ld Mayor 1464 and 1476, MP City London 1467, m twice, *dsp* 1480):

THOMAS JOCELYN, of High Roding, Essex; m Alice, dau of Lewis Duke, by Anne, dau of John Cotton, and had:

GEORGE JOCELYN, of High Roding; m Maud, dau of Edward Bardolfe, and had:

JOHN JOCELYN, of High Roding; m Philippa, dau of William Bradbury, and d 1525, leaving:

Sir THOMAS JOCELYN, KB 1547, of High Roding; m Dorothy, dau of Sir Geoffrey Gates, and d 1561, having had, with other issue, including two daus (Mary, m 1st John Kebell, m 2nd John Glascoke, of Noteley; Jane, m 1st Richard Kelton, m 2nd Roger Harlakenden):

RICHARD JOCELYN, of High Roding; m 1st Anne, dau of Sir Thomas Shelton; m 2nd Anne, dau of Thomas Lucas, of Bury St Edmunds, and d 1604, leaving by her:

RICHARD JOCELYN, of Hyde Hall, Herts; m 1st —, dau of Richard Barnes, DD, Bp Durham; m 2nd Joyce, dau of Robert Atkinson, of Stowell, Glos, and by her had:

Sir ROBERT JOCELYN, of Hyde Hall; b 1600; Sheriff Herts 1645; m Bridget, dau of Sir William Smith, of Hill Hall, Essex, and was bur 3 May 1664, having had a 3rd but est surv s:

Sir Robert Jocelyn, 1st Bt (E), so cr 8 June 1665, of Hyde Hall; Sheriff Herts 1677; *bapt* 14 Jan 1622/3; m 1650 Jane (*bur* 29 March 1706), dau and coheir of Robert Strange, of Somerford, Wilts, and was bur 12 June 1712, having had, with other issue:

1 **Sir Strange Jocelyn, 2nd Bt**; b 1651; educ Queens' Coll Cambridge (BA); m 1686 Mary (d 19 May 1731), dau of Tristram Conyers, of Copped Hall, Essex, and d 3 Sept 1734, having had surv issue:

(1) **Sir John Jocelyn, 3rd Bt**; barrister; *bapt* 4 Oct 1689; d unm 1 Nov 1741

(2) **Sir Conyers Jocelyn, 4th Bt**; Sheriff Herts 1745; *bapt* 19 July 1703; d unm 24 May 1778

(1) Mary; m John Bayley

2 Edward (Rev); BD; Fell Queens' Coll Cambridge, Rector High Roding, Essex; d unm Sept 1732

3 Thomas, of Sawbridgeworth, Herts; m Anne, dau of Thomas Bray, of Westminster, and had, with other issue:

(1) ROBERT JOCELYN, **1st Viscount Jocelyn**, so cr 6 Dec 1755, as also 29 Nov 1743 BARON NEWPORT OF NEWPORT, Co Tipperary (both I), PC (I 1739); b c 1688; MP (I Parl) Granard 1725–27 and Newtownards, Co Down, 1727–30, Ld Chllr Ireland 1739–56; m 1st c 24 July 1730 Charlotte (d 23 Feb 1747), dau and coheir of Charles Anderson, of Worcester, and had:

  1a ROBERT, **1st Earl**

(1) (cont.) The **1st Viscount** m 2nd 15 Nov 1754 Frances (*dsp* 25 May 1772), widow of 1st Earl of Rosse (qv) of the 1718 cr and dau of Thomas Claxton, and d 3 Dec 1756

(1) Sarah; m Ven Alexander Alcock, Archdeacon Lismore

(2) Anne; m 20 June 1730 Samuel Waller, of Newport, Co Tipperary, and d June 1800, leaving issue (see WALLER, Bt)

(3) Rebecca; m 1 Sept 1748 Henry Alcock, Clerk Irish H of C

4 George; Brig-Gen; Col Gds; m 14 Nov 1713 Catharine (d April 1730), widow of Sir Thomas Twysden, 4th Bt, of Roydon Hall, Kent (see 1967 edn), and dau and heiress of Sir Francis Wythers, Judge King's Bench, and d Nov 1727, having had:

(1) George; Lt-Col, Dep Govr Carlisle; d unm 14 July 1762

(2) John; Maj; d 16 Dec 1765

(3) Robert; Army Offr; m Oct 1763 Ann, dau of Simon Newport

(1) Jane; m (licence 28 Feb 1749) John Bloomfield, of Redwood, Co Tipperary, and had issue

1 Sarah; m Thomas Pickard and had issue (see SELBORNE, E)

The 1st VISCOUNT's only son,

Sir Robert Jocelyn, 5th Bt, as which s cousin 1778, and **1st Earl of Roden**, of High Roding, Co Tipperary (I), so cr 1 Dec 1771; *bapt* 31 July 1731; MP (I Parl) Old Leighlin 1743–56, Auditor-Gen Ireland 1750–97; m 11 Dec 1752 Anne (d 9 Jan 1818), er dau and heiress of 1st Earl of Clanbrassill of the 1756 cr by Henrietta, dau of 1st Earl of Portland (qv), and had, with other issue:

1 ROBERT, **2nd Earl**

2 George; b 7 Dec 1764; MP Dundalk 1783–98, Dep Auditor-Gen 1796; m Thomasine (d Dec 1818), dau of Henry Cole Bowen, of Bowen's Court, Kildorrey, Co Cork, and d April 1798, leaving:

(1) Harriet; *m* 1812 Rev Walter Hore (*d* 1843), Rector Ferns, s of Walter Hore, of Seafield, and gs of Walter Hore, of Harperstown, Co Wexford

(2) Georgiana; *m* 1813 Maj James Boyd, of Rosslare, Co Wexford, King's Dragoon Gds, and *d* 1819, leaving issue

(3) Louisa Joan; *m* 1st Rev and Hon Edward Wingfield (*see* POWERSCOURT, V) and had issue; *m* 2nd 2 Aug 1833, as his 2nd w, Robert Richard Tighe (*d* 20 July 1873) and *d* 17 June 1874

(4) Sophia; *m* 1818 Walter Steele and *d* 1856

(5) Anne; *m* 22 March 1817 Walter Newton, of Dunleckny, Co Carlow, and *d* 1857. He *d* 23 Aug 1853

(6) Thomasine Emily; *m* 16 March 1819 Sir Frederick Shaw, 3rd Bt, PC (*qv*), and *d* 30 Nov 1859, leaving issue

3 Percy (Rt Rev); DD, Bp Clogher; *d* Dec 1843

4 John, of Brockley Park; *b* 1769; MP Dundalk 1798–1800 and Co Louth 1800–10 and 1820–26; *m* 1795 Margaret, 3rd dau of Rt Hon Richard FitzGerald, of Mount Ophaley, and *d* 21 Jan 1828, leaving:

(1) Anne Charlotte; *m* 3 Aug 1820 5th Earl of Mayo (*qv*) and *d* 26 Jan 1867, leaving issue

1 Harriet; *m* 1780 4th Earl of Massereene and *d* 7 July 1831, leaving issue (*see* MASSEREENE and FERRARD, V)

2 Louisa; *m* 27 May 1800 Maj-Gen Orde, of Weetwood House, and *d* 1 Sept 1807

3 Emelia; *m* Gen John Straton and *d* 30 May 1845

The 1st EARL *d* 22 June 1797; his est son,

ROBERT JOCELYN, **2nd Earl of Roden**, KP (1806), PC (I 1797); *b* 26 Oct 1756; MP (I Parl) Maryborough (modern Portlaoise) 1776–78 and Dundalk 1783–97, Auditor-Gen Irish Exchequer 1797–1820, helped suppress 1798 Uprising as cdr First Fencible Light Dragoons at the encounter of Rathfarnham 25 May, also opposed a French landing in Ireland at the encounter called the 'Race of Castlebar' 27 Aug 1798; rep I peer 1801–20; *m* 1st 5 Feb 1788 Frances Theodosia (*d* 22 May 1802), est dau of Very Rev Robert Bligh, Dean Elphin, and n of 1st Earl of Darnley (*qv*), and *d* 29 June 1820, having had, with other issue (*d* unm):

1 ROBERT JOCELYN, **3rd Earl of Roden**, KP (1821), PC (1812); *b* 27 Oct 1788; *educ* Harrow; MP (Tory) Co Louth 1806–07 and 1810–20, Treasurer May–July 1812 and V-Chamberlain Household 1812–21, Auditor-Gen Exchequer Ireland 1820–22, Custos Rotulorum Co Louth 1820–49 (removed after an inquiry censured him following a riot at Dolly's Brae 12 July 1849 between Orangemen (of whom he was a supporter, being Grand Master of the Orange Soc) and RCs, in which quite a few people were killed); *cr* 17 July 1821 BARON CLANBRASSILL (UK); *m* 1st 9 Jan 1813 Maria Frances Catherine (*d* 25 Feb 1861), 2nd dau of 16th Lord (Baron) Le Despenser (*see* FALMOUTH, V), and had issue; *m* 2nd 16 Aug 1862 Clementina Janet (*d* 9 July 1903), widow of Capt Robert Lushington Reilly, of Scarvagh, Co Down, and dau of Thomas Andrews, of Greenknowe, Dumfriesshire, and *d* 20 March 1870, having had by his 1st w:

(1) Robert, *Viscount Jocelyn*; *b* 20 Feb 1816; MP (C, later Peelite) King's Lynn 1842–54, Sec Bd Control 1845–46; *m* 27 April 1841 Lady Frances Elizabeth Cowper, Extra Ldy Bedchamber to HM QUEEN VICTORIA, VA 2nd Cl (*d* 26 March 1880), yst dau of 5th Earl Cowper (*see* LUCAS OF CRUDWELL, B), and *d* 12 Aug 1854, leaving, with a dau (*d* unm):

1a ROBERT JOCELYN, **4th Earl of Roden**; *b* 22 Nov 1846; *educ* Eton and Trin Coll Cambridge; Ld-in-Waiting (C) 1874–80, Lt 1st Life Gds; *d* unm 9 Jan 1880

2a Frederick Spencer; *b* 11 July 1852; Page of Honour to HM QUEEN VICTORIA; *d* 12 Nov 1871

1a Edith; *m* 21 Feb 1865 5th Earl of Arran (*qv*) and *d* 3 Oct 1871, leaving issue

(2) JOHN STRANGE JOCELYN, **5th Earl of Roden**, DL (Co Down); *b* 4 June 1823; *educ* Harrow; Lt-Col Scots Fus Gds Crimea, cmded 2nd Jäger Corps Br German Legion, Chev Legn Hon; *m* 31 July 1851 Hon Sophia Hobhouse (*d* 3 Dec 1916), dau and coheir of 1st Baron Broughton (*see* HOBHOUSE, Bt), and *dspm* 3 July 1897, when the Barony of Clanbrassill expired, having had:

1a Violet Charlotte Julia Maria; *m* 1st 7 June 1880 (*divorce* 25 Nov 1901) Sir Reginald William Proctor-Beauchamp, 5th Bt (*qv*), and had issue; *m* 2nd 12 Dec 1906 Hugh Watt, of Knightsbridge, MP Glasgow, and *d* 22 Oct 1925. He *d* 16 March 1921

(3) William Nassau, CB; *b* 23 Oct 1832; Sec Legation Constantinople 1874–78, Chargé d'Affaires Hesse-Darmstadt 1878, Min Res Baden and Hesse-Darmstadt 1892; *m* 11 Oct 1866 Cecilia Mary (*d* 1 Jan 1894), yst dau of Adml Sir Sir George Elliot, KCB (*see* MINTO, E), and *dsp* 11 Nov 1892

(1) Elizabeth Frances Charlotte; *m* 1st 21 Jan 1836 6th Viscount Powerscourt (*qv*) and had issue; *m* 2nd 30 April 1846 4th Marquess of Londonderry (*qv*) and *d* 2 Sept 1884

(2) Frances; Ldy Bedchamber to HM QUEEN VICTORIA; *m* 25 July 1833 1st Earl of Gainsborough (*qv*) and *d* 12 May 1885, leaving issue

(3) Maria; *m* 11 June 1848 Hon Charles Robert Weld-Forester (*see* FORESTER, B) and *d* 17 March 1894

1 Frances Theodosia; *m* 7 Feb 1815 5th Viscount Powerscourt (*qv*) and *d* 10 May 1820, leaving issue

The **2nd Earl** *m* 2nd 5 July 1804 Juliana Anne (*d* 23 Nov 1856), yst dau of John Orde, of Weetwood, Northumberland, and by her had:

2 John; *b* July 1805; Capt 7th Hus; *m* 1st 18 July 1839 Emily (*d* 3 May 1845), 2nd dau of Henry Thompson, of Holgate Lodge, Yorks, and had:

(1) WILLIAM HENRY JOCELYN, **6th Earl of Roden**; *b* 5 Nov 1842; Capt RN (ret 1892); *d* unm 23 Jan 1910

(2) ROBERT JULIAN ORDE, **7th Earl**

2 (cont.) The Hon John Jocelyn *m* 2nd 16 Aug 1855 Helen (*d* 19 March 1890), dau of Capt Hill, and *d* 22 July 1869

3 Augustus George Frederick; *b* Dec 1811; Maj 6th Dragoon Gds; *m* 1st 19 Feb 1845 Cecilia (*d* 26 Aug 1847), 2nd dau of Gen Sir Neil Douglas, KCB, KCH, and had:

(1) Barbara Juliana Augusta; *m* 2 Oct 1861 John Allen Allen, of Erroll, and had issue. He *d* 24 June 1885

3 (cont.) Maj The Hon Augustus Jocelyn *m* 2nd 8 Jan 1851 Grace (*d* 24 Jan 1852), 2nd dau of Sir John MacNeill, LLD, and *d* 11 April 1887, having by her had:

(1) Julian Robert John, CB (1918); *b* 12 Jan 1852, Col, Cmdt Sch of Gunnery Shoeburyness 1905–09, War Office and Admlty 1914–19; *m* 1875 Euphemia Jessie (*d* 27 April 1906), dau of Major A Balderston, HEICS, and *d* 13 Sept 1929, having had:

1a Julian Robert MacNeill; *b* 13 June 1887; *d* 9 Feb 1888

1a Grace Helen; *b* 11 July 1882; *d* 19 April 1884

2a Isabella Jessie; *b* 20 Dec 1883; *m* 25 Sept 1907 Col Lewis St John Rawlinson Clutterbuck, OBE, RA (*d* 7 June 1965), only s of Col Lewis Alexander Clutterbuck, and *d* 31 March 1968, leaving issue

3a Gladys; *b* 31 May 1885; *m* 12 Aug 1907 Lt-Col David Allan Strachan, RA (Res) (*d* 7 Dec 1951), and *dsp* 8 April 1970

The 6th EARL's bro,

ROBERT JULIAN ORDE JOCELYN, **7th Earl of Roden**, JP Co Down and Cheshire, DL; *b* 19 April 1845; Lt-Col King's Liverpool Regt; *m* 7 Dec 1882 Ada Maria (*d* 18 Feb 1931), dau of Col Soame Gambier Jenyns, CB, and had:

1 ROBERT SOAME, **8th Earl**

1 Julian Mary; *b* 6 Dec 1885; *m* 19 April 1905 Roger Charlton Parr, JP, DL (*d* 7 Aug 1958), only s of Joseph Charlton Parr, JP, DL, and *d* 5 July 1973, leaving issue

2 Marcia Valda; *b* 23 Jan 1891; *m* 1st 28 July 1914 (*divorce* 1924) Maj Robert Barclay Black, DSO (*d* 31 Dec 1953), s of J Milne Black, and had issue; *m* 2nd 23 Aug 1924 Maj-Gen Eric Grant Miles, CB, DSO, MC, KOSB, 2nd s of George Herbert Miles, of Homestall, Welwyn, and *d* 18 March 1972, leaving further issue

The 7th EARL *d* 18 Dec 1915; his only s,

ROBERT SOAME JOCELYN, **8th Earl of Roden**, DL (Co Down); *b* 8 Sept 1883; Capt NI Horse WW I, rep I peer; *m* 19 July 1905 Elinor Jessie (*d* 11 Feb 1962), 2nd dau of Joseph Charlton Parr, JP, DL, of Grappenhall, Heyes, Cheshire, and Staunton Park, Staunton-on-Arrow, Herefs, and had:

1 ROBERT WILLIAM, **9th Earl**

2 John Charlton; *b* 29 Feb 1924; Midshipman RN WW II; *ka* in HMS *Barham* 25 Nov 1941

1 Elizabeth; *b* 28 Jan 1907; *m* 1st 3 Aug 1927 (*divorce* 1940) Gerald Francis Annesley (*see* ANNESLEY, E); *m* 2nd 31 Aug 1940 (*divorce* 1949) Hon Charles Dudley Anthony Ross (*see* DE ROS, B) and had further issue; *m* 3rd 15 April 1954 Cdr Warden Sydney Learmonth Gilchrist, RN (*d* 15 Sept 1958), s of S J Learmonth Gilchrist, of S Kensington; *m* 4th 11 July 1967 Brig (Edward) Maxwell Tyler, DSO, MC and bar, RA, s of Edward Ernest Tyler, of NSW

2 Mabel Kathleen; *b* 25 March 1915; *m* 1st 21 July 1937 (*divorce* 1959) Richard Neville Brooke, only s of Sir Richard Christopher Brooke, 9th Bt, of Norton Priory (*qv*); *m* 2nd 17 June 1960, as his 2nd w, Sir Nicolas John Alexander Cheetham, KCMG, only s of Sir Milne Cheetham, KCMG, and *d* 1985, having had issue by her 1st husb

The 8th EARL *d* 30 Oct 1956; his only surv s,

ROBERT WILLIAM JOCELYN, **9th Earl of Roden**, DL (Co Down 1961); *b* 4 Dec 1909; Capt RN WW II (despatches three times); *m* 21 Oct 1937 Clodagh Rose (*d* 1989), dau of Edward Robert Kennedy (*see* KENNEDY, Bt), and *d* 1993, leaving:

1 ROBERT JOHN JOCELYN, **10th and present Earl of Roden**

2 Thomas Alan; *b* 4 Oct 1941; *educ* Stowe and RNC Dartmouth; Lt-Cdr RN; *m* 12 Nov 1966 (*divorce* 1982) Fiona Alice, dau of Capt Rudland Dallas Cairns, DSC, RN, of Taghmon, Co Wexford; missing feared lost at sea 1991, leaving:

(1) +Charles Patrick; *b* 20 Oct 1978

(1) *Moira Anne; *b* 5 Nov 1969

(2) *Caragh Clodagh; *b* 28 Dec 1976

3 +James Michael [The Hon James Jocelyn, Glynsk, Cashel, Connemara, Co Galway, Ireland]; *b* 12 April 1943; *educ* Stowe and Trin Coll Dublin

RODGER OF EARLSFERRY

Creation: B. (LP, UK) 1992.

THE BARON RODGER OF EARLSFERRY, of Earlsferry, District of NE Fife (Alan Ferguson Rodger, PC (1992)) [The Rt Hon the Lord Rodger of Earlsferry PC, House of Lords, London SW1A 0PW]; *b* 18 Sept 1944; *educ* Kelvinside Acad Glasgow, Glasgow U (MA, LLB) and New Coll Oxford (DCL, MA, DPhil, Fell and Tutor Law 1970–72); Research Fellow Balliol Coll Oxford 1969–70, advocate 1974, Clerk Faculty Advocates 1976–79, Standing Jr Counsel (Scotland) DTI 1979, QC 1985, Advocate Depute 1985–88, Home Advocate Depute 1986–88, Slr-Gen Scotland 1989–92, Ld Advocate Scotland 1992–96, Ld Justice-Gen and Ld Pres Court Session 1996–; Member Mental Welfare Commn Scotland 1982–85; Hon Bencher Lincoln's Inn 1992, FBA 1991, FRSE 1992

Lineage: THOMAS FERGUSON RODGER, CBE, of Glasgow; Prof; *m* Jean Margaret Smith Chalmers and had:

ALAN FERGUSON, *cr* a **Baron**

RODGERS

Arms: Az. two bars gemel dancetty arg., overall two palm branches in saltire enfiled through an ancient crown or. **Crest:** Two raven's heads addorsed sa. and gu., both within a collar or, pendant therefrom a rose arg., barbed and seeded ppr. **Motto:** Παθηματα μαθηματα ('All experience is knowledge'). **Creation:** Bt. (UK) 29 June 1964.

SIR (ANDREW) PIERS WINGATE RODGERS, 3RD BT, of Groombridge, Co Kent [Sir Piers Rodgers Bt, 20 Princelet St, London E1 6QH]; *b* 24 Oct 1944; *s* bro 1997; *educ* Eton and Merton Coll Oxford (BA); with J Henry Schroder Wagg 1967–73 (PA to chm 1971–73); Dir ICOMOS (Sec UK Ctee 1981) Paris 1973–79, Consultant UNESCO Paris 1979–80, Sec RA, Chantrey Bequest and Br Inst Fund 1982–96, Dir RA Burlington Gdns Project 1996–97, memb: Bd Warburg Inst 1993– and Court of Assists Masons' Co 1982–, Freeman City London, memb Merchant Adventurers' Co York, FRSA 1973, Chev Arts et Lettres 1987, Ordre National de Merite 1991, Cavaliere Ufficiale Ordine al Merito Italy 1992; *m* 1979 *Marie-Agathe, dau of Charles-Albert Houette, Croix de Guerre, of Bléneau, France, and has:

1 +THOMAS; *b* 18 Dec 1979; *educ* Eton
2 +Augustus; *b* 1983

Lineage: CHARLES RODGERS, of York; *b* 1843; *educ* privately; *m* 1891 Maud Mary (*d* 1941), dau of James Hodgson, of Welburn, Yorks, and *d* 1909, leaving:

Sir John Charles Rodgers, 1st Bt (UK), so *cr* 29 June 1964, DL (Kent 1973); *b* 5 Oct 1906; *educ* St Peter's York, Keble Coll Oxford (BA 1928 MA 1948) and Ecole des Roches France; sub-warden Mary Ward Settlement London 1929, Lecturer and Admin Assist Hull U 1930, FO 1939 and 1944–45, Dir: Commercial Rels Div Min Info 1939–41 and Post-War Export Trade Devpt Dept Overseas Trade 1941–42, Dep Head Industl Info Div Min Production 1942–44, MP (C) Sevenoaks 1950–1976, PPS to Mins Works and Educn and BOT 1951–57, Jr Min BOT 1958–60, dep chm J Walter Thompson 1960, Fndr-Govr Admin Staff Coll, memb: Cncl Fndn Management Educn, BBC Gen Advsy Cncl 1946–52, Exec Ctee Br Cncl 1958; Govr BFI 1958, V-Chm Exec Ctee Political and Economic Planning 1960–68, Internat Pres European Centre for Documentation and Info 1960–68, memb Cncl RCA 1968–93, UK Del Gen Assembly Cncl Europe and WEU 1969–93, Pres IPA 1967–69, Master Masons' Co 1967–68, Soc for Individual Freedom 1970–73; Grand Cross Order Civil Merit Spain 1965 and Liechtenstein 1970, Cdr Order Dom Infante Henrique Portugal 1972, Grand Offr Order Leopold II Belguim 1978, Order Brilliant Star China 1979, Kt Cdr 1st Cl Roy Order N Star Sweden 1980, Cdr 1st Cl Order Lion Finland 1980, Medal of Merit Cncl Europe 1980; *m* 23 Dec 1930 Betsy JP, PhD (*d* May or June 1998), yst dau of Francis William Aikin-Sneath, JP, of Burleigh Court and Tibberton Court, Glos, and *d* 1993, leaving:

1 **Sir (John Fairlie) Tobias Rodgers, 2nd Bt**; *b* 2 July 1940; *educ* Eton and Worcester Coll Oxford; antiquarian book dealer, jnlst, publisher; *d* unm 19 Jan 1997
2 Sir (ANDREW) PIERS WINGATE RODGERS, **3rd and present Bt**

RODGERS OF QUARRY BANK

Creation: B. (LP, UK) 1992.

THE BARON RODGERS OF QUARRY BANK, of Kentish Town, London Borough of Camden (William Thomas Rodgers, PC (1975)) [The Rt Hon The Lord Rodgers of Quarry Bank PC, House of Lords, London SW1A 0PW]; *b* 28 Oct 1928; *educ* Quarry Bank High Sch Liverpool and Magdalen Coll Oxford; MP (Lab) Stockton-on-Tees 1962–74 and (Lab 1974–81, SDP 1981–83) Stockton Teesside 1974–83 (fought (Lab) Bristol W March 1957, (SDP/Alliance) Milton Keynes 1987), Parly U-Sec DEA 1964–67, FO (Leader UK Delegn Cncl Europe and WEU Assembly) 1967–68, Min State BOT 1968–69, Treasury 1969–70, MOD 1974–76, Sec State Tport 1976–79, Gen-Sec Fabian Soc 1953–60 (memb to 1981), V-Pres SDP 1982–87, Chm Expenditure Ctee Trade & Industry 1971–74 and ASA 1995–; Dir-Gen RIBA 1987–94, Leader Lib-Dems Ho Lds 1997–; author: *Hugh Gaitskell, 1906–1963* (ed, 1964), *The People into Parliament* (1966), *The Politics of Change* (1982), *Government and Industry* (ed, 1986); *m* 1955 *Silvia, dau of Hirsch Szulman, of London, and has three daus

Lineage: WILLIAM ARTHUR RODGERS, of Liverpool; *m* Gertrude Helen — and had:

WILLIAM THOMAS, *cr* a **Baron**

RODNEY

Arms: Or three eagles displayed, wings inverted purpure. **Crest:** On a ducal coronet or an eagle, wings displayed and inverted purpure.
Supporters: Two eagles, wings inverted purpure, beaked and membered or, each sustaining with the interior claw a banner of St George, the staves proper, enfiled each with a naval coronet gold.
Motto: *Non generant aquilæ columbas* ('Eagles do not beget doves').
Creations: Bt. (GB) 22 Jan 1764, B. (GB) 19 June 1782.

THE 10TH BARON RODNEY OF RODNEY STOKE, Co Somerset, and a **Baronet** (Sir George Brydges Rodney, Bt) [The Rt Hon The Lord Rodney, 38 Pembroke Rd, London W8 6NU]; *b* 3 Jan 1953; *s* f 1992; *educ* Eton; *m* 20 Aug 1996 *Jane, dau of Rowan Blakeney, of The Old Rectory, Hatherop, Glos

Lineage: RICHARD de RODENYE; *b c* 1270; acquired *temp* EDWARD I land at Rodney, nr Mark, in the Somerset levels, also land at Claverham; in EDWARD I's serv 1307 on, commr sea walls and dykes 1314 and 1316 at Hambury Salt Marsh, Glos, and Somerset coast; ktd 1316; Constable Bristol Castle 1322; *m* 1st Maud —; *m* 2nd Lucy —; *m* 3rd — and *d* by March 1323, having had by his 2nd w, with two yr sons (Richard; Thomas):

Sir WALTER de RODNEY; apparently ancestor of:

Sir JOHN RODNEY; inherited Rodney Stoke from his cousin Sir George Rodney; *m* Jane, dau of Sir Henry Seymour (*see* SOMERSET, D), and *d* 6 Aug 1612 aged 61, leaving, with other issue:

1 Edward (Sir), of Rodney Stoke; *m* Frances dau of Sir Robert Southwell, of Woodrising, Norfolk, and *d* 1657, leaving:

(1) Elizabeth
(2) Anne/Frances; *m* Sir Thomas Bridges/Brydges, of Keynsham Abbey, nr Bristol, and had, with other issue:

1a Harry; *m* 1st Lady Diana Holles, dau of 2nd Earl of Clare of the 1624 *cr*, and had a dau (Arabella, *m* John Mitchell, of Kingston Russell, Dorset); *m* 2nd — Freeman and by her had two more daus

2a George Rodney, of Avington, Hants; *m* by 24 June 1677 Lady Anna Maria Brudenell, dau of 2nd Earl of Cardigan (*see* AILESBURY, M) and widow of 11th Earl of Shrewsbury and Waterford (*qv*), and was *bur* 9 Feb 1713, leaving:

1b George Rodney, of Avington; inherited estates of his uncle Harry; MP Winchester 1714–51; *d* aged *c* 72 (found drowned in a stream running through his garden), leaving the bulk of his estates to his Bridges/Brydges relatives who became Dukes of Chandos (*see* TEMPLE OF STOWE, E) but his Alresford estate in Hants to **1st Baron Rodney** (*see* below)

(3) Penelope; *m* Sir Peter Gleane, Bt

2 George, of Lyndhurst, Hants; *b* 1608; *m* Anne, dau of Sir Thomas Lake and widow of 16th Lord (Baron) De Ros (*qv*) of Helmsley, and *d* 1630, having had:

(1) ANTHONY

3 William, of Morelinch, Somerset; *b* 1610; *m* Alice, dau of Sir Thomas Caesar, Baron Exchequer (bro of Sir Julius Caesar, Master Rolls, and Henry Caesar, Dean Ely, and s of Cesari Adelmare, of Padua, physician to QUEENs MARY and ELIZABETH I), and *d* 1669, having had:

(1) William; companion of the Quaker William Penn in America

Sir EDWARD RODNEY's n,

ANTHONY RODNEY; Capt in Col Leigh's Regt of Dragoons, Lt-Col Holt's Regt of Marines 1702; *m* Constantia, dau and coheir of Ralph Clarke, and was *k* 1705 in a duel at Barcelona, leaving:

HENRY RODNEY, of Walton-on-Thames, Surrey; *b* 1681; Cornet of Horse, Capt RM, cmdg GEORGE I's roy yacht (a post he owed to his cousin the Duke of Chandos's influence); *m* Mary, est dau and coheir of Sir Henry Newton, Envoy Extrdy to Tuscany, LLD, Judge Admlty Court, and *d* 1737, having had three sons and a dau; the 2nd but est surv s:

Sir George Brydges Rodney, 1st Bt (GB), so *cr* 22 Jan 1764, and **1st Baron Rodney of Rodney Stoke**, Co Somerset (GB), so *cr* 19 June 1782 (with £2,000 a year (nearly £94,000 a year in late-1990s terms) to himself and (from 1793) his successors), KB (1780); *bapt* 13 Feb 1718/9 (GEORGE I stood sponsor); *educ* Harrow; RN: joined 1732, Lt 1739, Cdr 1742, present at defeat of French off Finisterre 1747, Govr Newfoundland 1749–50, R-Adml May 1759, cmded successful bombardment of Le Havre and destruction of flotilla prepared there to invade England July 1759, C-in-C Leeward Islands Station 1761–63 (reduced Martinique 1762, captured Grenada, St Lucia and St Vincent), V-Adml 1763; defeated Spanish fleet 16 Jan 1780 off Cape St Vincent, taking the enemy cdr Adml Don Juan de Langara against the French off Martinique 17 April 1780; captured St Eustatius Jan 1781; routed French under Count de Grasse 12 April 1782 (Battle of the Saints), capturing de Grasse, the latter's flagship *Ville de Paris* of 110 guns, three other ships of 74 guns each and two ships of 64 guns each and sinking another of 74 guns (3,000 French killed, 6,000 wounded); he later captured four other enemy ships; as a result the British got much better terms at the Treaty of Versailles 20 Jan 1783 (which ended the War of American Independence) than they would otherwise have done following their disastrous performance in America culminating in the surrender of Cornwallis (*qv*) at Yorktown; MP Saltash 1751–54 (fought Camelford 1754), Okehampton 1759–61, Penryn 1762–68, Northampton 1768–74 and Westminster 1780–82, Govr Greenwich Hosp 1765–70, R-Adml GB 1771, C-in-C Jamaica Station 1771–74, Adml the White 1778; *m* 1st 31 Jan 1753 Jane (*d* Jan 1757), sis of 7th and 8th Earls of Northampton (*see* NORTHAMPTON, M), and had:

1 GEORGE, **2nd Baron**

2 James; Capt RN; lost at sea 1776 unm

The **1st Baron** *m* 2nd 1764 Henrietta (*d* March 1829 aged 90), dau of John Clies, merchant at Lisbon, by Margaretta, 5th dau of William Gower, of Glandovan, Cilgerron, Pembs, and *d* 24 May 1792, having by her had:

3 John; *b* 10 May 1765; Capt RN, Ch Sec to Govt Ceylon; *m* 1st 4 July 1784 Catherine (*d* 26 Feb 1794), only dau of 6th Earl of Westmeath (*qv*), and had:

(1) Catherine Henrietta; *m* 20 July 1810 Gen Hon Sir Patrick Stuart, GCMG (*d* 7 Feb 1855), and *d* 17 April 1870

(2) Fanny Mary; *m* 20 Feb 1813 11th Lord Blantyre (accidentally *k* at Brussels 22 Sept 1830; *see* 1900 edn) and *d* 19 Nov 1875, leaving issue

(3) Frances Rodney; *m* 4 Jan 1810 Thomas Eden (*d* 8 Nov 1844) and *d* 5 Jan 1879

3 (cont.) Capt The Hon John Rodney *m* 2nd 19 Oct 1799 Lady Louisa Martha Stratford (*d* 2 Dec 1814), est dau and coheir of 3rd Earl of Aldborough (*see* 1875 edn), and by her had, with a dau (*d* unm):

(1) John Stratford; *b* 14 May 1802; *m* 1st 22 March 1824 — Boyce, of Bombay (*dsp* 3 Feb 1825); *m* 2nd 23 Dec 1826 Eleanor, 3rd dau of Joseph Hume, and *d* 28 Dec 1854, leaving:

1a Tollemache Montagu Brydges; *dsp* 24 April 1858

1a Catherine Dora; *m* 8 May 1860 Adml Henry Craven St John and *d* 18 May 1914, leaving issue (*see* BOLINGBROKE and SAINT JOHN, V)

(2) Maitland Thomas; *b* 14 Oct 1810; Capt RN; *m* 10 Jan 1849 Elizabeth Frances (*d* 27 Oct 1886), 5th dau of Col Dickson, and *d* 18 July 1872

(4) Louisa Frederica; *m* 29 June 1818 Lord John George Lennox (*see* RICHMOND and GORDON, D) and *d* 12 Jan 1865, leaving issue

(5) Angela; *m* 8 Jan 1825 Col Alexander Browne, RE, and *d* 12 Feb 1897, leaving issue

(6) Eliza; *m* 22 March 1832 James Sedgwick Wetenhall (*d* 1872) and *d* 1860

(7) Emily Georgiana; *m* 19 Oct 1835 Lt-Col William Marsden Wetenhall (*d* 25 May 1847), 10th Regt, and *d* 2 Oct 1842

(8) Caroline Stuart; *m* 3 April 1830 Campbell Drummond Riddell (*d* 27 Dec 1858) and *d* Jan 1898

3 (cont.) Capt The Hon John Rodney *m* 3rd 7 June 1815 Antoinette (*d* 26 Nov 1868), only dau of Anthony Pierre Reyne, and *d* 9 April 1847, having by her had, with four daus (*d* unm):

(3) George Brydges, CB; *b* 7 Nov 1820; Lt-Gen RM, Chev Legn Hon, 5th Cl Medjidie; *m* 21 Jan 1856 Isabella Elizabeth (*d* 1 Aug 1915), 2nd dau of Gen Marcus Beresford, and *dsp* 8 July 1895

(4) Lennox George, JP (Hants); *b* 10 Dec 1837; Lt-Col RMLI, served Baltic Expdn 1855 (medal); *m* 3 July 1872 Julia Susan (*d* 26 Feb 1934), yr dau of Lt Phillip Hast, RN, and *d* 6 Aug 1913, leaving:

1a Lennox George Brydges; *b* 21 Sept 1875; Maj 1st Bn The Roy Irish Rifles, Boer War (Queen's medal, three clasps), WW I (wounded, 1914 star, two

medals); *m* 5 March 1917 Gwendolen Agnes Rodney Edwards (*m* 2nd Julian Edward), 2nd dau of Richard Whytock Leslie, MD, LLD, KGStJ, of St Heliers, Strandtown, Co Down, and *dsp* 11 July 1945

1a Isabel Mary; *b* 29 April 1878; *m* 8 Aug 1900 Albert Hillam Ozzard (*d* 18 Oct 1960 aged 94), s of Col A H Ozzard, RMLI, and *d* 29 Aug 1948

(9) Antoinette Anna Louisa; *m* 21 July 1832 Capt Robert F Bourchier (*d* 1837), 4th Bombay NI, and *d* 21 June 1898

4 Edward; *b* 18 June 1783; Capt RN; *m* 1807 Rebecca Geer (*d* 13 July 1840) and *d* 12 Nov 1828, leaving:

(1) George Brydges; *b* 5 March 1827; *d* 1834

(1) Henrietta Fraser; *m* 28 Oct 1845 Sir Hugh Owen Owen, 2nd Bt (*qv*), and *d* 17 July 1894, leaving:

1a, George Rodney; had:

1b Margaret; *m* 3 Nov 1900 Cdr Robert Burton Rodney, USN

1 Jane; *m* 6 July 1784 George Chambers

2 Margaret Anne; *d* 14 Oct 1858

3 Sarah Brydges; *m* 26 Nov 1801 Gen Godfrey Basil Meynell Mundy (*d* 14 March 1848) and *d* 17 July 1871 aged 91, leaving issue

The 1st BARON's est s,

GEORGE RODNEY, **2nd Baron Rodney of Rodney Stoke**; *b* 25 Dec 1753; Capt 3rd Foot Gds, Lt-Col 1783, MP (Tory) Northampton 1780–84; *m* 10 April 1781 Anne (*d* 15 Aug 1840), dau and coheir of Thomas Harley, PC, Ld Mayor London 1767–68 (3rd s of 3rd Earl of Oxford and Mortimer; *see* OXFORD AND ASQUITH, preliminary remarks), and *d* 2 Jan 1802, having had:

1 GEORGE RODNEY, **3rd Baron Rodney of Rodney Stoke**; *b* 17 June 1782; *educ* Ch Ch Oxford; DCL, Ld Lt Radnorshire 1805–42; *m* 27 Feb 1819 Charlotte Georgiana (*d* 19 Feb 1878), sis of 1st Baron Tredegar (*see* 1963 edn), and *dsp* 21 June 1842

2 THOMAS JAMES RODNEY later HARLEY-RODNEY (roy licence 4 Nov 1805), **4th Baron Rodney of Rodney Stoke**; *b* 12 April 1784; *d unm* 30 Oct 1843

3 Rev SPENCER RODNEY, **5th Baron Rodney of Rodney Stoke**; *b* 30 May 1785; *educ* Ch Ch Oxford (Fell All Souls 1807–44); Rector Elmley, Kent, 1805–18; *d unm* 15 May 1846

4 Robert; *b* 14 May 1786; Capt RN; *m* 20 July 1819 Anne (*d* 24 Feb 1824), yst dau and coheir of Thomas Dennett, of Lock Ashurst, Sussex, and *d* 20 July 1826, leaving:

(1) ROBERT DENNETT, **6th Baron**

(1) Anne; granted rank of baron's dau 1847; *m* 13 June 1844 Maj Manaton Pipon (*d* Sept 1881) and *d* 4 Nov 1878 aged 75

5 James Berkeley; *b* 8 Sept 1789; Lt-Col 3rd Gds; *d* 16 Dec 1831

6 Henry (Rev); *b* 30 Sept 1790; Preb Hereford; *d* Dec 1878

7 Mortimer; *b* 13 Dec 1791; *m* 27 April 1815 Sarah Burton (*d* 25 Feb 1853), dau of Robert Withy, and *d* 30 March 1856, leaving, with two other daus (*d* unm):

(1) Mortimer Harley; *b* 23 Feb 1817; Capt RN; *m* 3 June 1857 Emily Youart and *d* 14 Aug 1881, having had, with another dau (*d* unm):

1a Mortimer Harley Brydges; *b* 8 April 1861; *d* 1 March 1881

1a Mary Louisa; *d unm* March 1951

(2) Frederick James; *b* 16 May 1821; *m* 30 June 1852 Frances Philippa Catherine (*d* 21 Dec 1894), 2nd dau of Rev John Vesey Hamilton, Rector Little Chart, Kent, and *d* 23 Jan 1912, having had, with other issue:

1a Spencer Vesey; *b* 4 May 1863; *d unm* 7 April 1946

2a Edward Hamilton; *b* 19 Oct 1871; *d unm* March 1948

3a Reginald George; *b* 11 Oct 1873; *m* 1916 Patricia Lissette du Chastel (*d* 1964), dau of William James MacGrath, of Co Tipperary, and *d* 21 Nov 1933, leaving:

1b +Philip Harley Brydges [Philip Rodney Esq, 61 Knighton Rd, Wembury, Devon PL9 0EA]; *b* 17 Sept 1917; *m* Jan 1951 *Janet Barker and has:

1c *Julie Rose Patricia; *b* 25 May 1954; *m* 1976 *Andrew George Lewis Leftley and has:

1d *Ian Andrew Philip; *b* 1985

1d *Nicola Caroline; *b* 1979

2c *Faye Jessica Frances Corisande; *b* 23 March 1958; *m* 1991 *Graham George Tongue, and has:

1d *Martin Terence Philip; *b* 14 July 1994

1a Evelyn Augusta; *d unm* 8 Jan 1945

2a Bertha Vesina Rose; *d unm* 21 Dec 1945

3a Frances Maria; *d unm* 22 March 1955

4a Henrietta Mary; *m* 28 June 1905 William Crosbie Hamilton, MD, and *d* 16 May 1930

5a Clementina Laura; *d unm* April 1951

(3) Arthur Rueff; *b* 1 Nov 1832; *m* 11 May 1858 Alicia Hannah (*d* 30 July 1900), yst dau of Col Henry Salwey, of Runnymede Pk, Egham, Surrey, and *d* 22 April 1908, leaving, with a s (*d* unm):

1a Gertrude Alice; *b* 1859

2a Florence Leila; *b* 1862; *m* 25 Aug 1896 Edward Docker

(1) Frances Jane; *m* 16 Oct 1861 Baldwin John Pollexfen Bastard, DL (*d* 22 Oct 1905), of Kitley, Devon, and *dsp* 2 Feb 1914

8 William Powell, of Llanvihangel Court, Abergavenny, Mon, JP, DL; *b* 1 July 1794; High Sheriff 1860; *m* 26 Oct 1824 Elizabeth (*d* 10 March 1888 aged 84), dau of Thomas Brown, memb Supreme Cncl India, and *d* 27 Aug 1878, leaving, with two daus (*d* unm):

(1) William Powell; *b* 20 Sept 1829; *m* 11 Sept 1856 Diana Hotham (*d* 11 Oct 1917), 2nd dau of Sir John William Lubbock, 3rd Bt (*see* Avebury, B), and *d* 19 June 1868, having had issue, with three other daus (*d* unm):

1a Harley, JP (Mon); *b* 20 Nov 1858; *educ* Ch Ch Oxford (MA); Assist Keeper Public Records; *d* 5 Sept 1930

1a Anne Eliza

9 John; *b* 26 March 1798; *d* 4 Jan 1823

1 Anne Jane; *m* 22 Jan 1824 Edmund Pollexfen Bastard (*d* 8 June 1838), of Kitley, Devon, and *d* 25 April 1833, leaving issue

The 5th BARON's n,

ROBERT DENNETT RODNEY, **6th Baron Rodney of Rodney Stoke**; *b* 21 May 1820; Ensign Scots Gds 1838; *m* 3 Aug 1850 Sarah (*d* 1 Oct 1882), dau of John Singleton, and *d* 19 Aug 1864, leaving:

1 GEORGE BRIDGES HARLEY DENNETT, **7th Baron**

2 Robert William Henry; *b* 11 Aug 1858; *m* 14 Sept 1882 Henrietta Katherine Letitia (*d* 18 Nov 1948), dau of Henry Bertie Watkin Williams-Wynn (*see* WILLIAMS-WYNN, Bt), and *d* 29 Jan 1933, having had, with four other daus (*d* unm):

  (1) Dennett Bertie; *b* 16 Jan 1886; *d* 4 Sept 1887

  (2) Mervyn Harley; *b* 16 Aug 1890; *educ* Wellington; Lt-Cdr RNR; *m* 1st 16 Feb 1915 Dorothy (*d* 4 March 1917), only dau of Rev Benjamin Norton Thompson, Rector Weston-super-Mare, Preb Wells, and had:

    1a Nigel Robert Harley; *b* 21 Feb 1917; Cdr RN WW II (despatches four times); *m* 13 July 1946 *Patricia Ann Merlyn [Mrs Nigel Rodney, Ashen House, Northleigh, Colyton, Devon], dau of Lt-Col Harley Wentworth Ashburner, DSO, of Cheltenham, and *d* 1992, leaving:

      1b +Nicholas Simon Harley [Nicholas Rodney Esq, 17 rue de Labruyère, 78000 Versailles, France]; *b* 20 Dec 1947; *m* 1973 *Maïté Bernadette Edith, dau of Henri Pinet des Ecots, of Château de Curty, Imphy, France, and has:

        1c *Victoria Ségolène Jehanne Gwenaëlle; *b* 28 Nov 1997

      2b +Christopher Lossie Charles; *b* 3 April 1957

      1b *Julia Diana; *b* 27 May 1951

      2b *Susan Emma Gabrielle [Mrs Charles Guest, Glebe House, Southleigh, Colyton, Devon]; *b* 25 July 1952; *m* 1975 *Charles Ainslie Guest, s of Dennis William Guest, of Rye, Sussex, and has:

        1c *Henry Harley; *b* 1983

        2c *Charles Humphrey; *b* 1985

        3c *Oliver Hugo; *b* 1987

  (2) (cont.) Mervyn Rodney *m* 2nd 27 Jan 1921 (*divorce* 1956) Louise (*d* 27 May 1979 aged 83), only child of Prof Armand Halieux, and *d* 5 Oct 1964, having by her had:

    2a John Armand, MC; *b* 8 Dec 1921; *educ* Uppingham and Magdalen Coll Oxford; Capt Coldstream Gds WW II 1942–45; *m* 8 Sept 1951 *(Gertrude) Evelyn [Mrs John Rodney, 147 Gloucester Rd, London SW7 4TH], yr dau of Capt Simon John James, of Westcliff-on-Sea, and *d* 1992, leaving:

      1b +Peter Miles; *b* 3 March 1953; *educ* Radley; *m* 1980 *Marianne Hilary, dau of George Robert Downes, and has:

        1c *Lydia Jane Louise; *b* 1983

        2c *Katharine Amelia Laura; *b* 1985

      2b +David James [David Rodney Esq, 74 Cicada Rd, London SW18 3QN]; *b* 15 June 1965; *educ* Haileybury and RMA Sandhurst; 2nd Lt Coldstream Gds 1985; *m* 1989 *Sally L M, er dau of Dr David Norman Howell Owen, of Bryn-y-Mor, Fishguard, Pembs, and has:

        1c +Harry John Melville; *b* 1992

        2c +Oliver Hugh James; *b* 12 July 1994

  (3) Robert Henry Basil; *b* 9 June 1893; *educ* Clifton; *m* 1928 *Ellen [Mrs Robert Rodney, The Cottage, 55 Oakdale Rd, Mount Roskill, Auckland, New Zealand], dau of Henry Brimicombe, of Devon

  (4) Ivor Morgan, OBE (1945); *b* 19 June 1896; *educ* Repton; Capt Dorset Regt, WWs I and II, RAF 1915–43; in Psychological Warfare Br AFHQ MEF 1943–45, G/Capt, memb Ware RDC, chm ATC Ctee and Herts TA Ctee; *m* 27 May 1931 Althea Caroline Winifred (*d* 1978), er dau of Sir Gerald Woods Wollaston, KCB, KCVO, FSA, Garter King of Arms 1930–44, and *d* 16 June 1954, leaving:

    1a *Sarah Patience [Mrs Brian Woodard, 69 Bernham Rd, Hellesdon, Norfolk NR6 5QQ]; *b* 22 May 1933; SRN, SCM; *m* 19 Dec 1959 *Brian Charles Woodard, s of Charles Richard Woodard, of Norwich, and has:

      1b *Anthony John; *b* 27 March 1960

      2b *Paris Morgan; *b* 17 June 1962

      3b *Craig Charles; *b* 7 Dec 1963; *m* 1987 *Linda Christine Heasman and has:

        1c *Ritchie Craig; *b* 31 Dec 1990

        1c *Kimberley Linda; *b* 14 Oct 1988

      1b *Helen Mary; *b* 24 April 1961; *m* 1st 1979 (*divorce* 1985) Lloyd Haydn Anthony Evans, and:

        1c *Stephanie Sarah; *b* 29 Sept 1980

      1b (cont.) Mrs Helen Evans *m* 2nd 14 Feb 1994 *Gerard Martin Kavanagh, of Toronto, and by him has:

        1c *Ryan Francis; *b* 24 May 1996

        2c *Cheyenne Vaire; *b* 16 June 1995

    2a *Prudence Jane [Mrs Keith Wollaston, 1 Beach Ct, The Beach, Walmer, Deal, Kent CT14 7HN]; *b* 6 May 1936; *m* 20 Aug 1960 *Keith Hyde Wollaston, TD, s of Geoffrey Lester Wollaston, of Sale, Cheshire, and has:

      1b *Andrew James Rodney; *b* 2 July 1961; *m* 1991 *Alison Wishart and has:

        1c *George William Woods; *b* 27 Sept 1996

        1c *Amelia Grace Forsyth; *b* 24 March 1995

        2c *Olivia Lucy Hyde; *b* 1 Dec 1997

      1b *Rachel Althea Rodney; *b* 9 May 1963; *m* 1995 *Sam Hatfield and has:

        1c *India Rose Rodney; *b* 21 Oct 1995

        2c *Althea Georgina Catcheside; *b* 30 Sept 1997

      2b *Frances Jane Rodney; *b* 7 Nov 1964; *m* 1993 *Said El Moumni and has:

        1c *Sarah; *b* 27 July 1994

      3b *Catherine Mary Rodney; *b* 7 Nov 1964; *m* 1991 *Robert Dickson and has:

        1c *Wendy Elizabeth; *b* 1992

    3a *Alicia Henrietta Althea [Mrs David Pentin, 16 St Dunstan's Terrace, Canterbury, Kent CT2 8AX]; *b* 17 Oct 1937; *m* 11 June 1960 *David John Pentin, only s of Sydney Edward Pentin, of Canterbury, and has:

      1b *John Mark; *b* 11 Feb 1964; *m* 1995 *Sheena Nicolette Forster and has:

        1c *Natasha Alexandra; *b* 25 May 1997

      2b *Richard Harley; *b* 16 Aug 1969

      3b *Edward Michael; *b* 23 Feb 1971

      1b *Caroline Louise; *b* 23 April 1962; *m* 1987 *Mark Kendall Blamey and has:

        1c *Jacob John; *b* 12 April 1992

        2c *Joseph; *b* 29 May 1994

  (1) Grace Marion; *b* 18 July 1887; *m* 11 Sept 1918 Capt Maurice White, Rifle Bde (*d* 8 May 1925), 2nd s of Tyndale White, of Stondon Place, Essex, and *d* 20 Nov 1960

1 Patience Annie; *m* 17 Dec 1878 Robert William Daker Harley, DL (*d* 13 Nov 1907), of Brampton Bryan, Herefs, and *d* 14 May 1918

The 6th BARON's er s,

GEORGE BRIDGES HARLEY DENNETT RODNEY, **7th Baron Rodney of Rodney Stoke**, DL (Herefs); *b* 28 Feb 1857; *educ* Eton; Capt 1st Life Gds 1886–88, Capt Res Offrs 1889, Capt Salop Imp Yeo 1890–97, Lt-Col 16th Middx (London Irish) Rifle Vols 1898; *m* 1st 24 Jan 1891 (*divorce* 1902) Hon Corisande Evelyn Vere Guest, CBE (1918) (*d* 1 Sept 1943), dau of 1st Baron Wimborne (*see* WIMBORNE, V); *m* 2nd 28 Jan 1903 Charlotte Eugenia (*d* 5 Nov 1939), yst dau of Edmund Probyn, DL, of Huntley and Longhope, Glos, and *d* 29 Dec 1909, having had by his 1st w:

1 GEORGE BRIDGES HARLEY GUEST, **8th Baron**

2 James Henry Bertie, MC; *b* 29 March 1893; Capt 5th Bn Rifle Bde WW I (wounded twice, despatches), F/Lt RAF; *m* 1st 15 Sept 1923 (*divorce* 1928) Mrs Bertha Eveline Edith Finch-Noyes, dau of Frederick Jones; *m* 2nd 1928 *Frances Strickland Lovell [Mrs Alwyne Farquharson of Invercauld, Braemar, Aberdeenshire AB35 5TS] (*m* 2nd 5 July 1938 (*divorce* 1948) Capt Charles Gordon, Scottish Horse, yr s of Alexander Gordon of Pitlurg, and has issue; *m* 3rd 3 Feb 1949 Capt Alwyne Arthur Compton Farquharson of Invercauld, MC (*see* NORTHAMPTON, M), dau of Robert Pollard Oldham, of Seattle, USA, and *d* 9 Dec 1933

3 (Charles Christian) Simon, of Brizes Pk, Kelvedon Hatch, Essex; *b* 26 July 1895; *educ* Repton; Capt Gren Gds, WW I (POW) and WW II; *m* 7 Feb 1922 Gladys (*d* 22 Jan 1966), sis of 1st Viscount Greenwood (*qv*)

4 William Francis; *b* 2 Oct 1896; 2nd Lt Rifle Bde and RFC; *ka* 9 May 1915

The 7th BARON's est s,

GEORGE BRIDGES HARLEY GUEST RODNEY, **8th Baron Rodney of Rodney Stoke**; *b* 2 Nov 1891; *educ* Eton and Oriel Coll Oxford (BA 1913); Capt 2nd Dragoons, RSG, WW I (1914 star, two medals), emigrated to Canada and ran a 1,000-acre ranch, Silver Jubilee Medal 1935; *m* 15 Sept 1917 Lady Marjorie Lowther (*d* 29 July 1968), yr dau of 6th Earl of Lonsdale (*qv*), and *d* 18 Dec 1973, having had:

1 George William; *b* 16 Dec 1918; *educ* Stowe and McGill U; F/O RAF WW II; *ka* Sept 1942

2 JOHN FRANCIS, **9th Baron**

3 Michael Christopher; *b* 26 June 1926; *educ* St Peter's Ct, Upper Canada Coll and McGill U; *m* 1st 4 April 1953 (*divorce* 1973) Anne, dau of David Yuile, of Montreal; *m* 2nd 1974 *Penelope Jane [The Hon Mrs Michael Rodney, PO Box 11, Pender Is, BC V0N 2M0, Canada], dau of Capt Eric S Garner, of Easton, Northants, and *d* 1993, leaving by his 1st w:

  (1) *Patricia Anne; *b* 30 Aug 1955

  (2) *Jocelyn Marjorie; *b* 3 Oct 1959

  (3) *Jennifer Susan; *b* 26 Jan 1964

1 *Diana Rosemary [The Hon Diana Rodney, 5222 Sark Rd, Victoria, BC V8Y 2M3, Canada]; *b* 19 April 1924; *educ* McGill U (BA 1949); with WRCNS WW II

2 Sylvia Corisande; *b* 12 Jan 1930; *educ* McGill U (BA); *m* 5 May 1962 *Eric de Bellaigue [Eric de Bellaigue Esq, 5 Randolph Mews, Randolph Ave, London W9], er twin s of Pierre de Bellaigue, of New York, and Mrs William Ladd, of Knightsbridge, and *d* 10 Feb 1985, leaving:

  (1) *Nicholas Charles Rodney; *b* 15 Jan 1966

  (2) *Christopher; *b* 23 Sept 1971

The 8th BARON's est surv s,

JOHN FRANCIS RODNEY, **9th Baron Rodney of Rodney Stoke**; *b* 28 June 1920; *educ* Stowe and McGill; Lt Commandos Burma WW II (despatches), with Rootes Ltd 1946–52 (dir Rootes, Switzerland), with Vacumatic Ltd 1952– (mktg dir), chm Br Printing Machinery Assoc 1976–; *m* 3 Nov 1951 *Régine Elisabeth Lucienne Jeanne Thérèse Marie Ghislaine [The Rt Hon Régine Lady Rodney, 38 Pembroke Rd, London W8 6NU], yr dau of Chevalier Robert Egide Marie Ghislain Pangaert d'Opdorp, of Château Rullingen, Looz, Belgium, and *d* 1992, leaving:

1 GEORGE BRYDGES RODNEY, **10th and present Baron Rodney of Rodney Stoke**

1 *Anne [The Hon Anne Rodney, 3 Avenue Ct, Draycott Ave, London SW3]; *b* 27 June 1955; *m* 1st 1982 (*divorce* 19–) Hugh Lusted, PhD, of San Francisco; *m* 2nd 1991 *Alexander Constantine Basil D'Janoeff, s of Constantine V D'Janoeff, of Windsor, Berks, and has:

  (1) *Katya Alexandra; *b* 4 Jan 1994

ROGERS OF RIVERSIDE

Creation: B. (LP, UK) 1996.

THE BARON ROGERS OF RIVERSIDE, of Chelsea, Borough of Kensington and Chelsea (Sir Richard George Rogers) [The Rt Hon The Lord Rogers of Riverside, House of Lords, London SW1A 0PW]; *b* 23 July 1933; *educ* AA (AA Dipl), Yale (MArch), RIBA; architect (works include Centre Pompidou Paris, Lloyd's Building City London, Channel 4 HQ London); chm Richard Rogers Architects Ltd, dir River Cafe, Thames Wharf Studios, London First; ktd 1991, RA 1984 (ARA 1978); author: *Richard Rogers Architecture* (1985), *A U: Richard Rodgers 1978–88* (1988), *Architecture: a modern view* (1990), *A New London* (jt author 1992); *m* 1st 1961 Sue — and has three sons; *m* 2nd 1973 *Ruth Elias and by her has two sons

Lineage: NINO ROGERS; *m* Dada Geiringer and had:

RICHARD GEORGE, *cr* a **Baron**

ROLL OF IPSDEN

Creation: B. (LP, UK) 1977.

THE BARON ROLL OF IPSDEN, of Ipsden, Co Oxon (Sir Eric Roll, KCMG (1962, CMG 1949), CB (1956)) [The Rt Hon The Lord Roll of Ipsden KCMG CB, D2 Albany, Piccadilly, London W1V 9RD]; *b* 1 Dec 1907; *educ* Birmingham U (BCom, PhD); Prof Economics and Commerce U Coll Hull 1935–46, Special Rockefeller Fndn Fell USA 1939–41, Memb then Dep Head Br Food Mission N America, UK Dep Member and UK Exec Offr Combined Food Bd Washington 1941–46, Assist Sec Min Food 1946–47, U-Sec Treasury 1948, Min UK Delegn OEEC 1949, Dep Head UK Delegn NATO Paris 1952–53, U-Sec Min Ag 1953–57, Exec Dir Internat Sugar Cncl 1957–59, Chm UN Sugar Conf 1958, Dep Sec Min Ag 1959–61, Dep Leader UK Delegn negotiations EEC 1961–63, Ec Min and Head UK Treasury Delegn Washington, Exec Dir UK IMF and IBRD 1963–64, PUS DEA 1964–66, Dir Bank of England 1968–77, Chm then Hon Chm Book Devpt Cncl 1967–, dir Times Newspapers Ltd 1967–80 and Times Newspapers Hldgs 1980–83, ind memb NEDC 1971–80, Chllr Southampton U 1974–84, chm S G Warburg & Co and Mercury Securities 1974–84, Pres S G Warburg Gp 1987–95 (Sr Advsr 1995–), Hon DSc Hull, Hon DSoc Sci Birmingham, Hon LID Southampton; author: *An Early Experiment in Industrial Organization* (1930), *Spotlight on Germany* (1933), *About Money* (1934), *Elements of Economic Theory* (1935), *Organized Labour* (coauthor, 1938), *The British Commonwealth at War* (coauthor, 1943), *A History of Economic Thought* (1954), *The Combined Food Board* (1957), *The World After Keynes* (1968), *The Uses and Abuses of Economics* (1978), *The Mixed Economy* (ed, 1982), *Crowded Hours* (1985), *Where Did We Go Wrong?* (1995); *m* 1934 (Wini)Fred (*d* 28 Jan 1998), only dau of Elliott Taylor, and has:

1 *Joanna; *b* 1944

2 *Elizabeth; *b* 1946; *m* 1st 1970 (*divorce* 1975) Hon Robin James Greenhill (*d* 1986), yr s of Baron Greenhill of Harrow (*qv*); *m* 2nd 19– *Peter Foldes and by him has issue

Lineage: MATHIAS ROLL; *m* Fanny — and had:

ERIC, *cr* a **Baron**

ROLLO

Arms: Or a chevron between three boar's heads erased azure.
Crest: A stag's head couped proper. **Supporters:** Two stags proper.
Motto: *La fortune passe partout* ('Fortune makes way through everything'). **Creations:** L. (S) 10 Jan 1650/1, B. (UK) 29 June 1869.

THE 14TH LORD ROLLO OF DUNCRUB, Co Perth, and **Baron Dunning** of Dunning and Pitcairns, Co Perth (David Eric Howard Rollo) [The Rt Hon The Lord Rollo, Pitcairns, Dunning, Perthshire PH2 9BX]; *b* 31 March 1943; *s* f 1997; *educ* Eton; late Capt Gren Gds; *m* 18 Feb 1971 *Felicity Anne Christian, only dau of Lt-Cdr John Bruce Lamb, DSC, RN, of Barrow House, Cornwall, and has had:

1 +JAMES DAVID WILLIAM, *Master of Rollo* [The Master of Rollo, Acre's Farm, Bradfield, Berks RG7 6JH]; *b* 8 Jan 1972; *educ* Eton and Edinburgh U (BComm); banker

2 William; *b* 18 March, *d* 25 March 1974

3 +Thomas Stapylton; *b* 13 Feb 1975; *educ* Milton Abbey

4 +William Eric John; *b* 20 Sept 1978; *educ* Bradfield

Lineage: JOHN ROLLO(K), 1st of Duncrub, Perths, which was granted him (with other lands in Strathern) by 1st Earl of Stratheam of the 1357 *cr*, to whom he was Sec (grant confirmed 14 Feb 1380/1 by ROBERT II, the Earl's f); Baillie Perth 1361–66, Burgesses' rep at Parl held Perth Feb 1369/70; *d* 1390, leaving:

DUNCAN ROLLO, 2nd of Duncrub; Burgess Edinburgh, Auditor of Scotland 1410–19; *d c* June 1419; his s or gs:

ANDREW ROLLO, 3rd of Duncrub; granted by roy charter lands of Ardkelly, Methven, 1480/1; *d c* 1481; leaving:

ROBERT; *dvp c* 21 April 1471, leaving:

WILLIAM ROLLO, 4th of Duncrub; his lands erected into a free (territorial) barony 26 Aug 1511; *d* 28 Oct 1513, leaving an er s:

ROBERT ROLLO, 5th of Duncrub; *m* Jonet Grahame and was *ka* Flodden 9 Sept 1513, leaving:

ANDREW ROLLO, 6th of Duncrub; *m* Marion, dau and heiress of David Rollo of Manmure, and *d* Dec 1565, leaving, with other issue:

1 George, 7th of Duncrub; *m c* 1549 Isobel, dau of William Moncreiffe of that Ilk (see ERROLL, E), and *dsp* 6 May 1581

2 JAMES

3 Walter (Sir), of Petmady, Lawtoun and Garden; *m* 1st — and had two sons; *m* 2nd (contract 10 Oct 1591) Jean (*m* 2nd Sir Alexander Jardine of Applegirth), dau of 5th Lord Innermeath (see MORAY, E), and *d* 27 May 1603, having by her had issue

4 Peter; Bp Dunkeld, Ld Session; *m* 1st Christian, sis of Capt David Cant and widow of (a) Sir Henry Balfour and (b) Capt John Balfour; *m* 2nd Elizabeth Weston (*d* Oct 1621), widow of John Fairlie of Bruntesfield, and *dsp c* 30 June 1632

ANDREW ROLLO's 2nd son,

JAMES ROLLO(CK), 8th of Duncrub; *m* (contract 5 Jan 1569/70) Agnes (*m* 2nd Peter Oliphant), dau of Robert Collace of Balnamoon, Forfarshire, and *d* May 1584, having by her had, with another s:

1 ANDREW, **1st Lord**

1 Marion; *m* (contract 1 Jan 1608) Sir James Bruce and *d* 24 Dec 1642

2 Elizabeth; *m* (contract 31 July 1598) Sir James Stewart of Ballechin and had issue

JAMES ROLLO's er son,

Sir ANDREW ROLLO, **1st Lord Rollo of Duncrub** (S), so *cr* 10 Jan 1650/1, with remainder to heirs male whomsoever, 9th of Duncrub, JP (Perths 1613); *b* 1577; ktd by 1613, bought Kincladie 1615 and the lands of Kippans and others 1639, also got roy charters of the (territorial) Baronies of Rossie 1621 and Tilliecultrie, Clackmannanshire, 1644; MP Perths 1621 and 1630 and Clackmannanshire 1650–51, Sheriff Perths 1633; *m* Catherine, dau of 1st Lord Maderty (see PERTH, E), and *d* 22 May 1659, having had:

1 JAMES, **2nd Lord**

2 John (Sir), of Bannockburn; *b* 22 Feb 1602; *m* 1st (contract 10 Sept 1635) Isabella, dau of Sir William Cockburn of Langton; *m* 2nd Annabel, dau of Sir John Buchanan of that Ilk; *m* 3rd (contract 27 Aug 1654) Helen, dau of Sir William Sinclair of Rosslyn, and *dspm* 1666

3 Laurence, of Rossie; *b* 15 March 1604; *m* Catharine, dau of Alexander Peebles

4 Andrew; *b* March 1605; Min Dunning; *m* 1st Isabella, dau of David Lindsay, Bp Edinburgh; *m* 2nd 1654 Helen, dau of William Oliphant of Pitlochie and widow of Patrick Murray; *m* 3rd Helen Mercer, widow of James Crichton of Wester Aldie, and *d* May 1668, leaving issue

5 William (Sir); *b* March 1613; royalist Civil War; captured at Philiphaugh and beheaded 21 Oct 1645

1 Margaret; *m* Sir John Drummond of Carnock and had issue

2 Jean; *m* 1st 1652 John Rollo of Powhouse; *m* 2nd John Drummond of Pitkellony

3 Anne; *m* 1st 1633 William Mercer of Clavadge; *m* 2nd Maj Drummond of Pitcairns and *d* 21 Oct 1658, leaving issue by both husbs

4 Isabel; *m* William Halliday of Tullibole and had issue

The 1st LORD's est son,

JAMES ROLLO, **2nd Lord Rollo of Duncrub**; *b* 11 Dec 1600; ktd 1633; Covenater in Civil War period; *m* 1st 24 April 1628 Dorothea (*dsp* 16 May 1638), dau of 4th Earl of Montrose (see MONTROSE, D); *m* 2nd 20 March 1641/2 Mary, dau of 7th Earl of Argyll (see ARGYLL, D), and was *bur* 12 June 1669, leaving by her, with other issue, including a dau (Margaret, *m* (contract 7 Sept 1682) Sir George Oliphant of Newton):

ANDREW ROLLO, **3rd Lord Rollo of Duncrub**; *m* Nov 1670 Margaret (*d* 20 Oct 1734), dau of 3rd Lord Balfour of Burleigh (*qv*), and *d* 4 March 1701, having had, with other issue:

1 John, *Master of Rollo*; Cornet Col Cunningham's Regt of Dragoons; *dvp* unm 20 May 1695, *k* by Patrick Graham, Yr. of Inchbrakie, after a quarrel over whether to drink the health of JAMES VII (and II, he having by now vacated the throne)

2 ROBERT ROLLO, **4th Lord Rollo of Duncrub**; *b* 12 June 1679; joined in Jacobite Rising 1715, hence imprisoned 1716–17; *m* 4 June 1702 Mary (*d* 16 April 1765), dau of Sir Henry Rollo of Woodside, and *d* 8 March 1758, having had, with two other sons (*d* young) and two er daus:

(1) ANDREW ROLLO, **5th Lord Rollo of Duncrub**; b 18 Nov 1703; present Battle of Dettingen 1743, Capt 22nd Foot 1743, Maj 1750, Lt-Col 1756, Col 1762, Brig-Gen (present taking of Louisburg, Nova Scotia, 1758, Canada 1760 and Martinique 1762); m 1st 22 April 1727 Catharine (d 28 July 1763), est dau and coheir of Lord James Murray (see ATHOLL, D); m 2nd 16 Feb 1765 Elizabeth (dsp 6 May 1781), 2nd dau of James Moray, 13th of Abercairny, and dsps 2 June 1765, having had by his 1st w:

1a John, *Master of Rollo*; b 6 Dec 1736; Capt 77th Foot 1760; dvp unm 24 Jan 1762

1a Anna; b 24 Oct 1729; d 9 Dec 1746

(2) Henry; b 12 June 1705; m 25 July 1724 Anne, sis of 5th Lord Ruthven of Freeland (see CARLISLE, E), and dsp 2 July 1745

(3) JOHN, **6th Lord**

(4) Clement Sobieski; b 24 May 1720; m 4 Aug 1756 Mary Amelia, dau of John Irvine of Bonshaw, and d 14 Jan 1762, leaving, with other issue:

1a Robert; b 25 Nov 1758; Capt 42nd Regt; m Janet, dau of James Graeme of Garvock, and settled in America

(1) Isobel; m John Aytoun/Aytone of Inchdairnie, Fife, and had, with other issue:

1a Mary; m her cousin **7th Lord Rollo of Duncrub** and d 24 April 1817

The 5th LORD's bro,

JOHN ROLLO, **6th Lord Rollo of Duncrub**; b 6 Feb 1708; m 1st Cecilia (d 21 June 1746), dau of James Johnston(e), Edinburgh merchant; m 2nd Mary (dsp), dau of John Kennedy, Min Peterculter; m 3rd Jane (dsp 19 April 1784), dau of Alexander Watson, Aberdeen merchant, and d 26 March 1783, having had by his 1st w, with a dau (Joanne, m John Carmichael of Blairsroar):

JAMES ROLLO, **7th Lord Rollo of Duncrub**; b 8 March 1738; Offr RM, present capture of Pondicherry 1761 and Manila 1762; m 4 Dec 1765 his cousin Mary (see above) and d 14 April 1784, having had, with other issue:

1 JOHN, **8th Lord**

2 Roger; b 6 April 1777; Collector Customs Ayrshire; RA; m 24 Feb 1801 Eliza (d 12 Aug 1826), dau of Capt Hunt and gdau of John Bowman of Ashgrove, Ayrshire, and d 5 March 1847, having had:

(1) James; b 28 Dec 1801; Maj; m 21 April 1834 Mary Anne Keogh (d 18 July 1877) and d 15 Feb 1844, leaving, with other issue:

1a Andrew FitzJames Cuninghame ROLLO later ROLLO-BOWMAN-BALLANTINE of Ashgrove and Castlehill, Ayrshire; b 1 Feb 1835; m 16 March 1864 Anne Harriet Curzon (d Jan 1901), only child of Lt-Col John Chalmers, 32nd Native Inf, and d 1891, leaving:

1b James Cuninghame; b 6 Aug 1865; d unm 1892

1a Annabella; m 1862 William Vost, of Stirling (d 1895), and had issue

(2) John Ballantine; b 12 July 1803; m 1st 16 April 1833 Williamina (d 2 Jan 1838), dau of Robert Robertson, of Duncanziemere, Ayrshire, and had:

1a Williamina Eliza

(2) (cont.) John Rollo m 2nd 10 Feb 1839 Janet (d 23 June 1868), dau of John Gray, of Kilmarnock, and d 1887, having by her had:

1a John; b 20 Feb 1847; m 1888 Frances Annie, dau of William Payne, of Footscray, Victoria, Australia, and d 24 May 1918

2a Cecilia Anne; m 13 July 1869 James Thomson and d 29 June 1914, leaving issue

3a Jessie; m 3 April 1866 Archibald Currie, JP, and d 13 July 1923, leaving issue

4a Jemima

(3) Roger

(1) Mary Isabella; m 15 July 1836 Gen William McPherson and d 1882, leaving issue

(2) Margaret Bowman; m 1st 2 Jan 1841 Joseph Harriman, of Tivoli (d 4 April 1847), and had issue; m 2nd 1856 Charles Edouard Napoleon Dörr, gs of Countess de Mont Louis, and d his widow 5 Feb 1908

1 Jane; m 31 March 1795 Capt Patrick Hunter, Bengal NI, and d Oct 1838, leaving issue

The 7th LORD's est son,

JOHN ROLLO, **8th Lord Rollo of Duncrub**; b 22 April 1773; Ensign Scots Gds 1790, served Flanders 1793, 1794 and 1795, ret as Lt, rep S peer 1841–46, dir Commercial bank Scotland; m 12 June 1806 Agnes (d 3 Feb 1855), dau of William Greig, of Edinburgh, and d 24 Dec 1846, having had, with another s (d young):

1 James; b 15 May 1808; d 17 Sept 1812

2 WILLIAM, **9th Lord**

3 John; b 1812; m 1st 7 March 1854 Jane Hay (d June 1873), dau of James Paterson, of Carpow, Perthshire, and had, with other issue:

(1) John; b Feb 1856; m 29 April 1903 Mary (d 25 Dec 1933), dau of Lt-Col Maitland, 72nd Bengal NI, and d 7 Feb 1931

3 (cont.) The Hon John Rollo m 2nd 25 Sept 1876 Jane (d 7 March 1892), dau of Maj James Marshall, HEICS, and d 30 Nov 1876

4 Robert (Sir), KCB; b 26 May 1814; Col Black Watch, Mil Sec Canada, Gen; m 20 March 1851 Harriet Anne (d 23 Oct 1910), est dau of Gen Sir Henry Ferguson-Davie, 1st Bt (qv), and dsp 25 Feb 1907

1 Mary; m 27 March 1833 Lt-Col Robert Knox Trotter (d 11 July 1876), of Ballindean, Perthshire, and d 9 Oct 1886, leaving issue

2 Martha; m 20 Sept 1850, as his 1st w, Lt-Gen Richardson-Robertson, CB (see STEWART-RICHARDSON), and d 17 Sept 1857

The 8th LORD's est surv s,

WILLIAM ROLLO, **9th Lord Rollo of Duncrub**; b 28 May 1809; Cornet 1st Roy Dragoons 1827, Lt 1831, ret 1834, rep S peer 1847–52; m 21 Oct 1834 Elizabeth (d 10 June 1836), only dau of John Rogerson, and d 8 Oct 1852, leaving:

JOHN ROGERSON ROLLO, **10th Lord Rollo of Duncrub**, JP, DL (Perths and Dumfriesshire); b 24 Oct 1835; educ Trin Coll Cambridge; rep S peer 1860–68; cr 29 June 1869 BARON DUNNING, of Dunning and Pitcairns, Co Perth (UK); m 15 Oct 1857 his cousin Agnes Bruce (d 2 May 1906), est dau of Lt-Col Robert Knox Trotter (see above), and d 3 Oct 1916, having had:

1 WILLIAM CHARLES WORDSWORTH ROLLO, **11th Lord Rollo of Duncrub**, CB (1911), JP; b 8 Jan 1860; Capt Roy Co Archers, Lt-Col and Hon Col cmdg 3rd Bn Black Watch; m 21 March 1882 Mary Eleanor (d 24 June 1929), dau of Capt Beaumont Williams Hotham (see HOTHAM, B), and d 3 March 1946, leaving:

(1) Rosalind Mary Agnes; b 18 June 1896; d 30 April 1974

2 Eric Norman; b 17 Feb 1861; m 30 April 1888 Constance Maud (d 18 Dec 1939), yst dau of Henry Booth Hohler, DL, of Fawkham Manor, Kent, and d 12 April 1930, leaving:

(1) JOHN ERIC HENRY, **12th Lord**

(2) William Hereward Charles, MC; b 23 June 1890; educ Eton and Trin Coll Cambridge (BA 1911); granted Aug 1946 with sisters rank of Ld of Parl's dau/yr s; barrister Inner Temple 1914, F/O RAFVR, Capt RSG, WWs I and II, slr 1921 with Withers, Nicholl, Manisty & Co; m 1st 14 Feb 1917 (divorce 1946) Lady Kathleen Nina Hill (d 30 Nov 1960), only dau of 6th Marquess of Downshire (qv), and had:

1a +(Peter) Andrew, MBE (1946) [Andrew Rollo Esq MBE, Cold Blow, Oare, Marlborough, Wilts]; b 6 July 1919; Lt RN WW II; m 29 April 1953 Patricia Mary (d 1985), dau of Capt Charles Cairn Best, and has:

1b +William Raoul; b 1 Aug 1955; educ Eton; Maj Blues and Royals; m 1987 *Annabel Evadne, only dau of Lt-Cdr Sir Howard Christian Sheldon Guinness, VRD, RNR (see GUINNESS, Bt), and has:

1c +Andrew; b 17 March 1996

1c *Kate; b 1989

2c *Laura; b 1991

1b *Susan Rose; b 24 March 1957

1a Primula Susan; b 18 Feb 1918; m 21 Sept 1940 (James) David Graham Niven (d 29 July 1983, having m 2nd 1948 Hjordis Tessmeden, a former Miss Sweden), the actor, yr s of William Graham Niven and Lady Comyn Platt, of Carswell Manor, Berks, and d 21 May 1946 following an accident, leaving:

1b *David; b 1942; late film agent and producer (titles include *The Eagle Has Landed*); m 1993 *Barbara —

2b *James; b 1945; banker, auctioneer; m *Fernande Weatherill, of New York

(2) (cont.) The Hon William Rollo m 2nd 21 Nov 1946 *Diana Joan [The Hon Mrs William Rollo, Barley Thorpe, Oakham, Rutland], yr dau of Edward Castell Wrey (see WREY, Bt) and formerly w of Capt Jocelyn Abel-Smith, and was k out hunting 3 Oct 1962

(1) Torfrida Henrietta Louisa; WW II in FANY; Assist and Dep Matron Birmingham Gen Hosp; d unm 2 Oct 1978

(2) Gylla Constance Susan, OBE (1948); Swedish Order Vasa 1st Cl; memb Roy Fine Art Commn Scotland; m 23 Jan 1925 Capt Sir Malcolm Mac Gregor of Mac Gregor, 5th Bt, CB, CMG, RN (qv), and had issue

3 Herbert Evelyn; b 6 Oct 1864; d April 1893

4 Bernard Francis; b 19 Dec 1868; educ Trin Coll Cambridge (MA); dir Br Overseas Bank, Manager Nat Bank of Egypt Alexandria 1899–1900 and London 1901–06, ptnr Steer, Lawford & Co 1906–20; m 2 June 1917 (divorce Scotland 1928) Edith Catherine, dau of Laurence Currie, of Minley Manor, Hants, and d 7 Feb 1935

5 Gilbert de Ste Croix, JP; b 13 Aug 1872; S/Cdr RNAS, Maj RAF, memb Roy Co Archers; m 24 Aug 1904 Margaret Freda Evelyn (d 26 Oct 1959), 2nd dau of Robert Crawfurd Antrobus (see ANTROBUS, Bt), and d 12 Feb 1932, leaving:

(1) Malcolm Rogerson; b 26 Oct 1906; ARSM; Lt RE WW II (POW); d in a German hosp of wounds 5 Dec 1941

(2) Alexander David; b 26 Dec 1909; educ Trin Coll Cambridge; Lt Seaforth Highrs WW II (invalided), later in Merchant Navy and with Admlty Salvage (wounded); memb Roy Co Archers; m 1st 5 Jan 1934 (divorce 195–) Maud Mary Venn; m 2nd 25 June 1952 Margaret Valmai (d 17 May 1961), only dau of William Slaney Wilmot, of Claverdon, Warwicks, and d 11 June 1974, leaving by her:

1a +Calum John Slaney; b 20 Feb 1953; m 1980 *Lindsay Froggatt

(3) Robert Duncan; b 1 May 1911; Maj Suffolk Regt WW II; m 30 July 1936 *Violet Augustine, only dau of Russell Charles Stanhope (see HARRINGTON, E), and d 1986, leaving:

1a +Gilbert Mark; b 7 Oct 1937; m 1968 his 1st cousin once-removed *Paulette Beatrice, dau of Lt-Col Aubrey Charles Stanhope, USAF (see HARRINGTON, E), and has:

1b +Duncan Andrew; b 1971

1b *Catherine Ann; b 1969

2b *Clare Elizabeth; b 1976

3b *Caroline Jane; b 1979

2a +Charles William [Charles Rollo Esq, 21 Countess Rd, Amesbury, Wilts]; b 4 April 1950

1a *Mary Rose [Mrs John Curry, 2 Rosery Ct, Dinton, Wilts]; b 30 Dec 1938; m 1st 1960 Noel Keaveney, of Cork; m 2nd 1988 *John Curry and has by her 1st husb:

1b *Catherine Ruth; b 1961

2b *Deborah Maeve; b 1963

(1) Glory Evelyn; b 11 July 1905; m 10 Feb 1934 Capt Bernard Henry Esmé Howard, MC (see NORFOLK, D)

1 Agnes Catharine; m 31 Jan 1883 Rev Robert Melvill Gore Browne (d 1 Dec 1931), Rector Leckhampstead, Bucks, s of Rt Rev Edward Harold Browne, DD, Bp Winchester, and d 29 Jan 1948, leaving issue

2 Constance Agnes; d unm 19 Aug 1929

3 Cecily Agatha Agnes; d unm 8 Nov 1947

4 Elizabeth Theresa Agnes; b 23 June 1874; d 1 Sept 1875

The 11th LORD's n,

JOHN ERIC HENRY ROLLO, **12th Lord Rollo of Duncrub**; b 8 Jan 1889; educ Eton; Maj 1st Bn Black Watch WW I; m 1st 15 Feb 1915 Helen Maud (d 15 Aug 1928), only surv child of Frederick Chetwynd-Stapylton (see CHETWYND, V), and had:

1 ERIC JOHN STAPYLTON ROLLO, **13th Lord Rollo of Duncrub**, JP (Perths 1962); *b* 3 Dec 1915; *educ* Eton; Capt Gren Gds WW II; *m* 17 Sept 1938 *Suzanne [The Rt Hon Suzanne Lady Rollo, Flat 1, Pitcairns, Dunning, Perthshire PH2 9BX], 2nd dau of William Howard Brinton Hatton, of Broome Ho, Clent, Worcs, and *d* 25 Sept 1997, leaving:

(1) DAVID ERIC HOWARD ROLLO, **14th and present Lord Rollo of Duncrub**

(2) +James Malcolm; *b* 25 Sept 1946; *educ* Eton and Ch Ch Oxford (BA); banker; *m* 14 Sept 1968 *Henrietta Elizabeth Flora, only dau of Maj Alasdair David Forbes Boyle, CMG (*see* GLASGOW, E), and has:

1a +Malcolm Howard; *b* 13 Oct 1981

1a *Helen Beatrice; *b* 1985

(1) *(Erica) Helen Susan [The Hon Mrs Dillon, 45 Sandford Rd, Ranelagh, Dublin 6, Ireland]; *b* 12 Dec 1939; *m* 25 July 1970 *Valentine Edward Dillon, s of Michael Francis Dillon, of Clonsilla, Co Dublin

2 Norman Chetwynd, MC (1944); *b* 8 Jan 1918; *educ* Eton; Maj KOSB, SR Offrs WW II; *ka* NW Europe 14 Sept 1944

3 David Ian, MBE (1943), MC; *b* 29 July 1921; *educ* Eton; Capt Gren Gds WW II (wounded); *m* 30 Sept 1948 *Bridget Mary [The Hon Mrs David Rollo, 30 King St, Nairn, Scotland IV12 4PD], est dau of Brig James Erskine Stirling, DSO (*see* DEVONSHIRE, D), and *d* 1981, leaving:

(1) +(Norman) Hamish [Hamish Rollo Esq, Burn Brae, Burghclere, Berks RG20 9EB]; *b* 21 May 1955; *educ* Radley; Col RE 1996; *m* July 1979 *Nicole, yst dau of V J Sullivan, of Ashford, Kent, and has:

1a +Andrew David; *b* 14 Nov 1980

2a +Euan Christopher; *b* 19 June 1983

(1) *Joanna Mary [Ms Joanna Rollo, 3 Jenner Rd, London N16 7SB]; *b* 7 May 1949; has:

1a *Georgia Eloise Rollo PITTS; *b* 1989

(2) *Carolyn Louise [Mrs Ronald Mitchell, Bogside of Brodie, Auldearn, Nairn]; *b* 3 April 1952; *m* 1st 25 July 1973 Gordon Wilson and has:

1a *Kirsty Jane MITCHELL; *b* 1974; *m* 1996 *Paul Bigsby and has:

1b *Megan Carolyn; *b* 1997

(2) (cont.) Mrs Wilson *m* 2nd 1981 *Ronald Mitchell and by him has:

1a *Jake David; *b* 1984

2a *Abigail Betty; *b* 1982

(3) *Harriet Clarissa Jane [Mrs Julian Spencer, 12 Streathbourne Rd, London SW17 8QX]; *b* 1 Nov 1960; *m* 1983 *Julian P Spencer, er s of Michael Spencer, and has:

1a *George Hector; *b* 1990

2a *Alexander James; *b* 1993

3a *Edward Æneas; *b* 1997

1 *Jean Helen [The Hon Mrs Heywood-Lonsdale, Mount Farm, Churchill, Oxon OX7 6NP]; *b* 2 Dec 1926; WRNS 1944–46; *m* 7 Oct 1952 *Lt-Col Robert Henry Heywood-Lonsdale, MBE, MC, DL (*see* VALENTIA, V), and has:

(1) *Thomas Norman; *b* 4 July 1953; *educ* Eton; *m* 1987 *Sarah Lonsdale, dau of Strachan Bongard, of Toronto, and has:

1a *James Alexander; *b* 1989

2a *Oliver Robert (twin); *b* 1989

3a *Edward David; *b* 1990

(1) *Helen Jane; *b* 5 Aug 1957; *m* 1994 *David Cleave and has:

1a *Robert Oliver; *b* 1996

(2) *Clare Jean; *b* 15 July 1961; *m* 1987 *James Hugh Leslie Melville (*see* LEVEN and MELVILLE, E) and has issue

(3) *Emma Lucinda; *b* 28 June 1962; *m* 1989 *Matthew Donald Knight, est s of Nicholas P Knight, of Eltham, and has:

1a *Laura Emma; *b* 1991

2a *Sophie Lucinda; *b* 1993

3a *Martha Emily; *b* 1995

The **12th Lord** *m* 2nd 24 March 1930 (*divorce* 1936) Phyllis Carina, only dau of Bernard Sanderson, and by her had:

4 +John Dunning; *b* 16 July 1931

The **12th Lord** *m* 3rd 5 June 1937 Mrs Lily Marie Cockshut (*m* 3rd 17 May 1949 Richard Andrew Perceval Leach (*d* 1981), s of Rev Alfred Wynter Leach, and *d* 1989), dau of Max Seiflow, and *d* 3 Sept 1947, leaving by her:

5 +Simon David [The Hon Simon Rollo, 60 Green Leas, Sunbury-on-Thames, Middx TW16 7PG]; *b* 4 Oct 1939; *educ* Eton; *m* 8 Aug 1964 *Valerie Ernestine, yr dau of Robert William Gaspard Willis, of Newton Green, Suffolk, and has:

(1) *Michelle Leila; *b* 26 Jan 1971

(2) *Dominique Ruth; *b* 8 July 1977

ROMNEY

Arms: Arg. a lion passant in bend gu. between two bendlets az.
Crest: A lion's head erased gu. **Supporters:** Two lions az. semé of cross-crosslets or, each gorged with a naval coronet of the last.
Motto: *Non sibi sed patriae* ('For country not self'). **Creations:** Bt. (E) 12 or 16 Aug 1663, B. (GB) 22 June 1716, V. and E. (UK) 22 June 1801.

THE 7TH EARL OF ROMNEY, of The Mote, **Viscount Marsham**, **Baron of Romney**, Co Kent, and a **Baronet** (Sir Michael Henry Marsham, Bt) [The Rt Hon The Earl of Romney, Wensum Farm, W Rudham, Norfolk PE31 8SZ]; *b* 22 Nov 1910; *s* cousin 1975; *educ* Sherborne; Maj RA (TA) WW II; *m* 28 June 1939 Frances Aileen (*d* 2 Oct 1995), only dau of Lt-Col James Russell Landale, IA

Lineage: JOHN MARSHAM, of Stratton Strawless, Norfolk; *m* Agnes — and *d* 1473, leaving, with two yr sons (Robert; Andrew) and a dau (Matilda, *m* — Worme and had issue):

JOHN MARSHAM, of Stratton Strawless; *m* Ellyne — and *d* 20 April 1515, leaving, with an est s (Thomas, ancestor of the MARSHAMs of Stratton Strawless) and a yst s (James, Sheriff Norwich 1539):

JOHN MARSHAM; Mayor Norwich 1518; *m* Elizabeth Claxton (*d* 1563) and *d* 1525, leaving, with an er s and two daus:

RALPH MARSHAM; Norwich merchant; *m* 29 May 1541 Elizabeth Blackman and *d* 1579, leaving, with three er sons and three daus:

THOMAS MARSHAM; *b* 1556; London merchant; *m* Magdalen (*d* 1618), dau of Richard Springham, London merchant, and was *bur* 12 March 1624, leaving, with an est s, a yst s (Ferdinando, *b* 1610, Esq of the body to CHARLESes I and II, *d unm* 7 Nov 1681) and two daus:

Sir John Marsham, 1st Bt (E), so *cr* 12 or 16 Aug 1663, of Whorn's Place, Cuxton, Kent, which he bought *c* 1660; *b* 23 Aug 1602; *educ* Westminster, St John's Coll Oxford and Middle Temple; Clerk in Chancery Feb 1637/8–41 and 1660–80; royalist Civil War; MP Rochester April–Dec 1660, ktd 1660; antiquary and historian; *m* 13 Jan 1630/1 Elizabeth (*d* 24 Sept 1689), dau of Sir William Hammond, of St Alban's Court, Kent, and *d* 25 May 1685, having had, with other issue (*d* young):

1 **Sir John Marsham, 2nd Bt**, of Whorn's Place and the Mote, Kent; *b* 15 Sept 1637; *educ* Queen's Coll Oxford and Middle Temple; Sheriff Kent 1691–92; author of a projected history of England; *m* 1st 11 Jan 1664/5 Anne (*dsp* 1672), dau of Sir Samuel Danvers, 1st Bt, of Culworth, Northants; *m* 2nd 10 March 1674/5 Hester (*d* 1716), dau of Sir George Sayer, and *d* 31 Dec 1692, having by her had:

(1) **Sir John Marsham, 3rd Bt**, of Whorn's Place and the Mote; *b* 12 Oct 1679; *d unm* 13 May 1696

2 ROBERT (Sir), **4th Bt**

1 Elizabeth; *b* 23 Nov 1631; *m* 1st 4 Aug 1652 Stephen Penkhurst (*d* 1657) and had issue; *m* 2nd 1662 her cousin William Hammond (*d* 6 May 1685), of St Alban's Court, and *d* 1675, having had further issue

2 Margaret; *b* 9 Dec 1644; *m* 1667 Sir Roger Twisden, 2nd Bt, of Bradburne (*d* 28 Feb 1702/3; *see* 1841 edn), and *d* 30 Jan 1687, leaving issue

The 3rd Bt's unc,

Sir Robert Marsham, 4th Bt, of Whorn's Place, the Mote and Bushey Hall, Herts; *b* 16 Dec 1650; *educ* St John's Coll and Middle Temple; Clerk in Chancery 1680, MP Maidstone 1698–1702, ktd 1681; *m* 12 Dec 1681 Margaretta (*d* 1710), dau and heiress of Thomas Bosville, of Little Mote, Eynsford, Kent, and *d* 26 July 1703, having had:

1 ROBERT, **1st Baron**

1 Elizabeth; *b* 21 Sept 1683; *m* 18 Nov 1700 Sir Thomas Palmer, Bt, of Wingham, Kent (*d* 8 Nov 1723; *see* 1838 edn), and *d* 1714, leaving issue

2 Margaretta; *b* 4 Sept 1684; *m* 23 June 1707, as his 1st w, Sir Brook Bridges, 1st Bt (*d* 19 March 1728), and *d* 1719, leaving issue (*see also* FitzWALTER, B)

3 Mary; *b* 18 May 1698; *m* 22 June 1723 Sir Thomas Hales, 2nd Bt, of Beakesbourne (*d* 6 Oct 1762), and *d* 4 Aug 1769, leaving issue

The 4th Bt's only s,

Sir Robert Marsham, 5th Bt, and **1st Baron of Romney**, Co Kent (GB), so *cr* 22 June 1716; *b* 17 Sept 1685; *educ* St John's Coll Oxford; MP (Whig) Maidstone

1708–16, Lt-Govr Dover Castle 1717; m 19 Aug 1708 Elizabeth (m 2nd 1732, as his 1st w, 3rd Earl of Hyndford and d 17 Nov 1750), est dau and coheir of Adml Sir Cloudesley Shovell, and d 28 Nov 1724, having had, with other issue (d young or unm, bar Elizabeth, b 15 Aug 1711, who m 21 April 1741, as his 2nd w, 1st Viscount Folkestone and d 25 Sept 1782, leaving issue; see RADNOR, E):

ROBERT MARSHAM, 2nd Baron of Romney; b 22 Aug 1712; educ Eton and Ch Ch Oxford; DCL 1733, FRS 1757, Col W Kent Militia 1759, Pres Soc of Arts 1761–93 (V-Pres 1755–61, FSA 1762) and Marine Soc 1756–93; m 29 July 1742 Priscilla (d 27 Feb 1771), dau and heiress of Charles Pym, of St Kitts, and d 16 Nov 1793, having had (in remainder to btcy and Barony only), with other issue (d unm):

1 Robert Pym; b 28 April 1743; d unm 28 Nov 1762

2 CHARLES, **1st Earl**

3 Jacob (Rev); b 28 Feb 1759; DD, Canon Windsor, Preb Rochester and Wells; m 28 June 1784 Amelia Frances (d 30 March 1836), only dau and heiress of Joseph Bullock, of Caversfield, Oxon, and d 28 Jan 1840, leaving, with three other daus (d unm):

(1) Robert MARSHAM later BULLOCK-MARSHAM, of Caversfield; b 17 June 1786; DCL, Warden Merton Coll Oxford; m 27 March 1828 Janet (d 10 Nov 1881), dau of Maj-Gen David Dewar, of Gilston House, Fife, and widow of Sir John Carmichael Anstruther, 6th Bt (qv), and d 27 Dec 1880, having had, with a dau (d unm):

1a Charles Jacob, of Edgcott, Bucks, JP (Oxon); b 18 Jan 1829; d unm Aug 1901

2a Robert Henry; b 3 Sept 1833; educ Oxford (MA); barrister, Met Police Magistrate, Recorder Maidstone 1868–79; m 26 Jan 1871 Laura (d 25 July 1926), dau of George Field, of Ashurst Park, Tunbridge Wells, and d 5 April 1913, leaving:

1b Charles George BULLOCK-MARSHAM later FIELD-MARSHAM (deed poll 2 June 1920), TD, JP (Kent); b 3 Dec 1872; educ Eton and Merton Coll Oxford (BA 1895 MA 1900); Maj W Kent Yeo WW I; m 25 Oct 1904 Mary Dorothea (d 26 Jan 1970), only child of Edward Knight, of Keswick Old Hall, Norfolk, and d 7 Oct 1958, having had:

1c Robert Edward; b 3 Aug 1905; educ Eton and RMC Sandhurst; Maj The Bays WW II, MFH Bicester and Warden Hill 1936–42, Jt MFH Eridge 1947–61; m 1st 24 June 1936 (divorce 1950) Mrs Geraldine Hamilton, dau of Henry Wrohan; m 2nd 2 Oct 1950 Joan Helen (d 1988), widow of his bro Charles Austen (see below), and dsp 24 Nov 1996

2c Charles Austen; b 3 Nov 1910; educ Eton; Lt Life Gds WW II 1939–41; m 14 Feb 1935 Joan Helen (m 2nd her bro-in-law; see above), est dau of Percy Llewelyn Nevill (see ABERGAVENNY, M), and das Jan 1941, leaving:

1d +Rupert Charles Edward [Rupert Field-Marsham Esq, 29 Roxborough St West, Toronto, Canada]; b 5 Feb 1938; educ Eton and McGill; late 2nd Lt RAC; m 1st 20 Sept 1963 (divorce 1973) Marilyn Muriel, only dau of Dr George B Maugham, of Montreal, and has:

1e +Robert Scott; b 12 July 1964

2e +Rupert Charles; b 29 Jan 1968

1d (cont.) Rupert Field-Marsham m 2nd 15 June 1973 *Lindsay Ruth, dau of Robert Dale-Harris by Leslie, dau of Leslie Howard, the actor, and by her had:

3e +George Robert; b 4 April 1975

4e +Mark Austen; b 1977

5e +Jacob Edward; b 1979

1c Mary Elizabeth; b 20 Oct 1907

2b Robert Anstruther MARSHAM later MORRIS-MARSHAM (roy licence 8 March 1924); b 1 Jan 1875; educ Oxford (MA); barrister; m 7 June 1904 Jessie Dorothy (d 23 Jan 1931), est dau of Andrew Richard Motion, of Upton Ho, Warwicks, and d 25 Nov 1946, leaving:

1c Richard Henry Anstruther; b 28 Nov 1905; educ Eton and Merton Coll Oxford; m 1st 21 June 1929 (divorce 1951) Iris Rose Sophia, dau of Capt Dennis Larking, CMG, RN; m 2nd 26 Nov 1951 *Eileen Reba [Mrs Richard Morris-Marsham, Jacaranda, 4 Chiltley Lane, Liphook, Hants], only dau of Victor di Halfalla Nahum, of Italy, and former w of Neville Blond, CMG, OBE, and d 1975, leaving by his 1st w:

1d +David Charles Robert [David Morris-Marsham Esq, 32 Alderbrook Rd, London SW12 8AE]; b 27 July 1930; educ Eton and Merton Coll Oxford; m 1976 *Margaret Lindelia, dau of Robert Crawford, and has:

1e *Victoria Harriet; b 1978

2e *Charlotte Rose; b 1979

2d +Jack Richard [Jack Morris-Marsham Esq, Brookside, Ewen, Glos GL7 6BU]; b 1936; educ Eton; m 1st 7 Sept 1963 (divorce 1978) Agnes Margaret (Molly), yr dau of Maj-Gen Walter Rutherfoord Goodman, CB, DSO, MC, of Little Bealings Holt, Woodbridge, Suffolk; m 2nd 1978 Ann Christine Humphreys (d 1980), dau of Howard Sargent Backhouse; m 3rd 1983 *Serena Sybil Newmark, dau of G/Capt Geoffrey Kinglake Fairclough, and by his 1st w has:

1e +James Jonathan [James Morris-Marsham Esq, 6 Dairy Farm, Gosditch, Ashton Keynes, Wilts SN6 6NZ]; b 10 Nov 1964; m 1991 *Susan Marie, er dau of Henry Menzel, of Falmouth, Cornwall, and has:

1f *Jessica Rose; b 1993

2e +Dominic Rutherfoord; b 1 March 1967

1e *Tiffany Jane; b 21 March 1969

2c Antony Cuthbert; b 4 Nov 1909; educ Eton; m 11 July 1935 Camilla, yr dau of Charles Humphrey Style (see STYLE, Bt), and d 27 Nov 1975, having had:

1d Antony Patrick; b 8 March 1937; educ Eton; d unm 28 Nov 1962

1d Jacqueline; b 2 June 1939; m 23 July 1969 *Michael Raymond Coulman, er s of Col Edward Raymond Coulman, OBE, TD, and had:

1e *Robert Patrick Raymond; b 31 Jan 1973

1b Mary Evelyn; b 14 Jan 1874; d unm 19 July 1962

2b Leila Janet; b 14 April 1879; d unm 8 Oct 1962

3a Cloudesley Dewar (Rev); b 30 Jan 1835; educ Oxford (MA); Rector Harrietsham, Kent; m 1st 20 June 1876 his cousin Frances Penelope (d 8 Feb 1890), dau of Rev George Frederick John Marsham (see below); m 2nd 16 Feb 1897 Edith Matilda (d 10 June 1929), dau of Rev George Birch Reynardson, and d 2 March 1915, leaving by his 1st w:

1b Cloudesley Henry; b 10 Feb 1879; educ Oxford (BA); Capt W Kent Yeo; m 14 Feb 1911 Algitha, JP (d 14 April 1972 aged 91), er dau of Rev Hon Algernon Robert Parker (see MACCLESFIELD, E), and d 19 July 1928, leaving:

1c +Cloudesley George, TD, JP (Kent 1958) [Maj Cloudesley Bullock-Marsham TD JP, Horton Cottage, Rolvenden Lane, Cranbrook, Kent TN17 4WP]; b 1917; educ Eton; Maj 297th (Kent Yeo) Field Regt RA (TA) WW II (POW); m 15 April 1941 *Suzanne Kate, yr dau of Dudley Holloway

2c +Algernon James [Algernon Bullock-Marsham Esq, Langton House, 42 The Street, Appledore, Kent TN26 2BX]; b 14 Aug 1919; educ Eton and Ch Ch Oxford; Capt KRRC WW II (POW); m 19 May 1948 *Elizabeth, only dau of AVM Malcolm Henderson, CB, CIE, DSO, and has:

1d +Charles James Lessels; b 7 June 1950; educ Eton

1c Joan; b 6 Nov 1911; m 6 Feb 1935 Col Hubert Mortimer Allfrey, MC, TD, DL, Kent Yeo, 2nd s of Charles Moubray Allfrey, and d 20 Aug 1962, leaving issue

2c *Vere Frances; b 21 Feb 1913; m 7 June 1932 (George) Ronald Pigé Leschallas (d 1991), er s of Percy Leschallas, and has:

1d *Anthony George; b 1933; m 1954 *Marie-Louise Yvonne Renner and has:

1e *Anthony Simon; b 1955; m 1987 *Amanda Nanci, dau of Maj James Le Coq, of Seething, Norfolk, and has:

1f *Marie-Clair; b 1988

2e *William Henry; b 1963; m 1992 *Emma C, er dau of David Huxtable, of Bosham, W Sussex

1e *Marie-Louise Sophie; b 1957

2e *Joanna Clare; b 1960; m 1989 *Edward Anthony Morys Berry (see KEMSLEY, V) and has issue

2d *James Ronald Pigé; b 1943; m 1967 *Rosemary Elizabeth, only dau of Rev Hon Andrew Charles Victor Elphinstone, and has issue (see ELPHINSTONE, L)

1d *Lavinia Frances; b 1934; m 1965 *Christopher William Trelawny Hare and has:

1e *Henry William Trelawny; b 1966

2e *Jonathan Christopher Trelawny; b 1968

3e *James Frederick Trelawny; b 1971

2d *Suzanne Vere; b 1939; m 1965 *Gen Sir (Charles) Edward Webb Jones, KCB, CBE, and has:

1e *Hume Richard Webb; b 1967; Capt RGJ

2e *Benjamin Edward Webb; b 1978

1e *Jemma Suzanne; b 1971

2b Francis William, DSO (1918), MC; b 13 July 1883; educ Eton; Col 3rd Dragoon Gds, formerly 19th Hus, WW I (despatches), DAAG 1919, GSO(2) 1922, Cdr 5th Cav Bde TA 1931, T/Brig, cmded 1st Cav Bde 1932–36, Hon Brig 1938, ADC to TM GEORGE V, EDWARD VIII and GEORGE VI 1935–38; m 19 April 1922 Finovola Marianne Eleanor, dau of Sir Fitzroy Donald Maclean, 10th Bt, of Dowart, KCB (qv), and widow of Roger Cordy Simpson, and d 22 Dec 1971

1b Jessie Catherine; b 15 March 1880; d unm 29 April 1940

2b Constance Elizabeth; b 6 June 1881; d 18 Nov 1917

1a Jessie Elizabeth; b 13 March 1832; m 24 Sept 1867 Rev Charles Montague Style and d 1922, leaving issue (see STYLE, Bt)

(2) Charles (Rev); b 2 June 1781; Vicar Stoke Lyne and Caversfield, Oxon; d unm 24 Aug 1867

(3) Henry Shovell; b 28 Jan 1794; Adml; m 27 Feb 1838 his yr bro's sis-in-law Maria Sophia (d 21 Dec 1861), est dau of Walter Jones, of Hayle Place, Kent, and dsp 26 Oct 1875

(4) Jacob Joseph (Rev); b 8 Feb 1804; Vicar Shorne, Kent; d unm 23 Oct 1894

(5) George Frederick John (Rev); b 2 June 1806; Rector Allington, Kent; m 4 June 1833 Elizabeth Marcia (d 20 April 1849), dau and coheir of Walter Jones (see above), and d 29 Jan 1852, leaving, with two other daus (d unm):

1a George, CBE (1920), of Hayle Cottage, Maidstone, Kent, and Headfort, Co Leitrim, JP, DL; b 10 April 1849; educ Oxford (BA); d unm 2 Dec 1927

1a Catherine Elizabeth; b 12 Jan 1838; m 1st 23 Jan 1866 Rev William Gale Townley (dsp 4 Sept 1869), Rector Upwell, Norfolk; m 2nd 11 May 1880 Hon Edward Kenyon (see KENYON, B) and dsp 16 June 1903

2a Frances Penelope; b 28 Dec 1841; m 20 June 1876 her cousin Rev Cloudesley Dewar Bullock Marsham (see above) and d 9 Feb 1890, leaving issue

(1) Louisa Charlotte; b 14 May 1790; m 22 Dec 1814 Capt William Style, RN (see STYLE, Bt), and d 25 Oct 1866, leaving issue

(2) Emily Eleanor; b 10 Feb 1803; m 10 May 1831 Sir Charles Fitzroy Maclean, 9th Bt, of Dowart (qv), and d 12 April 1838, leaving issue

1 Charlotte; b 12 Nov 1761; m 4 July 1792 John Coker (d 14 Jan 1819) and d 16 Jan 1794, leaving issue

The 2nd BARON's er surv s,

  CHARLES MARSHAM, 1st Earl of Romney, so cr 22 June 1801, as also VISCOUNT MARSHAM (UK) ; b 28 Sept 1744; educ Eton and Ch Ch Oxford; MP (Whig to 1783, Pittite 1788 on) 1768–74 and Kent 1774–90, V-Pres Soc Arts, memb Bd Ag 1793, Pres Marine Soc 1793, Ld Lt Kent 1797–1808; m 30 Aug 1766 Lady Frances Wyndham (d 14 Jan 1795), yr dau of 2nd Earl of Egremont (see EGREMONT, LECONFIELD and, B), and d 30 June 1868, having had, with three daus (of whom two d unm and Frances, b 25 Oct 1778, m 17 June 1805 Sir John Buchanan Riddell, 9th Bt; qv):

CHARLES MARSHAM, **2nd Earl of Romney**; *b* 22 Nov 1777; *educ* Eton and Ch Ch Oxford; MP (Ind Tory) Hythe 1798–1802 and 1806–07 and Downton 1803–06, Lt-Col 1st E Kent Militia 1809; *m* 1st 9 Sept 1806 Sophia (*d* 9 Sept 1812), dau of William Morton Pitt, of Kingston Ho, Dorset, and had:

1 CHARLES, **3rd Earl**

1 Sophia; *b* 13 July 1807; *m* 17 April 1837 Peter Richard Hoare and *d* 4 June 1863, leaving issue (*see* HOARE, Bt, of Barn Elms)

2 Frances; *b* 9 Nov 1809; *m* 2 Aug 1838 Maj-Gen Edward Charles Fletcher (*d* 5 June 1877), of Kenward, Kent, and *d* 29 Dec 1901, leaving issue

3 Mary; *b* 15 April 1811; *m* 3 May 1836 Henry Hoare (*d* 16 April 1866), of Staplehurst Place, Kent, and *d* 23 Feb 1871, leaving issue

4 Charlotte; *b* 30 Aug 1812; *m* 20 April 1853 Rev George William Corker (*d* 9 June 1880), Vicar Stony Stratford, Bucks, and *dsp* 18 Nov 1879

The **2nd Earl** *m* 2nd 9 Feb 1832 Mary Elizabeth (*d* 25 Dec 1847), dau of 2nd Viscount Sydney of St Leonards (*see* TOWNSHEND, M) and widow of George James Cholmondeley (*see* CHOLMONDELEY, M), and *d* 29 March 1845, having by her had:

2 Robert MARSHAM later MARSHAM-TOWNSHEND (roy licence 27 March 1893), JP (Kent and London), DL; *b* 15 Nov 1834; *educ* Oxford (MA); FSA, FRGS, FGS, Dip Serv 1855–59, Lt Kent Militia Artillery 1859–69; *m* 5 April 1877 Clara Catherine (*d* 17 March 1931), 2nd dau of Rev George Barber Paley, JP, of Langcliffe, Yorks, and *d* 11 Dec 1914, leaving:

(1) Hugh Sydney, JP (Kent); *b* 9 Feb 1878; *educ* Eton and Ch Ch Oxford; Lt Scots Gds and 4th Bn Glos Regt WW I (wounded); *m* 1st 19 April 1904 Cecilia Frances Laura (*d* 30 Nov 1912), er dau of Sir Henry Charles John Bunbury, 10th Bt (*qv*), and had:

1a John; *b* 17 Jan 1905; *educ* Eton; joined Dip Serv 1932, Maj Scots Gds WW II; *d* unm 5 Nov 1975

(1) (cont.) Hugh Marsham-Townshend *m* 2nd 6 Dec 1913 his sis-in-law Laura Constance Elinor, OBE (*d* 26 June 1950), dau of Sir Henry Charles John Bunbury, 10th Bt (*qv*), and *d* 17 May 1967, having by her had:

2a Thomas; *b* 26 Dec 1915; *educ* Eton; Capt Scots Gds WW II; *m* 22 Jan 1940 Averil Innes (*m* 2nd 8 Aug 1945 Col John Robert Stephenson Clarke, OBE, MC, Scots Gds (*d* 1993), est s of Edmund Stephenson Clarke, of Pickwell, Bolney, Sussex, and *d* 1993), dau of Maj Lewis Frederic Innes Loyd, and *d* of wounds recd in action 24 Jan 1944, leaving:

1b *June [Lady Rankin, 63 Marlborough Place, London NW8 0PT]; *b* 30 June 1942; *m* 1st 18 June 1962 Bryan Montagu Norman, er s of Lt-Col Mark Richard Norman, OBE, of Moor Place, Much Hadham, Herts, and adopted:

*Emily Kate; *b* 1975

1b (cont.) Mrs Norman *m* 2nd 1980 *Sir Ian Niall Rankin, 4th Bt (*qv*), and has issue

2b *Susan (Suki) [Sga Piero Studiati-Berni, via del Fossetto 3, 56010 Molina di Quosa, Pisa, Italy]; *b* posthumously 13 May 1944; *m* 26 Jan 1972 *Dr Piero Studiati-Berni, s of Dr Cesare Studiati-Berni and has:

1c *Cesare; *b* 7 Sept 1972

1c *Viola; *b* 1975

(2) Ferdinand; *b* 17 April 1880; *educ* Eton and Ch Ch Oxford (BA); Lt Scots Gds; *ka* 16 May 1915

The 2nd EARL's er s,

CHARLES MARSHAM, **3rd Earl of Romney**; *b* 1 July 1808; *educ* Eton and Ch Ch Oxford; MP (C) W Kent 1841–45; *m* 7 Feb 1832 Lady Margaret Harriet Montagu-Scott (*d* 5 June 1846), 4th dau of 4th Duke of Buccleuch and (6th Duke of) Queensberry (*qv*), and *d* 3 Sept 1874, having had, with three other daus (*d* unm):

1 CHARLES, **4th Earl**

2 John (Rev); *b* 25 July 1842; *educ* Cambridge (BA); Rector Barton Seagrave Northants 1868–1908 and Haccombe Devon 1908–12; *m* 21 June 1866 Penelope Jane (*d* 1 May 1936), yst dau of Rev William Wheler Hume, and *d* 16 Sept 1926, having had:

(1) Keith Henry; *b* 30 April 1868; served WW I; *m* 3 Oct 1894 Annie Maud (*d* 8 Sept 1952), 2nd dau of Edward Miller, of Tolmers, Herts, and *dsp* 3 Dec 1955

(2) Walter John; *b* 24 Oct 1869; *m* 16 July 1908 Frances Leonora (*d* 16 Nov 1956), dau of Edward Philip Monckton (*see* GALWAY, V), and *d* 8 March 1945, leaving:

1a John Edward; *b* 31 Aug 1910; *m* 1st 23 Sept 1937 (*divorce* 1970) Jean Frances, dau of Reginald Cambden Clare Hayward; *m* 2nd 1970 *Mrs Evelyn Moore [Mrs John Marsham, 16 Barchester Rd, Langley, Bucks], dau of Lesley George Rush, and *d* 1990, leaving by his 1st w:

1b +Richard John; *b* 23 April 1946; *m* 1964 *Janet Anne Wilson and has:

1c +Gary Frederick; *b* 1964; *m* 1988 his cousin *Celine Margaret, dau of Donald James Griffin (*see* below), and has:

1d *Cassandra Dawn; *b* 1989

2c +Stephen John; *b* 1967

1c *Gillian Dawn [Mrs David Forisky, 1 Belmont Vale, Maidenhead, Berks]; *b* 3 Feb 1938; *m* 1st 1956 Donald Griffin (*d* 1960), of Mombasa, and has:

1d *Pauline Elizabeth; *b* 1956; has:

1e *Darrell Colin GRIFFIN; *b* 1981

2e *John BUSHNELL; *b* 1986

1e *Gillian Dawn GRIFFIN; *b* 1976

2d *Celine Margaret; *b* 1959; *m* 1988 her cousin *Gary Frederick Marsham and has issue (*see* above)

1c (cont.) Mrs Donald Griffin *m* 2nd 1961 (*divorce* 1964) Alan Henry Craig; *m* 3rd 1968 Abdul Hanif Rashid (*d* 1971); *m* 4th 19– (*divorce* 1979) Thomas William McConnell; *m* 5th 1980 (*divorce* 1985, *remarried* 1990) *David Alfred Forisky and by her 3rd husb has:

1d *AFTAB later KRIS (deed poll) Hanif; *b* 1970

1a Violet Leonora; *b* 6 Nov 1913; *m* 3 Aug 1940 George Anthony Batterbury, s of Geoffrey Richard Batterbury, of Dorset, and had:

1b *Adrian William George; *b* 14 Nov 1944

2b *Mark Richard George; *b* 19 July 1947; *educ* Victoria U BC (BA 1969)

3b *Edward Anthony George; *b* 5 Jan 1949; *educ* Victoria U BC (BSc 1970)

1b *Susan [Miss Susan Batterbury, 11–23 Avorimore Terrace, Mosman Pk, Western Australia 6012]; *b* 12 Nov 1941; *educ* Br Columbia U (BSc 1963)

(3) Cyril Montagu Charles; *b* 31 March 1871; Bengal Police, Capt S African Constabulary; *m* 14 Feb 1911 Gladys Helen Marie (*d* 17 April 1965 aged 85), 3rd dau of Douglas Kingsford, barrister Inner Temple, and *d* 14 Nov 1943, leaving:

1a +Peter, JP (Herefs) [Peter Marsham Esq JP, King's Acre, Coddington, Herefs HR8 1JJ]; *b* 28 Jan 1912; *educ* Clifton; *m* 19 Feb 1938 *Margaret, dau of Benjamin Harral, of Yorks, and has:

1b +John Kingsford, OBE (1993); *b* 24 July 1942; *educ* Bryanston and RMC Sandhurst; Lt-Col 3rd LI; *m* 1978 *Olwen, dau of Joshua Adamson, of Brisbane, Australia, and has:

1c +Robert Edward Harral; *b* 1981

1c *Anne Kingsford; *b* 1979

2b +Robert Harral [Robert Marsham Esq, King's Acre, Coddington, Herefs HR8 1JJ]; *b* 13 Aug 1946; *educ* Abbotsholme Sch

1b *(Marion) Caroline [Mrs Caroline Walton, King's Acre, Coddington, Herefs HR8 1JJ]; *b* 10 Oct 1939; *m* 1st 7 Oct 1961 (*divorce* 1978) Richard Naylor, yst s of Lt-Col James William Naylor; *m* 2nd 1981 (*divorce* 1989) Dr George Richard Castellain Walton and by her 1st husb has:

1c *Charles Gray Marsham; *b* 27 Sept 1962

2c *Michael Harry Richard; *b* 4 March 1970

1c *Margaret Kingsford; *b* 17 June 1964

2a +Richard Douglas Hollinshead [Richard Marsham Esq, Llwynglas, Penrhiwllan, Llandyssul, Dyfed]; *b* 15 Oct 1913; *educ* Clifton; Maj Worcs Regt WW II; *m* 1 Nov 1947 (*divorce* 1981) Shirley, dau of John Hannah, of The Mill Ho, Mathon, Worcs, and has:

1b +Richard Charles Hannay; *b* 20 Sept 1948

2b +David John Hollinshead; *b* 17 Nov 1954; *educ* Queen's Coll Taunton

1b *Catherine Elizabeth; *b* 1 Feb 1952

1a Ann Margaret Kingsford; *b* 20 Oct 1916; *m* 17 July 1945 John Grattan Geary, Capt IA, s of F J G Geary, ICS, and *d* 25 Sept 1961, leaving issue

(4) Hubert Wheler; *b* 24 Sept 1876; Lt-Col Glam Yeo; *m* 6 Sept 1904 Blanche Mary Frederica (*d* 31 March 1963), est dau of Charles Joseph Stonor (*see* CAMOYS, B), and *d* 6 May 1952, leaving:

1a Hubert Anthony Lucius, OBE (1942); *b* 29 June 1905; Cdr RN WW II; *m* 9 July 1953 Margaret Mary (*d* 7 Sept 1995), yr dau of Ambrose Joseph Devas, of Kilmeston, Hants, and had:

1b Harriet Mary; *b* 29 May and *d* 5 June 1954

1a Sylvia Mary Blanche; *b* 19 Dec 1910

(5) John Ralph Theodore; *b* 9 Dec 1885; Lt 11th Bn Worcs Regt WW I (wounded); *m* 1918 Olive Hill (*d* 14 Dec 1926) and *d* 27 Feb 1919, leaving:

1a Ralph John Theodore; *b* June 1919; P/O RAFVR WW II; *kas* 31 Oct 1940

(1) Mabel Pensie; *m* 7 Aug 1902 Rev Arthur Robertson Hoare (*d* 18 March 1941), Rector Ashill, Norfolk, 2nd s of Rev Walter Marsham Hoare, of Fakenham, and *d* 14 April 1928, leaving issue

(2) Violet Mary; *b* 10 Oct 1872; *m* 18 Aug 1910 Edward Francis Johns (*d* 23 Sept 1948), headmaster Winton Ho Sch, Winchester, s of Rev CA Johns

(3) Evelyn Florence; Forces Welfare worker WW II; *m* 21 Oct 1930 her bro-in-law Rev Arthur Robertson Hoare and *d* 24 June 1956

(4) Grace Margaret; *b* 17 Sept 1877; *m* 29 Sept 1904 1st Baron Cullen of Ashbourne (*qv*), and has issue

(5) Mary Verena; *d* unm 23 Oct 1966

(6) Olive Home; *d* 9 Feb 1954

3 Henry; *b* 26 March 1845; Lt Rifle Bde; *d* unm 1 July 1908

1 Harriet; *b* 17 July 1838; *m* 24 Sept 1863 Col Henry Charles Fletcher, CMG, Scots Gds (*d* 31 Aug 1879), and *d* 14 Nov 1886, leaving issue

The 3rd EARL's est s,

CHARLES MARSHAM, **4th Earl of Romney**, JP (Kent and Norfolk), DL; *b* 7 March 1841; *educ* Eton and Ch Ch Oxford; Hon Lt RN Artillery Vols 1879, Pres Marine Soc, Ld-in-Waiting 1889–92; *m* 30 July 1863 Lady Frances Augusta Constance Muir Campbell Rawdon-Hastings (*d* 1 Sept 1910), dau and coheir of 2nd Marquess of Hastings (*see* LOUDOUN, E), and *d* 21 Aug 1905, having had:

1 CHARLES MARSHAM, **5th Earl of Romney**, JP (Kent and Norfolk); *b* 25 Oct 1864; *educ* Eton; Maj and Hon Lt-Col Beds Regt, ADC to Govr Madras 1888, Pres Marine Soc; *m* 12 June 1890 Anne Louisa (*d* 5 Feb 1936), dau of Sir Edward Henry Scott, 5th Bt, of Lytchett Minster, Dorset (*see* 1959 edn), and *d* 13 March 1933, leaving:

(1) CHARLES MARSHAM, **6th Earl of Romney**, JP (Norfolk), DL (1939); *b* 9 July 1892; *educ* Eton; Lt-Col Coldstream Gds WW I (wounded), Cmdt Gds Depot 1928–31, cmded 2nd Bn 1934–36, WW II: Cmdt Gds Depot Sept 1939–Jan 1940, HQ Lond Dist to Aug 1945 as GSO(1) Cadets, Pres Nat Cncl YMCA 1956–66, Marine Soc and Debtors Relief Funds Charity; *m* 24 July 1918 Marie Henrietta Margaret (*d* 21 Jan 1976), er dau of Adml Sir Colin Richard Keppel, GCVO, KICE, CB, DSO (*see* ALBEMARLE, E), and *dsp* 6 Sept 1975

2 Reginald Hastings, OBE (1918); *b* 19 Dec 1865; Lt-Col 7th Hus, cmded a sqdn Remount Serv 1917–19; *m* 4 Feb 1908 Dora Hermione (*d* 14 Aug 1923), 4th dau of Charles North, DL (*see* GUILFORD, E), and had:

(1) MICHAEL HENRY MARSHAM, **7th and present Earl of Romney**

(1) *Anne Rhoda [The Lady Anne Marsham, Wensum Farm, W Rudham, Norfolk PE31 8SZ]; *b* 7 June 1909; Section Offr WAAF WW II, Kenya Police Reserve Offr during Emergency 1953–54, Dist Pass Offr Molo 1956–60

3 Douglas Henry; *b* 13 Nov 1871; Lt 4th Bn Beds Regt (seconded for serv Bechuanaland); *ka* Mafeking 31 Oct 1899

4 Sydney Edward; *b* 29 Dec 1879; *educ* Eton; Lt Gren Gds (SR) WW I; *m* 2 Feb 1911 Joan, DBE (1945) (*d* 13 March 1972), only dau of William Warry, of Shapwick, Somerset, and *d* 6 Jan 1952, leaving:

(1) Peter William, MBE (1940); *b* 8 June 1913; *educ* Eton and Trin Coll Cambridge (BA 1935); Lt-Col Gren Gds WW II; *m* 18 July 1946 *Hersey [Mrs Peter Marsham, Waterloo Cottage, Gayton, Norfolk], dau of Maj Hon Richard Coke (*see* LEICESTER, E), and *d* 3 Nov 1970, having had:

1a +JULIAN CHARLES [Julian Marsham Esq, Gayton Hall, King's Lynn, Norfolk]; *b* 28 March 1948; heir presumptive; *educ* Eton; *m* 6 Sept 1975 *Catriona Anne, dau of Robert Christie Stewart (*see* COCHRANE OF CULTS, B), and has:

1b +David Charles; *b* 18 April 1977

2b +Michael Julian; *b* 3 March 1979

1b *Laura Clare; *b* 18 March 1984

1a *Lavinia [Mrs Hamish Lockhart, The Lee, Crosshill House, Auchterarder, Perthshire]; *b* 6 Feb 1950; *m* 7 Sept 1973 *Simon James Macdonald Lockhart and has issue (*see* DUCIE, E),

2a *Sarah [Mrs Maxwell Ward, Stobshiel House, Humbie, E Lothian]; *b* 3 Oct 1954; *m* 17 April 1982 *Maxwell Colin Bernard Ward and has issue (*see* BANGOR, E)

3a Davina; *b* 13 Feb; *d* 22 May 1956

1 Florence Mary Constance; *b* 9 Feb 1868; *m* 3 Dec 1891 Sir George Ralph Leigh Hare, 3rd Bt (*qv*), and *d* 4 Oct 1954, leaving issue

ROOTES

PRORSUM IN FUTURUM

Arms: Ermine within an orle azure a bugle horn sable, garnished or, stringed gules. **Crest:** On a wreath argent and vert a cubit arm bendwise in armour or, the hand proper, grasping a spear in bend also proper, flying therefrom a forked pennon barry argent and azure semée of plates and bezants. **Supporters:** On either side a horse argent gorged with a chain, pendant therefrom a wheel or. **Motto:** *Prorsum in futurum* ('Forward into the future'). **Badge:** A horse's head erased argent gorged with a riband gules, pendant therefrom by a riband azure a bugle horn sable garnished or. **Creation:** B. (UK) 16 Feb 1959.

THE 3RD BARON ROOTES (Nicholas Geoffrey Rootes) [The Rt Hon The Lord Rootes, 2 Cedars Rd, London SW13 0HP]; *b* 12 July 1951; *s* f 1992; *educ* Harrow; jnlst, copywriter and author: *The Drinker's Companion* (1987) and *Doing a Dyson* (1996); *m* 29 March 1976 *Dorothy Anne, dau of Cyril Wood, of Swansea, and formerly w of Jonathan Burn-Forti, of Barnes, London SW

Lineage: EDWARD AYLWYN ROOTES; engr; *m* twice and *d* 26 March 1929, leaving:

WILLIAM ROOTES, of Hawkhurst, Kent; *b* 11 June 1869; *educ* Kendon's Sch Goudhurst; engr; *m* 3 Sept 1892 Jennie (*d* 25 June 1908), dau of William Catt, of Brede, Sussex, and *d* 24 Jan 1955, leaving:

1 WILLIAM EDWARD, **1st Baron**

2 Reginald Claud (Sir); *b* 20 Oct 1896; *educ* Cranbrook Sch; Pres Soc Motor Mfrs 1945–46 (Dep Pres 1940–45), ktd 1946, Pres Motor Industry Research Assoc 1952–56, V-Pres Engrg and Allied Employers' Nat Assoc 1952–56, chm Rootes Motors 1956–67; *m* 1st 8 Feb 1922 (*divorce* 1938) Ruth Joyce, dau of Harding Bensted; *m* 2nd 30 Sept 1938 Nancy Norris, dau of John Clayton Beadle, and had issue by his 1st w:

(1) *Timothy David [Timothy Rootes Esq, The Barn House, Alkerton, Oxon]; *b* 26 May 1925; *educ* Harrow; Capt 6th Airborne Armoured Reconnaissance Regt 1944–47, md GDR Hldgs

The er s,

WILLIAM EDWARD ROOTES, **1st Baron Rootes**, of Ramsbury, Co Wilts (UK), so *cr* 16 Feb 1959, GBE (1955), KBE 1942); *b* 17 Aug 1894; *educ* Cranbrook Sch; Lt RNVR WW I, memb: BOT Advsy Cncl 1931–34 and 1939–40, BOT Deptl Ctee on Gift Coupon Tdg Stamps 1933, Overseas Trade Devpt Cncl 1933–40, Nat Advsy Cncl for Motor Mfg Indust, Engrg Advsy Cncl and Cncl of Soc Motor Mfrs and Traders (Pres 1939–42, V-Pres 1934–36), Exec Ctee Br Cncl; chm: Motor Vehicles Maintenance Advsy Ctee 1941 and Supply Cncl Min Supply 1941–42, Rootes Motors Ltd, Rootes Ltd, W Hemisphere Exports Cncl (late Dollar Exports Cncl), U of Warwick Promotion Ctee; dir Humber Ltd, Hillman Motor Car Co, Sunbeam-Talbot Ltd, Singer Motors, Rootes (Scotland) Ltd, Commer Cars, Karrier Motors,

Thrupp and Maberley, British Light Steel Pressings and Tilling Stevens; Pres Royal Smithfield Club; *m* 1st 15 March 1916 (*divorce* 1951) Nora (*d* 19 Sept 1964), dau of Horace Press, of Gt Yarmouth, Norfolk; *m* 2nd 9 Aug 1951 Ruby Joy Ann (*d* 28 Dec 1968), formerly w of Sir Francis Henry Grenville Peek, 4th Bt (*qv*), widow of Sir Charles Thomas Hewitt Mappin, 4th Bt (*see* 1970 edn), and dau of Capt Gordon Duff, RGA, of Brighton, and *d* 12 Dec 1964, leaving by his 1st w:

1 (WILLIAM) GEOFFREY, **2nd Baron**

2 Brian Gordon; *b* 1 Oct 1919; *educ* Harrow; T/Major 12th Roy Lancers WW I; chm Prestair Ltd and Dallick Ltd, Rootes Ltd, Rootes Motors Overseas Ltd, V-Chm Internat Rd Fedn, dir Rootes Motors Ltd to 1967; *m* 5 Feb 1944 *Elizabeth Margaret [The Hon Mrs Brian Rootes, The Old Farmhouse, Ramsbury, Wilts], widow of Lt Norman Lewis Phillips (*see* DUCIE, E) and yst dau of Rev Humphrey Gordon Barclay, CVO, MC, Rector Southrepps, Norwich, and *d* 1 Jan 1971, leaving:

(1) +WILLIAM BRIAN [William Rootes Esq, Belhie House, Aberuthven, Perthshire PH3 1EH]; *b* 8 Nov 1944; heir presumptive; *educ* Lycée Jaccard Lausanne; *m* 8 Nov 1969 *Alicia, yst dau of Frederick Graham Roberts, OBE, of East Farm House, Piddlehinton, Dorset, and has:

1a *Talitha Alice Louise; *b* 19 Oct 1973

2a *Annabell Catherine Natasha; *b* 2 Jan 1976

The 1st BARON's er son,

WILLIAM GEOFFREY ROOTES, **2nd Baron Rootes**; *b* 14 June 1917; *educ* Harrow and Ch Ch Oxford; T/Major RASC WW II; chm Rootes Motors, Chrysler UK 1967–73, Game Conservancy 1975–79, memb Nat Advsy Cncl for Motor Mfg Industry, Cncl, Cncl CBI 1967–74 and Warwick U 1968–74, NEDC Motor Manufacturing Industry 1968–73, UK Cncl World Wildlife Fund 1979 and Management Ctee Soc Motor Mfrs and Traders (Pres 1960–61), Pres Inst Motor Industry and Motor Cycle, St John Ambulance Berks 1975 and Trades Benevolent Fund 1968–70, dir Joseph Lucas (Industs) 1973 and RHM 1973, V-Pres Br Field Sports Soc 1978; *m* 15 Aug 1946 *Marian, widow of W/Cdr James Hogarth Slater, AFC, RAF, and dau of Lt-Col Herbert Roche Haytor, DSO, and *d* 1992, leaving:

1 NICHOLAS GEOFFREY ROOTES, **3rd and present Baron Rootes**

1 *Sally Hayter [The Hon Mrs St John, Cul-na-Cloich, Glenalmond, Perthshire]; *b* 12 Sept 1947; *m* 30 March 1968 *Andrew Beauchamp St John (*see* SAINT JOHN OF BLETSO, B)

ROPNER of Preston Hall

FIDES · ET · FORTITUDO

Arms: Per fess indented sa. and or a pale with three mullets pierced two and one and as many roebuck's heads erased one and two all counterchanged. **Crest:** In front of three tilting spears, one erect and two in saltire or, as many mascles interlaced fesswise of the last, thereon a roebuck's head erased sa. **Motto:** *Fides et fortitudo* ('Faith and fortitude'). **Creation:** Bt. (UK) 20 Aug 1904.

SIR ROBERT DOUGLAS ROPNER, 4TH BT, of Preston Hall, Co Durham [Sir Robert Ropner Bt, Forest Ridge, Maresfield Park, Sussex]; *b* 1 Dec 1921; *s* f 1962; *educ* Harrow; late Capt RA; *m* 24 Nov 1943 *Patricia Kathleen, yr dau of William Edward Schofield, of Blair Lodge, W Malling, Kent, and has:

1 +ROBERT CLINTON; *b* 6 Feb 1949; *educ* Harrow

1 *Serena Gay; *b* 23 Nov 1952

Lineage: JOHN HENRY ROPNER, of Magdeburg, Prussia; *m* Emilie, dau of Alfred Bessel, of Dresden, Saxony, and *d* 1848, leaving an est s:

Sir (Emil Hugo Oscar) Robert Ropner, 1st Bt (UK), so *cr* 20 Aug 1904, JP N R Yorks, DL Co Durham; *b* 16 Dec 1838; High Sheriff Co Durham 1896, MP (C) Stockton-on-Tees 1900–10, Lt-Col and Hon Col cmdg 1st Vol Bn Durham LI, ktd 1902; *m* 26 July 1858 Mary Anne (*d* 20 Oct 1921), dau of John Craik, of Newton Stewart, Wigtownshire, and *d* 26 Feb 1924, having had:

1 Sir John Henry Ropner, **2nd Bt**, VD, JP, DL Co Durham; *b* 7 Sept 1860; High Sheriff Co Durham 1911, Lt-Col and Hon Col 1st Vol Bn Durham LI; *m* 26 Sept 1888 Margaret (*d* 13 April 1932), 2nd dau of John MacGregor, of Sheffield, and had:

(1) Margaret; *b* 22 Sept 1894; *m* 30 Sept 1918 Capt John Robert Anderson Stroyan, RA, er s of John Stroyan, DL, of Lanrick, Perthshire, and *d* 9 Aug 1927

(2) Mary Enid; *b* 4 Aug 1897; *m* 24 July 1923 her sis's bro-in-law Ronald Strathearn Stroyan, (*d* 17 Nov 1957), and had issue

2 Emil Hugo Oscar Robert, of Elton Hall, Elton, Co Durham, JP; *b* 21 Dec 1862; MINA, shipbuilder; *m* 28 Sept 1892 Jane Venetia (*d* Dec 1939), dau of Richard Corker Walker, of Sowerby, Yorks, and *d* 3 April 1933, leaving:

(1) (EMIL HUGO OSCAR) ROBERT (Sir), **3rd Bt**

(2) Richard, TD, DL (Ross and Cromarty 1966); *b* 22 April 1898; *educ* Harrow and Edinburgh U (MB and ChB 1931); Lt-Col RAMC (TA), MGC WW I, MO Scottish Horse 1937–41, WW II: cmded No 87 (E African) Gen Hosp 1943–44, Dir Army Med Serv Br Mil Mission Ethiopia 1944–45, County Pres BRCS 1949–55, County Scout Commr 1945–65 (County Pres 1965–67); *m* 28 March 1928 Margaret Forbes (*d* 7 Sept 1976), dau of John Gilfillan Ronald, MD, of Torwood Hall, Larbert, and *d* 20 July 1975, leaving:

1a +Richard John Ronald; *b* 13 April 1941; *educ* Harrow and Edinburgh U (MB, ChB 1965); DObst RCOG 1970), DPM 1972, MRCPsych 1973; *m* 21 Sept 1974 *Janet Elizabeth, MB, MRCS, er dau of Dr J W Fox, of Chislehurst, Kent, and has:

    1b +James Richard Alexander; *b* 11 Jan 1977

    1b *Victoria Elizabeth Louise; *b* 1979

1a *Alison Margaret [Mrs Gerald Savage, The Old Quarry, Bramley, Surrey]; *b* 20 Jan 1930; SRN; *m* 4 July 1957 *Gerald Robert Savage, only s of Victor Laurent Savage, China Consular Serv, and has:

    1b *Nichola Mary; *b* 16 May 1958

2a *Pamela Christine [Mrs Thomas Stuttaford, 8 Ipswich Rd, Norwich, Norfolk]; *b* 1931; *educ* Edinburgh U (MA 1951); *m* 1 June 1957 *(Irving) Thomas Stuttaford, MRCS, LRCP, medical correspondent *The Times*, 2nd s of Dr William Joseph Edward Stuttaford, MC, of Bure Ridge, Horning, Norfolk, and has:

    1b *Andrew Irving Ropner; *b* 22 March 1958

    2b *Thomas Richard Ropner; *b* 25 Jan 1961

    3b *Hugo John Ropner; *b* 12 Feb 1964; *m* 19– *Joanna M, only dau of Keith Davenport, and has:

        1c *Oliver George Watkin; *b* 1994

(3) (Cuthbert) Maurice; *b* 11 April 1905; *educ* Harrow; Capt KOSB WW II; *m* 26 Sept 1929 Dorothea Seymour (*d* 21 Sept 1994), dau of Rev Robert William Bell, Vicar Stamfordham, and was *ka* 11 May 1945, leaving:

1a +George Maurice [Maj George Ropner, Gallowshaw, Netherwitton, Morpeth, Northumberland NE61 4NL]; *b* 28 July 1934; *educ* Harrow; Maj Northumberland Hus (TA)

1a *Vivien Anne; *b* 19 July 1930; *educ* Durham U (MB, BS 1955)

2a *Caroline Jane; *b* 5 Feb 1945

3 William, of Thorp Perrow, Bedale, Yorks, and Ambleside, W Hartlepool, Co Durham, JP; *b* 17 Sept 1864; *m* 18 April 1894 Sarah Woolacott (*d* 15 Sept 1948), dau of Ebenezer Cory, of W Hartlepool, and *d* 16 March 1947, leaving:

(1) Sir LEONARD ROPNER, 1st Bt, of Thorp Perrow (*qv*)

(2) (William) Guy (Sir), JP N R Yorks; *b* 14 June 1896; *educ* Harrow; Maj RA (TA) WW I, Dir Convoy Section Min War Tport 1944–45 , ktd 1947, dir Sir R Ropner & Co, V-Pres Chamber Shipping 1949–50 (Pres 1950–51); *m* 22 June 1921 Margarita (*d* 1973), dau of Sir William Cresswell Gray, 1st Bt (*qv*), and *d* 2 May 1971, leaving:

1a +(William Guy) David [David Ropner Esq, 1 Sunningdale Gdns, Stratford Rd, London W8 6PX]; *b* 3 April 1924; *educ* Harrow; late Capt RHA; *m* 1st 10 Sept 1955 (Mildred) Malise Hare, yr dau of George Armitage, MC, TD, FRCS, of Newburgh House, Coxwold, York, and has:

    1b +Guy David Armitage [Guy Ropner Esq, North Stanmore Farm, Stanmore, Newbury, Berks RG20 8SR]; *b* 11 Aug 1959; *m* 1991 *Annabel Frances, er dau of Michael Odiarne Coates, of Gt Shoesmiths Farm, Wadhurst, E Sussex, and has:

        1c *Amy Grace Coates; *b* 17 May 1992

        2c *Molly; *b* 29 June 1996

        3c *Flora; *b* 29 June 1996

    2b +Roderick John; *b* 24 Feb 1962

    3b +Peter Gavin Malise; *b* 31 Dec 1964

    1b *Lucy Armitage; *b* 10 Nov 1957; *m* 1985 *Christopher Goelet, yst s of John Goelet, of New York, and has:

        1c *Eloise Ropner; *b* 1987

        2c *Isabelle Guestier; *b* 1989

        3c *Henrietta Zoe; *b* 1992

1a (cont) David Ropner *m* 2nd 1985 *Hon Charlotte Mary, dau of 2nd Baron Piercy (*qv*) and former w of Paolo Emilio Taddei, and by her has:

    4b +Nicholas David Piercy; *b* 11 Nov 1986

2a +Jonathan Gray [Jonathan Ropner Esq, Dalesend, Patrick Brompton, nr Bedale, Yorks]; *b* 1 May 1931; *educ* Harrow; late Lt Irish Gds; *m* 31 Oct 1953 *Edith Avril, yr dau of Charles Urie Peat, MC, MA, FCA, of Wycliffe Hall, Barnard Castle, Durham, and has:

    1b +(Jonathan) Mark; *b* 25 Sept 1954; *educ* Harrow; *m* 1985 *Madelyn K, only dau of W Stefanech, of San Luis Obispo, Calif., and has:

        1c *James; *b* 1986

        1c *Jasmine; *b* 1989

    2b +Charles Guy Corban; *b* 2 Feb 1959; *m* 1989 *Emma, yr dau of Richard Andrews, of Courtyard Ho, Westow, N Yorks, and has:

        1c +Richard Jonathan Charles; *b* 1 May 1995

        1c *Mary Rose Avril; *b* 1991

        2c *Eugenie Annabel Pearl; *b* 1993

    3b +Paul Benedict Peat; *b* 28 Jan 1965; *m* 1992 *Peggy A, dau of Willard A Ison, Warrant Offr USN, of Salt Lake City, Utah, and has:

        1c *Chloe; *b* 1993

    4b +Dominic Adam; *b* 8 May 1968; *m* 1991 *Abigail, dau of Peter de Barros Clay, of Richmond, Surrey, and has:

1c +Inigo Thomas Robert; *b* 1993

1c *Daisy Manina Debarros; *b* 1992

1b *Margarita Carey; *b* 10 May 1956; *m* 1979 *John Dickinson and has:

    1c *Toby Benedict; *b* 1981

    1c *Amelia Sophie; *b* 1983

    2c *Leila Florence; *b* 1989

1a *Rita Gray [Mrs Rita Hodson, 13 Old Palace Lane, Richmond, Surrey]; *b* 13 July 1922; *m* 11 Sept 1947 (*divorce* 19–) Alan Maskew Hodson (*see* HODSON, B) and has:

    1b *Alexandra Mary; *b* 1958

(3) John ('Jock') Raymond; *b* 8 May 1903; *educ* Harrow and Clare Coll Cambridge (BA); High Sheriff Co Durham 1958, Lt RA (TA), Order Orange-Nassau Netherlands, dir Sir R Ropner & Co, Provincial Bank and Eggar, Forrester and Verner & Co; *m* 24 July 1928 Joan ('Jill') (*d* 1993), dau of William Redhead, and *d* 10 Nov 1996, leaving:

1a +William David Jock; *b* 27 June 1929; *educ* Harrow; *m* 19 Sept 1961 (*divorce* 1966) Elizabeth Anne, est dau of Elmer Ellsworth Jones, of Knightsbridge

2a +Jeremy Vyvyan [Jeremy Ropner Esq, Firby Hall, Bedale, N Yorks DL8 2PW]; *b* 3 May 1932; *educ* Harrow and RNC Dartmouth; *m* 25 June 1955 *Sally, yr dau of Maj George Talbot Willcox, MC, of Cobham, Surrey (*see* below), and has had:

    1b Clive Vyvyan Peter; *b* 17 March 1957; *d* 1979

    2b +Simon Jock Wilks; *b* 22 June 1962

    1b *Sophia Sally [Mrs Christopher Mansfield, 53 Campana Rd, London SW6 4AT]; *b* 28 Sept 1959; *m* 1991 *Christopher John Mansfield, s of Kenneth Mansfield, of Quarry Ho, Malton, Yorks

    2b *Lisa Cleone Vivian; *b* 2 July 1964; *m* 1985 *Capt (Timothy) Mark Nicole, 4th/7th Dragoon Gds, s of Tom Nicole, of Slape Manor, Netherbury, Dorset, and has:

        1c *Edward Tom George; *b* 1990

        2c *George Charles Jeremy; *b* 1993

        3c *Oscar; *b* 14 June 1996

        1c *Lucy Sophia Catherine; *b* 1987

1a *Susan Carole [Mrs Peter Martel, The Manor House, Gayles, Richmond, N Yorks DL11 7JF]; *b* 18 Sept 1936; *m* 19 Oct 1957 *Maj (Charles) Peter Martel, only s of Lt Gen Sir Giffard Martel, KCB, KBE, DSO, MC, of Bulford Lodge, Camberley, Surrey, and has had:

    1b *Nicholas Charles Giffard; *b* 21 Dec 1960; *m* 1987 (*divorce* 1996) Sarah Jane Maxwell, only dau of J S M Barlow, of Minshull Hall, Nantwich, Cheshire, and has:

        1c *Charles; *b* 1988

        2c *Hugo; *b* 1993

    1b *Carole Valerie; *b* 9 Aug 1958; *m* 1985 *Ivo Tennant and has issue (*see* GLENCONNER, B)

    2b Virginia Jill; *b* 1 April 1964; *d* 1971

    3b *Sarah Charlotte; *b* 1973

(4) Robert Desmond (Sir); *b* 2 July 1908; *educ* Harrow and Clare Coll Cambridge (BA 1930); Capt RA (TA) WW II, shipowner, memb: Gen Cncl Br Shipping 1941 (chm 1958–59) and Min Tport Ships Licensing Ctee 1947, chm Tramp Shipping Sub-Ctee of Shipping Advsy and Allocations Ctee 1947, dir: Ropner Hldgs, Sir R Ropner & Co, Ropner Insur Brokers, Elton Stores, Airtech, BP Clyde Tanker, BP Tanker Co, Hozelock, Airvert, Croft Autodrome, Ropner Management, Mainsforth Investments and International Tonnage Stabilisation Assoc, chm North of England Protecting and Indemnity Assoc, memb: Exec Cncl Shipping Fedn, Cncl of Chamber of Shipping UK (V-Pres 1957–58, Pres 1958–59, Chm Deep Sea Tramp Section 1951–53), ktd 1959, memb Shipping Advsy Panel 1962; *m* 1st 26 Jan 1932 (*divorce* 1946) Dorothy Beecroft Sheila, dau of Sir Edmund Beecroft Lacon, 5th Bt (*qv*), and had:

1a +(Robert) Bruce Beecroft [Bruce Ropner Esq, Camp Hill, Kirklington, Bedale, Yorks]; *b* 13 April 1933; *educ* Harrow; late Lt Welsh Gds; *m* 9 July 1960 *Willow, only dau of James William Hare, of Fieldhead, Thorner, nr Leeds, and has:

    1b +Robert James Bruce; *b* 7 Nov 1962; *m* 1986 *Johanna Louise, yr dau of Colin Strathearn Ropner Stroyan (*see* above), of Teith, Doune, Perthshire, and has:

        1c +(Robert) Angus; *b* 1988

        2c +Max; *b* 1990

        1c *Poppy; *b* 1993

    1b *Nicola Molly; *b* 2 June 1965

2a +Garry Lacon Jock; *b* 7 Oct 1937; late 2nd Lt Welsh Gds; *m* 1st 20 March 1962 (*divorce* 1973) Antonia, yr dau of Maj-Gen Edward Charles Colville, CB, DSO (*see* COLVILLE OF CULROSS, V); *m* 2nd 1974 Mrs Julie Marie Swanwick, dau of O B Aarvold; *m* 3rd *Mrs Marie-Louise (Sally) Raynar, dau of Arthur Southcombe Brook, and has by his 1st w:

    1b *Emma Louise; *b* 21 July 1963

(4) (cont) Sir Robert *m* 2nd 8 Dec 1947 Sibyl (*k* car crash 23 June 1969), formerly w of Richard Stormont Hays, of Crosby Lodge, Crosby-on-Eden, nr Carlisle, and dau of Thomas O Carter, and *d* 31 Aug 1977

(1) Constance Winsome; *b* 15 March 1899; *m* 19 Oct 1922 Maj George Talbot Willcox, MC, MInstT, s of A Talbot Willcox, and has issue. He *d* 28 Nov 1968

4 Walter; *b* 11 July 1868; *m* 18 April 1894 Jane Constance (*d* 14 Feb 1951), dau of Ebenezer Cory, of W Hartlepool, and had:

(1) Geoffrey Vyvyan; *b* 18 July 1898; served WW I, Assist Commr Police Aden 1930–37, Dep Commr Police Aden 1937–40; *m* 2 May 1961 Edith Sophia, dau of Richard Joseph Shedal, and *dsp* 24 June 1962

(1) Kathleen Vera; *b* 9 May 1895

(2) Lorna; *m* 23 June 1928 Lt Col Ronald Allison Sparks, TD, s of Ernest Leonard Sparks, of Putney, and had:

1a *Hubert Jeremy; *b* 31 Jan 1936; *educ* Repton; F/Lt RAF, electronic engr EMI 1953–59; *m* 7 March 1964 *Anna Patricia Crothers and has:

1b *Tracey Heather; *b* 23 Jan 1965

1a *Shirley Heather; *b* 28 Aug 1929; *m* 23 Nov 1957 *Lt Col Rev Lewis David Malcolm Patterson, s of Alexander Cox Patterson, and has:

1b *Bruce Peter John; *b* 6 Oct 1959

5 Leonard, JP Co Durham; *b* 20 April 1873; Capt 1st Vol Bn Durham LI, Mayor Stockton-on-Tees 1924 and 1925, High Sheriff Co Durham 1937; *m* 17 Nov 1904 Georgina (*d* 23 Sept 1930), dau of Murdock Mackay, and *d* 4 Aug 1937, leaving:

(1) +Leonard Robert; *b* 31 Jan 1910; *m* 1934 *Agnes Deans Bennett

(1) Helen Mary; *b* 13 Sept 1905; *m* 24 Aug 1933 Hon Mr Justice Joseph Bushby Hewson, RD, High Court Judge, s of Wilfred Bushby Hewson, of Carlisle, and had:

(2) Jean Winifred; *b* 3 March 1908; *m* 16 July 1929 (*divorce* 1945) Victor Bremner Purvis, MB, BS, s of Rev John Bremner Purvis, Vicar Bedlington, Northumberland, and had issue

1 Amy; *b* 10 March 1867; *m* 20 June 1894 Cecil James Sadler, JP, 2nd s of Sir Samuel Alexander Sadler, JP, MP, and *d* 4 Jan 1967, leaving issue. He *d* 19 Dec 1936

2 Lilian; *b* 26 Oct 1874; *m* 25 Aug 1903 Rev Sidney Cecil Woods, Rector Church Stretton, Salop, 1914–23, Sec Schools Missions to Seamen 1923, and had issue. He *d* 10 June 1942

3 Evelyn; *b* 25 Jan 1876; *m* 23 June 1898 Sir Henry Charles Holder, 2nd Bt (*qv*), and *d* 5 July 1956, leaving issue

4 Mabel; *b* 24 March 1877; *m* 17 April 1902 Frederick Byers Watson and had issue. He *d* 28 Nov 1916

5 Elsa Bessel; *b* 1 Oct 1886; *d* unm 20 Dec 1908

Sir JOHN *d* 13 July 1936; his n,

Sir (Emil Hugo Oscar) Robert Ropner, 3rd Bt; *b* 8 Oct 1893; *educ* Harrow, Capt 5th Bn Durham LI WW I (despatches), Staff Capt Boulogne Base 1916–18 and with Min Munitions, WW II CD; *m* 1918 Lillian Rochfort (*d* 9 May 1976), dau of Col Rochfort Snow, of Christchurch, NZ, and *d* 5 May 1962, having had:

1 Sir ROBERT DOUGLAS ROPNER, **4th and present Bt**

1 *Diana Joan; *b* 6 July 1919; *m* 23 Aug 1941 John Randall Elliott, RA, only s of C T Elliott

2 *Patricia Elizabeth [Mrs Claude MacDonald-Hull, Forest Ridge, Maresfield Park, nr Uckfield, Sussex]; *b* 10 April 1923; *m* 8 Jan 1944 *Lt-Col Claude Macdonald-Hull, MC, s of Alfred Henry Hull, of Hereford, and has:

(1) *Susan Patricia Macdonald; *b* 11 Feb 1948

(2) *Fiona Elizabeth Macdonald; *b* 13 Aug 1950

1 +HENRY JOHN WILLIAM; *b* 24 Oct 1981

4 *Carolyn Esme; *b* 1971

5 *Annabel Mariella; *b* 20 March 1974

Sir JOHN *m* 3rd 6 April 1996 *Mrs Niki Tippett

Lineage: WILLIAM ROPNER, JP, of Thorp Perrow (*see* ROPNER, Bt, of Preston Hall), had an est s:

Sir Leonard Ropner, 1st Bt (UK), so *cr* 31 Jan 1952, MC (1918), TD, JP (1923); *b* 26 Feb 1895; *educ* Harrow and Clare Coll Cambridge (BA 1922); Maj RGA WW I, cmded Durham Heavy Bde RA 1919–28, memb Co Durham T&AFA 1920–61 (V-Chm 1948–52), Hon Col 426 Coast Regt RA (TA) 1928–56, shipowner, sr ptnr Sir R Ropner & Co, MP (C) Sedgefield 1923–29 and Barkston Ash 1931–64, PPS to Sec State War 1924–28, Hon Treas: C and U Films Assoc 1930–47 (Chm 1947–49), Forestry Commr 1936–45, T/Chm Ctees H of C 1945–58, Hon Treas Primrose League 1952–64, Assist Controller Timber Supply Min Supply 1939, memb Timber Supply Dept Forestry Commn 1940, Dep Dir Home Grown Timber Prodn Min Supply 1941, Lt-Col RA and Col 21st Army Gp Belgium and Germany WW II, Hon Col 132 Corps Engineer Regt TA 1956–58, KStJ, Co Commr St John Ambulance Bde N R Yorks 1950; *m* 23 June 1932 Esme (*d* 11 Dec 1996), yst dau of William Bruce Robertson, of Kensington, and *d* 12 Oct 1977, leaving:

1 Sir JOHN BRUCE WOOLLACOTT, **2nd and present Bt**

1 *Merle Aurelia; *b* 12 Oct 1939; *m* 1st 29 Sept 1960 (*divorce* 1968) Christopher John Spence, yr s of Brig Ian Fleming Morris Spence, OBE, MC, TD, ADC, of W Kensington, and has had:

(1) Jeremy Mark; *b* 23 Oct 1964; *d* 1982

(1) *Miranda Jane; *b* 6 Jan 1963; *m* 1989 *Patrick Robin Barran (*see* BARRAN, Bt)

1 (cont.) Mrs Merle Spence *m* 2nd 6 Sept 1968 *Maj Lawrence Hew Williams Barrington, only s of Richard Irving Williams Barrington, and has further issue (*see* BARRINGTON, Bt)

2 *Virginia June [Mrs John Henderson, Holly Hill, Well, Bedale, Yorks]; *b* 17 Aug 1941; *m* 1st 14 June 1962 (*divorce* 1973) Anthony David Arnold William Forbes, only s of Lt Col David Arthur Walter Forbes, MC, Coldstream Gds; *m* 2nd 1974 *Capt John Alexander Henderson (*see* FARINGDON, B) and by her 1st husb has:

(1) Jonathan David; *b* 16 June 1964; *m* 1993 *Sacha Louisa, dau of Hon Robin Charles Denison-Pender (*see* PENDER, B), and has:

1a *Jack; *b* 25 Oct 1996

(1) *Susanna Jane; *b* 1 Dec 1966; *m* 1993 *William M Amberg, yr s of Michael Amberg, of Ravenstone, Bucks

ROPNER of
Thorp Perrow

Arms: As for ROPNER of Preston Hall, a crescent for difference.
Creation: Bt. (UK) 31 Jan 1952.

SIR JOHN BRUCE WOOLLACOTT ROPNER, 2ND BT, of Thorp Perrow, Co York, DL (Co Durham 1955) [Sir John Ropner Bt DL, Thorp Perrow, Bedale, N Yorks]; *b* 16 April 1937; *s f* 1977; *educ* Eton and St Paul's Sch USA; late Lt 17th/21st Lancers, shipowner, dir: Ropner plc, Ropner Management Ltd, Ropner Insur Brokers, Elton Stores, High Sheriff N Yorks 1991; *m* 1st 10 June 1961 (*divorce* 1970) Anne Melicent (Milet), only child of Sir Ralph Hubert John Delmé-Radcliffe, JP, of Hitchin Priory, Herts, and has had:

1 *Jenny [Mrs Graham Simpson, Hungry Lodge, Downs Lane, Mapledurwell, Hants RG25 2LQ]; *b* 20 March 1963; *m* 1st 1985 William H Bullard, s of Gerald Bullard; *m* 2nd 1990 *Graham G D Simpson, s of Brig John Simpson, of Hants and Sydney, and has:

(1) *Alexander John Drysdale; *b* 1992

(1) *Miranda Lucy Araminta; *b* 1994

2 *Katherine; *b* 16 April 1964; *m* 1988 *Hon Henry Thurstan Holland-Hibbert, er s of 6th Viscount Knutsford (*qv*), and has issue

3 Lucinda; *b* 29, *d* 31 March 1967

Sir JOHN *m* 2nd 9 Nov 1970 (*divorce* 1993) Auriol Veronica, yst dau of Capt Graham Laurie Mackeson-Sandbach (*see* MACKESON, Bt), and has:

ROSE of Montreal and
Hardwick House

Arms: Or a boar's head couped gu. armed and langued az. between three water bougets sa., on a chief of the second three maple leaves of the first. **Crest:** A harp or stringed az. **Mottoes:** 1 (over the crest) *Audeo* ('I dare'), (below the shield) Constant and true. **Creations:** Bt. (UK) 9 Sept 1872 (of Montreal), 19 July 1909 (of Hardwick House).

SIR JULIAN DAY ROSE, 5TH BT, of Montreal, and **4TH BT**, of Hardwick House, Whitchurch, Co Oxford [Sir Julian Rose Bt, Hardwick House, Whitchurch, nr Reading, RG8 7RB]; *b* 3 March 1947; *s* kinsman 1979 as 5th Bt and *f* 1966 as 4th Bt; *educ* Stanbridge Earls Sch, Romsey, and RADA; actor and assist dir, co-fndr Inst for Creative Devpt, Antwerp, 1978–83, organic farmer, writer and broadcaster, memb: cncl Soil Assoc 1984–, Ag Panel Intermediate Technology Devpt Gp 1984–, BBC Rural and Ag Affrs Advsy Ctee 1991–, chm Assoc Rural Businesses in Oxon 1995–; *m* 1976 *Elizabeth Goode, dau of Derrol Johnson, of Columbus, Ohio, and has:

1 +LAWRENCE MICHAEL; *b* 6 Oct 1986

1 *Miriam Margaret; *b* 1984

Lineage: JOHN ROSE, of Turriff, Aberdeenshire; *b* 1749 (s of John Rose, of Kilravock, Nairn, and later of Edingight, Banffshire); *d* 1836, leaving:

WILLIAM ROSE, of Huntingdon, Canada; *b* Turriff 1792; *m* 1819 Elizabeth (*d* 1822), dau of Capt James Fyfe, and had, with a dau (Elizabeth, *m* 1835 George Blake, of Huntingdon, Canada):

Sir John Rose, 1st Bt (UK), so *cr* 9 Sept 1872, GCMG 1878 (KCMG 1870), PC (1886), QC (1851); *b* 2 Aug 1820; barrister Canada 1842, Slr-Gen 1859, Min Public Works 1860 and Finance 1867, Receiver-Gen Duchy Cornwall 1883; *m* 1st 3 July 1843 Charlotte (*d* 3 Dec 1883), dau of Robert Emmett Temple, of Rutland, USA, and had:

1 **Sir William Rose, 2nd Bt**; *b* 1 April 1846; barrister; *m* 2 Jan 1868 Katherine Elizabeth (*d* 16 Jan 1929), dau of Alexander Macalister, of Torresdale Castle, Argyll, and *d* 4 Oct 1902, leaving:

  (1) **Sir Cyril Stanley Rose, 3rd Bt**; *b* 13 July 1874; *m* 14 Oct 1905 Laetitia (*d* July 1932), dau of Émile Hippolyte Rouy, and *d* 11 July 1915, leaving:

    1a **Sir Francis Cyril Rose, 4th Bt**; *b* 18 Sept 1909; *educ* Beaumont; painter and author, artistic adviser to The Edinburgh Tapestry Co and Roosen Silks Ltd; RAF WW II 1940–42 (invalided); *m* 1st 22 Feb 1943 (*divorce* 1966) Frederica Dorothy Violet, author, widow of Darcy Sinclair Sproul-Boulton and dau of Maj-Gen Sir Frederick Carrington, KCB, KCMG; *m* 2nd 7 Feb 1967 Beryl, widow of S/Ldr (Actg G/Capt) Basil Montefiore Davis, MIEE, MBritIRE, FRSA, RAF, and dau of Alfred Norris, and *d* Nov 1979

2 **Sir Charles Day Rose, 1st Bt** (UK), so *cr* 19 July 1909, of Hardwick House, Whitchurch, Oxon, JP Cambs and Oxon; *b* 23 Aug 1847; MP (Lib) E Cambs 1903–Jan 1910 and Dec 1910–13, Capt Montreal Garrison Artillery and Middx (Duke of Cambridge's) Hus; *m* 29 June 1871 Eliza (*d* 4 Nov 1922), dau of John Robinson McLean, MP E Staffs, and *d* 20 April 1913, having had:

  (1) Charles Ernest; Capt RHG; *b* 11 Dec 1873; *ka* Boer War May 1900

  (2) Bertram Temple; *b* 24 April 1875; *das* unm Boer War 30 March 1900

  (3) **Sir Frank Stanley Di Rose, 2nd Bt**; Capt 10th Hus Boer War 1900–02 and WW I; *b* 27 April 1877; *m* 31 March 1910 Daphne, JP (*d* 15 Aug 1966), yr dau of Capt Henry Brooks Gaskell, of Kiddington Hall, Oxon, and was *ka* 26 Oct 1914, leaving:

    1a **Sir Charles Henry Rose, 3rd Bt**; *b* 13 Oct 1912; *educ* RNC Dartmouth; Midshipman RN; *m* 3 June 1937 *Hon Phoebe Margaret Dorothy Phillimore [The Hon Phoebe Lady Rose, 2 East Lodges, Hardwick, Whitchurch-on-Thames, Oxon RG8 7RB], dau of 2nd Baron Phillimore (*qv*), and *d* 8 April 1966, having had:

      1b Timothy, *b* 14 May, *d* 16 May 1939

      2b Peter Frank Charles; *b* 27 July 1941; *educ* Eton; *d* following a car crash 12 June 1964

      3b Sir JULIAN DAY ROSE, **4th and present Bt of Hardwick and 5th and present Bt of Montreal**

      1b *Margaret Minna [Mrs John Cochrane, Fairspear House, Leafield, Oxford OX8 5NT]; *b* 13 Feb 1938; *m* 26 Nov 1966 *John Alexander Cochrane (see COCHRANE OF CULTS, B) and has issue

      2b *Penelope Clare; *b* 29 March 1945; *m* 1 March 1975 *Francis A A Carnwath CBE, est s of Sir Andrew Carnwath, KCVO, and has had:

        1c *Alexander; *b* 12 Dec 1980

        1c *Flora Helen; *b* 1976

        2c Catriona Rose; *b* 1978; *d* 1984

    1a *Amy [Mrs Robert Beloe, The Hill House, Queen's Rd, Richmond, Surrey]; *b* 4 May 1911; *m* 4 April 1933 Robert Beloe, CBE (*d* 1984), est s of Rev Robert Douglas Beloe, Headmaster Bradfield, and has:

      1b *Robert Francis (Rev) [The Rev Robert Beloe, The Vicarage, Wicken, Cambs]; *b* 1939; *m* 1970 *Sheila Napier Millar and has:

        1c *Amy Margaret; *b* 1971

        2c *Christina Ruth; *b* 1973

      1b *Helen [Mrs Oliver Stutchbury, Gayles, Friston, E Sussex BN20 0BA]; *b* 1934; *m* 1955 *Oliver Piers Stutchbury and has:

        1c *Wycliffe Robert Trant; *b* 1965

        1c *Emma Jane; *b* 1955; has issue:

          1d *Ben Joseph; *b* 1978

          1d *Lucy; *b* 1980

        2c *Catharine Rose; *b* 1958; *m* 19– *Kevin Allen

        3c *Rosalind Amy; *b* 1960; *m* 19– *Derry Robinson and has:

          1d *Jessica Helen; *b* 1987

      2b *Clarissa Elizabeth [Mrs John Higginbotham, 16 Holmfield Ave, Stoneygate, Leics]; *b* 1936; *m* 1963 *John Eagle Higginbotham, Headmaster Leicester GS, and has:

        1c *Robert Charles Trant; *b* 1967

        1c *Lydia Clare; *b* 1964

    2a Helen Briar; *b* (posthumous) 23 June 1915; *m* 7 June 1939 Lt-Col John Granville (*d* 1984), Oxon and Bucks LI, yst s of Lt-Col Bernard Granville, DSO, JP, DL, of Wellesbourne, Warwicks, and *d* 1995, leaving:

      1b *Antony Lansdowne [Antony Granville Esq, Tachbrook House, Stourton, Shipston on Stour, Warwicks]; *b* 1945; *m* 1970 *Harriet Anne, dau of Sir John James Macdonald Horlick, 5th Bt (*qv*), and has:

        1c *Edward James; *b* 1972

        1c *Matilda Rose; *b* 1975

      2b *Charles; *b* 1949

  (4) Adrian; *b* 6 Nov 1878; Capt RHG Boer War 1900–02; *m* 7 Dec 1907 Nancy Lycett, OBE (1946, MBE 1918) (*d* 6 May 1970) (*m* 2nd 5 Jan 1911 4th Baron Vivian, *qv*), er dau of Sir Edward Lycett Green, 2nd Bt (*qv*), and *dsp* 25 March 1908

  (1) Muriel Lilian; *m* 1st 17 Aug 1907 (*divorce* 1919) William Harold Tribe (*d* 1926), of Broadwater Manor, Sussex, and *m* 2nd 16 June 1920 Jack Victor Ralph Nelder (*d* 2 Jan 1962), only s of George Nelder

3 Edward Temple; *b* 2 Nov 1855; Capt 10th Hus; *m* 28 July 1883 Lady Cecilia Cathcart (*d* 2 Oct 1932), dau of 3rd Earl Cathcart (*qv*), and *d* 1920

1 Mary Temple; *m* 15 Sept 1867 Maj-Gen Sir Stanley de Astel Calvert Clarke, GCVO, CMG, and *d* 28 March 1913, leaving issue. He *d* 29 Nov 1911

2 Charlotte Army; *m* 15 Aug 1866 Francis Sloane Stanley, of Tedworth House, Hants, and *d* 24 Jan 1917, leaving issue. He *d* 29 Aug 1904

Sir John *m* 2nd 24 Jan 1887 Julia Charlotte Sophia (*d* 17 May 1937, having *m* 3rd 2 Feb 1892 Maj Sir William Eden Evans Gordon, MP), widow of 9th Marquess of Tweeddale (*qv*) and dau of Keith Stewart Mackenzie of Seaforth (see GALLOWAY, E), and *d* 24 Aug 1888

ROSE of Rayners

Arms: Azure a chevron invected erminois, between three water bougets in chief and one in base argent. **Crest:** A stag argent collared and resting the dexter foreleg on a water bouget azure.
Motto: *Probitate ac virtute* ('By probity and valour').
Creation: Bt. (UK) 14 May 1874.

SIR DAVID LANCASTER ROSE, 4TH BT, of Rayners, Co Buckingham [Sir David Rose Bt, 20 Kingston Close, Seaford, Sussex]; *b* 17 Feb 1934; *s* second cousin 1982; *m* 1965 *Dorothy, dau of Albert Edward Whitehead, and has:

1 +PHILIP JOHN LANCASTER; *b* 1966

2 +Christopher David; *b* 1968

1 *Angela Mary; *b* 1967

Lineage: THOMAS ROSE, of Thame; *m* 1698 Mary Peck and had:

THOMAS ROSE; settled Chipping Wycombe (Mayor 1753); *m* 1st 11 Feb 1730 Martha Morris (*dsp* 2 Jan 1732); *m* 2nd 6 June 1733 Martha Hawgood (*d* 2 Sept 1737); *m* 3rd 2 May 1738 Elizabeth Peel and *d* 28 Oct 1768, leaving by her:

THOMAS ROSE, of Chipping Wycombe, Mayor 1767 and often afterwards; *b* 2 Feb 1739; *m* 19 Feb 1767 Honor Tett (*d* Oct 1778), of Chipping Wycombe, and *d* Oct 1809, leaving a 3rd s:

WILLIAM ROSE, Mayor High Wycombe 1814 and subsequently; Assist-Surgn IA; *b* 5 Feb 1776; *m* 5 June 1810 Charlotte (*d* 31 July 1869), dau of William Baly, of High Wycombe, and *d* 1 July 1846, having had a 3rd s:

Sir Philip Rose, 1st Bt (UK), so *cr* 14 May 1874, JP Bucks, DL Middx; *b* 12 April 1816; High Sheriff Bucks 1878, Treasurer County Court, Hon Sec to Hosp for Consumption Brompton (fndr 1841); Kt Cdr Medjidie; *m* 2 Jan 1840 Margaretta (*d* 13 March 1889), dau of Robert Ranking, of Hastings, and *d* 17 April 1883, leaving:

1 **Sir Philip Frederick Rose, 2nd Bt**, JP, DL Bucks; *b* 4 Nov 1843; *educ* Harrow; High Sheriff Bucks 1898; *m* 25 July 1866 Rosa Anne (*d* 7 May 1925), dau of Rev William Wollaston Pym, Rector Willian, Herts, and *d* 23 Oct 1919, having had:

  (1) Philip Vivian; *b* 25 March 1869; Staff Capt 63rd Inf Bde, Capt 3rd Bn Oxon LI, WW I (severely wounded, POW); *m* 10 Jan 1899 Maud Winifred (*d* 4 Oct 1958, having *m* 2nd 30 Oct 1923 F Dixon-Brown), 2nd dau of William Gillian, of Kensington, and *d* 25 April 1917 of wounds recd in action, leaving:

    1a **Sir (Philip) Humphrey Vivian Rose, 3rd Bt**; *b* 16 March 1903; *educ* Harrow; HAC WW II; *m* 5 July 1927 *Evelyn Joan Victoria Heastey, yr dau of Martin Richardson, MD, and *d* 1982, having had:

      1b Phillip Humphrey Peter; *b* 30 May 1928; *k* by enemy aircraft 15 May 1943

      1b *Petica Mary [Mrs Andrew Waley, Pleasure House, E Sutton, Kent ME17 3NW]; *b* 30 May 1929; *m* 3 Sept 1955 His Honour Judge (Andrew) Felix Waley, VRD, MA, QC (*d* 16 April 1995), only s of Guy Felix Waley, and has had:

        1c *Simon Felix; *b* 9 Sept 1964

        1c *Sarah Elizabeth; *b* 17 Feb 1958

        2c *Jane Felicity; *b* 27 Feb 1959

        3c *Juliet Anne; *b* 10 Feb 1960

        4c Victoria Mary; *b* 7 Jan 1961; *d* 13 Sept 1962

      2b *Susan Elizabeth Anne; *b* 26 July 1932

    1a Marjorie Winifred; *b* 21 Feb 1900; *m* 5 Sept 1927 Wilfred Gerald Eyre, yst s of Edward Eyre, of New York and Mayfair, and *d* 1994, leaving:

      1b *Richard Carmel Thomas More; *b* 22 July 1936; *m* 1965 *Josepha Mary Schretlen and has:

        1c *Richard Edward; *b* 1966

        1c *Andrea Marjorie; *b* 1967

        2c *Christina Maria; *b* 1969

        3c *Judith Mary; *b* 1971

1b *Vivian Mary Raymonde [Mrs John Sweeny, 533 W Hallam, Aspen, CO 81611, USA]; *b* 29 Aug 1928; *m* 1949 *John Sweeney and has:

   1c *Michael Eyre; *b* 1953

   2c *Timothy Andrew; *b* 1957

   3c *Edward Philip; *b* 1963

   4c *Mark McConnell; *b* 1965

   1c *Marna Therese; *b* 1950

   2c *Carol Mary; *b* 1958

   3c *Kathrine Ann; *b* 1960

2b *Elisa Virginia Mary [Mrs Christopher Brennan, PO Box 1793, 10th and Torres–7SW, Carmel, CA 93921, USA]; *b* 7 Sept 1932; *m* 1st 1952 (*divorce* 1963) Charles Bennett Cobb and has:

   1c *Charles Dennison; *b* 1955

   2c *Gerald Bennett; *b* 1956

   1c *Marguerite Elisa; *b* 1957

2b (cont.) Mrs Elisa Cobb *m* 2nd 1963 *Christopher Brennan and by him has:

   3c *Christopher Thomas; *b* 1972

3b *Jane Olga Mary [Mrs Bruce Schuster, 2800 50 University Blvd, #153, Denver, CO 80210, USA]; *b* 5 Dec 1934; *m* 4 June 1960 *(Albert) Bruce Schuster, s of Leo J Schuster, of Denver, and has:

   1c *Anthony Bruce, *b* 14 Jan 1964

   2c *Philip Andrew, *b* 11 Nov 1965

   3c *Christopher Paul, *b* 4 July 1969

   4c *Matthew Ainsworth; *b* 1972

   1c *Jane Eyre, *b* 6 Nov 1962

2a *June Dorothy [Mrs June Brennan, House of Rosthshild, 675 50 University Blvd, Denver, CO 80209, USA]; *b* 12 June 1913; *m* 1938 (*divorce*) Marcel Brennan and has:

   1b *Christopher; *b* 1939

(2) Cecil Guy; *b* 29 July 1877; MICE, Maj RE WW I; *m* 6 April 1907 Rosa Belle (*d* 13 April 1957), dau of Herbert Emmerson, of Scarborough, and *d* 8 Nov 1962

(3) John Philip Sebastian; *b* 4 Feb 1889; *d* unm 17 Aug 1904

(1) Margaret Edith; *d* 8 Jan 1869

(2) Mary Gertrude; *m* 7 Feb 1895 Albert Norman Henderson, MC, Maj (T/Lt-Col) 10th Serv Bn Roy Warwicks Regt (*ka* 23 July 1916), yst s of William Henderson, and *d* 21 Nov 1956

(3) Rose Annie Dorothy; *m* 29 Nov 1894 Edward Noel Napier Bartlett, JP (*d* 17 April 1915), and *d* as the result of enemy action 12 May 1941, leaving issue

(4) Violet Annie (twin with Rose); *m* 1 July 1897 (*divorce* 1923) Quiller Orchardson Gilbey Gold and *d* 5 Feb 1934, leaving issue. He *d* 22 March 1955

2 William Barker; *b* 1845; barrister; *dsp* 1872.

3 Robert Baxter; *b* 3 March 1847; *m* 20 June 1872 Geraldine Mary (*d* 5 May 1933), dau of John Connell, of Barbados, and *d* 8 April 1887, leaving:

(1) Ryves Gerald Lancaster; *b* 5 April 1873; *d* 4 Dec 1931

4 Harcourt Ranking; *b* 2 July 1850; Capt Border Regt; *m* 10 Aug 1887 Ellen Elizabeth, widow of William Townsend Hall, of Faversham, Kent, and *dsp* 25 Oct 1908

5 Bateman Lancaster; *b* 27 Feb 1852; MA Oxon; *m* 6 March 1906 Editha (*d* 28 Dec 1963), dau of Sir John Frederick Croft, 2nd Bt (*qv*), and *d* 11 May 1912, leaving:

(1) Ronald Paul Lancaster; *b* 31 July 1907; *m* 1st 1933 (*divorce* 1937) Shelagh Grant Lindsay, dau of Maj Joseph Lindsey Curtis, and had:

   1a Sir DAVID LANCASTER ROSE, **4th and present Bt**

(1) (cont.) Ronald Rose *m* 2nd 28 Aug 1938 Peggy Gleitzman; *m* 3rd 1948 Emily Lavender, widow of Tom E Montgomery and dau of Capt Henry Vivian Hare (*see* LISTOWEL, E), and *d* 1977

6 George Alfred Sainte Croix, JP Berks; *b* 31 Jan 1854; Capt Roy Bucks Militia; *m* 8 April 1880 Beatrice (*d* 4 Jan 1911), dau of Sir Richard Quain, 1st Bt, MD (*see* 1898 edn), and *d* 14 Feb 1926, leaving:

(1) Ivor Sainte Croix, OBE (1919); *b* 16 March 1881; *educ* Eton; Maj Gren Gds, late KRRC, served Boer War, Somaliland 1902–04, WWs I (wounded, despatches) and II (despatches); *m* 1st 5 March 1907 Etta Mabel (*d* 1918), yst dau of Cdr Sebastian Gassiot, RN, and had:

   1a Nancy Bertha Sainte Croix; *b* 16 Jan 1908; *m* 1st 10 Dec 1934 Capt Rupert St Aubyn Malleson, AFC, RN (*d* following a road accident 12 July 1960), 2nd s of Maj-Gen Sir Wilfrid Malleson, KCIE, CB; *m* 2nd 10 April 1961 Thomas Collyer Summers, FRCS, LRCP

(1) (cont.) Maj Ivor Rose *m* 2nd 30 May 1918 (*divorce* 1935) Nancy (*d* 1968), est dau of Arthur Conran Blomfield, and by her had:

   2a *Camilla Mary Sainte Croix; *b* 25 July 1919; WW II as 2nd Offr WRNS; *m* 9 Aug 1945 Richard Oliver MacMahon Williams, OBE, MC, WS (*d* 1981), s of Prof John Williams Williams, LLD, BLitt, and has:

      1b *Caroline Jane Sainte Croix; *b* 2 June 1947; *educ* St Andrews (MA); *m* 1983 *Jeremy Peter Marriage and has:

         1c *Frederick Peter Oliver; *b* 1986

         1c *Clare Felicity; *b* 1984

         2c *Lucy Diana; *b* 1989

      2b *Nicola Valentine Blomfield; *b* 8 Dec 1948; *m* 1972 *Brig Alistair Stuart Hastings Irwin, OBE, late Black Watch, and has:

         1c *George Ronald Valentine Hastings; *b* 1983

         1c *Mary Rose Elizabeth; *b* 1975

         2c *Laura Bridget; *b* 1978

      3b *Rosemary Anne MacMahon; *b* 9 Aug 1952; *m* 1973 (*divorce* 1969) Adrian Gerald Burns and has:

         1c *Thomas Michael MacMahon; *b* 1979

         1c *Emily Caroline; *b* 1981

      4b *Lorna Christine Allan; *b* 25 Nov 1954; *m* 1975 *Gareth Bowring Stoddart and has issue (*see* MALET, Bt)

(1) (cont.) Maj Ivor Rose *m* 3rd 10 Dec 1936 (*divorce* 1951) Ruth Elldale (*d* 1952), est dau of Richard White, of Labrador and Newfoundland, and *d* 5 Feb 1962, having by her had:

   1a +George Vivian Sainte Croix [George Rose Esq, 45 Woodfield Lane, Ashtead, Surrey]; *b* 5 Feb 1939; *educ* Eton; *m* 6 Feb 1960 *Audrey Rosamond, dau of Lawrence Frederick Barrow, and has:

      1b +Philip Vivian Sainte Croix, *b* 1961

      1b *Alison Charlotte [Mrs Adrian Rowe, 191 Downs Barn Blvd, Milton Keynes, Bucks]; *b* 1960; *m* 1979 *Adrian Christopher Rowe and has:

         1c *Katherine Nancy Charlotte, *b* 1991

(2) Harcourt George Sainte Croix; *b* 13 Aug 1883; *educ* Eton and Magdalen Coll Oxford (BA); slr, Maj Intell Corps and Capt Herts Regt WW I, Legn Hon; *m* 1st 8 July 1908 (*divorce* 1920) Florence Norah (*d* 1970), only dau of Arthur Elliot Deane, of Littleton House, Winchester, and had:

   1a Anthony Sainte Croix; *b* 17 Feb 1910; *educ* Trin Hall Cambridge (BA); barrister Lincoln's Inn 1937, P/O AAF WW II; *kas* 11 Sept 1939

   1a *Jean [Mrs Henry Hale, High View House, Langtree, Torrington, Devon EX38 8NG]; *b* 22 March 1915 ; WW II in WAAF; *m* 28 Sept 1953 Lt-Cdr Henry Francis Ormsby Hale, RN (*d* 1984), s of Henry Ormsby Hale, of Dryden House, Oundle, Northants

(2) (cont.) Maj Harcourt Rose *m* 2nd 21 Oct 1920 (*divorce* 1930) Freda Victoria, er dau of C A Keyser, of Sweden; *m* 3rd 30 July 1930 *Estelle Marie, widow of Col Geoffrey Trollope Lee and dau of Marquis of Sarzano, 8th KRI Hus, and *d* 1 Dec 1955

(1) Evelyn Beatrice Sainte Croix; *m* 15 Feb 1906 Maj Valentine Fleming, DSO (*ka* 20 May 1917), of Brazier's Park, Wallingford, Oxon, er s of Robert Fleming, of Nettlebed, Oxon, and *d* 27 July 1964, having had issue (*see* WYFOLD, B)

(2) Kathleen Mary Sainte Croix; *m* 10 July 1907 (*divorce* 1930, resumed maiden name 1931) Gerald Henry Deane, er s of Arthur Deane, of Winchester, and *d* 15 July 1967, leaving issue

7 Charles Marston; *b* 15 Jan 1858; barrister, Lt Roy Bucks Militia; *m* 28 July 1887 Diana Louisa (*d* 1949), 2nd dau of Richard Thomas Lee, JP, of Grove Hall, Yorks, and *d* 6 Dec 1924, leaving:

(1) Evelyn Margaret; *b* 8 June 1888; *d* unm 1964

(2) Gladys Mary; *b* 1889; *m* 17 Nov 1909 Reginald Mordaunt CUMBERLEGE later CUMBERLEGE-WARE (1947; *d* 1965), er s of Henry Mordaunt Cumberlege, of Walsted Place, Lindfield, and had issue

(3) Sybil Renée; *b* 1896; *m* 1st 18 April 1917 S/Ldr Charles John Wharton Darwin, DSO, RAF (*das* 26 Dec 1941), formerly Maj Coldstream Gds, er s of Col Charles Waring Darwin, CB, of Elston Hall, Notts, and London W1, and had issue; *m* 2nd 26 June 1947 Col Ronald Streeter Lambert, MC, Gren Gds, s of Streeter Lambert

1 Margaret Amelia; *d* 8 Oct 1882

2 Louisa Frances; *m* 14 May 1868 Col Alfred James Wake, RA (*d* 30 Sept 1927), and *d* 13 Jan 1942, leaving issue

3 Lucy; *m* 31 March 1880 Col Edward Medley Carter, 2nd Bn Border Regt, 2nd s of Sir James Carter, Ch Justice New Brunswick, and *d* 15 March 1904, leaving issue

ROSEBERY

Arms: Quarterly, 1st and 4th, vert three primroses within a double tressure flory counterflory or (for PRIMROSE); 2nd and 3rd, argent a lion rampant double-queued sable (for CRESSY). **Crest:** A demi-lion gules, holding in the dexter paw a primrose or, as in the arms. **Supporters:** Two lions or. **Motto:** *Fide et fiducia* ('By faith and trust'). **Creations:** Bt. (NS) 1 Aug 1651; L. (Primrose and Dalmeny) and V. (Rosebery) (S) 1 April 1700; L. (Dalmeny and Primrose), V. (Inverkeithing) and E. (S) 10 April 1703 (Rosebery); B. (UK) 26 Jan 1828 (Rosebery); B. (Epsom), V. (Mentmore) and E. (Midlothian) (all UK) 3 July 1911.

THE 7TH EARL OF ROSEBERY, Earl of Midlothian, Viscount of Rosebery, Viscount of Inverkeithing, Viscount Mentmore, of Mentmore, Co Buckingham, **Lord Primrose and Dalmeny**, **Lord Dalmeny and Primrose**, Baron Rosebery, of

Rosebery, Co Midlothian, **Baron Epsom**, of Epsom, Co Surrey, and a **Baronet** (Sir Neil Archibald Primrose, Bt, DL (Midlothian 1960)) [The Rt Hon The Earl of Rosebery DL, Dalmeny House, South Queensferry, W Lothian EH30 9TQ]; *b* 11 Feb 1929; *s f* 1974; *educ* Stowe and New Coll Oxford; *m* 22 Jan 1955 *(Alison Mary) Deirdre, est dau of Ronald William Reid (*see* CHAYTOR, Bt), and has:

  1 +HARRY RONALD NEIL, *Lord Dalmeny* [Lord Dalmeny, Dalmeny House, South Queensferry, W Lothian EH30 9TQ]; *b* 20 Nov 1967; *educ* Dragon Sch Oxford, Eton and Trin Coll Cambridge (BA Hons); dir Sotheby's 1996–; *m* 1994 *Caroline J, est dau of Ronald Daglish and Mrs William Wyatt-Lowe, of Hemel Hempstead

  1 +Lucy Catherine Mary [The Lady Lucy Garton, West Hyde House, W Hyde, Herts]; *b* 24 Dec 1955; *m* 22 May 1976 *(Anthony Gavin) Charles Luis Garton, 2nd s of Anthony Charles Garton, and has:

    (1) +James Anthony Leo; *b* 1986

    (1) +Camilla Mary Eva; *b* 12 Sept 1982

  2 +Jane Margaret Helen; *b* 11 July 1960; *m* 1989 *Michael S F Kaplan, s of R Kaplan, of Cambridge, Mass., and has:

    (1) +Felix Balthazar Inigo; *b* 1991

  3 +Emma Elizabeth Anne; *b* 12 Sept 1962; *m* 1984 *William G Lamarque, yr s of W G Lamarque, and has:

    (1) +Victor George; *b* 1986

    (1) +Francesca; *b* 1988

  4 +Caroline Sara Frances; *b* 20 Nov 1964

Lineage: HENRY PRIMROSE; *b c* 1490; *d* in or after 1543, leaving, with three er sons (William, Burgess Dysart, *m* Margaret Sardis and *d* 2 Dec 1592; Archibald, Chamberlain Culross, Firfe, *m* Alison Patt and *d* 1 March 1593/4, leaving issue; Duncan, Baillie Culross 1580, *m* Helen Smyth and had issue) and a dau (Mause, *m* Andrew Gibson of Culross and *d* Nov 1570):

DAVID PRIMROSE, of Culross; *m* Janet Blaw and *d* 1574, leaving:

  1 Henry; Burgess Culross; *m* (contract 19 May 1574) Margaret (*d* Feb 1619), dau and coheir of Peter Reidoch of Aberlednock, and *d* 31 Aug 1621, leaving issue

  2 Archibald; Clerk Taxations and of Mines; *m* 11 Oct 1598 Katherine Andro and was *bur* Aug 1629, leaving issue

  3 JAMES

  4 Gilbert; Min Bordeaux and London

  1 Katherine; *m* Andrew Clayhills, Min Monifieth

  2 Euphame; *m* Sir George Bruce of Carnock

The 3rd son,

JAMES PRIMROSE; Clerk PC 1599–1640; *m* 1st *c* 12 June 1593 Sibylla Miller and had, with seven other children:

  1 Gilbert; *b* 28 Sept 1595; Clerk PC jtly with f 1627–37; *m* 21 June 1621 Janet, dau of George Foulis of Ravelston, and *dvp* 1637, leaving issue

  2 Robert; Envoy Sweden 1627; *d* Dec 1631

  1 Alison; *m* 24 Aug 1609 George Heriot, goldsmith and fndr Heriot's Hosp, and *d* 1613

JAMES PRIMROSE *m* 2nd Catherine (*d* 1651), dau of Richard Lawson, Edinburgh bookseller and Burgess, and *d* 21 Feb 1640, having by her had, with 11 other children:

  3 ARCHIBALD (Sir), **1st Bt**

  4 James; *b* 28 Jan 1619; Clerk PC 1649–68; *m c* 1646 Nicola (*d* 1675), dau of Sir James Mercer of Aldie, and was *bur* 17 Sept 1668, having had:

    (1) Christian; *m* 6th Lord Torpichen (*qv*)

  2 Agnes; *m* 1638 Alexander Menteth (*see* STUART-MENTETH, Bt)

JAMES PRIMROSE's est s by his 2nd w,

  Sir Archibald Primrose, 1st Bt (NS), so *cr* 1 Aug 1651, of Carringham/Carrington; *b* 16 May 1616; Clerk PC 1641–49 and 1652, royalist Civil War, hence his estates sequestrated after Battle of Worcester 1651; Ld Clerk Register 1660–76, a Ld of Session Feb 1660/1–76 as Lord Carrington, Ld Justice-Gen 1676–78; bought various estates, including the (territorial) Barony of Barnbougle, Dalmeny, Co Linlithgow 1662 from 4th Earl of Haddington (*qv*) for 160,000 marks (some £430,000 in late-1990s terms); *m* 1st by 1641 Elizabeth, dau and coheir of Sir James Keith of Benholme (*see* KINTORE, E), and had, with a dau (*d* unm):

  1 James (Sir), of Barnbougle; *b* 5 Feb 1645; *m* Elizabeth, dau of Sir Robert Sinclair, Bt, of Longformacus, and *dvp c* 1671, having had two daus

  2 **Sir William Primrose, 2nd Bt**, of Carrington; *b* 14 Jan 1649, Clerk of Notaries 1666; *m* by 1677 Mary, 3rd dau of Patrick Scott of Thirlestane, Selkirkshire, and *d* 23 Sept 1687, having with other issue:

    (1) **Sir James Primrose, 3rd Bt** and 1st VISCOUNT PRIMROSE, so *cr* 30 Nov 1703, as also LORD PRIMROSE AND CASTLEFIELD (both S), with remainder to heir male (*sic* in the patent, 'heirs male' in the warrant, the subsequent interpretation of the remainder favouring the latter reading) of his body, in default of which to the heir(s) male of his f; *b c* 1680; MP Co Edinburgh 1703; *m* Eleanor (*m* 2nd 1714 2nd Earl of Stair (*qv*) and *d* 21 Nov 1759), yst dau of 2nd Earl of Loudoun (*qv*), and *d* 13 June 1706, having by her had, with other issue:

      1a **Sir Archibald Primrose, 4th Bt** and 2nd VISCOUNT PRIMROSE; *d* unm 19 June 1716

      2a **Sir Hugh Primrose, 5th Bt** and 3rd and last VISCOUNT PRIMROSE; *b c* 1703; Capt Inniskilling Dragoons 1727, served Imp Army against French (shot behind the ear, the bullet later issuing at an eye, in a skirmish with French irregulars nr Claussen 1735), Lt-Col Gen Dalziel's Regt; *m* 21 June 1739 Anne (*dsp* 3 Feb 1775), dau of Very Rev Peter Drelincourt, Dean Armagh, and *dsp* 8 May 1741, when his peerages apparently expired, but the btcy passed to the **2nd Earl**

      (1) Mary; *m* 3rd Lord Bargeny (*d c* 1712, for whose earlier ancestry *see* HAMILTON and BRANDON, D) and *d c* 1708, leaving issue

      (2) Elizabeth; *m* 12 Sept 1702 9th Lord Elphinstone (*qv*) and *d* 16 Feb 1738, leaving issue

    3 Gilbert; Col 24th Foot, Maj-Gen; *dsp* 3 Sept 1731

    1 Margaret; *m* 5 Sept 1661, as his 1st w of three, Sir John Foulis, 1st Bt (*qv*), and *d* 15 April 1690, having had issue

    2 Catherine; *m* (contract 29 Oct 1663) Sir David Carnegie, 1st Bt, of Pitarrow and was *bur* 9 Oct 1677, leaving issue (*see* FIFE, D)

Sir Archibald *m* 2nd Agnes (*bur* 15 Dec 1699), dau of Sir William Gray of Pittendrum and widow of Sir James Dundas of Newliston, and *d* 27 Nov 1679, having by her had, with another dau (*d* unm):

  4 ARCHIBALD PRIMROSE, **1st Earl of Rosebery**, so *cr* 10 April 1703, as also VISCOUNT OF INVERKEITHING and LORD DALMENY AND PRIMROSE, with remainder to heirs male of his body, in default of which to heirs female of his body, as also previously 1 April 1700 VISCOUNT OF ROSEBERY, LORD PRIMROSE AND DALMENY (all S), with remainder to the heirs male of his body, in default of which to heirs female of his body, in default of which to his heirs of entail in the lands of Rosebery, PC (S 1701 and 1703); *b* 18 Dec 1664; served Imp Army against Turks in Hungary 1680; Gentleman Bedchamber to PRINCE GEORGE OF DENMARK (husb of future QUEEN ANNE) 1688; MP (Whig) Edinburgh 1695–1700; Chamberlain Fife and Strathearn 1703–14, a Commr for Union of E and S Parls 1707, rep S peer 1707, 1708, 1710, and 1713; *m* (licence 3 Feb 1690/1) Dorothy, only child of Everingham Cressy, of Birkin, Yorks, and *d* 20 Oct 1723, having had, with other issue:

  (1) **Sir James Primrose, 6th Bt**, as which *s* cousin (3rd and last VISCOUNT PRIMROSE; *see* above) and **2nd Earl of Rosebery**; *b c* 1691; *m* Mary (*d* 11 May 1756), sis of 4th Duke of Argyll (*qv*), and *d* 26 Nov 1755, having had, with other issue:

    1a Archibald, Lord Dalmeny; *b* 31 March 1717; *d* young

    2a John, *Lord Dalmeny*; *b* 1725; *d* unm 11 Aug 1755

    3a NEIL, **3rd Earl**

    (1) Mary; *m* 19 Nov 1724 her cousin Sir Archibald Primrose, 2nd Bt (*see* FOULIS, Bt), and had issue

    (2) Margaret; *m* 15 Feb 1738 9th Earl of Caithness (*qv*) and *d* 7 Oct 1785, leaving issue

  3 Grisel; *b* 19 Sept 1661; *m* 1st 30 April 1681 8th Lord Sempill (*qv*); *m* 2nd 1693 Brig-Gen Richard Cunningham and *d* 22 June 1723

The 2nd EARL's only surv s,

NEIL PRIMROSE, **3rd Earl of Rosebery**, KT (1771); *b* 1729; engaged in trade in London; rep S peer 1768, 1774 and 1780; *m* 1st 19 May 1764 Susan (*dsp* 20 Aug 1771), dau and eventual heiress of Sir Edward Ward, 5th Bt, of Bixley, Norfolk; *m* 2nd 17 July 1775 Mary (*d* 9 March 1823), dau of Sir Francis Vincent, 7th Bt (*see* 1940 edn), and *d* 25 March 1814, having by her had:

  1 ARCHIBALD JOHN, **4th Earl**

  2 Francis Ward; *b* 13 Feb 1785; barrister; *m* 10 Nov 1829 Percy (*d* 30 Aug 1864), 3rd dau of Col Ralph Gore, of Barrowmount, Ireland, and *d* 26 May 1860, having had, with other issue:

    (1) Francis Neil; *b* 27 March 1832; *m* Henrietta (*m* 2nd 30 April 1867 Maj George E Halliday, 82nd Regt, and *d* Oct 1871), dau of John Sewell, of St Albans, Canada, and *d* 24 Nov 1864, leaving:

      1a Frances Ethel; *b* 21 March 1860; *m* 22 Jan 1884 Henry Stafford Tyndale Biscoe (*d* 8 July 1911), of Holton Pk, Oxon, and *d* 12 March 1926, leaving issue

    (2) Edward Montagu; *b* 24 Feb 1844; *m* 4 Oct 1870 Claudine Willie Bain (*d* 17 June 1906), yst dau of Samuel S Lamb, and *d* 11 May 1892, leaving:

      1a Ralph Gore; *b* 28 June 1875; *m* 18 Oct 1913 Agatha Vera, dau of David Moss Coulter, and with his dau Margaret was *k* by a cloud burst in British Columbia 28 Oct 1921, having had:

        1b Gerald Edward David; *b* 11 July 1914; *m* 16 Sept 1950 *Anne Loletta [Mrs Gerald Primrose, 350 La Prenda, Millbrae, CA 94030, USA], yst dau of James Ranney Broughton, of Atwood, Ontario, and *d* 1988, leaving:

          1c +James Ralph [James Primrose, 242 Sydney Dve, Alamo, CA 94507, USA]; *b* 27 May 1952; *m* 1983 *Jane Porter, dau of Lewis Weyburn Saxby, Jr, of Toledo, Ohio, and has:

            1d +Andrew Gerald; *b* 1988

            2d +Nicholas James; *b* 1991

        2b Neil; *b* 7 Dec 1918; BA 1943, BEd 1958; *m* 21 Aug 1944 *Margaret Verna, BA [Mrs Neil Primrose, 14560 Sunset Dve, White Rock, BC V4B 2V9, Canada], dau of Henry James Francis, of Portsmouth, and *d* 1979, leaving:

          1c +David Neil [David Primrose Esq, 2278 Midas St, Abbotsford, BC V2S 4R2, Canada]; *b* 1 July 1945; CGA; *m* 26 Feb 1966 *Anna Joyce, dau of Francis Charles Walters, of White Rock, BC, and has:

            1d +David Francis Neil; *b* 5 Oct 1966; CGA; *m* 1989 *Cynthia Lee, dau of Dennis C Rumpel, of Abbotsford, BC

            2d +Douglas James Baird; *b* 30 July 1970; BA, BEd; *m* 1994 *Tracey Michelle, dau of Ian Gillies, of Abbotsford, BC

          1c (cont.) Mr and Mrs David Primrose also adopted:

            *Amy Irene; *b* 1979

            *Tanya Margaret; *b* 1983

          1c +Margaret Jane Elizabeth [Mrs Robert Maikawa, 5382 Frances St, Burnaby, BC V5B 1T5, Canada]; *b* 1 May 1948; *m* 1971 *Robert Noboru Maikawa and has:

            1d +Paul Robert; *b* 1974

            2d +Steven Anthony; *b* 1976

            1d +Andrea Margaret; *b* 1990

          2c +Deirdre Katherine [Mrs Thomas Ruffen, 812 East 51st Ave, Vancouver, BC V5X 1E5, Canada]; *b* 16 Nov 1951; *m* 1971 *Thomas Kevin Ruffen and has:

            1d +Jessica Kirsten; *b* 1973

          3c +Ann Jennifer [Mrs Christopher Barber, Box 34 Morello Rd, RR1, Nanoose Bay, BC V0R 2R0, Canada]; *b* 13 Dec 1954; *m* 1973 *Christopher John Barber and has:

            1d +Matthew John; *b* 1975

            2d +Daniel Morgan; *b* 1977

            1d +Jennifer Erin; *b* 1978

        1b Margaret Enid; *b* 15 Jan 1916; *d* 28 Oct 1921

      2a Percy Bouverie; *b* 20 Dec 1879; *dsp* 24 Feb 1960

1a Claudine Louisa; *d* unm 9 Sept 1960

2a Maud Ethel; *d* young, 22 March 1893

(1) Percy; *b* 9 June 1839; *m* 26 April 1865 Rev George Collyer Harris (*d* 4 May 1874), Vicar St Luke's, Torquay, Preb Exeter, and *d* 27 July 1919, leaving issue

(2) Bellamira Emma; *b* 22 March 1846; *m* 1st 28 April 1864 Arthur Randolph MULLINGS later RANDOLPH, Capt 15th Hus, of Eastcourt, Wilts, and had issue; *m* 2nd 1876 Godfrey Darley Beswick and *d* 1882

1 Charlotte; *m* 1st 27 May 1800 1st Earl of Effingham (*qv*) and had issue; *m* 2nd 30 April 1858 Thomas Holmes and *d* 17 Sept 1864

2 Mary; *m* 11 April 1808 Henry John Shepherd, s of Rt Hon Sir Samuel Shepherd (*d* May 1855), Ld Ch Baron Exchequer Scotland, and *d* 7 Jan 1847

3 Dorothea Arabella; *m* 1 Sept 1801 William Hervey (*d* 5 May 1862) and *d* 16 Nov 1825

The 3rd EARL's er s,

ARCHIBALD JOHN PRIMROSE, **4th Earl of Rosebery**, KT (1840), PC (1831); *b* 14 Oct 1783; *educ* Pembroke Coll Cambridge (MA 1804, Hon LLD 1819); MP (Canningite Tory, later Whig) Helston 1805–06 and Cashel 1806–07, rep S peer 1818, 1820 and 1826; *cr* 26 Jan 1828 BARON ROSEBERY, of Rosebery, Co Midlothian (UK); Ld Lt Linlithgow 1843–63; *m* 1st 20 May 1808 (*divorce* 1815 for her adultery with Sir Henry St John-Mildmay, 4th Bt (*qv*), the widower of her sis Charlotte and subsequently her 2nd husb, for which the **4th Earl** won £15,000 (nearly £430,000 in late-1990s terms) damages) Harriet (*d* 9 Dec 1834), 2nd dau of Hon Bartholomew Bouverie (*see* RADNOR, E), and had, with a dau (*d* young):

1 Archibald, *Lord Dalmeny*; *b* 2 Oct 1809; MP (Lib) Stirling Burghs 1833–47, a Ld Admlty 1835–41, V-Lt Linlithgowshire 1844; *m* 20 Sept 1843 Lady Catherine Lucy Wilhelmina Stanhope (*m* 2nd 2 Aug 1854 4th Duke of Cleveland (*see* BARNARD, B) and *d* 18 May 1901), dau of 4th Earl Stanhope (*see* 1967 edn CHESTERFIELD and STANHOPE, E), and *dvp* 23 Jan 1851, leaving:

(1) ARCHIBALD PHILIP, **5th Earl**

(2) Everard Henry; *b* 8 Sept 1848; granted 30 May 1886 with sisters rank of earl's dau/yr s; Col Gren Gds, Mil Attaché Vienna; *d* unm 9 April 1885

(1) Mary Catherine Constance; *m* 8 Oct 1885 Henry Walter Hope and *d* 3 Sept 1935, leaving issue (*see* LINLITHGOW, M)

(2) Constance Evelyn; *m* 15 July 1867 2nd Baron Leconfield and *d* 27 June 1939, leaving issue (*see* EGREMONT, LECONFIELD and, B)

2 Bouverie Francis, CB, DL (Edinburgh); *b* 19 Sept 1813; Lt-Col Queen's City of Edinburgh Rifle Vol Bde; *m* 21 April 1838 Frederica Sophia (*d* 11 Oct 1867), sis of 1st Earl of Lichfield (*qv*), and *d* 20 March 1898, having had, with two daus (*d* unm):

(1) Francis Archibald; *b* 29 Oct 1843; *m* 12 Nov 1872 Jane (*d* 1 Nov 1921), dau of George King, of Waratah, Sydney, NSW, and *d* 4 Aug 1922, leaving:

1a Archibald Bouverie; *b* 23 June 1881; *m* 1st 7 May 1915 (*divorce* 1922) Diva Amelia, only dau of the Emilio Marolda, of Palermo; *m* 2nd 26 Nov 1924 (*divorce* 1945) Lilian Ruth, only dau of Charles Lowry, of New York; *m* 3rd 1951 Norah Lilian (*d* Jan 1970), dau of Edward Cannell, of Liverpool and Roscrea, Co Tipperary, and *dsp* 3 Sept 1969

1a Frederica Jane; *d* unm 13 Feb 1967

2a Dorothy; *m* 1894 Sir Thomas Peter Anderson Stuart, MD, LLD (*d* 29 Feb 1920), Prof Physiology U of Sydney, NSW, and Dean Medicine, s of Alexander Stuart, Dean of Guild, and *d* 21 Sept 1954, leaving issue

3a Louisa Wilhelmina; *d* unm 6 Jan 1962

4a Evelyn; *m* 20 June 1906 Col John Colpoys Connor, CMG, MB, RAMC (*d* 16 Nov 1936), s of John Connor, of Stoneyford, Co Antrim, and had:

1b John Richard, CBE (1954, OBE 1945); *b* 8 Oct 1908; *educ* Harrow and Emmanuel Coll Cambridge (BA 1931); Col RE

1b Evelyn Hazel; *b* 12 April 1907; *m* Sept 1935 William Hugh Trueman Fisher, OBE, s of W R Fisher, and had:

1c William Humphrey; *b* 23 Nov 1941; *d* 1 May 1962

1c Elizabeth Ruth; *b* 16 June 1938; *d* 23 March 1955

2c +Annette Clare; *b* 9 June 1940; *m* 1971 *John Alexander Kirkpatrick Millar

5a Constance Margaret; *m* 5 June 1907 Lt-Col James Macpherson, DSO, IA (*d* 11 March 1938), s of Lt-Col Robert Nasmyth Macpherson, and *d* 18 Aug 1967, leaving issue

6a Gwendolen Gertrude Maude

(2) Henry William (Sir), KCB (1899), CSI (1885), ISO (1904), PC; *b* 22 Aug 1846; Sec Office Works 1886–95, chm: Bd Customs 1895–99, Bd Inland Revenue 1899–1907, Pacific Cable Bd 1907–14; Commr Temporalities under Welsh Church Act 1914; *m* 2 Nov 1888 Helen Mary (*d* 11 June 1919), est dau of Gilbert McMicking (*see* DENMAN, B), and *d* 17 June 1923, leaving:

1a Archibald Henry Reginald; *b* 14 Dec 1889; Lt Scots Gds (SR); barrister Inner Temple 1912; *m* 1922 Anna Elizabeth Palliser (*d* 21 Jan 1962), dau of John Booth Dickenson, of Penistone, and *dsp* 20 Aug 1963

(3) Gilbert Edward; *b* 27 Feb 1848; *m* 13 May 1893 Jessie Katherine, dau of Lt Costelloe, of Lackeen Castle, Co Tipperary, and *d* 16 Feb 1935

(4) George Anson; *b* 21 Sept 1849; V-Adml; *m* 30 April 1889 Mary Cecelia (*d* 6 June 1941), dau of Thomas Kenny, MP, of Halifax, Nova Scotia, and *d* 6 Jan 1930, leaving:

1a Marjorie Frances; *b* 9 March 1890; *m* 11 Jan 1928 George Victor Evans, Nigerian Political Serv, 3rd s of Rev E Muirhead Evans, VD, and *dsp* 25 Oct 1967

2a Adela Blanche Margaret; *b* 5 Feb 1891; *m* 6 July 1921 Douglas Leslie Cox and *d* 24 Dec 1943, having had issue

(5) Arthur John; *b* 29 June 1853; Bengal CS; *d* unm 13 Sept 1888

(6) Edward Neil; *b* 19 Nov 1854; *d* 25 Feb 1910

(1) Alice Jane; *m* 1st 16 April 1868 George William Mercer Henderson, of Fordell, Fife (*dsp* 17 Oct 1881); *m* 2nd 27 Dec 1887 John Bellingham (*see* BELLINGHAM, Bt) and *d* 27 March 1930

(2) Charlotte Henrietta; *m* 10 Jan 1878 Cdr Carleton Tufnell, JP, DL, RN (*d* 10 Jan 1893), and *dsp* 13 Feb 1941

1 Harriet; *b* 13 Oct 1810; *m* 29 Dec 1835 Sir John Dunlop, 1st Bt (*d* 3 April 1839), and *d* 8 March 1876

The **4th Earl** *m* 2nd 12 Aug 1819 Anne Margaret (*d* 19 Aug 1882), est dau of 1st Viscount Anson (*see* LICHFIELD, E), and *d* 4 March 1868, having by her had, with another dau (*d* unm):

2 Anne; *m* 30 May 1848 as his 3rd w Henry Tufnell, PC, MP (*d* 15 June 1854), and *d* 17 Sept 1862, leaving issue

The 4th EARL's gs,

ARCHIBALD PHILIP PRIMROSE, **5th Earl of Rosebery**, KG (1892), KT (1895), VD, PC, JP (Bucks); *b* 7 May 1847; *educ* Eton and Ch Ch Oxford; Ld Lt Linlithgowshire 1873–1929 and Midlothian 1884–1929, Ld Rector Aberdeen U 1878–81, Edinburgh U 1882–83, Glasgow U 1899–1902 and St Andrews 1910–13, memb Cncl Scottish Educn 1881–1929, U-Sec (Lib) Home Dept 1881–83, Ld Privy Seal and First Commr Works Feb-June 1885, For Sec Feb-July 1886 and 1892–94, first Chm LCC 1889, 1890 and 1892, PM, First Ld Treasury and Ld Pres Cncl March 1894–June 1895 (Leader Libs till 1898), Pres Linlithgow and Midlothian TAA, Er Bro Trin Ho 1901, Hon Col 8th Bn Roy Scots and 1st Lowland Bde RFA (TA), Capt-Gen Roy Co Archers, Tstee Br Museum 1883, DCL Oxon 1893, LLD, FRS 1886, FBA, FSA 1876, Hon LLD Glasgow 1879, Aberdeen 1881, Edinburgh 1882, St Andrews 1885, Cantab 1888 and Liverpool 1910, High Steward Kingston-on-Thames 1901, Roy Victorian Chain; *cr* 3 July 1911 EARL OF MIDLOTHIAN, VISCOUNT MENTMORE, of Mentmore, Co Buckingham, and BARON EPSOM, of Epsom, Co Surrey (all UK); *m* 20 March 1878 Hannah (*d* 19 Nov 1890), only dau and heiress of Baron Mayer Amschel de Rothschild, of Mentmore, Bucks (*see* ROTHSCHILD, B), and *d* 21 May 1929, having had:

1 ALBERT EDWARD HARRY MAYER ARCHIBALD, **6th Earl**

2 Neil James Archibald, PC (1917), MC, JP (London); *b* 14 Dec 1882; *educ* Oxford (MA); CA London, Capt Bucks Hus WW I; MP (Lib) N Cambs 1910–17, U-Sec For Affrs 1915–16, Jt Parly Sec Treasury 1916–17; *m* 7 April 1915 Lady Victoria Alice Louise Stanley (*m* 2nd 10 June 1919 Capt Sir (Harold) Malcolm Bullock, 1st and last Bt, MBE, MA, MP, of Middlefield, Great Shelford, Cambs (*d* 20 June 1966), and *d* 26 Nov 1927), dau of 17th Earl of Derby (*qv*), and was *ka* 18 Nov 1917, leaving:

(1) Ruth Alice Hannah Mary; *b* 18 April 1916; *m* 25 April 1936 2nd Earl of Halifax (*qv*) and *d* 31 Aug 1989, having had issue

1 Sybil Myra Caroline; *m* 28 March 1903 Lt-Gen Sir Charles John Cecil Grant, KCB, KCVO, DSO, late Coldm Gds (*d* 9 Nov 1950), s of Lt-Gen Sir Robert Grant, GCB, and *d* 25 Feb 1955, leaving issue

2 Margaret Etrenne Hannah, CI (1911), JP (Co London); Legn Hon; *m* 20 April 1899 1st and last Marquess of Crewe, KG (*see* 1935 edn), and *d* 13 March 1967, leaving issue

The 5th EARL's er s,

ALBERT EDWARD HARRY MEYER ARCHIBALD PRIMROSE, **6th Earl of Rosebery**, KT (1947), PC (1945), DSO (1918), MC (1916), JP (Edinburgh); *b* 8 Jan 1882; *educ* Eton and RMC Sandhurst; 2nd Lt Gren Gds 1902–03, Capt Surrey Co Cricket XI 1905–07, played cricket for Scotland against Australia 1906, V-Chm Bucks TAA 1908, MP (Lib) Midlothian 1906–10, Sec State Scotland May-July 1945, WW I: Assist Mil Sec Ld Allenby's personal staff 1914–17, T/Lt-Col 1917 (wounded, despatches), Legn Hon, 514th (West Roy Lothian Scots) LAA Regt RA: Brig 1922–36, Hon Col 1949–74, Ld Lt Midlothian 1929–64, Lt Roy Co of Archers: Ensign 1936–45, Lt 1945–74, Capt 1948–74, Regnl Commr for Scotland 1941–45 (Dep Commr 1940–41), memb Roy Commn JPs 1946, memb Roy Fine Art Commn Scotland 1947–74 (Chm 1952–56), Chm Scottish Tourist Bd 1955–65, Pres: Thoroughbred Breeders' Assoc 1932–56, Roy Zoological Soc Scotland 1942–64, Surrey Co Cricket Club 1947–50, Roy Scottish Corp 1947–74, MCC 1953–54; Steward Jockey Club 1929–32 and 1945–48, MFH Whaddon Chase 1923–33 (Jt MFH 1934–40), chm Deptl Ctee Export and Slaughter Horses 1949; FRSE 1953, Hon LLD Edin 1953, Hon FRCSE 1955; *m* 1st 15 April 1909 (*divorce* 1919) Lady Dorothy Alice Margaret Augusta (*d* 11 Jan 1966), sis of 3rd Duke of Westminster (*qv*), and had:

1 Archibald Ronald, *Lord Dalmeny*; *b* 1 Aug 1910; 2nd Lt Gen List; *d* unm 11 Nov 1931

1 +Helen Dorothy [The Lady Helen Smith, The Old Rectory, Souldern, Bicester, Oxon]; *b* 1913; *m* 26 June 1933 Hon Hugh Adeane Vivian Smith, 3rd s of 1st Baron Bicester (*qv*), and has issue

The **6th Earl** *m* 2nd 24 June 1924 Eva Isabel Marian, DBE (1955), JP, LLD (Edinburgh) 1957 (*d* 1987), 3rd dau of 2nd Baron Aberdare (*qv*) and formerly w of 3rd Baron Belper (*qv*), and *d* 30 May 1974, having by her had:

2 NEIL ARCHIBALD PRIMROSE, **7th and present Earl of Rosebery**

2 Mary; *b* and *d* 15 March 1935

Seat: Dalmeny House, S Queensferry, W Lothian. Dalmeny is said to be the earliest neo-Gothic house in Scotland. It dates from the year before Waterloo (it contains a Napoleon Room, appropriately) and was designed by William Wilkins. Indeed it appears to be Wilkins's first attempt at the Gothic, for hitherto he had worked in neo-classical idiom. (The National Gallery in London, perhaps his best-known building, is typical of his later manner.) Much of the very fine collection of French furniture, paintings, porcelain and tapestries were acquired through the Rothschild connection and came from Mentmore.

ROSS

Arms: Per pale argent and sable a chevron between in chief a lion passant and in base an anchor, all counterchanged. **Crest:** A hawk rising sable between two branches of juniper, leaved and fructed proper. **Motto:** *Doucement* ('Softly'). **Creation:** Bt. (UK) 26 Jan 1960.

SIR (JAMES) KEITH ROSS, 2ND BT, of Whetstone, Co Middx, RD (1967) [Sir Keith Ross Bt RD, Moonhills Gate, Exbury Rd, Beaulieu, Hants SO42 7YS]; *b* 9 May 1927; *s f* 1980; *educ* St Paul's and Middx Hosp Medical Sch (MB, BS 1950, MS 1965); house surgn, registrar, sr registrar Middx Hosp 1950–67, Surgn-Lt Cdr RNR (ret 1972), Heller Fellowship San Francisco 1959, Registrar Brompton Hosp 1958, 1960, consultant thoracic surgeon: Harefield and Central Middx Hosps 1964–67 and Nat Heart Hosp 1967–72, consultant cardiac surgeon: Wessex Region 1972–90 and King Edward VII Hosp Midhurst 1978–1992, Hunterian Prof 1961, memb cncl RCS 1986–94, Pres Soc Cardiothoracic Surgeons 1988; FRCS 1956, FRCSE 1989; *m* 24 Nov 1956 *Jacqueline Annella, dau of Francis William Clarke, of Banstead, Surrey, and has:

1 +ANDREW CHARLES PATERSON [Capt Andrew Ross, RM, 4 Haven Villas, Ferry Rd, Topsham, Exeter, Devon EX3 0JW]; *b* 18 June 1966; *educ* Sherborne and Plymouth Poly (BSc); Capt RM; *m* 1 Nov 1997 *Dr Sarah Jean Murray, Surg Lt-Cdr RN, dau of Dennis Murray, of Curbar, Derbys

1 *Susan Wendy [Mrs Nigel Wolstenholme, The Oast House, Kings Somborne, Hants SO20 6QH]; *b* 28 Feb 1958; *m* 1983 *Nigel Timothy Wolstenholme

2 *Janet Mary [Mrs Timothy Morgan, Moonhills Gate Cottage, Exbury Rd, Beaulieu, Hants SO42 7YS]; *b* 20 Nov 1960; *m* 1990 *Timothy N Morgan, s of N V Morgan, of Dibden Purlieu, Hants

3 *Anne Townsend [Mrs Murray Anderson-Wallace, 20 Heathfield Terrace, Leeds LS6 4DE]; *b* 10 Sept 1962; *m* 1993 *Murray J S Anderson-Wallace

Lineage: JAMES ROSS; *b* 7 Nov 1865; *educ* Fodderty and Nairn; Pncpl Bank of England; *m* 12 July 1894 May (*d* 6 Dec 1941), dau of Kenneth Paterson, of Foulis Mains, Ross-shire, and *d* 16 July 1944, leaving, with three yr sons (Alexander, *educ* London U (BSc) 1920), *d* 1949; William, *educ* Reading U (BScAg 1924); Kenneth Macdonald, MB Lond 1931, FFA, RCS 1953):

Sir James Paterson Ross, 1st Bt (UK), so *cr* 26 Jan 1960, KCVO (1949); *b* 26 May 1895; *educ* Christ's Coll Finchley and London U (MB, BS 1920, MS 1928); Surgn-Lt RN WW I 1917–18, MRCS Eng and LRCP Lond 1917, FRCS Eng 1922, Reader Surgery London U 1931–35, Prof Surgery 1935–60, Prof Emeritus 1960, Surgn St Bartholomew's Hosp 1935–60, memb Cncl Roy Coll Surgns 1943 (Pres 1957–60), Surgn to HM THE QUEEN 1952–64, Hon Fell American Coll Surgns 1953, Hon Freeman Barbers' Co 1955 and Apothecaries' Soc 1956, Hon LLD Glasgow 1957, Hon FRACS 1957, Hon FRCS Edin 1959, Hon Fell Faculty Radiologists 1959, Hon FRPPS Glasgow 1959, Hon FRSM 1962, Hon FDSRCS 1964; *m* 5 July 1924 Marjorie Burton, dau of Capt Frederick William Townsend, of Curdridge, Hants, and *d* 5 July 1980, having had:

1 Ian Frederick; *b* 22 July, *d* 25 Aug 1925

2 Sir (JAMES) KEITH ROSS, **2nd and present Bt**

3 +Harvey Burton, RD [Harvey Ross Esq RD, Springvale, Brewery Common, Mortimer, Berks RG7 3JE]; *b* 1 Oct 1928; *educ* St Paul's and St Bartholomew's Hosp Medical Coll (MB, BS 1952); FRCS Eng 1957, MS Lond 1966, Surgn-Lt-Cdr RNR; *m* 1st 20 Oct 1962 Nancy Joan, only dau of Bentley Collingwood Hilliam; *m* 2nd 1988 *Susan Christine, dau of P M Blandy, of Reading, Berks, and by his 1st w has:

(1) +Edward Paterson; *b* 13 Nov 1963

(2) +James Hilliam; *b* 1972

(1) *Imogen; *b* 1970

ROSSE

Arms: Gules three leopard's faces argent. **Crest:** A demi-poleaxe erect gules, the point or. **Supporters:** Two leopards argent pelletté, each gorged with a collar gules charged with four bezants. **Motto:** *Pro Deo et rege* ('For God and king'). **Creations:** Bt. (I) 15 Dec 1677, B. (I) 25 Sept 1792, E.(I) 3 Feb 1806.

THE 7TH EARL OF ROSSE, Baron Oxmantown, Co Wexford, and a **Baronet** (Sir (William Clere Leonard) Brendan Wilmer Parsons, Bt) [The Rt Hon The Earl of Rosse, Birr Castle, Birr, Co Offaly, Ireland]; *b* 21 Oct 1936; *s f* 1979; *educ* Eton, L'Aiglon Coll Switzerland, Grenoble U and Ch Ch Oxford (BA 1961, MA 1964); UN official 1963–80 (admin offr UNTAB Ghana 1963–65, Assist Resident Rep Dahomey 1965–68, Area offr Mid-West Africa 1968–70, Assist Resident Rep Iran 1970–75, Dep Resident Rep Bangladesh 1975–78 and Algeria 1978–80), dir: Historic Irish Houses and Gardens Assoc 1980–91, Agency for Personal Service Overseas 1986–90, Birr Scientific and Heritage Fndn 1985– and Lorne Ho Tst 1993–, memb Irish Govt's Advisory Cncl on Devpt and Co-opn 1984–89, FRAS, Hon Fell Inst Engrs Ireland 1994; *m* 15 Oct 1966 *Alison Margaret, er dau of Maj John Davey Cooke-Hurle, JP, of Startforth Hall, Barnard Castle, Co Durham, and has:

1 +(LAURENCE) PATRICK, *Lord Oxmantown*; *b* 31 March 1969; *educ* L'Aiglon

2 +Michael John Finn; *b* 9 Nov 1981

1 *Alicia Siobhan Margaret Nasreen; *b* 11 Mar 1971 (for whom HRH THE PRINCESS MARGARET, COUNTESS OF SNOWDON, stood sponsor); *educ* Kingston U (BEng 1993)

Rosse, previous creations: Apart from the Earldom of the 1718 creation covered below, a Barony of Hervey of Rosse, Co Wexford, was created in the Irish peerage in 1620 for Sir William Hervey, 1st and last Bt (see BRISTOL, M). The Scottish Earls of Ross (see BOSVILLE MACDONALD, Bt) sometimes spelled themselves with a final 'e'.

Lineage: WILLIAM PARSONS, of Norfolk; seemingly f of:

1 Sir WILLIAM PARSONS, 1st Bt (I), so *cr* 10 Nov 1620; migrated *c* 1590 to Ireland, where Commr Plantations and granted extensive lands by the Crown; Surveyor-Gen Ireland 1602, Jt Supervisor Crown lands with his bro Laurence 1611; ktd 1620; MP (I Parl) Newcastle Co Dublin 1613–15 and Co Wicklow 1639–48, Jt Ld Justice Ireland 1640–43 (when dismissed and imprisoned for suspected treason); *m* Elizabeth, est dau of Alderman John Lany, of Dublin, and was *bur* 2 March 1649/50, having had, with other issue:

(1) Richard; MP (I Parl) Fethard 1634–39 and Wicklow 1639–42; *m* Lettice (*m* 2nd 1st Earl of Mount Alexander), dau of Sir Adam Loftus, of Rathfarnham, and *dvp* in or after 1639, leaving, with two daus:

1a Sir WILLIAM PARSONS, 2nd Bt, of Bellamont, Co Dublin; *m* Catherine Jones, est dau of 2nd Viscount Ranelagh (see CORK and ORRERY, E), and *d* 31 Dec 1658, having had an only surv s:

1b Sir RICHARD PARSONS, 3rd Bt, and 1st VISCOUNT ROSSE, Co Wexford, so *cr* 2 July 1681, as also BARON OXMANTOWN (both I), with remainder to the male line special, PC (I 1686); *b c* 1656; imprisoned Tower London Feb 1695/6 for high treason; *m* 1st by licence 27 Feb 1676/7 Anne (*dsp*), dau of Thomas Walsingham (see SUFFOLK and BERKSHIRE, E); *m* 2nd 14 Oct 1681 Catherine Brydges (*dsp*, *bur* 24 Aug 1682), dau of 6th Baron Chandos of Sudeley; *m* 3rd Dec 1685 Elizabeth, est dau of Sir George Hamilton, Count Hamilton (see ABERCORN, D), and *d* 30 Jan 1702/3, having by her had, with a yr s and three daus:

1c Sir RICHARD PARSONS, 4th Bt, and 1st EARL OF ROSSE (I), so *cr* 16 June 1718; *m* 1st 25 June 1714 Mary (*d* 15 Oct 1718), est dau of Lord William Paulet (see WINCHESTER, M), and had issue; *m* 2nd 1719 Frances (*m* 2nd 15 Nov 1754 1st Viscount Jocelyn (see RODEN, E) and *d* 24 May 1772), dau of Thomas Claxton, of Dublin, and *d* 26 June 1741, leaving an er s:

1d Sir RICHARD PARSONS, 5th Bt, and 2nd and last EARL OF ROSSE; *b c* 1718; *educ* Trin Coll Dublin; *m* 16 Feb 1754 Olivia (*m* 2nd 8 Oct 1770 John Bateman, 3rd s of Rowland Bateman, of Oakpark, Co Kerry), dau and coheir of Hugh Edwards, of Castle Gore, Co Tyrone, but *dsp* 27 Aug 1764, when his titles expired

(2) John; *m* Elizabeth, dau of Sir Walsingham Cooke, of Tornduffe, Co Wexford, and had, with a dau:

  1a Arthur, of Tornduffe; *m* 1st Eleanor (*dsp* 1 Dec 1667), dau of John Pennington, of Dublin; *m* 2nd Lady Bridget Feilding (*d* 20 July 1669), dau of 1st Earl of Desmond (*see* DENBIGH and DESMOND, E); *m* 3rd Mary, dau of Moyses Hill (*see* DOWNSHIRE, M), and by her had, with four daus:

    1b Michael, of Tornduffe; *m* Clotilda, 2nd dau of Christian Borr, of Drynogh, Co Wexford, and *d* 1700, leaving:

      1c Arthur; *dsp* Aug 1701

    2b William; *dsp* on or after 21 Feb 1705, leaving his estates to his 3rd cousin **Sir William Parsons, 2nd Bt**, of the 1677 *cr*

(1) Mary; *m* as his 2nd w Arthur Hill, of Hillsborough (*see* DOWNSHIRE, M), and had issue

2 Laurence (Sir); Attorney-Gen Munster 1612, ktd 1612; Jt Surveyor-Gen Ireland with bro 1620, 2nd Baron Exchequer 1624; *m* Jane Malham and *d* 8 Sept 1628, leaving an est s:

  (1) Richard, of Birr, King's Co; *dsp* 22 May 1634

  (2) William, of Birr; Govr 1641 territory of Ely O'Carroll; held Birr Castle 14–15 months before surrendering 20 Jan 1642/3 to the Confederate Irish; *m* 19 June 1636 Dorothy, dau of Sir Thomas Philips, of Newtown Limavady, Co Derry, and *d* 1653, leaving, with three yr sons and three daus:

    1a **Sir Laurence Parsons, 1st Bt** (I), so *cr* 15 Dec 1677, of Birr; *m* Frances (*d* 2 Nov 1701), yst dau and coheir of William Savage, of Rheban, Co Kildare, and *d* 1698, leaving an est s:

      1b **Sir William Parsons, 2nd Bt**; MP (I Parl) King's Co 1692–1741; *m* 1st Elizabeth (*d* 15 Nov 1701), dau of Sir George Preston, Bt, of Craigmillar, and had:

        1c William; *m* Feb 1705/6 Martha, dau of Thomas Pigott, of Chetwynd, Co Cork, and had, with other issue:

          1d **Sir Laurence Parsons, 3rd Bt**; *m* 1st 5 Sept 1730 Mary, est dau and coheir of William Sprigge, of Clognovoe, King's Co, and had:

            1e **Sir William Parsons, 4th Bt**; *b* 6 May 1731; MP King's Co, High Sheriff 1779; *m* 28 June 1754 Mary, only dau and heir of John Cleare, of Kilburry, Co Tipperary, and *d* 1 May 1791, leaving:

              1f LAURENCE, **2nd Earl**

              2f John Clere; *b* 1760; barrister, Ch Commr Insolvent Court Ireland; *m* Nov 1805 Mary Anne, dau of William Moore, and had, with two yr sons and two daus:

                1g Laurence; Clerk Peace King's Co; *m* Rebecca Catherine, dau of John Lawder, of Ashford, Co Roscommon, and had, with other issue:

                  1h Lawrence W, CB; BA; Col

              3f William (Rev); *b* 1764; *d* unm 1838

              4f Thomas Clere; *b* 1766; barrister, Chm King's Co QS; *d* unm 1825

          1d (cont.) **Sir Laurence** *m* 2nd 16 Feb 1742 Anne, only dau of Wentworth Harman, of Moyle, Co Carlow, and Newcastle, Co Longford, and *d* 1756, having by her had, with other issue:

            2e Wentworth; *b* Oct 1745; Army Capt; *m* Charlotte, 3rd dau of Paul Winter, of Dublin, and had:

              1f Anne; *m* R B Deverell

            3e LAURENCE HARMAN PARSONS later HARMAN, **1st Earl of Rosse**, so *cr* 3 Feb 1806, with remainder to heirs male of his body, in default of which to his n of the half-blood LAURENCE, **2nd Earl**, as also earlier 25 Sept 1792 BARON OXMANTOWN, Co, Wexford, with identical remainder, and 6 Oct 1795 VISCOUNT OXMANTOWN, Co Wexford (all I), with ordinary remainder to heirs male of his body, of Newcastle, Co Longford; *b* 26 July 1749; *educ* Trin Coll Dublin; MP (I Parl) Co Longford 1776–92, rep I peer 1801–07, Chllr Dublin U 1802–07; *m* 11 June 1772 Jane (*d* 27 Jan 1838), est dau of 1st Earl of Kingston (*qv*), and *dspm* 20 April 1807, when the Viscountcy expired, leaving:

            1f Frances; *m* 9 Dec 1799 1st Viscount Lorton of Boyle (*see* KINGSTON, E) and *d* 7 Oct 1841, leaving issue

          2d William, of Birr; *m* 1st — and had:

            1e William

            2e Laurence; Maj 7th Regt

            1e Mary; *m* Robert Weldon (*see* WELDON, Bt)

          2d (cont.) William Parsons *m* 2nd Elinor, dau of William Weldon (*see* WELDON, Bt), and *d* 1780, having by her had:

            2e Elizabeth; *m* Capt Baynton

            3e Martha; *m* 5 July 1793 Richard Creaghe, DL, of Castle Park, Garden, Co Tipperary, and *d* 26 July 1837, leaving issue

      1b (cont.) **Sir William** *m* 2nd by licence 10 Feb 1718/9 Elizabeth (*dsp* 6 Feb 1739/40), widow of Rev Dillon Ashe and est dau and coheir of Sir George St George, and *d* 17 March 1740/1

The 1st EARL's n,

LAURENCE PARSONS, **2nd Earl of Rosse**, PC (I 1805); *b* 21 May 1758; *educ* Trin Coll Dublin (BA, LLD); MP (I Parl) Dublin U 1782–90 and King's Co 1791–1800 and (Tory, UK Parl) 1801–07, opposed Union of GB and I Parls; Col King's Co Militia Regt 1791–98, a Ld Treasury Ireland 1805–09, Jt PMG Ireland 1809–31, rep I peer 1809–41, custos rotulorum King's Co 1828–41; *m* 1 May 1797 Alice (*d* 4 May 1867), er dau of John Lloyd, of Gloster, King's Co, and had:

1 WILLIAM, **3rd Earl**.

2 John Cleare; *b* 17 Aug 1802; *d* 10 Aug 1828

3 Laurence; *b* 3 Nov 1805; *m* 1st 10 May 1836 Elizabeth (*d* 9 Dec 1844), est dau of 2nd Earl of Norbury (*qv*), and had:

  (1) Laurence Hardress Hector; *b* 31 Jan 1839; Capt RA; *d* 2 Feb 1924

  (2) William; *b* 16 May 1840; Capt RN; *d* 6 March 1891

  (3) Hector Laurence (Rev); *b* 19 March 1843; *d* unm

  (1) Elizabeth Helen; *m* 18 Nov 1861 Fergusson Floyer Hogg, BCS, 3rd s of Sir James Weir Hogg, 1st Bt (*qv*), and *dsp* 4 Dec 1862

3 (cont.) The Hon Laurence Parsons *m* 2nd 11 April 1849 Jane (*d* 3 April 1901), est dau of 2nd Baron Feversham (*qv*), and *d* 22 Nov 1894, having by her had:

  (4) Albert William; *b* 25 April 1850; *d* unm 1929

  (5) Randolph Cecil (Rev); *b* 23 July 1852; *m* 12 Dec 1901 Florence Emily (*d* 26 Feb 1946), dau of William Ashton, and *d* 28 March 1941, leaving:

    1a John Cecil Lawrence; *b* 19 Feb 1905; *m* 1940 (*divorce* 1958) Mary Lovell and *d* 1978, leaving:

      1b Michael Charles [Michael Parsons Esq, 12 Addicott Road, Weston-super-Mare, Somerset]; *b* 12 May 1950

      1b *Cynthia; *b* 1 Dec 1948; *m* 1967 *John Ryman and has:

        1c *Julie Angela; *b* 1968

    1a *Joan Mary; *b* 8 Oct 1906; LRAM

  (2) Louisa Alice, of Thatched House Lodge, Richmond Park; *m* 23 Feb 1878 Maj-Gen 1st and last Baron Ranksborough, CB, CVO (*d* 28 Feb 1921; *see* 1970 edn BROCKLEHURST, Bt), and *d* 28 Oct 1937

  (3) Florence Helen Isabella; *m* 21 March 1881 Col Frederick Henry Harford, Scots Gds (*d* 20 Aug 1926), of Down Place, Windsor, and *d* 30 June 1931, leaving issue

1 Jane; *m* 12 Dec 1835 Arthur Edward Knox (*d* 23 Sept 1886), of Castle Rea, Co Mayo, and *d* 31 Dec 1883

2 Alicia; *m* 1837 Sir Edward Conroy, 2nd Bt (*see* 1900 edn), and *d* 21 Jan 1885 aged 70. He *d* 3 Nov 1869

The 2nd EARL *d* 24 Feb 1841; his est s,

WILLIAM PARSONS, **3rd Earl of Rosse**, KP (1845); *b* 17 June 1800; *educ* Trin Coll Dublin and Magdalen Coll Oxford (Hon Fell 1862–67); King's Co: MP (Whig) 1821–34, Ld Lt 1831–67, Col Militia 1834, High Sheriff 1839, rep I peer 1845–67, Chllr Dublin U 1862, distinguished astronomer who built the 'Leviathan of Parsonstown', a telescope with a 72-inch diameter reflector that because of the unparalleled amount of reflected light it gathered allowed the viewer to see further into space than any other instrument in the world until well into the 20th century; with it he discovered among other phenonena that many galaxies are spiral-shaped; PRS 1848–54 (FRS 1831, Roy Medallist 1851), LLD Cantab 1842 and Dublin 1863, Pres Br Assoc 1843, FSA 1854, memb Imp Acad Sciences St Petersburg 1853, Chev Legn Hon 1855; *m* 14 April 1836 Mary (*d* 22 July 1885 aged 72), est dau and coheir of John Wilmer Field, of Heaton Hall, Yorks, and had, with two other sons (*d* young) and a dau (*d* unm):

1 LAURENCE, **4th Earl**

2 Randal (Rev); *b* 26 April 1848; *educ* Trin Coll Dublin (MA); Rector Sandhurst, Berks, 1880–1921, Hon Canon Ch Ch Oxford; *m* 9 Aug 1876 Eleanor Victoria (*d* 2 Jan 1936), 2nd dau of Rt Rev J F Mackarness, DD, Bp Oxford, and *dsp* 15 Nov 1936

3 Richard Clere; *b* 21 Feb 1851; MA Dublin; *m* 21 Nov 1878 Agnes Elizabeth (*d* 19 Aug 1922), dau of John Frederic La Trobe Bateman, FRS, of Moor Park, Farnham, and *d* 26 Jan 1923, leaving:

  (1) William Frederic, DSO (1917); *b* 10 Nov 1879; *educ* Wellington; Lt-Col RA WW I (despatches, Brevet); *m* 23 Nov 1915 Clara Helena (*d* 1972), yst dau of Hon Edward Gerald Strutt, CH (*see* RAYLEIGH, B), and *d* 29 Jan 1956, leaving:

    1a +(Desmond) Richard [Richard Parsons Esq, Flat 5, 113 Ifield Rd, London SW10 9AS]; *b* 26 Aug 1916; *educ* Lancing and Trin Coll Cambridge (BA 1938); late 2nd Lt Essex Regt

    1a *Nancy Olivia; *b* 2 July 1919

  (2) Arthur David Clere; *b* 8 Nov 1881; *educ* Wellington and Trin Coll Cambridge (BA 1904); *m* 28 April 1914 Doris (*d* 27 Nov 1970), dau of Norman Charles Cookson, of Wylam, Northumberland, and *d* 10 July 1955, having had:

    1a +(Arthur) Christopher [Maj Christopher Parsons, Hatchwood House, Odiham, Hants]; *b* 2 June 1919; *educ* Harrow and Trin Coll Cambridge; Maj RA WW II; *m* 16 April 1945 *Veronica Rosetta de Courcy, er dau of Maj-Gen Sir Guy de Courcy Glover, KBE, CB, DSO, MC, and has:

      1b +John Christopher, LVO (1992) [John Parsons Esq LVO, The Old Stables, Kensington Palace, London W8 4PU]; *b* 21 May 1946; *educ* Harrow and Trin Coll Cambridge (BA); Dep Keeper Privy Purse and Dep Treas to HM THE QUEEN 1988–; *m* 1982 *Hon Anne Constance Manningham-Buller, yst dau of 1st Viscount Dilhorne (*qv*), and has:

        1c +Michael Reginald; *b* 1983

        2c +David Guy; *b* 1985

        1c *Lilah Veronica; *b* 1988

      1b *Rosemary Anne [Mrs John Burke, Western House, Lowick, Northumberland TD15 2UD]; *b* 12 May 1948; *m* 1975 *John Bernard Burke and has:

        1c *Edward Christopher Sandars; *b* 1981

        1c *Henrietta Celia Sandars; *b* 1979

        2c *Juliet Rosemary Sandars; *b* 1985

    2b *Daphne Phoebe [Mrs Hugh Oliver-Bellasis, Wootton House, Wootton St Lawrence, Hants RG23 8PE]; *b* 21 May 1951; *m* 7 Aug 1971 *Maj Hugh Richard Oliver-Bellasis and has issue (*see* BATES, Bt, of Bellefield)

  2a +Norman Charles [Norman Parsons Esq, Pigdon House, nr Morpeth, Northumberland NE61 3SE]; *b* 9 Feb 1925; *educ* Harrow and Trin Coll Cambridge (MA); *m* 7 Feb 1953 Katharine Alison (*d* 15 July 1992), 2nd dau of Col Henry Hamilton Gardiner, MC, RA, of Manor House, Newenden, Kent, and has had:

    1b Giles Randal; *b* 25 Sept 1957; *d* 13 March 1983

    1b *Deborah Anne [Mrs Timothy Martin, 154 Loughborough Rd, Nottingham NG2 7JE]; *b* 26 May 1954; *m* 1988 *Timothy Harvey Noel Martin and has:

      1c *Toby Charles Parsons; *b* 1991

      2c *Harry William Parsons; *b* 1994

    2b *Clare Elizabeth [Mrs Emanuele Trucco, 25 Dick Rd, Edinburgh EH9 2JH]; *b* 28 Dec 1959; *m* 15 Sept 1991 *Emanuele Trucco and has:

      1c *Emily Valeria Parsons; *b* 29 July 1994

      2c *Francesca Alison Parsons; *b* 27 Dec 1996

3b *Katharine Mary [Mrs Bruce Gentles, Montgomery House, Stukeley Park, Cambs PE17 5AQ]; *b* 2 Oct 1963; *m* 22 Oct 1987 *(Alexander) Bruce Gentles

1a *Theodora Phoebe [Mrs James Wainwright, Sycamore, Shamley Green, Surrey GU5 0UZ]; *b* 26 June 1915; *m* 23 Sept 1939 Lt-Cdr James Bertram Everard Wainwright, DSO, OBE, RN (*das* 19 Sept 1943), s of Dr George Bertram Wainwright, OBE, MD, BCh, of Winchester, and has had:

1b *Andrew Christopher James; *b* 1943

1b Susan Rosalind; *b* 1941; *m* 1967 *Richard Edward Dawson and *d* 1989

2a Rosalind Doris; *b* 27 July 1916; *d* 1 July 1917

3a *Phyllis Rosemary; *b* 8 April 1918; *m* 1st 12 July 1945 Ian Akers-Douglas (*d* following an accident 16 Dec 1952) and has issue (*see* CHILSTON, V); *m* 2nd 9 Oct 1965 *Maj John Anthony Cobham Shaw, MC, only s of Capt John Leslie Morton Shaw, of The Red House, Exeter, Devon

(3) Laurence Edmund (Rev Canon); *b* 22 July 1883; *educ* Winchester and Ch Ch Oxford (BA 1906, MA 1909); Curate St Bartholomew Armley, Yorks, 1908–11, Domestic Chaplain to Bp Southwark 1911–14, Missionary Shantung 1914–15, Curate Wimbledon 1915–16, Vicar Chippenham Wilts 1916–25, Dean Cape Town 1925–28, Vicar Coleman's Hatch 1931–32, Dir S African Ch Inst Westminster 1932–45, Commissary to Archbp Cape Town 1933–45, Hon Canon St George's Cathedral Cape Town 1937–45, Prov Canon 1945, Gen Sec SPCK 1945–54; *m* 22 July 1911 Lydia Dorothy (*d* 19 April 1964), yst dau of Frederic Foster La Trobe Bateman, and *d* 17 Dec 1972, leaving:

1a Mary Alice; *b* 31 March 1912

(4) John Randal; *b* 27 Dec 1884; *educ* Wellington and Trin Coll Cambridge (BA 1907); RNVR WW I, chm Gillett Bros Discount Co, Naval Attaché Petrograd 1917–18, Russian Orders St Stanislas 2nd Cl with Swords, St Anne 3rd Cl with Swords; *m* 29 Nov 1909 Hon Alice Esmeralda O'Neill, yst dau of 2nd Baron O'Neill (*qv*), and *dsp* 15 March 1967

(5) (Richard) Edward (Rev); *b* 16 Feb 1888; *educ* Wellington and Trin Coll Cambridge (BA 1910, MA 1923); Lt-Col RE WW I (despatches), Curate St Paul's Bedford 1923–27, Vicar Oxhey Herts 1927–36, Dir Religious Educn Nat Soc 1936–41, Canon York 1941, Sec Churches' Ctee Religious Educn HM Forces 1941–48, Rector Wotton 1943–49, Fndr Warden Moor Park College Christian Adult Educn 1949–61, Govr 1961; *m* 11 Oct 1917 Hester Katherine (*d* 17 June 1954), dau of Maj John William Ainslie Drummond (*see* PERTH, E), and *d* Oct 1971, leaving:

1a +Desmond John (Rev) [The Rev Desmond Parsons, The Vicarage, Limpsfield, Surrey RH8 0DG]; *b* 31 Oct 1925; *educ* Eton; late Lt Irish Gds, Gen Sec and Dep Warden Moor Park Coll 1949–63, Assist to Dir Richmond Fellowship 1963–65, Coll of Resurrection Mirfield 1965–66, Curate St Mark's Purley 1966, Rector Limpsfield and Titsey 1983–; *m* 27 April 1968 *Althea Hermione, only child of Charles Anthony Stanley Prowse by Esme Edith, only dau of Sir Geoffrey William Millais, 4th Bt (*qv*), and has:

1b +Benedict Desmond Drummond; *b* 31 Jan 1969

1b *Francesca Catherine; *b* 30 June 1972

1a *Agnes Mary; *b* 25 Nov 1918; *m* 6 Sept 1941 *Maj Cosmo Rex Ivor Russell (*see* AMPTHILL, B) and has issue

2a *Hester Clere; *b* 22 Feb 1920; *m* 8 June 1940 *David Hastings Gerald Russell (*see* AMPTHILL, B) and has issue

3a *Elizabeth Frances; *b* 14 April 1923; with BRCS 1941–48, Programme Offr YMCA for HM Forces Germany 1948–52

4a *Rachel Anne [Miss Rachel Parsons, 38 Ridgeway Rd, Farnham, Surrey]; *b* 19 Sept 1927

(6) Desmond Cleare; *b* 2 Feb 1890; *educ* Winchester and Trin Coll Cambridge (BA); Capt Irish Gds; *ka* 15 Sept 1916

4 Charles Algernon (Sir), OM, KCB, JP, of Ray Demesne, Kirkwelpington, Northumberland; *b* 13 June 1854; invented the steam turbine; High Sheriff Northumberland 1910, Hon Col Irish Fus, Pres Br Assoc 1919–20, Master Shipwrights' Co, FRS, DSc Cantab, Hon Fell St John's Coll Cambridge, Hon DSc Oxon, Dublin, Durham and Toronto, Hon DCL Glasgow, LLD Edin and Leeds, Hon DEng Liverpool, Copley Medal of Roy Soc 1928; *m* 1883 Katharine (*d* 16 Oct 1933), dau of William Bethell, of Rise, Hull, and *d* 11 Feb 1931, having had:

(1) Algernon George; *b* 19 Oct 1886; T/Maj RFA; *ka* 26 April 1918

(1) Rachel Mary; AINA, memb LCC 1922–25; *d* unm 1 July 1956

The 3rd EARL *d* 31 Oct 1867; his est s,

LAURENCE PARSONS, **4th Earl of Rosse**, KP (1890), JP Co Tipperary and W R Yorks; *b* 17 Nov 1840; *educ* Trin Coll Dublin; constructed a thermometer for gauging the moon's heat; FRAS 1867, FRS 1867, High Sheriff King's Co 1867, rep I peer 1868–1908, DCL Oxon 1870, LLD Dublin 1879, Chllr Dublin U 1885–1908, Pres RDS 1888–92, Ld Lt King's Co 1892–1908, PRIA 1896–1901, LLD Cantab 1900, memb Senate Roy U Ireland, Hon DSc Leeds; *m* 1 Sept 1870 Hon Frances Cassandra Harvey-Hawke (*d* 9 Dec 1921), only child of 4th Baron Hawke (*qv*) of Towton, and *d* 29 Aug 1908, having had, with another s (*d* an infant):

1 WILLIAM EDWARD, **5th Earl**

2 Geoffry Lawrence, JP Hants; *b* 24 May 1874; *educ* Winchester and Balliol Coll Oxford (BA 1897, MA 1900); Lt Gen List 1916–19, Renter Warden Shipwrights' Co 1950, Prime Warden 1951; *m* 5 Sept 1911 Margaret Betty (*d* 16 May 1952), est dau of Sir John Evelyn Gladstone, 4th Bt (*qv*), and *dsp* 13 May 1956

1 Muriel Frances Mary; *b* 13 Nov 1876; *m* 28 May 1906 Brig-Gen Harold Maxwell Grenfell, CMG, MVO, and *d* 10 April 1927, leaving issue (*see* GRENFELL, B)

The er s,

WILLIAM EDWARD PARSONS, **5th Earl of Rosse**; *b* 14 June 1873; *educ* Eton and Ch Ch Oxford (BA); Lt 4th Bn W Yorks Regt (Militia) 1896–97, Lt 1st Bn Coldstream Gds 1898–1900, Maj 1906, ret 1907 (served Boer War 1899–1900 (Queen's Medal, three clasps), rep I peer 1911, Irish Gds WW I (severely wounded), Ld Lt King's Co 1909–18; *m* 19 Oct 1905 (Frances) Lois (*m* 2nd 15 May 1920 5th Viscount de Vesci; *qv*), 2nd dau of Sir Cecil Edmund Lister-Kaye, 4th Bt (*qv*), and had:

1 (LAURENCE) MICHAEL HARVEY, **6th Earl**

2 Desmond Edward; *b* 13 Dec 1910; *d* 4 July 1937

1 (Mary) Bridget; *b* 27 Oct 1907; *d* unm 26 Jan 1982

The 5th EARL *d* 10 June 1918 from wounds recd in action; his er s,

(LAURENCE) MICHAEL HARVEY PARSONS, **6th Earl of Rosse**, KBE (1974, MBE 1945); *b* 28 Sept 1906; *educ* Eton and Ch Ch Oxford (BA 1929, MA 1931); Capt Irish Gds WW II, Pres Georgian Gp (Chm 1947–68), Chm Standing Commn Museums and Galleries, Dep Chm Nat Tst, Pres Ancient Monuments Soc, Tstee Hist Churches Preservn Tst, Chm Internat. Dendrology Soc, Hon LLD Dublin 1950, Belfast 1964, MRIA, FSA London, FSA Ireland, FRAS, FRSA, Hon ARIBA, Pro-Chllr Dublin U 1965–79 (V-Chllr 1949–64); *m* 19 Sept 1935 Anne, formerly w of Ronald Owen Lloyd Armstrong-Jones, MBE, QC (*see* SNOWDON, E), and only dau of Lt-Col Leonard Charles Rudolph Messel, OBE, TD, of Nymans, Staplefield, Sussex, and *d* 1 July 1979, leaving:

1 (WILLIAM CLERE LEONARD) BRENDAN WILMER PARSONS, **7th and present Earl of Rosse**

2 +(Desmond Oliver) Martin [The Hon Martin Parsons, Womersley Park, Doncaster, Yorks]; *b* 23 Dec 1938; *educ* Eton and L'Aiglon; *m* 22 May 1965 *Aline Edwina, only dau of George Alexander Macdonald, MB, ChB, of Gable End, Priors Marston, Warwicks, and has:

(1) +Rupert Alexander Michael; *b* 3 Sept 1966

(2) +Desmond Edward Richard; *b* 30 Oct 1968

Seat: Birr Castle, Birr, Co Offaly. The earliest part of the present building may well date back to before the Parsons' tenancy, which began in the 17th century, in other words to the time of the O'Carrolls, who were formerly the chief (native Irish) family in the area around Birr. What seems to have been an earlier barbican was converted during the 17th century to a family dwelling after something more like a proper fortress was set alight during the siege of the mid-1640s. Two separate towers were joined together also. The last remains of a separate O'Carroll building, the old keep and some outbuildings, were demolished in the last quarter of the 18th century to make way for the great expanse of grass that now stretches away from the main entrance. In the early years of the 19th century the **2nd Earl** built the neo-Gothic fortified gateway that fronts the end of Oxmantown Mall in the town of Birr and also did up much of the castle interior with groining and similar Gothic motifs. The result remains spectacular, particularly in the saloon, from where there is a breathtaking view out over the River Camcor, which just there forms a torrent and is spanned by a delicate iron bridge.

A generation later a third storey was added after a fire had badly damaged the roof. (A third fire in 1919 destroyed a coffered ceiling in the library.) There is a very fine staircase of polished yew which dates from the second half of the 17th century and some entrancing neo-neo-Gothic decorative effects in the bedrooms executed in the light-hearted manner of Rex Whistler by the late Anne Countess of Rosse. The grounds contain very fine tree and shrub specimens.

ROSSLYN

Arms: Quarterly, 1st, argent a cross engrailed sable (for ST CLAIR); 2nd, argent a pale sable (for ERSKINE); 3rd, azure a bend between six cross crosslets fitchée or (for MAR); 4th, argent on a chevron gules between three roses of the last barbed vert a fleur-de-lys of the field for difference (for WEDDERBURN). **Crests:** 1 A demi-phoenix in flames proper and over it the device 'Rinasco piu glorioso' ['I am reborn more glorious'], 2 An eagle's head erased proper with the words 'Illaeso lumine solem' ['[Enjoy] the sun with unimpaired light'] (for WEDDERBURN). **Supporters:** Dexter, an eagle wings inverted proper, gorged with a collar argent, thereon a fleur-de-lys gules; sinister, a griffin wings elevated proper. **Motto:** Fight. **Creations:** Bt. (NS) 30 April 1666, B. (GB) 31 Oct 1795, E. (UK) 21 April 1801.

THE 7TH EARL OF ROSSLYN, Co Midlothian, **7th Baron Loughborough**, Co Surrey, and a **Baronet** (Sir Peter St Clair-Erskine, Bt) [The Rt Hon The Earl of Rosslyn, House of Lords, London SW1A 0PW]; *b* 31 March 1958; *s* f 1977; *educ* Eton and Bristol U (BA); Met Police 1980–94, Thames Valley Police 1994– (Superintendent Slough area), tstee Dunimarle Mus, dir Ludgrove Sch Tst; *m* 1982 *Helen M, est dau of C R Watters, of Christ's Hospital, Sussex, and has:

1 +JAMIE WILLIAM, *Lord Loughborough*; *b* 28 May 1986

2 +A son; *b* 199–

1 *Alice; *b* 1988

2 *Lucia; *b* 1993

Lineage (of Wedderburn): Sir PETER WEDDERBURN of Gosford (*see* OGILVY-WEDDERBURN), which he bought 1639; *b* 1612; advocate 1642, Clerk to PC (S) 1660, a Ld of Session as Lord Glasford 1668; *m* 1st 1 Feb 1649 Christian Gibson and had a s (*d* young); *m* 2nd 1653 Agnes, dau of John Dickson of Hartree, a Ld of Session; *m* 3rd 1677 Elizabeth Goldman, widow of Robert Cheplane, and *d* 11 Nov 1679, having by her had no issue; by his 2nd w he had, with other issue:

1 John, of Gosford, PC (S); *b* 1657; Lt-Col 14th Dragoons; drowned off Calais 26 May 1688

2 Sir PETER WEDDERBURN later HALKETT, 1st Bt (NS), so *cr* 31 Dec 1697, of Gosford; *b* 1660; Capt Grenadiers, MP Dunfermline 1705–07 (S Parl) and 1707–08 (GB Parl); *m* by 1695 Janet, sis and heiress of Sir James Halkett, 2nd Bt (*dsp* 19 May 1705), whom he s in the Pitfirrane estate, Fifeshire, and *d* 20 March 1746, leaving:

(1) Sir PETER HALKETT, 2nd Bt, of Pitfirrane; *b* by 1695; MP Stirling burghs 1734–41, Lt-Col Battle of Gladsmuir 1745, when captured by Jacobites; cmded 44th Foot in America 1754; *m* Amelia, dau of 7th Earl of Moray (*qv*) and was *ka* 9 July 1755 in N America serving under Gen Braddock, leaving, with two other sons (*d* unm):

1a Sir PETER HALKETT, 3rd Bt, of Pitfirrane; *d* unm 1792

(2) Charles, of Gosford; *m* Mary, dau of Sir Henry Wardlaw, 3rd Bt (*qv*), and had, with other issue:

1a Sir JOHN WEDDERBURN later HALKETT, 4th Bt, of Pitfirrane; *b* 6 Aug 1720; Army Capt, present capture of Guadaloupe 1758; *m* 1st 1758 Elizabeth (*dspm* 18 Dec 1758), dau of Andrew Fletcher of Saltoun, Ld Justice Clerk, and had:

1b Elizabeth; *b* 12 Dec 1758; *m* Trophime Gérard, Marquis de Lally-Tollendal (*d* 1830), legitimated s of Count (Thomas Arthur) de Lally (the scapegoat executed to appease French public opinion for the nation's failure against the British in India in the 1750s and 1760s) and himself (the Marquis) an early but swiftly superseded Conservative leader in the opening stages of the French Revolution who later devoted himself to prison reform in Restoration France, and *d* 6 Feb 1850, leaving, with another dau:

1c A dau; *m* Henri Raymond, Count d'Aux de Lescont

1a (cont.) Sir JOHN *m* 2nd by 1764 Mary, dau of Hon John Hamilton (*see* HADDINGTON, E), and *d* 7 Aug 1793, leaving, with other issue:

1b Sir CHARLES HALKETT, 5th Bt, of Pitfirrane; *b* 1764; Capt Dunfermline troop Fife Yeo; *d* unm 26 Jan 1837

2b Sir PETER HALKETT, 6th Bt, GCH, of Pitfirrane; *b* 1765; Adml the Blue; *m* 14 Oct 1802 Elizabeth, dau of William Todd, of London, and *d* 7 Oct 1839, leaving:

1c Sir JOHN HALKETT, 7th Bt, of Pitfirrane; *b* 15 Jan 1805; Cdr RN 1837; *m* 8 April 1831 Amelia Hood, dau of Col — Conway, and *d* 5 Aug 1847, leaving, with other issue:

1d Sir PETER ARTHUR HALKETT, 8th Bt, JP, DL Fifeshire, of Pitfirrane; *b* 1 May 1834; *educ* Cheltenham; Ensign 81st Foot 1851, 42nd Foot 1853, served Crimean War (medal with three clasps), Capt 1855, tfd Light Dragoons 1856, Cdr Order Isabella la Catolica Spain; *m* 6 May 1856 his cousin Eliza Anna (*see* below) and *dspms* 8 March 1904, when the btcy expired or became dormant

1c Jane Margaret; *m* Capt Richard Kirwan Hill, 52nd Regt, and *d* 3 May 1857, having had, with other issue:

1d Rowley Richard Conway; *b* March 1841; Lt-Col 31st Regt; *m* 5 March 1878 Blanche, dau of Edward Cropper by Hon Margaret, *née* Denman (*see* DENMAN, B), and had issue

1d Eliza Anna; *m* 6 May 1856 her cousin Sir PETER ARTHUR HALKETT, 8th Bt, and had issue

3b Peter; *b* 1768; Govr Bahamas, 1st Commr WI Accounts; *m* 1st Anne (*dsp* 1805), dau of William Todd; *m* 2nd 1815 Katherine, dau of 4th Earl of Selkirk (*see* HAMILTON and BRANDON, D), and by her had five sons

4b Alexander (Sir), KCH; *b* 1776; Gen; *m* Georgiana, dau of Capt George Sprowle, 16th Regt, and *d* 24 Aug 1851, having had four sons and a dau

3 Alexander; Commr Excise Scotland; *m* Mary, dau of John Deas, of Coldingknows, Berwicks, and had, with two daus:

(1) PETER

(1) Mary; *m* 1716 George Cheape, of Preston Pans, 5th s of Henry Cheape, 2nd of Rossie, and had issue

The only s,

PETER WEDDERBURN, of Chesterhall, Haddingtonshire; Ld of Session as Lord Chesterhall 1755; *m* Janet (*d* June 1771), dau of David Ogilvie, Dragoons Capt, and *d* 11 Aug 1756, leaving:

1 ALEXANDER WEDDERBURN, **1st Earl of Rosslyn** (UK), so *cr* 21 April 1801, with remainder, failing heirs male of his body, to his sister's sons, as also earlier 31 Oct 1795 BARON LOUGHBOROUGH, of Loughborough, Surrey (GB), with like remainder, as also earlier still 17 June 1780 BARON LOUGHBOROUGH, of Loughborough, Co Leicester (GB), with usual remainder to the heirs male of his body only, PC (1780); *b* 13 Feb 1733; *educ* Edinburgh U and Inner Temple; advocate 1753–54, barrister Inner Temple 1757, MP (Tory) Ayr burghs 1761–68, Richmond (Yorks) 1768–69, Bishop's Castle 1770–74 and 1778–80 and Okehampton 1774–78, KC and Bencher Lincoln's Inn 1763, Slr-Gen 1771, Attorney-Gen 1778–80, Ld Ch Justice 1780–93, First Commr Gt Seal April–Dec 1783, Ld Chllr 1793–1801, LLD Dublin 1781, FRS and FSA 1787, Er Bro Trin House 1799–1805, Tstee Br Museum 1801–05; *m* 1st 31 Dec 1767 Betty Anne (*d* 15 Feb 1781), dau and heiress of John Dawson, of Morley, Yorks; *m* 2nd 12 Sept 1782 Charlotte (*d* 1826), dau of 1st Viscount Courtenay (*see* DEVON, E), and *dsps* 3 Jan 1805, having by her had a s (*d* in infancy), when the 1780 Barony expired

2 David; Col HEICS; *k* recapture of Barrock, India, 1773

1 Janet; *m* 1761 **Sir Henry Erskine, 5th Bt,** of Alva (*d* 7 Aug 1765; *see* **Lineage (of Erskine)** below), and had:

(1) Sir JAMES ERSKINE later ST CLAIR-ERSKINE (roy licence 9 June 1789 on inheriting the Dysart, Rosslyn and other estates from his cousin Col James ST CLAIR *see* SINCLAIR, L), **6th Bt,** and **2nd Earl of Rosslyn**, GCB (1820), PC (1829); *b* 6 Feb 1762; *educ* Edinburgh Acad and Eton; Cornet 1st Horse Gds, Lt 35th Foot, Lt 2nd Dragoons 1778, Capt 19th Light Dragoons 1780, tfd 14th Light Dragoons 1781, ADC to Ld Lt Ireland 1782, Maj 8th Light Dragoons 1783, Lt-Col 12th Light Dragoons 1792, ADC to GEORGE III 1792, Adj-Gen Corsican campaign 1793, Col 1795, Brig-Gen Portugal 1796, Maj-Gen 1798, C-in-C Mediterranean 1798–99, Col Sussex Fencible Cav, cmded a Div Scotland 1800–01, Col 9th Light Dragoons 1801, Lt-Gen 1805, cmded SW Dist Ireland to 1806, special mission Lisbon 1806, cmded a Div Denmark 1807, Walcheren Expdn 1809 and SE Dist 1812–14, Gen 1814; MP (Whig) Castle Rising 1781–84, Morpeth 1784–96, Kirkcaldy burghs 1796–1805, Dir Chancery Scotland 1785, Ld Lt Fifeshire 1828–37, Ld Privy Seal 1829–30, a Ld Treasury Nov–Dec 1834, Ld Pres Cncl 1834–35; *m* 4 Nov 1789 Henrietta Elizabeth (*d* 8 Aug 1810), est dau of Hon Edward Bouverie (*see* RADNOR, E), and had:

1a Henry Alexander; *b* 2 June 1792; *d* young

2a JAMES ALEXANDER, **3rd Earl**

3a Henry Francis; *b* 1804; Capt Coldstream Gds; *d* unm 24 May 1829

1a Janet; *m* 10 Nov 1829 Bethell Walrond, of Dulford Ho, Devon, and *d* 16 Nov 1880, leaving issue

(2) John; Comptroller Army Accounts; *m* 1802 Mary, dau of Sir John Mordaunt, 7th Bt (*qv*), and *d* 10 Feb 1817, leaving:

1a Mary; *m* 18 June 1856, as his 2nd w, Sir Thomas Dyke Acland, 11th Bt, of Columb John (*qv*), and *dsp* 14 May 1892

(1) Henrietta Maria; granted 1801 rank of earl's daul *d* unm 16 Feb 1820

The 2nd EARL *d* 18 Jan 1837; his 2nd s,

JAMES ALEXANDER ST CLAIR-ERSKINE, **3rd Earl of Rosslyn**, PC (1841); *b* 15 Feb 1802; *educ* Eton; Capt 9th Light Dragoons 1823, Lt-Col 1828, Lt-Gen 1859, Col 7th Hus 1864, Gen 1866; MP (Tory) Kirkcaldy burghs 1830–31 and Gt Grimsby 1831–32, Master Buckhounds 1841–46 and Feb–Dec 1852, U-Sec War March–June 1859, Maj 1st Fifeshire Mounted Rifles; *m* 10 Oct 1826 Frances (*d* 30 Sept 1858), dau of Lt-Gen William Wemyss, of Wemyss Castle (*see* WEMYSS and MARCH, E), and had:

1 James Alexander George, *Lord Loughborough*; *b* 10 May 1830; *educ* Eton; Lt 2nd Life Gds; *d* unm 28 Dec 1851

2 FRANCIS ROBERT, **4th Earl**

1 Harriet Elizabeth; *m* 22 Aug 1865 Prince Münster, Hereditary Marshal of Hanover, Amb UK, and *dsp* 28 Nov 1867. He *d* 28 March 1902

The 3rd EARL *d* 16 June 1866; his only surv s,

FRANCIS ROBERT ST CLAIR-ERSKINE, **4th Earl of Rosslyn**, PC (1886), DL Fifeshire; *b* 2 March 1833; *educ* Eton and Merton Coll Oxford; Ld HC Gen Assembly Ch Scotland 1874, 1878, 1879 and 1880, Capt Gentlemen-at-Arms 1886–90, Amb Spain for marriage of ALFONSO XII 1878; *m* 8 Nov 1866 Blanche Adeliza (*d* 8 Dec 1933), dau of Henry FitzRoy (*see* GRAFTON, D) and widow of Hon Charles Henry Maynard (*see* 1865 edn MAYNARD, V), and had:

1 JAMES FRANCIS HARRY, **5th Earl**

2 Alexander FitzRoy; *b* 22 April 1870; *m* 28 Oct 1905 Winifrede, dau of Henry William Baker, of California, and *d* 25 Feb 1914

1 Millicent Fanny; *b* 20 Oct 1867; Croix de Guerre, 1st Cl Belgian Red Cross; *m* 1st 20 Oct 1884 4th Duke of Sutherland (*qv*) and had issue; *m* 2nd 17 Oct 1914 (*divorce* 1919) Brig-Gen Percy Desmond Fitzgerald, DSO, 11th Hus (*d* 17 Aug 1933), s of Hon Nicholas Fitzgerald, of Turlough, Co Mayo, and Moira, St Kilda, Australia; *m* 3rd 27 Oct 1919 Lt-Col George Ernest Hawes, DSO, MC, Roy Fus (*d* 1946), s of George Hawes, of Coombe Pk, Bath, and *d* 29 Sept 1957

2 Sybil Mary; *b* 20 Aug 1871; *m* 28 May 1892 13th Earl of Westmorland (*qv*) and *d* 21 July 1910, leaving issue

3 Angela Selina Bianca; *b* 11 June 1876; *m* 27 April 1896 (*divorce* 1906, resumed maiden name by deed poll 1929) Lt-Col James Stewart Forbes and *d* 22 Oct 1950, having had issue (*see* FORBES, Bt, of Newe)

The 4th EARL *d* 6 Sept 1890; his er s,

JAMES FRANCIS HARRY ST CLAIR-ERSKINE, **5th Earl of Rosslyn**, JP, DL Fife; *b* 16 March 1869; *educ* Eton and Magdalen Coll Oxford; Lt 3rd Bn Northants Regt Militia 1886–90, 2nd Lt RHG 1890, Capt Fifeshire Light Horse Vols 1890–97, Thornycroft's Mounted Inf Boer War (present Relief Ladysmith, *Daily Mail* war correspondent 1900, Queen's Medal with two clasps), Priv Sec to Sec of State Scotland 1904, Maj KRRC WW I 1915–17; *m* 1st 19 July 1890 (*divorce* 1902) Violet Aline (*d* 17 Feb 1945), yr dau of Robert Charles de Grey Vyner (*see* LUCAS OF CRUDWELL, B), and had:

1 Francis Edward Scudamore, *Lord Loughborough*; *b* 16 Nov 1892; Capt KRRC and Lt RNVR WW I (wounded); *m* 27 Dec 1915 (*divorce* 1926) Margaret Sheila Mackellar (*d* 13 Oct 1969, having *m* 2nd Sir John Milbanke, 11th Bt, *qv*), dau of Harry Chisholm, of Sydney, NSW, and *d* 4 Aug 1929, leaving:

(1) ANTHONY HUGH FRANCIS HARRY, **6th Earl**

(2) Peter George Alexander; *b* 30 Oct 1918; *educ* Eton and RAF Coll Cranwell; P/O RAF; *kas* 8 Sept 1939

1 Rosabelle Millicent; *b* 30 Oct 1891; *m* 1st 12 Feb 1912 Lt David Cecil Bingham (*ka* 14 Sept 1914, *see* LUCAN, E) and had issue; *m* 2nd 20 May 1916 Lt-Col John Charles Brand, DSO, MC, and *d* 12 Dec 1956, leaving further issue (*see* HAMPDEN, V)

The 5th Earl *m* 2nd 20 March 1905 (*divorce* 1907) Anna (*d* 4 Oct 1917), dau of George Robinson, of Minneapolis; *m* 3rd 8 Oct 1908 Vera Mary ('Tommy'), BEM (*d* 24 Feb 1975), dau of Eric Edward Bayley, 17th Lancers, of Little Moyle, Co Carlow, and by her had:

2 James (Hamish) Alexander Wedderburn, MC (1943); *b* 23 Aug 1909; *educ* Eton and New Coll Oxford; Maj Coldstream Gds WW II 1939–42 (wounded, despatches twice, POW, escaped); *d* unm 17 Dec 1973

3 David Simon; *b* 18 Nov 1917; *educ* Ampleforth and Merton Coll Oxford (Scholar, BA 1938); Maj Roy Scots WW II (despatches); *m* 5 March 1948 (*divorce* 1958) Antonia Mary (*d* 13 Aug 1965), only dau of Adml of the Fleet Sir John Donald Kelly, GCB, GCVO, and *d* 1985, leaving:

(1) Jonathan Harry; *b* 8 Nov 1949; *educ* Guelph U Ontario and RMA Sandhurst; *m* 1980 *Mrs Christine Moore, dau of Frederick Inch, of Huntingdon, and *d* 3 Feb 1995

2 Mary Sybil; *b* May 1912; *m* 1st 19 July 1933 (*divorce* 1944) Philip Gordon Dunn (later 2nd Bt), only s of Sir James Hamet Dunn, 1st Bt (*see* 1970 edn), of Bathurst, and had issue; *m* 2nd 5 Oct 1946 (*divorce* 1958) Capt Robin Francis Campbell, DSO, only s of Sir Ronald Hugh Campbell, GCMG, PC; *m* 3rd 5 Oct 1962 (*divorce* 1969) Charles Raymond McCabe; *m* 4th 1969 her former husb Sir Philip Gordon Dunn, 2nd Bt (*d* 20 June 1976)

The 5th EARL *d* 10 Aug 1939; his gs,

ANTHONY HUGH FRANCIS HARRY ST CLAIR-ERSKINE, **6th Earl of Rosslyn**; *b* 18 May 1917; *educ* Eton and Magdalen Coll Oxford; WW II: Capt KRRC (Sec GHQ Liaison Regt), attd Canadian Army 1944–45 (despatches); dir R F Kershaw Ltd, underwriting memb Lloyd's; *m* 3 Aug 1955 (*divorce* 1962) Athenaïs de Mortemart, only dau of Louis Victor, Duc de Vivonne, by Mme Michael Valery Ollivier, of La Ferme Ste Barbe, Arcangues, BP, France, and *d* 22 Nov 1977, having had:

1 PETER ST CLAIR-ERSKINE, **7th and present Earl of Rosslyn**

1 *Caroline; *b* 7 June 1956; *m* 1991 *Michael Francis Marten, s of Lt-Col Francis William Marten, CMG, MC (*see* VERNON, B)

Lineage (of Erskine): Sir CHARLES ERSKINE of Alva (6th s of 18th/2nd Earl of Mar (*qv*) by his 2nd w); *m* (contract 10 Jan 1639) Mary, dau of Sir Thomas Hope, 1st Bt (*qv*), and *d* 8 July 1663, leaving a 3rd but est surv s:

Sir Charles Erskine, 1st Bt (NS), so *cr* 30 April 1666, of Alva; *b* 4 July 1643; MP Clackmannanshire 1665–67 and Stirling 1689–90; *m* 1670 Christian, dau of Sir James Dundas of Arniston (*see* 1970 edn DUNDAS, Bt, of Arniston), and *d* 4 June 1690, having had, with a dau:

1 **Sir James Erskine, 2nd Bt**; *ka* Battle of Landen 23 July 1693

2 JOHN (Sir), **3rd Bt**

3 Charles, of Tinwald, Dumfriesshire; advocate 1711, MP Dumfries 1722–41 and Kirkwall 1741, Slr-Gen Scotland 1725, King's Advocate 1737, a Ld of Session as Lord Tinwald 1742, Ld Justice Clerk 1748; *m* 1st 21 Dec 1712 Grizel Grierson, of Barjarg, Dumfriesshire; *m* 2nd 26 Aug 1753 Elizabeth (*d* 24 Oct 1806), widow of William Maxwell, MD, of Preston, and dau of William Harestanes of Craigs, Kirkcudbrightshire, and *d* 5 April 1763, having by his 1st w had:

(1) Charles; *b* 23 Oct 1716; MP Ayr burghs 1747–49, barrister; *d* unm 25 June 1749

(2) James, of Barjarg and Alva; *b* 20 June 1722; a Ld of Session 1761 as Lord Barjarg and later as Lord Alva; *m* 1st 19 June 1749 Margaret (*d* 1766), dau and coheir of Hugh Macguire of Drumdow, Ayrshire; *m* 2nd Jean, widow of Sir James Stirling, 3rd Bt, of Glorat (*see* 1970 edn), and dau of John Stirling, and *d* 13 May 1796, having had, with other issue:

1a John; *b* 30 Dec 1758; barrister, Clerk Commissary Ct; *m* 23 Aug 1786 Christian, dau of John Carruthers, and *d* 16 Jan 1793, having had, with other issue:

1b James, of Aberdona; *b* 20 Aug 1787; *m* his cousin —, dau of Lt-Col Patrick Tytler, and had:

1c Isabella; *m* 3 May 1832 Hon James Murray and *d* 11 April 1875, leaving issue (*see* ELIBANK, L)

1a Isabella *m* Lt-Col Patrick Tytler, s of William Tytler, of Woodhouselee, and had issue

4 Robert; MD, physician to the Tsar of Russia

The 2nd Bt's bro,

Sir John Erskine, 3rd Bt; MP (S Parl) Clackmannanshire 1700–02 and Burntisland 1703–07 and (GB Parl) 1707–08 and Clackmannanshire 1713–15; *m* Catherine, dau of 1st/10th Lord Sinclair (*qv*), and *d* 12 March 1739, leaving:

1 **Sir Charles Erskine, 4th Bt**; Maj Roy Scots Regt; *m* 1743 Henrietta, dau of Col Fraser of Dundalloch, and was *ka* Battle of Laffeldt 2 July 1747, leaving a dau

2 **Sir Henry Erskine, 5th Bt**; Lt-Gen, Col Roy Scots, MP Ayr burghs 1749–54 and Anstruther burghs 1754–61, Sec Order Thistle; *m* 1761 Janet (*d* June 1797), sis of **1st Earl of Rosslyn**, and had issue (*see* above)

ROSSMORE

POST · PRŒLIA · PRÆMIA

Arms: Quarterly, 1st and 4th, per bend or and arg. in chief a tree eradicated and in base a sea horse regardant naiant in waves, all ppr. (for WESTENRA); 2nd and 3rd, quarterly, 1st and 4th, az. three mullets within a bordure arg. (for MURRAY); 2nd and 3rd, gu. three martlets within a bordure or. (for CAIRNES). **Crest:** A lion rampant ppr. **Supporters:** Dexter, a trooper of the 5th Dragoons resting his right hand upon a drawn sword, point downwards, all ppr.; sinister, a horse of the 5th Dragoons, caparisoned ppr. **Motto:** *Post prœlia præmia* ('After battles, rewards'). **Creations:** B. (I) 19 Oct 1796 and (UK) 7 July 1838.

THE 8TH BARON ROSSMORE OF MONAGHAN (I) and **7th Baron Rossmore of Monaghan**, Co Monaghan (UK) (William Warner Westenra) [The Rt Hon The Lord Rossmore, Rossmore Park, Co Monaghan, Ireland]; *b* 14 Feb 1931; *s f* 1958; *educ* Eton and Trin Coll Cambridge (BA 1957); late 2nd Lt Somerset LI, photographer as Paddy Rossmore; *m* 1982 *Valerie Marion, dau of Brian Tobin, of Riverstown, Co Offaly, and has:

1 +BENEDICT WILLIAM; *b* 6 March 1983

Lineage: WILLIAM de CARNYS; had confirmatory roy charter 1363 of (territorial) Baronies of E and W Whitburn, Linlithgowshire, to him and his s; had:

1 Duncan; had an only dau and heiress (*m* Stephen de Crichton and was ancestor of the CRICHTONs of Cairns and CRICHTONs of Ruthven)

2 John; one of three Custumars (keepers of records of manorial customs and laws) of Linlithgow 1369–1401

3 William; Constable Linlithgow Castle 1369–79 and Edinburgh Castle 1379–1401; had, with other issue:

(1) John, of Cults, which he inherited from his unc; Custumar Linlithgow 1406–22 and Shield Bearer to Earl of Douglas; *d* 1456, leaving, with two yr sons:

1a JOHN

4 Alexander; Provost Lincluden Coll; granted by Earl of Douglas (*see* QUEENSBERRY, M) land in Galloway, including Cults, Carsluth and Strathans; *d* 1422

WILLIAM de CARNYS's ggs,

JOHN CAIRNIS of Cults and Orchardton; Custumar Linlithgow 1449–56; did mil service for JAMES II; *d c* 1493; his s or gs:

WILLIAM CAIRNIS of Orchardton; called to Parl as minor Baron 1527; *m* Margaret, dau of Patrick Agnew of Lochnaw (*see* AGNEW, Bt, of Lochnaw), and *d* 1555, having had, with other issue:

1 William, of Orchardton; outlawed 1527; *m* Janet, dau of Thomas Kennedy of Knocknalling, and *d* 1588, leaving three daus and coheirs who sold Orchardton

2 JOHN

3 Peter; ancestor of the CAIRNSes of Kipp

4 Henry; ancestor of the CAIRNSes of Torr

The 2nd s,

JOHN CAIRNIS of Cults; Esquire to MARY QUEEN OF SCOTS; *m* 1555 Margaret, dau of Alexander McCulloch of Killaster, and *d* 1568, leaving a 2nd s:

JOHN CAIRNIS of Cults; sold most of his estates; *m* Margaret Hamilton and *d* 1603, leaving:

ALEXANDER CAIRNIS of Blairboys; sold the rest of his estates; gen agent Ulster 1609 for Scottish plantation of Donegal; *d c* 1635, leaving an est s:

JOHN CAIRNES, of Parsonstown or Cecil, Co Tyrone, and Donoughmore, Co Donegal; MP Augher 1639 and 1640; *m* Jane, dau of James Miller, MD, of Millhugh, and had, with two daus:

1 Sir ALEXANDER CAIRNES, 1st Bt (GB), so *cr* 6 May 1708, with remainder in default of heirs male of his body to his yr bro, of Monaghan; banker in Dublin and London who was apostrophised by Swift; MP (I Parl) Co Monaghan 1709–27 and Monaghan town 1727–32, Keeper Phoenix Park 1712; *m* 17 Feb 1697/8 Elizabeth (*d* 4 June 1731), sis of Sir Nathaniel Gould, Turkey merchant, and *dspms* 30 Oct 1732, having had:

(1) William Henry; *d* unm *vp*

(1) Mary; *m* 1st Sept 1724, as his 2nd w, 7th Lord Blayney, Baron of Monaghan (*d* 19 March 1732/3; *see* 1874 edn); *m* 2nd 1734 Col John Murray, MP Co Monaghan (*d* 29 June 1743), and *d* 28 Aug 1790, having had:

1a Frances Cairnes; *b c* 1738; *m* 29 Feb 1752 William Henry Fortescue, 1st and last Earl of Clermont (*dspm* 30 Sept 1806), and *d* 3 Dec 1820

2a Elizabeth; *b c* 1734; *m* 29 May 1754 Gen ROBERT CUNNINGHAME, **1st Baron Rossmore of Monaghan** (I), so *cr* 19 Oct 1796, with special remainder, failing male issue, to his w's surv sisters' sons, PC (I 1782) (served 14th Foot at Culloden 1746, Capt and ADC to Archbp Armagh when latter Ld Justice Ireland 1751, Col cmdg 124th Foot 1762, Adj-Gen Ireland, Maj-Gen 1772, Col 14th Foot 1775, Lt-Gen 1777, Col 5th Roy Irish Dragoons 1787–99, C-in-C Ireland 1793, Gen 1793, MP (I Parl) Tulske 1751–60, Armagh 1761–68, Monaghan 1769–96 and (GB Parl) E Grinstead 1788–89, rep I peer Jan-Aug 1801; *dsp* 6 Aug 1801), s of Col David Cunninghame [*sic*], of Seabegs, Fort Maj Stirling Castle, and *d* 23 Dec 1824

3a Anne; *m* 1761 Rt Hon Theophilus Jones (*d* 8 Dec 1811) and *d* 1 Feb 1827, leaving a s (*d* unm)

4a Mary; *d* unm 1744

5a Harriet; *m* 29 Nov 1764 Henry Westenra (*see* **Lineage (of Westenra)** below) and had:

1b WARNER WILLIAM, **1st/2nd Baron**

2b Henry; *b* 1 June 1770; Lt-Col 8th Hus; *m* 1829 Anna (*dsp* 8 Jan 1831), yst dau of Isaac Corry, of Abbey Yard, Newry, Co Down

1b Mary Frances; *m* 16 Feb 1788, as his 3rd w, Sir John Craven Carden, 1st Bt, of Templemore (*qv*), and had issue

2b Harriet Esther; *m* 17 April 1797 Col Hon Edward Wingfield, 3rd s of 3rd Viscount Powerscourt (*qv*), and *d* 16 Dec 1858, leaving issue

2 William; Dublin merchant, MP (I Parl) Belfast 1703–6; *dsp, bur* 9 Aug 1707

3 Sir HENRY CAIRNES, 2nd and last Bt; London banker and merchant, MP (I Parl) Monaghan town 1732–43; *m* 10 July 1711 his sis-in-law's n Frances (*d* 8 March 1749/50), dau of John Gould, of Hackney, Middx, dir HEIC, and *dsp* 16 June 1743, when the btcy expired

The 1st BARON's w's er surv n,

WARNER WILLIAM WESTENRA, **2nd Baron Rossmore of Monaghan** and **1st Baron Rossmore of Monaghan**, Co Monaghan (UK), so *cr* 7 July 1838; *b* 14 Oct 1765; *educ* Trin Coll Dublin; Co Monaghan: MP (I Parl) Aug–Dec 1800 and (UK Parl) 1800–01, custos rotulorum 1805–42 and Ld Lt 1831–42; *m* 1st 3 Oct 1791 Mary Anne (*d* 12 Aug 1807), 2nd dau of Charles Walsh, of Walsh Park, Co Tipperary, and had, with other issue:

1 HENRY ROBERT, **2nd/3rd Baron**.

2 Richard; *b* 21 Feb 1796; *m* 8 June 1822 Henrietta (*m* 2nd April 1841 Lt-Col Arthur G Lewis (*d* 22 Sept 1869) and *d* 1860), only child of Henry Owen Scott, of Scotstown, Co Monaghan, and *d* 9 June 1838, leaving three daus

3 John Craven, of Sharavogue, King's Co; *b* 31 March 1798; King's Co: MP and High Sheriff 1863, Lt-Col Scots Fus Gds; *m* 1st 31 March 1834 Eleanor Mary (*d* 17 Dec 1838), dau of William Jolliffe; *m* 2nd 23 July 1842 Anne (*d* 5 July 1882), dau of Louis Charles Daubuz, and *d* 5 Dec 1874, having by her had:

(1) Mary Anne Wilmot; *m* 15 Aug 1867 14th Earl of Huntingdon (*qv*) and *d* 16 Dec 1894, leaving issue

The **2nd Baron** *m* 2nd 3 June 1819 Augusta (*d* 28 July 1840), sis of 7th Earl of Wemyss (*see* WEMYSS and MARCH, E), and *d* 10 Aug 1842

His est s,

HENRY ROBERT, **2nd/3rd Baron Rossmore of Monaghan**; *b* 24 Aug 1792; *educ* Westminster and Trin Coll Dublin; Co Monaghan: MP (Whig) 1818–30, 1831–32, May-July 1834 and 1835–42, Ld Lt 1843–52; *m* 1st 25 Jan 1820 Anne Douglas-Hamilton (*dsp* 20 Aug 1844), illegitimate dau of 8th Duke of Hamilton and (5th Duke of) Brandon (*qv*) by Harriet Pye Bennett, actress (w of (a) Lt James Esten, RN, and (b) Major John Scott-Waring, MP); *m* 2nd 19 May 1846 his cousin Josephine Julia Helen (*m* 2nd 18 June 1863 Lt-Col George William Stacpoole, 18th Regt (*d* 19 Nov 1894), and *d* 12 Sept 1912), 2nd dau of Henry Lloyd, of Farrinroy, Co Tipperary, by Harriet Amelia, dau of Sir John Craven Carden, 1st Bt, of Templemore (*qv*), and *d* 1 Dec 1860, having by her had, with two other daus (*d* unm):

1 HENRY CAIRNES WESTENRA, **3rd/4th Baron Rossmore of Monaghan**; *b* 14 Nov 1851; *educ* Eton; Lt 1st Life Gds 1871; *d* unm 28 March 1874 from a fall in the Guards' Cup race at Windsor Steeplechase eight days earlier

2 DERRICK WARNER WILLIAM, **4th/5th Baron**

3 Richard Hamilton; *b* 2 May 1854; Lt 9th Lancers; *d* 22 Dec 1880

4 Peter Craven, DL Co Monaghan; *b* 12 Sept 1855; Capt and Hon Maj 5th Bn Princess Victoria's Roy Irish Fus; *m* 30 April 1895 Innys Maud Eaglesfield (*d* 1 May 1943), 2nd dau of Lansdowne Daubeny, JP, of North Court, Norton Malreward, Somerset, and *d* 2 Jan 1932, leaving:

(1) Petronella Mary Kathleen; *b* 27 April 1897; *m* 2 Dec 1920 Capt Edward Theobald Walsh Church, RN, s of Maj Charles Theobald Walsh Church, Roy Sussex Regt, of Dawlish, S Devon, and *d* 18 March 1966, leaving issue. He *d* 3 March 1948

(2) Norah Muriel Patricia; *b* 16 March 1901; *d* unm 4 Oct 1964

1 Frances Kathleen; *m* 3 Aug 1870 Maj Henry Augustus Candy, 9th Lancers, of Somerby Grove, Oakham, and *d* 7 Aug 1925, leaving issue. He *d* 26 July 1911

2 Norah Josephine Harcourt; *m* 3 Dec 1873 Maj Gilbert Stirling, RHG and 9th Lancers, of Larbert, Stirling, and Sysonby Lodge, Melton Mowbray, and *d* 13 Sept 1934, leaving issue. He *d* 7 Aug 1915

The 3rd/4th BARON's bro,

DERRICK WARNER WILLIAM WESTENRA, **4th/5th Baron Rossmore of Monaghan**, *b* 7 Feb 1853; *educ* Rugby; Sub-Lt 9th Lancers 1872, tfd 1st Life Gds 1874, ret 1876, Hon Col Monaghan Militia, Ld Lt Co Monaghan 1897–1921, author: *Things I Can Tell* (1912); *m* 14 June 1882 Mittie, OBE (1920) (*d* 8 Feb 1953), dau of Richard Christopher Naylor, MFH Pytchley, of Hooton Hall, Cheshire, and had:

1 WILLIAM, **5th/6th Baron**

2 Richard; *b* 15 Oct 1893; Lt Irish Gds and RFC; *m* 1st 24 Nov 1919 (*divorce* 1936) Alice Florence (*d* 2 June 1975), only dau of Maxwell Vandeleur Blacker-Douglas, of Bellevue Park, Killiney, Co Dublin, and had:

(1) *Cynthia Zia Hester; *b* 7 Sept 1920; *m* 6 May 1947 (*divorce* 1957) Eric Miles, s of Aldred Shakespear Miles, of Buenos Aires, and has:

1a *Richard Christopher [Richard Miles Esq, 37 St Peter's Sq, London W6 9NW]; *b* 30 Sept 1952; *m* 1982 *Sarah Dawson and has:

1b *Robert Henry Shakespear; *b* 1988

2b *Henry Blacker Shakespear; *b* 1990

1b *Katharine Westenra; *b* 1985

1a *Caroline Rose [Mrs James Stansfeld-Huelin, La Vallonerie, La Blinerie, St Clements, Jersey, CI]; *b* 1948; *m* 30 May 1970 *James Peter Stansfeld-Huelin and has:

1b *Alicia Antoinette; *b* 1975

2b *Rosanna Arlette; *b* 1978

2a *Sylvia Claire [Mrs Guy Woods, Homestead, Rue De La Fontaine, St Lawrence, Jersey, CI]; *b* 1950; *m* 1979 *Guy Robert William Woods and has:

1b *Serena Sylvia; *b* 1982

2 (cont.) The Hon Richard Westenra *m* 2nd 12 Oct 1936 Margaret Cecilia Sullivan (*d* 1979), formerly w of Capt Arthur Trevor Hope and dau of Rev George Sullivan Edgcombe, and *d* 26 July 1944

1 Mary, DBE (1930); *b* 1 Dec 1890; Section Offr WAAF WW II; *m* 5 Sept 1911 Sir Abe Bailey, 1st Bt, KCMG (*qv*), and *d* 28 Aug 1960, leaving issue

The 4th/5th BARON *d* 31 Jan 1921; his er s,

WILLIAM WESTENRA, **5th/6th Baron Rossmore of Monaghan**; *b* 12 July 1892; *educ* Wellington; ADC Personal Staff WW I 1917, with Directorate of Air-Service Rescue Air Ministry, Lt RNVR WW II; *m* 8 Nov 1927 Dolores Cecil (*d* 1981), formerly w of Col Maurice George Lee, RFC, and dau of Lt-Col James Alban Wilson, DSO, IA, of W Burton, Yorks, and *d* 17 Oct 1958, leaving:

1 WILLIAM WARNER WESTENRA, **6th/7th and present Baron Rossmore of Monaghan**

1 *Brigid Mary; *b* 23 Sept 1928; *m* 16 Aug 1956 (*divorce* 1969, resumed maiden name) Hon Jonathan Alan Howard, yst s of 3rd Baron Strathcona and Mount Royal (*qv*), and has issue

Lineage (of Westenra): WARNER WESTENRA, of Dublin, where he settled from Holland *temp* CHARLES II and was naturalised 1662; bought 1667 from Col Grace the town and lands of Clonleagh, Breekennagh and Lyagh, King's County; *m* Elizabeth Wybrantz and *d* 1676, having had, with a dau (Elizabeth, *m* Simon Digby, DD, Bp Elphin):

HENRY WESTENRA; inherited estates of his kinsman Peter Westenra, MP Athboy; *m* 1700 Eleanor, sis of 1st Viscount Allen (*see* 1845 edn), and had, with other issue, including two daus (Elizabeth, *m* William Weldon; *see* WELDON, Bt; Jane, *m* 1734 1st Viscount Galway (*qv*) and *d* 1788):

WARNER WESTENRA; MP Maryborough (modern Portlaoise) 1728; *m* 13 Dec 1738 Lady Hester Lambart, 2nd dau of 4th Earl of Cavan (*qv*), and had, with other issue, including a dau (Castiliana, *m* 1st Capt Dodd, *m* 2nd 1792 Sir Edward William Crosbie, 5th Bt (*d* 1798), and had issue):

HENRY WESTENRA, of Rathleague, Queen's Co; *b* 12 Jan 1742; MP Monaghan, Seneschal King's Manors Ireland; *m* 1 Dec 1764 Harriet, dau of Col John Murray, MP Co Monaghan, by Mary, widow of 7th Lord Blayney, Baron of Monaghan, and dau and heiress of Sir ALEXANDER CAIRNES, 1st Bt (*see* above), and had:

WARNER WILLIAM WESTENRA, **1st/2nd Baron Rossmore of Monaghan**

ROTHERMERE

BENE · QUI · SEDULO

Arms: Az. two rolls of paper in saltire or, banded in the centre gu., between four bees volant of the second. **Crest:** A cubit arm erect, the hand holding a roll of paper fesswise ppr., between two ostrich feathers or. **Supporters:** On either side a gladiator fully habited and accoutred, the dexter holding in the exterior hand a sword, the sinister holding on the exterior arm a shield, all ppr., each charged on the breast with a fountain. **Motto:** *Bene qui sedulo* ('He who acts diligently acts well'). **Creations:** Bt. (UK) 14 July 1910, B. (UK) 17 Jan 1914, V. (UK) 17 May 1919.

THE 3RD VISCOUNT ROTHERMERE, of Hemsted, Co Kent, **Baron Rothermere**, Hemsted, Co Kent, and a **Baronet** (Sir Vere Harold Esmond Harmsworth, Bt) [The Rt Hon The Viscount Rothermere, 36 rue du Sentier, Paris 75002, France]; *b* 27 Aug 1925; *s* f 1978; *educ* Eton and Kent Sch Conn.; with Anglo-Canadian Paper Mills 1948–50, Assoc Newspapers 1951–92, launched new *Daily Mail* 3 May 1971 and *Mail on Sunday* 1982, chm: Associated Newspaper Hldgs 1970–, Daily Mail and Gen Tst 1978–, tstee Reuters, pres: Euromoney Publications plc, Cwlth Press Union 1983–89 (chm UK section 1976), London Press Club 1976–81, Cdr: Order Merit Italy 1977, Order Lion Finland 1978, Order Southern Cross Brazil 1993, Order White Rose Finland 1995, Order Merit Hungarian Republic Middle Cross with Star 1996, FRSA, FIMgt; *m* 1st 21 March 1957 (Patricia Evelyn) Beverley ('Bubbles') (*d* 1992), er dau of John William Matthews, FRCS, of Heathcroft, Hertford Heath, and formerly w of Christopher John Brooks (*see* CRAWSHAW, B); *m* 2nd 1993 *Maiko Joeong-shun Lee, of Kyoto, Japan, and by his 1st w has:

1 +(HAROLD) JONATHAN ESMOND VERE; *b* 3 Dec 1967; md Courier Printing and Publishing; *m* July 1993 *Claudia C, dau of Terence J Clemence, property developer, of Belgravia, and has:

  (1) +Vere Richard Jonathan Harold; *b* 20 Oct 1994

  (1) *Eleanor Patricia Margaret; *b* 17 Oct 1996

1 *Geraldine Theodora Mary Gabriel; *b* 25 July 1957; *m* 1981 (*divorce* 1990) David, *Lord Ogilvy*, er s of 13th Earl of Airlie (*qv*), and has issue; *m* 2nd 28 June 1997 *Glyn Maxwell, author and poet, s of Dr James Maxwell, and by him has:

  (1) *Alfreda Ceridwen Patricia Rose; *b* 13 March 1997

2 *Camilla Patricia Caroline; *b* 28 July 1964; *m* Oct 1989 *Andrew R Yeates and has:

  (1) *Sebastian Andrew Alexander Vere; *b* 1990

  (2) *Alexander Samuel Jonathan Vere; *b* 1993

  (1) *Imogen Camilla Patricia Geraldine; *b* March 1995

  (2) *India Charlotte Caroline Sarah; *b* June 1996

Lineage: THOMAS HARMSWORTH, of Baughurst, Hants; *b c* 1540; had:

THOMAS HARMSWORTH, of Baughurst, *d* by 1635, leaving:

RICHARD HARMSWORTH, of Baughurst; *d c* 1637, leaving:

RICHARD HARMSWORTH, of Baughurst; *d* by 1663; his 3rd s:

RALPH HARMSWORTH, of Baughurst; *d* 1728, leaving:

RICHARD HARMSWORTH, of Odiham, Hants; *m* Anne — and *d* 1742, leaving:

JOHN HARMSWORTH, of Odiham; *m* 3 Nov 1719 Mary Reding (*d* Nov 1742) and *d* March 1777; his 2nd s:

RICHARD HARMSWORTH, of Hillside, Odiham; *m* 6 Oct 1751 Martha Bust (*d* 1774) and *d* Nov 1770, leaving:

RICHARD HARMSWORTH, of N Warnborough, Hants; *b* Feb 1759; *m* 21 April 1783 Mary Martin (*d* 9 Feb 1833) and *d* 15 March 1823, having had, with other issue:

CHARLES HARMSWORTH, of London; *b* 17 June 1805; *m* Hannah Carter and *d* 1 Oct 1857, leaving:

ALFRED HARMSWORTH; *b* 3 July 1837; barrister Middle Temple; *m* 21 Sept 1864 Geraldine Mary (*d* 29 Aug 1925), dau of William Maffett, of Pembroke Place, Dublin, and *d* 16 July 1889, having had:

  1 Sir ALFRED CHARLES WILLIAM HARMSWORTH, 1st and last Bt, so *cr* 23 Aug 1904, and 1st and last VISCOUNT NORTHCLIFFE, of St Peter, Co Kent, so

cr 14 Jan 1918, as also previously 27 Dec 1905 BARON NORTHCLIFFE, of the Isle of Thanet, Kent (all UK), JP Cinque Ports; *b* 15 July 1865; *educ* Stamford GS; fndr *Answers* 1888, *Daily Mail* 1896, *Ladies' Mirror* (later renamed *Daily Mirror*) 1903, owner *The Times* 1908 on, Chm Br War Mission to US 1916, Dir Propaganda in Enemy Countries 1917–18, LLD Rochester U, NY, Lt-Col 3rd Vol Bn E Kent Regt; *m* 11 April 1888 Mary Elizabeth, GBE (1918), ARRC (1919), DGStJ, V-Patron Westminster Hosp (*d* 29 July 1963, having *m* 2nd 4 April 1923 Sir Robert Arundell Hudson, GBE (*d* 25 Nov 1927)), est dau of Robert Milner, of Kidlington, Oxon, and *dsp* 14 Aug 1922, when his titles expired

2 HAROLD SIDNEY, **1st Viscount**

3 CECIL BISSHOPP HARMSWORTH, *cr* BARON HARMSWORTH (*qv*)

4 Sir (ROBERT) LEICESTER HARMSWORTH, 1st Bt (UK), so *cr* 1 July 1918, of Moray Lodge, Kensington; *b* 1 Nov 1870; MP Caithness 1900–18 and Sutherland 1918–22, dir Amalgamated Press, Hon LLD Queen's U Ontario 1927; *m* 13 Feb 1892 Annie Louisa (*d* 1 Dec 1963 aged 95), est dau of Thomas Scott, of Cornard, Suffolk, and Clapham, and *d* 19 Jan 1937, leaving:

  (1) Sir ALFRED LEICESTER ST BARBE HARMSWORTH, 2nd Bt; *b* 26 Nov 1892; *educ* Westminster and Ch Ch Oxford; Capt 8th Bn Glos Regt WW I (wounded), chm Retford and Gainsborough Times Co; *m* 2 July 1936 (*divorce* 1939) Margaret Florence Ivy Hall, and *dsp* 1 March 1962

  (2) Harold Cecil Aubrey (Sir); *b* 13 June 1897; chm Harmsworth Press, The Western Morning News Co and West Country Publications, Lt RMA WW I, Hon Lt-Col Queen's York Rangers, ktd 1935; *d* unm 7 Sept 1952

  (3) Robert Lovel St John; *b* 29 Nov 1893; *d* unm 15 Sept 1920

  (4) Sir (ARTHUR) GEOFFREY ANNESLEY HARMSWORTH, 3rd Bt; *b* 29 March 1904; *educ* Harrow; chm Harmsworth Press, West Country Publications and Western Morning News, dir Daily Mail and Gen Tst, war correspondent 1939–40, S/Ldr RAFVR WW II, FSA; *d* unm 1980, when the btcy expired

  (1) Annie Mary Geraldine; *b* 4 May 1900; *m* 1 March 1921 Terry Colley Durham, est s of W A Durham, of Appomattox, Va., and had issue

  (2) Violet Lilian Rosemary; *b* 19 Aug 1902; *m* 25 Jan 1926 Alexander Godfrey Crosbie Collins (*d* 18 April 1932), est s of Sir Godfrey Pattison Collins, KBE, CMG, PC, MP, and had issue

  (3) Margaret Rosabelle Northcliffe; *b* 20 Aug 1911

5 Sir HILDEBRAND AUBREY HARMSWORTH, 1st Bt, of Freshwater Grove (*qv*)

6 Albert St John; *b* 19 May 1876; *educ* Ch Ch Oxford (BA); *d* unm 3 May 1933

7 Vyvyan George; *b* 16 April 1881; *educ* Charterhouse and Trin Hall Cambridge; T/Capt RASC WW I; *m* 6 June 1906 Constance Gwendolen Mary (*d* 17 March 1962), est dau of Charles William Catt, of The Outwoods, Duffield, Derbys, and *d* 14 July 1957, having had:

  (1) St John Bernard Vyvyan; *b* 28 Nov 1912; *educ* Harrow and New Coll Oxford (BA); barrister Middle Temple 1938, Lt-Cdr RNVR WW II, Met Magistrate 1961; *m* 22 July 1937 Jane Penelope (*d* 15 April 1984), est dau of Basil Tanfield Beridge Boothby (*see* BOOTHBY, Bt), and *d* 13 June 1995, leaving:

    1a *Penelope Georgina Mary; *b* 28 Aug 1938; *educ* Somerville Coll Oxford; *m* 17 April 1968 *Wyndham Parfitt, s of D W Parfitt, of Cirencester, Glos, and has:

      1b *Oliver; *b* 19–

    2a *Sarah Elizabeth; *b* 28 March 1941; *m* 9 Feb 1963 (*divorce* 1974) 9th Earl of Antrim (*qv*) and has issue

    3a *Laura Jane [Mrs David Montagu-Douglas-Scott, 19 Petworth St, London SW11]; *b* 24 Oct 1944; *m* 10 June 1967 *David Henry George Montagu-Douglas-Scott (*see* BUCCLEUCH and QUEENSBERRY, D) and has issue

  (2) (Charles Alfred St John) Peter; *b* 6 July 1914; Capt SR Offrs Welsh Gds WW II; *m* 16 Dec 1935 *Nancy, widow of John Parish Robertson, and was *ka* N Africa 9 April 1943, leaving:

    1a *Vyvyan Peter Wilfrid, MVO (1977); *b* posthumously 27 Aug 1943; *educ* Harrow; Maj Welsh Gds, T/Equerry to HRH THE DUKE OF EDINBURGH 1973–76; *m* 12 May 1977 *Alexandra, est dau of Princess Juliet Melikoff, of Chelsea

    1a *Gillian; *b* 24 Oct 1938; *m* 26 Sept 1959 *Brian Alexander Miller-Thomas, only s of William Miller-Thomas, of Peeblesshire and Edinburgh, and has:

      1b *Vyvyan Peter Alexander; *b* 18 Sept 1960

      2b *Brian Andrew William; *b* 18 Sept 1960

      1b *Catriona Gillian; *b* 22 May 1962

      2b *Melanie Pamela; *b* 16 Oct 1965

      3b *Diana Laura; *b* 10 July 1967

  (3) (Stanley George) Michael St John, TD, DL (Caithness 1965); *b* 13 Oct 1916; 2nd Lt 4th/5th Seaforth Highrs (TA), Capt IA; *m* 2 Nov 1937 Lady Jessamine Cécile Marjorie (*d* 14 April 1994), only dau of 3rd Marquess of Aberdeen and Temair (*qv*), and *d* 1981, having had:

    1a *Andrew Vyvyan Michael Istvan St John [Andrew Harmsworth Esq, Revayah, Wester Quarff, Shetland ZE2 9EZ]; *b* 31 May 1939; *educ* Harrow, RMA Sandhurst and RAC Cirencester; late Capt 1st Bn Queen's Own Highrs; *m* 9 Sept 1967 *Sarah Katharine Susan, est dau of Col William Innes Moberly, CBE, and has:

      1b *Alasdair William Michael Gordon; *b* 29 June 1971

      2b *Richard Andrew; *b* 1981

      3b *Gideon David; *b* 1985

      1b *Laura Jessamine; *b* 27 Aug 1969; *m* 1994 *Andrew Stone

    2a *Peter Michael Patrick John; *b* 8 Dec 1952

    1a *Marigold Ishbel Geraldine Mary Jessamine [Mrs Francis Pym, Bolney House, Bolney, W Sussex RH17 5QR]; *b* 6 Dec 1940; *m* 6 Dec 1963 *Rev (Victor) Francis Pym (*see* PYM, B, LP), and has had:

      1b Alexander Michael Francis; *b* 3 June 1970; Lt RN; *d* 9 Oct 1995 in a paragliding/drowning accident

      2b *John Andrew Dudley; *b* 15 Dec 1971

      1b *Rebekah Mary Jane; *b* 1 April 1975

      2b *Victoria Naomi Jessamine; *b* 2 May 1978

2a *Caroline Sophia [Mrs Petros Demetriades, Tompazi 75, Nicosia, Cyprus]; *b* 25 July 1946; *m* 1978 *Petros Demetriades and has:

  1b *Anastasia Marjorie; *b* 1980

  2b *Cecilia Laura; *b* 1982

  3b *Myria Ishbel; *b* 1986

  4b *Jessia Demetra Penelope; *b* 1988

3a *Angela Mary Cecile [Mrs Angela Sinclair of Thrumster, Thrumster Mains, Caithness]; *b* 22 Oct 1949; *m* 14 Jan 1970 (*divorce* 1997) Dennis Sinclair of Thrumster and has:

  1b *Peter Donald; *b* 1973

  2b *Michael Douglas William; *b* 1978

  3b *John; *b* 1979

  4b *William; *b* 1984

  1b *Fiona Gwendolen Isobel; *b* 1970

4a *Islay Jane Winifred; *b* 12 Jan 1951; *m* 1976 *Ruairidh MacLeod and has:

  1b *Andrew; *b* 1978

  2b *Hamish; *b* 1981

  1b *Catherine Mary; *b* 1977

  2b *Elizabeth; *b* 1979

  3b *Fiona Jane; *b* 1987

(1) *Gwendolen Violet Suzanne; *b* 17 March 1920; *m* 20 Dec 1947 *Maj John Roderick Mathieson, RA, er s of Col William Mathieson, of Nitonagh, Maidstone, and has:

  1a *William George Roderick; *b* 12 Oct 1951; *educ* Sherborne

  2a *Andrea Gwendolen Maree; *b* 13 Nov 1949

1 Geraldine Adelaide Hamilton; *m* 12 Feb 1891 Sir Lucas White King, SCI, LLD Trin Coll Dublin, ICD (*d* 23 Aug 1925), est s of Dep Surgn-Gen Henry King, of Dublin, and *d* 7 Oct 1945, leaving issue

2 Violet Grace; *m* 7 March 1906 Lt-Col Wilfrid Hubert Wild, DSO, OBE, JP, DL, Northumberland Fus, s of Rev Robert Louis Wild, Rector Hurstmonceux, and *d* 26 March 1961, leaving issue. He *d* 3 Jan 1953

3 Christabel Rose; *m* 14 June 1905 Lt-Col Percy Collingwood Burton, OBE, DL (*d* 20 May 1953), 2nd s of William George Burton, of Dalkey, Co Dublin, and *d* 11 June 1967 aged 87, leaving:

  (1) Percy Basil Harmsworth; *b* 27 July 1906; *educ* Repton and Trin Coll Cambridge (BA); Maj 1st Army and Gen Staff WW II (despatches); *m* 1st Vera, dau of Vladimir Poliakoff, and had:

    1a Richard St John Vladimir; ARIBA; *m* Mireille, dau of Joseph Dernbach, of St John's Wood, and had:

      1b *Mark; *b* 24 April 1957

      2b *David; *b* 6 Oct 1958

      3b *Jonathan; *b* 2 Jan 1960

      1b *Catherine; *b* 7 Jan 1962

  (1) (cont.) Percy Burton *m* 2nd Elizabeth, dau of Louis Alfred William Bouwens van der Boijen, and by her had:

    2a Patrick William Harmsworth; *b* 24 Feb 1949

  (2) Lucas John Harmsworth; *b* 4 Jan 1916; *educ* Stowe and Cambridge; MRCS, LRCP, DPH, FRSH, Capt RAMC WW II, Dir Centl Cncl for Health Educn 1949–58, MO WHO 1959 on; *m* 7 July 1947 Isabella, dau of Carlo de Marchi, of Italy, and had:

    1a *Gioia Cristabella Maria; *b* 3 May 1949

    2a *Cristabel Vera Maria; *b* 28 Aug 1950

(1) *Christabel Mary Harmsworth [Mrs Peter Bielenberg, Munny House, Tullow, Co Carlow, Ireland]; *b* 18 June 1909; author *The Past is Myself* (1968); *m* 29 Sept 1934 *Peter Bielenberg, of Hamburg, and has:

  1a *Nicholas Paul; *b* 2 Aug 1935; *m* 23 Aug 1958 *Countess Charlotte von der Schulenburg and has:

    1b *Andrew Detlof; *b* 10 Aug 1959

    2b *Kim Peter; *b* 21 June 1969

    1b *Jennifer Patricia; *b* 17 March 1964

  2a *John Peter; *b* 23 March 1937

  3a *Christopher Albrecht; *b* 10 Jan 1942; *m* 20 May 1966 *Countess Angela von der Schulenburg

(2) *Barbara Geraldine Northcliffe; *b* 28 Aug 1912; *m* 11 Sept 1933 Charles Ayrey MacDonald and has:

  1a *Kevin; *b* 1937

  1a *Carley; *b* 18 April 1935; *m* 6 June 1957 *Robin Brown and has:

    1b *Melanie; *b* 30 June 1958

    2b *Christabel; *b* 26 March 1960

  2a *(Barbara) Jill; *b* 17 March 1939; *m* *James Christie and has:

    1b *Anna Barbara; *b* 2 May 1964

The 2nd s,

Sir Harold Sidney Harmsworth, 1st Bt, and **1st Viscount Rothermere**, of Hemsted, Co Kent, so *cr* 14 July 1910 and 17 May 1919 respectively, as also 17 Jan 1914 BARON ROTHERMERE, of Hemsted, Co Kent (all UK), PC (1917), DL (Sutherland); *b* 26 April 1868; Dir-Gen Royal Army Clothing Dept 1916–17, Pres Air Cncl 1917–18, Hon Bencher Middle Temple 1928, owned *Daily Mail* and *Evening News*, chm Associated Newspapers, dir Amalgamated Press, fndr Harold Vyvyan Harmsworth Chair US History Oxford, King Edward VII Chair of English Lit and Vere Harmsworth Chair of Naval History Cambridge, Hungarian Order of Service 1st Cl; *m* 4 July 1893 Mary Lilian (*d* 16 March 1937), dau of George Wade Share, of Forest Hill, Surrey, and *d* 26 Nov 1940, having had:

1 Harold Alfred Vyvyan St George, MC (1918); *b* 2 Aug 1894; *educ* Eton and Oxford; Capt Irish Gds (SR) WW I (wounded twice); *d* 12 Feb 1918 of wounds recd in action

2 Vere Sidney Tudor; *b* 25 Sept 1895; Lt RNVR and Drake Bn RN Div WW I; *ka* 13 Nov 1916

3 ESMOND CECIL HARMSWORTH, **2nd Viscount Rothermere**; *b* 29 May 1898; *educ* Eton; Lt RMA WW I, ADC to PM Peace Conf 1919, MP (U) Isle of Thanet 1919–29, chm: Associated Newspapers, Daily Mail and Gen Tst, Newspaper Proprietors' Assoc 1934–61, Newsprint Supply Co 1940–59, Chm Trustee Reuters News Agency, Pres Newspaper Press Fund 1935–37, first Chllr Newfoundland U 1952–61; *m* 1st 12 Jan 1920 (*divorce* 1938) Margaret Hunam, dau of William Lancelot Redhead, of Carville Hall, Brentford, and had:

  (1) VERE HAROLD ESMOND HARMSWORTH, **3rd and present Viscount Rothermere**

(1) *Lorna Peggy Vyvyan [The Hon Lady Cooper-Key, Floralies, Ave de Grande Bretagne, Monte Carlo, Monaco]; *b* 24 Oct 1920; *m* 11 Jan 1941 Maj Sir (Edmund Mc)Neill Cooper-Key, MP, Irish Gds (*d* 1981), er s of Capt Edmund Moore Cooper-Key, CB, MVO, RN, of Landford, Fleet, Hants, and has had:

  1a Adrian Astley Vere; *b* 28 Feb 1942; *educ* Eton; *d* following a car crash Spain 9 Sept 1963

  2a (Kevin) Esmond Peter; *b* 16 July 1943; *educ* Le Rosey, Millfield and Carlton U Canada; *m* 1st 1971 (*divorce* 1976) Lady Mary-Gaye Georgiana Lorna Curzon, dau of 6th Earl Howe (*qv*), and had:

    1b *Pandora Lorna Mary; *b* 1973

  2a (cont.) Esmond Cooper-Key *m* 2nd 1980 *Anna (*m* 2nd 1987 Thomas C U M Lundstrom), dau of Count Wilhelm Wachmeister, Swedish Amb US, and *d* 1985, leaving by her:

    1b *Cosmo; *b* 1980

    2b *Cara; *b* 1981

  1a *Emma Charlotte, *b* 23 Dec 1958; *m* 1st 1985 (*divorce* 19–) Hilary Ord Chittenden, s of N G Chittenden; *m* 2nd 1989 *(Brian) James Douglas Collins and by him has issue (see MORTON, E)

(2) *Esme Mary Gabriel, CVO; *b* 6 July 1922; Ldy Bedchamber to HM THE QUEEN 1967–71, Extra Ldy 1974–93 and Extra Woman Bedchamber 1993–; *m* 1st 10 Jan 1942 3rd Earl of Cromer (*qv*) and has issue; *m* 2nd 1993, as his 2nd w, *(Reinier) Gerrit Anton van der Woude, late Capt Gren Gds

3 (cont.) The **2nd Viscount** *m* 2nd 28 June 1945 (*divorce* 1952) Ann Geraldine Mary (*d* 1981), widow of 3rd Baron O'Neill (*qv*) and est dau of Hon Guy Lawrence Charteris (see WEMYSS and MARCH, E); *m* 3rd 28 March 1966 Mary (*d* 1993), formerly w of Richard Ohrstrom, of The Plains, Va., and est dau of Kenneth Murchison, of Dallas, Tex., and *d* 12 July 1978, leaving by her:

  (2) +(Esmond) Vyvyan; *b* 18 June 1967

ROTHERWICK

Arms: Per chevron az. and arg. in chief two estoiles or and in base an ancient ship with three masts, sails furled sa., flags flying gu., on a chief invected of the third a rose also gu., barbed and seeded ppr., between two fleurs-de-lys of the first. **Crest:** A sea-lion erect ppr., gorged with a naval crown and holding in the dexter fin an estoile or. **Supporters:** Dexter, a lion; sinister, a Bengal tiger ppr., each gorged with a naval crown and supporting a flag-staff also ppr., flying therefrom a banner gu., thereon a lozenge arg. charged with a lion rampant of the field. **Motto:** *Caute sed impavide* ('Cautiously but fearlessly'). **Creations:** Bt. (UK) 29 Jan 1924, B. (UK) 8 June 1939.

THE 3RD BARON ROTHERWICK, of Tylney, Co Southampton, and a **Baronet** (Sir (Herbert) Robin Cayzer, Bt) [The Rt Hon The Lord Rotherwick, Cornbury Park, Charlbury, Oxon OX7 3EH]; *b* 12 March 1954; *s f* 1996; *educ* Harrow and RMA Sandhurst; late Lt Life Gds (T&AVR); Pres Gen Aviation Awareness Cncl; *m* 6 March 1982 *Sara, only dau of Robert James McAlpine (see McALPINE, Bt), and has:

1 +HERBERT ROBIN; *b* 10 July 1989

2 +Henry Alexander; *b* 1991

1 *Harriette Jane; *b* 1986

Lineage: Sir CHARLES WILLIAM CAYZER, 1st Bt, of Gartmore (*qv*); had a 5th s:

Sir Herbert Robin Cayzer, 1st Bt, and **1st Baron Rotherwick**, of Tylney, Co Southampton (both UK), so *cr* 29 Jan 1924 and 8 June 1939 respectively, DL (Hants 1936–50, Sussex 1948), JP (Hants 1905–44, Glasgow 1944–48); *b* 23 July 1881; *educ* Rugby; Maj QO Roy Glasgow Yeo WW I (despatches), cmdg 24th Div

Mounted Troops, MP (C) Portsmouth S 1918–22 and 1923–39, Chm H of C Shipping Ctee 1932–39 and Naval Ctee 1936–39, memb Select Ctee Estimates 1934–36, 1st Pres Gen Cncl Br Shipping, memb cncl Chamber Shipping UK (Pres 1941–42), first chm Br Cwlth Shipping Co, chm: Union Castle Mail Steamship Co, Clan Line Steamers, Cayzer, Irvine & Co, Scottish Shire Line, Turnbull, Martin & Co, B and SA Steam Navigation, Houstons (London) Ltd, Greenock Dockyard Ltd, Caledonian Investments, Sea Lion Investments, Scottish Lion Insur, Scottish Tanker Co and Br Ship Adoption Soc; dir: Suez Canal Co London, Gen Shipowners' Assoc, Liverpool Steamship Owners' Assoc, Shipowners' Assoc, English Coaling Co, Steamship Owners' Coal Assoc, Ceylon Wharfage Co and Thames Nautical Trg Coll; Hon Col Roy Signals (TA) 1939, raised and cmded 25th Bn (Rotherwick) HG 1940–43, MFH Garth 1922–26, Jt MFH 1931–39; *m* 18 Jan 1911 Freda Penelope (*d* 11 Feb 1961), 4th dau of Col William Hans Rathborne, of Scripplestown and Kilcogy, Co Cavan, and *d* 16 March 1958, leaving:

1 (HERBERT) ROBIN CAYZER, **2nd Baron Rotherwick**; *b* 5 Dec 1912; *educ* Eton and Ch Ch Oxford (BA 1935); Maj RSG (SR) WW II (1938 Middle East), dep chm Caledonia Investments, Br and Cwlth Shipping, dir Cayzer Steel Bowater Hldgs 1974–96, MFH Heythrop; *m* 4 April 1952 Sarah Jane (*d* 2 Aug 1978), only dau of Sir Michael Nial Slade, 6th Bt (*qv*), and *d* 11 June 1996, leaving:

(1) (HERBERT) ROBIN CAYZER, **3rd and present Baron Rotherwick**

(2) +Charles William [The Hon Charles Cayzer, Finstock Manor, Finstock, Oxon OX7 3DG]; *b* 26 April 1957; *educ* Harrow and RMA Sandhurst; late Lt Life Gds; dir Caledonia Investments plc; *m* 1985 *Amanda C S, 2nd dau of John Squire, of Marbella, Spain, and has:

   1a +(Charles) William; *b* 14 July 1991

   1a *Victoria Amanda; *b* 22 June 1989

(3) +Avon Arthur; *b* 13 Sept 1968

(1) *Robina Jane [The Hon Mrs Debarge, 62 Elm Park Rd, London SW3 6AU]; *b* 24 Jan 1953; *m* 4 July 1981 *Dr Oliver Debarge and has:

   1a *Alexandra Jane; *b* 1982

   2a *Iona Amelia; *b* 1986

2 (Michael) Anthony Rathborne; *b* 28 May 1920; *educ* Eton and RMC Sandhurst; Lt (T/Capt) RSG WW II (wounded, despatches), Pres Chamber Shipping UK 1967, dep chm Br and Cwlth Shipping Co, chm Liverpool Steamship Owners' Assoc 1956–57, Pres Inst Shipping and Forwarding Agents 1963 and 1964; *m* 1st 11 June 1952 Hon Patricia Helen Browne, est dau of 4th Baron Oranmore and Browne (*qv*), and had:

(1) *(Linda) Kinvara; *b* 28 March 1953; *m* 1st (*divorce* 1989) Timothy James Douro Hoare, est s of Michael Douro Hoare, of Downland Ct, Ditchling, Sussex; *m* 2nd *Alan Holder and by her 1st husb has:

   1a *Sam Patrick Douro; *b* 1981

(2) *Rosanne [The Hon Mrs Hugh Tollemache, Sandbourne House, Earl's Croome, Worcs WR8 9GD]; *b* 10 Sept 1956; *m* 1986 *Hon Hugh John Hamilton Tollemache, yr s of 6th Baron Tollemache (*qv*), and has issue

(3) *Verena Brigid; *b* 8 Feb 1961; *m* 1985 *R Ian Molson, 3rd s of William M Molson, of Montreal, and has had:

   1a *Edward Charles; *b* 1987

   1a Camilla Rose; *b* 1989; *d* 1995

   2a *Natasha; *b* 1995

   3a *Louisa; *b* 1996

2 (cont.) The Hon Anthony Cayzer *m* 2nd 14 May 1982 *Baroness Sybille de Selys Longchamps and *d* 1990

1 Pamela Penelope; *m* 17 July 1939 *Brig Hon Richard Gustavus Hamilton-Russell, MVO DSO and bar, 2nd s of 9th Viscount Boyne (*qv*), and *d* 1987, having had issue

2 *Molly Angela [The Hon Lady Wyldbore-Smith, Grantham House, Grantham, Lincs NG31 6SS]; *m* 1 April 1944 *Maj-Gen Sir (Francis) Brian Wyldbore-Smith, CB, DSO, OBE (*see* SMITH-MARRIOTT, Bt), and has issue

ROTHES

GRIP FAST

Arms: Quarterly, 1st and 4th, argent on a bend azure three buckles or (for LESLIE); 2nd and 3rd, or a lion rampant gules, debruised by a ribbon sable (for ABERNETHY). **Crest:** A demi-griffin proper. **Supporters:** Two griffins proper, beaked, armed and winged or. **Motto:** Grip fast. **Creations:** L. (S) 1445, E. (S) by 20 March 1457/8.

THE 21ST EARL OF ROTHES and **Lord Leslie and Ballinbreich** (Ian Lionel Malcolm Leslie) [The Rt Hon The Earl of Rothes, Tanglewood, West Tytherley, Wilts SP5 1LX]; *b* 10 May 1932; *s* f 1975; *educ* Eton; Sub-Lt RNVR 1953; *m* 8 July 1955 *Marigold, only dau of Sir David Martyn Evans-Bevan, 1st Bt (*qv*), and has:

1 +James Malcolm David, *Lord Leslie* [Lord Leslie, Littlecroft, West Milton, Dorset DT6 3SL]; *b* 4 June 1958; *educ* Eton; graduated Parnham House 1990

2 +Alexander John [The Hon Alexander Leslie, Whitefield House, Letham, Cupar, Fife KY15 7SB]; *b* 18 Feb 1962; *educ* Eton; *m* 24 Feb 1990 *Tina L, dau of Dr T E Gordon, of Orlando, Fla.

Lineage: BARTHOLOMEW/BARTOLF, probably a Hungarian nobleman who travelled to Scotland in the retinue of MARGARET, later MALCOLM III CANMORE's Queen; became her chamberlain after her marriage; apparently *m* Beatrix, sis of MALCOLM III, hence granted extensive lands, particularly in the Garioch district of Aberdeenshire at Lesslyn, whence the family name; ktd, Govr Edinburgh Castle; *d* 1121, leaving:

MALCOLM, whose lands were confirmed by charter from David, Earl of Huntingdon; Constable Inverurie Castle (subsequently a hereditary office); had:

NORMAN; *m* the dau of the (feudal) Lord of Lorn and *d* by 1248, leaving, with two yr sons:

NORINO; had:

NORMAN, 1st of Leslie; granted further lands in Fife, Fythkill, later Leslie; paid homage 1296 to EDWARD I, Sheriff Aberdeen; *m* Elizabeth Leith and *d* by 1317, leaving:

Sir ANDREW de LESLIE; *m* 1313 Mary, dau of Alexander Abernethy of that Ilk (*see* SALTOUN, L), thus aquiring Ballinbreich, Fife and Cairnie, Forfar, and *d* by 1324, leaving:

1 Andrew; *d* by 1353

2 Norino; envoy to France and Rome; *m* Margaret, gdau and heiress of Alexander of Lamberton, and *d* in the Crusades by 1366

3 JOHN

4 Walter; *m* by 13 Sept 1365, as her 1st husb, Euphemia, Countess of Ross in her own right and *d* 27 Feb 1381/2, being known as Earl of Ross in right of his w, leaving a s and two daus

5 George, 1st of Balquhain; had issue (*see* LESLIE, Bt, and LEVEN and MELVILLE, E)

The third son

JOHN de LESLIE, first heard of as 'of Rothes' April 1392; seemingly *b* 1318–20; *s* to great-nephew's territorial Barony of Ballinbreich Jan 1391/2; *d* by 24 Oct 1396, leaving:

Sir GEORGE LESLIE of Rothes; granted with his w Fythkill, Fife (which he renamed Leslie), by roy charter Feb 1397/8; nominal heir to Ballinbreich but kept out of possession by Sir Andrew's life-rent and the unexpected return of David Leslie; Sheriff Fife 1409; *m* Elizabeth, dau of Sir Thomas de la Haye, 7th of Erroll (*see* ERROLL, E) by Elizabeth, dau of ROBERT II (*see* MORAY, E), and *d* in or after Feb 1411/2, having had:

Sir NORMAN LESLIE of Rothes and Fythkill; *b c* 1380; *s* to Ballinbreich and the other entailed lands May 1439; *m c* 2 Sept 1416 Christian, dau of Sir John Seton of Seton (*see* EGLINTON and WINTON, E), and *d* after 19 May 1439 but before 3 Feb 1439/40, leaving:

GEORGE LESLIE, **1st Earl of Rothes**, so *cr* between 5 Nov 1457 and 20 March 1457/8, as also 1445 LORD LESLIE (both S), of Leven; had his lands in the Sheriffdoms of Aberdeen, Elgin, Perth, and Fife united into the (territorial) Barony of Ballinbreich 20 March 1457/8; *m* 1st *c* 1435 Margaret, dau of John Lundin of that Ilk, and had a dau (Margaret, *m* Alexander Comyn of Ernside); *m* 2nd 1440 Christian, dau of Walter Halyburton of Dirleton, and had issue; *m* 3rd(? or 2nd) Elizabeth Campbell and *d* between 31 Aug 1489 and 24 May 1490, having by Christian had:

  1 Andrew, *Master of Rothes*; ktd by late May 1459; *m* Lady Elizabeth Sinclair, dau of 1st Earl of Caithness (*qv*), who was also at one time 3rd Earl of Orkney, and *d* by 3 Aug 1473, leaving:

    (1) John, of Balmain; *m* 1476, as her 1st husb, Lady Janet Keith, dau of 1st Earl Marischal (*see* KINTORE, E), and *dsp* by 23 June 1481

    (2) GEORGE LESLIE, **2nd Earl of Rothes**; *d* unm March 1512/3

    (3) WILLIAM, **3rd Earl**

  2 Elizabeth; *m* 1485 3rd Earl of Erroll (*qv*)

  3 Christian; *m* 2nd Lord Sinclair (*qv*)

The 2nd EARL's bro,

  WILLIAM LESLIE, **3rd Earl of Rothes**; *m* Margaret, dau of Sir Michael Balfour of Monquhanny, and was *ka* Battle of Flodden 9 Sept 1513, leaving:

  1 GEORGE, **4th Earl**

  2 John, of Parkhill; aided in the murder of Cardinal Beaton 1546; *m* Euphemia, dau of Sir John Moncreiff, and *d* 1576, leaving two daus

  3 James; Min Rothes; *d* 1576

The 3rd EARL's est s,

  GEORGE LESLIE, **4th Earl of Rothes**, PC (S 1528); Extrdy Ld of Session and Sheriff Fife, Amb Denmark 1550; on the attainder of his s, the *Master of Rothes*, had a charter of the forfeited lands of Ballinbreich, which he alienated to his 3rd s Andrew; *m* 1st 1517 (*divorce* 27 Dec 1520) Margaret, illegitimate dau of 3rd Lord Crichton of Sanquhar (*see* BUTE, M) by Margaret, dau of JAMES III, and had:

  1 Norman, *Master of Rothes*, PC (S 1545); pncpl agent in murder of Cardinal Beaton 29 May 1546, for which he was attainted; later distinguished himself in the French service; *m c* Feb 1540/1 Isabel (*dsp*), dau of 5th Lord Lindsay of the Byres (*see* LINDSAY, E), and *dvp* of wounds recd at Battle of Renti 31 Aug 1554

  2 William; implicated in murder of Cardinal Beaton (pardoned 1548); passed over in his f's settlement of the Earldom but claimed it unsuccessfully 1564

  1 Elizabeth

The **4th Earl** *m* 2nd 5 June 1525 Elizabeth (*dsp*), dau of 2nd Lord Gray (*qv*) and widow of (a) 4th Lord Glamis (*see* STRATHMORE and KINGHORNE, E) and (b) 3rd Earl of Huntly (*see* HUNTLY, M); *m* 3rd by 29 Jan 1529/30 Agnes, dau of Sir John Somerville of Cambusnethan and widow of 2nd Lord Fleming, by whom he had:

  3 ANDREW, **5th Earl**

  4 Peter

  5 James; ancestor of the LESLIEs of Ballybay, Ireland

  6 John; living 1543

  2 Janet; *m* Crichton of Naughton

  3 Helen; *m* 1st Gilbert Seton of Parbroath; *m* 2nd Mark Ker (*see* LOTHIAN, M) and had issue

The **4th Earl** *m* 4th his 1st w Margaret and by her had:

  7 Robert, of Ardersier; claimed Earldom 1560; Capt St Andrews Castle 1565; *m* Janet, dau of 2nd Lord Elphinstone (*qv*), and *d* 22 Sept 1588

  4 Agnes; *m* 6th Earl of Morton (*qv*)

  5 Beatrix; *m* Bea(u)ton of Creich

  6 Euphemia; *m* Learmonth of Balcomie

  7 Margaret; *m* 25 Dec 1575 8th Earl of Angus (*see* HAMILTON and BRANDON, D)

The **4th Earl** *m* 5th by 10 April 1543 Isobel, widow of 8th Earl of Crawford (*see* CRAWFORD and BALCARRES, E) and dau of — Lundy and *d* Dieppe 28 Nov 1558 (possibly poisoned) while returning home from the marriage of MARY QUEEN OF SCOTS to the DAUPHIN, leaving in addition, by one or other of his ws, yet another dau (Janet, *m* 1st David Crichton of Waughton, *m* 2nd by 8 March 1557/8, as his 2nd w, John Grant, 4th of Freuchie (*see* STRATHSPEY, B), *m* 3rd 1589 James Elphinstone (*see* ELPHINSTONE, L) and *d* 17 Dec 1591):

His 4th son,

  ANDREW LESLIE, **5th Earl of Rothes**, so declared by a decreet arbitral of the Crown 15 Jan 1564/5, which obliged William (*see* above) to give up the title, the latter being made over to ANDREW and the heirs male of his body, whom failing, the title to go back to William, who was in any case to receive the Cairney estate, Perthshire; *m* 1st apparently in Dec 1547 Grizel, dau of Sir James Hamilton of Finnart, and had:

  1 James, *Master of Rothes*; *m* 1st *c* 11 Jan 1574/5 Margaret, dau of 6th Lord Lindsay of the Byres (*see* LINDSAY, E), and had two sons and four daus (including Grizel, *m* 1st Earl of Dunfermline); *m* 2nd 1594 Katherine, dau of 3rd Lord Drummond (*see* PERTH, E), and by her had:

    (1) JOHN, **6th Earl**

    (1) Jean; *m* Alexander Menzies of Weem

  2 Patrick; Commendator Lindores; ancestor of the LESLIEs Lords Lindores and LESLIEs Lords Newark

  3 Andrew (Sir), of Lumbanny; *dsp*

  1 Eupheme; *m* 7th Lord Lindsay of the Byres (*see* LINDSAY, E)

  2 Elizabeth; *m* 1st David, est s of Sir John Wemyss of Wemyss (*see* WEMYSS and MARCH, E); *m* 2nd 1st Earl of Findlater (*see* SEAFIELD, E)

The **5th Earl** *m* 2nd after 3 Oct 1573 Jean, dau of 3rd Lord Ruthven (*see* CARLISLE, E) and widow of 2nd Lord Methven (*see* MORAY, E), and by her had:

  3 Margaret; *m* Sir William Cunningham of Caprington

  4 Mary; *m* 1st Lord Melville of Raith

The **5th Earl** *m* 3rd *c* 1592 Janet, dau of David Durie of that Ilk, and by her had:

  4 George, of Newton; *d* unm

  5 John (Sir), of Newton; ancestor of the 5th and later Lords Lindores

  6 Robert; *dsp*

  4 Isabel; *m* James, Master of Sinclair, est s of 5th Lord Sinclair (*qv*)

The 5th EARL *d* 1611; his gs,

  JOHN LESLIE, **6th Earl of Rothes**, JP (Elgin and Forres); *b* 1596; *m* 1614 Lady Anna Erskine, dau of 18th/2nd Earl of Mar (*qv*), and *d* Aug 1641, having had:

  1 JOHN, **7th Earl**

  1 Margaret; *m* 1st Alexander Leslie, Lord Balgonie (*d* shortly after 1642), s and heir of 1st Earl of Leven (*see* LEVEN and MELVILLE, E); *m* 2nd 2nd Earl of Buccleuch (*see* BUCCLEUCH and QUEENSBERRY, D); *m* 3rd 13 Jan 1653 2nd Earl of Wemyss (*see* WEMYSS and MARCH, E) and *d* Feb 1688

  2 Mary; *m c* 17–24 Dec 1635, as his 2nd w, 7th Earl of Eglinto(u)n (*see* EGLINTON and WINTON, E)

The 6th EARL's son,

  JOHN LESLIE, **7th Earl of Rothes** and 1st and last DUKE OF ROTHES, so *cr* 29 May 1680, as also MARQUESS OF BAMBREICH, EARL OF LESLIE, VISCOUNT OF LUGTOUN, LORD AUCHMUTYE AND CASKIEBERRIE (all S), PC (E 1663); *b c* 1630; captured by English Battle of Worcester 3 Sept 1651 and held intermittently in the Tower of London and Edinburgh Castle; Pres Cncl S 1660, Extrdy Ld of Session Feb 1660/1, Ld High Treasurer Scotland 1663, Ld High Commr S Parl 1663, 1665 and 1666; Keeper Scottish Privy Seal 1664, Ld HC to Gen Assembly Ch Scotland 1664, Ld Chllr Scotland 1667; obtained 4 July 1663 a new charter of his ancestral titles (Earldom of Rothes and Lordship of Leslie, now regranted as Lordship of Leslie and Ballinbreich) and estates, with remainder to the heirs male of his body, whom failing, to the heirs female of his body, or of the body of his heirs male, with other remainders; *m c* Jan–Feb 1647/8 Anne, dau of John, Earl of Crawford and Lindsay, and *d* 26 July 1681, when the Dukedom and other title *cr* the year before expired, leaving, with a yr dau (Christian, *m* 1st 3rd Marquess of Montrose (*see* MONTROSE, D) and 2nd Sir John Bruce of Kinross, Bt):

  MARGARET Leslie, *suo jure* **Countess of Rothes**; *m* 8 Oct 1674 Charles HAMILTON, 5th Earl of Haddington (*qv*), and *d* 20 Aug 1700, leaving, with a yr s (Thomas; *s* to the Earldom of Haddington under a marriage contract between his parents):

  JOHN HAMILTON later LESLIE, **9th Earl of Rothes**; *b* 1675; Ld Privy Seal Scotland 1704–05, rep S peer 1708–10 and 1715–22, V-Adml Scotland 1715, Ld High Commr to Gen Assembly Ch Scotland 1715–21, helped suppress 1715 Uprising as cdr Horse Vols at Sheriffmuir, Govr Stirling Castle Feb 1717/8–22; *m* 29 April 1697 Lady Jean Hay (*d* 1731), dau of 2nd Marquess of Tweeddale (*qv*), and *d* 4 Sept 1731, having had:

  1 JOHN, **10th Earl**

  2 Charles; Col; *d* 1769

  3 Thomas; Equerry to the PRINCE OF WALES, Barrack-Master of Scotland, MP Perth 1743; *d* 1772

  4 James, of Milndean; advocate 1726, Sheriff Depute Fife; *d* 1761

  5 William; Maj; *d* 1764

  6 Andrew; Equerry to PRINCESS OF WALES; *d* 1776

The 9th EARL's son,

  JOHN LESLIE, **10th Earl of Rothes**, KT (1753), PC (I 1756); *b c* 1698; Maj-Gen Jan 1742/3, Lt-Gen staff Ireland 1751; rep S peer 1723–34 and 1747–67; in his time Leslie House was destroyed by fire 1763 and Ballinbreich sold to Sir Laurence Dundas; *m* 1st 1741 Hannah (*d* 1761), dau and coheir of Mathew Howard, of Thorpe, Norfolk, and had:

  1 JOHN LESLIE, **11th Earl of Rothes**; *b* 19 Oct 1744; *educ* Eton; *m* 4 April 1768 Jane (*m* 2nd 1774 Hon Patrick Maitland, s of 6th Earl of Lauderdale; *qv*), dau of Thomas Maitland of Soutra, and *dsp* 1773

  1 JANE ELIZABETH, **Countess of Rothes**

  2 Mary; *m* 1770 3rd Earl of Portmore (*see* 1835 edn) and *d* 1799

The **10th Earl** *m* 2nd 27 June 1763 Mary (*m* 2nd 1770 Bennet Langton, Prof of Ancient Lit at RA, of Langton, Lincs (*d* 1801), and *d* 7 Sept 1785, leaving issue), dau of Gresham Lloyd by Mary Holt, later Countess of Haddington (*qv*), and *d* 1767, having had no issue by her

The 11th EARL's sis,

  JANE ELIZABETH Leslie, **Countess of Rothes** in her own right; *b* 5 May 1750; her succession was unsuccessfully disputed by her uncle Andrew Leslie; *m* 1st 2 Jan 1766 George Raymond EVELYN (*d* 23 Dec 1770), 3rd s of William EVELYN-GLANVILLE later EVELYN, of St Clere, and had an only surv s:

  1 GEORGE WILLIAM, **13th Earl**

The **Countess** *m* 2nd 1772 Sir Lucas PEPYS, 1st Bt (*d* 1830; *see* COTTENHAM, E), and *d* 1810, having by him had, with another s and a dau (*d* in infancy):

  2 Sir CHARLES LESLIE later PEPYS, 2nd Bt; *d* 1832

  3 Rev Sir HENRY LESLIE, 3rd Bt; *m* 1816 Elizabeth Jane, dau of Rev James Oakes, and *dsp* 9 Dec 1849, when the btcy passed to the Earl of Cottenham (*qv*)

  1 Harriet; *m* 29 Nov 1804 10th Earl of Devon (*qv*) and *d* 16 Dec 1839, leaving issue

The COUNTESS's est s,

  GEORGE WILLIAM EVELYN later EVELYN-LESLIE, **13th Earl of Rothes**; *b* 28 March 1768; *educ* Eton and St John's (coll Cambridge); rep S peer 1812–17; *m* 1st 24 May 1789 Lady Henrietta Anne Pelham (*d* 1797), est dau of 1st Earl of Chichester (*qv*), and had, with two daus (*d* unm):

  1 HENRIETTA ANNE, **Countess of Rothes**

The **13th Earl** *m* 2nd 1798 Charlotte Julia (*d* 21 May 1846), dau of Col John Campbell of Dunoon, and *d* 1817, having by her had, with two other daus (*d* unm or in infancy):

  2 Elizabeth Jane; *m* 16 Dec 1830 Maj Augustus Wathen, 15th Hus (later 13th Light Dragoons) (*d* 3 May 1843), only s of Maj Wathen, and *d* 19 Jan 1861

The 13th EARL's est dau,

  HENRIETTA ANNE Evelyn-Leslie, **Countess of Rothes** in her own right; *b* 26 March 1790; *m* 1806 George GWYTHER later LESLIE, a gardener (*d* 24 March 1829), and *d* 30 Jan 1819, having had:

  1 GEORGE WILLIAM EVELYN GWYTHER later LESLIE, **15th Earl of Rothes**; *b* 8 Nov 1809; *m* 7 May 1831 Louisa (*d* 21 Jan 1886), 3rd dau of Col Henry Anderson later Anderson-Morshead, Col Cmdt RE, and *d* 10 March 1841, leaving:

    (1) GEORGE WILLIAM EVELYN LESLIE, **16th Earl of Rothes**; *b* 4 Feb 1835; *d* unm 2 Jan 1859

    (1) HENRIETTA ANDERSON-MORSHEAD Leslie, **Countess of Rothes** in her own right; *b* 1832; *m* 22 Jan 1861 Hon George WALDEGRAVE later

WALDEGRAVE-LESLIE, MP Hastings 1864–68 (*d* 8 July 1904), 3rd s of 8th Earl Waldegrave (*qv*), and *dsp* 10 Feb 1886

2 Thomas Jenkins; *b* 29 June 1813; Army Offr; *m* 25 Aug 1834 Honora Seward (*d* Oct 1879), only dau of Maj Thomas Burrowes, of Stradone House, Co Cavan, and *d* 13 July 1849

1 Henrietta Anne; *m* 16 Nov 1827 Charles Knight Murray, barrister, and *d* 14 April 1832

2 MARY ELIZABETH, **Countess of Rothes**

3 Anna Maria; *m* 6 Jan 1835 14th Earl of Devon (*qv*) and *d* 18 Feb 1897, leaving issue

4 Catherine Caroline; *m* 1841 John Parker (*d* 1847), Capt 66th Regt (*see* MORLEY, E), and *d* 11 Jan 1844

The COUNTESS's aunt,

MARY ELIZABETH Leslie, **Countess of Rothes** in her own right; *b* 9 July 1811; *m* 11 Aug 1835 Martin Edward HAWORTH later HAWORTH-LESLIE (roy licence March 1886; *d* 2 Nov 1886), Capt 60th Rifles, of Boreham Wood, Herts, and had, with two other sons and two other daus:

1 Martin Leslie HAWORTH later LESLIE (roy licence 1865); *b* 12 March 1839; *m* 10 June 1873 Georgina Frances (*d* 29 Jan 1934), dau of Henry Studdy, of Waddeton Court, Devon, and *dvm* 22 Dec 1882, leaving:

(1) NORMAN EVELYN, **19th Earl**

(1) Mary Eleanor; *b* 18 Oct 1875; granted with sisters rank of earl's daus 2 July 1898; *d* unm 20 Feb 1969

(2) Mildred Emily; *b* 22 Dec 1878; *d* unm 1971

(3) Georgina; *b* 11 Dec 1879; *m* 7 Nov 1908 William Blacklock Haden Corser, of Horsham, Sussex, s of Haden Corser, of Ingatestone, Essex, and *dsp* 6 June 1941

2 Edward Courtenay; *b* 2 July 1840; *m* 1 Oct 1890 Caroline Edith (*d* 10 March 1948), yst dau of Thomas Tregenna Biddulph, of Earee, Shoalhaven, NSW, and *d* 31 Jan 1911, leaving:

(1) Edward Biddulph; *b* 31 Jan 1895; with AIF WW I

(2) Martin Tregenna; *b* 2 May 1896; with AIF Egypt, Gallipoli and France WW I (wounded), Lt 1st Machine Gun Bn; *m* 1st 21 Dec 1928 Nettie Margaret (*d* 21 July 1943), dau of William Harper, of Napier, NZ, and had:

1a +Mary Haworth; *b* 30 Sept 1936

(2) (cont.) Martin Haworth-Leslie *m* 2nd 22 Dec 1945 *Joyce Enid, er dau of Rev Alfred James Gardner, of Chatswood, NSW, and widow of Rev L M Dunstan

(3) +Norman Evelyn; *b* 26 Jan 1898; *m* 29 Jan 1944 *Helen Thomson, dau of James Thomson Robertson, of Brisbane, Qld

(1) Mary Henrietta; *b* 26 Sept 1892; *d* unm 4 Jan 1914

(2) Alice Veronica; *b* 14 Aug 1901; *d* unm 2 May 1928

3 Lydston Horton; *b* 2 Sept 1849; *m* 28 June 1881 Elizabeth Anne (*d* 19 June 1898), dau of Robert Reece, and *dsp* 16 April 1890

1 Emily Louisa; *m* 25 April 1871 James Frederick Cherry (*d* 1883) and *d* 21 April 1936, having had:

(1) Charles Cameron; *dsp*

(1) Miriam Emily; *m* Herbert Owen-Taylor (*d* 1921) and *d* 18 Jan 1954, leaving:

1a +Leslie H; *m* 1937 *Vera Hutton and has:

1b +Allan; *b* 14 Nov 1946; *educ* Oundle and Bristol U; *m* 20 Dec 1969 *Rosalind Phyllis Muriel, dau of Sir Philip Harold Pilditch, 2nd Bt (*qv*)

1a +Miriam Audrey Leslie; *m* 1st 1928 R A P Corkery; *m* 2nd 1947 Col J Stuart-Usher; *m* 3rd July 1956 *Charles W Iliffe, only s of Rev Charles Iliffe, of Kirklington Rectory, Yorks

2a +Doreen; *b* 6 July 1907; *m* 10 Aug 1935 *Derick Hetherington Cooper and has:

1b +Michael Hetherington; *b* 24 May 1936; *educ* Ratcliffe Coll Leicester

(2) Gladys; *m* Maj G O S Pringle, RA (ret) (*d* 1952), and *d* 4 May 1965

2 Grace; *m* 10 April 1876 John Bazley-White (*d* 9 Feb 1927), MP Gravesend, and *d* 5 Oct 1933, leaving issue (*see* STYLE, Bt)

The COUNTESS *d* 19 Sept 1893; her gs,

NORMAN EVELYN LESLIE, **19th Earl of Rothes**, JP (Fife); *b* 13 July 1877; rep S peer 1906–23, Col Highland Cyclist Bn, formerly Capt Fife RFA, Lt 6th Vol Bn Black Watch and 4th Bn Devonshire Regt WW I (wounded); *m* 19 April 1900 (Lucy) Noël Martha (*m* 2nd 22 Dec 1927 Lt-Col Claud Macfie, DSO, Seaforth Highrs (*d* 23 Dec 1963), 3rd s of William Macfie, CB, of Airds, Argyll, and Uplands Hall, Preston, and *d* 12 Sept 1956), only child of Thomas Dyer Edwardes, of Prinknash Park, Glos, and had:

1 MALCOLM GEORGE DYER-EDWARDES, **20th Earl**

2 John Wayland; *b* 16 Dec 1909; *educ* Stowe and Corpus Christi Coll Cambridge; F/Lt RAFVR WW II (invalided 1943), memb Roy Co Archers; *m* 5 July 1932 *Coral Angela [The Hon Mrs John Leslie, The Dower House, Headbourne Worthy, Hants SO23 7JG], er dau of George Henry Pinckard, JP, of Combe Court, Chiddingfold, Surrey, and *d* 1991, leaving:

(1) +Alastair Pinckard, TD [Alastair Leslie Esq TD, Seasyde House, by Errol, Perthshire PH2 7TA]; *b* 29 Dec 1934; *educ* Eton; late Capt Roy Scots Fus (TA), memb Roy Co Archers and Court Clothworkers' Co (Prime Assist 1997–98); *m* 18 Dec 1963 *Rosemary, er dau of Cdr Hubert Wyndham Barry, RN (*see* BARRY, Bt), and has had:

1a David John; *b* 27 April 1967; *d* 1989

1a +Fiona Jane; *b* 24 Oct 1965; *m* 1990 *Richard Alan Patrick de Klee, yst s of Col Murray de Klee, OBE, of Auchnacraig, Isle of Mull, and has:

1b +Frederick Leslie Blair; *b* 27 Sept 1993

2b +Lachlan Richard John; *b* 5 March 1996

2a +Ann Mary; *b* 11 Oct 1973; *m* 12 July 1997 *Kelvin Mullins, s of Laurie Mullins

(1) +Amber Elizabeth [Mrs Beresford White, Dumpford Manor House, Trotton, Hants GU31 5JR]; *b* 5 May 1939; *m* 2 April 1964 *Beresford Robert Winder White, s of Robert White, of Gerrards Cross, Bucks, and has:

1a +Rupert Beresford; *b* 24 Nov 1966

2a +Alexander Richard Beresford; *b* 25 Oct 1968

The 19th EARL *d* 29 March 1927; his er s,

MALCOLM GEORGE DYER-EDWARDES LESLIE, **20th Earl of Rothes**; *b* 8 Feb 1902; *educ* Eton; rep S peer 1931–59; Maj Gen List, memb Roy Co Archers, Dir Tyres Min Supply 1942–45, dep chm BET, chm Nat Mutual Life Assur, Dir Omnium Investment; *m* 17 July 1926 Beryl Violet, only dau of James Lionel Dugdale (*see* CRATHORNE, B), and *d* 17 May 1975, leaving:

1 IAN LIONEL MALCOLM LESLIE, **21st and present Earl of Rothes**

1 +Jean, CBE (1991) [The Lady Jean Mackenzie CBE, Kingfisher House, Ampfield, Hants SO51 9BT]; *b* 26 Aug 1927; *m* 26 April 1949 *Roderick Robin Mackenzie, only surv s of Capt Roderick Kilgour Mackenzie, Seaforth Highrs, of Kincraig, Ross-shire

2 +Evelyn [The Lady Evelyn Mackworth-Young, Fisherton Mill, Fisherton de la Mere, Wilts BA12 0PZ]; *b* 11 March 1929; *m* 14 July 1949 Gerard William Mackworth-Young (*d* 1984) (*see* YOUNG, Bt, of Formosa Place) and has issue

ROTHSCHILD

Arms: Quarterly, 1st, or an eagle displayed sa., langued gu.; 2nd and 3rd, az. issuing from the dexter and sinister sides of the shield an arm embowed ppr., grasping five arrows, points to the base arg.; 4th, or a lion rampant ppr., langued gu., over all an escutcheon gu., thereon a target, the point to the dexter, ppr. **Crests:** 1 (centre) Issuant from a ducal coronet or an eagle displayed sa., 2 (dexter) Out of a ducal coronet or between open buffalo horns per fess or and sa. a mullet of six points or, 3 (sinister) Out of a ducal coronet or three ostrich feathers, the centre arg., the exterior ones az. **Supporters:** Dexter, a lion rampant or; sinister, a unicorn arg. **Motto:** *Concordia, integritas industria* ('Concord, integrity, industry'). **Creations:** Bt. (UK) 12 Jan 1847, B. (UK) 29 June 1885, B. (Austria) 29 Sept 1822.

THE 4TH BARON ROTHSCHILD, of Tring, Co Hertford, and a **Baronet**, also a **Baron** of the Austrian Empire (Sir (Nathaniel Charles) Jacob Rothschild, Bt, GBE (1998)) [The Rt Hon The Lord Rothschild GBE, 14 St James's Place, London SW1A 1NP; Stowell Park, Marlborough, Wilts]; *b* 29 April 1936; *s f* 1990; *educ* Eton and Ch Ch Oxford (BA); late 2nd Lt Life Gds; chm: St James's Place Capital (formerly J Rothschild Hldgs) plc 1971–96 (non-exec dir 1996–), Rothschild Investment Tst 1971–, Bd Tstees Nat Gallery 1985–, Nat Heritage Memorial Fund 1992–98 and Tstee Heather Tst for the Arts 1998–; dir N M Rothschild and Sons 1963–80, memb cncl RCA 1986– (Sr Fell 1992), Pres Inst Jewish Affrs 1992, Hon PhD Hebrew U Jerusalem 1992, Cdr Order Henry The Navigator Portugal 1985, Hadrian Award from World Monumnets Fund, NYC, for restoration and conservation 1995; *m* 20 Oct 1961 *Serena Mary, er dau of Sir Philip Gordon Dunn, 2nd Bt, of Bathurst (*see* 1970 edn), and has:

1 +NATHANIEL PHILIP VICTOR JAMES; *b* 12 July 1971; *educ* Wadham Coll Oxford; *m* 13 Nov 1995 *Annabelle, actress, dau of Max Neilson

1 *Hannah Mary; *b* 22 May 1962

2 *Beth Matilda; *b* 27 Feb 1964; *m* 1991 *Antonio Tomassini, s of Georgio Tomassini, and has:

(1) *Ferdinand; *b* 1992

(2) *Wardi; *b* 19–

(1) *Tess; *b* 5 Oct 1996

3 *Emily (Emmy) Magda; *b* 19 Dec 1967; *m* 24 June 1998 *Julian Freeman-Attwood, s of Maj Warren Freeman-Attwood and Mrs Liz Mostyn-Owen

Lineage: URI FEIBESCH; had:

ELCHANAN; *m* — Fogel (*d* 1550) and *d* 1550, leaving, with an est s (Moses) and four yr sons (Abraham, *d* 1564; David; Brendel; Uri Feibesch, *d* c 1588):

ISAAK ELCHANAN; *m* Esther — (*d* 1609) and *d* 1585, leaving, with an est s (Elchanen) and two yst sons (Raphael, *d* 1624; Fogel):

MOSES; *m* Gitchen (*d* 1640) and *d* 1635, leaving, with an est s (Uri Feibesch, *d* 1690) and a yst s (Isaak, *d* 1680):

NAPHTALI HERZ; *m* 1st Schönchen (*d* 1661); *m* 2nd Hannah (*d* 1686) and *d* 1685, leaving, with four other children (Moses; Isaak Itzik, *d* 1659; Rel, *d* 1655; Gutle, *d* 1678):

KALMON; *m* 1st Gitle (*d* 1668); *m* 2nd Bele (*d* 1712) and *d* 1707, leaving, with an est s (Meier, *d* 1747), a yst s (Salman, *d* 1750) and a dau (Esther, *d* 1747):

MOSES BAUER ('farmer') or ROTHSCHILD (from *rot schild*, or 'red shield', the sign outside the family's house in the Frankfurt ghetto in ISAAK ELCHANAN's time); *d* 1735, leaving, with a yr s (Herz Moses, *d* 1728):

AMSCHEL MOSES BAUER/ROTHSCHILD; *m* Schönche Lechnich (*d* 1756) and *d* 1755, leaving:

1 Mayer Amschel; *b* 23 Feb 1743/4; Imperial (HRE) Crown Agent 1800; *m* 1770 Gutle (Gertrude) (*d* 1849), dau of Salomon Baruch Schnapper, and *d* 19 Sept 1812, having had, with other issue (*d* young):

(1) Amschel Mayer; *b* 1773; *cr* 29 Sept 1822 with his four yr bros a Baron of Austria; continued the family business at Frankfurt; *m* 1796 Eva Hanau (*d* 1848) and *d* 1855; the business eventually passed into the hands of the Naples ROTHSCHILDs

(2) Salomon Mayer, of Vienna; *b* 1774; fnded Austrian branch of Rothschild's; *m* 1800 Caroline Stern (*d* 1854) and *d* 1855, leaving:

1a Anselm Salomon; *b* 1803; *m* 1826 his cousin Charlotte, est dau of Nathan Rothschild, of the UK branch, and *d* 1874, leaving:

1b Mayer Anselm Leon; *b* 1827; 1828

2b Nathaniel Mayer; *b* 1836; *d* 1905

3b Ferdinand James Anselm; *b* 1839; *m* 1865 his cousin Evelina, dau of Lionel Nathan de Rothschild, of the UK branch (*see below*) and *d* 17 Dec 1898

4b Salomon Albert Anselm; *b* 1844; *m* 1876 his cousin Bettina Caroline, dau of Alphonse de Rothschild, and *d* 1911, leaving:

1c George Anselme Alphonse; *b* 1877; *d* 1934

2c Alphonse Mayer; *b* 1878; *m* 1912 Clarice Sebag-Montefiore (*d* 1967) and *d* 1942, leaving:

1d Albert Anselm Salomon Nimrod; *b* 1922; *d* 1938

1d *Bettina Jemima; *b* 1924; *m* 1943 *Matthew James Looram

2d Gwendoline Charlotte Frances Joan; *b* 1927; *m* 1948 *Roland Henry Hoguet and *d* 1972

3c Louis Nathaniel; *b* 1882; *m* 1946 Hildegard Johanna Caroline Marie Auersperg (*d* 1981) and *d* 1955

4c Eugène Daniel; *b* 1884; *m* 1st 1925 Kitty Schönborn-Bucheim (*d* 1946); *m* 2nd 1952 Jeanne Stuart

5c Oscar Ruben; *b* 1888; *d* 1909

1c Charlotte Esther; *b* 1885

2c Valentine Noémi; *b* 1886; *m* 1911 Baron Sigismund von Springer (*d* 1928) and *d* 1969

1b (Caroline) Julie Anselme; *b* 1830; *m* 1850 her cousin Adolphe Carl de Rothschild and *d* 1907

2b Hannah Mathilde; *b* 1832; *m* 1849 her cousin Wilhelm Carl de Rothschild and *d* 1924

3b Sara Louise; *b* 1834; *m* 1858 Baron Raimondo Franchetti (*d* 1905) and *d* 1924

4b Alice Charlotte; *b* 1847; *d* 1922

1a Betty; *b* 1805; *m* 1824 her uncle James Mayer de Rothschild (*see below*) and *d* 1886

(3) NATHAN MAYER, for whom *see below*

(4) Carl Mayer; *b* 1788; fndr Naples branch, which after the unification of Italy returned to Frankfurt; *m* 1818 Adelheid Hertz (*d* 1853) and *d* 1855, having had, with another s (*d* young):

1a Mayer Carl; *b* 1820; *m* 1842 his cousin Louise Rothschild (*see below*) and *d* 16 Oct 1886, leaving, with two other daus (*d* unm):

1b Adèle Hannah Charlotte; *b* 1843; *m* 1862 her cousin Salomon James de Rothschild (*d* 1864) and *d* 1922

2b Emma Louisa; *b* 1844; *m* 1867 her cousin **1st Baron Rothschild** (*see below*) and *d* 1935

3b Laura Thérèse; *b* 1847; *m* 1871 her cousin Nathan James Edouard Rothschild (*see below*) and *d* 1931, leaving issue

4b Margaretha Alexandrine; *b* 1855; *m* 1878 Duke de Gramont (*d* 1925) and *d* 1905

5b Bertha Clara; *b* 1862; *m* 1882 Prince de Wagram (*d* 1911) and *d* 1903

2a Adolph Carl; *b* 1823; *m* 1850 his cousin (Caroline) Julie Anselme de Rothschild and *d* 1900

3a Wilhelm Carl; *b* 1828; *m* 1849 his cousin Hannah Mathilde, dau of Anselm de Rothschild, and *d* 25 Jan 1901, having had, with an est dau (*d* young):

1b Adelheid; *b* 1853; *m* 1877 Edmond James (*d* 1934) and *d* 1935

2b Minna Caroline; *b* 1857; *m* 1878 Maximilian Benedikt Heyum GOLDSCHMIDT later GOLDSCHMIDT-ROTHSCHILD (*d* 1940) and *d* 1903

1a Charlotte; *b* 1819; *m* 1836 her cousin Lionel de Rothschild (*see below*) and had issue

(5) JACOB later JAMES Mayer, of Paris; *b* 1792; fndr French branch of the family; *m* 1824 his niece Betty (*d* 1856) and *d* 1868, leaving:

1a Mayer Alphonse; *b* 1827; *m* 1857 his cousin Leonora, of the UK branch (*see below*) and *d* 26 May 1905, having had, with an er s (*d* unm):

1b Edouard Alphonse James; *b* 1868; *m* 1905 Germaine Alice Halphen (*d* 1975) and *d* 1949, having had, with an er s (*d* young):

1c *Guy Edouard Alphonse Paul [Baron Guy de Rothschild, 2 rue Saint-Louis-en-l'Isle, 75008 Paris, France]; *b* 1909; *educ* Lycées Condorcet et Louis le Grand, Facultés de Droit et des Lettres; Associé de MM de Rothschild Freres 1936–67, Pres Compagnie du Chemin de Fer du Nord 1949–68, Banque Rothschild 1968–78, Societé Imétal 1975–79, served WW II (Croix de Guerre), Chev du Mérite Agricole 1948, Offr Legn Hon 1959; author: *The Whims of Fortune* (1985); *m* 1st

1937 (*divorce* 19–) Alix Hermine Jeanette Schey von Koromla (*d* 1982) and has:

1d *David René James; *b* 1942; *m* 1974 *Olimpia Anna Aldobrandini and has:

1e *Alexandre Guy Francesco; *b* 1980

1e *Lavinia Anne Alix; *b* 1976

2e *Stephanie Anne-Marie Héelène; *b* 1977

1c (cont.) Baron Guy de Rothschild *m* 2nd 1957 Marie Hélène Naïla Stephanie Josina van Zuylen de Nyevelt (*d* 1996), formerly w of Count François de Nicolay, and by her has:

2d *Edouard Etienne Alphonse; *b* 1957; *m* *Mathilde Marie Alexe Christianne, dau of Etienne Coche de la Ferté and formerly w of Sir Valentine Abdy, 6th Bt (*qv*)

1c *Jacqueline Rebecca Louise; *b* 1911; *m* 1st 1930 Robert Paul Michel Calmann-Lévy; *m* 2nd 1937 Gregor Piatigorsky (*d* 1976)

2c *Bethsabée Louise Emilie Béatrix; *b* 1914; *m* 1948 Donald Bloomingdale (*d* 1954)

1b Bettina Caroline; *b* 1858; *m* 1876 her cousin Salomon Albert Anselm Rothschild

2b Charlotte Béatrix; *b* 1864; *m* 1883 Maurice Ephrussi (*d* 1916) and *d* 1934

2a Gustave Samuel James; *b* 1829; *m* 1859 Cécile Anspach (*d* 1912) and *d* 1911, having had, with two er sons (*d* unm):

1b Robert Philippe Gustave; *b* 1880; *m* 1907 Gabrielle Nelly Régine Beer (*d* 1945) and *d* 1946, leaving:

1c James Gustave Jules Alain; *b* 1910; *m* 1938 *Mary Germaine Nathalie Chauvin de Treuil and *d* 1982, leaving:

1d *Eric Alain Robert David; *b* 1940; *m* 1983 *Maria Beatrice Caracciolo di Forino

2d *Robert James; *b* 1947

1d *Béatrice Juliette Ruth; *b* 1939; *m* 1st 1962 Armand Angliviel de la Beaumelle (*d* 1964); *m* 2nd 1981 *Pierre Max Rosenberg

2c *Elie Robert; *b* 1917; *m* 1942 *Liliane Elisabeth Victoire Fould-Springer and has:

1d *Michel Nathaniel Robert Eugène; *b* 1946; *m* 1975 *Nili Limon and has:

1e *Raphael Benjamin Jacob; *b* 1976

1e *Esther Eva; *b* 1979

1d *Nelly Rachel Cécile; *b* 1947; *m* 1970 *Adam John Munthe and has issue (*see* REA, B)

2d *Elisabeth Clarice Esther Gustava; *b* 1952; *m* 1970 *March Ernest Leland

1c *Diane Cécile Alice Juliette; *b* 1907; *m* 1st 1932 (*divorce* 19–) Anatole Muhlstein (*d* 1957); *m* 2nd 1952 Giuseppe Benvenuti (*d* 1967)

2c *Cécile Léonie Eugénie Gudule Lucie; *b* 1913

1b Zoe Lucie Betty; *b* 1863; *m* 1882 Baron Leon Lambert (*d* 1919) and *d* 1916

2b Aline Caroline; *b* 1867; *m* 1887 Sir Edward Albert Sassoon (*d* 1912) and *d* 1909

3b Bertha Juliette; *b* 1870; *m* 1892 Baron David Emmanuel Leonino (*d* 1936) and *d* 1896

3a Salomon James; *b* 1835; *m* 1862 his cousin Adèle Hannah Charlotte (*d* 1922) and *d* 1864, leaving:

1b Hélène Betty Louise Caroline; *b* 1863; *m* 1887 Baron van Zuylen de Nyevelt (*d* 1934)

4a Edmond James; *b* 1845; fndr Rishon le Zion and Zichron Yaacov; *m* 1877 his cousin Adelheid, dau of Wilhelm Carl de Rothschild, and *d* 1934, leaving:

1b James (Jimmy) Armand Edmond, DCM, JP, DL, of Waddesdon Manor, Bucks, which he inherited from his cousin Alice; *b* 1878; *educ* Lycée Louis le Grand and Trin Coll Cambridge; settled UK; Maj Roy Fus WW I, MP (Lib) Isle of Ely 1929–45, Jt Parly Sec Min Supply 1945, Tstee Wallace Collection 1941–55; *m* 1913 Dorothy Mathilde, MBE, only dau of Eugene Pinto, and *d* 7 May 1957

2b Maurice Edmond Charles; *b* 1881; French Senator under Third Republic; *m* 1909 Noémi Claire Alice Palmyre Halphen (*d* 1968) and *d* 1957, leaving:

1c Edmond Adolphe Maurice Jules Jacques; *b* 30 Sept 1926; *educ* Geneva U; fndr La Compagnie Financière 1953, dir Banque Rothschild, Banque Privée Geneva and Château Clarke vineyard, chm Isrop, late Pres Israel Gen Bank Tel Aviv, head Israel Corp, Cdr Order Arts and Letters 1990 and Legn Hon 1994; *m* 1st 1958 (*divorce* 19–) Veselinka (Georgina ('Lina') Blanc) Vladova Gueorguieva; *m* 2nd 1963 *Nadine Nelly Jeannette Lhopitalier (the actress Nadine Tallier) [Baronne Edmond de Rothschild, Château de Pregny, Geneva, Switzerland] and *d* 3 Nov 1997, leaving:

1d *Benjamin Edmond Maurice; *b* 1963

1b Miriam Caroline Alexandrine; *b* 1881; *m* 1910 Albet Maximilian von Goldschmidt-Rothschild (*d* 1941) and *d* 1965

1a Charlotte; *b* 1825; *m* 1842 her cousin Nathaniel Rothschild (*see below*) and *d* 1899

(1) Schönge Jeannette; *b* 1771; *m* 1795 Benedict Moses Worms (*d* 1824) and *d* 1859

(2) Isabella; *b* 1781; *m* 1802 Bernhard Juda Sichel (*d* 1862) and *d* 1861

(3) Babette; *b* 1784; *m* 1808 Siegmur Leopold Dreyfus (*d* 1845) and *d* 1869

(4) Julie; *b* 1790; *m* 1811 Meyer Levin Beyfus (*d* 1860) and *d* 1815

(5) Henriette; *b* 1791; *m* 1815 Abraham Montefiore (*d* 1824), her bro Nathan's bro-in-law

2 Kalman Amschel; *m c* 1779 Bunle Schames and *d* 1782

3 Moses Amschel; *b* 1746; *m* 1762 Sorchen Lechnich (*d* 1799) and *d* 1794

1 Bele; *d* 1759

2 Gutelche; *b* 1755; *m* 1802 Salman Daniel Goldschmied Hameln (*d* 1813) and *d* 1812

The 3rd s,

NATHAN MAYER ROTHSCHILD, of London, where settled 1798 (naturalised 12 June 1804); *b* 16 Sept 1777; Austrian Consul London 1820 but did not assume the Austrian Barony; *m* 22 Oct 1806 Hannah, 3rd dau of Levi Barent Cohen (*see* WALEY-COHEN, Bt), and had:

1 LIONEL NATHAN

2 **Sir Anthony Nathan Rothschild, 1st Bt** (UK), so *cr* 12 Jan 1847, with remainder, failing heirs male of his body, to his er bro Lionel's sons; *b* 29 May 1810; *m* 30 March 1840 Louisa (*d* 22 Sept 1910), dau of Abraham Montefiore (grandfather of Sir Francis Montefiore, 1st and last Bt), and *dspm* 4 Jan 1876, leaving:

(1) Constance; *b* 1843; *m* 23 Nov 1877 1st and last Baron Battersea (*see* 1907 edn) and *dsp* 22 Nov 1931

(2) Annie; *b* 1844; *m* 12 Feb 1873 Hon Eliot Constantine Yorke, 4th s of 4th Earl of Hardwicke (*qv*), and *d* 21 Nov 1926

3 Nathaniel; *b* 2 July 1812; *m* 17 Aug 1842 his cousin Charlotte (*d* 20 June 1899), dau of James de Rothschild, of Paris, and *d* 19 Feb 1870, having had, with two yr sons and a dau (all *d* unm):

(1) Nathan James Edouard, of Paris; *b* 29 Oct 1844; *m* 11 Oct 1871 his cousin Laura Thérèse, dau of Mayer Carl Rothschild, of Frankfurt, and *d* 25 Oct 1884, leaving:

1a Henri James Nathaniel Charles; *b* 1872; *m* 1895 Mathilde Sophie Henriette de Weisweiller (*d* 1926) and *d* 1946, leaving:

1b James Nathaniel Charles Léopold; *b* 1896; *m* 1st 1923 Claude Dupont (*d* 1964); *m* 2nd 1966 *Yvette Choquet and *d* 1984, leaving by his 1st w:

1c *Nicole; *b* 1924

2c *Monique; *b* 1925; *m* 1st (*divorce* 19–) Jean-François Drach; *m* 2nd 1950 *Georges Halphen

2b Philippe; *b* 1902; *m* 1st 1935 Elisabeth de Chambure (*d* 1945); *m* 2nd 1954 Pauline Fairfax Potter (*d* 1976) and *d* 1988, leaving by his 1st w:

1c *Charles Henri; *b* 1937

1c *Philippine Mathilde Camille; *b* 1935; *m* 1961 *Jacques Sereys

1b Nadine Charlotte; *b* 1898; *m* 1919 Adrien Thierry (*d* 1961) and *d* 1958

4 Mayer ('Muffy') Amschel, of Mentmore, Bucks, DL; *b* 29 June 1818; MP Hythe; *m* 26 June 1850 his cousin Juliana (*d* 9 March 1877), est dau of Isaac Cohen (*see* WALEY-COHEN, Bt), and *d* 6 Feb 1874, leaving:

(1) Hannah; *m* 20 March 1878 5th Earl of Rosebery (*qv*) and *d* 19 Nov 1890, leaving issue

1 Charlotte; *m* her cousin Anselm Rothschild, s of Baron (Salomon Mayer) Rothschild, of Vienna, and *d* 17 May 1859, leaving issue

2 Hannah Mayer; *m* 29 April 1839 Hon Henry FitzRoy, yr s of 2nd Baron Southampton (*qv*), and *d* 2 Dec 1864, leaving issue

3 Louise; *b* 1820; *m* 6 April 1842 her cousin Mayer Charles Rothschild, of Frankfurt, and *d* 12 Dec 1894, leaving issue

NATHAN MAYER ROTHSCHILD *d* 28 July 1836; his est s,

BARON (LIONEL NATHAN) de ROTHSCHILD, of Gunnersbury Park, Isleworth, Middx; *b* 22 Nov 1807; *s* f as sr ptnr N M Rothschild and Sons; by roy licence 16 June 1838 was allowed with other heirs male of body of grantee to use title of Baron of Austria; elected MP (Lib) for City London 1847, 1849, 1852 and 1857, but only sat 1858–74 (insistence on full oath, to which he objected on religious grounds, having been dropped 1858); *m* 15 June 1836 his cousin Charlotte (*d* 13 March 1884), only dau of Baron Carl Mayer de Rothschild, of Naples, and had:

1 NATHAN MAYER (Sir), **2nd Bt**, and **1st Baron**

2 Alfred Charles, CVO, of Halton, nr Tring, DL London; *b* 20 July 1842; Tstee Nat Gallery and Wallace Collection, with N M Rothschild and Sons, Dir Bank of England 1836–90, Chev Legn Hon; *d* 31 Jan 1918; possibly the true f by Marie, w of Frederick Charles Wombwell (*see* WOMBWELL, Bt), of the latter couple's dau (Almina, Countess of Carnarvon; *qv*)

3 Leopold, CVO (1902), JP, DL Bucks; *b* 22 Nov 1845; *educ* Trin Coll Cambridge (BA 1867, MA 1870); Lt City London; *m* 19 Jan 1881 Marie, CBE (1920) (*d* 8 April 1837), dau of Achille Perugia, of Trieste, and *d* 29 May 1917, leaving:

(1) Lionel Nathan, OBE (1917), JP Bucks; *b* 25 Jan 1882; *educ* Harrow and Trin Coll Cambridge (MA); MP Aylesbury 1910–23; *m* 8 Oct 1912 Marie Louise Eugénie, Assoc CStJ (*d* 17 May 1975), yr dau of Edmund Beer, of Paris, and *d* 28 Jan 1942, leaving:

1a +Edmund Leopold, CBE (1997), TD [Edmund de Rothschild Esq CBE TD, Exbury House, Exbury, Hants SO4 1AF]; *b* 2 Jan 1916; *educ* Harrow and Trin Coll Cambridge (MA 1941); Maj RA (TA) WW II (wounded); merchant banker; dir Rothschild Continuation Ltd 1975–95 (chm 1970–75), dep chm British Newfoundland Corp 1963–69 and Churchill Falls (Labrador) Corp 1966–69; AUR Hydropower Ltd 1980–91; Pres: Assoc Jewish Ex-Servicemen and Women and Research Into Ageing; Govt Tstee Freedom from Hunger Campaign 1965–; V-Pres Queen's Nursing Inst; memb: Asia Ctee BNEC 1970–71 (Chm 1971) and Cncl Roy Nat Pension Fund for Nurses to 1996; Freeman City London; Liveryman Fishmongers' Co 1949–; Hon LLD Memorial U Newfoundland 1961, Hon DSc Salford, Order Sacred Treasure 1st Cl Japan, author: *Window on the World* (1949) and *A Gilt-Edged Life: Memoirs* (1998); *m* 1st 22 June 1948 Elizabeth Edith (*d* 1980), only dau of Marcel Lentner, of Vienna; *m* 2nd 1982 *Anne, widow of J Malcolm Harrison, and by his 1st w has:

1b +Nicholas David; *b* 10 Oct 1951; *educ* Harrow; *m* 1985 *Caroline Jeanne Lucy, dau of Lawrence Darvall, of Reading, and adopted:

*Chloe Alix Irina; *b* 1990

2b +(David) Lionel; *b* 28 Nov 1955; *educ* Harrow; author: *The Rothschild Gardens* (1996); *m* 1991 *Louise de C, dau of Dr P M de C Williams, of Boar's Hill, Oxford, and has:

1c +Leopold James; *b* 1994

2c *Amschel Nathaniel; *b* 3 Sept 1995

1c *Elizabeth Naomi; *b* 1992

1b *Katherine Juliette [Mrs Marcus Agius, 7 South Terrace, London SW7 2TB]; *b* 11 July 1949; *m* 10 July 1971 *Marcus Ambrose Paul Agius, yst s of Alfred Agius, of Kensington, and has:

1c *Marie-Louise Eleanor; *b* 27 Nov 1977

2c *Lara Sophie Elizabeth; *b* 1980

2b *Charlotte Henrietta; *b* 28 Nov 1955; *m* 1990 *Nigel S Brown, yr s of Michael G H Brown

1a (cont.) Edmund de Rothschild *m* 2nd 26 April 1982 *Anne Evelyn, JP, widow of Lt-Col J Malcolm Harrison, OBE, TD

2a +Leopold David, CBE (1985) [Leopold de Rothschild Esq CBE, New Court, St Swithin's Lane, London EC4P 4DU]; *b* 12 May 1927; *educ* Harrow and Trin Coll Cambridge; dir N M Rothschild and Sons 1970– and Bank of England 1970–83, chm: Cncl RCM 1988–, Tstee Sci Museum 1987–98, memb cncl Winston Churchill Meml Tst 1990–, Orders: Francisco de Miranda 1st Cl Venezuela, Merit Chile, Southern Cross Brazil, Aztec Eagle Mexico

1a *Rosemary Leonora Ruth [Mrs Antony Seys, 31 The Mansion, Albury Park, Guildford, Surrey GU5 9BB]; *b* 21 Sept 1913; *m* 1st 3 July 1934 (*divorce* 1942) Maj Hon Denis Gomer Berry and has issue (*see* KEMSLEY, V); *m* 2nd 18 Feb 1942 Maj (John) Antony Seys (*d* 1989), 2nd s of Godfrey William Seys, of Wirewoods Green, Glos, and by him has:

1b *David Godfrey Antony [David Seys Esq, Aston House, Blackheath, Surrey GU4 8RD]; *b* 16 Oct 1947; *educ* Harrow; *m* 1978 *Nicola Barrington Baird and has:

1c *Alexander Antony David; *b* 4 Aug 1980

2c *Philip Christopher Hugh; *b* 1984

2a *Naomi Louisa Nina [Mme Bertrand Goldschmidt, 11 Boulevard Flandrin, 75116 Paris, France]; *b* 22 Oct 1920; *m* 1st 2 Oct 1941 Jean Pierre Reinach (*ka* 31 May 1942), s of Adolphe Reinach, of Paris, and has:

1b *Jocelyne Marguerite Marie Louise; *b* 18 Oct 1942; *m* 18 March 1965 *Claude Brice, of Paris, s of Robert Brice, of Nancy, and has issue

2a (cont.) Mme Reinach *m* 2nd 26 Feb 1947 *Bertrand Léopold Goldschmidt, s of Paul Goldschmidt, of Paris, and by him has:

1b *Paul Lionel; *b* 4 Nov 1952; *m* 1982 (*divorce* 1997) Cynthia Hampton and has issue

2b *Emma Louise; *b* 25 Oct 1955; *m* 1987 *David Machover and has issue

(2) Evelyn Achille; *b* 6 Jan 1886; *educ* Trin Coll Cambridge (BA); Maj Bucks Yeo WW I (despatches); *d* 17 Nov 1917 of wounds recd in action

(3) Anthony Gustav, DL Bucks; *b* 26 June 1887; *educ* Harrow and Trin Coll Cambridge (BA 1910, MA 1913); Maj Bucks Yeo WW I (wounded, despatches), ptnr N M Rothschild and Sons; *m* 10 June 1926 Yvonne Lydia Louise (*d* 6 Jan 1977), est dau of Robert Cahen d'Anvers, of Paris, and *d* 5 Feb 1961, leaving:

1a +Evelyn Robert Adrian (Sir) [Sir Evelyn de Rothschild, Ascott, Wing, Bucks]; *b* 29 Aug 1931; *educ* Harrow (Govr 1976) and Trin Coll Cambridge; chm N M Rothschild and Sons, dir Charter Consolidated 1973–, chm: *Economist* 1972–89, Utd Racecourses 1977–94, Br Merchant Banking and Securities Houses Assoc 1985–89, ktd 1989, memb Prince of Wales's Inst of Architecture to Dec 1996, Hon BSc and BEcon Hull 1994; *m* 1st 30 Sept 1966 (*divorce* 1971) Jeannette Ellen Dorothy (*d* 1981), only dau of Ernest Bishop, of Hastings; *m* 2nd 1 July 1973 *Victoria Lou, dau of Lewis Schott, of New York, and by her has:

1b +Anthony James; *b* 30 Jan 1977; *educ* Harrow; record producer (fndr Bullion Records 1996)

2b +David Mayer; *b* 25 Aug 1978

1b *Jessica; *b* 5 June 1974; *educ* Edinburgh U; lit ed *Tatler*, model

1a *Renée Louise Marie [Mrs Peter Robeson, Fences Farm, Tyringham, Bucks]; *b* 23 March 1927; *m* 17 Feb 1955 *Peter David Robeson, equestrian, s of Gilbert Buxton Robeson

2a Anne Sonia; *b* 30 May 1930; *d* 1971

1 Leonora; *m* 4 March 1857 her cousin Baron Mayer Alphonse de Rothschild, of the French branch, and *d* 6 Jan 1911, leaving issue

2 Evelina; *m* 7 June 1865 her cousin Baron Ferdinand James de Rothschild, JP, of Lodge Hill, Bucks, 2nd s of Baron Anselm de Rothschild, of the Frankfurt branch, and *dsp* 4 Dec 1866

BARON (LIONEL NATHAN) De ROTHSCHILD *d* 3 June 1879; his est s,

Sir Nathan Mayer Rothschild, 2nd Bt, and **1st Baron Rothschild**, of Tring, Co Hertford (UK), so *cr* 29 June 1885, GCVO (1902), PC (1902); *b* 8 Nov 1840; *educ* Trin Coll Cambridge; MP (Lib) Aylesbury 1865–85, Ld Lt Bucks 1889–1915, Lt City London, Capt Bucks Yeo Cav, Hon LLD Cantab 1911; *m* 17 April 1867 his cousin Emma Louisa (*d* Jan 1935), dau of Baron Mayer Carl Rothschild, formerly of the Naples branch but by now of Frankfurt, and *d* 31 March 1915, leaving:

1 LIONEL WALTER ROTHSCHILD, **2nd Baron Rothschild**, JP, DL Bucks; *b* 8 Feb 1868; Maj Bucks Yeo, MP (Lib U) Aylesbury 1899–1910, Tstee Br Museum 1899, Lt City London, FRS, Hon PhD Giessen; *d* unm 27 Aug 1937

2 (Nathaniel) Charles, JP Northants; *b* 9 May 1877; *educ* Trin Coll Cambridge (MA); Lt City London, High Sheriff Northants 1905; *m* 6 Feb 1907 Rozsika (*d* 30 June 1940), 3rd dau of Capt Alfred von Wertheimstein, of Nagyvarad, Hungary, and *d* by his own hand 12 Oct 1923, leaving:

(1) NATHANIEL MAYER VICTOR, **3rd Baron**

(1) *Miriam Louisa, CBE (1982) [The Hon Mrs Miriam Lane CBE, Ashton Wold, Oundle, Northants PE8 5LZ]; *b* 5 Aug 1908; granted with sisters 15 March 1983 rank of baron's daus; Tstee Natural History Museum 1967–75, Visiting Prof Roy Free Hosp, FRS 1985, Hon DSc: Oxon, Leicester, Hull, Göteborg, N Western, OU and Essex; author: *Catalogue Rothschild Collection of Fleas* (vols I–VI 1953–83), *Fleas, Flukes and Cuckoos* (co-author 1952), *The Butterfly Garden* (co-author 1983), *Dear Lord Rothschild* (1983), *Atlas of Insect Tissue* (co-author 1985), *Animals & Man* (1986), *Butterfly Cooing Like a Dove* (1990), *Rothschild Gardens* (1996), *Rothschild Reserves: Time and Fragile Nature* (1997); *m* 14 Aug 1943 (*divorce* 1957) Col George Henry Lane, MC, The Buffs, er s of Ernest Lanyi, of Budapest, and has had, with another s and dau (*d* young):

1a *Charles Daniel; *b* 1948

1a *Mary Rozsiska; b 1945
2a *Charlotte Theresa; b 1951
3a *Johanna Miriam; b 1951
(2) Elizabeth Charlotte; b 5 Nov 1909
(3) Kathleen Annie Pannonica; b 10 Dec 1913; m 15 Oct 1935 (divorce 1956) Lt-Col Baron Jules de Koenigswarter, French Min Plen USA, s of Baron Louis de Koenigswarter, of Paris, and had issue
1 Charlotte Louisa Adela Evelina; b 3 April 1873; m 4 Oct 1899 Maj Clive Behrens, JP, DL (d 28 Aug 1935), of Swinton Grange, Malton, Yorks, s of Edward Behrens, of Manchester, and d 9 May 1947, having had issue

The 2nd BARON's n,
NATHANIEL MAYER VICTOR ROTHSCHILD, **3rd Baron Rothschild**, GBE (1975), GM (1944); b 31 Oct 1910; educ Harrow, and Trin Coll Cambridge (PhD and MA 1937, Fell 1935–39, Hon Fell 1961); ScD 1950, Assist Dir Research Dept Zoology Cambridge 1950–70, FRS 1953, Hon Fell: Wolfson Coll Cambridge 1966, Inst Biology 1971, Imp Coll 1975, City U 1972, Bath U 1978, Weizmann Inst Sci Rehovoth 1982, Bellairs Research Inst McGill 1968, Hon DSc Newcastle, Manchester, Technion Haifa, Lt-Col Intell Corps WW II (despatches), dir BOAC 1946–58, Hon PhD Tel Aviv 1971, Hebrew U Jerusalem 1975, Bar-ilon U Israel 1980, Hon DUniv York 1980, Chm Ag Research Cncl 1948–58, memb Cncl Sci Policy 1965–66, Centl Advsy Cncl for Sci and Tech 1969, v-chm Shell Research Ltd 1961–63, chm 1990; Research Co-ordinator Roy Dutch Shell Gp 1965–70, chm Shell Research NV 1967–70, dir Shell Internat Research 1965–70, Shell Chemicals UK, Shell Internat 1969–70, Dir-Gen CPRS 1970–74, memb BBC Gen Advsy Cncl 1952–56 and 1963–70, chm N M Rothschild and Sons 1975, Assoc KStJ, US Bronze Star 1948, US Legn Merit 1946; m 1st 28 Dec 1933 (divorce 1946) Barbara (d 1989, having m 2nd (divorce 19–) Rex Warner (d 1986), of the FO, m 3rd 1961 Nico Hadjikyriakou-Ghika), only dau of St John Hutchinson, KC, and had:

1 (NATHANIEL CHARLES) JACOB ROTHSCHILD, **4th and present Baron Rothschild**
1 *Sarah [The Hon Mrs Daniel, 72 Victoria Park, Cambridge]; b 13 Sept 1934; educ St Hilda's Coll Oxford; m 1st 19– (divorce 19–) James Douglas Henry, of London; m 2nd 19– *— Daniel and by her 1st husb has:
(1) *Thomas James DANIEL; b 19–; m 1993 *Emma Louise Gilmour, yr dau of John Robert Purvis, CBE, of Gilmerton, St Andrews, Fife
(1) *Sharon; b 19–; m 19– *Da'ad de Gunzbourg and has:
1a *Patrice; b 19–
2 *Miranda; b 25 Dec 1940; m 1st 1962 Boudjemaa Boumaza (d 1964); m 2nd *Iain Thomas Watson

The **3rd Baron** m 2nd 14 Aug 1946 Teresa (Tess) Georgina, MBE (1945), JP (d 29 May 1996), 2nd dau of Robert John Grote Mayor, CB, and great-niece of Beatrice Webb (see 1940 edn PASSFIELD, B), and d March 1990, having by her had:
2 Benjamin Mayor; b and d 16 May 1952
3 Amschel Mayor James; b 18 April 1955; educ Leys Sch Cambridge and City U London; ciculation manager Literary Review in 1970s, ch exec Rothschild Asset Management 1990–93 (chm 1993–96), dir Sun Alliance, tstee Hanadiv Fndn; m 8 Jan 1981 *Anita Patience [The Hon Mrs Amschel Rothschild, Rushbrook, Bury St Edmunds, Suffolk], 3rd dau of James Edward Alexander Rundel Guinness (see GUINNESS, Bt), and d by his own hand 8 July 1996, leaving:
(1) +James Amschel Victor; b 1985
(1) *Kate Emma; b 29 July 1982
(2) *Alice Miranda; b 29 Nov 1983
3 *Emma Georgina [The Hon Mrs Sen, King's College, Cambridge CB2 1ST]; b 16 May 1948; educ Somerville Coll Oxford (MA) and M I T, USA; Fell 1988– and Dir Centre for History and Economics 1992– King's Coll Cambridge, author: Paradise Lost: the decline of the auto-industrial age (1973); m 1991 *Prof Amartya Kumar Sen
4 *Victoria Katherine [The Hon Victoria Rothschild, 2b Addison Ave, London W11]; b 13 Aug 1953; educ Bedford Coll, London

ROWALLAN

Arms: Quarterly, 1st and 4th, arg. a key fessways, wards downwards, between two ravens sa. (for CORBETT); 2nd and 3rd, az. a chevron or between two bear's heads couped arg. muzzled gu. in chief, and in base a cross moline of the third (for POLSON). **Crest:** A branch of oak, thereon a raven sa. **Supporters:** Dexter, a salmon ppr. holding in its mouth a jewelled ring or; sinister, a seal ppr. **Motto:** (over crest) Deus pascit corvos ('God feeds the ravens'). **Creation:** B. (UK) 27 June 1911.

THE 4TH BARON ROWALLAN, of Rowallan, Co Ayr (John Polson Cameron Corbett) [The Rt Hon The Lord Rowallan, Meiklemosside, Fenwick, Ayrshire KA3 6AY]; b 8 March 1947; s f 1993; educ Eton and RAC Cirencester; chartered surveyor and farmer, C parly candidate twice in 1970s, dir: Rowallan Hldgs 1994–, Rowallan Ltd 1996– and Rowallan Activity Centre Ltd 1991–, chm Turner-Dundas 1989– and Loch Eoin Covenanters Tst 1977–; m 1st 6 Feb 1971 (divorce 1983) (Susan) Jane Dianne, dau of James A Green, of New Farm House, South Linden, Northumberland, and has:
1 +JASON WILLIAM POLSON CAMERON; b 21 April 1972; educ Glenalmond and RAC Cirencester
1 *Joanne Gwyn Alice Cameron; b 8 June 1974
The 4th BARON m 2nd 1984 (divorce 1994) Sandrew Filomena, dau of William Bryson, of Holland Green, Kilmaurs, Ayrshire, and by her has:
2 +(Jonathan Arthur) Cameron; b 1985
2 *Soay Mairi Cameron; b 1988
The 4th BARON m 3rd 1995 *Claire Dinning, dau of Robert Laidler, of Tyne and Wear

Lineage: LORIMER CORBETT, of Glasgow; Dr; had:
THOMAS CORBETT, of South Park, Cove, Dunbartonshire, JP; b 6 March 1822; m Sarah (d 1905), dau of Archibald Cameron, and had:
1 Thomas Lorimer, JP London; b 18 Dec 1854; MP N Down 1900–10, Dep Chm LCC 1899; m 1880 —, dau of John Connell, of Tooting Common, and dsp 6 April 1910
2 ARCHIBALD CAMERON, **1st Baron**
3 Harry, of Arngask, Perths; d unm
1 Jessie; m J P Curran, of St Andrews, and had issue
THOMAS CORBETT d 1 April 1880; his 2nd s,
ARCHIBALD CAMERON CORBETT, **1st Baron Rowallan**, of Rowallan, Co Ayr (UK), so cr 27 June 1911, JP Warwicks and Lanarks; b 23 May 1856; MP (first Lib, Lib U 1886–1908, Ind Lib thereafter) Glasgow Tradeston 1885–1911 (fought N Warwicks 1884); m 8 Oct 1887 Alice Mary (d 10 July 1902), only dau of John Polson, of Castle Levan, Gourock, and d 19 March 1933, leaving, with a yr s (Arthur Cameron, b 6 March 1898, F/Sub-Lt RNAS, ka 4 Dec 1916) and a dau (Elsie Cameron, d unm 13 Feb 1976):
THOMAS GODFREY POLSON CORBETT, **2nd Baron Rowallan**, KT 1957, KBE 1951, MC, (1917), TD; b 19 Dec 1895; educ Eton; Maj Ayrshire Yeo (TAR), Gren Gds SR, WW I (wounded), WW II as Lt-Col cmdg 6th Bn Roy Scots Fus, Ch Scout Cwlth and Empire 1945–59, Govr Tasmania 1959–63, Hon Col Roy Tasmania Regt 1960–63, Hon LLD McGill 1948, Glasgow 1952 and Birmingham 1957, Hon Freeman Edinburgh 1957, KStJ 1959; m 14 Aug 1918 Gwyn Mervyn, CStJ (d 14 Sept 1971), est dau of Joseph Bowman Grimond, and had:
1 ARTHUR CAMERON, **3rd Baron**
2 Thomas Anthony (Atty), MC (1946); Capt Gren Gds WW II (wounded twice, despatches), racehorse trainer; d car crash 27 Nov 1976
3 John Polson; b 9 Oct 1924; educ Eton; Lt Gren Gds WW II; ka July 1944
4 +Joseph Mervyn [The Hon Joseph Corbett, The Old Rectory, Coates, Glos]; b 22 April 1929; educ Eton and Corpus Christi Coll Cambridge (BA 1953); Lt Roy Scots Fus; m 20 Feb 1960 *Hon Catherine Lyon-Dalberg-Acton, 3rd dau of 3rd Baron Acton (qv), and has:
(1) +Sebastian Antony [Sebastian Corbett Esq, Chittlegrove, Rendcomb, Glos GL3 7DG]; b 23 Jan 1963; educ Eton and RAC Cirencester; m 1991 *Mrs Doran Elizabeth Ann McPherson, only dau of Alan Leary, and has:

1a +George Alan Cameron; *b* 1993

(1) *Victoria [Mrs Hugh Merrill, 21 Bristol Gdns, London W9 2JQ]; *b* 10 Jan 1961; *m* 1988 *Hugh Merrill, MVO, s of Eric Merrill, of Monkseaton, Tyne and Wear, and has:

    1a *James Joseph; *b* 1989

    2a *Guy Charles; *b* 1992

    3a *Thomas Hugh; *b* 1994

5 +Robert Cameron [The Hon Robert Corbett, Stair House, Stair, Ayrshire]; *b* 29 Nov 1940; *educ* Eton and Ch Ch Oxford;

1 *Fiona Elizabeth Cameron [The Hon Mrs Patterson, Kisby's Farm, Ecchinswell, Berks RG15 4TS]; *b* 14 Nov 1942; *m* 6 Aug 1966 (*divorce* 1972) David Henry Amherst Cecil and has issue (*see* AMHERST OF HACKNEY, B); *m* 2nd 1974 *William Garry Patterson, late Maj Life Gds, and by him has:

    (1) *Joseph Robert William; *b* 1981

The 2nd BARON *d* 30 Nov 1977; his est s,

ARTHUR CAMERON CORBETT, **3rd Baron Rowallan**, DL (1929); *b* 17 Dec 1919; *educ* Eton and Balliol Coll Oxford; Capt Ayrshire Yeo WW II (despatches), Croix de Guerre; *m* 1st 23 June 1945 (*divorce* 1962) Eleanor Mary (*m* 2nd 1963 Col (Richard) Derek Cardiff), only dau of George Frederic Boyle (*see* GLASGOW, E), and had:

1 JOHN POLSON CAMERON CORBETT, **4th and present Baron Rowallan**

1 *Sarah Elizabeth Cameron [The Hon Mrs Maclean, 8 Elthiron Rd, London SW6]; *b* 5 April 1949; *m* 17 April 1968 *(Lachlan) Roderick Maclean, er s of Maj Gordon Maclean, of N Warnborough, Hants, and has:

    (1) *Iona Charlotte; *b* 30 March 1969

    (2) *Sophy Emma; *b* 15 Feb 1972

2 *Anne Mary Cameron [The Hon Mrs Turner, Prescott House, Tiverton, Devon EX16 5NB]; *b* 3 Sept 1953; *m* 18 April 1972 *Rodney John Turner, s of R H Turner, of The Hall, Sonning, Berks, and has:

    (1) *James Antony; *b* 14 Aug 1975; *educ* Milton Abbey

    (2) *Charles Rory; *b* 12 Dec 1981; *educ* Eton

    (1) *Nicola Anne Maria; *b* 14 Feb 1974

    (2) *Arabella Mary Claire; *b* 16 Oct 1984

3 *Rosalind Eleanor Cameron [The Hon Mrs Sacher, 11 Lansdowne Crescent, London W11 2N]; *b* 2 Jan 1958; *m* 2 May 1977 *Jeremy Sacher, 2nd s of Michael Sacher, of Belgravia, and has:

    (1) *Harry; *b* 1987

    (1) *Chloe Emma; *b* 14 Aug 1979

    (2) *Charlotte Daisy; *b* 25 April 1982

The **3rd Baron** *m* 2nd 10 Sept 1963 (*annulled* 1970) April Ashley, *né(e)* George Jamieson, formerly with merchant Navy, issue of Frederick Jackson, of Liverpool, and *d* 1993

ROWLEY

Arms: Arg. on a bend engrailed between two Cornish choughs sa. three escallops of the field. **Crest:** A mullet pierced or. **Supporters:** Two Cornish choughs ppr., navally crowned or, each gorged with a riband, therefrom pendant a representation of the Order of Maria Theresa. **Motto:** *Ventis secundis* ('With favouring winds'). **Creation:** Bt. (GB) 27 June 1786 (of Tendring) and (UK) 21 March 1836 (of Hill House).

SIR CHARLES ROBERT ROWLEY, 7TH BT, of Hill House, Berkshire, and **8th Bt**, of Tendring, Suffolk [Sir Charles Rowley Bt, Naseby Hall, Northants NN6 6DP; 21 Tedworth Sq, London SW3 4DR]; *b* 15 March 1926; *s* f 1971 in btcy of Hill House and cousin 1997 in btcy of Tendring; *educ* Wellington; *m* 10 Dec 1952 *Astrid Pennington Cleife, only dau of Sir Arthur Massey, CBE, MD, of Kensington, and has:

1 +RICHARD CHARLES [Richard Rowley Esq, 15 Worfield St, London SW11 4RB]; *b* 14 Aug 1959; *educ* Eton and Exeter Coll Oxford (BA); *m* 1989 *(Elizabeth) Alison, dau of (Arthur) Henry Bellingham (*see* BELLINGHAM, Bt), and has:

    (1) +Joshua Andrew; *b* 1989

(2) +William Henry Stuart; *b* 1992

1 *Caroline Astrid; *b* 28 June 1955; *m* 1979 *Edwin Rudolph Joseph March Phillipps de Lisle and has:

    (1) *Alexander Edwin; *b* 1983

    (2) *Nicholas Charles; *b* 1991

Lineage: Sir WILLIAM ROWLEY, KB; Adml of the Fleet; served RN 1716–46; *m* by 21 July 1729 Arabella (*d* Feb 1784), dau and heir of Thomas Dawson (*k* Siege of Gibraltar 1705), s and heir of Thomas Dawson, of Castle Dawson, Co Londonderry, Capt Army, and had:

1 Thomas; *d* unm

2 JOSHUA (Sir), **1st Bt** (of Tendring)

3 Clotworthy; *b* 1731; barrister, MP Downpatrick; *m* 1766 Letitia (*d* 1776), dau of Samuel Campbell, of Bath and Mount Campbell, Co Leitrim, and *d* 1805, leaving:

    (1) William; Commr Customs, Recorder Kinsale, Co Cork; *d* unm 1811

    (2) Sir JOSIAS ROWLEY, 1st and last Bt (UK), so *cr* 2 Nov 1813, GCB, GCMG; Adml; *d* unm 10 Jan 1842, when the btcy expired

    (3) Samuel Campbell; *b* 19 Jan 1774; R-Adml the White; *m* 1st Mary, dau of — Thompson, of White Park, Co Fermagh; *m* 2nd 4 Nov 1830 Mary, only dau of Edmund Cronin, of Newtown, Co Kilkenny, and *dsp*

    (4) John (Rev); LLD, Preb Christ Church, Dublin; *m* 30 Sept 1826 Catherine, 2nd dau of Joseph Clarke, of Kilburn Priory, Middx, and had:

        1a Mary; *m* Charles Vigogne, of Wicklow, and had issue

4 William; Major-Gen; *d* unm

1 Arabella; *m* 1st Capt Martin, RN; *m* 2nd Col G Gibbs, of Horkesley Park, Suffolk

Sir WILLIAM *d* 1 Jan 1768; his 2nd s,

Sir WILLIAM Rowley, 1st Bt (GB), so *cr* 27 June 1786; *b* 1 May 1734; R-Adml the White; *m* 18 April 1759 Sarah (*d* 26 Dec 1812), dau and heiress of Bartholomew Burton, and *d* 26 Feb 1790, having had:

1 **Sir William Rowley, 2nd Bt;** *b* 10 Feb 1761; *m* March 1785 Susannah Edith (*d* 21 Jan 1850), dau of Adml Sir Robert Harland, Bt, of Sproughton, Suffolk (*see* 1834 edn), and *d* 20 Oct 1832, having had, with two daus (*d* unm):

    (1) William Barrington Harland; *b* 9 March 1787; *m* 1819 Marianne, dau of J Hart, and *dsp*

    (2) **Sir Joshua Ricketts Rowley, 3rd Bt;** V-Adml; *m* 10 Aug 1824 Charlotte (*d* 11 Dec 1862), only dau of John Moseley, of Great Glemham House, Suffolk, and *dsp* 18 March 1857

    (3) **Sir Charles Robert Rowley, 4th Bt;** *b* 5 May 1800; Capt Gren Gds; *m* 14 Sept 1830 Hon Maria Louis Vanneck (*d* 16 March 1878), only dau of 2nd Baron Huntingfield (*qv*), and *d* 8 Sept 1888, having had, with seven daus (*d* unm):

        1a William Arcedeckne; *b* 30 Dec 1836; *d* 20 Jan 1853

        2a **Sir Joshua Thellusson Rowley, 5th Bt,** VD, JP, DL; *b* 8 Feb 1838; Hon Col 5th Bn Suffolk Regt; *m* 19 Oct 1887 Hon Louisa Helene Brownlow (*d* 5 Dec 1922), Maid-of-Honour to HM QUEEN VICTORIA, dau of 2nd Baron Lurgan, KP (*see* 1970 edn), and *d* 23 April 1931, having had:

           1b **Sir Charles Samuel Rowley, 6th Bt,** OBE (1962), TD (1942), JP, DL; *b* 23 Dec 1891; *educ* Eton and Trin Coll Cambridge; Col cmdg 55th (Suffolk and Norfolk Yeo) Anti-Tank Regt, formerly 108th Field Bde, RA (TA), late Capt Gren Gds, served WW I and WW II; *m* 7 Jan 1920 Margery Frances (*d* 15 March 1977), est dau of Sir Nicholas Henry Bacon, 12th/13th Bt (*qv*), and *d* 19 Jan 1962, leaving:

              1c **Sir Joshua Francis Rowley, 7th Bt,** JP (Suffolk 1978), of Tendring Hall, Suffolk; *b* 31 Dec 1920; *educ* Eton and Trin Coll Cambridge; Dep Sec Nat Tst 1952–55, Suffolk: chm W Suffolk CC 1971–74, CC 1976–78, High Sheriff 1971, Ld Lt 1978–94 (V-Lt 1973–78, DL 1968–73), Capt Gren Gds WW II, Hon DCL UEA 1991; *m* 13 June 1959 Hon Celia Ella Vere Monckton (*d* 13 Dec 1997), 2nd dau of 8th Viscount Galway (*qv*), and *d* 21 Feb 1997, leaving:

                1d *(Susan) Emily Frances [Mrs Robert Holden, Sibdon Castle, Craven Arms, Salop SY7 9AQ; 94 Frithville Gdns, London W12 7JW]; *b* 6 Oct 1965; *m* 1988 *Robert David Holden (*see* POWIS, E) and has:

                  1e *Hubert Joshua Robert; *b* 10 March 1997

                  1e *Lucia Hermione Sophia; *b* 10 March 1997

             1c *(Alethea) Susan [Mrs Henry Townshend, Brook Hall, Bramfield, Suffolk]; *b* 27 Sept 1922; *m* 31 Dec 1949 *Henry Reginald Townshend, MBE, only s of Reginald Brooks Townshend, OBE, and has:

                1d *James Reginald; *b* 1954; *m* 1980 *Olivia Mora Matthey and has:

                  1e *Henry Roscoe; *b* 1984

                  1e *Georgina Hermione; *b* 1982

                2d *Robert Charles; *b* 1956; *m* 1983 *Fiona Elizabeth Mary Fraser and has:

                  1e *Hugh Charles; *b* 1984

                  2e *A son; *b* 1991

                  1e *Arabella Charlotte; *b* 1987

                1d *Albinia Jane; *b* 1952; *m* 1977 *James Anthony Stoddart Murray and has:

                  1e *Susannah Albinia Frances; *b* 1979

                  2e *Annabel Katharine Law; *b* 1981

              2c Prudence Louisa; *b* 10 Sept 1926; *m* 23 April 1954 *Hon Martin Denzil Fortescue, yr s of 6th Earl Fortescue (*qv*), and *d* 1992, having had issue

           2b Joshua Robert; *b* 1 March 1893; Capt HLI, attd 5th Bn Suffolk Regt; *ka* 2 Nov 1917

        3a Harland; *b* 30 Oct 1840; *d* 27 Aug 1854

        4a Charles Robert; *b* 29 Dec 1849; Col Gren Gds; *d* 5 April 1933

        1a Arethusa Marianne; *m* 11 May 1859 Col William Beeston Long, JP, DL, of Hurts Hall, Saxmundham, est s of William Long, JP, DL, of Hurts Hall, and *dsp* 18 Dec 1889. He *d* 2 Sept 1892

2a Charlotte Louisa; *m* 16 Aug 1867 3rd Baron Hatherton (*qv*) and *d* 19 Feb 1923, leaving issue

3a Edith Sophia; *m* 12 Aug 1874 Sir Hugh Cholmeley, 3rd Bt (*qv*), and *d* 26 Dec 1910, leaving issue

4a Katherine; *m* 29 Jan 1881 Rev Hon Cecil James Littleton (*see* HATHERTON, B) and *d* 16 April 1935

(1) Sarah Marianne; *m* 8 Sept 1815 Sir George Dashwood, 4th Bt (*qv*), of Kirtlington Park, and *d* 24 March 1877, leaving issue

(2) Susan Arabella; *m* 2 Nov 1820 Col Douglas Mercer and *d* 1862

(3) Georgiana; *m* 30 Nov 1841 John Blagrave, of Calcot (*d* 21 June 1867)

(4) Jane; *m* 31 March 1823 Charles Calvert, of Ockley Court, Surrey, and had issue. He *d* 8 Sept 1832

2 Bartholomew Samuel; *b* 10 June 1764; V-Adml the Blue, C-in-C Jamaica; *m* Arabella, widow of Benjamin Wade, of Newgrange, Yorks, and dau of Capt William Martin, RN, and *d* 7 Oct 1811

3 Joshua (Rev); *b* 16 Oct 1769; *m* 2 April 1799 Mary, dau of Henry Scourfield, and had issue

4 CHARLES (Sir), **1st Bt** (of Hill House)

1 Philadelphia; *m* 27 Feb 1798 Sir Charles Cotton, 5th Bt, of Landwade, Cambs (*see* 1863 edn), and *d* 5 April 1855, having had issue. He *d* 24 Feb 1812

2 Sarah; *m* William Martin, of Hemmingston Hall, Suffolk, and *d* 21 Dec 1841

3 Arabella; *m* Peter Godfrey, of Old Hall, Suffolk

The 1st Bt (of Tendring's) 4th s,

Sir Charles Rowley, 1st Bt (UK), so *cr* 21 March 1836, of Hill House, Berks, GCB, GCH; *b* 16 Dec 1770; Adml the White; *m* 7 Dec 1797 Elizabeth (*d* 11 Jan 1838), dau of Sir Richard King, Bt, and *d* 13 Oct 1845, having had:

1 **Sir Charles Rowley, 2nd Bt**, DL Suffolk; *b* 16 Feb 1801; Lt-Col; *m* 1st 31 Aug 1822 Frances (*d* 21 April 1834), only dau of John Evelyn, of Wootton, Surrey, and had, with a dau (*d* unm):

(1) Charles Evelyn; *b* 30 June 1824; Capt RN; *m* 11 May 1848 Grace Anna (*d* 29 Sept 1885), dau of John Ward Boughton Leigh, of Brownsover Hall, Warwicks, and *dsp* & *vp* 18 June 1879

(2) Albert Evelyn; Lt Gren Gds; *ka* Sebastopol 16 Oct 1854

(1) Sophia Frances Evelyn; *m* 15 July 1841 Edward Nourse Harvey, of Over-Ross, and *d* 15 July 1896. He *d* 1889

1 (cont.) **Sir Charles** *m* 2nd 5 April 1843 Peroline (*d* 23 July 1883), only child of Michel Marcowitz, of Lyons, France, and *d* 23 Nov 1884

2 Burton; Lt RN; *d* 1822

3 George; *b* 25 Feb 1805; Maj 2nd Bombay Cav; *m* 13 April 1830 Emily Isabella (*d* 19 Jan 1896), dau of Lt-Col Robert Honner, of Lee Mount, Co Cork, and *d* 13 April 1848, leaving:

(1) GEORGE CHARLES ERSKINE (Sir), **3rd Bt**

(1) Emilie Elizabeth Burton; *m* 9 Aug 1853 Lt-Col F W Knight and *d* 17 Jan 1902. He *d* 27 Aug 1902

(2) Florence Grosvenor; *m* 1st 18 June 1861 Capt Hon John Cranch Walker Vivian and had issue (*see* VIVIAN, B); *m* 2nd 3 July 1872 5th Marquess of Waterford (*qv*) and *d* 4 April 1873

(3) Louisa Sophia Isabella; *m* 26 Oct 1878 Lt-Col Lucius Falkland Brancaleone Cary, Rifle Bde, of Torre Abbey, Devon, and *d* 3 July 1934, leaving issue. He *d* July 1916

4 Richard Freeman; *b* March 1806; Capt RN; *m* 12 July 1828 Elizabeth Julia (*d* 18 Feb 1870), dau of John Angerstein, MP, of Weeting Hall, Norfolk, and Woodlands, Blackheath, Kent, and *d* 13 Aug 1854, leaving:

(1) Richard Brooke; *b* 13 May 1829; *m* 26 Feb 1874 Emily Margaret (*d* 18 June 1908), dau of William Anthony Harrison, and *dsp* 12 Nov 1906

(2) Charles John; *b* 24 Dec 1832; Adml, Naval ADC; *m* 9 May 1867 Alice Mary Arabella (*d* 27 Nov 1931), dau of George Cary Elwes, and *d* 11 Nov 1919, leaving:

1a Charles Pelham; *b* 26 April 1877; BA Oxon; Maj RGA; accidentally *k* 29 Oct 1916

2a Windsor Angerstein; *b* 2 Aug 1878; *d* unm 1 Nov 1946

1a May; *b* 11 May 1880; *d* unm 17 Feb 1965

(3) John Angerstein; *b* 20 Aug 1834; Capt 13th Foot; *m* 25 April 1860 Georgiana Augusta (*d* 1890) (*née* Catania), widow of Stewart Strogan, and *d* 26 May 1870, having had:

1a John Richard Frederick; *b* 16 Aug 1864; *m* 1897 Mary Hay (*d* 1902), dau of Rev William Hay Chapman, and *d* 1921, having had:

1b Charles John; *b* 1898; *m* 1 Dec 1917 Ronalda Bruce Margaret Wentworth (*d* 28 Dec 1979), est dau of Ronald Wentworth Beaumont (*see* ALLENDALE, V), and *d* 18 Jan 1927, leaving:

1c Vivian Charles Beaumont; *b* 15 April 1918; Roy Canadian Army 1st Div WW II (Canadian Volunteer Serv Medal with clasp); with Marine Div BC Govt to 1978; *m* 1st Marion Theodora Gibbs (*d* 14 July 1966 in a car accident); *m* 2nd Oct 1967 Elsie Kail (*d* 1991); *m* 3rd April 1989 *Connie Morris and *d* 24 Nov 1995, leaving by his 1st w:

1d +John Maylow, of Nelson, BC; *b* 7 April 1950; *m* 6 June 1984 *Pam Gravel and has:

1e +Charles Beaumont; *b* 5 Oct 1986

2e +Johnathon Adrian; *b* 18 May 1988

1d *Pauline Vivian, of Vancouver, BC; *b* 18 Feb 1946; *m* 19– (*divorce* 19–) Patrick Le May

2d *Pamela Jane [Mrs Frederick Hendy, #25–803 Hodgson Rd, Williams Lake, BC V2G 3R2, Canada]; *b* 18 Sept 1948; nurse; *m* 5 May 1972 *Frederick Wayne Hendy, Forest Ranger, and has:

1e *Michelle Renee; *b* 2 Feb 1974; BSc

2e *Cheryl Pauline; *b* 14 April 1977

1c *Evelyn [Mrs John Sutton, RR#3 S20 C13, Nelson, BC V1L 5P6, Canada]; *b* 1919; *m* *John H Sutton and has:

1d *Robert Hugh; *b* 20 June 1942; *m* — (*divorce*) and has:

1e *Benjamin Hugh; *b* 12 Aug 1984

1e *Tina Louise; *b* 15 July 1965

2d *Brian Rowley; *b* 26 Sept 1943; *m* 19– *Evelyn Cox and has:

1e *Scott; *b* 1974

1e *Nichoel Jean Edyth; *b* 21 April 1977

3d *John William; *b* 11 Sept 1951; *m* and has two sons

2c *June Iris Veronica; *b* 16 June 1921; *m* Thomas Cook (*d* 1974) and has:

1d *Thomas Barrie; *b* 2 Sept 1941; *m* three times and has four children

1d *Barbara Vivian; *b* 16 May 1943; *m* 19– *Bob Lomery and has:

1e *Christopher; *b* 6 Nov 1964

1e *Brenda; *b* 27 Aug 1963

2e *Kerri; *b* 2 Nov 1967

3e *Roberta; *b* 3 Sept 1970

2d *Bonnie Kathleen; *b* 6 Oct 1946; *m* (*divorce*) Rodney Patterson and has:

1e *Erin Kathleen; *b* 18 April 1972

3d *Rona Julie; *b* 8 Oct 1951; *m* and has two sons

4d *Valerie Colleen [Mrs Bruce Healey, Box 5 Site 94, Woods Rd RR#2, Summerland, BC V0H 1X0, Canada]; *b* 6 Feb 1954; *m* 19– *Bruce Healey and has:

1e *Mark Bruce

1e *Marni

2e *Mareena

5d *Victoria Ann [Mrs Bernie Wierbitzky, General Delivery, Anahim Lake, BC V0L 1C0, Canada]; *b* 28 July 1956; *m* 19– *Bernie Wierbitzky and has:

1e *Brant

1e *Katheryne

3c *(Olva) Diana [Mrs Keith Anderson, 1659 w 60th Ave, Vancouver, BC V6P 2A7, Canada]; *b* 2 July 1929; *m* 1st George Eldridge and has:

1d *Gary; *b* 1951

3c (cont.) Mrs Diana Eldridge *m* 2nd Barnett Auld and by him has:

1d *Bebbe; *b* 1959

2d *Rebecca Lynn; *b* 1960

3c (cont.) Mrs Diana Auld *m* 3rd *Keith Arnold Anderson and by him has:

2d *Karl Kelly; *b* 17 May 1964

1a Georgina Mina Julia Elizabeth Catania; *m* 1886 Stanley C T C Felgate and had issue

2a Florence Ellen Louisa; *m* 1881 Frank Hyde, of Hyde End, Berks, and *d* 1890, leaving issue

3a Evelyn Frederica Laila Agnese; *m* 1886 Percy St George Felgate and *d* 1888, leaving issue

(4) Julius Henry (Rev); *b* 29 Oct 1836; MA Cantab; Rector S Ockendon, Essex, 1879–1911; *m* 18 July 1861 Julia (*d* 2 Jan 1927), 4th dau of Rev Capel Molyneux (*see* 1940 edn MOLYNEUX, Bt), and *d* 22 Oct 1915, leaving:

1a Julius Richard Capel; *b* 19 May 1862; *m* 5 Oct 1886 Maude Agnes (*d* 18 Dec 1945), dau of John Cox Wallis, of NZ, and *d* 18 March 1935, leaving, with a dau (*d* young):

1b Charles Donovan, MBE (1918); *b* 2 Sept 1889; Capt RGA; *m* 14 Oct 1917 Hon Irene Evelyn Beatrice Molesworth (*d* 6 Sept 1949, having *m* 2nd 8 March 1941 Francis Henry Ash), er dau of 9th Viscount Molesworth (*qv*), and *d* 19 Jan 1935, having had:

1c Charles John; *b* 29 Nov 1920; *d* 3 Jan 1922

2c John Howard; *b* 5 Nov 1931; *educ* Gresham's and Reading U (BSc); *m* 9 Feb 1962 *Aileen Margery [Mrs John Rowley, Monk's Orchard, Blakeney, Norfolk], dau of Robert Clifford Freeman, of Gerrard's Cross, Bucks, and *d* 20 Dec 1997, leaving:

1d +Charles John Freeman; *b* 24 Jan 1969

1d *Irene Frances Elizabeth; *b* 18 Aug 1965

1c MARY DESTINE later ELISABETH GEM (deed poll 1944); *b* 26 Oct 1918; *m* 17 June 1940 Rev Edward Guy Betton Bright-Betton, Rector Narborough, Norfolk, s of Rev Edward Augustus Bright-Betton

2c *Nina Irene [Miss Nina Rowley, Camphill Village, Alpha Kalbaskraal, Western Cape 7302, S Africa]; *b* 6 Nov 1922; DPA London

3c *June Rose; *b* 16 June 1924; *m* 24 Dec 1954 *Thomas Opitz

4c *Julia May [Mrs Anthony Twist, Clements End, Conduit Head Rd, Cambridge]; *b* 7 Jan 1934; *m* 19 Feb 1955 *Anthony Frederick Twist, s of Capt Wilfred Twist, and has:

1d *Andrew Charles; *b* 2 Jan 1958; *m* 1st 1977 Bronwen Anne Bowden and has:

1e *Rebecca Catherine; *b* 1985

1d (cont.) Andrew Twist *m* 2nd 1987 *Sally Michael Mangos and by her has:

1e *Samuel Wilfred; *b* 1993

2d *Julian Richard; *b* 14 Feb 1960; *m* 1981 *Gillian Sandra Hooper and has:

1e *Jennifer Megan; *b* 1987

2e *Helen Victoria; *b* 1989

3e *Sarah Catherine; *b* 1991

3d *Philip Michael; *b* 2 Oct 1962; *m* 1983 *Elspeth Jane Barr and has:

1e *Lucy Alice; *b* 1987

2e *Emily Charlotte; *b* 1989

3e *Rosie Francesca; *b* 1993

1d *Catherine Julia; *b* 15 May 1956

*Mai Alison (adopted); *b* 1970

2b Julius Douglas Philip; *b* 14 Oct 1900; *educ* New York U (BA 1921)

3b Theodore John Capel; *b* 5 March 1905; *d* 9 July 1909

2a Julius Leigh; *b* 3 March 1864; *m* 1st 1890 Florence (*d* 1893), dau of Harry Coe, and had:

1b Robin Julius Leigh; *b* 11 April 1892; *educ* Palmers Coll; Life Gds WW I (wounded, despatches); *m* 3 April 1920 Edith May (*d* 1984), dau of Sidney Hugo Mumford, of Eton, and *d* 1974, having had:

  1c *Thelma Jeanne [Mrs René Lefèvre, Ivydene, East Drive, Bracklesham Bay, W Sussex]; *b* 14 Oct 1923; *m* 1 Jan 1946 *René Georges Lucien Paul Lefèvre, s of Georges Lefèvre, of Quibou-par-Canisy, Manche, France, and has:

    1d *Julian Howard Georges Alphonse [Julian Lefèvre Esq, World Food Programme, PO Box 25, Hanoi, Vietnam]; *b* 27 April 1949; *educ* Leeds U (BA)

    1d *Michelle Edith Germaine [Mrs Graziani, 20 Friars Way, London W3 6QE]; *b* 14 Nov 1946; *m* 19– *— Graziani

    2d *Christine Renée Jeanne [Mrs Bennett, 34 Oaktree Rd, Marlow, Bucks SL7 3EE]; *b* 7 March 1948; *m* 19– *— Bennett

    3d *Jacqueline Marguerite Frederica [Mrs Tavassoli, Cheum Des Novalles 4A, 1807 Blonay, Switzerland]; *b* 15 March 1951; *m* 19– *— Tavassoli

  2c *Audrey Frederica [Mrs Thomas Smith, Walnut Trees, Cemetery Lane, Woodmancote, Hants PO10 8QA]; *b* 3 Oct 1928; *m* 1949 *Thomas Arthur Smith and has:

    1d *Ivan Howard Lee [Ivan Smith Esq, Lordington Park, Lordington, W Sussex]; *b* 20 Aug 1952; *m* 1st 1978 Pamela Joan, dau of Ronald Janman, and has:

      1e *James Leigh Thomas; *b* 1983

      2e *Luke Robin Anthony; *b* 1984

    1d (cont.) Ivan Smith *m* 2nd *Jessica Jane, dau of David Rutland, and by her has:

      1e *Harriet Jane; *b* 1993

    2d *Stephen Frederick John [Stephen Smith Esq, Downs View, East Marden, W Sussex]; *b* 31 March 1955; *m* 1983 *Shona Joyce, dau of Peter McCall, and has:

      1e *Nicholas Edward Peter; *b* 1984

      1e *Charlotte Louise; *b* 1986

1b Frederica Mina Mabel; *b* 1894; *m* Harvey Anderson, of California, and had:

  1c *Bruce Milton; *b* 1922; *m* — and has:

    1d *Bruce Kenneth [Bruce Anderson Esq, 2503 171 St SE, Bothill, WA, USA]; *b* 1945

2a (cont.) Julius Leigh Rowley *m* 2nd 1899 Alma, dau of Harry Welch, and *d* 5 Jan 1943, having by her had:

  2b +Julius Henry; *b* 1905

  3b *Douglas Lionel; *b* 1916

  2b Norine Florence; *b* 1901; *m* — O'Leary and *d* 19–

  3b Violet Frances; *b* 1903; *m* — Fenwick

  4b *Geraldine Winifred; *b* 29 Jan 1909; *m* 9 July 1932 Clarence Arthur Allenden and has issue

  5b *Hildred Vivian; *b* 1912; *m* —Wycoft

  6b *Alma Julia; *b* 1915

3a Richard Molyneux Julius; *b* 12 May 1865; *m* 28 April 1900 Isabel Sophia (*d* 1951), dau of Oscar J Nelson, of Gothenberg, Sweden, and *d* 1948, leaving:

  1b Richard Julius Glenn; *b* 12 May 1903; *d* 1924

  2b Frederick Dunan Lorin; *b* 12 Sept 1912; *m* 1941 *Dale, dau of Joseph Antellini, and *d* 1968, having had:

    1c *Pamela Dale; *b* 16 May 1942

    2c *Loryn Lee; *b* 20 May 1946

  1b Constance Frederica Julia Christine; *b* 19 Feb 1901; *m* 1922 Burnell Hamilton De Vos and had:

    1c *Burnell Hamilton, Jr [Burnell Hamilton de Vos Jr, 1570 Charlton Rd, San Marino, CA, USA]; *b* 19 Jan 1927; *m* 11 June 1949 *Bonita Barrack and has:

      1d *Burnell Hamilton III; *b* 29 Jan 1954

      2d *Douglas Edwards; *b* 14 Feb 1956

    2c *Richard Glenn [Richard Hamilton De Vos Esq, 3558 Strathmoor Drive, Dayton, OH 45429, USA]; *b* 8 April 1932; *m* 16 June 1954 *Berneita Heyman and has:

      1d *Richard Glenn, Jr; *b* 28 March 1956

      2d *Duncan Wayne; *b* 15 March 1960

      1d *Julia Christine; *b* 11 Feb 1959

      2d *Katherine Eileen; *b* 24 July 1964

4a Howard Fiennes Julius, CBE (1919); *b* 14 Aug 1868; *educ* Roy Acad Gosport; Capt RN WW I (despatches), Ch Inspr RNLI 1919–30, US DSM; *m* 27 March 1900 Alice Udall (*d c* 1950), dau of William Paterson Muir, of Melbourne, Australia, and *d* 4 April 1948, having had:

  1b Geraldine Howard; *d* unm 27 Dec 1930

5a George Guy Singleton; *b* 24 Dec 1874; Remount Service WW I; *m* 1913 Sarah Turp, yst dau of Robert Bridge, and *d* 3 Oct 1935

1a Frederica Julia; *m* 1st 1 June 1893 (*divorce* 1901) John Rolland Singleton, of Hazeley, Winchfield, and Beaufort Park, Battle, Sussex, and had issue; *m* 2nd 17 July 1903 Lt William Edward Meade, 6th Bn Middx Regt, of Danehurst Lodge, Hordle, Hants, and *d* 23 Feb 1960, leaving further issue. He *d* 1919

(5) Henry Frederick; *b* 22 March 1839; Capt 78th Highrs; *m* 27 Sept 1870 Eveline (*m* 2nd 26 March 1881 Robert Wilberforce Oldham), 2nd dau of Innes Noad, of Fan Court, Lyne, Surrey, and *dsp* 8 April 1874

(1) Amelia Elizabeth; *m* 11 Dec 1880 Rev William Hay Chapman and *d* 9 Sept 1886, leaving issue

5 Robert Hibbert Bartholomew; *b* Dec 1817; Cdr RN; *m* 1845 Donna Juanita di Latzona and *d* Montevideo 2 July 1860, having had two sons and two daus

1 Elizabeth Sophia; *m* 1 July 1818 Peter Langford Brooke, of Mere Hall, Cheshire, and *dsp* 29 April 1835

---

2 Louisa; *m* 17 Aug 1824 10th Earl of Kinnoull (*qv*) and *d* 6 March 1885, leaving issue

The 2nd Bt's nephew,

Sir George Charles Erskine Rowley, 3rd Bt; *b* 26 Sept 1844; Lt-Col 1st Bn Roy Welch Fus; *m* 1st 27 Sept 1867 Alicia Augusta (*d* 25 Dec 1888), dau of Capt Hollis, 1st Dragoon Gds, and had, with a dau (*d* an infant):

1 **Rev Sir George Charles Augustus Rowley, 4th Bt**; *b* 18 March 1869; Rector Eastwick, Herts, 1899–1916; *m* 16 Dec 1891 Caroline (*d* 9 April 1953), only dau of Rev John Cuming, of The Grange, Shipton, Yorks, and *d* 7 Sept 1924, leaving:

  (1) **Sir George William Rowley, 5th Bt**; *b* 10 May 1896; *educ* Repton and RMC Sandhurst; Capt and Brevet Maj Essex Regt, WWs I (wounded) and II 1939–41; *m* 17 June 1939 Marjorie Alice (*d* 27 Dec 1973), formerly w of John Neville Parker and dau of John William Borcherds Blagrave, and *dsp* 8 Aug 1953

  (1) Dorothy Burton; *m* 13 May 1915 Rev Preb Charles Sigismund de Cerjat, s of Rev Charles Rowland Wynne de Cerjat, Rector Gt Hallingbury, Essex, and *d* 17 Feb 1965, leaving issue

  (2) Eleanor Caroline; *m* 15 Nov 1922 Harry Lindsay Molyneux, s of Thomas Molyneux, and had issue. He *d* Jan 1956

Sir George *m* 2nd 24 July 1890 Amy Isabel, OBE (1918) (*d* 22 Aug 1961 aged 94), 3rd dau of William Foster Batt, of Cae Kenfy, Abergavenny, and *d* 15 Jan 1922, having by her had:

2 WILLIAM JOSHUA (Sir), **6th Bt**

3 Charles Ronald; *b* 25 July 1893; *educ* Wellington; 2nd Lt Lancs Fus WW I; *ka* 10 July 1916

4 Reginald Frederick; *b* 15 Aug 1896; *educ* RMA Woolwich; Lt RFA WW I (wounded); *ka* 21 March 1918

The 5th Bt's unc,

Sir William Joshua Rowley, 6th Bt; *b* 15 April 1891; *educ* Wellington and RMC Sandhurst; Lt-Col Lancs Fus, WWs I (wounded) and II; *m* 1st 17 Dec 1917 (*divorce* 1940) Beatrice Gwendoline, dau of Rev Augustus George Kirby, Vicar S Weald, Essex, and had:

1 Sir CHARLES ROBERT ROWLEY, **7th and present Bt** (of Hill House) **and 8th and present Bt** (of Tendring)

2 +(Joshua) Christopher; *b* 10 Sept 1928; *educ* Canford

1 *Avice Gwendoline [Mrs John Latham, The Forge, Cawston, Norfolk]; *b* 14 May 1920; *m* 10 Oct 1953 *John Arderne Mere Latham, s of Capt Arderne Mere Latham, of Tomlyns, Hutton, Essex, and has:

  (1) *Mark Joshua Arderne; *b* 27 Aug 1955

  (2) *Robert William Mere; *b* 28 Oct 1956

Sir William *m* 2nd 27 Nov 1940 Margaret Sheila (*d* 12 May 1997), only dau of Harold Camp, of Stamford, Conn., and *d* 11 Nov 1971, having by her had:

2 *Felicity Margaret [Mrs Michael Slinger, Slaters House, Widdington, Essex CB11 3SN; 34 Hornton St, London W8]; *b* 28 Feb 1945; *m* 15 April 1967 *(Alexander) Michael Foulds Slinger, only s of Milton Slinger, of Spring Grove, Colne, Lancs, and has:

  (1) *Arabella Claire Felicity; *b* 1972

  (2) *Katharine Merianna Sarah; *b* 1977

3 *(Prudence) Elizabeth; *b* 25 Dec 1951; *m* 2 Sept 1972 *Simon Geoffrey Hull, s of Maj Geoffrey Hull, of Someries Stud, Newmarket, and has:

  (1) *Thomas Gresham; *b* 1975

  (1) *Louisa Claire; *b* 1977

ROXBURGHE

Arms: Quarterly, 1st and 4th grandquarters counter quartered, 1st and 4th, vert on a chevron between three unicorn's heads erased argent, armed and maned or, as many mullets sable (for KER); 2nd and 3rd, gules three mascles or (for WEAPONT); 2nd and 3rd grandquarters, argent three stars of five points azure (for INNES).
Crests: 1 A unicorn's head erased argent, armed and maned or (for KER), 2 A boar's head erased proper, langued gules (for INNES).
Supporters: Two savages, wreathed about the head and waist with laurel, each holding in their exterior hands a club, resting on the shoulder, all proper. **Mottoes:** 1 *Pro Christo et patria dulce periculum* ('For Christ and country danger is sweet'), 2 Be traist.
Creations: L. (S) 16 Nov 1600 (Roxburghe); L. (Ker of Cessford and Caverton) and E. (Roxburghe) (S) 18 Sept 1616; Bt. (NS) 28 May 1625; D., M., E. (Kelso) and V. (all S) 25 April 1707; E. (Innes) (UK) 11 Aug 1837.

THE 10TH DUKE OF ROXBURGHE, *Marquis of Bowmont and Cessford*, *Earl of Roxburghe*, *Earl of Kelso*, *Earl Innes*, *Viscount of Broxmouth*, *Lord Roxburghe*, *Lord Ker of Cessford and Caverton* and a *Baronet* (Sir Guy David Innes-Ker, Bt) [His Grace The Duke of Roxburghe, Floors Castle, Kelso, Roxburghshire TD5 7RW]; *b* 18 Nov 1954; *s f* 1974, also as 30th Feudal Baron of Innes; *educ* Eton, Magdalene Coll Cambridge (BA Land Economy 1980, MA 1984) and RMA Sandhurst (Sword of Honour 1974); Lt Blues and Royals (RHG/1st Dragoons) 1974, RARO 1977; memb Fishmonger's Co, Freeman City London 1983; *m* 1st 10 Sept 1977 (*divorce* 1990) Lady Jane Meriel Grosvenor (*m* 2nd Edward Dawnay; *see* DOWNE, V), yr dau of 5th Duke of Westminster (*qv*), and has:

> 1 +CHARLES ROBERT GEORGE, *Marquis of Bowmont and Cessford*; *b* 18 Feb 1981
>
> 2 +Edward Arthur Gerald; *b* 2 Feb 1984 (HRH THE DUKE OF YORK stood sponsor)
>
> 1 *Rosanagh Viola Alexandra; *b* 16 Jan 1979

The 10th DUKE *m* 2nd 1992 *Virginia Mary, er dau of David Wynn-Williams by Mrs Christopher Edwards, and by her has:

> 3 +George Alastair; *b* 20 Nov 1996
>
> 2 *Isabella May; *b* 7 Sept 1994

Lineage (of Ker): Sir ANDREW KER(R) of Cessford (*see* LOTHIAN, M); *k* 18 July 1526, leaving an est s:

Sir WALTER KER of Cessford; a commr to treat with the English 28 Aug 1559; supported JAMES VI 1567 against his mother MARY QUEEN OF SCOTS; *m* by 27 Sept 1543 Isabel (*d* 1 May 1585), dau of Sir Andrew Ker of Ferniehirst (*see* LOTHIAN, M), and *d* by 1583, having had:

> 1 Andrew (Sir), of Caverton; *dsp* & *vp* by March 1563/4
> 2 WILLIAM
> 3 Thomas; *dsp*
> 1 Agnes; *m* by 8 Dec 1558 John Edmondstone of Edmondstone
> 2 Isobel; *m* John Rutherford of Hunthill
> 3 Margaret; *m* by 4 Feb 1557/8, as his 1st w, 5th Lord Home (*see* HOME, E)

Sir WALTER's only surv s,

WILLIAM KER of Cessford; Warden Middle March; had charters of Ormistoun and Maxtoun 24 Jan 1592 and of the (territorial) Barony of Ernebeuch 20 July 1595; *m* (contract 3 March 1563/4) Janet, dau of Sir James Douglas of Drumlanrig (*see* QUEENSBERRY, M) and widow of James Tweedie of Drumelzier, and *d* Feb 1600, having had:

> 1 Sir ROBERT KER, **1st Earl of Roxburghe**, so *cr* 18 Sept 1616, as also LORD KER OF CESSFORD AND CAVERTON, to him and his heirs male, as also earlier 16 Nov 1600 LORD ROXBURGHE (all S), PC (S 1599), JP (Roxburghs 1610); *b c* 1570; ktd 1590; brought about the murder of his cousin William Kerr of Ancram and Woodheid 1590 (*see* LOTHIAN, M), for which his possessions were seized and he was obliged to leave the country, taking refuge in England; pardoned 1591; Warden Depute Middle March 1593, Commr Scottish Exchequer 1610, Ld Privy Seal Scotland 1637–Feb 1648/9 and again by Jan 1649/50; *m*

1st 5 Dec 1587 Margaret, dau of William Maitland of Lethington (*see* LAUDERDALE, E), and had:

> (1) William, *Lord Ker*; *d* unm & *vp* just prior to 9 March 1616/7
> (1) Jean; *m* (contract 28 Aug 1613) 2nd Earl of Perth (*qv*) and had, with other issue:
>> 1a John (Sir), of Logie Almond; ancestor of Sir William Drummond, one of the claimants to the titles on the death of **4th Duke of Roxburghe** (*see* below)
>> 2a WILLIAM DRUMMOND later KER, **2nd Earl of Roxburghe**, PC (S Feb 1660/1); Col Scots Bde in Holland; royalist Civil War; ktd by Feb 1648, Col Roxburgh and Selkirk Militia 1668; *m* (contract 17 May 1655, in fulfilment of the deed of nomination drawn up by the 1st Earl; *see* below) his cousin Jean, dau of Harry, *Lord Ker*, and *d* 2 July 1675, having had, with two other sons (*dsp*):
>>> 1b ROBERT KER, **3rd Earl of Roxburghe**, PC (S 1680), JP (Roxburghs 1680); *b c* 1658; Sheriff Pncpl Selkirk 1681; *m* 10 Oct 1675 Margaret (*d* 22 Jan 1753), dau of 1st Marquess of Tweeddale (*qv*); lost at sea off the coast of Yarmouth 6 May 1682 while accompanying the Duke of York from London to Scotland in the ship *Gloucester*, leaving:
>>>> 1c ROBERT KER, **4th Earl of Roxburghe**; *b c* 1677; *d* unm 13 July 1696
>>>> 2c JOHN KER, **1st Duke of Roxburghe**, so *cr* 25 April 1707, as also MARQUIS OF BOWMONT AND CESSFORD, EARL OF KELSO, VISCOUNT OF BROXMOUTH, and LORD KER OF CESSFORD AND CAVERTON (all S), with identical remainder to that of the Earldom of Roxburghe, KG (1722), PC (March 1708/9); *b c* 1680; Sec State Scotland 1704–05 and 1716–25, rep S peer 1707, 1708, 1715, 1727; Keeper Privy Seal Scotland 1714–16, fought against Jacobites Battle of Sheriffmuir 13 Nov 1715, Ld Lt Roxburghs and Selkirk 1715–Feb 1740/1; *m* 1 Jan 1707/8 Mary (*d* 21 Sept 1718), dau of 2nd Earl of Nottingham (*see* WINCHILSEA and NOTTINGHAM, E) and widow of William Saville, 2nd Marquess of Halifax, and *d* 27 Feb 1740/1, leaving:
>>>>> 1d ROBERT KER, **2nd Duke of Roxburghe**; *b c* 1709; *cr vp* 24 May 1722 BARON KER OF WAKEFIELD, Co York, and EARL KER OF WAKEFIELD, Co York (both GB); *m* 16 June 1739 his cousin Essex (*d* 7 Dec 1764), dau of Sir Roger Mostyn, 3rd Bt (*see* MOSTYN, B), and *d* 20 Aug 1755, having had:
>>>>>> 1e JOHN KER, **3rd Duke of Roxburghe**, KG (1801), KT (1768), PC (1796); *b* 23 April 1740; *educ* Eton; a Ld Bedchamber 1767–96, Ld Lt Roxburghs 1794–1804, Grooms Stole and First Ld Bedchamber 1796–1804; bibliophile, in commemoration of the sale of whose collection 1812 the Roxburghe Club was founded; *d* unm 19 March 1804, when the GB honours expired
>>>>>> 2e Robert; *b* 27 Aug 1747; Lt-Col 6th Dragoons; *d* 20 March 1781
>>>>>> 1e Essex; *b* 25 March 1744; *d* unm
>>>>>> 2e Mary; *b* 17 March 1746
>>>>> 3c William; Lt-Gen, MP Berwick and Dysart; *d* unm 7 Jan 1741
>> 2b JOHN KER later BELLENDEN, 2nd LORD BELLENDEN OF BROUGHTON; *m* 10 April 1683 Mary (*d* 17 March 1725/6), 2nd dau of 1st Earl of Drogheda (*qv*) and widow of 3rd Earl of Dalhousie (*qv*), and *d* March 1707, having had:
>>> 1c JOHN BELLENDEN, 3rd LORD BELLENDEN OF BROUGHTON; *b* 1685; *m* 3 Sept 1722 Mary (*d* 23 Nov 1792), dau of John Parnell, of Baldock, Herts, and *d* 16 March 1740/1, leaving, with other daus (*d* young or unm):
>>>> 1d KER BELLENDEN, 4th LORD BELLENDEN OF BROUGHTON; *b* 22 Oct 1725; Offr RN; *m* 13 March 1749 Elizabeth (*d* 21 Jan 1798), dau of Richard Brett, Clerk of Cheque Deptford Dockyard, and *d* 2 March 1753, leaving:
>>>>> 1e JOHN KER BELLENDEN, 5th LORD BELLENDEN OF BROUGHTON; *b* 22 Aug 1751; Ensign 25th Regt 1775; *m* 26 June 1787 Sarah (*d* 21 Nov 1794), widow of — Cumming, of Montego Bay, Jamaica, and *dsp* 20 Oct 1796
>>>> 2d ROBERT BELLENDEN, 6th LORD BELLENDEN OF BROUGHTON; *b* 7 April 1734; Capt 11th Foot 1761 and 68th Foot 1767; *d* unm 13 Oct 1797
>>>> 1d Jean; *b* 26 June 1724; *m* 8 Jan 1741 Ephraim Miller, of Hertingfordbury, and *d* 27 May 1763
>>>> 2d Caroline; *b* 29 March 1728; *m* 18 March 1760 John Gawler (*d* 24 Dec 1803), of Weyhill, Hants, and *d* 1 April 1802, leaving, with other issue:
>>>>> 1e John Bellenden GAWLER later BELLENDEN-KER (roy licence 5 Nov 1804), of Bishopsgate, London; *b c* 1765; Capt 2nd Life Gds, botanist; unsuccessfully claimed Bellenden estate or an annuity paid from it; *d* June 1842
>>>> 3d Maria; *b* 1 Aug 1729; *m* John Eatt, of Cambridge, and *d* 15 May 1805
>>>> 4d Diana; *b* 17 Dec 1731; *m* 6 Nov 1758 John Bulteel, of Membland, Devon, and *d* Feb 1799, having had issue
>>> 2c Robert; *b* 5 March 1689; *dsp*
>>> 3c William; *b c* 1702; Lt-Col 3rd Dragoon Gds; *m* by licence 16 April 1726 Jacomina Farmer, of Normanton, Lincs, and *d* 1759, having had, with a dau (Jacomina, *m* 4 April 1749 Thomas Orby Hunter, MP, of Waverley Abbey, Surrey):
>>>> 1d WILLIAM BELLENDEN later BELLENDEN-KER, 7th and probably last LORD BELLENDEN OF BROUGHTON, as which *s* cousin 1794, and **4th Duke of Roxburghe**, as which *s* another cousin 1804; *bapt* 20 Oct 1728; Capt 25th Foot 1757; *m* 1st 7 Dec 1750 Margaret (*dsps*), dau of Rev Dr Burroughs; *m* 2nd 29 June 1789 Mary (*m* 2nd 19 Aug 1806 John, s of Louisa, Countess of Dysart (*qv*) in her own right, and *d* 9 April 1838), dau of Capt Benjamin Bechenoe/Bechinoe, RN (*see* SMITH-MARRIOTT, Bt), and *dsps* 22 Oct 1805, when the Ldship of Parl of Bellenden probably expired (at the least became dormant), while the estates and other honours became dormant, the succession being contested by (a) Lady Essex Ker, the **3rd Duke's** er sis, as **1st Earl's** heir of line, (b) Maj-Gen Walter Ker (heir male of **1st Earl**), (c)

Rt Hon William Drummond of Logie Almond (heir male of **2nd Earl**) and (d) **Sir James Innes of that Ilk, 6th Bt** (heir general), in favour of the last of whom the Ho Lds decided 1812

4c James; had:

1d James, of Bigods, Essex; Capt 21st Foot; *dsp* by 28 Jan 1763

1d Elizabeth; *m* Edward Kelly, of Dublin

2d Jemima; *d* unm

3d Mary; *m* Sir Richard Murray, Bt

5c Henry (Sir); Gentleman Usher Black Rod; *dsp* 7 April 1761

1c Margaret; *d* unm

2c Mary; *m* 1720 4th Duke of Argyll (*qv*) and *d* 18 Dec 1736, having had issue

1b Jean; *m* 3rd Earl of Balcarres (*see* CRAWFORD and BALCARRES, E) and had issue

1a Jean; *m* (contract 10 March 1633) 3rd Earl of Wigtoun and had issue (her issue male died out 16 May 1747)

2a Lilias; *m* 3 June 1643 2nd Earl of Tullibardine (*see* ATHOLL, D)

(2) Isabel; *m* 4 Aug 1618 2nd Viscount Dudhope (*see* DUNDEE, E) and had issue

(3) Mary; *m* 1st Sir James Haliburton of Pitcur; *m* 2nd *c* 1660 2nd Earl of Southesk (*see* FIFE, D) and *d* 1650

1 (cont.) The **1st Earl** *m* 2nd 3 Feb 1613/4 Jean (*d* 7 Oct 1643), sis of 2nd Earl of Perth (*qv*; the **1st Earl**'s s-in-law by his 1st w), and by her had:

(2) Harry, *Lord Ker*; *m* 3 Feb 1638 Lady Margaret Hay (*m* 2nd (contract 20 Feb 1644/45) 6th Earl of Cassilis (*see* AILSA, M) and *d* April 1695), only dau of 10th Earl of Erroll (*qv*), and *d* 1 Feb 1642/3, having by her had:

1a Jean; *m* (contract 17 May 1655) her cousin **2nd Earl of Roxburghe**

2a Anne; *m* (contract 5 Dec 1660) 4th Earl of Wigtoun (*d* April 1668) and *d* Nov 1673, leaving:

1b Jean; *m* 23 Dec 1677 3rd Earl of Panmure (*d* 1 Feb 1686) and *dsp* April 1683 (*see* DALHOUSIE, E)

3a Margaret; *m* (contract 18 July 1666) **Sir James Innes, 3rd Bt**, of Innes (*see* **Lineage (of Innes)** below), and *d* 8 Jan 1681, having had:

1b Robert, Yr. of that Ilk; *dvp*

2b **Sir Henry Innes, 4th Bt**, of Innes; to whom his f conveyed his estates 1694; MP Elgin and Forres; opposed Union of S and E Parls; *ktd vp*; *m* Sept 1694 his cousin Jean, dau of Duncan Forbes of Culloden, and *d* 5 Nov 1721, having had:

1c Robert (Sir); *dvp*

2c Duncan; *b* 5 Oct 1697; *d* young

3c **Sir Henry Innes, 5th Bt**, of Innes; Conservator Morayshire; *m* 9 Oct 1727 Anne Drummouda (*d* 15 Feb 1771), sis of Sir Ludovic Grant, 7th Bt (*see* STRATHSPEY, B), and *d* 31 Oct 1762, having had, with five daus:

1d Henry, Yr. of Innes; *dvp* by 1759

2d JAMES (Sir), **6th Bt**, and **5th Duke**

3d Robert; Capt; *d* 9 Aug 1795, leaving:

1e Robert

4c John, of Inchbroom; *d* unm 18 Feb 1777

1c Margaret; *m* 1721 Capt George Innes (*see below*) and *d* 1771

2c Anne; *b* 1702; *m* James Stephen, Provost Elgin, and *d* 7 July 1771

3c Jean; *d* unm 1729

3b Hugh; Sgt in Col Munro's Regt; *dsp* Flanders

1b Marjorie; *m* MacDougall of Mackerstoun (*d* 1702)

2b Mary; *m* Rev John Urquhart, Min Urquhart (*d* 31 Oct 1721)

1 (cont.) The **1st Earl**, who on the death of his yr and only surv s Harry obtained 31 July 1646 a regrant of his titles and estates to the heirs male of his body, whom failing to any heirs he might nominate (choosing in a deed 23 Feb 1647/8 (ratified by Parl 20 May 1648) (a) his gs Sir William Drummond and the latter's issue in tail male by 'his spouse aforementioned', (b) three successive yr sons of his gdau Jean, Countess of Wigtoun, and their heirs male, provided the heir succeeding should marry the est (or failing the 2nd, 3rd or 4th) dau of his s-in-law Harry, *Lord Ker*, in default of which (c) to the daus of Harry, *Lord Ker* by primogeniture, in default of which (d) his own heirs male whatsoever; *m* 3rd Lady Isobel Douglas (*m* 2nd (contract 20 Dec 1656) 2nd Marquess of Montrose; *see* MONTROSE, D), dau of 7th Earl of Morton (*qv*), and *d* 18 Jan 1649/50, having by her had no issue

2 Mark (Sir), of Ormistoun; *dsp* Sept 1603

1 Margaret; *m* 1st James Pringle of Woodhouse; *m* 2nd Sir David Home of Wedderburn (*see* HOME, Bt, for earlier ancestry) and *d* 1589

2 Mary; *m* 1st Lord Scott of Buccleuch (*see* BUCCLEUCH and QUEENSBERRY, D)

3 Elizabeth; *m* 20 April 1601 Sir James Bellenden of Broughton (*d* 3 Nov 1606) and had:

(1) WILLIAM BELLENDEN, 1st LORD BELLENDEN OF BROUGHTON in Midlothian (S), so *cr* 10 June 1661, with remainder to the heirs male of his body, PC (S Feb 1660/1); *b* 1604/5; royalist Civil War; Treasurer Depute Scotland 1661, Heritable Usher Scottish Exchequer 1663, a Treasury Commr Scotland 1668; being childless he obtained a regrant of his peerage (confirmed 12 Dec 1673) with remainder to his cousin John, 4th s of **2nd Earl of Roxburghe**, and *d* unm 6 Sept 1671)

(1) Margaret; *m* after 14 Dec 1625 Henry Erskine, Master of Cardross, 3rd s of 1st Lord Cardross (*see* BUCHAN, E), who was also 18th/2nd Earl of Mar, and had issue

The 5th Bt's est surv s,

Sir JAMES INNES later INNES-NORCLIFFE (roy licence 31 May 1769 following his 1st marriage) later still INNES-KERR (following 1st w's death, when her estates were inherited by her nephew and it ceased to be politic to bear her name), **6th Bt**, of Innes, as which *s f*, and **5th Duke of Roxburghe**, as which *s* 4th cousin on being recognised as heir by Ho Lds 11 May 1812; *b* 10 Jan 1736; *educ* Leyden U; Capt 88th Foot 1759 and 58th Foot 1779; sold Innes estates 1767 to his cousin 2nd Earl Fife (*see* FIFE, D), rep S peer 1818–20; *m* 1st 19 April 1769 Mary

(*dsp* 20 July 1807), er dau of Sir John Wray, 12th Bt, of Glentworth, Lincs, by Frances, dau and heir of Fairfax Norcliffe, of Langton, E R Yorks; *m* 2nd 28 July 1807 (just over a week after his 1st w's death) Harriet (*m* 2nd 14 Nov 1827 Lt-Col Walter Frederick O'Reilly, CB, 41st Regt, and *d* 19 Jan 1855), dau of Benjamin Charlewood, of Windlesham, Surrey, and *d* 19 July 1823, having by her had, with a dau (*b* and *d* 1814):

JAMES HENRY ROBERT INNES-KER, **6th Duke of Roxburghe**, KT (1840); *b* 12 July 1816; *educ* Eton and Ch Ch Oxford; *cr* 11 Aug 1837 EARL INNES (UK), Lt-Gen Roy Co Archers, Govr Nat Bank Scotland, Ld Lt Berwicks 1873–79; *m* 29 Dec 1836 Susanna Stephania (*d* 6 May 1895), VA 3rd Cl, Ldy Bedchamber to HM QUEEN VICTORIA, only child of Lt-Gen Sir Charles Dalbiac, KCH, and *d* 23 April 1879, having had:

1 JAMES HENRY ROBERT, **7th Duke**

2 Charles John; *b* 31 Dec 1842; Lt-Col Scots Gds; *m* 15 Jan 1866 Blanche Mary (*d* 1 July 1914), 4th dau of Col Thomas Peers Williams, of Craig-y-Don and Temple Ho, Bucks, and *d* 19 Nov 1919, having had:

(1) Charles James; *b* 19 Jan 1867; Gentleman Usher to TM QUEEN VICTORIA to 1901 and EDWARD VII 1901–06; *d* unm 13 April 1906

(2) Bertram Harry; *b* 5 April 1870; *educ* Winchester; *d* unm 1 April 1951

1 Susan Harriet; *m* 5 Aug 1857 Sir James Grant Suttie, 6th Bt (*qv*), and *d* 13 Oct 1909, leaving issue

2 Charlotte Isabella; *m* 28 Oct 1862 George Russell and *d* 24 April 1881, leaving issue (*see* BEDFORD, D)

The 6th DUKE's er s,

JAMES HENRY ROBERT INNES-KER, **7th Duke of Roxburghe**, DL (Berwickshire); *b* 5 Sept 1839; *educ* Eton and Ch Ch Oxford (MA); Roxburghshire: MP (Lib) 1870–74, Ld Lt 1884–92, memb Roy Co Archers; *m* 11 June 1874 Lady Anne Emily Spencer-Churchill, OBE, VA (*d* 20 June 1923), Ldy Bedchamber and Mistress Robes to HM QUEEN VICTORIA, 4th dau of 7th Duke of Marlborough (*qv*), and *d* 23 Oct 1892, having had:

1 HENRY JOHN, **8th Duke**

2 Alastair Robert, CVO, DSO; *b* 2 Nov 1880; Lt-Col RHG (Blues), S/Cdr RFC; Boer War, WW I (wounded), Equerry-in-Ordinary to HM GEORGE V 1930–36; *m* 10 Oct 1907 Anne (*d* 30 Oct 1959), yr dau of William Lawrence Breese, of New York, and *d* 1 March 1936, leaving:

(1) Alastair James; *b* 4 Oct 1908; Lt 10th Canadian Armoured Regt WW II; *m* 7 Sept 1939 Benedicta, dau of Thomas Caverhill, of Montreal, and was *ka* Normandy July 1944

(2) David Charles; *b* 7 Jan 1910; *educ* Eton; Maj RA WW II (despatches); *m* 15 Nov 1939 (*divorce* 1948) Crista Irene Valentine, yr dau of Lt-Col Chandos de Paravicini, OBE, of Birkholme Manor, Corby, Lincs, and *d* 17 Aug 1957, leaving:

1a Mary Ann; *b* 29 April 1941

(1) Eloise Jean Horatia; *b* 1915; *m* 15 March 1940 *S/Ldr (Reginald) Baron (Barry) Black, RAF, s of Joseph Baron Black, of Belfast, and *d* 22 Jan 1996, leaving:

1a *Nicola Jean Anne [Mrs Archibald Orr Ewing, 13 Warriston Crescent, Edinburgh EH3 5LA]; *b* 1943; *m* 1972 *Archibald Donald Orr Ewing and has issue (*see* ORR EWING, Bt)

3 Robert Edward; *b* 22 July 1885; *educ* Eton; Maj Irish Gds, Equipt Offr RFC, Egyptian Army 1912, WW I (wounded), WW II as F/Lt RAFVR; *m* 1st 27 Oct 1920 (*divorce* Scotland 1935) Charlotte Josephine (Jose Collins, actress) (*d* 6 Dec 1958), dau of Stephen Patrick Cooney and formerly w of Leslie Chatfield; *m* 2nd 28 July 1939 Eleanor Marie (*d* 2 Feb 1958), dau of Aubrey Woodhead and formerly w of Hugh Christopher Hadley, and *dsp* 19 July 1958

1 Margaret Frances Susan; *b* 13 May 1875; *m* 25 July 1898 Maj James Alexander Orr Ewing (*ka* 28 May 1900) and *d* 15 Dec 1930, leaving issue (*see* ORR EWING, Bt)

2 Victoria Alexandrina; *b* 16 Nov 1877 (HM QUEEN VICTORIA stood sponsor); *m* 17 Aug 1901 Lt-Col Charles Hyde Villiers and *d* 22 May 1970, leaving issue (*see* CLARENDON, E)

3 Isabel; *b* 14 Jan 1879; *m* 23 June 1904 Hon Guy Greville Wilson, CMG, DSO, s of 1st Baron Nunburnholme (*qv*), and *dsp* 12 Oct 1905

4 Evelyn Anne, OBE (1902), JP (W R Yorks); *b* 7 Feb 1882; *m* 23 Nov 1907 Col William Fellowes Collins, DSO, RSG (*d* 15 Feb 1948), of Cundall Manor, Helperby, Yorks, and Knaresborough Ho, Yorks, and *d* 27 Sept 1957, leaving issue

The 7th DUKE's est s,

HENRY JOHN INNES-KER, **8th Duke of Roxburghe**, KT (1902), MVO (1901); *b* 25 July 1876; *educ* Eton and RMC Sandhurst; 2nd Lt 4th Bn Argyll and Sutherland Highrs (Militia) 1895, Lt RHG 1898–1904, Household Cav composite regt Boer war 1900, Lt RO 1905, Maj Lothians and Border Horse Imp Yeo 1906, V-Chm TFA Roxburghs 1908, served WW I (severely wounded) 1914–15, Ld Lt Roxburghs 1918, Lt Roy Co of Archers 1930, Chllr Order of Thistle; *m* 10 Nov 1903 Mary (*d* 26 April 1937), dau of Ogden Goelet, of New York, by May, dau of Richard T Wilson, of Newport, RI, and New York, and *d* 29 Sept 1932, leaving:

GEORGE VICTOR ROBERT JOHN INNES-KER, **9th Duke of Roxburghe**, JP, DL Roxburghs; *b* 7 Sept 1913 (TM GEORGE V and QUEEN MARY stood sponsor); *educ* Eton and RMC Sandhurst; Lt RO, RHG (Blues), memb Roy Co Archers; *m* 1st 24 Oct 1935 (*divorce* 1953) Lady Mary Evelyn Hungerford Crewe-Milnes, yst dau of 1st and last Marquess of Crewe, KG, PC (*see* 1940 edn); *m* 2nd 5 Jan 1954 Margaret Elisabeth (*m* 3rd 23 Feb 1976 as his 2nd w Jocelyn Olaf Hambro, MC (*see* HAMBRO, B), and *d* 1983), dau of Capt Frederick Bradshaw McConnel, Gordon Highrs, and formerly w of Lt-Col James Cunningham Church, MC, DL, Argyll and Sutherland Highrs, and *d* 26 Sept 1974, having had:

1 GUY DAVID INNES-KER, **10th and present Duke of Roxburghe**

2 +Robert Anthony [The Lord Robert Innes-Ker, Battlesden Park, Battlesden, Beds MK17 9HW]; *b* 28 May 1959; *educ* Gordonstoun; Lt Blues and Royals, served Falklands 1982 (despatches); head sales and small companies teams Kleinwort Benson; *m* 12 March 1996 *Dr Katherine Pelly, PhD (Oxon 1987) and has:

(1) *Eliza Henrietta; *b* 23 July 1997

Lineage (of Innes): BEROWALD FLANDRENSIS (*i.e.*, a Fleming); granted the (territorial) Barony of Innes, Morayshire, situated between the rivers Spey and Lossie, by MALCOLM IV 25 Dec 1160; had:

JOHN; had:

Sir WALTER de INEYS; ktd by 7 Aug 1235; confirmed in his possessions by charter of ALEXANDER II 20 Jan 1225; *s* by (his kinsman?):

Sir GREGOR de INSULA; had:

WILLIAM, of Innes; living 1263; *s* by (his kinsman?):

WILLIAM de INAYS; submitted to EDWARD I 17 July 1296; *s* by (his kinsman?):

WILLIAM de INNES, reckoned 7th of that Ilk; living 4 Dec 1330; *m* Margaret Leslie, sis of Walter, Earl of Ross, and had:

Sir ROBERT INNES, 8th of that Ilk; ktd by 18 Aug 1381; *m* (dispensation 29 Oct 1364) Christian de Barclay and had, with two est sons (Sir Walter, *d* young; John, Bp Moray 1407–14) and a yst (George; Scottish Provincial Trinitarian Order, *d* 1414):

Sir ALEXANDER de INNES, 9th of that Ilk; *m* Janet, dau and heiress of Sir David de Aberchirder of that Ilk, and *d* 28 April 1412, leaving:

Sir WALTER de INNES, 10th of that Ilk; had charters of lands through his mother 1426 and 1438; *m* 1st *c* 1408 Agnes/Euphemia, dau of Hugh Fraser, 4th of Lovat (*see* LOVAT, L), and widow of Lachlan Mackintosh, Capt of Clan Chattan, and had:

1 ROBERT

2 Berowald, of Halton; had:

(1) Isobel; may have been mother by James Dunbar, 4th Earl of Moray of the March 1371/2 *cr* (*see* MORAY, E, preliminary remarks, also DUNBAR, Bt, of Mochrum) of Elizabeth de Dunbar, Countess of Moray in right of her husb, 7th Earl of Douglas (*see* QUEENSBERRY, M)

(2) Margaret; *m* Sir Patrick Maitland of Netherdale

Sir WALTER *m* 2nd a dau of Sandilands of Calder (*see* TORPHICHEN, L) and *d* by 14 July 1456, having by her had:

3 John, of Ardmellie

His est s,

Sir ROBERT de INNES, 11th of that Ilk; *m c* 1436 a dau of Sir William Douglas, 2nd of Drumlanrig (*see* QUEENSBERRY, M), and *d* by 1 Feb 1464, having had, with two yr sons (Walter, of Innermarkie, had issue; *see* INNES, Bt, of Balvenie; Robert, of Drainie, ancestor of Father Lewis Innes, Jacobite Sec of State for Scotland and Father Thomas Innes, historian) and three daus (Margaret, *m* Sir James Ogilvy of Deskford and Findlater (*see* SEAFIELD, E); A dau, *m* Walter Barclay of Towie-Barclay; A dau, *m* James Douglas of Pittendreich):

Sir JAMES de INNES, 12th of that Ilk; Esq of the Body to JAMES III, present Battle of Blackness 1488; *m* 1st Lady Janet Gordon, dau of 1st Earl of Huntly (*see* HUNTLY, M), and had:

1 Alexander, 13th of that Ilk; *m* 1st 1493 Christian, dau of Sir James Dunbar of Westfield (*see* DUNBAR, Bt, of Mochrum), and *d* 1537, leaving:

(1) Alexander, 14th of that Ilk; *b* 1494; *m* 1st by 1529 Elizabeth, dau of 4th Lord Saltoun (*qv*) of Abernethy, and had:

1a William, 15th of that Ilk; one of the Protestant lesser Barons who sat in the Parl of 1560; *m* 1544 Elizabeth Hepburn (*m* 2nd by 1567 Alexander Hay of Fynesfield), of the family of Beinston, and *d* April 1565, leaving:

1b Alexander, 16th of that Ilk; *b c* April 1553; *m* 1st May 1574 Lady Barbara Sinclair (*d* July 1576), dau of 4th Earl of Caithness (*qv*) and formerly w of 13th Earl of Sutherland (*qv*); *m* 2nd Lady Jean Gordon (*m* 2nd Thomas, 9th s of 4th Earl of Huntly; *see* HUNTLY, M), dau of 12th Earl of Sutherland, and *dsp*, being beheaded at the Cross in Edinburgh 1 Jan 1577/8 for the murder of Walter Innes, bro of Thomas Innes of Pethnick

2b John, 17th of that Ilk; *b* 1556; *m* 1580 Elizabeth (*m* 2nd James Gordon of Auchenhieff), dau of 6th Lord Saltoun (*qv*) of Abernethy; resigned chiefship and estates 2 Dec 1578 in favour of his cousin Alexander Innes of Cromey; *dsp c* 1587 (allegedly murdered)

1b Elspeth; *dsp c* 1605

2b Marjorie; *m* Archibald Dewar

2a James, of Elrick, Culvie and Monbeens

(1) (cont) Alexander Innes, 14th of that Ilk, *m* 2nd by 1541 Elizabeth (*m* 3rd 1553/4 Alexander Dunbar of Conzie), dau of 6th Lord Forbes (*qv*) and widow of Gilbert Keith of Troup, and *d* Sept 1553, leaving by her:

1a Margaret; *m* June 1553 (*divorce* 1574) Robert Innes, 3rd of Innermarkie (*see* INNES, Bt, of Balvenie)

(2) James in Leuchars; had a dau (Margaret, *m* James Innes of Cromey; *see* below)

(3) Robert, of Moneddie

(1) Elizabeth; *m* 1st Alexander Sinclair of Dunbeath and Stemster, 2nd s of 2nd Earl of Caithness (*qv*); *m* 2nd Arthur Forbes of Putachie, 3rd s of 6th Lord Forbes (*qv*)

(2) Katharine; *m* Archibald Douglas of Pittendreich

(3) Lucretia; *m* William Leslie of Chapelton

2 ROBERT

1 Elizabeth; *m* 1st 3 May 1481 Sir George Meldrum of Fyvie; *m* 2nd by 1523 John Forbes of Pitsligo and had issue (*see* FORBES, Bt, of Newe)

2 Janet; *m* William Sutherland of Duffus (murdered *c* 1529/30)

Sir JAMES *m* 2nd *c* 1473 Margaret Culane, widow of William Roland, and *d c* 1491, having by her had:

3 William, of Cromey; had a s (Berowald)

4 George

5 James, of Rothiebrisbane

6 Thomas, of Balnacoul

3 Iona; *m* Robert Gordon of Udauch

His 2nd s,

ROBERT INNES of Rothmakenzie and Cromey; *m* 1st a dau of Sir William Meldrum of Fyvie and had:

1 JAMES

2 Alexander, wadsetter (conveyancer of land as security for a debt) of Blackhills; *m* a dau of Hay of Lochloy and *d* by 1547, leaving:

(1) John, in Blackhills; *m* Jeronissa, dau of John Gordon, 4th of Gight, and *d* by 1576, having had:

1a Alexander, of Cotts and Leuchars; Constable Spynie; *m* by 27 April 1587 Marjorie, dau of William Gordon of Gight, and *d* 1634, leaving:

1b John, of Leuchars; Hereditary Constable Spynie; *m* 8 Aug 1622 Elizabeth (*d* July 1655), dau of Archibald Douglas of Pittendriech, and *d* Sept 1645, leaving:

1c John, of Leuchars; Constable of Spynie; *m* Marjorie, dau of James Geddes of Auchinroath, and *d* 18 May 1677, leaving, with other issue:

1d John, of Leuchars; *m c* 1702 Elizabeth (*m* 2nd George Haldane), dau of Sir George Gordon of Edinglassie, and *d* Dec 1715, leaving:

1e John, of Leuchars; Capt 17th (Wynyard's) Regt; *dspl* Dec 1781, having settled Leuchars on John Innes of Dunkinty (*see* below)

2c Alexander; went to Ireland; *m* a dau of Rev Edward Brice, Rector Balligarry, and had, with three er sons (*dsp*):

1d William; *m* Jane, dau of Robert Brice, of Castle Chichester, Co Antrim, and had, with other issue:

1e William (Rev); *b* Dublin 1691; *m* Isabella, dau of Lt-Col James Simpson, and *d* 1735, leaving, with two other sons and five daus:

1f William, of Dromantine, Co Down; *m* 1744 Dorothea (*d* 1785), dau of Charles Brice, of Castle Chichester, and *d* 1785, leaving, with other issue:

1g Charles Brice, of Dromantine; High Sheriff Co Down 1775; *d* unm 1804

2g Arthur, of Dromantine; High Sheriff Co Down 1814; Capt 9th Dragoons; *m* 1796 Anne, dau of Edward Crow, of Tullamore, King's Co, and had, with other issue:

1h Arthur, of Dromantine, JP, DL; High Sheriff Co Down 1832; Lt 3rd Dragoon Gds; *m* 15 May 1829 Mary Jervis (*d* 24 Jan 1886), dau of William Wolseley, Adml the Red, and *d* 1835, leaving:

1i Arthur Charles INNES later INNES-CROSS, of Dromantine, JP, DL; *b* 25 Nov 1834; MP Newry 1865–68; *m* 1st 16 July 1858 Louisa Letitia Henrietta (*d* 27 Jan 1886), 2nd dau of James Brabazon, of Co Meath, and had:

1j Edith Clara Brabazon; *d* young

1i (cont.) Arthur INNES-CROSS *m* 2nd 21 Sept 1887 Sarah Jane Beauchamp (*m* 2nd 18 March 1907 Herbert Martin COOKE later COOKE-CROSS (roy licence 14 March 1908, *d* 30 July 1931), est s of Mason Cooke, of Ely, and *d* 16 Nov 1911), dau of Col William Cross, JP, DL, of Dartan, Co Armagh, and *d* 14 April 1902, having by her had:

1j Arthur Charles Wolseley INNES-CROSS later INNES, MC, of Dromantine; *b* 8 June 1888; Lt Irish Gds; *m* 15 March 1916 Etta Maud (*d* 1971), dau of William Bradshaw, of Ordleyhill, Hants, and *d* 12 Jan 1940, leaving:

1k Arthur Charles Sydney; *b* 19 May 1922; *educ* Eton; RAF WW II; *ka* 23 July 1943

2k *William Anthony Wolseley [William Innes Esq, 35 Whittingstall Rd, London SW6]; *b* 9 Nov 1935; *educ* Eton and RMA Sandhurst; Lt Scots Gds

1k *Anne; *b* 23 Jan 1929; *m* 31 Jan 1959 *Roger I C Ryland, s of Capt John Ryland, CIE, RN, of Royston, BC, Canada, and has:

1l *Charles John; *b* 1962; *m* 1990 *Jane M, er dau of Prof Charles Fowler Cullis, of Cuckfield, Sussex and has:

1m *Anna Elizabeth; *b* 1991

2m *Arabella Kate; *b* 1994

1l *Anna; *b* 1960

2j Sydney Maxwell; *b* 29 April 1894; *educ* Eton and RMC Sandhurst; 2nd Lt Roy Irish Rifles WW I; *ka* Ypres Oct 1914

2j Marian Dorothea; *m* 7 Sept 1912 Sir Richard Christopher Brooke, 9th Bt, of Norton Priory (*qv*), and *d* 13 Feb 1965, leaving issue

1i Mary Catherine; *d* unm 1916

2i Anne Northeske; *m* Col James Loftus Winniett Nunn, 80th Regt (*d* 16 May 1899), and *d* 1 March 1887

3i Emma Jean; *d* unm 23 Oct 1868

3c Robert; *k* at Leuchars by Covenanters, leaving:

1d John; living 1665

4c George

5c Samuel; Procurator Fiscal Regality of Spynie

2b Alexander (Sir); Cupbearer to CHARLES I; *m* Mary, dau of Sir Robert Jacob, Slr-Gen Ireland, and *d* 1646, having had, with two daus:

1c Charles

2c Gordon

3b Robert; royalist Capt and Intell Offr Civil War; *m* Margaret Strachan and had:

1c James; *b* 1 March 1620

4b Patrick, of Nether Meft; *m* Isabel, dau of Henry Buchan, and *d* 1676

5b George, of Calcotts; Capt Lord Spynie's Regt, Lt-Col Swedish Army; *m* Isabel, dau of Sir Adam Gordon of Pask, and *d* May 1686, leaving:

1c Alexander, of Dunkinty; *m* Jean, dau of Kinnaird of Culbin, and *d* Jan 1688, leaving:

1d David, of Dunkinty; Capt Collin's Regt; *ka sp* Ireland

2d George, of Dunkinty; Provost Elgin 1711–14; *m* —, dau of Samuel Tulloch, Parson of Spynie, and *d* 1740, having had:

1e David, Yr. of Dunkinty; *dsp* & *vp*

2e John, of Dunkinty; *b* 1697; heir of entail in Leuchars 1781; *m* Margaret (*d* 23 June 1793), dau of Alexander Strachan of Tarrie, and *dsp* 9 Sept 1788

3e James; Advocate-Gen Jamaica; *dspl* 1774

4e Robert; *m* 30 Dec 1736 Mary, dau of William Gordon of Farskane, and had issue, now extinct in male line; gf of Professor Cosmo Innes, historian

5e Archibald, of Calcotts; *m* Rebecca, dau of Robert Dunbar of Newton, and *d* by Nov 1780, leaving:

 1f George; living Jamaica 1782

2c John, of Dykeside; *m* Helen Dunbar and *dsp* 30 May 1714

3c Patrick; excommunicated for fratricide 11 April 1671

4c Charles; *k* by his bro 1671

6b James; Lt-Col Laird of Innes's Regt 1651; *d* 1658

7b William (Rev); Vicar Harwich-cum-Dovercourt; *m* Jane — and *d* 19 March 1638, leaving:

 1c Garburetts, of Thorp

 2c Robert, of Little Oakley

2a Adam, of Redhall; *m* Katharine Clerk and *d* after 1631, leaving:

 1b Robert, of Redhall 1630; had:

  1c Robert, 3rd of Redhall; WS; living 1693

 2b James; had:

  1c A dau; *m* Robert Douglas, s of Douglas of Tilquhillie

  2c Janet; *m* 1674 Govr Thomas Pitt (*d* 1726) and *d* 10 Jan 1727, leaving issue, among whom were the Earls of Chatham (*see* JERSEY, E)

 3b John, of Dipple and Lichnett; Lt-Col; *m* 1648 Jean, dau of John Campbell, Provost Dunbarton, and had:

  1c James, 2nd of Lichnett; *m* Jean Meason and *d* April 1707, leaving:

   1d James, 3rd of Lichnett; *m* 17 May 1699 Hon Marjorie Ogilvy, dau of 2nd Lord Banff (*see* 1900 edn), and *d* by 1728, leaving:

    1e George, 4th of Lichnett; living 1732

    1e Jean

   2d Robert

   3d David

   4d Alexander; living 6 Dec 1715

  2c John; living 1684

  3c Robert

  4c Hugh; *b* 1664; Min Mortlach, Banffshire; *m* 1 Nov 1702 Elizabeth (*d* 11 Sept 1757), dau of Abernethy of Maen, and *d* 18 March 1733, leaving:

   1d Alexander; apprentice apothecary Edinburgh 1729

   1d Isobel; *m* 11 July 1722 John Ramsay, Min Botarie

 4b Vincent; HEICS

 5b Edward; HEICS

 3a Robert; had:

  1b Robert (Sir); royalist QMG Civil War; *m* Elizabeth Pitt and *d* 1648, leaving:

   1c Richard; *b* 1640; apparently ktd; HEICS

 4a James; living 1588

 1a Agnes; *m* Patrick Dunbar of Tempillane

ROBERT INNES of Rothmakenzie and Cromey *m* 2nd the dau of MacCulloch of Plaidds, Heritable Baillie Sanctuary of St Duthac of Tain, Constable Orkney, and by her had:

3 Alexander, of Plaidds and Cadboll; Tutor (guardian) of Cromey, Heritable Baillie St Duthac of Tain, Constable Orkney, Capt Kirkwall Castle; *m* Isobel Innes and *d* by 1583, leaving:

 (1) Robert, of Redhall, which he sold 1583; *d* by 1598, leaving:

  1a James; heir to his gf 1598

 (2) William, of Blackhills; *d c* 1631, leaving:

  1a James, 2nd of Blackhills; *m* by 10 Nov 1627 Margaret, dau of Walter Innes of Auchintoul, and *d* 1642; ancestor of the INNESes of Blackhills

  2a Gilbert; tutor Blackhills 1655; in Whitewray 1631, Over Auchinroath 1664; had issue and was ancestor of the INNES-SMITHs

  3a William; living 1656

  4a Robert; living 1625

  1a Grizel; *m* 18 June 1611 Leonard Leslie, Min Rothes

 (3) Thomas, of Inche of Spynie; living 1607

 (1) Elspeth, of Edinglassie

4 John; Baillie Elgin 1551

ROBERT INNES of Rothmakenzie and Cromey *d* by 6 March 1536; his est s,

JAMES INNES of Cromey; *m* 1st *c* 1533 Catharine, dau of Sir William Gordon, 1st of Gight, and had:

1 ALEXANDER

2 John; living 8 Dec 1554; *m* and *dspm*

JAMES INNES of Cromey *m* 2nd 1543 Margaret (*m* 2nd Alexander Seton of Meldrum; *m* 3rd William Gordon of Arradoul), dau of James Innes of Leuchars, and was *ka* at Scottish defeat by English of Pinkie 1547, having had four more daus; his er s:

ALEXANDER INNES, 18th of that Ilk and 3rd of Cromey; *b* 1537; received from John Innes of that Ilk the chiefship and estates 2 Dec 1578; *m* 1st Beatrix, dau of Alexander Dunbar, Prior Pluscarden; *m* 2nd 1563 Janet, dau of Alexander Urquhart of Cromartie; *m* 3rd 18 Dec 1565 Isobel (*m* 2nd 1 Dec 1585 Sir David Lindsay of Edzell; *see* CRAWFORD and BALCARRES, E), dau and heiress of Arthur Forbes of Logie and Balfour, and was murdered at Aberdeen 13 April 1580 by Robert Innes of Innermarkie (*see* INNES, Bt, of Balvenie), having had, with a dau (Elisabeth, *m* 11 May 1585 William Meldrum of Montcoffer):

ROBERT INNES, 19th of that Ilk; *b c* April 1562; *m* 1 Oct 1582 Elisabeth (*d* 26 Feb 1613), 3rd dau of 3rd Lord Elphinstone (*qv*), and *d* 25 Sept 1596 (or 1606), having had:

1 ROBERT (Sir), **1st Bt**

2 John (Sir), of Cromey; *m* 1613 Elizabeth, dau of Sir James Sinclair of Murkle, and had:

 (1) Robert (Sir), of Muirton; *m* 1st Jean Cockburn; *m* 2nd his cousin Grisel, dau of **Sir Robert Innes, 1st Bt**, of that Ilk, and *d* 6 April 1667, leaving:

  1a Robert, 2nd of Muirton; *dsp* Jan 1678

  2a James, 3rd of Muirton, which he sold; living 1684

  3a Alexander; at King's Coll 1670

  4a John; living 1682

  1a Elizabeth; *m* Donald Campbell of Urchany

 (2) John, of Bomellie; Maj; *m* 29 March 1670 Jean Richardson (*d* 20 May 1696) and *dsp* March 1672

1 Anne; *m* Rev John Guthrie, Yr. of that Ilk (*dvp* 1643)

2 Marie; *m* 1st, as his 2nd w, Alexander Douglas, Bp Moray (*d* 11 May 1623); *m* 2nd 16 Oct 1624 John Urquhart of Laithers and Craigfintry (*d* 11 Dec 1632); *m* 3rd 21 Nov 1633, as his 2nd w, William Hay of Fetterletter, s of 8th Earl of Erroll (*qv*)

3 Margaret; *m* George Munro of Miltoun

ROBERT INNES's er s,

Sir Robert Innes, 1st Bt, of that Ilk (NS), so *cr* 28 May 1625, with remainder to his heirs male whomsoever, PC (1641); *b* 1583/4; MP Moray; *m* (contract 18 Dec 1611) Lady Grizel Stewart, dau of 2nd Earl of Moray (*qv*), and *d* 17 Nov 1658, having had:

1 ROBERT (Sir), **2nd Bt**

2 James, of Lichnett; *m* 9 May 1659 Isabella, dau of David Ross of Balnagowan and widow of Lt-Col John Sutherland (bro of Lord Duffus), and had:

 (1) Robert; living 1690

 (2) Peter

3 William, of Nether Dallachy; had, with an er s:

 (1) Andrew, of Broadgate, Bristol; *b* 1641; *m* 1st Jean Randall; *m* 2nd Elizabeth, dau of Jeremy Martin, of Redland Court, Bristol, and *d* 29 Dec 1723, having by her had, with five other sons (*dsp*) and six daus:

  1a Jeremy, of Redland Court; *d* 1764, leaving:

   1b Elizabeth; *m* 1742 Slade Baker, whose issue inherited Redland Court

  2a William, of North Stoke, Bristol; bookseller in London, Master Stationers' Co; *dsp* 1756

  3a John, of Redland Court; bookseller in London; *dsp* 1778

1 Elizabeth; *m* 1st John Urquhart of Craigston (*d* 30 Nov 1634); *m* 2nd 28 Oct 1635 Alexander, Lord Brodie (Ld of Session), and *d* 12 Aug 1640

2 Mary; *m* Sir James Stewart of Rosyth

3 Grizel; *m* Sir Robert Innes of Muirton and *d* 19 Aug 1664

4 Barbara; *m* 1st Robert Dunbar of Westfield, Sheriff Moray (*d* 1661); *m* 2nd Sept 1663 David Dunbar of Dunphail; *m* 3rd 31 March 1676 Robert Dunbar of Burgie and *d* 9 Dec 1681

5 Jean; *m* 13 Jan 1653 1st Lord Duffus and *dsp* 21 March 1653

6 Anne; *b* 22 April 1625

The 1st Bt's est s,

Sir Robert Innes, 2nd Bt, of that Ilk; MP Elgin and Forres 1661–78; *m* Jean, 3rd dau and coheir of 6th Lord Ross of Halkhead, and *d* Feb 1689, having had:

1 JAMES (Sir), **3rd Bt** (*see* **Lineage (of Ker)** above)

2 John; Lt Earl of Mar's Regt 1682; *d* young

3 William; Capt Scots Gds; *m* by 1670 — Durie and had:

 (1) George; *b* April 1671; Capt Roy Foot 1696; *m* 1721 Margaret (*d* 1771), dau of **Sir Henry Innes, 4th Bt**, of that Ilk, and had, with a dau (Harriet, *m* Thomas Ewing):

  1a Henry; Lt-Gen RM Chatham Div; *d* 18 Nov 1806

  2a George; *dspl*

1 Margaret; *m* Hugh Rose of Kilravock and *d* 20 May 1684

2 Marie; *m* Duncan Forbes of Culloden

3 Jean; *m* Alexander Rose of Clava and *d* 11 Feb 1684

4 Idonea; eloped with and *m* — Sutherland

5 Grizel; *b* 20 July 1654; *m* 1673 Sir James Calder of Muirton, 1st Bt

6 Elizabeth; *m* 4 Sept 1681 Arthur Forbes, 12th of Echt

Seat: Floors Castle, Roxburghs. Originally called Friars, which points to the original ownership of the estate by a religious house, then during the 16th and 17th centuries Fleurs (perhaps reflecting the importance of Franco-Scottish ties then), this palatial edifice dates in its present form from the early 18th century.

The **1st Duke**, who moved the site of his house to a position north of what appears to have been a castellated dwelling, initially erected a house in straightforward early Georgian idiom. It was not until the early 19th century that Floors's present appearance took shape, when William Henry Playfair was employed by the **6th Duke** to dress his house up into something like a Caledonian Blenheim. (Significantly, it was Vanbrugh, the designer of Blenheim, who had worked on Floors around 1718.)

Playfair was perhaps principally a neo-classicist. He designed much of the New Town in Edinburgh, also the Scottish National Gallery, and it has been suggested that Edinburgh's 19th-century sobriquet 'The Modern Athens' derived in large part from his embellishments to the city. But he had also shown signs of a talent for neo-Jacobethan stylistics in his work on Donaldson's Hospital between 1842 and 1848. The next year he started on Floors and studded it with finials, machicolation, parapets and turrets capped by shallow domes. The result successfully disguises Floors's sheer size, though even now the boast in its promotional literature that it is Scotland's largest inhabited castle comes as no particular surprise.

Floors was the location of HRH THE DUKE OF YORK's marriage proposal to the then Miss Sarah Ferguson.

ROYDEN

Arms: Vert three stag's heads erased in pale between two bugle horns stringed in fess, all or. **Crest:** A stag's head erased or, collared gemel vert, holding in the mouth a riband also vert, suspended therefrom an escutcheon of the arms of Royden.
Mottoes: *Comme je trouve* ('I take things as I find them').
Creation: Bt (U.K.), 29 July 1905.

SIR CHRISTOPHER JOHN ROYDEN, 5TH BT, of Frankby, Co Palatine of Chester [Sir Christopher Royden Bt, Flat 2, 8 Nevern Sq, London SW5 9NW]; *b* 26 Feb 1937; *s* f 1976; *educ* Winchester and Ch Ch Oxford (MA); late 2nd Lt 16th/5th Queen's Roy Lancers, assoc dir Gerrard Vivian Gray Ltd 1988–, Duncan Fox & Co Ltd 1960–71, Spencer Thornton & Co 1971–88 (ptnr 1974–86, dir 1986–88); *m* 28 Nov 1961 *Diana Bridget, only dau of Lt-Col Joseph Henry Goodhart, MC, 14th/20th Hus, of Keldholme Priory, Kirbymoorside, Yorks, by Evelyn Catherine Bridget, yst dau of Henry Ralph Beaumont, JP, DL, of Whitley Beaumont, Yorks, and has:

1 +JOHN MICHAEL JOSEPH; *b* 17 March 1965; *educ* Stowe and Reading U (LLB); *m* 1989 *Lucilla Mary, dau of John Ralph Stourton (*see* MOWBRAY, SEGRAVE and STOURTON, B), and has:
  (1) *Charlotte Alice Maude; *b* 1992
  (2) *A dau
2 +Richard Thomas Bland; *b* 20 March 1967
1 *Emma Mary Bridget; *b* 25 Jan 1971

Lineage: ALEXANDER ROYDEN, of Chester; had:

JOSEPH ROYDEN, of Chester; *m* Mary, dau of John Bennett, of Heswall, and *d* 1721, leaving:

JOHN ROYDEN, of Frankby and Caldy, Cheshire; *bapt* 16 June 1719; *m* 1st 1 Feb 1742/3 Elizabeth Linacre, of Barnston, Cheshire; *m* 2nd 30 May 1758 Elizabeth Guile (*bur* 3 July 1770) and *d* 15 March 1799, having had by her two sons and a dau and by his 1st w, four daus and a yr s (John, *bapt* 6 May 1752, *m* 4 April 1774 Mary (*bur* 27 Aug 1804), dau of Thomas Longworth, of Thurstaston, Cheshire, and *d* 22 March 1839):

JOSEPH ROYDEN, of Frankby; *b* 1745; *m* 30 April 1770 Martha (*d* 18 Nov 1819), dau of William Hankinson, of Chester, and *d* 8 Oct 1832, having had, with four er sons and three daus:

THOMAS ROYDEN, of Frankby; *b* 16 Feb 1792; *m* 14 April 1825 Nancy (*d* 22 June 1864), dau of Thomas Dean, of Scale Hall, Skerton, Lancs, and *d* 15 Sept 1868, having had, with a yr s (Joseph, of Roby, Lancs, *b* 6 May 1833, *m* 21 April 1853 Mary Elizabeth, dau of Thomas Ellis, of Wolverhampton, and *d* 7 July 1895, having had issue), two daus (Martha, *m* 6 Aug 1851 John Hays Wilson, of Lea Hall, Gateacre, Lancs, and *d* 27 Nov 1915; Anne Dean, *d* 30 Nov 1921 aged 92) and two other children (*d* in infancy):

Sir Thomas Bland Royden, 1st Bt (UK), so *cr* 29 July 1905, of Frankby, JP Liverpool, DL Cheshire; *b* 20 Feb 1831; Mayor Liverpool 1878–79, Alderman 1905, MP (C) W Toxteth 1885–92, High Sheriff Cheshire 1903; *m* 4 July 1865 Alice Elizabeth (*d* 20 March 1932), dau of Thomas Dowdall, of Liverpool, and *d* 29 Aug 1917, leaving:

1 **Sir Thomas Royden, 2nd Bt**, and 1st and last BARON ROYDEN, of Frankby, Co Palatine of Chester (UK), so *cr* 1944, CH (1919), JP Hants, DL; *b* 22 May 1871, *educ* Winchester (Fell 1940) and Magdalen Coll Oxford (MA); High Sheriff Hants 1917, MP (C U) Bootle 1918–22, dir Cunard Steamship Co, Cunard White Star Ltd, Midland Bank, Phoenix Assur and Shell Transport and Trading, Cdr Legn Hon and Order St Maurice and St Lazarus Italy, CStJ; *m* 20 April 1922 Quenelda Mary (*d* 17 Feb 1969 aged 95), widow of Charles James Williamson (*see* FORRES, B) and dau of Harry Clegg, JP, DL, of Plas Llanfair, Anglesey, and *dsp* 6 Nov 1950, when the Barony expired
2 ERNEST BLAND (Sir), **3rd Bt**
1 Alice Nancy; *m* 27 June 1889 Percy Lens Rooper, of Little Court, Speldhurst, Kent, and *d* 7 Jan 1952, leaving issue. He *d* 15 April 1930
2 Ethel Martha, OBE (1919); Dep Assist Dir WRNS WW I; *d* unm 30 Aug 1955

3 Mary Catherine; First Commr Cheshire Girl Guides; *d* unm 31 Jan 1966 aged 95
4 Mabel; *m* 8 Dec 1908 Hugh Neilson, of Chapeltoun, Stewarton, and *d* 8 July 1935, leaving issue. He *d* 7 June 1944
5 Evelyn Mary; *m* 5 April 1899 Hadden Todd, of Willaston Grange, Willaston, Cheshire, s of Hadden William Todd by Eleanor, 3rd dau of William Pilkington, JP, DL, of St Helens, and *d* 13 May 1971 aged 95, leaving issue He *d* 29 Nov 1942
6 (Agnes) Maude, CH (1930); *educ* Cheltenham Ladies' Coll and LMH Oxford; Assist Preacher City Temple 1917–20, Min Guildhouse Eccleston Sq, London SW1, religious author and broadcaster; Hon DD Glasgow 1931, Hon LLD Liverpool 1935, Dr Hum Lit Mills Coll Calif. 1937; *m* 2 Oct 1944 Rev George William Hudson Shaw (*d* 30 Nov 1944), Rector St Botolph's Bishopsgate, and *d* 30 July 1956, leaving an adopted dau

The 2nd Bt's bro,
Sir Ernest Bland Royden, 3rd Bt, JP Cheshire; *b* 30 Jan 1873; *educ* Winchester; High Sheriff Anglesey 1920; *m* 31 Oct 1901 Rachel Mary (*d* 20 Jan 1947), dau of Jerome Smith, of Frankby, Cheshire, and had:

1 JOHN LEDWARD (Sir), **4th Bt**
2 Thomas Jerome; *b* 16 Oct 1913; *educ* Winchester and Magdalen Coll Oxford; Br Min War Tport New York 1941–45, dir Phoenix Assur New York; *m* 1st 8 Sept 1937 Catherine Mary Denton (*d* 9 March 1970), dau of Charles Denton Toosey, of Oxton, Birkenhead, and had:
  (1) +Ernest Jerome [Ernest Royden Esq, 556 Forest View, Hudson, Quebec J0P 1J0, Canada]; *b* 7 July 1944; *m* 1974 *Suzanne Adams and has:
    1a *Catherine Helene; *b* 1992
  (2) Jonathan Bland; *b* Sept 1952; *d* 16 Jan 1962
  (1) *Anne Elizabeth Mary [Mrs Barry Gerken, 37 Woodside Dve, MA 01740, USA]; *b* 19 Sept 1945; *m* 1967 *Barry Lewis Gerken, est s of L J Gerken, of Chanute, Kans., and has:
    1a *Heather Kristin; *b* 19 Feb 1969
    2a *Stephanie Rebecca; *b* 1971
2 (cont.) Thomas Royden *m* 2nd 14 Nov 1970 *Lynn, dau of Lloyd Aspinwall Jr, of Mountain Lake, Lake Wales, Fla., and *d* 1991, having by her had:
  (3) +Thomas; *b* 1976
  (2) *Alexa; *b* 1972
1 *Rachel Nancy; *b* 7 Dec 1902; *m* 8 Jan 1931 Lt-Col John Forbes Batten, OBE, MC (*d* 1979), RA, er s of John Holgate Batten, of Woking, and has had:
  (1) Rachel Ann; *b* 10 Sept 1932; *m* 1st 1956 (*divorce* 1960) Peter Long; *m* 2nd 1963 Leslie Ernest Sutton (*d* 1992), DPhil, FRS, s of W Sutton, of London, and *d* 1987, having had issue
  (2) *Catherine Jean [Mrs Thomas Dowell, 64 Berkeley Rd, Westbury Pk, Bristol]; *b* 15 Nov 1934; *m* 12 Feb 1955 *Thomas Burtt Dowell, s of Dr Thomas Leslie Dowell, of Low Bentham, Lancs, and has issue
2 Alice Joan, MBE (1961); *m* 28 Sept 1935 her sis's bro-in-law Brig Stephen Alexander Holgate Batten, CBE, RE (*d* 10 Jan 1957), yr s of John Holgate Batten, of Woking, and had:
  (1) *Stephen Duval; *b* 2 April 1945; *educ* Uppingham and Pembroke Coll Oxford
  (1) *Anne Ledward; *b* 19 May 1940; *educ* London U (BSc 1966)
3 Mabel Dean; *d* 7 Feb 1912
4 Mary Elizabeth; *m* 1st 30 Sept 1936 (*divorce* 1957) Dr Clarence Laverne Johnson, s of Nels John Johnson, of Kewanee, Ill., and had:
  (1) *Nels Royden; *b* 27 Jan 1939; *m* 1961 *Barbara Joan, yr dau of M P Skillern, of Ealing, and has:
    1a *Christopher Matthew Laverne; *b* 29 Aug 1964
    1a *Carol Anne; *b* 19 Nov 1966
  (2) John Antony Royden; *b* 11 Nov 1941; *d* unm April 1965
  (1) *Mary Elizabeth Royden; *b* 3 Jan 1945; *m* 22 Sept 1966 *Hon Patrick Greville Howard, yst s of 20th Earl of Suffolk and (13th Earl of) Berkshire (*qv*), and has issue
  (2) *Sally Ann Royden; *b* 21 May 1948; *m* 25 July 1968 *Peter Grant Auguste Hennessy (*see* WINDLESHAM, B)
4 (cont.) Mrs Mary Johnson *m* 2nd 5 Feb 1957 Allan MacNeil Dyson (Neil) Perrins, only s of James Allan Dyson Perrins, MC, of Annaghbeg House, Nenagh, Co Tipperary. He *d* 27 May 1965
5 *Vera Katharine (twin with Mary Elizabeth); *b* 1915; *m* 23 April 1935 *Charles Gavin Clark, er s of Henry Gordon Clark, of Birkenhead, and has had:
  (1) David Gavin Bland; *b* 25 Feb 1944; *d* 1997
  (1) *Sonia Jennifer Jane [Mrs Antony Bevan, 12 Bramble Close, Holbury, Hants SO45 2JP]; *b* 22 May 1936; *m* 1st July 1956 (*divorce* 1965) John Cecil McGregor Cuthbert; *m* 2nd 5 Nov 1965 *Antony James Bevan and by her 1st husb has:
    1a *Michael John [Michael Cuthbert Esq, The Hunting Box, Patmore Heath, Herts]; *b* 1 Sept 1958; *m* and has issue
    2a *Andrew Charles [Andrew Cuthbert Esq, The Garden House, Carnell Estate, Hurlford, Ayrshire KA1 5JS]; *b* 28 Oct 1960; *m* *—
  (2) *Gillian Vera [Mrs Maldwin Drummond, Cadland House, Fawley, Hants]; *b* 15 Sept 1939; *m* 1st 20 March 1958 (*divorce* 1978) (Alexander) Graham Athol Turner Laing, only s of George Alec Turner Laing, of Little Common, Sussex, and has had:
    1a Alexander Hubert; *b* 1968; *d* 1971
    1a *Sophia Henrietta [Mrs Charles Comninos, 74 Denbigh St, London SW1V 2EX]; *b* 7 Sept 1960; *m* 30 May 1987 *Charles Comninos, s of Michael Comninos, of Staithe Ho, Chiswick, and has:
      1b *Alexander John; *b* 5 March 1989
      1b *Marina Catherine; *b* 14 Oct 1992
    2a *Ariane Sarah [Mrs Edward Koopman, 81 rue Corot, 92410 Ville D'Avray, France]; *b* 5 Jan 1963; *m* 1992 *Edward J Koopman, s of Hendrick Koopman, of St Didier au Mont d'Or, France, and has:
      1b *Henry Charles Bart; *b* 1997
      1b *Margaux Beatrix; *b* 1995

3a *Laura Catherine [Miss L Laing, 96 Auriol Rd, London W14 0SP]; b 20 Oct 1969

(2) (cont.) Mrs Gillian Laing m 2nd 1978 *Maldwin Andrew Cyril Drummond, JP, DL, and has further issue (see PERTH, E)

The 3rd Bt d 13 Oct 1960; his er s,

Sir John Ledward Royden, 4th Bt; b 31 Dec 1907; educ Winchester and Magdalen Coll Oxford; attd Willingdon Mission S America 1939–40, served Min Ec Warfare 1939–45, dir Duncan Fox and Co, S American Merchants, Order Merit Chile; m 30 June 1936 Dolores Catherine (d 1994), er dau of Cecil John George Coward, of Lima, Peru, and d 30 May 1976, leaving:

1 Sir CHRISTOPHER JOHN ROYDEN, **5th and present Bt**

2 +Thomas Cecil [Thomas Royden Esq, Netherfield Place Farm, Battle, Sussex]; b 26 July 1938; educ Winchester, Ch Ch Oxford, Maryland U, LSE, Utah State U (MSc) and California State Poly U Pomona; Master USA Ag, settlement manager Kitale, Tanzania, consultant Utah State U

1 *(Catherine) Anne; b 28 Feb 1945; m 14 July 1965 (divorce 1979) Christopher Synge Barton (see SYNGE, Bt) and has:

(1) *James Edward Synge; b 1974

(1) *Sarah Melissa Synge; b 1970

2 *(Quenelda) Jane [Mrs Robert Loder, Leonardslee Gdns, Lower Beeding, W Sussex]; b 21 April 1947; m 1 April 1967 *Robert Reginald (Robin) Loder and has issue (see LODER, Bt)

RUGBY

Arms: Erm. a fort with two towers ppr., issuant from the base a pile reversed sa., a chief dancettée or, surmounted by a pile az., charged with an increscent arg. **Crest:** A gauntlet fesswise grasping a lantern ppr. **Supporters:** On either side an Afghan hound ppr., gorged with a collar, the chain reflexed over the back or. **Motto:** Pass friend.
Creation: B. (UK) 10 Feb 1947.

THE 3RD BARON RUGBY, of Rugby, Co Warwick (Robert Charles Maffey) [The Rt Hon The Lord Rugby, Grove Farm, Frankton, Rugby CV23 9QG]; b 4 May 1951; s 1990; farmer; m 18 May 1974 *Anne Penelope, yr dau of David Hale, of Somerden, Chiddingstone, Kent, and has:

1 +TIMOTHY JAMES HOWARD; b 23 July 1975

2 +Philip Edward; b 1976

Lineage: NICHOLAS WILLIAM MAFFEY, of Leighton Buzzard; m Sophia — and had:

JOHN MAFFEY, of Leighton Buzzard; b 20 Sept 1811; d 1886, leaving:

THOMAS MAFFEY, of Rugby; b 23 April 1842; m Penelope Mary (d May 1899), dau of John Loader, of Thame, and d May 1917, leaving, with a dau (Grace Penelope, m 20 Nov 1917 Sir Frank Herbert Mitchell, KCVO, CBE (d 27 Nov 1951), and d 12 Sept 1959, leaving issue:

JOHN LOADER MAFFEY, **1st Baron Rugby** (UK), of Rugby, Co Warwick, so cr 10 Feb 1947, GCMG (1935), KCMG 1931), KCB (1934), KCVO (1921), CSI (1920), CIE (1916); b 1 July 1877; educ Rugby (Govr 1934–39) and Ch Ch Oxford (Hon Student); joined ICS 1899, tfd Political Dept 1905, Mohmand FF 1908 (medal and clasp), Political Agent Khyber 1909–12, Dep Commr Peshawar 1914–15, Dep Sec For and Political Dept Govt India 1915–16, Ch Political Offr Afghanistan NW Frontier FF 1919, Priv Sec to Viceroy 1916–20, Ch Sec to HRH THE DUKE OF CONNAUGHT 1921, Ch Cmmr NWFP India 1921–24, Govr-Gen Sudan 1926–33, PUS Colonies 1933–37, UK Rep Eire 1939–49, dir Imp Airways and Rio Tinto Ltd 1937–39, Grand Cordon Italy, Egyptian Order Ismail, Star Ethiopia; m 28 Aug 1907 Dorothy Gladys, OBE (1919) (d 3 Feb 1973), 2nd dau of Charles Lang Huggins, JP, of Hadlow Grange, Buxted, Sussex, by Agnes Maud Dingwall, and had:

1 ALAN LOADER, **2nd Baron**

2 +Simon Chelmsford Loader [The Hon Simon Maffey, Charterhouse, London EC1]; b 12 April 1919; educ Rugby; 2nd Lt Coldstream Gds 1937–43, WW II with Regt and Merchant Navy (wounded, invalided); m 1949 (divorce 1962) Andrée Norma, dau of George Middleton, of London, and has:

(1) *Penelope Anne; b 27 Dec 1950; m 1973 *Richard Patrick James Lacy and has issue (see TYRWHITT, Bt)

---

1 *Penelope Loader, MBE (1955), JP (Suffolk 1953) [The Hon Lady Aitken MBE JP, 2 North Court, Great Peter St, London SW1P 3LL]; b 2 Dec 1910; m 28 April 1938 Sir William Traven Aitken, KBE, MP (see BEAVERBROOK, B), and has issue

The 1st BARON d 20 April 1969; his er s,

ALAN LOADER MAFFEY, **2nd Baron Rugby**; b 16 April 1913; educ Stowe; F/Lt RAuxAF WW II, Liveryman Saddlers' Co (Key Warden 1977); m 14 April 1947 *Margaret [The Rt Hon Margaret Lady Rugby, Grove Farm, Frankton, Rugby CV23 9QG], dau of Harold Bindley, of Burton-on-Trent, and d 1990, having had:

1 John Richard; b 28 Aug 1949; educ Harrow; dsp Egypt 1981

2 ROBERT CHARLES MAFFEY, **3rd and present Baron Rugby**

3 +Christopher Alan [The Hon Christopher Maffey, Hamiltons Rd, RD4, Waiuku, Auckland, New Zealand]; b 20 Feb 1955; educ Malvern; m 1st 1977 (divorce 1981) Barbara Anne, yr dau of Guthrie Stewart, of Auckland, NZ; m 2nd 1982 (divorce 1991) Katherine, er dau of Viv Rutherfurd, of Waiuku; m 3rd 1995 *Sarah Louise, dau of Peter Solon, of NZ and by his 2nd w has:

(1) +Aaron John; b 1983

(2) +Leigh Alan; b 1984

4 +Mark Andrew [The Hon Mark Maffey, The Flat, Grove Farm, Frankton, Warwicks]; b 7 June 1956; educ Harrow and Ecole de Commerce Neuchâtel; m 1983 *Angela Mary, dau of Derek J Polton, of Draycote, Rugby, and has:

(1) +Thomas Henry; b 1988

(2) +Christopher James; b 1993

(1) *Georgina Louise; b 1986

1 *Selina Penelope [The Hon Selina Maffey, McDougal Rd, Julatten, Queensland 4880, Australia]; b 15 Nov 1952; has:

(1) *Tamas Henry; b 1990

(1) *Angelica Helena; b 1986

2 *Alicia Dorothy [The Hon Mrs Morton, Manor Farm, Draycote, Warwicks]; b 14 Jan 1960; m 1981 *Richard M Morton, 2nd s of John Morton, of Draycote, and has:

(1) *Samuel Richard; b 1986

(2) *John Alan Kynaston; b 1990

(1) *Eleanor Margaret; b 1984

RUGGE-PRICE

Arms: Quarterly, 1st and 4th, gules a lion rampant argent (for PRICE); 2nd and 3rd, sable on a chevron, invected argent, between three mullets or, pierced of the field, a unicorn's head erased of the first (for RUGGE). **Crests:** 1 A lion rampant argent, in the dexter paw a rose slipped proper (for PRICE), 2 A talbot passant argent, gorged with a collar, pendant therefrom an escutcheon sable, charged with the head of an ibex couped also argent (for RUGGE). **Motto:** Vive ut vivas ('Live [now] such that you may live [hereafter]').
Creation: Bt. (UK) 2 Feb 1804.

SIR (CHARLES) KEITH NAPIER RUGGE-PRICE, 9TH BT, of Spring Grove, Richmond, Surrey [Sir Keith Rugge-Price Bt, 2 Lorne Cres, St Albert, Alberta, Canada T8N 3R2]; b 7 Aug 1936; s f 1966; educ Middleton Coll Ireland and London Poly; served 5th Regt RHA 1954–59; m 12 June 1965 *Jacqueline Mary, yr dau of Maj Pierre Paul Loranger, MC, CD, of Quebec, and has:

1 +JAMES KEITH PETER; b 8 April 1967

2 +Andrew Philip Richard; b 6 Jan 1970

Lineage: RHYS WYNN Ap CADWALLADER bought 1583 lands in Hiraethog and elsewhere in Denbighs; m Margaret, dau of Ellizan ap William ap Griffith ap Jenkins, of Ryngoch, and d between 2 Oct 1596 and 2 Nov 1604, having had, with two other sons:

1 WILLIAM

2 Thomas Price/Thomas ap Rhys Wynn, of Geeler, Denbighs; High Sheriff 1623; m Lucy, dau and heiress of Robert Rodd, of Foxley, Herefs, and was ancestor of the PRICE Bts, of Foxley (see 1857 edn); also ggf of:

(1) Robert; Baron Exchequer 1714

The est s,

WILLIAM PRICE, of Geeler, Denbighs, and Bath, Somerset; bought 1590 from his uncle Robert lands called Athac Als Kair Haithe and others called Bryna, in Hierathog; gifted by his f 1591 the Geeler estate in Denbighs; m —, who brought him lands in West Hannan, Bittom, Glos, and had an est s:

Rev JOHN PRICE; Rector and patron Farnborough, Berks, 1606; m Jane — and d by 1646, leaving a 4th s:

Rev BARTHOLOMEW PRICE; bapt 13 July 1623; Rector Farnborough; m Mary (d 30 June 1686 aged 52), dau of Petley Garnham, of Farnborough, Serjeant counting-house of CHARLES II, and d 17 April 1677 aged 54, leaving a 6th s:

PETLEY PRICE, of The Ham, Wantage, Berks; bapt 27 Oct 1668; m 12 Jan 1706 Joan Smith, of Wroughton, Wilts, and was bur 10 Nov 1723, leaving a 5th s:

Rev RALPH PRICE; bapt 1 Nov 1715; Rector, patron and Vicar Lyminge, Kent, patron Farnborough; m 18 Feb 1739 Sarah (d 1780), dau and coheir of Richard Richardson, of Smalley, Derbys, and d 20 Nov 1779, leaving, with another s (d an infant):

1 Ralph, of Lyminge (Rev); b 18 May 1745; m 2 Nov 1775 Albinia (d 17 Aug 1827), dau of Rev George Woodward, BC, Rector E Hendred, by Albinia, dau of George Courthope, of Whiligh, Sussex, and d 7 July 1811; ancestor of the PRICEs of Lyminge

2 CHARLES (Sir), **1st Bt**

1 Mary; d unm 1764

2 Catharine; m 28 June 1775 Thomas Goodlake, of Letcombe Regis, Berks, and had issue

3 Sarah; m George Evans, of Balham

The 2nd surv s,

Sir Charles Price, 1st Bt (UK), so cr 2 Feb 1804, of Spring Grove, Richmond, Surrey; b 25 Jan 1748; MP London, Alderman, Ld Mayor 1803; m 16 Dec 1773 Mary (d 22 Feb 1838), dau and coheir of William Rugge, of Conduit St, London W1, and d 19 July 1818, having had, with another s (d young) and two daus (d unm):

1 CHARLES (Sir), **2nd Bt**

2 Ralph, of Sydenham, Kent; b 8 Feb 1780; m 3 Sept 1805 Charlotte Savery (d 2 April 1850), 2nd dau of Lt-Col Thomas Carteret Hardy, Col Cmdt York Fus, by Sarah Price, and d 3 April 1860, having had, with another s (d an infant) and dau (d unm):

(1) Ralph Charles, of Hill House, Carshalton, Surrey; b 25 July 1808; patron Farnborough; m 1 Oct 1835 his cousin Albinia Eliza (d 10 Aug 1886), 5th dau of **Sir Charles Price, 2nd Bt**, and d 1 March 1868, having had, with another s (d young) and three daus (d unm):

1a Edmund (Rev); b 11 Aug 1836; Rector and patron Farnborough; m 17 Oct 1867 Frances Augusta (d 12 Nov 1931 aged 92), dau of Edward Cockburn Kindersley, and dsp 15 Sept 1872

2a Ralph George, JP Essex; b 18 June 1838; m 13 Nov 1867 Annette Mary (d 11 Oct 1916), dau of Rev Simeon Burney Warner, and d 29 Sept 1904, having had:

1b Edith Mabel Warner; m 29 Jan 1889 Brig-Gen Frank Broadwood Matthews, CB, DSO, KOR Lancaster Regt (d 24 April 1940), of Old Raven House, Hook, Hants, s of Charles P Matthews, JP, of Havering-atte-Bower, Essex, and d 1 Jan 1940, leaving issue

2b Annette Maud Warner; m 30 July 1891 Sir Joseph Child Priestley, KC, JP, DL (d 9 June 1941), of Tatmore Place, Hitchin, Herts, 2nd s of Sir William Overend Priestley, MD, MP, of Edinburgh, and d 19 July 1946, leaving issue

3a Alfred Adams; b 9 Jan 1840; Capt 67th Regt; m 17 Jan 1867 Eliza Lockett (d 15 Dec 1901), dau of Thomas Taylor, ICS, and d 15 March 1917, having had:

1b Ernest Charles; b 19 Oct 1867; d unm 3 April 1900

2b Kenneth Alexander; b 2 Jan 1869; Capt 9th Canadian Mounted Rifles (Strathcona's Horse) WW I; m 6 July 1904 Helen Mary (d 1942), 2nd dau of William Baldwin George, and had:

1c Guy Adams; b 1 Jan 1907; d unm 11 Feb 1934

2c Alan Alfred; b Aug 1914; d 1915

3c +Arthur Basil; b 1916; m 1939 *Ethel Frances Brindle

4c +Douglas Leonard; b 1 Feb 1922; F/Lt RAF; m 1943 *Hazel Irene Boyles

1c *Ethel Marian; b 7 June 1905; m 1 March 1930 *Kenneth Couch and has issue

2c *Phyllis; b 14 Sept 1908; m 1941 *Leslie Henry, Canadian Army

3c Ralph Charles, of Forty Garry House; b 6 Dec 1873; served WW I; d unm 19 Feb 1919

1b Geraldine Mabel; m 1890 Maj Claude George Ironside Currie (d 3 Dec 1916), Dorset Regt, and d 24 March 1899, leaving issue

2b Kathleen Mary; m 7 March 1907 Robert George McCrea, 2nd s of Maj F Bradford McCrea, 8th King's Regt, and had issue

4a Alexander Smirke; b 30 Oct 1841; d 19 April 1917

5a Herbert Still; b 1 Dec 1845; Lt 4th Dragoon Gds; d unm 21 Aug 1900

6a Leonard Charles; b 12 Feb 1855; d unm 20 Jan 1946

1a Marian Frances; b 27 June 1847; m 13 May 1874 James Frederick Gaitskell (d 1895) and d 18 Dec 1931 aged 84

(2) Robert; b 13 July 1813; Capt 67th Regt Bengal NI; m 1st 25 Aug 1838 Ellen Anne Robinson (dsp 24 Nov 1838); m 2nd 29 Feb 1840 Sophia Catharine (d 8 Oct 1845), yst dau of Lt-Col Robert Leslie Anstruther, 6th Bengal Lt Cav, and had:

1a Ralph Anstruther; b 11 Aug 1842; Lt-Col BSC; m 2 July 1867 Fanny Hughes (d 30 June 1927), dau of James Lamb, and d 3 Dec 1914, having had:

1b Robert James Stafford; b 18 Feb 1870; d unm 8 Feb 1914

1b Mary Sophia; m 29 Aug 1908 Charles Rundall Cunningham (d 13 Aug 1932), s of Lt-Col Charles Cunningham, RE

(2) (cont.) Capt Robert Price m 3rd 16 May 1850 his 1st cousin Harriet (d 11 May 1880), 3rd dau of **Sir Charter Price, 2nd Bt**, and was ka 5 Feb 1853 at Donabue nr Rangoon

(3) Francis Lysons, of Surbiton Hill, Kingston, Surrey; b 27 Dec 1819; memb Gentlemen-at-Arms; m 28 Dec 1854 Louisa Georgina (d 1 March 1865), 2nd dau of Charles Burlton, 41st Regt, and had:

1a Louise Charlotte Mary; d unm 11 Feb 1899

(1) Sarah Anne; m 19 March 1829 Simon Adams Beck (d 1883) and d 14 March 1839, having had issue

(2) Laura Frances; m 27 Aug 1840 Robert Still (d 10 March 1875), of Sutton Hill, Surrey, est s of Rev John Still, of Barwick House, Wilts, and d 18 May 1863, having had issue

3 Richard, of The Lawn, Lambeth; b 1 June 1781; m 12 Oct 1805 Elizabeth Engel (d 5 March 1847), dau of Henry Heyman, of Queen Square House, Consul-Gen for the Hanse Towns, and d 15 Sept 1852, having had, with other issue (d young or unm):

(1) Augustus; b 14 June 1813; Lt-Col 4th Bombay Rifles; m 27 April 1852 Elizabeth Emma (d 21 Oct 1890), dau of Maj-Gen Christopher Hodgson, and d 17 May 1860, having had, with a dau (d unm):

1a Petley Lloyd Augustus; b 25 April 1856; BCS; m 26 Aug 1884 Mary Cotton (d 1946), dau of Capt Frederick Arthur Egerton, RN (see GREY EGERTON, Bt), and d 30 Dec 1910, leaving:

1b Augustus Robert Petley; b 4 May 1885; Capt IA (despatches); m 2 Dec 1922 Augusta Elsy Maud (d 1980), dau of Gilbert Wilkes, of Ganges, British Columbia, and d 27 June 1945, leaving:

1c +Augustus Robert Kenrick; b 2 May 1927

1c *Elsy Mary; b 10 Sept 1923; m 15 June 1963 *Raymond Perks and has:

1d *John Robert Raymond; b 10 Feb 1965

2d *David Raymond; b 18 May 1966

2b Harold Tudor Egerton; b 17 March 1888; m 2 July 1927 Margaret Frances, 2nd dau of Edward Fotheringham Layard, of Southsea, Hants, and d 22 July 1965, leaving:

1c +John Harold Petley; b 1928; m 14 Feb 1953 *Edith, dau of J Lee, of Victoria, BC

1c *Ruth Gladys; b 1930

3b Reginald; b 28 Aug 1889; d 24 Nov 1964

1b *Elizabeth Rosina May; b 7 Dec 1886; m 1915 Lt Alexander Thomas Benthall Charlesworth (ka 30 May 1917), RFC

2b Ada Marjorie; b 18 Oct 1890; m 1915 Lt Cecil Edward Archibald Leslie Ley, MC, RE, and had issue

2a Herman Chicheley Augustus, JP Somerset; b 14 June 1858; d 28 Aug 1933

1a Florence Engel Augusta; m 5 July 1911 Robert Brindley Wood (d 1914), of Kentville, Nova Scotia, and d 30 Sept 1938

(2) Edward Ralph; b 9 Nov 1818; d 22 March 1852

(3) Richard; b 5 March 1820; d unm 11 Jan 1865

(4) George Uvedale; b 3 April 1821; Gen Bombay SC; m 1st 3 July 1851 Elizabeth Palmer (d 15 July 1857), widow of Lt Arthur Edward Frere, 24th Regt, and dau of James Price, 24th Regt, and had, with a dau (d unm):

1a George Uvedale; b 10 Dec 1853; d 29 Oct 1929

2a Edward Augustus Uvedale; b 18 Oct 1854; Maj 4th Bn E Surrey Regt; m 27 Oct 1881 Elizabeth Henrietta (d 19 Nov 1905), dau of Henry John Philip Dumas, JP Surrey; lost with his wife in the wreck of the *Hilda* off St Malo 19 Nov 1905, leaving:

1b Reginald Henry Uvedale; b 23 Nov 1883; m 2 June 1909 Mabel Evelyn (m 2nd 4 March 1944 Dr Anthony McCall, who d 30 Sept 1954), er dau of Capt Ashley Mackenzie, E Yorks Regt, and dsp 28 May 1910

2b Geoffrey Uvedale; b 5 Feb 1885; Lt-Cdr RNVR WW I (despatches, wounded); m 28 Oct 1908 Winifred Ethel (d 1963), only dau of Edgar Lacey Price, of Putney, and d 3 Jan 1960, leaving:

1c *Vivienne Betty Henrietta; b 1 Feb 1910; m 2 Jan 1934 *Brig Maurice Rapinet Mackenzie, DSO, RA, s of Philip Rapinet Mackenzie, of Rome, and has:

1d *Michael Philip Uvedale Rapinet; b 26 June 1937; educ Downside and Lincoln Coll Oxford

1b Helen Rose Elizabeth; m 17 Sept 1908 Henry Edward Seccombe (d 24 Nov 1955), ARIBA, only s of Henry L Seccombe and gs of Sir T L Seccombe, GCIE, KCSI, CB, and d 21 March 1969, having had issue

2b Kathleen Janette; b 12 June 1886; m 7 Nov 1912 Capt Leslie Granville Waller, Intell Corps (d 25 Nov 1969), er s of R R Waller, of Calcutta, and had:

1c *Margaret Evelyn Henrietta [Mrs Jacques Lioni, Mr Sixlaan 3, Amstelveen, Netherlands]; b 5 Nov 1913; m 4 Nov 1939 *Jacques Lioni and has:

1d *David Alexander; b 22 Sept 1941

2d *John Christopher Granville; b 16 March 1945

1d *Helen Mary; b 17 Feb 1947

1a Catharine Rosina; m 19 Oct 1872 Thomas Henry Moore and had issue

(4) (cont.) Gen George Price m 2nd 22 Jan 1859 Harriette Anne Wilhelmina (d 25 March 1925), dau of Rev Charles Robert Gayer, and d 7 Dec 1891, having by her had:

3a Charles Henry Uvedale, CB (1914), DSO (1899); b 16 June 1862; Brig-Gen IA, served Burma and Uganda; m 1 Oct 1889 Ada Mary (d 30 July 1956), dau of John Orlando Hercules Norman Oliver, CSI, and d 22 Feb 1942, having had:

1b Ryswynn Uvedale; b 14 Aug 1890; d 10 March 1906

1b Merlyth Mary; b 21 May 1895

4a Cyril Uvedale, CMG (1916); b 13 May 1868; educ Utd Service Coll Westward Ho! and RMC Sandhurst; Lt-Col and Brevet-Col IA, formerly Royal Dublin Fus, Zhob Field Force 1890, Uganda 1897–99 (despatches, medal with clasp), China 1901 (medal), WW I (despatches, Brevet), Order St

Anne Russia 3rd Cl with swords; m 1st 11 Oct 1902 Ethel Maude (d 30 Sept 1916), dau of Capt William Henry Ashe, 18th Roy Irish Regt; m 2nd 7 May 1919 May Edith (d 1967), dau of Robert Lewis, of S Africa, and d 3 May 1956, having by her had:

1b +Roger Uvedale [Roger Price Esq, 27 Mariners Walk, Rustington, W Sussex BN16 2ER]; b 22 Jan 1921; Capt IA WW II; m 1946 *Angela Marcella Exton, dau of Brig — Wallis, IA, and has:

1c *Myfanwy Uvedale [Mrs Michael Payne, 22 Lansdown Rd, Angmering, W Sussex BN16 4JX]; b 12 Jan 1948; m 1st 1968 (divorce 1989) Peter John Penney and has:

1d *Ian Richard; b 1970

1d *Samantha Helen; b 1973

1c (cont.) Mrs Myfanwy Penney m 2nd 1992 *Michael John Payne

2a Mary Sophia; d unm 17 Dec 1947

(1) Mary; m 21 July 1836 her cousin **Sir Arthur James Rugge-Price, 5th Bt**, and d 22 Sept 1905, leaving issue

(2) Rosina Mary; m 8 Jan 1868 her cousin **Sir Frederick Pott Price, 4th Bt** and d 21 March 1904

(3) Frances Henrietta; m 15 April 1856 Patrick Stewart (d 18 May 1903), barrister Middle Temple, and dsp 6 Jan 1864

(4) Catherine Harriet; m 24 Jan 1850 Surgn-Gen Henry R D Marrett (d 7 Feb 1867), s of Maj-Gen — Marrett, of Bath, and d 27 Oct 1885, leaving issue

4 Thomas, of Clementhorpe, Yorks; b 4 Aug 1783; 4th Dragoon Gds; m 22 May 1814 Eliza (d 10 March 1857), dau and coheir of Hall Plumer, and d 29 Jan 1856, having had:

(1) Thomas Charles (Rev); b 4 Aug 1816; Vicar St Augustine's, Bristol; m 8 April 1847 Ellen (d 1878), 5th dau of John Taylor, of Liverpool, and d 8 Nov 1885, leaving, with two other sons (d young) and three daus (d unm):

1a Charles Chicheley, JP British Honduras; b 1 Oct 1854; m 19 March 1901 Mary Ethel Geraldine (d 20 June 1902), dau of Richard Henry Lambert, of Bristol, and dsp 4 Aug 1910

2a Ralph Mountague Rokeby; b 3 May 1860; m 1889 Emily Ada (d 1924), widow of Alexander Finlay Bowman, of British Honduras, and dau of William Jex and d 20 July 1905, leaving:

1b Ralph Chicheley Rokeby; b 1889; m 19 April 1921 Dora Mignon Shenstone, dau of Richard Simpson, and d with his wife and dau in a hurricane 10 Sept 1931, having had:

1c Phyllis Geraldine Rokeby; b 12 Sept 1924; d 10 Sept 1931

2b Arthur Mountague Rokeby; b 21 Aug 1892; m 9 Aug 1916 Eliza (d 1983), dau of Victor Kuylen, of Stann Creek, British Honduras, and d 6 June 1941, leaving:

1c +Ralph Mountague Rokeby [Ralph Price Esq, 4429 Kawanee Ave, Metairie, LA 70002, USA]; b 1917; Dep Colonial Sec British Honduras, Capt Caribbean Regt WW II, Colonial Police Medal for Meritorious Service 1957; m 31 Aug 1942 *Margarita Matilde Ernestina, dau of Nazario Cervantes, of Belize, and has:

1d +Ralph Mountague Rokeby; b 12 Oct 1946; m 1976 *Kim, dau of Harold Maranto Jr, of Louisiana, and has:

1e +Jared; b 1978

2e +Joshua; b 1980

3e +Andrew; b 1982

4e +Adam; b 1984

1e *Jennifer Leigh; b 1977

2d +Arthur Richard Rokeby [Arthur Price Esq, 41228 Elorado Dr, Hammond, LA 70403, USA]; b 3 Nov 1949; m 1972 *Elaine Sand and has:

1e +Jason Richard; b 1974

2e +Scott Richard; b 1979

3d David Francis Rokeby; b 16 July 1956; d 1986

4d Michael John Rokeby; b 30 Dec 1958; d 1987

1d *Patricia Elizabeth Rokeby [Mrs Marvin Sabido, 1905 Kent Ave, Metairie, LA 70001, USA]; b 25 Oct 1943; m 27 June 1963 *Marvin Robert Sabido, s of Lewis Sabido, of Belize, and has:

1e *Marvin Robert; b 17 Sept 1964

2e *David Andrew; b 3 March 1967

3e *Christopher Ian; b 10 April 1969

4e *Steven Scott; b 1975

2d *Alice Mae Rokeby [Mrs Lloyd Perrien, 2604 N Sibley St, Metairie, LA 70003, USA]; b 5 June 1948; m 1972 *Lloyd Perrien and has:

1e *Todd Andrew; b 1973

2e *Derek Lloyd; b 1976

3d *Margaret Joan Rokeby; b 23 Aug 1952

4d *Carolyn Mary Rokeby; b 20 June 1962

2c Arthur Victor Rokeby; b 1921; F/Sgt RAF WW II; m 1955 *Bridget Ellen [Mrs Arthur Price, 510 South Archer St, Anaheim, CA, USA], dau of Michael Austin Flynn, of Canada, and d 1964, leaving:

1d +Richard Arthur; b 1959

2d +Michael Craig (twin); b 1959

1d *Bridget Ellen b 1956

2d *Judith; b 1958

3d *Jennifer (twin); b 1958

4d *Margaret Mary; b 1962

5d *Sheila Rose; b 1963

6d *Elizabeth Ann; b 1964

1b Gladys Ethel Rokeby; b 1895; m 1917 Robert Albert Gegg Howard and had issue. He d 1963

3a Thomas Plumer; b 15 May 1861; m 1884 Elizabeth Laura Middleton (d 1946), dau of Capt Richard George Collins, 57th Regt, of Melbourne House, Cullompton, and d 15 Oct 1930, leaving:

1b Thomas Ralph Plumer; b 1 March 1885; slr 1907, Capt RGA (TF) WW I; m 31 July 1916 Ruth Beatrice (d 1978), dau of Sydney Harris, of Edgbaston, and d 3 Jan 1967, leaving:

1c +Richard Ralph Plumer [Richard Price Esq, 1–1019 Pemberton Rd, Victoria BC, V8S 3R5, Canada]; b 22 March 1926; m 1954 *Audrey Chrystal, dau of James Anderson Gray, of London, Ontario, and has:

1d +James Plumer [James Price Esq, 4919 48 Ave, Ladner, BC, V4K 1V4, Canada]; b 1957

2d +Norman Plumer [Norman Price Esq, 337 Richmond Rd, Victoria, BC, V8P 4P3, Canada]; b 1959; m 1979 *Bronwyn Anne, dau of Robert Fox, of Victoria, BC, and has:

1e *Tristan Christina; b 1980

1c *Ruth Rosemary Plumer [Mrs Ruth Sindall, 10 Garden Mews, Warsash, Hants SO31 9GW]; b 1920; m 1946 (divorce 1953) F/O Robert Alfred John Sindall, RAF, and has:

1d *David Robert Plumer; b 24 Jan 1947; educ Embley Park Sch; m 1978 *Susan Jane Humby

1d *Sally Ann [Mrs Roger Hogben, 21 Nutwick Rd, Denvilles, Havant, Hants]; b 23 Aug 1949; m 1st 22 Feb 1969 (divorce 1975) Stephen Philip Clarke, s of Philip Ernest Clarke, of Melbourne, Australia, and has:

1e *Rachel Melanie; b 1 Jan 1970

2e *Sarah Elizabeth; b 1972

1d (cont.) Mrs Sally Clarke m 2nd 1977 *Roger David Hogben and by him has:

3e *Helen Abigail; b 1977

1b Phyllis Joan Sinclair Plumer; b 16 June 1895; m 17 July 1918 Thomas Brunyée Harston (d 23 Sept 1951), LLB, slr, Capt King's Regt, and had:

1c *Anthony Plumer Brunyée; b 12 March 1924; educ Sedbergh and St Andrews; MB, ChB, MRCOG, Lt-Col RAMC

1c *Bridget Elizabeth Uvedale; b 11 Jan 1931

4a Hall Towrye, JP British Honduras; b 27 April 1864; barrister; m 1st 16 Oct 1888 Matilda Caroline (d 3 Nov 1920), dau of Richard Henry Bowen; m 2nd 1921 Edith Mabel, widow of R E Pommells, of Belize, and d 2 Nov 1931

1a Alice Ellen; m 1st 20 April 1882 Alexander Stanley Lowndes (d 1893); m 2nd 1895 Samuel Sunders (d 1905), of Calcutta; m 3rd 1906 Cyril Templeton King and d 30 Nov 1921

(2) Edwin Plumer, QC; b 13 March 1818; BA, Judge County Court No 32 1874–95, Recorder York; m 1st 15 June 1841 his cousin Lucy (d 1884), dau and coheir of John Harrison, of Ripley, by Lucy Henrietta, 2nd dau of **Sir Charles Price, 1st Bt**, and had, with a dau (d unm):

1a John Harrison; b 8 Dec 1848; d unm 11 Feb 1893

1a Georgiana Charlotte Elizabeth; m 22 Oct 1879 William Thomas Law, MD, FRCS, s of Henry Compton Law (dsps 6 Sept 1910), of Allington, Wilts, and d 13 March 1927

2a Beatrice Mary PLUMER-PRICE; d 20 June 1929

(2) (cont.) Judge Edwin Price m 2nd 1884 Agnes Mary (d 1888), widow of John Samuel Guy and dau of William Normanville; m 3rd 1889 Janet Louisa (d 1909), dau of J M Bird, and d 1 Aug 1899

(3) Spencer Cosby; b 19 Aug 1819; Capt 72nd Highrs; m 1st 19 Dec 1843 Sarah (d 12 Aug 1850), widow of William Cooke-Collis, of Castle Cooke, Co Cork, and est surv dau of John Hyde, DL, of Castle Hyde, Co Cork, and had:

1a Annie Eliza; m 8 June 1869 Hormuzd Rassam (d 15 Sept 1910), ICS, Br Envoy Abyssinia, and d 29 July 1924 aged 84, leaving issue

2a Louisa Mary; m 1st 16 May 1872 Henry Charles Cutcliffe; m 2nd 1875 Alfred Teevan, 55th Regt, and d 1911, leaving issue

3a Caroline Frances; m 24 Dec 1867 Col Henry George Saunders (d 1912), IA, and d 22 Oct 1914, leaving issue

(3) (cont.) Capt Spencer Price m 2nd 22 Sept 1857 (divorce 1873) Adelaide (d 4 Jan 1916), dau of George Baker; m 3rd 26 March 1873 Emily (d April 1875), dau of James Howe, and d 16 June 1892, having by her had:

1a Spencer Edward Cosby; b 23 Sept 1873; m 29 Dec 1894 his cousin Eleanor Anne, dau of Mark Watmore, and had:

1b +Spencer Kendrick Sydney; b 26 June 1902

1b Sydney Melita Cosby; b 2 June 1897; d 15 Jan 1900

2b Nesta Joan Cosby; b 24 Nov 1900

(4) Hall Rokeley; b 11 July 1821; Lt City London; m 12 May 1853 Fanny (d 20 Feb 1899), dau of Matthew Holland, and d 8 May 1903, leaving, with a dau (d unm):

1a Arthur Rokeby; b 5 March 1854; d unm 29 Oct 1912

2a Wilfrid Thomas Rokeby; b 16 Jan 1856; BA Oxon, slr; m 30 Oct 1888 Emily Catherine (d 7 Oct 1952), est dau of Charles Frederick Murray, of Woodcote Hall, Epsom, and d 15 Aug 1926, leaving:

1b Harold Rokeby, MC; b 27 July 1889; educ Winchester; Lt (Actg Capt) 2nd Bn Rifle Bde WW I (despatches, wounded); m 8 Aug 1932 *Angela Mary, only child of Rev Henry Johnson Treloar Bennetts, and dsp 4 June 1965

2b Murray Rokeby; b 29 Oct 1894; educ Gresham's; Indian Imp Police, Capt York and Lancaster Regt WW I, Inspr (wounded), Dep-Gen Police 1946–49, Indian Police Medal; d unm 24 Sept 1968

1b Freda Rokeby; m 1st 19 June 1915 Capt George Edgecombe Hellyer (d 22 Aug 1915 of wounds recd in action), 10th Bn Hants Regt; m 2nd 23 Jan 1917 Arthur William Montague Marshall (d 13 Jan 1957), s of John Marshall, of The Red House, Great Barr, Staffs, and had:

1c John Wilfrid; b 24 Feb 1918; Lt RN; ka 27 April 1941

1c *Jean Margaret; b 5 Dec 1919; m 4 April 1942 *Capt Thomas Hugh Peter Wilson, RN, s of Rev Thomas Erskine Wilson, of Bolney, Sussex, and has:

1d *Rosamond Margaret [Mrs David Wright, Vindelis, Old Hill, Portland, Dorset]; b 24 Feb 1943; m 18 Oct 1967 *Lt-Cdr David Wright, RN, stepson of Evelyn Wright, of Halifax, Yorks

2d *Veronica Ane; b 30 Oct 1944

3d *Felicity Jean; b 29 Aug 1949

2b Marjorie Rokeby

3b Olive Rokeby; d unm 16 Aug 1971

(5) Clement Uvedale; b 19 April 1825; d unm 25 Dec 1879

(1) Eliza Caroline; m 29 March 1855 Capt Robert Charles Holmes (d 17 April 1869), 10th Hus, and d 1881, leaving issue

(2) Araminta Mary; m 23 Nov 1848 Burkhardt Heinrich von Schmeling (d 14 Nov 1902), Gen Prussian Army, formerly 1st Regt of Gds, Govr Danzig, and d 16 Feb 1901, leaving issue

1 Mary Anne; m 24 Feb 1803, William Moore, of Doctors Commons, and d 18 July 1838, leaving issue

2 Lucy Henrietta; m 12 Nov 1807 John Harrison, only s of John Harrison, of Benningholme Hall and Ruisthorpe, Yorks, and Ripley Court, Surrey, and d 1809, leaving issue

3 Anne; m David Holmes, Army Offr, s of Robert Holmes, of Ballyadam, Co Limerick, and had issue

The 1st Bt's est son,

Sir Charles Price, 2nd Bt; b 3 Sept 1776; m 3 May 1798 Mary Ann (d 9 May 1847), dau of William King, of King St, Covent Garden, and d 26 April 1847, having had, with another s (d young) and three daus (d young or unm):

1 **Sir Charles Rugge Price 3rd Bt**; b 28 Sept 1801; d unm 3 July 1866

2 **Sir Frederick Pott Price, 4th Bt**; b 5 Sept 1806; m 8 Jan 1868 his cosin Rosina Mary, dau of Richard Price, and dsp 15 Nov 1873

3 ARTHUR JAMES (Sir), **5th Bt**

1 Mary; m 4 Nov 1823 William Pott (d 6 Dec 1878), of Southwark, and d 15 Aug 1870, leaving issue

2 Harriet; m 16 May 1850 her 1st cousin Capt Robert Price and d his widow 11 May 1880

3 Albinia Eliza; m 1 Oct 1835 her 1st cousin Ralph Charles Price and d 10 Aug 1886, having had issue

4 Emily Harriet; m 24 April 1845 Henry Currey (d 23 Nov 1900), of Sydenham, Kent, and d 1 March 1896, leaving issue

The 4th Bt's yr bro,

Sir ARTHUR JAMES PRICE later RUGGE-PRICE (roy licence 7 March 1874), **5th Bt**; b 22 Sept 1808; m 21 July 1836 his 1st cousin Mary, est dau of Richard Price, and had, with another s (d unm):

1 CHARLES (Sir), **6th Bt**

1 Mary Rugge; m 6 Dec 1860 Irving Frederick de Rougemont (d 9 Feb 1905) and d 21 March 1915, leaving issue

2 Augusta Rosina; m 4 Nov 1867 Rev Henry Dodwell Moore, Vicar Honington, Lincs, Canon Lincoln, and d 6 Feb 1901, leaving issue

Sir ARTHUR d 5 Jan 1892; his s,

Sir Charles Rugge-Price, 6th Bt; JP, DL; b 26 May 1841; Hon Col 3rd Vol Bn E Surrey Regt; m 11 April 1867 Antonia Mary (d 21 Jan 1918), 2nd dau of William James Harvey, JP, DL, of Carnousie, Banffshire, and had:

1 CHARLES FREDERICK (Sir) **7th Bt**

2 Arthur Rugge; b 10 Feb 1873; Lt 3rd Vol Bn E Surrey Regt; d 10 Dec 1897

1 Isobel Mary Engel

2 Gwendolen Amy; m 7 Oct 1896 Arthur Trevor O'Bryen Leslie (d 17 Aug 1939), MBE, s of Capt Thomas Leslie, of Kilmore, Co Cavan, and d 29 Feb 1912, having had issue

3 Edith Winifred; d unm 5 Sept 1944

4 Henrietta; m 4 June 1907 Richard Rawlinson (d June 1945), s of Thomas Rawlinson, and d March 1947, leaving issue

5 Gwladys Margaret; d unm 24 Sept 1954

Sir CHARLES d 4 May 1927; his s,

Sir Charles Frederick Rugge-Price, 7th Bt; b 5 Feb 1868; educ Cheltenham and RMA Woolwich; Lt-Col RAF Boer War 1900–01 (despatches, Queen's medal with four clasps) and WW I (despatches twice); m 15 Oct 1901 Isabella Napier Keith (d 26 Aug 1947), er dau of Maj-Gen Sir James Keith Trotter, KCB, CMG, DL, and had:

1 CHARLES JAMES NAPIER (Sir), **8th Bt**

2 Anthony Arthur Keith, CBE (1967); b 9 Nov 1914; educ Harrow; Col 13th/18th Hus WW II, OC 13th/18th Roy Hus 1956–58; m 1st 27 April 1939 (divorce 1948) Joan Lisette Douglas, yst dau of Alan Douglas Pilkington, of Dean Wood, Newbury, Berks, and Achvarasdal, Reay, Thurso, Caithness, and had:

(1) +(Anthony) Jeremy [Jeremy Rugge-Price, 60 Lincoln Ave, Purchase, NY 10577-2302, USA]; b 23 March 1940; educ Harrow; late Capt 13th/18th Roy Hus (QMO); m 20 July 1963 (divorce) Sarah Olivia Valentine, only dau of Maj Thomas Adam, of Denmore, Bridge of Don, Aberdeenshire, and has:

1a +Andrew Christian [Andrew Rugge-Price Esq, 499 King's Rd, London SW3 0TU]; b 21 Dec 1964; m 1991 *Sophie A, yr dau of A J Hind and Mrs W Hipwell, of Norwich

2a +Barnaby Douglas; b 17 Sept 1969

1a *Matilda Candide; b 25 Nov 1970

(1) (cont.) Jeremy Rugge-Price m 2nd 14 July 1972 (divorce) Beverly Ann, dau of Lt-Col L G Davidson Brett, of Corfe, Somerset, and by her has:

3a +Edward Jason Napier; b 29 Nov 1973

(1) (cont.) Jeremy Rugge-Price m 3rd 1981 *Carolyn Anne, only dau of Sir Richard Ashton Beaumont, KCMG, OBE, and formerly w of Michael Brodrick Hicks Beach (see ST ALDWYN, E), and has:

4a +Robert Jake; b 2 Jan 1982

(2) Andrew Douglas Napier; b 18 Jan 1943; d 1 Feb 1957

(3) +James Keith Alan [James Rugge-Price Esq, Stainswick Manor, Shrivenham, Wilts SN6 8LD]; b 10 Oct 1944; educ Harrow; m 1st 30 March 1967 (divorce 1972) Elizabeth Mary, only dau of Lt-Col James Innes (see WESTBURY, B), and has:

1a *Lucy Caroline; b 7 June 1969

(3) (cont.) James Rugge-Price m 2nd 26 April 1976 *Alexa, dau of Arthur Patrick Usher Crookshank, and by her has:

2a *Samantha; b 24 May 1979

3a *Kinvara; b 24 May 1979

4a *Alice; b 22 May 1985

2 (cont.) Col Anthony Rugge-Price m 2nd 1952 *Mrs (Mary) Joy Campbell [Mrs Anthony Rugge-Price, 47 Draycott Place, London SW3], dau of John Eric Horniman, and d 14 May 1997, having by her had:

(1) *Juliet [Mrs Thomas Hughes Hallett, 49 Eglantine Rd, London SW18]; b 23 Dec 1954; m 1979 *Thomas M S Hughes Hallett, yr s of Michael Hughes Hallett, of Barton-on-the-Heath, Glos, and has had:

1a *Archie James Arthur; b 1983

1a Emily; d 23 Oct 1982

2a *Grace Majorie; b 1986

1 Catherine Majorie; b 5 Jan 1904; m 9 Jan 1930 Lt-Gen Sir Philip Maxwell Balfour, KBE, CB, MC (d 4 Feb 1977), RA, er s of Charles Frederick Balfour, ICS, and d 14 Feb 1997

2 *Lois Mary Maitland; b 2 Oct 1911; m 20 Sept 1932 Lt-Col Aylmer Lochiel Cameron, DSO, MC, RA (d 1982), s of Maj Euan Duncan Cameron, RFA, and has:

(1) *Ewen Duncan, OBE; b 1935; Brig Black Watch (RHR); m 1973 *Joanna Margaret, dau of Maj James Malcolm Hay (see TWEEDDALE, M)

Sir CHARLES d 13 Feb 1953; his er s,

Sir Charles James Napier Rugge-Price, 8th Bt; b 4 Sept 1902; educ Harrow and RMA Woolwich; Maj RA WW II; m 2 Nov 1935 *Maeve Marguerite [Maeve Lady Rugge-Price, 3 Chagford House, Chagford St, London NW1], yst dau of Edgar Stanley de la Pena, of Hythe, Kent, and d 7 Nov 1966, leaving:

1 Sir (CHARLES) KEITH NAPIER RUGGE-PRICE, **9th and present Bt**

1 *Angela Muriel Frances; b 17 June 1938; m 3 Jan 1970 *Martyn Samuel, er s of H D Samuel, of St Leonards-on-Sea, and has:

(1) *Bernard Charles; b 20 July 1971

(2) *Edward Hugh; b 1974

2 *Jayne Marjorie Agnes [Mrs Jayne Tankard, Tangora, 20 Sea Way, Sea Lane, Middleton-on-Sea, Sussex]; b 6 June 1943; m 3 April 1965 (divorce 19–) Leslie Charles Tankard, yr s of A E Tankard, of 12 Gravesend Rd, London W12, and has:

(1) *Nigel Peter Stewart; b 1970

(1) *Wendy Julie Angela; b 10 Aug 1967

3 *Catharine Sarah Christine [Miss Catharine Rugge-Price, 8421 La Salle Boulevard, Montreal, PQ, Canada]; b 3 April 1948

RUGGLES-BRISE

Arms: Quarterly, 1st and 4th, gu. a cross between four mascles arg., all within a bordure sa., charged with eight quatrefoils of the second (for BRISE); 2nd and 3rd, arg. on a chevron gu., between three roses of the second, barbed, seeded, leaved and slipped ppr., as many estoiles or (for RUGGLES). **Crests:** 1 A demi-crocodile sa. (for BRISE), 2 In front of twelve arrows in saltire ppr., heads outward, a tower or, inflamed ppr. (for RUGGLES). **Motto:** Struggle. **Creation:** Bt. (UK) 31 Jan 1935.

SIR JOHN ARCHIBALD RUGGLES-BRISE, 2ND BT, of Spains Hall, Finchingfield, Co Essex, CB (1958), OBE (1945) TD, JP (Essex 1946) [Sir John Ruggles-Brise Bt CB OBE TD JP, Spains Hall, Finchingfield, Essex CM7 4PF]; b 13 June 1908; s f 1942; educ Eton; WW II in AA Cmd, cmded 1st 450 Mixed HAA Regt, formed and cmded 459th Mixed HAA Regt (TA), Essex: Ld Lt 1958–78, V-Lt 1947–58, DL 1945, Pres T&AFA 1958–66; Church Commr 1959–65, pres CLA 1958–1959 and Game Fair, chm Standing Cncl Baronetage 1958–63, Pro-Chllr Essex U 1964–79, Hon Freeman Chelmsford, former govr Felsted and Chigwell Schs, memb Lloyd's Underwriters, KStJ

Lineage: Col Sir SAMUEL RUGGLES-BRISE, KCB, of Spains Hall, Essex, JP (Essex), DL; had:

ARCHIBALD WEYLAND RUGGLES-BRISE, of Spains Hall; *b* 2 April 1853; barrister, Capt Suffolk Yeo; *m* 26 Sept 1876 Mabel (*d* 29 April 1929), est dau of Octavius Edward Coope, MP, of Rochetts, Essex, and *d* 30 July 1939, leaving:

1 EDWARD ARCHIBALD (Sir), **1st Bt**

2 Evelyn Coope; *b* 5 June 1888; *educ* Eton; Capt Norfolk Yeo WW I; *m* 11 Feb 1920 Mildred Dorothy, yr dau of Edward George Cubitt, of Honing Hall, Norfolk, and *d* 28 Sept 1977, leaving:

    (1) Stephen Evelyn; *b* 25 March 1921; *educ* Eton; Rifle Bde and RAOC WW II; *d* unm 31 Oct 1977

    (2) Thomas Oliver; *b* 18 Nov 1922; *educ* Eton and Trin Coll Oxford; Lt 2nd Armoured Bn Gren Gds WW II; *ka* France 18 July 1944

    (1) *Jane Mary; *b* 6 Jan 1925; *m* 16 May 1951 Anthony Addison Birley, 2nd s of Charles Fair Birley, of Jersey, and has:

        1a *Mary Eileen; *b* 16 March 1957

        2a *Susanna Jane; *b* 5 Nov 1958

3 Cecil Weyland; *d* young 1890

4 Harold Ralph, MC; *b* 18 Feb 1891; *educ* Winchester; RE WW I (Belgian Croix de Guerre), MLC Tanganyika Territory 1926–31, KAR WW II; *m* 25 June 1925 Cecily Jane, MBE (*d* 6 Jan 1958), dau of John Henry Gurney, JP, DL, of Keswick Hall, and *d* 23 April 1951, leaving:

    (1) *Alethea Mabel; *b* 29 May 1926; E African WTS WW II; *m* 8 May 1948 (*divorce* 1965) Ernest Mackenzie Waller, Lt Gren Gds, s of Ernest Waller, of Inglaterra, Tangier, and has:

        1a *Jeremy Mark Ralph [Jeremy Waller Esq, The Red House, 17 Nethergate St, Clare, Suffolk CO10 8NP]; *b* 6 Aug 1953; *educ* King's Sch Canterbury

        2a *Martin Christopher; *b* 4 Jan 1956; *educ* Eton

1 Marjory Mabel; *d* unm 22 Feb 1955

2 Emily Ada Pleasance, JP Norfolk; *m* 21 Nov 1911 Quintin Edward Gurney, TD, DL, of Bawdeswell Hall, Norfolk, and Keswick Hall, Norwich, and *d* 22 Oct 1972, leaving issue. He *d* 30 June 1968

3 Dorothy Clara; *m* 22 May 1913 Christopher Richard Gurney, of Northrepps Hall, Norwich, and *d* 27 Oct 1960, leaving issue. He *d* 27 Nov 1969

4 Octavia Florence; *m* 4 April 1922 Francis Guy Pym (*see* PYM, B) and had:

    (1) *Stephen Guy; *b* 18 Sept 1925; *m* 3 April 1947 *Florence Tereson, dau of Louis Bourassa, OBE, of Pearce River, Alberta, Canada, and has:

        1a *Charles Stephen Guy; *b* 15 Jan 1956

        2a *Michael Ruthven; *b* 11 Jan 1959

        1a *Coryn Barbara; *b* 14 March 1948

        2a *Jacqueline Margery; *b* 10 Feb 1950

        3a *Stephanie Louise; *b* 28 May 1951

        4a *Roxanne Marie; *b* 9 Sept 1953

The est s,

Sir Edward Archibald Ruggles-Brise, 1st Bt (UK), so *cr* 31 Jan 1935, MC, TD, JP, DL; *b* 9 Sept 1882; served WW I, MP (C) Maldon 1922–23 and 1924–42; Lt-Col cmdg Essex Yeo 1927–34, Brevet Col 1931; V-Lt Essex 1939, V-Chm Essex T&AFA; *m* 1st 25 June 1906 Agatha (*d* 2 April 1937), est dau of John Henry Gurney, JP, DL, of Keswick Hall, Norfolk, and had:

1 Sir JOHN ARCHIBALD RUGGLES-BRISE, **2nd and present Bt**

2 +GUY EDWARD, TD, DL (Essex 1967) [Guy Ruggles-Brise Esq TD DL, Housham Tye Manor, Harlow, Essex CM17 0QL; Ledgowan Lodge, Achnasheen, Wester Ross IV22 2EH]; *b* 15 June 1914; heir presumptive; *educ* Eton; High Sheriff Essex 1967, memb London Stock Exchange, sr ptnr Wontner, Colphin & Francis, dir The Investment Co 1972, consultant Brewin Dolphin & Co (stockbrokers), V-Chm Riding for Disabled Tst, late Capt 104th (Essex Yeo) Field Bde RA and Commando No 7 WW II (POW, escaped); *m* 1st 7 Dec 1940 Elizabeth (*d* 1988), only dau of James Knox, of Smithstone House, Kilwinning, Hants; *m* 2nd 1994 *Christine Margaret Fothergill-Spencer, only dau of Lt John A Fothergill, and by his 1st w has:

    (1) +Timothy Edward; *b* 11 April 1945; *educ* Eton; *m* 3 May 1975 *Rosemary, yr dau of J S Craig, of London NW3, and has:

        1a +Archibald Edward; *b* 1979

        2a +Charles Evelyn; *b* 1983

        3a +Iain; *b* 1989

        1a *Olivia Agnes; *b* 31 May 1977

        2a *Felicity Rose; *b* 1984

    (2) +James Rupert; *b* 22 June 1947; *educ* Eton

    (3) +Samuel Guy [Samuel Ruggles-Brise Esq, Mill House, Little Bardfield, Essex]; *b* 19 Jan 1956; *educ* Stowe; *m* 23 June 1979 *Katherine Margaret, dau of Brig R J Bishop, MBE, MC, RA (*see* THURSO, V), and has:

        1a +Edward James; *b* 30 July 1985

        1a *Camilla Jane; *b* 12 Aug 1983

1 *Violet Agatha [Mrs Hubert Barry, Flat 5, Sutton Manor Mews, Sutton Scotney, Hants SO21 3JX]; *b* 24 May 1907; *m* 19 Aug 1936 Cdr Hubert Wyndham Barry, RN (*see* BARRY, Bt), and has issue

2 Cecilia Margaret; *b* 21 Oct 1919; Section Offr WAAF WW II; *m* 28 Sept 1943 (John) Julian Riddick (*m* 2nd Ruth Milson and *d* 13 Jan 1997), est s of Col John Galloway Riddick, CBE, DSO, TD, JP, of Hanson House, Mobberley, Cheshire, and *d* 1991, leaving:

    (1) *Robert John Gurney; *b* 19 Jan 1951; *educ* Stowe

    (2) *Graham Edward Galloway; *b* 26 Aug 1955; *educ* Stowe

    (1) *Elspeth Marjorie; *b* 22 Sept 1952

Sir Edward *m* 2nd 14 March 1939 Lucy Barbara, MBE (1957), Sr Social Worker Boys' Prison Wormwood Scrubs 1945–64, yr dau of Rt Rev Walter Ruthven Pym (*see* PYM, B), and *d* 12 May 1942

Seat: Spains Hall, Finchingfield, Essex. The Ruggles, later Ruggles-Brise, family bought Spains in 1760. Previously it had belonged to a family called Kempe, who built the earliest part of the present house in the 15th century and greatly added to it in the late 16th. Around the time of its acquisition by Samuel Ruggles a further extension was made. 'Spains' is a corruption of 'de Ispania', the name of the family who held the manor at the time of the Domesday survey. It was acquired by the KEMPEs some two hundred years afterwards.

RUMBOLD

Arms: Or on a chevron gu. three cinquefoils of the field, a canton of the second, charged with a leopard's face erminois. **Crest:** A demi-lion rampant erminois. **Motto:** *Virtutis laus actio* ('The praise of virtue is action'). **Creation:** Bt. (GB) 27 March 1779.

SIR HENRY JOHN SEBASTIAN RUMBOLD, 11TH BT, of Woodhall, Watton, Hertford [Sir Henry Rumbold Bt, 19 Hollywood Rd, London SW10 9HT; Hatch House, Tisbury, Wilts SP3 6PA]; *b* 24 Dec 1947; *s f* 1983; *educ* Eton and William and Mary Coll Va.; slr, ptnr Dawson Cornwell & Co 1991–; *m* 6 Oct 1978 *Frances Ann (Holly), formerly w of Julian Berry and dau of Dr A Whitfield Hawkes and Mrs Alistair Cooke, of New York

Lineage: ROBERT RUMBOULD, of Burbage, Leics; *b* 1560; *m* Margery — (*d* 1627) and *d* Oct 1621, leaving, with other issue:

THOMAS RUMBOULD, of Burbage; royalist Civil War, captured Battle of Naseby 1645; *m* Catherine Riplinghame (*d* 1636) and had, with four daus:

    1 William, of Parson's Green, Fulham; *b* 1613; royalist Civil War, with office of the Great Wardrobe, took from London the Royal Standard set up at Nottingham 1642, fought Naseby, went to Cadiz, returned after 1649, Sec secret Cncl kept up in England during his exile, Comptroller Gt Wardrobe and Surveyor-Gen Customs 1660; *m* Mary, dau of William Barclay, Esq of the Body to CHARLES I, and *d* 27 May 1667, leaving:

        (1) Edward; *bapt* 5 June 1665; Surveyor-Gen Customs; *m* Anne, dau of 4th Viscount Grandison of Limerick (*see* JERSEY, E), and *dsp* 19 Aug 1729

        (1) Mary; *bapt* 26 Oct 1656; *m* 25 Aug 1680 James Sloane, MP Thetford, est bro of Sir Hans Sloane, 1st and last Bt

        (2) Jane; *bapt* 14 Nov 1663; *m* Richard Hosier, of Shrewsbury

    2 HENRY

    3 Thomas; *bapt* 28 Jan 1628; Consul Cadiz; *m* Rafaela de los Cameros, widow of Richard Crocker, and was *bur* 19 Jan 1706

The 2nd s,

    HENRY RUMBOLD; *bapt* 19 Jan 1618; merchant Puerto Sta Maria, Spain; active Royalist agent, Consul-Gen Andalucia 1660, Gentleman Privy Chamber Extraordinary; *m* 1st Isabel de Avila (*d* 1662) and had:

    1 Henry; volunteer at Tangier; *d* Dec 1688, leaving issue

HENRY RUMBOLD *m* 2nd 25 Jan 1663 Francisca Maria, dau of Brian I'Anson, Grandee of Spain, 2nd s of Sir Brian I'Anson, Bt, by Beatriz Rico, and *d* March 1690, having by her had:

    2 William; HEICS; *m* Elizabeth Mason and was *bur* 15 Sept 1728, leaving, with other issue:

        (1) WILLIAM

        (2) Henry; Sec Cncl Bengal; *m* 17 Aug 1731 Sarah Basnet and *d* 1 Sept 1743, leaving issue

The er s,

    WILLIAM RUMBOLD; HEIC's Naval Serv; *m* 8 Dec 1726 Dorothy, widow of John Mann and dau of Richard Cheney, of Hackney, and *d* 1745, being then 2nd in Council at Tellicherry, leaving, with another s (*d* young):

    1 William; *b* 1730; Lt Madras Army, present operations round Madura and Siege Trichinopoly; *d* unm 1 Aug 1757

    2 THOMAS (Sir), **1st Bt**

    1 Dorothy; *m* 1st Capt Northall, RA, and had issue; *m* 2nd 24 June 1762 John Taylor, of Townhead, Lancs, and had further issue

The 2nd surv s,

    Sir Thomas Rumbold, 1st Bt (GB), so *cr* 27 March 1779, of Woodhall Watton, Herts; *b* 15 June 1736; joined HEICS 1752, present recapture Calcutta, ADC to Clive of India (*see* POWIS, E) Battle of Plassey 1757 (severely wounded), Govr Madras, MP New Shoreham, Sussex, Melcombe Regis, Shaftesbury and Yarmouth, IoW, tea planter; *m* 1st 22 June 1756 Frances (*bur* 22 Aug 1764), only dau of James Berriman by Frances Aspinwall, and had:

    1 William Richard; *b* 1 March 1760; Capt 1st Foot Gds, ADC to Sir Hector Munro Siege Pondicherry Oct 1778, delivered despatches and colours of the fortress to GEORGE III, MP Melcombe Regis; *d* unm 14 June 1786

2 GEORGE BERRIMAN (Sir), **2nd Bt**

1 Frances; *b* 21 Sept 1762; *m* Col Francis Hale Rigby, of Mistley Hall, Essex, and had issue

Sir Thomas *m* 2nd 2 May 1772 Joanna (*d* 4 Jan 1823), dau of Rt Rev Edmund Law, DD, Bp Carlisle (*see* ELLENBOROUGH, B), and *d* 11 Nov 1791, leaving all his property to his children by her, for whose benefit he directed that his estate of Woodhall Watton, Herts, should be sold, having by her had, with other issue:

3 Charles Edmund, of Preston Candover, Hants; *b* 11 Aug 1788; MP Gt Yarmouth; *m* Harriet (*d* 6 Oct 1877), dau of John Gardner, of Ashford, Kent, and *d* 31 May 1857, leaving:

  (1) Charles James Augustus; *b* 6 Feb 1834; MA Cantab, FRGS; *m* 30 July 1863 Agatha Ellen (*d* 21 Sept 1897), dau of George Woodroffe Franklyn, MP, of Lovel Hill, Berks, and *d* 2 June 1900, leaving:

    1a Charles Edmund Arden Law; *b* 24 Aug 1872; Capt 2nd Dragoon Gds Queen's Bays Boer War 1901–02, WW I as Capt RE, Chev Ordre du Mérite Maritime 1936; *m* 1st 14 Feb 1906 Anne Christian (*d* 3 April 1928), 2nd dau of Hon Richard Anthony Nugent (*see* WESTMEATH, E), and had:

      1b Thomas Christian Nugent; *b* 1 Aug, *d* 20 Aug 1911

      2b Richard William John Nugent; *b* 24 June 1913; author and jnlst, P/O RAF WW II; *d* unm 10 March 1961

      1b Rosemary Christian Nugent; *b* 29 Oct 1916; *m* 18 Feb 1936 (*divorce* 1951, resumed maiden name) Don Jose Maria Puigcerver and *d* 9 Nov 1957, leaving issue

    1a (cont) Charles Rumbold *m* 2nd 17 May 1938 Yvonne Catherine Aurore Beatrice Garnon (*d* Dec 1956), dau of Alphonse Billot, and *d* 9 April 1943

    2a Christian Franklyn Hales; *b* 5 Sept 1873; Maj 4th Bn E Surrey Regt, attd 2nd Bn Norfolk Regt, Capt Roy Scots Fus, Boer War 1899–1902, Persian Gulf with IEF WW I; *ka* Ctesiphon 22 Nov 1915

    1a Agatha Mary Harriet; *m* 28 Jan 1897 Rev Harry Bathurst Norman and *d* 9 Nov 1906, leaving issue

  (2) Thomas Henry; *b* 26 March 1835; *m* 7 Nov 1872 Katherine Lucy (*d* 21 Aug 1932), dau of John Bott, of Coton Hall, Staffs, and *d* 1882, leaving:

    1a Anwer Thomas Law; *b* 27 Oct 1873; *educ* Winchester and Trin Coll Cambridge (BA, LLB 1895); *m* 7 May 1904 Ellen Mary, yst dau of Thomas Holt, of Crewkerne, Somerset, and *d* 1 Oct 1916

    2a William Richard, MC (1918); *b* 30 April 1877, *educ* Haileybury; T/Capt RE and Pioneer Sectn Nigeria Regt, RWAFF, WW I; *d* unm 29 Feb 1960

    3a Thomas Arthur; *b* 28 Feb 1882; Lt RE TF WW I (despatches); *m* 1st 21 Oct 1911 Evelyn Mary (*d* 25 May 1954), only dau of Walter Comyn Jackson, JP, of Swanley, Kent, and had:

      1b Thomas Michael; *b* 21 July 1914; Lt RNVR WW II (despatches posthumously); *m* 4 Nov 1939 *Rosemary Hazel (*m* 2nd 9 Oct 1944 Cdr Richard Gatehouse, DSC, RN, and has issue), est dau of J P Hampshire, of Wimbledon, and *das* at sea 21 Dec 1940

      1b *Elizabeth Anne, MBE (1975); *b* 25 Sept 1919; *m* 28 March 1940 *3rd Baron Hayter (*qv*) and has issue

    3a (cont) Thomas Rumbold *m* 2nd 2 June 1959 Elizabeth Kirkpatrick (*d* 23 Nov 1973), widow of Capt Warren Skeffington Wynne, of St Andrews, and dau of Rev Thomas MacDougal Brisbane Paterson, of Laighstone Hall, Hamilton, and *d* 4 May 1972

    1a Harriet Lucy Elizabeth; *m* 19 Sept 1908 Sydney Theodore Hudson, er s of Sydney Hudson, JP, of Meads Court, Eastbourne, and Manchester, and *d* 28 July 1959, leaving issue. He *d* 15 Feb 1949

    2a Katherine Cecilia; *d* unm 6 Aug 1972

  (3) Henry Edmund William; *b* 27 June 1837; Lt Roy Fus and Capt 3rd Bn Essex Regt; *m* 23 April 1871 Ellen Schaefer (*d* 10 March 1916), only child of Cumberland Dugan Hollins, of Baltimore, and *d* 26 Aug 1911, leaving:

    1a Cumberland Henry Collins; *b* 1 June 1872; Capt US Engrs; *m* 1st 25 June 1902 Emma (*d* 9 April 1934), dau of William Bowly Wilson, of Baltimore; *m* 2nd 22 Oct 1935 Gladys Rose (*d* 25 March 1967), dau of George Gorling, of Goring, Berks, and *dsp*

    2a Edmund Law Hollins; *b* 21 April 1876; Lt QM Dept USA WW I; *d* unm

    1a Ethel Law Hollins; *d* 1932

    2a Annie Law Hollins; *m* 1st 26 Nov 1907 Ernest Krewson Richardson (*d* 16 Aug 1910), of Germantown, Pa., and had issue; *m* 2nd 1916 S Brown Thompson, of Bath, Va.

2 Maria Augusta Dorothea; *m* 1st Col Frederick Manners, 96th Foot; *m* 2nd 9 June 1812 Sir Grenville Temple, 9th Bt (*d* 18 Feb 1829; *see* 1850 edn), and *d* 14 Feb 1852

The 1st Bt's est surv son,

  Sir George Berriman Rumbold, 2nd Bt; *b* 17 Aug 1764; Min Resident Hamburg to 1804; *m* Nov 1783 Caroline (*m* 2nd 1809 V-Adml Sir William Sidney Smith, GCB, and *d* 16 May 1826), only child of James Hearn, of Shanakill, Co Waterford, and had, with other issue:

1 WILLIAM (Sir), **3rd Bt**

1 Caroline; *b* 20 Feb 1786; *m* Col Adolphe de St Clair, of the Garde Royale, and *d* Feb 1848, leaving issue

2 Maria; *b* 10 May 178–; *m* R-Adml Arabin and *d* 31 Dec 1875. He *d* 1855

3 Emily; *b* 1790; *m* Ferdinand, Baron de Delmar, and *d* 15 Jan 1861

The 2nd Bt *d* 15 Dec 1807; his er s,

  Sir William Rumbold, 3rd Bt; *b* 22 May 1787; *m* 13 July 1809 Hon Harriet Elizabeth Parkyns (*b* 1 July 1789, *d* 8 Sept 1830), 2nd dau and coheir of 1st Baron Rancliffe (*see* 1850 edn), and *d* 24 Aug 1833, having had, with other issue:

1 **Sir Cavendish Stuart Rumbold, 4th Bt**; *b* 26 Aug 1815; *m* 1836 Mary Harcourt (*dsp* 1850), est dau of R-Adml Manby, of Northwold, Norfolk, and *d* 27 March 1853

2 **Sir Arthur Carlos Henry Rumbold, 5th Bt**; *b* 25 Sept 1820; Maj 70th Regt Crimean War, Order Medjidie 4th Cl, Col Imperial Ottoman Army, Pres and sr memb Exec Cncl Nevis 1857–63 and Virgin Is 1865–69; *m* 1st Jan 1846 Antoinette (*d* 27 Nov 1867), only child of Cmdt Antoine de Kerven; *m* 2nd 18 Aug 1868 Helen Eliza, Assist Gen Soc Sacred Heart (*d* 20 Sept 1921), est dau of Edward Hopewell, of The Grove, Walthamstow, and *d* 12 June 1869, leaving:

  (1) **Sir Arthur Victor Raoul Anduze Rumbold, 6th Bt**; *b* posthumously 24 July 1869; *dsp* 16 June 1877

3 **Sir Charles Hale Rumbold, 7th Bt**; *b* 12 Oct 1822; *m* and *dsp* 28 Aug 1877

4 HORACE (Sir), **8th Bt**

5 William; *b* 3 Sept 1830; Lt Gren Gds; *m* 25 Nov 1853 Nadine, Princesse Lobanov, of Rostov (*d* 1889), and *d* 26 Dec 1893

1 Emily Victorine Elizabeth; *b* 13 Oct 1824; *m* 1st 16 Oct 1848 (*divorce* 1866) Capt George Henry Cavendish, 1st Life Gds (*see* DEVONSHIRE, D); *m* 2nd 20 Aug 1870 Count Gaston de la Rochefoucauld and *d* 11 Sept 1904

The 7th Bt's bro,

  Sir Horace Rumbold, 8th Bt, GCB, GCMG, PC; *b* 2 July 1829; Dipl Serv: joined 1849, Min Chile 1872–78 and Berne 1878–79, Envoy Extrdy and Min Plen Argentina 1879–80, Sweden 1880–84, Greece 1884–88 and The Netherlands 1888–96, Amb Extrdy and Plen Austria-Hungary 1896–1900; *m* 1st 15 July 1867 Caroline Barney (*d* 26 Dec 1872), dau of George Harrington, of Washington, US Min Berne, and had:

1 HORACE GEORGE MONTAGU (Sir), **9th Bt**

2 William Edwin, CMG (1919); *b* 22 Oct 1870; Col RA, Belgian and French Croixs de Guerre; *m* 21 Feb 1903 Elizabeth Gordon (*d* 21 Feb 1948), dau of Rev Robert James Cameron, of Burntisland, Fife, and *d* 25 Jan 1947, leaving:

  (1) (Horace) Algernon Fraser (Sir), KCMG (1960, CMG 1953), CIE (1947); *b* 27 Feb 1906; *educ* Wellington and Ch Ch Oxford (BA 1927); India Office: Assist Pncpl 1929, Priv Sec to Parly U-Sec 1930–33, U-Sec 1933–34, Pncpl 1934, Assist Sec 1943, tfd to CRO 1947, Dep UK HC S Africa 1949–53, Assist U-Sec 1954, Dep U-Sec 1958–66; *m* 19 Jan 1946 *Margaret Adel [Lady Rumbold, Shortwoods, West Clandon, Surrey GU4 7UB], only dau of Arthur Joseph Hughes, OBE, of Pages, Chigwell Row, Essex, and *d* 1993, having had:

    1a *Sarah Josephine [Mrs Robert Owen, 2 Beverley Rd, London SW13 0LX]; *b* 7 Jan 1948; *m* 9 Aug 1969 *Robert Michael Owen, QC, s of Gwynne Llewellyn Owen, and has:

      1b *Thomas Llewellyn; *b* 1973

      2b *Huw Algernon; *b* 1976

    2a *Caroline Elizabeth [Mrs Richard Keevil, Cliffansty Farm, Clevancy, Calne, Wilts SN11 8ST]; *b* 15 March 1950; *m* 1981 *Richard James Keevil and has:

      1b *Katharine Elizabeth Adele; *b* 1982

      2b *Cordelia Jane; *b* 1988

  (2) Willam Robert; *b* 4 Feb 1912; *educ* Wellington and Ch Ch Oxford (MA 1944); F/O RAF WW II; *m* 1st 1942 (*divorce* 1952) Pamela Mary Dewe and had:

    1a *Cheryl Anne [Sga Cheryl Dotti, 5 Avenue Calas, 1206 Geneva, Switzerland]; *b* 22 June 1944; *m* 4 May 1968 (*divorce* 1979) Luca C Dotti, s of Dr Dominico Dotti and Paola Roberti (*née* Bandini), of Rome

  (2) (cont.) William Rumbold *m* 2nd 8 Aug 1957 *Sylvia Violet, only dau of Lawrence John Smith, of Lusaka, Zambia, and by her had:

    1a +CHARLES ANTON [Charles Rumbold Esq, 18 Blake Gdns, London SW6 4QB]; *b* 7 Feb 1959; heir presumptive; *m* 1987 *Susan, er dau of J M Tucker, of Melbourne, Australia, and has:

      1b *Eleanor; *b* 1995

    2a +Alexander Robert; *b* 1971

  (3) Alastair Gordon, OBE (1953), MC (1936); *b* 28 Oct 1914; *educ* Wellington; Lt-Col Cameron Highrs, Palestine 1936–39, WW II; *m* 1st 30 July 1941 (*divorce* 1952) Tania, dau of Michael Borzakovsky, and had:

    1a +Michael Alastair; *b* 6 July 1943; *educ* Wellington and Haute Ecole de Commerce Paris; *m* 1976 *Katharine Mary, dau of Donal John Cagney, of Broadstairs, Kent, and has:

      1b +Angus Michael; *b* 1982

      1b *Victoria Catherine; *b* 31 Dec 1977

      2b *Lucinda; *b* 1979

  (3) (cont.) Col Alastair Rumbold *m* 2nd 12 Sept 1958 *Auriol Cressida [Mrs Alastair Rumbold, 4 North St, Castle Cary, Somerset], dau of Col William Rixon Bucknall, of The Hatton, Redgorton, Perthshire, and Mrs J A Hopwood, and *d* 1992, having by her had:

    1a *Belinda Cressida; *b* 2 Oct 1962

  (1) *Violet Elizabeth [Mrs Andrew Atha, Abbotsfield, Exhall, Warwicks]; *m* 7 Nov 1934 Andrew Atha (*d* 23 Aug 1967), s of Charles Gurney Atha, and has:

    1a *Charles Antony; *b* 2 Aug 1937; *educ* Harrow and Worcester Coll Oxford

    1a *Elizabeth Ann Amanda [Mrs Michael Abrahams, Newfield, Mickley, Ripon, N Yorks]; *b* 8 Feb 1940; *m* 1 June 1967 *Michael Abrahams, CBE, DL, s of Alexander Abrahams, of Esher, Surrey

3 George; *b* 19 Oct 1871; Lt AOD, Hon Attaché The Hague 1892; in RN; *d* unm 1951

Sir Horace *m* 2nd 28 July 1881 Louisa Anne (*d* 8 Jan 1940), widow of Capt St George Francis Robert Caulfeild (*see* CHARLEMONT, V) and only dau of Thomas Russell Crampton, CE, and *d* 3 Nov 1913, having by her had:

4 Hugh Cecil Levinge; *b* 7 Feb 1884; Lt Rifle Bde Boer War 1902, Capt Gren Gds WW I (wounded, Chev Order Crown of Belgium); *m* 12 March 1932 Zoe (*d* 29 Oct 1958), dau of Thomas Jaspard Akins, of St Louis, Mo., by Sarah Elizabeth Green, and *d* 18 Nov 1932

Sir HORACE's est s,

  Sir Horace George Montagu Rumbold, 9th Bt, GCB (1934), GCMG (1923, KCMG 1917), MVO (1907), PC (1920); *b* 5 Feb 1869; Hon Attaché 1888, Attaché 1890, 3rd Sec 1893, 2nd Sec 1896, 1st Sec 1904, Counsellor Tokyo 1909–13 and Berlin 1913–14, FO 1914–16, Envoy Extrdy and Min Plen Berne 1916 and Poland 1919–20, HC and Amb Constantinople 1920–24, Amb Madrid 1924–28 and Berlin 1928–33 (ret), 2nd Br Plen Lausanne Conf 1922–23, Pncpl Br Del resumed Conf April 1923, memb Roy Commn Palestine 1937, Chm Centl VAD Cncl 1937; *m* 18 July 1905 Etheldred Constantia, CBE (1920), DGStJ (*d* 23 Oct 1964), yr dau of Sir Edmund Douglas Veitch Fane, KCMG, of Boyton Manor, Wilts, and had:

1 (HORACE) ANTHONY CLAUDE (Sir), **10th Bt**

1 *Constantia Dorothy [Mrs Hugh Farmar, Wasing Old Rectory, Aldermaston, Berks RG7 4NB]; *b* 1906, *m* 30 Nov 1944 Hugh William Farmar, MVO, LLD (*d* 1987), s of Col Harold Mynors Farmar, CMG, DSO, and has:

(1) *(Hugh Alexander) Peregrine [Peregrine Farmar Esq, Saltway House, Bibury, Glos]; *b* 28 Sept 1945; *educ* Eton and Keble Coll Oxford; *m* 1973 *Carole Mary Phillips and has:

 1a *Samuel Hugh Gregory; *b* 1977

 1a *Rebecca Lucy; *b* 1975

 2a *Georgina Frances; *b* 1980

 3a *Charlotte Felicity; *b* 1985

(2) *Francis (Frank) Edmund [Francis Farmar Esq, 1 Rectory Cottages, Sedgehill, Dorset SP7 9JH]; *b* 8 May 1948; *educ* Eton, St Martin's Coll Art and W of England Coll of Art; *m* 1982 (*divorce* 1997) Judith Madeline Povoas

2 Bridget Margherita; *b* 27 Sept 1914; *d* 19 July 1918

Sir HORACE *d* 24 May 1941; his only s,

 Sir (Horace) Anthony Claude Rumbold, 10th Bt, KCMG (1962, CMG 1953), KCVO (1969), CB (1955); *b* 7 March 1911; *educ* Eton and Magdalen Coll Oxford (BA 1934); Dip Serv: 3rd Sec 1936, 2nd Sec 1940, 1st Sec 1945, Counsellor 1949, Paris 1951–54, Pncpl Priv Sec to For Sec 1954–55, Assist U-Sec FO 1957, Min Paris 1961–65, Amb Thailand 1965–67, Austria 1967, Cdr St Olav Norway, Grand Cross Order Merit Austria; *m* 20 June 1937 (*divorce* 1974) Felicity Ann, yr dau of Lt-Col Frederick George Glyn Bailey, RA (*see* INCHCAPE, E), and had:

 1 Sir HENRY JOHN SEBASTIAN RUMBOLD, **11th and present Bt**

1 *Serena Caroline [Mrs Jeremy Lancaster, The Gables, Broadwell, Glos]; *b* 27 Jan 1939; *m* 18 July 1959 *Jeremy Lancaster, est s of Norman Gerald Lancaster, of Sparrow's Nest, Woodnorton, Worcs, and has:

 (1) *Nicholas Horace John; *b* 1 Jan 1966

 (1) *Emma Charlotte; *b* 14 Sept 1961

 (2) *Joanna Elizabeth; *b* 28 Aug 1963

 (3) *Frances Mary; *b* 29 June 1968

2 *Venetia Mary [Miss Venetia Rumbold, Juvenud Con Una Mision, Casilla 18, 1277 Mira Floreo, Lima, Peru]; *b* 8 Dec 1941

3 *Camilla Charlotte [Mrs Camilla Swayne, Elmbury Cottage, Sheepwash Lane, Wylye, Wilts BA12 0QX]; *b* 17 Aug 1943; *m* 1st 28 Feb 1962 (*divorce* 1970) Hon Christopher Baliol Brett, est s of 4th Viscount Esher (*qv*), and has issue; *m* 2nd 1972 (*divorce* 1983) Giles Oliver Cairnes Swayne, only s of Sir Ronald Oliver Carless Swayne, MC, and by him has:

 (1) *Orlando Benedict Carlos; *b* 1974

Sir Anthony *m* 2nd 14 Dec 1974 *Mrs Pauline Laetitia Graham [Pauline Lady Rumbold, Hatch Cottage, Coker's Frome, Dorset DT2 7SD], dau of Hon David Francis Tennant (*see* GLENCONNER, B), and formerly w of (a) Capt Julian Alfred Lane-Fox-Pitt-Rivers and (b) Euan Douglas Graham (*see* MONTROSE, D), and *d* 4 Dec 1983

RUNCIE

Arms: Arg. on a fess sa. between three roses gu. barbed and seeded ppr. as many crosses patoncées also arg. **Crest:** A horse statant arg., crined, maned, unguled and the tail sa., gorged with a chaplet of roses gu., barbed and seeded ppr., resting the dexter foreleg upon a millrind gold. **Creation:** B. (LP, UK) 1991.

THE BARON RUNCIE, of Cuddesdon, Co Oxford (Rt Rev Robert Alexander Kennedy Runcie, MC (1945), PC (1980)) [The Rt Rev and Rt Hon The Lord Runcie MC PC, 26a Jennings Rd, St Albans, Herts AL1 4PD]; *b* 2 Oct 1921; *educ* Merchant Taylors', BNC Oxford (MA) and Westcott House Cambridge (Dip Theol); Scots Guards WW II, Deacon 1950, Priest 1951, Curate All Saints Gosforth 1950–52, Chaplain and V-Pres Westcott House 1953–56, Dean Trin Coll Cambridge 1956–60 (Hon Fell 1975), Pncpl Cuddesdon Theol Coll 1960–70, Bp St Albans 1970–80, Archbp Canterbury 1980–91, High Steward Cambridge U 1991–, Assist Bp St Albans 1991–, Anglican Chm Anglican-Orthodox Jt Doctrinal Commn 1973–80, Teape Lecturer Delhi U 1962, Nobel Lecturer Harvard 1987, Hon Bencher Gray's Inn 1981, Hon DD Oxon 1980, Cantab 1981, St Andrews 1989, Yale 1989, London 1990, Hon DLitt Keele 1981, Hon DCL Kent 1982, Hon LittD Liverpool 1983, Freeman Cities London, Canterbury and St Albans and Merchant Taylors', Grocers' and Butchers' Cos, Roy Victorian Chain 1991, author:

Cathedral and City: St Albans Ancient and Modern (ed, 1978), *Windows onto God* (1983), *Seasons of the Spirit* (1983), *One Light for One World* (1988), *Authority in Crisis? An Anglican response* (1988), *The Unity We Seek* (1989); *m* 1957 *(Angela) Rosalind, dau of J W Cecil Turner, MC, of Cambridge, and has:

1 *James [The Hon James Runcie, 36 Liverpool Rd, St Albans, Herts AL1 3UJ]; *b* 1959; *educ* Marlborough and Trin Hall Cambridge (MA); *m* 1985 *Mrs Marilyn Elsie Kellagher, dau of John Campbell Imrie, of Redroofs, Markinch, Fife, and has:

 (1) *Charlotte Susan Elizabeth; *b* 1989

1*Rebecca [The Hon Mrs Tabor, 86B Broxash Road, London SW11 6AB]; *b* 1962; *educ* St Albans HS for Girls, Haileybury and St Mary's Coll Durham; *m* 1994 *T M Christopher Tabor, only s of G M Tabor, of South Cerney, Glos, and has:

 (1) *Matthew Alexander; *b* 22 Aug 1996

Lineage: ROBERT DALZIEL RUNCIE, of Crosby, Merseyside; *m* Anne — and had:

ROBERT ALEXANDER KENNEDY, *cr* a **Baron**

RUNCIMAN OF DOXFORD

Arms: Per fess or and az. a lymphad, oars in action, the sail charged with a thistle, leaved and slipped ppr., flags flying to the dexter gu. **Crest:** A sea-horse erect or, holding in fore-fins a thistle as in the arms. **Supporters:** On either side a sea-horse or, gorged with a chain, pendant therefrom a grappling-iron az. **Motto:** By sea. **Creations:** Bt. (UK) 23 July 1906, B. (UK) 17 Jan 1933, V. (UK) 10 June 1937.

THE 3RD VISCOUNT RUNCIMAN OF DOXFORD, of Doxford, Co Northumberland, **Baron Runciman**, of Shoreston, Co Northumberland, and a **Baronet** (Sir Walter Garrison (Garry) Runciman, Bt, CBE (1987)) [The Rt Hon The Viscount Runciman of Doxford CBE, 44 Clifton Hill, London NW8 0QG; Doxford, Chathill, Northumberland]; *b* 10 Nov 1934; *s f* 1989; *educ* Eton and Trin Coll Cambridge (Fell 1959–63 and 1971–); late 2nd Lt Gren Gds, chm: Walter Runciman Ltd 1976–90, Runciman Investments 1990–, Andrew Weir & Co 1991–, dep chm Fin Servs Authority, pres Gen Cncl Br Shipping 1986–87, chm Roy Commn Criminal Justice 1991–93, memb Social Science Research Cncl 1974–79, author: *Plato's Later Epistemology* (1962), *Social Science and Political Theory* (1963), *Relative Deprivation and Social Justice* (1966), *Confessions of a Reluctant Theorist* (1989), *A Treatise on Social Theory* (Vol I 1983, Vol II 1989, Vol III 1997) and *The Social Animal* (1998), Hon DSc (Soc Sci) Edinburgh, Hon D York U, FBA 1975; *m* 17 April 1963 *Ruth, DBE (1998, OBE 1991), chm Mental Health Act Commission, co-fndr Prison Reform Tst and chm Independent Inquiry into the Misuse of Drugs Act 1971 1997–, only dau of Joseph Hellman, of Johannesburg, and former w of Dennis Mack Smith, the historian of Italy, and has:

1 +DAVID WALTER; *b* 1 March 1967; *educ* Eton and Trin Coll Cambridge

1 *Lisa; *b* 18 Aug 1965

2 *Catherine; *b* 18 July 1969

Lineage: WALTER RUNCIMAN, of Cresswell, Northumberland; *m* Jean (*d* 1906), dau of John Finlay, of Dunbar, and *d* 1878, leaving a 4th s:

Sir Walter Runciman, 1st Bt, so *cr* 23 July 1906, as also 17 Jan 1933 **1st Baron Runciman**, of Shoreston, Co Northumberland (both UK), JP (Northumberland, Durham and Newcastle); *b* 6 July 1847; head Walter Runciman & Co, shipowners, chm Anchor Line, Glasgow, MP (Lib) Hartlepool 1914–18, Hon Cdre RNVSR 1937, Pres UK Chamber Shipping 1910–11, Tyne Improvement Commr 1900–20; *m* 27 March 1869 Ann Margaret (*d* 20 Feb 1933), dau of John Lawson, of Blakemoor, Northumberland, and *d* 13 Aug 1937, leaving:

WALTER RUNCIMAN, **1st Viscount Runciman of Doxford**, of Doxford, Co Northumberland (UK), so *cr* 10 June 1937, PC (1908), JP (Northumberland); *b* 19 Nov 1870; *educ* Trin Coll Cambridge (BA 1892, MA 1895); MP (Lib) Oldham 1899–1900, Dewsbury 1902–18, Swansea W 1924–29 and St Ives (Cornwall) 1929–37, Parly Sec Local Govt Bd 1905–07, Fin Sec Treasury 1907–08, Pres: Bd Educn 1908–11, Bd Ag and Fisheries, BOT 1914–16 and 1931–37 and UK Chamber Shipping 1926, Commr Woods, Forest and Land Revenues 1911–14, chm: UK Provident Instn 1920–31 and Internat Shipping Conf 1926, Master Shipwrights' Co 1926–27, head unofficial Br Mission Czechoslovakia 1938, Ld Pres Cncl 1938–39, Hon LLD Manchester 1910 and Bristol 1929, Hon DCL Oxon 1934, Er Bro Trin House; *m* 23 Aug 1898 Hilda, MP St Ives (Cornwall) 1928–29, JP Co London and Northumberland (*d* 28 Oct 1956), 5th dau of James Cochran Stevenson, MP, of Westoe, S Shields, and had:

1 WALTER LESLIE, **2nd Viscount**

2 +(James Cochran) Steven(son) (Sir), CH (1984) [The Hon Sir Steven Runciman CH, Elshieshields, Lockerbie, Dumfriesshire DG11 1LY]; *b* 7 July 1903; *educ* Eton and Trin Coll Cambridge (BA 1924, MA 1928, Fell 1927–38, Hon Fell 1965); Press Attaché Legation Sofia 1940–41, Min Info Cairo and Jerusalem 1941–42, Prof Byzantine Art and History Istanbul U 1942–45, Br Cncl Rep Greece 1945–47, ktd 1958, Gifford Lecturer U of St Andrews 1960–61, Tstee Br Museum 1960–68, Corresponding Memb Acad of Athens, CLit 1987, FBA 1957, FSA 1964, Hon Litt D Oxon and Cantab, Hon LLD Glasgow, Hon DLitt: Durham, London, St Andrews and Birmingham, Hon DD Wabash, Indiana and Ball State, Indiana, Hon DHL Chicago and New York, Hon DPhil Salonica, Kt Cdr Phoenix Greece, Order Madara Horseman 1st Cl Bulgaria, author: *The Emperor Romanus Lecapenus* (1929), *The First Bulgarian Empire* (1930), *Byzantine Civilization* (1933), *The Mediaeval Manichee* (1947), *The Crusades* (1951–54), *The Eastern Schism* (1955), *The Sicilian Vespers* (1958), *The White Rajahs* (1960), *The Fall of Constantinople* (1965), *The Great Church in Captivity* (1968), *The Last Byzantine Renaissance* (1970), *The Orthodox Churches and the Secular State* (1972), *Byzantine Style and Civilization* (1975), *The Byzantine Theocracy* (1977), *Mistra* (1980) and *A Traveller's Alphabet* (1991)

1 Margaret; *b* 23 Sept 1901; Capt ATA WW II; *m* 1st 15 July 1925 (*divorce* 1936) Roderick Sydney NETTLETON later KING-FARLOW, er s of Sir Sydney Charles Nettleton King Farlow, and had issue; *m* 2nd 1938 Capt Douglas Keith Fairweather, ATA (*das* April 1944), s of Sir Walter Fairweather, and *das* following an air crash 5 Aug 1944, leaving issue

2 Ruth; *b* 2 Aug 1907; *m* 1st 8 Jan 1936 (*divorce* 1948) George Alexander Holmden, only s of Sir Osborn George Holmden, KBE, and had:

  (1) *Philippa Ruth; *b* 28 Feb 1937; *m* 1 Feb 1966 *Lt-Col Edward Llewellyn Stocker, MC, er s of R-Adml Percy Stocker, OBE, of Chichester, Sussex

  (2) *Belinda Mary; *b* 16 Dec 1942

2 (cont) The Hon Mrs Ruth Holmden *m* 2nd 16 Feb 1950 Elliot Russell Karslake Bovill, s of Alfred Karslake Bovill, of S Walsham, Norfolk, and *d* 24 Jan 1971. He *d* 20 Jan 1969

3 *Katharine, JP [The Hon Lady Lyell JP, Puddephats Farm, Markyate, Herts]; *b* 4 Dec 1909; *educ* Girton Coll Cambridge (MA); *m* 1st 23 Oct 1931 4th Baron Farrer (*d* 24 Jan 1954; *see* 1963 edn); *m* 2nd 24 Sept 1955 Sir Maurice Legat Lyell (Hon Mr Justice Lyell), 7th s of Alexander Lyell, of Gardyne Castle, Angus. He *d* 27 May 1975

The 1st VISCOUNT *d* 14 Nov 1949; his er s,

WALTER LESLIE RUNCIMAN, **2nd Viscount Runciman of Doxford**, OBE (1946), AFC (1937), AE, DL (Northumberland 1961); *b* 26 Aug 1900; *educ* Eton and Trin Coll Cambridge (BA 1922, MA 1982); Er Bro Trin House 1973, Hon DCL Durham 1937, memb Master Mariners' Co, chm Walter Runciman & Co, dep chm Lloyds Bank 1962–71, Chm Tstees Nat Maritime Museum 1962–72, Cdre Roy Yacht Sqdn 1968–74, Pres RINA 1951–61, Chm N of England Shipowners Assoc 1931–32 and 1970–71 and Cncl Armstrong Coll U of Durham 1935–37, Dir-Gen BOAC 1940–43, Hon A/Cdre 607(F) Sqdn RAuxAF, A/Cdre and Air Attaché Teheran 1943–46, Pres UK Chamber Shipping, Chm Gen Cncl Br Shipping 1952, memb: Air Tport Advsy Cncl 1946–54 (V-Chm 1951–54) and Shipping Advsy Panel 1962, Chm: DTI Ctee Special Wrecks 1973 and Br Hallmarking Cncl 1974; *m* 1st 20 Dec 1923 (*divorce* 1928) Rosamond Nina (*d* 1990), the novelist, 2nd dau of Rudolph Chambers Lehmann, of Fieldhead, Bourne End, Bucks; *m* 2nd 11 April 1932 Katherine Schuyler (*d* 1993 aged 90), yst dau of William R Garrison, of New York, and *d* 1989, leaving:

WALTER GARRISON (GARRY) RUNCIMAN, **3rd and present Viscount Runciman of Doxford**

RUSSELL, Earl

Arms: Arg. a lion rampant gu., on a chief sa. three escallops of the field, over the centre escallop a mullet. **Crest:** A goat statant arg., armed and unguled or. **Supporters:** Dexter, a lion gu.; sinister, a heraldic antelope gu., armed, unguled and tufted, ducally gorged and chained, the chain reflexed over the back or, each supporter charged on the shoulder with a mullet arg. **Motto:** *Che sara sara* ('What will be, will be'). **Creations:** E. and V. (UK) 30 July 1861.

THE 5TH EARL RUSSELL, of Kingston Russell, Co Dorset and **Viscount Amberley**, of Amberley, Co Gloucester, and Ardsalla, Co Meath (Conrad Sebastian Robert Russell) [The Rt Hon The Earl Russell, Department of History, King's College, Strand, London WC2R 2LS]; *b* 15 April 1937; s half-bro 1987; *educ* Eton and Merton Coll Oxford (BA 1958, MA 1962); History Lecturer Bedford Coll Lond U 1960–74, Reader 1974–79, Prof History Yale 1979–84, Astor Prof Br History UCL 1984–90, Prof Br History King's Coll London 1990–, Sir Henry Savile Visiting Prof Merton Coll Oxford 1994–95, Ford Lecturer Oxford 1987–88, Trevelyan Lecturer Cambridge 1995; Lib Dem Social Security Spokesperson, FRHistS 1971, FBA 1991, author: *The Crisis of Parliaments: English History 1509–1660* (1971), *Parliaments and English Politics 1621–1629* (1979), *The Causes of the English Civil War* (1990), *Unrevolutionary England 1603–1642* (1990), *The Fall of the British Monarchies 1637–1642* (1991), *Academic Freedom* (1993); *m* 11 Aug 1962 *Elizabeth Franklin, est dau of Horace Sanders, of Chippenham, Wilts, and has:

1 +NICHOLAS LYULPH, *Viscount Amberley*; *b* 12 Sept 1968; *educ* William Ellis Sch Camden

2 +John Francis; *b* 19 Nov 1971; *educ* William Ellis Sch

Lineage: The 6th DUKE OF BEDFORD (*qv*); had a 3rd s:

JOHN RUSSELL, **1st Earl Russell**, of Kingston Russell, Co Dorset (such territorial designation relating to an attempt to commemorate a bogus descent by the Woburn Russells from a medieval family of Dorset Russells), so *cr* 30 July 1861, as also VISCOUNT AMBERLEY (both UK), of Amberley, Co Gloucester, and Ardsalla, Co Meath (the latter territorial designation commemorating a legacy of land at that place bequeathed Lord John by a totally unrelated admirer, the 3rd and last Earl Ludlow; *see* STEWART, Bt, of Ramelton), KG (1862), GCMG (1869), PC (1830); *b* 18 Aug 1792; *educ* Westminster and Edinburgh U; MP (Lib) Tavistock 1813–17, 1818–19 and 1830–32, Hunts 1820–26, Bandon 1826–30, S Devon 1832–35, Stroud 1835–41 and City London 1841–61, Home Sec 1835–39, Colonial Sec 1839–41 and 1855, For Sec 1852–53 and 1859–65, Ld Pres Cncl 1854–55, Commr to Vienna Congress, PM 1846–52 and 1865–66; *m* 1st 11 April 1835 Adelaide (*d* 1 Nov 1838), widow of 2nd Baron Ribblesdale (*see* 1925 edn) and dau of Thomas Lister, of Armitage Park, and had:

1 Georgiana Adelaide; *m* 15 Aug 1867 Archibald Peel and *d* 25 Sept 1922, leaving issue (*see* PEEL, E)

2 Victoria; *m* 16 April 1861 Rev Henry Montagu Villiers and *d* 9 May 1880, leaving issue (*see* CLARENDON, E)

The **1st Earl** *m* 2nd 20 July 1841 Lady Frances Anna Maria Elliot-Murray-Kynynmound (*d* 17 Jan 1898), dau of 2nd Earl of Minto (*qv*), and *d* 28 May 1878, having by her had:

1 John, *Viscount Amberley*; *b* 10 Dec 1842; MP Nottingham; *m* 8 Nov 1864 Katharine-Louisa (*d* 28 June 1874), dau of 2nd Baron Stanley of Alderley (*see* STANLEY OF ALDERLEY, SHEFFIELD and, B), and *d* 9 Jan 1876, having had:

  (1) JOHN FRANCIS STANLEY RUSSELL, **2nd Earl Russell**, JP Norfolk; *b* 12 Aug 1865; barrister, Lt Army Motor Res, Alderman LCC, Parly Sec Tport 1929, Parly U-Sec India Dec 1929–31; *m* 1st 6 Feb 1890 (*divorce* 1901) Mabel Edith (*d* 22 Sept 1908), yst dau of Sir Claude Scott, 4th Bt, by Maria Selina (sentenced 1897 to eight months imprisonment for libelling the 2nd Earl, her dau's husb); *m* 2nd 31 Oct 1901 (*divorce* 1915) Marion, dau of George Cooke, of Cumbernauld; *m* 3rd 1916 (*separated* 1919) Mary Annette, authoress (*d* 9 Feb 1941), widow of Count (Henning August) von Arnim, dau of H Herron Beauchamp and cousin of the short story-writer Katherine Mansfield, and *dsp* 3 March 1931

  (2) BERTRAND ARTHUR WILLIAM, **3rd Earl**

  (1) Rachel Lucretia; *b* 2 March 1868; *d* 3 July 1874

2 George Gilbert William; *b* 14 April 1848; BA Cantab; Lt 9th Lancers; *d* 27 Jan 1933

3 Francis Albert Rollo; *b* 11 July 1849; MA Oxon, FRMetS; *m* 1st 21 April 1885 Alice Sophia (*d* 12 May 1886), dau of Thomas Spragging Godfrey, of Balderton Hall, Notts, and had:

(1) Arthur John Godfrey; *b* 11 March 1886; *educ* Balliol Coll Oxford (BA); *m* 3 Sept 1914 Hilda, dau of William Foster, and *dsp* 9 March 1943

3 (cont) The Hon Francis Russell *m* 2nd 28 April 1891 Gertrude Ellen Cornelia (*d* 28 Oct 1942), est dau of Henry Joachim, of Highlands, Haslemere, and *d* 30 March 1914, having by her had:

(2) John Albert, MC; *b* 8 Oct 1895; Capt 2nd S Staffs Regt WW I (wounded); *m* 1928 Alice Ives and *dsp* 12 April 1931

(1) Margaret Frances; *b* 15 May 1894; *m* 18 Dec 1918 Edward Mayow Hastings Lloyd, CB, CMG, 3rd s of Edward Wynell Mayow Lloyd, of Hartford House, Winchfield, Hants, and had issue. He *d* 27 Jan 1968

3 (Mary) Agatha; *b* 1853; *d* unm 23 April 1933

The 2nd EARL's bro,

BERTRAND ARTHUR WILLIAM RUSSELL, **3rd Earl Russell** (the philosopher Bertrand Russell), OM (1949); *b* 18 May 1872; *educ* Trin Coll Cambridge (BA, 7th Wrangler 1893, 1st Class Moral Science 1894, Fell 1895, MA 1897, lecturer 1944); Dr honoris causa U of Aix-Marseilles 1949, Hon Assoc Nat Inst Arts and Letters USA 1953, Hon Fell LSE 1961, author: *German Social Democracy* (1896), *Essay on the Foundations of Geometry* (1897), *Philosophy of Leibniz* (1900), *Principles of Mathematics* (1903), *Philosophical Essays* (1910), *Problems of Philosophy* (1911), *Principia Mathematica* (with A N Whitehead, 1910), *Our Knowledge of the External World as a Field for Scientific Method in Philosophy* (1914), *Principles of Social Reconstruction* (1917), *Mysticism and Logic* (1918), *Roads to Freedom* (1918), *Introduction to Mathematical Philosophy* (1919), *The Practice and Theory of Bolshevism* (1920), *The Analysis of Mind* (1921), *The Problem of China* (1922), *The ABC of Atoms* (1923), *The Prospects of Industrial Civilisation* (with Dora Russell, 1923), *What I Believe* (1925), *The ABC of Relativity* (1925), *On Education* (1926), *The Analysis of Matter* (1927), *An Outline of Philosophy* (1927), *Sceptical Essays* (1928), *Marriage and Morals* (1929), *The Conquest of Happiness* (1930), *The Scientific Outlook* (1931), *Education and the Social Order* (1932), *Freedom and Organisation, 1814–1914* (1934), *In Praise of Idleness* (1935), *Which Way to Peace?* (1936), *The Amberley Papers* (with Patricia Russell, 1937), *Power: A New Social Analysis* (1938), *An Inquiry into Meaning and Truth* (1940), *History of Western Philosophy* (1946), *Human Knowledge, its Scope and Limits* (1948), *Authority and the Individual* (1949), *Unpopular Essays* (1950), *New Hopes for a Changing World* (1951), *The Impact of Science upon Society* (1952), *Satan in the Suburbs* (short stories, 1953), *Nightmares of Eminent Persons* (1954), *Human Society in Ethics and Politics* (1954), *Portraits from Memory* (1956), *Why I am not a Christian* (1957), *Common Sense and Nuclear Warfare* (1958), *My Philosophical Development* (1959), *Wisdom of the West* (1959), *Fact and Fiction* (1961), *Has Man a Future?* (1961), *Unarmed Victory* (1963), *Political Ideals* (1963), *War Crimes in Vietnam* (1967), *Autobiography* (3 vols: 1967, 1968, 1969), FRS 1908, Sylvester Medal RS 1934, de Morgan Medal London Mathematical Soc 1934, Nobel Prize Literature 1950; *m* 1st 13 Dec 1894 (*divorce* 1921) Alys Whitall Pearsall (*d* 21 Jan 1951), dau of Robert Pearsall Smith, of Friday's Hill, Haslemere, Surrey; *m* 2nd 27 Sept 1921 (*divorce* 1935) Dora Winifred, MBE, dau of Sir Frederick Black, KCB, and had:

1 JOHN CONRAD RUSSELL, **4th Earl Russell**; *b* 16 Nov 1921; *educ* Dartington Hall and California and Harvard Us; T/Sub-Lt RNVR and Br Admlty Delegn Washington WW II 1943–46, T/Assist Pncpl FAO Washington 1946–47 and Treasury 1947–48; *m* 28 Aug 1946 (*divorce* 1955) Susan Doniphan, dau of Nicholas Vachel Lindsay, the American poet, and had:

(1) *Sarah Elizabeth; *b* 16 Jan 1946

(2) Lucy Catherine; *b* 21 July 1948; *d* unm 11 April 1975

1 (cont.) The **4th Earl** *d* 1987, having adopted his wife's dau:

*Felicity Anne; *b* 2 Sept 1945

1 *Katherine Jane; *b* 29 Dec 1923; *m* 1948 *Rev Charles William Stuart Tait, s of Charles Herman Avis Tait, of Boston, Mass., and has:

(1) *David Alexander; *b* 1951

(2) *Jonathan Francis; *b* 1955

(3) *Andrew Michael Philip; *b* 1961

(4) *Benjamin Peter; *b* 1 April 1965

(1) *Anne Elizabeth; *b* 1953

2 *Harriet Ruth; *b* 8 July 1930

The **3rd Earl** *m* 3rd 18 Jan 1936 (*divorce* 1952) Patricia Helen, dau of Harry Evelyn Spence, and by her had:

2 CONRAD SEBASTIAN ROBERT RUSSELL, **5th and present Earl Russell**

The **3rd Earl** *m* 4th 15 Dec 1952 Edith (*d* 1 Jan 1978), dau of Edward Bronson Finch, of New York, and *d* 2 Feb 1970

RUSSELL, Bt, of Littleworth Corner

Arms: Arg. a lion rampant gu., on a chief sa. three escallops of the field, the whole within a bordure engrailed vert. **Crest:** A goat passant arg., armed or, charged with three trefoils slipped fesswise vert. **Motto:** *Che sara sara* ('What will be, will be'). **Creation:** Bt. (UK) 18 Jan 1916.

SIR CHARLES DOMINIC RUSSELL, 4TH BT, of Littleworth Corner, Burnham, Co Buckingham [Sir Charles Russell Bt, Flat 12, 39 Egerton Gdns, London SW3 2DD]; *b* 28 May 1956; *s f* 1997; *educ* Worth Abbey; *m* 1986 (*divorce* 1995) Sarah Jane Murray, only dau of Anthony Chandor, of Haslemere, Surrey, and has:

1 +CHARLES WILLIAM; *b* 8 Sept 1988

Lineage: CHARLES RUSSELL, of Killough, Co Down; *b* 2 Jan 1759 (s of George Russell, of Ballystrew, Co Down, and Elizabeth Norris); *m* 1st 1 Sept 1784 Rose McCoy (*d* 9 July 1785) and had issue; *m* 2nd Anne, dau of Thomas McEvoy, of Drogheda, and *d* 28 Feb 1828, having by her had issue; his est s by his 1st w:

ARTHUR RUSSELL, of Seafield House, Killowen, and Newry, Co Down; *b* 9 July 1785; *m* 17 Jan 1825 Margaret, widow of John Hamill, of Belfast, and dau of Mathew Mullan, of Belfast, and *d* 28 May 1845, having had an er s:

CHARLES RUSSELL, BARON RUSSELL OF KILLOWEN, Co Down (UK, LP), so *cr* 7 May 1894, GCMG (1893), PC (1894), DL (Surrey); *b* 10 Nov 1832; *educ* Castleknock and Trin Coll Dublin; barrister Lincoln's Inn 1859, QC and bencher 1872, Attorney-Gen 1886 and 1892–94, Counsel for GB Bering Sea Arbitration 1893, MP Dundalk 1880–85 and S Hackney 1885–92 and 1892–95, ktd 1886, Ld Appeal in Ordinary, Ld Ch Justice 1894; *m* 10 Aug 1858 Ellen (*d* 10 March 1918), dau of Joseph Stevenson Mulholland, MD, of Belfast, and *d* 10 Aug 1900, having had:

1 Arthur Joseph; *b* 19 Feb 1861; *educ* Oriel Coll Oxford (MA); barrister 1886, County Court Judge Wandsworth; *m* 7 Oct 1891 Florence (*d* 21 July 1933), only dau of James Cuming, MD, of Belfast, and *dsp* 22 Nov 1907

2 **Sir Charles Russell, 1st Bt** (UK), so *cr* 18 Jan 1916, with remainder to the heirs male of the body of his f, KCVO; *b* 8 July 1863; *educ* Beaumont; *m* 1888, fndr and ptnr Charles Russell & Co, slr for Br Agent Bering Sea Arbitration 1893, Canadian Govt and Stewards Jockey Club; memb LCC 1910–13, KGStJ; *m* 1889 Adah Walmsley (*d* 28 Jan 1939), dau of Lt William Williams, RN, of Glanmawddach, Dolgelly, by Adeline, yst dau of Sir Joshua Walmsley, JP, MP, of Waventree Hall, Lancs, Smilslea Park, Leics, and Hume Towers and Wolverton Park, Hants, and *dspm* 27 March 1928, leaving:

(1) Monica; *m* 1st 9 April 1917 (*divorce* 1932) her cousin **Sir Alec Charles Russell, 2nd Bt**, MC, and had issue (*see below*); *m* 2nd 11 Nov 1942 Brig John Victor Faviell, CBE, MC, s of Charles Victor Faviell, of Perceval House, Blackheath

3 Cyril; *b* 1865; *educ* Univ Coll Oxford (BA); *m* 25 Jan 1893 Helen Mary (*d* 22 Aug 1937), dau of Alexander George Pirie, of Leckmelm, Ross-shire, and *d* 14 May 1920, leaving:

(1) ALEC CHARLES (Sir), **2nd Bt**

(2) Gerald Cyril, MC; *b* 12 Jan 1896; *educ* Beaumont; T/Maj RFA WW I (despatches), slr 1921, sr ptnr Charles Russell & Co; *m* 3 Oct 1923 Barbara (*d* 1985), 3rd dau of Sir James Philip Reynolds, 1st Bt, DSO, MP (*qv*), and *d* 3 March 1962, leaving:

1a +Cyril [Cyril Russell Esq, The Covert, Aldeburgh, Suffolk]; *b* 2 Oct 1924; Lt Irish Gds, slr 1948, ptnr Charles Russell; *m* 30 June 1949 *(Eileen Mary) Elizabeth, dau of Maj William Douglas Grant Batten, 3rd Gurkha Rifles, by Eileen Mary, yr dau of Albert Willson, of Waldegrave Park, Twickenham, and has:

1b +Gerald William; *b* 21 May 1950; *educ* Beaumont and Ampleforth; *m* 1976 *Tessa, dau of Richard Rumsey, and has:

1c +James Alexander; *b* 1978

1c *Sophie Annabel; *b* 1980

2c *Lucy Victoria; *b* 1983

3c *Kate Elizabeth; *b* 1985

2b +Patrick James; b 11 May 1952; educ Ampleforth; m 1977 *Pamela Jill, dau of Philip Gordon, and has:

  1c +Oliver William Grant; b 1981

  1c *Jessica Helen; b 1984

  2c *Camilla Ellinora; b 1987

3b +Nicholas Alastair; b 8 Aug 1958; m 1986 *Heather B L, dau of Col John Burrell, of Ronay, Aldeburgh, Suffolk, and has:

  1c +Alastair Hamish; b 1987

  1c *Philippa; b 19–

2a (John) Alastair (Rev); b 13 Aug 1928; educ Beaumont; RC priest, Army Chaplain; d 8 May 1997

3a +Colin Patrick [Colin Russell Esq, Long Ford, Duntisbourne Leer, Cirencester, Glos GL7 7AS]; b 15 July 1944; educ Beaumont and Univ Coll Oxford (BA); slr 1970; m 1978 *Jessica Margaret, only dau of Ramsay William Rainsford-Hannay (see WISEMAN, Bt)

1a Moira; b 28 March 1927; nun; d 1992

2a *Clodagh Mary [Mrs David Reid, The Studio, Priors Hill Rd, Aldeburgh, Suffolk]; b 14 Sept 1933; m 1971 *Brig David William Reid, MBE, s of Sir Robert Neil Reid, KCSI, KCIE

(3) Denis Leslie, MBE (1945), TD; b 2 July 1909; educ Beaumont and Univ Coll Oxford (BA); Maj RA WW II (despatches), stockbroker, sr ptnr George Henderson & Co; m 6 Oct 1932 Verena (d 1995), yr dau of George Henderson, of Belgravia and The Orchard House, Crastock, Surrey, and d 1986, having had:

1a (Denis) Anthony; b 12 April 1934; educ Beaumont; stockbroker, ptnr George Henderson; m 27 Sept 1961 *Charlotte Mary (m 2nd 2 Jan 1970 John Watcyn Lewis, s of John Lewis, of Denison House, Little Gaddesden, Herts), yr dau of Lt-Col Sir Ian Frank Bowater, GBE, DSO, TD (see BOWATER, Bt, of Friston), and d 30 July 1966, leaving:

  1b +William Anthony Bowater; b 15 April 1965; m 1989 *Hilary Ann, only dau of John Chaplin, of Cambridge, and has:

    1c +Edward John Bowater; b 1992

  1b *Amanda Charlotte; b 4 June 1963; m 1987 *Charles Nicholas Yaxley, only s of John Yaxley, of Hong Kong, and has:

    1c *Thomas; b 1989

2a +David Ian [David Russell Esq, 25a Eddiscombe Rd, London SW10]; b 1 April 1943; educ Ampleforth; ptnr Rowe & Pitman Hurst-Brown; m 30 April 1976 *Hon Frances Marion, dau of Lt-Col Stuart Whitemore Chant-Sempill, OBE, MC, by Lady Sempill (qv), and has:

  1b *Katherine Ann; b 19 June 1980

1a *Sally Verena [Mrs William Weatherall, Shorndown, Mursley, Bucks]; b 20 Feb 1937; m 19 Oct 1956 *William Bertram Weatherall, s of Lt-Col Nigel Edward Weatherall, of Caldwell House, Gilling West, N Yorks, and has:

  1b *Michael William [Michael Weatherall Esq, 4 Hosack Rd, London SW17 7QP]; b 11 April 1958; m 1987 *Penelope Ann, dau of Frederick Wharton Askew, of Caroline Ho, Redhill, Surrey, and has:

    1c *Edward Frederick; b 1991

    2c *Toby William; b 1993

  1b *Annabel Jane; b 25 Dec 1960; m 1985 *William George Briscoe Bevan and has issue (see BROCKLEBANK, Bt)

  2b *Clare Victoria (twin); b 25 Dec 1960; m 1987 *James Bunten de Sales La Terrière, est s of Capt Ian Cameron de Sales La Terrière, of Dunalastair, Perthshire, and has:

    1c *Archie; b 1990

    2c *Dominic John; b 1993

    1c *Emma; b 1988

(4) (Cyril) Alan; b 5 Dec 1910; educ Beaumont; Lt-Col London Scottish, md J Henry Schroder Wagg, dir: Alexanders Discount, District Bank, Legal and General Assur, IBM UK, Schroders Ltd, Turner & Newall and Yorkshire Bank; m 1st 24 May 1937 Grace Evelyn (d 1 April 1943), est dau of William Thomas Moore, of New York, and had:

1a Genia Helen Kathleen; b 11 March 1938; m 20 June 1959 Jeremy Paterson-Fox, s of Alexander Peter Paterson-Fox, and had:

  1b *Alastair Mark; b 30 March 1960

  2b *Philip Alan; b 16 Dec 1965

  3b *Neil Jeremy; b 25 Feb 1968

  1b *Claire Emma; b 28 Nov 1961

(4) (cont.) Col Alan Russell m 2nd 2 May 1944 *Jean Patricia [Mrs Alan Russell, 23 Park Lane, Aldeburgh, Suffolk], widow of W/Cdr John Ryan Cridland, AAF, and er dau of Stafford Croom-Johnson, of Little Manor, West End, Nailsea, Somerset, and d 1986, having by her had:

1a +Michael Alan; b 16 Jan 1947; educ Beaumont; m 1972 *Penelope, yr dau of Lt-Col A R Dawe, OBE, of Wyke Lodge, Normandy, and has:

  1b +Toby Alan; b 1974

  1b *Michaela Katherine; b 1976

(1) Phyllis Helen; b 1 Nov 1897; m 27 Dec 1923 Sir Theobald Mathew, KBE, MC, s of Charles Mathew, KC, and had issue. He d 29 Feb 1964

(2) Eileen Valerie; b 15 Nov 1901; m 24 May 1930 (Albert Louis) Georges Gund, Chev Legn Hon, Croix de Guerre, yst s of Albert Gund, of Paris, and d 29 March 1963. He d 17 Nov 1965

4 FRANCIS (FRANK) XAVIER, BARON RUSSELL OF KILLOWEN, Co Down 1929 (LP, UK), so cr 18 Nov PC (1928); b 2 July 1867; educ Beaumont and Oriel Coll Oxford (Hon Fell 1928); barrister Lincoln's Inn 1893 (Treasurer 1936), KC 1908, bencher 1913, High Court Judge (Chancery) 1919, Ld Justice Appeal 1928, Ld Appeal in Ordinary; m 17 Feb 1900 Hon Mary Emily Ritchie (d 10 Nov 1956), 5th dau of 1st Baron Ritchie of Dundee (qv), and d 20 Dec 1946, leaving:

(1) CHARLES RITCHIE (Sir), BARON RUSSELL OF KILLOWEN, Co Down, (LP, UK), so cr 1975, PC (1962); b 12 Jan 1908; educ Beaumont and Oriel Coll Oxford (BA 1929, MA 1951, Hon Fell 1962); barrister Lincoln's Inn 1931, RA WW II (wounded, despatches, Croix de Guerre), QC 1948, Bencher 1952, Attorney-Gen Duchy of Cornwall 1951–60, High Court Judge (Chancery)

1960, ktd 1960, Pres Restrictive Practices Court 1961–62; m 1st 4 Aug 1933 Joan Elisabeth (d 14 June 1976), only child of James Aubrey Torrens, MD, FRCP, of 46 Wimpole St, London W1; m 2nd 1979 *Elizabeth Cecilia, dau of AVM William Foster Macneece Foster, CB, CBE, DSO, DFC, and widow of Judge Edward Hay Laughton-Scott, QC, and d 1986, having had by his 1st w:

1a *Valentine Francis Xavier Michael [The Hon Valentine Russell, CP51, 1631 Moléson, Fribourg, Switzerland]; b 12 May 1938; educ Beaumont and Oriel Coll Oxford

2a +(Francis) Damian [The Hon Damian Russell, 17 Lurline Gdns, London SW11]; b 8 June 1947; educ Beaumont and Trin Coll Dublin; m 1994 *Carole Myers, BSc, DPhil, of Hillsborough, S Yorks

1a *Julian Mary [The Hon Mrs Ullman, 1245 29th St NW, Washington DC, USA]; b 5 April 1935; m 1st 9 June 1955 (divorce 1974) Anthony Rodney Allfrey, er s of Capt Basil Holmsdale Allfrey, of Vienna; m 2nd *Dr Harlan Ullman and has by her 1st husb:

  1b *Charles Sebastian Holmsdale; b 29 March 1959

  1b *Arabel Mary; b 11 June 1956

  2b *Georgiana Rose; b 20 July 1957

2a Brigid Mary; b 21 Dec 1940; d 19 Nov 1941

(1) Mary Lilian Ritchie; b 22 Jan 1901; d unm 15 Feb 1956

(2) Eileen; d an infant 23 Aug 1904

(3) Margaret Mary; b 1 July 1905; m 16 Feb 1941 Milan Bratza Yovanovitch (d 16 Feb 1964), er s of Pantalemon Yovanovitch, of Novisad, Yugoslavia, and has:

1a *Nicolas Dusan Bratza; b 3 March 1945; educ Wimbledon Coll and BNC Oxford (BA); barrister Lincoln's Inn 1969

2a *Gregory Francis Pantalemon; b 6 Sept 1947; educ Wimbledon Coll

1a *Maria Dobrilla Cecilia [Mrs Bryant Ellis, 36 Craigside, Galsworthy Rd, Kingston-upon-Thames, Surrey]; b 4 May 1942; m 15 Nov 1969 Bryant Edward Ellis, only s of Edward Akin Ellis, of Wallasey and Broughton, Cheshire

5 Bertrand Joseph, DSO (1915); b 12 Aug 1876; educ Beaumont; Lt-Col RA, Bde-Maj RA 1916, Boer War 1900, WW I (wounded, despatches, Croix de Guerre Italy); m 1st 15 July 1902 Dorothy (d 24 Feb 1921), dau of John George Leeming, and had:

(1) Prudence; b 2 May 1904; m 1st 16 July 1929 (divorce 1943) Michael Chetwynd Ellison, only s of Charles Chetwynd Ellison, of Ashfield, Malton, Yorks; m 2nd 6 Feb 1951 James Gordon Findlay, yr s of William Findlay, of Birkdale, Lancs

(2) Ursula; b 28 May 1905; m 1 May 1929 Maj Stanford BUNN later BURN (deed poll 1933), Roy Scots, est s of Harry Hunter Bunn, and d India May 1942, leaving issue. He was ka Hong Kong Dec 1941

(3) Joan [Mrs Charles Brand, 1 Stanhope Mews East, London SW7]; b 5 April 1908; m 27 July 1933 Charles Gordon Brand, CBE (d 28 March 1966), er s of Sir Harry Francis Brand, of Harecomb, Crowborough, and has:

1a *Andrew Charles Ninian [Andrew Brand Esq, c/o Charles Russell & Co, Hale Court, Lincoln's Inn, London WC2]; b 7 Nov 1937; educ Stonyhurst; slr, ptnr Charles Russell; m 9 Oct 1965 *Dorothea Margaret Ann, er dau of John William Hill, of Norris End, E Preston, Sussex, and has:

  1b *Charles Matthew John; b 25 Aug 1966

2a *Duncan Valentine; b 14 Feb 1941; educ Stonyhurst and Brasenose Coll Oxford; m 24 Feb 1968 *Hilary, dau of A Peter Rivers, of Banstead, Surrey, and has:

  1b *Jeremy Charles Peter; b 12 Nov 1969

1a *Felicity Clare; b 25 July 1945; m 23 April 1976 *Dan Douglas, s of Mrs Joseph L Maas, of Homestead, Fla.

(4) *Clodagh [Mrs Thomas Haddon, Mole End, Hale House Lane, Churt, Farnham, Surrey GU10 2JG]; b 17 Nov 1912; m 5 Sept 1939 Brig Thomas Haddon, CBE, Border Regt (d 1993), s of Maj John Thomas Haddon, of Hamilton, Lanarks, and has:

1a *Paul Antony [Paul Haddon Esq, 36 Goodwyn's Vale, London N10 2HA]; b 16 Nov 1940; educ Beaumont and Campion Hall Oxford; m 7 June 1975 *Denise, only child of R O C King, and has:

  1b *Patrick Oliver; b 23 Aug 1981

  1b *Claire Elizabeth; b 26 Nov 1975

  2b *Laura Mary; b 29 Sept 1977

  3b *Juliet Annabel; b 17 Oct 1979

2a *Martin Thomas; b 8 Dec 1944; educ Beaumont and Worcester Coll Oxford

3a *John Richard; b 15 April 1947; educ Beaumont and Worcester Coll Oxford

5 (cont.) Lt-Col Bertrand Russell m 2nd 31 Oct 1922 (divorce 1936) Mavis Winifred, only dau of Frederick Hazell, of Frinton-on-Sea, and d 9 May 1960, having by her had:

(1) Michael Dudley, of East Grinstead, Sussex; b 22 Sept 1923; m 1st 6 Aug 1949 (divorce 1959) Jeanette, yr dau of Maj Arthur Sinclair Cannon, of Rangoon, and had:

1a +Christopher John; b 13 Nov 1951; educ Worth; m 1976 (divorce 1981) Nicola, only dau of James de Courcy Hughes, and has:

  1b +Dominic John; b 1979

  1b *Lucienne Eva; b 1977

1a *Julia Meryen [Mrs Timothy Ashworth, Old Marsham Farm, Pett, Sussex]; b 25 Aug 1954; m 1986 *Timothy Ashworth and has:

  1b *Camilla Eileen; b 1989

  2b *Elizabeth Annabelle; b 1990

(1) (cont.) Michael Russell m 2nd 27 Jan 1960 *Judy [Mrs Michael Russell, Meadow Court, Coombe Hill Rd, East Grinstead, W Sussex], yr dau of Dr M A W Roberts, of Kitale, Kenya, and d 1993, having by her had:

2a *Anna Katherine; b 8 May 1961

3a *Verena Grace [Mrs Andrew Weir, 105 Trentham St, London SW18 5DH]; b 1962; m 1989 *Andrew Bruce Weir and has:

  1b *Oliver Michael; b 1994

1b *Isobelle Katherine; *b* 1991

1 Lilian Frances; *b* 20 April 1859; *d* 2 Nov 1864

2 Eileen Mary; *b* 15 Jan 1865; *m* 4 Feb 1891 Douglas Lyon Holms, er s of John Holms, JP, MP, and *d* 6 April 1941, leaving issue. He *d* 30 Aug 1924

3 Mary Gertrude; *b* 3 March 1874; nun; *d* 1 Dec 1960

4 Lillian; *b* 17 Feb 1878; *m* 3 May 1906 Henry Olpherts Drummond, of Farr Lodge, Henley-on-Thames, yr s of James Drummond, MD, and *d* 9 Oct 1949, leaving issue. He *d* 29 March 1928

5 Margaret; *b* 21 April 1879; *d* unm 27 Oct 1945

The 1st Bt's n,

Sir Alec Charles Russell, 2nd Bt, MC; *b* 19 Dec 1894; *educ* Beaumont; Capt RA WW II (wounded, despatches); *m* 1st 9 April 1917 (*divorce* 1932) his cousin Monica (*d* 1978), only child of Hon Sir Charles Russell, 1st Bt, KCVO (*see* above), and had:

1 **Sir Charles Ian Russell, 3rd Bt**; *b* 13 March 1918; *educ* Beaumont and Univ Coll Oxford; Capt RHA WW II (despatches); slr 1947, sr ptnr Charles Russell & Co, Lincoln's Inn; *m* 18 Jan 1947 Rosemary (*d* 4 June 1996), er dau of Sir John Theodore Prestige, of Bourne Pk, Bishopsbourne, Kent, and *d* 26 Sept 1997, leaving:

(1) Sir CHARLES DOMINIC RUSSELL, **4th and present Bt**

(1) *Clare Harriet Faviell [Mrs Richard Shepherd, Stratton End, Cirencester, Glos]; *b* 30 March 1949; *m* 10 Jan 1974 *Richard James Shepherd, s of W J Shepherd, and has:

1a *Edward James; *b* 1977

2a *Andrew Charles; *b* 1979

3a *Thomas Richard; *b* 1982

1 Sheila Helen; *b* 28 Nov 1921; Jr Cdr ATS WW II; *m* 5 Oct 1946 Capt Lawrence Noel George Pace, Argyll and Sutherland Highrs, only s of Surg-Capt John Francis Pace, MB, ChB, RN, of York, and had:

(1) *Andrew Faviell; *b* 15 Dec 1948; *educ* Beaumont

(2) *Mark Faviell; *b* 23 March 1952; *educ* Worth

Sir Alec *m* 2nd 7 May 1936 Rowena Mary (*m* 3rd 24 Jan 1946 Alexander Smail, s of Henry Smail), formerly w of Maj Malcolm David Motion and dau of Richard Scott Lamb, of West Denton, Northumberland, and *d* 8 July 1938

RUSSELL, Bt, of Swallowfield

Arms: Arg. a chevron sa. between three cross-crosslets fitchée az. within a bordure engrailed gu., bearing alternate bezants and escallops or. **Crest:** A demi-lion rampant erm., charged with a fasces ppr. and bearing in his dexter paw a cross-crosslet fitchée sa. **Motto:** *Discite justitiam moniti* ('Be advised and learn justice'). **Creation:** Bt. (UK) 10 Dec 1812.

SIR (ARTHUR) MERVYN RUSSELL, 8TH BT, of Swallowfield, Berks [Sir Mervyn Russell Bt, 83 Wentworth Gdns, Exeter EX4 1NQ]; *b* 7 Feb 1923; s half-bro 1993; *m* 1st 1945 (*divorce* 19–) Ruth Holloway and has:

1 +STEPHEN CHARLES; *b* 12 Jan 1949

Sir MERVYN *m* 2nd 1956 *Kathleen Joyce Searle and by her has:

2 +A son; *b* 19–

Lineage: This family originated in Worcestershire and their arms, until slightly altered on the creation of the 1st Bt, were the same as those of the Russell Bts of Strensham, Worcs, a title that expired 1705.

MICHAEL RUSSELL, s of a Parliamentarian in the Civil War; settled Dover late 17th century; *m* Hester, dau of Thomas Scott, of Kent, and had, with Thomas (*dsp*):

MICHAEL RUSSELL, of Dover; *b* 1711; *m* Hannah (*d* 1 Sept 1796), dau of Henry Henshaw, of Dover, and *d* 23 Nov 1793, having had, with two er sons and a yst s:

Sir Henry Russell, 1st Bt (UK), so *cr* 10 Dec 1812, PC; *b* 19 Aug 1751; Ch Justice Supreme Court Bengal; *m* 1st 1 Aug 1776 Anne (*dsps* 25 Nov 1780), dau of John

Skinner, of Lydd, Kent; *m* 2nd 23 July 1782 Anna Barbara (*d* 1 Aug 1814), sis of 1st and last Earl Whitworth (*see* RAVENSDALE, B), and had, with a dau (*d* unm):

1 HENRY (Sir), **2nd Bt**

2 Charles; *b* 22 July 1786; *d* unm 1856

3 Francis Whitworth; *b* 30 Jan 1790; *m* 10 June 1823 Jane Anne Catherine (*d* 1867), 2nd dau of James Brodie, of Brodie, Morayshire, and *d* 26 March 1852, having had, with other issue:

(1) Francis Whitworth; *b* 1830; Maj 5th Bengal Cav; *m* 22 Sept 1851 Alice Mary (*d* 24 Sept 1892), er dau of Sir John Murray Naesmyth of Posso, 4th Bt (*see* 1928 edn), and *d* 1872, leaving:

1a Francis Whitworth; *b* 1854; *m* 1886 Maude Agnes, dau of Denis O'Brien, of Knockroe, Co Cork, and had:

1b Francis Whitworth; *b* 1888

2a Edward Stuart Marjoribanks Harley; *b* 1857; *m* 1882 Mary (*d* 2 Feb 1938), only dau of Capt W Phipps, and *d* 15 March 1926, leaving:

1b Alice

2b Rachel

3b Kate

1a Mary Rachel Katherine; *m* 17 Jan 1877 Robert Dundas Arthur Graham Fergusson and *d* 19 June 1923, leaving issue (*see* FERGUSSON, Bt)

(1) Elizabeth Gordon Brodie; *m* 19 Nov 1850 Sir James Naesmyth of Posso, 5th Bt (*see* 1928 edn), and *dsp* June 1887. He *d* 10 Oct 1896

4 Whitworth (Rev); *b* 17 Sept 1795; *m* 6 April 1824 Frances (*d* 1873), dau of V-Adml Carpenter, and *d* 2 Aug 1847, leaving:

(1) Henry; *b* 6 Feb 1827; *m* 1848 Maria Charlotte, dau of Henry Hammond Shelton, and *d* 21 Aug 1852, leaving:

1a Whitworth; *b* 1849; *m* 1886 Caroline Eleanor, dau of J P Armstrong, CE, and *d* 1893, leaving:

1b John Whitworth; *b* 1891; *m* Mary Alice (*d* 1985), dau of J R Anderson, and *d* 1982, leaving:

1c +Whitworth ATHELSTAN later ATHOL [Whitworth Russell Esq, 23 Ingleton Terr, Hamilton, New Zealand]; *b* 1918; MB, ChB, DCP; *m* 1946 *Marjory Ellen Ross and has:

1d +Anthony Whitworth [Anthony Russell Esq, 15 Iusoll Ave, Hamilton, New Zealand]; *b* 1951; *m* 1st 1971 (*divorce* 1986) Catherine Sylvia Bradley; *m* 2nd *Catherine Patricia Felicity Orange and has by his 1st w:

1e +James Whitworth; *b* 1979

1e *Joanna Alice; *b* 1976

2e *Claire Jennifer; *b* 1980

2d +Michael David; *b* 1959

1d *Juliet Ethne; *b* 1962; *m* 1983 (*divorce* 1990) Shaughan Bruce and has:

1e *Alexandra Ellen; *b* 1987

2c +Richard Hudson; *b* 1928

1c *Elizabeth Alison, BA [Mrs David Poswillo, Ferndale, 7 Oldfield Rd, Bickley, Kent BR1 2LE]; *b* 1934; *m* 1956 *David Ernest Poswillo, CBE, DDS, MD, DSc, Emeritus Prof UMDS, Guy's Hosp, U of London, and has:

1d *Stephen David; *b* 1962; *m* 1988 *Michelle Lynn Narcisse and has:

1e *Maxwell Stephen; *b* 1994

2d *Mark Geoffrey; *b* 1964

1d *Deborah Jane; *b* 1958, *m* *Robert William Caton and has:

1e *Harry James; *b* 1997

1e *Lucy Harriet; *b* 1994

2d *Mary Jill; *b* 1961, *m* 1987 *Robert William Gerald Battye and has:

1e *Alexander Robert; *b* 1989

1e *Emma Alice; *b* 1991

1b Charlotte; *b* 1887; *m* 1927 Arthur Westbrook and *d* 1987, leaving:

1c *Arthur Robert Whitworth [Arthur Westbrook Esq, 51 Redbourne Ave, London N3 2BP]; *b* 1928; *m* 1960 *Ida Hamilton, of Wellington, NZ, and has:

1d *Trudi; *b* 19–

2b Mary; *b* 1889; *m* 19– Benjamin Ward Burnett, of Wanganui, NZ and *d* 1944, leaving:

1c *Ward Benjamin; *b* 1927; *m* 1964 *Margaret Anne Head and has:

1d *Steven Russell; *b* 1967

1d *Rosalind Margaret; *b* 1965

1c *Mary Russell; *b* 19–

3b Naomi; *d* 1968

(2) Charles Whitworth; *b* 10 Aug 1828; Capt RN; *m* 28 Sept 1854 Maria Barnston (*d* 2 Dec 1915), yr dau of Gen Henry Daubeny, KH, JP, and *dsp* 30 Oct 1863

(1) Fanny; *m* 8 June 1848 Rev William Brassey Hole, Vicar Bray, Berks, and *d* Feb 1906, leaving issue. He *d* 1887

5 George Lake; *b* 19 June 1801; *m* 16 Feb 1832 Lady Caroline Alicia Diana Pery (*d* 11 Dec 1890), dau of 1st Earl of Limerick (*qv*), and *d* 16 Nov 1878, leaving:

(1) Cecil Henry; *b* 15 April 1833; MA Cantab, barrister and Bencher Lincoln's Inn, Treasurer 1907; *m* 18 Jan 1859 Katharine (*d* 22 Nov 1905), dau of Henry Porter, of Winslade, and *d* 16 June 1910, having had:

1a George Cecil; *b* 20 Oct 1861; *m* 1889 Alice Jane Evelyn (*d* 18 Sept 1949), dau of E W Mills, JP, of Wellington, NZ, and *d* 28 Oct 1915, having had:

1b Charles Lake Cecil; *b* 1889; *d* 1894

2b Evelyn Aylmer Cecil; *b* 1891; *m* 1st 1916 (*divorce* 1923) Alice Edith, dau of W H Wallis, of California Gully, Bendigo, Victoria, Australia, and had:

1c *Sadie Evelyn; *b* 1917; *educ* Melbourne U (BA 1917); *m* 21 Dec 1940 Harold William Halls, s of W J Halls, of Warragal, Victoria, and has:

1d *Peter John; *b* 1944; *m* 1969 *Marjorie, dau of Rev Maurice Padman, of Snowtown, S Australia, and has:

1e *Evelyn Marie; *b* 1972

2e *Joanne Michelle; *b* 1973

2d *Robin; *b* 1958; BCom, LLB

2b (cont.) Evelyn Russell *m* 2nd 24 May 1924 Irene, 2nd dau of John Brodrick, JP, of Nangana, Victoria, and *d* 1963, having by her had:

1c +William Henry Cecil [William Russell Esq, Strensham, Beaumont Rd, Berwick 3806, Victoria, Australia]; *b* 18 Feb 1927; *m* 1954 *Margaret Winifred, dau of Gordon Newton, of McKinnon, Victoria, and has:

1d +Mark Newton Cecil [Mark Russell Esq, Russmore, 30 Norbury Rd, Upper Beaconsfield, Victoria, Australia]; *b* 1959; *m* 1987 *Rosemary Anne, dau of Alan Moore, of E Bentleigh, Victoria, and has:

1e +William James Cecil; *b* 1994

1e *Briony Jane; *b* 1990

1d *Jane Elizabeth; *b* 1956; *m* 1976 *Timothy Leslie Moore, 2nd s of Lt-Col Colin Moore, of East Brighton, Victoria, and has:

1e *Jayce William; *b* 1980

1e *Ebby Margaret; *b* 1983

2d *Kim Margaret; *b* 1964; *m* 1989 *Mark Raymond Bloodworth, s of Raymond Bloodworth, of Rosanna, Victoria

2c +Harry Arthur Cecil, JP [Harry Russell Esq JP, Quarry Hill, 19 Belmont Ave, Upwey, Victoria 3158, Australia]; *b* 31 Aug 1931; *m* 1959 *Marjorie Ailsa, dau of Alfred Sutton, of Hawthorn, Victoria, and has:

1d +Ewen James Cecil; *b* 1967

1d *Sarah Anne Cecil; *b* 1962

2d *Virginia Kate Cecil (twin); *b* 1962; *m* 1992 *David Robert Edwards, s of Philip Edwards, of Hawthorn, Victoria, and has:

1e *Stephanie Kate; *b* 1996

3b Edmond Henry Cecil; *b* 1892; *educ* Haileybury; AIF WW I, Lt Roy Australian Engrs WW II, memb Berwicks CC 1921–29

4b John Hardress Cecil; *b* 1896; AIF WW I; *m* 19 April 1927 Doris Marion, only dau of Ernest Reginald Green, of Colac, Victoria, and had:

1c +John Alan Cecil [John Russell Esq, Protea Bowl, Gembrook VIC 3782, Australia]; *b* 15 Sept 1928; *m* 1955 *Patricia Mary Gordon, dau of Roddam Morris Douglas, of Emerald, Victoria, and has:

1d *Susan Patricia; *b* 1956

2d *Penelope Ann; *b* 1959

3d *Lynette Margaret; *b* 1963

4d *Diane Marion; *b* 1964

2a Henry Cecil; *b* 8 Oct 1863; *dsp* 25 April 1885

3a Edmond Cecil, OBE (1919); *b* 25 May 1876; *educ* Eton; *d* unm 17 Feb 1955

1a Rose Cecil; *b* 12 Nov 1859; *m* 16 Jan 1890 Hubert Arthur Strickland (*see* STRICKLAND-CONSTABLE, Bt) and *dsp* 30 Sept 1939

2a Augusta Cecil; *b* 9 Dec 1867; *d* unm 15 Aug 1888

3a Katharine Cecil; *b* 1 Jan 1873; *d* unm 24 Nov 1947

4a Diana Cecil; *b* 29 March, *d* 2 Oct 1878

1 Caroline; *m* 2 Nov 1824 Cdr Henry Fortescue (*see* FORTESCUE, E) and *d* 6 March 1869, leaving issue

2 Katharine; *m* 18 April 1816 Henry Jones, of Stapleton, Glos, and *d* Sept 1845

3 Henrietta; *m* Sept 1820 Thomas Greene, MP, of Slyne, Lancs, and Whittington Hall, Kirby Lonsdale

4 Rose Aylmer; *m* 27 July 1820 Henry Porter, of Winslade, Devon. He *d* June 1880

Sir HENRY *d* 18 Jan 1836; his est s,

Sir Henry Russell, 2nd Bt; *b* 27 May 1783; Br Resident Hyderabad; *m* 1st 20 Oct 1808 Jane Amelia (*d* 29 Dec 1808), 2nd dau of John Casamaijor, of Madras; *m* 2nd 13 Nov 1816 Marie Clotilde (*d* 31 Jan 1872), dau of Benoit Mottet de la Fontaine, Baron fieffé de St Corneille, Seigneur de la Motte et de la Fontaine, Picardy, and *d* 19 April 1852, having by her had, with a dau (*d* unm):

1 Henry; *b* 9 June 1819; *d* Cairo 20 Jan 1847

2 **Sir Charles Russell, 3rd Bt**, VC (1854); *b* 22 June 1826; MP (C) Berks 1865–68 and Warminster 1874–83, Lt-Col Gren Gds Crimean War, Legn Hon; *d* unm 14 April 1883

3 GEORGE (Sir), **4th Bt**

1 Mary; *m* 3 Sept 1856 Col Dawson Greene, of Whittington Hall, and Slyne, Lancs, and *d* 17 April 1894, leaving issue. He *d* 28 Jan 1897

2 Priscilla; *m* 25 April 1865 George Brackenbury, CMG, Consul Lisbon, and *d* 22 Nov 1924, leaving issue. He *d* 21 Jan 1895

Sir CHARLES's bro,

Sir George Russell, 4th Bt, DL; *b* 23 Aug 1828; barrister, Recorder Wokingham, Judge County Court (Circuit No 49) 1874–85, MP (C) E Berks; *m* 5 March 1867 Constance Charlotte Elisa (*d* 20 June 1925), est dau of Lord Arthur Lennox (*see* RICHMOND and GORDON, D) and *d* 7 March 1898, leaving:

1 **Sir George Arthur Charles Russell, 5th Bt**; *b* 28 June 1868; *d* unm 14 Jan 1944

2 ARTHUR EDWARD IAN MONTAGU (Sir), **6th Bt**

1 Marie Clotilde, DGStJ; *m* 15 July 1903 Hon Arthur Ernest Guinness (*see* IVEAGH, E) and *d* 22 July 1953, leaving issue

Sir GEORGE's bro,

Sir Arthur Edward Ian Montagu Russell, 6th Bt, MBE (1920); *b* 30 Nov 1878; *educ* Eton; Lt RE WW I, Pres Mineralogical Soc GB 1939–42, Hon DSc Oxford 1956; *m* 1st 22 June 1904 Aileen Kerr (*d* 17 Jan 1920), yst dau of Adml Mark Robert Pechell (*see* PECHELL, Bt), and had:

1 **Sir George Michael Russell, 7th Bt**; *b* 30 Sept 1908; *educ* Radley; *m* 20 Feb 1936 *Joy Frances Bedford, dau of W Mitchell, of Irwin, WAustralia, and *d* 1993, leaving:

(1) *Marie Clotilde; *b* 26 March 1939; *m* 1965 (*divorce* 1984) Nelson Grant Mews, s of P Mews, of Perth, W Australia, and has:

1a *Josephine Lucy; *b* 1974

(2) *Mary Christina; *b* 27 Nov 1944

1 Bettine; *b* 24 May 1905; *m* 9 Oct 1929 2nd Baron Broughshane (*qv*) and *d* 1994, having had issue

Sir Arthur *m* 2nd 7 June 1922 (*divorce* 1932) Cornélie, dau of Maj Jacques de Bruign, of Amsterdam, and by her had:

2 Sir (ARTHUR) MERVYN RUSSELL, **8th and present Bt**

Sir Arthur *m* 3rd 16 Dec 1933 *Marjorie Elizabeth Josephine, only dau of Ernest Rudman, of Foxhangers, Earley, Berks, and *d* 23 Feb 1964, leaving by her:

3 Christopher; *b* 22 Feb 1937; *educ* Charterhouse; *m* 1st 3 March 1962 (*divorce* 1983) Ann, only dau of Lt-Col Clifford Donald Battersby Campling, of Canterbury; *m* 2nd 1983 *Loveday Mary, widow of Cdr P D Davey, RN

RUSSELL OF LIVERPOOL

Arms: Per saltire sa. and or, in chief an estoile arg., two roses in fess gu., barbed and seeded ppr., and in base a thistle leaved and slipped of the second. **Crest:** An owl, wings expanded arg., beaked and legged or, resting the dexter claw on an estoile az. **Supporters:** On either side an owl arg., beaked and legged or, gorged with a chaplet of roses gu., leaved vert. **Motto:** More light.
Creation: B. (UK) 9 Oct 1919.

THE 3RD BARON RUSSELL OF LIVERPOOL, of Liverpool (Simon Gordon Jared Russell) [The Rt Hon The Lord Russell of Liverpool, House of Lords, London SW1A 0PW]; *b* 30 Aug 1952; *s* gf 1981; *educ* Charterhouse, Trin Coll Cambridge and INSEAD France; *m* 1984 *Dr Gilda F, yst dau of F Albano, of Salerno, Italy, and has:

1 +EDWARD CHARLES STANLEY; *b* 2 Sept 1985

2 +William Francis Langley; *b* 1988

1 *Leonora Maria Kiloran; *b* 1987

Lineage: EDWARD HASLINGDEN RUSSELL, of London; *b* 21 Jan 1809; *m* 1833 Mary Anne (*d* 1851), dau of William Crook, of Calne, Wilts, and *d* 1851, having had, with other issue:

EDWARD RICHARD RUSSELL, **1st Baron Russell of Liverpool**, Lancs (UK), so *cr* 9 Oct 1919; *b* 9 Aug 1834; ed *Liverpool Daily Post* 1869–1919, ktd 1893, 1st pres Liverpool Reform Club, memb Court Liverpool U, Govr U Coll Aberystwyth, pres IOJ, MP (Lib) Glasgow Bridgeton 1885–87; *m* 1st 16 Dec 1858 Eliza Sophia (*d* 22 Jan 1901), dau of Stephen Bradley, of Bridge, Kent; *m* 2nd 30 April 1902 Jean Stewart (*d* 16 March 1927), widow of Joseph McFarlane and dau of Alexander Macdonald, of Campbelltown, Argyll, and *d* 20 Feb 1920, having by his 1st w had:

1 Edward Haslingden; *b* 3 Dec 1859; *m* 16 Dec 1891 Maud (*d* 22 Nov 1930), dau of T W Robertson, and *dsp* 12 March 1906

2 Richard Henry Langley; *b* 1861; *m* 8 July 1893 Mabel (*d* March 1956, having *m* 2nd 19 Sept 1902 Henry Langdon Bruce, who *d* 4 Feb 1943), dau of Frederick Younge, and *d* 1899, leaving:

(1) EDWARD FREDERICK LANGLEY, **2nd Baron**

3 Sidney Pitt; *b* 1864; *d* 1866

The 1st BARON's gs,

EDWARD FREDERICK LANGLEY RUSSELL, **2nd Baron Russell of Liverpool**, CBE (1945, OBE 1943), MC (1916) and two bars (1918); *b* 10 April 1895; *educ* Liverpool Coll and St John's Coll Oxford; barrister Gray's Inn 1931, Brig King's Regt (Liverpool) and 20th Lancers (IA), Mil Assist to JAG 1934–43, DJAG 1943–51, Assist JAG 1951–54, served WWs I (wounded, despatches) and II (despatches, Offr Legn Hon 1961), author: *The Scourge of the Swastika* (1954), *Though the Heavens Fall* (1956), *The Knights of Bushido* (1958), *That Reminds Me* (1959), *If I forget Thee* (1960), *The Royal Conscience* (1961), *The Trial of Adolf Eichmann* (1962), *The Tragedy of the Congo* (1962), *South Africa Today — and Tomorrow?* (1963), *The Knight of the Sword* (1964), *Deadman's Hill* (1965), *Caroline the Unhappy Queen* (1967), *Return of the Swastika?* (1968), *Henry of Navarre* (1969), *The French Corsairs* (1970) and *Prisons and Prisoners in Portugal*; *m* 1st 1920 (*divorce* 1933) Constance Claudine (*d* 1974), yr dau of Col Philip Cecil Harcourt Gordon, CMG, RAMC, of Jersey, and had:

1 Langley Gordon Haslingden, MC (1945); *b* 14 Sept 1922; *educ* Charterhouse; Capt Gren Gds WW II; *m* 13 June 1951 *Kiloran Margaret [The Hon Mrs Lang-

ley Russell, Ash Farm, Stourpaine, Dorset DT11 8PW], er dau of Hon Sir Arthur Jared Palmer Howard, KBE, CVO, JP (see STRATHCONA AND MOUNT ROYAL, B), and d 16 Sept 1975, leaving:

(1) SIMON GORDON JARED RUSSELL, **3rd and present Baron Russell of Liverpool**

(2) +Adam Mark Haslingden; b 23 Oct 1957; granted 1983 with siblings rank of baron's dau/yr s

(3) +Daniel Charles Edward; b 8 March 1962

(1) *Emma Kiloran; b 15 June 1955

(2) *Annabel Tacy; b 29 Dec 1959; m 1987 *Lt-Col Mark Ralph Michael Eliot, 1st Queen's Dragoon Gds, s of Maj Morrell Geoffrey Eliot, MBE, and has:

   1a *Caspar Laurence Robin; b 1989

   2a *Ralph Morrell Arthur; b 1992

   3a *Barnaby Wynn Alexander; b 1995

(3) *Lucy Leonora Catherine; b 1968

1 *Anne Philippa [The Hon Mrs Warren, 15 Williams St, Taupo 2730, New Zealand]; b 13 Feb 1924; m 13 Nov 1947 Gershom Radcliffe Layton Warren (d 1991), Maj Canadian Army, only surv s of Herbert Brough Warren, JP, of Hortland House, Co Kildare

The **2nd Baron** m 2nd 5 July 1933 (divorce 1946) Joan Betty, dau of Dr David Ewart, OBE, MD, FRCS, of Chichester, and by her had:

2 *Crystal [The Hon Mrs Crystal Essington-Boulton, Ann Boleyn's Cottage, Grandmother's Rock Lane, Beach, Bittern, Avon]; b 4 Jan 1936; m 23 June 1955 (divorce 1969) John Mark Essington-Boulton, s of Maj Clive Essington-Boulton, of Turvey, Beds, and has:

(1) *James Clive; b 24 July 1958

(1) *Nicolette; b 24 March 1956

The **2nd Baron** m 3rd 27 May 1946 Alix (k car crash nr Dinard 8 Oct 1971), widow of Count Bernard de Richard d'Ivry and only dau of Marquis de Breviare d'Alaincourt; m 4th 3 Nov 1972 Selina (d 1977), widow of A W Brayley, of Grand Avenue, Hove, Sussex, and d 1981

RUSSELL-JOHNSTON

Creation: B. (LP, UK) 1997.

THE BARON RUSSELL-JOHNSTON, of Minginish, Highlands (Sir (David) Russell Johnston) [The Rt Hon The Lord Russell-Johnston, House of Lords, London SW1A 0PW]; b 28 July 1932; educ Carbost Public Sch, Portree High Sch and Edinburgh U; Intell Corps 1958, Moray House Coll of Educn 1958–61, taught Liberton Secondary Sch 1961–63, research assist Scottish Lib Party 1963–64 (V-Chm 1965–70, Chm 1970–74, Leader 1974–88), memb Roy Commn Local Govt Scotland 1966–69; MP (Lib) Inverness 1964–83 and (Lib to 1988, Lib Dem 1988–97) Inverness, Nairn and Lochaber 1983–97; Dep Leader Soc and Lib Dems 1988–92, Pres Scottish Lib Dems 1988–94, Memb UK Delgn European Parl 1973–74 and 1976–79 (V-Pres Political Ctee 1976–79), Cncl Europe and WEU 1988, Pres Cncl Europe Sub-Ctee Youth and Sport 1992–; Leader Lib Dem and Reform Gp Cncl Europe 1994; memb: Select Ctee Privileges 1988–92; Lib Dem Spokesman: For Affrs 1988–89, EC Affrs 1988–, East-West Rels 1992–94, Centl and E Europe 1994–; Chm All Party Scottish Gaelic Parly Gp; V-Chm Europe Gp; V-Pres: Lib Gp, European Lib Dem and Reform Parties 1990–92, Lib Internat 1994–; Sec: UK-Falkland Is Parly Gp, Br-Hong Kong Parly Gp; Treas All Party Photography Gp; V-Ch Camanachd Assoc 1987–90, ktd 1985; m 1967 *Joan Graham Menzies and has three sons

Lineage: DAVID KNOX JOHNSTON; m Georgina Margaret Gerrie Russell and had:

(DAVID) RUSSELL (Sir), cr a **Baron**

RUTLAND

POUR·Y·PARVENIR

Arms: Or two bars azure, a chief quarterly of the last and gules; in the 1st and 4th two fleurs-de-lys and in the 2nd and 3rd a lion passant guardant, all or. **Crest:** On a chapeau gules, doubled ermine, a peacock in its pride proper. **Supporters:** Two unicorns argent, armed, unguled, maned and tufted or. **Motto:** Pour y parvenir ('So as to accomplish it'). HENRY VIII gave permission for the features at the top of the shield to be used by the Earls of Rutland (a permission later inherited by the Dukes of Rutland) when he created Thomas Manners the 1st Earl. **Creations:** E. (E) 18 June 1525, B. (E) 30 April 1679 (Manners of Haddon) and (UK) 17 June 1896, D. and M. (E) 29 March 1703.

THE 10TH DUKE OR RUTLAND, Marquess of Granby, Co Nottingham, **Earl of Rutland**, Lord Manners of Haddon (barony cr by writ, hence heritable by heirs general, which can include females, so that the + against each living female Manners or Manners-Sutton and her issue indicates that she/they is/are in remainder to this peerage only, among all those held by the Dukes of Rutland) and **Baron Roos of Belvoir**, Co Leicester (Charles John Robert Manners, CBE (1962), JP, DL (Rutland 1950)) [His Grace The Duke of Rutland CBE JP DL, Belvoir Castle, Grantham, Lincs NG32 1PE]; b 28 May 1919; s f 1940; educ Eton and Trin Coll Cambridge (BA 1940); late Capt Gren Gds, MFH Belvoir 1940, Jt MFH 1947, chm: E Midland Ec Planning Cncl 1971–74 and Leics CC 1974–77, owns Rutland Hotels Ltd; m 1st 27 April 1946 (divorce 1956) Anne Bairstow, est dau of Maj William Cumming Bell, of Binham Lodge, Edgerton, Huddersfield, and has:

1 +Charlotte Louisa; b 7 Jan 1947

The 10th DUKE m 2nd 15 May 1958 *Frances Helen, only dau of Charles Sweeny, of Mayfair, and Margaret Duchess of Argyll (see ARGYLL, D), and by her has had:

1 +DAVID CHARLES ROBERT, Marquess of Granby [Marquess of Granby, Knipton Lodge, 35 Pasture Lane, Knipton, Lincs NG32 1RE]; b 8 May 1959; educ Wellesley House and Stanbridge Earls; dir: Belvoir Management and Belvoir Arms and Armour, agent for Elderkins Gunsmiths, of Spalding, Lincs, Freeman City London, Liveryman Gunsmiths' Co; m 1992 *Emma L, dau of John Watkins, of Heartsease, Knighton, Powys, and has:

(1) +Violet Diana Louise; b 1993

(2) +Alice; b 1995

(3) +Eliza Charlotte; b 17 July 1997

2 Robert George; b 18 June 1961; d 28 Feb 1964

3 +Edward John Francis [The Lord Edward Manners, Belvoir Castle, Belvoir, Grantham, Lincs NG32 1PE]; b 29 May 1965; educ Eton

2 +(Helen) Theresa Margaret [The Lady Theresa Chipman, 25 Westgate Terr, London SW10 9BT]; b 11 Nov 1962; late lead singer with pop group The Business Connection; m 28 June 1997 *Dr John Chipman

Earldom of Rutland: The first creation under this title was in 1390 by RICHARD II in favour of his cousin Edward, eldest son of Edmund Duke of York, who was in turn the fifth son of EDWARD III. The Earldom was conferred on Edward only while his father was alive, however, so that on the latter's death in 1402 it became extinct. The 1st Earl of Rutland of the 1390 creation was also made Sheriff of Rutland and granted the castle, lordship and town of Oakham to maintain the dignity of his new position. The fact that the new Earl was given these additional benefits suggests the creation should be seen as a transitional one between the earldoms of the immediate post-Conquest era, which were quasi-hereditary high offices with specific sources of income attached for their upkeep, and the modern state of affairs, under which an earldom is a personal title of honour (see also NORTHUMBERLAND, D).

The second creation seems to have taken place later in the first half of the 15th century. Edmund Plantagenet, was calling himself Earl of Rutland as early as 1454 (he was born in 1443). He was younger brother of the Earl of March (later EDWARD IV) and a great-nephew of the 1st and last Earl of Rutland of the 1390 creation. He was being officially acknowledged as Earl of Rutland by the time of his attainder in 1459, though this attainder was reversed the next year. He was killed in cold blood while in flight from the battlefield by the 9th Baron Clifford (see DE CLIFFORD, B), known as the 'Butcher' or 'Bloody Clifford' for precisely this sort of behaviour, following the Lancastrian victory of Wakefield in 1460, when the Earldom became extinct. His sister Anne's daughter by her 2nd husband, Sir Thomas St Leger, was another Anne. This second Anne married as her 2nd husband George Manners, 11th Lord (Baron) Ros (*see* DE ROS, B), and it was their son Thomas Manners who was made Earl of Rutland in the present creation in 1525. The 1st Manners Earl of Rutland was thus a great-nephew of EDWARD IV and a direct descendant of EDWARD III. This descent appears to be reflected in the present arms of the Dukes or Rutland (*see* above).

Lineage: A Manners family is first heard of in Etal, Northumberland, in 1232, when one ROBERT MANNERS was involved in a boundary dispute. Various spellings of the name — Maner, Mainer, Mesners — as well as Manners existed in Normandy over a century and a half from just before the Norman Conquest. But any connection with the Manners Dukes of Rutland is conjectural, as is any connection between ROBERT and WILLIAM below.

WILLIAM de MANNERS; *d* 1349; possibly f of:

Sir ROBERT (de) MANNERS, of Etal, Northumberland; had a grant of land in Northumberland 1329; mentions his f's and his own military service against the Scots in a petition to EDWARD III of 1331; possibly Constable of Norham Castle as early as 1333, certainly by 1345; MP Northumberland 1340; granted roy licence to fortify his mansion of Ethale (Etal) 1342, negotiated truce with Scots 1342, fought against Scots at English victory of Neville's Cross 1346; *m* according to some sources Joane, dau and heiress of Sir Henry Strother, of Newton Glendall, according to others *m* at least twice, one w being Margaret, another Ada, and *d* 1355; his s or possibly gs but certainly his heir:

Sir JOHN MANNERS; *b* 1355; *m* Alice, widow of William Whytchestre, of Whitchester, Northumberland, and had, with two other sons:

Sir JOHN MANNERS, of Etal; Sheriff Northumberland 1413; *m* Anne, dau of Sir John Middleton, and *d* 6 Sept 1438, having had, with a yr s (John, served under Richard Nevill(e), Earl of Warwick (*see* ABERGAVENNY, M), and *d* June 1492; may have been confused with his nephews John and/or Gilbert?):

Sir ROBERT MANNERS, JP (Norhamshire (a subdivision of Northumberland) 1438); *b* 1408; appointed to oversee the keeping of a truce with the Scots, Sheriff Northumberland 1454, MP Northumberland 1459; *m* Joane or Johanna (*d* 1488), dau of Sir Robert Ogle and sis of 1st Lord (Baron) Ogle (*see* DEVONSHIRE, D), and *d c* 1461, having had, with three yr sons (John, *d* 1492; Gilbert, described as one of the Earl of Warwick's retainers, presumably that Earl who was known as the 'Kingmaker' (*see* ABERGAVENNY, M); Thomas, of Etal):

Sir ROBERT MANNERS, JP (1485), of Etal; Sheriff Northumberland 1463, 1465 and 1485, ktd 1485; *m* (licence 13 June 1469) Eleanor (*d* 1487), est dau of 9th Lord (Baron) De Ros of Helmsley (*see* DE ROS, B), by which marriage Belvoir Castle, among other possessions, came to the Manners family, and *d* 1495, having had, with a yr s (Edward) and three daus (Elizabeth, *m* Sir William Fairfax, of Steeton Castle, Yorks, Justice Common Pleas (*see* FAIRFAX OF CAMERON, L); Dorothy, *m* Thomas Fairfax; Cicely, *m* Thomas Fairfax, bro of the Sir William Fairfax mentioned above):

GEORGE MANNERS, 11th LORD (Baron) DE ROS OF HELMSLEY, JP (Surrey 1512), of Belvoir and Hamlake (*i.e*, Helmsley, Yorks); *b* in or a little before 1470; *s* between 23 Oct 1508 and 21 Nov 1512 his unc in the Barony of De Ros by the death of his aunt Isabel Lady Lovel(l) (w of Sir Thomas Lovel(l), who was appointed guardian of his (Sir Thomas's) bro-in-law 10th Lord (Baron) De Ros of Helmsley due to the latter's incapacity 1492); ktd 1497, Commissioner of Oyer and Terminer (a precursor of the later Circuit Judge, though usually a layman) Sussex 1505, commissioner to review the army 1512, served in the campaign against the French 1513, being present at Battle of Thérouanne and Siege of Tournai; *m c* 1490 Anne (*b* 1476; *d* 21 April 1526), dau and heiress of Sir Thomas St Leger by Anne Plantagenet (*see* above in preliminary remarks on the Earldom of Rutland) and ?*das* 27 Oct 1513, having had issue, with two other sons and a dau (*d* unm):

1 THOMAS, **1st Earl**

2 Oliver (Sir)

3 Richard (Sir); had a grant of lands in Leics, Salop, Staffs and Worcs 1547; *m* 1st Margaret (*dsp* 1550), dau of Sir Robert Dymoke, of Scrivelsby, Lincs; *m* 2nd the widow of Sir William Coffyn and by her had:

(1) John

1 Anne; *m* Sir Henry Capel, of Raines, Essex, ancestor of the Earls of Essex (*qv*)

2 Eleanor; *m* as his 2nd w of three John Bourchier, 2nd Earl of Bath (*d* 1560) of the 1536 *cr*, and was *bur* 16 Sept 1547, having had issue (*see* WREY, Bt)

3 Elizabeth; *m* by 1513 Thomas Sandys, 2nd Baron Sandys of the 1523 *cr*, of The Vine, Hants, and had issue

4 Katherine; *m* Sir Robert Constable, of Everingham, Yorks

5 Margaret; *m* 1st Sir Henry Strangways; *m* 2nd, as his 2nd w, Robert Heneage, Auditor Duchy of Lancaster (*see* WINCHILSEA and NOTTINGHAM, E; also 1967 edn HENEAGE, B)

The est s,

THOMAS MANNERS, **1st Earl of Rutland** (E), so *cr* 18 June 1525, and 12th LORD (Baron) DE ROS OF HELMSLEY, KG (1525), PC (1536), JP (Essex, Herts, Leics, Lincs, Middx, Notts, Rutland, Surrey and E, N and W Ridings of Yorks 1524–26 and Essex, Lincs, Rutland, Surrey and W Riding Yorks 1542); *b* by 1492; Jt Constable Nottingham Castle (full Constable 1542) and Keeper Sherwood Forest 1519 (Warden 1524), one of the peers who tried Duke of Buckingham 1521 on a bill of attainder (*see* STAFFORD, B), Cupbearer to HENRY VIII Dec 1521, Steward of Pickering, Yorks, Jan 1522, Warden Eastern and Middle Marches towards Scotland April-Oct 1522, Keeper Enfield Chase 1526, one of those presiding at trial of QUEEN ANNE BOLEYN 1536, a cdr of the King's forces in suppressing the Pilgrimage of Grace 1536, Ld Chamberlain to QUEENs ANNE OF CLEVES and CATHARINE HOWARD 1539–41, Warden and Ch Justice and Justice in Eyre of forests beyond Trent 1540–43, Ld Warden Scottish Marches Aug-Sept 1542, got possession at the Dissolution of the Monasteries of Charley, Croxton, Garradon and the Manor of Muston, all Leics, the last of these formerly the possession of Osulveston Priory, also Belvoir, Eagle and Kyme, all in Lincs, and Beverley, Nunburnholme, Rievaulx and Warter, all in Yorks; *m* 1st (marriage settlement 21 Feb 1512/3) Elizabeth (*dsp* after 26 Oct 1513), dau of Sir Robert Lovel(l) and almost certainly niece of the Sir Thomas Lovel(l) mentioned above; *m* 2nd Eleanor (Ldy of the Privy Chamber to ANNE OF CLEVES; *d* 1551), dau of Sir William Paston, of Paston, Norfolk, and *d* 20 Sept 1543, having had (with another dau):

1 HENRY MANNERS, **2nd Earl of Rutland** and 13th LORD (Baron) DE ROS OF HELMSLEY, KG (1559), JP (Notts Feb 1553/4); *b* 23 Sept 1526; ktd 1544, envoy France 1546 and 1551, Constable Nottingham Castle and Warden Sherwood Forest 1547, Warden East and Middle Marches 1549–51, Jt Ld Lt Lincs and Notts 1551, Ld Lt: Notts 1552–63 and Rutland 1559–63; supported LADY JANE GREY on death of EDWARD VI and briefly imprisoned by MARY in consequence, but soon restored to favour; Adml 1556, Capt Gen Horse Picardy Jan 1557/8, Ld Pres Cncl of North Jan 1560/1, Ecclesiastical Commr Province of York 1561; *m* 1st 3 July 1536 Lady Margaret Nevill(e) (*d* 13 Oct 1559), dau of 4th Earl of Westmorland (*see* ABERGAVENNY, M), and had:

(1) EDWARD MANNERS, **3rd Earl of Rutland** and 14th LORD (Baron) DE ROS OF HELMSLEY, KG (1584); *b* 12 July 1549; *educ* Oxford (MA 1566) but also had an MA (presumably honorary) 1564 from Cambridge; Lt of Foot and memb Ld Lt's Cncl in suppression of Rebellion of Northern Earls 1569 (*see* NORTHUMBERLAND, D), Constable Nottingham Castle and Warden Sherwood Forest 1570, Memb Cncl of the North 1572, Ld Lt: Notts 1574 and Lincs 1585–87, Memb Ecclesiastical Commn Province of York 1577, Ch Commr Treaty of Berwick with Scots 1586, one of those presiding at trial of MARY QUEEN OF SCOTS 1586, Ld Chllr for two days April 1587, his term of office being cut short by death; *m c* 6 June 1573 Isabel (*b c* 1552; *d* 14 Jan 1605/6), dau of Sir Thomas Holcroft, of Vale Royal, Cheshire, and *d* 14 April 1587, leaving:

1a ELIZABETH MANNERS, BARONESS DE ROS OF HELMSLEY in her own right (*see* DE ROS, B) according to the doctrine beginning to evolve about this time; *m* 13 Jan 1588/9, as his 1st w, William Cecil, subsequently styled *Lord Burghley* and later still (substantive) 2nd Earl of Exeter (*see* EXETER, M), and *d* 1 May 1591 in child birth, leaving:

1b WILLIAM CECIL, 16th LORD (Baron) DE ROS OF HELMSLEY, his claim to which title as heir general was confirmed 22 July 1616 (*see* also below against 6th EARL OF RUTLAND); *b* May 1590; *m* 12 Feb 1615/6 Anne, dau of Sir Thomas Lake, and *dsp* and *vp* in Italy, where it is said he became a Catholic, 27 June 1618, when the Barony of De Ros passed to his cousin **6th Earl of Rutland**

(2) JOHN MANNERS, **4th Earl of Rutland**; *b* by 1552; *educ* St John's Coll Cambridge and Gray's Inn; Constable Nottingham Castle, Warden Sherwood Forest and Ld Lt Notts 1587–Feb 1587/8; *m* by 1575 Elizabeth (*bur* 24 March 1594/5), 4th dau of Francis Charlton, of Apley Castle, Salop (*see* MEYRICK, Bt), and *d* 24 Feb 1587/8, having had, with a dau (*d* unm):

1a Edward; *b* by 1576; *d* seven weeks after birth

2a ROGER MANNERS, **5th Earl of Rutland**, KB (1603); *b* 6 Oct 1576; *educ* Queens' and Corpus Christi Colls Cambridge (MA Feb 1594/5, also MA Oxon 1598), also Inner Temple and Gray's Inn; participated in the Azores Expedition of 1597, in which a force under the Earl of Essex, Lord Howard of Effingham, Sir Francis Vere and Sir Walter Raleigh narrowly failed to capture the Spanish treasure fleet; High Steward E Retford by Nov 1598, served Ireland as Capt of Foot under Earl of Essex 1599, ktd 1599, served Low Countries 1600, Constable Nottingham Castle and Warden Sherwood Forest 1600; participated in Essex's Rebellion Feb 1600/1 and was imprisoned in the Tower of London Feb 1600/1–Aug 1601, being fined £30,000 (some £1,010,000 in late-1990s terms), though this was later reduced to £10,000 (say £335,000 in late-1990s terms); Ld Lt Lincs and High Steward Grantham 1603, Steward Long Bennington and Mansfield 1609; *m* by 15 March 1598/9 Elizabeth (*bapt* 20 Nov 1585; *bur* by 11 Aug 1612), dau and heiress of Sir Philip Sidney (*see* DE L'ISLE, V), and *dsp* 26 June 1612

3a FRANCIS MANNERS, **6th Earl of Rutland**, KG (1616), KB (Jan 1604/5), PC (1617); *b* 1578; *educ* Christ's Coll Cambridge; involved in Essex's Rebellion but released from imprisonment on bail of £1,000 (over £30,000 in late–1990s terms) late March 1601, Jt Keeper Beskwood Pk 1607, Ld Lt Lincs 1612–29, Constable Nottingham Castle and Warden Sherwood Forest 1612–20; unsuccessfuly claimed Barony of De Ros (*see* above) but *cr* in compensation 22 July 1616 LORD (Baron) ROOS OF HAMLAKE (E), and *s* as 17th LORD (Baron) DE ROS OF HELMSLEY anyway on the death of his cousin William 27 June 1618; Ch Justice in Eyre beyond Trent 1619–32; rumoured to be a Catholic, and since his 2nd w was undoubtedly one some astonishment was expressed by contemporaries at his being honoured with the Garter; Steward Greenwich 1628; *m* 1st 6 May 1602 Frances (*d* by 26 Nov 1605), 3rd dau and coheir of Sir Henry Knyvett (*see* SUFFOLK and BERKSHIRE, E), of Charlton, Wilts, and widow of Sir William Bevill, of Kilkhampton, Cornwall, and had:

1b KATHERINE Manners, BARONESS DE ROS OF HELMSLEY in her own right according to the doctrine developing at this time, as which *s* f 17 Dec 1632; *m* 1st 16 May 1620 George VILLIERS, afterwards 1st Duke of Buckingham (assassinated 23 Aug 1628; *see* JERSEY, E), and had issue (*see* DE ROS, B); *m* 2nd by 12 April 1635, as his 1st w, 2nd Earl of Antrim (*qv*) of the Jan 1644/5 *cr* and 1st and last Marquess of Antrim (*dsp* 3 Feb 1682), and *d* late Oct 1649

3a (cont.) The **6th Earl** *m* 2nd after 26 Oct 1608 Cecily (*dsps* and was *bur* 11 Sept 1653), dau of Sir John Tufton, 1st Bt of the 1611 *cr* (*see* HOTHFIELD, B), of Hothfield, Kent, and sis of 1st Earl of Thanet, also widow of Sir Edward Hungerford, and *dspm* 17 Dec 1632 (when the Barony of De Ros passed to his dau KATHERINE, the Barony of Roos of Hamlake expired and the Earldom of Rutland passed to his bro), having had:

1b Henry; *dvp* an infant from alleged witchcraft and was *bur* 26 Sept 1613

2b Francis; *dvp* an infant from alleged witchcraft 5 March 1619/20

4a GEORGE MANNERS, **7th Earl of Rutland**; *b c* 1580; *educ* Christ's Coll Cambridge (MA 1612); involved in Earl of Essex's Rebellion but released from imprisonment on bail of £500 (some £175,000 in late-1990s terms) late March 1601, MP: Grantham 1603/4–10/11, 1614, 1623/4–25 and 1625 and Lincs 1619/20–21/2, Warden Sherwood Forest 1635; *m* 3 March 1605 Frances (*d* between 1 April 1644 and 1656 at a great age), dau of Sir Edward Carey, of Aldenham, Herts, and sis of 1st Viscount of Falkland (*qv*), also widow of Ralph Baesh, of Stanstead Abbots, Herts, and *dsp* 29 March 1641

5a Oliver (Sir); ktd 23 April 1608

1a Bridget; *m* Robert Tyrwhitt, of Kettleby, Lincs

2a Frances; *b* posthumously 22 Oct 1588; *m* (licence 4 Feb 1602/3) 3rd Baron Willoughby of Parham (*see* WILLOUGHBY DE ERESBY, B), through whose descendants the Barony of De Ros (*qv*) has passed to its present holder, and *d c* 1643, having had issue

3a Elizabeth; *m* by Michaelmas 1609 Emanuel Scrope, 11th Lord (Baron) Scrope, of Bolton, and 1st and last Earl of Sunderland (*b* 1 Aug 1584; *dspl* 30 May 1630), and *dsp*, being *bur* 16 March 1653/4

4a Mary; *d* unm

(1) Elizabeth; *m* 18 Jan 1572/3, as his 1st w, Sir William Courtenay, of Powderham Castle, Devon, and had issue (*see* DEVON, E)

1 (cont.) The **2nd Earl** *m* 2nd between Jan and March 1559/60 Bridget (*m* 3rd 1566, as his 2nd w, 2nd Earl of Bedford (*see* BEDFORD, D) and *dsp* 12 Jan 1600/1), est dau of 1st and last Lord (Baron) Hussey of the 1529 *cr* and widow of Sir Richard Morrison, and *d* 17 Sept 1563

2 John (Sir), of Haddon Hall, Derbys; *m* Dorothy (*d* 24 June 1584), dau of Sir George Vernon (*see* VERNON, B) whereby Haddon Hall came to the Manners family; *d* 4 June 1611, having had an est s:

(1) George (Sir), of Haddon Hall; *m* 1 Aug 1593 Grace, sis of Robert Pierrepont, 1st Earl of Kingston-upon-Hull (*see* 1953 edn MANVERS, E), and 2nd dau of Sir Henry Pierrepont by Frances (er dau of Sir William Cavendish, of Chatsworth, and sis of 1st Earl of Devonshire, *see* DEVONSHIRE, D), and *d* 23 April 1623, having had, with other issue:

1a JOHN, **8th Earl**

1a Elizabeth; *m* 1616 Robert Sutton, 1st Baron Lexinton of Aram (*d* 1668), and had issue (*see below*)

2a Eleanor; *m* 1622 1st Baron Rockingham and had issue (*see* 1970 edn FITZWILLIAM, E)

3a Frances; *m* 2nd Viscount Castleton (*see* SCARBROUGH, E) and had issue

3 Roger, of Uffington, Lincs; Esquire of the Body to QUEENs MARY and ELIZABETH I, benefactor to Corpus Christi Coll Cambridge; *d* 1607

4 Thomas (Sir); *m* Theodosia, dau of Sir Thomas Newton, and had:

(1) Anne; *m* William Vavasour (*see* VAVASOUR, Bt) and had issue

5 Oliver; served against the French at Newhaven; *d* 1563

1 Gertrude; *m* 28 April 1539, as his 1st w, 6th Earl of Shrewsbury and Waterford (*qv*) and was *bur* 16 Jan 1566/7, having had issue

2 Anne; *m* 3 July 1536, as his 1st w of three, 5th Earl of Westmorland of the 1397 *cr* (*see* ABERGAVENNY, M), and *d* on or after 27 June 1549, having had issue

3 Frances; *m* by 31 Jan 1555/6, as his 1st w, Henry Nevill(e), 4th Lord (Baron) Bergavenny (*see* ABERGAVENNY, M), and was *bur* Sept 1576, leaving issue

4 Catherine; *m* Sir Henry Capell, of Raines, Essex, by whom she was grandmother of 1st Baron Capell of Hadham (*see* ESSEX, E)

5 Elizabeth; *m* Sir John Savage, of Rock Savage, Cheshire; they were ancestors of the w of the 2nd s of the 2nd Earl of Cholmondeley, whence the title Earl of Rocksavage featuring among those conferred on the 1st Marquess of Cholmondeley (*qv*)

The 7th EARL's 2nd cousin,

JOHN MANNERS, **8th Earl of Rutland**; *b* 10 June 1604; *s* to Haddon estates held by his *f* 23 April 1623; *educ* Queens' (other sources say Trin) Coll Cambridge and Inner Temple; MP Derbys Feb 1625/6–June 1626 and April-May 1640, High Sheriff Derbys 1632, Ld Lt Derbys (Parly appointment) March 1641/2, apptd a Parly Commr to treat with Scots July 1643 and 1645 and a Parly Commr for Gt Seal Nov 1643 but managed to avoid serving in either capacity in 1643 on a plea of ill health, Memb Ctee: for Excise 1645 and Navy and Customs 1647, Ch Justice in Eyre north of Trent 1646–61, Ld Lt Leics Feb 1666/7–77; *m* 1628 Frances (*bapt* 8 Aug 1613; *d* 19 May 1671), 2nd dau of 1st Baron Montagu of Boughton (*see* MANCHESTER, D), and *d* 29 Sept 1679, having had, with other issue (including two er sons):

1 JOHN, **1st Duke**

1 Frances; *b* 2 Dec 1630; *m* 8 Dec 1646, as his 1st w, 4th Earl of Exeter and *d* 2 Dec 1669, leaving issue (*see* EXETER, M)

2 Grace; *b* 1632; *m* 1st by 1666 3rd and last Viscount Chaworth of Armagh (*see* BYRON, B, and MEATH, E), and had issue; *m* 2nd after 1694, as his 1st w, Sir William Langhorne, 1st and last Bt (*b c* 1634, *cr* a Bt 1668; *dsp* 26 Feb 1714/5, having *m* 2nd Mary Aston), of Charlton, Kent, and *d* 15 Feb 1699/1700

3 Margaret; *m c* 1665 3rd Earl of Salisbury and *d* just prior to 30 Aug 1682, having had issue (*see* SALISBURY, M)

4 Dorothy; *m* 22 Sept 1669 2nd Earl of Shaftesbury (*qv*) and *d* June 1698, leaving issue

5 Elizabeth; *m* (settlement 17 Sept 1669) 3rd Viscount of Valentia (*qv*), and *d* 7 Dec 1700, leaving issue

6 Anne; *b c* 1655; *m* April 1672, as his 1st w, 1st Viscount Howe (*see* HOWE, E) and had issue

The 8th EARL's 3rd but only surv s,

JOHN MANNERS, **1st Duke of Rutland**, so *cr* 29 March 1703, as also MARQUESS OF GRANBY and earlier (by writ, *vp*) 30 April 1679 LORD (Baron) MANNERS OF HADDON (all E); *b* 29 May 1638; Leics: MP 1661–79 and Ld Lt 1677–87 (dismissed by JAMES II 1687), 1698–1703 and May; one of the principal supporters of the Revolution in 1688, helping raise Notts for WILLIAM OF ORANGE (subsequently WILLIAM III) and sheltering JAMES II's dau Princess Anne (later QUEEN ANNE) at Belvoir when she fled from London; *m* 1st 13 July 1658 (*divorce* on grounds of adultery in Ecclesiastical Court 1666 and by Act of Parliament, which had the effect of making her issue illegitimate, 8 Feb 1667/8) Lady Anne Pierrepont (*bapt* 9 March 1630/1; two of the children she bore while *m* to her 1st husb, John Manners and Charles Manners, were alive on 11 May 1699; she ?*m* 2nd — Vaughan and *d* by Jan 1696/7), est dau and coheir of 1st and last Marquess of Dorchester of the 1645 *cr*; *m* 2nd 10 Nov 1671 Lady Diana Bruce (*dsps* in child birth 15 July 1672), est dau of 1st Earl of Ailesbury (*see* AILESBURY, M) and widow of Sir Seymour Shirley, 5th Bt (*see* FERRERS, E), and had:

1 Robert; *b* and *d* 15 July 1672

The **1st Duke** *m* 3rd 8 Jan 1673/4 Katherine (*b* 10 Aug 1657; *d* 24 Jan 1732/3), dau of 3rd Viscount Campden (*see* GAINSBOROUGH, E), and *d* 10 Jan 1710/1, having had, with a 3rd s and two daus:

2 JOHN MANNERS, **2nd Duke of Rutland**, KG (1714); *b* 18 Sept 1676; MP (Whig) Derbys Feb–June 1701, Leics 1701–02 and Nov 1710–Feb 1710/11 and Grantham 1705–10, a Commr for Union with Scotland 1706, Ld Lt Rutland 1712–15 and Leics 1714–16 and Leics 1714 1720/21; *m* 1st 17 Aug 1693 Catherine (*b* 23 Aug 1676; *d* 30 Oct 1711), sis of 2nd Duke of Bedford (*qv*), and had, with two other sons:

(1) JOHN, **3rd Duke**

(2) William; *d* 1772, having had illegitimately:

1a John, of Hainby Hall and Grantham Grange, Leics; MP; *m* Louise, Countess of Dysart (*qv*) in her own right, and had, with at least three other (er) daus:

1b Grace Louisa; *m* 15 Aug 1802, as his 2nd w, 6th Duke of Saint Albans (*qv*)

(1) Catherine; *m* 1726 Rt Hon Henry Pelham, yr bro of 1st Duke of Newcastle-under-Lyne (*see* CHICHESTER, E), and *d* 1780, having had issue

(2) Frances; *m* 2 Sept 1732 Richard Arundell (*d* 1759), 2nd s of 2nd Baron Arundell of Trerice

(3) Elizabeth; *m* as his 1st w 1st Viscount Galway (*qv*) and *d* 22 March 1730 aged 21, having had issue

2 (cont.) The **2nd Duke** *m* 2nd 1 Jan 1712/3 Lucy Sherard (*d* 27 Oct 1751 aged 66), dau of 2nd Baron Sherard of Leitrim and sis of 1st Earl of Harborough (*see* 1931 edn SHERARD, B), and *d* 22 Feb 1720/1, having by her had, with other issue:

(3) Robert; Gen; *m* 1 Jan 1756 Mary Digges (*d* 22 Feb 1829 aged 92), of Roehampton, Surrey, and had two sons and two daus

(4) Caroline; *m* 1st (licence 2 Oct 1734) Sir Henry Harpur, 5th Bt (*d* 7 June 1748), of Calke Abbey, Derbys, and had issue; *m* 2nd 18 July 1753, as his 2nd w, Sir Robert Burdett, 4th Bt (*see* LATYMER, B), and *d* without further issue 10 Nov 1769

(5) Lucy; *m* 28 Oct 1742 2nd Duke of Montrose (*qv*) and *d* 18 June 1788 aged 71, leaving issue

The 2nd DUKE's est s,

JOHN MANNERS, **3rd Duke of Rutland**, KG (1722), PC (1727); *b* 21 Oct 1696; *educ* ?Eton; MP (Whig) Rutland 1719/20–20/21, Ld Lt Leics 1721–29, a Ld Bedchamber 1721–27, Chllr Duchy Lancaster 1727–36, raised the infantry regt which his s (*see below*) commanded against the Jacobites 1745, Ld Steward Household 1755–61, a Ld Justice (Regt) of the Realm April-Sept 1755, Groom Stole 1761, Master Horse 1761–66; *m* 27 Aug 1717 Bridget Sutton (*b* 30 Nov 1699; *d* 16 June 1734), dau and eventually sole heiress of 2nd and last Baron Lexinton of Aram (*see* SUTTON, Bt), and *d* 29 May 1779 at Rutland House, Knightsbridge, now the site of Rutland Gate, having had, with other issue:

1 John, *Marquess of Granby*, PC (1760); *b* 2 Jan 1720/21; *educ* Eton and Trin Coll Cambridge (LLD 1769); MP (Whig) Grantham 1741–54 and Cambs 1754–70, Col his f's infantry regt (the 'Leicester Blues') against Jacobites 1745–46, accompanying the DUKE OF CUMBERLAND in the mopping up operations after Culloden, served Flanders 1747, Maj-Gen 1755, Col RHG 1758–70, commanded 1st Cav Bde N Germany 1758 at start of Seven Years' War (1758–65), Lt-Gen 1759, Temporary C-in-C Br Forces Germany, playing an important role at the Battle of Minden 1759 and leading a highly successful charge of heavy cavalry at the victory over the French of Warburg 1760, Col 21st Dragoons 1760–63, Ld Lt Derbys 1764–66, Master-Gen Ordnance 1763–70, C-in-C Land Forces GB 1766–70; it is this Marquess of Granby who is commemorated in the name of so many pubs; *m* 3 Sept 1750 Lady Frances Seymour (*b* 18 July 1728; *d* 25 Jan 1760/1), 4th dau of 6th Duke of Somerset (*qv*), and *dvp* 18 Oct 1770, having had, with two other daus and at least one illegitimate child, a dau, who *m* her 1st cousin (*see below*):

(1) John, styled (unjustifiably, since the representation of the Barony of De Ros by now was vested in another branch of the family) Lord Roos; *b* 29 Aug 1759; *dvp* 2 June 1760

(2) CHARLES, **4th Duke**

(3) Robert; *b* 6 Feb 1758; served RN: Lt 1778, Capt 1780, seeing action at Ushant 27 July 1778, Cape St Vincent 1779, Cape Henry 5 Sept 1781 and Dominica 12 April 1782, where he lost a leg and *d* some days afterward of tetanus

(1) Frances; *b* 24 March 1753; *m* 1st 9 July 1772 (*divorce* 1777), as his 1st w, George Carpenter, 2nd Earl of Tyrconnel (*see* WATERFORD, M); *m* 2nd 27 Oct 1777 Philip Leslie, alias Anstruther, 2nd s of Alexander Anstruther, the self-styled Lord Newark (*see* CARMICHAEL-ANSTRUTHER, Bt), and *d* 15 Oct 1792

2 Robert MANNERS later MANNERS-SUTTON (added on his inheriting the estates of his maternal gf Lord Lexinton of Aram); Lt-Col 21st Dragoons under his er bro Granby; *dsp* 1772, when those estates devolved upon his next brother:

3 George MANNERS later MANNERS-SUTTON (added on his inheriting the estates); *b* 8 March 1723; *m* 1st 5 Dec 1749 Diana (*d* 13 May 1767), only dau of Thomas Chaplin, of Blankney, Lincs (*see* 1970 edn CHAPLIN, V), and had:

(1) John; *b* 29 July 1752; MP, Gds Capt; *m* his cousin Anne, illegitimate dau of John, Marquess of Granby, and *d* 17 Feb 1826, having had, with other issue:

1a Frederick (Rev); *b* 1784; *m* 2 Sept 1821 Lady Henrietta Barbara Lumley (*m* 2nd 24 Aug 1837 John Lodge Ellerton, of Bodsilin, Caernarvne, and *d* 17 July 1864), yst dau of 7th Earl of Scarbrough (*qv*), and *d* 30 Aug 1826, leaving:

1b John Henry, of Kelham, Notts, JP, DL (Notts); *b* 4 Aug 1822; *educ* Eton; MP (C) Newark 1852–57, High Sheriff Notts 1863; *m* 21 April 1853 Mary Jemima (she obtained a judicial separation 1885 and *d* 17 March 1904), est dau of Rev Gustavus Burnaby, Rector St Peter's Bedford, Canon Middleham, and *d* 5 July 1898, leaving:

1c John Henry Evelyn, of Kelham Hall; *b* 28 March 1854; *d* unm 8 Aug 1906

1c Edith Mary; *b* 1855; *m* 25 Aug 1877 Robert Heathcote, of Lobthorpe, Lincs, and *d* 25 April 1924, leaving issue (*see* WILLOUGHBY DE ERESBY, B)

2b William (Rev); *b* 27 Dec 1824; *m* Sarah Anne Williams (*d* 9 Feb 1875) and *d* 29 Dec 1899, leaving:

1c Frederick William; *b* 19 Aug 1865; Lt 4th Bn E Surrey Regt; *m* 15 April 1902 Winifred Grace (*d* 1 Sept 1970), est dau of Dr Charles S Richardson, of Tasmania, and *d* 17 March 1946, leaving:

1d +John Lumley [John Manners-Sutton Esq, 3 Buckingham St, Gilberton 5081, Adelaide, S Australia, Australia]; *b* 2 Feb 1914; *educ* Melbourne C of E GS; served RAN 1943–46; *m* 4 Nov 1949 *Elizabeth Mary Gylda Eliot, dau of Archibald N G Irving, of Lesmurdie, W Australia, and has:

1e +John Frederick; *b* 17 Feb 1955, *educ* Ch Ch GS Claremont

1e +Elizabeth Marjorie Inez [Mrs Barry Clements, 61 Riley Rd, Dalkeith, WA 6009, Australia]; *b* 4 Aug 1950; *m* 1987 *Barry Spencer Clements, MB, ChB, MRCP, only s of Sydney Ernest Clements, of Johannesburg, and has:

1f +Christopher James; *b* 9 Feb 1989

2f +Michael Alexander; *b* 7 April 1992

2e +Melanie Grace [Mrs Robert Champion De Crespigny, 1 Edwin Terrace, Gilberton 5081, Adelaide, S Australia, Australia]; *b* 31 Oct 1952; *m* 1978 *Robert James Champion de Crespigny, s of Dr James V Champion de Crespigny, of Bentleigh, Melbourne, Australia and has:

1f +Stuart James; *b* 19 Sept 1980

2f +Angus Robert; *b* 14 Sept 1982

3f +Lachlan Thomas; *b* 18 Aug 1984

4f +James John; *b* 3 April 1987

1f +Georgina Melanie; *b* 31 Aug 1993

1d Violet Marjorie; *b* 14 Feb 1903; *d* unm 18 Sept 1933

2d Dorothy Joyce; *b* 19 June 1904; *m* 28 Sept 1926 John Bouverie Primrose, est s of Edwin Brown Primrose, of Melbourne, and *d* 26 July 1985, having had:

1e +John Robert Manners [John Primrose Esq, 1389 Geelong-Barwon Heads Rd, Connewarre, Victoria, Australia]; *b* 22 Aug 1927; Pentecostal Minister; *m* 1st 1977 Nancy Margaret Challis (*d* 1993), of Connewarre, Victoria; *m* 2nd 1994 *Olive Ashton Ross, of Drysdale, Victoria

2e Roger Bouverie Manners; *b* 29 Jan 1934; civil engr, MIE Aust; *m* 28 March 1964 Ann Lloyd (*d* 13 Jan 1991), est dau of William James Symons, of Holcombe, Devon, and *d* 15 Nov 1997, leaving:

1f +Guy William Orlando Manners [Guy Primrose Esq, 15 Phosphate Rd, N Shore, Victoria, Australia]; *b* 11 Oct 1965; *m* 19– *Joanne Mary Mackintosh, of North Shore, and has:

1g +Wesley James; *b* 6 Feb 1996

2g +Louis William; *b* 12 March 1997

1g *Sarah Louise; *b* 16 April 1993

2g *Alison Marie; *b* 11 June 1994

2f +Toby Giles Manners; *b* 11 Nov 1966

3f +John Miles Manners; *b* 14 April 1969

3e +Edwin Neil Manners [Edwin Primrose Esq, 1B Wattletree Ct, Maiden Gully, Victoria 3551, Australia]; *b* 30 Sept 1942; *m* 9 Jan 1965 *Jannetje, only dau of Jan Hendrik Bouhof, of Connewarre, Via Geelong, and has:

1f +Richard Neil [Richard Primrose Esq, 1A Wattletree Ct, Maiden Gully, Victoria 3551, Australia]; *b* 10 Nov 1966; *m* 30 April 1994 *Melissa Anne, only dau of Donald Ernest Campbell, of Belmont, Victoria, and has:

1g +Madelyn Joan; *b* 27 April 1997

1f +Tamara Jane [Mrs Neil Edwards, 27 Peppermint Grove, Noarlunga Downs, S Australia 5168]; *b* 6 June 1970; *m* 4 Dec 1993 *Neil Robert Edwards, yst s of Gordon Robert Edwards, of Adelaide, and has:

1g +Nelson Gilbert; *b* 8 Nov 1996

1g +Brittany Louise; *b* 24 March 1995

1e +Diana Marjorie Manners [Miss Diana Primrose, 295 Curlewis Rd, Wallington 3221, Via Geelong, Victoria, Australia]; *b* 16 Feb 1938; Dip Inst Mgmt, Dip Dietetics, TTTC, MDAA, APD

3d +Freda Grace [Mrs Keith Roberts, Bendon, 19 Fernhurst Grove, Kew, Melbourne, Australia]; *b* 21 Nov 1905; *m* 11 Feb 1925 Keith Lee Roberts (*d* 2 May 1949), 3rd s of John Roberts, and has:

1e +Christopher Manners [Christopher Roberts Esq, 184 Sladen Street, Cranbourne 3977, Victoria, Australia]; *b* 8 July 1932; *educ* Baptist GS, Geelong GS and Queensland U (BVSc); MRCVS; *m* 1964 *Beverley Ann Jensen, of Harvey, W Australia, and has:

1f +Andrew Lee Christian; *b* 28 July 1971

2f +Adam Keith Llewellyn; *b* 2 Nov 1972

2e +Antony John [Anthony Roberts Esq, Maranup, Roberts Rd, Leongatha, S Gipsland, Victoria, Australia]; *b* 7 March 1938; *m* 26 Nov 1960 *Margaret Mary Carra and has:

1f +Timothy Keith; *b* 3 July 1961

2f +Jonathan Antony; *b* 11 Sept 1963

1f +Caroline Margaret; *b* 1 April 1966

1e +Joanna Margaret [Mrs Keith Andrews, Treweeks Rd, Blampied, Victoria, Australia]; *b* 24 April 1935; *m* 4 Jan 1962 *Keith Clive Michael Andrews, BCom, DipEd (MU), MACE, DipEd Admin (MNE) 1967, s of Bernard Andrews, of Victoria, and has:

1f +Michael Keith; *b* 4 Jan 1963

2f +Christopher Bernard; *b* 13 March 1968

1f +Jane Elizabeth; *b* 6 Aug 1964

2f +Kerrie Anne; *b* 11 Feb 1966

4d +Evelyn Mabel; *b* 1 Jan 1909; *m* 2 Oct 1928 John Kenneth Finlay, MBE (*d* 23 May 1970), est s of John Henry Finlay, of Melbourne, and *d* 27 Aug 1994, leaving:

1e +Chester Manners [Chester Finlay Esq, GPO Box 824F, Melbourne, Australia]; *b* 3 Oct 1932; *educ* Melbourne C of E GS and Massey Ag Coll, NZ; agronomist with Chester Finlay Agronomic Servs Pty

2e +Warwick Henry [Warwick Finlay Esq, Campbells Bend, Murchison, Victoria, Australia]; *b* 7 Oct 1934; *m* 6 Jan 1973 *Anne Elizabeth, dau of J R Hughes Jones, of St Asaph, Wales, and has:

1f +Gareth John; *b* 1974

1f +Jocelyn Edwina; *b* 1976

3e +John Lexton [John Finlay Esq, Thalia, RMB 4067, Violet Town, Victoria 3669, Australia]; *b* 11 June 1936; *educ* Melbourne C of E GS; *m* 23 Jan 1961 *Sandra Marion, er dau of Donald Hugh Bayne, of Nagambie, Victoria, and has:

1f +Mark John; *b* 10 March 1966

1f +Sarah Elizabeth; *b* 20 May 1961

2f +Catherine Deborah; *b* 8 Oct 1963

2c Henry; *b* 1867; *d* unm 6 July 1950

1c Violet Henrietta; *m* 20 Dec 1906 Charles Varley and *d c* 1930, leaving issue

1b Harriet Georgiana Maria; *b* 1827; *m* 6 July 1852 Rev John Cruger Murray-Aynsley (*see* ATHOLL, D) and *dsp* 6 Aug 1898

2a Thomas (Rev); *b* 6 Aug 1795; Canon Residentiary and Sub-Dean Lincoln, Rector Kelham; *m* 23 Nov 1826 Lucy Sarah (*m* 2nd 14 July 1846 E Jarman), only child of Rev Hans S Mortimer, and *dsp* 27 Oct 1844

1a Mary Georgina; *m* 20 Jan 1812 Robert Nassau Sutton, s of Sir Richard Sutton, 1st Bt (*qv*), and *d* 8 Nov 1846, having had issue

(2) Charles (Most Rev); *b* 14 Feb 1755; *educ* Charterhouse and Emmanuel Coll Cambridge (BA 1777, 15th Wrangler, MA 1780, DD 1792); Rector Averham-with-Kelham, Norfolk, and Whitwell, Derbys, 1785, Dean Peterborough 1791, Bp Norwich 1792, Dean Windsor 1794, Archbp Canterbury 1805; *m* 3 April 1778 Mary (*d* 10 March 1832), dau of Thomas Thoroton, of Screveton, Notts, and *d* 21 July 1828, having had, with eight other daus:

1a CHARLES MANNERS-SUTTON, 1st VISCOUNT CANTERBURY of the city of Canterbury, so *cr* 10 March 1835, as also BARON BOTTESFORD OF BOTTESFORD, Co Leicester (both UK), GCB (1833), PC (1809); *b* 29 Jan 1780; *educ* Eton and Trin Coll Cambridge (BA 1802, MA 1805, LLD 1824); barrister Lincoln s Inn 1806 on (Bencher 1817), MP (Tory) Scarborough 1806–32 and Cambridge U 1832–35, JAG 1809–17, Speaker H of C 1817–35, Registrar Court Faculties of Archbp Canterbury 1827–34, High Commr for treating Canadian claims 1835; *m* 1st 8 July 1811 Lucy Maria Charlotte (*d* 7 Dec 1815), est dau of John Denison, of Ossington, Notts, and sis of John Denison, Speaker H of C 1857, and had:

1b CHARLES JOHN MANNERS-SUTTON, 2nd VISCOUNT CANTERBURY; *b* 17 April 1812; *educ* Eton; sat as C in Ho of Lds; *d* unm 13 Nov 1869

2b JOHN HENRY THOMAS MANNERS-SUTTON, 3rd VISCOUNT CANTERBURY, GCMG (1873), KCB (1866); *b* 27 May 1814; *educ* Eton and Trin Coll Cambridge (MA 1835); Registrar Court Faculties of Archbp Canterbury 1834–77, MP (Tory, later Peelite, later still Lib) Cambridge 1839–40 (unseated for bribery) and 1841–47, U-Sec Home Dept 1841–46, Lt-Govr New Brunswick 1854–61, Govr: Trinidad 1864–66 and Victoria (Australia) 1866–73; *m* 5 July 1838 Georgiana (*d* 14 Sept 1899), yst dau of Charles Tompson, of Witchingham Hall, Norfolk, and *d* 24 June 1877, having had:

1c HENRY CHARLES MANNERS-SUTTON, 4th VISCOUNT CANTERBURY, JP, DL (Norfolk); *b* 11 July 1839; *educ* Harrow and Magdalene Coll Cambridge; sat as Lib in Ho Lds; *m* 16 April 1872 Amy Rachel (*d* 23 Jan 1935), only dau of Hon Frederick Walpole, MP (*see* WALPOLE, B), and *d* 19 Feb 1914, leaving:

1d HENRY FREDERICK WALPOLE MANNERS-SUTTON, 5th VISCOUNT CANTERBURY, DL Norfolk; *b* 8 April 1879; *d* unm 22 Oct 1918

2c Graham Edward Henry, DL (Middx); *b* 7 Feb 1843; *m* 12 Feb 1867 Charlotte Laura (*d* 18 Nov 1905), only dau of Lt-Col Francis L'Estrange Astley, of Burgh Hall, Norfolk (*see* HASTINGS, B), and *d* 30 May 1888, leaving, with a dau (*d* unm):

1d Francis Henry Astley; *b* 10 Feb 1869; *d* unm 7 March 1916

2d CHARLES GRAHAM MANNERS-SUTTON, 6th and last VISCOUNT CANTERBURY, JP, DL (Norfolk); *b* 23 Jan 1872; Capt Submarine Miners RE, Boer War 1900–02 and WW I; *m* 15 June 1903 Ethelwyn (*d* 2 Dec 1957), dau of Charles Hindle, and *d* 26 Feb 1941, when his titles expired, having had:

1e Charlotte Ethelwyn; *b* 22 April 1904; *d* 5 Feb 1920

3c George Kett Henry; *d* 2 March 1856

4c John Gurney Henry

5c Robert Henry; *b* 12 April 1854; barrister Inner Temple from 1879; *d* unm 26 Feb 1899

1c Anna Maria Georgiana; *m* 25 June 1868 Charles Edward Bright, CMG (*d* 17 July 1915), of Manor House, Elstree, Herts, and *d* 26 Dec 1924, leaving issue

2c Mabel Georgiana

1b Charlotte Matilda; *m* 12 Feb 1833 Richard Sanderson, MP Colchester (*d* 29 Oct 1857), and *d* 14 May 1898, leaving issue

1a (cont.) The 1st VISCOUNT CANTERBURY *m* 2nd 6 Dec 1828 Ellen (*d* 16 Nov 1845), dau of Edmund Power, of Curragheen, Co Waterford, and widow of John Home Purves, of Purves, New Brunswick, and *d* 21 July 1845, having by her had:

2b Frances Diana; *b* 17 Dec 1829; *m* 8 Aug 1848 18th Baron Hastings (*qv*) and *d* 1 June 1874, leaving issue

2a Francis; *b* 5 July 1783; Lt-Col Coldstream Gds; *m* 27 July 1814 Mary (*d* 7 May 1843), est dau of Laver Oliver, of Brill House, Bucks, and *dsp* 5 March 1825

1a Mary; *m* 17 May 1856 Hugh Percy, Bp Carlisle (*see* NORTHUMBERLAND D), and *d* 4 Sept 1831

2a Charlotte; *m* 5 Oct 1812 Ven James Croft, Archdeacon Canterbury (*d* 9 May 1869), and *d* 14 Feb 1825

(3) THOMAS MANNERS later MANNERS-SUTTON, *cr* BARON MANNERS (*qv*)

(1) Louisa Bridget; *m* 15 June 1790 Edward Lockwood-Perceval (*d* 6 July 1804), of Bishop's Hall, Essex, and *d* 5 Feb 1800, leaving issue

(2) Charlotte; *m* 16 June 1789 Thomas Lockwood, s of Thomas Lockwood, and *d* 1827, leaving issue

3 (cont.) Lord George MANNERS-SUTTON *m* 2nd 5 Feb 1768 Mary, dau of Joshua Peart, and *d* 7 Jan 1783, having by her had:

(3) Mary; *m* 1799 Rev Richard Lockwood (*d* 1830), of Fifield, Essex, and *d* 20 Nov 1829

The 3rd DUKE's gs,

CHARLES MANNERS, **4th Duke of Rutland**, KG (1782), PC (1783); *b* 15 March 1754; *educ* Eton and Trin Coll Cambridge (MA 1774); MP (Whig, later Pittite Tory) Cambridge U 1774–79, Ld Lt: Leics 1779–87 and Ireland (in which capacity he was in favour of the Union, eventually effected 1800) 1784–87, Ld Steward of the Household Feb–April 1783 with a seat in the Cabinet, Ld Privy Seal Dec 1783–Feb 1784; *m* 26 Dec 1775 Lady Mary Isabella Somerset (*b* 1 Aug 1756; *d* 2 Sept 1831), yst dau of 4th Duke of Beaufort (*qv*), and *d en poste* in Dublin 24 Oct 1787, leaving:

1 JOHN HENRY, **5th Duke**

2 Charles Henry Somerset, KCB; *b* 24 Oct 1780; MP, Col 3rd Dragoons, Gen; *d* unm 25 May 1855

3 Robert William, CB; *b* 14 Dec 1781; Maj-Gen, Col 3rd Dragoons; *d* 15 Nov 1835

4 William Robert Albanac; *b* 1 May 1783; *d* 22 April 1793

1 Elizabeth Isabella; *m* 21 Aug 1798 Richard Norman, of Leatherhead, Surrey, and *d* 5 Oct 1853, leaving issue

2 Katherine Mary; *b* 29 April 1779; *m* 16 June 1800 1st Baron Forester (*qv*) and *d* 1 May 1829, leaving issue

The 4th DUKE's est s,

JOHN HENRY MANNERS, **5th Duke of Rutland**, KG (1803); *b* 4 Jan 1778; *educ* Ealing Sch and Trin Coll Cambridge (MA 1797); DCL, Ld Lt Leics 1799–1857, Col Leicestershire Militia, Cambridge: Recorder 1799–1800 and High Steward 1800–35, Recorder Grantham and Scarborough, Tstee Br Museum; *m* 22 April 1799 Lady Elizabeth Howard (*b* 13 Nov 1780; *d* 28 Nov 1825), dau of 5th Earl of Carlisle (*qv*), and *d* 20 Jan 1857, having had, with two est sons (*d* in infancy):

1 CHARLES CECIL JOHN MANNERS, **6th Duke of Rutland**, KG (1867); *b* 16 May 1815; *educ* Eton and Trin Coll Cambridge (MA 1835); MP (C) Stamford 1837–52 and N Leics 1852–57, very briefly leader of the Protectionist rump of the Peelite Tories Feb–March 1848, Ld of the Bedchamber to HRH PRINCE ALBERT 1843–46, Ld Lt: Lincs 1852–57 and Leics 1857–88, Hon Col 3rd Bn Leics Regt; *d* unm 3 March 1888

2 JOHN JAMES ROBERT, **7th Duke**

3 George John, of Cheveley Park, Cambs; *b* 22 June 1820; Col RHG, MP Cambs; *m* 4 Oct 1855 Lady Adeliza Matilda Howard (*d* 7 Feb 1904), yst dau of 13th Duke of Norfolk (*qv*), and *d* 8 Sept 1874, having had:

(1) Charles George Edmund John; *b* 26 Sept 1858; Capt Gren Gds, formerly 15th Hus, served 1st Boer War 1880–81; *d* unm 25 Sept 1911

(2) George Espec John (Sir), of Fornham Park, Bury St Edmunds, and Little Haddon Hall, Woodbridge, Suffolk, JP, DL (Suffolk); *b* 17 June 1860; *educ* Trin Coll Cambridge (BA); Cdr J Div Metropolitan Special Constabulary 1914–16, High Sheriff Suffolk 1915, Assist Provost Marshal 1916, attd 3rd Cyclist Bde for Coast Defence 1917–18, Bde Educn Offr 1919–20, Capt and Hon Maj 3rd Bn Leics Regt, ktd 1920; *m* 24 April 1884 Anna Sophia (*d* 30 Dec 1940), dau of George Gilstrap, of Winthorpe, and *dsp* 2 Sept 1939

(3) Fitzalan George John; *b* 27 Feb 1866; Maj Scots Gds; *d* unm 15 March 1901

(1) Cicely Elizabeth Adeliza; *b* 21 Nov 1856; *d* unm 29 March 1949

(2) Frances Geraldine; *b* 20 Aug 1864; *d* 6 March 1865

1 Elizabeth Frederica; *m* 7 March 1821 Andrew Robert Drummond, of Cadland, nr Southampton, and *d* 20 March 1886, leaving issue (*see* PERTH, E)

2 Emmeline Charlotte Elizabeth; poetess; *m* 17 Feb 1831 Hon Charles Stuart-Wortley-Mackenzie, 2nd s of 1st Baron Wharncliffe, and *d* 30 Oct 1855, leaving issue (*see* WHARNCLIFFE, E)

3 Katherine Isabella; *m* 1 Dec 1830 2nd Marquess of Bristol (*qv*) and *d* 20 April 1848, leaving issue

4 Adeliza Elizabeth Gertrude; *m* 22 Feb 1848 her cousin Rev Canon F J Norman (*d* 29 Dec 1888), Rector Bottesford, Leics, and *d* 26 Oct 1877, having had issue

The 6th DUKE's yr bro,

JOHN JAMES ROBERT MANNERS, **7th Duke of Rutland**, KG (1891), GCB (1880), PC (1852); *b* 13 Dec 1818; *educ* Eton and Trin Coll Cambridge (MA 1839, LLD 1862); MP (C, Protectionist after 1846) Newark 1841–47 (memb with Alexander Cochrane-Wishart-Baillie, better though incorrectly known as Baillie-Cochrane, afterwards 1st Baron Lamington of Lamington (*see* 1949 edn), Benjamin Disraeli, afterwards 1st and last Earl of Beaconsfield, and George Smythe, afterwards 7th Viscount Strangford, of the fanciful, backward-looking but socially concerned coterie known as Young England), unsuccessfully fought Liverpool 1847 and City of London 1849, MP (C Protectionist) Colchester 1850–57, N Leics 1857–85 and E Leics 1885–88, First Commr of Works and Public Bldgs with a seat in the Cabinet March-Dec 1852, 1858–59 and 1866–68, PMG 1874–80 and 1885–86, Chllr Duchy of Lancaster 1886–92, MFH Belvoir, DCL Oxford 1876, Hon Col 3rd Bn Leics Regt, High Steward Cambridge, Master Shipwrights' Co, chm Tithes Redemption Tst; *cr* 17 June 1896 BARON ROOS OF BELVOIR, Co Leicester (UK); author: *England's Trust, and other Poems* (1841), in which occur the celebrated lines 'Let wealth and commerce, law and learning die,/But leave us still our old nobility', the pamphlet *Plea for National Holydays* [sic] (1843), *Notes of an Irish Tour* (1849), *English Ballads* (1850), *A Cruise in*

Scotch Waters on board the Duke of Rutland's yacht 'Resolution' *in 1848* (1850) and the pamphlet *Church of England in the Colonies* (1851); *m* 1st 10 June 1851 Catherine Louisa Georgina (*b* 28 Jan 1831; *d* 7 April 1854), only dau of Lt-Col George Marlay, CB, of Belvedere, Co Westmeath, whose mother was Lady Catherine Butler, dau of Brinsley, 2nd Earl of Lanesborough (*qv*), and had:

1 HENRY JOHN BRINSLEY, **8th Duke**

The **7th Duke** *m* 2nd 15 May 1862 Janetta (*b* 8 Sept 1836; *d* 11 July 1899), est dau of Thomas Hughan, of Airds, Galloway, by Lady Louisa *née* Beauclerk, dau of 8th Duke of St Albans (*qv*), and *d* 4 Aug 1906, having by her had, with other issue:

2 Edward William John; *b* 5 Aug 1864; *educ* Wellington and RMC Sandhurst; Capt Rifle Bde, Maj 3rd Bn Leics Regt, MP (C) Melton 1895–1900, Field Master Belvoir hounds under his f; *d* 26 Feb 1903

3 Cecil Reginald John; *b* 4 Feb 1868; *educ* Charterhouse and Trin Hall Cambridge; Assist Priv Sec to Sec State India 1886–92, MP (C) Melton 1900–06; *k* by a train at Crowborough Station 8 Sept 1945

4 Robert William Orlando, CMG (1917), DSO (1900); *b* 4 Feb 1870; Maj KRRC and T/LT-Col cmdg 10th Bn Northumberland Fus, Isazai Expedition, Boer War (despatches) and WW I (despatches, wounded); *m* 15 Nov 1902 Mildred Mary, CBE (1920) (*d* 19 Jan 1934), dau of Rev Charles P Buckworth and widow of Maj Henry Edward Buchanan Riddell (*see* RIDDELL, Bt), and was *ka* 11 Sept 1917, leaving:

(1) Elizabeth Katharine Joan; *b* 1904; *m* 25 Jan 1932 Lt-Col John Norman Pulteney Lascelles and *d* 198–, having had issue (*see* HAREWOOD, E)

1 Elizabeth Emily; *b* 6 Feb 1878; *m* 30 April 1903 Lord George William Montagu-Douglas-Scott, 3rd s of 6th Duke of Buccleuch and (8th Duke of) Queensberry (*qv*), and *d* 22 July 1924, leaving issue

The 7th DUKE's est s,

HENRY JOHN BRINSLEY MANNERS, **8th Duke of Rutland**, KG (1918), TD; *b* 16 April 1852; *educ* Eton and Trin Coll Cambridge (Hon LLD 1924); Ld Lt Leics 1900–25, Pncpl Priv Sec to PM 1885–86 and 1886–88, MP E Leics 1888–95, Hon Col 3rd and 4th Bns Leics Regt and Pres Leics TA, called up to Ho of Lds *vp* 6 June 1896 in f's Barony of Manners of Haddon; *m* 25 Nov 1882 Marion Margaret Violet (*b* 7 March 1856; *d* 22 Dec 1937), dau of Col Hon Charles Hugh Lindsay, CB (*see* CRAWFORD and BALCARRES, E), and *d* 8 May 1925, having had:

1 Robert Charles John, styled *Lord Haddon*; *b* 8 Aug 1885; *d* 28 Sept 1894

2 JOHN HENRY MONTAGU, **9th Duke**

1 (Victoria) Marjorie Harriet; *b* 20 Dec 1883; *m* 3 Aug 1912 6th Marquess of Anglesey (*qv*) and *d* 3 Nov 1946, leaving issue

2 Violet Catherine; *b* 24 April 1888, *m* 1st 1 Feb 1911 Hugo Francis Charteris, Lord Elcho (*ka* 23 April 1916, *vp*), and had issue (*see* WEMYSS and MARCH, E); *m* 2nd 9 July 1921 Guy Benson (*d* 30 April 1975), est s of Robert Henry Benson, of Buckhurst, Sussex, and *d* 23 Dec 1971, leaving by him:

(1) Nicholas Robin; *b* 2 May 1922; *educ* Eton; Lt-Cdr RN (ret 1954) WW II; *m* 1 Oct 1949 *Muriel Joan Barbara, dau of Alfred Kitchiner, of Bournemouth, and *d* 19–, leaving:

1a +Robert Charles [Robert Benson Esq, Glebe House, Lowther, Penrith, Cumbria CA10 2HH]; *b* 17 Nov 1952; *educ* Eton and Southampton U (BSc); agent and sporting manager Lowther Estates 1976–, dir Lakeland Investment Co 1980–, chm: NW Br Field Sports Soc, Lowther Driving Trials and Country Fair, memb ctee: Timber Growers UK, CLA and Br Deer Soc; *m* 6 Dec 1978, as her 2nd husb, *Lady Jane Lowther, dau of 7th Earl of Lonsdale (*qv*), and has:

1b +Laura Jane; *b* 1980

2b +Sophie Camilla; *b* 1984

2a +Christopher Lindsay [Christopher Benson Esq, Aycote Farm, Rendcomb, Cirencester, Glos GL7 7EP]; *b* 26 Aug 1954; *educ* Eton

3a +Patrick Robin [Patrick Benson Esq, 42 Bloemfontein Rd, London W12 7BX]; *b* 5 Jan 1956; *educ* Eton

1a +Penelope Jane; *b* 26 June 1950

(2) +Giles Barnaby; *b* 18 Dec 1923; *educ* Eton and Balliol Coll Oxford; Capt KRRC WW II; *m* 5 Aug 1954 *Rosemary, dau of Clive Stuart Saxon Burt, QC, of Lower Ufford, nr Ipswich, and has:

1a +Carolyn Jane; *b* 15 July 1955

2a +Vanessa Robyn; *b* 7 Aug 1957

3a +Laura Francesca; *b* 25 June 1962

(3) +Jeremy Henry, OBE [Jeremy Benson Esq OBE, Walpole House, Chiswick Mall, London W4 2PS]; *b* 25 June 1925; *educ* Eton and AA; AADip, FRIBA; *m* 1 Aug 1951 *Patricia Ann, dau of Dr James Duff Stewart, of Seaton, Devon, and has:

1a +Guy Rupert; *b* 9 Jan 1955; *educ* Eton

2a +Martin James [Martin Benson Esq, 69 Netherwood Rd, London W14 0BP]; *b* 6 June 1957; *educ* Eton

1a +Anne Catherine; *b* 20 Feb 1953

2a +Elizabeth Jane; *b* 13 Aug 1959

3a +Sarah Henrietta; *b* 1 April 1961

3 Diana Olivia Winifred Maud; *b* to her mother 29 Aug 1892, Harry Cust (more correctly Henry John Cockayne-Cust, er bro of 5th Baron Brownlow, *qv*) being widely accepted by contemporaries of Lady Diana's parents, and seemingly by herself from c 1912, as the f; celebrated hostess, beauty and society figure featuring in virtually every collection of memoirs by anyone of importance from the 1920s to the 1960s, played the part of a statue of the Madonna which comes to life in Max Reinhardt's play without words *The Miracle* in several revivals from 1923 into the 1930s, author of three-part autobiography: *The Rainbow Comes and Goes* (1958), *The Light of Common Day* (1959) and *Trumpets from the Steep* (1960); *m* 2 June 1919 (Alfred) Duff Cooper, later 1st Viscount Norwich (*qv*; *d* 1 Jan 1954; she reverted to the name Lady Diana Cooper 8 Jan 1954), and *d* 1986, leaving issue

The 8th DUKE's only surv s,

JOHN HENRY MONTAGU MANNERS, **9th Duke of Rutland**; *b* 21 Sept 1886; *educ* Eton and Trin Coll Cambridge; Hon Attaché Rome 1909, Capt 4th Bn Leicester Regt, ADC on Personal Staff 1916, memb Roy Commn on Historical MSS. 1928, bore HM QUEEN ELIZABETH (subsequently THE QUEEN MOTHER)'s Sceptre with the Cross at the Coronation 1937; *m* 27 Jan 1916 Kathleen, JP (Leics Pres: BRCS and Girl Guides, held canopy of HM QUEEN ELIZA-BETH (subsequently THE QUEEN MOTHER) at Coronation 1937; *d* 4 Dec 1989), 3rd dau of Francis John Tennant, of Innes, Morayshire (*see* GLENCONNER, B), and *d* 22 April 1940, leaving:

1 CHARLES JOHN ROBERT MANNERS, **10th and present Duke of Rutland**

2 +John [The Lord John Manners, Reservoir Cottage, Knipton, Grantham, Lincs; Haddon Hall, Bakewell, Derbyshire]; *b* 18 July 1922; *educ* Eton and New Coll Oxford; late Capt Life Gds and 2nd SAS Regt, High Sheriff Leics 1973–74; *m* 12 June 1957 Mary Diana (*d* 12 Sept 1997), yst dau of Lt-Col Lancelot Geoffrey Moore, DSO, of Chelsea and S Rhodesia, and has:

(1) +Richard John Peveril; *b* 12 March 1963

(1) +Elizabeth ('Libby') Diana; *b* 4 Oct 1959; *m* 1986 *Alexander Russell and has issue (*see* BEDFORD, D)

(2) +Lucy Rachel; *b* 15 Feb 1961; Extra Ldy in Waiting to HRH THE DUCH-ESS OF YORK 1989–96

3 +Roger David [The Lord Roger Manners, Marsh End Farm, Heddington, Wilts; Belcombe Court, Bradford-on-Avon, Wilts]; *b* 23 Sept 1925; *educ* Eton; 2nd Lt Gren Gds; *m* 8 March 1965 *Finola St Lawrence, only dau of Thomas Edward Daubeney, of Easington Park, Ampney St Peter, Glos, and has:

(1) +Moira Violet Joanna; *b* 19 Aug 1966

(2) +Phoebe Constance Adeliza; *b* 4 April 1968

1 +Ursula Isabel [The Lady Ursula D'Abo, West Wratting Park, Cambridge CB1 5LR; 29 Kensington Square, London W8]; *b* 8 Nov 1916; one of HM QUEEN ELIZABETH (subsequently THE QUEEN MOTHER)'s trainbearers Coronation 1937; *m* 1st 25 July 1943 (*divorce* 1948) Lt-Cdr (A) Anthony Freire Marreco, RNVR, only s of Geoffrey Freire Marreco, of Old Court House, St Mawes, Cornwall; *m* 2nd 22 Nov 1951 Robert Erland Nicolai d'Abo (*d* 30 July 1970), er s of Gerard Louis d'Abo, of Coval Court, Sunningdale, Berks, and has:

(1) +John Henry Erland; *b* 7 Oct 1953; *educ* Eton

(2) +Richard Winston Mark; *b* 3 July 1956; *educ* Eton

(1) +Louisa Jane [The Hon Mrs John Ramsay, 1Kassala Rd, London SW11]; *b* 8 Jan 1955; *m* 1981 *Hon John Patrick Ramsay, yst s of 16th Earl of Dalhousie (*qv*), and has issue

2 +Isabel Violet Kathleen [The Lady Isabel Throckmorton, Coughton Court, Alcester, Warwicks; Molland, S Molton, N Devon]; *b* 5 Jan 1918; *m* 1st 24 Nov 1936 (*divorce* 1951), as his 2nd w, G/Capt Thomas Evelyn Bulkeley Guinness, OBE (*see* GUINNESS, Bt), and has issue; *m* 2nd 29 July 1953 Sir Robert George Maxwell Throckmorton, 11th and last Bt (*d* 1989; *see* 1970 edn)

Seats: Belvoir Castle, Grantham, Lincs; Haddon Hall, Derbys.

Belvoir (pronounced 'Beaver') was originally built shortly after the Conquest by Robert de Toeni or de Stafford (*see* STAFFORD, B). This structure was mostly destroyed during the Wars of the Roses. Its replacement, completed in 1555 by the **2nd Earl of Rutland**, only lasted till 1649, when it too was destroyed on the recommendation of the Council of State, the place having been held by Royalists for much of the Civil War. The **8th Earl of Rutland**, the then owner and a moderate Parliamentarian, was granted a derisory £1,500 (some £33,000 in late-1990s terms) compensation for the loss of his principal residence. Following the Restoration he started on a third version and completed it by 1668, but this too was pulled down, roughly a hundred years afterwards. Elizabeth, wife of the **5th Duke**, started construction of the present edifice, though she was assisted by James Wyatt and later her husband's chaplain after a catastrophic fire in 1816.

Haddon, a fortified manor house rather than a castle, is nevertheless more authentically medieval. Its origins are 12th-century. The banqueting hall is 14th-century, though restored early in the 20th century, and the dining room mid-16th-century. Haddon was abandoned by the MANNERSes from some time in the first half of the 18th century (the **3rd Duke** was the last to live there at that period) to just before World War I, when the **9th Duke**, whose ambition it had always been to make it his home, started to restore it, though he did not actually move in till 1927. The Haddon estate, however, was sold in 1920 for just over £350,000 (nearly £4,700,000 in late-1990s terms). It totalled 14,500 acres.

RYAN

Arms: Gu. in chief two griffins sejant respectant and combatant or, in base a garb of rye ppr. **Crest:** Upon a mount vert a griffin sejant sa., holding in the dexter claw a sword erect ppr. and resting the sinister on a sickle or. **Motto:** *Sans travail rien* ('Nothing without work'). **Creation:** Bt. (UK) 8 Sept 1919.

SIR DEREK GERALD RYAN, 4TH BT, of Hintlesham, Co Suffolk [Sir Derek Ryan Bt, 4618 South Austin St, Seattle, WA 98118, USA]; *b* 25 March 1954; *s f* 1990; *educ* Berkeley U Calif (BA Environmental Design 1977); architect; *m* 1st 1986 (*divorce* 1990) Maria Teresa, dau of Juan G Rodriguez, of Lexington, Ky.; *m* 2nd 27 Dec 1997 *Roberta Walker

Lineage: MICHAEL RYAN, of Kilkenny; had:

MICHAEL DESMOND RYAN; *m* Eliza Anne, dau of Joseph Allen, and had a 3rd s:

Sir Gerald Hemmington Ryan, 1st Bt (UK), so cr 8 Sept 1919, of Hintlesham, Suffolk, JP Norfolk and Co London; *b* 25 Jan 1861; chm Phoenix Assur, ktd 1911, High Sheriff Suffolk 1920; *m* 23 July 1885 Ellen Amelia (*d* 22 Nov 1935), only dau of Augustus Thomas Ellis, of Parkside, Cambridge, and had:

1 GERALD ELLIS (Sir), **2nd Bt**

2 Vivian Desmond; *b* 7 Sept 1893; *m* 1st 20 Sept 1917 Kathleen Frances (*d* 15 Nov 1945), dau of James William Helps, MInstCE, of S Croydon, and had:

(1) +DESMOND MAURICE [Desmond Ryan Esq, S15 C8 RR4, Gower Point Rd, Gibsons, BC V0N 1V0, Canada; 306–1626 West 10th, Vancouver, BC V6J 2A2, Canada]; *b* 16 Sept 1918; heir presumptive; *m* 19 Aug 1942 *Margaret Catherine, dau of A H Brereton, of Vancouver, and has:

1a +Barry Desmond; *b* 30 June 1943; *m* 1975 *Evodia Massemola, and has:

1b +Lerato; *b* 1979

2b +Andrew; *b* 1986

2a +Kevin Vivian; *b* 14 March 1951; *m* 1977 *Ellen Folkestad and has:

1b +Martin; *b* 1980

1b *Caralynn; *b* 1982

3a +Michael Brereton; *b* 1954; has:

1b *Aaron; *b* 1986

(2) +Adrian James [Adrian Ryan Esq, 8 Camden Studios, Camden Street, London NW1]; *b* 3 Oct 1920; *m* 1st 1941 (*divorce* 1950) Peggy Rose and has:

1a *Geraldine Daphne; *b* 1943

(2) (cont.) Adrian Ryan *m* 2nd 3 Sept 1952 Barbara Pitt; *m* 3rd 1977 *Susan Curnow and has by his 2nd w:

2a *Scarlett Kathleen; *b* 1954

3a *Vivien Frances; *b* 1957

(1) *Jeanette Daphne; *b* 2 Aug 1929; BA 1950

2 (cont.) Vivian Ryan *m* 2nd 11 April 1946 Nanny (*d* 1988), dau of Dixon Slater, of Skipton, Yorks, and *d* 25 Feb 1950, leaving:

(3) +John Desmond [John Ryan Esq, 11 Compton Rise, Pinner, Middx HA5 5HS]; *b* 1945; *m* 1969 *Tina, dau of Arthur Percy Gregory, and has:

1a *Nicola Jane; *b* 1972

2a *Rosalind Anne; *b* 1975

The 1st Bt *d* 27 May 1937; his est s,

Sir Gerald Ellis Ryan, 2nd Bt; *b* 17 Aug 1888; MA Oxon; barrister Inner Temple; *m* 17 Feb 1914 Hylda Winifryde (*d* 4 Jan 1925), dau of Maj Spencer John Herapath, and had:

1 Michael Erskine; *b* 9 April 1920; P/O RAF WW II; *ka* May 1940

2 DEREK GERALD (Sir), **3rd Bt**

1 Aileen Pamela; *b* 22 June 1916; *m* 19 April 1950 Peter James Frederick Green, er s of John Everard Green, of Hainault, Essex

The 2nd Bt *d* 1 Sept 1947; his only surv s,

Sir Derek Gerald Ryan, 3rd Bt; *b* 9 July 1922; *educ* Harrow; Lt Gren Gds WW II; *m* 1st 8 July 1947 (*divorce* 1971) Penelope Anne (*m* 2nd 28 Sept 1973 Walter Lennon), only dau of Reginald E (Rex) Hawkings, of New York; *m* 2nd 1972 *Katja

Edeltraud Hildegard [Katya Lady Ryan, 1m Marixgarten 21, 65343 Eltville, Germany], dau of Ernest Best, of Kassel, and d 1990, leaving by his 1st w:

1 Sir DEREK GERALD RYAN, **4th and present Bt**

1 *Anne Katherine [Mrs Steven Casciola, 909 N Palm Ave # 311, W Hollywood, CA 90069, USA]; b 28 July 1951; m 1st 1977 (divorce 1989) Edgard Puente; m 2nd 1989 *Steven Casciola

2 *Jenifer Hylda [Mrs Christopher Newall, 17 Lonsdale Sq, London N1 1EN]; b 28 March 1955; m 1985 *Christopher Stirling Newall, s of Peter Newall, of Crookham Westfield Farmhouse, Cornhill on Tweed, Northumberland, and has:

  (1) *Alfred Stirling; b 1987

  (2) *George Stirling; b 1990

3 *Caroline Sarah [Mrs Jeff Chase, 15 Brook Rd, Topsfield, MA 01983, USA]; b 23 June 1956; m 1990 *Jeff Chase and has:

  (1) *Perry; b 1994

  (1) *Monica Kristi; b 1991

  (2) *Liza (twin); b 1994

RYCROFT

Arms: Quarterly, 1st and 4th, per bend or and az. three griffin's heads erased counterchanged, on a chief erm. a fleur-de-lys between two roses gu. (for RYCROFT); 2nd and 3rd, party per pale or and sa. a chevron between three fleurs-de-lys all counterchanged (for NELSON). **Crest:** A griffin's head erased per bend or and az., charged with two fleurs-de-lys counterchanged. **Motto:** Faythe hathe no fear. **Creation:** Bt. (GB) 22 Jan 1784.

SIR RICHARD NEWTON RYCROFT, 7TH BT, of Calton, Co York [Sir Richard Rycroft Bt, Winalls Wood House, Stuckton, Hants SP6 2HQ]; b 23 Jan 1918; s f 1958; educ Winchester and Ch Ch Oxford (BA 1939); Maj Beds and Herts Inf, attd Special Services Balkans, WW II (despatches), Kt Cross Roy Order Phoenix Greece with swords; m 30 April 1947 *Ann, yr dau of Hugh Bellingham-Smith, of Alfriston, Sussex, by Mrs Harvey Boas Robarts, of Kensington, and has:

1 *Susan Marilda [Mrs Ian Martell, Wood House, Shotley Bridge, Co Durham DH8 9TL]; b 23 Jan 1948; educ Trin Coll Dublin (MA); m 1974 *Ian Martell and has:

  (1) *Jonathan Newton; b 1978

  (1) *Alice; b 1976

2 *Sally Ann [Viscountess FitzHarris, Greywell Hill, Greywell, Hants RG29 1DG]; b 14 March 1950; educ Magdalen Coll Oxford (MA 1991); m 14 June 1969 *James Carleton, Viscount FitzHarris, only s of 6th Earl of Malmesbury (qv), and has issue

Lineage: JOHN NELSON, of Calton; had an only surv s:

Rev Sir RICHARD NELSON later RYCROFT (roy licence 28 Dec 1758), **1st Bt** (GB), so cr 22 Jan 1784; Rector Penshurst, Kent; m 13 Feb 1759 Penelope (d 13 Feb 1821), yst dau of Rev Richard Stonehewer, LLD, Rector Houghton-le-Springs, Co Durham, and had, with three other sons (d young):

1 NELSON (Sir), **2nd Bt**

2 Henry (Sir); b 10 Jan 1766; Kt Harbinger; m 1794 Jane, widow of William D Naper, of Loughcrew, Co Meath, and dau of Ferdinando Tracy Travell, of Upper Slaughter, Glos, and dsp 3rd Oct 1846

1 Penelope; m 1791 Nathaniel Lee Acton, of Livermere Park, Suffolk, and d 1819

2 Margery; m 1793 James Bouwens and d 1835

3 Mary; m 1792 Rt Rev and Hon George Pelham, DD, Bp Lincoln, 3rd s of 1st Earl of Chichester (qv), and d 1837

4 Charlotte; m 1792 Charles Edward Pigou, of Shernfold, Sussex, and d March 1813

5 Esther; m 1806 H Harford, of Down Place, Berks, and d his widow 1853

6 Elizabeth; m 20 Oct 1831 Adam Askew, of Redheugh, Co Durham, and dsp his widow 1856

Sir RICHARD d 5 July 1786; his est s,

Sir Nelson Rycroft, 2nd Bt; b 15 Feb 1761; m 1st 11 July 1791 Charlotte (d 28 May 1803), dau of Henry Read, of Crowood, Wilts, and had:

1 William John Nelson; b 1792; d 1800

2 RICHARD HENRY CHARLES (Sir), **3rd Bt**

3 Henry (Rev); b 28 Feb 1797; Vicar Mumby, Lincs; d unm 6 April 1840

1 Charlotte; m 1842 Gen Sir John Hanbury, KCB, KCH, Col 99th Regt, bro of 1st Baron Bateman (see 1931 edn), and d his widow 1870

2 Harriet; m 15 Aug 1833 R-Adml Charles Hamlyn Williams, RN, 2nd s of Sir James Hamlyn Williams, 2nd Bt, and d 3 Sept 1882

Sir Nelson m 2nd 3 May 1808 Margaret (dsp 30 March 1837), yst dau of Robert Mandeville, and d 1 Oct 1827

His er surv s,

Sir Richard Henry Charles Rycroft, 3rd Bt; b 21 Dec 1793; m 18 May 1830 Charlotte Anne Josephine (d 3 Oct 1874), est dau of William Tennant, of Little Aston Hall, Staffs, and had:

1 NELSON (Sir), **4th Bt**

2 Charles Alfred William; b 18 Sept 1838; m 19 Jan 1875 Edith Maude (d 17 Nov 1912), yst dau of Capt Hugh Berners, RN, and d 23 April 1884, leaving:

  (1) Alfred Richard Hugh, DSO (1918); b 21 Feb 1876; Lt Roy Welch Fus Boer War 1899–1900, Maj W Kent Yeo, Tank Corps and Remount Service WW I (wounded, despatches); m 18 May 1901 Violet (d 28 Dec 1964), dau of Capt William Trevelyan Somerset Kevill-Davies, JP, 17th Lancers, and d 5 April 1944, having had:

    1a Lily Maud Phyllis; b 6 Nov 1902; m 20 Jan 1926 Maj Patrick Vincent, MC, 3rd/6th Dragoon Gds, s of Col Arthur Hare Vincent, of Summer Hill House, Castle Connell, Co Clare, and d 6 Aug 1936

  (2) Henry Frederick; b 26 Feb 1879; Capt 2nd Bn York and Lancaster Regt, Lt Wilts Regt; ka 7 Aug 1915

  (1) Charlotte Maud; m 9 Nov 1899 Fritz Ritter, Rittmeister Hanoverian Dragoons, and d 28 Feb 1943, having had issue

  (2) Aurea Louisa Harriet; m 10 Feb 1903 Lt-Col Edmund Stuart Eardley Wilmot Eardley-Russell, MVO, RFA, est s of Capt Theodosius Stuart Russell, of St John's, Wakefield, Yorks, and d 4 April 1948, having had isssue. He d 29 March 1918

3 Henry Richard; b 7 March 1840; d 13 Sept 1854

Sir RICHARD d 21 Oct 1864; his est s,

Sir Nelson Rycroft, 4th Bt, DL Hants; b 11 March 1831; High Sheriff 1881, Hon Col 3rd Bn Hants Regt; m 27 July 1858 Juliana (d 6 Jan 1917), est dau of Sir John Ogilvy, 9th Bt (qv), and had:

1 RICHARD NELSON (Sir), **5th Bt**

2 William Henry (Sir), KCB (1919), KCMG (1918); b 17 Feb 1861; served Egypt 1884 and 1887, Indian Frontier Expdn 1897, Boer War 1900–01, Somaliland 1903, Staff WW I (despatches seven times), Maj-Gen i/c Admin Br Army Black Sea 1918–20 and HQ Irish Command 1920–21, Govr Br N Borneo 1922–25, cmded 11th Hus, 4th Cl Medjidie, KGStJ, Grand Cdr Greek Order Redeemer, Grand Offr Star Romania, Serbian Order White Eagle 2nd Cl with swords, Greek Order Merit 2nd Cl, Cdr Legion Honour; m 28 Sept 1887 Grace Ronald Maria (d 8 Dec 1946), only child of Fletcher Norton Menzies of Menzies, and d 4 Nov 1925, leaving:

  (1) Julian Neil Oscar, DSO (1918), MC; b 22 Feb 1892; Personal Staff WW I (wounded, despatches, Croix de Guerre), Capt and Brevet Maj Black Watch, Bde Maj 1917, T/Lt-Col cmdg 1918, Adj Roy Hosp Chelsea 1924–25; m 20 Oct 1920 Elizabeth Mildred Louisa (d 11 Sept 1932), yr dau of Sir Ralph Anstruther, 6th Bt (qv), and d 12 Jan 1928, leaving:

    1a *Cynthia Margaret [Mrs Philip Stenning, Sunnyside, Elie, Fife KY9 1DN]; m 2 July 1949 *Col Philip Dives Stenning, RE, only s of Edgar Henry Stenning, of Bickley, Kent, and has:

      1b *Christopher John William [Christopher Stenning Esq, 15 Peterborough Rd, London SW6 3BT]; b 16 Oct 1950; educ Marlborough; m 1981 *Ruth, dau of George T C Draper, of Swaffham, Norfolk, and has:

        1c *Jonathan; b 1985

        1c *Rachel; b 1983

      2b *Nicholas Julian Seymour [Nicholas Stenning Esq, Medstead House, Medstead, Hants GU34 5LY]; b 24 Nov 1952; educ Marlborough and Pembroke Coll Oxford; m 1976 *Caroline, dau of Michael Livingstone-Learmont, MC, of Minchinhampton, Glos, and has:

        1c *Alexander; b 1985

        1c *Clare; b 1979

        2c *Emily; b 1981

      3b *Richard Neil [Richard Stenning Esq, Meadcroft, Sidmouth Rd, Colyton, Devon EX13 6NP]; b 12 Dec 1955; educ Marlborough and Nottingham U; m 1988 *Alison, dau of Mrs A E Hooper, and has:

        1c *Aisha; b 1989

        2c *Eliana Grace; b 1990

    2a *Evelyn Joanna Christian [Mrs Martin Claridge, St Martin's House, St Martin's Ave, Canterbury, Kent CT1 1QQ]; m 30 May 1953 *Martin Claridge, MCh, FRCS, s of Gerald Frank Claridge, of Bardleden, Smarden, Kent, and has:

      1b *Simon Julian; b 12 Nov 1954; m 19– (divorce) Marit McKerchar and has:

        1c *Rebecca Tatsachen; b 1987

        2c *Jessica; b 1989

      2b *Tobias James; b 25 Oct 1963; m 19– *Dr Victoria Hartnel and has:

        1c *Fergus; b 1994

        1c *Hester Lucy; b 1996

      1b *Anna Louise; b 8 April 1958

      2b *Katharine Georgina; b 1 April 1960; m 19– *Richard Fuller and has:

        1c *Caspar Furneau; b 1995

        1c *Matilda Grace; b 1997

  (1) Madalen Margaret; m 6 Sept 1921 Lt-Col Clarence Evelyn Gardner, Glos Regt, yr s of Col Alan Coulston Gardner, MP, of Clearwell Castle, Coleford, Glos (see BLYTH, B), and had issue. He d 9 March 1950

3 Edmund Hugh (Rev); *b* 3 Sept 1862; MA Cantab, Rector Penshurst, Kent; *m* 18 Nov 1902 Winifred Edith (*d* 30 Dec 1968), er dau of Adml of the Fleet Sir Arthur Dalrymple Fanshawe, GCB, GCVO, and *d* 18 July 1932, leaving:

(1) +Arthur John [Arthur Rycroft Esq, The Old Vicarage, Wilsford, Wilts]; *b* 23 Oct 1905; *educ* Radley and Corpus Christi Coll Oxford (BA 1927)

(2) David Hugh, OBE (1943); *b* 30 Dec 1907; *educ* Radley and RMC Sandhurst; psc, Col Staff KSLI WW II; *m* 1st 18 Dec 1930 (*divorce* 1934) Elizabeth Edith Dilys, only dau of Capt Miles Bertie Cunningham Carbery, 1st Roy Irish Fus, and had:

1a Julian Miles Wemyss; *b* 7 Nov 1931; *educ* RNC Dartmouth; Lt RN; *m* 14 Aug 1954 *Jennifer Margaret (*m* 2nd 19 July 1966 Sir John Ogilvy Rennie, KCMG, s of Charles Ogilvy Rennie, of Greenock), yr dau of Lt-Col John Gordon Wainwright, of Penn, Bucks, and was *k* in an accident in HMS *Sidon* 16 June 1955

(2) (cont.) Col David Rycroft *m* 2nd 31 July 1939 Cicely Phoebe Susanna (*d* 1980), yr dau of Lt-Col Robert Bruère Otter-Barry, OBE, Roy Sussex Regt, of Glazeley Hall, nr Bridgnorth, Salop, and was *ka* Dalmatia 13 Nov 1944, having by her had:

2a +Henry David; *b* 24 March 1943; *educ* Radley and St Andrews (BSc 1967); MB, BS; *m* 1st 1972 (*divorce* 1983) Nicole Elizabeth, dau of Maurice Kenig, MD; *m* 2nd 1983 *Mrs Dorothea Ann Joan Heaney, yr dau of Robert Eilliam Nicholson Evans (*see* LEES, Bt, of Blackrock), and has by his 1st w:

1b +Alexander Theophilus; *b* 1975

1a *Charlotte Susanna; *b* 14 June 1941; *educ* Girton Coll Cambridge (BA 1964); FCO: Amb (non-resident) Chad 1989

(1) Barbara Frances; *b* 30 Dec 1903; *educ* St Hugh's Coll Oxford (BA 1926)

4 Charles Michael Richard; *b* 29 Sept 1864; Capt Prince Albert's Somerset LI; *d* unm 31 Jan 1897

5 Evelyn George; *b* 6 Feb 1871; *d* unm 29 Dec 1920

1 Margaret Charlotte Henrietta (twin with Evelyn George); *d* unm 23 April 1949

Sir NELSON *d* 30 March 1894; his est s,

Sir Richard Nelson Rycroft, 5th Bt, DL Hants; *b* 12 Dec 1859; High Sheriff Hants 1899, Lt Rifle Bde, Capt 3rd Bn Hants Regt, Boer War with Imp Yeo 1899–1900 (despatches), Maj TFR, T/Maj Artists' Rifles WW I; *m* 1st 11 Feb 1886 Lady Dorothea Hester Bluett Wallop (*d* 29 Dec 1906), 4th dau of 5th Earl of Portsmouth (*qv*), and had:

1 NELSON EDWARD OLIVER (Sir), **6th Bt**

2 Newton Richard Valoynes; *b* 21 Dec 1892; *d* 13 March 1893

3 Richard Michael (Rev); *b* 27 Sept 1897; Lt 3rd Bn Hants Regt, Vicar Rolleston-on-the-Wark, Notts; *m* 26 Aug 1924 Evelyn Maud (*d* 31 Aug 1969), dau of Francis James Driscoll, of Jersey, and *d* 30 Jan 1968, leaving:

(1) *Jean Dorothea; *b* 10 Sept 1925; WW II 1943–45 in WRNS; *m* 25 Aug 1945 Charles Spencer Goldring, 3rd s of Wallace Goldring, of Ridgeville, Ontario, and has had:

1a *Paul Michael [Paul Goldring Esq, 4085 Rue Berri, Montreal, Quebec, Canada]; *b* 13 July 1947; *educ* St Mary's U Halifax (BA 1967); *m* 1983 *Ryoko Mine and has:

1b *Matthew John Wallace Yotaru Mine; *b* 1985

2b *Nathan Charles Toshiharu Mine; *b* 1987

2a *(James) Philip [Dr Philip Goldring, 618 Fraser Ave, Ottawa, Ontario K2A 2R5, Canada]; *b* 25 Sept 1948; *educ* St Mary's U Halifax (BA 1967), Dalhousie U (MA 1969) Halifax and London U (PhD 1978); *m* 1969 *Dr Marianne Louise McLean, PhD, and has:

1b *Andrew Michael Dmitri; *b* 27 May 1970

2b *Hugh Douglas Arthur; *b* 17 May 1986

3b *Alexander Charles McLean; *b* 27 Sept 1990

4b *Colin John Denison; *b* 30 Oct 1992

3a Hugh Charles; *b* 13 Nov 1951; *d* 21 April 1953

4a *Nicholas John; *b* 3 March 1954

5a *Hilary Adrian Jerome; *b* 22 Sept 1959; *educ* Ontario U (Bus Ad)

6a *Stephen Gerard; *b* 3 Aug 1961

7a *Christopher Septimus Denison; *b* 3 Aug 1961

1a *Felicity Jocelyn; *b* 26 May 1965; *educ* Dalhousie U (BSc)

(2) *(Mary) Elizabeth [Miss Elizabeth Rycroft, 8 Southcote Rd, London N19 5BJ]; *b* 23 Nov 1935; *educ* RCA (MA)

Sir Richard *m* 2nd 1 Feb 1911 Emily Mary (*d* 14 June 1982 aged 99), er dau of Col Hon Henry William Lowry-Corry (*see* BELMORE, E), and by her had:

4 Henry Richard, DSC (1943), OBE (1960); *b* 28 Dec 1911; *educ* RNC Dartmouth; Cdr RN (ret 1962) WW II (despatches); *m* 15 Nov 1941 *Penelope Gwendolen [Mrs Henry Rycroft, 19 Marcuse Fields, Bosham, W Sussex], dau of Lt-Col Charles Spenser Browne Evans-Lombe, Leinster Regt, of Beer, Devon, and *d* 1985, having had:

(1) +RICHARD JOHN [Richard Rycroft Esq, 14 Ship Rd, Burnham-on-Crouch, Essex]; *b* 15 June 1946; heir presumptive; *educ* Sherborne

(1) *Caroline Mary [Mrs Nicholas Meyrick, Church Farm House, Empingham, Rutland LE15 8PN]; *b* 9 Nov 1944; *educ* Downe House, Newbury, and U of Sussex (BSc); *m* 6 Aug 1966 *Capt Nicholas Wolryche Meyrick, RA, yr s of Cdr Michael Donston Capel Meyrick, DSO, OBE, RN, of The Coach House, Norton, Sussex, and has:

1a *Julian Timothy; *b* 2 May 1968; *educ* Univ Coll Oxford

2a *Oliver Michael; *b* 1 Feb 1978; *educ* BNC Oxford

1a *Hilary Jocelyn; *b* 22 June 1970; *educ* Queen's Coll Oxford

(2) *Philippa Eve [Mrs Peter Jenkinson, Fringford Cottage, Fringford, Oxon OX6 9DP]; *b* 5 May 1949; *educ* Downe House, Newbury; *m* 1981 *Peter Edward Jenkinson and has:

1a *Susanna Emily; *b* 1982

2a *Olivia Mary; *b* 1984

3a *Harriet Anne; *b* 1989

(3) *Jocelyn Penelope [Mrs Michael Lawton, Bryn Garw Lodge, Brynmenyn, Bridgend, Glam CF32 8UU]; *b* 9 Oct 1955; *educ* Wispers Sch, Haslemere; *m* 1984 *Michael Piers Lawton and has:

1a *Piers Simon George; *b* 1990

1a *Sarah Louise; *b* 1988

5 +Charles Frederick [Charles Rycroft Esq, 2 Modbury Gdns, London NW5 3QE]; *b* 9 Sept 1914; *educ* Wellington and Trin Coll Cambridge (BA 1936), MB, BS (Lond); *m* 1st 9 May 1947 (*divorce* 1963) Mrs Chloe Rosenfeld, er dau of Edouard Majolier and Mrs Peter Longton, of Springle House, Hertford; *m* 2nd 1977 *Jenny, dau of William Pearson, and by his 1st w has:

(1) +Francis Edward; *b* 4 Aug 1950; *educ* Gresham's; *m* 1975 *Cherry, dau of Kenneth Willmott, of School Farm Barn, Alburgh, Norfolk and has:

1a +Michael; *b* 1979

1a *Kelly; *b* 1977

(1) *Alice Julia [Mrs Ibrahim Jama, 3 Woodside Rd, Manchester 16]; *b* 21 Aug 1947; *educ* U of Kent (BA 1969); *m* 1978 *Ibrahim Jama and has issue

(2) *Catherine Ann [Mrs Christopher Merriman, Tankers' Row, S Clydach, Abergavenny, Gwent]; *b* 28 April 1949; *educ* U of Kent (BA); *m* 1970 *Christopher Piers Merriman and has:

1a *Roger Christopher; *b* 1975

1a *Chloe Catherine; *b* 1977

1 *Alice Juliana Rosamond [Mrs Patrick Harvey, The Paddock, 4 South Place, Lee on the Solent, Hants]; *b* 5 Dec 1915; *m* 1st 23 April 1938 Neil Malise Graham (*d* as the result of a motoring accident 9 June 1939), only s of Maj George Humphrey Irving Graham, Devonshire Regt and IA, and has:

(1) *Charles Edward Malise [Capt Charles Graham, Riccards Down House, Abbotsham, N Devon EX39 5BG]; *b* 4 April 1939; *educ* King's Coll Taunton, Sch of Navigation Southampton (Master Mariner) and Exeter U (LLB Hons); Yr Bro Hull Trin Ho; *m* 1976 *Lynn Marie, dau of Stanley Carter

(2) *Bruce Torquil Irving [Bruce Graham Esq, Penhoat Huon, Guimiliau, Landivisiau, France]; *b* 4 April 1939; *educ* King's Coll Taunton

1 (cont.) Mrs Neil Graham *m* 2nd 26 June 1943 Rev Patrick Roger Harvey, RN (*d* 1986), 2nd s of Reginald Hickman Harvey, of Reigate, and by him has:

(3) *Michael Timothy John [Michael Harvey Esq, 9 Rue Pierre Larousse, 69100 Villeurbanne, France]; *b* 6 Nov 1944; *educ* Worksop Coll, Keble Coll Oxford (BA 1966, MA 1993) and Lyons U, France

(1) *Diana Lavender Mary; *b* 27 Jan 1946; *educ* St Clare's Penzance; *m* 1970 *Robert Ian Fellows and has:

1a *Gregory Chad; *b* 5 Dec 1974

1a *Charlotte Claire; *b* 14 Aug 1976

(2) *(Primrose) Miranda Margaret [Mrs Michael Line, 19 Moorland Close, Locks Heath, Southampton SO31 6WD]; *b* 26 June 1953; *educ* St Clare's Penzance; *m* 1989 *Michael Robert Line and has:

1a *Harriet Clare; *b* 14 Nov 1992

2 *Eleanor Mary [Miss Eleanor Ryecroft, Resthaven, Pitchcombe, Stroud, Glos]; *b* 2 April 1918; WW II 1942–45 in WRNS

Sir RICHARD *d* 25 Oct 1925; his est s,

Sir Nelson Edward Oliver Rycroft, 6th Bt; *b* 19 Dec 1886; *educ* Winchester and Ch Ch Oxford (BA 1909); T/Lt Rifle Bde, Lt 11th Hus, WW I, MFH Vyne 1932–38, High Sheriff Hants 1938; *m* 1 June 1912 Ethel Sylvia (*d* 14 May 1952), dau of Robert Nurton, of Odcombe House, Yeovil, Somerset, and *d* 30 Aug 1958, having had:

1 Richard; *b* 7 Oct, 1913; *d* 28 March 1918

2 Sir RICHARD NEWTON RYCROFT, **7th and present Bt**

RYDER OF EATON HASTINGS

Creation: B. (LP, UK) 1975.

THE BARON RYDER OF EATON HASTINGS, of Eaton Hastings, Co Oxon ((Sydney Thomas) Don Ryder) [The Rt Hon The Lord Ryder of Eaton Hastings, House of Lords, London SW1A 0PW]; *b* 16 Sept 1916; *educ* Ealing County GS; ed *Stock Exchange Gazette* 1950–60, jt md Kelly Iliffe Hldgs and Associated Iliffe Press 1961–63; md 1961–63, dir IPC 1963–70; md Reed Paper Gp 1963–68 and chm and ch exec Reed Internat (formerly Reed Gp) 1968–75; Pres Nat Materials Handling Centre 1970–75; V-Pres RoSPA 1973–88, dir Metropolitan Estate and Property Corp 1972–75, memb Cncl BIM 1970–75, Br Gas Bd 1972–78 and Reserve Pension Bd 1973–75, UK-S Africa Trade Assoc 1974–75, Govt Ch Industl Advsr and chm NEB 1975–77, ktd 1972; *m* 1950 *Eileen, dau of William Dodds, and has:

1 *Michael John; *b* 1953

1 *Jill Patricia; *b* 1950

Lineage: JOHN RYDER; had:

(SYDNEY THOMAS) DON, *cr* a **Baron**

RYDER OF WARSAW

Creation: B. (LP, UK) 1978.

THE BARONESS RYDER OF WARSAW, of Warsaw, Poland, and Cavendish, Co Suffolk ((Margaret) Susan Ryder, CMG (1976), OBE (1957)) [The Rt Hon The Baroness Ryder of Warsaw CMG OBE, Sue Ryder Home, Cavendish, Sudbury, Suffolk CO10 8AY]; *b* 3 July 1923; *educ* Benenden; FANY and SOE WW II; fndr Sue Ryder Fndn for Sick and Disabled; co-fndr Ryder-Cheshire Fndn; Tstee Leonard Cheshire Fndn, World Meml Fund for Disaster Relief; Hon LLD: Liverpool 1973, Exeter 1980, London 1981, Leeds 1984, Cambridge 1989; Hon DLitt Reading 1982; Hon DCL Kent 1986, D Essex U 1993; Order Polonia Restituta: Officer's Cross 1965, Cdr's Cross 1992; Golden Order Merit Poland 1976; Medal of Yugoslav Flag with Gold Wreath and Dipl 1971; Polish Order of Smile 1980; author: *And the Morrow is Theirs* (1975); *Child of My Love* (1986); *m* 1959 Gp Capt (Geoffrey) Leonard Cheshire (Baron Cheshire), VC, OM, DSO, DFC (*d* 1992), and has:

1 *Jeremy Charles; *b* 1960
1 *Elizabeth Diana; *b* 1962

Lineage: CHARLES RYDER; *m* Elizabeth — and had:

(MARGARET) SUSAN, *cr* a **Baroness**

RYDER OF WENSUM

Creation: B. (LP, UK) 19 April 1997.

THE BARON RYDER OF WENSUM, of Wensum, Co Norfolk (Richard Andrew Ryder, (OBE 1981), PC (1990)) [The Rt Hon The Lord Ryder of Wensum OBE PC, House of Lords, London SW1A 0PW]; *b* 4 Feb 1949; *educ* Radley and Magdalene Coll Cambridge; ptnr M Ryder and Sons; Political Sec to: Leader Oppn 1975–79, PM 1979–81, MP (C) Mid-Norfolk 1983–97, Chm For and Cwlth Cncl 1984–89, PPS to: Fin Sec Treas 1984, For Sec 1984–86, Assist Govt Whip 1986–88, Parly U-Sec MAFF 1988–89, Ec Sec Treasury 1989–90, Paymaster Gen 1990, Parly Sec Treasury and Govt Ch Whip 1990–95; chm Eastern Counties Radio 1997–; *m* 1981 *Caroline, MBE, only dau of Sir David Stephens, and has had a dau and s (*d* young)

Lineage: RICHARD STEPHEN RYDER, JP, DL; *m* Margaret MacKenzie and has:

RICHARD ANDREW, *cr* a **Baron**

SAATCHI

Creation: B. (LP, UK) 1996.

THE BARON SAATCHI, of Staplefield, Co West Sussex (Maurice Saatchi) [The Rt Hon The Lord Saatchi, 36 Golden Sq, London W1R 4EE]; *b* 21 June 1946; *educ* LSE; co-fndr Saatchi & Saatchi 1970 (chm 1985–94), chm Megalomedia plc 1995–, ptnr M&C Saatchi Agency 1995–; *m* 1984 *Josephine Hart, novelist, and has a s

Lineage: NATHAN SAATCHI; *m* Daisy — and had:

1 *Charles; *b* 9 June 1943; *educ* Christ's Coll Finchley; fndr-dir Saatchi & Saatchi 1970–93, dir Crmer Saatchi 1968–70, assoc dir Collett Dickenson Pearce 1966–68, ptnr M&C Saatchi Agency 1995–; *m* *Kay — and has a dau
2 MAURICE, *cr* a Baron

SACKVILLE

JOUR · DE · MA · VIE

Arms: Quarterly, 1st and 4th, arg. a fess dancettée sa. (for WEST); 2nd and 3rd, quarterly or and gu. a bend vair (for SACKVILLE). **Crests:** 1 Out of a ducal coronet or a griffin's head az., beaked and eared gold (for WEST), 2 Out of a coronet composed of fleurs-de-lys or an estoile arg. **Supporters:** On either side a griffin az., gorged with a ducal coronet or, therefrom pendant on the dexter an escutcheon of the arms of WEST and on the sinister an escutcheon of the arms of SACKVILLE. **Motto:** *Jour de ma vie* ('Day of my life'). **Creation:** B. (UK) 2 Oct 1876.

THE 6TH BARON SACKVILLE OF KNOLE, Co Kent (Lionel Bertrand Sackville-West) [The Rt Hon The Lord Sackville, Knole, Sevenoaks, Kent TN15 0RP]; *b* 30 May 1913; *s* cousin 1965; *educ* Winchester and Magdalen Coll Oxford (BA 1934); Capt Coldstream Gds WW II 1939–42 (POW), memb Lloyd's 1949; *m* 1st 9 Oct 1953 Jacobine Napier (*d* 1971), yr dau of James Robert Menzies-Wilson, of Fotheringhay Lodge, Nassington, Peterborough, and widow of Capt John Hichens, RA, and has:

1 *Teresa [The Hon Mrs Marlow, 11 Gladstone St, London SE1 6EY]; *b* 29 Nov 1954; *m* 1979 *(Alastair) Rupert Marlow, s of Capt C N Marlow, RN, of Greenhill House, Upper Westwood, Wilts, and has:
  (1) *Sebastian Edward; *b* 8 May 1985
  (1) *Julia Catherine; *b* 8 April 1982
  (2) *Rebecca Clare; *b* 20 Nov 1983
2 *Catherine Jacobine [The Hon Mrs Catherine Sackville-West, 36 Iffley Rd, London W6]; *b* 10 March 1956; *m* 1980 (*divorce* 1984) Stuart Cooper Bennett, er s of H M Bennett, of Pasadena, Calif.
3 *Sophia Anne [The Hon Mrs Elliott, 11 Sinclair Gdns, London W14]; *b* 19 July 1957; *m* 1988 *Guy R Elliott, only s of Robert Elliott, of Little Ashley Farm, Bradford-on-Avon, Wilts
4 *Victoria Mary [The Hon Mrs Lang, 61 Richbourne Terrace, London SW8]; *b* 26 April 1959; *m* 1989 *Jonathan G F Lang, yr s of John Lang, of Nairobi, and has:
  (1) *Leo John Bertrand; *b* 1993
  (1) *Clementine Jacobine Eva; *b* 1991
5 *Sarah Elizabeth; *b* 14 Sept 1960; *m* 1992 *(Edward) Simon Rendall, yr s of Peter Godfrey Rendall, of Burford, Oxon, and has:
  (1) *Frederick Thomas Inigo; *b* 22 Sept 1994
  (2) *Edward Bertrand Montague; *b* 30 May 1996

The 6th BARON *m* 2nd 23 April 1974 (*divorce* 1983) Arlie Roebuck (*d* 1991), dau of Charles Woodhead, of Romany Rye, Brisbane, Qld, widow of Maj Hugh Dalzell Steward, W Yorks Regt, and formerly w of Maj-Gen Sir Francis Wilfred de Guingand, KBE, CB, DSO; *m* 3rd 2 Dec 1983 *Jean, dau of Arthur Stanley Garton, of Danesfield, Marlow, Bucks, and widow of Maj Sir Edward Imbert-Terry, 3rd Bt (*qv*)

Lineage: HERBRAND de SAUQUEVILLE, of a Norman family from Sauqueville, SW of Dieppe, held Fawley, Bucks, at the Domesday Survey 1086, having been granted it possibly as early as 1070; also feudal Ld of Sauqueville-sur-Scie, having presumably acquired that fief from Walter Giffard, an earlier feudal Ld of Sauqueville, to whom he was steward; HERBRAND's descendants held Buckhurst Bergholt in the early 13th century and were ancestors of:

JOHN SACKVILLE, of Chiddingly, Sussex; *m* Margaret, dau of Sir William Boleyn, KB (*see* 1970 edn ORMONDE, M) and *d* 27 Sept 1557, having had an est s:

Sir RICHARD SACKVILLE, PC; Chllr Court of Augmentation, U-Treasurer Exchequer, MP Kent and Surrey; *m* Winifred (*m* 2nd, as his 3rd w, 2nd Marquess of Winchester (*qv*) and *d* 1586), dau of Sir John Bru(g)ge(s)/Brydges, Ld Mayor London 1520, and *d* 21 April 1566, leaving, with at least two daus (Anne, *m* 10th Lord (Baron) Dacre (*qv*); Mildred, *m* as his 2nd w Sir William Fitzwilliam (*see* 1970 edn FITZWILLIAM, E) and had issue; *see* SHELLEY, Bt):

THOMAS SACKVILLE, 1st EARL OF DORSET, so *cr* 13 March 1603/4, as also earlier 8 June 1567 BARON OF BUCKHURST, Co Sussex (both E), KG (1589), PC (between 1582 and Feb 1595/6); *b* between 1527 and 1536; allegedly *educ* Hart

Hall Oxford and St John's Coll Cambridge; barrister Inner Temple, MP Westmorland 1557/8, E Grinstead 1559 and Aylesbury 1563–67, ktd 1567, Amb to States (foreunner of The Netherlands) in the Low Countries in revolt against Spain; Jt Ld Lt Sussex 1587–1608, Jt Commr Gt Seal 1591–92, Chllr Oxford U 1591–1608, Ld High Treasurer 1599–1608; author 'Induction' and the 'Complaint of Buckingham' in the 1563 edn of *A Mirror for Magistrates* (anthology of didactic poetry) and Acts IV and V (Thomas Norton being responsible for Acts I–III, or so the 1st edn of 1565 claims) of *Gorboduc* (first performed 1561), alleged to be the first English blank-verse tragedy and the first tragedy where some attempt is made at characterisation rather than personifications of virtues, vices, etc; *m* 1555 Cicely, 2nd dau of Sir John Baker, PC, of Sissinghurst Castle, Kent, Speaker H of C, and *d* 19 April 1608, having had, with another s:

1 ROBERT SACKVILLE, 2nd EARL OF DORSET; *b* 1561; *educ* Hart Hall Oxford; MP Sussex 1584–86, 1592–93, 1597–98, 1601 and 1604–08 and Lewes 1588–89; Jt Ld Lt Sussex 1608–09; *m* 1st *c* 4 Feb 1578/9 Margaret (*d* 4 Sept 1591), dau of 4th Duke of Norfolk (*qv*); *m* 2nd 4 Dec 1592 Anne, widow of (a) 1st Lord (Baron) Compton (*see* NORTHAMPTON, M) and (b) William Stanley, 3rd Lord (Baron) Monteagle (*see* DERBY, E), and dau of Sir John Spencer, of Althorp (*see* MARLBOROUGH, D), and *d* 27 Feb 1608/9, having had by his 1st w:

(1) RICHARD SACKVILLE, 3rd EARL OF DORSET; *b* 28 March 1589; *m* 25 Feb 1608/9 Anne, Baroness Clifford (*see* DE CLIFFORD, B) in her own right (*m* 2nd 4th Earl of Pembroke and (1st Earl of) Montgomery; *qv*), dau of 3rd Earl of Cumberland, and *dspms* 28 March (his birthday) 1624, having had:

1a Thomas, *Lord Buckhurst*; *bapt* 24 Feb 1619/20; *dvp* in infancy

1a Margaret; *m* 21 April 1629 2nd Earl of Thanet (*see* DE CLIFFORD, B) and had issue

2a Isabella; *m* 5 July 1647 3rd Earl of Northampton (*see* NORTHAMPTON, M) and *d* 22 Aug 1719

(2) EDWARD SACKVILLE, 4th EARL OF DORSET, KG (1625), KB (1616), PC (1626); *b* 1590; *k* 2nd Lord Bruce of Kinloss (*see* ELGIN and KINCARDINE, E) in a duel over a woman at Bergen-op-Zoom 1613; MP Sussex 1620–22, Jt Ld Lt Middx 1620–22 and 1628–42, Jt Ld Lt Sussex 1624–42, Chamberlain Household 1644–46; *m* by 2 March 1612 Mary, dau and heiress of Sir George Curzon, of Croxall, Derbys (*see* SCARSDALE, V), and *d* 18 July 1652, having had:

1a RICHARD SACKVILLE, 5th EARL OF DORSET; *b* 16 Sept 1622; MP E Grinstead 1640–44, Jt Ld Lt Middx 1660–70 and Sussex 1670–77; *m* 1637 Lady Frances Cranfield (*m* 2nd Henry Powle), yst dau of 1st Earl of Middlesex, and *d* 1667, having had, with other issue:

1b CHARLES SACKVILLE, 6th EARL OF DORSET and 1st EARL OF MIDDLESEX and BARON CRANFIELD, of Cranfield, Co Bedford (both E), so *cr* 4 April 1675 (following his inheritance of the estates of his maternal uncle the 3rd and last Earl of Middlesex of the 1621 *cr*), KG (Feb 1691/2), PC (Feb 1688/9); *b* 24 Jan 1637/8; MP E Grinstead 1661–75, Envoy to France 1669, Jt Ld Lt Sussex (with f) 1670–77 and solely 1677–87/8 and 1689–Jan 1705/6, Ld Chamberlain Feb 1688/9–97, Jt Ld Lt Somerset 1690–91, patron of the writers Dryden, Prior and Wycherley; *m* 1st June 1674 Mary, dau of Col Hervey Bagot and widow of Charles Berkeley, Earl of Falmouth (*see* FALMOUTH, V, preliminary remarks); *m* 2nd 7 March 1684/5 Mary, dau of 3rd Earl of Northampton (*see* NORTHAMPTON, M), and had, with a dau:

1c LIONEL CRANFIELD SACKVILLE, 7th EARL OF DORSET, 2nd EARL OF MIDDLESEX and 1st DUKE OF DORSET, so *cr* 13 June 1720, KG (1714), PC (1714); *b* 18 Jan 1688; *educ* Westminster; Ld Warden Cinque Ports 1708–12, 1714–17 and 1728–65, Groom Stole and 1st Ld Bedchamber 1714–17, Ld Steward Household 1725–30 and 1737–45, Ld Lt Ireland 1730–37 and 1751–55, Ld Pres Cncl Jan 1744/5–51, Master Horse 1755–57, Ld Lt Kent 1746–65; *m* Jan 1708/9 Elizabeth (*d* 12 June 1768), Maid of Honour to QUEEN ANNE and First Ldy Bedchamber and Mistress Robes to GEORGE I's QUEEN CAROLINE, dau of Lt-Gen Walter Philip Colyear and n of 1st Earl of Portmore (*see* 1833 edn), and *d* 10 Oct 1765, having had, with a dau (*d* young):

1d CHARLES SACKVILLE, 2nd DUKE OF DORSET, PC (1766); *b* 6 Feb 1710/1; *educ* Westminster and Ch Ch Oxford; MP (Whig) E Grinstead 1734–42 and 1761–65, Sussex 1742–47 and Old Sarum 1747–54, a Ld Treasury 1743–47, Ld Lt Kent 1766–69; *m* 30 Oct 1744 Hon Grace Boyle, Mistress Robes and a Ldy Bedchamber to PRINCESS OF WALES 1743–63 and allegedly mistress to FREDERICK PRINCE OF WALES, dau of 2nd and last Viscount Shannon (*see* CORK and ORRERY, E), and *dsp* 6 Jan 1769

2d John Philip; *b* 22 June 1713; *m* 1744 Frances, dau of lst Earl Gower (*see* SUTHERLAND, D), and *d* 1765, leaving:

1e JOHN FREDERICK SACKVILLE, 3rd DUKE OF DORSET, KG (nominated 1788 but never installed), PC (1782); *b* 25 March 1745; *educ* Westminster; MP (Whig) Kent 1768–69, Ld Lt Kent 1769–97, Col 1779, Capt Yeomen Gd 1782–83, Amb France 1783–89, Ld Steward Household 1789–99; *m* 4 Jan 1790 Arabella Diana (*m* 2nd 1st and last Earl Whitworth; *see* RAVENSDALE, B), dau and coheir of Sir Charles Cope, Bt, of Brewern, Oxon, and *d* 19 July 1799, leaving:

1f GEORGE JOHN FREDERICK SACKVILLE, 4th DUKE OF DORSET; *b* 15 Nov 1793; *educ* Harrow and Ch Ch Oxford; *k* hunting near Dublin 14 Feb 1815

1f Mary; *m* 1st 5 Aug 1811 6th Earl of Plymouth (*qv*); *m* 2nd 25 May 1839 1st Earl Amherst (*see* AMHERST OF HACKNEY, B, preliminary remarks), and *dsp* 20 July 1864

2f ELIZABETH, for whom *see* further below

1e Mary; *m* 30 Aug 1767 8th Earl of Thanet (*d* 10 April 1786; *see* LUCAS OF CRUDWELL, B) and had issue

3d GEORGE SACKVILLE later GERMAIN (Act of Parl 16 Feb 1770 under terms of will of Sir John and Lady Elizabeth Germain, of Drayton, Northants, neither of whom was in any way related to him), 1st VISCOUNT SACKVILLE, of Drayton, Co Northampton, so *cr* 11 Feb 1782, as also BARON BOLEBROKE, Co Sussex (both GB), PC (I 1751, GB 1758–60 and 1765); *b* 26 Jan 1715/6; *educ* Westminster and Trin Coll Dublin; barrister 1734, Clerk Irish PC, MP (I Parl) Portarlington 1733–61 and (GB Parl) Dover 1741–61, Hythe 1761–68 and E Grinstead 1768–82, Ch Sec to Ld Lt Ireland 1751–55, Jt V-Treasurer Ireland 1765–66, Capt Carabiniers 1737 (Col Jan 1749/50), Lt-Col 28th Foot 1740, ADC to GEORGE II 1743, fought Battle of Fontenoy 1745 (wounded), Col 1 June 1745, served Culloden Campaign under DUKE OF CUMBERLAND 1746, Col 20th Foot 1746, Col 12th Dragoons 1749, Maj-Gen 1755, Col 2nd Dragoon Gds and Lt-Gen Ordnance 1757–59, 2ic St Malo and Germany Expdny Forces 1758, C-in-C Br Forces Germany Oct 1758 till broken for disobeying orders by his superior offr Prince Ferdinand of Brunswick to advance with the cavalry at the Allied victory over the French of Minden 1 Aug 1759 (apparently out of a momentary failure of nerve, despite his bravery, particularly at Fontenoy, and his ability hitherto, though it has also been suggested, notably by Horace Walpole, that he wished to prevent total victory by Prince Frederick, even at the cost of his own reputation); rehabilitated by GEORGE III, who personally decided to ennoble him, Ld Commr Trade and Plantation 1775–79, Sec State N American Colonies 1775–82 (when his strict policy contributed to the British defeat in the War of American Independence); *m* 3 Sept 1754 Diana (*d* 15 Jan 1778), 2nd dau and coheir of John Sambrooke, and *d* 26 Aug 1785, having had, with two other daus:

1e CHARLES SACKVILLE, 2nd and last VISCOUNT SACKVILLE and 5th and last DUKE OF DORSET (as which s cousin), KG (1826), PC (1821); *b* 27 Aug 1767; *d* unm 29 July 1843, when all his titles expired

2e George; *b* 7 Dec 1770; *m* Dec 1814 Harriet Pearce (*d* 18 April 1835) and *d* 31 May 1836, leaving:

1f Caroline Harriet, of Drayton; *m* 2 June 1837 William Bruce Stopford (*see* COURTOWN, E) and *d* 16 Jan 1908, leaving issue

1e Diane; *b* 8 July 1756; *m* 26 Nov 1777 2nd and last Earl of Glandore, PC (I) (*see* 1832 edn BRANDEN, B), and *d* 29 Aug 1814

1d Elizabeth; *m* 6 Dec 1726 2nd Viscount Weymouth (*see* BATH, M) and *dsp* 9th June 1729

2d Caroline; *m* 27 July 1742 1st Earl of Dorchester of the 1792 *cr* (*see* PORTARLINGTON, E) and *d* 24 March 1775

1b (cont.) The 6th EARL OF DORSET *m* 3rd 27 Oct 1704 Anne, widow of — Roche, and *d* 29 Jan 1705/6

1b Mary; *b* 4 Feb 1646; *m* 6 Feb 1664/5 2nd Earl of Orrery and *d* 4 Nov 1710, leaving issue (*see* CORK and ORRERY, E)

2b Anne; *m* 4th Earl of Home (*qv*)

3b Frances; *b* 6 Feb 1655; *m* 11 Dec 1683 1st Viscount Lanesborough of the 1676 *cr* (*see* LANESBOROUGH, E, preliminary remarks) and had issue

2a Edward; *m* Bridget, *de jure* Baroness Norris in her own right (*see* LINDSEY and ABINGDON, E)

(1) Cecily; *m* Sir Henry Compton, KB (*see* NORTHAMPTON, M)

(2) Anne; *m* 1st Edward Seymour, Lord Beauchamp, KB, bro of 2nd Duke of Somerset (*qv*); *m* 2nd Sir Edward Lewes

2 William (Sir); *b c* 1570; ktd 1589; *k* France in Wars of Religion 1591

3 Thomas; fought against the Turks 1595

1 Anne; *m* Sir Henry Glemham, of Glemham, Suffolk

2 Jane; *m* Feb 1591 2nd Viscount Montague (*d* 23 Oct 1629) and had issue (*see* WINCHESTER, M)

3 Mary; *m* 7th Lord (Baron) Bergavenny (*see* ABERGAVENNY, M) and had issue

The 4th and penultimate DUKE OF DORSET's yr sis,

ELIZABETH SACKVILLE later SACKVILLE-WEST (roy licence 6 Nov 1843), BARONESS BUCKHURST OF BUCKHURST in her own right (UK), so *cr* 27 April 1864, with remainder to her 2nd surv s Reginald and the heirs male of his body, whom failing to her 3rd and subsequent sons by her then husb and the heirs male of their bodies, with a rider that if any heir inheriting the Barony also inherited the Earldom of De La Warr the Barony should pass to a yr bro, younger s or heir male of the body of any such, in other words the next heir to the Barony, should such a person exist (the idea being to prevent the Earldom and Barony being held by the same person — an intention which was frustrated; *see* DE LA WARR, E); *b* 11 Aug 1795; *m* 21 June 1813 5th Earl De La Warr (*qv*) and *d* 9 Jan 1870, having had, with three er sons and three daus:

1 MORTIMER WEST later SACKVILLE-WEST, **1st Baron Sackville of Knole**, Co Kent (UK), so *cr* 2 Oct 1876, with special remainder, in default of male issue, to his brothers; *b* 22 Sept 1820; unsuccessfully claimed Barony of Buckhurst of Buckhurst *cr* for his mother when his er bro, who had *s* their mother as 2nd Baron Buckhurst of Buckhurst in 1870, inherited the Earldom of De La Warr in 1873; the special 'jumping' remainder in the patent of creation was ajudged invalid but a like clause in the deed governing the inheritance of the Knole and other Sackville estates was ruled sound and he inherited them accordingly; his Barony of Sackville was conferred as a consolation prize; *m* 1st 14 Jan 1847 Fanny Charlotte (*d* 19 Jan 1870), dau of Maj-Gen William Dickson, CB, HEICS, of Beenham, Berks; *m* 2nd 12 June 1873 Elizabeth (*d* 23 Jan 1888), 2nd dau of Charles Wilson Faber, of Northaw House, Herts (*see* 1931 edn WITTENHAM, B), and *d* 1 Oct 1888

2 LIONEL SACKVILLE-WEST, **2nd Baron Sackville of Knole**, GCMG (1888, KCMG 1885), JP, DL Kent; *b* 19 July 1827; Dip Serv: joined 1847, Sec Legation Turin 1858–64 and Madrid 1864–67, Sec Embassy Berlin 1867 and Paris 1868–72, Envoy Extrdy and Min Plen Argentina 1872–78, Spain 1878–81 and USA 1881–88; *dspl* unm 3 Sept 1908, leaving by his mistress the Spanish dancer 'Pepita' (in reality Josefa, dau of Pedro Duran, a barber of Malaga, by Catalina Ortega, of gypsy extraction):

(1) Maximiliano De La OLIVA; documentation was drawn up stating him to be s of 'Pepita' by Juan Antonio de la Oliva, her official husband; hence he was prevented from claiming the Barony of Sackville of Knole on his biological f's death

(2) Ernest Henri Jean Baptiste SACKVILLE-WEST; claimed the Barony on his f's death, alleging his legitimacy; his petition failed in the High Court Probate Division Feb 1910

(1) Victoria Josefa; *b* 23 Sept 1862; acted as her f's hostess in Washington (*see* section ARTHUR, CHESTER A., p. 506, also p. 525, AMERICAN PRESIDENTIAL FAMILIES, 1994, Morris Genealogical Books SA); *m* **3rd Baron Sackville of Knole** (*see* below) and had issue

3 William Edward; *b* 27 Oct 1830; MA Oxon; Lt-Col Gren Gds; *m* 7 Aug 1860 Georgina (*d* 23 Feb 1883), yst dau of George Dodwell, of Kevinsfort, Co Sligo, and *d* 30 Sept 1905, leaving:

(1) LIONEL EDWARD SACKVILLE-WEST, **3rd Baron Sackville of Knole**, JP, DL Kent; *b* 15 May 1867; MA Oxon; Kent: Lt-Col (W) Yeo, V-Chm CC, Chm TAA WW I; *m* 17 June 1890 his cousin Victoria Sackville-West (*d* 30 Jan 1936), illegitimate dau of the **2nd Baron**, and *d* 28 Jan 1928, leaving:

1aVi(c)t(ori)a Mary, CH (1948), JP; *b* 9 March 1892; author (as Vita Sackville-West) of some 50 books, including: *Heritage* (1919), *Knole and the Sackvilles* (1922), *The Land* (1926, a poem, Hawthornden Prize 1927), *Andrew Marvell* (1929), *The Edwardians* (1930), *All Passion Spent* (1931), *Sissinghurst* (1933), *Pepita* (1937), *The Eagle and the Dove* (1943), *The Garden* (1946, Heinemann Prize 1947), DLitt Durham and Newcastle 1950, FRSL; *m* 1 Oct 1913 Hon Sir Harold George Nicolson, KCVO, CMG (*see* CARNOCK, B), and *d* 2 June 1962, leaving issue

(2) CHARLES JOHN SACKVILLE-WEST, **4th Baron Sackville of Knole**, KBE (1919), CB (1921), CMG (1915); *b* 10 Aug 1870; *educ* Winchester and RMC Sandhurst; Maj-Gen KRRC, served Manipur 1891 (despatches), Boer War 1899–1900 (despatches) and WW I (wounded twice, despatches), Br Rep Supreme War Cncl Versailles 1918–19, Mil Attaché Paris 1920–24, Lt-Govr Guernsey 1925–29, Legn Hon, US DSM, Croix de Guerre Italy and France, Grand Offr Order Crown Italy; *m* 1st 5 Jan 1897 Maude Cecelia (*d* 7 Dec 1920), dau of Capt Matthew John Bell, and had:

1a EDWARD (EDDIE) CHARLES SACKVILLE-WEST, **5th Baron Sackville of Knole**; *b* 13 Nov 1901; *educ* Eton and Ch Ch Oxford; music critic, author: *A Flame in Sunlight*; *d* unm 4 July 1965

1a Diana Joan; *b* 10 Oct 1906; *m* 1st 3 Dec 1929 (*divorce* 1944) 4th Baron Romilly (*see* 1970 edn); *m* 2nd 13 Jan 1951 Lt-Col Sir Douglas Montgomery Bernard Hall, 2nd Bt, DSO, of Burton Park (*qv*)

(2) (cont.) The **4th Baron** *m* 2nd 30 Jan 1924 Anne (*d* 8 Jan 1961), formerly w of Stephen Sohier Bigelow, of Boston, and dau of William Meredith, of New York, and *d* 8 May 1962

(3) Bertrand George; *b* 20 Nov 1872; *educ* Winchester and Ch Ch Oxford (BA 1894); Inspr Ottoman Public Debt Office Constantinople 1895–1921, Lt-Cdr RNVR WW I, Legn Hon; *m* 28 July 1908 Eva Adela Mabel Inigo (*d* 28 Feb 1936), dau of Maj-Gen Inigo Richmond Jones, CB, CVO, of Kelston Park, Somerset, and *d* 23 Aug 1959, leaving:

1a LIONEL BERTRAND SACKVILLE-WEST, **6th and present Baron Sackville of Knole**

2a +HUGH ROSSLYN INIGO, MC [Hugh Sackville-West Esq MC, Knole, Sevenoaks, Kent]; *b* 1 Feb 1919; heir presumptive; *educ* Winchester and Magdalen Coll Oxford (MA 1939); Capt RTR WW II (wounded), Overseas Serv Nigeria 1946–59, chartered land agent (QA) 1965, ARICS, Croix de Guerre 1945; *m* 29 June 1957 *Bridget Eleanor Ailsie, est dau of Capt Robert Lionel Brooke Cunliffe, CBE, RN (*see* CUNLIFFE, Bt), and has:

1b +Robert Bertrand [Robert Sackville-West Esq, Gardener's Cottage, Knole, Kent TN15 0RP]; *b* 10 July 1958; *m* 1st 1985 (*divorce* 1992) Catherine Dorothea, er dau of Geoffrey Bennett, of Smelthouses, N Yorks; *m* 2nd 1994 *(Margot) Jane, dau of Mark MacAndrew, of Holmwood House, Holmwood, Surrey, and has by her:

1c *Freya; *b* 6 Aug 1998

2b +William Lionel Cunliffe; *b* 9 Jan 1967; *m* 1993 *Annika, dau of Kurt Lennartsson, of Västeras, Sweden, by Birgitta Dellastrand, of Köping, Sweden

1b *Mary Cecilie; *b* 10 Sept 1960

2b *Elizabeth Anne; *b* 8 July 1962

3b *Jane Eleanor; *b* 16 April 1964

1a Cecilie Alice Maud; *b* 15, *d* 29 May 1909

2a *Elizabeth Margaret; *b* 4 March 1911; *m* 8 July 1943 Thomas Bradwall Barlow, 2nd s of Sir John Emmott Barlow, 1st Bt, of Bradwall Hall (*qv*), and has issue

(1) Mary Elizabeth; *m* 12 April 1898 John Tracey, of Ford, Bicknoller, Somerset, and *d* 13 Sept 1944. He *d* 13 Sept 1947

(2) Cecilie Victoria, CBE (1920); *m* 5 Jan 1901 Sir Robert Albert Cunliffe, 5th Bt (*qv*), and *d* 10 March 1955. He *d* 18 June 1905

Seat: Knole, Sevenoaks, Kent. The sheer size of Knole is staggering. The architectural historian Nigel Nicolson, whose mother was a daughter of the house, wrote in an essay of the early 1960s that it allegedly possessed a room for each day of the year. Even more staggering than the size is the thought that in over half a millennium nobody had prepared a definitive calculation of just how big the place was. But then Knole is more like a small town than a house, with seven courtyards counting wells and uncovered walkways. It is also extraordinarily homogeneous, being built entirely of the grey-brown stone that embellishes other traditional buildings across northeast Sussex, southeast Surrey and east Kent.

The first creator of Knole was apparently Thomas Bourchier, Cardinal-Archbishop of Canterbury and a younger brother of the 1st Bourchier Earl of Essex (*qv*, preliminary remarks). In 1455 he acquired the manor of Knole from Lord Saye and Sele (*qv*), though it is not clear if that manor was a house or administrative territorial unit, *i.e.*, estate. Bourchier spent the next 30 years building much of the present structure, including the gatehouse on the west facade and its two-storey flanks. (The charming Dutch gables were added by the 1st Earl of Dorset over a hundred years later.) He seems to have been something of a Renaissance cultural patron, entertaining extensively there. It was at Knole that he died in 1486. It subsequently became a kind of tied cottage on a vast scale inasmuch as the Primate of All England often resided there throughout the next four incumbencies. Perhaps only when one realises that Knole was planned by a prelate as a quasi-institutional dwelling that the collegiate layout of courtyard after courtyard seems entirely natural, though it must be said that this was a standard feature of laymens' houses at the time.

The last occupational inhabitant was Cranmer; the next owner HENRY VIII. Knole's takeover by the King was a microcosm of the national church's appropriation by the Crown. The transfer occurred in 1538, almost midway between the suppression of the lesser religious houses and that of the greater ones. Knole remained fundamentally in Tudor monarch hands till the end of the century, for though ELIZABETH I granted its reversion to her cousin Thomas Sackville in 1566, it did not become fully his till her death, 37 years later. No doubt that is why he did not start his massive enlargement work till then, though he was an extremely busy public figure in the intervening years and may have wanted to oversee the project personally, something he could not do till he had won a little leisure in old age.

Possibly too much is made of Sackville's kinship with the then sovereign when mentioning that she chose him to grant Knole to (just as it is easy to overstate HENRY VIII's acquisitiveness in wresting Knole from his Archbishop, given that it was not by then a personal possession of the Archbishop in question). It is often forgotten that Bourchier had been great-grandson of EDWARD III through his mother, Anne, daughter of Thomas of Woodstock, EDWARD's youngest son. Morever his brother Lord Essex married another of EDWARD III's granddaughters, making Essex, and at a pinch Bourchier, uncle by marriage to EDWARD IV, to whom in addition Bourchier's nephew William (sometimes styled Lord Bourchier) was brother-in-law. In comparison Sackville's relationship of second cousin to ELIZABETH I through her disgraced mother looks a bit threadbare.

Once in full control Lord Dorset (as Sackville had now become) got down to work. He inserted panelled and intricately plastered state rooms above the old archiepiscopal palace, erected a colonnade in the Stone Court opposite the Great Hall and began building up one of the finest assemblages of 17th-century furniture in England. The 'Knole' sofa, with its end flaps lashed to the back by cords round the finials, epitomises the style of an entire epoch in the popular mind. It is merely the best-known item. Augmented in the late 17th century, the collection became incomparable. At that date the development of the mansion itself more or less came to an end. The clock tower was built in the 18th century, some orangery windows inserted in the 19th, but essentially the entire gigantic edifice remains more or less as the poet Dryden, protégé of the 6th Earl of Dorset, would have known it when he wrote *Astraea Redux* in 1660 to clebrate the Restoration.

SAINSBURY

Creation: B (LP, UK) 3 May 1962.

THE BARON SAINSBURY, of Drury Lane in the Borough of Holborn (Alan John Sainsbury) [The Rt Hon The Lord Sainsbury, Stamford House, Stamford St, London SE1 9LL]; *b* 13 Aug 1902; *educ* Haileybury; J Sainsbury Ltd: joined 1921, jt pres 1967– (chm 1956–67), Lib candidate Sudbury 1929, 1931 and 1935 gen elections; served consultative ctees Min Food WW II; joined Lab Pty 1945 and SDP 1981; memb: Williams Ctee Milk Distbn 1947–48, Food Research Advsy Ctee 1960–70 (chm 1965–70), NEDC Distributive Trades Ctee 1964–68, Exec Ctee PEP 1970–76, V-Pres: Roy Soc Encouragement Arts, Mfres and Commerce 1962–66, Assoc of Ag 1965–73, Internat Vol Serv 1977–81, Parly Gp for World Govt 1982–; Pres: Pestalozzi Children's Village Trust 1963–, Multiple Shops Fedn 1963–65, Grocers' Inst 1963–66, Internat Assoc Chain Stores 1965–68, Roy Inst Public Health and Hygiene 1965–70, Distributive Trades Educn and Training Cncl 1975–83; Chm: Ctee Enquiry Relationship Pharmaceutical Industry and NHS 1965–68, Tstees Overseas Students Advsy Bureau 1969–, Tstees Uganda Asian Relief Trust 1972–74, NIESR; Govr City Lit Inst 1967–69, memb Court Essex U 1966–76, Hon Fell Inst Food Sci and Tech; *m* 1st 31 Oct 1925 (*divorce* 1939) Doreen Davan (*d* 1985), dau of Leonard Adams, and has:

1 *JOHN DAVAN SAINSBURY, BARON SAINSBURY OF PRESTON CANDOVER (*qv*)

2 *Simon David Davan [The Hon Simon Sainsbury, Stamford House, Stamford St, London SE1 9LL]; *b* 1 March 1930; *educ* Eton and Trin Coll Cambridge; late v-chm and dir J Sainsbury, Tstee: Wallace Collection 1977–, Nat Gallery 1991–

3 *Timothy Alan Davan (Sir), PC (1992) [The Rt Hon Sir Timothy Sainsbury PC MP, House of Commons, London SW1A 0AA]; *b* 11 June 1932; *educ* Eton and Worcester Coll Oxford (hon Fell 1982); dir J Sainsbury Ltd 1962–83 and 1994–, MP (C) Hove 1973–97, PPS to: Environment Sec 1979–83, Def Sec 1983; Govt Whip 1983–87, Parly U-Sec MOD 1987–89 and FCO 1989–90, Min State DTI 1990–94, Parly chm C Friends of Israel 1994–97, ktd 1995, Hon ARICS 1994, Hon FRIBA 1994; *m* 26 April 1961 *Susan Mary, dau of Brig James Alastair Harry Mitchell, CBE, DSO, and has:

(1) *(Timothy) James; *b* 3 Feb 1962; *educ* Worcester Coll Oxford; *m* 8 July 1995 *Margaret Martin

(2) *Alexander; *b* 17 Jan 1968

(1) *Camilla Davan; *b* 16 Dec 1962; *m* 1987 *Shaun Anthony Woodward, MP (C) Witney 1997–, yst s of Dennis Woodward, and has:

1a *Thomas Rory George; *b* 30 June 1989

1a *Eleanor Laura Davan; *b* 31 May 1991

2a *Olivia Mary Victoria; *b* 6 Oct 1993

3a *Katherine Matilda Rose; *b* 20 Sept 1996

(2) *Jessica Mary; *b* 4 March 1970; *m* 12 July 1972 *Peter de Lupis

The BARON SAINSBURY *m* 2nd 12 Sept 1944 Anne Elizabeth (Babette) (*d* 1988), dau of Paul Lewy, of Paris, and by her has:

1*Paulette Ann; *b* 2 March 1946; *m* *James Anderson and has:

(1) *Lindsey (dau)

Lineage: JOHN SAINSBURY, of Blackfriars; *b* 1781; hatter; *m* Sarah — and *d* 6 Oct 1850, leaving:

JOHN SAINSBURY, of Lambeth and Westminster; *b* c 1809; picture-framemaker; *m* Elizabeth Coomb(e)s and *d* 31 Jan 1863, having had, with three daus (Elizabeth Sarah, *b* 23 Oct 1840; Eliza Jane, *b* 13 Dec 1841, *d* unm 24 Dec 1866; Margaret Maria, *b* 17 Dec 1842, *d* 21 May 1846):

JOHN JAMES SAINSBURY; *b* 12 June 1844; opened grocer's in Drury Lane 1869; *m* 20 April 1869 Mary Ann (*d* 9 June 1927), dau of Benjamin Staples, and *d* 3 Jan 1928, leaving:

1 JOHN BENJAMIN

2 George; *b* 12 Oct 1872; *m* 1st 1 June 1898 Rose —; *m* 2nd Rhoda — and *d* 12 April 1964, having by her had:
  (1) *Cecil John
  (2) *Dudley George
  (1) *Irene
  (2) *Doris

3 Frank; *b* 11 Aug 1877; *d* 1955

4 Arthur; *b* 13 April 1880; *m* Winifred MacDonald (*d* 17 April 1976) and *d* 23 May 1962, leaving:
  (1) *James; *b* 18 June 1909
  (1) *Violet Sybil; *b* 3 March 1904
  (2) *Olive; *b* 3 Sept 1906

5 Alfred; *b* 7 March 1884; *m* Violette Dorothy (Dolly) Weldon (*d* 18 April 1976) and *d* 16 April 1965, leaving:
  (1) *(Alfred) Vernon
  (2) *(Ronald) Ivor
  (3) Michael; *d* 1944
  (1) *Valerie

6 Paul James; *b* 5 Dec 1890; *m* Constance Helen (*d* 14 June 1974) and *d* 27 Oct 1982, leaving:
  (1) *(John) Barry
  (1) *(Mary) Patricia
  (2) *Angela Helen

1 Mary Ann; *b* 29 Dec 1869; *d* 27 July 1870

2 Alice; *b* 7 Feb 1876; *m* 6 June 1899 — Symon and had three sons and a dau

3 Louise; *b* 31 Dec 1878; *m* — Hankey and *d* 29 Jan 1925, leaving three sons and two daus

4 Lilian; *b* 30 July 1882; *m* — Weldon and had a s

5 Elsie; *b* 29 April 1885; *d* unm

6 Dorothy Maud; *b* 15 July 1889; *m* 26 April 1929 — Love

The est s,
JOHN BENJAMIN SAINSBURY, of Little Common, Sussex; *b* 8 Jan 1871; chm J Sainsbury Ltd 1928–56; *m* 8 Jan 1896 Mabel Miriam (*d* 1941), dau of Jacob Van Den Bergh, and *d* 23 May 1956, leaving:

1 ALAN JOHN SAINSBURY, **present Baron Sainsbury**

2 *Robert James (Sir); *b* 24 Oct 1906; *educ* Haileybury, and Pembroke Coll Cambridge (MA, Hon Fell 1983); J Sainsbury Ltd: joined 1930, dir 1934, jt gen man 1938, dep chm 1956, chm 1967, jt pres 1969; Govr St Thomas's Hosp 1939–1968, Treas Inst Med Social Workers 1948–71, memb Arts Cncl Art Panel, Tstee Tate Gallery 1959–73 (v-chm 1967, chm 1969), fndr (with w) Sainsbury Centre for Visual Arts UEA 1978, memb management ctee Courtauld Inst 1979–82, pres Br Assoc Friends of Museums 1985–, ktd 1967, ACA 1930, FCA 1935, Hon FRIBA 1986, Hon DrRCA 1976, Hon LittD UEA 1977, Hon LLD Liverpool 1988; *m* 3 March 1937 his 2nd cousin *Lisa Ingeborg Vera, dau of Simon Van Den Bergh, and has had:
  (1) *DAVID JOHN SAINSBURY, BARON SAINSBURY OF TURVILLE (*qv*)
  (1) Elizabeth; *b* 19 July 1938; *m* 5 May 1962 *Roger Clark and *d* 14 Aug 1977, leaving:
    1a *James Jackson; *b* 23 Feb 1964
    2a *Alexander Simon; *b* 25 Feb 1966
  (2) *Cecilia; *b* 30 July 1945; *m* *Conrad C Blakey, only s of G B Blakey, and has:
    1a *Simon
    2a *Michael Robert; *b* 10 July 1975
  (3) *Annabel; *b* 22 Jan 1948

1 Vera Mabel; *b* 22 Dec 1896; *m* 1st Leonard Fletcher, s of Robert Fletcher; *m* 2nd 14 Oct 1938 Maj Charles B Toms and *d* 27 March 1969, leaving by her 1st husb:
  (1) *William John
  (1) *Wendy Mabel

2 Nora

SAINSBURY OF PRESTON CANDOVER

AD·EXCELLENTIAM·CONTENDERE

Arms: Azure on a fess dancetty between three cornucopiae bendwise or, as many lyres gules. **Crest:** A mural crown azure, thereon a leopard sejant proper supporting a corinthian column gold. **Supporters:** On either side rampant upon a cornucopia or a leopard proper, the compartment comprising a grassy mount all proper. **Motto:** *Ad excellentiam contendere* ('Striving for quality'). **Creation:** B. (LP, UK) 1989.

THE BARON SAINSBURY OF PRESTON CANDOVER, of Preston Candover, Co Hants (Sir John Davan Sainsbury, KG (1992)) [The Rt Hon the Lord Sainsbury of Preston Candover KG, Stamford House, Stamford St, London SE1 9LL]; *b* 2 Nov 1927; *educ* Stowe and Worcester Coll Oxford (Hon Fell 1982); dir: J Sainsbury plc 1958–92 (v-chm 1967–69, chm 1969–92, pres 1992–), ROH 1969–85 (Chm 1988–92), Friends of Covent Gdn 1969–81), *The Economist* 1972–80, ROH Tst 1974–84 and 1987–; Chm: Benesh Inst Choreology 1986–87, Dulwich Picture Gallery 1994–, Govrs Royal Ballet 1995– (Govr 1985– and Roy Ballet Sch 1965–76 and 1987–91); Jt Hon Treas European Movement 1972–75, Memb: Cncl Retail Consortium 1975–79, Nat Ctee for Electoral Reform 1976–85, President's Ctee CBI 1982–84; V-Pres Contemporary Arts Soc 1984– (Hon Sec 1965–71, V-Chm 1971–74); Tstee: Nat Gallery 1976–83, Westminster Abbey Tst 1977–83, Tate Gallery 1982–83, Rhodes Tst 1984–98, Prince of Wales Inst Architecture 1992– ; Pres: British Retail Consortium 1993–97, Sparsholt Coll, Hants, 1993– and Stoic Soc; ktd 1980; Hon Bencher Inner Temple 1985, Hon FIGD 1973, Hon DScEcon London 1985, Hon DLitt South Bank U 1992, Hon LLD Bristol 1993, Hon FRIBA 1993, Albert Medal RSA 1989; *m* 8 March 1963 *Anya (Anya Linden, Roy Ballet ballerina), formerly w of Igor Tamarin and dau of George Charles Eltenton, and has:
1 *(John) Julian; *b* 9 March 1966
2 *Mark Leonard; *b* 5 Feb 1969
1 *Sarah Jane; *b* 4 June 1964: *m* 1990 *Robert Joseph Neville Galmoye Butler-Sloss, er s of Hon Mr Justice (Joseph William Alexander) Butler-Sloss

Lineage: *see* SAINSBURY, B

SAINSBURY OF TURVILLE

Creation: B. (LP, UK) 2 Aug 1997.

THE BARON SAINSBURY OF TURVILLE, of Turville, Co Buckingham (David John Sainsbury) [The Rt Hon The Lord Sainsbury of Turville, c/o J Sainsbury plc, Stanford House, Stanford St, London SE1 9LL]; *b* 24 Oct 1940; *educ* King's Coll Cambridge and Columbia U NY; J Sainsbury: joined 1963, fin dir 1973–90, dep chm 1988–92, chm and ch exec 1992–97, chm 1997–98; memb: Ctee Review Post Office 1975–77, Governing Body London Business Sch 1985– (Chm 1991–); Tstee SDP 1982–90; Hon FEng 1994; Hon LLD Cantab 1997; memb IPPR Cmmn Public Policy and Br Business 1995–97; Parly U-Sec DTI 1998–; author: *Government and Industry: a new partnership* (1981), *Wealth Creation and Jobs* (with Christopher Smallwood, 1987); *m* 15 Nov 1973 *Susan Carole, er dau of K M Reid, of Ambleside, Westmorland, and has:
1 *Clare Natasha; *b* 20 Aug 1974
2 *(Anya) Lucy; *b* 12 May 1976
3 *Francesca Elizabeth; *b* 21 May 1978

Lineage: *See* SAINSBURY, B

SAINT ALBANS

AUSPICIUM · MELIORIS · ÆVI

Arms: Quarterly, 1st and 4th grand quarters, the arms of CHARLES II (1st and 4th, France and England, quarterly; 2nd, Scotland; 3rd, Ireland), over all a sinister baton gu., charged with three roses arg., barbed and seeded ppr.; 2nd and 3rd, quarterly gu. and or, in the 1st quarter a mullet arg. (for De VERE). **Crest:** On a chapeau gu. doubled erm. a lion statant guardant or, crowned with a ducal coronet per pale arg. and of the first, gorged with a collar of the last, thereon three roses also arg., barbed and seed ppr.
Supporters: Dexter, an antelope arg., armed and unguled or; sinister, a greyhound arg.; each gorged with a collar, as in the crest.
Motto: *Auspicium melioris ævi* ('A pledge of better times').
Creations: B. (Heddington) and E. (E) 27 Dec 1676, D. (E) 10 Jan 1683/4, B. (Vere of Hanworth) (GB) 28 March 1750.

THE 14TH DUKE OF SAINT ALBANS, Earl of Burford, Co Oxon, **Baron Heddington**, Co Oxon, and **Baron Vere of Hanworth**, Co Middx (Murray de Vere Beauclerk) [His Grace The Duke of Saint Albans, 3 St George's Court, Gloucester Rd, London SW7 4QZ]; *b* 19 Jan 1939; *s f* 1988, also as Hereditary Grand Falconer of England and Hereditary Registrar Court of Chancery; *educ* Tonbridge; chartered accountant 1962, ptnr Burford and Co, Chartered Accountants, 1981–, Freeman City London, Liveryman Drapers' Co 1969, Govr-Gen Roy Stuart Soc 1988–, Pres Beaufort Opera 1991–; *m* 1st 31 Jan 1963 (*divorce* 1974) Rosemary Frances, only dau of Francis Harold Scoones, JP, MRCS, LRCP, of W Kensington; *m* 2nd 29 Aug 1974 *Cynthia Theresa Mary, yst dau of Lt-Col William James Holdsworth Howard, DSO, and formerly w of (a) Henry George Arton, of Canada, and (b) Sir Anthony Robin Maurice Hooper, 2nd Bt (*see* 1970 edn), and by his 1st w has:

1 +CHARLES FRANCIS TOPHAM De VERE, *Earl of Burford* [Earl of Burford, c/o Otley Hall, Otley, nr Ipswich, Suffolk IP6 9PA]; *b* 22 Feb 1965; *educ* Eton, Sherborne, Hertford Coll Oxford (MA) and Edinburgh U; Pres and fndr De Vere Soc, V-Pres Roy Stuart Soc 1989–, Liveryman Drapers' Co 1990; *m* 29 Dec 1994 *Louise Ann Beatrice Fiona, est dau of Col Malcolm Vernon Robey, and has:

  1a +James Malcolm Aubrey Edward de Vere, *Lord Vere of Hanworth*; *b* 2 Aug 1995

1 *Emma Caroline de Vere [The Lady Emma Smellie, 1A Templar St, London SE5 9JB]; *b* 22 July 1963; *educ* Roedean, St John's Coll Cambridge (BA) and UEA; *m* 1991 *David Craig Shaw Smellie, s of Prof (Robert) Martin Stuart Smellie, of Hyndland, Glasgow, and has:

  (1) *Martha Lucy Rose; *b* 5 March 1997

Saint Alban(s), other creations: For the Viscountcy of Saint Alban, *see* BACON, Bt. For the Earldom of Saint Albans extant between 1628 and 1657, *see* SLIGO, M.

In 1660 Henry Jermyn, a younger son of Sir Thomas Jermyn, of Rushbroke, Suffolk, Comptroller of the Household to CHARLES I, was created Earl of St Albans, having been ennobled seventeen years earlier, at the start of the Civil War, as Baron Jermyn of St Edmundsbury (*i.e.,* Bury St Edmunds). He had been Ambassador to France and Holland during the Civil War and eventually ran HENRIETTA MARIA's household in France when she moved there permanently as the Civil War drew to a close. (He was also believed by at least one contemporary gossip to have secretly married her.)

After the Restoration he was again Ambassador to France as well as becoming Lord Chamberlain and a Knight of the Garter. On his death the Earldom expired but his Barony passed to his nephew under a special remainder drawn up at the time of its creation. On the Barony's extinction in 1708 the Jermyn estates passed to the 2nd Baron's daughters, among whom was Mary, wife of Sir Robert Davers, Bt. Their descendant Elizabeth Davers married in 1752 the 4th Earl of Bristol, whose son when promoted to the Marquessate of Bristol (*qv*) accordingly took as a subsidiary title that of Earl Jermyn of Horningsheath, the eldest son and heir of the Marquesses of Bristol being known by the abbreviated courtesy title Earl Jermyn ever since. An earlier link between the two families may have existed in that the 2nd Baron Jermyn of St Edmundsbury is sometimes said to have married

as his first wife a daughter of Sir William Hervey (or indeed Sir Thomas Hervey, though this latter is certainly mistaken).

Lineage (of Beauclerk): CHARLES II had illegitimately by Eleanor ('Nell') Gwynn (*d* 14 Nov 1687 aged 37, when allegedly on the point of being *cr* Countess of Greenwich), Ldy of QUEEN CATHERINE's Privy Chamber 1675, 2nd dau of Thomas Gwyn(e) by Eleanor/Helena, with a yr s (James, *Lord Beauclaire* (so designated by roy warrant 17 Jan 1676/7, with rank of an earl's est s), *b* 25 Dec 1671, *d* Sept 1680):

CHARLES BEAUCLERK, **1st Duke of Saint Albans**, so *cr* 10 Jan 1683/4, as also earlier 27 Dec 1676 BARON HEDDINGTON, Co Oxon, and EARL OF BURFORD, Co Oxon, with in the last two cases only remainder, failing male issue of his own body, to his bro, KG (1718); *b* 8 May 1670; Ch Ranger of Enfield Chase 1684, Hereditary Grand Falconer Jan 1684/5, Col 8th Horse 1687, served Imp Army at capture Belgrade 1688, also against French in Low Countries 1693, when present at Battle of Neerwinden, Capt Gentlemen Pensioners 1693–Jan 1711/2 and 1714–26, a Ld Bedchamber 1697–1702, Hereditary Registrar Court of Chancery 1698, Ld Lt Berks 1714–26, Freeman and High Steward Windsor 1716, High Steward Wokingham 1718, FRS 1722; *m* 17 April 1694 Lady Diana de Vere (*d* 15 Jan 1741/2), 1st Ldy of Bedchamber and Lady of the Stole to GEORGE I's w CAROLINE, est dau and eventually sole heiress of 20th and last Earl of Oxford (*see* **Lineage (of de Vere)** below), and *d* 11 May 1726, having had:

1 CHARLES BEAUCLERK, **2nd Duke of Saint Albans**, KG (1741), KB (1725); *b* 6 April 1696; *educ* Eton and New Coll Oxford; MP Bodmin (Whig) 1718–22 and Windsor 1722–26, Freeman Windsor 1722, Ld Lt Berks 1727–51, Constable and Govr Windsor Castle and Ld Warden Windsor Forest 1730–51, a Ld Bedchamber 1738–51, High Steward Windsor 1728; *m* 13 Dec 1722 Lucy (*d* 12 Nov 1752), est dau and coheir of Sir John Werden, 2nd and last Bt, of Cholmeaton, Cheshire, Leyland, Lancs, and Holyport, Berks, and *d* 27 July 1751, leaving:

  (1) GEORGE BEAUCLERK, **3rd Duke of Saint Albans**; *b* 25 June 1730; *educ* Eton; Ld Lt Berks 1751–60 and 1771–86, a Ld Bedchamber 1751, High Steward Windsor 1751; *m* 23 Dec 1752 Jane (*d* 16 Dec 1778), dau and coheir of Sir Walter Roberts, 6th Bt, of Glassenbury Park, Kent (*see* ROBERTS, Bt, of Glassenbury, Kent, Brightfieldstown, Co Cork, and City of Cork), and *dspl* 1 Feb 1786, having had illegitimately (at least one dau being his cook, according to Horace Walpole):

    1a A son; *b* 1748; *d* 30 Jan 1759

    2a George; *b* 20 Dec 1755; *bur* 11 Oct 1756

    3a A son; *b* Sept 1757; *d* Feb 1758

    1a Anne-Amelie; *b* 5 Dec 1756; *m* Simon Froment, of Brussels (*d* 20 Oct 1823), and *d* 3 Nov 1826

    2a (Mariette-Victoire-)Rosé; *b* 1 Dec 1758; *m* after 1785 Huberti Offhus, Brussels advocate, and had:

      1b Anne Amelie; *b* 1 Aug 1787

    3a Marie-Agnes; *b* 1 Dec 1758

  (1) Diana; *b* 20 Oct 1725; *m* 2 Feb 1761 Rt Rev Hon Shute Barrington, DD, DCL, Bp Durham, 5th s of 1st Viscount Barrington (*d* 25 March 1826; *see* 1970 edn), and *dsp* 28 May 1766

2 William; *b* 22 May 1698; *educ* Eton; Capt RHG, MP Chichester, V-Chamberlain Household 1728; *m* 13 Dec 1722 Charlotte (*d* 3 July 1770), 2nd dau and coheir of Sir John Werden, 2nd and last Bt, of Cholmeaton, Cheshire, Leyland, Lancs, and Holyport, Berks, and *d* 23 Feb 1732/3, leaving:

  (1) William; *b* 26 May 1726; *educ* Eton; *d* 28 Nov 1738

  (2) Charles; served 107th Foot, Page of Honour to DUKE OF CUMBERLAND 1740, Lt-Col 3rd Foot Gds 1761, Govr Pendennis Castle; *m* Elizabeth Jones (*d* 5 Dec 1768) and *d* 30 Aug 1775, leaving:

    1a GEORGE BEAUCLERK, **4th Duke of Saint Albans**; *b* 5 Dec 1758; Ensign 3rd Foot Gds 1775 (Capt-Lt 1778, Lt-Col 3rd 1786), served War American Independence; *d unm* 10 Feb 1787

  (1) Charlotte; *m* 22 Dec 1744 John Drummond and *d* 7 March 1793, leaving issue (*see* PERTH, E)

  (2) Caroline; *m* 23 Feb 1756 Maj-Gen Sir William Draper, KB (*d* 8 Jan 1787), and *dsp* 1778

3 VERE BEAUCLERK, **1st Baron Vere of Hanworth**, Co Middx (GB), so *cr* 28 March 1750; *b* 14 July 1699; RN: Capt 1721, Commr Navy 1732, a Ld of Admlty 1738–42 and 1744–49, R-Adml the Red 1745, V-Adml the Blue 1746, Adml the Blue 1748, ret 1749, MP (Whig) Windsor 1726–41 and Plymouth 1741–50, Ld Lt Berks 1761–71; *m* 13 April 1736 Mary (*d* 21 Jan 1783), er dau and coheir of Thomas Chambers (*see* BERKELEY, B), and *d* 21 Oct 1781, having had:

  (1) Vere; *b* 12 Jan 1736/7; *d* 26 Dec 1739

  (2) Chambers; *b* 22 Feb 1737/8; *educ* Westminster; *d* 16 July 1747

  (3) Sackville; *b* 12 April 1739; *bur* 25 April 1739

  (4) AUBREY, **5th Duke**

  (1) Elizabeth; *b* July 1742; *bur* 26 April 1746

  (2) Mary; *b* 4 Dec 1743; *m* 2 Oct 1762 Lord Charles Spencer (*see* MARLBOROUGH, D) and *d* 13 Jan 1812, leaving issue

4 Henry, of Foliejon Park, Winkfield, Berks, which he bought 1744, and Somerset House, London; *b* 11 Aug 1701; served 59th Foot (present Siege Gibraltar 1727), Col 31st Foot 1739, MP Plymouth 1740–41 and Thetford 1751–61; *m* 1st 21 April 1729 — (*dsp*), dau of Governor — Philips, of Stanwell, Middx; *m* 2nd 25 June 1739 Martha (*d* 5 March 1788), a Maid of Honour to QUEEN CAROLINE 1732, dau of 4th Baron Lovelace of Hurley (*see* LOVELACE, E, preliminary remarks), and *d* 5 Jan 1761, having by her had:

  (1) George; *b* 18 March 1739/40; *d* young

  (2) Henry (Rev); *b* 12 Aug 1745; *educ* Eton and Ch Ch Oxford (BA 1767, MA 1769); Ld Manor Leckhampstead, Bucks (as which s mother), Rector Greens Norton, Northants, and St Mary Somerset, London; *m* 23 Nov 1769 his 1st cousin once-removed Charlotte (*d* 20 March 1774), dau of John Drummond (*see* above), and *d* 8 Nov 1817, having had, with other issue:

    1a Henry; *bapt* 6 Sept 1770; *d* young

    2a John, of Leckhampstead and London; *b* 10 Feb 1772; *educ* Eton and Ch Ch Oxford (BA 1793, MA 1796); barrister Middle Temple 1793, Ld Manor and Patron Living Leckhampstead; *m* 14 Aug 1798 Mary, est dau of Thomas Fitzhugh, of Plâs Power, Denbighs, and Portland Place, London, and *d* 8 Jan 1840, leaving:

1b Henry William; *b* 15 Nov 1812; *educ* Harrow; Ld Manor and Patron Living Leckhampstead; *m* 1st 21 May 1838 Lady Katherine Frances Ashburnham (*d* 6 April 1839), 7th dau of 3rd Earl of Ashburnham, KG (*see* 1924 edn), and had:

1c Katherine Mary; *b* 19 March 1839; *m* 1 Aug 1864 Rev Sir Frederick Boyd, 6th and last Bt (*d* 13 Feb 1889), and *d* 3 Aug 1867, leaving a dau

1b (cont.) Henry Beauclerk *m* 2nd 11 Aug 1840 Louisa (*dsp* 28 Dec 1882), 3rd dau of Sir George Wombwell, 2nd Bt (*qv*), and *d* 8 June 1894

1b Charlotte Mary; *b* 21 May 1801; *d* unm 7 May 1852

2b Catharine; *b* 10 Sept 1814; *d* unm

(1) Diana; *b* 24 Jan 1741; Maid of Honour to QUEEN CHARLOTTE; *d* unm 13 Feb 1809

(2) Henrietta; *b* 26 Nov 1742

(3) Mary; *b* 25 Nov 1743; *m* Rev Walter Williams, Rector Harrow

(4) Charlotte; *b* 24 Oct 1746

(5) Martha; *b* 12 Dec 1747

(6) Anne; *b* 5 Oct 1749; *m* 23 May 1794 Rev George Talbot, bro of 1st Earl Talbot (*see* SHREWSBURY and WATERFORD, E), and *dsp* 1809

5 Sidney, PC (1740), of Windsor, Berks; *b* 27 Feb 1703; *educ* Eton and Trin Coll Oxford (MA 1727, DCL 1733); V-Chamberlain Household 1740–42, MP Windsor 1733–34, Tstee and Common Cllr Georgia Soc 1739, Master Harriers 1738; *m* 9 Dec 1736 Mary (*d* 20 Nov 1766), dau and heir of Thomas Norris, MP, of Speke Hall, Lancs, High Sheriff Lancs 1696, and *d* 23 Nov 1744, leaving:

(1) Topham (so named after Richard Topham, MP, whose estates his f had inherited), of Clewer Manor, Berks, Speke Hall, Lancs, and Great Russell St, Bloomsbury; *b* Dec 1739; *educ* Eton and Trin Coll Oxford; bibliophile, the friend of Dr Johnson; *m* 12 March 1768 Diana (*d* 1 Aug 1808), er dau of 3rd Duke of Marlborough (*qv*) and formerly w of 2nd Viscount Bolingbroke and (3rd Viscount) Saint John (*qv*), and *d* 11 March 1780, leaving:

1a Charles George, of St Leonards Lodge, Horsham, Sussex, which he bought 1801 having sold Speke 1797; *b* 20 Jan 1774; *educ* Ch Ch Oxford; MP Richmond 1796–98; *m* 29 April 1799 Emily Charlotte (*d* 22 Jan 1832), 2nd dau of William Ogilvie, of Ardglass Castle, Co Down (*see* RICHMOND and GORDON, D), and *d* 25 Dec 1845, having had:

1b Aubrey William, of Ardglass Castle and St Leonards Lodge; *b* 20 Feb 1801; Maj 99th Foot 1826, MP E Surrey 1832–37; *m* 1st 13 Feb 1834 Ida (*d* 23 April 1838), 4th dau of Sir Charles Foster Goring, 7th Bt (*qv*), and had:

1c Aubrey de Vere, of Ardglass Castle and Mayfair, JP Co Down; *b* 5 Oct 1837; *educ* Rugby, Cheltenham and Trin Coll Cambridge; High Sheriff Co Down 1863; *m* 1st 1 Dec 1858 (*divorce* 1895) his cousin Evelyn Georgiana Matilda (*d* 10 Jan 1931), 3rd dau of Henry FitzRoy (*see* GRAFTON, D), and had:

1d Sidney de Vere; *b* 8 May 1866; *educ* Eton and Trin Coll Cambridge (BA 1887); *d* unm 4 July 1903

1c (cont.) Aubrey de Vere Beauclerk *m* 2nd 16 Nov 1895 Katherine Lucy (*d* 23 Jan 1910), widow of Capt J Collier Tucker, RN, and *d* 9 July 1919

1c Ida; *b* 29 Jan 1835; *d* 1844

2c Diana Arabella; *b* 1836; *d* unm 26 May 1855

3c Augusta; *b* 1838; *m* 4 Jan 1866 Thomas Edward Howe, barrister, and had four sons and two daus

1b (cont.) Aubrey William Beauclerk *m* 2nd 7 Dec 1841 Rose Matilda (*d* 20 July 1878), dau of Joshua Robinson, and *d* 1 Feb 1854, having by her had:

4c Louisa Katherine, of Millbeck Cottage, Keswick, Cumberland; *d* unm 1929

5c Isabella Julia; *m* 19 Oct 1867 Surgn-Maj Chevalier George Albert Palatiano, MD (*d* 1910), of Corfu, and *d* 13 March 1930, leaving a s and two daus

1b (cont.) Aubrey William Beauclerk also had illegitimately:

2c Charles (Rev); *b* c 1823/4; Army Capt, Deacon 1860, Curate Saintfield, Co Down, 1860, Priest 1861, Perpetual Curate Dunsverick, Co Antrim, 1861–66 and Glencraig, Co Down, 1866–69, Vicar St Mary's, Belfast, 1869–75, Chaplain Holy Trinity Ch Boulogne 1875; *m* 8 Nov 1860 Elizabeth Maria (*d* 30 April 1888), 4th dau of Rev Henry Murphy, and *d* 27 Jan 1880, having had, with other issue (five of whom *d* in infancy):

1d Henry Wyndham; *b* 14 Dec 1869; *educ* Merchant Taylors'; settled in Canada 1906, with Canadian Pacific Rlwy, dir Bank of Montreal and Brompton Pulp and Paper Co; *m* 3 June 1911 Hon Alice Josephine (*d* 1963), est dau of 1st Baron Shaughnessy (*qv*), and *d* Jan 1937, leaving:

1e *Thomas

1e *Audrey

2d Ernest Octavius; *b* 22 Feb 1871; *educ* Clergy Orphans Sch Canterbury; artist, settled USA, served Boer War

3d Aubrey; settled USA; had a s and dau

4d Herbert Charles; *b* 7 Sept 1875; *educ* Clergy Orphans Sch Canterbury; with Merchant Navy; settled S Africa; had:

1e Wyndham, of Natal; living 1952

1d Amy Louisa; *b* 21 Oct 1861; *m* 1st — Bult, of S Africa; *m* 2nd Dr Edward Bromet, of Denewood Grange, Batheaston, Somerset, and *dsp* 1940

2d Frances Maude; *b* 30 April 1863; *m* Lt-Col William Henry Oliphert Kemmis, JP, DL, of Ballinacor, Co Wicklow, and Somerleaze Selwood, Somerset, High Sheriff Co Wicklow 1904, s of Col William Kemmis, JP, DL, of Clopoke, and *d* Feb 1941, leaving issue. He *d* 18 Dec 1939

3d Florence Elizabeth; *b* 1866; *m* 1891 Richard Garrett, of Leiston, Suffolk, and *d* 1954, leaving a s and (by Charlotte Bury) a dau (Charlotte Jane, *b* 1830, *d* unm Jan 1855)

2b Charles Robert, of St Leonards Lodge and London; *b* 6 Jan 1802; *educ* Halnaker, Sussex, and Gonville and Caius Coll Cambridge (BA 1823, MA 1827, Fell 1822–42); barrister Lincoln's Inn 1829; *m* March 1842 Joaquina (*d* 16 Nov 1881), 2nd dau of Don José M de Zamora, Ch Magistrate Cuba, and *d* 22 Feb 1872, having had:

1c Sidney Joseph; *b* 22 Dec 1848; *d* 7 Aug 1851

2c Ferdinand, of Dibden, Hants; *b* 15 Jan 1851; Capt RE, Maj cmdg Lakhimpur Vol Rifles, Afghan War 1879 (medal), WW I with Sussex Vol Training Corps, Pres W India Industl Assoc; Guardian, Tstee and Sec to Salar Jung Minors and Estates Hyderabad; *m* 9 Feb 1872 Emily Johanna Frances (*d* 1 Feb 1916), yst dau of Col Robert Clifford Lloyd, 68th Regt, and *dsp* 3 May 1920, having adopted:

Helen Mary Dorothea (actual dau of Maj Sydney Edwin Bellingham; *see* BELLINGHAM, Bt); novelist; *d* unm 8 July 1969

3c Charles Sidney (Rev), SJ; *b* 1 Jan 1855; *educ* Beaumont and Stonyhurst; ordained 1888, Rector Holywell Flints 1890–98, helped restore St Winefride's Well as RC shrine, also served at Boscombe, Roehampton, Malta, Clitheroe, Richmond and Accrington; *d* unm 22 Dec 1934

4c Henry Sidney (Rev), SJ; *b* 25 Nov 1857; *educ* Beaumont, and Stonyhurst; ordained 1890, missionary Barbados, British Guiana, Jamaica and Maryland, Vicar-Gen to Bp Galton and Superior SJ Guiana and Barbados; *d* unm 30 Sept 1909

5c Robert Sidney de Vere; *b* 14 Dec 1858; *educ* Beaumont; Headmaster Kenilworth Sch Cape Town, author: *Summary of English History to 1802*; *m* 30 Oct 1894 Beatrice Annie Elliot (*d* 14 Oct 1947), 2nd dau of Arthur Richard Holebone, and *d* 26 March 1934, having had:

1d Nevill Alfred de Vere; *b* 13 Oct 1895; T/2nd Lt 12th Bn Essex Regt; *ka* 17 June 1915

6c William Topham Sidney; *b* 3 July 1864; *educ* Beaumont; engr in Argentina; *m* 17 Dec 1910 Lola, Countess de Peñalver (*d* 9 Sept 1972), only surv child of Enrique, Count de Peñalver and Marqués de Arcos, in Spain, and *d* 5 May 1950, having had:

1d William Nicholas; *b* 12 June 1912; *educ* Beaumont; *d* unm 10 May 1948

2d Henry Topham; *b* 19 Nov 1913; *d* 7 March 1929

3d +Raphael Charles (Ralph), Marqués de Urria (Spain), MBE (1945) [Ralph Beauclerk Esq MBE, 20 Sunnyside, London SW19 4SH]; *b* 10 Aug 1917; *educ* Downside and in France; Capt Intell Corps attd SOE WW II (Croix de Guerre), with Hongkong and Shanghai Banking Corp to 1970 and Banque Privée Luxembourg to 1974; *m* 24 Aug 1957 Noirine Mary (*d* Jan 1997), est dau of James Bowen, of Bowen's Cross, Co Cork, and has:

1e +William Raphael [William Beauclerk Esq, 15 rue de Breteuil, 78670 Medan, France]; *b* 14 Aug 1961; *educ* Worth; Lt RN (ret), served in HMY *Britannia*; ARICS; *m* 1986 *Margaret Eleanor, dau of Lesley James Mountjoy, of Totteridge, London, and has:

1f +Alexander Charles; *b* 11 Feb 1990

2f +Cameron; *b* 25 March 1993

1f *Charlotte; *b* 24 July 1987

1e *Dolores Mary [Mrs Richard Makower, 6 Lache Lane, Chester CH4 7LR]; *b* 11 July 1958; SRN; *m* 1981 *Dr Richard M Makower, s of C S Makower, MC, and has:

1f *Timothy; *b* 27 Aug 1984

2f *Oliver William; *b* 12 March 1992

1f *Emily Elizabeth; *b* 11 March 1987

1d *Diana Mary Ildefonsa [Miss Diana Beauclerk, Villa Etchè Biskiak, 9 Ave des Chênes, Biarritz, France; *b* 1 May 1924; WRNS WW II

1c Mary; *b* 17 April 1861; *d* unm 17 Oct 1920

3b George Robert, of King's Castle, Ardglass, Co Down; *b* 28 Feb 1803; Capt 23rd Regt Roy Welch Fus, author *Beauclerk's Journey to Morocco*; *m* 2 June 1861 Maria Sarah (*d* 18 Oct 1923), yr dau of Ralph Lonsdale, and *d* 5 Dec 1871, having had:

1c Amelius George de Vere, of Stanway, Essex; *b* 1 Oct 1871; Lt 1st Vol Bn Suffolk Regt WW I; *m* 26 Aug 1918 Marguerite Olive Claire (Margot) (*d* 27 March 1978), dau of Louis Antoine Bertrand, of Matfield, Kent, and *d* 26 Aug 1939, leaving:

1d Anthony Amelius de Vere; *b* 6 July 1920; *educ* Bryanston; *d* unm 10 May 1962

1c Georgiana; *b* 10 July 1862; *d* unm 10 May 1942

2c Caroline Elizabeth; *b* 12 June 1865; *m* 24 April 1895 Rev Alfred Norris Cope, Vicar Dormington with Bartestree, Herefs, and *dsp* 8 Nov 1952. He *d* 4 Sept 1936

3c Emily Kathleen; *b* 25 Jan 1867; *m* 26 Dec 1917 George Duguay, of Ryde, IoW, and *dsp* 16 April 1953. He *d* 10 May 1944

4c Ida; *b* 7 June 1869; *m* 30 July 1891 George Francis Berney, of Croydon, Surrey, and *d* 5 Aug 1955, leaving two sons and two daus. He *d* 3 March 1931

4b Amelius; *b* 1809

5b Ferdinand; *b* 1811; Actg Cornet Bengal Light Cav; *d* unm 5 Oct 1829

6b Augustus; *b* 1813

1b Emily Frederica; *b* 1 March 1800; *d* 16 Sept 1816

2b Caroline Anne; *b* 12 Jan 1804; *m* 20 Oct 1829 Robert Aldridge, JP, DL, of New Lodge, Horsham, only s of Capt John Aldridge, MP, and *d* 11 Sept 1869, leaving issue. He *d* 26 May 1871

3b Georgiana; *b* 1805; *m* 10 Oct 1826 Sir John Dean Paul, 2nd Bt (*see* 1967 edn), and *d* 25 Dec 1847, leaving issue. He *d* 7 Sept 1868

4b Diana Olivia; *b* 21 June 1806; *m* 10 April 1823 Sir Francis Fletcher-Vane, 3rd Bt (*see* 1934 edn), and *d* 9 Feb 1875, leaving issue. He *d* 15 Feb 1842

5b Jane Elizabeth; *b* 1807; *m* 24 July 1830 Henry FitzRoy, JP and *d* 15 July 1892, leaving issue (*see* above and GRAFTON, D)

6b Isabella Elizabeth; *b* 10 Oct 1808; *m* 12 March 1840 Adml John William Montagu and *d* 21 July 1864, leaving issue (*see* MANCHESTER, D)

7b Katherine Katinka; *b* May 1812; *m* 5 April 1845 Sir George Ashley Maude, KCB, and *d* 2 June 1882, leaving issue (*see* HAWARDEN, V)

1a Mary; *b* 20 Aug 1766; *m* Count Jenison Walworth (*d* 1824), of Heidelberg, Grand Chamberlain of Household to King of Württemberg, est s of Francis Jenison, of Walworth, Co Durham, and had two sons and four daus

2a Elizabeth; *b* 20 Aug 1766; *m* 8 April 1787 her 1st cousin 11th Earl of Pembroke and (8th Earl of) Montgomery (*qv*) and *d* 25 March 1793, leaving issue

3a Anne Charlotte; *d* unm

(1) Charlotte; *d* unm

6 George, of Winchfield Ho, Hants, which he bought 1767; *b* 26 Dec 1704; Capt 1st Foot 1736, MP Windsor 1744, ADC to GEORGE II 1745, Col 8th Marines 1745–48, Col 19th Foot 1748, Lt-Govr Gibraltar 1753, Govr Landguard Fort Suffolk 1753, Maj-Gen 1755, Lt-Gen and C-in-C Scotland 1758, memb Roy Co Archers 1761, Ld Manor Winchfield; *m* Margaret (*d* 23 Oct 1792), dau of Thomas Bainbridge of Slale, Northumberland and *dsp* 11 May 1768

7 Seymour; *b* 24 June, *d* 1 July 1708

8 James (Rt Rev); *b* 1709; *educ* Queen's Coll Oxford (BA 1730, MA 1733, DD 1744); Preb Windsor 1733, Canon Windsor 1738, Chaplain in Ordinary to GEORGE II 1739, Dep Clerk Closet 1744, Bp Hereford 1746–87; *d* unm 20 Oct 1787

9 Aubrey; *b* 1711; RN: joined 1723, Capt: HMS *Ludlow* 1731, HMS *Dolphin* 1736, HMS *Weymouth* 1740 and HMS *Prince Frederick* 1740; *m* Catherine (*dsp* 27 Oct 1755), widow of Col Francis Alexander and dau of Sir Henry Newton, Envoy Tuscany and Genoa and an Admlty Judge, and was *ka* Battle of Cartagena 24 Feb 1740

1 Diana; *b* 1697; *d* unm after 1743

2 Mary *b* 1713; *d* unm

3 Anne; *b* 1716; *d* unm

The 4th DUKE's first cousin once-removed,

AUBREY BEAUCLERK, **5th Duke of Saint Albans**, as which *s* cousin, and **2nd Baron Vere of Hanworth**, as which *s* f 1781; *b* 3 June 1740; *educ* Westminster and Queen's Coll Oxford; MP (Whig) Thetford 1761–68 and Aldborough, Yorks, 1768–74; *m* 4 May 1763 Lady Catherine Ponsonby (*d* 4 Sept 1789), dau of 2nd Earl of Bessborough (*qv*), and *d* 9 Feb 1802, having had:

1 AUBREY BEAUCLERK, **6th Duke of Saint Albans**; *b* 21 Aug 1765; joined Foot Gds 1781, 34th Foot: Capt 1783, Lt-Col 1789, MP (Whig to 1794, Pittite thereafter, though Whig once again when a peer) Kingston-upon-Hull 1790–96; *m* 1st 9 July 1788 Jane (*dspm* 18 Aug 1800), dau of John Moses, of Hull, and had:

(1) Mary; *m* 6 Nov 1811 8th Earl of Coventry (*qv*) and *d* 11 Sept 1845, leaving issue

1 (cont.) The **6th Duke** *m* 2nd 15 Aug 1802 Grace Louisa Manners (*d* 19 Feb 1816), 4th dau of John Manners (*see* RUTLAND, D), and *d* 12 Aug 1815, leaving by her:

(1) AUBREY BEAUCLERK, **7th Duke of Saint Albans**; *b* 7 April 1815; *d* 19 Feb 1816 (three hours before his mother)

2 WILLIAM BEAUCLERK, **8th Duke of Saint Albans**; *b* 18 Dec 1766; RN: Midshipman 1782, Lt 1788, Cdr 1822, High Sheriff Denbighs 1803, Lincs 1808; *m* 1st 20 July 1791 Charlotte (*d* 19 Oct 1797), dau and heir of Rev Robert Carter Thelwall, of Redbourne Hall, Lincs, by Charlotte, dau of Sir John Nelthorpe, 5th Bt (*see* 1865 edn), and had a s (William Robert; *bapt* 11 May, *bur* 13 May 1794); *m* 2nd 4 March 1799 Maria Janetta (*d* 17 Jan 1822), only dau and heir of John Nelthorpe, of Little Grimsby Hall, Lincs, High Sheriff Lincs 1775, by Mary, 2nd dau of Robert Cracroft, of Hackthorn, and *d* 17 July 1825, having by her had (with a dau Julia *b* and *d* 1805):

(1) WILLIAM AUBREY DE VERE BEAUCLERK, **9th Duke of Saint Albans**; *b* 24 March 1801; *educ* Christ's Coll Cambridge (Hon LLD 1828); *m* 1st 16 June 1827 Harriot (*dsp* 6 Aug 1837), widow of Thomas Coutts, the banker, and dau of Matthew Mellon, Lt Madras Inf; *m* 2nd 29 May 1839 Elizabeth Catherine (*m* 2nd 10 Nov 1859 10th Viscount Falkland (*qv*) and *d* 2 Dec 1893), yst dau of Maj-Gen Joseph Gubbins, of Stoneham, Hants, and Kilfrush, Co Limerick, and *d* 27 May 1849, having by her had:

1a WILLIAM AMELIUS AUBREY DE VERE BEAUCLERK, **10th Duke of Saint Albans**, PC (1869), DL (Lincs 1860); *b* 15 April 1840; *educ* Eton and Trin Coll Cambridge; Hon Col 1st Notts (Robin Hood) Rifle Vols 1868, Capt Yeoman Gd 1868–74, Ld Lt Notts 1880–98, author: *Life of R B Osborne* (his f-in-law); *m* 1st 20 June 1867 Sybil Mary (*d* 7 Sept 1871), est dau of Lt-Gen Hon Charles Grey (*see* GREY, E), and had:

1b CHARLES VICTOR ALBERT AUBREY DE VERE BEAUCLERK, **11th Duke of Saint Albans**; *b* 26 March 1870 (HM QUEEN VICTORIA and HRH THE PRINCE OF WALES (later EDWARD VII) stood sponsor); *educ* Eton; 2nd Lt 1st Life Gds 1893, Capt S Notts Yeo 1898–1900, Lt 3rd Bn Roy Scots (Lothian) Regt; *d* unm 19 Sept 1934

1b Louise de Vere; *b* 12 April 1869 (HRH PRINCESS LOUISE DUCHESS OF ARGYLL stood sponsor); *m* 25 Oct 1890 1st Baron Wakehurst (*qv*) and *d* 15 Dec 1958, leaving issue

2b Sybil Evelyn de Vere; *b* 21 Aug 1871; *m* 4 Nov 1899 Maj William Frank Lascelles and *d* 20 Sept 1910, leaving issue (*see* HAREWOOD, E)

1a (cont.) The **10th Duke** *m* 2nd 3 Jan 1874 Grace (*d* 18 Nov 1926), dau and coheir of Ralph Bernal-Osborne, MP (*see* OSBORNE, Bt), and *d* 10 May 1898, having by her had:

2b OSBORNE DE VERE BEAUCLERK, **12th Duke of Saint Albans**, DL Co Waterford; *b* 16 Oct 1874; *educ* Eton; High Sheriff Waterford 1920, 17th Lancers Boer War 1899–02 (Capt 1901, despatches), ADC to FM 1st Earl Haig (*qv*) WW I; *m* 19 Aug 1918 Lady Beatrix Frances, GBE (1919), DGStJ (*d* 5 Aug 1953), widow of 6th Marquess of Waterford (*qv*) and 2nd dau of 5th Marquess of Lansdowne (*qv*), and *dsp* 2 March 1964

3b William Huddleston de Vere; *b* 16 Aug 1883; *educ* Eton; *d* unm 25 Dec 1954

3b Moyra de Vere; *b* 20 Jan 1876; *m* 30 July 1895 Lord Richard Frederick Cavendish (*see* DEVONSHIRE, D) and *d* 7 Feb 1942, leaving issue

4b Katherine de Vere; *b* 25 May 1877; *m* 1st 23 Jan 1896 (*divorce* 1920) Henry Charles Augustus Somers Somerset and had issue (*see* BEAUFORT, D); *m* 2nd 22 April 1921 Maj-Gen Sir William Lambton, KCB, CMG, CVO, DSO (*see* DURHAM, E), and *d* 1 Feb 1958

5b Alexandra de Vere; *b* 5 July 1878; *d* unm 16 April 1935

1a Diana de Vere; *b* 10 Dec 1842; *m* 18 Dec 1872 Hon Sir John Walter Huddleston, QC, MP, of The Grange, Ascot, Berks, last Baron Exchequer of Supreme Court, yst s of T Huddleston, RA, and *dsp* 1 April 1905. He *d* 5 Dec 1890

2a Charlotte

(2) John Nelthorpe; *b* 3 Dec 1805; *bur* 4 Aug 1810

(3) Frederick Charles Peter, of Little Grimsby Hall, JP Lincs; *b* 29 June 1808; *educ* RNC; Ld Manor and Patron Living Little Grimsby, RN: Midshipman 1823 (present Battle of Navarinoin HMS *Asia*), Cdr 1834, Capt 1856; *m* 16 Feb 1848 Jemima Eleanora (*d* 14 Oct 1877), 6th dau of James Raymond Johnstone of Alva (*see* JOHNSTONE, Bt), and *d* 17 Nov 1865, leaving:

1a William Nelthorpe, of Little Grimsby Hall, JP, DL (Parts of Lindsey); *b* 7 April 1849; *educ* Eton, Cheltenham and Trin Coll Cambridge (BA 1872, LLM 1875, LLD 1888); Ld Manor and Patron Living Little Grimsby, Envoy Extrdy and Min Plen Peru, Ecuador and Bolivia 1906 on, author: *Rural Italy* (1888); *m* 1st 27 April 1878 Jane Isabella (*d* 3 Jan 1888), 2nd dau of Rev James Rathborne, Rector W Tytherley, Hants, and had:

1b Aubrey Nelthorpe, of Little Grimsby Hall; *b* 24 March 1879; *educ* RMC Sandhurst; Ld Manor and Patron Living Little Grimsby, Maj N Staffs (POW's) Regt India 1911; *m* 21 Feb 1911 Vera Eileen May (*d* 4 April 1975, having *m* 2nd 29 April 1919 Capt Gerald Andrew Greig, Roy Scots Fus), only dau of Capt William Holcombe Francis, Glos Regt, and *d* 22 April 1916, leaving:

1c *Daphne Diana de Vere [Countess Claude Chauvin de Précourt, Kennards, Amberley, W Sussex]; *b* 26 Dec 1911; *m* 19 April 1933 Count Claude Antoine Chauvin de Précourt (*d* 5 Sept 1971), s of Count Charles Leschevin de Précourt, and has:

1d *François Charles Christian [Count François Chauvin de Précourt, 36 rue de la Résistance, 78150 Le Chesnay, France]; *b* 22 Feb 1936; *educ* Ecole St Martin France; late Lt (Cav) French Army; *m* 5 May 1962 *Sabine, dau of Count de Vautibault, and has:

1e *Claude Henri Aubrey; *b* 29 May 1963

2e *Rémy François Xavier; *b* 6 March 1972

1e *Ghislaine; *b* 15 Nov 1967; *m* 27 April 1991 *Jean du Puytison, of Versailles, and has

2d *Philippe Etienne [Count Philippe Chauvin de Précourt, 27 rue Borgnis Desbordes, 78000 Versailles, France]; *b* 19 Oct 1938; *educ* Ecole des Roches; ESSEC, Lt (Res Inf) French Army; *m* 1st 12 July 1961 Marie Noelle (*d* 17 Oct 1989), dau of (Gerard) René Gasquet, of Neuilly-sur-Seine; *m* 2nd 1992 *Catherine, dau of Robert Treppier, of Paris, and by his 1st w has:

1e *Aude Emilie; *b* 28 Jan 1962; *m* 20 May 1989 *Count Geoffrey de Monteynard, s of Count Jean de Monteynard, of Versailles, and has issue

2e *Laure Sabine Pierrette; *b* 23 Jan 1963; *m* 25 Nov 1995 *Dr Thierry Hano, of Versailles, and has issue

3e *Clarisse Agnes; *b* 20 Feb 1966; *m* 13 July 1991 *Nicolas Demont, of Versailles, and has issue

4e *Marguerite; *b* 21 May 1972; *m* 2 Sept 1995 *Baron Frédéric de Ravinel, of Sigy, France

3d *Jean Yves Xavier [Count Jean Chauvin de Précourt, Le Bouscatel, 30450 Ponteils Bresis, France]; *b* 31 May 1943; *educ* Ecole des Roches; Sub-Lt French Navy; *m* 1 Feb 1970 *Nathalie, dau of Dr — Dubel, and has:

1e *Blaise; *b* 1962

2e *Jerémie Adrian; *b* 1978

1e *Penelope; *b* 30 May 1971

1d *Anne Victoria; *b* 13 Dec 1944; *m* 20 July 1986 *Nigel Foxell

2c Hermione de Vere; *b* 30 Nov 1915; *m* 1 Oct 1939 James Dewar, MBE, GM (*d* 12 May 1983), AEA, FCA, F/Lt RAFVR, only s of James Evan Dewar, of Putney, and *d* 5 Nov 1969, having had:

1d A son; *b* and *d* 25 Oct 1940

2d *Peter de Vere DEWAR later BEAUCLERK-DEWAR (as which recognised by Lord Lyon Office 26 Oct 1965), RD (1980) and bar (1990), JP (Inner London) [Lt-Cdr Peter Beauclerk-Dewar RD JP RNR, 22 Faroe Rd, London W14 0EP]; *b* 19 Feb 1943; *educ* Ampleforth; Lt-Cdr RNR, memb Roy Co Archers Falkland Pursuivant Extrdy 1975, 1982, 1984, 1986, 1987, 1991, 1994, 1996 & 1997, Freeman City London 1965, Liveryman Haberdashers' Co 1967, OStJ, Kt SMO Malta 1971, Kt Sacred Mil Order Constantine St George 1981, Cdr Merit with Swords Pro Merito Melitensi 1989, FSAScot, FIMgt, FFA, Hon FHG, author: *The House of Nell Gwyn* (co-author 1974), *The House of Dewar* (1991) and *The Family History Record Book* (1991); *m* 4 Feb 1967 *Sarah Ann Sweet Verge, e dau of Maj Lionel John Verge Rudder, DCLI, of Bibury, Glos, and has:

1e *James William Aubrey de Vere [James Beauclerk-Dewar Esq, 1 Sterndale Rd, London W14 0HT]; *b* 30 Sept 1970; *educ* Ampleforth

1e *Alexandra Hermione Sarah; *b* 1 Aug 1972

2e *Emma Diana Peta; *b* 9 Sept 1973

3e *Philippa Caroline Frances; *b* 8 Aug 1982

1d *Gillian de Vere [Mrs Gillian Beauclerk, Lamberts, Stourton Caundle, Dorset DT10 2JJ]; *b* 20 March 1944; *m* 1st 24 Sept 1964 (*divorce* 1978) Peter John Lawrence Silley, MIMarE, of Park House, Eynsford, only s of Bernard Lawrence Silley, of Matching Green, Essex, by Mrs Claud Alexander (*see* HAGART-ALEXANDER, Bt); *m* 2nd 22 Dec 1978 (*divorce* 1990, took mother's maiden name) Robert Erskine Beveridge, MA, of Tunbridge Wells, Kent, only s of Charles Robert Beveridge, and by her 1st husb has had:

1e *Natasha Margaret; *b* 19 Nov 1965

2e Tanya Anne; *b* 11 July 1967; *d* 23 Aug 1984

2b Nelthorpe de Vere; *b* 1, *d* 2 Jan 1888

1b Isabella Eleanor; *b* 28 Sept, *d* 9 Oct 1881

2b Violet Mary; *b* 2 Nov 1883; served WW I (Mons Star with Ypres Bar), Poor Clare Nun (Sister Mary Seraphim) 1950–56, author: *The Book of Talbot* (1933, James Tait Black Memorial Prize); *m* 1 Feb 1907 John Talbot Clifton, JP, of Lytham Hall, Lancs, and Kildalton Castle, Port Ellen, Islay, Hebrides, and *d* 20 Nov 1961, leaving issue. He *d* 23 March 1928

3b Florence Frederica de Vere; *b* 8 Oct 1885; *m* 14 Nov 1912 Lt-Col Reginald Joseph Bentinck and *d* 4 June 1977, leaving issue (*see* PORTLAND, E)

1a (cont.) William Beauclerk *m* 2nd 5 Sept 1892 Evelyn Amy (*d* 10 June 1933), er dau of Sir Robert Hart, 1st Bt, GCMG (*see* 1967 edn), Inspr-Gen Customs China, and *d* 5 March 1908, having by her had:

4b Vera Louise; *b* 21 Sept 1893; *m* 28 April 1926 George Ramsay Acland Mills (*d* 1972), s of Rev Barton Reginald Vaughan Mills, and *dsp* 5 Jan 1942

5b Hilda de Vere; *b* 21 Jan 1895; *m* 21 June 1933 Miles Malcolm Acheson, BEd, Chinese Maritime Customs Serv, s of Guy Francis Hamilton Acheson, and *d* 16 Sept 1964, leaving two daus

2a Frederick Amelius; *b* 8 Oct 1851; *educ* Charterhouse and Cheltenham; Lt 60th Rifles, ret 1877; *m* 12 Jan 1881 Mary Harriett Isabella Cumberland (*m* 2nd 30 April 1898 Maj Robert FitzRoy Maclean Johnstone, IA (*see* JOHNSTONE, Bt), and *d* 18 Nov 1929), sis of 1st and last Baron Islington (*see* 1936 edn), and *d* 22 May 1887, having had:

1b Evelyn Eleanora; *b* 15 Feb, *d* 12 July 1883

(4) Henry; *b* 23 June 1812; Lt 87th Regt of Foot, Roy Fus, ret 1838; *d* unm 22 Jan 1856

(5) Charles, of Lower Winchfield House, Hants; *b* 10 Oct 1813; Capt 1st Foot, Maj Northumberland Militia; *m* 7 Sept 1842 Laura Maria Theresa (*d* 29 Sept 1858), dau and heir of Col Edward Stopford, Amb Spain, and *d* from injuries recd while trying to rescue a lifeboat crew off Scarborough 2 Nov 1861, leaving:

1a William Arthur Stopford de Vere, of Richmond, Surrey; *b* 3 Jan 1844; Bengal Cav IA; *m* 1st 3 July 1869 Mary Augusta (*d* 20 April 1870), only dau of Adml Sir George Augustus Westphal, and had:

1b George Montagu de Vere; *b* 4 April 1870; *educ* Eton; Lt Gren Gds, Capt 12th Bn KRRC; *m* 26 Jan 1905 May du Bois (*d* 4 Aug 1942), widow of Henry Vincent Holden and dau of Thomas A Meinell, and *d* 5 April 1931, leaving a dau

1a (cont.) William Beauclerk *m* 2nd 4 Nov 1874 Elizabeth Susan (*d* 25 May 1934), yr dau of Edward James, of Swarland Park, Northumberland, and *d* 11 Feb 1917, having by her had:

2b Charles Edward de Vere; *b* 10 Sept 1875; *educ* Clifton and RMC Sandhurst; Lt KRRC, Uganda Rifles 1898, ADC; *d* unm Uganda 14 Jan 1900

1b Sybil Evelyn de Vere; *b* 10 Dec 1876; *m* 15 March 1902 William Murray Thomas, of Lerryn, Cornwall, yr s of George Housman Thomas, and *dsp* 26 Dec 1902

2b Diana Lily de Vere, MBE (1918); *b* 27 Dec 1878; *m* 4 Jan 1912 Christian Hugh Septimus James, of Rudchester, Northumberland, 7th s of Thomas James, JP, DL, of Otterburn Tower and Rudchester, and *dsp* 30 Jan 1954

2a Thomas Wentworth Sydney, of Irasberg, Vt.; *b* 21 March 1847; *educ* Mil Inst Lexington, Ky., and Troy, NY; civ engr; *m* 1st 2 Jan 1872 Mary Frances (*d* 17 May 1873), dau of Hon Ira H Allen, and had:

1b May Frances; *b* 10 May 1873; *m* 1st William C Stetson and had two sons; *m* 2nd Dr Eben Gaynor and by him had a s

2a (cont.) Thomas Beauclerk *m* 2nd 1875 Elizabeth Porter Yates, of Utica, NY (*d* 1911), and *d* 29 Jan 1938, having by her had:

1b William Preston, of Concord, NH; *b* 9 June 1875; surgn; *m* 2 July 1894 Jennie Mabel Hayward (*d* 13 July 11 March 1959) and *d* 18 March 1921, having had:

1c Sydney Wentworth; *b* 10 Oct 1895; *educ* Syracuse U; 12th Aero Sqdn, 4th US Army Corps WW I; *ka* 29 Oct 1918

1c Barbara; *b* 4 Feb 1913; *educ* Syracuse U; *m* 29 May 1940 *Joseph John Betz, of Fort Lauderdale, Fla., and had issue

2b Harry Wentworth; *b* 19 Oct 1879; drowned 28 July 1887

2b Laura Maria Theresa; *b* 1878; *m* 8 Oct 1907 Dr Percy Charles Waller Templeton, of Irasberg, Vt., and *d* 29 Sept 1938, leaving four daus

3b Muriel

3a Aubrey Topham, of Aldeburgh, Suffolk; *b* 29 Oct 1850; served RHA; *m* 17 Sept 1913 Gwendolen Loftus (*d* 2 May 1958), 4th dau of Capt Sir Frederic Hughes, JP, DL, of Barnstown House, Co Wexford, and *d* 14 Jan 1933, leaving:

1b CHARLES FREDERIC AUBREY DE VERE, **13th Duke**

4a Herbert Augustus Corbett; *b* 3 Jan 1852; *d* unm 30 Aug 1904

5a George Robert Algernon; *b* 15 July 1854; *educ* Haileybury; *m* 1st 13 Nov 1873 Sarah (*dsp* 15 April 1903), dau of William Turner, of High Wycombe, Bucks; *m* 2nd 23 March 1912 Antoinette Jeanne Alice (*d* 1 March 1926), dau of Arni Jaquerod, of Geneva, and *dsp* 29 April 1927

1a Florence Emily Rachel; *b* 4 July 1845; *m* 24 April 1867 Rev John Hart-Davies, Vicar St Paul's Covent Garden, and *d* 3 April 1922, leaving five sons and two daus

2a Laura Maria Theresa; *b* 3 Jan 1849; *m* 10 Aug 1867 Viscount Milton, MP, est s of 6th Earl Fitzwilliam, KG, DCL (*see* 1970 edn), and *d* 20 March 1886, leaving issue

3a Blanche Evelyn; *b* 1 Oct 1855; *m* 29 July 1903 Rev David Evans, Vicar St James's, Croydon, Surrey, and *dsp* 30 Nov 1951. He *d* 20 Jan 1906

4a Valunga; *b* 21 March 1857; *d* unm 6 Dec 1939

(6) Amelius Wentworth, of Leiston Hall, Suffolk; *b* 16 Aug 1815; *educ* RNC; RN: joined 1830, Lt 1841, Cdr 1846, Capt 1864; ret 1864; *m* 27 July 1853 Frances Maria (*m* 2nd 2 Jan 1884 Lt-Gen John Walpole D'Oyly and *d* 9 Nov 1910), only dau and heir of Charles Harrison, of Bryanston Sq, London, and *d* 24 March 1879, having had:

1a Charles William Wentworth de Vere; *b* 8 May 1854; *educ* Eton and Trin Coll Cambridge (BA 1877, MA 1880); Capt 15th Hus; *m* 17 Jan 1908 Ida Stewart (*d* 7 Feb 1929), widow of Albert Edward Williamson Goldsmid, MVO, and est dau of Frederick Hendricks, and *dsp* 29 Dec 1912

2a Amelius Francis Ward; *b* 22 March 1857; *educ* Eton and Trin Coll Cambridge; barrister, Lincoln's Inn 1885; *d* unm 1 Jan 1935

3a William Abdy, of Tower Court, Ascot Berks; *b* 29 April 1859; *m* 20 Nov 1902 Emily Standbridge (*d* 3 June 1917), only dau of Thomas King, and *dsp* Dec 1912

1a Frances Maria Janetta; *b* 8 Sept 1855; *m* 19 June 1879 Maj George Paynter, of Gate Ho, Staffs, and Eaton Grange, Leics, 3rd s of William Paynter, JP, DL, of Camborne Ho, and *d* 6 May 1884, leaving issue. He *d* 18 July 1907

2a Amelia Frances Mary Eveligh; *b* 29 Dec 1860; *d* 15 Dec 1868

3a Maria Elizabeth Harriet Adele; *b* 10 July 1863; *d* 31 Jan 1865

4a Lilchen Agnes Georgiana; *d* young 23 May 1867

(7) George Augustus; *b* 14 Dec 1818; *educ* Charterhouse; with 10th Hus, Maj 6th Dragoon Gds, served Crimean War (medal); *d* unm 3 Jan 1880

(1) Maria Amelia; *b* 11 May 1800; *d* unm 9 July 1873

(2) Charlotte; *b* 4 April 1802 *d* unm 12 Aug 1842

(3) Caroline Janetta; *b* 28 June 1804; *m* 14 July 1825 6th Earl of Essex (*qv*) and *d* 22 Aug 1862, leaving issue

(4) Louisa Georgiana; *b* 20 Dec 1806; *m* 28 Dec 1835 Thomas Hughan of Airds and *d* 18 Feb 1853, leaving issue. He *d* 24 March 1879

(5) Georgiana; *b* 11 Sept 1809; *m* 10 Feb 1829 Sir Montague John Cholmeley, 2nd Bt (*qv*), and *d* 8 Jan 1880, leaving issue

(6) Mary Noel; *b* 28 Dec 1810; *m* 15 Dec 1837 Thomas George Corbett, of Elsham Hall, Lincs, and *d* 29 Nov 1850, leaving a dau. He *d* 5 July 1868

3 Amelius (Sir), GCB (1835, KCB 1815), GCH (1831), of Winchfield Ho, Hants; *b* 23 May 1771, Adml of the White, Principal Naval ADC to KING WILLIAM IV from 1830 and to QUEEN VICTORIA, Ld of the Manor of Winchfield, RN: joined 1782, Capt HMS *Nemesis* 1793 and HMS *Juno*, in which assisted at Blockade of Toulon 1794, Capt HMS *Argo* 1795, HMS *Dryad* 1796, HMS *Fortune* 1800, HMS *Majestic*, HMS *Saturn* 1805 and HMS *Royal Oak* 1809, Col RM 1810, R-Adml the Blue 1811, the White 1812 and the Red 1814, V-Adml the White 1819, C-in-C Lisbon and Portuguese Coast 1824–27, Adml the Blue 1830, C-in-C Plymouth 1836–39, FRS 1809; *dspl* unm 10 Dec 1846, leaving:

(1) Charles Frederick Augustus de Vere; *b* 1836; *m* 19 March 1859 Sarah Caroline, dau of James Paul, of Portsea, Hants, and *d* 11 April 1882, leaving:

1a Amelius Aubrey de Vere; *b* 1861; *educ* Liverpool Coll; Sec and Manager Manchester Dog Show Soc 1896, Manager Kennel Club Show; *m* 8 March 1892 Sarah Elizabeth (*d* 6 Sept 1838), dau of Thomas Newton, of Liverpool, and *d* 18 March 1910, leaving:

1b Amelius Aubrey de Vere, JP; *b* 20 Sept 1894; *educ* Liverpool Coll; RNVR 1914–15 and RFC 1915–19 WW I, Mayor Oswestry 1959–60; *m* 26 Dec 1923 Phoebe, dau of Joseph Davies, and had:

1c *Amelius Aubrey de Vere, JP [Amelius Beauclerk Esq JP, Grenston, Croeswylan Lane, Oswestry, Salop SY10 9PT]; *b* 3 March 1924; F/O RAFVR WW II; *m* 15 June 1946 Sydney Frances, dau of D C F Thomas, and has:

1d *Alan Aubrey de Vere; *b* 6 Feb 1954; *educ* U Coll of Wales (PhD 1978)

1d *Eleanor Frances de Vere; *b* 20 Feb 1950

1c *Marjorie Elizabeth de Vere; *b* 5 March 1926; *m* 20 June 1964 Ellis John Zinn, of Johannesburg. He *d* Aug 1966

2b Charles Ernest de Vere; *b* 12 March 1899; *m* 3 Dec 1923 Jennie Gertrude Howell and *d* 1971, leaving:

1c *Jean de Vere; *b* 24 Nov 1924; *m* *Alec John Hayward and has:

1d *Valerie Frances

2a Amelius Wentworth, sometime of Singapore; *b* 1861; *d* unm 1915

3a Frederick Wentworth; *b* 30 Jan 1864; US Consular Agent Surabaya, Dutch East Indies; took Dutch nationality 1896; *m* 1st Jane Ottolina Potter (*dsp*); *m* 2nd 14 May 1903 Jacoba Jeanette Charlotta (*d* 20 July 1961), dau of Jan Willem le Comte, of Surabaya, and *d* 24 Dec 1908, having by her had:

1b Charles Frederick; *b* 23 Sept 1904; *educ* Brighton Coll and Wadham Coll Oxford (MA); Colonial Admin Serv, DC Tanganyika 1929–56, Sr Maths Master Hove Coll, took Br nationality 1928; *m* 15 May 1930 Dorothy Charlton (*d* 7 July 1967), dau of John Lupton Lister, of Brighton, and had:

1c *Diana Charlton; *b* 30 March 1931; *m* 29 Sept 1956 *John Nicholas Lewis, s of Frederick Ernest Lewis, of Bournemouth, and has a s and dau

2b Aubrey Wentworth; *b* 4 Sept 1908; *educ* Hurstpierpoint; *m* 27 Oct 1938 *Joyce Muriel, dau of Horace Langdon, of London, and *d* 22 Nov 1983, leaving:

1c *Nicholas Wentworth [Nicholas Beauclerk Esq, 4 Cairngorm Pl, Cove, Farnborough, Hants GU14 9HU]; *b* 21 Feb 1940; *educ* Hurstpierpoint; *m* 11 Sept 1971 *Lynda Jean, dau of John Kirby, of London, and has:

1d *Christopher Charles Aubrey Wentworth; *b* 17 March 1985

1d *Nicola Jean; *b* 1 July 1977

2d *Gemma Louise; *b* 8 June 1980

2c *Charles Aubrey; *b* 17 March 1948; *educ* Hurstpierpoint

1a Sarah Toft Mallory; *b* 26 Jan 1860

2a Blanche de Vere; *b* 1863; *m* Arthur George Manifold, of Liverpool, and *dsp* 29 Nov 1952. He *d* 1908

3a Diana de Vere; *b* 24 Dec 1867; *m* Alfred Charles Manifold, of Liverpool, and *d* June 1968

4 Frederick (Rev), of Winchfield House; *b* 8 May 1773; *educ* Trin Coll Coll Cambridge (MA 1792, DD 1824); Ld Manor Winchfield, Curate Groton, Suffolk, 1795–97, Vicar Kimpton, Herts, 1797–1827 and Redbourn and St Michael's, St Albans, 1827–50; Pres MCC 1826; *m* 3 July 1813 Hon Charlotte Dillon (*d* 26 Sept 1866), 3rd dau of 12th Viscount Dillon (*qv*) of Costello-Gallin, and *d* 22 April 1850, leaving issue

(1) Charles William, of Winchfield House and Boulogne, JP, DL (Hants 1844); *b* 7 May 1816; *educ* Charterhouse and Ch Ch Oxford (BA 1838); Ld Manor Winchfield; *m* 15 Aug 1844 Penelope (*d* 15 April 1890), dau of Edward Hulkes, and *d* 23 May 1863, leaving:

1a Frederick Edward, JP, DL Hants; *b* 3 July 1852; *educ* Ch Ch Oxford; sold Winchfield House 1908; *d unm* 17 Nov 1919

2a Charles St John; *b* 10 Oct 1854; *educ* Marlborough; *d* 12 Sept 1921

1a Caroline Elizabeth; *b* 28 Aug 1845; *m* 16 April 1868 Rev Francis William Hudson, Vicar Gt Wilbraham, Cambs, and *d* 29 June 1915, leaving two sons. He *d* 10 June 1901

2a Penelope Sarah Blanche; *b* 25 Oct 1846; *m* 20 Oct 1869 Sir St Vincent Alexander Hammick, 3rd Bt (*qv*), and *d* March 1886, leaving issue

3a Charlotte Amelia; *b* 8 July 1848

4a Frederica Jane; *b* 17 Nov 1850; *m* 15 Nov 1870 Col John Ormsby Vandeleur, CB, Rifle Bde, of Ballinacourty Castle, Co Limerick (*d* 11 June 1900), and *d* 30 June 1926, leaving a s and four daus

5a Henrietta Mary; *b* 2 Nov 1856; *m* 7 Aug 1877 Edward Stisted Mostyn Pryce, of Gunley, Montgomeryshire (*d* 14 June 1932), and *d* 28 Sept 1932 having had issue

(2) Aubrey Frederick James; *b* 3 May 1817; *educ* Charterhouse; served Scots Fus Gds, Capt Roy Fus (7th Foot), ret 1847; *d unm* 3 Jan 1853

(1) Caroline Henrietta Frederica; *b* 19 April 1815; author; *m* 12 Dec 1851 Charles Eugene Leloup, of Brussels. He *d* 27 April 1878

(2) Henrietta Mary; *b* 1 July 1818; author with her sis of *Tales of Fashion and Reality* (1836); *m* 2 Aug 1842 Sir Edward Rokewood Gate, 9th and last Bt (*see* 1871 edn), and *dsp* Jan 1887. He *d* 3 Jan 1872

1 Catherine Elizabeth; *m* 1 Sept 1802 Rev James Burgess, Vicar Hanworth 1805–16, s of Rev James Burgess, and *dsp* July 1803. He *d* 27 Nov 1827

2 Caroline; *m* 16 Feb 1797 Hon Charles Lawrence Dundas and *d* 23 Nov 1838, leaving issue (*see* ZETLAND, M)

3 Georgiana; *b* 1776; *d* 17 Oct 1791

The 12th DUKE's second cousin,

CHARLES FREDERIC AUBREY DE VERE BEAUCLERK, **13th Duke of Saint Albans**, OBE (1945); *b* 16 Aug 1915; *educ* Eton and Magdalene Coll Cambridge (BA 1937, MA 1947); WW II: Somerset LI 1939–41, Mil Intell and PsyWar, Hon Col Intell Corps 1946, Controller Info Servs Allied Commn Austria 1946–50, Ch Books Ed COI 1951–58, Ch Films Prodn Offr 1958–60, Dir Films Div 1960–64, chm: Grendon Securities, Industl Midlands Investment, Travelworld Olympic Ltd, dir: Herbert Greaves Ltd, Amalgamated Developers Ltd, Monotype Corp 1973, memb Advsy Cncl Centre Educnl TV Overseas; *m* 1st 21 March 1938 (*divorce* 1947) Nathalie Chatham, dau of Percival Field Walker, and had:

1 MURRAY DE VERE BEAUCLERK, **14th and present Duke of Saint Albans**

The 13th Duke *m* 2nd 18 March 1947 *Suzanne Marie Adele [Her Grace The Dowager Duchess of St Albans, 64 West St, Newbury, Berks RG13 1BD], author *The Mimosa and The Mango* and *Paradise and Pestilence: Aspects of Provence* (1997), dau of Emile William Fesq, of Le Mas Mistral, Vence, France, and *d* 8 Oct 1988, having by her had:

2 +Peter Charles de Vere [The Lord Peter Beauclerk, 2726 Shelter Island Dve 332, San Diego, CA 92106, USA]; *b* 13 Jan 1948; *educ* Eton; RNR 1966–69; *m* 17 May 1972 (*divorce* 1978) Beverlie June, dau of Alva Edwin Bailey of California, and has had:

(1) Robin de Vere; *b* 24 Feb 1971; accidentally drowned 10 June 1973

(1) *Angela Grace de Vere; *b* 24 Dec 1974

3 +James Charles Fesq de Vere [The Lord James Beauclerk, Barn House, Midgham, Berks RG7 5UG]; *b* 6 Feb 1949; *educ* Eton

4 +John William Aubrey de Vere [The Lord John Beauclerk, c/o Save The Children Fund (Mongolia), 17 Grove Lane, London SE5 8SP]; *b* 10 Feb 1950; *educ* Eton; *m* 1986 *Caroline Ann Heath, dau of Mrs B Wilkinson, of IoW, and has:

(1) *Kiatsi Sofia; *b* 12 Oct 1984

4 (cont.) Lord John Beauclerk also has by *Maria Kolacinska:

(2) *Annamary; *b* 6 May 1998

1 *Caroline Anne de Vere [The Lady Caroline ffrench Blake, Barn House, Midgham, Berks RG7 5UG]; *b* 19 July 1951; *educ* Fritham House and Queen's Gate Sch; *m* 11 July 1970 (*divorce* 1986) Neil St John ffrench Blake, er s of Lt-Col R L V ffrench Blake, of Midgham Park Farm, Berks, and has:

(1) *Clare Eleanor de Vere ffrench; *b* 15 Jan 1972

(2) *Katherine (Kate) Julianna de Vere ffrench; *b* 25 May 1977

2 A dau; *b* and *d* 15 Nov 1963

Lineage (of de Vere): ALBERIC/AUBREY de VER (a place in the Côtentin Peninsula, Normandy), probably himself a Norman; *b* by 1040; by the Domesday Survey held numerous manors, chiefly in Cambs, Essex and Suffolk, Hedingham, Essex, being the chief one, but also in Hunts, Middx (including Cheniston, now Kensington) and Northants; references to him as Chamberlain occur *c* 1110; founded Earl's Colne Priory, Essex, where he and many of his descendants are buried; Sheriff Berks by 1106; *m* Beatrice — and *d* probably 1112, having had, with an est s (*dvp* 1106) and four yst sons (Geoffrey; Roger; Robert; William):

ALBERIC de VERE; *b* probably by 1090; described as King's Chamberlain by 1112; Sheriff London and Middx 1121 or 1122, Jt Sheriff 1125, often Sheriff Essex, Jt Sheriff Beds, Bucks, Cambs, Hunts, Norfolk, Suffolk and Surrey 1129 and Essex, Herts, Leics and Northants 1130; Master Chamberlain of England 1133; possibly Ch Justiciar of England 1139; *m* Alice, dau of Gilbert FitzRichard, Lord of Clare and Tunbridge, and sis of Gilbert, 1st Earl of Pembroke (*see* PEMBROKE and MONTGOMERY, E, preliminary remarks), and was *k* in a riot in London 15 May 1141, having had, with three yr sons (Robert, feudal Ld of Twywell, Northants; Geoffrey; William, Chllr of England) and three daus (Adeliza, *m* Henry de Essex; Juliana, *m* Hugh Bigod, Earl of Norfolk (*see* NORFOLK, D, preliminary remarks); Rohesia, *m* 1st Geoffrey de Mandeville, Earl of Essex (*d* 14 Sept 1144), and had issue, *m* 2nd Payne Beauchamp, of Bedford):

AUBREY de VERE, 1st EARL OF OXFORD (E), so *cr* 1142 by the EMPRESS MATILDA (*see also* OXFORD AND ASQUITH, E, preliminary remarks) and recognised as such by STEPHEN *c* 1152–53; *b* probably *c* 1110; Master Chamberlain of England, as which s f; *m* 1st *c* 1139 (*divorce* by 1146) Beatrice, gdau of Manas-

ses, Count of Guisnes, Northern France, whom he *s* in that fief late 1139 on doing homage to his overlord Thierry, Count of Flanders (though he was obliged to surrender it on his divorce); *m* 2nd by 1152 Eufeme (*dspm* (certainly and *dsp* probably) 1153 or 1154), dau of William de Cauntelo; *m* 3rd 1162 or 1163 Agnes, dau of Henry de Essex, feudal Ld of Rayleigh and Haughley, and *d* 26 Dec 1194, having by her had, with other issue:

1 AUBREY de VERE, 2nd EARL OF OXFORD; *b* in or after 1163; hereditary Master Chamberlain of England, Sheriff Essex and Herts 1208–13, Steward Forest of Essex 1213; *m* 1st Isabel (*dsp* 1206–07), dau and heiress of Walter de Bolebec, feudal Ld of Whitchurch; *m* 2nd Alice, dau of Roger Bigod, 2nd Earl of Norfolk (*see* NORFOLK, D, preliminary remarks), and *dspl* by Oct 1214, leaving illegitimately:

(1) Roger; *d* 1221

2 Ralph; *dvf*

3 ROBERT, 3rd EARL

3 William; Bp Hereford

1 Adeliza

2 Sarah

The 2nd EARL's bro,

ROBERT de VERE, 3rd EARL OF OXFORD; *b* probably after 1164; hereditary Master Chamberlain of England, one of the magnates appointed to enforce KING JOHN's observance of Magna Carta; Justice Itinerant 1220 and Justice in King's Court at Westminster 1221; *m* Isabel (*d* 3 Feb 1245), sis of Walter de Bolebec, aunt of his er bro's 1st w, and *d* by 25 Oct 1221, having had:

1 HUGH, 4th EARL

2 Henry (Sir), of Gt Addington, Northants; had:

(1) Robert (Sir); had:

1a Richard; *m* Isabel, dau and ultimate heiress of John Greene, of Drayton, through whom he acquired Drayton

1 Eleanor; *m* as his 1st w Ralph Gernon (*m* 2nd Hawise (?Tregoz) and *d* 1274)

The 3rd EARL's er s,

HUGH de VERE, 4th EARL OF OXFORD; *b c* 1210; hereditary Master Chamberlain of England; ktd 1233; *m* after 11 Feb 1222/3 Hawise, dau of Saher de Quincey, 1st Earl of Winchester (*see* WINCHESTER, M, preliminary remarks), and *d* by 23 Dec 1263, having had, with three daus (Isabel, *m* John de Courtenay (*see* DEVON, E) and had issue; Laura, *m* Reynold d'Argentine and *d* 1292, leaving issue; Margaret, *m* Hugh de Cressi):

ROBERT de VERE, 5th EARL OF OXFORD; *b c* 1240; hereditary Master Chamberlain of England; ktd 1264 (by Simon de Montfort, Earl of Leicester (*see* LEICESTER, E, preliminary remarks) on the eve of the Battle of Lewes); as a supporter of de Montfort's was unawares at Kenilworth 1 Aug 1265 and temporarily deprived of the Earldom till the provisions of the Dictum of Kenilworth (which among other things restored it to him) came into force 1266; the Chamberlainship, of which he had also been deprived, was not restored him though he appears to have been permitted to perfom its duties at EDWARD I's coronation 1274; *m* Alice, dau and heiress of Gilbert de Sanford, and *d* by 7 Sept 1296, having had:

1 ROBERT de VERE, 6th EARL OF OXFORD; *b* probably *c* 24 June 1257; fought against Scots Battle of Falkirk 1298; opposed EDWARD II's favourite Gaveston but fought for EDWARD against the rebel Earl of Lancaster 1322; that he tried unsuccessfully to have the office of Master Chamberlain restored him is further evidence that it had not been restored his f (*see* above); *m* Margaret (*d* 1296/7), sis of Edmund, 1st Lord (Baron) Mortimer, and *dsps* 17 April 1331, having had:

(1) Thomas; *b c* 1282; ktd 1306; fought for EDWARD II against Earl of Lancaster at Battle of Boroughbridge March 1321/2; *m* by 17 June 1315, possibly as his 2nd w, Agnes, allegedly dau of William de Ros, of Hamlake, and widow of Payn Tibetot, and *dsp* & *vp* by 12 May 1329

2 HUGH de VERE, 1st and last LORD (Baron) VERE/VEER (E), so *cr* (according to later doctrine) by writ of summons to Parl 6 Feb 1298/9; *b* probably between June 1257 and March 158/9; ktd by late Aug 1293; cmded English troops against French in Gascony Campaign 1294–97, subsequently negotiator with French for peace terms; also served against Scots, notably at Siege of Carlaverock 1300; *m* just after 12 June 1294 Denise (*dsp* by 13 April 1314), only dau and heiress of Sir William de Munchensy, and *dsp*, probably shortly after 22 May 1319, when his Barony expired

3 Alfonso (Sir); *m* allegedly Joan, dau of Sir Richard Foliot, and *d* just prior to 20 Dec 1328, leaving:

(1) JOHN, 7th EARL

4 Gilbert; *b c* 1264; *educ* U of Paris; clerk; *d unm* Sept 1289

5 Philip; *b c* 1266; *educ* U of Paris; clerk; *d unm*

6 John; *educ* U of Paris

1 Joan; *m* William de Warenne, s of 7th Earl of Surrey of the 1088 *cr*, and had, with other issue:

(1) Alice; *m* 1305 9th/2nd Earl of Arundel and had issue (*see* NORFOLK, D)

2 Hawise, living 1297; *dsp*

The 6th EARl's n,

JOHN de VERE, 7th EARL OF OXFORD; *b c* 12 March 1311/2; successfully claimed hereditary post of Master Chamberlain of England; campaigned against Scots and French, notably at victories of Crécy 1340 and Poitiers 1356; *m* by 27 March 1336 Maud, widow of Robert FitzPayn and dau of Bartholomew de Badlesmere, 1st Lord (Baron) Badlesmere, and *d* 23/24 Jan 1359/60 at Siege of Rheims, having had:

1 John; *b* probably *c* Dec 1335; *m* probably July 1341 Elizabeth (*d* 7 Aug 1395), dau of 2nd Earl of Devon (*qv*) of the Feb 1334/5 *cr*, and *dsp* & *vp* by 23 June 1350

2 THOMAS de VERE, 8th EARL OF OXFORD; *b* probably 1336 or 1337; hereditary Master Chamberlain of England; campaigned in France 1359–60 and 1369; *m* by 10 June 1350 Maud, dau of Sir Ralph de Ufford, Ch Justice Ireland and bro of 1st Earl of Suffolk (*see* SUFFOLK and BERKSHIRE, E, preliminary remarks), and *d* between 12 and 18 Sept 1371, leaving:

(1) ROBERT de VERE, 9th EARL OF OXFORD, KG (*c* 1385); *b* 16 Jan 1361/2; hereditary Master Chamberlain of England; ktd 1377, chief favourite of

RICHARD II, who *cr* him 1 Dec 1385 MARQUESS OF DUBLIN (E) for life plus the territory and Lordship of Ireland with virtually royal power, also 13 Oct 1386 (in lieu of the Marquessate, which was now withdrawn) DUKE OF IRELAND (E), also for life, together with the entire territory of Ireland and its own lesser islands and all other appurtenances; Ch Justice Chester and N Wales Sept and Oct 1387 respectively; *m* 1st by 5 Oct 1376 (*divorce* 1387) Philippa (*d* Oct 1411), dau and coheir of Enguerrand de Coucy, Earl of Bedford, by Isabel, dau of EDWARD III; *m* 2nd (papal *annulment* 1398) Agnes Lancerone/Landskron, an attendant (quite possibly of German origin) of RICHARD II's 1st w ANNE OF BOHEMIA, and after being forced to flee abroad due to the enmity his repudiation of his 1st w had aroused among RICHARD II's uncles (*see* OXFORD AND ASQUITH, E, preliminary remarks) *dsp* at Louvain 1392, when the Dukedom expired, having been declared guilty of treason and his honours and property forfeited

3 AUBREY de VERE, 10th EARL OF OXFORD, as which restored Jan/Feb 1392/3 (having got back his n's possessions (but neither then nor later the hereditary post of Chamberlain of England) on the latter's death 1392), PC (Nov 1378–Jan 1379/80); *b c* 1339; Sec to EDWARD THE BLACK PRINCE (est s of EDWARD III) 1371; Envoy to negotiate peace with France 1377 and 1383; Constable Hadleigh Castle Feb 1377/8, Chamberlain Roy Household by late Jan 1380/1; *m* Alice (*d* 29 April 1401), dau of 3rd Lord (Baron) Fitzwalter (*qv*), and had:

(1) RICHARD, 11th EARL

(2) John; *dsp*

(1) Alice; *m* 1st Guy d'Albon; *m* 2nd Sir John FitzLewis

4 Robert; *dvp* probably unm

1 Margaret; *m* 1st 3rd Lord (Baron) Beaumont and had issue (*see* BEAUMONT, Bt); *m* 2nd Sir Nicholas de Lovain; *m* 3rd Sir John Devereux

2 Maud; unm in 1359

3 Elizabeth; *m* 1st 1341 Sir Hugh de Courtenay (*see* DEVON, E) and had issue; *m* 2nd, as his 2nd w, 3rd Lord (Baron) Mowbray (*see* MOWBRAY, SEGRAVE and STOURTON, B); *m* 3rd 18 Jan 1368/9 Sir William de Cosynton and *d* Aug or Sept 1375

The 10th EARL *d* 23 April 1400; his er s,

RICHARD de VERE, 11th EARL OF OXFORD, KG (1416); *b* probably 1385; cmded troops in the Agincourt campaign 1415 and its follow-up 1416; *m* 1st by 1400 — (*dsp* young), very probably dau of John de Holand, 1st Duke of Exeter (*see* ZOUCHE, B), by Elizabeth (sis of HENRY IV); *m* 2nd 1406/7 Alice (*m* 3rd Nicholas Thorley), widow of Guy de St Aubyn and dau of Sir Richard Sergeaux, of Cornwall, by Philippa, dau of Sir Edmund de Arundel (bastardised s of 11th/4th Earl of Arundel; *see* NORFOLK, D), and *d* 15 Feb 1416/7, having had:

1 JOHN de VERE, 12th EARL OF OXFORD, PC (1431); *b* 23 April 1408; ktd Feb 1425/6; *m* between 22 May and 31 Aug 1425 Elizabeth, only dau and heiress of Sir John Howard (*see* NORFOLK, D), and was beheaded 26 Feb 1461/2 with his est s for treason, having had:

(1) Aubrey (Sir), JP (Suffolk 1458); *m c* April 1460 Anne, est dau of Humphry Stafford, 1st Duke of Buckingham (*see* STAFFORD, B), and *dsp* 1461, being beheaded six days before his f

(2) JOHN de VERE, 13th EARL OF OXFORD, as which restored by Jan 1463/4, KG (1485/6), KB (1465), PC (1485/6); *b* 8 Sept 1442; acted (though on behalf of his bro-in-law the ('Kingmaker') Earl of Warwick, then the official holder of the post) as Great Chamberlain of England at coronation of EDWARD IV's QUEEN ELIZABETH 1465; imprisoned Tower London 1468–69 suspected of conspiring with the Lancastrian party; fled abroad with members of the dissident Yorkist faction 1470 but returned to England 1471 and helped restore HENRY VI; Constable of England 1471; cmded Lancastrian left wing at Battle of Barnet, where the fog led his own side into confusing his armorial device with their opponent EDWARD IV's sun in its splendour; in the resulting panic the Lancastrians were routed; fled abroad again and turned privateer in the Channel; landed in Cornwall 1473 and held St Michael's Mount till obliged to capitulate, whereupon incarcerated at the Castle of Hammes, nr Calais, and attainted 1475; broke out of Hammes 1485, joined the future HENRY VII and led the latter's archers at Bosworth, following which his attainder was reversed and he was made Ld High Adml of England, Ireland and Aquitaine, High Steward Duchy Lancaster south of Trent and Constable Tower London; also had restored the hereditary post of Ld Gt Chamberlain of England; a cdr of HENRY VII's forces at Battles of Stoke 1487 and Blackheath 1497; *m* 1st Lady Margaret Neville, sis of Richard ('The Kingmaker'), 1st/16th Earl of Warwick (*see* ABERGAVENNY, M); *m* 2nd between 28 Nov 1508 and 10 April 1509 Elizabeth (*d* 26 June 1537), widow of 2nd Viscount Beaumont (*see* BEAUMONT, Bt) and dau of Sir Richard Scrope, and *dsp(s?)* 10 March 1512/3

(3) George (Sir); accompanied his er bro at Barnet and in the descent on Cornwall, being accordingly attainted too but as with his er bro only until the ascent of HENRY VII, when the attainder reversed; Ch Steward St Osyth's Priory Essex 1491; *m* Margaret, dau and heiress of Sir William Stafford, of Bishop's Frome, Herefs, and *d* 1503, leaving:

1a George; *dvp* 1498

2a JOHN de VERE, 14th EARL OF OXFORD, called 'Little John of Camps', certainly from his living at Camps Castle, Cambs, and supposedly from his small size, but more probably from his having *s* as a minor; *b* 14 Aug 1499; *m* Lady Anne Howard, dau of 2nd Duke of Norfolk (*qv*), and *dsp* 14 July 1526, when the post of Ld Gt Chamberlain reverted to the Crown

1a Dorothy; *m* as his 1st w 3rd Lord (Baron) Latymer (*qv*) and had issue

2a Elizabeth; *m* Sir Anthony Wingfield, KG, and had issue (*see* POWERSCOURT, V)

3a Ursula; *m* 1st George Windsor; *m* 2nd Sir Edmund Knightly and *dsp* 1560

(4) Richard (Sir); *m* as her 2nd w Margaret, dau of Henry Percy, of Atholl (*see* NORTHUMBERLAND, D)

(5) Thomas (Sir), *dsp* 1489

(1) Mary; nun at Barking

(2) J(o)ane; *m* Sir William Norreys, of Yattendon, and had issue (*see* LINDSEY and ABINGDON, E)

(3) Elizabeth; *m* William Bourchier, s of 1st Earl of Essex (*qv*, preliminary remarks) of the 1461 *cr*

2 Robert (Sir); *m* Joan, widow of Sir Nicholas Carew (*see* CAREW, Bt) and dau of Sir Hugh Courtenay (*see* DEVON, E), and had:

(1) John; *m* Alice, widow of Sir Walter Courtenay and dau of Sir Walter Colbroke or Kilrington, and had:

1a JOHN, 15th EARL

2 (cont.) Sir Robert de Vere, who was *ka* Battle of St Albans 1455, had illegitimately:

(2) John; ancester of the VERES later VERE-LAURIEs of Carlton Hall (*see* MASSEREENE and FERRARD, V)

The 14th EARL's 2nd cousin,

JOHN de VERE, 15th EARL OF OXFORD, KG (1527), PC (by late March 1530/1); Esq of Body to HENRY VII at latter's funeral 1509; ktd 1513, Sheriff Essex and Herts and Keeper Colchester Castle 1515–16, 1519–20 and 1524–25, Ld Gt Chamberlain for life only 1526; *m* 1st 1493/4 Christian (*dsp* by 4 Nov 1498), 3rd dau and heiress of Thomas Foderingey, of Brockley, Suffolk; *m* 2nd between 29 April 1507 and 4 July 1509 Elizabeth, dau and heiress of Edward Trussel, of Kibblestone, Staffs, and *d* 21 March 1539/40, having by her had:

1 JOHN de VERE, 16th EARL OF OXFORD, PC (1553); *b c* 1516; served Boulogne Campaign 1544; ktd Feb 1546/7, Jt Ld Lt Essex 1550–53, Ld Lt 1558 and 1559; acted as Ld Gt Chamberlain at MARY's coronation 30 Nov 1553, though after his f's death the post had been given to Thomas Cromwell and in 1547 the 16th EARL had been declared to have no right to the post; nevertheless recognised as hereditary Ld Gt Chamberlain by ELIZABETH I's coronation 15 Jan 1558/9, when he acted as such; *m* 1st 3 July 1536 Dorothy, dau of 4th Earl of Westmorland of the 1397 *cr* (*see* ABERGAVENNY, M), and had:

(1) Katherine; *m* 3rd Baron Windsor and had issue (*see* PLYMOUTH, E)

1 (cont.) The 16th EARL *m* 2nd 1 Aug 1548 Margery (*m* 2nd Charles Tyrrell and *d* 2 Dec 1568), dau of John Golding, and *d* 3 Aug 1562, having by her had:

(1) EDWARD de VERE, 17th EARL OF OXFORD (PC *c* 1603); *b* 12 April 1550; *educ* Queens' and St John's Coll Cambridge and Gray's Inn; hereditary Ld Gt Chamberlain; scholar and poet in his own right as well as literary patron (an activity which with his extravagance at Court and unfortunate investments in overseas explorations impoverished him); imprisoned Tower London March-June 1581, quite for what is unclear (possibly getting with child one Anne Vavasour), though it was not political; jt cdr English expdn to Low Countries 1585; *m* 1st 19 Dec 1571 Anne, dau of 1st Baron of Burghley (*see* EXETER, M), and had, with a s and 4th dau (both *d* as infants):

1a Elizabeth; *m* 26 June 1594 6th Earl of Derby (*qv*) and *d* 10 March 1626, leaving issue

2a Bridget; *m* 1598 2nd Baron Norris and had issue (*see* LINDSEY and ABINGDON, E)

3a Susan; *m* 27 Dec 1604 4th Earl of Pembroke and (1st Earl of) Montgomery (*qv*) and *d* Jan 1628, leaving issue

(1) The 17th EARL *m* 2nd after 4 July 1591 Elizabeth, a Maid of Honour to ELIZABETH I, dau of Thomas Trentham, of Rowcester Priory, Staffs, and *d* 24 June 1604, having by her had:

1a HENRY de VERE, 18th EARL OF OXFORD, KB (1610); *b* 24 Feb 1593; *educ* Inner Temple; hereditary Ld Gt Chamberlain; lived on the Continent for some years to economise; Capt of a regt fighting on the Protestant side (1620) and Col of another such (1624) in early phase of Thirty Years War; imprisoned Tower London 1622–23 for criticising the govt; *m* 1 Jan 1623/4 Lady Diana Cecil (*m* 2nd 1st Earl of Elgin; *see* ELGIN and KINCARDINE, E), dau of 2nd Earl of Exeter (*see* EXETER, M), and *dsp* between 2 and 9 June 1625 of wounds recd 15 May previously during Siege of Breda, The Netherlands

(2) Mary; *m* 1st between Christmas 1577 and 12 March 1577/8 (separated apparently by 20 April 1600) 13th Lord (Baron) Willoughby de Eresby (*qv*) and had issue (*see* LINDSEY and ABINGDON, E); *m* 2nd by 2 June 1605 (separated by 15 July 1622), as his 1st w, Sir Eustace Hart (*d* 18 Sept 1634), of London, and *d* probably 24 June 1624

2 Aubrey; *m* Margaret, dau of John Spring, of Lavenham, Suffolk, and had:

(1) Hugh; *m* Eleanor Walsh and had:

1a ROBERT, 19th EARL

1a Susan; *bur* 24 April 1580

2a Margery; *bur* 31 July 1583

3 Robert

4 Geoffrey, of Crepping Hall, Wakes Colne, Essex; *m* Elizabeth, dau of Richard Hardekyn, of Odewell and Wotton, Gestingthorpe, Essex, and had, with other issue:

(1) John, of Kisby Hall, Essex; *m* Thomasine Pater and had issue

(2) Francis (Sir); led English forces helping Dutch against Spain in Low Countries to 1604; Govr Brill; *dsps* 28 Aug 1609

(3) Geoffrey; *d* unm

(4) HORATIO VERE, 1st and last BARON VERE OF TILBURY, Co Essex (E), so *cr* 24 July 1625; *b* 1565; served from 1590 under the Dutch opposed to the Spanish Forces in Low Countries, cmded a company under his er bro Sir Francis 1591–94, wounded Siege of Steenwyck 1592, apptd Capt during Siege of Groningen 1594; served in English forces Expdn to Cadiz 1596, when ktd, Col 1599 when back in Low Countries, present Battle of Nieuwport 1600, wounded defending Ostend against Spaniards Jan 1601/2, Sr Col English forces Low Countries 1604, present taking of Sluys by Dutch 1604, ably conducted retreat at Mulheim 1605, thereby saving Dutch forces from Spaniards; Govr Brill following his er bro's death 1619–16; present Siege of Juliers 1610; Govr Utrecht 1618; Capt-Gen English forces Rhenish Palatinate Feb 1621/2 (apptd cdr 1620) in opening phase Thirty Years War; Master-Gen Ordnance March 1628/9–34; *m* Nov 1607 Mary, widow of William Hoby, of Hailes, Glos, and sis of 1st Viscount Tracy of Rathcoole (*see* SUDELEY, B), and *dspm* 2 May 1635, when the Barony expired, leaving:

1a Elizabeth; *m* John Holles, 2nd Earl of Clare of the 1624 *cr*, and had issue

2a Mary; *m* 1st Sir Roger Townshend, 1st Bt, and had issue (*see* TOWNSHEND, M); *m* 2nd 2nd Earl of Westmorland (*qv*) and was *bur* 18 Nov 1669, having had further issue

3a Catherine; *m* 1st Oliver St John (*see* BOLINGBROKE and SAINT JOHN, V); *m* 2nd 2nd Baron Poulett of Hinton St George (*see* 1970 edn POULETT, E)

4a Anne; *m* 3rd Lord Fairfax of Cameron (*qv*) and had issue

5a Dorothy; *m* John Wolstenholme (*dvp*), est s of Sir John Wolstenholme, Bt, of Nostell, Yorks

(1) Frances; *m* Sir Robert Harcourt and had issue (*see* VERNON, B)

1 Elizabeth; *m* 1st Baron Darcy of Chiche and had issue

2 Anne; *m* 1st by 31 Jan 1537/8 1st Baron Sheffield and had issue (*see* SHEF-FIELD, Bt); *m* 2nd, as his 1st w, John Brock, of Colchester, and was *bur* 14 Feb 1571/2

3 Frances; *m* Henry, Earl of Surrey, KG, only s of 3rd Duke of Norfolk (*qv*)

The 18th EARL's second cousin,

ROBERT de VERE, 19TH EARL OF OXFORD, as which recognised 5 April 1626 following a claim to the Earldom by 1st Earl of Lindsey (*see* LINDSEY and ABINGDON, E), who, however, successfully claimed the post of hereditary Ld Gt Chamberlain, as heir general of the 18th EARL; *b* 23 Aug 1575; Capt of Foot in Dutch serv 1626 and Lt-Col 1629–32; *ktd* 1629; *m* by 1626 Bauck/Beatrice, dau of Sijerck van Hemmema, of Berlikum, Friesland, and was *k* 7 Aug 1632 at Siege of Maastricht, leaving:

AUBREY de VERE, 20TH and last EARL OF OXFORD, KG (1660), PC (Jan 1669/70–79, Jan 1680/1, 1689 and 1702); *b* 28 Feb 1626/7; Serjeant-Maj in Col Knightley's Regt in Dutch serv 1644, Col 1646–50, imprisoned Tower London 1654 and 1659 as suspected royalist; unsuccessfully claimed right to act as Ld Gt Chamberlain at CHARLES II's coronation; Ld Lt Essex 1660–Feb 1667/8 and 1688–1703, Col Roy Regt Horse ('Oxford Blues') Jan 1660/1–88 and 1688–1703, Gentleman Bedchamber 1678–85 and 1689–97, Lt-Gen Horse and Foot 1678, Envoy Extrdy France 1680, Steward HAC 1682, fought for WILLIAM III Battle of the Boyne 1690, Speaker Ho Lds 1700–01; *m* 1st 18 June 1647 Anne (*dsp* 14 Sept 1659), dau and coheir of 2nd Viscount Bayning of Sudbury; *m* 2nd just prior to 12 April 1673 Diana, dau of George Kirke (*see also* VERNON, B), Groom Bedchamber to CHARLES I, and *dspms* 12 March 1702/3, when the Earldom expired, having by her had, with other issue (*d* young or unm):

Diana, eventual sole heiress of her father; *m* 13 April 1694 **1st Duke of Saint Albans**

SAINT ALDWYN

TOUT·EN·BON·HEURE

Arms: Quarterly, 1st and 4th, vair arg. and gu., a canton az. charged with a pile or (for BEACH); 2nd and 3rd, gu. a fess wavy between three fleurs-de-lys or (for HICKS). **Crest:** A demi-lion rampant arg., ducally gorged or, holding in the paws an escutcheon az., charged with a pile or (for BEACH). **Supporters:** Dexter, a knight armed cap-à-pie in English armour of the middle of the 14th century, his jupon charged with the arms of BEACH; sinister, a knight similarly vested, his jupon charged with the arms of HICKS. **Motto:** *Tout en bon heure* ('All in good time'). **Creations:** Bt. (E) 21 July 1619, V. (St Aldwyn) (UK) 6 Jan 1906, E. and V. (Quenington) (UK) 22 Feb 1915.

THE 3RD EARL SAINT ALDWYN, of Coln St Aldwyn, Co Glos, **Viscount Saint Aldwyn**, of Coln St Aldwyn, Co Glos, **Viscount Quenington**, of Quenington, Co Glos, and a **Baronet** (Sir Michael Henry Hicks Beach, Bt) [The Rt Hon The Earl St Aldwyn, Williamstrip Park, Coln St Aldwyn, Glos GL7 5AT; 17 Hale House, 34 De Vere Gdns, London W8 5AQ]; *b* 7 Feb 1950; *s f* 1992; *educ* Eton and Ch Ch Oxford (BA 1973, MA 1975); Chm Anglo-Brazilian Soc; *m* 16 April 1982 *Gilda Maria, only dau of Baron Saavedra, of Rio de Janeiro, and has:

1 *Atalanta Maria; *b* 6 Sept 1983

2 *Aurora Ursula; *b* 1988

Lineage: ROBERT HICKS, of Cheapside; *b c* 1524 (cousin of Richard Hicks, of Cromhall, Glos (*d by* 1558) and Morgan Hicks (*d by* 1565), sons of Thomas Hicks, of the Court House, Cromhall); mercer, Freeman Ironmongers' Co; *m* Julian (*d* 1592), dau of William Arthur, of Clapham, and *d by* 1557, having had, with three other sons (*d* in infancy):

1 MICHAEL (Sir)

2 Clement; Searcher of Customs at Chester; *d by* 1628

3 Sir BAPTIST HICKS, 1st and last Bt, so *cr* 1 July 1620, and 1st VISCOUNT CAMPDEN, Co Glos, also BARON HICKS OF ILMINGTON, Co Warwick (all E), the last two *cr* 5 May 1628 respectively, with in the case of the peerages only, special remainder to his s-in-law 1st Baron Noel of Ridlington, and the heirs male of the latter's body (*see* GAINSBOROUGH, E); *ktd* 1603; financial agent to JAMES I, MP Tavistock 1620–22 and Tewkesbury 1624–26 and March-May 1628; *m* 6 Sept 1584 Elizabeth, sis of Sir Humphrey May, Master of the Rolls 1629, and *d* 18 Oct 1629, when the btcy expired, leaving issue (*see* SHAFTES-BURY, E)

The est s,

Sir MICHAEL HICKS, of Beverston Castle, Glos, which he bought, and Ruck-holts, Essex; *b* 21 Oct 1543; barrister, Sec to 1st Baron of Burghley (*see* EXETER, M); *m* Elizabeth (*bur* 14 Feb 1634), widow of Henry Parvis, of Ruckholts, and dau of Gabriel Colston, of Forest Ho, Waltham, and *d* 15 Aug 1612, having had, with a yr s and a dau (Elizabeth, *m* 14 Dec 1619 Sir William A(i)rmine, 1st Bt (*d* 10 April 1651), of Osgodby, Lincs, and had issue; *see* KIMBERLEY, E):

Sir William Hicks, 1st Bt (E), so *cr* 21 July 1619, of Beverston Castle; *b* 1596; MP Marlow 1625–6, Tewkesbury 1628–29 and Gt Marlow 1640; *m* 8 Sept 1625 Margaret (*bur* 10 Sept 1652), dau of 4th Baron Paget (*see* ANGLESEY, M), and *d* 9 Oct 1680, leaving surv issue:

1 **Sir William Hicks, 2nd Bt**; *b* Dec 1629; High Sheriff Essex 1684–85; *m* 7 Feb 1661/2 Marthagnes (*d* 1723), est dau and coheir of Sir Henry Coningsby, of N Mymms Park, Herts, and *d* 22 April 1703, having had, with two daus:

(1) **Sir Henry Hicks, 3rd Bt**; *m* 1st Elizabeth (*d* 14 Jan 1705), dau of Adml Sir John Holmes, and had issue (*dvp*); *m* 2nd Barbara (*bur* 8 Aug 1746), dau of Joseph Johnson, of Walthamstow, and *d* 28 Oct 1755, having by her had, with a yr s (Michael, *dsp*):

1a **Sir Robert Hicks, 4th Bt**; blind; *d unm* 1768

(2) Charles, of Wild, Herts; *m* — Coningsby and *d* 1760, having had, with a dau:

1a **Sir John Baptist Hicks, 5th Bt**; *dsp* 23 Nov 1792

2 Michael (Sir), of Witcombe Park, Glos; *b* 1645; *m* Aug 1679 Susanna, widow of Samuel Beaumont Everard, of Middle Temple, and yst dau of Sir Richard Howe, and *d* 4 May 1710, having had surv issue, with a dau:

(1) Howe, of Witcombe Park; *m* Mary, dau of Jeffrey Watts, of Essex, and *d* 1723, leaving:

1a HOWE (Sir), **6th Bt**

1 Letitia; *bapt* 13 July 1626; *m* 1st 13 Aug 1651, as his 3rd w, 1st Earl of Donegall (*see* DONEGALL, M); *m* 2nd Sir William Franklyn, of Maverne, Beds, and was *bur* 15 May 1691, leaving issue

The 5th Bt's cousin,

Sir Howe Hicks, 6th Bt; *b* 8 Aug 1722; *m* 28 July 1739 Martha, dau of Rev John Browne, of Salperton Park, Rector Coberley, Glos, and *d* Aug 1801, having had, with three daus:

1 **Sir William Hicks, 7th Bt**; *b* 29 Oct 1754; High Sheriff Glos 1812–13; *m* 1st 12 May 1785 Judith (*dsps* 5 March 1787), 3rd dau and coheir of Edward Whit-combe, of Orleton; *m* 2nd 7 Oct 1793 Anne Rachel (*d* 13 April 1839), est dau of Thomas Lobb Chute, of The Vine, and *dspm* 23 Oct 1834, leaving by her:

(1) Anne Rachel; *m* 16 March 1816 Sir Lambert Cromie/Crumie, 2nd Bt (*see* 1841 edn), and *d* 23 Sept 1885 aged 91

2 Michael HICKS later HICKS-BEACH (roy licence 23 June 1790), of Beverston Castle and Williamstrip Park; *b* 11 April 1760; MP Cirencester 1794–1818; *m* 7 Oct 1779 Henrietta Maria (*d* 18 Oct 1837), only surv dau of William Beach, of Netheravon, Wilts, and *d* 5 Jan 1830, having had, with two daus:

(1) Michael, of Beverstone Castle, Williamstrip, Netheravon Ho and Keevil Manor, Wilts; *b* 22 Oct 1780; *m* 26 Jan 1809 Caroline Jane (*d* 4 May 1860), est dau of William Mount, of Wasing Place, Berks, and *dvp* 27 Sept 1815, leaving, with other issue:

1a MICHAEL (Sir), **8th Bt**

(2) William HICKS-BEACH later BEACH (roy licence 24 June 1838), of Oak-ley Hall, Hants, and Keevil Manor; *b* 24 July 1783; MP Malmesbury 1812–17; *m* 1 Feb 1826 Jane Henrietta (*d* 11 Aug 1831), dau of John Browne, of Salper-ton, Glos, and *d* 22 Nov 1856, leaving:

1a William Wither Bramston, PC, of Oakley Hall and Keevil Manor, JP, DL Hants; *b* 25 Dec 1826; MA Oxon; Maj Hants Yeo Cav, MP Hants 1857–85 and W Hants 1885–1901 (ultimately Father of the House), *m* 8 Oct 1857 Caroline Chichester (*d* 29 March 1918), yst dau of Col Augustus Cleveland, of Tapeley Park, Devon, and *d* 3 Aug 1901, leaving:

1b Archibald William Hicks, of Oakley Manor, Basingstoke, JP Hants; *b* 21 Oct 1859; Maj KRRC, extra ADC to Ld Lt Ireland 1886–89, FGS, PASI, Ld Manors of Deane and Oakley; *m* 5 Jan 1888 Violet Isabel (*d* 19 Sept 1891), only dau of Hon Slingsby Bethell, CB (*see* WESTBURY, B), and *d* 22 Jan 1924, leaving:

1c William Guy Hicks; *b* 23 July 1891; *educ* Eton; Lt Yeo; *m* 1st 3 Oct 1914 (*divorce* 1932) Fanny Muriel (*d* 19 Aug 1965), only dau of Ninian Bannatyne Stewart, of Wemyss Bay, Renfrewshire, and had:

1d Michael William Bramston, DSC; *b* 12 March 1919; *educ* Eton and Pembroke Coll Cambridge; Lt RNVR WW II; *m* 22 July 1940 Kathleen Edith Doreen Augusta (*d* 1985), yst dau of Sir Brodrick Cecil Hart-well, 4th Bt (*qv*), and *d* 1985, leaving:

1e Michael Brodrick; *b* 9 Jan 1942; *educ* Eton; *m* 1st 14 May 1970 (*divorce* 19–) Carolyn Anne, only dau of Sir Richard Ashton Beau-mont, KCMG, OBE, of Chelsea; *m* 2nd 1979 *Mrs Eugenia (Jenny) Anne Garton and *d* 31 Dec 1997

2d +Peter Stewart, OBE (1968) [Capt Peter Hicks-Beach OBE RN, Boscobel, Hamner Lane, Grayshott, Surrey GU26 6JD]; *b* 23 Sept 1924; *educ* RNC Dartmouth; served WW II (despatches); *m* 20 May 1950 Victoria Margaret (*d* 1986), yst dau of Ralph Victor Nelson, RN, of Horndean, Hants, and has had:

1e Richard Steward Nelson; *b* 22 July 1951; *d* 24 Jan 1966

1e *Sally Elizabeth; *b* 2 June 1953; *m* 1980 *Anthony Michael Farnfield and has:

1f *Johanna; *b* 1983

3d +Geoffrey Robert Wither [Geoffrey Hicks-Beach Esq, Cucumber Hall, Fressingfield, Suffolk]; *b* 14 Nov 1925; *educ* Charterhouse; *m* 19 July 1952 *Rosemary Wendy, dau of Harry Wolseley-Charles, of Maidenhead, and has:

1e +Nicholas Charles; *b* 6 Oct 1960; *educ* Charterhouse and Bristol U; scriptwriter *Eastenders*

1e *Fiona Susan [Mrs Anthony Edwards, 107 Mycanae Rd, London SE3]; *b* 2 June 1955; *m* 1981 *Anthony Arthur Edwards, s of A A Edwards, of Swansea, and has:

1f *Benjamin Nicholas Owen; *b* 1984

2f *Samuel Dafydd William; *b* 1989

1f *Rosamund Margretta Victoria; *b* 1986

1d Patricia Isabel; *b* 22 April, *d* 3 Oct 1922

1c (cont.) William Beach *m* 2nd 14 Dec 1932 Beatrice Mary Swetenham (*d* 24 March 1975), formerly w of Desmond Percival FitzGerald Uniacke and only dau of Arthur Oliver Johnstone, Indian Police, and *d* 8 Feb 1953

1c Cicely Caroline Hicks; *b* 1 Nov 1888; *m* 8 Sept 1914 Walter Scott MacLellan (*d* 8 April 1959), er s of George S MacLellan, of West Lodge, Glasgow, and had:

1d *Roderick George Scott; *b* 1918; *m* 1954 *Jennifer, dau of Lt-Col Stanley Casson, and has issue

1d *Violet Maude; *b* 1915; *m* 1945 Col Robert Andrew Alexander Scarth Macrae, MBE, DL, Seaforth Highrs, and has issue

2c Winifred Violet Hicks; *b* 7 Oct 1889; *m* 1 Nov 1922 William Henry Murray, 2nd s of David Alexander Bruce Murray, of Winnipeg, Canada, and *d* 8 Dec 1961

2b Ellice Michael Hicks, JP Hants; *b* 31 March 1875; *educ* Eton; 1st Sec Dip Serv; *d* unm 6 Sept 1948

1b Alice Margaret; *m* 19 July 1890 William Graham Nicholson, PC, of Basing Park, Hants, and *d* 8 May 1935, leaving issue. He *d* 29 July 1942

1a Mary Jane; *m* 19 April 1849 Sir Wyndham Spencer Portal, 1st Bt (*qv*), and *d* 4 Nov 1903, leaving issue

2a Henrietta Maria; *m* 22 June 1852 Col Sir John Williams Wallington, KCB, of Keevil Manor, Wilts, and *d* 26 Oct 1905, leaving issue. He *d* 23 March 1910

The 7th Bt's great-nephew,

Sir Michael Hicks-Beach, 8th Bt; *b* 25 Oct 1809; MP E Glos 1854; *m* 14 Aug 1832 Harriett Vittoria (*d* 20 Jan 1900), 2nd dau of John Stratton, of Farthinghoe Lodge, Northants, and had (male-line descendents of the yr s being in remainder to the Btcy only):

1 MICHAEL EDWARD, 1st Earl

2 William Frederick, of Witcombe Park, Glos, JP; *b* 14 July 1841; CA Glos, MP Tewkesbury 1916–18; *m* 1st 5 July 1865 Elizabeth Caroline (*d* 22 Jan 1901), dau of Thomas Tyrwhitt Drake, of Shardeloes, and had:

(1) William; *b* 12 July 1866; Capt 4th Bn Gloucester Regt; *d* unm 20 July 1906

(2) Michael; *b* 8 Aug 1872; *m* 20 Dec 1907 Helene (*d* 29 May 1941), dau of Arthur Des Fosses, of Montreal, and *d* 6 July 1952, leaving:

1a Michael, of Bedford Hills, NY, USA; *b* 20 May 1909; Sr Master Sgt SAC USAF; *m* 1st 26 May 1932 (*divorce* 1958) Dorothy, dau of Robert Stratton, of Clinton, Conn., and *d* 9 Sept 1994, leaving:

1b *Heather Dianne [Mrs Heather Hicks-Beach, 417 Hampton Court, Falls Church, VA 22046, USA]; *b* 3 Aug 1935; *m* 20 Jan 1957 (*divorce* 1970, resumed maiden name) Edward Lionel Peck, US For Serv, Amb (ret), only s of Alexander George Peck, of Los Angeles, and has:

1c *Brian Michael; *b* 2 Nov 1960; *m* 1996 *Sachiko Kono, dau of Michihisa Kono, of Tokyo

1c *Heather Anne; *b* 1 March 1959; *m* 1989 *Michael Lindner and has:

1d *Noah William; *b* 1994

1d *Jamie Sarah; *b* 1998

1a (cont.) Michael Hicks-Beach *m* 2nd 27 May 1944 Eunice W (*d* 1973), dau of Rudolph J Thanisch, of Boston, Mass.; *m* 3rd 1974 Grace Vera (*d* 1996), dau of Henry Moos, Sr, of Union City, NJ, and widow of Charles Arthur Rankin

2a Frederick Edward; *b* 30 Dec 1911; Lt-Cdr USN; *m* 1st 1941 (*divorce* 1947) Harriet (*m* 2nd 1947 Oren Clark Burt), dau of — Green, of Brooklyn, and had:

1b *Frances Helene [Ms Frances Hicks-Beach, 934 E 40th St, Brooklyn, NY 11210, USA]; *b* 2 Sept 1942; has:

1c *Liam Christopher; *b* 1981

2a (cont.) Lt-Cdr Frederick Hicks-Beach *m* 2nd 5 April 1947 Lois (*d* 1988), dau of John W Lainhart, of Washington, DC, and *d* 14 Sept 1972

3a John Hugh; *b* 24 May 1915; *m* 21 July 1945 *Jeanne Potter [Mrs John Hicks-Beach, 55 Clinton Rd, Bedford Hills, NY, USA], dau of Herbert McGuhy, of Bedford Hills, and *d* 1982, leaving:

1b +John Hugh; *b* 18 Dec 1960

1b *Lucinda [Mrs Timothy Quinn, 21 Sunset Place, N Salem, NY 10560, USA]; *b* 16 Feb 1948; *m* 6 May 1971 *Timothy F Quinn and has:

1c *Tressan Lucinda; *b* 1977

2c *Holly Bebhinn; *b* 1979

2b *Priscilla; *b* 31 Dec 1950; *m* 1982 *Ferdinand Travis Hopkins IV

(3) Ellis; *b* 22 April 1874; *educ* Charterhouse; Ch Chancery Registrar Supreme Court Judicature, 2nd Lt Welsh Gds and Lt 2nd Vol Bn Gloucester Regt; *m* 24 Sept 1903 Nancy (*d* 7 Sept 1942), only child of Spencer Whitehead, Master Supreme Court, and *d* 27 Sept 1943, having had:

1a William Whitehead, TD, DL (Glos 1963); *b* 23 March 1907; *educ* Eton and Magdalene Coll Cambridge; slr 1932, ptnr Payne, Hicks Beach and Co 1933, Maj Roy Glos Hus (TA), MP (C) Cheltenham 1950–64; *m* 12 Sept 1939 *Diana, dau of Christopher Gurney Hoare, of Gateley Hall, Elmham, Norfolk, and *d* 1 Jan 1975, leaving:

1b Mark William; *b* 8 Feb 1943; *educ* Eton; *m* 25 March 1966 *Cecilia Ruth [Mrs Mark Hicks Beach, Witcombe Farm, Great Witcombe, Glos

GL3 4TR], er dau of Douglas Allan Wright, of Ashford, Kent, and *d* 7 Feb 1998, having had:

1c Jonathan Ellis; *b* 1967; *d* 26 April 1967

2c +Andrew William; *b* 1970

3c +Frederick David; *b* 1980

1c *Lucinda Jane; *b* 1975

1b *Elizabeth Anne [Mrs Simon Clarke, Pennybridge Farm, Mayfield, Sussex]; *b* 17 Aug 1940; *m* 19 May 1962 *Simon Ernest Houlston Clarke, only s of Thomas G Clarke, DSO, of Knightsbridge, and Mrs C T Miller, of Chelsea, and has:

1c *Martin; *b* 24 Nov 1963

2c *Timothy; *b* 14 Oct 1965

2b *Rosemary Gillian [Mrs Murray Naylor, South Warnborough Manor, Hants RE25 1RR]; *b* 3 June 1944; *m* 31 July 1965 *Maj-Gen (David) Murray Naylor, Scots Gds, yr s of Thomas Humphrey Naylor, of The Grange, Ashton, Cheshire (*see* 1940 edn HOLT, Bt), and has:

1c *Nicholas John; *b* 13 March 1967

2c *Duncan Hugh; *b* 17 Oct 1968

3c *Christopher William; *b* 1972

2a Spencer Ellis; *b* 7 May 1911; *d* unm 30 Nov 1969

3a John; *b* 4 May; *d* 15 June 1913

1a Rachel; *b* 17 July 1904; *m* 10 April 1934 Col Edward Roderick Hill, DSO, Coldstream Gds, only s of Capt Roderick Tickell Hill, of St Arvan's Court, Chepstow, and had issue

2a Anne; *b* 30 March 1908; *m* 27 April 1931 4th Baron Leigh (*qv*) and *d* 1977, having had issue

3a *Letitia [Mrs John Grover, 57 Lyndhurst Grove, London SE15]; *b* 16 Oct 1909; *m* 1st 7 Aug 1931 (*divorce* 1939) Horace Alfred Townsend, only s of William Alfred Townsend, and has:

1b *John [John Townsend Esq, 23 Aldersmead Rd, Beckenham, Kent]; *b* 1934; *m* 1957 *Andrina Hume

1b *Tomazin [Mrs Stanley Geller, 120 Harwich Rd, Mistley, Essex CO11 2DG]; *b* 1933; *m* 1953 *Stanley John Geller

3a (cont.) Mrs Letitia Townsend *m* 2nd 20 Jan 1947 (*divorce* 1960) George Rufus Miles, s of George Rufus Miles, of Greenwich, and has by him:

2b *George Rufus [George Miles Esq, Garden Cottage, Rookery Rd, Downe, Herts]; *b* 20 Feb 1949; *educ* The Friends Sch Saffron Walden

3b *Richard Josef [Richard Miles Esq, Great Mollands Farmhouse, South Ockenden, Essex]; *b* 31 Jan 1951; *educ* The Friends Sch Saffron Walden

3a (cont.) Mrs Letitia Miles *m* 3rd 10 Nov 1960 *John Messent Grover, s of Douglas Walter Grover, of Culver End, Amberley, Glos

(4) Edward Howe; *b* 7 Dec 1875; *educ* Marlborough; *m* 2 Sept 1903 Alberta Louise (*d* 8 Oct 1946), dau of William Penn Jaynes, of Vancouver, and *d* 21 April 1967, leaving:

1a +Edward Adryan [Edward Hicks-Beach, PO Box 1373, La Pine, OR 97739, USA]; *b* 21 Oct 1915; *m* 1st 30 Dec 1936 (*divorce* 1940) Evelyn Jane, dau of Clarence Hiram Dale, of Los Angeles; *m* 2nd 13 Oct 1940 *Linnéa Maria, dau of Andrew Holst, and by her has:

1b +Edward Erick [Edward Hicks-Beach, RR1 Box 60Y, Custer, SD 57730, USA]; *b* 4 Sept 1941; *m* 13 Aug 1991 *Betty May Snider, dau of Henry C Snider, of Johnson Co, Iowa

2b +Frederick Howe [Frederick Hicks-Beach, 5181 Heil Ave, Huntington Beach, CA 92649, USA]; *b* 21 June 1944; *m* 12 Dec 1970 *Kathleen Mary, dau of Roy Edward Fincher, and has:

1c *Chad Edward; *b* 12 Dec 1977

1c *Clara; *b* 19 Jan 1983

1a Clara Violet Louise; *b* 1905; *m* 12 Dec 1954 *Ralph Ehner Wilson, 2nd s of Harry Ehner Wilson, of El Monte, California

2a Doris Margaret; *b* 1910; *m* 21 July 1934 Harry Roderic Theodore Marble (*d* 7 May 1993), only s of Daniel Arthur Marble, of Southgate, California, and *d* 2 Sept 1991 leaving:

1b *Harry Arthur [Harry Marble, 3221 21st Street, Santa Monica, CA, USA]; *b* 29 June 1936; *m* 1st 29 Jan 1966 (*divorce*) Marilyn Frances, dau of Francis A Schneider, of Oxford, Iowa; *m* 2nd Dec 1996 *Sylvia —, and by his 1st w has:

1c *Daniel Edward [Daniel Marble Esq, 3822 College Ave, Culver City, CA, USA]; *b* 29 Oct 1966; *m* Aug 1996 *Nicola Van Dam

2c *Timothy John; *b* 26 Feb 1968

3c *Joseph Harry; *b* 1975

1c *Karen Margaret; *b* 1971

2b *William Edward [William Marble, 175 Toho Trail, Flagstaff, AZ, USA]; *b* 28 Jan 1947

3b *Michael Stephen; *b* 28 Jan 1947

1b *Linnea Louise [Mrs Garrith Perrine, 4266 Saratoga Dr, Redding, CA 96002, USA]; *b* 20 Aug 1940; *m* 1st 6 June 1959 (*divorce* 1977) Charles Bartl Adams, s of Walter John Adams, of Santa Monica; *m* 2nd 1977 *Garrith Dale Perrine and by her 1st husb has:

1c *Gregory Walter [Gregory Adams Esq, 1916 Alexis Court, Redding, CA, USA]; *b* 27 Nov 1962; *m* 10 Sept 1988 (*divorce* 1994) Kathryn, dau of Harold Willoughby, of Corning, Calif, and has issue

2c *Brian Roderic; *b* 27 Feb 1965

3c *Steven Edward; *b* 10 Sept 1969; *m* 7 Oct 1995 *Amy Elizabeth, dau of Warren Magee, of Napa, Calif, and has issue

(5) Charles; *b* 5 Jan 1878; *d* unm 13 March 1961

(1) Violet Elizabeth; *m* 3 Dec 1907 1st and last Earl Loreburn and *d* 5 Feb 1931. He *dsp* 30 Nov 1923

(2) Margaret Agnes; *m* 21 Oct 1908 Joseph Dillworth Crewdson, yst s of Theodore Crewdson, of Syde, Glos, and *d* 8 March 1943. He *d* 15 Aug 1946

(3) Myrtle Ardina; *d* 17 June 1937

2 (cont.) William Hicks-Beach *m* 2nd 25 Nov 1903 Susan (*d* 17 Nov 1958), dau of Adml Henry Christian, MVO, and *d* 7 Sept 1923

1 Carolina Julia; *m* 7 May 1861 Sir John Talbot Dillwyn-Llewelyn, 1st Bt (*see* DILLWYN-VENABLES-LLEWELYN, Bt) and *d* 3 March 1917, leaving issue

2 Emily Georgina Jane; *m* 28 Jan 1864 George Pargiter Fuller and *d* 30 Dec 1930, leaving issue (*see* FULLER, Bt)

3 Alice Mary; *m* 10 Aug 1865 William Henry Barneby, DL, of Longworth & Brockington Grange, Herefs, 2nd s of John Barneby, MP, of Brockhampton Park, Herefs, and *d* 27 Jan 1933, having had issue. He *d* 6 July 1914

4 Henrietta Maria; *m* 7 Jan 1873 Rev Robert Lowbridge Baker, of West Hay, Somerset, Rector Wilcote-cum-Ramsden, Oxon, and *d* 25 Feb 1932, leaving issue. He *d* 3 Jan 1904

5 Laura Harriet; *m* 19 Nov 1872 Arthur Charles Mitchell, of High Grove, Tetbury, Glos, and *d* 6 March 1874, leaving issue. He *d* 25 March 1917

6 Mary Ethel; *m* 12 Oct 1882 2nd Baron Crawshaw (*qv*) and *d* 1 Oct 1914, leaving issue

The 8th Bt *d* 22 Nov 1854; his er son,

Sir Michael Edward Hicks-Beach, 9th Bt, and **1st Earl Saint Aldwyn**, of Coln St Aldwyn, Glos, so cr 22 Feb 1915, as also VISCOUNT QUENINGTON, of Quenington, Co Glos, as also earlier 6 Jan 1906 VISCOUNT SAINT ALDWYN, of Coln St Aldwyn, Co Glos (all UK); PC (GB and I 1874), JP, DL Glos; *b* 23 Oct 1837; *educ* Eton and Ch Ch Oxford (BA 1858, MA 1861, Hon DCL 1878); MP (C) E Glos 1864–85 and W Bristol 1885–1906, Parly Sec Poor Law Bd 1868, U-Sec Home Dept 1868, Ch Sec Ireland 1874–78 and 1886–87, Colonial Sec 1878–80, Chllr Exchequer 1885–86 and 1895–1902, Pres BOT 1888–92, Church Estates Commr 1892–95 and 1908, High Steward Gloucester, Ind Chm S Wales Coal Trade Conciliation Bd; *m* 1st 6 Jan 1864 Caroline Susan (*dsp* 14 Aug 1865), dau of John Henry Elwes, of Colesbourne Park, Glos; *m* 2nd 3 Sept 1874 Lady Lucy Catherine (*d* 17 March 1940), 3rd dau of 3rd Earl Fortescue (*qv*), and by her had:

1 Michael Hugh, *Viscount Quenington*, JP Glos; *b* 19 Jan 1877; *educ* Eton and Ch Ch Oxford (BA 1901, MA 1904); MP Tewkesbury 1906–16, Lt and Adj Roy Glos Yeo, Capt 4th Bn Gloucester Regt; *m* 28 Sept 1909 Marjorie (*d* 4 March 1916), dau of Henry Dent Brocklehurst, of Sudeley Castle, Glos, bro of 1st and last Baron Ranksborough, and was *ka* Egypt 23 April 1916, leaving:

  (1) MICHAEL JOHN, **2nd Earl**

  (1) *Delia Mary; *b* 2 Aug 1910; granted rank of earl's dau 12 Jan 1920; *m* 3 Dec 1934 Brigadier Sir Michael Dillwyn-Venables-Llewelyn, 3rd Bt (*qv*), and has issue

1 Eleanor Lucy; *b* 29 Oct 1875; *m* 14 Feb 1907 Lt-Col Sir John Keane, 5th Bt (*qv*), and *d* 1 Dec 1960, leaving issue

2 Susan Evelyn, JP Glos; *b* 15 June 1878; *d* unm 17 Feb 1965

3 Victoria Alexandrina; *b* 12 Sept 1879 (HM QUEEN VICTORIA stood sponsor); *d* unm 29 April 1963

The 1st EARL *d* 30 April 1916 (a week after his s's death); his gs,

MICHAEL JOHN HICKS-BEACH, **2nd Earl Saint Aldwyn**, KBE (1964), TD, PC (1959), JP (Glos 1952), DL (1950); *b* 9 Oct 1912; *educ* Eton and Ch Ch Oxford; Parly Sec Min Ag and Fish 1954–58, Capt Gentlemen at Arms and Govt Ch Whip Ho Lds 1958–64 and 1970–74, Opposition Ch Whip Ho Lds 1964–70 and 1974–78, Maj Roy Glos Hus (TA), GCStJ 1978, Chllr OStJ 1978 (V-Chllr 1969–78); *m* 26 June 1948 Mrs Diana Mary Christian Smyly, DStJ (*d* 10 July 1992), only dau of Henry Christian George Mills (*see* 1970 edn HILLINGDON, B), and *d* 29 Jan 1992, having had:

1 MICHAEL HENRY HICKS BEACH, **3rd and present Earl Saint Aldwyn**

2 Peter Hugh; *b* 21 May 1952; *educ* Eton; painter; *d* unm 1990

3 +DAVID SEYMOUR [The Hon David Hicks Beach, The Upper Mill, Coln St Aldwyns, Glos GL7 5AJ]; *b* 25 May 1955; heir presumptive; *educ* Eton and RAC Cirencester; Page of Honour to HM THE QUEEN 1969–72, proprietor The Bones Dogalogue (mail order accessories for dogs); *m* 1993 *Katrina (Kate) Louise Susannah, dau of Michael Henriques, of Winson Manor, Cirencester, and has:

  (1) *Lucy Susan; *b* 31 Oct 1996

ST CLAIR-FORD

Arms: Per pale gu. and or two bends vair, on a canton of the second a greyhound courant sa. **Crest:** A greyhound's head sa., erased gu., muzzled or. **Motto:** *Omnium rerum vicissitudo* ('All things are subject to change'). **Creation:** Bt. (GB) 22 Feb 1793

SIR JAMES ANSON ST CLAIR-FORD, 7TH BT, of Ember Court, Surrey [Sir James St Clair-Ford Bt, 161 Sheen Lane, London SW14 8NA]; *b* 16 March 1952; *s* f 1991; *educ* Wellington and Bristol U; *m* 1977 (*divorce* 1985) Jennifer Margaret, yr dau of Cdre J Robin Grindle, RN, of Drake House, Devonport; *m* 2nd 1987 *Mary Anne, er dau of His Hon Judge (Nathaniel Robert) Blaker, QC, DL, of Winchester

Lineage: THOMAS FORD, of The Ridge, Barbados (descended from a royalist family in Devon); *m* 24 July 1690 Eleanor Austin and had:

FRANCIS FORD; *bapt* 6 Feb 1693; Memb Assembly Barbados; *m* Martha, dau of Smithell Matson and widow of Capt John Hooper, and had:

FRANCIS FORD, of Lears, Barbados; *b* 24 Feb 1717; Memb Barbados Assembly; *m* 28 Jan 1758 Elizabeth (*bur* 18 April 1764), widow of Samuel Osbourne and dau of Birch Hothersall, both of Barbados, and *d* 1772, having had, with three daus (Martha, *m* W Becher, of Howbury, Beds; Anne, *m* John Swinfen, of Swinfen Hall, Staffs; Elizabeth, *m* 14 Oct 1790 9th Lord Colville of Culross (*qv*) and *dsp* 19 Aug 1839):

Sir Francis Ford, 1st Bt (GB), so cr 22 Feb 1793, of Ember Court, Surrey; *b* 15 Nov 1758; Memb Cncl Barbados, MP (GB Parl) 1790; *m* 22 Jan 1785 Mary (*d* 20 Jan 1837), est dau of George ANSON formerly ADAMS (*see* LICHFIELD, E), and *d* Barbados 17 June 1801, having had, with other issue:

1 **Sir Francis Ford, 2nd Bt**; *b* 15 Feb 1787; *m* 4 Sept 1817 Eliza (*d* 20 May 1875), only dau of Henry Brady, of Limerick, and *d* 13 April 1839, having had, with another **s** (*d* unm):

  (1) **Sir Francis John Ford, 3rd Bt**; *b* 14 Aug 1818; *m* 31 Oct 1846 Cornelia Maria (*d* 21 May 1896), est dau of Gen Sir Ralph Darling, GCH, and *d* 26 Nov 1850, having had, with other issue:

    1a **Sir Francis Colville Ford, 4th Bt**; *b* 11 June 1850; *m* 25 March 1873 his cousin Frances Colville, est dau of William Ford, CSI (*see* below), and *d* 16 Nov 1890, leaving:

      1b **Sir (Francis Charles) Rupert Ford, 5th Bt**; *b* 5 April 1877; *m* 3 Sept 1918 Katharine Olive, 2nd dau of James Charles Yorke (*see* HARDWICKE, E), and *dspm* 28 Feb 1948, leaving:

        1c (Beryl) Cicely; *b* 16 Dec 1921; *m* 27 Oct 1951 *James Arthur Peter Peirce, MB, ChB, BSc [James Peirce Esq, St Annes, 4 Hill Road, Swanage, Dorset], s of Cyril Hubert Newport Peirce, of Cascais, Portugal, and *d* 15 April 1995, leaving:

          1d *Martin Charles Arthur; *b* 17 Nov 1952; *educ* Tonbridge

          1d *Sarah Jane Charlotte; *b* 4 April 1955

        2c *Janetta Olive [Mrs David Pullinger, 16 Hollow Oak Road, Stoborough, Dorset BH20 5AH]; *b* 20 Nov 1925; *m* 2 May 1964 *David Ryland Pullinger, s of Sidney Russell Pullinger, of Swanage

      2b Francis Walter Barton (Rev); *b* 5 April 1877; MA Dunelm; Minister private chapel of S Richard de Wych, Ashdown Park, nr Tunbridge Wells; Vicar Dunton Green, Kent, 1904–06, Ganton 1919–20 and Dorney, Windsor, 1927–30; *m* 21 Sept 1909 Louisa Gann, 2nd dau of Robert McKenzie Nish, and *d* 27 June 1939, leaving:

        1c Francis Colville McKenzie; *b* 15 Oct 1911; Gunner RA WW II; *ka* 1943

      1b Frances Elsie; *m* 10 Sept 1900 Raymond Carpmael, MICE, MIME, of Reading, s of Deanston Carpmael, of Little Thurrock Hall, Grays, Essex, and *d* 21 Jan 1931

      2b Helena Blanche Colville; *d* unm 21 Nov 1930

      3b Cornelia Caroline; *m* 5 April 1915 Reuben Ball and *d* 9 Oct 1946, leaving issue

  (2) William, CSI, of Ford Park, Chagford; *b* 29 Nov 1821; BCS 1842–69 (a bar and medal for good service at Delhi during Indian Mutiny); *m* 27 Oct 1845 Catherine Margaret (*d* 23 Oct 1869), est dau of Maj-Gen John Anthony Hodgson, HEICS, of Bishop Auckland, and *d* 18 June 1905, having had:

    1a Frances Colville; *m* 25 March 1873 her cousin **Sir Francis Colville Ford, 4th Bt** (*see* above), and *d* 9 June 1911, leaving issue

    2a Edith Mary; *m* 26 Aug 1875 Edward Penrose Arnold-Forster, DL, s of William Delafield Arnold and adopted s of W E Forster, PC, MP, and *d* 16 Dec 1942, leaving issue. He *d* 19 Jan 1927

  (3) St Clair FORD later ST CLAIR-FORD (1878); *b* 6 Jan 1830; Capt Bombay Staff Corps; *m* 27 Nov 1862 Eliza Jane (*d* 4 March 1919), est dau of Thomas Smalley Potter, of East Court, Charlton Kings, Glos, and *d* 31 Jan 1896, leaving:

    1a Anson St Clair; *b* 7 Oct 1864; Capt 1st Garrison Bn Leicester Regt, Glos Yeo Boer War 1900–01; *m* 18 Feb 1903 Isabel Maria Frances (*d* 26 Oct 1955), 2nd dau of Francis Adams, of Llyfnant, Cheltenham, and *d* 6 May 1940, having had:

      1b AUBREY (Sir) **6th Bt**

    2b Peter (Sir), KBE (1961, CBE 1953), CB (1954), DSO (1943) and bar (1944); *b* 25 Nov 1905; *educ* Dover Coll and RMC Sandhurst; Maj-Gen KOYLI WW II, Malaya 1951–52, Training Advsr Pakistan Army 1952–54, GOC(1) Fedn Malaya 1955–57, Dep Ch Staff ALFCE 1958–60 (ret), Gen Sec Offrs Assoc 1963; *d* 14 May 1989

    3b Drummond; *b* 16 Dec 1907; Lt-Cdr RN WW II; *m* 26 Aug 1933 *Norah Elizabeth (*m* 2nd 3 July 1945 R-Adml Peter Noel Buckley, CB, DSO (*d* 1988), of Sway, Hants), only dau of Capt Charles James Astley Maberly, 17th Lancers, of Compton, Hants, and was *ka* cmdg HM Submarine *Traveller* Dec 1942, leaving:

      1c +COLIN ANSON [Colin St Clair-Ford Esq, Honeysuckle Cottage, E Lambrook, S Petherton, Somerset TA13 5HW]; *b* 19 April 1939; heir presumptive; *educ* Nautical Coll Pangbourne; *m* 18 April 1964 *Gillian Mary, est dau of R-Adml Peter Skelton, CB, of Beaconsfield, Bucks, and has:

        1d *Kate Mary; *b* 6 March 1967; *m* 1993 *Jonathan Paul Weatherall, s of Ian Weatherall, of Purley, Surrey

        2d *Fiona Elizabeth; *b* 11 March 1969

      2c +Robin Sam [Robin St Clair-Ford Esq, 4 Wardie Rd, Edinburgh EH5 3QD]; *b* 6 June 1941; *educ* Nautical Coll Pangbourne and RMA Sandhurst; Capt The Light Infantry; m 13 Dec 1980 *Alison Frances, yr dau of William Dickson, of Corsham, Wilts, and has:

1d +(William) Sam; b 24 Jan 1982

2d +Peter James; b 17 Feb 1984

1c *Elizabeth Jane [Lady James, West Bucknowle House, Bucknowle, Dorset BH20 5PQ]; b 29 May 1937; m 18 Nov 1961 *Sir John Nigel Courtenay James, KCVO, CBE, est s of Frank James, of Little Garth, Lilliput, Dorset, and has:

1d *Simon Drummond Courtenay; b 12 Nov 1966

1d *Annabel Clare; b 4 Feb 1964

4b Francis; b 29 July, d 4 Sept 1909

5b Vernon John, MBE (1940); b 24 June 1918; Cdr RN WW II; m 20 Nov 1947 *Patricia Mary (m 2nd 27 Nov 1954 Lt-Cdr Michael Lionel Yeoward Ainsworth, RN (d 1978); m 3rd 1984 *Richard Patrick Beeny, of Whitewater Lodge, Riseley Mill, Berks), dau of Frederick Gordon Hay Bedford, of Petersfield, Hants, and d 18 Aug 1952, leaving:

1c +Timothy Bedford; b 7 July 1948; educ Bradfield and UEA; m 19– *Jennie Hemsley and has:

1d *Emma; b 1977

2d *Charlotte; b 1979

2c +Gordon Sam; b 12 Dec 1950; educ Bradfield and Southampton U; m 1979 *Hilary Jean, dau of Maj H Charlesworth, of Wokingham, Berks, and has:

1d +Rufus; b 1980

2d +Joseph; b 1981

1d *Theresa; b 1984

1b Daphne Jane, OBE (1972); b 3 April 1914; m 1 Dec 1934 Col Geoffrey William Preston, RE (d 1976), only child of John Harrison Preston, and d 12 Oct 1997, leaving:

1c *Roger St Clair, CBE (1986, OBE 1979) [Brig Roger Preston CBE, Whitegrounds, Thornthorpe, Malton, N Yorks YO17 9LX]; b 24 Oct 1935; educ Eton and RMA Sandhurst; Brig LI (late KOYLI); m 29 Aug 1964 *Polly Mary, dau of Robin Marriott, of Malton, N Yorks, and has:

1d *Mark Robin; b 20 Jan 1968; m 27 Aug 1997 *Katherine, dau of Robert Whittaker, of Ravensmoor, Nantwich, Cheshire

2d *Hugh Geoffrey; b 21 Oct 1970

1d *Sarah Jane; b 5 March 1966; m 30 Aug 1994 *Alexander Guthe, s of Digby Guthe, of Silton Hall, Thirsk, N Yorks, and has:

1e *Annabel Mathilda; b 13 Feb 1998

1c *Judith Mary; b 15 July 1946; m 16 Sept 1967 (divorce 1992) Lt Adrian Charles Estcourt, Parachute Regt, s of Maj-Gen Edward Noel Keith Estcourt, DSO, OBE, of The Vyne, Sherborne St John, Basingstoke, Hants

2a Beauchamp St Clair; b 7 April 1867; Lt-Col E Yorkshire Regt, Boer War 1901–02; m 1911 Alzbeta Wolencova (d 25 Jan 1970 aged 90), dau of Antonino Wolencz, of Weinberge, Bohemia, and d 12 Nov 1938

3a Leicester St Clair, MBE (1919); b 1879; T/Capt RASC; m 12 June 1906 Hildred Carlyle (d 8 May 1962), 3rd dau of Rowland Ticehurst, of Cheltenham and Crickley, Glos, and d 24 Feb 1938

1a Eva St Clair; m 21 July 1898 Henry Cecil Donald, s of William Donald, of Victoria, and d 4 July 1934. He d 27 Oct 1904

2a Ada St Clair; m 29 July 1893 Archibald Hamilton Donald, yr s of Colin Dunlop Donald, of Glasgow, and had issue. He d 1919

(1) Mary; m 28 Jan 1840 Rev Sir William Lionel Darell, 4th Bt (qv), and dsp 9 March 1842

(2) Eliza Caroline; m 1st 28 Sept 1849 Lt-Col Christopher Simpson Maling, 68th Regt (d March 1860); m 2nd 12 Feb 1866 Lt-Col William Charles Newhouse, 5th Fus, and d 5 Jan 1879

(3) Anna Maria; m 13 Aug 1851 Gen Sir David Scott Dodgson, KCB, Bengal Army, and d 14 Feb 1881, leaving issue. He d 26 May 1898

2 Charles (Rev); b 1797; Rector Billingford and Postwick; m 9 May 1839 Catherine, est dau of Henry Stuart (see LICHFIELD, E), and d 9 May 1863, leaving, with other issue:

(1) Henry Stuart; b 1 Oct 1843; Lt RA; m 1873 Sophia Sarah (dsp 9 Aug 1881), dau of E Gregory; m 2nd 8 Sept 1883 Mary, dau of Thomas Wells, and d 8 Oct 1895, having by her had, with a dau (d young):

1a Reginald Severne; Lt 1st/9th Bn Hants Regt

(2) William Vernon; b 2 Oct 1847; m 1878 Lydia, dau of H C Price, and d 1890

(3) Charles Primrose (Rev); b 27 May 1849; BA Cantab; Chaplain E R Mental Hosp; m 2 Sept 1875 Mary Jane (d 26 Feb 1830), dau of Rev I B Turner, and d 27 Nov 1922, leaving, with other issue:

1a Roger Anson (Rev); b 5 July 1878; BA Cantab; Capt 25th Bn Royal Fus, Priest in Charge St Margaret's Corstorphine, Edinburgh; m 27 July 1916 Kathleen Orme, dau of Montague Torridge Morris, Colonial CS, and d 23 June 1932, leaving:

1b Peter Roger Anson; b 12 May 1917; W/Cdr RAF WW II; ka 20 June 1944

2b +Montague Patrick; b 14 Dec 1918; BSc, MRCVS, Sr Veterinary Offr Colonial Service N Nigeria 1958; m 1st 12 April 1951 (divorce 1967) Rosalind Elizabeth, dau of Lt-Col Thomas Harold Barnes, of Castle Cary, Somerset; m 2nd 1969 *Ivy Lillian Lowden, dau of William Bucknell, and by his 1st w has:

1c *Sara Kathleen; b 5 April 1959

3b Francis Orme; b 16 Oct 1920; Capt RM Commandos WW II; ka Sicily 1943

4b +Charles Primrose [Charles Ford Esq, The Old Rectory, Skidbrooke, Lincs LN11 7DQ]; b 31 Dec 1922; educ Trin Coll Glenalmond; F/Lt RAF (ret); m 30 April 1949 *Margaret Watson and has:

1c *Victoria Primrose; b 21 Dec 1953

1b *Dorothy Vernon; b 1930

2a Charles Stuart, JP, b 7 Oct 1879; Maj RO 38th Bn Ottawa Highrs, Commr Ottawa; m 17 Nov 1916 Alice Elizabeth (d 21 May 1941), dau of Thomas Deavy, and dsp 10 Jan 1944

1a Margaret Vernon; b 8 Oct 1880; m 1Sept 1904 Capt Reginald Tavernor Johnson, 5th N Staffs Regt (ka 13 Oct 1915), of The Upper House, Barlaston, Staffs, s of H J Johnson, and d 7 April 1960

2a Alice Constance; b 15 Sept 1885; m 17 July 1907 Cuthbert Bailey and had issue

(1) Catherine Mary; m 12 April 1864 Henry Prescott Green and d 27 Oct 1900. He d 1892

1 Mary; m 1st 24 Feb 1807 Peter Touchet; m 2nd 20 July 1816 Capt Henry Elton, RN (see ELTON, Bt), and d 12 May 1872, leaving issue

2 Georgiana; m 4 March 1816 I E F Welch, of Edworth Park, Glos, and d April 1879

3 Sophia Catherine; m 19 Feb 1822 Col John Palmer Chichester, of Arlington, Devon, and dsp 29 April 1847. He d 5 Nov 1823

4 Caroline; m John Hyde, of Hardwick, Lancs, and d 24 Sept 1882

5 Anne; m 20 July 1844 Robert Bertram Mitford, yr bro of John Philip Osbaldeston Mitford, JP, of Mitford Castle, Northumberland, and d 29 June 1870. He dsp 1 Dec 1880

The 5th Bt's cousin,

Sir Aubrey St Clair-Ford, 6th Bt, DSO (1942) and bar (1942); b 29 Feb 1904; educ RNCs Osborne and Dartmouth; Capt RN WW II (despatches twice), Korea 1951 (despatches twice), Offr US Legn Merit 1954; m 10 May 1945 *Anne [Dowager Lady St Clair-Ford, West Winds, Woodgreen, Fordingbridge, Hants SP6 2AU], dau of Harold Cecil Christopherson, of Penerley Lodge, Beaulieu, Hants, and d 8 April 1991, leaving:

1 Sir JAMES ANSON ST CLAIR-FORD, **7th and present Bt**

1 *Julia Mary [Mrs Patrick Hunter-Jones, North Green Farm, Sibton, Saxmundham, Suffolk]; b 11 March 1954, m 1st 1977 (divorce 1983) John E Kerr; m 2nd 17 Sept 1992 *Patrick Hunter-Jones and by him has:

(1) *Charles Alexander Aubrey; b 3 Aug 1995

(2) *Lucy Claire; b 1 May 1994

SAINT DAVIDS

Arms: Argent a lion rampant sable, ducally gorged and chained or, langued and taloned gules. **Crest:** A lion as in the arms.
Supporters: Dexter, a knight vested in chain armour, his jupon charged with the arms of PHILIPPS and resting his exterior hand upon the hilt of his sword; sinister, a knight vested in plate-armour, his jupon charged with the arms of WOGAN (or, on a chief sable three martlets of the field) and resting his exterior hand upon the hilt of his sword, both standing upon a battlemented wall, all proper. **Motto:** Ducit amor patriæ ('Love of country motivates (me)').
Creations: B. (E) 26 Sept 1299 (Strange), 7 Jan 1425/6 (Hungerford), 13 Jan 1444/5 (Moleyns) and (UK) 6 July 1908 (St Davids); Bt. (E) 9 Nov 1621; V. (UK) 17 June 1918.

THE 3RD VISCOUNT SAINT DAVIDS, of Lydstep Haven, Co Pembroke, **Lord** (Baron) **Strange** (of Knokyn), **Lord** (Baron) **Hungerford**, **Lord** (Baron) **Moleyns** (the + against each living female or her issue or the living issue of a deceased female refers to the fact that the Baronies of Strange, Hungerford and Moleyns only are heritable by and through females as well as males), **3rd Baron Saint Davids**, of Roch Castle, Co Pembroke, and a **Baronet** (Sir Colwyn Jestyn John Philipps, Bt) [The Rt Hon The Viscount Saint Davids, House of Lords, London SW1A 0PW]; b 30 Jan 1939; s f 1991; educ Haverfordwest GS, Sevenoaks Sch, George Taylor and Staff Melbourne, Australia, and King's Coll London (Cert Advanced Musical Studies 1989); with Securities Agy 1957–58 (trainee) and 1960–65, 2nd Lt Welsh Gds Nat Serv 1958–60, memb Stock Exchange 1965, investment analyst Maguire Kingsmill & Co 1965–68, ptnr Kemp-Gee (subsequently Scrimgeour Kemp-Gee) 1971, dir: Citicorp Scrimgeour Vickers 1985–88 and Greig Middleton 1989–90 (consultant 1991–92), Ld-in-Waiting (Govt Whip) 1992–94, a Dep Speaker Ho Lds 1995–; memb Baden-Powell Fellowship 1985–,

Liveryman Musicians' Co 1971–; *m* 7 Dec 1965 *Augusta Victoria Correa Larrain*, dau of Don Estantislao Correa Ugarte, of Santiago, Chile, and has:
  1 +RHODRI COLWYN; *b* 16 Sept 1966; *educ* Worth
  2 +Roland Augusto Jestyn Estantislao; *b* 9 April 1970; *educ* Downside

Lineage (of Philipps): CYDIFOR FAWR, of Blaen Cuch, N Dyfed; *m* Elinor, allegedly of Cilsant, Llanwinio, Carmarths, dau of Llwch Llawen Fawr, and *d* 1091, having had:

BLEDRI LATIMER, of Cilsant, called 'Latimer', or 'Interpreter', because he understood the language of the Normans who about now began their advance into S Wales and could help the Welsh communicate with them; living 1116; *m* Clydwen, dau of Gruffudd ap Cydrych, and had:

RHYS Ap BLEDRI; did homage to HENRY II, by whom he was made Ld Justice of S Wales; *m* Angharad, dau of Llywelyn Ddiriaid, s of Rhys ap Tewdwr, Prince Deheubarth (technically Seisyllwg and Dyfed) 1153–97, and had, with a dau (*m* Edmund Vychan, Ld of Erygyath, Steward and Ch Counsellor to PRINCE LLYWELYN (presumably the one known as 'THE GREAT', who reigned 1190–1240)):

Sir ARON (AARON) Ap RHYS; attended RICHARD I on Crusade 1190 and for his gallantry against the Saracens is said to have been made a Kt of the Sepulchre of Our Saviour; *m* Gwenllian, dau of Ednynet Fychan, Steward to LLYWELYN THE GREAT, and had:

GWILLYM Ab ARON, of Cilsant; *m* Jonet, dau of Meurig ap Trahaearn, of Berriew, Montgomeryshire, and had:

MADOG Ap GWILYM; *m* Jonet, dau of Gruffudd ab Ivor, of Castleddwm, and had:

IEUAN Ab MADOG; *m* Catherine, dau of Elidir Ddu, and had:

MADOG Ab IEUAN; had:

PHILIP Ap MADOG; *m* Elen, dau of Gwilym ap Caradog, and had:

MAREDUDD Ap PHILIP Ap MADOG, of Cilsant; Bailiff itinerant Carmarthen 1423–26; living 1438/9; *m* 1st Jonet, dau of Ieuab ap Llywelyn, of Corrws, Cards; *m* 2nd Gwerful, dau of Gronwy ap Ieuan, of Gwynfryn, Llanystumdwy, Caernarvs, and by his 1st w had:

PHILIP Ap MAREDUGG, of Cilsant; Bailiff Carmarthen 1417–18, 1325–26 and 1437–38, Bailiff itinerant Carmarthen 1437–38; *m* Jonet, dau of Jenkin Llwyd, of Pwll Dyfarch, and *d* in or after 1441, leaving:

Sir THOMAS PHILIPPS, of Picton, Pembs; Esquire of the Body to HENRY VII, ktd 1513, Sheriff Pembs 1516; *m* by Oct 1491 Joan, dau and coheir of Henry Dwnn (*d* 1469), of Picton Castle, Pembs, whose ancestor, Sir John Wogan, of Wiston, lived *temp* HENRY III and *m* the dau and heiress of Sir William Picton, of Picton, whose ancestor came to Dyfed with Arnulph de Montgomery (first Norman conqueror of Dyfed) and was granted the manor and castle of Picton, and *d* 1520, leaving:

JOHN PHILIPPS, of Picton, Slebech, Pembs; sheriff Pembs 1542 and Carmarths 1544 and 1547; *m* 1st Elizabeth, est dau of Sir William Griffith (*c* 1480–1531), of Penrhyn, Chamberlain N Wales, by Jane, dau of Thomas Stradling, of St Donat's, Glam; *m* 2nd Ann, dau of John Voel, of Longridge, and *d* 14 Nov 1551, leaving by his 1st w:

1 William, of Picton Castle; *b c* 1530; Sheriff Pembs 1564, MP Pembroke Jan-May 1559 and 1572–73; *m* Jane, dau of Sir Thomas Perrott, of Haroldston, Pembroke, and *d* 1573, having had:
  (1) Elizabeth; *m* George Owen, of Henllys, Ld of Kemaes and an antiquary
  (2) Mary; *m* Alban Stepney and had issue
2 Morgan; Sheriff Pembs 1576; *m* 1st Ann, dau of Richard Morris, of Caswilia; *m* 2nd Elizabeth (*d* 9 March 1585), dau of Richard Fletcher, of Bangor, Caernarvs, and *d* 8 July 1585, leaving by her:
  1a **Sir John Philips, 1st Bt** (E), so *cr* 9 Nov 1621, of Picton Castle; *b c* 1566; Sheriff Pembs 1594–95 and 1610–11 and Cards 1622–23, MP Pembs 1597–98 and Oct–Dec 1601; *m* 1st on or after 11 Nov 1585 Anne, dau of Sir John Perrott, of Haroldston, Pembs, Ld Deputy Ireland (allegedly an illegitimate s of HENRY VIII); *m* 2nd Margaret (*m* 2nd Henry Crowe), dau of Sir Thomas Dennis, sometimes described as of Picton but also as of Bicton, Devon, and *d* 27 March 1629, having by his 1st w had, with other issue:
    1b **Sir Richard Philipps, 2nd Bt**; *b c* 1594; Sheriff Pembs 1632–33 and Carmarths 1640–41; royalist Civil War, garrisoned Picton Castle; *m* 1st by 1613 Elizabeth, est dau of Sir Erasmus Dryden, 1st Bt (*qv*), and had, with other issue:
      1c **Sir Erasmus Philipps, 3rd Bt**; *b c* 1623; Sheriff Carmarths 1649–50 and Pembs 1655–56, MP Pembs 1654–55 and Jan-April 1659, Custos Rotulorum Pembroke, Mil Commr S Wales 14 March 1654, Commr for Pembs, Cards and Carmarths 16 Aug 1655; *m* 1st Lady Cicely Finch, dau of 2nd Earl of Winchilsea (*see* WINCHILSEA and NOTTINGHAM, E), and had, with a s (*d* young):
        1d Anne; *m* 1st Thomas Bowen (*dsp*), of Trelloyne; *m* 2nd Thomas Heyward, of Rudbaxton
      1c (cont.) **Sir Erasmus** *m* 2nd Katherine, est dau and coheir of Edward D'Arcy, of Dartford, Kent, by Lady Elizabeth Stanhope, yr dau of 1st Earl of Chesterfield (*see* 1967 edn CHESTERFIELD and STANHOPE, E), and *d* 18 Jan 1696/7, having had, with other issue:
        1d Edward; *m* Elizabeth (*m* 2nd, as his 2nd w, Simon Harcourt (*d* 21 March 1724), of Pendley, Aldbury, Herts, and *d* 17 Aug 1706), dau and heiress of John Cannon, of Cilgetty, Pembs, and *dsp* & *vp* 15 April 1694
        2d **Sir John Philipps, 4th Bt**; MP Pembroke 1695–1702 and Haverfordwest 1718–22, Custos Rotulorum Pembs; *m* 12 Dec 1697 Mary, dau and heiress of Anthony Smith, E India merchant, and *d* 5 Jan 1736/7, having had, with three daus (*d* unm):
          1e **Sir Erasmus Philiips, 5th Bt**; *b c* 1701; *educ* Pembroke Coll Oxford and Lincoln's Inn; MP Haverfordwest 1726–43, Sheriff Carmarthen 1727, memb Common Cncl Haverfordwest 1737, economist and author: *An Appeal to Common-sense; or some Considerations offered to restore Publick Credit* (1720–21), *The State of the Nation in respect to her Commerce, Debts, and Money*

(1725), *The Creditor's Advocate and Debtor's Friend* (1731) and *Essays* (1751); *d* unm by accidental drowning in the Avon nr Bath 7 Oct 1743
          2e **Sir John Phillips, 6th Bt**, PC (1763); *b c* 1701; *educ* Pembroke Coll Oxford; barrister, Mayor Haverfordwest 1736, MP: Carmarthen 1741–47, Petersfield 1754–61 and Pembs 1761–64, Ld Commr BOT and Plantations 1744–45, DCL Oxford 1744, Custos Rotulorum Haverfordwest 1761–64; *m* 22 Sept 1725 Elizabeth, dau of Henry Shepherd, of London, and *d* 23 June 1764, leaving, with four daus:
            1f **Sir Richard Philipps, 7th Bt**, and 1st and last BARON MILFORD in Ireland (I), so *cr* 22 July 1766 (allegedly as a sop by the PM, Lord North (*see* GUILFORD, E), to console him for being refused permission to cut a carriage road up to the front door of his London house); *b* 1744; *educ* Pembroke Coll Oxford; MP (Whig) Pembs 1765–70 and 1786–1812, Plympton 1774–80 and Haverfordwest 1784–86, Custos Rotulorum Haverfordwest 1764–70, Ld Lt Haverfordwest 1770–1823, Ld Lt Pembs 1786–1823; *m* 2 June 1764 his cousin Mary (*d* 26 Aug 1815), dau and heiress of James Philips, of Pontypark, Pembs, and *dsp* 28 Nov 1823, when the Barony expired and Picton Castle passed to his cousin Richard Bulkely Philipps Grant (*see* 1959 edn FOLEY-PHILIPPS, Bt)
            3e Bulkeley, of Abercover, Carmarths (*see* 1959 edn FOLEY-PHILIPPS, Bt)
          1d Margaret; *m* Rev Griffith Jones (*d* 8 April 1761), Rector Llanddowror, and *d* 5 Jan 1755/6
          2d Elizabeth; *m* John Shorter, s of Sir John Shorter, Ld Mayor London, and had, with at least one yr dau:
            1e Catherine; *b c* 1682; *m* 30 July 1700, as his 1st w, 1st Earl of Orford (*see* WALPOLE, B), and *d* 20 Aug 1737, having had issue
  1b (cont.) **Sir Richard** *m* 2nd Catherine (*m* 4th Gen Philip Skippon, of Norfolk), dau of Daniel Oxenbridge, MD, and widow of (a) John Fowler (*d* 14 Dec 1642) and (b) George Henley (*d* by 1645), and *d* 1648, having by her had a dau
  2b Hugh, of Martletywe or Martletywo, and Sandyehaven, Pembs; *m* Anne (*d* 1652), dau of Roger Lort, of Stackpoole Court, Pembs, and *d* Jan-March 1651/2, leaving:
    1c Richard; *m* Frances, dau of Edward Noel, bro of Sir Verney Noel, 1st Bt, and had:
      1d Charles; *m* 1st Anne, dau of William Philips, of Haythogg (this branch died out in the male line on the death 1798 of William Philip(p)s, whose sis Anne *m* Joseph Allen, of Gilleswick, Pembs, and had issue); *m* 2nd Philippa, dau of Rowland Laugharne, of St Bride's, and by her had:
        1e Rowland; *m* Martha, dau of John Edwards, and *d* 1768, leaving, with other issue:
          1f Rowland PHILIPPS later PHILIPPS-LAUGHARNE; *m* 1750 Ann(i)e, dau of Rev James Laugharne, and had, with two daus (*d* unm):
            1g John, of Orlandon, Pembs; *m* 1783 Elizabeth, dau of Joseph Allen, and had, with two daus:
              1h Sir ROWLAND HENRY PHILIPPS-LAUGHARNE later PHILIPPS-LAUGHARNE-PHILIPPS (apparently added on inheriting btcy 1823), **8th Bt**; *b* Jan 1788; *m* 21 Jan 1812 Elizabeth (*d* 26 Aug 1834), dau of James Frampton, of Frome, Somerset, and *dsp* 23 April 1832
              2h Sir WILLIAM PHILIPPS-LAUGHARNE later PHILIPPS-LAUGHARNE-PHILIPPS (added on inheriting btcy 1832), **9th Bt**; *b* 2 Oct 1794; *educ* Jesus Coll Oxford; *m* 13 Oct 1829 Elizabeth (*b* 1 Nov 1808; *d* 1865), dau of George White, and *d* 17 Feb 1850, having had, with four daus:
                1i **Sir Godwin Philipps-Laugharne-Philips, 10th Bt**; *b* 10 Jan 1840; *d* unm 12 Feb 1857
    2d Richard; *b c* 1660; Lt-Gen, Govr Nova Scotia 1720–30; *m* 1st Jan 1691/2 Elizabeth (*d* 1739/40), dau of Alexander Cosby, of Stradbally Hall, Queen's Co; *m* 2nd Catherine, dau of Sir John Statham, of Wigwell, Derbys, and widow of Benjamin Bagshawe, of Ridge Hall, Derbys, and *d* 14 Oct 1750, leaving by his 1st w, with a dau (*d* unm):
      1e Cosby; Army Capt; *m* Teresa —, of Minorca, and *d* 1736, leaving, with a dau (*d* unm):
        1f William; Capt RN; *m* 28 Oct 1756 Ann Pedder and had:
          1g William Hollingworth; *b* 17 Dec 1757; Capt Notts Militia; *m* 29 March 1786 Harriet (*d* 15 March 1845), dau of Anthony Fonblanque, London merchant, and *d* 9 May 1839, leaving:
            1h William Thomas (Rev); *b* 18 Aug 1787; BD, Fell Magdalen Coll Oxford, Rector Fittleton, Wilts; *d* unm 28 Sept 1854
            2h **Sir James Evans Philips, 11th Bt**; *bapt* 16 Nov 1793; *educ* Queen's Coll Oxford (BA 1817, MA 1820); Vicar Osmington, Dorset, 1832–73; *m* 4 July 1822 Mary Anne (*d* 20 March 1833), dau of Benjamin Bickley, Bristol merchant, and *d* 14 Feb 1873, having had, with two daus (*d* young or unm):
              1i JAMES ERASMUS (Sir), **12th Bt**
            1i Emily Fonblanque; *m* 4 Jan 1848 Rev Harry Jones (*dsp* 30 Sept 1900), of Bartonmere, Suffolk, Vicar St Philip, Regent Street, Preb St Paul's, and *d* 6 Sept 1904
            2i Harriet Fonblanque; *m* 2 Feb 1858 Rev W Francis Tregarthen (*d* 1884), Schs Inspr, and *d* 15 Feb 1899
            3h Henry (Rev); *b* 19 Dec 1796; MA Oxon; *m* 30 March 1842 Margaret Eleanor (*d* 9 Jan 1867), dau of Maj Christopher Vowell, and *dsp* 13 Dec 1892
          1e Alethea; *m* 23 April 1729 Sir Peter Soame, 4th and last Bt of the Feb 1684/5 *cr*, of Heydon, Essex (*dspms* 7 Sept 1798), and *d* March 1745

1b Dorothy; *m* c 1608, as his 1st w, 1st Viscount Valentia (*qv*) and *d* 3 May 1624, leaving issue

2b Jane; *m* as his 3rd w 1st Viscount Claneboye (*see* DUFFERIN AND CLANEBOYE, B) and *d* in or after March 1644, leaving issue

3b Frances; *m* as his 1st w Sir Hugh Owen, 1st Bt (*qv*), of the 1641 *cr* and *dsp* 1629

The 11th Bt's only s,

Rev Sir James Erasmus Phillips, 12th Bt, of Picton, Pembs; *b* 23 Oct 1824; *educ* Ch Ch Oxford (BA 1847, MA 1853); Vicar Warminster 1859–97, Warden St Boniface's Missionary Coll Warminster, Preb Salisbury 1870; *m* 5 May 1859 Mary Margaret Best (*d* 5 Sept 1913), sis of 5th Baron Wynford (*qv*), and *d* 21 Feb 1912, having had:

1 JOHN WYNFORDt, **1st Viscount**

2 Ivor (Sir), KCB (1917), DSO (1900), JP (Pembs and Haverfordwest); *b* 9 Sept 1861; *educ* Felsted; served Militia 1881–83 and IA 1883–1903 (Lt 1883, Capt 1894, Maj 1901: Burmese War 1887–89 (medal and two clasps), Chin Lushai Expdn 1889, Miranzai Expdn 1891 (clasp), Isazai Expdn 1892, NW Frontier India 1896 (medal and two clasps), Tirah Campaign 1896–97 (despatches twice, clasp) and China 1900–01 (Relief Peking following Boxer Rising; despatches, medal and clasp), V-Lt and CA Pembs, MP (Lib) Southampton 1906–22, Lt-Col 1908 and Hon Col 1909 Pembroke Yeo, Govr Pembroke Castle 1908–12, WW I: GSO(2) 1914, Brig-Gen cmdg 115th Bde 1914–15, Parly Sec (Mil) Min Munitions 1915, T/Maj-Gen cmdg 38th (Welsh) Div (which he raised) 1915–16 and Hon Maj-Gen July 1916 following service at Somme, Ld Manors of E and W Pembroke, KJStJ, author: *The Issue of Orders in the Field* (1900); *m* 9 Sept 1891 Marian Isobel, OBE (1920), DGStJ (*d* 3 July 1945), dau of James Buchanan Mirrlees, of Redlands, Glasgow, and *d* 15 Aug 1940, leaving:

(1) Marjorie Elsie; *b* 1892; *m* 30 Oct 1925 Lt-Col (Vincent) Basil Ramsden, DSO, MC (*d* 6 April 1936), Res of Offrs, S Wales Borderers, s of Richard Ramsden, of Siddinghurst, Surrey, and *d* 197–, having had issue

3 OWEN COSBY PHILIPPS, 1st and last BARON KYLSANT, of Carmarthen, Co Carmarthen, and of Amroth, Co Pembroke (UK), so *cr* 14 Feb 1923, GCMG (1918–31, KCMG 1909–31); *b* 25 March 1863; apprenticed to a Newcastle shipping firm and later (1886) worked in shipping in Glasgow, fndr King Line (shipping co) The Clyde 1888, chm and md Roy Mail Steam Packet Co 1902 on (engineered acquisition of Pacific Steam Navigation Co, Lamport & Holt, Nelson Line, Elder Dempster, Glen and Shire Line, Union-Castle Mail Steamship Co 1912, Harland & Wolff (Belfast) 1924, Oceanic Steam Navigation Co (White Star Line) 1927, imprisoned for circulating a false prospectus 1931), Pres: Chamber of Shipping, London Chamber Commerce and Fedn Chambers of Commerce of Br Empire, High Sheriff Pembs 1904–05, MP (Lib) Pembroke and Haverfordwest 1906–10, MP (U) Chester 1916–18 and City of Chester 1918–22, Chm Wales and Mon U Cncl 1921–31, Grand Cross Spanish Red Cross 1912, MFH Carmarthenshire 1912–16, Hon Capt RNR 1914, KJStJ 1916–31, Ld Lt Haverfordwest 1924–31, V-Adml N Wales and Carmarthenshire 1929, Ld Manor Llanstephan; *m* 16 Sept 1902 Mai Alice Magdalene, CBE (1920), DJStJ, Order of Mercy (*d* 14 Dec 1952), er dau and coheir of Thomas Morris, DL, of Coomb, Llangain, Carmarths, by Alice, dau of James Lloyd, of Bronwydd, Carmarths, and *dspm* 5 June 1937, when the Barony expired, leaving:

(1) Nesta Donne, TD (1947), DL (Carmarthenshire 1965); *b* 20 Nov 1903; Ch Cdr ATS WW II; *m* 1st 17 Sept 1921 10th Earl of Coventry (*ka* May 1940; *qv*) and had issue; *m* 2nd 17 Jan 1953 Maj Terrance Vincent Fisher-Hoch, RA (*d* 1978), s of John Henry Fisher-Hoch, of Basle, Switzerland, and *d* 29 April 1997

(2) *Olwen Gwynne, JP (N R Yorks 1955) [The Hon Mrs Barker JP, Orchard House, High St, Nawton, Yorks YO6 5TT]; *b* 1905; *m* 1st 21 Feb 1925 (*divorce* 1937) 7th Baron Suffield (*qv*); *m* 2nd 22 Dec 1937 Lt-Col Frank Richard Barker, TD, RA (*d* 1974), s of Christopher Barker, of Oakhyrst Grange, Caterham, Surrey, and has by him:

1a *Timothy Gwynne [Timothy Barker Esq, Thorpe Morieux Hall, Thorpe Morieux, Suffolk IP30 0NW]; *b* 8 April 1940; *educ* Eton and Jesus Coll Cambridge; *m* 14 July 1964 *Philippa Rachel Mary, dau of Brig Mervyn Christopher Thursby-Pelham, OBE, of Ridgeland House, Finchampstead, Berks, and has:

1b *Christopher Gwynne; *b* 19 Jan 1970

1b *Camilla Gwynne; *b* 27 Feb 1968

3a Honor Chedworth; *m* 1st 2 June 1927 (*annulled* 1931) 2nd Baron Faringdon (*qv*); *m* 2nd 5 Feb 1936 *(Charles) Vere Pilkington [Vere Pilkington Esq, Casal da Nora, Colares, Portugal], est s of Charles Carlisle Pilkington, and was *k* in a car crash in Spain 18 July 1961, leaving a s

4 Alfred Perrott; *b* 10 Nov 1864; *d* 8 Aug 1889

5 Bertram Erasmus, JP Wilts, Northumberland and NZ; *b* 24 Aug 1870; Capt Northumberland Imp Yeo, Govr Salisbury Infirmary, memb Wilts Standing Jt and Ag Ctees, served Red Cross Mediterranean 1915–17, High Sheriff Wilts 1923; *m* 23 June 1914 Florence (*d* Feb 1947), yst dau of William Donaldson Cruddas, DL, MP, of Haughton Castle, Northumberland, and *d* 10 Feb 1947

6 Sir LAURENCE RICHARD PHILIPPS, 1st Bt, and 1st BARON MILFORD (*qv*)

1 Cicely; *b* 12 July 1866; *m* 1st 9 Aug 1892 William Donald Smallpiece, LRCP (*d* 2 June 1927), and had issue; *m* 2nd 29 June 1930 Capt William Charles Godsal (*d* 5 Aug 1938), of Haines Hill, Berks, and *d* 1 Feb 1952

2 Grace Mary; *d unm* 29 July 1918

3 Elsbeth; Fell Newnham Coll Cambridge 1898, Assist Dir Milk Min Food WW I; *m* 28 Aug 1902 Marcus Southwell Dimsdale (*d* 28 July 1919), of Coton Court, Coton, Cambs, and The Corner House, Cambridge, 4th s of Robert, 6th Baron Dimsdale (*see* 1956 edn Foreign Titles Section), and *d* 3 Oct 1949, leaving issue

4 Violet Mary; *m* 29 April 1903 Rev Cyril Frederic Parry Burnett (*d* 17 May 1947), of Perfeddgoed, Caernarvs, Vicar St Barnabas, Marylebone, and *d* 19 March 1954, leaving issue

5 Gladys; *d* 13 Jan 1886

The 12th Bt's est s,

Sir John Wynford Philipps, 13th Bt, and **1st Viscount Saint Davids**, of Lydstep Haven, Co Pembroke, so *cr* 17 June 1918, as also earlier 6 July 1908 BARON ST DAVIDS, of Roch Castle, Co Pembroke (both UK), GBE (1922), PC (1914), JP, DL; *b* 30 May 1860; *educ* Felsted and Keble Coll Oxford (BA 1882, MA 1885); barrister Middle Temple 1886, MP (Lib) Mid-Lanarks 1888–94 and Pembs 1898–1908, chm: Lib Pty Fund, Costa Rica Railway Co, Buenos Ayres & Pacific Railway 1900, memb Investments Ctee set up under Insur Act 1913, chm Unemployment Grants Ctee 1920–32, memb Rds Bd, Pres Organisation for Employment of Retired Offrs and Pembs TAA 1911–32, Capt Pembroke Imp Yeo, Ld Lt Pembs 1920–32; *m* 1st 14 Feb 1888 Nora (*d* 30 March 1915), yr dau of Isidor Gerstenberg, of Stockleigh House, Regent's Park, London, fndr and chm Cncl Foreign Bondholders, by Fanny Alice, dau of Abraham Bauer, of Hamburg and London, and had:

1 Colwyn Erasmus Arnold; *b* 11 Dec 1888; Capt RHG WW I (despatches); *ka* 13 May 1915

2 Roland Erasmus, MC, JP (Pembs); *b* 27 Feb 1890; *educ* New Coll Oxford (BA); Capt 9th (Serv) Bn City of London Regt 1914–16 (despatches); *ka* 7 July 1916

The **1st Viscount** *m* 2nd 27 April 1916 Lady Elizabeth Frances Rawdon-Hastings (granted by roy warrant 9 Oct 1920 rank of earl's dau; declared by Ho of Lds resolution 17 Dec 1920 coheir to Baronies of Botreaux, Hastings (of Hastings), Hungerford, Moleyns, Stanley and Strange (of Knokyn); *s* her unc 23 Feb 1921 as **Baroness Hungerford**, **Baroness Moleyns** and **Baroness Strange** (of Knokyn) in her own right on termination of the abeyance in those titles; *d* 12 Dec 1974), 2nd dau and coheir of Hon Paulyn Francis Cuthbert Rawdon-Hastings (n of 4th and last Marquess of Hastings; *see* below) and sis of Countess of Loudoun (*qv*) in her own right, and *d* 28 March 1938, leaving by her:

3 JESTYN REGINALD AUSTEN PLANTAGENET, **2nd Viscount**

1 Lelgarde De Clare Elizabeth; *b* 23 Sept 1918; *m* 19 June 1950 (*divorce* 1967) Colin Charles Evans, s of Maj William Sandford Evans, Welch Regt, of Rosehill Cottage, Cosheston, Pembroke Dock, and *d* 1984, leaving:

(1) +Roland Anthony Christopher [Roland Evans Esq, 78 Dundela Pk, Sandycove, Dublin, Ireland]; *b* 15 July 1951; *educ* Portora Roy Sch; *m* 1978 *Annette Matilda, dau of Alfred Hunter, of Carrick Henry, Co Sligo, and has:

1a +Rebecca Lara; *b* 1982

(2) +William Harold Sandford [William Evans Esq, Aglish, The Curragh, Castlebar, Co Mayo, Ireland]; *b* 14 April 1953; *educ* St George's Sch Nenagh, Co Tipperary; *m* 1979 *Elizabeth Ann, dau of Sean James Smith, of Castlebar, and has:

1a +Billy Sean; *b* 1980

1a +Kayleigh Elizabeth; *b* 1988

2a +Bronwyn Mary; *b* 1990

(1) +(Lorna) Susan [Miss Susan Evans, 11 Fairoak Chase, Brockla, Whitchurch, Bridgend, Mid Glamorgan]; *b* 14 April 1953

The 1st VISCOUNT's only surv s,

JESTYN REGINALD AUSTEN PLANTAGENET PHILIPPS, **2nd Viscount Saint Davids**, as which s f 1938, and **22nd Lord** (Baron) **Hungerford**, **21st Lord** (Baron) **Moleyns** and **14th Lord** (Baron) **Strange** (of Knokyn), as which *s* mother 1974; *b* 19 Feb 1917; *educ* Eton and Trin Coll Cambridge; Lt RNVR WW II, patron and fndr Pirate Club, Floating Youth Club for Boys and Girls; *m* 1st 5th May 1938 (*divorce* 1954) Doreen Guinness (*d* 19 Oct 1956), only dau of Capt Arthur Craven Jowett, of Coverdale, Toorak, Vict, Australia, and had:

1 COLWYN JESTYN JOHN PHILIPS, **3rd and present Viscount Saint Davids**

1 +Rowena Frances [The Hon Mrs Rowena Elford, 418 Wellington St, Clifton Hill, 3068 Victoria, Australia]; *b* 7 Aug 1940; *m* 31 Oct 1959 (*divorce* 1977) David Elford, s of Richard Elford, of Melbourne, Australia, and has:

(1) Richard David; *b* 24 Feb 1962; *educ* St Kevin's Coll Toorak; *d* 1990

(1) +Wendy Doreen Mary; *b* 23 Aug 1960

(2) +Suzanne; *b* 20 Oct 1963

(3) +Leone; *b* 12 March 1965

2 +Myfanwy Ann [The Hon Mrs Smith, 23 Pyrland Rd, London N5]; *b* 28 Oct 1944; *m* 2 Nov 1968 *John Frederick Smith, er s of Harry Smith, of Lea Royd, Ossett, Yorks, and has:

(1) +Tobias Peter John; *b* Nov 1971

(2) +Benjamin Cosby; *b* 1 June 1973

3 +Rhiannon Elisabeth [The Hon Mrs Rhiannon Chapman, 106 Prince of Wales Rd, London NW5 3NE]; *b* 21 Sept 1946; *educ* Tormead Sch and King's Coll London (LLB); FIPM, personnel dir International Stock Exchange 1980–90, dir Industl Soc 1991–, memb: Universities Funding Cncl and Employment Appeal Tbnl; *m* 7 June 1974 (*divorce* 1991) Donald Hudson Chapman, s of Francis Robert Chapman, of Ipswich

4 +Eiddwen Sara [The Hon Mrs Owen, 4 Quarry Rd, Kenilworth, Warwicks CV8 1AE]; *b* 28 June 1948; *m* 1986 *Clive Geoffrey Owen and has:

(1) +David James; *b* 1987

(2) +Philip Michael; *b* 1990

The **2nd Viscount** *m* 2nd 15 Oct 1954 (*divorce* 1959) Elisabeth Joyce, er dau of Dr Eleazar Alec Woolf, of Hove, Sussex; *m* 3rd 19 Oct 1959 *Evelyn Marjorie [The Rt Hon Marjorie Viscountess St Davids, 15 St Mark's Crescent, London NW1 7TS], BA UCL, only dau of Dr John Edmund Guy Harris, of The Heritage, Bray-on-Thames, Berks, and *d* 1991

Lineage (of Strange (of Knokyn)): ROALD 'Le STRANGE' or 'EXTRANEUS' may have been a Breton and was of a family that seems to have migrated from Brittany to England (hence his second name, whether in its French or Latin form). But it is less certain that his family were actually of Breton origin. He testified to a charter before 1122 and was a tenant of Alan fitz Fleald (*see* MORAY, E) in Mileham, Norfolk; also held land in Hunstanton, Norfolk; *m* Maud, dau of Ralph fitz Herlewin or Ralph de Hunstanton, and was in all probability dead by 1158, having had, with two other but not necessarily yr sons (Hamon, held land in Cheswardine, Salop, *d* by 1163/4; Guy, granted land in Alveley, Salop, Sheriff Salop 1159–60, had at least two daus):

JOHN (I) LESTRANGE; granted land by HENRY II in Ness, Salop, 1158 and Staffs 1168–69; *m* Hawise — and *d* by Michaelmas 1178, leaving:

JOHN (II) LESTRANGE; had dealings with his female cousins (Guy's daus) over land at Knockin, Salop, 1196/7; negotiator on behalf of KING JOHN with LLYWELYN THE GREAT PRINCE OF NORTH WALES 1204 and 1214; Sheriff Salop and Staffs 1216; granted manor of Kidderminster 1216; *m* Amice — and *d* by 20 Jan 1233/4, leaving:

JOHN (III) LESTRANGE; old enough to attend on KING JOHN in 1213 and to undertake mil service against the French 1214; granted by HENRY III the manor of Wrockwardine, Salop, 25 May 1231; played a part in negotiations between HENRY III and PRINCE LLYWELYN THE GREAT 1232; Constable Montgomery Castle 1235 and Bridgnorth, Chester and Shrewsbury Castles 1233–40, Sheriff: Salop and Staffs 1236–48 and Cheshire 1241–42, Justice Chester 1240 or 1241; supported HENRY III against Simon De Montfort (unlike? his s; see below); *m* (?)Lucy, dau of Robert Tregoz, and *d* by 26 March 1269, having had:

1 JOHN, for whom see further below

2 Hamon; granted manor of Ellesmere by HENRY III 1266/7, Sheriff Hants, granted Chawton, Hants, by the end of 1271; *m* 1272 Isabella d'Ibelin, widow of HUGH II, KING OF CYPRUS of the Lusignan dynasty, and *d* apparently while on crusade with EDWARD I (who, however, had returned to England 1272) in the Holy Land 1274/5

3 ROGER LESTRANGE, 1st and last LORD (Baron) STRANGE (of Ellesmere) (E), so *cr* by writ of summons (according to later doctrine) to the Parl at Westminster 24 June 1295 and again 1 Nov 1295 and yet again 26 Jan 1296/7, though not thereafter; Sheriff Yorks 1272–74, Justice of the Forest south of Trent 1283–96, served in EDWARD I's Welsh campaigns from 1276; *m* 1st, as her 2nd husb, Maud (*d* by April 1273), est dau of William de Beauchamp, feudal Baron of Bedford (*i.e.*, not as a peer of Parl), and widow of Roger de Mowbray (*see* MOWBRAY, SEGRAVE and STOURTON, B); *m* 2nd Maud — (*d* on or after 8 April 1331) and *dsps* 31 July 1311, when whatever Barony may be deemed to have existed expired

4 Robert; acquired Chawton after death of his bro Hamon and Wrockwardine in the latter's lifetime; *m* Eleanor, dau and coheir of William de Blancminster (modern Whitchurch, Salop), and predeceased her 12 Oct 1276, leaving:

(1) John; *d* by 18 June 1289

(2) FULK LESTRANGE, 1st LORD (Baron) STRANGE (of Blackmere) (E), so *cr* by writ of summons (according to later doctrine) 4 March 1308/9; *b c* 1267; served in EDWARD I's and EDWARD II's Scottish campaigns 1298–1323; Seneschal Aquitaine 1322; *m* Eleanor (predeceased her husb), dau of John Giffard, of Brimsfield, Glos, 1st Lord (Baron) Giffard, and *d* by 23 Jan 1323/4, leaving:

1a JOHN LESTRANGE, 2nd LORD (Baron) STRANGE (of Blackmere), JP (Salop 1332); *b c* 1305; fought at Crécy 1346; *m* as her 1st husb Ankaret (*m* 2nd Sir Thomas de Ferrers and *d* 8 Oct 1361), dau of William Boteler, of Wem, Salop, and *d* 21 July 1349, leaving:

1b FULK LESTRANGE, 3rd LORD (Baron) STRANGE (of Blackmere); *b c* 1330; *m* (contract 12 March 1346/7), as her 1st husb, Lady Elizabeth de Stafford (*b* c 1334; *m* 2nd Sir John de Ferrers, 4th Lord Ferrers of Chartley (*see* HEREFORD, V); *m* 3rd Reynold de Cobham, 2nd Lord Cobham of the 1347 *cr* (*see* BURGH, B), and *d* 7 Aug 1375), dau of Ralph, 1st Earl of Stafford of the March 1350/1 *cr* (*see* STAFFORD, B), and *dspm* 30 Aug 1349, leaving issue (among whose descendants, if any, the representation of the Barony of Strange (of Blackmere) is still extant, the Barony in question being held by later legal doctrine to have fallen into abeyance from 1349):

1c Joan; *m* John Car(e)les(s)

2c Eleanor; *m* Edward de Acton

2b JOHN LESTRANGE, 1st LORD (Baron) STRANGE or LESTRANGE of a new *cr* by writ of summons 3 April 1360, JP (Salop 1360); *b* 1332; *m* Lady Mary FitzAlan (*d* 29 Aug 1396), dau of 10th/3rd Earl of Arundel (*see* NORFOLK, D), and *d* 12 May 1361, leaving:

1c JOHN LESTRANGE, 2nd LORD (Baron) STRANGE or LESTRANGE of the 1360 *cr*; *b c* 1353; *m* as her 1st husb Isabel, dau of 11th Earl of Warwick (*see* WARWICK, BROOKE and, E) of the 1088 *cr*, and *dspm* while still under age 3 Aug 1375, leaving:

1d ELIZABETH Lestrange, according to later legal doctrine BARONESS STRANGE in her own right; *b* 6 Dec 1373; seems to have *m* as his 1st w 15 March 1382/3 Thomas de MOWBRAY, 1st DUKE OF NORFOLK of the 1397 *cr* (*see* MOWBRAY, SEGRAVE and STOURTON, B), and *dsp* 23 Aug 1383

1c ANKARET Lestrange; *s* her er niece 1383 according to later legal doctrine as BARONESS STRANGE in her own right; *b c* 1361; *m* 1st by 23 Aug 1383 Sir Richard TALBOT (*d* 7/8 Sept 1396), who was called to Parl as LORD (Baron) TALBOT (of Blackmere) between 3 March 1383/4 and 17 Dec 1387, but this is usually seen as a fresh *cr* rather than as a summons to attend Parl as a peer in right of his w, and had issue; *m* 2nd between 8 March 1400/1 and 4 July 1401, as his 2nd w, Thomas NEVILL(E), 6th LORD (Baron) FURNIVALL(E) in right of his 1st w (he *dspm* 14 March 1406/7), and *d* 1 June 1413, leaving four sons (*see* SHREWSBURY and WATERFORD, E, for subsequent history of the Baronies of Furnivall(e), Strange (of Blackmere) of the 1360 *cr* and Talbot)

1 Hawise; *m* before 1241 Gruffydd ap Gwenwynwyn (s and h of GWENWYNWYN PRINCE OF SOUTH POWYS or POWYS WENWYNWYN; *d* after 21 Feb 1286 but before the end of 1287), Ld (*i.e.*, feudally) of Arwystli, Caereinion, Cyfeiliog, Mawddwy, Upper Mochnant and Y Tair Swydd by grant of HENRY III 1241, though he later supported LLYWELYN THE LAST, PRINCE OF WALES, and *d* 1310, having had, with six other sons and a dau:

(1) Owen Ap GRUFFYDD Ap GWENWYNWYN *alias* de la POLE (*i.e.*, of Welshpool); allegedly surrendered the principality of Powis to EDWARD I in the late 13th century, though the principality had already been the subject of constant fighting and dispute between the Kings of England and LLYWELYN THE LAST, PRINCE OF WALES, receiving from EDWARD I in return the same area as a free Baron of England (*i.e.*, as Ld of a feudal barony); *m* as her 1st husb Joan or Joanna (*m* 2nd between 18 Aug 1295 and 22 Nov 1298 Sir Roger Trumwyne and *d* by Michaelmas 1348), dau of Sir Robert Corbet, of Wattlesburgh and Moreton Corbet (*see* 1970 edn CORBET, Bt), and *d* by 15 Oct 1293, leaving an only s:

1a Gruffydd Ap OWEN or de la POLE; *b c* 1291; *m* as her 1st Ela (*m* 2nd by 12 Dec 1309 Sir James de Perrers; *m* 3rd by 10 July 1322 Piers Corbet and *d* between 5 March 1324/5 and 9 June 1325), dau of Nicholas de Audley, and *dsp* by 25 June 1309

1a Hawise, called *Gadarn* or 'The Hardy'; *b* apparently 25 July 1290; Ldy of Powis in her own right; *m* 1309 John Cherleton, 1st Lord (Baron) Cherleton, who was confirmed by EDWARD II 1313–14 in his tenure of the Powis estates through his w, and *d* between Aug 1345 and 1353, being ancestress with her husb of the succeeding 2nd, 3rd, 4th and 5th Lords Cherleton, the Barony falling into abeyance according to later legal doctrine March 1420/1on the death *spm* of 5th Lord (Baron) Cherleton, among whose daus' descendants any representation in the Barony may be held to exist

JOHN (III) LESTRANGE's est s,

JOHN (IV) LESTRANGE; may have been a supporter of Simon de Montfort (*see* LEICESTER, E, preliminary remarks) in his disputes with HENRY III; was at any rate instructed by the King to surrender his possession of Montgomery Castle 1261 and 1263, it having been ordered to be made over to him 1260; a royal order for its restoration to him (JOHN (IV) LESTRANGE) was also made 1265, suggesting that any support by him for Simon de Montfort was now ended; *m* Joan (predeceased her husb), dau of Roger de Somery by Nichole, dau and coheir of William de Aubigny, Earl of Arundel (*see* NORFOLK, D), and *d* by 26 Feb 1275/6, leaving:

JOHN (V) LESTRANGE, **1st Lord** (Baron) **Strange** (of Knokyn) (E), so *cr* by writ 26 Sept 1299 onwards (first as EXTRANEUS (STRANGE) then 4 March 1308/9 onwards as STRANGE OF KNOKYN); *b c* 1253; served in EDWARD I's Welsh campaigns 1276–87 and Scottish campaigns 1298–1308; *m* 1st Alienore, dau of Joan (widow of Stephen de Somery; *d c* 1240) and a subsequent husb of Joan's, perhaps Godfrey de Crawcumbe; *m* 2nd Maud, dau and heiress either of Roger de Deyville, of Walton Deyville, Warwicks, or of Ebles de Montibus, of Ketton, Rutland, and *d* by 8 Aug 1309, leaving (presumably by his 2nd w, since her putative paternity would account for the unusual forename Ebles being given to the 2nd s):

1 JOHN (VI), **2nd Lord**

2 EBLES LESTRANGE, 1st LORD (Baron) STRANGE, so *cr* 3 Dec 1326 by writ of summons (according to later doctrine), although also occasionally referred to in contemporary documents as EARL OF LINCOLN, presumably in right of his w (husb and w were the subject of an order decreeing that they should be paid the stipend derived from Lincs revenues traditionally associated with the upkeep of the earldom of a county (*see* RUTLAND, D, and NORTHUMBERLAND, D, for discussion of earldoms at this period); moreover, he, his w and their heirs were apptd Keepers Lincoln Castle 1331 and he made Keeper of Lincs 1332; he was, however, never summoned to Parl as EARL OF LINCOLN); supported Thomas, 2nd Earl of Lancaster (est s of Edmund Crouchback, 1st Earl of Lancaster, 2nd s of HENRY III) in opposing and encompassing the death of Piers Gaveston, EDWARD II's favourite; pardoned for this 1313; Kt Banneret 1326; called up for mil service against Scots 1327 and 1332/3; *m* by 10 Nov 1324, as her 2nd husb, LADY ALICE de LACY, COUNTESS OF LINCOLN AND SALISBURY in her own right (*b* 25 Dec 1281; *m* 1st c 1294 Thomas, 2nd Earl of Lancaster (*see* above; he seems to have been called EARL OF LINCOLN also, again presumably in right of his w; *divorce* 1318 following Lady Alice's abduction 1317 by a knight, who also claimed the Earldom of Lincoln, together with that of Salisbury, in right of an alleged intimacy with her before her 1st marriage such that he was her actual husb, this being done allegedly with the knowledge of EDWARD II so as to heap obloquy on the Earl of Lancaster); *m* 3rd Hugh de Fre(y)ne, Lord (Baron) Frene, following a second abduction, and dsp 2 Oct 1348, when the Earldom of Lincoln of the 1232 *cr* expired), dau of 3rd Earl of Lincoln of the 1232 *cr* by his w Margaret, heiress of her grandmother Ela Countess of Salisbury, and *dsp* 8 Sept 1335, when the Barony expired

3 Hamon (Sir), ancestor of the Le STRANGEs/L'ESTRANGEs of Hunstanton, Norfolk (*see* HASTINGS, B)

1 Katherine; *m* 1st Sir Alan de Gloseley; *m* 2nd, as his 2nd w, Sir William de Wrottesley (*see* WROTTESLEY, B)

The 1st LORD (Baron) STRANGE (of Knokyn)'s s,

JOHN (VI) LESTRANGE, **2nd Lord** (Baron) **Strange** (of Knokyn); *b c* 1282; *m* Iseult (*d* on or after 18 May 1324) and *d* by 6 Feb 1310/1, leaving:

1 JOHN (VII) LESTRANGE, **3rd Lord** (Baron) **Strange** (of Knokyn); *b c* 1296; *m* Maud (*d* on or after 1 April 1324) and *d* by 28 May 1323

2 ROGER LESTRANGE, **4th Lord** (Baron) **Strange** (of Knokyn); *b* 15 Aug 1301; Kt Banneret Jan 1326/7; inherited estates of his unc EBLES LESTRANGE, 1st and last LORD (Baron) LESTRANGE of the 1326 *cr*; in 1347 was serving abroad in Hundred Years War; *m* 1st Maud — and had:

(1) ROGER, **5th Lord**

2 (cont.) The **4th Lord** *m* 2nd by 25 March 1344, as her 1st husb, Joan de Ingham, Baroness Ingham in her own right according to later doctrine (*m* 2nd 1350–51, as his 2nd w, Sir Miles de Stapleton and *d* 1360–65), dau and eventual heiress of Oliver, 1st Lord (Baron) Ingham of the 1328 *cr*, and *d* without having had further issue 29 July 1349

His s by his 1st w,

ROGER LESTRANGE, **5th Lord** (Baron) **Strange** (of Knokyn); *b c* 1326; served Hundred Years War in France; *m* by 1338 Lady Al(a)ine FitzAlan (*d* 20 Jan 1385/6), dau of 9th/2nd Earl of Arundel (*see* NORFOLK, D), and *d* 23 Aug 1382, having had (with at least one dau, Lucy, *m* by 23 April 1383, as his 1st w, 5th Lord (Baron) Willoughby de Eresby; *qv*):

JOHN LESTRANGE, **6th Lord** (Baron) **Strange** (of Knokyn); *b c* 1352; *m* as her 1st husb Maud de Mohun (*m* 2nd Sir Nicholas Hauberk and *d* 20 Sept 1400), 3rd and yst dau and coheir of 2nd Lord (Baron) Mohun, KG, of the 1299 *cr*, and *d* 28 July 1397, leaving:

RICHARD LESTRANGE, **7th Lord** (Baron) **Strange** (of Knokyn) and through his mother 3rd LORD (Baron) MOHUN according to later doctrine, he having *s* to that title on the death *sp* 1431 of his mother's sis Philippe (*m* 1st Sir Walter FitzWalter, 4th Lord (Baron) FitzWalter (*see* FitzWALTER, B); *m* 2nd Sir John Golafre; *m* 3rd Edward, 1st Earl of Rutland of the 1390 cr (*see* RUTLAND, D) and 2nd Duke of York, gs of EDWARD III), last surv dau of his maternal gf 2nd Lord (Baron) Mohun (*see* above), when the notional abeyance (according to later doctrine) in the Barony of Mohun was terminated; *b* 1 Aug 1381; *m* 1st after 9 Oct 1408 Joan or Constance (*dsp* on or after 28 March 1438), allegedly dau of Lord De Grey (of Ruthin?); *m* 2nd by 26 Aug 1439 Elizabeth (*d* by 17 March 1453/4), allegedly est dau of Sir Reynold or Reginald (de) Cobham, putative 3rd (Baron) Lord Cobham (*see* BURGH, B), of Sterborough Castle, Kent, and *d* 9 Aug 1449, leaving:

JOHN LESTRANGE, **8th Lord** (Baron) **Strange** (of Knokyn) and 4th LORD (Baron) MOHUN; *b c* 1444; a prominent Yorkist; *m* 1st by 27 March 1450 (?Lady) Jacquette (?Woodville), allegedly 4th dau of 1st Earl Rivers of the 1466 *cr* and sis of ELIZABETH, w of EDWARD IV; *m* 2nd Anne (?)Nevill(e), yst dau of 1st Lord (Baron) Bergavenny (*see* ABERGAVENNY, M), and *dspm* 16 Oct 1479, leaving an only child and heiress, who according to later legal doctrine *s* in her own right to the Baronies of Strange (of Knokyn) and Mohun:

JOAN Lestrange, **Baroness Strange** (of Knokyn) and BARONESS MOHUN; *b c* 1463; *m* by 26 Feb 1480/1 Sir George STANLEY, est s of 1st Earl of Derby (*qv*), who was called up to Ho Lds 15 Nov 1482 *vp* in his w's Barony as **9th Lord** (Baron) **Strange** (of Knokyn) and *dvp* 4 or 5 Dec 1503; she *d* 20 March 1513/4, leaving:

THOMAS STANLEY, **10th Lord** (Baron) **Strange** (of Knokyn) and 6th LORD (Baron) MOHUN; *s* his paternal gf 1504 as 2nd EARL OF DERBY, and had, with other issue:

EDWARD STANLEY, **11th Lord** (Baron) **Strange** (of Knokyn), 3rd EARL OF DERBY and 7th LORD (Baron) MOHUN; *d* 24 Oct 1572, having by his 1st w had:

HENRY STANLEY, **12th Lord** (Baron) **Strange** (of Knokyn) (as which called up to Ho Lds 23 Jan 1558/9 *vp*), 4th EARL OF DERBY and 8th LORD (Baron) MOHUN; had, with other issue:

1 FERDINANDO STANLEY, **13th Lord** (Baron) **Strange** (of Knokyn) (as which called up to Ho Lds 19 Feb 1592/3 *vp*), 5th EARL OF DERBY and 9th LORD (Baron) MOHUN; *dspm* 16 April 1594, when the Earldom of Derby passed to his yr bro William and the Barony of Strange (of Knokyn), together with those of Mohun and Stanley, fell into abeyance among his three daus and coheirs:

(1) Anne; *b* 1580; *m* 1st 28 Feb 1607/8 5th Baron Chandos of Sudeley (*see* TEMPLE OF STOWE, E); *m* 2nd 22 July 1624 2nd Earl of Castlehaven (*see* 1970 edn AUDLEY, B) and was *bur* 11 Oct 1647

(2) Frances; *b* May 1583; *m c* 1601 1st Earl of Bridgwater (*see* GREY EGERTON, Bt, also SUTHERLAND, D) and *d* 11 March 1635/6, leaving issue

(3) ELIZABETH Stanley; *b* 6 Jan 1587/8; *m* 15 Jan 1601 5th EARL OF HUNTINGDON (*qv*), who was also 10th LORD (Baron) BOTREAUX, 7th LORD (Baron) HASTINGS (of Hastings), **9th Lord** (Baron) **Hungerford** and **7th Lord** (Baron) **Moleyns** (*see below* **Lineage (of Hungerford and Moleyns)**) and *d* 20 Jan 1632/3, leaving:

1a FERDINANDO HASTINGS, 11th LORD (Baron) BOTREAUX, 8th LORD (Baron) HASTINGS (of Hastings), **10th Lord** (Baron) **Hungerford**, **8th Lord** (Baron) **Moleyns** and 6th EARL OF HUNTINGDON; called up to Ho of Lds *vp* 1640 in his f's Barony of Hastings; had, with other issue:

1b THEOPHILUS HASTINGS, 12th LORD (Baron) BOTREAUX, 9th LORD (Baron) HASTINGS (of Hastings), **11th Lord** (Baron) **Hungerford**, **9th Lord** (Baron) **Moleyns** and 7th EARL OF HUNTINGDON; had, with other issue:

1c GEORGE HASTINGS, 13th LORD (Baron) BOTREAUX, 10th LORD (Baron) HASTINGS (of Hastings), **12th Lord** (Baron) **Hungerford**, **10th Lord** (Baron) **Moleyns** and 8th EARL OF HUNTINGDON; *d unm* 22 Feb 1704/5

1b (cont.) The **11th Lord Hungerford** and **9th Lord Moleyns** etc *m* 2nd 8 May 1690, as her 2nd w of three, Frances, dau of Francis Fowler, and *d* 30 May 1701, leaving by her:

2c THEOPHILUS HASTINGS, 14th LORD (Baron) BOTREAUX, 11th LORD (Baron) HASTINGS (of Hastings), **13th Lord** (Baron) **Hungerford**, **11th Lord** (Baron) **Moleyns** and 9th EARL OF HUNTINGDON; had, with other issue:

1d FRANCIS HASTINGS, 15th LORD (Baron) BOTREAUX, 12th LORD (Baron) HASTINGS (of Hastings), **14th Lord** (Baron) **Hungerford**, **12th Lord** (Baron) **Moleyns** and 10th EARL OF HUNTINGDON; *d unm* 2 Oct 1789, when the Earldom of Huntingdon became dormant

2d ELIZABETH Hastings, BARONESS BOTREAUX, BARONESS HASTINGS (of Hastings), **Baroness Hungerford** and **Baroness Moleyns** in her own right; *b* 23 March 1731; *m* 26 Feb 1752, as his 3rd w, John RAWDON, 1st Earl of Moira (*see* LOUDOUN, E), and *d* 11 April 1808, leaving an est s:

1e FRANCIS RAWDON later RAWDON-HASTINGS, 1st MARQUESS OF HASTINGS (*see also* LOUDOUN, E) and 14th LORD (Baron) HASTINGS (of Hastings), also *de jure* 17th LORD (Baron) BOTREAUX, 13th LORD (Baron) HASTINGS (of Hungerford), 16th LORD (Baron) HUNGERFORD and 14th LORD (Baron) MOLEYNS, since among the medieval Baronies only his claim to be LORD HASTINGS (of Hastings) was admitted; *b* 7 Dec 1754; *m* 12 July 1804 Flora Countess of Loudoun in her own right (*qv*) and *d* 28 Nov 1826, leaving:

1f GEORGE AUGUSTUS FRANCIS RAWDON-HASTINGS, 2nd MARQUESS OF HASTINGS and 15th LORD (Baron) HASTINGS (of Hastings), also from 1840 7th EARL OF LOUDOUN, also *de jure* 18th LORD (Baron) BOTREAUX, 14th LORD (Baron) HASTINGS (of Hungerford), 17th LORD (Baron) HUNGERFORD and 15th LORD (Baron) MOLEYNS; *b* 4 Feb 1808; *m* 1 Aug 1831, as her 1st husb, Barbara, Baroness Grey (of Ruthin) (*see* GREY, B) in her own right (*m* 2nd 9 April 1845 Adml Sir Hastings Reginald HENRY later YELVERTON, GCB (*d* 24 July 1878), and by him had a dau Barbara; *see* CHURSTON, B), and *d* 13 Jan 1844, leaving:

1g PAULYN REGINALD SERLO RAWDON-HASTINGS, 3rd MARQUESS OF HASTINGS, 8th EARL OF LOUDOUN, 16th LORD (Baron) HASTINGS (of Hastings) and *de jure* 19th LORD (Baron) BOTREAUX, 15th LORD (Baron) HASTINGS (of Hungerford), 18th LORD (Baron) HUNGERFORD and 16th LORD (Baron) MOLEYNS; *b* 2 June 1832; *d unm* 17 Jan 1851

2g HENRY WEYSFORD CHARLES PLANTAGENET RAWDON-HASTINGS, 4th and last MARQUESS OF HASTINGS, also 9th EARL OF LOUDOUN, 17th LORD (Baron) HASTINGS and *de jure* 20th LORD (Baron) BOTREAUX, 16th

LORD (Baron) HASTINGS (of Hungerford), 19th LORD (Baron) HUNGERFORD and 17th LORD (Baron) MOLEYNS, also from 1858 (when *s* mother in that title) 21st LORD (Baron) GREY (of Ruthin); *b* 22 July 1842; *m* 16 July 1864, as her 1st husb, Lady Florence Paget, dau of 2nd Marquess of Anglesey (*qv*), and *dsp* 10 Nov 1868, when the Marquessate of Hastings and all his other titles *cr* in the 18th or early 19th centuries expired, but the Earldom of Loudoun and associated creations in the peerage of Scotland passed to his est sis as heir of line, while the medieval Baronies in the peerage of England or right thereto fell into abeyance between his four full sisters, *i.e.*, those born of both his f and mother, with the exception of the Barony of Grey (of Ruthin), to which as well as his full sisters his half-sis on his mother's side Barbara (who *m* 2nd Baron Churston; *qv*) was coheir

1g EDITH MAUD Rawdon-Hastings, COUNTESS OF LOUDOUN, as which *s* er bro 1868, and on the termination 6 Nov 1871 of the abeyance of those titles in her favour BARONESS BOTREAUX, BARONESS HASTINGS (of Hastings), **Baroness Hungerford** and **Baroness Moleyns**, all in her own right; *b* 10 Dec 1833; *m* 30 April 1853 Charles Frederick CLIFTON later ABNEY-HASTINGS (Act of Parl 1859 following inheritance of the estates of Sir Charles Abney-Hastings, 2nd Bt, gs through an illegitimate descent of 10th Earl of Huntingdon; *cr* 4 May 1880 BARON DONINGTON, of Donington Park, Co Leicester (UK); *d* 24 July 1895, and *d* 23 Jan 1874, leaving, with other issue (*see* LOUDOUN, E):

1h CHARLES EDWARD HASTINGS ABNEY-HASTINGS later RAWDON-HASTINGS (roy licence 8 April 1887), 11th EARL OF LOUDOUN, 21st LORD (Baron) BOTREAUX, 19th LORD (Baron) HASTINGS (of Hastings), **21st Lord** (Baron) **Hungerford** and **19th Lord** (Baron) **Moleyns**; *b* 5 Jan 1855; *dsp* 17 May 1920, when the Baronies of Botreaux, Hastings (of Hastings), Hungerford and Moleyns fell once more into abeyance, the Scottish peerages passed to his niece Edith Maud as heir of line and the UK Barony of Donington passed to his only surv bro Gilbert (*see below*)

2h Paulyn Francis Cuthbert ABNEY-HASTINGS later RAWDON-HASTINGS (roy licence 1887); *b* 21 Oct 1856; *m* 20 Dec 1881 Lady Maud Grimston (*d* 3 Sept 1929), dau of 2nd Earl of Verulam (*qv*), and *d* 19 Oct 1907, leaving, with other issue (*see* LOUDOUN, E):

1i ELIZABETH FRANCES; *b* 19 June 1884; *s* 1921 her unc Charles on termination of abeyance in her favour as **Baroness Hungerford** and **Baroness Moleyns** and her remote ancestor the 5th Earl of Derby as **Baroness Strange** (of Knokyn) all in her own right; *m* **1st Viscount Saint Davids** (*see* above)

3h GILBERT THEOPHILUS CLIFTON ABNEY-HASTINGS later CLIFTON-HASTINGS-CAMPBELL (roy licence 2 Jan 1896), 3rd and last BARON DONINGTON; *b* 29 May 1859; Maj 3rd Bn Sherwood Foresters; *m* 12 July 1894 Maud Kemble, only surv child of Sir Charles Edward Hamilton, 1st and last Bt (*see* 1928 edn), and *d* 31 May 1927, when his Barony expired, having had, with other issue (*see* LOUDOUN, E):

1i Margaret Selina Flora Maud; *b* 7 July 1895; *m* 15 July 1917 Capt Sir Edward Orde MacTaggart-Stewart, 2nd and last Bt, JP, DL (Wigtownshire) (*d* 19 Oct 1948) and *d* 27 Feb 1975, having had:

1j Jean Susanna Flora; *b* 26 June 1918; *m* Desmond Snowden and *d* 6 May 1993, leaving:

1k *Peter [Peter Snowden Esq, Heugh Park Cottage, Auchenmalg, Glenluce, by Newton Stewart DG8]; *m* 19– (*divorce*) Penelope Salter, and has:

1l *Nicholas; *b* 1975

1k *Wendy; *m* *Dr Tom Frisch

2k *Devorguilla [Mrs Donald Baxter, 14 Radinden Manor Rd, Hove BN3 6NH]; *m* *Donald Baxter and has:

1l *Edward

2l *James

1l *Susanna

2j Faith Agnes Devorguilla; *b* 23 March 1926; *m* 1949 Henry John Brewis, MP (C) Galloway 1959–74 (*d* 1989; *see* WALKER, Bt, of Sand Hutton and WILLIAMS-WYNN, Bt), and *d* 26 May 1998, leaving:

1k +Francis Roger MacTaggart [Francis Brewis Esq, Ardwell House, Ardwell, Stranraer, Wigtownshire DG9 9LY]; *b* 30 Jan 1950; *educ* Eton; *m* 12 Dec 1981 *Marion Teresa, dau of Robert Anderson, and has issue

2k +(Ralph Michael) Rodney; *b* 17 May 1951; *m* 10 Feb 1979 *Valerie Anne, dau of Alexander Simpson Gerard, of Glasgow, and has:

1l +Katharine Anne; *b* 24 Aug 1981

2l +Mairi Fiona; *b* 26 Oct 1983

3k +Christopher Mark John [Christopher Brewis Esq, 10 Beresford Pk, Sunderland, Tyne and Wear SR2 7JU]; *b* 7 Dec 1956; *m* 3 July 1982 *Aileen Teresa, dau of David Rowland, of Newcastle, and has:

1l +David John; *b* 16 March 1988

1l +Catherine Flora; *b* 19 April 1985

1k +Sylvia Katharine Moira; *b* 13 Dec 1952; *m* 1st 1978 Timothy Harrison (*d* 1981), s of Wesley Harrison, of Taunton, and has:

1l +Wesley John; *b* 27 Nov 1979

1l +Abigail Katharine; *b* 3 June 1981

1k (cont.) Mrs Timothy Harrison m 2nd 1986 *Murray Michael Thomas Lloyd Watson, s of Alexander Watson, of Trull, Taunton, Devon, and by him has:

    2l +Alexander Guy Timothy Michael; b 22 Aug 1989

    2l +Alice Charlotte Pamela; b 15 Aug 1987

2g BERTHA LELGARDE Rawdon-Hastings, BARONESS GREY (of Ruthin) in her own right, as which recognised on termination of abeyance in her favour 29 Dec 1885; b 30 April 1835; m 11 Dec 1855 her er sister's bro-in-law Augustus Wykeham CLIFTON (d 9 May 1915), of Warton Hall, Lancs, yst bro of 1st BARON DONINGTON (see above), and d 15 Dec 1887, leaving:

    1h RAWDON GEORGE CLIFTON, 23rd LORD (Baron) GREY (of Ruthin), JP (Co Galway); b 14 Nov 1858; m 1 Sept 1892 Evelyn Isobel Ida Charlotte, only dau of James Foster, of Cranbourne Hall, Windsor Forest, and dsps & vp 31 Aug 1912

    2h CECIL TALBOT CLIFTON, 24th LORD (Baron) GREY (of Ruthin); b 9 Jan 1862; rancher in Montana; dsp 21 May 1934, when the Barony fell into abeyance between his nephew and niece (see below)

    1h Ella Cicely Mary; b 22 Nov 1856; m 30 July 1879 Lancelot George Butler-Bowdon (d 12 Sept 1909), of Barlborough House, Chesterfield, and d 2 July 1912, leaving:

        1i JOHN LANCELOT WYKEHAM BUTLER-BOWDON, 25th LORD (Baron) GREY (of Ruthin), on termination of abeyance in his favour 1940 following death of other co-heir, JP (Derbys); b 25 Oct 1883; educ Mount St Mary's Coll Spinkhill; d unm 25 Oct 1963, when the Barony fell once more into abeyance

        1i Lelgarde Harry Florence; b 16 Feb 1870; DGStJ; m 11 June 1895 Sir Alan Henry Bellingham, 4th Bt (qv), and dsp 15 Oct 1939

3g Victoria Mary Louisa; b 1837; m 1859 John Forbes Stratford Kirwan, of Moyne, Co Galway (b 1836; High Sheriff Co Longford 1860; d 1892), only s of Joseph Kirwan, of Hillsbrook (d 1852), and d 30 March 1888, having had issue (among whom any living descendants are in remainder to the Scottish peerages and medieval English ones):

    1h Euseby John; b 1864; d by 1886?

    2h George Augustus; b 1871

    1h Bertha Emily Evelyn; m 1895 Count Louis Lubienski Bodenham, JP, DL, of Rotherwas and Bullingham Manor, Herefs, and had, with an er s:

        1i Stanislas; had:

            1j Charles Henry; b 1935; m 1964 *Lia, dau of Giuseppe Zappala, of Rome, and d 1987, leaving:

                1k +Paul; b 1965

                1k +Elizabeth; b 1972

                2k +Monica (twin); b 1972

    2h Flora Sibyl (alias Mary Sybil Gertrude Kirwan, who d 18 July 1886 aged 23)

    3h Flora Amy

4g Frances Augusta Constance; b posthumously 16 March 1844; m 30 July 1863 4th Earl of Romney (qv) and d 1 Sept 1910, leaving issue

2 WILLIAM STANLEY, 6th EARL OF DERBY; had, with four daus:

(1) JAMES STANLEY, 1st LORD (Baron) STRANGE of the 1628 cr (being called up to Ho Lds 7 March 1627/8 vp in what was mistakenly thought to be his f's Barony of that name (i.e., Strange (of Knokyn)) and was given that Barony's precedency of 1299, although the Barony had in fact fallen into abeyance (according to a doctrine which only came to fruition in the late 17th century) between his female cousins on his unc's death so that in effect a new Barony of Strange was now cr), also 7th EARL OF DERBY; had, with other issue:

    1a CHARLES STANLEY, 2nd LORD (Baron) STRANGE of the 1628 cr and 8th EARL OF DERBY; d 21 Dec 1672, leaving:

        1b WILLIAM GEORGE RICHARD STANLEY, 3rd LORD (Baron) STRANGE of the 1628 cr and 9th EARL OF DERBY; dspms 5 Nov 1702, when the Barony of Strange cr 1628 fell into abeyance between his two daus, having had, with other issue:

            1c HENRIETTA MARIA, de jure BARONESS STRANGE of the 1628 cr in her own right on death of her yr sis 1714; b c 1687; m 1st 21 May 1706 4th Earl of Anglesey (dspms 18 Sept 1710; see VALENTIA, V) and had a dau (Elizabeth, d unm by 1718); m 2nd 24 July 1714 1st Earl of Ashburnham of the 1730 cr (d 10 March 1736/7) and dspm 26 June 1718, leaving by him, with other issue:

                1d HENRIETTA BRIDGET ASHBURNHAM, de jure BARONESS STRANGE of the 1628 cr in her own right; d unm 8 Aug 1732

    2b JAMES STANLEY, 6th LORD (Baron) STRANGE of the 1628 cr, as which s great-niece 1732, and 10th EARL OF DERBY; dspms 1 Feb 1735/6

    1a Amelia Sophia; m 5 May 1659 1st Marquess of Atholl and d 22 Feb 1702/3, leaving, with other issue:

        1b 1st DUKE OF ATHOLL (qv); had:

            1c 2nd DUKE OF ATHOLL; called up to Ho Lds 14 March 1736/7 vp as 7th LORD (Baron) STRANGE (see separate article STRANGE, B)

Lineage (of Hungerford and Moleyns)

(Note: The Hungerfords have often given the same forename to more than one member of a single generation. This makes the task of differentiating between them especially hard, particularly in the 17th century.)

WALTER (I) de HUNGERFORD; m Maude de Heytesbury and had:

WALTER (II) de HUNGERFORD; fl 1308; had:

1 Robert (Sir); MP Wilts 1316, commr 1327–28 to investigate extent of property held by the Despensers (see FALMOUTH, V); m ?1st Joan(e) —; m ?2nd, as her 2nd husb, Geva, widow of Adame de Stokke, and dsp 1354

2 Walter (Sir); MP Wilts 1331–32, 1333–34 and 1336; m Elizabeth, dau of Sir Adam FitzJohn, of Cherill, Wilts, and had:

(1) Thomas (Sir), of Farleigh Montford (later Farleigh Hungerford) and Wellow, Somerset, and Heytesbury, Wilts; MP: Wilts 1357, 1360, 1362, Jan 1376/7, 1380, 1383, 1386 and Jan 1392/3, Somerset 1378, 1382, 1388 and 1390, Wilts and Someset 1384 and Jan 1389/90, ktd by 1377, 1st formally constituted Speaker H of C 1377, Ch Steward to JOHN OF GAUNT (s of EDWARD III), Forester Selwood 1380, Constable Grosmount and Monmouth Castles; m 1st Eleanor, dau and heiress of Sir John Strug, of Heytesbury; m 2nd, as her 2nd husb, Joan (d 21 March 1411/2), dau and coheir of Sir Edmund Hussey, of Holbrook, Somerset, and widow of John Whyton, and d 3 Dec 1397, having had, with three er sons (Robert; Thomas; John, all dspm):

    1a Sir WALTER HUNGERFORD, KG (1421), **1st Lord** (Baron) **Hungerford** (E), so cr by writ 7 Jan 1425/6; b c 22 June 1378; ktd 1399, MP: Wilts 1400, 1404, 1407, 1413 and 1414 and Somerset 1409, Speaker H of C 1414, Sheriff: Wilts 1406 and Somerset and Dorset 1414; envoy to the HOLY ROMAN EMPEROR SIGISMUND 1414 and subsequently SIGISMUND's Master of the Household when the latter visited England 1416; served Hundred Years War: allegedly won a duel against CHARLES VI OF FRANCE before Calais 1401, fought at Agincourt 1415 (the spoils arising from which he allegedly used to restore Farleigh Castle, though he may also have raised the money from ransoming the eight distinguished Frenchmen he took prisoner after the Agincourt Campaign), cmded naval force which in 1416 relieved Harfleur (captured by HENRY V the previous year in the campaign that culminated in Agincourt) from a French blockade, envoy to negotiate with Archbp of Cologne 1417 and present at successful Siege of Rouen by HENRY V 1418; Steward Household to HENRYs V and VI, Constable Windsor Castle 1417, Memb Cncl of Regency 1422, Ld High Treasurer 1426–32; m 1st by 18 Sept 1402 Katherine (d on or after 14 June 1426), yr dau and coheir of Thomas Peverell, of Cornwall, and had:

        1b Walter (Sir); dvp France by 18 Feb 1432/3

        2b ROBERT, **2nd Lord**

        3b Edmund (Sir); ktd 1426, m just before 8 Nov 1416 Margaret (b c 1405), dau and coheir of Edward Burnell (ka vp Agincourt 25 Oct 1415) and gdau of 2nd Lord (Baron) Burnell, between whom and her two sisters the Barony of Burnell is by later doctrine held to have fallen into abeyance on the 2nd Lord Burnell's death in 1420 (see SHREWSBURY and WATERFORD, E), and d 1484, having had, with six daus:

            1c Thomas (Sir); ancestor of:

                1d Anthony, of Down Ampney, Glos; m Bridget, dau of John Shelley and gdau of Sir William Shelley, Judge Common Pleas (see SHELLEY, Bt), and had:

                    1e Anthony (Sir), DL (Wilts c 1608? to 1624), of Down Ampney, Glos, and Black Bourton, Oxon; b 1564; educ St John's Coll Oxford(?) (MA(?) 1594); ktd Feb 1607/8; m 1st Lucy, dau of Sir Walter Hungerford, of Farley (see below), and had:

                        1f Edward (Sir), DL (Wilts 1624); b 1596; inherited Hungerford estates on death 1607 of his maternal gf's half-bro (see below); MP Chippenham 1620 and 1640, KB 1625, Sheriff Wilts 1632, cmded Parly forces in Wilts in Civil War (fought at Lansdown Hill (narrow royalist victory) 5 July 1643 and Roundway Down (royalist victory) 13 July 1643, also besieged his half-bro Col John Hungerford in Farleigh Castle till it surrendered 1645); m (license 26 Feb 1619/20) Margaret, dau of William Hollidaie or Haliday, Alderman and Ld Mayor London (dsp 1672), and dsp 1648

                        2(?)f Anthony; Col Parly forces Civil War, served Ireland 1647–50 (Col Drogheda 1648); m Trisagon — (living 1658) and d 9 June 1657

                    1e (cont.) Sir Anthony Hungerford m 2nd Sarah, dau of John Crouch, of London, and d 1627, having by her had:

                        2/3f Anthony, of Black Bourton, Oxon; MP Malmesbury 1640 and in CHARLES I's Oxford Parl Dec 1643–March 1644; s his half-bro Edward in the Hungerford estates generally but as owner of Farleigh Castle allegedly only in 1653 (possibly because of confusion as to who was its rightful owner arising from the Civil War); m Rachel (d 1679/80), dau of Rice Jones, of Astall, Oxon, and d 18 Aug 1657, having had, with 10 other children (none of whom, if male, seem to have m and left surv male issue):

                            1g Edward (Sir), KB (1661), DL(?) (Wilts? to 1681); b 20 Oct 1632; MP Chippenham 1660,1661, 1678, 1679 and 1681, New Shoreham 1685, 1688 and 1690 and Steyning 1695, 1698, 1700 and 1702; resided when in London at Hungerford House, on the site of the present Charing Cross Station (and the northern bank of the Thames end of Hungerford Bridge, hence its name) until this was burnt down 1669, Lt-Col Regt of Archers 1661 and Col 1682; dissipated his family's once vast landed wealth, selling 30 manors, plus the manor of Farleigh, together with Farleigh Castle itself (the last two for £56,000 — roughly £4,000,000 in late-1990s terms); allegedly ended his days living on charity as a Kt of Windsor; m 1st Jane (d 18 May 1664), dau of Sir John Hele, of Devon, and had:

                              1h Edward; m Lady Alathea Compton (b 14 March 1661; d 14 Oct 1678), dau of 3rd Earl of Northampton (see NORTHAMPTON, M), and dsp Sept 1681

                            1h Rachel; b c 1662; m (licence 7 Jan 1679/80 and 9 March 1679/80) 3rd Viscount Massereene (see MASSEREENE and FERRARD, V) and d 2 Feb 1731/2, having had issue

                          1g (cont.) Sir Edward Hungerford m 2nd Jane Culme (d 1674) and had issue(?); m 3rd Jane Digby (d 23 Nov 1692) and was bur 8 July 1711, having had further issue(?); a s of Sir Edward's either by his 2nd or 3rd w d at Black Bourton, Oxon, 1748, when according to some sources the male representation of the Hungerfords died out, although a branch seems to have settled in Ireland around the mid-17th century and to have flourished there till well into the 20th

2g Anthony; b c 1635; worked clandestinely as a Royalist agent in England under the Protectorate 1655 and perhaps afterwards; d 7 June 1703

3/4f John; royalist Col Civil War, when held Farleigh Castle (see above)

1f? Another Sir Anthony Hungerford, of Down Ampney, Glos, m Elizabeth, dau of Sir Thomas Lucy, and d 1637, leaving an only dau and heiress:

1g Bridget; m by 1639 Edmund Dunch (b 1602; bur 4 Aug 1678), s of Sir William Dunch by Mary née Cromwell, aunt of The Protector OLIVER CROMWELL, who cr Edmund by Letters Patent 26 April 1658 BARON BURNELL OF EAST WITTENHAM, supposedly in reference to descent from the medieval Lords Burnell (see above), and had issue

2c Edward (Sir) m Anne, dau of Sir Edward Grey (see GREY, B), called to Parl from 14 Dec 1446 in right of his w as LORD (Baron) FERRERS (of Groby); ancestor of the HUNGERFORDs of Cadenham, Wilts

3c Walter; m Margaret, dau of Sir John St Leger

1b Elizabeth; m Sir Philip Courtenay and had issue (see DEVON, E)

2b Margaret; m Sir Walter Rodney

1a (cont.) The 1st Lord (Baron) Hungerford m 2nd by 8 May 1439 Eleanor (d 1 Aug 1455), dau of Sir John Berkeley, of Beverstone, Glos (see BERKELEY, B), and widow of (a) 13th/6th Earl of Arundel (see NORFOLK, D) and (b) Sir Richard Poynings, and d without having had further issue 9 Aug 1449

His est surv s by his 1st w,

ROBERT HUNGERFORD, 2nd Lord (Baron) Hungerford; b between c 1409 and c 1413; served Hundred Years War; m c 1420 Margaret de Botreaux, Baroness Botreaux in her own right according to later doctrine (d 7 Feb 1477/8), dau of 3rd Lord (Baron) Botreaux, and d 18 May 1459, having had, with two yr sons (Arnulph; William) and two daus (including Katherine, m by 10 June 1451 7th Lord (Baron) La Warre (see DE LA WARR, E) and d 12 May 1493, having had issue):

ROBERT HUNGERFORD, 3rd Lord (Baron) Hungerford and 1st Lord (Baron) Moleyns (E), so cr 13 Jan 1444/5 by writ vp; b by 1429; taken prisoner at the Battle of Castillon or Châtillon (the last battle — a catastrophic defeat for the English — of the Hundred Years War) 1453; on his return to England some six years later he supported the Lancastrian party in the Wars of Roses, being attainted 4 Nov 1461 on the ascendancy of the Yorkists under EDWARD IV after their victory of Towton, where he fought for HENRY VI; m by 5 Nov 1440, as her 1st husb, Eleanor (m 2nd c March 1468/9 Sir Oliver Manyngham and d 1476), dau and heiress of Sir William de Moleyns, of Stoke Poges, Bucks, and after being taken prisoner by the victorious Yorkists at the Battle of Hexham 15 May 1464 was executed at Newcastle 16 May 1464, having had:

1 Thomas (Sir); m by 16 Oct 1460, as her 1st husb, Lady Anne Percy, dau of 2nd Earl of Northumberland of the March 1415/6 cr (see NORTHUMBERLAND, D), and although he initially supported the Yorkists under EDWARD IV participated in the plot to restore HENRY VI in 1469 and was attainted and hanged, drawn and quartered at Bymerton (modern Bemerton?), nr Salisbury, 18 Jan 1468/9, leaving an only child and heiress:

(1) MARY Hungerford, BARONESS BOTREAUX, as which s her f's f's mother Margaret Feb 1477/8, and Baroness Hungerford and Baroness Moleyns, as which s her f's f and f respectively on the reversal 7 Nov 1485 of the respective attainders of 1461 and 1469, all three in her own right; b c 1467; m 1st by 18 Feb 1480/1 Sir Edward HASTINGS, cr by writ 15 Nov 1482 vp LORD HASTINGS (of Hungerford) (E), who s his f as 2nd LORD HASTINGS (of Hastings) the next year (13 June 1483) and d 8 Nov 1506, having had issue (see Lineage (of Strange (of Knokyn)); also the separate articles LOUDOUN, E, and HUNTINGDON, E; m 2nd 1 May 1509 Sir Richard Sacheverell (d 15 April 1534) and d by 10 July 1533, leaving by her 1st husb:

1a GEORGE HASTINGS, 1st EARL OF HUNTINGDON, 3rd LORD (Baron) HASTINGS (under which title he was called to Parl 1509) and 2nd LORD (Baron) HASTINGS (of Hungerford), also on his mother's death deemed by later doctrine to have become 6th LORD (Baron) BOTREAUX, 5th Lord (Baron) Hungerford and 3rd LORD (Baron) Moleyns; had, with other issue:

1b FRANCIS HASTINGS, 7th LORD (Baron) BOTREAUX, 4th LORD (Baron) HASTINGS, 3rd LORD (Baron) HASTINGS (of Hungerford), 6th Lord (Baron) Hungerford, 4th Lord (Baron) Moleyns and 2nd EARL OF HUNTINGDON; had, with other issue:

1c HENRY HASTINGS, 8th LORD (Baron) BOTREAUX, 5th LORD (Baron) HASTINGS, 4th LORD (Baron) HASTINGS (of Hungerford), 7th Lord (Baron) Hungerford, 5th Lord (Baron) Moleyns and 3rd EARL OF HUNTINGDON; dsp 14 Dec 1595

2c GEORGE HASTINGS, 9th LORD (Baron) BOTREAUX, 6th LORD (Baron) HASTINGS, 5th LORD (Baron) HASTINGS (of Hungerford), 8th Lord (Baron) Hungerford, 6th Lord (Baron) Moleyns and 4th EARL OF HUNTINGDON; had:

1d Francis, Lord Hastings; dvp 17 Dec 1595, leaving:

1e HENRY HASTINGS, 10th LORD (Baron) BOTREAUX, 7th LORD (Baron) HASTINGS, 6th LORD (Baron) HASTINGS (of Hungerford), 9th Lord (Baron) Hungerford, 7th Lord (Baron) Moleyns and 5th EARL OF HUNTINGDON; m 15 Jan 1601 Lady Elizabeth Stanley (d 20 Jan 1633), yst dau of 5th Earl of Derby (qv), and d 14 Nov 1643, having had issue (see above against Lineage of Strange (of Knokyn))

2 Walter (Sir), PC (1485 or 1486); MP Wilts 1477; initially pro-Lancastrian but pardoned by RICHARD III (by now the Yorkist leader) 1483; detained by RICHARD, however, on the news of the arrival of the Earl of Richmond (later HENRY VII) but escaped and fought for Richmond at Bosworth 1485, where he k his former commanding offr Sir Richard Brackenbury, Lt Tower London; ktd by HENRY VII on the field of Bosworth; envoy to the Pope 1493; helped suppress Perkin Warbeck's attempt on the throne 1497; m Jane, dau of Sir William Bulstrode, and d 1516, leaving an only s:

(1) Edward (Sir); served in HENRY VIII's French campaign 1513, ktd at Tournai 1513, Sheriff Wilts 1517 and Somerset and Dorset 1518; m 1st Jane La

Zouche, dau of 7th(?) Lord (Baron) Zouche (of Haryngworth) (see ZOUCHE, B), and had:

1a WALTER HUNGERFORD, 1st and last LORD (Baron) HUNGERFORD of Heytesbury (E), so cr by writ 27 April 1536; b c 1502; Squire of the Body to HENRY VIII c 1522 or 1523, Sheriff Wilts 1533; a close associate of Thomas Cromwell; m 1st Susan, dau of Sir John Danvers, of Culworth, Northants, and had, with two other daus:

1b Walter (Sir), called 'The Knight of Farley'; b 1532; had his estates restored 1554 on his 1st marriage but not the peerage, Sheriff Wilts 1557; m 1st c 1554 Anne Basset, Maid of Honour to QUEEN MARY; m 2nd c 1558 Anne (whom he unsuccessfully accused 1570 of having tried to poison him back in 1564, also of adultery with one William Darrell, of Littlecote; she d 1603), dau of Sir William Dormer, of Ascot, Berks, and had:

1c Edmund; dvp 1587

1c Susan; m 1st Michael Ernley, of Cannings, Wilts; m 2nd John Moring; m 3rd Sir Crew Reynolds

2c Lucy; m 1st Sir John St John, of Lydiard, and had issue (see BOLINGBROKE and SAINT JOHN, V); m 2nd, as his 2nd w, Sir Anthony Hungerford (see above)

3c Jane; m 1st Sir John Carne, of Ewenny, Glam

1b (cont.) Sir Walter Hungerford went through a form of marriage (despite his 2nd w still being alive) c 1595 with his mistress Margery Brighte, by whom he had already had at least two sons, but dspms 1596

1a (cont.) The 1st LORD (Baron) HUNGERFORD of Heytesbury m 2nd 1527 or 1528 Alice Sandys, dau of 1st Baron Sandys of the 1523 cr, and had:

2b Edward (Sir); s to the Hungerford estates 1596 on the death of his half-bro Sir Walter; Gentleman Pensioner to ELIZABETH I; m 1st Jane, widow of William Foster; m 2nd Cecily (m 2nd 6th Earl of Rutland; see RUTLAND, D), dau of Sir John Tufton, 1st Bt of the 1611 cr, and dsp 1607

1b (?)Eleanor; m William Masters

2b Mary; m 1st Thomas Baker; m 2nd Thomas Shaa

3b Anne

1a (cont.) The 1st LORD (Baron) HUNGERFORD of Heytesbury m 3rd Oct 1532, as her 1st husb, Elizabeth Hussey (m 2nd by 4 July 1544 Sir Robert Throgmorton and d 23 Jan 1553/4), dau of 1st Lord (Baron) Hussey of the 1529 cr, and was attainted 16 July 1540 for sodomy, sorcery and subversion, being beheaded along with Thomas Cromwell 28 July 1540, when the Barony was forfeited

(1) (cont.) Sir Edward Hungerford m 2nd, as her 2nd husb, Agnes, widow of James Cotell (for having murdered whom 26 July 1518, by strangulation in Farleigh Castle with the help of two local yeomen, she was executed 5 Feb 1522/3) and d 24 Jan 1521/2, bequeathing her his entire personal property

3 Leonard

1 Frideswide; nun at Sion, Middx

St George

FIRMITAS IN CŒLO

Arms: Arg. a chief az., over all a lion rampant gu., ducally crowned or, armed and langued of the second, a crescent for difference. **Crest:** A demi-lion rampant gu., ducally crowned or, armed and langued az. **Motto:** *Firmitas in cœlo* ('Stability in heaven'). **Creation:** Bt. (I) 12 March 1766.

SIR JOHN AVENEL BLIGH ST GEORGE, 10TH BT, of Athlone, Co Westmeath [Sir John St George Bt, 23 Burton St, Loughborough, Leics LE11 2DT]; b 18 March 1940; s f 1995; dir IRM Ltd and Hub Developments & Finance Ltd; m 1st 30 June 1962 (divorce 1979) Margaret, dau of John Leonard Carter, MBE, of Mayes Park House, Warnham, Sussex, and has:

1 *Elinor Jane Bligh [Mrs Richard Newbold, 4 St Leonards Rd, Claygate, Surrey]; b 6 Oct 1963; m 1990 *Richard Newbold and has:

(1) *Cameron; b 1991

(1) *Georgia; b 1993

2 *Catherine Bligh; b 3 Feb 1966

Sir JOHN m 2nd 1981 *Linda, dau of Robert Perry, of Glasgow, and by her has:

1 +ROBERT ALEXANDER BLIGH; *b* 17 Aug 1983

2 +Benjamin Bligh; *b* 1986

Lineage: The ST GEORGEs, who held the Hatley St George or Hungre Hatley estate, Cambs, from at least *temp* HENRY II to *temp* CHARLES II, were a cadet branch of a French family of the same name who held the fief of St Georges near Limoges.

BALDWIN; allegedly settled in England *temp* WILLIAM I (THE CONQUEROR); *d* in or after 1113, having had, with a dau (Albreda, nun in Clerkenwell):

WILLIAM ST GEORGE; living *temp* HENRY II; *m* —, dau of Bancis(?), of Kingston, and had, with a dau Mabilia (nun in Clerkenwell):

BALDWIN ST GEORGE; living 1199; had:

1 BALDWIN

2 William; living 1223

3 Robert de Hailesweston; *m* Agnes, dau and heiress of William de Alneto and widow of Hugo de Ardres, and had two sons (Baldwin; William) and two daus (Albreda, living 1245; Agnes, *m* William de Graffham)

4 Henry; *b by* 1223; *m* 1249 Alicia — and had three daus (Alicia, *m* Walter Gifford; Joan, *m* Robert Bozon; Rosamund)

The est s,

BALDWIN ST GEORGE; *b by* 1216; had, with a dau (Amicia, *m* Philip de Abingdon and had issue):

WILLIAM ST GEORGE; living 1243; had:

BALDWIN ST GEORGE; living 1256; *m* Basilia de Soham, of Mepham, Isle of Ely, widow of Eymond de Turenberd, Constable Tower London (by whom she had, with three other daus and coheirs, Margaret; *see* below) and *d* 1282, leaving:

Sir WILLIAM ST GEORGE; *m* his step-sis Margaret de Turenberd (*see* above) and *d by* 1312, having had, with a dau (Margery, *m* Robert Haringall, of Yorks):

BALDWIN ST GEORGE; *m* Johanna — (living 1340) and *dvp*, having had, with a dau (Basilia):

Sir WILLIAM ST GEORGE; living 1348; had:

Sir BALDWIN ST GEORGE; MP and Sheriff Cambs and Hunts; *m* Elizabeth, dau and coheir of Sir John Argentine, and had, with three yr sons (Thomas; Giles, at school 1393; John) and a dau (Elizabeth):

Sir BALDWIN ST GEORGE, JP; MP Cambs; *m* Joan, dau and coheir of Sir John Engaine, and *d* 18 Feb 1425, having had, with two yr sons (Baldwin; William):

JOHN ST GEORGE; *m* Matilda, dau and heiress of Sir William de Coggeshall, and *dvp*, leaving:

Sir WILLIAM ST GEORGE; MP Cambs; *m* 1st Alianora, dau and coheir of Sir Richard Arundel, and had a s (Thomas, *dvm* unm); *m* 2nd Katherine, dau of Sir John Manningham, and *d* 1472, having had by her:

Sir RICHARD ST GEORGE; *b* 1446; *m* Ann, dau of Thomas à Burgoine, of Impington, Cambs, and *d* 1485, having had:

THOMAS ST GEORGE; *b* 1473; *m* 1st Alice (*d by* 1512), dau of Sir John Rotherham, of Somerham, and had a s (George, *m* 1512 Joan, dau of William Mordaunt, and *dsp*) and two daus (Ann, *m* John Doowra; Catherine, *m* Richard Marshall); *m* 2nd Etheldreda, dau of Clement Higham, of Giffards, Suffolk, and *d* 1540, having by her had:

FRANCIS ST GEORGE, of Hatley St George; *b c* 1525; *m by c* 1540 Rose, dau of Thomas Hutton, of Drydrayton, Cambs, and had:

1 John, of Hatley St George; *m* Mary, dau of Peter Grey, of Rugcourt, Beds, and had:

  (1) John, of Hatley St George; fined £625 (some £25,200 in late-1990s terms) for royalism 1648; *m* Dorothy, dau of John Legatt, of Horn Court, Essex, and was *bur* 30 Dec 1652, having had, with three other sons (Thomas; William; Anthony):

    1a John; *m* 1st Clara Gage (*dsp*); *m* 2nd Margaret, dau of Francis Perkins, of Berks, and had:

      1b Mary; *m* F Harris

      2b Margaret; *m* — Segrave and *dsp* 1720

    2a Richard; *m* Susanna, dau of Anthony Thomson, of Cambridge, and had, with two daus (*d* unm):

      1b John; *m* Sarah, dau of Edward Norman, of London, and *d* 6 Oct 1690, having had, with another s (Elkin) and a dau (*d* in infancy):

        1c Edward; *m* Alicia, dau of Gabriel Selden, of Kinsale, Co Cork, and had seven sons and a dau (all *dsp*)

  (2) William

  (3) Henry

  (4) Peter

  (5) Thomas; *m* Frances, dau of John Shelbury, of High Holborn and Perivale, Middx, and *d* Nov 1637, having had a s (Baldwin) and dau (Margaret, nun in Paris)

2 Richard (Sir); ktd 1616, Norroy King of Arms 1603–23, Clarenceux King of Arms 1623–35; *m* Elizabeth, dau of Nicholas St John (*see* BOLINBROKE and SAINT JOHN, V), and *d* 17 May 1635, having had:

  (1) William; *ka* aged 22 helping suppress the native Irish at Lough Foyle *temp* ELIZABETH I

  (2) John; *k* fighting against native Irish

  (3) Henry (Sir); *b* 27 Jan 1581; Norroy King of Arms 1635–44, Garter King of Arms April-Nov 1644, DCL; *m* 1614 Mary, dau of Sir Thomas Dayrell, of Lillington Dayrell, Bucks, and *d* 5 Nov 1644, having had:

    1a Thomas (Sir), of Woodford, Essex; *b* 1615; Norroy King of Arms Jan 1679/80–85/6, Garter King of Arms Feb 1685/6–1702/3; *m* 1st Clara (*d* 1691) dau of Rev John Pymlowe; *m* 2nd Ann (*d* 7 Feb 1730), dau of Sir John Lawson, and *d* 6 March 1702/3, having by her had a dau (Isabella, *b* 4 Sept 1693) and by his 1st w:

      1b Thomas; lay Rector Bexley; *m* Damaris, dau and coheir of Robert Renter

      1b Elinor; *m* Thomas Dare, of Taunton

      2a William; royalist Col Civil War; *k* storming of Leicester 21 May 1645

      3a Henry (Sir); Norroy King of Arms 1677–78/9, Clarenceux King of Arms 1678/9–1703, Garter King of Arms 1703–15; *m* Elizabeth Wingfield (*d* 1704) and *d* 1715 aged 91, having had two daus

      4a Richard; Ulster King of Arms 1660–83; *m* Mary, dau of Henry Hastings, of Bramston, and *dsp*

      1a Elizabeth; *m* Col R Bourke

      2a Mary; *m* Ferdinand Hastings (*d* 1692/6), of Clement Danes, and had issue

      3a Frances; *m* George Tucker

      4a Rebecca; *m* George Cooke

(4) George (Sir), of Carrickdrumrusk, Co Leitrim; *b* 13 Jan 1583; MP; *m* Catharine, dau of Capt Richard Gifford, of Ballymagarrett, Co Roscommon, and *d* Headford, Co Galway, 5 Aug 1660, leaving an er s:

  1a Sir OLIVER ST GEORGE, 1st Bt (E possibly also I), so *cr* 5 Sept 1660, of Carrickdrumrusk; ktd Feb 1658/9 by Henry Cromwell, Ld Dep Ireland, and again 1660 by CHARLES II; Commr Irish Affrs 1660, MP (I Parl) Galway 1661–65 and 1692–93; *m by* 1651 Olivia, dau of Michael Beresford, of Coleraine, and widow of George Thornton, and *d* Oct 1695, leaving:

    1b Sir GEORGE ST GEORGE, 2nd and last Bt, and 1st and last BARON SAINT GEORGE OF HATLEY SAINT GEORGE, Cos Roscommon and Leitrim (I), so *cr* 18 April 1715, with remainder in default of heirs male of his own body to those of his f, PC (I 1715); *b c* 1658; *educ* Trin Coll Dublin; MP (I Parl) Co Roscommon 1692–93, 1695–99 and 1703–15, V-Adml Connaught; *m* 29 Nov 1681 Margaret, dau of 2nd Viscount Massereene (*see* MASSEREENE and FERRARD, V), and *dspm* 4 Aug 1735, when his titles expired, leaving:

      1c Mary; *m* 20 Dec 1714 John Usher, MP, V-Adml Connaught, and had:

        1d St George USHER later ST GEORGE (roy licence 25 May 1734), 1st and last BARON SAINT GEORGE OF HATLEY SAINT GEORGE, Cos Roscommon and Leitrim (I), so *cr* 19 April 1763; *b c* 1715; Sheriff Co Roscommon 1737, MP (I Parl) Carrick-upon-Shannon 1741–63; *m* 18 July 1752 Elizabeth, dau of Christopher Dominick, of Dublin, and *dspms* 2 Jan 1775, when the Barony expired, having had, with a s (*d* young):

          1e Emilia Olivia; *m* 7 Nov 1775 2nd Duke of Leinster (*qv*) and had issue

        1d Olivia; *m* Arthur Finch, of Tyrone, Co Galway, and had issue, who took the name ST GEORGE

      2d Judith; *m* George Lowther, of Kilone, Co Meath

    1a Eleanor; *m* Sir Arthur Gore, 1st Bt, of the 1662 *cr* (*see* ARRAN, E)

(5) Richard; *b* 27 March 1590; Capt in Ireland; Govr Athlone; *m* 1st 20 Feb 1625 Ann, dau of Michael Pinnock, of Turrock, Co Roscommon; *m* 2nd 1644 Dorothy, widow of Hamon L'Estrange and dau of Sir John Moore, and *d* 24 April 1667, having by her had a dau and by his 1st w, with two daus and two er sons:

  1a Henry, of Athlone; *b* 15 Oct 1638; Army Offr Ireland *temp* CHARLES II; granted the Woodsgift estate, Co Kilkenny, 1666; *m* 3 June 1669 Anne, dau of Ridgeley Hatfield, Dublin Alderman, and had, with other issue:

    1b Arthur; ancestor of the ST GEORGEs of Wood Park

  2b George, of Woodsgift; *b* 2 July 1682; MP; *m* Elizabeth, sis of 1st Earl of Darnley (*qv*), and *d* 23 Sept 1762, having had a 2nd s:

    1c **Sir Richard St George, 1st Bt** (I), so *cr* 12 March 1766, of Woodsgift, Co Kilkenny; *m* 27 July 1764 Sarah, only dau of Robert Persse, of Roxborough, Co Galway, and had, with other issue:

      1d RICHARD BLIGH (Sir), **2nd Bt**

      2d George (Rev); *m* Frances (*d* 24 Nov 1837), dau of Rev Thomas Grady, of Capercullen and Elton, and *d* 24 Nov 1824, leaving three daus

      3d Thomas Bligh; *m* 11 June 1804 Hannah, 3rd dau of Sir Hercules Langrishe, 1st Bt (*qv*), and *d* 1859, leaving, with other issue:

        1e Hercules Langrishe, JP Co Kilkenny; *b* 1810; High Sheriff Co Kilkenny 1848; *m* 1848 Margaret, dau of Alexander Taylor, and *d* 1860, leaving a dau

        2e Francis de Montmorency (Rev); *b* 1812; Rector St Anne, Shandon, Co Cork; *m* Catherine Jemina, dau of Thomas Newcomen Edgeworth, and *d* 1882, leaving:

          1f Annette; *m* 18 Oct 1877 Joseph Rawlins, of Dollarward, Cirencester, and *d* 3 Feb 1933, leaving issue. He *d* 1924

The 1st Bt *d* 1789; his est s,

Sir Richard Bligh St George, 2nd Bt; *b* 5 June 1765; Sec Order St Patrick; *m* 1st 10 Feb 1799 Harriet, dau of Rt Hon Mr Justice Kelly, of Kellyville, Queen's Co, and had three daus; *m* 2nd April 1807 Bridget (*d* Dec 1866), est dau of Theophilus Blakeney, of Abbert, Co Galway, and by her had, with another s and dau (*d* young):

1 THEOPHILUS JOHN (Sir), **3rd Bt**

2 Robert; *b* 18 Nov 1811; *m* 1841 Sophia Madelina Olivia (*d* 31 March 1901), 2nd dau of Very Rev James Mahon, Dean Dromore, and *d* 28 June 1893, having had, with other issue:

  (1) Robert James Ker; *b* 6 Nov 1843; *educ* Trin Coll Dublin (BA); *m* 5 Feb 1874 his cousin Katherine (*d* 1934), dau and coheir of Christopher St George, DL, of Tyrone, Co Galway, MP Co Galway, and *d* 6 Oct 1905, having had:

    1a Richard Christopher Bligh; *b* 14 Aug 1875; *m* 6 Sept 1916 Alice Rosabel (*d* 1964), dau of Lt-Col Hugh Latimer Donovan, of S Yardley, Worcs, by Rosabel Sinclair, dau of Andrew Samuel Kirkwood, of Cloongoonagh, Co Roscommon, and *d* 1945, leaving:

    1b *Catherine Harriette Mary Bligh [Miss Catherine St George, 1346 Coventry Rd, Yardley, Birmingham B25 8AN]; *b* 1917

  2a Arthur French; *b* 14 Sept 1878; *d* 2 Nov 1907

  3a Robert Charles Cecil; *b* 6 June 1883; *m* 5 May 1917 Lillian, dau of Thomas Hunt Talmadge, of Tuxedo Park, NY, and *d* 1948, leaving:

1b Robert Charles Cecil; *b* 1920; *m* 1943 *Priscilla, dau of John Tillerton Painter, of Pittsburgh, and *d* 1963, leaving:

  1c +Christopher; *b* 1946

1a Rosamund Frances Catherine

2a Gladys Alienora; *m* 3 July 1913 Henry Beechey, barrister, of Lahore, s of Frederick Beechey and gs of Sir William Beechey, PRA

3a Josephine; *d* unm 27 July 1969

(2) Howard Bligh, JP Cos Galway and Dublin; *b* 12 March 1857; *m* 26 May 1891 Florence Evelyn (*d* 16 Sept 1936), dau of George F Baker, of New York, and *d* 16 Feb 1937, having had:

1a George Baker Bligh; *b* 19 March 1892; *educ* Eton and Trin Coll Cambridge; *m* 14 April 1917 Katharine Delano, memb US Congress 1946, dau of H Price Collier, of Tuxedo Park, NY, and *d* 5 Oct 1957, leaving:

  1b *Priscilla Avenel [Mrs Priscilla Ryan, Box 201 Meetetse, WY 82433, USA]; *b* 1919; *m* 1st 2 Jan 1936 (*divorce* 1939) Angier Biddle Duke and has:

    1c *Angier St George Biddle; *b* 1938; *m* 1st 1959 Jeanne S Farmer; *m* 2nd 19– *Mary Ellen, dau of Ora Cecil Haga, and by his 1st w has:

      1d *George St George; *b* 1960

      2d *Benjamin Buchanan; *b* 1963

  1b (cont.) Mrs Priscilla Duke *m* 2nd June 1941 (*divorce*) Allan A Ryan and by him has:

    1c *Katherine Delano [Mrs Aldrich, Goodhap, Barrytown, NY 12507, USA]; *b* 1943; *m* 19– *— Aldrich

2a Howard Avenel Bligh; *b* 16 Dec 1894; *educ* Eton; Lt 1st Life Gds; *ka* 15 Nov 1914

3a Frederick Ferris Bligh, CVO (1953); *b* 25 March 1908; *educ* Eton; Col Life Gds, memb Gentlemen-at-Arms 1957, High Sheriff Glos 1959; *m* 4 Oct 1932 Meriel Margaret, JP (*d* 23 March 1966), yr dau of Lt-Col William Scott Warley Radcliffe, of Esseborne Manor, Hurstbourne Tarrant, Hants, and *d* 4 April 1970, leaving:

  1b *Meriel Jane Bligh [Miss Meriel St George, 424 E 52 St, Apt 2A, New York, NY 10022, USA]; *b* 5 Nov 1933; *m* 17 Dec 1966 (*divorce* 1971, resumed maiden name) Benjamin Brandreth McAlpin, est s of Benjamin Brandreth McAlpin, of Greenwich, Conn.

  2b *Sally Elizabeth Bligh [Mrs John Alford, Hammatethy House, St Breward, Bodmin, Cornwall]; *b* 13 June 1936; *m* 27 Nov 1965 *John Richard Alford, er s of Gerard George Alford, BSc, of The Rock House, Chalford, Glos, and has:

    1c *Charles William; *b* 22 Feb 1972

    1c *Julia Meriel Bligh; *b* 5 March 1967

    2c *Nicola Jane Bligh; *b* 29 May 1969

  3b *Diana Gillian Bligh [Lady Earle, Abington Rectory, Murroe, Co Limerick, Ireland]; *b* 24 March 1939; *m* 24 Jan 1967 *Sir (Hardman) George Algernon Earle, 6th Bt (*qv*), and has issue

1a *Evelyn (Gardenia) Bligh, OBE (1944); *b* 9 Oct 1897; dir Residential Nurseries Anglo-American Relief Fund 1941–46; *m* 18 Oct 1917 Maj Sir Derrick Wellesley Gunston, 1st Bt, MC (*qv*), and has issue

2a Vivien Antonia Bligh; *b* 1 Jan 1912; *m* 1st 7 June 1932 Alexander Frank Stanley Clarke, 14th/20th Hus, s of Lt-Col Albert Edward Stanley Clarke, DSO, MVO, Scots Gds (*d* 1947), and had issue; *m* 2nd 1950 Dr William Winch (*d* 25 Sept 1964); *m* 3rd 22 Sept 1966 Charles Patrick Ranke Graves, jnlst, 5th s of Alfred Percival Graves and bro of the author Robert Graves, and *d* 24 April 1975. He *d* 21 Feb 1971

(1) Sophia Madelina; *m* 1888 Rev William Shepperd, Vicar Baydon, Wilts, and *d* his widow 24 Sept 1931

(2) Josephine Louisa; *m* 7 Aug 1873 Henry Vesey Seymour Vesey-Fitzgerald, BCS, of Kilnacourt, Portalington, s of Rt Hon Sir Seymour Vesey-Fitzgerald. He *d* 16 March 1925

(3) Elizabeth Olivia; *m* 14 April 1874 Charles O'Hara Trench, of Clonfert, Co Galway, and *d* 1930, leaving issue. He *d* 1927

(4) Georgina Harriet; *d* 20 June 1937

(5) Madelina Ker; *d* 1871

(6) Henrietta Maude; *m* 23 July 1884 Arthur Hugo de Burdet Burdett, of Coolfinn, King's Co, and *d* 4 July 1934, leaving issue. He *d* 4 Dec 1917

3 William Oliver; *b* 19 March 1813; *m* 23 Nov 1846 Sarah (*d* 8 June 1881), dau of Michael Quirk, of Woodsgift, Co Kilkenny, and *d* 1 Nov 1884, having had:

(1) Richard Oliver; *b* 15 Aug 1847; *d* unm 12 April 1870

(2) William Henry; *b* 16 Feb 1849; *d* unm 5 Feb 1875

(3) George Edward; *b* 22 Nov 1854; *m* 13 Nov 1894 Henrietta (*d* 8 March 1907), dau of George Simms, of Ottawa, and *d* 29 July 1902, leaving:

1a Leslie George; *b* 5 Feb 1896; *m* 12 Feb 1918 Gladys (*d* 4 Nov 1941), dau of Alfred McGillivray, of Ottawa, and *d* 17 Dec 1968, leaving:

  1b +Leslie Richard [Leslie St George Esq, 3 Goodwin Ave, Nepean, Ontario K2E 5C4, Canada]; *b* 8 May 1924; RCAF Reserve Section (CVSM); *m* 3 June 1946 *Muriel Winnifred, dau of John Edwards, of Ottawa, and has:

    1c +Barry Edward; *b* 13 April 1949; *m* 1978 *Catherine Jean, dau of George P Campbell, of Ottawa, and has:

      1d +Joshua Adam; *b* 1980

      1d *Lauren Ashley; *b* 1982

    2c *Leslie Timothy; *b* 15 Oct 1961; *m* 1986 *Janet Lee, dau of Robert Ross Wilson, of Nepean, Ontario, and has:

      1d *Lindsay Blair; *b* 1989

      2d *Laura Leigh; *b* 1991

    1c *Gayle Mary; *b* 8 Jan 1953

    2c *Beverley Ann; *b* 16 Jan 1954; *m* 1979 *Kerry Patrick Scullion, of Ottawa, and has:

      1d *Timothy Patrick Pearse; *b* 1983

      2d *Rory Joseph Anthony; *b* 1987

  2b +Robert John; *b* 4 Nov 1941; *m* 20 July 1968 (*divorce* 1984) Vivien Jill, dau of David Walters, of London, and has:

1c +Christian Robert David; *b* 1974

1c *Catherine Lesley; *b* 1970

1b *Mary Audrey [Mrs John Scarcella, 1308–1701 Kilborn Ave, Ottawa, Ont K1H 6M8, Canada]; *b* 3 Jan 1927; *m* 12 March 1949 John Scarcella (*d* 1989), s of Louis Scarcella, of Ottawa, and has:

  1c *Byron Michael; *b* 21 Dec 1949; *m* 1973 *Annette, dau of Lionel Aucoin, of Ottawa, and has:

    1d *Lisa Marie; *b* 1977

  2c *David Louis Anthony *b* 14 May 1955

  3c *Gordon Kenneth John; *b* 17 Jan 1960

1a Jane Ellen; *b* 8 May 1900; *m* 29 July 1918 John Mallen (*d* 1973), s of James Walsh Mallen, of New York, and had:

  1b John Leslie, AM, DFC; *b* 4 Oct 1921; Maj USAAF; *m* 3 July 1944 *Shirley Ann, dau of Harold Winnick, of Rochester, NY, and was *k* in a mid-air collision of mil aircraft off Bermuda 29 June 1964, leaving:

    1c *John William; *b* 6 Jan 1948

    1c *Leslie Ann; *b* 20 April 1946

    2c *Sharyl Jean; *b* 12 March 1949

  2b *Richard William; *b* 7 Oct 1927; *m* 1st 18 April 1953 Lois Ann (*d* 1 June 1961), dau of Walter H Taylor, of Rochester, NY; *m* 2nd 2 Nov 1962 *Marlene E Green and by her has:

    1c *Michelle Ann; *b* 17 March 1965

  3b *Thomas James; *b* 12 Feb 1938; *m* 21 June 1958 *Sharon Holland, dau of Bernard J Douthwaite, of Rochester, NY, and has:

    1c *Thomas Richard; *b* 3 July 1959

    2c *Joseph Roycroft; *b* 19 March 1963

(4) Robert; *b* 22 Aug 1856; *m* 28 Feb 1881 Elizabeth Agatha (*d* 4 Dec 1935), dau of Thomas Tovey, of Perth, Ontario, and *d* 7 Dec 1939, having had:

1a Richard Bligh; *b* 22 Sept 1886; *m* 6 Aug 1920 (*divorce* 1930) Ada Mary Barr

2a Robert Oliver; *b* 13 Nov 1888; *d* unm 15 June 1925

3a George Edgar; *b* 6 March 1892; *m* 1 Feb 1929 Ruth Mary, dau of Harold Richardson, of Ottawa, and had:

  1b George Edgar II; *b* 12 Oct 1929; *m* 19– *Lise Lamothe and *d* 1992, leaving:

    1c +Eddie; *b* 19–

    2c +Richard; *b* 19–

    1c *Suzanne; *b* 19–

    2c *Julie; *b* 19–

  2b +Richard Bligh Harold; *b* 5 Oct 1935

  3b +Michael; *b* 19–

  4b +Tovey; *b* 19–

  1b *Ruth Mary Madora; *b* 18 April 1931

1a Lily Madora; *b* 11 April 1882; *m* 20 May 1908 Edgar Charles Coleman, s of Dr Arthur O F Coleman, of Ottawa, and had issue

2a Daisy Mary Evelyn; *b* 17 Dec 1884; *m* 16 Oct 1933 Dominic F Scanlon (*d* 4 March 1947)

3a Margaret Pearl; *b* 19 July 1895 ; *d* unm 24 July 1948

(5) Theophilus John; *b* 7 July 1861; *d* unm 9 July 1877

(6) James Howard; *b* 17 June 1864; *m* 1 Aug 1890 Catherine (*d* 5 March 1914), dau of Michael Burns, of Ottawa, and *d* 30 Jan 1939, having had:

1a James Howard; *b* 23 April 1893; *m* 17 Aug 1927 Elizabeth (*d* 21 Sept 1964), dau of William Belch, of Ottawa, and *d* 11 Feb 1962, having had:

  1b Howard Keith; *b* 1 Jan 1929

  1b *Constance June; *b* 16 May 1930; *m* 1955 *Robert Carl Bocieck, MD, and has:

    1c *Robert Gregory; *b* 1961

    2c *James Andrew *b* 1964

    1c *Virginia Elizabeth; *b* 1956

    2c *Beverley Ann; *b* 1959

2a William Oliver; *b* 19 July 1898; *d* 24 April 1914

1a Violet Catherine; *b* 5 Jan 1892; *d* 1894

2a Hazel Gertrude; *b* 12 Nov 1901; *m* 15 Jan 1924 George H Reinhardt

(7) Hercules Frank; *b* 4 Nov 1867; *m* 5 Aug 1895 Rosaline (*d* July 1901), dau of John Dunn, of Gaspé, Quebec, and *d* 2 June 1938, having had:

1a Hercules Frank, of Ottawa; *b* 19 Sept 1896; *m* 24 April 1939 *Marie Adeline Juliette, dau of Eugene Larocque, of Ottawa

2a Richard Bligh; *b* 3 Oct 1897; *d* unm 21 Feb 1935

(8) John Arthur; *b* 4 Nov 1867; *m* 22 Dec 1900 Lily Belle, dau of John Magladry, and *d* 21 June 1912, leaving:

1a +William John; *b* 5 Sept 1907

1a *Gladys Ellen; *b* 28 Aug 1901

2a *Marjorie Ellen; *b* 14 Jan 1903; *m* 19–*Lawrence J Desjardins

3a *Fanny Evelyn; *b* 17 Feb 1905

4a *Sarah Alice; *b* 7 Nov 1909

(1) Fanny Victoria; *b* 7 June 1852; *m* 6 March 1878 James Burn, of Ottawa, and *d* 30 May 1926, leaving issue. He *d* 9 April 1911

(2) Margaret; *b* 30 March 1859; *m* 22 June 1880 Charles Cole, of Ottawa, and *dsp* Aug 1882

(3) Marian Theodosia; *b* 31 May 1871; *d* 8 Dec 1876

4 James Cuffe, JP; *b* 1814; *m* 15 May 1856 Jane Grey (*d* 24 Jan 1892), only dau of Capt Arthur Loftus, RN (*see* ELY, M), and *d* 14 March 1891, leaving:

(1) Loftus; *b* 28 June 1858; Lt Q R W Surrey Militia; silver medal of Nat Shipwreck Relief Soc of NSW, Australia, for life-saving; *m* 25 March 1893 Marguerite Isabel Clifford (*d* 31 March 1956), dau of Clifford Fortescue Borrer, of Pickwell, Cuckfield, Sussex, and *d* 14 Dec 1952, leaving:

1a Clifford Fortescue Loftus, CBE (1948); *b* 22 July 1894; *educ* Eastbourne Coll and Merton Coll Oxford (MA); 4th Bn Roy Sussex Regt, TF, WW I; Clerk Jnls Ho Lds (ret 1960); *m* 29 July 1931 Gwen Marjorie Chisholm (*d*

1982), yst dau of Rev William Edward Dalton, Vicar Glynde, Sussex, and *d* 1 June 1966, having had:

  1b +John [John St George Esq, Warren Farm, Wilmington, E Sussex BN26 6RL]; *b* 21 Feb 1942; *educ* Michael Hall, Forest Row, Sussex; *m* 1st 1965 (*divorce* 1975) — and has:

    1c +William; *b* 1967

    1c *Lucy; *b* 1969

    2c *Marina; *b* 1970

  1b (cont.) John St George *m* 2nd 1975 *Elizabeth Jane, er dau of Herbert Westgate, of Berwick, Sussex

  1b Mary; *b* 14 July 1936; *d* 26 June 1939

  1a Aline Mary Loftus; *b* 10 March 1897; *m* 1st 19 Dec 1918 (*divorce* 1933) Lt Ernest Charles William Vane-Tempest, DSC, RNVR (*see* LONDONDERRY, M), and had issue; *m* 2nd 7 Nov 1933 (*divorce* 1948) Michael Ceely Sandford Pakenham and had further issue (*see* LONGFORD, E)

  2a Kathleen Adeline Jane Loftus; *b* 13 June 1898; *m* 25 April 1923 John Philip Stephenson Clarke (*d* 30 Nov 1969), 3rd s of Col Stephenson Robert Clarke, CB, of Borde Hill, Cuckfield, Sussex, and had issue

  3a *Violet Marguerite Loftus [Violet Lady Jackson, 38 Oakley St, London SW3]; *b* 11 March 1904; *m* 15 July 1931 Sir Hugh Nicholas Jackson, 2nd Bt (*d* 1979), of Eagle House (*qv*), and has issue

    (1) Florence Charlotte Jane; *b* 9 March 1857; *m* 17 July 1884 Alan Rudolph Grant, 2nd s of John Grant, of Kilgraston, and *d* 21 July 1920. He *d* 16 Oct 1925

  1 Grace Anne; *m* 6 Feb 1832 Rt Rev Charles Caulfeild (*see* CHARLEMONT, V) and *d* 1 Dec 1896

  2 Theodosia Elizabeth; *m* 6 June 1850 Rev James Freke and had issue

The 2nd Bt *d* 29 Dec 1851; his est surv s,

  Sir Theophilus John St George 3rd Bt; *b* 5 Oct 1810; RM Port Natal, First Col Natal Carbineers, served 12th Lancers; *m* 1st 11 Jan 1836 Caroline Georgiana (*d* 1842), 2nd dau of Joseph Andrew de Lautour, DL, JP, of Hexton Ho, Herts, and had:

  1 **Sir Richard de Lautour St George, 4th Bt**; *b* 2 April 1837; Capt Bengal Artillery; *d* unm 14 Oct 1861

  2 William Edward; *b* 7 July 1838; *d* 12 April 1847

  1 Caroline de Lautour; *m* 20 Feb 1858 Horatio Senftenberg Ross, BCS, and had issue. He *d* 11 Aug 1898

Sir Theophilus *m* 2nd 11 Nov 1847 Maria (*d* 5 Sept 1893), est dau of John Power, of Churchtown, Co Waterford, and *d* 23 July 1857, having by her had, with two other daus (*d* unm):

  3 **Sir John St George, 5th Bt**; *b* 3 April 1851; *educ* Oscott and Trin Coll Dublin; Lt 71st Highland LI; *m* 1 Dec 1894 Rose (*d* 13 May 1938), 3rd dau of Sir George Berkley, KCMG, and *dsp* 21 Dec 1938

  4 Arthur; *b* 12 April 1852; *m* 3 June 1892 Elizabeth Mary (Elsie) (*d* 29 March 1927), dau of Gerald Fitzgerald, JP, and *d* 14 Oct 1927, leaving:

    (1) Elsie Olivia Bligh; *b* 1893; *m* 9 May 1921 (*divorce* 1949) Capt Arthur Cecil Jocelyn, CVO, RFA, only s of Rev Nathaniel Jocelyn. He *d* 26 March 1959

    (2) Maria Frances Bligh; *b* 1894

    (3) Patricia Grace Bligh; *b* 1896

  5 THEOPHILUS JOHN (Sir), **6th Bt**

  6 Charles ST GEORGE later ST GEORGE-POWER; *b* posthumously 6 Jan 1858; *d* 4 Dec 1922

  2 Maria; *m* 18 April 1873 Charles Robert Glyn (*see* GLYN, Bt, of Ewell and Gaunts) and *d* 18 March 1926, leaving issue

The 5th Bt's bro,

  Sir Theophilus John St George, 6th Bt; *b* 25 Feb 1856; Assist Master Supreme Court Natal; *m* 7 Feb 1889 Florence Emma (*d* 14 Oct 1953), dau of John Vanderplank, of Natal, and *d* 19 Aug 1943, having had:

  1 Richard Theophilus, MM and bar; *b* 4 Feb 1892; Intell Offr S Africa and France WW I (wounded twice); *d* unm May 1923

  2 John Christopher, MM; *b* 23 Dec 1894; Natal Mounted Rifles German S W Africa and 2nd S African Inf France WW I; *d* 15 Oct 1916 of wounds recd in action Somme

  3 **Sir Robert Alan St George, 7th Bt**; *b* 20 March 1900; Lt RAF, Trooper 4th S African Armoured Car Regt (POW), WW II 1939–42; Religious Lay Brother Oblates of Mary Immaculate; *d* unm 1983

  4 **Rev Sir Denis Howard St George, 8th Bt**; *b* Sept 1902; RC priest; *dsp* 1989

  5 **Sir George Bligh St George, 9th Bt**; *b* 23 Sept 1908; *educ* Natal U (BA); Lt Roy Natal Carabiniers and Tech Serv Corps WW II, Natal Prov Admin 1929–73, dep dir admin Addington Hosp Durban; *m* 1935 *Mary Somerville [Mary Lady St George, Hatley Cottage, 28 Waterfall Gardens Village, Private Bag X01, Link Hills, Natal 3652, S Africa], dau of John Francis Fearly Sutcliffe, of Durban, and *d* 1995, leaving:

    (1) Sir JOHN AVENEL BLIGH ST GEORGE, **10th and present Bt**

    (2) +Peter Bligh [Peter St George Esq, 99 Castelnau, London SW13]; *b* 23 July 1946; MBA Cape Town, CA SA; dir County Natwest Investment Bankers; *m* 1974 *Elizabeth Meyrick, er dau of Alan Meyrick Williams, of Newport, Gwent, and has:

      1a +William Bligh; *b* 1984

      1a *Caroline Bligh; *b* 1976

      2a *Alice Mary Bligh *b* 1981

    (1) *Elizabeth Margaret Bligh [Mrs Peter Baikie, 21 Garrard Rd, Banstead, Surrey]; *b* 20 Feb 1936; *m* 3 Sept 1962 *Peter Ivor Bailie and has:

      1a *David Peter; *b* 2 Aug 1963

      2a *Derek John; *b* 1973

      1a *Fiona Margaret; *b* 15 April 1965

      2a *Linda Jeanne; *b* 14 Nov 1969

    (2) *Catherine Mary [Mrs John Walker, 33 Fourth Ave, Houghton, Johannesburg 2198, S Africa]; *b* 1937; *m* 11 April 1964 *John Douglas Walker, MB, BCh (Rand), ChB, Dip Mid COG (SR), MRCOG, and has:

      1a *John Paul Douglas; *b* 3 April 1968

      1a *Jane Philippa Douglas; *b* 7 Oct 1966

      2a *Felicity Mary Douglas; *b* 1974

    (3) *Angela Bligh; *b* 1952; *educ* Natal U (BEd)

  1 Emma Felice Mary *b* 1893; Matron Chronic Sick Hosp Natal

  2 Maria Edith; *b* 1896

  3 Anne Rose; *b* 1898; *m* 4 Dec 1926 William Farquhar Ogilvie (*d* Dec 1963), s of Alexander Ogilvie, and had:

    (1) *John Alexander; *b* 17 Nov 1927; *educ* Natal U S Africa, CA SA and R; *m* 13 Nov 1954 *Pamela Betty, dau of Frederick Thomas Brown, of Pietermaritzburg, and has:

      1a *Marion; *b* 10 Aug 1955

      2a *Helen Margaret; *b* 28 July 1957

      3a *Alison; *b* 17 Nov 1958

      4a *Clare; *b* 27 Jan 1963

    (2) *Angus; *b* 3 Jan 1930; *m* 1953 *Heather Wright and has four sons

    (1) *Margaret; *b* 23 June 1933; *m* 3 April 1961 *David George Kerby and has:

      1a*Carol Elizabeth; *b* 30 Dec 1965

  4 Florence Caroline; *m* 15 Nov 1930 Rudolph Gerrard du Preez, s of R G du Preez, of Ermelo, Transvaal, and had:

    (1) *Christopher Ralph (Rev); *b* 13 Oct 1931; *educ* Witwaterstrand U (CSc 1959); RC Priest

    (2) *David Raye (Rev) [Rev David du Preez, St Joseph's Scholasticate, PO Cedara, Natal, S Africa]; *b* 20 July 1934; missionary

  5 Patricia Margaret; *m* 7 June 1930 Michael John Power (*d* 2 Jan 1966), s of W M Power, MEC Natal, and had:

    (1) *Michael St George; *b* 1931

    (2) *Richard William St George; *b* 1942; *m* 1974 *Susan Dorothy Peiser and has:

      1a *Richard John *b* 1975

      1a *Catherine *b* 1978

    (1) *Jane St George; *b* 1934; *m* 1953 Gerald Malcolm Stewart, s of E M Stewart, and has:

      1a *Simon Malcolm; *b* 12 March 1957

      1a *Kim Louise; *b* 13 Oct 1953

SAINT GERMANS

Arms: Arg. a fesse gu. between two bars gemel wavy az. **Crest:** An elephant's head couped arg., collared gu. **Supporters:** Two eagles regardant, wings expanded ppr., each charged on the breast with an ermine spot. **Motto:** *Præcedentibus insta* ('Press close upon those in the lead'). **Creations:** B. (GB) 13 Jan 1784, E. (UK) 28 Nov 1815.

THE 10TH EARL OF SAINT GERMANS, Co Cornwall, and **Baron Eliot of St Germans**, Co Cornwall (Peregrine Nicholas Eliot) [The Rt Hon The Earl of Saint Germans, Port Eliot, St Germans, Cornwall]; *b* 2 Jan 1941; *s* f 1988; *educ* Eton; *m* 1st 9 Oct 1964 (*divorce* 1989) Hon Jacquetta Jean Frederika Lampson, 3rd dau of 1st Baron Killearn (*qv*); *m* 2nd 1992 (*divorce* May 1996) Elizabeth (Liz) Dorothy Williams, photographer, and by his 1st w has:

  1 +JAGO NICHOLAS ALDO, *Lord Eliot*; *b* 24 March 1966; *educ* Millfield

  2 +Louis Robert; *b* 11 April 1968; *educ* Eton; lead singer and lyricist with pop gp Rialto

  3 +Francis Michael; *b* 11 Nov 1971; *educ* Eton and Manchester U

Lineage: JOHN ELIOT; *m* Joan, dau of John Bonvile, of Chute, Devon, and had:

EDWARD ELIOT, of Cotelands, Devon; *m* Alice, dau of Robert Guye, and had (as well as a 4th s) an est s (John, of St Germans), a yst s (Robert, *d* 1562) and a 2nd s:

THOMAS ELIOT; *m* Joan, dau of John Norbrooke, and had:

RICHARD ELIOT, of Port Eliot, Cornwall (formerly a property belonging to the Augustinian Priory of St Germans, which he exchanged 1553 with the CHAMPERNOWNEs, its earlier owners following the Dissolution of the Monasteries, for property at Cotelands); *m* Bridget, dau and coheir of Nicholas Carswell, of Hatch, and *d* 1609, leaving:

Sir JOHN ELIOT, of Port Eliot, JP Devon to 1626; *b* by 20 April 1590; *educ* Exeter Coll Oxford and one of the Inns of Court; MP St Germans 1614 and 1626, Newport 1624 and 1625 and Cornwall 1628, ktd 1618, V-Adml Devon 1619–26; leader of early Parliamentary oppn to the Crown, in particular impeachment of 1st Duke of Buckingham (*see* JERSEY, E), originally a friend of his youth; several times imprisoned, notably 1629 to his death after he had defended Parliamentary privilege as to free speech; for this he was also fined £2,000 (nearly £97,000 in late-1990s terms); author: *The Monarchy of Man* (political philosophy, not printed till 1879), *An Apology for Socrates* (self-vindication, not printed till 1881), *Negotium Posterorum* (a Parliamentary history, not printed till 1881), *De Jure Majestatis, a political treatise of government* (not printed till 1882) and *Letterbook of Sir John Eliot* (not printed till 1882); *m* 1611 Rhadagund (*d* 1628), dau and coheir of Richard Gedie, of Trebursye, Cornwall, and *d* 27 Nov 1632, leaving, with three other sons and three other daus:

1 John; MP St Germans 1640 and 1660–78; *m* Honora, dau of Sir Daniel Norton, of Southwick, Hants, and *d* 1685, leaving:

(1) Daniel; MP; *d* 28 Oct 1702, leaving:

1a Katharine; *m* 1707 Browne Willis, of Whaddon, Bucks

2 Nicholas (5th s); had:

(1) —; had:

1a Edward, of Port Eliot; *m* 1st Susan, dau of Sir W Coryton; *m* 2nd Elizabeth, dau and ultimate coheir of James Craggs, PC, Sec State 1718–21, and *d* 1722, leaving:

1b James; *d* unm 1742

2a Richard, of Port Eliot; MP, Auditor and Receiver-Gen Duchy Cornwall; *m* 4 March 1726 Harriot (*m* 2nd 13 Oct 1749 Capt John Hamilton, RN, and had issue; *see* ABERCORN, D), illegitimate dau of his er bro's f-in-law James Craggs, and *d* 1748, having had, with other issue:

1b EDWARD ELIOT later CRAGGS-ELIOT (roy licence 15 April 1789), **1st Baron Eliot of Saint Germans**, Co Cornwall (GB), so *cr* 13 Jan 1784; *b* 8 July 1727; *educ* St Mary Hall Oxford; MP St Germans 1748–68 and 1774–75, Liskeard 1768–74 and Cornwall 1775–84, Receiver-Gen Duchy Cornwall 1751, a Ld of Trade 1760–76; *m* 25 Sept 1756 Catherine, only dau and heiress of Edward Elliston, of Gestingthorpe, Essex, and 1st cousin of the historian Edward Gibbon (*see* also ACTON, B), and *d* 17 Feb 1804, having had, with another s (*d* young):

1c Edward James; *b* 24 Aug 1758; MP St Germans 1780–84 and Liskeard 1784–97, a Ld Treasury 1782–83, King's Remembrancer Court of Exchequer 1785, a Commr Indian Affrs 1793; *m* 24 Sept 1785 Lady Harriot Pitt (*d* 1786), dau of 1st Earl of Chatham (*see* JERSEY, E), and *dvp* just prior to 20 Sept 1797, leaving:

1d Hester Harriet Pitt; *m* Lt-Gen Sir William Henry Pringle, GCB, MP, and *d* 5 Oct 1842, leaving issue. He *d* 1840

2c JOHN CRAGGS-ELIOT later ELIOT, **1st Earl of Saint Germans** (UK), so *cr* 28 Nov 1815, with remainder, in default of male issue of his own body, to his bro; *b* 30 Sept 1761; *educ* Pembroke Coll Cambridge; MP (Tory) Liskeard 1784–1804, Col E Cornwall Militia 1808 and Lt-Col Cmdt 1810; *m* 1st 8 Sept 1790 Caroline, est dau of Hon Charles Yorke (*see* HARDWICKE, E); *m* 2nd 19 Aug 1819 Harriet (*d* 4 March 1877), 2nd dau of Reginald Pole Carew, PC (*see* POLE, Bt, of Shute House), and *dsp* 17 Nov 1823

3c WILLIAM, **2nd Earl**

1b Elizabeth; *m* 2 Aug 1759 1st Baron Somers (*qv*) and *d* 1 Jan 1771, leaving issue

1 Elizabeth; *m* Col Nathaniel Fiennes and had issue (*see* SAYE AND SELE, B)

The 1st EARL's bro,

WILLIAM ELIOT, **2nd Earl of Saint Germans**; *b* 1 April 1767; *educ* Pembroke Coll Cambridge; MP (Tory) St Germans 1791–1802 and Liskeard 1802–23, Sec Legn Berlin 1791–93, Sec Embassy and Min Plen The Hague 1793–94, Min Plen to Elector Palatine and Diet of Ratisbon 1796–98, a Ld Admlty 1800–04, U-Sec For Affrs 1804–05, a Ld Treasury 1807–12; *m* 1st 30 Nov 1797 Lady Georgiana Augusta Leveson-Gower (*d* 24 March 1806), sis of 1st Duke of Sutherland (*qv*), and had, with another dau (*d* unm):

1 EDWARD GRANVILLE, **3rd Earl**

1 Susan Caroline; *m* 8 July 1824 4th Earl Beauchamp (*see* 1970 edn) and *d* 15 Jan 1835

2 Charlotte Sophia; *m* July 1825 Rev George Martin, Canon and Chllr Exeter Diocese, and *d* 8 July 1839, leaving issue. He *d* 27 Aug 1860

The **2nd Earl** *m* 2nd 13 Feb 1809 Letitia (*dsp* 20 Jan 1810), sis of 1st Baron Heytesbury (*qv*); *m* 3rd 7 March 1812 Charlotte (*dsp* 3 July 1813), dau of Lt-Gen John Robinson (*see* POWIS, E); *m* 4th 30 Aug 1814 Susan (*dsp* 5 Feb 1830), yst dau of Sir John Mordaunt, 7th Bt (*qv*), and *d* 19 Jan 1845

His only s,

EDWARD GRANVILLE ELIOT, **3rd Earl of Saint Germans**, GCB (1857, CB 1848), PC (GB and I 1841), DL (Cornwall 1841); *b* 29 Aug 1798; *educ* Westminster and Ch Ch Oxford; Attaché The Hague, Sec Legn Madrid 1823, MP (Tory) Liskeard 1824–32 and E Cornwall 1837–45, a Ld Treasury 1827–32, Envoy Extrdy Spain 1834–37 during the Carlist War there, bringing about a truce between the opposing sides called 'The Eliot Convention', Ch Sec Ireland 1841–45, PMG 1845–46, Special Dep Warden Stannaries 1852, Ld Lt Ireland 1853–55, Ld Steward Household 1857–58 and 1859–66; *m* 2 Sept 1824 Lady Jemima Cornwallis (*d* 2 July 1856), 3rd dau and coheir of 2nd and last Marquess Cornwallis (*see* CORNWALLIS, B), and *d* 7 Oct 1877, having had, with another dau (*d* young):

1 Edward John Cornwallis, *Lord Eliot*; *b* 2 April 1827; *educ* Eton and Ch Ch Oxford; Capt 1st Life Gds 1852; *dvp* unm 26 Nov 1864

2 Granville Charles Cornwallis; *b* 9 Sept 1828; Capt Coldstream Gds; *ka* Battle of Inkerman 5 Nov 1854

3 WILLIAM GORDON CORNWALLIS ELIOT, **4th Earl of Saint Germans**; *b* 14 Dec 1829; *educ* Eton; Attaché Hanover 1849, Madrid 1850, Lisbon 1851, 2nd Attaché Berlin 1853, 1st Attaché Constantinople 1857 and St Petersburg 1858, Sec Legn Rio de Janeiro 1859 and 1861 (Chargé d'Affaires March–Aug 1863), Sec Legn Athens 1859 (Chargé d'Affaires 1860–61), Lisbon 1864, Actg Sec Legn Washington 1863–64, resigned from Dip Serv 1865, MP (Lib) Devonport 1866–68, called up to Ho Lds *vp* in f's Barony 14 Sept 1870; *d* unm 19 March 1881

4 Ernest Cornwallis; *b* 28 April 1831; *d* 16 Jan 1832

5 HENRY CORNWALLIS ELIOT, **5th Earl of Saint Germans**, JP, DL Cornwall; *b* 11 Feb 1835; *educ* Eton; RN 1848–53, FO 1855–81 (Jr Clerk London 1855, Sec to Special Mission St Petersburg 1867, Assist Clerk London 1872–81); *m* 18 Oct 1881 Hon Emily Harriet Labouchere (*d* 18 Oct 1933), yst dau and coheir of 1st and last Baron Taunton (*see* 1869 edn), and *d* 24 Sept 1911, having had:

(1) Edward Henry John Cornwallis, *Lord Eliot*; *b* 30 Aug 1885; *educ* Eton and Magdalene Coll Cambridge; 2nd Lt Coldstream Gds 1908–09; *dvp* by his own hand of gunshot wounds 24 Aug 1909

(2) JOHN GRANVILLE CORNWALLIS ELIOT, **6th Earl of Saint Germans**, MC, DL; *b* 11 June 1890; *educ* RMC Sandhurst; Capt Res Offrs 2nd Dragoons (RSG) WW I (despatches, wounded); *m* 11 June 1918 Lady Blanche Linnie Somerset (*d* 30 Aug 1968, having *m* 2nd 15 July 1924 Capt George Francis Valentine Scott Douglas, 15th Hus, s of Francis John Douglas; *see* 1967 edn DOUGLAS, Bt, of Springwood), dau of 9th Duke of Beaufort (*qv*), and *d* 31 March 1922, leaving:

1a Rosemary Alexandra; *b* 26 Feb 1919; *m* 1st 2 Sept 1939 Capt Edward Christian Frederick Nutting, RHG (*das* Jan 1943; *see* NUTTING, Bt), and had issue; *m* 2nd 24 Feb 1945 (*annulled* 1949) Lt-Cdr David Frederick Hew Dunn, RN, yr s of Cecil de Sivrac Dunn, of Rowley Cottage, Iford, Wilts; *m* 3rd 22 Dec 1949 Col Ralph Alexander (Sascha) Rubens, Sherwood Foresters, only s of Capt Joshua Ernest Rubens, of Henley-in-Arden, Warwicks, and *d* 20 April 1963, leaving by him a dau

2a Cathleen Blanche Lily; *b* 29 July 1921; *m* 1st 15 Nov 1946 (*divorce* 1956) John Beeton Seyfried, RHG, only s of John Frederick Seyfried, of S Kensington, and had:

1b *David John [David Seyfried Esq, 39 Chiddingstone St, London SW6 3TQ]; *b* 3 March 1952; *educ* Harrow; coheir with cousin Michael Hudson to abeyant Barony of Botetourt and Herbert (*see* BEAUFORT, D); *m* 1975 *Jane Angela Bishop and has:

1c *Oliver Richard; *b* 1976; *educ* Harrow

1c *Charlotte Sophia Caroline; *b* 1977

1b *Sarah Diana [Mrs Peter Smith, 4 Childs Place, London SW5]; *b* 6 April 1949 *m* 1975 *Peter Michael Smith, s of P W Smith, of Reading, Berks

2a (cont.) Lady Cathleen Seyfried *m* 2nd 7 Jan 1957 Sir Havelock Henry Trevor Hudson (*d* Nov 1996), chm Lloyd's 1975–77, s of Savile Hudson, of Lincoln's Inn, London WC2, and *d* 1994, having by him had:

2b *Michael Guy Havelock; *b* 14 March 1962

2b *Louise Deborah; *b* 2 Dec 1958

6 Charles George Cornwallis, CVO, JP, DL Cornwall; *b* 16 Oct 1839; Capt Gren Gds, Hon Col 3rd Bn DCLI, Equerry to TRH PRINCE AND PRINCESS CHRISTIAN 1869–96 (Treas and Comptroller Household 1896–1901), Groom Privy Chamber 1871–99, Gentleman Usher 1899–1901, Order of Albrecht Saxony 2nd Cl; *m* 26 Oct 1865 Constance Rhiannon, Ldy-in-Waiting to HRH PRINCESS FREDERICA OF HANOVER (*d* 22 March 1916), sis of 1st Baron Wimborne (*see* WIMBORNE, V), and *d* 22 May 1901, leaving:

(1) GRANVILLE JOHN ELIOT, **7th Earl of Saint Germans**; *b* 22 Sept 1867; *educ* Charterhouse; *d* unm 20 Nov 1942

(2) MONTAGUE CHARLES, **8th Earl**

(3) Christian Edward Cornwallis, OBE (1919); *b* 17 July 1872; granted with siblings 7 March 1923 rank of earl's dau/yr s; *educ* Charterhouse; Lt-Col Res Offrs RM, Order Crown Belgium; *m* 1st 3 July 1897 Laura Grey (*d* 22 Jan 1938), dau of Lt-Col Sir George Chetwode, 6th Bt (*see* CHETWODE, B), and had:

1a Christian Philip Charles; *b* 27 Feb 1903; *educ* Eton; *m* 15 July 1933 Nina Wilcox Putnam Ogle and *dsp* 18 June 1948

1a (Frederica) Betty Cornwallis; *b* 4 Oct 1900; *m* 1st 10 May 1923 (*divorce* 1929) Capt Robert Wigram Crawford, KRRC, er s of John Henry Crawford; *m* 2nd 17 July 1942 Maj Sir Charles Markham, 2nd Bt (*qv*)

2a Ann Rosemary Bridget; *b* 5 Aug 1907; *m* 14 Sept 1933 Lt-Col Alexander Erskine Lawrence, MC, KRRC, s of Brig-Gen Richard Charles Bernard Lawrence, CB, CMG, 1st Dragoon Gds. He *d* 6 May 1956

(3) (cont.) The Hon Christian Eliot *m* 2nd 12 Feb 1938 Daisy Blossom (*d* 7 Jan 1965), widow of John Roberts and dau of Alexander Elkan, and *d* 20 Oct 1940

(4) Arthur Ernest Henry; *b* 13 July 1874; trooper Kitchener's Horse Boer War 1900–01, Capt and APM SW Dist Cape Colony, WW I (1914 medal with clasp); *m* 1st 23 May 1895 (*divorce* 1902) Florence Maude, dau of Capt Charles Egerton Parks-Smith; *m* 2nd 11 Oct 1911 Elizabeth (*d* 1 Nov 1913), widow of William A C Cornell and dau of M Marshall; *m* 3rd 26 April 1919 Mrs Mabel Louisa Atherton (*d* 9 July 1919), 3rd dau of Sir Edward John Dean Paul, 4th Bt (*see* 1967 edn); *m* 4th 23 Sept 1933 Elinor Whyte Hughes (*d* 22 March 1976), dau of James Andrew Brownlee, of Dundee, and *d* 8 Oct 1936

(5) Edward Granville; *b* 3 Jan 1878; *educ* Charterhouse and Magdalen Coll Oxford (BA 1900); Lt RNVR, Capt RGA, slr 1904, ptnr Kennedy, Ponsonby and Prideaux; *m* 3 Dec 1907 Clare Louisa (*d* 20 Sept 1927), yst dau of William Robert Phelips, DL, of Montacute, Somerset, and *d* 10 Feb 1952, leaving:

1a Peter Charles (Ven), MBE (1945), TD; *b* 30 Oct 1910; *educ* Wellington and Magdalene Coll Cambridge (BA 1931, MA 1935); slr 1934, Lt-Col 297th (Kent Yeo), Lt AA Regt RA, cmdg 1949–52, Deacon 1954, Assist Curate St Martin in-the-Fields 1954–57, Vicar Cockermouth 1957–61, Vicar Cropthorne with Charlton 1961–65, Archdeacon Worcester 1961–75, Residentiary Canon Worcester 1965–75; *m* 12 July 1934 *Lady Alethea Constance Dorothy Sydney Buxton [The Lady Alethea Eliot, The Old House, Kingsland, Herefs HR6 9QS], yst dau of 1st and last Earl Buxton (*see* BUXTON, Bt), and *d* 1995

1a *Margaret Augusta [Mrs Richard Asher, 6A Hillbury Rd, London SW17 8JT]; *b* 26 Feb 1914; Oboe Prof RAM; *m* 27 July 1943 Richard Alan John Asher, MD, FRCP (*d* by his own hand 25 April 1969), 2nd s of Rev Felix Asher, and has:

1b *Peter [Peter Asher Esq, 6 Phillimore Gdns, London W8 7QD]; *b* 22 June 1944; *educ* Westminster; sr v-pres Sony Music; *m* 1st Oct 1971 (*divorce* 19–) Elizabeth Doster; *m* 2nd 1983 *Wendy Worth and has:

1c *Victoria Jane; *b* 1984

1b *Jane [Jane Asher, c/o ICM, Oxford Ho, 76 Oxford St, London W1R 1RB]; *b* 5 April 1946; actress (stage appearances include both Wendy in *Peter Pan* 1961 and Peter in the same vehicle 1979; films include *Green-gage Summer* and *Alfie*), owns Jane Asher's Party Cakes Shop Chelsea, memb BBC Gen Advsy Ctee, Govr Molecule Theatre, memb BAFTA, assoc RADA, FRSA; author; *m* 19– *Gerald Scarfe, artist, and has:

1c *Alexander David; *b* 1981

2c *Rory Christopher; *b* 1983

1c *Katie Geraldine; *b* 1974

2b *Clare [Mrs John Gillies, 6 Hillbury Rd, London SW17 8JT]; *b* 3 Dec 1948; *m* 5 April 1975 *John Gillies and has:

1c *Sarah; *b* 6 April 1978

2c *Helen; *b* 7 Dec 1980

2a Susan; *b* 17 July 1921; *m* 17 Dec 1943 her er sis's bro-in-law Thomas George Horsey Asher (*d* 17 Dec 1966), yst s of Rev Felix Asher, and *d* 19 June 1992, leaving:

1b *John [John Asher Esq, 34 Starfield Rd, London W12 9SW]; *b* 12 Jan 1945; *educ* Harrow and Ch Ch Oxford

2b *Charles; *b* 16 July 1948; *educ* Harrow

3b *James; *b* 4 Sept 1950; *educ* Harrow

1b *Anne; *b* 12 April 1946

(1) Blanche Elizabeth; *b* 18 Aug 1866 *m* 27 May 1909 Stephen Ormston Eaton, of Tolethorpe Hall, Rutland, est s of Charles Ormston Eaton, of Tolethorpe Hall, and *d* 11 Sept 1929. He *d* 30 May 1911

(2) Evelyn Radigund; *b* 31 Jan 1869; *d* unm 25 May 1920

1 Louisa Susan Cornwallis; *m* 15 Jan 1850 7th Earl of Bessborough (*qv*) and *d* 15 Jan 1911, leaving isssue

The 7th EARL's bro,

MONTAGUE CHARLES ELIOT, **8th Earl of Saint Germans**, KCVO (1934, CVO 1928, MVO 1923), OBE (1919); *b* 13 May 1870; *educ* Charterhouse and Exeter Coll Oxford (BA 1893); barrister Inner Temple 1895, Lt-Cdr RNVR 1914–19, Gentleman Usher to TM EDWARD VII 1901–08 (Groom-in-Waiting 1908–10) and GEORGE V 1910–36 (Groom Robes 1920–36, Extra Groom-in-Waiting 1924–36), Extra Groom-in-Waiting to TM EDWARD VIII 1936, GEORGE VI 1937–52 and THE QUEEN 1952–60, Offr Order Leopold Belgium; *m* 22 June 1910 Helen Agnes (*d* 1 Sept 1962), dau of Arthur Post, of New York, by Elizabeth, later Lady Barrymore, and had:

1 NICHOLAS RICHARD MICHAEL, **9th Earl**

2 (Montague) Robert Vere; *b* 28 Oct 1923; *educ* Eton and Ch Ch Oxford; Page of Honour to HM GEORGE VI 1934–40, Coronation Medal 1937, Capt Gren Gds WW II 1944–45 (wounded) and Palestine 1945–48, memb Westminster City Cncl 1953–62; *m* 1983 *Marie Frances Richmond [The Hon Mrs Robert Eliot, Brightor House, Tideford, Cornwall], dau of Geoffrey Mervyn Cooper (*see* COOPER, Bt, of Woollahra) and widow of A R Lusk, of Comrie, Perthshire, and *d* 16 May 1994

1 (Germaine) Elizabeth Olive; *b* 13 April 1911; *m* 17 March 1932 (*divorce* 1940) Thomas James (*see* NORTHBOURNE, B); *m* 2nd 21 March 1950 (*divorce* 1963) Hon (Kenneth) George Kinnaird, yr s of 12th Lord Kinnaird, KT, KBE (*see* 1970 edn)

The 8th EARL *d* 19 Sept 1960; his er s,

NICHOLAS RICHARD MICHAEL ELIOT, **9th Earl of Saint Germans**; *b* 26 Jan 1914; *educ* Eton; Capt DCLI WW II; *m* 1st 25 April 1939 (*divorce* 1947) Helen Mary (*d* 6 Dec 1951), yr dau of Lt-Col Charles Walter Villiers, CBE, DSO (*see* CLARENDON, E), and had:

1 PEREGRINE NICHOLAS ELIOT, **10th and present Earl of Saint Germans**

1 *Frances Helen Mary; *b* 6 March 1943; *m* 9 Oct 1965 (*divorce* 1987) Charles Maurice, Earl of Shelburne, and has issue (*see* LANSDOWNE, M)

The **9th Earl** *m* 2nd 27 May 1948 (*divorce* 1959) Margaret Eleanor (*d* 2 Aug 1967), formerly w of (a) Hugh Wharton Earle and (b) Basil Francis Eyston and only dau of Lt-Col William Francis George Wyndham, MVO, of Heathfield Lodge, Midhurst, Sussex; *m* 3rd 15 Nov 1965 (Mary) Bridget (*d* 26 Dec 1998), formerly w of Lt-Col Jack Leslie Harry Lotinga and only child of Sir (Thomas) Shenton Whitelegge Thomas, GCMG, OBE, and *d* 1988

SAINT HELENS

Arms: Or three piles sa., each charged with a fountain. **Crest:** A dexter arm charged with a fountain, the hand grasping an arrow, all ppr. **Supporters:** Dexter, a wolf gu.; sinister, a griffin sa., each charged on the shoulder with a portcullis. **Motto:** Press through. **Creation:** B. (UK) 30 Dec 1964.

THE 2ND BARON SAINT HELENS, of St Helens, Co Palatine of Lancaster (Richard (Rory) Francis Hughes-Young) [The Rt Hon The Lord Saint Helens, Marchfield House, Binfield, Berks RG12 5EB]; *b* 4 Nov 1945; *s* f 1980; *educ* Nautical Coll Pangbourne; *m* 1983 *Mrs Emma R Talbot-Smith and has:

1 +HENRY THOMAS; *b* 7 March 1986

1 *Lara Elizabeth; *b* 1987

Lineage: WILLIAM YOUNG; *m* Jane Hunter and had:

WILLIAM YOUNG, of Galgorm, Co Antrim; MD; *m* 1st 1823 Anne (*d* 1835), dau of William Gihon, of Hillhead, Co Antrim, and had issue; *m* 2nd Jane Crawford (*d* 1844); *m* 3rd Maria Miller and *d* 1854, having by his 1st w had, with a yr s (William Alexander, *b* 1829, *m* Margaret Gihon and *d* 1894, leaving issue) and a dau (Jane, *b* 1831, *d* 1845):

JOHN YOUNG, PC (I 1887), of Galgorm Castle, Ballymena, Co Antrim, JP, DL Co Antrim; *b* Dec 1826; *educ* Trin Coll Dublin (MA); High Sheriff Co Antrim 1863, Hon LLD Roy U Ireland 1909; *m* 1st Jan 1855 Grace Charlotte (*d* 1876), 2nd dau of Lt-Col Patrick Savage, 13th Light Dragoons, and had:

1 William Robert, PC (I 1921), DL Co Antrim, of Galgorm Castle; *b* 1856; *m* 28 Aug 1893 Mary Alice (*d* 9 May 1946), er dau of Sir Francis Edmund Workman Macnaghten, 3rd Bt, PC (*qv*), and *d* 12 Sept 1933, leaving:

(1) Hilda Grace, of Galgorm Castle; *b* 22 June 1896; *m* 31 July 1924 Lt-Col Arthur O'Neill Cubitt Chichester, OBE, MC, and had issue (*see* O'NEILL, B)

2 Patrick Savage; *b* 1858; *m* 1st 1884 Flora (*d* 1892), yst dau of Sir Charles Lanyon, of The Abbey, Belfast; *m* 2nd Emily (*d* 1940), dau of William Walter, and *d* 1926, having by her had:

(1) John; *b* 25 Sept 1902; *d* 1912

(1) Elizabeth; *m* E Ritson

3 John Robert; *b* 1868; *d* 1869

4 HENRY GEORGE

5 John William Alexander; *b* 1873; *d* 1954

6 George Charles Gillespie; *b* 1876; *d* 1939

1 Anne Charlotte Maria; *b* 1857; *d* unm 17 April 1900

2 Maria; *b* 1880; *m* 23 Dec 1892 R-Adml John Casement (*d* 8 June 1910), 3rd s of John Casement, of Magherintemple, Co Antrim, and *d* 3 April 1943, leaving a dau

3 Grace Cottenham; *b* 1862; *m* 25 July 1890 Ogilvie Blair Graham (*d* Oct 1928), er s of Ogilvie Blair Graham, of Larchfield, Lisburn, Co Down, and *d* 21 Oct 1953, leaving three sons

4 Charlotte Elizabeth Rose; *b* 1864; *d* 1949

5 Rose Maud; *b* 1865; *d* 1947

6 Janet Henrietta; *b* 1867; *m* 12 Sept 1900 Alexander Miller (*d* 1939), s of Sir Alexander Edward Miller, CSI, KC, LLD, of Ballycastle, Co Antrim, and *d* 1944, leaving two daus

7 Ethel Margaret; *b* 1872; *m* 1st 8 March 1902 John Stevenson (*d* 1912), s of John Stevenson, of Middlesbrough; *m* 2nd 1919 her er sis's bro-in-law V-Adml Charles Blois Miller, CB (*d* 14 July 1926), and *dsp*

JOHN YOUNG *m* 2nd July 1878 Rose (*d* 12 June 1894), 2nd dau of Alexander Miller, of Ballycastle, and *d* 1915

The 4th s,

HENRY GEORGE YOUNG, CIE (1921), DSO (1917), of Skeffington Lodge, Antrim, DL Co Antrim; *b* 7 March 1870; *educ* Harrow and RMC Sandhurst; Brig-Gen IA (Chitral Relief Force 1895, NW Frontier Campaign 1897–98, Boer War 1902, WW I (despatches five times, Croix de Guerre), ret 1921), Serjeant-at-Arms NI Parl 1921–51; *m* 9 July 1908 Adelaide Mary Glencairn (*d* 2 Jan 1965), dau of Colin Glencairn Campbell by Octavia Helen, yr dau of Sir Edmund Charles Workman Macnaghten, 2nd Bt (*qv*), and *d* 15 Aug 1956, leaving:

MICHAEL HENRY COLIN YOUNG later HUGHES-YOUNG, **1st Baron Saint Helens**, of St Helens, Co Palatine of Lancaster (UK), so cr 30 Dec 1964, MC (1944); b 28 Oct 1912; educ Harrow and RMC Sandhurst; joined Black Watch 1932, attd French Army 1934, seconded KAR 1935, Abyssinia and WW II (wounded twice), ret as Lt-Col 1947, with C Centl Office 1948–55, C candidate St Helens 1951 gen election, MP (C) Wandsworth Centl 1955–64, PPS to Min State BOT March–April 1956, Assist Whip 1956–58, a Ld Commr Treasury 1958–62, Dep Govt Ch Whip 1959–64, Treasurer Household 1960–64; m 31 July 1939 Elizabeth Agnes (d 2 Oct 1956), yr dau of Richard Blakiston-Houston, JP, DL (see BLAKISTON, Bt), and d 27 Dec 1980, having had:

1 Patrick Michael; b 30 April 1942; educ Eton; Capt 11th Hus; d following a riding accident 11 March 1970

2 RICHARD FRANCIS HUGHES-YOUNG, **2nd and present Baron Saint Helens**

1 *Henrietta Maria [The Hon Mrs Stevens, Sutton Warbingtron, Long Sutton, Hants]; b 29 May 1940; m 5 Dec 1970 *Brian Turnbull Julius Stevens, est s of John Osmond Julius Stevens, of Montgomerys Farm, Farnham, Surrey, and Mrs Kathleen Bacon, of Duncrieff, Moffat, Dumfriesshire, and has:

(1) *Matilda Flora Julius; b 25 Feb 1973

(2) *Harriet Maria Julius; b 11 Jan 1975

(3) *Lousia Elizabeth Julius; b 15 Sept 1976

2 *Selina Lilian [The Hon Mrs Peto, Bealings House, Woodbridge, Suffolk IP13 6NP]; b 13 March 1944; m 28 May 1969 *Jonathan Basil Morton Peto and has issue (see PETO, Bt, of Barnstaple)

3 *Louisa Nina [The Hon Mrs Arbuthnott, Stone House Cottage, Stone, Worcs]; b 31 Aug 1949; m 20 July 1974 *Maj James Francis Arbuthnott and has issue (see ARBUTHNOTT, V)

SAINT JOHN OF BLETSO

Arms: Argent on a chief gules two mullets or. **Crest:** On a mount vert a falcon rising or, belled of the last, ducally gorged gules. **Supporters:** Two monkeys proper. **Motto:** *Data fata secutus* ('Having followed the fate allotted me'). **Creations:** B. (E) 13 Jan 1558/9, Bt. (E) 28 June 1660.

THE 22ND BARON SAINT JOHN OF BLETSO and a **Baronet** (Sir Anthony Tudor St John, Bt) [The Rt Hon The Lord St John of Bletso, 97 Cadogan Gdns, London SW3 2RE; Woodlands, Llanishen, Gwent NP6]; b 16 May 1957; s f 1978; educ Diocesan Coll Cape Town, Cape Town U (BA, BSc), U of S Africa (BProc) and London U (LLM); consultant, Smith New Court and Merrill Lynch; dir Brainware Europe; Tstee: Tusk, TVE, SAN Fndn and Earth 2000; chm Eurotrust Internat and MathEngine plc, Extra Ld-in-Waiting 1998–; m 1994 *Dr Helen-Westlake and has:

1 +OLIVER BEAUCHAMP; b 11 July 1995

2 +Alexander Andrew; b 29 Aug 1996

1 *Athene Emma; b 24 Feb 1998

Lineage: ALEXANDER de ST JOHN, of Instow, Devon; fl 1340; ancestor of:

WILLIAM de ST JOHN, of Fonmon, Glam; ancestor of:

Sir OLIVER ST JOHN, of Bletso, Beds; m as her 1st husb Margaret (m 2nd c 1442 1st Duke of Somerset (dspm 1444) of the 1443 cr (see BEAUFORT, D); m 3rd c April 1447 6th Lord (Baron) Welles (k Battle of Towton 29 March 1461) and had issue; see WILLOUGHBY DE ERESBY, B), dau and heiress of John Beauchamp (d c 1412), of Bletso (s of Sir Roger Beauchamp (c 1363–1406), gs of Roger Beauchamp, 1st and last Lord (Baron) Beauchamp (of Bletso), held according to later doctrine to have been cr by writ 1363, although none of his descendants were summoned to Parl as Lord Beauchamp; see, however, MORDAUNT, Bt) by Edith, dau of Sir John Stourton (see MOWBRAY, SEGRAVE and STOURTON, B), and d 1437, having had, with other issue:

1 JOHN (Sir)

2 Oliver; had issue (see BOLINGBROKE and SAINT JOHN, V)

1 Elizabeth; godmother to EDWARD V; m 1st by 2 April 1450, as his 2nd w, 5th Lord (Baron) Zouche (qv); m 2nd by 10 Dec 1471, as his 2nd w, 5th Lord (Baron) Scrope (of Bolton) and d between 1488 and 9 Feb 1490/1, having had by him:

(1) Mary; m Sir William Conyers

2 Edith; m Sir Geoffrey Pole, of Medmenham and Ellesborough, Bucks (d 4 Jan 1491), and had, with other issue:

(1) Richard (Sir), KG (1499); Esq of the Body to HENRY VII by 22 Oct 1485, Constable Harlech Castle and Sheriff Merioneths Feb 1485/6, ktd by late Aug 1487, Chamberlain to ARTHUR PRINCE OF WALES (HENRY VII's est s) by 20 March 1492/3; m between 1491 and 1494 Lady Margaret Plantagenet, later Countess of Salisbury in her own right, and d by 18 Dec 1505, having had issue (see ABERGAVENNY, M)

The er s,

Sir JOHN ST JOHN, KB, of Bletso; m Alice, dau of Sir Thomas Bradshaigh, of Haigh, Lancs, and had, with three daus:

Sir JOHN ST JOHN, KB, of Bletso; m Sibyl, dau of Morgan ap Jenkyns ap Philip, and had an est s:

Sir JOHN ST JOHN, of Bletso; granted by HENRY VIII the manor of Abbots Ripton, Hunts, which remained a St John possession till 1640; m Margaret, dau of Sir William Waldegrave, KB, of Smallbridge, Suffolk, and had, with four daus (including Margaret, Ldy of Honour to either MARY or ELIZABETH I, m 1st Sir John Gostwick, m 2nd, as his 2nd w, 2nd Earl of Bedford (see BEDFORD, D) and d 27 Aug 1562, having had issue):

OLIVER ST JOHN, **1st Baron Saint John of Bletso**, Co Bedford (E), so cr 13 Jan 1558/9, JP (Beds Feb 1553/4); MP Beds 1547–52, High Sheriff Beds and Bucks 1551, Commr Musters (local defence force) c mid-1560, Lt in Beds for resistance against Northern Rebellion 1569; m 1st by 8 Feb 1542/3 Agnes (b c 1520), dau of Sir John Fisher and gdau and heiress of Sir Michael Fisher, of Elstow, Beds; m 2nd by 28 Aug 1572, as her 4th husb, Elizabeth (d after 8 Dec 1602), dau of Geoffrey Chamber, of Gt and Little Stanmore, Middx, and widow of (a) Reynold Conyers (d 1558–59), (b) Sir Francis Stonor (d c 1566) and (c) Edward Griffin, Attorney-Gen 1552–59 (d c 1569), and d by 23 May 1582, having by his 1st w had:

1 JOHN ST JOHN, **2nd Baron Saint John of Bletso**; MP Beds Jan-May 1559 and 1562/3–66/7; m by 28 Feb 1574/5 Catherine (d 23 March 1614/5), sis of 1st Baron Dormer (qv) of Wyng, and dspms 23 Oct 1596, leaving:

(1) Anne; m 7 Feb 1596/7 3rd Baron Howard of Effingham (see EFFINGHAM, E) and d 7 June 1638, having had issue

2 OLIVER, **3rd Baron**

3 Thomas; had:

(1) Oliver, of Cayshoe, Beds; m Sarah, dau of Edward Buckley, of Odell, Beds, and had:

1a Oliver; b 1598?; educ Queens' Coll Cambridge; barrister Lincoln's Inn 1626; having informed 4th Earl of Bedford (see BEDFORD, D), who put much business his way, of certain of JAMES I's plans for curbing Parl, he was imprisoned in the Tower of London 1629, as a result of which he became hostile to the Stuart Court; defended the celebrated John Hampden (see BUCKINGHAMSHIRE, E) in his refusal to pay CHARLES I's Ship Money 1637; MP Totnes 1640 ('Short' Parl) and 1641 on ('Long' Parl) and soon became a Parly leader with Bedford, Hampden and Pym; Slr-Gen 1641–43, acted as Parl's substitute Attorney-Gen and a Parly Commr to have custody of the Gt Seal 1643–46, one of closest allies of OLIVER CROMWELL (to whom he was related by marriage; see below) 1644–48, though less so thereafter, Ch Justice Common Pleas 1648, apptd a Commr to try CHARLES I but declined to act, Memb Cncl of State under Commonwealth (i.e., to 1653 but not under the Protectorate till after OLIVER CROMWELL's death) and 1659, envoy to negotiate alliance with Utd Provinces (modern Netherlands) 1651, Chllr Cambridge U 1651, a Parly Commr to impose ordered administration on Scotland and promote its unification with England 1651–52, nominal Commr of Treasury 1654; by the assistance he gave General Mon(c)k (see MONCK, V) and other judicious manoeuvres he escaped punishment at the Restoration apart from permanent disqualification from public office; m 1st Jo(h)anna, dau of Sir James Altham, of Marks Hall, Latton, Essex, by Elizabeth, dau of Sir Francis Barrington by Joan (dau of Sir Henry Cromwell, of Hinchinbrook, Hunts (unc of OLIVER CROMWELL and John Hampden), and had:

1b Francis; MP Peterborough 1656 and 1659

2b William

1b Jo(h)anna; m c 1651 her cousin Sir Walter St John, 3rd Bt, and d by Feb 1705, leaving issue (see BOLINGBROKE and SAINT JOHN, V)

2b Catherine; m Henry St John, yr bro of Sir Walter St John, 3rd Bt

1a (cont.) Oliver St John m 2nd 21 Jan 1638 his 1st w's grandmother's 1st cousin Elizabeth, dau of Henry Cromwell, of Upwood, another unc of OLIVER CROMWELL (who was close to his cousin, the 2nd Mrs St John), and by her had:

3b Oliver; m Elizabeth, dau of William Hammond

3b Elizabeth; m 26 Feb 1655/6 John Bernard, of Huntingdon

1a (cont.) Oliver St John m 3rd 1 Oct 1645, as her 2nd husb, Elizabeth (m 3rd Sir Humphrey Sydenham, of Cholworthy, Somerset), dau of Daniel Oxenbridge, MD, of Daventry, Northants, and widow of Caleb Cockcroft, and d on the Continent of Europe, where he had lived some ten years, 31 Dec 1673

The 2nd BARON's yr bro,

OLIVER ST JOHN, **3rd Baron Saint John of Bletso**; b by(?) 1542; High Sheriff Beds 1585, Ld Lt Hunts 1596–1618; m Dorothy (bur 28 Nov 1605), dau and heir of John Read, of Boddington, Glos, and d 1618, having had:

1 OLIVER ST JOHN, **4th Baron Saint John of Bletso** and 1st EARL OF BOLINGBROKE (E), so cr 28 Dec 1624, KB (1610); b c 1584; MP Beds 1601 and 1603–04, Jt Ld Lt Hunts 1619, Ld Lt Beds (apptd by Parl) Feb 1642/3 and a Commr Admlty, Lay Memb (Westminster) Assembly of Divines, Jt Commr Gt Seal 1643–46; m April 1602 Elizabeth (bur 26 Oct 1655), dau and heiress of William Paulet (gn of 1st Marquess of Winchester, qv), of Ewalden, Somerset, and d June 1646, having had, with two other sons:

(1) OLIVER ST JOHN, **5th Baron Saint John of Bletso**, KB (Feb 1625/6); MP Beds 1625–26 and 1628–29, called up to Ho of Lds 14 May 1641 vp in f's Barony; seized and fortified Hereford for Parl Oct 1642 and refused CHARLES I entry; m by March 1628 Lady Arabella Egerton (bur 1669), dau of 1st Earl of Bridgwater (see GREY EGERTON, Bt), and dvp & spm of wounds recd while

in flight from the Battle of Edgehill 23 Oct 1642, following which he was taken prisoner, leaving, with three er daus:

1a Dorothy; *m* Francis Charlton, of Apley Castle, Salop, and had issue (*see* MEYRICK, Bt)

(2) Paulet (Sir), KB; *bapt* 24 July 1608; *m* (licence 10 Dec 1632) Elizabeth (*b c* 1615), dau and heiress of Sir Rowland Vaughan, of Shoreditch, and *dvp* between 3 May and 27 June 1638, having had:

1a OLIVER ST JOHN, **6th Baron Saint John of Bletso** and 2nd EARL OF BOLINGBROKE; *b* 1634; custos rotulorum Beds 1667–March 1687/8; *m* 24 Nov 1654 Lady Frances Cavendish (*d* 15 Aug 1678), 3rd dau of 1st Duke of Newcastle-upon-Tyne of the March 1664/5 *cr* (*see* DEVONSHIRE, D) by his 1st w, and *dsp* 18 March 1687/8

2a PAULET ST JOHN, **7th Baron Saint John of Bletso** and 3rd and last EARL OF BOLINGBROKE; MP Bedford 1663–81, Recorder Bedford, custos rotulorum Beds 1689–1711; *d unm* 5 Oct 1711, when the Earldom expired

2 Anthony (Sir); *educ* Queens' Coll Cambridge; *m* Aubrey, widow of Sir William Herbert, and *dsp*

3 Alexander (Sir); *educ* Queens' Coll Cambridge; MP Bedford; *m* Margaret (*dsp* 27 Aug 1666), dau of John Trye

4 Rowland (Sir), KB; *educ* Queens' Coll Cambridge; MP Beds; *m* Sybilla or Sybella, dau of John Vaughan, of Hargast, Herefs, and *d* Aug 1645, leaving:

(1) **Sir Oliver Saint John, 1st Bt**, of Woodford, Northants, (E), so *cr* 28 June 1660; *b c* 1624; *m c* 1648 Barbara, 3rd and yst dau and coheir of John St Andrew, of Gotham, Notts, and E Haddon, Northants, and *d* 3 Jan 1661/2, leaving an est s:

1a **Sir St Andrew St John, 2nd Bt**; *b c* 1650; *m* 10 March 1680/1 Jane (*b c* 1666; *d* after 23 Jan 1710/11), only dau of Sir William Blois (*see* BLOIS, Bt) by his 2nd w Jane, and *d* 1708, leaving:

1b **Sir St Oliver St John, 3rd Bt**; *b c* 1683; *d unm c* 1710

2b **Sir St Andrew St John, 4th Bt**; *b c* 1685; *m* Anne (*d* 10 Jan 1739), dau of Sir William James, of Korlings, Suffolk, and Kensington, and *d* early 1711, leaving a posthumous s:

1c **Sir Paulet St Andrew St John, 5th Bt**, and **8th Baron Saint John of Bletso**; *b* early 1711; *d* 10 May 1714

3b A son; *d* by 19 May 1714

4b WILLIAM ST JOHN, **9th Baron Saint John of Bletso**; *d unm* 11 Oct 1720

5b ROWLAND ST JOHN, **10th Baron Saint John of Bletso**; *d unm* 4 July 1722

6b JOHN ST JOHN, **11th Baron Saint John of Bletso**; Recorder Bedford, DCL Oxon 1724; *m* 6 March 1724/5 Elizabeth (*bapt* 24 Dec 1702; *d* 24 Oct 1769), 5th dau of Sir Ambrose Crowley, of Greenwich, and *d* 24 June 1757, having had:

1c JOHN, **12th Baron**

2c St Andrew (Very Rev); *b* 17 Jan 1732; DD, Dean Worcester; *m* Sarah, dau of Thomas Chase, of Bromley, Kent, and *d* 23 March 1795, leaving, with a dau (*dsp*):

1d Ambrose; *b* 27 Sept 1760; *m* 22 Feb 1790 Arabella (*d* 1805), dau of Sir James Hamlyn, 1st Bt (*see* 1861 edn WILLIAMS, Bt, of Clovelly), and *d* Nov 1823, leaving, with other issue:

1e St Andrew; *b* 28 June 1794; Capt 9th Foot; *m* 13 April 1820 Margaret (*d* 6 June 1875), est dau of Philip Moore, of Balla More, Peel, IOM, and *d* Orillia, Ontario, 25 Feb 1838, leaving:

1f Jane Margaret; *m* 25 Jan 1860 Lucius Richard O'Brien (*dsp* 13 Dec 1899), of Toronto, Pres Roy Canadian Acad Art, and *d* 10 Nov 1886

2f Sarah Ann; *m* 21 June 1845 Alpheus Todd, CMG (*d* 22 Jan 1884), Hon LLD Queen's Coll Kingston, Librarian to Dominion Ho of Parl, Ottawa, and *d* 14 Dec 1882, leaving issue

3f Arabella Diana Hamlyn; *m* 17 Jan 1849 George Hallen (*d* 7 April 1898), of Toronto, and had issue

1e Jemima; *m* by Aug 1824 William Kershaw, of Douglas, IOM, and had issue

2d John Francis Seymour; *b* 15 Nov 1761; Preb Worcester, Rector Severnstoke; *m* 26 May 1788 Frances, only dau of Richard Fleming and gdau of Dr Stukeley, antiquary, and *d* 4 Dec 1832, leaving, with other issue:

1e John Fleming, of Dinmore Manor, Herefs; *b* 9 April 1789; Rector Spondon, Derbys; *m* 5 June 1828 Cassandra (*d* 7 Aug 1848), 3rd dau of Francis Hurt, of Alderwasley, Derbys, and *dsp* 3 Aug 1848

2e Henry St Andrew (Rev); *b* 30 Nov 1796; Vicar Hilton and Addingham, Cumberland; *m* 12 May 1835 Emily Murray (*d* 27 Nov 1875), 2nd dau of Andrew Belcher, and *d* 2 Dec 1874, leaving:

1f Richard Fleming St Andrew; *b* 12 Sept 1839; Lt 60th Rifles, Hon MA Wadham Coll Oxford, Dep Commr Burma; *m* 1st 17 Oct 1871 Julia Louisa (*d* 20 Sept 1898), est dau of Rev William Churchill, of Muston and Colliton House, Dorset, and had:

1g Winstan St Andrew; *b* 28 July 1872; MRCS and LRCP London 1898, Fell Entomological Soc, CstJ; *m* 18 Dec 1909 Violet Julia Louise, 2nd dau of Henderson James Twigg, of Hawks Bay, NZ, and *d* 1962, leaving:

1h +Orford Henderson St Andrew; *b* 13 Dec 1910; *educ* Wellington and Hertford Coll Oxford (BA 1932); Capt Gen List WW II

2g Richard Stukeley, CB (1927), CIE (1919), DSO (1917); *b* 15 Jan 1876; IA: NW Frontier India 1897–98, China 1900 and WW I (wounded, despatches), T/Brig-Gen 1917, Embarkation Cmdt Bombay 1917–19, Lahore Base 1919–21, Col 1920, DA and QMG AHQ India 1921–22 cmdg Lahore Bde Area 1922–26, Maj-Gen 1926 DAQMG and QMG N Cmd India 1926–29, ret 1929, India and China medals, Order Sacred Treasure Japan and Karageorge Serbia 4th Cl with swords; *m* 14 Sept 1905 Edwardine Annie Georgina (*d* 2 Dec 1963), dau of Capt Louis A Jourdier, French Dragoons, and *dsp* 6 June 1959

3g Edward Churchill; *b* 13 Oct 1878; MIEE, Ch Engr Madras Electric Supply Co 1906–13, Lt RNVR (Tech) 1919, attd RNAS, Maj RFA 1918, tfd to Directorate Works and Buildings (A Ministry) as Supt Engr, ret 1938, Dep Assist Dir Fortifications and Works War Office 1939 as Maj RE, GO2, ret at own request 1942; *m* 18 April 1906 Irene (*d* 24 June 1956), dau of Col Charles Edward Shepherd, IA, and *d* 20 Aug 1956, leaving:

1h Edward Richard Gordon; *b* 17 May 1911; Lt-Col RA WW II; *m* 15 May 1943 Mary Aderyn (*d* 1993), dau of Rev H Jones-Davies, and *d* 1986, leaving:

1i *Catherine Aderyn [Mrs Friedrich Kuebart, 463 Bochum, Plasshofstrasse 21, Germany]; *b* 9 June 1944; *m* 1968 *Friedrich Kuebart

2i *Margaret Joan (Maggie) [Ms Maggie St John, 19 Selwyn Rd, Birmingham B16 0SH]; *b* 8 Jan 1949; *m* 1979 *Tony Dudley-Evans

1h *Catherine Margaret [Miss Catherine St John, 22 Greenway, Crediton, Devon]; *b* 21 Oct 1907

4g Arthur Beauchamp; *b* 24 May 1884; Cdr RN WW I (despatches); *m* 26 Nov 1914 Lucinda Mary Stanley (*b* 1888), dau of Hon John French (*see* DE FREYNE, B), and *d* 11 April 1948, leaving:

1h *Œnone Mary; *b* 15 May 1917; *m* 1st 1943 John Francis Elton Watkins and has:

1i *Mary Veronica [Mrs Donald Hodder, c/o Standard Bank, Cecil Sq, Harare, Zimbabwe]; *b* 27 Aug 1946; *m* 3 May 1969 *Donald Hodder

1h (cont.) Mrs John Watkins *m* 2nd 1 Sept 1953 *Leslie James Ashton, yst s of William Henry Ashton, of Birmingham

2h *Deidre Mary [Mrs Harold Leach, PO Box 1409, Port Shepstone 4240, Natal, S Africa]; *b* 22 Nov 1919; *m* 1944 *Harold Drummond-Hay Oxenham Leach and has:

1i *Susan Mary [Mrs Christopher Johnson, PO Box 125, Fort Victoria, Zimbabwe]; *b* 12 May 1945; *m* 1965 *Christopher Forbes Johnson, s of A/Cdre A F Johnson, DFC, by Enone Rashleigh, and has:

1j *Russell Forbes; *b* 28 July 1968

1j *Catherine Amber; *b* 31 Jan 1966

2i *Peta Mary [Mrs Clive Lilford, Landsend Farm, PO Box 26, Norton, Zimbabwe]; *b* 22 Sept 1947; *m* 1967 *Clive Charles Lilford and has:

1j *Grant Charles; *b* 13 May 1968

1j *Karen; *b* 17 Feb 1970

3i *Lucinda Margaret; *b* 31 Aug 1950

4i *Mary Louise [Mrs Birrell, Neptune Farm, Arctucus, Box HG481, Highlands, Harare, Zimbabwe]; *b* 8 Nov 1951; *m* 11 March 1972 *— Birrell

1g Julia Margaret; *b* 17 Oct 1877; *d unm* 29 March 1956

2g Catherine Frances Muriel; *b* 14 July 1882; *m* 3 July 1906 Charles Bernard Catt (*d* 15 Dec 1915), est s of Charles William Catt, of The Outwoods, Derby, and *d* 4 March 1962, leaving issue

1f (cont.) Richard St John *m* 2nd 19 March 1907 Lillian Margaret Rothwell, yr dau of Charles Tertius Burton, of Feltham, and *d* 6 Feb 1919

2f Edward Charles; *b* 28 May 1844; *d* 28 May 1878

3f Henry Beauchamp (Rev); *b* 8 Aug 1850; Lt 11th Foot (Devonshire Regt), Rector Ninfield, Sussex; *m* 26 Sept 1878 Emily Anne (*d* 2 Jan 1923), dau of Charles Bailey, of Redhill, Surrey, and *d* 16 Oct 1931, having had:

1g Emily Gladys; *b* 5 May 1882; *m* 17 Dec 1907 Edward Bradish, manager Roy Bank Canada, s of James Bradish, of Strandfield, Wexford, and *d* 1927, leaving issue

2g Barbara Esmée; *b* 11 Sept 1885; *d unm* on service as Red Cross nurse France 12 Oct 1916

1f Emily Sophia Mercy; *d unm* 14 Jan 1935

2f Margaret Grace Barbara; *d unm* 7 Dec 1938

3e George (Rev); *b* 25 Dec 1798; Rector Warndon, Worcs; *m* 5 July 1831 Marianne (*d* 1896), 4th dau of John Seymour Biscoe, of Clifton, Glos, gs of 8th Duke of Somerset (*qv*), and *d* 9 July 1877, leaving, with two daus (*d unm*):

1f George Beauchamp Fleming; *b* 9 Nov 1845; *m* 1880 Sarah Letitia (*d* 1950), dau of G B Abrey, of Canada, and *d* 25 Sept 1908, having had:

1g George Herbert; *b* 1881; *d* 1890

2g Harry Beauchamp; *b* 4 May 1886; *m* 1919 Mary Katherine (*d* 1947), dau of M H Fitzhardinge, of Sydney, NSW, and *d* 27 May 1957, leaving:

1h *Barbara Margaret [Miss Barbara St John, Unit 20 Chatswood Garden Village, 5 Hart St, Lane Cove, NSW 2066, Australia]; *b* 6 Feb 1920

2h *Gladys [Mrs Norman Fairfax, 133 Woodburn St, Evans Head, NSW 2473, Australia]; *b* 12 Nov 1922; AWAS WW II; *m* 1945 Norman Wycliffe Fairfax (*d* 1986) and has:

1i *John Beauchamp; *b* 1949

1i *Helen Margaret; *b* 1947

3g Oliver Nugent; *b* 1889; *d* 1890

1g Helen Barbara; *b* 11 Aug 1882; *d* 30 Nov 1967

2f John Seymour (Rev); *b* 3 March 1849; Rector Pencombe, Worcs; *m* 25 Aug 1880 Marian (*d* 15 July 1929), dau of Rev C S Grueber, and *d* 24 May 1922

1f Louisa Mary; *m* 31 May 1866 Ven William Walters, Archdeacon Worcester (*d* 23 Sept 1912)

2f Annie Barbara

3f Frances Fleming; m 5 Dec 1872 John Edward Sale (d 1897), of Marple, Cheshire, and d 24 Aug 1905

4e Fleming, of Henwick Grange, Worcs, and Dinmore, Herefs; b 25 March 1801; m 15 May 1832 Mary (d 1891), 4th dau of John Freeman, of Gaines, Herefs, and d 18 May 1857, leaving:

1f Harris Fleming (Rev), of Dinmore Manor, Herefs; b 14 Dec 1833; educ Trin Coll Cambridge (MA); m 29 June 1878 Gertrude Margaret (d 22 June 1923), est surv dau of Charles E Ward, of Clifton, and d 16 Aug 1903, leaving:

1g Oliver Stukeley Fleming; b 1 Aug 1881; educ Marlborough; Lt KSLI 1916–19; m 1st 1913 Agnes Margaret Jane (d 25 Jan 1916), dau of Arthur Jenkins, of Pencombe, Herefs, and had:

1h Richard Stukeley Fleming; b 20 July 1914; d unm 27 April 1940

1h *Evelyn Mary Fleming [Mrs Daniel Reidy, 31 Mayfield Rd, Crouch End, London N8]; b 5 Dec 1915; m 31 Aug 1943 Daniel Reidy (d 20 Aug 1969), only s of Daniel Patrick Reidy, of Highgate, and has:

1i *Richard Daniel Kenneth; b 19 Aug 1944

1g (cont.) Oliver St John m 2nd 26 June 1924 Elizabeth Sarah (d 8 Aug 1933), only dau of John Ross, of Dinmore, and d 19 April 1955, having by her had:

2h John Fleming; b 10 Aug 1926; d 14 May 1927

3h +Paul Fleming [Paul St John Esq, 6 Kinsella St, Joondanna, Perth, WA 6060, Australia]; b 29 Jan 1928; m 14 Feb 1953 *Lesley Patricia, yst dau of Albert Edwin Marsh, of Perth, W Australia, and has:

1i +Brian Fleming; b 27 March 1954

2i +Peter Michael St John; b 12 June 1957; m 1981 *Loretta Anne-Marie, er dau of John Toniolo, of Perth

1i *Nola Margaret; b 22 June 1955; m 1980 *Stewart Parkinson, yr s of John Parkinson, of Perth, and has:

1j *Hannah Jane; b 1983

2i *Pauline Maree Teresa; b 9 April 1960; m 1979 *Graham Leslie Waddell, of Perth

3i *Julie Frances; b 17 July 1964

4h +Oliver Peter Fleming (Rev) [The Rev Oliver St John, St Joseph's Presbytery, PO Box 45, Kulin, WA 6535, Australia]; b 19 June 1929; educ Melbourne U (BA) and W Australia U (Dip Ed)

5h +Michael Fleming [Michael St John Esq, 9 Victoria Ave, London N3]; b 28 June 1932; m 1958 *Teresa Josephine, dau of Thomas W Murphy, of Finchley, and has:

1i +Nicholas Fleming; b 15 April 1961; m 1989 *Catherine Clare, dau of James Smith, of Westcliff-on-Sea, Essex

2i +Andrew Thomas; b 9 May 1963

3i +Philip Ambrose; b 16 May 1965; m 1986 his cousin *Catherine Anne, dau of Stanley John Simpson, of Perth, W Australia (see below)

4i +Robert Oliver; b 1968

2h *Joan Fleming [Mrs Stanley Simpson, 13 Byron St, Leederville, Perth, W Australia 6007, Australia]; b 29 May 1925; m 7 June 1947 *Stanley John Simpson and has:

1i *Christopher John; b 25 June 1950; m 19– *Rosemary Anne, dau of Marcus Clarke

2i *Peter James [Peter St John Esq, Flat 2, Lorina Flats, Fairway, Nedlands, W Australia]; b 5 Sept 1952; m 19– *Irene Esther, dau of Antonino Margio, of Geraldton, W Australia

1i *Pauline Mary [Mrs Kenneth Glasgow, c/o BP Australia, Port-Hedland, W Australia]; b 17 Aug 1948; m 1968 *Kenneth Gerald Glasgow and has:

1j *Gerald

2i *Catherine Anne; b 1966; m 1986 her cousin +Philip St John (see above)

2g St Andrew Fleming (Rev); b 17 Nov 1887; educ Haileybury and Keble Coll Oxford (BA 1909); Rector Peakirk and Glinton, Peterborough, Chaplain Gen Community of St John the Divine, Pietermaritzburg; d 4 March 1976

3g Fleming (Rev); b 30 Jan 1891; educ Haileybury and St John's Coll Cambridge (BA 1912, MA 1933); Prior Provincial English Dominican Province

4g Charles Edward Fleming, RD; b 22 Aug 1893; Cdr RNR, WWs I and II as Maj SAAF; m 1st 20 April 1927 Eira (d 28 June 1950), only dau of Rev William Edward Humphreys, Rector Braunston, Rugby, and had:

1h Margaret Elinor Fleming; b 9 June, d 13 June 1929

4g (cont.) Cdr Charles St John m 2nd 1951 Nancy Milner (d 29 Dec 1995), dau of Instr-Capt Broadbent, RN, and widow of T Robyns, and d 14 Jan 1972

1g Mary Fleming; b 29 Aug 1879; m 25 April 1911 Rev Francis Williams Allen, Rector Culworth, Northants, yst s of T W Allen, of Hereford, and d 2 March 1963, leaving issue

2g Maud Fleming; b 20 Dec 1883; m 26 Feb 1924 Rev Owen Llewellyn Williams (d 14 Sept 1947), Vicar Bisham, Berks, yst s of Llewellyn Williams, and d 14 Jan 1965

3g Gertrude Fleming; b 26 Nov 1885; d unm 11 April 1974

1f Mary Elizabeth; b 6 July 1835; Sister of Mercy; d 28 April 1910

1e Barbara; m 1st John Baker, of Waverley House, Worcs (dsp); m 2nd 1 May 1819 John Balguy, QC, JP, DL, of Duffield, Derbys, Recorder Derby, and had issue

3d Thomas; b 19 May 1765; m 1st 26 July 1796 Frances (d 15 Nov 1810), dau of G Lavie, and had:

1e Thomas; b 7 June 1797; m 6 July 1822 Anne (m 2nd 22 Jan 1849 John Beresford Turner (d 2 Aug 1855) and dsp 28 July 1883), dau of Joseph Shelton, of Worcester, and dsp 19 Dec 1833

2e Oliver; b 6 Aug 1803; Capt HEIC's Madras Army; m 5 Nov 1835 Helen (d 14 Dec 1881), dau of John Young and widow of Henry Anson Nutt, and d 15 Nov 1844, leaving:

1f Oliver Beauchamp Coventry (Sir), KCSI (1882, CSI 1879); b 21 March 1837; educ Norwich GS and HEIC's Sch Addiscombe; 2nd Lt Bengal Engrs 1856, Lt 1858, Capt 1869, Maj 1876, Lt-Col 1880, Abyssinian War as Dir Field Telegraph and Army Signalling Dept 1867–68 (despatches, medal), Afghan War 1878–81 (despatches, thanked by Viceroy, medal with clasp), Sec to Govt Commr Baluchistan 1871, Pnccpl Mayo Coll Ajmir 1875, HM's Resident S Afghanistan 1881, FRGS, FRZS; m 23 Sept 1869 Janette (d 16 June 1921), 4th dau of James Ormond, of Abingdon, and d 4 June 1891, leaving:

1g Henry Beauchamp (Sir), KCIE (1930), CBE (1920); b 26 Aug 1874; educ RMC Sandhurst; Lt-Col IA (IPS ret), Agent to Govr-Gen Punjab States 1925–27, Agent and Ch Commr Baluchistan 1927–30; m 6 Feb 1907 Olive Amy (d 5 Nov 1963), 2nd dau of Col Charles Herbert, CSI, and d 5 Oct 1954, leaving:

1h Oliver Charles Beauchamp, CMG (1963); b 22 Oct 1907; educ Charterhouse and Sandhurst; Lt-Col IA (For and Political Serv), Sec to Govr NW Frontier Prov, FO from 1948; m 1st 2 Nov 1935 Elizabeth Mary (d 7 Sept 1957), er dau of Philip Octavius Lambton, of Gables, Rotherfield, Sussex, and had:

1i +Simon Lambton Beauchamp; b 3 Aug 1941; educ Dover Coll; m 1971 *Margaret Lee, step-dau of Percy Leslie Owen, of Tampa, Fla., and has:

1j +Ryan Christopher Beauchamp; b 1972

1j *Erin Elizabeth; b 1975

1i *Sarah Mary [Mrs Sarah Mayhew, 23 Fir Tree Close, Aldrington Rd, London SW16 1TF]; b 2 Aug 1937; m 7 Sept 1957 (divorce 1980) Michael Geoffrey Morvaren Mayhew, 2nd s of Maj Geoffrey Dixon Mayhew, of Speldhurst, Kent, and has:

1j *Nicholas Morvaren; b 17 Feb 1959; Lt Cdr RN; m 1987 *Katherine Anne

2j *Charles Geoffrey; b 27 March 1966; m 1989 *Michele Crosby and has:

1k *Joshua Charles; b 1991

1k *Emily Victoria; b 1992

3j *Hamish St John; b 1968; m 1993 *Julia A Jarvis

1j *Amanda Elizabeth; b 31 Jan 1962

2i *Victoria Anne [Mrs Brian Easton, 17 Abbots Way, Beckenham, Kent]; b 27 Aug 1942; m 1983 *Brian Richard Easton

3i *Vanessa Margaret [Mrs Nicholas Connolly, Monks Gate Cottage, Monks Gate, Horsham, Sussex]; b 26 Nov 1944; m 2 March 1964 *Nicholas John Connolly, est s of Wilfrid John Connolly, of Wimbledon, and has:

1j *Rupert St John; b 11 Oct 1965; educ Oxford (MA) and Warwick Us (MSc)

1j *Philippa Joan; b 1 April 1964; educ Leeds and Penn State Us (MEng, CEng MICE, MIStructE)

2j *Victoria Maria; b 25 April 1967; educ Oxford U (MA)

1h (cont.) Lt-Col Oliver St John m 2nd 18 Jan 1966 *Mary, dau of Capt John Jameson Kelvynge Greenway, RA, Govr Bristol Prison, and widow of John Gillum Maxwell-Gumbleton, and d 4 April 1976

2h Neville Tudor; b 8 Sept 1912; d 27 Sept 1937

1g Olive Helen; m 16 Sept 1911 Maj Henry Bingham Whistler Smith-Rewse, RFA (ka 21 Nov 1914), est s of Col Henry Whistler Smith-Rewse, CB, CVO, RE, and d 196–

2g Muriel; m 21 Oct 1902 Lt-Col Arthur Frederick Heaton (d 3 May 1926), RAMC, er s of Frederick Luxmore Heaton, of Plâs Elwy, St Asaph, Flintshire, and d 6 Sept 1962, having had issue

2f St Andrew; b 25 May, 1841; Maj RMLI; d 10 Nov 1896

1f Helen Frances; d unm 16 Sept 1906

2f Anne Olivia; d unm 26 Aug 1930

3f Sophia Margaret Beauchamp; m 14 Aug 1868 Capt W F McIlwaine, RMLI, and d 17 Aug 1911, leaving issue

4f Jane Matilda; m 12 Oct 1880 Col Charles Mitchell Smith (d 7 Oct 1920), RA, and had issue

3e Robert; b 13 Aug 1805; Lt-Gen; m 18 Jan 1845 Jesse Arabella (d 1897), dau of Col Charles Whitehill and widow of Maj Henry Crawshaw Teesdale, and d 9 Oct 1874, having had, with a s (d an infant):

1f Oliver Henry Beauchamp; b 15 Nov 1847; Col 95th Regt; m 14 Oct 1880 Bertha Frederica (d 12 March 1936), dau of Col John Scriven, DL, and d 16 Jan 1917, leaving:

1g Oliver; b 30 July 1881; Imp Yeo Boer War 1901, Maj 19th Hyderabad Regt, IA; d 18 Dec 1925

2g Henry Beauchamp; b 10 Jan 1883; Capt S Lancs Regt; m 7 March 1906 Ethel Emily (m 2nd 1930 Basil Henry Hayes and d 1968), dau of Capt A G Scriven, Oxfordshire LI, and d 9 Feb 1923

3g Robert; b 27 Sept 1884; m 1st 1912 Dorothy (d 31 March 1958), dau of Daniel Willink (see WILLINK, Bt), and had:

1h Oliver Moubray; b 10 Sept 1921; m 28 Sept 1968 Margaret Elunid Corbett (d 1984), dau of William John Jones, of Pont-Newynydd, Mon, and d 1994

3g (cont.) Robert St John m 2nd 5 March 1959 *Dorothy Kathleen [Mrs Robert St John, 8 Alderton Court, W Parade, Bexhill-on-Sea, E Sussex TN39 3HF], dau of A L Beardsley, of Bognor Regis, and *d* 27 Sept 1968, having adopted

   *Howard Kevin Willink; *b* 1950

   *Lesley Frances Willink; *b* 1947; *m* 19– *John Shotton

4g Ernest Perkins (Rev), MC; *b* 16 July 1886; CF 1915–18, Chaplain RAFVR 1940–46, Proctor in Convocation Diocese Southwark, Rector Sheering, Essex, 1952–53; *d* unm 19 Jan 1953

5g Philip George; *b* 12 March 1890; IARO; *m* 1920 Lois Irene, MBE (*d* 1965), dau of Rev Robert Peel Willock, and *d* 7 Dec 1942, leaving:

   1h Anthony Philip; *b* 1925; Lt RA WW II; *m* 1st 1947 (*divorce* 1951) Elizabeth Dawes and had:

      1i +David Warren [David St John Esq, 4 Nottingham Rd, Somercotes, Derbys DE55 4JJ]; *b* 1950; *m* 1977 *Dawn Yvonne, dau of John Barry Price, of Derby

   1h (cont.) Anthony St John *m* 2nd 4 Feb 1959 *Shelagh Marie James [Mrs Anthony St John, Christophers, Budleigh Salterton, Devon] and *d* 1990, having by her had:

      2i +Oliver Philip; *b* 26 Nov 1959

      1i *Trudie Sophia; *b* 16 Jan 1962

      2i *Katherine Emma; *b* 1963

1g Selina Barbara; *m* 21 Feb 1914 John Felix Fielding, s of Felix Fielding

2g Frances Beatrice Clara; *m* 1921 Thomas Agnew Ansdell (*d* 23 Jan 1966) and *d* 29 May 1957, leaving issue

2f Robert Newell; *b* 29 Dec 1850; *m* 14 April 1886 Gertrude (*d* 6 Nov 1930), dau of J H Brooke, of Yokohama, and widow of W H Smith, and *d* 9 Oct 1897, leaving:

   1g Robert St Andrew; *b* 1887; merchant, Lt Chinese Labour Corps WW I 1916–18; *m* 1st 17 July 1918 (*divorce* 1921) Joan Hartland; *m* 2nd 11 Feb 1929 *Hannah Sophia Marcia, dau of Rev Arthur Ronald Handyside

   2g Herbert Newell; *b* 1888; Private 15th Canadian Expdny Force 1915; *ka* 22 May 1915

3f Thomas Charles St Andrew; *b* 29 Jan 1853; Cdr RN; *m* 13 Aug 1877 Cecilia (*d* 24 Dec 1950), est dau of Maj Henry Lavie, Bombay Army, and *d* 11 March 1920, having had:

   1g Robert Henry Beauchamp; *b* 29 Oct 1878; Paymaster-Lt RNVR 1914–19; *m* 1st 1 Oct 1901 Agnes Mary Sybil (*d* 31 July 1915), dau of Capt Shelton, Argyll and Sutherland Highrs, and had:

      1h *Dorothy Mary Beaufort [Mrs Magnus Friman, 24 Sheepfold Lane, Amersham, Bucks]; *b* 10 July 1902; *m* 15 Oct 1962 *Magnus Carl Olof Friman, s of — Friman, of Gothenberg, Sweden

   1g (cont.) Robert St John *m* 2nd 9 Sept 1916 Edith Mary (*m* 2nd 16 May 1957 Hugh Nevill Drummond Whall), dau of Capt Cape Hutton, of Iver, Bucks, and *d* 1 Feb 1956, having by her had:

      1h Peter Cape Beauchamp; *b* 25 May 1917; F/O RAF 1939–40; *ka* Battle of Britain 22 Oct 1940

      2h Margaret Mary; *b* 30 April 1919; *m* 11 April 1940 W/Cdr David Vere George Mawhood, OBE, RAF, s of L P Mawhood by Mary Clare, actress, and *d* 197–, having had:

         1i *Martin David St John; *b* 4 Jan 1945

         2i *Simon St John; *b* 17 Dec 1947

   2g Aubrey Rochfort St Andrew; *b* 23 April, *d* 10 May 1882

   3g Newell St Andrew; *b* 18 May 1884; *m* 27 Oct 1910 Mary Audrey (*d* 1957), dau of Charles Ernest Hicks, of N Battleford, Canada, and *d* 1962, leaving:

      1h +Andrew Charles [Andrew St John Esq, 2295 W 6th Ave, Vancouver 9, BC, Canada]; *b* 16 Oct 1927; *m* 1952 *Cecile Marie, dau of W J Calnan, of Vancouver, and has:

         1i *Marie Patricia; *b* 195–

         2i *Janet Mary; *b* 1956

         3i *Jillian Eleanor; *b* 25 Aug 1966

      1h *Mary Cecilia; *m* 16 Nov 1932 Walter Davidson, s of Walter Davidson, and has had issue

      2h *Ella Monica; *b* 26 Sept 1917; *m* 27 Feb 1942 *William Howard Davis, s of Austin Davis, and has had:

         1i Jeffrey Howard; *b* 18 March 1943; *d* unm 13 Aug 1963

         2i *Ralph Austin; *b* 14 March 1947

         1i *Marion Elizabeth; *b* 20 March 1950

         2i *Anne Roberta; *b* 18 Dec 1954

      3h *Hilda Margaret; *b* 16 Dec 1926; *m* 1949 *Victor Leon and has:

         1i *Kenneth Lawrence; *b* 10 Sept 1960

         1i *Susan Hilda; *b* 22 July 1952

         2i *Catherine Ann; *b* 16 May 1962

4g Bertram Oliver; *b* 2 June 1885; Assist Paymaster RNR; *d* 27 July 1921

1g Helen Cecilia Mary; *b* 18 Aug 1880; *m* 1 May 1905 Henry J Hailey (*d* 26 July 1939), 3rd s of Henry J Hailey, of Clare, and had issue

2g Cecilia Margaret Beaufort; *b* 19 April 1883; *m* 21 April 1903 Thomas Rowan Ronald, s of Thomas Robert Ronald, of Welling, Kent, and *d* 5 Jan 1905, leaving issue

4f William Nugent; *b* 12 Oct 1858; *d* unm 18 June 1903

1f Frances Emily Elizabeth; *m* 15 June 1870 Rev E G Crane and *d* 28 Nov 1875

2f Anne Mary Barbara; *m* 6 Jan 1872 Maj-Gen William John Gillespie (*d* 3 July 1931), Berks Regt, of St Margaret's, Twickenham, and *d* 11 April 1930, leaving issue

3d (cont.) Thomas St John *m* 2nd 8 June 1816 Sarah Brookes (*m* 2nd John Hill) and *d* 1827, having by her had a dau

4d St Andrew; *b* 31 Oct 1766; LLD; *m* 9 March 1799 Anne (*d* 1807), dau of Samuel Hardwicke, and *d* 1836, leaving, with three daus (*dsp* or unm):

   1e St Andrew; *b* 11 Dec 1801; *m* 7 Aug 1830 Dorcas Serrell (*d* Sept 1842), yst dau of A Iremonger, of Guernsey, and *d* 1843, leaving a s (*dsp*)

   2e John Beauchamp; *b* 15 Jan 1803; *m* 19 Sept 1842 Katherine Maria (*d* 17 Sept 1847), dau of Lt-Col Steward, of Leamington, and *d* 15 Feb 1845, leaving:

      1f Edward Beauchamp; *b* 7 July 1843; Lt-Col Roy Sussex Regt; *m* 9 June 1870 Eleanor Frances Alti Maria Robinson (*d* 24 Nov 1893), dau of Rt Hon Sir Hercules Robinson, later (1896) 1st Baron Rosmead, GCMG (*see* 1933 edn), and *d* 14 Dec 1902, leaving a dau (*d* unm)

      2f Oliver Beauchamp; *b* 8 Oct 1844; Capt 58th Foot; *d* 7 May 1912

5d Harry; *b* 2 Jan 1768; *m* 21 April 1797 Catherine (*d* 23 July 1856), dau of Rev Henry Wigley, and *d* 20 Aug 1833, leaving:

   1e Frederick; *b* 24 Jan 1809; Surveyor-Gen Customs; *m* 17 July 1845 Mary Anne (*d* 4 July 1883 aged 63), dau of Edward Bramah, and *d* 4 Nov 1863, leaving, with two daus (*d* unm):

      1f Frederick; *b* 18 July 1849; *d* 5 Dec 1882

      2f Beauchamp; *b* 24 Oct 1850; *d* 11 June 1885

      3f Henry, of Norwood, Rawdon Is, Hastings River, NSW; *b* 5 March 1852; *m* 12 Dec 1877 Jessie Cameron, yst dau of Donald Macdonald, of Port Macquarie, NSW, and *d* 23 July 1939, leaving:

         1g Frederick de Porte (Rev); *b* 16 Nov 1879; Vicar Quirindi, NSW, Canon Armidale Cathedral; *m* 16 June 1908 Hannah Phoebe Mabel (*d* 12 April 1950), dau of Samuel Lucas Charles Pyrke, JP, of Bowling Alley Point, Tamworth, NSW, and *d* 4 July 1963, leaving:

            1h Oliver Beauchamp; *b* 6 May 1909; *d* 15 Feb 1993

            2h Roland Tyrwhitt, MBE (1968); *b* 16 Dec 1914; BEc Sydney 1941, BA Qld 1949, Lt AIF, Registrar Diocese of Brisbane and Province of Queensland; *m* 1st 30 July 1949 Margaret (*d* 1972), only dau of Ven Archdeacon Reginald Beatty Massey, and *d* Oct 1991, leaving:

               1i +David Henry [David St John Esq, 7 Raine Terrace, Winthrop, W Australia 6150, Australia]; *b* 1 Sept 1951; *educ* Queensland U (BSc, PhD); research manager material science CRA Advanced Tech Devpt Perth; *m* 1976 *Helen Jennifer, dau of Donald McLeod, of Brisbane, and has:

                  1j +Andrew Timothy; *b* 1980

                  2j +Robin Thomas; *b* 1983

               2i +Paul Michael [Paul St John Esq, 2/170 Dornoch Terrace, Highgate Hill, Queensland 4101, Australia]; *b* 4 June 1953; *educ* Queensland U (BSc); *m* 1987 *Frances Julia, dau of John Thompson McDonald, of Toowoomba

               3i +Nigel Alexander; *b* 2 Dec 1958; *educ* Queensland Inst Technology (BAppSc)

               4i +Julian Andrew; *b* 4 Aug 1963

               1i *Philippa Robin [Mrs Kim Grady, 15 Delville Ave, Moorooka, Queensland 4015, Australia]; *b* 18 April 1955; *educ* Queensland U (BA); *m* 1988 *Kim Graham Grady and has:

                  1j *Alicia St John; *b* 1988

             3h Edward (Ted) Henry, QC (1956); *b* 15 Aug 1916; *educ* Sydney U (BA 1937, LLB 1940); barrister 1940, Capt AIF Middle East 1941–43 and New Guinea 1943–44, Memb Ho Reps (Lib) for Warringah 1966–69 (fought next election unsuccessfully as Ind), chm Australian Section Int Commn of Jurists 1961–73, memb Int Commn Jurists Geneva 1966, Visiting Fell U of NSW, author: *A Time to Speak* (1969) and *Judgement at Hiroshima* (1995); *m* 1st 3 Aug 1940 Sylvette (*d* 13 Aug 1954), er dau of Jean Meer Cargher, of Strasbourg, Alsace, and had:

               1i *Madeleine [Mrs Madeleine St John, 53e Colville Gdns, London W11 2BA]; *b* 12 Nov 1941; *educ* Sydney U (BA); *m* 1965 (*divorce* 1972, resumed maiden name 1972) Christopher Roger Tillam, s of Roger Tillam, of Sydney

               2i *Colette; *b* 23 Dec 1944; *m* 1980 *Stephen Louis Lippincott, and has:

                  1j *Aaron; *b* 1985

             3h (cont.) Edward St John *m* 2nd 25 Oct 1955 *Valerie Erskine, dau of Henry John Winslow, and *d* 24 Oct 1994, having by her had:

               1i +Oliver Winslow; *b* 31 Aug 1956

               2i +Edward Erskine; *b* 21 Oct 1960; *m* 1988 *Susan Elizabeth, dau of Sydney Young, of Albury, NSW, and has:

                  1j +Henry William; *b* 1993

               3i +Patrick Graeme; *b* 4 Nov 1963; *educ* NSW U (BComm, LLB); *m* 1992 *Karen Leanne, dau of Peter John Reginald O'Loughlin, of Sydney

            1h Margery Patricia; *b* 31 Oct 1910; teacher; *m* 27 Sept 1952 Maj Maitland Buckeridge, The Buffs (*d* 1977), yr s of Alfred Buckeridge, and *d* 18 May 1993

            2h Marion; *b* 7 Dec 1911; *m* 2 Jan 1936 Rev Harold William Baker, BA (Sydney), BEd (Melb), assist master and chaplain King's Sch Parramatta, late Chaplain RAAF (*d* 12 Nov 1966), only s of Rev Canon Harold Napier Baker, and *d* 2 May 1984, having had:

1i *Richard St John [Richard Baker Esq, 18 Gordon Rd, Bowrab, NSW 2576, Australia]; *b* 30 Nov 1937; *m* 8 April 1964 *Virginia Dale, dau of Eric D Craig, of Warawee, NSW, and has:

1j *Andrew William St John [Andrew Baker Esq, 246 Kissing Point Rd, Turramurra, NSW 2074, Australia]; *b* 23 Sept 1967; *educ* NSW, Monash (BBus); assoc dir Rothschild Australia Asset Management; *m* 17 Oct 1992 *Helen Sinclair, dau of Adam Smith, of Lemon Tree Passage, NSW, and has:

1k *Tom St John; *b* 8 July 1994

1j *Miranda Alice [Mrs Peter Shoppee, 10 Currong Place, Turramurra, NSW 2074, Australia]; *b* 24 April 1968; *educ* Sydney U (BA); *m* 12 Feb 1994 *Peter John Shoppee, s of John O Shoppee, of St Ives, NSW, and has:

1k *Harrison John; *b* 3 April 1998

2j *Camilla Lucy [Miss Camilla Baker, 39 Bathurst St, Woollhara, NSW 2025, Australia]; *b* 19 Dec 1972; *educ* Sydney U

1i *Felicity Ruth [Ms Felicity Baker, 37 Nevern Sq, London SW5 9PE]; *b* 12 July 1940; *educ* Sydney (BA), Paris and Geneva Us; lecturer in French Pennsylvania U 1967–69, UCL 1969; Reader in French London U 1994–

2i *Priscilla Marion [Mrs David Maxwell, 31 Bradford St, Balmain, NSW 2041, Australia]; *b* 27 Dec 1948; *educ* NSW U (BA); *m* 1971 *David Maxwell

3h Margaret; *b* 19 Jan 1919; *m* 20 Jan 1940 Edward John Minchin, Assist Crown Slr NSW (*d* 21 April 1993), er s of Cyril Forde Minchin, JP, of Albury, NSW, and *d* 24 Dec 1973, leaving:

1i *Antony St John [Antony Minchin Esq, 20 Arthur Circle, Forrest, ACT 2603, Australia]; *b* 23 Sept 1942; *educ* NSW U (BCom 1967) and Australian Nat U (MEc) 1972, FCPA, Assist Auditor Gen; *m* 26 Aug 1970 *Elizabeth Hume, BA, DipEd, MA, PhD, Sr lecturer Classics ANU, dau of Armand Gunner, and has:

1j *Thomas Edward; *b* 10 July 1972; *educ* ANU (BA 1994, BSc 1996)

2j *William Bruno; *b* 26 May 1978

1i *Mary Annabel [Mrs Michael Ritchie, 74 Baroona Rd, Northbridge, NSW 2073, Australia]; *b* 8 Oct 1948; *m* 24 March 1972 *Michael William Ritchie, s of William Ritchie, of Northbridge, and has:

1j *Angela Margaret; *b* 1974

2j *Cecilia Elizabeth; *b* 1978

4h *Florence Anne [Mrs Frank Heller, 84 Wood Vale, London N10 3DN]; *b* 2 May 1924; *educ* Sydney U (Diploma Social Studies 1948) and Antioch Int U (MA); WRANS WW II; *m* 9 Dec 1955 *Frank Heller, BSc (Econ), PhD (London), only s of Maximilian Heller, of Hampstead, and has:

1i *Michael Guy St John; *b* 29 Dec 1957; *educ* Sussex U Inst Devpt Studies (MPhil, PhD)

1i *Juliet Margarethe; *b* 13 Oct 1961; *educ* Sussex U (BA)

2i *Clare Andrea; *b* 7 Sept 1964; *educ* Exeter U (BA); barrister Inner Temple 1991

5h *Pamela Mary [Mrs Pamela St John, River Glen, 1/590 Riversdale Rd, Camberwell, Victoria 3124, Australia]; *b* 1 Nov 1925; *educ* Melbourne (BA, BEd) and Adelaide Us (Cert KTC); Diploma Advanced Studies in Educn; lecturer Inst Early Childhood Devpt Melbourne 1967–84; *m* 1st 12 Feb 1946 (*divorce* 1959) Ronald Fry, late RN (*d* 1971), only s of William Fry, of Southampton, Hants, and has:

1i *Jeremy William St John FRY later ST JOHN [Jeremy St John Esq, 21 Tara Ave, Kew, Melbourne, Victoria 3101, Australia]; *b* 19 Sept 1952; *educ* Melbourne U (LLB); slr 1975, barrister 1983; *m* 1st 1978 (*divorce* 1985) Christine Fay Barrow and has:

1j *Emily Catherine; *b* 1980

2j *Polly Louise; *b* 1982

1i (cont.) Jeremy St John 2nd 1990 *Jillian Margaret Rivers and by her has:

1j *Thomas Rivers; *b* 1994

3j *Phoebe Rivers; *b* 1991

1i *Jennifer Jane; *b* 15 March 1949; *educ* Melbourne U, TITC Melbourne (BEd Special Educn) and TTCTD Melbourne; *m* 1977 *Jonathan Hugh Beverley Crosskill and has:

1j *Nicholas William; *b* 1980

2j *Richard Campbell; *b* 1982

3j *Edward Daniel; *b* 1982 (twin)

2i *Catherine Mary; *b* 11 Sept 1957; *educ* Melbourne U (Bed); *m* 1st 1978 (*divorce* 1981) David Kenneth Hitchcock; *m* 2nd 1981 (*divorce* 1992) Kim Leigh Mark Savery and by him has:

1j *Elliot Henry; *b* 1986

1j *Amelia Kate; *b* 1983

5h (cont.) Mrs Pamela Fry resumed the name St John 1972 and *m* 2nd 1976 (*divorce* 1977) Edward John Minchin, sl, retaining the name St John

2g Henry Beauchamp (Rev); *b* 3 June 1889; gunner AIF WW I, Chaplain RAAF WW II, Rector Morpeth, NSW, Canon Newcastle Cathedral, NSW; *d* unm 14 July 1964

3g Ambrose; *b* 21 Sept 1896; *m* 1925 Mary Kathleen, dau of Peter Gaffney, of Sydney, and *d* 1968, leaving:

1h +Kevin Joseph [Kevin St John Esq, 34 Kemp St, Port Macquarie, NSW 2444, Australia]; *b* 1926

2h +Desmond Henry; *b* 1932; *m* 19– *Mavis Duncan, of Rockhampton, Qld, and has:

1i *Lorelle

2i *Deborah

3i *Sandra; *b* 1963

1h *Marlene Illina [Mrs David Steuart, 6/25 Banksia Rd, Caringbah, NSW 2229, Australia]; *b* 1936; *m* 1962 *David Steuart and has:

1i *Jason; *b* 1967

1i *Nicole; *b* 1963

1g Maud Charlotte; *m* 30 Jan 1907 Roger Williamson Wilson (*d* 1948), of Willesboro, Rollands Plains, NSW, and *d* 1969, leaving issue

2g Ivy; *d* 1882

3g Violet Jessie

4g Mary Ella; *b* 14 May 1885; *d* unm 18 July 1952

5g Alma Zilla; *b* 14 Oct 1887; *d* unm 19 Oct 1961

4f Edward (Rev); *b* 1 Dec 1855; Canon St George's Cathedral Southwark; *d* 12 June 1934

5f Oliver; *b* 27 Sept 1857; *m* 18 Nov 1891 Alice, dau of Samuel Richardson, of Ingatestone, Essex, and had:

1g Oliver Beauchamp; *b* 1895; *m* 1st 1921 (*divorce* 19–) Winifred Lyndall Fox (*d* 1966), of Hastings, Sussex, and had:

1h *Patricia Jocelyn [Mrs John McCarter, 3171 Henderson Rd, Victoria, BC, Canada]; *b* 1922; *m* 27 Dec 1941 *Prof John Alexander McCarter, MA, PhD, Dir Cancer Research Inst U of W Ontario, s of Alexander McCarter, of Almonte, Ontario, and has:

1i *David Graham [David McCarter Esq, 511 Hibiscus Ave, London, Ontario, Canada]; *b* 5 Jan 1946; *m* 17 Aug 1968 *Janice Evelyn, dau of R E Yates, of Walkerton, Ontario, and has:

1j *Robert Alexander; *b* 1974

2i *Robert Malcolm; *b* 22 March 1948; *educ* Guelph U and Dept Zoology U of BC; *m* 1971 *Bonnie Gail, dau of Lorne E Davis, of London, Ontario

3i *William Alexander; *b* 23 Jan 1955

1i *Patricia Lyndall; *b* 19 April 1953

2h *Josephine Lyndall; *b* 1925; *m* 1947 (*divorce* 1974) Walter H Cudmore and has:

1i *Rodney William; *b* 1949; *m* 1972 *Leonora Marie, dau of Mrs Violet Edith Dixon

2i *Donald Mackenzie; *b* 1953

3i *Richard Michael; *b* 1957

1i *Diane Louise; *b* 1962

1g (cont.) Oliver St John *m* 2nd 1944 Josephine Lorna (*d* Aug 1969), dau of W Kurtze, of Saskatoon, and *d* 28 Nov 1970

1g Olive Alice; *b* 1892; *m* 1913 Gordon Thomson and had:

1h *Jack; *b* 19–; *m* 19– and has issue

2h *David; *b* 1920; *m* 19– and has issue

1h *Margaret; *b* 1915; *m* 1934 *A Ambridge, of Ottawa, and has issue

2h *Ruth; *b* 1918; *m* 19 — and has issue

3h *Beth; *b* 1920; *m* 19– and has issue

2g Constance Muriel; *b* 1893; *m* 1914 Bernard Freeman and had:

1h *John Lynn [John Freeman Esq, 3316 Ivanhoe Rd, Pittsburgh, PA, USA]; *b* 19–; *m* 19– and has:

1i *Jack; *b* 1952

2i *Richard; *b* 1955

2h *Bernard Keith; *m* 1st 1939 (*divorce* 1971) Florence Pozzi and has:

1i *Ronald Keith; *b* 1942; *m* 19– and has issue

2h (cont.) Bernard K Freeman *m* 2nd 1971 *Mildred Stockton

3h *Oliver Franklin [Oliver Freeman Esq, 437 Princeton Ave, Ventura, CA, USA]; *b* 1922; *m* 1946 *Marjorie Smith and has:

1i *Kim Donna; *b* 1954

2i *Cindy; *b* 1955

1h *Constance Mary; *b* 1924; *m* 1948 *John A Pusateri and has:

1i *John Freeman; *b* 1952

2i *Keith David; *b* 1957

1i *Marilyn; *b* 1949; *m* 19– and has issue

2i *Kathleen Alice; *b* 1950; *m* 19–

31 *Jill Anne; *b* 1964

4i *Lisa Mary; *b* 1966

3g Evelyn Victoria

1f Catherine; *m* 26 May 1870 Cdr Philip Nathaniel Tyrwhitt, RN (*d* Nov 1918), and had issue

2e Ambrose (Rev); *b* 29 June 1815; RC priest; *d* 24 May 1875

1e Catherine Wigley; *m* 30 Sept 1824 Robert Philip Tyrwhitt, barrister

2e Sarah; *m* 27 Aug 1831 Robert Burnett Brander, of W Grinstead, Sussex, and *d* 7 March 1876, leaving issue

3c Henry; Capt RN; *m* Mary Schuyler, of New York (*d* 6 Nov 1786), and *d* April 1780, leaving:

1d Henry; *m* a dau of Lt Logic, RN, and *d* 5 March 1834, leaving an est s:

1e James Henry; Capt RA; *m* and had issue

4c Ambrose (Rev); *b* 7 Oct 1743; *m* 17– and *d* 18 July 1775, leaving issue

1c Barbara; *m* 27 Sept 1764, as his 2nd w, 6th Earl of Coventry (*qv*) and *d* 25 Nov 1804, leaving issue

1b Elizabeth; *m* by 1650 Sir Thomas Alston, 1st Bt (*cr* 1642; extinct 1791 but title irregularly assumed till 1853 by a s and gs of the estranged w of the penultimate Bt by another man), of Odell, Beds, and *d* 8 Sept 1677, having had issue

5 Henry; *educ* Queens' Coll Cambridge

6 Beauchamp (Sir); *educ* Queens' Coll Cambridge; MP Bedford; *m* Rebecca —, of Tilbrook, Beds, and *d* 1631

1 Anne; *m* 1st Sir Robert Corbet (*d* 1583; *see* 1970 edn CORBET, Bt); *m* 2nd Sir Rowland Lytton (*see* LYTTON, E) and had issue

The 11th BARON's est s,

JOHN ST JOHN, **12th Baron Saint John of Bletso**; *b* 15 Nov 1725; *educ* Winchester and New Coll Oxford; FSA; *m* 13 Dec 1755 Susanne Louise (*b c* 1725; *d* 17 Oct 1805), dau and coheir (with her sis Louisa, w of Sir John Trevelyan, 4th Bt, of Nettlecombe, *qv*) of Peter Simond, a London merchant of Huguenot origin, and *d* 20 April 1767, having had, with two other daus:

1 John Peter; *b* 11 Nov 1756; *dvp* 21 Oct 1760

2 HENRY BEAUCHAMP ST JOHN, **13th Baron Saint John of Bletso**; *b* 2 Aug 1758; FLS; *m* 2 Dec 1780 Emma Maria Elizabeth (*d* 10 July 1825), 2nd dau of Samuel Whitbread, brewer, of Cardington, Beds, and *dspms* 18 Dec 1805, having had:

(1) A son; *b c* 1784; *dvp* March 1791

(1) Emma; *m* 1806 Rev John Foster, Rector Sarratt, Herts, and *d* his widow 23 July 1865

(2) Augusta; *m* as his 1st w Rt Hon Sir John Vaughan (*d* 1839), Serjeant-at-Law and Baron Exchequer, and *d* 30 Jan 1813, leaving issue

(3) Margaret Letitia Matilda; *m* 20 April 1813 Sir Albert Pell (*d* 6 Sept 1832), Judge Bankruptcy Court, and *d* 5 March 1868, leaving issue (*see* PYM, B)

(4) Barbara; *m* 20 July 1813 Rev Thomas Bedford (*d* 9 March 1816), of Haynes, Beds, and *d* 15 May 1855

3 ST ANDREW ST JOHN, **14th Baron Saint John of Bletso**; *b* 22 Aug 1759; barrister Lincoln's Inn; MP (Whig) Beds 1780–84 and 1784–1805, U-Sec to PM, Lord North (*see* GUILFORD, E), 1783, Capt Gentlemen Pensioners 1806–07; *m* 16 July 1807 Louisa (*b* 1785; *m* 2nd 4 Aug 1823, as his 2nd w, her late husb's niece's widower Rt Hon Sir John Vaughan (*see* above) and *d* 9 July 1860), est dau of Sir Charles William Rouse-Boughton, 9th Bt (*see* 1963 edn), and *d* 15 Oct 1817, having had:

(1) ST ANDREW BEAUCHAMP, **15th Baron**

(1) Louisa Barbara; *m* 15 July 1837, as his 1st w, Norman Macleod of Macleod, 25th Chief (*b* 18 July 1812; *d* 5 Feb 1895), and *d* 27 Oct 1880, having had issue

4 George; *b* 19 Oct 1764; Col; *m* 10 May 1795 Lavinia, dau of William Breton-Wolstenholme, and had, with other issue (of whom four were drowned with their parents on their passage from Bombay 1802):

(1) Edward Beauchamp (Rev); *b* 26 March 1795; Rector Ideford, Devon; *m* 1st 25 July 1820 Jane (*d* 3 June 1831), dau of James Slade, and had:

1a Henry Beauchamp Trefusis; *b* 1822; Lt Madras Army; *d* unm 1845

2a St Andrew; *b* 1827; Lt RE; *d* unm 21 Sept 1854

1a Lavinia Barbara; *m* 15 Nov 1843 John James Wynne, RM, and *d* 20 April 1880, leaving issue

2a Laura; *m* 11 Sept 1844 Francis Adolphus Moschzisker and had issue

3a Jane; *m* 28 Oct 1849 Samuel Arthur Walker (*d* 1894) and had issue

4a Eliza; *m* 1st 1858 Rev Lionel Rich (*dsp*); *m* 2nd 1 April 1875 Rev Hugh Thomas Downman; *m* 3rd 1882 Rev Paul M Walker (*d* 1897), Vicar Stopsley, Beds, and *d* 22 May 1911

5a Matilda; *m* 24 May 1855 Capt Edwin L Scott, 21st Bombay NI, 3rd s of Robert Scott, of Oaklands, nr Plymouth, and *d* 24 Dec 1866, leaving issue

(1) (cont.) The Rev Edward St John *m* 2nd 28 Nov 1844 Mary (*dsp* 31 Dec 1879 aged 91), 4th dau of Robert Lovell Gwatkin, of Killiow, Cornwall, and n of Sir Joshua Reynolds, and *d* 4 April 1856

(1) Elizabeth Barbara; *m* 31 March 1796 Sir Henry Vaughan Halford, 1st Bt (*d* 9 March 1844; *see* 1897 edn), and *d* 17 June 1833, leaving issue

The 14th BARON's only s,

ST ANDREW BEAUCHAMP ST JOHN, **15th Baron Saint John of Bletso**; *b* 8 Nov 1811; sat as Tory in Ho Lds; *m* 12 March 1838 Eleanor (*d* 28 Nov 1899), 2nd dau of V-Adml Sir Richard Hussey Hussey, formerly Moubray or Mowbray, GCMG, KCB, of Wood Walton, and *d* 27 Jan 1874, having had:

(1) ST ANDREW ST JOHN, **16th Baron Saint John of Bletso**; *b* 5 Oct 1840; sat as C Ho Lds; *m* 25 April 1868, as her 1st husb, Ellen Georgiana (*m* 2nd 1889 F S H Judd, of Rickling, Essex (*d* 12 May 1933), and *d* 26 Dec 1890), dau of Edward Senior, and *dspm* 2 Nov 1887, leaving:

1a Ellen Sydney; *b* 16 Oct 1869; *m* 11 Feb 1902 Maximilian Gowran Townley, JP (*d* 12 Dec 1942), MP Mid-Beds 1918–22, 5th s of Charles Watson Townley, of Fulbourn, Cambs, and *d* 15 Jan 1959

2a Margaret Beaufort; *b* 18 Jan 1875; *m* 2 June 1896 Arthur Francis Anderdon Weston (*d* 26 Jan 1937), only s of Alexander Anderdon Weston, JP, of Holme Grange, Berks, and *dsp* 2 Jan 1949

(2) BEAUCHAMP MOUBRAY, **17th Baron**

(3) Edmund Tudor (Rev); *b* 17 Sept 1848; Rector Bletso, Beds; *m* 11 July 1877 Adeline (*d* 28 Sept 1937), 3rd dau of Adml Sir Arthur Farquhar of Drumnagesk, KCB, and *d* 30 Sept 1884, having had:

1a Edmund Farquhar, CMG (1919), DSO (1917) and bar (1918); *b* 27 Feb 1879; Col RHA, Boer War 1899–1902 (despatches medal with four clasps), WW I 1914–17 (despatches), WW II (AA and QMG at GHQ Home Forces 2 Sept 1939), Croix de Guerre; *m* 1 June 1921 Henrietta Frances, only dau of Col James Alexander Dalmahoy, MVO, WS, and *d* 24 April 1945, leaving:

1b +(Edmund) Oliver [Oliver St John Esq, Spittal, Biggar, Lanarks]; *b* 13 Oct 1927; *educ* Trin Coll Glenalmond; WS 1953; *m* 17 April 1959 *Eliza-

beth Frances, only dau of Lt-Col Henry Rice Nicholl, Rifle Bde, of Lipwood Hall, Haydon Bridge, Northumberland, and has:

1c +Charles Henry Oliver; *b* 4 Dec 1963; *m* 1991 *Emma Catherine Sewell, er dau of Henry Moore, of Shucknall Court, Herefs, and has:

1d *Poppy Rebecca Harriet; *b* 31 Oct 1995

1c *Nicola Rosemary; *b* 8 Sept 1960

2c *Emma Harriet; *b* 28 April 1968

1b *Frances Dalmahoy [Miss Frances St John, Bletsoe, 26 St Andrew's St, Brechin, Angus]; *b* 25 July 1931

2a Beauchamp Tudor; *b* 17 July 1880; Maj Roy Northumberland Fus, Pncpl Clerk H of C 1916–40; *m* 31 March 1910 Madeleine Ethel (*d* 1982), est dau of J Ellis Goodbody, of Thornville, Limerick, and *d* 5 April 1965, leaving:

1b Roger Ellis Tudor, CB (1965), MC (1944); *b* 4 Oct 1911; *educ* Wellington and RMC Sandhurst; joined 5th Fus 1931, WW II Hong Kong, UK and NW Europe (Bde Maj 11th Armoured Div 1944–45, despatches), cmded 1st Bn Roy Northumberland Fus 1953–55 (despatches) Mau Mau Emergency and 11th Inf Bde Gp BAOR 1957, Assist Cmdt Staff Coll Camberley 1960–62, Cdr Br Army Staff and Mil Attaché Washington, DC, 1963–65, Pres Army Regular Commissions Bd 1965–67, ret 1967, personnel administrator Urwick Orr & Ptnrs (management consultants) 1967–73; *m* 20 Nov 1943 *Rosemary Jean Douglas [Mrs Roger St John, Harelaw, Gorse Hill Rd, Virginia Water, Surrey GU25 4AS], yst dau of Ronald Vickers, of Scaitcliffe, Englefield Green, and *d* 15 Oct 1998, leaving:

1c +Henry Edward Tudor [Henry St John Esq, 29 Windmill Heights, North Leigh, Oxon OX8 6ZD]; *b* 2 Jan 1949; *educ* Eton and Coll of Estate Management (BSc, FRICS); ptnr Cluttons Daniel Smith; *m* 21 May 1983 (*divorce* 1997) Kerra, est dau of John Lockhart, of Calgary, Alberta, and has:

1d +Oliver Tudor Lockhart; *b* 19 May 1984

1d *Atalanta Victoria; *b* 13 Jan 1987

1c *Angela Lucy [Mrs Christopher Delacombe, Southolme, Heather Way, Chobham, Surrey GU24 8RA]; *b* 29 Sept 1944; *m* 25 April 1970 *Maj Christopher Rohan Delacombe, Roy Scots, only s of Maj-Gen Sir Rohan Delacombe, KCMG, KCVO, KBE, CB, DSO, of Shrewton Manor, Salisbury, Wilts, and has:

1d *Caroline May; *b* 1971

2d *Sophie Clare; *b* 1973

3d *Katharine Joyce; *b* 1975

2c *Jane Margaret; *b* 22 Oct 1946

3c *Alice Rosemary [Mrs Hugh Williams, Lower Willsworthy, Peter Tavy, Devon PL19 9NB]; *b* 8 May 1950; *m* 5 Sept 1974 *Hugh Martyn Williams, yr s of Cdr A M Williams, of Werrington Park, Launceston, Cornwall, and has:

1d *Patrick; *b* 1986

1d *Emily; *b* 1979

2d *Florence; *b* 1980

3d *Martha; *b* 1985

4d *Veronica; *b* 1991

2b *Michael Beauchamp, DSC (1943) [Cdr Michael St John DSC RN, The Old Thatch, Leggs Lane, Heyshott, W Sussex]; *b* 13 May 1915; *educ* RNC Dartmouth; WW II in submarines; *m* 7 Oct 1944 *Pamela Patience, only dau of Sir Arthur Rundell Guinness, KCMG (*see* GUINNESS, Bt), and has:

1c +Andrew Beauchamp [Andrew St John Esq, Cul-na-Cloich, Glenalmond, Perthshire]; *b* 27 Aug 1945; *educ* Winchester; *m* 30 March 1968 *Hon Sally Hayter Rootes, only dau of 2nd Baron Rootes (*qv*)

1c *Clare Pamela [Mrs David Astor, Bruern Grange, Milton-under-Wychwood, Oxon]; *b* 28 May 1947; *m* 19 Sept 1968 *David Waldorf Astor, CBE (*see* ASTOR V), and has issue

2c *Hermione Patience [Mrs William Owen, Merriscourt Farm House, Churchill, Oxon OX76 6QX]; *b* 14 April 1951; *m* 1 March 1973 *William Stanhope Owen, yr s of Stanhope Owen, of Weeks Farm, Egerton, Kent, and has:

1d *Sam Arthur Stanhope; *b* 1975; *educ* Eton and Oxford U

1d *Georgina Hermione; *b* 1974; *educ* Bristol U (BA) and Courtauld Inst

3a St Andrew Oliver, DSO (1919); *b* 18 March 1882; Cdr RN, served China 1900, WW I 1914–19 (despatches, Croix de Guerre) and WW II 1940–44 as Res Naval Offr; *d* unm 17 Oct 1967

4a Richard; *b* 10 July 1883; Cdr RN, served WW I (despatches); *m* 1st 3 June 1909 (*divorce* 1913) Eda Meriel (*d* 4 April 1971), only child of Lt-Col Neil Benjamin Edmonstone (*see* EDMONSTONE, Bt); *m* 2nd 30 July 1913 Margaret Louise Causton (*d* 25 May 1957) and *d* 9 Oct 1967, having by her had:

1b John Richard; *b* 7 Feb 1917; *educ* Wellington; Capt RM; *m* 1st 1943 (*divorce* 1951) Helen, dau of H O Coleman, and had:

1c +Tudor Richard; *b* 7 Aug 1946; *m* 1977 *Marlyn, only dau of G Foster

1c *Lucinda Jill [Mrs Andrew Cameron-Beaumont, Tideford Farmhouse, Tideford, Cornwall]; *b* 19 March 1944; ARCM; *m* 24 Feb 1968 *Andrew Jon Cameron-Beaumont, FRICS, and has:

1d *Richard Peregrine; *b* 1973

1d *Charlotte Lucinda; *b* 1971

1b (cont.) John St John *m* 2nd 10 Oct 1952 *Diana Elwell [Mrs John St John, 40 Arkwright Rd, London NW3 6BH], yst dau of Col Edward Stockley Sinnott, CMG, TD, and *d* 2 Dec 1988, leaving by her:

2c *Clare Sylvia; *b* 21 July 1955

3c *Katharine Elinor Margaret; *b* 21 Oct 1957; *m* 1st 1976 (*divorce* 1986) Erik Austin Flakoll; *m* 2nd 1993 *Albert Sidney Griffin, of Kentucky

1a Eleanor Louisa; *m* 21 Jan 1874 Lt-Col Herman Wayne, 10th Foot, of Kelso House, Bath, and *d* 26 Feb 1923, leaving issue

(2) Laura; *m* 8 June 1867 Conolly Thomas McCausland, JP, DL (*d* 25 June 1902), of Drenagh, Co Londonderry, and *d* 21 Oct 1919, leaving issue

The 16th BARON's yr bro,

BEAUCHAMP MOUBRAY ST JOHN, **17th Baron Saint John of Bletso**; *b* 4 Dec 1844; Offr 74th Highrs, ret 1867, Ld Lt Beds 1905–12, Chm Bedford QS, Pres Beds TFA, sat as C in Ho of Lds; *m* 1st 4 Feb 1869 Helen Charlotte (*d* 23 March 1909 aged 60), 2nd dau of Harry Thornton, of Kempston Grange, Beds, and had:

1 HENRY BEAUCHAMP OLIVER ST JOHN, **18th Baron Saint John of Bletso**, JP, DL (Beds); *b* 24 June 1876; *d* unm 17 Oct 1920

2 MOUBRAY ST ANDREW THORNTON ST JOHN, **19th Baron Saint John of Bletso**, JP, DL (Beds); *b* 5 Nov 1877; Capt KOSB Boer War 1899–1902, Memb Ecclesiastical Ctee Houses of Parl 1925–31; *m* 1st 4 Oct 1905 Evelyn Geraldine (*d* 7 Dec 1918), yr dau of Capt Andrew Hamilton Russell, of The Heath House, Petersfield, 58th Regt, and had:

(1) JOHN MOUBRAY RUSSELL ST JOHN, **20th Baron Saint John of Bletso**; *b* 3 Aug 1917; *d* 13 April 1976

(1) Helen Evelyn; *b* 4 Oct 1906; *d* 24 Aug 1996

(2) *Katherine Barbara [The Hon Mrs Uttley, 44 Heath Crescent, Free School Lane, Halifax HX1 2PW]; *b* 15 Oct 1907; Section Offr WAAF WW II; *m* 10 June 1945 F/Lt George William Uttley, RAF (*d* 1986), only s of William Henry Uttley, of Mearclough House, Sowerby Bridge, Yorks, and has:

1a *Alathea St John; *b* 1947

(3) Margaret Beaufort; *b* 5 Oct 1909; BSc; *m* 10 Oct 1934 Charles Somerville Carmichael, er s of D L Carmichael, of Druidsmere, Blairgowrie, Perthshire, and *d* 198–, leaving:

1a *Margaret Mary [Miss Margaret Carmichael, Old Mill House, Newton Blossomville, Turvey, Beds]; *b* 1 Feb 1940; GGSM, ARCM

(4) Gertrude Eleanor Rosemary; *b* 23 Sept 1910; *m* 22 Feb 1935 Friedrich Max Hagedorn, only s of Otto Karl Albert Hagedorn, and *d* 3 April 1960, leaving issue

(5) Sybilla Laura Russell; *b* 26 Oct 1915; *m* 24 April 1943 Howard Ernest Churchill Fey, only s of E J Fey, of High Barton, Marford Hill, Wrexham, and *d* 198–, leaving:

1a *Margaret Angela; *b* 1945; *m* 1971 *Anthony Norman Carter

2a *Deborah Susan; *b* 1947; *m* 1969 *William Ronald Nicholson

2 (cont.) The **19th Baron** *m* 2nd 26 Sept 1923 Elizabeth May (*d* 25 Oct 1978 aged 93), dau of Lloyd Walter Griffith, of Hurst Court, Ore, Sussex, and widow of Col Edward Charles Ayshford Sanford, CMG, JP, of Nynehead Court, Wellington, Somerset, and *d* 28 Oct 1934

3 Rowland Tudor; *b* 1 May, 1882; *educ* Winchester and RMC Sandhurst; Lt-Col Durham LI WWs I (despatches) and II; *m* 17 Oct 1912 Katherine Madge (*d* 24 Nov 1954), dau of Sir Frank Lockwood, QC, MP, and *d* 17 Nov 1948, having had:

(1) Oliver John Frank Lockwood (Rev), DSC and bar; *b* 31 March 1914; *educ* RNC Dartmouth, RN Engrg Coll Keyham and Ripon Hall Theological Coll; Cdr RN WW II, ordained June 1958, Vicar St George's, Tyldesley, Manchester 1960–72; *m* 29 Dec 1938 *Elva Rosemary [Mrs Oliver St John, 29 Bay Rd, Alverstoke, Hants], dau of Alfred John Skinn, MB, ChB, of Hong Kong, and *d* 6 Aug 1972, leaving:

1a *Vyvian Elaine [Mrs Patrick Maudsley, 18 Tudor Way, Wellingborough, Northants]; *b* 19 June 1940; *m* April 1972 *Patrick Nelson Maudsley, er s of K N Maudsley, of Ashtead, Surrey, and has:

1b *Ruth Claire; *b* 1973

2a *Juliet Rosemary [Mrs Brian Johnson, 131 Grosvenor Ave, London N5]; *b* 11 May 1943; SRN; *m* 2 Sept 1967 *Brian William Ellis Johnson, ARIBA, s of Henry George Eric Johnson, of Bournemouth, Hants, and has:

1b *George St John; *b* 22 Sept 1969

2b *Hugh William Nicholas; *b* 1979

1b *Katherine Alice; *b* 22 Sept 1969

3a *Diana Hazel Susan [Mrs Ewart Holmes, Harpers Cottage, Main St, Avebury, Wilts SN8 1RF]; *b* 10 June 1946; BA; *m* June 1970 *Ewart John Holmes, ARIBA, MRTPI, s of Wendell Holmes, of Derby, and has:

1b *Rowland St John; *b* 1973

2b *Oliver John; *b* 1975

1b *Genevieve Anne; *b* 1979

4a *Margaret Vanessa Lucy; *b* 26 March 1948; *m* 2 Aug 1969 *George Marlay Spencer, s of Marlay Spencer, of Liverpool, and has:

1b *Rachel Marlay; *b* 1972

2b *Abigail; *b* 1974

(2) Stephen Rowland, MC; *b* 25 June 1915; Maj 5th RHA WW II; *ka* Italy 31 Oct 1943

(3) ANDREW BEAUCHAMP, **21st Baron**

(1) *Elaine Julia Barbara [The Hon Mrs Whidborne, Holly Mount, Pethybridge, Lustleigh, Devon TQ13 9TG]; *b* 19 June 1921; raised 1977 to rank of baron's dau; *m* 25 Aug 1939 *Lt-Col John Francis Whidborne, RA, only s of John Herbert Whidborne, of Stockleigh English, Devon, and has had:

1a Stephen Barham; *b* 6 Aug 1940; *educ* Blundell's; *d* unm July 1965

2a *Richard St John, MBE (1973) [Richard Whidborne Esq MBE, 14 Berrylands, Liss Forest, Hants GU33 7DB]; *b* 20 Jan 1942; *educ* Blundell's and RMA Sandhurst; Maj AAC (ret), with Air Accidents Investigation Branch, FRAeS 1993; *m* 1st 21 Aug 1965 Linda Beverley (*d* 21 April 1975), adopted dau of Cyril Trevor Sherwood, of The White Cottage, Salfords, Surrey; *m* 2nd 4 Feb 1978 *Jennifer Mary, RGN, SCM, dau of Frank Eric Gould, of Sempringham, and by his 1st w has:

1b *Nicholas St John; *b* 19 Feb 1969

1b *James Oliver St John; *b* 27 June 1973

1a *Julia Lauretta; *b* 18 Dec 1943

4 Charles Paulet; *b* 11 Oct 1886; *m* 18 April 1914 Noreen Mary Ilay (*d* 28 Aug 1977), only dau of Maj Robert Francis Ladeveze Napier (see NAPIER, Bt, of Merchistoun), and *dsp* 21 June 1945

1 Helen Mary; *b* 8 Oct 1869; *m* 30 April 1907 Capt Francis George Courthope Mansel Morgan, JP (*d* 22 Dec 1937), of Plâs Coed Môr, Anglesey, Govr Dartmoor Prison, and *d* 7 Feb 1947, leaving issue

2 Alice Gertrude; *b* 26 Jan 1873; *m* 21 June 1922 Capt Francis Geach Crossman (*d* 10 June 1944), Cape CS, s of Col William Henry Crossman, IA, and *dsp* 14 Jan 1954

3 Mabel Eleanor; *b* 8 July 1874; *m* 19 July 1922 Henry William de Salis (*d* 1949), s of Col de Salis, and *d* 27 Aug 1953

4 Barbara Ethel; *b* 27 June 1875; *d* unm 10 Oct 1954

5 Edith Laura; *b* 8 Sept 1879; Co Commr Girl Guides, Beds, V-Chm City of London Pensions Sub-Ctee, Order of Mercy with bar; *m* 4 Dec 1902 1st Baron Luke (*qv*) and *d* 2 Aug 1941, leaving issue

6 Emily Caroline Emma; *b* 29 Nov 1880; Ldy Pres League of Mercy, Beds, Order of Mercy with bar; *d* unm 27 Nov 1969

7 Eva; *b* 25 Jan 1884; *m* 17 Dec 1913 Lt-Col George Gerald Montague Tyrrell, DSO, JP, 5th Lancers (*d* 28 April 1951), only s of George Gerald Tyrrell, of Kilmacrew, Co Down, and *d* 7 Dec 1948, leaving issue

8 Margaret; *b* 24 Nov 1887; nun All Saints' Community, Colney, St Albans, Herts

The **18th Baron** *m* 2nd 26 April 1911 Ethel Susan (*d* 3 Jan 1945), 2nd dau of John Hablington Lutley, JP, DL, of Brockhampton Park, Hereford, and *d* 10 May 1912

The 20th BARON's 1st cousin,

ANDREW BEAUCHAMP ST JOHN, **21st Baron Saint John of Bletso**, TD (1952); *b* 23 Aug 1918; *educ* Wellington; IA WW II, Lt-Col RA (TA); *m* 10 Dec 1955 *Katherine [The Rt Hon Katherine Lady St John of Bletso, By The Sea, Kalk Bay, CP, S Africa], yst dau of Alfred G Berg, of London SW15, and *d* 11 Feb 1978, leaving:

1 ANTHONY TUDOR ST JOHN, **22nd and present Baron Saint John of Bletso**

ST JOHN OF FAWSLEY

Arms: Tierced in fess az., gu. and az. per pale counterchanged, in the az. an open crown or, in the gu. a lion passant guardant gold, armed and langued az. **Crest:** A fallow deer's head erased ppr., in the mouth a chaplet of laurel vert, the attires per fess, the dexter az. and gu., the sinister gu. and az. **Supporters:** Dexter, a monkey ppr.; sinister, a lion arg., winged or, both crowned with a crown rayonny also or and each rampant on a grassy mount, the dexter having a primrose growing therefrom, the sinister a lily, all ppr. **Motto:** *Deus nobiscum* ('God be with us'). **Creation:** B. (LP, UK) 1987.

THE BARON ST JOHN OF FAWSLEY, of Preston Capes, Co Northampton (Norman Antony Francis St John-Stevas, PC (1979)) [The Rt Hon The Lord St John of Fawsley PC, The Old Rectory, Preston Capes, Northants NN11 6TE; 7 Upper Harley St, London NW1 4PS]; *b* 18 May 1929; *educ* Ratcliffe, Fitzwilliam House (later Coll) Cambridge (Pres Union 1950, Hon Fell 1991, LittD 1994), Ch Ch Oxford, its promotion to collegiate status being largely Lord St John of Fawley's doing when Min State DES (Dlitt 1994), and Yale (Fell Law Sch 1957, SSD 1960); barrister Middle Temple 1952, lecturer Southampton U 1952–53, SSD King's Coll London 1953–56, PhD Lond 1957, jurisprudence tutor Ch Ch and Merton Coll Oxford 1953–55 and 1955–57 respectively, jnlst *Economist* 1959–64, C candidate Dagenham 1951 gen election, MP (C) Chelmsford 1964–87, DES: Parly U-Sec 1972–73 and Min State 1973–74, Oppn Spokesman Arts 1974 and Educn 1975–78, Shadow Min Arts 1979–81, Chllr Duchy Lancaster, Min for Arts and Leader H of C 1979–81; chm Booker Prize 1985, memb cncl Nat Soc for Dance 1983–, Nat Youth Theatre 1983– and RCA 1985–, V-Pres Theatres Advsy Cncl 1983–, dir N M Rothschild Tst 1990– (chm), Tstee Philharmonic Orchestra 1988–, Decorative Arts Soc 1984–, Master Emmanuel Coll Cambridge 1991–96 (Life Fell 1996–), Chm Roy Fine Art Commn 1985–, OStJ 1980, Order Merit Italy 1965, FRSL 1966; author: *Obscenity and the Law* (1956), *Walter Bagehot* (1959), *Life, Death and the Law* (1961), *The Right to Life* (1963), *Law and Morals* (1964), *Walter Bagehot's Works* (ed, 15 vols., 1966–86), *The Agonising Choice* (1971), *Pope John Paul II, his travels and mission* (1982), *The Two Cities* (1984)

Lineage: STEPHEN SPIRO STEVAS (whose gf, called Stevens, had settled in the Ionian Islands when they were under British rule and married a Contessa Rasi, his surname becoming Hellenised to 'Stevas'); civil engr, property developer and hotel owner; *m* Kitty St John O'Connor and had:

1 NORMAN ANTONY FRANCIS PANAGIA ST JOHN STEVAS later NORMAN ANTONY FRANCIS ST JOHN-STEVAS, *cr* a **Baron**

1 *Juno; actress as Juno Alexander

2 *Diana Maria; *m* *George Teeling Smith

ST JOHN-MILDMAY

Arms: Arg. three lions rampant az. **Crest:** A lion rampant guardant az. **Motto:** *Alla ta hara* ('God my help').
Creation: Bt. (GB) 9 Oct 1772.

SIR WALTER JOHN HUGH ST JOHN-MILDMAY, 12TH BT [Sir Walter St John-Mildmay Bt, 9 Lansdown Cresc, Bath BA1 5EX]; *b* 3 Sept 1935; *s* fourth cousin twice-removed on termination of dormancy 1997; *educ* Wycliffe Coll, Emmanuel Coll Cambridge, Hammersmith Coll of Art and Building and RAC Cirencester

Lineage (of Mildmay): HUGH de MILDME; living 1147; ancestor of:

Sir ROBERT de MILDMAY; *m* Matilda le Rous and had, with another s (Herbert, *dsp*):

ROGER MILDMAY, of Hambledon; living *c* 1294; had:

Sir ROGER MILDMAY, of Hambledon; living *c* 1322; *m* Matilda de Eltham and had:

HENRY MILDMAY, of Herefs; living 1371; had:

RAYFFE MILDMAY; living 1372; had:

RANULPHE MILDMAY; had:

HENRY MILDMAY, of Stonehouse, Glos; living 1390; had:

ROBERT MILDMAY, of Stonehouse; living *c* 1394; had:

ROBERT MILDMAY, of Stonehouse; living 1402; had:

THOMAS MILDMAY; living *c* 1439; *m* Anne Kingscote and had:

THOMAS MILDMAY; living *temp* EDWARD IV; *m* Margery, dau and heiress of John Cornish, of Much Waltham, Essex, and had, with a yr s (John):

WALTER MILDMAY, of Writtle, Essex; living 1483; *m* Mary Everard, of Much Waltham, and had:

THOMAS MILDMAY, of Chelmsford; yeoman and merchant; *m* Agnes Reade and *d* 1547, having had:

1 Thomas, of Moulsham Hall, nr Chelmsford, which he bought 1540, also of Bishop's Hall; Offr Court Augmentations 1536, Commr to visit Essex religious houses; High Sheriff Essex and Herts 1558; *m* Avicia, dau of William Gunson, of London, and *d* by 29 Jan 1566/7, leaving:

(1) Thomas (Sir); *m* Frances, dau of 11th Lord (Baron) FitzWalter (*qv*), and had issue

2 William, of Springfield Barnes, Essex, where granted land previously belonging to Coggeshall Abbey 1548; *m* 1st Elizabeth, dau of John Paschall, of Gt Baddow; *m* 2nd 7 June 1563 Annis, widow of Adam Winthrop, of Groton, Suffolk, and *d* 13 Feb 1570/1, leaving by his 1st w:

(1) Thomas (Sir), of Springfield Barnes; Sheriff Essex 1597, ktd 1603; *m* 12 June 1563 Alice (*d* 8 Nov 1607 aged 68), dau of Adam Winthrop, of Groton, Suffolk, and *d* 15 Dec 1612, having had, with other issue:

1a William; *m* 11 June 1590 Margaret (*d* Feb 1605), dau of Sir George Hervey, of Marks, Essex (*see* BRISTOL, M), and *dvp* 6 Feb 1615, leaving:

1b Thomas (Sir), of Springfield Barnes; *m* —, dau of John Ernle, of Whetham, Wilts, and had:

1c William, of Springfield Barnes; *m* Sibilla, dau of Sir Thomas Palmer, Bt, of Wingham, Kent (*see* 1850 edn), and had:

1d William; HEICS; *m* Sarah Wilcox and had:

1e Sir WILLIAM MILDMAY, 1st and last Bt (GB), so *cr* 5 Feb 1765; inherited Moulsham from his distant cousin 19th Lord (Baron) FitzWalter (*qv*); *dsp* 8 Aug 1771, when the btcy expired

2b Carew Hervey, of Marks, which inherited from his maternal uncle; *b* 2 Feb 1595; Groom Jewel Office 1625, High Sheriff Essex, MP Essex 1654–55 and 1656–58; *m* 25 Sept 1626 Dorothy (*bur* 16 May 1667), sis of Sir Gilbert Gerard, 1st Bt, of Harrow, Middx, and was *bur* 8 Aug 1676, leaving:

1c Francis Hervey, of Marks; *bapt* 28 Oct 1630; Groom Jewel Office; *m* 14 Sept 1656 Mary (*d* March 1717 aged 78), only child of Matthew Honeywood, and was *bur* 7 Aug 1703, leaving:

1d Carew Hervey, of Hazlegrove, which inherited from his cousin Humphrey Mildmay (for whose branch *see* below), and Marks; *bapt* 23 Nov 1658; High Sheriff Essex 1712; *m* 1 May 1688 Anne, dau of Richard LENNARD later BARRETT (2nd s of 13th Lord (Baron) Dacre; *qv*), and was *bur* 1 May 1743, leaving:

1e Carew Hervey, of Hazlegrove and Marks; *bapt* 6 March 1690; MP Harwich; *m* 1st 6 Jan 1718 Dorothy (*d* 23 Jan 1742), dau and heiress of John Eastmont, of Sherborne, Dorset, and had issue (*d* young or unm); *m* 2nd 17 May 1744 Edith (*dsp* 12 Oct 1772), dau and coheir of Sir Edward Phelips, of Montacute, Somerset, and *d* 16 Jan 1784 aged 93, leaving his estates to his great-niece Jane, w of Sir HENRY PAULET ST JOHN later ST JOHN-MILDMAY, **3rd Bt**, MP (*see* below)

2e Humphrey Hervey; *bapt* 6 April 1692; *m* 20 Aug 1706 his cousin Letitia (*d* 2 Oct 1749), dau and heiress of Halliday Mildmay (*see* below), and *d* 9 July 1761, having had, with other issue:

1f Carew, of Shawford House and Mildmay Park; *b* 1717; *m* 1 Feb 1761 Jane (*d* 2 May 1799), dau of William Prescod, Recorder Winchester, by Jane, later 3rd w of Sir Paulet St John, 1st Bt, MP (*see* below), and *d* 29 June 1768, leaving:

1g JANE, of Hazlegrove, Mildmay Park, Marks, Moulsham Hall and Shawford House; *m* 22 June 1786 Sir HENRY PAULET ST JOHN later ST JOHN-MILDMAY, **3rd Bt**, MP (*see* below)

2g Anne; *m* 15 Nov 1794 John Clerke (*d* Oct 1842), of Worthy, Hants, and *d* 1820, leaving issue

3g Letitia; *m* 4 Nov 1791 George William Ricketts, of Lainstone, Hants, 27th child of George Ricketts, of Jamaica, and *d* 29 March 1839

1f Anne; *m* Sir William Mildmay, 1st and last Bt (*dsp* 8 Aug 1771), of Moulsham Hall, Essex, and *d* 28 March 1796

3 John, of Cretingham, Suffolk; ancestor of the extinct MILDMAYs of Terling

4 Walter (Sir), KG, PC, of Apethorpe, Northants, Danbury Place, Essex, and Hazlegrove, Queen Camel, Somerset; MP Northants, Chllr Exchequer *temp* ELIZABETH I, fndr Emmanuel Coll Cambridge; *m* 25 May 1546 Mary (*d* 16 March 1576), sis of Sir Francis Walsingham, Sec State to ELIZABETH I, and *d* 31 May 1589, leaving:

(1) Anthony (Sir), of Apethorpe; Amb Paris; *m* Grace (*d* 27 July 1620), dau of Sir Henry Sherington, of Lacock, Wilts, and *d* 11 Sept 1617, leaving:

1a Mary; *b c* 1582; *m* just after 15 Feb 1598/9 1st Earl of Westmorland (*qv*) and *d* 9 April 1640, leaving issue

(2) Humphrey, of Danbury Place and Hazlegrove; MP Peterborough, High Sheriff Essex 1594; *m* 10 July 1586 Mary (*d* 12 Oct 1633 aged 73), dau of Sir Henry Capell (*see* ESSEX, E), and *d* 9 Aug 1613, leaving:

1a Humphrey (Sir), of Danbury Place and Hazlegrove; *m* July 1616 June, 3rd dau of Sir John Croftes, of W Stow and Saxham Parva, and had issue, now extinct

2a Anthony; attended CHARLES I during his imprisonment by Parl; had issue, now extinct

3a Henry (Sir), of Wanstead, Essex, and Shawford House, Twyford, Hants; MP Maldon, Sewer, Master Jewel House and Ch Steward Maldon *temp* JAMES I and CHARLES I; *m* 6 April 1619 Anne (*d* 12 March 1656/7), dau and coheir of William Halliday, London Alderman, of Stoke Newington, by Susan (dau of Sir Henry Rowe, Ld Mayor London, and later w of 2nd Earl of Warwick of the 1618 *cr*), and *d c* 1664/5, having had:

1b Henry, of Shawford House and Stoke Newington; High Sheriff Hants 1669; *m* 30 Aug 1674 Alice (*d* 20 Jan 1691/2), dau of Sir Moundiford Bramston, and *d* by 14 March 1704, having had:

1c Halliday; *b* 1675; *educ* Balliol Coll Oxford; *m* Ann (*d* between 20 July 1698 and 15 Feb 1699), dau of Sir John Bawden, and *dvp, bur* 21 Nov 1696, leaving:

1d Letitia, of Shawford House and Mildmay Park, Stoke Newington; *bapt* 17 Aug 1694; *m* her cousin Humphrey Hervey Mildmay and had issue (*see* above)

1 Maria; *m* Sir William Brouncker, of Wilts

2 Winifred; *m* Sir William Fitzwilliam (*d* 1618), of Milton, Northants, and Gaines Park, Essex, and *d* 10 Aug 1597 leaving issue (*see* 1970 edn FITZWILLIAM, E)

3 Christian; *m* 1st 1578 Charles Barrett (*dvp* 8 Aug 1584), s of Edward Barrett, of Belh(o)us(e), Aveley, Essex, and had:

(1) Sir EDWARD BARRETT, 1st and last Bt (NS), and 1st and last LORD BARRETT OF NEWBURGH (S), so *cr* 2 Oct 1628 and 17 Oct 1627 respectively (*i.e.*, made a Bt after having been made a peer, possibly a unique occurrence), PC (1628); *b* 21 June 1581; *educ* Queen's Coll Oxford and Lincoln's Inn; ktd 1608, MP Whitchurch 1614 and Newport, Cornwall, 1621–22, Amb Paris 1625, Chllr Exchequer 1628–29, Chllr Duchy Lancaster 1629–44, a Ld Treasury 1641–43, royalist Civil War; *m* 1st between 22 April and 3 May 1608 Jane (*dspm, bur* 2 Jan 1632/3), sis of 1st Viscount of Falkland (*qv*); *m* 2nd Aug 1635 Catharine, dau of Hugh Fenn, of Wotton-under-Edge, Glos, and widow of Hugh Perry, London Alderman, and *dsps* and was *bur* 2 Jan 1644/5, when his titles expired, leaving his Essex and Norfolk properties to his cousin Richard LENNARD later BARRETT (*see* above, also DACRE, B)

3 (cont.) Mrs Barrrett *m* 2nd Sir John Leveson and had issue (*see* SUTHERLAND, D)

Lineage (of St John): WILLIAM ST JOHN (s by his 2nd w of John St John, of Lydiard Tregoze and Farley Chamberlayne; *see* BOLINGBROKE and SAINT JOHN, V); *b* 1 Aug 1538; MP Stockbridge, High Sheriff Hants 1588; *m* Barbara (*bur* 3 Jan 1613/4), dau and heiress of Thomas Gore, of Nether Wallop, Hants and widow of Thomas Twyne, of Norton St Valery, Wonston, and *d* 18 April 1609, leaving:

HENRY ST JOHN, of Farley Chamberlayne and Norton St Valery; *b* 1586–69; MP Stockbridge 1588–89; *m* Ursula, dau of Hugh Stukeley, of Marsh, Dunster, Somerset, and *d* by 21 June 1621, leaving:

1 John, of Farley Chamberlayne and Norton St Valery; *m* Susanna (*d* 5 May 1628), dau of Sir Richard Gifforde, of King's Somborne, and *d* 7 Sept 1627, having had a s (*d* an infant 26 Feb 1627/8)

2 Oliver, of Farley Chamberlayne; *b* 27 Feb 1608; *m* Constance (*d* 14 Sept 1666), est dau of Walter Dawley, of Ibsley, Hants, and *d* 31 July 1665, leaving:

(1) Oliver, of Farley Chamberlayne; MP Stockbridge 1688–89; *m* Margery (*d* 27 June 1681), dau and coheir of Francis Rivet, of King's Somborne, MP Stockbridge, and *d* 26 Aug 1689, leaving a s (Oliver, *b* 8 Feb 1678/9, *educ* Balliol Coll Oxford, *d* unm 20 May 1699) and dau (Frances, *m* her cousin Ellis Mew(y)s; *see* below)

(1) Christian; *bapt* 16 Oct 1643; *m* 4 Oct 1666 Ellis Mew(y)s (*d* 12 Feb 1680), Recorder Romsey, Mayor Winchester 1685–86, s of Richard Mews, of Winchester, and was *bur* 26 June 1709, leaving:

1a Ellis MEW(Y)S later ST JOHN (Act of Parl 1701); *b* 1670; *m* 1st 6 Dec 1699 his 1st cousin Frances (*dsp* 15 March 1700; *see* above); *m* 2nd 31 Jan 1703 Martha (*bur* 8 March 1725), dau and eventual heiress of Edward Goodyear, Ld Manor Dogmersfield, Hants, and by her had, with other issue:

1b PAULET (Sir), **1st Bt**

2b Ellis (Rev); *b* 28 Feb 1705; Rector Finchampstead, Ld Manor Finchampstead W Court; *m* Elizabeth (*d* 1797), dau of John Pollen (*see* POLLEN, Bt), and *d* 17 Feb 1786, leaving issue

3b Goodyer; *b* 1719; High Sheriff Hants 1775; *d* 1778/9, ancestor of the extinct ST JOHNs of Mottisfont

1b Hester; *b* 1707; *m* John Pollen and had issue (*see* POLLEN, Bt)

1a (cont.) Ellis ST JOHN *m* 3rd 1726 Sarah, Ldy Manor of Marsh, Dunster, Somerset (*m* 3rd Capt Francis Townshend, Coldstream Gds, and was *bur* 27 April 1760 aged 76), 2nd dau of Sir Hugh Stukeley, 2nd Bt, of Hinton Ampner, Hants, and Marsh, and widow of Rev John Cobb, DD, Warden Winchester Coll, and *d* 19 Jan 1729, leaving no issue by her

His est s,

Sir Paulet St John, 1st Bt (GB), so *cr* 9 Oct 1772; *b* 7 April 1704; High Sheriff Hants 1728, MP Winchester 1734–41 and 1751–54 and Hants 1741–47, Mayor Winchester 1771; *m* 1st 17 Aug 1731 Elizabeth (*dsp* 21 Dec 1733), dau and heiress of Sir James Rushout, 2nd Bt (*see* 1887 edn NORTHWICK, B); *m* 2nd 1 Oct 1736 Mary (*d* 17 Dec 1758), widow of Sir Halswell Tynte, 3rd Bt (*see* WHARTON, B), and dau and heiress of John Waters, of Brecknock; *m* 3rd 27 Jan 1761 Jane (*dsp* 26 Jan 1791 aged 85), dau and heiress of Roger Harris, of Silksted, Hants, MP Southampton, and widow of William Pescod, Recorder Winchester, and *d* 9 June 1780, leaving by his 2nd w, with other issue:

Sir Henry Paulet St John, 2nd Bt; *b* July 1737; *educ* New Coll Oxford (MA); ktd 1760, MP Hants 1772–80; *m* 27 Oct 1763 Dorothy Maria (*d* 26 May 1768 aged 26), dau and eventual heiress of Abraham Tucker, of Betchworth Castle, Surrey, and *d* 7 Aug — leaving:

Sir HENRY PAULET ST JOHN later ST JOHN-MILDMAY (roy licence 8 Dec 1790), **3rd Bt**; *b* 30 Sept 1764; *educ* St John's Coll Cambridge (MA 1785); High Sheriff Hants 1787, MP Westbury 1796–1802, Winchester 1802–07 and Hants 1807–08, Mayor Winchester 1798; *m* 22 June 1786 Jane (*d* 6 May 1857 aged 92), est dau and coheir of Carew Mildmay (*see* **Lineage (of Mildmay)**) above), and *d* 11 Nov 1808, having had, with other issue:

1 **Sir Henry St John Carew St John-Mildmay, 4th Bt**; *b* 15 April 1787; MP Winchester 1807–18, Mayor Winchester 1808, Kt Order St Joachim; *m* 1st 7 Aug 1809 Charlotte (*d* 5 Aug 1810), est dau of Hon Bartholomew Bouverie (*see* RADNOR, E), and had:

(1) **Sir Henry Bouverie Paulet St John-Mildmay, 5th Bt**, JP, DL Hants; *b* 31 July 1810; Maj 2nd Dragoon Gds, Col Hants Yeo, High Sheriff Hants 1862; *m* 6 Feb 1851 Hon Helena Shaw-Lefevre (*d* 15 Sept 1897), 2nd dau of 1st and last Viscount Eversley (*see* 1888 edn), and *d* 16 July 1902, leaving:

1a **Sir Henry Paulet St John-Mildmay, 6th Bt**, JP Hants; *b* 28 April 1853; Maj Gren Gds, Egypt 1882 (medal and clasp), Suakim Expdn 1885 (despatches); *d* unm 24 April 1916

2a Sir GERALD ANTHONY ST JOHN-MILDMAY later SHAW-LEFEVRE-ST JOHN-MILDMAY (roy licence 20 Feb 1900 under terms of will of his gf 1st and last Viscount Eversley), **7th Bt**, JP; *b* 30 Oct 1860; Lt Hants Yeo Cav; *m* 19 Oct 1892 his cousin Isabel Emily (*d* 8 April 1950), 2nd dau of Rev Charles Arundell St John-Mildmay (*see* below), and *d* 22 Feb 1929, having had:

1b Sir ANTHONY SHAW-LEFEVRE-ST JOHN-MILDMAY later ST JOHN-MILDMAY (deed poll 15 Dec 1921), **8th Bt**, MC; *b* 13 Aug 1894; *educ* Eton and RMC Sandhurst; Capt Res Offrs Gren Gds WW I (wounded twice); *m* 1st 18 Dec 1920 (*divorce* 1933) Violet Vane (*d* 9 Nov 1981 aged 84), dau of Col Arthur William Henry Hay-Drummond of Cromlix (*see* KINNOULL, E); *m* 2nd 26 May 1934 (*divorce* 1942) Mrs Beatrice May Dickeson and *d* 3 Oct 1947, leaving by his 1st w:

1c **Sir Henry Gerald St John-Mildmay, 9th Bt**; *b* 17 April 1926; *educ* Eton; Lt Gren Gds; *d* unm 4 Nov 1949

2b Peter Henry Arundell; *b* 1, *d* 21 Jan 1905

1b Helena; *m* 28 April 1930 Col Michael Wallington, MC, Roy Sussex Regt, and *d* 19 March 1943

3a Carew Hervey Mary; *b* 30 March 1863; *educ* Trin Coll Cambridge (MA); Rector Aldham, Essex, and St Mary's, Stamford, Lincs, CF Boer War 1901–02 (medal); turned RC 1923; *m* 14 Aug 1912 Elizabeth Catherine (*d* 18 Jan 1942), yst dau of Sir Henry Roper (*see* TEYNHAM, B), and *d* 21 Nov 1937

1a Jane Emma; *b* 12 Dec 1851; *m* 24 April 1889 James Martin Carr-Lloyd (*d* 8 June 1919), of Lancing Manor, Sussex, and *dsp* 29 April 1928

2a Helena Charlotte; *b* 18 Dec 1854; *d* 4 April 1867

3a Laura Catherine; *b* 18 June 1856; *d* 29 April 1866

4a Constance Mary; *b* 30 March 1859; *m* 1st 5 April 1888 John Arthur Beach Wallington (*d* 6 Nov 1901), est s of Col Sir John Wallington, KCB, and had issue; *m* 2nd 17 April 1912 Lt-Col Algernon Forbes Randolph, CMG, DSO, DL (*d* 7 Feb 1953), yst s of Canon Randolph, Chllr York Minster, and *d* 17 Dec 1930

1 (cont.) **Sir Henry** *m* 2nd 1815 at Stuttgart, by special permission of the KING OF WURTTEMBERG, his deceased w's sister Harriet (*d* 9 Dec 1834), and *d* 17 Jan 1848 , having by her had:

(2) Edmond Henry; *b* 1815; Equerry to TRH 1st and 2nd DUKEs OF CAMBRIDGE 1844–50 and 1850–1904 respectively, served Radetzky's Hus Austrian Army, Br Commr Austrian Army HQ (Austrian War Medal) 1859, Cdr Order of Dannebrog; *m* 1st 8 March 1851 Louisa Josephine (*d* 27 Jan 1865), widow of Clarence Wigney, and had, with other issue:

1a Edmond Cecil Henry Arundell; *b* 14 April 1858; *m* 27 Sept 1888 Edith May Agnew (*m* 2nd 1 Feb 1917 Richard Rodney Pope), yst dau of John Macaulay, of Red Hall, Co Antrim, and *dsp* 15 Sept 1889

1a Henrietta Louisa Horatia; *b* 1852; *m* 15 Feb 1876 Rev Thomas Legh Claughton (*d* 13 Oct 1915), Canon Worcester, bro of Sir Gilbert Claughton, 1st Bt (*see* 1920 edn), and *d* 16 Sept 1927, leaving issue

2a Alice Grace Josephine; *b* 30 Nov 1855; *m* 26 April 1887 Rev Winslow Sutherland Stayner (*d* 30 Oct 1932), of The Manor House, Ebford, Devon, and *d* 22 Dec 1943, leaving issue

(2) (cont.) Edmond St John-Mildmay *m* 2nd 11 May 1867 his cousin Augusta Jane (*d* 14 July 1892), est dau of Ven Carew Anthony St John-Mildmay and widow of William Coesvelt Kortright, and by her had, with two sons:

3a Evelyn Augusta; *m* 22 Aug 1892 her cousin Maj Charles Beague St John-Mildmay and *d* 7 Dec 1927, leaving issue (*see* above)

(2) (cont.) Edmond St John-Mildmay *m* 3rd 18 Feb 1896 Elizabeth Mary, only child of George Hall, CE, of Norwich, and *d* 8 Oct 1905 aged 90

(3) Horace Osborne; *b* 1817; Offr 5th of Hus Austrian Army; *m* 30 Jan 1844 Jane (*d* 10 Jan 1878), dau of Stephen Dornbach, Offr Austrian Army, and *d* 5 May 1866, having had, with three other sons:

1a Edward Stephen; *b* 29 Sept 1845; *m* 29 April 1875 Leopoldine (*d* 23 Sept 1915), dau of Gishert Kapp, Austrian State Counsellor, and *d* 18 July 1917, leaving:

1b Henry Edward; *b* 18 July 1877; barrister Milan Court Appeal and Supreme Court Rome, Cdr Order Crown Italy; *m* 8 March 1924 Felicie Gerdy Neumann, of Rome, and *dsp* 4 Dec 1944

2b Walter Richard; *b* 20 Dec 1888; *d* 30 July 1905

1b Helen Jane; *d* an infant 17 June 1885

2b Mary Fanny Lucy; *b* 21 Jan 1886; *m* 30 Nov 1907 (*divorce* 1912, resumed maiden name) Raoul Stucchi and *d* 5 June 1973

(4) Augustus Fitzwalter; Offr 7th Imp Hus; *d* unm 8 March 1839

2 Paulet; *b* 8 April 1791; Ld Manors Farley Chamberlayne, Hazlegrove and Queen Camel, Lt Coldstream Gds, Mayor Winchester 1818, MP Winchester 19 years; *m* 12 March 1813 Anna Maria Wyndham (*d* 11 Dec 1864), yst dau of Hon Bartholomew Bouverie, MP (*see* RADNOR, E), and *d* 19 May 1845, having had, with other issue:

(1) Paulet Henry, of Hazlegrove; *b* 26 Oct 1814; *m* 13 Nov 1849 Caroline Adela Catherine Valencia (*d* 8 Oct 1906), dau of Rowland Standish, and *dsp* 16 April 1858

(2) Hervey George, of Hazlegrove; *b* 19 April 1817; Capt RN; *m* 1st 22 Feb 1859 Hon Elizabeth Shaw-Lefevre (*d* 23 Dec 1867), yst dau of 1st and last Viscount Eversley, GCB (*see* 1888 edn), and had:

1a Florence Wyndham; *m* 1 June 1886 Rev Carleton Rashleigh (*d* 29 April 1938) and *d* 10 May 1906, having had issue

(2) (cont.) Hervey St John-Mildmay *m* 2nd 14 July 1875 Augusta Frances (*dsp* Feb 1910), est dau of Rev Richard Seymour (*see* CULME-SEYMOUR, Bt), and *d* 21 May 1882

(3) Charles Arundell (Rev), JP, of Hazlegrove; *b* 21 June 1820; MA Oxon, Fell Merton Coll Oxford; *m* 17 Jan 1854 Harriet Louisa (*d* 21 April 1907), dau of Very Rev Hon George Neville-Grenville (*see* BRAYBROOKE, B), and *d* 5 March 1904, leaving:

1a Wyndham Paulet, of Hazlegrove, JP; *b* 21 Jan 1855; Capt N Somerset Yeo Cav and Rifle Bde, Afghan War 1878–9, medal and clasp for Ali Musjed; *m* 27 July 1889 Hon Alice Katharine Hamilton-Russell (*d* 17 Nov 1959 aged 96), est dau of 8th Viscount Boyne (*qv*), and *d* 2 March 1934

2a George, JP Somerset; *b* 24 Feb 1856; *educ* Corpus Christi Coll Oxford (BA); barrister, Maj Somerset LI, Staff Capt 61st Bde and S Cmd, Maj Labour Corps WW I; *m* 3 Aug 1898 Grace Mary (*d* 20 Dec 1920), est dau of Percival L Hambro (*see* HAMBRO, B), and *dsp* 19 April 1931

3a Arundell Glastonbury (Rev); *b* 25 Feb 1859; *educ* Magdalene Coll Cambridge (MA); Vicar Old Wolverton, Bucks, RD Burnham Norfolk 1893–1901; *m* 2 Feb 1898 Alys (*d* 19 Feb 1947), yst dau of Philip Pleydell-Bouverie (*see* RADNOR, E), and *d* 19 June 1925, having had:

1b Bouverie Walter; *b* 25 Feb 1899; 2nd Lt RAF; *ka* 16 April 1918

4a Walter Hervey; *b* 19 April 1860; *educ* Charterhouse; Maj Assam Valley LH, Brevet Maj RFA WW I; *m* 25 Nov 1909 Cecil Frances, OBE (1920) (*d* 17 Nov 1951), yr dau of Cecil Francis Gwyer, and *dsp* 21 Oct 1929

5a Paulet Bertram; *b* 27 June 1862; *educ* Winchester and Oxford; Lt 1st Vol Bn Wilts Regt WW I; *m* 30 Aug 1893 Selina Jane (*d* July 1925), dau of Rev Evelyn Harcourt-Vernon (*see* VERNON, B), and *dsp* 10 April 1943

6a **Rev Sir (Aubrey) Neville St John-Mildmay, 10th Bt**; *b* 14 Feb 1865; *educ* Winchester and New Coll Oxford (Scholar 1884, BA 1888, MA 1895); Vicar Pentleton, BC, 1906–07, Lecturer Classics and Philosophy U of BC Vancouver 1917–24, versifier and theological writer; *m* 24 Feb 1902 Louisa Jane (*d* 16 Feb 1940), formerly w of — Oliver and yr dau of John Barrett Maunder, of Johannesburg, and *d* 30 March 1955, having had:

1b Neville Arundell; *b* 4 May; *d* 18 May 1903

2b Walter Maunder; *b* 4 May, *d* 19 May 1903

3b VERUS ARUNDELL MAUNDER, *de jure* 11th Bt; *b* 6 Jan 1906; *m* 7 May 1943 *Marian [Mrs Verus St John-Mildmay, 5480 Blenheim St, Vancouver, BC, Canada], dau of Murdock Ross, and *dsp* 29 Nov 1965 without having claimed the btcy

1b Grace Audrey Louisa; *b* 19 Dec 1900; *m* 4 June 1931 John Christie, CH, MC (*d* 4 July 1962), of Glyndebourne, Sussex, only s of Augustus Langham Christie, of Glyndebourne and Tapley Park, Devon, and *d* 31 May 1953, leaving issue

7a Humphrey; *b* 28 July 1868; *d* 22 May 1872

1a Charlotte Agnes; *b* 1858; *d* unm 9 March 1882

2a Isabel Emily; *m* 19 Oct 1892 her cousin Sir GERALD ANTHONY SHAW-LEFEVRE-ST JOHN-MILDMAY, **7th Bt**, and *d* 8 April 1950, having had issue

3a Meriel Hariet Caroline; *d* unm 13 Oct 1937

3 George William; *b* 20 April 1792; Capt RN; *m* 28 April 1832 Mary (*d* 17 Jan 1892 in her 90th year), widow of John Morritt, of Rokeby Park, and dau of Peter Baillie of Dochfour, MP (*see* BURTON, B), and *d* 14 Feb 1851, leaving:

    (1) Herbert Alexander, MVO; *b* 20 July 1836; Lt-Col Rifle Bde; *m* 7 May 1884 Susan Margaret Stackpole (*d* 27 May 1918), dau of Hon John Lothrop Motley, DCL, US Min to UK, and *d* 21 Oct 1922

    (1) Geraldine Mary; *m* 5 Jan 1858 Alfred Buckley (*d* 15 Dec 1900), of New Hall, Wilts, est s of Maj-Gen — Buckley, MP, and *d* 13 Dec 1912, leaving issue

4 Humphrey; *b* 11 July 1794; Capt Coldstream Gds Peninsular War, MP Southampton, Dir Bank England; *m* 1st 27 Sept 1823 Hon Anne Eugenia Baring (*d* 8 March 1839), est dau of 1st Baron Ashburton (*qv*), and had:

    (1) Humphrey Francis ; *b* 25 Dec 1825; MP Herefs 1859 on; *m* June 1861 Sybella Harriet (*d* 10 June 1869 4th Lord Lyttelton, Baron of Frankley (*see* COBHAM, V), and *d* 9 Dec 1900), er dau of George Clive, MP, of Perrystone Court, Herefs, and *dsp* 29 Nov 1866

    (2) Henry Bingham ST JOHN-MILDMAY later MILDMAY, JP, DL (Kent, Devon), of Shoreham Place, Kent, and Flete, Devon; *b* 19 June 1828; High Sheriff Devon 1886; *m* 24 July 1860 Georgiana Frances (*d* 2 July 1899), dau of John Crocker Bulteel, of Flete, by Lady Elizabeth Grey, dau of 2nd Earl Grey (*qv*), and *d* 1 Nov 1905, having had:

        1a FRANCIS BINGHAM MILDMAY, 1st BARON MILDMAY OF FLETE, of Totnes, Co Devon (UK), so *cr* 20 Nov 1922, TD, PC (1916), JP Devon; *b* 26 April 1861; *educ* Eton and Trin Coll Cambridge (BA 1885); MP Totnes 1885–1922, Lt-Col W Kent Yeo, Boer War 1900 and personal staff WW I (despatches four times), dir GWR, Pres Roy Ag Soc England 1932, memb: Managing Bd Middx Hosp, Exec Ctee Nat U Assoc, Cncl and Revenue Ctee King Edward's Hosp Fund London and Nat Hunt Ctee 1937, memb and treas Medical Research Cncl, Ld Lt Devon 1928–36; *m* 26 July 1906 Alice Lilian, OStJ (*d* 22 March 1960), 2nd dau of Charles Seymour Grenfell (*see* GRENFELL, B), and *d* 8 Feb 1947, leaving:

            1b ANTHONY BINGHAM MILDMAY, 2nd and last BARON MILDMAY OF FLETE; *b* 14 April 1909; *educ* Eton and Trin Coll Cambridge (BA 1930); memb Nat Hunt Ctee 1938, gentleman rider, Capt RA (TA), Welsh Gds, WW II (despatches), Govr Roy Vet Coll, memb Cncl Roy Ag Soc England; drowned unm while bathing 12 May 1950, when the Barony expired

            1b *Helen Winifred, JP (Devon 1952) [Mrs John Mildmay-White, Pamflete, Holbeton, Devon]; ARRC; *m* 29 Sept 1945 Lt-Cdr (Richard) John Bramble WHITE later MILDMAY-WHITE (deed poll March 1958), RNR (*d* 10 Dec 1969), s of Cdr (S) Richard Ernest White, RN, of Bickington, Devon, and has:

                1c *Anthony John Bramble; *b* 10 Feb 1948; *educ* Eton

                1c *Richard Francis Bingham; *b* 17 Oct 1949; *educ* Eton; *m* 10 Nov 1973 *Sara J, 2nd dau of I K Cleland, of Southbury Farm, Colesbourne, Glos

                1c *Elizabeth Georgiana; *b* 3 Jan 1947; *m* 16 Sept 1967 (John) Valentine Lewthwaite (*d* 1990; *see* LEWTHWAITE, Bt) and has issue

        2a Robert; *b* 16 Feb, *d* 9 March 1864

        3a John; *b* 24 April 1868; *educ* Eton and Trin Coll Cambridge; *d* unm 2 Jan 1947

        4a Alfred; *b* 10 Aug 1871; sr ptnr Baring Bros; *d* unm 26 Oct 1944

        5a Alexander Richard; *b* 5 March 1873; Capt KRRC Boer War; *ka* 17 Sept 1901

        1a Helen Georgiana; *bapt* 1862; *d* 16 July 1871

        2a Mary Elizabeth; *b* 17 Sept 1866; *d* 1 Jan 1867

        3a Beatrice; *b* 11 Aug 1876; *d* unm 8 Dec 1952

4 (cont.) Humphrey St John-Mildmay *m* 2nd 20 Sept 1843 Marianne Frances (*d* 13 Feb 1873), only dau of Granville Harcourt-Vernon, MP (*see* VERNON, B), and *d* 9 Aug 1853, having by her had:

    (1) Lucy Frances Jane; *m* 15 Sept 1868 Capt James Thomas Richard Lane Fox, JP, DL, Gren Gds (*d* 26 Feb 1906), of Bramham Park, Yorks, and *d* 19 March 1920, leaving issue

    (2) Emily Mary; *d* 13 Sept 1920

    (3) Alice Catherine; *m* 23 Oct 1873 Capt Hon Henry Hervey Molyneux, RN (*dsp* 23 Sept 1915), s of 3rd Earl of Sefton (*see* 1970 edn), and *d* 12 Sept 1934 aged 82

5 John Francis; *b* 8 Dec 1795; Capt RN; *d* 1 Sept 1823

6 Edward; *b* 7 July 1797; Cornet 22nd Light Dragoons, Capt 10th Foot; *m* 1st 11 June 1818 (*divorce* July 1830) Marianne Catherine, dau of R Sherson, and had:

    (1) Edward Wheatley; *b* 24 Sept 1822; *d* 16 July 1840

    (2) Arthur George; *b* 3 Feb 1824; *m* 1st 6 Nov 1848 Louisa Latham (*d* 5 May 1855), dau of Capt Henry Gough Ord, RA, and had:

        1a Edward Arthur; *b* 8 Nov 1852; *educ* Trin Coll Cambridge (BA 1875); *d* unm 8 Dec 1876

    (2) (cont.) Arthur St John-Mildmay *m* 2nd Aug 1856 Charlotte Mary (*d* 1 June 1908), widow of Maj John Douglas Halkett, 4th Light Dragoons, and dau of Charles Heard Beague, RE, of Hollam House, Somerset, and *d* 8 March 1883, having by her had:

        2a Charles Beague, JP, DL Somerset; *b* 13 Jan 1861; Capt RA Boer War 1900–01 (medal with clasps), Maj Somerset RHA; *m* 22 Aug 1892 Evelyn Augusta (*d* 7 Dec 1927), dau of Capt Edmond St John-Mildmay (*see* below), and *d* 27 Sept 1923, having had:

            1b Dorothy; *d* 18 Dec 1908

            2b Letitia; *b* 1895; *m* 14 Oct 1922 (*divorce* 1952) Cdr Denys Shoppee, DSC, RN, s of Gerald Shoppee, LLD, and *dsp* 31 July 1968

        3a John Walter Paulet; *b* 1 Nov 1866; *educ* Emmanuel Coll Cambridge (BA); *m* 22 Aug 1894 Bertha Mabel (*d* 24 May 1950), 2nd dau of Joachim Theodor Satow, and *d* 16 Jan 1913, leaving:

1b Michael Paulet; *b* 6 May 1901; *educ* Emmanuel Coll Cambridge (BA 1923, MA 1927); *m* 2 Aug 1933 Joan Elizabeth (*d* 29 Jan 1977) dau of Brig-Gen Hugh Roderick Stockley, CIE, of Alkerton Grange, Eastington, Glos, and *d* 1993, leaving:

    1c Sir WALTER JOHN HUGH ST JOHN-MILDMAY, **12th and present Bt**

    2c +MICHAEL HUGH PAULET [Michael St John-Mildmay Esq, Drakestone House, Stinchcombe, Dursley, Glos]; *b* 28 Sept 1937; heir presumptive; *educ* Wycliffe Coll and Emmanuel Coll Cambridge (BA 1961); peripatetic teacher Bilingual Sch Cameroon and U of Libya, Tripoli; *m* 26 Sept 1965 *Crystal Margaret — and has:

        1d +Henry Walter; *b* 1971

        2d +Oliver James; *b* 1973

        1d *Emilia Alice Joan; *b* 1977

    2c (cont.) MICHAEL ST JOHN-MILDMAY also adopted his w's dau by her former husb — Ludlow:

        *Erica Greer

    1b Lorna Winifred; *b* 1895

    1a Alice Frances; *b* 23 May 1857; *d* 9 July 1922

    2a Edith Charlotte; *m* 2 Nov 1889 James Archibald Gordon Hamilton (*d* 21 Dec 1906), barrister, and *dsp* 25 Oct 1940

    3a Emma Magdalen; *m* 14 June 1894 Albert Edward Bles (*d* 1943), yr s of David Joseph Bles, of The Hague, and *dsp* 30 March 1949

    4a Letitia Elizabeth; *b* 29 Dec 1867; *d* unm 21 June 1903

    (1) Marianne Jane; *m* 22 April 1847 Charles George Barnett and *d* 1883

    (2) Jane Catherine; *m* 19 April 1849 Rev Evelyn Harcourt-Vernon (*d* 26 Jan 1890) and *d* 15 May 1891, leaving issue (*see* VERNON, B)

6 (cont.) Edward St John-Mildmay *m* 2nd 30 July 1835 Frances Lucy Penelope (*d* 23 Jan 1862), dau of Edward Lockwood Percival, of Dews Hall, Essex, and *d* 16 May 1868, having by her had:

    (3) Fanny Percival; *d* March 1845

7 Walter (Rev); *b* 12 Oct 1798; Rector Mottistone and Shorwell, IOW, Rector Dogmersfield, Hants; *m* 17 July 1834 Kitty Anne (*d* 6 April 1884 aged 87), only dau of Charles Warde, of Westerham, Kent, and *d* 31 July 1835

8 Carew Antony (Ven); *b* 2 Feb 1800; Rector Shorwell and Chelmsford, Essex, Vicar Burnham-on-Crouch, Archdeacon Essex; *m* 16 Dec 1830 Hon Caroline Waldegrave (*d* 7 Jan 1878), dau of 1st Baron Radstock (*see* WALDEGRAVE, E), and *d* 13 July 1878, leaving, with other issue:

    (1) Augusta Jane; *m* 1st William Coesvelt Kortright (*d* July 1863); *m* 2nd Capt Edmond Henry St John-Mildmay (*see* above) and *d* 14 July 1892

    (2) Horatia Louisa; *m* 5 Oct 1858 Pascoe Charles Glyn (*see* WOLVERTON, B) and *d* 15 Nov 1858

1 Jane Dorothea; *b* 11 April 1788; *m* 31 July 1810 1st Baron Methuen (*qv*) and *d* 15 March 1846

2 Maria; *b* 2 April 1790; *m* 3 June 1812 her distant cousin 4th Viscount Bolingbroke and (5th Viscount) St John (*qv*) and *d* 21 Dec 1836

3 Judith Anne; *b* 2 April 1790; *m* 24 May 1814 3rd Earl of Radnor (*qv*) and *d* 27 April 1851

SAINT LEVAN

Arms: Erm. on a cross gu. five bezants, a bordure wavy of the second. **Crest:** A rock, thereon a Cornish chough rising ppr., debruised by a bendlet wavy sinister erm. **Supporters:** On either side a lion or, each gorged with a chain sa., therefrom pendant an escutcheon, the dexter per fess az. and arg., in chief a naval crown encircled by two branches of oak in saltire slipped or and in base a ship in frame ppr., the sinister sa. charged with five bezants in cross. **Motto:** *In se teres* ('Exact in himself'). **Creations:** Bt. (UK) 31 July 1866, B. (UK) 4 July 1887.

THE 4TH BARON SAINT LEVAN OF SAINT MICHAEL'S MOUNT, Co Cornwall, and a **Baronet** (Sir John Francis Arthur St Aubyn, Bt, DSC (1944)) [The Rt Hon The Lord St Levan DSC, St Michael's Mount, Marazion, Cornwall TR17 0HT]; *b* 23 Feb 1919; *s f* 1978; *educ* Eton and Trin Coll Cambridge (BA 1940); Lt

RNVR WW II, slr 1948, Cornwall: High Sheriff 1974, V-Lt 1992–94 (DL 1977–92), Pres: Friends Plymouth City Museums and Art Gallery 1985–, St Ives Soc of Artists, Cornwall Maritime Tst 1995–, Cornwall Ch Action for the Unemployed 1978–, Cornwall Br Isles of Scilly District Scouts 1990–, W Cornwall Br Sail Training Assoc 1994– and Penwith Nat Tst Assoc 1987–; V-Pres: Roy Bath and SW Cos Soc 1984– (Pres 1983), Roy Cornwall Ag Assoc 1980– (Pres 1979); Patron: Cornwall Br-Normandy Veterans Assoc 1996– and Penzance Sea Cadets 1992–; author *Illustrated History of St Michael's Mount*; Bard of Cornwall; KStJ 1997, FRSA 1974; *m* Dec 1970 *Susan Mary Marcia, yr dau of Maj-Gen Sir John Noble Kennedy, GMCG, KCVO, KBE, CB, MC (*see* EXETER, M)

Lineage: GEOFFREY ST AUBYN; living *temp* HENRY IV; *m* Elizabeth, dau of Piers Kymyel, of Clowance, Cornwall, and had:

GEOFFREY ST AUBYN, of Clowance; gf of:

THOMAS ST AUBYN, of Clowance; Sheriff Cornwall *c* 1546; *m* Mary, dau of Sir Thomas Grenville, of Stow, Cornwall, and had:

JOHN ST AUBYN, of Clowance; Sheriff Cornwall *c* 1567; *m* Blanche, dau of Thomas Whittington, and had:

THOMAS ST AUBYN, of Clowance; *m* — Mal(l)et and had an est s:

JOHN ST AUBYN; *b* 1610; High Sheriff Cornwall *c* 1635; *m* Catharine, dau of Sir John Arundell, of Trerice, and had an est s:

JOHN ST AUBYN, of Clowance; *b c* 1610; MP, High Sheriff Cornwall 1666–67; *m* Catharine, dau of Francis Godolphin, of Treveneage, Cornwall, and *d* Aug 1684, having had an est s:

Sir JOHN ST AUBYN, 1st Bt (E), so *cr* 11 Dec 1671; *b* 6 April 1645; *educ* Exeter Coll Oxford; MP St Michael 1679–81; *m* 14 Nov 1665 Anne (*m* 2nd 15 Oct 1696 William Spencer, of Lancs; *m* 3rd 22 July 1708 Richard Page, of Harrow, and *d* by 1712), dau of James Jenkyn, of Trekenning, Cornwall, and *d* 1687, leaving, without other issue:

Sir JOHN ST AUBYN, 2nd Bt, of Clowance; *bapt* 13 June 1670; MP Helston 1689–95, High Sheriff Cornwall 1704–05; *m* 22 May 1695 Mary, dau of Peter Delahay, and *d* 20 June 1714, leaving, with other issue:

Sir JOHN ST AUBYN, 3rd Bt, of Clowance; *b c* 1703; *educ* Exeter Coll Oxford; MP Cornwall 1722–44; *m* 3 Oct 1725 Catherine, dau of Sir Nicholas Morice, 2nd Bt, of Wetherington, Devon (*see* PEMBROKE and MONTGOMERY, E), and was *bur* 28 Aug 1744, leaving, with four daus (Catharine, *d* unm; Mary, *m* John Buller, of Morral; Margaret, *m* Francis Bassett; Barbara, *m* Sir John Molesworth, 5th Bt, and had issue; *see* MOLESWORTH-ST AUBYN, Bt):

Sir JOHN ST AUBYN, 4th Bt, of Clowance; *b* 12 Nov 1726; *educ* Oriel Coll Oxford; MP Launceston 1747–54 and 1758–59 and Cornwall 1761–72; *m* 4 June 1756 Elizabeth (*m* 2nd 5 Oct 1782 John Baker, of Orsett, Essex), dau of William Wingfield, of Washington, Co Durham (*see* WILLIAMSON, Bt), and *d* 12 Nov 1772, having had:

1 Sir JOHN ST AUBYN, 5th and last Bt, of Clowance; *b* 17 May 1758; High Sheriff Cornwall 1781–82, MP Truro Feb–March 1784, Penrhyn 1784–90 and Helston 1807-12, FRS, FSA, FLS; *m* 1 July 1822 Juliana Vinicombe and *dspl* 10 Aug 1839, when the btcy expired, having had by her before their marriage, with three er sons, two yst sons and another dau:

(1) **Sir Edward St Aubyn, 1st Bt** (UK), so *cr* 31 July 1866, of St Michael's Mount, JP Cornwall; *b* 6 Nov 1799; inherited much of his f's estates; *m* 26 Jan 1828 Emma (*d* 3 March 1887 aged 81), dau of Gen William Knollys (*see* KNOLLYS, V, also below), and had issue (whose male-line males are in remainder to the btcy only):

1a JOHN, **1st Baron**

2a William; *b* 18 May 1831; *d* 6 Dec 1832

3a William (Rev); *b* 18 Jan 1834; Rector Stoke Damerell, Preb Exeter; *m* 29 Oct 1868 Edith Emily (*d* 19 April 1920), dau of Edward Johnston, of Silwood Lodge, Berks, and *dsp* 5 July 1894

4a Edward, JP Devon, DL Cornwall; *b* 8 March 1837; BA Cantab; Col 3rd Bn DCLI, barrister, Dep Special Warden Stannaries; *m* 1st 19 April 1866 Edith (*d* 25 April 1875), 2nd dau of V-Adml Hon Keith Stewart, CB (*see* GALLOWAY, E), and had, with another s and a dau (*d* young):

1b Guy Stewart, OBE (1919); *b* 21 Nov 1870; Col KRRC, Isazai Expdn 1892, Mashonaland 1896, Boer War 1899–1900; *m* 4 July 1899 Florita Catherine (*d* 7 Sept 1925), yst dau of Pascoe Du Pré Grenfell (*see* GRENFELL, B), and *d* 25 April 1924, leaving:

1c Edward FitzRoy; *b* 12 March 1907; S/Ldr AAF, Lt Gren Gds Res Offrs, WW II; *m* 28 Sept 1933 Eileen Margaret (Nancy) (*d* 21 Dec 1959), 3rd dau of Ferdinand Richard Holmes Meyrick, MD, of Kensington, and was *ka* off the coast of Holland 27 May 1943

1c Barbara Edith; *b* 25 March 1904; *m* 10 Oct 1924 Maj Donald Victor Charles McBarnet, Scots Gds, s of Alexander McBarnet, and had issue. He was *ka* 28 Feb 1944

2c *Juliet Mary; *b* 16 Sept 1905; *m* 6 Oct 1925 Maj William Eustance Pitt Miller, Gren Gds (Res), only s of Capt William Pitt Miller, of Thistleton, Lancs, and has:

1d *Robin; *b* 15 Feb 1928; *educ* Eton; late Lt Gren Gds, coauthor musicals *Vanity Fair, Dames At Sea*, etc

2d *Timothy Hugh; *b* 5 June 1937; *educ* Eton; late Lt Gren Gds

3c *Violet Susan May [Mrs Raymond Lort-Phillips, Camellia Cottage, Gorey Hill, Jersey, CI]; *b* 24 Feb 1909; *m* 17 Oct 1929 Capt Raymond Lort-Phillips, Scots Gds (*d* 1980), only s of Maj Frederick William Alfred Herbert Lort-Phillips, of Down Grange, Basingstoke, Hants, and has:

1d *Guy Stewart [Capt Guy Lort-Phillips, 6 Les Champs Farm, Grouville, Jersey, CI JE3 9AN]; *b* 21 Oct 1930; *educ* Eton and RMA Sandhurst; late Capt Welsh Gds, Count HRE; *m* 1st 21 Sept 1956 Norah Eugenie (*d* 1986), dau of Baron Hans Rodolphe de Jenner, of Château Landshüt, Berne, Switzerland, and formerly w of Patrick O'Leary; *m* 2nd 1996 *Jennifer Mary, dau of George Henry Darlow, of Kempstone, Beds, and formerly w of Robin Rumboll, and by his 1st w has:

1e *Piers Wickham; *b* 9 Aug 1957; *m* 1986 *Virginia, dau of Ronald Hodgson, of Vaucluse, Sydney, NSW, and has:

1f *Harry Burgess; *b* 1991

2e *Giles Raymond; *b* 18 Oct 1958; *m* 1985 *Kathleen, dau of Sydney Miles, of Randfontein, S Africa, and has:

1f *Guy Dylan; *b* 1986

2f *Ben Raymond; *b* 1988

3e *Edward St Aubyn; *b* 6 July 1966

2d *Peregrine Edward Grenfell; *b* 1937; *educ* Charterhouse and Trin Coll Cambridge (BA); slr 1962; *m* 1st 27 July 1963 (*divorce* 1981) Carolyn Diana Brougham, dau of George Andrew Brougham Docker; *m* 2nd 1984 his cousin *Lamorna (*m* 3rd 1990 Michael F Good), dau of Roger St Aubyn and formerly w of Capt David Julian Cotton, and *d* 1988, leaving by his 1st w:

1e *Penelope Samantha [Mrs Campbell Gordon, 8 Gerald Rd, London SW1W 9EQ]; *b* 17 Feb 1964; *m* 1994 *Campbell Gordon, yst s of Donald Gordon, CC, CMG, of Montreal, and has:

1f *Edward Peregrine Lysander; *b* 6 Nov 1997

2e *Venetia Nike; *b* 16 June 1968; *m* 22 Nov 1996 *Andrew Robin Eliot, yr s of Robin Francis Eliot, of Crowborough, E Sussex

3d *Anthony Frederick Fitzroy [Anthony Lort-Phillips Esq, 28 Midvale Rd, St Helier, Jersey, CI]; *b* 14 Oct 1944; *educ* Eton and RMA Sandhurst; Capt Gren Gds; *m* 1st 1971 Saranne Frances (*d* 1984), dau of James Harold Alexander, of Co Dublin, and formerly w of 10th Baron Calthorpe (*see* 1970 edn); *m* 2nd 1995 *Melanie Susan Clara Dargie, of Bryanston, S Africa, and by her has:

1e *Michaela Susan Alexandra; *b* 4 June 1991

4a (cont.) Col Edward St Aubyn *m* 2nd 25 Oct 1879 Eugenia Susannah (*d* 12 March 1886), widow of George Henry FitzRoy (*see* GRAFTON, D) and 2nd dau of David Barclay Chapman, and by her had:

2b Edward Geoffrey, DSO (1919), JP, DL Hants; *b* 10 Aug 1880; *educ* Eton and Trin Coll Cambridge; Col KRRC, Brig-Gen 1918–19, Col cmdg 128th Inf Bde 1928–32, served Boer War 1901–02, WW I (despatches), WW II with 8th (ND) Bn Hants Regt, Col cmdg New Forest Sector HG 1941–45, Chm Hants TAFA 1948, Croix de Guerre; *m* 4 July 1905 Beatrice Rosa Andalusia (*d* 16 April 1968), dau of John Edmond Audley Harvey, of lckwell Bury, Beds, and *d* 10 Dec 1960, leaving:

1c Roger; *b* 9 June 1906; *educ* Eton and RMC Sandhurst; Lt 4th Hus, MRCS Eng, LRCP Lond 1946; *m* 1st 26 June 1939 (*divorce* 1957) Baroness Sophie Helene von Puthon, 2nd dau of Baron Heinrich von Puthon, of Schloss Mirabell, Salzburg, and had:

1d *Lamorna Alice [Mrs Michael Good, Brick Kiln Cottage, Outwick, Hants SP6 2BT]; *b* 11 Feb 1944; *m* 1st 16 Jan 1965 (*divorce* 1983) David Julian Cotton, est s of Sir John Richard Cotton, KCMG, and has issue; *m* 2nd 1984 Peregrine Edward Grenfell Lort-Phillips (*d* 1988); *m* 3rd 5 April 1990 *Michael Frankland Good and by her 1st husb has:

1e *Caroline Mary Sophie [Mrs Julian Chamberlen, 11 Glenrosa St, London SW6 2QY]; *b* 20 Feb 1966; *m* 8 June 1990 *Julian Chamberlen, est s of Nicholas Chamberlen, and has:

1f *Ralph Hugo; *b* 4 April 1997

2d *Diana Mary [Mrs Daniel Romer-Lee, 35 Napier Ave, London SW6 3PS]; *b* 16 Nov 1945; *m* 1970 *Daniel Romer-Lee and has:

1e *Christopher Daniel; *b* 25 May 1972

1e *Serena Isabel Hilaria; *b* 20 March 1974

1c (cont.) Roger St Aubyn *m* 2nd 4 Aug 1957 (*divorce* 1968) Lorna, er dau of Capt Alastair Mackintosh, and *d* 1985, leaving by her:

1d +Edward [Edward St Aubyn Esq, Le Petit Canadeau, Le Plan du Castellet, Var 83330, France]; *b* 14 Jan 1960; *m* 1987 (*divorce* 1990) Nicola (*m* 2nd 1990 5th Marquess of Normanby, *qv*), yr dau of Milton Shulman

3d *Alexandra; *b* 11 Sept 1958

4a (cont.) Col Edward St Aubyn *m* 3rd 9 July 1891 Ada Mary (*d* 25 May 1948), only dau of Col Sir Robert Thomas White Thomson, KCB, of Broomford Manor, Devon, and *d* 11 Jan 1914, having by her had:

3b Morice Julian, MC; *b* 25 April 1892; Maj KRRC WW I (despatches); *ka* 23 March 1918

4b Erskine Knollys Heveningham, DSC; *b* 25 Sept 1898; Cdr RN, WW I (despatches), WW II; *ka* Battle of Java Sea March 1942

1b Hildegarde Ada; *b* 14 July 1894; *m* — Bruce

2b Bridget Catherine; *b* 16 May 1901; *m* 17 Oct 1922 Rev Arthur Gerald Sayer, Preb Bodmin, only s of Arthur Sayer, of Pett Place, Charing, Kent, and had issue

5a Edmund (Rev); *b* 9 May 1841; BA Oxon; Rector Babworth, Notts; *m* 21 Jan 1869 Alice Mary (*d* 3 June 1913), 3rd dau of Arthur Bastard Eastabrook Holdsworth, JP, of Widdicombe Ho, Devon, and *d* 2 April 1908, having had:

1b Edmund Holdsworth; *b* 24 May 1876; *d* 15 Feb 1877

2b Mervyn Launcelot; *b* 30 July 1877; Assist Inspr Bd Ag, served Boer War 1900; *d* unm 1 June 1910

1b Alice Muriel; *b* 3 March 1872; *m* 1st 30 July 1896 (*divorce* 1915) William Henry Mason, JP, DL (*dsp* 17 May 1936), of Morton Hall, Retford; *m* 2nd Henry Constable Curtis, of Budleigh Salterton, and *d* 12 March 1953

2b Elaine Rosalie; *b* 20 May 1874; *d* unm 23 July 1949

3b Margery Lettice; *b* 18 Oct 1883; *m* 21 April 1910 Edwin Routh Tomlinson and *d* 16 May 1958

4b Enid Gwendolen; *b* 12 Aug 1896; *d* unm 20 July 1955

1a Emma; *m* 19 Feb 1860 Adml Charles Wake (*see* WAKE, Bt) and *d* 15 March 1920, leaving issue

2a Juliana; *d* unm 17 Sept 1933

3a Catherine; *m* 14 April 1874 Sir Hereward Wake, 12th Bt (*qv*), and *d* 18 Jan 1944, leaving issue

(1) Elizabeth; *m* 1830 Gen William Knollys (*see* KNOLLYS, V) and had, with other issue:

    1a Emma; *b c* 1806; *m* her cousin **Sir Edward St Aubyn, 1st Bt** (*see* above), and had issue

2 Richard Thomas (Rev); *m* 1813 Frances, 2nd dau of Rev Fleming St John

1 Elizabeth; *m* Henry Prideaux and *d* 1804

2 Catherine; *m* 1790 Rev John Molesworth and had:

    (1) John MOLESWORTH later MOLESWORTH-ST AUBYN (Rev); inherited his unc the 5th and last Bt's estates; had issue (*see* MOLESWORTH-ST AUBYN, Bt)

3 Anne; *m* Robert White

4 Dorothy; *m* 1787 Sir Thomas Barrett-Lennard, 1st Bt (*qv*), and had issue

The 1st Bt *d* 30 Nov 1872; his est s,

JOHN ST AUBYN, **1st Baron Saint Levan of Saint Michael's Mount**, Co Cornwall (UK), so *cr* 4 July 1887, JP, DL Cornwall; *b* 23 Sept 1829; *educ* Eton and Trin Coll Cambridge; Special Deputy Warden of the Stannaries, MP W Cornwall 1858–85 and St Ives 1885–87, Hon Col 3rd Bn DCLI, Cdre Western Yacht Sqdn, Mayor Devonport 1890–91 and 1891–92; *m* 15 July 1856 Lady Elizabeth Clementina Townshend (*d* 18 Nov 1910), dau of 4th Marquess Townshend (*qv*), and *d* 14 May 1908, leaving:

1 JOHN TOWNSHEND ST AUBYN, **2nd Baron Saint Levan of Saint Michael's Mount**, CB (1908), CVO (1905), JP, DL Cornwall; *b* 23 Sept 1857; *educ* Eton and Trin Coll Cambridge; Gren Gds: joined 1878, ADC Egypt and Sudan (despatches, medal with clasp, bronze star) 1883–85, Suakin Epdn 1884, Nile Expdn 1884–86 (despatches, two clasps), ADC to Govr Hong Kong 1889–90, Capt and Brevet Maj 1890, Mil Sec to Govr-Gen Canada 1892–93, Lt-Col 1902, Cmded Gren Gds 1904–08, Col 1905, T/Brig-Gen WW I 1914–16, Hon Brig-Gen 1917, Staff Lt 1917–18, Hon Col Devon and Cornwall Heavy Bde RA, Hon Col Cornwall RGA, Dep Warden Stannaries, Order Red Eagle Prussia 2nd Cl; *m* 1st 23 June 1892 Lady Edith Hilaria Edgcumbe (*d* 3 April 1931), yst dau of 4th Earl of Mount Edgcumbe (*qv*), and had:

    (1) Marjory Katharine Elizabeth Alexandra; *b* 18 July 1893; *m* 27 Nov 1919 Hon John Holford Parker, 3rd s of 3rd Earl of Morley (*qv*), and had issue

    (2) Hilaria Lily; *b* 1 Nov 1894; *d* unm 29 Jan 1983

1 (cont.) The **2nd Baron** *m* 2nd 29 April 1933 Julia Georgiana Sarah (*d* 7 Feb 1938), widow of 2nd Earl of Dartrey (*see* 1933 edn) and dau of Sir George Orby Wombwell, 4th Bt (*qv*), and *d* 10 Nov 1940

2 Edward Stuart; *b* 30 Oct 1858; served Egypt 1882 (medal, bronze star), Boer War 1899–1900 (despatches twice, medal with three clasps), Maj Res Ofrs KRRC, Lt-Col cmdg 12th Bn, GSO 1914–15 WW I, KGStJ; *d* unm 30 Dec 1915, drowned in HMS *Persia*

3 Francis Michael; *b* 3 Nov 1859; Capt Rifle Bde Burmese War; *d* unm March 1895

4 Arthur James Dudley Stuart; *b* 5 Oct 1867; *m* 30 June 1894 Helen Kate (*d* 10 March 1948, having *m* 2nd 6 Oct 1904 Patrick James Crichton-Stuart; *see* BUTE, M)), dau of Dr J C Phillippo, of Jamaica, and *d* 30 Sept 1897, leaving:

    (1) FRANCIS CECIL, **3rd Baron**

5 Piers Stewart, JP Cornwall; *b* 11 April 1871; 2nd Lt KRRC, Boer War 1900, WW I; *d* of wounds recd in action 31 Oct 1914

6 Lionel Michael, MVO (1919); *b* 26 Feb 1878; *educ* Eton and Trin Coll Cambridge (BA 1900); Hon Attaché 1904–08, Equerry to HRH THE DUCHESS OF ALBANY 1910–22, Capt KRRC WW I (despatches), Chev Order Dannebrog, Cdr Luxemburg Order Oaken Crown; *m* 18 March 1915 Lady Mary Theresa Parker (*d* 2 Nov 1932), only dau of 3rd Earl of Morley (*qv*), and *d* 17 Sept 1965, having:

    (1) Michael John, MC; *b* 7 Jan 1916; Capt Oxon and Bucks LI WW II; *ka* Anzio 16 Feb 1944

    (2) Geoffrey Piers; *b* 11 April 1922; Lt-Cdr RN, WW II, Korea; *m* 17 May 1958 Valerie Elizabeth (*k* air crash 29 Feb 1964), only dau of W/Cdr Bertram William Trelawny Hare, RAF, of Curtisknowle, Totnes, S Devon, and was *k* with his w 29 Feb 1964, leaving:

        1a +Michael Piers; *b* 25 Feb 1959; *m* 1987 *Astrid E, dau of Richard Edward Walter Lumley, of Windlesham, Surrey, and has:

            1b +Thomas Piers; *b* 1991

            1b *Matilda Elizabeth; *b* 1994

            2b *Isabella Astrid; *b* 18 July 1996

        2a +Rupert Trelawny; *b* 21 Feb 1963

        1a *Camilla Elizabeth; *b* 14 Jan 1961; *m* 1988 *Jonathan Chaim Elichaoff, er s of Michael Elichaoff, of Finchley

    (3) +Thomas Edward, CVO (1993), DL (1984) [Maj Thomas St Aubyn CVO DL, Dairy House Farm, Ashford Hill, Berks RG19 8BL]; *b* 13 June 1923; *educ* Eton; Maj 60th Rifles WW II and Sudan Defence Force 1948–52; memb Gentlemen-at-Arms 1973 (Lt 1990–93), High Sheriff Hants 1979; *m* 21 Nov 1953 *Henrietta Mary, only dau of Sir Henry Gray Studholme, 1st Bt, CVO, MP (*qv*), and has:

        1a *Sarah Elizabeth; *b* 28 June 1955; *m* 1983 *Hugh Adrian Bethell (*see* RADNOR, E)

        2a *Caroline Mary [Mrs Andrew Llewellyn, Church Acre, Rhode Lane, Uplyme, Dorset]; *b* 12 Sept 1957; *m* 1980 *Andrew H Llewellyn

        3a *Judith Clare; *b* 14 Sept 1962

1 Elizabeth Blanche Emma; *m* 22 July 1891 Capt Hon Otway Seymour Cuffe, Rifle Bde, of Sheestown Lodge, Kilkenny (*dsp* 3 Jan 1912), 3rd s of 3rd Earl of Desart (*see* 1935 edn) and *d* 18 Dec 1941

2 Evelyn Catherine; *d* young 22 Oct 1862

3 Audrey Catherine; *m* 10 June 1893 Sydney Alexander Ponsonby and *d* 11 Sept 1936, having had issue (*see* BESSBOROUGH, E)

4 Evelyn Ethelreda; *m* 25 Sept 1895 Nelson Chapman Alcock, s of Henry Alcock (*d* 13 June 1900), of Berscote, Warwicks, and *d* 7 Oct 1934, leaving issue

5 Eleanor Clementina; *m* 2 Jan 1896 4th Earl Amherst (*see* 1970 edn) and *d* 17 Sept 1960, leaving issue

6 Mabel Georgina; *m* 7 Feb 1905 Ernest Mallet, of Paris, and *d* 18 Sept 1944, leaving issue

---

7 Gwendoline Juliana Dorothy Vere; *d* young 29 July 1874

The 2nd BARON's n,

FRANCIS CECIL ORD ST AUBYN, **3rd Baron Saint Levan of Saint Michael's Mount**, JP (Cornwall 1942), DL (Cornwall 1961); *b* 18 April 1895; *educ* Eton and RMC Sandhurst; Maj Gren Gds, WW I (wounded twice), WW II 1939–41, Col cmdg W Cornwall Sector HG 1942–44; *m* 6 Oct 1916 Hon (Clementina) Gwendolen Catharine Nicolson, JP (*d* 30 May 1995), only dau of 1st Baron Carnock (*qv*), and *d* 10 July 1978, leaving:

1 JOHN FRANCIS ARTHUR ST AUBYN, **4th and present Baron Saint Levan**

2 +(OLIVER) PIERS, MC (1944) [The Hon Piers St Aubyn MC, Hogus House, Ludgvan, Penzance, Cornwall TR20 8EZ]; *b* 12 July 1920; *educ* Wellington and St James' Sch, Maryland, USA; Capt Para Regt WW II (despatches), High Sheriff E Sussex 1982–83; *m* 8 Dec 1948 Mary Bailey (*d* 1987), est dau of Bailey Southwell, of Crocodile Leap Farm, Olievenhoutpoort, S Africa, by Erica, dau of D'Urban Barry, of Umtali, S Rhodesia, and has:

    (1) +James Piers Southwell [James St Aubyn Esq, Tredrea Manor, St Erth, Cornwall TR27 6JS]; *b* 6 June 1950; *educ* Eton and Magdalen Coll Oxford; *m* 1981 *Mary Caroline, yst dau of Peter Ward Bennett, OBE, of Dene House, Glynde, Sussex, and has:

        1a +Hugh James; *b* 14 June 1983

        2a +Felix John; *b* 16 Jan 1992

        1a *Clemency Lara; *b* 8 Feb 1985

        2a *Louisa Mary; *b* 18 Sept 1987

    (2) +Nicholas Francis [Nicholas St Aubyn Esq MP, House of Commons, London SW1A 1AA]; *b* 19 Nov 1955; *educ* Eton; MP (C) Guildford 1997–; *m* 1980 *Jane Mary, only dau of William F Brooks, of Bishopswood House, Bishopswood, Herefs, and has:

        1a +Henry Francis; *b* 1981

        2a +Edward Nicholas; *b* 5 July 1995

        1a *Katharine Mary; *b* 1983

        2a *Alice Jane; *b* 1986

        3a *Camilla Bailey; *b* 1990

    (1) *Fiona Mary [The Hon Mrs Robert Boyle, 30 Durand Gdns, London SW9 0PP]; *b* 11 July 1952; *m* 1987 *Hon Robert William Boyle and has issue (*see* CORK and ORRERY, E)

3 +Giles Rowan, LVO (1977) [The Hon Giles St Aubyn LVO, Cornwall Lodge, Cambridge Pk, St Peter Port, Guernsey, CI]; *b* 11 March 1925; *educ* Wellington, Glasgow U and Trin Coll Oxford (MA); Ordinary Seaman RNVR WW II 1944 (invalided), late house master Eton, author: *Lord Macaulay* (1952), *The Art of Argument* (1957), *A Victorian Eminence* (1957), *The Royal George* (1963), *A World to Win* (1968), *Infamous Victorians* (1971), *William of Gloucester: Pioneer Prince* (1977), *Edward VII: Prince and King* (1979), *The Year of Three Kings* (1983) and *Queen Victoria: a portrait* (1991); FRSL

1 *Jessica Gwendolen [The Hon Mrs Koppel, Goodworth House, Goodworth Clatford, Hants SP11 7QX]; *b* 8 Feb 1918; *m* 5 Sept 1939 Maj John Patrick Koppel, Welsh Gds (*d* 1995), only s of Percy Alexander Koppel, CMG, CBE, by Dorothy, dau of John Conrad im Thurn, and has:

    (1) *(Patrick) Anthony [Anthony Koppel Esq, Box 108, Route 1, Brookshire, TX 77423, USA]; *b* 24 May 1944; *educ* Eton; late 2nd Lt Welsh Gds; *m* 10 May 1st 1967 (*divorce* 1971) Jacqueline Ann, only dau of J N Fairrie; *m* 2nd 1974 Jerry, dau of Cecil White; *m* 3rd 1996 *Deborah Brister

    (1) *Lamorna Jessica [Mrs Alastair Hyde Villiers, 17 Lansdowne Crescent, London W11]; *b* 11 Dec 1940; *m* 1st 7 Nov 1964 (*divorce* 1974) Ian Clinton Elliot, late Welsh Gds, yst s of Ian Frederick Letsom Elliot, and has:

        1a *Patrick Ian; *b* 3 July 1965

        2a *Shane Robert; *b* 27 Oct 1970

    (1) (cont.) Mrs Lamorna Elliot *m* 2nd 1974 *Alastair Michael Hyde Villiers (*see* CLARENDON, E) and by him has:

        1a *Katherine Alexandra Hyde; *b* 1979

    (2) *Susan Catherine Dorothy [Mrs Richard Noel Dobbs, 19 Haygarth Place, Wimbledon Village, London SW19 5BX]; *b* 17 June 1942; *educ* Froebel Educnl Inst; *m* 12 Oct 1963 *Richard Noel Dobbs, ACA, est s of Lt Richard Arthur William Dobbs, RN, by Mrs A E McCaw, and has:

        1a *Richard Francis Conway; *b* 5 March 1966

        2a *Alexander Noel; *b* 13 June 1967

        1a *Jessica Katherine Anne; *b* 1971

2 *Philippa Catherine [The Hon Mrs Hulbert-Powell, Old Place Farm Bungalow, Mayfield, Sussex TN20 6PN]; *b* 19 June 1922; *m* 20 July 1948 Evelyn Charles Lacy Hulbert-Powell (*d* 1985), barrister, only s of Canon Charles Lacy Hulbert-Powell, FSA, of Burrell's Field, Cambridge, and has:

    (1) *Charles George Lacy [Charles Hulbert-Powell Esq, Old Place Farm, Mayfield, E Sussex]; *b* 15 Feb 1952; *educ* Eton; *m* 1978 *Sara Mary, er dau of Michael Walter Bonn (*see* BUXTON, Bt), and has:

        1a *John Charles Lacy; *b* 1984

        1a *Catherine Mary Lacy; *b* 1980

        2a *Emma Sara Lacy; *b* 1982

        3a *Victoria Elizabeth Lacy; *b* 1987

    (2) *Francis Peter Lacy; *b* 19 Jan 1961

    (1) *Elizabeth Catherine Lacy; *b* 29 July 1950; *m* 9 Oct 1976 *Lt-Cdr Richard Charles Harden, RN, and has issue (*see* INGRAM, Bt)

    (2) *Veronica Mary Lacy [Mrs John Maclean, Westfield House, Spynie, Morayshire]; *b* 16 June 1954; *m* 1979 *John Robert Maclean, DL, and has:

        1a *Hugh Charles; *b* 1980

        1a *Charlotte Louise; *b* 1982

        2a *Anastasia Mary; *b* 1986

    (3) *Teresa Philippa Lacy; *b* 19 Nov 1956; *m* 1993 *Paul H C T Isolani-Smyth, only s of C T Isolani, CBE, LVO

Seat: St Michael's Mount, Marazion, Cornwall. Shortly after the Conquest the Benedictine mother foundation of Mont Saint Michel in Normandy acquired St Michael's Mount by gift from Robert, Count of Mortain, who himself had been granted it only a few years before. In the first half of the following century the Abbot of Mont Saint Michel ordered a church to be constructed on the peak of the 300-foot rock in western England that so startlingly resembled his western French one. The original building fell down after an earth tremor some 150 years later and a replacement was put up the next century. The year before Agincourt the French proprietors were dispossessed and in HENRY VI's reign St Michael's Mount was made over to the Bridgettine nuns at Isleworth (*see* section **Seat** under NORTHUMBERLAND, D).

By the time of the Dissolution of the Monasteries in the 1530s the number of religious at St Michael's had dwindled to a handful, much as is the case at Mont Saint Michel today. But the rock had for long been of more temporal than spiritual significance. Before the advent of accurate artillery pieces its sea-girt local position, to say nothing of its wider strategic importance as a site for the defence or invasion of England's southwesternmost arm, made it a highly desirable military prize.The capture of it in the late 15th century by the 13th Earl of Oxford (*see* SAINT ALBANS, D) is only one of a number of episodes in which it was hotly contended for.

After being bought from ELIZABETH I by Robert Cecil, 1st Earl of Salisbury, and passing through the hands of a royalist commander in the Civil War, one Francis Basset, it was acquired in 1657 by John St Aubyn, father of the 1st Baronet of the 1671 creation. The new owners used it as no more than a temporary summer retreat for the next two hundred years, though they 'improved' such features as the old Lady Chapel by judicious gothicising during the first half of the 18th century — an extremely early exercise in the style, given that Horace Walpole himself only embarked on Strawberry Hill some seven years later. Just as the last quarter of the 19th century began the **1st Baron Saint Levan** (as he was to become 12 years later) called in a cousin of his, Piers St Aubyn, architect of the Temple Church off Fleet Street in London, and commissioned a thorough refurbishment, one which would give the family a proper dwelling there. Piers St Aubyn left the original ecclesiastical building at the very summit of the rock more or less alone but adroitly grafted onto its southeast flank a commodious mansion in light grey granite, carefully ensuring that the addition at no point interfered with the skyline view from afar of the old church. Internally the decoration is widely admired, notably (as well as the Lady Chapel already mentioned) the Chevy Chase Room, which was formerly the refectory when the monks lived there.

SAINT OSWALD

Arms: Erm. on a fess vert, three eagles displayed or. **Crest:** A demi-eagle displayed or, ducally gorged erm. **Supporters:** Two dragons regardant vert, each gorded with a ribbon or, pendant therefrom an escutcheon gu., charged with a rose arg. (the white rose of York). **Motto:** *Tout pour Dieu et ma patrie* ('All for God and my country'). **Creation:** B. (UK) 6 July 1885.

THE 5TH BARON SAINT OSWALD OF NOSTELL, in the West Riding of Co York (Derek Edward Anthony Winn, DL (W R Yorks 1987)) [The Rt Hon The Lord St Oswald DL, Nostell Priory, Wakefield, W Yorks WF4 1QE]; *b* 9 July 1919; *s* bro 1984; *educ* Stowe; served 60th Rifles, 2nd Lt KRRC 1938, Capt Para Regt WW II N Africa (wounded), ADC to Govr-Gen NZ 1943–45, Malayan Police Serv 1948–52, film producer 1953–67, farm owner, Pres: Wakefield Hospice 1985–, Wakefield MS Soc 1985–; author *I Served Caesar* 1972; *m* 10 June 1954 *Denise Eileen Charlotte, only dau of Wilfrid Haig Loyd (*see* OAKELEY, Bt), and has:

1 +CHARLES ROWLAND ANDREW; *b* 22 July 1959; *educ* The New Sch, Kings Langley, Herts; *m* 1985 *Louise Alexandra, dau of Stewart MacKenzie Scott, and has:

   (1) +Rowland Charles Sebastian Henry; *b* 15 April 1986

   (1) *Henrietta Sophia Alexandra; *b* 1993

1 *Geva Charlotte Caroline [The Hon Mrs Blackett, Clunie Cottage, Braemar, Aberdeenshire AB35 5QX]; *b* 15 Sept 1955; *m* 1987 *(John) Simon Blackett and has issue (*see* BLACKETT, Bt)

Lineage: GEORGE WYNN, allegedly descended from the WYNNS of Gwydir; draper to ELIZABETH I; granted arms 1604; *b c* 1560; *m* Margaret Green, of London, and *d* 1610, leaving:

EDMUND WINN, of Thornton Curteis, Lincs; *b* 1583; *m* Mary, dau of Rowland Berkeley, of Worcester, and sister of Sir Robert Berkeley, Judge King's Bench, and *d c* 1645, having had, with two yr sons (Rowland, *b* 1609, London Alderman, *d* 1676; Mark, of Little Warley, Essex, *b* 1611, *d* 1699, leaving issue) and five daus:

Sir GEORGE WYNNE, 1st Bt (E), so *cr* 3 Dec 1660, of Nostell, Yorks; *b c* 1607; High Sheriff Lincs 1657, royalist Civil War; *m* 1st Rachel (*dsp* by 1643), dau of John Turner, of Ham, Surrey; *m* 2nd *c* 1643 Elizabeth, dau of Robert Jeffreys, London Alderman (possibly identical with the Sir Robert Jeffreys who was Ld Mayor London 1685–86); *m* 3rd 16 April 1654 Anne (*bur* 18 Jan 1701/2), dau of Sir William Pelham (*bur* 18 July 1667, having by her had no issue; by his 2nd w he had, with three other sons:

1 Sir EDMUND WINN, 2nd Bt, of Nostell, Thornton Curteis and Huntwick, Yorks; *b c* 1644; *m* 1st (licence 11 Dec 1668) his stepmother's yr sis Elizabeth, dau of Sir William Pelham; *m* 2nd by 1674 Catharine — (*bur* 15 Nov 1704) and was *bur* 30 Aug 1694, leaving by her, with other issue:

   (1) Sir ROWLAND WINN, 3rd Bt, of Nostell, Nostell and Thornton Curteis; *bapt* 1 July 1675; *m* (licence 18 April 1702) Laetitia, dau and coheir of William Harbord, of Grafton Park, Northants, and was *bur* with her 6 March 1721/2, leaving, with other issue:

      1a Sir ROWLAND WINN, 4th Bt, of Huntwick, Nostell and Thornton Curteis; *b c* 1706; Sheriff Yorks 1731–32, Parly candidate for Yorks 1733; *m* 29 Aug 1729 Susanna (*bur* 24 March 1741/2), dau and coheir of Charles Henshaw, of Wellhall, Eltham, Kent, and *d* 23 Aug 1765, leaving, with other issue:

         1b Sir ROWLAND WINN, 5th Bt, of Huntwick, Nostell and Thornton Curteis; *bapt* 24 Feb 1739; briefly MP Pontefract 1738 (unseated Nov); *m* by 1768 Sabine Louise (*bur* 21 Sept 1798), only dau and heir of Jacques Philippe, Baron d'Hervert, Govr Vevey, Switzerland, and *d* 20 Feb 1785, leaving:

           1c Sir ROWLAND WINN, 6th Bt, of Nostell and Thornton Curteis; *b* 13 June 1775; High Sheriff Yorks 1799–1800; *d unm* 14 Oct 1805

           1c Esther Sabina; *b* 26 Nov 1768; *m* Jan 1793 John Williamson and *d* Dec 1803, leaving, with a dau (*d unm*):

              1d John WILLIAMSON later WINN (on inheriting Nostell from his maternal uncle); *dsp* 17 Nov 1817

              2d Charles WILLIAMSON later WINN, of Nostell; *m* 16 June 1819 Priscilla (*d* 19 Nov 1884 aged 88), dau of Sir William Strickland, 6th Bt (*see* STRICKLAND-CONSTABLE, Bt), and had, with three daus (*d unm*):

                1e ROWLAND, **1st Baron**

                2e Edmund John; *b* 23 Aug 1830; *m* 1863 Frances Jane Edith, dau of Stepney St George, of Headford Castle, Co Galway, and *d* 12 Oct 1908, leaving issue

                1e Cecilia Isabella; *b* 6 Oct 1821; *m* Sept 1848 Robert Manners Croft, est s of Ven James Croft, Archdeacon Canterbury, and had issue

                2e Esther Louisa; *b* 7 April 1824; *m* 15 Jan 1862 Rev Henry Sigismund de Cerjat, est s of Col Charles Sigismund de Cerjat, 1st Roy Dragoons, of Rovereaz, Vaud, Switzerland

                3e Katherine Matilda; *b* 5 Aug 1825; *m* 19 Aug 1846 William Assheton Cross, of Red Scar, Lancs, and *d* 16 April 1871, leaving issue

         2b Edward, of Bramham, Yorks; *bapt* 1 April 1740; *d unm* 13 Sept 1782

         1b Ann; *m* 12 April 1765 1st LORD HEADLEY, BARON ALLANSON AND WINN OF AGHADOE (*see* below)

   (2) Edmund, of Ackton in Featherstone, Yorks; *bapt* 2 Dec 1678; *d* Feb 1743, having had:

      1a Thomas, of Ackton; *b c* 1714; *m* 11 Dec 1753 Mary, dau of Humphrey Duncalf, of Highgate, Middx, and *d* 7 May 1780, leaving:

         1b Sir EDMUND MARK WINN, 7th Bt, of Nostell; *bapt* 16 Sept 1762; *d unm* 1 June 1833

   (3) George; *bapt* 19 Aug 1680; Smyrna merchant; *d unm* 1708

   (1) Elizabeth; *m* 1st Joseph Taylor; *m* 2nd Dr Charles Trimnell, Bp Winchester

2 George, of S Ferraby, Lincs; *b c* 1645; *m* Sarah, dau of Charles Pelham, of Brocklesby, Lincs (*see* YARBOROUGH, E), and had:

   (1) Pelham, of S Ferraby; Army Offr; *m* Elizabeth, dau of Rev Gilbert Wighton by Elizabeth, sis of William Allanson, of Syon, Middx, and had:

      1a Sir GEORGE WINN later ALLANSON-WINN (roy licence 20 Feb 1777), 1st Bt (GB), of Little Warley, Co Essex, and 1st LORD HEADLEY, BARON ALLANSON AND WINN OF AGHADOE, Co Kerry (I), so *cr* 14 Sept 1776 and 27 Nov 1797 respectively; *b* 1725; barrister Lincoln's Inn 1755, Baron Court Exchequer Scotland 1761–76; inherited 1763 the estate of his cousin, Mark Winn, of Little Warley, and 1775 that of his cousin, Charles Allanson, of Bramham Biggin, Yorks (only s of William Allanson; *see* above); MP Ripon (Pittite) 1789–98; *m* 1st 12 April 1765 his cousin Anne (*d* 9 Oct 1774), 6th dau of Sir ROWLAND WINN, 4th Bt, of Nostell, and had a dau (Georgiana Anne, *b* 1769, *d* 1782); *m* 2nd 24 June 1783 Jane (*d* 1825), est dau and heiress of Arthur Blennerhassett, of Ballyseedy, Co Kerry, and *d* 9 April 1798, having had, with two daus:

         1b Sir ALLANSON-WINN later WINN-ALLANSON, 8th Bt, of Nostell, as which *s* cousin June 1833, 2nd Bt, of Little Warley, and 2nd LORD HEADLEY, BARON ALLANSON AND WINN OF AGHADOE; *b* 25 June 1784; *educ* Eton; MP (Tory) Ripon 1806–07, Malton 1807–08 and Ludgershall 1811–12; *m* 19 Nov 1825 Anne Matthews (*d* 16 Feb 1863) and *dsp* 9 April 1840

         2b George Mark Arthur Way; *b* 14 Aug 1785; MP Maldon, Essex; *m* 27 April 1807 Elizabeth Mary (*d* 18 April 1863), est dau of Lewis Majendie, of Hedingham Castle, Essex, and *d* 5 Nov 1827, having had, with five other sons (*d* young unm):

           1c CHARLES ALLANSON-WINN, 3rd LORD HEADLEY, BARON ALLANSON AND WINN OF AGHADOE, DL (Essex); *b* 25 June 1810; rep I peer 1868–77; *m* 29 June 1841 Maria Margaret (*d* 24 April 1894), est dau of Major d'Arley, and *d* 30 July 1877, having had:

              1d Rowland William; *b* 18, *d* 20 June 1842

              2d CHARLES MARK ALLANSON-WINN, 4th LORD HEADLEY, BARON ALLANSON AND WINN OF AGHADOE, JP, DL (Co Kerry), JP (Essex and Middx); *b* 4 Dec 1845; *educ* Harrow and Univ Coll Oxford; Capt HAC 1881–85, rep I peer 1883, bankrupt 1886; *m* 31 Oct

1867 Elizabeth (Bessie) Houssemayne (*d* Oct 1928), dau of Rev John Blennerhassett, Rector Ryme, Dorset, and had *d* 13 Jan 1913, leaving:

1e Avis Millicent Blennerhassett; *m* 1st 27 April 1896 Herbert Dudley Hinton Crosse (*d* 18 Oct 1908), of Newell House, Sherborne, Dorset, and had issue; *m* 2nd 29 April 1911 Llewelyn Jones Llewellyn, MB, MRCS, LRCP (*d* 19 April 1934), and *d* 29 April 1936, having had further issue

1d Laura Jane; *m* 5 Feb 1874 St Lawrence Robert Morgan Tighe, DL (*d* 2 April 1895), and *d* 26 Oct 1923, having had issue

2d Millicent Julia; *m* 22 April 1876 Rev Richard John Livingstone, Rector Pencombe-cum-Marston Stannett, Herefs, Hon Canon Liverpool (*d* 14 Oct 1907), and *d* 13 July 1933, leaving issue

3d Marion Sybil; *m* 1st 25 Feb 1875 Capt Alexander Francis Powell, JP, DL (*d* 14 Dec 1886), of Hurdcott House, Wilts, and had issue; *m* 2nd 13 Nov 1890 Rev Benjamin Whitefoord, DD, Vicar Potterne, Wilts, Preb Salisbury, Pncpl Salisbury Theol Coll (*d* 1910), and *d* April 1934

2c Rowland; *b* 5 June 1816; granted with sis rank of baron's dau/yr s; *m* 28 March 1854 Margaretta Stephana (*d* 10 March 1871), 2nd dau of George Walker, of Overhall, Essex, and *d* 8 May 1888, leaving:

1d ROWLAND GEORGE ALLANSON-WINN, 5th LORD HEADLEY, BARON ALLANSON AND WINN OF AGHADOE, JP Kerry; *b* 19 Jan 1855; *educ* Trin Coll Cambridge (BA); MICEI, FSE (Pres 1921), Pres Br Muslim Soc (made pilgrimage to Mecca July 1923), Order Nahda 1st Cl 1923; *m* 1st 27 Oct 1899 Teresa St Josephine (*d* 23 Oct 1919), yst dau of W H Johnson, Govr Leh and Jummu, India; *m* 2nd 11 Feb 1921 Barbara Janet Ainsleigh (*d* 1929), 7th dau of Robert Lawrence Kilpatrick, of Co Kerry, by Elizabeth, widow of Thomas Baynton, of Darlington; *m* 3rd 28 July 1929 Catharine, fndr/chm Stonehenge Woollen Industry Ltd (*d* 6 Jan 1947), widow of Major Lindsay Bashford, OBE, RAOC, and dau of Joseph William Lovibond, of Lake House, Wilts, and *d* 22 June 1935, leaving by his 1st w:

1e ROWLAND PATRICK JOHN GEORGE ALLANSON-WINN, 6th LORD HEADLEY, BARON ALLANSON AND WINN OF AGHADOE; *b* 22 May 1901; *educ* privately; WW II: F/Offr RAFVR 1939–43 and Lt RNR 1943–45; *m* 18 Aug 1936 Edith Jane, yst dau of Rev George Dods, BD, Min Barry, Ayrshire, and *dsp* 17 Dec 1969

2e CHARLES ROWLAND ALLANSON-WINN, 7th and last LORD HEADLEY, BARON ALLANSON AND WINN OF AGHADOE; *b* 19 May 1902; *educ* Bedford Sch; *m* 8 Feb 1927 Hilda May, est dau of Thomas Wells Thorpe, of 52 Redington Rd, London NW, and *d* 1994, when all his titles expired, leaving:

1f John Rowland; *b* 14 Oct 1934; *educ* Canford

1f *Pamela Jean; *b* 25 March 1928; *m* 8 Oct 1949 Ivan Beshoff, s of J Beshoff, of Dublin, and has:

1g *David Rowland; *b* 8 July 1950

2f *Janet Diana [The Hon Mrs Webb, Springs, Rookery Dve, Westcott, Surrey]; *b* 13 April 1932; *m* 1st 24 Sept 1955 (*divorce* 1969) Antony John Vlassopulos, LLB, FICS, barrister, only s of J N Vlassopulos, of L'Angelina, Cros-de-Cagnes, Alpes Maritime, France, and has:

1g *Christopher John Antony, *b* 6 Nov 1958

2g *Mark Charles Antony; *b* 27 Nov 1959

2f (cont.) The Hon Mrs Janet Vlassopoulos *m* 2nd 1975 *David Walter Webb

3f *Susan Ethel; *b* 26 May 1936

3e Thomas Frederick George, *b* 3 Aug 1903, *d* 15 Aug 1904

4e John Valentine; *b* 31 Oct 1904; *educ* Bedford Sch; AIF WW II; *m* 23 Nov 1942 Barbara Muriel, dau of Owen Sparks, of Bridgetown, W Australia

5e Owain Gwynedd; *b* 15 Feb 1906; *educ* Bedford Sch; with Sudan Plantations Syndicate 1930–46; *m* 29 Oct 1938 *Ruth [The Hon Mrs Owain Allanson-Winn, PO Box 4340, George East, S Africa], formerly w of Harry Stuart Pearson and 2nd dau of Cecil Orpin, of Strand House, Youghal, Co Cork, and *d* 1993

1e Anne; *b* and *d* 15 Feb 1908

1d Helen Margaretta; granted with her sisters 19 Aug 1913 rank of baron's daus; *d* unm 28 Feb 1941

2d Stephanie; *m* 6 Oct 1886 George Maryon Wilson (*d* 26 July 1941), of Searles, Fletching, Sussex, 2nd s of Sir Spencer Maryon-Wilson, 10th Bt (*see* 1970 edn), and *d* 1 April 1940, leaving issue

3d Margaretta Anne; *d* unm 22 June 1951

1c Jane Mary; *d* unm 13 Nov 1884 aged 72

CHARLES WILLIAMSON later WINN *d* 17 Dec 1874 aged 79; his er s,

ROWLAND WINN, **1st Baron Saint Oswald of Nostell**, in the West Riding of Co York (UK), so cr 6 July 1885, DL; *b* 19 Feb 1820; MP (C) N Lincs 1868–85, a Ld Treasury 1874–80; *m* 21 March 1854 Harriet Maria Amelia (*d* 6 June 1926), 2nd dau of Col Henry Dumaresq (*see* LANESBOROUGH, E), and had:

1 ROWLAND, **2nd Baron**

2 Charles Cavendish; *b* Sept 1858; Maj Rifle Bde, ADC to Gen cmdg Bde at Gibraltar; *d* unm Jan 1898

3 Algernon James; *b* 12 Jan 1861; *d* unm 7 Aug 1894

4 George William Phipps; *b* 4 July 1863; *m* 15 Oct 1907 Mary Cecily (*d* 8 May 1959), 3rd dau of Col Edward Mashiter Dansey, OBE (*see* GIFFORD, B), and *dsp* 2 March 1952

5 Cecil Henry; *b* 27 Oct 1866; *m* 10 July 1913 Alice Marjorie Iris (*d* 15 Oct 1964), dau of Henry Darley, DL, JP, of Aldby Park, Yorks, and *d* 23 March 1934, leaving:

(1) (Henry) John, DSO (1951), MC; *b* 22 April 1914; Maj Roy Northumberland Fus WW II (wounded twice), Korea 1950–51 (wounded, despatches) and Kenya 1953–55 (despatches); *m* 10 May 1960 *Pamela Sylva [Mrs John Winn, Exelby House, Exelby, N Yorks DL8 2HB], only dau of Ernest Charles

de Rougemont, CBE, of Coldharbour Park, Hildenborough, Kent, by Mrs Erica Gardner, and *d* 1991, leaving:

1a +Martin John [Martin Winn Esq, 93 Palace Rd, London SW2 3LB]; *b* 12 March 1961; *m* 1986 *Caroline Anne, dau of Douglas da Costa, of Maida Vale, and has:

1b +Hugo John; *b* 1991

1b *Hannah Louise; *b* 1993

2b *Eleanor Mary Heather; *b* 12 Oct 1997

1a *Fiona Jane [Mrs Bruce Moriarty, 7 Habgood St, E Fremantle, WA 6158, Australia]; *b* 9 July 1962; *m* 1988 *Bruce J Moriarty, s of Donald Moriarty, of Halifax, Nova Scotia, and has:

1b *Ryan James; *b* 28 Sept 1996

(2) +(Geoffrey) Mark Victor [Mark Winn Esq, Aldby Park, Buttercrambe, York]; *b* 8 Aug 1918; Capt RE WW II; *m* 1st 17 Sept 1958 Alice Alexandra (*d* 1991), 4th dau of Peter Haig Thomas (*see* NORMANTON, E), and has:

1a +Geoffrey George WINN later WINN-DARLEY (roy licence 1985); *b* 2 Aug 1966

1a *Rosemary Alice [Mrs Christopher Nenadich, The Mole Hole, Ocle Pychard, Herefs]; *b* 26 Aug 1960; *m* 1993 *Christopher Milan Nenadich and has:

1b *Megan Rose; *b* 1993

2a *Iris Alexandra; *b* 5 Aug 1964

(2) (cont.) Mark Winn *m* 2nd 3 Sept 1994 *Patsy, formerly w of H Macmillan

1 Laura Sophia Priscilla; *m* 23 Jan 1883 4th and last Baron Cloncurry (*d* 12 Feb 1928; *see* 1928 edn) and *d* 29 Oct 1891, leaving issue

2 Emily Louisa; *d* unm 16 Nov 1927

3 Maud Julia Mary; *m* 31 May 1900 Lt-Gen Hon Sir (Alan) Richard Montagu-Stuart-Wortley, KCB, KCMG, DSO (*see* WHARNCLIFFE, E), and *d* 17 June 1938, leaving issue

The 1st BARON *d* 20 Jan 1893; his er s,

ROWLAND WINN, **2nd Baron Saint Oswald of Nostell**, JP, DL W R Yorks; *b* 1 Aug 1857; MP (C) Pontefract 1885–93, Capt Coldstream Gds; *m* 10 Oct 1892 Mabel Susan (*d* 14 Feb 1919), 3rd dau of Sir Charles Forbes, 4th Bt (*see* FORBES, Bt, of Newe), and had:

1 ROWLAND GEORGE, **3rd Baron**

2 Charles John Frederick; *b* 6 Oct 1896; *educ* Eton and RMC Sandhurst; F/O AAF, Lt 10th Hus 1914–22, WW I 1914–17 (wounded), ADC to Br Mil Rep at Marshal Foch's HQ 1918, F/O 616 Yorks Aux (F) Sqdn 1938, S/Ldr 1943, with Br Air Commn Washington, USA; *m* 1st 16 July 1919 (*divorce* 1925) Hon Olive Cecilia Paget (*d* 1974), est dau of 1st and last Baron Queenborough (*see* ANGLESEY, M), and had:

(1) *Pauline Katherine; *b* 18 July 1920; *m* 1st 30 Nov 1940 (*divorce* 1947) G/Capt Hon Edward Frederick Ward (*see* DUDLEY, E); *m* 2nd 28 Oct 1948 (*divorce* 1958) Norman Frank Paul Butler, s of Paul Butler, of Old Oak Brook, Hinsdale, Ill., and Palm Beach, Fla. and has:

1a *Sandra Pauline Whitney; *b* 29 July 1949; *m* *Timothy J Heise

2a *Paget; *b* 6 Feb 1953; *m* *Baron Ernest von Wedel

(1) (cont.) Mrs Pauline Butler *m* 3rd 12 Sept 1960 *Boyd de Brossard, of New York

(2) *Susan Mary Sheila [Mrs Edward Remington-Hobbs, 3 Lyall Mews, London SW1; Leeds Castle, Kent]; *b* 27 April 1923; *m* 1st 29 July 1946 (*divorce* 1971) Capt Hon Geoffrey Denis Erskine Russell and has had issue (*see* AMPTHILL, B); *m* 2nd 19 Dec 1972, as his 4th w, Lt-Col Edward Remington-Hobbs, DSO, OBE (*d* 29 July 1997)

2 (cont.) The Hon Charles Winn *m* 2nd 1929 (*divorce* 1938) Katherine, dau of Henry van Heukelom, and by her had:

(1) +Michael Peter Anthony [Michael Winn, 301 East 69th St, New York, NY 10021, USA]; *b* 12 Oct 1933; *m* 1963 *Caroline Knowlton, dau of Charles T Lipscomb, of Charleston, SC, and has:

1a +Charles Michael Anthony; *b* 1967

2 (cont.) The Hon Charles Winn *m* 3rd 17 Aug 1938 Theodora (*d* 1978), formerly w of W Palmer Dixon and dau of Warren Thorpe, of New York, and *d* 1 May 1968

3 Reginald Henry; *b* 4 Sept 1899; *educ* Eton and Ch Ch Oxford; Maj Gren Gds, WWs I and II; *m* 24 March 1924 *Alice, dau of Moncure Perkins, of Virginia, and *d* 1985, having had:

(1) Reginald David Alexander; *b* 27 July 1937; *educ* Eton and Ch Ch Oxford; accidentally drowned 15 Sept 1963

(1) *Elizabeth Susan [Miss Elizabeth Winn, Neville Ho, 15 Onslow Gdns, London SW7 3AW]; *b* 25 Jan 1925

(2) *Anne [The Hon Mrs Anne Wyndham, Thatched Cottage, Chilson, Charlbury, Oxon OX7 3HU]; *b* 1926; *m* 21 Jan 1947 (*divorce* 1982) Capt Hon Mark Hugh Wyndham, MC, 12th Lancers, and has issue (*see* EGREMONT, LECONFIELD and, B)

4 Anthony Edmund; *b* 4 Jan 1909; Capt Queen's Westminsters, KRRC, WW II; *ka* in Egypt, Nov 1942

1 Edith Victoria Blanche; *b* 12 Jan 1895; *m* 10 July 1916 Lt-Col Guy Randolph Westmacott, DSO, Gren Gds, only s of Maj-Gen Sir Richard Westmacott, KCB, DSO, and *d* 5 June 1966, leaving issue

The 2nd BARON *d* 13 April 1919; his est s,

ROWLAND GEORGE WINN, **3rd Baron Saint Oswald of Nostell** ; *b* 29 July 1893; *educ* Eton and RMC Sandhurst; Capt Res of Offrs, Coldstream Gds and Staff Offr RAF, WW I (wounded, 1914 star, two medals); *m* 29 Oct 1915 Evie Carew (*d* 9 June 1976), dau of Charles Greene, and *d* 25 Feb 1957, leaving:

1 ROWLAND DENYS GUY WINN, **4th Baron Saint Oswald of Nostell**, MC (1952), DL (W R Yorks 1962); *b* 19 Sept 1916; *educ* Stowe and Us of Bonn and Freiburg; Reuter's correspondent Spain 1935, *Daily Telegraph* war correspondent 1936 (condemned to death 1936), WW II with 8th King's Roy Irish Hus (despatches), volunteer Korea 1950–52, Ld in Waiting 1959–62, Jt Parly Sec Min Ag 1962–64, PPS to Ld Privy Seal 1970, Pres: Soc of Yorkshiremen in London and the Yorkshire Soc 1960–61, Yorkshire YCs 1965, Anglia Polish Soc 1980, Gt Yorkshire Show 1968–69; MEP 1973–79, Hon Col 150th (Northum-

brian) Regt RCT (V) 1967, V-Chm Centl & E European Commn of European Movement, Chev Order Leopold Belgium with Palm, Belgian Croix de Guerre with Palm 1951, Legn Hon and Croix de Guerre with palm France 1945, Grand Cross Order Polonia Restituta 1977, Grand Cross Isabel la Católica Spain 1980, author: *Lord Highport Dropped at Dawn* (1949), *My Dear It's Heaven* (1950), *Carmela* (1954); *m* 1st 8 May 1952 (*divorce* 1955) Laurian, only dau of Sir Roderick Jones, KBE, of Rottingdean, Sussex; *m* 2nd 24 June 1955 Marie Wanda (*d* 14 Feb 1981), yr dau of Sigismund Jaxa-Chamiec, of Filtrowa, Warsaw, and *d* 1984

2 DEREK EDWARD ANTHONY WINN, **5th and present Baron Saint Oswald of Nostell**

Seat: Nostell Priory, Wakefield, W Yorkshire. This is one of James Paine's first works, dating from the 1730s. Thirty years later it was added to by Robert Adam, who built on a wing. He also decorated the interior. The state rooms, with their exquisite plasterwork, are particularly fine examples of the Scottish architect's work and are enhanced by the Chippendale furniture specially designed to be seen in the high-18th-century setting he created at Nostell.

SAINT VINCENT

Arms: Sa. a chevron erm. between three martlets arg. **Crest:** Out of a naval crown or, enwrapped by a wreath of laurel vert, a demi-pegasus arg., maned and hoofed of the first, winged az., charged on the wing with a fleur-de-lys gold. **Supporters:** Dexter, an eagle, wings elevated and addorsed, holding in the sinister claw a thunder-bolt, all ppr.; sinister, a pegasus arg., maned and hoofed or, winged az., charged on the wing with a fleur-de-lys gold. **Motto:** Thus. **Creation:** V. (UK) 27 April 1801.

THE 7TH VISCOUNT SAINT VINCENT OF MEAFORD, Co Stafford (Ronald George James Jervis, JP (Somerset 1950)) [The Rt Hon The Viscount St Vincent JP, Les Charrières, St Ouen, Jersey, CI]; *b* 3 May 1905; *s* f 1940; *educ* Sherborne; Actg Lt Cdr RNVR WW II 1943–45; *m* 2 Oct 1945 *(Constance) Phillida Anne, only dau of Lt-Col Robert Hector Logan, OBE, Loyal Regt, of Taunton, Somerset, and has:

1 +EDWARD ROBERT JAMES [The Hon Edward Jervis, Colinas Verdes 26, Bensafrim, Lagos 8600, Algarve, Portugal]; *b* 12 May 1951; *educ* Radley; *m* 10 Feb 1977 *Victoria Margaret, only dau of Wilton J Oldham, of St Peter, Jersey, and has:

  (1) +James Richard Anthony; *b* 1982

  (1) *Emma Margaret Anne; *b* 13 Sept 1980

2 +Ronald Nigel John [The Hon Ronald Jervis, The Brooms, Congleton, Cheshire]; *b* 4 April 1954; *educ* Eton and Durham U (BSc 1976); *m* 1983 *Gillian Lois, dau of Geoffrey Sharp, and has:

  (1) +David Stephen; *b* 1988

  (1) *Sarah Frances; *b* 1986

  (2) *Ruth Margaret; *b* 1991

1 *Cassandra Phillida Anne [The Hon Mrs Cassandra Ringsell, O'Quintal, 8500 Mexhiloera Grande, Portimao, Algarve, Portugal]; *b* 30 April 1949; *m* 1st 24 Jan 1970 (*divorce* 1975) Martyn Leslie Ringsell, s of Raymond Ringsell, of Jersey; *m* 2nd 1 June 1979 (*divorce* 1981, resumed former name) James Edward Mcleod Colbeck-Welch, only s of AVM Edward Lawrence Colbeck-Welch, CB, OBE, DFC, RAF, of Jersey, and by her 1st husb has:

  (1) *Brett George Jervis; *b* 6 Jan 1972

  (2) *Christopher Charles Robert; *b* 6 Jan 1974

Lineage: JOHN JERVIS, of Ollerton, Salop; *m* Oct 1590 Helena Whittington and had:

JOHN JERVIS, of Ollerton; *m* Elizabeth, dau and sole heiress of John Jervys, of Chatcull, Eccleshall, Staffs, and *d* 1670, having had, with five daus, two er sons (William, of Meaford, bought Darlaston Hall, Staffs, from the COLLIERs; Sir Humphrey, Ld Mayor Dublin, ancestor of the WHITE JERVIS Bts of Bally Ellis) and a yst one (Peter, of Croxton), a 3rd s:

JOHN JERVIS, of Chatcull; *b* 1631; *m* Elizabeth Wakelyn and *d* 1680, having had, with a yr s:

JOHN JERVIS, of Darlaston; *b* 12 April 1670; High Sheriff Staffs; *m* 14 July 1692 Mary, only dau and heiress of John Swynfen, of Swynfen, Staffs, and had, with a dau (Mary, *m* James Bayley):

1 John; ancestor of the JERVISes of Darlaston

2 William (Rev); Rector Stone, Staffs; had:

  (1) Mary; *m* Slade Nash, of Martley, Worcs

3 Benjamin, of Trowbridge, Wilts; *b* 9 Dec 1697; *d* unm 1758

4 Thomas; ancestor of the JERVISes of Darlaston and Chatcull

5 SWYNFEN

6 Matthew, of Trowbridge, Wilts; ancestor of the JERVISes of Eccleshall

JOHN JERVIS *d* 3 Jan 1746; his 5th s,

SWYNFEN JERVIS, of Meaford, Staffs; *b* Nov 1700; barrister; *m* 1727 Elizabeth, dau of George Parker, of Park Hall, and sis of Rt Hon Sir Thomas Parker, Ch Baron Exchequer (*see* PARKER, Bt, of Shenstone Hall), and *d* 19 Nov 1771, leaving, with a dau (*dsp*):

1 William; *bapt* 22 May 1728; Gentleman Usher Privy Chamber; *m* 28 May 1771 Jane (*d* 29 April 1817), yst dau of Thomas Hatrell, of Newcastle-under-Lyme, and *dsp* 6 March 1813

2 JOHN JERVIS, **1st Viscount Saint Vincent of Meaford** (UK), so *cr* 27 April 1801, with remainder, in default of male issue, to his nephews William and Edward successively then his niece Mary, Countess of Northesk, and the heirs male of her body, as also earlier 23 June 1797 EARL OF SAINT VINCENT and BARON JERVIS OF MEAFORD, Co Stafford (both GB), but with ordinary remainder to the heirs male of his body, GCB (1815, KB 1782), PC (1801); *b* 9 Jan 1734/5; *educ* Burton-on-Trent GS; joined RN Jan 1748/9, Midshipman 1752, Lt 1755, Post Capt 1760, R-Adml 1787, V-Adml 1793, C-in-C W Indies 1793–95, Adml the Blue 1795, C-in-C Mediterranean 1795–97, during which at Battle of Cape St Vincent 14 Feb 1797 he defeated with 15 ships 27 Spanish ships of the line (thanks of both Houses Parl 3 and 8 March 1797 and granted £2,000 (over £73,000 in late-1990s terms) p.a.), quelled mutiny at the Nore and Spithead 1797–98, Adml the White 1799 and Red 1805, Lt-Gen Marines 1800–14, C-in-C Channel 1800–01, First Ld Admlty 1801–04, Actg Adml of the Fleet and C-in-C Channel 1806–07, Gen Marines 1814–23, Adml of the Fleet 1821; MP (Whig) Launceston 1783–84, Gt Yarmouth 1784–90 and Chipping Wycombe 1790–94; *m* 5 June 1783 his 1st cousin Martha (*d* 8 Feb 1816), dau of Lord Ch Baron Sir Thomas Parker, and *dsp* 13 March 1823, when the Earldom and Barony expired

1 Mary; *m* 19 April 1757 William Henry Ricketts (*d* 5 Oct 1799), Bencher Gray's Inn, of Longwood, Hants (23rd of his mother's 27 children), and *d* 12 March 1828, leaving:

  (1) William Henry RICKETTS later JERVIS (roy licence 10 June 1801); *b* 4 Nov 1764; Capt RN; *m* 9 Nov 1793 (*divorce* 1799) Lady Elizabeth Jane Lambart, dau of 6th Earl of Cavan (*qv*), and was drowned by the upsetting of his barge 26 Jan 1805, leaving two daus

  (2) EDWARD, **2nd Viscount**

  (1) Mary; *m* 9 Dec 1788 7th Earl of Northesk (*qv*) and *d* 20 Nov 1835, leaving issue

The 1st VISCOUNT's nephew,

EDWARD JERVIS RICKETTS later JERVIS (roy licence 7 May 1823), **2nd Viscount Saint Vincent of Meaford**; *b* 1 April 1767; *educ* Winchester and Ch Ch Oxford; barrister 1797; *m* 1st 29 Jan 1790 (*divorce* 1799) Mary Cassandra, 2nd dau of 7th Lord (Baron) Saye and Sele (*qv*), and had:

1 William Jervis; *b* 11 Oct 1794; *m* 28 July 1815 Sophia (*d* 8 Nov 1828), dau of George Narbonne Vincent, through whom Lord St Vincent inherited the Clarges property, and *dvp* 1839, leaving surv issue:

  (1) CARNEGIE ROBERT JOHN, **3rd Viscount**

  (2) William Monk, of Quarndon Hall, Derbys, JP, DL; *b* 25 Jan 1827; CA Derbys; granted with sis Feb 1860 rank of viscount's dau/yr s; Capt 3rd King's Own Staffs Militia, BCL Oxon, barrister; *m* 1st 21 April 1864 Harriet Wilmot (*d* 22 Jan 1875), dau of Robert Sacheverell Wilmot-Sitwell, of Stainsby House, Derbys; *m* 2nd 18 April 1876 his cousin Mary Maude (*d* 19 Jan 1879), est dau of Hon Edward Swynfen Parker-Jervis, of Aston Hall, Warwicks (*see* below); *m* 3rd 25 April 1882 Mary (*d* 28 Dec 1930), widow of Capt Herbert Herbert-Stepney, 79th Highrs, and dau of Edward Atkinson, DL, of Scafield, Donabate, and Carrick Brenan, Co Dublin, and *dsp* 25 March 1909

  (1) Caroline Mary Frances; *d* unm 28 May 1917 aged 93

1 Maria; *m* 25 Oct 1833 George Wilkie, MD, and *d* 13 Feb 1869. He *d* 4 March 1876

The **2nd Viscount** *m* 2nd 1810 Mary Anne (*d* 3 Jan 1855), 2nd dau of Thomas Parker, of Park Hall, Staffs (*see* PARKER, Bt, of Shenstone Hall), and by her had, with another s (*d* young):

2 Edward Swynfen JERVIS later PARKER-JERVIS (roy licence 1861), of Aston Hall, Sutton Coldfield, Staffs, and Park Hall, Staffs; *b* 3 Feb 1815; *m* 1st 12 March 1838 Mary (*d* 24 June 1884), dau of J Barker, and had, with other issue:

  (1) Edward John; *b* 18 Feb 1839; *m* 12 Dec 1861 Grace Catherine (*m* 2nd June 1873 William T Locker (*d* 1885), of Tillington House, Staffs, and *d* 3 March 1930), yr dau of Ch Justice Sir John Jervis, and *d* 31 July 1868, having had:

    1a Edward St Vincent; *b* 29 Sept 1863; Lt 3rd Bn Durham LI; *m* 11 March 1889 Winifred Maria (*d* 29 Aug 1915), only child of Walter Reynolds, and *d* 1941, having had:

      1b St Vincent John; *b* 21 July 1891; Lt RNVR; *m* 1917 Marianita (*m* 2nd John Frederick Harker), yr dau of C T Roller, of Burnham, Bucks, and *d* 16 Aug 1930, leaving:

        1c +Antony St Vincent [Anthony Parker-Jervis Esq, 3549 Cardiff Place, Victoria, BC, Canada]; *b* 21 Aug 1919; *educ* Ampleforth; Capt RCHA WW II; head Mathematics Dept St George's Sch, BC, 1961; *m* 6 June 1942 *Doris Beauchamp, er dau of George Beauchamp Taverner, of Roehampton and Middleton-on-Sea, Sussex, and has had:

          1d +Nicholas St Vincent [Nicholas Parker-Jervis Esq, 6474 109th St, Delta, BC, Canada V4E 1H3]; *b* 13 Nov 1943; *educ* U of BC (BA 1965), Oxford (DipEd 1966); *m* 1st 17 June 1967 (*divorce* 1976) Patsy K, dau of Masao Hayashi, of Steventon, BC; *m* 2nd 1976 *Hazel Anne, dau of

Edward Lester Pierrot and widow of Robert Frank Wright, and by her has:

    1e +John St Vincent; *b* 1980

    1e *Laura Anne; *b* 1978

  2d +Antony Leigh; *b* 28 Sept 1947; *m* 1981 *Lisa Robbyn Marie, dau of George Edmond Joseph Ayotte, and has:

    1e *Sarah Marie Grace; *b* 1983

  1d Mary; *b* 26 Dec, *d* 29 Dec 1948

  2d *Hilary Anne; *b* 20 Oct 1950

2c +Noel John; *b* 25 Dec 1920; *educ* Ampleforth and U BC (BA); Lance-Bombardier RCA, Prof U of Alberta; *m* 1st 1950 (*divorce* 1954) Jean Mary Columbus; *m* 2nd 28 Sept 1956 *Betty, 3rd dau of Jasper Rutherford, of Cumberland, BC, and adopted:

  *Jonathan Rutherford; *b* 5 Nov 1962

2b Geoffrey Walter; *b* 31 July 1893; *d* 1894

1b Dorothy St Vincent; *b* 11 Feb 1890; *m* 29 Aug 1916 (*divorce* 1922) George Thomas Cavendish Paget (*see* ANGLESEY, M) and *d c* 1945

2b Grace Winifred; *b* 9 July 1892; *m* 1947 Gilbert Edward George Devonshire

1a Katherine Dorothea; *b* 30 Sept 1864; *m* 2 Nov 1885 Rev Frederick Mortimer Harvey, Rector Bolnhurst, and *d* 14 April 1911, leaving issue

2a Gertrude Mary; *b* 30 Dec 1865; *m* 10 July 1888 Horatio Mainwaring, 12th s of Rowland Mainwaring, JP, DL, of Whitmore and Biddulph, Staffs (*d* 20 July 1913), and *dsp* 5 Feb 1956

3a Amy; *b* 12 Feb 1867; *m* 28 April 1892 Maj George Alexander Chapman, 98th Regt, of Tremlett Hill, Wellington, Somerset, and *d* 15 Feb 1906, leaving issue

4a Annie Theodora; *b* 2 Nov 1868; *m* 6 Feb 1895 Rev Cecil Edward Weston, Vicar St Mark's, Peterborough (*d* 1918), and *d* 1957

(2) John St Vincent, JP; *b* 25 Sept 1840; *m* 20 April 1876 Anne, only dau of Rev Edwin Hotham (*see* HOTHAM, B), and *dsp* 4 Jan 1892

(3) William Robert, of Meaford, Stone, and Park Hall, Longton, Staffs, JP, DL Staffs; *b* 11 Dec 1841; High Sheriff Staffs 1911, Lt 47th Regt and Capt 3rd Stafford Militia; *m* 24 July 1877 Ethel Mary (*d* 14 July 1932), est dau of Rev Charles Henry Mainwaring, JP, Rector Whitmore, and *d* 7 May 1919, leaving:

1a William Swynfen Whitehall, DSO (1915); *b* 27 Aug 1879; Lt-Col KRRC Boer War 1899–1902 (two medals, eight clasps) and WW I (despatches, brevet); *d* 18 Nov 1936

2a Edward Mainwaring, MC ; *b* 15 Oct 1880; Maj RA (TF) WW I (despatches); *m* 21 Feb 1906 Eleanor Dora (*d* 18 Sept 1955), yr dau of Alfred Charles Lyon, of Albrighton Hall, and *d* 6 Sept 1935, leaving:

1b Robert St Vincent; *b* 23 May 1908; *educ* Charterhouse and RMC Sandhurst; Capt Cheshire Regt; *m* 1st 2 Sept 1936 (*divorce* 1946) Lucy (*d* 20 March 1966), only dau of Maj William Edward Burrill, of The Green, Masham, Yorks, and had:

  1c *Diana Elizabeth; *b* 15 Oct 1937; *m* 24 June 1958 her cousin *Roger Parker-Jervis, yst s of George Parker-Jervis (*see* below), and has issue

1b (cont.) Robert Parker-Jervis *m* 2nd 31 July 1946 Pamela Violet (*d* 1981), formerly w of Lt Col Lennox John Livingstone-Learmonth, DSO, MC, RHA, and dau of Capt Alexander Moore Vandeleur, JP, Life Gds, of Kilrush and Cahircon, Ennis, Co Clare, and *d* 23 Jan 1973, having by her had:

  2c *Linda [Mrs Michael Lord, Orchard Farm, Tutts Clump, nr Reading, Berks RG7 6LB]; *b* 9 Oct 1946; *m* 31 Oct 1970 *Brig Michael Lord, s of Maj-Gen W A Lord, of Redfields Home Farmhouse, Church Crookham, Hants, and has:

    1d *Simon James Austin; *b* 27 Oct 1972

    2d *Guy Robert Thomas; *b* 26 Oct 1974

    3d *Patrick Michael Jervis; *b* 1977

  3c *Sally Anne [Mrs John Parsons, Townsend House, Corfe Castle, Dorset]; *b* 30 Oct 1947; *m* 1981 *John William Parsons, CBE, s of Frederick John Parsons, of Wareham, and has:

    1d *Timothy John Jervis; *b* 1987

  4c *Angela [Mrs Jeremy Payne, 50 Narbonne Ave, London SW4 9JT]; *b* 8 Aug 1949; *m* 1984 *(Peter) Jeremy Woodland Payne, s of Dr R F Payne, of Huxtable Farm, Devon, and has:

    1d *Christopher William; *b* 1992

    1d *Emily Louise; *b* 1989

2b Edward Carstairs; *b* 29 Dec 1910; Capt RWF WW II; *ka* 27 May 1940

1b *Rosemary Eleanor [Mrs Francis Barclay, Little Dunham Lodge, King's Lynn, Norfolk]; *b* 16 Feb 1914; *m* 15 Aug 1940 Brig Francis Peter Barclay, DSO, MC, Roy Norfolk Regt (*d* 1992), er s of Francis Hubert Barclay, and has had:

  1c Robin Peter; *b* 1943; *educ* Harrow and RMA Sandhurst; 2nd Lt 1st E Anglian Regt; *d* 1964 following a mountain accident while serving Aden

  1c *Christopher Thomas; *b* 1946; *educ* Harrow

3a Evelyn St Vincent; *b* 8 Nov 1833; *m* 9 Feb 1916 Lilac Gwendolen (*d* 22 Feb 1956), dau of Lt-Col Arthur Henry Armytage (*see* ARMYTAGE, Bt), and *d* 26 Dec 1957

1a Ethel Mary, OBE (1918), JP; *b* 6 May 1878; Cmdt Sandon Hall Aux Hosp 1915–18, medal of Queen Elisabeth of Belgium; *d* unm 5 Nov 1956

(4) Augustus Whitehall; *b* 2 Aug 1845; *d* 19 Aug 1887

(5) Charles Edward; *b* 25 July 1850; Lt-Col Durham LI; *m* 24 June 1878 Mary Isabella (*d* 30 May 1923), yst dau of William Henry Scott, of St Oswin's, Tynemouth, and *d* 10 Aug 1914, leaving:

1a Mary St Vincent; *b* 23 July 1880; *d* unm 20 April 1950

2a Violet Mabel; *b* 9 Aug 1881; *m* 21 Jan 1913 Lt-Col Robert Ellis Key, OBE, JP, York and Lancaster Regt, only surv s of Capt William Henry Key, of Fulford Hall, Yorks, and *dsp* 30 Dec 1968. He *d* 4 June 1961

(6) Thomas Swynfen; *b* 8 Dec 1852; *m* 17 Jan 1883 Bridget Harriet (*d* 27 Jan 1930), dau of Francis Baring Atkinson, DL, of Morland Hall, Westmorland, and *d* 16 Nov 1936, having had:

1a Thomas; *b* 20 Feb 1888; *educ* Eton and Oxford; Lt and T/Capt SR Gren Gds WW I; *d* 10 Feb 1924 of wounds recd 1918

2a Humphrey; *b* 23 July 1889; *educ* Radley; Lt and T/Capt Rifle Bde and Capt RAF WW I (despatches); *m* 23 May 1922 Helen Frances (*d* 10 Jan 1998), dau of Sir John Ralph Starkey 1st Bt (*qv*), and *d* 30 June 1948, leaving:

1b John Humphrey; *b* 16 March 1923; *educ* Radley; Capt (E) RE WW II; *m* 20 Oct 1956 *Elizabeth Margaret [Mrs John Parker-Jervis, The Mill Barn, Longworth, Oxon OX13 5EP], yr dau of Richard Durant Trotter, of Brin House, Flichity, Inverness, and *d* 1989, leaving:

  1c +Simon Humphrey; *b* 10 March 1961

  2c +George; *b* 19–

  1c *Fiona Mary; *b* 2 Feb 1965

  2c *Mary Clare; *b* 1 April 1966; *m* 1993 *Andrew Hank Shaw, s of Stephen Shaw, of Crockham Hill, Kent

2b +Christopher Thomas [Lt-Cdr Christopher Parker-Jervis RN, Lane Cottage, Watledge, Glos GL6 0AY]; *b* 20 Dec 1929; *educ* Radley; *m* 5 Sept 1959 *Gillian, dau of A Bowden and Mrs Rennie Mozley, of Keighley, Yorks, and has had:

  1c +Edward Christopher [Edward Parker-Jervis Esq, The Lodge, Foxes Lane, Kingsclere, Berks RG15 8QE]; *b* 21 Aug 1960; *educ* Abingdon and St Catherine's Coll Oxford; *m* 1990 *Sarah Jane, only dau of Rev John Musgrave Shorrock, of Bredgar Vicarage, Kent, and has:

    1d *Helen Alexandra; *b* 17 April 1995

  2c Patrick; *b* 6 Jan, *d* 7 Sept 1963

  3c +William Thomas; *b* 2 Aug 1965; *educ* Abingdon and Aberdeen U

  1c *Sarah Belinda; *b* 17 May 1967

3a George; *b* 19 Sept 1895; *educ* Eton and Magdalene Coll Cambridge (BA 1926, MA, 1934); Lt 2nd/6th N Staffs Regt WW I (despatches); *m* 25 Oct 1924 Ruth Alice (*d* 1990), dau of Charles Edward Farmer, and *d* 25 Dec 1973, leaving:

1b +James [Lt-Cdr James Parker-Jervis RN, Templewood, Brechin, Angus DD9 7PT]; *b* 10 May 1926; *educ* Eton; *m* 7 April 1956 *Sybil Anne, widow of Hon John Michael Inigo Cross (*see* CROSS, V) and dau of Maj Thomas Prain Douglas Murray, MBE, TD, DL, JP, of Templewood, Brechin, Angus, and has:

  1c +Andrew Swynfen [Andrew Parker-Jervis Esq, Home Farm House, Little Walden, Essex, CB4 1XE]; *b* 10 Oct 1959; *educ* Eton and Edinburgh U (BSc 1981); *m* 1990 *Victoria L, yst dau of Rowan B Hutchinson and Mrs D Allen, of Rendham Court, Saxmundham, Suffolk, and has:

    1d +Rowan; *b* 6 Oct 1995

    2d +Clovis George Balfour; *b* 24 Sept 1997

    1d *Holly Audrey; *b* 20 Oct 1993

  1c *Harriet Anne [Mrs Frederick Gibson, The Paphle, Cleish, Kinross KY13 7LR]; *b* 16 April 1957; *m* 1985 *Frederick Gibson, s of F W Gibson, and has:

    1d *James Frederick; *b* 7 Dec 1989

    1d *Rosie Alice; *b* 23 Aug 1993

2b +Nicholas [Nicholas Parker-Jervis Esq, The Manor House, South Littleton, Evesham, Worcs WR11 5TJ]; *b* 4 Nov 1927; *educ* Eton and Magdalene Coll Cambridge (BA 1949, MA 1979); *m* 17 Sept 1960 *Elisabeth Henley, dau of John Trevil Morgan, MBE, JP, and has:

  1c +George Rhidian; *b* 29 Oct 1961

  2c +Thomas Fabyan; *b* 1 April 1974

  1c *Catherine Elisabeth [Mrs Harry Crossley, Trafalgar House, Nelson St, Stroud, Glos GL5 2HN]; *b* 26 Jan 1964; *m* July 1995 *Harry Martin Crossley, est s of Martin Crossley, of Auchtermuchty, Fife, and has:

    1d *Barnaby Horace; *b* 15 May 1996

3b +Roger, DL [Roger Parker-Jervis Esq DL, The Old Schoolhouse, Brill, Bucks HP18 9RU]; *b* 11 Sept 1931; *educ* Eton and Magdalene Coll Cambridge; *m* 24 June 1958 his cousin *Diana Elizabeth, est dau of Capt Robert St Vincent Parker-Jervis (*see* above), and has:

  1c +(Edward) Swynfen [Swynfen Parker-Jervis Esq, No 1 Lodge, Great Hampden, Great Missenden, Bucks HP16 9RD]; *b* 28 Feb 1959; *m* 19– *Alison Kingsbury and has:

    1d +Edward John; *b* 1996

    1d *Juliet Elizabeth; *b* 1997

  2c +Guy [Guy Parker-Jervis Esq, 11 William St, W Hobart 7000, Tasmania, Australia]; *b* 29 Dec 1960; *m* 1985 (*divorce*) Linda Johnston

  1c *Lucy Alice; *b* 26 Sept 1966; *m* 1989 *Julian Guy Rutherford, yr s of Ian Rutherford, of Chidwickbury, Herts, and has:

    1d *Laura Diana; *b* 1992

    2d *Chloe Jane Lucy; *b* 1994

1a Bridget; *m* 10 May 1905 Maj Arthur Joseph Clay, 6th Bn N Staffs Regt, of Grangewood, Netherseal, est s of Charles John Clay, JP, of Staffs, and has issue. He *d* 18 Feb 1915

2a Evelyn, twin with Bridget; *m* 11 Feb 1914 Arthur Victor Negus, Staffs Yeo, s of Thomas Addison Negus, of Shenstone Lodge, Staffs, and *d* 9 Dec 1932, leaving issue. He *d* 15 June 1943

3a Dorothy; *m* 11 July 1916 Capt John Tillie Coryton, Rifle Bde (*d* 30 Nov 1965), est s of William Coryton, DL, of Pentillie Castle, Cornwall, and *d* 25 Dec 1972, leaving issue

(7) Arthur Ricketts; *b* 4 Sept 1857; *m* 1st 1889 Edith Adams; *m* 2nd 10 June 1898 Eliza Jane, dau of David Shaw, and *d* 22 Nov 1903, having by his 1st w had:

1a Edith; *m* 19– D M McWhirter, of Dumfriesshire, and *dsp* 30 May 1963

(8) Hubert de Gotham, Capt Staffs Yeo Cav; *b* 29 Dec 1858; *m* 20 Aug 1885 Florence (*d* 30 Jan 1928), dau of William Henry Scott, of St Oswin's, Tynemouth, and *d* 5 April 1894, leaving:

1a Yolande; *b* 10 Dec 1886; *m* 2 Oct 1918 Samuel Key Ferrier, RGA (*d* 8 March 1954), s of Thomas Henry Ferrier, WS, and *dsp* 11 Jan 1966

(1) Mary Maude; *m* 18 April 1876 her cousin Hon William Monk Jervis and *dsp* 19 Jan 1879

2 (cont.) Edward Parker-Jervis *m* 2nd 15 July 1886 Maude (*d* 17 Dec 1924), dau of Rev Charles Henry Mainwaring, JP, Rector Whitmore, and *d* 3 Jan 1896

2 Mary Anne; *m* 1st 26 Sept 1840 David Ochterlony Dyce Sombre, of Sirdhanah, Hindustan (who inherited the private possessions of HH the Begum of Sombre Sirdhanah and *d* 1 July 1851); *m* 2nd 1862 3rd Baron Forester (*qv*) and *d* 7 March 1893 aged 80

The 2nd VISCOUNT *d* 25 Sept 1859; his gs,

CARNEGIE ROBERT JOHN JERVIS, **3rd Viscount Saint Vincent of Meaford**; *b* 12 Aug 1825; *educ* Winchester and Eton; *m* 14 March 1848 Lucy Charlotte (*d* 3 April 1900), yst dau of John Baskervyle-Glegg, of Withington Hall, Cheshire, and *d* 19 July 1879, having had:

1 JOHN EDWARD LEVESON JERVIS, **4th Viscount Saint Vincent of Meaford**; *b* 3 April 1850; *educ* Harrow; Capt 16th Lancers, Lt 7th Hus, served Zulu War 1879, Afghan War 1880, 1st Boer War 1881, Egypt 1882; *d* unm 23 Jan 1885 from wounds recd Battle of Metamneh 17 Jan 1885

2 CARNEGIE PARKER JERVIS, **5th Viscount Saint Vincent of Meaford**, JP Lincs; *b* 5 April 1855; *educ* Harrow; Capt Princess Charlotte of Wales's Berks Regt; *m* 17 Oct 1885 (*divorce* 1896) Rebecca May, only surv dau of James Baston, of Manchester and Barrow-in-Furness, and *dsp* 22 Sept 1908

3 RONALD CLARGES, **6th Viscount**

4 Cecil Leonard; *b* 30 Dec 1861; *m* 1884 Laura Evelyn, dau of Joseph Davey, of Exeter, and *dsp* 1941

5 St Leger Henry, DSO; *b* 7 Sept 1863; T/Lt-Col cmdg a Bn Manchester Regt 1916–18, Hon Lt-Col 1918, Maj and Hon Lt-Col 3rd Bn Norfolk Regt, Maj KRRC, Boer War 1900–02 (severely wounded, despatches twice); *m* 14 June 1905 Hilda Maud (*d* 25 Jan 1942), only dau of Thomas Collier, of Bayswater, and *d* 11 April 1952, leaving:

(1) *Crystal Guina Lucy; *b* 16 April 1906; *m* 1st 11 Oct 1927 Brig Thomas James Bolle Bosville, CBE, DSO, MC, Rifle Bde (*d* 5 July 1945), only s of Thomas Bolle Bosville, JP, of Gate Helmsley Ho, Yorks, and had issue; *m* 2nd 8 July 1946 George Henderson Macnab

(2) Hilda Violet Ursula; *b* 7 April 1909; *m* 21 Nov 1934 (*divorce* 1949) 3rd Viscount Goschen (*qv*)

6 Lionel; *b* 4 June 1865; *d* unm 23 Jan 1946

1 Alice Maude; *m* 17 March 1868 John Liell Francklin, of Gonalston, Notts; *d* 28 Nov 1929, leaving issue. He *d* 27 Oct 1915

2 Lucy Ada, CI, JP; *m* 8 July 1874 4th Baron Harris (*qv*) and *d* 12 Feb 1930, leaving issue

3 Constance Helena; *d* unm 14 Jan 1867

4 Emily Violet; *m* 1st 30 June 1877 William Hargrave Pawson (*d* 13 Jan 1892), of Shawdon, Northumberland, and had issue; *m* 2nd 12 March 1896 John Howard, DL, JP, of Sibton Park, Lyming, Kent, MP Faversham, and *d* 1 March 1920, leaving further issue. He *d* 5 Oct 1911

The 5th VISCOUNT's bro,

RONALD CLARGES JERVIS, **6th Viscount Saint Vincent of Meaford**; *b* 3 Dec 1859; Capt and Hon Maj 5th Bn Northumberland Fus; *m* 13 Sept 1894 Marion Annie (*d* 17 Dec 1911), dau of James Broun, of Orchard, Carluke, Lanarks, and 16 Feb 1940, having had:

1 John Cyril Carnegie, MC (1919), Capt KRRC, ADC to Govr-Gen Canada 1926–28; *b* 10 July 1898; *k* in a seaplane accident 20 June 1929

2 RONALD GEORGE JAMES JERVIS, **7th and present Viscount Saint Vincent of Meaford**

1 Ivy Lorna; *b* 20 July 1895; *m* 22 April 1920 W Laurence Whittemore, MC, MA, s of Luther H Whittemore, of Toronto, and has issue

SALISBURY

Arms: Quarterly, 1st and 4th, barry of ten, argent and azure, over all six escutcheons sable, three, two and one, each charged with a lion rampant of the first; a crescent for difference (for CECIL); 2nd and 3rd, argent, on a pale sable, a conger's head erased and erect or, charged with an ermineot (for GASCOYNE). The arrangement three, two and one of the six lions rampant in the first and fourth quarters is reminiscent of the lions used by William Longespee Earl of Salisbury of the 12th-century creation on his shield. The latter were or on an azure field. **Crests:** 1 Six arrows in saltire or, barbed and flighted argent, girt together with a belt gules, buckled and garnished gold, over the arrows a morion cap proper, 2 A conger's head, erased and erect or, charged with an ermine spot.
Supporters: Two lions ermine. **Motto:** *Sero sed serio* ('Late but in earnest'). **Creations:** B. (E) 13 May 1603, V. (E) 20 Aug 1604, E. (E) 4 May 1605, M. (GB) 25 Aug 1789.

THE 6TH MARQUESS OF SALISBURY, **Earl of Salisbury**, **Viscount Cranborne**, Co Dorset, and **Baron Cecil of Essendon**, Co Rutland (Robert Edward Peter Gascoyne-Cecil, DL (Dorset 1974)) [The Most Hon The Marquess of Salisbury DL, Hatfield House, Hatfield, Herts AL9 5NF]; *b* 24 Oct 1916; *s f* 1972; *educ* Eton; MP (C) Bournemouth W Feb 1950–Jan 1954, Capt Gren Gds WW II, High Steward Hertford 1972–, Pres: Monday Club 1974–81 and Roy Assoc Br Dairy Farmers, memb edtl bd *Salisbury Review* 1982–, patron seven livings; *m* 18 Dec 1945 *Marjorie (Mollie) Olein, Pres Tradescant Tst, 2nd dau of Capt Hon Valentine Wyndham-Quin, RN (*see* DUNRAVEN and MOUNT-EARL, E), and has had:

1 +ROBERT MICHAEL JAMES CECIL, BARON CECIL OF ESSENDON (*qv*)

2 Richard Valentine; *b* 26 Jan 1948; *educ* Eton; Capt Gren Gds (despatches 1973); *k* Rhodesia 20 April 1978 while on a journalistic assignment

3 +Charles Edward Vere [The Lord Charles Cecil, 21 Hollywood Rd, London SW10 9HT]; *b* 13 July 1949; *educ* Eton and Ch Ch Oxford; md Berkeley Govett (UK), Pres Herts Assoc Youth Clubs, V-Chm Rambert Dance; *m* 1993 *Virginia Edith, yr dau of Paul Zervudachi, of Morges, Switzerland, and Levanto, Italy

4 +Valentine William [The Lord Valentine Cecil, 11 Shalcomb St, London SW10 0HZ]; *b* 13 May 1952; *educ* Eton; Page of Honour to HM QUEEN ELIZABETH THE QUEEN MOTHER 1966–67, Maj Gren Gds

5 Henry; *b* 3 May, *d* 6 May 1955

6 +Michael Hugh [The Lord Michael Cecil, Hatfield House, Hatfield, Herts AL9 5NF]; *b* 23 March 1960; *educ* Eton; Gren Gds 1980–; *m* 1986 *Camilla Julia, yr dau of Maj Richard Jervoise Scott, TD (*see* SCOTT, Bt, of Rotherfield Park), and has:

(1) +Hubert George; *b* 1992

(2) +Edward William James; *b* 29 June 1996

(1) *Daisy Alice Julia; *b* 23 Oct 1989

1 *Rose Alice Elizabeth; *b* 11 Sept 1956; artist; *m* 1st 9 Feb 1985 (*divorce* 1992) Mark Flawn-Thomas (*m* 2nd 31 Oct 1996 Hon Clare Lowther, dau of 2nd Viscount Ullswater; *qv*), yst s of Peter Flawn-Thomas, of Shortbridge Mill, Piltdown, Sussex; *m* 2nd 9 Oct 1996 *Malachy Dunne, landscape gardener

Earldom of Salisbury: The first creation of this title took place some time between June 1142 and 1147, when the EMPRESS MAUD, HENRY I's daughter, made Patrick de Salisbury an Earl. He is sometimes referred to as Earl of Wiltshire and sometimes as Earl of Salisbury, usually the latter. At this time an earldom was an official position rather than title of honour, but was often held by successive members of the same family (*see* NORTHUMBERLAND, D, preliminary remarks), though not necessarily by right. Patrick was descended from a line of men who had been Sheriffs of Wiltshire from shortly after the Norman Conquest and who may even have been of English rather than Norman origin. Patrick's son succeeded him as Earl but died leaving an only child, a daughter called Ela or Isabel. RICHARD I arranged her marriage to William Longespee ('Long Sword'), his illegitimate half-brother by HENRY II out of either Rosamund/Rosamond Clifford (the 'Fair Rosamond' of tradition) or a woman of obscure antecedents called Hikenai or Ykenai. (Longespee may, however, have been born of some other woman altogether.)

William Longespee thus became Earl of Salisbury in right of his wife, as was customary then. In his hands the Earldom of Salisbury began to count for much more both nationally and internationally. He was an envoy to France and various German potentates; went with KING JOHN to Ireland in 1210; acted as intermediary in the dispute between JOHN and the Pope; as Marshal of the King of England organised military operations against the French in Flanders, northern France and Gascony, also participating in naval action against the French in home waters; sided with JOHN at the time of Magna Carta but later submitted to LOUIS VIII of France when the latter invaded England at the request of the nobles ranged against JOHN; and with his wife laid two of the principal foundation stones of what was then the new cathedral at Salisbury.

Although William Longespee held the Earldom of Salisbury, albeit in right of his wife, his eldest son and heir Sir William (I) Longespee did not succeed to the dignity. Nor did Sir William's son, Sir William (II) Longespee. The position was complicated by the fact that Ela/Isabel outlived both her son and grandson. Accordingly after her death in 1261 her great-granddaughter, Sir William (II)'s daughter Margaret, came to be regarded by much later writers as *de jure* Countess of Salisbury, although she was referred to by that title in at least two documents dating from 1311, five years at most after her death. Yet neither Margaret nor her husband Henry de Lacy, Earl of Lincoln, styled themselves Countess/Earl of Salisbury.

The Earl and Countess (Henry and Margaret) of Lincoln were survived by a single child, a daughter Alice, who married Thomas Earl of Lancaster (see SAINT DAVIDS, V, section **Lineage (of Strange)**). Even before Alice's death, which took place in 1348, EDWARD III had in 1337 granted a new creation of the Earldom of Salisbury to a completely unrelated person, acting on the assumption that the dignity had previously reverted to the Crown. This assumption seems to have been based partly on the fact that Alice's husband Lancaster had been attainted and thus suffered a judicial corruption of blood, partly on the fact that Alice had been compelled to surrender her inherited estates to the Crown on the occasion of the aforesaid attainder. As late as the 14th century the notion that an earldom was closely connected with the possession of lands for its upkeep still held sway (see also RUTLAND, D, section **Earldom of Rutland**).

The 1st Earl of Salisbury of the second (1337) creation was the 3rd Lord (Baron) Montagu, a leading diplomat and military man under EDWARD III during the early stages of the Hundred Years War (he was made Marshal of England for life in 1338). The 2nd Earl of this creation fought at Crécy and Poitiers and was a founder Knight of the Garter, outliving all his fellow first-generation KGs. He also went through a form of marriage and subsequently cohabited as husband with Joan 'The Fair Maid of Kent'. Joan later married as her 3rd husband the Black Prince, was mother of RICHARD II and may well have been the lady who inspired the naming of the Order of the Garter. The next two Montagu Earls of Salisbury were also Knights of the Garter, though only one was appointed a Marshal of England as well. The 4th Earl of the 1337 creation has been called the most distinguished English commander of the phase of the Hundred Years War that followed the death of HENRY V in 1422 and beat the French at Cravant (1423) and Verneuil (1424). The latter was considered by contemporaries as important as Agincourt. He had literary leanings, being a patron of the poet John Lydgate, and a more famous literary connection through his second wife, who was Chaucer's granddaughter.

The 4th Earl of Salisbury of the 1337 creation died in 1428. He left a daughter, who married Richard Nevill(e) (see ABERGAVENNY, M). Nevill(e) was allowed to assume the title of (5th) Earl of Salisbury in right of his wife and served as Constable of England at the coronation of HENRY VI as King of France in 1431. He was also made Chancellor in 1454 and Great Chamberlain of England for life in 1460. He was a Yorkist in the Wars of the Roses and lost his life just after the Battle of Wakefield, one of the chief Lancastrian victories, in late 1460. His son and heir, who actually inherited the Earldom of Salisbury from his mother, the 5th Earl's widow, in 1462, is better known as the famous Earl of Warwick ('The Kingmaker'). On 'Kingmaker' Warwick/Salisbury's death the Earldom of Salisbury reverted once more to the Crown.

EDWARD IV created his brother George Plantagenet, Duke of Clarence, Earl of Salisbury in 1472, the year after 'Kingmaker' Warwick/Salisbury's death. George had married the late 'Kingmaker' Warwick/Salisbury's daughter but was nevertheless created Earl in his own right entirely, not recognised as being Earl of Salisbury in right of his wife, as had been the case before. He was attainted in Feb 1477/8, whereupon the Earldom was forfeited. EDWARD IV conferred a new creation of Earl of Salisbury a week later on his nephew Edward Plantagenet, son of Richard Duke of Gloucester (later RICHARD III). Edward the new Earl of Salisbury's mother (and RICHARD III's wife) Anne was the younger of 'Kingmaker' Warwick/Salisbury's two daughters but again the grant was to Edward rather than a recognition of his right to the title through his maternal ancestry, though doubtless this played a part, for example in the selection of the place name of which he was made Earl. Edward Earl of Salisbury of the 1477/8 creation died the year before his father RICHARD III was defeated and killed at Bosworth, and the Earldom of Salisbury accordingly became extinct.

After the accession of the Tudors Margaret Plantagenet, daughter of that George Plantagenet who had been created Earl of Salisbury in 1472, successfully petitioned HENRY VIII to reverse her brother's attainder. She was declared to be Countess of Salisbury but was later attainted and executed, whereupon any further extension of the creation of 1472 or even of 1337 (Margaret had actually claimed the latter) became forfeited.

Lineage: Other great families have been closely involved with high politics. None has continued that involvement so late into the modern age as the Salisbury CECILs. The **1st Earl** played a crucial role in smoothing the transition from ELIZABETH I's reign to JAMES I's, and with such secrecy that the very suspicion of a correspondence between the two men only arose two centuries later. Thereafter the family produced no statesman of major importance for over 250 years. But from the 1860s, while comparable dynasties began to be eased out of top-level politics, a second flowering occurred. The **3rd Marquess** was Prime Minister three times and for sheer staying power has never been equalled since Lord Liverpool (see JENKINSON, Bt). In the mid-20th century the position of the **5th Marquess**, a member of the 'Magic Circle' (Iain Macleod's (see MACLEOD OF BORVE, B) phrase) that chose Conservative Party leaders, recalled that earlier Lord Salisbury, better known as 'Warwick the Kingmaker' (see ABERGAVENNY,

M), who had dominated 15th-century politics. The **5th Marquess**'s grandson, the present Lord Cecil of Essendon (*qv*), helped engineer the survival of John Major as Prime Minister in mid–1995. His role as adviser during the 1997 election was less successful and his attempt to negotiate with the Labour Prime Minister behind his own leade'rs back over keeping hereditary peers in the House of Lords led in late 1998 to his dismissal from the Oppoition front bench. Nonetheless the retention of around 91 hereditaries that he had brokered looked likely to succeed, albeit temporarily.

The Salisbury CECILs' famous devotion in modern times to throne and altar (the Church of England), to say nothing of Conservatism, was a good deal less solid in the more distant past. The **1st Earl**, Robert Cecil, made the fatal mistake of starting the process whereby the royal prerogative was turned into a bargaining counter in negotiations with Parliament over finance, with ultimate erosion of the Crown's prestige. His son the **2nd Earl** opposed CHARLES I during the Civil War, though he balked at signing the instrument approving CHARLES's beheading together with the sweeping away of the monarchy and House of Lords. Nevertheless he held high office under Cromwells' Protectorate, though he became a fawning royalist after the Restoration.

The **2nd Earl**'s son and expected successor was also a leading Parliamentarian in the Civil War. The latters' son the **3rd Earl** had regicidal tendencies and thought Protestant solidarity should override the claims of the legitimate heir to the throne. The **4th Earl** turned Catholic, but in such a confessedly cynical fashion as to call his sincerity in doubt.

The **3rd Marquess** was one of the most gifted politicians intellectually of the 19th century. He was one of the founders of modern Conservative thought in recognising that Conservatism must be based on property-ownership and practical materialism rather than ties of duty, deference to social superiors or even cloudier mysticisms, such as old-fashioned Tories revered. He nevertheless saw many of the causes that were closest to his heart lost, notably over parliamentary reform, the disestablishment of the Church of Ireland and the abolition of the practice of buying promotion in the army, all of which he opposed, and (for the time being) the introduction of life peers to the House of Lords, which rather surprisingly he supported. Even his principal achievement in diplomacy, the Treaty of Berlin and his handling of the events that led up to it, had no lasting effect and he later expressed doubt as to the wisdom of the policy which lay behind it.

He was in fact a master of the rearguard action and his brand of Conservatism, embodying just such an ultimately defensive strategy, dominated his party's strategic thinking for three generations until the advent of Margaret Thatcher (see THATCHER, B), who like him had taken up the study of chemistry when younger and was elected a Fellow of the Royal Society but who unlike him took a less pessimistic view of public affairs.

The **3rd** and **5th Marquesses** also made history in constitutional as opposed to party political terms. The former conceived the idea of the mandate which, unlike its meaning today, stated that the will of the people and that of the House of Commons were not necessarily identical. Accordingly the House of Lords might have a duty to reject controversial bills, *e.g.*, proposed constitutional changes, even though they had passed the Commons, on the grounds that the people could then express a direct view, for instance in a general election. From 1945, when the **5th Marquess** (as Lord Cecil of Essendon) was Conservative Leader in the Lords, the earlier theory evolved in to the Salisbury Doctrine. This argues that the Lords should not reject a measure specifically set out in the Government's general election manifesto.

The 1st BARON BURGHLEY (see EXETER, M) had by his 2nd w Mildred an est surv s:

ROBERT CECIL, **1st Earl of Salisbury**, so *cr* 4 May 1605, as also earlier 13 May 1603 BARON CECIL OF ESSENDON, Co Rutland, and 20 Aug 1604 VISCOUNT CRANBORNE, Co Dorset (all E), KG (1606), KB (Jan 1604/5), PC (2 Aug 1591); *b* 1June 1563; *educ* Gray's Inn and St John's Coll Cambridge (MA Oxon 1605); in suite of 4th Earl of Derby (*qv*) when latter sent to negotiate at Ostend with Alexander of Parma (chief of PHILIP II OF SPAIN's land forces) 1587/8 shortly before the Armada, MP Westminster 1586–87 and Herts 1588–89, 1592–93, 1597–98 and 1601, ktd 1591, Pncpl Sec of State 1596–1612, Chllr Duchy Lancaster 1597–99, envoy to France Feb-April 1598 to prevent a Franco-Spanish alliance and to States Gen (modern The Netherlands) July 1598, Keeper Privy Seal and Signet 1603, Ld High Treasurer 1608–12; High Sheriff Herts 1589, High Steward: Cambridge U 1591, Kingston-upon-Hull 1603, St Martin-le-Grand *c* 1603, Lewisham by 1606 and Winchester Coll 1612, Bailiff City London and Liberties of Westminster *c* 1598, Recorder Colchester 1599, Master Court of Wards for life 1599–1612, Chllr Cambridge and Dublin Us 1601–12, Warden Cinque Ports 1603, Ld Lt Herts 1605–12, Jt Ld Lt Dorset 1611–12, author: *An Answer to Certain Scandalous Papers scattered abroad under Colour of a Catholick Admonition* (1606) and *The State and Dignitie of a Secretaire of Estate's Place* (1642); *m* 31 Aug 1589 Elizabeth Brooke (*b* 1 Jan 1562/3; Ldy of ELIZABETH I's Privy and Bed Chamber; *d* 24 Jan 1596/7), dau of 10th Lord (Baron) Cobham (*qv*), and *d* 24 May 1612, having had, with two daus (Frances, *m* 25 July 1610 5th Earl of Cumberland (see DE CLIFFORD, B) and *d* 14 Feb 1643/44; Catherine):

WILLIAM CECIL, **2nd Earl of Salisbury**, KG (1624), KB (Jan 1604/5), PC (1626); *b* 28 March 1591; *educ* Westminster(?), Sherborne, St John's Coll Cambridge (MA 1605, MA Oxon 1605), in Paris and Gray's Inn; MP Weymouth 1610–11 and (in CROMWELL's Lower House, though a peer) King's Lynn 1649–53 and 1656–58, Ld Lt Herts 1612, Ranger Enfield Chase 1622–61(?), Capt Gentlemen Pensioners 1635–42, Parliamentarian Civil War: Parly Lt Herts, Dorset and (town of) Poole March 1641/2, Commr: to hold Courts Martial 1644, Uxbridge Conference Jan 1644/5 and Ctees for Excise June 1645 and Admlty Oct 1645, Foreign Plantations March 1645/6, Gt Seal July-Oct 1646, Newport Conference 1648, Memb: Ctee for Navy and Customs 1647 and Cncl of State Feb 1648/9–51 and 1652–53, voted a marquessate by Parl 1645, High Steward St Albans 1663; *m* 1 Dec 1608 Lady Catherine Howard (*bur* 27 Jan 1672/3), yst dau of 1st Earl of Suffolk (see SUFFOLK and BERKSHIRE, E), and *d* 3 Dec 1668, having had, with other issue (*d* young or unm):

    1 James, *Viscount Cranborne*; *b* March, *bapt* 15 June (JAMES I stood sponsor), *d* late Oct 1616

    2 Charles, *Viscount Cranborne*, KB (Feb 1625/6); *bapt* 15 July 1619; *educ* St John's Coll Cambridge; MP Hertford April and Nov 1640, Parliamentarian Civil War: Commr: Weekly Assessment Herts Feb 1642/3, Sequestration Estates of

Delinquents 1643, Levying Money 1643, Gen Assessment Wilts and Herts 1644, for executing New Model Ordinance Herts Feb 1644/5, Prevention Abuses in Heraldry March 1645/6, to Determine Scandalous Offences 1646, Assessment Dorset and Wilts 1647 and for Settling Militia Dorset and Wilts 1648, cmded Herts vols 1643, memb ctee to raise money for def Wilts 1644; *m* 2 April 1639 Lady Diana Maxwell (*b c* 1619; *d* June 1675), yr dau and coheir of 1st and last Earl of Dirletoun, and *dvp* Dec 1660, having had, with other issue (*d* young or unm):

(1) JAMES, **3rd Earl**

(1) Catherine; *m* 3rd Earl of Kinnoull (*qv*) and had issue

(2) Frances; *m* 24 Dec 1679 Sir William Bowyer, 2nd Bt (*see* 1949 edn), MP, and *d* 15 June 1723, leaving issue

3 Robert; *m* Catherine Hopton

4 Philip; *m* Ursula Allen

5 William; *m* Elizabeth, dau of Sir Thomas Lawley, 1st Bt, and had issue (*see* 1932 edn WENLOCK, B)

6 Algernon; MP Old Sarum *temp* CHARLES II; *m* Dorothy, dau of Sandford Nevile, of Chevet, Yorks, and *d* Nov 1676, leaving:

(1) Diana; *m* — Turnor, est s of Sir Edmond Turnor

7 Edward

1 Anne; *m* 4th Earl of Northumberland (*see* NORTHUMBERLAND, D) and had issue

2 Elizabeth; *b c* 1620; *m* 4 March 1638/9 3rd Earl of Devonshire (*see* DEVONSHIRE, D) and *d* 19 Nov 1689, leaving issue

3 Diana; *b* 1622; *d* 1633

4 Catherine; *m* 19 May 1645 Philip Sidney, 3rd Earl of Leicester of the 1618 *cr* (*see* DE L'ISLE, V), and *d* 18 Aug 1652, leaving issue

5 Mary; *b c* 1631; *m* 1st/6th Baron Sandys of the 1523/1660 *cr* (*dsp* between 12 March 1667/8 and 16 Jan 1668/9; *see* SANDYS, B, preliminary remarks) and *d* in or after 1676–78(?)

The 2nd EARL's gs,

JAMES CECIL, **3rd Earl of Salisbury**, PC (3 Jan 1678/9–18 Jan 1680/1); *b* by 27 March 1646; *educ* St John's Coll Cambridge(?); claimed maternal gf's Scottish Lordship of Parl of Innerwick Oct 1661, served 2nd Dutch War (1665–67) aboard HMS *Royal Charles* 1666, MP Herts April-Dec 1668, one of the peers apptd to interogate 1st and last Viscount Stafford (*see* STAFFORD, B) regarding the Popish Plot Jan 1678/9, enthusiastic Whig and Exclusionist (advocate of JAMES II's being excluded from the succession because he was RC), imprisoned Tower London 16 Feb 1676/7–1 June 1677 for in effect questioning CHARLES II's right to prorogue Parl, participant Rye House Plot (plan by ultra-Whigs and unreconstructed Cromwellians to assassinate CHARLES II and his bro Duke of York (later JAMES II)) April 1683; *m c* 1665 Lady Margaret Manners (*d* by 30 Aug 1682), dau of 8th Earl of Rutland (*see* RUTLAND, D), and *d* May 1683, having had:

1 JAMES, **4th Earl**

2 Robert; MP Wotton Basset 1708; *m* Elizabeth, dau and heiress of Isaac Meynell, of Meynell Langley, Derbys, and widow of Richard Hale, of King's Walden, Herts, and *d* Feb 1715/6, leaving:

(1) Charles; Bp Bangor

(1) Margaret; *m* Sir Robert Brown

3 William

4 Charles

5 George

1 Catharine; *m* 12 July 1683 Sir George Downing, 2nd Bt, and *d* 13 Aug 1688, leaving issue

2 Frances; *m* 1692 Sir William Halford, 1st Bt (*d* 1 March 1708/9), of Welham, Leics, and *d* 1698

3 Mary; *m* Sir William Forester, of Dothill, Salop, and *d* 29 March 1739/40, leaving issue (*see* LEIGHTON, Bt)

4 Margaret; *bapt* 16 April 1672; *m* 1st 1691 2nd Baron Stawell of Somerton (*dspm* 30 Nov 1692); *m* 2nd 9 Jan 1695/6, as his 2nd w, 1st Earl of Ranelagh (*dspms* 5 Jan 1711/2) and *d* 21 Feb 1727/8

5 Mildred; *m* 1st 14 Aug 1693 Sir Uvedale Corbet, 3rd Bt (*d* 15 Oct 1701; *see* 1970 edn), of Leighton, Montgomeryshire; *m* 2nd Sir Charles Hotham, 4th Bt (*see* HOTHAM, B), and *d* 18 Jan 1726/7, leaving issue

The 3rd EARL's est s,

JAMES CECIL, **4th Earl of Salisbury**; *bapt* 25 Sep 1666; *educ* St John's Coll Cambridge; High Steward Hertford, Gentleman Bedchamber, turned RC 1688 two or three months before the flight of JAMES II and arrival of WILLIAM III, later lamenting his bad timing in matters of religion, Col of a regt of horse Nov 1688, impeached for high treason after false information laid against him 26 Oct 1689 and incarcerated Tower London till June 1692, when released on bail; *m* 13 July 1683 Frances (*b* 20 Oct 1670; *d* 8 July 1713), dau and coheir of Simon Bennett (*see* TANKERVILLE, E) and *d* 24 Oct 1694, leaving:

JAMES CECIL, **5th Earl of Salisbury**; *b* 8 June 1691; *educ* Ch Ch Oxford (MA 1707); Ld Lt Herts 1712–14, politically a Tory; *m* 12 Feb 1708/9 Lady Anne Tufton (*b* 9 Aug 1693; *d* 22 March 1757), 2nd dau of 6th Earl of Thanet and coheir following his death to the Barony of De Clifford (*qv*), while through her mother, a coheir to the Barony of Ogle (*see* DEVONSHIRE, D), the subsequent Earls and later Marquesses of Salisbury inherited the representation; *d* 9 Oct 1728, leaving, with other issue, including two daus (Anne, *m* William Strode, MP, of Ponsbourne Hall, Herts, and *d* 3 July 1752; Catharine, *b* 15 Aug 1719, *m* 15 Feb 1736/7, as his 1st w, 2nd Earl of Egmont (*qv*) and *d* 16 Aug 1752, leaving issue):

JAMES CECIL, **6th Earl of Salisbury**; *b* 20 Oct 1713; *educ* Westminster; High Steward Hertford 1735–80, Govr Foundling Hosp 1739; *m* 28 Jan 1744/5 Elizabeth (*b c* 1721; *d* 3 Feb 1776), dau of Edward Keet, of Canterbury, said by a contemporary source to have been a barber and tourist guide, sis of Rev John Keet, Rector Hatfield, and niece of the Earl's steward, and *d* 19 Sept 1780, leaving, with two daus (*d* unm):

JAMES CECIL, **7th Earl** and **1st Marquess of Salisbury** (GB), so *cr* 25 Aug 1789, KG (1793), PC (1780); *b* 4 Sept 1748; *educ* Eton; Ld Lt Herts 1771–1823 and High Steward Hertford 1780, Col Herts Militia 1773–1815, MP (Tory) Gt Bedwyn 1774–80 and Launceston 8–19 Sept 1780, Treasurer Household 1780–82, Ld Chamberlain 1783–1804, DCL 1773, FSA April 1784, FRS May 1784, Col 1794, Jt PMG 1816–23; *m* 2 Dec 1773 Lady Mary Hill (*b* 16 Aug 1750; her wit, grace and intelligence are said to have won for her husb from Pitt the Younger his promotion to the post of Ld Chamberlain together with the Marquessate; her personal qualities suggested to the govt the notion of putting her forward as a Tory great lady to woo the masses in competition with Georgiana Duchess of Devonshire (*see* DEVONSHIRE, D) during the notorious Westminster Election of 1784, which after a great struggle and obstruction by the authorities resulted in the return of Charles James Fox (*see* ILCHESTER, E) to the H of C; she hunted her husb's pack of hounds into her late seventies or early eighties and *d* 27 Nov 1835 in a fire that destroyed the west wing of Hatfield House), dau of 1st Marquess of Downshire (*qv*), and *d* 13 June 1823, having had:

1 JAMES BROWNLOW WILLIAM, **2nd Marquess**

1 Georgiana; *b* 20 March 1786; *m* 27 Feb 1816, as his 2nd w, 1st Baron Cowley of Wellesley (*see* COWLEY, E) and *dspm* 18 Jan 1860

2 Emily; *b* 14 July 1789; Extra Ldy of the Bedchamber to QUEEN ADELAIDE; *m* 29 May 1812 (*divorce* 1827), as his 1st w, 1st and last Marquess of Westmeath (*see* WESTMEATH, E) and *d* 21 Jan 1858, leaving issue

3 Caroline; *d* young

The 1st MARQUESS's only s,

JAMES BROWNLOW WILLIAM CECIL later GASCOYNE-CECIL (roy licence 22 March 1821), **2nd Marquess of Salisbury**, KG (1842), PC (1826); *b* 17 April 1791; *educ* Eton and Ch Ch Oxford (MA 1813, DCL 1834); MP (Tory) Weymouth 1813–17 and Hertford 1817–23, Col Herts Militia 1813, Commr Indian Affrs 1818–27, High Steward Hertford 1823, Provincial Grand Master Freemasons Herts 1833–44 and Dep Grand Master Utd Grand Lodge England 1841–44, Ld Lt Middx 1842–68, Ld Privy Seal March-Dec 1852, Ld Pres Cncl 1858–59; *m* 1st 2 Feb 1821 Frances Mary (*b* 25 Jan 1802; *d* 15 Oct 1839), dau and heiress of Bamber Gascoyne, of Childwall Hall, Lancs, and had:

1 James Emilius William Evelyn, *Viscount Cranborne*; *b* 29 Oct 1821; historian; *dvp* unm 14 June 1865

2 Arthur George Villiers; *b* 15 Dec 1823; *d* 25 April 1825

3 ROBERT ARTHUR TALBOT, **3rd Marquess**

4 Eustace Brownlow Henry (GASCOYNE-)CECIL, JP (Dorset, Essex and Middx), of Lytchett Heath, Poole, Dorset; *b* 24 April 1834; *educ* Harrow and Sandhurst; 43rd LI Cape and India, Coldstream Gds Crimea 1855–56 (Lt-Col 1861, ret 1863), Surveyor-Gen Ordnance 1874–80, MP S Essex 1865–68 and W Essex 1868–85, CA Dorset, chm For and Colonial, American, For and Gen, and Alliance Tst Cos, dir GER; *m* 18 Sept 1860 Lady Gertrude Louisa Scott (*d* 30 April 1919), 4th dau of 2nd Earl of Eldon (*qv*), and *d* 3 July 1921, leaving:

(1) EVELYN GASCOYNE-CECIL, 1st BARON ROCKLEY (*qv*)

(2) Algernon; *b* 31 Jan 1879; *educ* Eton and New Coll Oxford (BA 1901, MA 1905, Pres Oxford Union 1901); barrister Inner Temple 1905, served Min Munitions, Admlty Intell and FO WW I, Kt Justice SMO Malta 1938, FRHistS; *m* 17 July 1923 Lady Guendolen Fanny Godolphin Osborne (*d* 25 Feb 1933), est dau of 10th Duke of Leeds (*see* 1963 edn), and *dsp* 13 April 1953

(1) Blanche Louise; *b* 2 April 1872; *d* unm 21 Jan 1945

1 Mildred Arabella Charlotte; *m* 7 July 1842 Alexander James Beresford Beresford-Hope, PC, DL, MP Cambridge U (*d* 3 Sept 1887) and owner of the *Saturday Review* in which his bro-in-law the future **3rd Marquess of Salisbury** both cultivated a reputation as leading commentator on public affairs and earned money that was badly needed due to his f's disapproval of his marriage, and *d* 18 March 1881, leaving issue (*see* STRATHEDEN and CAMPBELL, B and ULLSWATER, V)

2 Blanche Mary Harriet; *m* 15 Aug 1843 James Maitland Balfour and *d* 16 May 1872, leaving issue (*see* BALFOUR, E)

The **2nd Marquess** *m* 2nd 29 April 1847 Lady Mary Catherine Sackville-West (*b* 23 July 1824; *m* 2nd 5 July 1870 15th Earl of Derby (*qv*); *d* 6 Dec 1900), 2nd dau of 5th Earl De la Warr (*qv*), and by her had:

5 Sackville Arthur; *b* 16 March 1848; MA; *d* unm 29 Jan 1898

6 Arthur, JP (Hants); *b* 3 July 1851; *educ* Trin Coll Cambridge (MA); Capt 4th Vol Bn Hants Regt; *m* 1st 8 Jan 1874 Elizabeth Ann (*d* 11 Oct 1901), est dau of Joseph Wilson, of Woodhorn Manor, Northumberland, and had:

(1) Arthur William James, JP; *b* 4 April 1875; *educ* Winchester and Trin Coll Cambridge; Capt Gren Gds Boer War; *m* 1 Dec 1906 Hon Beatrice Susan Theodosia Stuart Wortley (*d* 30 Dec 1973), er dau of 1st and last Baron Stuart of Wortley (*see* WHARNCLIFFE, E), and *d* 26 Sept 1936, leaving:

1a James Charles; *b* 3 May 1915; *educ* Eton and Magdalene Coll Cambridge (BA1937); Lt KRRC WW II; *m* 18 Oct 1941 (*divorce* 1947) Elizabeth Hope, only dau of William Priestley Caton-Woodville, and *dsp* 6 April 1964

2a Robert Arthur; *b* 16 Jan 1921; *educ* Winchester; Capt KRRC WW II, Assist to Dir Wallace Collection 1946 on; *d* unm 29 May 1994

1a Mary Elizabeth; *b* 18 March 1908; *m* 23 Sep 1935 Noel Charles Douglas Wilkey (*d* 20 Oct 1970), s of Francis Douglas Wilkey, and had issue

(2) Reginald Edward, DSO (1918), JP (Hants); *b* 15 Nov 1878; *educ* Winchester and Trin Coll Cambridge; a Verderer New Forest, Lt-Col 21st Lancers WW I (despatches); *m* 1 Feb 1902 Mary Beatrice (*d* 27 Jan 1940), dau of Henry Drayson Pilcher, of S Kensington, and *d* 22 Dec 1931, leaving:

1a Lionel; *b* 26 July 1907; *educ* Eton and Trin Coll Cambridge (BA 1930, MA); Capt Roy Scots Greys (SR), MFH Wilton and Old Berkeley; *m* 1941 *Marion Elizabeth Jessie (*m* 2nd 18 July 1966 4th Baron Romilly; see 1970 edn), er dau of Charles M Clover, of Pilgrims Way, Blewbury, Berks, and *dsp* 31 March 1963

1a Margaret Mary; *b* 31 July 1903; *m* 27 Sept 1941 George Heriot Pitt, FRCS, er s of George Newton Pitt, OBE, FRCP, and *d* 3 Sept 1950

2a (Catherine) Angela; *b* 17 Sep 1909; Lt-Col WRAC WW II; *d* unm 17 Sept 1969

6 (cont.) Lord Arthur Gascoyne-Cecil *m* 2nd 4 Nov 1902 Frederica (*m* 2nd 29 April 1922 Arthur Leigh Barker; *d* 17 March 1941), er dau of Baron Otto von Klenck, of Gmunden, Austria, and *d* 16 July 1913

7 Lionel; *b* 21 March 1853; *educ* Cambridge (BA); Maj and Hon Lt-Col 5th Bn Northumberland Fus; *d* unm 13 Jan 1901

3 Mary Arabella Arthur; *b* 26 April 1850; *m* 25 March 1872 10th Earl of Galloway (*qv*) and *d* 18 Aug 1903

4 Margaret Elizabeth; *d* unm 11 March,1919

The 2nd MARQUESS's est surv s,

ROBERT ARTHUR TALBOT GASCOYNE-CECIL, **3rd Marquess of Salisbury**, KG (1878), GCVO (1902), PC (1866), JP (Middx), DL (Kent and Middx); *b* 3 Feb 1830; *educ* Eton, Ch Ch Oxford (BA 1850, MA 1853, Sec and Treasurer Oxford Union, Fell All Souls 1853, DCL 1869, Hon Student Ch Ch 1894) and Lincoln's Inn; MP (C) Stamford 1853–68, Sec State India 1866–67 and 1874–78, Special Amb Constantinople Conf 1876–77, For Sec April 1878–April 1880, 1885–86, 1887–92 and 1895–1900, Jt Amb (with Disraeli) Congress of Berlin June-July 1878, PM June 1885–Jan 1886 (offered a dukedom by QUEEN VICTORIA after his first premiership but refused it on the grounds of insufficient wealth), July 1886–92 and 1895–1902, 1st Ld Treasury 1886–87, 1st Ld Privy Seal 1900–02, Tstee Nat Portrait Gallery 1856–69, chm: GER 1868–72 and Herts QS 1868–76, Hon Col 4th Bn Beds Regt and 1st Cinque Ports Rifle Vols, Chllr Oxford U 1869–1903, Er Bro Trin Ho 1885–1903, LLD Cantab 1888, PBA 1894, Ld Warden Cinque Ports 1896–1903, High Steward Westminster and Gt Yarmouth, FRS; *m* 11 July 1857 Georgina Charlotte, VA, CI (*d* 20 Nov 1899), dau of Sir Edward Hall Alderson, Baron Exchequer, and *d* 22 Aug 1903, having had:

1 JAMES EDWARD HUBERT, **4th Marquess**

2 (Rupert Ernest) William (GASCOYNE-)CECIL (Rt Rev); *b* 9 March 1863; *educ* Eton and Univ Coll Oxford (DD); ordained 1887, Curate Gt Yarmouth 1887–88, Rector Bishops Hatfield 1888–1916, RD Hertford 1904–16, Hon Chaplain to HM EDWARD VII 1909, Hon Canon St Albans 1910, Bp Exeter 1916–36, author: *Science and Religion*, *Changing China* (1910) and *Difficulties and Duties*; *m* 16 Aug 1887 Lady Florence Mary Bootle Wilbraham (*d* 17 May 1944), dau of 1st Earl of Lathom (*see* SKELMERSDALE, B), and *d* 23 June 1936, having had:

(1) Randle William GASCOYNE-CECIL; *b* 28 Nov 1889; Lt Warwickshire RHA WW I 1915–17 (wounded); *m* 1st 26 June 1914 (*divorce* 1915) Dorothy May, dau of Edward Janaway; *m* 2nd 2 June 1916 Elizabeth Claire (*d* 1972), dau of George Turner, and was *ka* 1 Dec 1917, having by her had:

1a William; *b* and *d* 1917

1a *Anne Mary [Mrs David Wilson, 371 Daly Ave, Ottawa, Canada K1N 6G8]; *b* posthumously 29 July 1918; 2nd Offr WRNS WW II; *m* 18 June 1945 *Lt-Cdr David Bryce Wilson, RCNVR, Canadian For Serv, s of Dr David Bruce Wilson, of Toronto, and has:

1b *Andrew David Randle [Andrew Wilson Esq, 13 Lynhaven Crescent, Nepean, Ontario, Canada K2E 5K3]; *b* 30 Nov 1956; Canadian For Serv; *m* 1988 *Susan Blyth-Schofield

1b *Elizabeth Anne [Mrs Bruno Fascinato, 52 Manitoba St, Guelp, Ontario, Canada N1E 3B9]; *b* 23 June 1946; *m* 1982 *Bruno Fascinato and has:

1c *Francesco Bruno Bruce; *b* 1980

2c *David Tullio Charles; *b* 1986

2b *Carolyn Susan Mary; *b* 26 Nov 1948; *m* 1972 *Simon Roger Williams [Simon Williams Esq, c/o Canadian High Commission, Canberra, Australia]

3b *Jennifer Laura Eve; *b* 13 July 1951; *m* 1982 (*divorce* 1994) Nyle Belkov

4b *Deborah Rosalind Louise [Ms Deborah Wilson, 702 Parkdale Ave, Ottawa, Ontario K1Y 1J4, Canada]; *b* 14 Aug 1952

(2) Victor Alexander GASCOYNE-CECIL, JP (Essex 1939), DL (1951–68); *b* 21 May 1891; *educ* Westminster and RMC Sandhurst; Maj Hants Regt and Tank Corps WW I (twice wounded), NW Frontier India 1922 and WW II, High Sheriff Essex 1949; *m* 25 Nov 1915 Fairlie Estelle Caroline (*d* 1980), er dau of Lt-Col Arthur Watson, Suffolk Regt, and *d* 17 Jan 1977, leaving:

1a +Rupert Arthur Victor GASCOYNE-CECIL later CECIL (deed poll 1955), DFC and bar; *b* 1 May 1917; *educ* Stowe and Balliol Coll Oxford (MA 1945, DPhil 1949); W/Cdr RAFVR WW II, V-Pncpl Linacre Coll Oxford; *m* 1st 12 Oct 1940 (*divorce* 1974) Helen Moira Rosemary Phillips, only child of Col Roland Luker, CMG, DSO, of Uffington Cottage, Stamford, and has:

1b +Desmond Hugh, CMG (1995) [Desmond Cecil Esq CMG, 38 Palace Rd, E Molesey, Surrey KT8 9DL]; *b* 19 Oct 1941; *educ* Magdalen Coll Sch, Queen's Coll Oxford (BA 1965, MA 1968), with Prof Max Rostal and Berne U; with FCO, Counsellor Vienna, U-Sec FCO 1992–95; *m* 20 June 1964 *Ruth Elizabeth, yr dau of Dr Werner Sachs, and has:

1c +Thomas Desmond; *b* 8 Dec 1966

2c +Nicholas David; *b* 15 Jan 1968

1c *Sarah Ruth; *b* 1972

2b +Timothy Rupert [Timothy Cecil Esq, 27 King's Rd, Flitwick, Bedford]; *b* 21 Feb 1944; *educ* Magdalen Coll Sch, Exeter Coll Oxford (BA 1966) and Munich U; *m* 1977 *Ursula Margaret, dau of John Christopher Rotton, of Compton, Sussex, and has:

1c +Robert; *b* 1977

2c +Thomas; *b* 1979

1b *June Elizabeth [Mrs June Robb, 4 Pleasant Place, Bathford, Bath BA1 7TL]; *b* 13 July 1946; *m* 3 Aug 1968 (*divorce* 1994) Michael Durnford Robb, s of Michael Anthony Moyse Robb, of Hampstead, and has:

1c *Geoffrey Edward; *b* 1972

1c *Joanna Frances; *b* 1970

1a (cont.) Dr Rupert Cecil *m* 2nd 19– *Anna Theresa, dau of Donald Hodson (*see* ARBUTHNOTT, V), and by her has:

2b *Flora; *b* 1971

3b *Maud; *b* 1972

2a Anthony Robert; *b* 25 May 1921; *educ* Felsted; *m* 1st 4 July 1944 (*divorce* 1951) Mary Hood, only dau of Rev Ernest James Simpson, of Great Burstead Vicarage, Billericay, Essex, formerly of S Rhodesia, and had:

1b +Michael Anthony [Michael Gascoyne-Cecil Esq, 12 School Rd, Downham, Essex]; *b* 13 Jan 1946; *educ* Felsted; *m* 1969 (*divorce* 1990) Carol Ann, only dau of Samuel Oxford, and has:

1c +Jonathan Michael; *b* 1971

2c +Christopher Anthony; *b* 1973

1c *Victoria Ruth; *b* 1976

2c *Elizabeth Carol; *b* 1980

1b *Jennifer Jean Mary [Mrs John Mills, Thorington Hall, Wherstead, Suffolk]; *b* 7 Oct 1947; *m* 1981 *John Warwick Mills and has:

1c *George Frederick Cecil; *b* 1986

1c *Eleanor Mary Cecil; *b* 1984

2a (cont.) Anthony Gascoyne-Cecil *m* 2nd 12 May 1952 *Alison Julia [Mrs Anthony Gascoyne-Cecil, Woodlands, Butts Green, Sandon, Chelmsford, Essex], only dau of Herbert Cecil Foster, of Little Baddow, Essex, and *d* 28 June 1998, leaving by her:

2b +Richard David [Richard Gascoyne-Cecil Esq, Chestnut Cottage, Butts Green, Sandon, Chelmsford, Essex]; *b* 30 Oct 1953; *educ* Felsted; *m* 1978 *Judith Westhorp, only dau of Geoffrey Roberts, OBE, of Chester, and has:

1c +James Anthony; *b* 1981

2c +Andrew Peter; 1985

1c +Helen Elizabeth; *b* 1982

2b *Caroline Alison; *b* 20 Dec 1955

3b *Rosalind Julia [Mrs David Platt, 2 Ilgars Cottage, Mosses Lane, S Woodham Ferrers, Chelmsford, Essex]; *b* 2 Feb 1962; *m* 1993 *David Platt, s of Malcolm Platt, of The Wirral

(3) John Arthur GASCOYNE-CECIL, MC (1918); *b* 28 March 1893; Capt RFA, Adj 1915; *ka* 27 Aug 1918

(4) Rupert Edward; *b* 20 Jan 1895; Lt 4th Bn Bedfordshire Regt; *ka* 11 July 1915

(1) Eve Alice; *b* 13 Jan 1900; *m* 16 April 1929 V-Adml Richard SHELLEY later BENYON (deed poll 1964), CB, CBE, 2nd s of Sir John Shelley, 9th Bt (*qv*), and *d* 1994, leaving issue

(2) Mary Edith; *b* 13 Jan 1900; *m* 29 Jan 1921 4th Baron Manners (*qv*) and *d* 1994, leaving issue

(3) Anne; *b* 8 Oct 1906; *d* 23 Oct 1924

3 (EDGAR ALGERNON) ROBERT (GASCOYNE-)CECIL, 1st and last VISCOUNT CECIL OF CHELWOOD, of Grinstead, Co Sussex (UK), so *cr* 24 Dec 1923, PC (16 June 1915), QC (1899), JP (Herts); *b* 14 Sept 1864; *educ* Eton and Univ Coll Oxford (MA, Hon Fell, Hon DCL 1919); Priv Sec to his f when PM 1886–88, barrister Inner Temple 1887, memb Gen Cncl Bar, Bencher Inner Temple 1910, chm Herts QS 1911–20, Chllr Consistory Ct and Vicar-Gen Archbishopric York 1915, MP (C) E Marylebone 1906–10, stood (C) for Blackburn and N Cambridge 1910, MP (Ind C) Hitchin 1911–23, For Affairs: Parly U-Sec 1915–18 and Assist Sec 1918–19, Min of Blockade 1916–18, Ld Privy Seal 1923–24, Chllr Duchy Lancaster 1924–27, Ch Br Delegate Opium Conf Geneva 1925, Chm later Pres League of Nations Union, Nobel Peace Prize 1937, Chllr Birmingham U 1918–44, Rector Aberdeen U 1924–27, Hon LLD: Aberdeen, Athens, Cambridge, Columbia, Liverpool, Manchester, Princeton and St Andrews; author: *The Principles of Commercial Law* (1891) and *The Way of Peace* (1928); *m* 22 Jan 1889 Lady Eleanor Lambton (*d* 24 April 1959), dau of 2nd Earl of Durham (*qv*), and *dsp* 24 Nov 1958, when the title expired

4 Edward Herbert (GASCOYNE-)CECIL, KCMG (1913), DSO (1898); *b* 12 July 1867; joined Gren Gds 1887, served: Dongola Expdn 1896 (despatches, Brevet Maj, 4th Class Medjidie, Br Medal, Khedive's Medal, two clasps), special mission to KING MENELIK OF ABYSSINIA 1897, Nile Expdn 1898 (Atbara: despatches; Khartoum: despatches and two clasps) and Boer War 1899–1901 (despatches, Brevet Lt-Col, Queen's Medal, two clasps), Agent-Gen Sudan Govt and Dir Intell Cairo 1904–06, Egypt: U-Sec War 1906 and Finance 1907–13 and Fin Advsr 1912–18, Grand Cordon Order Nile 1915; *m* 18 June 1894, as her 1st husb, Violet Georgina, DGStJ (Chev Legn Hon, ed *National Review* 1932–48, author *My Picture Gallery*; *m* 2nd 26 Feb 1921 1st and last Viscount Milner, KG, GCB, GCMG, PC (*d* 13 May 1925; *see* 1925 edn), and *d* 10 Oct 1958), 2nd dau of Adml Frederick Augustus Maxse (*see* BERKELEY, B), and *d* 13 Dec 1918, having had:

(1) George Edward GASCOYNE-CECIL; *b* 9 Sept 1895; 2nd Lt Gren Gds; *ka* 1 Sept 1914

(1) Helen Mary; *b* 11 May 1901; author; *m* 8 Feb 1921 2nd Baron Hardinge of Penshurst (*qv*) and *d* 1979, leaving issue

5 HUGH RICHARD HEATHCOTE (GASCOYNE-)CECIL, 1st and last BARON QUICKSWOOD, of Clothall, Co Hertford (UK), so *cr* 25 Jan 1941, PC (16 Jan 1918); *b* 14 Oct 1880; *educ* Eton and Univ Coll Oxford (BA 1891, MA 1894, Hon DCL1924); Assist Priv Sec to his f when For Sec 1891–92, MP (C) Greenwich 1895–1906 and Oxford U 1910–37, Lt RFC WW I, memb House of Laity Ch Assembly 1919–45, Provost Eton 1936–44, Tstee London Library, Hon DCL Durham, Hon LLD: Edinburgh 1910 and Cantab 1933, Hon Fell: Hertford Coll Oxford (Fell 1891–1936) and New Coll Oxford 1944; *d* unm 10 Dec 1956, when the title expired

1 Beatrix Maud, JP (Hants); Pres C and U Women's Franchise Assoc; *m* 27 Oct 1883 2nd Earl of Selborne (*qv*) and *d* 27 April 1950, leaving issue

2 Gwendolen (GASCOYNE-)CECIL; author *The Life of Robert, Marquis of Salisbury* (2 vols 1921); *d* unm 28 Sept 1945

3 Fanny Georgina Mildred; *d* 24 April 1867

The 3rd MARQUESS's est s,

JAMES EDWARD HUBERT GASCOYNE-CECIL, **4th Marquess of Salisbury**, KG (1917), GCVO (1909), CB (1900), PC, JP (Herts), DL; *b* 23 Oct 1861; *educ* Eton and Univ Coll Oxford (BA 1885, MA 1889, Hon Fell 1923, Hon DCL 1926); MP (C) NE Lancs 1885–92 and Rochester 1893–1903, Parly U-Sec For Affrs 1900–03, Ld Privy Seal 1903–05 and 1924–29, Pres BOT March-Dec 1905, Ld Pres Cncl and Dep Ldr Ho Lds 1922–24, Chllr Duchy Lancaster 1922–23, Leader Ho Lds 1925–29; Hon Col: 86th E Anglian Herts Yeo Bde, RFA (TD) and 48th (S Midland) Div RE (TA), Col cmdg 4th Bn Bedfordshire Regt, Col Hertfordshire Vol Regt and 4th Bn Essex Regt Boer War 1900, Chm Herts QS, High Steward: Westminster 1903 and Hertford 1905, ADC to TM EDWARD VII 1903–10 and GEORGE V 1910–29, Chm Canterbury Ho of Laymen 1906–11, Ld High Steward Coronation 1937; *m* 17 May 1887 Lady Cecily Alice Gore, JP (Herts) (*b* 15 July 1867; Ldy Bedchamber to HM QUEEN ALEXANDRA 1907–10, OStJ; *d* 5 Feb 1955), 2nd dau of 5th Earl of Arran (*qv*), and *d* 4 April 1947, leaving:

1 ROBERT ARTHUR JAMES, **5th Marquess**
2 (Edward Christian) David (GASCOYNE-)CECIL, CH (1949); *b* 9 April 1902; *educ* Eton and Ch Ch Oxford (BA 1924, MA 1927, Hon Student 1981); Fell: Wadham Coll Oxford 1924–30, New Coll Oxford 1938–69 (Hon Fell thereafter), Hon LittD: Leeds 1950, Hon DLitt London 1957, Hon DLitt Glasgow 1962, Hon LLD: St Andrews 1951 and Liverpool 1951, Cambridge: Leslie Stephen Lecturer 1935, Clark Lecturer 1941, Rede Lecturer 1956, Goldsmiths' Prof Eng Lit Oxford 1948–69, Tstee Nat Portrait Gallery 1937–51, Pres: Poetry Soc 1947–48 and Jane Austen Soc 1966–86, Hawthornden Prize 1930, James Tait Black Memorial Prize 1930, Medal RSL 1930, CLit 1972, author: *The Stricken Deer* (1929), *Sir Walter Scott* (1933), *Early Victorian Novelists* (1934), *Jane Austen* (1935), *The Young Melbourne* (1939), *Hardy, the Novelist* (1943), *Two Quiet Lives* (1948), *Poets and Story-Tellers* (1949), *Lord M* (1954), *The Fine Art of Reading* (1957), *Max* (1964), *Visionary and Dreamer: Two Poetic Painters — Samuel Palmer and Edward Burne-Jones* (1969), *The Bodley Head Max Beerbohm* (ed, 1970), *A Choice of Tennyson's Verse* (1971), *The Cecils of Hatfield House* (1973), *Library Looking-glass* (1973), *A Portrait of Jane Austen* (1978) and *A Portrait of Charles Lamb* (1983); *m* 13 Oct 1932 Rachel (*d* 29 July 1982), only dau of Sir Desmond MacCarthy, the critic, and *d* 1 Jan 1986, leaving:

(1) +Jonathan Hugh [Jonathan Cecil Esq, c/o Kate Feast Management, Primrose Hill Studios, 43a Princess Rd, London NW1]; *b* 22 Feb 1939; *educ* Eton, New Coll Oxford (BA) and LAMDA; jnlst and actor: *A Heritage and its History* (1965), *The Ruling Class* (1969), *Lulu* (1971), *Cowardy Custard* (1972), *Uncle Vanya* (1988), *The Dressmaker* (1990), *The Seagull* 1995, *Pride and Prejudice* 1996 (theatre); *The Great St Trinians Train Robbery* (1965), *Otley* (1968), *Barry Lyndon* (1973), *History of the World Pt I* (1980), *E La Nave Va* ('And The Ship Sails On', 1983), *The Fool* (1991) (cinema); also TV; *m* 1st July 1963 (*divorce* 19–) Vivien Sarah Frances, actress, est dau of David G Heilbron, TD, of Glasgow; *m* 2nd 3 Nov 1976 *Anna Sharkey, actress and singer

(2) +Hugh Peniston [Hugh Cecil Esq, 18 Warwick Ave, London W9 2PT]; *b* 29 Dec 1941; *educ* Eton and New Coll Oxford (BA 1964); history lecturer Leeds U; author: *The Flower of Battle* (1996) and (with Mirabel Cecil) *Clever Hearts* (1990, Duff Cooper Memorial Prize and Marsh Biography Award); *m* 20 Oct 1972 *Mirabel, writer, dau of Richard Walker, of Withington, Glos, and has:

1a +Conrad Richard James; *b* 4 Oct 1973

2a +David Edward Hugh; *b* 1978

1a *Clementine Rachel; *b* 22 Oct 1975

2a *Stella Gweadden Anna; *b* 22 June 1984

(3) *(Alice) Laura; *b* 29 Nov 1947; *m* 11 Jan 1975 *Angelo Hornak, s of Hermann Hornak and Mrs Albert Hourani, and has:

1a *Leo David; *b* 1979

1a *Francesca Rachel; *b* 1982

1 Beatrice Edith Mildred, DCVO (1947); *b* 10 Aug 1891; Ldy Bedchamber to HM QUEEN ELIZABETH (later THE QUEEN MOTHER) 1946, Extra Ldy Bedchamber 1946; *m* 12 April 1913 4th Baron Harlech (*qv*) and had issue
2 Mary Alice, GCVO (1955), CBE (1946); *b* 29 July 1895; Mistress Robes to HM THE QUEEN 1953–66, Hon LLD: Leeds 1954 and Exeter 1956, Chllr Exeter U 1956–71; *m* 21 April 1917 10th Duke of Devonshire (*qv*) and had issue

The 4th MARQUESS's er s,
ROBERT ARTHUR JAMES GASCOYNE-CECIL, **5th Marquess of Salisbury**, KG (1946), PC (1940), JP (Herts 1921, Dorset 1928), DL (Herts 1937, Dorset 1946); *b* 27 Aug 1893; *educ* Eton and Ch Ch Oxford (Hon DCL 1951); Lt Gren Gds (SR) WW I 1915–18 (Croix de Guerre, Chev Order Crown Belgium); MP (U) Dorset S 1929–41, Parly Sec to Ld Privy Seal 1934, Parly U-Sec For Affrs 1935–38, Paymaster-Gen May–Oct 1940, Sec State Dominion Affrs Oct 1940–42 and 1943–45, Sec State Colonies Feb–Nov 1942, Ld Privy Seal Nov 1942–43, Ldr Ho Lds 1942–45 and 1951–57, Ld Privy Seal 1951–52, Sec State Cwlth Rels May–Dec 1952, Ld Pres Cncl Dec 1952–57, Actg For Sec June-Oct 1953, called up to Ho of Lds 1941 *vp* in f's Barony, Chllr: Order Garter 1960–72, Liverpool U Nov 1951–71, Hon LLD: Toronto 1949, Birmingham 1950, Liverpool 1951, Cambridge 1954, Manchester 1954, London 1955, Hon DLitt Exeter 1956, Hon LLD St Andrews 1953, dir Westminster Bank, memb Roy Commn Historical MSS. 1928, Freedom of Salisbury, S Rhodesia, 1956, Pres: ESU 1943–51, U Coll SW, Exeter, 1945–56, High Steward Hertford 1947, FRA 1957, chm Roy Commn Historical Monuments 1957, Tstee Nat Gallery 1960–66; *m* 8 Dec 1915 Elizabeth Vere (*d* 5 June 1982), est dau of Lord Richard Cavendish (*see* DEVONSHIRE, D), and *d* 23 Feb 1972, having had:

1 ROBERT EDWARD PETER GASCOYNE-CECIL, **6th and present Marquess of Salisbury**

2 Michael Charles James; *b* 21 Oct 1918; *d* 27 Oct 1934

3 Richard Hugh Vere; *b* 31 Jan 1924; *educ* Eton; Sgt-Pilot RAF WW II; *d* following an accident 12 Aug 1944

Seat: Hatfield House, Hatfield, Herts. Up till 1607 Theobalds, also in Hertfordshire, was the principal residence of the Salisbury CECILs. But JAMES I took a fancy to it and offered Hatfield in exchange. The **1st Earl** prudently concurred. He spent the rest of his life first demolishing half the old palace at Hatfield (the other half still survives), then building the present structure. It was a much more symbolic act than just another late-Renaissance testimony to a family's wealth and power. Hatfield old palace was where the **1st Earl**'s former sovereign ELIZABETH I had been brought up and in the hall of which she had actually appointed his father her principal secretary three days after succeeding to the throne. The new house was only finished after the **1st Earl** had died.

He has been called his own architect but the detailed work was done by Robert Lemming, Limminge or Lyminge, the clerk of the works, who later worked on Blickling Hall, Norfolk (*see* also BUCKINGHAMSHIRE, E). According to some sources Lemming/Limminge/Lyminge was helped by Thomas Wilson, a servant of the **1st Earl**'s, who was later knighted, and Simon Basil, Surveyor of the King's Works.

SALT of Saltaire

Arms: Az. a chevron indented between two mullets in chief and a demi-ostrich displayed holding in the beak a horse-shoe in base or. **Crest:** Upon a rock an alpaca statant ppr. **Motto:** *Quid non Deo juvante* ('What can one not accomplish with God helping?'). **Creation:** Bt. (UK) 30 Oct 1869.

SIR PATRICK MACDONNELL SALT, 7TH BT, of Saltaire, Co York [Sir Patrick Salt Bt, Hillwatering Farmhouse, Langham, Suffolk IP31 3ED]; *b* 25 Sept 1932; *s* bro 1991; *educ* Stowe; memb Lloyd's, dir Cassidy Davis Members Agency 1983–92; *m* 1 July 1976 *Ann Elizabeth Mary, dau of Dr Thomas Kay Maclachlan and widow of Denys Kilham Roberts, OBE

Lineage: TITUS SALT; *d* 7 March 1804, leaving:

DANIEL SALT, of Bradford, Yorks; *m* 5 July 1802 Grace (*d* 10 Nov 1854), dau of Issac Smithies, of The Manor House, Morley, and *d* 28 Dec 1843, having had, with other issue:

Sir Titus Salt, 1st Bt (UK), so *cr* 30 Oct 1869, of Saltaire and Crow Nest, Yorks, DL and JP Yorks; *b* 20 Sept 1803; Sr Alderman Bradford, MP (Lib) Bradford 1848–50, pioneer of model towns for working people; *m* 21 Aug 1830 Caroline (*d* 20 April 1893), dau of George Whitlam, of Great Grimsby, Lincs, and had, with another s (*d* young) and three daus (*d* unm):

1 WILLIAM HENRY (Sir), **2nd Bt**

2 George; *b* 22 April 1833; *m* 1875 Jennie Louisa Fresco, of Florence (*d* Aug 1923), and *d* 8 May 1913

3 Edward, of Bathampton House, Bath, DL and JP Yorks; *b* 3 April 1837; *m* 1st 10 July 1861 Mary Jane Susan (*dsp* 9 Oct 1870), est dau of Samuel Elgood, of Leicester; *m* 2nd 1 Nov 1871 Sarah Amelia (*d* 31 July 1929), er dau of William Rouse, of Burley House, York, and *dsp* 24 Oct 1903

4 Herbert; *b* 17 April 1840; *m* 1st 1889 Elizabeth (*d* 1898), dau of John Douglas Farrell, and had:

(1) Lois Alexandrina Caroline; *b* 1892; *m* 1921 Victor Drogez, and has issue. He *d* 1945

4 (cont.) Herbert Salt *m* 2nd 1899 Margaret (*d* 28 March 1910), widow of Christopher Robert de Lacey, and *d* 21 July 1912

5 Titus, DL and JP Yorks; *b* 28 Aug 1843; *m* 15 March 1866 Catherine (*d* 22 Jan 1930), est surv dau of Joseph Crossley, of Broomfield, Halifax, Yorks, and niece of Sir Francis Crossley, 1st Bt (*see* SOMERLEYTON, B), and *d* 19 Nov 1887, leaving issue:

(1) Gordon Locksley; *b* 17 Dec 1866; *educ* Trin Coll Cambridge (BA); *m* 29 April 1903 Florence Mary (*d* 14 Jan 1959), dau of Rev James Williams Scarlett, Rector of Rossington, Doncaster, and *d* 12 April 1938, leaving:

1a John Scarlett Alexander; first Dir Bdcasting to Europe and N American Dir BBC WW II, Programme Dir N Region BBC, Lt RE; *b* 8 June 1905; *educ* Trin Coll Cambridge (BA 1927, MA 1939); *m* 14 July 1939 Olive Mary (*m* 2nd 31 Oct 1952 Christopher Bellhouse Gorton (*d* 2 Nov 1959)), only dau of William Gilbert Shapley, and *d* 26 Dec 1947, leaving:

1b +DANIEL ALEXANDER [Daniel Salt Esq, c/o British Airways, PO Box 190104, Anchorage, AK 99519–0104, USA]; *b* 15 Aug 1943, heir presumptive; *educ* Cheadle Hulme Sch; *m* 26 Aug 1968 Mehrchide (*d* 15 Feb 1998), only dau of Dr Ahmad Emami, of Teheran, Iran, and has:

1c *Firoozeh Katherine; *b* 7 Aug 1971

2c *Maryam Rachel; *b* 6 Oct 1974

2b +Nicholas John [Nicholas Salt Esq, Ty-Llottyn, Llawrynglyn, Caersurs, Powys, SY17 5RJ]; *b* 7 Dec 1945; *educ* Sedbergh; *m* 1971 *Catherine Kimerling, dau of Charles Grun, of New York, and has:

1c +Aaron; *b* 3 July 1972

1b *Christina Mary [Mrs Anthony Hart, 106A Raglan St, Mosman, NSW 2088, Australia]; *b* 11 May 1947; *m* 8 May 1976 *Anthony Hart and has:

1c *Adam John; *b* 7 Aug 1981

1a Sythe Margaret Isabella; *b* 20 March 1904; *d* unm 22 May 1977

2a Nesta Katharine; *b* 5 April 1909; *d* unm 8 Feb 1989

(2) Harold Crossley; *b* 2 Aug 1868; *educ* Cambridge (BA); *m* 16 Aug 1906 Grace Ethel Muriel, eldest dau of Rev Henry Madan Pratt, and gdau of Sir Matthew Wilson, 2nd Bt (*qv*), of Eshton Hall, and *d* 26 Dec 1943, having had:

 1a +Denys Geoffrey Crossley [Denys Salt Esq, Flat 6, 38 Holland Park, London W11]; *b* 4 May 1918; *educ* Marlborough and St Edmund Hall Oxford (MA); *m* 1st 5 May 1956 (*divorce* 1962) Patricia Lee, dau of Lt-Col D C Pope, MC, of Red House, Sutton Montis, Somerset; *m* 2nd 1 July 1989 *Eva Kiesling, of Graz, Austria

 2a +Peter Hubert Wharton, in India 1944–45 with Intell Corps; *b* 20 March 1920; *educ* Cheltenham and St Edmund Hall Oxford (MA); *m* 15 Sept 1951 Gillian Caryl (*d* 2 March 1983), dau of John Hill, of Westhill, Ledbury, and has:

  1b +Jonathan Wharton; *b* 18 April 1953; *m* 1981 *Susan Lee Jeanette, dau of William McGann, of Brighton, and has:

   1c *Benjamin Wharton; *b* 21 Nov 1982

   1c *Kate Alicia Gillian Samantha; *b* 22 April 1986

  1b *Miranda Elisabeth Caryl [Mrs Carteret Maunsell, 19 Velmore Rd, Chandlers Ford, Hants]; *b* 22 April 1955; *m* 27 Sept 1980 *Carteret Hunter Maunsell and has:

   1c *Mark Hugo; *b* 25 July 1986

   1c *Hannah Caryl; *b* 30 Dec 1982

   2c *Cara Alison; *b* 3 May 1984

 1a Marjorie Doreen; *b* 7 Dec 1911; *d* unm 1 May 1953

 2a Rosalind Diana; *b* 5 Sept 1915; *d* unm 8 April 1936

(3) Lawrence Titus Whitlam; *b* 8 Sept 1874; *d* unm 14 Dec 1946

(1) Mary Isabel; *b* 16 Sept 1876; *d* unm 21 May 1968

1 Amelia; *m* 2 April 1873 Henry Wright, JP, of Kensington, and *d* 1914. He *d* Aug 1893

2 Ada; *m* 11 July 1883 Edmund Herbert Stevenson, MICE, and *d* 22 Nov 1935, leaving issue. He *d* 1918

Sir TITUS *d* 29 Dec 1876; his est s,

Sir William Henry Salt, 2nd Bt, DL and JP Leics, High Sheriff 1879; *b* 5 Dec 1831; *m* 7 Dec 1854 Emma Dove Octaviana (*d* 1 July 1904), only child of John Dove Harris, MP, of Ratcliffe Hall, Leics, by Emma, dau of Arthur Shirley, of Tamworth, Staffs, and gdau of Richard Harris, MP, and had:

1 SHIRLEY HARRIS (Sir)

1 Constance Dove; *m* 20 April 1887 Rev Arthur FitzGerald Evans, Vicar Gt Maplestead, Essex, RD Hedingham, and *d* 1912, leaving issue

Sir WILLIAM *d* 7 July 1892; his only s,

Sir Shirley Harris Salt, 3rd Bt, JP Leics and Breconshire; *b* 4 May 1857; *educ* Trin Coll Cambridge (MA); barrister Inner Temple; *m* 9 Sept 1880 Charlotte Jane (*d* 13 June 1925), only dau of Very Rev John Cotter MacDonnell, DD, Canon Peterborough, Dean Cashel, and had:

1 JOHN WILLIAM TITUS (Sir), **4th Bt**

2 Robert Shirley MacDonnell; *b* 1888; *m* 1st 22 April 1914 (*divorce* 1942) Sybil Stella, dau of H G Marquis; *m* 2nd 14 March 1942 Gertrude Ada Elizabeth Emma, dau of Rev Robert Phillips, Vicar of Manthorpe, Lincs, and *dsp* 24 April 1943

3 Shirley Edward Philip; *b* 19 Sept 1891; *d* 23 Dec 1895

1 Dorothy Dove; *d* unm 19 Dec 1968

2 Kathleen Mary; *m* 23 April 1908 Hon Herbert Crawshay Bailey, 4th s of 1st Baron Glanusk (*qv*), and *d* 2 May 1948, leaving issue. He *d* 13 April 1936

Sir SHIRLEY *d* 11 Feb 1920; his est son,

Sir John William Titus Salt, 4th Bt; *b* 30 Nov 1884; *educ* Eton; Cdr RN, Orders Nile 4th Cl, El Nahda 4th Cl; *m* 1st 11 Sept 1913 (*divorce* 1926) Dorothy Baker (*d* 25 Oct 1952), dau of Brig-Gen William Baker Brown, CB, RE; *m* 2nd 25 June 1926 Stella Houlton (*d* 2 Aug 1974), 2nd dau of Richard Houlton Jackson, MRCS, LRCP, of Bakewell, Derbys, and *d* 22 Jan 1953, leaving issue:

1 **Sir David Shirley Salt, 5th Bt**; *b* 14 June 1930; *educ* Stowe; *m* 3 Dec 1955 (*divorce* 1974) Margaret Gillian, dau of Hugh Alwyn Lenox, of 31 Markham Square, London SW3, and *dsp* 3 Dec 1978

2 **Sir Anthony Houlton Salt, 6th Bt**; *b* 15 Sept 1931; *educ* Stowe; memb London Stock Exchange; *m* 29 June 1957 *Prudence Mary Dorothea Francis [Prudence Lady Salt, Dellow House, Ugley Green, Bishop's Stortford, Herts GM22 6HN], yst dau of Francis Ralph Meath Baker, JP, of Hasfield Court, Glos (*see* WESTMORLAND, E), and *d* 1991, leaving issue:

 (1) *Fenella Mary Houlton; *b* 10 Dec 1959; *m* 4 March 1995 *Nicholas de Satgé, yr s of Canon John de Satgé, and has:

  1a *Davina Mary Valentine; *b* 14 Dec 1996

 (2) *Rebecca Madeleine Harris; *b* 28 Oct 1961; *m* 1993 *Alexander I M Kennedy, 2nd s of John Kennedy, of Kensington, and has:

  1a *Edward Anthony Maxwell; *b* 3 July 1996

  2a *James Titus Maxwell; *b* 4 Feb 1998

 (3) *Lucinda Mary Harriet; *b* 8 Sept 1964; *m* 26 Oct 1996 *Stuart Feast, yr s of D Feast, of Lower Skemsdale, Kirk Michael, IOM

 (4) *Charlotte Lavinia Francis; *b* 13 Jan 1967; *m* 1993 *Christopher James Walter Trower, 3rd s of Anthony Gosselin Trower, of Stansteadbury, Ware, Herts, and has:

  1a *Arabella Olivia Francis; *b* 6 Nov 1995

  2a *Zara Rose Catherine; *b* 27 April 1998

3 Sir PATRICK MacDONNELL SALT, **7th and present Bt**

Arms: Arg. a chevron rompu between three mullets in chief and a lion rampant in base sa. **Crest:** Three annulets interlaced sa., thereon a dove holding in the beak an olive branch ppr. and charged on the neck with a chevron also sa. **Motto:** *In sale salus* ('Safety in salt'). **Creation:** Bt. (UK) 8 Aug 1899.

SIR (THOMAS) MICHAEL JOHN SALT, 4TH BT, of Standon and Weeping Cross [Sir Michael Salt Bt, Shillingstone House, Shillingstone, Dorset DT11 0QR]; *b* 7 Nov 1946; *s* f 1965; *educ* Eton; *m* 20 May 1971 *Caroline, er dau of Henry Robert John Hildyard, of Kensington, and has:

1 *Henrietta Sophia Meriel; *b* 1978

2 *Alexandra Georgia May; *b* 1 May 1982

Lineage: THOMAS SALT (s of James Salt, of Rugeley, Staffs); *bapt* 27 Dec 1651; *m* 6 April 1678 Elizabeth Averne and was *bur* 7 Nov 1892, leaving, with other issue:

JOSEPH SALT; *bapt* 2 July 1679; *m* 20 Aug 1699 Katherine Whiston and was *bur* 9 Jan 1720, leaving, with other issue:

JOSEPH SALT, of Sutton Coldfield, Warwicks; *bapt* 11 Sept 1702; *m* Mary Thomas and had, with other issue:

THOMAS SALT; *b* Oct 1732; merchant Birmingham; *m* 27 Jan 1767 Elizabeth (*m* 2nd 31 July 1792 Thomas Dibbs, of Bush Hill, Edmonton, Middx, and *d* 24 Aug 1829), 2nd dau of John Stevenson, of Stafford, Ld Manor Standon, Staffs, and *d* 17 Sept 1788, leaving, with a dau:

JOHN STEVENSON SALT, of Standon and Bloomsbury, JP Staffs; *b* 25 June 1775; High Sheriff 1838; banker; *m* 7 Jan 1880 his 1st cousin Sarah (*d* 13 Oct 1848), dau of William Stevenson, and *d* 16 Aug 1845, leaving, with other issue (including a 3rd s, William, antiquary, whose collection formed the basis of the William Salt Library, Stafford) an est s:

THOMAS SALT, of Standon and Weeping Cross, Staffs, JP, DL; *b* 20 Jan 1802; banker; *m* 12 Aug 1829 Harriet Letitia (*d* 26 April 1883), est dau of Rev John Hayes Petit, and *d* 21 March 1871, leaving, with three daus (Harriet, *b* 12 May 1830, *d* unm 8 Dec 1934; Sarah, *m* 25 Sept 1873 Rev Percy Brent and *d* 8 April 1914; a 3rd dau, *d* an infant):

Sir Thomas Salt, 1st Bt (UK), so *cr* 8 Aug 1899, of Standon and Weeping Cross, JP, DL Staffs; *b* 12 May 1830; *educ* Rugby and Balliol Coll Oxford (BA 1853, MA 1856); Capt 2nd Staffs Militia, MP (C) Stafford 1859–65, 1869–80, 1881–85 and 1886–92, Parly Sec Local Govt Bd 1875–80, 2nd Church Estates Commr 1879–80, Chm Lunacy Commn 1886–92, Public Works Loan Commr 1875–1904, Ecclesiastical Commr 1880–1904, Chm N Staffs Rlwy Co 1883–1904 and Lloyds Bank 1886–98; *m* 24 July 1861 Emma Helen Mary (*d* 23 March 1925), dau and eventual coheir of John Lavicount Anderdon, of Chislehurst, Kent, and Henlade House, Somerset, by Anna Maria, est dau of William Manning, MP (bro of Cardinal Manning), and had:

1 THOMAS ANDERDON (Sir), **2nd Bt**

2 Herbert Edward SALT later ANDERDON (deed poll 1923); *b* 20 Dec 1870; *m* 25 July 1899 Ethel Menie (*d* 12 May 1966 aged 95), yr dau of Henry Manisty, of S Kensington, and *d* 10 Nov 1938, having had:

 (1) +Henry Manisty; *b* 10 Nov 1900; *educ* Haileybury ; Capt Wilts Regt WW II; *m* 30 Nov 1929 *Sybilla Marjory, only dau of Lt-Col Reginald Holden Steward, OBE, Wilts Regt, of Rockley House, Devizes, and has:

  1a +John Nigel Steward [Cdr John Anderdon RN, Nursling House, Nursling, Hants]; *b* 24 May 1931; *educ* RNC Dartmouth; served Fleet Air Arm; *m* 3 Nov 1961 *Mavis Marjorie, only child of Lester Gibson, of Henleaze, Bristol, and has:

   1b +Alexander Philip; *b* 25 Dec 1963

  1a (cont.) Cdr and Mrs John Anderdon also adopted:
   *James; *b* 15 Dec 1954

  2a +Ian George Carlyle [Ian Anderdon Esq, Henlade House, Taunton, Somerset]; *b* 23 April 1936; *educ* Packwood Haugh, Salop

 (1) Dorothy Mary; *b* 4 April 1902; *d* 17 March 1937

 (2) Helen Katharine; *b* 4 April 1902; *d* unm 8 April 1969

(3) Rachel Elinor, MBE (1965); *b* 17 April 1909

3 George Edmund Stevenson; *b* 19 Feb 1873; Lt 1st Bn Roy Welch Fus Boer War (despatches); *das* unm 3 April 1900

4 Reginald John; *b* 2 March 1874; *educ* Charterhouse and New Coll Oxford; manager Lloyds Bank Leamington, fruit farmer in US; *m* 19 June 1901 Maud Fanny (*d* 13 June 1962), yst dau of Robert Wigram (*see* WIGRAM, Bt), and *d* 19 Oct 1963, having had:

(1) *Laura Enid; *b* 30 March 1902; *educ* Oxford; ed: *The Oxford Junior Encyclopedia*

(2) Barbara, DBE (1962, CBE 1959); *b* 30 Sept 1904; with UK Mission UN, Perm UK Rep ECOSOC New York, Minister Disarmament Conf Geneva and Counsellor and Consul Gen Tel Aviv, FO 1963–70

(3) Olive Mary; *b* 13 Aug 1910; *educ* UCL; *m* 25 Aug 1939 Richard Archibald Fawcett Wallis, OBE, Dip Serv, only s of Henry Richard Wallis, CMG, CBE, of Cheltenham, Glos, and *d* 3 Sept 1959, leaving issue

5 William Manning (Rev); *b* 22 April 1876; *educ* Pembroke Coll Cambridge (BA 1906, MA 1910); Vicar St Giles Shrewsbury, Preb Emeritus Lichfield, RD Shrewsbury; *m* 2 Jan 1907 Mildred Nairne (*d* 8 June 1926), dau of Lt-Col Charles Henry Edward Graeme, and *d* 12 Nov 1947, leaving:

(1) *Joan Mildred, JP (Mon 1960) [Mrs Frederick Tanner JP, The Vaga, Monmouth]; *b* 24 April 1908; *m* 11 May 1938 *Frederick Newman Tanner, s of Rev Charles Newman Tanner

(2) Rosemary; *b* 15 March 1911; *m* 31 July 1934 Leslie Louis Samuel Lowe, TD, JP, BLitt, Headmaster RCT Schs, Hatch End, Middlesex (*d* 16 Nov 1959)

(3) *Elizabeth [Miss Elizabeth Salt, Elmbridge, Church Rd, North Newton, Somerset]; *b* 30 May 1915

6 Walter Petit; *b* 5 Oct 1878; Capt 1st Bn Lancashire Fus WW I (despatches); *ka* 27 Oct 1916

7 Harold Francis, CB (1932), CMG (1919), DSO (1918); *b* 30 Dec 1879; *educ* Cooper's Hill; Maj-Gen RA, CRA 54th (E Anglian) Div TA 1930–31, Cdr AD Formation TA 1931–35, DAG India 1935–36, DQMG India 1936–39 (ret), WW I in Gallipoli, the Balkans, Palestine and Syria (despatches three times), with Air Min, Min Aircraft Production, Min Works WW II, Order Nile 3rd Cl; *m* 3 Aug 1914 Phyllis Dulcie (*d* 9 Nov 1965), dau of Maj Ewan Duncan Cameron, RFA, and *d* 10 Aug 1971, leaving:

(1) *Primrose Phyllis [Mrs James Niall, 99 Empire Circuit, Deakin, Canberra ACT 2603, Australia]; *b* 19 April 1915; *m* 1st 14 Nov 1935 Maj Anthony Hope Osborne, The Queen's Bays (*ka* 8 March 1943), only s of Hamilton Hope Osborne, of Widgeongully, NSW, and has:

1a *Duncan Norton Hope [Duncan Salt Esq, Douglas, Bungendore, NSW, Australia]; *b* Nov 1936; *educ* Wellington and Sydney U (BAg)

(1) (cont.) Mrs Anthony Osborne *m* 2nd 6 Oct 1944 (*divorce* 1948) Capt Philip Quellyn Roberts, RN, only s of Ambrose Oakes Roberts, of Uffington House, Chester, and by him has:

2a *Paul Quellyn; *b* 23 Aug 1945

(1) (cont.) Mrs Primrose Roberts *m* 3rd 15 Aug 1962 *James Mansfield Niall, est s of K M Niall, of Macedon, Vict, Australia

(2) *Babette Irene [Lady Millais, Elizabeth Court, 47 Milmans St, London SW10 0DA]; *b* 11 Oct 1922; *m* 1st 28 June 1941 Maj John de Grey Tatham Warter, MC, 2nd Dragoon Guards (*ka* El Alamein Nov 1942), er s of Henry de Grey Tatham Warter, of Broadwindsor House, Dorset; *m* 2nd 13 July 1946 Victor William Henry Sefton-Smith, of Pacific, Hayes Lane, Hayes, Kent, and by him has had:

1a *Ewan Victor William; *b* 27 Nov 1950; *educ* Eton

2a Francis; *b* and *d* 15 Feb 1955

1a *Susan Jane [Mrs David Hyman, 101 Flood St, London SW3 2DY]; *b* 13 May 1948; *m* 1st 21 Sept 1970 (*divorce* 1976) John Henry Deen; *m* 2nd 1976 (*divorce* 1987) John Leslie McClue; *m* 3rd 1987 *David Hyman and has by her 2nd husb:

1b *Linsey Jane; *b* 1976

2b *Laura Leslie; *b* 1977

2a *Lucy Annabelle [Mrs Richard Moore, 11 Chelsea Park Gdns, London SW3 6AF]; *b* 21 Dec 1952; *m* 30 April 1977 *Richard Hobart John de Courcy Moore, s of Hobart Moore, and has:

1b *Francis Richard Hobart de Courcy; *b* 1985

1b *Natalie Elizabeth Victoria de Courcy; *b* 1993

(2) (cont.) Mrs Babette Sefton-Smith; *m* 3rd 18 Feb 1975, as his 3rd w, Sir Ralph Regnault Millais, 5th Bt (*qv*)

1 Laura Helen; *m* 12 April 1887 1st Viscount Hanworth (*qv*) and *d* 16 Feb 1954, having issue

2 Mary Louisa; *m* 21 Jan 1889 Joseph William Young Howison Lavies, LFPS Glasgow (*dsp* 23 Feb 1900), and *d* 21 May 1901

3 Violet Blanche; *d* an infant, 1868

4 Helen Frances; *m* 30 Sept 1896 Maj John Cecil Grant McFerran, DL, JP, RE (TF), of Rickerscote, Staffs (*d* 25 Feb 1930), and *d* 7 Aug 1950, leaving issue

Sir THOMAS *d* 8 April 1904; his est s,

Sir Thomas Anderdon Salt, 2nd Bt, DSO (1917), JP, DL Staffs 1901–29, JP Dorset; *b* 8 Jan 1863; *educ* Clifton, Oriel Coll Oxford and RMC Sandhurst; W Coast Africa 1887–88 (despatches, medal with clasp), Punjab Frontier 1897 (medal with clasp), Boer War 1902 (medal with two clasps), WW I France, Balkans, Palestine, suppression Easter Rising Ireland 1916 (despatches, Order Nile 4th Cl, 1914 star and two medals), Maj 11th Hus, Lt-Col cmdg 3rd City London Yeo 1916–18 and 103rd MGB 1918–19, Hon Col 23rd (London) Armoured Car Co 1932–39, High Sheriff Staffs 1909; *m* 17 Jan 1905 Elinor Mary (*d* 11 Jan 1974 aged 92), 2nd dau of Sir Henry Arthur Wiggin, 2nd Bt (*qv*), and had:

1 THOMAS HENRY (Sir), **3rd Bt**

2 George Stevenson; *b* 16 Jan 1908; Lt-Cdr RN WW II; *m* 8 Nov 1935 *Lilian Bridget [Mrs William Lamb, Brookway, Rhinefield Rd, Brockenhurst, Hants SO42 7SR] (*m* 2nd 27 Nov 1948 Capt William John Lamb, CVO, OBE, RN, 2nd s of Sir Richard Amphlett Lamb, KCSI, CIE, ICS), dau of Frederick Stewart Francis, of Thakeham, Sussex, and was *ka* cmdg HM Submarine *Triad* Oct 1940, leaving:

(1) +James Frederick Thomas George, CB (1991) [Rear-Admiral James Salt CB, Salterns, Lock Lane, Birdham, W Sussex PO20 7BB]; *b* 19 April 1940; *educ* Wellington and RNC Dartmouth; RN: cmded HM Subs *Finwhale* and *Dreadnought*, HMS *Sheffield* (sunk Falklands Campaign), HMS *Southampton*, ACOS Ops to C-in-C Fleet 1984–85, Dir Def Intell 1986–87, ACNS (Gulf War) 1990–91, Mil Dep Def Export Serv 1992–97; *m* 5 April 1975 *Penelope M, only dau of W A Walker, of Wall Garth, Holcot, Northants, and has:

1a +George William; *b* 7 June 1977

2a +Charles James; *b* 3 July 1979

3a +Thomas Edward; *b* 20 May 1983

4a +John Philip; *b* 4 June 1986

(1) *Joanna Elizabeth; *b* 10 Dec 1937; *m* 4 May 1963 *Sir Robert Arnold Spencer-Nairn, 3rd Bt (*qv*), and has issue

1 Patience Elinor; *b* 5 July 1910; *m* 6 June 1936 (*divorce* 1947) G/Capt Geoffrey Francis, RAF, er s of Frederick Stewart Francis, of Thakeham, Sussex, and has:

(1) *Jessica Patience; *b* 31 Dec 1942; *m* 15 Oct 1966 Howard Finn Fetherstonhaugh, s of Harold Fetherstonhaugh, of Bridport

Sir THOMAS *d* 22 June 1940; his er s,

Sir Thomas Henry Salt, 3rd Bt, JP 1952 Dorset, DL 1949; *b* 26 Nov 1905; *educ* Eton and RMC Sandhurst; Lt-Col DCLI, ADC to Govr and C-in-C Malta 1931–34, Assist Def Security Offr Malta 1934–36, served WW II, Co Commr Boy Scouts Dorset 1944–54, High Sheriff Dorset 1954–55; *m* 20 Nov 1943 *Meriel Sophia Wilmot [Meriel Lady Salt, Shillingstone House, Shillingstone, Dorset], only dau of Capt Berkeley Cole Wilmot Williams, JP, DL, of Herringston, Dorchester, and *d* 15 Aug 1965, leaving:

1 Sir THOMAS MICHAEL JOHN SALT, **4th and present Bt**

2 +ANTHONY WILLIAM DAVID; *b* 5 Feb 1950, heir presumptive; *educ* Milton Abbey; *m* 1978 *Olivia Anne, yr dau of Martin Morgan Hudson, of Yokehurst Farm, S Chailey, Sussex, and has:

(1) +Edward James Stevenson; *b* 11 June 1981

(2) +Henry Martin Morgan; *b* 17 Dec 1983

1*Sarah Meriel [Mrs Malcolm Coombs, 10 The Close, Rickmansworth, Herts]; *b* 17 Sept 1944; *m* 15 Oct 1977 *Malcolm D Coombs, s of L G Coombs, of Ruislip, and has:

(1) *Dominic Nathaniel Thomas; *b* 1986

(1) *Augusta Elinor Lettice; *b* 1979

(2) *Octavia Alexandra Elizabeth; *b* 1981

2 *Jennifer Mary; *b* 9 Aug 1951; *m* 1977 *John Joseph William Clark, of Moyston, Vict, Australia, and has:

(1) *Thomas William; *b* 12 July 1979

(1) *Anthea Mary; *b* 1981

SALTOUN

Arms: Azure three fraises argent. **Crests:** Dexter, on a mount a flourish of strawberries leaved and fructed proper; sinister, an ostrich holding in its beak a horse-shoe proper. **Supporters:** Two cherubims with wings expanded and vested in long garments or. **Mottoes:** 1 Dexter (over crest) All my hope is in God, 2 sinister (over crest) In God is all. **Creation:** L. (S) 28 June 1445.

LADY SALTOUN OF ABERNETHY, 21st holder of title (Flora Marjory Fraser) [The Rt Hon The Lady Saltoun, Inverey House, Braemar, Aberdeenshire AB35 5YB]; *b* 18 Oct 1930; *s* f 1979, also as Ch of Clan Fraser; Sec Assoc Scottish Peers; *m* 6 Oct 1956 *Capt Alexander Arthur Alphonso David Maule Ramsay of Mar (*see* DALHOUSIE, E) and has:

1 +KATHARINE INGRID MARY ISABEL [The Hon Mrs Nicholson, Cairnbulg Castle, Fraserburgh, Aberdeenshire AB43 8TN]; *b* 11 Oct 1957 (HM QUEEN INGRID OF DENMARK and HRH THE late PRINCESS ROYAL stood sponsors); took name and arms of Fraser by warrant of Lord Lyon King of Arms 1973; *m* 3 May 1980 *Capt Mark Malise Nicolson, Irish Gds, only s of Malise Allen Nicolson, MC, of Frog Hall, Tilston, Cheshire, and has:

(1) +Alexander William Malise FRASER; *b* 5 July 1990

(1) +Louise Alexandra Patricia; *b* 1984

(2) +Juliet Victoria Katharine; *b* 1988

2 +Alice Elizabeth Margaret; b 8 July 1961 (HRH THE DUCHESS OF GLOUCESTER stood sponsor); m 1990 *David Ramsey, yr s of Ronald Ramsey, of St James, Barbados, and has:

(1) +Alexander David; b 1991

(2) +George Arthur Oliver Henry; b 28 Sept 1995

(3) +Oliver Henry; b 28 Sept 1995

(1) +Victoria Alice; b 1994

3 +Elizabeth Alexandra Mary; b 15 April 1963

Lineage (of Abernethy): MALCOLM III, KING OF SCOTS; had:

EDELRAD, apparently EARL OF FIFE, who fl early 12th century and was also Abbot of Dunkeld; possibly the same person as Eth, who was f of:

GILLEMICH(A)EL MACDUFF, EARL OF FIFE c 1129; d c 1133–36, leaving apparently:

EOGHIN/HUGH; hereditary Abbot of Abernethy, on the River Tay; had:

ORM; had 1172/3 a charter feudalising the abbacy; had:

LAURENCE de ABERNETHY; last hereditary Abbot, from whom the ecclesiastical functions were transferred to the Abbey of Arbroath; m Devorgulle and had:

1 Patrick; d by 1254

2 Hugh Abernethy of that Ilk; m by 5 April 1281, as her 3rd w, (m 4th by 10 April 1299, as his 2nd w, William FitzWarin and d by 10 Oct 1303), dau of Ewen of Argyll and widow of (a) MAGNUS, KING OF THE ISLE OF MAN (d 1265), and (b) Malise, 5th Earl of Stratheam (d by 23 Nov 1271), and d soon after 1291, leaving:

(1) Alexander Abernethy of that Ilk; d between 1315 and 1317, leaving:

1a Margaret; m John Stewart, 1st Earl of Angus of the 1329 cr (see MORAY, E), and had issue by him

2a Mary; m 1st 1313 Sir Andrew de Leslie of Leslie (see ROTHES, E) and had issue; m 2nd c 1325 Sir David de Lindsay and had further issue (see CRAWFORD and BALCARRES, E)

3 William, 1st of Saltoun; m Margaret — and d by 1290, leaving:

(1) William, 2nd of Saltoun; submitted to EDWARD I 1290 but asserted independence from the English by 1320; had:

1a William (Sir), 3rd of Saltoun; ka at Scottish defeat by English of Halidon Hill 1333, leaving a 2nd s:

1b George (Sir), 4th of Saltoun; m Alicia Wishart and had:

1c George, 5th of Saltoun; apparently ka at Scottish victory over English of Otterburn 1388, leaving:

1d William, 6th of Saltoun; m a dau of Robert Stewart, 1st Duke of Albany of the 1398 cr (see MORAY, E), and d 1420, having had an est s:

1e William, Yr. of Saltoun; m Margaret, dau of Sir William Borthwick (see BORTHWICK, L), and dvp, k Battle of Harlaw 24 July 1411, leaving:

1f William, 7th of Saltoun; hostage in England for JAMES I; dsp by 1428

2f LAURENCE ABERNETHY, **1st Lord Saltoun of Abernethy** (S), so cr 28 June 1445, of Saltoun and Rothiemay; b probably c 1400; Justiciar 1445; m by 1448 Margaret — and d by 13 March 1460/1, having had, with two daus:

1g WILLIAM ABERNETHY, **2nd Lord Saltoun of Abernethy**, PC (S by 20 March 1482/3); Sheriff Banffshire Feb 1458/9; m 1st — and had two daus (the er (name unknown) m Walter Ogston of that Ilk; Christian, m 1468 Sir John Wemyss of that Ilk; see WEMYSS and MARCH, E); m 2nd by 1464 Isabella Borthwick and dspm June 1488, perhaps at the Battle of Sauchieburn in which JAMES III was overthrown by rebels led by his own son and successor

2g JAMES, **3rd Lord**

3g George

4g Archibald

The 2nd LORD's bro,

JAMES ABERNETHY, **3rd Lord Saltoun of Abernethy**; served heir 10 Oct 1488 but had a long lawsuit with the heirs of line till this settled by arbitration; m — and d 1504 or 1505, having had:

1 ALEXANDER, **4th Lord**

1 Margaret; m John Stirling of Craigbernard

2 Janet; m Alexander Ogilvy of Deskford and Findlater and had issue (see SEAFIELD, E)

3 Elizabeth; m 31 May 1510 Alexander Hay of Delgaty and Ardendraught and had issue (see HAY, Bt, of Park)

4 Helen; m Thomas Urquhart of Fischerie and had issue

The 3rd LORD's only s,

ALEXANDER ABERNETHY, **4th Lord Saltoun of Abernethy**, PC (by Sept 1514); fought at Scottish rout by English of Flodden 1513, bought much land in Banffshire in the years 1514–17; m —, dau of 1st Earl of Buchan (qv) and d by 25 July 1527, having had:

1 WILLIAM, **5th Lord**

2 Laurence

3 John, of Balcors; m Elizabeth, dau of 6th Lord Glamis (see STRATHMORE AND KINGHORNE, E), and d 14 Nov 1581, leaving issue

4 Thomas; had issue

1 Beatrix; m Alexander Forbes of Pitsligo and had issue (see FORBES, Bt, of Newe)

2 Elizabeth; m as his 1st w Alexander Innes, 14th of that Ilk, and had issue (see ROXBURGHE, D)

The 4th LORD's est s,

WILLIAM ABERNETHY, **5th Lord Saltoun of Abernethy**; m by 23 July 1512 Lady Elizabeth Hay (d Oct 1574), dau of 4th Earl of Erroll (qv), and d Dec 1543, having had:

1 ALEXANDER, **6th Lord**

2 William; ancestor of the extinct ABERNETHYs of Birnes

1 Agnes; m William Crichton of Frendraught

2 Elizabeth; m 1st William Meldrum of Fyvie; m 2nd 11 April 1561 8th Lord Glamis (see STRATHMORE AND KINGHORNE, E) and d by May 1581

The 5th LORD's er s,

ALEXANDER ABERNETHY, **6th Lord Saltoun of Abernethy**, PC (S 1553); m 1st c 28 Aug 1550 Lady Alice/Alison Keith (d Aug 1567), dau of 3rd Earl Marischal (see KINTORE, E); m 2nd in or after 1572 Jean (m 3rd by 1589 William Kerr of Ewinstoun; see LOTHIAN, M), dau of James Johnstone, Yr. of Johnstone (see ANNANDALE AND HARTFELL, E), and widow of William, Master of Carlyle and d April 1587, having had by his 1st w:

1 GEORGE, **7th Lord**

2 Alexander, of Wester Saltoun; m (contract 7 Nov 1589) Elizabeth, dau of Sir James Crichton of Frendraught, and d 10 April 1603

3 John; ancestor of the extinct ABERNETHYs of Barrie and Mayen

1 Elizabeth; m 1st 1580 John Innes, 17th of that Ilk (see ROXBURGHE, D); m 2nd James Gordon of Auchenhieff

2 Margaret; m 1582 George Meldrum of Drumbreck

3 Jean; m 1st 1579 Alexander Seton of Meldrum (see SETON, Bt, of Pitmedden); m 2nd John Urquhart, s of Alexander Urquhart of Cromarty

4 Isobel; m 1593 John Cumming, Y.r of Earnside

The 6th LORD's est s,

GEORGE ABERNETHY, **7th Lord Saltoun of Abernethy**, PC (S by 15 Jan 1588/9); b c 1555; Sheriff Banffshire; m by 3 Aug 1574 Lady Margaret Stewart, dau of 4th Earl of Atholl (see MORAY, E), and d 27 April 1590, having had:

1 JOHN ABERNETHY, **8th Lord Saltoun of Abernethy**, PC (S 1600); b c 1577 or 1578; sold the Rothiemay estate 1612 to pay debts; m 1st after 30 Sept 1601 Magdalen (dspm 4 April 1603), dau of Henry Urquhart, Yr. of Cromarty, and had a dau (d young); m 2nd (contract 20 April and 5 Aug 1605) Lady Elizabeth Stewart (dsp 1608), dau of 2nd Earl of Moray (qv); m 3rd by 11 Jan 1608/9 Anne Stewart (mother illegitimately by 2nd Marquess of Hamilton of a dau Margaret, who m 1st Lord Belhaven and Stenton; qv), dau of 1st Lord Blantyre (see 1900 edn), and d between 30 June and 13 July 1612, having by her had:

(1) ALEXANDER ABERNETHY, **9th Lord Saltoun of Abernethy**; b 26 March 1611; sold the Saltoun estate 1643; d unm, bur 17 or 18 Dec 1668

(1) Anne; b 19 Nov 1609; d an infant

(2) MARGARET, de jure LADY SALTOUN OF ABERNETHY in her own right; b posthumously 2 Feb 1613; d unm after 9 March 1669

1 Margaret; m (contract 19 Dec 1595) Alexander Fraser, 9th of Philorth, and had, with two daus (see below **Lineage (of Fraser)**):

(1) ALEXANDER, **11th Lord**

2 Jean; m 1st 1608 Sir John Lindsay of Kinfauns; m 2nd George Gordon of Gight

3 Joneta; m Patrick Livingston

Lineage (of Fraser): UDARD FRASER; living second half of 12th century; m a sis of Oliver Fraser of Oliver Castle, Peeblesshire, on the River Tweed, s of Kylvert Fraser, and was probably f of:

1 Bernard (Sir); Sheriff Stirling 1234; m a sis of Nesius de London and d (apparently sp) c 1250

2 Adam; inherited the lands of Hales from his unc Oliver; m Constantia — and had:

(1) Laurence; at one point apparently feudal Ld of Drumelzier, which a certainn Sir William Fraser (his s?, n?) surrendered to ROBERT I (THE BRUCE) 1326; inherited North Hales from his unc Bernard but sold it

3 Gilbert (Sir), of Oliver Castle; b by 1214; Sheriff Tweeddale 1233–59; m Christian Lascelles (probably cognate with Leslie) and d c 1263, having had:

(1) John; m by 1243 Alicia, dau of William de Conigburg, feudal Ld of Stapilgorton, and dvp, leaving:

1a Richard (Sir), of Touchfraser; Sheriff Berwick 1292; d probably after 1307, leaving apparently:

1b Andrew (Sir), Yr. of Toucfraser; Sheriff Stirling; m Beatrix —, an heiress, probably of the Le CHENs of Duffus, and d by 1306, leaving:

1c ALEXANDER (Sir), for whom see further below

2c Andrew; k English victory over Scots of Halidon Hill 19 July 1333

3c Simon (Sir), of Brotherton and 1st of Lovat (see LOVAT, L)

4c James; ka Halidon Hill

2a Alexander, of Cornton, Stirlingshire; alleged ancestor of:

1b Michael, of Muchall, Stanywood and Kinmundy, Aberdeenshire; m Isobel, dau of Duncan Forbes of Monymusk, and d 1588, leaving:

1c ANDREW FRASER, 1st LORD FRASER (S), so cr 29 June 1633, with remainder to heirs male whatsoever; m 1st c 1592 Elizabeth, yst dau of the Countess of Buchan in her own right by Robert Douglas, 4th Earl of Buchan (qv) in right of his w, and had issue; m 2nd after 20 May 1624 Anne, dau of 3rd Lord Drummond (see PERTH, E) and widow of Patrick Barclay, of Towie, and d 10 Dec 1636; his s by his 1st w:

1d ANDREW FRASER, 2nd LORD FRASER; m 1st 1618 Margaret, est dau of 1st Lord Balmerinoch (see ELPHINSTONE, L) by his 2nd w, and had two sons (d young); m 2nd by 31 July 1637 Anne (d c 1640), dau of James Haldane of Gleneagles; m 3rd c 21 Aug 1644 Elizabeth Crichton, sis of 1st Viscount Frendraught, and d between July 1656 and July 1658, leaving by his 2nd w, with an er s (Thomas of Cairnbulg, d young, leaving a dau, Margaret, who m 2 Dec 1699 Sir James Innes 5th Bt, of Balvenie; qv):

1e ANDREW FRASER, 3rd LORD FRASER; m 1st 17 Oct 1658 Catherine (d 18 Oct 1663), dau of 7th Lord (Fraser of) Lovat (qv) and widow of (a) Sir John Sinclair of Dunbeath and (b) 1st Viscount of Arbuthnott (qv); m 2nd Jean, dau of 2nd Earl of Seaforth (see CROMARTIE, E) and widow of 20th/4th Earl of Mar (qv), and d 21 May 1674, leaving an only s by his 1st w:

1f CHARLES FRASER, 4th LORD FRASER; b by Sept 1662; stayed faithful to JAMES VII and II at the Glorious Revolution but soon capitulated to Williamite forces; nevertheless fined £200 (well over £10,000 in late-1990s terms) for Jacobitism (actually just drinking JAMES VII and II's health) 1693; took an oath of loyalty to new regime 1695 and supported Union of E and S parls 1700 but joined in 1715 Uprising, though he was not attainted since he managed to evade capture; *m* Sept 1683 Marjory/Mary, est dau of 7th Earl of Buchan (*qv*) and widow of Simon Fraser of Inveralloochy (*see* LOVAT, L), and *dsps* 12 Oct 1716 in a fall from a cliff at Pernan, Banffshire, when the title expired or became dormant of the FRASERs of Muchall

(2) Simon (Sir), of Oliver Castle; Kt Banneret, Keeper Roy Forest of Ettrick, Sheriff Traquair and Peebles; *d c* 1280, leaving:

  1a Simon (Sir), of Oliver Castle; Sheriff Traquair and Peebles, Keeper Selkirk and Traquair Forests; *m* Maria — (*m* 2nd Richard Siward) and *d* 1291, leaving, with other issue:

    1b Simon (Sir), of Oliver Castle and Neidpath; Kt Banneret; taken prisoner by English after Battle of Dunbar 27 April 1296 but set free to fight for EDWARD I in Flanders; Warden Selkirk Forest 1298; participated on English side Siege Carlaverock 1300 but by 1301 had switched sides to the Scots again; taken prisoner by the English 1306 and hanged, drawn and quartered in London; had:

      1c Margaret; *m* Sir Gilbert de Haya of Locherwort and had issue (*see* TWEEDDALE, M)

      2c Joan; *m* Sir Patrick Fleming of Biggar and was ancestor of the Earls of Wigtoun

(3) Andrew (Sir); *m* Beatrice — and *dsp*

(4) William; Bp St Andrews, Chllr Scotland, Regent for N of Scotland; *d* overseas 1297

Sir ANDREW FRASER of Touchfraser's est s,

  Sir ALEXANDER FRASER of Touchfraser and Cowie; Chamberlain Scotland 1319, Sheriff Kincardine and Stirling, granted extensive lands for loyalty to ROBERT I (THE BRUCE); *m* 1316 Lady Mary Bruce (*d c* 1323), sis of ROBERT I and widow of Sir Neil Campbell of Lochow, and was *k* at defeat of Scots by an invading host of English lords at Dupplin 12 Aug 1332, having had:

1 John of Touchfraser; *d* young, leaving a dau and heir:

  (1) Margaret; *m* Sir William Keith, Marshal of Scotland (*see* KINTORE, E), and had issue

2 William (Sir), of Cowie and Durris; *b c* 1318; *m* Margaret (living 1364), allegedly dau of Sir Andrew Moray of Bothwell, and was *k* Battle of Durham (Scottish invasion of England) 17 Oct 1346, having had:

  (1) ALEXANDER

  (2) John, of Auchinschogill; *m* Marjory, dau of Sir John — of Monymusk, and had by her a s (John, *dsp*) and two illegitimate sons (Andrew; William)

The er s,

  ALEXANDER FRASER of Cowie and Durris, 1st of Philorth; Sheriff Aberdeen; *m* 1375 Joanna, 2nd dau of William de Ross, 5th Earl of Ross, through whom he got Philorth; *m* 2nd by 1400 Elizabeth, allegedly dau of Sir David Hamilton, 3rd of Cadzow (*see* ABERCORN, D), and *d c* 1411, having had, with another s (Alexander, of Durris, probably illegitimate, ancestor of the FRASERs of Durris (now Dores) and FRASERs of Forest) and by his 2nd w:

Sir WILLIAM FRASER, 2nd of Philorth; sold the (territorial) Baronies of Cowie and Durris; *m* Elinor Douglas, thought to have been illegitimate dau of 2nd Earl of Douglas (*see* QUEENSBERRY, M), and *d* by 1441, having had, with two daus (Agnes, *m* 24 July 1423 William Forbes of Kinaldie, bro of 1st Lord Forbes (*qv*); Isabel, *m* Gilbert Menzies of Findon):

Sir ALEXANDER FRASER, 3rd of Philorth; *b* by 1410; *m* by 1430 his cousin Marjorie, dau of Gilbert Menzies of Findon, and *d* 7 April 1482, having had, with five yr sons (James, ancestor of the FRASERs of Memzie; William, living 1464; John, of Ardglassie, living 1464; Andrew, living 1464; George, living 1464):

ALEXANDER FRASER, 4th of Philorth; *m* (*m* 2nd Sir Gilbert Keith of Inverugie; *m* 3rd Jan 1499/1500 Sir Robert Douglas of Lochleven; *see* MORTON, E), dau of 1st Earl of Erroll (*qv*), and *d c* 1486, having had, with an est s (Sir Alexander, 5th of Philorth, simpleton, *dsp c* 1500), a yst s (George) and a dau (Janet, *m* — Baird of Ordinschives):

Sir WILLIAM FRASER, 6th of Philorth; *b* 1473; *m c* 1494 Elizabeth, dau of Sir Gilbert Keith of Inverugie, and *d* by 13 Nov 1513, leaving, with a dau (Christian, *m* Andrew Chalmers of Strichen):

ALEXANDER FRASER, 7th of Philorth; *m* 1st *c* 1516 Catharine, dau of Patrick Barclay of Gartly; *m* 2nd by July 1532 Catherine, dau of Gilbert Menzies of Findon and widow of Alexander Stratton of that Ilk, and *d* Nov 1569 aged 70, having had:

1 Alexander, Yr. of Philorth; *m* (papal dispensation 15 June 1534) Beatrice, dau of Robert Keith, Master of Marischal, and *dvp* 1564, leaving, with four yst sons (Alexander; of Tyrie; Hector; James; William):

  (1) ALEXANDER (Sir), 8th of Philorth

  (2) Walter, allegedly of Rathillock and Crechie; had two sons (Andrew; Alexander)

  (3) John, of Quarrelbuss; had a s (John, of Quarrelbuss and possibly Crechie; obtaine possession of the lands of Aberdour)

2 William, of Techmuiry, which property remained with his descendants till 1686, when it passed to James Gordon, husb of Alexander Fraser of Techmuiry's only dau Jane (*see also below*, however, against the dau by his 1st w of **11th Lord**)

3 Thomas, of Strichen, which he bought from Alexander Chalmers; *m* Isobel (*m* 2nd Thomas Fraser of Knockie later of Strichen; *see* LOVAT, L), allegedly dau of a man called John (more probably James) Forbes of Corsindae

4 Simon; *d* unm by Dec 1561

5 John; Rector U of Paris; *d* 1609

6 James, of Skatterty

1 Christina; *m* William Crawfurd of Fedderat

2 Elizabeth; *m c* 4 Nov 1566 William Gordon, Yr. of Awdiale

3 Margaret; *m* 1st Alexander Cumyn of Inverallochy; *m* 2nd Alexander Annand of Octerellon and *d* 1602

ALEXANDER FRASER, 7th of Philorth's gs,

  Sir ALEXANDER FRASER, 8th of Philorth; *b c* 1537; Commr S Parl for Aberdeenshire, built the town of Fraserburgh but obliged to sell a large part of his estates to various Fraser cousins; *m* 1st *c* 1559 Magdalen, dau of Sir Walter Ogilvie of Dunlugas; *m* 2nd (contract 31 May 1606) Elizabeth, est dau of Sir John Maxwell by Lady Herries of Terregles (*qv*) and widow of Sir John Gordon of Lochinvar, and *d* July 1623, having by his 1st w had:

1 ALEXANDER, 9th of Philorth

2 William; *d* unm

3 James, of Tyrie; had, with a dau (Jean):

  (1) Alexander, of Tyrie; had:

    1a James, of Tyrie, which he sold 1725 to Leslie of Iden; *m* Christian, dau of Sir Alexander Abercromby, 1st Bt (*qv*)

4 Simon; living 1613

5 Thomas; ancestor of a line of FRASERs who settled in Finland

1 Magdalen; *m* Patrick Cheyne of Esselmont

2 Anna/Margaret; *m c* 14 May 1606 William Hay of Ury and *d* July 1663

3 Elizabeth; *m* Sir Robert Keith of Ackergill

4 Barbara; *m* George Ogilvy of Carnousie

ALEXANDER FRASER, 8th of Philorth's est s,

  ALEXANDER FRASER, 9th of Philorth; *b c* 1579; *m* 1st (contract 19 Dec 1595 and 4 Jan 1595/6) Margaret, dau of **7th Lord Saltoun of Abernethy** (*see* above), and *d c* 1637, having had a s and two daus (Anna/Mary, *m* (contract 14 Oct 1616) George Baird of Auchmeddan; Magdalen, *m* James Forbes of Blackton); *m* 2nd Isabel, dau of Sir Robert Gordon of Lochinvar, and by her had another s (John, *dsp* by 1630); his s by his 1st w:

ALEXANDER FRASER, **11th Lord Saltoun of Abernethy**; *b* March 1604; *educ* King's Coll Aberdeen; Covenanter by 1638, cmded a regt in the Scots intervention in the English Civil War on behalf of CHARLES I; MP (S Parl) Aberdeenshire 1648 and 1661–63, fought for CHARLES II (to whom he made over a great deal of money) Battle of Worcester 3 Sept 1651; *m* 1st Isabel, dau of William Forbes of Tolquhoun, and had a dau (Janet, *m* her cousin Alexander Fraser of Techmuiry); *m* 2nd (contract 27 June 1634) Elizabeth, dau of Alexander Seton of Meldrum (*see* SETON, Bt, of Pitmedden) and widow of John Urquhart of Craigfintrie, and *d* 11 Aug 1693, having by her had:

1 Alexander, *Master of Saltoun*; *b c* 1630; *educ* King's Coll Aberdeen; *m* 1st *c* 11 Jan 1651/2 Lady Ann Kerr (*d* 30 Aug 1658), sis of 1st Marquess of Lothian (*qv*), and had:

  (1) Alexander; *b* 1653; *d* unm by 9 Dec 1672

  (2) WILLIAM, **12th Lord**

1 (cont.) The *Master of Saltoun m* 2nd 29 Oct 1660 Marion (*dsp* by Jan 1660/1), dau of 8th Earl of Glencairn (*see* CUNINGHAME, Bt) and widow of 1st Earl of Findlater; *m* 3rd 5 Aug 1663 Lady Sophia Erskine (*dsp*), sis of 2nd Earl of Kellie (*see* MAR and KELLIE, E), and *dvp* Nov 1682

The 11th LORD's gs,

WILLIAM FRASER, **12th Lord Saltoun of Abernethy**; *b* 21 Nov 1654; *educ* King's Coll Aberdeen; suspected, it would seem wrongly, of Jacobitism; *m* 11 Oct 1683 Margaret (*d* 1734), 2nd dau of Dr James Sharp, Archbp St Andrews (*see* 1970 edn SHARP-BETHUNE, Bt), and *d* 18 March 1715, having had:

1 ALEXANDER, **13th Lord**

2 William, of Fraserfield; *b* 19 Nov 1691; *m* 25 Oct 1724 Lady Katherine Anne Erskine (*d* 5 March 1733), dau of 9th Earl of Buchan (*qv*), and *d* 23 March 1727, leaving:

  (1) William, of Fraserfield; *b* 28 Sept 1725; *m* 5 Jan 1752 Rachel (*d* 3 June 1800), dau of Rev Hugh Kennedy, of Rotterdam, and *d* 31 Oct 1788, having had:

    1a William, of Fraserfield; *d* unm 1789

    2a Alexander, of Fraserfield; *b* 8 Jan 1761; HEICS; *m* 20 April 1795 Mary Christina (*d* 12 Sept 1813), est dau of George Moir, and *d* 18 July 1807, leaving:

      1b Margaret, of Fraserfield; *m* 27 May 1816 Henry David Forbes-Mitchell of Balgownie and *d* 19 Aug 1839, leaving issue (*see* SEMPILL, L)

      2b Rachel; *m* 15 July 1828 William Maxwell

      3b Katherine Isabella; *d* 1867

      4b Mary; *m* 1825 William Urquhart of Craigston, Aberdeenshire (*d* 1847), and had issue

    3a Henry David; *b* 27 April 1762; Army Offr; *m* 6 Oct 1800 Mary Christina, dau of John Forbes of Skellater, Aberdeenshire, Marshal-Gen in serv of King of Portugal, Kt Orders of Avis of Portugal and CARLOS III of Spain, and *d* 4 Aug 1810, leaving:

      1b William John; *b* 11 July 1801; Col in Russian serv; *d* unm 1864

      2b John Henry David; *b* 27 Dec 1803; Sec of Legation; *d* Florence 1839

      1b Sophia Maria Jane; *m* 1827 Count Henri François de Bombelles (*d* 1850) and had issue

      2b Margaret Alexia; *m* Marquis de Gargallo

      3b Mary Anne; *d* 1877

    4a Hugh (Rev); *b* 25 Dec 1764; Rector Woolwich; *m* 25 June 1803 Mary, dau of Richard Lloyd, and *d* 12 April 1837, having had:

      1b William Erskine; *b* 11 Jan 1806; *d* young

      1b Mary Wright; *d* unm

    5a Erskine, of Woodhill; *b* 23 June 1766; Col; *m* 3 May 1793 Elizabeth (*d* 18 Aug 1813), dau of Thomas Forbes of Ballogie, and *d* 2 Jan 1804, leaving:

      1b William, of Woodhill; *b* 21 Nov 1796; Lt-Col; *m* 20 Aug 1833 Mary Elizabeth, dau of Thomas Starkie Shuttleworth, of Ashton, Lancs, and *d* 13 July 1872, leaving:

        1c Elizabeth; *d* 21 Jan 1925

    1a Margaret; *m* 15 Oct 1771 11th Earl of Buchan (*qv*) and *dsp* 12 May 1819

    2a Katherine Anne; *m* 27 March 1777 Duncan Forbes-Mitchell of Thainstone and *d* 27 Dec 1836, leaving issue (*see* SEMPILL, L)

3 James, of Lonmay; m March 1726 Eleanor (d 7 Aug 1735), dau of 3rd Earl of Balcarres (see CRAWFORD and BALCARRES, E), and d 10 Aug 1729, having had:

(1) William; Cornet Stair's Regt of Dragoons; d unm

1 Helen; m 1709 James Gordon, er s of Sir John Gordon of Park, Banffshire

2 Henrietta; m 1718 John Gordon of Kinellar, s of Sir James Gordon of Lesmoir, and d 26 Feb 1751, leaving issue (see below against **15th Lord**)

3 Mary; m William Dalmahoy of Ravelrig

4 Isabella; m Rev David Brown, Min Belhavie, and d 27 April 1772

The 12th LORD's est s,

ALEXANDER FRASER, **13th Lord Saltoun of Abernethy**; b 1684; educ Oxford(?); m 26 Oct 1707 Mary, 3rd dau of 1st Earl of Aberdeen (see ABERDEEN AND TEMAIR, M), and d 24 July 1748, having had, with two daus (Ann, d unm 18 April 1807; Sophia, d unm 4 April 1784):

1 ALEXANDER FRASER, **14th Lord Saltoun of Abernethy**; b 1710; d unm 10 Oct 1751

2 William; advocate 1736; d unm 22 Nov 1748

3 GEORGE FRASER, **15th Lord Saltoun of Abernethy**; b 10 Oct 1720; Lt RM; m 5 June 1756 his cousin Eleanor (d 13 Sept 1800), dau of John Gordon of Kinellar, and d 30 Aug 1781, having had, with two other sons and two other daus (all d young or unm):

(1) ALEXANDER, **16th Lord**

(2) George; b 20 March 1763; Capt 59th Regt; d unm 8 Jan 1799

(1) Eleonora; m 1st 29 Aug 1786 Sir George Ramsay, 6th Bt, of Banff (d 16 April 1790, see 1970 edn); m 2nd 6 July 1792 Lt-Gen Duncan Campbell of Lochnell, Argyll (d 9 April 1837), and d c 1821

The 15th LORD's est s,

ALEXANDER FRASER, **16th Lord Saltoun of Abernethy**; b 27 June 1758; educ Lincoln's Inn; advocate 1780, Hon Burgess Banff 1791; m 9 June 1784 Marjory (d 15 Nov 1851), dau of Simon Fraser, of Ness Castle, Dir HEIC, and d 13 Sept 1793, having had:

1 ALEXANDER GEORGE FRASER, **17th Lord Saltoun of Abernethy**, KT (1852), KCB (1842, CB 1815), GCH (1837); b 22 April 1785; educ Eton; Ensign 35th Foot April 1802, Lt Sept 1802, Lt 42nd Foot 1803, Lt and Capt Gren Gds 1804, served Sicily 1806–07, Spain 1808–09 (present Corunna), Walcheren Expdn 1809, Cadiz 1811, Peninsular War 1811–14, Waterloo Campaign 1815 (when defence of orchard at Hougoumont made him famous), China 1841–44, rep S peer 1807–53, ADC to GEORGE IV and WILLIAM IV 1825–37, Maj-Gen 1837, Lt-Gen 1846, Col 55th Foot Feb–Aug 1846 and 2nd Foot 1846–53; Pres Madrigal Soc London, Chm Musical Union, Kt Maria Theresa Austria and St George Russia 4th Cl; m 6 March 1815 Catharine Thurlow (dsp 9 July 1826), illegitimate dau of 1st Baron Thurlow (qv), and dsp 18 Aug 1853

2 Simon; b 31 Aug 1787; d unm 10 Feb 1811

3 William; b 12 Oct 1791; W India merchant; m 9 April 1818 Elizabeth Graham (d 5 May 1853), 2nd dau of David Macdowall Grant of Arndilly, Banff, and d 21 March 1845, leaving:

(1) ALEXANDER, **18th Lord**

(2) David Macdowall (Sir), GCB; b 2 March 1825; granted with surv siblings Aug 1853 rank of Ld of Parl's daus/yr sons; Col cmdg RHA, Kt Medjidie; m 3 Jan 1854 Mary Georgina (d 7 Sept 1909), dau of Edward Gonne Bell, of Streamstown, Co Mayo, and d 25 Feb 1906, leaving:

1a Alexander David; b 30 Oct 1854; Capt 2nd Bn Gordon Highrs; das S Africa 28 April 1901

2a Edward Hay; b 2 Dec 1855; d 25 March 1915

3a David Macdowall; b 13 Oct 1857; Lt Cape Mounted Rifles; d at Krugersdorp of wounds recd while with Dr Jameson's force 11 Jan 1896

1a Maria Elizabeth Florence; m 10 Nov 1909 Sir Francis William Stronge, KCMG (see STRONGE, Bt), and d 13 Sept 1924

2a Catherine Frances Graham; m 28 Nov 1916 5th Baron Poltimore (qv) and dsp 9 April 1938

(3) Simon; b 19 Jan 1827; Lt Madras Cav; d unm 8 June 1845

(4) William Murray; b 6 April 1831; Maj Bengal SC; d 21 Sept 1872

(5) James Hay; b 24 March 1833; Col Bengal SC; m 1st 10 Aug 1864 Marian Stirling (d 16 Dec 1872), 5th dau of John Dundas, of Edinburgh, and had:

1a William; b 1866

1a Eleanor Katharine; d 29 March 1925

2a Laura Violet Jemima; d unm 28 May 1900

(5) (cont.) Col James Fraser m 2nd 12 Oct 1876 Emily Caroline (d 19 July 1925), 3rd dau of Col John Vandeleur, 10th Hus, of Mannister, Co Limerick, and d 24 March 1886

(6) Charles Julian; b 27 Feb, d 6 April 1838

(1) Mary Eleanor; d unm 20 March 1858

(2) Marjorie; d unm 28 June 1853

(3) Elizabeth; m 13 Oct 1853 Maj-Gen Hamilton Forbes (d 4 June 1891), of Ham, Surrey, Bengal SC, and d 20 Sept 1904, leaving issue

(4) Margaret Eleanora Georgina; m 12 March 1853 her unc's bro-in-law Capt John Arthur Evans, of Dean House, Oxon, and N Tuddenham, Norfolk, and d 13 Dec 1879, having had issue

(5) Eleanora Alexandrina; m 1 Feb 1858 Henry William Forester (see FORESTER, B) and d 12 May 1914, leaving issue

(6) Catharine Thurlow; m 28 Nov 1860 John Stewart Menzies (d 25 April 1867), of Chesthill, Aberfeldy, Perthshire, and d 4 April 1917, leaving issue

1 Margaret; d unm 14 Aug 1845

2 Eleanora; m 5 Dec 1825 William Macdowall Grant of Arndilly and d his widow, 26 Sept 1832, having had issue

The 17th LORD's n,

ALEXANDER FRASER, **18th Lord Saltoun of Abernethy**; b 5 May 1820; Ensign 96th Foot 1837, Capt 28th Foot 1845, Maj 1852, Lt-Col Aberdeenshire

Militia 1854–55, Brig-Gen Roy Co Archers, rep S peer 1859–86; m 25 April 1849 Charlotte (d 11 June 1890), 2nd dau of Thomas Browne Evans, of Dean House, Oxon, and N Tuddenham, Norfolk, and d 1 Feb 1886, having had:

1 ALEXANDER WILLIAM FREDERICK, **19th Lord**

2 Arthur Hay David; b 19 Aug 1852; Capt Scots Gds; m 9 Nov 1877 Lucy Jane (m 2nd 25 April 1887 Francis John Stuart Hay-Newton (see TWEEDDALE, M) and d 10 March 1939), only dau of Maj Robert Duncan Fergusson (see FERGUSSON, Bt), and d 27 Jan 1884, leaving:

(1) Helen Charlotte Isabella, GBE (1929, DBE 1919, CBE 1918); DSc Lond 1907, Hon LLD Glasgow 1919, Ch Controller QMAAC BEF 1917–18 (despatches), Cmdt WRAF 1918–19, Prof London U 1921–44, Prof Emeritus 1944–67, Fell Linnaean Soc, King's Coll Lond and Birkbeck Coll, Dir ATS 1939–41; m 7 Dec 1911 Prof David Thomas Gwynne-Vaughan, FRSE (d 4 Sept 1915), er s of Henry Gwynne-Vaughan, of Cynghordy, Breconshire, and dsp 26 Aug 1967

(2) Lucy Marjorie Kathleen, OBE (1919, MBE 1918); Adminr and Controller QMAAC BEF 1917–18 (despatches), Assist Cmdt and Dept Cmdt WRAF 1918–19, Ch Cmdt ATS 1939–41; m 1 Oct 1907 (divorce 1922) Edward Pratt-Barlow (d 1 Dec 1940), 60th Rifles, er s of Frank Pratt-Barlow, of Lynchmere Ho, Sussex, and d 12 Jan 1952

3 Thomas Henry Day; b 22 Oct 1853; d 12 Jan 1854

1 Charlotte Elizabeth Eleanor; m 1st 10 July 1873 William Henry Augustus Keppel and had issue (see ALBEMARLE, E); m 2nd 5 Dec 1903 Adml Sir Henry Frederick Stephenson, GCVO, KCB (d 16 Dec 1919), s of H F Stephenson, and d 25 Feb 1923

2 Marjorie Alexandrina Louisa; d young 19 May 1869

3 Annie Mary Eleanor; m 1st 15 July 1875 (divorce 8 Dec 1876) 15th Lord (Baron) Zouche (qv) (of Haryngworth); m 2nd 30 Aug 1893 2nd Baron Trevor (qv) of Brynkinhalt and dsp 10 May 1895

4 Alexandrina Charlotte Hannah; d an infant 23 Nov 1861

5 Alexandra Catherine May; m 29 March 1883 John Houblon Forbes and d Nov 1939, leaving issue (see STUART-FORBES, Bt)

The 18th LORD's est s,

ALEXANDER WILLIAM FREDERICK FRASER, **19th Lord Saltoun of Abernethy**, CMG (1917), DL (Aberdeenshire); b 8 Aug 1851; educ Eton; Capt Roy Co Archers, Lt-Col Gren Gds 1880, ret 1886, Maj 3rd Bn Gordon Highrs 1890–99, rep S peer 1890–1933, Hon Brig-Gen 1917; m 7 July 1885 Mary Helena (d 8 Oct 1940), sis of Sir Henry Christopher Grattan Bellew, 3rd Bt (qv), and d 19 June 1933, having had:

1 ALEXANDER ARTHUR, **20th Lord**

2 George, DSO (1920); b 4 March 1887; R-Adml, served WW I (despatches), WW II; m 1st 11 June 1920 (divorce 1934) Margaret Elizabeth Ida FRASER-SPENCER-STANHOPE (roy licence 1945, d 31 Jan 1964), only child of John Montague Spencer Stanhope, of Cannon Hall, Yorks, and had:

(1) +Simon Walter [Simon Fraser Esq, Mains of Tillyfoure, Monymusk, Aberdeenshire AB51 7JB]; b 24 Aug 1924; educ Eton; Argyll & Sutherland Highrs WW II 1942–46, Lt RA 1946–48; m 1st 21 June 1950 (divorce 1962) Jean Madeline Frances, er dau of Prof John Masson Gulland, FRS, of Edinburgh, and has:

1a +Isabel Madeline; b 31 Dec 1951

2a +Elspeth Caroline; b 8 July 1954

(1) (cont.) Simon Fraser m 2nd 1 Dec 1962 (divorce 1971) Yvonne, only dau of Edwin Valère-Newby, of Leeds, Yorks, and by her has:

1a +Alistair John; b 3 Nov 1963; m 1989 *Marie-Catherine Elizabeth, dau of James Sigston, of Prenton, Wirral, and has:

1b +Alexander James Walter; b 2 July 1995

2b +Robert Conrad; b 18 June 1997

3a +Deborah Gail; b 19 July 1965

(1) (cont.) Simon Fraser m 3rd 1971 (divorce 1976) Cheryl Mary Eleanor, dau of David McNeil Williams, of Summerfield Ho, Cheshire, and formerly w of Richard Charles Sheffield (see SHEFFIELD, Bt), and by her has:

2a +James David; b 1971

3a +William Alexander; b 1972

(1) (cont.) Simon Fraser m 4th 1976 (divorce 1983) Meryl, dau of John Ingham of Halifax, Yorks; m 5th 1987 Marjorie (d 1995), dau of Sydney Donaldson and widow of Neil W Cameron, MD, ChB; m 6th 1995 *Avice Moira Alexander, dau of James Finlayson Cunningham, MB, ChB, of West Park, Eyemouth, Berwicks

2 (cont.) The Hon George Fraser m 2nd 2 Oct 1934 *Margaret Elizabeth [The Hon Mrs George Fraser, Luxilyan, 15 Louw Ave, Somerset West, CP, S Africa], 2nd dau of Reginald Barnes, of St Ermin's, Westminster, and d 13 June 1970, having by her had:

(2) +Robert Andrew Gerard [Robert Fraser Esq, Suikerbos, Gordons Bay, CP, S Africa]; b 30 July 1935; educ Diocesan Coll Rondebosch and Cape Town U; m 31 Oct 1964 *Sarah Elizabeth, dau of Brig Gerald Edward Peck, CBE, DSO, of Piper's Plot, Lockeridge, Wilts, and has:

1a +David Alexander George; b 1966

1a +Fiona Elizabeth; b 1965

(3) +Patrick George [Patrick Fraser Esq, Silverhill, Kenilworth, CP, S Africa]; b 22 March 1938; educ Diocesan Coll Rondebosch and Cape Town U; m 1975 *Patricia Aletta, dau of Dr Peter John Frost, and has:

1a +Alexandra Nelle; b 1979

2a +Sophie Elizabeth; b 1981

3a +Camilla Mary; b 1981

3 Simon; b 7 Sept 1888; Lt 3rd Bn Gordon Highrs; ka 29 Oct 1914

4 William, DSO (1918), MC; b 5 July 1890; educ Charterhouse; Brig Gren Gds, formerly Gordon Highrs, Mil Attaché Brussels 1931–35 and Paris 1938–39, WW I (wounded), WW II (despatches, wounded), Head UNRRA Paris; m 22 Dec 1919 Pamela Cynthia (d 20 Oct 1975), 2nd dau of Cyril, Francis Maude (see HAWARDEN, V) and widow of Maj William La Touche Congreve, VC, DSO, MC, and d 11 Nov 1964, having had:

(1) +David William (Sir), GCB (1980, KCB 1973), OBE (1962) [Gen Sir David Fraser GCB OBE, Vallenders, Isington, Alton, Hants GU34 4PP]; b 30 Dec 1920; educ Eton and Ch Ch Oxford, Hon DLitt, Reading 1992; served WW II, Gen Gren Gds, cmdg 4th Div 1969–71, Malaya 1948, Cyprus 1958, Cameroun 1961, Borneo 1964, Maj-Gen (1969), ACDS (policy) 1971–73, VCGS 1973–75, UK Mil Rep NATO 1975–77, Comdt RCDS 1977–80, ADC (Gen) 1977–80, Col Roy Hants Regt 1981–87; Chm Treloar Tst and Govg Body Treloar Coll 1982–93, V-Lt Hants 1988– (DL 1982–88); m 1st 26 Sept 1947 (divorce 1952) Anne, yr dau of Brig Edward William Sturgis Balfour, CVO, DSO, OBE, MC (see BALFOUR, E), and has:

1a +Antonia Isabella; b 6 April 1949; m 1st 1972 (divorce 1975) Thomas Harney; m 2nd 1975 (divorce 1979) Thomas Bantock and by him has:

1b +Amaryllis Eva; b 1975

1a (cont.) Mrs Antonia Bantock m 3rd 1981 *Timothy Hanbury and by him has:

1b +Edan William Samson; b 1985

(1) (cont) Gen Sir David Fraser m 2nd 11 Oct 1957 *Julia Frances, yr dau of Maj Cyril James Oldridge de la Hey, of Northwick Hall, Worcs, and by her has:

1a +(Alexander) James; b 30 June 1960; m 12 April 1997 *Stephanie, est dau of Alastair Struthers, of Craigmaddie, Milngavie

2a +Simon William David [Simon Fraser Esq, Mountfield Court, nr Battle, E Sussex]; b 7 Dec 1963; m 1991 *Lucinda Anne, er dau of Thomas Edward Sydney Egerton, of Newbury, Berks, and has:

1b +Hector; b 1994

2b +Caspar; b 1996

2a +Arabella Katherine; b 15 Sept 1958; m 1984 *Lt-Col Gordon Thomas Riddell Birdwood (see BIRDWOOD, B) and has:

1b *Katie; b 9 Sept 1993

3a +Lucy Caroline [The Hon Mrs Alexander Baring, 109 Portobello Rd, London W10]; b 7 April 1965; m 1992 *Hon Alexander Nicholas John Baring, yr s of 7th Baron Ashburton, KCVO (qv), and has:

1b *Olive

2b *A dau

(2) Alastair Grattan Maude; b 3 March 1926; d 7 May 1932

1 Mary Alexandra; b 11 Dec 1891; m 1st 3 Jan 1918 Lt-Cdr John Robert Auber Codrington, RN (d Nov 1918), yst s of R-Adml William Codrington, CB (see HAMBLEDEN, V), and had issue; m 2nd 11 Sept 1928 Maj Arthur Balcarres Wardlaw-Ramsay, JP, DL (d 26 June 1956), 21st of Whitehill, Midlothian, and of Tillicoultry, Clackmannanshire, Argyll and Sutherland Highrs SR (see HOGG, Bt), and d following a car crash 11 Aug 1969, having by him had:

(1) +Euphan Mary [Lady Hanbury-Tenison, Clytha Park, Abergavenny, Gwent NP7 9BW]; b 1931; m 1955 *Sir Richard Hanbury-Tenison, KCVO, JP (see SUDELEY, B), and has:

1a +John Wardlaw; b 6 Dec 1957; educ Eton and Magdalen Coll Oxford (PhD); m 1 May 1993 *Laura Katharine, only dau of Sir Robert Lucian Wade-Gery, KCMG, KCVO

2a +William Ayscough; b 23 Oct 1962; educ Eton and Peterhouse Cambridge; m 23 May 1997 *Mina, dau of Rev W Choi, of New York

3a +Capel Thomas; b 2 Feb 1965; educ Blundell's and RAC Cirencester; m 1992 *(Beatrice) Hannah, est dau of Alan Hutchison, of Wern y Cwm, Abergavenny, and has:

1b +William Augustus; b 1992

1a +Sarah; b 27 March 1956; educ Exeter U, Munich and Queens' Coll Cambridge; m 9 June 1984 *Dr Martin S Tolley, er s of Canon George Tolley, of Dore, Sheffield, and has:

1b +Thomas; b 1986

2b +Isaac Adrian; b 1995

1b +Sophia Margaret; b 1989

2b +Ruth Felicity; b 1993

2a +Laura Mary; b 1 Sept 1966; educ Monmouth Girls' Sch; m 31 Aug 1991 *Abioudun John Femi-Ola, s of Femi Clement Femi-Ola, of London, and has:

1b +Benedict John Olusei; b 1995

(2) +Elizabeth Mary [Mrs Simon Walker-Heneage, The Old Rectory, Wanstrow, Somerset BA4 4TQ]; b 1934; m 1955 *Simon Anthony Helyar Walker-Heneage and has:

1a +James Arthur [James Walker-Heneage Esq, Buddens House, Bowerchalke, Wilts SP5 5BN]; b 1957; m 1987 *Charlotte Elizabeth, dau of Roland Shott, of North Farm, Ashmore, Wilts, and has:

1b +Alexander George; b 25 Sept 1995

1b +Eliza Mary; b 19 May 1993

2b *Georgia Madeline; b 22 June 1997

1a +Celia Mary [Mrs Paul Gurowich, 6 Loder Rd, Brighton, E Sussex BN1 6PJ]; b 1956; m 1990 *Paul Maxwell Gurowich, s of Peter Gurowich, of Winchester, and has:

1b +Timothy Peter; b 24 April 1991

2b +Aaron Finbar Simon; b 12 Dec 1994

2a +Arabella Jane [Mrs Nicholas Hoare, 66 Winchedon Rd, London SW6 5DR]; b 1959; m 1985 *Nicholas David Douro Hoare, s of Michael Douro Hoare, of Downsland Court, Ditchling, Sussex, and has:

1b +Thomas James Douro; b 23 July 1988

1b +Charlie Benjamin Douro; b 17 Nov 1997

3a +Sophia Dionysia; b 1962; m 1988 *Nicholas John Gibson Wright, s of David John Vernon Wright, of Oxford, and has:

1b +Flora Clemence Elizabeth; b 4 Nov 1990

1b +Lily Dionysia; b 13 June 1992

3b +Isobel Artemis; b 14 Jan 1997

4a +Sarah Phoebe; b 1974; has:

1b *Poppy Lauren Dean; b 2 May 1997

The 19th LORD's est s,

ALEXANDER ARTHUR FRASER, 20th Lord Saltoun of Abernethy, MC, JP, DL Aberdeenshire; b 8 March 1886; educ Eton and New Coll Oxford (MA); Capt and Hon Maj 3rd Bn Gordon Highrs WW I (POW), memb Roy Co Archers, rep S peer 1935–63; m 8 June 1920 Dorothy Geraldine (d 1985), est dau of Sir Charles Glynne Earle Welby, 5th Bt, CB (qv), and d 31 August 1979, having had:

Alexander Simon, Master of Saltoun, MC; b 12 Dec 1921; Lt Gren Gds WW II; ka Feb 1944

FLORA MARJORY FRASER, present Lady Saltoun

Seat: Cairnbulg Castle, Fraserburgh, Aberdeenshire. Cairnbulg was originally called Philorth (see **Lineage (of Fraser)** above) and the oldest part of the Castle, the massive square tower keep, was probably built in the 11th century at the time the property came to the Frasers with the marriage of Alexander Fraser and the Ross heiress Joanna. It is vaulted at ground level, has a great hall on the floor above and above that chambers which have been turned into guest bedrooms. The present name was given the Castle when Sir Alexander, 8th of Philorth, sold off much of his lands to his cousins.

Confusingly, the **11th Lord Saltoun of Abernethy** a couple of generations later built another house only a mile from the Castle at the little town of Philorth, and this structure was given the old name. Philorth House, as it was known, was destroyed by fire during World War I. Meanwhile Cairnbulg had passed into other hands, notably those of an Aberdeen shipbuilder, Sir John Duthie, who in the late 19th century restored what was by now something of a ruin. Cairnbulg was bought back by the Frasers in 1934. As well as the old keep there is a round tower crowned by a double crenellation and a purely domestic wing, the only hint of its castle status being the stepped gables above the top-floor windows.

SALUSBURY-TRELAWNY

Arms: Quarterly, 1st and 4th, argent a chevron sable (for TRELAWNY); 2nd and 3rd, gules a lion rampant per bend sinister argent and erminois ducally crowned between three crescents or, on a canton of the last a bear's head erased sable muzzled argent (for SALUSBURY). **Crests:** 1 A wolf proper (for TRELAWNY), 2 A demi-lion rampant per bend sinister argent and erminois, holding between the paws a shield or charged with a bear's head as in the arms (for SALUSBURY). **Mottoes:** 1 Sermoni consona facta ('Deeds agreeing with words'), 2 Virtus patrimonio nobilior ('Virtue is more noble than patrimony'). **Creation:** Bt. (E) 1 July 1628.

SIR JOHN BARRY SALUSBURY-TRELAWNY, 13TH BT, of Trelawny, Cornwall, JP (Kent 1973) [Sir John Trelawny Bt JP, Beavers Hill, Rectory Lane, Saltwood, Kent CT21 4QA]; b 4 Sept 1934; s f 1956; educ HMS Worcester; late 2nd Offr Merchant Navy, Sub-Lt RNVR, FInstM 1974, dir The Martin Walter Group Ltd 1971–74, jt dep md Korn Ferry Internat Inc 1981–83, dir Goddard Kay, Rogers Assoc 1984–95 (chm 1993–95), Pres London Cornish Assoc 1997–; m 4 Jan 1958 *Carol Knox, yr dau of Charles Francis Knox Watson, of Saltwood, and has:

1 +JOHN WILLIAM RICHARD [John Trelawny Esq, 278 Seabrook Rd, Hythe, Kent]; b 30 March 1960; m 1st 1980 (divorce 1986) Anita, yr dau of Kenneth Snelgrove, and has:

(1) +Harry John; b 10 Dec 1982

(1) +Victoria Hayley; b 31 Aug 1981

1 (cont.) JOHN TRELAWNY m 2nd 1987 (divorce 1993) Sandra Patricia, dau of Joseph Thompson, of Hythe, and by her has:

(2) +Thomas Jonathon; b 23 March 1989

1 *Jane Louise; b 5 Sept 1958; m 1977 *Maj John R Martin, Parachute Regt, and has:

(1) *James Jonathan; b 12 Feb 1982

(1) *Emma Jane; b 7 July 1980

2 *Amanda Sarah; b 28 July 1961; m 1980 *Capt Alan M Startin, Devonshire and Dorset Regt, and has:

(1) *Matthew Guy; b 24 Aug 1982

(2) *Benjamin Marcus; b 24 April 1984

(3) *Hamish William; b 1 April 1988

(1) *Pollyanna Knox; b 19 Aug 1992

3 *Emma Mary; b 22 April 1966; m 1988 *William Ernle Hardy Vernon (see HARROWBY, E) and has issue

Lineage: HAMELIN; held Treloen or Trelawny, parish of Altarnun, Cornwall, from Robert Count of Mortain (half-bro of WILLIAM I (THE CONQUEROR)) 1086; had:

RICHARD; had:

WILLIAM; held a kt's fee from Reginald de Botrell; had

JOHN; m —, dau of his f's overlord Reginald de Botrell, and had:

WILLIAM; m Joan Trewynnick; had:

JOHN; living temp EDWARD I; m Laura, dau of Sir Richard Sergaux/Serjeaux, and had:

WILLIAM; MP Launceston c 1326; m Margery de Riparüs/Rivers, and had:

WILLIAM; m Joan Douggall and had:

Sir JOHN; living c 1367; m Matilda Mynwenyke and had:

Sir JOHN TRELAWNY; MP and Coroner Cornwall; granted pension of £20 (just under £500,000 in late-1990s terms) p.a. by HENRY V for mil servs in Hundred Years War, following which the TRELAWNYs long bore on their coat of arms an augmentation of three oak or laurel leaves; m Agnes Trogodeck and had, with an er s (Sir Richard, MP Liskeard 1422, dspm):

JOHN TRELAWNY; MP Truro 1449, Sheriff Cornwall temp EDWARD IV; m Joan, heiress of Heligan, and d after 1485, leaving:

Sir JOHN TRELAWNY; m Jane Powna and had, with a yr s (John, m Florence, sis of 1st Earl of Devon (qv) of the 1485 cr):

WALTER TRELAWNY; had:

JOHN TRELAWNY; MP Liskeard 1553; m 1st Margery Lamelion and had issue; m 2nd Lora Trecarrel and d c 1537, having had another s (John, m Beatrice Trevanion); his s by his 1st w:

JOHN TRELAWNY, DL (Cornwall); MP Lostwithiel and Cornwall; paid £6 (over £37,000 in late-1990s terms) to avoid being ktd; twice Sheriff temp ELIZABETH I; m Anne Reskymer and had a 2nd s:

Sir JONATHAN TRELAWNY; MP Liskeard c 1593 and Cornwall c 1597 and 1603, High Sheriff Cornwall c 1595, ktd 1597; m Elizabeth, 2nd dau of Sir Henry Killigrew, and d 21 June 1604, having had, with three daus and a yr s (Edward, of Coldrenick, Cornwall):

Sir John Trelawny, 1st Bt (E), so cr 1 July 1628, of Trelawny; b 24 April 1592; Sheriff Cornwall c 1631; m 1st Elizabeth, dau of Sir Reginald Mohun, 1st Bt, of Boconnock; m 2nd Douglas, widow of Sir William Courtenay and dau and coheir of Tristram Gorges, and was bur 16 Feb 1664, having had, with other issue, including a yr s (Francis, m Margaret, dau of Sir Edward Seymour, 2nd Bt; see SOMERSET, D) and a dau (Margaret, m Amos, s of Sir Francis Fulford), an est s:

Sir Jonathan Trelawny, 2nd Bt; MP Cornwall 1661–78 and E Looe 1678–79; m Mary, dau of Sir Edward Seymour, 2nd Bt (see SOMERSET, D), and was bur 5 March 1680/1, having had, with other issue (d unm):

1 John; m Catherine, 3rd dau of James Jenkyn, and dsp & vp

2 **Rt Rev Sir Jonathan Trelawny, 3rd Bt;** b 24 March 1650; Bp Bristol 1685 (one of the Seven Bishops committed to the Tower by JAMES II), Exeter and 1707 Winchester; Prelate Order Garter; m 1684 Rebecca (d 11 Feb 1710), dau and coheir of Thomas Hele, of Bascombe, Devon, and d 19 July 1721, having had, with other issue:

(1) **Sir John Trelawny, 4th Bt;** MP Liskeard and W Looe; m Agnes Blackwood (d 8 April 1777) and dsp 1756

(2) Edward; b 1699; Commr Victualling Office, Govr Jamaica; m 1737 —, dau of John Crawford, and dsp

(3) Hele (Rev); DD, Rector S Hill and Landreath, Cornwall; dsp 1740

(1) Letitia; m her cousin **Sir Harry Trelawny, 5th Bt** (see below)

3 Henry; Brig-Gen, Govr Plymouth; m Rebecca, dau and coheir of Mathew Hales, and d 1702, having had:

(1) **Sir Harry Trelawny, 5th Bt;** bapt 15 Feb 1687; MP, ADC to 1st Duke of Marlborough (qv); m 1720 his cousin Letitia (bur 6 June 1775) and d 7 April 1762, having had, with a s (dvp) and two other daus (d unm):

1a Letitia; m her cousin **Sir William Trelawny, 6th Bt** (see below)

(2) William; bapt 13 Nov 1696; Army Capt; m Mary, est dau of William Bisset, of St Margaret's, Westminister, and Southampton, and had:

1a WILLIAM (Sir), **6th Bt**

2a Harry; Gen, Govr Landguard Fort; m 1752 Mary Dormer and d 28 Jan 1800, leaving:

1b Charles TRELAWNY later BRERETON-TRELAWNY, of Shotwick Park, Cheshire; m 1786 Maria, only sis of Sir Christopher Hawkins, 1st and last Bt (see 1828 edn), and d 19 June 1860, leaving:

1c Harry, of Shotwick; b 1792; Capt Gren Gds; m 1818 Caroline (d 23 Jan 1879), dau of Capt Monk, RN, and d 19 June 1869, having had:

1d Harry; Capt Gren Gds; dsp 1851

2d Horace Dormer BRERETON-TRELAWNY later TRELAWNY, of Shotwick, JP, DL Cheshire; b 22 Sept 1824; Capt RHG; m 28 April 1859 Hon Maria Katherine Walsh (d 23 Jan 1910), est dau of 1st Baron Ormathwaite (see 1970 edn), and d 15 April 1906, leaving:

1e Florence; m 7 June 1898 Francis Edward Rooper, JP, of Bronydd, Glynceirog, Denbighs, and d 22 March 1938, leaving issue

2e Maud; d unm 3 Feb 1928

3e Hilda; m 13 July 1892 John Herbert UPTON-COTTRELL-DORMER later UPTON (deed poll 1907), of Ingmire Hall, Sedbergh, Yorks, 4th s of Clement Cottrell-Dormer, of Rousham Hall, and d 10 June 1919, leaving issue. He d 13 Nov 1930

4e Lilian; m Aug 1920 Baron Bernardo Quaranta di San Severino, Italian Consul at Adalia, Turkey, and d Brisbane, Qld, 4 May 1961. He d 12 Feb 1934

5e Miny; m 30 July 1903 (divorce 1928, resumed maiden name 1943) Reginald Ashton Rigby, est s of Col Rigby, and d 15 Dec 1947, leaving issue

3d Clarence BRERETON-TRELAWNY later TRELAWNY; b 20 Dec 1826; served Austrian Army; m 15 Nov 1870 Mary (d 23 March 1930), dau of W S Campbell, US Consul Dresden, and d 28 Nov 1902, leaving:

1e Rose; m 21 Nov 1895 George Cameron Day, of Quennington Court, Fairford, Glos, and d 23 Sept 1921, leaving issue

2e Elma Agnes; m 28 Aug 1906 Launcelot Woods Creagh, est s of Lt Launcelot Stewart Creagh, RN, and d 23 Sept 1920. He d 1919

3e Violet Mary; m 1st 12 June 1899 Maj Bernard Robert Liebert, 7th Hus (ka 13 May 1915), and had issue; m 2nd 19 Feb 1917 Sir Robert Stanton Woods, MD, FRCP, MRCS, s of Robert Woods, JP, of Stewartstown, Co Tryone, and d 8 Sept 1964, leaving further issue. He d 18 Nov 1954

4e May

5e Ruby; m 26 Nov 1913 Brig Gen Henry Brewster Percy Lion Kennedy, CMG, DSO, KRRC, s of V-Adml J J Kennedy, CB, and had issue. He d 8 Dec 1953

1d Agnes Caroline; m 1st 1 July 1849 John James Calley (dsp 16 Jan 1854), of Burderop, Wilts; m 2nd 1857 Hedworth David Barclay, of Eastwick Park, Surrey, and d 14 July 1915, leaving issue. He d 25 Aug 1873

The 5th Bt's n and s-in-law,

Sir William Trelawny, 6th Bt; Offr RN, Govr Jamaica; m his cousin Letitia (d 24 Aug 1772; see above) and d 11 Dec 1772, having had, with a dau (Letitia Anne, m Paul Treby Treby, of Plympton, Devon, and d 1 Dec 1845, leaving issue):

Rev Sir Harry Trelawny, 7th Bt; bapt 26 June 1756; MA Oxon, Preb Oxford; m 28 Feb 1778 Anne (d 18 Nov 1822), dau of Rev James Brown, Rector Portishead, Vicar Kingston, Somerset, and d 24 Feb 1834, having had, with other issue, including a yr s (Hamelin, b 16 Oct 1782, Army Offr Peninsular War, Col RA, Govr St Helena, m 1806 Martha (d 6 Jan 1864), dau of J Rogers, of Sea View, Co Cork, and d 3 May 1856, leaving a s (d unm) and four daus), an est surv s:

Sir WILLIAM LEWIS TRELAWNY later SALUSBURY-TRELAWNY (roy licence 11 Dec 1802), **8th Bt;** b 4 July 1781; MP E Cornwall, Ld Lt Cornwall; m 24 Aug 1807 Patience Christian (d 20 June 1857), dau of John Phillips Carpenter, of Mount Tavy, Devon, and had, with other issue:

1 JOHN SALUSBURY, **9th Bt**

2 Harry Reginald, of Poltair, Penzance, JP, DL; b 12 Dec 1826; 6th Dragoons; m 14 July 1853 Juliana (d 28 Sept 1914), dau of Arthur Kelly, of Kelly, Devon, and d 24 Oct 1883, leaving:

(1) Harry; b 1 July 1858; m 15 May 1907 Winifred Mary, dau of Henry Saunderson, of Plymouth, and dsp 20 Oct 1908

(2) John; b 8 May 1860; m 2 April 1891 Florence (d 4 Jan 1946), dau of John Michael Williams, of Caerhays Castle, Cornwall, and d 14 April 1920, leaving:

1a John Maitland, MC; b 26 Jan 1892; educ Winchester; AMICE, Maj RE (RO) WW I (despatches three times) and WW II 1940–44, in Rlwy Dept India; m 18 March 1919 Louisa Frederica (d 1985), yst dau of Capt Guy Mainwaring, RN, and d 2 Nov 1954, leaving:

1b +John Guy; b 28 Dec 1919; educ Bradfield and RMC Sandhurst; Capt DCLI WW II (wounded, POW 1942–43); m 12 May 1948 *Ruth Gertrude, er dau of Edward Richard Marker (see BAGOT, B), and has:

1c +Richard John SALUSBURY-TRELAWNY later MARKER (deed poll 1974) [Richard Marker Esq, Combe, Honiton, Devon]; b 7 Aug 1953; m 1978 *Petronela Johana van der Mortel, of Victoria, BC, and has:

1d *Karissa Ann; b 1980

2d *Stephanie Michelle; b 1984

3d *Angela Nicole; b 1986

4d *Joanna Petronela; b 1988

2c +Peter Michael; b 25 March 1956

3c +Patrick Charles; b 13 Feb 1958

1c *Daphne Ann; b 23 Feb 1950

2c *Jill Margaret; b 14 Oct 1951

2b +Philip Michael, MC; b 11 Nov 1921; educ Winchester; Lt-Col LI WW II; m 23 March 1946 Jean Mary (d 1948), F/O WAAF, only dau of Col Herbert Cecil Fraser, DSO, OBE, TD, of Redlands, Myddelton, Ilkley, Yorks, and has:

1c +Simon Jonathan [Simon Salusbury-Trelawny Esq, 120 Earlsfield Rd, London SW18]; b 30 June 1948; educ Nautical Coll Pangbourne; commissioned SCLI; m 1st 5 Sept 1974 (divorce 1978) Caroline Margaret, only dau of Sir Nigel John Douglas Vernon, 4th Bt (qv); m 2nd 1978 *Marian Janet, dau of John MacAulay, of Poplar Hall, Ramsey, Essex, and has:

1d +Edward John; b 1979

2d +Harry Philip; b 1980

1c *Diane Jane [Mrs Robert Blake, Harrington House Farm, Spilsby, Lincs]; b 4 March 1947; m 11 April 1970 *Robert Jessop Blake, er s of James B Blake, of Clumber Lane Farm, Worksop, Notts, and has:

1d *James Trelawny; b 9 Sept 1971

2d *Jonathan Jessop; b 1973

1b *Laetitia Ann; b 14 Aug 1924; m 11 April 1953 *David Neil Courtenay McWatters, only s of Lt-Col Gerald McWatters, OBE, TD, of Brotherswood, Almondsbury, Glos, and has:

1c *Jonathan Courtenay; b 16 Sept 1954; educ Kelly Coll

1c *Victoria Courtenay; b 1 March 1956

2c *Jennifer Laetitia; b 16 Jan 1962,

2a Harry Reginald; *b* 7 May 1893; *d* 10 April 1921

(3) Arthur; *b* 31 May 1864; *d* 15 April 1927

(4) Hamelin William; *b* 22 March 1870; drowned India 15 July 1900

(1) Beatrice Laetitia; *d unm* 29 March 1907

(2) Edith, *d unm* 5 Feb 1889

(3) Eleanor; *m* 17 June 1890 Rev George Lincoln Gambler Lowe, Rector Throwleigh, Devon, and *d* 25 Jan 1936, leaving issue. He *d* 29 May 1933

(4) Florence; *m* 24 Oct 1895 Walter Gordon Deedes and *d* 19 March 1947, having had issue. He *d* 3 April 1924

1 Elizabeth; *m* 9 Jan 1834 Rev Henry John Morshead, JP, Rector Kelly, Devon, and *d* 22 March 1888, leaving issue. He *d* 25 Sept 1881

2 Caroline; *m* 13 Aug 1851 Ven Archdeacon Reginald Hobhouse, Rector St Ives and Archdeacon Bodmin, and *d* 1880, leaving issue. He *d* 27 Jan 1894

Sir WILLIAM *d* 15 Nov 1856; his er surv s,

Sir John Salusbury Salusbury-Trelawny, 9th Bt, DL; *b* 2 June 1816; Capt Roy Cornwall Rangers, Dep Warden Stannaries, MP Tavistock 1843–52 and 1857–65 and E Cornwall 1868–74; *m* 1st 25 Jan 1842 Harriet Jane (*d* 5 Nov 1879), est dau of J H Tremayne, of Heligan, Cornwall, and had:

1 WILLIAM LEWIS (Sir), **10th Bt**

1 Caroline Matilda; *m* 3 Oct 1863 Maj-Gen John Barton Sterling, Coldstream Gds, only surv s of Rev John Sterling, and *d* 2 Nov 1917, leaving issue. He *d* 5 Dec 1926

2 Florence; *m* 29 Nov 1871 Sir Jonathan Edmund Backhouse, 1st Bt (*qv*), and *d* 11 Oct 1902, leaving issue

Sir John *m* 2nd 19 May 1881 Harriet Jacqueline (*d* 13 Nov 1904), widow of Col Edward George Walpole Keppel (*see* ALBEMARLE, E) and dau of Sir Anthony Buller, of Pound, Devon, and *d* 4 Aug 1885A*

Sir JOHN's only s,

Sir William Lewis Salusbury-Trelawny, 10th Bt, JP, DL Cornwall; *b* 26 Aug 1844; Sheriff Cornwall 1891 and 1895, Capt Roy Cornwall Rangers; dropped use of 'Salusbury-' for all except formal purposes, e.g. legal documents, as have his male-line descendants; *m* 1st 14 July 1868 Jessy Rose Mary (*d* 23 Nov 1871), only dau of John Murray, of Philiphaugh, and had:

1 JOHN WILLIAM (Sir), **11th Bt**

1 Florence Rose Mary; *m* 17 Nov 1891 Edward Sydenham Fursdon (*d* 13 Feb 1930), of Fursdon, Devon, and *d* at sea by enemy action 25 Sept 1941, leaving issue.

Sir William *m* 2nd 17 Dec 1872 Harriett Buller (*d* 9 March 1932), est dau of Rev James Buller Kitson, Vicar Morval, and by her had:

2 James Edward Salusbury, OBE (1919); *b* 14 Sept 1873; Maj and Brevet Lt-Col DCLI, Adj 4th Bn 1908–10, WW I (severely wounded); Staff Capt War Office 1915, Assist Mil Sec 1917; *m* 1st 28 Nov 1907 (*divorce* 1930) Winifred Eveline (*d* 27 Dec 1937), dau of William Edward Dorrington, of Chelsea, and had:

(1) James Reginald Dorrington; *b* 6 Oct 1908; *educ* Westminster; slr 1931, Capt DCLI; *m* 1st 29 July 1932 Muriel Mary (*d* 25 April 1970), est dau of Sir Eustace William Windham Wrixon-Becher, 4th Bt (*qv*), and had:

1a +Jonathan William, OBE (1976); *b* 25 Feb 1934; *educ* Charterhouse; Col Coldstream Gds; *m* 1st 4 Dec 1959 (*divorce* 1969) Jill Rosamonde, only dau of Maj-Gen Cecil Benfield Fairbanks, CB, CBE, of Candy Lane House, Nayland, Suffolk; *m* 2nd 15 Aug 1970 (*divorce* 197–) Gillian Anne, only child of Richard John Radcliff, of Fossebridge House, Fossebridge, Glos, and by her has:

1b *Katherine Sophie; *b* 1972

1a *Mary Letitia [Mrs Procter Naylor, 17 Chapel St, Bildeston, Suffolk IP7 7EP]; *b* 11 Dec 1937; *m* 23 Sept 1966 *Procter Naylor, OBE, 3rd s of Frank Armitage Naylor, of Leeds, and has:

1b *Edward Trelawny Procter; *b* 13 May 1969; *m* 19 Aug 1996 *Barbara, er dau of Bernard Thole, of Amsterdam

2b *William James; *b* 18 March 1977

1b *Harriet Mary; *b* 12 Dec 1967

(1) (cont.) James Salusbury-Trelawny *m* 2nd 8 May 1971 *Vieno Helinä, yr dau of Väinö Junno, of Kemi, Finland, and *d* 1980

2 (cont.) James Salusbury-Trelawny *m* 2nd 15 Nov 1930 Edith Janetta (*d* 23 June 1961), dau of Nicholas Cornock, and *d* 27 Jan 1940

3 Lewis Dormer St Aubyn; *b* 6 Oct 1886; *educ* Eton; Maj KRRC; *m* 1st 8 May 1915 Adèle (*d* 9 Jan 1952), dau of Robert Nathaniel Netterville; *m* 2nd 8 Oct 1954 *Kathleen Marie Taylor *née* Keohane and *dsp* 27 June 1958

2 Rebecca Harriet Buller; *m* 5 Jan 1898 Arthur Francis Basset, s of Gustavus Lambart Basset, JP, DL, of Tehidy, Cornwall,, and *d* 27 Nov 1947, leaving issue. He *d* 30 May 1950

3 Dolores Olga; *m* 1st 28 April 1914 Henry Harcourt Willams (*d* 8 Sept 1927), of Pencalenick, Cornwall, s of Michael Henry Williams, and had issue; *m* 2nd 27 Oct 1931 6th Baron Rendlesham (*qv*) and *d* 5 Aug 1959

Sir WILLIAM *d* 30 Nov 1917; his est s,

Sir John William Salusbury-Trelawny, 11th Bt; *b* 6 May 1869; Lt 3rd Bn Welch Regt, Manitoba LI, Canadian Militia and 7th Bn Somerset LI; *m* 1st 9 Dec 1891 (*divorce* 1905) Agnes Hedvig Helga (*d* 3 March 1959 aged 87), est dau of William Bampfield Braddick, of Charlton Park, Blackheath, and had:

1 Violet Agnes Laetitia; *b* 23 Sept 1892; *m* 15 Jan 1912 Algernon Edward Percy Littleton (*d* 30 June 1943) and had issue (*see* HATHERTON, B); resumed maiden name by deed poll 1 Jan 1959

Sir John *m* 2nd 24 July 1905 Catherine Penelope (*d* 23 Jan 1930), formerly w of William Crewdson Howard and dau of Ambrose Sneyd Cave-Browne-Cave (*see* CAVE-BROWNE-CAVE, Bt) ; *m* 3rd 1 Feb 1936 Andrée Fanny Alexandra Allès, of Algiers (*d* 26 Jan 1944), and *d* 7 Feb 1944, leaving by his 2nd w:

1 **Sir John William Robin Maurice Salusbury-Trelawny, 12th Bt**; *b* 16 Jan 1908; F/Lt RAFVR WW II; *m* 1st 18 June 1932 (*divorce* 1935) Glenys Mary (*d* 1985), dau of John Cameron Kynoch, and had:

(1) Sir JOHN BARRY SALUSBURY-TRELAWNY, **13th and present Bt**

1 (cont.) **Sir John** *m* 2nd 20 Feb 1937 *Rosamund Helen (*m* 2nd 1990 *Christopher R V Bell, OBE) [Mrs Christopher Bell, 32 Harvest Close, Lindfield, W Sus-

sex RH16 2LW], yst dau of Arthur Reed Ropes (Adrian Ross, author and playwright), and *d* 28 Nov 1956, leaving by her:

(2) +William Hamelin [William Trelawny Esq, Southtown House, Southtown, W Pennard, Somerset BA6 8NS]; *b* 18 May 1942; *educ* Steyning GS Sussex; *m* 20 Sept 1967 Meline Martha Katharina (*d* 20 June 1969), dau of Dr Cornelius PA Zeijlmans van Emmichoven, of The Hague

(1) Elizabeth Ann; *b* 12 Aug 1940; *m* 28 Oct 1961 Peter McEwen Tillman, MD, er s of Wolf George Tillman, MD, MRCS, MRCP, of Glebe Cottage, W Grinstead, Sussex, and *d* 1974, leaving:

1a *Laetitia Elizabeth; *b* 13 Feb 1963

2a *Josephine Ann; *b* 10 May 1966

SAMUEL, Viscount

Arms: Or a bend between two caps of liberty gu., on a chief sa. a balance of the first. **Crest:** In front of a sun rising or a dove, wings elevated and addorsed, holding in the beak an olive branch ppr. **Supporters:** On either side a lion or, the dexter gorged with a collar gu. and resting the anterior hind leg on a stump of oak eradicated and sprouting ppr., the sinister gorged with an eastern crown also gu. and resting the interior hind leg on a stump of olive eradicated and sprouting, also ppr. **Motto:** Turn not aside. **Creation:** V. (UK) 8 June 1937.

THE 3RD VISCOUNT SAMUEL, of Mount Carmel, and of Toxteth, in the City of Liverpool (David Herbert Samuel, OBE (1996)) [Prof The Rt Hon The Viscount Samuel OBE, 1/4 Pinhas Rosen St, Herzlia 46590, Israel]; *b* 8 July 1922; *s* f 1978; *educ* Balliol Coll Oxford (MA 1948) and Hebrew U (PhD 1953); Capt RA WW II (despatches) UK, India, Burma and Sumatra 1942–46, Research Fell: Harvard 1957–58 and U of Calif Berkeley 1965–66, faculty Weizmann Inst Science Rehovot 1957–; Sherman Prof, Dean Chemistry Faculty 1971–73, Dir Centre for Neurosciences and Behavioural Research 1970–85, Sherman Prof Physical Chemistry 1968–87; memb US-Israel Educnl Fndn Bd 1969–74 (chm 1974–75), Chm Bd Studies Chemistry Feinberg Graduate Sch, memb Bd Israel Science Teaching Centre and Weizmann Science Press, Visiting Prof Sch of Molecular Studies Warwick U 1967–, Visiting Roy Soc Prof MRC Neuro-immunology Unit UCL 1974–75, Visiting Prof Pharmacology Dept Yale Sch Medicine 1983–84, memb Advsy Bd Bat-Sheva de Rothschild Fndn for Advancement of Science in Israel 1970–83, memb Israel Exec Ctee America-Israel Cultural Fndn 1978–88 (chm 1985–88), Govr Tel-Aviv Museum 1980–, memb Cncl Anglo-Israel Assoc London 1982–, titular memb ctee for Chemical Education of Internat Union of Pure and Applied Chemistry 1982–91, memb Advsy Ctee and Bd Tstees Israel Inst for Psychobiology 1973– and Bd Tstees Menninger Foundation Topeka, USA, co-ed *Aging of the Brain* (1983), memb editorial Bd: *Journal of Labelled Compounds and Radiopharmaceuticals*, *Alzheimer Disease and Associated Disorders* and *Brain, Behaviour and Immunity*; CChem, FRSC; *m* 1st 5 May 1950 (*divorce* 1957) Esther, yr dau of Jacob Berelowitz, of Cape Town, and has:

1 *Judith [The Hon Mrs Daliot, 5 Lipsky St, Tel Aviv, Israel]; *b* 29 Jan 1951; *educ* Technion-Israel Inst of Technology and AA London (BArch 1972); *m* 1987 *Dr Daniel Daliot, MD, and has:

(1) *Jonathan; *b* 1988

(2) *Talya; *b* 1990

The 3rd VISCOUNT *m* 2nd 14 Dec 1960 (*divorce* 1979) Rinna, dau of Meir Grossman, of Herzliyah, Israel, and formerly w of Reuben Dafni; *m* 3rd 1980 (*divorce* 1993) Veronika Engelhardt Grimm, dau of Ernest Engelhardt, of Toronto; *m* 4th 8 July 1997 *Mrs Eve Black and has by his 2nd w:

2 *Naomi Rachel [The Hon Mrs Wilf, 10 Bikurim St, Haifa 34576, Israel]; *b* 27 May 1962; *educ* Hebrew U Jerusalem Law Sch (LLB 1987); Legal Dept Israel Police Force 1990–; *m* 1992 *Nir Wilf and has:

(1) *Itamar; *b* 1994

(2) *Amit; *b* 1996

Lineage: LOUIS SAMUEL, of 40 Hunter St, Brunswick Sq, London, formerly of Liverpool; *b* 1794; *m* 17 Nov 1819 Henrietta (*d* 14 March 1860), dau of Israel Israel, of Bury St, St Mary Axe, and *d* 24 Aug 1859, having had, with other issue, including a yr s (*see* SWAYTHLING, B):

EDWIN LOUIS SAMUEL, of Claremont, Princes Park, Liverpool, later 9 Kensington Gore, London; *b* 19 Sept 1825; banker; *m* 24 Oct 1885 Clara (*d* 1 Nov 1920), dau of Ellis Samuel Yates, of Liverpool, and *d* 28 March 1877, leaving:

  1 Sir STUART MONTAGU SAMUEL, 1st and last Bt (UK), so *cr* 8 July 1912, of Chelwood Vetchery, Maresfield, Co Sussex, JP (Co London); *b* 24 Oct 1856; MP (Lib) Whitechapel 1900–13 and 1913–16, ptnr Samuel Montagu & Co, Bankers; *m* 10 April 1893 Ida Bessie Evaline (*d* 19 Sept 1941), dau of Alphonse Mayer, and *dspm* 13 May 1926, when the btcy expired, having had:

    (1) Vera Evelyn; *m* 22 April 1914 Major Sir (Jack Benn) Brunel Cohen, KBE (*d* 11 May 1965), s of Louis S Cohen, JP, of Liverpool, and had:

      1a *George Stuart Brunel COHEN later BRUNEL-COHEN (deed poll 1948), TD, JP; *b* 18 Nov 1918; *m* 15 Oct 1948 *Shelagh, widow of Lt J R McCosh, RNVR, and dau of Dr Michael Garry, of Formby, Lancs, and has:

        1b *Mark Patrick; *b* 8 Aug 1949; *educ* Downside and RMA Sandhurst

        2b *Edward Stuart; *b* 9 March 1952; *educ* Downside

        1b *Lucy Louise; *b* 8 Feb 1955

      2a *John Louis Brunel; *b* 13 June 1922; *m* 4 March 1951 Simone Dolores Everitt (*d* 22 Jan 1969), dau of Robert L de Vegriette, of Paris, and has:

        1b *Richard Stuart Brunel; *b* 17 Aug 1954; *educ* Winchester

        2b *David John Brunel; *b* 17 Aug 1954; *educ* Winchester

        1b *Jane; *b* 24 May 1952; *m* 19 Nov 1969 (*divorce* 19–, resumed maiden name) Philip Spira, of Berkeley, Calif.

      1a *Pamela May Brunel; *b* 1915

    (2) Eileen Victoria; Hon FRCOG; *m* 18 Sept 1923 Gilbert Harold Edgar, CBE, s of Edgar Samuel Edgar, and had issue

  2 Dennis Edwin; *b* 5 March 1858; *m* 21 Nov 1900 Katie Lilian (*d* 1 Dec 1935), dau of Abraham Lewis Lazarus, and *d* 30 May 1909, leaving:

    (1) Donald Edwin Lewis; *b* 19 July 1903; Hon Maj RAPC WW II, Samuel Montagu & Co, dir St Margaret's Tst 1965, Consultant St Margaret's Gp 1968, chm Waverley Manor (The Maurice and Samuel Lyon Home), Hendon; *m* 5 May 1932 *Rosemary Daphne Juliet, dau of Fernand René Lang, and had:

      1a *Dennis Eric [Dennis Samuel Esq, 15 Lansdowne Ct, Lansdowne Rise, London W11]; *b* 10 July 1936; *educ* Charterhouse and Balliol Coll Oxford (BA 1959, MA 1964)

      1a *Diana Bridget Lilian; *b* 26 July 1939; *m* 25 June 1963 *R R Aron and has:

        1b *Jeremy Andrew; *b* 17 Aug 1964

        1b *Katherine Esther; *b* 24 March 1966

      2a *Jane Rosemary; *b* 17 March 1943; *m* 16 May 1967 *Kenneth John Price, s of Bernard Price, of Derby

      3a *Judith Dorothea; *b* 24 July 1946

    (2) *Esmond; *b* 14 May 1906

    (1) Clara; *m* 30 Dec 1925 Percy Herbert Schwarzschild, s of Jacob Schwarzschild, and *d* 19 Nov 1963

    (2) *Dorothea; *m* 19 Oct 1938 Alan Henry Isaacs, yst s of Henry Isaacs. He *d* 22 Aug 1968

  3 Gilbert Ellis; *b* 30 June 1859; *m* 24 Sept 1889 Louise Victoria, DBE (1920) (*d* 13 Oct 1925), dau of Isaac Stiebel, and *d* 22 Oct 1926, having had:

    (1) Wilfrid Gilbert; *b* 3 Sept 1890; T/Lt Suffolk Regt; *ka* 21 Sept 1918

    (1) Norah Gilbert; *m* 12 March 1913 Donald van den Bergh, JP, est s of Henry van den Bergh, of Kensington, and had issue

  4 HERBERT LOUIS, **1st Viscount**

  1 Mabel Henrietta; *m* 8 Dec 1880 Marion Harry Alexander Spielmann and *d* 1 May 1938, leaving issue

The yst s,

  HERBERT LOUIS SAMUEL, **1st Viscount Samuel**, of Mount Carmel, and of Toxteth in the City of Liverpool (UK), so *cr* 8 June 1937, GCB (1926), OM (1958), GBE (1920), PC (1908); *b* 6 Nov 1870; *educ* Univ Coll Sch and Balliol Coll Oxford (BA 1893, MA 1897, Hon Fell 1935, Visitor 1946–57); MP (Lib) Cleveland 1902–18 and Darwen 1929–35, Parly U-Sec Home Dept 1905–09, Chllr Duchy Lancaster 1909–19 and PMG 1910–14 and (both) 1915–16, Pres Local Govt Bd 1914–15, Home Sec Jan–Dec 1916 and Aug 1931–Sept 1932, Br Special Commr Belgium 1919, HC Palestine 1920–22 and (also C-in-C) 1922–25, Pres: Roy Inst Philosophy 1931–63, English Assoc 1941, Roy Statistical Soc 1918–20, Chm Roy Commn Coal Industry 1925–26, Pres Parly and Scientific Ctee 1943–45 and 1950–52, Leader Libs H of C 1931–35 and Ho Lds 1944–55, Assoc KStJ, Hon DCL Oxon 1935, Hon LLD Cantab 1947, Liverpool 1949, Hon LittD Leeds 1953, Hon PhD Jerusalem 1959, Hon FRIBA 1948, author: *Liberalism: its Principles and Proposals*, *Belief and Action*, *Memoirs*, *A Book of Quotations*, *In Search of Reality*, *A Threefold Cord: Philosophy, Science, Religion* (with Prof Herbert Dingle), Grand Offr Order Leopold Belgium, *m* 17 Nov 1897 Beatrice Miriam (*d* 13 Sept 1959), yst dau of Ellis Abraham Franklin, and had:

  1 EDWIN HERBERT, **2nd Viscount**

  2 Philip Ellis Herbert; *b* 23 Dec 1900; *educ* Westminster and Trin Coll Cambridge; Hong Kong Vol Def Corps WW II (POW 1941–45); *d* 1996

  3 Godfrey Herbert, CBE (1969); *b* 12 Jan 1904; *educ* Westminster and Balliol Coll Oxford (BA 1926, MA 1947); FRIBA, AMTPI, Hon Lt-Col RE WW II, Sec Roy Fine Art Commn 1948–69; *d* unm 11 Dec 1982

  1 *Nancy Adelaide [The Hon Mrs Salaman, 45 Havenfield, Cambridge]; *educ* Somerville Coll Oxford (BA 1928, MA 1955); *m* 24 June 1935 Arthur Gabriel Salaman, MA, MB, BCh, MRCS, LRCP, Surgn attd ARP and HG WW II (*d* 31 Oct 1964), s of Redcliffe Nathan Salaman, FRS, of Barley, Royston, Herts, and has:

    (1) *John Redcliffe [John Salaman Esq, 5 Brooklyn Close, Rhiwbina, Cardiff CF4 6VT]; *b* 14 Oct 1937; *educ* Bedales, Clare Coll Cambridge and London Hosp; MA, MB, MChir, FRCS, LRCP, Prof Transplant Surgery Cardiff (ret 1994); *m* 4 Nov 1961 *Patricia Faith, dau of Edward George Burkett, of Enfield, Middx, and has:

      1a *Robert Arthur; *b* 13 Feb 1965

      2a *Paul William; *b* 1971

      1a *Janet Susan; *b* 1967

      2a *Mary Elizabeth; *b* 1969

    (2) *William Herbert; *b* 14 March 1940; *educ* Bedales and Clare Coll Cambridge (MA); *m* 30 March 1963 *Alison Spears, dau of Dr Phillipe Sidney de Quetteville Cabot, of Puddavine House, Totnes, Devon, and has:

      1a *Clare Rachel; *b* 23 March 1966

      2a *Rachel Isabel; *b* 21 Feb 1968

      3a *Anna; *b* 19–

    (1) *Susan Caroline [Mrs Susan Salaman, 23a High St, Littleport, Ely, Cambs CB6 1HE] (resumed maiden name); *b* 29 April 1936; *m* 5 Oct 1960 Reginald Valentine Clery (*d* Sept 1996), only s of Claud Valentine Clery, of Bray, Co Wicklow, and has:

      1a *Daniel Philip; *b* 9 Jan 1964

      1a *Emma Juliet; *b* 6 April 1962

      2a *Louisa Caroline; *b* 30 Sept 1967

    (2) *Juliet Miriam [Mrs Yaela Ben-Josef, Moshar Givat-Joat, Golan Heights, Israel]; *b* 21 May 1942; *m* 9 Dec 1961 *Reuben Ben-Josef, s of Joseph Selek, of Israel, and has:

      1a *Gull; *b* 1963

      2a *Oren; *b* 1965

      1a *Netta; *b* 1971

      2a *Tal; *b* 1979

The 1st VISCOUNT *d* 1963; his est s,

  EDWIN HERBERT SAMUEL, **2nd Viscount Samuel**, CMG; *b* 11 Sept 1898; *educ* Westminster, Balliol Coll Oxford (BA 1920) and Columbia U New York (Cwlth Fell 1961–62); 2nd Lt RFA WW I 1917–19, Colonial Admin Service Palestine 1920–48, Pncpl Israel Inst Public Admin Jerusalem 1947, Visiting Prof Middle East Govt and Admin Dropsie Coll Philadelphia 1948–49, Visiting Prof Graduate Sch Public Affrs State U of New York 1963, Sr Lecturer Br Institutions Hebrew U Jerusalem 1954–69, Mellon Fell U of Pittsburgh, author: *Problems of Government in the State of Israel*, *British Traditions in the Administration of Israel*, *A Cottage in Galilee*, *A Coat of Many Colours*, *My Friend Musa*, *The Cucumber King*, *His Celestial Highness* (last four being collections of short stories) and *A Lifetime in Jerusalem: Memoirs of Edwin Herbert, Viscount Samuel*; *m* 6 Dec 1920 Hadassah, dau of Judah Goor, of Tel Aviv, and *d* 14 Nov 1978, leaving:

  1 DAVID HERBERT SAMUEL, **3rd and present Viscount Samuel**

  2 +DAN JUDAH [The Hon Dan Samuel, 154 Hillspoint Rd, Westport, CT06880, USA; The Barns, Old Mill Farm, Mill Hamlet, Sidlesham, Sussex]; *b* 25 March 1925; heir presumptive; *educ* Rugby, Balliol Coll Oxford (MA 1950) and Sch of Advanced Internat Studies Washington, DC (1950–51); Maj late Yorks Hus, with Shell 1952, gen manager Shell Thailand 1962–66, with Shell Oil USA 1966–67, Pres Belgian Shell 1967, gen manager Regnl Mktg Shell Internat Chemical Co London 1971–72, mktg co-ordinator 1972–76, gp personnel co-ordinator 1976–77, regl co-ordinator W Hemisphere 1977–81, Dir Shell Internat Petroleum Co London 1973–81, Pres and Ch Exec Offr Scallop Corp NY 1981–86, business consultant, V-Pres Belgian Petroleum Fedn 1969, Chm Bd Management SEATO Graduate Sch Engrg Bangkok 1964–66, Tstee Asian Inst Technology 1966–68 and 1971–91, a Dir Cncl of the Americas NY 1981–86, dir: Witco Corp, Canadia Overseas Packaging Industries, Measurement Specialities, Br American Educnl Fndn and Asian Inst of Technology Fndn, Cdr Order Crown Thailand 1965, Offr Order Crown Belgium; *m* 1st 14 July 1957 (*divorce* 1977) Nonni (Esther), dau of Max Gordon, of Johannesburg, and has:

    (1) +Jonathan Herbert; *b* 17 Dec 1965; *m* 1995 *Bridget Mahoney

    (1) *Lia Miriam; *b* 9 March 1961; *m* 1987 *Glenn H Album

    (2) *Maia Tessa; *b* 24 Feb 1963

  2 (cont.) The Hon Dan Samuel *m* 2nd 1981 (*divorce* 1992) Heather, dau of Angus Cumming, of Haywards Heath, and by her has:

    (2) +Benjamin Angus; *b* 1983

    (3) *Sasha Tamar; *b* 1982

SAMUEL, Bt

Arms: Per chevron arg. and gu. two wolf heads erased in chief sa. and in base as many squirrels sejant addorsed, each cracking a nut of the first. **Crest:** Upon a rock ppr. in front of three spears, one in pale and two saltirewise arg., a wolf courant sa., pierced in the breast by an arrow of the second, flighted or. **Motto:** A pledge of better times. **Creation:** Bt. (UK) 8 March 1898.

SIR JON (JOHN) MICHAEL GLEN SAMUEL, 5TH BT, of Nevern Square [Sir John Samuel Bt, Dean House, Vernham Dean, Hants SP11 0LA]; *b* 25 Jan 1944; *s f* 1962; *educ* Radley and UCL (BSc); dir: Enfield Automotive 1967–70, Advanced Vehicle Systems Ltd 1971–78, chm: Electric Auto Corp (USA) 1978–83, Whisper Electric Car A/S (Denmark) 1984–88, Clean Air Transport Hldgs 1992–94; *m* 1st 24 Sept 1966 Antoinette Sandra, dau of Capt Antony Hewitt, RE (2nd SAS Regt), and Mrs K A H Casson, of Frith Farm, Wolverton, Hants; *m* 2nd 1982 *Mrs Elizabeth Ann Molinari, yst dau of Maj R G Curry, of Bournemouth, and by his 1st w has:

1 +ANTHONY JOHN FULTON; *b* 13 Oct 1972
2 +Rupert Casper James; *b* 9 March 1974

Lineage: EDWARD SAMUEL; *m* 1780 Hannah — (*d* 31 Dec 1821) and *d* 15 May 1810, leaving:

SAMPSON SAMUEL, of London; *m* Lydia — (*d* 31 March 1865) and *d* 2 Oct 1820, having had, with another s (Louis, *d* unm 27 Feb 1867):

Sir Saul Samuel, 1st Bt (UK), so *cr* 8 March 1898, KCMG, CB; *b* posthumously 2 Nov 1820; Agent Gen London for NSW; *m* 1st 16 Dec 1857 Henrietta Matilda (*d* 5 June 1864), dau of Benjamin Goldsmid Levien, of Geelong, Victoria, and had:

1 Louis, of Sydney; *b* 6 Jan 1861; *educ* Sydney GS; engr; *m* 2 March 1886 Mary Ruth (*d* 1941, having *m* 2nd 5 Oct 1892 Alfred Butler Trow, of Gloucester Terrace, London W (*d* 12 July 1923) and 3rd 20 March 1924 Herbert Bingham (*d* 13 March 1936)), dau of Silas Fowler, and *d* 29 Nov 1887, leaving:

  (1) Vera Henrietta Ruth; *b* 15 Dec 1886; *m* 1910 Henry Ernest Morriss and *d* 27 Nov 1954, leaving issue. He *d* Sept 1951

  (2) Lilly Louis; *b* posthumously 10 May 1888; *m* 30 Nov 1912 Harold Lawrence Slocock (*d* 19 Oct 1968), 2nd s of Rev Frederick Henry Slocock, and *d* 24 March 1962, having had:

    1a Harold Gilbert; *b* 16 Aug 1925; RAF; *d* unm 7 Feb 1945
    1a *Suzanne; *b* 20 Oct 1913; *m* 19– John Wade, MC, and has:
      1b *Charles Laurence; *b* 16 July 1937
      2b *Ian Denis; *b* 26 Jan 1939
      1b *Lauren; *b* 8 July 1946
    2a *Pamela; *b* 13 Jan 1915; *m* Edward Hood, AFC, and has:
      1b *Joanna; *b* 10 Oct 1943
    3a Josephine Ruth; *b* 22 May 1918; *d* 1920
    4a *Jean Yvonne; *b* 2 March 1922; *m* Lancelot Martin, AFC, and has:
      1b *Victoria Evelyn; *b* 22 May 1945
      2b *Drusilla; *b* 15 June 1948

2 **Sir Edward Levien Samuel, 2nd Bt**; *b* 28 April 1862; *m* 30 Sept 1891 Ray (*d* 26 Feb 1958), yst dau of Abraham Cowan, of Hampstead, and *d* 24 Nov 1937, leaving:

  (1) **Sir Edward Louis Samuel, 3rd Bt**; *b* 6 Nov 1896; *educ* Repton; RFA WWI, Maj RA WW II, Bursar Prince of Wales's Endowment Fund of Toc H 1928–40; *d* unm 25 April 1961

  (1) Vera Leah Henrietta; *m* 24 Sept 1925 Geoffrey Noel HOLT later HILLIER-HOLT (deed poll April 1930; *d* 14 Nov 1951), s of Hillier Holt, and had issue

3 Henri Saul; *b* 28 May 1864; Lt-Col APD, Lt Roy Munster Fus, Maj and Staff Paymaster APD; *m* 10 April 1895 Eva (*d* 25 Jan 1958), dau of Joseph Fulton, of The Glen, Paisley, and *d* 3 Jan 1935, leaving:

  (1) Gerald Glen; *b* 31 Dec 1895; *educ* Radley; Lt RFC WW I; *m* 1927 Hélène (*d* March 1966), widow of Paul Benedek, of New York, and dau of Jaques Nungne, of St Germain, France, and *dsp* 28 Feb 1957

  (2) JOHN OLIVER CECIL (Sir), **4th Bt**

  (1) *Eva Elizabeth; *b* 3 May 1905; *m* 22 Oct 1934 George Brian Stafford Cothay (*d* 1983), s of Stafford Cothay, of New Romney, Kent, and has:

    1a *Charlotte Ann Stafford [Mrs John May, Woodside, Eastergate, Chichester, W Sussex PO20 6SB]; *b* 3 Feb 1936; *m* 22 Dec 1962 *Cdr John Anthony May, LVO, s of F E May, of Portsmouth, and has:
      1b *Alexandra Louise Stafford; *b* 26 Sept 1965

  1 Lydia Eliza; *m* 14 Dec 1884 Walter Edward Thompson and *d* 30 Nov 1915, leaving issue. He *d* 1 May 1896

  2 Florence Fanny; *d* unm 30 May 1937

Sir Saul *m* 2nd 31 Oct 1877 Sara Louise (*d* 4 Nov 1940), dau of Edward Isaac, JP, of Auckland, and *d* 29 Aug 1900, having by her had:

  4 Randolph John; *b* 25 Aug 1878; *educ* Harrow; Capt RE WW I, civil engr; *d* unm 20 March 1948

The 3rd Bt's cousin,

  Sir John Oliver Cecil Samuel, 4th Bt; *b* 24 June 1916; *educ* Radley; F/Lt RAFVR WW II; *m* 23 Sept 1942 *Charlotte Mary [Mrs Heremon Desmond, The Old School House, West Horsley, Surrey] (*m* 2nd 2 Nov 1966 Heremon James Patrick Desmond (*d* 1971), s of Patrick Desmond, of Cork), dau of Robert Heber Hoyt, of Calgary, Alberta, and *d* 24 Oct 1962, leaving:

  1 Sir JON MICHAEL GLEN SAMUEL, **5th and present Bt**

  1 *Jane Lesley [Mrs John Newman, Gilson Court, Old Windsor, Berks SL4 2JL]; *b* 19 May 1947; *m* 20 Aug 1966 *John Henry Newman, est s of John Leonard Newman, of Kettering, Northants, and has:

    (1) *James Michael; *b* 19 Nov 1969
    (2) *Timothy John Hoyt; *b* 1972

SAMUELSON

Arms: Sable three piles wavy, two issuant from the chief and one from the base, or, each charged with a phoenix in flames proper. **Crest:** A phoenix in flames holding in the beak a torch fired proper, each wing charged with a scroll argent. **Motto:** *Post tenebras lux* ('Light after darkness'). **Creation:** Bt. (UK) 29 July 1884.

SIR (BERNARD) MICHAEL FRANCIS SAMUELSON, 5TH BT, of Bodicote, Banbury, Co Oxford [Sir Michael Samuelson Bt, Harborne, Hailsham Rd, Stone Cross, Pevensey, E Sussex BN24 5AS]; *b* 17 Jan 1917; *s f* 1981; *educ* Eton; Burma with RA and Leics Regt WW II (despatches); *m* 26 April 1952 *Janet Amy, yr dau of Lt-Cdr Laurence Garrett Elkington, RN, of Chelsea, and has:

1 +JAMES FRANCIS [James Samuelson Esq, 3 Manor Cottages, Buckhorn Weston, Dorset SP8 5HH]; *b* 20 Dec 1956; *educ* Hailsham; *m* 1987 *Caroline Anne Woodley and has:

  (1) *Miranda Alice; *b* 1990
  (2) *Naomi Harriet; *b* 1992

2 +Edward Bernard; *b* 1967; *educ* Hailsham

1 *Nancy Amy; *b* 1 Feb 1953

2 *Angela Margaret; *b* 1964

Lineage: HENRY SAMUELSON, of London; *b* 4 April 1764; *m* Rebecca Alexander (*d* 1843) and *d* 9 Sept 1813, leaving:

SAMUEL HENRY SAMUELSON, of Liverpool; *b* 4 Sept 1789; *m* 21 June 1815 Sarah Hertz (*d* 1875) and had:

1 BERNHARD (Sir), **1st Bt**

2 Edward, of Liverpool, JP; *m* 3 April 1850 Mary Anne, dau of John Jones, of Plas Yssa, nr Corwen, and *d* 1898, having had issue

3 Martin, of Hessle, nr Hull; *m* 1st Sarah, dau of Robert Croome, of Middleton Cheney; *m* 2nd Kate, dau of A Bannister, and *d* 26 Feb 1903, leaving issue

4 Alexander; *b* 20 July 1826; MICE; *m* Mary Anne (*d* 17 May 1892), dau of James Dosser, of Kingston-upon-Hull, and *d* 4 Sept 1873, leaving issue

5 James; *m* Fanny, dau of Rev W Worsley, and had issue

6 Newton; *m* Sarah (*d* 22 Aug 1911), dau of R J Hardman, and *d* Sept 1907, leaving issue

SAMUEL SAMUELSON *d* 18 June 1863; his est s,

  Sir Bernhard Samuelson, 1st Bt (UK), so *cr* 29 July 1884, PC, JP (Oxon); *b* 22 Nov 1820; CA Oxon, FRS, MP (Lib) Banbury 1859 and 1865–85 and Oxon N 1885–95, fndr and chm Sir B Samuelson and Co, of Middlesbrough, chm Roy

Commn Technical Instruction 1881; *m* 1st 20 July 1844 Caroline (*d* 17 April 1886), dau of Henry Blundell, JP, and had:

1 Sir Henry Bernard Samuelson, 2nd Bt, JP Somerset and Devon; *b* 30 Sept 1845; Capt 3rd Bn Gloucestershire Regt, MP (Lib) Cheltenham 1868–74 and Frome 1876–85, Chev Legn Hon, KGStJ; *m* 7 July 1874 Emily Maria (*d* 1 July 1930), widow of Capt Arthur Paulet Butler (*see* DUNBOYNE, B) and dau of John Goodden, JP, DL, of Over Compton, and *dsp* 14 March 1937

2 FRANCIS ARTHUR EDWARD (Sir), **3rd Bt**

3 Godfrey Blundell, JP Kent; *b* 3 June 1863; MP Forest of Dean 1887–92; *m* 1st 22 Sept 1887 Annie Jane (*d* 6 April 1920), 3rd dau of Rev Weston Brocklesby Davis; *m* 2nd 20 Aug 1923 May, widow of J Paterson Parkin and dau of William Stevens, of Saxham, Suffolk, and *d* 1941, having had by his 1st w:

(1) Bernard Godfrey; *b* 17 Oct 1888; *educ* Eton and Trin Coll Oxford; Capt Gren Gds WW I; *m* 1st 29 Oct 1910 Hon Evelyn Amy Akers-Douglas (*d* 13 July 1914), 4th dau of 1st Viscount Chilston (*qv*), and had:

  1a +Peter Bernard; *b* 1912; *educ* Eton; *m* 1935 (*divorce* 1949) Wilhelmina Blaaderen and has:

    1b +Jean Paul; *b* 18 Oct 1939; *educ* in Holland; *m* 15 June 1962 *Annette Louie, dau of Hubertus Johannes Richardus Ponjee, and has:

      1c +Dennis John; *b* 30 Sept 1963

      2c +Nicolas Andrew; *b* 12 Feb 1966

      3c +Quentin Jeremy; *b* 20 April 1969

      1c *Natasha Nicole; *b* 1972

    1b *Bridget; *b* 9 Oct 1935

    2b *Xandra Serafina; *b* 6 June 1937

(1) (cont.) Capt Bernard Samuelson *m* 2nd 1938 *Patricia Christobel, dau of William Wildash, and *d* 13 Nov 1954

(2) Guy Weston; *b* 15 Dec 1890; *educ* Radley; Capt 4th Bn Yorks Regt, F/O RAFVR; *m* 1st 2 April 1913 (*divorce* 1927) Naomi, er dau of Alfred Leney, JP, of The Garden House, Saltwood, Kent; *m* 2nd 9 Dec 1927 Frances Crawley, dau of Charles Lyne, and had by his 1st w:

  1a Rowland Guy Blundell; *b* 30 June 1914; *educ* Radley; F/O RAFVR

  2a John Peel Weston, MC (1939); *b* 13 Sept 1917; *educ* Sherborne and RMC Sandhurst; AIBAE, Lt-Col The Buffs Palestine 1938–39 (despatches) and WW II (despatches), Assist Sec (Mil) Cabinet and War Offices 1945–47; *m* 1st 15 Sept 1943 (*divorce* 1951) Pamela (*d* 1989), est dau of Cecil Esdaile Winter, of Surrenden Dering, Pluckley, Kent, and had:

    1b +Nigel John Esdaile [Nigel Samuelson Esq, Fronwen, Alexandra Rd, Brecon, Powys]; *b* 7 Sept 1944; *educ* Cokethorpe and Bristol U (LLB 1966); slr; *m* 1971 *Angela Margaret, dau of Bruce Samways, of Bleadon, Weston-super-Mare, and has:

      1c +Alistair Paul; *b* 1976

      2c +Robert Ernest; *b* 1979

      1c *Diana Helen Esdaile; *b* 1973

    2b +Christopher Richard Leney [Christopher Samuelson Esq, PO Box 472, Gibraltar]; *b* 9 July 1946; *educ* Sherborne; *m* Dec 1968 (*divorce* 1980) Catherine Elizabeth, er dau of Dr George M Cooper, of S Africa, and has:

      1c +John Michael Winter; *b* 1974

    2b (cont.) Christopher Samuelson *m* 2nd 1980 *Diana Margaret, dau of Richard Lewis, of Lahore, and by her has:

      1c *Nicola Robyn; *b* 1981

      2c *Lucy Anne; *b* 1986

  2a (cont.) Lt-Col John Samuelson *m* 2nd 20 June 1952 *Grace Eleanor, er dau of Richard Cecil Dawson, of Ball Hill, Newbury, Berks, and *d* 1988, having by her had:

    3b Robin Dawson; *b* 18 Oct 1953; *educ* Stowe; *d* 1978

    1b *Eleanor Clare; *b* 19 Sept 1958

  3a Henry Bernhard; *b* 21 July 1919; *educ* Sherborne; Lt Roy W Kent Regt TA 1938–41, served WW II, Freeman City London; *m* 1st 27 May 1947 (*divorce* 1949) Evelyn Patience, dau of John Nairn Burt, of Ashwell House, Knaresborough, Yorks; *m* 2nd 19– (*divorce* 1961) Barbara Crossley, of Sydenham; *m* 3rd 1961 *Anita Jill Waring, yst dau of Frederick William Guard, of Barnstaple, Devon, and *d* 1988, having by her had:

    1b +Francis Peel Waring [Francis Samuelson Esq, 8 Burrows Close, Braunton, Devon]; *b* 1961

    2b +Godfrey Weston Rhodes; *b* 1962

    3b +Kevin Guard Leney; *b* 1965

    4b +Clive Bernard Waring; *b* 1967

    5b +Henry Rhodes Hulke; *b* 1974

(3) Carol Hubert Francis; *b* 8 April 1899; *educ* Eton; Gren Gds WW I 1917–19; *m* 1st 12 April 1920 Doris (*d* 3 June 1959), yr dau of Capt John George Edmund Templer, of Lindridge, Bishops Teignton, Devon; *m* 2nd 1961 *Marjorie Hilda Donisthorpe [Mrs Carol Samuelson, Strand House, Ringmore, Shaldon, Devon] and *d* 1984, having had by his 1st w:

  1a *Eleanor Caroline [Mrs Marc Kerr, Windrush, Pollimore, Devon]; *b* 13 Aug 1921; *m* 16 Dec 1946 *Capt Marc Anderson Kerr, MBE, IA, s of Capt William John Wilmot Kerr, of Maer Craig, Exmouth, and has:

    1b *Vyvien Frances; *b* 10 Sept 1947; *m* 1972 *John Charles Gundry and has:

      1c *Mark Alexander; *b* 1983

    2b *Fiona Charlotte Eleanor; *b* 10 Sept 1953; *m* 1978 *Anthony Garne Fraser Peal and has:

      1c *Alastair Mark Fraser; *b* 1980

      2c *Nicholas Hugh Anderson; *b* 1983

4 Herbert Walter (Sir), KBE (1922); *b* 23 Jan 1865; *educ* Rugby; Chm and Treas U Coll Hosp 1927–37, KStJ; *m* 15 Feb 1896 Sybil Charlotte Eleanor, OBE (1920) (*d* 20 Jan 1961), only dau of Maj Hon Walter Harbord (*see* SUFFIELD, B), and *d* 5 Sept 1952, having had:

(1) Geoffrey Bernard FitzRoy, MC; *b* 26 Jan 1897; Lt Coldstream Gds WW I (despatches); *ka* 27 Nov 1917

(2) Rupert Eric Herbert; *b* 18 Oct 1899; *educ* Eton and RMC Sandhurst; Maj Coldstream Gds, WWs I and II; *m* 19 Nov1930 *Eileena Jane [Mrs Rupert

Samuelson, 10 Cadogan Square, London SW1], only dau of Arthur Reece-Jones, of Cefn-y-Parc, Barry, Glam, and *d* 1993, having had:

  1a *Doriel Sybil; *b* 4 Dec 1931; *m* 1st 29 April 1955 (*divorce* 1972) Andrew Charles Cecil Ridgway, only s of George E Ridgway, of Nicosia, Cyprus; *m* 2nd 1972 (*divorce* 1981) Aldwin David James Hall and has by her 1st husb:

    1b *Peter Eric; *b* 16 Oct 1958

    1b *Amanda Jane; *b* 7 Nov 1956

    2b *Joanna Kate; *b* 13 July 1962

    3b *Charlotte Rose; *b* 8 Feb 1965

  2a *Philippa Margaret; *b* 23 Oct 1934

1 Caroline, MBE, JP Dorset; *m* 19 May 1875 Col John Robert Phelips Goodden, DL, JP, and *d* 28 Feb 1940, leaving issue. He *d* 4 Feb 1929

2 Camilla; *m* 2 Jan 1883 Capt Arthur Stephens Phillpotts, RN, and *d* 1951. He *d* 12 Aug 1920

3 Florence Adelaide; *b* 9 Nov 1857; *d* 14 Oct 1881

4 Alice Gertrude; *b* 25 March 1862; *m* 8 Oct 1890 Capt Henry Pennell Tate, RM, and *d* 30 Dec 1955, leaving issue. He *d* 15 June 1896

Sir Bernhard *m* 2nd 6 April 1889 Lelia Mathilda (*d* 18 June 1915 while nursing wounded at Rouen), widow of William Denny, of Dumbarton, and dau of Chevalier Leon Serena, and *d* 10 May 1905

The 2nd Bt's bro,

  Sir Francis Arthur Edward Samuelson, 3rd Bt, JP; *b* 26 Feb 1861; BA Oxford, High Sheriff Yorks 1917–19, Chm: Tees Conservancy Commn, Sir B Samuelson & Co, Middlesbrough, and Samuelson & Co, Banbury; Pres Iron and Steel Inst; *m* 24 April 1888 Fanny Isabel (*d* 17 July 1897), er dau of William Merritt Wright, of St John, New Brunswick, and *d* 1983, having had:

1 FRANCIS HENRY BERNARD (Sir), **4th Bt**

1 Gertrude Evelyn Frances; *b* 15 Feb 1889; *d* unm 1951

2 Phyllis Mary; *b* 5 Sept 1891; *m* 31 July 1913 Edward Hamilton McCormick, 2nd s of L Hamilton McCormick, of Chicago and Mayfair, and had issue

3 Muriel Gertrude; *b* 24 June 1893; *m* 24 April 1915 Col Bassett Fitzgerald Wilson, MC, KRRC, s of Maurice Fitzgerald Wilson, and had issue

Sir FRANCIS *d* 3 Jan 1946; his only s,

  Sir Francis Henry Bernard Samuelson, 4th Bt; *b* 22 Feb 1890; *educ* Eton and Trin Coll Cambridge; Capt Yorks Hus WW I; *m* 2 July 1913 Margaret Kendall, only dau of H Kendall Barnes, of Orpington, Kent, and had:

1 Sir (BERNARD) MICHAEL FRANCIS SAMUELSON, **5th and present Bt**

2 +Christopher Blundell; *b* 7 Nov 1920; *educ* Eton and Trin Coll Cambridge; WW II with Staffs Yeo

3 +Richard [Richard Samuelson Esq, 11 Heath Rd, Petersfield, Hants]; *b* 2 May 1925; *educ* Eton; Lt Fleet Air Arm WW II 1943–46

1 Isabel Muriel; *b* 31 May 1915; *m* 1 Dec 1950 Richard Ward, s of Arthur Ward, of Horsham

2 *Diana Frances [Mrs William Blacklock, Little Lodge, Jarvis Lane, Steyning, Sussex BN44 3GL]; *b* 30 July 1922; *m* 11 Sept 1943 William Ord Blacklock (*d* 9 July 1958), s of Robert Russell Ord Blacklock, of Newcastle, and has:

(1) *Catherine Margaret; *b* 2 June 1945; *m* 1970 *Alistair Donald Mant, of Sydney, NSW, and has:

  1a *Eleanor Frances; *b* 1972

  2a *Isabel Catherine; *b* 1975

(2) *Frances Elizabeth; *b* 3 Nov 1946; *m* 1st 1970 (*divorce* 1981) Dennis Thomas Conroy; *m* 2nd 1990 *Allan Jarvis, of Perth, W Australia, and by her 1st husb has:

  1a *Thomas Liam; *b* 1974

  1a *Joanna Mary; *b* 1971

  2a *Alice Frances; *b* 1973

  3a *Kate Diana May; *b* 1980

(3) *Stephanie; *b* 16 May 1952; *m* 1972 *Barrie Weir and has:

  1a *Adam James; *b* 1976

  1a *Gemma Fay; *b* 1974

  2a *Natasha Hope; *b* 1977

SANDBERG

Creation: B. (LP, UK) 2 Aug 1997.

THE BARON SANDBERG, of Passfield, Co Hants (Sir Michael Graham Ruddock Sandberg, CBE (1982, OBE 1977)) [The Rt Hon The Lord Sandberg CBE, 100 Piccadilly, London W1V 9FN; Domaine de la Haute Germaine, Ste Marguerite, Le Broc, Alpes Maritime, France]; *b* 31 May 1922; *educ* St Edward's Sch Oxford; 6th Lancers IA and 1st Dragoon Gds 1945; joined Hong Kong and Shanghai Banking Corp 1949, Chm 1977–86; Memb Hong Kong Exec Cncl 1978–86; Steward Roy Hong Kong Jockey Club 1972–86 (Chm 1981–86); Treas Hong Kong U 1977–86; Chm Br Bank of the Middle East 1980–86, ktd 1986; FCIB (FIB 1977, V-Pres 1984–87), FRSA 1983, Freeman City London; Liveryman Clockmakers' Co, Hon LLD: Hong Kong 1984, Pepperdine 1986; *m* 1954 *Carmel Mary Roseleen Donnelly and has two sons and two daus

Lineage: GERALD ARTHUR CLIFFORD SANDBERG; *m* Ethel Marion — and had:

MICHAEL GRAHAM RUDDOCK, *cr* a **Baron**

SANDERSON

Arms: Az. a maunch between three annulets or. **Crest:** Between two wings or a sinister arm embowed in chain mail armour grasping a scimitar ppr., pommelled and hilted or. **Motto:** *Sans Dieu rien* ('Without God nothing'). **Creation:** Bt. (UK) 26 June 1920.

SIR FRANK LINTON SANDERSON, 3RD BT, of Malling Deanery, in the Parish of South Malling, Co Sussex [Sir Frank Sanderson Bt, Grandturzel Farm, Burwash, E Sussex TN19 7DE]; *b* 21 Nov 1933; *s f* 1992; *educ* Stowe and Salamanca U; RNVR 1950–65, J H Minet and Co Ltd 1956–93 (dir 1985–93), dir: Knott Hotels Co of London 1965–75 and Humber Fertilisers plc 1972–88, memb: Lloyd's 1957–97 and Chichester Diocesan Synod 1980–93, Master Curriers' Co 1993–94; *m* 4 April 1961 *Margaret Ann (Margot), only dau of John Cleveland Maxwell, of New York, and has:

1 +DAVID FRANK; *b* 26 Feb 1962; *educ* Stowe and Sussex U (BA); barrister Inner Temple 1985; *m* 1990 *Fiona Jane, dau of Robert Bruce Ure and Mrs Barbara Michael, of Bristol, and has:

(1) *Hannah Clare; *b* 9 June 1997

2 *Michael John; *b* 1 March 1965; *educ* Stowe

1 *Caroline Anne; *b* 29 June 1966; *m* 1996 *Simon John Kennedy, s of Donald Kennedy, of Kennington, Kent, and has:

(1) *Amy Elizabeth; *b* 16 April 1998

2 *Nina Margaret; *b* 23 Aug 1968

3 *Katherine Claire; *b* 23 Aug 1968; *m* 21 Dec 1996 *James M D Thomson, s of Paul Thomson and Mrs Michael Cuddigon, of Aldeburgh, Suffolk, and has:

(1) *Bronwen Olivia; *b* 6 May 1998

Lineage: WILLIAM SANDERSON, of Hull, Yorks; *b* 18 Sept 1796; *m* 17 Sept 1921 Elizabeth (*d* 23 Oct 1877), dau of George Linton, and *d* 2 Dec 1876, having had a 7th s:

JOHN SANDERSON, of Hull; *b* 20 March 1837; *m* 10 March 1863 Anne Elizabeth (*d* 17 Feb 1915), dau of William Barrett, of Saddlebow, Lynn, Norfolk, and *d* 10 July 1906, leaving a 7th s:

Sir Frank Bernard Sanderson, 1st Bt (UK), so *cr* 26 June 1920; *b* 4 Oct 1880; Controller Min Munitions 1915–19, MP (U) Darwen (Lancs) 1922–23 and 1924–29 and Ealing E 1931–50, fndr Wray Sanderson and Co, chm: Salts (Saltaire) Ltd and J and J Crombie Ltd Aberdeen 1923–85, Humber Fishing Co 1924–65, Standing Fin Ctee Inter-Parliamentary Union Geneva 1949, memb: Public Accounts Ctee H of C 1942–50 and Lloyd's, Tstee Stowe Sch, Pres King Edward VII Memorial Hosp Ealing; *m* 1st 8 Sept 1904 Amy Edith (*d* 13 Sept 1949), dau of David Wing, of Scarborough, Yorks, and had:

1 FRANK PHILIP BRYAN (Sir), **2nd Bt**

2 Derek Maxwell; *b* 31 March 1914; *educ* Harrow; *m* 14 Nov 1936 *Daphne [Mrs Derek Sanderson, Peyrières, 82150 Montaigu de Quercy, Tarn et Garonne, France], est dau of Frederick Ernest Bayard Elton (*see* ELTON, Bt), and *d* 1983, having had:

(1) +John Maxwell [J Maxwell Sanderson Esq, Brook House, Tinkers Lane, Blackboys, E Sussex TN22 4EU]; *b* 15 March 1938; *educ* Nautical Coll Pangbourne; *m* 28 July 1962 *Susan Elizabeth, WVSM, er dau of Brig Randall Thomas Kellow Pye, DSO, OBE, of Avenings, Danehill, Sussex, and has:

1a +Christian Maxwell; *b* 20 April, 1966; *educ* Wellington and U of the West of England (BA Hons)

1a *Charlotte Jane; *b* 20 Oct 1964; *educ* Downe House

(2) +Richard Bryan [Richard Sanderson Esq, Finca Argaga, La Gomera, Canary Islands]; *b* 25 April 1942; *educ* Harrow; Coldstream Gds 1960–63; *m* 7 Aug 1964 *Narina, yr dau of Louis Jonquier, of Lausanne, Switzerland, and has:

1a +Mark Bryan; *b* 1967

2a +Caspar Jason Manfred Henrique; *b* 1969

(3) +Christopher Derek [Christopher Sanderson Esq, 37 Glendavis Crescent, Toronto ONT ME4 16X, Canada]; *b* 15 Oct 1948; *educ* Milton Abbey and Dalhousie U (BA)

(1) *Sally Greet [Mrs Anthony Hindley, The Vicarage, S Malling, E Sussex BN7 2JA]; *b* 14 Dec 1939; *m* 1st 11 Feb 1966 Lother John; *m* 2nd 1988 *Rev Anthony Talbot Hindley and by her 1st husb has:

1a *Rolf Peter Jonni; *b* 19 Dec 1967

1a *Dominique; *b* 9 Nov 1969

1 *Pearl; *b* 30 July 1906; *m* 1st 20 Dec 1928 (*divorce* 1937) Gerald Melville Donner (*d* 19 Nov 1968), s of Edward Oscar Donner (*see* MACNAGHTEN, Bt); *m* 2nd 27 Nov 1947 Maj Alan Sherman James, RA (*d* 5 May 1963), yr s of Reginald William James, of Cheltenham, and by her 1st husb has:

(1) *John Melville [John Donner Esq, Heddon Oak House, Crowcombe, Somerset TA4 4BJ; 39 Bramerton St, London SW3]; *b* 18 July 1930; *educ* Stowe and RMA; Coldstream Gds 1948–53 and 1956 (Suez), underwriting memb Lloyd's 1964–94, md Fenchurch Insur Hldg plc 1969–74, chm DUA Ltd 1974–90 (Pres 1991–94), Queen's Award Export 1983, 1988; *m* 22 July 1952 *Patricia Mary, dau of Barnet Thomas Jenkins, of Bickleigh, S Devon, and has:

1a *Rupert Melville; *b* 28 July 1955; *educ* Stowe and Exeter U (BA)

1a *Annabel Elizabeth; *b* 5 Feb 1958; *educ* Benenden and Exeter U (BA); *m* 27 May 1995 *Michael R S Vernon

(1) *Gillian Pearl (twin) [Mrs Kenneth Coburn, The Coach House, Underhill Lane, Clayton, W Sussex BN6 0PJ]; *b* 18 July 1930; *m* 1963 Cdr Kenneth Coburn, USN (*d* 1971), and has:

1a *John Bruce; *b* 17 Oct 1967; *educ* Tonbridge

1a *Kimberly Gillian [Mrs Garth Kirkland, 315 Hudson Pde, Clareville, NSW 2107, Australia]; *b* 16 Dec 1965; *m* 4 July 1992 *(John) Garth Kirkland and has:

1b *Poppy Anne; *b* 5 Jan 1995

(2) *Rosita Ann [Mrs Michael Burtenshaw, Bottle Cottage, Reigate Heath, Surrey]; *b* 17 Aug 1933; *m* 1954 Michael Beresford Burtenshaw (*d* 1994)

Sir Frank *m* 2nd 14 Feb 1951 Joan Julia (*d* 1995), only dau of Harry Cubberley, of Ealing, and *d* 18 July 1965

His er s,

Sir (Frank Philip) Bryan Sanderson, 2nd Bt; *b* 18 Feb 1910; *educ* Stowe and Pembroke Coll Oxford; Lt-Cdr (A) RNVR WW II, memb Lloyd's, chm Humber Fishing and Fish Manure Co; *m* 22 Feb 1933 Annette Irene Caroline (*d* 2 Sept 1967), dau of Col Vincent Korab-Laskowski, of Warsaw, and gdau of Gen Count de Castellaz, and *d* 1992, leaving:

1 Sir FRANK LINTON SANDERSON, **3rd and present Bt**

2 +Peter Bryan [Peter Sanderson Esq, Hole Farm, N Chailey, E Sussex BN8 4EJ]; *b* 25 Feb 1946; *educ* Stowe and Salamanca U; *m* 1970 *Elizabeth Magdalena, dau of John Grün, of Hove, Sussex, and has:

(1) *Roberta Caroline; *b* 1974; *educ* St Leonards, Mayfield, Stowe and Southampton U (BSc)

1 *Merry Claire [Mrs David Lyle, Yew Tree Cottage, Scaynes Hill, Sussex]; *b* 5 Oct 1936; *m* 11 April 1959 *David Archibald Evelyn Lyle, Capt 16th/5th Queen's Roy Lancers, yst s of Capt Robert Charles Lyle, MC, of Lingfield, Surrey, and has:

(1) *James Robert Bryan; *b* 31 July 1961; *educ* Charterhouse and St Edmund Hall Oxford (BA)

(2) *Robert Giles; *b* 30 April 1964; *educ* Charterhouse and LSE (BA)

(3) *Edward Hugh; *b* 29 April 1970; *educ* Hurtwood Ho and London U (BA)

SANDERSON OF AYOT

Arms: Paly of six arg. and az., on a bend sa. a mullet arg. between two annulets or. **Crest:** A talbot passant arg., pied and eared sa., resting the dexter forepaw on an annulet or. **Supporters:** On either side a talbot sejant. **Motto:** *Semper fidelis* ('Always faithful'). **Creation:** B. (UK) 4 July 1960.

Alan Lindsay Sanderson [Dr Alan Sanderson, 2 Caroline Close, London W2]; *b* 12 Jan 1931; *s f* as 2nd Baron 15 Aug 1971, disclaimed Barony for life 28 Sept 1971; *educ* Uppingham; MB, BS (London 1954), MRCP (London 1959), MRCPsych; *m* 1959 *Gertrude Boschler and has:

1 +MICHAEL; *b* 6 Dec 1959; *educ* St Paul's, York U (BA) and The Wharton Sch, Pa. (MBA)

1 *Evelyn; *b* 1961

2 *Frances; *b* 1963

3 *Andrea; *b* 1964

4 *Stephanie; *b* 1970

Lineage: Sanderson or Saunderson was the surname of numerous families living in the North and North Midlands and their original surname of de Biddick or de Bydick seems to have been derived from land owned in Co Durham.

ALEXANDER de BIDDICK; had:

JAMES de BIDDICK later SANDERSON; ggf of:

JOHN SANDERSON, of Tickhill Castle, Yorks; had:

JOHN SANDERSON, of Stanby; had:

HENRY SANDERSON, of Stanby; had, with two yr sons (John, of Midthorpe; Nicholas, of Gonehill):

ROBERT SANDERSON, of Stanby, Ewes and Maltby, Yorks; *m* — Middlethwaite, of Penistone, and had , with two yr sons (Christopher, of Sterap, *m* Dionisia Barber, of Rowley, and had three sons; Henry):

JOHN SANDERSON, of Langsett, Stainton, Ewes and Maltby; *b* 1490; *d* by 21 June 1565, leaving with six daus, an est s (John, of Thurleston, left issue) and yst s (Nicholas), a 2nd s:

WILLIAM SANDERSON, of Stainton, Ewes, Maltby and Langsett; *b* 1526; *bur* 15 Oct 1606, leaving, with two daus and two yr sons (Thomas; Lawrence, *m* Anne Smith and was *bur* 19 Aug 1637):

JOHN SANDERSON, of Stainton; *m* Margaret — and *d* 1631, leaving, with two daus:

JOHN SANDERSON, of Stainton; *m* Mary — and *d* 1662, having had, with two yr sons (Thomas; George, *d* 1660) and a dau (Mary, *d* 1660):

JOHN SANDERSON; *b* 1631; *d* 1714, leaving, with two daus (Mary, *d* 1766; Dorothy, *d* 1714):

RICHARD SANDERSON, of Stainton and Tickhill; *b* 1680; Town Clerk Stainton; *d* 1772, leaving, with three yr sons (Richard, *d* 1721;Thomas, *d* 1723; William, *d* 1727):

JOHN SANDERSON, of Stainton and Armthorpe; *b* 1708; *d* 18 July 1785, leaving, with two er sons (John, of Armthorpe and London, *b* 1749, fndr Sanderson, Fry, Fox, tea merchants, *m* Margaret Shillitoes (*d* 1795) and had issue; Thomas, of Armthorpe and Hull, *bapt* 16 April 1751, *m* Sarah Priestman, of Scarborough (*d* 26 Oct 1810)):

RICHARD SANDERSON, of Balby, Yorks; *b* 1754; tanner and leather merchant Doncaster; *m* Sarah Birks (*d* 1834) and *d* 16 April 1835, having had, with six er sons (Joshua, *b* 15 July 1778, *bur* 16 March 1864; Richard, *b* 29 June 1779, *d* young; John, *b* 1 Dec 1780, *d* young; William, *b* 31 Jan 1782, *dvp* leaving issue; Thomas, *b* 4 June 1784, *m* and had a son Richard, who *d* America; John, *b* 26 Nov 1789, *d* 31 Dec 1837, having had issue), two yst sons (Edward, *b* 14 June 1795, *d* young; Charles, *b* 10 July 1800, *m* thrice and *d* 1884, having had issue) and four daus (Anne, *b* 23 May 1787, *m* — Amory, of Doncaster, and *d* 30 Nov 1854; Mary, *b* 2 Feb 1792, *d* young; Mary, *b* 8 May 1798, *dvp* unm; Sarah, *b* 29 Sept 1802, *m* — Marsden, of Thorne), a 7th s:

JOSEPH SANDERSON, of Hull; *b* 6 April 1793; *m* 30 Sept 1815 Elizabeth Rheam, of Hull, and *d* 6 April 1877, having had, with an est s (Edward Rheam, *b* 16 Dec 1818, *m* Elizabeth Wilson, of Hull, and *d* 10 Nov 1856, leaving issue), a yst s (Arthur, *b* 28 March 1834, Surgn-Maj, *m* Maria Iona Burnie (*d* 1911) and *dsp*) and two daus (Ellen, *b* 27 Oct 1816, *d* unm 18 May 1858; Anna Mary, *b* 15 Nov 1820, *m* Rev Alfred Rivet and *d* March 1910, having had four daus), a 2nd s:

RICHARD SANDERSON, of London, formerly of Birkenhead and New York; *b* 14 June 1831; *m* 1st 19 June 1855 Eliza Palmer Zara (*d* 17 March 1889), dau of Capt Thomas Hicks, HEICS, by Thomasina, dau of Capt Thomas Cookson; *m* 2nd Nara Burnett and *d* April 1921, having had by his 1st w:

1 Richard; *b* 9 Jan 1858; *m* 20 Oct 1886 Clare Otey and *d* 11 July 1942, leaving a son

2 HAROLD ARTHUR, of whom presently

3 Oswald, of Hull; *b* 3 Jan 1863; *m* 8 Feb 1888 Beatrice Bedall, of New York, and *d* 25 Dec 1936, leaving three sons and a dau

4 George Alfred; *b* 15 March 1865; *m* 1906 Katherine Lazarus and *d* 18 Feb 1911, leaving a s and dau

5 Lloyd Bowen, of New York; *b* 2 April 1866; *m* 20 April 1886 Ottilie Force (*d* April 1968) and *d* 24 Oct 1926, leaving two sons

6 Percy Robert; *b* 17 Aug 1867; *m* 1st 9 Dec 1906 Millie Taylor; *m* 2nd her sis Maude Alice Taylor (*d* 18 Dec 1941) and *dsp* 6 Jan 1946

1 Zara Frances; *b* 6 May 1856; *m* 9 Jan 1879 F M Walford and *d* 30 Jan 1890, leaving issue

2 Ada Christiana; *b* 28 Dec 1861; *m* 4 Feb 1891 Joseph B Duckworth and *d* 4 Aug 1931, leaving issue

3 Bertha Margaret; *b* 23 Jan 1864; *m* 1896 G H Dugdale, of Roanoke, Va., and *d* 28 Feb 1943, leaving issue

The 2nd s,

HAROLD ARTHUR SANDERSON, of Jenkyn Place, Bentley, Hants; *b* 20 Oct 1859; Pres Internat Mercantile Marine Co, chm White Star Line, dir Shaw, Savill and Albion, ptnr Sanderson and Son, New York, Hon Capt RNR; *m* 9 March 1885 Maud Blood (*d* 23 June 1927), of New York, and *d* 26 Feb 1932, leaving:

1 Harold Winchester; *b* 12 July 1892; Capt Gren Gds; *m* 24 Feb 1938 (*divorce* 1948) Beryl Susan (*d* 10 July 1976), formerly w of Claude A Cutbill and yst dau of Hon Frederic William Anson, JP (*see* LICHFIELD, E), and *dsp* 22 March 1955

2 BASIL, **1st Baron**

1 Lee; *b* 18 Dec 1886; *m* J A Ballard and *d* June 1941, leaving issue

2 Olga; *b* 23 Oct 1890; *m* 1917 T Barrett Blacket (*d* 1932) and *d* 1926, leaving issue

The 2nd s,

BASIL SANDERSON, **1st Baron Sanderson of Ayot**, of Welwyn, Co Hertford (UK), so *cr* 4 July 1960, MC and bar; *b* 19 June 1894; *educ* Rugby and Trin Coll

Oxford (Hon BA 1914); WW I: Maj Duke of Lancaster's Own Yeo, GSO(3) lst Inf Div, Bde Maj 126th Inf Bde and GSO(2) 41st Inf Div (despatches twice, Belgian Croix de Guerre, Brevet Maj); chm: London Gen Shipowners Soc 1933–34, Nat Cncl Port Labour Employers 1934–40, Shipowners side of Nat Maritime Bd 1946–51; Pres: Internat Shipping Fedn 1934–51, Br Employers' Confedn 1938–39, Shipping Fedn 1950–63 (chm 1934–50); Dir Shipping in Port Min Shipping 1939–41, Head Port Transit Control Min War Tport 1941–45; dir: Dalgety and NZ Loan Ltd 1946–64, Furness, Withy and Co Ltd 1945–65, Bank of England 1946–65, Ford Motor Co 1948–65, Shaw, Savill and Albion 1949–68 (chm 1947–63), Br Maritime Tst and Finance Corp for Industry 1953–66, memb Ec Planning Bd 1957–62, memb Council of Shipping 1962–68, High Sheriff London 1948, US Medal of Freedom with Silver Palm; *m* 27 Jan 1927 Evelyn Constance (*d* 9 Aug 1940), yr dau of Joseph Bruce Ismay, of The Lodge, Costelloe, Co Galway, and Mayfair, and *d* 15 Aug 1971, leaving:

1 ALAN LINDSAY SANDERSON, **briefly 2nd Baron Sanderson of Ayot**

2 +Murray Lee [The Hon Murray Sanderson, PO Box 20516, Kitwe, Zambia]; *b* 12 Jan 1931; *educ* Rugby, Trin Coll Oxford and King's Coll Cambridge; Admin Offr Kenya 1956–63; *m* 1st 30 April 1966 (*divorce* 1972) Muriel, dau of George Williams; *m* 2nd 1973 *Eva, dau of Rev David Simfukwe, and by her has:

(1) +Basil; *b* 1974

(1) *Constance; *b* 1976

1 *Pauline Maud; *b* 12 Feb 1929; *educ* LMH Oxford (MA 1950); Docteur de l'Université de Paris 1959; *m* 24 July 1952 Robert Henri Matarasso (*d* 1982), s of Dr I Matarasso, of Athens, and has:

(1) *Pascale; *b* 1955

(2) *Antoine; *b* 1957

(1) *François; *b* 1958

(2) *Véronique; *b* 1964

SANDERSON OF BOWDEN

Arms: Per pale, dexter bendy sable and or, sinister azure, a chevron per pale azure and or, in dexter chief a ram's head affronté argent horned gules, in sinister chief a fleur-de-lys issuant from a crescent argent. **Crest:** A cock or, armed, crested and wattled sable, supporting in the dexter claw a buckle of the first.
Supporters: Dexter, a Connemara pony proper; sinister, a Cashmere goat proper. **Motto:** Persevere. **Creation:** B. (LP, UK) 1985.

THE BARON SANDERSON OF BOWDEN, of Melrose, District of Ettrick and Lauderdale (Sir (Charles) Russell Sanderson, DL (Ettrick and Lauderdale 1989)) [The Rt Hon The Lord Sanderson of Bowden DL, Becketts Field, Bowden, Roxburghs TD6 0ST]; *b* 30 April 1933; *educ* Trin Coll Glenalmond (Memb Cncl 1982–), Scottish Coll of Textiles Galashiels (Govr 1980–87) and Bradford Coll; 2nd Lt Roy Signals 1952, 51 (Highland) Inf Div Signal Regt (TA) 1953–56, KOSB (TA) 1956–58; ptnr Chas P Sanderson 1958–87; Cllr Gen Assembly Ch Scotland 1972; Chm Centl & S Area Scottish C and U Assoc 1974–75 (V-Pres 1975–77, Pres 1977–79), V-Chm Nat Union C Assocs 1979–81 (Memb Exec Ctee 1977–, Chm 1981–86), ktd 1981, Memb C Party Policy Ctee 1979–86; Govr St Mary's Sch Melrose 1977–87; Chm: Edinburgh Fin Tst 1983–87, Shires Investment Tst 1984–87 and Glenalmond Coll Cncl 1994–; Memb: Scottish Cncl Ind Schs 1984–87, Ctee Governing Bodies Assoc 1984–87 and Court Napier U 1995–; Min State Scottish Office 1987–90, Chm Scottish C Party 1990–93; chm: Hawick Cashmere Co 1991–, Scottish Mortgage and Tst 1993– (dir 1991–), Scottish Pride plc 1994–97; dir Clydesdale Bank 1985–87 and 1994– (dep chm 1996–), Woolcombers Ltd 1991–94, United Auctions Ltd 1992–, Watson & Philip plc 1993–, Edinburgh Woollen Mills Ltd 1993–97, Morrison Construction Co 1995–; *m* 1958 *Frances Elizabeth, dau of Donald Alfred Ramsden Macaulay, of Rylstone, Skipton, Yorks, and has had:

1 *(Charles) David Russell [The Hon David Sanderson, Deansyde, Denholm Hawick, Roxburghshire]; *b* 1960; *educ* Glenmond and Leeds U (BA); *m* 1990 *Laura, yr dau of H G Purdie, of Coatbridge, Lanarks

2 Andrew Bruce Plummer; *b* 1968; *educ* Glenalmond; *d* 1991

1 *(Evelyn) Claire; *b* 1961; *educ* St Leonard's Sch, Newnham Coll Cambridge (BA) and Edinburgh U; MB, ChB; *m* 1986 *Thomas M Walker, only s of K P Walker, of Glenairlie, Kilmacolm

2 *(Frances) Georgina; *b* 1963; *educ* St Leonard's Sch and Queen Margaret's Coll Edinburgh; *m* 1990 *Peter James Holland Riley, s of Maj J C Riley, of Chislehurst, Kent

Lineage: CHARLES PLUMMER SANDERSON; *m* Martha Evelyn, dau of Joseph Gardiner, of Glasgow, and had:

(CHARLES) RUSSELL, *cr* a **Baron**

SANDFORD

Arms: Az. a cross couped and pointed between in chief two lions combatant and in base as many swan's wings elevated and addorsed respectant, all or. **Crest:** In front of a portcullis or a dexter arm embowed in armour fesswise, the hand clenched ppr. **Supporters:** On either side a pikeman of the Honourable Artillery Company armed and accoutred, supporting with the exterior hand a pike erect ppr., the dexter charged with a portcullis chained or, the sinister with an oak tree eradicated and fructed also ppr., the trunk pierced by three arrows or flighted az. (badge of the EDMONDSONs). **Motto:** *Cuicunque ferienti aperietur* ('It will be opened to whoever bears'). **Creation:** B. (UK) 14 July 1945.

THE 2ND BARON SANDFORD, of Banbury, Co Oxford (John Cyril Edmondson, DSC) [The Rev The Rt Hon Cdr The Lord Sandford DSC, 27 Ashley Gdns, Ambrosden Ave, London SW1P 1QD]; *b* 22 Dec 1920; *s f* 1959; *educ* Eton, RNC Dartmouth and Westcott Ho Theological Coll Cambridge; served WW II (wounded twice), Cdr RN (ret 1956), ordained 1958, Curate St Nicholas Harpenden 1958–63, on staff Bishop St Albans 1963–68, C Whip Ho Lds 1966–70, Parly U-Sec Environment 1970–73 and DES 1973–74, chm Westminister Cncl Social Servs, Pres Anglo-Swiss Soc 1974–84, Cncl Environmental Educn 1975–84 and Assoc Dist Cncls 1980–86 (thereafter V-Pres), Chm Ch Army Bd 1969–70, Community Task Force 1975–82, Conf on S E Regnl Planning 1981–89 and Redundant Churches 1982–89, V-Pres YHA 1977–89, dir Ecclesiastical Insur Grp 1978–89, Church Commr 1981–88, Fndr Sandford Award for Heritage Educn and Heritage Educn Tst; *m* 4 Jan 1947 *Catharine Mary, dau of Rev Oswald Andrew Hunt, of Itchen Abbas, Hants, and had:

1 +JAMES JOHN MOWBRAY [The Hon James Edmondson, 1023 East 21st St, Vancouver, BC V5V IS6, Canada]; *b* 1 July 1949; *educ* Eton and York U; sch counsellor; *m* 1st 1973 (*divorce* 1986) Ellen, dau of Jack Shapiro, of Toronto, and has:

  (1) *Sarah Juliette; *b* 22 June 1977

1 (cont.) The Hon James Edmondson *m* 2nd 1986 *Linda, dau of Michael Wheeler, of Nova Scotia, and by her has:

  (1) +Devon John; *b* 1986

2 +Nicholas Mark [The Hon Nicholas Edmondson, 237 Abbotsfield Rd, Pitsmoor, Sheffield]; *b* 7 June 1956; *educ* Eton; *m* 1983 (*separated* 1995) *Joanna, dau of Gordon Snee, of Willingham, Lincs, and has:

  (1) *Rachel Alice; *b* 1986

  (2) *Amber May; *b* 1989

1 *Margaret Catharine [The Hon Mrs Holland, Barncroft, Brightwell-cum-Sotwell, Oxon]; *b* 7 Nov 1947; *educ* Downe Ho Sch, Trin Coll Dublin and Bristol U; social worker; *m* 1977 *(Alan) Simon Charles Holland and has:

  (1) *Hereward Julian; *b* 1984

  (1) *Hannah Catharine; *b* 1979

  (2) *Venetia Frances; *b* 1981

2 *Frances Mary [The Hon Mrs Wharton, Vorgebirgstrasse 5, 50677 Köln, Germany]; *b* 4 June 1953; *educ* Downe Ho Sch and Bristol U; research scientist; *m* 1979 *Geoffrey Wharton, er s of Robert Wharton, of Grand Forks, ND, USA, and has:

  (1) *Lionel Thomas; *b* 1982

  (2) *John Lorenz; *b* 1984

Lineage: JAMES EDMONDSON, of Weston; *m* Isabelle Hitchens (*d* 20 Feb 1941) and *d* 7 Aug 1931, leaving, with a dau (Elsie, *m* 20 July 1920 Charles Edgar Farr, JP, of Westonbury, Herts, yst s of Albert Hart Farr, and *d* 1 March 1956, having had issue):

(ALBERT) JAMES EDMONDSON, **1st Baron Sandford**, of Banbury, Co Oxford (UK), so *cr* 14 July 1945, DL (Oxon); *b* 29 June 1886; *educ* Univ Coll Sch; Maj HAC WW I (RAH) and staff, MP (C) Banbury 1922–45, PPS to Parly Sec Min Pensions and Min Pensions 1924–29 and 1931–34, Priv Sec to Ch Civil Commr 1926, Assist Govt Whip 1937–39, a Ld Treasury 1939, V-Chamberlain Household 1939–42, Dep Ch Whip 1942–45, CC Oxon 1922–37, CStJ, ktd 1934, High Steward Oxford 1948; *m* 20 June 1911 Edith Elizabeth (*d* 19 March 1946), dau of James George Freeman, and *d* 16 May 1959, having had:

1 JOHN CYRIL EDMONDSON, **2nd and present Baron**

2 +Anthony James Kinghorn [The Hon Anthony Edmondson, Linley Lodge, East Knoyle, Wilts SP3 6BW]; *b* 20 July 1924; *educ* Eton and Harvard; Capt Gren Gds WW II; *m* 1st 26 April 1947 (*divorce* 1969) his er bro's sis-in-law Olivia Charlotte, yst dau of Rev Oswald Andrew Hunt, and has:

  (1) +Charles Anthony [Charles Edmondson Esq, Burhill, Buckland, Worcs WR12 7LY]; *b* 17 Feb 1949; *educ* Shrewsbury; *m* 1978 (*divorce* 1989) Isabella, dau of Thomas Wright, of Glasgow, and has:

    1a +Andrew James; *b* 1982

    1a *Sarah Isabella; *b* 1979

    2a *Gemma Lavinia; *b* 1981

  (1) (cont.) Charles Edmondson also has by Rhian Cowles:

    2a *Toby Benjamin; *b* 1994

  (2) +Simon Andrew [Simon Edmondson Esq, Conde de Aranda 3 – piso 4, 28001 Madrid, Spain]; *b* 29 Aug 1955; *educ* Shrewsbury; MA, MFA; *m* 1981 (*divorce* 1988) Louise Caroline Marion, dau of Donald Alistair Blair, of Brighton; *m* 2nd 1992 *Maria Martin Hernandez-Cañizares, dau of Cristobal Martin Garcia, of Madrid

  (3) +Anthony James [Anthony Edmondson Esq, Friday Island, Poole Keynes, Glos GL7 6ED]; *b* 13 Sept 1957; *m* 1987 (*divorce* 1993) Olivia, 5th dau of Dr Charles Dansie, of Welwyn, Herts, and has:

    1a +James Anthony Harry; *b* 1989

    1a *Charlotte Emily; *b* 1988

  (1) *Elizabeth Anne [Mrs Elizabeth Urquhart, 14 Davies Dve, Bishops Cannings, Wilts SN10 2RL]; *b* 31 March 1951; *m* 1979 (*separated*) Nigel A Urquhart, er s of Sir Andrew Urquhart, KCMG, MBE

2 (cont.) The Hon Anthony Edmondson *m* 2nd 21 Aug 1969 *Hilary Pauline, only child of Col Edward Shirley Trusler, OBE, and by her has had:

  (4) Rupert James Kinghorn; *b* 8 Feb 1972; *d* 1979

1 Margaret Ursula; *d* after a bathing accident 1934

SANDHURST

Arms: Arg. on a chevron embattled az. between three maunches sa. an eastern crown or, on a chief engrailed of the third a lion of the fourth combatant with a tiger cowed ppr. **Crest:** Out of an eastern crown arg. a gryphon's head sa., beaked or, between two branches of laurel ppr. **Supporters:** Dexter, a horse arg., mane and tail sa., charged on the shoulder with a rose gu., barbed and seeded ppr., holding in the mouth a branch of laurel vert; sinister, a tiger cowed ppr., gorged with a collar, therefrom a chain reflexed over the back sa. **Motto:** Steadfast. **Creation:** B. (UK) 28 March 1871.

THE 5TH BARON SANDHURST OF SANDHURST, Co Berks ((John Edward) Terence Mansfield, DFC (1944)) [The Rt Hon The Lord Sandhurst DFC, La Volière, Les Ruisseaux, St Brelade, Jersey JE3 8DD, CI]; *b* 4 Sept 1920; *s f* 1964; *educ* Harrow; F/Lt RAFVR, served 149, 419 (RCAF) and 12 Sqdns Bomber Cmd WW II, Met Special Constabulary 'C' Div (Sgt 1949–52, Long Serv Medal 1955), md Leslie Rankin Ltd, Hon ADC to Lt-Govr Jersey 1969–74; *m* 1st 7 Nov 1942 (*divorce* 1946) Priscilla Ann (*d* 1970), 2nd dau of J Fielder Johnson; *m* 2nd 3 April 1947 *Janet Mary, er dau of John Edward Lloyd, of New York, and by her has:

1 +GUY RHYS JOHN, QC (1994) [The Hon Guy Mansfield QC, 1 Crown Office Row, Temple, London EC4Y 7HH]; *b* 3 March 1949; *educ* Harrow and Oriel Coll Oxford (MA); barrister Middle Temple (Winston Churchill Award 1972), Recorder Crown Court 1993–, memb Gen Cncl Bar 1998–, chm Legal Aid & Fees Ctee 1998–; *m* 5 June 1976 *Philippa St Clair, er dau of Digby Everard Verdon-Roe, of Le Cannet, France, and has:

  (1) +Edward James; *b* 12 April 1982; *educ* Eton

(1) *Alice Georgina; *b* 4 Feb 1980; *educ* Wycombe Abbey

1 *Victoria Elizabeth [The Hon Mrs Bentley, South Fen House, Fen End, Warwicks CV8 1NQ]; *b* 30 Jan 1957; *educ* Benenden and Bordeaux U; *m* 4 Nov 1978 *(Charles) James Sharp Bentley, 2nd s of Kenneth Bentley, of Balmuir, by Dundee, and has:

(1) *James William Nicholas; *b* 17 Nov 1982

(1) *Sophie Katharine; *b* 1985

Lineage: — MANFIELD; had, with a yr s (Richard):

EDWARD MANFIELD; living 1625; had, with two yr sons (John James; Richard) and two daus (Mary, *m* Thomas Lyne; Sarah):

EDWARD MANFIELD; *m* Frances — and *d* by 1706, leaving, with two daus (Elizabeth, *m* Thomas Smithson; Frances):

JAMES MANFIELD, of Southampton; *m* Elizabeth — and *d* by 1706, leaving, with a dau (Ann, *m* — Martin, of Seaborough Court, Crewkerne, Somerset):

JOHN JAMES MANFIELD later MANSFIELD, of Ringwood Manor House, Hants; Under Sheriff Hants; *m* 1st 1730 Elizabeth Fezard (*bur* May 1740) and had issue; *m* 2nd Grace Benyon (*bur* Sept 1747) and was *bur* 29 Oct 1762, having by her had issue also; his son by his 1st w:

JAMES MANSFIELD (Sir); *b* 1733; Fell King's Coll Cambridge 1754, MA 1758, barrister Middle Temple, KC 1772, Slr-Gen 1780–82 and 1783, MP Cambridge U 1779–84, Ld Ch Justice Common Pleas 1804–14; *d* 23 Nov 1821, leaving:

JOHN EDWARD MANSFIELD, of Diggeswell House, Herts; *m* 1809 Mary Buchanan (*d* Nov 1868), dau of Gen Samuel Smith, of Baltimore, and *d* 7 July 1841, having had:

1 James; *d* 1849 aged 37, leaving two daus

2 John Smith, JP Middx and London; *b* 22 May 1813; BA Cantab, Fell Trin Coll, barrister Middle Temple 1842, Met Police Magistrate Marylebone 1860–88; *m* 10 Aug 1866 Françoise Julie, dau of Florent de Grairer, of Steine, France, and *d* 20 June 1905, leaving issue

3 Samuel, CSI (1866); Bombay CS, Memb Cncl Bombay; *d* 1894

4 Henry; Lt RN; *d* unm 1838

5 WILLIAM ROSE, **1st Baron**

6 Horatio; *b* 1821; *educ* Trin Coll Cambridge (MA); barrister Inner Temple; *m* 4 July 1871 Emma Georgiana Christina (*d* 25 Nov 1908), widow of Lt-Col Henry Wedderburn Cumming and dau of Sir William Clay, 1st Bt (*qv*), and *dsp* 1887

7 Charles Edward (Sir), KCMG; *b* 11 Oct 1828; Col 33rd Regt Crimea and Indian Mutiny, Consul-Gen Warsaw 1865, Bucharest 1876 and Bogota 1878, Min Resident Caracas 1883 and Lima 1884 (ret 1894); *m* 13 June 1859 Annie Eliza Margaret (*d* 21 Feb 1922), dau of Lt-Col Hon Augustus Frederick Ellis, MP (*see* HOWARD DE WALDEN, B), and *d* 1 Aug 1907, leaving issue

1 Margaret; *d* unm

2 Charlotte Henrietta; *m* Baron Vincent de Tuyll de Serooskerken and *d* 9 Feb 1869

3 Emily; *m* 13 July 1843 Sir John Ralph Milbanke-Huskisson, 8th Bt, and *d* 19 Dec 1905, leaving issue (*see* 1949 edn MILBANKE, Bt)

4 Isabella; *m* 3 Aug 1848 Hon Ralph Heneage Dutton, DL, MP, of Timsbury Manor, Hants, 3rd s of 2nd Baron Sherborne (*see* 1970 edn), and *d* 27 Feb 1895, leaving issue. He *d* 8 Oct 1892

The 5th s,

WILLIAM ROSE MANSFIELD, **1st Baron Sandhurst**, of Sandhurst, Berks (UK), so *cr* 28 March 1871, GCB (1870, KCB 1858), GCSI (24 May 1866, KSI 12 Feb 1866), PC (I 1870); *b* 21 June 1819; *educ* RMC Sandhurst (passed out top, which entitled him to a commission free of charge (this did not stop him opposing the abolition of promotion by purchase when a peer, however); he commemorated this earliest triumph in his choice of title over a third of a century later); Ensign 53rd Foot 1835, Capt 1843, served 1st Sikh War 1845–46 (ADC to C-in-C Battle of Sobraon 1846), Maj 1847, cmded 53rd Foot Punjab War 1848–49 (fought Battle of Gujerat 1849), Lt-Col 1851, served Peshawar frontier 1851–52, Brevet Col 1854, DAG Dublin 1855, Mil Advsr to Constantinople Embassy as Brig-Gen 1855, Consul-Gen Warsaw 1856–57, Ch Staff to Sir Colin Campbell with local rank of Maj-Gen Indian Mutiny 1857, substantive Maj-Gen 1858, recd thanks of Parliament 1859, C-in-C Bombay Army 1860–65, C-in-C India 1865–70, Col 38th Foot 1862–76, Lt-Gen (1864) cmdg Forces Ireland 1870–75, DCL; *m* 2 Nov 1854 Margaret (*d* 7 Jan 1892), dau of Robert Fellowes, of Shotesham Park, Norfolk, and *d* 23 June 1876, leaving:

1 WILLIAM MANSFIELD, **2nd Baron Sandhurst of Sandhurst** and 1st and last VISCOUNT SANDHURST OF SANDHURST, Co Berks (UK), so *cr* 1 Jan 1917, GCVO (1917), GCSI (1900), GCIE (1895), PC (1907); *b* 21 Aug 1855; *educ* Rugby; Lt Coldstream Gds 1875 (ret 1879), Ld in Waiting (Lib) 1880–85, Parly U-Sec War Feb–Aug 1886 and 1892–94, Govr Bombay 1895–1900, Ld Chamberlain 1912–21, Treas Bart's Hosp 1908–21, Grand Offr Legn Hon, Grand Cordon Dannebrog and Rising Sun Japan, KStJ]; *m* 1st 20 July 1881 Lady Victoria Alexandrina Spencer, CI (*d* 13 March 1906), dau of 4th Earl Spencer (*qv*), and had:

(1) John Robert; *b* 4, *d* 5 Sept 1882

(1) Elizabeth; *b* 9 June, *d* 17 Oct 1884

1 (cont.) The **2nd Baron** *m* 2nd 5 July 1909 Eleanor Mary Caroline, OBE (*d* 5 Dec 1934), widow of Hon Armine Wodehouse, CB, MP (*see* KIMBERLEY, E), and dau of Matthew Arnold, and *dspm* 2 Nov 1921, when the Viscountcy expired

2 JOHN WILLIAM, **3rd Baron**

3 Henry William; *b* 2 Dec 1860; Lt-Col 2nd Co of London Yeo, Maj 1st Dragoons; *m* 9 June 1885 Katharine Rachel (*d* 23 Feb 1928), dau of James Charles, of Kennet Ho, Harrow, and *d* 19 March 1933, leaving:

(1) William Henry Charles, DSO (1915); *b* 3 Oct 1887; *educ* Wellington and RMC Sandhurst; Hon Lt-Col, Maj Res Offrs Salop LI, W/Cdr RFC and RAF WW I (despatches twice), WW II in KRRC and cmdg 56th Essex Bn HG; *d* unm 18 May 1961

(2) James Cleland, JP Norfolk; *b* 20 Feb 1890; entered HMS *Britannia* 1905, served WW I (despatches), Capt RN (ret 1928), recalled 1939, served WW II, Assist Dir Mercantile Movement Admlty 1939–43, Ch Staff London Naval Cmd 1944, Russian Order St Stanislas 3rd Cl with swords, Italian medal for

valour, Offr US Legn Merit, CC Norfolk 1938–46; *m* 5 Aug 1914 Marjorie Frances, dau of John Field, and *dsp* 23 Oct 1964

(3) John Hamilton; *b* 12 Sept 1893; *educ* Wellington and Pembroke Coll Cambridge; Maj Coldstream Gds, served WWs I and II 1939–43; *m* 1st 15 April 1916 Phyllis Colvin (*d* 9 Aug 1930), dau of Col John M Burt, RA; *m* 2nd 19 March 1932 Rose Marion Carola Holms-Kerr, dau of Arthur Heaton, of Sutton Coldfield, and *d* 19 Feb 1967

(1) Katharine Rose; *b* 2 May 1886; *m* 12 Feb 1919 Capt Joseph Herbert Mayne, Beds Regt, s of Joseph Mayne, of Catherine Lodge, Warrenpoint, Co Down, and had issue. He *d* 18 Aug 1950

4 James William; *b* 12 Feb 1862; *educ* Trin Coll Cambridge (BA); *d* 17 June 1932

1 Margaret Louisa; *d* unm 19 Jan 1931

The 2nd BARON's bro,

JOHN WILLIAM MANSFIELD, **3rd Baron Sandhurst of Sandhurst**, JP Norfolk; *b* 10 July 1857; *educ* Trin Coll Cambridge (MA); barrister, Legal Chancery Visitor of Lunatics 1910–28; *m* 11 Sept 1888 Edith Mary (*d* 1 Nov 1939), 2nd dau of John Higson, of Oakmere Hall, Cheshire, and had:

1 RALPH SHELDON, **4th Baron**

1 Edith Margery; *b* 10 July 1889; *m* 1st 12 Oct 1910 Lt Charles Francis Nunneley, Northumberland Fus (*ka* 26 Oct 1914), s of Rev Frederick Barham Nunneley, and had:

(1) * Robin M C [Robin Nunneley Esq, 23 Hendre Rd, Holt, Norfolk NR25 6RR]; *b* 1912

1 (cont.) The Hon Mrs Nunneley *m* 2nd 28 Feb 1918 Maj John Edward Svensson, Argyll and Sutherland Highrs (*d* 8 July 1969), of The White House, Little Hautbois, Norwich, 2nd s of J C Svensson, of Leith, and *d* 12 Dec 1936, leaving by him:

(2) *John [John Svensson Esq, Park Cottage, S Wraxall, nr Bradford-on-Avon, Wilts]; *b* 1920

2 Olive; *b* 12 Oct; *d* 30 Dec 1895

3 Frances Hilary; *b* 11 Jan 1898; *d* 6 Feb 1901

The 3rd BARON *d* 6 Jan 1933; his only s,

RALPH SHELDON MANSFIELD, **4th Baron Sandhurst of Sandhurst**, OBE (1918); *b* 19 July 1892; *educ* Winchester and Trin Coll Cambridge (BA); Lt RE 1914, later Capt, WW I (despatches twice), Lt-Col Roy Signals WW II, served MI5, chm Br Rd Fedn 1946–54, pres Hatch Mansfield & Co; *m* 8 Feb 1917 Morley Victoria (*d* 17 June 1961), only child of Edward Berners Upcher, of Kirby Cane, Sheringham, Norfolk, and *d* 28 Oct 1964, leaving:

1 (JOHN EDWARD) TERENCE MANSFIELD, **5th and present Baron Sandhurst of Sandhurst**

2 Ralph Geoffrey Knyvet; *b* 8 Nov 1926; *educ* Haileybury; served Fleet Air Arm 1944–47, md Hatch Mansfield & Co, Dir Oxon St John Ambulance Assoc; *m* 1st 1 March 1952 (*divorce* 1960) Hélène Gertrude (*d* 1975), only dau of James Montague Coutts Duffus of Dalclaverhouse, of Claverhouse, by Dundee, and had:

(1) *(Penelope) Sara Helene [Mrs Neale Muir, Lot 16, Allen Rd, Forrest Dale, WA 6112, Australia]; *b* 11 March 1953; *m* 1983 *Dr C Neale Muir

(2) *Trudé Charlotte Victoria [Mrs Timothy Borrett, Beckwith Farm, Great Holland, Essex CO13 0ET]; *b* 15 April 1955; MPS; *m* 1983 *M Timothy Borrett and has:

1a *Alexandra Victoria; *b* 21 May 1984

2a *Katherine Frances; *b* 21 Dec 1986

(3) *Tessa Emily Henrietta [Mrs Steven Williams, 16 Marn Rd, Middleton Cheney, Banbury, Oxon OX17 2ND]; *b* 12 Jan 1959; *m* 1981 *Steven John Williams and has:

1a *James Matthew Thomas; *b* 29 Nov 1995

2 (cont.) The Hon Ralph Mansfield *m* 2nd 18 Sept 1961 *Evelyn Cecil [The Hon Mrs Ralph Mansfield, Wendover, 40 Old Rd, Frinton-on-Sea, Essex CO13 9BZ], yr dau of Sir Ronald (Barry) Keefe, of Boyton House, Ipswich Rd, Norwich, and *d* 1983, leaving by her:

(4) *Morley Rafael Kate [Mme Bernard Reignier, Château Malard, 33370 Pompignac, Bordeaux, France]; *b* 5 Nov 1965; *m* 1988 *Bernard Reignieur, engr, and has:

1a *Sheldon Camille; *b* 1 April 1992

2a *Tom Samuel; *b* 29 Oct 1994

1 Valerie; *b* 25 Dec 1918; *m* 18 June 1938 8th Earl of Macclesfield (*qv*) and *d* June 1995, leaving issue

SANDWICH

Arms: Quarterly, 1st and 4th, arg. three fusils conjoined in fess gu. within a bordure sa. (for MONTAGU); 2nd and 3rd, or an eagle displayed vert, beaked and membered gu. (for MONTHERMER). **Crest:** A griffin's head, couped or, beaked sa., wings addorsed of the last. **Supporters:** Dexter, a triton, holding over his right shoulder a trident, all ppr., crowned with an Eastern crown or; sinister, an eagle, wings addorsed, vert. **Motto:** *Post tot naufragia portum* ('After so many shipwrecks, a haven'). **Creation:** E., V. and B. (E) 12 July 1660.

THE **11TH EARL OF SANDWICH**, Co Kent, **Viscount Hinchingbrooke**, Co Huntingdon, and **Baron Mountagu of St Neots**, Co Huntingdon (John Edward Hollister Montagu) [The Rt Hon The Earl of Sandwich, Mapperton, Beaminster, Dorset DT8 3NR]; *b* 11 April 1943; *s f* 1995; *educ* Eton and Trin Coll Cambridge (BA 1965); editor and researcher; Christian Aid: Info Offr 1974–85, Research Offr 1985–86; ed Save the Children Fund 1987–92, consultant CARE Britain 1987–93, Govr Beaminster Sch 1996–; author: *The Book of the World* (1971), *Prospects for Africa's Children* (1990), *Children at Crisis Point* (1992); *m* 1 July 1968 *(Susan) Caroline, only dau of Canon Perceval Ecroyd Cobham Hayman, of Beaminster, Dorset, and has had:

  1 +LUKE TIMOTHY CHARLES, *Viscount Hinchingbrooke*; *b* 5 Dec 1969

  2 +Orlando William; *b* 16 Jan 1971; *m* 3 Aug 1996 *Laura Ann, dau of Richard Roundell (see DARTMOUTH, E)

  1 *Jemima Mary; *b* 14 Oct 1973

Lineage: Sir EDWARD MONTAGU (*see* MANCHESTER, D), of Boughton, Northants; had a 6th s:

Sir SYDNEY MONTAGU, KB (1616), of Hinchingbrooke, Hunts (originally a Benedictine convent, sold for £3,000 (over £14,500,000 in late-1990s terms) 1620 by Sir Oliver Cromwell, uncle of the more famous OLIVER, to the 1st Earl of Manchester, who sold it on to his yr bro); Groom Bedchamber to JAMES I, Master Court Bequests to CHARLES I, MP Hunts 1640 (expelled and imprisoned Tower London 1642 for opposing a pro-Parly Army resolution on eve of Civil War; *m* Paulina, 3rd dau of John Pepys, of Cottenham, Cambs (see COTTENHAM, E), and great-aunt of the diarist, and *d* 25 Sept 1644, having had, with an er s (Henry, *b* 16 May 1622, drowned in the moat at Barnwell, Northants, 28 April 1625) and a dau (Elizabeth, *m* Sir Gilbert Pickering, Bt, of Titchmarsh, Northants):

Sir EDWARD MONTAGU, **1st Earl of Sandwich**, Co Kent, so *cr* 12 July 1660, as also BARON MOUNTAGU [sic] OF SAINT NEOTS, Co Huntingdon, and VISCOUNT HINCHINGBROOKE, Co Huntingdon (all E), KG (1660), PC (1657), DL (Hunts (Parly appointment) 1643); *b* 27 July 1625; MP Hunts 1645–48, 1653, 1654–55 and 1656–58 and Weymouth April–July 1660, Parliamentarian Civil War (fought Marston Moor and Naseby), memb Cncl State 1653 (Ld Pres Nov), Commr Treasury 1654–59 and Admlty 1655, Jt Gen-at-Sea Jan 1656/7 (Jr Cdr of Fleet), memb CROMWELL's 'Other House' 1657, Gen of the Fleet 1660 (in which capacity brought it over to CHARLES II), Jt High Adml, Master Gt Wardrobe 1660–70, Adml of the Narrow Seas March 1660/1, V-Adml 1664 (July), Adml of the Blue 1664 (Nov), fought sea Battle of Lowestoft 2nd Dutch War June 1665, C-in-C July 1665, Amb Extrdy Madrid 1666–68, Pres Cncl for Plantations 1670; *m* 7 Nov 1642 Jemima, dau of 1st Baron Crew of Stene, and *d* apparently by drowning when he jumped from his flagship the *Royal James* (which had been set alight by Dutch fireships), being one of the last to leave her, during the Battle of Sole Bay in the Third Dutch War 28 May 1672, in which he had been cmdg the Blue Sqdn, leaving:

  1 EDWARD, **2nd Earl**

  2 Sydney MONTAGU later WORTLEY-MONTAGU; MP Hunts; *m* Anne, dau and heiress of Sir Francis Wortley, 2nd Bt, of Wortley, Co York, and *d* 11 Nov 1727, leaving:

    (1) Edward; *m* Lady Mary Pierrepont (the celebrated diarist and letter-writer Lady Mary Wortley Montagu), dau of 1st Duke of Kingston (see KINGSTON, E, preliminary remarks), and had issue (see BUTE, M, also WHARNCLIFFE, E)

  3 Oliver; MP Hunts, Slr Gen to the Queen 1685; *d* unm 1693 aged 38

  4 John, Master Trin Coll Cambridge 1683, V-Chancellor 1687, Dean Durham 1699, Master Sherburn Hosp; *d* unm 25 Feb 1728/9 aged 73

  5 Charles; *m* 1st Elizabeth, dau of Francis Forster, of Belford, Northumberland, and had:

    (1) James, of Newbold Verdon, Leics; MP Camelford; *bur* 8 Nov 1748

  5 (cont.) Charles Montagu *m* 2nd Sarah Rogers, of Newcastle-upon-Tyne, and by her had:

    (2) Edward, of Newbold Verdon; *m* Elizabeth, dau of Matthew Robinson, of Mount Morris, Kent, and *d* 1775

    (3) John; Lt-Col; *d* unm

    (1) Jemima

  6 James; *d* unm

  1 Jemima; *m* Sir Philip Carteret (*ka* Battle of Sole Bay 28 May 1672) and had:

    (1) GEORGE CARTERET, 1st BARON CARTERET OF HAWNES (*see* GRANVILLE, E, preliminary remarks)

  2 Paulina; *d* unm

  3 Anne; *m* 1st Sir Richard Edgcumbe, KB (*see* MOUNT EDGCUMBE, E); *m* 2nd her cousin Christopher Montagu, brother of Charles, 1st Earl of Halifax (*see* MANCHESTER, D), and *d* 14 March 1729

  4 Catherine; *m* Nicholas Bacon, s and heir of Sir Nicholas Bacon, KB, of Shrubland Hall, Suffolk (*see* BACON, Bt)

The 1st EARL's est s,

EDWARD MONTAGU, **2nd Earl of Sandwich**; *b* 3 Jan 1647/8; MP Dover 1670–72, Amb Lisbon 1678, Ld Lt Hunts by Feb 1680/1–85 and Cambs 1685–87; *m* Jan 1667/8 Anne (*d* 14 Sept 1671), 4th (but *see* 3rd) dau of 2nd Earl of Cork (and 1st Earl of Burlington, *see* CORK and ORRERY, E), and *d* by 29 Nov 1688, having had, with a yr s (Richard, MP Huntingdon, *d* unm 19 April 1697 aged 26) and a dau (Elizabeth, *d* unm):

EDWARD MONTAGU, **3rd Earl of Sandwich**; *b* 10 April 1670; *educ* Eton and Trin Coll Cambridge; DCL Oxon, LLD Cantab, Ld Lt and custos rotulorum Hunts; *m* by 11 July 1689 Elizabeth (*d* 27 July 1757), 2nd dau of 2nd Earl of Rochester, and had:

  1 Edward Richard, *Viscount Hinchinbroke*; *b* 7 July 1692; MP (Whig) Huntingdon 1713–22, Col 1st Foot Gds, Ld Lt Hunts; *m* 12 April 1707 his cousin Elizabeth (*m* 2nd 30 July 1728 Francis Seymour (*see* SOMERSET, D) and *d* 20 March 1761), only dau of Alexander Popham, of Littlecote, Berks, by Anne, only dau of 1st Duke of Montagu (*see* MANCHESTER, D), and *dvp* 3 Oct 1722, having had, with another s and dau (*d* young):

    (1) JOHN, **4th Earl**

    (2) William; Capt RN, MP Huntingdon; *m* Charlotte, dau of Francis Maylor, of Offord D'Arcy, Hunts, and *dsp* 10 Feb 1757

    (1) Elizabeth; *m* Sept 1737 Kelland Courtenay, 2nd s of Sir William Courtenay

  1 Elizabeth; *d* an infant

The 3rd EARL *d* 20 Oct 1729; his gs,

JOHN MONTAGU, **4th Earl of Sandwich**, PC (Feb 1748/9); *b* 13 Nov 1718; *educ* Eton and Trin Coll Cambridge; a Ld Admlty 1744–46, 1st Ld Admlty Feb 1748/9–51, April–Aug 1763 and 1771–82; Min Plen Breda Confs 1748; Sec State N Dept 1763–65 and 1770–71; Jt PMG 1768–70; Gen 1772; gave name to Sandwich Is (discovered by Capt Cook, whose voyages he sponsored) and the bread-based comestible, which he invented (but which makes especially ironic his death from a digestive disorder); *m* 3 March 1740/1 Dorothy (*d* 17 July 1797), dau of 1st Viscount Fane, and *d* 30 April 1792, having had, with two yr sons (Edward, *b* 30 June 1744, *d* 1752; William Augustus, *d* unm 1776), three illegitimate sons (including Basil, 1770–1851, and Adml Robert, *d* 1830), some or all of whom were by the 4th Earl out of Margaret/Martha Ray, a talented amateur singer with whom he cohabited at Hinchingbrooke and who was fatally shot through the head by the Rev James Hackman after turning down his persistent offers of marriage, and a dau (Mary, *b* 23 Feb 1747/8, *d* unm 1761):

JOHN MONTAGU, **5th Earl of Sandwich**, PC (1771); *b* 26 Jan 1743/4; *educ* Eton; Capt 3rd Foot Gds 1761, MP (Tory, but supported North-Fox coalition 1783) Brackley 1765–68 and Hunts 1768–92, Master Buckhounds 1783–1806; *m* 1st 8 March 1766 his cousin Elizabeth (*d* 1 July 1768), only surv child of 2nd Earl of Halifax of the 1715 *cr* (*see* MANCHESTER, D), and had:

  1 John George, *Viscount Hinchinbroke*; *b* 3 April 1767; MP Huntingdon 1790; *m* 2 March 1790 Dorothy Charlotte (*dsp* 10 Aug 1821), only dau of Stephen Beckingham, of Bourne Place, Kent, and *dvp* 29 Nov 1790

  1 Caroline; *d* July 1782

The **5th Earl** *m* 2nd 25 April 1772 Lady Mary Powlett (*d* 30 March 1779), dau and coheir of 6th and last Duke of Bolton (*see* WINCHESTER, M), and by her had:

  2 GEORGE JOHN, **6th Earl**

  3 Francis Charles; *d* unm

  2 Mary; *m* 7 Oct 1796 1st Viscount Templetown (*d* 21 Sept 1846; *see* 1970 edn) and *d* 4 Oct 1824, leaving issue

  3 Henrietta Susannah; *d* unm

The **5th Earl** also had an illegitimate dau Harriet, who *m* James Grant (*see* GRANT, Bt, of Dalvey)

He *d* 6 June 1814; his only surv s,

GEORGE JOHN MONTAGU, **6th Earl of Sandwich**; *b* 4 Feb 1773; *educ* Eton and Trin Coll Cambridge; MP (Tory) Hunts 1794–1814; *m* 9 July 1804 Lady Mary Ann Julia Louisa Harriet (*d* 19 April 1862), dau of 1st Earl Belmore (*qv*), and had:

  1 JOHN WILLIAM, **7th Earl**

  1 Harriet Mary; *m* 12 April 1823 2nd Baron Ashburton (*qv*) and *dsp* 4 March 1857

  2 Catherine Caroline; *m* 1 Dec 1831 Count Alexander Walewski, illegitimate s of NAPOLEON I by Marie Walewska and Min For Affrs under the Second Empire of his cousin NAPOLEON III, and *d* 30 April 1834, leaving issue. He *d* 27 Sept 1868

The 6th EARL *d* 21 May 1818; his only s,

JOHN WILLIAM MONTAGU, **7th Earl of Sandwich**, PC (1852); *b* 8 Nov 1811; *educ* Eton and Trin Coll Cambridge; Ld Lt Hunts 1841–84, Col 5th Bn KRRC,

Gren Gds, cmded Hunts Militia, Capt Gentlemen-at-Arms Feb–Dec 1852, Master Buckhounds 1858–59, ADC to HM QUEEN VICTORIA; *m* 1st 6 Sept 1838 Lady Mary Paget (*d* 20 Feb 1859), dau of 1st Marquess of Anglesey (*qv*), and had issue; *m* 2nd 27 Dec 1865 Lady Blanche Egerton (*d* 20 March 1894), dau of 1st Earl of Ellesmere (*see* SUTHERLAND, D), and *d* 3 March 1884, leaving by his 1st w:

1 EDWARD GEORGE HENRY, **8th Earl of Sandwich**, KCVO (1906), JP Dorset; *b* 13 July 1839; *educ* Eton; Col Gren Gds 1881, Ld Lt Hunts 1891–1916, special mission Constantinople 1858, attached Embassy Berlin and Konigsberg 1861, mission to Morocco 1875, High Steward Huntingdon, Chm Hunts CC, Mayor Huntingdon 1896–98, Col Gren Gds, Hon Col 5th Bn KRRC and Hunts Cyclist Bn TF, MP (C) Huntingdon 1876–84, KStJ; *d unm* 26 June 1916

2 Victor Alexander, CB; *b* 20 April 1841; joined RN 1853, served Crimean War (Crimean Medal, Sardinian Medal, Order of Medjdie), Canton River ops and Battle of Fatschan Creek 1857 (China War medal), Naval Bde Indian Mutiny 1857–59, Mediterranean and WI as Post Capt 1870–84, ret as R-Adml 1884; *m* 28 Nov 1867 Lady Agneta Harriet Yorke (*d* 12 March 1919), Ldy Bedchamber to HRH PRINCESS HELENA, dau of 4th Earl of Hardwicke (*qv*), and *d* 30 Jan 1915, leaving:

  (1) GEORGE CHARLES, **9th Earl**

  (1) Mary Sophie; granted with sisters by roy warrant 1917 rank of earl's daus; *d unm* 31 Jan 1946

  (2) Olga Blanche; *d unm* 4 Aug 1951

  (3) Helena Leopoldine; *m* 13 Aug 1904 Sir Thomas Alexander Vans Best, KCMG, KBE, s of Alexander Vans Best, FRCP, FRCS, of Aberdeen, and *d* 14 Dec 1958, leaving issue. He *d* 24 Nov 1941

3 Sydney; *b* 12 Aug 1842; *d* 4 April 1860

4 Oliver George Paulet; *b* 18 Oct 1844; Col RHG; *d* 24 Jan 1893

1 Emily Caroline; *m* 30 May 1870 Rt Hon Sir William Hart Dyke, 7th Bt (*qv*), and *d* 8 Aug 1831, leaving issue

2 Anne Florence Adelaide; *m* 5 Dec 1876 Capt Alfred Charles Duncombe, 1st Life Gds (*see* FEVERSHAM, B), and *dsp* 16 Jan 1940

The 8th EARL's n,

GEORGE CHARLES MONTAGU, **9th Earl of Sandwich**, JP Hunts; *b* 29 Dec 1874; *educ* Winchester and Magdalen Coll Oxford (BA 1897, MA 1925); MP S Hunts 1900–06, Hunts: CA, Chm CC 1933–46, Ld Lt, Pres TA 1922–46; dir Exchange Telegraph Co 1902–61, Tstee Tate Gallery 1934–41 and Nat Maritime Museum Greenwich 1937–47, Assist Priv Sec to Pres Bd Ag 1898–1900, Priv Sec to Pres Local Govt Board 1900–03, Chm Centl Prisoners of War Ctee 1918, memb Fine Arts Ctee Br Cncl; Chm Bishop's Advsy Ctee Ely, author: *Ten Years of Loco-motive Progress* (1907), *Windows* (verse, 1924), *The Bridle Way* (1925), *In a Green Shade* (1928), *Boyhood, an Autobiography* (1951), *Gleanings* (1955), *British and Foreign Naval Medals*; *m* 1st 25 July 1905 Alberta, JP Hunts (*d* 23 Oct 1951), dau of William Sturges, of New York, and had issue; *m* 2nd 12 Dec 1952 Ella Lilian (Amiya) (*d* 1986), formerly w of Seymour Douglas Corbin and dau of George Sully, of N Petherton, Somerset, and *d* 15 June 1962, leaving by his 1st w:

1 (ALEXANDER) VICTOR EDWARD PAULET, **10th Earl**

2 William Drogo Sturges; *b* 29 May 1908; F/O RAuxAF WW II; *m* 1st 19 Feb 1931 (*divorce* 1935) Tanis Eva Bulkeley (*d* 1993), dau of Benjamin Seymour Guinness (*see* GUINNESS, Bt), and had:

  (1) +(John) Dru [Dru Montagu Esq, Hall Place, W Meon, Hants GU32 1LX]; *b* 22 May 1932; Lt RNR; *m* 1st 24 May 1958 Sarah Maria (Sari), dau of Manolo de Palacio, of Madrid, and has:

    1a *Sophie Maria; *b* 4 March 1959

    2a *Bridget Doon; *b* 2 Jan 1961

    3a *Claire Mary; *b* 1962

    4a *Sarah Tanis; *b* 6 May 1965

  (1) (cont.) Dru Montagu *m* 2nd 1977 *Maria Elena (Minna), est dau of Rich-ard Guy Buckmaster, and by her has:

    1a +Paul Patrick Drogo; *b* 1979

    4a *Kyra; *b* 1978

2 (cont.) The Hon William Montagu *m* 2nd 5 March 1935 *Hon Janet Gladys (*m* 3rd 11 July 1942 Maj Thomas Edward Dealtry Kidd, MBE, RCA, er s of Hon Lt-Col Canon William Ennis Kidd, MC, MA, of Kingston, Ontario), formerly w of 11th Duke of Argyll (*qv*) and dau of 1st Baron Beaverbrook (*qv*), and was *kas* in a plane crash 26 Jan 1940, having by her had:

  (2) +William Drogo [William Montagu Esq, Garland Cottage, Beard's Yard, Langport, Somerset]; *b* 9 Feb 1936; *educ* Eton; *m* 1969 *Edna Maud Ahlers and has:

    1a *Michael Drogo; *b* 19–

    1a *Nicola Lilian; *b* 1971

    2a *Monette Edna; *b* 1973

1 (Mary) Faith; *b* 1 May 1911; *m* 1st 5 Feb 1938 (*divorce* 1940) Philip Booth Nes-bitt (*d* 1953), of Wilderness House, Carmel, Calif., s of Norman Hill Nesbitt, of Boston, USA, and had:

  (1) *(Caroline) Gemma [Mrs Best, The Studio, 14 Priory Rd, London W4]; *b* 1 June 1939; *m* 10 Jan 1964 (*divorce* 1976) Andrew Best, s of Ailwyn Best, of W Kensington, and has:

    1a *Matthew Thomas; *b* 24 Jan 1966

    1a *Anna Josephine; *b* 21 Feb 1965

1 (cont.) Lady Faith Nesbitt *m* 2nd 18 March 1948 Cdr Sir Michael Culme-Seymour, 5th Bt (*qv*), and *d* 16 Feb 1983, having had further issue

2 *Elizabeth [The Lady Elizabeth Montagu, 11 York Mansions, Prince of Wales Dve, London SW11 4DN]; *b* 4 July 1917; novelist

The 9th EARL's est s,

(ALEXANDER) VICTOR EDWARD PAULET MONTAGU, **10th Earl of Sand-wich**; *b* 22 May 1906; *s f* 1962 but disclaimed titles for life 24 July 1964; *educ* Eton and Trin Coll Cambridge (BA 1928, MA 1941); Lt 5th Bn Northants Regt (TA) 1926, served France 1940, later Maj, Gen Staff; dir Northern and Employers Assur, Priv Sec to 1st Earl Baldwin of Bewdley (*qv*) 1932–34, Treasurer Jr Imp League 1934–35, MP (C) Dorset S 1941–62, fndr chm Tory Reform Ctee H of C 1943–44, Pres: Anti-Common Market League 1962–84 and Samuel Pepys Club, Chm Conservative Trident Gp 1973; author: *Essays in Tory Reform* (1944), *The Conservative Dilemma* (1970); *m* 1st 27 July 1934 (*divorce* 1958) (Maud) Rose-

mary, only dau of Maj Ralph Harding Peto (*see* PETO, Bt, of Somerleyton), and had:

1 JOHN EDWARD HOLLISTER MONTAGU, **11th and present Earl of Sand-wich**

2 +(George Charles) Robert [The Hon Robert Montagu, The Old Manor, Ever-shot, Dorset DT2 0JR]; *b* 25 Nov 1949; *educ* Eton; *m* 1970 *Marzia Brigante Colonna and has:

  (1) +Oliver Drogo; *b* 1974

  (2) +Cosimo Ralph; *b* 1988

  (1) *Fiamma Fleur; *b* 1971

  (2) *Bona Frances; *b* 1972

1 *Sarah Jane Helen (has dropped courtesy title); *b* 25 Aug 1935; *m* 21 July 1959 (*divorce* 1971) Alessandro Enrico Ballarin, s of Dr Mario Ballarin, of Bari, Italy, and has:

  (1) *Caterina Teresa; *b* 19 Jan 1960

  (2) *Antonia Barbara; *b* 10 March 1964

2 *(Elizabeth) Anne (has dropped courtesy title); *b* 8 Feb 1937; *m* 8 July 1961 *Torquil Patrick Alexander Norman (*see* NORMAN, Bt) and has issue

3 Henrietta Mary; *b* 14 Jan, *d* 17 Feb 1940

4 *Katharine (Kate) Victoria [The Lady Kate Hunloke, The Old Rectory, Poul-shott, Wilts SN10 1RJ]; *b* 22 Feb 1945; *m* 15 July 1965 *Nicholas Victor Hun-loke, yr s of Lt-Col Henry Philip Hunloke, of St Catherine's Lodge, Bearwood Rd, Wokingham, Berks, by Lady Anne Montagu (*see* below), and has:

  (1) *Edward Perceval; *b* 1 Nov 1969

  (1) *Henrietta Yvery; *b* 14 May 1968

  (2) *Matilda Anne; *b* 25 July 1972

5 Julia Frances; *b* 12 April 1947; *m* 1st 20 Dec 1972 (*divorce* 1976) Martin Lee-Oakley, only s of Kenneth Lee-Oakley, of Wakefield, Yorks; *m* 2nd 1976 *Peter Gerald Edward Body [Peter Body Esq, The Beck, Wexham, Slough, Bucks] and *d* 19 May 1995, leaving by him:

  (1) *Timothy MONTAGU (deed poll 1995); *b* 4 May 1982

The **10th Earl** *m* 2nd 7 June 1962 (*annulled* 1965) Lady Anne, MBE (1952), JP (*d* 19 May 1995), yst dau of 9th Duke of Devonshire (*qv*), formerly w of Lt-Col Henry Philip Hunloke and widow of Christopher John Holland-Martin, MP, and *d* 25 Feb 1995

SANDYS

Arms: 1st and 4th, or a fess dancettée between three cross-crosslets fitchée gu. (for SANDYS); 2nd and 3rd, sa. on a fess arg. between three leopards passant guardant or, spotted of the field, as many escallops gu. (for HILL). **Crests:** 1 A griffin segreant per fess or and gu. (for SANDYS), 2 A stag's head couped gu., attired and collared or (for HILL). **Supporters:** Two griffins per fess or and gu., collared dancettée of the last. **Motto:** *Probum non pœnitet* ('The honest man has not to repent'). **Creation:** B. (UK) 19 June 1802.

THE 7TH BARON SANDYS, of Ombersley, Co Worcester (Richard Michael Oliver Hill, DL (Worcs 1968)) [The Rt Hon The Lord Sandys DL, Ombersley Court, Droitwich, Worcs WR9 0HH]; *b* 21 July 1931; *s f* 1961; *educ* RNC Dart-mouth; Lt RSG 1950–55, Ld-in-Waiting Jan–March 1974, C Whip Ho Lds 1974–79, Dep Ch Whip and Capt Yeomen Gd 1979–83, FRGS, patron of one liv-ing; *m* 16 Sept 1961 *Patricia Simpson, er dau of Capt Lionel Hall, MC, of Park Gate, Lower Beeding, Sussex

Sandys, Barony of, previous creation: In 1523 William Sandys, whose family had held The Vyne, Sherborne St John, Hants, since the late 14th century, was created Baron Sandys, probably by letters patent but since these were not enrolled a belief grew up in the next century that the creation was by writ. Had this been so it would have made the Barony heritable by heirs general, which could include females and their issue. Accordingly after Elizabeth Sandys, half-sister of the 4th Baron, in 1586 married Sir Edwin Sandys, who was of a com-pletely different family despite their identical surnames, there was some doubt in contemporaries' minds whether she might not eventually have transmitted right to the title to her grandson. The latter, William Sandys, was allowed to sit in the House of Lords from 1660, having claimed the Barony of 1523 but in effect, it would seem, being the grantee of a fresh creation conferred at the later date of 1660.

The 1st Baron of the 1523 creation was a powerful figure in early-Tudor Hampshire, governing Southampton, being appointed Constable of its Castle and building up sizeable land holdings elsewhere in the county as well as other estates in the West Country. He took part in HENRY VIII's French forays, acquiring a high reputation as a campaigner, and was given the Garter in 1518. Eight years later he became Lord Chamberlain. His great-grandson, the 3rd Baron, was involved in Essex's insurrection but got off with a massive fine and imprisonment in the Tower. The putatively 6th, though more probably 1st, Baron Sandys allowed a seat in the House of Lords as a result of the 1660 judgment, in 1653 sold The Vyne to Chaloner Chute, Speaker of the House of Commons, with members of whose family it remained till well into the 20th century. On the death without issue in March 1684/5 of Edwin Sandys, conceivably 8th but more probably 3rd Baron Sandys, the peerage either fell into abeyance or expired, almost certainly the latter.

Lineage: WILLIAM SANDYS; had:

GEORGE SANDYS; *m* Margaret, dau of John Dixon, of London, and had six sons; the 3rd s:

Most Rev EDWIN SANDYS; DD, Archbp York 1578–88; *m* 1st —; *m* 2nd Cecilia, dau of Sir Thomas Wilford, of Cranbrook, Kent, and by her had:

1 SAMUEL (Sir)

2 Edwin (Sir); *educ* Merchant Taylors'; *m* 1st Margaret, dau of John Eveleigh, of Devon, and had:

(1) Elizabeth; *m* Sir Thomas Wilsford, of Heding, Kent

2 (cont.) Sir Edwin Sandys *m* 2nd Anne, dau of Thomas Southcott, and by her had a dau; *m* 3rd Elizabeth (*dsp*), dau of Thomas Nevinson, of Eastrey; *m* 4th Catharine (*d* 1640), dau of Sir Richard Bulkeley, of Anglesey, and by her had, with other issue:

(1) Edwin, of Northbourne Court; Col Parly Army Civil War; *m* Catharine, dau and heiress of Richard Champneys, of Hall Place, Kent, and *d* of wounds recd Battle of Worcester Sept 1651, leaving:

1a Richard (Sir), of Northbourne Court; *m* Mary, er dau of Sir Henry Heyman, 1st Bt, and was accidentally *k* while hunting 1669, leaving:

1b Sir RICHARD SANDYS, 1st and last Bt (E), so *cr* 15 Dec 1684; said to have been *b* 6 Jan 1670, but if so was *cr* a Bt aged 14; *m* 1st *c* 12 April 1694 Jane, dau of Rev Thomas Ward, Preb Salisbury; *m* 2nd Mary, dau and coheir of Sir Francis Rolle, of Shapwick, Somerset, and *dspm* 5 May 1726, when the btcy expired, having had, with four other daus (*d* young):

1c Priscilla; *m* her 3rd cousin Henry Sandys, of Down, Kent, and had:

1d Richard, of Northbourne Court; *d* 1763, leaving issue

2c Mary; *m* William Roberts, of Harbledown, Kent

3c Anne; *m* Charles Pyott (*dspm* 1789)

3 Sir MYLES SANDYS, 1st Bt (E), so *cr* 25 Nov 1611, of Wilberton, Cambs; *b* 29 March 1563; *educ* Merchant Taylors'; ktd 1603, MP Cambridge U 1614, Huntingdon 1621–22 and Cambs 1628–29, Sheriff Cambs and Hunts 1615–16; *m* 1st Elizabeth, dau of Edward Cooke, of N Cray, Kent and had seven sons (all *dsp*); *m* 2nd 28 Nov 1626 Mary West, widow, and *d* 1645, leaving an est s:

(1) Sir MYLES SANDYS, 2nd and last Bt, of Wilberton; ktd *vp* 1626; *m* Elizabeth, dau and coheir of Thomas Park, of Wisbech, Cambs, and was *bur* 23 Feb 1653/4, when the btcy expired

4 George; traveller and poet; *d* 1643

The est s,

Sir SAMUEL SANDYS; *educ* Merchant Taylors'; leased Manor of Ombersley, Worcs, 1594–1610 and 1614 on; Sheriff Worcs *temp* JAMES I; *m* Mercy, only dau of Martin Colpeper, and *d* 18 Aug 1623, having had, with other issue, including a dau (Anne, *m* Sir Francis Wenman and had issue):

EDWIN SANDYS, of Ombersley; *m* Penelope, dau of Sir Richard Bulkeley, and *d* 6 Sept 1623, having had, with other issue, including a yr s (Richard, *k* Battle of Edgehill 23 Oct 1642):

SAMUEL SANDYS, of Ombersley; Army Offr, Govr Evesham, MP Worcs; *m* 1st Mary, only dau of Dr Hugh Barker, Dean of Arches; *m* 2nd Elizabeth, widow of Col Henry Washington (*see* Section Washington AMERICAN PRESIDENTIAL FAMILIES, 1994, Morris Genealogical Books SA) and dau of Sir John Pakington, 1st Bt (*see* HAMPTON, B), and *d* 1685, leaving an est s:

SAMUEL SANDYS, of Ombersley; MP; *m* Elizabeth, only dau of Sir John Pettus, and *d* 4 Aug 1701, having had, with other issue:

1 Edwin; MP Worcs; *m* Alice, dau of Sir James Rushout, 1st Bt, of Northwick Park, Brockley, Worcs (*see* 1887 edn NORTHWICK, B), and *dvp* 1699, leaving:

(1) SAMUEL SANDYS, 1st LORD SANDYS, BARON OF OMBERSLEY, Co Worcester (GB), so *cr* 20 Dec 1743, PC (Feb 1741/2); *b* 10 Aug 1695; *educ* New Coll Oxford; MP Worcester 1718–43, Chllr Exchequer and a Ld Treasury Feb 1741/2–43, Cofferer Household 1743–44, Treas Chamber 1747–55, Warden and Ch Justice Eyre S of Trent 1756 and 1759–61, Speaker Ho Lds 1756, 1st Ld Trade 1761–63; *m* 9 June 1725 Laetitia (*d* May 1779), er dau and coheir of Sir Thomas Tipping, 1st Bt, of Wheatfield, Oxon, and *d* 21 April 1770, having had, with other issue:

1a EDWIN SANDYS, 2nd and last LORD SANDYS, BARON OF OMBERSLEY; *b* 18 April 1726; *educ* Eton and New Coll Oxford; MP (Whig, later Court Party) Droitwich 1747–54, Bossiney 1754–61 and Westminster 1762–70, a Ld Admlty April–July 1757, DCL Oxon; *m* 26 Jan 1769 Anna Maria (*d* 1 Nov 1806), widow of William Payne King, of Fineshade Abbey, Northants, and sis of Sir James Colebrooke, 1st Bt, of Gatton, Surrey (*see* 1939 edn COLEBROOKE, B), and *dsp* 11 March 1797, when the Barony expired

2a Martin; *b c* 1729; Col, Equerry to DUKE OF CUMBERLAND; *m* 1760 Mary (*d* 1769), only child and heiress of William Trumbull, of Easthampstead Park, Berks (only s and heir of Sir William Trumbull, Sec State *temp* WILLIAM III, by Lady Judith Alexander, sis and coheir of 5th Earl of Stirling), and *d* 26 Dec 1768, having had, with two sons (*d* young):

1b MARY Sandys, **Lady Sandys, Baroness of Ombersley**, Co Worcester (UK), so *cr* 19 June 1802, with initial remainder to her four yr sons and

their male issue, in default of which to her est s; *b* 19 Sept 1764; *m* 29 June 1786 2nd Marquess of Downshire (*qv*) and *d* 1 Aug 1836, leaving, with other issue:

1c ARTHUR MOYSES WILLIAM HILL, **2nd Lord Sandys, Baron of Ombersley**; *b* 10 Jan 1792; *educ* Eton; Cornet 10th Light Dragoons 1809, Lt 1810, served Peninsular War (fought Battles of Vittoria and Pamplona), Staff Offr Waterloo Campaign 1815, Lt-Col 1819, Lt-Col 2nd Dragoons (Scots Greys) 1832–37, Col 1837, Maj-Gen 1846, Col 7th Dragoon Gds 1853–58, Col 2nd Dragoons 1858–60, MP (Whig) Co Down 1818–36; *d unm* 16 July 1860

2c ARTHUR MARCUS CECIL HILL later SANDYS (roy licence 11 Feb 1861), **3rd Lord Sandys, Baron of Ombersley**, PC (1841); *b* 28 Jan 1798; *educ* Eton and Edinburgh U; Attaché Madrid 1816, Précis Writer to For Sec 1822, attd UK Mission Congress Verona 1822, Attaché Paris 1823, Sec Legation Florence 1824, Sec Embassy Lisbon 1825, Rio de Janeiro 1825, St Petersburg 1827, MP (Lib) Newry, Co Down, 1832–34 and Evesham 1837–52, Comptroller Household June–Sept 1841 and 1846, Treas Household 1847–52, Kt Cdr Mil Order Tower and Sword Portugal; *m* 12 April 1837 Louisa (*d* 6 April 1886), yst dau of Joseph Blake (descended from Joseph, bro of Adml Blake), and *d* 10 April 1863, having had:

1d AUGUSTUS FREDERICK ARTHUR HILL later SANDYS, **4th Lord Sandys, Baron of Ombersley**, JP, DL (Worcs); *b* 2 March 1840; Ensign 96th Foot 1859, Lt 1862, Lt 2nd Life Gds 1863, ret 1868, Hon Col Queen's Own Worcester Imp Yeo, patron living Ombersley; *m* 3 Aug 1872 Augusta Anne (*d* 24 Jan 1903), 9th dau of Sir Charles des Voeux, 2nd Bt (*see* 1940 edn, also WINCHESTER, M), and *dsp* 26 July 1940

2d Marcus Windsor George; *b* 28 Sept 1849; Lt-Col 3rd Bn Duke of Edinburgh's Wilts Regt; *d unm* 14 May 1897

3d MICHAEL EDWIN MARCUS SANDYS, **5th Lord Sandys, Baron of Ombersley**, JP Worcs; *b* 31 Dec 1855; memb London Stock Exchange; *m* 1886 Marjorie Clare Pentreath (*d* 8 Oct 1929), dau of John Morgan, of Brighton and Wales, and *dsp* 4 Aug 1948

4d Edmund Arthur Marcus; *b* 9 March 1860; *m* 1884 Ida Marie (*d* 23 July 1926), dau of Maxwell Jones, of New York, and *dsp* 1 Sept 1914

1d Mary Georgiana Caroline; *m* 21 Oct 1858 Sir Edmund Filmer, 9th Bt, of East Sutton (*d* 17 Dec 1886; *see* 1916 edn), and *d* 18 March 1903, leaving issue

2d Anna Maria Frances; *m* 25 Aug 1868 Sir Herbert Hay Langham, 12th Bt (*qv*), and *d* 27 May 1876, leaving issue

3d Cecil Josephine; *d* 1 Sept 1935

4d Charlotte Blundell; *d* 24 Aug 1854

5d Rosa Louisa Vernon; *m* 14 Oct 1874 Capt William Duberly, Gren Gds, of Gaynes Hall, Hunts, and *d* 19 Sept 1943, having had issue. He *d* 18 Dec 1888

6d Nina Violet America; *m* 27 Nov 1880 Ambrose Charles Lisle March-Phillipps De Lisle, of Garendon Park, Leics, and *d* 18 Nov 1905, leaving issue. He *d* 27 Nov 1883

3c Arthur Augustus Edwin; *b* 13 Aug 1800; *d* 10 July 1831

4c George Augustus; *b* 9 Dec 1801; Maj; *m* 1st 21 Oct 1834 Cassandra Jane (*d* 14 March 1842), yst dau of Edward Knight, of Godmersham Park, Kent, and had:

1d Arthur Blundell George Sandys, of Gweedore, Co Donegal; *b* 13 May 1837; Capt Rifle Bde Indian Mutiny, Battle of Cawnpore, Siege of Lucknow, Oudh and Centl India Campaigns with Camel Corps, Inspr Prisons Ireland; *m* 16 Feb 1871 Helen Emily (*d* 25 June 1935), 3rd dau of Most Rev Richard Chenevix Trench (*see* ASHTOWN, B), and *d* 16 June 1923, leaving:

1e ARTHUR FitzGERALD SANDYS, **6th Baron**

2e Richard Augustus Sandys (Sir), KCB (1941, CB 1933); *b* 2 April 1880 Somaliland Campaign 1902–04 (medal), WW I, ADC to HM GEORGE V 1930, Sr Naval Offr Yangtze 1931–33, WW II, Cdre Convoys, Flag-Offr W Scotland, V-Adml; granted with surv siblings rank of baron's dau/er s 1950; Cdr Legn Hon, Croix de Guerre with Palms, US Legn Merit; *d unm* 5 July 1954

3e George Chenevix; *b* 4 May 1887; *educ* Haileybury and RMC Sandhurst; Duke of Edinburgh's Regt WW I (despatches three times, Croix de Guerre with Palms), RAF WW II; *m* 14 Dec 1921 Hon Patricia Irene Wilmot Tufton, dau of 2nd Baron Hothfield (*qv*), and *d* 12 Oct 1963, leaving:

1f Marcus Tufton; *b* 15 March 1931; *educ* Eton and St John's Coll Cambridge

1e Cicely Mary Isabel; *m* 22 April 1911 Hon Sackville Philip Tufton, 2nd s of 1st Baron Hothfield (*qv*), and *dsp* 26 June 1912

2e Madeline Edith; *m* 12 Jan 1917 John Edward Fowler Sclater, JP, of Kilwarlin House, Hillsborough, Co Down, and *d* 20 March 1921. He *d* 17 June 1918

3e Mary Cassandra; *m* 24 Nov 1909 Edgar John Chippindale (*d* 14 Sept 1937), yr s of William Chippindale, of Reigate, and *d* 10 Sept 1968, leaving a s

4e Dorothy Frances; *d unm* 10 April 1945

2d Augustus Charles Edward; *b* 9 March 1839; *d unm* 9 Dec 1908

1d Norah Mary Elizabeth; *m* 26 April 1859 Capt Hon Somerset Ward, 5th s of 3rd Viscount Bangor (*qv*), and *d* 24 April 1920, leaving issue

2d Cassandra Jane Louisa; *d unm* 16 Aug 1901

4c (cont.) Lord George Hill *m* 2nd 11 May 1847 his deceased w's sis Louisa (*d* 29 July 1889), 4th dau of Edward Knight, and *d* 6 April 1879, having by her had:

3d George Marcus Wandsbeck; *b* 9 April 1849; barrister Inner Temple; *d unm* 22 March 1911

1a Anne; *m* Christopher Bethell

2 Martin; Fell New Coll Oxford, barrister; *m* Elizabeth Burton and had issue

1 Mary; *m* 9th Viscount Hereford (*qv*) and *d* 14 Jan 1728/9, leaving issue

The 5th BARON's 1st cousin once-removed,

ARTHUR FITZGERALD SANDYS, **6th Lord Sandys, Baron of Ombersley**, DL (Worcs 1941); *b* 4 Dec 1876; *educ* Haileybury; Lt-Col RE, Tibet Expdn 1904, WW I; *m* 10 April 1924 Cynthia Mary (*d* 1990), only dau of Col Frederick Richard Trench-Gascoigne, DSO (*see* ASHTOWN, B), and *d* 24 Nov 1961 following a car crash, having had:

1 RICHARD MICHAEL OLIVER SANDYS, **7th and present Lord Sandys, Baron of Ombersley**

1 Patricia Mary Gwendolen; *b* 29 March 1926; *m* 9 July 1955 John Laurence Pepys Cockerell, Colonial Admin Serv, only *s* of Lt-Col Frederick William Pepys Cockerell, OBE, MC, and *dsp* 8 Jan 1957

2 *(Cynthia) Meriel [The Hon Mrs Wingfield, Barrington Park, Burford, Oxon]; *b* 29 April 1929; *m* 9 Oct 1954 *Charles Talbot Rhys Wingfield (*see* POWER-SCOURT, V) and has issue

Seat: Ombersley Court, Droitwich, Worcs. The 1st Lord Sandys of the 1743 creation commissioned Francis Smith in the mid-1720s to build him a country house in replacement of the old manor house which had previously stood on his property. This was smoothed over on the outside around 80 years later, so much so as to create a rather bland effect, the architects being J Webb and John Nash. Internally things are very different, the chief features being spectacular ceilings to the hall and principal staircase, panelled rooms of wood on the ground-floor western front and of Chinese silk on upper storeys and a fine chimney-piece in the saloon.

SAVILE

Arms: Argent on a bend sable three owls affrontée of the first, within a bordure wavy of the second. **Crest:** An owl affrontée argent, debruised by a bend sinister wavy sable. **Supporters:** Two talbots ermine, each gorged with a collar wavy sable, pendent therefrom a shield or, charged with a popinjay vert, collared gules. **Motto:** Bee fast. **Creation:** B. (UK) 27 Oct 1888.

THE 3RD BARON SAVILE OF RUFFORD, Co Nottingham (George Halifax Lumley-Savile, JP (Dewsbury 1955), DL (W R Yorks 1954)) [The Rt Hon The Lord Savile JP DL, Walshaw, Hebden Bridge, Yorks HX7 7AX; Gryce Hall, Shelley, Huddersfield Yorks HD8 8LP]; *b* 24 Jan 1919; *s* f 1931; *educ* Eton; WW II in Duke of Wellington's Regt (W R) (attd 1st Bn Lincs Regt Burma 1943–44), CStJ 1982

Lineage: The 8th EARL OF SCARBROUGH (*qv*) had illegitimately by Agnes, apparently a Frenchwoman who had been turned out of doors by her husband and who took the name Lumley (though all her sons by the Earl are presumed to have been originally called SAVILE-LUMLEY):

1 George Frederick; *b* 23 Sept 1812; *d* May 1816

2 JOHN SAVILE-LUMLEY later SAVILE (roy licence 28 May 1887 on inheriting the Rufford estate from his yst bro), **1st Baron Savile of Rufford**, Co Nottingham (UK), so *cr* 27 Oct 1888, with special remainder, in default of male issue, to his n John, GCB (1885, KCB 1878, CB 1873), PC (1883); *b* 6 Jan 1818; FO 1841–88: Attaché Berlin 1842, St Petersburg 1849, Sec Legation Washington 1854, Sec Embassy Madrid 1858–59, St Petersburg 1859–60 and 1865–66 and Constantinople April–Dec 1860, Envoy Extrdy and Min Plen Dresden June–Nov 1866, Berne 1867–68 and Brussels 1868–83, Amb Rome 1883–88; *d* unm 28 Nov 1896

3 Frederick (Rev); *b* 15 March 1819; *educ* Oxford (BA 1846); Rector Billsthorpe, Notts, 1847; *m* 29 May 1849 Mary (*d* 22 May 1922), only dau of Robert Castle Jenkins, of Beachley, Mon, and *d* 1859, leaving:

(1) JOHN, **2nd Baron**

(1) Amy Louise; granted with her sis 5 Nov 1904 rank of baron's daus; *m* 1st 1885 John Ferguson Goodfellow (*dsp* 1897); *m* 2nd 27 Feb 1906 Harry Fitzmaurice Huntsman, of Lound Hall, Notts, *s* of Benjamin Huntsman, DL, of W Retford Hall, and *d* 4 Feb 1943. He *d* 22 March 1929

(2) Minnie Emma Susan; *d* unm 28 May 1946

4 Henry SAVILE-LUMLEY later SAVILE (under terms of will of his f, who bequeathed him the Rufford and Thornhill estates worth £37,000 (some £1,060,000 in late-1990s terms) p.a. on condition he took the name SAVILE); *b* 2 Aug 1820; Capt 2nd Life Gds, High Sheriff Notts 1861; owner: *Cremorne* (won Derby 1872, Ascot Cup 1873, Grand Prix Paris 1872) and *The Ranger* (Grand Prix Paris 1863); *dsp* 28 Aug 1881

5 Augustus William SAVILE-LUMLEY later SAVILE (1881), of Rufford Abbey, which he inherited from his er bro; *b* 5 Dec 1828; Assist Master Ceremonies 1881–87; *dsp* Cannes 13 April 1887

The 1st BARON's n,

JOHN SAVILE LUMLEY later SAVILE-LUMLEY (roy licence 1898), **2nd Baron Savile of Rufford**, KCVO (1904, CVO 1903), JP, DL Notts; *b* 20 Sept 1853; *educ* Eton; Attaché 1873, Attaché Brussels 1874, 2nd Sec Athens 1879, FO 1882, ret 1889, Maj Notts Imp Yeo 1891, Hon Col 4th Bn Duke of Wellington's (W R) Regt 1900; *m* 1st 3 Nov 1894 Gertrude Violet (*d* 16 Oct 1912), widow of Horace Augustus Helyar, of Coker Court, Somerset, and only dau of Charles Francis Webster-Wedderburn (*see* OGILVIE-WEDDERBURN, Bt); *m* 2nd 1 Feb 1916 Esmé Grace Virginia, JP (Notts) (*d* 18 Jan 1958), formerly *w* of Capt Claud E Levita and only dau of John Wolton, and *d* 3 April 1931, leaving:

1 GEORGE HALIFAX LUMLEY-SAVILE, **3rd and present Baron Savile**

2 +HENRY LEOLINE THORNHILL; *b* 2 Oct 1923; heir presumptive; *educ* Eton; Lt Gren Gds WW II 1942–44 (wounded); *m* 1st 1 March 1946 (*divorce* 1951) Presiley June, only dau of Maj Geoffrey Herbert Elliot Inchbald, of Halebourne House, Chobham, Surrey, and has:

(1) +John Anthony Thornhill; *b* 10 Jan 1947

2 (cont.) The Hon Henry Lumley-Savile *m* 2nd 4 Jan 1961 Caroline Jeffie (*d* 14 Oct 1970), only dau of Peter Julian Clive, of California; *m* 3rd 31 July 1972 *Margaret Ann, ARCM, dau of Edward Matthew Phillips, of Vancouver, Canada, and widow of Peter Bruce (*see* ELGIN and KINCARDINE, E), and by her has:

(2) +James George Augustus; *b* 30 April 1975

(3) +Peter Edward Henry; *b* 30 April 1975

(4) +Robin William Matthew; *b* 30 April 1975

1 *Deirdre Barbara Elland [The Hon Mrs Parrot, 5506 Grove St, Chevy Chase, MD 20815, USA]; *b* 12 Sept 1928; *m* 21 Oct 1948 Col Kent Kane Parrot, USAF (*d* 28 April 1995), only *s* of Kent Kane Parrot, of Santa Barbara, Calif., by Mrs Mary O'Hara Alsop, authoress, of Chevy Chase, and has:

(1) *Jonathan Kent [Jonathan Parrot, 483 Peregrine Dve, Indialantic, FL 32903, USA]; *b* 7 July 1950; *m* 1976 *Theresa Marie Mell

(2) *Richard Halifax [Richard Parrot, 443 North Palm Dve, Apt E, Beverly Hills, CA 90210, USA]; *b* 20 July 1952

(1) *Barbara Elland [Mrs Howard Katz, 5507 Grove St, Chevy Chase, MD 20815, USA]; *b* 7 March 1959; *m* 1982 *Howard R Katz

SAVILLE OF NEWDIGATE

Creation: B. (LP, UK) 4 July 1997.

BARON SAVILLE OF NEWDIGATE, Co Surrey (Sir Mark Oliver Saville, PC (1994) [The Rt Hon The Lord Saville of Newdigate, House of Lords, London SW1A 0PW]; *b* 20 March 1936; *educ* Rye GS and BNC Oxford; 2nd Lt Roy Sussex Regt 1954–56, barrister Middle Temple 1962, Bencher 1983, QC 1975, High Court Judge Queen's Bench 1985–93, ktd 1985, Ld Justice Appeal 1994–97, Ld Appeal in Ordinary 1997–; *m* 1961 *Jill Gray and has two sons

Lineage: KENNETH VIVIAN SAVILLE; *m* Olivia Sarah Frances Gray and had:

MARK OLIVER, *cr* a **Baron**

SAYE AND SELE

Arms: Quarterly, 1st and 4th, az. three lions rampant or (for FIENNES); 2nd and 3rd, arg. a chevron between three moles sa. (for TWISLETON). **Crests:** 1 A wolf sejant ppr., ducally gorged and chained or (for FIENNES), 2 An arm embowed and vested sa., cuff arg., the hand ppr. holding a mole-spade or, headed and armed of the second (for TWISLETON). **Supporters:** Two wolves arg., gorged and chained as the crest. **Motto:** *Fortem posce animum* ('Put forwards a stout heart'). **Creation:** B. (E) 9 Aug 1603.

THE 15TH BARON SAYE AND SELE (Nathaniel Thomas Allen TWISLETON-WYKEHAM-FIENNES later FIENNES (deed poll 1965), DL (Oxon 1979)) [The Rt Hon The Lord Saye and Sele DL, Broughton Castle, Banbury, Oxon OX15 5EB]; *b* 22 Sept 1920; *s f* 1968; *educ* Eton and New Coll Oxford; Maj Rifle Bde 1941–49 (despatches twice), Tstee Ernest Cook Tst 1960–95 (Chm Tstees 1965–92), Fell Winchester Coll 1967–83, chartered surveyor (ptnr Laws and Fiennes); *m* 4 Dec 1958 *Mariette Helena DL (1997), only dau of Maj-Gen Sir Guy Salisbury-Jones, GCVO, CMG, CBE, MC, Coldstream Gds, (*d* 1985) of Mill Down, Hambledon, Hants, by Hilda, dau of Sir Maurice de Bunsen, 1st and last Bt, GCMG, GCVO, CB, PC (*see* 1932 edn), and has had:

1 +RICHARD INGEL [The Hon Richard Fiennes, Broughton Castle, Banbury, Oxon OX15 5EB]; *b* 19 Aug 1959; *educ* St David's Coll Llandudno

2 +Martin Guy; *b* 27 Feb 1961; *m* 28 Sept 1996 *Pauline Kang Chai Lian, only dau of Kang Tiong Lam, and has:

(1) +Guy; *b* 8 March 1997

3 Thomas Nathaniel; *b* 11 Oct 1965; *d* following an accident 3 Sept 1968

4 +William John; *b* 7 Aug 1970

1 +Susannah Hersey; *b* 27 Feb 1961; writer and painter

Lineage: It has been suggested that the family derived its name from Sai, about two miles SE of Argentan in Normandy, though there is no substantial evidence for this. Certainly WILLIAM de SAY, possibly a Norman, *m* by 1098 Agnes, dau of Hugh de Grentmesnil.

But the known pedigree originates with another WILLIAM de SAY; granted his (probably dead) f's lands in a charter of the EMPRESS MAUD between Christmas 1141 and June 1142; joined his bro-in-law Geoffrey de Mandeville, 1st Earl of Essex of the 1140 *cr* (*see* ESSEX, E, preliminary remarks), in rebellion against STEPHEN 1144; *m* Beatrice (*d* 19 April in 1197 or some year before it), dau of William de Mandeville, sis of 1st Earl of Essex and divorced w of Hugh Talebot, and was allegedly *k* in an attack on Burwell Castle, Cambs, along with his bro-in-law 1st Earl of Essex Aug 1144, though he may well have *d* later, leaving:

1 William, of Kimbolton, Hunts, and Saham, Norfolk; *m* — and *dspm* just prior to 1 Aug 1177, leaving:

(1) Beatrice; *m* by 25 Jan 1184/5 Geoffrey fitz Piers, 3rd Earl of Essex (*qv*) of the Jan 1155/6 *cr*, and *d* by 19 April 1197, leaving issue

(2) Maud; *m* William de Boclande (of Buckland), half-bro of her sis's husb, and *d* just prior to 28 March 1222, having had three daus

2 Geoffrey; *b* probably by 1135; involved in financial transactions and law suits against his cousin and n by marriage Geoffrey fitz Piers to gain the lands of the Mandeville Earls of Essex; *m* 1st Alice, dau of Hugh Maminot and widow of Ralph de Cahaines; *m* 2nd Alice or Adeliza (*b* after 1163; *d* in or after 1214), dau of 1st Earl of Oxford (*see* SAINT ALBANS, D) by his 3rd w Agnes, and *d* between 1212 and 1214, having by his 1st w had, with an est s (William, *d* by 1 Jan 1198/9?) and a yst (Ingram, in Ireland with his bro Geoffrey):

(1) Geoffrey; *b c* 1155; in 1210(?) was in Ireland with KING JOHN's army, one of the barons (magnates rather than peers of Parl) opposed to JOHN and one of the 25 assigned to see that Magna Charta was observed, pilgrim to Holy Land 1219; *m* 1st Alice, dau(?) of John de Chesney and widow of Hugh de Periers; *m* 2nd in or after 1225 Margery (*divorce* 12–), sis of William Briwere and widow of (a) — de la Ferté and (b) Eudes de Dammartin (*d* 1225), and *d* in Poitou just before Aug 1230, leaving (presumably by his 1st w), (?)with a yr s (?)Geoffrey(?):

1a William; accompanied his f to France April 1230, witnessed treaty between HENRY III and ALEXANDER II (of Scotland) 1237, accompanied HENRY III to France 1242 and 1253–54 and captured seven French prisoners in a skirmish at Saintes 22 July 1242; fought for HENRY III Battle of Lewes 1264; *m* 1st Sibyl (*d* in or after Oct 1250), dau(?) of John Marshal, of Lenton; *m* 2nd, as her 1st husb, Mary — (*m* 2nd by May 1273 Robert de Ufford, ancestor of the Earls of Suffolk of the March 1336/7 *cr* (*see* SUFFOLK and BERKSHIRE, E, preliminary remarks) and *d* by 12 Feb 1271/2, leaving:

1b William; *b* 20 Nov 1253; summoned to serve against Welsh 1277, 1282 and 1283, also to an embryonic form of Parl 1283; *m* Elizabeth — and *d* by 16 Sept 1295, leaving:

1c GEOFFREY de SAY, 1st LORD (Baron) SAY (E), so *cr* by writ of summons to Parl 26 July 1313; *b* 1279 or 1281; called up for mil service against Scots 1310 and 1311; *m* Idonia/Idoine de Leyburn, dau and through her issue ultimate heir of 1st Lord (Baron) Leyburn, and *d* by 3 March 1321/2, having had:

1d GEOFFREY de SAY, 2nd LORD (Baron) SAY, JP (Kent 1357); *b c* 1305; Adml King's Fleets from mouth of Thames to western ports 1336, Capt Fleet towards the west 1337, fought at Crécy 1346, Constable Rochester Castle for life 1355; *m* Lady Maud de Beauchamp (*d* 28 July 1369), dau of 10th Earl of Warwick of the 1088 *cr* (*see* WARWICK, BROOKE and E), and *d* 26 June 1359, having had:

1e WILLIAM de SAY, 3rd LORD (Baron) SAY; *b* 17 June 1314; ktd Oct 1361; *m* Beatrice de Brewes, dau of 1st and last (no descendant of his was summoned to Parl in this so-called peerage) Lord (Baron) Breouse/Brewes/Brewose, and *d* by 7 Aug 1375, leaving:

1f JOHN de SAY, 4th LORD (Baron) SAY; *b c* 1373; *dsp* 27 July 1382

1f ELIZABETH, BARONESS SAY and BARONESS LEYBURN in her own right according to later doctrine; *b* 24 Feb 1365/6; *m* 1st between 27 July and 26 Sept 1382, as his 2nd w(?), Sir John de Falvesl (of Fawsley, Northants) (called to Parl 20 Aug 1383 as LORD (Baron) FALVESLE or LORD (Baron) SAY; *dsp* 1392 or 1393); *m* 2nd by 13 Nov 1393 Sir William Heron (called to Parl 13 Nov 1393 as LORD (Baron) HERON or LORD (Baron) SAY; Steward Household to HENRY IV; *dsp* 30 Oct 1404) and *dsp* 8 July 1399, when according to later doctrine the Baronies of Say and Leyburn fell into abeyance between the representatives of the 3rd Lord Say's sisters (*see* immediately below)

1e Idonea; *m c* 1350, as his 1st w, 3rd Lord (Baron) Clinton (*qv*) and had issue (their gs 4th Lord (Baron) Clinton styled himself Lord Say from 1399, as did his successors till the 17th century, while their gggs 6th Lord (Baron) Clinton *m* his cousin Elizabeth Fiennes, ggdau of Sir William Fiennes by his w Joan; *see* immediately below)

2e JOAN de Say; *m* Sir William FIENNES (*d* 1359), s of John de Fiennes (*d* 1351) and Maud de Monceux, and had, with an er s (*d* young):

1f William (Sir), of Herstmonceux, Sussex (the manor of which he inherited through his paternal grandmother); *b* 1 Aug 1357; Sheriff Surrey and Sussex 1396; *m* Elizabeth, dau and heir of William Batesford/Batisford, of Sussex, and *d* 18 Jan 1402/3, leaving:

1g Roger (Sir); ktd by 8 June 1422, MP Sussex, Treasurer Household 1439–46, built Herstmonceux Castle with spoils from Hundred Years War; *m* Elizabeth, sis of Sir John Holland, of Northants, and had:

1h RICHARD FIENNES (Sir), called to Parl from 9 Oct 1459 as 7th LORD (Baron) DACRE (*qv*) in right of his w; *m c* June 1446 Joan, Baroness Dacre in her own right according to later doctrine, and had issue

2g JAMES, 1st LORD

3e Elizabeth; *m* Sir Thomas de Aldoun and had:

1f Maud; *m* Thomas Besenho (predeceased his w)

2f Mary; *m* Otho de Worthyngton

2d Roger

3d Ralph

1d Katharine; *m* 3rd Lord (Baron) Saint John of Lageham

2d Juliane; *m* Sir Roger de Nothwode

3d Isabel/Elizabeth; *m* John de Chaumpaigne

Sir WILLIAM FIENNES's 2nd s,

JAMES FIENNES, 1st LORD (Baron) SAYE AND SELE (E), so *cr* by Letters Patent probably by 24 Feb (writ of summons 3 March) 1446/7, PC (1447), JP (Kent 1433); *b c* 1395; served Hundred Years War in France, where granted lordship of Court-le-Comte by HENRY V, Capt (*i.e*, govr town of) Arques and Capt-Gen towns along the Seine; built Knole, Kent, with spoils from Hundred Years War, Sheriff Kent 1436, Esq of the Body and Kt of the Body to HENRY VI by 28 Aug 1437 and 9 Oct 1444 respectively, Sheriff Surrey and Sussex 1438, MP Kent 1439–40, 1442, 1445–46 and 1447, Constable Rochester Castle March 1442–Feb 1442/3, King's Serjeant by 24 April 1443, Constable Dover Castle and Warden Cinque Ports Feb 1446/7–50, King's Chamberlain April 1447, Constable Tower Aug 1447, Treasurer England 1449–50 (removed by HENRY VI when accused by H of C of treason as scapegoat for loss of French possessions towards close of Hundred Years War; later imprisoned in Tower by HENRY VI, again as scapegoat, on rising of Jack Cade); *m* Emiline/Emmeline Cro(w)mer (*d* 5 Jan 1451/2), of Willingham, and was beheaded by a lynch mob led by Jack Cade 4 July 1450, leaving:

WILLIAM FIENNES, 2nd LORD (Baron) SAYE AND SELE, PC (March 1453/4), JP (Kent 1461 and Hants Jan 1463/4); *b c* 1428; Kt of the Body by 18 Dec 1450, Constable Porchester Castle 1461–71, Keeper New Forest 1461–Feb 1466/7, fought winning Yorkist side Battle of Northampton 1460, V-Adml to the 'Kingmaker' Earl of Warwick (*see* ABERGAVENNY, M) when latter High Adml of England 1462, fled with EDWARD IV to Flanders 1470 and returned with EDWARD 1471, shortly after which he was *k* Battle of Barnet (Yorkist victory) 14 April 1471; *m* as her 1st husb Margaret (*m* 2nd John Hervey and *d* just prior to 30 May 1477), dau and heir of William Wykeham *alias* Perrott, of Broughton Castle (which thus came to the FIENNESes), s and heir of Sir Thomas Wykeham *alias* Parrott, 3rd s of William Parott by Alice, dau of William Champneys by Agnes, sis of William of Wykeham, Bp Winchester and fndr Winchester Coll and New Coll Oxford, and had, with an er s (Richard, *d* young):

HENRY FIENNES, *de jure* 3rd LORD (Baron) SAYE AND SELE; *b c* 1460; never called to Parl; *m* Anne, dau of Sir Richard Harcourt (*see* VERNON, B) by his 1st w, and *dvm* 1 Aug 1476, leaving an only s:

RICHARD FIENNES, *de jure* 4th LORD (Baron) SAYE AND SELE; *b* 1471; never called to Parl; *m* as her 1st husb Elizabeth (*m* 2nd William/Richard West and *d* 29 March 1527), dau of Richard Croft, of Chaffing (*i.e.*, Chipping) Norton, Oxon, and *d* 30 Sept/1 Oct 1501, leaving an only s:

EDWARD FIENNES, *de jure* 5th LORD (Baron) SAYE AND SELE; *b c* 1500; never called to Parl and seems not even to have continued use of the title after coming of age; *m c* 1518, as her 1st husb, Margaret (*m* 2nd by 1539, as his 3rd w of three, Sir Thomas Nevill, of Holt, Leics, and *d* in or after 1541), dau of Sir John Danvers, of Dauntsey, Wilts, and *d* 7 March 1527/8, leaving an only s:

Sir RICHARD FIENNES, *de jure* 6th LORD (Baron) SAYE AND SELE, JP (Oxon 1545 and 1547); *b c* 1520; never called to Parl and did not use title, Sheriff Oxon 1550 and 1557 and Bucks 1550 and 1558, ktd between 1567 and 1569; *m* Ursula, dau of Richard Fermor (*see* HESKETH, B), and *d* 3 Aug 1573, leaving an only s:

Sir RICHARD FIENNES, *de jure* 7th LORD (Baron) SAYE AND SELE of the Feb 1446/7 *cr*, a title he had for some time claimed, winning recognition from JAMES I but with in effect a new creation 9 Aug 1603 as **1st Baron Saye and Sele** (E) by letters patent, though with remainder to heirs general (*i.e.*, so as to include females and their issue), whereas the 1446/7 one had been almost certainly with remainder to heirs male only; *b c* 1557; *educ* Winchester; ktd 1592–93, Sheriff Oxon 1594, envoy with his cousin 2nd Earl of Lincoln of the 1572 *cr* (*qv*) to Landgrave of Hesse 1596; Keeper Banbury Castle Oct 1603; envoy in suite of 1st Earl of Hertford of the Jan 1558/9 *cr* (*see* SOMERSET, D), Amb to Archduke Albert of Austria at Brussels April-May 1605; *m* 1st *c* 1581 Constance (*d* in or after April 1587), dau of Sir William Kingsmill, of Sydmonton, Hants; *m* 2nd Elizabeth (*dsp* by 1632), dau and coheir of Henry Codingham and widow of William Paulet, of Ewalden, Somerset, and *d* just prior to 6 Feb 1612/3, leaving by his 1st w, with a dau (*m* Sir William Villiers, 1st Bt; *see* JERSEY, E) an only s:

WILLIAM ('Old Subtlety') FIENNES, **2nd Baron Saye and Sele** and 8th LORD (Baron) SAYE AND SELE of the Feb 1446/7 *cr*, also 1st VISCOUNT OF SAYE AND OF SELE (E), so *cr* 7 July 1624 (allegedly at the prompting of the 1st Duke of Buckingham (*see* JERSEY, E), his sister's cousin-in-law, in an attempt to retrieve his (Buckingham's) popularity outside Court circles), PC (Feb 1640/1 and again 1660); *b* 28 May 1582; *educ* Winchester and New Coll Oxford (Fell 1600); ktd *vp*;

able memb of the anti-Court faction in JAMES I's last years and throughout much of CHARLES I's reign, chiefly in expressing opposition to the irregular means of raising money those Kings employed, and doing so by among other means the peers' right of protest, a long-standing privilege he is credited with putting to contemporary use; involved in colonisation schemes in New World, including Caribbean, an area in what is now New Hampshire and another one on the Connecticut River whose principal settlement was called in his honour Say(e)brook (subsequently Seabrook); apptd by CHARLES I Master Court of Wards 1641–42 and a Ld of Treasury 1641–42 in an attempt to propitiate him, High Steward Oxford U 1641–43 and (Parly appointment) 1646–60; Ld Lt Cheshire, Oxon and Glos 1642 (Parly appointment), Col Parly foot regt 1642 and temporarily took Oxford though his own house of Broughton was captured by the Royalists after Edgehill (1642); Parly Commr to negotiate with CHARLES I March 1643, Memb: Ctee Safety of Kingdom by 16 Feb 1642/3, Westminster Assembly of Divines June 1643, Ctee Both Kingdoms Feb 1643/4, Ctee for Plantations 1660 and Ctee to settle govt of New England 1661; leading spirit in passing Self-Denying Ordinance 1645, Parly Commr to negotiate with Scots 1646 and CHARLES I (Treaty of Newport) 1648; *m c* 1602 Elizabeth (*d* 1648), dau of John Temple (*see* TEMPLE OF STOWE, E), and *d* 14 April 1662, having had, with five daus:

1 JAMES FIENNES, **3rd Baron Saye and Sele**, 9th LORD (Baron) SAYE AND SELE and 2nd VISCOUNT OF SAYE AND OF SELE; *b c* 1603; *educ* Queens' and Emmanuel Colls Cambridge and Lincoln's Inn; MP Banbury 1625 and Oxon 1626, 1628–29, March–May 1640, Oct 1640–Dec 1648 and 1660, Ld Lt Oxon Feb 1667/8–March 1673/4, Freeman City of Oxford 1668; *m* by 1631, as her 1st husb, Frances Cecil (*m* 2nd 1675 Rev Joshua Sprigge, MA, and *d* July 1684), dau and coheir of 1st and last Viscount Wimbledon (*see* EXETER, M), and *dspms* 15 March 1673/4, when the Barony of the 1603 *cr* fell into abeyance between his three surv daus, while the Barony of Feb 1446/7, together with the Viscountcy, passed to his nephew (*see* below), having had:

(1) James; *d* in infancy

(2) William; *d* in infancy

(3) William; drowned in the Seine while on a visit to France unm and under age

(1) ELIZABETH Fiennes; *b c* 1631; *m c* May 1649, as his 3rd w of four, Col Sir John TWIS(T)LETON (*d* 4 Dec 1682), 1st and last Bt (CROMWELL *cr* of 10 April 1658; forfeited at Restoration 1660), Kent Militia, of Horsman's Place, Dartford, Kent, and Barley (later Barlow) Hall, nr Selby, Yorks, and *d* 28 March 1674, leaving:

1a CECIL TWIS(T)LETON, *de jure* BARONESS SAYE AND SELE on the death of her cousin Frances (*see* below), whereby the abeyance in the Barony of the 1603 *cr* was naturally terminated inasmuch as there remained only one heir rather than two or more coheirs, though she (Cecil) did not assume the title; *m* 1st *c* 1669 George TWIS(T)LETON (*b* 6 Dec 1652(?)), of Wodhall, Wormsley, Yorks, s(?) of Lt-Col George Twis(t)leton, of the Parly Army in the Civil War and sometime Govr Denbigh Castle; *m* 2nd Robert Mignon and *d* 1723, leaving by her 1st husb:

1b FIENNES TWIS(T)LETON, *de jure* 5th BARON SAYE AND SELE, *b c* 1670; Ensign 9th Foot 1688, Capt 1695, Col and Adj-Gen Army in America March 1710/1, also serving Flanders, Ireland and Spain; *m* 1692 Mary Clarke, of an Irish family, and *d* 4 Sept 1730, leaving an only s:

1c JOHN TWIS(T)LETON, *de jure* 6th BARON SAYE AND SELE; *bapt* 16 Jan 1697/8; petitioned unsuccessfully for recognition as holder of the peerage; *m* 30 Dec 1733 Anne (*d* 14 Jan 1769), dau of William Gardner, of Little Bourton, Oxon, and *d* 1763, having had:

1d John; *b c* 1734; Lt-Col Coldstream Gds; *ka vp* and unm Battle of Brückmühle, nr Cassel, Germany, in Seven Years War 21 Sept 1762

2d THOMAS, **7th Baron**

3d Francis TWIS(T)LETON later THOMPSON (took w's name 1758); *b* 1736; Capt 3rd Regt Foot Gds 1758; *m* Elizabeth Thompson, of Hull, and *d* 1793

2a Frances; *m* Andrew Ellis, of Alrey, Flintshire, and had:

1b Cecill/Cicely; *m* 1st 13 March 1672/3 Sir Richard Langley (*d* 8 Feb 1677/8); *m* 2nd her cousin William Fiennes (*see* below) and *dsp* 22 July 1715

2 Nathaniel; *b c* 1608; *educ* Winchester and New Coll Oxford (perpetual Fell 1624 as fndr's kin); MP Banbury 'Short' (April–May 1640) and 'Long' (1640–60) Parls (though excluded from H of C in 'Pride's Purge' Dec 1648, but MP again for Oxon 1654 and Oxford U 1656), anti-episcopalian, Memb (Parly) Ctee of Safety 1642 and 1648, fought for Parl at Battle of Edgehill (draw, 1642), held Bristol for Parl till 26 July 1643 (Govr Bristol from 1 May 1643), Memb: Ctee of Army 1647 and OLIVER CROMWELL's Cncl of State 1654, Jt Keeper Gt Seal 1655 (Ch Commr 1658 and 1659), one of those who urged CROMWELL to accept the crown, Memb CROMWELL's 'Upper House' 1657; *m* 1st 11 Aug 1636 Elizabeth (*b* 1616), dau of Sir John Eliot (*see* ST GERMANS, E), and *d* 16 Dec 1669, leaving, with at least one dau (to whom admon was granted following the death of the 3rd VISCOUNT):

(1) Nathaniel; *dsp*

(2) WILLIAM FIENNES, 10th LORD (Baron) SAYE AND SELE and 3rd VISCOUNT OF SAYE AND OF SELE; *b c* 1641; Freeman City of Oxford Feb 1685/6; *m* 1st *c* April 1674 his cousin Mary (*b c* 1653; *d* in childbirth 23 Oct 1676), dau of Richard Fiennes by his 1st w; *m* 2nd 7 Sept 1685 Catherine (*dsp*), dau of Edward Walker, of Banbury, and *d* an imbecile 9 Dec 1698, leaving by his 1st w:

1a NATHANIEL FIENNES, 11th LORD (Baron) SAYE AND SELE and 4th VISCOUNT OF SAYE AND OF SELE; *b* 23 Oct 1676; *educ* Winchester and New Coll Oxford; sat as Whig in Ho of Lds; *d* unm 2 Jan 1709/10

2 (cont.) Nathaniel Fiennes *m* 2nd Frances (*b c* 1621; *d* 17 Oct 1691), dau of Richard Whitehead, of Tuderley, Hants, and *d* 16 Dec 1669, having had by her three daus

3 John; Col Parly regt of horse 1643, fought Naseby 1645, MP Morpeth 1645, Memb CROMWELL's Ho of Lds 1657; *m* Susannah (*b c* 1657; *d* 22 July 1715), dau and heiress of Thomas Hobbs, of Great Amwell, Herts, and had an only surv s:

(1) William; *m* as her 2nd husb his cousin Cecill/Cicely

(2) LAWRENCE FIENNES, 12th LORD (Baron) SAYE AND SELE and 5th VISCOUNT OF SAYE AND OF SELE; *d* unm 27 Dec 1742

4 Richard, of Ixworth, Suffolk; *m* 1st Margaret, dau and heir of Andrew Burrell, of Isle of Ely, and had, with four other daus:

(1) Pharamus; *dsp*

(2) William; *dsp*

(1) Mary; *m* her cousin 3rd VISCOUNT OF SAYE AND OF SELE (*see* above)

4 (cont.) Richard Fiennes *m* 2nd Susanna, dau of William Cobb, of Adderbury, Oxon, and *d c* 1674, having by her had, with four daus, an only surv s:

(3) Richard (Rev); *b c* 1674; MA, Fell: New Coll Oxford 1693–1704 and Winchester Coll 1713, Rector Akeley, Bucks, 1704; *m* 30 Oct 1705 Penelope, dau of George Chamberlayne, of Wardington, Oxon, and *d* 1722, leaving:

1a RICHARD FIENNES, 13th and last LORD (Baron) SAYE AND SELE and 6th and last VISCOUNT OF SAYE AND OF SELE; *bapt* 8 July 1716; *educ* Winchester and New Coll Oxford (Fell 1737–43, BCL 1743, DCL 1756); *m* 13 Nov 1753 Christobella (*d* 23 July 1789), dau and coheir of Sir Thomas Tyrrell, 2nd and last Bt, and widow of (a) John Knapp, of Cumnor, Berks, and (b) John Pigott, of Doddershall, Bucks, and *dsp* 29 July 1781, when the Viscountcy and Barony of the Feb 1446/7 expired, as also it seems the FIENNESes in the male line

The 6th and last VISCOUNT's 2nd cousin three-times removed,

THOMAS TWISLE(T)ON, **7th Baron Saye and Sele** *de jure* from his f's death in 1763 and *de facto* from 29 June 1781, when his claim to the 1603 *cr* was allowed; *b c* 1735; Ensign Scots Gds 1754, Lt and Capt 1758, also saw action at Brückmühle (*see* above against his er bro), Col 1777, Col 9th Foot June 1782–88, Maj-Gen Nov 1782; *m* 14 Dec 1767 Elizabeth (*bapt* 19 Feb 1740/1; *d* 1 April 1816), est dau of Sir Edward Turner, 2nd Bt, of Ambrosden, Oxon (*see* DRYDEN, Bt), and *d* by his own hand 1 July 1788, having had:

1 GREGORY WILLIAM TWIS(T)LETON later TWIS(T)LETON-FIENNES (roy licence 14 Feb 1825) and very little later still EARDLEY-TWIS(T)LETON-FIENNES (roy licence 16 March 1825), **8th Baron Saye and Sele**; *b* 14 April 1769; Ensign Coldstream Gds 1765, Lt 1790, ret 1794; *m* 8 Sept 1794 Hon Maria Marow(e) Eardley formerly Gideon (*b* 22 Nov 1767; *d* 5 Oct 1834), est dau and coheir of 1st and last Baron Eardley of Spalding by Maria, dau of Sir John Eardley Wilmot, Ld Ch Justice Common Pleas (*see* EARDLEY-WILMOT, Bt), and *d* 13 Nov 1844, having had:

(1) WILLIAM THOMAS TWIS(T)LETON later EARDLEY-TWIS(T)LETON-FIENNES, **9th Baron Saye and Sele**; *b* 24 April 1798; *educ* Eton; Provincial Grand Master Masons Kent 1829–47; *d* unm 31 March 1847

(1) Maria Elizabeth; *m* 31 Aug 1825 George Ernest, Count von Gersdorff, Chamberlain to King of Prussia; *dsp, bur* 15 Aug 1826

2 Thomas James (Ven); *b* 28 Sept 1770; DD, Vicar Blakesley, Northants, Archdeacon Colombo; *m* 1st 4 Nov 1788 (separated by deed 17 June 1794, *divorce* 26 May 1798) Charlotte Ann Frances (actress after her separation; had issue by John Stein, with whom she lived after her separation, one Charles Twis(t)leton, *b* 5 Jan or 30 March 1797, who claimed the Barony but had his claim rejected by the Ho Lds Ctee of Privileges on grounds that he was Stein's s), dau of John(?) Wattel(l), and had, with four er sons (*d* young):

(1) Charles

(1) Julia Eliza; *m* 18 April 1808 Capt James Brown (*d* 17 Nov 1810) and *d* 28 March 1832, leaving an only s

2 (cont.) Dr Thomas Twis(t)leton *m* 2nd 17 June 1798 Anne or Anna, dau and coheir of Benjamin Ash(e), of Bath, and *d* 15 Aug 1824, having by her had, with other issue (*d* young), including five er sons:

(1) FREDERICK, **10th Baron**

(2) Charles Samuel (Rev); *b* 4 July 1806; granted with his siblings rank of baron's dau/yr s; MA, Rector Ashow, Warwicks; *m* 1st 26 Sept 1837 Caroline (*d* 20 Sept 1873), est dau of Ralph Carr, of Tannington, Northumberland; *m* 2nd 24 Jan 1878 Dorothea Susan (*d* 21 Nov 1933), yst and only surv dau of Hon John Thicknesse Touchet (*see* 1970 edn AUDLEY, B), and *dsp* 13 Sept 1890

(3) Edward Turner Boyd; *b* 24 May 1809; Ch Commr: Poor Laws Ireland, Improvement of Oxford U, public schs and Civ Serv examination; *m* 19 May 1852 Ellen (*d* 17 May 1862), dau of Hon Edward Dwight, JP Massachusetts, and *dsp* 5 Oct 1874

(1) Mary Elizabeth; *m* 1st 6 Dec 1818 William Gisborne (*d* 1 Jan 1839) and had issue; *m* 2nd Capt R Twynham and *d* 17 Dec 1873

1 Julia Judith; *m* 8 Dec 1786 James Henry Leigh, of Adlestrop House, Glos, and Stoneleigh Abbey, Warwicks, and *d* 8 Feb 1843, leaving issue (*see* LEIGH, B)

2 Mary Cassandra; *b* 11 June 1774; *m* 1st 29 Jan 1790 (*divorce* 1799) 2nd Viscount St Vincent (*qv*); *m* 2nd 30 Jan 1806 Richard Charles Head Graves and *d* June 1843

The 9th BARON's 1st cousin,

FREDERICK BENJAMIN TWIS(T)LETON later TWIS(T)LETON-WYKEHAM-FIENNES (roy licence 14 Feb 1849), **10th Baron Saye and Sele**; *b* 4 July 1799; *educ* Winchester (Fell 1817–26) and New Coll Oxford (BCL 1825, DCL 1832); ordained 1823, Rector Broadwell and Adlestrop, Glos, 1825–52, Preb Hereford 1825, Treasurer 1832 and Canon Residentiary 1840 Hereford Cathedral, High Steward Banbury 1849; *m* 1st 4 June 1827 Hon Emily Wingfield, dau of 4th Viscount Powerscourt (*qv*), and had issue; *m* 2nd 18 Aug 1857 Hon Caroline Leigh (*d* 21 July 1909), 3rd dau of 1st Baron Leigh (*qv*) of Stoneleigh, and *d* 26 May 1887, having had by his 1st w:

1 JOHN, **11th Baron**

2 Cecil Brownlow (Rev); *b* 20 Aug 1831; MA, Rector Hamstall Ridware, Staffs, and Ashow, Warwicks; granted with his siblings rank of baron's dau/yr s; *m* Paris 17 Dec 1861 Maria Louisa (*d* 30 Jan 1871), est dau of John Hardy, Br Consul St Jago de Cuba, and *d* 30 March 1870, leaving:

(1) Henry Edward; *b* 3 March 1866; Capt 9th Lancers, Maj Roy E Kent Yeo; *d* 12 Oct 1932

(2) Cecil John; *b* 8 Sept 1867; Cdr RN; *d* unm 22 Dec 1899

(1) Emily Cecilia; *b* 24 Sept 1862; *d* unm 9 Nov 1934

3 Ivo de Vesci Edward, CB; *b* 16 Jan 1833; Lt-Col 9th Lancers; *m* 26 July 1864 Isabella Emily (*m* 2nd 20 Aug 1902 Eugene Stock (*d* 7 Sept 1928); *d* 22 Dec 1930), only dau of Charles Francis Gregg, and *d* 23 Nov 1875, leaving:

(1) Bertram Ralph Ivo; *b* 20 June 1865; Lt 1st Bn S Staffs Regt; *d* unm 9 July 1886

(2) Nathaniel Ivo Edward, DSO (1917); *b* posthumously 28 March 1876; *educ* Pembroke Coll Oxford; Maj RA WW I Mesopotamia and Palestine (despatches) and Mesopotamia (Arab Rebellion) 1920 (wounded); *m* 31 Oct 1901 Elizabeth (*d* 5 Dec 1968 aged 90), dau of Col Frederick Jacob Ponsonby Hill, Roy Scots, and *d* 29 Nov 1963, having had:

1a Geoffrey Ivo Frederick (Rev); *b* 1 Jan 1906; *educ* Winchester and Trin Coll Oxford (BA 1927, MA 1931); missionary Centl Africa 1932–64, Canon Emeritus Lusaka, Warden St Mark's Coll Mapanza, Zambia; *d* 1981

1a Idonea Cicely de Vesci; *b* 31 Aug 1902; *d* 29 Jan 1912

2a Elizabeth Margaret; *b* 16 Feb 1916; SRN; *m* 22 June 1950 John Ley Greaves, MD, MRCP, and *d* 198–, leaving:

1b +Francis Fiennes Ley; *b* 5 June 1952; *educ* Repton

2b +Peter Fiennes Ley; *b* 5 Oct 1955; *educ* Repton

1b +Elizabeth Anne Fiennes; *b* 10 April 1951; *m* 1974 *Timothy Somerset Charrington

2b +Jane Katherine Fiennes; *b* 5 Oct 1955

(1) Dorothy Margaret Isobel; *b* 8 July 1868; *m* 15 Oct 1893 Most Rev John Charles Wright, DD, Archbp Sydney (*d* 24 Feb 1933, s of Rev J Farrall Wright, Vicar Ch Ch Bolton, and *d* 14 Nov 1961, leaving issue

(2) Eva Caroline; *b* 1 July 1873; missionary SPG; *d* unm 18 March 1963

4 Wingfield Stratford (Rev); *b* 1 May 1834; MA, Fell New Coll Oxford, Rector Milton Keynes, Bucks; *m* 6 Oct 1863 Alice Susan (*d* 17 Feb 1922), 2nd dau of Very Rev Hon Grantham Munton Yorke (*see* HARDWICKE, E), and *d* 1923, having had:

(1) Gerard Yorke, CBE (1920); *b* 18 July 1864; *educ* New Coll Oxford (BA); *m* 28 June 1905 Gwendolen (*d* 20 Jan 1968 aged 92), dau of Francis Gisborne, of Holme Hall, Bakewell, Derbys, and *d* 13 Jan 1926, leaving:

1a Gerard Francis Gisborne, OBE (1957); *b* 7 June 1906; *educ* Winchester and Hertford Coll Oxford (BA 1929, MA); FRSA, MInstT, dir Hargreaves Gp, broadcaster, OStJ, author: *I Tried to Run a Railway*; *m* 1st 22 Dec 1934 Norah (*d* 24 Dec 1960), est dau of Thomas Davies, of Llangollen, and had:

1b +Jeremy [Jeremy Twisleton-Wykeham-Fiennes Esq, 36 Montpelier Grove, London NW5 2XE]; *b* 9 March 1937; *educ* Winchester and Clare Coll Cambridge; *m* 1st 1962 (*divorce* 19–) Else Brekke, dau of Niels Larsen, of Denmark; *m* 2nd — and by his 1st w has:

1c +Sine; *b* 1962

2c +Nicole Juana; *b* 1968

2b +Michael Wynn [Michael Twisleton-Wykeham-Fiennes Esq, Burcott Manor, nr Wells, Somerset BA5 1NH]; *b* 8 Sept 1941; *educ* Winchester, New Coll Oxford (MA 1968) and Harvard (MBA 1968); *m* 8 July 1966 *Rosalie Ruth, dau of Stanley Sheppard, of Street, Somerset, and has:

1c +Rupert Yorke; *b* 20 March 1969

2c +Hugo Barnabas; *b* 31 March 1971

3c +Joshua Gisborne; *b* 9 May 1974

4c +Ivo Martindale; *b* 21 Sept 1978

3b +Gerard Ivor; *b* 19 Feb 1946; *educ* Winchester and Hertford Coll Oxford; *m* 1973 *Jane, dau of Neil Digney, of Wimbledon, and has:

1c +David Gerard; *b* 1982

1c +Clare Elizabeth; *b* 1976

1b +Joslin Mary [Mrs Pierre Landells-Mills, 2954 Macomb St, NW Washington, DC 20008, USA]; *b* 11 May 1939; *educ* Newnham Coll Cambridge; *m* 1964 *Pierre Landell-Mills, s of Thomas Landell-Mills, of Devon, and has:

1c +Julius Paul; *b* July 1965

2c +Nicholas Vladimir; *b* 19 Dec 1967

1c +Natalia Norah; *b* 1972

2b +Bronwen Margaret [Mrs Oliver Addis, 389 Bobbin Head Rd, N Turramurra, NSW 2074, Australia]; *b* 7 July 1944; *m* 1967 *Oliver Addis, yr s of Robert Addis, of The Old Rectory, Hertingfordbury, Herts, and has:

1c +Thomas Oliver; *b* 1 March 1970

1c +Helen Mary; *b* 16 Feb 1968

2c +Harriet Jane; *b* 10 March 1972

3c +Sarah Elizabeth Ruth; *b* 22 May 1975

1a (cont.) Gerard Twisleton-Wykeham-Fiennes *m* 2nd 15 Dec 1962 *Jean [Mrs Gerard Twisleton-Wykeham-Fiennes, 29 Wentworth Rd, Aldeburgh, Suffolk], dau of James Valentine, of Essex, and formerly w of — Kerridge, and *d* 1985

2a Richard Nathaniel; *b* 26 Nov 1909; *educ* Winchester and Magdalene Coll Cambridge (BA 1935, MA 1953); MRCVS, Sr Lecturer Dept of Ag U of Gold Coast 1954; *m* 1st 15 Oct 1941 (*divorce* 1948) Mary Morwenna Daphne, only dau of Rev James Rashleigh Hale; *m* 2nd 19 Aug 1948 Alice Isobel (*d* 1986), dau of William Cowie, of Singapore, and formerly w of Robert Tremlett, of Mbale, Uganda, and *d* 1988, leaving by her:

1b +(Richard) George; *b* 17 July 1950; *educ* Winchester and Coll of Estate Mangement (BSc); ARICS; *m* 1974 *Julia, only dau of Raymond Humphrey, of Winchester, and has:

1c +Felix George; *b* 23 June 1978

1c +Eleanor Florence; *b* 1 June 1983

2c +Isobel Joanna; 1986

3c +Arabella Julia; *b* 1988

1b +Frances Elizabeth, JP [Mrs Michael Beatty JP, Tixall Farmhouse, Tixall, Staffs ST18 0XT]; *b* 1947; *educ* St Paul's and York U (BA); *m* 13 Dec 1969 *Col Michael P K Beatty, CBE, TD, DL (Staffs 1980), High Sheriff Staffs 1994–95, late Roy Mercian and Lancastrian Yeo, er s of Dr G K Beatty, and has:

1c +Geraldine Alice Martindale; *b* 30 Dec 1971; *educ* Abbots Bromley; *m* 1997 *Andrew Swinton, s of Rex Swinton, of Sydney, NSW

2c +Rosanna Mary Gisborne; *b* 17 March 1973; *educ* Millfield and Durham U (BA)

3c +Katherine Margaret Barrett; *b* 1980; *educ* Millfield

4c +Caroline Diana Charlotte; *b* 1986

3a John Saye Wingfield (Sir), KCB (1970, CB 1953), QC (1972); *b* 14 April 1911; *educ* Winchester and Balliol Coll Oxford (BA 1934); barrister Middle Temple 1936, Bencher 1969, Assist Parly Counsel Treasury 1939, Parly Counsel 1946, 2nd Parly Counsel 1956–68, 1st Parly Counsel 1968–72, Parly Counsel Malaya under Colombo Plan 1962–63, Hon Johan Mangku Negara (Malaysia 1963); *m* 1 Sept 1937 Sylvia Beatrice (*d* 1979), dau of Rev C R McDowall (*see* BURDETT, Bt), and *d* 21 April 1996, leaving:

1b +Nicholas John [Nicholas Twisleton-Wykeham-Fiennes Esq, 21 Chalfont Rd, Oxford OX2 6TL]; *b* 25 July 1940; *educ* Winchester and Merton Coll Oxford; *m* 1st 5 April 1969 (*divorce* 1990) Vicki Karen, dau of W A Thomas, of Stourbridge, Worcs, and has:

1c +Alexander William; *b* 22 May 1971

2c +John Edward; *b* 15 Feb 1973

1c +Katherine Margaret; *b* 2 Oct 1974

1b (cont.) Nicholas Twisleton-Wykeham-Fiennes *m* 2nd 24 Sept 1993 *Angela Helen, only dau of Rev Geoffrey Ellison, of Withington, Glos

2b +William Gerard [William Twisleton-Wykeham-Fiennes, April Cottage, Main St, Clanfield, Oxon OX18 2QH]; *b* 24 Jan 1946; *educ* Winchester, New Coll Oxford and Imp Coll London; *m* 29 Dec 1976 *Rosalind Dalzel, est dau of W D Pritchard, of Alderton, Glos, and has:

1c +Timothy Gerard; *b* 1985

1c +Lucy Anne; *b* 13 May 1981

1b +Judith Mary [Miss Judith Twisleton-Wykeham-Fiennes, 5 Parliament Court, Parliament Hill, London NW3 2TS]; *b* 6 June 1938; *educ* St Andrews

4a Michael Yorke; *b* 1 July 1912; *educ* Winchester and New Coll Oxford (BA); Capt RA (Indian Field Battery) WW II 1940–43, Co dir; *m* 16 Feb 1957 *Jacqueline [Mrs Michael Twisleton-Wykeham-Fiennes, Woodcote, 25 Oaks Rd, Tenterden, Kent TN30 6RD], 2nd dau of Rev Edward Montmorency Guilford, of Herstmonceux, Sussex, and *d* 1989, leaving:

1b +Toby Jonathan [Toby Fiennes Esq, 18 Shrublands Rd, Berkhamsted, Herts HP4 3HY]; *b* 25 March 1961; *m* 1989 *Hilary Linda, er dau of D T McGladdery, of Newton Abbot, Devon, and has:

1c +Thomas Michael; *b* 12 July 1995

1c +Emily Leonora; *b* 12 July 1995

2c +Caroline Leandra; *b* 12 July 1995

2b +Peter Guilford [Peter Fiennes Esq, 9 Hillier Rd, London SW11 6AX]; *b* 24 Jan 1963; *m* 1993 *Anna, only dau of Martin Graham, of Highgate, and has:

1c +Alexander Dylan; *b* 4 Jan 1995

1c +Natalie Geraldine; *b* 5 May 1991

5a David Eustace Martindale, CBE (1964); *b* 7 March 1916; *educ* Winchester and New Coll Oxford (BA 1937, MA 1964); FRSA, MBIM, Lt Malayan RNVR (wounded) WW II; *d* unm 198–

(2) Alberic Arthur; *b* 4 Sept 1865; *m* 9 Oct 1895 Gertrude Theodosia (*d* 12 Nov 1934), yst dau of Henry Fitz George Colley (*see* HARBERTON, V), and *d* 28 Sept 1919, leaving:

1a Maurice Alberic (Sir); *b* 1 March 1907; *educ* Repton and Armstrong Coll Newcastle; MIMechE, CEng, gen works dir Brush Electrical Engineering 1942, md: Davy and United Engrg 1945 and Davy-Ashmore 1960 (and chm 1961–69); *m* 1st 2 June 1932 (*divorce* 1964) Sylvia Joan (*d* 11 April 1996), dau of Maj David Finlay, 7th Dragoon Gds, and had:

1b +Mark [Mark Fiennes Esq, 29 Therapia Rd, London SE22 0SF]; *b* 11 Nov 1933; *educ* Eton; *m* 14 April 1962 Jennifer Anne Mary Alleyne (*d* 1993), dau of Brig Henry Alleyne Lash, IA, and has:

1c +Ralph Nathaniel [Ralph Fiennes, c/o Larry Dalzell Assocs, 91 Regent St, London W1R 7TB]; *b* 22 Dec 1962; *educ* St Kieran's Coll Kilkenny, Bp Wordsworth Sch Salisbury, Chelsea Sch of Art and RADA; actor: roles include title role in *Romeo and Juliet*, Lysander *A Midsummer Night's Dream* (both Open Air Theatre 1986), title role in *Henry VI* and *Troilus and Cressida* (RSC 1988–91), films: *A Dangerous Man* (played T E Lawrence), *Wuthering Heights* (Heathcliff), *Strange Days*, *The Quiz Show*, *The English Patient*, *Oscar and Lucinda* and *The Avengers*; *m* 1993 (*divorce* 28 Oct 1997) Alex(andra) Elizabeth, actress, dau of Anthony Kingston, of Betchworth, Surrey

2c +Magnus Hubert; *b* 21 Nov 1965; composer

3c +Jacob (Jake) Mark; *b* 1970; gamekeeper on the Raveningham Hall estate of Sir Nicholas Bacon, Bt (*qv*)

4c +Joseph Alberic; *b* 1970 (twin); actor

1c +Martha Maria; *b* 5 Feb 1964; film dir

2c +Sophia Victoria; *b* 12 Feb 1967; photographer

2b +Alberic George; *b* 26 July 1947; *educ* Lyceum Alpinum Zuoz, Switzerland; MS, FRCS; *m* 1985 *Louise Emily Jane, est dau of Gordon Bidlake, of Dorking, and has:

1c +Emily Elizabeth; *b* 29 Aug 1989

2c +Alice Henrietta; *b* 1991

1b +Elizabeth; *b* 28 May 1935; *m* 24 March 1965 Lt-Col Richard James Heslop Randall, Queen's Roy Irish Hus (*d* 1984), s of Maj Basil Fitzherbert Randall, Skinner's Horse, and has:

1c +William Basil; *b* 12 April 1966

2c +Matthew Michael Shaun; *b* 4 Jan 1968

2b +(Antonia Susan) Maria; *b* 5 June 1939 *m* 15 May 1970 (*divorce* 1989) John Houlton Ewing Mocatta, er s of Frederick Noel Mocatta, of Dalby, Qld, Australia

3b +Henrietta Celia [Mrs Stephen Molivadas, 4701 Willard Ave, Suite 703, Chevy Chase, MD 20815, USA]; *b* 20 Feb 1943; *m* 1987 *Stephen Molivadas, DFC, s of Constantine Molivadas, of Corfu

1a (cont.) Sir Maurice *m* 2nd 16 Oct 1967 *Erika Hueller, dau of Dr Herbert Hueller von Huellenried, of Vienna, and *d* 14 Sept 1994

1a Winifred Joan; *b* 13 Aug 1897; *m* 15 Nov 1928 Capt Maurice Charles Prendergast Vereker, MC, and had issue (*see* GORT, V)

2a Audrey Gertrude; *b* 26 March 1899; *d* 6 Aug 1995

3a +Celia Mary [Mrs Noel Rooke, The Green, Culworth, Banbury, Oxon]; *b* 10 March 1902; *m* 31 Dec 1932 Noel Rooke (*d* 5 Oct 1953), only s of Thomas Matthews Rooke, of Chiswick

(3) Caryl Wentworth, JP Co Dublin; *b* 29 May 1869; Maj ROAC WW I, Dep Assist Dir Ordnance Servs 47th Div (TA) 1919–26; *m* 27 Jan 1897 Kathleen Isabella (*d* 1 April 1961), dau of James Staple Hawkins, JP, of St Fentons, Baldoyle, Co Dublin, and *d* 9 May 1948, leaving:

1a Cecil Wingfield; *b* 24 Nov 1897; *educ* Marlborough; Maj RM, WW I (despatches) and WW II; *m* 1st 14 Dec 1920 Margaret Annie (*d* July 1921), yst dau of Philip Robinson, of Eggington, Derbys; *m* 2nd 20 Dec 1923 (*divorce* 1936) Jessie Mary Goddard, dau of Nicholas Goddard Jackson, of Duddington, and by her had:

1b Anthony Patrick; *b* 5 July 1927; *educ* Stowe; with Australian Broadcasting Commn; *m* 24 Feb 1966 *Prudence Jane [Mrs Anthony Twisleton-Wykeham-Fiennes, Manor Farm, Duddington, Lincs], est dau of G W Pearce, of Perth, W Australia, and *d* 1989, leaving:

1c +Nicholas Mark; *b* 2 Oct 1969

2c +Nathaniel Woodward; *b* 24 June 1973

1b +(Kathleen) Patricia [Mrs Richard Shedden, Bowers Barn, Iwerne Minster, Dorset DT11 8LE]; *b* 20 Nov 1925; *m* 4 July 1959 Richard Graham Shedden, MC (*d* 4 Feb 1997), yr s of Capt Lindesay Harry Compton Shedden, of Somerby, Melton Mowbray, and has:

1c +Simon Rory Lindesay; *b* 6 Jan 1963; *m* 19– (*divorce*) Juliet, dau of J C Lawley, of Foreward Green, Stowmarket, London and Africa

1c +Emma Lavinia, of Domaine de l'Orangerie, Antibes, France; *b* 18 Dec 1959; *m* 1 Oct 1994 *Patrick Robert Mant, s of David Mant, of Chapel Cottage, Symond's Yat, and has:

1d +Alexandra Remington; *b* 10 March 1996

1a (cont.) Maj Cecil Twisleton-Wykeham-Fiennes *m* 3rd 1940 (*divorce*) Elizabeth Stockton (*d* 18 Feb 1961), dau of George Perry Fiske, of New York; *m* 4th 27 May 1959 *Pauline Compelly Cabot and *d* 21 July 1972

1a Marjorie Alice; *b* 5 June 1899

2a Barbara Winifred; *b* 6 July 1908; *m* 17 Feb 1937 Thomas Herbert Sholl, Dip Ag, 2nd s of Edward Sholl, of Perth, W Australia, and *d* 24 June 1965

(4) John Temple; *b* 20 Jan 1877; Lt-Col Roy W Kent Regt, Boer War 1899–1902 (medal and clasps) and WW I (despatches, brevet); *m* Sept 1929 Constance Astbury (*d* 1939), dau of John Ross, of Hollywood, Belfast, and *d* 30 April 1970, leaving:

1a +Bridget Susan Winifred; *b* 12 Feb 1935; *m* 9 Oct 1956 *Melvin Marriott, yr s of L M Marriott, of Salisbury, S Rhodesia, and has:

1b +Crispin John Fiennes; *b* 1966

1b +Josephine Susan; *b* 1957

2b +Esmeralda Jane; *b* 1959

3b +Prudence Ann; *b* 1964

4b +Samantha Sara; *b* 1968

(1) Winifred Emily Cecil; *m* 1st 18 Oct 1894 (*annulled* 1909) Rev Percy Riddel Allnutt; *m* 2nd 16 Dec 1913 Brig John Stuart Omond, MBE, MC, RAOC, s of G W T Omond, MA, of The White Cottage, Mitcham, and *d* 22 Nov 1945

5 Frederick Nathaniel Fiennes; *b* 8 June 1836; Capt 23rd Royal Welch Fus, Mil Kt Windsor; *m* 16 Aug 1887 Isabella Margaret (*d* 17 Aug 1924), est dau of Thomas Martinson Richardson, of Hibaldstowe Cliff, Lincs, and *dsp* 26 Sept 1896

1 Emily Wingfield; *m* 1st 7 Aug 1849 Thomas Guy Gisborne, of Yoxall Lodge, Staffs (*d* 12 Sept 1869); *m* 2nd 2 April 1872 John Harward Griffiths (*d* 16 Sept 1885), of The Weir, Herefs, and *d* 11 Oct 1917 aged 90

2 Isabella Elizabeth Catherine; *m* 11 June 1857 Col Richard F Webb, DL, of Donnington Hall, Herefs, and *d* 11 Dec 1915, having had issue

The 10th BARON's est s,

JOHN FIENNES TWISLETON-WYKEHAM-FIENNES, **11th Baron Saye and Sele**, JP, DL Oxon, JP Middx, Warwicks and Westminster; *b* 28 Feb 1830; Capt Oxon Yeo Cav, CA Oxon; *m* 24 April 1856 Lady Augusta Sophia Hay (*d* 23 July 1915), yst dau of 11th Earl of Kinnoull (*qv*), and had:

1 GEOFFREY CECIL, **12th Baron**

2 Sir EUSTACE EDWARD TWISLETON-WYKEHAM-FIENNES, 1st Bt (*qv*)

3 Ivo Henry John (Rev); Rector Yaverland, Brading, IoW 1913–20; *m* 1 Oct 1901 Mabel (*d* 12 May 1948), 2nd dau of W F Blandy, of Reading, and *dsp* 8 Feb 1947

4 William Cecil (Rev); *b* 1 Aug 1879; *educ* Queen's Coll Oxford (BA); Deacon 1903, Priest 1905, Curate St Mark, Portsmouth; *d* unm 22 Sept 1906

1 Beatrice Emmeline Augusta; *m* 11 Jan 1881 Capt Moulbray Allfrey, 15th Hus, of Hillside, Sunningdale, est s of Frederick Allfrey, of Stanbury, Berks, and *d* 16 July 1929, leaving issue

2 Edwyna Susan Elizabeth; *m* 20 Aug 1889 Col Herbert Frecheville Ramsden, CBE, JP, and *d* 11 April 1931, leaving issue (*see* RAMSDEN, Bt)

3 Edith Ellen Louisa; *m* 21 Jan 1896 Rev Gibbs Payne Crawfurd, Vicar Sonning, Berks, s of Rev Charles W Payne Crawfurd, of Ardmillan, E Grinstead, and *d* 8 Jan 1929, leaving issue. He *d* 9 May 1932

4 Alexandra Caroline Frances; *m* 1 Feb 1900 Col John Edward Broadbent, CB (*see* BROADBENT, Bt), and *d* 3 Feb 1938

5 Maud Mary; Sister Community St Mary the Virgin Wantage;, *d* 26 June 1937

6 Gertrude Emily; *m* 14 Jan 1897 Rev Edward Pell Edmonds, Rector Whittington, Salop, RD, s of Rev Richard Edward Pell Edmonds, and *d* 6 Aug 1948, leaving issue. He *d* 8 Aug 1932

The 11th BARON *d* 8 Oct 1907; his est s,

GEOFFREY CECIL TWISLETON-WYKEHAM-FIENNES, **12th Baron Saye and Sele**; *b* 3 Aug 1858; Capt Roy Scots Fus, Hon Col 3rd Bn Roy Scots Fus, Lt-Col 3rd Bn Middx Co Regt, served Zulu War 1879–80 and WW I as Area Cmdt Flanders; Comptroller Household 1912–15, High Steward City of Oxford 1930; *m* 20 Feb 1884 Marion Ruperta Murray (*d* 27 July 1946), dau of Major Robert Bartholomew Lawes, DL, of Old Park, Kent, and *d* 2 Feb 1937, having had:

1 GEOFFREY RUPERT CECIL TWISLETON-WYKEHAM-FIENNES, **13th Baron Saye and Sele**, JP Oxon; *b* 27 Dec 1884; *educ* Harrow and New Coll Oxford (BA 1910); barrister Inner Temple 1911, Maj QO Oxon Hus WW I, CC Oxon; *d* unm 18 Feb 1949

2 IVO MURRAY, **14th Baron**

3 Laurence John Evelyn; *b* 4 Oct 1890; *educ* Harrow; WW I in RFC and RAF (despatches, wounded), Air Attaché Washington 1930–33, G/Capt RAF (ret 1938, recalled 1939), ARIBA 1945, Chev Leopold Belgium; *d* unm 16 May 1962

4 Ingelram Robert Nathaniel; *b* 5 Jan 1895; *d* 28 Dec 1896

5 Allen Rupert Ingelram, MC (1918); *b* 25 Sept 1897; Lt RFA (SR) WW I (despatches); accidentaly *k* 10 Oct 1920

1 Evelyn Idonia Cicely; *b* 12 Jan, *d* 28 July 1887

2 Cicely Marion Violet Joan; *b* 22 Nov 1900; *m* 3 July 1928l John William Dunne, Wilts Regt, s of Gen Sir John Hart Dunne, KCB, and had issue. He *d* 24 Aug 1949

The 13th BARON's brother,

IVO MURRAY TWISLETON-WYKEHAM-FIENNES, **14th Baron Saye and Sele**, OBE (1961), MC, DL Oxon; *b* 15 Dec 1885; *educ* Harrow and RMA Woolwich; Lt-Col RA WW I (despatches, Croix de Guerre), served WW II 1939–41, CC Oxon; *m* 16 Oct 1919 Hersey Cecilia Hester (*d* 31 Oct 1968), dau of Capt Sir Thomas Dacres Butler, KCVO, Yeoman Usher Black Rod Ho Lds, and *d* 21 Oct 1968, having had:

1 NATHANIEL THOMAS ALLEN FIENNES, **15th and present Baron Saye and Sele**

2 Ingelram Ivo; *b* 4 July 1922; *educ* Eton; Sgt/Pilot RAFVR WW II; *ka* Middle East Aug 1941

3 +Oliver William (Very Rev) [The Very Rev The Hon Oliver Twisleton-Wykeham-Fiennes, Home Farm House, Colsterworth, Lincs NG33 5HZ]; *b* 17 May 1926; *educ* Eton, New Coll Oxford (MA 1955) and Cuddesdon Theological Coll; Chaplain Clifton Coll 1958–63, Rector Lambeth 1963–69, Dean Lincoln 1969–89, Preb Aylesbury 1969–98, Dean Emeritus 1989–, Ch Commr 1977–88 (Board 1983–88), Fell Thanksgiving Sq, Dallas 1980, Nat Patron ESU of USA 1986, late Lt Rifle Bde; ChStJ 1970, KStJ 1997; *m* 26 June 1956 *Juliet, yr dau of Dr Trevor Heaton, of Chichester, and has:

(1) +Adam Hugh; *b* 13 July 1961

(2) +James William; *b* 13 July 1964; *m* 1 June 1996 *Caroline, er dau of John Newton-Davies, of Sundridge, Herts, and Mrs Diana Whiteside, of Chailey, Sussex, and has:

1a +Georgina Lucy; *b* 10 Nov 1998

(1) +Celia Ruth; *b* 8 April 1957; *m* 1979 *James Long-Howell, only s of Lt-Col J D Howell, of Dyfed, and has:

1a +George David Henry; *b* 22 April 1992

1a +Emily Myfanwy; *b* 25 June 1987

2a +Charlotte Angharad; *b* 26 Jan 1990

(2) +Laura Charlotte; *b* 12 Sept 1959; *m* 1988 *Roger Hughes, yr s of Gordon Hughes, of Chapeltown, Lancs, and has had:

1a +Charles Oliver Edmund; *b* 12 Nov 1989

2a Robert Roger; *b* and *d* 1992

1a +Lucy Venetia; *b* 7 Oct 1994

Seat: Broughton Castle, nr Banbury, Oxon. Not a castle at all but a manor house, albeit moated, Broughton was completed externally in MARY's reign in the middle of the 16th century and internally in the last years of ELIZABETH I's at its end. Some of the interior dates back to the 14th century, however. Besides two rare 16th-century chimney pieces the house has some 18th-century plasterwork, but is otherwise pretty much an organic late-medieval entity, untouched by later improvements.

SCANLON

B. (LP, UK) 1978.

THE BARON SCANLON, of Davyhulme, Co Greater Manchester (Hugh Parr Scanlon) [The Rt Hon The Lord Scanlon, 23 Seven Stones Dve, Broadstairs, Kent]; *b* 26 Oct 1913; *educ* Stretford Elementary Sch and Nat Cncl of Lab Colls; AEU: Divnl Organiser Manchester 1947–63, memb Exec Cncl 1963–67, Pres 1967–78; Memb: TUC Gen Cncl and Ec Cncl 1968–78, NEDC 1971–, Metrication Bd 1977–79, NEB 1977–79, Br Gas Corp 1977–, Govt Ctee Inquiry Teaching Maths Primary and Secondary Schs England and Wales 1978–; Chm Engrg Industry Training Bd 1975–82; V-Pres Internat Metalworkers' Fedn 1969–78; Pres European Metal Workers' Fedn 1974–78; Hon DCL Kent U 1988; *m* 1943 *Nora, dau of James Markey, and has two daus

Lineage: HUGH SCANLON; had:

HUGH PARR, *cr* a **Baron**

SCARBROUGH

MURUS · AENEUS · CONSCIENTIA · SANA

Arms: Arg. a fess gu. between three popinjays vert, collared of the second (the arms of the THWENGs, apparently assumed by Marmaduke de Lumley (1341–65) instead of the original arms of the LUMLEYs, which were six popinjays). **Crest:** A pelican in piety in her nest, all ppr. **Supporters:** Two parrots, wings addorsed and inverted vert. **Motto:** *Murus aeneus conscientia sana* ('A sound conscience is a wall of brass'). **Creations:** V. (I) 12 July 1628 (Lumley of Waterford), B. (E) 31 May 1681, V. (E) 10 April 1689, E. (E) 15 April 1690.

THE 12TH EARL OF SCARBROUGH, Viscount Lumley of Lumley Castle, Co Durham, **Viscount Lumley of Waterford** and **Baron Lumley of Lumley Castle**, Co Durham (Richard Aldred Lumley) [The Earl of Scarbrough, Sandbeck Park, Maltby, S Yorks S66 8PF]; *b* 5 Dec 1932; *s f* 1969; *educ* Eton and Magdalen Coll Oxford; 2nd Lt 11th Hus 1951–52, Lt Q O Yorks Dragoons 1952–56, ADC to Govr and C-in-C Cyprus 1956, Hon Col 1st Bn Yorks Vols 1975–88, Tstee Leeds Castle Fndn 1983–, Pres: Northern Area Roy Br Legion 1984–93, York Georgian Soc 1985–92, memb Roy Commn Historical MSS. 1994–, (V-Lt S Yorks 1996– (V-Lt 1990–96, DL 1974–90); *m* 9 July 1970 *Lady Elizabeth Anne Ramsay, Ldy Bedchamber to HM QUEEN ELIZABETH THE QUEEN MOTHER 1994–, er dau of 16th Earl of Dalhousie (*qv*), and has had:

1 +RICHARD OSBERT, *Viscount Lumley*; *b* 18 May 1973
2 Frederick Henry; *b* 27 Aug 1975; *d* 28 Aug 1975
3 +Thomas Henry; *b* 1980
1 *Rose Frederica Lily; *b* 1981

Lineage: ROBERT de LUM(E)LEY(E) (*i.e.*, of Lumley, on the River Wear, Co Durham); living 1133–40; UCHTRED de LUMLEY; and OSBERN de LUMELEIE; were presumably kin to:

Sir WILLIAM de LUMLEY; *m* —, probably dau and coheir of Sir William de Audre, and had:

Sir ROGER de LUMLEY, of Little Lumley; apparently ktd by 1268; *m* Sybil, est dau and coheir of Hugh de Morwick, and *d* by 1279, leaving, with at least one yr s (Roger):

Sir ROBERT de LUMLEY; *b c* 1272; ktd by 1306; *m* Mary, dau of John FitzMarmaduke by Isabel (dau of Robert de Bruce, seemingly identical with ROBERT I (THE BRUCE) KING OF SCOTS), and *d* by 13 July 1308, leaving:

Sir ROBERT de LUMLEY; ktd by 1316; *m* 1st(?) Lucy, one of three sisters and coheirs of William, Robert, and Thomas de Thweng, respectively 2nd, 3rd and 4th Lords (Barons) Thweng; *m* (?)2nd and(?) Joan — and *d* by 20 July 1325, having by his 1st w had, with at least one yr s (William):

MARMADUKE de LUMLEY, JP (Northumberland 1346); *b* 4 Sept 1341; *m* 1st — (*d* 1343); *m* 2nd Margaret de Holand *d* 26 Sept 1365, having by her had, with an er s (Robert, *b c* 1354–57, *d* unm 12 or 24 Dec 1374):

Sir RALPH de LUMLEY, 1st and last LORD (Baron) LUMLEY, so *cr* (according to later doctrine) by writ of summons 28 Sept 1384, JP (N R Yorks 1394 and 1397); *b c* 1360; ktd by 1384; captured by Scots Battle of Otterburn (*see* NORTHUMBERLAND, D, for details of battle) but released by 1389, Capt Berwick-upon-Tweed 1391; took part 1399 in attempt by the Earl of Huntingdon to restore RICHARD II (his half-bro) and was beheaded by the citizens of Cirencester Jan 1399/1400, being posthumously attainted and his peerage forfeited March 1400/1; *m* Eleanor, dau of 3rd Lord (Baron) Neville (of Raby) (*see* ABERGAVENNY, M), and had, with, 11 other children (including an est s, Thomas *d* 31 May 1400, and a 4th, Marmaduke, Master Trin Hall Cambridge, Chllr Cambridge U, Bp Carlisle 1430 and Lincoln 1451 and Treasurer of England 1446):

Sir JOHN de LUMLEY; *b* 2 Feb 1382/3; ktd by 1400; restored as to name and right to inherit f's and er bro's possessions 1411 but not it would seem the title; *m* Felicia, dau of Sir Matthew Redman, of Newcastle, and widow of John Wodecok, London mercer, and was *ka* Battle of Beaugé 22 March 1421 during Hundred Years War, leaving:

Sir THOMAS de LUMLEY, 1st LORD (Baron) LUMLEY, so *cr* (according to later doctrine) by writ of summons 26 July 1461; *b* 29 Sept 1408; ktd by late 1436, Jt

Commissary-Gen W Marches 1346, Constable Scarborough Castle 1455, Yorkist Wars of Roses; managed to get gf's attainder reversed 1461 (*after* he had been *cr* a peer afresh by writ of summons, thereby apparently becoming 2nd LORD (Baron) LUMLEY of the 1384 *cr* as well); cmded troops Newcastle 1461–62, helped take the Lancastrian-held Bamburgh Castle Dec 1462; *m* Margaret, dau of Sir James Harington, and *d* 1 April 1485, leaving, with possibly a dau who *m* Adam Tyrwhitt, of Kettleby, Lincs (*see* BERNERS, B):

Sir GEORGE de LUMLEY, 2nd/3rd LORD (Baron) LUMLEY, KB (1482); *b c* 1445; Jt Constable Scarborough Castle 1461, Sheriff Northumberland 1461–63 and 1467–71, MP Northumberland 1467, Ld Lt Northumberland 1480–81; made his peace with HENRY VII after Bosworth and was apptd a Commr of Array Yorks late Sept 1485; *m* Elizabeth, dau and heiress of Roger Thornton, merchant Newcastle-upon-Tyne, by Elizabeth, dau of 4th Lord (Baron) Greystoke, and *d* 13 Nov 1507, having had:

THOMAS LUMLEY; allegedly *m* Elizabeth, illegitimate dau of EDWARD IV by Lady Elizabeth Lucy, and *dvp* 1487, leaving, with three other sons and three daus:

RICHARD LUMLEY, 3rd/4th LORD (Baron) LUMLEY; *b c* 1477; *m* Anne, dau of Sir John Conyers, KG, of Hornby Castle, Yorks, and sis of 1st Lord (Baron) Conyers (*see* YARBOROUGH, E), and *d* 26 May 1510, having had:

1 Sir JOHN LUMLEY, 4th/5th LORD (Baron) LUMLEY, JP (Co Durham 1516); *b c* 1492; fought Battle of Flodden 1513, after which ktd; took part in Pilgrimage of Grace 1536 but pardoned; *m* Joan, dau of Henry, (probably 7th) Lord (Baron) Scrope (of Bolton), and *d* 1544 or 1545, when the Barony/-ies (whether of 1384 or 1461 or both) was forfeited due to the attainder of his er s:

(1) George; *m* Jane, 2nd dau and coheir of Sir Richard Knightley, of Upton, Northants, was attainted for treason following his participation in a second outbreak of North-Country opposition to the Dissolution of the Monasteries (and other religious innovations, also perhaps enclosures and various purely temporal causes of dissatisfaction) Jan 1536/7 and beheaded 2 June 1537, leaving:

1a Sir JOHN LUMLEY, 1st and last BARON LUMLEY, so *cr* 1547, when also restored in blood but not in honours (or so subsequent doctrine, as expressed by the Ho Lds Privileges Ctee report 23 March 1723/4 when commenting on the claim of Dr Robert Lloyd (*see* below) would have it; to contemporaries it was probably a restoration of the 1461 (?and/or 1384) creation, for the Act of Parl conferring the 1547 Barony assigned precedence of the older date (1461? 1384?), though with remainder in tail male, but the later detail signifies nothing either way since at that date the doctrine of baronies by writ being heritable by heirs general, which could include female and their issue, had not evolved), KB (1553); *b c* 1533; *educ* Queens' Coll Cambridge; High Steward Oxford U 1559–1609; imprisoned Tower London 1569–73 on suspicion of complicity in his bro-in-law the 4th Duke of Norfolk's (*qv*) matrimonial designs on MARY QUEEN OF SCOTS but was certainly never convicted of any associated crime and appears not even to have been tried; a Commr several state trials thereafter (showing he was again in favour), notably of MARY QUEEN OF SCOTS herself 1586; granted 1593 a charter of Hartlepool, where built a jetty, subsequent mariners from which port named Lumley's Inlet on Hudson's Bay after him; *m* 1st Lady Jane Fitz Alan, er dau and coheir of 19th/12th Earl of Arundel (*see* NORFOLK, D); *m* 2nd 1582 Elizabeth, dau of 2nd Baron Darcy of Chiche, but *dsps* 11 April 1609, when the Barony expired, leaving Lumley Castle, Co Durham, and other property to his cousin **1st Viscount Lumley of Waterford**

1a Jane; *m* Geoffrey Markham and *dsp*

2a Barbara; *m* 1st Humphrey Lloyd, antiquary and historian, of Denbigh, and had issue; her descendant the Rev Dr Robert Lumley Lloyd unsuccessfully claimed the 1547 Barony of Lumley 1723; *m* 2nd, as his 2nd w, William Williams, of Lochwillan (*see* WILLIAMS-BULKELEY, Bt)

(2) Percival; *m* 1543 Elizabeth Hussey

2 Anthony; *m* —, dau of Richard Gray, of Northumberland, and had:

(1) Roger; *m* Anne Kurtwich and had, with other issue:

1a RICHARD LUMLEY, **1st Viscount Lumley of Waterford** (I), so *cr* 12 July 1628; *bapt* 7 April 1589; ktd 1616; garrisoned Lumley Castle for the King in Civil War; royalist cdr in West of England at time of Bristol's capitulation to Parl 1645; *m* 1st Frances, widow of William Holland, of Chichester, Sussex, and dau of Henry Shelley (*see* DE L'ISLE, V), and had, with a dau:

1b John; *m* Mary, dau and eventually coheir of Sir Henry Compton, KB, of Brambletye, Sussex (*see* NORTHAMPTON, M), and was *bur* 10 Oct 1658, leaving, with other issue:

1c RICHARD, **1st Earl**
2c Henry

1a (cont.) The **1st Viscount** *m* 2nd 11 May 1630 Elizabeth (*bur* 2 Feb 1657/8), widow of Sir William Sandys and dau of Sir William Cornwallis, of Brome, Suffolk (*see* CORNWALLIS, B), and *d* by 12 March 1662/3, having by her had no issue

His gs,

RICHARD LUMLEY, **1st Earl of Scarbrough**, so *cr* 15 April 1690, as also earlier 31 May 1681 BARON LUMLEY, of Lumley Castle, and 10 April 1689 VISCOUNT LUMLEY (all E) (with remainder, in default of male issue, to his brother Henry), PC (Feb 1688/9); *b c* 1650; helped suppress Duke of Monmouth's rebellion (*see* BUCCLEUCH and QUEENSBERRY, D) Battle of Sedgemoor 1685, Col 6th Dragoon Gds 1685–87, a pncpl supporter of WILLIAM III (OF ORANGE) 1688, Capt 1st Life Gds 1689–99, Ld Lt Northumberland 1689–1712 and 1715–21 and Co Durham same dates, a Ld Treasury by Nov 1689, served under WILLIAM III Battle of the Boyne 1690, Maj-Gen 1692, Lt-Gen 1694 (ret 1697) but apptd Lt-Gen all forces March 1701/2, Chllr Duchy Lancaster March 1715/6–17, V-Treas 1717; *m* 17 March 1684/5 Frances, only dau and heir of Sir Henry Jones, of Aston, Oxon, by Frances, sis of Thomas, 2nd Viscount Fauconberg of Henknowle, and *d* 17 Dec 1721, having had, with an er s (Henry, *dvp* 1710):

1 RICHARD LUMLEY, **2nd Earl of Scarbrough**, KG (1724), PC (1727); *b c* 1688; *educ* Eton and King's Coll Cambridge; MP (Whig) E Grinstead 1708–10 and Arundel 1710–15, called up to Ho Lds 4 March 1714/5 *vp* in f's Barony ; fought against Jacobites Preston 1715, Ld Lt Northumberland 1721–39/40, Col Cold-

stream Gds 1722–39/40, Master Horse 1727–34, Maj-Gen 1735, Lt-Gen 1739; *d* unm 29 Jan 1739/40 by shooting himself through the roof of the mouth, possibly through a mental disorder arising from a knock on the head when involved in an accident in his carriage a few days previously, though another story relates that he killed himself the day before he was due to marry the famous beauty Isabella (Belle), widow of the 1st Duke of Montagu (*see* MANCHESTER, D)

2 THOMAS LUMLEY later LUMLEY-SAUNDERSON (by Act of Parl 1723 on inheriting estates of cousin James Saunderson, Earl of Castleton), **3rd Earl of Scarbrough**, KB (1725); *b c* 1691; *educ* apparently at Eton; Lt-Col Lord Hinchinbroke[*sic*]'s Regt of Foot 1717 and Ancaster's Regt of Foot 1745, Clerk to Cncl Duchy Lancaster 1716–31, Envoy Extrdy Lisbon 1722–24, MP (Whig, though opposing Walpole) Arundel 1722–27 and Lincs 1727–40, Equerry to GEORGE II 1727–30; *m* 27 June 1724 Frances (*d* 27 Oct 1772), dau and coheir of 1st Earl of Orkney (*qv*), and *d* 15 March 1752, leaving, with other issue:

(1) RICHARD LUMLEY-SAUNDERSON, **4th Earl of Scarbrough**, PC (1765); *b c* May 1725; *educ* Eton and King's Coll Cambridge; Dep Earl Marshal 1765–77; *m* 26 Dec 1752 Barbara, yr sister and heiress of Sir George Savile, Bt, of Rufford, Notts, and Thornhill, Yorks (title merged 1682–1700 with Marquessate of Halifax, for whose early ancestry *see* MEXBOROUGH, E, and HALIFAX, E, preliminary remarks), and *d* 12 May 1782, having had:

1a GEORGE AUGUSTA [*sic*] LUMLEY-SAUNDERSON, **5th Earl of Scarbrough**; *b* 22 Sept 1753; *educ* Eton and King's Coll Cambridge; MP (Whig) 1774–80; *d* unm 5 Sept 1807

2a RICHARD LUMLEY later LUMLEY-SAVILE (on inheriting the estate of his unc Sir George Savile, 8th Bt, 10 Jan 1784) later still LUMLEY-SAUNDERSON (after acquiring the Saunderson estates), **6th Earl of Scarbrough**; *b* 16 April 1757; *educ* Eton; Capt 86th Foot 1779 and 3rd Dragoons 1780–84; MP (Whig) Lincoln 1784–90, Sheriff Notts 1793, Capt Rufford Yeo 1803–08; *m* 14 June 1787 Henrietta (*d* March 1846), dau of 5th Baron Middleton (*qv*), and *dsp* 17 June 1832

3a Thomas Charles; Capt RN; *b* 1758; *k* aboard the *Isis* 3 Sept 1782

4a Rev JOHN LUMLEY later LUMLEY-SAVILE (roy licence 28 Sept 1807), **7th Earl of Scarbrough**; *b* 15 June 1760; *educ* Eton and King's Coll Cambridge; ordained 1785, Preb York 1785–1835, Rector Wintringham Lincs 1784 and Thornhill Yorks 1793; *m* 5 Nov 1785 Anna Maria (*d* 17 March 1850), dau of Julines Herring, of Jamaica, and *d* 21 Feb 1835 in a fall from his horse while hunting, having had, with other issue (*d* young):

1b JOHN LUMLEY later LUMLEY-SAVILE (roy licence 14 Oct 1836), **8th Earl of Scarbrough**; *b* 18 July 1788; MP (Whig) Notts 1826–32 and N Notts 1832–35, Ld Lt and custos rotulorum Notts 1839–56; *dspl* (*see* SAVILE, B) unm 29 Oct 1856

1b Anna Maria; *b* 1791; *d* 5 May 1840

2b Louisa Frances; *b* 1794; *m* 25 Sept 1825 Rev Thomas Cator, yr bro of John Cator, of Beckenham Place, Kent, and *d* 7 Jan 1885 aged 90, leaving issue. He *d* 24 Aug 1864

3b Henrietta Barbara; *b* 1796; *m* 1st 2 Sept 1821 Rev Frederick Manners Sutton (*see* RUTLAND, D); *m* 2nd 24 Aug 1837 John Lodge Ellerton, of Bodsilin, Caernarvs, and *d* 27 July 1864

5a Frederick; *b* 17 Oct 1761; *m* 1st 20 Feb 1786 Harriet Anne (*d* 20 July 1810), dau of John Boddington, and had:

1b Frederick LUMLEY later LUMLEY-SAVILE (Act of Parl 1834), of Tickhill Castle, Yorks; *b* 14 Jan 1788; *m* 2 May 1812 Charlotte Mary (*m* 2nd 20 July 1839 Robert Henry Southwell; *see* SOUTHWELL, V), dau of Rt Rev George de la Poer Beresford, Bp Kilmore (*see* WATERFORD, M), and *d* 27 Feb 1837, leaving:

1c RICHARD GEORGE, **9th Earl**

1c Frances Charlotte Arabella, of Tickhill Castle; granted with her sisters rank of earl's dau; *m* 8 March 1836 Col Charles John Hill (*d* 22 May 1867), of Cotgrave, Notts, and *d* 3 Aug 1879, leaving:

1d Georgina Mary; *m* 29 April 1867 Sir Henry William Gore-Booth, 5th Bt (*qv*), and *d* 23 Jan 1927, leaving issue

2c Henrietta Susan Beresford; *m* 5 Nov 1835 Edmund L'Estrange, of Tynte Lodge, Co Leitrim, yst s of Col L'Estrange, of Moystown, King's Co, and *d* 22 Dec 1904, leaving issue. He *d* Aug 1866

3c Anne Georgina; *m* 16 April 1844 Sir William Mordaunt Edward Milner, 5th Bt (*qv*), and *d* 2 Feb 1877, leaving issue

5a (cont.) The Hon Frederick Lumley *m* 2nd 25 March 1819 Jane (*dsp* 9 June 1825), 2nd dau of Adml Bradby, of Hamble, Hants, and *d* 20 Sept 1831

6a Savile Henry; *b* 18 June 1768; *m* 13 Dec 1806 Mary Henrietta (*d* 5 July 1869), dau of Henry Tabourdin, of Sydenham, Kent, and *dsp* 14 Nov 1846

7a William (Sir), KCB; *b* 28 Aug 1769; Gen, Col 1st Dragoon Gds, cmded cavalry Battle of Albuera Peninsular War; *m* 1st 3 Oct 1804 Mary (*dsp* July 1807), dau of Thomas Sutherland, of Ulverstone; *m* 2nd 3 March 1817 Louisa Margaret (*d* 11 Sept 1859), widow of Colonel Lynch Cotton and dau of John Robbins, and *d* 15 Dec 1850

1a Frances Barbara Ludlow; *d* an infant

2a Mary Arabella; *b* 1763; *m* 12 June 1792 Francis Ferrand Foljambe (*see* LIVERPOOL, E) and *dsp* 1 May 1817

3a Louisa; *b* 1773; *m* 26 Feb 1798 Winchcombe Henry Hartley and *d* 1811

4a Sophia; *b* 1777; *d* unm 1832

(1) Frances; *m* 26 June 1735 1st Earl Ludlow (*see* STEWART, Bt, of Ramelton) and *d* 20 March 1796, leaving issue

The 8th EARL's cousin,

RICHARD GEORGE LUMLEY, **9th Earl of Scarbrough**; *b* 7 May 1813; *educ* Eton; Lt-Col W Yorks Yeo Cav; *m* 8 Oct 1846 Frederica Mary Adeliza (*d* 2 April 1907), 2nd dau of Andrew Robert Drummond (*see* PERTH, E), and *d* 5 Dec 1884, having had:

1 Lyulph Richard Granby William, *Viscount Lumley*; *b* 7 June 1850; *d* unm 23 Aug 1868

2 ALDRED FREDERICK GEORGE BERESFORD LUMLEY, **10th Earl of Scarbrough**, KG (1929), GBE (1921), KCB (1911); *b* 16 Nov 1857; *educ* Eton; Ld Lt and custos rotulorum W R Yorks 1892–1904, T/Maj-Gen and Dir-Gen TVF 1917–21, Hon Maj-Gen 1921, Lt 7th Hus and Col Yorks Dragoons and Yorks

Mounted Bde (TD) Boer War 1900, ADC to HM EDWARD VII 1902, Bailiff Grand Cross and Sub-Prior of OStJ; *m* 8 April 1899 Lucy Cecilia, DGStJ (*d* 24 Sept 1931), widow of Robert Ashton and est dau of Cecil Dunn Gardner, and *d* 4 March 1945, leaving:

(1) *Serena Mary Barbara, JP (Richmond, Yorks, 1945) [The Lady Serena James JP, St Nicholas, Richmond, N Yorks]; *b* 30 March 1901; DStJ; *m* 23 July 1923 Hon Robert James, 3rd s of 2nd Baron Northbourne (*qv*), and has issue

3 Osbert Victor George Atheling, CMG; *b* 18 July 1862; Col 11th Hus, Inspr Cav, cmded 2nd Res Cav Bde WW I 1915–19, Hon Brig-Gen 1919; *m* 3 May 1892 Constance Ellinor, OBE, OStJ (*d* 21 Nov 1933), est dau of Capt Eustace John Wilson Patten, 1st Life Gds, s of 1st and last Baron Winmarleigh (*see* 1892 edn), and *d* 14 Dec 1923, having had:

(1) Richard John; *b* 30 July 1894; 2nd Lt 11th Hus; *ka* 17 Oct 1914

(2) LAWRENCE ROGER, **11th Earl**

(1) Sibell Evelyn; *b* 28 Jan 1893; *d* 21 Nov 1898

(2) Lilian Mary Theodora; *b* 22 May 1900; granted 1945 rank of earl's dau; *m* 14 Feb 1927 Col Clive Grantham Austin, Res of Offrs, RA, only s of Selwyn Percy Austin, of Roundwood, Micheldever, Hants, and had issue (*see* STANLEY OF ALDERLEY, SHEFFIELD and, B)

1 Algitha Frederica Mary; *m* 13 Aug 1868 4th Baron Bolton (*qv*) and *d* 23 June 1919, leaving issue

2 Ida Frances Annabella; DGStJ; *m* 7 Sept 1869 4th Earl of Bradford (*qv*) and *d* 22 Aug 1936, leaving issue

3 Lilian Selina Elizabeth; DGStJ; *m* 3 Aug 1871 1st Marquess of Zetland (*qv*) and *d* 24 Dec 1943, leaving issue

4 Sibell Mary; DJStJ; *m* 1st 3 Oct 1874 Earl Grosvenor (*d* 1884), est s of 1st Duke of Westminster (*qv*); *m* 2nd 7 Feb 1887 George Wyndham, PC, MP, and *d* 4 Feb 1929, having had issue (*see* EGREMONT, LECONFIELD and, B)

The 10th EARL's n,

LAWRENCE ROGER LUMLEY, **11th Earl of Scarbrough**, KG (1948), GCSI (1943), GCIE (1937), GCVO (1953), TD, PC (1952), DL (Co Durham); *b* 27 July 1896; *educ* Eton, RMC Sandhurst and Magdalen Coll Oxford (BA 1921); Capt 11th Hus, Capt and Brevet Maj Yorkshire Dragoons, WW I 1916–19 (wounded), Hon Maj-Gen WW II 1943–44; Ld Chamberlain 1952–63, Perm Ld-in-Waiting 1963–69, Ld Lt and custos rotulorum W R Yorks and City of York 1948–69, Hon DCL Durham 1949, Hon LLD Sheffield and Leeds 1951, London 1953, Hon Col Queen's Own Yorks Yeo 1956–62, PPS to: Parly U-Sec Colonies 1923–24, For Sec 1925–26 and 1935–37, Fin Sec Treasury 1931–32, Home Sec 1932–35, Min League Nations Affrs June–Dec 1935; Govr Bombay Sept 1937–March 1943, Parly U-Sec India and Burma May–July 1945, MP Kingston-upon-Hull E 1922–29 and York 1931–37, Pres: Roy Asiatic Soc 1946–49, E India Assoc 1946–51, Roy Centl Asian Soc 1954–60; Chm: Interdeptl Commn Oriental, Slavonic, E European and African Studies 1944–46, Govrs SOAS London U 1951–59, Ch Court U of Durham 1946–57 (Chllr 1958–69), chm Cwlth Scholarships Commn 1960–63, Pres Soc Yorkshiremen in London and Yorkshire Soc 1954, Dep Grand Master English Freemasons 1947 (Grand Master 1951–67), KStJ, Roy Victorian Chain 1963; *m* 12 July 1922 Katharine Isobel, DCVO (1962), JP (Co Durham 1944) (*d* 1979), Extra Ldy Bedchamber to HM QUEEN ELIZABETH THE QUEEN MOTHER, DStJ, Kaisar-i-Hind Gold Medal, dau of Robert Finnie McEwen (*see* McEWEN, Bt), and *d* 29 June 1969, leaving:

1 RICHARD ALDRED LUMLEY, **12th and present Earl of Scarbrough**

1 Mary Constance, OBE (1974); *b* 20 April 1923; DStJ; *m* 23 Aug 1952 Roger Fleetwood Hesketh, OBE, TD, DL (*see* BIBBY, Bt), and *d* 23 Jan 1998, having had:

(1) *Robert Fleetwood; *b* 10 June 1956; *educ* Eton; *m* 1990 *Hon Catherine Ingrid Guinness, est dau of 3rd Baron Moyne (*qv*) and formerly w of Lord Neidpath (*see* WEMYSS and MARCH, E), and has issue

(1) *Laura [Mrs Anthony Blond, 9 rue Thiers, 87300 Bellac, France]; *b* 4 July 1953; *m* 1981, as his 2nd w, *Anthony Blond, publisher and author, s by his 1st w (*see* ROMNEY, E) of Neville Blond, CMG, OBE (*see also* MARKS OF BROUGHTON, B, and STRACHEY, Bt), and has an adopted s:

*Ajith Charminda; *b* 1981

(2) Sarah Frances; *b* 12 Oct 1954; *m* 1980 *Patrick Anthony Ewen Bellville and *d* 1984

2 *Elizabeth, DCVO (1995, CVO 1983) [The Lady Grimthorpe DCVO, Westow Hall, York YO6 7NE]; *b* 22 July 1925; Ldy Bedchamber of HM QUEEN ELIZABETH THE QUEEN MOTHER 1973; *m* 17 Feb 1954 4th Baron Grimthorpe (*qv*) and has issue

3 *Anne Katharine Gabrielle [The Viscountess Ridley, Blagdon, Seaton Burn, Northumberland]; *b* 16 Nov 1928; *m* 3 Jan 1953 *4th Viscount Ridley (*qv*) and has issue

4 *(Jane Lily) Serena [The Lady Serena Wiley, Oak Hill, Palmyra, VA, USA]; *b* 5 Oct 1935; *m* 14 Nov 1963 *Hugh Wiley, s of William Howard Wiley, of Towson, Md., and has:

(1) *Justin Hugh; *b* 3 Dec 1964

(2) *Marcus Thomas; *b* 2 Nov 1966

(3) *Peter Alexander; *b* 25 July 1971

SCARMAN

Creation: (LP, UK) 1977.

THE BARON SCARMAN, of Quatt, Co Salop (Sir Leslie George Scarman, OBE (1945), PC (1972)) [The Rt Hon The Lord Scarman OBE PC, House of Lords, London SW1A 0PW]; *b* 29 July 1911; *educ* Radley and BNC Oxford (MA); barrister Middle Temple 1936, W/Cdr RAFVR WW II, QC 1957, Bencher 1961, ktd 1961, Judge Probate Divorce and Admlty Div 1961–72, Chm Law Commn 1965–72, Ld Justice Appeal 1973–77, Ld Appeal in Ordinary 1977–86; Chm: Cncl Legal Educn 1973–76, London U Court 1970–86; Pres: Senate Inns Court and Bar 1976–79, RIPA 1981–89, Constitutional Reform Centre 1984–, Citizen Action Compensation Campaign 1988–; Chllr Warwick U 1977–89; Hon Fell: BNC Oxford 1966, Imp Coll 1975, UCL 1985, LSE 1985, Leeds 1987, Brunel 1988; Hon LLD Exeter 1965, Glasgow 1969, London 1971, Keele 1972, Freiburg 1973, Warwick 1974, Bristol 1976, Manchester 1977, Kent 1981, Wales 1985, Queen's U Belfast 1990, Dundee 1990; Hon DCL: City 1980, Oxon 1982; author: *Pattern of Law Reform* (1967), *English Law: The New Dimension* (1975); *m* 1947 *Ruth Clement, dau of Clement Wright ICS, and adopted:

*John Clement; *b* 1946

Lineage: GEORGE CHARLES SCARMAN; *m* Ida Irene — and had:

LESLIE GEORGE, *cr* a **Baron**

SCARSDALE

Arms: Arg. on a bend sa. three popinjays or, collared gu. **Crest:** A popinjay rising or, collared gu. **Supporters:** Dexter, the figure of Prudence, represented by a woman habited arg., mantled az., holding in her sinister hand a javelin, entwined with a remora (*i.e*, serpent) ppr., sinister, the figure of Liberality also represented by a woman habited arg., mantled purpure, holding a cornucopia ppr. **Mottoes:** 1 Let Curzon holde what Curzon helde, 2 *Recte et suaviter* ('Justly and mildly'). **Creations:** Bt. (NS) 18 June 1636 and (E) 11 Aug 1641, B. (GB) 9 April 1761, V. (UK) 2 Nov 1911.

THE 3RD VISCOUNT SCARSDALE, of Scarsdale, Co Derby, **Baron Scarsdale**, Co Derby, and a **Baronet** (Sir Francis John Nathaniel Curzon, Bt) [The Rt Hon The Viscount Scarsdale, Kedleston Hall, Derby DE22 5JH; Tullich, Strathcarron, Ross-shire]; *b* 28 July 1924; *s* cousin 1977; *educ* Eton; late Capt Scots Gds; *m* 1st 3 July 1948 (*divorce* 1967) Solange Yvonne Palmyre Ghislaine (*d* 4 July 1974), yr dau of Oscar Ghislain Hanse, of Belgium, and has:

1 +PETER GHISLAIN NATHANIEL; *b* 6 March 1949; *educ* Ampleforth; *m* 1983 (*divorce* Jan 1996) Mrs Karen Osborne [Mrs Karen Curzon, Battle Barn Farm, Sedlescombe, Sussex] and has:

  (1) *Danielle Solange; *b* 1983

1 (cont.) The Hon PETER CURZON *m* 2nd 1996 *Michelle Reynolds, of Torquay

2 +David James Nathaniel [The Hon David Curzon, 33 Lingfield Rd, London SW19]; *b* 3 Feb 1958; *educ* Stowe; *m* 1981 *Ruth, dau of John Ernest Linton, of Wavertree, Liverpool, and has:

  (1) +Andrew Linton Nathaniel; *b* 1986

  (1) *Emma Rachel; *b* 1983

1 *Annette Yvonne [The Hon Mrs Latief, 12 Kaab Malek St, Hegaz Sq, Heliopolis, Cairo, Eygpt]; *b* 28 Oct 1953; *m* 1979 *Capt Hani Talaat Latief and has:

  (1) *Sagi; *b* 20 March 1982

  (2) *Shadi; *b* 11 Aug 1989

The 3rd VISCOUNT *m* 2nd 5 June 1968 *Helene Gladys Frances, only dau of Maj William George Ferguson Thomson, of Kinellar, Aberdeenshire, and formerly w of John Lubbock (*see* AVEBURY, B), and by her has:

4 +Richard Francis Nathaniel; *b* 30 Jan 1969; *educ* Shiplake and RAC Cirencester

5 +James Fergus Nathaniel; *b* 12 Sept 1970; *educ* Eton and Edinburgh U (MA)

Scarsdale, previous creation: Between 1645 and 1736 an Earldom of Scarsdale was held by the Lekes, Sir Francis Leke or Leake, the grantee, having been MP for Derbyshire at the end of ELIZABETH I's reign and one of the Baronets made on the founding of the order in 1611. This 1st Earl of Scarsdale ruined himself in the royal cause during the Civil War. His son the 2nd Earl, a Parliamentarian, was equally unlucky in money matters, being imprisoned for debt early in 1650. The 3rd Earl held numerous court appointments under CHARLES II, JAMES II and WILLIAM III, which argues a certain flexibility, though he was suspected of high treason in the reign of the last of these. He nevertheless attended QUEEN ANNE's coronation in an official capacity. His nephew the 4th and last Earl was imprisoned in the Tower of London at the time of the 1715 Jacobite Uprising on suspicion of disaffection. The title expired with his death.

Lineage: The name Curzon is said to derive from Courson, Normandy, either the Courson southeast of Coutances or Nôtre-Dame-de-Courson near Lisieux.

GERALINE/GIRALINE de CURZON, however, is said to have been a Breton; feudal Ld of Locking, Berks, and Fishead, Oxon, at the time of the Domesday Survey 1086; had, with an er s (Robert, held land 1086 at Uggeshall, Staffs, of Hugh, Earl of Chester; ancestor of the French branch of the family):

HUBERT de CURZON, of Fauld, Staffs, in 1086; *m* a sis and heiress of Roger de Croxall and *d* 1089, leaving:

1 ROBERT

2 Hubert; *dsp* in or after 1097, naming as heir his n Stephen

3 Stephen, of Fauld and Diseworth, Leics; living 1097; had:

  (1) Geraline, of Fauld; *d* 1165, leaving:

    1a Geraun (corruption of Geraline?); *dsp* in or after 1206

  (2) Stephen, of W Locking; *s* unc at Fauld and Diseworth; held two knights fees 1166; *m* Afuca [*sic*], dau of OLAF, KING OF THE ISLE OF MAN and THE ISLES and had:

    1a Stephen, of Fauld; *m* Aline — and *dsp* by 1202

    2a Jerome (Sir), of Fauld; living 1202; *m* Amicia, dau and heiress of Giles Mompesson, and had:

      1b Stephen, of Fauld; *m* Joan, dau of Sir Henry de Rolleston, of Rolleston, Staffs, and had:

        1c John, of Fauld; *d* unm

        1c Agnes; *m* Nicholas de Burton, who held Fauld in right of his w

      2b Robert

    2a Thomas, of Tutbury, Staffs

    1a Sarra [*sic*]

    2a Maud

HUBERT de CURZON's est s,
  ROBERT de CURZON, of Croxall, then Derbys now Staffs; *m* Beatrix, dau and heiress of Gilbert d'Aufay, of Kedleston, and *d* 1135, leaving:

1 Richard, of Croxall; *d* 1166, leaving:

  (1) Robert, of Croxall; also held Kedleston and other lands making a total of four kts' fees; *m* Alice — (*m* 2nd Alan de Somerville) and had:

    1a Richard, of Croxall; *m* Petronilla, sis and heiress of Roger de Camville, and was ancestor of the CURZONs of Croxall, whose heiress *m* 1612 4th Earl of Dorset (*see* SACKVILLE, B)

  (2) Robert; Cardinal; *d* 1218

2 THOMAS

3 William, of Stanfield and Besthorpe, Norfolk; living between 1189 and 1208; ancestor of the CURZONs of Norfolk

The 2nd s,
  THOMAS de CURZON; *m* 1186 Sybil — and had:

THOMAS de CURZON; held by 1198/9 a single kt's fee at Kedleston of his cousin Richard; *d* in or after 1242, having had, with a yr s (William) and a dau (Margery, *m* William le Burgilon, of Weston Underwood):

Sir ENGELHARD de CURZON, of Kedleston; living between 1247 and 1278; had, with a yr s (William, Rector Kedleston 1327):

RICHARD de CURZON, of Kedleston, where had charter of free warren 1305; *m* Joan — and *d* in or after 1330, leaving:

ROGER de CURZON; living between 1347 and 1380; had:

JOHN de CURZON, of Kedleston; *m* Eleanor, dau of Sir Robert de Twyford, of Twyford, and *d* 1406, leaving:

JOHN CURZON, PC, JP, of Kedleston; MP Derbys, Escheator (official implementing reversions of tenancies to the Crown) Derbys and Notts, Steward Honour (administrative centre of a feudal territorial unit) of Tutbury 1399, Constable Horsley Castle 1401; *m* Margaret, dau of Sir Nicholas Montgomery, of Cubley, and widow of Sir Ralph Brailsford, of Brailsford, and had, with a yr s (Thomas, JP, *m c* 1420 the dau and heiress of — Bulcote, of Bulcote, Notts, thus acquiring that Manor, and *d* 1462, leaving a dau and heiress, who *m* Alured Berwick, of Bulcote) and a dau (Margaret, *m* 1st Thomas Okeover, of Okeover (*see* WALKEROKEOVER, Bt), and 2nd Thomas Kniveton, of Bradley):

JOHN CURZON, called 'John with the White Head', of Kedleston, JP; *b* 1394; MP Derbys, High Sheriff Notts and Derby 1437, Escheator Notts and Derbys 1430, 1435 and 1440; *m* Joan, dau of Sir John Bagot, of Blithfield (*see* BAGOT, B), and *d* 1456, having had, with two yr sons (Robert; Henry, Bailiff of Duchy of Lancaster at Burton-on-Trent 1475, *m* Anne Mortimer and was ancestor of the CURZONs of Beckhall, Boram, Norfolk) and five daus (Thomasine, *m* Thomas Statham, of Morley; Joan, *m* Ralph Sacheverell, of Hopwell; Isabel, *m* John Bird, MP, of Nether Locke; Anne, *m* John Ireton, of Ireton Parva (*see* FERRERS, E, and CULLEN OF ASHBOURNE, B); Catherine, *m* Sir Nicholas Griffin, of Leics):

JOHN CURZON, JP, of Kedleston; Keeper Worcester Castle, High Sheriff Derbys and Notts 1472; *m* Joan FitzHerbert and *d* 1492, leaving, with three yr sons (Walter, of Water Perry, Northants, *m* Agnes de Cambridge and was ancestor of the COURSON, Bts, of Water Perry, who became extinct 1750, but whose name was perpetuated by John Barnewall-Curson (*see* TEYNHAM, B); Henry; Philip, of Letheringsett, Norfolk, *m* Agnes, dau and heiress of John Laville, and was ancestor of the CURZONs of Letheringsett) and a dau (Cecily, *m* William Frussell, of Seymour's Place, Egginton, Derbys):

RICHARD CURZON, of Kedleston; *m* Alice, dau of Sir Robert Willoughby, of Wollaton, Notts, and *d* 1496, leaving, with a yr s (Henry, *m* Margaret, dau of John Dethick, of Newkall, Derbys) and a dau (Elizabeth, Prioress King's Mead):

JOHN CURZON, of Kedleston; Sheriff Derbys *c* 1474, *c* 1484 and *c* 1487; *m* Elizabeth, dau of Stephen Eyre, of Hassop, and *d c* 1513, leaving:

RICHARD CURZON, of Kedleston; *b* 1505; *m* Eleanor, dau of German Pole, of Radborne, Derbys, and *d* 1546, leaving, with an est s (John, *dsp c* 1549) and two yst sons (Richard; Christopher):

FRANCIS CURZON, of Kedleston; *b c* 1524; *m* Eleanor, dau and coheir of Thomas Vernon, of Stokesay (*see* VERNON, B), and had, with three yr sons (Thomas; Francis, *bur* 30 May 1630; George, *bur* 25 June 1652, leaving a s Francis, ancestor of the Buckinghamshire CURZONs):

JOHN CURZON, of Kedleston; *b* 1551; High Sheriff Derbys 1609; *m* Millicent, widow of Anthony Gell, of Hopton, and dau of Sir Ralph Sacheverell, of Stanton, Derbys, and *d* 1632, leaving, with a yr s (Richard, ancestor of the CURZONs of Breedon and Lockington) and a dau (Eleanor, *m* Richard Boothby, of Marston, Leics):

Sir John Curzon, 1st Bt (NS), so *cr* 18 June 1636 and (E) 11 Aug 1641, of Kedleston; *b* 3 Nov 1598; *educ* Magdalen Coll Oxford; MP Brackley 1628–29 and Derbys April–May 1640 and 1640–48, ktd 15 June 1636, Sheriff Derbys 1638–39, Receiver Gen Duchy Lancaster estates, Parliamentarian Civil War; *m* Patience (*d* 30 March 1642), sis of 1st Baron Crewe of Stene, and *d* 13 Dec 1686, having had, with two daus (Eleanor, *m* Sir John Archer, Judge Common Pleas; Jane, *m* John Stanhope, of Elvaston, and *d* 14 April 1652, leaving issue; *see* HARRINGTON, E), as well as other issue (*dsp*):

Sir Nathaniel Curzon, 2nd Bt; *b* 17 Jan 1635; London merchant by 1671, Sheriff Derbys 1691–92; *m* by licence 5 July 1671 Sarah (*d* 4 Jan 1727/8), dau of William Penn, of Penn Manor, Bucks, and *d* 4 March 1718/9, having had, with four daus:

1 **Sir John Curzon, 3rd Bt**; *b c* 1674; *educ* Trin Coll Oxford (BA) and Inner Temple; MP Derbys 1701–27; *d* unm 6 Aug 1727

2 NATHANIEL (Sir), **4th Bt**

3 Francis; *d* unm

4 William; MP Clitheroe

5 Charles; DCL; *dsp*

The 3rd Bt's bro,

Sir Nathaniel Curzon, 4th Bt; *b* 1676; *educ* Trin Coll Oxford; barrister Inner Temple 1700, MP Derby 1713–15, Clitheroe 1722–27 and Derbyshire 1721–54; *m* 19 Feb 1716 Mary (*d* 18 March 1776), dau and coheir of Sir Ralph Assheton, 2nd Bt, of Middleton, Lancs (for whose early ancestry *see* CLITHEROE, B), acquiring through her the Whalley Abbey estate, Lancs, which passed to his yr s, and *d* 16 Nov 1758, having had, with a 3rd but 2nd surv s (ASSHETON, *cr* VISCOUNT CURZON OF PENN; *see* HOWE, E):

Sir Nathaniel Curzon, 5th Bt, and **1st Baron Scarsdale**, Co Derby (GB), so *cr* 9 April 1761; *b* 23 Dec 1726; *educ* Ch Ch Oxford; MP (Tory) Clitheroe 1748–54 and Derbys 1754–61; Chm Ctees Ho Lds 1775–90 and Ctee of whole House on State of Nation 1778; *m* 27 Oct 1750 Lady Caroline Colyear (*d* 7 Feb 1812), est dau of 2nd Earl of Portmore (*see* 1833 edn), and *d* 6 Dec 1804, having had, with four yr sons (Charles William, *b* 1758, served Army, *d* 1804; John, *b* 1759, served RN, *d* 1794; Rev David Francis, *b* 18 July 1761, *d* 1832; Henry, *b* 24 May 1765, Adml RN, *d* 2 May 1846) and two daus (*d* unm):

NATHANIEL CURZON, **2nd Baron Scarsdale**; *b* 16 Sept 1751; *educ* Ch Ch Oxford (MA); MP (Tory) Derbys 1775–84; *m* 1st 11 Aug 1777 Hon Sophia Susannah Noel (*d* 28 June 1782), 3rd dau of 1st Viscount Wentworth, and had, with two daus (LYTTON, E):

1 NATHANIEL CURZON, **3rd Baron Scarsdale**; *b* 3 Jan 1781; *d* unm 12 Nov 1856

The **2nd Baron** *m* 2nd 18 Nov 1798 Félicité Anne Josèphe (*d* 16 Dec 1850), dau of François Josèphe de Wattines, of Cambrai, France, and *d* 26 Jan 1837, having by her had:

2 Alfred (Rev); *b* 17 April 1801; MA Oxon; Rector Kedleston 1832–50; *m* 14 July 1825 Sophia (*d* 9 Feb 1890), dau of Robert Holden, of Nuttall Temple, Notts, and *d* 12 Jan 1850, leaving:

(1) George Nathaniel; *b* 5 Oct 1826; *k* by a fall from his horse 17 June 1855

(2) ALFRED NATHANIEL HOLDEN, **4th Baron**

(1) Sophia Félicité; granted with her sister rank of baron's dau; *m* 7 Sept 1854 W Hatfield De Rhodes, of Barlborough Hall, Derbys, and *dsp* 2 April 1889. He *d* 1833

(2) Mary Catherine; *m* 15 April 1858 1st Baron Trevor (*qv*) and *d* 20 Aug 1911, having had issue

3 Francis James; *b* 25 April 1803; barrister; *m* Louisa — (*dsp* 6 Nov 1840) and *d* 24 May 1851

2 Mary Elizabeth; *m* 29 Aug 1825 John Beaumont, of Barrow, Derbys, and *d* 11 Oct 1868, having had issue. He *d* 11 March 1834

3 Caroline Esther; *m* 13 Feb 1827 William Drury-Lowe, of Locko Park, Derbys, and *d* 16 Oct 1886, having had issue. He *d* 26 Feb 1877

The **2nd Baron** also had illegitimately, with other such issue:

Félicité Anne Josèphe; *d* unm 10 April 1844

The 3rd BARON's n,

Rev ALFRED NATHANIEL HOLDEN CURZON, **4th Baron Scarsdale**, JP (Derbys); *b* 12 July 1831; *educ* Rugby and Merton Coll Oxford; Rector Kedleston 1856–1916, CA Derbys; *m* 3 July 1856 Blanche (*d* 4 April 1875), 2nd dau of Joseph Pocklington Senhouse, of Netherhall, Cumberland, and *d* 23 March 1916, having had:

1 GEORGE NATHANIEL CURZON, **1st Viscount Scarsdale**, of Scarsdale, Co Derby, so *cr* 2 Nov 1911, with remainder, in default of male issue, to his f and the latter's heirs male of the body, as also EARL CURZON OF KEDLESTON, Co Derby, with remainder to the heirs male of his body, and BARON RAVENSDALE OF RAVENSDALE, Co Derby (all UK), with remainder in default of male

issue to his est dau and the heirs male of her body, in default of which to his other daus by primogeniture and the heirs male of their bodies, as also earlier 11 Nov 1898 BARON CURZON OF KEDLESTON, Co Derby (I), and 28 June 1921 MARQUESS CURZON OF KEDLESTON (UK), with in both the last cases remainder to the heirs male of his body, KG (1916), GCSI, GCIE (1898), PC (1895); *b* 11 Jan 1859; *educ* Eton and Balliol Coll (Hon Fell 1907) Oxford (Pres Union 1880, Fell All Souls 1883, Hon DCL 1904, Chllr 1907); Assist Priv Sec to 3rd Marquess of Salisbury (*qv*) 1885, MP (C) Southport 1886–98 (fought S Derbys 1885), U-Sec India 1891–92 and For Affrs 1895–98, Viceroy India 1898–1904 and 1904–05, rep I peer 1908, Ld Privy Seal 1915–16, Pres Air Bd 1916, Ld Pres Cncl and memb War Cabinet 1916–19, For Sec 1919–24, Leader Ho Lds 1916–24, Ld Pres Cncl and Leader Ho Lds 1924–25, Ld Warden Cinque Ports 1904–05, Tstee Nat Gallery and Br Museum, Pres RGS 1911–14, Roy Victorian Chain, Hon LLD Cantab 1907, Manchester 1908 and Glasgow 1911, Ld Rector Glasgow U 1908; *m* 1st 22 April 1895 Mary Victoria, CI, Kaisar-i-Hind gold medal (*d* 18 July 1906), dau of Levi Zeigler Leiter, of Washington, DC, and had issue (*see* RAVENSDALE, B); *m* 2nd 2 Jan 1917 Grace Elvina, GBE (*d* 29 June 1958), widow of Alfred Duggan, of Buenos Aires, and dau of J Monroe Hinds, US Min Brazil, and *dspm* 20 March 1925, when the Marquessate, Earldom and Irish Barony expired

2 Alfred Nathaniel; *b* 12 March 1860; Maj TF, Lt-Col and Hon Col cmdg 3rd Bn Sherwood Foresters, Notts and Derbys Regt; *m* 29 April 1891 Henrietta Mary (*d* 7 Dec 1954, having *m* 2nd 3 Aug 1922 Brig-Gen Claude Julian Hawker, CMG, CBE (*d* 13 Sept 1936)), dau of Hon Spencer Dudley Montagu, 4th s of 4th Baron Rokeby of Armagh (*see* 1883 edn), and *d* 20 Sept 1920, leaving:

(1) RICHARD NATHANIEL CURZON, **2nd Viscount Scarsdale**, TD; *b* 3 July 1898; *educ* Eton and RMC Sandhurst; 2nd Lt RSG, Capt Derbys Yeo, served WWs I and II, memb Derbys TAA, Hon Col RA (TA), Hon Attaché Rome 1923, CStJ, Dir Derbys StJ Assoc, V-Pres: StJ Bde, Br Boxing Bd Control, Pres: Amateur Diving Assoc and Amateur Boxing Assoc, dir Arthur Woollacott Ltd; *m* 1st 14 April 1923 (*divorce* 1946) Mildred Carson (*d* 18 May 1969), dau of William Roland Dunbar, and had:

1a *Anne Mildred; *b* 1923; ATS WW II; *m* 17 Oct 1942 (*divorce* 1960) Maj Walter James Latimer Willson, DSO, Gren Gds (*d* 1994), er s of Sir Walter Willson, of Kenward, Tonbridge, Kent, and has had:

1b *Simon James Curzon; *b* 28 Sept 1942; *educ* Eton; *m* 1st 1968 Sarah, er dau of Douglas Ferris Hewat Jaboor, MB, of Jersey (*see* AYKROYD, Bt); *m* 2nd 1979 *Sandra, dau of Harold Singer, of Tillsonburg, Canada, and by his 1st w has:

1c *Alexander James Alfred Curzon; *b* 1969

2c *Benjamin William Curzon; *b* 25 June 1971

2b Nicholas William Curzon; *b* 12 April 1951; *educ* Eton

1b *Jacqueline Anne Curzon; *b* 12 May 1945; *m* 1967 *Anthony Julian Bavin

2a Gloria Mary; *b* 1927; *m* 31 March 1951 John Garland Bearman, Capt Gen List, 2nd s of Frank Charles Bearman, of Stanmore, Middx, and *d* 21 July 1979 aged 52, leaving:

1b *Christopher Charles; *b* 6 May 1952; *educ* Charterhouse

2b *Anthony Richard; *b* 12 Feb 1955; *educ* Harrow

3a *Juliana Eveline [The Hon Mrs Roberts, Castledown, Portroe, Nenagh, Co Tipperary, Ireland]; *b* 1928; *m* 1st 12 April 1948 (*divorce* 1952) George Derek Stanley Smith, Lt RNVR (*d* 12 July 1963), only s of Col George Edward Stanley Smith, DSO, of Trevella, St Erme, Cornwall, and has had:

1b *Charles Peregrine; *b* 5 Feb 1952; *educ* Eton

1b Charlotte Vanessa; *b* 2 Nov 1948; *d* 31 July 1949

2b *Venetia Mary; *b* 27 Dec 1950

3a (cont.) Mrs Juliana Smith *m* 2nd 14 May 1953 (*divorce* 1956) Frederick Nettlefold, only s of Frederick John Nettlefold, of Chelwood Vachery, Sussex, and by him has:

3b *Caroline Anne; *b* 28 Feb 1954; *m* 1979 *Ivor, Viscount Windsor, er s of 3rd Earl of Plymouth (*qv*)

3a (cont.) Mrs Juliana Nettlefold *m* 3rd 3 July 1956 (*divorce* 1962) Sir Dudley Herbert Cunliffe-Owen, 2nd Bt (*qv*), and has further issue; *m* 4th 3 March 1962 (*divorce* 1972) John Roberts and has further issue (*see* ROBERTS, Bt, of Milner Field)

4a *Diana Geraldine [The Hon Diana Curzon, 623 Av Jose Antonio, Barcelona, Spain]; *b* 1934

(1) (cont.) The **2nd Viscount** *m* 2nd 10 Aug 1946 Ottilie Margarete Julie (*d* 18 Jan 1998), Ensign FANY WW II, formerly w of James Harris and est dau of Charles Pretzlik, of Lowfield Park, Crawley, Sussex, and *dspm* 1977

(1) Magdalen Blanche; *b* 10 March 1892; granted 17 Jan 1930 with her sis rank of viscount's daus; *m* 1st 25 June 1919 (*divorce* 1932) Maj Hugh Percy Gillilan, KAR (*d* Jan 1967), yr s of W Gillilan, of Kensington; *m* 2nd 26 Jan 1939 Lt-Col Geoffrey Henry Julian FitzPATRICK formerly SKEFFINGTON SMYTH, DSO (*d* 11 March 1939), 9th Lancers, yr s of Edward Randal Skeffington Smyth, JP, DL, of Mount Henry; *m* 3rd 7 Oct 1944 Thomas Simpson-Pedler, LLB, barrister, s of William Henry Pedler, of Barnstaple, N Devon, and *d* 5 Nov 1973

(2) Rosamond Mary; *b* 24 Dec 1893; *m* 30 April 1924 Sir Robert Archibald Cary, 1st Bt, MP (*qv*), and had issue

3 Francis Nathaniel; *b* 15 Dec 1865; *educ* Eton and Balliol Coll Oxford (BA); dir: Westminster Bank, Gen and Commercial Tst, chm National Mutual Life Assur Soc, Govr: London Hosp, London Poly and City Parochial Fndn, Life Pres St Moritz Tobogganning Club; *m* 27 April 1922 Winifred Phyllis (*d* 6 April 1961), formerly w of Robert Lambart Dunville and dau of Capt Christian Combe, RHG (*see* CONYNGHAM, M), and *d* 8 June 1941, leaving:

(1) FRANCIS JOHN NATHANIEL CURZON, **3rd and present Viscount Scarsdale**

(1) *(Christian) Avril [The Hon Avril Curzon, The House of the Pines, Virginia Ave, Virginia Water, Surrey]; *b* 24 April 1923; granted rank of viscount's dau 1980

4 Assheton Nathaniel; *b* 10 May 1867; *educ* Cheltenham; *m* 20 July 1897 Mercy Lilian (*d* 16 Oct 1936), dau of Haughton Charles Okeover (*see* WALKER-OKEOVER, Bt), and *d* 20 Aug 1950, having had:

(1) Ralph Okeover Nathaniel; *b* 24 July 1904; Capt Derbys Yeo WW II; *kas* while flying 10 July 1940

(1) Joan Doreen; *b* 13 June 1898; MA Oxon, FSA; *m* 9 June 1945 Lawrence Edward Tanner, CVO, FSA, Librarian Westminster Abbey, yr s of Ralph Tanner, of Westminster School

(2) Rhona Lillian; *b* 5 Nov 1900; *m* 28 Jan 1930 Lt-Col Patrick Richard Butler, DSO, Roy Welch Fus, est s of Lt-Gen Sir William Francis Butler, GCB, PC, and *d* 11 July 1979, leaving issue. He *d* 14 Dec 1967

(3) Vera Lillian; *b* 5 Nov 1900; *d* unm 2 May 1976

1 Sophia Caroline; *b* 20 Nov 1857; *m* 17 Jan 1882 Rev Charles MacMichael, Rector Walpole St Peter, Wisbech, and *d* 12 March 1929, leaving issue. He *d* 22 Dec 1905

2 Blanche Felicia; *b* 18 April 1861; *d* unm 23 April 1928

3 Mary Eveline; *d* an infant 4 May 1862

4 Eveline Mary; *b* 16 Feb 1864; *m* 19 Jan 1893 Sir James Percy Miller, 2nd Bt, DSO (*see* 1902 edn), and *dsp* 15 June 1934. He *d* 22 Jan 1906

5 Elinor Florence; *b* 13 Feb 1869; *d* unm 11 March 1939

6 Geraline Emily; *b* 8 May 1871; *m* 28 Feb 1901 William Tower Townshend, of Myross Wood, Co Cork, and *d* 17 May 1940, leaving issue. He *d* 6 Feb 1943

7 Margaret Georgina; *b* 23 Dec 1873; *m* 26 Jan 1899 Hardress John Waller, s of Bolton J Waller, of Moystown, King's Co, and *d* 19 July 1957, leaving issue. He *d* 14 July 1944

Seat: Kedleston Hall, Derby. The Curzons had already held the Manor of Kedleston for several centuries when the present mansion of that name was erected between 1759 and 1765. An earlier house demolished to make way for it dated from *c* 1700. It was clearly the **1st Baron**'s intention to rebuild on a very magnificent scale right from the start since he transplanted the local village to a new site about a mile distant and had a nearby turnpike road re-routed, procuring an Act of Parliament to do so, an expensive undertaking at that time. Though Kedleston is most famously associated with Robert Adam, whose masterpiece it is often reckoned as being, the idea of a Palladian villa plan was originally introduced by Matthew Brettingham, who had worked at Holkham (*see* LEICESTER, E), and modified by James Paine after Brettingham's dismissal.

It was Brettingham who conceived the idea of a central block with four lesser pavilions at the end of quadrants. It was also he who built the northeast wing in which the family lived while the old house was razed to the ground and where the present family lives. His two planned southern extensions were never added, probably for lack of money.

Paine took over from Brettingham in 1759 and built the northwest wing which housed the kitchen and servants' quarters and the eastern portion of the central block. He also produced designs in the Palladian style for that central block's north front, with its portico reached by an external double-flighted staircase on either side. But he had no time to put them into execution as he was replaced only a year later by Adam.

Adam was introduced to the **1st Baron** in 1758. He had originally been engaged to carry out the interior designs of the rooms and was at first chiefly employed on embellishments to the gardens and park such as the Piranesi-esque bridge across the lake and the boat house at its western end. In recognition of his extraordinary versatility he was soon put in charge of building operations as well. It was accordingly he who built most of the central block, modifying Paine's north front design by incorporating roundels and niches for statues instead of windows. The design for the south front was entirely his and here he used a more romantic style with a feeling of what he called 'movement'. This he achieved by combining curves and projections in the semblance of a triumphal arch (derived specifically from the Arch of Constantine in Rome) between the dome above and the double staircase with its voluptuous curves below.

Inside Adam was again the dominant decorative influence, although the Great Hall just inside the north entrance, modelled on the 'Egyptian Hall' of Vitruvius as interpreted by Palladio, is usually attributed to Brettingham on the grounds that it strongly recalls Holkham. Here a central space is separated from niches for statuary let into the walls by numerous Corinthian columns in Nottinghamshire alabaster. The **1st Baron**, who was closely involved in every aspect of the operations, had them fluted some years later, finding the original surfaces too smooth and shiny for his liking. He also added murals, a stucco ceiling and fireplaces surmounted by lightly draped females (allegedly virgins) striking gracefully complaisant attitudes.

The ceiling in the Great Hall is by George Richardson, who was in charge of finishing Kedleston. He employed a more elaborate decorative scheme involving filigree, which by now was coming into fashion. He was Adam's principal draughtsman, however, so that there was no very violent contrast with what had gone before. The trinity of rooms leading off the Great Hall on the eastern side are assuredly by Adam. They are said to have been dedicated to the arts respectively of literature, music and painting. Also by Adam is the central Saloon, the Domenico Bartoli pilasters in green scagliola either side of each doorframe and the paintings by Biagio Rebecca being to his designs. This is a circular chamber ultimately inspired by the Pantheon in Rome and like the Great Hall essentially a space in which to house statuary. The four state rooms on the western side of the house are the other principal parts of Kedleston by Adam. The furniture is incomparable.

The **3rd** and present **Viscount Scarsdale** made Kedleston over to the National Trust in 1987. A grant from the National Heritage Memorial Fund has enabled not just the house to be kept up but the retention of the collection within it.

SCOTLAND OF ASTHALL

Creation: B. (LP, UK) 2 Aug 1997.

THE BARONESS SCOTLAND OF ASTHALL, of Asthall, Co Oxon (Patricia Janet Scotland, QC (1991)) [The Rt Hon The Baroness Scotland of Asthall, 1 Gray's Inn Sq, London WC1R 5AG]; *educ* London U; barrister Middle Temple 1977, Bencher 1997; memb: Commn Racial Equality, Antigua Bar, Millennium Commn 1994–; *m* 1985 *Richard Mawhinney and has two sons

SCOTT of Beauclerc

Arms: Per chevron az. and or in chief two bees volant, and in base a crescent, all counterchanged. **Crest:** A crescent sa., issuant therefrom a bee volant ppr. **Motto:** *Invitum sequitur honor* ('Honour follows when unsought'). **Creation:** Bt. (UK) 27 July 1907.

SIR (WALTER) JOHN SCOTT, 5TH BT, of Beauclerc, Bywell St Andrews, Co Northumberland [Sir John Scott Bt, Darned House, Gifford, E Lothian EH14 4PJ]; *b* 24 Feb 1948; *s* f 1992; *educ* privately; farmer; *m* 1st 5 July 1969 (*divorce* 1971) Lowell Patria, dau of S/Ldr Pat Vaughan Goddard, of Auckland, NZ, and has:

1 *Rebecca; *b* 20 March 1970

Sir JOHN *m* 2nd 1977 *Mary Gavin, only dau of Alexander Fairly Anderson, of Gartocharn, Dunbartonshire, and by her has:

1 +WALTER SAMUEL; *b* 6 Dec 1984

2 *Diana Helen Rose; *b* 1977

Lineage: SAMUEL SCOTT, of Holm Cultram, Cumberland; *m* 25 Dec 1824 Mary Martin (*d* 10 Feb 1877), of Holm Cultram, and *d* 30 Aug 1833, leaving:

Sir Walter Scott, 1st Bt (UK), so *cr* 27 July 1907, of Beauclerc, Bywell St Andrews, Northumberland, JP; *b* 17 Aug 1826; *m* 1st 17 Nov 1853 Ann (*d* 11 June 1890), dau of John Brough, of Bromfield, Cumberland, and had:

1 **Sir John Scott, 2nd Bt**; *b* 23 Aug 1854; *m* 1st 6 Sept 1882 Elizabeth (*d* 13 Dec 1911), dau of Mark Garbutt, of Saltburn, Yorks; *m* 2nd 1919 Emily (*d* 24 May 1939), dau of Thomas Coates, of Benwell, Darlington, and *dsp* 29 April 1922

2 Walter; *b* 1 Nov 1858; *d* unm 23 Sept 1880

3 Joseph Samuel; *b* 6 Aug 1863; *m* 25 Jan 1893 Mary Hannah (*d* 24 Oct 1916), dau of Robert Appleby Oswald, of Kellow, Co Durham, and *d* 1 April 1906, having had:

(1) WALTER (Sir), **3rd Bt**

(1) Millie Oswald; *b* 10 Oct 1897; *m* 19 Jan 1922 Lt-Col Alan Wood, MC, RA, s of Philip Sleigh Wood, of Ravenscroft, Westhole, Co Durham, and had issue

4 Mason Thompson; *b* 29 Dec 1865; *m* 30 Nov 1899 Flora Alice (*d* 6 Dec 1903), dau of Joseph Williams, of Putney, and *d* 1 June 1916, leaving:

(1) William Walter Brough; *b* 27 Oct 1902; *educ* Harrow and RMC Sandhurst; T/Maj The Royals WW II, MFH: United 1927–28, (Jt) Portman 1928–32 and 1949–52, N Cotswold 1932–47, W Waterford 1947–49 and (Jt) Old Berks 1957–65; *m* 1st 1 July 1926 (*annulled* 1937) Bridget Margaret, dau of Charles Leigh Clay, of Wyndcliffe Court, Chepstow; *m* 2nd 25 Sept 1937 Pamela (*d* 2 May 1992), dau of Sir Charles William Fielding, KBE (*see* DENBIGH and DESMOND, E), and *d* 1980, leaving:

1a +(Charles) Martin Fielding [Martin Scott Esq, Mawley Farm House, Quenington, Glos GL7 5BW]; *b* 27 March 1945; *educ* Harrow and RMA Sandhurst; late Lt Roy Dragoons, Jt MFH Tiverton 1969–76 and VWH 1977–85, with Hambro Life 1981–91 and J Rothschild Assur 1992–; *m* 27 April 1970 *Mrs Jill Woodward, dau of W/Cdr Marcus Mowbray Hutchinson, AFC, AAF, and has:

1b *Camilla Jane; *b* 1971

1a *Maxine Ling Elizabeth [Mrs Edward Northey, 10 Linden Rd, Swanage BH19 1JH]; *b* 4 Oct 1939; *m* 1st 29 Oct 1966 (*divorce* 1975) Manuel Diaz-Camacho and has:

1b *Roderigo Manuel; *b* 1967

1b *Carolina del Rocio; b 1969

1a (cont.) Mrs Maxine Diaz-Camacho m 2nd 1975 (divorce) Edward Martin Anthony Northey and by him has:

2b *Andrew Edward William; b 1978

2b *Lucinda Elizabeth; b 1976

(1) Flora Brookbank; b 7 Oct 1903; m 3 Feb 1925 Brig Christopher Anthony White, KRRC (d 4 July 1969), only s of Anthony White, of Woolverstone Ho, nr Ipswich, and d 31 Oct 1982, having had:

1a *Jeremy Anthony [Maj Jeremy White, West Wing, Thornton Hall, Thornton, Bucks MK17 0HB]; b 13 Jan 1926; educ Eton; Maj late RSG; m 24 Jan 1951 *Elizabeth Catherine Denise, dau of John Adrian Frederick March Phillipps de Lisle, of Stockerston Hall, Uppingham, Leics, and has:

2b *Anthony John [Anthony White Esq, Leckhampstead House, nr Buckingham MK18 5NU]; b 8 Jan 1958; educ Milton Abbey; m 19– *Tessa Marian, dau of Lt-Col Sir John Hugo, KCVO, OBE, of Hilltop House, Vines Cross, Heathfield, and has:

1c *Zara Elizabeth Hugo; b 21 Dec 1987

2c *Charlotte Antonia; b 24 May 1989

3c *Serena Isabel; b 16 June 1992

1b *Phillippa Elizabeth White [Miss Phillippa White, The Stables, Bulls Lane, Thorpe Mandeville, Oxon OX17 2HX]; b 12 June 1952; Sec Grafton Hunt; Sec and Co-Fndr Union Country Sports Workers 1997–

2b *Juliet Anne [Mrs Peter Fenton, Merchants Farm, Long Newnton, Glos GL8 8RP]; b 15 Feb 1955; m 7 May 1983 *Peter Anthony Fenton, s of Mark Powell Fenton, of Cape Province, S Africa, and has:

1c *Christopher Belmont; b 8 July 1988

1c *Emily Victoria; b 26 Jan 1986

3b *Annabel Mary [Mrs Edward Montgomerey, The Plans, 38 The Longshott, Ballyclare, Co Antrim BT39 9SA]; b 1 Jan 1962; educ North Foreland Lodge and Exeter U; m 28 Aug 1990 *(Hugh) Edward John Montgomery, s of Hugh James Montgomery, of Benvarden, Dervock, Co Antrim, and has:

1c *Alexander Charles; b 4 July 1993

2c *James Anthony; b 29 Oct 1995

1a Gillian; b 9 April 1929; m 1st 2 July 1949 (divorce 1961) Ian Francis Coleridge Cole (d 12 Feb 1996), s of Coleridge Cole, of Knotty Green, Beaconsfield, and had:

1b *Christopher Ian [Christopher Coleridge Cole Esq, 8/F Yau Shun Bldg, 46–50 D'Aguilar St, Central, Hong Kong]; b 14 Nov 1950; educ Lancing; m 1st 30 June 1976 (divorce 1983) Anna Bouverie, dau of Keith Lyle, and has:

1c *Georgina Anoushka; b 3 Nov 1981

1b (cont.) Christopher Coleridge Cole m 2nd 18 Dec 1985 *Belinda Helen, dau of Gabriel Constantine Nassif, and by her has:

1c *Benjamin Ian; b 21 Sept 1986

2c *Freddie Ian William; b 21 Feb 1989

2c *Alexa Rosamunde; b 21 Oct 1993

1a (cont.) Mrs Gillian Cole m 2nd 20 March 1964 *Col Anthony Derek Swift Mangnall, OBE, s of Capt A R Mangnall, MC, of Christleton Grange, nr Chester and d 6 Aug 1989

5 Charles Thomas; b 4 March 1868; Capt Gloucester Yeo; m 13 June 1893 Jane Davidson (d 17 July 1958), dau of James Milvain, of Newcastle, and d 14 Jan 1953, having had:

(1) Charles Brough; b 4 Jan 1896; educ Harrow and RMC Sandhurst; Lt 1st Roy Dragoons; ka 20 Nov 1917

(2) Mason Hogarth; b 11 Aug 1900; educ RNCs Osborne and Dartmouth; Capt RN, Naval Attaché Madrid 1944–46, Chm Rahere Assoc (Friends of St Bart's Hosp), Jt MFH N Cotswold 1961–65; m 11 June 1924 Hon Irene Florence Seely (d 1976), 2nd dau of 1st Baron Mottistone (qv), and d 25 May 1971, leaving:

1a +Mason Charles; b 28 June 1930; educ Radley and RMA Sandhurst; late Capt Scots Gds; m 7 Nov 1953 *Judith Alison, dau of Capt M R Dalgliesh, of Truro, Cornwall, and has:

1b +Mason Stapleton; b 12 Aug 1954

2b +Adam; b 20 April 1963; m 1991 *Louise Sinclair Maddocks and has:

1c +Rory Sinclair; b 1992

1c *Laura Sinclair; b 1993

1b *Emma Jane; b 1957

2a +(John) Brough [Brough Scott Esq, Meadow House, Ewhurst, Surrey GU6 9PL]; b 12 Dec 1942; educ Radley and Corpus Christi Coll Oxford; former Nat Hunt jockey (100 winners), racing jnlst, edtl dir Racing Post 1988–, ch presenter Channel 4 Racing 1985–, ch sports writer Sunday Telegraph 1995–, author: World of Flat Racing (1983), On and Off the Rails (1984), Front Runners (1991), Up Front — Willie Carson (1994); m 3 Nov 1973 *Susan E, dau of R G MacInnes, of Meadow Ho, Ewhurst, Surrey, and has:

1b +Charles Ronald Brough; b 1976

2b +James Seely; b 1979

1b *Sophie Diana; b 1974

2b *Tessa Irene; b 1984

1a *Jane Emily [Lady Gow, 18 Ann St, Edinburgh EH4 1PJ]; b 12 March 1925; m 3 Oct 1946 Gen Sir (James) Michael Gow, GCB, Scots Gds, s of J C Gow, and has:

1b *Roderick Charles [Roderick Gow Esq, 49 Grahampton Lane, Greenwich, CT 06830, USA]; b 9 Sept 1947; educ Winchester and Trin Coll Cambridge; late Capt Scots Gds; m *Anne Bayart and has:

1c *Andrew Jonathan; b 8 March 1978

2c *Neil James; b 1981

1b *Susan Jane [Mrs Malcolm Ross, Netherhall, Bridge of Dee, Kirkcudbrightshire DG7 2AA]; b 7 March 1949; m 31 Jan 1969 *Lt-Col (W H) Malcolm Ross, CVO, OBE, late Scots Gds, er s of W J M Ross, and has:

1c *Hector Walter James; b 1983

1c *Tabitha Alice; b 1970

2c *Flora Jane Josephine; b 1974

2b *Anna Katharine [Mrs Anna Hunter, 12 Oakthorpe Rd, Oxford OX2 7BG]; b 12 April 1952; m 1977 (divorce 1991) Charles Hunter and has:

1c *Timothy Michael; b 1981

2c *Patrick James Simon; b 1984

1c *Sophie Irene; b 1977

3b *Belinda Catriona [Mrs Julius Drake, 21 Creighton Rd, London NW6 6EE]; b 3 June 1958; m 1987 *Julius M Drake, est s of Michael Drake, of Hampstead, and has:

1c *Katherine Molly Myrtle; b 12 Feb 1992

2c *Lydia Beatrice Elizabeth; b 14 Oct 1994

4b *Clunie Fiona Mary [Mrs Samuel Phipps, 5 Gillespie St, Edinburgh EH3 9NH; b 16 Nov 1964; m 1990 *Samuel Cornelius Dominic Phipps and has issue (see NORMANBY, M)

2a *(Irene) Jill; b 16 Feb 1928; m 14 June 1951 *John Gore Phillimore, CMG, and has issue (see PHILLIMORE, B)

3a *Janet Sylvia [Mrs Simon Chamberlayne, Oakham, Little Compton, Glos]; b 22 Nov 1941; m 20 April 1963 *Simon John Chamberlayne, er s of Lt-Col John Edward Stanes Chambelayne, of The Elm, Chipping Norton, Oxon, and has:

1b *Edward Charles; b 26 April 1966; m 1990 *Zoë E Cursham

1b *Sarah Caroline; b 10 June 1964

2b *Laura; b 1972

4a *Jennifer Teresa [Mrs Patrick Scott, 23 Caroline Terrace, London SW1]; b 16 Oct 1945; m 29 July 1967 *(Alexander) Patrick Scott, yr s of Col Alexander Brassey Jonathan Scott, DSO, MC, of Lasborough, Tetbury, Glos, and has:

1b *Emily Mary; b 1968

2b *Catherine Charlotte; b 1970

6 William Martin; b 27 March 1870; m 19 May 1906 Janie (d 10 Sept 1954), dau of James Birrell Campbell, of London, and dsp 26 Feb 1944

1 Annie Mary; b 14 Oct 1856; m 10 Dec 1891 Col John Victor Walton Rutherford, MB, of Briarwood, Newcastle, and d 13 June 1922

2 Fanny Elizabeth; b 30 July 1861; m 10 Jan 1888 George Brook, FLS, of Edinburgh, and d 23 Sept 1917, leaving issue. He d 1893

Sir Walter m 2nd Jan 1892 Helen (d 31 Oct 1936), widow of James Meikle, of Newcastle, and dau of John Dykes, of Avondale, Lanarks, and d 8 April 1910

His n,

Sir Walter Scott, 3rd Bt; b 31 March 1895; educ Charterhouse and Jesus Coll Cambridge; Maj RASC, served WW I and WW II; m 1st 10 Nov 1915 Nancie Margaret (Margot) (d 10 May 1944), dau of Samuel Herbert March, of Cannes; m 2nd 4 Oct 1949 Dorothea Cara (d 3 Nov 1970), widow of John Francis Crisp and dau of Col Francis John Fox, RHA, and d 8 June 1967, leaving by his 1st w:

Sir Walter Scott, 4th Bt, JP (E Sussex 1963), DL (1975); b 29 July 1918; educ Eton and Jesus Coll Cambridge; Maj 1st Royal Dragoons WW II; m 1st 15 Jan 1944 Diana Mary (d 1985), only dau of James Richard Owen, JP, of Holly Hill, Coleman's Hatch; m 2nd 1991 *Anna-Louise [Dowager Lady Scott, Newhouse West, Church Lane, Ripe, Sussex BN8 6AS], dau of Aubrey Derwent Healing, of Lewes, and d 1992, leaving by his 1st w:

1 Sir (WALTER) JOHN SCOTT, 5th and present Bt

1 Sarah Jane; b 28 Oct 1945; m 23 June 1972 (divorce 1987) 15th Duke of Hamilton and (12th Duke of) Brandon (qv) and d 1994, leaving issue

SCOTT of Rotherfield

Arms: Per pale indented arg. and sa. a saltire counterchanged. **Crest:** Out of a circlet of pales or a cubit arm erect habited gu., cuffed erm, the hand ppr. holding a paper scroll arg. **Motto:** In Christo salus ('In Christ alone is salvation'). **Creation:** Bt. (UK) 16 Feb 1962.

SIR JAMES JERVOISE SCOTT, 3RD BT, of Rotherfield, Co Southampton [Sir James Scott Bt, Rotherfield Park, Alton, Hants GU34 3QL]; b 12 Oct 1952; s f 1993; educ Eton and Trin Coll Cambridge (MA); land-owner, ag jnlst 1977–88, ed

Big Farm Weekly 1984–88; *m* 1982 *Judy Evelyn, formerly *w* of Andrew Lyndon-Skeggs and dau of Brian Sadler Leigh Trafford by Hon Audrey Evelyn Taylor, er dau of Baron Taylor of Hadfield (LP, *cr* 1983, *extinct* 1995), of Tismans, Rudgwick, W Sussex, and has:

  1 +ARTHUR JERVOISE TRAFFORD; *b* 2 Feb 1984; *educ* Eton

  1 *Alexandra Lilian; *b* 21 March 1986

Lineage: WILLIAM SCOTT, of Stapleford Tawney, Essex; held Manors of Wolfhampton, Ovesham, Guynge and Laytons 1476 and Manor of Stapleford by 1485; *m* Margaret/Margery (*d* 14 Oct 1505), dau and heir of Thomas Swynbourne, of York, and *d* 3 Nov 1491, leaving six sons and two daus; the 4th s:

JOHN SCOTT, of Hatfield Regis, Essex; *m* 1st —; *m* 2nd Johan — and *d* between 30 Dec 1558 and 28 Jan 1558/9, leaving, with four sons:

CHRISTOPHER SCOTT, of Hatfield Regis; yeoman; *d* between 1 April and 3 Aug 1640, leaving, with a yr s and three daus:

JOHN SCOTT, of Bishop Stortford, Herts; yeoman; *m* Rebecca — and *d* between 29 March 1661 and 23 March 1662, leaving three sons and three daus; the 2nd s:

SAMUEL SCOTT, of Little Hadham, Essex; yeoman; *m* 1st Marie — and had seven sons and three daus; *m* 2nd Margaret — (*d* between 22 June 1687 and 15 April 1689) and *d* between 5 Aug 1672 and 20 May 1687; his 2nd s by his 1st w:

THOMAS SCOTT, of Hadham Hall, Little Hadham; yeoman; *m* 1st Sarah — (*bur* 18 Aug 1685) and had issue; *m* 2nd Mary (*d* 5 Aug 1729), dau of Zachariah Nicholls, of Little Hadham, and was *bur* 6 Aug 1717, leaving:

SAMUEL SCOTT, of Fulham, Middx; brickmaker; *m* Sarah — and *d* 25 May 1719, leaving, with other issue:

THOMAS SCOTT, of Walham Green, Fulham; brickmaker; *m* by licence 24 Aug 1720 Anne Whittle, of Hackney, and *d* 19 Oct 1749, leaving, with other issue:

WILLIAM SCOTT, of Hammersmith and Grosvenor Place, Mayfair; *b* 29 Oct 1729; *m* 16 April 1764 Mary (*d* 28 May 1835 aged 92), dau of Richard Jeffreys, London merchant, and *d* 20 Dec 1785, leaving, with other issue:

JAMES SCOTT, of Hammersmith, Rotherfield Park, Hants, which he bought from the Marquess of Winchester 1808, and Shepperton Manor, Middx, JP Middx; *b* 1776; MP Bridport, High Sheriff Hants 1821; *m* 1st 5 Oct 1797 Martha (*d* 16 May 1815), dau of Thomas Bradbury Winter, of Shenley, Herts; *m* 2nd 29 Jan 1819 Margaret (*dsp* 5 Jan 1850 aged 68), dau of William Snell, of Salisbury Hall, Herts, and *d* 28 Feb 1855, leaving:

JAMES WINTER SCOTT, of Rotherfield Park, JP, DL Hants; *b* 26 May 1799; MP N Hants 1832–37, High Sheriff Hants 1864; *m* 24 Jan 1828 Lucy (*d* 19 Jan 1901 aged 90), yst dau of Rev Sir Samuel Clarke Jervoise, 1st Bt, of Idsworth Park (*see* 1933 edn), and *d* 4 Jan 1873, leaving:

  1 George Arthur Jervoise, of Rotherfield Park, Hants, JP, DL Hants; *b* 2 Nov 1833; *educ* Eton and Ch Ch Oxford (MA 1859); barrister Inner Temple, Fell All Souls, CA Hants; *m* 1 Sept 1875 Lady Mary Angela Wellesley (*see* WELLINGTON, D) and *dsp* 4 March 1895

  2 Walter Jervoise, JP Qld; *b* 3 April 1835; *educ* Eton and Merton Coll Oxford (BA); barrister Inner Temple, Sec to Govr Mauritius; *d* unm 26 June 1890

  3 Charles James (Rev), of Rotherfield Park and Forres, Morayshire; *bapt* 2 April 1837; *educ* Eton and Merton Coll Oxford (MA); Rector E Tisted, Hants; *m* 23 April 1874 Ruth, dau of Robert Caldwell, of Charleston, SC, and *dsp* 10 May 1899

  4 ARCHIBALD EDWARD

  1 Lucy Gertrude; *d* 28 June 1892 aged 63

  2 Katharine Maria; *bapt* 16 May 1830; *m* 9 April 1850 Sir Charles Hayes Miller, 7th Bt, of Chichester (*qv*), and *d* 11 Dec 1909, leaving issue

  3 Elinor; *bapt* 15 July 1832; *m* 5 June 1867 Maj-Gen Sir Charles Walters D'Oyly, 9th Bt (*qv*), of Newlands, Dorset, and *dsp* 3 Dec 1914

  4 Dora Caroline; *b* 12 March 1842; *m* 10 Oct 1861 Capt Richard William Spicer, 16th Lancers, and *d* 20 Feb 1919, leaving issue. He *d* 1892

The 4th s,

ARCHIBALD EDWARD SCOTT, of Rotherfield Park, JP Hants; *b* 17 Jan 1851; *educ* Eton and Merton Coll Oxford; Ld Manors of Rotherfield, E Tisted and Noar; *m* 22 Nov 1888 Cecilia Maria (*d* 11 July 1931), dau of William Bolitho, of Polwithen, Cornwall, and *d* 8 Jan 1924, leaving:

  1 JERVOISE BOLITHO (Sir), **1st Bt**

  2 Oswald Arthur (Sir), KCMG (1951), DSO (1918); *b* 17 June 1893; *educ* Eton and Magdalen Coll Oxford; Maj 10th Bn Hants Regt WW I (despatches), Dip Serv: joined 1919, 1st Sec Madrid 1933, Counsellor Baghdad 1937, Lisbon 1938, FO 1940–47, Min Finland 1947–51, Amb Peru 1951–53; *m* 1st 19 May 1917 (*divorce* 1933) Hermione Monica, dau of William Ferrand, of St Ives, and had:

    (1) Edward Jervoise Ferrand; *b* 8 Feb 1918; *educ* Eton and Magdalene Coll Cambridge; 2nd Lt KRRC 1940, Mil Attaché Kabul 1942–45; *m* 1st 24 Aug 1949 (*divorce* 1966) Diana Madeleine, formerly w of John Francis George Perceval and dau of Lt-Cdr Vyvyan Whitmore Pearce, RN, of Cape Town, and had:

      1a *James Richard; *b* 6 May 1950; *educ* Eton

      2a *Roland Edward; *b* 6 May 1950; *educ* Eton

      3a *Nicholas Arthur; *b* 3 July 1952; *educ* Eton

      4a *Anthony Vyvyan; *b* 3 July 1952; *educ* Eton; *m*

    (1) (cont.) Edward Scott *m* 2nd 30 Sept 1966 *Anne, dau of Percy William Elliott, of Alton, Hants

    (2) Richard Oswald; *b* 4 April 1920; 2nd Lt KRRC WW II; *ka* Calais 25 May 1940

    (3) Thomas Roland; *b* 13 Oct 1923; P/O RAFVR WW II; *k* on flying ops 22 Oct 1942

    (1) *Monica Cecilia, JP (Suffolk 1969) [Mrs Hugh Philbrick JP, Turnstall Hall, Woodbridge, Suffolk]; *b* 20 Dec 1925; *m* 23 July 1949 *Hugh Ludlow Philbrick, s of Alan Nelson Philbrick, of Seckford House, Woodbridge, and has:

      1a *Richard Hugh; *b* 27 Dec 1950; *educ* Marlborough and Newcastle U

      2a *David Roland Scott; *b* 28 May 1952; *educ* Marlborough

      1a *Sarah Monica Loveday; *b* 20 Nov 1954

    2a *Clare Ludlow; *b* 5 July 1957

  2 (cont.) Sir Oswald *m* 2nd 3 Jan 1934 Ursula Margaret, yst dau of Rev Henry Bazeley Wolryche-Whitmore, of Royal Hill, Tewkesbury, Glos, and *d* 19 May 1960

  3 Geoffrey Thomas Archibald; *b* 24 Feb 1895; *educ* RNCs Osborne and Dartmouth; Cdr RN, served WWs I and II 1942; *m* 29 Oct 1932 Geraldine Amelia, only child of Lt-Col Alexander Fitzgerald Watt, DSO, of Hemingford Grey House, Hunts, and *d* 5 Nov 1958, leaving:

    (1) *John Jervoise Fitzgerald; *b* 12 Aug 1933; *educ* Eton and RMA Sandhurst; Lt-Col Blues and Royals, formerly Roy Dragoons; *m* 24 April 1957 *Susan Valerie, est dau of Lt-Col Sir Ranulph Twisleton-Wykeham-Fiennes, 2nd Bt (*qv*), and has:

      1a *Arabella Caroline; *b* 15 April 1959; *m* 1986 *Francis D Wiliams

      2a *Venetia Lucy; *b* 25 June 1963

    (2) *David Robert Geoffrey; *b* 7 Jan 1943; *educ* Eton

    (1) *Cecilia Caroline Georgina; *b* 16 Jan 1936; *m* 11 March 1959 Maj Philip Walter Frank Arkwright, Blues and Royals, formerly Roy Dragoons, yr s of Lt-Col Francis Godfrey Bertram Arkwright, DSO, MC, 12th Roy Lancers, and has:

      1a *Dominic Geoffrey Philip; *b* 16 March 1961

      2a *Francis Jocelyn Philip; *b* 8 March 1965

      1a *Annabel Georgia; *b* 16 May 1962

    (2) *Rosamond Geraldine; *b* 6 June 1938; *m* 21 Feb 1968 Robert Donald Harman, s of Herbert Donald Harman, and has:

      1a *Davina Rose; *b* 28 June 1969

  1 Margaret Lucy; *b* 8 Aug 1890; *m* May 1919 Capt Robert Francis Hanbury, 14th Bn Beds Regt, only s of Edmund Smith Hanbury, DL, of Poles, Herts, and *d* 10 March 1966, leaving issue. He *d* April 1960

The est s,

Sir Jervoise Bolitho Scott, 1st Bt (UK), so *cr* 16 Feb 1962, JP (Hants 1926), DL (1936); *b* 3 Feb 1892; *educ* Eton and Magdalen Coll Oxford (BA 1913); Capt 7th QOH WW I, ret 1925, WW II: Pioneer Corps 1942, Col 1944, Dep Dir Labour SHAEF 1944, Palestine 1945, Jt MFH Hampshire 1925–29, Hants: CC 1932, High Sheriff 1936, CA 1949, Chm Alton Petty Sessions 1932–39 and 1946–65, Official Verderer New Forest 1950–64; *m* 31 Jan 1924 Kathleen Isabel, yr dau of Godfrey Walter, of Malshanger, Hants, and had:

  1 JAMES WALTER (Sir), **2nd Bt**

  2 +Samuel Arthur [Samuel Scott Esq, Thatched Cottage, E Tisted, Hants]; *b* 17 June 1926; *educ* Eton and RMC Sandhurst; 7th QOH 1946–48, 8th KRI Hus Korea 1950–51, 21st SAS (Artists) TA 1951–52; *m* 28 Sept 1952 *Juliet Modwena, er dau of Samuel Ranulph Allsopp, CBE, DL (*see* HINDLIP, B), and has:

    (1) +Henry Samuel Jervoise; *b* 25 Nov 1955; *educ* Eton and RMA Sandhurst; Maj Life Gds; *m* 1979 *Joanna Sarah, dau of James Brownlow, of The Old Rectory, Kelling, Norfolk, and has:

      1a +Geoffrey James Ranulph; *b* 1980

      2a +Rory Samuel Jervoise; *b* 1982

  3 Richard Jervoise, TD; *b* 23 May 1929; *educ* Eton, New Coll Oxford and Belfast Tech; Rifle Bde 1947–49, Maj Queen's Roy Rifles (TA), memb London Stock Exchange, attended Admin Staff Coll Henley 1965; *m* 19 Jan 1955 *Julia Maud, yr dau of Brig Sir Henry Robert Kincaid Floyd, 5th Bt, CB, CBE (*qv*), and had:

    (1) *Victoria Kathleen; *b* 30 Jan 1956; *m* 1977 *Charles Herbert Parker and has:

      1a *Thomas Richard; *b* 1982

      2a *Samuel George; *b* 1984

      1a *Emma Louise; *b* 1987

    (2) *Camilla Julia *b* 17 April 1958; *m* 1986 *Lord Michael Hugh Cecil, yst s of 6th Marquess of Salisbury (*qv*), and has issue

The 1st Bt *d* 21 June 1965; his est s,

Sir James Walter Scott, 2nd Bt; *b* 26 Oct 1924; *educ* Eton;) Life Gds, Gren Gds 1943–60: France and Germany WW II 1944–45, Palestine 1945–46, ADC to Viceroy India 1946–48, Malaya 1948–49, Adj Gds Depot 1949–51, psc 1954, Adj RMA Sandhurst 1956–58, Cyprus 1958, Mil Assist to Gen Sir Dudley Ward 1959–60, tfd Life Gds 1960, Cyprus 1964, Malaysia 1966, ret as Lt-Col 1969, Ld Lt Hampshire 1982–93; underwriting memb Lloyd's 1954, Master Mercers' Co 1977 (Liveryman 1969, Renter Warden 1973), Lt of Gentlemen at Arms 1993 (memb 1977–93); *m* 8 Dec 1951 *Anne Constantia [Anne Lady Scott, The Knapp, Colemore, Hants GU34 3RX], est dau of Lt-Col Clive Grantham, Austin, DL, of Roundwood, Micheldever, Hants, and *d* 1993, having had:

  1 Sir JAMES JERVOISE SCOTT, **3rd and present Bt**

  2 +Charles Clive [Charles Scott Esq, Manor Farm, Colemore, Alton, Hants GU34 3RX]; *b* 31 July 1954; *educ* Eton and Trin Coll Cambridge; *m* 1979 *Caroline Frances, dau of Hugh Grahame Jago, of Old Cottage, Campfield Pl, Leith Hill, Surrey, and has:

    (1) *Eleanor Gabriel; *b* 1981

    (2) *Rose Loveday; *b* 1983

    (3) *Alice Olivia; *b* 1987

  3 Alex(ander) Archibald; *b* 8 Feb 1960; *educ* Eton and Queens' Coll Cambridge; racehorse trainer (won 164 races and trained two champions in six years); *m* 1986 *Julia Mary Mackenzie [Mrs Alexander Scott, Glebe House, Cheveley, Suffolk CB8 9DG], est dau of Patrick William Mackenzie Dean, of E Mere, Lincs, and was *k* 1994, leaving:

    (1) +Daniel Fitzroy; *b* 1987

    (2) +Rupert Patrick; *b* 1992

    (1) *Emily Rosanna; *b* 1990

  1 Mary Anne Louise; *b* 29 May 1957; *d* 15 Dec 1962

  2 *Susannah Maria [Mrs James Kelly, Ardovie House, by Brechin, Angus DD9 6ST]; *b* 2 Oct 1963; *m* 1990 *Maj James Richard Kelly, Scots Gds, only s of John Kelly, of Barnes, London SW, and has:

    (1) *Archibald Clive; *b* 3 Jan 1992

    (2) *George Claude; *b* 15 May 1993

    (3) *James Charles; *b* 22 Jan 1995

SCOTT of Witley

Arms: Arg. pelletée, in base a lymphad sa., pennons flying to the sinister gu., in chief two crescents az. **Crest:** An ancient cannon firing to the dexter ppr. **Motto:** Aim straight. **Creation:** Bt. (UK) 3 Feb 1913.

SIR ANTHONY PERCY SCOTT, 3RD BT, of Witley, Surrey [Sir Anthony Scott Bt, Longbarrow, Goodworth Clatford, Hants SP11 7SE]; *b* 1 May 1937; *s* f 1984; *educ* Harrow and Ch Ch Oxford (MA); barrister Inner Temple 1960, chm and md L M (Moneybrokers) Ltd 1986–95; *m* 2 June 1962 *Caroline Theresa Anne, er dau of (William Charles) Edward Bacon, of Hill Ho, Mobberley, Cheshire, and has:

1 +HENRY DOUGLAS EDWARD [Henry Scott Esq, 59 Church Path, London W4 5BH]; *b* 26 March 1964; *educ* Harrow; *m* 1993 *Carole Ruth, er dau of Derek Maddick and Mrs E Roberts, of Auckland, NZ

2 +Simon James (Rev); *b* 31 March 1965; *educ* Harrow, Ch Ch Oxford and Wycliffe Hall Oxford; ordained 1991

1 *Miranda Claire; *b* 6 Dec 1967

Lineage: JAMES SCOTT; Dr; had:

MONTAGU SCOTT; had:

Sir Percy Moreton Scott, 1st Bt (UK), so *cr* 3 Feb 1913, KCB (1910, CB 1900), KCVO (1906, CVO 1902); *b* 10 July 1853; *educ* UCL and RNC Greenwich: RN: joined 1866, served Ashanti War 1873–77 (despatches, medal), Congo Expdn 1875 (despatches, promotion), Egypt 1882 (despatches, medal, bronze star), R-Adml 1895, Boer War 1899–1900 (medal, despatches), China 1900 (medal), ADC to HM EDWARD VII 1900–05, V-Adml 1908, Adml 1913 (ret but returned to active serv Nov 1914); invented signalling lamps, targets and other gunnery appliances, also gun carriages used in the Chinese Expdn and Boer War and the technique called 'director firing', LLD Cantab, Kt Cdr St Olav Norway and Medjidie 3rd Cl; *m* 1st 10 Jan 1893 (*divorce* 1911) Teresa Roma (*d* 20 March 1928), est dau of Sir Frederick Dixon-Hartland, 1st and last Bt (*see* 1909 edn), and had:

1 John D'Urban; *b* 12 Feb 1900; Midshipman RN; *ka* Battle of Jutland 31 May 1916

2 DOUGLAS WINCHESTER (Sir), **2nd Bt**

1 Rosemary; *b* 21 Oct 1903; *m* 27 Nov 1926 Col Sir John Frederick INGLEFIELD later CROMPTON-INGLEFIELD (deed poll 15 Dec 1930), TD, DL, Derbys Yeo, est s of Adml Sir Frederick Samuel Inglefield, KCB, and *d* 19 Aug 1978, leaving:

(1) *Patricia Jane, JP Staffs; *b* 29 Nov 1929; *m* 23 June 1951 Michael Christopher Bagshawe, TD, 2nd s of Francis Ernest Gisborne Bagshawe, JP, DL, of Snitterton Hall, Matlock, Derbys, and has:

1a *John Nicholas Samuel; *b* 4 Dec 1954; *educ* Stowe

1a *Albinia Sarah; *b* 5 Feb 1953

(2) *Isma Rosemary; *b* 18 May 1931; *m* 21 Dec 1953 Lt-Cdr John Anthony Stuart Crawford, RN (*d* car crash 29 Jan 1967), only s of Capt John Stuart Crawford, RN, and has:

1a *Alistair John Stuart; *b* 16 Jan 1959

1a *Alison Jane; *b* 9 Nov 1957

(3) *Caroline Sarah [Mrs Thomas Kilner, Oakhanger Cottage, Oakhanger, Hants]; *b* 16 Nov 1936; *m* 11 Feb 1961 *Thomas Anthony Alistair Kilner, only s of George Casson Kilner, of Belgravia, and has:

1a *Toby Jonathan Casson; *b* 17 Feb 1966

Sir Percy *m* 2nd 23 March 1914 Fanny Vaughan Johnston (*d* 22 June 1936), formerly w of Col Arthur Pole Welman and 3rd dau of Thomas Ramsay Dennis, and *d* 18 Oct 1924

His only surv s,

Sir Douglas Winchester Scott, 2nd Bt; *b* 4 Feb 1907; *educ* Harrow and RMC Sandhurst; Staff Capt June 1939, WW II: 1st Armoured Div 1940, cmded 3rd Hus 1944, 9th Queen's Roy Lancers 1947, ret as Lt-Col, Hon Col 3rd Hus 1955–58 and Queen's Own Hus 1962–65, Treas Thomas Coram Fndn 1958–70 (V-Pres 1970–84); *m* 22 July 1933 Elizabeth Joyce, 2nd dau of Archibald Lloyd Glanley, and *d* 1984, leaving:

1 Sir ANTHONY PERCY SCOTT, **3rd and present Bt**

2 +Alastair John Douglas [Alastair Scott Esq, Church House, Broome, Worcs]; *b* 14 April 1940; *educ* Harrow and McGill U; *m* 15 Jan 1965 *Virginia Mary, 2nd dau of John Gaynor, of Pyrford Woods, Surrey, and has:

(1) +William Douglas; *b* 2 Nov 1966

(1) *Sarah Victoria; *b* 27 Nov 1969

(2) *Penelope Mary; *b* 1974

1*Diana Jean [Mrs John Fraser-Mackenzie, Lone Cow Estate, PO Box 22, Mutorashanga, Zimbabwe]; *b* 9 Nov 1934; *m* 5 Oct 1956 *John Peter Fraser-Mackenzie, yr s of John Ord Alistair Fraser-Mackenzie, MBE, of Bunchrew, Inverness-shire, and has had:

(1) *Robert Douglas [Robert Fraser-Mackenzie Esq, Lone Cow Estate, PO Box 22, Mutorashanga, Zimbabwe]; *b* 7 July 1959; *m* 1991 *Phillipa Mary, est dau of Harold Jones, and has:

1a *Jamie Anthony; *b* 17 May 1993

1a *Eliza Christabel; *b* 20 Jan 1996

(2) Alastair Thomas; *b* 20 March, *d* 25 April 1962

(1) *Elizabeth Henrietta [Countess Ahlefeldt-Laurvig-Lehn, Paulpetersenvej 8, 2820 Gentofte, Denmark]; *b* 3 May 1958; *m* 1988 *Count Thomas Ahlefeldt-Laurvig-Lehn and has:

1a *Frederick Peter; *b* 7 Oct 1989

2a *Eric Douglas; *b* 2 April 1991

(2) *Georgina Ann; *b* 19 Sept 1963; *m* 1989 *Maj Charles P H Knaggs, Irish Gds, s of George H Knaggs, of Hales, Salop, and has:

1a *Arthur John Huntley; *b* 6 Nov 1991

2a *Robert George Huntley; *b* 27 March 1993

3a *Edmund Douglas Huntley; *b* 29 Jan 1997

(3) *Catherine Beatrice [Lady Calum Graham, The Old Rectory, Akeley, Bucks MK18 5HJ]; *b* 28 March 1966; *m* 1991 *Lord Calum Ian Graham, yst s of 7th Duke of Montrose (*qv*)

SCOTT of Yews

Arms: Az. a greyhound courant arg., collared gu. and attached by a line of the second to a sphere in chief or. **Crest:** A sphere or encircled by four feathers erect severally arg., az., gold and gu. **Motto:** *Le Dieu le Fort l'Eternel parleray* ('I will speak of God as Strength and Eternity personified'). **Creation:** Bt. (UK) 27 July 1909.

SIR OLIVER CHRISTOPHER ANDERSON SCOTT, 3RD BT, of Yews, Undermillbeck, Co Westmorland [Sir Oliver Scott Bt, 31 Kensington Sq, London W8 5HH]; *b* 6 Nov 1922; *s* f 1960; *educ* Charterhouse and King's Coll Cambridge (BA 1942, MB, BCh 1946, MA 1947, MD 1976); High Sheriff Westmorland 1966, trained St Thomas's Hosp (MRCS, LRCP 1946), Surg-Lt RNVR 1947–49, memb Sci Staff Br Empire Cancer Campaign 1954–69, dir Provincial Insur 1955–64 and BECCR Research Unit Radiobiology Mount Vernon Hosp Northwood 1966–69, chm Fin Ctee Br Cancer Cncl 1970–, Hon Consultant Inst Cancer Research 1974–82, memb cncl Cancer Research Campaign 1978–91, radiobiologist St Thomas's Hosp London 1982–88; *m* 19 May 1951 *Phoebe-Anne, er dau of Desmond O'Neill Tolhurst, of The Gateways, London SW3, and has:

1 +CHRISTOPHER JAMES; *b* 16 Jan 1955; *educ* Bryanston, Trin Coll Cambridge and INSEAD; *m* 1988 *Emma Jane, only dau of Michael John Boxhall, of Chichester, Sussex, and has:

(1) +Edward James Saim; *b* 25 Oct 1990

(2) +Charles James Michael; *b* 26 May 1994

(1) *Oenone Jennifer Katharine; *b* 16 Feb 1992

(2) *Cressida Jane Phoebe; *b* 24 July 1997

1 *Hermione Mary; *b* 7 March 1952; *m* 1978 *Dr Miles Richard Stanford, yr s of K J Stanford, of Langton Matravers, Dorset, and has:

(1) *Emma; *b* 1984

(2) *Harriet; *b* 1986

(3) *Olivia; *b* 1989

2 *Camilla Nancy; *b* 11 Sept 1956; *m* 1990 *David Bruce Withington, yr s of James Withington, of Competa, Spain, and has:

(1) *Oliver; *b* 1991

(2) *Samuel Peter; *b* 1993

Lineage: HEINRICH SC(H)OT, of Eysenrodt, Nassau; living 12th century and holding leases of iron mines; allegedly descended from natives of Scotland who had settled in a Franconian village called after them Schotten; allegedly ancestor of families called SCHOTT of Schottenstein, Strasburg and Braunfels in Solms. The pedigree of the last family of SCHOTTS begins, however, only with:

MATTHIAS SCHOTT, of Braunfels; gf of:

EMMERICH SCHOTT, of Braunfels; Seneschal County of Solms 1451–84; m Hedwig Heltrau and had five sons (of whom the yst, Thomas, m Anna von Reinol and had a s Jean Schotte or Johann Schott von Schottenborn, of Hadonville, Lorraine, b 1541, Archer of the Guard, granted by CHARLES II of Lorraine noble status, author of *Genealogia* (1587), *dsp*, leaving his papers to the descendants of his uncle JOHANN, for whom *see* below):

JOHANN SCHOTT, of Dutenhofen in Huttenberg, Nassau; had a 2nd s:

ADAM SCHOTT, of Nieder-Kleen in Huttenberg; living 1562, Sheriff of a division of Nassau 28 years; m Christine Endstein von Dotzenheim and had:

PETER SCHOTT; s f as Sheriff; m Anne, dau of Lorentz Stephani, and had:

JOHANN MARTIN SCHOTT, of Glessen U, Protestant Pastor; m 4 Nov 1617 Maria Margaretha, dau of Tobias Weber, PhD, Superintendent/Bp Idstein, Nassau, and d 1621, leaving:

JOHANN FRIEDRICH SCHOTT, of Idstein; b 15 Dec 1621; Treas Consistory; m 1st Anna Christina — (d 23 Feb 1663); m 2nd 25 Nov 1663 Apollonia Forst and d 5 July 1684, having by her had:

JOHANN CHRISTOPHER SCHOTT, of Idstein; b 20 Dec 1668; Councillor; m 29 Jan 1695 Maria Dorothea Sattler (d 8 Feb 1751) and d 31 March 1733, leaving:

WILHELM LEONHARD SCHOTT, of Idstein; b 16 Feb 1709; Councillor and Justice; m 22 Nov 1735 Susana Margaretha (d April 1772), dau of Johann Matthaus Schlosser, and d 15 Feb 1787, leaving:

JOHANN DANIEL SCHOTT; b 10 Nov 1739; Maj White Russian Hus 1769–75; m 28 April 1778 Anna Catharina (d 8 Feb 1798), widow of Johann Heinrich Schenck, Patrician of Frankfurt, and d 15 Dec 1814, leaving:

JOHANN DANIEL SCHOTT, b 22 July 1787; Frankfurt merchant; m 21 March 1813 Margarethe Christiana (d 13 Nov 1835), dau of Johann Georg Nopp, and d 29 May 1874, leaving:

JOHN GEORGE SCHOTT, of Prestwich, Lancs; b 23 April 1815; merchant, naturalised Briton; m 3 Aug 1840 Sarah Ann (d 6 April 1895), dau of James Kinder, of Manchester, gs of Ralph Kinder, of Staley Hall, Cheshire, and d 4 March 1858, leaving:

1 Samuel; b 15 Sept 1842; d unm 13 March 1868

2 JAMES WILLIAM (Sir), **1st Bt**

3 George Frederick SCHOTT later SCOTT, JP, DL Merioneths; b 23 Jan 1852; High Sheriff Merioneths 1908, Hon Lt-Col 3rd Bn Cheshire Regt; m 9 April 1885 Beatrice Mary (d 1912), only dau and heiress of John Leigh Taylor, DL, of Penmaenucha and Arthog Hall, Merioneths, and d 31 Oct 1916, leaving:

  (1) Sybil Mary Gella; m 26 March 1915 Maj Charles Llewelyn Wynne-Jones, 17th Lancers, only s of Very Rev Llewelyn Wynne-Jones, Dean St Asaph, and had issue

4 Edward Daniel, of Disley, Cheshire; b 7 Feb 1853; Maj 4th Vol Bn Cheshire Regt; d unm 26 July 1900

1 Margaretha Christiana; d 2 Feb 1926

The 2nd s,

Sir JAMES WILLIAM SCHOTT later SCOTT (roy licence for him and siblings), **1st Bt** (UK), so cr 27 July 1909, of Yews, Undermillbeck, Co Westmorland, JP Westmorland and Lancs; b 23 June 1844; m 16 April 1874 Anne Jane (d 30 April 1922), dau and heiress of John Haslam, JP, textile mfr and merchant, of Gilnow Hall, Bolton-le-Moors, Lancs, and Yewbarrow Hall, Grange-over-Sands, thus acquiring control of his f-in-law's enterprises, and had:

1 SAMUEL HASLAM (Sir), **2nd Bt**

2 Francis Clayton; b 6 Aug 1881; educ Oriel Coll Oxford (BA 1903); High Sheriff Westmorland 1934, chm Provincial Insur, fndr and chm Brathay Hall Centre Ambleside; m 31 Aug 1911 Gwendolen Frieda Martha, 2nd dau of George Jager, of Lingdale, Birkenhead, and had:

  (1) +Peter Francis, CBE (1982) [Peter Scott Esq CBE, 58 Cumberland St, London SW1]; b 21 Sept 1917; educ Winchester and Oriel Coll Oxford (BA 1939); Capt KRRC (SR), chm Provincial Insur; m 21 Sept 1953 *Prudence Mary, dau of Capt Grenville Milligan, RN, and has:

    1a +Francis Alexander; b 11 Oct 1959

    1a *Charlotte Rose; b 3 Oct 1954

    2a *Madeleine Mary; b 16 May 1957

    3a *Rebecca Anne; b 24 Oct 1960

  (1) *Joan Frieda [Dr Joan Trevelyan, 21B, Inverleith Place, Edinburgh EH3 5QD]; b 19 Aug 1912; BM, BCh; m 1 June 1949 (*divorce* 1959) John Trevelyan, CBE (*see* TREVELYAN, Bt, of Nettlecombe), and has issue

1 Jane Millicent, OBE (1920); m 4 Aug 1904 Capt Edward Gwynne Eardley-Wilmot, RWF, and d 11 Dec 1964, leaving issue (*see* EARDLEY-WILMOT, Bt)

The 1st Bt d 4 Aug 1913; his er s,

Sir Samuel Haslam Scott, 2nd Bt, JP Westmorland; b 7 Aug 1875; educ Oriel Coll Oxford (BA 1900, MA 1902); dir Provincial Insur and chm 1913–46, High Sheriff Westmorland 1926; m 1st 4 April 1905 Carmen Estelle (d 8 Feb 1919), 2nd dau of Edmund Heuer, of Dunham Knoll, Dunham Massey, Cheshire, and had:

1 James Philip Edmund; b 13 Aug 1915; Capt KRRC WW II; d of wounds recd in action 31 May 1942

1 Mary Margareta; m 4 July 1946 Frank Sargent, MD, MRCP, and d 9 March 1960, leaving issue

2 *(Anne) Katharine Sibella [Mrs Jocelyn Morton, 13 Acacia Gdns, London NW8 6AH]; b 1912; RIBA; m 20 Sept 1944 Jocelyn Wiseman Fagan Morton (d 1987), yr s of Sir James Morton, LLD, of Daiston Hall, nr Carlisle, and has:

  (1) *Eleanor Katharine Mary; b 11 Aug 1948; m 1977 *Ali Resa Afsari and has:

    1a *Anna Rose; b 29 Oct 1979

  (2) *Frances Anne Marylee; b 14 Sept 1950; m 1972 *Benjamin Charles Ruck Keene and has:

    1a *Alexander Charles Edward; b 1976

    2a *Dominic Nicholas John; b 1982

    1a *Hermione Katharine Mary; b 1978

  (3) *(Beatrice) Emily Margareta [Mrs Reginald Norton, The Hideaway, Hatfield Down, Faringdon, Oxon SN7 8JH]; b 8 May 1952; m 1980 *Reginald Henry L R Norton and has:

    1a *Thomas Henry Jocelyn; b 21 Sept 1981

    1a *Natalia Beatrice Adelaide; b 4 Feb 1985

  (4) *Lucia Katharine Fagan; b 26 April 1954; m 1975 *Andrew Francis King and has:

    1a *Robert Morton; b 27 Oct 1985

    1a *Rosalind Frances; b 8 Sept 1981

    2a *Carmel Katharine; b 7 Oct 1983

    3a *Frances Sibella; b 29 Nov 1987

Sir Samuel m 2nd 18 March 1920 Nancy Lilian (d 15 Aug 1935), dau of William Charles Anderson, of Hill House, Keston, Kent, and by her had:

2 Sir OLIVER CHRISTOPHER ANDERSON SCOTT, **3rd and present Bt**

Sir Samuel m 3rd 7 Jan 1937 Marion Dorothy (d 21 Dec 1978), er dau of Charles Garnett, of Hall Garth, nr Carnforth, Lancs, and d 23 June 1960

SEAFIELD

Arms: Quarterly, 1st and 4th grand quarters, quarterly, 1st and 4th, argent a lion passant guardant gules, crowned with an imperial crown or; 2nd and 3rd, argent, a cross engrailed sable (for OGILVIE); 2nd and 3rd grand quarters, gules three antique crowns or (for GRANT). **Crests:** 1 (dexter), a lady richly attired from the waist upwards proper wearing a pointed 15th-century head-dress argent (for OGILVIE); 2 (sinister), a burning hill between two Scots pine saplings proper (for GRANT). **Supporters:** Dexter, a lion rampant guardant or, armed gules; sinister, a savage or naked man bearing on his shoulder a club proper and wreathed about the head and middle with a laurel vert. **Mottoes:** 1 (under arms) Stand fast, 2 (over dexter crest) *Toutjours* ('Ever'), 3 (over sinister crest) *Craigellachie aye* ('Craigellachie for ever'). **Creations:** L. (S) 24 June 1698 (Ogilvy of Cullen), V. (S) 24 June 1698 (Seafield), L. (S) 24 June 1701 (Deskford and Cullen), V. (S) 24 June 1701 (Reidhaven), E. (S) 24 June 1701.

THE 13TH EARL OF SEAFIELD, Viscount Seafield, Viscount of Reidhaven, Lord Ogilvy of Cullen and **Lord Ogilvy of Deskford and Cullen** (Ian Derek Francis Ogilvie-Grant) [The Rt Hon The Earl of Seafield, Old Cullen, Cullen, Buckie, Banffshire AB56 4XW]; b 20 March 1939; s mother 1969; educ Eton; m 1st 5 Oct 1960 (*divorce* 1971) Mary Dawn Mackenzie, er dau of Henry George Coats Illingworth, of Bayswater; m 2nd 27 July 1971 *Leila, dau of Mahmoud Refaat, of Cairo and by his 1st w has:

1 +JAMES ANDREW, *Viscount Reidhaven* and *Master of Seafield*; b 30 Nov 1963; educ Harrow

2 +Alexander Derek Henry; b 26 Jan 1966; educ Eton

Lineage (of Ogilvy of Deskford and Findlater): Sir WALTER OGILVY of Lintrathen (*see* AIRLIE, E); d 1440, having had by his 2nd w:

WALTER OGILVY; m Margaret, dau and heiress of Sir John Sinclair of Deskford and Findlater, got a charter of those territorial Baronies to himself and his w 1440, and had, with a yr s (Sir Walter, of Boyne, ancestor of the Lords Banff (dormant 1803)):

Sir JAMES OGILVY; s mother in Deskford and Findlater; m 1st Margaret, dau of Sir Robert de Innes, 11th of that Ilk (*see* ROXBURGHE, D); m 2nd Margaret Chaumes (m 2nd Alexander Irvine of Drum and d c 19 May 1532) and d 13 Feb

1509/10, leaving by one or other of his ws at least one dau (Muriel, *m* John Grant, Yr. of Freuchie; *see* STRATHSPEY, B); his est s by his 1st w:

JAMES OGILVY of Deskford and Findlater; *m* Agnes, dau of 2nd Earl of Huntly (*see* HUNTLY, M), and *dvp* 1 Feb 1505/6, having had, with other issue, including a dau (Elizabeth, *m* Sir James Dunbar of Westfield, for whose predecessors *see* DUNBAR, Bt, of Mochrum):

ALEXANDER OGILVY of Deskford and Findlater; resigned his lands to the Crown, which united them into the territorial Barony of Ogilvy and entailed the new entity on him and his heirs; *m* 1st Janet, dau of 3rd Lord Saltoun (*qv*) of Abernethy; *m* 2nd by 1535 Elizabeth (*m* 2nd John Gordon of Ogilvy, 3rd s of 4th Earl of Huntly; see HUNTLY, M) illegitimate dau of Adam Gordon, Dean of Caithness, s of 1st Earl of Huntly (*see* HUNTLY, M); his est s by his 1st w:

JAMES OGILVY of Cardell; disinherited by his f in favour of that f's 2nd w's 2nd husb John Gordon (*see* above), sparking a feud between GORDONs and OGILVYs that ended with the defeat of the former 1562 and reinstatement of JAMES OGILVY in lands of Findlater and Deskford 1567; *m* 1st Janet, 3rd dau of Sir Robert Gordon of Lochinvar (for whose predecessors *see* GORDON, Bt); *m* 2nd (contract 30 Oct 1558) Marion Livingston (*dsp* 13 Feb 1577), sis of 6th Lord Livingston, and *d* after 19 Feb 1574, having had by his 1st w:

ALEXANDER OGILVY of Collard; *m* by 1557 his distant cousin Barbara (*m* 2nd John Parton of Pitmeddan), dau of Sir Walter Ogilvy of Boyne, and *dvp* by 27 June 1562, having had, with a dau (Marjorie):

Sir WALTER OGILVY of Deskford and Findlater, 1st LORD OGILVY OF DESKFORD (S), so *cr* 4 Oct 1615; m 1st Agnes (*dspm*), dau of 3rd Lord Elphinstone (*qv*), and had a dau (Christian, *m* John Forbes of Pitsligo (*see* FORBES, Bt, of Newe) and had issue); *m* 2nd 1582 Lady Mary Douglas, 3rd dau of 6th Earl of Morton (*qv*), and *d* between 6 July 1625 and 14 Feb 1627, having by her had, with a yr s (Alexander, of Kempcairn, *m* Katherine, dau of John Grant of Freuchie (*see* STRATHSPEY, B), and had issue) and two more daus (Margaret, *m* 1st 1598 5th Earl of Buchan (*qv*) and 2nd 1603 7th Lord Gray (*qv*); Mary, *m* (contract 11 Dec 1613) Sir John Grant, 6th of Freuchie (*see* STRATHSPEY, B), and had issue):

JAMES OGILVY, 2nd LORD OGILVY OF DESKFORD and 1st EARL OF FINDLATER (S), so *cr* 20 Feb 1638, with remainder to the heirs male of his body succeeding to his estates, PC (S 1637 and 1641); *m* 1st (contract 13 Feb 1610) Elizabeth, dau of 5th Earl of Rothes (*qv*) by his 1st w and widow of David Wemyss, Yr. of Wemyss (*see* WEMYSS and MARCH, E); *m* 2nd Lady Marion Cuninghame (*m* 2nd Alexander Fraser, Master of Saltoun; *see* SALTOUN, L), dau of 8th Earl of Glencairn (*see* CUNINGHAME, Bt), and, having no sons (indeed no issue at all by his 2nd w), got a regrant of his titles 18 Oct 1641 with remainder to his er dau's husb Sir Patrick Ogilvy and the latter's heirs male provided Sir Patrick styled himself Lord Deskford and Inchmartine in his f-in-law's lifetime, and *dspm* 1652, leaving by his 1st w, with a yr dau (Anne, *m* (contract 5 April 1637) 9th Earl of Glencairn (*see* CUNINGHAME, Bt) and had issue):

ELIZABETH Ogilvy; *m* her distant cousin PATRICK OGILVY of Inchmartine, 2nd EARL OF FINDLATER (*see* below)

Lineage (of Ogilvy of Inchmartine): Sir ALEXANDER OGILVY of Auchterhouse (bro of Sir Walter Ogilvy of Lintrathen; *see* above and AIRLIE, E); had a 2nd s:

Sir ANDREW OGILVY of Inchmartine, Perths; *m* by 29 Feb 1439/40 Marjory, dau and coheir of Sir John Glen of Balmuto and sis of Isobel, 2nd w of Sir Walter Ogilvy of Deskford (*see* AIRLIE, E, and above against **Lineage (of Ogilvy of Deskford and Findlater)**), and *d* after 1461, leaving:

Sir DAVID OGILVY of Inchmartime; *m* Mariota Hay and *d* by 6 Jan 1506, having had:

JAMES OGILVY of Balgally and later Inchmartine, of which had a charter from his parents 13 Aug 1500; *m* Isabella Oliphant and was *ka* Flodden 1513, leaving an est s:

PATRICK OGILVY of Inchmartine; *m* 1st Mariota Stewart, dau of 2nd Lord Innermeath (*see* MORAY, E); *m* 2nd Elizabeth, dau of Andrew Kinnaird of that Ilk, and had an est s:

WILLIAM OGILVY of Inchmartine; served heir to his f 25 May 1535; *m* Janet (*m* 2nd by 7 June 1566 James Sandilands of Cravie; *see* TORPHICHEN, L), dau of 4th Lord Gray (*qv*), and *d* after 31 March 1556, having had an est s:

PATRICK OGILVY of Inchmartine; MP Perth, served heir to his f 14 May 1566; *m* 1st (dispensation 2 April 1561) Marion (*d* June 1582), dau of 5th Lord Gray (*qv*) and widow of Patrick, Master of Ruthven (*see* CARLISLE, E), and had issue; *m* 2nd Elizabeth Butter (*d* May 1590), widow of Patrick Stewart of Stuikis; *m* 3rd Geills Seton (*d* 5 Feb 1601) and *d* by 24 May 1623; his est s:

PATRICK OGILVY, Yr. of Inchmartine; *m* Margaret (*m* 2nd 1st Earl of Kinnoull; *qv*), dau of Sir James Halyburton of Pitcur, and *dvp* 21 Nov 1592, having had an er s:

Sir PATRICK OGILVY of Inchmartine, which he sold 1650 to the 2nd Earl of Leven (*see* LEVEN and MELVILLE, E), who rechristened the estate Inchleslie; *m* (contract 20–25 Feb 1609) Anne, 3rd dau of Sir Duncan Campbell of Glenorchy (for whose early ancestry *see* ARGYLL, D), and *d* 30 March 1651, leaving, with a yr s and a dau (Margeret, *m* Frederick Lyon of Brigton, MP, 4th s of 1st Earl of Kinghorne, and had issue; *see* STRATHMORE AND KINGHORNE, E):

PATRICK OGILVY, 2nd EARL OF FINDLATER; *m* Elizabeth, est dau and heiress of 1st Earl of Findlater (*see* above), and *d* May 1659, leaving, with a dau (Elizabeth):

JAMES OGILVY, 3rd EARL OF FINDLATER; *m* 1st *c* 1658 Lady Anne Montgomerie (*d* Aug 1687), only child by his 1st w of 7th Earl of Eglinto(u)n (*see* EGLINTON and WINTON, E) and widow of Robert Seton; *m* 2nd Oct 1703 Mary (*dsp* by Aug 1705), dau of 2nd Duke of Hamilton (*qv*) and widow of (a) 2nd Earl of Callendar and (b) Sir James Livingston, Bt, of Westquarter (*see* 1862 edn), and *d* 1711, having by his 1st w had:

1 Walter, *Lord Deskford*; *b c* 1660; *dvp* unm May 1669

2 JAMES OGILVY, 4th EARL OF FINDLATER and **1st Earl of Seafield**, so *cr* 24 June 1701, as also VISCOUNT OF REIDHAVEN and LORD OGILVY OF DESKFORD AND CULLEN (all S), with remainder to 'other heirs of entail succeeding him in his lands and Baronies' and earlier 24 June 1698 VISCOUNT OF SEAFIELD and LORD OGILVY OF CULLEN (both S), with remainder to 'other heirs of tailzie, to be contained in the Charter of his (the grantee's) lands, Baronies, and others, conform to a Signature, under his (the King's) Royal hand of the date of these presents', KT (Feb 1703/4), PC (1707–14 and 1723–30); *b* 11 July 1663; advocate 1685, MP Cullen 1689–95, Slr-Gen Scotland 1693, ktd 1695, Sec State Scotland Jan 1695/6–1702 and 1704–05, Pres S Parl 1698, FRS 1698, High Commr to Gen Assembly Ch Scotland 1700, 1703, 1724 and 1727, Ld High Chllr Scotland 1702–04 and 1705–08, rep S peer 1707–10, 1712–15 and 1722–30, Ld Ch Baron Scotland 1708–10, Keeper Gt Seal 1713–14; *m* 1687 Anne (*d* 14 Aug 1708), dau of Sir William Dunbar, 1st Bt, of Durn (*qv*), and *d* 15 Aug 1730, having had:

(1) JAMES OGILVY, **2nd Earl of Seafield** and 5th EARL OF FINDLATER; *b c* 1689; incarcerated Edinburgh Castle as a suspected Jacobite sympathiser during 1715 Uprising, a Ld of Police Scotland 1734–42, rep S peer 1734–61, V-Adml Scotland 1737/8–64; *m* 1st *c* 1714 Lady Elizabeth Hay, dau of 7th Earl of Kinnoull (*qv*), and had:

1a JAMES OGILVY, **3rd Earl of Seafield** and 6th EARL OF FINDLATER; *b c* 1714; Commr Customs Scotland, 1754–61, Chllr King's Coll Aberdeen 1761–70, a Ld Police Scotland 1765–70; *m* 9 June 1749 Lady Mary Murray (*d* 29 Dec 1795), 18th child of 1st Duke of Atholl (*qv*), and committed suicide 3 Nov 1770, leaving an only surv s:

1b JAMES OGILVY, **4th Earl of Seafield** and 7th EARL OF FINDLATER; *b* 10 April 1750; *educ* Ch Ch Oxford; *m* 1779 Christina Teresa Josepha (*d* 24 May 1813), dau of Sir Joseph Murray, 3rd Bt, of Melgund (*see* 1882 edn), Count Murray of Melgum (HRE), and *dsp* 5 Oct 1811, when the Earldom of Findlater and Ldship of Parl of Ogilvy of Deskford became dormant

1a MARGARET Ogilvy; *m* 31 Oct 1735, as his 2nd w, Sir Ludovic GRANT later COLQUHOUN later still GRANT again, 7th Bt (*see* STRATHSPEY, B), and *d* 20 Feb 1757, having had, with four other daus (*d* unm):

1b Sir JAMES GRANT of Grant, 8th Bt; *b* 19 May 1738; *m* 4 Jan 1763 Jean (*d* 15 Feb 1805), only child of Alexander Duff, of Hatton, Aberdeenshire, and *d* 18 Feb 1811, leaving, with two yst sons (Robert Henry, *b* 5 Aug 1783, *d* unm 11 Feb 1862; Alexander Hope, *b* 21 Aug 1784, *d* 22 Aug 1793) and six daus (Anne Margaret, *d* unm 3 Nov 1827; Margaret, *m* 10 June 1795 Maj-Gen Francis Stewart of Lesmurdie and *d* 3 Dec 1830, leaving issue; Jane, *d* unm 22 May 1809; Penuel, *d* unm 27 Jan 1844; Christina Teresa, *d* unm 16 July 1793; Magdalene, *d* unm; Mary Sophia, *d* unm 26 Feb 1788):

1c Sir LEWIS ALEXANDER GRANT later GRANT-OGILVY, 9th Bt, and **5th Earl of Seafield**; *b* 22 March 1767; *educ* Westminster, Edinburgh U and Lincoln's Inn; Provost Forres 1788, advocate 1789, MP (Tory) Elginshire 1790–96, FRS 1791; *d* unm 26 Oct 1840

2c Alexander; *d* an infant 21 March 1772

3c James Thomas; *b* 10 Aug 1776; Magistrate Furruckabad, India, Registrar Provincial Court Benares 1802; *d* unm 28 July 1804

4c FRANCIS WILLIAM, **6th Earl**

1b Penuel Ogilvy; *m* 6 Jan 1776 Henry Mackenzie and *d* 3 April 1835

2b Anne Hope; *m* 3 April 1781 Very Rev Robert Darley Waddilove, DD, Dean Ripon, and *d* 1797, leaving issue

3b Helen; *m* 9 Sept 1773 Sir Alexander Penrose Cumming Gordon, 1st Bt (*see* GORDON CUMMING, Bt), and *d* 1 Jan 1832, leaving issue

2a Anne; *m* 14 Sept 1733 2nd Earl of Hopetoun and *d* 8 Feb 1759, leaving issue (*see* LINLITHGOW, M)

(1) (cont.) The **2nd Earl** *m* 2nd Dec 1723 Sophia (*dsp* 25 April 1761), dau of 1st Earl of Hopetoun (*see* LINLITHGOW, M), and *d* 9 July 1764

(2) William; *d* young

(3) George; advocate; *d* unm Jan 1732

(1) Elizabeth; *m* by 15 July 1710 6th Earl of Lauderdale (*qv*) and *d* 24 Sept 1778, leaving issue

(2) Janet; *m* 1st Hugh Forbes, Yr. of Craigievar (*see* FORBES, Bt, of Craigievar); *m* 2nd 1719 1st Earl of Fife (*see* FIFE, D) and *d* 1722

3 Patrick, of Lonmay and Inchmartine; Col, MP Cullen 1702–08 and Elgin Burghs 1708–10; *m* 1st Elizabeth, dau of Sir James Baird of Auchmedden and widow of Sir Alexander Abercromby, 1st Bt (*qv*); *m* 2nd his cousin Elizabeth (*d* 29 June 1753), dau of Hon Francis Montgomerie, 2nd s of 7th Earl of Eglinton (*see* EGLINTON and WINTON, E), and *d* 20 Sept 1737, leaving issue

1 Anna; *m* (contract 19 Oct 1692) George Allardice of that Ilk and *d* 27 Aug 1735, leaving issue

The 5th EARL's bro,

FRANCIS WILLIAM GRANT later OGILVY-GRANT, **6th Earl of Seafield**; *b* 6 March 1778; served Strathspey Fencibles 1793, Capt 97th or Strathspey Regt 1794, Lt-Col 3rd Argyll Fencibles 1799, MP (Tory) Elgin Burghs 1802–06, Inverness Burghs 1806–07, Elginshire 1807–32 and Nairn 1832–40, Ld Lt Inverness-shire 1809, rep S peer 1841–53; *m* 1st 20 May 1811 Mary Anne (*d* 27 Feb 1840), only dau of John Charles Dunn, of Higham Ho, Sussex, and had:

1 James; *b* 16 April 1812; *d* 15 March 1815

2 Francis William, *Master of Grant*; *b* 5 Oct 1814; MP Inverness-shire 1838–40; *d* unm 11 March 1840

3 JOHN CHARLES OGILVY-GRANT, **7th Earl of Seafield**, KT (1879); *b* 4 Sept 1815; Midshipman RN 1828–40, rep S peer 1853–58; *cr* 14 Aug 1858 BARON STRATHSPEY OF STRATHSPEY in the counties of Inverness and Moray (UK); *m* 12 Aug 1850 Hon Caroline Stuart (who *s* to the Grant and Seafield estates 1884 and *d* 6 Oct 1911, having left them in trust for the **11th Earl** and his successors in the title), yst dau of 11th Lord Blantyre (*see* 1900 edn), and *d* 18 Feb 1881, leaving:

(1) IAN CHARLES OGILVY-GRANT, **8th Earl of Seafield**, DL (Banffshire and Inverness-shire); *b* 7 Oct 1851; *educ* Eton; Cornet 1869, Lt 1871 1st Life Gds, ret 1877; *d* unm 31 March 1884, when the Barony expired

4 JAMES, **9th Earl**

5 Lewis Alexander; *b* 18 Sept 1820; Lt RHG (Blues); *m* 15 Aug 1849 Georgina (*d* 6 March 1885), dau of Robert George Maunsell, and *d* 24 Dec 1902, leaving:

(1) Alexander Lewis Henry; *b* 1 Aug 1854; *m* 30 Oct 1889 Hilda Annie, dau of Sir Thomas Erskine Perry, Ch Justice Bombay, and *dsp* 3 March 1904

(2) Robert George; *b* 10 Oct 1856; *d* July 1888

(1) Mary Louisa Eleanora; *m* 28 July 1885 Henry Maitland Sperling (*d* 1951), of Coombe Trenchard, Lew Down, N Devon, and *d* 6 May 1952

(2) Maria Jane Anne; *d* unm 12 Feb 1932

6 George Henry Essex, of Easter Eichies, Craig Ellachie; *b* 13 Feb 1825; Capt 42nd Highrs; *m* 2 Oct 1855 Eleanora (*d* 5 April 1889), 4th dau of Sir William Gordon Cumming, 2nd Bt (*qv*), and *d* 31 May 1873, leaving:

(1) Henry Oswin; *b* 2 April 1859; 2nd W India Regt; *d* 21 Sept 1919

(2) William Robert; *b* 25 March 1863; Assist Keeper Zoological Dept Natural History Museum; *m* 1 Oct 1890 Maud Louisa (*d* 31 Dec 1937), est dau of Adml Mark Robert Pechell (*see* 1970 edn PECHELL, Bt), and *d* 26 July 1924, leaving:

1a (Charles Randolph) Mark, of Kew Green and Athens; *b* 15 March 1905; *educ* Eton and Trin Coll Oxford (BA 1929); Hon Attaché Cairo, Maj Scots Gds WW II (POW, despatches), Mil Mission Greece 1946, Inf Dept Greek Emb London 1947–69; *d* unm 13 Feb 1969

1a Eleanora; *b* 22 Sept 1892; *m* 1st 14 July 1913 (*divorce* 1926) Lt-Cdr Reginald William Blake, RN (*d* 20 June 1927), s of Col Arthur Maurice Blake, CB, DL, of Danesbury, Herts, and had:

1b +Pamela Rosemary [Mrs Leslie Beuttler, Finca Villordo, Benalmadena-Pueblo, Malaga, Spain]; *b* 1916; *m* 1937 Col Leslie Brindley Beuttler, OBE, Duke of Wellington's Regt (*d* 1978), and has had:

1c Michael Simon Brindley Bream; *b* 1940; *d* 1988

2c +Nicholas Randolph Kerr [Nicholas Beuttler Esq, Route des Guiols, 83310 La Môle, France]; *b* 1943; *m* 1979 *Martine Andriveau

1c +(Caroline) Jane [The Hon Mrs Alan Clark, Saltwood Castle, Hyth, Kent CT21 4QU]; *b* 1942; *m* 1958 *Hon Alan Kenneth McKenzie Clark, PC, MP, s of Baron Clark (LP, extinct 1983), and has:

1d +James Alasdair Kenneth; *b* 1960; *m* 1st 1985 (*divorce* 1988) Sarah Marian, yst dau of A Dawes, of Fulmer, Bucks; *m* 2nd 1988 Sally Ruth, dau of Peter Smith, of Codsall, Staffs; *m* 3rd July 1995 *Julie —

2d +Andrew McKenzie; *b* 1962; *m* 1993 *Sarah G, dau of Nigel Harris, of Muscat

2b +Lavinia Elizabeth [Mrs Charles Morton, The Old Stables, Hollybush Park, Newborough, Staffs DE13 8SF]; *b* 1921; *m* 1954 Lt-Col Charles Edward Morton, TD (*d* 1988), and has:

1c +Roger Thomas [Roger Morton Esq, Green Lanes, Gt Coxwell, Oxon]; *b* 1957

1c +Louise Jean [Miss Louise Morton, Cuckoo Cage Farm, Rangemore, Staffs DE13 9RX]; *b* 1955

1a (cont.) Mrs Eleanora Blake *m* 2nd 15 Dec 1926 Sir Roger Thomas Twysden, 10th Bt (*qv*), and *d* 16 Dec 1956

2a Marjorie Elspeth; *b* 25 June 1894; *m* 30 June 1921 Capt Ronald Fitz-Hardinge Speir, RE (*d* 7 April 1961), yst s of Robert Thomas Napier Speir (*see* GIFFORD, B), and *d* 24 Nov 1967, leaving:

1b +(John Hugh) Anthony [Anthony Speir Esq, PO Box 5389, Cresta 2118, S Africa]; *b* 1925; Capt S African Inf Corps; *m* 1st 1946 (*divorce* 1952) Isobel, dau of James Snart, of Leicester; *m* 2nd 1974 *Joan Margaret, dau of A Valentine, of Krugersdorp, and has by his 1st w:

1c +Helen Joanna [Mrs Helen Thomson, 5 Belmont Ave, Madison, NJ 07940, USA]; *b* 1948; *m* 1969 (*divorce* 1997) David George Thomson and has:

1d +Iain James Speir; *b* 1973

1d +Caroline Louise Speir; *b* 1976

2c +Fiona Margaret [Mrs Michael Haughey, 11 Blenheim Rd, London W4 1UB]; *b* 1951; *m* 1973 *Michael John Haughey and has:

1d +Barnaby Michael FitzHardinge Speir; *b* 1975

2d +Tobias John Thomas Speir; *b* 1983

3d +Michael Gabriel Bartholomew Speir; *b* 1986

1d +Rachel Mary Speir; *b* 1974

2d +Bethany Joy Speir; *b* 1978

3d +Tamara Jane Speir; *b* 1979

1b +Elizabeth Jean [Miss Elizabeth Speir, Flat 5, 13 Upper Phillimore Gdns, London W8 7HF]; *b* 1922

2b +Diana Marigold [Miss Diana Speir, 1 North St, St Andrews, Fife]; *b* 1932

3a Alison Jean; *b* 6 March 1896; *m* 20 Dec 1923 Capt Reginald Cordwallis Hargreaves, MVO, MC, Rifle Bde (*d* 1974), only surv s of Charles Reginald Hargreaves, 13th Hus, and *d* 17 Oct 1970, leaving:

1b +Basil John Alexander, JP (N Westminster 1968) [Basil Hargreaves Esq JP, c/o National Westminster Bank, 19 High St, Heathfield, E Sussex]; *b* 7 April 1925; *educ* Eton; *m* 1st 22 April 1960 (*divorce* 1972) Anne Mary Beatrice, er dau of Philip Stacey, of Smithy Cottage, W Knighton, Dorset, and has:

1c +Charles John Cornwallis; *b* 22 Dec 1966

1b (cont.) Basil Hargreaves *m* 2nd 1980 *Barbara Ann Baker, *née* Court

1b +(Alison) June [Mrs Ronald Burns, Swallowfield, Enton Green, Surrey]; *b* 16 June 1928; *m* 1978 *Ronald Burns

(3) George Randolph Seymour; *b* 20 June 1866; *m* 22 Feb 1909 Carmen, er dau of José Tomas Errazuriz, of Bryanston Sq, London W, and *d* 1958, having had:

1a Randolph Anthony; *b* 29 April 1915; *d* 17 March 1921

1a +Hester Marie; *b* 16 June 1924

(1) Alice Elizabeth; *m* 6 July 1889 Lord Walter Gordon-Lennox and *d* 7 March 1946, leaving issue (*see* RICHMOND and GORDON, D)

(2) Muriel Frances Charlotte; *m* 2 June 1892 Geoffrey Apsley St Quintin (*d* 25 April 1913), yst s of Lt-Col M C D St Quintin, 17th Lancers, of Scampston Hall, Yorks, and *d* 5 May 1929, leaving issue

7 Edward Alexander; *b* 17 June 1833; *d* 1844

1 Jane; *m* 20 July 1843 Gen Sir Edward Walter Forestier-Walker, KCB, and *d* 16 Sept 1861, leaving issue (*see* FORESTIER-WALKER, Bt)

The **6th Earl** *m* 2nd 17 Aug 1843 Louisa Emma (*m* 2nd 31 Jan 1856 Maj Godfrey Hugh Massey, 19th Foot (*d* 4 June 1862); *m* 3rd 5 July 1864 (*divorce*) Lord Henry Loftus (*see* ELY, M) and *d* 2 Aug 1884 aged 66), 2nd dau of Robert George Maunsell, of Limerick, and *d* 30 July 1853

The 8th EARL's unc,

JAMES OGILVY-GRANT, **9th Earl of Seafield**, DL; *b* 27 Dec 1817; *educ* Harrow; Capt 42nd Foot, MP (C) Elginshire and Nairnshire 1868–74, Lt-Col Elginshire Vols; *cr* 17 June 1884 BARON STRATHSPEY OF STRATHSPEY, Cos Inverness and Moray (UK); *m* 1st 6 April 1841 Caroline Louisa (*d* 6 Feb 1850), 2nd dau of Eyre Evans (*see* CARBERY, B); *m* 2nd 13 April 1853 Constance Helena (*d* 13 Feb 1872), 4th dau of Sir Robert Abercromby, 5th Bt (*qv*), and by her had a s (Robert Abercromby, *b* 4 Sept 1855, Capt Gordon Highrs, Hon Maj, Afghan War 1879–80, 1st Boer War 1881, Nile Expdn 1884–85, WW I, T/Lt-Col RASC 1916, *m* 26 April 1911 Evelyn Maud (*d* 27 Feb 1939), dau of H Hilton, of Kensington, and widow of Maj Frederick David Milward, Lancs Fus, and *d* 11 April 1925); *m* 3rd 15 Dec 1875 Georgiana Adelaide (*d* 7 Sept 1903), dau of Gen Frederick Nathaniel Walker, KCH, of Manor House, Bushey, and widow of William Stuart, of Aldenham Abbey, Herts, and Tempsford Hall, Beds, and *d* 5 June 1888, leaving by his 1st w:

FRANCIS WILLIAM OGILVY-GRANT, **10th Earl of Seafield**; *b* 9 March 1847; *m* 24 Nov 1874 his 1st cousin Anne Trevor Corry (Nina) (*d* 16 Oct 1935), only dau of Maj George Evans (*see* CARBERY, B), and *d* 3 Dec 1888, leaving:

1 JAMES OGILVIE-GRANT [*sic*], **11th Earl of Seafield**, DL (Banffshire and Inverness-shire); *b* 18 April 1876; Lt Canterbury Yeo Cav NZ Forces, Capt 3rd (attd 5th) Bn Queen's Own Cameron Highrs WW I; *m* 22 June 1898 (Mary Elizabeth) Nina (*d* 22 Jan 1962), er dau of Joseph Henry Townend, JP, MD, of Christchurch, NZ, and *d* 12 Nov 1915 of wounds recd in action, leaving:

(1) NINA CAROLINE Ogilvie-Grant, **Countess of Seafield** in her own right; *b* 17 April 1906; Pres Banffshire League Mercy; *m* 24 Jan 1930 (*divorce* 1957) Derek Herbert STUDLEY later OGILVIE-GRANT-STUDLEY-HERBERT (deed poll 1939, *d* 26 March 1960), s of John Tatchell Studley, of Seaborough Court, Dorset, by Beatrice Frances, er surv dau of Dudley Raikes de Chair, and *d* 30 Sept 1969, having had:

1a IAN DEREK FRANCIS OGILVIE-GRANT-STUDLEY-HERBERT later OGILVIE-GRANT (recognised by warrant of Lord Lyon 1971), **13th and present Earl of Seafield**

1a +Pauline Anne [The Lady Pauline Nicholson, Revack Lodge, Grantown-on-Spey, Morayshire]; *b* 26 May 1944; *m* 1st 11 March 1964 (*divorce* 1970) her bro-in-law James Henry Harcourt Illingworth, only s of Henry George Coats Illingworth, of S Kensington; *m* 2nd 1972 (*divorce* 1976) Sir William Gordon Gordon Cumming, 6th Bt (*qv*); *m* 3rd 1976 Hugh Richard Sykes; *m* 4th 1989 *David John Nicholson and by her 3rd husb has:

1b +Harry Peter Derek; *b* 1977

2 Sir TREVOR OGILVY-GRANT, 16th Bt, and 4th BARON STRATHSPEY (*qv*) OF STRATHSPEY, as which s bro

3 John Charles; *b* 1887; *d* 1893

1 Caroline Louisa; *b* 9 May 1877; *d* unm 11 Jan 1945

2 Sydney Montagu; *b* 23 July 1882; *m* 9 April 1912 Rev William Rice (*d* 1919) and *d* 23 July 1944

3 Ina Eleanora; *b* 23 July 1882; *d* 1893

4 Nina Geraldine; *b* 8 June 1884; DGStJ; *m* 12 Aug 1915 Sir Lees Knowles, 1st and last Bt, CVO, OBE, TD, DL, MA, LLM (*dsp* 7 Oct 1928), and *d* 21 Jan 1951

SEALE

Arms: Or two barrulets az. between three wolf heads erased sa., in the fess point a mural crown gu. **Crest:** Out of a crown vallery or a wolf's head arg., the neck encircled with a wreath of oak vert. **Motto:** *In cœlo salus* ('In heaven is salvation'). **Creation:** Bt. (UK) 31 July 1838.

SIR JOHN HENRY SEALE, 5TH BT, of Mount Boone, Devon [Sir John Seale Bt, Slade, nr Kingsbridge, Devon TQ7 4BH]; *b* 3 March 1921; *s f* 1964; *educ* Eton and Ch Ch Oxford; Capt RA WW II, RIBA, architect, sr lecturer Plymouth Sch of Architecture; *m* 27 June 1953 *Ray Josephine, er dau of Robert Gordon Charters, MC, of Christchurch, NZ, and has:

  1 +(JOHN) ROBERT CHARTERS [Robert Seale Esq, 7 Lime Tree Close, Mattishall, Norfolk NR20 3PP]; *b* 17 Aug 1954; *educ* Eton; *m* 8 Sept 1996 *Michelle, dau of Kevan Taylor, of Mattishall

  1 *Elizabeth Margaret Anne; *b* 1 Sept 1956

Lineage: LEONARD SEALE, of St Brelade, Jersey; *b* 1425; *m* Carterette, dau of Richard Pipon, and had:

JOHN SEALE; *b* 1450; *m* Catherine Fiott and had:

GERMAIN SEALE; *b* 1484; *m* Mary de Carteret and had:

COLLAS SEALE; *b* 1513; *m* Sarath, dau of Stephen Baudayn, and had:

GERMAIN SEALE; *b* 1537; *m* 1563 Collette, dau of Clement Estur, and had, with three yr sons and a dau:

JOHN SEALE; *b* 1564; Constable St Brelade 1615–21; *m* 1596 Denise, dau of Thomas Pipon, and *d* 1621, leaving, with three other sons (including two er ones, Germain, had a s (*dsp*); Thomas, *b* 1605, Jurat 1644–46, *m* 1635 Anne de Carteret and had issue) and two daus:

JOHN SEALE; *b* 1606; Constable St Brelade 1644–51; *m* 1st 1635 Susan, dau of James Le Goupil; *m* 2nd Elizabeth Bailhache and *d* 1670, having by her had issue and by his 1st w:

JOHN SEALE; *b* 1640; *m* 1660 Elizabeth, dau of Philip Benest, and had, with an er s (John, *b* 1667, merchant in Bilbao and London, *d* 1714) and two daus:

THOMAS SEALE, of Jersey; *b* 1669; *m* 1692 Elizabeth Pipon and had:

JOHN SEALE; *b* 1705; acquired Mount Boone; *m* 1st 1734 Mary, only dau of Charles Hayne, of Lupton and Fuge, Devon; *m* 2nd 1743 Elizabeth, dau of John Fownes, of Nethway; *m* 3rd Anna Maria, sis of Sir John Rogers, Bt (*see* 1889 edn BLACHFORD, B), and *d* 7 Sept 1777, having by his 2nd w had an only surv s:

JOHN SEALE, of Mount Boone; *b c* 1753; *m* 1775 Sarah (*d* 4 Nov 1815), dau of Charles Hayne, of Lupton, and sis and coheir of Charles Hayne, of Lupton and Fuge House, and had:

  1 JOHN HENRY (Sir), **1st Bt**

  2 Robert; *d unm* 1819

  3 Charles Henry; *b* 1790; Capt RN; *m* 23 July 1827 Eliza (*d* 2 Sept 1878), dau of Sir William Jervis Twysden, 7th Bt, of Roydon Hall (*see* 1967 edn), and *d* 9 Feb 1856, having had:

    (1) Charles Twysden; *b* 1827; *m* 1856 Susan, 2nd dau of Adml Carthew, and *dsp* 1868

    (1) Margaret E F; *m* 1850 Maj-Gen John George Boothby, RA, and *d* 10 April 1909, leaving issue (*see* BOOTHBY, Bt)

  1 Elizabeth Maria; *m* George Kekewich

  2 Harriet Anne; *m* Thomas Lister, of Armytage Park, Staffs

JOHN SEALE *d* 23 May 1824; his est s,

  Sir John Henry Seale, 1st Bt (UK), so *cr* 31 July 1838; *b* 25 Dec 1780; MP (Lib) Dartmouth 1832–44; *m* 4 June 1805 Paulina Elizabeth (*d* 17 April 1862), only child of Sir Paul Jodrell, MD, and had:

  1 HENRY PAUL (Sir), **2nd Bt**

  2 Charles SEALE later SEALE-HAYNE, of Fuge House, Dartmouth; *b* Dec 1808; *m* 1 Dec 1832 Louisa (*m* 2nd 9 Sept 1856 James Buller, of Dunley, Devon, and *d* 23 April 1879), dau of Richard Jennings, of Portland Place, and *d* 31 Oct 1842, leaving:

    (1) Charles Hayne, PC, of Fuge and Pitt Houses and Kingswear Castle, Devon, JP; *b* 22 Oct 1833; MP Mid Div Devon 1885–1903, Hon Col 3rd Bn Devonshire Regt, Paymaster-Gen 1892–95; *d unm* 22 Nov 1903

  3 Edward Taylor (Rev); *b* 26 Dec 1811; Rector Moreleigh, Devon; *m* 9 Dec 1841 Amelia Anne, est dau of George Templer, of Sandford Orleigh, and *d* 1893, leaving:

    (1) Edward; *b* 12 Sept 1842; RN; *dsp* 1881

    (2) George Thomas; *b* 29 Sept 1845; *m* 1 Sept 1871 Marion Edith (*d* 1929), dau of W J Wentworth Cookson, of Christchurch, NZ, and *d* 1922, leaving:

      1a George Edward Dugald; *b* 1872; *m* 1905 Beatrice Agatha Tipping Lanauze and *d* 1937, leaving:

        1b Henry Dugald Cranstoun; *b* 1910; *m* 1948 *Elsie Joyce Neilson and *d* 1986

      2a Frederick Hayne; *b* 1878; *m* 1903 Ethel Lenore (*d* 1959), dau of Joseph Nathan, and *d* 1931, leaving:

        1b Richard Wentworth; *b* 1904; *m* 1927 Edith Hazel (*d* 1990), dau of William Brown Birch, and *d* 1972, leaving:

          1c +Richard Laurie [Richard Seale Esq, 32 Kincardine Crescent, Floreat Park, WA 6014, Australia]; *b* 1930; *m* 1956 *Paula Cathleen, dau of Carl Bruechle, and has:

            1d +Richard Beaumont; *b* 1966

            1d *Stacey Jennifer; *b* 1958

            2d *Leanda Jane; *b* 1960

            3d *Petrina Louise; *b* 1962

        2b Gordon Frederick; *b* 1906; *m* 1936 *Eva Vera [Mrs Gordon Seale, 37 Marlow St, Wembley, W Australia], dau of Charles Adams, and *d* 1985, having had:

          1c *Elizabeth Lenore; *b* 1939; *m* 1961 *Horace Charles Kennedy and has:

            1d *Shane Brett; *b* 1967

            1d *Natalie Lisa; *b* 1965

          2c *Carolyn Margaret; *b* 1943

        3b Walter Douglas; *b* 1907; *m* 1st 1935 (*divorce* 1967) Mona Carruthers, dau of Sidney Herbert Reidy-Crofts; *m* 2nd 1974 Barbara Topping (*d* 1993) and *d* 1989, having had by his 1st w:

          1c +John Digby; *b* 1937; *m* 1st 1960 Roslyn Edith, dau of David Englander; *m* 2nd 1980 *Ann, dau of James Thomas Collingwood Mullner

          1c *Felicity Jane [Mrs Sidney Bradshaw, 156 Hensman Rd, Subiaco WA 6008, Australia]; *b* 1939; *m* 1st 1961 Evan Owen, s of Vaughan Owen, of Rockingham, WA; *m* 2nd 1987 *Sidney Donald Bradshaw and has by her 1st husb:

            1d *Simon Llewellyn; *b* 1963

            1d *Sarah Alexandra; *b* 1967

            2d *Sophia Jane; *b* 1971

        4b Alan Dudley; *b* 1911; *m* 1947 *Ilma Ruth [Mrs Alan Seale, 25 Fortune St, S Perth, WA 6151, Australia], dau of Edward John Barrett, and *d* 1989, having had:

          1c +Philip Gregory; *b* 1948; *m* 1st 1978 (*divorce* 1981) Cheryl Davis; *m* 2nd 1991 *Adele Sharam

          2c +Brian Wentworth [Brian Seale Esq, 23 Lofoten Way, Ferndale, WA 6155, Australia]; *b* 1950; *m* 1970 *Cheryl Lynne, dau of Stanley Rear Gibb, and has:

            1d +Paul Langdon Wentworth; *b* 1973

            1d *Belynda Ruth; *b* 1971

            2d *Rebekah Michaela Alyse; *b* 1976

          1c *Marlene Ruth [Mrs Lance Rattigan, 13 Roseberry Ave, S Perth, WA 6151, Australia]; *b* 1952; *m* 1974 *Lance Rattigan and has:

            1d *Jeremy Lance; *b* 1977

            2d *Timothy Neal; *b* 1979

            3d *Andrew Stephen; *b* 1982

        1b *Grace Mildred [Mrs Brian Schofield, Newholme, Lower Shiplake, Oxon RG9 3JS]; *b* 1909; *m* 1946 V-Adml Brian Betham Schofield, CB, CBE (*d* 1984), s of Thomas Dodgson Schofield, of Alderley Edge, and has:

          1c *Elizabeth Virginia; *b* 1948

          2c *Rosemary Victoria [Mrs Stephen Willis, 48 Westbourne Park Rd, London W2 1PH]; *b* 1950; *m* 1982 *Stephen Mark Willis and has:

            1d *Anthony Brian; *b* 1987

            1d *Alexandra Rose; *b* 1985

            2d *Olivia Grace; *b* 1990

      1a Marguerite Louise; *b* 1881; *m* 1906 George Stewart and had issue. He *d* 1923

      2a Olive Isabel; *b* 1883; *m* 1915 Walter Humphries and *d* 14 Sept 1965, leaving issue

    (3) Frederick Fortescue; *b* 17 March 1851

  4 Robert Bewick; *b* 12 Feb 1815; *d* 1881

  5 Thomas Fownes; *b* 27 May 1817; Capt 94th Regt; *d* 1849

  6 George Augustus; *b* 7 Feb 1819; RN; *d* 11 Feb 1844

  7 Frederick Southcote; *b* 22 Feb 1827; Capt RA; *m* 24 April 1851 Harriet, 2nd dau of J A Harvey, Ordnance Store Keeper in Canada, and *d* 30 Sept 1861

  1 Elizabeth; *b* 20 Aug 1813; *m* 1843 10th Lord Cranstoun (*d* 18 June 1869; see 1869 edn) and *d* 31 Dec 1899, leaving issue

  2 Jane; *b* 1823; *d* 1844

The 1st Bt *d* 29 Nov 1844; his est s,

  Sir Henry Paul Seale, 2nd Bt, JP, DL; *b* 17 Feb 1806; *m* 4 Aug 1840 Emily (*d* 19 Oct 1898), yst dau of Col I R Hartman, Coldstream Gds, and had, with three other daus (*d unm*):

  1 JOHN HENRY (Sir), **3rd Bt**

  1 Lucy Clara; *m* 18 March 1869 Capt Arthur Woodall Gillett, RN, 2nd s of Rev G E Gillett, Rector Waltham, Leics, and *d* 22 Feb 1881

2 Margaret Amélie; *m* 30 Oct 1902 Cecil Vandeleur Keighly-Peach, 4th s of Capt H P Keighly-Peach, of Stratford-on-Avon, and *d* 24 Jan 1944

The 2nd Bt *d* 17 Dec 1897; his only s,

Sir John Henry Seale, 3rd Bt, JP, DL Devon and Mon; *b* 14 Nov 1843; barrister; *m* 1st 21 May 1879 Mary Henrietta (*d* 31 Aug 1882), only surv child of Arthur Hyde Dendy, of Rock House, Torquay, and Parkfield, Paignton, and had:

1 JOHN CARTERET HYDE (Sir), **4th Bt**

2 Henry Dendy; *b* 13 Aug 1882; *educ* Eton and Ch Ch Oxford (BA 1904); T/Maj MGC 1918 WW I, Order St Stanislas Russia; *m* 12 Dec 1914 Lora May (*d* 1974), 2nd dau of Cecil Hurst Bisshopp, of Fernlea, Oban, Argyllshire, and *d* 31 Dec 1974, leaving:

(1) *Mary Désirée [Mrs George Hutchison, 2 Canvin Rue, Apt 211, Kirkland, Quebec H9H 4B5, Canada]; *b* 1 Nov 1915; *educ* Toronto U (BA 1936); Capt RCAMC WW II 1942–46; *m* 1st 2 Nov 1946 Stanley James Meyers (*d* 1974), 3rd s of James Christie Meyers, of Montreal; *m* 2nd 1978 Charles Eastman Adams (*d* 198–); *m* 3rd 198– *George Hutchison and by her 1st husb has:

1a *Linda May [Mrs Linda Giroux, 12 St Johns, Pointe Claire, Quebec H9S 4Z1, Canada]; *b* 23 April 1948; *m* 1973 (*divorce* 1981) Robert Donald Giroux and has:

1b *Sean Robert; *b* 1975

2b *Scot Donald; *b* 1977

1 Edith Mary; *b* 1 March 1880; *m* 12 July 1904 Rev Francis Russell Benedict Simpson (*d* 1970), Vicar Dartmouth 1914–34, est s of Francis Charles Simpson, of Maypool, S Devon, and *d* 7 Aug 1961, leaving:

(1) Christopher Francis Russell; *b* 1908; *m c* 1949 Winifred Pomeroy (*d* 1975) and *d* 1985

(1) *Joan Mary [Miss Joan Simpson, Waye, Bovey Tracey, Newton Abbot, Devon TQ13 9LF]; *b* 1910

(2) *Anne Catherine Meyrick [Miss Anne Simpson, Waye, Bovey Tracey, Newton Abbot, Devon TQ13 9LF]; *b* 1912

Sir John *m* 2nd 2 June 1885 Adela (*d* 29 June 1929), sis of Sir Alfred Jodrell, 4th Bt (*see* 1929 edn), and *d* 29 July 1914

His er s,

Sir John Carteret Hyde Seale, 4th Bt; *b* 23 July 1881; *educ* Eton and Ch Ch Oxford; barrister Inner Temple 1907; *m* 18 Jan 1917 Margaret (*d* 4 June 1960), dau of Lt-Col William Herring, JP, 27th Inniskillings, of Narborough House, Norfolk, and *d* 22 May 1964, leaving:

1 Sir JOHN HENRY SEALE, **5th and present Bt**

2 +Richard Styleman [Richard Seale Esq, Conduit Rise, Conduit Head Rd, Cambridge CB3 0EY]; *b* 11 April 1924; *educ* Eton and Pembroke Coll Cambridge (MA); *m* 5 June 1963 *Elizabeth Vazeille, only dau of Thomas Binstead Bright, of Silverdale, Lancs, and has:

(1) +William Thomas Carteret; *b* 29 July 1964

(1) *Margaret Rachel Vazeille; *b* 12 Aug 1966; *m* 1991 *Paul Atputhakumar Jebarajasingam Supramaniam, of London and Singapore, and has:

1a *James Timothy Bright Aiyathuraisingam; *b* 1993

2a *Matthew Edward Herring Jeyathuraisingam; *b* 1998

1*Mary Paulina [Mrs George More, Bazzleways, Milborne Port, Dorset DT9 5EH]; *m* 20 Nov 1945 Col George Robert Melville Harvey More, MC, RE (*d* 1991), s of Capt George Irwin Sanctuary More, OBE, RN, of Sherborne, and has:

(1) *Robert Harvey [Robert More Esq, Harpar House, 85A Pickwick Rd, Corsham, Wilts SN13 9BY]; *b* 17 Oct 1946; *educ* Sherborne; *m* 1989 *Claire, dau of Cdr C H H Harwood, RN, of Rowde, Wilts, and has:

1a *Caspar George Harvey; *b* 15 Dec 1992

1a *Harriet Caroline Eaton; *b* 1 Nov 1990

2a *Marina Elisabeth Eaton; *b* 7 Oct 1994

(2) *Henry Sanctuary [Henry More, 1436 Miramonte Ave, Los Altos, CA 94024-5601, USA]; *b* 21 Nov 1948; *educ* Sherborne and Bristol U (BSc (Eng)); *m* 1977 *Adelle Anne, dau of Harold Mackenzie Smith, of Sacramento, Calif., and has:

1a *Paul Henry; *b* 13 June 1979

2a *Stephen Henry; *b* 22 Aug 1981

1a *Susannah Mary; *b* 18 Feb 1993

(3) *John William [John More Esq, 2 Allée des Charmilles, 77420 Champs-sur-Marne, France]; *b* 25 July 1953; *educ* Sherborne; *m* 1987 *Martine Frédérique Micheline, dau of Jacques Wolf, of Paris, and has:

1a *Ludéric Norman James; *b* 6 June 1994

1a *Noëlie Joanna; *b* 27 Feb 1991

(1)*Sarah Frances [Miss Sarah More, Bazzleways, Milborne Port, Dorset DT9 5EH]; *b* 16 Jan 1952; *educ* Sherborne Sch for Girls and Roy Vetinary Coll London; MRCVS

SEBRIGHT

Arms: Arg. three cinquefoils sa. **Crest:** A tiger sejant arg., maned and crowned or. **Motto:** *Servare mentem* ('Preserving equanimity'). **Badge:** A garb of oats or, band az. inscribed with the motto *Pro Rege* ('For the King'). **Creation:** Bt. (E) 20 Dec 1626.

SIR PETER GILES VIVIAN SEBRIGHT, 15TH BT, of Besford, Co Worcester [Sir Peter Sebright Bt, 6 Finchley Rd, Auckland Park, Johannesburg 2092, S Africa]; *b* 2 Aug 1953; *s f* 1985; *m* 1st 1977 (*divorce* 19–) Regina Maria, dau of Francis Steven Clarebrough, of Melbourne, Australia, and has:

1 +RUFUS HUGO GILES; *b* 31 July 1978

Sir PETER *m* 2nd 1987 *Madeleine — and by her has:

2 +Dashiell; *b* 1987

Lineage: WALTER SEBRIGHT, of Sebright Hall, Much Baddow, Essex; lived *temp* HENRY II; *m* Elizabeth, dau and sole heiress of Sir Henry de Ashe, and had:

STEPHEN SEBRIGHT; had:

WALTER SEBRIGHT; *m* Margery, widow of Geoffrey de Panimer and 2nd dau and coheir of Robert Mascall, of Great Baddow, and had:

PETER SEBRIGHT, of Sebright Hall, which he held by service of keeping the King's saddle-horse 40 days at the King's charge for whenever he visited the locality; lived late 13th century; had, with an er s (Giles, of Sebright Hall, whose issue died out *temp* HENRY VIII):

MABELL [*sic*] SEBRIGHT, of Brooke's Place, Essex; lived *temp* EDWARD I; *m* Katherine, dau and heiress of Ralph Cowper, of Blakes Hall, Wolverley, Worcs, and was ancestor of:

JOHN SEBRIGHT, of Blakes Hall; sold Brooke's Place 1491; had:

HUMPHREY SEBRIGHT, of Blakes Hall; *m* Katherine Ridge, of Ridge, Staffs, and had:

EDWARD SEBRIGHT, of Blakes Hall; *m* Joyce, dau of William Grosvenor, of Bubington, Staffs, and had, with a yr s (William, of Besford, Worcs, MP Droitwich 1572–83, Town Clerk London 1573–1612, *m* Elizabeth, dau of James Morley, of London, but *dsp* 27 Oct 1620) and a dau (Eleanor, *m* 21 Nov 1576 Thomas Austin, of Oxley, Staffs):

JOHN SEBRIGHT, of Blakes Hall; *m* Anne (*m* 2nd Thomas Walsh, of Stockton, Worcs), dau of Richard Bullingham, and had, with an er s (William, *dsp*) and three daus (Judith, *m* Edward Broad, of Dunelme Park, Worcs; Sarah, *m* by 1606 1st Baron Coventry (*see* COVENTRY, E); Anne, *m* John Burnell, of London):

Sir Edward Sebright, 1st Bt (E), so *cr* 20 Dec 1626, of Besford Court, Worcs; *b c* 1585; *educ* BNC Oxford; Sheriff Worcs 1621, ktd 1627, royalist Commr Array Battle of Edgehill 1642; *m* 1st by 1611 Theodosia, dau of Gerard Whorwood, of Compton, Staffs, and had two sons (William, *dvp*; John, *b* 1611, *dvp*) and a dau (Elizabeth, *m* Sir John Repington); *m* 2nd *c* 1638 Elizabeth, widow of Sir Lewis Ma(u)nsel(l), 2nd Bt, of the 1611 *cr* (*see* MANSEL, Bt) and est dau of 1st Earl of Manchester (*see* MANCHESTER, D), and *d* by 11 Feb 1657/8, leaving by her:

Sir Edward Sebright, 2nd Bt, of Besford Court; *b c* 1645; *educ* St John's Coll Oxford; *m* (licence 15 Feb 1664/5) Elizabeth (*d* 30 Sept 1685), dau of Sir Edward Knightley, KB, of Fawsley, Northants, and *d* 11 Sept 1679, leaving, with a yr s (Richard, of Croxton, Norfolk, *dsp* 1733):

Sir Edward Sebright, 3rd Bt, of Besford Court; *b* 1668; *educ* Jesus Coll Oxford; Sheriff Worcs 1685; *m* (licence 24 March 1687/8) Anne (*m* 2nd Charles Lyttelton (*see* COBHAM, V) and *d* 25 Dec 1718), dau and heiress of Thomas Saunders, of Beechwood, Herts, and *d* 15 Dec 1702, leaving, with a yr s (Edward, of Croxton, murdered 20 Sept 1723 nr Calais) and two daus (Anne, *m* 1721 Sir Charles Buck, 3rd Bt (*d* 20 June 1729), and 18 Sept 1764; Ada, *m* John Coke, of Whiteparish, Wilts):

Sir Thomas Saunders Sebright, 4th Bt, of Beechwood and Besford Court; *b* 11 May 1692; *educ* Jesus Coll Oxford (DCL 1732); MP Herts 1715–36; *m* Henrietta (*d* 21 March 1771/72), dau of Sir Samuel Dashwood, Ld Mayor London 1702–03 (*see* DASHWOOD, Bt, of West Wycombe), and *d* 12 April 1736, leaving:

1 **Sir Thomas Saunders Sebright, 5th Bt**, of Beechwood and Besford Court; *bapt* 21 Dec 1723; *educ* Westminster and Ch Ch Oxford; *d* unm 30 Oct 1761

2 **Sir John Sebright, 6th Bt**, of Beechwood and Besford Court; *bapt* 19 Oct 1725; *educ* Westminster; Col 18th Foot, Lt-Gen, MP Bath 1763–68; *m* 15 May 1766 Sarah (*bur* 4 Jan 1813), dau of Edward Knight, of Wolverley, Worcs, and had:

(1) JOHN SAUNDERS (Sir), **7th Bt**

(2) Edward Amherst Saunders; Lt-Col Gren Gds; *d* 1795

(1) Henrietta; *m* 3 Sept 1794 2nd Earl of Harewood (*qv*) and *d* 15 Feb 1840, leaving issue

(2) Mary; *m* Nicholas Lewis Fenwick, of Terrington, Norfolk, and *d* his widow 4 Dec 1854

Sir JOHN *d* 23 Feb 1794; his er s,

Sir John Saunders Sebright, 7th Bt, of Beechwood and Besford Court; *b* 23 May 1767; Herts: Sheriff 1797–98, MP 1807–35; *m* 6 Aug 1793 Harriet (*d* Aug 1826), only dau and heiress of Richard Crofts, of W Harling, Norfolk, and *d* 15 April 1846, having had, with eight daus (including Frederica Anne Saunders, *m* 1822 Frederick Franks (*d* 1822) and *d* 2 Nov 1864):

Sir Thomas Gage Saunders Sebright, 8th Bt, of Beechwood and Besford Court; *b* 1802; *m* 1st 17 Nov 1842 Sarah Anne (*d* 14 Feb 1846), 2nd dau of Capt Hoffman, RN, and had:

1 **Sir John Gage Saunders Sebright, 9th Bt**, JP, of Beechwood and Besford Court; *b* 20 Aug 1843; *educ* Ch Ch Oxford; Ensign 4th Herts Rifle Vols 1860, High Sheriff Herts 1874, Maj 4th Bn Beds Militia 1881; *m* 27 March 1865 Hon Olivia Amy Douglas Fitzpatrick (*d* 22 May 1895), yst dau of 1st Baron Castletown (*see* 1937 edn), and *d* 15 Nov 1890, having had:

(1) **Sir Egbert Cecil Saunders Sebright, 10th Bt**, DL Herts, of Beechwood; *b* 12 June 1871; *d unm* 1 April 1897

(1) Olive Marion Constance Elinor; *b* 17 April 1875 ; *d* 22 Dec 1882

Sir Thomas *m* 2nd 17 July 1850 Olivia (*d* 27 June 1859), yst dau of John Joseph Henry (*see* LEINSTER, D), and *d* 29 Aug 1864, having by her had:

2 Walter Charles Saunders; *b* 1852 ; *d* 25 June 1859

3 **Sir Edgar Reginald Saunders Sebright, 11th Bt**, JP, DL Herts, of Beechwood; *b* 27 May 1854; *educ* Eton and Magdalen Coll Oxford; Equerry to HRH PRINCESS MARY ADELAIDE DUCHESS OF TECK 1882–97, ADC to Govr and C-in-C Victoria 1892–94, Priv Sec to Govr S Australia 1894–95, High Sheriff Herts 1904, Maj and Hon Lt-Col 4th Bn Beds Militia; *d unm* 25 Dec 1917

4 **Sir Guy Thomas Saunders Sebright, 12th Bt**, JP Herts; *b* 19 Aug 1856; Lt Coldstream Gds; *m* 27 June 1882 Olive Emily (*d* 14 Dec 1951), dau of Arthur Thomas Frederick (*see* FREDERICK, Bt), and *dsps* 11 Sept 1933, having had:

(1) Guy Ivo; *b* 1883; *m* 1st 1904 (*divorce* 1906) Mary Louisa, dau of Capt Arthur Rodney Blane, RN; *m* 2nd 13 March 1907 Vera Florence Annie (*m* 2nd 8 May 1918 (*divorce* 1926) 2nd Baron Terrington (*qv*) and 3rd 28 March 1949 Max W Lensvelt, of Johannesburg), dau of Henry George Bousher, of London, and *dsp* 12 July 1912

5 Arthur Edward Saunders; *b* 30 March 1859; Lt 4th Bn Beds Regt; *m* 1st 1889 Emily Eva (*d* 2 Sept 1921), widow of W Ingram and dau of John Bowen; *m* 2nd 1922 Mrs Alice Marion Lampson, dau of Albert Fairweather Luke, of Exeter, and *d* 22 Aug 1933, leaving by his 1st w:

(1) **Sir Giles Edward Sebright, 13th Bt**, CBE (1954), JP Herts; *b* 12 Nov 1896; *educ* Wellington; CC Herts, Capt Herts Regt (TA) and 4th Dragoon Gds, Lt-Col cmdg 2nd Herts Regt, WWs I and II, Equerry to HRH THE DUKE OF YORK 1922–23, Steward Br Boxing Bd of Control; *m* 1929 Margery Hilda, JP (Devon 1954), formerly w of Raymond Massey, the actor, and dau of Adml Sir Sydney Robert Fremantle, GCB, MVO (*see* COTTESLOE, B), and *d* 9 Dec 1954, leaving:

1a **Sir Hugo Giles Edmund Sebright, 14th Bt**; *b* 2 March 1931; *m* 1st 6 Dec 1952 (*divorce* 1964) Deirdre Anne (*m* 2nd 1965 Anthony Melbourne-Hart (*d* 1988)), only dau of Maj Vivian Lionel Slingsby Bethell (*see* WESTBURY, B), and had:

1b Sir PETER GILES VIVIAN SEBRIGHT, **15th and present Bt**

1a (cont.) **Sir Hugo** *m* 2nd 7 Jan 1965 Sheila Mary Howard, widow of Maj Edward George Hervey (*see* BRISTOL, M) and dau of Walter Howard Rocke, of Salisbury, Rhodesia; *m* 3rd 1984 *Victoria Rosamond [The Dowager Lady Sebright, BP3, Clarensac 30870, France], dau of Capt Richard Taylor White, DSO, RN (*see* WHITE, Bt, of Wallingwells), and formerly w of David Ashton Ashton-Bostock, and *d* 1985

SECCOMBE

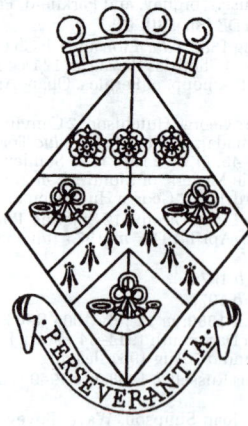

Arms: Per pale gules and vert a chevron ermine between three bugle horns argent, stringed or, on a chief per pale vert and gules three roses argent barbed or, on each another rose gules barbed and seeded proper. **Motto:** *Perseverantia* ('Perseverance').
Creation: B. (LP, UK) 1991.

THE BARONESS SECCOMBE, of Kineton, Co Warwicks (Dame Joan Anna Dalziel Owen, DBE (1984), JP Solihull (1968)) [The Rt Hon The Baroness Seccombe DBE JP, Linden Cottage, The Green, Little Kineton, Warwicks CV35 0DH]; *b* 3 May 1930; *educ* St Martin's Sch Solihull; Chm Ld Chllr's Advsy Ctee Solihull 1975–93, Chm Bench 1981–84; memb Heart of Eng Tourist Bd 1977–81, Women's Nat Commn 1984–90; W Midlands CC 1977–81 (Chm Trading Standards Ctee 1979–81); Chm: C Women's Nat Ctee 1981–84, Nat Union of C and U Assocs 1987–88 (V-Chm 1984–87); V-Chm C Party 1987–; Govr Nuffield Hosps 1988–; Chm Tstees Nuffield Hosps Pension Fund; *m* 1950 *Henry Lawrence Seccombe and has:

1 *Philip Stanley; *b* 1951; *educ* Rugby and RAC Cirencester; *m* 1977 *Isabel Elizabeth Urquhart and has:

(1) *Charles Stanley; *b* 1981

(1) *Olivia Elizabeth; *b* 1984

2 *Robert Murray; *b* 1954; *educ* Stowe and BNC Oxford; *m* *Tatyana Karpenko and has:

(1) *Anna Tatyana; *b* 1995

Lineage: ROBERT JOHN OWEN; *m* 12 July 1924 Olive Barlow and had:

1 *John Arthur Dalziel [Hon Sir John Owen, Royal Courts of Justice, Strand, London WC2 2LL]; *b* 22 Nov 1925; *educ* Solihull Sch and BNC Oxford (MA, BCL 1949); commnd 2nd KEO Goorkha Rifles 1946; barrister Gray's Inn 1951, bencher 1980, QC 1970, Dean of the Arches of Canterbury and Auditor Chancery Court of York 1980–, Judge High Court of Justice, Queen's Bench Divn 1986–; *m* 1952 *Valerie, dau of W Ethell and has:

(1) *James Alexander Dalziel; *b* 1 June 1966

(1) *Melissa Clare; *b* 12 Nov 1960; actress (films include *Four Weddings and a Funeral*); *m* 1 June 1985 (*divorce* 1997) Hon Michael John Ulick Knatchbull, s of 7th Baron Brabourne (*qv*) and Countess Mountbatten of Burma (*qv*), and has issue

1 JOAN ANNA DALZIEL, *cr* a **Baroness**

SEELY

Arms: Az. three ears of wheat, banded or, between two martlets in pale and as many wreaths of roses in fess arg. **Crest:** In front of three ears of wheat banded or the trunk of a tree fesswise, eradicated and sprouting to the dexter ppr. **Motto:** I ripen and die yet live. **Creation:** Bt. (UK) 19 Feb 1896.

SIR NIGEL EDWARD SEELY, 5TH BT, of Sherwood Lodge, Arnold, Notts, and Brooke House, Isle of Wight [Sir Nigel Seely Bt, 3 Craven Hill Mews, London W2 3DY]; *b* 28 July 1923; *s* f 1980; *educ* Stowe; *m* 1st 8 July 1949 Loraine, only dau of Wilfred Lindley-Travis, of Gatehead, Fulstone, Yorks; *m* 2nd 1984 *Trudi, novelist, dau of Sydney Pacter, of Tunbridge Wells, and by his 1st w has:

1 *Charlotte Alexandra Mary; *b* 19 Nov 1954; *m* 1st 1980 (*divorce* 19–) Paul Arthur Schwartz, of New York; *m* 2nd 1988 *Allen Lawrence Levy and by him has:

  (1) *Emily Rose; *b* 1989

2 *Catherine Lucy Emily; *b* 24 Nov 1957; *m* 1994 *William Gatacre and has issue (*see* PAGET, Bt, of Cranmore Hall)

3 *Henrietta Louisa; *b* 12 Oct 1962

Lineage: CHARLES SEELY, of Lincoln, *bapt* 27 March 1768; *m* 11 June 1798 Ann (*d* 20 June 1863), dau of Jeremiah Wilkinson, of Lincoln, and *d* March 1809, having had, with a dau:

CHARLES SEELY, of Brooke House, Brooke, IoW, and S Kensington, JP Hants, Lincs and Surrey, DL Lincs; *b* 3 Oct 1803; MP Lincoln 1847–48 and 1861–85, High Sheriff Hants 1860; *m* 28 June 1831 Mary (*d* 20 Aug 1884), yst dau of Jonathan Hilton, of Newcastle, and *d* 21 Oct 1887, having had, with two other sons (*d* infants):

1 CHARLES (Sir), **1st Bt**

1 Mary; *m* 20 July 1860 Rev Thomas Renwick, Rector Mottistone and Vicar Sherwell, IOW, and had issue. He *d* 12 Oct 1874

2 Frances Anne; *m* 6 June 1861 Benjamin Temple Cotton, of Afton House, Freshwater, IOW, and *d* 19 Nov 1869, leaving issue

3 Jane Anne; *m* 10 April 1882 Col Henry George Gore-Browne, VC, JP, and *d* 3 April 1913, having had issue (*see* SLIGO, M)

His only surv s,

Sir Charles Seely, 1st Bt (UK), so *cr* 19 Feb 1896, of Sherwood Lodge, Arnold, Notts, and Brooke House, IOW, JP Derbys, Hants and Notts, DL Notts; *b* 11 Aug 1833; MP (Lib) Nottingham 1869–74 and 1880–85 and W Nottingham 1885–86 and 1892–95, High Sheriff Notts 1890, Lt-Col 1st Notts (Robin Hood) Rifle Vols, KGStJ; *m* 11 Aug 1857 Emily (*d* 8 Dec 1894), dau of William Evans, of Crumpsall Grange, Lancs (*see* 1970 edn EVANS, Bt, of Tubbendens), and had:

1 CHARLES HILTON (Sir), **2nd Bt**

2 Arthur; *b* 1, *d* 2 June 1860

3 Frank Evelyn, TD, JP, DL Notts; *b* 5 July 1864; *educ* Trin Coll Cambridge (BA); Lt-Col S Notts Yeo, WW I in Egypt and Gallipoli, ADC Personal Staff; High Sheriff Notts 1922; *m* 1st 8 Aug 1899 Leila Eliza (*d* 16 Feb 1903), dau of Rev Henry Charles Russell (*see* BEDFORD, D), and had:

  (1) (Frank) James Wriothesley; *b* 28 Aug 1901; High Sheriff of Notts 1939, MFH S Notts, Capt 107th (S Notts Hus Yeo) Bde (TA), 2nd Lt 15th/19th Hus, WW II as Maj Notts and Derby Regt (Sherwood Foresters); *m* 5 Feb 1925 Vera Lilian, 3rd dau of Col Charles Wilfred Birkin, CMG (*see* BIRKIN, Bt), and *d* 5 Aug 1956, leaving:

    1a Michael James; *b* 20 Aug 1926; *educ* Eton; racing jnlst on *The Times* and *The Field*; *m* 1st 6 Sept 1952 (*divorce* 1966) (Barbara) Patricia Callaghan; *m* 2nd 14 April 1966 Patricia Ann Auchterlonie (*d* 1990), only dau of George Percy Wright, of Daresbury, Cheshire; *m* 3rd 1993 *Irene Heath and *d* 1993, leaving by his 2nd w:

      1b *Rachel; *b* 17 July 1967

    2a +Timothy Ward; *b* 10 June 1935; *educ* Eton; actor; *m* 1960 (*divorce* 19–) Anne Henrietta Maria St Paul, formerly w of James Dugdale Berridge and only dau of Horace George St Paul Butler, of High Humbledon, Wooler, Northumberland, and has:

      1b +Hugo Michael David St Paul; *b* 1961; *m* 1991 *J Caroline, er dau of Dr A Milner, of Islip, Oxon, and has:

        1c *India Grace St Paul; *b* 1992

      3a +James Richard Francis [James Seely Esq, Mill Cottage, East Bergholt, Suffolk CO7 6US]; *b* 29 Jan 1940; *educ* Harrow; *m* 30 Jan 1960 *Wendy Mary, est dau of George Russell Hutchinson, of Bristol, and has:

        1b +Christian James Russell; *b* 17 Dec 1960

        2b +Jonathan Sebastian; *b* 11 Dec 1962

    1a Clare Elizma; *b* 26 March 1929; *m* 3 Dec 1949 Christopher John Filmer-Sankey (*d* 25 Nov 1957), yr s of William Filmer-Sankey, and had:

      1b *Dominic Hugh; *b* 26 June 1950

      2b *Christopher John Timothy; *b* 18 March 1958

    2a Cherry Angela Mary; *b* 2 Aug 1931; *m* 2 Feb 1955 Desmond Barnaby O'Brien (*see* INCHIQUIN, B) and *d* 1992, having had issue

  (2) William Evelyn; *b* 16 Oct 1902; Lt-Col S Notts Hus WW II, MFH S Notts; *m* 28 Sept 1927 Irene Lavender (*d* 30 Sept 1977, having *m* 2nd 28 June 1943 Maj-Gen Sir Miles William Arthur Peel Graham, KBE, CB, MC (*d* 8 Feb 1976)), only dau of Richard Francklin, of The Manor House, Oxton, Notts, and was *ka* N Africa 6 June 1942, leaving:

    1a +Richard Evelyn, JP [Richard Seely Esq JP, 33 Upper Park Rd, London NW3]; *b* 28 Sept 1928; *educ* Eton; barrister Gray's Inn 1961; *m* 9 Jan 1960 *Hildegard Helga, dau of Wilhelm Schnarr, of Mainz, Germany, and has:

      1b +Philip Frank Evelyn; *b* 13 Sept 1963; *educ* Harrow

      2b +Robert William Henry; *b* 1 June 1966; *educ* Harrow

    2a +Charles William [Charles Seely Esq, Rendham Barnes, Saxmundham, Suffolk IP17 2AB]; *b* 31 Dec 1935; *educ* Eton; *m* 4 Jan 1958 *Morvyth, dau of George Arthur St George, of Brighton, and has:

      1b *Amy Jane Lavender; *b* 1 Dec 1969

      2b *Camilla Rose; *b* 14 Oct 1972

      3b *Joanna Matilda; *b* 20 July 1974

  (1) Leila Emily; *b* 24 Aug 1900; *m* 26 July 1923 4th Viscount Hampden (*qv*) and had issue

3 (cont.) Frank Seely *m* 2nd 2 Oct 1907 Gertrude Fanny, OBE, JP Notts (*d* 9 July 1967), dau of Henry Edward Thornton, of The Wymeshead, Kegworth, Derbys, and *d* 16 April 1928, having by her had:

  (2) *Sheila Katherine; *b* 25 Sept 1908; *m* 28 Feb 1933 Richard Eustace Talbot (*see* SHREWSBURY and WATERFORD, E), and has had issue

  (3) *Nina Mary Aline; *b* 23 Nov 1911; *m* 28 Aug 1939 W/Cdr Michael James Beaumont Young, DFC and bar, RAF, yst s of Maj Reginald Young, Sherwood Foresters, and has:

    1a *Michael Patrick William; *b* 18 Aug 1944; *educ* Milton Abbey

    2a *David Richard James; *b* 23 Oct 1949; *educ* Worth; South Notts Hus

    1a *Mary Andrea; *b* 6 May 1943; *m* 1 Sept 1962 John Russell Frears, lecturer Loughborough U of Tech, s of Dr Russell Edward Frears, of Nottingham, and has:

      1b *Naomi Mary Frances; *b* 3 March 1963

      2b *Nina Katherine; *b* 15 March 1964

      3b *Lucy May Leila; *b* 16 March 1966

4 JOHN EDWARD BERNARD SEELY, *cr* BARON MOTTISTONE (*qv*)

1 Florence Mary; *d* unm 9 March 1933

2 Emily; *m* 31 Oct 1888 Sir John Ralph Starkey, 1st Bt (*qv*), and *d* 24 Nov 1944, leaving issue

3 Annie; *m* 24 May 1884 Col Reginald Pemberton Leach, CMG, JP, RFA (*d* 27 Feb 1929), 6th s of Lt-Col Sir George Archibald Leach, KCB, RE, and *d* 20 Aug 1943, leaving issue

4 Lilian; *m* 7 June 1888 Col Philip Hugh Dalbiac, CB, TD, MP N Camberwell, 3rd s of Henry Eardley Aylmer Dalbiac, JP, DL, of Durrington Manor, Sussex, and *d* 24 Jan 1956, leaving issue. He *d* 28 April 1927

5 Mary; *m* 14 Jan 1895 William Hollins, JP, of Berry Hill, Mansfield, Notts, and *d* 1947, having had issue. He *d* 1918

6 Sylvia Ruth; *m* 25 June 1901 Aubrey Augustus Henley Wykeham, JP, DL, of Tythrop Ho, Oxon, and Pitt Place, IoW, and *d* 22 April 1951, leaving issue. He *d* 22 May 1947

The 1st Bt *d* 16 April 1915; his est s,

Sir Charles Hilton Seely, 2nd Bt, JP Hants and Notts, DL Notts; *b* 7 July 1859; *educ* Harrow and Trin Coll Cambridge (MA); MP (Lib U) Lincoln 1895–1906 and Mansfield 1916–18, High Sheriff Notts 1912, Capt 1st Notts Rifle Vols, Co Cmdt IOW Vol Regt, Lt-Col 5th Vol Bn Hants Regt, KGStJ; *m* 9 Dec 1891 Hilda Lucy (*d* 24 Aug 1939), est dau of Richard Tassell Anthony Grant, JP, of W Cowes, IoW, and *d* 26 Feb 1926, having had:

1 Charles Grant; *b* 29 Nov 1894; Capt 8th Hants Regt (IOW Rifles) TF WW I (wounded); *ka* 19 April 1917

2 **Sir Hugh Michael Seely, 3rd Bt**, and 1st and last BARON SHERWOOD, of Calverton, Co Nottingham (UK), so *cr* 14 Aug 1941, JP (Notts 1926); *b* 2 Oct 1898; *educ* Eton; Lt Gren Gds and S Notts Hus, S/Ldr cmdg 504 (Co of Nottingham) (F) Sqdn RAuxAF (Hon A/Cdre 1947), MP (Lib) E Norfolk 1922–24, and Berwick-upon-Tweed 1935–41, Assist Lib Whip 1935, PPS to Sec State Air 1940, Jt U-Sec Air 1941–45, Hon Treas Lib Centl Assoc 1941, High Sheriff Notts 1925; *m* 1st 23 March 1942 (*divorce* 1948) Hon Molly Patricia, widow of Capt Roger Charles George Chetwode (*see* CHETWODE, B) and 3rd dau of 1st Viscount Camrose (*qv*); *m* 2nd 16 March 1970 Catherine Thornton (*d* 13 Sept 1974), widow of John Osborne Ranger, and *d* 1 April 1970, when the Barony expired

3 VICTOR BASIL JOHN (Sir), **4th Bt**

4 Nigel Richard William; *b* 13 Nov 1902; S/Ldr AAF WW II; *m* 24 March 1937 Isabella Elinor Margarete (*m* 2nd 24 Jan 1949 Edward Bromley-Davenport (*d* 1990), 3rd s of Walter Arthur Bromley-Davenport, of The Kennels, Capesthorne, Cheshire, and *d* 17 Jan 1957), only dau of Eugene von Rieben, and *das* 10 May 1943, leaving:

  (1) +Charles John Howell [Charles Seely Esq, La Bosnière, Cussay, France]; *b* 3 Nov 1937; *educ* Eton

(2) +Hilton Nigel Matthew [Hilton Seely Esq, 45 Sterndale Rd, London W14 0HT]; *b* 2 March 1940; *educ* Eton; *m* 1st 27 Jan 1971 Leonie M, dau of Brig George Taylor, and has:

  1a +Charles Hilton; *b* 1972

  2a +Dominic Edward; *b* 1975

(2) (cont.) Hilton Seely *m* 2nd 1993 *Denise M, dau of Thomas Muckle, of Rothbury, Northumberland, and by her has:

  3a +Max Anthony Philip; *b* 1993

(1) *Elinor Ivy; *b* 22 Feb 1941; *m* 1st 10 Dec 1968 Maj Martin Vyvyan Carleton-Smith, Irish Gds, 3rd s of Lt-Col Dudley Lance Guy Carleton-Smith, King's Dragoon Gds; *m* 2nd 1990 *Ian V Fletcher, of Johannesburg, and has by her 1st husb:

  1a *Robin Francis Popham; *b* 1972

  1a *Camilla Alison; *b* 11 Dec 1969

(2) *Isabella Frances [Mrs Anthony Covill, 97 Arthur Road, London SW19]; *b* 22 Feb 1941; *m* 1st 15 May 1961 (*divorce* 1966) Simon James Scrimgeour, yr s of Stuart Scrimgeour, of S Kensington, and has:

  1a *Lucilla Jane; *b* 10 March 1963

(2) (cont.) Mrs Isabella Scrimgeour *m* 2nd 14 June 1966 *Anthony Piers Covill, s of Frederick Charles Covill, of Chelsea, and by him has:

  1a *Piers Anthony Charles; *b* 26 June 1967

  2a *Joseph William Edward; *b* 7 Aug 1969

1 Violet Lucy Emily; *m* 20 July 1921 2nd Viscount Allendale (*qv*) and had issue

2 Ivy Angela, MBE (1944)

The 3rd Bt's bro,

Sir Victor Basil John Seely, 4th Bt; *b* 18 May 1900; *educ* Eton and Trin Coll Cambridge; Lt S Notts Yeo, Maj 9th Queen's Own Lancers RAC WW II (POW 1941–43, escaped), Master Gunmakers' Co 1957 and 1964, dir Securities Agency and various Investment Tsts; *m* 1st 22 Sept 1922 (*divorce* 1931) Sybil ('Nancy') Helen (*d* 12 July 1994, having *m* 3rd 1931 Baron Paget of Northampton, PC, QC (LP, *d* 1990), dau of Sills Clifford Gibbons, of Scaynes Hill, Sussex, and widow of Sir John Bridger Shiffner, 6th Bt (*qv*), and had:

1 Sir NIGEL EDWARD SEELY, **5th and present Bt**

Sir Victor *m* 2nd 16 Jan 1931 Hon Patience (*d* 13 Feb 1935), formerly w of Brig Christian George Maude, DSO, OBE, MC (*see* HAWARDEN, V), and er dau of 1st Baron Rochdale (*see* ROCHDALE, V), and by her had:

1*Victoria [Mrs Victoria Bray, Bridgewater, Spy Lane, Loxwood, W Sussex RH14 0SS]; *b* 6 Sept 1933; *m* 23 July 1954 (*divorce* 1975) (Francis Arthur) Michael Bray, DSC, 3rd s of Francis Evelyn Bray, of Woodham Grange, Horsell, Woking, Surrey, and has:

  (1) *Charles Michael Francis [Charles Bray Esq, 61 Fentiman Rd, London SW8 1LH]; *b* 1957; *m* 1992 *Elspeth J, yr dau of Alastair Moncrieff, of Old Bosham, Sussex, and has:

    1a *Alastair Charles Michael; *b* 1993

  (1) *Mariana Victoria Magdalen [Mrs Richard Sampson, Manor House, Calton, Staffs ST10 3JX]; *b* 1956; *m* 1985 *Maj Richard C B Sampson, Life Gds, s of Maj Richard C Sampson, of Norwich, and has:

    1a *George Edward Richard; *b* 1986

    2a *Charles Michael Henry; *b* 1988

    3a *Hugo Miles Evelyn; *b* 1991

  (2) *Amelia Mary; *b* 1962; *m* 1985 *Andrew James Randolph Macpherson, er s of Colin Macpherson, of Martyr Worthy, Hants, and has:

    1a *Matilda Mary; *b* 1987

    2a *Cluny Amelia; *b* 1991

    3a *Ottilie Elizabeth; *b* 1993

Sir Victor *m* 3rd 8 June 1937 *Mary Frances Margaret, er dau of William Ronald Collins, of S Kensington, and d 1980, leaving by her:

2 +VICTOR RONALD [Maj Victor Seely, Newlands Farm, Farfield, Glos GL11 5HE]; *b* 1 Aug 1941; heir presumptive; *educ* Eton and RMA Sandhurst; Maj Roy Hus (POWO) and Wilts Yeo, seconded Sultan of Oman's armed forces 1970–71; *m* 6 June 1972 *Annette Bruce, dau of Lt-Col J A D McEwen, of Salperton Ho, Salperton, Glos, and has:

  (1) +William Victor Conway; *b* 16 sept 1983

  (1) *Natasha Wilhelmina Annette; *b* 1979

2 *Alexandra Mary Hilda; *b* 16 Sept 1938; *m* 21 Nov 1966 *Henry Charles Seymour (*see* HERTFORD, M) and has issue

SEFTON OF GARSTON

Creation: B. (LP, UK) 1978.

THE BARON SEFTON OF GARSTON, of Garston, Co Merseyside (William Henry Sefton) [The Rt Hon The Lord Sefton of Garside, House of Lords. London SW1A 0PW]; *b* 5 Aug 1915; *educ* Duncombe Rd Sch Liverpool; Liverpool CC 1953 (Leader 1964,), Chm and Leader Merseyside CC 1974–77 (Oppn Leader 1977–79), Runcorn Devpt Corp: joined 1964, Dep Chm 1967, Chm NW Ec Planning Cncl 1975–89, V-Chm and Bd Memb Warrington and Runcorn Devpt Corp 1981–85 and Chm Runcorn Devpt Corp 1974–81 (Bd Memb 1964–81); *m* 1940 *Phyllis Kerr

Lineage: GEORGE SEFTON; *m* Emma — and had:

WILLIAM HENRY, *cr* a **Baron**

SELBORNE

Arms: Arg. on two bars sa. three trefoils slipped of the first, in chief a greyhound courant of the second, collared or. **Crest:** On a mount vert a greyhound sejant sa., collared or, charged on the shoulder with a trefoil, slipped arg. **Supporters:** On either side a greyhound sa., collared and charged on the shoulder with a trefoil, slipped arg. **Motto:** *Palma virtuti* ('Let the palm be awarded to virtue'). **Creations:** B. (UK) 23 Oct 1872, E. and V. (UK) 30 Dec 1882.

THE 4TH EARL OF SELBORNE, Co Southampton, **Viscount Wolmer of Blackmoor**, Co Southampton, and **Baron Selborne of Selborne** (Sir John Roundell Palmer, KBE (1987), JP (Hants 1971), DL (Hants 1982)) [The Rt Hon The Earl of Selborne KBE JP DL, Temple Manor, Selborne, Hants GU34 3LR]; *b* 24 March 1940; *s* gf 1971; *educ* Eton and Ch Ch Oxford (MA); CC Hants 1967–74, V-Chm Apple and Pear Devpt Cncl 1971–73, Treas Bridewell Roy Hosp (King Edward's Sch, Witley) 1972–83, Chm: Hops Mktg Bd 1978–82, Ag and Food Research Cncl 1983–89, Master Mercer's Co 1989, chm jt Nature Conservation Ctee 1991–97, Ho Lds Select Ctee Sci and Tech 1993–97, memb Govt Panel on Sustainable Devpt 1994–97, Pres: S of England Ag Soc 1984, Inst Ag Management, Roy Ag Soc England 1988, RGS 1997–, Parly and Sci Ctee 1997–, memb: Roy Commn Environmental Pollution 1993–, Chllr Southampton U 1996–, FRS, FIBiol, FRAgS, Hon LLD Bristol 1989, Hon DSc Cranfield 1991, Hon ScD UEA 1996; *m* 19 Dec 1969 *Joanna Van Antwerp, MA, PhD, yr dau of Evan Maitland James, of Upwood Pk, Abingdon, Oxon, and has:

1 +WILLIAM LEWIS, *Viscount Wolmer*; *b* 1 Sept 1971; *educ* Eton and Ch Ch Oxford, Inst Devpt Studies Sussex U 1996–

2 +George Horsley; *b* 12 March 1974; *educ* Eton and Leeds U

3 +Luke James; *b* 12 March 1974; *educ* Eton and Goldsmiths' Coll London

1 *Emily Sophia; *b* 27 April 1978; *educ* Bryanston and Edinburgh U

Lineage: THOMAS PALMER, of Marston, Staffs; *b c* 1470; *m* Margaret — (*d* after 1532) and *d* after 1532, leaving:

RALPH PALMER, of Marston; *b c* 1495; *m* Alice (*d* 1561), dau of Richard Weston, and *d* 1559, having had, with a yr s (William, *b* 1525, *d* after 1558) and three daus (Thomasina, *b c* 1522, *m* James Deane and *d* after 1560, leaving issue; Agnes, *b c* 1523, *m* Thomas Sale and *d* 1560, leaving a dau (Alice); Margaret, *b c* 1526, *m* John Cotton and *d* after 1560, leaving issue):

THOMAS PALMER, of Marston; *b c* 1524; *m* Joan, dau of William Fox, of Hopton, Staffs, and was *bur* 21 Feb 1593, having had, with two daus (Thomasina, *b* 1560, *m* Thomas Cooke; Catherine, *b* 1565, *m* William Crompton):

  1 Robert, of Hill, Beds; *b c* 1557; *m* 10 June 1595 Marie (*d* after 1636), dau of Walter Craddock, and *d* 12 Aug 1630, being ancestor of the PALMER-MOREWOODs of Alfreton and leaving:

    (1) William (Sir), of Warden

  2 WILLIAM

  3 John (Rev); *b* 1561; Rector St Mary's Stafford; *d* 6 July 1639

  4 Thomas; *b* 1561; *m* 12 Oct 1591 Jane (*d* March 1628), dau of Matthew Dorington, and *d* Jan 1628, leaving issue

The 2nd s,

WILLIAM PALMER, of Wanlip Hall, which he bought 1625, and Ladbroke, Warwicks, an estate he bought 1633; *bapt* 24 Dec 1559; merchant, memb Haberdashers' Co 1626, Govr Bart's Hosp; *m* Barbara (*d* 17 April 1651), dau of Thomas Archdale, of Wycombe, Bucks, and *d* 20 Sept 1636, having had, with an est s (Thomas, *b* 1606, *dsp* by 1636), five yr sons (John, *b* and *d* 1613; William, *d* by 1636; Sir William, of Hill, Beds, *b* 1615, *s* to Ladbroke 1636 but exchanged 1642 for that of his cousin Sir William Palmer (*see* above) at Hill, ktd 1642 after Battle of Edgehill, Carver-in-Ordinary to CHARLES I 1645, *m* Margaret (*d* 1671), dau of Sir Thomas Gardner, Recorder London, by Rebecca Child, and *d* 1671, leaving eight sons and a dau; John, of Aldermanbury, *b* 1618, haberdasher, *m* Mary, dau of Michael Biddulph, of Elmhurst, Staffs (ancestor of the BIDDULPHs of Ledbury), and *d* after 1692; Henry, *d* by 1636) and a dau (Elizabeth, *dsp*), a 2nd s:

ARCHDALE PALMER, of Wanlip; *b* 1610; *educ* Sidney Sussex Coll Cambridge; Leics: High Sheriff 1641, Ld Lt; *m* Martha (*d* 1678), dau of Thomas Smith, and *d* 6 Aug 1673, having had, with five yr sons (Rev Archdale, *b* 1638, *educ* Sidney Sussex and Pembroke Colls Cambridge, Curate St Andrew's Hertford, *m* Ann (*d* after 1673), dau of Bartholomew Cradock, and had two daus (Martha; Anne), *m* 2nd 24 Oct 1678 Mary, dau of Thomas Joyce, of Warwick, and *d* Sept 1686, leaving by her two further daus (Barbara, *m* her cousin John Palmer (*see* below); Mary); John, *b* 1643, *d* by 1672; Samuel, of London, *b* 1635, linen draper, *m* Grisell Ewres, of Waltham Cross, and *d* after 1729, leaving a s (George); Joshua, of St Botolph's, Bishopsgate, *b* 9 April 1658, *educ* St Catharine's Coll Cambridge and Leyden U (MD 1683), LRCP, *d c* 1708) and three daus (Dorcas, *b* 1644, *d* by 1672; Barbara, *b* 1647, *d* after 1673; Martha, *b* 1651, *m* Richard Lloyd and *d* after 1673):

WILLIAM PALMER, of Wanlip; *b* 1636; *m* 1st 20 Aug 1660 Elizabeth (*d* 1 Feb 1669), dau of William Danvers, of Swithland, Leics, by Elizabeth Babington, and had, with two yst sons (John, *b* 1666, *d* an infant; Henry, *b* 1667, West India merchant, *d* unm 28 May 1740) and a dau (Elizabeth, *b* 1669, *d* 1670):

1 ARCHDALE

2 Thomas; *b* 1664; settled New England; *m* 29 Jan 1697 Abigail, dau of Eliakim Hutchinson, of Boston, Mass., and *d* 1740, leaving five sons and four daus

3 William; *b* 1665; *educ* Leyden U (MD *c* 1692); *m* Mary Hough and *d* 1713, leaving:

(1) Mary; *m* Dr Coote Molesworth, FRS (*see* MOLESWORTH, V)

WILLIAM PALMER *m* 2nd Martha, dau of Col Thomas Hunt, of Boreatton, Salop, and *d* 18 April 1692, having by her had, with three more daus (Martha, *b* after 1671, *d* 1745; Barbara; Mary; both *d* young):

4 Samuel; *b c* 1671; *m* Elizabeth — and *d* by 1744, leaving a s and two daus

5 John; *b c* 1672; lawyer Middle Temple; *m* his cousin Barbara (*d* by 1738), dau of Thomas Palmer, of Newark, and *d* 1738, leaving two daus

The est s,
ARCHDALE PALMER, of Wanlip; *b* 1661; *educ* Gray's Inn; MP Leicester 1695–98; *m* 1st 21 April 1684 Mary (*d* 12 June 1695), dau of Joseph Dawson, and had ten sons and a dau, including:

1 John; *b* 1685; *m* Anne (*d* 1765), dau of Samuel Danvers, of Swithland, by Elizabeth Moreward, and *d* 1727, leaving:

(1) Anne

2 William; *m* 1714 Elizabeth Bucknell and *d* 19 April 1739, leaving issue (now extinct)

3 Joseph; *b* after 1684; *d* unm 1723

1 Elizabeth; *m* John Bakewell and had three daus (Elizabeth; Mary; Anne)

ARCHDALE PALMER *m* 2nd 19 Dec 1698 Anne (*d* 1764), dau of Nicholas Charlton, and by her had nine further sons and six further daus, including:

4 Henry, of Wanlip; *b* 12 Oct 1703; merchant; *m* 29 July 1740 Elizabeth Borrett and was *bur* 26 March 1773, having had, with two sons and two yr daus:

(1) Catherine Susanna; *b* March 1742; *m* 8 March 1766 Sir Charles Grave Hudson, 1st Bt, and had issue (*see* PALMER, Bt, of Wanlip Hall)

5 Samuel; *b* 17 Sept 1704; *bur* 22 June 1713

6 THOMAS

7 Archdale; *b* 13 March 1713; *bur* 22 April 1752

8 Charlton; *b* 29 March 1714; *m* 1st 23 April 1743 Mary Dawson and had an only dau (Susannah, *m* Rev Thomas Pollok, Rector Grettleton, Wilts, and had issue); *m* 2nd June 1767 Louisa Chapman (*dsp* by 12 Sept 1822), of Chiswick, and *d* 29 July 1797

2 Martha; *b* 18 Feb 1706/7; *m* 2 Oct 1732 Benjamin Lewis and had issue

3 Mary; *b* 20 April 1708; *m* 1733 William Faris and had a s

ARCHDALE PALMER *d* 15 Sept 1732; his 6th s here mentioned,
THOMAS PALMER, of Cheshunt, Herts, and London; *b* 11 April 1706; merchant, Mercers' Co: Freeman 1729, Master 1773; *m* 26 Feb 1731 Rebecca (*d* 18 May 1782), dau of Thomas Pickard, of Cheshunt, by Sarah Jocelyn (*see* RODEN, E), and *d* 31 Aug 1789, having had, with two yr sons (Archdale, HEICS, *d* unm 1786; Thomas, of Cheam, Surrey, *b* 1736, *m* 18 June 1767 Sarah (*d* 23 Dec 1815), dau of John Wathen, of Clapham, and *d* 8 Jan 1814, leaving issue, now extinct in the male line) and a dau (Sarah, *d* unm 1766):
WILLIAM PALMER, of Nazeing Park, Essex, JP; *b* 1737; London merchant, High Sheriff Essex, Master Mercers' Co 1795; *m* 22 July 1766 Mary (*d* 3 July 1824), dau of Rev John Horsley, Rector Thorley and Newington Butts, and *d* 25 June 1821, having had:

1 George, JP, of Nazeing Park; *b* 11 Feb 1772; *educ* Charterhouse; Master Mercers' Co 1820; involved in fndg RNLI (Dep Chm 1828–53), designed lifeboat in gen use 1826–58); MP S Essex 1836–47; *m* 29 Dec 1795 Anna Maria (*d* 13 Oct 1856), dau and coheir of William Bund, of Wick Episcopi, Worcs, and *d* 12 May 1853, leaving three sons and two daus

2 Thomas; *b* 6 May 1773; *educ* Charterhouse; writer HEICS; *d* unm 24 Sept 1799

3 WILLIAM JOCELYN (Rev)

4 John Horsley, of Hurlingham; *b* 7 July 1779; *educ* Charterhouse; Bank England: Dir 1811–57, Govr 1830–32, Master Mercers' Co 1826; *m* 1st 16 Nov 1810 Elizabeth (*d* 22 June 1839), dau of John Belli, of Southampton, by Elizabeth Stuart Cockerell, of Westbourne Ho, Middx, and *d* 7 Feb 1858

5 Edward; *b* 6 July 1781; *educ* Charterhouse; Post Capt HMS *Nautilus*; *d* unm 8 Jan 1807 when she was wrecked in the Mediterranean

6 Ralph (Sir); *b* 11 April 1783; *educ* Charterhouse and Ch Ch Oxford; memb Mercers' Co, Ch Justice Madras 1825–35; *m* 2 Nov 1829 Margaret Elizabeth (*d* 14 March 1867), est dau of Maj-Gen Robert Bryce Fearon, CB, and *d* 25 Jan 1838, leaving issue

The 3rd s,
Rev WILLIAM JOCELYN PALMER; *b* 5 Feb 1778; *educ* Charterhouse and BNC Oxford; BD, Rector Mixbury and Finmere, Oxon 1802–52, memb Mercers' Co; *m* 10 Sept 1810 Dorothea Richardson (*d* 1 Dec 1867), yst dau of Rev William Roundell, of Gledstone, Skipton-in-Craven, Yorks, and *d* 28 Sept 1853, having had, with two other daus (*d* unm):

1 William; *b* 12 July 1811; *educ* Rugby and Magdalen Coll Oxford (Fell 1832–55); Deacon 1836, advocated Greek Orthodox and RC intercommunion, turned RC 1855; *d* 5 April 1879

2 ROUNDELL, **1st Earl**

3 Henry Roundell; *b* 10 July 1816; *educ* Rugby; lost at sea off Halifax, Nova Scotia, Dec 1834

4 George Horsley (Rev), of Coldhayes, Hants; *b* 10 July 1822; *educ* Charterhouse and Exeter Coll Oxford; Rector Mixbury 1852–81, memb Mercers' Co; *m* 3 Aug 1852 Elizabeth Frances (*d* 23 Oct 1921), only child of Rev Francis Horsley, of Matching, Essex, and *d* 17 May 1890

5 Edwin (Ven); *b* 18 July 1824; *educ* Charterhouse and Balliol Coll Oxford (Fell 1846–57), also Hon Fell; DD 1878, Archdeacon Oxford and student Ch Ch 1877–95, Prof Latin Oxford U 1870–78, Hon Fell Balliol and Corpus Christi Colls, memb Mercers' Co; *m* 19 Sept 1867 Henrietta (*d* 20 Jan 1915), yst dau of Rev James Riddell (*see* RIDDELL, Bt), and *d* 17 Oct 1895, having had:

(1) Edwin James (Rt Rev); *b* 10 Jan 1869; *educ* Winchester and Balliol Coll Oxford (BA 1891, Fell and Tutor 1891–1908, MA 1894, DD 1908); Bp Bombay 1908–29, Assist Bp Gloucester 1929, Sub-Prelate OStJ 1918, Hon Canon Gloucester 1932–36; *m* 7 Oct 1912 Hazel (*d* 6 Feb 1931), dau of Col Edward Hanning Hanning-Lee, 2nd Life Gds, of Bighton Manor, Alresford, Hants, and *dsp* 28 March 1954

(1) Mary Henrietta; *b* 30 Nov 1871; *m* 9 July 1917 Rev Canon Arthur Nesham Bax, Vicar Moseley, Birmingham, Hon Canon Birmingham, s of Capt Bonham Ward Bax, RN, and *d* 26 Nov 1951. He *d* 18 March 1960

(2) Lucy Dorothea; *b* 25 Aug 1873; *d* unm 22 March 1964

1 Eleanor; *m* 18 Feb 1851 Rev Cyril William Wood, Rector Stogursey, Somerset, and *d* 25 Dec 1873, having had two sons. He *d* 1870

2 Emily Frances; Mother Superior St Cyprian's Sisterhood; *d* unm 20 Jan 1906

The 2nd s,
ROUNDELL PALMER, **1st Earl of Selborne**, Co Southampton, so *cr* 30 Dec 1882, as also VISCOUNT WOLMER OF BLACKMOOR, Co Southampton, and earlier 23 Oct 1872 BARON SELBORNE OF SELBORNE, Co Southampton (all UK), PC (1872); *b* 27 Nov 1812; *educ* Rugby, Winchester (Fell 1875–95) and Ch Ch (Hon Student 1867) Oxford (Pres Union 1832, Fell 1834–38 and Hon Fell 1862 Magdalen Coll, Dep Steward and Counsel to U 1861–63, DCL 1862, High Steward 1892); barrister Lincoln's Inn 1837 (Bencher 1849, Treas 1864), MP (Peelite to 1857, Lib thereafter) Plymouth 1847–52 and 1853–57 and Richmond 1861–72, QC 1849, Slr-Gen 1861–63, ktd 1861, Attorney-Gen 1863–66, Ld Chllr 1872–74 and 1880–85, FRS 1860, Master Mercers' Co 1876, Chm Us Commn 1876–80, Ld Rector St Andrews U 1877, Pres Wordsworth Soc 1886, Hon LLD Cantab 1888; *m* 2 Feb 1848 Lady Laura Waldegrave (*d* 10 April 1885), 2nd dau of 8th Earl Waldegrave (*qv*), and had:

1 WILLIAM WALDEGRAVE, **2nd Earl**

1 Laura Elizabeth; *b* 16 March 1849; *m* 26 Oct 1876 Rt Rev George Ridding, DD, 1st Bp Southwell, and *d* 22 May 1939. He *dsp* 30 Aug 1904

2 Mary Dorothea, DBE; *b* 25 March 1850; *m* 5 Aug 1874 9th Earl Waldegrave (*qv*) and *d* 8 Nov 1933, leaving issue

3 Sophia Matilda; *b* 14 Nov 1852; *m* 16 Feb 1903 Amable Charles Franquet, Count de Franqueville, LLD, memb Institut de France, of Château de la Muette, Passy, Paris, and Château de Bourbilly, Semur en Auxois, Côte d'Or, France, and *d* 28 Oct 1915. He *d* 28 Dec 1919

4 Sarah Wilfreda; *b* 3 Oct 1854; *m* 3 Oct 1883 George Tournay Biddulph and *d* 4 Oct 1910, leaving issue (*see* BIDDULPH, B)

5 Beatrix Maud Cecil; *b* 11 April 1858; *d* 27 April 1950

The 1st EARL *d* 4 May 1895; his only s,
WILLIAM WALDEGRAVE PALMER, **2nd Earl of Selborne**, KG (1909), GCMG (1905), PC (1900), JP Hants; *b* 17 Oct 1859; *educ* Winchester (Fell 1904 and Warden 1920–25) and Univ Coll Oxford (DCL 1911); Assist Priv Sec to Chllr Exchequer 1882–85, MP (Lib to 1886, Lib U thereafter) E Hants 1885–92 and W Edinburgh 1892–95, U-Sec Colonies 1895–1900, 1st Ld Admlty 1900–05, HC S Africa and Govr and C-in-C Transvaal and Orange River Colony 1905–10, Pres Bd Ag 1915–16, LLD Cantab 1910, High Steward Winchester 1929–42, Fell Roy Empire Soc, Er Bro Trin Ho, Chm Ho Laity Ch Assembly, Hon Col 3rd Bn Hants Regt, CA Hants; *m* 27 Oct 1883 Lady Beatrix Maud Cecil, JP (Hants) (*d* 27 April 1950), dau of 3rd Marquess of Salisbury (*qv*), and had:

1 ROUNDELL CECIL, **3rd Earl**

2 Robert Stafford Arthur; *b* 26 Sept 1888; *educ* Oxford; barrister Inner Temple, Capt 6th Bn Hants Regt; *ka* Mesopotamia 21 Jan 1916

3 (William Jocelyn) Lewis, JP (Hants 1941); *b* 15 Sept 1894; *educ* Winchester and Ch Ch Oxford (MA 1919); Hants: CC 1945, CA 1957–67, Capt 6th Bn Hants Regt, FLS, Treas RHS 1953–65, Master Mercers' Co 1950–51 and 1955–56; *m* 13 May 1922 Hon Dorothy Cicely Sybil Loder (*d* 1986), est dau of 1st Baron Wakehurst (*qv*), and *d* 6 June 1971, leaving:

(1) Stephen Roundell (Rev); *b* 17 March 1923; *educ* Eton and Ch Ch Oxford (MA 1954); Hon Capt RE WW II, ordained 1953; *m* 20 Sept 1952 *Joyce [Mrs Stephen Palmer, 21 Windy Ridge, Beaminster, Dorset DT8 3SP], dau of Rev Walter Darling Topping, Vicar Gt Saling, Essex, and *d* 1990, leaving:

1a +William Jocelyn; *b* 21 July 1953; *educ* Lancing and Bedford Coll London; *m* 19– *Catherine, dau of Jean Pierre Hossen Iopp; and has:

1b *Sophie Juliette; *b* 3 June 1992

2b *Chloe Celine; *b* 5 May 1994

2a +Andrew Nicholas; *b* 18 March 1955; *educ* Lancing and Worcester Coll Oxford (MA, DPhil); Lecturer Eastern Christian Studies SOAS London; *m* 1980 (*divorce* 1996) Anne Marie, dau of Joseph Foster, and has:

1b *Thomas John; *b* 29 March 1986

1b *Rebecca Louise; *b* 7 Nov 1982

2b *Frances Mary Laura; *b* 6 Aug 1984

3b *Alice Rose; *b* 31 Aug 1987

4b *Isobel Margaret Jane; *b* 30 July 1989

5b *Catherine Anna Sophia; *b* 9 Jan 1992

(1) *Penelope Jane [Mrs David Jamison, Les Fontenelles, Forest, Guernsey, CI GY8 0BL]; *b* July 1925; WRNS WW II; *m* 19 May 1965 David George Jamison, BM, Fell Corpus Christi Coll Oxford, s of David Jamison, MD, of Newtownards, Co Down

1 Mabel Laura Georgiana, CBE (1919), JP; *b* 6 Oct 1884; *m* 16 June 1906 5th Earl Grey (*qv*) and *d* 15 July 1958, leaving issue

The 2nd EARL *d* 26 Feb 1942; his est s,
ROUNDELL CECIL PALMER, **3rd Earl of Selborne**, CH (1945), PC (1929), JP (Hants 1911); *b* 15 April 1887; *educ* Winchester and Univ Coll Oxford (MA 1909); MP (Lib) Newton 1910–18 and Aldershot 1918–40, PPS to U-Sec For Affrs 1916, Maj 3rd Bn Hants Regt, Assist Dir War Trade Dept 1916–18, Parly Sec BOT 1922–24, Assist PMG 1924–29, Dir Cement Min Works and Bldgs 1940–42, called up to Ho Lds *vp* in f's barony 1940, Min Ec Warfare 1942–45, memb Ho Laity Ch Assembly 1920, Pres Ch Army 1949, Master Mercers' Co 1948, chm Nat Provincial Bank 1951–53, dep chm Boots 1951–64; *m* 1st 9 June 1910 Hon Grace Ridley (*d* 22 Sept 1959), 3rd dau of 1st Viscount Ridley (*qv*); *m* 2nd 3 March 1966 Valerie Irene (*d* 5 Dec 1968), formerly w of Bryan Henry Bevan, s of Edmund Henry Bevan, JP, of Hilston Park, Mon (*see* GRANTLEY, B), and yr dau of Joseph Anthony Nicholas de Thomka de Thomkahaza, late Sec of State Hungary, and *d* 3 Sept 1971, having by his 1st w had:

1 William Matthew, *Viscount Wolmer*; *b* 27 May 1912; *educ* Winchester and Balliol Coll Oxford (BA 1933); Capt Hants Regt WW II; *m* 16 July 1936 *Priscilla [Mrs Frederick Fryer, Vernon Hill House, Bishop's Waltham, Hants] (*m* 2nd 6 July 1948 4th Baron Newton (*qv*); *m* 3rd 1994, as his 2nd w, Frederick Charles Horace Fryer; *see* PEEL, E), yr dau of Capt John Egerton Warburton (*see* GREY EGERTON, Bt), and was accidentally *kas* by a shell 2 Oct 1942, having had:

(1) JOHN ROUNDELL PALMER, **4th and present Earl of Selborne**

(2) +Henry William [The Hon Henry Palmer, Burhunt Farm, Selborne, Hants GU34 3LP]; *b* 12 July 1941; *educ* Eton and Ch Ch Oxford (BA 1963, MA 1967); granted with sis rank of earl's dau/yr s 1985, dir Centre for Interfirm Comparison 1985–, FIMgt, Master Mercers' Co 1992, dep chm St Paul's Girls' Sch 1995–; *m* 5 Oct 1968 *(Patricia) Minette, er dau of Sir Patrick William Donner, of Hurstbourne Park, Whitchurch, Hants, and has:

1a +Benjamin Matthew; *b* 20 July 1970 *educ* Eton

2a +Robert Henry; *b* 28 Nov 1972; *educ* Eton, St John's Coll Oxford and Gray's Inn

3a +Charles William; *b* 31 Oct 1978; *educ* Eton and Edinburgh U

1a *Laura Cecilia; *b* 8 April 1976; *educ* St Mary's Ascot and New Coll Oxford

(1) Rosemary Laura; *b* 26 May 1937; *d* 30 April 1938

(2) *Katherine Elizabeth [The Lady Katherine Nall-Cain, Ballacleator, St Judes, IOM]; *b* 24 July 1938; *m* 16 June 1958 *Hon David Lawrence Robert Nall-Cain, yr s of 2nd Baron Brocket (*qv*), and has issue

2 John Ralph Roundell; *b* 11 May *d* 13 Nov 1914

3 Robert Jocelyn, MC (1944), JP (Hants 1951); *b* 9 Jan 1919; *educ* Winchester and Balliol Coll Oxford; Maj Coldstream Gds WW II (despatches twice), CC Hants 1954; *m* 11 May 1950 Anne Rosemary, Baroness Lucas of Crudwell (*qv*) and Lady Dingwall and *d* 30 Nov 1991, leaving issue

4 Edward Roundell; *b* 10 April 1926; *educ* Winchester, Ch Ch Oxford (MA) and Madrid U; FRHS; *m* 18 May 1957 *Joanna Constance, est dau of Lt-Col Sir Edmund Castell Bacon, 13th and 14th Bt (*qv*), and *d* 1 Aug 1974, leaving:

(1) +Francis Mark Bacon; *b* 21 June 1958

(2) +Matthew Roundell; *b* 12 Feb 1965

(1) *Henrietta Cecilia; *b* 12 May 1960

(2) *Lucinda Beatrice; *b* 26 Jan 1962

1*Anne Beatrice Mary [The Lady Anne Brewis, Benham's House, Benham's Lane, Blackmoor, Hants]; *b* 26 March 1911; *educ* Somerville Coll Oxford (BA 1934); *m* 3 July 1935 Rev John Salusbury Brewis (*d* 1972), s of George Robert Brewis, of Oxford (*see* 1970 edn DUCKWORTH-KING, Bt), and has:

(1) *Thomas William [Thomas Brewis Esq, West Garth, Bailes Lane, Normandy, Surrey GU3 2AX]; *b* 27 Aug 1937; *educ* Eton and New Coll Oxford; *m* 1983 *Susan Alison Virginia, dau of Lt-Col J A Mackay

(2) *Robert Salusbury [Robert Brewis Esq, Benham's Farm, Benham's Lane, Blackmoor, Hants]; *b* 21 May 1939; *educ* Eton and Magdalen Coll Oxford; *m* 21 April 1965 *Irena, er dau of Wiktor Grubert, and has had:

1a *Paul William Salusbury; *b* 11 Nov 1966

2a John Wiktor; *b* 16 Sept 1967; *d* 22 Feb 1968

3a *Edward George; *b* 4 March 1969

1a *Eleanor Anne; *b* 1975

(1) *Mary Elizabeth Maud [Mrs David Tweedie, 31 Oxberry Rd, London SW6]; *b* 11 April 1947; *m* 24 Oct 1970 *David Allison Osborne Tweedie, slr, est s of Dr D Reid Tweedie, of Malaysia and Farnham, Surrey, and has:

1a *Jeannie Anne Cecilia; *b* 1973; *educ* Exeter U

2a *Katherine Grace; *b* 1975; *educ* St Andrews U

(2) *Susan Amy [Mrs Edward Martineau, Moorland, Box End Rd, Bromham, Beds MK43 8LU]; *b* 21 June 1949; *educ* King's Coll London; *m* 31 May 1975 *Edward Crispin Akers Martineau, yr s of Anthony Adeane Martineau, of The Palace House, Bishops Waltham, Hants, and has:

1a *Frederick Phelips; *b* 1979

1a *Flora Felicity; *b* 1981

2 *Laura Mary [The Lady Laura Eastaugh, 9 Blackmoor House, Blackmoor, Hants GU33 6DA]; *b* 29 Aug 1915; Dipl Theology Lambeth 1944, Chaplain's Assist ATS 1944–46, Hants Sec Women's Land Army 1940–42; *m* 1 April 1948 Rt Rev Cyril Eastaugh, MC, Bp Peterborough 1961–72 (*d* 1988), s of Robert Wilgress Eastaugh, and has:

(1) *Andrew Nathaniel [Andrew Eastaugh Esq, South Cove House, Wrentham, Suffolk NR34 7JD]; *b* 15 Sept 1954; *educ* Eton; MB, BS, MRCS Eng, LRCP Lond 1978, MRCP, MRCGP; *m* 19– *Alice M, yr dau of Cyril Hopkins, of Glutières, Switzerland, and has:

1a *Rose Frances; *b* 1983

2a *Charlotte Laura; *b* 1985

3a *Sophia Mary; *b* 1988

(1) *Laura Jane Catherine [Mrs Giichi Inoue, Apt 111, 4–3–16 Nakarokugo, Ota-Ku, Tokyo 144, Japan]; *b* 29 June 1949; *m* 1st 19 Aug 1972 William McDonell Eddis, yr s of Arthur McDonell Eddis, of Warren House, Aldeburgh, Suffolk, and has:

1a *Nathalie; *b* 1973

(1) (cont.) Mrs Eddis *m* 2nd 1981 *Giichi Inoue and by him has:

2a *Marina; *b* 1984

(2) *Elisabeth Mary [Mrs Mark Bryant, 365 Walsgrave Rd, Coventry CV2 4BG]; *b* 7 Oct 1951; *educ* St Aidan's Coll Durham; *m* 7 Feb 1976 *Rev Canon Mark Bryant, est s of Canon Douglas Bryant, of Egham, Hythe, Kent, and has:

1a *Simon Mark; *b* 1978

2a *Christopher Nathaniel; *b* 1984

1a *Helen Elisabeth; *b* 1981

3 *Mary Sophia [The Lady Mary Gore, Grove Farm, Stoke-by-Nayland, Essex CO6 4SL]; *b* 6 Sept 1920; Ldy-in-Waiting to HRH PRINCESS ELIZABETH 1944–47, Extra Ldy-in-Waiting 1947–49; *m* 1st 11 Nov 1944 Maj Hon (Thomas) Anthony Edward Towneley Strachey, only s of 3rd Baron O'Hagan (*qv*), and has issue; *m* 2nd 1981, as his 2nd w, *(Francis) St John Gore, CBE (*see* GORE, Bt)

SELBY

Arms: Or a lion rampant sa. between four escallops two and two fesswise gu., on a chief of the last as many escallops of the field. **Crest:** A cubit arm vested sa., cuff arg., the hand grasping a sword erect ppr. between two wings each per pale nebuly, the dexter of the last and gu., the sinister gu. an owl sa. **Supporters:** Dexter, an owl sa. charged with a balance or; sinister an eagle sa., charged with a portcullis gold. **Motto:** *Nec temere nec tarde* ('Neither rashly nor slowly'). **Creation:** V. (UK) 6 July 1905.

THE 5TH VISCOUNT SELBY, of the City of Carlisle (Edward Thomas William Gully) [The Rt Hon The Viscount Selby, House of Lords, London SW1A 0PW]; *b* 21 Sept 1967; *s* f 1997; *educ* Harrow; *m* 1992 Charlotte Catherine (*d* 1995), yr dau of Rolph Brege, of Lomma, Sweden, and has:

1 +CHRISTOPHER ROLF THOMAS; *b* 18 Oct 1993

Lineage: DANIEL GULLY, of Sheffield, Jamaica, and Liverpool; coffee planter; had:

JAMES MANBY GULLY, of the Priory, Gt Malvern; *b* 14 March 1808; MD; *m* 9 June 1831 Frances (*d* 1838), dau of Thomas Court, and *d* 1883, leaving:

WILLIAM COURT GULLY, **1st Viscount Selby**, of the City of Carlisle (UK), so *cr* 6 July 1905, PC (1895); *b* 29 Aug 1835; *educ* Trin Coll Cambridge (Pres Union 1855, BA 1856, MA 1859, Hon LLD 1900); barrister Inner Temple 1860 (Bencher 1879), QC 1877, Recorder Wigan 1886–95, MP (Lib) Carlisle 1886–1905, Speaker H of C 1895–1905, Hon DCL Oxon 1904; *m* 15 April 1865 Elizabeth Anne Walford (*d* 15 Nov 1906), est dau of Thomas Selby, of Whitley and Wimbish, Essex, and had:

1 JAMES WILLIAM HERSCHELL, **2nd Viscount**

2 Edward Walford Karslake, CB; *b* 21 Oct 1870; Sec to his f and successor as Speakers H of C 1895–1911 and to Caledonian Canal Commrs 1899–1911, Examiner Private Bills and Taxing Office for H of C 1911–27, T/Lt RNVR 1915; *m* 4 Dec 1901 Ada (*d* 6 Dec 1957), er dau of Robert Symon, of Mayfair, and *d* 8 Nov 1931, leaving:

(1) Sheila; *b* 1 Sept 1902; Chm Appeals Ctee DGAA, Chm Queen Mary's Guild Needlework; *m* 6 Dec 1921 25th Lord (Baron) Mowbray, (26th Lord (Baron)) Segrave and (22nd Lord (Baron)) Stourton (*qv*) and *d* 19 Feb 1975, leaving issue

(2) Joan Marcia; *b* 26 Dec 1905; *m* 6 Dec 1933 John William St John Whitehead, 2nd s of Sir Beethom Whitehead, KCMG, and *d* 2 July 1937

1 Gertrude Annie; *m* 17 May 1888 His Hon Judge James Aloysius Scully, 3rd s of James Scully, of Co Tipperary, and *d* 12 April 1949, leaving issue. He *d* 5 Feb 1929

2 Florence Julia; *m* 12 Nov 1892 Sir William Guy Granet, GBE, s of William Augustus Granet, of Genoa, and *d* 17 Sept 1949, leaving issue. He *d* 11 Oct 1943

3 Mary Honorah Rhoda; *m* 17 March 1894 Sir Adrian Donald Wilde Pollock, KCMG, and *d* 21 Aug 1961, leaving issue (*see* POLLOCK, Bt)

4 Elizabeth Kate Shelley; *m* 1st 24 July 1902 (annulled 1907) Capt Carleton Salkeld, 10th Roy Hus (*d* 30 March 1959), s of Lt-Col Louis Carruthers Salkeld, JP, of Holme Hill and Hawksdale Hall, Cumberland; *m* 2nd Dec 1907 Capt Hon Edward Brabazon Meade, yst s of 4th Earl of Clanwilliam (*qv*), and *dsp* 26 July 1908

The 1st VISCOUNT *d* 6 Nov 1909; his er s,
JAMES WILLIAM HERSCHELL GULLY, **2nd Viscount Selby**; *b* 4 Oct 1867; *educ* Winchester and Balliol Coll Oxford; barrister Inner Temple 1892; *m* 1st 9

June 1893 (*divorce* 1909) Ada Isabel (*d* 5 March 1931), dau of Alexander George Pirie, of Stoneywood Ho, Aberdeen, and Leckmelm, Ross-shire, and had:

  1 Lesley; *b* 26 Oct 1897; *d* unm 5 June 1946

The **2nd Viscount** *m* 2nd 5 Aug 1909 Dorothy Evelyn (*d* 22 July 1951), yst dau of Sir William Grey, KCSI (*see* GREY, E), and by her had:

  1 THOMAS SUTTON EVELYN, **3rd Viscount**

  2 Signe Evelyn; *b* 10 Nov 1909; *m* 24 Oct 1938 MAX BRANDENSTEIN later MARK LESLIE BRANDON (naturalised UK citizen 1945), yr s of Ludwig Brandenstein, of Munich, and *d* 12 May 1997, having had:

    (1) *Lionel Roderick Evelyn; *b* 1939

    (1) *Vanessa Maxine [Mrs Gilbert Thompson-Royds, Seymour House, Market St, Charlbury, Oxford OX7 3PJ]; *b* 1947; *m* 1976 *Gilbert Thompson-Royds and has issue (*see* THOMPSON, Bt, of Park Gate)

    (2) Audrey; *d* young

  3 Helen Janice Patricia; *b* 18 March 1915

  4 Elizabeth Millicent; *b* 8 Feb 1917; *m* 1947 Clarence Henry Quainton McConnell, s of Charles James McConnell, of Pylle, Somerset, and had issue

The 2nd VISCOUNT *d* 2 Feb 1923; his only s,

  THOMAS SUTTON EVELYN GULLY, **3rd Viscount Selby**; *b* 16 Feb 1911; *educ* Bradfield and Chillon Coll Switzerland; Lt-Cdr (S) RNVR WW II; *m* 31 May 1933 Veronica Catherine (*d* 7 Sept 1996), er dau of Albert Joseph George by Mrs Briscoe-George, of Aldford House, Park Lane, London W1, and Starbotton, Yorks, and *d* 18 Sept 1959, leaving:

  1 MICHAEL GUY JOHN GULLY, **4th Viscount Selby**; *b* 15 Aug 1942; *educ* Harrow; FCA, memb Inst Taxation; *m* 29 May 1965 *Mary Theresa [The Rt Hon Mary Viscountess Selby, Ardfern House, by Lochgilphead, Argyll], dau of Capt Thomas Folliott Powell, of S Kensington, and *d* 10 Jan 1997, leaving:

    (1) EDWARD THOMAS WILLIAM GULLY, **5th and present Viscount Selby**

    (1) *Catherine Mary Albinia; *b* 17 March 1971

  2 +(James) Edward Hugh Grey [The Hon Edward Gully, Island of Shuna, Arduaine, by Oban, Argyll; Dunmore, Easdale, Isle of Seil, by Oban, Argyll]; *b* 17 March 1945; *educ* King's Canterbury; *m* 4 Dec 1971 *Fiona Margaret, only dau of Ian Straithaird Mackenzie, of Invervyne Lodge, Lochgilphead, and Isle of Iona, Argyll, and has:

    (1) +James Ian Mackenzie; *b* 1975

    (2) +Andrew Donald Mackenzie; *b* 1977

  1 *(Helen) Alexandra Briscoe [The Hon Lady Roche, Bridge House, Starbotton, N Yorks BD23 5HY; 36 Coniger Rd, London SW6 3TA]; *b* 8 June 1934; *m* 1st 15 Nov 1952 (*divorce* 1966) Roger d'Hautville Moreton Frewen (*d* 1972), est s of Hugh Moreton Frewen, JP, by Princess Maria di Mignano, and has:

    (1) *Jonathan Briscoe Moreton; *b* 4 Nov 1953; *m* 1979 *Anita Louise, yr dau of Nils J L Grebstad, of Norway, and has:

      1a *Antonia; *b* 1987

    (2) *Robert Edward Jerome [Capt Robert Frewen, Park Hall, Healaugh, N Yorks DL11 6UL]; *b* 10 May 1957; *educ* Eton, RMA Sandhurst and RAC Cirencester; Capt Irish Gds; ARICS; *m* 1989 *Rolline Charlotte, yr dau of Alexander Fergus Forbes Williamson (*see* FORRES, B), and has:

      1a *Jerome Fergus d'Estoutville; *b* 12 Jan 1995

      1a *Jennie Selina McMorrough; *b* 17 Nov 1992

    (3) *Charles Grey Justin; *b* 13 Feb 1959; *educ* Eton

    (1) Selina Veronica Clara; *b* 3 May 1955; *k* car crash 1972

  1 (cont.) The Hon Mrs Alexandra Frewen also has by John Foster:

    (2) *Emma Catherine Gully; *b* 1964; *m* 1985 *Jonathan Colin Fraser Bower, only s of Colin Bower, of Fulham

  1 (cont.) The Hon Mrs Alexandra Frewen *m* 2nd 24 June 1971 *Sir David O'Grady Roche, 5th Bt, and has further issue (*see* ROCHE, Bt)

  2 Audrey Lucille Veronica; *b* 18 Jan 1936; *m* 4 Aug 1955 Henry William Edward Briscoe, yr s of Dr H C Briscoe, of Natal, S Africa, and had:

    (1) *Charles Hylton William; *b* 12 April 1960

    (2) *Robert Michael England; *b* 28 July 1962

    (1) *Catherine Sarah Susan; *b* 24 May 1956

    (2) *Elizabeth Judith Audrey; *b* 23 Oct 1958

    (3) *Joy Joanna; *b* 22 Jan 1965

SELKIRK OF DOUGLAS

Arms (of Earls of Selkirk): Quarterly, 1st and 4th grand quarters, argent a heart gules imperially crowned proper, on a chief azure three mullets argent (for DOUGLAS); 2nd grand quarter, counter-quartered, 1st, azure a lion rampant argent, crowned or (for GALLOWAY); 2nd, or a lion rampant gules, surmounted of a riband sable (for ABERNETHY); 3rd, argent three piles gules (for JEDFOREST); 4th, or a fess chequy azure and argent, surmounted of a bend gules charged with three buckles or (for STEWART); 3rd grand quarter, counter-quartered, 1st and 4th, gules three cinquefoils ermine (for HAMILTON); 2nd and 3rd, argent a lymphad, sails furled sable, flagged gules (for ARRAN); over the grand quarters at the fess point a crescent sable. **Crest:** On a chapeau gules, doubled ermine, a salamander in flames proper. **Supporters:** Dexter, a savage wreathed about the head and middle with laurel, holding in his exterior hand a club, resting in a brandished posture on his shoulder, all proper; sinister, an antelope argent, armed and unguled or, gorged with an earl's coronet proper and having a chain reflexed over the back, also or. **Mottoes:** 1 *Jamais arriere* ('Never behind'), 2 *Firmior quo paratior* ('Steadier because readier'). **Creations:** L. and E. (S) 4 Oct 1646, regrant 6 Oct 1688, B. (LP, UK) 1997.

THE BARON SELKIRK OF DOUGLAS (Lord James Alexander Douglas-Hamilton, PC (1996), QC (1996) [The Rt Hon The Lord Selkirk of Douglas PC QC, House of Lords, London SW1A 0PW]; *b* 31 July 1942; *s* unc as 11th Earl of Selkirk 24 Nov 1994 (as adjudged by Lyon Court decree 14 March 1996), disclaimed peerages for life 28 Nov 1994; *educ* Eton, Balliol Coll Oxford (Boxing Blue 1961, Pres Oxford U C Assoc 1963 and Union 1964, MA) and Edinburgh U (LLB); Capt (RARO) Cameronians Co 2nd Bn Lowlands Vols TA, Hon A/Cdre No 2 (City of Edinburgh) Maritime HQ Unit 1994–; advocate 1968, memb Murrayfield-Cramond Cncl Edinburgh 1972, MP (C) Edinburgh West 1974–97, Assist Govt Whip (Scottish C MPs) 1977, Ld Commr Treasury 1979–81, PPS to: FCO Min 1983–86 and Sec State Scotland 1986–87, Parly U-Sec Home Affrs and Environment 1987–92, Educn and Housing Scottish Off 1992–95, Min State Home Affrs and Health Scottish Off 1995–97; Hon Pres Scottish Amateur Boxing Assoc 1975, Pres Roy Cwlth Soc Scotland 1979–87, Scottish Cncl UNA 1981–87; author: *Motive for a Mission: The Story behind Hess's Flight to Britain* (1971), *The Air Battle for Malta: the diaries of a fighter pilot* 1981 (2nd edn 1990), *Roof of the World: man's first flight over Everest* (1983), *The Truth About Rudolph Hess* (1993); *m* 24 Aug 1974 *Hon (Priscilla) Susan Buchan, only child of 2nd Baron Tweedsmuir (*qv*) and Baroness Tweedsmuir of Belhelvie (LP, *d* 1978), and has:

  1 +(JOHN) ANDREW, *Lord Daer, Master of Selkirk*; *b* 8 Feb 1978

  2 +Charles Douglas; *b* 20 June 1979

  3 +James Robert; *b* 1981

  4 +Harry Alexander (twin); *b* 1981

Lineage: The 1st MARQUESS OF DOUGLAS (*see* HAMILTON and BRANDON, D, and throughout for further details); had by his 2nd w an est s:

WILLIAM DOUGLAS later DOUGLAS-HAMILTON, **1st Earl of Selkirk**, so *cr* 4 Aug 1646, as also LORD DAER AND SHOTCLEUCH, with remainder to heirs male (resigned by him and regranted 6 Oct 1688 to his son Charles), KG (1682), PC (S Feb 1660/1, E 1687); *b* 24 Dec 1634; had, with other issue:

  1 JAMES HAMILTON, 4th DUKE OF HAMILTON and 1st DUKE OF BRANDON; had:

    (1) JAMES HAMILTON, 5th DUKE OF HAMILTON and 2nd DUKE OF BRANDON; had by his 1st w:

      1a JAMES HAMILTON, 6th DUKE OF HAMILTON and 3rd DUKE OF BRANDON; had:

        1b JAMES GEORGE HAMILTON, 7th DUKE OF HAMILTON and 4th DUKE OF BRANDON; *d* unm

        2b DOUGLAS HAMILTON, 8th DUKE OF HAMILTON and 5th DUKE OF BRANDON

(1) (cont.) The 5th/2nd DUKE had by a 2nd w:

1a ARCHIBALD HAMILTON, **9th DUKE OF HAMILTON** and **6th DUKE OF BRANDON**; had:

  1b ALEXANDER HAMILTON, **10th DUKE OF HAMILTON** and **7th DUKE OF BRANDON**; had:

    1c WILLIAM ALEXANDER ANTHONY ARCHIBALD HAMILTON, **11th DUKE OF HAMILTON** and **8th DUKE OF BRANDON**; had:

      1d WILLIAM ALEXANDER LOUIS STEPHEN HAMILTON later DOUGLAS-HAMILTON, **8th Earl of Selkirk**, also **12th DUKE OF HAMILTON** and **9th DUKE OF BRANDON**; *dspm*

      2d CHARLES GEORGE ARCHIBALD DOUGLAS-HAMILTON, **7th Earl of Selkirk**; *b* 18 May 1847; Lt 11th Hus; *dsp* 2 May 1886

2 CHARLES HAMILTON later DOUGLAS, **2nd Earl of Selkirk**

3 JOHN HAMILTON, **3rd Earl of Selkirk**

4 Basil; drowned Minnick Water, Galloway, 27 Aug 1701, having had, with other issue:

  (1) Basil; had, with other issue:

    1a DUNBAR HAMILTON later DOUGLAS, **4th Earl of Selkirk**; *b* 1 Dec 1722; *educ* Yorks and Glasgow U (DCL 1745); supported Govt in 1745 Jacobite Rising, Rector Glasgow U 1766–68; had, with other issue:

      1b Basil William, *Lord Daer*; *b* 16 March 1763; *educ* privately and Edinburgh U; in Paris during early days of French Revolution, with which sympathised, memb Scots 'Friends of the People' Soc, prominent in Edinburgh Convention 1793; *dvp* unm of TB Ivybridge, Devon, 9 Nov 1794 after Madeira voyage

      2b John, *Lord Daer*; *b* 24 May 1765; advocate 1787; *d* unm Florence 9 July 1797

      3b Dunbar; *b* 9 July 1766; Cdr RN; *d* of yellow fever St Christopher's, WI, 29 Oct 1796

      4b Alexander; *b* 12 Dec 1767; Capt 38th Foot; *d* of yellow fever Guadaloupe 7 June 1794

      5b David; *b* 8 Sept 1768; *d* 7 May 1770

      6b THOMAS DOUGLAS, **5th Earl of Selkirk**; *b* 20 June 1771; visited Canada 1803–04, fnded settlements: Prince Edward I, Gulf St Lawrence, 'Baldoon', Upper Canada, and Red River (now Winnipeg) after grant of land from Hudson's Bay Co 1811, FRS 1808; *m* Inveresk 24 Nov 1807 Joan, only surv dau of James Wedderburn-Colville, and *d* Pau, France, 8 April 1820, leaving:

        1c DUNBAR JAMES DOUGLAS, **6th Earl of Selkirk**; *b* London 22 April 1809; *educ* Eton and Ch Ch Oxford (BA 1830, MA 1834); FRS 1831; *dsp* 11 April 1885

(1) Anne (named after his f's god-mother QUEEN ANNE); *b* 12 Oct 1709; *m* Oct 1742 Anna Charlotte Maria Powell and *d* 25 Dec 1748, leaving, with other issue:

  1a Charles Powell; *b* 26 Dec 1747; Adml; *m* May 1777 Lucretia, dau of George Augustus Prosser, and *d* 12 March 1825, leaving, with other issue:

    1b Augustus Barrington Price Anne Powell; *b* 22 May 1781; *m* 2 April 1805 Maria Catherine, dau of John Hyde, and *d* 27 Aug 1849, having had, with other issue:

      1c Charles Henry; *b* 7 Oct 1808; *m* 2nd 31 Jan 1860 Elizabeth Ann Hill and by her had:

        1d ALFRED DOUGLAS DOUGLAS-HAMILTON, **9th Earl of Selkirk** (which held in fiduciary fee), also **13th DUKE OF HAMILTON** and **10th DUKE OF BRANDON**; *b* 6 March 1862; *m* 4 Dec 1901 Nina Mary Benita Poore and *d* 16 March 1940, having had:

          1e DOUGLAS DOUGLAS-HAMILTON, **14th DUKE OF HAMILTON** and **11th DUKE OF BRANDON**; *b* 3 Feb 1903; *m* 2 Dec 1937 *Lady Elizabeth Ivy Percy, er dau of 8th Duke of Northumberland (*qv*), and *d* 1973, having had:

            1f +ANGUS ALAN DOUGLAS DOUGLAS-HAMILTON, **15th DUKE OF HAMILTON** and **12th DUKE OF BRANDON**

            2f JAMES ALEXANDER DOUGLAS-HAMILTON, **briefly 11th Earl of Selkirk and present Baron Selkirk of Douglas**

          2e GEORGE NIGEL DOUGLAS-HAMILTON, **10th Earl of Selkirk**, KT (1976), GCMG (1959), GBE (1963, OBE 1941), AFC (1938), PC (1955), QC (1959); *b* 4 Jan 1906; *s* f 16 March 1940 (as adjudged by Lyon Court decree 11 May 1945, confirmed 11 Sept 1945); *educ* Eton, Balliol Coll Oxford (MA 19 33), Edinburgh (LLB 1933), Paris (Sorbonne), Bonn and Vienna Us; advocate 1935; G/Capt RAuxAF, cmded No 603 (City of Edinburgh) Bomber Sqdn 1934–38, WW II (despatches twice); Capt 44th Co Boy's Bde 1932–38, memb Edinburgh Town Cncl 1935–40 and Gen Bd Control Scotland 1936–39, Dep Keeper Palace Holyrood House 1937–94, Commr Special Areas Scotland 1937–39, memb Roy Co Archers; de S peer 1945–63, Ld-in-Waiting (C) 1951–53, Paymaster-Gen 1953–55, Chllr Duchy Lancaster 1955–57, 1st Ld Admlty 1957–59, HC Singapore and Commr-Gen SE Asia 1959–63, UK Rep SEATO 1960–63, Chm: C Cwlth Cncl 1965–72 and Victoria League 1971–77; Pres: Bldg Socs Assoc 1965–82, Ski Fedn GB 1964–68, Anglo-Swiss Soc 1965–74, Roy Soc Asian Affairs 1966–76, Assoc Ind U Peers 1967–79; Freedom of Hamilton, Lanarks, 1938, Hon Ch Saulteaux Indians 1967, Hon Citizen Winnipeg, Selkirk and Manitoba; *m* 6 Aug 1949 Audrey ('Wendy') Durell (*d* 21 Dec 1994), only dau of Maurice Drummond-Sale-Barker, and *dsp* 24 Nov 1994

SELSDON

Arms: Parted per pale arg. and gu. a stag's head cabossed between three mascles, all counterchanged. **Crest:** A hand couped ppr. grasping a cross crosslet fitchée in bend sinister gu. **Supporters:** Two sea-horses ppr., crined sa., finned or. **Motto:** *Deus providebit* ('God will provide'). **Creations:** Bt. (UK) 26 Sept 1900, B. (UK) 14 Jan 1932.

THE 3RD BARON SELSDON, of Croydon, Surrey and a **Baronet** (Sir Malcolm McEacharn Mitchell-Thomson, Bt) [The Rt Hon The Lord Selsdon, House of Lords, London SW1A 0PW]; *b* 27 Oct 1937; *s* f 1963; *educ* Winchester; Sub-Lt RNVR, Del Cncl of Europe and WEU 1972–78, with C T Bowring 1972–76, local dir Singer and Friedlander 1972; Midland Bank Gp 1976–90, chm Ctee Middle East Trade 1979–86, Pres Br Exporters Cncl 1990–; *m* 1st 2 June 1965 Patricia Anne, dau of Donald Smith, of Chase Farm, Haslemere, Surrey, and has:

  1 +CALLUM MALCOLM McEACHARN; *b* 7 Nov 1969

The 3rd BARON *m* 2nd 1995 *Gabrielle Tesseron, *née* Williams

Lineage: ANDREW THOMSON, of Alloa, Clackmannanshire; *b* 3 Aug 1787; *m* 8 April 1808 Joan (*d* 21 March 1856 aged 70), dau of John Forrester, and *d* 10 Dec 1829, leaving an est s:

ANDREW THOMSON, of Seafield, Alloa; *b* 30 April 1809; Commr Supply Clackmannan; *m* 2 Feb 1835 Janet (*d* 11 June 1888), dau of William Mitchell, of Alloa (*see* 1970 edn MITCHELL, Bt), and *d* 26 Oct 1871, leaving:

  1 Andrew, of Edinburgh, JP; *b* 1 Nov 1837; *m* 25 April 1866 Martha, dau of William Wilson, of St Ninians, Stirling, and *d* 31 May 1893, leaving issue

  2 William Mitchell; *b* 1 Aug 1841; *d* 27 March 1845

  3 Alexander, of Edinburgh, JP; *b* 9 Jan 1843; *m* 1st 14 Dec 1870 Beatrice (*d* 17 Dec 1871), dau of Benjamin Taberer, of Burton-on-Trent, Staffs, and had issue; *m* 2nd 29 Jan 1874 Mary Ann, dau of William Mitchell, of Cupar, Fife, and *d* 5 Nov 1899, having by her had issue

  4 MITCHELL (Sir), **1st Bt**

  1 Janet Wingate; *b* 3 Sept 1839; *m* 25 Sept 1860 John Guthrie Smith (*d* 22 Jan 1895), advocate, and *d* 1921, leaving issue

The 4th s,

Sir MITCHELL THOMSON later MITCHELL-THOMSON (roy licence 27 Sept 1900), **1st Bt** (UK), so *cr* 26 Sept 1900, JP, DL Edinburgh, JP Peeblesshire, of Polmood, Peebles; *b* 15 Dec 1846; Ld Provost Edinburgh 1897–1900, memb Roy Co Archers, FSA Scot, FRSE, KGStJ; *m* 1st 5 July 1876 Eliza Flowerdew (*d* 17 May 1877), dau of William Lowson (*see* LOWSON, Bt), and had:

  1 WILLIAM LOWSON, **1st Baron**

Sir Mitchell *m* 2nd 29 Sept 1880 Eliza Lamb (*d* 4 Dec 1926), dau of Robert Cook, of Leith, and *d* 16 Nov 1918, leaving by her:

  1 Janet Barclay Mitchell; *b* 7 Oct 1881; *d* unm 16 May 1959

  2 Mary Violet Mitchell; *b* 27 Feb 1883; *m* 18 Nov 1913 John Edwards Osborne, Maj Oxon and Bucks LI, only s of John Osborne, of Clifton, Bristol, and *d* 25 May 1923, leaving issue

The only s,

Sir William Lowson Mitchell-Thomas, 2nd Bt, and **1st Baron Selsdon**, of Croydon, Co Surrey (UK), so *cr* 14 Jan 1932, KBE (1918, CBE 1918), PC (1924); *b* 15 April 1877; *educ* Winchester, Balliol Coll Oxford (BA) and Edinburgh U (LLB); advocate 1903, MP (C) NW Lanarks 1906–10, N Down 1910–18, Glasgow Maryhill 1918–22 and Croydon S 1923–32, Dir Restriction Enemy Supplies Dept 1916–18, Br Rep Supreme Ec Cncl Paris 1919, Parly Sec Min Food 1920–21 and BOT 1921–22, PMG 1924–29; V-Chm Roy Commn Wheat Supplies 1921, Ch Civil Commr Gen Strike 1926, Chm TV Advsy Ctee 1935, memb Roy Co Archers, Hon Lt RNVR WW I, Legn Hon, Order Crown Italy; *m* 1st 1909 (*divorce* Scottish Courts 1932) Anne Madeleine (*d* 1946), yr dau of Sir Malcolm Donald McEacharn, of Galloway House, Wigtownshire; *m* 2nd 18 Jan 1933 Effie Lilian (*d* 12 April 1956), formerly w of Walter Harte Loder Johnson and dau of Lt-Col Charles Brennan, of Mullingar, Co Westmeath, and *d* 24 Dec 1938, leaving by his 1st w:

PATRICK MITCHELL-THOMSON, **2nd Baron Selsdon**, DSC (1943); *b* 28 May 1913; *educ* Winchester; Lt RNVR WW II; *m* 1st 12 Nov 1936 (*divorce* 1944) Phoebette (*d* 1991), er dau of Crossley Swithinbank, of Donnington Grove, Newbury, Berks, and had:

  1 MALCOLM McEACHARN MITCHELL-THOMSON, **3rd and present Baron Selsdon**

    1 *(Mary) Gail; *b* 11 Oct 1939; *m* 1963 *Patrick John Joseph O'Kelly, MB, BCh, only s of Patrick O'Kelly, of Dublin, and has:

      (1) *Sebastian Patrick Sean; *b* 20 Aug 1964

      (2) *Shane; *b* 1968

      (3) *Niall; *b* 1970

The **2nd Baron** *m* 2nd 29 Aug 1944 Dorothy (Bettie) (*m* 2nd 1972 Charles Larking and *d* 1988), est dau of Frederick John Greenish, of Honnington Hall, Lincs, and *d* 7 Feb 1963, leaving by her:

  2 *Petrina Frances Anne [The Hon Mrs Pugh, Whitelands, Rudford, Glos GL2 8ED]; *b* 7 April 1945; *m* 5 May 1967 *James Geoffrey Lennox Pugh, Gren Gds, s of Geoffrey Pugh, of Temple Guiting House, Glos, and has:

    (1) *Henry William Geoffrey; *b* 23 April 1974

    (1) *Emma; *b* 27 May 1969

SEMPILL

Arms: Argent a chevron chequy gules and of the field between three hunting horns sable, garnished and stringed of the second. **Crest:** A stag's head argent, attired with ten tines azure and gorged of a Prince's crown or. **Supporters:** Two greyhounds argent, collared gules. **Motto:** (Over the crest) Keep tryst. **Creation:** L. (S) by 10 Nov 1488.

THE 21ST LORD SEMPILL (James William Stuart Whitmore Sempill) [The Rt Hon The Lord Sempill, 3 Vanburgh Place, Leith, Edinburgh EH6 8AE]; *b* 25 Feb 1949; *s* mother 1995; *educ* Oratory Sch, St Clare's Hall Oxford (BA) and Hertford Coll Oxford; with Gallaher Ltd 1972–80, Sentinel Engrg Pty Johannesburg 1980–81, manager TWS PR Johannesburg 1982–83, mktg manager S African Breweries 1983, account dir Nates Wells Pty 1986, ptnr in ad agency Johannesburg 1988–90, client serv dir Ogilvy & Mather Cape Town 1990–92, dir: Scottish and Newcastle Breweries (trade mktg 1993–95, special projects 1995–), Scotch Embassy Ltd 1995–; *m* 9 Sept 1977 *Josephine Ann Edith, er dau of Joseph Norman Rees, of Johannesburg, and has:

  1 +FRANCIS HENRY WILLIAM; *Master of Sempill*; *b* 4 Jan 1979

  1 +Cosima; *b* 20 April 1983

Lineage: ROBERT de SEMPILL; Steward feudal Barony of Renfrew; living between *c* 1280 and *c* 1309; had an er s:

ROBERT de SEMPILL; had:

WILLIAM de SEMPILL; Steward Renfrew; acquired the lands of Eliotstoun, Renfrewshire, by 13 April 1344; ancestor of:

Sir THOMAS SEMPILL of Eliotstoun; Sheriff Renfrew; *m* Elizabeth Ross, possibly dau of 1st Lord Ross of Halkhead, and was *ka* Battle of Sauchieburn 11 June 1488, in which JAMES IV's supporters (of which Sir THOMAS was probably one, hence his son's ennoblement) overthrew his f JAMES III, leaving:

Sir JOHN SEMPILL, **1st Lord Sempill** (S), so *cr* by 10 Nov 1488; Envoy England 1492; *m* 1st by 9 Sept 1501 Margaret (*d* shortly after 21 April 1504), dau of Sir Robert Colville of Hiltoun and Ochiltree (*see* COLVILLE OF CULROSS, V); *m* 2nd by 16 Feb 1505/6 Margaret (*dsp* by him), dau of James Crichton of Ruthvendenny and widow of Sir William Stirling of Keir, and was *ka* Flodden 9 Sept 1513, leaving by his 1st w, with a yr s (Gabriel, ancestor of the SEMPILLs of Cathcart):

WILLIAM SEMPILL, **2nd Lord Sempill**, PC (S 1514); Sheriff Renfrew, Justiciar Regality of Paisley; *m* 1st by 20 July 1517 Margaret, dau of 1st Earl of Eglinto(u)n (*see* EGLINTON and WINTON, E); *m* 2nd by 12 Feb 1522/3 Elizabeth, dau of John Arnot of Arnot, Fife, but had no issue by her; *m* 3rd Marion (*m* 3rd John Campbell of Skipinche/Skipnish; *see* ARGYLL, D), dau of Hugh Montgomerie of Hazlehead (*see* EGLINTON and WINTON, E) and widow of Thomas Crawford of Auchinames, and *d* 3 June 1552, having by her also had no issue but leaving by his 1st

w, with four yr sons (David, of Craigenfeoch, living 1553, had issue; Ninian, of Clook, Renfrewshire, living 1563, *dsp*; William, of Thirdpart of Auchinames, *dsp* 3 Dec 1576; Peter, Constable Edinburgh Castle 1544) and two daus (Helen, *m* 3rd Lord Cathcart (*see* CATHCART, E; Mary, *m* Sir John Stirling of Keir):

ROBERT SEMPILL, **3rd Lord Sempill**, PC (S 1571); *b c* 1505; Govr and Constable Douglas Castle 1533, Sheriff Renfrew Jan 1543/4, Bailiff Regality of Paisley 1544; captured by English at their victory over Scots of Pinkie 10 Sept 1547; stabbed dead 5th Lord Crichton of Sanquhar (*see* BUTE, M) and imprisoned for it in Edinburgh Castle but his dau Grizel's influence with the Archbp of St Andrews, whose mistress she was, saved him from almost certain execution; supported MARY QUEEN OF SCOTS, hence Sempill Castle captured by her opponents 1560; later supported JAMES VI (and I of England), though remaining RC, and fought against MARY Battle of Langside 1568; Jt Lt western ports 1568; Lt-Gen and Justiciar Lanark and Renfrew 1572; *m* (1st?) by 7 April 1538 Isabel, dau of William Hamilton of Sanquhar; allegedly *m* 2nd Elizabeth Carlile, perhaps an Englishwoman, had by her a s (John) and two daus (Jonet; Dorothy), originally illegitimate but legitimated 24 Aug 1546, and *d* between 1 Aug 1573 and 17 Jan 1575/6, having by Isabel had, with two other sons (*dsp*):

  1 Robert, *Master of Sempill*; supported MARY QUEEN OF SCOTS; *m* 1st (contract 27 May 1543) Elizabeth, illegitimate dau of James Hamilton, 1st Earl of Arran of the 1503 *cr* (*see* ABERCORN, D); *m* 2nd by 30 April 1569 Barbara (*m* 2nd Robert Mure of Caldwell), dau of Archibald Preston of Valleyfield, Perths, and *dvp* by 16 Dec 1569, leaving by her:

    (1) ROBERT, **4th Lord**

  2 Andrew; *m* by 30 Nov 1565 Margaret, dau of George Stirling of Craigbernard, and had issue

  1 Grisel; *m* by 10 March 1539/40 (*divorce* by 21 Feb 1545/6) James Hamilton of Stonehouse (*d* 1548), er s of James Hamilton of Raploch, and *d* Oct 1575, leaving issue

  2 Margaret; *m* 1st by 7 Oct 1545 David Hamilton of Broomhill (*ka* Pinkie 1547) and had issue; *m* 2nd by Jan 1553/4 John Whitefoord of Whitefoord and *d* Nov 1580, leaving issue

The 3rd LORD's gs,

ROBERT SEMPILL, **4th Lord Sempill**, PC (S 1597); had made over to him by his gf 1572 posts of Justiciar and Baillie Regality of Paisley; Amb Spain 1595; *m* 1st (contract 11 Sept 1583) Agnes, dau of 3rd Earl of Eglinto(u)n (*see* EGLINTON and WINTON, E), and had:

  1 HUGH, **5th Lord**

  2 William; *b* by 11 Jan 1591; *d* by 11 June 1618

  3 James; living 11 June 1618

  1 Anne; *m* (contract 8 June 1603) Sir Archibald Steward of Castlemilk (*d* Dec 1631) and had issue

  2 Barbara; *m* by 19 Jan 1610 Sir Coll Lamont of Inneryne (*d c* 1634, leaving issue)

  3 Grisel; *m* John Logan of Raiss and had issue

  4 Jean; *m* April 1612 John Brisbane of Bishopstoun and *d* after 23 May 1626, leaving issue

The 4th Lord *m* 2nd *c* 13 Sept 1604 Johanna (*m* 3rd Capt Patrick Craufurd, of Tredonnell, Co Donegal; *m* 4th Sir George Marbury and *d* 14 June 1638), dau of Levimus Everard of, Cncllr of State in Spanish Netherlands Province of Mechlin, and widow of Sir John Hamilton, bro of 1st Earl of Abercorn (*see* ABERCORN, D), and by her had:

  4 William (Sir), of Letterkenny, Co Donegal, JP; *m* Anne, dau of Sir William Stewart, 1st Bt, of Ramelton (*qv*), and had:

    (1) Catherine/Francescina; *m* as his 1st w Sir Charles Hamilton, 2nd Bt (*d* by 9 May 1689), of Castle Hamilton, Co Cavan, and had:

      1a Sir FRANCIS HAMILTON, 3rd Bt, of Castle Hamilton; attainted by JAMES II's I Parl 1689; MP (I Parl) Co Cavan 1692–93, 1695–99 and 1703–13, Sheriff Co Donegal 1694; *m* 1st *c* 1685 Lady Catherine Montgomery, dau of 1st Earl of Mount Alexander; *m* 2nd 26 March 1695 Anne (*m* 2nd 17 Dec 1718, as his 2nd w, Lord Archibald Hamilton; *see* HAMILTON and BRANDON, D), dau and heiress of Claud Hamilton (perhaps bro of his son-in-law's gf the 1st Bt), and *dsps* 4 Feb 1713/4, leaving an illegitimate dau (Frances Tweedy)

The 4th LORD *d* 25 March 1611; his est s,

HUGH SEMPILL, **5th Lord Sempill**, JP (Ayrshire Jan 1613/4, Renfrewshire 1616); Burgess Glasgow 1618; alienated hereditary posts of Shrievalty of Renfrew and Bailliedom of Paisley; *m* 1st (contract 7 Nov 1611) Anne, dau of 1st Earl of Abercorn (*see* ABERCORN, D), and had:

  1 Marion; *m* (contract 4 May 1636) Sir George Preston, 1st Bt, of Valleyfield (*see* 1873 edn), and had issue

  2 Anne; *m* — Hamilton and *d* on or after 3 Feb 1651, having had issue

The 5th Lord *m* 2nd (contract 27 Nov 1620) Elizabeth (*m* 2nd by 20 May 1643 1st Lord Mordington; *see* HAMILTON and BRANDON, D), dau of 9th Earl of Erroll (*qv*), and *d* 19 Sept 1639, having by her had:

  1 FRANCIS SEMPILL, **6th Lord Sempill**; *b c* 1622; *m* (contract 25 March 1640) Isabel, dau of 3rd Earl of Winto(u)n (*see* EGLINTON and WINTON, E), and *dsp* 3 Nov 1644

  2 William; *dsp* by 3 Nov 1644

  3 ROBERT, **7th Lord**

  4 Archibald, of Dykehead; *b c* 1635; had, with two daus:

    (1) Robert; seemingly recognised 1712 as (9th) Lord Sempill (being heir male to **8th Lord**) by titular James III; *b* 1672; *educ* Scots Coll Douai; Cadet Normandois Inf French Army by 1688, Ensign Scottish Gds 1689, Capt Ld Galmoye's Inf Regt 1708, tfd Dillon Regt Feb 1714/5 (all French Serv); *m* Elizabeth Abercromby and *d* by 11 Nov 1737, leaving:

      1a Francis, also recognised by Jacobites as (10th) Lord Sempill; *educ* Scots Coll Douai; titular James III's agent Paris from prior to 1738; apparently *m* Mary, dau of 4th Earl of Seaforth (*see* CROMARTIE, E) and widow of John Caryll, of Harting, Sussex, and *d* 9 Dec 1748

  5 James (Rev); SJ; *d* Madrid

3 Elizabeth; *m* 2nd Lord Mordington and had issue (*see* HAMILTON and BRANDON, D)

4 Jean; *m* (contract 13 May 1668) William Menzies, of Pitfoddles

The 6th LORD's bro,

ROBERT SEMPILL, **7th Lord Sempill**; Commr War Renfrewshire 1648; entailed (Crown confirmation 25 July 1685) his lands and title on his er dau in default of heirs male of his body; *m* after 8 Feb 1647/8 Anne, only dau of 1st Lord Mordington (*see* HAMILTON and BRANDON, D), and *d* 8 Sept 1675, having had:

1 Robert, *Master of Sempill*; *b c* 1655; *educ* Scots Coll Madrid; *dvp* unm 1670

2 James; *educ* Scots' College Douai and Madrid; *dvp*

3 FRANCIS SEMPILL, **8th Lord Sempill**; *b c* 1660; *educ* Glasgow U, Capt Lanark Militia 1683, Commr Excise Renfrew 1683; *m* 30 April 1681 Grizel (*m* 2nd 1693 Brig-Gen Richard Cunningham and *d* 22 June 1723), sis of 1st Earl of Rosebery (*qv*), and *dsp* 4 April 1684

1 ANNE Sempill, **Lady Sempill** in her own right; got a regrant of the title 16 May 1688 with remainder to (a) heirs male of her and her husb's bodies, (b) heirs female ditto, (c) heirs male then female of her body by any other husb and (d) anybody chosen by her and her husb and finally to heirs and assigns whatsoever; *m* (contract 6 Aug 1675) Francis ABERCROMBY, of Fetterneir, Aberdeenshire, *cr* 5 July 1685 LORD GLASFOORD (S) for life (*m* 2nd 27 March 1699 Christabella, widow of Sir Giles Eyre, and was *bur* 23 Nov 1703, having *d* in the Fleet debtor's prison), and *d* 1695, having had issue (who bore their mother's surname), with a dau (*d* unm):

(1) FRANCIS SEMPILL, **10th Lord Sempill**; *b c* 1685; Commr Supply 1704, Capt Lord Carmichael's Regt of Dragoons 1711 and Grant's Foot Regt 1715; *d* unm by 4 Aug 1716

(2) Robert; Army Capt; *ka* abroad

(3) JOHN SEMPILL, **11th Lord Sempill**; opposed Jacobites 1715, Burgess Glasgow 1721; *d* unm 17 Feb 1727

(4) Alexander; *d* young

(5) HUGH, **12th Lord**

2 Jean; *m* Alexander St Clair of Rosslyn (for whose early ancestry *see* CAITHNESS, E) and had issue

3 Elizabeth; *dsp*

The 11th LORD's bro,

HEW SEMPILL, **12th Lord Sempill**; *b* just after 16 May 1688; Adj 26th Foot (Cameronians) 1708, Ensign 1709 (fought Battle of Malplaquet (pyrrhic Br Victory over French in War of Spanish Succession) 1709), Capt 1712, Lt-Col 19th Foot 1731, Col 43rd Highrs (later 42nd Highrs, Black Watch) 1741–45, Col 25th Foot (KOSB) 1745 (fought British defeat by French of Fontenoy 1745), Brig-Gen 1745, cmded left wing of Hanoverian army at final defeat of Jacobites of Culloden 16 April 1746, Burgess Glasgow 1714 and Edinburgh 1739, appointive Govr Barbados 1746 (did not take up post); sold the Eliotstoun and Sempill estates 1727; bought the N Barr estate 1741; *m* 13 May 1718 Sarah (*d* 17 April 1749), dau and coheir (with her sis Rebecca, mother of 1st Baron Clive of Plassey; *see* POWIS, E) of Nathaniel Gaskell, of Manchester, and had, with other issue (*d* young or unm):

1 JOHN, **13th Lord**

2 George; Col HEICS; *m* 1st Catherine (*d* 5 Feb 1762), dau and heiress of Arthur Gordon of Wardhouse; *m* 2nd 1 Dec 1766 his cousin Anne, sis of 1st Baron Clive of Plassey; *m* 3rd 15 June 1775 Jane, dau and heiress of Thomas Butterworth and widow of Francis Joddrell, of Yeadsley, and *dsp* 18 Dec 1979

3 Hugh; Capt RM; *d* 1764

1 Sarah; *m* 28 April 1750 Patrick Crawford of Auchinames and Drumsoy, MP, and *d* 25 April 1751, leaving a dau (*d* unm)

2 Anne; *m* 16 Sept 1754 Adam Austin, MD (*d* 1 Dec 1773), of Edinburgh, and *d* 27 Nov 1793, having had, with eight daus:

(1) Hugh Austin; Judge at Burdwan; *dsp* 1784

The 12th LORD *d* 25 Nov 1746; his est s,

JOHN SEMPILL, **13th Lord Sempill**; *m* 10 March 1755 Janet (*d* 26 June 1809), dau and heiress of Hugh Dunlop, of Bishoptoun, Renfrewshire, and *d* 15 Jan 1782, leaving:

1 HUGH SEMPILL, **14th Lord Sempill**; *b* 1 July 1758; Ensign 3rd Foot Gds 1777, Lt and Capt 1781 (stripped of commission 1792 for contact with French Jacobins); *m* (licence 25 Jan 1787) Mary (*d* 16 Sept 1806), dau of Charles Mellish, of Ragnal, Notts, and *d* 25 Jan 1830, having had, with a 3rd s (*d* young):

(1) SELKIRK SEMPILL, **15th Lord Sempill**; *b* 12 Feb 1788; Capt Renfrewshire Militia; *d* unm 4 May 1835

(2) Francis; *d* unm 2 Jan 1823

(1) MARIA JANET Sempill, **Lady Sempill** in her own right; *b* 1790; *m* 14 Jan 1836 Edward CANDLER later SEMPILL (roy licence 23 Aug 1853) (*d* 7 April 1871), of Callan, Co Kilkenny, Dun Edin and Belwood, Midlothian, and Morton Pinkey, Northants, and *dsps* 5 Sept 1884

(2) Sarah; *d* unm 18 Nov 1866

1 SARAH Sempill; *m* 4 June 1780 Sir William FORBES, 5th Bt, of Craigievar (*qv*), and *d* 8 Sept 1799, having had, with other issue:

(1) Sir ARTHUR FORBES, 6th Bt, of Craigievar; *d* unm 1823

(2) Sir JOHN FORBES, 7th Bt, of Craigievar; *m* 15 Sept 1825 Charlotte Elizabeth, dau of 18th Lord Forbes (*qv*), and *d* 16 Feb 1846, having had, with other issue:

1a Sir WILLIAM FORBES later FORBES-SEMPILL, 8th Bt, as which *s f* 1846, and **17th Lord Sempill**, as which *s* 1st cousin once-removed 1884, VD, JP, DL (Aberdeenshire); *b* 20 May 1836; *educ* Eton; Ensign Coldstream Gds 1854 (ret 1857), Capt later Hon Col 9th Aberdeenshire Rifle Vols 1859–61; *m* 1st 23 June 1858 (*divorce* Dec 1861) Caroline Louisa (*m* 2nd 19 June 1862 Septimus E Carlisle, of Belmont, Staffs, and *d* 11 Dec 1872), only dau of Sir Charles Forbes, 3rd Bt, of Newe (*qv*), and had:

1b Katherine Charlotte Elizabeth Stewart, MBE; *m* 5 Dec 1907 George Muirhead, LLD, of Speybank, Fochabers (*d* 29 Jan 1928), and *d* 22 March 1938

1a (cont.) The **17th Lord** *m* 2nd 18 Nov 1862 Frances Emily (*d* 13 May 1887), yst dau of Sir Robert Abercromby, 5th Bt (*qv*); *m* 3rd 30 April 1890 Mary Beresford (*d* 18 Dec 1930), yst dau of Henry Sherbrooke formerly

Lowe, of Oxton, Notts, and *d* 21 July 1905, having by his 2nd w had, with other issue (*see* FORBES, Bt, of Craigievar):

1b Sir JOHN FORBES-SEMPILL, 9th Bt, and **18th Lord Sempill**, JP (Aberdeenshire); *b* 21 Aug 1863; *educ* Eton; 3rd Bn Gordon Highrs 1883, Lt Argyll and Sutherland Highrs 1885, tfd Cameron Highrs 1886, served Sudan 1885–86, tfd RASC 1889, Capt 1891, Hazara Expdn 1889, tfd Black Watch 1894 (ret as Capt 1904), Lovat Scouts (wounded, medal, five clasps) Boer War 1901–02, cmded 8th Black Watch WW I 1914–15 (severely wounded, despatches, three medals), rep S peer 1910–34, Aberdeenshire: Chm TAA, V-Lt, ADC to HM GEORGE V, Hon Col 5th Bn Gordon Highrs; *m* 22 June 1892 Gwendolen Emily Mary (*d* 2 March 1944), er dau of Herbert Prodgers, of Kington St Michael, Wilts, and *d* 28 Feb 1934, having had, with other issue (*see* FORBES, Bt, of Craigievar):

1c WILLIAM FRANCIS, **19th Lord**

1b Evelyn Courtenay; *b* 4 Oct 1868; *m* 7 June 1894 Lt-Col Duncan Vernon Pirie, OBE, JP, DL, formerly Capt 3rd Hus (*d* 11 Jan 1931), est s of Gordon Pirie, of Waterton, Aberdeenshire, and *d* 1 March 1934, leaving:

1c Patrick Taldo, MC (1918); *b* 17 March 1897; *educ* Winchester; Gordon Highrs 1915–47, WW I (despatches) and WW II (despatches), ret as Col; *m* 25 Nov 1938 *Christine Barbara, dau of Charles Edward de Lacepede (later Cahill), and *dsp* 29 April 1965

2c Alexander William; *b* 20 Aug 1899; Lt 3rd Bn Seaforth Highrs; *m* 30 Nov 1935 *Annie Ridley, dau of Herbert Joseph Richardson, and *d* 24 Nov 1993, having had:

1d Ridley Gordon; *b* 28 Aug 1936; *m* 1962 *Eva Maria Lenel [Mrs Ridley Pirie, 28 Hubert Rd, Winchester, Hants] and *d* 27 April 1984, leaving:

1e +Edward Duncan; *b* 1968

1e +Fernanda; *b* 1964

3c +Douglas Gordon [Douglas Pirie Esq, The Old House, Milland, Liphook, Hants; 70 Pelham Ct, Fulham Rd, London SW3]; *b* 21 Oct 1910; *educ* Winchester and Edinburgh U; Priv Sec and ADC to Govr Mauritius 1937–40, Lt-Col Coldstream Gds WW II (despatches, Legn Hon), Priv Sec to Govr Kenya 1946–47, Colonial Office 1947–50, FO 1950–53, memb Roy Co Archers; *m* 24 Sept 1954 *Jean Frances Caroline Alicia Dorothea Grant, yst dau of Evelyn George Massey Carmichael of Carmichael, OBE, JP, FSA (*see* COLQUHOUN, Bt), and has had:

1d Douglas Alastair Carmichael; *b* 23 June 1957; *d* unm 8 April 1989

1c Evelyn Jean-Gordon; *b* 1895; *m* 1926 Col Owen Evelyn Wynne, OBE, RE (*d* 1974), s of Gen Sir Arthur Singleton Wynne, GCB, and *d* 1981, leaving:

1d +Robert Owen [Robert Wynne Esq, 18 Britten St, London SW3]; *b* 1930; *educ* Wellington and RMA Sandhurst; Lt KOYLI Malaya 1950–51

1d +Evelyn Valérie [Mrs Thomas Drew, Fossens House, Methill Rd, Alyth, Perthshire]; *b* 1928; *educ* St Andrews (MA 1950); *m* 1957 *Thomas Syme Drew, s of Maj-Gen Sir James Syme Drew, KBE, CB, DSO, MC, and has:

1e +Rachel Jean [Mrs John Barstow, Thorpe Hall, Ampleforth, N Yorks]; *b* 1961; *m* 1986 *John David Barstow and has:

1f +Marcus Thomas James; *b* 1990

1f +Julia Victoria; *b* 1992

2c +Valérie Marguerite [Mrs Henry Spry, Old Rectory House, Coombe Bissett, Wilts]; *b* 1906; *m* 1962 Henry Ernest Spry, CBE (*d* 1967)

1a Elizabeth; *m* 25 July 1854 Robert Grant of Druminnor, Aberdeenshire (*d* 1 Jan 1894), and *d* 29 Dec 1890, leaving:

1b Charlotte Elizabeth Henrietta; *m* 1886 Philip Alexander HOLLAND, who with her took 1896 the name GRANT of Druminnor, and had:

1c Alexander Philip Foulerton, MBE; *b* 1887; *m* 1916 Maud Annie (*d* 1963), dau of John Dyer, of Cheltenham, and *d* 1961, leaving:

1d +Rachel Ann; *b* 1922; *m* 1941 *Maurice Richard Pope and has:

1e +Richard John; *b* 1953

1e +Diana Mary Ann [Mrs Laramy Day, Tuckerton Farm, N Newton, Somerset]; *b* 1955; *m* 1978 *Laramy Walter Badcock Day

2a Sarah; *m* 14 April 1852 her cousin Duncan Forbes, JP (*see* FORBES, Bt, of Craigievar), and *d* 6 Oct 1891, leaving, with two daus (*d* unm):

1b John; *b* 24 March 1855; *d* unm 14 April 1908

2b Duncan; *b* 30 Sept 1856; *dsp* 1895

3b Alexander Mansfield; *b* 28 April 1858; *m* 13 Aug 1887 Mary Antoinette (*d* 3 June 1860 aged 97), er dau of Alexander Forbes, of Galleries, Aberdeen, and *d* 27 Feb 1932, leaving:

1c Duncan Alexander; *b* 13 May 1888; 11th Bn Argyll and Sutherland Highrs WW I (wounded); *m* 15 Jan 1918 Sybil Dorothy (*d* 27 May 1948), dau of John Mitchell, of Kotagala, Ceylon, and *d* 24 Jan 1964, leaving:

1d Duncan, MC; *b* 19 May 1922; *educ* Haileybury and Clare Coll Cambridge; Seaforth Highrs WW II, Fell Clare Coll Cambridge, Emeritus Reader History Modern Political Thought Cambridge; *m* 21 Aug 1947 *Sheila [Mrs Duncan Forbes, 18 Thornton Close, Girton, Cambridge CB3 0NQ], dau of Rev Clement John Morton, and *d* 3 Dec 1994, leaving:

1e +Duncan Alastair [Duncan Forbes Esq, 80 Southfield Rd, Oxford OX1 4PA]; *b* 22 Aug 1949; *educ* Leys Sch Cambridge; Fell and Bursar Mansfield Coll Oxford; *m* July 1971 *Angela, dau of Francis Ralph Sargent, and has:

1f +Joy Mary; *b* 1972

2f +Katherine Dorothy; *b* 1976

2e +Ian [Ian Forbes Esq, Peat Hill, Westgate, Bishop Auckland, Co Durham DL13 1PG]; *b* 22 Aug 1949; *educ* Perse Sch Cambridge; *m* 1973 *Pamela, dau of Dr Douglas Bailey, and has:

1f +Nicholas Iain; *b* 1973

1f +Helen Catherine; *b* 1977

2f +Susan Claire; *b* 1980

1e +Helen Morag [Mrs Mark Fitton, 17 Bowood Cres, Leeds LS7 2PY]; *b* 17 June 1954; *m* 1986 *Mark Fitton and has:

  1f +Jessica Elisabeth; *b* 1990

  2f +Ruth; *b* 1992

1d Jean Mhari; *b* 3 May 1919; *d* Nov 1982

2d +Katharine Ann [Mrs Katharine Cook, Inveroy, Roy Bridge, Inverness-shire]; *b* 3 June 1926; *m* 14 Aug 1947 (*divorce* 1956) Albert Cook and has:

  1e +Rosemary Ann [Mrs Timothy Skipper, Gyfeile, Maesymeillion, Llandysul, Dyfed]; *b* 27 Oct 1948; *m* 1979 *Timothy Cresswell Skipper and has:

    1f +Andrew James; *b* 1979

    2f +Peter Timothy; *b* 1983

  2e +Valerie [Mrs Timothy Dix, 2 Drimsdale, S Uist, Western Isles]; *b* 19 May 1952; *m* 1986 *Timothy Dix and has:

    1f +Alasdair John; *b* 1987

    2f +Iain Timothy; *b* 1989

2c Mansfield Duval; *b* 1 Nov 1889; Fell Clare Coll Cambridge; *d* unm 28 Jan 1936

1c Mhari Margaret; *b* 19 Feb 1891; *m* 1st 26 Aug 1918 (*divorce* 1935) Arthur Haydn Parry (*d* 1944) and had:

  1d +Mhari Elisabeth Forbes [Miss Mhari Parry, Broadmead Copse, Wanborough, Surrey]; *b* 3 Sept 1921; singer, lecturer, manager Opera Players Ltd

1c (cont.) Mrs Mhari Parry *m* 2nd 16 Oct 1935 Maj Stuart Frederick Maxwell Ferguson, MC, RA (*d* 1975)

4b William Henry; *b* 26 Aug 1860; *d* 26 Feb 1931

3a Caroline Ann; *m* 11 June 1862 Rev Frederick Walter Robberds (*d* 30 April 1898), Rector Salford, Bristol, and *d* 19 March 1896, leaving:

1b Walter John Forbes (Rev); DD; had:

  1c Ethel Margaret; *b* 1901; *m* 1938 John Whitehead (*d* 1985) and *d* 1984, leaving:

    1d +Janet Margaret [Mrs Peter Low, 21 Corbar Rd, Buxton, Derbys]; *b* 1939; *educ* St Andrews (MA); *m* 1968 *Peter John Low and has:

      1e +Caroline Margaret; *b* 1969

      2e +Elizabeth Hilary; *b* 1971

      3e +Polly Alexandra; *b* 1973

2c Katharine Frances; *b* 1904; *m* 1924 Francis David Jefferson Buist (*d* 1980),and *d* 1980, leaving:

  1d +Mary [Mrs William Drysdale, Beech Cottage, 1 Glen Ct, Dunblane, Perthshire FK15 0DY]; *b* 1926; *m* 1st 1945 (*divorce* 1966) Roland Sydney Hill (*d* 1972); *m* 2nd 1967 William James Drysdale (*d* 1979) and by her 1st husb has:

    1e +Andrew Forbes [Andrew Hill Esq, Leask Cottage, Collieston, Aberdeenshire]; *b* 1955; MA Edinburgh; FSA Scot; *m* 1983 *Linda Joan Knox

    2e +David Jefferson; *b* 1957

    1e +Susan Frances [Mrs Donald Drysdale, Ardlochan, 49 Roselea Dve, Milngavie, Glasgow]; *b* 1946; *m* 1969 *Donald Drysdale, CA, and has:

      1f +Michael Christopher; *b* 1972

      2f +Alastair Nicholas; *b* 1974

      1f +Lisa Jane; *b* 1977

    2e +Alison Margaret [Mrs Eugene O'Neale, 23 Warriston Cres, Edinburgh EH3 5LB]; *b* 1949; MA Edinburgh; *m* 1st 1971 Iain Taylor Carruthers (*d* 1986); *m* 2nd 1988 *Eugene Charles Henry O'Neale and by her 1st husb has:

      1f +Angus St John Hornsby; *b* 1983

      1f +Catherine Lucy Forbes; *b* 1974

      2f +Jessica Rose; *b* 1977

2d +Margaret Brora [Mrs Richard Butterworth, Maus House, Hilton, Dornoch, Sutherland IV25 3PW]; *b* 17 Nov 1930; *m* 1954 *(Charles) Richard Butterworth and has:

  1e +Emma Mary [Mrs Emma Murray, Ardmore House, By Edderton, Tain, Ross-shire IV19 1LB]; *b* 26 Sept 1955; *m* 1980 (*divorce* 1998) Francis Anderson Murray and has:

    1f +Angus Francis Hugh; *b* 11 Sept 1984

    2f +Frederick Richard Finnbarr; *b* 11 May 1987

    1f +Lucy Anne; *b* 26 Feb 1983

  2e +Charlotte Clunes [Mrs Gordon Dickie, Poundland, Moniaive, Dumfriesshire]; *b* 1958; *m* 1981 *Gordon Bruce Dickie and has:

    1f +Alice Katharine Brora; *b* 1983

    2f +Arabella Rose; *b* 1984

    3f +Flora Sophia Elizabeth; *b* 1988

2 Janet; *d* 6 June 1858 aged 90

3 Joanna; *d* 10 July 1840

The 18th LORD's er s,

Sir WILLIAM FRANCIS FORBES-SEMPILL, 10th Bt (*see also* FORBES, Bt, of Craigievar), and **19th Lord Sempill**, AFC; *b* 24 Sept 1893; *educ* Eton; *m* 1st 20 Feb 1919 Eileen Marion (*d* 18 July 1935), only dau of Sir John Lavery, RA, and formerly w of James Dickinson, KC, and had:

1 ANN MOIRA Sempill, **Lady Sempill** in her own right; *b* 19 March 1920; Petty Offr WRNS WW II; *m* 1st 25 Oct 1941 (*divorce* 1945) Capt (Arthur) Eric HOLT, Manchester Regt, yst s of Arthur Holt, of Oxford, and had:

  (1) +Frances Marion [The Hon Mrs Russell, 4 Westover Rd, London SW18 2RG]; *b* 1942; *educ* France and Madrid U; *m* 30 April 1976 *David Ian Russell (*see* RUSSELL, Bt, of Littleworth Corner) and has issue

1 (cont.) **Lady Sempill** *m* 2nd 28 Oct 1948 Lt-Col Stuart Whitemore CHANT later CHANT-SEMPILL (Lyon Court decree 1966), OBE, MC (*d* 1991), Gordon Highrs and No 5 Commando, s of Norman James Whitemore Chant, and *d* 1995, leaving by him:

(1) JAMES WILLIAM STUART WHITEMORE SEMPILL, **21st and present Lord Sempill**

(2) +Ian David Whitemore [Lt-Col The Hon Ian Chant-Sempill, The Bell House, Sutton Veny, Wilts BA12 7AW]; *b* 2 April 1951; *educ* Oratory Sch; Lt-Col Gordon Highrs; *m* 1980 *Amanda, yr dau of Anthony Dallas, of Blackmoor, Burghfield, Berks, and has:

  1a +Hamish Anthony Stuart; *b* 14 Aug 1987

  1a +Clementine Ann Constance; *b* 10 July 1985

2 June Mary; *b* 17 June 1922; WVS WW II; *k* by enemy action 11 May 1941

The **19th Lord** *m* 2nd 1 Feb 1941 Cecilia Alice (*d* 1984), er dau of Bertram Edward Dunbar-Kilburn, of Ledwell, Sandford St Martin, Oxon, and *d* 30 Dec 1965, having by her had:

3 +Janet Cecilia [The Hon Janet Forbes-Sempill, Keil Cottage, Muir of Fowlis, nr Alford, Aberdeenshire]; *b* 4 May 1942; *educ* Colchester Coll of Art

4 +Kirstine Elizabeth [The Hon Mrs Daranyi-Forbes-Sempill, Flat 8, 17–20 Embankment Gdns, London SW3]; *b* 9 Aug 1944; *m* 1st 1 June 1968 (*divorce* 1989) (John) Michael CABLE later FORBES-CABLE (deed poll 1968), est s of Richard Victor Cable, of Woodhill, Compton, Staffs; *m* 2nd 1990 *Béla Peter de Daranyi and by her 1st husb has:

  (1) +William Richard Craigievar; *b* 27 Feb 1970

  (2) +Malcolm Dunbar Craigievar; *b* 1972

5 +Brigid Gabriel; *b* 14 Dec 1945; *educ* RCA; *m* 27 May 1983 (*divorce* 19–) Hon Jeremy Menuhin, yr s of Baron Menuhin (*qv*), and has:

  (1) +Petroc Forbes; *b* 1988

  (1) +Nadja Cecilia; *b* 1985

SEROTA

Creation: B. (LP, UK) 1967.

THE BARONESS SEROTA, of Hampstead in Greater London (Dame Beatrice Katz, DBE (1992), JP (Inner London) [The Rt Hon The Baroness Serota DBE JP, The Coach House, 15 Lyndhurst Terr, London NW3 5QA]; *b* 15 Oct 1919; *educ* John Howard Sch and LSE (BSc Econ); Cncllr Hampstead Borough 1945–49; LCC (Brixton) 1954–65 (Chm Children's Ctee 1958–65), GLC (Lambeth) 1964–67; Memb: Advsy Cncl Child Care and Central Training Cncl in Child Care 1958–68; Roy Commn Penal System 1964–66, Latey Ctee on Age of Majority 1965–67, Advsy Cncl on Penal System 1966–68, 1974–79 (Chm 1976–79), Seebohm Ctee on Organisation of Local Authority Personal Social Services 1966–68, Community Rels Commn 1970–76, BBC Complaints Commn 1975–77; Chm Health Educn Cncl 1967–69, Baroness-in-Waiting 1968–69, Min State DHSS 1969–70; V-Pres Nat Cncl for One Parent Families 1971–, fndr-chm Commn Local Admin (Local Ombudsman Serv) 1974–82; Govr BBC 1977–82; Dep Speaker Ho Lords 1985–; Hon Fell LSE 1976; Hon DLitt Loughborough 1983; *m* 1942 *Stanley Serota, FICE, and has:

1 *Nicholas Andrew (does not use courtesy title); *b* 1946; *educ* Haberdashers' Askes Sch, Christ's Coll Cambridge (BA) and Courtauld Inst of Art (MA); Dir Whitechapel Art Gallery 1976–88 and Tate Gallery 1988–, Tstee Public Art Devpt Tst 1983–88; *m* 1st 1973 (*divorce* 1995) Angela Mary Beveridge (*m* 2nd, as his 2nd w, Alexander Bernstein, chm Granada to 1996, n of late Baron Bernstein); *m* 2nd 22 March 1997 *Teresa Gleadowe and by his 1st w has:

  (1) *Anya Rowena; *b* 1975

  (2) *Beth Alexandra; *b* 1976

1 *Judith Alexandra Anne; *b* 1948; *educ* Royal Manchester Coll of Music; *m* 1973 *Francis John Pugh and has:

  (1) *Rebecca Sarah; *b* 1975

  (2) *Ellen Martha; *b* 1978

Lineage: ALEXANDER KATZ; had:

BEATRICE, *cr* a **Baroness**

SETON of Abercorn

Arms: Quarterly, 1st and 4th, or three crescents within a double tressure, flory counterflory gu. (for SETON); 2nd and 3rd, argent three inescutcheons gu. (for HAY). **Crest:** A boar's head couped or, armed and langued az. **Supporters:** Two greyhounds ppr. **Motto:** Forward ours. **Creation:** Bt. (NS) 3 June 1663.

SIR IAIN BRUCE SETON, 13TH BT, of Abercorn, Linlithgowshire [Sir Iain Seton Bt, Bellavista, PO Box 253, Bridgetown, WA 6255, Australia]; *b* 27 Aug 1942; *educ* Colchester and Chadacre Ag Inst; *s* f 1988; *m* 29 Aug 1963 *Margaret Ann, only dau of Walter Charles Faulkner, of Gt Horkesley, Essex, and has:

1 +LAURENCE BRUCE; *b* 1 July 1968; *m* 6 Oct 1990 *Rachel, dau of Jeffrey Woods, of Bridgetown, and has:

  (1) *Rowan Ann; *b* 25 Feb 1996

  (2) *Sarah Jane; IbI 22 Sept 1998

1 *Amanda Jane; *b* 4 May 1971

Lineage: The 1st EARL OF HUNTLY (*see* HUNTLY, M); had by his 1st w an est s (excluded from succession to the Earldom and estates):

Sir ALEXANDER SETON of Touch; apptd Hereditary Armour Bearer to JAMES IV 1488; *m* Elizabeth, dau of *de jure* 13th Earl of Mar (*qv*), and had:

Sir ALEXANDER SETON of Touch; *m* Elizabeth, dau of 1st Lord Home (*see* HOME, E) by his 2nd w, and was *ka* Battle of Flodden 1513, leaving:

Sir NINIAN SETON of Touch; *m* as her 2nd husb Janet (*m* 3rd Sir James Towers of Inverleith), dau of Sir Edward Chisholm of Cromlix and widow of Sir Alexander Napier of Merchistoun (*see* NAPIER, Bt, of Merchistoun), and had, with at least one dau (Janet, *m* 1548 Robert Galbraith, 1st of Blairquhois (*see* STRATHCLYDE, B):

Sir WALTER SETON of Touch; *m* Elizabeth, sis of *de jure* 16th Earl of Mar (*qv*), and had:

JAMES SETON, of Touch; *m* 1st Janet, dau of Sir William Cranstoun of that Ilk, and had a s (John, of Touch, whose gggs Archibald, of Touch, had a s James, of Touch, the last male of his line, and a dau Elizabeth); *m* 2nd Jean, dau of Edmondstoun of Ednam, Roxburghshire, and by her had:

Sir ALEXANDER SETON of Gargunnock, Stirling; Ld of Session as Lord Kilcreuch; *m* Marion, dau and est coheir of William Maule of Glaster, and *d* in or after 1612, having had, with other issue:

ALEXANDER SETON of Kilcreuch; MP Stirling 1612; *m* Margaret, dau of Walter Cornwall of Bonhard, Linlithgow, and *d* in or after 1636, leaving:

Sir Walter Seton, 1st Bt (NS), so *cr* 3 June 1663, apparently with remainder to his heirs male whatsoever, of Northbank, having sold *c* 1672 to the HOPEs the territorial Barony of Abercorn, Linlithgowshire, of which he had had charter 1662; MP Linlithgowshire 1665, 1667 and 1669–74; *m* Christian, dau of George Dundas of Dundas, and *d* 20 Feb 1692, leaving, with other issue:

Sir Walter Seton, 2nd Bt, of Northbank; advocate 1635, Commissary Clerk Edinburgh; *m* (contract 6 Sept 1702) Euphemia, dau of Sir Robert Murray of Priestfield and Melgum, and *d* 3 Jan 1708, leaving:

Sir Henry Seton, 3rd Bt, of Northbank; *m* Barbara, dau of Sir John Wemyss, 2nd Bt, of Bogie (*see* WEMYSS and MARCH, E), and *d* 1751, having had, with other issue:

Sir Henry Seton, 4th Bt, of Culbeg, Stirlingshire; Capt 17th Foot, Collector Customs Bowness; *m c* 1770 Margaret (*d* 2 March 1809), dau of Alexander Hay of Drumelzier (*see* TWEEDDALE, M), and *d* 29 June 1788, leaving:

Sir Alexander Seton, 5th Bt; *b* 4 May 1772; Offr HEICS; *m* 20 May 1795 Lydia (*d* 23 Feb 1851), 5th dau of Sir Charles William Blunt, 3rd Bt (*qv*), and *d* 4 Feb 1810, having had, with other issue:

1 **Sir Henry John Seton, 6th Bt**; *b* 4 April 1796; Capt 52nd Regt and 5th Dragoon Gds Peninsular War, Groom-in-Waiting to HM QUEEN VICTORIA; *d* unm 21 July 1868, run over by a London cab

2 **Sir Charles Hay Seton, 7th Bt**; *b* 14 Nov 1797; Capt 5th Dragoon Gds; *m* 19 May 1829 Caroline (*d* 17 Nov 1868), dau of Walter Parry Hodges, Receiver-Gen Dorset, and *d* 11 June 1869, leaving:

  (1) **Sir Bruce Maxwell Seton, 8th Bt**, DL Tower Hamlets; *b* 31 Jan 1836; Priv Sec to Ld Pres Cncl 1867–74, Pncpl Clerk WO to 1882; *m* 30 Jan 1886 Helen (*d* 18 July 1922), dau of Gen Richard Hamilton, CB, Madras Army, and *dsp* 12 March 1915

3 Bruce; *b* 25 June 1799; Col HEICS; *m* 1st 17 June 1825 Jane, dau of John Elphinstone; *m* 2nd 1839 Emma Orton (*d* 25 Sept 1889) and *d* 27 Nov 1876, leaving by her:

  (1) Alexander Reginald; *b* 25 May 1840; Lt-Col RE; *m* 18 Sept 1862 Emma Elizabeth, dau of Lt-Col William Loch, 1st Bombay Lancers, and *d* 12 Nov 1887, leaving:

  1a **Sir Bruce Gordon Seton, 9th Bt**; *b* 13 Oct 1868; CB, Lt-Col, Brevet Col IMS, NWF India 1894 (severely wounded, medal with clasp), Tochi Valley 1897 (medal with clasp), WW I (despatches, medals); *m* 18 March 1895 Elma (*d* 24 Nov 1960), dau of Lt-Col Frank Hugh Armstrong, RASC, and *d* 3 July 1932, having had:

  1b **Sir Alexander Hay Seton, 10th Bt**; *b* 14 Aug 1904; *educ* Trin Coll Glenalmond; Carrick Pursuivant Arms 1935–39, Lt Roy Scots, F/Lt RAFVR; *m* 1st 12 March 1927 (*divorce* 1939) Zeyla Daphne (*d* 20 Nov 1963), dau of John Sanderson, of Muirhouse, Davidson's Mains, and had:

  1c *Egidia Hay [Mrs Norman Haynes, 35 St Maur Rd, London SW6]; *b* 5 July 1928; *m* 1st 1948 (*divorce* 1949) her cousin Andrew George Seton Arnot (*d* 1988), only s of Lt Reginald George Arnot, RN (ret) (*see above*); *m* 2nd 18 Jan 1953 *(Frederick) Norman Haynes, s of Frederick Haynes, of Edinburgh, and by him has:

  1d *Hamish Norman Seton [Hamish Haynes Esq, 40 Jessica Rd, London SW18]; *b* 20 Sept 1956; *m* 1982 *Carmella Milne-Buckley

  2d *Alasdair Frederick Seton [Alasdair Haynes Esq, 2 Old Palace Terrace, The Green, Richmond, Surrey TW9 1NB]; *b* 28 Jan 1960; *m* 1993 *Jane Elizabeth Bridgman

  1b (cont.) **Sir Alexander** *m* 2nd 17 June 1939 (*divorce* 1958) Mrs Flavia de Pinto (*d* 13 Oct 1959), yr dau of Lt-Col James Stewart Forbes (*see* FORBES, Bt, of Newe); *m* 3rd 30 July 1962 *Julia, OBE, VMH [Dowager Lady Seton OBE VMH, 122 Swan Court, Chelsea Manor St, London SW3 5RU], author, dau of Frank Clements, OBE (1989), and *d* 7 Feb 1963

  2b **Sir Bruce Lovat Seton, 11th Bt**; *b* 29 May 1909; *educ* Edinburgh Acad and RMC Sandhurst; 2nd Lt Black Watch, Maj Cameronians (Scottish Rifles), WW II; actor; *m* 1st 7 March 1937 (*divorce* 1940) Tamara Desni, dau of Jacob Brodsky and formerly w of Hans Wilhelm; *m* 2nd 14 Feb 1940 (Florence) Antoinette Glossop, dau of François (Frank) Cellier, of Surrey, and *dspm* 28 Sept 1969, having had:

  1c *Lydia Antoinette Gordon [Mrs Norman Vine, 21B Ailsa Rd, Twickenham, Middx]; *b* 14 Nov 1941; *m* 1st 1966 (*divorce* 1981) Peter S Spratt; *m* 2nd 1982 *Norman Victor Vine and by him has:

  1d *Antony Patrick Seton; *b* 1982

  1b Jean Gordon; *m* 1st 7 Dec 1922 (*divorce* 1947) Capt Reginald George Arnot, RN, s of Cdr G H Arnot, RN, of Rockferry, Cheshire, and had issue; *m* 2nd Aug 1947 Brig-Gen Nicholas Hamner Cobb, US Army, of Fla.

  2b Marie de Seton; *m* 1st 7 Nov 1925 (*divorce* 1943) Capt Ian Reddie Hamilton Black, CBE, RN, est s of Cdr Henry Somes Black, RIM, of Dysart, Fife, and had issue; *m* 2nd 26 Oct 1943 1st Baron Tedder (*qv*) and *d* 3 Jan 1965, leaving further issue

  2a Alexander Maxwell; *b* 30 Sept 1875; Capt RA; *d* unm 11 Oct 1904

  3a Charles Monteach; *b* 30 March 1880; Benedictine monk; *d* 5 Nov 1945

  4a Walter Warren; *b* 4 Oct 1882; DLit Lond, DJuris Padua, PhD Prague, FSA, Sec, Fell and lecturer Scottish history UCL, Kt Order Redeemer Greece, Order Crown Italy; *d* unm 26 Jan 1927

  1a Katharine Marion; *d* unm 2 Feb 1951

  2a Elsie Madeline; *m* 8 May 1901 Algernon James Pollock and *d* 24 March 1946, leaving issue

  3a Aileen Mary; *m* 22 Sept 1899 Frank Binford Hole, of Sutton, Surrey, and had issue

  (2) Bruce Outram; *b* 7 May 1841; Lt-Col RE; *m* 21 July 1880 Louisa Harriet Manderson (*d* 31 March 1886), dau of Surgn-Gen Charles Thomas Paske, IMS, and *d* 29 July 1901, leaving:

  1a Evelyn; *m* 1 Oct 1902 Brig-Gen Sir Percy Molesworth Sykes, KCIE, CB, CMG (*d* 11 June 1945), only s of Rev William Sykes, and had issue (*see* 1949 edn SYKES, Bt, of Cheadle)

  2a Ruth Mary; *m* 15 Feb 1905 Marmaduke Brian Sunderland (*d* 29 Jan 1930), only child of Lt-Col — Sunderland, and *d* Sept 1967, leaving issue

  3a Violet Adela; WW II: CD, BRCS, Cmdt Conington Castle EMS Hosp 1941–45 (Greys, Kelvedon, Essex); *m* 1st 18 May 1904 her cousin Charles Henry Seton and had issue (*see below*); *m* 2nd 1921 William Neilson, of Kilmacolm (*d* 13 Nov 1952), and by him had:

  1b *William Gordon; *b* 26 Nov 1922; Col Roy Signals, apptd Def and Mil Attaché to KING FAISAL OF SAUDI ARABIA 1969; *m* 28 July 1961 *Ann, est dau of Col David Charles Belton, OBE, and has:

  1c *Charles Andrew Seton; *b* 12 April 1962; *m* 20 Aug 1988 *Caroline Anne Murray, of Canterbury, and has:

  1d *Toby William; *b* 18 June 1990

  2d *Harry George; *b* 29 Dec 1993

  1b *Jean Seton; *b* 12 July 1925; *m* 21 Dec 1957 *Maj Charles James Eyre, RM, of Hayling Island, Hants, and has:

  1c *Caroline Elizabeth Margaret; *b* 25 Sept 1958; *m* 3 June 1989 *Roger John Gray and has:

  1d *Robert John; *b* 10 July 1990

  1d *Emma Louise; *b* 24 Jan 1994

  2c *Jennifer Mary Seton; *b* 20 Oct 1961; *m* 13 July 1991 *Quentin Kean and has:

  1d *Reuben James Seton; *b* 30 April 1997

(3) William Bowman; *b* 1 Sept 1843; Lt-Col Bombay SC; *m* 7 Sept 1878 Elizabeth Frances Maria, dau of Maj-Gen George Swiney, Bengal SC, and *d* 1886

(4) Charles Compton; *b* 24 July 1846; Lt RE; *m* 30 July 1868 Phœbe Elizabeth (*d* 3 Dec 1873), dau of Sir Henry William Ripley, 1st Bt (*qv*), and *d* 18 Nov 1923, having had:

1a Charles Henry; *b* 28 Aug 1869; *m* 18 May 1904 his cousin Violet Adela Seton (*see above*) and *d* 29 July 1917, leaving:

1b CHRISTOPHER BRUCE (Sir), **12th Bt**

1b Joyce Phoebe; *b* 3 Aug 1906; *m* 19 Jan 1932 Eric Charles Edward Garnett (*d* 15 April 1955), of Glatton, Hunts, and *d* 22 Dec 1934, leaving issue

2b Violet Beechie; *b* 16 Jan 1917; *m* 21 May 1937 Wilfred Barnard (*d* 8 May 1982), of Felixstowe, and *d* 14 June 1995, having had:

1c *Christopher John; *b* 3 March 1938; *educ* Stamford Sch; 46 Sqdn RASC (LCT) 1961–64, Borneo 1963–64, Capt LCT Agebadia; *m* 5 March 1966 *Diana Eileen, only dau of Peter James Wise, of Southampton, and has:

1d *David Charles; *b* 27 Feb 1972

1d *Charlotte Diana; *b* 8 June 1967; *m* 24 March 1990 *George Hamish Nicol and has:

1e *(George) Alasdair Buchanan; *b* 28 Dec 1991

2e *Callum Fraser; *b* 4 April 1993

2d *Joanna Suzanne; *b* 25 Sept 1968

2c David Seton; *b* 2 Sept 1942; *educ* Stamford Sch; *k* by lightning in S Africa 1971

1c *Jane Mary; *b* 11 May 1944; *m* 19– (*divorce*) Michael Gorton and has:

1d *Bruce; *b* 8 Feb 1971

1d *Hedy; *b* 6 May 1972

2c *Jean Suzanne; *b* 26 Jan 1946; *m* 10 June 1967 *James Alec Williamson and has:

1d *Emma Jane; *b* 31 Jan 1969; *m* 5 Oct 1991 *Glen Andrew James Symons and has:

1e *William Jack Douglas; *b* 20 Nov 1993

1e *Megan Emily Kathleen; *b* 26 Jan 1996

2a Bruce Hugh; *b* 6 Nov 1871; *d unm* 8 June 1899

1a Margaret Annie Phœbe; *m* 12 Oct 1898 (*divorce* 1934) Maj Arthur Pelham Frankland, DSO, and *d* 2 Feb 1953, leaving issue (*see* ZOUCHE, B)

(5) Henry James; *b* 27 Aug 1854; Maj Roy Irish Rifles Boer War (severley wounded, medal with two clasps); *m* 1st 6 Dec 1888 Elizabeth (*dsp* 2 Sept 1897), dau of Henry James Byron (*see* BYRON, B); *m* 2nd 3 May 1899 Marie Bowles (*m* 2nd 19 Jan 1922 Sir Charles George Walpole (*see* WALPOLE, B) and *d* 5 Feb 1928), dau of Percy Hale Wallace, and *d* 26 Oct 1920, leaving:

1a Marie; *b* 1910; author; *m* 1942 (*divorce* 1958) Donald Louis Hesson

(1) Emma Alice; *m* 18 July 1876 Henry Ripley (*see* RIPLEY, Bt) and *d* 10 Jan 1884, leaving issue

4 James; *b* 2 Oct 1803; HEICS; *d unm* India 1834

5 Alexander; *b* 14 Dec 1805; HEICS; *d unm* India 1831

The 11th Bt's cousin,

Sir Christopher Bruce Seton, 12th Bt; *b* 3 Oct 1909; *educ* Magdalene Coll Cambridge (BA 1931); *m* 23 Sept 1939 *Joyce Vivian [Joyce Lady Seton, Flat 1B Papillon House, Balkerne Gdns, Colchester, Essex CO1 1PR], SRN, SCM, er dau of Oliver George Barnard, of Lockington House, Stowmarket, and *d* 1988, leaving:

1 Sir IAIN BRUCE SETON, **13th and present Bt**

2 +Michael Charles [Michael Seton Esq, Fingringhoe, Colchester, Essex]; *b* 25 Sept 1944; *educ* Colchester Tech; *m* 6 Sept 1973 *Vida Millicent, dau of Sidney Clarence Smith, of Boxted, Essex, and has:

(1) +Philip Charles; *b* 12 May 1975

(1) *Helen Mary; *b* 28 Feb 1978

1 *Sarah Ann [Mrs Sarah Good, Box 433, Belton, MO 64012, USA]; *b* 25 Sept 1944; *m* 1st 4 May 1968 (*divorce* 1970) Thomas Charles Usher, 2nd s of Thomas Clemens Usher, of Toronto, by Mrs R D Swan, of Wycliffe, Barnard Castle, Co Durham; *m* 2nd 1974 (*divorce* 1988) Ferdinand Winston Good

2 *Joanna Mary [Mrs Peter Gillespie, Vicarage Farm, Halliford Rd, Sunbury-on-Thames, Middx TW16 6DW]; *b* 8 Sept 1946; *m* 20 April 1983 *Peter Gillespie and has:

(1) *Giles Peter Seton; *b* 30 June 1986

SETON of Pitmedden

Arms: Quarterly, 1st and 4th, or three crescents, in the centre a man's heart distilling blood, the whole within a double tressure flory counterflory gules (for SETON); 2nd and 3rd, argent a demi-otter sable, crowned or, issuing out of a bar wavy of the second (for MELDRUM). **Crest:** A demi-man in military habit, holding the banner of Scotland with the motto on an escroll above *Sustento sanguine signa* ('I sustain the standard with my blood'). **Supporters:** Dexter, a deerhound argent, collared gules, charged with crescents or; sinister, an otter sable. **Motto:** *Merces hæc certa laborum* ('This is the sure reward of labour'). **Creation:** Bt. (NS) 15 Jan 1683/4.

SIR JAMES CHRISTALL SETON, 12TH BT, of Pitmedden, Aberdeenshire [Sir James Seton Bt, Otterbein Home, 585 North State, Route 741, Lebanon, OH 45036–9551, USA]; *b* 21 Jan 1913; *s* kinsman 1993; Corp US Army WW II 1943–46; *m* 1939 *Evelyn, dau of Ray Hafer

Lineage: Sir ALEXANDER SETON; had by Elizabeth Gordon (*see* HUNTLY, M) a 2nd s:

WILLIAM SETON; *m* Elizabeth, dau and heiress of William Meldrum of that Ilk, thus acquiring the (territorial) Barony of Meldrum and other estates, and was *ka* fighting under his bro the 1st Earl of Huntly (*see* HUNTLY, M) at the Battle of Brechin May 1452, leaving:

ALEXANDER SETON; *m* a dau of Alexander Sutherland of Duffus, was ancestor of the Lords Duffus (*see* SUTHERLAND, E), and had:

WILLIAM SETON of Meldrum; *m* Elizabeth (*m* 2nd John Collison, of Aberdeen), dau of Alexander Leslie, 1st of Wardis (*see* LESLIE, Bt), and *dvp*, leaving:

ALEXANDER SETON of Meldrum; served heir to his gf 1512; *m* 1st Agnes, dau of Patrick Gordon of Methlic and Haddo (*see* ABERDEEN AND TEMAIR, M), and had issue; *m* 2nd Janet (Im 2nd James Gordon, 3rd of Abergeldie (*ka* Scots defeat by English of Pinkie 10 Sept 1547), and had issue, dau and coheir of George Leith, 7th of Barnis, and was murdered *c* 1526 by the Master of Forbes (*see* FORBES, L), leaving an est s by his 1st w:

WILLIAM SETON of Meldrum; *m* 1st Janet, dau of James Gordon of Lesmoir, and had:

1 Alexander, of Meldrum; *m* 1st Elizabeth, 2nd dau of Alexander Irvine of Lonmay; *m* 2nd Jean, dau of 6th Lord Saltoun (*qv*) of Abernethy

2 John, of Lumphard, Broomhill (confirmed by Crown charter 1575) and Mounie, Aberdeenshire (confirmed by Crown charter 1597); *m* Marjory, dau of Panton of Pitmedden, and had:

(1) William, of Mounie

3 William, of Slattie

WILLIAM SETON *m* 2nd Margaret, dau of Innes of Leuchars, and by her had:

4 George; Chllr Aberdeen Cathedral; *dsp*

5 James, of Bourtie; acquired the lands of Pitmedden, Aberdeenshire; *m* Margaret, gdau of William Rolland, Master Aberdeen Mint *temp* JAMES V, and had:

(1) Alexander, of Pitmedden; *m* Beatrix, sis of 1st Lord Banff, and had, with seven daus:

1a John, of Pitmedden; royalist Civil War; *m* 1633 Elizabeth (*m* 2nd 1st Earl of Hartfell; *see* ANNANDALE AND HARTFELL, E), dau of Sir Samuel Johnstone, 1st Bt, of Elphinstone, and was shot through the heart by a cannonball at the Battle of the Bridge of Dee June 1639 while carrying CHARLES I's standard, hence his descendants' heart with drops of blood issuing from it in their coat of arms, leaving:

1b James, of Pitmedden; served RN; *d* 1667 of wounds recd in enemy attack on Chatham in Second Dutch War

2b **Sir Alexander Seton, 1st Bt** (NS), so *cr* 15 Jan 1683/4 in recognition of f's servs, of Pitmedden; ktd 1664, MP Aberdeenshire 1681–82 and 1685–86, Ld of Session 1677 as Lord Pitmedden; *m* 1673 Margaret (*d* 19 Oct 1733), dau and heiress of William Lauder, and had, with other issue:

1c WILLIAM (Sir), **2nd Bt**

2c George, of Mounie; *m* 1st Anne, dau of Sir Alexander Gibson, Bt, of Pentland, and had:

    1d Helen; *m* Alexander Leslie of Warthill

2c (cont.) George Seton *m* 2nd Anne, dau of John Leslie of Tochar, and by her had issue

3c Alexander; MD; physician forces under Duke of Marlborough

1c Elizabeth; *m* Sir Alexander Wedderburn, 2nd Bt (*see* OGILVY-WEDDERBURN, Bt), and had issue

2c Margaret; *m* Sir John Lauder, 3rd Bt, of Fountainhall (*see* DICK-LAUDER, Bt), and had issue

Sir ALEXANDER *d* 1719; his est s,

  Sir William Seton, 2nd Bt; *bapt* 6 March 1673; MP Aberdeenshire 1702–08, Commr for Union S and E Parls; *m* 1702 Katherine (*d* 1749), dau of Sir Thomas Burnett, 3rd Bt, of Leys (*see* 1956 edn), and *d* 1744, having had, with three other daus:

1 **Sir Alexander Seton, 3rd Bt**; *b* 19 Jan 1703; Capt Gds; *d* unm 21 July 1750

2 **Sir William Seton, 4th Bt**; *d* unm 11 Oct 1774

3 Thomas; MD; *m* a dau of Sir John Paterson and *dsp*

4 **Sir Archibald Seton, 5th Bt**; Lt RN; *dsp* 26 May 1775

5 Charles; had:

    (1) WILLIAM (Sir), **6th Bt**

1 Margaret; *m* Sir John Paterson, Bt

The 5th Bt's n,

  Sir William Seton, 6th Bt; *m* 23 Nov 1775 Margaret, est dau of James Ligertwood, of Tillery, and had, with two daus:

1 James; Maj 92nd Highrs, Peninsula gold medal; *m* Frances, dau of Capt George Coote, n of Sir Eyre Coote (*see* COOTE, Bt), and *dvp* 1814 from wounds recd in Peninsular War, leaving, with two daus (*d* unm):

    (1) WILLIAM COOTE (Sir), **7th Bt**

2 William; *d* in India

The 6th Bt *d* 16 Feb 1818; his gs,

  Sir William Coote Seton, 7th Bt, JP, DL Aberdeenshire; *b* 19 Dec 1818; advocate 1831; *m* 26 Nov 1834 Eliza Henrietta (*d* 24 April 1873), 2nd dau of Henry Lumsden of Cushney, Aberdeenshire, dir HEIC, and widow of Capt John Wilson, HEICS, and *d* 30 Dec 1880, leaving:

1 **Sir James Lumsden Seton, 8th Bt**; *b* 1 Sept 1835; Capt 102nd Regt, Abyssinia and Burma campaigns, Indian Mutiny (medals), Order Iron Cross 2nd Cl Prussia for saving life on battlefield Franco-Prussian War 1870; *m* 20 Oct 1870 Elizabeth (*d c* 1934), dau of George Castle, of Oxford, and *dsp* 28 Sept 1884

2 **Sir William Samuel Seton, 9th Bt**, JP, DL Aberdeenshire; *b* 22 May 1837; served Indian Navy, Col IA, Persian Campaign 1856 (medal with clasp), Afghan War 1880 (medal with clasp); *m* 15 March 1876 Eva Kate St Leger (*d* 12 Feb 1927), only dau of Gen Sir Henry Hastings Affleck Wood, KCB, and *d* 5 March 1914, leaving:

    (1) **Sir John Hastings Seton, 10th Bt**; *b* 20 Sept 1888; *educ* Bedford Sch; Lt Durham Roy Field Res Artillery, Capt 2nd (formerly with 6th) Gordon Highrs, WWs I and II; *m* 18 June 1923 (*divorce* 1950) Alice Ida, CBE (1949) (*d* 28 July 1995), Gp Offr WRAF WW II, dau of Percy C Hodge, Cape CS, and *d* 21 June 1956, leaving:

        1a **Sir Robert James Seton, 11th Bt**; *b* 20 April 1926; *educ* HMS *Worcester*; Midshipman RNVR WW II; *d* 1993

        1a *Alice Eva Elizabeth; *b* 16 May 1924; WRNS WW II 1942–46; *m* 3 April 1954 *John Herbert Warner, only s of Sidney Herbert Warner, of Acton, and has:

            1b *Sylla Elizabeth; *b* 4 Sept 1955

    (1) Eva Sophia; *m* George Porrel Hornsen and *dsp*

    (2) Mary Christian; *m* — Tawse

    (3) Hilda Magdalene; *m* P Williams and had a dau

    (4) Ethel Susanna; *m* 1916 Peter Hunter and *d* 28 May 19–, leaving a s and two daus

    (5) Florence Kate Agnes

3 Henry (Rev); *b* 1839; *d* unm 18 June 1867

4 Matthew; *b* 26 May 1844; barrister; *m* 11 Sept 1877 Thérèse Prudence Rose (*d* 2 Sept 1931), only dau of Pierre Bonnet, of Paris, and *d* 25 June 1887, leaving issue:

    (1) Robert Coote; *b* 11 March 1881; served WW I 1916–19 with Australian Forces; *d* unm 5 Aug 1952

    (1) Rose Henrietta Lumsden

    (2) Violet Thérèse

    (3) Lily Mackenzie; *d* unm 21 April 1966

5 Charles; *b* 24 Oct 1847; Capt 9th Norfolk Regt, served in Jowaki Afridi Campaign 1877 (medal with clasp), Afghan War 1879–81 (medal with clasp); *m* 17 May 1882 Elizabeth (*d* 13 Oct 1930), dau of James O'Neil, and *d* 22 March 1926, having had issue:

    (1) Christall Dougall; *b* 24 Sept 1883; *m* 27 June 1909 Sara Johnson (*d* 7 Jan 1958), dau of Wallace Moore, and *d* 28 May 1969, leaving issue:

        1a Sir JAMES CHRISTALL SETON, **12th and present Bt**

        2a Charles Wallace, US Bronze Star, Purple Heart, and Silver Star, Sgt 1st Cl US Army, served in Korea; *b* 1915; *m* 1943 *Joyce [Mrs Charles Seton, 798 Dinner St, Palm Bay, Florida 32905, USA], dau of Stephen F Perdunn, and *d* 1975, leaving:

            1b +CHARLES WALLACE [Charles Seton Esq, 7008 Santa Rosa Parkway, Fort Pierce, Florida 34951, USA], heir presumptive; *b* 25 Aug 1948; *m* 1974 *Rebecca, dau of Robert Lowery

            2b +Bruce Anthony; *b* 29 April 1957; *m* 19– *Paula, dau of Emmett Harper

            1b *Judith Allen; *b* 1944

            2b *Marsha Ann; *b* 1947; *m* 1981 (*divorce* 1984) Glen Duffy, and has issue:

                1c *Steven Seton; *b* 1968

3b *Terri Michele [Mrs William Dick 7418 Zimmerman Ave, Apt 2, Delair, NJ 08110, USA]; *b* 10 June 1958; *m* 1984 *William Dick, son of William Dick, Sr, and has issue:

    1c *David; *b* 1985

    2c *Thomas; *b* 1987

    1c *Desire Michelle; *b* 1983

3a (Robert) Benjamin; *b* 1917; *m* 1940 Martha Mae (*d* 1974), dau of Fred Minich, and *d* 1993, leaving issue:

    1b *Karen Louise [Mrs Michael Conrad, 878 Viewland, Rochester Hills, Michigan 48309, USA]; *b* 1941; *educ* Ohrollmir, and Ohio U (BSc (Ed)); *m* 1963 *Michael Conrad, and has issue:

        1c *Dennis Michael; *b* 5 May 1964; *m* 1993 *Bridgett, dau of John George Heal III

    2b *Dorothy Jean; *b* 1947

1a *Dorothy Kathryn; *b* 1910; *m* 1st 6 Feb 1937 (*divorce* 1940) George B Leonard, of Cleveland, Ohio, USA; she *m* 2nd 1947 *Kenneth M James, and has issue:

    1b *Susan Kay; *b* 13 Aug 1949

(1) Dorothy Beatrix, Nursing Serv of USA, served WW I; *b* 12 Sept 1885; *d* 8 Feb 1920, from effects of service in France

1 Eliza; *m* 23 Jan 1873 David Dyce Brown, MA, MD, and *d* 14 Dec 1903, leaving issue

2 Magdalene Frances; *m* 6 Oct 1870 Arthur Talbot Bevan (*d* 9 July 1918), of Bessels Green, Sevenoaks, 5th son of Charles James Bevan, of Bryanston Sq, and *d* 18 Aug 1918

3 Frances; *d* unm 29 May 1925

SEWEL

Creation: B. (LP, UK) 18 Nov 1995.

THE BARON SEWEL, of Gilcomstoun, District of City of Aberdeen (John Buttifant Sewel, CBE (1984)) [The Rt The Lord Sewel CBE, House of Lords, London SW1A 0PW]; *b* 15 Jan 1946; *educ* Hanson Boys' GS Bradford, Durham U, U Coll Swansea (research assist Sociology and Anthropology Dept 1967–69) and Aberdeen U (research Fell Politics Dept 1969–72, Educn and Political Economy Depts 1972–75, Lecturer 1975, Sr Lecturer 1988, Prof Regnl Centre Study Ec and Social Policy 1991–97, Dean Ec and Social Scis 1988–95 and Social Scis and Law 1995–96, V-Pncpl 1994–96); memb Aberdeen DC 1974–78 (Leader 1977–80), Accounts Commn Scotland 1987– and Scottish Constitutional Commn 1994–95, Pres COSLA 1982–84, Parly U-Sec Scottish Office 1997–; author: *Colliery Closure and Social Change* (1975), *Education and Migration* (1976), *The Politics of Independence: a study of a Scottish town* (with F W Bealey 1981) and *The Rural Community and the Small School* (co-author 1983); *m* 1st 1968 (*divorce* 1986) Rosemary Christine Langeland; *m* 2nd 1987 *Leonora Mary Harding and by his 1st w has a s and dau

Lineage: LEONARD BUTTIFANT SEWEL; *m* *Hilda Ivy Brown and had:

JOHN BUTTIFANT, *cr* a **Baron**

SHAFTESBURY

Arms: Quarterly, 1st and 4th, arg. three bulls statant sa., armed and unguled or (for ASHLEY); 2nd and 3rd, gu. a bend engrailed between six lions rampant or (for COOPER). **Crest:** On a chapeau gu. doubled erm. a bull statant sa., ducally gorged, armed and unguled or. **Supporters:** Dexter, a bull sa., armed, unguled and ducally gorged, line reflexed over the back or; sinister, a talbot az. ducally gorged or. **Motto:** Love, serve. **Creations:** Bt. (E) 4 July 1622, B. (E) 20 April 1661, B. and E. (E) 23 April 1672.

THE 10TH EARL OF SHAFTESBURY, **Baron Ashley of Wimborne St Giles**, Co Dorset, **Baron Cooper of Pawlett**, Co Somerset, and a **Baronet** (Sir Anthony Ashley-Cooper, Bt) [The Rt Hon The Earl of Shaftesbury, St Giles's House, Wimborne, Dorset BH21 5NH]; *b* 22 May 1938; *s* gf 1961; *educ* Eton and Ch Ch Oxford; late Lt 10th Roy Hus, dir PKL Gp 1989–, Hon Pres Shaftesbury Soc, chm London Philharmonic Orchestra Cncl 1966–80, Hon Citizen S Carolina 1967, patron seven livings; *m* 1st 21 July 1966 (*divorce* 1976) Bianca Maria, dau of Gino de Paolis, of Rome, and formerly w of Jack Le Vien, film producer; *m* 2nd 15 Dec 1976 *Mrs Christina Eve Casella, dau of Nils Montan, and by her has:

1 +ANTHONY NILS CHRISTIAN, *Lord Ashley*; *b* 24 June 1977

2 +Nicholas Edmund Anthony; *b* 3 June 1979

Lineage: RICHARD COOPER; *s* his f and bro in large estates in Hants and Sussex; bought *c* 1532 Manor of Paulett from Sir Amyas Paulet (*see* WINCHESTER, M); *m* June, dau of John Kingsmill, of Sydmonton, Hants, and *d* 8 May 1566, leaving:

Sir JOHN COOPER; MP Whitchurch, Hants, 1586; *m* Martha, dau of Anthony Skutt, of Stanton Drew, Somerset, and *d* 1610, leaving:

Sir John Cooper, 1st Bt (E), so cr 4 July 1622, of Rockbourne, Hants; *m* 1st Anne, dau and sole heiress of Sir Anthony Ashley, 1st Bt, of Wimborne St Giles, Dorset, Sec at War *temp* ELIZABETH I, by Jane, dau of Philip Okeover (*see* WALKER-OKEOVER, Bt); *m* 2nd Mary, widow of Sir Charles Morrison and dau and coheir of Baptist Hicks, 1st Viscount Campden (*see* SAINT ALDWYN, E, also GAINS-BOROUGH, E), and *d* 23 March 1631, leaving by his 1st w, with a yr s and a dau:

Sir Anthony Ashley Cooper, 2nd Bt, and **1st Earl of Shaftesbury**, so cr 23 April 1672, as also BARON COOPER OF PAWLETT, Co Somerset, and earlier 20 April 1661 BARON ASHLEY OF WIMBORNE ST GILES, Co Dorset (all E), PC (1660–74); *b* 22 July 1661; *educ* Exeter Coll Oxford and Lincoln's Inn (Bencher 1673); MP Tewkesbury March-May 1640, Downton Dec 1640 and Wilts 1653, 1654–55, 1656–58 and 1659–60; Civil War: royalist Col of Foot and Capt of Horse, Govr Weymouth and Portland, Sheriff Dorset 1643, turned Parliamentarian Feb 1643/4, cmded a Parly Bde Aug 1643, FM Gen and C-in-C Parly forces Dorset Oct 1643, Sheriff Wilts 1646, Memb: CROMWELL's Cncl of State 1653, LORD PROTECTOR's Cncl 1653–54 and Rump Parl's Cncl of State 1659 and Feb 1659/60; took charge of Tower of London on Parl's behalf and one of seven Army Commrs Dec 1659, Col Fleetwood's Horse Jan 1659/60, Govr IoW and Capt of Foot there Feb 1659/60; one of a delegn of 12 deputed by H of C to seek CHARLES II's return from exile in Holland May 1660; obtained a pardon for his anti-monarchist activities June 1660; memb Ctee Plantations July 1660; Chllr Exchequer 1661–72 and U-Treas 1661–67, FRS 1663, a Ld of Treasury 1667–72, memb CHARLES II's coterie of acronymic advsrs called the CABAL (his name being commemorated in one of the As); Ld Lt Dorset Jan 1671/2–74, High Steward Salisbury 1672, Pres Cncl Trade and Plantations 1672–76, Ld Chllr 1672–73; after being relieved of office 1673 he led the anti-court party in Parl, especially in its antipapistical utterances; imprisoned Tower of London Feb 1676/7–Feb 1677/8 for opposing Parl's prorogation for more than one year; Pres Cncl April-Oct 1679 (apptd in an attempt by CHARLES II to conciliate his opponents), as which introduced Habeas Corpus Bill; may be regarded as fndr of the Whig tradition in England, perhaps even the Whig Party itself; again imprisoned Tower of London 1681 on charge of high treason, a charge that would have been true a few months later when with the Duke of Monmouth (*see* BUCCLEUCH and QUEENSBERRY, D) he did in fact plan an uprising to ensure a Protestant succession; fled to Holland Nov 1682 and *d* 21 Jan 1682/3 in exile in Amsterdam, having *m* 1st 25 Feb 1638/9 Margaret (*dsp* 11 July 1649), dau of 1st Baron Coventry of Aylesborough (*see* COVENTRY, E); *m* 2nd 15 April 1650 Frances (*d* 1654), dau of 3rd Earl of Exeter (*see* EXETER, M); *m* 3rd 30 Aug 1655 Margaret (*dsp* 1693), sis of 1st Earl of Sunderland (*see* MARLBOROUGH, D), and by his 2nd w had, with an er s (Cecil, *d* young 1651) and a dau:

ANTHONY ASHLEY COOPER, **2nd Earl of Shaftesbury**; *b* 16 Jan 1651/2; *educ* Trin Coll Oxford; MP (Whig) Weymouth and Melcombe Regis 1670–79 and 1679/80–83, V-Adml Dorset 1679 and March 1684/5–99; *m* 22 Sept 1669 Dorothy (*d* June 1698), dau of 8th Earl of Rutland (*see* RUTLAND, D), and *d* 10 Nov 1699, having had, with other issue, including a yr s (Maurice, *b* 14 April 1675, scholar, *m* Catharine (*d* 31 March 1721), dau of William Popple, and *dsp* 21 Oct 1726) and a dau (Elizabeth, *m* 20 April 1707 James Harris and had issue; *see* MALMESBURY, E):

ANTHONY ASHLEY COOPER, **3rd Earl of Shaftesbury**; *b* 26 Feb 1670/1; *educ* Winchester; MP (Whig) Poole 1695–98, V-Adml Dorset 1701–02; author: *Characteristics of Men, Manners, Opinions, Times* (1711) and *Second Characters* (not published till 1914), called by Voltaire the boldest English philosopher, bracketed by Montesquieu with Plato, Malebranche and Montaigne as the human race's four leading poets, and only a little less revered by Diderot, Herder, Leibniz, Lessing and Moses Mendelssohn; *m* 29 Aug 1709 Jane (*d* 23 Nov 1751), dau of Thomas Ewer, of Bushey Hall and the Leas, Watford, Herts (*see* MANCHESTER, D), and *d* Naples 15 Feb 1712/3, where he had settled a little over a year before for his health's sake, leaving:

ANTHONY ASHLEY COOPER, **4th Earl of Shaftesbury**, PC (1761); *b* 9 Feb 1710/1; *educ* New Coll Oxford; Ld Lt Dorset March 1734/5–71, Recorder Shaftesbury 1756, High Steward Dorchester 1757, Brig-Gen Dorset Militia 1761, Govr Levant Co 1766–71, FRS 1754, FSA 1767; *m* 1st 12 March 1724 Susannah (*dsp* 20 June 1758), dau of 3rd Earl of Gainsborough (*qv*); *m* 2nd 20 March 1759 Mary (*d* 12 Nov 1804), sis of 1st Earl of Radnor (*qv*), and *d* 27 May 1771, leaving by her:

1 ANTHONY ASHLEY COOPER, **5th Earl of Shaftesbury**; *b* 17 Sept 1761; *educ* Winchester and Ch Ch Oxford; FRS 1785; *m* 17 July 1786 Barbara, dau and heiress of Sir John Webb, 5th Bt (*see* 1874 edn), of Oldstock House, Wilts, and *dspm* 14 May 1811, leaving:

(1) Barbara; *m* 8 Aug 1814 1st Baron de Mauley of Canford (*qv*) and *d* 5 June 1844, leaving issue

2 CROPLEY ASHLEY, **6th Earl**

1 Mary Anne; *m* 14 April 1788 Charles Sturt, MP (*d* 12 May 1812), of Crichel House, Dorset, and *d* 8 July 1854, leaving issue (*see* 1940 edn ALINGTON, B)

The 5th EARL's bro,
CROPLEY ASHLEY COOPER, **6th Earl of Shaftesbury**, PC (1814); *b* 21 Dec 1768; *educ* Winchester and Ch Ch Oxford; Lt Dorset Militia 1790 (Capt 1794), MP (Tory) Dorchester Jan–June 1790 and Nov 1790–1811, Capot 1st Regt Fencible Cav 1794, High Steward Dorchester 1798, Clerk Deliveries Ordnance 1804–06 and March–July 1807, Clerk Ordnance 1807–11, Chm Ctees Ho Lds 1814–51; *m* 10 Dec 1796 Anne (*d* 7 Aug 1865 in her 91st year), dau of 4th Duke of Marlborough (*qv*), and had:

1 ANTHONY, **7th Earl**

2 (Anthony) William; *b* 4 Oct 1803; Master St Catherine's Hosp, DCL; *m* 8 March 1831 Maria Anne (*d* 10 Jan 1891), est dau of Col Hugh Duncan Baillie, of Tarradale, and *dsp* 18 April 1877

3 (Anthony) Henry; *b* 5 May 1807; MP Dorchester, Army Capt; *m* 2 Oct 1835 Jane Frances (*d* 1893), only dau of Robert Pattison, of Wrackleford, Dorset, and *d* 30 Nov 1858, leaving, with a dau (*d* unm):

(1) Emily Frances; *m* 20 Aug 1885 Henri de Satgé (*d* 12 Jan 1907), 3rd s of Vicomte de Satgé

4 (Anthony) John, QC; *b* 21 Dec 1808; *m* 17 March 1840 Julia (*d* 10 April 1907), est dau of Henry John Conyers, of Copt Hall, Essex, and *dsp* 1 Jan 1867

5 Anthony Francis; *b* 1810; *d* 1825, following a fight at Eton

6 Anthony Lionel; *b* Jan 1813; RN; *d* 14 Jan 1836

1 Caroline Mary; *m* 1 Jan 1831 Joseph Neeld, of Grittleton, Wilts, MP, and *d* 11 June 1869. He *d* 24 March 1856

2 Harriet Anne; *m* 18 March 1830 Henry Thomas Lowry-Corry, PC, MP (*see* BELMORE, E), and *d* 25 March 1868, leaving issue

3 Charlotte Barbara; *m* 1824 Henry Lyster (*d* 12 Dec 1863), of Rowton Castle, Salop, and *d* 11 Dec 1889

The 7th EARL *d* 2 June 1851; his est s,

ANTHONY ASHLEY-COOPER, **7th Earl of Shaftesbury**, KG (1862); *b* 28 April 1801; *educ* Harrow and Ch Ch Oxford (DCL 1841); MP (Tory to 1831, moderate C 1831–51) Woodstock 1826–30, Dorchester 1830–31, Dorset 1831–46 and Bath 1846–51, Commr Indian Affrs 1828–30, Met Lunacy Commr 1828–85 and Chm Lunacy Commn 1829–85, as which engineered reforms in lunacy laws, the first of his numerous philanthropical deeds, a Ld Admlty 1834–35, an Ecclesiastical Commr 1841–47, Pres Statistical Soc 1843–45, Br and For Bible Soc 1851–85, memb Gen Bd Health 1848–54, Ld Lt Dorset 1856–85, Freedom City London 1884; *m* 10 June 1830 Emily Caroline Catherine Frances (*d* 15 Oct 1872), dau of 5th Earl Cowper (*see* LUCAS OF CRUDWELL, B), and had, with other issue:

1 ANTHONY, **8th Earl**

2 (Anthony) Evelyn Melbourne ASHLEY-COOPER later ASHLEY, PC, of Classiebawn, Mullaghmore, Co Sligo, and Broadlands, Romsey, Hants, JP (Dorset, Hants and Co Sligo), DL (Hants); *b* 24 July 1836; MA Cantab; barrister, Priv Sec to Lord Palmerston, MP (Lib) Poole 1874–80 and IOW 1880–85, Sec BOT 1880–82, Ch Estates Commr 1880–85, U-Sec Colonies 1882–85, Official Verderer New Forest, Mayor Romsey 1898–1903; *m* 1st 28 July 1866 Sybella Charlotte (*d* 31 Aug 1886), 2nd dau of Sir Walter Rockcliffe Farquhar, 3rd Bt (*qv*), and had, with a dau (*d* young):

(1) WILFRID WILLIAM ASHLEY, 1st and last BARON MOUNT TEMPLE, of Lee, Co Southampton (UK), so cr 13 Jan 1932, PC (1924), JP, DL Hants; *b* 13 Sept 1867; *educ* Harrow and Magdalen Coll Oxford; Ayrshire Militia 1886–89, Gren Gds 1889–98 (Hon Lt-Col), Hants Militia 1899–1903, MP (C) Blackpool 1906–18, Fylde 1918–22 and New Forest and Christchurch 1922–32, Parly Sec Min Tport 1922–23, U-Sec War 1923–24, Min Tport 1924–29, Maj 3rd Bn Hants Regt and Lt-Col cmdg 20th Bn King's Liverpool Regt 1914–15, Chm Navy League, Comrades of Gt War and Anti-Socialist Union, CA Hants, High Steward Romsey, Pres Anglo-German Fellowship to 1938; *m* 1st 4 Jan 1901 Amalia Mary Maud (*d* 5 Feb 1911), only child of Sir Ernest Cassel, GCB, GCMG, GCVO, PC, and had:

1a Edwina Cynthia Annette, CI (1947), GBE (1947), DCVO (1946); *b* 28 Nov 1901 (HM EDWARD VII stood sponsor), Supt-in-Ch St John Ambulance Bde (despatches 1946), GCStJ, Hon LLD Edinburgh 1954, Freedom City Edinburgh 1954, Order Brilliant Star China, 1st Cl Belgian and Netherlands Red Cross; *m* 18 July 1922 1st Earl Mountbatten of Burma (*qv*), and *d* 21 Feb 1960, leaving issue

2a (Ruth) Mary (Clarisse); *m* 1st 12 May 1927 (*divorce* 1940) Capt Alec Stratford Cunningham-Reid, DFC (*d* 26 March 1977), s of Rev Arthur M Cunningham-Reid, and had issue; *m* 2nd 3 Sept 1940 (*divorce* 1943) Laurie Gardner, only s of Sir Ernest Gardner, of Maidenhead, Berks; *m* 3rd 15 June 1944 (*divorce* 1955) 4th Baron Delamere (*qv*)

(1) (cont.) The 1st and last BARON *m* 2nd 29 Aug 1914 Muriel Emily (*d* 24 June 1954), formerly w of R-Adml Hon Arthur Lionel Ochoncar Forbes-Sempill (*see* FORBES, Bt, of Craigievar) and er dau of Rev Walter Spencer, of Fownhope Court, Herefs, and *dspm* 3 July 1939, when the title expired

(1) Lilian Blanche Georgiana; *b* 27 June 1875; *m* 16 Nov 1895 Col Hercules Arthur Pakenham, CMG, and *d* 14 Sept 1939, leaving issue (*see* LONGFORD, E)

2 (cont.) The Rt Hon Evelyn Ashley *m* 2nd 30 June 1891 Lady Alice Cole (*d* 25 Aug 1931), 3rd dau of 3rd Earl of Enniskillen (*qv*), and *d* 15 Nov 1907, leaving by her:

(2) Anthony Henry Evelyn; *b* 25 Feb 1894; Capt Coldstream Gds; *m* 6 March 1920 Albinia Mary (*m* 3rd 3 Feb 1923 ACM Sir Edgar Rainey Ludlow-Hewitt, GCB, GBE, CMG, DSO, RAF (*d* 15 Aug 1973), of Westbrook House, Bromham, Wilts, and *d* 16 April 1972), widow of Francis William Talbot Clerke (*see* CLERKE, Bt) and er dau of Maj Edward Henry Evans Lombe, of Thickthorn and Marlingford Hall, Norwich, and *d* 14 Jan 1921

(3) (Anthony) Lionel George, DL (Dorset); *b* 7 Sept 1838; MA Cantab; *m* 12 Dec 1868 Francis Elizabeth (*d* Aug 1875), yr dau of Capel Hanbury-Leigh (*see* SUDELEY, B), and *dsp* 18 Aug 1914

(4) (Anthony) Cecil, DL (Dorset); *b* 8 Aug 1849; MA Cantab; *d* unm 23 Sept 1932

(2) Victoria Elizabeth; *m* 8 Jan 1873, as his 2nd w, 2nd Baron Templemore (*see* DONEGALL, M) and *d* 15 Feb 1927, leaving issue

The 7th EARL *d* 1 Oct 1885; his est s,

ANTHONY ASHLEY-COOPER, **8th Earl of Shaftesbury**; *b* 27 June 1831; *educ* Rugby; joined RN 1848, served Black Sea and baltic Crimean War, MP (Lib) Hull 1857–59 and Cricklade 1859–65; *m* 22 Aug 1857 Harriet Augusta Anna Seymourina (*d* 14 April 1898), only dau of 3rd Marquess of Donegall (*qv*), and committed suicide 13 April 1886 by shooting himself in a cab in Langham Place, London W, having deluded himself that he was ruined, leaving:

1 ANTHONY, **9th Earl**

1 Margaret Emily; *b* 28 Sept 1858; *m* 27 May 1884 Theophillus Basil Percy Levett, of Belgravia, est s of Theophilus John Levett, of Wychnor, Staffs, and *d* 16 Oct 1931. He *d* 26 May 1929

2 Evelyn Harriet; *b* 27 June 1865; *m* 1st 23 Oct 1889 2nd Baron Magheramorne and had issue (*see* HOGG, Bt); *m* 2nd 1 March 1905 Hon Hugo Baring, OBE, 6th s of 1st Baron Revelstoke (*qv*), and *d* 22 Jan 1931

3 Mildred Georgiana; *b* 25 Feb 1867; *m* 16 July 1895 Hon George Higginson Allsopp, MP, 3rd s of 1st Baron Hindlip (*qv*), and *d* 4 March 1958, leaving issue

4 Susan Violet; *b* 18 July 1868; *m* 14 July 1892 12th Earl of Mar and (14th Earl of) Kellie (*qv*) and *d* 16 Dec 1938, leaving issue

5 Ethel Maud; *b* 16 Dec 1870; *m* 6 Feb 1894 V-Adml Sir George John Scott Warrender, 7th Bt, KCB, KCVO, and *d* 3 Sept 1945, leaving issue (*see* BRUNTISFIELD, B)

The 8th EARL's only s,

ANTHONY ASHLEY-COOPER, **9th Earl of Shaftesbury**, KP (1911), GCVO (1924, KCVO 1906), CBE (1919), PC (1922), JP (Dorset); *b* 31 Aug 1869; *educ* Eton and RMC Sandhurst; 2nd Lt 10th Hus 1890, Lt 1891, Capt 1898, ret 1899, Mil Sec to Govr Victoria 1895–98, memb London Sch Bd 1901–03, Commr Congested Districts Bd Ireland 1903–14; Belfast: HM Lt 1903–11 (and Co Antrim 1911–16), Ld Mayor 1907, Chllr Queen's U 1909–23 (and Hon LLD); Chamberlain to HM QUEEN MARY 1901 (when PRINCESS OF WALES) and 1910–22; WW I: Col Cmdg 1st SW Mtd Bde TF 1913–16, Brig-Gen 1914, Hon Brig-Gen 1919, Hon Col NI Horse, Lt-Col and Hon Col Antrim RGA; Dorset: Ld Lt 1916–52, Chm CC 1924–46; Devpt Commr 1920–49, Chm: Nat Advsy Cncl Min Labour on Juvenile Employment 1928–31, Devpt Commn 1946; Yr Bro Trin Ho 1920, Ld Steward Household 1922–36, Bailiff Grand Cross OStJ, Grand Offr Legn Hon; *m* 15 July 1899 Lady Constance Sibell Grosvenor, DJStJ (*d* 8 July 1957), Extra Lady Bedchamber to HM QUEEN MARY, er dau of Earl Grosvenor (*see* WESTMINSTER, D), and *d* 25 March 1961, having had:

1 *Lord Ashley*, JP, DL Dorset; *b* 4 Oct 1900; *educ* Eton, RMC Sandhurst and Gonville and Caius Coll Cambridge; ADC to Govr Bombay 1929–30 and C-in-C India 1930–31, Maj Roy Wilts Yeo (TA) 1941, OStJ; *m* 1st 3 Feb 1927 (*divorce* 1935) (Edith Louise) Sylvia (*d* 30 June 1977), actress, dau of Arthur Hawkes; *m* 2nd 31 March 1937 *Françoise [Mme François Goussault, 6 Square d'Astorg, Residence St Honoré, 78150 Le Chesnay, France] (*m* 2nd 12 Aug 1947 Col François Goussault, French Air Force (*d* 1984), s of Col Maurice Goussault, of Le Mans), est dau of Georges Soulier, of Rouen, and *d* 8 March 1947, leaving:

(1) ANTHONY ASHLEY-COOPER, **10th and present Earl of Shaftesbury**

(2) *Frances Mary Elizabeth [The Lady Frances Ashley Cooper, La Combe, 30126 Tavel, Gard, France]; *b* 9 April 1940; granted rank of earl's dau Dec 1962

2 (Anthony) John Percy Hugh Michael; *b* 5 Oct 1915; *educ* Eton and Trin Coll Oxford (MA); Maj Life Gds WW II 1939–41 (POW), OStJ; *m* 5 Jan 1946 *Julian, est dau of Maj George Gerald Petherick (*see* RADNOR, E), and *d* 1986, leaving:

(1) *Susan Mary Jeane; *b* 11 Nov 1946

(2) *Caroline Sibell; *b* 14 Sept 1948; *m* *Keith Brian and has:

1a *Victoria; *b* 28 Sept 1983

(3) *Elizabeth Julian; *b* 12 Sept 1950

(4) *Mary Patricia; *b* 12 March 1953; *m* 1984 *Robert John Elkington, s of J D R Elkington, of Haworth House, Kintbury, Berks, and has:

1a *Edwina Amy Charlotte; *b* 1989

1 Mary Sibell; *b* 3 Oct 1902; *m* 27 Nov 1928 3rd and last Baron Alington (*d* 17 Sept 1940; see 1940 edn) and *d* 2 Aug 1936, leaving issue

2 Dorothea Louise; *b* 29 April 1907; OStJ; *m* 23 July 1935 1st Viscount Head (*qv*) and *d* 1987, leaving issue

3 Lettice Mildred Mary ; *b* 12 Feb 1911; Flt/Offr WAAF (despatches) WW II, OStJ

SHAKERLEY

Arms: Arg. a chevron vert between three hillocks of the second. **Crest:** A hare ppr., resting her forefeet on a garb or. **Motto:** *Moriendo vivam* ('By dying I will live'). **Creation:** Bt. (UK) 30 July 1838.

SIR GEOFFREY ADAM SHAKERLEY, 6TH Bt, of Somerford Park, Co Chester [Sir Geoffrey Shakerley Bt, 57 Artesian Rd, London W2 5BD]; *b* 9 Dec 1932; *s f* 1970; *educ* Harrow and Trin Coll Oxford (BA 1956); 2nd Lt KRRC 1952–53, dir Photographic Records Ltd 1970–; author: *Henry Moore Sculpture in Landscape* (1978), *The English Dog at Home* (1986); *m* 1st 3 July 1962 Virginia Elizabeth (*d* 25 Jan 1968), est dau of William Eric Brands Maskell, of Little Down, Duncton, W Sussex, by Mrs J R Hawkins, and has:

1 +NICHOLAS SIMON ADAM; *b* 20 Dec 1963

2 +Peter Jonathan; *b* 9 Feb 1966

Sir GEOFFREY *m* 2nd 27 July 1972 *Lady Elizabeth Georgiana, sis of 5th Earl of Lichfield (*qv*), and by her has:

1 *Fiona Elizabeth Fenella; *b* 18 Aug 1973

Lineage: GEOFFREY SHAKERLEY, of Shakerley, Lancs; living *temp* HENRY VII; *m* 1st Joan, sis of Robert Langley, of Edgecroft; *m* 2nd Anne (*dsp* by him), widow of John Legh, of Booths, Cheshire, and dau of Sir William Booth, of Dunham Massey, Cheshire, and had by his 1st w, with a yr s (William; living 1536) and a dau (Margaret, *dsp*):

PETER SHAKERLEY, of Shakerley; living *temp* HENRY VIII; *m* Elizabeth, dau and heiress of John Legh, of Booths (s of John Legh, of Booths, by Elizabeth, dau and coheir of Robert Grosvenor, of Hulme, Cheshire), and had:

GEOFFREY SHAKERLEY, of Hulme; *m* 1st —, dau of Lawrence Holland; *m* 2nd Isabella, dau of Thomas Venables, Baron (a local dignity [not a peerage of Parliament] found in the Palatinate of Chester) of Kinderton, and *d* 5 June 1547, having had, with five yr sons and four daus:

PETER SHAKERLEY, of Hulme; *m* Elizabeth, dau and coheir of Sir Randal Mainwaring, of Over Peover, Cheshire, and *d* 6 Jan 1553, leaving an est s:

GEOFFREY SHAKERLEY, of Hulme; Sheriff Cheshire 1610; *m* Jane, dau of Sir George Beeston, of Beeston, Cheshire, and *d* 1618, having had, with other issue:

HUGH SHAKERLEY; *m* Margaret, dau of Thomas Bunbury, of Stanney, and *dvp*, leaving:

PETER SHAKERLEY, of Hulme; *m* Margaret (*m* 2nd William Vernon, the Cheshire antiquary), dau of William Oldfield, of Bradwell, and had:

Sir GEOFFREY SHAKERLEY, of Hulme; *b c* 1618; royalist Civil War; *m* 1st Katherine (*d* 4 April 1673), dau of William Pennington, of Muncaster, Cumberland (*see* 1917 edn MUNCASTER, B), and had two sons (Peter, of Hulme, Govr Chester, *m* Elizabeth, dau of Sir Thomas Mainwaring, 1st Bt, of Over Peover (*see* 1934 edn), and *dsp* 1726; Geoffrey, *m* Frances, dau of Francis Keynell, of the Island of Nevis, and *dsp*) and two daus; *m* 2nd Jane, dau of John Dolben, of Segroyt, Denbighs, and *d* 1696, having by her had, with a yst twin s (John, *dsp* 1709):

GEORGE SHAKERLEY, of Hulme and Gwersyllt; *m* Anne (*d* 1767), dau of Sir Walter Bagot, of Blythfield, Staffs, and *d* 2 Feb 1756, having had, with three other sons, including an er s (Geoffrey, *b* 1706, *m* Anne (*m* 2nd 11 Jan 1738 10th Viscount Kilmorey and had issue; *see* KILMOREY, E), dau and coheir of John Hurleston, of Newton, Cheshire, and *dsp* 1733), and a dau (Frances, *m* 1748 Sir Watkin Williams-Wynn, 3rd Bt; *qv*):

PETER SHAKERLEY, of Hulme; *m* 1st Ann, dau of John Amson, of Lees; *m* 2nd 13 March 1765 Margaret (*dsp* by him), dau of Roger Morris, of Netherby, and by his 1st w had:

ELIZABETH Shakerley; *m* 20 March 1764 Charles BUCKWORTH (*d* 22 Aug 1783), of Park Place, Berks, and *d* 27 Sept 1811, having had, with other issue, including two yr sons (Peter Everard, of Englefield Green, Surrey, *b* 11 Aug 1768, *m* Julia, dau of Sir Thomas Blackhall, and *d* Jan 1840, having had issue; Joseph Francis, of Wootton, Beds, *b* 30 Jan 1770, *m* Mary, dau of Sir Philip Monoux, 5th Bt, and *d* 1846):

CHARLES WATKIN JOHN BUCKWORTH later SHAKERLEY (Act of Parl 1788), of Somerford Park, Cheshire; *b* 15 June 1767; High Sheriff Cheshire 1791; *m* Dorothy (*d* 1820), dau of Jacob Moreland, of Copplethwaite Hall, Westmorland, and *d* 20 Sept 1834, leaving, with a yr s (Geoffrey Joseph, of Whatcroft Hall, Cheshire, *b* 25 March 1800, *m* 25 April 1827 Eleanor Maria (*d* 16 Oct 1889), dau of Rev James Webster, of Ashfield, Co Longford, and *d* 14 May 1878, leaving issue) and a dau (Frances Margaretta, *m* 1st 26 Nov 1816 Vigors Hervey (*d* 25 Aug 1828), of Killiane Castle, Co Wexford, and 2nd 1832 Thomas Read Kemp, MP, and *d* his widow 28 Aug 1860):

Sir Charles Peter Shakerley, 1st Bt (UK), so cr 30 July 1838, of Somerford Park; *b* 27 Dec 1792; *m* 1st 26 Feb 1819 Laure Angelique Rosalba, dau of the Duke d'Avaray; *m* 2nd 20 Dec 1831 Jessie Matilda (*d* 8 Aug 1902), dau of James Scott, of Rotherfield Park, Hants (*see* SCOTT, Bt, of Rotherfield), and *d* 14 Sept 1857, leaving, with a dau (Gertrude, *m* 11 Dec 1860 Lt-Col Charles Milligan (*d* 18 Nov 1902), of Caldwell Hall, Derbys, and *d* 26 Jan 1912, leaving issue):

Sir Charles Watkin Shakerley, 2nd Bt, KCB, JP, DL Cheshire; *b* 27 March 1833; High Sheriff Cheshire 1863; *m* 14 July 1858 Georgiana Harriett (*d* 16 Jan 1907) er dau and coheir of George Holland Ackers, of Moreton Hall, Cheshire, and *d* 20 Oct 1898, leaving:

1 **Sir Walter Geoffrey Shakerley, 3rd Bt**, CBE (1919); *b* 26 Nov 1859; Lt KRRC, Hon Col 7th Bn Cheshire Regt, cmded 7th Bn 1891–1909 and 2nd/7th Bn WW I 1914–16; *m* 7 Jan 1885 Hilda Mary, CBE (1920), DGStJ (*d* 19 March 1927), only dau of Henry Hodgson, of Currarevagh, Co Galway, and *d* 11 Jan 1943, leaving:

(1) Mabel Beatrice; *b* 4 Aug 1889; *m* 16 Dec 1913 Oswald James Walter Napier, s of Arthur Sampson Napier, DLitt, PhD, of Merton College, Oxford. He *d* 9 Jan 1966

(2) Marguerite Irene; *b* 18 Feb 1893; *m* 3 Jan 1923 Walter Nigel Usher Dunlop, ICS, er surv s of David Jugurtha Dunlop, and *d* 2 Sept 1965, leaving issue

(3) Sylvia Mary; *b* 26 July 1900; *m* 1st 16 July 1924 (*divorce* 1939) Sir Arthur Wynne Morgan Bryant, CBE, est s of Sir Francis Morgan Bryant, CVO, CBE, ISO; *m* 2nd 17 Jan 1942 Frank Derek Chew, RA, and *d* 1950

(4) Moira Veronica; *b* 12 Sept 1901; *m* 22 April 1924 Cdr Douglas Samuel Loram, RD, RNR, only s of Edwin Loram, of Okehampton, Devon, and had:

1a *Roy; *b* 21 Feb 1926; *m* 25 April 1953 *Susan Anne Dennys Parry, dau of William Llywelyn Parry de Winton, and has:

1b *Anthony David John; *b* 7 Oct 1957

2b *William Geoffrey Walter; *b* 16 June 1961

3b *Peter Henry James; *b* 12 Oct 1962

1b *Amanda Philippa Anne; *b* 15 Nov 1954

2a *Ronald Geoffrey; *b* 22 May 1927; late Lt RN; *m* 19 Oct 1963 *Caroline Jennifer, est dau of Henry Bartlett, of W Kirby, Cheshire, and has:

    1b *Richard William Geoffrey; *b* 15 Feb 1967

    1b *Annabel Elizabeth; *b* 27 Jan 1965

    2b *Mary Caroline; *b* 18 Jan 1970

2 GEORGE HERBERT (Sir), **4th Bt**

3 Ernest Alfred SHAKERLEY later SHAKERLEY-HOWELL (roy licence 29 Jan 1927), of Ethy, Lostwithiel, Cornwall, JP W R Yorks and Liberty of Ripon; *b* 20 Sept 1866; Maj DCLI Boer War 1899–1902 (despatches, Queen's medal with four clasps, King's medal with two clasps), Staff-Capt Rlwy Tport 1914; *m* 7 Sept 1905 Rhoda Mary Louisa (*d* 23 March 1934), er dau of Francis Buller Howell, DL, of Ethy (*see* HEYWOOD, Bt), and *d* 22 Feb 1934, leaving:

(1) Peter Francis SHAKERLEY-HOWELL later SHAKERLEY, OBE (1945); *b* 29 July 1906; *educ* Clifton; Hon Col RA WW II (despatches twice), Order Orange Nassau; *m* 10 March 1934 Alison May (*d* 1992), dau of Alexander Sands, of Aberdeen, and *d* 1994, leaving:

    1a +(Geoffrey) Clive Howell [Clive Shakerley Esq, Tredudwell Manor, Lanteglos-by-Fowey, Cornwall]; *b* 5 Aug 1935; *educ* Radley and St Edmund Hall Oxford (BA 1959); *m* 20 March 1965 *Rosanna Ruth, yr dau of Thomas Philip Barneby, of The Hill, Duloe, Cornwall, and has:

       1b +Alastair Justin Charles; *b* 3 April 1972

       1b *Alison Clare; *b* 17 April 1970

    2a +(Peter) Gavin David [Maj Gavin Shakerley, Pont House, Lanteglos-by-Fowey, Cornwall PL23 1LX]; *b* 18 June 1950; *educ* Radley and Durham U (BA 1975); Maj Irish Gds; *m* 1976 *Margaret Ann, dau of Bernard Hammond, of Chichester, and has:

       1b +(Charles) Alaister; *b* 1981

       1b *Antonia Elizabeth; *b* 1983

    1a *Angela Madeleine; *b* 12 March 1938; *m* 1st 23 Aug 1958 (*divorce* 1978) William Trevor Stephens, of Australia, s of William Frederick Stephens, of Toxteth Park, Liverpool, and has:

       1b *Richard Gwyn; *b* 25 May 1961

       2b *John Angelo; *b* 12 Nov 1963

       3b *David Paul; *b* 22 March 1965

       1b *Teresa Madeline; *b* 29 June 1959

    1a (cont.) Mr and Mrs William Stephens also adopted:

       *Patrick Joseph; *b* 8 May 1962

       *Sandie Patricia; *b* 5 June 1966

    1a (cont.) Mrs Angela Stephens *m* 2nd 1978 Harry Dudley Phillips (*d* 1982) and by him has:

       4b *Harry Sydney; *b* 1977

    2a *Dawn Michelle Alison [Mrs Dawn Knight, 21d Russell Cres, Rotarua 3201, New Zealand]; *b* 30 March 1942; *m* 1 May 1965 *Peter Joseph Knight, s of William Joseph Botolph Knight, of Penzance, Cornwall, and has:

       1b *Timothy William Francis; *b* 11 April 1968

       1b *Karen Francesca; *b* 18 Feb 1966; *m* 26 July 1986 *Richard Mallinson and has:

          1c *James Sean; *b* 15 April 1992

          1c *Kate Judith; *b* 7 Aug 1994

       2b *Sarah Melody Foye; *b* 21 Aug 1969; *m* 23 Nov 1991 *Christopher Bramwell Jans and has:

          1c *Danielle Frances; *b* 16 Oct 1989

          2c *Zöe Rose; *b* 26 Sept 1995

(1) Denise Marian; *b* 3 Sept 1907; *m* 26 Nov 1935 James Leslie Byrne Perceval (*d* 1945), only s of James Byrne Perceval, of Sydney, NSW, and *d* 24 Sept 1994, leaving:

    1a *Francis James [Francis Perceval Esq, 146 Matthew Flinders Dve, Cooee Bay, Rockhampton 4073, Australia]; *b* 15 Jan 1937; *educ* James Cook U N Qld; Capt Australian Army (ret 1984), Vietnam 1971–72; *m* 1st 12 Nov 1960 (*divorce* 1980) Judith Ann, yr dau of S F Spinks, of Langley Burrell, Chippenham; *m* 2nd 1987 *Patricia Almond and by his 1st w has:

       1b *Christiaan Byrne Joseph Perceval; *b* 27 July 1968

       1b *Antoinette Mary; *b* 3 Feb 1962

       2b *Lucinda Eleanor; *b* 31 Dec 1963

    2a *Anthony Ernest [Anthony Perceval Esq, 7 Waverley Rd, St Albans, Herts AL3 5PB]; *b* 1 Aug 1938; *educ* Lincoln Coll Oxford; *m* 5 June 1965 (*divorce* 1981) Jennifer, er dau of Charles Cyril Mason, of Drake's Court, Fishers Pond, Hants, and has:

       1b *Jane Lucinda; *b* 13 April 1966

       2b *Katherine; *b* 9 July 1969

    3a John Adrian; *b* 31 March 1945; *d* 1987

    1a *Sara Mary [Mrs Robert Baker, Lucehayne, Widworthy, Devon EX14 9JS]; *b* 1 Aug 1942; *m* 1982 *Robert Edward Nicolas Baker, barrister

(2) *Kathleen Dorothy [Mrs Robert Hall, 14 Hill Lands, Wargrave, Berks RG10 8JY]; *b* 12 June 1914; *m* 20 June 1942 Robert Arnold Hall (*d* 19 May 1962), er s of Arnold Percy Hall, of Wimbledon, and has:

    1a *Peter Arnold [Peter Hall Esq, Maple Tree House, Finch Lane, Knotty Green, Bucks HP9 2TL]; *b* 7 April 1943; *educ* Harrow; slr 1969; *m* 1971 *Gillian Mary Stuart, only dau of John Clark, of Gillan Cove House, Gillan, Cornwall, and has:

       1b *Nicholas Robert Stuart Arnold; *b* 1974

       1b *Camilla Jane Kathleen; *b* 1976

       2b *Venetia Juliet Antonia; *b* 1981

    2a *Jeremy Arnold [Jeremy Hall Esq, 11 Egerton Rd, Wallingford, Oxon OX10 0HP]; *b* 13 Nov 1949; *educ* Bearwood Coll; *m* 1971 (*divorce* 1989) Julia Rosa, only child of Frank Alexander, of Reading, and has:

       1b *Laurence Alexander; *b* 1977

       1b *Charlotte Louise; *b* 1979

1a *Juliet Rosalind [Mrs Juliet Perkins, Flat 6, 30 Church Lane, London SW19 3HQ]; *b* 19 Feb 1946; *m* 1971 (*divorce* 1987) Christopher Charles Perkins and has:

    1b *Daniel Robert; *b* 1977

    1b *Esther Catherine; *b* 1979

The 3rd Bt's bro,

    Sir GEORGE HERBERT SHAKERLEY later SHAKERLEY-ACKERS (roy licence 8 Jan 1908) later still SHAKERLEY, **4th Bt**, of Duddleswell Manor, Uckfield, Sussex, JP Cheshire; *b* 27 Sept 1863; Lt KRRC, Capt and Hon Maj 5th Vol Bn Cheshire Regt; *m* 22 Jan 1891 Evelyn Mary (*d* 20 June 1953), 2nd dau of Col Charles Hosken France-Hayhurst, DL, JP, of Bostock Hall, Cheshire, and *d* 7 Aug 1945, having had, with three daus (Gladys Mary, *b* 19 Feb 1892, *d* 22 May 1978; Isabel Violet, *b* 5 Nov 1893, *d* 26 Nov 1989; Phyllis Evelyn, *b* 26 July 1903, *d* unm 25 May 1972):

Sir Cyril Holland Shakerley, 5th Bt, JP (W Sussex 1937), DL (Sussex 1949); *b* 28 Feb 1897; *educ* Harrow and RMC Sandhurst; Lt KRRC, Maj 4th Bn Cheshire Regt, RFC and RAF, WWs I and II; *m* 26 June 1928 Elizabeth Averil (*d* 28 Aug 1990), MBE (1955), er dau of Edward Gwynne Eardley-Wilmot (*see* EARDLEY-WILMOT, Bt), and *d* 21 Aug 1970, leaving:

1 Sir GEOFFREY ADAM SHAKERLEY, **6th and present Bt**

2 +Charles Frederick Eardley [Charles Shakerley Esq, Cudworth Manor, Newdigate, Surrey RH5 5BH]; *b* 14 June 1934; *educ* Harrow, Ch Ch Oxford (BA 1956, MA) and U of Pennsylvania; ptnr Sheppards & Chase, chm Provincial Insur and Provincial Life Assur 1977; *m* 27 Feb 1962 *Lucy Carolyn, er dau of Francis St George Fisher, of Cragg, Cockermouth, Cumberland, and has:

    (1) *Eleanor Jane; *b* 24 Sept 1963

    (2) *Victoria Lee; *b* 7 March 1966; *m* 1990 *Maj Charles William Nepean Crewdson, 9th/12th Roy Lancers, s of John Crewdson, of Sinster House, Winster, Cumbria

    (3) *Philippa Patricia Alice; *b* 14 March 1970; *m* 17 Dec 1997 *Maj William Grace, yr s of Antony Grace

1 *Jane Eve [Mrs David Phillips, The Old Rectory, Stedham, Sussex GU29 0NQ]; *b* 6 April 1930; *m* 1 May 1963 *David William Phillips, yr s of Capt Percival Phillips, of Paignton, Devon, and has:

    (1) *Katherine Elizabeth; *b* 16 Feb 1966; *m* 1992 *Leonard J Wadstein, of Cannes, and has:

       1a *Alexander James; *b* 19 March 1996

       1a *Georgina Kate; *b* 6 June 1994

SHAKESPEARE

Arms: Or on a bend between in chief a portcullis and in base an anchor sa. a spear of the field. **Crest:** In front of a portcullis sa. an eagle rising, grasping with the dexter claw a spear or, barbed arg. **Creation:** Bt. (UK) 11 July 1942.

Thomas (Tom) William Shakespeare [Dr Tom Shakespeare, 13 Wood Terrace, Bill Quay, Gateshead, Tyne and Wear NE10 0UD]; *b* 11 May 1966; s f 1996 (does not use title); *educ* Radley, Pembroke Coll Cambridge (BA 1987, MA 1990) and King's Coll Cambridge (MPhil 1991, PhD 1995); lecturer sociology Sunderland U 1993–95, Research Fell Sociology Leeds U 1996–; co-author *The Sexual Politics of Disability* (1996), ed *The Disability Reader* (1998)

Lineage: HUMPHREY SHAKESPEARE, of Feckenham, Worcs, and Ipsley, Warwicks; *m* 28 March 1649 Elinor Scale and was *bur* 28 March 1689, leaving:

1 Humphrey, of Ipsley; *bapt* Nov 1651; *m* 3 July 1689 Anne Raber (*bur* 8 July 1690) and was *bur* 10 Jan 1700/1

2 John, of Ipsley; *bapt* 24 June 1655; *bur* 14 Nov 1694

3 William SHAKESPEARE *alias* SHAKSBY, of Ipsley; *bapt* 28 Dec 1656; *m* Ursula — and was *bur* 4 Oct 1711, having had issue

4 Charles; *bapt* 30 Dec 1660; *bur* 1662

5 Henry; *bapt* 19 Oct 1662

6 Thomas, of Ipsley and Studley, Warwicks; *bapt* 25 June 1665; *m* Jane — (*bur* 22 May 1709) and *d* in or after 1700, leaving, with three daus:

    (1) John; living 1700

    (2) WILLIAM, of whom presently

(3) Humphrey; *bapt* 24 March 1704; *bur* 1709

1 Ursula; *bapt* 27 March 1653; *m* 17 Aug 1676 John Turner *alias* Bant and was *bur* 2 Dec 1702, having had issue

The gs,

WILLIAM SHAKESPEARE, of Studley and later Preston Bagott, Warwicks; *bapt* 1 Feb 1696; *m* Elizabeth — (*d* by 23 March 1767) and was *bur* 10 March 1767, having had, with a yr s (Thomas, *bapt* 8 April 1733, witnessed his bro's marriage, *bur* 7 Dec 1759):

JOHN SHAKESPEARE, of Preston Bagott; *bapt* 30 Aug 1730; yeoman; *m* 26 Oct 1756 Mary Mugg (living 1769) and was *bur* 6 Nov 1768, having had, with two yr sons (John, of Preston Bagott, *bapt* 21 Aug 1759, *m* Nov 1797 Hannah Padge (*d* 21 Aug 1841 aged 70) and *d* 13 Jan 1840, having had issue; Thomas, *bapt* 8 April 1761):

WILLIAM SHAKESPEARE, of Henley-in-Arden, Warwicks; *bapt* 4 May 1757; *m* 27 Nov 1776 Mary Hancox (*bur* 28 Feb 1821 aged 70) and had seven sons and a dau; the 2nd s:

WILLIAM SHAKESPEARE, of Henley-in-Arden and Beaudesert; *bapt* 29 Nov 1778; *m* Charlotte — (*d* 23 April 1852 aged 66) and was *bur* 31 May 1822, having had, with two er sons (William, *bapt* 20 March 1808, *bur* 20 June 1830; George, *bapt* 6 May 1810, *bur* 26 Oct 1824) and three daus:

Rev BENJAMIN SHAKESPEARE, of Kilham, Yorks, and St Mark's Crescent, Regent's Park, London; *b* 5 May 1817; Baptist min; *m* 1st — but had no issue; *m* 2nd 21 Nov 1854 Mary Ann (*d* 10 July 1886 aged 61), dau of Rev John Hithersay, Baptist min, of Kilham, and *d* 20 Dec 1887, having by her had, with an er s (Alfred William, of Chatham Close, Golders Green, *b* 14 Nov 1855, *m* 4 Jan 1888 Ethel Maud (*d* 12 Nov 1939 aged 85), dau of Samuel Culley, of Norwich, and *dsp* 9 Sept 1940) and a dau (Charlotte Ellen, *b* 23 Oct 1859, *m* Henry Deshayes):

Rev JOHN HOWARD SHAKESPEARE, of Finchley; *b* 16 April 1857; MA Lond, DD Glasgow; Baptist min, 1st Moderator Free Ch Fed Cncl; *m* 5 Sept 1883 Amy Gertrude, dau of Rev William Goodman, of Finchley, and *d* 12 March 1928, leaving:

1 William Goodman; *b* 24 April 1890; MRCS, LRCP, MO Wychcrest Sch, Med Ref Min Labour Malvern, Maj RAMC, Medaille de la Reconnaissance Française; *m* 1 Jan 1927 Ruth Maude, yr dau of William Etty Potter, of Old BurslEdon, Hants, and had:

(1) *John William Richmond, MVO (1968); *b* 11 June 1930; *educ* Winchester and Trin Coll Oxford (MA); Lt Irish Gds (RARO), Br Embassy Staff Rio de Janeiro 1966–69; *m* 15 April 1955 *Lalage Ann, 3rd dau of Stuart Petre Brodie Mais, FRSA, of Bliss House, Finches Gdns, Lindfield, Sussex, and has:

1a *Nicholas; *b* 3 March 1957; *educ* Shrewsbury and Cambridge; jnlst, broadcaster, lit ed *Daily Telegraph*, author: *The Vision of Elena Silves* (novel, 1989)

2a *Christopher; *b* 22 June 1962

3a *Sebastian; *b* 18 June 1965

1a *Amanda Juliet Rosalind; *b* 30 Jan 1960

(1) *Anne; *b* 15 Jan 1934; *m* 12 March 1960 *Patrick Bernard Turner, s of Capt Evelyn Lennox Turner, IA, and has had:

1a Jeremy Patrick; *b* 14 May, *d* 14 June 1962

2a *Dominic Timothy Patrick; *b* 14 Jan 1964

3a *Benjamin Patrick; *b* 7 Jan 1967

1a *Annabel Lee; *b* 19 Feb 1961

2 GEOFFREY HITHERSAY (Sir), **1st Bt**

3 John Hope; *b* 2 Sept 1906; *d* 20 Jan 1940

1 Mary Arden; *b* 8 May 1896; *m* 1928 Donald Saxby McWilliams and had:

(1) *Mary Joanna; *b* 23 Oct 1929; *m* 1957 *José Mira, of Madrid

(2) *Jane Shakespeare; *b* 25 May 1932; *m* 1956 *Ladis Kristof, of Chicago

The Rev JOHN SHAKESPEARE's 2nd s,

Sir Geoffrey Hithersay Shakespeare, 1st Bt (UK), so *cr* 11 July 1942, PC (1945); *b* 23 Sept 1893; *educ* Highgate Sch and Emmanuel Coll Cambridge (BA and LLB 1920, MA 1921, Pres Union 1920); barrister Middle Temple 1921, Capt 5th Bn Norfolk Regt WW I, MP (Lib) Wellingborough 1922–23 and Norwich 1929–45, Priv Sec to PM 1921–22, Jr Ld Treasury and Lib Nat Ch Whip 1931–32, Parly Sec Min Health 1932–36 and Bd Educn 1936–37, Parly and Fin Sec Admlty 1937–40, Parly Sec Dept Overseas Trade April–May 1940, U-Sec Dominion Affrs and Chm Children's Overseas Reception Bd 1940–42, V-Chm Govrs Westminster Hosp 1948–63, Pres Soc Br Gas Industs 1953–54, Chm Industl Co-Partnership Assoc 1957; *m* 1st 16 Sept 1926 Aimée Constance (*d* 14 Feb 1950), widow of Cdr Sir Thomas Fisher, KBE, RN, and dau of Walter Loveridge, of Cobham, Staffs, and had:

1 **Sir William Geoffrey Shakespeare, 2nd Bt**; *b* 12 Oct 1927; *educ* Radley, Clare Coll Cambridge (MA 1957) and St George's Hosp (MB and BChir 1958); DCH 1961, GP Aylesbury 1968–87, paediatric registrar Roy Bucks and assoc Hosps, clinical assist Dermatology Dept Roy Bucks Hosp, hosp practitioner Manor Ho Hosp Aylesbury 1972–96, Snowdon Working Party (Integration of Handicapped) 1974–76, V-Pres Nat PHAB 1977 and RGA 1982–96, medical advsr Bucks Adoption Panel 1987–96, Tstee Shakespeare Globe Tst 1992–96; *m* 3 June 1964 *Susan Mary [Lady Shakespeare, Manor Cottage, Stoke Mandeville, Bucks HP22 5XA], 2nd dau of A Douglas Raffel, of Colombo, Ceylon, and *d* 12 March 1996, leaving:

(1) THOMAS WILLIAM SHAKESPEARE, **3rd and present Bt**

(2) +JAMES DOUGLAS GEOFFREY; *b* 12 Feb 1971; heir presumptive; *educ* Radley and Fitzwilliam Coll Cambridge (BA 1993)

1 Judith Anne; *b* 9 May 1931; *educ* North Foreland Lodge; *d* 31 Oct 1949

Sir Geoffrey *m* 2nd 29 Feb 1952 *Elizabeth [Elizabeth Lady Shakespeare, Flat 6, Great Ash, Lubbock Rd, Chislehurst, Kent BR7 5JZ], Section Offr WAAF 1940–45 (despatches, Bronze Star USA), Freeman City London 1974, er dau of Brig Robert William Hare, CMG, DSO, DL (*see* LISTOWEL, E), and *d* 1980

SHANNON

VIVIT · POST · FUNERA · VIRTUS

SPECTEMUR · AGENDO

Arms: Per bend crenellé arg. and gu. a crescent for difference. **Crest:** Out of a ducal coronet or a lion's head erased per pale crenellée arg. and gu., a crescent for difference. **Supporters:** Two lions, per pale crenellée, the dexter gu. and arg., the sinister arg. and gu., each charged with a crescent for difference. **Mottoes:** 1 *Vivit post funera virtus* ('Virtue lives after death'), 2 *Spectemur agendo* ('Let us be judged by our actions'). **Creations:** E. V. and B. (Castle Martyr) (I) 17 April 1756, B. (GB) 6 Aug 1786 (Carleton).

THE 9TH EARL OF SHANNON, Viscount Boyle of Bandon, Co Cork, **Baron of Castle Martyr**, Co Cork, and **Baron Carleton**, of Carleton, Co York (Richard Bentinck Boyle) [The Rt Hon The Earl of Shannon, Pimm's Cottage, Man's Hill, Burghfield Common, Berks RG7 3BD]; *b* 23 Oct 1924; *s f* 1963; *educ* Eton; late Capt Irish Gds, dir Conf Industl Research Assoc and Ctee Dirs Research Assoc, chm and md J Starkie Gardner Ltd 1960–69, Pres Architectural Metal Craftsmens' Assoc 1966–69, fndr chm Fndn Science and Technology 1977–83, Provincial Grand Master Masonic Province of Surrey 1967–; FRSA, FIMgt, FBHI; *m* 1st 17 Sept 1947 (*divorce* 1955) Donna Catherine Irene Helen (Katie Boyle, broadcaster), dau of Marquis Demetrio Imperiali di Francavilla; *m* 2nd 25 May 1957 (*divorce* 1979) Susan Margaret Rogers, dau of John Percy Russell Hogg and step-dau of Lt-Col Wilfrid Edmund Rogers; *m* 3rd 1994 *Almine, dau of Rocco Catorsia de Villiers, of Cape Town, and by his 2nd w has:

1 +RICHARD HENRY JOHN, *Viscount Boyle*; *b* 19 Jan 1960

1 *Georgina Susan; *b* 7 Feb 1961

2 *Caroline Mary Victoria [The Lady Caroline Waters, Snowberry Cottage, Somerswey, Shalford, Surrey GU4 8EQ]; *b* 12 Oct 1965; *m* 1990 *Mark Nowell Waters, only s of P N Waters, of Guildford, and has:

(1) *Oliver Robert Nowell; *b* 1991

(2) *Max Alexander; *b* 1993

Previous creations: The **1st Earl of Shannon**'s uncle had been created in 1660 Viscount Shannon and his first cousin Lord Clifford of Lanesborough's second son (who through the **2nd Earl of Shannon**'s mother was also the latter's great-uncle) had been created in 1714 Baron Carlton (*see* CORK and ORRERY, E). The former title expired with the death of the grantee's grandson in 1740; the latter was even shorter-lived, expiring with its original grantee and only holder in 1725.

Two other Baronies of Carleton have existed. The earlier, under its full name 'Carleton of Imbercourt', was conferred in 1626 on Sir Dudley Carleton, a Privy Counsellor and official at CHARLES I's court who was promoted Viscount Dorchester two years later and died three and a half years later still, when both peerages expired. The later creation, the Barony of Carleton of Anner to give it its full name, was conferred on Hugh Carleton, son of a Corkonian merchant, in 1789. Eight years later he was promoted Viscount Carleton of Clare, chiefly to bribe him into supporting the Union of British and Irish Parliaments (both these late-18th-century creations were in the Irish peerage). On his death without issue in 1826 his titles expired with him.

Lineage: The 1st EARL OF ORRERY (*see* CORK and ORRERY, E) had a 2nd s:

HENRY BOYLE, of Castle Martyr, Co Cork; *m* Lady Mary O'Brien, dau of 1st Earl of Inchiquin (*see* INCHIQUIN, B), and *d* 1693 on campaign in Flanders, having had:

1 Roger; *d* unm 1705

2 HENRY, **1st Earl**

3 Charles; Capt RN cmdg HMS *Bristol*

4 William; Capt Schomberg's Horse, Commr Appeals Ireland; *m* Martha Beaufoy, dau and heiress of Sir Samuel Garth, Physician Forces Ireland, and *d* 1725, leaving:

(1) Henry; Capt of Horse; *d* 14 Feb 1756

(2) Robert; *dsp*, when his estates in Berks, Norfolk and Oxon passed to his sisters

1 Beaufoy; *m* 11 June 1736 John Wilder, of Nunhide, Berks

2 Henrietta; *m* 9 Dec 1736 William Nichols, of Froyle, Bucks

3 Elizabeth; *m* 9 Oct 1736 Matthew Graves, of Chiswick, and had issue

The 2nd s,

HENRY BOYLE, **1st Earl of Shannon**, so *cr* 17 April 1756, as also BARON OF CASTLE MARTYR, Co Cork, and VISCOUNT BOYLE OF BANDON, Co Cork (all I), PC (I 1733); *b c* 1686; *educ* Ch Ch Oxford; MP (I Parl) Midleton 1707–11, Kilmallock 1713–15 and Co Cork 1715–56, Speaker I H of C 1733–56, Chllr I Exchequer 1733–35 and 1739, Commr Revenue Ireland 1735–39, LLD Trin Coll Dublin 1735; *m* 1st 1715 Catherine (*dsp* 5 May 1725), dau of Chidley Coote, of Kilmallock (*see* COOTE, Bt); *m* 2nd Sept 1726 his cousin Henrietta (*d* 13 Dec 1746), yst dau of 3rd Earl of Cork (*see* CORK and ORRERY, E), and by her had:

1 RICHARD, **2nd Earl**

2 Henry BOYLE later BOYLE-WALSINGHAM; *m* Lucy (*m* 2nd 20 March 1760 1st Viscount Clifden (*see* 1970 edn) and *d* 26 July 1802), est dau of Col John Martin, and *d* 1756, having had:

(1) Henry; *d* 1757

3 William; *d* 1748

4 Charles; *m* 1755 Henrietta, only dau of James Price, and *d* 1758, leaving:

(1) John, of Bafford Hall, Co Dublin; *b* 1758; *m* 1799 Eleanor, dau of R Taylor, and *d* 1809, having had, with a dau (Alice Mary, *d* an infant 1802):

1a William Edwin; *b* 1801; *m* 1839 Mary, dau of Thomas Redfern, of Leicester, and *d* Dec 1840, leaving:

1b William Richard; *b* 12 Oct 1840; *m* 1861 Elizabeth (*d* 1874), dau of H Bates, of Nottingham, and *d* 10 July 1902, leaving:

1c Charlotte Mary; *m* 1884 James Martin-Langley and had issue

2c Dora; *b* 15 Feb 1878

5 Robert BOYLE later BOYLE-WALSINGHAM; *b* 1736; MP Dungarvan, Knaresborough and Fowey; *m* 17 July 1759 Charlotte (*d* 1790), 2nd dau and coheir of Sir Charles Hanbury-Williams, KB (*see* SUDELEY, B), and was lost aboard the man-of-war *Thunderer*, which he cmded, in a West Indian hurricane Oct 1779, having had:

(1) Richard; *b* 1762; *d* 1788

(1) CHARLOTTE, BARONESS DE ROS (*qv*) OF HELMSLEY in her own right

1 Juliana; *m* 18 May 1745 1st Earl of Carrick (*qv*) and *d* 22 Feb 1804, leaving issue

The 1st EARL *d* 28 Dec 1764; his est s,

RICHARD BOYLE, **2nd Earl of Shannon**, KP (1783), PC (I 1763–70 and 1774); *b* 30 Jan 1727/8; *educ* Trin Coll Dublin; MP (I Parl) Dungarvan 1749–60 and Co Cork 1761–64, Master Gen Ordnance Ireland 1766–70, Muster Master and Clerk Cheque Armies in Ireland 1774–81, V-Treas Ireland 1781–89; *cr* 6 Aug 1786 BARON CARLETON, of Carleton, Co York (GB); *m* 15 Dec 1763 Catherine (*d* 30 Jan 1827), sis of 1st Baron Ponsonby of Imokilly (*see* BESSBOROUGH, E), and *d* 20 May 1807, leaving, with a dau (Catherine Henrietta, *m* 12 Feb 1784 1st Earl of Bandon (*d* 26 Nov 1830) *see* 1970 edn) and *d* 8 July 1815, leaving issue):

HENRY BOYLE, **3rd Earl of Shannon**, KP (1808), PC (I 1809); *b* 8 Aug 1771; *educ* Winchester; MP (I Parl) Cloghnikelty 1794–97, Co Cork 1797–1800 and (UK Parl as Tory) 1801–07 and Bandon 15–20 May 1807, Co Cork: custos rotulorum 1807–42 and Ld Lt 1831–42, Clerk Pells Ireland 1808–22; *m* 7 June 1798 Sarah (*d* 6 Sept 1820), 4th dau of John Hyde, of Castle Hyde, Co Cork, and had, with six daus (*d* unm):

1 Richard, *b* 22 Feb 1802; *d* aged *c* 12 months

2 RICHARD, **4th Earl**

3 Henry Charles; *b* 10 Nov 1815; Army Offr; *m* 22 Sept 1841 Catherine Sophronia Jane (*d* 15 July 1844), 2nd dau of James Ede, of Ridgway Castle, Hants, and *dsp* 6 April 1846

4 Robert Francis; *b* 6 Oct 1818; Capt RN; *m* 2 Oct 1858 Elizabeth (*d* 18 Dec 1889), only dau of Capt W Hole, RN, of Bideford, Devon, and *dsp* 20 Jan 1883

The 3rd EARL *d* 22 April 1842; his est surv s,

RICHARD BOYLE, **4th Earl of Shannon**; *b* 12 May 1809; MP (Whig) Co Cork 1830–32; *m* 28 May 1832 Emily Henrietta (*d* 1 Dec 1887), yst dau of Lord George Seymour (*see* HERTFORD, M), and *d* 1 Aug 1868, having had, with a yr s (Frederick James, *b* 16 Sept 1835, RN, *d* 10 Oct 1861):

HENRY BENTINCK BOYLE, **5th Earl of Shannon**; *b* 22 Nov 1833; *educ* Eton; Attaché Frankfurt 1852 and Vienna 1852–53, Hon Col 2nd Bde S Irish Div RA; *m* 1st 12 July 1858 Lady Blanche Emma Lascelles (*d* 26 Dec 1863), 3rd dau of 3rd Earl of Harewood (*qv*), and had:

RICHARD HENRY, **6th Earl**

2 Henry George; *b* 10 Feb 1862; Lt 3rd Bn Yorks Regt; *d* unm 16 Dec 1908

3 Robert Francis, MVO; *b* 12 Dec 1863; served Egypt 1882, W Africa 1894 and WW I, V-Adml; *m* 3 Aug 1899 Cerise (*d* 7 April 1951), 2nd dau of Sir Claude Champion de Crespigny, 4th Bt (*see* 1953 edn), and *d* 11 Sept 1922, leaving:

(1) Vivian Francis; *b* 9 Jan 1902; Cdr RN; *m* 25 June 1929 Margaret Ruth Howard, er dau of Charles Howard Tripp, of Timaru, NZ, and *d* 21 Sept 1962, leaving:

1a +Robert Francis [Robert Boyle Esq, 3 McDowell Street, Rotorua, New Zealand]; *b* 15 Aug 1930; logging consultant; *m* 2 April 1956 *Janet Eleanor, only dau of Selwyn Ashley Cooper, of Rotorua, and has:

1b +David de Crespigny; *b* 2 Sept 1959

2b +Robert Andrew; *b* 18 July 1961

1b *Judith Eleanor; *b* 19 June 1957; *m* 1987 (*divorce* 1992) Abid Ilahi

1a *Moyra Anne [Mrs William Leonard, 4 Gifford St, St Heliers Bay, Auckland 5, New Zealand]; *b* 11 Jan 1936; *m* 26 Feb 1960 William Francis Leonard (*d* 24 Sept 1997), s of William Alan Emmerson Leonard, of Mission Bay, Auckland, and has:

1b *Mark Francis; *b* 1961; by Julie Sigley has:

1c *Ruby Innes LEONARD; *b* 3 Jan 1994

2c *Frances Rose LEONARD; *b* 10 Oct 1995

1b *Zucchi Philippa Jane; *b* 1962; *m* 1988 *Alastair Salmond, of Wellington, and has:

1c *Oscar William; *b* 25 May 1991

1c *Hannah June; *b* 5 Aug 1992

2b *Virginia Anne; *b* 1965; *m* 22 Aug 1992 *Kenneth Cooke, of Auckland

(2) Robin Lascelles; *b* 13 Nov 1915; Lt Roy Welch Fus WW II; *ka* June 1940

(1) Moyra Blanche; *b* 19 Feb 1903; *m* 10 Oct 1929 Capt Hercules Bradshaw Moorhead, 7th QOH, er s of Wickham Hercules Bradshaw Moorhead, DL, of Newry, Co Down

(2) Bridget Cérise; *b* 13 March 1908; *m* 24 June 1933 Lt-Col John Rowson Saynor, only s of John Edward Saynor, and *d* 3 March 1968, leaving issue. He *d* 30 Jan 1965

The **5th Earl** *m* 2nd 14 Jan 1868 Julia Charlotte (*d* 27 Dec 1921), yst dau of Sir William Edmund Cradock-Hartopp, 3rd Bt (*qv*), and by her had:

4 Walter John Harry, CBE (1930); *b* 11 March 1869; Sr Official Receiver Bankruptcy 1922–34; *m* 25 April 1900 Ethel Horatia (*d* 8 April 1949), yst dau of Edward Rowe Fisher-Rowe, of Thorncombe, and *d* 24 Feb 1939, leaving:

(1) Walter Julian Algernon; *b* 26 Nov 1918; *educ* Westminster; Lt RNVR WW II; *m* 30 July 1941 *Anita Diana, er dau of Wilfred Harry Greenhow, and had:

1a Clive Richard; *b* 7 March, *d* 30 March 1953

(1) Patricia Beaufoy; *b* 17 March 1901; *d* unm 24 June 1968

(2) *Helena Diana Victoria; *b* 20 Nov 1907; *m* 27 Sept 1932 (*divorce* 1961) Edward Locker Delmar-Morgan, AMIEE (*d* 29 Jan 1975), er s of John Godfrey Yule Delmar-Morgan, of Chelsea, and has:

1a *John Oliver Julian; *b* 30 May 1934; *educ* Eton; Sub-Lt (S) RNR; *m* 5 May 1962 *Penelope Jane, only dau of Eaton Woodhouse, of Alderley Edge, Cheshire, and has:

1b *Susannah Clare; *b* 10 March 1963

2b *Rebecca Jane; *b* 10 July 1965

1a *Patricia Jane [Mrs Peter Fowler, 2730 West 13th Ave, Vancouver 8, BC, Canada]; *b* 23 July 1941; *m* 23 July 1966 Peter George Edmund Fowler, er s of Cdr George Charles Willoughby Fowler, RN, of Froxfield, Hants, and Ashby Manor, Spilsby, Lincs, and has:

1b *Patrick Michael Thomas; *b* 4 Aug 1968

5 Edward Spencer Harry; *b* 8 Oct 1870; Boer War 1900, Actg Cdr RNC Osborne 1914–18, Capt RN; *m* 12 Dec 1904 Lily (*d* 4 April 1953), est dau of William Sanderson Beaumont Gardner, of Palermo, and *d* 8 Oct 1937, leaving:

(1) Patrick Spencer; *b* 31 Oct 1905; *educ* RNCs Osborne and Dartmouth; Lt-Cdr RNVR WW II; *m* 1st 20 Aug 1932 Vera Maude Radcliffe Agnew (*d* 4 Feb 1940), er dau of Daniel Radcliffe, JP, LLD, of Pen-y-lan, Cardiff, and had:

1a +Michael Patrick Radcliffe, DL (Hants 1982) [Michael Boyle Esq DL, Saint Cross House, Whitchurch, Hants RG28 7AS]; *b* 25 Jan 1934; *educ* Eton; late Capt Irish Gds, OStJ, Hants: Commr St John Ambulance Bde, CC 1970; *m* 28 July 1962 *Lady Nell Carleton Harris, yr dau of 6th Earl of Malmesbury (*qv*), and has:

1b +Robert Algernon Radcliffe; *b* 10 Jan 1963; *educ* King's Sch Bruton; Capt Irish Gds; *m* 1987 *Fiona Elisabeth Maule, yst dau of Col George Patrick Maule Ramsay (*see* DALHOUSIE, E)

2b +Rupert; *b* 20 Feb 1968

1b *Maria; *b* 26 Oct 1964

(1) (cont.) Lt-Cdr Patrick Boyle *m* 2nd 5 Aug 1940 *Rita Sylva [Mrs Patrick Boyle, 13 Springfield, E Oakley, Hants RG23 7DR], yr dau of Cecil Berens, JP, of Kent, and *d* 1978, having by her had:

2a *David Spencer [David Boyle Esq, The Dower House, Heythrop, Oxon OX7 5TL]; *b* 23 April 1942; *educ* Winchester and Pembroke Coll Cambridge; *m* 1980 *Melanie Georgiana, only dau of William Robert Brudenell Foster (*see* AILESBURY, M), and has:

1b +James Patrick; *b* 1983

1b *Fenella; *b* 1982

6 Algernon Douglas Edward Harry (Sir), KCB (1924, CB), CMG (1918), MVO (1901); *b* 21 Oct 1871; served WW I (despatches, Legn Hon), ADC to HM GEORGE V 1918–19, 4th Sea Ld 1920–24, Adml, memb PLA 1925–29, Russian Order of St Anne 2nd Cl with swords, 3rd Cl Order Rising Sun Japan, Croix de Guerre, Cdr Order Crown Belgium; *d* unm 13 Oct 1949

The **5th EARL** *d* 8 Feb 1890; his est s,

RICHARD HENRY BOYLE, **6th Earl of Shannon**; *b* 15 May 1860; *educ* Eton; Lt Rifle Bde 1880–82, moved to Canada 1883, where took to ranching and served as memb Canadian Parl, Sgt RNWMPC; *m* 19 Aug 1895 Nellie (*d* 10 April 1910), dau of Charles Thompson, of Bookham, Surrey, and *d* 11 Dec 1906, having had:

1 Richard Charles; *b* 10, *d* 23 July 1896

2 RICHARD BERNARD BOYLE, **7th Earl of Shannon**; *b* 13 Nov 1897; 2nd Lt Roy Fus 1916 WW I; *ka* 13 April 1917

3 ROBERT HENRY BOYLE, **8th Earl of Shannon**; *b* 1 Feb 1900; *educ* Malvern and RMC Sandhurst; ADC to Govr Madras 1923, Lt Roy Fus, Capt IA, WW II; *m* 27 Dec 1923 Marjorie (*d* 1981), dau of Septimus Augustus Walker, of Ootacamund, India, and *d* 29 Dec 1963, leaving:

(1) RICHARD BENTINCK BOYLE, **9th and present Earl of Shannon**

1 Helen; *b* 24 Sept 1898; *m* 20 Sept 1922 (*divorce* 1933) Maj Cyril Bouchier Barlow, IA, s of Brig-Gen John Arthur Barlow, and had:

(1) *Michael Roderick; *b* 22 June 1929; *educ* Rugby and Trin Coll Cambridge

SHARP of Heckmondwike

Arms: Az. on a fess engrailed arg. between two plates a torteau between two pheons gu. **Crest:** In front of a pheon sa. an eagle's head erased az., charged with a cross-crosslet or. **Motto:** *Nitor donec supero* ('I strive till I overcome'). **Creation:** Bt. (UK) 28 June 1920.

SIR SAMUEL CHRISTOPHER REGINALD SHARP, 4TH BT, of Heckmondwike, West Riding, Co York; *b* 25 April 1936; *s* cousin 1996; *educ* Rugby; *m* 1st 1958 (*divorce* 1967) Sheila Moody; *m* 2nd 1968 *Anna M P Rossi, of Rome

Lineage: JOSEPH SHARP, of Stone Chair, Shelf, Yorks; *d* 8 April 1856, leaving:

JAMES SHARP, of Shirley Manor, Wyke, Yorks; *b* 31 Dec 1828; *m* 8 Oct 1853 Hannah (*d* 30 Oct 1903), dau of Joseph Gaunt, of Batley, Yorks, and *d* 11 May 1911, leaving, with a yr s (James, *b* 6 Feb 1863, *m* Charlotte Elizabeth (*d* 22 May 1928)) and two daus:

Sir Milton Sheridan Sharp, 1st Bt (UK), so *cr* 28 June 1920; *b* 30 Jan 1856; chm Bradford Dyers Assoc; *m* 10 April 1879 Annie (*d* 22 Nov 1919), dau of James Turner, of Low Moor, Yorks, and *d* 22 May 1924, having had:

1 **Sir Milton Sharp, 2nd Bt**; *b* 22 April 1880; *educ* Shrewsbury and Trin Hall Cambridge (BA 1902); *m* 1909 Gertrude Clara Louisa (*d* 30 Aug 1940), dau of William Robert Albert Earl, and *d* 17 Dec 1941, leaving:

  (1) **Sir Milton Reginald Sharp, 3rd Bt**; *b* 21 Nov 1909; *educ* Shrewsbury and Trin Hall Cambridge; Maj RA (TA); *m* 1st 1935 Dorothy Mary, yr dau of Bernard R McCarrick, of Kilglass House, Ballina, Co Mayo; *m* 2nd 1951 *Marie-Louise de Vignon [Marie-Louise Lady Sharp, c/o Messrs Redfearns, Midland Bank Chambers, Heckmondwike, Yorks], of Paris, and *dsp* 4 May 1996

  2 Charles George Gordon; *b* 7 July 1885; *educ* Shrewsbury and Trin Hall Cambridge; *m* — and *d* 31 Jan 1961, leaving:

    (1) *Elizabeth; *b* 19–

  3 Reginald; *b* 8 Sept 1888; *m* 1st (*divorce*) Janet Hilda Clapham; *m* 2nd 12 May 1933 Mrs Doris Eve Faulder (*d* 1958), dau of — Heath, and by her had:

    (1) Sir SAMUEL CHRISTOPHER REGINALD SHARP, **4th and present Bt**

    (1) *Caroline Eve; *b* 22 Nov 1944

    (2) *Rosemary Anne; *b* 2 March 1946

  3 (cont.) Reginald Sharp *m* 3rd *Marguerite Louise Eugenie, dau of — Ondoux, of Cagnicourt, France, and *d* 4 Jan 1969

  4 Herbert; *b* 28 Feb 1891; *m* —, and *d* 3 Aug 1952, leaving:

    (1) +JOHN HERBERT; *b* 5 Aug 1920; heir presumptive; formerly with BBC

  5 Henry Edward; *b* 6 Aug 1893; *d* unm 3 July 1965

  6 Harold (Jack); *b* 2 July 1895, *m* — Lister and *d* 11 May 1965, leaving:

    (1) +Jack; *b* 15 Sept 1932

    (1) *Barbara Elizabeth; *b* 3 Jan 1931

  1 Lucy; *d* 17 Jan 1921

SHARP of Warden Court

Arms: Arg. on a fess indented between two falcon's heads erased sa. three pheons or. **Crest:** Upon a mount vert a falcon rising ppr., belled and resting the dexter claw upon a pheon or. **Motto:** *In veritate victoria* ('Victory in truth'). **Creation:** Bt. (UK) 23 June 1922.

SIR ADRIAN SHARP, 4TH BT, of Warden Court, Maidstone, Co Kent [Sir Adrian Sharp Bt, 27 Donkin Ave, Tableview, Cape Town 7441, S Africa]; *b* 17 Sept 1951; *s f* 1985; *educ* Boxhill Sch and Nat Business Coll Cape Town; exec manager Toyota Motor Co; *m* 1st 1976 (*divorce* 1986) Hazel Patricia, only dau of James Trevor Wallace, of Pietersburg, S Africa, and formerly w of William Ian Barrett Bothwell; *m* 2nd 1994 *Denise, only dau of Percy Edward Roberts, of Ironbridge, Salop, and by her has:

1 +HAYDEN SEAN; *b* 27 Aug 1994

Lineage: JAMES SHARP, of Maidstone; *m* Mary Ann, dau of Edmund Deal, of Maidstone, and had:

Sir Edward Sharp, 1st Bt (UK), so *cr* 23 June 1922; *b* 13 May 1854; fndr/chm Edward Sharp & Sons, confectioners, of Maidstone, Maj Cadet Bn Roy W Kent Regt; *m* 1st 2 July 1878 Clara (*d* 30 Nov 1925), er dau of James Betts, of Maidstone; *m* 2nd 6 Nov 1928 Rose May (*d* 18 Oct 1947), widow of Albert Edward Harding, of Ashford, and dau of W Davies, and had by his 1st w:

1 HERBERT EDWARD (Sir), **2nd Bt**

2 Wilfred James; *b* 5 Aug 1880; Army Capt; *m* 12 June 1909 Ada Frances (*d* 16 Oct 1936), dau of George Meek, of Beckenham, Kent, and *d* 2 Dec 1945, having had:

  (1) Edward Harold Wilfred; *b* 22 Sept 1910; late chm Edward Sharp & Sons; *d* 19–

  (2) George Herbert Bryan; *b* 15 Feb 1914; *d* 26 March 1923

  (3) +John Rayner Edgar [John Sharp Esq, The Old Mill, Sutton Valence, Kent]; *b* 19 July 1917; *educ* Malvern and Harvard Business Sch; late chm Edward Sharp & Sons

The 1st Bt *d* 23 Aug 1931; his er s,

  Sir Herbert Edward Sharp, 2nd Bt; *b* 25 April 1879; dir Edward Sharp & Sons; *m* 1st 12 Sept 1908 (*divorce* 1927) Winifred Elizabeth Cheevers, dau of William Cheevers Peverley, of Dover; *m* 2nd 5 Feb 1927 Ray Alice Mary (*m* 2nd 1937 Kenneth Brian Downey, s of J T Downey, of Felixstowe), dau of Frederick George Bloomfield, of Kensal Rise, London, and *d* 16 June 1936, leaving:

Sir Edward Herbert Sharp, 3rd Bt; *b* 3 Dec 1927; *educ* Haileybury; *m* 19 April 1949 *Beryl Kathleen, yr dau of Leonard Simmons-Green, of Shirley, Worcs, and *d* 1985, leaving:

1 Sir ADRIAN SHARP, **4th and present Bt**

2 +Owen [Owen Sharp Esq, PO Box 486, Ballito 4420, S Africa; 17 Ipahla Lane, Chakas Rock, 4390 Natal, S Africa]; *b* 19 Sept 1956; *educ* Waterford, Swaziland and Durham U; *m* 1980 *Caroline, dau of Jerrard Collings van Beuge, of Durban, and has:

  (1) +Declan; *b* 21 July 1980

  (2) +Lyndall; *b* 3 Oct 1983

1 *Terry; *b* 10 March 1950; *m* 1969 *Ian Wilson, of Durban, s of Ennis Wilson, of Ashtead, Surrey, and has:

  (1) *Karen; *b* 1969

  (2) *Tracey; *b* 1971

  (3) *Lee; *b* 1972

SHARPLES

SHAUGHNESSY

Arms: Argent a chevron vert between in chief two copper beech trees eradicated and in base a white tailed tropic bird (*Phaethon lepturus*) volant proper (for SHARPLES), on an escutcheon of pretence the arms of NEWALL, *viz.*, per saltire argent and gules a crozier in fess or between three bustards, wings elevated and addorsed, counterchanged. **Supporters:** On either side a Great Dane dog, resting the interior hind foot proper on a portcullis or.
Creation: B. (LP, UK) 1973.

Arms: Per fess gu. and az. in chief two millrinds and in base an ancient harp or, within a bordure engrailed erm. **Crest:** Issuing from an antique crown a dexter cubit arm in armour and gauntleted, grasping a two-headed battle-axe, all ppr. **Supporters:** Dexter, an Irish wolf hound ppr., collared arg., charged with three trefoils vert; sinister, a beaver ppr., collared arg., charged with three maple leaves gu. **Motto:** *Manu forti* ('With a strong hand').
Creation: B. (UK) 25 Jan 1916.

THE BARONESS SHARPLES, of Chawton, Hampshire (Pamela Newall) [The Rt Hon The Baroness Sharples, 60 Westminster Gdns, Marsham St, London SW1P 4JG; Well Cottage, Higher Coombe, Shaftesbury, Dorset SP7 9LR]; *b* 11 Feb 1923; *educ* Southover Manor Lewes and Florence; WAAF 1941–46; Memb Review Body Armed Forces Pay 1979–81; Dir TVS 1981–90, 1991–93; *m* 1st 1946 Sir Richard Christopher Sharples, KCMG, OBE, MC, Govr Bermuda (*assassinated* Bermuda 1973); *m* 2nd 1977 Patrick David de Laszlo (*d* 1980); *m* 3rd 1983 Robert Douglas Swan (*d* 1995) and has by her 1st husb:

1 *Christopher John [The Hon Christopher Sharples, 72 Elm Park Rd, London SW3 6AY]; *b* 1947; chm GNI 1994–; *m* 1975 *Sharon, er dau of Robert Sweeny, of Montague Sq, London W1, and has issue

2 *David Richard; *b* 1955; *m* 1981 (*divorce* 1988) Anna(bel), 2nd dau of Col Thomas Armitage Hall, OBE (*see* DUFFERIN ADN CLANBOYE, B)

1 *Fiona; *b* 1949; *m* 1981 (*divorce* 1982) Alexander Paterson and has:

 (1) *Natalie Louise; *b* 1975

2 *Miranda [The Hon Mrs Larkins, Can Xifra, Rivdarenes, 17421 Gerona, Spain]; *b* 1951; *m* 1981 *Nicholas Larkins, er s of Dr N Larkins, of Sydney, NSW, and has:

 (1) *Harry Claud; *b* 1985

 (1) *Amelia Kate (Kitty); *b* 1989

Lineage: Lt-Cdr KEITH WILLIAM NEWALL; *m* Violet Ruby Ashton and had:

PAMELA, *cr* a **Baroness**

THE 3RD BARON SHAUGHNESSY, of Montreal, Canada, and Ashford, Co Limerick (William Graham Shaughnessy, CD (1955)) [The Rt Hon The Lord Shaughnessy CD, House of Lords, London SW1A 0PW]; *b* 28 March 1922; *s f* 1938; *educ* Bishop's Coll Sch, Bishop's U Quebec (BA 1941) and Columbia U New York (MSc 1947); Maj Canadian Gren Gds WW II 1941–45 (despatches), exec assist to Canadian Min Fin 1949–51, Pres Roy Cwlth Soc Montreal 1959–61, dir: Canada-UK Chamber of Commerce 1981–, Arbor Memorial Services Inc (Toronto) 1972– and Eurogas Corp (Calgary) 1995–, memb Ho Lds Jt Select Ctees: Statutory Instruments 1985–, Delegated Powers Scrutiny 1992–96, Tstee: The Last Post Fund, Canada Memorial Fndn (UK); *m* 18 March 1944 *Mary, only dau of John Whitley, of Copthorne House, Letchworth, Herts, and has had:

1 Patrick John; *b* 23 Oct 1944; *d* 1982

2 +MICHAEL JAMES; *b* 12 Nov 1946

1 *Brigid Mary; *b* 30 Jan 1948

2 *Marion Kathleen; *b* 2 May 1951

Lineage: THOMAS SHAUGHNESSY, of Ashford, Co Limerick, later of Wisconsin; had:

THOMAS GEORGE SHAUGHNESSY, **1st Baron Shaughnessy**, of Montreal, Canada, and Ashford, Co Limerick (UK), so *cr* 25 Jan 1916, KCVO (1907); *b* 6 Oct 1853; with Milwaukee and St Paul Rlwy 1868, Canadian Pacific Rlwy 1882–1923 (Assist to Gen Manager 1884 and to Pres 1889–91, V-Pres and Dir 1891–99, Pres 1899–1918), ktd 1901, Hon MInstCE, Hon LLD Dublin 1911, McGill and Dartmouth, KGStJ, Order Sacred Treasure Japan; *m* 12 Jan 1880 Elizabeth Bridget (*d* 8 May 1937), dau of M Nagle, of Milwaukee, and had:

1 WILLIAM JAMES, **2nd Baron**

2 Alfred Thomas; *b* 18 Oct 1887; Capt 60th Canadian Inf; *m* 30 April 1912 Sarah Polk (*d* 17 Oct 1955, having *m* 2nd 15 Nov 1920 Lt-Col Hon Sir Piers Walter Legh, GCVO, CMG, CIE, OBE; *see* NEWTON, B), dau of Judge James C Bradford, of Nashville, Tenn. (*see* Section Polk AMERICAN PRESIDENTIAL FAMILIES, 1994, Morris Genealogical Books SA), and was *ka* 31 March 1916, leaving:

(1) Thomas Bradford; *b* 14 Jan 1915; *educ* Eton, Oxford (BA 1937) and McGill (BCL 1947); Welsh Gds and SAS WW II, memb Montreal Bar 1947, slr with Canadian Industries Ltd; *m* 18 June 1949 Margot (*d* 1991), only dau of William Daney Chambers, of Westmount, Montreal, and *d* 1994, leaving:

 1a *Amanda Marguerite Polk; *b* 14 Feb 1951

 2a *Roxane Elizabeth; *b* 30 Sept 1952; *m* 1984 *Thomas Herbert McGreevy, s of John McGreevy, of Quebec City, and has:

  1b *Julian Thomas Gray; *b* 1989

  1b *Sarah Paige; *b* 1986

  2b *Madeleine Claire Elizabeth; *b* 1989

 3a *Tara Evelyn [Mrs Alain Du Bois, 50 Tunstall Ave, Senneville, Quebec H9X 1T2, Canada]; *b* 15 Nov 1954; *m* 1983 *Alain Du Bois, s of Leopold Du Bois, of Magog, Quebec, and has:

  1b *Louis Shaughnessy; *b* 1985

  1b *Chella Evelyn; *b* 1988

(2) +Alfred James; *b* posthumously 19 May 1916; Capt Gren Gds (Res), TV writer, script ed *Upstairs, Downstairs*, playwright; *m* 18 Sept 1948 *Jean Margaret, only dau of George Lodge, of Kirkella, Yorks, and has:

 1a +Charles George Patrick; *b* 9 Feb 1955; *educ* Eton; *m* 1983 *Susan, dau of Sydney Fallender, of Los Angeles, and has:

  1b *Jenny Johanna; *b* 1990

2a +David James Bradford; *b* 3 March 1957; *m* 1985 *Anne-Marie, dau of Thomas Schoettle, of Indianapolis, and has:
    1b *Amy Jean; *b* 1990
    2b *Kathryn Anne; *b* 1992
(1) *Elizabeth Sarah Polk [Mrs Derek Lawson, 78 Melton Court, Old Brompton Rd, London SW7 3JH]; *b* 23 Jan 1913; *m* 1st 25 July 1932 (*divorce* 1946) 2nd Baron Grenfell (*qv*) and has issue; *m* 2nd 26 Jan 1946 Maj Berkeley Buckingham Howard Stafford, KRRC (*d* 30 Oct 1966), er s of Berkeley Howard Stafford, of Sway Place, Hants; *m* 3rd 2 May 1969 (*divorce* 1975) Trevor Walton (Rex) King, s of William Samuel King, MBE; *m* 4th 1983 Cdr (Arnold) Derek Arthur Lawson, RN (*d* 1984)
1 Alice Josephine *b* 28 Oct 1880; *m* 3 June 1911 Henry Wyndham Beauclerk, of Montreal, and *d* 1963, leaving issue (*see* ST ALBANS D)
2 Marguerite Kathleen; *b* 23 June 1891; *d* unm 15 May 1958
3 Edith Mary; *b* 11 July 1892; *m* 3 June 1914 Maj René Martin Redmond, DSO, 60th Bn Canadian Inf, s of William H Redmond, of Montreal, and *d* 8 Dec 1964, leaving issue. He *d* 21 July 1955

The 1st BARON *d* 10 Dec 1923; his er s,
WILLIAM JAMES SHAUGHNESSY, **2nd Baron Shaughnessy**, KC (Canada 1920); *b* 29 Sept 1883; *educ* Bishop's Coll Sch Lennoxville, McGill, Trin Coll Cambridge and Laval U Montreal (LLM); barrister Canada 1910, WW I: Capt Irish Canadian Rangers, ADC personal staff, GSO 1917 (despatches), Lt-Col cmdg 199th Canadian Bn, Lt-Col Canadian Militia, V-Pres Roy Empire Soc, dir: Canadian Pacific Rlwy, Canadian Bank of Commerce, Canadian Salt Co, Canadian NW Land Co, Lake of the Woods Milling Co, chm Canadian Bd Yorkshire Insur; *m* 16 Nov 1911 Marion (*d* 18 March 1936), dau of Robert Kilgour Graham, of Montreal, and niece of 1st and last Baron Atholstan, and *d* 4 Oct 1938, leaving:
1 WILLIAM GRAHAM SHAUGHNESSY, **3rd and present Baron Shaughnessy**
1 Margaret Helena Graham; *b* 30 Oct 1912; *d* unm 24 Sept 1966
2 Hazel Marion; *b* 16 April 1914; *m* 1938 James R Ballantyne and had issue
3 Bridget Ann; *b* 16 Feb 1916

SHAW

TE·IPSUM·NOSCE

Arms: Or on a chevron engrailed between three eagles displayed sa. as many trefoils slipped of the field. **Crest:** A hind's head couped az., the neck transpierced by an arrow in bend or, flighted arg. **Motto:** *Te ipsum nosce* ('Know thyself'). **Creation:** Bt. (UK) 17 Aug 1821.

SIR ROBERT SHAW, 7TH BT, of Bushy Park, Co Dublin [Sir Robert Shaw Bt, 234 40th Ave, Calgary, AB T2S 0X3, Canada]; *b* 31 Jan 1925; *s f* 1969; *educ* Harrow, Oklahoma U (BS Civil Engrg) and Missouri U (MS Civil Engrg); Lt RN WW II 1943–45, design engr Shaw Consulting, Alberta, memb Engineering Inst Canada; *m* 6 Oct 1954 *Jocelyn Mary, only dau of Andrew W McGuffie, of Mbabane, Swaziland, and has:
1 *Grania; *b* 31 July 1955
2 *Reinet; *b* 12 Nov 1960

Lineage: WILLIAM SHAW; *b* Hants *c* 1651 but of Scottish descent; Capt Michelburn's Foot Battle of the Boyne 1690; *m* Elizabeth — (*d* 1738) and *d* 1734, having had, with three yr sons and a dau:

RICHARD SHAW, of Ballinderry, Co Tipperary; *b* 1673; *m* Jan 1696 Judith, dau of Edward Briscoe, of Timakilly, Co Kilkenny, and *dvp* 1729, having had, with five yr sons and three daus:

ROBERT SHAW, of Sandpitts, Co Kilkenny; *b* 1698; *m* 1736 Mary, dau of Bernard Markham, of Fanningstown, Co Kilkenny, and *d* 1758, having had, with other issue:
1 William, of Sandpitts; *m* — English and had:
    (1) Robert (Rev); Rector St John's, Kilkenny
    (2) John
    (3) Bernard, of Kilkenny; *m* 1 April 1802 Frances, dau of Rev E Carr, and *d* 3 Feb 1826, leaving:
        1a George Carr, of Dublin; *m* 17 June 1852 Lucinda Elizabeth, dau of Walter Gurly, and had:

1b (George) Bernard, of Ayot St Lawrence, Herts; *b* 1856; author of over 50 plays, also novels and political, economic and critical works; Nobel Prize Literature 1925; *m* 1898 Charlotte, of Denny, Co Cork, er dau and coheir of Horace Payne-Townshend, JP, DL, and *dsp* 2 Nov 1950
2 Thomas, of Clonmel; *m* Susanna — and had issue
3 ROBERT
1 Rebecca; *m* 1755 William Briscoe

The 5th s,
ROBERT SHAW; Dublin merchant, Accountant-Gen Post Office; *m* 1st Mary Higgins, of Higginsbrook, Co Meath, and had:
1 ROBERT (Sir), **1st Bt**
2 Bernard; *b* June 1755; Collector of Cork; *m* Jane, dau of Michael Westropp, and *d* 1808, leaving, with other issue:
    (1) Robert Bernard, of Monkstown Castle, Co Cork; *m* 1st Rebecca, dau of Edward Hoare Reeves, of Castle Kevin and Ballyglissane, and had a 3rd s:
        1a Eyre Massey Shaw (Sir), KCB, DL; *b* 17 Jan 1828; Chief Offr London Fire Bde 1861–91; *m* Anna (*d* 12 Dec 1897), dau of Murto Dove, of Lisbon, and *d* 25 Aug 1908, leaving issue
3 Ponsonby; *b* 15 July 1784; Dublin banker; *m* Alice (*d* May 1841), dau of Jonathan Eade, of Stoke Newington, and *d* 19 Dec 1871, leaving issue
4 Thomas; Capt 25th Lt Dragoons
5 John; *m* 19 April 1809 Harriet, dau of Jonathan Eade, and had, with other issue:
    (1) Joseph, of Melbourne, Australia; *b* 10 July 1825; Customs Offr Ireland; *m* 4 Sept 1862 Ellen Neale (*d* 21 June 1912), dau of Charles Cresswell, of Worcester, and *d* Nov 1880, leaving:
        1a Joseph; *b* 1863; *d* 1864
        2a Robert de Courcy, of Victoria, Australia; *b* 19 May 1866; *m* 3 Sept 1889 Edith Shields (*d* 27 June 1910), of Gippsland, and *d* 9 July 1950, leaving issue:
            1b Robert Mervyn; *educ* Melbourne U (BS); Capt AAMC WW I; had:
                1c *Robert Richard; PhD Oxon (Rhodes Scholar 1948), ch aeronautical engr IATA Montreal
                2c *John Mervyn; ch engr Gas and Fuel Corp Victoria, Australia
                3c Robert de Cowrey; MD
                4c *Maxwell Thomas; has issue
            2b Joseph; *m* 7 Nov 1928 Margery Hore and had:
                1c *Geoffrey de Courcy; *b* 19 Feb 1934; *m* 26 Jan 1957 *Jeannette Galt and has:
                    1d *Alexander Geoffrey; *b* 10 Nov 1966
                    1d *Fiona Louise; *b* 9 Aug 1959
                    2d *Karen June; *b* 1 Feb 1961
                    3d *Heather Margery; *b* 10 Nov 1966
                1c *June Margery; *b* 30 June 1931
                2c *Elizabeth Ann [Mrs John Black, 38 Gladwyn St, East Bentleigh, Vic 3165, Australia]; *b* 4 Jan 1936; *m* 1 May 1965 *John Black and has:
                    1d *Richard Mason; *b* 24 Oct 1967
                    2d *Simon James; *b* 11 June 1970; *m* 3 Sept 1994 *Katherine Menzies and has:
                        1e *Harrison John; *b* 17 Jan 1998
            3b Winston Cresswell
            4b Leonard Cornwall
            1b Eileen Florence; *m* Frank Gooch (*d* 1941), of Kyneton, Victoria, and had two sons
            2b Dorothy Ellen Edith; *m* Erik Gunnersen, of Balwyn, Victoria, and had issue
        1a Josephine Harriet; *m* 27 Nov 1896 Rev Edgar Ward-Thomas, Vicar Lorne, Victoria, and had issue
        2a Blanche Ellen; *m* 19 March 1885 Maj John Buchan, of Melbourne, Victorian Militia, and had issue. He *d* 15 Dec 1922
        3a Emily Florence; *d* 27 March 1936
        4a Mabel Anne; *m* 30 April 1897 Percy Brereton-Colquhoun, slr, of Sydney, and *d* 25 July 1914, leaving issue
1 Mary; *m* 4 Feb 1800 John Cathcart Lees (*see* LEES, Bt, of Blackrock) and had issue
2 Charlotte; *m* Sir William McMahon, 1st Bt, of Dublin (*see* 1926 edn)

ROBERT SHAW *m* 2nd Priscilla Cecilia (*m* 2nd 7 Nov 1798 Hugh Moore, of Eglantine, Co Down), dau of Col Armitage, of Ross-on-Wye, Herefs, and *d* 2 July 1796, having by her had:
6 George; *m* Maria, dau of William Chipendall
7 Lees; *m* Caroline, dau of William Chipendall
3 Caroline; *m* Sir James Caleb Anderson, Bt, and *d* 24 Dec 1859
4 Sylvia; *m* — Viennot, French Army Offr

His est s,
Sir Robert Shaw, 1st Bt (UK), so cr 17 Aug 1821; *b* 29 Jan 1774; Col Roy Dublin Militia, MP New Ross and Dublin 1804–26, High Sheriff Co Dublin 1806; *m* 1st 7 Jan 1796 Maria (*d* 28 March 1831), dau and heiress of Abraham Wilkinson, of Bushy Park, Co Dublin; *m* 2nd 2 July 1834 Amelia (*d* 11 Jan 1860), only dau of Benjamin Spencer, and *d* 10 March 1849, leaving by his 1st w, with two other daus:
1 **Sir Robert Shaw, 2nd Bt**, DL Co Dublin; *b* 28 Sept 1796; *d* unm 19 Feb 1869
2 FREDERICK (Sir), **3rd Bt**
3 Beresford William; *b* 31 Oct 1806; 5th Regt, later Maj Dublin Militia, RM Co Tipperary; *d* 20 Oct 1847
4 George Augustus (Rev); *b* 16 Dec 1814; *d* 4 Sept 1838
5 Charles, QC; *b* 27 July 1817; Chm Co Monaghan Bench; *m* 4 Oct 1845 Mary (*d* 17 March 1865), dau of William Barton, of Grove, and *d* 9 Dec 1870, having had, with three daus (*d* unm):
    (1) Robert Barton; *b* 2 Dec 1847; *m* Dec 1895 Caroline Anna (*dsp* 1 Feb 1910), 3rd dau of S de la Cherois-Crommelin, of Carrowdore, Co Down, and *d* 10 Dec 1923

(2) Charles Barton (Rev Canon); *b* 24 June 1853; *d* 18 Oct 1934

(3) William; *b* 5 Jan 1857; *m* 14 March 1889 Roxanna Massie, dau of James Henry Bowles, and *d* 9 Jan 1939, having had:

1a William Henry; *b* 31 July 1890; *d* unm 17 Aug 1914

1a Emily Newell; *b* 20 May 1902; *m* 9 Feb 1921 Charles Franklin Jenners and had:

1b *Charles Franklin; *b* 1924

2b *Stuart Barton; *b* 1929

1b *Barbara Claire; *b* 1932

(4) Thomas Barton; *b* 27 May 1858; Inspr Bd Educn, Assist Sec Tech Instn Ireland, Capt RE; *d* 1915

(1) Caroline; *d* unm 29 March 1944

(2) Alice Arabella; *d* unm 13 Nov 1955 aged 93

1 Charlotte; *m* Augustus Frederick Wynne and *d* 1859, leaving issue

The 2nd Bt's bro,

Sir Frederick Shaw, 3rd Bt, PC; *b* 11 Dec 1799; Recorder Dublin, MP Dublin 1830–32 and U of Dublin 1832–48; *m* 16 March 1819 Thomasine Emily (*d* 30 Nov 1859), dau of Hon George Jocelyn (*see* RODEN, E), and had, with two other daus (*d* unm):

1 ROBERT (Sir), **4th Bt**

2 George, CB; *b* 21 Dec 1822; Maj-Gen RA; *m* 1st 27 Oct 1846 Marie (*d* Feb 1871), dau of E Desfontaines, of Mauritius, and had, with two daus (*d* unm):

(1) Frederick; *b* 13 June 1850; *m* 1873 Ella Jane (*d* 27 May 1926), dau of William Willis, of USA, and *d* 1928, having had:

1a George Jocelyn; *b* 17 Dec 1877; *d* unm 1912

2a William Edward; *b* 8 Sept 1879; *d* unm 1920

1a Flora Alice; *d* unm 16 June 1961

2a Emily Marie; *m* 1910 John Frisbourne Herriford and *d* 1955. He *d* 1939

3a Cora Desfontaines; *m* 1909 Charles Abner Howard, LLD

(2) George Jocelyn; *b* 23 Jan 1857; Col IA; *m* 2 July 1883 Elizabeth Harriette (*d* 15 July 1956), dau of Col Horatio Samuel Court, Madras SC, and *d* 18 June 1928, leaving:

1a Percy Jocelyn; *b* 30 April 1893; *educ* Lancing and Dulwich; 2nd Leics Regt Mesopotamia and Palestine WW I, RAPC WW II; *m* 28 March 1931 Ivy Muriel, dau of William Thomas Seager, of London

2a Edward Wingfield, DSO; *b* 19 Feb 1895; Capt Middx Regt WW I (despatches); *d* 7 Dec 1916 from wounds recd in action

1a Elsie Marie, MBE (1919); VAD WW I; *d* unm 2 Aug 1963

(3) Edward Wingfield; *b* 31 March 1858; *dsp* 2 Jan 1895

(4) Robert; *b* 10 March 1864; *d* 30 Dec 1894, leaving issue

(1) Emilie Marie; *m* 9 Aug 1870 Capt Edward Fenwick Brackenbury, RA, of Skendleby Hall, Lincs, and *d* 20 May 1898

(2) Flora Louise, DBE; colonial ed *The Times*, jt fndr War Refugees Ctee WW I, fndr Lady Lugard Hospitality Ctee; *m* 11 June 1902 1st and last Baron Lugard, GCMG, CB, DSO, PC (*d* 11 April 1945; *see* 1940 edn), and *d* 25 Jan 1929

(3) Marie Harriet; *d* unm 4 Aug 1951

(4) Thomasine Caroline; *m* 1st 29 July 1882 Maj Charles Aloysius Ryan, RA (*d* 17 March 1879), and had issue; *m* 2nd 9 Nov 1901 Brig-Gen Edward Parry Lambert, CB, CMG, RA, and *d* 21 Nov 1953. He *d* 26 May 1932

(5) Louisa; *m* 23 Jan 1901 John Philip Bagwell, s of Richard Bagwell, DL, of Marfield, Clonmel, CoTipperary, and *d* 13 March 1948, having had issue. He *d* 22 Aug 1946

2 (cont.) Gen George Shaw *m* 2nd 1 Oct 1872 Ellen (*d* 1900), widow of Surgn-Maj James Somerville Little, RA, and dau of Rev Charles Porter, DD, of St Leonards, Exeter, and *d* 12 Oct 1892

3 Frederic; *b* 1824; Bengal CS, U-Sec For Dept Govt India Bengal; *m* 1852 Sophia Anne (*d* 20 July 1906), dau of James Johnstone, of Dromore Lodge, Co Monaghan, and *dsp* 13 Dec 1856

4 Edward Wingfield; *b* 1827; Capt RN, Lt-Govr Malacca; *m* 30 June 1858 Louise (*d* 16 June 1920), dau of Col Sir Stephen John Hill, KCMG, CB, and *d* 24 May 1879, leaving:

(1) Edward Wingfield; *b* 9 June 1867; *m* 12 March 1908 Gladys May (*d* 1942), yst dau of William Berridge, of Windsor, Berks, and *d* 21 Oct 1925, leaving:

1a Jack Wingfield; *b* 10 May 1919; *m* 12 June 1945 *Wanda Patricia Ross, of Victoria, BC, and had:

1b +Michael Wingfield; *b* 11 March 1948

(1) Marian Louisa; *m* 29 Jan 1898 John Crowe Dwyer and *d* 31 Oct 1918

(2) Edith Constance; *m* 1st 7 Oct 1880 (*annulled* 1884) Charles Buckley; *m* 2nd Dec 1884 Maj Archibald Francis Campbell-Johnson, The Buffs, and *d* Aug 1941. He *d* 25 Sept 1937

5 Wilkinson Jocelyn; *b* 4 July 1834; MA Dublin, Lt-Col Roy Dublin Fus, Kt Dannebrog; *m* 5 April 1873 Lavinia Mary (*d* 11April 1937), dau of Edward Barrington de Fonblanque, and *d* 13 April 1911, leaving:

(1) Jocelyn Frederick de Fonblanque; *b* 28 Feb 1874; Maj RA; *m* 27 Dec 1921 May Alberta Bevan (*d* 1930), dau of Robert Cecil Kenward, and *d* 28 June 1936, leaving:

1a +Jocelyn Frederick Basil; *b* 4 Oct 1923; *educ* Wellington, King's Coll London, RNEC Keyham and Miami U (BSc Engrg); Sub-Lt RNVR WW II 1944–46, owner Shaw and Assocs, consulting engrs, Fell American Soc Civil Engrs, chartered civ engr, lecturer Miami U, author; *m* 21 Nov 1964 (*divorce* 1971) Carolyn Ann, dau of Samuel Bexon Guynes, of Waco, Texas, and heiress of W P Walker, of Longmont, Colo., and has:

1b +Jocelyn Robert Guynes; *b* 27 June 1965

2b +John Frederick Darin; *b* 13 May 1967

3b +Edward Henry David; *b* 9 Sept 1969

(1) Esme Mary; *b* 10 Sept 1883; VAD WW II; *d* unm 6 Oct 1967

1 Thomasine Harriot; *m* 10 June 1851 Sir John Floyd, 3rd Bt (*qv*), and *dsp* 16 Feb 1856

The 3rd Bt *d* 30 June 1876; his est s,

Sir Robert Shaw, 4th Bt, DL Co Dublin; *b* 3 Aug 1821; High Sheriff Co Dublin 1848, Lt-Col Dublin Militia; *m* 10 June 1852 Catherine Grace (Kate) (*d* 15 Dec

1902), dau of William Barton, of Grove, Co Tipperary, and *d* 16 May 1895, leaving:

Sir Frederick William Shaw, 5th Bt, DSO, JP, DL; *b* 15 March 1858; Lt 1st Roy Dragoons Boer War 1900 (despatches), Lt-Col and Hon Col cmdg 5th Bn Roy Dublin Fus 1907–13, 8th Service Bn Roy Dublin Fus WW I 1914–16 and 2nd Garrison Bn Roy Irish Regt 1916–18; *m* 9 July 1885 Eleanor Hester (*d* 13 Feb 1946), dau of Maj F H de Vere, RE, and had:

1 ROBERT DE VERE (Sir), **6th Bt**

2 Frederick Charleton, OBE; *b* 17 Jan 1895; Lt-Col 3rd KAR, WWs I (despatches) and II (despatches); *m* 6 Nov 1922 Angela (*d* 1978), formerly w of William Sewall and dau of Ricardo de Acosta, of New York, and *das* following a car crash in Germany 23 July 1945, leaving:

(1) Frederick Miguel; *b* 25 May 1924; Lt (E) RN; lost in HM Submarine *Affray* 17 April 1951

(1) *Mercedes Eily [Mrs Miles Hudson, The Priors Farm, Mattingley Green, Hants]; *b* 11 Sept 1926; late WRNS; *m* 19 May 1956 Capt Miles Matthew Lee Hudson, 12th Roy Lancers, only s of Brig Charles Edward Hudson, VC, CB, DSO, MC, of Denbury Manor, Newton Abbot, S Devon, and has:

1a *Mark John Frederick; *b* 24 Feb 1957

2a *Peter Charles; *b* 25 Aug 1960

3a *Richard Miles; *b* 9 June 1966

1a *Veronica Mary; *b* 1 June 1958

1 Annie Kate; *m* 20 Dec 1910 Col Cyril de Putron, Lancs Fus, of Lower Bertozerie, Guernsey, 2nd s of John Augustus de Putron, of Elstree, Herts, and *d* 18 Jan 1962, leaving issue. He *d* 5 July 1941

2 Mary Margaret, MBE (1920); *d* unm 30 Nov 1968

3 Grace Eleanor; *m* 9 Oct 1912 Maj Guy Vernon Goodliffe, MC, Roy Fus, 2nd s of Walter Francis Goodliffe, and *d* 16 April 1964, leaving issue. He *d* 29 May 1966

4 Eily de Vere; *d* unm 27 April 1949

The 5th Bt *d* 15 July 1927; his er s,

Sir Robert de Vere Shaw, 6th Bt, MC and bar; *b* 24 Feb 1890; *educ* Harrow and RMA Woolwich; Hon Lt-Col RA, WWs I and II 1940–44 (invalided), MLC Kenya 1934–38; *m* 14 March 1923 Dorothy Joan (*d* Oct 1967), dau of Thomas Cross, of Insetton House, Belbroughton, Worcs, and *d* 26 March 1969, having had:

1 Sir ROBERT SHAW, **7th and present Bt**

2 John Frederick de Vere; *b* 8 May 1930; Lt RA; *m* 6 Aug 1955 *Penelope Ann [Mrs Hougham Mills, P O Box 628, Umtentweni, 4235 Natal, S Africa] (*m* 2nd Hougham Robert Mills, s of R N Mills, of Somerset East, CP), er dau of Maj Denis William Powlett Milbank (*see* MILBANK, Bt), and was *k* in a car crash 30 Oct 1960, leaving:

(1) +CHARLES DE VERE [Maj Charles Shaw, Pigeon Farmhouse, Greenham, Berks RG14 7SP]; *b* 1 March 1957; heir presumptive; *educ* Michaelhouse S Africa; Maj 5th R Inniskilling Dragoon Gds 1975–87; businessman; *m* 1985 *Sonia, er dau of Thomas Geoffrey Eden, of Surrey, and has:

1a +Robert Jonathan de Vere; *b* 7 Aug 1988

1a *Alexandra Frances; *b* 1986

(1) *Jane Frances; *b* 19 Nov 1958

(2) *Ann Vivian; *b* 28 Sept 1960

SHAW OF NORTHSTEAD

Creation: B. (LP, UK) 1994.

THE BARON SHAW OF NORTHSTEAD, of Liversedge, Co W Yorks (Sir Michael Norman Shaw, JP (Dewsbury 1955), DL (W Yorks 1977) [The Rt Hon The Lord Shaw of Northstead JP DL, Duxbury Hall, Liversedge, W Yorks WF15 7NR]; *b* 9 Oct 1920; *educ* Sedbegh; CA, MP (Lib and C) Brighouse and Spenborough March 1960–64, (C) Scarborough and Whitby 1966–74 and Scarborough 1974–92, PPS to Min Labour 1962–63, Sec State DTI 1970–72 and Chllr Duchy Lancaster 1973, memb UK Delegn Euro Parl 1974–79, FCA, ktd 1982

Lineage: NORMAN SHAW; had:

MICHAEL NORMAN, *cr* a **Baron**

SHAWCROSS

Arms: Per pale az. and gu. on a saltire between four annulets arg. an ermine spot sa. **Crest:** Upon the battlements of a tower ppr. a martlet gu., holding in the beak a cross patée fitchée or. **Supporters:** Dexter, a lion arg., gorged with a chain sa., pendant therefrom an escutcheon, also sa., charged with a balance or; sinister, a griffin sa., armed and langued az., gorged with a chain, pendant therefrom a portcullis or. **Creation:** B. (LP, UK) 14 Feb 1959.

THE BARON SHAWCROSS, of Friston, Co Sussex (Sir Hartley William Shawcross, GBE (1974, OBE (1945)), PC (1946), QC (1939), JP (Sussex 1941)) [The Rt Hon The Lord Shawcross GBE PC QC JP, Friston Place, Sussex BN20 0AH; Anchorage, St Mawes, Cornwall TR2 5DR; 60 Victoria Embankment, London EC4Y 0JP]; *b* 4 Feb 1902; *educ* Dulwich and Geneva U; barrister Gray's Inn 1925, Bencher 1939, Treas 1955, memb Bar Cncl (Chm 1952–57), Hon Memb American and NY Bars, Hon Fell American Bar Fndn, Sr Law Lecturer Liverpool U, Recorder Salford 1941–44 and Kingston-upon-Thames 1946–61, MP (Lab) St Helens 1945–58, Attorney-Gen 1945–51, Pres BOT April–Oct 1951, Pncpl UK Del UN Assemblies 1945–49, Ch UK Prosecutor Nuremberg Trials 1945–46, UK memb Perm Court Arbitration The Hague 1950–67; Chm: Justice 1956–72, Roy Commn on Press 1961–62, MRC 1965–65, City Panel on Take-Overs and Mergers 1968–80, Upjohn (UK) Ltd, Thames TV 1969–74, Dominion Lincoln Assoc Co, Internat Advsy Cncl Morgan Guaranty Tst Co NY 1967–74, European Enterprises Devpt, Catering Wages Commn 1943–45, Bd Govrs Dulwich Coll, Nat Assoc CD Offrs, Internat Law Section Br Inst Internat and Comparative Law Sussex, Discharged Prisoners' Aid Soc 1962–66, Press Cncl 1974–78; Pres: London Police Court Mission (now Rainer Fndn), Br Hotels and Restaurants Assoc, Soc Sussex Downsmen and Fedn Sussex Amenity Socs, dir: Shell Tport and Trading, Hawker-Siddeley Gp, EMI, Caffyns Motors, Times Newspapers, Observer Newspapers, RHM, Morgan et C (Paris), Morgan et Cie (Internat), memb: Cncl Internat Chamber Commerce, Dep Regnl Commr SE Regn 1940–42, Regnl Commr NW Regn 1942–45, Cncl Eastbourne Coll, Court London U and Chllr and Cncl Sussex U 1965–85, V-Pres The Pilgrims 1977–, Steward RAC, Hon LLM Liverpool 1934, Hon LLD Columbia U 1954, Bristol U 1954, Michigan U 1959, Leigh U USA 1965, Sussex U 1966, London, Liverpool and New Brunswick 1968, Hon DCL Liverpool 1969, New Brunswick and Hull, Hon Memb Roy Coll Surgeons and Roy Coll Obstetricians and Gynaecologists, ktd 1945, author: *Life Sentence* (1995); *m* 1st 24 May 1924 Alberta Rosita (*d* by her own hand 30 Dec 1943), dau of William Shyvers, of Upminster Lodge, Essex; *m* 2nd 21 Sept 1944 Joan Winifred (*k* in a riding accident 26 Jan 1974), dau of Hume Mather, of Carlton Lodge, Tunbridge Wells; *m* 3rd 18 April 1997 *Susanne Monique, formerly w of Bob Huiskamp, and by his 2nd w has:

1 *William Hartley Hume [The Hon William Shawcross, 46 Blomfield Rd, London W9]; *b* 28 May 1946; *educ* Eton and Univ Coll Oxford; jnlst and author, with *Sunday Times*, *New Statesman*, *Washington Post* and *Spectator*; *m* 1st 31 Jan 1972 (*divorce* 1980) Marina Sarah, est dau of Esmond Warner, TD, of Summerhill, Lolworth, Cambridge, and has:

  (1) *Conrad Hartley Pelham; *b* 26 April 1977

1 (cont.) The Hon William Shawcross *m* 2nd 1981 (*divorce* 19–) Michal E, dau of A J Levin, of London; *m* 3rd 1993 *Hon Mrs Olga Polizzi, est dau of Baron Forte (*qv*), and by his 2nd w has:

  (1) *Eleanor Joan Georgina; *b* 1983

2 *Hume; *b* 19 March 1953; *educ* Eton

1 *Joanna [The Hon Mrs Peck, Pond Cottage, Friston Place, Sussex BN20 0AG]; *b* 20 Sept 1948; *educ* Benenden and St Bartholomew's Hosp Med Sch; *m* 1986 *Charles Russell Peck, est s of Russell Peck, of Cambridge, Mass., and has:

  (1) *Henry Russell Hartley; *b* 1988

  (1) *Alice Joan; *b* 1989

Lineage: JOHN SHALCROSSE, of Shawtown, nr Flixton; *b* 1535; *m* Anne — (*bur* 1590) and had:

JOHN SHAGHCROSSE/SHAWCROSS, of Flixton, nr Manchester; *b* 1575; *m* 1610 Ellen — (*bur* 1638) and had:

JOHN SHALCROSSE/SHAWCROSS; *b* 1613; *m* 1631 Margaret Fernhead and had:

JOHN SHAWCROSS; *b* 1634; *m* 1653 Anne Coupe and had:

JOHN SHAWCROSS; *b* 1655; *m* 1677 Ellen Davenport and had:

JOHN SHAWCROSS; *b* 1681; *m* 1703 Mary — and had:

JOHN MATHEW SHAWCROSS, of Flixton and later Gorton Hall; *m* Mary — and *d* 1748, leaving, with two yr sons (Peter; Matthew):

JOHN SHAWCROSS, of Gorton Hall; *b* 1716; *m* Mary — (*d* 1793) and *d* 15 Nov 1789, leaving, with an er s (John):

PETER SHAWCROSS, of Droylesden, nr Manchester; *b* 1744; *m* 31 Dec 1772 Mary (*d* 1785), dau of Samuel Beswick, and *d* by 1800, leaving, with other issue:

WILLIAM SHAWCROSS, of Droylesden; *b* 1774; *m* 1st Mrs Martha Smith; *m* 2nd Elizabeth Wainewright and *d* 1845, having had, with two yr sons (Edward, *b* 1800, *d* unm 1872; Richard, *b* 1802, *m* 1834 Louisa Carrighan and *d* 1886, having had issue) and two daus (Louisa; Julia Sidney, *d* 1849):

JOHN SHAWCROSS, of Droylesden; *b* 1798; *m* 1824 Mary Tuer (*d* 1867) and *d* 1845, leaving, with three yr sons (Henry, *b* 1826, *m* 1859 Anne, dau of E Willmer; John Harbour, *b* 1832, *d* unm 1868; Reginald, *b* 1834, *m* Laura Ravenscamp, of New Orleans, and *d* 1892):

WILLIAM TUER SHAWCROSS, of Foxholes, Rochdale; *b* 1825; Mayor Rochdale; *m* 1854 Elizabeth Eckersley and *d* 1884, leaving:

1 Harold, JP (Lancs 1907); *b* 1855; *m* 1896 Rachel, 3rd dau of Thomas Henry Huxley, PC, FRS, and had:

  (1) Anthony Tuer; *b* 1900; *m* 5 May 1927 *Mary, sis of Baron Donaldson of Kingsbridge (LP; *see* 1970 edn), and has had:

    1a *David Stuart; *b* 29 April 1929; late Eton housemaster; *m* 17 Nov 1951 *Elizabeth Anne, dau of Alexander Daniels, of Little Bealings, Woodbridge, Suffolk, and has:

      1b *Christopher Anthony; *b* 7 Dec 1956

      1b *Penelope Clare; *b* 4 Feb 1955

    2a Simon Anthony; *b* 1937; *d* following an accident 25 May 1959

    1a *Elizabeth Vere; *b* 4 March 1928; ARIBA; *m* 1954 *S R Hill-Smith

  (1) Betty; *d* 1923

2 Oliver; *b* 1859; *d* 1884

3 Arthur William; *b* 1863; *d* 1895

4 Philip; *b* 1865; *m* Mary Yule, of London, and *d* 1936, leaving:

  (1) Cecil

  (2) Tony

5 Herbert Tuer, JP (Berks 1914); *b* 1870; *educ* Giggleswick GS; *m* 1912 Mabel Paddon (*d* 1942), dau of Rev T K Higgs, of Greenacres, Oldham, and *d* July 1961, leaving:

  (1) *Edith Paddon; *b* 25 March 1913; *educ* St Hilda's Coll Oxford (BA 1935); *m* 1943 *Edward N Hall and has:

    1a *David Barnet; *b* 30 March 1944

    2a *Jonathan Shawcross [Jonathan Hall, Box 2, Dept of Chemistry, Haverweyer Hall, Columbia U, New York, NY 10027, USA]; *b* 16 March 1947

    1a *Sheila Margaret; *b* 8 March 1954

6 John; *b* 17 Sept 1871; *educ* Clifton and Univ Coll Oxford (MA 1896); *m* 20 Sept 1900 Hilda Constance (*d* 22 April 1942), dau of G Asser, and *d* 9 Feb 1966, leaving:

  (1) HARTLEY WILLIAM, *cr* a **Baron**

  (2) Christopher Nyholm, QC (1949); *b* 20 June 1905; *educ* Dulwich and Univ Coll Oxford; barrister Gray's Inn 1931 (Bencher 1954), WW II: RNVR Special Branch 1940, Cdr 1944, legal advsr to chm BOAC 1944–45, MP (Lab) Widnes 1945–50, Recorder Nottingham 1950–61; *m* 1st 1931 (*divorce* 1949) Doreen Adeline Teresa, dau of R A Burrows, of London; *m* 2nd 17 Aug 1949 *Maridel, only dau of Dr Robert Maxwell Chance, of Mayfair, and *d* 18 Aug 1973, leaving:

    1a *Timothy; *b* 8 Feb 1953; *educ* Eton and Univ Coll Oxford (BA 1972)

    1a *Christabel Anne; *b* 27 Oct 1951

SHAW-STEWART

Arms: Quarterly, 1st and 4th, or a fess checky az., over all a lion rampant gu. (for STEWART of Blackhall); 2nd and 3rd, az. three covered cups or (for SHAW of Greenock). **Crests:** 1 A lion's head erased gu., armed and langued az. (for STEWART of Blackhall), 2 Holding a club over his shoulder ppr., a demi-savage wreathed about the head and middle with a laurel vert (for SHAW of Greenock). **Supporters:** Dexter, a lion rampant gu., armed and langued az., gorged with a collar checky arg. and az.; sinister, a savage holding a club over his shoulder, all ppr., wreathed round the middle with laurel-leaves vert. **Mottoes:** (over crests) 1 *Spero meliora* ('I hope for better things'), 2 I mean well. **Creation:** Bt. (NS) 27 March 1667.

SIR HOUSTON MARK SHAW-STEWART, 11TH BT, of Greenock and Blackhall, Renfrewshire, MC (1950), TD [Maj Sir Houston Shaw-Stewart Bt MC TD, Ardgowan, Inverkip, Renfrewshire PA16 0DW]; *b* 24 April 1931; *s* bro 1980; *educ* Eton; 2nd Lt Roy Ulster Rifles Korea 1950–51, Maj Ayrshire Yeo, Hon Col A (Ayrshire Yeo) Sqdn Queen's Own Yeo RAC (TA) 1984–87, memb Roy Co Archers, V-Lt Strathclyde Region 1980–95 (DL Renfrewshire 1970–74, Strathclyde Regn 1974–80); *m* 1982 *Lucinda Victoria, yr dau of Alexander K H Fletcher, of the Old Vicarage, Wighill, N Yorks, and has:

1 +LUDOVIC HOUSTON; *b* 12 Nov 1986

Lineage: ROBERT III (*see* MORAY, E); had illegitimately:

Sir JOHN STEWART; had charters from his f of the lands of Auchingoun 1390, Blackhall 1395 and Ardgowan 1403, all Renfrewshire; ancestor of:

JOHN STEWART of Blackhall and Ardgowan; got roy charter 1508 confirming earlier charters; ancestor of:

JAMES STEWART of Ardgowan; got roy charter 1576 erecting his lands of Auchingoun, Blackhall and Ardgowan into a (territorial) Barony; *m* Margaret, dau of William Wallace of Johnston, and had:

JOHN STEWART; *m* Margaret, dau of Archibald Stewart of Castlemilk, and *d* 1598, leaving:

Sir ARCHIBALD STEWART of Blackhall, PC; MP, Commr to Parl for Renfrewshire; *m* 1st 1613 Margaret (*d* Aug 1621), dau of Bryce Blair of that Ilk; *m* 2nd 1624 Margaret, dau of George Home, *de jure* 3rd Earl of Dunbar (*see* HOME, Bt), and *d* 1665, leaving by his 1st w:

1 John; *m* 1633 Mary, dau of Sir James Stirling of Keir, and *dvp* by 1658, leaving, with other issue:

  (1) John; *m* Barbara (*m* 2nd Sir William Drummond of Hawthornden), dau of Sir William Scott of Clerkington by his 2nd w Barbara Dalmahoy, and *dsp* 1658

  (2) ARCHIBALD (Sir), **1st Bt**

  (1) Mary; *m* Sir Alexander Cuninghame, 1st Bt (*qv*), and had issue

2 Archibald, of Scotston; *m* Margaret, dau and heiress of John Hutcheson of Scotston

3 Walter, of Pardovan; *m* Elizabeth, dau and heiress of Robert Stewart of Pardovan, and had:

  (1) Walter

1 Annabella; *m* 1646 Sir George Maxwell of Auldhouse and Pollok (*d* April 1677) and had issue (*see* HERON-MAXWELL, Bt)

2 Margaret; *m* Sir David Boswell of Auchinleck

Sir ARCHIBALD's gs,

Sir Archibald Stewart, 1st Bt (NS), so *cr* 27 March 1667, of Blackhall; MP Renfrewshire 1667; *b* probably *c* 1635; *m* 1st Anne, *er* dau and coheir of Sir John Craufurd, 1st Bt, of Kilbirnie (*see* CUNINGHAME, Bt); *m* 2nd Agnes (*dsp*), probably dau of Sir Alexander Dalmahoy of that Ilk; *m* 3rd Mary Douglas and *d c* 1722, leaving further issue by her and by his 1st w, with an *er* s (*dsp*):

---

1 John; advocate 1692, MP Renfrewshire 1700–04; *m* 13 March 1700 Rebecca (*bur* 21 May 1740), dau of Michael Wallace, of Glasgow, physician, and *dvp* April 1713, leaving, with other issue:

  (1) **Sir Archibald Stewart, 2nd Bt**, of Blackhall; advocate 1718; *d* unm April 1724

  (2) MICHAEL (Sir), **3rd Bt**

  (1) Anne; *m* her cousin Archibald Steuart of Steuart Hall

2 Walter STEWART later STEUART of Steuart Hall, nr Stirling; Slr-Gen Scotland 1720; *m* 1st Barbara Kay; *m* 2nd Barbara, dau of — Scott of Malleny, and had, with other issue:

  (1) Archibald, of Steuart Hall; *m* 29 Nov 1727 his cousin Anne (*see* above) and had:

    1a David, of Steuart Hall, WS; *b* 1744; *m* Margaret (*d* 1806), dau of Robert Ramsay of Camno, and *d* 2 May 1823, leaving, with other issue:

      1b Robert, of Steuart Hall; *b* Oct 1776; *m* 16 April 1827 Helen (*d* 24 March 1859), dau of Walter Buchanan and widow of Boyd Dunlop, and *d* 14 March 1844, leaving:

        1c David, of Steuart Hall; *b* 19 March 1830; Maj 34th Regt; *m* 17 Jan 1861 Dorothy Emily (*d* 18 Feb 1910), only dau of Rev John Cox, and *d* 16 Dec 1890, leaving:

          1d Robert John Archibald; *b* 10 Oct 1863; *d* 27 Oct 1932

          1d Mary Helen; *m* Sept 1909 Col William George Lyddon, CMG, RA, and *d* 31 Oct 1926

      2b George Mackenzie; *b* 10 Dec 1786; Lt-Gen HEICS; *m* 25 Dec 1820 Mary (*d* 24 June 1869), dau of Murray Babington, and *d* 23 June 1855, leaving, with other issue:

        1c George; *b* 3 Oct 1821; Brig-Gen Roy Co Archers; *m* 9 Nov 1865 Susan Alexander (*d* 14 March 1921), dau of James McAlpine and widow of Lt Henry Goodwyn, Bengal Engrs, HEICS, and *d* 5 Oct 1893, leaving:

          1d George Mackenzie, WS; *b* 10 Dec 1866; *m* 24 April 1919 Mary Dorothea, only dau of Adml F S Clayton, of Ross-on-Wye, Herefs, and *dsp* 20 March 1942

          2d James McAlpine; *b* 2 March 1868; Capt 4th Bn S Staffs Regt; *m* 28 April 1921 Mary, dau of Capt John Edward Compton-Bracebridge, of Atherstone Hall, Warwicks, and *d* 18 Oct 1946, leaving:

            1e *Mary Veronica [Mrs Donald Goldberg-Steuart, Street Ashton House, Stretton-under-Fosse, Rugby, Warwicks CV23 0PJ]; *b* 27 June 1926; *m* 21 April 1950 *Donald Arthur GOLDBERG later GOLDBERG-STEUART (deed poll)

          3d Murray Babington; *b* 21 Feb 1872; MB, CM, Chm Galloway U Assoc 1931–46; *m* 17 Oct 1904 Maud Ann Sophia, MBE (1920) (*d* 13 Dec 1962), 2nd dau of Lt-Gen Charles Samuel Steward, Madras Army, by Eliza Ducarol Constance Hamilton (*see* HAMILTON, Bt, of Silverton Hill), and *d* 29 Dec 1964, leaving:

            1e Ducarol Anne Katherine; FANY, ATS, WW II

          1d Janet Alexander; *m* 29 July 1899 Very Rev Llewelyn Wynne-Jones (*d* 23 Feb 1936), Dean Emeritus St Asaph, only s of Rev Canon Llewelyn Wynne-Jones, of Llanymynsch, Mon, and *d* 11 Nov 1959

        2c John Shaw; *b* 21 Oct 1832; Maj Madras Artillery; *m* 20 June 1867 Mary Babington Ball (*d* 21 Sept 1916), dau of Robert Ball Steele, and *d* 15 June 1872, leaving:

          1d Jane West Babington; *m* 31 Oct 1893 Lt-Col Oliver Goldsmith Ievers (*d* 11 Feb 1916), Indian Staff Corps, only s of Lt Henry Rogers Ievers, RA, and *d* 4 Aug 1933, leaving issue

        1c Mary; *m* 2 Jan 1849 Maj-Gen Sir Frederick John Goldsmid, KCSI, CB (*d* 12 Jan 1908), Madras Army, and *d* 21 July 1900, leaving issue

        2c Dora; *m* 16 Oct 1855 Yeats H Goldsmid (*dsp* 21 Nov 1878) and *d* Dec 1900

        3c Alice; *m* 11 April 1867 Very Rev T B W Niven, DD, and *d* July 1905, leaving issue

  (1) Barbara; *m* Aug 1727 Sir John Maxwell, 2nd Bt, of the 1682 *cr* and had issue (*see* HERON-MAXWELL, Bt)

1 Margaret; *m* 1685 John Brisbane of Bishopton and with him was ancestor of the BRISBANEs of that Ilk

Sir ARCHIBALD's bro,

Sir Michael Stewart, 3rd Bt, of Blackhall; *b c* 1712; advocate 1735; *m* June 1738 Helen (*d* 19 July 1746), est dau of Sir John Houston, 3rd Bt, of Houston, by Margaret, dau of Sir John Shaw, 2nd Bt, of Greenock, by Eleanor, *er* dau and coheir of Sir Thomas Nicolson, 3rd Bt, of Carnock (*see* CARNOCK, B), and *d* 20 Oct 1796, having had, with other issue:

1 Sir JOHN STEWART later SHAW-STEWART (on inheriting 1752 the Greenock, Easter Greenock and Finnart estates from his great-uncle Sir John Shaw, 3rd Bt, of Greenock), **4th Bt**, of Greenock and Blackhall; *b* probably *c* 1740; MP Renfrewshire 1780–83 and 1786–96; *m* April 1786 Frances (*d* 21 March 1818), dau of Robert Colhoun, of St Christopher, WI, and widow of Sir James Maxwell, 6th Bt, of the 1682 *cr* (*see* HERON-MAXWELL, Bt), and *dsp* 7 Aug 1812

2 Houston STEWART later STEWART-NICOLSON (on inheriting 1752 the Carnock estate from Sir John Houston, 4th Bt); *m* 19 March 1765 Margaret, dau of Boyd Porterfield of that Ilk, and *d* 1785, leaving:

  (1) Sir MICHAEL STEWART-NICOLSON later SHAW-STEWART (on inheriting 7 Sept 1812 the Greenock estate), **5th Bt**; *b* 10 Feb 1766; Ld-Lt of Renfrewshire; *m* 24 Sept 1787 his cousin Catharine (*d* 10 May 1849), yr dau of Sir William Maxwell, 3rd Bt, of Springkell (*see* HERON-MAXWELL, Bt) and *d* 25 Aug 1825, having had, with other issue:

    1a MICHAEL (Sir), **6th Bt**

    2a Houston (Sir), GCB; *b* 2 Aug 1791; Adml of the Fleet, a Ld Admlty; MP, Govr Greenwich Hosp; *m* Feb 1818 Martha (*d* 17 April 1870), dau of Sir William Miller, 2nd Bt, of Glenlee (*qv*), and *d* 10 Dec 1875, having had, with other issue:

      1b William Houston (Sir), GCB; *b* 7 Sept 1822; Adml, Controller Navy 1881–85, C-in-C Devonport; *m* 1st 20 Feb 1850 Catherine Elizabeth (*d* 23 Nov 1867), est dau of Eyre Coote (*see* COOTE, Bt), and had:

        1c Houston; *b* 6 June 1854; Lt RN; *k* Sudan 1884

2c Archibald William Houston; *b* 18 Nov 1864; *m* 17 Dec 1891 Flora Sarah Anne (*d* 1 Jan 1950), only dau of Thomas Beeson, of Stonewall, Manitoba, and *d* 29 May 1946, having had:

1d William Houston; *b* 19 Feb 1893; served WW I; missing, presumed *d* 26 May 1917

1d Catherine Grace; *b* 4 Aug 1898

1c Grace; *m* 22 April 1879 Capt Marie Louis Emile Renet (*d* 25 March 1895), 13th Dragoons, French Army, and *d* 21 July 1887, leaving issue

2c Catherine Coote; *d* unm 19 Aug 1930

3c Louisa Mary; *d* unm 29 Dec 1914

1b (cont.) Sir William Shaw-Stewart *m* 2nd 11 Jan 1872 Blanche Caroline (*d* 17 Sept 1927), 3rd dau of Adml Hon Keith Stewart, CB (*see* GALLOWAY, E), and *d* 13 Nov 1902, having by her had:

3c Blanche Nina Mary; *d* unm 8 May 1947

4b John Erskine Douglas; *b* 13 Jan 1832; *m* 17 Jan 1854 Julia (*d* 17 Sept 1899), dau of Rev Henry Turton, and *d* 2 Aug 1870, having had, with other issue:

1c Michael Patrick; *b* Oct 1860; *m* 1886 Fanny Montgomery (*d* 1947), dau of G V Stewart (*see* STEWART, Bt, of Athenree), and *d* 1921, having had:

1d John Houston Douglas; *b* 1890; *d* 1903

2d George Archdale; *b* 1893; *m* 1921 Myrtle (*d* 1971), dau of John Wheeler, of Auckland, NZ, and *d* 9 July 1959, leaving:

1e *Lois Frances [Miss Lois Shaw-Stewart, Unit 4, 8 Bowling Ave, Epsom, Auckland, New Zealand]; *b* 1925

3d Donald Erskine; *b* 1905; *m* 1936 Ailsa Violet Annie (*d* 1970), dau of John Forbes, of Auckland, NZ, and had:

1e +Donald Michael [Donald Shaw-Stewart Esq, 699 Mt Eden Rd, Mt Eden, Auckland, New Zealand]; *b* 1944; *m* 1970 (*divorce* 1979) Jill Mary Smith and has:

1f +Bradley James; *b* 1970

2f +Jonathan Paul; *b* 1973

1f *Joanne Clare; *b* 1975

1d Angela Julia Isabel; *m* 1920 Ernest Conway Bennett and had issue

2d Nina Margaret; *m* 1910 Charles Gunson and *d* 1934, leaving issue

3d Muriel Frances; *m* 1925 Cyril Lester and had issue

1c Harriet Nina; *m* 18 March 1876 Hugh Fletcher Campbell, yst s of H F Campbell, of Boloquhan, Stirling, and *d* 24 Dec 1906

3a John Shaw; *b* 24 July 1793; advocate, Sheriff Stirling; *m* 15 Aug 1827 Jane Stuart (*d* 27 Dec 1886), dau of Sir John Shaw Heron-Maxwell, 4th Bt (*qv*), and *d* June 1840, leaving, with other issue:

1b Michael John Maxwell; *b* 24 Nov 1828; *m* 11 April 1867 Julia (*d* 10 June 1899), dau of Augustus Hermann Kindermann, and *d* 3 April 1894, leaving:

1c Michael John; *b* 22 Sept 1870; *d* 4 July 1938

1c Margaret Veronica; *b* 20 March 1869; *d* unm 11 June 1936

2b John Heron Maxwell; *b* 9 Sept 1831; Maj-Gen RE; *m* 7 Sept 1871 Mary Catherine Bedingfeld (*d* 22 Dec 1909), only dau of Col George Chancellor Collyer, RE, and *d* 6 July 1908, leaving:

1c Basil Heron, CMG (1918), DSO (1917); *b* 8 Dec 1877; *educ* Marlborough and RMA Woolwich; Col RA, Bde-Maj 1916, WW I (despatches); *m* 9 Nov 1916 Vera, yst dau of William Henry Caldwell, of Morar, Inverness-shire, and *d* 7 April 1939, leaving:

1d Patrick Hugh; *b* 9 July 1921; *educ* Eton; Lt Scots Gds WW II; *ka* Italy Jan 1944

2d +Michael [Michael Shaw-Stewart Esq, Linthill, Melrose, Roxburghshire]; *b* 17 Nov 1925; *educ* Eton and King's Coll Cambridge (MA); ARIBA, AA Dipl, FRIAS; Lt Scots Gds 1944–47; *m* 15 Dec 1951 *Grizel Margaret Lighton, only dau of Maj Alexander Caldwell Stewart, MC (*see* LIGHTON, Bt), and has:

1e +Archibald John [Archibald Shaw-Stewart Esq, Drummore, Doune, Perthshire]; *b* 21 Nov 1953; *educ* Eton; *m* 1983 *Judy, er dau of Maj Robert Courage, CVO, MBE, of Windlesham, Surrey, and has:

1f +Robert Houston; *b* 1986

1f *Mary Ann; *b* 1987

2f *Phoebe Kate; *b* 1990

2e +Robert Hugh; *b* 24 June 1960

1e *Helen Katharine; *b* 8 June 1959; *m* 8 Oct 1995 *Alastair George Bradstock (*see* HAWARDEN, V)

3d +John William Archibald [John Shaw-Stewart Esq, Traigh House, Arisaig, Inverness-shire]; *b* 28 Jan 1929; *educ* Eton; *m* 11 June 1955 Vora June Douglas (*d* 30 April 1998), 2nd dau of Charles Whistler Mackintosh (*see* HAMILTON and BRANDON, D), and has:

1e +David Hugh [David Shaw-Stewart Esq, Hailes, By Haddington, E Lothian]; *b* 25 July 1956; *educ* Eton; *m* 1984 *Linda Mary Catherine, er dau of Terence Malin Dare Sorby, CBE, of the Old Vicarage, Markbeech, Kent, and has:

1f +Lachlan Hugo Terence; *b* 1988

2f +Guy Philip; *b* 1990

1f *Alexandra Linda Vora; *b* 1986

2e +Patrick Douglas; *b* 7 Feb 1958

3e +Alexander Malcolm; *b* 14 July 1960

1e *Mairi Hermione Margaret; *b* 2 Sept 1962; *m* 19– *Barry Hextall and has:

1f *Lily Vera; *b* 16 Jan 1999

2c Patrick Houston; *b* 17 Aug 1888; *educ* Balliol Coll Oxford (BA); poet, Fell All Souls 1910, Lt-Cdr RNVR WW I (Chev Legn Hon, Croix de Guerre); *ka* nr Metz 30 Dec 1917

1c Mary Winifred; *d* unm 21 Jan 1937

2c Katharine Bedingfeld, MBE (1943); *d* unm 10 July 1959

1b Mary Elizabeth; *m* 6 March 1856 James Howden and *d* 13 Jan 1909, having had issue

2b Helenora Grace; *m* 18 May 1870 Capt Ian Dalrymple Clark (*d* 1870), 8th Madras Light Cav, and *d* 2 Feb 1922, leaving issue

4a Patrick Maxwell; *b* 1795; MP Lancaster 1831–37 and Renfrewshire 1841; *d* 30 Oct 1846

5a William Maxwell; *d* July 1869

1a Margaret; *m* 28 July 1836 11th Duke of Somerset (*qv*) and *dsp* 18 July 1880

2a Catharine; *m* Capt John Osborne, 6th Inniskilling Dragoons (*d* 1879), and *d* 7 Nov 1883, leaving issue

3a Helenora; *m* 10 June 1833 Sir William Maxwell, 6th Bt, of Monreith (*qv*), and *d* 27 Oct 1876, having had issue

3 Archibald; *k* 1779 defending Tobago against American privateers

1 Margaret; *m* 1764 Sir William Maxwell, 3rd Bt, of Springkell (*d* 4 March 1804), and *d* March 1816, having had issue (*see* HERON-MAXWELL, Bt)

The 5th Bt's est s,

Sir Michael Shaw-Stewart, 6th Bt, of Greenock; *b* 1788; *educ* Ch Ch Oxford and Lincoln's Inn; MP Lanarks 1827–30 and Renfrewshire 1830–37; *m* 16 Sept 1819 Eliza Mary (*d* 25 Jan 1852), only child of Robert Farquhar, of Newark, Renfrewshire, and *d* 19 Dec 1836, having had, with other issue:

1 MICHAEL ROBERT (Sir), **7th Bt**

2 John Archibald, JP Middx, JP, DL Renfrewshire; *b* 15 Sept 1829; MA Oxon; *m* 1st 27 Aug 1857 Helenora Margaret Angela (*d* 24 Jan 1865), only dau of Boyd Alexander of Ballochmyle and Southbar; *m* 2nd April 1881 Isabella Barbara (*d* 1883), dau of T C Hume and widow of Capt J H T Alexander, CB, RN, of Southbar; *m* 3rd 21 Jan 1886 Constance Mary (*d* 12 Oct 1910), dau of Edward Johnston, and *d* 25 May 1900, leaving by his 1st w:

(1) Archibald Claud; *b* 10 Dec 1859; *d* 9 June 1938

(1) Helenora; *b* 16 July 1858; *m* 20 April 1882 Sir Francis Gore-Browne, KC, JP (*d* 2 Sept 1922), s of Col Sir Thomas Gore-Browne, KCMG, CB, and *d* 18 Dec 1946, leaving issue

(2) Constance Angela; *b* 24 Feb 1862; *d* unm 7 Nov 1942

3 Robert Farquhar; *b* 3 March 1836; Scots Fus Gds; *m* 10 Feb 1859 Isabella Jane (*d* 21 Sept 1916), est dau of Hon Charles William Warner, CB, Attorney-Gen Trinidad, and *d* 29 Oct 1911, having had:

(1) Robert Michael; *b* 17 Feb 1860; *d* 10 Jan 1890

(2) Francis Charles; *b* 30 June; *d* 9 Aug 1869

(3) Charles Edward; *d* an infant

(4) Patrick Francis; *b* 13 Feb 1872; Lt 2nd Vol Bn Roy Scots Fus; *m* 19 April 1928 Mrs Nancye Reece (*d* 14 Feb 1965), dau of Ernest Wilcox, MD, of Hambrook Court, Glos, and *dsp* 15 June 1952

1 Mary Isobel; *d* unm 2 Sept 1911

2 Agnes Ethel; *d* unm 18 Feb 1959

3 Olive Margaret; *m* 17 April 1917 Rev Thomas John Hardy (*d* 8 March 1944), Warden St Mary's House of Retreat, Regent's Park

1 Katharine Mary, VA; Bedchamber Woman to HM QUEEN VICTORIA; *m* 2 May 1848 Maj-Gen Hon Robert Bruce (*see* ELGIN and KINCARDINE, E) and *dsp* 3 Dec 1889

The 6th Bt's est s,

Sir Michael Robert Shaw-Stewart, 7th Bt, of Greenock; *b* 26 Nov 1826; *educ* Eton and Ch Ch Oxford; Offr 2nd Life Gds 1845–46, MP Renfrewshire 1855–65, Lt-Col 1st Renfrew Vols 1860–1903, Sheriff Wilts 1883, Ld Lt Renfrewshire, Hon Col 1st Vol Bn Argyll & Sutherland Highrs; *m* 28 Dec 1852 Lady Octavia Grosvenor (*d* 29 May 1921), 6th dau of 2nd Marquess of Westminster (*see* WESTMINSTER, D), and *d* 10 Dec 1903, having had:

1 **Sir (Michael) Hugh Shaw-Stewart, 8th Bt**, KCB (1933, CB 1916), TD, JP Renfrewshire, of Greenock; *b* 11 July 1854; *educ* Eton and Ch Ch Oxford; Capt 4th Bn Argyll & Sutherland Highrs, MP E Renfrewshire 1886–1906, Hon Col 5th/6th Bn, Ld Lt Renfrewshire, Hon LLD Glasgow 1936, Chm CC and TA Renfrewshire; *m* 14 Nov 1833 Lady Alice Emma Thynne, CBE, JP Renfrewshire (*d* 26 Jan 1942), dau of 4th Marquess of Bath (*qv*), and *dsp* 29 June 1942

2 Charles Robert (Rev); *b* 9 July 1856; *educ* Ch Ch Oxford (MA); Rector Cowden, Kent; *m* 2 Jan 1890 Ida Fannie Caroline (*d* May 1940), 3rd dau of H W Afken, of Oldenburg, and *d* 28 Feb 1932, leaving:

(1) Una Mary; *b* 10 Oct 1890; *m* 5 June 1916 Walter Rupert Reynell (*d* 21 March 1948), MD, FRCP, s of Walter Reynell, of Reynella, S Australia, and had:

1a *Peter Carew; *b* 1917

2a *Anthony Charles; *b* 1930

1a *Joan Katherine; *b* 1918

2a *Anne Lenore; *b* 1923

(2) Katharine; *b* 4 July 1893; *m* 1st 24 Jan 1912 Maj Robert Alexander (*d* 22 June 1928), est surv s of Lt-Col Boyd F Alexander, Rifle Bde; *m* 2nd 22 Sept 1928 Edward Arthur Courthope (*d* 16 Sept 1963), s of William John Courthope, CB, and by her 1st husb had:

1a Boyd; *b* 4 Nov 1913; *educ* Radley and Magdalen Coll Oxford (BA); *m* 1941 *Frederica Emma, dau of F M Graham, of Yankalilla, S Australia, and widow of R A Brown, of Brussels

1a *Mary; *b* 29 Oct 1914; *m* 7 Aug 1935 Cdr Rev Eric Hart Dyke, RN, and has issue (*see* DYKE, Bt)

3 Walter Richard, MBE (1920), JP, DL Wilts; *b* 27 June 1861; Capt 1st Wilts Vol RC and 4th Bn Argyll & Sutherland Highrs, CC Wilts 1889–1920, High Sheriff 1919–20; *m* 24 Oct 1891 Mary Beatrice Sydney, OBE (1920) (*d* 11 Sept 1943), dau of Sidney Leveson Lane, and *d* 25 Sept 1934, leaving:

(1) (WALTER) GUY (Sir), **9th Bt**

(2) Niel; *b* 7 July 1894; Lt 1st Bn and 3rd Bn Rifle Bde, WW I; *ka* Guillemont 21 Aug 1916

(3) Michael Sidney; *b* 29 June 1905; accidentally shot dead 11 July 1936

(1) Mary Sibell Agnes; *b* 3 April 1896; ARRC; *m* 14 Sept 1932 Lt-Col Ian Rose Innes Forbes, DSO (*d* 18 Sept 1957), and *dsp* 5 March 1957

(2) Irene Beatrice, JP Wilts; *b* 11 Oct 1901; *m* 1 April 1926 Brig Reginald Gordon Ward Rimington, RTR, 6th Dragoons (*d* from wounds April 1941), only s of Lt-Gen Sir Michael Rimington, KCB, CVO, and *d* 2 Jan 1971, leaving:

1a *Niel William; *b* 1 Feb 1928; *educ* Ampleforth and Ch Ch Oxford

1a *Rosemary Monica; *b* 12 Jan 1927; *m* 4 April 1960 *Kenneth James and has:

   1b *Henry Christopher; *b* 5 April 1962

   1b *Helen Mary; *b* 8 April 1961

2a *Gillian Margaret Mary; *b* 5 June 1931; *m* Aug 1961 *Maj E Makoui, Imperial Iranian Air Force, and has issue

3a *Bridget Clare; *b* 23 March 1937

4a *Mary Marcia; *b* 8 Sept 1938; *m* 3 Sept 1966 *Bernard Kennedy Lane, of Shaftesbury, Dorset, and has:

   1b *John Reginald; *b* 11 July 1969

   1b *Mary Margaret; *b* 27 Oct 1967

4 Archibald William; *b* 6 July 1865; *d* 5 Dec 1927

5 Houston Michael, DSO; *b* 3 Oct 1871; Capt 17th Lancers; *d* 28 July 1901

1 Evelyn Margaret; *d* an infant 1 Feb 1859

2 Eliza Mary; *d* 3 May 1875

3 Helen; *b* 18 July 1859; *m* 28 Sept 1880 4th Earl Manvers (*d* 17 July 1926; *see* 1953 edn) and *d* 11 March 1939, leaving issue

4 Agnes Caroline; *b* 25 June 1862; *m* 15 Sept 1898 Hon Henry Stuart Littleton (*see* HATHERTON, B) and *d* 4 July 1935

The 8th Bt's n,

Sir (Walter) Guy Shaw-Stewart, 9th Bt, MC, of Greenock and Blackhall, JP Renfrewshire; *b* 10 Aug 1892; *educ* Eton; 2nd Coldstream Gds WW I (wounded twice), Maj Res Offrs Coldstream Gds, memb Renfrew TAA 1933–76, Lt-Col and Brevet Col 5th/6th Bn Argyll & Sutherland Highrs (TA) 1934, cmded 6th Argyll & Sutherland Highrs WW II France 1940, Renfrewshire: Ld Lt 1950–67 (DL 1944–50), Convener CC 1950–76; *m* 1st 31 July 1915 Diana (*d* 22 April 1968), est dau of John George Bulteel, of Pamflete, Devon; *m* 2nd 9 Aug 1949 his former sis-in-law Elizabeth Sofia, JP (Renfrewshire 1955) (*d* 28 April 1931), dau of John George Bulteel and widow of Maj-Gen Alan Geoffrey Charles Dawnay, CBE, DSO (*see* DOWNE, V), and *d* 26 April 1976, having by his 1st w had:

1 Ian Niel; *b* 28 April 1918; *d* 2 Oct 1925

2 **Sir Euan Guy Shaw-Stewart, 10th Bt**; *b* 11 Oct 1928; *educ* Eton; *m* 1st 26 Sept 1953 (*divorce* 1956) Mary Louise, 2nd dau of Lt-Col Geoffrey Reginald Devereux Shaw, of Scottow Hall, Norwich, and had, with twin sons (*b* and *d* 7 Jan 1955):

   (1) *Fiona Mary Onyx; *b* 4 May 1954; *m* 1981 *Guy Nicholas John Jewers, s of Maj J S Jewers, RM, of Home Farm, Swailcliffe, Oxon

2 (cont.) **Sir Euan** *m* 2nd 22 Sept 1962 (*divorce* 1969) Victoria Anne [Victoria Lady Shaw-Stewart, 42 Sheridan Rd, London SW19], yr dau of W Fryer, of London, and *d* 30 Jan 1980, having by her had:

   (2) *Claudia Mary; *b* 26 Nov 1963

3 **Sir HOUSTON MARK SHAW-STEWART, 11th and present Bt**

1 Lavinia Mariqueta; *b* 6 May 1919; *m* 1st 27 Nov 1940 (*divorce* 1947) Capt George Hubert Wyndham Clark, Welsh Gds, only s of Wyndham Clark, and had issue; *m* 2nd 1947 (*divorce* 1961) Robert Barry Chambers and had further issue; *m* 3rd 7 Oct 1961 Cedric Alan Smith, only s of Harry Smith, and *d* 4 March 1971

2 Cynthia Mary; *b* 5 Feb 1922; *d* unm 19 Oct 1946

SHEFFIELD

Arms: Arg. a chevron engrailed between two garbs in chief gu. and in base a sheaf of five arrows ppr. banded, also gu. **Crest:** A boar's head erased at the neck or between two arrows, points downwards ppr. **Motto:** *Comiter sed fortiter* ('Composedly but determinedly'). **Creation:** Bt. (GB) 1 March 1755.

SIR REGINALD ADRIAN BERKELEY SHEFFIELD, 8TH BT, of Normanby, Co Lincoln, DL (Humberside 1985) [Sir Reginald Sheffield Bt DL, Normanby Park, Normanby, S Humberside DN15 9HS]; *b* 9 May 1946; *s* unc 1977; *educ* Eton; CC Humberside 1985–93, md Normanby Estate Co, memb Lloyd's 1977–, v-chm S Humberside Business Advice Centre 1984–; *m* 1st 11 Nov 1969 (*divorce* 1975) Annabel Lucy Veronica, dau of Timothy Angus Jones (*see* ASTOR, V, and CLIFFORD OF CHUDLEIGH, B), and has:

1 *Samantha Gwendoline; *b* 18 April 1971; *educ* Bristol U; *m* 1 June 1996 *David W D Cameron, yr s of Ian Cameron

2 *Emily Julia; *b* 1973

Sir REGINALD *m* 2nd 1977 *Victoria Penelope, dau of Ronald Clive Walker, DFC, by Mrs Paul Luxmoore-May, and by her has:

1 +ROBERT CHARLES BERKELEY; *b* 1 Sept 1984

3 *Alice Daisy Victoria; *b* 1980

4 *Lucy Mary; *b* 1981

Lineage: ROBERT SHEFFIELD; MP Lincs 1442 and 1445–46; had:

ROBERT SHEFFIELD; MP Bedwin 1467–68 and Ludgershall 1472–75; had:

Sir ROBERT SHEFFIELD; Recorder London 1495–1508, Speaker H of C 1510 and 1512; had:

Sir ROBERT SHEFFIELD; *m* 1st Jane, sis of 2nd Earl of Derby (*qv*); *m* 2nd Margaret (*m* 2nd — Cavendish), dau of Sir John Zouche, of Codnor, Derbys (*see* GREY, B, and ZOUCHE, B), and *d* 15 Nov 1531, leaving by his 1st w:

EDMUND SHEFFIELD, 1st BARON SHEFFIELD, of Butterwick, Co Lincoln (E), so *cr* 16 Feb 1546/7; *b* 22 Nov 1521; memb Thomas Cromwell's entourage 1538, served French Campaign 1544, an envoy to France 1546; *m* by 31 Jan 1537/8 Anne, 2nd dau of 15th Earl of Oxford (*see* SAINT ALBANS, D), and was *k* Norwich 31 July 1549 while a memb of the govt forces sent to suppress Kett's Rebellion, leaving:

JOHN SHEFFIELD, 2nd BARON SHEFFIELD, KB (Jan 1558/9); *b c* 1538; *m c* 1562 Douglas (*m* allegedly 2nd 1573 Robert Dudley, Earl of Leicester, and 3rd(?) 29 Nov 1579, as his 2nd w, Sir Edward Stafford, Amb France 1583–90, and was *bur* 11 Dec 1608), dau of 1st Baron Howard of Effingham (*see* EFFINGHAM, E), and *d* 10 Dec 1568, leaving:

EDMUND SHEFFIELD, 3rd BARON SHEFFIELD and 1st EARL OF MULGRAVE, Co York (E), so *cr* 5 Feb 1625/6, KG (1593); *b* 7 Dec 1565; *educ* Ch Ch Oxford; served English fleet against Spanish Armada 1588, ktd 1588, absentee Govr Brill, Low Countries, Jan–July 1598, Ld Lt Yorks 1603–19, Ld Pres Cncl in N 1603–19, V-Adml Yorks 1616; *m* 1st by 13 Nov 1581 Ursula (*d* by 4 Aug 1618), dau of Sir Robert Tyrwhitt (*see* BERNERS, B), of Kettleby, Lincs; *m* 2nd 4 March 1618/9 Mariana, dau of Sir William Erwin/Irwin, and *d* Oct 1646, having by his 1st w had, with at least two other sons (drowned with their est bro; *see* below):

Sir JOHN SHEFFIELD; *m* Grizel, dau of Sir Edmund Anderson, Ch Judge Common Pleas, and was drowned Dec 1641 *vp* in the Humber, leaving:

EDMUND SHEFFIELD, 2nd EARL OF MULGRAVE; *b c* Dec 1611; V-Adml Yorks 1646 (Parly apptmt), Cncllr State 1649–50 and 1654–58, nominated memb of CROMWELL's 'Other House' but did not take his seat; *m c* 13 April 1631 Lady Elizabeth Cranfield (*m* 2nd, as his 1st w, 1st Baron Ossulston; *see* TANKERVILLE, E), 2nd dau of 1st Earl of Middlesex, and *d* 24 Aug 1658, leaving:

JOHN SHEFFIELD, 3rd EARL OF MULGRAVE and 1st DUKE OF THE COUNTY OF BUCKINGHAM AND OF NORMANBY, so *cr* 24 March 1702/3, as also earlier 10 May 1694 MARQUESS OF NORMANBY, Co Lincoln (both E), KG (1674), PC (1685–Feb 1688/9, 1694–March 1695/6, 1702–08 and 1710–124); *b* 8 Sept 1647; served RN (present victory over Dutch of Sole Bay 1672), Gentleman Bedchamber 1673–82 and May–Oct 1685, Col Holland Regt 1673–82 and 1684–85, also cmded forces Tangier, Govr Hull 1679–82, Ld Lt E R Yorks 1679–82, 1687–88 and 1711–13, Ld Chamberlain 1685–88, V-Adml Yorks and Northumberland 1687–89, Ld Privy Seal 1702–05, Ld Lt N R Yorks 1702–05 and 1711–14, a Commr Union of S and E Parls 1706, Ld Steward Household 1710–11, Ld Pres Cncl 1711–14, Ld Lt Middx 1711–14; poetaster; *m* 1st 18 March 1685/6 Ursula (*d* 13 Aug 1697), dau of George Stawell, of Cothelstone, Somerset, and widow of 1st and last Earl of Conway (*see* HERTFORD, M, preliminary remarks), but had no issue by her; *m* 2nd 12 March 1698/9 Katherine (*d* 7 Feb 1703/4), dau of 5th Baron Brooke (*see* WARWICK, BROOKE and, E) and widow of 2nd Earl of Gainsborough (*qv*), but had no issue by her; *m* 3rd 16 March 1705/6 Catherine, illegitimate dau of JAMES II by Catherine Sedley (*see* MEXBOROUGH, E), Countess of Dorchester, and widow of 3rd Earl of Anglesey of the 1661 *cr* (*see* VALENTIA, V, also NORMANBY, M), and *d* 24 Feb 1720/1, having by her had, with at least two er sons (*d* infants):

   1 EDMUND SHEFFIELD, 2nd and last DUKE OF THE COUNTY OF BUCKINGHAM AND OF NORMANBY; *b* 3 Jan 1715/6; *educ* Queen's Coll Oxford; ADC to Duke of Berwick (*see* JERSEY, E), his mother's half-bro, in Germany 1734; *d* unm 30 Oct 1735, when his titles expired

The 1st DUKE had illegitimately by Frances, *née* Stewart, at that time or perhaps afterwards w of Oliver Lambart, yr s of 3rd Earl of Cavan (*qv*):

   2 Sir CHARLES HERBERT later SHEFFIELD (under terms of f's will, which proved 28 March 1721), **1st Bt** (GB), so *cr* 1 March 1755, of Normanby; *b* probably *c* 1706; inherited a large portion of the Sheffield lands, including the Normanby estate, Lincs; *m* 25 April 1741 Margaret Diana (*d* 6 Jan 1762), dau of Gen Joseph Sabine, Govr Ghent and Gibraltar, and *d* 5 Sept 1774, having had, with two other daus (*d* unm):

      (1) **Sir John Sheffield, 2nd Bt**, of Normanby; *b c* 1743; *educ* Ch Ch Oxford; *m* 3 April 1784 Charlotte Sophia (*d* 15 Dec 1835), dau of Very Rev Hon William Digby (*see* DIGBY, B), and *dsp* 4 Feb 1815

      (2) Charles; *d* unm, *bur* 31 May 1790

      (3) ROBERT (Sir), **3rd Bt**

      (1) Anne Diana; *m* Lt-Gen Thomas Cox

The 1st DUKE also had illegitimately, by an unknown woman (possibly Frances mentioned above):

   1 Mary; took surname Sheffield; *m* 22 July 1707, as his 2nd w, 4th Baron Altham (*see* VALENTIA, V) and *d* 26 Oct 1729

The 2nd Bt's bro,

Rev Sir Robert Sheffield, 3rd Bt, of Normanby; *b c* 1758; *educ* Ch Ch Oxford; Rector Flixborough, Lincs, Vicar Burton, Lincs; *m* 1st by 1785 Penelope (*d* 22 June 1787), dau of Sir Abraham Pitches, of Streatham, Surrey, and had, with a dau (*d* unm):

   1 ROBERT (Sir), **4th Bt**

The **Rev Sir Robert** *m* 2nd by 1797 Sarah Anne (*d* 14 Sept 1858), dau of Rev Brackley Kennet, DD, and by her had:

2 Charles (Rev); *b* 19 Oct 1797; Rector Flixborough; *m* 20 Nov 1820 Lucy (*d* 15 Feb 1857), dau of Col Smelt, and *d* 20 Feb 1882, having had, with three other daus (*d* young or unm):

(1) Caroline Alice; *m* 20 April 1841 Rev Canon Charles Lloyd, Rector Chalfont St Giles, and *d* 29 June 1893, leaving issue. He *d* 29 April 1883

(2) Lucy Emily; *m* 9 May 1848 Rev Henry George Middleton Pretyman, Vicar Lowick, and *dsp* 21 Aug 1878, leaving issue. He *d* 11 May 1870

1 Agnes Anne; *m* 31 Aug 1824 Rev Henry Lyttelton Neave (*see* NEAVE, Bt)

2 Margaret Jane; *m* 24 Nov 1831 Cdr Rose Henry Fuller, RN, and *d* 25 Feb 1852

3 Mary Emily; *m* 1st 1820 Samuel Fortnum Cox, of Sandford Park, Oxon; *m* 2nd 1859 Adam Schoales, of Southampton, and *d* 19 Jan 1872

4 Maria Ursula; *m* 16 Oct 1827 Rev R Fitzherbert Fuller

5 Charlotte Cecilia; *m* 1st 15 Nov 1830 H H Jackson, of Hartfield, Sussex; *m* 2nd 11 Dec 1845 Bernard Hale and *d* 16 May 1883

The 3rd Bt *d* 26 Feb 1815; his er s,

Sir Robert Sheffield, 4th Bt, of Normanby; *b* 25 Feb 1786; High Sheriff Lincs 1817–18, Chm Kirton QS; *m* 8 Dec 1818 Julia Brigida (*d* 28 Oct 1875), dau of Sir John Newbold, Ch Justice Bengal, and had:

1 ROBERT (Sir), **5th Bt**

2 Henry Digby; *b* 30 Jan 1833; *m* 7 July 1877 Evelyn Diana Turner Fairchild and *dsp* 22 Sept 1888

3 John Charles, of Caradoyne, Claremorris, Co Mayo, JP; *b* 9 Sept 1834; Capt 21st Fus; *m* 1st 24 July 1861 Mary Sarah (*d* 16 April 1899), est dau of Thomas Butler Stoney, of Portland Park, Co Tipperary, and had:

(1) John William Bowes; *b* 10 Oct 1862; *d* 14 Nov 1875

(2) Robert Stoney SHEFFIELD later OLIPHANT-SHEFFIELD, of Broadfield, Cumberland, JP; *b* 25 July 1864; *m* 25 Sept 1901 Mary Beatrice (*d* 28 Oct 1933), only child of George Henry Hewitt Oliphant-Ferguson, of Broadfield, and *d* 11 Sept 1937, leaving:

1a Edmund George OLIPHANT-SHEFFIELD later SHEFFIELD; *b* 2 June 1913; *educ* Harrow; Lt RNVR; *m* 1 March 1939 Eva May (*d* 1988), est dau of Charles Blood Mulville, of Hampstead, and *d* 1976, leaving:

1b +John Robert [John Sheffield Esq, Broadfield, Southwaite, Cumbria CA4 0LR]; *b* 11 July 1941; *educ* Harrow; *m* 1st 3 Aug 1967 (*divorce* 1971) Valerie Jean, dau of Capt George Ernest Towill, of Carlisle; *m* 2nd 1978 Elizabeth Helen (*d* 1991), dau of James Turner; *m* 3rd 1994 *Jean Ann, dau of Charles Edward Lomas, and by his 1st w has:

1c +Edward John; *b* 9 Oct 1968

2c +Andrew George; *b* 1970

2b +Richard Charles [Richard Sheffield Esq, Davaar, Connel, Argyll PA37 1PT]; *b* 18 Jan 1944; *educ* Harrow; *m* 1st 14 Jan 1966 (*divorce* 1972) Cheryl Mary Eleanor, only dau of David Lloyd McNeil Williams, of S Croydon; *m* 2nd 1972 (*divorce* 1982) Caroline Alison, dau of Everett Ryshworth Unwin, of Lelant, Cornwall; *m* 3rd 1986 *Mary Morrice, dau of Charles Maclay Scott, of Bearsden Glasgow

3b +George Henry Oliphant; *b* 21 Jan 1948; *educ* Rannoch; *m* 1974 *Christine Holdsworth

1a Penelope Mary Elinor; *b* 22 Aug 1904

2a Barbara Cecily; *b* 19 March 1907; *m* 25 April 1942 Maj Cornwallis Philip Wykeham-Martin, RE, of Burnham, Bucks, s of Maj Robert Fiennes Wykeham-Martin, MBE (for whose earlier ancestry *see* CORNWALLIS, B), and *dsp* 24 June 1949

3 (cont.) John Sheffield *m* 2nd 8 May 1901 Marie Louise Westcott (*d* 8 March 1937), dau of L J A Papineau, of Quebec, Canada, and *d* 12 Nov 1903

4 George; *b* 13 Sept 1836; *educ* Oxford; Dip Serv 1859–88 (Priv Sec to UK Amb Paris 1867–87); *d* unm 10 Oct 1898

5 Frank (Rev); *b* 3 Dec 1838; *educ* Cambridge; Rector Brayesworth, Eye; *m* 15 Oct 1896 Constance Mary (*d* 28 Jan 1943), dau of Rev Hon Arthur Allen Bateman-Hanbury (*see* 1931 edn BATEMAN, B), and *d* 22 Dec 1903, leaving:

(1) Arthur Digby (Rev); *b* 14 July 1897; *educ* Shrewsbury and Ch Ch Oxford (BA 1920, MA 1937); Vicar Chaddleworth 1932–44 and Clewer Berks 1944–56; *m* 3 May 1932 Alice Katharine (*d* 1982), dau of Donald Malcolm Scott, of London W1, and *d* 1975, leaving:

1a +Nigel Digby [Nigel Sheffield Esq, The Rookery, Earl Soham, Suffolk IP13 7RU]; *b* 24 May 1933; *educ* Eton and Ch Ch Oxford (BA 1955, MA 1958); *m* 17 Sept 1960 *Helen Jane Ann, est dau of Lt-Col Bernard Russell-French, DSO, of Edgeworth, Glos, and has:

1b +Timothy John Digby *b* 19 Aug 1966; *m* 1994 *Alexandra C, dau of Nicholas Butterworth, of St Leonards, Herts, and has:

1c +Frederick Arthur Digby; *b* 2 Nov 1997

1b *Ann Margot; *b* 23 March 1963; *m* 6 Dec 1988 *John Underwood

2b *Susan Margaret; *b* 29 May 1965; *m* 6 June 1992 *Michael Lock and has:

1c *Thomas Hugo; *b* 19–

1c *Alice Jane; *b* 19–

(2) Oswald Frank; *b* 22 May 1900; *educ* Shrewsbury and Wadham Coll Oxford (BA 1922); Maj York and Lancaster Regt

1 Julia Maria; *m* 26 Oct 1847 Sir John Trollope, 7th Bt (*qv*), and *d* 2 Nov 1876, leaving issue

2 Sophia Penelope; *m* 1st 21 June 1857 4th Earl of Ilchester (*qv*); *m* 2nd 19 Jan 1867 1st Baron Hylton (*qv*) and *d* 27 Aug 1882

3 Louisa; *m* 30 March 1848 Thomas Wynn Hornby and *d* 4 Aug 1904, leaving issue. He *d* 6 April 1906

The 4th Bt *d* 7 Nov 1862; his er s,

Sir Robert Sheffield, 5th Bt, of Normanby, JP, DL; *b* 8 Dec 1823; *educ* Eton and Ch Ch Oxford; RHG: joined 1842, Capt 1849, ret as Maj 1861, High Sheriff Lincs 1872; *m* 30 Jan 1867 Priscilla Isabella Laura (*m* 2nd 15 March 1890 Lt-Col Thomas Astell St Quintin, 8th Hus, and *d* 30 May 1900), dau of Lt-Col Henry Dumaresq (*see* LANESBOROUGH, E), and had:

1 BERKELEY DIGBY (Sir), **6th Bt**

1 Gwendoline Sophia Alice; *m* 24 April 1889 6th Earl of Lonsdale (*qv*) and *d* 4 Nov 1921, leaving issue

2 Helen, JP Cheshire; RRC; *m* 12 April 1893 Lord Arthur Hugh Grosvenor (*see* WESTMINSTER, D) and *d* 12 July 1950, leaving issue

3 Dorothy Marie Isolde; *m* 16 July 1902 7th Viscount Portman (*qv*) and *d* 21 May 1964, leaving issue

The 5th Bt *d* 23 Oct 1886; his only s,

Sir Berkeley Digby George Sheffield, 6th Bt, of Normanby, JP, DL Lincs; *b* 19 Jan 1876; *educ* Eton; High Sheriff Lincs 1905, CA Lindsey CC, Charter Mayor Scunthorpe 1936, memb Lincs TAA, MP Brigg 1907–10 and 1922–29, dir Gt Centl Rlwy 1908–23, Hon Attaché Paris 1897, Clerk FO 1917, Actg Priv Sec Allied Mission Russia 1917, attd Supreme War Cncl 1918, Capt Lincs Yeo, TFR, DAQMG 62nd Div 1915–17, ADC 1916, Lt Westmorland and Cumberland Yeo Cav, Lt 4th Bn Lincs Regt, Capt Lincs Imp Yeo; *m* 19 July 1904 Julia Mary, OBE (1920), DGStJ, despatches twice for services during WW I (*d* 14 July 1952), est dau of Baron de Tuyll, of The Hague, Holland, and *d* 26 Nov 1946, leaving:

1 **Sir Robert Arthur Sheffield, 7th Bt**; *b* 8 Oct 1905; *d* unm 2 June 1977

2 (Edmund Charles) Reginald , JP (Lincs 1954), DL (1951); *b* 24 Oct 1908; *educ* Eton; Maj 1st Northants Yeo (TA) WW II 1939–44 (wounded, despatches); *m* 12 Nov 1931 Nancie Miriel Denise (*d* 10 Feb 1997), widow of Lt-Cdr (George Pearson) Glen Kidston, RN, and yst dau of Edward Roland Soames, of Belgravia, by Eleanor Corisande, 2nd dau of Sir John Dugdale Astley, 2nd Bt (*see* 1970 edn ASTLEY, Bt), and *d* 6 March 1977, having had:

(1) Robert Charles Reginald Francis; *b* 9 Nov 1935; *d* in a fire 23 Jan 1945

(2) Sir REGINALD ADRIAN BERKELEY SHEFFIELD, **8th and present Bt**

(1) Serena Mary; *b* 4 Oct 1932; *d* unm 14 July 1997

(2) *Fiona Mary; *b* 14 March 1939; *m* 1 Aug 1961 2nd Baron Inchyra (*qv*) and has issue

3 George Berkeley; *b* 23 Oct 1910; *educ* Eton and Magdalene Coll Cambridge (MA); Capt Gren Gds, Maj Yorks Dragoons TA, WW II; *m* 1st 3 Oct 1935 Psyche Isabel Joan, Cmdt MTC (*d* 2 Jan 1945), only dau of Capt Edward Altham, CB, RN; *m* 2nd 21 April 1949 Hon Agnes Wilson (*d* 11 March 1976), formerly w of Maj Dermot Ralph Daly, Scots Gds, and yr dau of 1st Baron McGowan (*qv*), and *d* 2 July 1968, having by her had:

(1) *Laura Diana [Mrs Paul Sednaoui, Ramsden House, Ramsden, Oxon]; *b* 26 Nov 1949; *m* 1st 4 Nov 1969 (*divorce*) George William Pilkington, yst s of Thomas Alec Pilkington, of Wimbledon; *m* 2nd 1990 *Paul Sednaoui and by her 1st husb has:

1a *Harry George; *b* 5 Feb 1971

1a *Martha Mary; *b* 1972

(2) *Davina Mary; *b* 1 March 1951; *m* 21 Dec 1981 *Jonathan Derek Morley, yst s of Brig Michael Frederick Morley, MBE, of Marlborough, Wilts, and has:

1a *Thomas George Jonathan; *b* 1983

2a *William Frederick Duncan; *b* 1984

3a *Henry Quintus; *b* 1987

4 +John Vincent, CBE (1941) [John Sheffield Esq CBE, New Barn House, Laverstoke, Whitchurch, Hants RG28 7PF]; *b* 11 Nov 1913; *educ* Eton and Magdalene Coll Cambridge (MA); Sec Bd Salvage Min Supply 1941–42, Dep Dir Emergency Works and Recovery Min Works 1942–43, Priv Sec to Min Works 1943–44, fndr Norcros Ltd 1956, chm Portals Ltd 1969–80 and BEC 1980–83, High Sheriff Lincs 1944, OStJ; *m* 1st 21 April 1936 Anne Margaret (*d* 8 Feb 1969), 2nd dau of Sir Lionel Lawson Faudel-Phillips, 3rd and last Bt (*see* 1940 edn); *m* 2nd 11 Oct 1971 *France Mary Agnes, of Park Walk, Chelsea, dau of Brig-Gen Goland Clarke, CMG, DSO, and formerly w of Maj Ivor Crosthwaite, and by his 1st w has:

(1) +(John) Julian Lionel George [Julian Sheffield Esq, Spring Pool, Laverstoke, Hants RG28 7PD]; *b* 28 Aug 1938; *educ* Eton and Christ's Coll Cambridge (MA); dir Norcros 1974, High Sheriff Hants 1998–99; *m* 14 July 1961 *Carolyn Alexandra, er dau of Brig Sir Alexander Abel Smith (*see* SOMERSET, D), and has:

1a +John David; *b* 8 Feb 1963

2a +Simon Robert Alexander; *b* 22 March 1964

3a +Lionel Julian; *b* 18 Feb 1969

1a *Nicola Elizabeth Anne; *b* 12 Feb 1973

(1) *Jane Armyne, LVO [Mrs Jane Stevens LVO, The Mill House, Sutton Courtenay, Abingdon, Oxon OX14 0NH]; *b* 4 March 1937; Ldy-in-Waiting to HRH PRINCESS MARGARET, COUNTESS OF SNOWDON 1970; *m* 14 June 1956 (*divorce* 1979) Sir Jocelyn Edward Greville Stevens, CVO, s of Maj Charles Greville B Stewart-Stevens, of Balnakeilly, Pitlochry, Perthshire, and has had:

1a *Charles Greville Vincent; *b* 8 Aug 1957; *m* 1980 *Delphine S, dau of John Dove, of Wadham Ho, Abbey Woods, Tromode, IoM, and has:

1b *Nicholas John; *b* 1988

1b *Leonora Mary; *b* 1985

2b *Amanda Julia; *b* 1992

2a (Rupert) Sebastian Greville; *b* 8 Feb 1964; *d* 1989

1a *Pandora Anne [Mrs Charles Delevingne, Paddock House, 9 Spencer Park, London SW18]; *b* 28 June 1959; *m* 18 June 1983 *Charles Hamar Delevingne and has issue (*see* GREENWOOD, V)

2a *Melinda Armyne; *bapt* 29 April 1972

(2) *Diana Anne [Mrs David Norman, Burkham House, Alton, Hants GU34 5RS]; *b* 15 May 1942; *m* 9 July 1966 *David Mark Norman, yr s of Lt-Col Mark Richard Norman, OBE, of Moor Place, Much Hadham, Herts, and has:

1a *Jonathan Mark Ronald; *b* 1972

1a *Anna Helen; *b* 31 Dec 1967

2a *Isabella Julia; *b* 1971

3a *Davina Penelope; *b* 1981

(3) *Angela Margaret [Mrs Anthony Burrows, The Hall, Barham, Ipswich, Suffolk]; *b* 10 May 1947; *m* 6 Oct 1966 *Anthony Richard Brocas Burrows, er s of Lt-Gen Montagu Brocas Burrows, CB, DSO, MC, of Oakendene, Cowfold, Sussex, and has:

1a *(Edward) Brocas; *b* 1975

1a *Carey Jane; *b* 24 March 1968

2a *Joanna Molly Anne; *b* 21 Nov 1969

3a *(Angela) Petra; *b* 1972

1 Diana Mary; *b* 17 Jan 1907; *m* 11 Dec 1928 Hon Robert Henry Digby (*see* DIGBY, B) and *d* 17 July 1969, leaving issue

SHELLEY

COMME·JE·TROUVE

Arms: Sa. a fess engrailed between three whelk-shells or. **Crest:** A gryphon's head, erased arg., ducally gorged or. **Motto:** *Comme je trouve* ('As I find'). **Creation:** Bt. (E) 22 May 1611.

John Richard Shelley [Dr John Shelley, Shobrooke Park, Crediton, Devon EX17 1DG]; *b* 18 Jan 1943; *s* gf 1992 and established claim but does not use title; *educ* King's Sch Bruton, Trin Coll Cambridge (MA, MB, BCh) and St Mary's Hosp London (DObst RCOG, MRCGP); ptnr Drs Shelley, Doddington and Gibb; memb Exeter Diocesan Synod 1976–79; *m* 28 Aug 1965 *Clare, dau of Claud Bicknell, OBE, of Newcastle, and has:

1 *Diana Elizabeth; *b* 16 Oct 1970; *m* 1993 *John S Moule, s of B J Moule, of Wellington, Salop

2 *Helen Ruth; *b* 1972; *m* 1994 *Amos Storkey, s of Alan Storkey, of Ealing

Lineage: JOHN SHELLEY; MP Rye 1417 on, also Sandwich; *m* Beatrice, dau and heir of Sir John Hawkwood, and had:

JOHN SHELLEY; *m* Elizabeth, dau and heiress of John Michelgrove, of Michelgrove, Sussex, which he thus acquired, and *d* 1526, leaving, with three yr sons (Edward, of Worminghurst Park (*see* DE L'ISLE, V); Richard, of Patcham, ancestor of the SHELLEYs of Pateham and SHELLEYs of Lewes, whose last male heir Henry *d* unm 1811, leaving his four sisters coheiresses (the 3rd Eleanor *m* 1806 George John Dalbiac); Sir John, *k* at capture of Rhodes by the Ottoman Turks):

Sir WILLIAM SHELLEY; Judge Court Common Pleas, ktd 1529; *m* Alice, est dau of Sir Hamon Belknap, of Maskelbury, Essex, by Joan Boteler, coheir (according to later doctrine) to the Barony of Sudeley/Suleye of the 1299 *cr* (abeyant, again according to later doctrine, 1473), thus acquiring estates in Warwicks, and had, with four yr sons and three daus:

JOHN SHELLEY, of Michelgrove; *m* Mary, dau of Sir William Fitzwilliam (*see* SACKVILLE, B, and 1970 edn FITZWILLIAM, E), and *d* 16 Dec 1550, leaving a 2nd s:

JOHN SHELLEY, of Michelgrove; *m* Eleanor, dau of Sir Thomas Lovell, of E Harling, Norfolk, and had an est s:

Sir John Shelley, 1st Bt (E), so *cr* 22 May 1611, of Michelgrove; ktd 1612; sold *c* 1612 his Warwickshire lands and bought others in Sussex; *m* Jane, dau of Sir Thomas Reresby, of Thribergh, Yorks, and *d* by 14 Nov 1644, having had, with a yr s (John, *m* Mary, dau and heiress of George Bailey, and *dsp*):

Sir WILLIAM SHELLEY, of Michelgrove; ktd 1636; *m* Christiana Maria, dau of Sir James Vantelet, and *dvp* by 22 Nov 1639, leaving:

Sir Charles Shelley, 2nd Bt; *m* 1st 2 March 1651/2 Elizabeth, dau of Benjamin Weston, 4th s of 1st Earl of Portland of the Feb 1632/3 *cr* (*see* PORTLAND, E, preliminary remarks); *m* 2nd Mary (*bur* 14 Nov 1699), widow of 9th Lord (Baron) (A)Bergavenny (*see* ABERGAVENNY, M) and sis of Sir Henry Gifford, Bt, of Burstall, Leics of the 1660 *cr*, and *d* 1681, having by his 1st w had four sons and two daus, who all *dsp* except his 3rd s:

Sir John Shelley, 3rd Bt; *m* 1st his stepmother's dau Mary/Bridget/Winifred (*bapt* 24 May 1687), only dau of 9th Lord (Baron) (A)Bergavenny, and had a dau (Frances, *m c* 26 Feb 1703/4 5th Viscount FitzWilliam of Merrion (*see* 1833 edn) and was *bur* 18 Nov 1771 aged 99, leaving issue; *m* 2nd *c* 1690 Mary (*m* 2nd George Mathew, of Thurles, Co Tipperary and *d* by 1722), dau and coheir of Sir John Gage, 4th Bt (*see* GAGE, V), and *d* 25 April 1703, having by her had, with a yr s (Richard, Commr Stamp Office, *m* Mrs Fleetwood and had issue; *see* RAVENSDALE, B) and three daus (Mary, *m* by 1712 Sir John Lawson, 3rd Bt, of Brough, Yorks (*see* 1834 edn); Elizabeth, *m* Edward Sheldon; Catherine, *m* George Mathew and had issue; *see* 1833 edn LANDAFF, E):

Sir John Shelley, 4th Bt; *b* 5 March 1691/2; *m* 1st 21 May 1717 Katherine, dau of Sir Thomas Scawen, London Alderman, and had two daus (Catherine; Mary); *m* 2nd 16 March 1726/7 Margaret (*d* 23 Nov 1758), sis of 1st Duke of Newcastle-

under-Line (*see* CHICHESTER, E, and LINCOLN, E), and *d* 6 Sept 1771, having by her had, with three further daus (Henrietta, *m* 26 June 1763 1st Earl of Onslow (*qv*); Elizabeth, *m* James Cannon; Tryphena, *m* Charles Polhill):

Sir John Shelley, 5th Bt, PC; MP, Keeper Records Tower London, Clerk of the Pipe, Treas Household; *m* 1st Wilhelmina (*d* 1772), dau of John Newnham, of Maresfield Park, Sussex; *m* 2nd 1775 Elizabeth, dau of Edward Woodcock, and *d* 11 Sept 1783, having by her had three daus (*d* unm) and by his 1st w:

Sir John Shelley, 6th Bt; *b* 3 March 1772; *m* 4 June 1807 Frances (*d* 24 Feb 1873), only dau and heiress of Thomas Winckley, of Brockholes, Lancs (*see also* HESKETH, B), and *d* 28 March 1852, leaving:

1 **Sir John Villiers Shelley, 7th Bt;** *b* 18 March 1808; MP Westminster 1852–65; *m* 13 Aug 1832 Louisa Elizabeth Anne (*d* 15 March 1895), only child of Rev Samuel Johnes Knight, of Henley Hall, Salop, and *d* 26 Jan 1867, leaving:

(1) Blanche Henrietta Johnes; *m* 13 Nov 1874 Hervey Charles Pechell (*see* 1970 edn PECHELL, Bt) and *d* 12 April 1898

2 FREDERICK (Sir), **8th Bt**

3 Adolphus Edward; *b* 2 March 1812; *m* 23 April 1836 Amelie, only dau of Henry John Hinchliffe, and *d* 25 May 1854, leaving:

(1) Arthur John; *b* 26 Jan 1837; *d* 7 Sept 1880

(2) Harry Byam; *b* 14 Nov 1838; 31st Regt Madras LI; *d* 14 May 1865

(3) Montagu Adolphus; *b* 11 Feb 1842; served RN

(1) Katherine Cecilia; *m* 1st 3 March 1859 James Bontein (*d* 16 Oct 1884), Gentleman Usher to HM QUEEN VICTORIA, and had issue; *m* 2nd 1885 Maj-Gen Francis Edward Drewe, of Grange, Devon, and *d* 5 Sept 1902. He *d* 20 Feb 1891

4 Spencer; *b* 24 Dec 1813; with Treasury; *m* 1 Feb 1843 Susanna (*d* 1 May 1920), er dau of Stephen Ralph Martin-Leake, of Thorpe Hall, Essex, and *d* 10 March 1908, leaving:

(1) Spencer, JP Glos; *b* 24 Oct 1843; *m* 1st 10 Feb 1876 Mary Renny (*d* 1 Feb 1914), dau of Thomas Watson, and had:

1a Spencer, of Huntley Court, Huntley, Glos; *b* 26 Sept 1878; *m* 17 Sept 1917 Gladys (*d* 16 May 1947), only dau of Edric Thetis Mulligan, of Sydney, NSW, and *d* 30 Oct 1942, having had:

1b +Spencer, JP (Glos) [Spencer Shelley Esq JP, Tigh-na-Sithe, Dalginross, Comrie, Perthshire PH6 2HE]; *b* 14 April 1920; *educ* Cheltenham; Lt RNVR WW II; *m* 29 June 1946 *Maureen, late WRNS, est dau of Cdre Trevor Lewis Owen, OBE, RD, Er Bro Trin Ho, and has:

1c *Elizabeth Grey [Mrs Michael Oakley, Wingates Farm, Mayhill, Longhope, Glos GL17 0RF]; *b* 28 May 1948; *m* 1976 *Michael D R Oakley and has had:

1d James Spencer; *b* 1981; *d* 5 Feb 1998

1d *Laura Elizabeth; *b* 1978

2c *Anna Frances; *b* 30 Jan 1950; *m* 27 June 1983 *Edward Osborne Cavendish and has issue (*see* DEVONSHIRE, D)

3c *Katherine Jane [Mrs Roger Keyworth, Tuateawa, Kennedy Bay Rd, Coromandel, New Zealand]; *b* 28 Sept 1954; *m* 1981 *Roger David Keyworth and has:

1d *Billy Finn Shelley; *b* 1988

1d *Moana Grace Shelley; *b* 1986

2b +Charles Francis [Charles Shelley Esq, Little Conigere, Jubilee Rd, Mitcheldean, Glos GL17 0EE]; *b* 26 Dec 1925; *educ* Cheltenham; Sub-Lt RNVR WW II; *m* 1st 6 Jan 1951 Elizabeth Jane (*d* 1992), only child of Brig Sir Francis Smith Reid, CBE, of Berden Hall, nr Bishops Stortford, Herts; *m* 2nd 3 Sept 1995 *Mary Anne Gough, er dau of Edward Savidge, of Wharton, Western under Penyard, Herefs, and by his 1st w has:

1c *Sarah Jane; *b* 2 Feb 1952

2c *Julia Frances; *b* 7 July 1954; *m* 1980 *Charles Brereton Frater and has:

1d *George Kenneth Charles; *b* 1987

1d *Rebecca Jane; *b* 1984

3c *Caroline Ruth; *b* 29 Sept 1957

3b +Frederick Norman [Frederick Shelley Esq, 2 Ferguson St, Alfred Cove 6154, Perth, W Australia]; *b* 26 Dec 1925; *educ* Cheltenham; CEng, AMIMechE; *m* 12 April 1958 *Ruth Mary, only dau of Rowland Colley Skitt, of Baraket, Sudan, and has:

1c +Stephen Spencer [Stephen Shelley Esq, 11 Peacock St, Burwood 3125, Victoria, Australia]; *b* 23 Oct 1959; *m* 1990 *Heidi, 2nd dau of Heinz Kaupert, formerly of Silesia, and has:

1d +James Spencer; *b* 7 Jan 1991

2d +Thomas Joseph; *b* 12 July 1993

3d +Guy William; *b* 23 Jan 1997

2c +Philip Norman; *b* 22 Dec 1960; *m* 1992 *Anna Uszko, of Kew, Melbourne, Australia

3c +William Rowland; *b* 23 July 1964

1c *Anne Lucy; *b* 5 Jan 1963; *m* 1988 *Peter James Franklin, of Perth, W Australia

1b Patricia Mary; *b* 18 Jan 1918; *d* 18 July 1921

2b *Cynthia Kathleen [Mrs Richard Hayes, Four Ashes, Cosheston, Pembroke Dock, Dyfed SA72 4TX]; *b* 27 July 1921; WRNS WW II; *m* 17 Aug 1943 *Lt Richard Michael Lloyd Hayes, RN, DL, KStJ, CEng, FIMechE, FRINA, FIMarE, High Sheriff Pembs, s of Raymond Stanley Hayes, JP, of Bryngarow House, Bridgend, Glam, and has:

1c *Sylvia Josephine Ruth [The Hon Mrs Andrew Lawson Johnston, Inverernan House, Strathdon, Aberdeenshire AB3 87A]; *b* 8 May 1945; *m* 22 June 1968 *Hon (George) Andrew Lawson Johnston, 3rd s of 2nd Baron Luke (*qv*)

2c *Frances Patricia Jane [Mrs Julian Seddon, The Old Vicarage, 26 Wandle Rd, London SW17 7DW]; *b* 3 Sept 1948; *m* 1971 *Julian Dyson Seddon and has:

1d *Alexander James Dyson; *b* 2 May 1973

1d *Zoe Louisa; *b* 8 May 1974

3c *Anne Wendy Felicity [Mrs Peter Cartwright, Harfield Farm House, Curdridge, Botley, Hants]; *b* 11 June 1950; *m* 1972 *Peter A Cartwright and has:

    1d *Thomas Aubrey; *b* 1975

    2d *William Cloudesley; *b* 1989

    1d *Emma Juliet; *b* 1973

2a William Archibald Douglas; *b* 1889; *d* 16 Aug 1902

1a Margaret Ruth; *m* 1st 7 Sept 1915 William Renny Watson (*d* 12 Dec 1918), Nigerian Marine Service, s of Ernest Watson, of Los Angeles; *m* 2nd 3 Feb 1921 Rev Neville Dundas, s of Col Dundas, of Stirlingshire. He *d* 16 Oct 1935

(1) (cont.) Spencer Shelley *m* 2nd 20 June 1916 Ghita (*d* 1942), dau of W H H Hutchinson, of Cottingham Hall, nr Hull, and *d* 17 Nov 1932

(2) Francis Hesketh; *b* 2 March 1854; *d* unm 27 Jan 1908

(1) Georgiana Fanny; *m* 8 Aug 1867 (*divorce* Dec 1877) Richard Saul Ferguson, DL, and had issue. He *d* 1900

(2) Florentia; *m* 15 July 1870 James Henry Davidson, of Aldeburgh, Suffolk

(3) Rosamond Blanche Isabel; *m* 27 Jan 1892 Herbert Fullarton Dent, of Chestnut Lodge, Surbiton, and Canton, China, and *d* 22 April 1917, leaving issue

1 Fanny Lucy; *m* 19 May 1834 Hon George Edgcumbe, yst s of 2nd Earl of Mount Edgcumbe (*qv*), and *d* 11 May 1899, leaving issue

2 Cecilia Victorine; *m* 11 Aug 1842 Thomas Fassett Kent, barrister, and *dsp*

The 7th Bt's bro,

Rev Sir Frederick Shelley, 8th Bt; *b* 5 May 1809; Rector Beerferris, Devon; *m* 4 Feb 1845 Charlotte Martha (*d* 20 May 1893), dau of Rev Henry Hippisley, of Lambourne Place, Berks, and had:

1 JOHN (Sir), **9th Bt**

2 Frederick, JP (Devon); *b* 31 Aug 1849; *m* 1 June 1882 Lady Margaret Stafford Northcote (*d* 20 July 1947), yst dau of 1st Earl of Iddesleigh (*qv*), and *d* 21 Jan 1925, leaving:

    (1) Pastorella Cecilia Martha; *b* 28 Jan 1886; *d* unm 26 May 1964

1 Charlotte Frances; *b* 21 May 1855; *m* 18 July 1883 5th and last Baron Haldon (*dsp* 11 Jan 1939; *see* 1939 edn) and *d* 12 Jan 1931

The 8th Bt *d* 19 March 1869; his er s,

Sir John Shelley, 9th Bt, JP, DL Devon; *b* 31 Aug 1848; *educ* Univ Coll Oxford (BA); High Sheriff of Devon 1895, Lt-Col cmdg Roy 1st Devon Yeo (TD), Hon Col 1902–22; *m* 29 June 1882 Marion Emma (*d* 30 March 1948), est dau of Richard Benyon, of Englefield House, Berks, and had:

1 JOHN FREDERICK (Sir), **10th Bt**

2 Richard SHELLEY later BENYON (deed poll 14 March 1964 on inheriting Englefield estate from his cousin Sir Henry Benyon, 3rd and last Bt (*see* 1959 edn); also roy licence 1967 for himself and er s), CB (1946), CBE (1942); *b* 18 Jan 1892; served RN WW I and II, V-Adml; Bucks: High Sheriff 1958, V-Lt 1961–68; *m* 16 April 1929 Eve Alice (*d* 3 Feb 1994), twin dau of Rt Rev Lord William Rupert Ernest Cecil (*see* SALISBURY, M), and *d* 13 June 1968, leaving:

    (1) +William Richard (Sir), JP (Berks 1962), DL (Berks 1970) [Sir William Benyon JP DL, Englefield House, nr Reading, Berks RG7 5EN]; *b* 17 Jan 1930; RN 1947–56, MP (C) Buckingham 1970–83 and Milton Keynes 1983–92, PPS to Min Housing and Construction 1972–74, C Whip 1974–76 , ktd 1992, High Sheriff Berks 1995; *m* 24 Aug 1957 *Elizabeth Ann, yr dau of V-Adml Ronald Hamilton Curzon Hallifax, CB, CBE (*see* HUGHES, Bt), and has:

      1a +Richard Henry Ronald [Richard Benyon Esq, The Lambdens, Beenham, Berks RG7 5LD]; *b* 21 Oct 1960; *m* 8 Oct 1988 *Emma Helen, yr dau of Capt Anthony Henry Heber Villiers (*see* CLARENDON, E), and has:

        1b +Harry Charles William; *b* 12 July 1990

        2b +Thomas Anthony Edward; *b* 6 June 1992

        3b +Frederick Richard; *b* 14 March 1994

      2a +Edward William [Edward Benyon Esq, Lovegroves Farm, Mortimer-West End, Berks]; *b* 23 May 1962 (HM QUEEN ANNE MARIE OF THE HELLENES stood sponsor); *m* 17 June 1989 *Katy E M, yr dau of Robin Crofts, of Nethercote Ho, Flecknoe, Warwicks, and has:

        1b +Charles; *b* 20 Aug 1991

        1b *Victoria; *b* 11 April 1993

      1a *Catherine Rose Ingrid; *b* 15 Nov 1958 (HM QUEEN INGRID OF DENMARK stood sponsor); *m* 22 Sept 1984 *Peter Ian Haig, s of Maj Andrew Haig, of Norfolk, and has:

        1b *William Robin; *b* 17 Jan 1988

        1b *Georgiana Elizabeth; *b* 27 Dec 1989

        2b *Rachel Louisa; *b* 22 May 1992

      2a *Mary Elizabeth; *b* 4 July 1965; *m* 9 June 1990 *Capt Thomas R P Riall, 15th/19th King's Roy Hus, s of Maj Patrick Riall, of Knockbawn, Kilmacanogue, Co Wicklow, and has:

        1b *Phineas Patrick; *b* 28 Oct 1993

        2b *Mathew Thomas William; *b* 26 April 1996

        1b *Rosanna Eleanor; *b* 29 June 1992

      3a *Susannah Eve; *b* 17 May 1969; *m* 18 May 1996 *George Neville McBain

    (2) +James Edward, CBE [James Shelley Esq CBE, Mays Farm House, Ramsdell, Hants RG26 5RE]; *b* 18 June 1932; *educ* Eton and Univ Coll Oxford (MA 1961); *m* 16 June 1956 *Judith, only dau of George Grubb, of Gerrards Cross, Bucks, and has:

      1a +Timothy James; *b* 14 Sept 1966; *m* 1993 *Emma Jane, est dau of David Dinkeldein, of Whiteway Farmhouse, nr Newbury, and has:

        1b *Jemima Louise; *b* 1996

      2a +Philip John; *b* 14 Sept 1966; *m* 1994 *Joanne Marie, dau of Stewart England, of Ravenshead, Notts, and has:

        1b +Jack Alexander Stewart; *b* 1995

        1b *Genevieve Mary; *b* 1997

      1a *Alison Jane; *b* 10 April 1959; *m* 1990 *Anthony Clavane, s of Emile Clavane, of Leeds, and has:

        1b *Rosa; *b* 1992

        2b *Miriam; *b* 1994

2a *Penelope Sarah; *b* 8 June 1960

(3) +Andrew Thomas Rupert [Andrew Shelley Esq, Oakfield, Cox Green, W Sussex RH12 3DD]; *b* 18 Nov 1933; *educ* Eton and RMA Sandhurst; Maj RGJ; *m* 11 Dec 1971 *Joanna Margaret, only dau of Adm Sir (Randolph Stewart) Gresham Nicholson, KBE, CB, DSO, DSC, of The Toll House, Bucks Green, W Sussex, and has:

    1a +Nicholas Charles; *b* 1978

    1a *Sarah Lucy; *b* 18 March 1974

(4) +David Robert [David Shelley Esq, Church End Cottage, Kensworth, Beds LU6 3RA]; *b* 2 April 1937; *educ* Eton and Univ Coll Oxford (BA 1961); *m* 30 Aug 1971 *Elisabeth Rhoda, yr dau of Gilbert Graham Balfour (*see* HALSEY, Bt), and has:

    1a +Peter David; *b* 5 Nov 1972

    2a +Jonathan Rupert; *b* 3 Feb 1974

1 Elizabeth Marion; *b* 14 June 1883; *m* 29 April 1911 Kenneth Loder Cromwell Prescott, of Arborfield Court, Reading, and *d* 19 Nov 1949, leaving issue. He *d* 3 Dec 1922

2 Constance May; *b* 5 May 1890; *m* 14 April 1921 Capt Noel Arthur Godolphin Quicke, JP, Duke of Cornwall's LI Res Offrs, of Newton St Cyres, Devon, and *d* 1 Nov 1971, leaving issue. He *d* 16 Dec 1943

3 Mary; *b* 16 Sept 1895; *d* 1898

The 9th Bt *d* 29 March 1931; his er s,

Sir John Frederick Shelley, 10th Bt , JP (Devon 1922), DL (1939); *b* 14 Oct 1884; *educ* Winchester and Trin Coll Cambridge; Maj Roy 1st Devon Yeo (TA) WW I, Devon: CA, High Sheriff 1938, Chm CC 1946–55, Coronation Medal 1937; *m* 1st 17 April 1912 Nora Coleridge (*d* 13 May 1953), only dau of Francis James Coleridge Boles, JP, of Redcliffe, Exmouth, S Devon, and had:

1 John; *b* 31 Dec 1915; *educ* Charterhouse and Trin Coll Cambridge, FLAS; *m* 6 July 1940 *Dorothy Irvine [Mrs John Shelley, Westacott, Shobrooke, Devon], er dau of Arthur Irvine Ingram, slr, of Bath, and *d* 12 Jan 1974, leaving:

    (1) Sir JOHN RICHARD SHELLEY, **11th and present Bt**

    (2) +THOMAS HENRY; *b* 3 Feb 1945; heir presumptive; *educ* King's Sch Bruton and Trin Coll Cambridge (BA); *m* 1970 (*divorce* 1992) Katharine Mary Holton and has:

      1a *Kirsten Rachel Irvine; *b* 1973

      2a *Victoria Juliet; *b* 1974

      3a *Benita Mary; *b* 1978

2 +Philip Spencer [Philip Shelley Esq, East Lodge, Shobrooke Park, Crediton, Devon EX17 1DG]; *b* 8 March 1921; *educ* Bradfield and Reading U; late F/O RAF; *m* 1st 29 July 1947 (*divorce* 1963) Pamela Grace, only dau of Lt-Col Henry Nigel Kermack, RE, and has:

    (1) +Nigel Anthony; *b* 27 May 1948; *m* 1972 *Pamela Mary Inder and has:

      1a *Alexandra Margaret; *b* 1975

    (2) +Malcolm Frederick; *b* 5 Oct 1953; *m* 1974 *Lynne Sharon Buckingham

    (1) *Marian Pamela; *b* 19 Sept 1950

2 (cont.) Philip Shelley *m* 2nd 27 Sept 1968 (*divorce* 1978) Elizabeth Philippa, dau of Leonard George Edward Llewellyn, of Nairobi, and by her has:

    (2) *Nora Elizabeth; *b* 10 Nov 1969

    (3) *Gillian Philippa; *b* 1971

1 *Mary Nora [Mrs Robin Paige, Tanglewood, Louth Rd, Horncastle, Lincs LN9 6EN]; *b* 1 Feb 1913; *m* 7 Oct 1940 Maj Robin Paige, MC, TD (*d* 29 Oct 1969), s of William Robert Paige, of Sheffield, and has:

    (1) *Michael Robert [Michael Paige Esq, Rose Cottage, Low Hameringham, Lincs LN9 6PG]; *b* 12 July 1941; *educ* Loretto; *m* 4 June 1966 *Patricia Margaret, dau of Montague Eric Appleby, slr, of Radcliffe-on-Trent, Notts, and has:

      1a *Nicholas Robert; *b* 1972

      1a *Catherine Mary; *b* 3 Nov 1968; *m* 1994 *Dr Alexander Grey, s of Colin Grey, of Halton Holegate, Lincs

      2a *Sarah Jane; *b* 1970; *m* 1998 *Max Frick, s of Peter Frick, of Thimbleby, Lincs

    (2) *Timothy John; *b* 12 July 1941; *educ* privately

    (3) *Christopher David [Maj Christopher Paige TD, 2 Mallard Close, Thorpe Hesley, Rotherham S Yorks S61 2TW]; *b* 29 April 1945; *educ* Giggleswick; Maj RE (TA); *m* 1970 *Cynthia Ann Ison and has:

      1a *David Hugh; *b* 1976

      1a *Joanne Lesley; *b* 1983

2 *Frances Elizabeth [Mrs Henry Rusbridger, St Crispins, Brampford Speke, Exeter, Devon]; *b* 27 Feb 1914; *m* 25 Oct 1938 Rev Henry John Allen Rusbridger (*d* 1985), est s of Rev Henry Rusbridger, of Tedburn St Mary, Exeter, and has:

    (1) *Peter Henry James; *b* 20 Sept 1941; *educ* Exeter Sch; *m* 16 Aug 1969 *Geraldine Elisabeth, only dau of Robert Johnston, of Achnasmeorach, Kilchrenan, by Taynuilt, Argyll, and has:

      1a *Charles Peter James; *b* 1971

      1a *Lucy Victoria; *b* 1973

    (1) *Elizabeth Jean; *b* 8 Aug 1939; *m* 18 May 1963 Rev Preb Michael Hubert Venn Bowles, of Stanmore, Middx, s of Maurice Hubert Bowles, of Willand, Cullompton, Devon, and has:

      1a *Jeremy Michael; *b* 15 May 1966

      1a *Catherine Elizabeth; *b* 21 July 1964

      2a *Jennifer Susan; *b* 1974

    (2) *Margaret Anne; *b* 20 Sept 1941; *m* 1st 14 Sept 1965 (*divorce* 1976) Arthur William Frederick Sacheverel Pulford, s of Rev Walter William Pulford, of Smallburgh, Norfolk; *m* 2nd 1979 *Kenneth E R Hawkins and by her 1st husb has:

      1a *Claire Frances; *b* 17 Aug 1966

3 *Gillian Hester [Mrs Michael Howard, Southern Wood, Peter Tavy, Devon]; *b* 3 June 1918; *m* 5 May 1949 Capt Michael William Howard, MC (*see* CARLISLE, E)

Sir John *m* 2nd 28 Oct 1953 Marianne (*d* 18 Feb 1974), widow of Capt John Theodore Martin Mee and only dau of Maj Wolstan Francis, DCLI, of The Mill House, Quy, Cambridge, and *d* 8 March 1976

SHEPHERD

Creation: B. (UK) 28 June 1946.

THE 2ND BARON SHEPHERD, of Spalding, Co Lincoln, PC (1965) (Malcolm Newton Shepherd) [The Rt Hon The Lord Shepherd PC, 29 Kennington Palace Court, Sancroft St, London SE11 5UL]; *b* 27 Sept 1918; *s* f 1954; *educ* Friends' Sch Saffron Walden; Lt RASC (Special Forces) WW II, dir Mitchell Cotts & Co 1946–50, chm and md Fielding, Brown and Finch 1950–64, Capt (Ch Govt Whip Ho Lds) Gentlemen-at-Arms 1964–67, Dep Speaker Ho Lds 1964, Min State Cwlth Office 1967–70, Dep Leader Ho Lds 1968–70, Ld Privy Seal and Ldr Ho Lds 1974–76, dep chm Sterling Gp 1976–86, chm: Practice and Procedure Select Ctee Ho Lds 1976–78, MRC 1973–79, Civ Serv Pay Research Unit Bd 1978–81, Packaging Cncl 1978–82 and NBC 1979–84, Pres: Ho Lds Ctee EC Affrs, Telecom-Transport-Energy 1987–89, Chequepoint Internat 1989–, internat consultant: Sun Hung Kai Securities, Sun Hung Kai Bank Hong Kong; *m* 15 Nov 1941 Alison (*d* 3 Feb 1998), dau of Patrick Redmond, of Edinburgh, and has:

  1 +GRAEME GEORGE; *b* 6 Jan 1949; *m* 1971 *Eleanor — and has:

    (1) +Patrick Malcolm; *b* 19–

  2 +Douglas Newton; *b* 23 Sept 1952

Lineage: GEORGE ROBERT SHEPHERD, of Spalding, Lincs; *m* Helen Sophia — and had:

GEORGE ROBERT SHEPHERD, **1st Baron Shepherd**, of Spalding, Co Lincoln, (UK), so *cr* 28 June 1946, PC (1951); *b* 19 Aug 1881; *educ* Spalding Bd Sch; shop assistant, memb Nat Union Shop Assistants, Warehousemen and Clerks, memb and first chm Nat Union Lab Organisers and Election Agents, Lab Party agent: Dundee 1909–13, Blackburn 1931–20, Assist Nat Agent Lab Party 1920–29, Nat Agent 1929–46, Ld-in-Waiting 1948–49, Capt Yeomen Gd 1949, Capt Gentlemen-at-Arms (Ch Govt Whip Ho Lds) 1949–51, Ch Oppn Whip Ho Lds 1951, Dep Speaker Ho Lds 1951, memb Parly Ctee PLP; *m* 4 Aug 1915 Ada (*d* 1975), dau of Alfred Newton, of Halstead, Essex, and *d* 4 Dec 1954, leaving:

  1 MALCOLM NEWTON SHEPHERD, **2nd and present Baron Shepherd**

  1 *Margaret Eleanor [The Hon Mrs Bates, Justacott, 3 Victoria Cottages, Lydiate Lane, Lynton, N Devon]; *b* 14 Feb 1922; *educ* Friends' Sch Saffron Walden; ATS and RASC WW II; *m* 7 May 1949 *Theodore Leonard Bates, s of Theodore Leonard Bates, of St John's Wood, and has:

    (1) *Andrew Michael; *b* 24 Nov 1952

    (1) *Suzanne Katherine Michele; *b* 24 Oct 1960

SHEPPARD OF DIDGEMERE

Creation: B. (LP, UK) 1994.

THE BARON SHEPPARD OF DIDGEMERE, of Roydon, Co Essex (Sir Allen John George Sheppard, KCVO (1998)) [The Rt Hon The Lord Sheppard of Didgemere KCVO, House of Lords, London SW1A 0PW]; *b* 25 Dec 1932; *educ* Ilford County Sch and LSE (Govr 1989–); with Ford 1958–68, Rootes/Chrysler 1968–71, BL 1971–75, Grand Met 1975–96, dir later chm UBM Gp 1981–85, chm: Mallinson-Denny Gp 1985–87, McBride Ltd 1993–, Gp Tst 1994–, Unipart 1996–, GB Rlwys 1996–, BITC 1994–97, Prince's Tst Cncl 1995–, London First 1992–; dep chm: Meyer Internat 1992–94, Brightreasons Gp 1994–96; part-time memb BR Bd 1985–90, dir: Bowater 1993–94; memb cncl Animal Health Tst 1992–, co-chm London Pride Ptnrship 1995–, memb Bd management C Party 1993–98, ktd 1990; author: *Your Business Matters* (1958) and *Maximum Leadership* (1995); *m* 1st 1959 (*divorce* 1980) Peggy Damaris Jones; *m* 2nd 1980 *Mary Stewart

Lineage: JOHN BAGGOTT SHEPPARD; *m* Lily Marjorie Palmer and had:

ALLEN JOHN GEORGE, *cr* a **Baron**

SHEPPARD OF LIVERPOOL

Creation: B. (LP, UK) 31 Dec 1997.

THE BARON SHEPPERD OF LIVERPOOL, of West Kirby, Co Merseyside (Rt Rev David Stuart Sheppard) [The Rt Rev and Rt Hon The Lord Sheppard of Liverpool, House of Lords, London SW1A 0PW]; *b* 6 March 1929; *educ* Sherborne and Trin Hall Cambridge (Capt Cricket Team 1952) and Ridley Hall Theological Coll; Assist Curate St Mary's Islington 1955–57, Warden Mayflower Family Centre Canning Town 1957–69, Bp Suffragan Woolwich 1969–75, Chm Evangelical Urban Training Project 1968–75, Peckham Settlement 1969–75, Martin Luther King Fndn 1970–75, Urban Ministry 1970–75, Area Bd Merseyside MSC 1978–85, Centl Religious Advsy Ctee BBC and IBA 1989–93, Gen Synod Bd Social Responsibility 1991–96, Nat Pres Family Serv Units 1987–97; played cricket for Sussex 1947–62 (Capt 1953), England 1950–63, Bp Liverpool 1975–97; author: *Parson's Pitch* (1964), *Built as a City* (1974), *Bias to the Poor* (1983), *The Other Britain* (1984), *Better Together* (with D Worlock 1988), *With Christ in the Wilderness* (1990), *With Hope in Our Hearts* (1994); *m* 1957 *Grace Isaac and has a dau

Lineage: STUART MORTON WINTER SHEPPARD; slr; *m* Barbara — and had:

DAVID STUART, *cr* a **Baron**

SHERFIELD

Arms: Arg. on a fess embattled counter-embattled gu., between in chief two falcons ppr., belted or, and in base a lion's face of the second, an annulet or between two bezants. **Crest:** A dexter arm embowed in armour ppr., encircled by an annulet or and holding a flagstaff, therefrom flowing a banner arg., charged with a lion's face gu. **Supporters:** Dexter, a lion sa., pendant from a chain about the neck or a bezant charged with a model representing an atom of Lithium 6 sa.; sinister, a bald headed eagle rising ppr., adorned likewise about the neck, the bezant charged with a lawn tennis racquet erect gu. **Motto:** *In lumine luce* ('Shine forth in glory').
Creation: B. (UK) 29 June 1964.

THE 2ND BARON SHERFIELD, of Sherfield-on-Loddon, Co Southampton (Christopher James Makins) [The Rt Hon The Lord Sherfield, 3034 P St NW, Washington DC 20007, USA]; *b* 23 July 1942; *s* f 1996; *educ* Winchester and New Coll Oxford, Fell All Souls' Oxford 1963; Dip Serv 1964–75; *m* 1976 *Wendy Cortesi and has:

  1 *Marian; *b* 198–

Lineage: Sir ERNEST MAKINS, KBE, CB, DSO (*see* MAKINS, Bt); had an est s:

ROGER MELLOR MAKINS, **1st Baron Sherfield**, of Sherfield-on-Loddon, Co Southampton (UK), so *cr* 29 June 1964, GCB (1960, KCB 1953), GCMG (1955, KCMG 1949, CMG 1944), DL (Hants 1978); *b* 3 Feb 1904; *educ* Winchester (Fell 1963–79, Warden 1974–79) and Ch Ch (Hon Student) Oxford (Hon DLC 1957, Fell All Souls 1925–39, Distinguishd Fell 1957–96); barrister Inner Temple 1927, Dip Serv: joined 1928, Chargé d'Affaires Oslo 1934, Assist Advsr League Nations Affrs 1937, Sec Intergovernmental Ctee Refugees 1938, Head Western Dept 1939, Dip Rep with Min Resident W Africa 1942, Assist to Min Resident Allied HQ Med 1943–44, Min Washington 1945–47, Assist U-Sec FO 1947–48, Dep U-Sec 1948–52, Amb Washington 1952–56, Jt Perm Sec Treasury 1956–60, Chm: UKAEA 1960–64, Govrs Imp Coll Sci and Tech 1962–74, Industl and Commercial Fin Corp 1964–74, Marshall Aid Commemn Commn 1965–73, Hill Samuel and Hill Samuel Gp 1966–70, Finance for Industries (ret 1974), A C Cosser 1968–82, Raytheon Europe 1970–82 and Wells-Fargo 1972–84, Pres Parly and Sci Ctee 1969–72, Br Standards Inst 1970–72, Centre Internat Briefing 1972–85, Ho Lds Select Ctee Sci and Tech 1984–87, Dep Chm Ditchley Fndn, Tstee Kennedy Meml Fund, V-Pres Pilgrims 1977–96, Hon LLD: Sheffield and London 1975, Hon DLitt Reading, Hon DL N Carolina U, Hon FICE, Chllr Reading U 1970–92, Chllr Emeritus 1992–96, FRS 1986; author: (ed) *Economic and Social Consequences of Nuclear Energy* (1972); *m* 30 April 1934 Alice Brooks (*d* 1985), dau of Hon Dwight Filey Davis, AB, LLB, Govr Fedl Reserve Bank and The Philippines, Sec War in Pres Coolidge's administration and donor of the Davis Cup for tennis, of Washington, DC, and *d* 9 Nov 1996, leaving:

  1 CHRISTOPHER JAMES MAKINS, **2nd and present Baron Sherfield**

  2 +DWIGHT WILLIAM [The Hon Dwight Makins, 37 Hamilton Gdns, London SW7]; *b* 2 March 1951; heir presumptive; *educ* Winchester and Ch Ch Oxford; stockbroker with Vickers da Costa, dir: King & Shaxson, Wistech Hldgs, md John Govett 1985–88; *m* 1983 *Penelope Jane, dau of Donald R L Massy Collier

  1 *Mary [The Rt Hon The Viscountess Norwich, 24 Blomfield Rd, London W9]; *b* 11 July 1935; *m* 1st 11 July 1959 (*divorce* 1984) Hon Hugo John Laurence Philipps, only s of 2nd Baron Milford (*qv*), and has issue; *m* 2nd, as his 2nd w, *2nd Viscount Norwich (*qv*)

  2 *Cynthia [The Hon Mrs Colman, 7 Tor Gdns, London W8]; *b* 11 July 1935; *m* 4 March 1967 *Oliver James Colman, yr s of Sir Jeremiah Colman, 2nd Bt (*qv*), and has issue

  3 *Virginia [The Hon Mrs Shapiro, 14 Woodstock Rd, London W4 1UE]; *b* 15 Jan 1939; *educ* LMH Oxford; *m* 20 July 1972 *David Shapiro, s of I A Shapiro, and has:

    (1) *Adam Geoffrey; *b* 4 Dec 1973

    (2) *Jacob Roger; *b* 16 Feb 1976

    (3) *Jeremy Paul; *b* 29 April 1979

  4 *Patricia [The Hon Mrs Sagan, 717 Costa Rica Ave, San Mateo, CA 94402, USA]; *b* 28 Jan 1946; *m* 1st 15 Oct 1966 Michael Ordway Miller, of Muir Beach,

Calif., s of Albert G Miller, of Carmel, Calif.; *m* 2nd 1980 *Loring Sagan and has by him:

(1) *Colin; *b* 29 April 1981

(1) *Ana; *b* 198–

SHERSTON-BAKER

Arms: Arg. a saltire sa. charged with five escallops erminois; on a chief az. a lion passant of the third, armed and langued gu.
Crest: A demi-lion rampant per fess indented erminois and pean, supporting in his paws an escallop arg. charged with an erm. spot.
Motto: *Fidei coticula crux* ('The cross is the test of faith').
Creation: Bt. (GB) 14 May 1796.

SIR ROBERT GEORGE HUMPHREY SHERSTON-BAKER, 7TH BT, of Dunstable House, Richmond, Surrey [Sir Robert Sherston-Baker Bt, Wealden House, North Elham, Kent CT4 6UY]; *b* 3 April 1951; *s* f 1990; *m* 1991 *Vanessa R A, yst dau of C E A Baird, of Grouville, Jersey, and has:

1 +DAVID ARBUTHNOT GEORGE; *b* 24 Nov 1992

1 *Amy Margaret; *b* 1994

Lineage: JAMES BAKER, of Buckland House, nr Taunton, Somerset; Ld Manors of Cogload and Sampford Arundel, Somerset, also of Nicholas Hayne and Hale, Culmstock, Devon; *m* Sarah — and had, with three er sons (Christopher, *b c* 1685, High Sheriff Somerset 1724, *dsp* 15 Dec 1729; James, *dsp* 31 July 1747; George, of Brockenhurst House, Hants, barrister, Bencher Inner Temple, *m* 1 Aug 1728 Elizabeth, widow of Robert Vansittart, of Shottesbrooke, and dau of Sir Peter Vandeput, and *dsp* 21 Dec 1770):

JOHN BAKER, of Richmond, Surrey; MD; *m* Sarah, dau and coheir of Robert Wood, and had, with two er sons and a dau (Sarah, *d* young):

Sir Robert Baker, 1st Bt (GB), so *cr* 14 May 1796 (for raising and maintaining a 500–strong cavalry troop, 'The Richmond Rangers'), of Dunstable House, Surrey, and Nicholas Hayne, Devon; *b* 1757; *educ* Inner Temple; *m* Aug 1783 Dinah (*d* March 1805), dau and sole heiress of George Hayley, Alderman, Sheriff and MP City London, by Mary, sis of John Wilkes, the famous MP for Middx, and *d* Feb 1826, having had, with other issue:

1 Robert; *b* 1785; *d* 1802

2 **Sir Henry Loraine Baker, 2nd Bt**, CB; *b* 3 Jan 1787; joined RN 1797, V-Adml; *m* 27 June 1820 Louisa Anne (*d* 12 Sept 1861), only dau of William Williams, MP Weymouth (*see* WILLIAMS, Bt, of Bridehead), and *d* 2 Nov 1859, having had, with other issue:

(1) **Rev Sir Henry Williams Baker, 3rd Bt**; *b* 27 May 1821; Vicar Monkland, Herefs, helped compile *Hymns Ancient and Modern*; *d* unm 12 Feb 1877

3 George Augustus (Rev); *b* 27 Jan 1788; Rector Ibstone-cum-Fingest, Oxon; *m* 9 May 1812 Sophia (*d* 7 July 1857), yst dau of Peter Sherston, of Stoberry Hill, Somerset, and *d* 4 March 1866, having had:

(1) Henry Sherston; *b* 20 May 1814; barrister; *m* May 1842 Maria Martha (*d* 9 March 1897), dau of John Burke, of York Place, and *d* 26 April 1875, leaving:

1a GEORGE SHERSTON (Sir), **4th Bt**

2a Robert Henry Sherston; *b* 4 Aug 1848; Lt-Col RA; *m* 29 Jan 1890 Mabel (*m* 2nd Capt F G G Morris, Border Regt), 4th dau of Maj-Gen Albert Henry Bamfield, of Exmouth, Devon, and *dsp* 14 Aug 1904

3a John Chicheley Sherston; *b* 30 July 1850; Maj and Hon Lt-Col Submarine Miners, Capt 3rd Bn Middx Regt; *m* 1 July 1884 Louisa Constance (*d* 28 Jan 1936), dau of Sir Thomas George Bernard Dancer, 6th Bt (*see* 1933 edn), and *d* 1 Oct 1913, leaving:

1b Henry Chicheley Dancer Sherston; *b* 1893; *educ* Queen Elizabeth's GS Wimborne; Lt 3rd Bn Queen's Roy W Surrey Regt; *m* Deidri Veronica Doreen, only dau of Lt-Col Edwin Bailey Stuart-Rattray, RE, of Ricksmansworth, Herts, and *dsp* 10 Nov 1978, having adopted:

Ann

Peter

1b Winifred Violet Sherston

2b Georgiana Sophia; *m* 18 July 1877 Freeman Leopold Bagnall, of Curzon Park, Chester, and *d* 27 April 1911. He *dsp* 1897

The 3rd Bt's 1st cousin once-removed,

Sir George Sherston Baker, 4th Bt, JP Lincs, Great Grimsby, Boston, Barnstaple and Bideford; *b* 19 May 1846; Recorder Helston 1886–89, Barnstaple and Bideford 1889, Examiner Preliminary Exams four Inns of Court 1894–1901, Revising Barrister Cornwall 1898–1901, Co Court Judge Circuit No 17 1901–23, ed *Law Magazine* 1895–98; *m* 1st 3 June 1873 Jane Mary (*d* 26 May 1909), dau of Frederick James Fegen, CB, RN, of Ballinlonty, Co Tipperary, and had:

1 DODINGTON GEORGE RICHARD SHERSTON (Sir), **5th Bt**

2 John Dunstan Sherston; *b* 3 Jan 1882; slr 1907, attorney High Court Bombay 1911; *m* 27 Nov 1915 Anna Josephine (*d* 8 May 1952), 3rd dau of Alexander Wood, FSA, and *d* 28 Aug 1940, leaving:

(1) +Peter Sherston, MC [Maj Peter Baker MC, 3D Sheen Gate Gdns, London SW14 7PD]; *b* 7 Aug 1918; *educ* Downside; Maj RA WW II (despatches), Queen's Messenger 1964–77; *m* 15 March 1947 *Elizabeth, yr dau of Walter Hugh Barham, of Tunbridge Wells, and has:

1a *Veronica [Mrs Veronica Fulton, 243 Waldegrave Rd, Twickenham TW1 4SY]; *b* 27 April 1948; *m* 1969 (*divorce* 1989) Christopher Carlton Fulton, s of F J A Fulton, of Nelson, NZ, and has:

1b *Guy Charles Jeffreys; *b* 1970

1b *Robyn Frances Jeffreys; *b* 1973

2a *Josephine [Mrs John Chambers, 26 Shalstone Rd, London SW14 7HR]; *b* 26 May 1950; *m* 19 July 1975 *John Gordon Chambers, s of Norman Henry Chambers, of St Albans, Herts, and has:

1b *Oliver Henry Sherston; *b* 27 June 1979

3a *Gabrielle [Mrs Geoffrey Tuff, 21 Redwood Dve, Writtle, Essex CM1 3LY]; *b* 20 Dec 1954; *m* 1977 *Geoffrey Tuff, s of Col Charles Reginald Tuff, and has:

1b *Rebecca; *b* 1981

1b *Alice; *b b* 1983

(1) *Loraine Josephine [Comtesse Alexandre du Bouzet, 21 Avenue de Parc St James, 92200 Neuilly-sur-Seine, Paris, France]; *m* 8 Jan 1938 Comte Alexandre Gaston Pierre du Bouzet (*d* 1989), er s of Comte du Bonzet, and has:

1a *Jean Pierre; *b* 1938

2a *Patrick Peter [M Patrick du Bouzet, 10 Cité Rougemont, 75009 Paris, France]; *b* 1939; *m* 1968 *Susan, dau of Ake Böhn, of Stockholm, and has:

1b *Alexandre; *b* 1971

2b *Mikaël; *b* 1974

3a *Christian Xavier; *b* 1942

4a *Jean François; *b* 1950

1a *Marguerite Loraine; *b* 1940; *m* 1964 *(Andrew) Ivan Bruce [Ivan Bruce Esq, 10 Calle Romero de Torres, 29600 Marbella, Spain], s of William Douglas Bruce, and *d* 1991, leaving:

1b *Douglas Ivan; *b* 1967

1b *Christina Loraine; *b* 1970

2b *Marina Yolanda; *b* 1978

2a *Anne France [Mrs Peter Meakin, 4 Violet Rd, Claremont 7700, S Africa]; *b* 1943; *m* 1966 *Peter Meakin and has:

1b *Vanessa Claire; *b* 15 May 1967; *m* 1992 *Matthias Grone and has:

1c *Sebastian Karl; *b* 21 Oct 1993

1c *Francesa Loraine; *b* 2 June 1996

2b *Natacha Clarissa; *b* 21 April 1970

3a *Chantel [Mme Jean David, 21 Avenue de Parc St James, 92200 Neuilly-sur-Seine, Paris]; *b* 1946; *m* 1967 *Jean François David, s of Jean David, and has:

1b *Oliver Charles; *b* 1968

2b *Christophe Pierre André; *b* 1970

1b *Ingrid Antoinette Loraine; *b* 1973

4a Béatrice Marie Madeleine; *b* 1958; *m* 1988 *Gilles Bouhours, s of Louis Bouhours, and *d* 1993, leaving:

1b *Amoury; *b* 1988

2b *Cédric; *b* 1990

3 Michael Frederick Sherston (Rev); *b* 8 Aug 1884; RC priest; *d* 7 Aug 1905

1 Mary Louisa Sherston; *m* 14 June 1898 James McCarthy, Dir-Gen Survey Siam, s of Denis McCarthy, and *d* 20 Aug 1911, leaving issue. He *d* 23 Sept 1919

2 Henrietta Catherine Sherston; *m* 24 Nov 1904 Walter George Chapman, T/Maj Middx Regt, dir Associated Portland Cement Mfrs, only s of Frank Chapman, of Beech Hill House, Wadhurst, and *d* 4 Nov 1964, having had issue

3 Emily Margaret Sherston; *m* 8 Oct 1910 Arthur Oldham, s of Edwin Oldham, Town Clerk Stockport, and *d* 12 Dec 1964, leaving issue. He *d* 23 Sept 1938

4 Georgiana Jane Sherston; *m* 28 Sept 1912 Percy King Padday, FFA, s of Percy Clement Padday, of Larut Hall, Penang. He *d* 27 Jan 1968 aged 93

Sir George *m* 2nd 19 Feb 1912 Mary Josephine (*d* 9 Dec 1919), yr dau of Henry Bacchus, of The Manor House, Lillington, Warwicks; *m* 3rd 4 Aug 1920 Emmeline Margaret Rose (*d* 13 Dec 1950), dau of James Andrews, MICE, and *d* 15 March 1923

His est s,

Sir DODINGTON GEORGE RICHARD SHERSTON BAKER later SHERSTON-BAKER (deed poll 18 April 1923), **5th Bt**; *b* 22 July 1877; Lt-Col IMS, LRCP, MRCS, WW I, Orders Nile 4th Cl and El Nahda Hedjaz 4th Cl; *m* 15 Dec 1906 Irene Mary Roper (*d* 12 May 1950), yst dau of Col Sir John Roper Parkington, DL, and *d* 18 Nov 1944, leaving, with a dau (Irene Mary Magdalen):

Sir Humphrey Dodington Benedict Sherston Sherston-Baker, 6th Bt; *b* 13 Oct 1907; *educ* Downside and Christ's Coll Cambridge (BA 1929); *m* 26 Jan 1938 (*divorce* 1952) Margaret Alice, only dau of Henry William Binns, of Kensington and Blythburgh, Suffolk, and *d* 1990, leaving:

1 Sir ROBERT GEORGE HUMPHREY SHERSTON-BAKER, **7th and present Bt**

1 *Margaret Elizabeth; *b* 11 Sept 1939; *m* 18 April 1969 Peter Leggatt, s of Harry Leggatt and Mrs Gerald Cobb, of Meonstoke, Hants

2 *Sarah Loraine; *b* 5 Nov 1940; *m* 18 April 1963 *Christopher Charles Jervis Johnson-Ferguson (*see* JOHNSON-FERGUSON, Bt) and has issue

3 *Jane Magdalen; *b* 6 April 1948

SHIFFNER

Arms: Az. a bend sinister, in chief two estoiles in like bend or, in base the end and stock of an anchor gold, issuing from waves of the sea ppr. **Crest:** An estoile or, between the rays six annulets az. **Motto:** *Non est mortale quod opto* ('I place my faith in the hereafter'). **Creation:** Bt. (UK) 16 Dec 1818.

SIR HENRY DAVID SHIFFNER, 8TH BT, of Coombe, Sussex [Sir Henry Shiffner Bt, PO Box 90, St Helier, Jersey, CI]; *b* 2 Feb 1930; *s f* 1941; *educ* Rugby and Trin Hall Cambridge (BA); company dir; *m* 1st 8 Feb 1949 (*divorce* 1956) Dorothy, dau of W G Jackson, of Coventry, and has had:

  1 Lesley Dorothy; *b* 19 March 1950; *d* Oct 1955
  2 *Elizabeth Marilyn; *b* 4 Dec 1953

Sir HENRY *m* 2nd 18 Feb 1957 (*divorce* 1970) Beryl, dau of J George Milburn, of Saltdean, Sussex; *m* 3rd 1970 *Joaquina Ramos Lopez, of Madrid, and by his 2nd w has:

  3 *Linda Mary; *b* 12 Dec 1957

Lineage: HENRY SHIFFNER, of Pontrilas, Herefs; MP Minehead; *m* Mary, dau of John Jackson, Govr Bengal 1748, and had an est s:

Sir George Shiffner, 1st Bt (UK), so *cr* 16 Dec 1818; *b* 17 Nov 1762; *m* 31 Oct 1787 Mary (*d* 1 June 1844), dau and heir of Sir John Bridger, of Coombe, Sussex, and *d* Feb 1842, having had, with two other daus (*d* unm):

  1 John Bridger; *b* 26 Aug 1788; Capt 3rd Foot Gds; *d* 15 April 1814 of wounds recd at Battle of Bayonne the preceding day
  2 **Sir Henry Shiffner, 2nd Bt**; *b* 4 Nov 1789; V-Adml; *m* 9 July 1825 Emily (*d* 9 March 1878), 2nd dau of Thomas Brooke, of Church Minshull, Cheshire, and *dsp* 18 March 1859
  3 GEORGE (Sir) **3rd Bt**
  4 Thomas, of Westergate, Sussex, JP, DL; *b* 8 Aug 1796; *m* 3 Aug 1841 Mary (*d* 19 Nov 1894), dau of James Brown, of Harehills Grove, Leeds, and *d* 1872, leaving:
    (1) Emily Charlotte; *m* 6 Nov 1889 Adml Sir Francis Charles Bridgeman, GCB, GCVO, and *d* 25 Nov 1922 (*see* BRADFORD, E)
    (2) Annie Mary; *m* 24 July 1876 Sir Reginald Graham, 8th Bt, of Norton Coners (*qv*), and *d* 16 Dec 1917, leaving issue
  1 Rebecca Frances; *m* 3 April 1819 Rev Charles Edmund Ruck Keene, of Swyncombe House, Oxon, and *d* 1880
  2 Henrietta Louisa; *m* 15 Jan 1834 George Hoper, of Thornhill, Sussex

The 2nd Bt's bro,

Sir George Shiffner, 3rd Bt; *b* 17 May 1791; Canon Res Chichester, Vicar Amport, Hants; *m* 10 July 1817 Elizabeth (*d* 3 Nov 1861), est dau of Rev Croxton Johnson, of Wilmslow, Cheshire, and had:

  1 GEORGE CROXTON (Sir), **4th Bt**
  2 John; *b* 15 Sept 1824; Capt 34t Regt; *ka* Sebastopol 18 June 1855
  3 Edward Thomas; *b* 18 April 1828; Lt-Col 54th Foot; *d* 8 Sept 1883
  4 Bertie; *b* 3 Sept 1830, Maj 61st Foot; *m* 27 Oct 1877 Louisa Anne (*d* 27 June 1910), widow of Capt Charles Egerton Harcourt Vernon, RN (*see* VERNON, B), and dau of Capt Garth, RN, of Haines Hill, Berks, and *dsp* 22 May 1900
  1 Frances Mary; *m* 26 Oct 1872 Adml Brunswick Popham, of Cardean, Perthshire, and *d* 30 May 1881. He *d* 6 Feb 1878
  2 Louisa Emily; *m* 26 Oct 1858 Thomas Best, of Redrice, Hants, and *d* 7 Aug 1908, leaving issue. He *d* 1886

The 3rd Bt *d* 14 Dec 1863; his est s,

Rev Sir George Croxton Shiffner, 4th Bt; *b* 21 Aug 1819; MA Oxon; Rector Hamsey, Sussex, RD Lewes 1867; *m* 26 Oct 1854 Elizabeth (*d* 8 June 1897), dau and heiress of John Greenall, of Myddleton Hall, Lancs; and had:

  1 JOHN (Sir), **5th Bt**
  2 George Bridger, JP W R Yorks; *b* 2 Dec 1866; *educ* Radley; Cdr Doncaster Div W R Yorks Special Constabulary 1915–37, Special Constabulary Medal with two bars, Silver Jubilee Medal 1935; *m* 12 Sept 1893 Georgiana Mary (*d* 5 Oct 1931), dau of Lt-Col William James Scarlett (*see* ABINGER, B), and *d* 31 March 1949, leaving:

(1) George Edward; *b* 10 March 1901; *educ* Wellington and RMC Sandhurst; Capt Oxon and Bucks LI WW II; *m* 5 March 1935 Kathleen Patricia (*d* 1978), only dau of Lt-Col Sir Edward Boscawen Frederick, 9th Bt, CVO (*qv*), and *d* 10 July 1956, leaving:
  1a +GEORGE FREDERICK [George Shiffner Esq, 14 Coggeshall Rd, Braintree, Essex CM7 6BY; Searles, Alderford St, Sible Hedingham, Essex]; *b* 3 Aug 1936; heir presumptive; *educ* Wellington; *m* 1961 *Dorothea Helena Cynthia, dau of T H McLean, and has:
    1b +Michael George Edward; *b* 5 March 1963
    1b *Penelope Ann Dorothy; *b* 2 Feb 1962
  1a *Susan Georgiana [Mrs Michael Scales, Culverdown, Great Henny, Sudbury, Suffolk CO10 7LY]; *b* 27 March 1938; *m* 1st 20 Aug 1963 Henry Pickup (*d* 1975), s of Henry Pickup, of Scarborough, Yorks; *m* 2nd 1975 *Michael Scales and by him has:
    1b *Timothy Michael Edward; *b* 1977
(2) John Scarlett; *b* 21 Aug 1910; *educ* RNC Dartmouth and RNEC Keyham; Capt RN (despatches), AMIMechE; *m* 11 Jan 1940 *Margaret Harriet [Mrs John Shiffner, 10 Malvern Ct, Onslow Sq, London SW7], 2nd dau of George Smith Tullis, of StratHenry, Leslie, Fife, and *d* 1980, leaving:
  1a +John Robert, CB (1995) [Rear-Adml John Shiffner CB, c/o Lloyds Bank, 2 Spithead, Dartmouth, Devon]; *b* 30 Aug 1941; *educ* Sedbergh, RNC Dartmouth and Manadon (BSc, CEng); RN 1959–95, Capt BRNC Dartmouth 1989–91, ADC to HM THE QUEEN 1989–91, Ch Staff to C-in-C Naval Home Cmd 1991–93, Dir Gen Fleet Support (Equipt and Systems) MoD 1993; FIMarE, MInstD; *m* 2 Aug 1969 *Rosemary Anne Creyghton, yr dau of Brig Alfred Tilly, CBE, DL, of Pump Cottage, Newton St Cyres, Devon, and has:
    1b +John Edward; *b* 1971
    2b +Henry Charles Alexander; *b* 1975
    1b *Caroline Mary Tilly; *b* 1973
  2a +Charles Tullis; *b* 6 Feb 1944; *educ* Sedbergh and St Andrews (MA); *m* 1978 *Rosamund Mary, dau of James London, of Woods Hill, W Chiltington, W Sussex, and has:
    1b *Robin John Landon; *b* 1982
    1b *Katherine Landon; *b* 1979
    2b *Elizabeth Margaret Mary; *b* 1981
  1a *Priscilla Mary Scarlett; *b* 31 March 1949
(1) Dorothy Mary; *b* 3 Aug 1894; *m* 3 Aug 1938 Hon Henry George Godolphin Pelham, 2nd s of 5th Earl of Chichester (*qv*)
(2) Eleanor Barbara Georgina, artist; *b* 8 March 1896; *educ* Roy Academy Schs (Landseer scholarship)
(3) Mary Bridger; *b* 4 Jan 1898; *d* unm 23 Sept 1948
(4) Marion Frances; *b* 10 April 1914; *d* unm 30 Jan 1947
1 Emily; *b* 6 Jan 1856; *m* 16 July 1889 Croxton S Johnson, of Aldwick, Bognor, and Wellshurst, Hellingly, Sussex, and *d* 12 Feb 1929. He *dsp* 18 Jan 1902
2 Mary Louisa; *b* 11 Dec 1859; *m* 6 June 1895 Herbert Arthur Scawen Blunt, of Hurst Barns, nr Lewes, s of Rev Henry Blunt, Rector St Andrew's Holborn, and *dsp* 14 Jan 1909. He *d* 23 March 1907
3 Elizabeth Frances; *b* 6 March 1863; *d* unm 14 June 1944
4 Eleanor Isabella; *b* 29 Oct 1868; *d* unm 27 July 1953

The 4th Bt *d* 3 Jan 1906; his er s,

Sir John Shiffner, 5th Bt, JP Sussex; *b* 8 Aug 1857; Capt RA Zulu War 1879; *m* 11 Jan 1894 Elsie, OBE (1920), JP (Sussex), DGStJ, dau of Ogden Hoffman Burrows, of Newport, RI, and *d* 5 April 1914, leaving:

  1 **Sir John Bridger Shiffner, 6th Bt**; *b* 5 Aug 1899; 2nd Lt Roy Sussex Regt; *m* 16 July 1918 Sybil ('Nancy') Helen (*d* 12 July 1994, having *m* 2nd 22 Sept 1922 (*divorce* 1931) Sir Victor Basil John Seely, 4th Bt (*qv*), and 3rd 21 Sept 1931 Baron Paget of Northampton, PC, QC (LP, *d* 1990)), dau of Sills Clifford Gibbons, of Scaynes Hill, Sussex, and was *ka* 24 Sept 1918
  2 **Sir Henry Burrows Shiffner, 7th Bt**, OBE; *b* 29 July 1902; *educ* Wellington and RMA Woolwich; ADC to Govr and C-in-C Uganda 1926–29, Maj RA WW II; *m* 8 May 1929 Margaret Mary, er dau of Sir Ernest Arthur Gowers, GCB, GBE, of Rondle Wood, Liphook, Hants, and was *ka* 22 Nov 1941, leaving:
    (1) Sir HENRY DAVID SHIFFNER, **8th and present Bt**
  1 Elizabeth Mary; *b* 9 Dec 1894; *m* 1st 20 March 1915 Maj Gerard David Tidmarsh, MC, RA (*das* 9 Nov 1944), er s of David Tidmarsh, of Lota, Limerick, and had:
    (1) *Betty Mary; *b* 15 May 1916; *m* 7 March 1946 Aleksander Leon Suchanek and has:
      1a *Silas Waldo Gerard; *b* 6 Feb 1951
      2a *Konrad Aleksander Bridger; *b* 8 Sept 1952
  1 (cont.) Mrs Gerard Tidmarsh *m* 2nd 25 Jan 1950 Lt-Col Osmund John Fooks, 14th/20th King's Hus, s of Edward John Fooks, of Langton Green, Kent

SHORE OF STEPNEY

Creation: B. (LP, UK) 19 April 1997.

THE BARON SHORE OF STEPNEY, of Stepney in the London Borough of Tower Hamlets (Peter David Shore, PC (1967)) [The Rt Hon The Lord Shore of Stepney PC, 23 Dryburgh Rd, London SW15 1BN]; *b* 20 May 1924; *educ* Quarrybank GS Liverpool and King's Coll Cambridge; Head Lab Research Dept 1959–64, MP (Lab) Stepney 1964–74, Stepney and Poplar 1974–83, Bethnal Green and Stepney 1983–97, PPS to PM 1965–66, Jt Parly Sec: Min Technology 1966–67 and DEA 1967, Sec State: Ec Affrs 1967–69, Trade 1974–76, Environment 1976–79; Min without Portfolio 1969–70, Dep Leader H of C 1969–70, Oppn Spokesman: Europe 1971–74, For Affrs 1979–80, Treasury and Ec Affrs 1980–83, Trade and Industry 1983–84, Shadow Leader H of C 1984–87; memb: Select Ctee For Affairs 1987–97, Ctee on Standards in Public Life 1994; author: *Entitled to Know* (1966), *Leading the Left* (1993); *m* 1948 *Dr Elizabeth Catherine Wrong, CB (1980), dau of Edward Murray Wrong and Rosalind Grace Smith, Dep Ch Med Offr DHSS 1977–84, Dean Postgrad Medicine NW Thames Regn 1985–93, Dean Postgrad Med Educn N Thames Regn 1993–95, and has, with another s (*d* young):

1 *Crispin Nicholas; *b* 31 March 1959; has by *Fiona Graham a s and dau
   1 *Thomasina; *b* 24 May 1951; *m* 1981 *Peter Miles and has three sons
2 *Tacy Susan; *b* 5 Oct 1953; *m* 1982 *Robert Lee Smith and has four daus

SHREWSBURY and WATERFORD

Prest d'accomplir

Arms: Quarterly, 1st and 4th, gu. a lion rampant within a bordure engrailed or (for TALBOT); 2nd and 3rd, az. a chevron between three mullets or (for CHETWYND). **Crests:** 1 On a chapeau gu. doubled erm. a lion statant or, the tail extended (for TALBOT), 2 A goat's head erased arg. attired or (for CHETWYND). **Supporters:** Two talbots arg. **Motto:** *Prest d'accomplir* ('Ready to accomplish'). **Badge:** A talbot passant arg. **Creations:** E. (E) 20 May 1442 (Shrewsbury), (I) 17 July 1446 (Waterford) and (GB) 3 July 1784 (Talbot of Hensol), B. (GB) 5 Dec 1733 (Talbot of Hensol), V. (GB) 3 July 1784.

THE 22ND EARL OF SHREWSBURY, **Earl of Waterford**, **Earl Talbot of Hensol**, Co Glamorgan, **Viscount Ingestre**, Co Stafford, and **Baron Talbot of Hensol**, Co Glamorgan (Charles Henry John Benedict Crofton Chetwynd Chetwynd-Talbot, DL (Staffs 1994)) [The Rt Hon The Earl of Shrewsbury DL, Wanfield Hall, Kingstone, Staffs ST14 8QT]; *b* 18 Dec 1952 (HRH THE DUKE OF GLOUCESTER stood sponsor); *s f* 1980, also as Premier Earl of England and Ireland and Hereditary Ld High Steward of Ireland (Hereditary Gt Seneschal); *educ* Harrow; dir: Britannia Bldg Soc 1984–92 (dep chm 1987–89, jt dep chm 1989–92), memb exec ctee: Staffs Assoc Boys' Clubs 1981–, Staffs Br Game Conservancy Tst 1988, Pres: Staffs Soc 1989–91, Bldg Socs Assoc 1993–97, Chm Firearms Consultative Ctee (advises Home Office) 1988–, Chllr U of Wolverhampton 1993–, Hon LLD Wolverhampton 1994; *m* 5 Jan 1974 *Deborah Jane, only dau of Noel S Hutchinson, of Ellerton Ho, Sambrook, Salop, and has:

1 +JAMES RICHARD CHARLES JOHN, *Viscount Ingestre*; *b* 11 Jan 1978
2 +Edward William Henry Alexander; *b* 18 Sept 1981
   1 *Victoria Jane; *b* 7 Sept 1975

Shrewsbury, Earldom of: In early December 1074 Roger de Montgomery was created Earl of Shropshire or Shrewsbury. As with other medieval earldoms (*see* WINCHESTER, M, preliminary remarks, for a discussion of this point), little distinction was then made between the county town and county proper when designating a specific name for a title, chiefly because an earl, who was then more or less an official, albeit often hereditary, was inconceivable except as earl of a county.

Roger was son of another Roger de Montgomery, seigneur of the Norman places (St Germain-de-Montgomery and Ste-Foy-de-Montgomery) of that name in the Calvados region. He was a prominent member of the nobles grouped around WILLIAM (later WILLIAM I of England, THE CONQUEROR) OF NORMANDY well before the 1066 invasion of England but stayed behind in Normandy during the actual enterprise. The year after Hastings he went to England and received land grants in Sussex. He is thought to have constructed the Castle at Montgomery (now in Powys, but formerly named Montgomeryshire after his family), doing so shortly before the Domesday Survey.

His son, the 2nd Earl of Shrewsbury (or Shropshire) of the 1074 creation, was killed by a missile launched from a Norse (or conceivably Irish) raiding party off the Anglesey coast while riding along the forshore on that island trying to fend them off. He was accounted gentle by the English and Normans but a Hammer by the Welsh. Under the system then prevailing the Earldom passed to an elder brother, Robert de Bellême, who constructed Bridgnorth Castle and continued the family policy of harrying the Welsh. He rebelled against HENRY I and in 1102 was deprived of the Earldom of Shrewsbury/Shropshire, together with his English and Welsh estates.

Lineage: RICHARD TAL(E)BOT; granted manors of Eccleswall and Linton, Herefs, from the Crown by 1155/6; *d* by Michaelmas 1175, leaving:

GILBERT TALBOT; ktd by Feb 1207/8; *d* by 13 Feb 1230/1, leaving:

RICHARD TALBOT; *m* between 1219 and 1224 Aline, widow of Drew de Montagu (*dvp* by 1216; ancestor of the Montagu Earls of Salisbury; *see* SALISBURY, M, preliminary remarks) and dau of Alan Basset, of Wycombe, Bucks, by Aline, dau and coheir of Philip de Gai, and was probably f of:

GILBERT TALBOT; of age by 1242/3; Justice Chester 1255, Custodian Castles of Grosmont, Skinfrith and White Castle (modern Whitchurch, Salop) 1260; *m* Gwenthlian, dau and eventual heir of Rhys Mechyll, feudal Ld of Dynevor, s of Rhys Grig, feudal Ld of Ystrad Tywi and Dynevor, yr s of Rhys ap Griffith, Prince of South Wales, and *d* just before 8 Sept 1274, leaving:

RICHARD TALBOT; *b c* 1250; Custodian Cardiff 1297, Sheriff Glos 1299–1301; allegedly *m* after 7 Jan 1268/9 Sarah, sis of William de Beauchamp, Earl of Warwick (*see* WARWICK, BROOKE and, E, preliminary remarks), and *d* just before 3 Sept 1306, leaving, with a yr s (Richard, of Richard's Castle, Herefs, whose line appears to have expired on the death without issue of his ggs in 1388; *see* ZOUCHE, B):

Sir GILBERT TALBOT, 1st LORD (Baron) TALBOT (E), so *cr* by writ of summons to Parl (according to later doctrine) 27 Jan 1331/2, KB by 16 March 1321/2; *b* 18 Oct 1276; pardoned for involvement in death of Piers Gaveston 1313; also opposed the Despensers (*see* FALMOUTH, V) and EDWARD II in person at Battle of Boroughbridge March 1321/2, Keeper Gloucester 1322, King's Chamberlain March 1327/8, Justice S Wales 1330, Keeper Builth Castle 1330, also Bwlch-y-Dinas, Bllaenllyfni (both Breconshire) and Newcastle Emlyn (Carmarths) Castles 1333, together with Carmarthen Castle Jan or Feb 1339/40; allegedly *m* Anne, dau of William Le Botiler, of Wem, Salop, and *d* 24 Feb 1345/6, leaving:

Sir RICHARD TALBOT, 2nd LORD (Baron) TALBOT, KB by 1338; *b c* 1305; asserted his right to estates in Scotland through his w and participated in Edward Balliol's descent on Scotland 1332, helping defeat the Scots at Battle of Dupplin Moor 12 Aug 1332; captured by the Scots 1334 but ransomed 1335; Keeper Berwick-upon-Tweed 1337–55, Ch Keeper Southampton Feb 1339/40, Ch Justice Glos and Worcs 1341, a Capt in the English army that defeated the French Battle of Morlaix 30 Sept 1342 during opening phase of Hundred Years War, Steward King's Household 1345, present Battle of Crécy and Siege Calais 1346–47, Keeper Pembroke and Tenby Castles and Pembs Jan 1349/9–51; *m* between 24 July 1326 and 23 March 1326/7 Elizabeth, dau and coheir of John Comyn, Lord of Badenoch, by Joan, sis of Aymer de Valence, Earl of Pembroke (*see* PEMBROKE and MONTGOMERY, E, preliminary remarks), and *d* 23 Oct 1356, leaving:

GILBERT TALBOT, 3rd LORD (Baron) TALBOT; *b c* 1332; *m* 1st by 8 Sept 1352 Lady Pernel Butler (*d* allegedly 1386), dau of 1st Earl of Ormond (*see* MOUNTGARRET, V), and had an only son; *m* 2nd by 16 Nov 1379 Joan, widow of 2nd Lord (Baron) Cherleton and dau of Ralph de Stafford, 1st Earl of Stafford (*see* STAFFORD, B), and *d* allegedly 24 April 1387, leaving by his 1st w:

Sir RICHARD TALBOT, 4th LORD (Baron) TALBOT, also 1st LORD (Baron) TALBOT (of Blackmere), so *cr* by writ of summons (according to later doctrine) *vp* 3 March 1383/4, seemingly as a fresh creation albeit the territorial designation of the writ was worded as though in right of his w (*see* SAINT DAVIDS, V); *b c* 1361; ktd 1377; *m* by 23 Aug 1383 Ankaret (*m* 2nd as his 2nd w Thomas Nevill(e), 5th Lord (Baron) Furnivall(e)/Nevill of Halumshire (*see* ABERGAVENNY, M), and *d* 1 June 1413), sis and eventually sole heiress of John, 5th Lord (Baron) Strange (of Blackmere), thus becoming according to later doctrine BARONESS STRANGE (of Blackmere) in her own right, and *d* 8 or 9 Sept 1396, leaving, with other issue:

1 GILBERT TALBOT, 5th LORD (Baron) TALBOT, KG (1408 or 1409) and through his mother 5th or 6th LORD (Baron) STRANGE (of Blackmere) according to later doctrine; *b* 1383; defeated Welsh Battle of Grosmount 11 March 1404/5, captured Harlech Castle after a siege Dec 1408–Jan 1408/9, Ch Justice Cheshire 1413, Capt Caen Castle Normandy 1418, besieged and captured Domfront and Caudebec July and Sept 1418 respectively; (?)m 1st(?) (certainly betrothed to) Joan (*dsp* seemingly prior to consummation of the marriage (if any) 16 Aug 1400), 2nd dau of Thomas (of Woodstock), Duke of Gloucester, yst son of EDWARD III; *m* 2nd(?) *c* 1415 Beatrix, of Portugal, possibly a memb of the prominent Pinto family but possibly also of a line descended illegitimately from ALFONSO III of Portugal, and *dspm* 19 Oct 1418, leaving:

  (1) ANKARET TALBOT, de jure BARONESS TALBOT and STRANGE (of Blackmere); *b c* 1416; *d* 13 Dec 1421
2 JOHN, **1st Earl**
3 Richard; Archbp Dublin 1417–49, Ld Chllr Ireland 1423–April 1426 and Oct 1426–31, Ld Justice Ireland, Ld Dep Ireland 1435–36, 1437 and 1447–49
  1 Eleanor; *m* Thomas, s of 1st and last Baron Sudeley (*qv*) of the 1441 *cr*

The 2nd s,

Sir JOHN TALBOT, **1st Earl of Shrewsbury** (technically the Earldom was designated as being of 'Salop' or 'Shropshire' but ever afterwards, indeed in the grantee's own lifetime, its bearers have been known as Earls of 'Shrewsbury') (E) and **1st Earl of Waterford** (I), so *cr* 20 May 1442 and 17 July 1446 (when also made Hereditary Steward of Ireland) respectively, though called to Parl 26 Oct 1409 by writs made out to LORD (Baron) De FURNYVALL/De HALOMSHIRE (*see* PETRE, B) in right of his 1st w (*see* below) during her lifetime and as LORD (Baron) TALBOT (of Hallamshire) afterwards, also according to later doctrine 7th LORD (Baron) TALBOT and 7th or 10th LORD (Baron) STRANGE (of Blackmere) on his niece ANKARET's death 1421, KG (1424), JP (Derbys Feb 1407/8, Salop and Staffs March 1409/10); *b c* 1384; King's Esq 1407, ktd by 1413, King's Lt Ireland Feb 1413/4 and March 1444/5, Justiciar Ireland Jan-April 1425, campaigned Hundred Years War: Battle of Verneuil 1424, took Laval March 1427/8, also Nogent-le Roi and was at Siege of Orleans 1428–29, cdr Battle of Patay June 1429 (captured but subsequently ransomed), took Patay 1433, Joigny 1434, Beaumont-sur-Oise May 1434, Creil June 1434 and Clermont, *cr* by HENRY VI COUNT OF CLERMONT en Beauvoisis (part of a policy pursued by HENRYs V and VI of making their chief commanders nobles in English-occupied France with French fiefs), present Siege of Saint-Denis Sept 1435, retook Pays de Caux 1436, won Battle of Ris (nr Rouen) late 1436, took Ivry and Pontoise Jan-Feb 1436/7, held Le Croty 1437, Marshal of France by 6 April 1437, took Longueville 1438, reinforced Meaux 1439 and Pontoise several times, destroyed Poissy 1441, conducted Siege of Dieppe 1442, Keeper Porchester Castle and Govr Portsmouth Feb 1451/2, Lt of Aquitaine 1452, retook Bordeaux Oct 1452, took Fronsac March 1452/3, finally killed with his 4th s (3rd here noticed; *see* below) at the rout of Castillon (the last battle of the Hundred Years War) 17 July 1453; *m* 1st by 12 March 1406/7 Maud, BARONESS FURNIVALL(E) in her own right according to later doctrine (*d c* 1423), dau and heiress of Thomas Nevill(e), 5th Lord (Baron) Furnivall(e) (*see* above, also ABERGAVENNY, M) in right of his 1st w, and had surv issue:

1 JOHN, **2nd Earl**

2 Christopher (Sir); Lancastrian Wars of Roses; *ka* Battle of Northampton (Yorkist victory) 10 July 1460

The **1st Earl** *m* 2nd 6 Sept 1425 Lady Margaret Beauchamp (*d* 14 June 1467), est dau and coheir of Richard, Earl of Warwick (*see* WARWICK, BROOKE and, E) by his 1st w Elizabeth (only child of 5th Lord (Baron) Berkeley (*qv*) of the 1295 *cr*, and deemed by later doctrine to have been Baroness Berkeley and Baroness Lisle in her own right, though on her death they would have fallen into abeyance between her three daus and coheirs even by the same later doctrine), and by her had:

3 Sir JOHN TALBOT, 1st VISCOUNT LISLE, also 1st LORD AND BARON OF LISLE, so *cr* 30 Oct 1451 and 26 July 1444 respectively , with remainder in the latter case to his heirs being Lords of the Manor of Kingston Lisle, Berks, with precedence of 1357, PC (1453), JP (Salop 1444); *b c* 1426; served in France under his f; *m* Joan, dau and coheir of Thomas Chedder and widow of Richard Stafford, and was *ka* Battle of Castillon 17 July 1453, leaving, with two daus:

(1) Sir THOMAS TALBOT, 2nd and last VISCOUNT LISLE; *b c* 1443–48; ktd 1465; *m* Sept 1466 Margaret, dau of William Herbert, 1st Earl of Pembroke (*see* PEMBROKE and MONTGOMERY, E, also POWIS, E), and *dsps* 20 March 1469/70 in a skirmish between his followers and those of William, Lord (Baron) Berkeley (*qv*), with whose family the Talbots had been feuding for some time, when the Viscounty expired, but the Barony of Lisle, inasmuch as it went with possession of the manor of Kingston Lisle according to the terms of the patent of creation, became dormant

4 Humphrey (Sir); Marshal of Calais, *dsp* 1492

5 Lewis (Sir), of Penyard, Herefs

1 Joan; *m c* 25 July 1457, as his 3rd or 4th w, 1st Lord (Baron) Berkeley (*qv*); *m* 2nd 1487 Edmund Hungerford

2 Elizabeth; *m* by 27 Nov 1448 4th and last Duke of Norfolk of the 1397 *cr* (*see* MOWBRAY, SEGRAVE and STOURTON, B) and had issue

The 1st EARL's est s,

JOHN TALBOT, **2nd Earl of Shrewsbury** and **Waterford**, KG (1457), KB (1426), PC (1453), JP (Derbys 1441, W R Yorks March 1441/2, Herts and Notts 1443); *b c* 1413; Ld Chllr Ireland 1446, Treasurer England 1456–58; *m* by March 1444/5 Lady Elizabeth Butler (*d* 8 Sept 1473), only dau of 4th Earl of Ormonde (*see* 1970 edn ORMONDE, M), and was *ka* with his bro Sir Christopher at Battle of Northampton 10 July 1460, having had, with other issue:

1 JOHN TALBOT, **3rd Earl of Shrewsbury** and **Waterford**, JP (Salop 1466 and Derbys, Notts and Staffs Feb 1466/7); *b* 12 Dec 1448; ktd Feb 1460/1; on Lancastrian side Battle of Towton 29 March 1461 but in EDWARD IV's entourage Dec 1461; Ch Justice N Wales 1471; a man of literary tastes (composed a poem to Margaret of Anjou); *m c* 1467 Lady Katharine Stafford (*d* 26 Dec 1476), 5th dau of Humphrey, 1st Duke of Buckingham (*see* STAFFORD, B), and *d* 28 June 1473, leaving an er s:

(1) GEORGE TALBOT, **4th Earl of Shrewsbury** and **Waterford**, KG (1488), KB (1475), PC (1512), JP (Derbys, Herefs, Notts, Salop, Staffs, Worcs and E R and W R Yorks 1486); *b* 1468; fought Battle of Stoke 1487, Steward Household 1506–38, Lt Gen Army invasion of France 1513, fought Battle of the Spurs 16 Aug and took Thérouanne 22 Aug, Lt Gen of the North 1522, played an important role in suppressing the Pilgrimage of Grace 1536; *m* 1st by 27 June 1481 Anne, dau of William, 1st Lord (Baron) Hastings (of Hastings) (*see* HUNTINGDON, E), and had six sons and five daus; *m* 2nd *c* 1512 Elizabeth, dau and coheir of Sir Richard Walden, of Erith, Kent, by whom he had one surv dau (Anne; *m* 1st Peter Compton, s and heir of Sir William Compton (*see* NORTHAMPTON, M); *m* 2nd 1st Earl of Pembroke; *see* PEMBROKE and MONTGOMERY, E), and *d* 26 July 1538, leaving a 2nd but est surv s:

1a FRANCIS TALBOT, **5th Earl of Shrewsbury** and **Waterford**, KG (1545), PC (by Jan 1548/9); *b* 1500; called up to Ho Lds *vp* as LORD (Baron) TALBOT 17 Feb 1532/3; Pres Cncl of the North 1549, Ld Lt Derbys and Yorks 1551; *m* 1st by 30 Nov 1523 Mary, dau of 2nd Lord (Baron) Dacre (*qv*) (of Gilsland), and had issue; *m* 2nd by Aug 1553 Grace, widow of Francis Carless and dau of Robert Shakerley, of Little Langdon, Derbys, and *d* 25 Sept 1560, leaving by his 1st w:

1b GEORGE TALBOT, **6th Earl of Shrewsbury** and **Waterford**, KG (1561), KB (Feb 1546/7), PC (1571), JP (Derbys 1547); *b c* 1522; called up to Ho Lds *vp* as LORD (Baron) TALBOT 5 Jan 1552/3; Jt Lt Gen North 1565, Ld Lt Derbys, Notts, Yorks 1565, apptd to keep watch on MARY QUEEN OF SCOTS at Tutbury and Sheffield Castles Feb 1568/9–Sept 1584, Earl Marshal 2 Jan 1572/3 following trial of Duke of Norfolk (*qv*) the previous year, when he was Ld High Steward, Ld Lt Derbys and Staffs 1585; *m* 1st 28 April 1539 Lady Gertrude Manners (*d* 1566), dau of 1st Earl of Rutland (*see* RUTLAND, D), and had four sons and three daus; *m* 2nd 9 Feb 1567/8 Elizabeth ('Bess of Hardwick'), dau and coheir of John Hardwick, of Hardwick, and widow of (a) Sir William St Loe, (b) Sir William Cavendish (*see* DEVONSHIRE, D) and (c) Robert Barlow, of Barlow, Derbys, and *d* 18 Nov 1590, having had:

1c Francis, *Lord Talbot*; *b c* 1550; *educ* St John's Coll Oxford; *m* 17 Feb 1562/3 Lady Anne Herbert, dau of 1st Earl of Pembroke (*see* PEMBROKE and MONTGOMERY, E), and *dsp* & *vp* and was *bur* 3 Sept 1582

2c GILBERT TALBOT, **7th Earl of Shrewsbury** and **Waterford**, KG (1592), PC (1601 and 1603); *b* 20 Nov 1552; *educ* St John's Coll Oxford and U of Padua; MP Derbys 1572–83, called up to Ho Lds *vp* as LORD (Baron) TALBOT 28 Jan 1588/9; Amb France 1596, fndr Shrewsbury Hosp Sheffield; *m* 9 Feb 1567/8 (the same day as his f *m* his stepmother) Mary, dau of his stepmother by Sir William Cavendish and sis of 1st Earl of Devonshire (*see* DEVONSHIRE, D), and *dspms* 8 May 1616, when the Baronies of Talbot, Furnivall(e) and Strange (of Blackmere) fell into abeyance until Alathe(i)a (*see* below) inherited them on outliving her er sisters (*see* PETRE, B), leaving, with two sons (*d* young):

1d Mary; *m* 4 Nov 1604 3rd Earl of Pembroke (*see* PEMBROKE and MONTGOMERY, E) and *dsp* March 1649

2d Elizabeth; *m* 16 Nov 1601 8th Earl of Kent (*see* GREY, B) and *dsp* 7 Dec 1651

3d ALATHE(I)A, BARONESS TALBOT, FURNIVALL(E) and STRANGE (of Blackmere) in her own right according to the doctrine evolving about this time; god-daughter of ELIZABETH I; *m* by 24 Sept 1606 Thomas HOWARD, 21st/14th Earl of Arundel, 3rd Earl of Surrey and 1st Earl of Norfolk, and *d* 24 May 1654, having had issue (*see* NORFOLK, D, and PETRE, B)

3c EDWARD TALBOT, **8th Earl of Shrewsbury** and **Waterford**; *bapt* 25 Feb 1561; *educ* Magdalen Coll Oxford; MP Northumberland 1586–87; *m* 1583 Jane (*bur* 7 Jan 1625/6), dau and coheir of 7th Lord (Baron) Ogle, and *dsps* 8 Feb 1617

2 James (Sir); *dsp* 2 Sept 1471

3 Christopher; Rector Christchurch, Salop; living 1474

4 Gilbert (Sir), KG (1496), KB (1487), PC, of Grafton, Worcs; High Sheriff Salop *temp* RICHARD III, but fought for HENRY VII Battle of Bosworth 1485, cmdg the right wing; ktd 1485; cdr Battle of Stoke 1487, when Lambert Simnel and his followers were defeated; Deputy Calais; *m* 1st Elizabeth, widow of 5th Lord (Baron) Scrope (of Masham) and dau of Ralph de Greystoke, 5th Lord (Baron) Greystoke, and had:

(1) Gilbert (Sir), of Grafton; Sheriff Worcs *c* 1540; *m* 1st Anne, dau and coheir of Sir William Paston; *m* 2nd Elizabeth Wynter and *d* 22 Oct 1542, having by his 1st w had, with two sons (*dsp*):

1a Margaret; *m* Sir Robert Newport

2a Elizabeth; *m* Sir John Lyttelton and had issue (*see* COBHAM, V)

3a Mary; *m* Sir Thomas Astley, of Patshull, and had issue (*see* 1970 edn ASTLEY, Bt)

(2) Humphry (Sir), *dsp* in the Holy Land

4 (cont.) Sir Gilbert Talbot *m* 2nd Etheldreda (Audrey), widow of (a) Thomas Barton and (b) Richard Gardiner, Ld Mayor London, and dau of William Landwade Cotton, of Landwade, Cambs, and *d* 19 Sept 1518, having by her had:

(3) John (Sir), of Albrighton, Salop, and later Grafton; High Sheriff Salop 1528, 1538 and 1542; *m* 1st Margaret, dau and heiress of Adam Troutbeck, of Mobberley, Cheshire, and had:

1a John (Sir), of Grafton and Albrighton; *m* Frances, dau of Sir John Giffard, and *d* 6 June 1555, having had:

1b John (Sir), of Grafton; *m* 1st Catherine, dau of Sir William Petre (*see* PETRE, B); *m* 2nd Margaret, dau of 5th Lord (Baron) Windsor (*see* PLYMOUTH, E), and by his 1st w had:

1c GEORGE TALBOT, **9th Earl of Shrewsbury** and **Waterford**, of Grafton; *b* 19 Dec 1566; *educ* Amiens and Rouen; RC priest; *d* unm 2 April 1630

2c John, of Longford, Salop; *m* Eleanor, dau and coheir of Sir Thomas Baskerville, of Brinsop, Herefs, and *d* 1607, having had, with other issue (*d* unm):

1d JOHN TALBOT, **10th Earl of Shrewsbury** and **Waterford**; *b* by 1601; royalist Civil War, as which, being also RC, he had his estates sequestrated by the Ctee for Compounding 1647; *m* 1st by 1619 Mary, dau of Sir Francis Fortescue, KB, of Salden Hill; *m* 2nd by 15 Feb 1647/8 Frances (*d* on or after 2 May 1652), dau of 1st Baron Arundell of Wardour (*see* 1940 edn), and *d* 8 Feb 1653/4, having by her had further issue and by his 1st w:

1e George, *Lord Talbot*; *b c* 1620; *m* Jan 1639 Mary, dau of 2nd Baron Powis (see POWIS, E), and *dsp* & *vp* 7 March 1642

2e FRANCIS TALBOT, **11th Earl of Shrewsbury** and **Waterford**; *b c* 1623; Capt royalist armies Civil War, fought Battle of Worcester 1651, Treasurer and Gen Receiver Ireland 1661; *m* 1st Anne, dau and heiress of Sir John Conyers (*see* VAUX OF HARROWDEN, B), and had an only surv dau (*see* CAMOYS, B) and two sons (*d* young); *m* 2nd 10 Jan 1658/9, as her 1st husb, Lady Anna Maria Brudenell, dau of 2nd Earl of Cardigan (*see* AILESBURY, M), and *d* 16 March 1667/8 of wounds received in a duel with George Villiers, 2nd Duke of Buckingham (*see* JERSEY, E), the lover of his 2nd w (who is said to have slept with the Duke while he wore the bloodstained shirt he had killed her husb in and to have held his horse, disguised as a page, while the duel was in process), having by her had an only surv s:

1f CHARLES TALBOT, **12th Earl of Shrewsbury** and **Waterford** and 1st and last DUKE OF SHREWSBURY, so *cr* 30 April 1694, as also MARQUESS OF ALTON, Co Stafford, KG (1694), PC (Feb 1688/9–92, 1710 and 1714); *b* 24 July 1660 (godson of CHARLES II); served in wars in Flanders 1678, abjured Catholicism for C of

E 1679, Ld Lt Staffs 1681–87, Col 7th Horse (5th Dragoon Gds) 1685–Jan 1686/7, one of the seven magnates who invited WILLIAM III to England 1688; Sec State for N Feb 1688/9–90 and S March 1693/4–98, Ld Lt: Herts March 1688/9–91, Worcs March 1688/9–Feb 1717/8, Anglesey, Caernarvs, Denbighs, Flints, Herefs, Merioneths and Montgomerys 1694, also Salop 1712–14, Chamberlain Household 1699–1700 and 1710–14, Amb Extrdy France 1712–14, Ld Lt Ireland 1713–14, last Ld High Treas July–Oct 1714 during the close of QUEEN ANNE's reign (she delivered the wand of office into his hands on her death bed) and the interim until GEORGE I (whose proclamation he signed, thus helping smooth the succession), having been a Whig earlier but a Tory from at least 1710, Groom Stole and Keeper Privy Purse 1714, Chamberlain Household 1714–15; *m* 9/20 Sept 1705 Adelaide, widow of — Roffeni and yr dau of Andrea, Marquis Paleotti, of Bologna, by his 2nd w Maria Cristina, 5th dau of Carlo Dudley, titular Duke of Northumberland (*qv*), but *dsps* 1 Feb 1717/8, when the Dukedom and Marquessate expired

3e Gilbert; *b c* 1631; *m* Jane, dau of William(?) Flatsbury, and was *bur* 11 April 1702, leaving:

1f GILBERT TALBOT (but took name GREY), 13th EARL OF SHREWSBURY and WATERFORD but never assumed titles; *b* 11 Jan 1672/3; *educ* Coll English Jesuits St Omer, joined SJ 1694, RC priest *c* 1700, memb English Mission Coll of St Aloysius (Lancs Dist), Chaplain Conventual Chapel Inst of Mary at York 1701, Missionary Father Coll St Aloysius 1704 and Rector 1711 and 1734–38 (at Coll St Ignatius London Dist meanwhile), sometime chaplain to Lord Petre and Lady Stourton; *d* unm 22 July 1743

2f George; *m* 11 March 1719 Hon Mary FitzWilliam (*d* 20 Sept 1752), dau of 4th Viscount FitzWilliam of Merrion (*see* 1833 edn) by Elizabeth, sis of George Pitt, of Stratfield Saye, Berks, and *d* 12 Dec 1733, having had, with other issue:

1g GEORGE TALBOT, **14th Earl of Shrewsbury** and **Waterford**; *b* 11 Dec 1719; *m* 21 Nov 1743 Elizabeth, dau of 7th Baron Dormer (*qv*) of Wyng, and *dsp* 21 July 1787

2g Charles, of Horecross in Yoxall, Staffs; *m* 1st 23 May 1749 Mary (*d* 8 June 1750), dau and coheir of Robert Alwyn, of Trayford, Essex, and had a dau (*d* unm); *m* 2nd 7 April 1752 Mary, dau of Sir George Mostyn, 4th Bt, of Talacre (*qv*), and *d* 11 April 1766 aged 44, having by her had, with other issue:

1h CHARLES TALBOT, **15th Earl of Shrewsbury** and **Waterford**; *b* 8 March 1753; *educ* Univ Coll Oxford; RC, FSA 1811; *m* 23 Sept 1792 Elizabeth (*d* 13 Feb 1847), est dau of James Hoey, a Dublin printer, and *dsp* 6 April 1827

2h George Joseph; *b* 23 Nov 1763; *dsp* 7 July 1789

3h John Joseph; *b* 9 June 1765; *m* 1st 29 May 1789 Catherine (*d* May 1791), dau of Thomas Clifton, of Lytham, Lancs, and had:

1i Charles; *b* 1790; *d* 1802

2i JOHN TALBOT, **16th Earl of Shrewsbury** and **Waterford**; *b* 18 March 1791; *educ* Old Hall and Stonyhurst; Hon Memb Pontifical Acad St Luke Rome; *m* 27 June 1814 Maria Theresa (*d* 8 June 1856), est dau of William Talbot, of Castle Talbot, Co Wexford, and *dspms* 9 Nov 1852, having had, with a s (*d* an infant):

1j Mary Alethea Beatrix; granted rank of Princess by LUDWIG I OF BAVARIA; *m* 4 April 1839 Philip Andrew, Prince Doria Pamphili-Landi, of Rome, and *d* 18 Dec 1858, leaving issue. He *d* 19 March 1876

2j Gwendoline Catherine; *m* 11 May 1835 Marcantonio Aldobrandini, Prince of Sulmona, later Prince Borghese, of Rome, and *d* 27 Oct 1840, leaving issue

3h (cont.) John Joseph Talbot *m* 2nd 4 May 1797 Harriet Anne (*m* 2nd 13 Dec 1815 15th Baron Teynham (*qv*) and *d* 7 June 1839), dau of Rev Bacon Bedingfeld (*see* BEDINGFELD, Bt), and *d* 8 Aug 1815, having by her had, with other issue:

2i George Henry; *m* 6 April 1829 Augusta Jones (*m* 2nd 10 Sept 1839 Hon Craven FitzHardinge Berkeley (*d* 1 July 1855; *see* BERKELEY, B) and *d* 25 May 1841), dau of Sir Horace St Paul, Bt (*see* 1850 edn), and *d* 19 June 1839, having had:

1j John; *b* 18 Feb 1830; *d* 23 April 1846

2j Augusta; *b* 5 June 1831; *m* 22 July 1851 1st Baron Howard of Glossop (*see* NORFOLK, D) and *d* 3 July 1862

1i Harriet; *m* 19 Oct 1829 John W Searle and *d* 9 Oct 1866. He *d* 1861

2i Charlotte; *m* 19 Aug 1830 12th and last Earl of Roscommon (*dsp* 15 May 1850; *see* 1850 edn) and *d* 21 Nov 1843

1h Barbara; *b* 1 July 1756; *m* 9 April 1780 Francis Fortescue Turville, of Husband's Bosworth, Leics, and *d* 4 Jan 1806

2h Juliana; *b* 3 March 1759; *m* 7 June 1784 Michael Bryan, author *The Biographical Historical Dictionary of Painters and Engravers*, and *d* 19 Feb 1801, leaving issue

3h Theresa; *b* 31 July 1761; *m* 5 Feb 1793 Robert Selby, yst s of Thomas Selby, of Biddleston, Northumberland, and *d* 1 Jan 1823, leaving issue

3g Francis, of Witham Place, Essex; *b* 1727; *m* 1st 20 April 1761 Lady Anne Belasyse (*dsp* 13 Sept 1768), dau of 1st Earl of Fauconberg of Newborough; *m* 2nd 18 May 1772 Margaret Frances, only dau of William Sheldon, of Weston, Warwicks, and *d* 22 Nov 1813, leaving by her, with other issue:

1h Charles Thomas; *b* 24 Nov 1782; Lt-Col; *m* 1 Feb 1830 Julia (*m* 2nd 10 Jan 1839 John Hubert Washington Hibbert, of Bilton Grange, Warwicks, and *d* 4 June 1892), 3rd dau of Sir Henry Tichborne, 8th Bt (*see* 1967 edn DOUGHTY-

TICHBORNE, Bt), and *d* 30 April 1838, having had, with an er s (*d* young):

1i BERTRAM ARTHUR TALBOT, **17th Earl of Shrewsbury** and **Waterford**; *b* 11 Dec 1832; V-Adml Chester 1854, Kt Cdr SMO Malta, Kt Grand Cross Order of Pius IX, High Steward Albrighton; *d* unm 10 Aug 1856

1i Annette Mary; granted 1854 rank of earl's dau; *m* 17 Jan 1855 Sir Humphrey de Trafford, 2nd Bt (*qv*), and *d* 1 July 1922, leaving issue

2i Gwendoline Elizabeth; *m* 29 Oct 1857 Edward Henry Petre (*see* PETRE, B) and *d* 3 Sept 1910, leaving issue

1h Maria; *b* 4 Oct 1779; *m* 22 Sept 1802 James Wheble, of Woodley Lodge, Berks, and *d* 25 April 1814

1g Barbara; *m* 30 June 1742 5th Lord Aston of Forfar (*dspm* 1751, when his title became dormant) and *d* 9 Nov 1759, leaving issue

2g Mary; *m* 9 Aug 1759 8th Baron Dormer (*qv*) of Wyng and *d* 18 May 1753, leaving issue

1b Bridget; *m* Sir John Talbot, of Castlering, Co Louth (*see* TALBOT OF MALAHIDE, B)

1a Anne; *m* Thomas Needham, of Shenton

(3) (cont.) Sir John Talbot *m* 2nd Elizabeth (*d* 10 May 1558), dau of Walter Wrottesley (*see* WROTTESLEY, B) and *d* 10 Sept 1549, having had:

2a John (Sir), of Salwarp, Worcs; *m* 13 Sept 1574 Olive, dau and coheir of Sir Henry Sherrington, of Lacock, Wilts, and *d* 9 Dec 1581, having had:

1b Sherrington, of Salwarp and Lacock; *m* 1st Elizabeth, dau of Sir Thomas Leighton, of Feckingham, Worcs, Govr Guernsey, and had, with four daus:

1c Sherrington; *m* 13 Oct 1627 Jane, sis of Sir Thomas Lyttelton, 1st Bt (*see* COBHAM, V), and *d* 1677, leaving:

1d John (Sir), of Lacock; *m* 1st Elizabeth, dau of Sir John Keyt, 1st Bt, of Ebrington, and had a s (*dsp*); *m* 2nd Barbara, dau of Sir Henry Slingsby, 1st Bt, of Scriven, Yorks, and by her had, with other issue:

1e Anne; *m* Sir John Ivory and had issue

2e Barbara; *b c* 1671; *m* 11 July 1689 1st Viscount de Longueville (*see* GREY, B) and had issue

2c Gilbert (Sir), Master Jewel Office *temp* CHARLES II; *d* unm

1b (cont.) Sherrington Talbot *m* 2nd Mary, dau of John Washbourne, of Wichinford, Worcs, and *d* 1642, having by her had, with other issue:

3c George, of Rudge, Salop; had:

1d Catherine; *m* Sir Clement Clerke, of Launde Abbey, Leics

4c William, of Whittington and Stourton Castle, Staffs; *m* Mary (*d* 1661), dau of Thomas Doughty, of Whittington and Kinver, Staffs, and *d* 27 March 1686, leaving:

1d William (Rt Rev); *bapt* 2 July 1658; *educ* Oriel Coll Oxford (MA 23 June 1680); Ld Lt and custos rotulorum Co Durham, Dean Worcester 1691, Bp Oxford 1699–1715, Bp Salisbury 1715–22, Bp Durham 1722; *m* Catherine, dau of Richard King, London Alderman, and had, with other issue:

1e CHARLES, **1st Baron Talbot of Hensol**

2e Edward; *b* 1693; MA Oxon; Archdeacon Berks; *d* 9 Dec 1720

3e Sherrington; *b* 1699; Maj-Gen; *m* 1st Elizabeth, dau of Henry Medgett, and had:

1f William (Rev); *b* 1718; MA Oxon; Rector St Giles's Reading; *d* 2 March 1774

2f Sir CHARLES HENRY TALBOT, 1st Bt (GB), so *cr* 31 May 1790, of Mickleham, Surrey, and Belfast; *m* 1749 Anne, only child of Thomas Hassel, and *d* 30 June 1798, having had, with four daus:

1g Sir CHARLES TALBOT, 2nd Bt; *d* unm Nov 1812

2g Sir GEORGE TALBOT, 3rd and last Bt; *b* 14 March 1763; *m* 1787 Anna, dau of Rev Thomas Preston, of Swainston, Co Meath, and *dspm* 10 June 1850, when the btcy expired

3e (cont.) Maj-Gen Sherrington Talbot *m* 2nd Eleanor (*dsp*), dau of William Higford Dixton, *m* 3rd Charlotte, dau of Thomas Freeman, of Antigua, and by her had:

1f Indiana; *m* 9 Feb 1773 Lewes Peake Garland, of Michaelstow, Essex, and had issue. He *d* 1780

2f Henrietta Maria; *m* Rt Rev Charles Trimnell, DD, Bp Winchester

1d Catherine; *m* 1st Walter Littleton (*see* HATHERTON, B) and had issue; *m* 2nd Lancelot Blackburn, DD, Archbp York

2d Frances; *m* Samuel Jewkes, of Wolverley, Worcs

2b John, of Badgworth; *m* Mary, dau and heiress of Thomas Trimnel, of Okeley, Worcs, and had:

1c John, of Okely; *m* Margaret, dau of Thomas Gower, of Droitwich, Worcs

3b Thomas, of Worvill, Salop; *m* Magdalen, dau of Sir Marmaduke Wyvill, and had:

1c Robert, of Worvill; *m* Anne, dau of William Sheldon, of Broadway, Worcs, and had:

1d Thomas, of Worvill

2d Gilbert

3d George

1 Anne; *m* Sir Henry Vernon, KB, PC (*see* VERNON, B)

The Rt Rev WILIAM TALBOT *d* 10 Oct 1730; his est s,

CHARLES TALBOT, **1st Baron Talbot of Hensol**, Co Glamorgan (GB), so *cr* 5 Dec 1733, PC (1733); *bapt* 22 Dec 1685; *educ* Eton and Oriel Coll Oxford (Fell All Souls 1704); barrister Inner Temple 1710 (Treas 172627) and Lincoln's Inn Jan 1718/9 (Bencher both Inns 1726), Slr-Gen to PRINCE OF WALES 1717, MP (Whig) Tregony 1720–22 and Durham 1722–23, Slr-Gen 1726–33, Ld Chllr 1733–Feb 1736/7; *m* 1709 Cecil (*d* 13 June 1720), dau and heiress of Charles Matthews, of Castell-y-Mynach, Glamorgan, and ggdau of David Jenkins, of Hensol, and *d* 14 Feb 1736/7, leaving:

1 WILLIAM TALBOT, **2nd Baron Talbot of Hensol** and 1st and last EARL TALBOT (GB), so *cr* 10 March 1761, also 1st BARON DYNEVOR (*qv*), of Dinevor, Co Carmarthen (GB), so *cr* 17 Oct 1780, with in the latter case only remainder to his dau and heirs male of her body, PC (1761); *b* 16 May 1710; *educ* Eton and Exeter Coll Oxford; MP (Whig) Glamorgan 1734–37, Co Glam Militia 1760, Ld Steward Household 1761–82; *m* 21 Feb 1733/4 Mary (*d* 5 April 1787), only dau and heiress of Adam de Cardonnel, of Bedhampton Park, Hants, and *d* 27 April 1782, when the Earldom expired, leaving:

  (1) CECIL Talbot, BARONESS DINEVOR; *m* 16 Aug 1756 George RICE, MP, of Newtown, Carmarths, and had issue (*see* DYNEVOR, B)

2 John, MP; *m* 1st May 1737 Henrietta Maria (*dsp* Dec 1747), dau and coheir of Sir Matthew Decker, 1st and last Bt; *m* 2nd Aug 1748 Catherine (*d* 20 Jan 1785), est dau and eventual heir of 2nd Viscount Chetwynd (*qv*), through whom he acquired the Ingestre estate comprising Ingestr(i)e Hall and over 10,500 acres of Staffs, and *d* 22 Sept 1756, having by her had, with two other sons (*d* unm):

  (1) JOHN CHETWYND TALBOT later CHETWYND-TALBOT (roy licence 19 April 1786), **1st Earl Talbot of Hensol**, Co Glamorgan, so *cr* 3 July 1784, as also VISCOUNT INGESTRE, Co Stafford (both GB); *b* 5 Jan 1749/50; *educ* Eton and Magdalen Coll Oxford; MP (Tory) Castle Rising 1777–82, a Ld Trade and Plantations 1781–82; *m* 7 May 1776 Lady Charlotte Hill (*d* 17 Jan 1804), dau of 1st Marquess of Downshire (*qv*), and *d* 19 May 1793, leaving:

    1a CHARLES, **2nd Earl**

    2a John (Rev); *b* 4 April 1779; *d* 8 Feb 1825

  (2) George (Rev); *m* Anne, dau of Lord Henry Beauclerk (*see* SAINT ALBANS, D), and *dsp*

3 George (Rev); DD, Vicar Guiting, Glos; *m* 3 Jan 1761 Anne (*d* 31 Dec 1813), est dau of 1st Viscount Folkestone (*see* RADNOR, E), and *d* 19 Nov 1782, leaving, with two daus:

  (1) George, of Temple Guiting, Glos; *b* 25 March 1763; *m* 4 Jan 1789 Charlotte Elizabeth (*d* 1817), dau and coheir of Rev Thomas Drake, DD, and *d* 7 April 1836, leaving, with two other daus (*d* unm):

    1a Mary Anne; *m* 18 May 1815 Sir Francis Lawley, 7th Bt (*see* 1932 edn WENLOCK, B), of Middleton Hall, Warwicks. He *dsp* 30 Jan 1851

    2a Charlotte; *m* 27 June 1818 William Mount and had issue (*see* MOUNT, Bt)

  (2) Charles (Very Rev); *b* 26 Oct 1769; DD, Dean Salisbury; *m* 27 June 1796 Elizabeth (*d* 5 May 1836), dau of 5th Duke of Beaufort (*qv*), and *d* 28 Feb 1823, leaving, with other issue:

    1a Henry George (Rev); *b* 28 June 1798; Rector Michel Troye, Glos; *m* 1 Aug 1835 Mary Elizabeth (*d* 14 Sept 1838), dau of Maj-Gen Hon Sir William Ponsonby, KCB (*see* BESSBOROUGH, E), and *d* 10 March 1867, leaving:

      1b Henry Charles; *b* 29 June 1838; Capt 43rd Foot; *m* 16 Oct 1867 Juliana Augusta (*d* 22 Jan 1928), dau of Capt Hugh Berners, RN, of Woolverstone Park, Ipswich, and *d* 31 March 1901, leaving, with a dau:

        1c Henry Arthur Charles (Rev); *b* 17 Aug 1868; Lt 4th Bn Oxon LI, RC priest, Chaplain Magistral Obedience SMO Malta; *d* unm 16 March 1939

        2c Henry FitzRoy George, DSO; *b* 24 Feb 1874; Capt RN, Nile Expdn 1898 (despatches, medal with clasp, Egyptian medal), Boer War 1899–1900 (medal) and WW I (despatches); *m* 4 June 1904 Susan Blair Athol (*d* 19 March 1951), only dau of William Allison, of Kilvington, Thirsk, Yorks, and *d* 3 July 1920 of disease contracted through the war on active service, leaving:

          1d (Arthur Allison) FitzRoy (Sir), KBE (1964), CB (1961), DSO (1940) and bar (1943), DL (Somerset 1973); *b* 22 Oct 1909; RN: served WW II (wounded), Flag Offr: Middle East 1960–62, S Atlantic and S America 1963–65; C-in-C Plymouth 1965–67, V-Adml; *m* 1st 28 Sept 1940 Joyce Gertrude (*d* 1981), er dau of Frank Edwin Linley, of Fowey, Cornwall; *m* 2nd 6 Jan 1983 Elizabeth (*d* 4 Dec 1995), dau of Rupert Handley Ensor, widow of Sir Esmond Otho Durlacher and formerly w of Capt Richard Steel, RN and *d* 16 June 1998, leaving by his 1st w:

           1e *Anthea Jane [Mrs James Charrington, 10 Gainsborough Dve, Sherborne, Dorset DT9 6DR]; *b* 7 June 1944; *m* 6 Sept 1969 *James Arthur Hubert Charrington, er s of Peter Ronald Lethbridge Charrington, MC, of Brookes Hall, Horsington, Somerset, and has:

              1f *Melissa Clare; *b* 16 July 1970

              2f *Lucinda Rose; *b* 26 Feb 1973

           2e *Elizabeth Ann; *b* 4 Sept 1945; *m* 10 May 1969 *Michael John Philip Ashton Shuttleworth, RM, est s of Lt-Cdr John Ashton Shuttleworth, RN, of Nether Hall, Hathersage, Derbys, and has:

              1f *Ashton FitzRoy; *b* 1972

              2f *Henry Ashton; *b* 1974

          1d Nesta Cecil; *b* 6 April 1905; *m* 14 Dec 1929 Capt John Hext Lewes, OBE, RN, JP (*d* 14 March 1992), Ld Lt Cards 1956–74 and Dyfed 1974–77, only s of Col John Lewes, RA, of Llanllyr, Cards, and *d* 16 June 1994, leaving:

           1e *John William Talbot [Lt-Cdr John Lewes RN, Penny Cottage, Llansawel, Llandeilo, Dyfed SA19 7JU]; *b* 22 Jan 1931; *educ* RNC Dartmouth; Lt-Cdr RN Korea 1950–51; *m* 1st 3 April 1954 (*divorce* 1962) Mary Georgiana (*d* 1992), dau of Pascoe Anthony George Glyn (*see* WOLVERTON, B), and has:

              1f *John Pascoe; *b* 25 April 1955; *educ* Shrewsbury

              2f *James Glyn; *b* 18 Feb 1959; *m* 1984 *Helen Lohmann, of Reading, Pa., and has:

                1g *Maxwell John Pascoe; *b* 1985

              1f *Alice Mary Rhianon; *b* 12 Dec 1957

           1e (cont.) Lt-Cdr John Lewes *m* 2nd 9 Jan 1967 *Margaret Jane, dau of Owen Fenner Clayton, of Sydney, NSW, and by her has had:

              3f *Owain Vaughan; *b* 9 July 1967

              2f Sian Frances Louisa; *b* 31 July; *d* 21 Sept 1969

              3f *Angharad Hope; *b* 1972; *m* 1st 1992 (divorce 1998) Ian McCartney; *m* 2nd 1998 *Brian Willis, and by her 1st husb has:

           1g *Felix James; *b* 22 May 1993

           1g *Francesca Rose; *b* 16 Sept 1994

         1e *Loveday Elisabeth Talbot [Mrs Robert Gee, Llanllyr, Talsarn, Lampeter, Dyfed]; *b* 1 Nov 1932; *m* 1 Dec 1956 *Robert George Gee, s of George Gee, of London W1, and has:

           1f *Mathew George Cooper; *b* 30 April 1960

           2f *Patrick Robert Cooper; *b* 25 Nov 1963; *m* 1991 *Miranda Whitelaw Dunn and has:

              1g *William Benedict Robert Cooper; *b* 21 Feb 1992

              2g *Benedict Thomas Lewes; *b* 23 Jan 1995

           1f *Emma Louise Moya; *b* 23 Oct 1962; *m* 1990 *Nicholas Eric Hugh Barran and has issue (*see* BARRAN, Bt)

          2e *Gwenllian Anne Talbot [Mrs John Kidd, Llanfair, Llandyssul, Dyfed]; *b* 19 June 1934; *m* 10 Dec 1955 *Capt John Franklin Kidd, RN, s of John Kidd, of Perry Heath, Herts, and has:

           1f *John Christopher William; *b* 4 Feb 1957

           1f *Elizabeth Ceridwen; *b* 8 Aug 1958

         1c Gwendoline Mary Elizabeth; *b* 5 Nov 1870; *m* 8 Jan 1891 Hon Louis Vanden-Bempde-Johnstone, s of 1st Baron Derwent (*qv*), and *d* 16 Nov 1969, leaving issue

        2c Cecil Maud; *m* 17 July 1900 Andrew Holford Pitcairn, of Northam Lodge, Northam, N Devon, s of Col Pitcairn, of Pitcullo, Fife, and *d* 12 April 1954. He *d* 11 March 1938

      2a Charles (Sir), KCB; *b* 1 Nov 1801; Adml; *m* 11 Dec 1838 Charlotte Georgiana (*d* 7 Sept 1883), widow of Lt-Col Stapleton and sis of 3rd Baron Ponsonby of Imokilly (*see* BESSBOROUGH, E), and *d* 8 Aug 1876, leaving:

        1b Charles William TALBOT later TALBOT-PONSONBY (roy licence with arms 1866 under terms of will of his uncle 3rd Baron Ponsonby of Imokilly), of Inchiquin, Youghal, Co Cork, JP Co Cork and Hants; *b* 29 May 1843; Lt RN; *m* 15 Jan 1868 Constance Louisa (*d* 23 March 1933), yst dau of Frederick Peter Delmé-Radcliffe, of Hitchin Priory, Herts, and *d* 23 July 1927, having had:

          1c William Charles Francis; *b* 14 Oct 1868; *d* 1870

          2c John Seymour William, Lt RN; *b* 1 May 1870; *d* 15 Jan 1895

          3c Edward Frederick; *b* 21 Oct 1872; Maj RHA Boer War 1899–1902, MFH Kildare; *m* 26 Sept 1899 Marion Theodora (*d* 1 Jan 1970 aged 96), dau of William Nicholson (*see* NICHOLSON OF WINTERBOURNE, B), and *d* 27 July 1946, leaving:

           1d John Arthur; *b* 10 March 1907; Capt 7th Hus, Lt-Col RAC (TA), MFH Warwickshire; *m* 1st 9 April 1931 (*divorce* 1956) Frances Elizabeth (*d* 1980), only dau of Douglas Henry Fraser, of Wardington Ho, nr Banbury, Oxon (*see* 1970 edn FRASER OF LONSDALE, B), and had:

            1e +Michael Clement [Michael Talbot-Ponsonby Esq, Hinton Manor, Hinton Parva, Wilts SN4 0DW]; *b* 3 Jan 1932; *educ* Eton; *m* 28 Jan 1956 Judith Katharine (*d* 1985), yst dau of Rt Rev Theodore Sumner Gibson, Bp Kimberley, S Africa, and has:

              1f *Caroline Frances; *b* 19 Oct 1958; *m* 1990 *Patrick E F Pilkington, est s of Maj Nigel Pilkington, of Purley, Surrey, and has:

                1g *Hubert Edward; *b* 1991

                2g *John Nigel; *b* 1993

                3g *Patrick Cecil; *b* 1994

                4g *Oliver George; *b* 12 Sept 1997

              2f *Charlotte Jane [Mrs William O'Leary, Upper House, Knucklas, Knighton, Powys LD7 1PN]; *b* 5 Feb 1963; *m* 1992 *William M E O'Leary, est s of David O'Leary, literary agent, of Oxon and Notting Hill, and has:

                1g *Arthur Valentine; *b* 15 Feb 1997

                1g *Lettice; *b* 6 Nov 1994

              3f *Lucy Elizabeth, of The Seychelles; *b* 6 Nov 1965; has:

                1g *Loic; *b* 27 April 1994

                1g *Florence; *b* 20 Dec 1995

              4f *Katherine Louisa; *b* 1 Nov 1967; has:

                1g *Barnaby; *b* 23 June 1996

            2e +Peter William [Peter Talbot-Ponsonby Esq, Tocknells House, Painswick, Glos GL6 6TR]; *b* 10 July 1938; *m* 1st 12 July 1962 (*divorce* 1988) Sarah Vansittart, yr dau of Sir Eric Vansittart Bowater (*see* BOWATER, Bt, of Hill Crest), and has:

              1f *Nina Karen; *b* 22 May 1964; *m* 19–

              2f *Jessica Evelyn [Mrs Andrew Saunders, 19 Ensor Mews, London SW7]; *b* 7 Oct 1965; *m* 1987 *Andrew J Saunders and has issue

              3f *Eila; *b* 13 April 1972; *m* and has issue

            2e (cont.) Peter Talbot-Ponsonby *m* 2nd 1988 *Jane Faye, dau of Jean Lancelot d'Espeissis, of Perth, W Australia, and by her has:

              1f +Frederick James; *b* 1990

           1d (cont.) Lt-Col John Talbot-Ponsonby *m* 2nd 7 March 1957 Daphne (*m* 3rd 4 Aug 1972 Capt Thomas Francis Jeune Hanbury, MC, Life Gds, and *d* 7 Dec 1976), formerly w of Capt Jack Brittain-Jones, CBE, and er dau of Percival Augustus Duke, OBE, of The Island, Walton-on-Hill, Surrey, and *d* out hunting 29 Dec 1969

          1d Marion Constance; *b* 19 Jan 1904; *m* 15 Nov 1923 Col Ernest Elliot Buckland Mackintosh, DSO, RE, Dir Science Museum 1933–46, s of Ernest Alexander Buckland Mackintosh, and had issue. He *d* Nov 1957

          4c Charles George; *b* 1 May 1874; BA Oxon, barrister; *m* 22 Jan 1914 Violet Mary (*d* 26 June 1945), only dau of Capt Raymond William Parr, of Belgravia, and *d* 16 Jan 1937, leaving:

           1d Edward ('Jimmy') FitzRoy; *b* 22 Aug 1916; *educ* Harrow; *m* 1st 3 March 1938 (*divorce* 1960) (Bertha) Marie-Louise Muriel (*d* 21 Jan 1999), er dau of Horatio Claude Barber, of Trinity Hill, Jersey, and had:

            1e +Nigel Edward Charles [Nigel Talbot-Ponsonby Esq, Langrish Lodge, Langrish, Petersfield, Hants]; *b* 24 Sept 1946; *educ* Harrow;

m 16 April 1977 *Robina Helen, er dau of Lt-Cdr Henry Victor Bruce, RN (*see* ELGIN and KINCARDINE, E), and has:

1f +Charles Henry FitzRoy; *b* 3 Dec 1981

2f +James Nigel Edward; *b* 1986

3f +Alexander John Bruce; *b* 1987

1e *Suzanne Molly; *b* 23 Aug 1939; *m* 5 Oct 1957 (*divorce* 1973) Lt-Cdr James Granville Lucas, RN, and has issue (*see* LUCAS, Bt)

1d (cont.) Edward Talbot-Ponsonby *m* 2nd 9 May 1960 (*divorce* 1967) Mrs Shirley Rhona Mearns; *m* 3rd 27 July 1967 *Anja Edith Boudewijn [Mrs Edward Talbot-Ponsonby, East Lodge, Rogate, Hants], of Cowes, and *d* 22 June 1996

5c Frederick William; *b* 19 Jan 1879; Cdr RN, Chev Legn Hon; *m* 26 June 1913 Hannah (*d* 6 Jan 1952), yst dau of John Ritchie Findlay, DL, of Aberlour, Banffshire (*see* 1970 edn FINDLAY, Bt), and *d* 12 Nov 1930, leaving:

1d Evelyn John; *b* 18 Sept 1915; *educ* Harrow and Trin Coll Cambridge (BA 1937, MA 1941); Lt RNVR WW II; *m* 17 April 1943 *Hilary [Mrs Evelyn Talbot-Ponsonby, 38 Kitsbury Rd, Berkhamsted, Herts HP4 3EA], only dau of Thomas Kingsley Curtis, of Highgate, and *d* 23 April 1997, leaving:

1e +Andrew (Rev Preb) [The Rev Preb Andrew Talbot-Ponsonby, Leintwardine Rectory, nr Craven Arms, Salop SY7 0LL]; *b* 26 Feb 1944; *educ* Harrow and Leeds U (Dip Theol 1966); ordained 1968; *m* 1st 27 July 1968 Alice Margaret (*d* 1989), er dau of Raymond Whittier Baldwin, of Alderley Edge, Cheshire, by Penelope Sophia, yr dau of Sir Thomas Dalmahoy Barlow, GBE (*see* BARLOW, Bt, of London); *m* 2nd 1991 *Rev Jill, dau of Cecil Frank Robert Sims, of Shirley, Hants, and by his 1st w has:

1f +Daniel Frederick; *b* 25 Oct 1971; *educ* Shrewsbury and Oriel Coll Oxford (MA, DPhil)

2f +Thomas Martin; *b* 9 April 1973; *educ* Shrewsbury and Clare Coll, Cambridge (MA)

3f +William Peter; *b* 18 Aug 1975; *educ* Shrewsbury and Oriel Coll Oxford (MPhys)

4f +Henry James; *b* 5 Nov 1981

2e +Christopher; *b* 23 May 1950; *educ* Harrow

3e +Simon [Simon Talbot-Ponsonby Esq, West Barns, Home Farm, Abbots Leigh, Bristol BS8 3QF]; *b* 11 June 1952; *educ* Harrow and Nottingham U (BSc); CEng; *m* 1st 31 July 1976 (*divorce* 1990) Hilary, dau of Eric Cropper; *m* 2nd 11 May 1998 *Mrs Anne Christine Bruce, dau of William Harold Wakely, of Portsmouth

1e *(Elizabeth) Hannah [Mrs John Beck, 4 St Mary's Ave, Harrogate, Yorks]; *b* 30 Nov 1945; *educ* North London Collegiate Sch and U of Kent (BA); *m* 4 Jan 1969 *Dr John Michael Beck, only s of Frank L Beck, of Bradford, and has:

1f *Mark Thomas Coulton; *b* 1972

2f *George Samuel Curtis; *b* 1975

3f *Charles Edward Frank; *b* 1979

1f *Tess Adwoa Margaret Nora; *b* 1970

2f *Ruth Mary Ann; *b* 1977

2e *Celia; *b* 6 Sept 1947; *m* 1971 *David McTeer, G/Capt RAF, and has:

1f *Stuart Paul; *b* 1973

2f *Ian James; *b* 1975

3f *Philip John; *b* 1977

1d *(Felicity) Philippa [Lady Scott, The New Grounds, Slimbridge, Glos GL2 7BS]; *b* 22 Nov 1918; *m* 7 Aug 1951, as his 2nd w, Sir Peter Markham Scott, CH, CBE, DSC (*d* 1989, *see* BRUCE, Bt, of Downhill), and has:

1e *(Richard) Falcon [Falcon Scott Esq, The Chalet, Weeton Lane, Dunkeswick, Leeds LS17 9LP]; *b* 2 June 1954; *educ* Millfield; *m* 1st 1981 (*divorce* 1992) Jillian Elizabeth Gomersall and has:

1f *Lucy Jane Elizabeth; *b* Dec 1983

1e (cont.) Falcon Scott *m* 2nd 1995 *Jane Frances, dau of Noel Schofield, of Harrogate, Yorks, and by her has:

1f *Christopher Robert; *b* 1996

1e *Dafila Kathleen [Mrs Timothy Clutton-Brock, White Roses, The Hythe, Reach, Cambs CB5 0JQ]; *b* 9 June 1952; *m* 1980 *Prof Timothy Clutton-Brock and has:

1f *Peter; *b* 1983

1f *Amber; *b* 1981

6c Arthur Hugh Brabazon; *b* 4 Sept 1885; Maj 9th Bn Hants Regt, Pres Land Agents' Soc 1938, CC Hants 1929–34, Commr to 16th Duke of Norfolk 1935; *m* 24 July 1913 Alianore Rachel (*d* 29 May 1974), dau of Sir Edward Stafford Howard, KCB (*see* NORFOLK, D), and *d* 24 Oct 1952, leaving:

1d Alathea Rachel Constance; *b* 13 May 1914; *m* 1st 15 June 1935 Maj Guy Richard Tufnell Gillett, RA (*kas* 29 Nov 1942), er s of Col Charles Richard Gillett, DSO, of Maida, Camberley, and has:

1e *Aurea June; *b* 26 June 1936; *m* 25 Sept 1964 Timothy Edward Pritchard Thornycroft, MA, MIMechE, AMRINA, of Southampton, IOW and S of England Royal Mail Steam Packet Co, only s of John Ward Thornycroft, of IOW, and has:

1f *John FitzRoy; *b* 26 Aug 1965

2f *Benjamin Delmé; *b* 16 June 1968

2e *Julia Geraldine; *b* 18 Jan 1939; *m* 4 April 1964 Ivor Russell, er s of Godfrey Russell, of Forthampton Ho, Forthampton, Glos

1d (cont.) Mrs Guy Gillett *m* 2nd 20 March 1944 Peter Delmé-Radcliffe, er s of Arthur Henry Delmé-Radcliffe, of The White Cottage, Branksome Park, Hants, and *d* 24 July 1976

1c Evelyn Mary Georgiana; *b* 22 Feb 1876; *d* unm 23 Feb 1915

2c Constance Emma; *b* 18 Nov 1882; *m* 28 Dec 1937 (*annulled* 1940) Alfred Frederick Kaufmann, resumed maiden name by deed poll 1941 and *dsp* 9 March 1949

2b Francis Arthur Bouverie; *b* 27 Sept 1851; Maj Oxon LI; *m* 16 Nov 1878 Alice Mary Beatrice (*d* 1 March 1944), dau of Maj-Gen Edward Melville Lawford, 4th Madras Cav, and *d* 20 May 1916, leaving:

1c Frank Eustace George; *b* 6 Oct 1879; *educ* Haileybury; Col IA, China 1900 (medal) and WW I (Brevet Maj and Lt-Col); *m* 17 July 1909 Ruth Leslie (*d* 2 Sept 1939), dau of Col Edmund William Creswell, RE, and *dsp* 25 Sept 1958

2c Edward Charles; *b* 9 April 1881; Capt 47th Sikhs, IA, Boer War 1900–02 (Queen's medal with three clasps, King's medal with two clasps), WW I; *m* 30 Sept 1908 Dorothy Maynard (*d* 28 Dec 1947), dau of Sir William Gibbons, KCB (*see* GIBBONS, Bt), and *d* 29 April 1915 of wounds recd in action, leaving:

1d Patricia Mary; *b* 23 Dec 1909; *m* 17 July 1937 Brig Denys Edward Osbert Thackwell, CBE, RE (*d* 1990), Pres Int Cartographical Assoc 1964–68, only s of Brig-Gen Osbert Montague Roche Thackwell, RE, and *d* 1986, having had:

1e *William Talbot Roche [Maj William Thackwell, 273 Bexley Rd, Maidstone, Kent]; *b* 21 Feb 1947; *educ* Sherborne and RMA Sandhurst; Maj RE

1e *Sara Charlotte [Mrs John Turnbull, Thornhill, Holt, nr Wimborne, Dorset BH21 7DJ]; *b* 8 May 1938; *m* 29 Aug 1959 Capt John Grey Turnbull, RA, er s of Rev Peveril Hayes Turnbull, of The Cottage, Brandeston, Suffolk, by Lady Jane Grey, only dau of 9th Earl of Stamford (*see* 1970 edn), and has:

1f *Mark Robert; *b* 8 Oct 1961; *m* 16 Sept 1995 *Philippa, dau of Lt-Col Colin Heggie

2f *Christopher John; *b* 9 July 1963; *m* 1991 *Clare, dau of Christopher Green

3f *Anthony Lawrence; *b* 27 March 1965; *m* 9 July 1994 *Dr Amanda Varnava, dau of Anthony Varnava

1f *Elizabeth Frances; *b* 12 July 1960; *m* 30 July 1983 *Timothy Lowth

2f *Alison Jane; *b* 8 May 1967; *m* 6 Dec 1997 *Simon Chesters-Thompson

2e *Catherine Patricia [Mrs Gerard Delaney, Witherenden Hill House, Burwash, Sussex]; *b* 20 Sept 1939; *m* 30 Jan 1965 *Gerard Anthony Delaney, s of William Delaney, of Purley, Surrey, and has:

1f *Rachel Ann; *b* 2 Dec 1965; *m* 1991 *James de Candole

2f *(Alexandra) Ruth; *b* 10 Sept 1967; *m* 1995 *Hamish Macdonald

2d Iris Nonie; *b* 26 Dec 1913; *m* 14 Sept 1939 Robert Rushton Henshaw, s of Richard Henry Henshaw, of Mossley Hill, Liverpool, and *d* 27 April 1965, leaving issue

3c Cecil Ponsonby (Sir), KCB (1947), KBE (1939), DSO (1915) and bar (1917); *b* 31 Aug 1884; *educ* Bedford Sch and HMS *Britannia*; WW I (submarines) (despatches), Head Naval Air Section Admlty 1926, Naval ADC to HM GEORGE V 1931, Dir Naval Equipment 1932–34, R-Adml Submarines 1934–36, Dir Dockyards Admlty 1937–46, bronze medal of Roy Humane Soc, Grand Offr Order Orange Nassau, Chev Legn Hon; *m* 14 Aug 1912 Bridget (*d* 1 Aug 1960), dau of Robert Bateson Dixon Bradshaw, of Barrow-in-Furness, and *d* 17 March 1970, having had:

1d Francis Robert Cecil; *b* 6 Dec 1913; Lt RN WW II; *ka* in HM Submarine *Thames* July 1940

2d Edward Bartle; *b* 23 July 1915; Lt RN WW II; *ka* in HM Submarine *Snapper* Feb 1941

3d *John [Lt-Col John Talbot, Lodge House, Smeeth, Kent TN25 6QZ]; *b* 17 Aug 1925; *educ* Radley; Lt-Col RA, MA to CINCENT 1966, Def Attaché: Sofia 1969 and Vienna 1972; *m* 29 July 1954 *Janet Wyndham, yr dau of Lt-Gen Sir William Wyndham Green, KBE, CB, DSO, MC, DL, of Little Gables, New Romney, Kent, and has:

1e +David John; *b* 26 Jan 1960; *m* 1983 *Margaret Manson, dau of Douglas Gordon McKenzie Cameron, of Dunfermline, Fife, and has:

1f +Charles Edward Cameron; *b* 1987

2f +James Alexander St John; *b* 1989

3f +Sholto Richard John; *b* 1993

2e +Anthony Francis Wyndham [Anthony Talbot Esq, 23 Wandle Rd, London SW17 7DL]; *b* 21 Sept 1961; *m* 1989 *Melody Jane, dau of Peter Sidney Hallett, of NSW, and has:

1f *Imogen Primrose Claire; *b* 1993

2f *(Samantha) Jasmine; *b* 6 May 1995

3f *Bridget Eleanor Wyndham; *b* 6 March 1997

3e +Peter Charles [Peter Talbot Esq, 85 Hewlett St, Bronte, NSW 2024, Australia]; *b* 3 Sept 1964; *m* 1990 *Jacqueline Margaret, dau of David Parkes, of The Old Rectory, Wrington, Bristol, and has:

1f *Ella Parkes; *b* 2 Jan 1995

2f *Mia Parkes; *b* 28 March 1997

1d Barbara Bridget; *b* 25 Jan 1919; *m* 21 Dec 1940 Cdr Richard Molyneux Favell, DSC, JP, DL, RN, High Sheriff Cornwall 1963, er s of Richard Vernon Favell, of St Buryan, Cornwall, and *d* 7 June 1996, having had:

1e *Frances Barbara Molyneux [Lady Banham, Penberth, St Buryan, N Penzance, Cornwall TR19 6HJ]; *b* 6 Feb 1943; *m* 30 Oct 1965 *Sir John Michael Middlecott Banham, er s of Terence Middlecott Banham, of Cornwall, and has:

1f *Mark Richard Middlecott; *b* 30 April 1968

1f *Serena Frances Tamsin; *b* 24 May 1970

2f *Morwenna Bridget Favell; *b* 14 Sept 1972

2e *Bridget Alathea [Mrs David Hugh-Jones, The Thatched Cottage, Penberth, St Buryan, Cornwall]; *b* 9 Feb 1946; *m* 8 Aug 1970 *David Llewelyn Hugh-Jones, yst s of Llewelyn A Hugh-Jones, of Camberley, and has:

  1f *Tristan Llewelyn; *b* 1973

  2f *Rupert Favell; *b* 1977

  1f *Demelza Alice; *b* 18 May 1971

  2f *Carenza Bridie; *b* 1978

3e *Julia Alice [Mrs Derek Bryant, Chynance, Penberth Valley, St Buryan, Cornwall]; *b* 3 June 1949; *m* 1976 *Derek Robin Bryant and has:

  1f *Frank Favell Ingram; *b* 12 Dec 1981

  1f *Rebecca Sophie; *b* 7 Aug 1978

  2f *Rachel Jessica; *b* 8 Dec 1980

4c *Reginald FitzRoy; *b* 21 Sept 1886, 2nd Lt Mil Wing RFC, manager Bukit Jelutong Estate, FMS; *m* 17 Oct 1913 Marguerite (*d* 24 June 1968), yst dau of Harry John, of Bombay, and was *ka* 26 Aug 1916

3b George Ponsonby; *b* 29 April 1853; *m* 29 Sept 1887 Blanche (*d* 19 March 1922), dau of Adml Hon George Douglas (*see* MORTON, E), and *d* 28 Feb 1924, leaving:

1c Arthur George, CB (1945), DSO (1939), and bar (1944); *b* 31 March 1892; V-Adml, served WW I and WW II (despatches three times), ADC to HM GEORGE VI 1943, Sr Br Naval Offr Greece 1946, Head Br Naval Mission to Greece 1947 , Offr Order Redeemer Greece, Cdr US Legion of Merit, Legn Hon, Croix de Guerre; *m* 7 Dec 1918 Doris (*d* 1972), Ch Offr WRNS, est dau of Charles Fremantle Branson, of Putney Heath, and *d* 15 Oct 1960, leaving:

1d Diana Maud Ponsonby; *b* 5 Jan 1921; *m* 7 Feb 1942 Maj Leslie Alban Harris, OBE, DSC, RM, FAA (*d* 19 June 1995), s of Albert Edward John Harris, ISO, of Mellersh Cottage, Wonersh, Surrey, and *d* 4 June 1997, leaving:

1e *Nicholas Graham Talbot [Lt-Cdr Nicholas Harris RN, The Granary, Milborne Port, Sherborne, Dorset DT9 5ED]; *b* 18 May 1947; *educ* Sherborne and RNC Dartmouth; Lt Cdr RN; *m* 6 Nov 1971 Jennifer Jane Stuart, dau of Justin Mallinson, of Bredy, Burton Bradstock, Dorset, and has:

  1f *Charles Justin Talbot; *b* 1983

  1f *Antonia Diana Stuart; *b* 1975

  2f *Francesca Louise Talbot; *b* 1979

1c Hylda Alice; *b* 2 July 1889; *d* 5 Dec 1977

1b Georgy Melosina Mary Elizabeth; *m* 14 April 1874 Cdr Francis Augustus Delmé-Radcliffe, RN, DL, of Hitchin Priory, Herts, and *d* 26 Jan 1917. He *dsp* 22 Dec 1916

2b Fanny Charlotte Emma; *m* 6 June 1861 Capt Duncan McNeill, Scots Greys, of Oransay Priory, Argyll, 3rd s of Alexander McNeill, of Colonsay and Gigha, and *d* 31 Oct 1913, leaving issue. He *d* 10 June 1924

3b Edith; *m* 2 March 1878 Maj Charles Davis Sherston, JP, 1st Bn Rifle Bde, of Evercreech, Somerset, and *d* 1 May 1918, leaving issue. He *d* 26 March 1916

4b Rose (twin with Edith); *d* 24 May 1922

3a George, Col 43rd Regt; *b* 19 Aug 1809; *m* 1st 26 June 1836 Frances (*d* 30 July 1861), est dau of Lt-Col F Ralph West, 33rd Regt, and had:

1b FitzRoy Somerset; *b* 22 Dec 1837; Maj-Gen RA; *m* 21 Aug 1869 Mary Elizabeth (*d* 22 Dec 1915), dau of W H Nicholson, and *d* 4 Nov 1906, leaving:

1c George Reginald FitzRoy, TD; *b* 19 June 1870; Capt RHA, NW Frontier 1897–98 (despatches), Boer War 1899–1902 and India in WW I (despatches), Hon Col 56th Wessex Bde RFA TA; *m* 21 Aug 1902 Eleanor Morwenna (*d* 25 March 1949), only dau of Rev Roger Granville, Sub-Dean and Preb Exeter, and *d* 27 Nov 1931, leaving:

1d Granville FitzRoy; *b* 3 March 1908; *educ* Kelly Coll and RMA Sandhurst; Col RTR WW II; *m* 22 Oct 1938 *Kathleen Betty [Mrs Granville Talbot, Lapworth Cottage, Elstead, Surrey], only dau of Gerald Townend, of Woking, Surrey, and *d* 1978, leaving:

1e +John FitzRoy [Dr John Talbot, Daggers House, Market Place, Hope, Derbys S33 6RH]; *b* 1 Oct 1945; *educ* Uppingham and St Thomas's Hosp London; MB, BS, FRCS, FRC Oph, LRCP, consultant opthalmic surgeon and Hon Lecturer Sheffield Med Sch; *m* 1972 *Esmé Gillian, JP, yst dau of Dr R de Brath Ashworth, of Holdfast Hall, Warfield, Berks (*see* RAVENSDALE, B), and has:

  1f *Fleur Katharine FitzRoy; *b* 1978

  2f *Emily Sarah FitzRoy; *b* 1980

  3f *Ann Adele FitzRoy; *b* 1987

1d Gwendoline Betty Alice; *b* 6 June 1905; *d* May 1990

3a (cont.) Col George Talbot *m* 2nd 29 April 1863 Angelina, widow of Henry Daniel, and *d* 2 Feb 1871

1a Frances Cecil; *m* 31 Dec 1829 Hon Philip Abbot (*see* 1917 edn COLCHESTER, B) and *d* his widow 7 Nov 1855

2a Maria Charlotte; *m* 16 May 1826 Lt Henry Every, est s of Sir Henry Every, 9th Bt (*qv*), and *d* 26 Aug 1827

3a Georgiana Elizabeth; *m* 4 Sept 1828 Rev Augustus Philip Clayton, s of Sir William Clayton, 4th Bt (*qv*), and *d* 23 June 1885, leaving issue

The 1st EARL TALBOT OF HENSOL's er s,

CHARLES CHETWYND CHETWYND-TALBOT, **2nd Earl Talbot of Hensol**, KG (1844), KP 1821–44), PC (1817); *b* 25 April 1777; *educ* Ch Ch Oxford (MA); Ld Lt: Staffs 1812–49, Ireland 1817–21, FRS, FSA; *m* 28 Aug 1800 Frances Thomasine (*d* 30 Dec 1819), est dau of Charles Lambart, of Beaupark, Meath (*see* 1970 edn LAMBART, Bt), and had:

1 Charles Thomas, *Viscount Ingestre*; *b* 11 July 1802; accidentally *k* Vienna 23 May 1826

2 HENRY JOHN CHETWYND, **3rd Earl Talbot of Hensol** and **18th Earl of Shrewsbury** and **Waterford**

3 Arthur (Rev), RD, Rector Church Eaton and Ingestre, Staffs; *b* 12 Nov 1805; *m* 1st 17 July 1832 Harriet (*d* 6 Feb 1845), dau of Henry Charles Hervey-Aston, of Aston Hall, Cheshire, and had:

(1) Charles Arthur TALBOT; *b* 11 May 1834; Capt Rifle Bde; *m* 24 Jan 1857 Mary Matilda (*d* 1 Dec 1873), dau of Richard John Whitman, and *d* 8 Aug 1869, leaving:

1a Algernon Charles; *b* 16 Jan 1859; *m* 19 Jan 1886 Edith Ellen (*d* 23 Jan 1951), dau of William Bunce Greenfield, DL, JP, of Beechwood Park, Herts, and *d* 27 July 1888, leaving:

1b Edith Mary; *m* 2 June 1927 Maj George Rupert Mather, TD, s of Rev H S Mather, and had:

1c John Rupert Stephen; *b* 1928; Capt and Adj Somerset LI, attd 3 (K) Bn KAR (despatches); *d* of wounds in Malaya 27 June 1953

2a Arthur Hervey, JP (Cheshire); *b* 13 March 1863; Lt-Col 5th Bn Cheshire Regt, Brig-Gen cmdg a Div Cheshire TF WW I; *m* 1882 Olympia Annette (*d* 28 March 1938), dau of T J Clarke, and *d* 13 March 1927, leaving:

1b Douglas Hervey, DSO (1918), MC, of Aston Hall, Cheshire; *b* 1882; Lt-Col 17th/21st Lancers, Boer War 1901–02, WW I (despatches, Croix de Guerre, Order St Maurice and St Lazarus of Italy); *m* 23 July 1914 Dorothy Helen (*d* 1978), dau of William Roylance Court, JP, of The Manor House, Middlewich, and *d* 23 March 1927, leaving:

1c +Bryan Hervey [Bryan Talbot Esq, Aston Lodge, Aston Runcorn, Cheshire]; *b* 15 Jan 1916; *educ* Marlborough; F/Lt RAFVR WW II; *m* 3 Feb 1940 Katherine (*d* 1977), dau of Robert John Hughes, of Llandudno, and has:

1d +Andrew Hervey [Andrew Talbot Esq, White Cottage, Aston Heath, Runcorn, Cheshire]; *b* 15 Jan 1946; *educ* Marlborough; *m* 1st 28 Jan 1972 (*divorce* 1976) Hilda Margaret Priscilla Williams, SRN; *m* 2nd 1979 *Danielle Claude, yst dau of Roger Basil Boulay, of France, and has:

1e *Jessie Sarah; *b* 1983

2d +Howard Douglas [Howard Talbot Esq, Burnt Thatch, Aston, Cheshire]; *b* 22 Feb 1948; *educ* Marlborough; *m* 28 July 1972 *Christine Ann, dau of W A A Dutton, of Hoole Bank, Chester, and has:

1e +Charles Aston Hervey; *b* 1981

1e *Bridget Louisa; *b* 1975

2e *Sophie Katharine; *b* 1977

1d *Marie-Luize [Mrs John Haycraft, The Pipings, Pebworth, Warwicks]; *b* 16 June 1942; MSR, SRR; *m* 1 Oct 1966 *John Bernard Haycraft, s of Bernard Gottfried Haycraft, of Long Crendon, Bucks, and has:

1e *Alexander Richard; *b* 5 May 1969

2e *Oliver Talbot; *b* 1972

3e *Simon Hervey; *b* 1973

2d *Wendy Robina Roylance [Mrs Rodger Price, Hilltop, Sutton Weaver, Runcorn, Cheshire]; *b* 7 July 1949; *m* 1973 *Rodger Price and has:

1e *Hannah Roylance; *b* 1975

2e *Madeleine Kate; *b* 1977

2b John Victor Chetwynd; *b* 1887; *educ* Haileybury; Lt Gren Gds; *m* 28 March 1914 Mrs Edith Muriel Potter (*d* 5 Jan 1957) and *dsp* 27 Jan 1955

1b Gwendolen Ida; *m* 27 June 1905 Arthur Lacy Compton Clarke, 8th s of Stephenson Clarke, of Brook House, Ardingly, Sussex, and *d* 28 July 1925. He *d* 8 Sept 1933

2b Cecil Muriel; *b* 6 Nov 1890; *b* 21 Nov 1902

3a Charles Aston; *b* 24 July 1864; *m* 22 March 1893 Elizabeth Mary (*dsp* 11 Jan 1895), dau of Thomas Best, of Eltville House, nr Manchester

1a Harriet Cecil; *m* 23 Jan 1878 William Henry Gramshaw, of Warlingham, Surrey, and *d* 25 Aug 1937, leaving issue

2a Gwendolen Mary; Pres and Chm Hastings BRCS, Chm Hastings C Assoc; *m* 8 June 1880 Harry Wyndham Jefferson and *d* 25 Feb 1948, leaving issue. He *d* 18 June 1918

3a Muriel Ethel; *m* 10 June 1890 the Duke d'Angelo Gavotti-Verospi and *d* 29 Aug 1890

(2) Hervey Arthur TALBOT, of Aston Grange, Cheshire; *b* 3 Oct 1838; Col 3rd and 4th Bns S Staffs Regt; *m* 23 June 1874 Eva Julietta (*d* 1888, having *m* 2nd 27 Oct 1887 Capt George Capel Fenwick, Roy Welch Fus, of Plas Fron, Wrexham (*d* 28 March 1909)), dau of Henry Crawshay, of Oaklands Park, Glos, and *d* 11 Sept 1884, leaving:

1a Arthur Aston; *b* 5 March 1881; Lt Suffolk Regt; *m* 13 April 1912 Mary Winifred (*d* 1964), dau of A Battiscombe, of Hinton Court, Herefs, and *das* E Africa Nov 1918, leaving:

1b +Patrick Edward Aston; *b* 13 Sept 1913; late RAF and Royal Aircraft Establishment 1933–46; CEng, MRAeS; *m* 21 July 1936 *Gwyneth, yr dau of Lt-Col H G Sargeaunt, RA, and has:

1c +David Nugent Aston, of Ontario, Canada; *b* 14 April 1939; *m* 1st 1962 (*divorce* 1971) Carole, dau of Oakley Pawson, of Ontario, and has:

1d +John Oakley Aston; *b* 1964

1d *Jeanne Davida; *b* 1962

2d *Rachel Millicent; *b* 1966

1c (cont.) David Talbot *m* 2nd 1979 Rachel (*d* 1988), yr dau of Dr Frank Edmund Hampton, of Grimsby, Lincs, and by her has:

3d *Georgina Amy; *b* 1980

1c *Maryan Gwyneth [Mrs M Talbot-Roberts, 2 Douro Terrace, St Helier, Jersey, CI]; *b* 24 Jan 1938; BA Hons 1959, Chev Ordre Artes et Lettres; *m* 1974 *John Roberts

1a Muriel Marguerita; *b* 25 Sept 1875; *m* Percy Logan

(1) Blanche; *m* 15 Aug 1854 (*divorce* 1865) William Henry Chetwynd and *d* 1898, leaving issue (*see* CHETWYND, Bt)

(2) Frances Jessy; *m* 1st 19 June 1867 Capt Walter de Winton, DL, JP, 1st Life Gds (*d* 24 May 1878), of Maesllwch Castle; *m* 2nd 9 Dec 1880 Capt Hon Geoffrey Richard Clegg Hill (*see* HILL, V) and *d* 20 Oct 1918

3 (cont.) The Rev and Hon Arthur Chetwynd-Talbot *m* 2nd 19 Oct 1854 Mary Elizabeth (*d* 30 Sept 1896), only dau of John Masterman, of Hull, and *d* 13 Jan 1884, having by her had:

(3) Arthur Henry (Rev); *b* 27 Sept 1855; Preb Lichfield, Rector Edgmond, Salop, Provost Denstone Coll Uttoxeter; *m* 6 Aug 1903 Eveline Mary (*d* 28 July 1952), dau and coheir of Col Charles James Ashton, of Little Onn Hall, Staffs, and *d* 26 Nov 1927, leaving:

1a John Arthur, AFC; *b* 14 March 1905; *educ* Harrow and Sidney Sussex Coll Cambridge (BA 1928); AMIMechE, S/Ldr RAFVR WW II; *m* 1st 6 July 1929 (*divorce* 1963) Helen Mary (*d* 17 Aug 1969), est dau of V-Adml Cyril Samuel Townsend, CB, and had:

1b +John Edward [John Chetwynd-Talbot Esq, 46 Swan St, Kingsclere, Newbury, Berks]; *b* 29 Oct 1934; *educ* Harrow; Sub-Lt (A) RNVR 1955–57; *m* 1st 3 April 1959 (*divorce* 1964) Sonja Ann, dau of Roger Walker, of South Corner, Duncton, W Sussex, and has:

1c *Jane Sonja [Mrs Simon Barkes, Fawler End, Kingston Lisle, Oxon]; *b* 8 April 1960; *m* 1984 *Simon Barkes, s of B R Barkes, of Wimbledon, and has:

1d *Benjamin; *b* 1989

1d *Harriet Maria Eleanora; *b* 1987

2d *Serena Jane; *b* 1991

2c *Sarah Ann; *b* 2 Feb 1962; *m* 1983 *Michael W Morris, s of M E Morris, of Myrtle Cottage, Llandogo, Gwent, and has:

1d *Rebecca Sarah; *b* 1984

2d *Chloe; *b* 1985

1b (cont.) John Chetwynd-Talbot *m* 2nd 4 April 1967 *Belinda Bess, dau of Maj Euan James Leslie Warren Gilchrist, MC, DFC, RA, of Monk Sherborne House, nr Basingstoke, Hants, and by her has:

1c +Edward John; *b* 2 April 1969

3c *Mary Rowena, *b* 31 Jan 1968

4c *Prudence Ankaret; *b* 2 April 1969

1b *Susan Mary [Mrs William Thomson, Holt Valley Farm, Clayton, Hassocks, Sussex]; *b* 30 June 1930; *m* 11 Sept 1954 *William Byars Thomson, only s of Charles Binney White Thomson, of Bournemouth, and has:

1c *Geoffrey Charles Byars; *b* 17 March 1958

2c *Richard William Byars (Rev); *b* 1960

1c *Mary Rose Byars [Mrs Peter Shears, 109 Bonchurch Rd, Brighton, Sussex]; *b* 24 Jan 1962; MB, BS; *m* 1987 *Peter George Shears

2b *Ankaret Helen; *b* 26 July 1932; *m* 10 Sept 1955 *John Orcheston Dean, s of S S Dean, of Johannesburg, and has:

1c *John Anthony; *b* 1962

1c *Joanna Elizabeth [Mrs David Wilson, 60 Evelyn Ave, Ottawa, Ontario, Canada]; *b* 1956; *m* 1979 *David Knight Wilson and has:

1d *Lucas Knight; *b* 1983

1d *Amanda Helen; *b* 1981

2c *Philippa Ankaret [Mrs Russel Pedley, RR1, S Slocan, BC, Canada]; *b* 1958; *m* 1979 *Russel Ray Pedley and has:

1d *Sidney Matthew; *b* 1982

1d *Jasmine Ankaret; *b* 1981

3c *Louise Helen [Mrs Douglas Moody, 354 Queen St, Midland, Ontario, Canada]; *b* 1960; *m* 1979 *Douglas William Moody and has:

1d *Jonathan William; *b* 1979

2d *Adam Douglas; *b* 1982

3d *Simon Jeffrey; *b* 1984

1a (cont.) John Chetwynd-Talbot *m* 2nd 21 Sept 1963 *Betty Verral [Mrs John Chetwynd-Talbot, Stoke End Cottage, Stoke Green, Stoke Poges, Bucks], yst dau of Rev Augustus George Allton, and *d* 1993

2a Arthur Charles Ashton (Rev); *b* 28 Dec 1907; *educ* Harrow and Ch Ch Oxford (BA 1929, MA 1944); Vicar Wantage 1953–60, Rector Catsfield Sussex 1960; *m* 15 May 1945 *Pamela Mountjoy [Mrs Arthur Chetwynd-Talbot, Flat 2 Park Lodge, 2 Blackwater Rd, Eastbourne BN21 4JE], dau of Hugh John Say, of Dartford, Kent, and *d* 1987, leaving:

1b *Clare Eveline [Mrs Clare Green, 29 Holloway, Bath BA2 4PT]; *b* 31 Dec 1946; *educ* Nottingham U (BA 1968); *m* 18 Oct 1968 (*divorce* 1976) Malcolm Garfield Green, s of John Garfield Green, of E Molesey, Surrey, and has:

1c *Timothy Ashton Garfield; *b* 1969

1c *Caroline Anne; *b* 4 Feb 1971

3a Richard Michael Arthur; *b* 28 Sept 1911; *educ* Harrow and Magdalene Coll Cambridge (BA 1933, MA 1948); barrister Middle Temple 1936, Maj KSLI WW II, Dep Chm Salop QS 1950, Chm 1968, Recorder Banbury 1955, Bencher Middle Temple 1962

4a Ellis Edward Arthur, GC, MBE; *b* 22 March 1920; Lt RE WW II; *k* while on special duty with RAF in Malta Oct 1941

1a Mary Eveline; *b* 13 Aug 1906; *m* 16 July 1929 Lt-Gen Sir Richard Wakefield Goodbody, GCB, KBE, DSO, RHA, est s of Gerald Ernest Goodbody, of Woodsdown, Lisnagry, Co Limerick, and had issue

2a Anne Elizabeth; *b* 16 Jan 1910; *educ* St Anne's Coll Oxford (BA 1932); WRNS WW II

4 John CHETWYND TALBOT, QC; *b* 31 May 1806; Attorney-Gen to HRH THE PRINCE OF WALES (HM EDWARD VII) and Recorder Windsor; *m* 30 Aug 1830 Caroline Jane (*d* 12 June 1876), dau of 1st Baron Wharncliffe (*see* WHARNCLIFFE, E), and *d* 26 May 1852, leaving:

(1) John Gilbert, PC, JP (Sussex, Middx and London), DL, of Falconhurst, Edenbridge, Kent; *b* 24 Feb 1835; MA Oxon; CA Kent, Chm W Kent QS, DCL, MP W Kent 1868–78 and Oxford U 1878–1910; *m* 19 July 1860 Hon Meriel Sarah Lyttelton (*d* 22 April 1925), est dau of 4th Baron Lyttelton (*see* COBHAM, V), and *d* 1 Feb 1910, having had:

1a George John (Sir), PC (1937), KC (1906); *b* 19 June 1861; MA, Fell All Souls; barrister 1887, Bencher Inner Temple 1914 (Treas 1936), High Court Judge 1923–37, ktd 1924; *m* 3 June 1897 Gertrude Harriott (*d* 4 May 1941), dau of Albemarle Cator, of Woodbastwick Hall, Norfolk, and *d* 11 July 1938, having had:

1b John Bertram; *b* 10 June 1900: *d* 16 Aug 1922

2b Thomas George, CB (1960), QC (1954); *b* 21 Dec 1904; *educ* Winchester and New Coll Oxford (BA); barrister Inner Temple 1929, Capt Scots Gds WW II, Dep Parly Counsel Treasury 1944–53, Counsel to Chm Ctees Ho Lds 1953, Bencher Inner Temple 1960; *m* 14 Dec 1933 Hon Cynthia Edith Guest (*d* 30 April 1994), yr dau of 1st Viscount Wimborne (*qv*), and *d* 8 Feb 1992, leaving:

1c +Charles John [Charles Talbot Esq, Falconhurst, Markbeech, Kent TN8 5NR]; *b* 13 April 1947; *educ* Eton; barrister; *m* 1st 1978 (*divorce* 1992) Phyllida R, est dau of Rev Michael McCormick, and has:

1d +Richard Charles; *b* 3 Oct 1980

2d +Francis Michael; *b* 12 May 1982

3d +Hugo Peter; *b* 29 June 1983

1c (cont.) Charles Talbot *m* 2nd 1993 *Nicola Mary, dau of George Boulton, of Otford, Kent, and by her has:

4d +George Thomas; *b* 9 Oct 1992

1d *Henrietta Meriel; *b* 16 April 1995

1c *Meriel Cornelia [Mrs Robert Boyd, The Stone House, Adlington, Macclesfield, Cheshire SK10 4NU]; *b* 27 Jan 1935; *m* 1 April 1966 *Prof Robert David Hugh Boyd, MB, MRCP, 2nd s of Prof James Dixon Boyd, Prof Anatomy Cambridge, and has:

1d *Thomas Dixon; *b* 14 Feb 1967

1d *Diana Charlotte; *b* 15 March 1969

2d *Lucy Madeleine; *b* 16 Sept 1974

2c *Joanna [Mrs Alan Smith, Edells, Markbeech, Kent TN8 5PB]; *b* 3 April 1938; *educ* Cheltenham Ladies' Coll and LMH Oxford (BA); *m* 30 Sept 1964 *Alan Malcolm Smith, only s of Ernest Smith, of High View Lodge, Charlbury, Oxon, and has:

1d *Bertram Thomas; *b* 1 Feb 1967

1d *Emily Mary; *b* 27 Sept 1965; *m* 1994 *David Conway Turner and has:

1e *Meriel Sarah Anna; *b* 17 Dec 1996

2d *Flora; *b* 1971

3c *Mary Gertrude [Miss Mary Talbot, 13 Ufton Grove, London N1]; *b* 1 Feb 1942

1b Mary Meriel Gertrude; *b* 18 Jan 1903; *m* 3 July 1929 Hon Geoffrey John Orlando Bridgeman, MC, MB, FRCS, LRCP, 2nd s of 1st Viscount Bridgeman (*qv*), and *d* 5 July 1974, leaving issue

2a Bertram, JP Roxburghs; *b* 27 April 1865; Convener Roxburghshire CC, memb Educnl Endowments Commn Scotland 1929, Clerk H of C; *m* 21 Feb 1903 Lady Victoria Alexandrina (*d* 19 June 1938), widow of 9th Marquess of Lothian (*qv*) and est dau of 5th Duke of Buccleuch and (7th Duke of) Queensberry (*qv*), and *d* 5 May 1936

3a John Edward; *b* 14 March 1870; BA Oxon, Assist Sec Bd Educn; *m* 27 April 1898 Mabel (*d* 10 March 1949), dau of Archibald Balfour, of Chelsea, and *d* 30 May 1937, leaving:

1b Evan Arthur Christopher, MBE (1945); *b* 31 May 1903; *educ* Eton; Lt-Col Gren Gds WW II; *m* 11 Jan 1926 Félicité Annette Cynthia (*d* 1965), dau of Lt-Col William Edward Long, of Hurts Hall, Saxmundham, and *d* 1975, leaving:

1c +Christopher Michael Edward; *b* 29 Sept 1928; late Lt RN, stockbroker, ptnr Grenfell & Co; *m* 6 Oct 1962 *Suzanne Barbara, er dau of Arthur Dulley, and Mrs Peter Ollard, of Broom Close, Haslemere, Surrey, and has:

1d *Sarah Josephine; *b* 31 July 1964; *m* 1990 *Hugh S Muirhead, s of Richard Muirhead, of Plumpton, Sussex, and has:

1e *Archie Patrick Talbot; *b* 10 Nov 1995

2e *Jack Richard Caradoc; *b* 19 May 1998

1e *Madeleine; *b* 19–

2d *Miranda Meriel; *b* 26 May 1966

3d *Alice Elizabeth; *b* 27 April 1969; *m* 26 April 1997 *Adam C Dickens, s of Rev Harry Dickens

1c *Catherine [Mrs Catherine Kelly, 11 rue Maitre Cornille, 13990 Fontvieille, France]; *b* 6 March 1930; *m* 12 Feb 1958 (*divorce* 1978) Clement Francis Kelly, s of Clement Patrick Kelly, of Dublin, and has:

1d *Anthea Jane; *b* 1959; *m* 1981 (*divorce* 1991) C Coulson

2d *Felicity Ankaret; *b* 1962; *m* 1992 *Gordon Jones

2b Richard Eustace; *b* 11 Feb 1907; *educ* Eton; *m* 28 Feb 1933 *Sheila Katherine, 2nd dau of Lt Col Frank Seely (*see* SEELY, Bt), and had:

1c Julia; *b* and *d* 10 Aug 1934

1b Anne Meriel; *b* 9 Aug 1899

2b Joan Ankaret; *b* 3 March 1901; *m* 11 Dec 1928 Capt Eric Hyde Villiers, DSO, and had issue (*see* CLARENDON, E)

4a Eustace; *b* 1 Sept 1873; MA, MB Cantab; *d* unm 26 May 1905

1a Mary; *m* 14 April 1896 Rt Rev Winfrid Oldfield Burrows, Bp Chichester, and *d* 25 May 1897, leaving issue. He *d* 12 Feb 1929

2a Caroline Agnes; *m* 13 Oct 1891 Talbot Baines and *d* 26 March 1930, leaving issue. He *d* 29 Nov 1927

3a Meriel Lucy, DBE (1920); Dir Women's Branch Min Ag 1917–21, memb Govt Overseas Settlement Ctee, Chm BBC Appeals Advsy Ctee, memb BBC Gen Advsy Cncl and Roy Commn on Police 1928; *d* unm 15 Dec 1956

4a Evelyn (twin with Eustace); *d* unm 15 Nov 1962 aged 89

5a Gwendolen; *m* 6 Dec 1905 Sir Guy Stephenson, CB (*d* 17 Oct 1930), er s of Sir Augustus Keppel Stephenson, KCB, and *d* 26 July 1960, leaving issue

6a Margaret Isabel; *m* 2 July 1904 7th Earl of Antrim (*qv*) and *d* 19 April 1974 aged 95, leaving issue

(2) Edward Stuart (Rt Rev); *b* 19 Feb 1844; DD, Bp Rochester, Southwark and Winchester 1911–23; *m* 29 June 1870 Hon Lavinia Lyttelton (*d* 9 Oct 1939), 3rd dau of 4th Baron Lyttelton (*see* COBHAM, V), and *d* 30 Jan 1934, having had:

1a Edward Keble (Rev), MC; *b* 31 Dec 1877; *educ* Winchester and Ch Ch Oxford (BA 1900, MA 1906); Superior Community Resurrection Mirfield Yorks, WW I (despatches), Chaplain to TM GEORGE V 1920–36, EDWARD VIII 1936 and GEORGE VI 1937–49, Hon CF 1920; *d unm* 21 Oct 1949

2a Neville Stuart (Rt Rev), MC; *b* 21 Aug 1879; *educ* Haileybury and Ch Ch Oxford (MA, DD 1920); Lt Rifle Bde Boer War 1899–1902, Fell and Chaplain Balliol Coll Oxford 1909–14, CF WW I (despatches), Assist Chaplain Gen 1918, Hon Chaplain 1921, Bp Pretoria 1920–33, Vicar St Mary's Nottingham, RD Nottingham 1933–43; *m* 13 April 1918 Cecil Mary (*d* 9 Sept 1921), dau of William Seymour Eastwood, of W Stoke House, Sussex, and *d* 3 April 1943, leaving:

1b Gilbert Seymour Wyndham; *b* 31 Aug 1921; Capt Rifle Bde WW II; *kas* France June 1944

1b *Elizabeth, JP (Herts 1960) [Mrs Ronald Chalk JP, 3 Wildwood Court, Cedars Estate, Dog Kennel Lane, Chorleywood WD3 5GG]; *b* 17 Dec 1919; F/O WAAF WW II (despatches); *m* 23 Feb 1946 F/Lt Ronald Arthur Chalk (*d* 1993), s of Arthur Chalk, of Watford, Herts, and has:

1c *Gilbert John [Gilbert Chalk Esq, 103 Elgin Cres, London W11 2JF]; *b* 21 Sept 1947; *educ* Lancing; *m* 1975 *Gillian Frances Audrey, only dau of Sir Gervase Ralph Edmund Blois, 10th Bt (*qv*), and formerly w of Hugh Christopher Riddle, and has:

1d *Alexander John Gervase; *b* 8 Aug 1976

2d *Christopher Harry Gilbert; *b* 22 May 1985

1d *Nicola Elizabeth; *b* 26 Feb 1978

1c *Sarah Elizabeth; *b* 23 Feb 1950; *m* 1982 *Nicholas John Squire and has:

1d *Guy Charles; *b* 1985

2d *Hugo Edward John; *b* 1987

1d *Amanda Elizabeth; *b* 1984

2d *Octavia Clare; *b* 1991

3a Gilbert Walter Lyttelton; *b* 1 Sept 1891; Lt 7th (Service) Bn Rifle Bde; *ka* 30 July 1915

1a Mary Catherine; *b* 2 Oct 1875; *m* 6 April 1904 Very Rev Lionel George Bridges Justice Ford (*d* 27 March 1932), Dean York, Headmaster Harrow 1910–25, s of William Augustus Ford, and *d* 2 Sept 1957, leaving, with other issue:

1b *Edward William Spencer (Sir), GCVO (1998, KCVO 1957, MVO 1949), KCB (1967, CB 1952), ERD (Northants 1972) [Sir Edward Ford GCVO KCB ERD DL, Canal House, 23 Blomfield Rd, London W9 1AD]; *b* 24 July 1910; *educ* Eton and New Coll Oxford; tutor to KING FAROUK of Egypt 1936–37, barrister 1937, 2nd Lt SR Gren Gds 1936, Lt 1939, WW II: Bde Maj 10th Inf and 24th Gds Bdes, Instr Staff Coll Haifa 1944–45, Assist Priv Sec to TM GEORGE VI 1946–52 and THE QUEEN 1952–67, Extra Equerry to HM THE QUEEN 1955, Sec and Registrar OM 1975–, Sec Pilgrims Tst 1967–75, Tstee York Glaziers' Tst 1977–, Memb Ct Assist Goldsmiths' Co 1970–, High Sheriff Northants 1970; *m* 1949 Virginia (*d* 1995), er dau of 1st and last Baron Brand (*see* 1963 edn) and widow of John Metcalfe Polk, of New York, and has two sons (*see* TATE, Bt)

2a Lavinia Caroline; *b* 15 April 1882; *d unm* 30 Sept 1950

5 (George) Gustavus CHETWYND-TALBOT (Rev); *b* 19 March 1810; MA, Rector Withington, Glos; *m* 25 June 1842 Emily Sarah (*d* 21 Nov 1876), 2nd dau of Henry Elwes, of Colesbourne House, Glos, and *d* 8 Sept 1896, having had, with two daus (*d unm*):

(1) George Canning TALBOT, of Prescott, Glos, JP; *b* 18 March 1845; Capt 1st Stafford Militia; *m* 30 Sept 1875 Edith Mary (*d* 13 May 1932), only dau of William Coare Brocklehurst, MP, of Butley Hall, Cheshire, and *d* 8 Sept 1891, leaving:

1a John Arthur William; *b* 26 June 1876; Maj TFR Yeo and Glos Yeo; *m* 25 April 1906 Barbara Grace (*d* 30 April 1938), dau of Rowland Ticehurst, of Crickley, Witcombe, Glos, and *d* 1 Nov 1918, leaving:

1b *Lettice Mary [Mrs George Miller, Berrywood House, Donhead, Shaftesbury, Dorset]; *b* 9 Dec 1907; *m* 22 Aug 1934 George Butt Miller, Gren Gds (*d* 12 Aug 1958), er s of Thomas Butt Miller, of Kingscote Park, nr Tetbury, and has:

1c *Thomas Butt [Thomas Miller Esq, La Planque, Torteval, Guernsey, CI]; *b* 7 Nov 1935; *educ* Eton and New Coll Oxford (BA 1961, MA 1966); slr 1966; *m* 20 March 1965 *Jane Mary, only dau of Charles Collingwood Roberts, of The Old Rectory, Bepton, Midhurst, Sussex

2c *Robert Cottrell Butt [Robert Miller Esq, 80 Alderney St, London SW1]; *b* 4 May 1947; *educ* Worksop Coll, Trin Coll Dublin (BA) and Edinburgh U (M Litt); *m* 1971 *Patricia Georgina, dau of Dr George C McBrien, of Ansdown, Bath, and has:

1d *George Talbot; *b* 1974; *educ* Sherborne and Reading U

1d *Caroline Mary; *b* 1978

3c *John Richard Butt [John Miller Esq, The Gleve House, Kilninor, Gorey, Co Wexford, Ireland]; *b* 16 Sept 1950; *educ* Stanbridge Earls Sch and Duke U N Carolina

1c *Barbara Blanche; *b* 9 July 1938

2c *Mary Ruth [Mrs George Blaug, Calebrook House, Charlton Musgrove, Somerset]; *b* 20 Dec 1939; *m* 1989 *George Blaug

(2) Gustavus Arthur CHETWYND-TALBOT, of Marchwood Ho, Hemel Hempstead, Herts; *b* 24 Dec 1848; MP Hemel Hempstead, MLC Ceylon; *m* 22 Jan 1880 Susan Frances (*d* 8 May 1934), 2nd dau of Robert Elwes, JP, DL, of Congham Hall, Norfolk, and *d* 16 Oct 1920, having had:

1a Reginald George, CBE (1919); *b* 25 Jan 1881; Lt-Col RAF, Cdr RN; *m* 11 Nov 1909 Mary Helen Charlotte (*d* 29 Sept 1922), yr dau of Hon Henry Robert Hepburne-Scott (*see* POLWARTH, L), and *d* 11 Sept 1939, having had:

1b John Reginald; *b* 14 Aug 1910; *d* 4 March 1920

1b Alethea Cecil; *b* 9 Sept 1913; *m* 22 Feb 1940 Brig Sir Harry Ripley Mackeson, 1st Bt (*qv*), and had issue

2a Gilbert Gustavus; *b* 25 Jan 1888; *d unm* 2 Jan 1945

3a Humfrey Richard; *b* 11 Sept 1889; Lt 3rd Dragoon Gds; *ka* 13 Nov 1914

1a Cecil Emily; *m* 24 Jan 1907 Sir Hugh Steuart Gladstone, DL, of Capenoch, Dumfriesshire, and *d* 6 July 1949, leaving issue. He *d* 5 April 1949

2a Constance Evelyn Mary; writer, artist, diarist; Pres Coll of Psychic Science; *m* 23 Aug 1912 Brig-Gen William Henry Sitwell, CB, DSO, of Barmoor Castle, Lowick, Northumberland, and *d* 21 Aug 1974, leaving issue. He *d* 7 Sept 1932

3a Olave Dorothy; *b* 29 April 1891; *d* 26 June 1893

(1) Emily Margaret; *m* 15 Dec 1864 John Habington Barneby Lutley, DL, of Brockhampton, Herts, and *d* 18 Nov 1886, leaving issue. He *d* 2 Sept 1906

(2) Adela Henrietta; *b* 9 Aug 1856; *m* 24 Jan 1888 Rev Charlton G Lane, Rector Little Gaddesden, and *d* 17 March 1936, leaving issue. He *d* 2 Nov 1892

6 William Whitworth (Rev); *b* 17 Jan 1814; Rector Bishop's Hatfield, Herts; *m* 4 July 1843 Eleonora Julia (*d* 15 Dec 1897), est dau of Hon William James Coventry (*see* COVENTRY, E), and *d* 3 July 1888, leaving:

(1) Adelbert Cecil (Sir), KCIE; *b* 3 June 1845 (QUEEN ADELAIDE stood sponsor in person); Lt-Col IA, Res Kashmir 1896–1900; *m* 28 April 1870 Agnes Mary (*d* 16 March 1894), dau of Rev W Clarke, Vicar Swinderby, and *d* 28 Dec 1920, leaving:

1a Adelbert William James; *b* 6 Feb 1876; *educ* Eton and Magdalen Coll Oxford (BA 1899); ICS; *m* Edith — and *d* 6 April 1950

1a Guendolen Beatrix Nesta; *m* 24 Sept 1896 Lt Col Stuart Hill Godfrey, CIE, IA, s of John R R Godfrey, and *d* 6 Oct 1947, leaving issue. He *d* 29 Nov 1941

2a Muriel Agnes Eleanora; *m* 31 Oct 1908 Percy Brown, Indian Educnl Service, and *d* 26 Jan 1943, leaving issue

3a Esmé Mary Dorothea; *m* 15 Sept 1900 Lt-Col Sir Armine Brereton Dew, KCIE, CSI, Ch Commr Baluchistan, and *d* 22 April 1951, leaving issue. He *d* 7 June 1941

(2) William James; *b* 20 Sept 1847; Sub-Lt RN; *d* 8 March 1872

(3) Gerald Francis, JP Kent and Essex; *b* 23 Nov 1848; Lt-Col Staffs Imp Yeo, served 2nd Dragoons Prussian Army 1870, Lt City London; *m* 1 June 1870 Henrietta Clarissa Noyes (*d* 23 Dec 1928), est dau of Henry M Bradhurst, of New York, and *d* 2 Jan 1904, having had:

1a Henry Augustus; *b* 9 April 1871; *d* 20 Oct 1875

2a Victor Adelbert William Gerald; *b* 23 July 1872; 2nd Lt RASC; *d* 22 Aug 1932

3a Bertram William Chetwynd; *b* 15 Dec 1876; *m* 19 Oct 1904 Edith Marian, only dau of Lt-Gen Sir Charles Knight Pearson, KCMG, CB, and *d* 12 June 1941, leaving:

1b Marian Adelaide; *b* 7 Dec 1908; *m* 3 Jan 1929 John Raymond Micklethwait, only s of John Leonard Micklethwait, of Newlays Hall, nr Leeds. He *d* 19 Jan 1966

4a Stafford Cecil; *b* 3 May 1880; *educ* Cheltenham; *m* 30 Oct 1905 Ethel Lilian Caroline Leslie (*d* 1963), 3rd dau of Robert Leslie Gault, of Montreal, and *d* 16 Sept 1950, leaving:

1b *Charlotte Henrietta Dorwin [Mrs Richard Powys-Smith, Church Place, E Hendred, Oxon]; *b* 19 Sept 1908; *m* 1935 *Richard Charles Powys-Smith and has:

1c *Richard Talbot; *b* 1941; *m* 1970 *Lavinia Susan Sanderson and has:

1d *James Robert Talbot; *b* 1972

2d *Mark William Talbot; *b* 1975

5a Gerald Francis (Sir), KCVO, CMG, OBE; *b* 21 Aug 1881; Cdr RNVR, Naval Attaché Athens; *m* 15 June 1920 Helene (*d* 27 May 1975), widow of Capt Charles Labouchere, Army of France, and dau of S Jarislowsky, of Paris, and *d* 17 April 1945, leaving:

1b *Isobel Helen Henrietta [Mrs Anthony Mackenzie Smith, Backfields End, Winchelsea, Sussex TN36 4AB]; *b* 12 May 1923; *m* 1 Sept 1942 *Antony Mackenzie Smith, OBE, MC, yr s of John Mackenzie Smith, of Madras, and has:

1c *Peter; *b* 1946; *m* 1973 *Sandra Gay-French and has:

1d *Helen Sarah; *b* 1974

2d *Alexandra Anne; *b* 1976

3d *Harriet Isobel; *b* 1981

2c *Duncan John Gerald [Duncan Mackenzie Smith Esq, 10c Windsor Rd, London W5 5PD]; *b* 1951

1c *Jane Elizabeth; *b* 1947; *m* 1972 *Robin Martin and has:

1d *James Benedict; *b* 1973

2d *Edward Barnaby; *b* 1975

3d *Peter Nicholas; *b* 1983

2c *Catherine Isobel [Mrs Simon Hawke, Corner House, High St, Islip, Oxon OX5 2RX]; *b* 1957; MD Sydney 1982; *m* 1979 *Dr Simon Hawke and has:

1d *Henrietta; *b* 1984

2d *Charlotte; *b* 1986

1a Louise Victoria Gisela, MBE; *b* 6 March 1885; *m* 18 Sept 1917 Maj Ernest Sotham, MC, Manchester Regt, and *d* 30 April 1950, leaving issue

7 Gilbert Chetwynd (Rt Rev Monsignor); *b* 28 April 1816; DD, Canon of Rome; *d* 13 Dec 1896

8 Wellington Patrick Manvers CHETWYND-TALBOT (Sir), KCB; *b* 12 Dec 1817; Army Capt, Hon Col 3rd and 4th Bns S Staffs Regt, Serjeant-at-Arms Ho Lds 1858–98; *m* 11 Oct 1860 Lady Emma Charlotte (*d* 23 Aug 1928), only dau of 14th Earl of Derby (*qv*), and *d* 23 Sept 1898, having had:

(1) Charles Stanley; *b* 31 Jan 1862; Lt S Staffs Regt; *d unm* 20 Oct 1890

(2) Frederick Gilbert, DSO (1900); *b* 1 May 1868; *educ* Wellington; Lt-Col Rifle Bde, Boer War 1900–02 (wounded, despatches twice), WW I; *d unm* 25 Dec 1948

(3) Walter Stanley, CIE; *b* 4 Nov 1869; ISS; *d* 3 July 1935

(4) Henry Arthur; *b* 23 Aug 1872; *d* 15 July 1920

(5) Gilbert Edward; *b* 4 Sept 1876; *educ* Wellington; Lt 4th Bn S Staffs Regt; *m* 5 Jan 1905 Geraldine Mary (*d* 12 Feb 1953), 2nd dau of Rev Canon Frederick William Murray (*see* ATHOLL, D), and *d* 26 March 1950, leaving:

1a Patrick Gilbert Murray; *b* 14 Oct 1905; *educ* Haileybury; Maj RA (TA); *m* 2 June 1928 Audrey (*d* 26 Jan 1995), yst dau of Julius Ernst Guthe, JP, of Kepwick Hall, Northallerton, Yorks, and *d* 9 Jan 1979, leaving:

1b +Humphrey John Patrick [Humphrey Chetwynd-Talbot Esq, The Three Horseshoes, 31 Staploe, St Neots, Cambs PE19 4JA]; *b* 11 Jan 1930; *educ* Winchester and Univ Coll Oxford (BA 1952, MA 1958); *m* 11 April 1953 *Anne, twin dau of Capt Edward Glyn de Styrap Jukes-Hughes, CBE, RN, of Stourbridge Ho, Milton-on-Stour, Dorset, and has:

1c *Kathryn Helen Anne; *b* 8 March 1957; *m* 1979 *Sydney Anthony George Abrahams and has:

1d *Thomas Anthony Talbot; *b* 1985

1d *Annika Kathryn Anne; *b* 1983

2d *Harriett Laila; *b* 1988

2c *Jennifer Mary; *b* 2 Nov 1958; *educ* St Hugh's Coll Oxford (MA), MBA, 2nd Lt WRAC 1979; *m* 1983 *Martin Paul Rigby, late Capt RGJ, s of John Rigby, of Camberley, Surrey, and has:

1d *Dominic John Vaughan; *b* 1992

1d *Eloise Jennifer; *b* 1989

2d *Alice Helen Elizabeth; *b* 1992

3c *Annabel Jean; *b* 21 May 1961; *educ* Exeter U (B Ed Hons)

2b +Michael Gilbert [Michael Chetwynd-Talbot Esq, Sunny Lawn, Tweentown, Cheddar, Somerset BS27 3JE]; *b* 18 June 1931; *educ* Eton and RMA Sandhurst; late Capt RA; *m* 1st 27 Oct 1956 (*divorce* 19–) Bridget Adèle, yr dau of Sidney Terence Evelyn Pook Ennion, of Colbourne, IOW; *m* 2nd 19– *Muriel Ramadan and by his 1st w has:

1c +Rupert Edward Terence Gilbert; *b* 4 Sept 1962; *m* —

2c +Tobias John Michael; *b* 26 Aug 1963; *m* —

1c *Juliet Emma Serena; *b* 26 April 1958

1b *Janet Ivory Audrey [Mrs Donald Robertson, 35 Gloucester Rd, Kew Green, Surrey]; *b* 28 Nov 1932; *m* 4 Sept 1954 *Donald Craufurd Robertson, s of James Craufurd Robertson, of Parkstone, Dorset, and has:

1c *James Craufurd; *b* 20 April 1958; *m* —

2c *William Alexander; *b* 8 Oct 1959

3c *David Kenneth Craufurd; *b* 17 May 1964

2a (Edward) Hugh Frederick, MBE (1945); *b* 19 Jan 1909; *educ* Haileybury; Capt RA WW II; *m* 27 July 1935 *Cynthia Phoebe Duncan [Mrs Hugh Chetwynd-Talbot, Mead Acre, Milton Lilbourne, Pewsey, Wilts SN9 5LQ], er dau of Noel McGrigor Phillips, of Stoke D'Abernon Manor, Surrey, and *d* 8 March 1998, leaving:

1b +Mark Patrick [Mark Chetwynd-Talbot Esq, Scencliffe Grange, Coxwold, York YO6 4BR]; *b* 24 June 1941; *educ* Wellington and RMA Sandhurst; Maj Coldstream Gds 1971; *m* 1970 *Elizabeth Ann, dau of Sacheverel O F Bateman, of Mortham Tower, Barnard Castle, Co Durham, and has:

1c +Nicholas John [Nicholas Chetwynd-Talbot Esq, 6 Hilary Close, London SW6]; *b* 31 Dec 1971; *educ* Wellington and Durham U; *m* 1997 *Penelope Jane, dau of Michael Toulmin, of Thorpe Arch Hall, Wetherby, N Yorks

1c *Lara Katherine; *b* 10 Nov 1973

1b *Anthea [Mrs Simon Anthill, The Old School House, Scofton, Worksop, Notts]; *b* 15 Oct 1939; *m* 25 May 1963 (Philip) Simon Antill (*d* 1996), yst s of Walter Samuel Antill, of Rose Cottage, Lindrick Dale, Worksop, Notts, and has:

1c *Vanessa Cicely; *b* 26 May 1964; *m* 1989 *Andrew Robinson and has:

1d *Thomas; *b* 1992

1d *Abigail; *b* 1994

2c *Juliet Willa; *b* 18 April 1966; *m* 1995 *Neil Goodwin and has:

1d *Sophie Lara; *b* 1997

3c *Helen Meriel; *b* 18 May 1969

4c *Jemima Louise; *b* 1971

2b *Meriel [Mrs Mark Wyndham-Baker, The Old School, Fyfield, Abingdon, Oxon]; *b* 17 March 1944; *m* 30 July 1964 *Mark Alexander Wyndham-Baker, er s of Lt-Cdr Alexander Arthur Wyndham-Baker, RN, of Bonny Farm, Bindura, Rhodesia, and has issue (*see* MACNAGHTEN, Bt)

(1) Cecil Emma; *b* 6 April 1864; *m* 1 June 1886 William Seymour Eastwood, of W Stoke House, Chichester, and *d* 26 Jan 1934, having had issue. He *d* 24 Feb 1946

(2) Edith Constance Louisa; *b* 24 June 1865; *m* 6 Sept 1888 William Arthur Wigram and *d* 11 Nov 1941, leaving issue (*see* WIGRAM, Bt)

(3) Helen Ivory; *b* 14 April 1880; *d* unm 10 May 1956

9 Gerald CHETWYND-TALBOT; *b* 3 Oct 1819; Dir-Gen Mil Store Dept India Office; *m* 1840 Margaret (*d* 8 Dec 1894), dau of Capt Alexander Mackay, and *d* 13 Feb 1885, leaving, with two daus:

(1) Charles Alexander Price; *b* 22 March 1842; Consul Gen Boston, Consul Galicia, the Asturias and Leon, Lt 14th Hus; *m* 22 March 1876 Maud (*d* 22 Oct 1922), dau of Quentin Fleming, of Chapelville, Liverpool, and *d* Dec 1903, leaving:

1a Charles Fleming Chetwynd; *b* 8 April 1879; T/Capt King's Regt, Boer War 1900–02, WW I; *m* 31 Dec 1906 Margaret Dorothy (*d* 17 Aug 1969), only dau of Lt Col Dunbar Fraser Huyshe, RA, and *d* 8 June 1933, leaving:

1b Charles John Huyshe Chetwynd; *b* 10 Dec 1910; *educ* Eton; Reuter's Ch Correspondent Ethiopia, first Br war correspondent accredited to Marshal Tito Yugoslavia 1944 (POW); *m* 3 Jan 1939 Jane Vaughan (*d* 1989) (took VAUGHAN by deed poll), dau of David Wheldon Jones, of Plas Blaenddol, Ffestiniog, Merioneths, and *d* 1991, leaving:

1c +John Vaughan Chetwynd [John Chetwynd-Talbot Esq, 8 Kinecroft, Wallingford, Oxon]; *b* 4 Dec 1941; *educ* Eton; Page to Earl of Shrewsbury Coronation 1953

1c *Frances Elizabeth [Mrs Peter Mayes, Blakenhall Lodge, The Green, Barton-under-Needwood, Staffs; Mansion Basement, Albany, Piccadilly, London W1]; *b* 2 June 1947; *m* *Peter Henry Mayes, s of H D Mayes, of Cheltenham, Glos, and has:

1d *Tomasine Lucy; *b* 14 May 1977

2d *Rebecca Jane; *b* 6 July 1979

2b +Gilbert Alexander Lucius Chetwynd [Lt-Col Gilbert Chetwynd-Talbot, Pleasant Cottage, Brightwell-cum-Sotwell, Wallingford, Oxon OX10 0RJ]; *b* 23 March 1918; *educ* Eton; Lt-Col 14th/20th King's Hus WW II (despatches), Sec to Albany, Piccadilly, 1967–83

1b *Geraldine Cecil Barbara [Miss Geraldine Chetwynd-Talbot, Pleasant Cottage, Brightwell-cum-Sotwell, Wallingford, Oxon OX10 0RJ]; *b* 1907; Subaltern FANY

2a Nicholas Gerald Chetwynd; *b* 15 Nov 1884; 10th Roy Fus WW I; *m* 26 May 1927 Violet Winter (*m* 2nd 23 March 1953 Canon Richard Lewellin Rhys (*d* 21 Aug 1956)), 2nd dau of Albert Coad, of Sutton, Surrey, and *dsp* 5 Oct 1946

3a Gilbert Patrick Chetwynd; *b* 13 July 1886; Lt W R Regt; *m* 12 Oct 1921 (*divorce* 1929) Alice Alethea, er dau of C H Christopher Moller, of Chelsea, and *d* Dec 1958, having had:

1b +Christopher Patrick Chetwynd [Christopher Chetwynd-Talbot Esq RD, Mulberry House, Whitsbury, Fordingbridge, Hants SP6]; *b* 31 Aug 1922; *educ* Harrow and Corpus Christi Coll Cambridge; Lt RNVR WW II, Lt-Cdr RNR 1957–81; *m* 29 Jan 1955 *Rosalind Mary, yr dau of AVM Christopher Neil Hope Bilney, CB, CBE, of Ashorne, Leckford, Hants, and adopted:

*Patrick Nicholas Chetwynd; *b* 12 Jan 1958

*Harriet Susan; *b* 23 Dec 1959

2b Gerald Nicholas Chetwynd; *b* 21 May 1924; *d* 30 Aug 1933

1b Barbara Maud Mary (twin with her brother Gerald); *educ* Benenden; *m* 25 Feb 1949 *(Thomas) Douglas Scott, s of James Scott, of Fearn, Ross-shire, and *d* March 1995

4a William Alexander Chetwynd; *d* an infant 19 Sept 1890

1a Maud Margaret Anne Geraldine; *b* 1877; *d* unm

2a Cecil Katherine; *b* 22 March 1878; *m* 1904 Thomas Guyatt, Consul Vigo, and *d* leaving issue. He *d* 4 Feb 1924

3a Alice Edith Palgrave; *b* 7 Jan 1881; *m* 27 April 1918 William Porter Palgrave Archdale, CBE, 2nd s of Sir Edward Mervyn Archdale, 1st Bt (*qv*), and *d* 17 June 1963, leaving issue

4a Matilda Charlotte Palgrave; *b* 22 April 1882; *m* 26 Sept 1907 Augustus Neal Rantoul, of Ipswich, Mass., and *d* leaving issue. He *d* 1 July 1934

(2) Gerald Henry; *b* 25 Sept 1843; 60th Rifles; *m* 1880 Frieda Amanda Sophia (*d* 25 Jan 1921), dau of Wilhelm von Segelken, of Oldenburg, Germany, and *dsp* 26 March 1910

1 Frances Charlotte; *m* 5 April 1820 4th Earl of Dartmouth (*qv*) and *d* 4 Oct 1823, leaving issue

2 Cecil Chetwynd; *m* 19 July 1831 7th Marquess of Lothian (*qv*) and *d* 13 May 1877, leaving issue

The 2nd EARL TALBOT OF HENSOL *d* 10 Jan 1849; his est surv s,

HENRY JOHN CHETWYND-TALBOT, **3rd Earl Talbot of Hensol** and **18th Earl of Shrewsbury** and **Waterford**, as which *s* distant cousin 10 Aug 1856 (right to title allowed 1 June 1858), CB (1827), PC (1858); *b* 8 Nov 1803; RN: joined 1817, Lt 1824, Cdr 1826, cmdg HMS *Philomel* Battle of Navarino 1827, Capt 1827, R-Adml 1854, V-Adml 1861, Adml 1865, MP (C) Hertford 1830–31, Armagh May–Aug 1831, Dublin 1831–33 and S Staffs 1837–49, Ld in Waiting May–Dec 1852, Naval ADC to HM QUEEN VICTORIA 1852–54, Capt Gentlemen-at-Arms 1858–59, Kt St Louis and Kt 2nd Cl St Anne Russia, Kt Redeemer Greece 1833 KSI; *m* 8 Nov 1828 Lady Sarah Elizabeth Beresford (*d* 13 Oct 1884), only surv dau of 2nd Marquess of Waterford (*qv*) by Susan (dau of 2nd Earl of Tyrconnel; *see* below), and had:

1 CHARLES JOHN, **19th Earl**

2 Walter Cecil CHETWYND-TALBOT later CARPENTER (roy licence with arms 1 June 1868 under terms of will of Sarah, widow of John Carpenter, 4th and last Earl of Tyrconnel and Walter's great-uncle), of Kiplin, Northallerton, JP (Staffs and N R Yorks); Adml, ADC to HM QUEEN VICTORIA, MP Co Waterford 1859–65; *b* 27 March 1834; *m* 1st 27 Oct 1869 Maria Georgiana (*d* 25 April 1876), 4th dau of Sir Robert Miller Mundy, KCMG, of Hollybank, Hants, Lt-Govr Grenada, and had:

(1) Sarah Marie Talbot; *b* 21 April 1876; *m* 7 Aug 1907 Christopher Hatton Turnor, of Stoke Rochford, Lincs, and *d* 21 Sept 1957. He *d* 19 Aug 1940

2 (cont.) Walter Carpenter *m* 2nd 10 Feb 1887 Hon Beatrice de Grey (*d* 16 Oct 1927), 2nd dau of 5th Baron Walsingham (*qv*), and *d* 13 May 1904

3 Reginald Arthur James (Sir), KCB, JP Bucks; *b* 11 July 1841; MP Stafford 1869–74, served Zulu War, Egyptian Campaign and Nile Expdn, ADC to HM QUEEN VICTORIA 1889–96, Lt-Col cmdg 1st Life Gds, Maj-Gen cmdg Forces Egypt 1898–1903, Col 3rd Dragoon Gds 1903–20, Govr Victoria 1904–08, Cdr Legn Hon; *m* 8 May 1877 Margaret Jane (*d* 6 Oct 1937), 2nd dau of Rt Hon James Stuart-Wortley (*see* WHARNCLIFFE, E), and *d* 15 Jan 1929

4 Alfred; *b* 14 Sept 1848; MA Oxon; *m* 28 June 1882 Hon Emily Augusta Louisa de Grey (*d* 26 Jan 1912), est dau of 5th Baron Walsingham (*qv*), and *d* 9 May 1913, leaving:

(1) Humphrey John; *b* 8 Oct 1883; BA Oxon; Lt RASC, attd RGA, Assist Priv Sec to Govr Victoria 1907–08; *d* unm 6 Feb 1944

(2) Geoffrey Richard Henry; *b* 29 March 1888; F/Lt RNAS; *kas* 29 June 1916

(1) Bridget Elizabeth, OBE (1920), Croce de Guerra 1917, memb Nat Labour Cncl Inquiry into Merchant Service Conditions 1938; *d* unm 29 Nov 1971

(2) Kathleen, MBE (1943); VAD WW I (despatches); *d* unm 2 July 1958

1 Victoria Susan; *d* unm 8 June 1856

2 Constance Harriet Mahonesa; *m* 12 Aug 1857 8th Marquess of Lothian (*qv*) and *d* 10 Oct 1901

3 Gertrude Frances; *b* 21 March 1840; *m* 19 Aug 1874 13th Earl of Pembroke and (10th Earl of) Montgomery (*qv*) and *d* 30 Sept 1906

4 Adelaide; *m* 22 June 1868 3rd Earl Brownlow (*see* BROWNLOW, B) and *dsp* 16 March 1917

The 18th/3rd EARL *d* 4 June 1868; his est s,

CHARLES JOHN CHETWYND-TALBOT, **19th Earl of Shrewsbury** and **Waterford** and **4th Earl Talbot of Hensol**, PC (1875); *b* 13 April 1830; *educ* Eton and Merton Coll Oxford; Cornet 1st Life Gds 1851, Lt 1853, MP (C) Stafford 1857–59, N Staffs 1859–65 and Stamford 1868, Maj QOR Staffs Yeo 1864, High Steward Stafford 1868, Capt Gentlemen-at-Arms 1875–77; granted by roy warrant 1871 privilege of carrying a White Wand at the appropriate ceremonies in Ireland as symbol of his Ld High Stewardship of Ireland; *m* 15 Feb 1855 (Anna) Theresa (*d* 29 July 1912), est dau of Cdr Richard Howe Cockerell, RN, by Theresa (afterwards Countess of Eglinton (*see* EGLINTON and WINTON, E)), one of eight illegitimate children by Thomas Gleadowe-Newcomen, 2nd and last Viscount Newcomen, by Harriet Holland, and had:

1 CHARLES HENRY JOHN, **20th Earl**

1 Theresa Susey Helen; *m* 2 Oct 1875 6th Marquess of Londonderry (*qv*) and *d* 16 March 1919, leaving issue

2 Guendolen Theresa; *m* 1st 18 Jan 1877 Col Edward Chaplin, MP Lincoln (*d* 23 Dec 1883), and had issue (*see* 1870 edn CHAPLIN, V); *m* 2nd 4 Oct 1887 Maj Archibald Cosmo Little, 5th Lancers, of Upton House, Tetbury, Glos, and *d* 20 Jan 1937, leaving further issue. He *d* 8 Jan 1934

3 Muriel Frances Louisa; *m* 1st 23 Dec 1876 Viscount Helmsley (*see* FEVERSHAM, B) and had issue; *m* 2nd 6 June 1885 Hugh Darby Annesley Owen, of Bettws Hall, Montgomeryshire, and *d* 2 March 1925. He *d* 12 March 1908

The 19th/4th EARL *d* 11 May 1877; his only s,

CHARLES HENRY JOHN CHETWYND-TALBOT, **20th Earl of Shrewsbury** and **Waterford** and **5th Earl Talbot of Hensol**, KCVO (1907); *b* 13 Nov 1860; *educ* Eton; High Steward Stafford, Staff Offr to GOC Mersey Defences from 10 Oct 1915, Hon Maj RWF, Maj Remount Dept 1914–15, formerly Lt Staffs Yeo; owned a large fleet of hansom cabs; *m* 21 June and 26 July 1882 Ellen Mary (*d* 23 Aug 1940), formerly w of Alfred Edward Miller Mundy, of Shipley Hall, Derby, and dau of Charles Rowland Palmer-Morewood, of Ladbroke Hall, Warwicks, and Alfreton Park, Derbys, by Georgina, dau of 7th Baron Byron (*qv*), and had:

1 Charles John Alton, *Viscount Ingestre*, MVO (1907); *b* 8 Sept 1882; *educ* Eton; 2nd Lt RHG 1900, Lt 1902, T/Capt WW I; *m* 23 April 1904 Lady Winifred Constance Hester Paget (*d* 18 April 1965, having *m* 2nd 2 Aug 1917 Richard Edmands [*sic*] Pennoyer (*d* 17 Nov 1968) and had further issue), sis of 6th Marquess of Anglesey (*qv*), and *dvp* 8 Jan 1915, leaving:

(1) JOHN GEORGE CHARLES HENRY ALTON ALEXANDER CHETWYND, **21st/6th Earl**

(1) Ursula Winifred; granted with sisters by roy warrant 15 Nov 1921 rank of earl's daus; *b* 12 Sept 1907; *m* 1st 8 Nov 1930 Hector Stewart (*d* 6 March 1935), of Fifield Manor, Fifield, Oxon, er s of Charles E Stewart, of Lady Mede, Kimble, Bucks; *m* 2nd 22 April 1942 (*divorce* 1952) Lt-Cdr (A) Michael Burton Stewart, RNVR (*d* 16 May 1962), yr s of Lt-Col William Burton Stewart, Lothian and Border Horse, of Alnmouth, Northumberland; *m* 3rd 10 April 1954 Patrick Hamilton (*d* 23 Sept 1962), author of *Gaslight*, *Hangover Square* etc, s of Walter Bernard Hamilton; *m* 4th 14 Dec 1964 Dr William Leonard James, OBE, s of William Richard James, of Torquay, and was *k* with him in an air accident 26 Aug 1966

(2) *(Victoria) Audrey Beatrice; *b* 13 March 1910; *m* 1st 3 March 1932 (*divorce* 1936) 6th Baron Sheffield (*see* STANLEY OF ALDERLEY, SHEFFIELD and, B) and has issue; *m* 2nd 20 Dec 1945 Gwyn Rhyse Francis Morris, QC (*d* 1982), s of William John Morris, of Pembroke

(3) Joan; *b* 30 Oct 1911; *m* 27 May 1937 W/Cdr Francis Howard Bickerton, RAF, s of Jones Bickerton, and *d* 2 June 1974, leaving issue. He *d* 21 Aug 1954

1 (Nellie) Viola Castalia Florence; *b* 3 July 1885; *m* 1st 19 Dec 1907 (*divorce* 1916) Cdr Reginald Edward Gore, RN (*d* 12 Sept 1963), only s of Lt-Gen Edward Arthur Gore, DL; *m* 2nd 16 Aug 1916 Capt Walter Arnold Conduitt, s of Henry Walter Conduitt, and *dsp* 23 July 1951. He *d* 1956

The 20th/5th EARL *d* 7 May 1921; his gs,

JOHN GEORGE CHARLES HENRY ALTON ALEXANDER CHETWYND CHETWYND-TALBOT, **21st Earl of Shrewsbury** and **Waterford** and **6th Earl Talbot of Hensol** , JP (Staffs 1943), DL (1946–62); *b* 1 Dec 1914 (TM GEORGE V and QUEEN MARY stood sponsors); *educ* Eton; Pres Assoc of Ag 1936–60, Capt RA (TA) WW II, CC 1945 Staffs, Hon A/Cdre (3509 Fighter Control Unit) RAAF from 1949; *m* 1st 24 Feb 1936 (*divorce* 1963) Nadine Muriel, yr dau of Brig-Gen Cyril Randell Crofton (formerly Crofton Atkins), CBE, of Trobridge, Crediton, Devon; *m* 2nd 18 Oct 1963 (Doris) Aileen Mortlock (*d* 1993), dau of Sandes Alexander Mortlock, and *d* 1980, leaving by his 1st w:

1 CHARLES HENRY JOHN BENEDICT CROFTON CHETWYND CHETWYND-TALBOT, **22nd and present Earl of Shrewsbury** and **Waterford** and **7th Earl Talbot of Hensol**

2 +Paul Alexander Anthony Bueno [The Hon Paul Chetwynd-Talbot, Gunville House, Grateley, Hants SP11 8JQ]; *b* 25 Nov 1957; *educ* Eton and Ch Ch Oxford (BA); *m* July 1982 *Sarah Elizabeth, dau of Simon Hildebrand Melville Bradley (*see* HAMPDEN V), and has:

(1) +Harry; *b* 1985

(2) +Jack; *b* 1987

(3) +Rory Arthur; *b* 22 July 1995

1 *Charlotte Sarah Alexandra [The Lady Charlotte Cavazza, San Felice del Benaco, Brescia, Italy]; *b* 18 Nov 1938; *m* 20 July 1965 Camillo Cavazza dei Conti Cavazza (*d* 1981), yst s of Count Alessandro Cavazza, of Isola del Garda, Brescia, Italy, by Princess Livia Borghese, and has:

(1) *Sigmar; *b* 2 Jan 1966

(2) *Eric; *b* 12 Feb 1969

(3) *Cristian; *b* 5 Oct 1979

(4) *Lars-Patrick; *b* 5 Oct 1979

(1) *Livia; *b* 25 Sept 1967

(2) *Ilona *b* 31 Oct 1972

(3) *Alberta; *b* 6 May 1977

2 *(Josephine) Sylvia-Rose [The Lady Sylvia-Rose Saint, Ledburn Farm, Ledburn, Beds]; *b* 23 May 1940; *m* 24 April 1965 *Stafford Antony Saint, twin s of Dr Stafford Eric Saint, CVO, of Iver, Bucks, and has:

(1) *Stafford Alexander Antony Talbot; *b* 4 Nov 1970

(1) *Helen Elizabeth Charlotte; *b* 20 April 1966

(2) *Victoria Nadine Mary; *b* 6 Feb 1968

3 *Catherine Laura [The Lady Catherine Chamberlain, Stocks Farm, Burley Street, nr Ringwood, Hants BH24 4BZ]; *b* 4 Aug 1945; LRAM; *m* 10 Oct 1966 *Richard Sebastian Endicott Chamberlain, est s of Lawrence Endicott Chamberlain, of The Dairy House, Tonerspuddle, Dorset, and has:

(1) *Thomas Endicott; *b* 9 July 1973; *educ* Radley

(1) *Sophie Anne Zacyntha; *b* 26 Sept 1968

(2) *Caroline Amy; *b* 13 May 1971

4 *Marguerite Mary [The Lady Marguerite Wynne, 18 Campbell Dve, Beaconsfield, Bucks HP9 1TF]; *b* 12 June 1950; *m* 1st 21 July 1970 Guy William Brisbane, only s of W/Cdr Guy Maxwell Brisbane, RAF, of Greystokes, Weyborne, Norfolk; *m* 2nd 1984 *Andrew Wynne and by her 1st husb has:

(1) *Duncan Guy Talbot; *b* 1975; *educ* Berkhamsted

SHUCKBURGH

Arms: Sa. a chevron between three mullets arg. **Crest:** A blackamoor couped at the waist ppr. with a dart in his hand, point downwards or. **Motto:** *Hæc manus ob patriam* ('This hand for my country'). **Creation:** Bt. (E) 25 June 1660.

SIR RUPERT CHARLES GERALD SHUCKBURGH, 13TH BT, of Shuckburgh, Co Warwick [Sir Rupert Shuckburgh Bt, Shuckburgh Hall, Daventry, Northants NN11 6DT]; *b* 12 Feb 1949; *s f* 1988; *educ* Worksop Coll; *m* 1st 8 May 1976 (*divorce* 1987) Judith M, dau of William Gordon Mackaness, of Paddock Lodge, Everdon, Northants; *m* 2nd 1987 *Margaret Ida, dau of William Evans, of Middleton, Derbys, and by his 1st w has:

1 +JAMES RUPERT CHARLES; *b* 4 Jan 1978

2 +Peter Gerald William; *b* 1982

Lineage: JOHN SHUCKBURGH, of Shuckburgh, Warwicks; *m* Joan, dau of Adam Napton, of Napton, Warwicks, and had an est s:

WILLIAM SHUCKBURGH, of Shuckburgh; *m* Jane, dau of John Fulwood, of Tamworth, Staffs, and had an est s:

THOMAS SHUCKBURGH, of Shuckburgh; *m* Jane, dau and coheir of Thomas Sidenhall, and had an est s:

THOMAS SHUCKBURGH, of Shuckburgh; *m* Philippa, dau of Nicholas Vaux, and had an est s:

THOMAS SHUCKBURGH, of Shuckburgh; *m* Isabella, dau of Benedict Medley, of Whitnash, Warwicks, Clerk Signet to HENRY VII, and had an est s:

THOMAS SHUCKBURGH, of Shuckburgh; *m* —, dau of George Smyth, and had an est s:

ANTHONY SHUCKBURGH, of Shuckburgh; Sheriff Warwicks 1568; *m* 1st Anne, dau of Thomas Foxley, of Foxley, Northants, and had issue; *m* 2nd Anne Skeffington and *d* 1 April 1594, leaving an only surv s:

JOHN SHUCKBURGH, of Shuckburgh; *b* 1563; *m* Margaret (*d* 22 March 1629), est dau of Richard Middlemore, of Edgbaston, and *d* 20 March 1631, leaving an est s:

Sir RICHARD SHUCKBURGH, of Shuckburgh; MP Warwick 1641, ktd after Battle of Edge Hill 22 Oct 1642; captured by Parly forces after defending his seat of Shuckburgh; *m* 1st 1627 Mary (*d* 1629), widow of William Crompton, of Stone, Staffs, and 2nd dau of Ralph Sneyde, of Keele, Staffs; *m* 2nd 1631 Elizabeth, dau of Sir Robert Lee, of Billesley, Warwicks; *m* 3rd 1634 Grace (*m* 2nd 27 Oct 1659 John Keating, of Norraghmore, Co Kildare, Ld Ch Justice Common Pleas Ireland, and *d* 12 April 1677), dau of Sir Thomas Holt, 1st Bt, of Aston, and *d* 13 June 1656, having by her had, with three yr sons (Richard, *dsp*; George, had issue; Charles, ancestor of the SHUCKBURGHs of Downton, Wilts) and three daus

(Anne, *m* Henry Edmonds, of Preston Hall, Northants; Grace, *m* 1st (licence 30 Aug 1670) Sir John Bernard, 2nd Bt, of Huntingdon, and 2nd — Marrett, and *d* 1721; Elizabeth, *m* as his 2nd w Sir Richard Waldo):

Sir John Shuckburgh, 1st Bt (E), so *cr* 25 June 1660, of Shuckburgh; *b* 1635; *m* 18 Dec 1656, as her 1st husb, Catherine, dau of Sir Hatton Fermor (*see* HESKETH, B), and *d* 1661, leaving:

Sir Charles Shuckburgh, 2nd Bt; *b* 1659; High Sheriff Warwicks 1685–87, MP 1698–1705, Master Buckhounds to QUEEN ANNE; *m* 1st (licence 19 Sept 1679) Catherine (*d c* 1683), dau of Sir Hugh Stewkley/Stukeley, 2nd Bt, of Hinton, Hants, and had:

1 **Sir John Shuckburgh, 3rd Bt**; *b* 18 Aug 1683; *m* 1705 Abigail (*d by* 1659), dau of George Goodwin, of Latchford, Oxon, and *d* 19 June 1724, having had, with eight other daus:

(1) **Sir Stewkley Shuckburgh, 4th Bt**; *d unm* 10 March 1759

(1) Grace; *m* 1st Sir Edward Boughton, 5th Bt, and had issue (*see* 1963 edn ROUSE BOUGHTON, Bt); *m* 2nd 1723 Matthew Lister (*d* Jan 1786) and had issue

(2) Elizabeth; *m* Christopher Jeaffreson, of Dullingham, MP for Cambridge, and *d* 1776

1 Catherine; *m* as his 2nd w Sir William Boughton, 4th Bt (*d* 22 July 1716; *see* 1963 edn ROUSE BOUGHTON), and *d* 1725, leaving issue

2 Sarah; *m* Charles Bentley, of Kineton, Warwicks, and *d* 1726

Sir Charles *m* 2nd (licence 26 Oct 1684) Diana (*d* 28 Sept 1725), dau of 11th Lord (Baron) Willoughby de Broke (*qv*), and *d* 2 Sept 1705, having by her had, with three daus:

2 Charles, of Longborough, Glos, and Farthingstone, Northants; *b* 1694; *m* 1718 Sarah, dau of Col Henry Hunt, of Blockley, Worcs, and *d* 1752, leaving:

(1) **Sir Charles Shuckburgh, 5th Bt**; *bapt* 17 March 1721/2; MA All Souls Oxford; *m* 5 May 1749 Anne (*d* 8 Oct 1776), widow of Campbell Price, of Westbury, Bucks, and dau of — Robinson, and *dsp* 10 Aug 1773

(2) Richard; Lt-Col; *m* 1750 Sarah, widow of Edward Bate and dau of Capt Hayward, RN, and *d* 2 Sept 1773, having had:

1a Sir GEORGE AUGUSTUS WILLIAM SHUCKBURGH later SHUCKBURGH-EVELYN (added on f-in-laws death 1793), **6th Bt**; *educ* Balliol Coll Oxford (BA); MP Warwicks 1780–1804, FRS; *m* 1st 1782 Sarah Johanna (*dsp* 10 April 1783), dau of John Darker, of Gayton, Northants; *m* 2nd 6 Oct 1785 Julia Annabella (*bur* 23 Sept 1797), dau and sole heiress of John Evelyn, of Felbridge, Surrey, and *d* 11 Aug 1804, leaving by her:

1b Julia Evelyn Medley; *m* 19 July 1810 3rd Earl of Liverpool (*qv*) and *d* 8 April 1814, leaving issue

2a STEWKLEY (Sir), **7th Bt**

1a Sarah; *m* J Clevland, MP, of Tapeley, Devon

3 Richard; Army Capt; *d unm* 1724

4 Edward (Rev); *educ* Ch Ch Oxford (BA); Rector Bromsall, Staffs; *d unm* Feb 1729/30

The 6th Bt's bro,

Sir Stewkley Shuckburgh, 7th Bt; *m* 5 Sept 1786 Charlotte Catherine (*d* 18 Feb 1837), dau of Thomas Tydd, of Airdworth, Worcs, and had, with seven other daus:

1 FRANCIS (Sir), **8th Bt**

2 Thomas Stewkley; *b* 13 July 1791; *d* 23 Aug 1824

3 Charles Robert; *b* 14 Oct 1794; Lt-Col; *m* 1st Feb 1826 Emma (*d* 1838), dau of James Butler, and had:

(1) Augusta; *b* 1835; *d* 1844

3 (cont.) Lt-Col Charles Shuckburgh *m* 2nd Oct 1842 Mariana (*d* 1 Aug 1881), dau of Maj Travers, Rifle Bde, and *d* 17 Jan 1873

4 Henry Adolphus; *b* 25 Nov 1800; Col 40th Bengal NI; *m* 1st 16 Nov 1843 Sarah Elizabeth (*dsp*), dau of William Dwarris, of Golden Grove, Jamaica; *m* 2nd 5 May 1854 Catherine Dorothy (*d* 17 April 1866), est dau of Daniel J Cloete, High Sheriff Cape Town, and *d* 22 Dec 1860, leaving by her, with two daus (*d unm*):

(1) Henry James; *b* 25 Feb 1855; Maj 2nd Bn Norfolk Regt; *m* 25 Nov 1886 Ida Florence Geraldine (*d* 12 Jan 1906), widow of **Sir George Shuckburgh, 9th Bt** (*see* below), and dau of Rev F W Robertson, and *dsp* 9 Feb 1895

(2) George Stewkley; *b* 5 Aug 1860; Cdr RN; *m* 9 Sept 1898 Amy Mary (*d* 2 Oct 1962, having *m* 2nd 27 Sept 1913 Charles Adalbert Tucker), dau of John Robertson, of Colac, Victoria, Australia, and *d* 8 March 1912, leaving:

1a Mabel Evelyn; *b* 19 Aug 1899

2a Lorna May; *b* 29 Aug 1900

1 Mary Amelia; *b* 17 April 1793; *m* 1820 Cdr T L P Laugharne, RN, and *d* 19 Feb 1858

2 Emily Almeria; *b* 31 Oct 1808; *m* 5 June 1867 Rev Samuel Sampson, of Colyton Grove, Devon, and *d* 24 March 1895. He *d* 1875

The 7th Bt *d* 21 July 1809; his est s,

Sir Francis Shuckburgh, 8th Bt; *b* 12 March 1789; FRS; *m* 27 Oct 1825 Anne Maria Draycott (*d* 8 Nov 1846), dau of Peter Denys (*see* HESKETH, B), and *d* 29 Oct 1876, having had, with a dau (Charlotte Georgiana Amelia, *b* 21 Aug 1826; *m* 24 April 1860 Rev John Richard Errington (*d* 4 Oct 1882), Rector Ladbroke, Warwicks, Hon Canon Worcester, and *d* 11 June 1902, leaving issue) and another dau (*d* young):

Sir George Thomas Francis Shuckburgh, 9th Bt, JP, DL; *b* 23 July 1829; Maj Scots Fus Gds, Chev Legn Hon and of Medjidie; *m* 24 June 1879 Ida Florence Geraldine (*m* 2nd 25 Nov 1886 Maj Henry James Shuckburgh (*see* above) and *d* 12 Jan 1906), only dau of Rev Frederick William Robertson and gdau of Sir George Denys, 1st Bt (*see* 1956 edn) and *d* 12 Jan 1884, leaving:

1 **Sir Stewkley Frederick Draycott Shuckburgh, 10th Bt**; *b* 20 June 1880; *d unm* 17 Nov 1917

2 **Sir Gerald Francis Stewkley Shuckburgh, 11th Bt**, JP Warwicks; *b* 28 Feb 1882; High Sheriff Warwicks 1921; *m* 2 March 1908 Honor Zoë, OBE (1920), JP (Warwicks 1940), dau of Neville Thursby, of Harlestone, Northants, and had:

(1) CHARLES GERALD STEWKLEY (Sir), **12th Bt**

(2) Basil James Stewkley; *b* 25 July 1916; *educ* Trin Coll Oxford (BA); 2nd Lt KRRC WW II (despatches); *ka* Middle East June 1941

(1) Evelyn Honor, JP Hants; *b* 21 Feb 1910; *m* 8 Feb 1940 Maj Anthony John Burrows, TD, RA (*d* 24 May 1949 as a result of war service), yr s of E P Burrows, of Heatherside, Keston, and *d* 3 Nov 1958, leaving issue

The 11th Bt *d* 3 Aug 1939; his er s,

Sir Charles Gerald Stewkley Shuckburgh, 12th Bt, TD (1946), JP (Warwicks 1946), DL (1965); *b* 28 Feb 1911; *educ* Harrow and Trin Coll Oxford; High Sheriff 1965; Maj 11th (City of London Yeo) LAA Bde RA (TA); *m* 1st 11 Dec 1935 Remony Dorothy (*d* 2 May 1936), only dau of Frederick Norman Bell, of Buenos Aires; *m* 2nd 22 May 1937 Nancy Diana Mary, OBE (*d* 1984), only dau of Capt Rupert Egerton Lubbock, RN (*see* AVEBURY, B), and *d* 1988, having had:

1 Robin James Stewkley; *b* 7 Dec 1941; *d* 20 March 1944

2 Sir RUPERT CHARLES GERALD SHUCKBURGH, **13th and present Bt**

1 *Remony Charmian [Mrs Michael Taylor-Downes, 60 Shingham, Swaffham, Norfolk PE37 8AY]; *b* 27 April 1938; *m* 1st 5 Oct 1963 (*divorce* 1978) Hugo Macdonald Price, s of Donald Frances Price, of St Michael's-on-Wyre, Lancs; *m* 2nd 1983 Michael Taylor-Downes (*d* 15 May 1991) and by her 1st husb has:

(1) *Robin Macdonald; *b* 16 Aug 1970

(2) *Justin Bryan; *b* 30 May 1973

2 *Amanda Maria [Miss Amanda Shuckburgh, The Gate House, White Colne, Essex CO6 2PW]; *b* 15 July 1946

SHUTTLEWORTH

KYND·KYNN·KNAWNE·KEPE

Arms: Quarterly: 1st and 4th, arg. three weaver's shuttles sa., tipped and furnished or (for SHUTTLEWORTH); 2nd and 3rd, arg. three ermine spots within two bendlets sa., the whole between as many crescents az (for KAY). **Crests:** 1 A cubit arm in armour ppr., grasping in the gauntlet a shuttle as in the arms (for SHUTTLEWORTH), 2 On a crescent az. a goldfinch ppr. (for KAY). **Supporters:** Dexter, a weaver ppr., holding in his exterior hand a shuttle as in the arms; sinister, a sailor holding in his exterior hand a ship's lantern ppr. **Motto:** *Kynd Kynn Knawne Kepe* ('Keep kind kin when known'). **Creations:** Bt. (UK) 22 Dec 1849, B. (UK) 16 July 1902.

THE 5TH BARON SHUTTLEWORTH, of Gawthorpe, Co Palatine of Lancaster, and a **Baronet** (Sir Charles Geoffrey Nicholas Kay-Shuttleworth, Bt, JP) [The Rt Hon The Lord Shuttleworth JP, Leck Hall, Carnforth, Lancs LA6 2JF; 14 Sloane Ave, London SW3 3JE]; *b* 2 Aug 1948; *s f* 1975; *educ* Eton; FRICS, ptnr Burton, Barnes and Vigers, chartered surveyors 1977–96, chm: Rural Devpt Commn 1990–97, Nat and Provincial Bldg Soc 1994–96 (dep chm 1983–94), Lancs Small Industries ctee CoSIRA 1978–83, Lancs Youth Clubs Assoc 1980–86 (pres 1986–), dir: Burnley Bldg Soc 1978–82, Rank Fndn 1993–, dep chm and dir Abbey National plc 1996–, cncl memb: Lancaster U 1990–93, CBI 1993–95, Pres Roy Lancs Ag Soc 1985–86, Govr Giggleswick Sch 1981– (Chm 1984–97), Ld Lt and custos rotulorum Lancs 1996– (DL 1986), memb Cncl Duchy Lancaster 1998–; Hon Fell U of Central Lancashire 1996, Hon Col 4th (vol) Bn Queen's Lancashire Regt 1996 KStJ; *m* 25 Oct 1975 *Ann Mary, yr dau of Maj James Dunbar Whatman MC, of Northcote Hill, Shamley Green, Surrey, and formerly w of Daniel Henry Barclay, and has:

1 +THOMAS EDWARD; *b* 29 Sept 1976

2 +David Charles; *b* 29 Aug 1978

3 +William James; *b* 29 Nov 1979

Lineage (of Shuttleworth): HENRY de SHUTTLEWORTH; *m* 1330 Agnes, dau and heiress of William de Hacking, and had:

UGHTRED de SHUTTLEWORTH, of Gawthorpe; living *c* 1389; presumably ancestor of:

HUGH SHUTTLEWORTH; had:

LAWRENCE SHUTTLEWORTH, of Gawthorpe; living 1463; *m* Elizabeth, dau of Richard Worsley, of Mearley, and had:

NICHOLAS SHUTTLEWORTH, of Gawthorpe; *b c* 1460; *m* 1503 Anne/Helen, dau of Christopher Parker, of Radholme Park, Yorks, and had:

HUGH SHUTTLEWORTH, of Gawthorpe; *b* 1504; *m* 1540 Anne, dau of Thomas Grimshaw, of Clayton, and was *bur* 26 Dec 1596, having had, with two er sons (Sir Richard, of Gawthorpe, Serjeant-at-law, Ch Justice Chester *c* 1589, *m* Margaret, widow of Robert Barton, of Smithells, and dau of Peter Legh, of Lyme, and *dsp* 4 Nov 1599; Rev Lawrence, of Gawthorpe Hall, which he built to plans by his er bro, BD, Rector Whitchford, Warwicks, *bur* unm 22 Feb 1607/8) and two daus:

THOMAS SHUTTLEWORTH, of Smithells; *m* Anne, dau of Richard Lever, and had:

RICHARD SHUTTLEWORTH, of Gawthorpe Hall; *b* 1592; Sheriff Lancs 1618 and 1638, MP Preston 1641 and 1656, Col Parly Army Civil War; *m* 24 April 1612 Fleetwood (*d* 1664), dau and heiress of Richard Barton, of Barton (the last of a Lancs family who descended uninterruptedly from Geoffrey de Barton *c* 1200), and *d* June 1669, having had, with 11 other children (five sons fighting for Parl Civil War):

RICHARD SHUTTLEWORTH; MP Clitheroe 1640 and in Long Parl; Col Parly Army Civil War; *m* Jane, dau of John Kirke, of London, and *dvp* 1648, leaving:

RICHARD SHUTTLEWORTH, of Gawthorpe and Barton, also Forcett, Yorks; *b* 19 Sept 1644; Sheriff Yorks 1678; *m* 28 July 1664 Margaret (*bur* 23 May 1683), dau of John Tempest, of Old Durham, and was *bur* 5 March 1680/1, leaving:

Sir RICHARD SHUTTLEWORTH, of Gawthorpe Hall and Forcett; *b* 1664; ktd 1684; *m* 1682 Catherine (*d* between 19 Aug 1727 and 1 March 1728), dau and heiress of Henry Clerke, DD, Pres Magdalen Coll Oxford, and *d* 27 July 1687, leaving:

RICHARD SHUTTLEWORTH, of Gawthorpe; *bapt* 3 Sept 1683; MP Lancs 1707–49, Father of the House; *m* Emma (*bur* 26 Oct 1725), dau of William Tempest, of Old Durham, and was *bur* 3 Jan 1749/50, leaving, with a yr s (William, ancestor of the SHUTTLEWORTHs of Hathersage Hall):

JAMES SHUTTLEWORTH, of Gawthorpe and Forcett, also Barton Lodge; *bapt* 6 Dec 1714; MP Preston 1741–54 and Lancs 1761–68, High Sheriff Yorks 1760; *m* Mary, dau and heiress of Robert Holden, of Aston, Derbys, and *d* 28 June 1773 aged 58, leaving, with a 4th s (Rev Charles Edward SHUTTLEWORTH later HOLDEN (roy licence 1791), ancestor of the HOLDENs of Aston) an est s:

ROBERT SHUTTLEWORTH, of Gawthorpe; *m* 15 May 1776 Anne (*d* 23 April 1801), dau of Gen Desaguliers, Equerry to GEORGE III, and *d* 29 Jan 1816, leaving, with an er s (ancestor of the SHUTTLEWORTHs of Collyers, Petersfield):

ROBERT SHUTTLEWORTH, of Gawthorpe; *b* 1784; Chm Preston QS, barrister; *m* 5 Nov 1816 Janet (*m* 2nd 16 June 1825 Frederick North, MP (*see* GUILFORD, E), and *d* 17 Jan 1855), est dau of Sir John Marjoribanks, Bt, of Lees, Berwicks (*see* 1888 edn), and *d* 6 March 1818, leaving:

JANET Shuttleworth, of Gawthorpe Hall; *b* 9 Nov 1817; *m* 24 Feb 1842 Sir James Phillips KAY later KAY-SHUTTLEWORTH, **1st Bt** (*see* below), and *d* 14 Sept 1872, leaving issue

Lineage (of Kay): JAMES KAY, of Basslane, *m* Sarah — (*d* 9 March 1748) and *d* 19 Dec 1744 aged 74, leaving:

ARTHUR KAY; *b* 25 Oct 1700; had:

JAMES KAY, of Basslane, Walmesley; *b* 1731; *m* Mary Kay (*d* 3 Sept 1809 aged 72), of Birtle, and *d* 16 Feb 1802, leaving:

ROBERT KAY, of Brookshaw, Bury; *b* 30 May 1768; *m* 22 Sept 1803 Hannah, dau of James Phillips, and *d* 25 April 1834, leaving:

1 JAMES PHILLIPS (Sir), **1st Bt**

2 Robert, of Rochdale; *b c* 1808; *m* Rachel Woodcock (*d* 1870) and *d* 31 Dec 1873, leaving:

  (1) Frederick; *b* 1839; *m* Alice Woodcock and *dsp*

  (1) Fanny; *b* 1837; *d* unm

3 Joseph, of Fredley, Dorking, QC; *b* 28 Feb 1821, Judge Manchester and Salford Palatine Court; *m* 21 April 1863 Elizabeth Mary, dau of Thomas Drummond, and *dsp*

4 Edward Ebenezer (Sir), PC, QC 1866, JP; *b* 2 July 1822; *educ* Trin Coll Cambridge (MA 1847); barrister Lincoln's Inn 1847, chm Norfolk QS, High Court Judge Chancery Div 1881, Ld Justice Appeal; *m* 2 April 1850 Mary Valence (*d* 10 Oct 1889), dau of Rev William French, Master Jesus Coll Cambridge, Canon Ely, and *d* 1897, leaving two daus (both *d* unm)

5 Thomas; had issue (settled NZ)

1 Hannah; *d* unm 16 June 1869 aged 63

The est s,

Sir JAMES PHILLIPS KAY later KAY-SHUTTLEWORTH (roy licence 1842), **1st Bt** (UK), so *cr* 22 Dec 1849, JP, DL Lancs; *b* 20 July 1804; MD and Hon DCL Oxford, High Sheriff Lancs 1864, Sec Ctee Cncl on Educn; *m* 24 Feb 1842 Janet Shuttleworth (*see* above) and had:

1 UGHTRED JAMES, **1st Baron**

2 Robert; *b* 20 Oct 1847; *m* 22 Jan 1896 Ethel Clementina (*d* 29 April 1962), dau of Alfred John Freeman, MD, of San Remo, Italy, and *d* 30 July 1934, having had:

  (1) John; *b* 13, *d* 16 Jan 1907

  (1) Helen Victoria; *b* 4 May 1905; *m* 26 May 1936 Maj Wynyard Montagu Hall, WYorks Regt (*d* 24 Dec 1949), s of Col Montagu Hall, Roy Munster Fus, of Ryde, IOW, and *d* 19—

3 Lionel Edward; *b* 14 Feb 1849; MA Cantab, MRCS, UK V-Consul San Remo; *m* 21 Dec 1877 Charlotte Mary (*d* 5 April 1925), 5th surv dau of Capt Charles Walcott, RN, of Portlooe House, Cornwall, and *d* 11 Dec 1900, having had:

  (1) Charles Ughtred; *b* 3 March 1879; *d* 11 March 1895

  (1) Janet Walcott; *b* 10 Feb 1881; served WW I (Special Service Cross BRCS); *d* unm 28 Oct 1958

4 Stewart Marjoribanks; *b* 8 Nov 1851; *d* unm 7 July 1887

1 Janet Elizabeth; *b* 6 May 1843; *d* unm 17 May 1914

The 1st Bt *d* 26 May 1877; his est s,

UGHTRED JAMES KAY-SHUTTLEWORTH, **1st Baron Shuttleworth**, of Gawthorpe, Co Palatine of Lancaster (UK), so *cr* 16 July 1902, PC (1886), JP Westmorland and Lancs; *b* 18 Dec 1844; *educ* Harrow and London U; MP (Lib) Hastings 1869–80 and Clitheroe 1885–1902, memb London Sch Bd 1880–82, U-Sec India Feb-April 1886, Chllr Duchy Lancaster April-Aug 1886, Chm Public Accounts Ctee 1888–92, Parly Sec Admlty 1892–95, Chm Roy Commn Canals and Waterways 1906–11, Ld Lt and custos rotulorum Lancs 1908–28, Pres Lancs TAA 1908–28, Hon Col 93rd E Lancs Bde RAF (TA), Hon LLD Manchester 1912; *m* 1 July 1871 Blanche Marion (*d* 10 June 1924), yst dau of Sir Woodbine Parish, KCH, JP, FRS, FRGS, FGS, of Quarry House, St Leonard's-on-Sea, Sussex, and *d* 20 Dec 1939, having had:

1 Lawrence Ughtred; *b* 21 Sept 1887; barrister Inner Temple 1913, unsuccessful Lib parly candidate Altrincham 1913, Priv Sec to Walter Runciman, PC (*see* RUNCIMAN OF DOXFORD, V) 1914–16, Capt and Adj RFA WW I (despatches); *m* 1 Feb 1913 Selina Adine (*m* 2nd 31 Jan 1920 Maj-Gen William Birchall Macauley King, CMG, DSO, VD (*d* 23 June 1950), of Montreal, and resumed her 1st husb's name), only dau of Gen Hon Francis Charles Bridgeman (*see* BRADFORD, E), and was *ka* 30 March 1917, leaving:

  (1) RICHARD UGHTRED PAUL KAY-SHUTTLEWORTH, **2nd Baron Shuttleworth**, JP Lancs; *b* 30 Oct 1913; *educ* Eton and Balliol Coll Oxford (BA); CC Lancs 1937, F/O RAFVR WW II; *ka* Battle of Britain 8 Aug 1940

  (2) RONALD ORLANDO LAWRENCE KAY-SHUTTLEWORTH, **3rd Baron Shuttleworth** ; *b* posthumously 7 Oct 1917; *educ* Eton and Balliol Coll Oxford; Capt RA (TA) WW II; *ka* N Africa 17 Nov 1942

  (1) Rosemary Florence Angela; *b* 12 Sept 1915; granted rank of baron's dau 21 June 1940

2 Edward James; *b* 16 March 1890; barrister Inner Temple, T/Capt 7th Bn Rifle Bde 1915, S/Capt 1916, WW I; *m* 5 Dec 1914 Sibell Eleanor Maud (*m* 2nd 11 May 1920 Rev Hon Charles Frederick Lyttelton, MC (*see* COBHAM, V); *m* 3rd 27 Sept 1937 Roger Fulford, s of Canon F J Fulford), dau of Charles Robert Whorwood Adeane, CB, of Babraham Hall, Cambs, and was accidentally *k* 10 July 1917, leaving:

  (1) CHARLES UGHTRED JOHN, **4th Baron**

  (1) Pamela Catherine Mabell; *b* 17 Sept 1915; *m* 1st 7 Aug 1935 (*divorce* 1940) Lt Hon William Keith Rous, RN, 2nd s of 3rd Earl of Stradbroke (*qv*), and had issue; *m* 2nd 25 June 1942 Maj Hon Sir Thomas Frankland, 11th Bt (*see* ZOUCHE, B), and had further issue; *m* 3rd 29 June 1946 (*divorce* 1968) Michael Barclay, er s of Rev Humphrey Gordon Barclay, CVO, of Southrepps Rectory, Norwich, and had further issue; *m* 4th Maj Robert Hugh Pardoe, RE, yr s of John Huben Pardoe, FLAS, and *d* 1972

1 Angela Mary; *b* 18 Sept 1872; *m* 30 Dec 1899 Col Bernard Ramsden James, JP, DL, Roy Warwicks Regt, 4th s of John Henry James, JP, of Watford, Herts, and *d* 20 Dec 1967, leaving a s and three daus. He *d* 30 April 1938

2 Nina Louisa; *b* 31 March 1879; *m* 21 Dec 1910 His Hon Eustace Gilbert Hills, KC, County Court Judge (*d* 17 Oct 1934), and *d* 11 April 1948, having had issue (*see* 1956 edn HILLS, Bt)

3 Rachel Beatrice, MBE (1949), JP Lancs 1934; *b* 17 Feb 1886; County Commr NE Lancs Girl Guides 1916–49 (V-Pres 1950), memb Lancs CC Records Ctee and Lancs County Magistrates Ctee 1952; *d* unm 20 April 1967

4 Catherine Blanche; *b* 7 April 1894; *m* 22 Aug 1917 Charles Symonds Leaf, JP, FSA, late Lt RM and Actg Capt E Kent Regt, only s of Walter Leaf, LittD, DLitt, and *d* 18 Oct 1963, leaving issue. He *d* 19 Feb 1947

The 3rd BARON's cousin,

CHARLES UGHTRED JOHN KAY-SHUTTLEWORTH, **4th Baron Shuttleworth**, MC (1940), JP (Lancs 1944), DL (1956); *b* 24 June 1917; *educ* Eton and Magdalene Coll Cambridge (BA 1938, MA 1953); T/Maj RHA WW II 1939–42 (wounded twice, invalided); *m* 5 Nov 1947 Anne Elizabeth (*d* 1991), er dau of Col Geoffrey Phillips, CBE, DSO (*see* RIDLEY, V), and *d* 5 Oct 1975, leaving:

1 CHARLES GEOFFREY NICHOLAS KAY-SHUTTLEWORTH, **5th and present Baron Shuttleworth**

2 +Robert James; *b* 27 May 1954; *educ* Eton and RMA Sandhurst; Lt Coldstream Gds 1974; *m* 18 Aug 1995 *(J) Claire, est dau of Michael Pridham, of Pudleston, Herefs

3 +Edward Roger Noël; *b* 28 June 1962; *educ* Eton; *m* 5 June 1996 *Noemi, yr dau of Delfin Cortez, of The Philippines, and has:

  (1) *Ellen Anne; *b* 9 Jan 1998

1 *Sarah (Sally) Rachel Jane; *b* 18 July 1950; *m* 1st 31 Oct 1970 (*divorce* 1984) Richard Francis Foster, yr son of William Foster, of Lexham Hall, King's Lynn, Norfolk (*see* AILESBURY, M), and has:

  (1) *Edward William Thomas; *b* 1978

  (1) *Henrietta Victoria; *b* 1973

  (2) *Georgina Pamela; *b* 1975

1 (cont.) The Hon Mrs Sally Foster *m* 2nd 1988 *Peter Figgins and by him has:

  (2) *Tom; *b* 1990

Seat: Leck Hall, Cowan Bridge, Lancs. The **4th Baron** moved out of the original family seat, Gawthorpe Hall, in 1953 and gave it to the National Trust in 1970. As a replacement he bought Leck, which lay conveniently close to his Barbon estate near the county boundary with what was then Westmorland. Despite having been pressed into service as a boys' prep school earlier it retains some beautiful features, such as marble chimney pieces, plaster cornices and tropical hardwood doors. It was built by John Webb around 1800, although remains of an earlier 17th-century structure are detectable to the rear. Also to the rear are noteworthy ancillary buildings such as the Dutch barn and Tuscan-style orangery. In addition to the internal decorative features already mentioned the main house contains a central hall with an imposing staircase rising two floors, the whole being lent a sense of space by arches, the work of Francis Johnson. Outside the visual effect would be somewhat stark but for the lovely setting. The main facade, for instance, consists of four rectangular bays on each floor either side, that is to say two-by-two, of a three-bay central window on the first floor and a portico with ionic columns at ground level.

SIDMOUTH

LIBERTAS·SUB·REGE·PIO

Arms: Per pale erm. and ermines on a chevron five lozenges all counterchanged between three fleurs-de-lys or. **Crest:** A cat-a-mountain sejant guardant ppr. bezantée, his dexter paw resting upon a shield az. charged with a mace erect, surmounted with a regal crown, or within a bordure engrailed arg. **Supporters:** On either side a stag, the dexter ermines, the sinister erm., each attired and gorged with a chain, pendant therefrom a key, all or.
Motto: *Libertas sub rege pio* ('Liberty under a pious king').
Creation: V. (UK) 12 Jan 1805.

THE 7TH VISCOUNT SIDMOUTH, of Sidmouth, Co Devon (John Tonge Anthony Pellew Addington) [The Rt Hon The Viscount Sidmouth, 12 Brock St, Bath BA1 2LW]; *b* 3 Oct 1914; *s f* 1976; *educ* Downside and BNC Oxford; Colonial Service E Africa 1938–54, dir Joseph Rochford & Sons, memb cncl and Chm Glasshouse Ctee NFU 1962–69, memb: Ag Research Cncl 1969–74, Centl Cncl Ag Co-opn 1970–73, Select Ctee ECs 1984–87, Pres Nat Cncl Inland Tport 1978–84, Kt SMO Malta 1962; *m* 1st 20 Jan 1940 Barbara Mary Angela (*d* 1989), est dau of Bernard Rochford, OBE, of S Kensington; *m* 2nd 1993 *(Marie) Thérèse, dau of His Hon Sir Joseph (Alfred) Sheridan and widow of Francis Anthony Baring Pollen (*see* POLLEN, Bt), and by his 1st w has had:

1 Christopher John; *b* 10 April 1941; *educ* Downside and BNC Oxford; *m* 28 July 1963 Clio Mona (*d* 8 April 1986), only dau of Dr John Peristiany, of Athens, and *d* 2 June 1986

2 +JEREMY FRANCIS [The Hon Jeremy Addington, Highway Manor, nr Calne, Wilts SN11 8SR]; *b* 29 July 1947; *educ* Ampleforth; *m* 1st 20 March 1970 Grete Henningsen, dau of Paul Walter Henningsen, of Denmark, and has:
  (1) +Steffan; *b* 26 Oct 1966
  (1) *Laura Grete; *b* 15 May 1975
2 (cont.) The Hon Jeremy Addington *m* 2nd 1986 *Una, est dau of James Coogan, of Compton Bassett, Wilts, and Mrs Susanna Newman, and by her has:
  (2) +John; *b* 29 Nov 1990
  (3) *Anna Frances; *b* 1988

1 *Veronica Mary [The Hon Mrs Hodges, 54a Cornwall Gdns, London SW7 4BG; Lawn Cottage, Tisbury, Wilts SP3 6SG]; *b* 9 Nov 1944; *m* 1st 17 July 1982 (*annulled* 1987) Allan (George) Mainds, of Bishopstone, Bucks, er s of George Mainds; *m* 2nd 1989 *Michael Jeremy Hodges, only s of Capt Michael Hodges, RN, and has:
  (1) *Philippa Clare ADDINGTON; *b* 1969
2 *Susan Barbara [The Hon Mrs Kimpton, 27 Ellerby St, London SW6]; *b* 17 Dec 1945; *m* 1st 16 Dec 1965 (*divorce* 1975) Count Giovanni Paolo Giacomo Alessandro Camillo Manassei di Collestate, er s of Count Alessandro Augusto Giovanni Giacinto Barnaba Manassei di Collestate by Lady Maryel de Wichfeld (*see* PERTH, E); *m* 2nd 1990, as his 2nd w, *Anthony Andrew Ward Kimpton (*see* HAZLERIGG, B) and by her 1st husb has:
  (1) *Hugo Alexander; *b* 12 Dec 1969
  (1) *Marina Catherine; *b* 14 Nov 1967
3 *Janet Theresa; *b* 4 Oct 1949; *m* 24 March 1972 *Anthony Goodman, s of Isaac Harris Goodman, of London, and has:
  (1) *Joanna Louìse; *b* 31 Jan 1973
  (2) *Frances Julia; *b* 24 July 1975
  (3) *Isabel Alice; *b* 2 Nov 1979
4 *Pauline Rosemary [The Hon Mrs Clare, Maes Yr Eglwys, Aberarth, Dyfed]; *b* 18 Feb 1951; *m* 18 Aug 1973 *Paul Christopher Clare, s of George William Clone, of Putney, and has:
  (1) *Tomas Aeron; *b* 22 Feb 1980
  (2) *John Joseph; *b* 1988
  (1) *Jennifer Rose; *b* 1982
5 A dau; *b* and *d* 12 May 1955
6 *Mary Margaret (Kidge) [The Hon Mrs Burns, 51 Brynmaer Rd, London SW11 4EN]; *b* 29 June 1956; *m* 15 April 1978 *James Alexander John Burns, yst s of Thomas Ferrier Burns, and has:
  (1) *Julia Isabel; *b* Feb 1985

  (2) *Miriam Janet; *b* Dec 1985

Lineage: JOHN ADDINGTON, of a family settled in 1350 at Pottersbury, otherwise Estpiry, Northants, was living 1473; *m* Alys — (*d* 1515) and *d* 1514, leaving six sons; the 3rd:

RALPH ADDINGTON; *m* Elizabeth — and *d* 1542, leaving a 2nd s:

ROBERT ADDINGTON, of Pottersbury; *m* Margery — and *d* 1555, leaving, with other issue:

WILLIAM ADDINGTON, of Fringford, Oxon; *m* Katharine, dau of Hugh Humfrey, and was *bur* June 1600, leaving, with other issue:

HENRY ADDINGTON, of Fringford; *b c* 1582; *m* —, dau of Henry Watson, of Hethe, Oxon, and was *bur* 7 April 1676, leaving, with other issue:

WILLIAM ADDINGTON; *m* Christian, dau of Rev Robert Sharrock, of Adstock, Bucks, and *d* 1680, having had, with other issue:

HENRY ADDINGTON, of Fringford; *bapt* 10 July 1659; *m* 1st 10 May 1696 Elizabeth (*d* 1702), dau of Henry Markham, of Tingewick, Bucks; *m* 2nd Elizabeth, dau of Anthony Watts, of Sulgrave, Northants, and *d* 5 March 1729, leaving, with other issue:

ANTHONY ADDINGTON, of Fringford; *b* 13 Dec 1713; *educ* Trin Coll Oxford (MD); London GP, his patients including Pitt the Elder (*see* JERSEY, E) and GEORGE III; Ld Manors of Up Ottery and Rawridge, Devon; *m* 22 Sept 1745 Mary (*d* 7 Nov 1778), dau and heiress of Rev Haviland John Hiley, of Reading, and had:
  1 HENRY
  2 John Hiley, PC, of Langford Court, Somerset; MP Truro 1787–90, Winchelsea 1794–96, Wendover 1796–1802, Bossiney 1802–03 and Harwich 1803–18, a Ld Treasury 1800, Paymaster-Gen Forces; *m* 25 Oct 1785 Mary (*d* 3 Sept 1833), dau of Henry Unwin, and *d* 11 June 1818, leaving, with a dau (*d* unm):
    (1) Haviland John; *b* 20 Nov 1787; *dsp*
    (2) Henry Unwin, PC; *b* 24 March 1790; Envoy Extrdy and Min Plen Spain, U-Sec For Affrs 1842–54; *m* 10 Nov 1836 Eleanor Anne (*d* 17 Oct 1877), dau of T G Bucknall Estcourt, MP, and *dsp* 6 March 1870
  1 Anne; *m* 2 June 1770 William Goodenough, MD, and *d* 12 June 1806
  2 Eleanor; *m* 1 Aug 1771 James Sutton, of New Park, Wilts. and had issue. He *d* 1801
  3 Elizabeth; *m* Aug 1782 William Hoskyns, of North Perrot, Somerset, and *d* 26 June 1827, leaving issue. He *d* 1813
  4 Charlotte; *m* 1 Aug 1788 Charles BRAGGE later BATHURST, PC, Treas Navy, of Lydney Park, Glos, and *d* 27 May 1839, leaving issue (*see* BLEDISLOE, V)

Dr ANTHONY ADDINGTON *d* 21 March 1790; his er s,

HENRY ADDINGTON, **1st Viscount Sidmouth**, of Sidmouth, Co Devon (UK), so *cr* 12 Jan 1805, PC (1789); *b* 30 May 1757; *educ* Winchester and BNC Oxford (DCL 1814); barrister Lincoln's Inn 1784, Recorder Devizes 1784, MP (Tory) Devizes 1784–1805, Speaker H of C 1789–1801, PM, First Ld Treasury and Chllr Exchequer 1801–04, Ld Pres Cncl Jan–July 1805, 1806–07 and April–June 1812, Ld Privy Seal Feb-Oct 1806, Home Sec 1812–22 (possibly the most repressive in British history), retained Cabinet seat till 1824; Govr Charterhouse 1802, High Steward Westminster 1813–42, Er Bro Trin Ho 1818–44, Dep Ranger Richmond Pk, FSA 1791; *m* 1st 19 Sept 1781 Ursula Mary (*d* 28 June 1811), dau and coheir of Leonard Hammond, of Cheam, Surrey, and had, with another dau (*d* unm):
  1 Henry; *b* 30 Sept 1786; *educ* Winchester and Ch Ch Oxford; Clerk of the Pells 1802; *d* unm and insane 30 1823 after at least one suicide attempt, in 1805
  2 Charles Anthony; *d* an infant, *bur* 20 Aug 1789
  3 WILLIAM LEONARD, **2nd Viscount**
  1 Frances; *m* 20 June 1820 Very Rev Hon George Pellew (*see* EXMOUTH, V) and *d* 27 Feb 1870
  2 Charlotte; *m* 1838 Rev Horace Gore Currie and *d* 1870
  3 Henrietta; *m* 1838 Capt Thomas Barker Wall and *d* 12 Aug 1868

The **1st Viscount** *m* 2nd 29 July 1823 Marianne (*d* 26 April 1842), widow of Thomas Townshend, of Honington, Warwicks, and only dau of 1st and last Baron Stowell of Stowell Park (*see* ELDON, E), and *d* 15 Feb 1844

His only surv s,

Rev WILLIAM LEONARD ADDINGTON, **2nd Viscount Sidmouth**; *b* 13 Nov 1794; *educ* Westminster and Ch Ch Oxford; Rector Poole, 1821–44; *m* 20 April 1820 Mary (*d* 17 Jan 1894 in her 100th year), dau of Rev John Young, Rector Thorpe Malsor, Northants, and had, with two other sons (*d* young and unm):
  1 WILLIAM WELLS, **3rd Viscount**
  2 Leonard Allen, DL Devon; *b* 11 May 1828; Maj RA, DAQMG Bengal, Hon Lt-Col 1st Devon Artillery Vols; *m* 16 July 1853 Laetitia Anne (*d* 12 May 1889), 3rd dau of Erving Clark, of Efford Manor, Devon, and *d* 4 June 1888, leaving:
    (1) William Leonard; *b* 12 Aug 1856; Maj Roy W Surrey Regt; *m* 11 June 1890 Augusta (*d* 16 Jan 1942), dau of Rev Hayter George Hayter-Hames, of Chagford, Devon, and *d* 15 Dec 1919, leaving:
      1a Leonard George, DSC; *b* 18 Aug 1892; Cdr RN; *m* 11 July 1939 Sheena, dau of Hector Forbes of Culloden
      1a Mary Beatrice; *d* unm 3 Dec 1938
      2a Stella Laetitia
    (2) Hiley Reginald; *b* 2 Aug 1861; Maj KRRC; *m* 7 June 1893 Nelly (*d* 29 Dec 1956), 2nd dau of Osmond de Lancey Priaulx, of The Mount, Guernsey, and *d* 15 May 1940, leaving:
      1a Rupert Hiley Priaulx ; *b* 23 June 1898; Maj RA, WW I 1916–18 (twice wounded, two medals); WW II (wounded, despatches, present Dunkirk Evacuation); *m* 9 July 1935 Margaret Penrose, formerly w of Lt-Col Oliver Barry Rupert Dickey, RASC, and dau of Lt-Col William Lambert Penrose Mark-Wardlaw, N Staffs Regt, and *d* 15 Aug 1989
    (1) Laetitia Anne; *m* 9 Jan 1880 Maj William Bicknell Coney, Sherwood Foresters, and *d* 8 Oct 1912, leaving issue
    (2) Maud Florence, OBE (1920); *d* unm 17 Feb 1936
    (3) Blanche Mary; *m* 15 Jan 1890 Capt John Ravenhill Prescott, Sherwood Foresters, of Dalton Grange, Lancs, er s of John Prescott, JP, DL, of Dalton Grange, and *d* 14 Aug 1957, leaving issue. He *d* 1915

(4) Beatrice Cordelia; *m* 9 Jan 1906 Henry Dawson Were, of Sidmouth, *s* of T B Were, of Broad Clyst, Devon, and *d* 1 Feb 1939, having had issue

(5) Barbara Marion; *m* 26 Aug 1897 Maj-Gen Sir James Marshall Stewart, KCB, KCMG, 5th Roy Gurkha Rifles, and *d* 4 May 1962, leaving issue. He *d* 20 July 1943

3 Hiley Robert; *b* 4 April 1830; HEICS, 74th Punjab Inf; *k* Indian Mutiny 11 May 1857

4 Charles John; *b* 17 March 1832; 38th Regt Crimea (severely wounded) and Indian Mutiny, Lt-Col cmdg 100th Regt 1871–77, Col cmdg 35th Regtl Dist 1877–83, AA&QMG 1884–85, Col cmdg troops Shorncliffe 1885–86, Col Devonshire Regt, Maj-Gen; *m* 5 Aug 1862 Nelly Hindmarsh (*d* 27 June 1912), 2nd dau of Alfred Miller-Mundy, of Shipley Hall, Derbys, and *dsp* 11 Sept 1903

1 Mary Ursula; *m* 15 April 1841 Miles Charles Seton, of Treskerby Cornwall, *est s* of Col William Carden Seton, CB, and *d* 11 Oct 1899, leaving issue. He *d* 18 Sept 1877

2 Louisa Charlotte; *m* 29 April 1862 Thomas Goldie Dickson, of Edinburgh, and *d* 30 Dec 1899, leaving issue. He *d* 28 July 1905

3 Caroline Penelope; *m* 15 Sept 1853 Newdigate Hooper Kearney Burne and *d* 19 Dec 1923, having had issue. He *d* 3 May 1898

4 Frances Sophia; *m* 1 Sept 1861 David Scott Dickson and *d* 2 Feb 1934, having had issue. He *d* 14 Feb 1900

The 2nd VISCOUNT *d* 25 March 1864; his est surv s,

WILLIAM WELLS ADDINGTON, **3rd Viscount Sidmouth**, JP, DL Devon, JP Somerset; *b* 25 March 1824; Lt RN 1846 (ret 1848), MP (C) Devizes 1863–64; *m* 28 Sept 1848 Georgiana Susan (*d* 2 Jan 1896), est dau of Very Rev Hon George Pellew (*see* EXMOUTH, V), and had, with another dau (*d* young):

1 GERALD ANTHONY PELLEW BAGNALL, **4th Viscount**

2 Herbert Hiley Stafford; *b* 12 March 1859; Capt Roy Fus, Maj Res Offrs; *d* unm 17 April 1943

3 Harold William; *b* 24 May 1860; Col RFA, Uganda 1898, Boer War 1901, WW I; *m* 1887 Constance, dau of A J Clairmonte, of Lakelands, Nova Scotia, and *dsp* 27 Dec 1941

4 Francis Charles Bathurst; *b* 14 June 1861; Capt RN; *d* unm 12 Feb 1905

1 Alice Mary; *m* 6 March 1894, as his 2nd w, James Johnstone Bevan, JP, of Northgate House, Bury St Edmunds, 3rd *s* of Charles Bevan, and *d* 23 Sept 1929. He *dsp* 5 Nov 1898

2 Ursula Georgiana; *m* 12 Feb 1879 Francis John Helyar, of Bath, and *d* 17 Dec 1947, leaving issue. He *d* Dec 1918

3 Eveline; *m* 15 Sept 1875, as his 2nd w, Francis Arkwright, JP, of Overton, Marton, NZ, and Coton House, Warwicks, and *dsp* 25 July 1944. He *d* 1 March 1915

4 Mabel; *m* 30 Oct 1879 Sir Archibald Ernest Orr Ewing, 3rd Bt (*qv*), and *d* 30 March 1942, having had issue. He *d* 14 Feb 1900

The 3rd VISCOUNT *d* 28 Oct 1913; his est s,

GERALD ANTHONY PELLEW BAGNALL ADDINGTON, **4th Viscount Sidmouth**, JP Devon; *b* 29 Nov 1854; *educ* Rugby and Merton Coll Oxford; *m* 27 July 1881 Ethel Mary (*d* 18 Dec 1954), only dau of Capt Louis Charles Henry Tonge, RN, of Highway, Wilts, and *d* 25 March 1915, leaving:

1 GERALD WILLIAM ADDINGTON, **5th Viscount Sidmouth**, JP; *b* 19 Aug 1882; *educ* Eton and abroad; chm Honiton RDC, Capt 6th Bn Devonshire Regt (TA), WW I in India, Mesopotamia, Aden and Salonica, a Govr Allhallows' Sch, Rousdon, Devon; Coronation Medal 1937; *m* 2 Oct 1915 Mary Murdoch (*d* 20 Dec 1983 aged 91) only dau of Sir Donald Campbell Johnstone, ICS, Ch Judge Lahore, and *dsp* 4 April 1953

2 RAYMOND ANTHONY, **6th Viscount**

1 Ursula Mary; *m* 3 Nov 1909 Lt James Hope-Wallace (*see* LINLITHGOW, M) and *d* 24 Aug 1962, leaving issue

2 Marjorie Ruth; *m* 20 Oct 1910 Col Oscar Mark Harris, DSO, RHA, 2nd *s* of Henry Harris, of Jersey, and has issue. He *d* 11 Aug 1965

The 5th VISCOUNT's bro,

RAYMOND ANTHONY ADDINGTON, **6th Viscount Sidmouth**; *b* 24 Jan 1887; *educ* Cheltenham and RMC Sandhurst; Maj 26th KGO Light Cav, IA, WW I Flanders 1914–16, S Persia 1918–19, NWF 1919–20; *m* 26 Aug 1913 Gladys Mary Dever (*d* 14 April 1983 aged 97), dau of Thomas Francis Hughes, Commr Chinese Customs, and *d* 7 Feb 1976, leaving:

1 JOHN TONGE ANTHONY PELLEW ADDINGTON, **7th and present Viscount Sidmouth**

2 +Hiley William Dever [Lt-Cdr The Hon Hiley Addington RN, 1420 Sylvan Court, Sarnia, Ontario, Canada N7S 4A3]; *b* 31 Oct 1917; *educ* RNC Dartmouth; AMIMechE, Lt-Cdr (E) RN WW II and as Pilot FAA; *m* 1st 15 Dec 1942 Brenda Swanney (*d* 1990), 2nd dau of Prof Robert Charles Wallace, CMG, PhD, DSc, Pncpl Queen's U, Kingston, Ontario; *m* 2nd 1993 *Rita, widow of Alec T Cousins, and by his 1st w has:

(1) +Robert Hiley; *b* 15 Oct 1944

(2) +Charles Haviland; *b* 10 April 1949

(1) *Frances Clare; *b* 17 Sept 1947

3 +Raymond Thomas Casamajor, MC (1944) [Maj The Hon Raymond Addington MC, Strattons, Highway, Wilts SN11 8SR]; *b* 7 Jan 1919; *educ* Downside and RMA Woolwich; Maj RHA WW II Commandos and Paratroops; *m* 2 Oct 1947 Veronique (*d* following an accident 9 April 1970), yst dau of Emile Wirtz, of Antwerp, and has:

(1) +Peter John Gerald [Peter Addington Esq, Highway Farm, Calne, Wilts SN11 8SR]; *b* 2 Aug 1948; *educ* Downside and RAC Cirencester; *m* 9 July 1977 *Rosemary Anita, er dau of Richard Anthony Lamb, of Knighton Manor, Broadchalke, Wilts, and has:

  1a +Paul Anthony; *b* 6 June 1979

  2a +Michael Peter; *b* 1980

  3a +Edmund John; *b* 1983

  4a +Raleigh Thomas; *b* 1987

(2) +Donald Emile [Donald Addington Esq, 216 Varsity Estates Link, Calgary, Alberta, Canada T3B 4C9]; *b* 6 Dec 1949; *educ* Downside and London U; *m* 1973 *Jean Margaret, dau of David Alexander Baikie, and has:

  1a +Jack Alexander; *b* 1974

  2a +Leo Nicholas; *b* 1976

  3a +Oliver Thomas; *b* 1979

  1a *Zoe Veronica; *b* 1977

(3) +Francis Henry; *b* 24 April 1955; *educ* Downside

(1) *Lucy Anne; *b* 17 Jan 1952

(2) *Carol Jacqueline; *b* 2 Dec 1953

(3) *Antonia Veronica; *b* 16 Oct 1956

(4) *Edwina Gillian; *b* 1959; *m* 1983 *Yokinobu Mori, of Tokyo and Riyadh, Saudi Arabia, and has:

  1a *Henry Addington; *b* 1984

  2a *George Addington; *b* 1987

4 +Gurth Louis Francis [The Hon Gurth Addington, 11 Edwin St, Fairlight, NSW 2094, Australia]; *b* 26 Feb 1920; *educ* RNC Dartmouth, Downside and BNC Oxford (MA); bomber navigator RAF WW II; *m* 10 May 1950 *Patience Gillian, 2nd dau of Lt-Col L E Travers, RE, of Travers Point, Metung, Victoria, and has:

(1) +Martin Gerald Francis [Martin Addington Esq, 6 Palm Ave, Palmerston North, New Zealand]; *b* 6 April 1952; *m* 1978 *Lynne Elizabeth Mautner and has:

  1a +Benjamin Richard Francis; *b* 1980

  1a *Lauren Elizabeth; *b* 1982

(2) +David Anthony Brian [David Addington Esq, 32 Aitken Ave, Queenscliff, Sydney, NSW 2096, Australia]; *b* 18 May 1955; *m* 1979 *Mary-Anne Delmont and has:

  1a +Daniel Anthony Travers; *b* 1985

  1a *Emma Teresa; *b* 1982

(3) +Mark Nicholas Guy; *b* 27 Aug 1957

(1) *Mary Clare; *b* 8 Feb 1951; *m* 1975 *Trevor Roberts and has:

  1a *Dafydd Wynn; *b* 1982

  2a *Owen Wynn; *b* 1986

  3a *Gareth Wynn; *b* 1988

  1a *Halina Clare; *b* 1980

(2) *Catherine Dorothy [Mrs Richard Lumley, 3 Edwards Bay Rd, Mosman, Sydney, NSW 2088, Australia]; *b* 11 May 1953; *m* 1975 *Richard James Lumley and has:

  1a *Roger Gurth; *b* 1988

  1a *Justine Molly; *b* 1982

  2a *Rebecca Patience; *b* 1984

  3a *Philippa Catherine; *b* 1986

(3) *Deirdre Anne [Mrs Derek Trow, 370 Lords Place, Orange, NSW 2800, Australia]; *b* 18 May 1955; *m* 1981 *Derek Trow and has:

  1a *Gareth Michael Addington; *b* 1986

  1a *Miriam Johanna Addington; *b* 1987

(4) *Monica Jane [Mrs Glenn Batchelor, 33 Piedmont St, Box Hill South, Melbourne, Vic 3128, Australia]; *b* 27 Aug 1957; *m* 1983 *Glenn Richard Batchelor and has:

  1a *Richard Mark; *b* 1989

  1a *Kate Betty; *b* 1986

  2a *Jessica Patience; *b* 1988

(5) *Barbara Mary [Mrs John Waugh, 7 Wisdom Place, Hughes, ACT 2605, Australia]; *b* 10 Aug 1961; *m* 1987 *John William Waugh and has:

  1a *Henry William Addington; *b* 1990

  1a *Olivia Charlotte; *b* 1988

  2a *Cecilia Jane; *b* 1992

(6) *Jane Margaret [Mrs Stephen Hill, 199 Onewa Rd, Birkenhead, Auckland, New Zealand]; *b* 17 Feb 1964; *m* 1984 *Stephen Hill and has:

  1a *Edward James; *b* 1989

5 +Leslie Richard Bagnall, DFC (1952) [Lt-Col The Hon Leslie Addington DFC, Polebridge, Sutton Veny, Warminster, Wilts BA12 7AL]; *b* 20 Sept 1923; *educ* Downside; 2nd Indian Airborne Div WW II, Pilot AOP Malaya 1948 and Korea 1951–52, Lt-Col RHA cmdg Essex Yeo 1965–66; *m* 25 June 1955 *Anne, er dau of Capt Trevor Hume (*see* LACY, Bt), and has:

(1) +William Leslie Hume; *b* 8 Aug 1956; *educ* Downside; *m* 1981 *Sally Jane, dau of Brig D G Russell, of Fletching, Sussex, and has:

  1a +Alexander William Russell; *b* 1987

  2a +Jason Robin Mark; *b* 1989

(1) (cont.) Mr and Mrs William Addington also adopted:

  *Jessica Louise Susan; *b* 12 Oct 1991

  *Sasha Elizabeth Anna; *b* 17 Aug 1993

(2) +Richard Charles Raymond; *b* 22 May 1958; *m* 1989 *Deryn Victoria, dau of Col R H Johnson, of San Antonio, Tex., by Mrs Joan Pepita Nell Brown, of Bourton-on-the-Hill, Glos, and has:

  1a +Raleigh; *b* 15 Aug 1990

  1a *Constance Victoria Nell; *b* 1993

  2a *Honor; *b* 15 Aug 1996

(1) *Sarah Anne Clare; *b* 12 Jan 1961

(2) *Alice Mary Cynthia; *b* 16 March 1964; *m* 1992 *Julian Guy er s of Lt-Cdr Wyndham Julian Rogers-Coltman, OBE, RN (ret), of Berryburn, Ancroft, Northumberland, and has:

  1a *Charles Wyndham; *b* 1994

  2a *Hugh Leslie; *b* 1997

6 Raleigh Hugh Leonard (Rev); *b* 4 April 1926; *educ* Downside and Pembroke Coll Cambridge; Lt Rifle Bde WW II; joined the Oratory 1950; *d* 27 June 1980

1 *Prudence Mary; *b* 11 June 1916; *m* 1 July 1939 Lt-Cdr Hugo Edward Forbes Tweedie, DSC, RN (*d* 1986), er s of Adml Sir Hugh Justin Tweedie, KCB, of Wraxall House, Wraxall, Somerset, and has had:

(1) *Alexander Hugh Carmichael [Alexander Tweedie Esq, Harewood Cottage, Ugley Green, Herts CM22 6HW]; *b* 13 May 1942; *educ* Downside,

Christ's Coll Cambridge (BA Ag) and Stanford U (MA Ag Ec); *m* 1966 *Wendy, dau of Basil Henry Francis Templer, and has:

1a *Michael Hugh Quarter; *b* 1970
2a *Richard; *b* 1976
1a *Lisa Ann; *b* 1967; *m* 1997 *Guy Franklin
2a *Jessica Margaret; *b* 1968; *m* 1994 *Adrian Stone

(2) *Dominic James Drumelzier; *b* 24 July 1945; *educ* Downside; *m* 1st 1972 Maia Knoetzer; *m* 2nd 1975 Dr Judith Atkinson; *m* 3rd 19– *Shanthie Naidoo and by his 2nd w has:

1a *James; *b* 1975
2a *Hugh; *b* 1976

(3) *Julian Michael Forbes [Julian Tweedie Esq, Mombiti, Manston Rd, Sturminster Newton, Dorset DT10 1BQ]; *b* 5 May 1947; *educ* Downside; *m* 1970 *Shirley, dau of Leslie Mousley, of Machakos, Kenya, and has:

1a *Nicola; *b* 1976
2a *Zoe; *b* 1990

(4) Richard Anthony Quarter; *b* 12 Nov 1949; *d* 13 March 1951
(5) *Stephen John Oliver; *b* 1 June 1952; *educ* Downside and Leeds U (BA); *m* 1987 *Ruth Lowery and has:

1a *Owen; *b* 13 Dec 1987
2a *Benedict; *b* 6 Oct 1989
3a *Martin; *b* 21 Feb 1992
1a *Julia; *b* 26 Aug 1994

(1) *Teresa Frances [Mrs Nicolas Garratt Carp, Wonham House, Bampton, Tiverton, Devon EX16 9JZ]; *b* 14 May 1940; *m* 23 May 1964 *Nicolas Alexander Victor Garratt Carp, ACA, only s of 2nd Lt Victor Alexander Carp, RTR, by Mrs M J Nolan, of Tunbridge Wells, and has:

1a *Sarah Frances; *b* 24 April 1965
2a *Juliet Anne; *b* 6 Dec 1967
3a *Victoria Teresa; *b* 23 April 1970; *m* 1995 *Waleed Khalid Yousif Al-Hussaini
4a *Lucy Beatrice; *b* 1972

(2) *Monica Mary [Mrs Ian Newbery, 17 Braidley Rd, Bournemouth, Dorset BH2 6JX]; *b* 5 May 1954; *educ* St Mary's Convent Shaftesbury and Hull U (BA); *m* 12 Aug 1978 *Ian Richard Newbery and has:

1a *Guy Francis; *b* 31 Jan 1983
2a *John Forbes; *b* 5 March 1985

(3) *(Prudence) Margaret; *b* 16 Oct 1956; SRN; *m* 1992 *Dr Malcolm Courts
2 *Mary Octavia [The Hon Mrs Ingall, Santiani c/Campanet 29, Moscari, 07314 Mallorca, Spain]; *b* 17 April 1927; *m* 1st 24 Oct 1953 (*divorce* 1959) David Christopher Leeming, 2nd s of John Fishwick Leeming, of Bowden, Cheshire, and has:

(1) *David Tobias (Toby); *b* 19 Jan 1955; *m* 19– *Teresa
2 (cont.) The Hon Mrs Mary Leeming *m* 2nd 2 May 1959 David Tilling Wroth (*d* 1986), s of Leslie Allan Wroth, JP, of W Farm House, Collingbourne Ducis, Wilts; *m* 3rd 1989 Maj R William Ingall, DSO, 2nd/6th Gurkha Rifles (*d* 1993)
3 *Elizabeth Clare [The Hon Elizabeth Addington, Coachmans Cottage, Church St, Pewsey, Wilts SN9 5DL]; *b* 4 Aug 1928]

SIEFF OF BRIMPTON

Arms: Sable a lion rampant argent crowned with an eastern crown and holding between the forepaws two triangles interlaced and eradiated or, on a chief argent a lyre azure between two pairs of paintbrushes in saltire proper. **Crest:** A demi-lion as in the arms supporting a caduceus or. **Supporters:** Dexter, a lion holding aloft two interlaced triangles or, depressing a cornucopia replenished proper and gorged with a plain collar sable tied about with a fishing line knotted in front, pendant therefrom a grey wulf trout fly proper; sinister, an owl proper gorged with a like collar tied about with a fishing line knotted in front, pendant therefrom a red wulf trout fly proper. **Motto:** *Senza sapienza niente capire* ('Without knowledge there is no understanding'). **Creation:** B. (LP, UK) 1980.

THE BARON SIEFF OF BRIMPTON, of Brimpton, Co Berks (Sir Marcus Joseph Sieff, OBE (1944)) [The Rt Hon The Lord Sieff of Brimpton OBE, Michael House, 47 Baker St, London W1A 1DN]; *b* 2 July 1913; *educ* Manchester GS, St Paul's and Corpus Christi Coll Cambridge (BA); Col RA WW II; Marks and Spencer: dir 1954, assist md 1965–67, v-chm 1965, jt md 1967–83, dep chm 1971, chm 1972–84, pres 1984–85, hon pres 1985–, ktd 1971; chm First Internat Bank of Israel Tst Ltd 1983–, non-exec chm *The Independent* 1986–93, non-exec dir: Wicks plc 1986–93, Sock Shop Internat plc 1987–89; memb BNEC 1965–71; chm Export Ctee for Israel 1965–68; v-pres Policy Studies Inst 1975–; Tstee Nat Portrait Gallery 1986–92; Hon Pres: Anglo-Israel Chamber Commerce 1975–, Jt Israel Appeal 1984–; Hon LLD St Andrews 1983, Hon FRCS 1984, Hon Dr Babson Coll Mass. 1984, Hon DLitt Reading 1986, D Stirling U 1986, Hon Master Bench Inner Temple 1987, Hon Dr Laws Leicester 1988; author: *Don't Ask the Price* (1987), *Marcus Sieff on Management* (1990); *m* 1st 1937 (*divorce* 1947) Rosalie Fromson and has:

1 *David Daniel; *b* 1939; *educ* Repton; *m* 1962 *Jennifer, dau of H Walton of Salford Priors, Worcs, and has:

(1) *Simon Marcus; *b* 1965; *m* 14 Feb 1995 *Mrs Diana Ward
(2) *Jonathan David; *b* 1966; *educ* King's Sch Bruton; dir Global Inc (clothing co); *m* 22 Oct 1995 *Hayley, dau of Elliott Bernerd, and has:

1a *Jack Elliott; *b* 21 July 1996

BARON SIEFF OF BRIMPTON *m* 2nd 1951 (*divorce* 1953) Elsie Florence Gosen; *m* 3rd 1956 (*divorce* 1962) Brenda Mary Beith and by her has:

1 *Amanda Jane; *b* 1958

BARON SIEFF OF BRIMPTON *m* 4th 1963 Mrs Pauline Lily Moretzki (*d* 28 Feb 1997), da of Friedrich Spatz, and by her has:

2 *Daniela Frederica; *b* 1965

Lineage: *See* MARKS OF BROUGHTON, B

SILKIN

Creation: B. (UK) 4 July 1950.

Arthur Silkin [Arthur Silkin Esq, 33 Woodnook Rd, London SW16 6TZ]; *b* 20 Oct 1916; *s* 11 May 1972 but disclaimed peerage for life 18 May 1972; *educ* Dulwich and Peterhouse Cambridge (BA 1938); with Min Labour and Nat Serv 1939, F/O RAF WW II, For and Cwlth Serv 1953–57 and 1960–66 (1st Sec HC's Office Calcutta 1960–61, Dakar 1962–64, Kinshasa 1964–66), Dept Employment and Productivity 1966–76, lecturer public admin CS Coll Sunningdale 1971–76; *m* 13 Sept 1969 *Audrey, dau of Thomas Bennett, of Newark, Notts

Lineage: LEWIS SILKIN, **1st Baron Silkin**, of Dulwich, Co London (UK), so *cr* 4 July 1950, CH (1965), PC (1945); *b* 14 Nov 1889; *educ* London U; slr 1920, memb LCC 1925, MP (Lab) Peckham 1936–50, chm Town Planning Ctee LCC 1940–45, Min Town and Country Planning 1945–50; *m* 1st Aug 1915 Rosa Neft (*d* 29 Dec 1947) and had:

1 ARTHUR SILKIN, **briefly 2nd Baron Silkin**
2 SAMUEL CHARLES SILKIN, BARON SILKIN OF DULWICH (LP, UK), so *cr* 1985, PC (1974), QC (1963); *b* 6 March 1918; *educ* Dulwich and Trin Hall Cambridge (BA 1939); barrister Middle Temple 1941, Bencher 1970, Lt-Col RA WW II (despatches), memb Camberwell Met Borough Cncl 1953–59 (chm Planning Ctee 1954–58, Dep Leader 1953–57), MP (Lab) Camberwell 1964–74 and Southwark, Dulwich 1974–85, Attorney Gen 1974–79, memb Roy Commn Penal System 1965–66, Recorder Bedford 1966–71, chm Select Ctee Parly Privilege 1966–67, memb Privileges Ctee 1974–85, chm PLP's Gps Common Market and Euro Affrs 1966–70, chm Legal Affrs Ctee Consultative Assembly Cncl Europe 1966–70, EFTA Parliamentarians 1968–69, Soc Lab Lawyers 1964–71 (V-Pres 1971–88) and Br Inst Human Rights 1972–74, dep chm BPCC 1982–88, Govr Roy Bethlem and Maudsley Hosps 1970–74, Pres Alcohol Educn Centre 1972–88 and Southwark Playgrounds Tst; *m* 1st 31 Jan 1941 Elaine Violet (*d* 1984), dau of Arthur Stamp, of London; *m* 2nd *Sheila Marian [The Rt Hon The Lady Silkin, The Croft, The Green, East End, North Leigh, Oxon], dau of A E Jeal and widow of Walter Swanston, and *d* 1988, leaving by his 1st w:

(1) +CHRISTOPHER LEWIS [The Hon Christopher Silkin, New Buildings, Clyro, Herefs HR3 5SQ]; *b* 12 Sept 1947; heir presumptive; *educ* Dulwich and Chepstow Coll Art and Tech (LLB London 1974); slr 1977; by *Carolyn Theobald has:

1a *Jacob Lewis; *b* 16 Aug 1988
1a *Bethany Elaine; *b* 13 Oct 1986

(2) +Peter David Arthur; *b* 28 Dec 1952; *educ* Dulwich and Sussex U (Pres Union 1977–78, V-Pres NUS 1979–80, BA 1974, MA 1975); memb Inst Public Finance and Accountancy 1985; *m* 1st 8 June 1974 (*divorce* 19–) Frances, dau of Dr Patrick Kemp, of Woking, Surrey; *m* 2nd 1977 *—, of Addis Ababa, Ethiopia

(1) *Charlotte Ann [The Hon Mrs Josephs, Manor Grounds, Noke, Oxford OX3 9TX]; *b* 20 Nov 1944; *educ* James Allen's Girls Sch, Wheatley Coll Further Educn Oxon and Lady Spencer Churchill Coll Oxford (BEd); *m* 10 July 1965 *Francis Josephs, s of Joseph Josephs, of Beckenham, Kent, and has:

1a *Thomas Daniel; *b* 19 Dec 1972
1a *Anna Frances; *b* 15 Dec 1975

(2) *Patricia Jane [The Hon Mrs Patricia Johnson, 31 Victoria Rd, London N4 3SJ]; *b* 12 Sept 1947; *educ* James Allen's Girls Sch and Sussex U (BA 1969); *m* 1970 (*divorce* 1997) Dr Michael Johnson, PhD

3 John Ernest, PC (1966); *b* 18 March 1923; *educ* Dulwich and Trin Hall Cambridge (BA 1944, LLB 1946, MA 1949); Lt RNVR WW II; slr 1950, MP (Lab) Deptford 1963–87, a Ld Treasury (Govt Whip) 1966, Dep Ch Whip 1966, Parly Sec Treasury and Govt Ch Whip 1966–69, Min Planning and Local Gvt 1974, Min Ag, Fisheries and Food 1976–79; *m* 21 April 1950 *Rosamund John [The Hon Mrs John Silkin, 25 Westminster Gdns, Marsham St, London SW1P 4JD], actress, formerly w of Lt-Cdr Russell Lloyd, RNVR, and dau of Frederick Jones, and *d* 1987, leaving:

(1) +Rory Lewis [Rory Silkin Esq, 48 Fontarabia Rd, London SW11 5PF]; *b* 14 March 1954; *m* 30 July 1983 *Mary Vesper Shaw and has:

1a *Anna Rosamund Isobel; *b* 25 May 1990

2a *Natasha Catherine Elizabeth; *b* 24 Aug 1993

The **1st Baron** *m* 2nd 5 Oct 1948 Frieda M (*d* 24 June 1963), widow of J F Fielder Johnson and dau of Rev Canon Pilling, of Norwich; *m* 3rd 26 March 1964 Marguerite Schlageter (*d* 15 Dec 1975) and *d* 11 May 1972

SILSOE

Arms: Sa. two swords points upwards in saltire arg., pommels and hilts or, on a chief of the second a closed book gu., garnished of the third, between two torteaux. **Crest:** Issuant from a mural crown or an apple tree fructed, the trunk entwined by a serpent. **Supporters:** On either side a Kashmir goat arg., horned, winged and gorged with a mural crown or. **Motto:** *Eloquentia virtus evocant* ('Virtue by eloquence'). **Creations:** Bt. (UK) 18 Jan 1943, B. (UK) 18 Jan 1963.

THE 2ND BARON SILSOE, of Silsoe, Co Bedford, and a **Baronet** (Sir David Malcolm Trustram Eve, Bt, QC (1972) [The Rt Hon The Lord Silsoe QC, Neals Farm, Wyfold, Berks RG4 9JB]; *b* 2 May 1930; *s f* 1976; *educ* Winchester, Ch Ch Oxford (BA 1953, MA 1957) and Columbia U NY; 2nd Lt 1st Bn Roy Welch Fus 1949–50, Lt Queen Victoria's Rifles (TA) 1950–53, tstee Roy Welch Fus Regtl Museum, barrister Inner Temple 1955, Bar Auditor Inner Temple 1965–70, Bencher 1970; *m* 15 June 1963 *Bridget Min, only dau of Sir Rupert Charles Hart-Davis, publisher and author, of The Old Rectory, Marske-in-Swaledale, N Yorks, and has:

1 +SIMON RUPERT TRUSTRAM; *b* 17 April 1966

1 *Amy Janet Trustram; *b* 13 June 1964

Lineage: RICHARD EVE, of Willingale Doe, The Rodings, Essex; *b c* 1580; Yeoman of Chambers to the King; *m* Anne Gethinge and *d* 1630, leaving, with two yr sons (Adam, *b c* 1610, *m* Anne —; Seath) and two daus (Sara; Anne):

RICHARD EVE; *b c* 1608; living abroad 1629; either he or his bro Adam was f of:

RICHARD EVE, of Aythorp Roding, Essex; *b c* 1640; *m* 1st Mary — (*d* bearing twins); *m* 2nd Anne — (*d* 1701) and *d c* 1700, having by her had, with a dau:

RICHARD EVE, of Aythorp Roding; *b* 12 Dec 1664; had:

RICHARD EVE, of Aythorp Roding; *b* 1696; *m* 30 April 1732 Esther Lee (*d* 1 June 1751) and *d* 12 Nov 1747, leaving, with a yr s (Charles, of Aythorp Roding, *b* 5 Feb 1737, *m* 1761 Phoebe Knight (*d* 13 Aug 1779) and had issue) and a dau (Esther, *b* 17 March 1734, *m* 1753 Adam Eve and had issue):

RICHARD EVE, of Aythorp Roding and later Berners/Bundish Hall, Berners Roding, Essex; *b* 18 March 1733; *m* 1st 22 Feb 1753 Mary Boltwood; *m* 2nd 15 July 1758 Elizabeth (*d* 16 Oct 1794), widow of — Clift, and *d* 11 Jan 1794, having by her had two sons (Henry, of Berners Hall and Chigwell Row, Essex, *b* 24 Feb 1760, *m* 31 Oct 1781 Mary Long (*d* 17 June 1837) and *d* 15 Feb 1833, leaving issue; William, of Shelley Hall, Essex, *b* 1765, *m* 6 Dec 1788 Mary Scruby and had issue) and by his 1st w, with two sons (Charles, of Nettleswell Bury and Diggins Fyfield, Rodings, *b* 21 Jan 1755, *m* 4 Feb 1778 Sarah Clift, of Berners Roding, and had issue; Richard, *b* 2 May 1756, *d* an infant):

RICHARD EVE, of Lanark Farm, Weston, Herts, and later Tillingham Hall, Childerditch, Essex; *b* 10 June 1757; regained the Manor of Keeres (lost by the EVEs under the Commonwealth); *m* 1st 1781 Mary Jeeves; *m* 2nd 27 Oct 1785 Hannah Foster (*d* 1816), of Wymondly, Herts, and *d* 1803, having by her had:

1 RICHARD

2 Henry Weston, of Maldon; *b* 1790; *m* 8 Nov 1834 Mary Douglas Thorp (*d* 9 Sept 1875) and *d* 26 Dec 1854, leaving issue

3 Charles; *b* 1792

4 William, of Bundish Hall, Berners Roding; *b* 1793; *m* Mary Chaplin (*d* 24 Feb 1873) and *d* 10 Feb 1853, leaving three daus

1 Mary; *b* 1787; *m* 1st 1825 Frederick Gostelow, of Clophill; *m* 2nd Henry Pestell and *d* 1857

2 Hannah; *b* 1789; *m* 1st William Eve, of Berners Hall and Aythorp Roding, and had issue; *m* 2nd Stephen Algar Green and *d* 21 May 1863

3 Lydia; *b* 1795; *m* Robert Eve, of Bundish Hall, and *d* 25 Aug 1846, leaving issue

The est s,

RICHARD EVE, of West End Farm, Silsoe, Beds; *b* 3 Aug 1788; Churchwarden Silsoe 70 years; *m* 1st 1807 Sarah Caton (*d* 1817), niece of West End Farm's previous tenant, and had:

1 Richard (Rev); *b* 8 March 1810; Vicar Beauchamp Roding; had issue

2 Charles, of Newport Pagnell, Bucks; *b* 18 March 1811; had issue

3 Henry Thomas, of Maldon; *b* 14 Dec 1814; *m* Mary D'eath Burls (*d* 28 April 1895) and had issue

1 Charlotte Caton; *b* 15 June 1808; *m* 1833 William Langford

2 Hannah Sarah; *b* 5 Jan 1813; *m* 22 June 1836 John Tapp

3 Mary Ann; *b* 5 Nov 1816; *m* -

4 Sarah; *b* 8 July 1818; *m* 11 Oct 1854 Samuel Knight

RICHARD EVE *m* 2nd 11 Sept 1828 Mary (*d* 30 May 1885), dau of John Trustram, of Shillington, Beds, and *d* 6 Nov 1885, having by her had:

4 JOHN RICHARD

5 William; *b* 15 March 1835; FSI; *m* 2 July 1861 Caroline Hannah Todd (*d* 31 Jan 1924) and *d* 13 Feb 1916, leaving issue

5 Eliza; *b* 19 Aug 1832; *m* 18– —

The 4th s,

JOHN RICHARD EVE, of Elmhurst, Bedford; *b* 6 July 1833; *m* 5 Jan 1859 Frederica Somers (*d* 5 March 1915) and *d* 15 Aug 1902, having had:

1 Frederick Somers; *b* 28 April 1861; *m* 1 June 1895 Maude Davies and *d* April 1900

2 Arthur Stewart, CBE; *b* 22 Nov 1862; Col, Dean Faculties McGill U Montreal, FRS; *m* 22 April 1905 Elizabeth Brooks, of Montreal, and *d* 24 March 1948

3 HERBERT TRUSTRAM (Sir)

4 Percy Somers; *b* 23 Feb 1869; *d* 17 June 1870

5 Frank Cecil; *b* 15 Feb 1871; MD; *m* 3 June 1911 Sally Byers and *d* 7 Dec 1952

6 Charles Gerald; *b* 9 Dec 1872; PPRICS; *d* 29 Oct 1946

1 Emily; *b* 8 Feb 1860; *m* 1st 6 Aug 1885 J H Eagles and had issue; *m* 2nd 1894 Dr Llewellyn Williams

The 3rd s,

Sir HERBERT TRUSTRAM EVE, KBE (1918), of Silsoe, Beds, and later Earls Court; *b* 4 June 1865; *educ* Bedford Sch; Maj 5th Bn Vol Beds Regt, chm Forage Ctee War Dept WW I, FSI, FAI; *m* 6 April 1893 Fanny Jean, JP (*d* 1 Feb 1934 aged 71), est dau of Rev John Robert Turing (*see* TURING, Bt), and had:

1 (ARTHUR) MALCOLM TRUSTRAM, **1st Baron**

2 John Douglas Trustram; *b* 6 Dec 1897; *educ* Winchester; Maj Herts Regt WW I 1916–19, re-employed WW II 1939–42, FLAS, FAI, PRICS 1960–61; *m* 1st 11 Dec 1924 (*divorce* 1933) Hon Nancy Atkin, 4th dau of Baron Atkin, PC (LP, *see* 1940 edn); *m* 2nd 7 Sept 1934 Sheila (*m* 2nd Jimmy Salter and *d* 27 Oct 1995), yr dau of Allister Macmillan, FRGS, FRSA, of Thorpeness, Suffolk, and Johannesburg, and by her had:

(1) *(Douglas) John Richard Trustram; *b* 30 April 1936; *educ* Winchester; FRICS, QALAS, FAI; *m* 5 May 1961 *Pipyn Elizabeth, er dau of Reginald Beale, of Lower House Farm, Nantyderry, Abergavenny, and has:

1a *Charles Edward; *b* 17 May 1962

2a *(Anthony) David; *b* 8 Oct 1963; *m* 19– *Jayne — and has:

1b *Sarah Elizabeth; *b* 2 Aug 1996

1a *Charlotte Louise; *b* 24 June 1968

(2) *William (Bill) Peter Trustram; *b* 25 June 1943; *educ* Winchester and Lausanne Hotel Sch; hotelier

3 (Raymond) Alister Trustram, CBE (1945); *b* 14 Jan 1900; *educ* Winchester and RMC Sandhurst; WW II: CO Rifle Depot and 11th Bn KRRC 1941–42, on Staff 25 Corps 1943 and BML (Greece), Brig 1943, ret 1955, Regtl Sec KRRC 1958–68; *m* 22 Oct 1925 Margaret Florence, yst dau of Donald Nicoll, of Martyr Worthy, Hants, and *d* 15 March 1982, having had:

(1) Patrick Raymond Trustram; *b* 31 Jan 1928; *d* 5 April 1929

(2) *(John) Roy Trustram [Maj Roy Trustram Eve, Kellinghams, Waltham St Lawrence, Berks RG10 0JJ]; *b* 19 Dec 1931; *educ* Winchester and RMA Sandhurst; 2nd Lt KRRC 1952, Capt and Adjt Kenya Regt (TF) 1955–58, Adj 1st Bn KRRC 1958–59, Queen's Roy Rifles (TA) and GSO(3) 56th Inf Bde 1962, Maj 1963, DAA&QMG 1964–66, 2i/c 5th (T) Bn RGJ 1967–69; md William Grant and Sons (Standfast) 1966–89, md: Business in the Community 1989–92, The Civic Tst 1992–97, High Sheriff Berks 1997–98, OStJ 1963; *m* 15 Dec 1962 *Mary Alice, only dau of Sir Ian Fraser, DSO, OBE, DL, MD, MCh, DSc, FRCS (Eng), FRCSI, FRCS (Ed), FACS, of Belfast, and has:

1a *James Luke; *b* 9 July 1968

2a *Ian Patrick; *b* 1 Sept 1972

1a *Catherine Margaret; *b* 11 April 1965; *m* 18 April 1998 *Donald Glenn Trotman, s of Jack Trotman, of Angmering, W Sussex

(3) *Alexander (Alec) James Trustram; *b* 3 June 1937; *educ* Stowe; 2nd Lt KRRC 1955–57, Lt Queen's Westminster Rifles, Capt 1961, Queen's Roy Rifles 1967, 5th Bn RGJ, memb London Stock Exchange, ptnr Laurie Milbank & Co; *m* 22 Sept 1967 *(Evelyn) Belinda, yr dau of David Maurice Dean, VRD, MB, BS, MRCS, LRCP, of King's Lynn, Norfolk, and has:

1a *Toby Alexander; *b* 4 May 1971

1a *Annabel Victoria; *b* 11 Feb 1969

2a *Emily Sarah; *b* 5 Aug 1972

1 Jean Dorothy; *b* 10 April 1896; *m* 1st 24 July 1919 Antony Gibbons Grinling, s of Gibbons Grinling, of Hampstead, and had a s; *m* 2nd 2 Aug 1933 John Gore Barrow, s of Percy Herbert Aggett Barrow, of Hollist House, Midhurst, Sussex, and *d* 1 July 1954, leaving a s by him

2 Joan Christine Turing; *b* 3 May 1904; *d* 15 Aug 1905

Sir HERBERT *d* 11 Nov 1936; his est s,

Sir (Arthur) Malcolm Trustram Eve, 1st Bt, and **1st Baron Silsoe**, of Silsoe, Co Bedford (both UK), so *cr* 18 Jan 1943 and 18 Jan 1963 respectively, GBE (1950), MC, TD and 3 clasps, KC (1935); *b* 8 April 1894; *educ* Winchester and Ch Ch

Oxford (BA 1919, MA 1927); barrister Inner Temple 1919, Bencher 1942, Reader 1965, Treas 1966; Brig TA WW I, WW II with 53rd (Welsh) Div, chm: Air Tport Licensing Authority 1938–39, War Damage Commn 1941–49, Building Apprenticeship Trng Cncl 1943–47, Local Govt Boundary Commn 1945–49, War Works Commn 1945–49, Centl Land Bd 1947–49, St George's Hosp Med Sch 1948–54, St George's Hosp 1952–54, Burnham Ctees on Teachers' Salaries 1950–53, Cncl on Police Salaries 1951, Ld Mayor's Nat Flood and Tempest Distress Fund 1953, Road Haulage Disposal Bd 1953–56, Electoral Boundaries Commn Mauritius 1957, Fiji Sugar Inquiry Commn 1961; memb Church Assembly 1952–57, 3rd Church Estates Commr 1952–54, 1st Church Estates Commr 1954–69, 1st Crown Estates Commr 1954–62, dir: Yorkshire Insur 1949–66, New River Co 1954–70; hon memb: RICS, Chartered Auctioneers and Estate Agents Inst; indep chm Cement Makers' Fedn 1951–70, Pres W European Cement Assoc 1952–70, Govr Peabody Tst 1957–65, Commr Fiji Coconut Industry Inquiry 1963, Gentleman Usher Purple Rod Order Br Empire 1960–69, Hon V-Pres Town Planning Inst, Hon Fell: Inst Builders, Inst Municipal Treasurers and Accountants; m 1st 23 Aug 1927 Marguerite (d 25 Dec 1945), yst dau of Sir Augustus Meredith Nanton, of Winnipeg, Canada, and had:

1 DAVID MALCOLM TRUSTRAM EVE, **2nd and present Baron Silsoe**

2 +Peter Nanton Trustram (twin), OBE (1978) [Col The Hon Peter Trustram Eve OBE, Barton End Hall, Nailsworth, Glos GL6 0QQ; Flat D, 163 Pavilion Rd, London SW1]; b 2 May 1930; educ Winchester and Ch Ch Oxford (BA 1953, MA 1960); 2nd Lt Roy Welch Fus 1949–50, Lt Queen Victoria's Rifles (TA) 1950–53, Lt RGJ 1953, Capt 1954, Lt-Col RGJ 1973, Col (ret), US Armed Forces Staff Coll 1972, Br Army Staff Washington 1972–73, cdg offr Oxford U OTC 1973–75, Def and Mil Attaché Brussels 1980–83; gen manager Churchill Hosp, Oxford, 1985–88; m 29 April 1961 *Petronilla Letiere Sheldon, dau of Jannion Steele Elliott, of Dowles Manor, Bewdley, Worcs, and has:

(1) +Richard Malcolm Jannion Trustram; b 9 March 1963; m 1988 *(Albinia) Julia, er dau of Maj Christopher Wyndham Diggle (see THOMPSON, Bt, of Park Gate), and has:

1a +Alexander Christopher Peter Trustram; b 1993

2a +James Arthur Richard Trustram; b 15 May 1996

(2) +Nicholas Dominic Peter Trustram; b 14 Nov 1965

The **1st Baron** m 2nd 31 Oct 1946 Margaret Elizabeth (Maisie) (d 1993), yst dau of Henry Wallace Robertson, of Milbrae, Ayton, Berwicks, and d 3 Dec 1976

SIMEON

Arms: Per fess sa. and or a pale counterchanged, in chief an ermine-spot of the first between two trefoils slipped of the second and in base a like trefoil between two like ermine spots. **Crest:** A fox passant regardant ppr., in the mouth a trefoil slipped vert. **Supporters:** Dexter, a fox regardant ppr., in the mouth a trefoil slipped vert; sinister, a lion gu. ducally crowned or. **Mottoes:** Serviendo ('By serving'), Nec temere, nec timide ('Neither rashly nor timidly'). **Creation:** Bt. (UK) 22 May 1815.

SIR JOHN EDMUND BARRINGTON SIMEON, 7TH BT, of Grazeley, Berks [Sir John Simeon Bt, c/o Jerome & Co, 98 High St, Newport, IoW PO30 1BD]; b 1 March 1911; s f 1957; educ Eton and Ch Ch Oxford; F/Lt RAF WW II 1939–43 (invalided), civ serv Min Ag 1943–51 and BC Dept Social Welfare 1951–75; m 10 July 1937 *Anne Robina Mary, er dau of Hamilton Dean, and has:

1 +RICHARD EDMUND BARRINGTON [Prof Richard Simeon, 20 Biggar Ave, Toronto, Ontario M6H 2N4, Canada]; b 2 March 1943; educ St George's Sch Vancouver, BC U (BA) and Yale (MA 1966, PhD 1968); Assist Prof Political Studies Queen's U Kingston Ontario 1968–, Prof Political Sci and Law Toronto U, Dir Inst Intergovernmental Rels 1976–83 and Sch Public Admin 1986–90, V-Chm Ontario Law Reform Commn 1989–; m 1st 6 Aug 1966 (divorce 1989) Agnes Joan, only dau of George Frederick Weld, of W Vancouver; m 2nd 1993 *Maryetta Cheney and by his 1st w has:

(1) +Stephen George Barrington; b 29 Oct 1970

(1) *Rachel Elizabeth; b 1973

1 *Anne Emily Philippa [Mrs Nigel Gow, 6129 Highbury, Vancouver, BC, Canada]; b 18 Oct 1938; m 26 May 1962 *Nigel Leonard Harper Gow, only s of Alan Harper Gow, of The Plough, Oddington, Glos, and has:

(1) *Ian Harper; b 18 Jan 1968

(1) *Lisa Harper; b 15 July 1965

2 *Sara Alexandra [Mrs Christopher Foster, 134 Caprice Heights, Salt Spring Island, Canada]; b 5 Nov 1946; m 1st 1967 (divorce 1994) Anthony John Williams; m 2nd 7 Dec 1996 *Christopher John Foster, late of Headcorn, Kent, and by her 1st husb has:

(1) *Derek John; b 1973

(2) *Trevor Michael; b 1975

(1) *Adria Elizabeth; b 1971

Lineage: Sir John Simeon, **1st Bt** (UK), so cr 22 May 1815; MP, Sr Master Chancery; m Rebecca (d 21 Oct 1830), est dau of John Cornwall, of Hendon House, Middx, and had:

1 RICHARD GODIN (Sir), **2nd Bt**

2 Edward, of Carshalton House, Surrey; b 1788; m 1st Sept 1814 Sophia Charlotte, 2nd dau of Philip Lybbe Powys, of Hardwicke House, Oxon; and m 2nd 22 Sept 1836 Eliza, widow of Philip Thomas Wykeham, of Tythrop, Oxon, and dau of Fiennes WYKEHAM later WYKEHAM-MARTIN (see CORNWALLIS, B), and dsp 16 Oct 1851

3 Charles; b 7 July 1791; R-Adml; m 5 July 1821 Frances (d 8 Dec 1882), dau of Capt Thomas Woore, and d 12 Nov 1858, leaving, with a dau (d unm):

(1) Charles; b 25 July 1822; m Madeline Sophia Emma, dau of Ernest Noltz, and had three daus

(2) Richard Godin; b 3 July 1823; Lt-Col Bengal Cav; m 11 Oct 1847 Charlotte, dau of Lt-Col William Henry Earle, HEICS, and d 1 July 1867, leaving:

1a John Edward; b 7 June 1851; m 12 June 1871 Mary, dau of Maj Macpherson

2a Charles; b 14 Feb 1860

1a Charlotte Frances; m 12 Dec 1867 R J Johnson and d 18 Sept 1872, leaving issue

2a Eliza Jane; m 15 Feb 1871 Lt-Col Alfred Edward Garnault

3a Emily Sophia

4a Gertrude

(3) Edward; b Dec 1824; Lt-Col RA; m 1860 Lavinia (d 1919), dau of Maj Jeffery Amherst Willows, and d 11 July 1898, having had:

1a Edward Archibald; b 1860; MRCS, LRCP; m 1888 Rose Beaumont (d 18 Nov 1933), dau of Charles Eddowes, MRCS, and d 15 Dec 1930, leaving:

1b Charles Edward Barrington (Sir), KBE (1945), CB (1943); b 24 Dec 1889; RN: served WWs I and II 1939–45 (despatches), Dir Naval Ordnance Admlty 1936–39, cmded HMS Renown 1939–41, ADC to HM GEORGE VI 1940, Dep Controller Admlty 1941–46, V-Adml, Gd Offr Orange Nassau Netherlands; m 31 July 1918 Gladys (d 1983), 3rd dau of Benjamin Arkle, of Spital, Cheshire, and d 16 Nov 1955, having had:

1c John Edward; b 18 Jan 1921; Lt Rifle Bde WW II; ka Libya 28 May 1942

2c +(Hugh) Michael [Michael Simeon, 3 Westview Lane, S Norwark, CT 06854, USA]; b 1 Nov 1926; educ RNC Dartmouth and Harvard (MBA 1965); RN WW II; m 16 April 1966 *Ilona-Maria, dau of Prof Dr Med Gustav Schimert, of Munich, and has:

1d +George Edward; b 13 Feb 1969

2d +John David; b 15 June 1971

1d *Diana Maria; b 16 April 1967; m 3 July 1995 *Robert John Spadoni

3c +William Martin [William Simeon Esq, Lot 49, Condor Dve, Nikenbah, 4655 Qld, Australia]; b 19 Aug 1936; Rifle Bde; m 29 April 1959 (divorce 1965) Doreen Mary Wren; m 2nd 1971 *Jane Naik and by her has:

1d *Kathryn Mary Anne; b 1972

2d *Samantha Mervena; b 1974

1c Joan Denise; b 1919; m 4 Sept 1947 Reginald James Pringle, MBE, ICS (d 1980), yr s of Sir James (Scott) Pringle, KCB, OBE, and d 1996, leaving:

1d *James Edward; b 20 Jan 1949; educ Cambridge (MA, PhD); astronomer; m 1974 *Alison May, dau of Richard Leonard Sturge, of Saffron Walden, Essex, and has:

1e *Edmund Richard James; b 1980

2e *Christopher Charles Theodore; b 1983

2d *Reginald Denys; b 20 Sept 1951; educ Southampton U (BA), DPhil Oxon; historian and archaeologist, FSA

3d *Richard Charles; b 9 March 1954; educ York U (BA), MSc London Business Sch; m 1980 *Jeanine Ghislaine, dau of George Romarin, of Falisole, Belgium

1d *Anne Denise; b 5 Sept 1958; m 1986 *Andrew Charles Ellis, only s of Charles Matthew Ellis, of Abbeywood, London

2c *Marguerite Gladys [Mrs Peter Adams, 3 Farmhill Rd, Waltham Abbey, Essex EN9 1NE]; b 1922; 3rd Offr WRNS WW II; m 9 March 1946 Maj Peter Rainier Adams, RA, er s of Lt-Col Henry Rainier Adams, DSO, of Hythe, Kent, and has:

1d *John Rainier; b 4 Aug 1947; flautist

2d *Hugh Robert; b 14 Jan 1949; educ Chingford High Sch; engr

3d *Charles David; b 8 March 1951; educ Chingford High Sch and Bristol U

3c *Josephine Osyth [Mrs Thomas Kennedy, Hill House, Berecourt Rd, Pangbourne, Berks RG8 8JU]; b 23 July 1932; m 3 Aug 1956 *Lt-Cdr Thomas David Alexander Kennedy, RN, yr s of S D Kennedy, of Bushey, Herts, and has:

1d *Martin Charles; b 20 Jan 1958; m 1985 *Suzanne Jayne, er dau of Ronald Charles Brown, of Ayr, and has:

1e *Peter Charles; b 1997

1e *Lucy Joanne; b 1994

2d *Ian David; b 25 Jan 1965

1d *Fiona Osyth; b 22 Sept 1960; m 1st (divorce 1988) Dominic James Shaw and has:

1e *Katurah Osyth; b 1987

1d (cont.) Mrs Fiona Shaw m 2nd 1989 (divorce 1997) Hugh Anstruther Rance and by him has:

2e *Eleanor Yaiah Tara; b 1990

3e *Saskia Leah Channah; b 1992

4e *Demelza Chloe-Mae; b 1995

2a George Ernest, of Auckland, NZ; b 1862

3a Herbert Richard; b 1865; m 1892 Effie Dean Florence (d 1938), dau of Walter Moss, of Ashburton, NZ, and d 1926, leaving:

1b Richard Walter Ernest; b 1895

2b Percival Edward Ralph; b 1898

1b Dorothy Florence Marguerite; b 1896; m 1922 Harold Stevenson, of Gisborne, NZ, and had issue

2b Beatrice Lavinia Amy; b 1900; m 1927 Edward Franklin Jones and had issue

(4) Thomas Woore, RN; b 18 Dec 1834; m 20 Dec 1868 Matilda, 2nd dau of Edward Kemp, of Bury St Edmunds, and dsp

(5) Henry Scott; b 16 March 1836; Capt 27th Regt; m 3 Dec 1861 Isabel Maria (d 31 May 1912), dau of Daniel Chambers Macreight, of Hauteville, Jersey, and d 2 April 1897

(6) John; b 22 Jan 1841; Lt 54th Regt; had issue

(7) Albert; b 26 Nov 1841; Lt 40th Regt; had issue

(1) Catherine Thomasine; m Capt Jean Charles Edouard Pigeard, Hon CB, French Naval Attaché UK, and d 1911

(2) Harriet; m April 1849 Maj James Le Quesne and had issue

(3) Letitia; m 5 July 1869 Henry Charles Hamilton, CSI (see HAMILTON, Bt, of Silvertonhill), and dsp 28 June 1917

(4) Augusta Wilhelmina; m 1st 1849 Giffard Nicholas le Quesne (d 30 Jan 1877), Cdr Roy Jersey Artillery, and had issue; m 2nd 12 Jan 1880 Maj Thomas Mayhew, RA, and d 12 March 1907

(5) Eliza; m 14 Jan 1862 Rev Charles Elrington McKay, Vicar Laracor, and had issue. He d 1906

1 Eleanora Elizabeth; m Col Webber Smith, RA

2 Charlotte; m Thomas Browne Evans, of Tuddenham, Norfolk, and d 4 Sept 1860

3 Harriet; m July 1814 Sir Frederick Francis Baker, 2nd Bt, of Loventor, Devon, and d 15 Nov 1845, leaving issue (see BAKER-WILBRAHAM, Bt)

Sir JOHN d 4 Feb 1824; his est s,

Sir Richard Godin Simeon, 2nd Bt; b 21 May 1784; m 8 April 1813 Louisa Edith (d 12 April 1847), est dau and heiress of Sir Fitzwilliam Barrington, 10th Bt, of Barrington Hall, Essex, and Swainston, IoW (see 1833 edn), and had, with another dau (d unm):

1 JOHN (Sir), **3rd Bt**

2 Charles, of Hursley, Winchester; b 9 Dec 1816; Capt 75th Regt; m 5 May 1842 Sarah Jane (d 3 April 1903), only child of Philip Williams, KC, Recorder Winchester, and d 29 May 1867, having had, with another s (d young) and five daus (d unm):

(1) Philip Barrington (Rev); b 12 Dec 1845; educ Ch Ch Oxford (MA 1871); MA Cape U 1892, Vicar Milverton Warwicks 1913–23; m 31 Aug 1899 Lucy Ann (d 6 April 1929), dau of John William Woodcock, Bombay CS, and d 9 Dec 1926

(2) Algernon Barrington (Rev); b 20 Feb 1847; educ Ch Ch Oxford (MA 1872); Rector Bigbury Devon 1893–1904 and Yattendon Berks 1904–25, Warden St Edward's Sch Oxford 1869–92; m 16 Jan 1883 Beatrice Emma (d 17 May 1949), dau of Rev Frederick Paget Wilkinson (see CAMPBELL-ORDE, Bt), and d 12 March 1928, leaving:

1a Lionel Barrington; b 1 March 1885; 2nd Lt HLI; m 1st 13 May 1909 (divorce 1928) Dorothy, yr dau of James Henry Breach, MRCS, of Yattendon, and had:

1b Richard Charles Barrington; b 26 Feb 1914; engr; d 10 Dec 1966

1b *Elizabeth Audrey Barrington; b 19 Oct 1910; m 1st 6 July 1948 George Ross Bancroft (d 1961); m 2nd 22 Aug 1966 *Jason Lucas, writer

2b Sheila Rosemary Barrington; b 17 Dec 1915; d 13 Aug 1916

1a (cont.) Lionel Simeon m 2nd 1928 Dorothy Ashton (d 14 June 1959), er dau of James Crofts Ingram, of Chailey, Sussex, and d 13 Aug 1939

2a Charles; b 11 May 1886; d 15 Nov 1912

1a Violet Barrington; b 30 Nov 1883; Carmelite nun; d 7 April 1966

2a Rosalind Barrington; b 24 April 1887; d unm June 1963

3a Mary Felicia Barrington; b 30 April 1891; d unm

(3) Geoffrey Barrington (Rev); b 9 March 1848; MA Oxon 1874; Vicar Dunster, Somerset, Rector Littleham, Devon; m 10 Feb 1886 Janetta Nina (d Oct 1931), dau of Rev Robert Sutton (see SUTTON, Bt), and d 2 March 1906, leaving:

1a Geoffrey Nelthorpe; b 20 April 1888, Imp Forest Serv; m 11 Aug 1919 Henrietta Mary Collingwood (d 1989), er dau of Rev William Collingwood Carter, and d 27 Dec 1923, leaving:

1b +Geoffrey John Barrington [Lt-Cdr Geoffrey Simeon RN, Maple House, Chilbolton, Hants SO20 6BQ]; b 2 Aug 1923; FRICS; m 20 March 1954 *Elizabeth Frances Richenda, dau of Rev Robert Clifford Rham, BD, AKC, of Feock, Cornwall, and has:

1c +Charles Richard Barrington; b 11 May 1958; educ Sherborne

1c *Sarah Richenda Barrington; b 18 Jan 1956

2c *Elizabeth Anne Barrington [Mrs Anthony Harrison, 11 Chilton Candover, Alresford, Hants SO24 9TX]; b 9 May 1960; m 25 April 1987 *Anthony George Harrison, s of G G Harrison, of St Ives, Cornwall, and has:

1d *George Geoffrey; b 22 June 1988

2d *Robert William; b 25 Feb 1990

1b Janetta Mary Barrington; b 22 July 1920; WAAF WW II; m 31 Aug 1946 Cdr John Pemberton Mosse, DSC, RN, s of Capt Harry Tylden Mosse, RN, of Bourne Tap, Aldington, Kent, and d 10 April 1986, leaving:

1c *Peter John [Cdr Peter Mosse RN, Lower Peak, Warnford, Hants SO2 1LA]; b 21 June 1947; educ Sherborne and RNC Dartmouth; Cdr RN; m 1975 *Sarah Francesca Macphail and has:

1d *Patrick Tylden Rutherford; b 9 Jan 1977

2d *Andrew David b 1979

3d *Simon Rupert b 1981

1d *Georgina Elaine b 1981

2c *Martin Barrington [Martin Mosse Esq, Drogo, 1 Grenfield Ct, Emsworth, Hants PO10 7SA]; b 15 May 1950; educ Sherborne and New Coll Oxford (BA 1974); m 1988 *Barbara Corey

1a Joan Barrington; b 26 July 1890; d unm 4 May 1954

2a Eleanor Blachford; b 21 April 1892, d unm 25 Sept 1950

(4) Lionel Barrington; b 6 Nov 1852; Lt RN, engr PWD India 1876–96; m 3 Aug 1876 Elizabeth (d 31 July 1929), dau of Sir John Wither Awdry, QC, of Notton, Wilts, and d 30 Aug 1896, leaving, with another s (d an infant) and two daus (d unm):

1a Charles John; b 6 July 1878; m 7 Sept 1910 Elinor Yorke (d 7 Sept 1940), dau of Gen Charles King, of Milwaukee, and d 2 Nov 1946, leaving:

1b *Elizabeth [Mrs Richard Copleston, 34 Old Towne Rd, Cheshire, CT 06410, USA]; b 4 Aug 1917; m 8 July 1948 *Maj Richard Guillemard Copleston, RE, s of W E Copleston, of Wincanton, Somerset

1a Edith Frances; b 2 Oct 1882; d unm 30 May 1965

2a Margaret Alice; b 15 Dec 1885; d unm 24 Nov 1961

3a Catherine Isabel; b 23 Sept 1887; m 6 Aug 1914 Maj Alfred Russel Marshall, DSO, MC, MA, RE (SR), and d 11 Dec 1951, leaving issue

4a Mary Leonora; b 24 April 1891; d unm 13 Jan 1969

(5) Hugh Barrington (Rev); b 12 Jan 1858; educ Keble Coll Oxford (MA); Rector Edburton, Sussex; m 13 May 1886 Beatrice (d 24 July 1930), yst dau of Henry Anthony Littledale, of Bolton Hall, Yorks, and d 21 Jan 1941, leaving:

1a Guy Barrington; b 19 Jan 1887; educ Ch Ch Oxford (MA); m 10 April 1912 Mary Mitford (d 19 Nov 1962), dau of James Wilmot Bowker, Assist Commr Basutoland, and d 19 Jan 1917

1a Beatrice Edith; b 6 July 1888; nun (Sister Beatrice, Community of the Resurrection)

2a Mildred Eleanor; b 8 May 1890; m 11 Feb 1914 Geoffrey Courthope Bosanquet , yr s of Sir Frederick Albert Bosanquet, KC, and had issue. He d 27 Dec 1971

(1) Emma Mary; b 28 Oct 1856; m 4 Sept 1883 Rt Rev Alfred Willis, DD, Bp Honolulu, and d 7 Feb 1933. He d 14 Nov 1920

(2) Mabel Selina; b 26 Aug 1860; m 30 Dec 1879 Rev Herbert Andrew Dalton, DD, Headmaster Felsted, and d 11 Jan 1935, leaving issue. He d 18 May 1928

3 Cornwall; b 5 Feb 1820; barrister Lincoln's Inn; m 1 Jan 1861 Mary (d 13 July 1921), dau of Thomas Browne Evans, of N Tuddenham, Norfolk, and Dene, Oxon, and d 18 March 1880, having had, with two other sons (d young) and two daus (d unm):

(1) Perceval Barrington; b 22 Sept 1862; educ Marlborough; m 3 Nov 1885 Annie Caroline (d 23 April 1929), dau of Henry Harrison, MRCS (Eng), and d 12 Oct 1951, leaving:

1a Cornwall Barrington ; b 19 Sept 1889; educ King's Canterbury and Trin Coll Oxford (BA 1913); Capt Roy Mon RE (SR) WW I (despatches); m 1st 18 July 1928 (divorce 1947) Ellaline Margery Mary (d 11 Aug 1966), er dau of Arnold le Poer Power, of Clonmel, Co Tipperary, and had:

1b +John Power Barrington, OBE (1978) [John Simeon Esq OBE, 4 Cliff Rd, Dovercourt, Essex CO12 3PP]; b 15 Nov 1929; educ Beaumont and RMA Sandhurst; late Dip serv; 1st Sec Colombo 1967, Bonn 1968–70, Port of Spain 1970–73 (Actg HC), FCO 1973–75, Dep HC and Head Post Ibadan Nigeria 1975–79 (counsellor 1978), Consul Gen: Berlin 1979–81 and Hamburg 1981–84; m 1st 16 Sept 1951 (divorce 1955) Margaretta Valborg Johanna, only dau of Erik Ahlstrom, of Norrmark, Finland; m 2nd 20 Oct 1966 Norma Fill (d 16 Dec 1969), er dau of Capt Norman Herbert Dopson, RA, of Nottingham; m 3rd 1970 *Carina Renate Elisabeth, dau of Michael Schüller, of Bonn, and by his 2nd w has:

1c +Charles John Barrington [Charles Simeon Esq, 15 Varna Rd, London SW6 7LB]; b 1 May 1967; educ King's Canterbury; m 19 July 1997 *Sarah Catherine, yr dau of David Keith Youngman, of Chipstead, Surrey

1b Ann Ella Mary; b 10 Feb 1931; m 1st 1961 (divorce 1984) Bryan Reginald Baxter; m 2nd 1984 *S/Ldr Terence William Devey Smith, RAF (ret), and d 20 June 1987, leaving by her 1st husb:

1c *Robert Bryan; b 1962; m 1988 *Jacqueline, dau of John Rupert Godfrey, of Monbulk, Victoria, Australia, and has:

1d *Jack Godfrey; b 1989

2d *Timothy Reginald; b 1964; BA

1a (cont.) Cornwall Simeon m 2nd 23 July 1947 Violet, MBE (1920) (d 3 Aug 1979), widow of Lt-Col Neal William Douglas-Matheson, DSO and bar, MC, RE, and only dau of Algernon Hodson, of Hove, and d 31 March 1957

1a Ella Dorothea Barrington; b 3 Aug 1886; d unm 23 April 1966

(2) John Pole (Rev); b 30 Sept 1872; educ Wellington and Selwyn Coll Cambridge (BA 1902, MA 1906); Vicar Tolleshunt D'Arcy, Essex, served Boer War and WW I (despatches); m 17 Sept 1908 Dorothy (d 11 Nov 1955), dau of Rev Sidney Benjamin Field, and d 2 June 1951, leaving:

1a *Joan Edith Barrington; b 24 June 1909; m 1st 25 Nov 1938 (divorce 1945) Richard William Barnes Clarke; m 2nd 1945 Wenzel Jaksch (d 27 Nov 1966) and by him has:

1b *George Barrington; b 10 Dec 1945; m 1974 *Carmen Julia, dau of Don Constantino Torres, of Colombia, and has:

1c *David Wenzel; b 1977

1c *Sandra Mary; b 1978

1b *Mary Dorothy Plantagenet; b 18 Nov 1947; m 1981 *Uwe Grodd, s of Reinhold Grodd, of Stuttgart, and has:

1c *Sebastian Wenzel; b 1981

(1) Evelyn Mary; *m* 7 Oct 1905 Maurice Simeon McKay, er s of Rev Charles Elrington McKay (*see* above), and *d* 1 Nov 1952. He *d* 25 June 1939

1 Jane Elizabeth; *m* June 1846 Rev Robert Sumner, 3rd s of Rt Rev Charles Richard Sumner, DD, Bp Winchester, and *d* 23 April 1851, leaving issue

Sir RICHARD *d* 4 Jan 1854; his est s,

Sir John Simeon, 3rd Bt; *b* 5 Feb 1815; MP IOW; *m* 1st 26 Nov 1840 Jane Maria (*d* 24 Aug 1860), only dau of Sir Frederick Francis Baker, 2nd Bt (*see* BAKER WILBRAHAM, Bt), and had, with another s (*d* an infant) and three daus (*d* unm):

1 **Sir John Stephen Barrington Simeon, 4th Bt,** JP (Hants), DL (IoW); *b* 31 Aug 1850; Rifle Bde, Hon Col Hants RGA, CA IoW, MP Southampton 1895–1906; *m* 18 June 1872 Isabella Mary (*d* 4 Nov 1936), only child of Hon Ralph Heneage Dutton (*see* 1970 edn SHERBORNE, B), and *dsp* 26 April 1909

2 EDMUND CHARLES (Sir), **5th Bt**

3 Stephen Louis; *b* 9 Nov 1857; Clerk H of C 1880–1917, Pncpl Clerk Ctees and Private Bills 1913–17; *m* 12 Nov 1885 Louisa Augusta Eardley (*d* 2 June 1925), er dau of Hugh Culling Eardley Childers, PC, MP, and *d* 25 April 1937, having had:

  (1) Leonard Stephen Barrington, MC; *b* 10 June 1891; *educ* Eton and Trin Coll Cambridge (BA 1912, MA 1918); Offr i/c Admlty Works E Anglia Dist, T/Lt 1st Bn Roy Fus, WW I; *m* 16 Oct 1924 Ella Hazel Powys (*d* 1980), only dau of Col Powys Lane, IA, of Upper Ward, Bonchurch, IoW, and *d* 1978, leaving:

    1a +Miles Powys Barrington [Miles Simeon Esq, Dalte's Farm, St Osyth, Essex]; *b* 19 Oct 1927; *m* 29 Dec 1956 *Joan Mary, only dau of Laurence Frederick Underhay, of Clacton-on-Sea, and has:

      1b +Michael John Barrington; *b* 29 Oct 1957

      2b +Robert Miles [Robert Simeon Esq, Dalte's Farm, St Osyth, Essex CO16 8SA]; *b* 24 Dec 1959; *m* 1988 *Carol Ann Newcombe and has had:

        1c +John Robert; *b* 1992

        2c +James Kenneth Barrington; *b* 1996

        1c Laura Ann; *b* and *d* 1988

        2c *Samantha Ann; *b* 1989

    1a *Anne Primrose Louise [Mrs John Adams, Gable End, Rickinghall, Suffolk]; *b* 15 Sept 1925; *m* 1st 20 July 1944 (*divorce* 1959) Louis Gustav Julian Strauss, s of Maurice Strauss; *m* 2nd 1959 Leonard Townsend (*d* 1971); *m* 3rd 1973 G/Capt John Michael Skelton Adams, RAF, CEng, FIEE, FIMechE (*d* 1993), and by her 1st husb has:

      1b *Linda Evelyn; *b* 1947; *m* 1974 *Thomas Kennedy Nelson and has:

        1c *Hamish Kennedy; *b* 1975

        2c *Robin Simon; *b* 1977

      2b *Caroline Louise; *b* 1948; *m* 1974 (*divorce* 1981) Nicholas John de Jongh

      3b *Diana Margaret; *b* 1955; *m* 1978 (*divorce* 1984) Peter Gilbert Marsland and has:

        1c *Christopher Barrington; *b* 1981

  (1) Marjorie Lovis Tennyson; *m* 15 Jan 1914 William Edward Frank Macmillan, only surv s of George Macmillan, and *d* 24 Jan 1934, leaving issue. He *d* 11 May 1954

  (2) Ursula Mary; *d* unm 10 Dec 1949

1 Louisa Edith; *m* 29 Oct 1872 Richard Ward, only surv s of Francis R Ward, and *d* 10 July 1895, leaving issue

Sir John *m* 2nd 2 Oct 1861 Hon Catherine Dorothea Colville (*see* COLVILLE, V) and *d* 21 May 1870, having by her had, with a s (*d* young):

  2 Catherine Dorothea Mary; *m* 25 Oct 1887 Hon Algernon Henry Grosvenor, 4th s of 1st Baron Ebury (*qv*), and *d* 18 Feb 1917, leaving issue

The 4th Bt's bro,

Sir Edmund Charles Simeon, 5th Bt; *b* 11 Dec 1855; *m* 26 Sept 1883 Laura Jane (*d* 8 March 1949), er dau of Capt Walter Mountiford Westropp-Dawson (*see* CLAY, Bt), and *d* 18 June 1915, leaving

1 **Sir John Walter Barrington Simeon, 6th Bt;** *b* Jan 1886; *educ* Eton and Ch Ch Oxford, Capt 8th Bn Hants Regt, Assist Equipment Offr RFC; *m* 22 April 1909 Adelaide Emily (*d* 3 Sept 1934), er dau of Col Hon Edward Alexander Holmes-à-Court (*see* HEYTESBURY, B), and *d* 24 June 1957, leaving:

  (1) Sir JOHN EDMUND BARRINGTON SIMEON, **7th and present Bt**

  (1) *Elizabeth Jane; *b* 3 March 1916; Subaltern ATS WW II; *m* 4 July 1943 (*divorce* 1952) Sub-Lt Thomas Arthur Ratcliffe, RN, est s of George Edwin Ratcliffe, of Plumstead, Kent, and has:

    1a *Donal Arthur; *b* 1946

SIMON

Arms: Gu. three lotus flowers in pale ppr. between two flaunches or, each charged with a lion rampant of the field. **Crest:** Upon a well ppr. an eagle rising or. **Supporters:** Dexter, a guillemot; sinister, a monal ppr. **Motto:** *J'ai ainsi mon nom* ('Such is my name'). **Creation:** V. (UK) 20 May 1940.

THE 3RD VISCOUNT SIMON, of Stackpole Elidor, Co Pembroke (Jan David Simon) [The Rt Hon The Viscount Simon, House of Lords, London SW1A 0PW]; *b* 20 July 1940; *s f* 1993; *educ* Westminster, Southampton U Sch of Navigation and Sydney Tech; *m* 1969 *Mary Elizabeth, dau of John Joseph Burns, of Sydney, NSW, and has:

  1 *Fiona Elizabeth Christine; *b* 15 May 1971

Lineage: Rev EDWIN SIMON; Congregational Min Bath; *m* Fanny, yst dau of William Pole Allsebrook, of Thurvaston Hall, Derbys, and had, with a dau (Margaret Pole, *m* Daniel Morgan *d* 1961)):

JOHN ALLSEBROOK SIMON, **1st Viscount Simon**, of Stackpole Elidor, Co Pembroke (UK), so *cr* 20 May 1940, GCSI (1930), GCVO (1937, KCVO 1911), OBE (1919), PC (1913); *b* 28 Feb 1873; *educ* Fettes and Wadham Coll (Hon Fell 1912) Oxford (Pres Union 1896, Fell All Souls 1897, Hon DCL 1912, High Steward 1948); barrister Inner Temple 1899, KC 1908, Treas 1930–31 (also memb Middle Temple), Bencher 1910, Standing Counsel Oxford U 1909–10, MP (Nat Lib) SW Essex 1906–18 and Spen Valley 1922–40, Slr-Gen 1910–13, Attorney-Gen 1913–15, Home Sec 1915–16 and 1935–37 (also Dep Ldr H of C), For Sec 1931–35, Chllr Exchequer 1937–40, Ld Chllr 1940–45, Leader Lib Nat Party to 1940, WW I: Staff Capt RFC 1917, T/Maj 1917, Hon Maj 1918 (despatches),KGStJ, Chm Indian Statutory Commn 1927–30 and Population Commn 1943–46, Pres R101 Airship Inquiry 1930–31 and Nat Union Lib Clubs; ktd 1910, Hon LLD: Edin 1927, Cambridge 1928, McGill, Toronto, and Columbia 1929, Manchester 1930, Leeds 1933, St Andrews 1937 and Sheffield 1939; *m* 1st 24 May 1899 Ethel Mary (*d* 12 Sept 1902), dau of Gilbert Venables, and had:

  1 JOHN GILBERT, **2nd Viscount**

  1 Margaret Elizabeth; *b* 7 March 1900; *m* 2 Oct 1924 Geoffrey Richard Edwards, OBE (*d* 10 Dec 1961), s of Richard Edwards, and *d* 18 Feb 1966, leaving issue (*see* TRYON, B)

  2 Joan Angel Allsebrook, JP (Hants 1942); *b* 8 Aug 1901; *m* 11 Feb 1924 Capt John Allan Bickford-Smith, RN, s of Roandu Albert Henry Bickford-Smith, and had issue. He *d* 8 May 1970

The **1st Viscount** *m* 2nd 18 Dec 1917 Kathleen, DBE (1933), DGStJ (*d* 27 March 1955), widow f Thomas Manning, MD, and dau of Francis Eugene Harvey, of Wexford, and *d* 11 Jan 1954

His only s,

JOHN GILBERT SIMON, **2nd Viscount Simon**, CMG (1947); *b* 2 Sept 1902; *educ* Winchester and Balliol Coll Oxford; with Min War Tport 1940–47, md P&O Steam Navigation Co 1947–58, Pres: Chamber Shipping UK 1957–58, Roy Inst Naval Architects 1961–71, chm PLA 1958–71, Hon Er Bro Trin Ho 1975, Offr Order Orange Nassau; *m* 22 Dec 1930 *(James) Christie [The Rt Hon The Dowager Viscountess Simon, 2 Church Cottages, Abbotskerswell, Devon TQ12 5NY], dau of William Stanley Hunt, and *d* 1993, leaving:

  1 JAN DAVID SIMON, **3rd and present Viscount Simon**

  1 Gemma Louise; *b* 26 Oct 1934; *educ* Moira House Sch Eastbourne and Sch Slavonic Studies London U (BA); *m* 29 May 1956 *Brian Read Hunter, s of Norman Hunter, of London, and *d* 11 Oct 1994, leaving:

    (1) *Ian; *b* 24 Jan 1957

    (2) *Alan; *b* 24 Nov 1958

SIMON OF GLAISDALE

Arms: Per saltire sable and ermine a pair of scales or between in fess two roses argent barbed and seeded proper and in pale two crescents ermine. **Crest:** A cock's head erased azure combed and wattled gules between two palm branches vert, holding in the beak two roses argent, clipped, leaved, barbed and seeded proper. **Supporters:** Dexter, a man habited in the robes of a Doctor of Civil Law in the University of Cambridge proper, holding in his dexter hand a book or; sinister, a man habited in the robes of the President of the Probate Divorce and Admiralty Division of the High Court proper. **Motto:** *Si monent tubae paratus* ('If the trumpets sound, be ready'). **Creation:** B. (LP, UK) 1971.

THE BARON SIMON OF GLAISDALE, of Glaisdale, N Riding, Co York (Sir Jocelyn Edward Salis Simon, PC (1961)) [The Rt Hon The Lord Simon PC, House of Lords, London SW1A 0PW]; *b* 15 Jan 1911; *educ* Gresham's and Trin Hall Cambridge; barrister Middle Temple 1934, WWII: Maj RTR 1939, RAC Madagascar 1942, Lt-Col 1945; KC 1951, Bencher 1958; MP (C) W Middlesbrough1951–62; Jt Parly U-Sec Home Office 1957–58, Fin Sec Treasury 1958–59, ktd 1959, Slr-Gen 1959–62, Pres Probate Divorce and Admlty Div High Court 1962–71, Ld Appeal in Ordinary 1971–77; *m* 1st 1934 Gwendolen Helen (*d* 1937), dau of E J Evans; *m* 2nd 1948 *Fay Elizabeth Leicester, JP, dau of Brig H Guy A Pearson, of Jersey, and by her has:

1 *Peregrine Charles Hugo, QC (1991) [The Hon Peregrine Simon QC, Midge Hall, Glaisdale, Whitby, N Yorks]; *b* 1950; *educ* Westminster and Trin Hall Cambridge (MA); barrister Middle Temple 1973; *m* 1980 *Francesca, dau of Maj T W E Fortescue Hitchins, of Border Lodge, Brewham, Somerset, and has:
  (1) *Alexander Edward Orlando; *b* 1986
  (2) *Ferdinand William Hugo; *b* 1989
  (1) *Polly Harriet Artemis; *b* 1982
  (2) *Lucy Persephone Frances; *b* 1984
2 *(Benedict) Mark Leicester [The Hon Mark Simon, 33 South Parade, Oxford]; *b* 1953; *educ* Marlborough, Trin Hall Cambridge (MA) and Wolfson Coll Oxford (BLitt); *m* 1980 *Patricia, dau of Ricardo Hernandez Arnozurrutia, of Mexico City, and has:
  (1) *Isaak David; *b* 1989
  (1) *Jael Daniela; *b* 1984
3 *(Dominic) Crispin Adam [The Hon Crispin Simon, Cotte Farm, Coombe Hay, Bath, Avon]; *b* 1958; *educ* Westminster and Lincoln Coll, Oxford (MA); *m* 1983 *Georgina Frances, dau of R G Brown, of Chestnut House, Albrighton, Salop, and has:
  (1) *Freddie; *b* 1991
  (1) *Clementine; *b* 1993

Lineage: FRANK CECIL SIMON, of Hampstead; *m* Claire Evelyn — and had:
JOCELYN EDWARD SALIS, *cr* a **Baron**

SIMON OF HIGHBURY

Creation: B. (LP, UK) 7 May 1997.

THE BARON SIMON OF HIGHBURY, of Canonbury in the London Borough of Islington (Sir David Alec Gwyn Simon, CBE (1991)) [The Rt Hon The Lord Simon of Highbury CBE, House of Lords, London SW1A 0PW]; *b* 24 July 1939; *educ* Christ's Hosp, Gonville and Caius Coll Cambridge and INSEAD (MBA); BP 1961–97 (md 1986–95, dep chm 1990–95, chm 1995–97), a Dir Bank of England 1995–97, ktd 1995, Min State DTI 1997–, Hon Degree U of Bath 1998; *m* 1st 1964 (*divorce* 1987) Hanne Mohne and has two sons; *m* 2nd 1992 *Sarah Roderick Smith

Lineage: ROGER ALBERT DAMAS JULES SIMON; *m* Barbara Hudd and had:
DAVID ALEC GWYN (Sir), *cr* a **Baron**

SIMON OF WYTHENSHAWE

Creation: B. (UK) 17 Jan 1947.

Roger Simon [Roger Simon Esq, Oakhill, Chester Ave, Richmond, Surrey TW10 6NP]; *b* 16 Oct 1913; *s f* 1960 but does not use title; *educ* Gresham's and Gonville and Caius Coll Cambridge (BA 1935, MA 1939); served WW II; *m* 18 July 1951 *(Anthea) Daphne, dau of Sidney George William May, of Milford-on-Sea, Hants, and has:

1 +MATTHEW; *b* 10 April 1955; *educ* St Paul's and Balliol Coll Oxford (BA, PhD); lecturer, CEng, MIMechE
1 *Margaret; *b* 31 March 1953; *educ* St Paul's Girls' Sch and Manchester U

Lineage (of Simon): HENRY SIMON, of Lawnhurst, Didsbury, Manchester; *b* 7 June 1835; MICE; *m* Emily Stoehr (*d* 7 Nov 1920) and *d* 22 July 1899, leaving:

1 ERNEST DARWIN, **1st Baron**
1 Eleanor Aristodora; *m* 8 May 1906 Sir George Hamilton, 1st Bt, of Ilford (*d* 12 Jan 1947; see 1970 edn), and *d* 6 May 1958, leaving:
  (1) Sir PATRICK GEORGE HAMILTON, 2nd and last Bt; *b* 17 Nov 1908; *educ* Eton and Trin Coll Oxford (BA 1931, MA 1936); Dir Propeller Production Min Aircraft Production 1942–44, Chm: Advsy Ctee Commercial Info Overseas BOT 1957–59, N Western Tport Users Consultative Ctee 1957–64, Centl Middx Gp Hosp Management Ctee, Dep Chm Export Publicity Cncl BOT 1959, memb: Cncl London Chamber Commerce 1959–62 and ITA 1964–69, Treas Fedn Cwlth and Br Chambers Commerce 1962–64; *m* 17 Oct 1941 *Winifred Mary (Pix), OBE (1957) [Lady Hamilton, Flat 7, 39 Hyde Park Gate, London SW7 5DS; 21 Madingley Rd, Cambridge CB3 0EG], formerly w of Prof John Richard Nicholas Stone, CBE, and only dau of Hammon Beaconsfield Jenkins, of Maddings, Hadstock, and *d* 1992, when the btcy expired
  (1) Lindisfarne Christodora; *m* 15 April 1937 (Richard Lawrence) Christopher Hippisley (*d* 23 June 1969), 2nd s of Lt-Col Arthur Hippisley, OBE, RGA, and had issue
2 Margaret Antonia; *m* 30 Oct 1914 R-Adml Tufton Percy Hamilton Beamish, CB, of Chelworth, Chelwood, Gate, Sussex, 4th s of R-Adml Henry Hamilton Beamish, CB, and *d* 27 Dec 1956, leaving issue. He *d* 2 May 1951

His son,
ERNEST DARWIN SIMON, **1st Baron Simon of Wythenshawe**, of Didsbury, City of Manchester (UK), so *cr* 17 June 1947; *b* 9 Oct 1879; *educ* Rugby and Pembroke Coll Cambridge (BA 1901, MA 1920), Hon LLD, Manchester 1944, eng and contractor, MInstCE, MIMechE, pres: Henry Simon Holdings Ltd, Simon Carves Ltd, memb Manchester CC 1912–25 (chm Housing Ctee 1919–23, Ld Mayor Manchester 1921–22, MP (Lib) Withington 1923–24, and 1929–31, Parl Sec Min Health Sept–Oct 1931, memb Ec Advsy Cncl 1932, chm Cncl Manchester U 1941–57 (Treas 1932–41), Chm and Govr BBC 1947–52, Chm Area Board, and Area Offr Min Aircraft Production 1940–42, Dep Chm Centl Cncl Works and Buildings 1941–44, Chm Fuel and Power Advsy Cncl 1944–46, chm Ctee Inquiry Distribution Building Materials 1946–47, author: *The Smokeless City, How to Abolish the Slums, A City Council from Within, Physical Science of Flour Milling, The Smaller Democracies, The Rebuilding of Manchester, The Anti-Slum Campaign, Rebuilding Britain: a Twenty-Year Plan*; *m* 22 Nov 1912 Shena Dorothy (*d* 17 July 1972), CC Manchester, memb Fin Ctee and chm Educn Ctee, Freewoman (1964), author: *Three Schools for One* and *A Century of City Government*, educationalist, dau of John Wilson Potter, of Westminister, and *d* 3 Oct 1960, leaving:

1 ROGER SIMON, **2nd and present Baron Simon of Wythenshawe**
2 +Brian [The Hon Brian Simon, 11 Pendene Rd, Leicester]; *b* 26 March 1915; *educ* Gresham's and Trin Coll Cambridge; served WW II 1940–45; *m* 12 Feb 1941 *Joan Home, dau of Capt Home Peel, DSO, MC (*see* RENNELL, B), and has had:
  (1) Alan; *b* 7 May 1943; *educ* The Gateway Sch Leicester and Balliol Coll Oxford; *d* 1991
  (2) +Martin [Martin Simon Esq, 38 Amersham Rd, High Wycombe, Bucks]; *b* 29 Nov 1944; *educ* The Gateway Sch Leicester and Hull U; *m* *— and has:
    1a +A son
    1a *A dau
1 Antonia; *b* 21 Aug 1917; *d* 8 Sept 1929

Lineage (of Hamilton): Rt Rev HUGH HAMILTON, of Newtown Hamilton, Co Armagh; Bp Ossory 1798–1805, DD, FRS; had a 3rd s:

HENRY HAMILTON, JP, of Tullylish House, Co Down, JP; *b* 24 Nov 1780; *m* 1808 Sarah (*d* 28 Nov 1871), dau of Rev Michael Sandys, Rector Powerscourt, Co Wicklow, and *d* 7 Dec 1834, having had a 3rd s:

Ven GEORGE HANS HAMILTON, JP; *b* 1823; DD, Archdeacon Northumberland, Canon Durham; *m* 1st 9 May 1848 Arabella Sarah (*d* 1860), only dau of John Best, HEICS, and had two sons and a dau; *m* 2nd 1 June 1869 Lady Louisa Frances Clements (*d* 31 Aug 1939), sis of 4th Earl of Leitrim (*see* 1949 edn), and *d* 23 Sept 1905, having by her had, with two er sons (George Francis Clements, *b* 24 March 1870, *d* 1900; Robert Charles Clements, *b* 15 May 1871, *d* 1901) and a dau (Louisa Lindisfarne Clements, *m* 29 May 1902 William Whitaker Maitland, CVO, OBE (*d* 5 Nov 1926), of Loughton Hall, Essex, and *d* 3 March 1952, leaving issue):

Sir (COLLINGWOOD) GEORGE CLEMENTS HAMILTON, 1st Bt (UK), so *cr* 10 June 1937, of Ilford, Co Essex, JP Cheshire and Suffolk; *b* 1 Nov 1877; MP Altrincham 1913–23, Ilford 1928–37, PPS to Min Pensions 1919–21, Maj Queen's Westminster Rifles and TAR, RFC WW I 1917, electrical engr, Controller Enrolment Nat Serv 1916 and Contract Claims Min Munitions 1918, ktd 1922; *m* 8 May 1906 Eleanor Christodora Simon (*see* above) and had issue

SIMPSON OF DUNKELD

Creation: B. (LP, UK) 2 Aug 1997.

THE BARON SIMPSON OF DUNKELD, of Dunkeld in Perth and Kinross (George Simpson) [The Rt Hon The Lord Simpson of Dunkeld, House of Lords, London SW1A 0PW]; *b* 2 July 1942; *educ* Morgan Acad Dundee and Dundee Inst Tech; sr accountant gas industry Scotland 1962–69, centl audit manager BLMC 1969–73, fin controller Leyland Truck and Bus Div 1973–76, accounting dir Leyland Cars 1976–78, fin and systems dir Leyland Trucks 1978–80, md: Coventry Climax 1980–83, Freight Rover 1983–86, Rover Gp 1989–91 (ch exec 1991–92, chm 1991–94), GEC 1996–; ch exec offr Leyland DAF 1986–88, dep ch exec BAE 1992–94 (dir 1990–94), chm: Ballast Nedam Construction 1992–94, Arlington Securities 1993–94; ch exec Lucas Industs 1994–96, memb supervisory bd and non exec dir: Pilkington plc 1992–, Northern Venture Capital 1992–, Pro Share 1992–, ICI 1995–; memb exec ctee SMMT 1986– (v-pres 1986–95, pres cncl 1995–96); FCCA, FIMI, FCIT; *m* 1964 *Eva Chalmers and has a s and dau

Lineage: WILLIAM SIMPSON; *m* Elizabeth — and has:

GEORGE, *cr* a **Baron**

SINCLAIR, Lord

Arms: Argent a cross engrailed azure. **Crest:** A swan, wings expanded and elevated proper, gorged with a ducal coronet and chained or. **Supporters:** Two gryphons sable, armed, beaked and winged or. **Motto:** *Feight*. **Creation:** L. (S) *c* 1449.

THE 8TH/17TH LORD SINCLAIR (Charles Murray Kennedy St Clair, CVO (1990, LVO 1953)) [Maj The Rt Hon The Lord Sinclair CVO DL, Knocknalling, St John's Town of Dalry, Castle Douglas, Kirkcudbrightshire DG7 3ST]; *b* 21 June 1914; *s* f 1957; *educ* Eton and Magdalene Coll Cambridge (BA 1936); Maj Coldstream Gds (ret 1947), Palestine 1937–39 (wounded, despatches), WW II with Gds Armoured Div; memb Roy Co Archers, Portcullis Pursuivant of Arms 1949–57, York Herald 1957–68, Hon Genealogist Roy Victorian Order 1960–68, Extra Equerry to HM QUEEN ELIZABETH THE QUEEN MOTHER 1953–, rep S peer 1959–63; Ld Lt Dumfries and Galloway Region (Dist of Stewartry) 1982–89 (V-Ld Lt 1977–82, DL Kirkcudbrightshire 1969–74 and Dumfries and Galloway 1974–77); *m* 6 Jan 1968 *Anne Lettice, yr dau of Sir Richard Charles Geers Cotterell, 5th Bt (*qv*), and has:

1 +MATTHEW MURRAY KENNEDY, *Master of Sinclair*; *b* 9 Dec 1968

1 *Laura Anne; *b* 25 June 1972

2 *Annabel Lettice; *b* 27 June 1973

Lineage (of Sinclair): The 1st EARL OF CAITHNESS (*qv*) had an est s:

WILLIAM SINCLAIR, **2nd Lord Sinclair**; tried to get his virtual disinheriting by his f reversed, ultimately surrendering to his half-bro Sir Oliver the territorial Barony of Rosslyn but getting in exchange Ravenscraig Castle, lands in Dysart and other territory; *m c* 29 April 1458 Christian, dau of 1st Earl of Rothes (*qv*), with whom he got a charter of lands of Newburgh 1459, and *d* 1487, having been ajudged 1482 incapable of managing his own affrs for 16 years past, leaving an est s:

HENRY SINCLAIR, **3rd Lord Sinclair**, as which confirmed by Act of Parl 26 Jan 1488/9; granted by charter 13-year lease (renewed for 19 years 1501) of Orkney and Shetland, the Justiciarship thereof and Kirkwall Castle 1489; Master of Artillery March 1510/1, Capt ship *Great Michael* 1512; *m* by 4 Dec 1488 Margaret, sis of 1st Earl of Bothwell (*see* BUCHAN-HEPBURN, Bt), and was *ka* at Scots rout by English of Flodden 9 Sept 1513, leaving, with three daus (Katherine, *m* as his 1st w Sir David Wemyss of Wemyss (*see* WEMYSS and MARCH, E); Helen, *m* 4th Lord Ogilvy of Airlie (*see* AIRLIE, E); Jean, *m* Alexander Lindsay, Master of Crawford; *see* CRAWFORD and BALCARRES, E):

WILLIAM SINCLAIR, **4th Lord Sinclair**; *m* 1st(?) just after 17 April 1524 Elizabeth (*d* after 24 Nov 1549) , dau of 2nd Earl Marischal (*see* KINTORE, E) and widow of Colin, Master of Oliphant; apparently *m* 2nd Agnes/Mariota Bruce and *d* after 17 July 1570, leaving by his 1st w, with at least one yr s (Magnus, *m* Mariota Bruxce):

HENRY SINCLAIR, **5th Lord Sinclair**, PC (S by late 1573); *b* 1527 or 1528; *m* 1st *c* June 1547 Janet (*d* 8 April 1569), dau of 5th Lord Lindsay of the Byres (*see* LINDSAY, E), and had, with other issue:

  1 James, *Master of Sinclair*, PC (S by 26 Feb 1592/3); *b c* 1557; *m* 1577 Isabel, dau of 5th Earl of Rothes (*qv*), and *dvp* 9 May 1593, leaving:

    (1) HENRY SINCLAIR, **6th Lord Sinclair**; *b* March 1581; *d* unm 1602

    (2) JAMES SINCLAIR, **7th Lord Sinclair**; *d* unm 1607

    (3) PATRICK, **8th Lord**

    (1) Margaret; *m* William, Lord Berriedale (*see* CAITHNESS, E)

  2 Patrick; ancestor of the SINCLAIRs of Balgreggie (male line extinct on death of John Sinclair of Balgreggie 1710)

The **5th Lord** *m* 2nd well before 26 March 1588 Elizabeth, dau of 7th Lord Forbes (*qv*), and *d* 21 Oct 1601, having by her had, with other issue:

  3 Laurence

  1 Elizabeth; *m* Sir Duncan Campbell of Glenorchy (for whose early ancestry *see* ARGYLL, D)

The 7th LORD's bro,

PATRICK SINCLAIR, **8th Lord Sinclair**; imprisoned Edinburgh Castle Dec 1614 for debt and other offences; *m* Margaret, dau of Sir John Cockburn of Ormiston, Ld Justice Clerk, and *d* 1615 or 1617, leaving an est s:

JOHN SINCLAIR, **9th Lord Sinclair**, PC (S 1641, Feb 1660/1 and 1674); *bapt* 29 Oct 1610; originally a Covenanter but supported CHARLES I 1646 and joined CHARLES II's expedn to England, where captured by CROMWELL's forces Battle of Worcester 3 Sept 1651 and held prisoner Windsor Castle to 1660; *m c* July 1651 Lady Mary Wemyss, dau of 1st Earl of Wemyss (*see* WEMYSS and MARCH, E), and *dspm* 10 Nov 1674, having settled his estates on his only dau's est s and apparently having expressed a desire that the title should go with them, but he having omitted to make a formal resignation of it some doubt subsequently arose as to the validity of the instrument of 1677 regranting the title to the **10th Lord** inasmuch as heirs might exist other than those mentioned in the 1677 instrument, thereby giving rise to the existence of two separate Ldships of Parl of Sinclair, having had:

CATHERINE Sinclair, *Mistress of Sinclair*; *m* 15 April 1659 her extremely distant cousin (*see* CAITHNESS, E) John ST CLAIR of Herdmanston, Haddingtonshire (*d* after 22 Aug 1672), and *dvp* 3 July 1666, leaving an est s:

HENRY ST CLAIR, **1st/10th Lord Sinclair** (S), as which confirmed (or *cr* anew?) 1 June 1677, with precedence of the earlier title and remainder, in default of heirs male of his body, to his bro John and the latter's heirs male, in default of which to his f's bros Robert, George and Matthew successively and the heirs male of their bodies, in default of which to the nearest heir male whatsoever of the grantee/confirmee Henry; *bapt* 3 June 1660; sole peer to object to the Scottish Parl settling the Crown on WILLIAM III and MARY 1689 following the flight of JAMES II; *m* 30 Dec 1680 Barbara, est dau of Sir James Cockburn, 1st Bt, of Cockburn (*qv*), and was *bur* 14 March 1722/3, having had:

  1 John, *Master of Sinclair*; *bapt* 5 Dec 1683; MP (Tory) Dysart Burghs 1708 (election pronounced invalid since he est s of a peer), Capt-Lt Preston's Regt 1708 (obliged to resign Oct 1708 following his killing of two bros called Schaw in affrays which were called duels, although no seconds were present), entered service of Prussia till granted roy pardon back in Britain for the deaths he had caused there; Jacobite 1715, fought Battle of Sheriffmuir 13 Nov 1715, hence attainted and the title he would have inherited from his f forfeited, though an Act of Parl 1736 allowed him to inherit property, whereupon his yr bro James made over to him the family estates which he had held since their f's death; author: *Memoirs of the Rebellion*; *m* 1st *c* Aug 1733 Margaret (*dsps* 22 July 1747), dau of 5th Earl of Galloway (*qv*) and widow of 5th Earl of Southesk (*see* FIFE, D); *m* 2nd 24 April 1750, as her 1st husb, Amelia, sis of 3rd Duke of Atholl (*qv*), and *dsp* 2 Nov 1750

  2 James; Ensign 1st Bn Roy Regt 1694, 1708, Capt 3rd Foot Gds 1714, 2nd Maj 1722, 1st Maj and Brevet Col 1723, OC 22nd Foot 1734, Col Roy Scots 1737–62, Brig-Gen 1739, Maj-Gen 1741, QMG Br Forces Flanders 1745, Lt-Gen 1745, C-in-C expdn which destroyed French fortifications Quiberon 1746, Gen 1761, MP (Whig) Dysart Burghs 1722–34 and 1747–54, Sutherland 1736–47 and Fifeshire 1754–62, envoy Vienna and Turin 1748, Govr Co Corkn; bought 1735 Rosslyn Castle and the Dysart and Ravenscraig estates from the last heir of a cadet branch of the ST CLAIRS, leaving them to his sisters' heirs male; *m* Janet (*d* 1766), yst dau of Hon Sir David Dalrymple, 1st Bt, of Hailes (*see* STAIR, E) and widow of Sir John Baird, 2nd Bt, of Newbyth, of the Feb 1679/80 *cr* (*see* BAIRD, Bt, of Saughton Hall), and *dsp* 30 Nov 1762

  1 Grizel; *m* John Paterson, of Prestonhall, Fifeshire, est s of Archbp Glasgow, and *d* 22 Aug 1737, having had:

(1) James PATERSON later ST CLAIR; Col; *s* to the Dysart and Rosslyn estates; *d* unm 14 May 1789, leaving them to his cousin 2nd Earl of Rosslyn (*qv*)

(1) Margaret; *m* 1744 John Thomson of Charleton, Fife, and had:

1a Grizel Maria; *s* to Charleton; *m* Col John Anstruther, 2nd *s* of Sir Philip Anstruther, 2nd Bt, of Balcaskie (*qv*), and had issue

2 Catherine; *m* Sir John Erskine, 3rd Bt, of Alva and had issue (*see* ROSSLYN, E)

3 Mary; *m* as his 2nd *w* Sir William Baird, 1st Bt, of Newbyth, of the Feb 1679/80 *cr* and *dsp* 23 Oct 1756

4 Elizabeth; *m* (contract 5 July 1716) 4th Earl of Wemyss (*see* WEMYSS and MARCH, E) and *d* 1721, leaving issue

Lineage (of St Clair): HENRY ST CLAIR; *vicecomes* (effectively lieutenant) to Richard de Morville, Constable of Scotland; got 1162 charter of lands of Herdmanston; companion in arms of ROBERT I (THE BRUCE), who for his servs at the victory over the English of Bannockburn 1314 gave him a sword whose blade was engraved *Le Roi me donne, St Clair me Porte* ('The King gives me; St Clair wears me'); presumably ancestor of:

Sir JOHN ST CLAIR of Herdmanston; living 1389; *m* Elizabeth Polwarth, heiress of Polwarth; *gf* of:

Sir JOHN ST CLAIR of Herdmanston and Polwarth; living 1444; had, with an er *s* (Sir John, of Herdmanston and Polwarth, whose two daus and coheiresses took large estates to the HOMEs of Wedderburne (*see* HOME, Bt) and the Earls of Marchmont; *see* POLWARTH, L):

Sir WILLIAM ST CLAIR of Herdmanston; ancestor in the 5th generation of:

Sir JOHN ST CLAIR of Herdmanston; *m* Elizabeth, dau of Sir John Sinclair, Bt, of Stevenson, and had, with five other sons:

1 John; *m* Catherine, *Mistress of Sinclair*, only dau of **9th Lord Sinclair** (*see* above against **Lineage (of Sinclair)**), and had:

(1) HENRY ST CLAIR, **1st/10th Lord Sinclair**

2 Matthew; mentioned as one of those in remainder under the 1677 instrument; *m* Elizabeth, dau of Sir Thomas Carr of Cavers, Roxburghshire, and was *bur* 11 Nov 1728, leaving:

(1) CHARLES ST CLAIR of Herdmanston, *de jure* 2nd/11th LORD SINCLAIR (never assumed title); *b* 25 Jan 1691/2; advocate 1722; *m c* 1 April 1731 Elizabeth, dau of Sir Andrew Hume of Kimminghame (*see* POLWARTH, L), and *d* 4 Jan 1775, having had:

1a Matthew; *b* 17 March 1732; *dvp* young

2a ANDREW ST CLAIR of Herdmanston, *de jure* 3rd/12th LORD SINCLAIR (never assumed title); *b* 30 July 1733; Edinburgh merchant; *m* 28 Dec 1763 Elizabeth, dau of John Rutherford, Yr. of Edgerston, Roxburghs (*see* ELIOTT, Bt), and *d* 16 Dec 1775, having had an est s:

1b CHARLES ST CLAIR, **4th/13th Lord Sinclair**, as which recognised by Ho Lds 25 April 1782; *b* 30 July 1768; Ensign 2nd Bn 1st Foot (Roy Scots) 1784, Lt 17th Foot 1788, recruited an company 1790 but tfd to 15th Foot, Capt 1791, Maj 1795, Lt-Col 1799, ret 1802, Lt-Col Berwicks Militia 1803–05, rep S peer 1807–59; *m* 1st 13 Feb 1802 Mary Agnes (*d* 16 July 1814), only dau of James Chisholm of Chisholm, Roxburghs, and had, with another *s* (*d* unm):

1c JAMES, **5th/14th Lord**

2c Charles, of Eyemouth, Berwicks; *b* 8 June 1811; Cdr RN; *m* 1st 29 Sept 1840 Isabella Jane (*d* 22 June 1852), 4th dau of W Foreman Home, of Wedderburn, Berwicks, and had:

1d William Home Chisholm; *b* 9 Sept 1841; Adml; Yr Bro Trin Ho, ADC to HM QUEEN VICTORIA 1893–96; *m* 1 July 1869 Emma Searle (*d* 13 Oct 1925), dau of Julian Slight, FRCS, and *d* 16 Nov 1905, leaving:

1e Charles Home Douglas; *b* 3 June 1873; Maj ASC, Boer War (medal with four clasps), WW I (despatches); *m* 13 June 1911 Agatha Mary (*d* 17 April 1954), yr dau of E Bowyer-Jacks, of Houndiscombe, Plymouth, and *d* 31 March 1921

2e Frederic Cathcart Guy; *b* 29 May 1878; Capt RN, Kt Order St Stanislas Russia; *m* 17 May 1912 Maude Sophie Childers (*d* 23 July 1962), yr dau of Capt Stephen Henry Childers Thompson, RN, of Taplow, Bucks, and *d* 21 March 1931, leaving:

1f +Derek Charles ST CLAIR later ST CLAIR-STANNARD (deed poll 1939), MBE (1945) [Derek St Clair-Stannard Esq MBE, The Priory, 33 Church St, Godalming, Surrey GU7 1EL]; *b* 16 Aug 1919; *educ* Ottershaw; Lt RNVR WW II, For Serv 1947–54, PRO Roy Ag Soc England 1955–70, MIPR, dir Derek Stannard PR 1970–85; *m* 4 April 1953 *Elisabeth Ann, only dau of Douglas Charles Baskett, and has:

1g +Matthew Peter; *b* 2 Jan 1954; *educ* Westminster; *m* 1981 *Sally Elizabeth, est dau of Capt R Heptinstall, RN, and has:

1h +Guy Roger; *b* 1982

2h +Oliver Simon Charles; *b* 1984

1h *Chloe Elizabeth; *b* 1989

1g *Lucie; *b* 27 Sept 1955; *m* 1981 *Richard John Shelbourne, yr *s* of G R Shelbourne, of Langore, Cornwall, and has:

1h *Frederick John Philip; *b* 1988

1h *India Lucie; *b* 1982

2h *Arabella Frances; *b* 1984

3h *Tatiana Francesca Sophia; *b* 1993

2g *Sophie Alexandra; *b* 1 Dec 1958; *m* 1985 *Richard Sean de Courcy O'Grady, est *s* of Patrick de Courcy O'Grady, and has:

1h *Ludovic Patrick; *b* 1989

1h *Harriet Rose; *b* 1987

3g *Josephine Camilla; *b* 9 Nov 1965; *m* 1996 *John Maurice Owen, *s* of David Owen, of Milnrow, Lancs

1f *Enid Joyce; *b* 23 Feb 1913; *m* 5 Jan 1943 *W/Cdr James FISCHER-SOBELL later ST CLAIR-SOBELL (deed poll 1945),

RAF, PhD, FRSC, *s* of Otho Sobell, of Melbourne, Australia, and has:

1g *Guy James; *b* 12 May 1944

2d Charles James Chisholm; *b* 19 Jan 1844; RN; *d* 4 Aug 1861

3d Matthew John, of Nangoorie, Glen Innes, NSW; *b* 30 May 1845; *m* 23 April 1869 Charlotte Fraser (*d* 1921), dau of D M Sinclair, Police Magistrate, of Warwick, Qld, and *d* 22 May 1926, having had:

1e Charles Matthew Duncan; *b* 2 March 1886; Gunner 1st Bde Australian Field Artillery; *kas* 24 July 1917

2e William Archibald; *b* 4 Oct 1888; *d* 15 Jan 1889

1e Carlie May; *b* 1870; *m* 1889 Henry William Russell Hughes and *d* 1948, leaving issue

2e Isabella Louisa Home; *b* 1872; *m* 1896 James Henry McCausland, of Sydney, and *d* 1927, leaving issue

3e Eva Pringle; *b* 1873; *m* 1905 John Conynham McCausland (*d* 1953) and *d* 1964, leaving issue

4e Violet Jane Hamilton; *b* 1883; *d* unm 1939

5e Beatrice Cerise; *b* 1891; *m* 1914 Ralph Bernard Bolitho Snowdon (*d* 1936), of Glen Innes, NSW, and had issue

4d Adolphus Frederick; *b* 2 Dec 1847; Capt RN; *d* 6 May 1895

5d James Andrew; *b* 31 Dec 1851; *m* Frances Harriett, dau of Christopher Dawson Fenwick, and *d* 1914, leaving:

1e Percival James; *b* 1876; *m* Violet Christina (*d* 1922), dau of Percival Bowes Frederick, and *d* 1945, leaving:

1f Rodney Samuel; *b* 1919; *m* 1942 *Beatrice Wyatt Walker [Mrs Rodney St Clair, Trefusis, Boomi, nr Moree, NSW, Australia], and *d* 1964, leaving:

1g +Malcolm Clive; *b* 1943; *m* 29 Sept 1971 *Julie Murphy and has:

1h +Rodney James; *b* 1973

2h +Timothy; *b* 1975

1g *Rosslyn Violet; *b* 1947; *m* April 1971 *Iain Boyd Couper and has:

1h *Samuel Boyd; *b* 11 Nov 1971

1h *Rachel Kate; *b* 1974

2g *Lynda Helen; *b* 1953; *m* 1974 *Ronald Coulton and has:

1h *Christopher Ronald; *b* 1980

1h *Sarah Jane; *b* 1977

2e Charles Archibald; *b* 1878; *m* 1912 Madeline Smith and *d* 1917, leaving:

1f *Joan Madeline; *b* 1914

3e Harold; *b* 1880

4e Christopher Fenwick St Clair; *b* 1882; *m* 1914 Ethel Maud Cheesbrough and was *ka* in France 1918, leaving:

1f Christopher Ian; *b* 1914

1f *Erica Webster [Mrs Duncan McConnel, Cressbrook, Toogoolawah, Qld, Australia]; *b* 3 Nov 1916; *m* 19 March 1940 *Duncan Cannon McConnel, only *s* of Edgar Cannon McConnel, and has:

1g *Christopher David; *b* 22 March 1951; *m* 1984 *Susan Jane Underdown and has:

1h *Caitlin Jane St Clair; *b* 1990

1g *Rosemary Robina St Clair; *b* 2 Dec 1941; *m* 1987 *Graham Kensley Neumann

2g *Dianna Rose; *b* 8 Dec 1946; *m* 1968 *Arthur Edmund de Norbury Rogers and has:

1h *Andrew de Norbury; *b* 1970

2h *Scott McConnel; *b* 1972

3h *James McConnel; *b* 1974

1e Helen Muriel; *b* 19 Sept 1879; *m* Wilfred John Corbett Lawson (*d* 19 Aug 1936), of Sydney, NSW, and *d* 29 Nov 1963, leaving issue

1d Mary Jane; *m* 4 April 1877 Rev Frederick George Stapleton (*d* 13 Feb 1927), Vicar Seamer, York, 2nd *s* of Augustus Granville Stapleton, of Warbrook, Hants, and *d* 9 July 1918, having had issue

2d Isabella Home; *m* 2 Aug 1883 Watkin William Jones, MD (*d* 23 Jan 1929), and *d* 5 Aug 1936, leaving issue

2c (cont.) Cdr The Hon Charles St Clair *m* 2nd 1 July 1854 Anne Crawfurd (*d* 15 Dec 1899), 4th dau of Sir John Pringle, 5th Bt (*qv*), and *d* 8 Feb 1863, having by her had:

6d John Pringle; *b* 12 April 1862; *m* 5 July 1902 Clara, 3rd dau of Henry Chapman

3d Susan Eva; *m* 11 Oct 1899 Henry Edward Cousans (*d* 20 May 1909), of Shipbourne, Tonbridge, and *d* 29 May 1928

1c Susan; *m* 6 Aug 1829, as his 1st *w*, Francis Dennis Massy-Dawson (*see* MASSY, B) and *d* 17 Sept 1856, leaving issue

1b (cont.) The **4th/13th Lord** *m* 2nd 18 Sept 1816 Isabella Mary (*d* 5 Jan 1875), yst dau of Alexander Chatto, of Mainhouse, Roxburghshire, and *d* 30 Sept 1863, having had, with other issue:

2c Jane Elizabeth; *m* 6 Sept 1853 Rev William Leyland Feilden (*d* 16 Jan 1907), Rector Rolleston, Lancs, 3rd *s* of Joseph Feilden, of Witton Pk, Lancs, and *d* 1 July 1904, leaving issue

3a Elizabeth; *m* 2 Sept 1773 Lt-Col James Dalrymple, 2nd *s* of Sir James Dalrymple, 2nd Bt, of Hailes (*see* STAIR, E)

The 4th/13th LORD's est s,

JAMES ST CLAIR, **5th/14th Lord Sinclair**; *b* 3 July 1803; *educ* Winchester; Ensign Gren Gds 1822, Lt and capt 1826, Maj 92nd Foot 1827, rep S peer 1868–80; *m* 14 Sept 1830 Jane (*d* 12 June 1887 aged 75), est dau of Achibald Little, of Shabden Pk, Surrey, and *d* 24 Oct 1880, having had, with other issue:

1 CHARLES WILLIAM, **6th/15th Lord**

2 Lockhart Matthew, CIE, CBE; *b* 25 July 1855; *educ* Wellington and RIE Coll Coopers Hill; MInstCE, PWD India 1876–1904 (Superintending Engr), Sec to

Govt CP 1902–04, cmded Div Met Special Constabulary 1916; *m* 30 July 1881 Ellen Mary Margaret (*d* 1 Feb 1931), dau of Surgn-Maj-Gen William Roche Rice, CSI, MD, and *d* 22 July 1930, having had:

(1) James Chisholm Rice; *b* 22 March 1882; *d* 11 Aug 1883

(2) William Lockhart, DSO (1918); *b* 22 June 1883; Maj RFA, Togoland and Cameroons 1914, WW I (despatches); *m* 4 Oct 1919 Dorothy Kate, yst dau of Victor Leopold Northam, and *d* 23 Feb 1920

(3) George James Paul, CB (1945), CBE (1944), DSO (1917), DL (Glos 1953); *b* 29 June 1885; WW I (wounded, despatches): Bde-Maj 1916 and 1918, GSO(2), 42nd (E Lancs) Div 1929–33, AAG War Off 1937, WW II: Maj-Gen RA, High Sheriff Glos 1954; *m* 11 Nov 1911 Charlotte Theresa Orme (*d* 5 Feb 1961), only child of Maj Archibald Cosmo Little (*see* SHREWSBURY and WATERFORD, E), and *d* 13 Nov 1955, having had:

1a +Malcolm Archibald James, TD [Lt-Col Malcolm St Clair TD, The Priory, Long Newnton, Tetbury, Glos]; *b* 16 Feb 1927; *educ* Eton; farmer; Lt-Col cmdg Roy Glos Hus (TA) 1967–69; MP (C) Bristol SE 1961–63, having fought seat 1959 and at by-election 1961 against Viscount Stansgate (*qv*), being awarded seat after Election Petition; *m* 11 June 1955 *Mary-Jean Rosalie Alice, only child of W/Cdr Caryl Liddell Hargreaves (*see* RAVENSWORTH, B), and has:

1b +Hugh Alan Charles [Hugh St Clair Esq, Thurgarton Lodge, Thurgarton, Norfolk]; *b* 28 Feb 1957; *educ* Eton and USA; writer; *m* 1988 *Raffaella F, er dau of George Barker, of Itteringham, Norfolk, and has:

1c +Roman George; *b* 1988

2c +Lorne Alexander; *b* 1991

1c *Esme Topaz Alice; *b* 19–

2b +Andrew David Paul; *b* 12 Feb 1960; *educ* Eton

1b *Vanessa Alice Rosabelle; *b* 1971; *educ* St Mary's Calne and Manchester U (BA)

1a Helen Mary Orme; *b* 6 March 1918; *m* 11 July 1951 George Bradshaw Emslie, MBE, yst s of George McNeill Emslie, of Dalston, Cumberland, and had issue

2a *Rosabelle Evelyn Theresa; *b* 10 June 1919

3a *Guendolen Helen Charlotte [Mrs Maurice Cleaver, Berkley House, The Chipping, Tetbury, Glos]; *b* 22 Dec 1920; *m* 19 March 1966 Maurice Owen Griffith Cleaver (*d* 1975), only s of Lt-Col Douglas Whyte Cleaver, DSO, of Park Palace, Monte Carlo

4a Lavender Margaret Pauline; *b* 18 Aug 1924; *d* unm 27 Oct 1947

(4) Lockhart Frederick Charles; *b* 5 Oct 1896; *educ* Wellington and RMC Sandhurst; WW I: Lt 21st Lancers and with RFC (wounded); *m* 1st 24 April 1919 (*divorce* 1933) Evelyn Mary Josephine (*d* 18 May 1956), dau of Nicholas Joseph Synnott, JP, of Furness, Naas, Co Kildare, and had:

1a *Jean Margaret Alice; *b* 23 Sept 1920; *m* 1st 5 June 1941 (*divorce* 1950) Cecil Geoffrey Monson, er s of Frederick George Monson, of Castlemoate, Swords, Co Dublin; *m* 2nd 18 July 1952 (*divorce* 1969) Jack Mervyn Frank Baer, yr s of Frank Baer, of Pyrford, Surrey, and has:

1b *Lucy Alix St Clair; *b* 22 July 1959

(4) (cont) Lockhart St Clair *m* 2nd 1934 (*divorce* 1944) Sylvia Violet Francina, dau of Maj Marwood Elton Lane, of Haloowella, Norwood, Ceylon, and *d* 9 Nov 1960

The 5th/14th LORD's est son,

CHARLES WILLIAM ST CLAIR, **6th/15th Lord Sinclair**, JP Berwicks; *b* 8 Sept 1831; *educ* RMC Sandhurst; Ensign 57th Foot 1848, Lt 1851, Capt 1854, Maj 1856, served Crimea (severely wounded attack on Redan), AAG Forces Bosphorus 1855–56, served Indian Mutiny 1857, N Z War 1861–62, Lt-Col 1868, Hon Col 1879, rep S peer 1885–1922; *m* 6 Oct 1870 Margaret Jane (*d* 4 Dec 1935), yr dau of James Murray, of Ancoats Hall, and *d* 25 April 1922, having had:

1 ARCHIBALD JAMES MURRAY, **7th/16th Lord**

2 Charles Henry Murray; *b* 19 Dec 1878; Capt Seaforth Highrs, Kt Order Saxe-Ernestine Saxe Coburg and Gotha, memb Roy Co Archers, served Boer War (despatches), WW I (despatches); *ka* nr La Bassée 20 Dec 1914

1 Ada Jane; *d* unm 24 Feb 1959

2 Margaret Helen; *m* 1 Oct 1902 Capt Alick Christian Fraser, DL (*d* 29 Oct 1959), 2nd s of Alexander Caspar Fraser, JP, DL, of Mongewell Pk, nr Wallingford, and *d* 6 Feb 1939, leaving issue

3 Georgina Violet; *m* 19 Jan 1910 Lt-Col Harry Miller Davson, CMG, DSO (*see* DAVSON, Bt), and *d* 28 Dec 1957, leaving issue

The 6th/15th LORD's er s,

ARCHIBALD JAMES MURRAY ST CLAIR, **7th/16th Lord Sinclair**, MVO (4th Cl 1918), JP Kirkcudbrightshire; *b* 16 Feb 1875; *educ* Eton; 2nd Lt 2nd Dragoons (Scots Greys) 1896, Lt 1899, Capt 1901, Boer War 1899–1902, WW I, Extra Equerry to HRH PRINCE ARTHUR OF CONNAUGHT 1914–38, rep S peer 1923–57, memb Roy Co Archers, Order Rising Sun Japan; *m* 31 Jan 1906 Violet Frances (*d* 8 Nov 1953), only child of Col John Murray Kennedy, MVO, of Knockalling, Kirkcudbrightshire, and *d* 25 Nov 1957, having had:

1 CHARLES MURRAY KENNEDY ST CLAIR, **8th/17th and present Lord Sinclair**

1 Patricia Mary; *b* 17 March 1912; *m* 15 March 1940 Lt-Col Charles Archibald Richard Coghill, OBE, Scots Gds (*d* 28 Jan 1975), s of Norman Alfred Coghill, of Almington Hall, Market Drayton, and *d* 13 Dec 1996, leaving:

(1) *Hugh Murray Charles [Hugh Coghill Esq, Lodge Farm, Castle Acre, King's Lynn, Norfolk]; *b* 30 Dec 1950; *educ* Eton; *m* 1973 *(Elizabeth Ann) Edwina, yr dau of Rev Mark Wynn-Eyton Wells, and has:

1a *Charles Edward Mark; *b* 1976

2a *Harry Robert Murray; *b* 1978

3a *Benjamin Michael Richard; *b* 1981

(1) *Sarah; *b* 14 Jan 1948; *m* 1972 *Peter Grosvenor Hopkins, only son of F G Hopkins, of Wellesbourne, and has:

1a *James Richard Grosvenor; *b* 1972

1a *Laura Sarah; *b* 1975

2a *Catherine Jane; *b* 1978

(2) *(Patricia) Jane [Mrs Graham Merrison, Ivy Cott, Iden Green, Benenden, Kent]; *b* 12 Sept 1949; *m* 12 Sept 1970 *Graham Merrison, er s of James Merrison, of Reading, and has:

1a *Rupert Alexander James; *b* 1973

2a *Alexander Toby Charles; *b* 1974

3a *Edward Nicholas Harry; *b* 1976

1a *Annabel Sophie Louise; *b* 1978

SINCLAIR, Bt

Arms: Quarterly, 1st, az. a ship at anchor, oars in saltire or, flagged gu., within a double tressure counterflory of the second; 2nd and 3rd, or a lion rampant gu., armed and langued az.; 4th, az. a ship under sail or, sails arg. and flags gu., over all, dividing the quarters, a cross engrailed sa. (for SINCLAIR), the whole within a bordure parted per pale, the dexter side indented gu., the sinister erm.
Crest: A cock ppr. **Motto:** *Fidelitas* ('Fidelity').
Creation: Bt. (NS) 12 Oct 1704.

SIR PATRICK ROBERT RICHARD SINCLAIR, 10TH BT, of Dunbeath, Caithness-shire [Sir Patrick Sinclair Bt, 5 New Square, Lincoln's Inn, London WC2A 3RJ]; *b* 21 May 1936; *s* cousin 1990; *educ* Winchester and Oriel Coll Oxford; Sub-Lt RNR, barrister Lincoln's Inn 1961, Bencher 1994; *m* 14 Sept 1974 *Susan Catherine Beresford, est dau of Geoffrey Clive Davies, OBE (*see* KNOWLES, Bt), and has:

1 +WILLIAM ROBERT FRANCIS; *b* 27 March 1979

1 *Helen Margaret Gwendolen; *b* 1984

Lineage: ALEXANDER SINCLAIR of Latheron, Caithness (*see* CAITHNESS, E); *m* Jean, dau of John Cunningham of Lambrughton and Caprington, and had, with other issue:

1 William, of Dunbeath, Latheron and Geanies; MP Caithness 1661–63; *m* 1656 his cousin Elizabeth (*d* 1722), dau of Sir James Sinclair, 1st Bt, of Mey (*see* CAITHNESS, E), and *d* 1690, having had, with other issue:

(1) John, of Dunbeath and Latheron; sold Geanies; *m* Isabel, dau of Mackenzie of Ardlock, and had, with other issue:

1a James; of Latheron; *m* 1728 his cousin Frances, dau of John Sinclair of Ratter (*see* CAITHNESS, E), and *d* 1775, leaving:

1b James, of Latheron; *d* unm 1788

(2) William, of Stemster; *m* Helen, dau of Gen Sir George Munro of Culraine (*see* MUNRO, Bt, of Foulis-Obsdale, Bt) and widow of Joseph Mackay of Bighouse, and *dsp* 1699

(3) **Sir James Sinclair, 1st Bt** (NS), so *cr* 12 Oct 1704, with remainder to heirs male for ever, of Dunbeath; MP Caithness 1703–07; *m* 1st Isabel, dau and coheir of Sir Archibald Muir of Thornton, Ayrshire, Ld Provost Edinburgh, and had, with other issue:

1a **Sir William Sinclair, 2nd Bt**; sold Dunbeath to William Sinclair of Freswick (*see* CAITHNESS, E); Baptist Min Keiss and (1755) Edinburgh; *m* Charlotte, dau of Hon Sir James SUTHERLAND later DUNBAR, 1st Bt, of Hempriggs (*qv*), and *d* 2 Aug 1767, having had:

1b Alexander; *m* Elizabeth, dau of Eric Sutherland, only son of 3rd Lord Duffus (*see* DUNBAR, Bt, of Hempriggs), and *dvp*, leaving:

1c **Sir Alexander Sinclair, 3rd Bt**; Lt 88th Foot; *dsp* 1786

2a **Sir Benjamin Sinclair, 4th Bt**; sold Stemster, which his f had made over to him 31 Jan 1740; *m* Jean, dau of John Sinclair of Assery, and *d* 26 Oct 1796, leaving, with other issue:

1b **Sir John Sinclair, 5th Bt**; Lt-Gen HEICS Artillery Serv; *m* 1st 8 Dec 1802 Mary Anne Notley (*d* Oct 1806) and had:

1c John Notley; *d* young

1c Jane; *m* Patrick Wallace, HEICS, and *d* Oct 1892

1b (cont.) **Sir John** *m* 2nd 1825 Sarah Charlotte Carter (*dsp* 26 Dec 1866) and *dspms* 1 Oct 1842

(3) (cont.) **Sir James** *m* 2nd Isabel, dau of John Lumsden, Aberdeen shipmaster, and *d* 28 Dec 1742, having by her had:

1a Jean; *m* Robert Campbell

(1) Jean; *m* 1682 Sir George Sinclair of Clyth

(2) Catherine; *m* Sir Patrick Dunbar, 3rd Bt, of Northfield (*qv*)

2 John, of Brabster; *m* Elizabeth, dau of Patrick Sinclair of Ulbster (*see* THURSO, V), and had, with other issue:

(1) Alexander, of Brabster; *m* Margaret, dau of John Sinclair of Ratter (*see* CAITHNESS, E), and had:

1a George, of Brabster; *m* Janet, dau of James Sutherland of Langwell, and had, with other issue:

1b Anne; *m* 1762 Robert Sutherland of Langwell, whose descendants *s* to Brabster

3 George, of Barrock, nr Wick, Caithness; *m* 1st Anne, dau of John Dunbar of Hempriggs (*see* DUNBAR, Bt, of Northfield), and had:

(1) John, of Barrock; *m* 1st Anne, dau of Robert Sinclair of Durran, and had:

1a Alexander, of Barrock; *m* Jean, dau of William Sinclair of Freswick, and had:

1b John, of Barrock; Army Capt; *m* Anne, dau of Thomas Longmire, of Penrith, and had:

1c JOHN (Sir), **6th Bt**

2b William

(1) (cont.) John Sinclair of Barrock *m* 2nd Janet (*m* 2nd Harry Innes, of Borlum and Sandside), dau of Sir James Dunbar, 1st Bt, of Hempriggs (*qv*), and had:

2a John, of Sibster

3 (cont.) George Sinclair *m* 2nd Elizabeth, dau of David Murray of Clarden and widow of William Innes, and had two sons, who had issue; *m* 3rd Elizabeth, dau of William Cumming, and by her had a dau

1 Margaret; *m* Sir William Dunbar, 1st Bt, of Hempriggs, and had issue (*see* DUNBAR, of Northfield, Bt)

The 5th Bt's second cousin once-removed,

Sir John Sinclair, 6th Bt, of Barrock; *b* 16 Sept 1794; *m* July 1821 Margaret (*d* 29 Nov 1879), yst dau of John Learmonth, of Edinburgh, and *d* 21 April 1873, having had, with other issue:

1 John; *b* 2 May 1822; Capt 39th Madras NI; *ka* cmdg 3rd Regt Hyderabad Contingent capture of Jhansi 5 April 1858

2 Alexander Young; *b* 16 Feb 1824; Lt-Col Bombay Army; *m* 26 June 1861 Margaret Crichton (*d* 12 March 1909), dau of James Alston, and *dvp* 3 Feb 1871, having had, with other issue:

(1) **Sir John Rose George Sinclair, 7th Bt**, DSO, VD, JP; *b* 10 Aug 1864; cmded 62nd (Middx) Imp Yeo Boer War (despatches), WW I with King's (Liverpool) Regt, Hon Col and Lt-Col cmdg Caithness Vol Artillery, V-Lt of Caithness; *m* 7 Jan 1885 Edith (*d* 10 June 1934), dau of Lt-Col William Matthew Dunbar, memb Gentlemen-at-Arms, and *dsp* 3 Nov 1928

(2) Norman Alexander; *b* 29 July 1869; *m* 29 Jan 1898 Edith Lilian (*d* 28 April 1951), dau of Col Robert William Hamilton (*see* BELHAVEN AND STENTON, L), and *d* 11 May 1904, leaving:

1a **Sir Ronald Norman John Charles Udny Sinclair, 8th Bt**, TD, JP, DL Caithness; *b* 30 June 1899; *educ* Wellington and RMC Sandhurst; Maj 4th/5th Bn Seaforth Highrs (TA); *m* 5 Jan 1926 Reba Blair, Co Cmdt ATS 1938–41 (*m* 2nd 12 Aug 1957 Lt-Col Henry Richard Hildreth, MBE, 2nd s of Lt-Col Harold Crossley Hildreth, DSO, OBE, FRCS, RAMC), est dau of Anthony Inglis, MD, of Lismore, Ayr, and *d* 19 Oct 1952, leaving:

1b **Sir John Rollo Norman Blair Sinclair, 9th Bt**; *b* 4 Nov 1928; *educ* Wellington; Lt Intelligence Corps, dir Lucis Tst 1957–61; *d* unm 1990

1b *Georgina Margaret Snowdrop [Mrs Georgina Sinclair, The Mount, Brewood, Staffs]; *b* 1932; *m* 3 Dec 1955 (*divorce* 1968, resumed maiden name) John Leonard Maddocks and has:

1c *John Alexander Sinclair [John Maddocks Esq, 202 Battersea Bridge Rd, London SW11]; *b* 21 March 1960

1c *Margaret Louise Sinclair [Mrs Adam Scott, Barrock House, Lyth, Caithness KW1 4UD]; *b* 21 Jan 1962; *m* 1991 *Adam Piers Scott and has:

1d *Rory Alexander Sinclair; *b* 1991

2d *Oliver Roderick Archibald Sinclair; *b* 1995

3d *Timothy Charles Sinclair; *b* 1997

1d *Laura Rose Sinclair; *b* 1993

2b *SUSAN LILIAN PRIMROSE, *cr* BARONESS MASHAM OF ILTON (*qv*)

2a Alexander Robert; *b* 26 Sept 1901; *educ* Winchester; *m* 7 July 1928 Vera Mabel, 2nd dau of Walter Stephings Baxendale, of Sevenoaks, and had:

1b Sir PATRICK ROBERT RICHARD SINCLAIR, **10th and present Bt**

1b Roona Fidelity; *b* 12 Sept 1932; *m* 11 July 1959 *Ernle Money-Kyrle, MICE, est s of Roger Ernle Money-Kyrle, JP, PhD, of Whetham, Calne, Wilts, and had:

1c *Charles Ernle Robin; *b* 10 Dec 1961

2c *Andrew Richard William; *b* 30 March 1965

(1) (cont.) *m* 4 Nov 1884 George Felix Standish Sinclair (*d* 10 June 1943), yr s of Sir John George Tollemache Sinclair, 3rd Bt, of Ulbster, and *d* 2 July 1932, leaving issue (*see* THURSO, V)

3 George; *b* 29 Jan 1826; Capt Bengal Army; *m* 15 June 1859 Agnes (*d* 17 March 1876), only dau of John Learmonth, of Dean, Edinburgh, and *d* 23 March 1871, leaving:

(1) JOHN SINCLAIR, 1st BARON PENTLAND, of Lyth, co Caithness (UK), so *cr* 15 Feb 1909, GCSI (1918), GCIE (1912), PC (1905); *b* 7 July 1860; *educ* Edinburgh Acad, Wellington and RMC Sandhurst; 2nd Lt 5th Roy Irish Lancers 1879, Sudan Expdn 1885 (medal with clasp), ADC to Ld Lt Ireland 1886, ret as Capt 1887, memb LCC 1889–92, MP (Lib) Dunbartonshire 1892–95 and Forfarshire 1897–1909 (fought Ayr Burghs 1886), Scottish Lib Whip, Sec to Govr-Gen Canada 1896–97, Sec for Scotland 1905–12, Govr Madras 1912–19, LLD Glasgow, Aberdeen and St Andrews; *m* 12 July 1904 Lady Marjorie Adeline Gordon, DBE (1917), DGStJ (1904), only dau of 1st Marquess of Aberdeen and Temair (*qv*), and *d* 11 Jan 1925, leaving:

1a HENRY JOHN SINCLAIR, 2nd and last BARON PENTLAND; *b* 6 June 1907; *educ* Wellington and Trin Coll Cambridge (BA and Pres Union 1929); AMICE, MAIEE; *m* 11 Sept 1941 *Lucy Elisabeth [The Rt Hon The Lady Pentland, 4670 Independence Ave, Riverdale, NY 10471, USA], dau of Sir

Henry Babington Smith, GBE, CH, KCB, CSI (*see* ELGIN and KINCARDINE, E), and *d* 1984, when the Barony expired, leaving:

1b *Mary [The Hon Mrs Rothenberg, 131 East 66 St, New York, NY 10021, USA]; *b* 21 Nov 1942; *educ* Mt Holyoke USA (BA 1964); *m* 1976 *Jon Anderson Rothenburg and has:

1c *Laura Elizabeth; *b* 3 Feb 1981

1a Margaret Ishbel; BA Girton Coll Cambridge

(2) Charles George; *b* 1862; *d* 17 March 1935

(3) George Henry; *b* 1866; *d* 10 Jan 1922

SINCLAIR OF CLEEVE

Arms: Or a cross engrailed sa., in the first quarter a sword erect ppr., on a chief also sa. three martlets gold. **Crest:** In front of a saltire arg. a dove ppr., beaked and legged gu., in the beak an olive branch, also ppr. **Supporters:** Dexter, a griffin sa.; sinister, a unicorn arg., each gorged with a chaplet of white may, leaved and flowered ppr. **Motto:** *Credo* ('I believe'). **Badge:** A cross engrailed, couped sa., within a wreath of olive or. **Creation:** B. (UK) 22 Jan 1957.

THE 3RD BARON SINCLAIR OF CLEEVE, of Cleeve, Co Somerset (John Lawrence Robert Sinclair) [The Rt Hon The Lord Sinclair of Cleeve, House of Lords, London SW1A 0PW]; *b* 6 Jan 1953; *s f* 1985; *educ* Winchester, Bath U and Manchester U; sch master

Lineage: ROBERT DUNBAR SINCLAIR, of Lybster, Caithness; *b* 18 May 1824; *m* 23 March 1848 Hannah (*d* 6 July 1908), dau of Robert Gunn, of Aubery Cottage, Lybster, and *d* 31 May 1899, leaving:

ROBERT HENRY SINCLAIR, JP; *b* 1 July 1851; dir James Finlay & Co Ltd, of Glasgow; *m* 26 Feb 1891 Margaret (*d* Aug 1917), dau of John Macwhannell, of Glasgow, and *d* 23 Oct 1923, leaving:

ROBERT JOHN SINCLAIR, **1st Baron Sinclair of Cleeve**, of Cleeve, Co Somerset (UK), so *cr* 22 Jan 1957, KCB (1946), KBE (1941, MBE 1918); *b* 29 July 1893; *educ* Glasgow Acad (Govr 1952) and Oriel Coll Oxford (BA 1914, MA 1918, Hon Fell 1959); WW I: Gallipoli (wounded, despatches), Lt 5th Bn KOSB 1916–19, seconded Min Munitions (Dep Dir Inspection), joined Imperial Tobacco Co 1919 (assist sec 1920, sec 1927, dir 1933, dep chm 1939, chm 1947–59, pres 1959–67), Dir-Gen Army Requirements War Office 1939–42, memb Supply Cncl 1939–42 and Army Cncl 1940–42, Dep for Min Production on Combined Production and Resources Bd Washington 1942–43, Ch Exec Min Production 1943–45, dir: BAT 1944–64, Fin Corp for Industry 1945–49 and 1951–69 (chm 1960–64), Bristol Waterworks 1946 (chm 1960), Tobacco Securitites Tst 1948–69, Dollar Exports Bd 1949–51, Dollar Exports Cncl 1951–54, Cwlth Devpt Fin Co 1953–69, Nat Provincial Bank 1958–69, Debenture Corp 1959, Gen Accident Fire and Life Assur 1959, memb UK Perm Security Commn 1965, Pro-Chllr Bristol U 1946 (Hon LLD 1959), High Sheriff Somerset 1951, Pres FBI 1949–50, Master Soc Merchant Venturers 1952–53, Tstee *The Economist* 1953, Chm Ctee Inquiry Financial Structure Colonial Devpt Corp 1959, US Medal of Freedom with Gold Palm 1947; *m* 18 Sept 1917 Mary Shearer, dau of Robert Shearer Barclay, of Randfontein, S Africa, and had:

1 JOHN ROBERT KILGOUR, **2nd Baron**

2 David Barclay; *b* 29 July 1922; *educ* Winchester; Lt 51st Highland Div Reconnaissance Corps WW II; *ka* El Alamein 27 Oct 1942

The 1st BARON *d* 4 March 1979; his only s,

JOHN ROBERT KILGOUR, **2nd Baron Sinclair of Cleeve**, OBE (1963, MBE 1954); *b* 3 Nov 1919; *educ* Winchester and RMC Sandhurst; Lt QO Cameron Highrs WW II 1939–45 (despatches), Capt 1946, Maj 1951, French Staff Coll 1953–54, GSO(2) War Office 1957, Lt-Col 1960, UK Mil Attaché Leopoldville Congo 1960–63, Mil Assist to Dep SACEUR SHAPE 1964–67, MOD 1967–69; *m* 12 April 1950 *Patricia, dau of Lawrence Hellyer, of The Hawke, Lockerbie, Dumfriesshire, and *d* 1985, leaving:

1 JOHN LAWRENCE ROBERT SINCLAIR, **3rd and present Baron Sinclair of Cleeve**

1 *Juliet; *b* 16 Oct 1951; *m* 1 June 1983 *A Philip Wallis, only s of A P Wallis, of Beaumont, nr Clacton, Essex

2 *Jane [The Hon Mrs Holliday, Larkfield, Hawstead, Suffolk]; *b* 13 July 1955; *m* 17 April 1982 *Robert Anthony John Holliday, *s* of R F Holliday, of Ash-wellthorpe, Norfolk, and has:

    (1) *James Robert Sinclair; *b* 1984

    (1) *Fiona Jane; *b* 1987

SINCLAIR-LOCKHART

Arms: Quarterly, 1st and 4th, arg. a man's heart ppr. within a fetterlock sa., on a chief az. three boar's heads erased arg., all within a bordure erm., charged with three crosses patée gu.; 2nd and 3rd, arg. on a saltire engrailed gu. five bezants. **Crest:** A boar's head erased arg. **Motto:** *Corda serrata fero* ('I bear a locked heart').
Creation: Bt. (NS) 18 June 1636.

SIR SIMON JOHN EDWARD FRANCIS SINCLAIR-LOCKHART, 15TH BT [Sir Simon Sinclair Lockhart Bt, 13 Franklin Terrace, Havelock North, Hawkes Bay, New Zealand]; *b* 22 July 1941; *s f* 1985; *m* 24 Jan 1973 *Felicity Edith, formerly w of Cdr Michael Waymouth, RNZN and only dau of Ivan Lachlan Campbell Stewart, of Havelock North, and has:

    1 +ROBERT MUIR; *b* 12 Sept 1973

    2 +James Lachlan; *b* 12 Sept 1973

    1 *Fiona Mary; *b* 1979

Lineage: MATTHEW SINCLAIR, 9th of Longformacus, Berwicks; *m* Elizabeth, dau of Sir John Swinton of Swinton by Margaret, dau of David Home of Wedderburn (for whose early ancestry *see* HOME, Bt), and had a yr s:

Sir John Sinclair, 1st Bt (NS), so *cr* 18 June 1636; Edinburgh merchant; bought the Stevenson estate, Haddingtonshire, 1624; *m* Marion McMath and *d c* 1649, having had an est s:

JOHN SINCLAIR; *m* Isabel (*m* 2nd Sir John Grierson of Lag), dau of Robert, Lord Boyd, and *dvp* 1643, leaving:

    1 **Sir John Sinclair, 2nd Bt**; *d* unm *c* 1652

    2 **Sir Robert Sinclair, 3rd Bt**, PC; Sheriff Haddington, Baron Exchequer, MP Haddingtonshire 1689–1702; had his lands erected into a (territorial) Barony 1663; *m* 1st 1663 Helen, dau of John, Earl of Crawford and Lindsay, and had issue; *m* 2nd Anne (*dsp*), dau of Sir William Scott of Ardross, and *d* July 1713, leaving:

        (1) **Sir John Sinclair, 4th Bt**, MP Lanark 1703–07; *m* 1698 Martha (*d* 15 May 1752), widow of Cromwell Lockhart, of Lee, Lanarks, and dau and ultimate heiress of Sir John Lockhart of Castlehill, a Ld Session, and had, with five other sons and five daus:

            1a ROBERT (Sir), **5th Bt**

            2a James SINCLAIR later LOCKHART; *m* Charlotte, dau of James Boyle, and had three daus

            3a George SINCLAIR later LOCKHART of Castlehill; Ld of Session as Lord Woodhall; *dsp* 5 May 1764

Sir JOHN *d* 1752; his est s,

Sir Robert Sinclair, 5th Bt; *m* Sept 1733 Isabella, only dau of Col James Ker, and *d* 1754, having had four sons and four daus, of whom:

    1 **Sir John Sinclair, 6th Bt**; inherited the Murkle and other estates from Alexander, 9th Earl of Caithness (*qv*); *m* Mary, yst dau of of William Blair of that Ilk, and *d* 13 Feb 1789, leaving an est s:

        (1) **Sir Robert Sinclair, 7th Bt**; Lt-Govr Fort St George; *m* 2 April 1789 Madeline (*m* 2nd 25 Nov 1805 Charles Fyshe Palmer and *d* 31 May 1847), 2nd dau of 4th Duke of Gordon (*see* RICHMOND and GORDON, D), and *d* 4 Aug 1795, leaving:

            1a **Sir John Gordon Sinclair, 8th Bt**; *b* 31 July 1790; served RN 63 years: Midshipman HMS *Victory* under Nelson, cmded HMS *Redwing* Mediterranean at actions of Morjean and Cassis, Capt 1814, Adml 1861; *m* 15 June 1812 Anne (*d* 23 Sept 1857), n of 26th Baron Kingsale (*qv*), and *d* 13 Nov 1863, having had, with three other daus (*d* unm):

                1b **Sir Robert Charles Sinclair, 9th Bt**, of Murkle, Caithness, and Stevenson, Haddingtonshire, JP, DL; *b* 25 Aug 1820; Capt 38th Regt, Hon Col 1st Caithness Artillery Vols, Vol Offr's Decoration; *m* 1st 1851 Charlotte

Anne (*d* 7 July 1874), dau of Lt John Coote, 71st Regt; *m* 2nd 5 Dec 1876 Louisa (*d* 29 Jan 1931), est dau of Roderick Hugonin, of Kimmylles House, Inverness, and *dsp* 5 May 1899

            2b John Michael De Courcy; *b* 22 Nov 1823; Capt RA; *d* India 15 June 1862

            3b Gordon Cornwallis; *b* 13 Aug 1835; Lt RN; *d* 21 March 1866

            1b Madalina; *m* 15 Oct 1839 Capt Hon Dudley Pelham, RN (*d* 13 April 1851), inherited the Sinclair estates from her bro 1899, added the name SINCLAIR and *d* 11 Nov 1910, leaving issue (*see* YARBOROUGH, E)

            2b Susan Hay; *m* 12 June 1867 Gen Wilbraham Oates Lennox, VC, KCB (*see* RICHMOND and GORDON, D), inherited the Sinclair estates from her sis, added by deed poll the name SINCLAIR and *d* 6 April 1912, leaving issue

2 James SINCLAIR later LOCKHART, of Castlehill, Lanarks, which inherited 1764 from his unc George Lockhart, Lord Woodhall (*see* above); *m* 1773 Mary Amelia, dau of Walter Nisbet, of Nevis, and had:

    (1) Robert, of Castle Hill, Cambusnethen and Stonehouse; *m* 1st 9 Oct 1804 Eliza (*d* April 1816), dau of Richard Newman Newman, of Thurnbury Park, Glos, and had, with three sons and an est dau (*d* unm):

        1a Eliza Anne; *m* 1825 John Piercy Henderson, of Foswell Bank, Perths

        2a Susan; *m* William Dalglish and had issue

        3a Anne Nisbet; *m* Thomas McCall and had issue

    (1) (cont.) Robert Lockhart *m* 2nd 30 June 1817 Charlotte Simpson (*d* 18 March 1869), dau of Capt William Mercer, of Potterhill, and *d* 2 Nov 1850, having by her had, with four other daus:

        1a William Mercer; *b* 1818; drowned 1849

        2a Sir GRAEME ALEXANDER LOCKHART later SINCLAIR-LOCKHART, **10th Bt**, CB, JP, DL, of Castle Hill; *b* 23 Jan 1820; Col 78th Regt, Persian Campaign, Indian Mutiny, Maj-Gen; *m* 1861 Emily Udny (*d* 8 June 1904), dau of James Brebne, advocate, of Aberdeen, and *dsp* 20 March 1904

        3a George Duncan; *b* 1821; *m* Elizabeth Amanda, dau of Dr Thomas, of Clifton, and had:

            1b ROBERT DUNCAN (Sir), **11th Bt**

            1b Charlotte Elizabeth Mercer; *m* 14 March 1883 Edward Richardson, of Canterbury, NZ, and *d* 19 Jan 1884, leaving issue. He *d* 23 March 1915

5 Charlotte, *m* James Baird, of Camberusdoon

6 Louisa, *m* her cousin Col McGrigor, IA, and had issue

7 Barbara Forbes; *m* 1859 Alexander Whitelaw, of Gartshore, Dunbartonshire, and *d* 1909, leaving issue. He *d* 1 July 1879

The 10th Bt's n,

Sir Robert Duncan Sinclair-Lockhart, 11th Bt; *b* 12 Nov 1859; *m* 26 Dec 1895 Flora Louisa Jane Beresford Nation (*d* 9 Aug 1937), dau of Capt Edward Henry Power, LLD, DSc, of Darlinghurst, N Sydney, NSW, and *d* 7 Nov 1918, leaving:

1 **Sir Graeme Duncan Power Sinclair-Lockhart, 12th Bt**; *b* 29 Jan 1897, *educ* Wanganui Collegiate Sch NZ and Pembroke Coll Cambridge; 2nd Lt Scottish Horse (Scouts), TAR, WW I with NZ Mounted Rifles, Russo-Finnish War 1939–40, WW II 1942–46; *m* 9 May 1932 (*divorce* 1947) Jeanne Hamilton, only child of Capt John Ferguson, and *dsp* 15 Feb 1959

2 **Sir John Beresford Sinclair-Lockhart, 13th Bt**, ED; *b* 4 Nov 1904, *educ* King's Coll Auckland, NZ U and Sidney Sussex Coll Cambridge (BE (Civil), BSc (Physics)); civ engr NZ, Colonial Admin Serv Kenya 1934–63, Maj RA WW II; *m* 22 Oct 1949 Winifred Ray, 4th dau of Tom Ray Cavaghan, of Aglionby Grange, Carlisle, and *dsp* 11 March 1970

3 **Sir Muir Edward Sinclair-Lockhart, 14th Bt**; *b* 23 July 1906; *m* 18 May 1940 *(Olga) Ann [Ann Lady Sinclair-Lockhart, Haunui, RD7, Feilding, New Zealand], dau of Claude Victor White-Parsons, of Hawkes Bay, and *d* 1985, leaving:

    (1) Sir SIMON JOHN EDWARD FRANCIS SINCLAIR-LOCKHART, **15th and present Baronet**

    (1) *Sara Ann May; *b* 13 Nov 1942; *m* 21 Aug 1968 (*divorce*, resumed maiden name) Nicholas Welcome Willcock, *s* of Douglas Brian Willcock, of Little Brookfield, Belbroughton, Worcs

4 Robert Nation; *b* 3 March 1910; *d* 1944

5 Bruce; *b* 20 Feb 1911; LLM U of NZ, slr; *m* 23 Dec 1940 (*divorce* 1949) Joan Marian Belle, only dau of Brig Ronald Henry Quilliam, CBE, QC, and *d* 14 Nov 1965, leaving:

    (1) *Sally Elizabeth; *b* 28 Feb 1942; *m* 21 Nov 1964 *Stuart William Veitch, *s* of Richard Brandon Veitch, of Gisborne, NZ, and has:

        1a *Guy Bruce; *b* 8 April 1966

        2a *William Ronald; *b* 4 Jan 1968

        3a *Michael Richard; *b* 1970

        1a *Katie Jane; *b* 1973

1 Elizabeth Sinclair; *b* 26 Feb 1903; *m* 1929 Walter Raleigh Grace (*d* 26 Sept 1950), yst s of Ven Archdeacon T S Grace, of Marlborough, NZ, and had:

    (1) Bryan Raleigh; *b* 26 Feb 1930; *d* unm 18 April 1953

    (1) *Angela Elizabeth; *b* 30 Aug 1933; *m* 19 Jan 1957 *Keith Grace McKenzie, MB ChB (NZ), DTM, HMRCGP, s of Alan Roy Mckenzie, of Invercargill, NZ, and has:

        1a *Heather Grace; *b* 27 March 1958

        2a *Jennifer Grace; *b* 1 April 1960

        3a *Elizabeth Grace; *b* 25 May 1965

SINHA

JATA · DHARMA · STATA · JAYA

Arms: Arg. on a chevron erm., between in chief two lotus flowers and in base an adjutant bird all ppr., three fountains. **Crest:** A demi-tiger supporting with its paws a fasces erect ppr. **Supporters:** On either side an adjutant bird ppr., collared or. **Motto:** *Jata dharma stata jaya* ('He who believes in Dharma always has success in life'). **Creation:** B. (UK) 14 Feb 1919.

THE 5TH BARON SINHA, of Raipur, Residency of Bengal [The Rt Hon The Lord Sinha, 2 Highfield Rd, Billericay, Essex CM11 2PF]; *b* 18 May 1930; *s* nephew 1992; *educ* Charterhouse; former sales manager with Unilever then Pilkington; *m* 1965 *Lolita, dau of Deb Kumar Das, and has, with a yr s and two daus:

  1 +ARUP KUMAR SINHA; *b* 23 April 1966

Lineage: SITA KANTHA SINHA, of Raipur, Birbhum, Bengal; had:

SATYENDRA PRASANNA SINHA, **1st Baron Sinha**, of Raipur, Residency of Bengal (UK), so *cr* 14 Feb 1919, KCSI (1921), PC (1919), KC (1918), barrister Lincoln's Inn (Hon Bencher 1927) and Calcutta 1886, Advocate-Gen Bengal 1906, legal memb Govr-Gen's Cncl 1909–10, ktd 1915, Advocate-Gen and MEC Bengal 1916–17, Indian rep Special War Confs 1917 and 1918, U-Sec India 1919–20, Govr in Cncl Bihar and Orissa 1920–21, memb PC Judicial Ctee 1926; *m* 15 May 1880 Govinda Mohini (*d* Oct 1938), dau of Kristo Chunder Mitter, and had:

  1 ARUN KUMAR, **2nd Baron**

  2 Sisir K; *b* 22 Aug 1890; barrister; *m* 1917 — and *d* 1950, leaving:
    (1) +Indrajit; *b* 18 Aug 1918; *m* 22 April 1951 *Sunanda, dau of S Seu, of Calcutta, and has:
      1a *Premola; *b* 23 March 1954
    (1) *Anita; *b* 1921

  3 Sushil Kumar; *b* 9 June 1894; *educ* Balliol Coll Oxford and Pembroke Coll Cambridge; ICS, Ch Presidency Magistrate Calcutta; *m* 1st Oct 1919 — (*d* Dec 1919), dau of Sir Atul Chandra Chatterjee, GCIE, KCSI, ICS; *m* 2nd 1921 Romola, dau of Dr S K Mullick, and *d* 1968, leaving:
    (1) +Arun; *b* 13 Sept 1939; nuclear physicist in US
    (1) *Leila; *b* 15 June 1937

  4 Tarun K; *b* 9 Feb 1899; *educ* Hertford Coll Oxford (BA); with Fin Dept Govt India

  1 Kamala; *b* 1892; *m* 1st 1910 (*divorce* 1943) Ashoke Chandra Gupta, OBE, Accountant-Gen Centl Revenue India; *m* 2nd 1943 J Burnier, of Paris, and by her 1st husb had:
    (1) *Anil Kumar; *b* 1918

  2 Romola; *m* 1913 (*divorce* 1930) N N Gupta, barrister, and had issue

  3 Bijoli; *m* 1918 Runge Lall Dutt and had issue

The 1st BARON *d* 5 March 1928; his est s,

ARUN KUMAR SINHA, **2nd Baron Sinha**; *b* 22 Aug 1887; barrister; *m* 1st 1916 Pryatana (*d* 1919), er dau of Rai Bahadur Lalit Mohan Chatterjee, and had:
  1 *Bina; *b* May 1917
  2 *Gita; *b* 17 Nov 1918

The **2nd Baron** *m* 2nd 1919 Nirupama, yr dau of Rai Bahadur Lalit Mohan Chatterjee (*see* above), and *d* 11 May 1967, leaving by her

  1 SUDHINDRO PROSANNO SINHA, **3rd Baron Sinha**; *b* 29 Oct 1920; *educ* Bryanston; chm and md McNeill Barry Ltd Calcutta; *m* 1945 *Madhabi, dau of Monoranjan Chatterjee, of Calcutta, and *d* 1989, leaving:
    (1) SUSANTA PRASANNA SINHA, **4th Baron Sinha**; *b* 1953; tea broker; *m* 1972 *Patricia Orchard *d* 1992, having had:
      1a Shane Patrick; *b* 1974; *d* 1978
      1a *Caroline; *b* 1973
      2a Sharon Patricia; *b* 1975; *d* 1978
    (1) *Manjula; *b* 1947; *m* 19– (*divorce* 19–) Tobgye Dorji, s of Jigme Dorji, PM Bhutan, and has:
      1a *Jigme Tobgye; *b* 19–
    (2) *Anjana Lahiri; *b* 1950
  2 ANINDO KUMAR SINHA, **5th and present Baron Sinha**
  3 *Sheila; *b* 6 June 1923

SITWELL

Arms: Barry of eight or and vert three lions rampant sa. **Crest:** A demi-lion rampant, erased sa., holding between the paws an escutcheon per pale or and vert. **Motto:** *Ne cede malis* ('Yield not to misfortune'). **Creation:** Bt. (UK) 3 Oct 1808.

SIR (SACHEVERELL) RERESBY SITWELL, 7TH BT, of Renishaw, Co Derby, DL (Derbys 1984) [Sir Reresby Sitwell Bt DL, Renishaw Hall, nr Sheffield S31 9WB; 4 Southwick Place, London W2 2TN]; *b* 15 April 1927; *s* f 1988; *educ* Eton and King's Coll Cambridge; Lt Gren Gds (RARO) BAOR 1946–48, advertising and public relations exec 1948–60, vending machine business 1960–70, wine merchant 1960–75, High Sheriff Derbys 1983, Freeman City London 1984, Ld Manors of Eckington and Barlborough, Derbys, and Whiston and Brampton-en-le-Morthen, Yorks; *m* 31 Oct 1952 *Penelope, yr dau of Col Hon Donald Alexander Forbes, DSO, MVO (*see* GRANARD, E), and has:

  1 *Alexandra Isobel Susanna Edith; *b* 24 March 1958; *m* 1991 *Richard A Hayward, er s of Sir Jack Hayward, OBE, and has:
    (1) *Jack Osbert Reresby Sitwell (Bertie); *b* 1994
    (1) *Rosaleen Catriona Sitwell; *b* 1993

Lineage: WALTER de BOYS/de BOSCO/del WODE (*i.e.*, 'of the wood'); *d* by 1301 en route to the Holy Land, leaving:

SIMON SITEWELL, of Ridgeway, Eckington, Derbys; presumably kin to:

ROGER CYTEWELL; a fndr 1310 guild of St Mary of Eckington; presumably kin to:

JOHN CYTEWELL; thought to be f of a 4th s:

ROGER SYTWELL; living 1424; had:

ROBERT SYTWELL; had:

WILLIAM SYTWELL; *m* Elizabeth, dau, and coheir of Thomas Patte, and had:

ROBERT SYTWELL, of Staveley Netherthorpe; living 1588; *m* Elizabeth — (*m* 2nd Roland Eyre, of Hassop, ancestor of the titular Earls of Newburgh) and *d* 1599; presumably kin to:

FRANCIS SITWELL, of Eckington, Derbys; *m* Ellen, dau of Robert Bright, of Dore, Derbys, and was *bur* 9 March 1605, leaving, with two yr sons (Francis, *bapt* 26 Aug 1565, f of Robert (*dsp* 1599); William, *bapt* 23 Oct 1574) and three daus (Grace, *m* 3 Feb 1594 Thomas Crofte; Frances, *m* 1 Oct 1593 Richard Treeton; Alice, *d* unm):

GEORGE SITWELL, of Eckington; *bapt* 23 Sept 1569; bought back ROBERT SYTWELL's estates; *m* Mary (*m* 2nd Henry Wigfall, of Carter Hall), dau of Thomas Walker, of Derby, and was *bur* 23 April 1607, leaving:

GEORGE SITWELL, of Renishaw, Eckington, where he took up residence 1626; *bapt* 15 March 1600/1; royalist Civil War but Sheriff Derbys during Interregnum 1653; *m* 17 July 1627 Margaret, dau of Hugh Childers, of Car House, nr Doncaster, and was *bur* 2 Aug 1667, having had, with six yr sons (George, merchant at Seville 1662, of London by 1706, *m* Elizabeth, dau of Ralph Hawtrey, of Ruislip, Middx, and *d* 1708; Robert, merchant at Leghorn 1662, of London by 1684, *m* Elizabeth — and *d* by Sept 1684; John, of Derby, apprentice tailor, living 1667; William; two other sons *d* young) and four daus (Mary, *m* 1656 William Revel, of Ogston, Derbys; Elizabeth, *m* 1659 Robert Copley, of Nether Hall, Doncaster; two other daus *d* young):

FRANCIS SITWELL, of Renishaw; *bapt* 18 Jan 1630/1; Sheriff Derbys 1671; *m* 1656 Catherine, sis of William Sacheverel, the politician, of Barton and Morley, and *d* 1671, leaving, with three other sons and three daus (all *dsp* or unm):

  1 George, of Renishaw, JP, DL; *b* 23 Aug 1657; a Commr for Ld Ltcy London after 1689; *m* 20 May 1680 Anne, dau and heiress of Thomas Kent, of Povey, Dronfield, and was *bur* 24 Feb 1722/3, leaving, with two yr sons (*d* unm) and two daus (*dsp* or unm):
    (1) Francis, of Renishaw, DL; High Sheriff Derbys 1735; *d* unm 20 May 1753

  2 William, of Sheffield; *bapt* 16 Oct 1662; attorney; *m* 21 Sept 1693 Mary, dau and eventual heiress of Leonard Reresby, of Ecclesfield, one of the RERESBYs of Thribergh, and had, with three sons (Francis, attorney in Sheffield, *d* unm;

William, ironmonger in London, *d* unm; Henry, *d* unm) and another dau (*d* unm):

(1) Catherine; *bapt* 20 Aug 1702; *m* after 9 Nov 1725 Jonathan Hurt, of Sheffield, *s* of Valentine Hurt, of Hesley Hall, and had, with a dau (*d* young):

1a Francis HURT later SITWELL (roy licence 7 March 1777); *bapt* 29 April 1728; inherited 1791 his cousin Samuel Phipps's estates; *m* Mary (*d* 13 July 1792), sis to Col Warneford, of Warneford Place, and *d* 16 Aug 1793, having had:

1b SITWELL (Sir), **1st Bt**

2b Francis, of Barmoor Castle, Northumberland; MP Berwick and Carlisle; *m* 21 Sept 1795 Anne, dau of Sir Ilay Campbell, 1st Bt, of Succoth (*qv*), and *d* 10 Feb 1813, leaving, with another dau (*d* young):

1c Francis, of Barmoor Castle; *b* 1797; *m* 1818 Harriet Augusta Manners and *dsp* 1865

2c William Hurt, of Barmoor Castle and Yeavering; *b* 10 Sept 1803; Maj; *m* 29 Jan 1828 Sarah Honoria, dau of J Sisson Cooper, Comptroller-Gen Stamp Dept Ireland, and *d* 17 Jan 1865, having had, with three other sons and three other daus (*d* young or unm):

1d William Henry; *b* 23 May 1829; Lt 1st Bengal Inf; *ka* India 11 Jan 1850

2d Francis Henry Massey, of Barmoor Castle; *b* 9 Feb 1831; Maj, ADC to Sir James Outram, 1st Bt (*qv*), Persian Expdn and Indian Mutiny; *m* 1859 Elizabeth Maria, dau of Ogle d'Olier, and had two sons (William Henry; Francis Honorius Sisson)

3d Albert Hurt; *b* 1834; Rector St Peter's London, Chaplain to HM QUEEN VICTORIA; *m* Frances Featherstonehaugh and had two sons

1c Mary Amelia; *m* 30 April 1824 John Tait, advocate, Sheriff Perths, and *d* 1844 or 1845, leaving issue

2c Anne Jane; *m* 12 July 1824 her cousin John Campbell and had issue (see CAMPBELL, Bt, of Succoth)

3b Hurt, of Thurcroft and Ferney Hall, Salop; *m* Anne, dau of Simon Francis Hardy, of Huntingdon, and *d* 3 March 1803, leaving:

1c Francis Hurt, of Ferney Hall; *m* 1826 Harriet (*d* Oct 1827), dau of Sir Joseph Wallis Hoare, 3rd Bt, of Annabella (*qv*), and *d* 22 Aug 1835, leaving:

1d William Willoughby Hurt, of Ferney Hall; *b* 2 Oct 1827; *m* 1st 29 Sept 1853 Harriet Margaret (*d* May 1855), dau of William H Harford, of Barley Wood, Somerset, and had:

1e Willoughby Harford; *b* 18 May 1855

1d (cont.) William Sitwell *m* 2nd Eliza Harriet, dau of Richard Burton Phillipson, of Dunston House, Staffs, and by her had:

2e Francis Hurt; *b* 14 Jan 1860

1e Elinor Harriet; *m* 16 Sept 1884 Sir William Grenville Williams 4th Bt, of Bodelwyddan (*qv*), and *d* 30 April 1894, leaving issue

1b Mary; *m* 1 July 1790 Sir William Wake, 9th Bt (*qv*), and *d* 22 Nov 1791, leaving issue

The est s,

Sir Sitwell Sitwell, 1st Bt (UK), so *cr* 3 Oct 1808, of Renishaw, JP Derbys, Yorks; *b* Sept 1769; MP W Looe 1796, High Sheriff Derbys 1807; *m* 1st 1 Aug 1791 Alice (*d* 3 May 1797), dau of Thomas Parke, of Highfield Ho, Lancs, and sis of 1st and last Baron Wensleydale (*see* 1868 edn); *m* 2nd 23 July 1798 Sarah Caroline (*m* 2nd 19 Aug 1821 John Smith Wright, of Bulcote and Rempstone Hall, Notts, and *d* 2 Nov 1860), yst dau of James Stovin, of Whitgift Hall, and *d* 14 July 1811, having by her had a dau (*d* young), and by his 1st w, with two daus (Mary Alice, *m* 28 Aug 1815 Sir Charles Wake, 10th Bt (*qv*), and *dsp* 3 Sept 1816; Anne Elizabeth, *m* 1815 Gen Sir Frederick Stovin, KCB (*d* 16 Aug 1865), and *d* 3 April 1856):

Sir George Sitwell, 2nd Bt, of Renishaw; *b* 20 April 1797; High Sheriff Derbys 1828; *m* 1 June 1818 Susan Murray (*d* 13 May 1880), est dau of Crawford Tait, of Harvieston, Clackmannanshire, and sis of Archbp Archibald Tait of Canterbury, and had, with two other sons and five other daus (*d* young or unm):

1 SITWELL RERESBY (Sir), **3rd Bt**

2 George Frederick; *b* 7 July 1828; Capt 1st Life Gds, 85th Salop LI and 3rd Light Dragoons; *m* 3 Dec 1857 Cecilia Fanny (*d* 1 Nov 1873), dau of Henry FitzRoy (*see* GRAFTON, D), and *d* 1884, leaving:

(1) Claude George Henry, DSO (1899); *b* 18 Oct 1858; 85th Salop LI, Capt Manchester Regt, Lt-Col Roy Dublin Fus, V-Consul Uganda; *m* 1887 Amy Elizabeth Barrington (*d* 23 April 1890), dau of Robert Barrington Cooke, of Scarborough, and was *ka* Boer War 22 or 23 Feb 1900, leaving:

1a Cecilia Dorothy Charlotte; *m* 1st Sept 1910 (*divorce*) Maj Percy John Harris, Army Vet Corps, and had issue; *m* 2nd 1919, as his 2nd w, Frederick Laine Maunsell, slr, yst *s* of Rev Frederick Webster Maunsell, of Shrule, Queen's Co, Rector Symondsbury, Dorset. He *d* 30 May 1921

(2) Cecil Frederick; *b* 26 May 1860; Sec and ADC to Govr Windward Islands, Govt Commr to Gambia Tribes; *k* Gambia 14 June 1900

(3) Herbert Wellington; *b* 1 Aug 1861; Lt 4th Bn Sutherland and Argyll Highrs; *m* 1st 15 Jan 1885 (*divorce* 1901) Julietta Fisher, dau of Maj Robert Cary, Confederate States Army; *m* 2nd 1914 Eva (*d* 1920), widow of Richard C Worthington and dau of Stephen Putney, of Richmond, USA, and *d* 23 Jan 1922, having had by his 1st w:

1a Herbert Cecil FitzRoy; *b* 20 Jan 1896; Capt US Army; *m* 1st 1921 Helen (*d* 1955), dau of William E Barlow, PhD, of Cambridge, and had:

1b George FitzRoy; *b* 1923; Lt-Col US Army; *m* 1945 (*divorce* 1971) Elizabeth, dau of Paul Freed, of Waynesboro, Va., and *d* 198–, leaving:

1c *Elizabeth; *b* 1951; *m* Nov 1969 *Alfred Townsend Truitt, of Bradenton, Fla., and has:

1d *Anne; *b* 1972

1a (cont.) Herbert C Sitwell *m* 2nd 14 May 1961 *Phronsie Irene, formerly w of (a) W L Filmer and (b) Erik Solling Monberg, of Copenhagen, and dau of Peter Addison Marsh, of Campbell Co, Va., and *d* 15 Aug 1965

1a Juliet Evelyn Fay; *b* 12 Dec 1888

1 Susan Alice; *m* 29 July 1844 2nd Viscount Combermere (*qv*) and *d* 12 Aug 1869, leaving issue

---

2 Mary Elizabeth Anne; *m* 20 May 1871 Sir George Robert Osborn, 6th Bt (*qv*), and *dsp* 20 Feb 1909

3 Georgiana Caroline; *m* 7 Oct 1856 Archibald Campbell Swinton, of Kimminghame, Berwicks, and *d* 2 Feb 1900, leaving issue. He *d* 27 Nov 1890

4 Lucy Charlotte Hurt; *m* 18 Aug 1860 Herwald Crawford Wake, CB, 4th *s* of Sir Charles Wake, 10th Bt (*qv*), and *d* 17 Aug 1907, leaving issue

The 2nd Bt *d* 12 March 1853; his est s,

Sir Sitwell Reresby Sitwell, 3rd Bt, of Renishaw; *b* 6 Oct 1820; Lt 1st Life Gds; *m* 20 Aug 1857 Louisa Lucy (*d* 31 Oct 1911), 4th dau and coheir of Col Hon Henry Hely-Hutchinson (*see* DONOUGHMORE, E), and *d* 12 April 1862, leaving, with two daus (*d* unm):

Sir George Reresby Sitwell, 4th Bt, JP (Scarborough and Derbys); *b* 27 Jan 1860; Capt Yorks Dragoons, Lt-Col and Hon Col cmdg 2nd Vol Bn Yorks Regt, MP Scarborough 1885–86 and 1892–95, High Sheriff Derbys 1898; *m* 23 Nov 1886 Lady Ida Emily Augusta Denison, dau of 1st Earl of Londesborough (*qv*), and *d* 9 July 1943, leaving:

1 **Sir (Francis) Osbert Sacheverell Sitwell, 5th Bt**, CH (1958), CBE (1956), JP (Derbys 1939); *b* 6 Dec 1892; *educ* Eton; Capt Gren Gds (SR), poet and prose writer, Hon LLD St Andrews 1946, Hon DLitt Sheffield 1951, FRSL, Hon FRIBA 1957, won the first award of the *Sunday Times* prize for literature 1947, chm Management Ctee Authors' Soc 1944–45, 1946–48 and 1952; *d* unm 4 May 1969

2 SACHEVERELL (Sir), **6th Bt**

1 Edith Louisa, DBE (1954); poet, Hon LittD: Leeds 1948, Durham 1948, Oxon 1951, Sheffield 1954, V-Pres RSL 1958; *d* unm 9 Dec 1964

The 5th Bt's bro,

Sir Sacheverell Sitwell, 6th Bt, CH, JP (Northants 1943); *b* 15 Nov 1897; *educ* Eton and Balliol Coll Oxford; Lt Gren Gds (SR), *s* to Weston Hall 1923, High Sheriff Northants 1948; poet, author over 70 books, including *For Want of the Golden City* (1973); *m* 12 Oct 1925 Georgia, yr dau of Arthur Doble, of Montreal, by Georgie, dau of George Hyde, of Truro, Nova Scotia, and *d* 1988, leaving:

1 Sir (SACHEVERELL) RERESBY SITWELL, **7th and present Bt**

2 +FRANCIS TRAJAN SACHEVERELL [Francis Sitwell Esq, Weston Hall, Towcester, Northants NN12 8PU]; *b* 17 Sept 1935; heir presumptive; *educ* Eton; Sub-Lt RNVR 1954–56, Roy Dutch Shell Group 1956–66, advertising, public affairs and PR consultant, memb: Cncl London Philharmonic Orchestra 1965–84 (V-Chm 1983–84), Byam Shaw Sch Art 1975–91, WWF 1985–89, dir Sadlers Wells Theatre 1995–96, exec dir Westminster Forum 1997–; City Liaison Gp 1988–; *m* 21 June 1966 *Susanna Carolyn, 3rd dau of Rt Hon Sir Ronald Hibbert Cross, 1st and last Bt, KCMG, KCVO, PC (*see* 1959 edn), and has:

(1) +George Reresby Sacheverell; *b* 22 April 1967

(2) +William Ronald Sacheverell; *b* 2 Oct 1969; theatre critic *Daily Express* to 1997

(1) *Henrietta Louise Vereker; *b* 10 June 1973

SKELMERSDALE

Arms: Quarterly, 1st and 4th, arg. three bendlets wavy az. (for WILBRAHAM); 2nd and 3rd, gu. on a chevron engrailed, between three combs arg., as many crosses patées-fitchées of the field (for BOOTLE). **Crests:** 1 A wolf's head erased arg. (for WILBRAHAM), 2 A demi-lion regardant ppr., holding between his paws an escutcheon gu., charged with a cross-flory arg. (for BOOTLE). **Supporters:** Dexter, a wolf arg. gorged with a collar az., therefrom pendant an escutcheon, the field az., charged with two bars arg., a canton sa., thereon a wolf's head erased of the second (for WILBRAHAM); sinister, a wolf ppr. collared or, therefrom pendant an escutcheon as the dexter. **Motto:** *In portu quies* ('In a haven is rest'). **Creation:** B. (UK) 30 Jan 1828.

THE 7TH BARON SKELMERSDALE, of Skelmersdale, Co Lancaster (Roger Bootle-Wilbraham) [The Rt Hon The Lord Skelmersdale, House of Lords, London SW1A 0PW]; *b* 2 April 1945; *s f* 1973; *educ* Eton and Lord Wandsworth Coll; market gardener, breeder of a new strain of daffodil, V-Chm Cncl for Enviromental Conservation 1979–81, md Broadleigh Nurseries Ltd 1973–78 and dir 1991–,

Ld in Waiting (Govt Whip) 1981–86, Parly U-Sec: DOE 1986–87, DHSS 1987–88, DSS 1988–89, NI 1989–90, adviser politics and Parly affrs 1990–, dep chm Ctees Ho Lds 1991–, Dep Speaker 1996–; Pres: Somerset Tst for Nature Conservation 1980, Br Naturalists Assoc 1980–93, Chm Stroke Assoc 1993–, Govr Taunton Sch 1993–; *m* 5 Feb 1972 *Christine Joan, only dau of Philip Roy Morgan, of Ever-creech, Somerset, and has:

1 +ANDREW; *b* 9 Aug 1977
1 *Carolyn Ann; *b* 6 Oct 1974

Lineage: Sir RICHARD de WILBURGHAM; feudal Ld of Wymincham, Sheriff Cheshire *c* 1259; *m* 1st Margery, dau and coheir of Warine Vernon, Baron of Shipbrook (*see* VERNON, B), and had a *s* (*dsp*) and two daus (*m* respectively Richard de Lostock and Robert de Winnington); *m* 2nd Letitia, 2nd dau and coheir of Sir William Venables, of Wymincham, and *d c* 1274, having by her had:

WILLIAM de WILBURGHAM; feudal Ld of Radnor; *m* twice but had issue only by his 1st w Christiana, sis and coheir of Richard Crosley of Preston, Lancs; his est s:

WILLIAM de WILBURGHAM; feudal Ld of Radnor; *d c* 1353, leaving:

RALPH de WILBURGHAM; feudal Ld of Radnor; *m* 1st Felicia, dau of John de Hulme; *m* 2nd Matilda, dau of Robert Leigh, of Addington, by Matilda, dau of Sir Thomas de Norley, and *d c* 1388, leaving by his 1st w:

THOMAS de WILBURGHAM; feudal Ld of Radnor; *b c* 1366; *m* Margery, dau of Thomas de Leighes, and *d c* 1410, leaving:

THOMAS de WILBURGHAM; feudal Ld of Radnor; *m* Margaret, dau and heir of John Golborne, feudal Ld of Woodhey, thus acquiring that manor, and had, with three other sons:

1 Thomas; feudal Ld of the united manors of Radnor and Woodhey; *m temp* HENRY VI Margaret, dau of Thomas de Swettenham by Alice, sis and heiress of Roger de Overton, and *d c* 1492, leaving an est s:

(1) William WILBRAHAM, of Woodhey; *m* Helena, dau of Philip Egerton, of Egerton, and had, with several daus:

1a Thomas, of Woodhey; *m* Margaret, dau of Sir John Mainwaring, of Peover, and *dsp* 1558

2a Richard, of Woodhey; MP Cheshire, Master Jewel House and Revels to QUEEN MARY; *m* Dorothy, dau of Richard Grosvenor (*see* WESTMIN-STER, D), and had:

1b Thomas, of Woodhey and Tiltson; *m* 1st Frances, dau of Sir Hugh Cholmondeley, of Cholmondeley, and *d* 1610, having had:

1c Sir RICHARD WILBRAHAM, 1st Bt (E), so *cr* 1621, of Woodhey; *m* Grace, sis of 1st Viscount Savage, and *d* 1643, leaving an est s:

1d Sir THOMAS WILBRAHAM, 2nd Bt; royalist Civil War; *m* his cousin Elizabeth, dau and coheir of Sir Roger Wilbraham, of Bridge-more, Cheshire (*see* below), and *d c* 1660, having had, with an only dau (*m* 27 May 1657 Mytton Davies, of Gwynsanney, Sheriff Flint-shire 1670) and several other sons (all *dsp*):

1e Ralph, of Newbottle, Northants; *m* Christiana, dau of Edward Leigh, of Bagulegh, and *dvp*, having had, with an only dau and heir-ess (Elizabeth, *m* Sackville Tufton, ancestor of the Earls of Thanet; *see* DE CLIFFORD, B), an est s:

1f Sir THOMAS WILBRAHAM, 3rd and last Bt; *m* Elizabeth, dau and heiress of Edward Mytton, and *dspm* 1692, when the btcy expired, while his estates were shared by his daus as coheirs:

1g Elizabeth; *m* Sir Thomas Middleton, Bt, of Chirk Castle
2g Grace; *m* 3rd Earl of Dysart (*qv*)
3g Mary; *m* 2nd Earl of Bradford (*qv*) of the 1694 *cr*

2 Randulph; *m* Alice — and *d* 2 March 1548, leaving an est s:
(1) Ralph; *m* Elizabeth Sandford, of Lancaster, and had:
1a Randulph; Bristol merchant; *dsp* 1581
2a RICHARD
3a Thomas; barrister, Recorder City London, Attorney Court Wards; *m* Bar-bara, dau of Robert Chudleigh, of Middx, and *d* 1573
1a Margaret; *m* Thomas Clutter, of Nantwich

RALPH WILBRAHAM *d* 1552; his 2nd s,
RICHARD WILBRAHAM, of Nantwich; *b* 1528; *m* 1st Eliza, dau of Thomas Maisterson, of Nantwich; *m* 2nd Margaret, widow of Alexander Elerch, and had:

1 Richard; barrister, Common Serjeant City London; *m* 1584 Elizabeth, dau of Sir Thomas Puleston, Ld Mayor London, and *dvp* 13 Sept 1601, leaving, with other issue:
(1) THOMAS

2 Roger; Slr-Gen Ireland, Master Court Requests 1600; *dspm* 1616, leaving:
(1) Elizabeth; *m* her cousin Sir THOMAS WILBRAHAM, 2nd Bt (*see* above)

3 Thomas; *m* Anne Pyerson and had issue
4 Ralph; fœdary Cheshire and Flintshire, ancestor of the WILBRAHAMs of Dorfold

RICHARD Sr *d* 1612; his gs,
THOMAS WILBRAHAM, of Nantwich; *m* 1619 Rachel, dau and sole heiress of Joshua Clive (*see* POWIS, E), and had, with other issue:

ROGER WILBRAHAM, of Nantwich; *b* 1623; one of the intended Kts of the Royal Oak (an order mooted, but never founded, in CHARLES II's time), his estate being then valued at £1,000 (over £40,000 in late-1990s terms) p.a.; *m* his cousin Alice, dau of Roger Wilbraham, of Dorfold, and gdau maternally of Thomas Ravenscroft, of Bretton, and had, with two daus (Alice, *m* her cousin Ralph Wil-braham, of Dorfold; Grace, *m* Sir Thomas Brooke; *see* BROOKE, Bt, of Norton Pri-ory), and several yr sons:

RANDLE WILBRAHAM, of Nantwich; Sheriff Cheshire 1714; *m* Mary, dau of Sir Richard Brooke, 2nd Bt, of Norton (*qv*), and *d* 1732, having had, with an est s (Roger, of Nantwich, ancestor of the WILBRAHAMs of Delamere), two yst sons (Thomas, LLD, FRS, Fell All Souls, *dsp*; Rev Henry William, Rector Shelford, *d* unm) and three daus, a 2nd s:

RANDLE WILBRAHAM, LLD, of Rode Hall, Cheshire, which his gf ROGER had bought from a cousin, Randle Rode, in 1669; Dep-High Steward Oxford U, MP; *m*

---

24 Aug 1722 Dorothy, only dau of Andrew Kenrick, of Chester, and *d* 1770, leav-ing an only surv s:

RICHARD WILBRAHAM later WILBRAHAM-BOOTLE (added under terms of will of his w's unc, Sir Thomas Bootle (*d* 1753), Chllr to FREDERICK, PRINCE OF WALES, who had bought the manor of Lathom in 1725 and the Skelmersdale estate 1751, although the BOOTLEs had been landed proprietors in Melling as early as 1317), of Rode; MP Chester; *m* Mary, dau and sole heiress of Robert Bootle, of Lathom House, Lancs, and had:

1 EDWARD, **1st Baron**

2 Randle, of Rode, JP; *b* 10 Jan 1773; High Steward Congleton; *m* 1st 5 Dec 1798 Letitia (*d* 30 March 1805), dau and heiress of Rev Edward Rudd, Rector Haughton-le-Skerne, by Lætitia, dau of John Arden, of Alvanley, and had issue; *m* 2nd 9 Feb 1808 Sybella (*d* 30 May 1868), dau of Philip Egerton, and *d* 12 Jan 1861, having had further issue (*see* BAKER-WILBRAHAM, Bt)

1 Anne Dorothea; *m* 1784 1st Baron Alvanley (*see* 1857 edn) and *d* 17 Jan 1825
2 Mary; *m* 26 Oct 1780, as his 2nd w, William Tatton Egerton, of Tatton Park, and Wythenshawe, Cheshire, and *d* 13 Nov 1784, leaving issue. He *d* 21 April 1806
3 Francisca Alicia; *m* 1783 Anthony Hardolph Eyre, of Grove, Notts, and *d* 3 Sept 1810
4 Sibylla Georgiana; *m* 16 June 1791 William ffarington, of Worden, Lancs, and *d* 22 Nov 1799
5 Emma; *m* 1 June 1794 Sir Charles Edmonstone, 2nd Bt (*qv*), and *d* 30 Nov 1797, leaving issue
6 Elizabeth; *m* 1821 Rev W Barnes, Rector Brixton Doverill, Wilts, and *d* 17 Dec 1841

The est s,
EDWARD WILBRAHAM-BOOTLE later BOOTLE-WILBRAHAM (roy licence 8 Dec 1814), **1st Baron Skelmersdale**, of Skelmersdale, Co Lancaster (UK), so *cr* 30 Jan 1828; *b* 7 March 1771; *educ* Eton and Ch Ch Oxford; MP (Tory) Westbury 1795–96, Newcastle-under-Lyme 1796–1812, Clitheroe 1812–18 and Dover 1818–28; *m* 19 April 1796 Mary Elizabeth (*d* 2 June 1840), dau of Rev Edward Taylor, of Bifrons, Kent, and *d* 3 April 1853, having had, with a dau (*d* unm):

1 Richard; *b* 27 Oct 1801; MP; *m* 22 May 1832 Jessy (*d* 18 July 1892), 3rd dau of Sir Richard Brooke, 6th Bt, of Norton Priory (*qv*), and *dvp* 5 May 1844, leaving:

(1) EDWARD BOOTLE-WILBRAHAM, **2nd Baron Skelmersdale** and 1st EARL OF LATHOM, Co Lancaster, so *cr* 3 May 1880, GCB (1892), PC (1874), JP, DL Lancs; *b* 12 Dec 1837; *educ* Eton and Ch Ch Oxford; Ld-in-Waiting 1866–68, Capt Yeomen Gd 1874–80, Ld Chamberlain 1885–Feb 1886, Aug 1886–92 and 1895–98, Hon Col Lancs Hus; *m* 16 Aug 1860 Lady Alice Villiers (*d* 23 Nov 1897), 2nd dau of 4th Earl of Clarendon (*qv*), and *d* 19 Nov 1898, having had, with two daus (*d* unm):

1a EDWARD GEORGE BOOTLE-WILBRAHAM, **3rd Baron Skelmersdale** and 2nd EARL OF LATHOM, JP Lancs; *b* 26 Oct 1864; Maj and Hon Lt-Col Lancs Hus, Cdr RNVR (Liverpool Div), Hon Col 2nd Lancs RE Vols, Maj RHG; *m* 15 Aug 1889 Lady Wilma Pleydell-Bouverie, CBE (*m* 2nd 16 Nov 1912 Lt-Gen Sir Henry Merrick Lawson, KCB (*d* 2 Nov 1933), and *d* 10 Feb 1931), only surv dau of 5th Earl of Radnor (*qv*), and *d* 15 March 1910, hav-ing had, with another dau (*d* unm):

1b EDWARD WILLIAM BOOTLE-WILBRAHAM, **4th Baron Skelmers-dale** and 3rd and last EARL OF LATHOM; *b* 16 May 1895; Capt Lancs Hus Yeo, ADC to Govr-Gen Bombay; *m* 2 June 1927 (Marie) Xenia (*d* 5 Sept 1974), formerly w of Ronald William Morison and dau of E E de Tunzelman, of Singapore, and *dsp* 6 Feb 1930, when the Earldom expired

1b Helen Alice; *b* 12 Aug 1890; *m* 1st 29 Jan 1913 (*divorce* 1922) Hugh Sartorius Whitaker, yst s of William Ingham Whitaker, JP (*d* 24 Jan 1971), of Pylewell Park, Hants, and had issue; *m* 2nd 10 June 1925 Maj-Gen Henry William Newcome, CB, CMG, DSO, RA, s of Maj Henry George Newcome, RA (*d* 25 Feb 1963), and *d* 2 Aug 1929, having had fur-ther issue

2b Barbara Ann; *b* 2 May 1893; *m* 21 Dec 1914 Francis Seymour (*see* HERTFORD, M) and *d* 31 Oct 1949

3b Rosemary Wilma; *b* 1 Oct 1903; *m* 1st 26 July 1930 Vincent Francis Cassidy (*d* 19 May 1931), of S Kensington; *m* 2nd Capt T H Bird (*d* 1954) and *d* 10 March 1968, leaving issue

2a Villiers Richard; *b* 17 April 1867; Lt Rifle Bde (Prince Consort's Own); *m* 25 Oct 1900 Violet Inez de Romero (*dsp* 27 Dec 1908) and *d* 6 June 1913
3a Randle Arthur; *b* 6 April 1868; Sub-Lt RN; *d* 11 July 1889
4a Reginald Francis; *b* 26 July 1875; *m* 18 Dec 1903 Lilian Mary (*m* 2nd 2 March 1917 Richard Mountford Wood, of Aldbury, Herts, and Les Cigales, Agay, France), 2nd dau of Maj William Lyster Holt, and *dsp* 21 June 1912
1a Alice Maud, OBE (1920) (HRH PRINCESS ALICE stood sponsor); *d* 28 Oct 1922
2a Florence Mary; *m* 16 Aug 1887 Rt Rev Lord William Gascoyne-Cecil, Bp Exeter (*see* SALISBURY, M), and *d* 17 May 1944, leaving issue
3a Bertha Mabel; Woman Bedchamber to HM QUEEN MARY 1907–35, Extra Woman Bedchamber 1935–43; *m* 9 May 1903 Maj Arthur Frederick Dawkins, Northumberland Fus, s of Clinton George Augustus Dawkins, and *d* 12 Nov 1943, leaving issue. He *d* 27 March 1905

(1) Adela Mary; granted with her sisters rank of baron's daus; *d* 22 April 1881
(2) Jessy Caroline; *m* 4 Oct 1865 John Bateman, of Brightlingsea Hall, Essex, and *d* 18 Oct 1925, leaving issue. He *d* 12 Oct 1910
(3) Edith; *m* 7 Sept 1859 Ynyr Henry Burges, of Parkanaur, Co Tyrone, and *d* 2 Feb 1894, leaving issue. He *d* 14 Aug 1908
(4) Rose; *d* unm 20 May 1918

2 Edward; *b* 22 Dec 1807; Col Coldstream Gds; *m* 8 July 1841 Emily (*d* 20 Dec 1899), 4th dau of James Ramsbottom, and *d* 17 Dec 1882, leaving:
(1) Arthur, DL; *b* 9 Sept 1842; Lt Coldstream Gds, Lt-Col 1st Vol Bn Manches-ter Regt; *m* 19 July 1875 Elizabeth Jane (*d* 2 Feb 1925), n of Sir William Jar-dine, 7th Bt, of Applegirth (*qv*), and *d* 21 May 1897, leaving:

1a ARTHUR GEORGE BOOTLE-WILBRAHAM, **5th Baron Skelmersdale**, MC; *b* 21 May 1876; *educ* Wellington and Freiburg (Saxony) Sch of Mines; Capt RE (SR) WW I (despatches); *d* unm 9 Feb 1969

2a Evelyn Caryl, OBE (1918); *b* 8 June 1877; *educ* Clifton and Leipzig U (PhD 1904); FIC, MIChemE, Min Munitions WW I; *m* 31 Oct 1924 (Sylvia) Joan (*d* 8 April 1995), only dau of Hugh Reeves, of Tillingham, Hartfield, Sussex, and *d* 3 Feb 1955

3a Claude; *b* 8 June 1877; Maj RASC WW I (despatches); *m* 1st 17 Feb 1921 (*divorce* 1932) Frances May Pile; *m* 2nd 18 Aug 1932 Hilda Marguerite, dau of Michael Knockton, and *dsp* 25 July 1955

(2) Lionel; *b* 19 Jan 1853; Maj Princess Victoria's Roy Irish Fus; *m* 9 April 1895 Lavinia (*d* 31 Aug 1930), dau of Abraham Wilson, of Downshire House, Newry, Co Down, and *d* 4 Jan 1914, leaving:

  1a LIONEL, **6th Baron**

  1a Yvonne

(1) Emma Violet; *d* 1846

(2) Ada Constance; *m* 11 July 1867 Onorato Caetani, 15th Duke di Sermoneta, Senator of Italy and sometime Min For Affrs, and *d* 16 Sept 1934, leaving issue. He *d* 2 Sept 1917

(3) Emily Florence; *m* 22 July 1869 26th Earl of Crawford and (9th Earl of) Balcarres (*qv*) and *d* 15 Jan 1934, leaving issue

(4) Evelyn Adela; *m* 30 Oct 1877 Sir John Gordon Kennedy, KCMG, and *d* 28 Nov 1939, leaving issue (*see* AILSA, M)

1 Emma Caroline; *m* 21 May 1825 14th Earl of Derby (*qv*) and *d* 26 April 1876, leaving issue

The 5th BARON's cousin,

LIONEL BOOTLE-WILBRAHAM, **6th Baron Skelmersdale**, DSO (1940), MC (1917); *b* 23 Sept 1896; *educ* Wellington and Cheltenham; Brig, Lt-Col Coldstream Gds, ADC to Govr Madras 1924–27, Mil Sec 1929–32, served WWs I and II (despatches), Dir Assoc Br Oil Engines (Export) Ltd; *m* 1 Oct 1936 Ann (*d* 1974), 2nd dau of Percy Cuthbert Quilter (*see* QUILTER, Bt), and *d* 21 July 1973, leaving:

1 ROGER BOOTLE-WILBRAHAM, **7th and present Baron Skelmersdale**

1 *Lavinia [The Hon Mrs Massey, Waterstone House, Itchenor, W Sussex]; *b* 1 Aug 1937; *m* 12 July 1969 *Robert Brian Noel Massey, only s of Noel Armstrong Edmonds Massey, of Brighton, by Mme Arnaud des Chaffons, of Amboise, France, and has:

  (1) *Harry; *b* 1975

  (2) *Archibald Edmonds; *b* 1977

2 *Olivia [The Hon Mrs Olivia Lowsley-Williams, Villa Rosa, 36 Paseo de Coca, Los Barrios, Cadiz, Spain]; *b* 31 Dec 1938; *m* 29 July 1961 (*divorce* 1975) Anthony John Hoole Lowsley-Williams (*see* MAKINS, Bt), 2nd s of Maj Francis Saville Hoole Lowsley-Williams, 16th/5th Lancers, and Lady Greene, of Wickham Ho, Newbury, Berks, and has:

  (1) *Richard Edward; *b* 16 Aug 1962

  (2) *(Hugh) Sebastian; *b* 22 July 1964

  (3) *Benjamin Christopher; *b* 25 Dec 1968

3 *Daphne [The Hon Daphne Wilbraham, 1 Canynge Sq, Clifton, Bristol BS8 3LA]; *b* 1946; *m* 1980 (*divorce* 1992, resumed part of maiden name) Jocelyn Peter Gore Graham, s of Brig Peter Alastair John Gore Graham, of Chalkpit Cottage, Blewbury, Oxon, and has:

  (1) *Tamsin Christobel; *b* 1985

SKIDELSKY

Creation: B. (LP, UK) 1991.

THE BARON SKIDELSKY, of Tilton, Co East Sussex (Robert Jacob Alexander Skidelsky) [The Rt Hon The Lord Skidelsky, Tilton House, Firle, E Sussex BN8 6LL]; *b* 25 April 1939; *educ* Brighton Coll and Jesus Coll Oxford (MA, DPhil, Hon Fell 1997); Research Fellow Nuffield Coll Oxford 1965–68, Br Acad 1968–70, Assoc Prof History Johns Hopkins U USA 1970–76, Head Dept of History, Philosophy and European Studies N London Poly 1976–78, Prof Internat Studies Warwick U 1978–90, Prof Political Economy Warwick U 1990–, Chm Charleston Tst 1987–92, Memb Policy Ctee SDP 1988–90 and Ld Chllr's Advsy Cncl Public Records 1988–93, Chm Social Market Fndn 1989–, Pres Hands Off Reading Campaign 1994–97, FRHistS 1973, FRSL 1978, FBA 1994; Hon DLitt Buckingham U 1997; author: *Politicians and the Slump* (1967), *English Progressive Schools* (1969), *Oswald Mosley* (1975), *John Maynard Keynes* (vol I 1883–1920: 'Hopes Betrayed' (1983), vol II 1921–1937: 'The Economist as Saviour' (1992)), *Interests and Obsessions* (1993), *The World After Commmunism* (1995); *m* 1970 *Augusta Mary Clarissa, dau of John Humphrey Hope, of E Harptree, Somerset, and has:

1 *Edward; *b* 1973; *educ* Eton

2 *William; *b* 1976; *educ* Eton

1 *Juliet; *b* 1983

Lineage: BORIS JACOB SKIDELSKY, of Vladivostok, Russia; *m* Galia Sapelkin and had:

ROBERT JACOB ALEXANDER SKIDELSKY, *cr* a **Baron**

SKINNER

Arms: Erm. on a bend or, between in chief a port between two towers ppr., flying therefrom to the sinister two pennons gu., and in base an ancient ship of the second, three maple leaves, slipped vert.

Crest: A griffin's head couped vert, the neck or, between two dragon's wings gu. **Motto:** *Nec timeo nec sperno* ('I neither fear nor despise'). **Creation:** Bt. (UK) 9 Feb 1912.

SIR (THOMAS) KEITH HEWITT SKINNER, 4TH BT, of Pont Street, Chelsea [Sir Keith Skinner Bt, Wood Farm, Reydon, Suffolk IP18 6SL]; *b* 6 Dec 1927; *s f* 1972; *educ* Charterhouse; md Thomas Skinner & Co (Publishers) 1952–60, dir: Iliffe and Co 1958–65, Iliffe-NTP Ltd, Reed Internat 1980–90, chm and ch exec Reed Publishing Ltd and Reed Regional Publishing 1982–90, chm: Business Press Int 1970–84, Industrial Trade Fair Hldgs 1977–; *m* 29 April 1959 *Jill, dau of Cedric Ivor Tuckett, of Yardley Gables, Tonbridge, Kent, and has:

1 +(THOMAS) JAMES HEWITT; *b* 11 Sept 1962

2 +Ian Ivor; *b* 11 Sept 1964

Lineage: JAMES SKINNER, of Bristol; had:

Sir Thomas Skinner, 1st Bt (UK), so *cr* 9 Feb 1912, of Pont Street, Chelsea, JP Middx; *b* 23 Nov 1840; dir Canadian Pacific Rlwy, Bank of Montreal and Commercial Cable Co; fndr/ed *Stock Exchange Year Book* and *The Directory of Directors*; *m* 1st 17 March 1866 Sarah Margaret (*d* 6 Feb 1902), dau of Jonas Barnett Hewitt, of London and Macclesfield, and had:

1 (THOMAS) HEWITT (Sir), **2nd Bt**

2 Ernest; *b* 18 Aug 1880; *m* 2 Sept 1903 Leonie Mercedes (*d* 19 Sept 1964), 3rd dau of Henry William Doll, of Lancing, Sussex, and *d* 9 March 1919, leaving:

  (1) *(Eva) Jacqueline Leonie [Miss Jacqueline Skinner, 8 Taring Gate, St Lawrence Ave, Worthing, Sussex]; *b* 26 May 1914

3 John; *b* 12 Feb 1882; *m* 16 June 1904 Angela (*d* 16 July 1958), only dau of Walter Dunn, of Maida Vale, London, and *d* 21 June 1939, leaving:

  (1) +John Reginald; *b* 5 Dec 1909; *m* 2 April 1949 *Shirley Evelyn, dau of James Roddick, of Melbourne, Australia, and has:

    1a *Dawn Rosalyn; *b* 31 May 1952

4 Charles Henry; *b* 28 April 1886; *m* 8 Feb 1910 Violet Muriel, only dau of Herbert Furber, of Hampstead and Frinton, Essex, and *d* 15 April 1966, having had:

  (1) (Charles) David Evelyn; *b* 17 July 1916; *educ* Cheltenham; *m* 11 March 1940 *Pamela [Mrs David Skinner, The Pound, Yarmouth, IoW PO41 0PY], dau of Dr Samuel Barrett Couper, of Blaby, Leics, and *d* 1987, leaving:

    1a +Peter David [Peter Skinner Esq, Elm Tree House, Kemble, Glos]; *b* 25 Feb 1941; *educ* Sherborne; late RAF; *m* 14 March 1964 *Susan Mary, er dau of Keith Francis Thompson, of Worcester, and has:

      1b +Mark David Francis; *b* 10 Feb 1966

      2b +James Nicholas Peter; *b* 1982

      1b *Sarah Lucinda; *b* 8 Dec 1968

    1a *Carol; *b* 1 Jan 1944; *m* 1st 5 Dec 1967 (*divorce* 19–) Peter De Villiers; *m* 2nd 1993 *Alwyn Landman

    2a *Susan Pamela [Mrs Robert Webb, The Manor House, Walton-in-Gordano, Somerset]; *b* 23 Aug 1945; *m* 27 Feb 1965 *Robert Webb

  (1) Violet Elizabeth Furber; *b* 20 Dec 1913; *m* 15 June 1935 Albert Ryan Wood, only s of T R Wood, of Green Tiles, Ufford, Suffolk, and *d* 4 Sept 1965, leaving issue

1 Margaret Maude; *m* 16 May 1888 Sydney Wallis Leleux, of Brixton, and *d* 28 Jan 1911, leaving issue

2 Lynette; *m* 3 July 1895 Alfred William Attneave, of Highbury, and *d* 3 Feb 1939, having had issue. He *d* 8 March 1936

3 Elsie Winifred; *m* 9 June 1898 George Sibley Berry (*d* 15 March 1916), of Enfield, Middx, and had:

  (1) Kenneth Frank; *b* 14 July 1899

  (2) George Duncan; *b* 17 Sept 1901

4 Dorothy; *m* 4 Dec 1906 James Brewer, of London, and *d* 22 Sept 1963

Sir Thomas *m* 2nd 26 May 1903 Martha Lauretta (*d* 31 Jan 1924), widow of Charles James Williamson, of New York, and dau of Job Long, of New York, and *d* 11 May 1926

The er s,

Sir (Thomas) Hewitt Skinner, 2nd Bt; *b* 12 June 1875; *educ* Cheltenham; chm and md Thomas Skinner & Co; *m* 21 March 1899 Nellie Constance (*d* 17 Nov 1955), er dau of James Hay Hall, of Highgate, and had:

1 (THOMAS) GORDON (Sir), **3rd Bt**

2 Stanley Hewitt; *b* 13 March 1911; W/Cdr AAF WW II; *m* 19 April 1941 *Joyce (*m* 2nd 8 Nov 1945 Lt-Col Louis de Loriol, RA (*d* Aug 1966); *m* 3rd 8 Nov 1969 Lt-Col George Cecil Pim, s of George Pim, of Brenanstown, Co Dublin), yr dau of Rodney de Levis Prizer, of London and New York, and was *kas* 19 Aug 1942

1 Constance Irene; *b* 29 April 1901; *m* 28 Oct 1936 Claude Harry Mills (*d* 1971), 3rd s of William Henry Mills, JP

2 Nellie Gwendoline; *b* 23 June, *d* 7 July 1904

3 Marie Vivien; *b* 23 Dec 1908; *m* 1st 12 Oct 1933 (*divorce* 1950) Robert Archibald Hugh Collum, only s of Hugh Fraser Collum, of Surbiton, and has:

(1) *Hugh Robert; *b* 29 June 1940; *educ* Eton; ACA; *m* 24 July 1965 *Elizabeth Noel, yr dau of Henry Gordon Stewart, of Moor Cottage, Binfield, Berks, and has:

1a *Lucinda Elizabeth; *b* 13 June 1967

2a *Melissa Jane; *b* 6 Sept 1969

(1) *Juliet Vivian; *b* 17 April 1942; *m* 15 June 1963 *Andrew John Mack Huntley, only s of William Mack Huntley, of Bristol, and has:

1a *Amanda Juliet; *b* 2 July 1968

2a *A dau; *b* 8 May 1971

3 (cont.) Mrs Marie Collum *m* 2nd 19 Aug 1950 Haydon Dorman Bradshaw, son of Richard Goodwin Bradshaw, of Coombe Warren, Kingston Hill, Surrey

Sir HEWITT *d* 4 Oct 1968; his er and only surv son,

Sir (Thomas) Gordon Skinner, 3rd Bt; *b* 29 Dec 1899; *educ* Charterhouse and Exeter Coll Oxford; RAF (despatches) WWs I and II, dir and manager Thomas Skinner & Co 1937–51; *m* 1st 5 June 1926 (*divorce* 1953) Mollie Barbara (*d* 21 Oct 1965), er dau of Herbert William Girling, of Frostenden, Suffolk, and had:

1 Sir (THOMAS) KEITH HEWITT SKINNER, **4th and present Bt**

2 +Gordon Michael Hewitt [Gordon Skinner Esq, PO Box 16526, Nairobi, Kenya]; *b* 24 July 1930; *educ* Charterhouse; *m* 1st 8 Oct 1955 (*divorce* 1960) Josephine Dawn, dau of Dudley S Redman, of Bleak Hall, Biggleswade, Beds, and has:

(1) +Dudley Mark Hewitt; *b* 22 Sept 1956

2 (cont.) Gordon Skinner *m* 2nd 2 April 1961 (*divorce* 1968) Eve, dau of Vernon John Fullforth, of London SW1, and by her has:

(1) *Sarah Patricia; *b* 11 Oct 1963

2 (cont.) Gordon Skinner *m* 3rd 5 Oct 1968 Jean Margaret Helen (*d* in a car accident 1 March 1995), widow of Robin Vetch and dau of Donald Sharp, of Kenya; *m* 4th 27 Nov 1995 *Pamela Savage, widow of Keith Savage and dau of Charles H Rowbottom

3 +Peter Girling Hewitt [Peter Skinner Esq, Highway Model Farm, Downside, Cobham, Surrey KT11 3JZ]; *b* 4 Dec 1938; *educ* Clayesmore; *m* 4 June 1966 *Jennifer Dingley, dau of John Corbett, of Perry Mill, Bradley Green, Worcs, and has:

(1) +Justin Mark Thomas; *b* 12 Sept 1968

(2) +Peter Dominic Thomas; *b* 1970

(1) *Gemma Sophia Nicola; *b* 1977

Sir Gordon *m* 2nd 4 July 1953 *Jeanne Marie Louise, only dau of François de Launoit, of Brussels, and *d* 22 Nov 1972

SKIPWITH

Arms: Arg. three bars gu., in chief a greyhound courant sa., collared or. **Crest:** A turnstile ppr. **Motto:** *Sans Dieu je ne puis* ('Without God I am not able'). **Creation:** Bt. (E) 20 Dec 1622.

SIR PATRICK ALEXANDER D'ESTOTEVILLE SKIPWITH, 12TH BT, of Prestwould, Co Leicester [Sir Patrick Skipwith Bt, 76 rue de Pont-aux-Moines, 45450 Donnery, France]; *b* 1 Sept 1938; *s* gf 1950; *educ* Harrow, Trin Coll Dublin (MA) and Imperial Coll London (DIC, PhD); marine geologist Tasmania 1966–67, Malaysia 1967–69, W Africa 1969–70, with Directorate Gen Mineral Resources Jeddah Saudi Arabia 1970–71 and 1972–73, geological ed Bureau de Recherches Géologiques et Minières Jeddah 1973–86, dir Immel Publishing 1987–95 and md 1988–89, consultant ed and translator (GeoEdit) 1986–96, head translation BRGM Orléans 1996–; *m* 24 June 1964 (*divorce* 1970) Gillian Patricia, adopted dau of Charles Frederick Harwood, of White Barn Ho, Alderley Edge, Cheshire, and has:

1 ALEXANDER SEBASTIAN GREY D'ESTOTEVILLE; *b* 9 April 1969; *educ* Harrow and Kent U; md Pepper Head Design

1 *Zara Alexandra Jane d'Estoteville; *b* 8 April 1967

Sir PATRICK *m* 2nd 1972 (*divorce* 1997) Ashkhain, dau of Bedros Atikian, of Calgary, Canada; *m* 3rd 1997 *Martine Sophie, dau of Joseph de Wilde, of Theillay, France, and by her has:

2 +Grey Camille d'Estoteville; *b* 17 July 1997

3 +Louis Peyton d'Estoteville; *b* 17 July 1997

Lineage: PATRICE de SKIPWIC, possibly yr s of ROBERT d'ESTOUTEVILLE (gs of ROBERT (*Grandboelle*) d'ESTOUTEVILLE, Sire d'Estouteville, Normandy, a companion of WILLIAM I (THE CONQUEROR)), feudal Ld Cottingham (*d* 1183), by whom PATRICE was granted the feudal Ldship of Skipwith, E R Yorks, after 1166; *m* Beatrix, dau of Pagan de Langton, and had:

GEOFFREY de SKIPWIC; living by 1199; *m* Margaria (*m* 2nd Adam de Mariscis), dau and heir of William Menethorpe, and had, with two yr sons (Gerald; Ralph de Thorpe):

REGINALD de SKIPWIC; feudal Ld Skipwith by 1205; *m* —, dau of John de Bella Aqua/Bellew, of Carlton, Yorks and had, with a yr s (Richard de Thorpe, *dsp*):

Sir WILLIAM de SKIPWITH; feudal Ld Skipwith by 1252; *m* Alice, dau of John and sis and heir of Sir William Thorpe, feudal Ld Kettleby Thorpe and Bigby, Lincs, and had, with two daus (Anne, *m* Sir John d'Isney, of Norton Disney, Lincs; Catherine, *m* Sir Robert Constable, of Flamborough, Yorks, MP Yorks):

Sir JOHN de SKIPWITH; held 1282 a Kt's fee in Skipwith, Little Weighton, Kettleby Thorpe and Bigby; feudal Ld Wrauby in right of his w; *m* Isabella, dau and heir of Robert de Arches, and *d* 1349, having had, with two other sons (William, *dsp*; Robert, *dsp*) and a dau (Elizabeth, *m* as his 1st w Sir John Babthorpe, of Babthorpe, Yorks):

JOHN de SKIPWITH; *m* Margaret, 3rd dau and coheir of Sir Walter de la Lynde, feudal Ld Bolebroke, Sussex, and Laceby, Lincs, and *dvp*, leaving, with a yr s (John, feudal Ld Haburgh, Lincs, ancestor of the SKIPWITHs of Haburgh, who died out 1560, and of St Albans, who died out 1663):

Sir WILLIAM de SKIPWITH; *m* 1st Margaret, dau of Sir Ralph fitz Simon, feudal Ld Ormsby and sis and heir of Sir Simon fitz Ralph; *m* 2nd — and *d* by 1369, leaving by her a dau (Margaret, *m* 1st 1378 Sir Alexander Surtees, of N Gosford (*d* 1380), *m* 2nd Sir Robert Constable, MP, of Flamborough, thrice Sheriff Yorks, and had issue by both) and by his 1st w, with two er sons (Ralph, *d* young; John, *d* unm 1326):

Sir WILLIAM de SKIPWITH, KB (1360); *b c* 1314; MP York 1348, Justice of Assize 1351, King's Serjeant 1354, Justice City London 1357, Judge King's Bench 1359, Ld Ch Baron Exchequer 1363, Ld Ch Justice Ireland 1370, Ch Justice N and S Wales 1376, Judge Common Pleas 1376, Ld Ch Justice 1378–88; *m* Alice, only child of Sir William de Hiltoft, feudal Ld Middle and S Hiltoft in Ingoldmells, also Mumby, Covenham, Calthorpe and Uphall, Lincs, and *d* after 1398, having had:

1 William, JP Lincs and Yorks; Commr Array Yorks 1376 and Parts of Lindsey 1382, Escheator (*roy official implementing reversion of land to Crown in event of previous holder having d without heirs*) Lincs and Yorks 1380, Alnager

Yorks 1394; *m* 1st Catharine (*dsp*), dau of Roger Aswardby, of Aswardby; *m* 2nd Catherine, dau of Edmund (?) d'Averinges and widow of Sir Thomas Bosville, of Cavill, and *d* 1401, having had by her:

   (1) William; *dvp*

   (1) Elizabeth; *m* George Monboucher, s and heir of Asir Nicholas Monboucher, of Gamelton, and *dsp* 1412/3

2 JOHN (Sir)

3 Stephen; Rector Beningworth, Ingoldmells and Rand, Canon Lincoln, Master Peterhouse Cambridge; *d* 1397

4 Patrick; *m* ?Agnes, dau of John Langholme, of Conisholme, and had:

   (1) Barnaby

5 Thomas; Kt Hospiotaller Superior Preceptory of Ribston, Yorks, after 1408

1 Alice; *m* 4th Lord (Baron) Willoughby de Eresby (*qv*)

2 Margaret; *m* 1st Hugh de Cressy, s and heir of Sir John de Cressy, of Hodstock; *m* 2nd Sir Henry Vavasour, of Haslewood (*see* VAVASOUR, Bt)

3 Anne; *m* Sir John Lascelles, of Escrick, and had issue

The 2nd s,

Sir JOHN SKIPWITH; Sheriff Lincs 1394, 1397 and 1399, ktd 1399, MP Lincs 1406, 1407 and 1414; *m* Alice, dau of Sir Frederick Tilney, of Tilney, Norfolk, and Boston, Lincs, and *d* 15 July 1415, having had, with an est s (William, *dsp* & *vp*) and two yr sons (William, of Louth, living 1472; Patrick, MP Lincs 1427 and 1433, *m* Agnes, dau and heir of Sir Thomas Hawley, of Utterby, Lincs, and *d* 1471, being ancestor of the SKIPWITHs of Utterby; who died out *c* 1650, and the SKIPWITHs of Snore, Norfolk, who died out after 1660):

Sir THOMAS SKIPWITH; fought in Hundred Years War, ktd 1417; *m* Margaret, dau of 5th Lord (Baron) Willoughby de Eresby (*qv*), and *d* 1417, leaving:

Sir WILLIAM SKIPWITH; *b* 1417; Sheriff Lincs 1458 and 1465; *m* 1st Joan (*dsp*), dau of Sir Edmund/Robert Mortimer; *m* 2nd Agnes, widow of Thomas St Quintin, of Harpham, and dau of Sir John Constable, of Burton Constable, and *d c* 1485, leaving, with two daus (Joan, Prioress Greenfield, *d* 1518; Alice, *m* Sir John Markham, of Cotham, and had issue):

Sir JOHN SKIPWITH; Sheriff Lincs 1492, fought Battles of Stoke 1487 and Blackheath 1497, ktd 1497; *m* 1478 Catherine, dau of Sir Richard FitzWilliam, of Wadworth, and *d* 1518, leaving:

1 WILLIAM (Sir)

1 Catherine; Gentlewoman to QUEEN ANNE OF CLEVES; *m* Sir Thomas Heneage, of Hainton, Lincs, and had:

   (1) Catherine; *m c* 1535, as his 1st w, 1st Baron Willoughby of Parham (*see* WILLOUGHBY DE ERESBY, B)

2 Elizabeth; *m* 1st Anthony Rygge, of Boothby Pagnell and Cumberworth; *m* 2nd Matthew Thyimelby, of Poolham and Tetford, and had issue by both husbs

3 Agnes; *m* Charles/Richard Yarborough, of Yarborough, Lincs

The only s,

Sir WILLIAM SKIPWITH; ktd 1526, Sheriff Lincs 1527, MP Lincs 1529; involved in Pilgrimage of Grace, a rebellion sparked off by a mob attacking his bro-in-law Sir Thomas Heneage; *m* 1st Elizabeth, dau of Sir William Tyrwhitt (*see* BERNERS, B), and had:

1 William (Sir); fought Battle of Musselburgh 1547, after which ktd; Lincs: MP 1547 and 1553, Sheriff 1553 and 1563; *m* Elizabeth, dau and heir of Sir Richard Page, PC, Chamberlain to EDWARD VI, and half-sis of Anne, Duchess of Somerset (*qv*), and was ancestor of the SKIPWITHs of Newbold, Warwicks, and Metheringham, Lincs

Sir WILLIAM *m* 2nd Alice, dau and coheir of Sir Lionel Dymoke, of Mareham-on-the-Hill, Lincs, and *d* 1547, leaving by her:

2 Lionel, of Covenham, Calthorpe and Mareham-on-the-Hill; *m* 1st Margaret, dau and heiress of John Barnardiston, yr s of Sir Thomas Barnardiston, of Great Cotes, and had three daus; *m* 2nd Jane, dau and coheir of William Bracebridge, of Kingsbury, Warwicks

3 John, of Walmesgate; *m* Eleanor, dau of John Kingston, of Great Grimsby, Lincs, and had:

   (1) Lionel; MP Grimsby; *m* Margaret, dau of Thomas Towthby, of Towthby, Lincs, and *dspm* 1616, leaving three daus

4 George, of Cotham, Lincs; *m* 1st Margaret (*d* 1594), dau of Thomas Gibson and widow of Edward Ayscough, Cupbearer to HENRY VIII; *m* 2nd Eleanor — and *d* 1601, leaving:

   (1) Gertrude; *m* 1596 George Foljambe

5 HENRY

1 Eleanor; *m* Richard Bolle, of Haugh, Lincs, and had issue

2 Mary; *m* Sir George FitzWiliam, of Mablethorpe, Lincs, and had issue

3 Emma; *m* Sir Tristram Tyrwhitt (*see* BERNERS, B)

4 Dorothy; *m* Andrew Gedny, of Bay Enderby (*d* 1591), and *d* 1591, leaving issue

5 Elizabeth; *m* Thomas Clifford, of Brackenburgh, Lincs, and *d* 1595, leaving issue

6 Margaret; *m* 1st between 26 April and 15 May 1539 2nd Lord (Baron) Tailboys (*dsp* just prior to 6 Sept 1540; *see* CLINTON, B); *m* 2nd 20 Feb 1546/7 Sir Peter Carew (*dsp* 27 Nov 1575), of Mohun's Ottery, Devon (for whose earlier ancestry *see* CAREW, Bt); *m* 3rd 20 July 1579, as his 3rd w, Sir John Clifton, of Barrington, Somerset, and *d* 6 May 1583

7 Anne; *m* William Hatcliffe, of Hatcliffe, Lincs

8 Bridget; Maid of Honour and Gentlewoman to ELIZABETH I; *m* as his 2nd w Brian Cave (*see* CAVE-BROWN-CAVE, Bt)

The yst s,

HENRY SKIPWITH; bought Prestwould, Leics, and other manors (including possibly Beaumont Leys, Leics, of which he was certainly Ld) from his step-daus; Equerry to ELIZABETH I, MP Leics; *m* Jane, widow of Francis Hele, of Prestwould, and dau of Francis Hall, MP Grantham, Lincs, and *d* 1588, leaving:

1 WILLIAM (Sir)

2 Francis; *d* unm 1589

3 Henry, of Tugby and Knightthorpe; *m* Joan, dau of Leonard Aston, of Longdon, Staffs, 2nd s of Sir Edward Aston, of Tixall, and *d* 1639, leaving a dau

4 George; served English forces Low Countries aiding Protestants there; *k* Bommell, Netherlands, unm

1 Ursula; *m* Edward Ayscough, of Cotham, s of Edward Ayscough, and had issue

2 Catherine; *m* 1st Walter Desborough; *m* 2nd Sir Walter Ayscough, of Blyborough, Lincs

3 Anne; *m* Henry Smith, of Withcock, Lincs, and had:

   (1) Henry; one of the Regicides responsible for the execution of CHARLES I

4 Jane; *m* Sir William Samwell, of Upton, Northants, and had issue (*see* HARINGTON, Bt)

5 Bridget; *m* Walter Ayscough, of Washington, Lincs, unc of her bro-in-law Sir Walter Ayscough (*see above*), and *dsps*

6 Dorothy; *m* Thomas Woodward, of Butlers Marston, Warwicks, and had issue

7 Elizabeth; *m* Thomas Harington, of S Witham and Boothby Pagnell, Lincs, and *dsp*

8 Margaret; *m* Sir Matthew Saunders, of Shangton, Leics, and had issue

The est s,

Sir WILLIAM SKIPWITH; Leics: Sheriff 1597, MP 1601 (and Leicester 1605), ktd 1603; *m* 1st Margaret, dau of Roger Cave (*see* CAVE-BROWN-CAVE, Bt); *m* 2nd Jane, dau and heiress of John Roberts, of Wollaston, and widow of (a) John Walpole, of Whaplode, and (b) John Markham, of Sedgebrook, and *d* 3 May 1610, leaving by his 1st w:

1 HENRY (Sir), **1st Bt**

2 George; *b* 1592; *d* unm Denmark 1609

3 Thomas; *b* 1594; *m* Anne, dau of John Bluett, of Harloxton, Lincs, and had male issue

1 Jane; *m* Sir George Throckmorton, of Fulbrook, Oxon, gs of 1st Baron Vaux of Harrowden (*qv*), and *dsps*

2 Anne; *m* Edward Pate, of Eye Kettleby, Leics, Sheriff Leics 1640, and *dsp*

3 Elizabeth; *m* as his 1st w her er sis's husb's yr bro Sir John Pate, 1st and last Bt (*d* 1652), of Sisonby, Leics, and *d* 17 Aug 1628 aged 37, leaving issue

The est s,

Sir Henry Skipwith, 1st Bt (E), so *cr* 20 Dec 1622, of Prestwould; *educ* Queens' Coll Cambridge; ktd 1609, Leics: Sheriff 1636, DL 1641, Commr Array, Gentleman Privy Chamber to CHARLES I, royalist Civil War, declared a delinquent by Parl and fined £1,114 (some £45,000 in late-1990s terms), the Prestwould estate being declared forfeit and acquired by Christopher Packe; *m* 1st Anne (*d* 1631), dau and coheir of Sir Thomas Kempe, of Olantigh and Chilham Castle, Kent; *m* 2nd Blandina (*d* 1660), dau of John Pennen, of Badgeworth, Somerset, and widow of John Acton, of Elmley Lovat, Worcs, goldsmith to CHARLES I, and by his 1st w had, with an est s (William, *b* 1613, *dsp*) and three daus (Elizabeth, emigrated to Virginia, as did her next sis; Diana, *m* Maj Edward Dale, four times High Sheriff Lancaster Co, Va.; Anne, *d* unm 1696):

1 **Sir Henry Skipwith, 2nd Bt**; *d* unm

2 **Sir Grey Skipwith, 3rd Bt**; emigrated to Middlesex Co, Va., during the Commonwealth; *m* Anne, widow of Edmund Kempe, royalist emigrant from Norfolk, and had, with a dau (Cassandra, *m* Philip Coale, High Sheriff Baltimore, Md.):

   (2) **Sir William Skipwith, 4th Bt**, High Sheriff Middlesex County, Va.; *m* Sarah, dau of John Peyton, of Va., a descendant of the Peytons of Isleham, Cambs (*see* Sections Washington, Jefferson and W H Harrison, AMERICAN PRESIDENTIAL FAMILIES, 1994, Morris Genealogical Books SA, for possible Peyton connections), and had:

      1a **Sir Grey Skipwith, 5th Bt**; *b* 2 Aug 1705; *d* unm Va. 1740

      2a WILLIAM (Sir), **6th Bt**

      3a Robert; *b* 1712

      4a Henry; *b* 1714; *d* unm 1736

      5a Fulwar, of Dinwiddie County, Va.; *b* 1720; *m* Martha, dau of Francis Waldron, and had, with a dau:

         1b Fulwar; US Consul-Gen France, 1st Govr of US Florida; *m* Countess Evelina Barlie van den Clooster and had, with a dau:

            1c Grey; *d* unm

            1c Lelia; *m* 1st Thomas Bolling Robertson, Govr and Senator Louisiana (*d* 1828); *m* 2nd Humberston Skipwith, of Prestwould, Va. (*see* below)

The 5th Bt's bro,

Sir William Skipwith, 6th Bt, of Greencroft Plantation, nr Blandford, Va.; *b* 1707; *m* 1733 Elizabeth, only dau of John Smith, High Sheriff Middlesex Co, Va., yst s of John Smith, of Purton, Glos Co, Va., by Mary, dau of Col Augustin Warner, they being great-grandparents of Pres GEORGE WASHINGTON (*see* AMERICAN PRESIDENTIAL FAMILIES, 1994, Morris Genealogical Books, SA) and *d* 25 Feb 1764, having had:

1 William; *dvp* unm 1750 in England

2 PEYTON (Sir), **7th Bt**

3 Henry, of Hors du Monde, Va.; Col Cumberland Militia Battle Yorktown, memb Va. Ho Dels, Lt and Sheriff Cumberland Co; *m* 1st Tabitha, dau of John Wayles of Charles City, Va.; *m* 2nd Elizabeth, dau of William Byrd III, of Westover, Va., and by his 1st w had:

   (1) Henry; *m* Anne, dau of Judge John Robertson, memb US Congress, Lt Govr of Va., and had issue

   (1) Martha; *m* Edmund Harrison, of Amelia Co

   (2) Mary; *m* Thomas Randolph, of Dungeness, Va.

4 Robert; *m* Anne, dau of John Wayles and sis of Anne Wayles (*see* above) and of Martha Wayles, who *m* Thomas Jefferson, 3rd President of the USA (*see* AMERICAN PRESIDENTIAL FAMILIES, 1994, Morris Genealogical Books SA) and had:

   (1) George, of Hickory Hall; *m* Mary, dau of William Murray, and had:

      1a Robert; *m* 1st Jane Rolfe, dau of William Bolling, of Bolling Hall

      2a William; *ka* American Civil War

3a George; *m* Maria Brooks and had issue

4a Thomas Bolling; *m* Emma Devereux and *d* 1873, leaving issue

1a Cornelia; *m* James Whittle

1 Mary; *m* 1st William Randolph, of Chatsworth, Va.; *m* 2nd Col Richard Meade, ADC to Gen GEORGE WASHINGTON

2 Jane; *m* Edmund Ruffin, of Evergreen, Va., and had issue

3 Elizabeth; *m* William Short V and had issue

4 Sarah; *m* Richard Kenman, of Mount Pleasant, Va., and had issue

The 2nd s,

Sir Peyton Skipwith, 7th Bt; *b* 13 March 1743; *educ* in England; added greatly to his American estates, building a new seat called Prestwould in Mecklenburg Co, Va.; tried for treason as a loyalist at the time of the American War of Independence but acquitted; *m* 1st 1764 Anne (*d* 1779), dau of Hugh Miller, of Blandford, Va., and a descendant of the Indian Princess Pocahontas, and had:

1 GREY (Sir), **8th Bt**

2 Peyton, of Cotes, Ga.; *m* Cornelia, dau of Gen Nathaniel Greene, 2ic to Gen GEORGE WASHINGTON, and *d* 1808/9, leaving:

(1) George, of Hinds Co, Miss.; *m* Mary, dau of William Newsome, of Mauny Co, Tenn., and had issue

(2) Peyton Horatio; *m* 1st Catherine Anderson; *m* 2nd Frances, dau of Rt Rev Leonidas Polk, Bp Tennessee and Lt-Gen Confederate Army (*see* Section Polk, AMERICAN PRESIDENTIAL FAMILIES, 1994, Morris Genealogical Books SA)

(3) Grey; *m* Virginia, dau of Col Miles Cary, of Oakhill, Va.

1 Lelia; *m* 1st George Carter, of Shirley Plantation, Va.; *m* 2nd St George Tucker, memb 1st US Congress and a Judge for nearly 50 years

Sir Peyton *m* 2nd 1788 Jean, sis of his 1st w, and by her had:

3 Humberstone; inherited most of the American estates; *m* 1st Sarah Nevison, of Norfolk, Va., and had:

(1) Helen; *m* Rt Rev John Wilmer, Bp Louisiana

(2) Sarah; *m* S Wilmer Carrell, of Philadelphia

3 (cont.) Humberstone Skipwith *m* 2nd Lelia, dau of Fulwar Skipwith, of Baton Rouge, La. (*see* above), and by her had, with other issue:

(1) Fulwar; *m* Anne, dau of Austin Ledyard, of Mobile, Ala., and had:

1a Austin; sold Prestwould

4 Horatio Brontë; *d* unm 1805

2 Helen; *m* Tucker Coles, of Tallwood, Albemarle Co, Va., bro of John (*see* below)

3 Selina; *m* John Coles, of Enniscorthy, Albemarle Co, a noted Virginia statesman

Sir PEYTON *d* 9 Oct 1805 in Virginia; his est s,

Sir Grey Skipwith, 8th Bt; *b* 17 Sept 1771; *educ* Trin Coll Cambridge; remained in England there on inheriting the estates of his kinsman Sir Thomas Skipwith, 4th and last Bt, of Newbold; MP Warwicks and Chm Warwicks QS; *m* 22 April 1801 Harriet (*d* 7 July 1830), 3rd dau of Gore Townsend, of Honington Hall, Warwicks, by Elizabeth, dau of 4th Earl of Plymouth (*qv*), and had, with two daus (*d* unm):

1 THOMAS GEORGE (Sir), **9th Bt**

2 William; *b* 2 Dec 1807; *educ* Rugby and Ch Ch Oxford; Capt 47th Regt; *m* 8 Sept 1843 Louisa (*d* 2 May 1908), 3rd dau of Edward Morant Gale, of Upham Ho, Hants, and *d* 25 Sept 1907 in his 100th year, having had, with a dau (*d* unm):

(1) William; *b* 1844; Lt RN; *d* unm 8 July 1873

3 Fulwar; *b* 18 Feb 1810; *educ* Rugby; Judge with HEIC; *m* 2 July 1835 Mary Philadelphia (*d* 23 June 1895), est dau of Rev Thomas Coker Adams, and *d* 22 June 1883, leaving, with a dau (*d* unm):

(1) Grey Townsend, of Loversal Hall, Doncaster, JP Kent; *b* 2 Nov 1838; Col RE; *m* 1st 3 Dec 1867 Elizabeth Helen (*d* 27 Dec 1878), dau of Maj James Wemyss, Bengal Army (*see* WEMYSS and MARCH, E), and had, with a dau (*d* young):

1a Fulwar Estoteville; *b* 9 June 1874; *educ* Haileybury; Ch Engr Bombay, Baroda and Centl India Rlwy, Capt Indian Def Force WW I; *m* 24 Aug 1905 Kathleen Alice Georgina (*d* 17 Dec 1967), yst dau of Rev John Adams, Vicar Offchurch, Warwicks, and *d* 23 Dec 1963, leaving:

1b Grey Henry; *b* 29 Dec 1908; *d* 6 April 1978

1b Elizabeth Kathleen; *b* 24 July 1907; *d* 12 Oct 1990

2a James Wemyss, of Alveston Ho, Warwicks; *b* 25 Nov 1875; *educ* Wellington and RMA Woolwich; Lt-Col RE Boer War 1900 (medal with three clasps), WW I (twice wounded, despatches); *m* 10 June 1911 Estelle (*d* 31 Oct 1961), 3rd dau of Robert Henderson, of Liss, Hants, and *d* 5 Nov 1950, leaving:

1b +Patrick James Townsend [Lt-Col Patrick Skipwith, North End, Chiddingfold, Surrey GU8 4UU]; *b* 8 Oct 1915; *educ* Shrewsbury and RMA Woolwich; Lt-Col RA WW II (POW); *m* 24 Feb 1941 Beryl Daisy (*d* 13 Jan 1999), yr dau of Arthur A Fair, of Montree, Athlone, Co Westmeath, and has:

1c +Michael James Grey [Michael Skipwith Esq, Swyncombe Old School, Cookley Green, nr Nettlebed, Oxon RG9 6EN]; *b* 25 Nov 1951; *educ* Bradfield; *m* 1988 *Jacqueline, dau of J Ould, of Coventry, Leics, and has:

1d *Oliver James Grey; *b* 6 July 1991

2d *Charlie Mo John; *b* 31 Oct 1993

1c *Susan Virginia; *b* 2 April 1947; *m* 1988 *Christopher James Frederick Blumer (*see* LAUDERDALE, E)

2c *Bridget Anne [Mrs John Macaskill, 12 Sheep Lane, LI, New York, NY 11560, USA]; *b* 5 Aug 1948; *m* 1981 *John Macaskill, s of Dr John Macaskill, of Edinburgh, and has:

1d *John; *b* 1984

2d *Ben; *b* 1986

2b John Granville Wemyss; *b* 12 Feb 1921; *educ* Shrewsbury and RMA Woolwich; Maj RA WW II; *m* 1st 10 June 1947 Margaret Lettice Mary (*d*

22 Oct 1968), only dau of Col William Paget-Tomlinson, DSO, 7th QO Hus, of Biggins House, Kirkby Lonsdale, Lancs; *m* 2nd 1977 Eva Agnes (*d* 7 April 1997), dau of George Cooper Ingall, of Croft End, Kendal, and widow of Maj James Cameron Campbell, RE, and *d* 1991, leaving by his 1st w:

1c +Guy Paget Grey [Guy Skipwith Esq, 107 Cheshire St, Market Drayton, Salop]; *b* 22 Feb 1951; *educ* Shrewsbury and Nottingham U; *m* 1972 *Pamela Jane, dau of Thomas N Foster, of Salop, and has:

1d +Thomas Grey; *b* 21 July 1979

2d +Robert John; *b* 1985

1d *Judith Lakshmi; *b* 1988

2c +Philip James Henderson [Philip Skipwith Esq, Biggins Grange, Kirkby Lonsdale, Lancs]; *b* 29 Oct 1957; *educ* Shrewsbury

1b *Margaret Virginia; *b* 21 July 1912; *m* 1st 20 Feb 1937 Gordon Kenneth Luker Gourlay (*d* 10 Jan 1946), yr s of Francis Thornborough Gourlay, of Anagach Lodge, Grantown-on-Spey, Morayshire, and has:

1c *Jean Margaret; *b* 21 May 1940; *m* 22 Dec 1962 *Vagn Aage Pedersen, s of Ange Pedersen, of Bogeso, Denmark, and has:

1d *Julie Christine; *b* 31 July 1969

2c *Hazel Anne Virginia; *b* 9 Sept 1943; *m* 6 Feb 1965 *David John Bowen Moody, s of C H Moody, of Hermanus, S Africa, and has:

1d *Christopher Gordon; *b* 22 June 1966

1d *Bridget Elizabeth; *b* 11 Nov 1968

1b (cont.) Mrs Gordon Gourlay *m* 2nd 22 Feb 1947 Lt-Col Ian Robert Grimwood, BSc, Frontier Force Regt, IA, s of Arthur John Grimwood, of Welwyn Garden City, and by him has:

3c *Elisabeth Josephine Nisbet; *b* 13 Sept 1948

3a Frederick ; *b* 23 Dec 1877; *educ* Haileybury and RMC Sandhurst; Lt-Col Gurkha Rifles, served China 1900, Tibet Mission 1904, Zakka Khel Expdn 1908, WW I (despatches); *m* 7 May 1916 Lily Spence (*d* 1979), dau of Lt-Col John Garvie, MD, IMS, and *d* 17 April 1964, leaving:

1b David James; *b* 6 Feb 1917; *educ* Wellington and Corpus Christi Coll Oxford (BA 1938, MA 1947); Bimbashi Sudan Defence Force, Capt SOE, Long Range Desert Gp WW II (POW), housemaster Bloxham 1948–56, St Andrew's Coll Grahamstown S Africa 1956–58, Headmaster Shiplake 1960–66; *d* unm 6 June 1966

1b *Wendy Elisabeth [Mrs Thomas Crane, Bridge Cottage, Well Lane, Midhurst, Sussex GU29 9QQ]; *b* 16 Aug 1927; *m* 15 Aug 1955 *Capt Thomas Peter Robin Crane, RASC, s of Thomas Taversham Crane, of Maidenhead, and has:

1c *Jennifer Anne [Mrs David Corner, 105 Listria Park, London N16 5SP]; *b* 8 July 1958; *educ* Midhurst G S, Bedales and St Martin's (BA Hons); TV ed and dir; *m* 1988 *David Michael Corner, s of Frederick Ord Corner, of Dorking, Surrey, and has:

1d *Susan Daisy Ashley; *b* 26 Feb 1993

2c *Caroline Virginia; *b* 1969

1a Mary Effie; *b* 16 Jan 1872; *d* unm 17 Oct 1945

(1) (cont.) Col Grey Skipwith *m* 2nd 21 Sept 1887 Sophia Flora, OBE (*d* 19 Dec 1940), dau of Col Charles Cooke-Yarborough, CB (*see* COOKE, Bt), and *d* 12 Aug 1900, having by her had, with a dau (*d* unm):

4a Charles Grey Yule, of Loversall Hall, JP (W R Yorks); *b* 20 April 1890; *educ* Wellington; Capt IA WW I (despatches twice), Coronation Medal 1937; *m* 20 Feb 1926 Althea Kathleen Joyce (*d* 10 June 1973), yst dau of Charles Samuel Hunting, JP, of Slaley Hall, Slaley, Northumberland, and *d* 29 Jan 1967, leaving:

1b +Michael Charles [Michael Skipwith Esq, Lotus Pottery, Stoke Gabriel, S Devon]; *b* 9 Aug 1928; *educ* Wellington; 2nd Lt Roy Sigs 1946–49; *m* 15 April 1957 *Mary Elizabeth, est dau of Richard Barthram Wood, of Croft House, Kirby Moorside, Yorks, and has:

1c +Jonathan Charles d'Estoteville [Jonathan Skipwith Esq, The Palms, Venn Grove, Plymouth, Devon]; *b* 19 April 1962; BSc; *m* 1993 *Gina, dau of M P Ferrigno, of Dournazac, France

1c *Joanna Lisette; *b* 6 Feb 1960

5a Granville Arthur; *b* 17 June 1893; Lt RFA; *ka* 16 June 1915

2a Flora Blanche; *b* 10 Feb 1889; *m* 21 Nov 1923 Capt Reginald Wellington Ross, MC, Seaforth Highrs, yst s of Rev J C Ross and gs of Adml Sir James Ross, Polar explorer, and *d* 6 Sept 1965, leaving issue. He *d* 10 Feb 1964

3a Frances Helen; *b* 10 Feb 1889; *m* 18 Sept 1917 Lt-Col George Kingston Sullivan, OBE, MC, DL, KOYLI, s of Thomas Kingston Sullivan, of Glanmire Ho, Co Cork, and *d* 19 July 1979. He *d* 14 Dec 1961

(1) Mary Wilhelmina; *m* 2 June 1877 Sir Henry Yule, KCSI, CB, and *d* 26 April 1881. He *d* 30 Dec 1889

4 Grey; *b* 10 April 1811; *educ* Rugby; Capt RN; *m* 1st 26 April 1853 Louisa Maria (*d* 2 March 1864), sis of Sir Richard Temple, 1st Bt (*qv*), and had:

(1) Grey; *b* 31 Jan 1855; Maj and Brevet Lt-Col RMLI, Zulu War 1879, Egyptian Campaign 1882; *d* unm 6 Feb 1909

(1) Sophia Mary; *m* 16 Nov 1897 Rev Gray Granville, Vicar Wasperton, Warwicks, only s of Rev Granville John Granville, Vicar Stratford-on-Avon, and *d* 28 June 1955, leaving issue. He *d* 11 Dec 1913

4 (cont.) Capt Grey Skipwith *m* 2nd 27 April 1867 Fanny Elizabeth (*d* 2 Feb 1912), 2nd dau of Henry Tudor, of Portland Place, London, and *d* 1894, having by her had:

(2) Harry Louis Estoteville, CMG (1919); *b* 23 Jan 1868; V-Adml WW I; *m* 27 April 1905 Ethel Maura (*d* 6 Dec 1946), yst dau of John Henry Sharp, JP, of Hove, Sussex, and *d* 13 March 1955

(3) Frederick George, CMG (1919); *b* 31 Aug 1870; *educ* Wellington; Col 1st Bn Roy Warwicks Regt, Sudan Expdn 1898, Boer War 1901–02, WW I (despatches); *m* 1st 16 June 1903 Bertha Sylvia (*d* 12 Jan 1944), er dau of Charles Augustus Chapman, of Chicago; *m* 2nd 8 March 1954 Nora (*d* 8 Jan 1958), widow of Maj Charles Hacket and dau of Edward Johnson Lorking, and *dsp* 29 Jan 1964

5 Peyton; *b* 1812; *d* unm 1814

6 Henry; *b* 13 June 1815; *educ* Rugby and Eton; Col 43rd Regt; *m* 30 May 1862 Horatio Charlotte (*d* 6 March 1910), dau of Rev Horace Robert Pechell (*see* 1970 edn PECHELL, Bt), and *dsp* 1 Aug 1886

7 Lionel, of Doctors' Commons; *b* 5 Aug 1816; *educ* Rugby; *m* 9 Nov 1852 Nannette (*d* 1877), 4th dau of Thomas Walker, of Ravenfield, Yorks, and *d* 18 April 1886, having had:

(1) Archibald Peyton; *b* 27 Aug 1853; *m* 3 June 1880 Edith (*m* 2nd 31 Jan 1888 Lt-Col Reginald Curtis Toogood, Roy Scots Fus (d 3 June 1939), and *d* 20 Jan 1943), 4th dau of Rev Canon Francis Coulman Royds, Rector Coddington, and *d* 28 Dec 1883, leaving:

1a Frank Peyton; *b* 28 Feb 1881; Maj 7th Bn Roy Scots Fus WW I; *m* 9 Nov 1909, as her 1st husb, Hon Bridget Vera Byng, only dau of 8th Viscount Torrington (*qv*), and was *ka c* Sept 1915, leaving:

1b Nannette Elizabeth; *b* 5 Aug 1910; *m* 17 March 1954 Lt-Col John Raymond Louis Dennis Brett, Colonial Admin Service and Roy Garwhal Rifles, s of Maj Raymond George Brett, of Rising Tide, Portrush, NI

2b Cynthia; *b* 30 July 1912; *m* 15 June 1933 Desmond Louis Shaw Smith, only s of Louis Shaw Smith, of Ballawley Park, Dundrum, Co Dublin, and had issue

1a Nora; *b* 30 April 1882; *m* 12 July 1906 Cdr Lord George Frederick Seymour, RN, 4th s of 6th Marquess of Hertford (*qv*), and *d* 23 Sept 1959, leaving issue

(2) Frederick Charles; *b* 22 Sept 1857; *m* 1893 Mary Annie, dau of George Frederick Cremer, of NZ, and *d* 1940, leaving:

1a Gore Peyton Lewis, of Auckland, NZ; *b* 1894

2a Lionel Ernest; *b* 1896; *m* 21 March 1929 Eva May, dau of J Hopkins, of Auckland, NZ, and had:

1b +Ronald Hugh; *b* 14 Aug 1930

(3) Robert Windsor; *b* 7 Jan 1860; *m* 12 Oct 1904 Clara Mildred (*d* 20 Feb 1952), widow of Cecil Wynne Parry and 2nd dau of Col Thomas Edward Vickers, CB, and *dsp* 3 April 1949

(4) Francis; *b* 10 Feb 1861; Lt 4th Bn Beds Regt; *m* 25 April 1899 Marjory (*d* 14 April 1957, having *m* 2nd 10 May 1939 Lt-Col Hugh de Putron, who *d* 6 May 1949), dau of Capt Thomas Francis Rolt, Coldstream Gds, of Christleton, Cheshire, and *d* 6 June 1934, leaving:

1a Robert Grey; *b* 2 Feb 1900; *m* 1 Aug 1937 *Annemarie, dau of Hans Evers, of Ratzeburg, Germany, and *d* 1989, leaving:

1b +Francis Grey [Francis Skipwith Esq, Crosfields School, Shinfield, Reading]; *b* 12 May 1940; *educ* Plumtree Sch, Rhodesia, Cape Town U and King Alfred's Coll Winchester; *m* 31 Aug 1968 *Jacqueline Ann, er dau of Charles Albert Frederick Kettley, of Whitchurch Hill, Berks, and has:

1c +Andrew William Grey; *b* 14 Nov 1969; *educ* Charterhouse and Trin Coll Cambridge

2c +Timothy Edward; *b* 1972; *educ* Charterhouse

3c +Barnaby James; *b* 1974; *educ* St Edward's Sch Oxford

2b +Robert Frederick [Robert Skipwith Esq, PO Box 327, Kwe Kwe, Zimbabwe]; *b* 11 Sept 1941; *m* 1st 1965 (*divorce* 1971) Patricia Ann Saville and has:

1c +Charles Robert; *b* 1969

2b (cont.) Robert Skipwith *m* 2nd 1971 *Judith Ann, dau of Thomas Stephen Johnson, and by her has:

2c +Thomas Stephen; *b* 1975

3c +James Grey; *b* 1976

2a Lionel Peyton; *b* 23 June 1902; Capt RN WW II (despatches twice); *m* 21 July 1926 Thelma Westwood (*d* 1988), only child of Surgn-Cdr Adrian A Forrester, RN, and *d* 1978, leaving:

1b *Venetia Forrester; *b* 10 May 1932; *m* 28 July 1951 (*divorce* 1991) Cdr James Michael Burnard Walkey, RN, only s of R-Adml Howarth Seymour Walkey, CBE, of Lowden Lodge, Chippenham, Wilts, and has:

1c *Anthony Charles d'Estouteville; *b* 1955

2c *Justin Robert Chichester; *b* 1957

3a William Estouteville; *b* 16 June 1904; *educ* RNCs Osborne and Dartmouth; *m* 1st 17 Feb 1934 Margaret Joan (*d* Jan 1965), yst dau of Ernest Mark Shattock, and had:

1b +Mark; *b* 26 Dec 1944; *educ* Marlborough and Southampton U; *m* Denise — and has:

1c +Stephen

2c +James

3c +Peter; *b* 2 June 1979

1c +Juliet

1b *Sara Anne; *b* 9 April 1947

3a (cont.) William Skipwith *m* 2nd 11 Dec 1968 Joan Emma (*d* 1998), formerly w of Aubrey Gordon Leacock, CBE, FRCS, and dau of Joseph William Teale, of Farnham Common, Bucks, and *d* 1976

4a Francis Humberston; *b* 6 Aug 1909; *d* unm 1976

(5) Granville Gore (Rev); *b* 29 July 1865; *educ* Jesus Coll Cambridge (BA 1891, MA 1897); Rector Englefield 1904–21; *m* 12 July 1899 Violet Mary (*d* 20 Jan 1957), dau of George Walter Tyser, JP, of Mortimer, Berks (*see* 1970 edn PARKYNS, Bt), and *d* 7 March 1955 aged 90, leaving:

1a Philip Lionel D'Estouteville SKIPWITH later SKIPWITH-TYSER (roy licence 1958); *b* 1 May 1904; *educ* Eton and Trin Coll Cambridge; Lt RE WW II (despatches, POW); *m* 22 June 1932 *Elsie Barbara [Mrs Philip Skipwith-Tyser, Greywell House, Midlington, Droxford, Hants], er dau of Col Arthur Edward Phillips, DSO, of Elm House, Winterbourne Dauntsey, Wilts, and *d* 1991, having had:

1b +Richard Peyton [Richard Skipwith Esq, Old House Hotel, Wickham, Hants]; *b* 13 Oct 1937; *educ* Eton; *m* 12 Feb 1963 *Annie Carmen Angele Marie, est dau of André Bonnor, of Château Leyran, Villenave d'Ornon, Gironde, France, and has:

1c +Julian Alexandre d'Estouteville; *b* 25 Jan 1972

1c *Anouk Barbara Hélène; *b* 1974

2b +Charles Fulwar [Charles Skipwith Esq, Cobbett's Restaurant, The Square, Botley, Hants]; *b* 13 April 1946; *educ* Wellington; *m* 12 July 1969 *Lucie Louise, dau of Maurice Othon, of Cursan, France, and has:

1c *Naomi Barbara Marie-Françoise; *b* 1972

2c *Alissa Caroline Marie-Thérèse; *b* 1975

3c *Georgina Marie-Louise Selina; *b* 1979

1b *Noel Camilla [Mrs Anthony Benda, The Old Vicarage, Crondall, Hants]; *b* 25 Dec 1934; *m* 30 Jan 1959 *Capt Anthony Charles Alston Benda, 1st Queen's Dragoon Gds, s of Charles Kenneth Benda, of Kensington, and has:

1c *Nicholas James Alston; *b* 30 Dec 1960

2c *Jonathan Charles Alston; *b* 22 May 1962

3c *William Philip Alston; *b* 1 June 1966

2a +Osmund Humberston [The Rev Prebendary Osmund Skipwith, 23 Heathdene Manor, Grandfield Ave, Watford, Herts]; *b* 28 Feb 1906; *educ* Harrow and New Coll Oxford (BA 1928, MA 1933); Rector N Cadbury, Somerset, CF Kenya, UMCA Missionary 1935–41, CF 1941–54; *m* 6 Feb 1946 *Philippa Katharine Jane, 2nd Offr WRNS, only dau of Richard Edward Skipwith, MBE, of Ruddington, Notts, and has:

1b +Peter Michael [Peter Skipwith Esq, 25 The Ridgeway, Watford, Herts WD1 3TH]; *b* 3 May 1947; *educ* Lancing and U Coll of N Wales (BSc 1968); *m* 1970 *Patricia Mary, BA, ARICS, dau of David Allan, of Penrith, and has:

1c *Susan Katharine; *b* 1972; BA

2c *Rebecca; *b* 1974; BA

1a Barbara Nannette; *b* 1902; *m* 23 June 1928 Col Gerald William Kenyon-Slaney and *d* 1995, leaving issue (*see* KENYON, B)

(1) Helen; *m* 4 June 1878 Howard Gilliat, JP, of Abbots Ripton Hall, Hunts, and *d* 27 Nov 1934, leaving issue. He *d* 3 Dec 1906

(2) Dora Mary, *d* unm 16 Dec 1947

(3) Mabel Georgiana; *m* 17 June 1885 William Henry Perry Leslie, of Bryntanat, Oswestry, and had issue. He *d* 23 May 1926

(4) Nannette Ida; *d* unm 17 April 1938

8 Francis Robert d'Estouteville; *b* 16 June 1820; *educ* Rugby and Magdalen Coll Oxford; emigrated to NZ; *m* 1859 Emily Morshed Symons; had issue by Hinenui Te Po, dau of the Maori Ch Matenga Te Matai, and *d* 21 Sept 1855

9 Frederick; *b* 1821; *d* 1823

10 Randolph (Rev); *b* 22 Nov 1822; *educ* Rugby and Trin Coll Cambridge; Rector Whilton, Northants; *m* 2 Sept 1846 Mary Holden (*d* 20 Dec 1904), only dau of Rev Henry Steward, and *d* 11 March 1899, leaving:

(1) Ernest d'Estouteville; *b* 1847; *m* 1874 Catherine (*d* 12 April 1936), dau of Capt Adam Peebles, and *d* 1894, leaving:

1a Randolph Bruce d'Estouteville; *b* 1880; *m* 1906 Adelia L Warnken (*d* 1938) and *d* 1939, leaving:

1b *Margery Louise; *b* 1908; *m* 1936 Earle Sydney Chard and has:

1c *Carole Elizabeth; *m* 1958 *Gordon Lorne Down

2b *Lorraine Gladys; *b* 1909; *m* 1936 Herbert Roberts Adams (*d* 1983) and has:

1c *Donald Bruce; *b* 1942

1a Constance Mary; *b* 1879; *m* 1905 Wilfred Healy and had issue

2a Alice Peebles; *b* 1882; *d* unm 1952

3a Emilie Beatrice; *b* 1885; *m* 1916 Capt Hugh Brymer Bowman and had issue. He *d* 6 June 1951

(1) Constance Laura; *m* 5 Sept 1872 Rev George Spencer Leigh-Bennett, Vicar St James's, Long Sutton, Lincs, and *d* 30 March 1928, leaving issue. He *d* 11 Dec 1906

11 Humberston (Rev); *b* 8 Dec 1823; *educ* Rugby and Trin Coll Cambridge; BCL Cantab; Rector Hampstall Ridware, Lincs; *m* 1st 26 Oct 1865 Adelaide Emma (*d* 27 March 1869), only child and heiress of Rev Henry Biddulph (*see* BIDDULPH, Bt), and had:

(1) Alice Louisa; *d* unm 20 March 1954

11 (cont.) The Rev Humberston Skipwith *m* 2nd 18 April 1871 Louisa Mary (*d* 11 Aug 1917), 2nd dau of Rev Arthur Robert Kenney-Herbert, Rector Bourton-on-Dunsmore, RD, and *d* 7 Jan 1911

12 Sidmouth Stowell; *b* 29 March 1825; *educ* Rugby; Cdr RN; *m* 10 Sept 1861 Charlotte (*d* 18 Nov 1897), 6th dau of James Backwell Praed, of Tyringham, and *d* 4 Sept 1872, leaving:

(1) Reginald; *b* 7 Oct 1866; *educ* Eton; *m* 2 March 1897 Kathleen Agatha (*d* 16 Feb 1959), 4th dau of Arthur Phillip Lloyd (*see* BRADFORD, E), and *d* 8 June 1931, leaving:

1a Geoffrey Reginald; *b* 16 May 1900; *educ* Gresham's; 2nd Lt King's Salop LI; *d* unm 9 Feb 1961

2a Arthur Grey; *b* 13 Jan 1902; *m* 15 Aug 1933 Sara Hope (*d* 20 Nov 1994), yst dau of Maj Alfred James Fraser, DSO, of Hardingstone, Northants, and *d* 7 Aug 1997, having had:

1b Thomas Reginald Grey; *b* 30 March 1935; *d* 18 Dec 1937

2b +(William) Grey; *b* 18 Oct 1938; *educ* Bryanston

1b *(Sara) Jane [Mrs John Robins, Manor Farm, Longbridge Deverill, Wilts BA12 7EA]; *b* 25 March 1943; *m* 2 Sept 1967 *Capt John William Finlay Robins, 10th Roy Hus (PWO), s of Maj Frank Finlay Robins, MC, and Mrs Alfred Martyn Williams, of Werrington Park, Launceston, Cornwall, and has:

1c *Ian Finlay; *b* 16 June 1970

1c *Isabella Ruth Sara; *b* 3 Aug 1972

2b *(Rosemary) Anne [The Rt Hon The Lady Iliffe, Yattendon Park, Yattendon, Berks RG18 0UT]; *b* 25 March 1943; *m* 16 July 1966 *3rd Baron Iliffe (*qv*) and has issue

1a Rosemary Gwendolen; *b* 30 April 1907; *d* unm 26 June 1967

(2) Gerald; *b* 15 July 1869; *d* unm 16 Oct 1932

(1) Eva; *m* 26 April 1898 Edmund Henry Whitmore (*see* WHITMORE, Bt) and *d* 19 April 1944

1 Anna; *m* 1st 21 Dec 1824 Rev John Thomas Parker (*d* 26 Oct 1852), of Newbold-upon-Avon, and had issue; *m* 2nd Rev William James (*dsp* 11 Nov 1861) and *d* 1878

2 Selina; *m* 3 May 1824 James Lenox William Naper, MP, DL, of Loughcrew, Co Meath, and *d* 12 Sept 1880, having had issue. He *d* 2 Sept 1868

3 Harriett; *m* 24 June 1828 Henry Christopher Wise, MP, DL, of Woodcote, Warwicks, and *d* 15 June 1858, having had issue

4 Louisa; *m* 27 March 1827 John Fullerton, of Thrybergh Park, Yorks, and *d* 19 Sept 1875, having had issue. He *d* 6 March 1871

5 Marianne; *m* 16 April 1839 Rev Granville John Granville, Vicar Stratford-on-Avon, and *d* 26 April 1871, having had issue. He *d* 1878

6 Lelia Sophia; *m* 3 Jan 1855 Adml Robert Tryon and *d* 25 Aug 1889, leaving issue (*see* TRYON, B)

Sir GREY *d* 13 May 1852; his est s,

Sir Thomas George Skipwith, 9th Bt, DL, of Newbold Hall, Warwicks; *b* 9 Feb 1803; Capt 4th Dragoon Gds, Col Warwicks militia, MP N Warwicks; *m* 1st 15 July 1840 Emma (*dsp* 14 June 1842), dau of Thomas Hatton, of Liverpool; *m* 2nd 21 May 1853 Jane (*d* 3 May 1862), 2nd dau of Hubert Butler Moore, of Shannon Grove, Co Galway (and gdau of the Dowager Lady Dunboyne; *see* DUNBOYNE, B), and *d* 30 Nov 1863, having by her had, with a yr s (Grey Hubert, *b* 2 July 1860, *educ* Trin Coll Oxford, *d* unm 1 April 1917) and a dau (*d* unm):

Sir Peyton d'Estoteville Skipwith, 10th Bt, DL; *b* 12 Feb 1857; Hon Maj 4th Bn Warwicks Regt; *m* 5 Feb 1879 Alice Mary (*d* 20 March 1947, having *m* 2nd 1 June 1892 John Hugh Ward-Boughton-Leigh, Hon Maj 4th Bn Roy Warwicks Regt, who *d* 24 Oct 1924, and had issue), only dau of Maj-Gen B B Herrick, RMLI, and had:

1 GREY HUMBERSTON d'ESTOTEVILLE (Sir), **11th Bt**

1 Carrie d'Estoteville; *b* 16 March 1880; *m* 2 Aug 1906 Lt-Col Lewis Egerton Hopkins, DSO, OBE, RE, 3rd s of Thomas Hopkins, of Limber Grange, Lincs, and *d* 16 Jan 1938, leaving issue

2 Violet Jane; *b* 31 Oct 1881; *m* 15 Nov 1909 Alexander Vere Nicoll, 2nd s of Thomas Vere Nicoll, of S Kensington, and *d* 16 Feb 1968, leaving issue. He *d* 6 Dec 1960

Sir PEYTON *d* 12 May 1891; his only s,

Sir Grey Humberston d'Estoteville Skipwith, 11th Bt, JP (Warwicks and Worcs); *b* 4 Dec 1884; *educ* Harrow and Trin Coll Cambridge; Capt TAR, 23rd Bn City of London Regt, 2nd Lt Warwicks Yeo; *s* to Honington estates on death of cousin Col Frederick Townsend, but subsequently sold them; *m* 1st 20 Jan 1910 (*divorce* 1928) Elsie Maude (*d* 28 April 1971), yr dau of Maj Robert Allison-Browne, and had:

1 Grey d'Estoteville Townsend; *b* 23 March 1912; F/O RAFVR WW II; *m* 21 July 1937 *Sofka, formerly w of Leo Zinovieff and dau of Prince Peter Alexandro-vitch Dolgorouky, and was *ka* on air operations over Dusseldorf May 1942, leaving:

(1) Sir PATRICK ALEXANDER d'ESTOTEVILLE SKIPWITH, **12th and present Bt**

1 *Audrey Elsie Townsend [Mrs Anthony Negretti, Thornborough Thatch, Sutton March, Sutton Scotney, Hants SO21 3JX]; *b* 1911; *m* 2 Jan 1943 *(Paul) Antony Negretti, Maj Black Watch, er s of Paul Negretti, of Lane House, Lodsworth, Sussex, and has:

(1) *(Antony) Simon Timothy [Simon Negretti Esq, Taynton Mill, Taynton, Oxon OX18 4UH]; *b* 2 Dec 1945; *educ* Eton; *m* 4 Sept 1981 *Lucinda Gay, yst dau of Guy Lawrence, and has:

  1a *Guy Simon; *b* 28 Aug 1983

  1a *Melissa Gipsy; *b* 22 March 1989

(1) *Annelise Audrey [Mrs Alexander Kemp, Homewood Farm, Mulgowie, Qld 4341, Australia]; *b* 24 Sept 1948; *m* 28 June 1975 *Alexander George Munro Kemp, s of James Kemp, of Qld, and has:

  1a *Simon James; *b* 6 April 1977

  1a *Emma Bay; *b* 23 Sept 1979

Sir **Grey** *m* 2nd 16 Oct 1928 Cynthia Egerton (d 9 Aug 1995), yr dau of Egerton Leigh, JP, DL, of Jodrell Hall, Cheshire, and *d* 3 Feb 1950, having by her had:

2 +Egerton Grey d'Estoteville [Egerton Skipwith Esq, Langton Old Rectory, Langton Long, Dorset DT11 9HS]; *b* 8 Feb 1935; *educ* Canford; late 13th/18th Roy Hus; *m* 1997 *Deidre Veronica, yst dau of Richard Guinness (*see* GUINNESS, Bt) and formerly w of Alberto Heyra, of Lima, Peru

3 +Peyton Stephen [Peyton Skipwith Esq, c/o The Fine Art Society plc, 148 New Bond St, London W1Y 0JT]; *b* 30 June 1939; *educ* Canford; fine arts author; *m* 10 Oct 1971 *Anne, dau of Capt C E Barren, of Seasalter, Kent, and has:

(1) +Grey Egerton d'Estoteville; *b* 1981

(1) *Selina; *b* 1972

(2) *Amber Louise; *b* 1974; *m* 1996 *Jason Selvey, s of Stanley Selvey of Birmingham, and has:

  1a *Megan Louise; *b* 1997

SLADE

Arms: Per fess arg. and sa. a pale counterchanged and three horse's heads erased two and one of the second; a chief erm., thereon two bombs fired, ppr. **Crest:** On a mount vert a horse's head erased sa., encircled with a chain in form of an arch gold. **Mottoes:** 1 *Fidus et audax* ('Faithful and bold'), 2 *A bon droit* ('With good right'). **Creation:** Bt. (UK) 30 Sept 1831.

SIR BENJAMIN JULIAN ALFRED SLADE, 7TH BT, of Maunsel House, Somerset [Sir Benjamin Slade Bt, Maunsel Grange, North Newton, Somerset TA7 0BU]; *b* 22 May 1946; *s f* 1962; *educ* Millfield; chm: Shirlstar Container Tport Ltd 1973– (also md) and Pyman Bell Hldgs, memb Ironmongers' Co, Freeman City London 1979; *m* 1977 (*divorce* 1991) Pauline Carol, er dau of Maj Claude Myburgh, of Inholmes Ct, Hartley Wintney, Hants

Lineage: HENRY SLADE, of Burstock, Dorset; *m* Hannah, dau of James Colmer, of Drimpton, Dorset, and had:

HENRY SLADE; *m* Mary Case and had:

JOHN SLADE, of Maunsell House, Somerset, JP, DL; Commr Victualling Bd; *m* 16 Aug 1775 Charlotte, yst dau of Henry Portal, of Freefolk (*see* PORTAL, Bt), and *d* 1801, leaving, with two daus (Charlotte, *m* Alexander Cobham, of Shinfield Place, Berks, and *dsp*; Sophia, *m* 1789 her cousin William Portal, of Ashe Park, Hants, and *d* 19 Jan 1857, leaving issue; *see* PORTAL, Bt):

Sir John Slade, 1st Bt (UK), so *cr* 30 Sept 1831, GCH; *b* 31 Dec 1762; Cornet 10th Hus 1780, served Peninsula War, fought Battle of Corunna, cmded Cav Bde 1809–13, twice thanked by Parl, recd gold medal and clasp for Corunna and Fuentes d'Onoro, silver medal with two clasps for Sahagun and Busaco, Col 4th Dragoon Gds, Gen, Equerry to DUKE OF CUMBERLAND 1800; *m* 1st 20 Sept 1792 Anna Eliza Dawson (*d* 24 Dec 1819) and had:

1 John Henry, Lt-Col 1st Dragoon Gds; *b* 8 July 1796; *m* Feb 1837 Fanny (*m* 2nd 25 April 1848 R-Adml Aylmer Paynter (*d* 17 Dec 1876)), only child of Henry Chapman M'Veagh, of Bath, and *d* 30 Oct 1843, leaving:

(1) Louisa; *m* 15 July 1858 Alan Cameron Bruce-Pryce, JP, barrister, gs of J Bruce-Pryce, of Duffryn, Glam, and n of 1st Baron Aberdare (*qv*), and *d* 11 June 1868, leaving issue

2 Charles George; Maj 3rd Light Dragoons; *dsp* 10 Feb 1839

3 FREDERICK WILLIAM (Sir), **2nd Bt**

4 Marcus John; *b* 22 Jan 1801; Lt-Gen, Col 50th Foot, Lt-Govr Guernsey; *m* 7 April 1842 Charlotte (*d* 22 Feb 1909), yst dau of Hon Andrew Ramsay (*see* DALHOUSIE, E), and *d* 7 March 1872, having had:

(1) John Ramsay (Sir), KCB; *b* 16 March 1843; Maj-Gen, Col Cmdt RA 1912, Gentleman Usher to TM EDWARD VII 1901–03 and 1905–10 and GEORGE V 1910, ADC to HM QUEEN VICTORIA, Kt SS. Maurice and Lazarus, Grand Offr Crown Italy, served Afghanistan, S Africa and as Mil Attaché Italian campaign Africa; *m* 1st 9 Sept 1871 Lucia Aurora (*d* 21 Oct 1872), dau of Don Vicente di Ramos, and had:

  1a Victor Marcus; *b* 16 Oct 1872; *d* 21 Jan 1873

(1) (cont.) Maj-Gen Sir John Slade *m* 2nd 7 Nov 1882 Janet Little (*d* 17 June 1935), dau of Gen R Blucher Wood, CB, and *d* 4 Sept 1913, having by her had:

  1a Lucia, CBE (1920); *b* 23 Aug 1883; *m* 2 Sept 1909 Sir Charles Murray Marling, GCMG, CB, Dip Serv, 2nd s of Sir William Henry Marling, 2nd Bt (*qv*), and *d* 11 Sept 1927, leaving issue

(2) Arthur Maitland; *b* 27 Nov 1846; *d* 1847

(3) Montagu Maule; *b* 16 Jan 1849, Maj 10th Hus; *ka* Battle of El Teb 29 Feb 1884

(4) Frederick George, CB; *b* 17 Dec 1851; FRGS, Lt-Gen RA, Inspr-Gen RGA at HQ 1902–06, served Kaffir War 1878, Zulu War 1879, Transvaal 1881, Egypt 1882, Sudan 1884, Nile Expdn 1884–85; *m* 8 Aug 1885 Emmeline Charlotte Delap (*d* 30 March 1919), dau of Maj Wadham Wyndham Bond, of Armagh, and *d* 16 Aug 1910, having had:

  1a Marcus Wyndham Frederick; *b* 21 July, *d* 5 Aug 1886

  1a Marie Ruby Eileen (Mimi); *b* 4 July 1889; *d* unm 14 April 1949

  2a Victoria Olga Edwine; *b* 28 Oct 1891; *m* — and *d c* 1942

(1) Fanny Maule; *m* 10 Sept 1870 George Sackville Lane Fox, of Bramham, Yorks (*see* 1949 edn BINGLEY, B), and *d* 28 April 1875, leaving issue. He *d* 24 March 1918

(2) Helen Grace; *m* 28 April 1903 Francis Robert Gregson (*das* 15 May 1917), of Murton and Burdon, Co Durham, and *dsp* 7 April 1932

5 Adolphus (Sir), KCB; *b* 22 May 1802; V-Adml Turkish service with title of Ferik and appellation Muschaver Pasha, Kt 2nd Cl Order Medjidie and Osmanieh; author: *Turkey and the Crimean War*; *d* unm 13 Nov 1877

6 Ernest Augustus; *b* 30 June 1805; Offr 40th and 54th Foot, Burma medal, CS NSW; *m* twice and *d* 5 March 1868

7 Alfred Robert; Lt RN; *d* unm 20 Dec 1829

1 Charlotte Susan; *m* 6 April 1823 Henri, Marquis de Faverges, of Italy, and *d* 17 Nov 1878, leaving issue

2 Anna Eliza; *m* 1 March 1821 Wadham Penruddock Wyndham, MP, of The College, Salisbury, and *d* 7 May 1872. He *dsp* 22 Oct 1843

Sir John *m* 2nd 17 June 1822 Matilda Ellen (*d* 12 Sept 1868), 2nd dau of James Dawson, of Fork Hill, Co Armagh, by Olivia, dau of Matthew Daly, and by her had:

8 Herbert Dawson; *b* 28 May 1824; Maj-Gen 1st King's Dragoon Gds, ADC to Gen Sir J K Scarlett, GCB (*see* ABINGER, B), Crimea; *m* 2 June 1851 Harriet Augusta (*d* 13 Feb 1905), dau of Chichester Francis Bolton, of Tullydonnel, Co Louth, and *d* 15 June 1900, having had:

(1) Gerald; *b* 20 Aug 1851; *d* unm 5 Nov 1897

(1) Maud Evelyn; *m* 1st 1887 Morley Humphrey; *m* 2nd 1897 Thomas Barton Higson, of Shanghai

9 Wyndham, of Montys Court, Somerset, JP, DL; *b* 27 Aug 1826, BA Oxon; Met Police Magistrate 1877–1901; *m* 10 Feb 1863 Cicely (*d* 11 May 1920), dau of Sir Digby Neave, 3rd Bt (*qv*), and *d* 13 March 1910, leaving:

(1) Wyndham Neave, of Montys Court; *b* 17 Sept 1867; *educ* Eton and Balliol Coll Oxford (MA); barrister, Recorder Bridgwater 1897; *m* 16 Nov 1898 Evelyn Mary (*d* 1941), dau of William Clarence Watson, JP, DL, of Colworth, Beds, and *dsp* 11 Feb 1941

(1) Cicely Maud; *b* 29 April 1864; *m* 1 June 1886 Col William Kenyon Mitford, CMG, CVO, of Pitshill, Petworth, and *d* 18 March 1960, leaving issue. He *d* 20 Sept 1943

(2) Mary Arundell; *b* 10 Sept 1865; *m* 17 Feb 1887 Col Rowland Burdon, CBE, DL, of Castle Eden, Co Durham, and *d* 20 Feb 1930, having had issue. He *d* 1 Aug 1944

(3) Olive; *b* 29 Oct 1870; *m* 28 July 1894 Maj Charles James Anstruther and *d* 16 Oct 1935, leaving issue (*see* ANSTRUTHER, Bt)

10 William Hickes; *b* 9 Dec 1829; Lt-Col 5th Lancers; *m* 13 July 1861 Cecilia Louisa (*d* 14 March 1931), dau of Sir Charles Des Voeux, 2nd Bt (*see* 1940 edn), and *d* 28 July 1884, leaving:

(1) Cecil William Paulet; *b* 22 Nov 1803; Capt 3rd Bn Wilts Regt and Br S African Police Mashonaland 1890 (medal and clasp), on HQ Staff (Musketry) Aldershot 1915–19, FRGS, FZS; *d* unm 5 Nov 1943

(2) Reginald Robert; *b* 24 Oct 1868; Lt 3rd Res Bn Wilts Regt, Lt 4th Bn Suffolk Regt, WW I; *m* 4 Sept 1924 Lilian Florence, dau of Samuel J Reynolds, of Upton, Cheshire, and *dsp* 5 Feb 1946

(3) Frederick Rupert; *b* 5 May 1870; Lt 4th Bn Sherwood Foresters; *m* 14 Feb 1900 Hilda Marion Morell, 2nd dau of Sir Morell Mackenzie, and *d* 14 April 1915

(1) Alice Mary; *d* unm

11 George FitzClarence (Rev); *b* 13 Sept 1831; MA Oxon; Rector Buckland, Surrey, RD Reigate, Fell All Souls; *m* 16 June 1858 Eleanor Frances (*d* 6 Dec 1901), est dau of Henry Warre, of Bindon, Somerset, and *d* 23 Dec 1904, leaving:

(1) Edmond John Warre (Sir), KCIE, KCVO; *b* 20 March 1859; Adml, ADC to HM, C-in-C E Indies Station 1909–12, served Egypt; *m* 26 Oct 1887 Florence Madelena (*d* 11 July 1931), est dau of James Carr Saunders, of Milton Heath, Dorking, and *d* 20 Jan 1928, leaving:

1a Rhona Warre; *m* 17 Sept 1913 Harold Anselm Bellamy Vernon, CSI, CIE, ICS, s of Rev Preb J R Vernon, and *d* 7 April 1938, leaving issue. He *d* 8 Dec 1945

2a Madeleine Warre

(2) Marcus Warre, KC (Hong Kong); *b* 10 Sept 1865; *educ* New Coll Oxford (BA); barrister; *m* 8 Aug 1902 Josephine Isabella, est dau of Rev Henry Savill Young (*see* YOUNG, Bt, of North Dean), and *d* 27 Nov 1941, leaving:

1a Marcus George Savill; *b* 30 Sept 1906; *educ* Clifton and New Coll Oxford; RA WW II; *m* 1 Feb 1944 (*divorce* 1953) Rita Annie, WAAF, dau of William James Motton, of Plymouth, and *d* 1972, leaving:

1b *Susan Rebecca [Miss Susan Slade, 2 Walton House, Walton St, London SW3]; *b* 22 Nov 1945; painter

1a Muriel Rebecca, OBE (1947); *b* 23 June 1902; *m* 1 July 1924 Evelyn Stewart Lansdowne Beale, yr s of Bertram Beale, and *d* Oct 1993, having had issue

2a Eleanor Isabella; *b* 11 Jan 1904; Flt/Capt ATA WW II; *kas* 13 July 1944

(3) Henry Adolphus Warre; *b* 17 Jan 1869; *m* 1 Nov 1898 Beatrice Isobel Hilda (*d* 25 Sept 1940), yr dau of David Alexander Gordon (*see* GORDON, Bt), and *d* 6 Jan 1936, leaving:

1a Gerald Gordon; *b* 27 Oct 1899; Cdr RN, served WWs I and II; *m* 27 July 1932 Netta Kathleen, only child of Richard Edward Lloyd Maunsell, CBE, of Northbrooke, Ashford, Kent

2a Maurice Gordon; *b* 26 April 1902; *educ* Winchester; *m* 24 March 1934 Margaret (*d* 1980), dau of Hew Congreve Kennedy, and *d* 7 March 1971, leaving:

1b *Primrose; *b* 20 Dec 1934; *m* 12 Oct 1957 *Lt-Col John Patrick Roger Heather Hayes, RE, s of Cecil John Hayes, and has:

1c *Phoebe; *b* 1960

(1) Margaret Philippa Rose; *b* 8 April 1876;, MB, ChB; *m* 14 Aug 1907 Dr Job Posthuma, of Groot Bentveld, Zandvoort, Holland, s of Dr Suardus Posthuma, and *d* 18 March 1961. He *d* 30 Sept 1914

3 Sophia Louisa; *b* 14 Aug 1837; *m* 11 June 1863 Lt-Col Adolphus William Desart Burton, CB, bro of Sir Charles William Cuffe Burton, 5th Bt (*see* 1902 edn), and had issue. He *d* 11 Feb 1882

4 Gertrude Matilda; *b* 18 April 1841; *d* 8 May 1919

Sir JOHN *d* 13 Aug 1859; his est surv s,

Sir Frederick William Slade, 2nd Bt, QC; *b* 21 Jan 1801; Bencher Middle Temple; *m* 23 Dec 1833 Barbara Browne-Mostyn (*see* MOSTYN, Bt) and had:

1 ALFRED FREDERICK ADOLPHUS (Sir), **3rd Bt**

2 Charles George; *b* 1836; Col Rifle Bde, Cdr Sch of Musketry 1890–94; *d* unm 6 Sept 1897

3 Harry Hubert de Merve; *b* 18 Sept 1845; *m* 29 March 1879 Evelyn Juliet Marguerite, 2nd dau of Capt Frederick Sayer (*see* NORMANBY, M), and *d* 21 Oct 1932

4 Marcus; *b* 13 May 1847; *d* unm 1905

1 Maria Lucinda; *m* Nov 1850 Charles William Tinling (*d* 1885)

2 Harriet Georgiana; *m* 1858 John Staniforth, of Pimlico, and *d* 8 June 1916, leaving issue. He *d* 1894

3 Caroline Georgiana; *m* 27 Sept 1859 John Daniel King, barrister, and *d* 1 Feb 1894, leaving issue. He *d* 13 Oct 1884

4 Florence Barbara; *m* 20 June 1863 Alexander Gordon Breton, yst s of Rev Edward Breton, Rector Charmouth, Dorset, and *d* 6 March 1895

Sir FREDERICK *d* 8 Aug 1863; his est s,

Sir Alfred Frederic Adolphus Slade, 3rd Bt; *b* 28 May 1834; Receiver-Gen Inland Revenue, Hon Col 2nd Somerset Vol, Capt 57th Foot, served Siege Sebastopol and Indian Mutiny; *m* 6 Sept 1860 Mary Constance (*d* 20 March 1894), 2nd dau of William Cuthbert, of Beaufront Castle, Hexham, Northumberland, and had:

1 CUTHBERT (Sir), **4th Bt**

2 Basil Alfred; *b* 29 May 1865; *m* 1st 29 March 1891 (*divorce* 1925) Louisa Mary, dau of William Clements, of Kingsclere, and had:

(1) Frederick William Patrick; *b* 19 Jan 1892; Lt-Cdr RNVR, Assist Agent Port Sudan, submarines Dardanelles 1915, Assist Naval Tport Offr 1922–23 (despatches three times), Chev Order Redeemer Greece, Greek MC; *m* 2 May 1914 Marie, dau of Edouard Perruche, and *d* 14 May 1928, leaving:

1a *Mary Magdalen Althea; *b* 1915; *m* 8 Feb 1937 *Olivier Lopez-y-Royo, s of Duke of Taurisano, and has:

1b *Diego; *b* 1939

2b *Francis; *b* 1942

1b *Maria José; *b* 1937

2b *Isolda Dolores; *b* 1943

(1) Iris Mary

2 (cont.) Basil Slade *m* 2nd 6 Nov 1925 Grace Joanna, dau of Edward Harrison Tame, of Whitecote, nr Halstead, Essex, and *d* 21 July 1930

1 Violet Mary; *m* 2 Nov 1887 Lt-Col John Anstruther Smith-Cuninghame, DL, of Caprington Castle, Ayrshire, and *d* 21 Dec 1917, leaving issue. He *d* 17 Dec 1921

2 Irene Marguerite; *m* 13 July 1892 Capt Charles Henry Halford, Gren Gds, of East Bergholt, Suffolk, and *d* 5 May 1943. He *d* 26 Feb 1922

3 Constance Maud; *d* unm June 1941

Sir ALFRED *d* 19 July 1890; his er s,

Sir Cuthbert Slade, 4th Bt, JP W Somerset; *b* 10 April 1863; Capt Scots Gds; *m* 2 Dec 1896 Kathleen (*d* 14 Jan 1930), dau of Rowland Scovell, of Fairholme, Co Dublin, and *d* 9 Feb 1908, leaving:

1 **Sir Alfred Fothringram Slade, 5th Bt**; *b* 17 Jan 1898; *educ* Eton; Capt Res Offrs Scots Gds, served WWs I and II, MFH Avon Vale 1933–37; *m* 29 April 1922 Freda Mary, yr dau of Sidney Meates, of Whitehall, Maidenhead, and *dsp* 28 Oct 1960

2 **Sir Michael Nial Slade, 6th Bt**; *b* 30 July 1900; *educ* Cheltenham and RMC Sandhurst; Capt Somerst LI; *m* 7 May 1928 Angela Clare Rosalind (*d* 4 Sept 1959), dau of Orlando Chichester (*see* CHICHESTER, Bt), and *d* 15 April 1962, having had:

(1) Robert Orlando Michael Cuthbert; *b* 21 April 1936; *educ* Malvern; *d* accidentally 10 March 1958

(2) Sir BENJAMIN JULIAN ALFRED SLADE, **7th and present Bt**

(1) Sarah Jane; *b* 13 Sept 1930; *m* 4 April 1952 2nd Baron Rotherwick (*qv*) and *d* 1978, leaving issue

1 Barbara Constance; *m* 1 June 1931 Nathaniel Alexander Lindley, er s of Hon Lennox Hannay Lindley (*see* 1921 edn LINDLEY, B), and *d* 1981, leaving issue

SLEIGHT

Arms: Per chevron or and sa., in chief two cross-crosslets and in base a lymphad with sail hoisted counterchanged. **Crest:** A mast with sail hoisted arg., charged with three cross-crosslets sa. **Motto:** Serve all, slight none. **Creation:** Bt. (UK) 29 June 1920.

SIR RICHARD SLEIGHT, 4TH BT, of Weelsby Hall, Co Lincoln [Sir Richard Sleight Bt, c/o National Westminster Bank, 22 George St, Richmond, Surrey TW9 1JW]; *b* 27 May 1946; *s* f 1990; *m* 1978 *Marie-Thérèse, only dau of O M Stepan, of Bromley, Kent and has:
- 1 +JAMES ALEXANDER; *b* 5 Jan 1981
- 2 +Nicholas Edward; *b* 1985

Lineage: CHARLES GEORGE SLEIGHT, of Clee, Lincs; *b* 1663; *m* 1687 Agnes Seymour and *d* 1711, leaving, with an est s, three yst s and three daus:

JOHN HENRY SLEIGHT, of Clee; *b* 1692; *m* 1717 Caroline Hamby and *d* 1749, leaving, with two daus:

WILLIAM ROBERT SLEIGHT; *b* 1723; *m* 1744 Jane Rawster and *d* 1791, leaving, with other issue:

WILLIAM SLEIGHT; *b* 1745; *m* 1763 Mary Appleby and *d* 1810, having had, with three yr sons (Richard, *bapt* 4 Nov 1768; William, *b* 21 Feb 1772; Matthew, *b* 20 June 1782, *d* 22 June 1783) and three daus (Hannah, *b* 11 Feb 1770, *m* 26 Nov 1795 Cuthbert Ridley, of Sprotley in Holderness, Yorks; Lutitia, *b* 31 March 1774; Mary, *b* Oct 1780):

ROBERT SLEIGHT, of Clee; *b* 1766; *m* 1796 Elizabeth Skelton (*d* 16 Nov 1858) and *d* 28 Feb 1840, having had, with three est sons (Thomas, *bapt* 14 Sept 1797, *d* unm 1864; Robert, *bapt* 9 June 1806, *bur* 21 Nov 1829; Benjamin, *bapt* 30 Nov 1807, *bur* 21 Oct 1826), a yst s (William, *bapt* 10 Feb 1817, *m* Mary — and *d* 1885, leaving three sons) and four daus (Mary, *bapt* 3 July 1799; Anne, *bapt* 13 Oct 1801; Elizabeth, *bapt* 9 Sept 1804; Rebecca, *bapt* 22 May 1810) a 4th s:

JOSEPH SLEIGHT, of Clee; *b* 20 June 1813; *m* 8 Dec 1834 Ann (*b* 1815, *d* 1891), est dau of John Dannatt, of The North Hall, Binbrook, Lincs, and *d* 24 March 1902, having had, with two est sons (Joseph, *b* 10 Aug 1845, *m* Mary Jane Turner and *d* 1898, leaving two sons and two daus; Robert, *b* 31 Dec 1851, *m* Helen Brewster, and *d* 1932), a yst s (Henry, *b* 24 March 1857, *m* Ann Chapman, of Binbrook, Lincs, and *d* 14 Feb 1911) and nine daus (including Allas, *b* 16 Feb 1849, *m* Charles Lancaster; Helen, *b* 7 March 1861, *m* Sydney Hawdon and *d* 1955, leaving issue; Ruth, *b* Oct 1863, *m* George Parker and *d* 1855, leaving issue), a 3rd s:

Sir George Frederick Sleight, 1st Bt (UK), so cr 29 June 1920, JP (Parts of Lindsey); *b* 26 March 1853; *m* 21 Nov 1872 Rebecca (*d* 29 May 1921), dau of John Longden, of Beesby, Alford, Lincs, and had, with two daus (*d* unm):
- 1 ERNEST (Sir), **2nd Bt**
- 2 Rowland, JP; *b* 18 March 1877; *educ* Rugby; Maj Boer War 1899–1902, Qld Def Force, WW I with Lincs Yeo; *m* 1 Nov 1906 Phoebe Lambert (*d* 6 Feb 1962), dau of Alderman Henry Smethurst, JP, of Grimsby, and *d* 13 May 1947, leaving:
  - (1) +(Rowland) Derek Lambert [Derek Sleight Esq, The White House, Quidenham, Norfolk NR16 2PB]]; *b* 9 May 1908; *educ* Rugby; *m* 21 Aug 1939 *Winifred, dau of Calvert Hunt, of London, and has:
    - 1a *Lesley Svea [Mrs Crispin de Boos, The Bakehouse, Banham, Norfolk NR16 2HW]; *b* 7 June 1943; *m* 1980 *Crispin de Boos
  - (1) Florence Barbara Longden; *m* 10 June 1936 Rex Bletcher, s of George Bletcher, JP, of Greetwell Hall, Manton, Lincs, and *d* 2 March 1968, leaving two sons
  - (2) Phoebe Patricia
- 3 Nelson; *b* 30 Dec 1883; *m* 21 April 1915 Edith Mary (*d* 19 Jan 1966), dau of Christopher Dewick Charles Hunt, of Gainsborough, and *d* 21 Dec 1940, leaving:
  - (1) +Peter, DFM, AE [S/Ldr Peter Sleight DFM AE, Corner Cottage, Hawerby, Humberside]; *b* 16 Oct 1920; *educ* St James's GS Grimsby; S/Ldr RAF WW II; *m* 15 March 1947 *Joyce Elizabeth, est dau of John Henry Dale, of The Longmore, Wold Newton, Lincs, and has:
    - 1a +John Nelson [John Sleight Esq, 51 Park Dve, Grimsby, S Humberside]; *b* 15 Nov 1947; *educ* Havelock GS Grimsby; *m* 2 Dec 1974 *Susan Jennifer, dau of J C Hewson, of Tetney, S Humberside, and has:

- 1b *Lucy Margaret; *b* 1979
- 2b *Sophie Elizabeth; *b* 1982
- 1a *Diana Margaret [Mrs James Atkinson, Chartwell House, Messingham Lane, Scawby, S Humberside]; *b* 28 March 1950; *m* 5 Oct 1974 *James Stewart Atkinson, s of Charles Atkinson, of Scunthorpe, and has:
  - 1b *Charles William James; *b* 1977
  - 1b *Charlotte Diana; *b* 1980
  - 2b *Louise Joanna (twin); *b* 1980
- (1) *Violet Mary [Mrs Frederick Redshaw, 64 Moorgate, Acomb, N Yorks]; *b* 1917; *m* 10 Aug 1938 Frederick Ousey Redshaw (*d* 1930), s of Frederick Redshaw, of Grimsby, and has:
  - 1a *Pamela Mary; *b* 6 Oct 1942; *m* 23 March 1968 *George Bryan O'Toole and has:
    - 1b *Laurence James; *b* 15 May 1969
    - 2b *Howard Charles; *b* 1975
    - 1b *Stella Elizabeth; *b* 1971
    - 2b *Lucy Alicia; *b* 1978
- 4 George Frederick; *b* 18 June 1890; *educ* Repton; *m* 22 May 1915 Edith Mary (*d* 19 July 1963), dau of Edwin James Brockway, JP, of Oakham, Rutland, and *d* 17 Sept 1954, leaving:
  - (1) +George Frederick; *b* 17 June 1917; *educ* Rugby; RAFVR Training Branch WW II; *m* 17 Sept 1949 *Nancy Lilian, only dau of Henry Elliott, of Anfield, nr Liverpool
  - (2) +Michael Marcus [Michael Sleight Esq, Binbrook Hall, Binbrook, Lincs LN3 6BW]; *b* 12 Aug 1924; *educ* privately and Cambridge; ROC WW II
  - (1) *Edith Mary [Mrs James Davey, Kelstern Hall, nr Louth, Lincs]; *b* 1918; *m* 20 June 1947 *James Davey, of Limber Hill, Habrough, and has:
    - 1a *Veronica Mary; *b* 10 Aug 1950
    - 2a *Caroline Frances; *b* 2 Nov 1954
- 1 Eleanor; *d* unm 22 Dec 1966 aged 88
- 2 Violet; *m* 30 Sept 1915 Ferdinand Henri Martin Koch, Swiss Consul, and *d* 23 Dec 1925, leaving issue
- 3 Gladys; *b* 1894; *m* 2 Feb 1916 Gerald Noel Sowerby, 2nd s of Francis Sowerby, of Hawerby Hall, Grimsby, and had issue. He *d* 20 June 1959

Sir GEORGE *d* 19 March 1921; his est s,

Sir Ernest Sleight, 2nd Bt, OBE, TD, JP, DL Lincs; *b* 14 Oct 1873; Maj 5th Bn Lincoln Regt (TA), memb Mil Serv (Hardship) Ctee, dir Fishing Vessels Mutual War Risk Assoc Ltd; memb Nat Serv Ctees Lincs (Parts of Lindsey) and Grimsby, served WW I (1914–15 star, two medals), High Sheriff Lincs 1946; *m* 5 Oct 1898 Margaret (*d* 30 Dec 1976), dau of Charles Frederick Carter, JP, of The Limes, Grimsby, and had:
- 1 Arthur Ernest; *b* 27 Dec 1905; *d* unm 16 July 1928
- 2 JOHN FREDERICK (Sir), **3rd Bt**
- 1 Eleanor Mary; *b* 15 July 1899; *d* 11 Feb 1900
- 2 Margaret; *b* 13 Dec 1900, *d* 29 Sept 1901
- 3 Joan Winifred; *b* 16 May 1904; *m* 1st 22 Oct 1924 Ernest Addison (*d* 18 Sept 1951), 4th s of Matthew Addison, of Riby Grove, Lincs, and had issue; *m* 2nd 17 Sept 1957 Alfred Frank Culham, 3rd s of James Samuel Culham, of Virginia House, Gayton, Norfolk

Sir ERNEST *d* 16 July 1946; his only surv s,

Sir John Frederick Sleight, 3rd Bt; *b* 13 April 1909; *educ* Brighton Coll; *m* 1942 *Jacqueline Margaret [Jacqueline Lady Sleight, Surfers Paradise, Qld 4217, Australia], widow of Ronald Mundell and est dau of Maj H R Carter, of Brisbane, Qld, and *d* 1990, leaving:

Sir RICHARD SLEIGHT, **4th and present Bt**

SLIGO

SUIVEZ · RAISON

Arms: Sa. three lions passant in bend arg. between four bendlets of the last. **Crest:** An eagle displayed vert. **Supporters:** Dexter, a talbot ppr., gorged with a baron's coronet; sinister, a horse arg. **Motto:** *Suivez raison* ('Follow the right'). **Creations:** B. (I) 10 Sept 1760 (Monteagle) and (UK) 20 Feb 1806 (Monteagle of Westport), V. (I) 24 Aug 1768, E. (I) 4 Dec 1771 (Altamont) and (I) 29 Dec 1800 (Clanricarde), M. (I) 29 Dec 1800.

THE 11TH MARQUESS OF SLIGO, Earl of Altamont, Co Mayo, **Earl of Clanricarde**, Co Galway, **Viscount Westport** of Westport, Co Mayo, **Baron Monteagle** of Westport, Co Mayo, and **Baron Monteagle of Westport**, Co Mayo (Jeremy Ulick Browne) [The Most Hon The Marquess of Sligo, Westport House, Westport, Co Mayo, Ireland]; *b* 4 June 1939; *s f* 1991; *educ* St Columba's Coll and RAC Cirencester; *m* 26 Oct 1961 *Jennifer June Lushington, only dau of Maj (George) Derek Cooper, MC, Life Gds, of Dunlewey, Gweedore, Co Donegal, by his 1st w Pamela (later Mrs Cyril Heber Percy), est dau of Kinmont Willie Armstrong-Lushington-Tulloch, of Shanbolard, Moyard, Co Galway, and has:

1 *Sheelyn Felicity; *b* 1 June 1963
2 *Karen Lavinia; *b* 3 July 1964; *m* 19– *Kevin —
3 *Lucinda Jane; *b* 18 May 1969; *m* 199– *Alan —
4 *Clare Romane; *b* 23 Dec 1974
5 *Alannah Pamela Josephine Grace; *b* 1 March 1980

Lineage: Sir JOHN BROWNE, 1st Bt, of The Neale, Co Mayo (*see* KILMAINE, B), had a 2nd s:

JOHN BROWNE, of Kinturk and Westport, Co Mayo; Col in JAMES II'S army in Ireland; barrister Connaught 1680; helped draft Treaty of Limerick 1691; *m* 1st —; *m* 2nd Maud Bourke, yr dau of 3rd Viscount (Bourke of) Mayo (*see* MAYO, E, preliminary remarks), and *d* 1712, having had, with a yr s (Valentine, of Mount Browne, Co Mayo, *m* Bridget, dau of Col James Talbot, of Mount Talbot and Templeoge, and had a dau Mary, *m* John Lynch, of Clogher, Co Mayo) and three daus (Bridget, *m* as his 2nd w 13th Lord (Baron) Athenry (*d* 3 May 1709) and *d* 13 Jan 1702, leaving issue; Elizabeth, *m* John Bermingham, of Kellbrack (or Ross), Co Mayo, and had issue; Mary, *m* 8 July 1702, as his 1st w, her cousin 6th Viscount (Bourke of) Mayo (*d* 1741) and had issue):

PETER BROWNE, of Westport; *m* Mary, widow of John Moore/O'Moore, of Cloghan, and er dau of Denis Daly, of Caragh, Co Galway, Judge Court Common Pleas Ireland, and *d* between 12 July 1718 and 20 June 1724, leaving:

JOHN BROWNE, **1st Earl of Altamont**, Co Mayo, so *cr* 4 Dec 1771, as also earlier 10 Sept 1760 BARON MONTEAGLE (otherwise known as Croagh Patrick, a 2,510-ft high mountain nr Westport) of Westport, Co Mayo, and 24 Aug 1768 VISCOUNT WESTPORT of Westport, Co Mayo (all I); *b c* 1709; *educ* Ch Ch Oxford; Sheriff Co Mayo 1731, MP (I Parl) Castlebar 1744–60, Govr Mayo; *m* Dec 1729 Anne (*d* 7 March 1771), est dau of Sir Arthur Gore, 2nd Bt (*see* ARRAN, E), and had:

1 PETER, **2nd Earl**
2 Arthur, PC, of Leixlip Castle and Newtown, Co Roscommon; *b* 1731; Col 28th Foot, present Battle of Quebec 1759, MP Co Mayo; *m* 1766 Anne (*d* July 1807), dau of Silvester Gardiner, MD, of Boston, Mass., and *d* 21 July 1779, having had, with other issue:
  (1) John, of Athleague House and Newtown, Co Roscommon; *b* 1756; Maj 67th Regt; *m* 1st 1784 Rosa Mary, dau of Adml Sir Richard Hughes, 2nd Bt (*qv*), and had:
    1a Arthur, of Newtown and Roxborough House, Co Roscommon; *b* 1785; *m* 3 Jan 1814 Anna Elizabeth (*d* 23 April 1867), only dau of Capt Richard Clements, HEICS, and *d* 18 Oct 1870, having had, with other issue:
      1b Henry George BROWNE later GORE-BROWNE (deed poll 1904), VC, JP, DL Hants; *b* 29 Sept 1830; Col 100th Foot, Dep Govr IoW 1912; *m* 10 April 1864 Jane Anne (*d* 3 April 1913), sis of Sir Charles Seely, 1st Bt (*qv*), and *d* 15 Nov 1912, having had:
        1c Charles Henry Arthur; *b* 1876; *m* 1898 Daisy, dau of William Dow, and *dvp* 11 Aug 1910, leaving:

        1d Geoffrey George; *b* 28 Aug 1899; Midshipman RN; *ka* lost in HMS *Aboukir* 22 Sept 1914
        1c Annie Mary Claudine; *m* 18 April 1901 Walter John Langton, of Wootton Lodge, IOW, and had issue
      1b Claudine Adelaide; *m* 11 March 1854 George Sandes Graves, RIC, and *d* 5 April 1877, leaving issue
      2b Emily Alice; *m* 22 June 1841 James Arthur Browne, of Browne Hall, Co Mayo, and had issue. He *d* 27 Dec 1868
      3b Ellen Cummins; *m* May 1856 her cousin Henry Browne, 2nd s of George Browne, of Mount Browne, Co Roscommon (*see below*), and had issue
      4b Mary
      5b Annie
  (1) (cont.) Maj John Browne *m* 2nd Elizabeth, widow of — Bernard and dau of Judge Sullivan, and *d* 24 Aug 1819, having by her had, with other issue:
    2a John; Judge Court Bankruptcy Ireland; *m* —, dau of Gen Stafford, and had:
      1b Hugh; Ensign; *k* Delhi in Indian Mutiny
    3a George, of Mount Browne House, Coolmeen, Killicloghan and Dacloon, Co Roscommon;, barrister; *m* 1825 May, dau of Col Kenny, and *d* 15 May 1865, leaving:
      1b Robert, of Strokestown, Co Roscommon; *b* 21 Nov 1826; slr; *d* 1870
      2b Henry, of Corteen, Co Longford, and Corgarrow and Dacloon, Co Roscommon; *b* 14 June 1829; barrister; *m* May 1856 his cousin Ellen Cummins, 4th dau of Arthur Browne, of Newtown (*see above*), and *d* 1869, having had, with two daus:
        1c George Kenny, *dsp c* 1920–30
        2c Ernest Henry; *b* 1863; *m c* 1916 Beatrice Brownrigg (*d* 13 Dec 1964) and *d* 8 Dec 1928, leaving:
          1d +Ernest Henry; *b* 1913
          1d *Beatrice Mary [Miss Beatrice Browne, 92 Cabra Park, Phibsborough, Dublin, Ireland]; *b* 1911
        3c Arthur Kenny, of Newtown and Ballinhurly
      3b Arthur, of Mount Browne, Co Roscommon, JP; *b* 16 Jan 1837; LLB; *m* 1st 1866 Frances, dau of Maj Long, of Co Cork, and had:
        1c Frances; *d unm*
      3b (cont.) Arthur Browne *m* 2nd 16 March 1891 Marie Cecilia (*d* 28 Aug 1893), widow of Patrick George Browne, of Clonfad, and dau of — Hanly, and by her had:
        1c Arthur Marie John George Joseph, of Mount Browne, Killicloghan and Cordrummin, Co Roscommon; *b* 24 Feb 1892; *d* 195–
      3b (cont.) Arthur Browne *m* 3rd Dec 1893 Bridie Jane Georgina (*m* 2nd 26 Aug 1907 Walter Alfred Jones, JP, PhD), dau of Robert ffrench, JP, of Larchgrove, Co Roscommon, s of Robert Henry ffrench, of Frenchlawn, Co Roscommon, and Carney Castle, Fethard, Co Tipperary, and *d* 29 Dec 1899
(2) George Townsend; *b* 1760; *m* — Fleetwood and *d* 4 June 1856, leaving, with four daus:
  1a John Denis (Rev); *b* 1807; Vicar Braintree, Essex; *m* Mary Ruth (*d* 1893), dau of William Lacy, and *d* 17 Feb 1864, leaving, with a dau (*d unm*):
    1b Valentine John Augustus later Valentine Denis (deed poll) (Rev); *b* 18 Sept 1843; served 7th Fus, Rector Nuffield, Oxon, 1897–1929; *m* 8 Jan 1884 Frances Elizabeth (*d* 11 June 1939), 3rd dau of William Rose, barrister, and *d* 22 Dec 1933, leaving:
      1c Rosalind Frances; *b* 1885
  2b Alfred Denis; *b* 5 Dec 1845; *d unm* 4 April 1902
  1b Florence Isabella; *m* 12 April 1904 Clement Stephens, of St Leonards-on-Sea, s of J C Stephens, of Maidstone, and *d* 18 April 1931. He *d* 1920
(1) Augusta Louisa; *m* 1803 Lt-Col Dominick Browne, of Browne Hall, Co Mayo, and *d* 1850, leaving issue
3 George; *m* Dorcas, dau and coheir of James Moore, of Newport, and had:
  (1) Margaret; *m* 20 Aug 1784 Dominick Geoffrey Browne and *d* 29 May 1838, having had issue (*see* ORANMORE AND BROWNE, B)
4 James; Prime Serjeant Ireland; *d unm* 1790
5 Henry; Ensign 22nd Regt 1756, Lt 1756, Lt Louisburg Gren, fought Battle of Quebec 1759, Capt 5th Roy Irish Dragoons 1764, ret 1771; *m* Anna, yr dau of Sir Henry Lynch, 5th Bt (*see* LYNCH-BLOSSE, Bt), and *dsp* March 1812
6 John; *m* 1st Mary Cocks and had (with a s):
  (1) Emily; *m* 8 Jan 1788 Dominick Browne, of Ashford, Co Galway, and had issue
  (2) Mary; *m* 14 May 1800 Peter Blake, of Corbally Castle, Co Galway
6 (cont.) The Hon John Browne *m* 2nd Rosalinda (*d* 30 April 1812), dau of Eneas Gilker, and by her had, with other issue:
  (3) Louisa; *m* 26 Aug 1807 George Moore, of Moore Hall, Co Mayo, and had issue, being grandmother of the novelist George Moore (1852–1933)
1 Anne; *m* 12 Oct 1762 Ross Mahon, of Castlegar, Co Galway (*see* MAHON, Bt), and *d* 21 Feb 1815, leaving issue

The 1st EARL *d* 4 July 1776; his est s,
PETER BROWNE later BROWNE-KELLY (added on marriage), **2nd Earl of Altamont**; *b c* 1731; *educ* Ch Ch Oxford; MP (I Parl) Co Mayo 1761–68; *m* 16 April 1752 Elizabeth, only dau and heiress of Denis Kelly, Ch Justice Jamaica, of Lisduffe, Co Galway, and had, with a dau (*d unm*):

1 JOHN DENIS, **1st Marquess**
2 Denis, PC, MP; *b* 1763; *m c* 7 Dec 1790 his cousin Anne (*d* 30 Dec 1833), dau of Ross Mahon, of Castlegar, Co Galway, and *d* 14 Aug 1828, leaving, with other issue:
  (1) James, of Claremont House, Co Mayo; *b* 15 June 1793; MP Co Mayo; *m* 1st Oct 1820 Eleanor Catherine (*dsp* Dec 1823), 3rd dau of John Wells, JP, DL, MP, of Bickley Hall, Kent; *m* 2nd 17 March 1825 Elizabeth (*d* 1867), dau of John Puget, JP, of Pointer's Grove, Totteridge, Herts, and *d* 23 Dec 1854, leaving a s and three daus (*d unm*)

(2) Peter; *b* 1794; MP Rye, Chargé d'Affaires Copenhagen; *m* 4 July 1822 Catherine Esther, dau of John Puget, of Pointer's Grove, and *d* 7 April 1872, having had, with a dau (*d* unm):

1a Peter Denis; *b* 11 March 1825; *m* 20 June 1865 Emily (*d* 25 June 1896), est dau of Col Richard Beauchamp (*see* PROCTOR-BEAUCHAMP, Bt), and *d* 17 Nov 1883, leaving:

1b Beauchamp Denis; *b* 1 Oct 1871; *d* unm 28 March 1910

1b Sophia Esther Maria; *m* 1896 her cousin Silvio Camillo, Marquis of Casanova, of San Remigio, Pallanza, Italy, and *d* 12 Jan 1960, leaving issue

1a Esther Jane; *m* 3 April 1860 Marquis of Casanova and had issue

2a Eleanor Isabella; *m* 10 Aug 1867 Agosto Satori

(3) Denis (Very Rev); *b* 12 Oct 1795; Vicar Santry, Rector Enniscorthy, Dean Emly; *m* 7 June 1824 Anne Alicia (*d* 26 Oct 1876), dau of Thomas William Filgate, of Arthurstown, Co Louth, and *d* 14 March 1864, leaving, with three daus (*d* unm):

1a Denis Howe; *b* 6 Oct 1826; *m* 28 July 1884 Louisa, widow of Rev Francis Browne, and *d* 13 March 1912, having had:

1b Ernest Charles Denis; *b* 1885; *d* 1904

2a William Denis; *b* 3 June 1836; *m* 18 Feb 1879 Louisa (*d* 31 Dec 1926), dau of Thomas Hackett, of Moor Park, King's Co, and *d* 16 May 1916, leaving:

1b Denis Robert Howe, OBE (1919); *b* 19 Dec 1879; *educ* Malvern and King's Coll London; Lt-Col IARO WW I Mesopotamia 1916–19; Indian Serv Engrs, Ch Engr and Sec Govt Bombay PWD 1926–30, attd RE Min Supply Cardiff 1940–45; *d* unm 25 July 1954

2b William Charles Denis; *b* 3 Nov 1888; Sub-Lt Hood Bn RND; *ka* Dardanelles 4 June 1915

1b Emily Alice; *b* 3 Dec 1880; *m* 24 Oct 1911 Sir Stephen James Murphy, ICS (*d* 21 Oct 1950), Judge High Court Bombay, er s of Lt-Col Patrick Murphy, IMS, and *d* Jan 1969, having had issue

2b Louisa Muriel; *b* 21 March 1882; *m* 24 April 1906 Edward Mansell, FRIBA (*d* 11 March 1941), s of Thomas Henry Mansell, of Melbury, Boscombe, Bournemouth, and *d* 20 March 1956, leaving issue

3b Helen Ethel; *b* 26 July 1884; *m* 21 Nov 1905 Cdr Edward Mathew Hale, RN (*d* 19 Jan 1921), s of Rt Rev Mathew Blagden Hale, DD, Bp Brisbane, and *d* 30 June 1958, leaving issue

(4) John Denis, of Mount Browne, Co Mayo; *b* 1798; *m* 25 Aug 1832 Esther (*d c* 1883) est dau of John Wells, JP, DL, MP, of Bickley Hall, Kent, and *d* 21 May 1862, having had:

1a Henry Burdett; *b* 1837; *d* at sea 1857

2a Percival Altamont, of Mount Browne and Hanworth, Middx; *b* 1 Aug 1841; Capt Bombay SC; *m* 3 Jan 1871 Caroline Maude (*d* 20 Feb 1937), yst dau of James Hunt, of Brighton, and *d* 2 Aug 1919, leaving:

1b Percy Frederick; *b* 25 Aug 1872; Capt S African Constabulary, Commr Police Tanganyika 1920–29; *m* 27 April 1904 Ruth (*d* 16 Sept 1957), yr dau of John Reynolds Warren, of Berea, Durban, and *d* 5 May 1959, having had:

1c Patrick Warren; *b* 14 Feb 1908; Maj King's Regt WW II; *m* 24 April 1936 *Ada Elizabeth Minnie Barnes [Mrs Ada Browne, 3 Cardigan Rd, London SW13] (*m* 2nd 10 April 1946 (*divorce* 1954 resumed 1st hub's name) Charles Edward Halton Duprez) and *d* 15 Dec 1944, leaving:

1d +Michael Lewis; *b* 28 May 1940

2d +(Philip) Anthony [Anthony Browne, 111E 75th St, New York, NY 10021, USA]; *b* 29 Nov 1941; *educ* Boxgrove Sch Guildford

1d *Patricia Ruth [Mrs David Heather, 113 Redland Rd, Redland, Bristol]; *b* 19 April 1937; *m* 19– *David Heather and has:

1e *Lucy; *b* 19–

1c *Nancye Maud [Mrs Aubrey Rous, The Cottage, 12 Mayfair Ave, Newlands 7700, Cape Town, S Africa]; *b* 13 June 1905; *m* 22 Aug 1945 Maj Aubrey James Rous (*d* 23 April 1969), s of William James Rous, of London, and has:

1d *Patrick James [Patrick Rous, Happy Hollow Lane, Austin, Tx 78703, USA]; *b* 21 Jan 1947; *educ* Ottershaw

2c *Moya Lennox [Mrs Richard Birtwistle, 1005–2012 Fullerton Ave, N Vancouver, BC V7P 3P3, Canada]; *b* 31 Dec 1917; *m* 2 March 1944 Richard Read Birtwistle (*d* 1983), s of Henry Haydock Birtwistle, of Whalley, Lancs, and has:

1d *Susan Lennox [Mrs Dan Koch, 1945 Russel Way, W Vancouver, BC V7V 3B3, Canada]; *b* 7 May 1947; *m* 1972 *Capt Dan Collinson Koch and has:

1e *Michael Richard Collinson; *b* 1975

2e *Christopher John Collinson; *b* 1978

3e *James Daniel Collinson; *b* 1990

2b Burdett; *b* 18 Oct 1875; Capt Special List; *m* 19 Oct 1925 Winifred Lilian (*d* 22 Sept 1944), dau of Charles Woodbridge, of Henley-on-Thames, and *d* 28 Feb 1956

3b Denis Howe; *b* 20 Dec 1876; *d* 9 June 1920

4b Herbert; *b* 23 Sept 1878; *d* unm 1967

1b Kathleen Maude; *b* 3 Nov 1879; *d* unm 26 Jan 1951

2b Nora Catherine; *b* 15 Oct 1880; *d* 5 Sept 1883

3b Muriel; *b* 4 Nov 1886; *m* 6 April 1918 Horace Muir Lyster and had issue

4b Ethel Mildred; *b* 12 June 1892; *d* unm 1965

1a Esther Charlotte; *m* 4 Jan 1862 Thomas Bingham and *d* 1912, leaving issue. He *d* 1885

2a Louisa Anne; *m* 31 Jan 1866 Col Frederick Augustus Le Mesurier, CB, RE, of Oxford, and *d* 10 April 1912, leaving issue. He *d* 9 June 1926

3a Julia Sophia; *m* 31 Jan 1872 Maj John Otway Wemyss, The Buffs, of Danesfort, Co Kilkenny, and *d* 13 Sept 1926. He *dsp* 1891

4a Caroline Catherine; *m* 18 Jan 1862 Lt-Col Eugene Hay Cameron, RA, and *d* 21 Dec 1934, leaving issue. He *d* 1885

(5) George (Rev); *b* 29 May 1803; Vicar Lenton, Notts; *m* 1828 Elizabeth Anne (*d* 8 Dec 1870), dau of Rev Edward Day, of Beaufort Ho, Co Kerry, and *d* 1886, having had, with other issue:

1a George Robert, of Cahirdown, Co Kerry, JP; *b* 10 Oct 1833; High Sheriff Co Kerry 1889; *m* 1 Oct 1862 Emma Frances (*d* 26 Oct 1932), only dau of Wilson Gun, DL, of Rattoo, Co Kerry, and *d* 24 March 1904, leaving:

1b George Denis Gun; *b* 5 July 1874; *educ* Trin Hall Cambridge; *m* 23 March 1901 Gertrude Bessy (*d* 1953), yst dau of John Robert Sutton Hudson, and *d* 1946, leaving:

1c +Denis George Robert Anthony Gun; *b* 9 Aug 1907; *m* 15 Dec 1960 *Violet Ailsa, dau of Karl Stewart-Hess, of Wallasey, Cheshire

1c *Gertrude Frances Hester Gun [Mrs Roger McCulloch, PO Box 200, Selukwe, Zimbabwe]; *b* 1905; *m* 1st 1931 George Ryder Runton (*d* 1935) and has:

1d *Aileen Frances; *b* 1932; *m* 1950 John Geoffrey Harrison (*d* 1975) and has:

1e *Michael John; *b* 1952

1e *Rosemary Ann; *b* 1954

1c (cont.) Mrs George Runton *m* 2nd 1945 *Roger Sydney McCulloch and by him has:

2d *Jane Ann Louise; *b* 1946; *m* 1968 *Marie Denise Guiot-Pascau, of Natal, and has:

1e *Daniel François; *b* 1973

2e *Grant Ivan; *b* 1975

3e *Heal Gregory; *b* 1977

1b Gertrude Georgina; *m* 19 April 1895 Archibald Denis Hay Cameron and *d* 16 Jan 1948, having had issue. He *d* 20 Dec 1946

2b Emmeline Elizabeth; *m* 27 March 1897 David George Plunkett, of Alberta, Canada, and *d* 18 May 1933, leaving issue

3b Hester Harriet; *m* 6 April 1899 Henry Middleton and *d* 17 March 1910, leaving issue

4b Elizabeth Frances

5b Kathleen Emilia; *m* 15 March 1904 Sidney Burd Leigh-Taylor, s of William Taylor, of Westbourne, Bolton-le-Moor, Lancs, and Arthog Hall, Merioneths, and *d* 3 Sept 1938, leaving issue

6b Henrietta Ethne; *m* 1 June 1901 Hon William Henry Ernest Robert Turlough O'Brien and *d* 18 Dec 1950, leaving issue (*see* INCHIQUIN, B)

2a Robert (Rev); *b* 19 March 1835; Rector Fawley, Hants; *m* 5 April 1866 Ellen Richenda (*d* 2 Aug 1916), yst dau of Rev Daniel Wilson, Vicar Islington, and *d* 27 Aug 1900, leaving:

1b Robert Denis; *b* 21 Feb 1867; *m* 16 Dec 1905 Beatrice (*d* 8 Jan 1957), dau of Henry John Batson, of Hampstead, and *d* 7 April 1937, leaving:

1c Robert John Denis; *b* 20 March 1907; MRCS, LRCP, Surgn-Lt RNVR WW II; *m* 9 July 1949 *Norah Mary [Mrs Robert Browne, 1536 Pershore Rd, Stirchley, Birmingham, W Midlands], dau of David Haywood, of Burton-on-Trent, and *d* 1985, leaving:

1d +Stephen Denis; *b* 4 May 1950; *educ* George Dixon GS and Birmingham U; MRCGP; *m* 1978 *Patricia Marian, dau of William George Delahaye, of Birmingham, and has:

1e *Elizabeth Anne; *b* 1979

2e *Sarah Jayne; *b* 1981

2d +Anthony David; *b* 10 Sept 1958; MSc; *m* 1983 *Susan Elizabeth, dau of John Frederick Hole, of Stourbridge, and has:

1e +David Alexander; *b* 1989

2e +Daniel Benjamin; *b* 1991

1d *Margaret; *b* 8 March 1952; *m* 1973 *John Charles Williams and has:

1e *Rachel; *b* 1977

2e *Ruth Emma; *b* 1979

2c Terence Francis Denis; *b* 6 Nov 1910; RTR WW II; *m* 28 Sept 1947 Avril Honor (*d* 1973), dau of William T Thompson, of Rustington, Sussex, and *d* 1987, leaving:

1d +Peter Malyon Denis; *b* 9 Feb 1953; *educ* Monkton Combe Sch

2d +Ian Anthony Denis [Ian Browne Esq, 20 Woodfield Lane, Ashtead, Surrey KT21 2BE]; *b* 25 July 1956; *educ* Monkton Combe Sch

2b Cyril George Denis (Rev); *b* 18 Sept 1873; Rector Sombra, Ontario; *m* Nov 1906 Sarah (*d* 13 Nov 1943), dau of Charles Crooks Higby, and *d* 14 Sept 1952, leaving:

1c Cyril Theodore Martin (Rev); *b* 6 July 1912; Rector Tilston and Shocklach; *d* 19 July 1996

1c Muriel Eunice Myra; *b* 9 Sept 1908; *d* 31 Jan 1984

3b Ambrose George Denis; *b* 6 Oct 1875; Lt Army Ordnance Dept WW I; *m* 1st 27 Oct 1915 Alice Winifred (*d* 18 April 1938), only dau of Sir William White, KCB, Dir Naval Construction and Assist Controller RN 1885–1902, and had:

1c +William Robert Anthony Denis [William Browne Esq, 22 West Cliff Park Drive, Dawlish, Devon EX7 9EA]; *b* 31 Dec 1924; FRICS, RM WW II; *m* 1st 1949 (*divorce* 1967) Eileen Beatrice Louise, dau of Horace Hugh Percival Hunt, of High Ham, Somerset, and has:

1d +James Anthony Ulick Denis [James Browne Esq, 41 Cambridge Rd, Ely, Cambs CB7 4HJ]; *b* 20 June 1956; *educ* Clifton and Ecole Hotelière, Lausanne, Switzerland; *m* 22 Sept 1988 *Linda, dau of Maj John James Patrick Brennen, of Bath, and has:

1e +Dominic Oscar James; *b* 9 Dec 1993

1e *Natalie Louise; *b* 23 Nov 1990

1d *Caroline Elizabeth Anne Denis [Mrs John Perou, Marlpost, Chaddleworth, Berks RG20 7EH]; *b* 17 April 1952; *m* 10 May 1975 *John Christopher Perou, s of John Disney Perou, of London, and has:

1e *Edmund Arthur James; *b* 27 June 1989

1c (cont.) William Browne *m* 2nd June 1967 *Hildegard, dau of Johann Cremer, of Dorsten, Germany, and by her has:

  2d +Andrew Christopher Denis; *b* 8 Nov 1972

1c *Winifred Anne Denis [Mrs John Bateman, 24 Manstone Mead, Sidmouth, Devon]; *b* 2 Jan 1921; *m* 1950 John Henry Bateman (*d* 1997), s of Capt H Vernon Bateman, Munster Rifles, of Cambridge

3b (cont.) Ambrose Browne *m* 2nd 20 Dec 1941 *Gertrude Mary Anna (*d* 1973), yr dau of Rev John Kipling Quarterman, of London SE3, and *d* 11 Aug 1954

1b Lucy Muriel; *b* 13 Nov 1868; *d* unm 25 Nov 1943

2b Elizabeth Richenda; *b* 28 Jan 1870; *d* unm 19 Jan 1944

3b Harriette Rowan; *b* 6 Aug 1871; *m* 27 Aug 1906 William Horace Salmon, s of William Salmon, of Reading, and *d* 22 March 1951, leaving issue. He *d* 27 June 1955

3a Francis (Rev); *b* 17 April 1844; incumbent Christ Church, Trent, Enfield; *m* 15 Oct 1873 Louisa, only dau of Rev William Filgate, of Arthurstown, Co Louth, and *dsp* 8 Aug 1879

(1) Harriet Mary; *m* June 1829 Rev Robert Pakenham and *d* 23 May 1865, leaving issue (*see* LONGFORD, E)

1 Anne; *m* 18 Aug 1785 1st Earl of Desart (*see* 1935 edn) and *d* 15 Aug 1814, leaving issue. He *d* 9 Aug 1804

2 Elizabeth; *m* 6 Aug 1786 Sir Ross Mahon, 1st Bt (*qv*), of Castlegar, Co Galway, and *d* 24 Feb 1795, leaving issue

3 Charlotte; *m* 9 Jan 1794 John Mahon, of Besborough, Co Tipperary, and *d* 23 Jan 1849, leaving issue (*see* MAHON, Bt)

The 2nd EARL *d* 28 Dec 1780; his er s,

JOHN DENIS BROWNE, **1st Marquess of Sligo** (I), so *cr* 29 Dec 1800, as also 20 Feb 1806 BARON MONTEAGLE OF WESTPORT, Co Mayo (UK), KP (1800), PC (I 1785); *b* 11 June 1756; *educ* Eton; Sheriff Co Mayo 1779, MP (I Parl) Jamestown 1776–80, rep I peer 1801; *m* 21 May 1787 Lady Louisa Catharine Howe (*m* 2nd and last Baron Stowell of Stowell Park (*see* 1836 edn), and *d* 1817), yst dau of 1st and last Earl Howe (*qv*) of the 1788 *cr*, and *d* 2 June 1809, leaving:

HOWE PETER BROWNE, **2nd Marquess of Sligo**, KP (1810), PC (I 1809, GB 1834); *b* 18 May 1788; *educ* Eton; Ld Lt Co Mayo 1831–34 and 1842–45, Govr and V-Adml Jamaica 1833–36, Col S Mayo Militia; *m* 4 March 1816 Lady Hester Catherine de Burgh (*d* 17 Feb 1878), dau of 13th Earl of Clanricarde (*see* below), and *d* 26 Jan 1845, having had, with another s (*d* young) and four daus (*d* unm):

1 GEORGE JOHN BROWNE, **3rd Marquess of Sligo**; *b* 31 Jan 1820 (GEORGE IV stood sponsor); *educ* Eton and Trin Coll Cambridge; Hon Col 3rd Bn Connaught Rangers 1841; *m* 1st 3 May 1847 Ellen Sydney (*d* 23 Nov 1852), dau of 6th Viscount Strangford, and had a dau (*d* young); *m* 2nd 20 July 1858 Lady Julia Catherine Anne Nugent (*d* 25 June 1859), est dau of 9th Earl of Westmeath (*qv*), and by her had a dau (*d* young); *m* 3rd 6 June 1878 Isabelle Raymonde (*d* 26 May 1927), 3rd dau of Vicomte de Peyronnet, and *d* 30 Dec 1896, having by her had:

  (1) Mary Isabel Peyronnet; *b* 6 Nov 1881; *d* unm 18 Dec 1948

  (2) Isabel Mary Peyronnet, OBE (1918); *b* 6 Nov 1881; FLS; *d* unm 8 June 1947

2 James de Burgh; *b* 1823; Cornet 9th Lancers 1843, Lt 10th Hus 1846, served 1st Sikh war, ADC to 1st Viscount Gough (*qv*) Battle of Sobraon 1846; *d* 6 April 1847

3 JOHN THOMAS BROWNE, **4th Marquess of Sligo**, JP, DL Co Mayo; *b* 10 Sept 1824; Lt RN, MP (Lib) Mayo 1857–68; *d* unm 30 Dec 1903

4 HENRY ULICK, **5th Marquess**

5 Richard Howe; *b* 6 Aug 1834; Maj 96th Regt Crimea; *m* 16 Dec 1863 Agnes Elizabeth (*d* 17 Jan 1885 aged 41), dau of Dr Joseph Amesbury, of Brighton, and *d* 28 Oct 1912, having had, with twin daus (*d* infants):

  (1) Arthur Richard; *b* 10 March 1866; *m* 3 May 1892 Jessie Bernice (*m* 2nd 26 July 1910 Lt-Col Bernard High Wilbraham, DSO (*d* 2 May 1942) and *d* 21 April 1947), dau of James Seagrave, of Tasmania, and *d* 24 April 1900, leaving:

    1a Arthur Richard Howe; *b* 7 March 1893; Lt RFC; *ka* 22 Feb 1916

  (2) Percy Howe; *b* 4 Dec 1868; Staff Capt and Brevet Maj WW I (despatches three times), Cdr Order Avis Portugal, Chev Order Leopold Belgium; *m* 16 Feb 1897 Alice Tremlett, dau of Capt Charles Henry Mariller, and *d* 16 Dec 1940, leaving:

    1a Anthony Howe; *b* 30 June 1905; Lt-Cdr RN WW II; *m* 6 Oct 1931 Joyce Mary Le Roy (*m* 2nd 1946 S/Ldr Graham Doody, ACA (*d* 1981), and *d* 1981), only dau of John Collin, of Trumpington, Cambs, and was *ka* 14 Oct 1940, leaving:

      1b +Patrick Ulick Anthony Howe [Patrick Browne Esq, The Bury, Foxton, Cambs CB2 6RP]; *b* 29 Jan 1935; *educ* Eton and Magdalene Coll Cambridge; late RN; *m* 1st 28 July 1962 (*divorce* 1985) Gerd, er dau of Anders Hamer, of Norway, and has:

        1c +Patrick Alexander Howe; *b* 11 Nov 1965

        2c +Anthony Howe; *b* 19 Jan 1967

        1c *Cecilie Howe; *b* 1 June 1963

      1b (cont.) Patrick Browne *m* 2nd 6 July 1991 *Emily Rutherford, dau of Marvin Langley, of Skaneateles, NY

      2b +Michael John Le Roy [Michael Browne Esq, PO Box 651799, Benmore 2010, S Africa]; *b* 30 July 1936; *educ* RNC Dartmouth and Natal U; late RN; *m* 19 Dec 1959 (*divorce* 1969) Sarah Ruth, er dau of James Edward Kenneth Sprot, of Hillcrest, Natal, and has:

        1c +Richard Howe; *b* 6 June 1962

        2c +Jeremy Ulick; *b* 16 Oct 1963

    1a Margaret Kathleen; *b* 22 June 1898; *m* 8 April 1924 Almeric Hugh Seymour, CBE, ICS (*d* 7 Jan 1950), s of Dr Seymour, of Oxford, and had:

      1b Timothy Hugh; *b* 12 Dec 1928; *m* 19 April 1958 *Elisabeth Valerie, dau of Dr Rayner Thrower, and *d* 30 July 1997, leaving:

        1c *Meryl Penelope Jane; *b* 7 May 1959

        2c *Elizabeth Anne Peronel; *b* 17 June 1961

        3c *Catherine Fiona Margaret; *b* 5 Aug 1964

4c *Joanna Melanie Ruth; *b* 5 Aug 1964; *m* 14 Oct 1989 *Robert Mark Longden

1b Ruth Meryl; *b* 30 Jan 1925; *d* 9 April 1939

2b *Elizabeth Jennifer Jane; *b* 20 Oct 1934; *m* 23 Aug 1957 Capt Rhoderick Stewart Cochrane-Dyet, 9th/12th Queen's Roy Lancers, s of Col J C Cochrane-Dyet, and has:

  1c *Charles Nicholas; *b* 4 Oct 1958

  2c *Christopher James Richard; *b* 19 April 1963

  1c *Amanda Jane; *b* 17 March 1961

(3) Cyril Edward, OBE (1949); *b* 15 July 1873; *educ* Marlborough and Trin Coll Cambridge (BA 1895, MA 1899); Dir in Eire of Irish Sailors' and Soldiers' Land Tst 1924–49, Inspr Audits Local Govt Bd Ireland; *m* 30 April 1902 Alice Christina (*d* 11 Jan 1962), dau of Frederick Thomas Lewin, DL, of Castlegrove, Co Galway, and *d* 29 Aug 1960, leaving:

  1a Peter Raleigh Howe; *b* 22 Jan 1918; 2nd Lt Roy Irish Fus WW II (despatches); *ka* 23 May 1940

  1a Dorothy Lucy Agnes; *b* 6 June 1911; *d* unm 12 Aug 1932

  2a *Phyllis Marion Alice [Mrs Kingsmill Pennefather, Elsinore, Delgany, Co Wicklow, Ireland]; *b* 17 Feb 1913; *educ* Trin Coll Dublin (BA 1936); *m* 1st 29 May 1941 Harold Hugh Brodie Ind, BSc (*d* 1977), only s of Algernon Edward Brise Ind, of Bath; *m* 2nd 1982 *Kingsmill Pennefather and by her 1st husb has:

    1b *Peter Lewin Brodie [Peter Brodie Esq, 18 Oak Apple Close, Cowfold, W Sussex]; *b* 3 Aug 1944; *educ* Eton and Trin Coll Dublin (BA 1967); *m* 1982 *Peta Mary Wildbore, *née* Butler, and has:

      1c *Lisa Peta Alice; *b* 1983

    1b *Christina Isabel Mary [Mrs Robin Scott, Throstlenest, Summer Bridge, Harrogate, Yorks]; *b* 2 Oct 1942; *educ* Trin Coll Dublin (BA) and Inst of Educn London (PGCE); *m* 21 Feb 1970 *W/Cdr Robin Worthington Scott, yr s of Lt-Col Claude Worthington Scott, and has:

      1c *Gervase Roderick John; *b* 1971; *educ* Repton and Edinburgh U

      2c *Nicholas Hugo Howe; *b* 1972; *educ* Repton and Edinburgh U

  2b *Miranda Eleanor Phyllis [Mrs John O'Connor, Ashleagh, Knockroe, Co Wicklow, Ireland]; *b* 15 Oct 1946; *m* *Prof John Morris O'Connor, PhD, Assist Prof Philosophy, Case Western U, Ohio, and has:

    1c *Amanda Evelyn Alice; *b* 1974

3a *Marjory Maud [Mrs Charles Doyne, Cotes des Vallées, Castel, Guernsey, CI]; *b* 31 Jan 1916; *m* 19 June 1954 *Charles Hastings Doyne, s of Dermot Doyne, of Wells, Co Wexford, and has:

  1b *Charles Philip [Charles Doyne Esq, Greenside House, Hampsthwaite, N Yorks HG3 2 EU]; *b* 11 April 1955; *educ* Sherborne and Aston U (BSc); *m* 1987 *Sarah Mary, dau of Michael S Benson, of Dane Hill, Sussex, and has:

    1c *Samuel Charles Michael; *b* 1992

    1c *Alice Sarah Mary; *b* 1990

(1) Helen Augusta; *b* 17 Aug 1867; *m* 19 Sept 1901 Hon George Mitchell, PM S Rhodesia, s of William Mitchell, of Ayrshire, and *d* 1964, leaving issue. He *d* 4 July 1937

(2) Marion Agnes; *b* 13 Feb 1871; *d* unm 29 July 1947

1 Louisa Catherine; *m* 18 May 1839 Charles Knox, of Castle Lacken, Co Mayo, and *d* 14 Dec 1891 aged 75, leaving issue. He *d* 14 March 1867

2 Harriet; *m* 31 March 1853 Sir Robert Lynch-Blosse, 10th Bt (*qv*), and *d* 29 June 1904, leaving issue

3 Hester Georgiana; *m* 7 Aug 1858 Col Hon Shapland Francis Carew and *d* 10 Jan 1925, leaving issue (*see* CAREW, B)

4 Marian; *m* 2 June 1868 Hugh Wilbraham, JP, of Old Head Ho, Co Mayo, and *d* 30 March 1916, leaving issue. He *d* 19 July 1890

The 4th MARQUESS's bro,

HENRY ULICK BROWNE, **5th Marquess of Sligo**, DL Co Mayo; *b* 14 March 1831; BCS 1851–86; *m* 25 Oct 1855 Catherine Henrietta (*d* 26 Nov 1914), dau of William Stephens Dicken, Dep Inspr-Gen IMS, and *d* 24 Feb 1913, having had:

1 GEORGE ULICK BROWNE, **6th Marquess of Sligo** and **4th Earl of Clanricarde**, as which s 2nd Marquess of Clanricarde (*see* below) 1916; *b* 1 Sept 1856; Ld Lt and custos rotulorum Co Mayo, Capt 12th Bengal Cav Afghan War 1879–80 (medal and clasp), FSA, FZS, FRGS; *m* 12 Oct 1887 Agatha Stewart (*d* 4 Jan 1965), dau of James Stewart Hodgson, of Lythe Hill, Haslemere, and *d* 26 Feb 1935, leaving:

  (1) ULICK De BURGH BROWNE, **7th Marquess of Sligo**, MC; *b* 30 March 1898; Capt and Adj 2nd Dragoons WW I 1917–18; *d* unm 7 Jan 1941

  (1) Eileen Agatha; *b* 3 Sept 1889; *m* 16 April 1921 7th and last Earl Stanhope, KG, PC, DSO, MC (*see* 1967 edn CHESTERFIELD and STANHOPE, E), and *dsp* 18 Sept 1940. He *d* 15 Aug 1967

  (2) Moyra Melisande; *b* 22 Sept 1892; *m* 15 Feb 1912 Allan William George Campbell, Coldstream Gds, only s of Allan Campbell, of Mayfair, and *d* 7 March 1974, leaving issue. He *d* 20 Sept 1914 from wounds recd in action Battle of the Aisne

  (3) Doreen Geraldine, CI (1937); DStJ; *m* 22 Jan 1919 5th Baron Brabourne (*qv*) and was murdered by terrorists (allegedly the IRA) 27 Aug 1979 off the coast of Co Sligo, having had issue

2 Herbert Richard; *b* 11 Oct 1858; Capt BSC Afghan War (medal) 1879–80, Political Offr Lushai Hills 1890; *kas* 9 Sept 1890

3 ARTHUR HOWE BROWNE, **8th Marquess of Sligo**, KBE, CB; *b* 8 May 1867; 2nd Lt 3rd S Staffs Regt 1887, joined 1st Roy Munster Fus 1889, Adj 2nd Bn 1895–99, SSO and Cantonment Magistrate Fatehgarh 1892–93 and Dum-Dum 1895–96, ATO Tirah Expdny Force 1898 (medal with clasp), Actg DAAG and QMG Malakand Field Force and Swat Moveable Column 1898–99, Boer War 1901–02 (medal with five clasps), SSO Kimberley Dist 1901–02, Assist DAAG Sirhind Dist 1903, Instr RMA Woolwich 1905–09, ret as Maj 1909, Sec Imp War Graves Commn 1919–30, S Africa 1901–02, Staff War Office WW I (Brevet Lt-Col Col, Legn Honour, Grand Offr Order Christ), Col Roy Munster Fus; dir Birmid Industs and Birmingham Aluminium (1903) Casting Co, FZS, FRHS; *m* 18 Nov 1919 Lilian Whiteside (*d* 13 Aug 1953), widow of Maj Arthur Frederick Mann and dau of Charles Chapman, Dep Commr Oudh, and *dsp* 28 May 1951

4 TERENCE MORRIS BROWNE, **9th Marquess of Sligo**; *b* 28 Sept 1873; Supt Bengal Police; *d* unm 28 July 1952

5 Alfred Eden, DSO (1918); *b* 30 Nov 1878; Lt-Col RFA, Capt Res Offrs RA WW I (despatches); *m* 2 April 1908 Cicely (*d* 16 Aug 1918), yst dau of Edward Wormald, of Sheepwell Ho, Herts, and Mayfair, and was *ka* 27 Aug 1918, leaving:

(1) DENIS EDWARD BROWNE, **10th Marquess of Sligo**; *b* 13 Dec 1908; *educ* Eton; *m* 12 Nov 1930 *José, dau of William Gauche, and *d* 1991, leaving:

1a JEREMY ULICK BROWNE, **11th and present Marquess of Sligo**

(2) Ulick; *b* 16 Jan 1915; *educ* Eton; Capt RA WW II; granted 2 May 1953 with siblings rank of marquess's dau/yr s; *m* 1st 3 Jan 1942 Mrs Elma Valerie Warren (*d* 21 Sept 1959), yr dau of Capt Andrew Burmanoff, Russian Hus; *m* 2nd March 1962 *Fiona Glenn [The Lady Ulick Browne, 32 The Little Boltons, London SW10], dau of John Glenn, of E Grinstead, Sussex, and *d* 21 Oct 1979, having by her had:

1a +SEBASTIAN ULICK; *b* 27 May 1964; heir presumptive; *educ* Rugby; *m* 1984 (*divorce* 1992) Christina Maria, yst dau of Luis Suaznabar, of Bolivia, and has:

1b +Christopher Ulick; *b* 14 Nov 1988

1b *Camilla; *b* 1986

1a *Ulicia Catherine; *b* 28 Nov 1962; *m* 1993 *Giles P T Edwards, only s of Peter Guy Edwards, of Low Walworth Hall, Darlington, Co Durham, and has:

1b *Charlotte; *b* 19–

2b *Emily Jill; *b* 9 Oct 1996

(1) *Sheelah Annette [The Lady Sheelah Treherne, Long Meadow, Hasketon, Suffolk]; *b* 13 Dec 1908; *m* 2 Jan 1930 John Dalrymple Winn Treherne (*d* 1972), s of Apsley Treherne, and has:

1a Roland Dalrymple; *b* 21 July 1935; *educ* Eton; *d* 1992

1a *Oona Cicely [Mrs Oona Methuen-Campbell, Long Meadow, Hasketon, Suffolk]; *b* 4 Oct 1930; *m* 31 Oct 1950 (*divorce* 1973) Christopher Paul Mansel Campbell Methuen-Campbell and has issue (*see* METHUEN, B)

(2) *Noreen [The Lady Noreen Branson, 46 Southwood Ave, London N6]; *b* 16 May 1910; *m* 1 June 1931 Clive Ali Chimmo Branson, s of Maj L H Branson (*ka* Far East 1944), and has:

1a *Rosa [Mrs Henry Hooper, 46 Southwood Ave, London N6]; *b* 1933; *m* 1st 1954 (*divorce* 1966) Alan Hopkins; *m* 2nd 1971 Henry Joseph Hooper (*d* 1990) and by her 1st husb has:

1b *Michael Stephen; *b* 1958; *m* 1986 *Eileen Jane Eccles

1b *Peggy Anne [Mrs Anthony Godfrey, 10 Colmans Court, 46 Morris Rd, London E14 6NQ]; *b* 11 July 1955; *m* 1st 1975 (*divorce* 1983) Thomas Aquinas Prendeville; *m* 2nd 1987 *Anthony George Francis Godfrey and by him has:

1c *Joel Nathaniel John; *b* 22 Aug 1994

1c *Isolde Iona Hephzibah; *b* 4 July 1989

1 Catherine Elizabeth; *d* 13 Feb 1874 aged 16

2 Edith Hester; *b* 12 March 1860; *m* 4 June 1881 John George Charles, BCS, and *d* 6 March 1936, leaving issue. He *d* 25 Oct 1915

3 Florence Marion; *b* 13 Jan 1863; *m* 23 Oct 1886 Col William Randal Hamilton Beresford-Ash, DL, Roy Welch Fus, of Ashbrook, Co Londonderry, and *d* 22 Nov 1946, leaving issue (*see* WATERFORD, M)

4 Norah (twin with Terence); *m* 29 June 1904 Thomas Jasper Mutton More, OBE, JP, of Linley Hall, Bishop's Castle, and The Old Rectory, The More, Bishop's Castle, Salop, and *d* 28 Dec 1948, leaving issue. He *d* 15 Jan 1947

5 Alice Evelyn; *b* 31 March 1877; *m* 19 Oct 1898 John FitzGerald Mahon and *d* 6 Aug 1970, leaving issue (*see* MAHON Bt)

Lineage (Earldom of Clanricarde): The de Burgh Earls of Ulster, so created around 1264, died out in the direct male line in 1333. A cadet branch (heads of which were known as MacWilliam Eighter (meaning 'nearer', 'southern' or 'upper') as opposed to those of another branch called MacWilliam Oughter (meaning 'further', 'northern' or 'lower'); *see* also MAYO, E) was represented by:

ULICK BURKE; feudal Ld of Clanricarde, *i.e.*, an area of Connaught comprising the territorial Baronies of Athenry, Clare, Dunkellin, Kiltartan or Killtaraght, Leitrim and Loughrea, Co Galway, between 1467 and 1487; gf of:

RICHARD BURKE MacWILLIAM; Chief of Clanricarde; *m* 1st a dau of Murrough O'Madden; *m* 2nd Lady Margaret Butler, dau of 8th Earl of Ormond and (1st Earl of) Ossory (*see* 1970 edn ORMONDE, M), and *d* April 1530, leaving by her a s (William Burke of Rahaly) and by his 1st w:

ULICK *Negan* ('Ulick of the Heads', from his habit of beheading enemies in battle) BURKE or De BURGH, 1st EARL OF CLANRICARDE, AND BARON OF DUNKELLIN (I), so *cr* 1 July 1543, 9th Chief of Clanricarde 1541–44 following the overthrow of his f's cousin Sir Ulick Bourke, Govr Connaught; granted monastic lands in the diocese of Clonfert, together with the advowsons and donations of rectories etc in Clanricarde and Dunkellin, which had formerly belonged to the monastery of de Vice Nova; *m* 1st (separated but marriage upheld 1550) Grace/Grania, dau of Maolrona O'Carroll, Prince of Ely, and divorced w of O'Melaghlin, and had issue; *m* 2nd (later separated) his cousin Honora, dau of Rickard *Og* ('The Younger') MacWilliam, of Clanric(k)ard(e); *m* 3rd (in the lifetime of his 1st w) Maria Lynch (whose s by him, John Bourke, claimed the Earldom 4 Feb 1568) and *d* 19 Oct 1544, leaving, with at least three illegitimate sons (Thomas 'the Athlete', chosen his f's successor as Chief of Clanric(k)ard, but overthrown and *k* 1545; Redmond 'of the Broom', *d* 1595, f of Ulick (who *k* George Bingham (*see* LUCAN, E, and CLANMORRIS, B) at Sligo 1595); Edmund, of Ballylee, *d* 1597):

RICHARD *Sassanagh* ('The Saxon' since declared his f's heir according to English law rather than by acclaim of the clansmen, also for having helped the English put down native Irish in 1548, 1552 and 1553) BURKE/De BURGH, 2nd EARL OF CLANRICARDE, AND BARON OF DUNKELLIN; *m* 1st 1548 (*divorce* on grounds of legal stumbling block and her witchcraft against him) Lady Margaret O'Brien, dau of 1st Earl of Thomond (*see* INCHIQUIN, B); *m* 2nd 24 Nov 1553 Lady Margaret O'Brien (*d* 1568), dau of 2nd Earl of Thomond; *m* 3rd 1568 Cecilia or Gille (*d* by *c* 1572), dau of Cormac *Og* MacCarty, of Muskerry, and widow of 1st Baron Dunboyne (*qv*); *m* 4th Sawne, dau of MacHugo; *m* 5th Julian Browne, of Galway; *m* 6th Honora (*d* 1594), dau of Mac I Brien, of Arra, by whom he had a s (Richard *Og* Burke, ancestor of the BOURKEs of Meelick, Co Galway), all of whom he divorced in turn; *m* 7th Margaret Burke and having petitioned the English 15 Feb 1559 that his s by his 1st w should succeed him notwithstanding their divorce, *d* 24 July 1582, leaving, with three other sons (including John 'of the Shamrocks', *cr* BARON LEITRIM 6 May 1583 and murdered *spl* 11 Nov 1583) and a dau by his 3rd w, an only s by his 1st w:

ULICK BURKE/De BURGH, 3rd EARL OF CLANRICARDE, AND BARON OF DUNKELLIN; supported English during Earl of Tyrone's Uprising 1598–1601; *m* 25 Nov 1564 Honora, dau of John *Og* Burke, of Clogheroka and Tullyra, Co Galway; and *d* 20 May 1601, having had, with a legitimate er s (*d* an infant) and a dau (Margaret, *m* Sir John Burke, of Derrymaclaughna):

1 RICHARD 'of Kinsale' (from the battle there 24 Dec 1601, where he played an important role in the defeat of the native Irish under the Earl of Tyrone) BURKE/De BURGH, 4th EARL OF CLANRICARDE, AND BARON OF DUNKELLIN, also *cr* 3 April 1624 BARON OF SOMERHILL and VISCOUNT TUNBRIDGE, Kent, and 23 Aug 1628 EARL OF ST ALBANS, Co Hertford (all E), and BARON OF IMANNEY AND VISCOUNT GALWAY, in the Province of Connaught (I), with in the last case (*i.e.*, the Barony of Imanney and Viscountcy of Galway) remainder to heirs male of his f; Ld Pres Connaught 1604–16, Govr Galway 1616; *m* by 8 April 1603 Frances, widow of (a) Sir Philip Sidney (*see* DE L'ISLE, V) and (b) 3rd Viscount Hereford (*qv*) and dau and heiress of Sir Francis Walsingham, and *d* 12 Nov 1635, leaving, with another dau, an only s:

(1) ULICK BURKE/De BURGH, 5th EARL OF CLANRICARDE, AND BARON OF DUNKELLIN, also 2nd EARL OF ST ALBANS and 1st MARQUESS OF CLANRICARDE (I), so *cr* 21 Feb 1645/6, PC (I 1645); either he or the 6th EARL OF CLANRICARDE was the probable successor to their cousin as 3rd VISCOUNT BOURKE OF CLANMORIES (*see* below); *b* by 8 Dec 1604; Govr Galway 1636, ktd 1638, Lt-Gen and C-in-C Connaught 1644, Ld Dep Gen Ireland 1650–52; *m* Dec 1622 Lady Anne Compton (*d* 17 Aug 1675), yr dau of 1st Earl of Northampton (*see* NORTHAMPTON, M), and *dspm* July 1657, when the Marquessate and his English peerages expired, while the Irish peerages (with the exception of the Viscountcy of Galway, which to all intents and purposes seems to have become dormant) passed to his cousin, leaving:

1a Margaret; *m* after 2 March 1659 Charles Maccarty, Viscount Muskerry (*dvp* 3 June 1665), s and h of 1st Earl of Clancarty of the 1658 *cr* (*see* CLANCARTY, E, preliminary remarks); *m* 2nd 1676 Robert Villiers *alias* Danvers, self-styled Viscount Purbeck (*d* 1684); *m* 3rd Col Robert Feilding, MP Gowran, known as 'Beau Feilding', and *d* Aug 1698. He *d* 12 May 1712

(1) Honora; *m* 1st Garratt McCoghlan; *m* 2nd by 4 Oct 1633, as his 2nd w, 5th Marquess of Winchester (*qv*)

2 Thomas (Sir); *m* Ursula, widow of Capt Anthony Brabazon, of Ballinasloe, and dau of Sir Nicholas Malby, Ch Commr Connaught, and *dsp*

3 JOHN BURKE, 1st VISCOUNT BOURKE OF CLANMORIES [*sic*], Co Mayo (I), so *cr* 20 April 1629, with remainder, in default of his own male issue, to his f's male issue; of Dunsandle; *m* Katherine, dau of Capt Anthony Brabazon, of Ballinasloe, and *d* 16 Nov 1633, leaving:

(1) THOMAS BURKE, 2nd VISCOUNT BOURKE OF CLANMORIES; *m* Margaret Fleming (m 2nd Sir Edmund Burke, 2nd Bt, of Glinsk; see 1850 edn), dau of Christopher, 12th Lord (Baron) Slane, and *dsp* Sept 1642

4 William (Sir); *m* Joan (*m* 2nd Teig O'Brien; *see* INCHIQUIN, B), dau of Sir Dermot O'Shaughnessy, of Gort, Co Galway, and *d* 2 Feb 1625/6, having had, with three daus:

(1) RICHARD BURKE, 6th EARL OF CLANRICARDE, AND BARON OF DUNKELLIN; *m* Lady Elizabeth Butler, dau of 11th Earl of Ormonde and (3rd Earl of) Ossory (*see* MOUNTGARRET, V), and *dspm* Aug 1666, having had:

1a Mary; *m* 1st Sir John Burke, of Derrymaclaughna; *m* 2nd, as his 1st w, Edward, 13th Lord (Baron) Athenry, and *d* 1685

2a Margaret; *m* Col Garret Moore and *d* 1671

(2) WILLIAM, 7th Earl

5 Edmund, of Kilcornan, Co Galway; *m* Katherine, dau of Thomas St Lawrence, of Co Kilkenny, and *d* 22 June 1639; ancestor of the BURKEs of Kilcornan and BURKEs of Greenfield, Co Galway

The 6th EARL's bro,

WILLIAM BURKE, 7th EARL OF CLANRICARDE, AND BARON OF DUNKELLIN, PC (I 1681); Lt Co Galway 1680, Ch Govr Co Galway 1687; *m* 1st Lettice (*bur* 25 Sept 1655), only dau of Sir Henry Shirley, 2nd Bt (*see* FERRERS, E), and had:

1 RICHARD BURKE, 8th EARL OF CLANRICARDE, AND BARON OF DUNKELLIN, PC (I 1689); cdr Jacobite Inf Regt 1689, Govr Galway till its capitulation to Williamite forces 1691, outlawed 11 May 1691; *m* (?)1st(?) 22 Jan 1669/70 Elizabeth, yst dau of — Bagnall, Page to JAMES II, and had, with other issue:

(1) Dorothy; *m* Alexander Pendarves, of Roscrowe, Cornwall

1 (cont.) The 8th EARL (?)*m* 2nd(?) Anne, dau of Sir Thomas Cheeke, of Pirgo, Essex, by his 2nd w Essex (dau of Robert Rich, 1st Earl of Warwick of the 1618 *cr*; *see* WARWICK, BROOKE and, E) and widow of (a) Robert Rich, 3rd Earl of Warwick of the 1618 *cr* and (b) Richard Rogers, of Bryanston, Dorset; *m* 3rd Bridget, dau of 8th Viscount Dillon (*qv*), and *dspms* 2 Feb 1709, having by her had:

(2) Mary; *m* July 1713, as his 1st w, Patrick Bellew (*dsp* & *vp*), est s of Sir John Bellew, 2nd Bt (*see* BELLEW, B), and *d* 12 Jan 1713/4

2 JOHN, 9th EARL

The 7th EARL *m* 2nd Lady Helen (*m* 3rd Col Thomas Burke and *d* 15 Feb 1732), dau of Donough Maccarty, 1st Earl of Clancarty of the 1658 *cr* (*see* CLANCARTY, E, preliminary remarks) and widow of John Fitzgerald, of Dromana, Co Waterford, and *d* 4 Oct 1687, having by her had, with another s (*dsp*):

3 Thomas; *k* 1686 Buda, Hungary

4 ULICK BURKE, 1st and last VISCOUNT OF GALWAY and BARON OF TYAQUIN, Co Galway (both I), so *cr* 2 June 1687; *b c* 1670; *m* 30 July 1688 Frances Lane (*m* 2nd Henry Fox and was ancestor with him of the LANE-FOXes), dau of 1st Viscount Lanesborough (*see* LANESBOROUGH, E), and *dsps*, *k* fighting for JAMES II Battle of Aughrim 12 July 1691, when his titles expired (he was in any case outlawed either before the battle or posthumously)

1 Margaret; *m* 1st 1689 5th Viscount Magennis of Iveagh (*dsp* 1693); *m* 2nd Col Thomas Butler, of Kilcash

2 Honor; *m* 1st *c* 9 Jan 1689/90 1st titular Earl of Lucan of the Jacobite *cr* of Jan 1690/1 (*see* LUCAN, E, preliminary remarks); *m* 2nd 26 March 1695, as his 1st w, 1st Duke of Berwick-upon-Tweed (*see* MARLBOROUGH, D) and *d* 1698, leaving issue

The 8th EARL's bro,

JOHN BURKE, 9th EARL OF CLANRICARDE, AND BARON OF DUNKELLIN, also 1st BARON BOURKE OF BOPHIN, Co Galway (I), so *cr* by JAMES II 2 April 1689 after his having been deemed to have vacated the throne of England but before his deposition as King of Ireland; *b* 1642; Jacobite Col of Foot Battle of Aughrim 1691, at which he was captured, then attainted (but restored 1702); *m* Oct 1684 Mary, dau of James Talbot, of Templeogue, Co Dublin, and had:

1 William; *d* 1703 aged 17

2 MICHAEL, 10th EARL

3 James, on whom his father settled Clondagoff and other lands in Co Galway; *m* Mary, only dau and heiress of John Burke, of Clogheroka, and *dspm* Aug 1718

4 Richard; *d* young

5 Ulick; *dsp* Sept 1763

6 Thomas, of Lackan, Co Roscommon; *m* Mary, dau of Alexander Eustace, and *dspm* 1764

7 Edward; Gen in Spanish Service; *d* unm 7 March 1743 of wounds recd Battle of Campo Santo

8 John; *d* 1718 aged 22

9 William; in French service; *ka* Battle of Fontenoy 11 May 1745

1 Letitia; *m* Sir Festus Burke, of Glinsk

2 Bridget; *m* 1720 9th Viscount Dillon (*qv*) of Costello-Gallen and *d* 16 July 1779, leaving issue

3 Honora; *m* John Kelly, of Cloonlyon, Co Galway

4 Margaret; *d* young

5 Margaret; *m* Garett Moore, of Cloghan, and *d* 1735

The 9th EARL *d* 17 Oct 1722; his est s,

MICHAEL BURKE, 10th EARL OF CLANRICARDE, AND BARON OF DUN-KELLIN, PC (I 1726); *b c* 1686; *educ* Eton, conformed to C of E; called up 3 Aug 1711 to Ho Lds *vp* in f's Barony of Dunkellin; *m* 19 Sept 1714 Anne (*d* 1 Jan 1732/3), widow of Hugh Parker and est dau and coheir of John Smyth, Commr Excise, and *d* 28 Nov 1736, having had, with an er s and two daus (including Anne, *m* Denis Daly, er s of James Daly, of Raford):

JOHN SMITH BURKE later De BURGH (roy licence 13 May 1752), 11th EARL OF CLANRICARDE, AND BARON OF DUNKELLIN, PC (I, 8–16 July 1761); *b* 11 Nov 1720; *educ* Winchester; *m* 1 July 1740 Hester Amelia (*d* 29 Dec 1804), yst dau of Sir Henry Vincent, 6th Bt (*see* 1940 edn D'ABERNON, V), and *d* 21 April 1782, having had, with two daus:

1 HENRY De BURGH, 12th EARL and 1st and last MARQUESS OF CLANRI-CARDE (I), so *cr* 17 Aug 1789, KP (1783), PC (I 1783); *b* 8 Jan 1742/3; MP (I Parl) Co Galway 1768–69, Govr Co Galway 1782; *m* 17 March 1785 Lady Urania Anne Paulet (*m* 2nd 28 Oct 1799 Col Peter Kington (*k* Buenos Aires 6 July 1807); *m* 3rd 22 May 1813 Hon Sir Joseph Sidney Yorke, KCB (*see* HARD-WICKE, E), and *d* 27 Dec 1843), dau of 12th Marquess of Winchester (*qv*), and *dsp* 8 Dec 1797, when the Marquessate of Clanricarde of the 1789 *cr* expired

2 JOHN THOMAS De BURGH, 13th and last EARL OF CLANRICARDE, AND BARON OF DUNKELLIN, but **1st Earl of Clanricarde**, Co Galway (I), so *cr* 29 Dec 1800, with special remainder, failing male issue, to the heirs male of their bodies, PC (I 1801); *b* 22 Sept 1744; Lt-Col 68th Foot, Maj-Gen 1793, Lt Gen 1798, Gen 1803, Govr Hull 1801–08, rep I peer 1801–08; *m* 17 March 1799 Elizabeth (*d* 26 March 1854), dau of Sir Thomas Burke, 1st Bt (*qv*), of Marble Hill, Co Galway, and *d* 27 July 1808, having had:

(1) ULICK JOHN De BURGH, **2nd Earl of Clanricarde** and 1st MARQUESS OF CLANRICARDE (I), so *cr* 26 Nov 1825, as also BARON SOMERHILL, of Somerhill, Co Kent (UK) 13 Dec 1826, KP (1831), PC (1830); *b* 20 Dec 1802; Parly U-Sec For Affrs 1826–27, Capt Yeomen Gd 1830–34, Ld Lt Co Galway 1831–74, V-Adml Connaught, Amb St Petersburg 1838–41, PMG 1846–52, Ld Privy Seal three weeks in Feb 1858 (his resignation as which was precipi-tated by the revelation that he had fathered an illegitimate s by a Mrs Hand-cock); *m* 4 April 1825 Harriet (*d* 8 Jan 1876), sis and heiress of Earl Canning and only dau of Viscountess Canning by the statesman George Canning (*see* GARVAGH, B), and *d* 10 April 1874, having had:

1a Ulick Canning, *Lord Dunkellin*; *b* 12 July 1827; MP Co Galway 1857–65, Lt-Col Coldstream Gds, Kt Order Medjidie; *d* unm 16 Aug 1867

2a HUBERT GEORGE De BURGH later De BURGH-CANNING (roy licence 9 July 1862), **3rd Earl of Clanricarde** and 2nd and last MARQUESS OF CLANRICARDE, DL Co Galway; *b* 15 Dec 1832; *educ* Harrow; in Dip Serv at Turin 1852–63, MP (Lib) Co Galway 1867–71; *d* unm 12 April 1916, when all his titles expired bar the Earldom of Clanricarde *cr* 29 Dec 1800, which passed to his cousin, **6th Marquess of Sligo**

1a Elizabeth Joanna; *m* 17 July 1845 4th Earl of Harewood (*qv*) and *d* 26 Feb 1854, leaving issue

2a Emily Charlotte; *m* 20 July 1853 9th Earl of Cork and (9th Earl of) Orrery (*qv*) and *d* 10 Oct 1912, leaving issue

3a Catherine; *m* 8 Aug 1850 John Weyland, of Woodeaton, Oxon, and Woodrising, Norfolk, and *d* 9 April 1895, having had issue. He *d* 5 April 1902

4a Margaret Anne; *m* 6 March 1856 1st Baron Allendale and *d* 31 March 1888 aged 56, leaving issue (*see* ALLENDALE, V)

5a Harriet Augusta; *m* 3 March 1859 Thomas Frederick Charles Vernon-Wentworth and *d* 18 Jan 1901, having had issue. He *d* 1 Jan 1902

(1) Hester Catherine; *m* 4 March 1816 **2nd Marquess of Sligo** (*see* above) and had issue

(2) Emily; *m* 9 Jan 1826 3rd Earl of Howth (*see* 1909 edn) and *d* 5 Dec 1842, leaving issue. He *d* 5 Feb 1874

Seat: Westport House, Westport, Co Mayo, Ireland. An O'Malley castle originally occupied the site of the present house, the O'Malleys being the ancestors of the Brownes (*see* above, also KILMAINE, B). Nothing remains of it apart perhaps from the cellars, and even their continued existence (as part of the early

18th-century core, designed by Richard Castle) is conjectural. The house Castle designed was extended in the late 1770s in such a way that it formed one flank of a rectangular structure, with a space in the centre which in the late 1850s was covered to form the present library. Castle's block still provided the main entrance, however. Finishing touches to the internal parts of the enlarged struc-ture, notably the dining-room, were added by James Wyatt in the time of the **1st Marquess**, although externally the **2nd Marquess** extended two small wings in the form of a terrace over basement and incorporated a library (burnt down 1826 but restored after 1845).

The internal decorations of the entrance front comprise the only entire scheme by Richard Castle in existence (although Russborough, Co Wicklow, contains many individual items by him). They include a Doric frieze and a coffered and arched ceiling.

SLIM

Arms: Gules semée of swords erect argent a lion rampant or, on a canton quarterly azure and argent a mullet of seven points gold.
Crest: Out of a crown vallary or a peacock in its pride proper, gorged with a collar, the line reflexed over the back gold.
Supporters: Dexter, a British soldier in jungle-green battle dress with web equipment, the exterior hand supporting a rifle with bayonet affixed; sinister, a Gurkha rifleman in North-West Frontier dress with web equipment, the exterior hand supporting a rifle, all proper. **Motto:** *Merses profundo pulchrior evenit* ('Defeat into victory'). **Creation:** V. (UK) 15 July 1960.

THE 2ND VISCOUNT SLIM of Yarralumla, Capital Territory of Australia, and Bishopston in the City and Co of Bristol (Lt-Col John Douglas Slim, OBE (1973), DL (Gtr London 1988)) [Lt Col The Rt Hon The Viscount Slim OBE DL, House of Lords, London SW1A 0PW]; *b* 20 July 1927; *s f* 1970; *educ* Prince of Wales Roy Indian Mil Coll Dehra Dun; commnd IA 6th Gurkha Rifles, Lt-Col (ret) Argyll and Sutherland Highrs, GSO(2) HQ Middle East Cmd 1966–67, Cdr 22 SAS Regt 1967–70, GSO(1) UKLF 1972; chm and ch exec Peek plc (formerly Peek Hldgs) 1976–91 (dep chm 1991–), dir Trailfinders Ltd 1984–, Pres Burma Star Assoc 1971–, V-Pres Britain-Australia Soc 1988 (Chm 1978–84), V-Chm Arab-Br Chamber Commerce and Industry 1977–96, Master Clothworkers' Co 1995–96, Exec V-Pres SAS Assoc, FRGS 1983; *m* 18 July 1958 *Elisabeth, dau of Arthur Rawdon Spinney, CBE, of Kyrenia, Cyprus, and has:

1 +MARK WILLIAM RAWDON; *b* 13 Feb 1960; *educ* Eton and Bristol U; *m* 1992 *Harriet Laura, yr dau of Jonathan Harrison, of Beds, and has:

(1) +Rufus William Rawdon; *b* 15 April 1995

2 +Hugo John Robertson; *b* 28 Aug 1961; *educ* Eton and St John's Coll Oxford (MA); sr research offr Save The Children Fund, FRGS; *m* 1991 *M B Rebecca, dau of Prof Philip Abrams and Mrs Derek Greenwood, of Bristol, and has:

(1) +Solomon Joseph Abrams; *b* 15 June 1997

(1) *Jessica Charlotte Abrams; *b* 1 Nov 1994

1 *Mary Ann; *b* 13 Nov 1964; *educ* King's Coll London (BA)

Lineage: JOHN SLIM, of Bristol; *b* 1851; *m* Charlotte (*d* 1951), dau of Charles Tucker, of Burnham, Somerset, and *d* 1916, leaving, with an er s (Charles John, MRCS Eng, LRCP London 1922):

WILLIAM JOSEPH SLIM, **1st Viscount Slim**, of Yarralumla in the Capital Terri-tory of Australia, and of Bishopston in the City and Co of Bristol (UK), so *cr* 15 July 1960, KG (1959), GCB (1950, KCB and CB 1944), GCMG (1952), GCVO (1954), GBE (1946, CBE 1942), DSO (1943), MC (1917); *b* 6 Aug 1891; *educ* King Edward's Sch Birmingham; IA, commnd 6th Gurkha Rifles, Roy Warwicks Regt WW I (wounded twice), WW II (wounded, despatches), Cmdt: 2nd/7th Gurkha Rifles 1937 and Sr Offrs' Sch India 1939, cmded 10th India Inf Bde 1939, 10th India Div 1940, Burma Corps 1942, 15th India Corps 1942, 14th Army 1943 and Allied Land Forces SE Asia 1945, Cmdt IDC 1946, ADC-Gen to HM GEORGE VI 1947, Dep Chm Rlwy Exec Jan-Nov 1948, CIGS 1948–52, Govr-Gen and C-in-C Australia 1953–60, Dep Constable and Lt-Govr Windsor Castle 1963–64, Constable and Govr 1964–70, Col 7th Gurkha Rifles 1944–56, Col W Yorks Regt 1947–56, Col 1st Gurkha Rifles 1949–56, Master Clothworkers' Co 1962, Jt Pres Dalgety and NZ Loan Ltd, London, dir: Nat Bank of Australasia and London Assur, ICI, Ch Cdr US Legion of Merit, Hon LLD Cambridge, Birmingham,

Sydney, Adelaide, Leeds and Melbourne, Hon DCL Oxford 1947, Hon DLitt New England 1955, Hon DSc NSW 1959, Hon FRCS Edin, Hon FRACP, KStJ 1953; *m* 1 Jan 1926 Aileen (*d* 1994), DStJ, Kaisar-i-Hind Medal, dau of Rev John Robertson, of Edinburgh, and *d* 14 Dec 1970, leaving:

1 JOHN DOUGLAS SLIM, **2nd and present Viscount Slim**

1 *Una Mary [The Hon Mrs Rowcliffe, Bramson, Puddington, Devon]; *b* 1 Dec 1930; *m* 1st 17 Jan 1953 (*divorce* 1979) Maj Peter Nigel Stewart Frazer, Gren Gds, yr s of Col Donald Frazer, DSO, of Puddington Lodge, Tiverton; *m* 2nd 1980 *Ronald Rowcliffe and by her 1st husb has:

  (1) *Sarah Juliet; *b* 15 Dec 1953; *m* 1978 *Robert M Whyte

  (2) *(Jennifer) Jane; *b* 23 Nov 1956; *m* 1989 *Colin P G Farrant, s of Michael Farrant, of Crawley, Hants, and has:

    1a *Luke; *b* 1991

    1a *Annabel Mary; *b* 1993

  (3) *Emma Mary; *b* 23 July 1965

SLYNN OF HADLEY

Arms: Argent on a chevron gules, between three leopard's heads proper, as many garbs or, on a chief azure three saltires couped argent. **Crest:** Within a crest coronet or a tawny owl, holding in the dexter claw a quill erect proper, the leg ringed or. **Motto:** *Conari intellegere* ('Trying to understand'). **Creation:** B. (LP, UK) 1992.

THE BARON SLYNN OF HADLEY, of Eggington, Co Bedford (Gordon Slynn, PC (1992)) [The Rt Hon The Lord Slynn of Hadley PC, House of Lords, London SW1A 0PW]; *b* 17 Feb 1930; *educ* Sandbach Sch, Goldsmiths' Coll and Trin Coll Camb; barrister Gray's Inn 1956 (Treasurer 1988), Recorder 1971, Hon Recorder Hereford 1972–76, Jr Counsel Treasury 1968–74, QC 1974, Leading Counsel Treasury 1974–76, High Court Judge Queen's Bench 1976–81, Pres Employment Appeal Tbnl 1978–81 and Bar Assoc for Commerce, Finance and Industry 1999–, Advocate-Gen Court Justice EC 1981–88, Judge 1988–92, Ld Appeal in Ordinary 1992–, Visiting Prof Law Durham 1981–88, U of Tech Sydney 1990– and Nat U India, Ch Steward Hereford 1978–, Govr Internat Students' Tst 1979–85 and 1992–, Chm Exec Cncl Internat Law Assoc 1988–, Master Broderers' Co 1994, Commandeur d'honneur de Bontemps de Medoc et des Graves, Commandeur Confrerie de St Cumbert, Chevalier de Tastevin, author: *Introducing a European Legal Order*, ktd 1976, Hon Fell Buckingham U 1982, St Andrew's Coll Sydney U 1991, Liverpool Poly 1992 and Goldsmiths' Coll 1993, Hon LLD Birmingham 1983, Buckingham 1983, Exeter 1985, U of Technology Sydney 1991, Bristol Poly 1992, Sussex 1992, Stetson USA 1993, Staffordshire 1994, Pace NY 1995, Pondicherry 1997, Kingston 1997, Hon DCL Durham 1989, Durham City 1994, Hon Decanus Legis Mercer U USA 1986, Hon Fell American Coll Trial Lawyers 1992, Memb American Law Inst 1993, Fell King's Coll London 1995–; *m* 1962 *Odile Marie Henriette, dau of Pierre Boutin

Lineage: JOHN SLYNN; *m* Edith — and had:

1 GORDON, *cr* a **Baron**

2 *Geoffrey; *b* 25 May 1933; *m* 19– *Pauline Ruscoe and has:

  (1) *Richard Mark Slynn; *b* 23 Nov 1961; *m* 19– *Nicola O'Ferral and has:

    1a *Jeremy Frederick Gordon; *b* 4 April 1993

    2a *William Patrick Geoffrey; *b* 27 June 1995

  (1) *Gillian Margaret Slynn; *b* 5 May 1964

SMILEY

Arms: Quarterly, 1st and 4th, per bend az. and or a lion rampant erm. between three pheons counterchanged (for SMILEY); 2nd and 3rd, gu. on a chevron arg. two mullets az., in base a fusil of the second (for KERR). **Crest:** A lion's gamb erased, holding by the shaft a pheon, point downwards, or. **Motto:** *Industria virtus et fortitudo* ('By industry, valour, and fortitude'). **Creation:** Bt. (UK) 13 Oct 1903.

SIR JOHN PHILIP SMILEY, 4TH BT, of Drumalis, Larne, Co Antrim, and Gallowhill, Paisley, Renfrewshire [Lt-Col Sir John Smiley Bt, Cornerway House, Chobham, Surrey GU24 8SW]; *b* 24 Feb 1934; *s f* 1990; *educ* Eton and RMA Sandhurst; Lt-Col Gren Gds Cyprus 1958–59, ADC to Govr Bermuda 1961–62, ret 1986; with Russell Reynolds Assocs 1986–89, memb Ct Assists Grocers' Co (Master 1992–93); *m* 2 Nov 1963 *Davina Elizabeth, est dau of Denis Charles Griffiths, of Orlingbury Hall, nr Kettering, Northants, and has:

1 +CHRISTOPHER HUGH CHARLES; *b* 7 Feb 1968; *educ* Eton and Edinburgh U (MA); *m* 16 Oct 1998 *Clare Annabel, yst dau of Maj Henry Charles Blosse-Lynch (*see* 1940 edn YATE, Bt) and formerly w of — Barr Smith

2 +William Timothy John; *b* 27 May 1972; *educ* Eton and Bristol U (BSc); Capt Gren Gds

1 *Melinda Elizabeth Eirène [Mrs Jonathon Baker, Lovel House, Upton Noble, Somerset BA4 6BA]; *b* 26 June 1965; *m* 1991 *Jonathon Mark Midelton Baker, s of John Baker, of Monmouth House, Yenston, Somerset, and has:

  (1) *Archie John Midelton; *b* 12 Jan 1993

  (2) *Herbert Douglas Midleton; *b* 11 Jan 1995

Lineage: THOMAS SMAILLIE, of Bradsheilburne, Cambusnethan, Lanarks; *b* c. 1554; *d* July 1627, having had, with an er s (William, of Bradsheilburne, *d* by 1649, leaving issue):

THOMAS SMAILLIE, of Cambusnethan and later Glasgow; *m* Margaret Ranking and had a yst s:

ROBERT SM(A)ILLIE; *b* 1619; Burgess Glasgow; *m* Elizabeth Ramsey and *d* Nov 1662, leaving, with an er s and two daus:

ROBERT SMILLIE, of Skerry and Dunard, Co Antrim; *b* 1645; *d* 1712, leaving:

SAMUEL SMILEY; had:

JOHN SMILEY, of Invermore, Co Antrim; *m* Margaret — and *d c* 1748, having had, with a yr s and a dau:

SAMUEL SMILEY, of Inver, Co Antrim; *b* 1720; *m* Christiana, dau of Guy Robinson, of Fox Hall, Cairncastle, Co Antrim, and *d* 27 Dec 1797, having had an est s:

JOHN SMILEY, of Larne, Co Antrim; *m* Martha, dau of Robert Love, and *d* Dec 1833, leaving, with two er sons (Robert Love, of Islandmagee; Samuel) and two daus (Mary; Christiana):

JOHN SMILEY, of Larne, Co Antrim; *b* 26 Dec 1796; *m* 10 Dec 1824 Ann (*d* 3 April 1868), dau of John Reid, and *d* 5 April 1878, leaving, with three other sons (including an est, John MacCullough, *d* 1916, a yst, Robert, *m* Mary Taylor and *d* 1876, having had a dau, Annie Taylor (*dsp*) and another s, who *d* young) and five daus (Sarah, *m* James Coey and *d* 24 Feb 1904; Margaret Thompson, *m* Charles Howden and *d* 14 Dec 1907; Martha Love, *m* John A Bowman and *d* 1 Jan 1904; Annie, *m* Stewart Clark, MP, DL, and *d* 21 March 1910, leaving issue (*see* STEWART-CLARK, Bt); and another dau, who *d* young), a 2nd s:

Sir Hugh Houston Smiley, 1st Bt (UK), so *cr* 13 Oct 1903, of Drumalis, Larne, Co Antrim, and Gallowhill, Paisley, Renfrewshire, JP, DL Co Antrim, JP Renfrewshire; *b* 5 Jan 1841; High Sheriff Co Antrim 1899; *m* 9 Sept 1874 Elizabeth Anne (*d* 14 July 1930), only child of Peter Kerr, of Gallowhill, and had:

1 JOHN (Sir), **2nd Bt**

2 Peter Kerr SMILEY later KERR-SMILEY; *b* 22 Feb 1879; Lt 21st Lancers Boer War 1901–02, MP N Antrim 1910–22, Hon Maj Roy Irish Rifles WW I; *m* 5 July 1905 Maud (*d* 28 May 1962), only dau of Ernest Louis Simpson, of New York, and *d* 23 June 1943, leaving:

  (1) Cyril Hugh, TD; *b* 15 April 1906; *educ* Eton and Magdalen Coll Oxford; Hon Lt-Col Suffolk Regt WW II; *m* 25 April 1933 Agnes (*d* 1986), er dau of Lt-Col George Cecil Minett Sorel Cameron, CBE, of Gorthleck Ho, Gorthleck, Inverness-shire, and *d* 1980, leaving:

1a +Peter Simon [Lt-Col Peter Kerr-Smiley, Towranna Farm, Huntingfield, Suffolk IP19 0QP]; *b* 9 June 1934; *educ* Ampleforth and RMA Sandhurst; QO Cameron Highrs 1954–61, QO Highrs (Seaforth and Camerons) 1961–84, Arabian Peninsula 1956–57, ADC Govr Malta 1959–61, Lt-Col 1974, CO Scottish Inf Depot (Bridge of Don) 1974–76, Queen's Messenger 1984–96; *m* 15 Jan 1960 (*divorce* 1981) Jennifer Guise, only dau of Lt-Col Thomas Guise Tucker, MC, Roy Hants Regt, of Malta, and has:

  1b +Mark Alexander [Mark Kerr-Smiley Esq, 15 Granard Rd, London SW12 8UJ]; *b* 30 March 1961; *educ* Ampleforth; *m* 1988 *Manuela Marie, dau of S M Raquez, of Brussels, and has:

    1c +Frederick Hugh; *b* 25 March 1992

    1c *Isabella Louise; *b* 19 Feb 1990

    2c *Eloise Olivia; *b* 13 May 1995

  2b +Justin Robert; *b* 25 April 1965; *educ* Ampleforth and Newcastle U (BA)

  1b *Emma Caroline Hyde; *b* 28 Feb 1963; *m* 1994 *Euan D Nicolson, yr s of Timothy Nicolson, of Kintbury, Berks, and Mrs Nicholas Embiricos, of Kirdford, Sussex

2a +Hector Robert [Hector Kerr-Smiley Esq, Elms Hall, Colne Engaine, Essex CO6 2JL]; *b* 26 Aug 1937; *educ* Ampleforth; late Lt QO Cameron Highrs; *m* 29 March 1962 *Eleanor Jill, er dau of Cdr Peter van Breda Wadlow, RN, of Stanton Hill, Godalming, Surrey, and has:

  1b +Simon Alastair Hugh [Simon Kerr-Smiley Esq, 47 Littleton St, London SW18 3SZ]; *b* 27 July 1964; *educ* Gordonstoun; *m* 19 Dec 1992 *Nony Mary Louise, dau of Sir Richard John Uniacke Barrow, 6th Bt (*qv*), and has:

    1c *Eleanor Sophie Frances; *b* 9 July 1994

    2c *(Fiona) Emma Victoria; *b* 28 June 1996

  2b +Christopher Peter Nicholas [Christopher Kerr-Smiley Esq, Elms Hall, Colne Eugaine, Colchester, Essex CO6 2JL]; *b* 22 Jan 1967; *educ* Eton and Bristol U (BA 199–); slr 1995

  1b *Charlotte Elizabeth; *b* 17 Jan 1963; *m* 1990 *Christopher Hugh Courtney Smith, s of Sir Robert Courtney Smith, CBE, and has:

    1c *George Hector Courtney; *b* 29 July 1993

    1c *Harriet Rose Constance; *b* 13 July 1995

3a +Nicholas Ernest; *b* 3 Dec 1940; *educ* Ampleforth and Kalgoorlie Sch of Mines (MAusIMM); *m* 1973 *Georgina Jane, er dau of Maj Sir George Andrew Dick-Lauder, 12th Bt (*qv*), and has:

  1b *Samantha Fiona Marguerite; *b* 1976

(1) *Elizabeth Maud [Mrs Christopher Hussey, Scotney Castle, Lamberhurst, Kent TN3 8JD]; *b* 16 April 1907; *m* 23 April 1936 Christopher Edward Clive Hussey, CBE, FSA (*d* 20 March 1970), architectural historian, only s of Maj William Clive Hussey, CVO

3 Hubert Stewart; *b* 5 June 1883; Capt Roy Fus; *m* 15 June 1909 Elsie Hope (*m* 2nd 25 Oct 1922 Lt-Col John Charles Denton Carlisle, DSO, OBE, MC), only dau of Sir Charles Frederick Gill, KC, and *d* 15 April 1922, leaving:

(1) (Charles) Michael; *b* 25 June 1910; *educ* Eton; Maj Rifle Bde WW II 1939–40 (POW); *m* 15 Sept 1939 Lavinia (*d* 1991), 2nd dau of Hon Bernard Clive Pearson (*see* COWDRAY, V), and *d* 1991, leaving:

  1a +James Robin Clive [James Smiley Esq, 50 Martin Rd, Centennial Park, Sydney, NSW 2021, Australia]; *b* 27 June 1947; *educ* Gordonstoun; *m* 1981 *Jane Suzanne, dau of James Gorrie, of Killara, NSW, and has:

    1b +Alexander Orlando Charles; *b* 1981

    2b +Thomas Robin James; *b* 1983

  2a +Andrew Michael [Andrew Smiley Esq, Upper Easton Pierry Farm, Kingston St Michael, Chippenham SN14 6JU]; *b* 30 Nov 1952; *educ* Eton; served Gren Gds; *m* 1975 *(Sarah) Caroline, dau of Lt-Col C C Coade, and has:

    1b *Charlotte Sarah; *b* 1983

    2b *Sarah Miranda; *b* 1986

  1a *Miranda Daphne Jane; *b* 19 Aug 1940; *m* 12 March 1963 (*divorce* 1984) 3rd Earl of Iveagh (*qv*) and has issue

(1) Bridget Eileen Suzanne; *m* 1st 25 Oct 1939 (*divorce* 1951) Maj John Monsell Christian, MC, TD, 60th Rifles, s of Adml Arthur Christian; *m* 2nd 31 Jan 1952 (*divorce* 1966) Maj (Edward) Peter Godfrey Miller Mundy, MC, only s of Godfrey Edward Miller Mundy, of Shipley Hall, Derbys

1 Eileen Margaret Kerr; *b* 31 Jan 1895; *m* 29 July 1922 Rev Alfred James Elgar, s of Alfred Elgar, of Canterbury, and had issue. He *d* 13 Aug 1963

The 1st Bt *d* 3 March 1909; his est s,

Sir John Smiley, 2nd Bt; *b* 28 Oct 1876; Lt 4th Argyll and Sutherland Highrs, Capt NI IY, Boer War 1899–1900 and 1902 (Queen's medal, three clasps, King's medal, two clasps), Maj 6th Dragoon Gds (Carabiniers) WW I; *m* 26 Nov 1903 Valerie (*d* 1 Sept 1978 aged 95), yst dau of Sir Claude Champion de Crespigny, 4th Bt (*see* 1953 edn), and *d* 13 April 1930, leaving:

1 **Sir Hugh Houston Smiley, 3rd Bt**, JP (Hants 1952); *b* 14 Nov 1905; *educ* Eton and RMC Sandhurst; Capt Gren Gds WW II, Hants; High Sheriff 1959, V-Ld Lt 1973–82 (DL 1962–73); *m* 18 Jan 1933 *Nancy Elizabeth Louise Hardy [Nancy Lady Smiley, Ivalls, Bentworth, Hants GU34 5JU], er dau of Ernest Walter Hardy Beaton and sis of Cecil Beaton, the photographer, and *d* 1 Nov 1990, leaving:

(1) **Sir JOHN PHILIP SMILEY, 4th and present Bt**

2 John Claude; *b* 10 March 1910; *educ* Eton and Pembroke Coll Oxford; Hon Capt Middx Yeo (TAR) WW II; *m* 1st 4 Dec 1936 (*divorce* 1942) Lady Cecilia Katherine Wellesey (*d* 30 Sept 1952), yr dau of 3rd Earl Cowley (*qv*), and had:

(1) +David Valerian [Maj David Smiley, Meadwell House, Meadwell, Lifton, Devon PL16 0HJ]; *b* 1 April 1938; *educ* Wellington; Maj RHG Cyprus 1958; *m* 1st 7 Sept 1962 Rose-Ann, est dau of Col David Greig, of Borland, Kilmarnock, Ayrshire; *m* 2nd 1988 *Jill Velia, dau of Cdr John Kershaw, DSO, & widow of Lionel William (Robin) Huntington, MC, and by his 1st w has had:

  1a +Patrick Valerian; *b* 16 Nov 1965; *educ* Trin Coll Glenalmond and Durham U (BA); *m* 21 Feb 1998 *Arabella Faith, dau of Brian Chapman

  2a Thomas Edward de Crespigny; *b* 7 Dec 1967; *educ* Kiel Sch; *d* 24 Nov 1989

1a *(Katherine) Cecilia [Mrs Tom Varcoe, 77 Winchester St, Overton, Hants]; *b* 4 Nov 1963; *m* 1990 *Tom Julian Beaumont Varcoe, yr s of Beaumont Varcoe, of Nanscawen, Par, Cornwall, and has:

  1b *Thomas Anthony Beaumont; *b* 23 Jan 1991

  2b *Xan John Felix; *b* 15 July 1992

2 (cont.) John Smiley *m* 2nd 17 Jan 1947 Sheila (*d* 1978), formerly w of Francis William Frederick Otter-Barry and yr dau of Hon Stanhope A Tollemache (*see* TOLLEMACHE, B), and *d* 22 Aug 1995

3 +David de Crespigny, LVO (1952), OBE (1946), MC (1943) and bar (1944) [Col David Smiley LVO OBE MC, 30 Kensington Mansions, Trebovir Rd, London SW5 9TQ]; *b* 11 April 1916; *educ* Nautical Coll Pangbourne and RMC Sandhurst; served WW II (despatches), Col cmdg RHG 1951–54, Br Mil Attaché Stockholm 1955–58, Cdr Sultan of Muscat and Oman's Armed Forces 1958–61, memb Gentlemen-at-Arms 1966–68, Kt Cdr Order Sword Sweden, Grand Cordon Order Skanderbeg Albania, author: *Arabian Assignment* (1975), *Albanian Assignment* (1984) and *Irregular Regular* (1994); *m* 28 April 1947 *Moyra Eileen, widow of Maj Hugo Douglas Tweedie, Scots Gds, and yr dau of Lt-Col Lord Francis George Montagu Douglas Scott, KCMG, DSO (*see* BUCCLEUCH and QUEENSBERRY, D), and has:

(1) +Xan de Crespigny [Xan Smiley Esq, 68 Lonsdale Rd, Oxford OX2 7EP]; *b* 1 May 1949; *educ* Eton and New Coll Oxford; ed *Africa Confidential* 1977–81, leader writer *The Times* 1982–83, foreign specialist 1983–86 and political editor *Economist* 1992–, Moscow correspondent *Daily Telegraph* 1986–89, Washington correspondent *Sunday Telegraph* 1990–92; *m* 26 Aug 1983 *Hon Jane, formerly w of Charles Thomas Pugh and yst dau of 3rd Baron Acton (*qv*) of Aldenham, and has:

  1a +Ben Richard Philip de Crespigny; *b* 1983

  2a +Adam David Emerich; *b* 1988

(2) +Philip David [Philip Smiley Esq, 157 Mount Pleasant Rd, Singapore 298345]; *b* 26 Aug 1951; *educ* Eton and St Andrews (MA); Solomon Islands Govt 1974–80, Hong Kong Govt 1980–85, W I Carr (Far East) 1985–90, md Jardine Fleming Internat Securities 1990–; *m* 1995 *Sohyung, dau of Gen Young Woo Kim, of Seoul, Korea, and has:

  1a +Francis Hugh Kim; *b* 13 Jan 1996

  2a +Dominic David; *b* 14 Dec 1998

1 *Patricia Margaret [Mrs Charles Dalby, 3 The Lilypool, Melbourne, Derbys]; *b* 1907; *m* 1st 22 Oct 1931 Rupert Douglas Tollemache (*see* TOLLEMACHE, B); *m* 2nd 27 March 1941 Col Charles Dalby, CBE, 60th Rifles (*d* 1981), yr s of Maj John Dalby, of Castle Donington, Leics, and by him has:

(1) *(Charles) Gerald [Gerald Dalby Esq, Dalbie House, Castle Donington, Derby DE74 2PP]; *b* 6 Feb 1942; *educ* Eton; Arch Assoc Dipl, ARIBA; *m* 1980 *Kathleen Margaret, er dau of Stanley Hodson (*see* HODSON, Bt), and has:

  1a *Edward Charles Gerald; *b* 15 Sept 1982

  1a *Lucy Margaretta Hyacinthe; *b* 8 April 1981

(2) *Patrick Claude John [Patrick Dalby Esq, 40 Chester Row, London SW1W 8JP]; *b* 6 Feb 1948; *educ* Rugby; late 2nd Lt RGJ; ptnr Cazenove & Co, stockbrokers

SMITH of Crowmallie

Arms: Or on the waves of the sea a three-masted ship in full sail ppr., flagged gu., on a chief engrailed vert a flame of fire between two horseshoes of the first. **Crest:** A sea-horse arg.
Badge: A sea-horse as in the crest displayed on a standard of his liveries, viz., or and vert. **Motto:** *Per undas* ('Through the waves').
Creation: Bt. (UK) 21 June 1945.

SIR ROBERT HILL SMITH, 3RD BT, of Crowmallie, Co Aberdeen [Sir Robert Smith Bt MP, Crowmallie House, Pitcaple, Inverurie, Aberdeenshire AB51 5HR]; *b* 15 April 1958; *s* 1983; *educ* Merchant Taylors' and Aberdeen U; SDP Lib Alliance Parly candidate Aberdeen N 1987, Lib Dem memb Aberdeenshire Unitary Cncl 1995–97, V-Chm Grampian Jt Police Bd 1995–97, MP (Lib Dem) Aberdeenshire W and Kincardine 1997–; *m* 13 Aug 1993 *Fiona Anne Cormack and has:

1 *Helen Rosemary; *b* 9 Aug 1994

2 *Kirsty Diana; *b* 8 Oct 1997

Lineage: JAMES SMITH, of Saltcoats, Ayrshire, later of Glasgow; *b* 8 Jan 1777; fndr City (shipping) Line (later Ellerman City Line); *m* 1798 Margaret, dau of Robert Workman, of Belfast, and *d* 1867, leaving a yr s:

GEORGE SMITH, of Mountblow, Pollokshields, Glasgow; *b* 20 Aug 1803; chm City Line; *m* 2nd 21 March 1837 Ellen Service and *d* 4 March 1876, leaving:

GEORGE SMITH, of Glenmorag, Dunoon, Argyll; *b* 11 Sept 1845; *educ* Glasgow Acad; chm City Line; *m* 31 July 1867 Mary (*d* 8 Jan 1883), dau of Robert Workman, of Ceara, Belfast, and *d* 2 Nov 1899, having had:

1 George, of Pittodrie, JP Aberdeenshire; *b* 2 Jan 1871; Capt 6th Bn Gordon Highrs; *m* 14 April 1896 Kathleen Marion (*d* 15 Jan 1964), er dau of William Workman, of Nottinghill, Belfast, and was *ka* 13 March 1915, leaving:

　(1) George; *b* 1898; *d* 1921

　(2) Robert Laidlaw, of Pittodrie, Pitcaple, JP (Aberdeenshire 1954); *b* 1906; *educ* Eastbourne Coll; *m* 3 Jan 1935 *Margaret Erica, dau of William Parkin-Moore, of Whitehall, Cumberland, and *d* 6 June 1959, having had:

　　1a *George Robert Theodore; *b* 23 Jan 1950

　　1a Margaret Andrea Katherine; *b* 14 June 1938; *d* 28 March 1945

　　2a *Daphne Helena; *b* 26 Feb 1943

　(1) Mary Kathleen; *b* 1900; *m* 24 March 1926 Baron Balerno, CBE, TD, JP, DL (LP, *d* 1983), and *d* 12 Aug 1947, leaving:

　　1a George Adam (Rev); *b* 4 March 1929; *educ* Edinburgh Acad, Trin Coll Glenalmond, Edinburgh U (MA 1951) and Union Theological Seminary New York (BD 1955); housemaster Fettes; *m* 4 Sept 1961 *(Isobel Angela) Margaret [The Hon Mrs George Buchanan-Smith, Woodhouselea, Milton Bridge, Penicuik, Midlothian], widow of Stuart McIntosh and dau of Edward Bowden, of Oxshott, Surrey, and *d* 24 Feb 1983, leaving:

　　　1b *(George) Adam Edward; *b* 22 July 1964

　　　2b *Stuart Hunter; *b* 7 May 1966

　　　1b *Fiona; *b* 19–

　　　2b *Hannah Mary; *b* 30 June 1962

　　2a Alick Laidlaw, PC (1984); *b* 8 April 1932; *educ* Edinburgh Acad, Trin Coll Glenalmond, Pembroke Coll Cambridge (BA 1954) and Edinburgh U; MP (C) N Angus and Mearns 1964–91, Parly U-Sec Home Affrs and Ag 1970–74, Capt Reserve of Offrs Gordon Highrs; Min State Ag Fisheries and Food 1979–83, and Dept Energy 1983–87; *m* 17 Aug 1956 *Janet Delahoy, CBE (1993) [The Hon Mrs Alick Buchanan-Smith CBE, Cockeden, Cockburn, Balerno, Midlothian EH14 7JE], dau of Thomas Lawrie, CBE, and *d* 1991, leaving:

　　　1b *James Colquhoun; *b* 12 Aug 1962

　　　1b *Jean Marjorie; *b* 29 July 1957

　　　2b *Margaret Workman; *b* 10 Aug 1960

　　　3b *Fenella Delahoy; *b* 20 Feb 1965

　　3a *Robin Dunlop (Rev) [The Rev and Hon Robin Buchanan-Smith, Isle of Eriska, Ledaie, Oban, Argyll]; *b* 1 Feb 1936; *educ* Edinburgh Acad, Trin Coll Glenalmond, Pembroke Coll Cambridge (BA 1957), New Coll Edinburgh and Princeton Theological Seminary USA (ThM 1961); Fulbright Scholar; Min Christ's Ch Dunollie Oban 1962–66, Chaplain 8th Bn Argyll and Sutherland Highrs (TA) 1963–67, St Andrews U 1966–73 and U OTC 1967, 3rd Bn Argyll and Sutherland Highrs 1966 and Highland Vols 1966–67, BCC Preacher USA 1968, Chllr's Assessor St Andrews 1981–85, dir Scottish TV 1982–96; Tstee Carnegie Tst for Universities of Scotland 1988–, chm Cross Tst 1989–, Tstee Scottish Orthopaedic Research Tst into Trauma 1993–; *m* 13 July 1966 *Sheena Mary, yr dau of Alexander W Edwards, of Duncraggan, Oban, Argyll, and has:

　　　1b *Beppo Robert; *b* 4 Dec 1968

　　　2b *Chay Alexander; *b* 6 Sept 1971

　　4a *Jock Gordon [Prof The Hon Jock Buchanan-Smith, Pitcaple Farm, RR2, Cambridge, Ontario N3C 2V4, Canada]; *b* 9 March 1940; *educ* Edinburgh Acad, Trin Coll Glenalmond, Aberdeen U (BSc Ag 1962), Iowa State U (BS 1963), Texas Tech U (MS 1965) and Oklahoma State U (PhD 1969); Lt Gordon Highrs 1963, Assist Prof Guelph U; *m* 26 Aug 1964 *Virginia Lee, dau of James S Maxson, of Dallas, and has issue

　　1a *Mary Drummond, DBE (1993) [The Hon Dame Mary Corsar DBE, Burg, Torloisk, Ulva Ferry, Isle of Mull PA74 6NH]; *b* 8 July 1927; *educ* Edinburgh U (MA 1949); Dep Ch Commr Girl Guides Scotland 1972–77, Govr Fettes 1982, Chm WRVS 1988–93, memb Parole Bd Scotland 1982–89, chm TSB Fndn Scotland 1994–97; *m* 25 April 1953 *Lt-Col Charles Herbert Kenneth Corsar, LVO, OBE, TD, JP, DL, Roy Scots, s of Kenneth Corsar, of Cairniehill, and has had:

　　　1b *George Kenneth Drummond; *b* 26 June 1954; BSc MS

　　　2b *David Charles Buchanan; *b* 4 Sept 1957

　　　1b Kathleen Mary Herdman

　　　2b *Katharine Martha Hutcheson; *b* 31 July 1961

　　　3b *Mary Grizel Dunlop; *b* 30 May 1965; BSc, CA; *m* 1989 *Edward Guest

2 **Sir Robert Workman Smith, 1st Bt** (UK), so *cr* 21 June 1945, JP; *b* 7 Dec 1880; *educ* Glasgow Acad and Trin Coll Cambridge (BA 1905); barrister Inner Temple 1908, T/Lt RASC WW I 1916–19, MP (C) Aberdeen Centl and Kincardine 1924–45, ktd 1934; *m* 6 Dec 1911 Jessie Hill, yr dau of William Workman, of Nottinghill, Belfast, and *d* 6 Dec 1957, leaving:

　(1) **Sir (William) Gordon Smith, 2nd Bt**, VRD; *b* 30 Jan 1916; *educ* Westminster and Trin Coll Cambridge (BA 1937); barrister Inner Temple 1939, Lt-Cdr RNR WW II (despatches); *m* 1st 29 Oct 1941 (*divorce*) Diana Gundreda, dau of Maj Charles Horace Malden, RMLI, of Aquahorthies, Aberdeenshire, by Lilian Robertson, yr dau of Ernest Bagshaw, JP, of Ford Hall, Derbys; *m* 2nd 1958 *Diana May Violet Peel Goodchild [Diana Lady Smith, Crowmallie, Pitcaple, Aberdeenshire], formerly w of G Ian Young, of Burnham-on-Crouch, Essex, and *d* 20 May 1983, leaving by her:

　　1a Sir ROBERT HILL SMITH, **3rd and present Bt**

　　2a +CHARLES GORDON [Dr Charles Smith, 21 Kimberley Rd, Cambridge CB4 1HG]; *b* 21 April 1959; heir presumptive; *educ* Merchant Taylors', St Andrews, U of Oregon and Trin Hall Cambridge (PhD); Lecturer Physics

Cambridge; *m* 29 Aug 1990 *Ann Maria (PhD), dau of Joseph Kennedy, of Ballycastle, Co Antrim, and has:

　　　1b *Samuel Gordon; *b* 11 Nov 1993

　　　2b *Rory Donal; *b* 23 Feb 1996

　(2) +Robert Alexander [Robert Smith Esq, East Crowmallie, Pitcaple, Aberdeenshire]; *b* 6 March 1920; *educ* Stowe, Westminster and Trin Coll Cambridge; Lt RNVR WW II; *m* 15 Dec 1945 *Marianne, widow of George Paloutine, of Philippeville, Algeria, and dau of Serge Denisieff, and has:

　　1a +Andrew Alexander; *b* 2 Nov 1946; *educ* Gordonstoun

　　2a +Robert Serge; *b* 2 Nov 1948; *educ* Gordonstoun

SMITH of Eardiston

Arms: Sa. a cross-flory or, on a chief engrailed erm. a demi-lion issuant between two cross-crosslets gu. **Crest:** A greyhound couchant sa., collared and line reflexed over the back or, the body charged with a cross-crosslet of the last, the dexter paw resting upon a cross-flory as in the arms. **Creation:** Bt. (UK) 23 Sept 1809.

SIR CHRISTOPHER SYDNEY WINWOOD SMITH, 5TH BT, of Eardiston, Co Worcester [Sir Christopher Smith Bt, Junction Rd, via Grafton, NSW 2460, Australia]; *b* 20 Sept 1906; *s f* 1953; *m* 1932 *Phyllis Berenice, yst dau of Thomas Robert O'Grady, of Waterford, Ireland, and Grafton, NSW, and has had:

1 Christopher Sydney Winwood; *b* 1933; *d* 5 Aug 1937

2 +ROBERT SYDNEY WINWOOD [Robert Smith Esq, 13 Siren St, Port Maquarie, NSW, Australia]; *b* 1939; *m* 1971 *Roslyn Nellie, est dau of James Keith McKensie, of Sydney, NSW, and has:

　(1) +Craig Robert Winwood; *b* 1974

　(1) *Robyn Louise Winwood; *b* 1978

3 +Hugh William Standish Winwood [Hugh Smith Esq, 15 Jordan St, Fairfield, NSW 2169, Australia]; *b* 1942; *m* 1966 *Clare Philomena, est dau of Leslie Arthur Stinson, of Sydney, and has:

　(1) +Christopher Hugh Winwood; *b* 1966

　(2) +Gregory Robert Winwood; *b* 1971

　(1) *Catherine Anne Winwood; *b* 1969

　(2) *Julie Stella Winwood; *b* 1973

4 +Terence John Winwood; *b* 1944; *m* 1967 *Helen June, dau of Donald W McLeod, of Cootamundra, NSW, and has:

　(1) +Ian James Winwood; *b* 1969

　(2) +Richard Charles Winwood; *b* 1972

　(1) *Jaqueline Nicole Winwood; *b* 1975

5 +Matthew Roy Winwood; *b* 1947; *m* 1975 *Janette Lefevre, est dau of John Truman, of Sydney, and has:

　(1) +Michael Winwood; *b* 1977

6 +David Anthony Winwood; *b* 1949; *m* 1976 *Judith Chaffey, of Grafton, NSW, and has:

　(1) +Simon Winwood; *b* 1976

　(2) +Steven Winwood; *b* 1977

7 +Ronald James Thomas Winwood; *b* 1951; *m* 1976 *Rhonda Jean, est dau of Ronald Raine, of Sydney, and has:

　(1) +Gary Winwood; *b* 1978

　(2) +Benjamin Winwood; *b* 1981

　(1) *Megan Winwood; *b* 1984

1 *Villette Mary Winwood; *b* 1935; *m* 1961 *Roger Hore and has:

　(1) *Andrew; *b* 1962

2 *Helen Eve Winwood; *b* 1936; *m* 1957 *Arthur Sydney Macalpine and has:

　(1) *Arthur David; *b* 1959

　(2) *Ian Christopher; *b* 1961

　(1) *Alison Helen; *b* 1965

　(2) *Jillian Elizabeth; *b* 1969

3 *Frances Caroline Winwood; *b* 1941; *m* 1973 *Kenneth James Hebblewhite and has:

　(1) *Mark Kenneth; *b* 1976

　(2) *Simon James; *b* 1978

(1) *Rebecca Frances; *b* 1978

Lineage: THOMAS SMITH, of Burwarton, Salop; *m* Letitia, dau of Edward Morris, of Burford, Salop, and had an est s:

Sir William Smith, 1st Bt (UK), so *cr* 23 Sept 1809, of Eardiston; *m* 10 Oct 1780 Mary, dau of Edward Wheeler of Lambswick, Worcs, and *d* 1821, leaving, with a dau (Cecilia Maria, *m* 2 May 1816 V W Wheeler, of Kyrewood Ho, Worcs, and *d* 2 March 1821):

Sir Christopher Sidney Smith, 2nd Bt; *b* 14 May 1798; *m* 1st 30 Dec 1822 Mary (*d* 1 Dec 1833), dau of Rev Robert Foley; *m* 2nd Dec 1837 Mrs Harriette Murphy (*dsp* April 1840), only dau of Thomas Lee, of Headingley, nr Leeds, and *d* 7 Aug 1839 having had, with a yr s (Edward, *b* 28 Oct 1826, *d* unm) and three daus (ary Sidney, *m* 27 Aug 1846 Rev Samuel John Heathcote, and *d* 1885, leaving issue (*see* HEATHCOTE, Bt, of Hursley); Elizabeth, *m* 23 Sept 1853 Charles Gabriel Shaw and *d* 11 Jan 1900; another dau, *d* unm):

Sir William Smith, 3rd Bt, DL; *b* 5 Oct 1823; *m* 1st 5 May 1843 Susan (*d* 30 April 1892), 4th dau of Adml Sir William George Parker, 2nd Bt, of Harburn (*see* 1902 edn), and had, with four other sons (*d* young or unm):

1 Christopher Sydney Winwood; *b* 24 Jan 1846; *m* 10 Aug 1877 Caroline, only child of William Holland, of Fitzroy, Queensland, and *dvp* 1886, leaving:

  (1) WILLIAM SYDNEY WINWOOD (Sir), **4th Bt**

  (1) Maud Agnes Winwood

  (2) Dorothy Winwood

2 William Arthur Winwood; *b* 3 Nov 1854; *m* 6 Oct 1886 Harriet (*d* 5 Nov 1942), dau of John Lethbridge Cowland, and *d* 22 May 1928, leaving:

  (1) Christopher William Winwood; *b* 28 March 1893; Instr-Cdr RN; *m* 1916 Alice Muriel (*d* 20 April 1969), dau of Capt W F Garside, of Morden, Seaford, and *d* 6 April 1969, leaving:

    1a Antony Winwood, DFC; *b* 1920; RAF WW II; *d* 1993

    1a *Pauline Muriel Winwood [Mrs Richard Archer, 7 Laurel Dve, Southmoor, Abingdon, Oxon OX13 5DG] ; *b* 1918; *m* 1st 1949 James Mayhew and adopted:

      *Marilyn Carol; *b* 27 March 1952

      *Juliet Mary; *b* 24 Dec 1953

    1a (cont.) Mrs Mayhew *m* 2nd 1977 *Richard Tudor Archer

  (1) Constance Evelyn Winwood, MBE (1918); PA to Dir Supplies Air Min WW I; *m* 6 June 1921 Leonard Tolcher Tracey, OBE, MC, est surv s of Dr H E Tracey, of Willand, Devon, and had issue

  (2) Gladys Pauline Winwood; *d* unm 2 Dec 1947

1 Mary Agnes Winwood; *m* 1st 20 April 1881 Rev Sir Thomas Collingwood Hughes, 8th Bt (*qv*); *m* 2nd Nov 1890 Robert Halliday Gunning, MD, LLD, of W Kensington, and *d* 19 Oct 1932. He *d* 22 March 1900

2 Elizabeth Ellen Winwood; *m* 27 Oct 1892 Col Edward Vincent Vashon Wheeler, OBE, of Newnham Court, Tenbury, Worcs, and *d* 5 Jan 1955, leaving issue. He *d* 21 May 1933

Sir William *m* 2nd 1892 Helen Agnes (*dsp* 4 May 1914), dau of William Houseman, of Woodchester Ho, Glos, and *d* 4 Jan 1893

His gs,

Sir William Sydney Winwood Smith, 4th Bt; *b* 1 April 1879; *m* 27 July 1905 Caroline (*d* 1938), only dau of James Harris, of Queenstown, Co Cork, and *d* July 1953, leaving:

1 Sir CHRISTOPHER SYDNEY WINWOOD SMITH, **5th and present Bt**

2 +Rupert William Winwood; *b* 4 Sept 1908; *m* 17 Aug 1940 *Nancia Jean Margaret, dau of John Bailey Cave, of Coffs Harbour, NSW, and has:

  (1) +Geoffrey Stirling Winwood; *b* 20 June 1945; *m* 1972 *Stephanie Sue, er dau of W Kelly, of Cabarlah, Qld, and has:

    1a +Nicholas William Winwood; *b* 1977

    2a +Hugh Stirling Winwood; *b* 1981

  (2) +Adrian John Winwood; *b* 1955; *m* 1984 *Lucinda Tranquilla, dau of A Gastaldo, of Adelaide, S Australia

  (1) *Merran Joy Winwood; *b* 23 Dec 1942; *m* 1977 *Virgil Joseph Hull, PhD, of Keyser, W Va., USA, and has:

    1a *Meredith Fleur Winwood; *b* 1980

SMITH of Keighley

Arms: Tierced in pale reversed arg., gu. and az., in chief two roses counterchanged, barbed and seeded ppr., and in base a London pride plant, flowered and eradicated, all ppr. **Crest:** Upon a rock a moorcock rising, resting the dexter foot on a double convex lens, all ppr. **Motto:** Think and act. **Creation:** Bt. (UK) 28 Nov 1947.

SIR CHARLES BRACEWELL SMITH, 4TH BT, of Keighley, Co York [Sir Charles Smith Bt, The Hermitage, 7 Clarence Gate Gdns, Glentworth St, London NW1 6AY]; *b* 13 Oct 1955; *s* bro 1983; *educ* Harrow; fndr Homestead Charitable Tst, author: *On the Song of the Saints*; *m* 1st 1977 Carol Vivien (*d* 1994), dau of Norman Hough, of Cookham, Berks; *m* 2nd 1996 *Nina Kakkar

Lineage: SAMUEL SMITH, of Keighley, Yorks; had:

Sir Bracewell Smith, 1st Bt (UK), so *cr* 28 Nov 1947, KCVO (1948), of Keighley, Co York; *b* 29 June 1884; *educ* privately and Leeds U (BSc 1908, Hon LLD 1948); memb Finsbury and Holborn Bd Guardians 1919–22, Cllr and Alderman Holborn 1922–37, memb LCC 1925–28, Mayor Holborn 1931–32, MP (C) Dulwich 1932–45, Lt City London, Alderman Lime St Ward 1938, Sheriff 1943–44, Ld Mayor 1946–47, underwriting memb Lloyd's, chm: Park Lane Hotel Ltd, Ritz Hotel London Ltd, Ritz Devpt Co, Carlton Hotel Ltd, Practical Press Ltd, Earls Court Ltd, Wembley Stadium Ltd, Carpac Ltd and Hotel and Catering Exhibition Ltd; dir: Ritz Hotel Paris Ltd, Parkland Mfg Co and Assoc Rediffusion Ltd, Life Pres Arsenal Football Club, Past Master Spectacle Makers', Bakers', Glaziers' and Framework Knitters' Cos, memb Court Carmen's Co, Liveryman Pattenmakers' Co, Pres London Schs Athletic Assoc, Hon V-Pres FA, Hon Treas Reedham Sch, Almoner Christ's Hosp, Hon Freeman Keighley 1957, ktd 1945; *m* 29 Dec 1909 Edith Smith (*d* 21 March 1953), dau of George Whitaker, of Bingley, Yorks, and *d* 12 Jan 1966, leaving:

1 **Sir George Bracewell Smith, 2nd Bt**, MBE (1946); *b* 5 Nov 1912; *educ* Wrekin Coll and Emmanuel Coll Cambridge (BA 1932, MA); chm Park Lane Hotel Ltd, Ritz Hotel London Ltd, Ritz Hotels Devpt Co and Practical Press Ltd 1966–76; *m* 8 Oct 1951 Helene Marie (*d* 15 April 1975), dau of John Frederick Hydock, of Philadelphia, and *d* 18 Sept 1976, leaving:

  (1) **Sir Guy Bracewell Smith, 3rd Bt**; *b* 12 Dec 1952; *educ* Harrow; *d* 1983

  (2) Sir CHARLES BRACEWELL SMITH, **4th and present Bt**

1 Eileen; *b* 22 March 1911; *m* 1st April 1933 F/Lt Harry Lascelles Carr (*d* 17 Aug 1943), s of Sir Emsley Carr, of Walton-on-the-Hill, Surrey, and had:

  (1) *Clive Emsley Bracewell Lascelles; *b* 29 May 1934; *m* 5 Oct 1963 *Isabel, MA, only dau of Vicomte Devezeaux de Rancougne, of Paris

  (2) *Richard Charles Lascelles; *b* 22 July 1938; *m* 11 June 1960 *Edda, dau of Paul Armbrust, of Bremen

  (1) *Carol Mary Lascelles; *m* 15 Jan 1955 *Francis Geoffrey Hooton, s of Reginald Hooton, of Winnipeg, Canada

1 (cont.) Mrs Harry Carr *m* 2nd 9 Sept 1948 James Shelley Phipps Armstrong, Ontario Agent-Gen UK, s of Joseph E Armstrong, MP, of Petrolia, Ontario, and by him had:

  (2) *Sarah Margaret Phipps; *b* 19 May 1951

SMITH of Stratford Place

Arms: Quarterly, or and gu. a fret between three fleurs-de-lys all counterchanged. **Crest:** A fret gu. issuant therefrom a fleur-de-lys or. **Motto:** *Dabit qui dedit* ('He will give who hath given'). **Creation:** Bt. (UK) 6 Sept 1897.

SIR (THOMAS) GILBERT SMITH, 4TH BT, of Stratford Place, London [Sir Gilbert Smith Bt, PO Box 654, Masterton, New Zealand]; *b* 2 July 1937; *educ* Huntley Sch and Nelson Coll; *s f* 1961; *m* 20 Jan 1962 *Patricia Christine, 3rd dau of David James Cooper, of Paraparaumu, NZ, and has:

  1 +ANDREW THOMAS; *b* 17 Oct 1965
  2 +Alistair Blair; *b* 13 July 1969
  1 *Janne Fiona; *b* 24 Feb 1963; *m* 1988 *David Carl Finlayson, of Leoin, NZ

Lineage: BENJAMIN SMITH, of Edgbaston, Warwicks, and Camberwell; *b* 1764; *m* 1st 1788 Mary Adams; *m* 2nd 1802 Mary Shiers (*d* 1812) and *d* 28 Aug 1823, having by her had a dau and by his 1st w, with three yr sons and three daus:

BENJAMIN SMITH, of Great Lodge, Tonbridge, and Blackheath; *b* 1793; *m* 1817 Susannah, dau of Apsley Pellatt, of The Friars, Lewes, and *d* 1850, leaving, with two daus (*d* unm):

  1 Benjamin Frederick (Ven); *b* 1819; *educ* Trin Coll Cambridge (MA); Archdeacon Maidstone, Canon Canterbury; *m* 1846 Harriet Anne (*d* 27 Dec 1906), only dau of Thomas Ward, of Moreton Morrell, Warwicks, and *d* 25 March 1900, leaving issue
  2 Stephen; *b* 1822; *m* 1847 Mary Sophia (*d* 20 Nov 1906), 5th dau of John Greaves, of Radford, Warwicks, and *d* 1890, having had issue
  3 Henry; *b* 1823; *m* 1852 Rosa Sophia (*d* 1893), dau of Robert Knaggs, MD, of Melbourne, and *d* 1896, having had issue
  4 Apsley; *b* 1825; *m* 1849 Emma Elizabeth (*d* 1893), dau of George Richards Elkington, of Woodbrooke, Northfield, Worcs, and *d* 1905, having had issue
  5 George Maberly (Rev); *b* 1831; *educ* Gonville and Caius Coll Cambridge (MA); Rector Penshurst, Kent, Hon Canon Canterbury; *m* 1863 Emily Harriet, est dau of Maxwell Macartney, MD, of Rosebrook, Co Armagh, and had issue
  6 THOMAS (Sir), **1st Bt**
  7 Joseph Brandram; *b* 1835; *d* unm
  8 Herbert Jowett; *b* 1837; *m* 10 June 1862 Emily, dau of Rev William Wilson, and *d* 1899, leaving issue
  1 Mary; *m* 1854, as his 2nd w, Rudolph Meisheimer, and *d* 22 Jan 1906. He *d* 1869

The 6th s,

Sir Thomas Smith, 1st Bt (UK), so *cr* 6 Sept 1897, KCVO, of Stratford Place, London; *b* 23 March 1833; FRCS, Surgn-Extrdy to HM QUEEN VICTORIA, Hon Serjeant-Surgn to HM EDWARD VII, Consulting Surgn St Bart's Hosp and King Edward VII's Hosp for Offrs; *m* 27 Aug 1862 Ann Elisa (*d* 9 Feb 1879), 2nd dau of Frederick Parbury, of Bayswater, and *d* 1 Oct 1909, leaving:

  1 **Sir (Thomas) Rudolph Hampden Smith, 2nd Bt**, CBE (1920); *b* 24 Jan 1869; *educ* Winchester; MRCS and LRCP London 1892, MA, BC, and MB Cambridge 1894, FRCS London 1895; *m* 14 June 1897 Anne Ellen (*d* 26 Sept 1928), dau of Joseph William Sharpe, and *dsp* 25 June 1958
  2 Gilbert; *b* 28 Nov 1874; *educ* Marlborough; MRCS 1896, FRCS, LRCP 1899, MD (Dunelm) 1900; *m* 1 Aug 1900 Elizabeth Adeline (*d* 22 June 1954), 3rd dau of William Carson, of Bryn Estyn, Chester, and *d* 22 June 1950, leaving:
    (1) THOMAS TURNER (Sir), **3rd Bt**
    (2) Gilbert Patrick; *b* 17 May 1906
    (3) Michael Carson Lyndon, MC; *b* 11 Jan 1908; *educ* London U (MB, BS 1934); Lt-Col IMS, MRCS, LRCP 1934; *m* 31 Oct 1936 Mary Pauline (*d* 1988), dau of Charles Rowlatt, of Headley, Hants, and *d* 21 March 1961, leaving:
      1a +Patrick Charles Gilbert; *b* 5 June 1939; *educ* Marlborough, Sidney Sussex Coll Cambridge (MA) and St Bartholomew's Hosp (MB); BCh, DPM
      1a *Sarah Gillian; *b* 10 Nov 1937; *m* 1st 6 Dec 1958 (*divorce* 1988) Capt Antony Gibbon Chater, 9th/12th Roy Lancers, yst s of Lt-Cdr J D G Chater, of Kenya, and has:
        1b *James Michael Douglas; *b* 1 Nov 1959
        2b *Giles Addison; *b* 3 Oct 1961

        3b *Piers Antony Rowlatt; *b* 20 March 1963
      1a (cont.) Mrs Sarah Chater *m* 2nd 21 April 1967 (*divorce* 1992) Sir Peter Wilfred Giles Graham Moon, 5th Bt, of Portman Sq (*qv*), and has further issue
      2a *Elizabeth Caroline; *b* 7 Dec 1940; *m* 1967 *Christopher Ravenscroft and has:
        1b *Michael Jack; *b* 1973
      3a *Alexa Pauline Lovedy; *b* 31 Dec 1945; *m* 19– *John Davenport
      4a *Joanna Esmée; *b* 3 Oct 1948; *m* 1969 *John Alexander Broom and has:
        1b *Alexander Rui Tomas; *b* 1972
        2b *Daniel John; *b* 1978
        1b *Orlanda Maria; *b* 1974
    (4) Felix Martin; *b* 3 Oct 1911; *m* 5 Sept 1936 *Freda, yr dau of Frederick W Blackall, of Kenley, Surrey
    (1) *Jean Elisabeth [Mrs Andrew Fergus, Buffbeards, Hindhead Rd, Haslemere, Surrey GU27 1LH]; *b* 10 Sept 1901; *m* 30 Nov 1929 *Andrew Naismith Fergus, BSc, MB, ChB, FRFPS, DPH Cambridge, DO Oxford, late T/Maj RMAC, s of John F Fergus, MD, of Glasgow, and has:
      1a *John Naismith; *b* 8 Feb 1934; *educ* Oxford (MA, MB); FRGS (Edin), FRCS, late Capt RAMC, Consultant Surgn; *m* 18 July 1970 *Mrs Catherine Isabel Wake, MRCS, LRCP, MB, dau of David Cazes, of Guernsey, and has:
        1b *Robert David Wenley; *b* 1977
        2b *Adam Andrew Wake; *b* 1978
      1a *Margaret Elizabeth, 23 June 1931
      2a *Sheena Mary; *b* 2 June 1939; MVO
      3a *Helen Kay [Mrs Ingo Evers, Coton Hall, Bridgnorth, Salop WV15 6ES]; *b* 4 Nov 1947 PhD, BSc, MSc; *m* 1974 *Ingo Evers, MPhil, and has:
        1b *Andrew Dominic Lothar; *b* 1981
    (2) *Madeleine Lovedy; *b* 16 June 1909

3 Martin Turner; *b* 29 June 1876; BA Oxon; *d* unm 27 Nov 1953
1 Laura Elizabeth; *m* 27 May 1886 Sir Archibald Edward Garrod, KCMG, MD, FRS, Regius Prof Medicine Oxford, s of Sir Alfred Baring Garrod, MD, FRS, and *d* 21 Feb 1940, having had issue. He *d* 28 March 1936
2 Annie Parbury; *m* 18 Feb 1896 Charles Percival Crouch, MB, FRCS, of Clifton, Bristol, and *d* 11 Nov 1961, leaving issue. He *d* 25 June 1926
3 Ada Marion; *m* 1895 Charles Ernest Baker, MB, FRCS, and *d* 3 Jan 1922, leaving issue. He *d* 28 March 1909
4 Gertrude; *b* 5 Oct 1870; *d* unm 1 Oct 1959
5 Grace Margaret; *d* unm 24 April 1946
6 Mildred; *m* 17 July 1902 Thomas Alfred Mayo, MB, FRCS, s of Alfred Charles Mayo, JP, of Great Yarmouth, and *d* 26 Dec 1968 aged 89, leaving issue. He *d* 1 Nov 1950

The 2nd Bt's n,

Sir Thomas Turner Smith, 3rd Bt; *b* 28 June 1903; *educ* Oundle; *m* 20 July 1935 *Agnes [Agnes Lady Smith, 118 Liverpool St, Wanganui, New Zealand], only dau of Bernard Page, of Wellington, NZ, and *d* 11 May 1961, leaving:

1 Sir THOMAS GILBERT SMITH, **4th and present Bt**
2 +Denis Michael; *b* 1945; *m* 1967 *Janet, dau of Leslie Raymond Eckoff, of Ambarwood, RD3, Drury, NZ, and has:
  (1) +Richard Michael; *b* 12 March 1968
  (1) *Joanna Marie; *b* 1 Oct 1969
1 *Barbara Elizabeth; *b* 1939; *m* 1967 *Selwyn Lloyd Harris, of Sanson, NZ, s of Boyd Harris, of Sanson, and has:
  (1) *Boyd John; *b* 11 March 1968
  (2) *Peter Thomas; *b* 1970
  (3) *Quentin Patrick; *b* 1972
  (4) *Zane Gilbert; *b* 1974
2 *Gillian Madeleine; *b* 1941; *m* 1978 *Michael Nicholas McCarthy, JP, of Wanganui, NZ, and has:
  (1) *Samuel Thomas O'Meara; *b* 1980
  (1) *Trinity Madeleine; *b* 1979

SMITH OF CLIFTON

Creation: B. (LP, UK) 2 Aug 1997.

THE BARON SMITH OF CLIFTON, of Mountsandel, Co Londonderry (Sir Trevor Arthur Smith) [The Rt Hon The Lord Smith of Clifton, University of Ulster, University House, Coleraine, Co Londonderry BT52 1SA]; *b* 14 June 1937; *educ* LSE; sch master LCC 1958–59, assist lecturer Exeter U 1959–60, research offr Acton Soc Tst 1960–62, lecturer politics Hull U 1962–67, Visiting Assoc Prof California State U 1969, Lecturer and Sr Lecturer Political Studies Queen Mary Coll 1967–83 (Head Dept 1972–85, Dean Social Studies 1979–82, Prof 1983–91, Pro-Pncpl 1985–87, Sr Pncpl 1987–89, Sr V-Pncpl 1989–91), V-Chllr Ulster U; memb: Lib Party Exec 1958–59, Willesden Area Synod 1985–88, Senate London U 1987–91, Tower Hamlets DHA 1987–91, Unservile State Gp 1987–92, UK Socrates Cncl (chm 1996–), Edtl Bd Govt and Opposition 1995–, Bd A Taste of Ulster 1996–, Bd Opera NI 1997–, Admin Bd Internat Assoc Universities 1995–; dir: Job Ownership Ltd 1978–85, New Society Ltd 1986–88, Statesman and Nation Publishing Co 1988–90 (chm 1990), G Duckworth & Co 1990–, Government and Opposition 1995–; V-Pres: Patients' Assoc 1988–, Political Studies Assoc UK 1989–91 and 1993 (chm 1988–89, Pres 1991–93); ktd 1996, Pres Belfast Civic Tst 1995–; Tstee: Joseph Rowntree Reform Tst 1975– (chm 1987–), Acton Soc Tst 1975–87, Employment Inst 1987–92; V-Chm Govrs Princess Alexandra and Newham Coll of Nursing and Midwifery 1990–91; Govr: Sir John Cass and Redcoats Sch 1979–84, Haifa U 1985–91, Bell Educnl Tst 1988–93; Hon Memb Senate Fachhochschule Augsburg 1994; CIMgt (CIBM 1992); Hon Prof Ulster U 1991; Hon LLD Dublin 1992, Hull 1993, LLD Belfast 1995, NUI

1996; author: *Training Managers* (with M Argylle 1962), *Town Councillors* (with A M Rees 1964), *Town and County Hall* (1966), *Anti-Politics: consensus and reform* (1972), *The Fixers* (with A Young 1995); *m* 1st 1960 (*divorce* 1973) Brenda Eustace and has two sons; *m* 2nd 1979 *Julia Bullock and by her has a dau

Lineage: ARTHUR SMITH; *m* Vera — and had an er s:

TREVOR ARTHUR, *cr* a **Baron**

SMITH OF GILMOREHILL

Creation: B. (LP, UK) 1995.

THE BARONESS SMITH OF GILMOREHILL, of Gilmorehill, District of City of Glasgow (Elizabeth Margaret Bennett, DL (Edinburgh 1996) [The Rt Hon The Baroness Smith of Gilmorehill DL, House of Lords, London SW1A 0PW]; *b* 4 June 1940; *educ* Hutchesons' Girls' GS and Glasgow U; GB-USSR Assoc: admin assist 1962–64, Scottish Sec 1982–88; French teacher 1964–68, memb Press Complaints Commn 1995–, Chm Edinburgh Festival Fringe 1995, dir Scottish Media Gp plc 1995–, memb governing body Br Assoc for Centl and E Europe 1996–, Oppn Spokesman Tourism 1996–97; *m* 1967 John Smith, PC, QC (*d* May 1994), Leader Lab Pty 1992–94, and has:

1 *Sarah; *b c* 1971; BBC TV producer to 1996, with Channel 4's *Here and Now* 1996–97, news reporter Channel 5 1997–

2 *Jane; *b c* 1972; Lab Pty worker 1996–

3 *Catherine; *b c* 1973; *educ* Glasgow U

Lineage: FREDERICK WILLIAM MONCRIEFF BENNETT; *m* Elizabeth Waters Irvine Shanks and had:

ELIZABETH MARGARET, *cr* a **Baroness**

SMITH-DODSWORTH

Arms: Quarterly, 1st and 4th, argent a bend engrailed sable between three annulets gules (for DODSWORTH); 2nd and 3rd, per saltire argent and sable, two trefoils slipped in pale gules (for SMITH).
Crests: 1 A dexter cubic arm in chain mail or, the hand proper, grasping a broken tilting-spear, the broken part imbued gules (for DODSWORTH), 2 Out of a ducal coronet or a boar's head, couped at the neck azure, crined and tusked gold (for SMITH).
Motto: *Pro lege senatuque rege* ('For King, law and Parliament').
Creation: Bt. (GB) 22 Jan 1784.

SIR JOHN CHRISTOPHER SMITH-DODSWORTH, 8TH BT, of Newland Park and Thornton Watlass, Co York [Sir John Smith-Dodsworth Bt, Thornton Watlass Hall, Ripon, Yorks]; *b* 4 March 1935; *s* f 1940; *educ* Ampleforth and RAC Cirencester; jt author: *New Zealand Ferns and Allied Plants* (1989), *New Zealand Native Shrubs and Climbers* (1991); *m* 1st 5 Aug 1961 (*divorce* 1971) Margaret Anne, dau of Alfred William Sainsbury Jones, of Ruardean, Glos, and has:

1 +DAVID JOHN; *b* 23 Oct 1963; *educ* Ampleforth

1 *Cyrilla Denise; *b* 1 July 1962

Sir JOHN *m* 2nd 1972 Margaret Theresa (*d* 1990), dau of Henry Grey, of Auckland, NZ, and by her has:

2 +Daniel Leui'i; *b* 1974

Sir JOHN *m* 3rd 1991 *Lolita, dau of Romeo Pulante, of The Philippines, and by her has:

3 +A son; *b* 199–

2 *Joanna Marie; *b* 1993

Lineage: JOHN SMITH, of Ecclesfield; *m* Priscilla Silvester and had:

JOHN SMITH, of Newland Hall, W R Yorks; *m* 1st Ann Sculthorp (*dsp*); *m* 2nd Ann, dau of Christopher Hodgson, of Westerton, and *d* 1746, leaving, with a dau (Elizabeth, *m* Robert Dalway Haliday, of Belfast):

Sir John Silvester Smith, 1st Bt (GB), so *cr* 22 Jan 1784, of Newland Park and Birthwait, Yorks; *m* 20 July 1761 Henrietta Maria, dau of John Dodsworth, of Thornton Watlass, and *d* 15 June 1789, having had, with four daus:

1 Sir EDWARD SMITH later DODSWORTH (roy licence 1821 in compliance with terms of will of his uncle Rev Frederick Dodsworth, DD, Canon Windsor), **2nd Bt**; *b* 13 Aug 1768; *m* 22 Sept 1804 Susannah (*d* 13 March 1830), yst dau of Col Henry Dawkins, of Standlynch, Wilts, and *dsp* 31 Dec 1845

2 George (Rev); *b* 25 Sept 1772; Vicar Erchefont, Alderbury and Farley, Wilts; *d* unm 1811

3 Sir CHARLES SMITH later DODSWORTH (roy licence 1846), **3rd Bt**; *b* 22 Aug 1775; Lt-Col 22nd Light Dragoons; *m* 8 June 1808 Elizabeth (*d* 12 June 1853), only child of John Armstrong, of Lisgoole, and gdau of 9th Baron Blayney (*see* 1874 edn), and had, with other issue:

  (1) MATTHEW (Sir), **4th Bt**

  (2) Frederick; *b* 18 Feb 1822; *m* 4 May 1848 Jane Rebecca (*d* 13 Oct 1899), dau of John Young, of Westridge, IoW, and *d* 11 Oct 1885, leaving:

    1a Rosa Alexandrine Elizabeth Maria; *m* 9 Feb 1891 Aymar de Seyssel d'Aix, Marchese di Sommariva (*d* 1896), and *d* 9 Dec 1930

Sir CHARLES *d* 28 July 1857; his s,

Sir Matthew Smith-Dodsworth, 4th Bt; *b* 6 Feb 1819; Capt RA; *m* 23 Sept 1852 Anne Julia (*d* 26 Feb 1890), dau of Col — Crowder, KH, of Brotherton, Yorks, and *d* 30 April 1858, having had:

1 **Sir Charles Edward Smith-Dodsworth, 5th Bt**, DL; *b* 27 June 1853; *m* 5 March 1889 Blanche (*d* 28 Aug 1949), 3rd dau of Hon George Edwin Lascelles (*see* HAREWOOD, E), and *dsp* 5 Aug 1891

2 MATTHEW BLAYNEY (Sir), **6th Bt**

3 Frederick Cadwallader; *b* 15 Aug 1858; 11th Foot; *m* 1888 Hannah Elizabeth (*m* 2nd 1901), dau of T Harrison, of Little Rock, Osceola, Iowa, and *d* 7 Jan 1900, leaving:

  (1) Dorothy; *b* 5 Nov 1891; *m* 1st 14 Jan 1913 Geoffrey Hoyer Millar (*see* INCHYRA, B) and had issue; *m* 2nd 1919 Sir Eugene Goossens, the conductor, and had further issue; *m* 3rd 1930 Daniel Joseph Reagan, of US Legation, Berne

1 Henrietta, OBE (1918); *m* 23 Jan 1886 Sir Henry Monson de la Poer Beresford-Peirse, 3rd Bt (*qv*), and *d* 1 Nov 1926, leaving issue

The 5th Bt's bro,

Sir Matthew Blayney Smith-Dodsworth, 6th Bt, OBE; *b* 26 Oct 1856; *educ* Univ Coll Oxford; *m* 5 Nov 1887 Agnes Eliza (*d* 8 July 1926), only dau of John Crowder, and had:

1 CLAUDE MATTHEW (Sir), **7th Bt**

1 Violet Agnes; *b* 17 Dec 1889; *m* 10 April 1915 Rt Rev Henry Townsend Vodden (*d* 24 Aug 1960), Bp Suffragen Hull, s of Rev Harry Vodden, of Brixton, Devon, and *d* 7 Feb 1964, leaving issue

2 Hilda Monica, JP (1959) Caithness; *b* 26 Sept 1903; *m* 19 June 1930 Lt-Col (Herbert) Brian Taylor, OBE, TD (*d* 22 July 1957), est s of Capt Herbert Anderson Taylor, of Sutton Hall, Thirsk, and had:

  (1) *David Jenneson [David Taylor Esq, Box 141, Kericho, Kenya]; *b* 21 May 1937; *educ* Gordonstoun; *m* 15 Jan 1966 *Anne, dau of A B Doyle, of Nevis, West Indies, and has:

    1a *Anita; *b* 1966

  (2) *Simon Brian [Simon Taylor Esq, Ardgilzean House, Elgin, Moray IV30 3XT]; *b* 30 June 1939; *educ* Winchester; Capt late 1st Bn QO Highrs; *m* 29 April 1970 *Amalia Zoe, yr dau of Patrick Butler-Henderson (*see* FARINGDON, B), and has:

    1a *Emma Amalia Jane; *b* 26 July 1971; *m* 1994 *Tsewang Topgyal and has issue

    2a *Amanda Katherine Zoe; *b* 14 April 1973

    3a *Hilda Penelope Beatrice; *b* 5 Jan 1976

  (3) *Christopher Dodsworth; *b* 14 Jan 1951; *educ* Winchester

Sir MATTHEW *d* 8 Dec 1931; his s,

Sir Claude Matthew Smith-Dodsworth, 7th Bt; *b* 12 Aug 1888; Lt Yorks Regt; *m* 6 Feb 1932 Cyrilla Marie Louise, JP (*d* 1984), 3rd dau of William Ernest Taylor, of Linnet Lane, Liverpool, and *d* 18 May 1940, leaving:

1 Sir JOHN CHRISTOPHER SMITH-DODSWORTH, **8th and present Bt**

1 *Mary Cyrilla [Mrs Mary Clacy, Thornton Watlass Hall, Ripon, Yorks]; *b* 13 May 1933; *m* 1978 (*divorce* 1993) Gresham Clacy, of Arizona

2 *Julia Agnes [Mrs Brian Maccelari, 98 Napier Ave, Hillside, Bulawayo, Zimbabwe]; *b* 20 March 1938; *m* 31 Jan 1963 *Brian Carlo Maccelari and has:

  (1) *Douglas Charles Dodsworth; *b* 25 July 1965

  (2) *Jeremy Christopher Dodsworth; *b* 25 July 1965

  (1) *Mary Frances Dodsworth; *b* 10 Nov 1963

  (2) *Angela Josephine Dodsworth; *b* 1969

SMITH-GORDON

Arms: Quarterly, 1st and 4th, per fess azure and gules two barrulets engrailed ermine between three boar's heads erased or (for GORDON); 2nd and 3rd, argent on a bend cotised between two unicorn's heads erased azure three fusils or, a canton gules, thereon a sword erect proper, pommel and hilt gold, the blade encircled by an eastern crown of the last (for SMITH). **Crests:** 1 Issuant from the battlements of a tower a stag's head affrontée proper, all between two palm branches vert (for GORDON), 2 (for augmentation) A representation of the ornamental silver centre piece of the service of the plate presented to Lt-Gen Sir Lionel Smith by his European and native friends at Bombay, all proper (for SMITH), 3 Out of an eastern crown or a dexter arm embowed in armour encircled by a wreath of laurel, the hand grasping a sword, all proper (for SMITH). **Mottoes:** (over 1st crest) *Animo non astutia* ('By courage not by craft'), (over 3rd crest) *Mea spes in Deo* ('My hope is in God'). **Creation:** Bt. (UK) 19 July 1838.

SIR (LIONEL) ELDRED PETER SMITH-GORDON, 5TH BT [Sir Eldred Smith-Gordon Bt, 13 Shalcomb Street, London SW10 0HZ]; *b* 7 May 1935; *s f* 1976; *educ* Eton and Trin Coll Oxford; *m* 2 Feb 1962 *Sandra Rosamund Ann, yr dau of W/Cdr Walter Ronald Farley, DFC, and Mrs Dennis Poore, of Kensington, and has:

1 +LIONEL GEORGE ELDRED [Lionel Smith-Gordon, c/o J P Morgan & Co, 60 Wall St, New York, NY 10260-0060, USA]; *b* 1 July 1964; *educ* Eton, Westfield Coll and King's Coll London; v-pres J P Morgan Singapore; *m* 10 April 1993 *Kumi, only dau of Masahi Suzuki, of Urawa, Saitama, Japan

1 *Isobel Charlotte Laura; *b* 17 Aug 1966; *m* 30 Aug 1997 *Thomas Magee, yst s of Hugh F Magee, of Santa Rosa, Calif., and Mrs Jack Smith, of Grants Pass, Oregon

Lineage: RICHARD SMITH, of Islington, Middx, of which held the advowson; *b* 1707; *m* —, widow of Nathaniel Crow, of Barbados, and had:

1 Richard (Rev); Rector Islington; *m* — Mapp and had:

(1)Richard (Rev); Rector Sutton, Sussex; *m* —, dau of Richard Acklom, of Wiseton Hall, Notts

(1) A dau; *m* Capt Robert Allen, 91st Highrs, of The Grove, Lymington, Hants, and had issue

2 BENJAMIN

1 Eleanor; *m* Anthony Todd and had:

(1) Eleanor; *m* 15 Aug 1782 8th Earl of Lauderdale (*qv*)

2 Elizabeth; *m* John Robinson, Sec Treasury, of Wyke House, Middx, and had:

(1) Mary; *m* 1781 2nd Earl of Abergavenny (*see* ABERGAVENNY, M)

3 Mary; *m* 1st William Berney, of Barbados; *m* 2nd 29 Nov 1768 Thomas Dyer, s of Sir Thomas Dyer, 5th Bt (*qv*), and *d* Aug 1775, leaving issue

RICHARD SMITH's 2nd s,

BENJAMIN SMITH, of Lys, Hants; Sheriff Hants 1777; *m* 23 Feb 1765 Charlotte (the novelist Charlotte Smith), est dau of Nicholas Turner, of Bignor Park, Sussex, and Stoke House, Surrey, and *d* 1806, leaving, with other issue:

1 William Towers; *b* 1766; Judge Morrshedabad, India; *m* 1798 Catherine Maria, dau of Andrew Morris (*see* KILLANIN, B), and *d* 1826, leaving:

(1) Seton Lionel; *b* 1817; Maj 54th Regt; *m* 1848 Frances Catherine (*d* 1896), dau of Thomas Fane Uniacke, of Lymbury Lodge, Co Westmeath, and *d* 1887, leaving:

1a Mordaunt Kirwan SMITH later MORDAUNT-SMITH; *b* 1857; *m* 1895 Ethel Blanche (*d* 15 Aug 1915), 3rd dau of Rev Theodosius Ward-Boughton-Leigh, of Brownsover Hall, nr Rugby and *d* 1906, leaving:

1b Bridgeman Rochfort; *b* 1899; Lt RIN and Warwickshire Yeo, Lt RNVR WW II; *m* 4 Jan 1938 *Elsie Horatia Rosemary Maunsell Baldwin (*m* 2nd 29 March 1967 Patrick Birkett Harris, er s of George Grinling Harris, of Summer House, Southwold, Suffolk), est dau of Rev Horace Fitzhenry Waller-Bridge, and *d* 6 Sept 1943, leaving:

1c *Dawn Theodosia Eileen; *b* 28 Feb 1940; *m* 9 July 1964 *John Malcolm Robb, est s of Hugh Boulton Robb, MC, AFC, of Highway House, Lower Froyle, Hants, and has:

1d *Camilla Theodosia; *b* 1965

2d *Sarah Dawn; *b* 1968

2b Cotterell Boughton; *b* 1902; 2nd Lt Welsh Gds and Warwicks Yeo, Maj Welsh Regt (GSO(3) 1940–43) WW II; *m* 24 June 1926 Hon Kathleen Marcia Browne, dau of 3rd Baron Oranmore and Browne (*qv*), and *d* 5 Feb 1956, leaving:

1c *Michael Cotterell Geoffrey David; *b* 30 June 1927; *educ* Lancing; Lt Black Watch Palestine 1945–47; *m* 23 May 1959 *Diana Katherine, yr dau of Joseph John Edward Potter, of The Great House, Cheshunt, Herts, and has:

1d *Michael Joseph Cotterell Nicholas; *b* 27 Sept 1962

1c *Olwen Marcia Blanche; *b* 7 Dec 1923; *m* 1st 12 June 1952 Wayne Ewing Harriss (*d* 1958), s of Richard T Harriss, of New York and Whitehall Plantation, Louisiana; *m* 2nd 25 Oct 1960 *Hugh Dearman Janson, yst s of Charles Wilfrid Janson (*see* SUTHERLAND, E)

1b Eileen Frances; *m* 1922 Llewellyn Pryse Lloyd, of Glangwill, Carmarths, and *d* 1946, leaving issue

2 LIONEL (Sir), **1st Bt**

1 Augusta; *m* the Chevalier de Foville and *d* 1792

BENJAMIN SMITH's 5th s,

Sir Lionel Smith, 1st Bt (UK), so *cr* 19 July 1838, GCB, GCH; *b* 9 Oct 1778; ADC to HRH THE DUKE OF KENT, Lt-Gen, Col 40th Foot, Govr-Gen Jamaica and Mauritius; *m* 1st Ellen Marianne (*d* 1814), dau of Thomas Galway, of Killery, Co Kerry, and had:

1 Ellen Maria; *m* John Warden, memb Cncl Bombay, and *d* 1 Oct 1829, leaving issue

2 Marianne; *m* 24 Oct 1826 Robert Luard, Judge in India, and had issue

Sir Lionel *m* 2nd 20 Nov 1819 Isabella Curwen (*d* 5 Jan 1842), yst dau of Eldred Curwen Pottinger, of Mount Pottinger, Co Down, by Anne, dau of Robert Gordon, of Florida, Co Down, and *d* 2 Jan 1842, having by her had:

1 LIONEL ELDRED (Sir), **2nd Bt**

1 Isabella; *d* young

2 Augusta; *m* 5 May 1841 Lt-Col Walter Warde (*d* 4 May 1861), s of Gen Sir Henry Warde, GCB, and *d* 17 Dec 1893, leaving issue

3 Isabella; *m* 21 June 1845 Sir George Floyd Duckett, 3rd and last Bt (*dsp* 13 May 1902), and *d* 31 Dec 1901

4 Agnes Letitia; *d* 1936

5 Charlotte Anne; *m* 8 Nov 1859 Edward Maxwell Brownlow, of Exe View, Alphington, Devon, and *dsp* 10 Feb 1863

Sir LIONEL's only s,

Sir Lionel Eldred SMITH later SMITH-GORDON (roy licence 5 Feb 1868), **2nd Bt**; *b* 2 April 1833; Capt 71st LI Crimea and Indian Mutiny (medal and clasps); *m* 12 April 1854 his cousin Fanny (*d* 13 Jan 1906), dau of Thomas Pottinger, of Mount Pottinger, and *d* 1 Dec 1905, having had:

1 **Sir Lionel Eldred Pottinger Smith-Gordon, 3rd Bt**; *b* 22 March 1857; *m* 1883 Sophia Annie (*d* 27 Feb 1943), only dau of Robert James Scott, BSC, and *d* 10 Jan 1933, leaving:

(1) **Sir Lionel Eldred Pottinger Smith-Gordon, 4th Bt**; *b* 25 Nov 1889; *educ* Eton and Trin Coll Oxford; RNVR 1940–43, chm Jencons (Scientific) Ltd; *m* 1st 1 Dec 1913 (*divorce* 1933) Ellen, er dau of Senator Fletcher, of Jacksonville, Fla.; *m* 2nd 4 July 1933 *Eileen Laura, only dau of Capt Harry George Adams-Connor, CVO, DL, of Carisbrooke, IoW, and *d* 1976, leaving by his 2nd w:

1a Sir (LIONEL) ELDRED PETER SMITH-GORDON, **5th and present Bt**

1 Eliza Isabella; *m* 10 Aug 1876 William Moss, of Oak Braes, Godalming, Surrey, and *d* 10 Sept 1898, leaving issue

2 Charlotte Maria; *m* 12 July 1895 George Barnes (*d* 1916), of Down Hall, Wembdon, Somerset, and *d* 1922

3 Julia Anne; *d unm* 31 Dec 1938

SMITH-MARRIOTT

Arms: Quarterly, 1st and 4th, barry of six or and sa., in chief two escallops gu. (for MARRIOTT); 2nd and 3rd, sa. a fess erminois, cotised or, between three martlets of the last, each charged with an erm. spot (for SMITH). **Crests:** 1 A mount vert, thereon a talbot passant sa., guttée de larmes, collared and a line reflexed over the black or (for MARRIOTT), 2 A greyhound sejant gu., collared and a line reflexed over the back or, charged on the shoulder with a mascle arg. **Motto:** *Semper fidelis* ('Ever faithful').
Creation: Bt. (GB) 1 June 1774.

SIR HUGH CAVENDISH SMITH-MARRIOTT, 11TH BT, of Sydling St Nicholas, Co Dorset [Sir Hugh Smith-Marriott Bt, 26 Shipley Rd, Westbury-on-Trym, Bristol BS9 3HS]; *b* 22 March 1925; *s* f 1987; *educ* Bristol Cathedral Sch; md Drawing Office Co 1956, gp mktg exec Bryan Bros Gp 1976, PR and mktg exec dir HSM Mktg, Bristol, 1988–; *m* 18 July 1953 Pauline Anne (*d* 1985), only dau of Frank Fawcett Holt, of Abbotsway, Bristol, and has:

1 *Julie Anne [Mrs David Graveney, 6 Southover Close, Westbury-on-Trym, Bristol]; *b* 2 Sept 1958; *m* 1978 *David Anthony Graveney and has:
  (1) *Adam Hugh Francis; *b* 1982
  (1) *Charlotte Pauline; *b* 1986

Lineage: JOHN SMITH, of Holditch, Devon; yeoman, though of a merchant family established in Exeter since HENRY VI's time; *m* 1st Alice, dau of Alexander Muttlebury, of Jordans, Ilminster; *m* 2nd — and by his 1st w had a 3rd s:

NICHOLAS SMITH; *d* 1596; ancestor of the:
1 George (Sir), of Madford/Madeworthy, Devon; High Sheriff Devon 1615; *m* 1st — and had:
  (1) Elizabeth; *m* Sir Thomas Monck, of Potheridge, Devon, and had:
    1a GEORGE MONCK, 1st DUKE OF ALBEMARLE of the 1660 *cr* (see MONCK, V)
1 (cont.) Sir George *m* 2nd — and *d* 1619, leaving by her:
  (2) A dau; *m* Sir Bevil Granville (see GRANVILLE, E, preliminary remarks)
2 — ; had:
  (1) Robert, of Ilminster; *d* Oct 1656, having had, with three daus:
    1a Edmund, of Ilminster; *b* 1619; Capt RN; had, with other issue:
      1b William; merchant on Tenerife, Canary Islands; had:
        1c Charles, of Waddon, Surrey; *m* Rebecca, dau of Capt Marrener, and had:
          1d Charles, of Stratford, Langthorne, Essex; *m* Judith, dau of Isaac Lefevre and great-aunt of 1st and last Viscount Eversley (see 1888 edn) of Heckfield, GCB, and had:
            1e Charles, of Suttons, Stapleford Tawney, Essex; *b* 1757; MP Westbury; *m* 1798 Augusta, 3rd dau of Joshua Smith, of Erlstoke Park, Wilts, and had issue (see SPENCER-SMITH, Bt)
    2b Edmund; ancestor of the BOWDEN-SMITHs
  2a George, of W Dowlish, Somerset, which he inherited from his f; *b* 1624; *d* 11 Jan 1700, leaving a 2nd s:
    1b John, of W Dowlish; *b c* 1659; *m* Mary — (*d* 22 Oct 1729) and *d* 2 Feb 1729, having had:
      1c Henry, of Chard; *dspm* 1750
      2c George, of Wapping; starch-maker; *m* Elizabeth — (*d* 1740) and *d* 1730, leaving, with an est s, a yst s and a dau:
        1d Henry, of Wapping and Windsor, Berks; *b c* 1714; *m* Mary (*d* 1787), dau of John Hill, and *d* 31 Jan 1768, leaving:
          1e JOHN (Sir), **1st Bt**
          2e William; *d* a minor by 1760
          3e Edmund; LLD, Rector Godmanstone and Melcombe Horsey, Dorset; Fellow Magdalene Coll Cambridge; *d* 17 Nov 1814
          4e George
          1e Susanna; *m* Capt Benjamin Bechenoe/Bechinoe, RN, and *d* 30 Nov 1804, leaving:

1f Mary; *m* 1st 29 June 1789, as his 1st w, 4th Duke of Roxburghe (*qv*); *m* 2nd 19 Aug 1806 John, s of Louisa, Countess of Dysart (*qv*) in her own right, and *d* 9 April 1838
2e Elizabeth; *m* George Gould, of Upwey, Dorset
3c John, of Honiton, Devon; *m* 1st Mary (*d* 5 March 1741), dau of Rev George Passiner Clerk, and had issue; *m* 2nd Rebecca (*dsp* 17 Feb 1759), only dau of Robert Smith, of Langham, Somerst, and *d* 3 Dec 1757
1c Mary; *m* Josiah Anstice, of S Petherton, Somerset
3a Robert, of Ilminster; *b* 1629, ancestor of the extinct SMITHEs of Horsham Park
4a William, of Lyme Regis; *b* 1631; merchant; *d* 16 Aug 1677, leaving:
  1b Robert, of Langham, Chard; had:
    1c William (Sir), of Sydling St Nicholas
5a Thomas, of Exeter; *b* 1634; *d* 1709, leaving issue

HENRY SMITH's est s,

Sir John Smith, 1st Bt (GB), so *cr* 1 June 1774; *b* 10 April 1744; inherited as a boy the estates of his kinsman Alderman Sir William Smith, of London and Sydling St Nicholas, Dorset; FRS, Hon DCL, Sheriff Dorset 1772; *m* 1st 18 Feb 1768 Elizabeth (*d* 13 Feb 1796), dau and heiress of Robert Curtis, of Wiltsthorpe, Lincs, by Elizabeth, sis and coheir of Mathew Wyldbore, MP, of Peterborough; *m* 2nd Anna Eleonora, est dau of Thomas Morland, of Court Lodge, Kent, and *d* 13 Nov 1807, having had no issue by her but leaving by his 1st w, with two daus (Elizabeth, *d* unm 6 Nov 1811; Amelia, *m* Hon Richard George Quin (see DUNRAVEN and MOUNT-EARL, E) and *d* 18 May 1845):

Sir John Wyldbore Smith, 2nd Bt, of Sydling St Nicholas and The Down House, Blandford; *b* 19 May 1770; Sheriff Dorset 1814; *m* 13 May 1797 Elizabeth Anne (*d* 27 Feb 1844 aged 77), 2nd dau and coheir of Rev James Marriott, DCL, of Horsmonden, Kent, and *d* 29 Feb 1852, having had:

1 **Sir John James Smith, 3rd Bt**; *b* 10 April 1800; *m* 11 Nov 1828 Frances (*d* 1 June 1895 aged 92), dau of John Frederick Pinney, of Somerton Erleigh, and *dsp* 3 Sept 1862
2 WILLIAM (Sir), **4th Bt**
3 George Roxburgh; *b* 15 Oct 1804; *d* 24 May 1805
4 Henry Curtis (Rev); *b* 25 Jan 1806; Rector Rushton, Dorset; *m* 25 Oct 1832 Elizabeth (*m* 2nd 6 Dec 1846 Robert Parry Nisbett, of Southbroome, Wilts), only surv dau of Edward Green, of Hinxton Hall, Cambs, and *d* 19 Dec 1834
5 Reginald Southwell (Rev); *b* 18 Aug 1809; Rector W Stafford, Dorset, Canon Salisbury; *m* 25 Feb 1836 Emily Genevieve (*d* 1877), dau of Henry Hanson Simpson, of Bitterne Manor House, Hants, and *d* 28 Dec 1895, leaving, with other issue:
  (1) Henry John; *b* 11 Jan 1838; *m* 20 Jan 1874 his yr bro's sis-in-law Alice Bertha, 5th dau of Rev Edmund Dawe Wickham, Vicar Holmwood, Surrey, and *dsp* 10 Nov 1879
  (2) Reginald Bosworth, JP Dorset; *b* 28 June 1839; assist master Harrow, Fell Trin Coll Oxford; *m* 9 Aug 1864 Flora (*d* 6 March 1927), 4th dau of Rev Edmund Dawe Wickham, and *d* 17 Oct 1908, having had:
    1a Gerard Hugh Bosworth; *b* 28 April 1868; *m* 1893 Olive, dau of B Yates, and *d* 1940, having had:
      1b +Reginald Claude Bosworth; *b* 10 April 1899; *m* 1929 *Evelyn Whittington, of Panama City, Fla., and has:
        1c +Reginald Claude; *b* 1930
        2c +Wayne Edward; *b* 1932
        3c James Lee; *b* 1939
        1c *Evelyn Joan; *b* 1935
        2c *Geraldine; *b* 1942
      1b Flora Bosworth; *b* 1893; *d* 1896
      2b *Ellinor Joan Bosworth; *b* 2 March 1896
      3b *Vera Bosworth; *b* 18 Oct 1904; *m* 1st 1921 (*divorce* 1923) Manuel M Paula and has issue; *m* 2nd 1925 Daniel Joseph Keene and has further issue
      4b *Bertha Bosworth; *b* 30 April 1908; *m* 1926 Roy Bronson and has issue
    2a Alan Wyldbore Bosworth; *b* 13 April 1870; Lt RN; *m* 1899 Mary, widow of Dr F F Brown, LLD, and dau of Maurice Kennedy, and *dsp* 18 Sept 1901
    3a Reginald Montagu Bosworth, CBE (1929); *b* 23 Jan 1872; Govt Sec Basutoland (ret 1930); *m* 1st 1905 Agnes Val (accidentally *k* 4 May 1915), dau of G Val Davies, and had:
      1b Kathleen Flora Bosworth; *b* 22 Dec 1907; *m* 1932 Frederick Herbert Yoxall Bamford, stockbroker, and had:
        1c *Alan Peter; *b* 19 March 1936
        1c *Sally Anne; *b* 16 Nov 1937; *m* 27 Feb 1960 *Ian Wilson Dixon, mining engr, and has:
          1d *Mark Christopher; *b* 8 Dec 1961
          2d *Colin Bruce; *b* 12 March 1967
    2b *Daphne Evangeline Bosworth [Mrs John Cottrell, Red Cross Home, 302 Main Rd, Walmer 6070, Port Elizabeth, CP, S Africa]; *b* 4 Sept 1909; BA 1928; *m* 1932 John Awdry Cottrell, OBE, Dir African Educn N Rhodesia 1948–58, and has:
      1c *Christopher Bosworth [Christopher Cottrell Esq, Transvaal Museum, PO Box 413, Pretoria 0001, S Africa]; *b* 26 Sept 1934; *educ* Rhodes U (BSc 1954) and Queens' Coll Cambridge; Jr Research Fell Churchill Coll Cambridge 1960–61, Research Fell U Coll Rhodesia and Nyasaland 1961, Prof Zoology U of Zimbabwe 1980–86, Head Curator Lepidoptera Transvaal Museum 1986–; *m* 1962 *Meriol Lesley, dau of Col L N Millard, of Taunton, Somerset, and has:
        1d *John Gray; *b* 27 Feb 1964
        2d *Christopher Noel; *b* Dec 1966
      2c *Richard Gray [Richard Cottrell Esq, PO Box 2356, Johannesburg, S Africa]; *b* 26 Nov 1935; CA 1956, ptnr Cooper & Lybrand Johannesburg; *m* 1971 *Moya Ann, dau of George R English, of Rochford, Essex, and has:
        1d *Edward Christopher; *b* 1974

2d *Peter Richard; b 1975

3c *Gilbert Reginald James [Gilbert Cottrell Esq, The Corporate Consulting Gp (Pty) Ltd, 604 Boland Bank Building, Lower Burg St, Cape Town, S Africa]; b 28 Nov 1944; educ Falcon Coll Rhodesia, Queens' Coll Cambridge (BA) and Columbia U New York (MBA); late mktg planning analyst Internat Paper Co New York; m 1971 *Phoebe Madelaire, dau of Dr Tage Madelaire Nielsen, of New London, Conn., and has:

    1d *Ariel Daphne; b 1974

    2d *Miranda Claire; b 1977

3b *Ursula Gwendolin Bosworth [Mrs William Scott, 21 2nd Ave, Linden, Johannesburg 2195, S Africa]; b 6 April 1911; m 1st 1934 (divorce 1947) Arnold Lingen Watson, slr, and has:

    1c *Toni Elaine [Mrs Jeremy Frere, 21 2nd Ave, Linden, Johannesburg 2195, S Africa]; b 26 March 1936; m 18 May 1957 *Maj Jeremy Alexander Keble White Frere, 1st Roy Anglian Regt, yr s of Brig Jasper Gray Frere, DSO, OBE, MC, and has:

        1d *Martin Adrian; b 26 Feb 1958; educ Witwatersrand U (BSc); m 1987 *Anabel, dau of Patrick Warren-Gash, of Worthing, Sussex

3b (cont.) Mrs Ursula Watson m 2nd 1947 William Patrick Temple Scott (d 1971)

3a (cont.) Reginald Smith m 2nd 1916 Kate Evelyn, dau of Frederick Charles Pardoe Radclyffe, of Birmingham, and d 18 Oct 1944, having by her had:

1b Reginald Bosworth; b 7 July 1917; LLB, attorney E London, S Africa, Trooper 6th S African Armoured Div WW II 1942–45; m 11 Dec 1965 *Helen Margaret, dau of Ernest R Stidworthy, of E London, and d 1996

2b Alan Bosworth; b 13 May 1919; CA (SA), FSAA, Gunner S African Artillery WW II; m 2 April 1949 *Helen Noble, dau of John Noble Mackenzie, of Johannesburg, and d 6 Nov 1996, leaving:

    1c +Michael John Bosworth; b 21 April 1951; BA, Bcom, CA S Africa; m 1st 1982 (divorce 1985) Colleen May Hauptfleisch; m 2nd 1985 *Elizabeth Ann Ringstead and by her has:

        1d *Matthew Edward; b 1988

    1c *Pamela Anne Bosworth [Mrs Keith Butler-Wheelhouse, The Orchard, Sudbury Hill, Harrow on the Hill, Middx HA1 3NA]; b 11 Aug 1953; BA; m 1973 *Keith Oliver Butler-Wheelhouse and has:

        1d *Duncan; b 1981

        2d *Andrew; b 1985

4a Bertrand Nigel Bosworth; b 20 June 1873; educ Harrow and Magdalen Coll Oxford (BA 1897); ICS; m 3 June 1912 (divorce 1932) Mary Constance (d 21 Sept 1961 aged 87), yst dau of David Inches Bett, of New Hall, Forfarshire, and d 19 Feb 1947, leaving:

1b *Mary Nigella; b 26 Nov 1913; m 6 Aug 1946 (divorce 1959) Peter de Lande Long, FRICS, FLAS, only s of Lt-Col Albert de Lande Long, DSO, DL, of Lisle Court, Wootton Bridge, IoW, and has:

    1c *Ian Bartholomew de Lande; b 10 March 1949; educ Winchester and York U; m 1970 *Marjorie, dau of Dr Hamilton, of Dublin

    2c *Jonathan de Lande; b 8 Feb 1951; educ Winchester and London U; ACA; m 1978 *Marianne Skuzinski

    3c *Peter Graeme de Lande; b 4 Nov 1952; educ Winchester and Trin Coll Cambridge; MICE

2b *Janet Wickham [Mrs Claude Nicol, 40 Ferncroft Ave, London NW3]; b 23 Aug 1916; m 1939 *Col Claude Scott Nicol, TD, MD, FRCP, RAMC (TA), and has:

    1c *Alasdair Gordon; b 25 Oct 1944; m 1974 *Julie Mayston Collings, of Melbourne, Australia, and has:

        1d *Stuart; b 1977

    1c *Judy [Mrs John Rochfort, White Ways, Thornford Rd, Headley, Newbury, Berks]; b 19 Jan 1943; m 25 June 1966 *John Diggory de Bourbel Rochfort and has:

        1d *Christopher Michael de Bourbel; b 5 Aug 1969

        2d *Jeremy; b 1971

        3d *James; b 1974

    2c *Melany; b 3 Dec 1946; m 1973 *Piers Hayward Hughes and has:

        1d *Robert; b 1976

        2d Katherine Melany; b 1974

5a Mervyn Henry Bosworth; b July 1878; m 1st 1914 (divorce 1919) Sophie, dau of John Warmington, of Ninnes, Lelant, Cornwall; m 2nd 1920 (divorce 1926) Mary Annette Morcom, of Johannesburg, and by her had:

1b Anthony Mervyn Bosworth; b 17 Sept 1925; m 10 Jan 1951 *Jean Rosemary [Mrs Anthony Smith, Blesbok Ridge, PO Box 132, Nottingham Rd, Kwa Zulu, Natal, S Africa 3280], dau of A Peerman, of Johannesburg, and d 30 Nov 1992, leaving:

    1c +Mervyn Nigel Bosworth; b 9 Feb 1957; educ Natal U (BSc Civ Engrg 1981); m 14 July 1984 *Maryna Elizabeth van Niekerk and has:

        1d *Sadie Elizabeth; b 14 April 1987

        2d *Jessica Danielle; b 19 Sept 1989

        3d *Antonia Emma; b 25 Aug 1997

    1c *Gwen Bridget [Mrs Ian Watson, Blesbok Ridge, PO Box 132, Nottingham, Kwa Zulu, Natal, S Africa 3280]; b 21 Aug 1953; m 7 March 1981 *Ian Watson and has:

        1d *Cameron Nicholas; b 9 May 1983

        2d *Oliver Hylton; b 31 Dec 1986

5a (cont.) Mervyn Smith m 3rd 31 Dec 1927 *Sarah Aletta, est dau of H W Fourie, of Johannesburg, and d 2 Feb 1950

6a Nevil Digby Bosworth, CB (1946); b 17 Feb 1886; educ Harrow and Pembroke Coll Cambridge (BA 1907); Priv Sec to Ld Pres Cncl and Pres Bd Educn 1916, Chm Exec Br Cncl Welfare Spastics, U-Sec Min Educn; m 15 July 1913 Gladys (d 29 March 1965), dau of John Francis Wood, of Uffculme, and d 17 June 1964, having had:

1b John Bosworth; b 3 Feb 1918; d 31 Aug 1923

2b Michael Digby Bosworth; b 14 Nov 1920; educ Harrow and Trin Coll Oxford (BA 1941); Lt RA WW II; ka Burma 10 March 1945

3b +Richard Nevil BOSWORTH later BOSWORTH-SMITH (deed poll 1969) [Richard Bosworth-Smith Esq, 7 Hillside Rd, Northwood, Middx]; b 26 Oct 1926; educ Harrow and Balliol Coll Oxford (BA 1950, MA 1952); m 3 Sept 1960 *Anne, er dau of John Ree, of Pinner, Middx, and has:

    1c +Nevil John Bosworth; b 1 Sept 1961

    1c *Mary Margaret Bosworth; b 24 Oct 1964

1b Bridget Laura Bosworth; b 2 July 1915; educ St Felix and St Hugh's Coll Oxford (BA 1936); m 1st 23 April 1938 (divorce 1951) James Guy Bramwell, yr s of Capt Guy Bramwell, Cameronians, and had:

    1c *Crispin John SMITH later SPEAIGHT (deed poll 1957); b 25 Oct 1945; educ Ampleforth; ACA 1969

    1c *Teresa Clare; b 18 June 1939; m 1st 15 July 1961 (divorce 1966) Hon Alexander Davison, only s of 2nd Baron Broughshane (qv), and has issue; m 2nd 22 Sept 1967 *Alexander Newman, s of Michael Newman, of Exmouth

1b (cont.) Mrs Bridget Bramwell m 2nd 28 May 1951 Robert William Speaight, CBE, FRSL, est s of Frederick William Speaight, of Goodrich House, Hatfield, Herts

1a Ellinor Flora Bosworth; m 1st 1894 Sir Harry Langhorne Thompson, KCMG (d 28 April 1902); m 2nd 25 Sept 1907 Sir Edward Ion Beresford Grogan, 2nd Bt, CMG, DSO (d 11 July 1927; see 1927 edn), and dsp 10 May 1948

2a Emily Winifred Bosworth; m 7 Oct 1907 Dr August Gustav Heisler and d 13 May 1919, leaving issue

3a Lorna Lawrence Bosworth; m 27 Feb 1906 Edwin Ellen Goldmann, Prof Surgery Freiburg, and d 29 Sept 1919, leaving issue. He d 12 Aug 1913

4a Bertha Joan Bosworth; m 1st 9 Aug 1911 Lt-Col Charles Sinclair Shephard, DSO (d 31 Dec 1930), s of John Shephard, of Castle Hill, Surrey; m 2nd 9 Jan 1939 Capt Royal Cochrane, MGC, s of W J Cochrane, of Belfast. He d 1951

(3) Walter William Mariott, CBE (1918); b 21 Dec 1846; Col RA; m 6 Aug 1874 Alice Mary (d 1 Aug 1932), 2nd dau of John H Ley, of Trehill, Devon, and d 1944, leaving:

1a Harry Reginald Walter Marriott (Sir), KCB (1942), CBE (1928), DSO (1916), JP, DL Dorset 1938; b 1 Aug 1875; educ Repton (Govr 1935); Nile Expdn 1898, Boer War 1900–02 (despatches), WW I (twice wounded, despatches), Dep Dir Armaments India 1919–23 (later Dir Artillery), ADC to HM GEORGE V 1930–32, Pres Ordnance Ctee (ret 1934), Chm Dorset TAA 1936–43, Maj-Gen RA; m 12 Sept 1906 Dorothy Herbert, dau of H Herbert Smith, JP, of Buckhill, Calne, Wilts, and dsp 3 Nov 1955

1a Alice Emily Marriott; m 1st 1 Sept 1904 Lt-Col Francis William Egerton (see GREY EGERTON, Bt); m 2nd 30 April 1929 George Henry Blore, est s of Rev Canon G J Blore, DD, and d 5 April 1958

2a Henrietta Rose Marriott; m 1st 21 April 1903 (divorce 1908) Lt-Col Frederick John Stewart Cleeve, RFA (d 1916), s of Col S A Cleeve; m 2nd 1909 Lt-Col Philip Walter Beresford Henning, DSO, RA, and d 19 Oct 1961, leaving issue. He d 7 April 1962

3a Constance Gertrude Marriott; m 1 Dec 1921 Lt-Col John Whinfield Parrington, RFA, est s of M W Parrington, of Carley Lodge, Sunderland, and had issue. He d 10 June 1961

4a Vera Rose Marriott; b 22 Oct 1887; m 20 Nov 1912 Brig Geoffrey Cathcart Gowlland, RE, s of Richard Gowlland, and had issue

(4) Edward Floyer Noel (Rev); b 9 Dec 1850; Vicar St Mary Tottenham; d unm 14 March 1908

(1) Emily Anne; m 8 July 1863 Rev John S Thomas and d 1879

(2) Evangeline Frances; d unm 1945

(3) Caroline Blanche; m 21 Oct 1884 Col Caledon Philip Egerton and d 28 March 1912, leaving issue (see GREY EGERTON, Bt)

6 Francis (Rev); b 28 Dec 1810; educ Winchester and Balliol Coll Oxford (MA); Rector Tarrant Rawston and Tarrant Rushton, Dorset; m 22 Nov 1838 Mary Isabella (d 1878), dau of Capt Richard Bogue, RHA, and d 29 Dec 1851, leaving:

(1) (Francis) Alfred (Rev); b 16 Oct 1841; Rector Tarrant Rushton; m 14 Jan 1868 Elinor Mary Frances (d 28 March 1913), yst dau of Rev William Moss King, Rector Long Crichel, Dorset, and d 15 July 1877, leaving:

1a Hugh Francis Wyldbore SMITH later WYLDBORE-SMITH (roy licence 1903), of Broadstone, Dorset; b 15 Feb 1869; Capt RN; m 19 Nov 1903 Kate Beatrice (d 16 Jan 1959), dau of William Henry Deane, JP, DL, of Fareham House, Hants, and d 8 May 1919, leaving:

1b Hugh Deane; b 15 Feb 1907; Lt-Cdr RN, Fleet Signals and Wireless Offr E Indies Station, WW II; m 5 June 1937 *Rachel Caroline Lucy [Mrs Hugh Wyldbore-Smith, The White House, Husborne Crawley, Beds], er dau of Rev Edward Yarde Orlebar, of Crawley Park, Bletchley, Bucks, and was kas in HMS Hood 24 May 1941, leaving:

    1c +Nicolas Hugh [Nicolas Wyldbore-Smith Esq, The Courtiers, Clifton Hampden, Oxon]; b 23 May 1938; educ Wellington and St James's Md.; dir Ind Coope Ltd (ret 1988), Clerk Girdlers' Co 1991–95; m 18 July 1964 *Gillian Mary, yr dau of Leslie Boland Carman, of Fareham, Hants, and has:

        1d +Alexander Hugh Nicolas; b 9 Aug 1969; educ Dragon Sch Oxford, Bryanston and Oxford Brooks U (BSc)

        2d +James William; b 1971; educ Dragon Sch Oxford, Radley, Bristol U (BSc) and City U

    2c Piers; b 22 July 1939; educ Eton, New Coll Oxford and London U (BA); schoolmaster; d 28 Dec 1987

2b Alfred Reginald; b 16 July 1910; d 13 April 1911

3b John Henry; b 11 Sept 1916; educ Charterhouse; Lt RNVR WW II, memb London Stock Exchange; m 15 April 1939 Robina (d 1993), dau of Capt Francis Welsford Ward, of Bosloe, Cornwall, and d 4 May 1982, leaving:

    1c +William Francis [William Wyldbore-Smith Esq, Bremhill Manor, Calne, Wilts]; b 15 Jan 1948; educ Marlborough; m 27 Dec 1974 *Mrs

Prisca Faith Jenney, er dau of Rev Peter Nourse, of Eardisland, Herefs, and has:

   1d *Philippa; b 15 April 1977

1c *Robina Ann; b 3 Oct 1943; m 25 June 1977 *(Richard Robert) Bindon Plowman, est s of R G Plowman, of Boulter End, Bucks, and has:

   1d *Andrew John Napier; b 11 Jan 1979

   1d *Felicity Frances Robina; b 1980

1c *Susan Elizabeth; b 15 Aug 1950

1b Kathleen Elinor; m 3 June 1936 Algernon Spencer (d 1965), yst s of William Stacey Spencer, of The Mount, Stansted, Essex, and had:

   1c *Charles Peter [Charles Spencer Esq, 18 Kiaat St, Rand Park Ridge Ext 1, Randburg 2194, S Africa]; b 1937; m 19– *Sharpy — and has issue

   2c *David Wyldbore [David Spencer Esq, PO Box 328, Bergulei, 2012, Johannesburg, S Africa]; b 1939; m 1st 19– Cynthia Raulo and has issue; m 2nd 19– *Linda — and has further issue

   3c *Hugh Mark [Hugh Spencer Esq, 38 Kildare Ave, Park View, Johannesburg, S Africa]; b 1941

   4c *Simon Francis [Simon Spencer Esq, PO Box 2880, North Cliff, 2115 Johannesburg, S Africa]; b 1946

   5c *Christopher Audley [Christopher Spencer Esq, PO Box 1277, Fonteinbleu, 2032 Johannesburg, S Africa]; b 1948; m 19– *Moira — and has issue

2a William Reginald Wyldbore (Rev); b 26 March 1874; educ Pembroke Coll Cambridge (MA); Vicar Coleshill, Warwicks, and Grindon, Co Durham, Domestic Chaplain to Marquess of Londonderry; m 20 June 1905 Dorothy (d 13 June 1969 aged 92), dau of George Green, of Watford, and d 26 June 1943, leaving:

   1b (Reginald) Anthony Wyldbore, JP (Warwicks 1962); b 22 May 1909; educ Shrewsbury and Pembroke Coll Cambridge (BA); Staff of Dir Naval Armaments WW II and of Birmingham U, memb Meriden RDC; m 30 Sept 1933 Honor Christine Dyott (d 1984), yr dau of George Dyott Willmot, and d 1987, leaving:

      1c +Michael Anthony Wyldbore SMITH later WYLDBORE-SMITH (deed poll 1969) [Michael Wyldbore-Smith Esq, Moat Cottage, Berkswell, W Midlands CV7 7BX]; b 6 Sept 1944; educ Cheltenham; m 24 June 1967 *Sheila Margaret, dau of Ewart Charles Harold Organ, OBE, of Kenilworth, Warwicks, and has:

         1d *Sarah; b 5 July 1969

         2d *Nicola; b 27 April 1971

         3d *Claire; b 26 April 1977

2b +(Francis) Brian Wyldbore SMITH later WYLDBORE-SMITH (deed poll June 1966) (Sir), CB (1965), DSO (1943), OBE (1945) [Sir Brian Wyldbore-Smith CB DSO OBE, Grantham House, Grantham, Lincs NG31 6SS]; b 10 July 1913; educ Wellington and RMA Woolwich; 15th/19th King's Roy Hus WW II, cmded 15th/19th Hus 1954, Malaya 1955 (despatches), Staff Coll Camberley 1957–58, Ch Staff to C-in-C Far East 1962–64, GOC 44th Home Counties Div and Dep Constable Dover Castle 1965–68, ret as Maj-Gen 1968, ktd 1980; m 1 April 1944 *Hon Molly Angela Cayzer, yr dau of 1st Baron Rotherwick (qv), and has:

   1c +(Brian) Robin; b 4 Sept 1957; educ Eton

   1c *Carolyn Molly; b 11 Dec 1944; m 2 Nov 1968 *Harry O Ditson, s of L Ditson, of New York, and has:

      1d *Sam Lennie; b 1984

      1d *Lucy Rebecca; b 1975

      2d *Melissa Martha; b 1978

   2c *Angela Maureen [Mrs Barrie Giffard-Taylor, Barnbridge Farm, E Tytherton, Wilts]; b 24 Feb 1947; m 1975 *Barrie Giffard-Taylor, s of William Taylor, of Beauport House, Pinkney's Green, Berks, and has:

      1d *James William; b 1982

      1d *Jemima Alice; b 1 Aug 1977

      2d *Emily Victoria; b 1979

   3c *Penelope Ann; b 2 May 1948; m 18 Oct 1973 *James Emerson Herdman, only s of John Patrick Herdman, of Carricklee House, Strabane, Co Tyrone, and has:

      1d *Emerson John; b 1979

      1d *Katherine Louise; b 1977

   4c Nicola Jane; b 22 Aug 1952; d 30 June 1996

3a Edmund Charles Wyldbore (Sir); b 15 Jan 1877; FSS, V-Consul Tangier 1900, Chargé d'Affaires 1905, V-Consul Canea Crete 1907–10, Consul-Gen 1908–10, seconded to Exhibition Branch BOT 1910, Dir Internat Commn Supplies for Allies 1914–17, Assist-Sec BOT 1917, Dir Suez Canal Co 1919, V-Pres Compagnie International des Wagons-Lits, Fedn Br Industs, Chm Thomas Cook & Son, ktd 1916, Grand Cordon Order St Anne Russia, Grand Offr Order Crown Italy and Romania, Ofcr Legn Hon, Cdr Orders Leopold Belgium and George I Greece, 3rd Cl Order Sacred Treasure Japan and Order St Sava Serbia; m 14 Oct 1901 Evadne Maude (d 25 April 1960), dau of John Talbot Kellett (see KELLETT, Bt), and d 18 Oct 1938, leaving:

   1b Jocelin Evadne; m 11 Feb 1929 Lt-Col Sir John Duckett Floyd, 6th Bt (qv), and d 17 Jan 1976, leaving issue

   2b Monica Elizabeth; m 1st 28 April 1930 Capt Evan Llewellyn Gibbs, Coldstream Gds (see ALDENHAM and HUNSDON OF HUNSDON, B), and had issue; m 2nd 24 Oct 1957 Lt-Col Walter Pearce-Serocold, DSO, TD, yr s of Col Oswald Pearce-Serocold, CMG, JP, DL, of Taplow Hill, Bucks, and d 8 July 1973

   1a Ursula Gertrude; d 20 June 1922

   2a Sybil Bertha; d unm 29 Sept 1934

(2) Edmund Hanson; b 13 April 1846; m 1870 Sophie Marcella Poole (d 1925) and d 1896, leaving

   1a Eleanor Fanny; m 1894 Rev Frank Benet Phillips, Rector Buckland, Herts, and had issue

(3) Arthur; Capt 1st Royals; d unm 1878

(1) Mary Anna Marriott; m 22 June 1859 Very Rev Philip Frank Eliot, KCVO, DD, Dean Windsor, 3rd s of William Eliot, DL, of Weymouth, and d 1881, leaving issue. He d 1 Nov 1917

(2) Julia Emily; d unm 1880

(3) Fanny Isabella; m 7 Aug 1866 Rev Cyril FitzRoy Wilson, Rector Stowlangtoft, Suffolk, and d 1886, leaving issue (see WILSON, B)

(4) Ella Henrietta; m 30 Jan 1873 Rev Hugh Bellamy, Chaplain RN, and d 19 Feb 1921, having had issue. He d 3 Nov 1904

(5) Gertrude Floyer; m 24 June 1879 16th Earl of Moray (qv) and d 15 March 1928

7 Edward Heathcote; b 18 May 1813; Maj 76th Regt; m 29 Jan 1839 Christina (d 1894), dau of William Mackintosh, of Geddes, and d 26 Nov 1870, having had, with other issue:

(1) Edward John Algernon; b 1840; Offr 97th Regt, formerly RN, served Sebastopol; d unm 20 Dec 1864

(2) William Henry Curtis; b 2 Sept 1843; Lt 104th Regt; m 28 May 1867 Annie (m 2nd Capt Mosley Mayne), dau of Rev A Wilkinson, and d 17 Aug 1872

(3) Amelius Morland; b 30 Jan 1845; 18th Hus, Assist Colonial Sec NZ; m 30 May 1877 Louisa (d 31 Dec 1942), dau of Henry Howorth, barrister, of Dunedin, and d 27 May 1929, leaving, with two sons (d unm):

   1a Christine Mary Louise; b 22 Sept 1880; m 13 Sept 1927 Charles Webb-Bowen

(4) Heathcote (Rev); b 19 Dec 1847; Vicar Kingweston, Somerset, then St Michael's, Princetown, Dartmoor; m 1st 1 May 1873 Clara Jane (d March 1898), yst dau of John Ross Soden, and had, with other issue:

   1a Clifford Edward SMITH later HEATHCOTE-SMITH (deed poll 1930) (Sir), KBE (1943), CMG (1936); b 26 March 1883; educ Pembroke Coll Cambridge; Levant Consular Service 1906 on, Consul-Gen Alexandria 1924–43, T/Cdr RNVR 1918–19, Order Redeemer Greece; m 27 March 1909 Helene (d 28 March 1967), dau of John R Spiegelthal, and d 3 Jan 1963, leaving:

      1b +Clifford Bertram Bruce, CBE (1963) [Clifford Heathcote-Smith Esq, 4 Britts Farm Rd, Buxted, E Sussex]; b 2 Sept 1912; educ Malvern and Pembroke Coll Cambridge; Dip Serv: Dep HC Madras 1965; Actg Sr Clerk H of C; m 13 April 1940 *Thelma Joyce, dau of Carl Victor Engström, of Tientsin, China, and has:

         1c +Charles Clifford Ralph; b 24 Jan 1949; educ Malvern

         2c +Max Christopher; b 16 Dec 1950; educ Malvern; m 1982 *Drusilla Mary Derrick

      1b Jocelyn Elaine Laura; m 28 Aug 1939 Capt Sir Anthony Henry Thorold, 15th Bt, OBE, DSC, RN (qv), and d 1993, leaving issue

      2b *Elaine Mary Elisabeth [Mrs Roger Wellby, 17 Honeybanks, Wendover, Bucks HP22 6NA]; m 18 April 1936 R-Adml Roger Stanley Wellby, CB, DSO, DL, s of Dr Stanley Wellby, and has:

         1c *Michael Anthony; b 21 Oct 1939; educ Nautical Coll Pangbourne and Melbourne U; m 15 Jan 1966 *Kate Frances, er dau of William Francis Willett Ram, of Berkhamsted, Herts, and has:

            1d *Anthony William; b 4 Dec 1969

            1d *Kate D'Esterre; b 26 Jan 1968

         2c *Christopher Mark; b 8 March 1943; educ Scotch Coll Melbourne, Berkhamsted and Ch Ch Oxford (MA); ACA; m 1982 *Barbara, dau of Frank Elston, of Liverpool, and has:

            1d *Peter Nicholas Elston; b 1986

            2d *Jack William Heathcote; b 1988

         3c *Peter Martin; b 9 Jan 1946; educ Scotch Coll Melbourne, Berkhamsted and Ch Ch Oxford; m 1988 *Helen Matson

   1a Frances Ethel Heathcote; b 1877; m 10 June 1904 Archibald Lestock Hales, yr s of Francis Richard Hales, of Catford

(4) (cont.) The Rev Heathcote Smith m 2nd 17 Oct 1899 Louisa Floyd (d 22 Dec 1956), dau of George White, of Gt Missenden, Bucks, and d 1914, having by her had:

   2a Cecil Roland Heathcote, MBE (1945); b 6 Oct 1901; Capt Intelligence Corps WW II, UK V-Consul Guayaquil, Ecuador, 1945–48

   2a Stephanie Cecilia Heathcote; b 8 Jan 1904

(1) Jane Elizabeth Anna

(2) Eleonora Frances; m 11 Oct 1865 Edward James Castle, KC, Recorder Bristol (d 27 April 1912) and had issue

1 Anne Eliza; b 11 May 1803; m 20 April 1826 Rev John Digby Wingfield and d 22 July 1859, having had issue. He d 24 Jan 1878

2 Lydia Bosworth; b 6 March 1808; m Henry Lees, MD, and d 10 Aug 1876

The 3rd Bt's bro,

Rev Sir WILLIAM MARRIOTT SMITH later SMITH-MARRIOTT (roy licence 15 Feb 1811), 4th Bt; b 31 Aug 1801; Rector and Patron Horsmonden, Kent; m 1st 29 Dec 1825 Julia Elizabeth (d 11 March 1842), 4th dau of Thomas Law Hodges, of Hemsted, Kent; m 2nd 11 April 1844 Frances (dsp 30 Sept 1900), dau of Robert Radclyffe, of Foxdenton, and d 4 Oct 1864, leaving by his 1st w:

   1 Sir William Henry Marriott Smith-Marriott, 5th Bt, JP Dorset, of The Down House; b 7 Aug 1835; High Sheriff Dorset 1875; m 12 Dec 1868 Elizabeth Dorothy (d 25 March 1904), dau of Hon Richard Cavendish (see WATERPARK, B), and d 30 Nov 1924, leaving:

      (1) Sir William John Smith-Marriott, 6th Bt, JP Dorset; b 6 Nov 1870; d unm 24 May 1941

      (2) Sir John Richard Wyldbore Smith-Marriott, 7th Bt; b 7 Dec 1875; d unm 5 Feb 1942

      (1) Dorothea Anna; d unm 26 March 1949

      (2) Mabel Alice, of The Manor House, Blandford St Mary, Dorset; m 25 Jan 1910 Maj Arthur Hamilton Cooper, DL (d 25 May 1973), 2nd s of Sir William Charles Cooper, 3rd Bt, of Woollahra, and d 20 June 1973, leaving issue

   2 John Bosworth; b 13 Oct 1837; m 17 July 1862 Julia Frances (d 15 Feb 1910), 2nd dau of Charles James Radclyffe, of Foxdenton Hall, Lancs, and Hyde, Dorset, and d 18 Feb 1900, leaving:

(1) **Sir William Smith-Marriott, 8th Bt**; *b* 5 Aug 1865; *educ* Ch Ch Oxford (MA); barrister; *m* 1st 19 April 1887 Charlotte Marianne (*d* 23 March 1910), est dau of John Francis Austen, of Capel Manor, Horsmonden, Kent (*see* BLG), and had:

  1a Mary Charlotte; *m* 1st 29 Nov 1913 Heathfield Dodgson and had issue; *m* 2nd 27 Jan 1927 Allan Hugh Harrison (*d* 1943)

(1) (cont.) **Sir William** *m* 2nd 5 Dec 1911 Elinor Louisa (Nora) (*d* 19 June 1941), widow of Harry William Stronge (*see* STRONGE, Bt) and dau of Ludlow Eustace Maude (*see* HAWARDEN, V), and *d* 21 Dec 1943, leaving by her:

  2a *Rosemary Kathleen; *b* 10 Aug 1916; *m* 16 Sept 1944 Henry Everett, er s of Henry B Everett (*see* GALLOWAY, E), and has:

    1b *William Marriott [William Everett Esq, Roughfield Farm, Hurst Green, Sussex TN19 7QY]; *b* 1946; ARICS, ABIAC, ACIArb; *m* 1976 *Caroline Dawn Colley and has:

      1c *George Henry Arthur; *b* 1978

      1c *Cecilia Hermione Rosemary; *b* 1985

    1b *Barbara Rosemary [Mrs John Crowell, 22 All Farthing Lane, London SW18]; *b* 1948; *m* 1st 1968 Timothy James Gerard Dyas; *m* 2nd 1972 John Derek Hall; *m* 3rd 1980 *John Lawrence Crowell

    2b *Helen Rosalind [Mrs Jonathan Barnes, 7 Priory Walk, London SW10]; *b* 1954; *m* 1984 *Jonathan David Batrick Barnes

(2) Charles Ernest; *b* 2 April 1872; *educ* Trin Coll Cambridge (BA); *m* 2 June 1900 (*divorce* 1915) his cousin Frances Julia Elizabeth (*d* 14 Sept 1955), dau of Rev Hugh F Smith-Marriott (*see below*), and *d* 31 Dec 1919, leaving:

  1a Ernest John Bosworth; *b* 8 March 1902; *d* 3 Aug 1929 in a plane crash

(1) Hilda Maria; *m* 1st 1887 Rev William Nepean Peareth (*d* 1901), of Lidwells, Kent, and had issue; *m* 2nd 1904 Rev Augustus William Frederick Theodore de Spallier and *d* 22 May 1937. He *d* 12 Feb 1937

3 Hugh Forbes (Rev), JP Kent; *b* 10 Oct 1840; educ Trin Coll Cambridge (MA); Rector Horsmonden; *m* 17 Nov 1864 Frances Catherine Mary (*d* 4 Dec 1920), 2nd dau of Adml Hon George Cavendish (*see* WATERPARK, B), and *d* 14 Aug 1922, leaving:

  (1) **Rev Sir Hugh Randolph Cavendish Smith-Marriott, 9th Bt**; *b* 4 Oct 1868; *educ* Magdalene Coll Cambridge (BA); Rector Horsmonden 1922–44; *d* unm 21 March 1944

  (2) George Rudolph Wyldbore; *b* 6 Dec 1869; *m* 1897 Dorothy Magdalene, dau of Rev John Parry, Vicar Llanarmon, and *d* 20 Dec 1926, having had:

    1a Hugh John Wyldbore; *b* 1898

    2a **Sir Ralph George Cavendish Smith-Marriott, 10th Bt**; *b* 16 Dec 1900; *educ* Cranleigh; *m* 1st 1924 Phyllis Elizabeth (*d* 24 Sept 1932), dau of Richard Kemp, Govr Bristol Prison, and had:

      1b Sir HUGH CAVENDISH SMITH-MARRIOTT, **11th and present Bt**

      2b +PETER FRANCIS [The Paddock, 88 Maiden Hall, Highnam, Glos]; *b* 14 Feb 1927; heir presumptive; *m* 28 Oct 1961 *Jean Graham Martin, only dau of James Sorley Ritchie, of Salisbury, S Rhodesia, and has:

        1c +Martin Ralph; *b* 30 Dec 1962

        2c +Neil Hugh; *b* 22 March 1964

        3c +Ian Peter; *b* 22 March 1967

        4c +Mark Nicholas; *b* 1974

        5c +Paul Graham (twin); *b* 1974

      1b *Doris Mary [Mrs Alexander MacCaig, 11 Shipley Road, Westbury-on-Trym, Bristol BS9 3HR]; *b* 9 Feb 1929; *m* 24 Aug 1957 *Alexander Stewart MacCaig, est s of Alexander Neilson MacCaig, of Hale, Cheshire, and has:

        1c *Helen Mary; *b* 9 Oct 1958; *m* 1985 *John Michael Burton and has:

          1d *Thomas Michael; *b* 1989

          2d *Andrew Jack; *b* 1992

          1d *Kathryn Anne; *b* 1986

        2c Susan Jane; *b* 23 Jan 1961; *m* 1988 *Dr David Richardson and *d* 4 June 1996, leaving:

          1d *Polly Francesca; *b* 1991

          2d *Maisie Jane; *b* 1994

        3c *Anne Elizabeth; *b* 29 Sept 1964

    2a (cont.) **Sir Ralph** *m* 2nd 28 Oct 1933 Doris Mary (*d* 27 Sept 1951), er dau of R L C Morrison, of Tenby, Dyfed; *m* 3rd 12 May 1966 *Barbara Mary [Dowager Lady Smith-Marriott, 28a Westover Rd, Westbury-on-Trym, Bristol], dau of G C Brown and widow of Lt J A Cantlay, DLI, and *d* 1987

    3a Francis Patrick Parry; *b* 1906; *m* 1932

(1) Frances Julia Elizabeth; *b* 11 July 1871; *m* 2 June 1900 (*divorce* 1915) her cousin Charles Ernest Smith-Marriott and had issue (*see above*)

1 Anna Rebecca; *m* 23 Sept 1852 Edward John Briscoe, of Riverdale, Killucan, Co Westmeath, and *d* 1935, having had issue. He *d* 1 May 1911

2 Catherine Twisden; *m* 30 July 1861 Rev Pierce Butler and *d* 3 Nov 1904, leaving issue (*see* CARRICK E)

3 Charlotte Lydia Peareth; *m* 18 May 1865 Rev Horace Meeres, Rector Bradwell, Glos, and *d* 31 Aug 1926, leaving issue. He *d* 5 July 1907

SMYTH

Arms: Ermine on a bend between two unicorn's heads erased az. three lozenges or. **Crest:** A demi bull rampant, issuing from a ducal coronet or, armed and horned or and gorged with a collar az., charged with three lozenges and rimmed or. **Motto:** *Nec timeo nec sperno* ('I neither fear mine enemy nor do I despise him'). **Creation:** Bt. (UK) 23 Jan 1956.

SIR TIMOTHY JOHN SMYTH, 2ND BT, of Teignmouth, Co Devon [Dr Sir Timothy Smyth Bt, PO Box 571, N Sydney, NSW 2059, Australia]; *b* 16 April 1953; *s* gf 1983; *educ* NSW U; MB, BS (1977); MBA (AGSM) 1985, LLB 1987, FRACMA 1985, Medical Administrator Prince Henry Hosp Sydney 1980–86, ch exec offr Sydney Health Serv 1986–88, gen manager St George Hosp Sydney 1988–91, ch exec offr Hunter Area Health Serv 1992–97, Dep DG NSW Health 1997–; *m* 1981 *Bernadette Mary, dau of Leo Askew, and has:

  1 +BRENDAN JULIAN; *b* 4 Oct 1981

  2 +Gerard Timothy; *b* 1988

  1 *Kathryn Mary; *b* 1983

  2 *Emma Louise; *b* 1985

Lineage: RICHARD SMYTH, of Myreshaw, Yorks; *b* 1594; *m* 1st Margaret Hodgson, of Bolton; *m* 2nd Lucretia Pearson (*d* 31 Jan 1688/9 aged 84), of Bradford, and *d* 1656, having by his 1st w had, with other issue:

JOHN SMYTH, of Myreshaw; *b* 1623; *m* Isabell (*d* 26 Sept 1711 age 83), dau of Randall Wood by Alice Margetson, sis of James Margetson, Archbp Armagh and Primate Ireland, and *d* 9 Oct 1685, having had, with other issue:

JOHN SMYTH, JP W R Yorks, of Heath, nr Wakefield, Yorks, an estate he bought 1709; *bapt* 27 Sept 1654; *m* 1st 11 Oct 1683 Hannah (*d* 28 Jan 1693), dau and heiress of Richard Harrison, of Wakefield; *m* 2nd Mary (*d* 22 April 1700), widow of John Mitchell and dau and heiress of William Wilton, of Stead Sike, Yorks; *m* 3rd 19 Sept 1708 Henrietta Catharine (*dsp* 1740), widow of John Batt, of Oakwell Hall, Yorks, and dau of William Metcalfe, of Northallerton and Sand Hutton, Yorks, and *d* 25 Dec 1729, having by his 1st w had a 2nd s:

JOHN SMYTH, JP W R Yorks, of Heath and Myreshaw; *b* 13 Sept 1715; *m* 6 May 1746 Bridget (*d* 17 Feb 1800), dau and sole heiress of Benjamin Foxley, of London, and *d* 10 April 1771, leaving:

JOHN SMYTH, PC; *b* 12 Feb 1748; a Ld Admlty and Treasury, Master of the Mint, MP Pontefract 25 years; *m* 4 June 1778 Lady Georgiana FitzRoy (*d* 10 Jan 1799), est dau of 3rd Duke of Grafton (*qv*), and *d* 12 Feb 1811, having had, with other issue:

JOHN HENRY SMYTH, of Heath Hall, Yorks; *b* 20 March 1780; MP Cambridge U; *m* 1st 25 July 1810 Sarah Caroline (*dsp* 29 May 1811), dau of Henry Ibbotson, of St Antony's Northumberland; *m* 2nd 16 April 1814 his cousin Lady Elizabeth Anne FitzRoy, 2nd dau of 4th Duke of Grafton, and *d* 20 Oct 1822, having had, with an er s (John George, JP, DL, of Heath Hall, *b* 5 Feb 1815, MP York, Col 2nd W York Militia, *m* 25 April 1837 Hon Diana Bosville-Macdonald, dau of 3rd Baron Macdonald (*qv*), and *d* 10 June 1859, having had four daus):

HENRY SMYTH, CB; *b* 5 April 1816; Maj-Gen, Legn Hon; *m* 28 June 1865 Rebecca Mary (*d* 7 Oct 1889), est dau of Thomas Peirce, and had:

WILLIAM JOHN SMYTH; *b* 2 May 1869; *educ* Balliol Coll Oxford (BA); ICS; *m* 25 Feb 1893 Lilian May (*d* 22 July 1956), dau of Capt Henry Clifford, RN, and *d* Burma, leaving:

  1 JOHN GEORGE (Sir), **1st Bt**

  2 Herbert Edward FitzRoy, MC (1915); *b* 12 Sept 1896; *educ* Repton and RMC Sandhurst; 2nd Lt Oxon and Bucks LI 1915; WW I Mesopotamia and N Russia, Lt-Col 1st Bn KOYLI 1939, Brig WW II France, Norway, Burma and Middle East (wounded twice); *m* 2 June 1938 *Peggy Warren, est dau of Col Guy Warren Meade, DSO, MC, and had:

    (1) *Anne Faith; *b* 10 July 1939; *m* 7 Jan 1961 Robert Edward Blois Johnson, s of William Blois Johnson, of Fords Hill, Bolney, Sussex, and has:

      1a *Fiona Jane Blois; *b* 24 Nov 1962

      2a *Clare Anne; *b* 2 Jan 1964

      3a *Rebecca Louise; *b* 30 Oct 1969

3 Henry Malcolm, OBE; *b* 1 Dec 1898; *educ* St Bees Sch, Pembroke Coll Oxford and RMC Quetta; 9th Gurkhas 1917, Capt 1922, Army student of Russian 1930–31, Russian Interpreter 1931, Shanghai Internat Police: Assist Commr 1932, Dep Commr 1938, Actg Commr 1941, MI6 1943–44, Lt-Col 1943, Berlin Mil Govt 1945–46, Special Police Corps Germany 1946–49; *d* unm 8 July 1963

The est s,

Sir John George Smyth, 1st Bt (UK), so *cr* 23 Jan 1956, VC (1915), MC (1920), PC (1962); *b* 24 Oct 1893; *educ* Repton, and RMC Sandhurst; 2nd Lt IA 1912, WW I (despatches, Order St George Russia): Senussi Campaign W Egypt 1915–16, Mohmand Expdn India 1916, Afghan War 1919, Waziristan Frontier Expdn 1919–20 (despatches), Mesopotamian Insurrection 1920–21 (despatches), NWF 1930 (despatches), Mohmand 1935 (despatches), Brevet Maj 1928, Brevet Lt-Col 1933, Col 1936, Instr Staff Coll Camberley 1931–34, Cmdt 45th Rattray's Sikhs 1936–39, WW II: GSO(1) 2nd London Div 1939–40, cmded 127 Inf Bde Flanders (despatches), Actg Maj-Gen 1941, raised 19th Div India, cmded 17th Div Burma, ret Nov 1942, Hon Brig 1943; mil correspondent Kemsley Newspapers 1943–44, *Daily Sketch* and *Sunday Times* 1945–46, tennis correspondent *Sunday Times* 1946–51, Comptroller Roy Alexandra and Albert Sch 1948–63, MP (C) Norwood 1950–66, Parly Sec Min Pensions 1951–53, Jt Parly Sec Min Pensions and NI 1953–55, Govr: Queen Mary's Hosp Roehampton 1956–62, Freeman City London, Liveryman Farriers' Co 1951 (Master 1961–62), author: *Defence is our Business* (1945), *Lawn Tennis* (1953), *The Game's the Same* (1955), *Burma Road* (play with Ian Hay) (1945), *Until the Morning* (play with Ian Hay) (1950), *Before the Dawn* (1957), *Paradise Island* (1958), *The Only Enemy* (autobiography, 1959), *Trouble in Paradise* (1959), *Ann Goes Hunting* (1960), *Sandhurst* (1961), *The Story of the Victoria Cross* (1962), *Beloved Cats* (1963), *Blue Magnolia* (1964), *Behind the Scenes at Wimbledon* (with Col Macaulay, 1965), *Ming* (1966), *The Rebellious Rani* (1966), *The Life of General Sir Lashmer Whistler* (1967), *The Story of the George Cross* (1968), *In This Sign Conquer* (1968), *The Will to Live* (1970), *The Valiant* (1970), and *The History of the Not Forgotten Association* (1970); *m* 1st 22 July 1920 (*divorce* 1940) Margaret, dau of Charles Lawrence Dundas (*see* ZETLAND, M); *m* 2nd 12 April 1940 Frances Mary Blair Read, only dau of Lt-Col Robert Alexander Chambers, OBE, IMS, and *d* 1983, leaving by his 1st w:

1 John Lawrence; *b* 6 Nov 1921; *educ* Ampleforth; Lt Queen's Roy Regt; *ka* Kohima 7 May 1944

2 Julian; *b* 16 Oct 1923; *educ* Ampleforth; T/Actg Lt RNVR WW II; *m* 9 July 1952 *Phyllis Philomena Mary [Mrs Julian Smyth, 22 Ina Gregory Court, Conder, ACT 2906, Australia], yst dau of John Francis Cannon, and *d* 29 April 1974, leaving:

(1) Sir TIMOTHY JOHN SMYTH, **2nd and present Bt**

(2) +Christopher Charles; *b* 26 June 1954

(3) +John George; *b* 7 April 1957

(4) +Simon Gerard; *b* 28 Sept 1961

(5) +Andrew; *b* 13 July 1964

(1) *Margaret Mary; *b* 11 May 1955

(2) *Clare Marie; *b* 30 March 1960

3 Robin; *b* 5 Dec 1926; *educ* Ampleforth and Trin Coll Oxford (BA 1951); Rifle Bde WW II 1944–45, Capt 1948; *m* 3 Jan 1961 *Joan Harrison [Mrs Robin Smyth, 4 rue Villehardouin, Paris 75003, France], dau of W J Williams, of Worthing, Sussex, and *d* 1992, leaving:

(1) +John Julian; *b* 23 Sept 1961

1*Jillian Margaret [Mrs David Firth, 98 Sussex Way, London N7]; *b* 23 April 1929; *educ* Convent of Sacred Heart Roehampton; *m* 20 July 1968 *David George Firth, s of Harold Firth

SNOWDON

Arms: Sa. on a chevron arg., between in chief two fleurs de lys and in base an eagle displayed or, four pallets gu. **Crest:** A stag statant gu., attired, collared and unguled or, between two arms embowed in armour, the hands ppr., each grasping a fleur de lys gold. **Supporters:** Dexter, a griffin; sinister, an eagle, each with wings elevated and addorsed or. **Motto:** *Anoddo duw anoddir* ('What God wills will be'). **Creation:** E. and V. (UK) 6 Oct 1961.

THE 1ST EARL OF SNOWDON and **Viscount Linley**, of Nymans, Co Sussex (Sir Antony Charles Robert Armstrong-Jones, GCVO (1969)) [The Rt Hon The Earl of Snowdon GCVO, 22 Launceston Place, London W8 5RL]; *b* 7 March 1930; *educ* Eton and Jesus Coll Cambridge (coxed winning U Boat-race crew 1950); joined

Staff Cncl Industl Design 1961 (consultant 1962–87), ed advsr *Design* magazine 1961–87, artistic advsr *Sunday Times* 1962–90, Constable Caernarvon Castle 1963–, designed Snowdon Aviary, London Zoo, TV film producer (*e.g., Don't Count the Candles* (1968); two Hollywood Emmy Awards and St George Prize Venice); memb: cncl Nat Fund Research Crippling Diseases, Prince of Wales Advsy Ctee Disability; Chm Working Party Integrating Disabled , photographer *Telegraph Magazine* 1990–; Pres: Contemporary Arts Soc Wales, Welsh Theatre Co, author: *London* (1958), *A View of Venice* (1972), *The Sack of Bath* (1972), *Inchcape Review* (1977), *Personal View* (1979), *Tasmania Essay* (1981), *Sittings* (1983), *Stills* (1984–87), *Israel, a First View* (1986), *My Wales* (with Viscount Tonypandy 1986), *Public Appearances 1987–91* (1991), *Wild Flowers* (1995), *Snowdon on Stage* (1996), *Wild Fruit* (1997); Liveryman Clothworkers' Co 1959, Hon Fell: Inst Br Photographers 1961, Manchester Coll Art and Design 1967 and Roy Photographic Soc GB 1968, Hon Dr Bradford 1989, Hon LLD Bath 1989, Hon DLitt Portsmouth 1994, RDI 1978, FCSD, FRSA, Sr Fell RCA 1986 and Provost 1995–, 1st Hon Pres ADAPT (Access for Disabled People to Arts Premises Today) 1995–; *m* 6 May 1960 (*divorce* 1978) HRH THE PRINCESS MARGARET ROSE (*see* ROYAL FAMILY) and has issue; *m* 2nd 13 Dec 1978 *Lucy Mary, only dau of Donald Brook Davies, of Enniskerry, Co Wicklow, and formerly w of Michael Lindsay-Hogg (*see* LINDSAY-HOGG, Bt), and by her has:

2 *Frances; *b* 17 July 1979

The 1st EARL has by *Melanie Jane, dau of Sir Patrick Desmond William Cable-Alexander, 6th Bt (*qv*):

2 *Jasper; *b* 30 April 1998

Lineage: JOHN RICHARD, of Ty Newydd, Llandecwyn, Merioneths; *b c* 1743; *m* 1st 15 May 1765 Jane Roberts, of Penbryn Isaf, Llandecwyn; *m* 2nd Margaret Owen and *d* by 23 July 1822, having by her had a s (William) and by his 1st w (all bore surname JONES), with two est sons (Robert, *dvp* 1818, leaving issue; Richard, *dvp*, leaving issue; a yst s (John) and four daus (Anne, *m* — Owen and *dvp*, leaving issue; Gwen; Eleanor; Jane) a 3rd s:

THOMAS JONES, of Cefnmeusydd Uchaf, Caernarvs; *bapt* 20 May 1787; Master Mariner; *m* 5 May1820 Elizabeth, dau and heiress of Richard Thomas, of Cefnmeusydd Uchaf, and *d* 19 Aug 1843, leaving, with two er sons (Richard Thomas, *bapt* 5 Aug 1821, *m* 10 Oct 1846 Louisa Baron and *d* 21 Jan 1857; John Richard, *bapt* Aug 1825, *d* 17 March 1870):

Rev THOMAS JONES, of Cefnmeusydd and Eisteddfa, Criccieth; *b* 2 Dec 1826; *m* 1855 Jane Elizabeth (*d* 8 Dec 1904), dau of Robert Jones, of Eisteddfa, formerly Aberkin, and *d* 25 Aug 1896, leaving, with three daus:

1 ROBERT ARMSTRONG

2 Richard Thomas; *b* 1859; *d* 7 July 1899

3 Thomas; *b* 2 June 1862; *d* 17 Jan 1919

4 John Lloyd Thomas; *b* 8 Sept 1864; Lt-Col IMS, Assay Master Indian Mint; *d* 11 Nov 1925

5 David Fowden; *b* 1870; *m* Mary, dau of Rev John Hughes, Vicar Tydweiliog, and *d* 4 May 1942, leaving:

(1) *Dorothy Mary Catherine; *m* 20 Dec 1947 Noel Cameron Barnes (*d* 26 Feb 1956)

(2) *Marjorie Duffy; *b* 17 Jan 1908; *m* 17 Oct 1942 Sydney Courtenay Kirkby, s of Capt David William Kirkby, of Maesyneuadd, Talsarnau, Merioneth. He *d* 6 Aug 1953

The est s,

Sir ROBERT JONES later ARMSTRONG-JONES (deed poll), CBE (1918), JP Essex, Caernarvs and London, DL Caernarvs and London; *b* 2 Dec 1857; *educ* London U and St Bartholomew's Hosp; MD Lond 1883, FRCS Eng 1885, FRCP London 1907, T/Lt-Col RAMC 1916, ktd 1917, Hon DSc Wales 1920, FSA, High Sheriff Caernarvonshire 1929; *m* 4 Nov 1893 Margaret Elizabeth (*d* 2 May 1943), dau of Sir Owen Roberts, JP, DL, LLD, DCL, of Plas Dinas, Caernarvs, which he thus acquired, and *d* 30 Jan 1943, leaving:

1 RONALD OWEN LLOYD

1 Elaine Margaret; *b* 28 April 1895; *m* 8 July 1920 Col Charles Edward Wauchope, MC, RA, s of Edward Wauchope, of Goldings Manor, Loughton, Essex, and *d* 27 July 1965, leaving two sons and two daus. He *d* 16 July 1969

2 Gwendolen Jane; *b* 2 July 1905; *m* 23 July 1932 Hon Mr Justice (Sir Denys) Buckley, 4th s of 1st Baron Wrenbury (*qv*), and *d* 1985, leaving issue

The only s,

RONALD OWEN LLOYD ARMSTRONG-JONES, MBE (1945), QC (1954), JP (1939), DL (1961), of Plas Dinas; *b* 18 May 1899; *educ* Eton and Magdalen Coll Oxford (MA 1922); barrister Inner Temple 1922, 2nd Lt RA WW I, High Sheriff Caernarvs 1936, Maj KRRC WW II (invalided 1945), Dep Judge Advocate FM Montgomery's staff Normandy and Airborne HQ 1944–45, Ld Chllr's Visitor (Legal) 1955, memb Industl Disputes Tbnl 1955–59, Govr St Bartholomew's Hosp, memb Court Assistants Clothworkers' Co; *m* 1st 22 July 1925 (*divorce* 1934) Anne (*m* 2nd 19 Sept 1935 6th Earl of Rosse (*qv*) and had further issue), only child of Lt-Col Leonard Charles Rudolph Messel, OBE, TD, of Cuckfield, Sussex, and had:

1 ANTONY CHARLES ROBERT ARMSTRONG-JONES, **1st and present Earl of Snowdon**

1 Susan Anne; *m* 20 May 1950 6th Viscount de Vesci (*qv*) and *d* 1986, having had issue

Maj RONALD ARMSTRONG-JONES *m* 2nd 18 June 1936 (*divorce* 1959) (Gwendoline) Carol Akhurst (*k* in a car crash 4 Oct 1966), dau of Sir Thomas Melrose Coombe, of Glenelg, S Australia; *m* 3rd 11 Feb 1960 *Jenifer (*m* 2nd 10 June 1969 John Walter Skelsey, MC, s of John Clifford Skelsey, of Harrogate, Yorks), dau of Basil Unite, and *d* 27 Jan 1966, leaving by her:

2 *Peregrine Thomas Owen Llewellyn [Peregrine Armstrong-Jones Esq, 39 Addington Sq, London SE5 7LB]; *b* 15 Nov 1960; *educ* Eton and RAC Cirencester; *m* 29 Oct 1987 *Caroline Therese Bloy, Dame SMO Malta, and has:

(1) *India Sophie; *b* 22 Feb 1997

SOMERLEYTON

OMNE·BONUM·AB·ALTO

Arms: Gu. a chevron indented erm. between two cross-crosslets in chief and a saltire in base or. **Crest:** A demi-hind erased ppr., charged with two bars and holding between the feet a cross-crosslet or. **Supporters:** On either side a hind ppr., semée of cross-crosslets or. **Motto:** *Omne bonum ab alto* ('All good is from above').
Creation: Bt. (UK) 23 Jan 1863, B. (UK) 26 June 1916.

THE 3RD BARON SOMERLEYTON, of Somerleyton, Suffolk, and a **Baronet** (Sir Savile William Francis Crossley, Bt, GCVO (1998, KCVO 1994), JP (Suffolk 1964), DL (Suffolk 1964)) [The Rt Hon The Lord Somerleyton GCVO JP DL, Somerleyton Hall, Lowestoft, Suffolk NR32 5QQ]; *b* 17 Sept 1928; *s* f 1959; *educ* Eton and RAC Cirencester; farmer, Capt Coldstream Gds (ret 1956), CC E Suffolk 1961–73, Ld in Waiting 1979–92, Master of the Horse 1991–, dir: E Anglian Water 1961–, Essex and Suffolk Water plc 1994–, chm: E Anglia regional br HHA, Assoc Masters Harriers and Beagles, Pres E Region YMCA, Govr Lowestoft Coll Further Educn; *m* 14 Oct 1963 *Belinda Maris, OBE (1997), dau of Vivian Graham Loyd, of Kingsmoor, Ascot, Berks, and Mrs Gerald Critchley, of Belgravia, and has:

1 +HUGH FRANCIS SAVILE; *b* 27 Sept 1971; Page of Hon to HM THE QUEEN 1983–84

1 *Isabel Alicia Claire; *b* 27 Sept 1964; *m* 1991 *Mark Cator (see STOREY, Bt)

2 *Camilla Mary Lara; *b* 27 June 1967; *m* 1993 *William Aldwin (Sandy) Soames, est s of Robert Harold Soames, of Toppesfield, Essex

3 *Alicia Phyllis Belinda; *b* 9 April 1969; *m* 28 Nov 1998 *Robert Pawson, only s of Michael Pawson, of Windsor Forest, Berks

4 *Louisa Bridget Vivien; *b* 20 Feb 1974

Lineage: JOHN CROSSLEY, of Halifax; *m* Martha Turner and had:

Sir Francis Crossley, 1st Bt (UK), so *cr* 23 Jan 1863; *b* 26 Oct 1817; carpet mfr, MP (Lib) Halifax 1852–59 and NW R Yorks 1859–72; *m* 11 Oct 1845 Martha Eliza (*d* 21 Aug 1891), dau of Henry Brinton, and *d* 5 Jan 1872, leaving:

Sir Savile Brinton Crossley, 2nd Bt, and **1st Baron Somerleyton**, of Somerleyton, Suffolk (UK), so *cr* 26 June 1916, GCVO (1922, KCVO 1909), PC (1902), JP, DL Suffolk, JP Norfolk; *b* 14 June 1857; *educ* Eton and Balliol Coll Oxford; MP (U) N Suffolk 1885–92 and Halifax 1900–06, High Sheriff Suffolk 1896, Imp Yeo Boer War 1899–1901, Paymaster-Gen Forces 1902–05, Hon Col and Col Col cmdg PWO Norfolk RGA 1906–09, Maj 1st Suffolk Yeo 1915–16, Ld-in-Waiting 1918–24, Hon Sec King Edward VII's Hosp Fund, KGStJ; *m* 14 Dec 1887 Phyllis, CBE (1918) (*d* 22 Nov 1948), yst dau of Gen Sir Henry de Bathe, 4th Bt, KCB (see 1940 edn), and had:

1 FRANCIS SAVILE, **2nd Baron**

2 John de Bathe, JP Suffolk; *b* 3 Feb 1893; Capt 108th Suffolk and Norfolk Field Bde (TAR) WW I Gallipoli, Palestine and Flanders; *m* 1st 10 Sept 1918 (*divorce* 1930) Dorothy Frances (*d* 28 Feb 1955), est dau of Capt Sir George Everard Arthur Cayley, 9th Bt (*qv*), and had:

(1) +Anthony Everard Savile [Anthony Crossley Esq, Milima, MSF 115 Gympie, Qld 4570, Australia]; *b* 30 July 1920; *m* 4 April 1956 *Jean Margaret Gillian, er dau of David Oliphant Russell, of Kipkarren River, Kenya, and has:

1a +John de Bathe; *b* 22 May 1958; *m* 1982 *Yvonne van Tongeren

2a +Timothy Elgon Savile; *b* 1963

1a *Marguerite; *b* 10 Feb 1957; *m* 1982 *William Anthony Peat Darbyshire

2a *Julia; *b* 2 Jan 1960

(2) +Charles John [Charles Crossley Esq, Linda Cruises, Cosgrove Lock, Milton Keynes, Bucks MK19 7JR]; *b* 23 Dec 1921; *educ* Nautical Coll Pangbourne; Lt RNR WW II; *m* 2 March 1957 *Catherine Adelaide Anne, formerly w of John Henry Mark Fane, MBE (see CLINTON, B), and dau of Gabriel Noel Dyer, of Paris (see LEGARD, Bt)

2 (cont.) Capt The Hon John Crossley *m* 2nd 27 Nov 1930 Sybelle Winifred Louisa, JP, CC Hants, SSStJ (*d* 26 June 1963), formerly w of Gerald James Pixley and dau of Cyril Augustus Drummond (see PERTH, E), and *d* 24 June 1935, having by her had:

(1) *(Elizabeth) Belinda [Belinda Lady Montagu of Beaulieu, New Farm House, Longdown, Marchwood, Hants SO40 4UH]; *b* 11 Jan 1932; *m* 11 April 1959 (*divorce* 1974) 2nd Baron Montagu of Beaulieu (*qv*) and has issue

3 William George Francis; *b* 14 Nov; *d* 4 Dec 1903

1 Phyllis Patty, MBE (1942), JP (Norfolk 1934); Jr Cdr ATS; *m* 3 July 1917 Capt Evelyn Hugh Barclay, Scots Gds (SR), of Colney Hall, Norwich, only surv s of Hugh Gurney Barclay, MVO, JP, and had issue. He *d* 4 Sept 1956

2 Monica Victoria; *m* 19 Sept 1918 Lt-Gen Sir Arthur Francis Smith, KCB, KBE, DSO, MC, Coldstream Gds, only surv s of Col Granville Roland Francis Smith, CB, CVO, of Duffield Hall, Derbys, and had:

(1) Geoffrey Arthur Granville; *b* 4 June 1926; *educ* Eton and RMC Sandhurst; Capt Coldstream Gds; *d* following an accident 18 Sept 1953

(1) *Auriol Blanche; *b* 25 July 1919; *m* 13 Oct 1944 Maj Michael Warren Ingram, Gren Gds, yr s of Sir Herbert Ingram, 2nd Bt (*qv*), and has issue

(2) *Susan Monica; *b* 17 June 1921; *m* 30 March 1943 Capt Thomas Gillespie Browne, RE, s of Hugh Browne, of Warlingham, Surrey, and has:

1a *Jennifer Anne; *b* 19 Feb 1944; *m* 25 June 1965 John Patrick Michael Hugh Evelyn, s of Maj Peter George Evelyn, Gren Gds, of Wotton, nr Dorking, Surrey

2a *Hilary Jane; *b* 25 Oct 1945; *m* 18 Dec 1965 Julian Alexander Ludovic James, est s of Capt Christopher Alexander James, RN, of Warroch House, Milnathort, Kinross-shire, and has:

1b*Christopher Mark William; *b* 18 Feb 1967

2b*David Hugh Geoffrey; *b* 31 May 1969

3a *Monica Jean; *b* 21 July 1949. *m* 12 April 1970 *David R M James-Duff and has:

1b *; *b* 16 Sept 1971

(3) *Hazel Charlotte; *b* 6 Aug 1924; *m* 18 Aug 1943 Maj Peter Gordon Rowley, RA, s of Gordon Rowley, of Surabaya, Java, and has:

1a *David Gordon; *b* 21 July 1946; *educ* Bryanston; *m* 27 March 1971 *Jeane Angela, er dau of Maj I A Hargroves, of Woking, Surrey

1a *Wendy Drusilla; *b* 21 Sept 1950

2a *Hazel Jane; *b* 14 Jan 1959

The 1st BARON *d* 25 Feb 1935; his est s,

FRANCIS SAVILE CROSSLEY, **2nd Baron Somerleyton**, MC (1915), JP, DL Suffolk; *b* 1 June 1889; *educ* Eton; Maj 9th Lancers WW I 1914–15 (despatches) and 108th (Suffolk and Norfolk) Field Bde TA 1924–35, chm Lowestoft Water Co; *m* 1 July 1924 Bridget, MBE (1944), JP (Suffolk 1937) (*d* 26 Dec 1983 aged 84), 3rd dau of William Douro Hoare, CBE, JP, of Guessens, Welwyn, Herts, and *d* 15 July 1959, leaving:

1 SAVILE WILLIAM FRANCIS CROSSLEY, **3rd and present Baron Somerleyton**

2 +(Richard) Nicholas, TD (1973), DL (N Yorks 1988) [Col The Hon Nicholas Crossley TD DL, Westfield Farm, Norton, N Yorks YO17 9PL]; *b* 24 Dec 1932; *educ* Eton and RMA Sandhurst; Capt 9th Queen's Roy Lancers (ret 1961), Hon Col Queen's Own Yeo (TA) 1991–94, Col Gen Staff (TA) 1978, ADC TAVR to HM THE QUEEN 1980, High Sheriff N Yorks 1989, Lt-Col Yorks Yeo, memb Gentlemen-at-Arms; *m* 1st 30 April 1958 Alexandra Anne Maitland (*d* 1990), only dau of W/Cdr Charles Donald Graham Welch, of Perrot Farm, Graffham, Sussex, and has:

(1) +John Dickon Francis; *b* 16 Dec 1966; *educ* Eton and RMA Sandhurst; Capt 9th/12th Lancers; *m* Oct 1997 *Sarah, dau of Maj John Freeland, of Holt Lodge, Kintbury, Berks

(1) *Amanda Carolyn; *b* 14 April 1960; *m* 1st 1984 Patrick James Auchinleck Darling, only s of Gerald Ralph Auchinleck Darling, RD, QC, of Crevanagh, Omagh, Co Tyrone, and has:

1a *Shaunagh Edwina Auchinleck; *b* 1986

(1) (cont.) Mrs Darling *m* 2nd 1992 *Edward P U Mead, s of Humphrey Mead, of Normandy, and Mrs Peter Cadbury, of Alresford, Hants, and by him has:

1a *Arthur Silas; *b* 1993

2a *Leila Alexandria; *b* (twin) 1993

(2) *Lucinda Mary; *b* 5 May 1962; *m* 1980 *Masood Oloumi, of Yazdi, and has:

1a *Lily; *b* 1985

2a *Rose; *b* 1989

2 (cont.) Col Nicholas Crossley *m* 2nd 1995 *Priscilla Ann Kennedy, dau of Maj Alastair Graham, of Norton Conyers, Northallerton

1 *Mary, JP (Huntingdon and Peterborough 1966) [The Hon Mrs Birkbeck JP, Bainton House, Stamford, Lincs PE9 3AF]; *b* 3 Feb 1926; *m* 7 July 1950 *Maj William Birkbeck, DL, Coldstream Gds, yst s of Maj Henry Anthony Birkbeck, MC, JP, DL, of Westacre, Norfolk, and has:

(1) *Anthony William Savile; *b* 4 April 1956; *educ* Eton; *m* 1991 *Hon Davina Mary Bewicke-Copley, yr dau of 6th Baron Cromwell (*qv*), and has:

1a *Elizabeth (Beth); *b* 1993

2a *Katherine (Kate); *b* 29 July 1994

(1) *Victoria Mary; *b* 24 Sept 1951; *m* 1981 (*divorce* 1995) Adauto Santos, of Rio de Janeiro

(2) *Priscilla Bridget; *b* 18 Sept 1952; *m* 1987 *John Kenneth Scott Moncrieff, er s of David Charles Scott Moncrieff, CVO, TD, WS, of Edinburgh, and has:

1a *Robert David; *b* 1991

1a *Iona Mary; *b* 1988

2a *Isabel Ann; *b* 1989

(3) *Rosetta Sybil; *b* 16 June 1958; *m* 1987 *Iain James Russell, only s of James Russell, of Croyard Ho, Beauly, Inverness-shire, and Seafield, Co Waterford, and has:

1a *Oliver George Seckham; *b* 1988

2a *Alastair William James; *b* 1991

3a *Patrick Alexander Bazaine; *b* 1993

4a *Douglas Anthony Iain; *b* 18 Dec 1997

Seat: Somerleyton Hall, Lowestoft, Suffolk. In origin a 17th-century house of brick and stone, Somerleyton was made drastically bigger, as well as being added to in a different stone, the Caen type, in the late 1840s. The architect was John Thomas, who was first and foremost a sculptor. He had helped embellish the rebuilt Houses of Parliament and it was probably through his Westminster connections that the clock tower at Somerleyton came to house a time-piece by Vulliamy that had been designed for the Parliament buildings but turned down by Government on grounds of cost. The man who commissioned Thomas at Somerleyton was the speculative builder and railway constructor Sir Samuel Peto, 1st Bt, of Somerleyton (qv), who added a model village nearby as well as commissioning a rural Crystal Palace protecting a winter garden as adjunct to the main house. It was largely dismantled at the beginning of World War I but an elaborate conservatory survives. (Long before that Peto had got into financial difficulties and in 1863 sold the place to **Sir Francis Crossley, 1st Bt**.)

Homage was paid to the 17th century in the predominant architectural style, which is Jacobethan, though infused with a strong Gallo-Italian flavour. The three-storey south portico, for instance, may evoke Burghley, but is overwhelmed by the very French-looking dormer windows and the bright scarlet brick. Internally, though the Victorian love of ornamentation was allowed a free rein, a greater sense of the 17th century is achievable. This is due to the predominance of panelling, which is particularly noteworthy in the Staircase Hall. As regards the Oak Parlour wainscot it is genuinely of the period, while the Library's oak bookshelves are by J M Willcox, who although a Victorian executed good pastiche Tudor woodwork at Warwick Castle and Charlecote as well.

The Library was once a banqueting hall whereas the present Dining Room was once a library. The chief features here are a pair of paintings of Napoleonic War episodes by Clarkson Stanfield. Much of the panelling has marble slabs or paintings such as these (others are by Landseer) let into it and what with elaborate fireplaces and of course statuary, reflecting Thomas's principal profession, the *tout ensemble* in the end confirms that this is a High Victorian house not a Jacobethan one.

SOMERS

Arms: Quarterly, 1st and 4th, sa. a chevron between three stag's attires arg. (for COCKS); 2nd and 3rd, vert a fess dancette erm. (for SOMERS). **Crests:** 1 On a mount ppr. a stag lodged regardant arg., attired sa. (for SOMERS), 2 A bay tree ppr., suspended therefrom by a strap gu. a cuirass with epauliers and tasces arg., charged with an ermine spot sa. (for COCKS). **Supporters:** On each side a lion erm., gorged with collar indented vert. **Motto:** *Prodesse quam conspici* ('To be useful, rather than conspicuous'). **Creations:** Bt. (GB) 7 Oct 1772, B. (GB) 17 May 1784.

THE 9TH LORD SOM(M)ERS, BARON OF EVESHAM, Co Worcester, and a **Baronet** (Sir Philip Sebastian Somers Cocks, Bt) [The Rt Hon The Lord Somers, 19 Kempson Rd, London SW6 4PX]; *b* 4 Jan 1948; *s* cousin 1995; *educ* Elston Hall Newark and Craig-y-Parc Cardiff

Lineage: THOMAS COCKS, of Bishop's Cleeve, Glos; *m* Elizabeth Holland, of Lancs, and *d* 1601, having had, with an est s, eight yr sons and three daus:

RICHARD COCKS; bought Castleditch, Herefs; *m* Judith, dau and coheir of John Eliot, of the City of London, and had, with a yr s (Sir RICHARD COCKS, 1st Bt, of Dumbleton, Glos, so *cr* 7 Feb 1661/2 (expired on death 4 April 1765 of 4th Bt)):

THOMAS COCKS, of Castleditch; *m* Anne, dau of Ambrose Elton, of Ledbury, Herefs, and had, with two intermediate sons and three daus:

1 John, of Castleditch, *d* unm

2 Thomas (Rev), of Castleditch; *d* 1724, leaving:

  (1) Mary; *m* her cousin John Cocks (*see* below) and *d* 4 Feb 1779

3 Charles; MP Worcester 1692 and Droitwich; *m* Maria, dau of John Somers, of Clifton-upon-Severn, Worcs, and sis and coheir of John Som(m)ers, 1st and last Baron Som(m)ers of Evesham (*b* 4 March 1650/1, MP (Whig) Worcester 1689–93, Slr-Gen 1689–92, Attorney-Gen 1692–93, Ld Chllr 1697–1700, Ld Pres Cncl 1708–10, *d* unm 26 April 1716), and had, with a dau (*d* unm):

  (1) James, of Bruckmans, Herts; MP Reigate; *m* 1st 1718 Lady Elizabeth Newport (*dsp*), 2nd dau of 2nd Earl of Bradford (*qv*) of the 1694 *cr*; *m* 2nd Anne, yst dau of 4th Baron Berkeley of Stratton (*see* BERKELEY, B), and had:

    1a James; *kas* on the French coast 1758

  (2) John, of Castleditch, which he inherited with other estates from his n James (*see* immediately above), as well as the estates of the 4th and last Cocks Bt, of Dumbleton, Glos, in 1765 (*see* above); *m* 3 Sept 1724 his cousin Mary (*see* above) and had, with other issue:

    1a CHARLES, **1st Baron**

    2a John (Rev); *bapt* 14 April 1731; Rector Suckleigh, Worcs, Preb Bristol; *d* unm

    3a Joseph; *bapt* 14 Jan 1732; barrister; *m* 1758 Margaret, dau of John Thorniloe, and *d* 4 April 1775, leaving two daus

    4a James; *b* 22 June 1734; *m* 5 Nov 1772 Martha, dau of R-Adml Charles Watson, and had issue

    5a Philip (Rev); *bapt* 25 Feb 1735; Rector Acton, Preb Lincoln; *d* unm 17 Sept 1797

    6a Thomas Somers; *b* 3 Dec 1737; banker at Charing Cross; *m* 29 Aug 1768 Ann, dau of Alexander Thistlethwayte, and *d* 15 Nov 1796, leaving issue

1 Catherine; *m* 3 Aug 1704 James Harris (*see* MALMESBURY, E) and *d* 13 June 1705

2 Elizabeth; *d* unm

3 Margaret; *m* 1st Earl of Hardwicke (*qv*) and *d* 10 Sept 1761

JOHN COCKS *d* 24 June 1771; his est s,

Sir Charles Cocks, 1st Bt, and **1st Lord Sommers, Baron of Evesham,** Co Worcester, so *cr* 7 Oct 1772 and 17 May 1784 respectively (both GB); *b* 29 June 1725; *educ* Worcester Coll Oxford and Lincoln's Inn; barrister 1750; MP (Whig to *c* 1770, thereafter Tory or once ennobled a Pittite) Reigate 1747–84; *m* 1st 8 Aug 1759 Elizabeth (*d* 1 Jan 1771), sis of 1st Baron Eliot of St Germans (*see* ST GERMANS, E), and had, with two daus (*d* unm):

1 JOHN SOMMERS COCKS, **2nd Lord Sommers, Baron of Evesham,** also *cr* 17 July 1821 VISCOUNT EASTNOR of Eastnor Castle, Co Hereford, and EARL SOMMERS; *b* 6 May 1760; *educ* Westminster and St Alban's Hall Oxford; MP (Pittite, later Whig and as a peer Tory) W Looe 1782–84, Grampound 1784–90 and Reigate 1790–1806, Recorder Gloucester 1811, Ld Lt Herefs 1817–41, High Steward Hereford; *m* 1st 19 March 1785 Margaret (*d* 9 Feb 1831), only dau of Rev Treadway Russell Nash, DD, and had, with a dau (*d* unm):

  (1) Edward Charles; *b* 27 July 1786; Maj; *d* unm 8 Oct 1812 during the assault on Burgos

  (2) JOHN SOMMERS COCKS later SOMERS-COCKS (roy licence 27 April 1841), **3rd Lord Sommers, Baron of Evesham** and 2nd EARL SOMMERS; *b* 19 March 1788; *educ* Westminster; Lt 16th Light Dragoons 1805, Capt 2nd Dragoon Gds 1807, served Peninsular War 1812, ret 1813, Maj Worcs Yeo Cav 1813–27, Lt-Col Herefs Militia 1831 (Col 1836), MP (Tory) Reigate 1812–18 and 1832–41 and Hereford 1818–32, Ld Lt Herefs 1845–52; *m* 4 Feb 1815 Lady Caroline Harriet Yorke (*d* 27 May 1873), dau of 3rd Earl of Hardwicke (*qv*), and *d* 5 Oct 1852, having had, with two daus (*d* young or unm):

    1a CHARLES SOMERS COCKS later SOMERS-COCKS, **4th Lord Sommers, Baron of Evesham** and 3rd and last EARL SOMMERS; *b* 14 July 1819; *educ* Ch Ch Oxford; MP (C) Reigate 1841–47; *m* 2 Oct 1850 Virginia (*d* 29 Sept 1910), dau of James Pattie, BCS, and *d* 26 Sept 1883, when the Earldom and Viscountcy expired, having had:

      1b Isabella Caroline; *m* 6 Feb 1872 Lord Henry Richard Charles Somerset, PC, 2nd s of 8th Duke of Beaufort (*qv*), and *d* 12 March 1921, leaving issue

      2b Adeline Marie, GBE; *m* 24 Oct 1876 10th Duke of Bedford (*qv*) and *d* 12 April 1920

      3b Virginia; *d* young 9 Jan 1859

    1a Caroline Margaret; Maid of Honour to HM QUEEN VICTORIA; *m* 20 June 1849 Rev Hon Charles Leslie Courtenay (*see* DEVON, E) and *dsp* 14 Nov 1894

    2a Harriet Catherine; *m* 22 April 1850 Francis Richard Wegg-Prosser, of Belmont, Herefs, and *d* 6 May 1893, leaving issue. He *d* 16 Aug 1911

  (3) James Somers; *b* 9 Jan 1790; Preb Hereford, Canon Worcester; *d* 5 July 1856

1 (cont.) The **2nd Baron** *m* 2nd 3 June 1834 his cousin Jane (*d* 3 Nov 1868), widow of Rev George Waddington and dau of James Cocks, and *d* 5 Jan 1841

2 Edward Charles; drowned when a pupil at Westminster 1781

The **1st Baron** *m* 2nd 20 May 1772 Anne (*d* 1833), dau of Reginald Pole (*see* POLE, Bt, of Shute), and *d* 30 Jan 1806, having by her had:

3 Philip James; *b* 2 Dec 1774; Lt-Col Gren Gds; *m* 29 Nov 1812 Frances (*d* Dec 1870), dau of Arthur Herbert, of Brewsterfield, Killarney, and *d* 1 April 1857, leaving:

  (1) Charles Richard Somers; *b* 22 April 1814; Vicar of Wolverley, Worcs, and Neen Savage, Salop; *d* unm 4 Feb 1876

  (2) PHILIP REGINALD COCKS, **5th Lord Sommers, Baron of Evesham;** *b* 22 Aug 1815; Col RA; *m* 14 Dec 1859 Camilla Sophia Anne (*d* 8 Dec 1904), dau of Rev William Newton, Vicar Old Cleeve, Somerset, and *dsp* 30 Sept 1899

  (3) Arthur Herbert, CB; *b* 18 April 1819; BCS; *m* 15 April 1847 Anna Marion Jessie (*d* 3 Sept 1914), dau of Lt-Gen James Eckford, CB, Bengal Army, and *d* 29 Aug 1881, having had:

    1a John Patrick Somers; *b* 31 May 1848; 67th Regt; *d* unm 24 Sept 1879

    2a Herbert Haldane Somers; *b* 5 May 1861; Lt Coldstream Gds and 1st Kent Vol Corps, Capt 4th Bn Worcs Regt; *m* 26 June 1883 Blanche Margaret Standish (*d* 26 Dec 1895), dau of Maj Herbert Clogstoun, VC, RE, and *d* 26 Dec 1894, leaving issue

    1b ARTHUR HERBERT TENNYSON COCKS, **6th Lord Sommers, Baron of Evesham,** KCMG (1926), DSO (1919), MC; *b* 20 March 1887; *educ* Charterhouse and New Coll Oxford; Lt-Col Res Offrs Life Gds, Hon Col 13th Australian Light Horse, 52nd Australian Inf Bn and Herefs Regt, WW I (despatches, Legn Hon), Ld-in-Waiting 1924–26, Govr Victoria 1926–31, Actg Govr-Gen Australia 1930, Ld Lt Herefs 1933–44, Dep Ch Scout GB 1936–41, Ch Scout UK and Cwlth 1941–44; *m* 20 April 1921 (Daisy) Finola, CBE (1950), Ch Commr Girl Guides Assoc 1943–49, yr dau of Capt Bertram Charles Christopher Spencer Meeking, 10th Hus, and *d* 14 July 1944, leaving:

1c Elizabeth Violet Virginia; *b* 24 Oct 1922; 3rd Offr WRNS; *m* 28 Feb 1947 Maj Benjamin Alexander Frederick Hervey-Bathurst, DL, Gren Gds, s of Sir Frederick Hervey-Bathurst, 5th Bt (*qv*), and had issue

1b Isabel Joan; *b* 21 Oct 1884; *d* 4 Nov 1885

2b Adeline Verena Ishbel, JP; *b* 1886; DGStJ, Hon LLD Witwatersrand U 1937; *m* 5 Aug 1905 6th Earl of Clarendon (*qv*) and *d* 6 Feb 1963, having had issue

3a Henry Lawrence Somers (Rev); *b* 1 Nov 1862; Rector Instow, N Devon; *m* 14 Jan 1891 Deas Thusnelda (*d* 21 Dec 1945), dau of Llewellyn Haskell, of USA, and *d* 6 Jan 1940, having had:

1b Reginald Somers, MC (1918); *b* 24 July 1894; Capt 17th Bn Somerset LI attd HQ Inf Bde WW I (despatches); *m* 16 Jan 1918 Flora Margaret (*m* 2nd 22 July 1925 Stephen Legassicke Hancock), 2nd dau of Henry King Sturdee, of Norton Manor, Somerset, and was *ka* 24 April 1918

4a ARTHUR PERCY SOMERS COCKS, 7th Lord Sommers, Baron of Evesham; *b* 23 Nov 1864; *educ* Charterhouse; Canadian Forces WW I 1915–17; *m* 1896 Benita (*d* 29 May 1950), dau of Maj Luther Sabin, of USA, and *d* 8 Feb 1953, leaving:

   1c JOHN PATRICK SOMERS COCKS, 8th Lord Sommers, Baron of Evesham; *b* 30 April 1907; *educ* privately and RCM (BMus, ARCM); Dir Music Epsom Coll 1949–53, Prof Theory and Composition RCM 1967–77; *m* 1st 15 Aug 1935 Barbara Marianne (*d* 11 Sept 1959), dau of Charles Henry Southall, of Norwich; *m* 2nd 28 July 1961 Dora Helen (*d* 1993), dau of John Mountfort, of Sydney, NSW, and *d* 15 Feb 1995

   1c Dorothy Helen; *d* unm 25 May 1963

   2c Helen Judith; *m* 1st 20 May 1949 T Everett Malen (*d* 1 July 1961), s of John S Malen, of Gloucester, Mass.; *m* 2nd 27 Sept 1965 Earl G Henry, s of George Henry, of Belmont, Winconsin

1a Frances Rhoda; *m* 1st 13 Nov 1872 Edward Wallace Evans (*d* 28 Dec 1901), of Alfrick Court, nr Worcester, and had issue; *m* 2nd 24 Feb 1903 Frederic de Burgh Newington, of The Rookery, Newbury, Berks, and *d* 18 Feb 1931

2a Caroline Yorke; *b* 1854; granted 23 April 1948 with her sis rank of baron's dau; *m* 7 April 1880 Robert William Banner and *d* 2 June 1949, leaving issue. He *d* 8 Nov 1903

3a Mary Dorothy; *b* 1857; *m* 3 Jan 1895 Rt Rev John Reginald Harmer, DD, Bp Rochester 1905–30, s of Rev G Harmer, Vicar Maisemore, Glos, and *d* 13 April 1949, leaving issue. He *d* 9 March 1944

(4) John James Thomas Somers; *b* 18 Aug 1820; granted rank of baron's yr s 1888; *m* 15 April 1858 Ann (*d* 21 July 1899), dau of Rev Joseph Simpson, Rector Horsted, Sussex, and *d* 21 Sept 1906, having had:

1a Philip Alphonso Somers, CMG (1911); *b* 22 Nov 1862; Consul Lisbon 1907–18, Consul-Gen Naples 1918–26; *m* 19 April 1906 Gwenllian Blanche (*d* 29 July 1957), dau of David Williams, of Ty Bruce, Hirwain, Glam, and *d* 26 March 1940, leaving:

   1b John Sebastian Somers, CVO (1961), CBE (1959); *b* 6 Feb 1907; *educ* Ampleforth and Balliol Coll Oxford (BA 1929); Laming Travelling Fell Queen's Coll Oxford 1929, Consul-Gen Munich 1954–59 and Naples 1959–64; *m* 27 Dec 1946 *Marjorie Olive [Mrs John Somers Cocks, 19 Kempson Rd, London SW6 4PX], dau of Arthur Julius Weller, Ch Inspr Schs Malaya, and *d* 25 May 1964, leaving:

      1c PHILIP SEBASTIAN SOMERS COCKS, 9th and present Lord So(m)mers, Baron of Evesham

      1c *Anne (Anna) Gwenllian [The Hon Anna Somers Cocks, 57 Fentiman Rd, London SW8 1LH]; *b* 18 April 1950; *educ* St Anne's Coll Oxford (MA) and Courtauld Inst London U (MA); V&A: Assist Keeper Dept Metal Work 1973–85, Dept Ceramics 1985–87, ed: *Apollo Magazine* 1987–90 and *The Art Newspaper* 1990–94 (chm 1995–), granted, with her sis, rank of Baron's dau in or after April 1995, author: *The Victoria and Albert Museum, the making of the collection* (1980); *m* 1st 11 Sept 1971 (*divorce* 1972) Martin Alan Walker, jlst *The Guardian*, only s of T M Walker, of Wembley, Middx; *m* 2nd 29 June 1978 (*divorce*) John Julian Savile Lee Hardy; *m* 3rd 1991 *Umberto Allemandi, publisher, of Turin, and by her 2nd husb has:

         1d *Maximilian John Lee; *b* 1980

         1d *Katherine Isabella Eugenia; *b* 1982

      2c *Frances Mary Somers [The Hon Frances Somers Cocks, 39 Rylett Rd, London W12]; *b* 7 April 1953; *educ* Somerville Coll Oxford

2a Charles Sebastian Somers, CMG (1903); *b* 20 Jan 1870; *educ* Oratory Sch Edgbaston; FO 1894, Assist Sec For Dept Govt India 1904–06, Priv Sec to U-Sec For Affrs; *d* unm 10 Feb 1951

1a Agnes Mary; *m* 8 July 1884 William Philip Arkwright, of Thorn, nr Plymouth, and *d* 26 Sept 1940. He *d* 19 Feb 1925

2a Frances Pauline Somers; *m* 6 July 1882 Francis Egerton Harding, of Old Springs, Staffs, and *d* 26 Oct 1887, leaving issue. He *d* 13 May 1937

3a Jane Margaret Somers; nun

4a Anne Hariot Mary Somers; *m* 22 March 1892 Baron Despine, of Aix-les-Bains, and *d* Oct 1953, having had issue. He *d* 1917

(1) Frances; *m* 7 Oct 1847 Philip Allen, of Liscongill, Co Cork, and *d* 4 March 1895. He *d* 1866

4 Reginald; *b* 14 Jan 1777; *m* 21 Dec 1802 his cousin Anne (*d* 19 March 1810), 2nd dau of James Cocks, and *d* 19 Nov 1805, leaving:

(1) Henry Somers (Rev); *b* 16 Dec 1803; *m* 1 Jan 1829 Frances Mercy, dau of Henry Bromley, of Abberley Lodge, Worcs, and *d* 25 Nov 1856, having had, with other issue:

1a Henry Bromley (Rev); *b* 19 June 1831; Vicar Sydenham, Christchurch, NZ, and Leigh, Worcs; *m* 25 July 1861 Harriet Elizabeth (*d* 1920), yst dau of Col Philip Wodehouse (*see* KIMBERLEY, E), and *d* 1894, leaving:

   1b Reginald Wodehouse; *b* 31 Aug 1863; *m* 1883 Mary Thompson, of New Orleans, and *d* 17 Nov 1926

   2b Henry Somers; *b* 16 June 1865; *d* 1897

   3b Philip John (Rev Canon); *b* 31 Oct 1866; Rector Clovelly, Devon, and Waimate, S Canterbury, NZ, Canon Christchurch; *m* 1895 Mary Hannah (*d* 5 Sept 1951), dau of John Gebbie, and *d* 23 Oct 1938, having had:

1c Henry Bromley; *b* 1896; NZ Forces WW I; *m* 1922 Edith Hazel (*d* 1976), yst dau of F H Melville Walker, of Christchurch, NZ, and *d* 4 Nov 1967, leaving:

1d +ALAN BROMLEY [Alan Cocks Esq, 55 La Trobe St, Pakuranga, Auckland, New Zealand]; *b* 1930; heir presumptive; *m* 15 Oct 1955 *Pamela Fay, dau of A H Gourlay, of Christchurch, NZ, and has:

   1e +Martin Bromley [Martin Cocks Esq, 10 Clipper Place, Cockle Bay, Auckland, New Zealand]; *b* 14 Sept 1957; *m* 1982 *Carol Anne, dau of A K White, of Auckland, and has:

      1f +Jonathan Bromley; *b* 1985

      2f +Stephen Michael; *b* 1987

   1e *Lynette Marguerite [Mrs Kevin Steadman, 13 Darcy Place, Royal Heights, Auckland, New Zealand]; *b* 28 April 1960; *m* 1981 *Kevin Mark Steadman and has:

      1f *Ryan David; *b* 1990

      1f *Rachel Marguerite; *b* 1993

   2e *Gillian Fay [Mrs Christean Mitchell, 3602 Flagstone Dve, Carrollton, TX 75007, USA]; *b* 20 Oct 1962; *m* 1989 *Christean Lenard Mitchell and has:

      1f *Tyler Christean; *b* 1994

   3e *Judith Grace Somers [Judith Cocks, 4 Wood St, Papakura, Auckland, New Zealand]; *b* 1973; BSc Auckland U

1d *Pamela Somers [Mrs Allan Hall, 6 Ann St, Gisborne, New Zealand]; *b* 1927; *educ* Canterbury (NZ) Coll (BA 1948, MA 1949, Diploma NZ Library Sch 1949]; *m* 1968 *Allan John Hall, slr, s of Ralph Hall, of Gisborne, and has:

   1e *Veronica Ann; *b* 6 Jan 1970; *educ* Victoria U (BA, LLB)

   2e *Rosemary Megan; *b* 1972; *educ* Otago U (MB, ChB)

2c John Reginald; *b* 1898; *m* 1920 Mary Dillworth (*d* 1973), only dau of Charles Dillworth Fox, of Christchurch, NZ, and *d* 1973, leaving:

1d +John Alexander [John Cocks Esq, RD, Turua, New Zealand]; *b* 21 Sept 1921

2d +Timothy Charles [Timothy Cocks Esq, 3 Leal Place, Manly, Whangaparaoa 1463, New Zealand]; *b* 28 Nov 1923; *m* 19 Feb 1949 *June Alice, only dau of John C Fantham, of Remuera, Auckland, and has:

   1e +Ross Basil [Ross Cocks Esq, RD1, Bruntwood, Cambridge, New Zealand]; *b* 13 Oct 1951; *m* 1972 *Janice Evelyn, yst dau of Pat Russell, of Silverdale, and has:

      1f +Wayne Gregory; *b* 1976

      2f +Michael Bryce; *b* 1977

      1f *Joanna Caron; *b* 1982

   2e +Barry John [Barry Cocks Esq, 58 Citrus Ave, Wahi Beach, Auckland, New Zealand]; *b* 2 June 1954; *m* 1980 *Raewyn Louisa, dau of R P Gavin, of Tuakau, and has:

      1f +Philip Gavin; *b* 1984

      2f +Ryan John; *b* 1987

   1e *Helen Julie [Mrs William McCready, c/o 3 Leal Place, Manly, Whangaparaoa 1463, New Zealand]; *b* 17 Feb 1958; *m* 1984 *William Roy McCready and has:

      1f *Richard James; *b* 1987

      2f *Daniel Thomas; *b* 1992

      1f *Carol Anne; *b* 1985

1d *Kathleen Mary [Mrs Archibald Gray, 22 Hillcrest St, Tirau, Waikato, New Zealand]; *b* 26 Sept 1922; *m* 23 Feb 1946 *Archibald Stewart Gray, est s of Archibald Gray, of Tirau, NZ, and has:

   1e *Peter Stewart [Peter Gray Esq, Parapara Rd, Tirau, Waikato, New Zealand]; *b* 9 Dec 1946; *m* 1984 *Mary Elizabeth, dau of Robert Hyndman, of Hamilton, NZ, and has:

      1f *Simon Peter; *b* 1988

      2f *Timothy Stephen; *b* 1996

   2e *Sidney Charles [Sydney Gray Esq, Long Gully, Takitimu, RD1, Te Anau, South Island, New Zealand]; *b* 3 June 1948; *m* 1976 *Susan Mary, 2nd dau of Robin Sim, of Queenstown, NZ, and has:

      1f *Rebekah Susan; *b* 1978

      2f *Catherine Amy; *b* 1980

   1e *Mary Kathleen [Mrs John Bray, PO Ahaura, West Coast, South Island, New Zealand]; *b* 28 Oct 1949; *m* 1971 *John Edward Bray and has:

      1f *Rachael Janine; *b* 1975

      2f *Helen Mary; *b* 1977

      3f *Carissa Anne; *b* 1979

   2e *Barbara Elizabeth [Mrs Ian Goodall, 48 Orakei Rd, Remuera, Auckland 5, New Zealand]; *b* 19 May 1951; *m* 1974 *Ian Goodall and has:

      1f *Elizabeth Anne; *b* 1976

      2f *Hilary Jean; *b* 1978

2d *Phoebe Somers [Mrs Roland Hunter, 7B Waerenga Rd, Otaki, New Zealand]; *b* 8 April 1925; *m* 18 April 1949 Roland Hunter (*d* 11 Oct 1994), yst s of J Hunter, of Wellington, NZ, and has:

   1e *James Reginald [James Hunter Esq, PO Box 53, Putaruru, New Zealand]; *b* 3 June 1953; *m* 1 Nov 1975 *Anna Margaret, only dau of Michael Malanchak, of Lower Hutt, and has had:

      1f James Michael Roland; *b* 12 March, *d* 8 Oct 1977

      2f *David James Robert; *b* 1 Jan 1979

      3f *Brian Benjamin; *b* 17 Dec 1980

      1f *Roseanna Marie; *b* 1985

   2e *Roger Paul [Roger Hunter Esq, RD Turua, New Zealand]; *b* 1 Sept 1956; *m* 7 July 1984 *Stephanie Gaye, yst dau of Colin William Wallace, and has:

      1f *Donee Kirsten; *b* 4 Nov 1997

1e *Ann Helen [Mrs Peter Spicer, 26 Hogg Crescent, Masterton 5901, New Zealand]; *b* 19 June 1950; *m* 1st 1970 (*divorce* 1987) Brian Edward Turner; *m* 2nd 31 Oct 1987 *Peter Terrance Spicer and by her 1st husb has:

  1f *Pamela Ann [Mrs Roger Nelson, 46 Guthrie St, Lower Hutt, New Zealand]; *b* 19 April 1972; *m* 11 Nov 1995 *Roger Keith Nelson, er s of Keith Nelson, of Masterton

  2f *Melanie Rose; *b* 31 Dec 1973

2e *Janet Claire [Mrs Randall Papworth, 11 Colenso Place, Otaki, New Zealand]; *b* 27 Nov 1951; *m* 20 March 1971 *Randall John Papworth and has:

  1f *Michael Randall; *b* 21 Feb 1974 and has:

    1g *Michaela; *b* April 1993

  1f *Susanne Mary; *b* 31 July 1971 and has:

    1g *Kisha; *b* 6 Nov 1992

  2f *Elizabeth Carol; *b* 25 July 1972 and has:

    1g *Jaimee Carol; *b* 31 Aug 1997

3e *Peggy Jane [Mrs Steven Mathie, 2 Bermer Rd, Belmont, Lower Hutt, New Zealand]; *b* 19 Feb 1958; *m* 19 Feb 1977 *Steven Daryl Mathie and has:

  1f *Bruce Thomas; *b* 28 Nov 1981

  1f *Jennifer Louise; *b* 20 Sept 1983

3c Edgar Basil; *b* 1899; BE (NZ), AMInstCE; *m* 1932 Violet Marion (*d* 29 March 1969), dau of Henry John Purvis, of Beckenham, Kent, and *dsp* 3 Feb 1967

4c Hubert Maurice (Ven); *b* 1901; *educ* Canterbury (NZ) Coll (BA 1923, MA 1924); BC Melbourne 1948, Vicar Papanui, Archdeacon Christchurch, Vicar-Gen, Assist to Bp Christchurch 1964; *m* 1928 *Mary Madeline, only dau of Charles Dearden Matson, of Christchurch, and had:

  1d +Michael Dearden Somers (Rev) [The Rev Michael Somers Cocks, Robbs Rd, Whitecliffs, RD Coalgate, New Zealand]; *b* 1928; *educ* Canterbury (NZ) Coll (MA 1951), and Oxford (BA 1953, MA 1957); Curate Merivale Christchurch 1953–58, Vicar Ross and S Westland 1958–63, St Martin's Christchurch 1963 and Hororata Canterbury; Anglican Chapln W Sweden 1993–98; *m* 1st 1958 Barbara Phyllis, er dau of Hector Frank Allan, of Nelson, NZ, and has:

    1e +Richard Martin; *b* 1966

    1e *Charlotte Elizabeth; *b* 1959

    2e *Andrea Jane; *b* 1961

    3e *Stephanie Anne; *b* 1963

  1d (cont) Michael Somers *m* 2nd 1983 *Gertrud Birgitta, dau of Johan Axel Ewald Svarén of Sjösa, Sweden

  2d +Jonathan Somers [Jonathan Somers Cocks Esq, 113 Worcester St, Ashhurst, Manawatu, New Zealand]; *b* 1933; *m* 1st 1962 Audrey Geraldine (*d* 1987), dau of Aubrey William Scott, of Burnham, NZ; *m* 2nd 1991 *Jennifer Marianne, dau of William Rudd Pratt, of Apiti, NZ, and by his 1st w has:

    1e +Jeremy Andrew Somers; *b* 1964; *m* 1996 *Angela Merle, dau of O Fox, of Palmerston North

    1e *Jennifer Mary; *b* 1963

1c Mary Ethel Somers; *d* an infant 1898

2c *Edith May Somers; *b* 1905; Nursing Sister NZ Forces WW II 1939–43

4b Frederick Armine; *b* 27 Jan 1871; *m* 1899 Mary Louisa (*d* 9 Dec 1951), yst dau of Capt Parsons, of Rangiora, NZ, and *d* 22 Dec 1966, having had:

1c Douglas Edgar West; *b* 1899; *m* 1925 Olive May, dau of Joseph Messines, and *d* 1981, leaving:

  1d +Peter Douglas [Peter Cocks Esq, Adams Rd, RD6, W Melton, Christchurch, New Zealand]; *b* 1937; *m* *Joan, dau of Brentnall Lees, of Christchurch, NZ, and has:

    1e +Paul Brentnall; *b* 1964

    1e *Sheryll Anne; *b* 1962

  1d *Patricia Somers [Mrs Walter Ussher, 6 Burrows Ave, Karori, Wellington, NZ]; *b* 1927; *m* 1953 *Walter Percival Ussher, s of Percival Ussher, of Christchurch, NZ, and has:

    1e *Simon Walter; *b* 1957

    1e *Julie Helen; *b* 1960; *m* 1983 *Paul Raymond Quinn and has:

      1f *Jarrod Jeffrey; *b* 1984

      2f *Alistair Paul; *b* 1986

      3f *Bradley David; *b* 1988

  2d *Helen Marion Somers [Mrs Helen Barr, 4 Roberta Dve, Spreydon, Christchurch 2, New Zealand]; *b* 1930; *m* 1952 (*divorce* 1976) Kenneth William Barr, s of William Barr, of Christchurch, NZ, and has:

    1e *Deborah Jane; *b* 1956; *m* 19– *Stuart Stephenson and has:

      1f *Dominic Robert; *b* 1988

      2f *Simon Salvatore; *b* 1990

      3f *Tobias Douglas Stuart; *b* 1993

    2e *Janine Patricia; *b* 1959; *m* 1988 *Alastair James

    3e *Elizabeth Kaye; *b* 1962; *m* 1989 *Beat Gasser

2c Armine Christopher Somers; *b* 1903; *m* 1936 *Ella, dau of J S Buzan, of Oamaru, and had:

  1d +Robin Fraser [Robin Cocks Esq, 17 Ashbrook Lane, Lower Cashmere, Christchurch 2, New Zealand]; *b* 1943; *m* 1969 *Anita Josephine, dau of K A J Smith, of Christchurch, and has:

    1e +Rodney Somers; *b* 1969

    2e +Calvin James; *b* 1972

    1e *Penelope Jane; *b* 1974

2d +Denis Somers [Denis Cocks Esq, 97 Mount Pleasant Rd, Mount Pleasant, Christchurch 8, New Zealand]; *b* 1947; BA; *m* 1971 *Allison Elspeth, dau of W H Cook, of Dacre, Southland, NZ, and has:

  1e +Bede Somers; *b* 1979

  1e *Gretchen Emma; *b* 1976

1d *Diane Beverley; *b* 1939; *m* 1962 *Douglas Bernard Charles Williams, s of Douglas Cameron Williams, of Christchurch, NZ, and has:

  1e *Shane Douglas; *b* 1962

  2e *Brent Charles; *b* 1965

2d *Juliet Elizabeth [Mrs Donald Stirton, 7 Searells Rd, Christchurch 5, New Zealand]; *b* 1940; SRN; *m* 1964 *Donald Martin Stirton, s of Donald Stirton, of Island Bay, Wellington, and has:

  1e *Rachel; *b* 1972

  2e *Sally Somers; *b* 1976

3c Charles John Somers; *b* April 1904; *m* 1932 *Hazel, dau of William Steel, of Christchurch, NZ, and *d* 1975, leaving:

  1d +Geoffrey Somers; *b* 1934; *m* 1st 1959 Madeline Mary (*d* 1980), dau of R J Coulter, of Ashburton, NZ; *m* 2nd 1985 *Sharon May Fountain and by his 1st w has:

    1e +Richard Somers; *b* 1962

    2e +Mark Somers; *b* 1967

    1e *Elizabeth Mary; *b* 1968

    2e *Charlotte Ann; *b* 1972

  2d +Ian Somers [Ian Cocks Esq, 12 Andover St, Herivale, Christchurch 1, New Zealand]; *b* 27 May 1940; APANZ; *m* 1961 *Beverley Claire, dau of G W Kearney, of Christchurch, and has:

    1e *Tracey Jane; *b* 1962; *m* 1987 Peter Leon Roborgh, s of Dr Rudolf Roborgh of Motueka, NZ, and has:

      1f *Zoë Alexandra; *b* 1989

      2f *Lydia Francesca; *b* 1991

      3f *Molly Victoria; *b* 1994

      4f *Georgina Sylvie; *b* 1996

    2e *Sarah Hilary; *b* 1964; *m* 1997 *Andrew Murray Watson, s of Oliver Watson of Seddon, Marlborough, NZ

1d *Sandra Christine [Mrs Thomas Keenan, 7 St Andrews Sq, Christchurch New Zealand]; *b* 27 Dec 1944; *educ* Canterbury U, NZ (BA); *m* 1968 *Thomas Desmond Keenan, MB ChB, and has:

  1e *Timothy James; *b* 1969

  1e *Caroline Mary; *b* 1971

4c +Patrick Somers [Patrick Somers Cocks Esq, 20B Glenharrow Ave, Avonhead, Christchurch, New Zealand]; *b* Sept 1905; *m* 1943 *Evelyn May, dau of Lealand Bertram Iles, and has:

  1d *Barbara Mary [Mrs Graeme Wynn, 3550 W 19th Ave, Vancoouver, BC, Canada]; *b* 1944; SRN; *m* 1975 *Graeme Clifford Wynn and has:

    1e *Jonathan Blakeley Somers; *b* 1984

    1e *Louise Jane; *b* 1978

  2d *Yvonne Dawn; *b* 1946; *m* 24 June 1967 (*divorce* 1983) Leonard Astley Newton, s of Edward Isaac Newton, of Norco, Calif., and has:

    1e *John Patrick; *b* 1975

    1e *Roxanne Leah; *b* 1972

  3d *Cynthia Joan; *b* 1950

  4d *Marion Elizabeth [Mrs Dennis Young, 23 Meadowville Ave, Spreydon, Christchurch, New Zealand]; *b* 1952; *m* 1st 1970 (*divorce* 1978) Kenneth Michael Tate and has:

    1e *Rachael Marion; *b* 1971

  4d (cont.) Mrs Marion Tate *m* 2nd 1979 *Dennis Erwyn Young and by him has:

    2e *Heather Jane; *b* 1980

5b Edgar Bromley; *b* 8 July 1872; *d* 1900

6b Charles Richard; *b* 31 Dec 1877; *m* 1926 Fanny (*d* 27 Dec 1968), dau of S E Hubbard, of Dunedin, NZ, and *d* 1944, leaving:

1c +Charles Bromley [Charles Cocks Esq, 71 Garden Rd, Fendalton, Christchurch, New Zealand] *b* 5 Aug 1928; *educ* Canterbury Coll, NZ (LLB 1956)

7b Arthur Eustace; *b* 23 Dec 1882; Cpl HAC; *d* unm Sept 1956

1b Lucy Elizabeth; *d* young 26 Nov 1877

2b Frances Mercy; *b* 21 June 1864; *m* 1894 Walter Septimus Fisher and *d* c 1932, leaving issue

3b Harriet Lydia Muriel; *b* 26 Nov 1874; *d* unm June 1953

4b Mary Millicent; *b* 25 May 1876; *d* unm 2 Aug 1906

5b Katherine Agatha; *b* 24 June 1879; *d* unm 18 April 1957

6b Monica; *b* 1881; Coronation Medal 1937; *d* unm 1964

1 Anna Maria; *m* 4 Dec 1797 Rev Philip Yorke (see HARDWICKE, E) and *d* 27 July 1835, leaving issue

SOMERSET

Arms: Quarterly, 1st and 4th, or on a pile gu. between six fleurs-de-lys az. three lions of England (coat of augmentation granted by HENRY VIII on his marriage with Lady Jane Seymour); 2nd and 3rd, gu. two wings conjoined in lure, the tips downwards, or (for SEYMOUR). **Crest:** Out of a ducal coronet or a phoenix of the last, issuing from flames ppr. **Supporters:** Dexter, a unicorn arg., armed, maned and tufted or, gorged with a ducal coronet per pale az. and gold, to which is affixed a chain of the last; sinister, a bull az., ducally gorged, chained, hoofed and armed or. **Motto:** *Foy pour devoir* ('Faith for duty'). **Creations:** B. and D. (E) 15 Feb 1546/7, Bt. (E) 29 June 1611.

THE 19TH DUKE OF SOMERSET, **Baron Seymour**, and a **Baronet** (Sir John Michael Edward Seymour, Bt, DL (Wilts 1993)) [His Grace The Duke of Somerset DL, Berry Pomeroy, Totnes, S Devon]; *b* 30 Dec 1952; *s* 1984; *educ* Eton; FRICS; *m* 20 May 1978 *Judith-Rose, est dau of John F C Hull, of Kensington, and has:

1 +SEBASTIAN EDWARD, *Lord Seymour*; *b* 3 Feb 1982
2 +Charles Thomas George; *b* 1992
1 *Sophia Rose; *b* 1987
2 *Henrietta Charlotte; *b* 1989

Somerset, other titles: A certain William de Moion (a name that later came to be known as Mohun), whose father had arrived in England from Normandy in WILLIAM I (THE CONQUEROR)'s time and been made Sheriff of Somerset, was created Earl of Somerset by the EMPRESS MAUD in 1141. He died by 1155 and his appointment as Earl (for such was the relatively utilitarian nature of earldoms then; *see* NORTHUMBERLAND, D, and RUTLAND, D, preliminary remarks) was renewed neither to him by STEPHEN before his death nor by HENRY II to any of his (Earl William's) six sons after it.

Two and a half centuries later RICHARD II created the eldest of John of Gaunt's bastards by Catherine Swynford John Beaufort Earl of Somerset. He was later promoted Marquess of Somerset, though degraded from the rank in the early part of HENRY IV's reign. Both before and after the deposition of RICHARD he was a prominent military figure, chiefly in France during the Hundred Years War. The latter conflict continued to provide the Beaufort Earls of Somerset with opportunities: the 3rd Earl, one of John's younger sons, was promoted Duke of Somerset in 1443 following various military operations in Normandy, Anjou and Maine, though these were competently executed rather than conspicuously triumphant. Probably his close kinship with HENRY VI was chief cause of his leap in the peerage, for his mother Margaret was daughter of Thomas Earl of Kent, a descendant of EDWARD I. It is this Duke of Somerset's daughter who was mother of HENRY VII.

The Dukedom of Somerset created in 1443 expired with the death of the grantee in 1444. His brother inherited as 4th Earl of Somerset, however, and in 1448 was promoted Duke, despite a military career of relative failure during the last phase of the Hundred Years War. He died fighting on the Lancastrian side at the 1st Battle of St Albans in 1455. The 2nd Duke of Somerset of the 1448 creation, initially a Lancastrian like his father, was attainted in 1461, restored by EDWARD IV in blood and honours in 1463, deserted EDWARD IV later the same year and was executed (and the act of restoration annulled) after the Lancastrian defeat of Hexham 1464, only to be posthumously pardoned once HENRY VII had ascended the throne in 1485. This Duke's younger brother Edmund Beaufort was regarded by Lancastrians as rightful Duke of Somerset after 1464 and indeed so styled himself, but he died in 1471, having in any case been attainted six years earlier. The Beaufort Earls and Dukes of Somerset thus came to an end.

HENRY VII's third son Edmund is said to have been created Duke of Somerset but no independent documentary evidence for the claim has been found. He died an infant without issue in any case. HENRY VIII created his only publicly acknowledged illegitimate son Duke of Richmond and Somerset in 1525, but the lad died without issue aged about 17. Lastly, during the century between 1552 and 1660 during which the Seymour Dukedom of Somerset lay under attainder, Robert Carr or Ker (*see* LOTHIAN, M), one of JAMES I's two most notorious favourites (the other being George Villiers, Duke of Buckingham; *see* JERSEY, E), was created Earl of Somerset. This took place in 1613. He and his Countess, the still more notorious Frances, divorced wife of the 3rd Devereux Earl of Essex (*see* HEREFORD, V), were involved in Sir Thomas Overbury's murder in 1613 and though both were found guilty were let off. He died without issue in 1645 and the title expired. There was an attempt by the 2nd Marquess of Worcester in 1646 and again at the Restoration to pass off forged documents as instruments creating him Duke of Somerset, but the imposture deceived few and he withdrew the claim. For the Viscountcy of Somerset of Cashel, *see* BEAUFORT, D.

Lineage: Sir RICHARD ST MAURO acquired the estates of Woundy, Penhow, etc, Mon, and lived at Penhow; his est s:

Sir ROGER de ST MAURO; *d c* 1300, leaving:

Sir ROGER de ST MAURO; living *c* 1315; *m* Joan, heiress, of Damarel, Devon, and allegedly had, with an er s (John, *d c* 1359, leaving a s Roger, whose dau and heiress conveyed the inheritance to the BOWLAYs of Penhow, who bore the Seymour arms; a BOWLAY heiress *m* Sir George Somerset, 3rd s of 1st Earl of Worcester; *see* BEAUFORT, D):

Sir ROGER de ST MAURO; *m* Cicely (*b c* 1321; *m* 2nd by 1383 Richard Turberville and *d* 7 June 1394, having had issue by both husbs), er sis and in her issue sole heiress of John Beauchamp, 3rd Lord (Baron) Beauchamp (of Hatch, Somerset), and *d* by 1361, leaving:

Sir WILLIAM SEYMOUR; attended THE BLACK PRINCE to Gascony *c* 1359 in opening phase of Hundred Years War; *m* Margaret, dau and heiress of Simon de Brockbury, of Herefs, by Joan, sis and heiress of Sir Peter de la Mare, and *dvm* 25 Aug 1391, leaving:

ROGER SEYMOUR; *b c* 1367; became heir of his grandmother Cicely in 1394 and thereby according to later doctrine *de jure* 4th Lord (Baron) Beauchamp (of Hatch); *m* Matilda (who brought Wolf Hall into her husb's family), dau and coheir of Sir William Esturmy, of Chadham, Wilts, Speaker H of C 1405, and had:

JOHN SEYMOUR; Sheriff Hants *c* 1431 and Wilts *c* 1432; *m* 30 July 1424 Isabel, dau and heiress of Mark William, Mayor Bristol, and had:

JOHN SEYMOUR; Sheriff Wilts *c* 1458; *m* Elizabeth, dau and heiress of Sir Robert Coker, of Lawrence Lydiard, Somerset, and *dvp c* 1464, leaving, with a yr s (Humphrey, of Evenswinden, Wilts, *m* Elizabeth, dau and coheir of Thomas Winslow, of Burton, Oxon, and had a s, Simon, of Burton, ancestor of the SEYMOURs of Burton):

JOHN SEYMOUR; *s* his gf aged 14; *m* 1st Elizabeth, dau of Sir George Darrell, of Littlecote, Wilts (*see* MOWBRAY, SEGRAVE and STOURTON, B), and had four sons and four daus; *m* 2nd —, dau of Robert Hardon, and had another s (Roger, *dspm*); his est s:

Sir JOHN SEYMOUR, KB (1513), of Wolf Hall, Wilts; a cdr against the Cornish rebels 1497, Sheriff Dorset, Somerset and Wilts; *m* Margery (*d* 1550), 2nd dau of Sir Henry Wentworth, KB (*see* LYTTON, E), and *d* 21 Dec 1536, having had, with an est s:

1 EDWARD, **1st Duke**
2 Henry (Sir), KB, of Marwell, Hants; *m* Barbara, dau of Thomas Morgan, and had, with other issue (now extinct in the male line):
    (1) Jane; *m* Sir John Rodney (*see* RODNEY, B)
3 THOMAS SEYMOUR, 1st and last BARON SEYMOUR OF SUDELEY, Co Gloucester (E), so *cr* 16 Feb 1546/7 (on the accession of his n EDWARD VI), KG (Feb 1546/7), PC (Jan 1546/7), JP (Berks, Devon, Essex); *b c* 1508; Gentleman Privy Chamber 1536, Jt Amb to Regent Netherlands 1543, Master Ordnance 1544, Adml of the Fleet 1544, Ld High Adml Feb 1546/7; *m c* May 1547 CATHERINE (Parr) (*d* 5 Sept 1548), widow of HENRY VIII and *dspm*, being beheaded 20 March 1548/9 following his attainder and conviction of high treason, when the Barony was forfeited, leaving:
    (1) Mary; *b* Aug-Sept 1548; *m*(?) Sir Edward Bushel(?)
1 JANE; *m* 20 May 1536 HENRY VIII and *d* 14 Oct 1537, leaving:
    (1) EDWARD VI
2 Elizabeth; *m* 1st Sir Anthony Oughtred; *m* 2nd by 1538 1st Baron Cromwell of the 1540 *cr* (*see* CROMWELL, B, preliminary remarks), s of the Thomas Cromwell who at one time was HENRY VIII's principal minister, and had issue; *m* 3rd 2nd Marquess of Winchester (*qv*)
3 Dorothy; *m* 1st Sir Clement Smith; *m* 2nd Thomas Leventhorpe

Sir JOHN's est s:

  Sir EDWARD SEYMOUR, **1st Duke of Somerset**, so *cr* 16 Feb 1546/7, with a special remainder to his male issue by his current (2nd) w, then to his 2nd s (by his 1st w) and the latter's heirs male of the body, and finally to the heirs male of his own body by any subsequent wife, as also 15 Feb 1546/7 BARON SEYMOUR with an identical reminder and previously 5 June 1536 VISCOUNT BEAUCHAMP with remainder to heirs male of his body to be begotten from that moment on (*i.e.*, ignoring his sons by his 1st w, which has been taken to suggest he had at that time suspicions of their paternity, especially in the case of the eldest) and 18 Oct 1537 EARL OF HERTFORD (all E), with remainder to present or future heirs male of his body by his current (2nd) w, KG (1540/1), PC (1537); *b c* 1500; *educ* Oxford and Cambridge (?); Page of Honour to MARY TUDOR QUEEN CONSORT OF FRANCE 1514, Esq of the Body in the wars in France 1523, ktd 1523, accompanied Wolsey on his embassy to France 1527, Esq of the Body 1530, Capt Island of Jersey 1536, Jt Chllr N Wales 1536, Warden Scottish Marches Oct–Dec 1542, Ld High Adml Dec 1542–Jan 1542/3, Gt Chamberlain 1542/3–Feb 1546/7, Lt-Gen in N of England 1544, when he led an army into Scotland, capturing Edinburgh and Leith and ravaging Haddingtonshire; defeated French outside Boulogne Feb 1544/5; one of the executors of HENRY VIII's will, following whose death 26 Jan 1546/7 he was made Govr of the person of EDWARD VI and Ld High Steward for the Coronation; Earl Marshal 17 Feb 1547, PROTECTOR OF THE REALM with plenary powers 12 March 1546/7–13 Oct 1549; Capt-Gen of England 11 Aug 1547; defeated the Scots Battle of Pinkie (Musselburgh) 10 Sept 1547; *m* 1st probably by 1519 (*divorce* 1535) Katherine, dau and coheir of Sir William Fillol, of Fillol's Hall, Essex, and had:
1 John; *bur* 19 Dec 1552
2 Edward (Sir), of Berry Pomeroy, Devon; served with his f Battle of Pinkie (Musselburgh) 10 Sept 1547, ktd 18 Sept 1547; after his f's attainder he was restored in blood by an Act of Parl 1553, which enabled him to inherit land; granted 6 Sept 1553 Manors of Walton, Shedder and Stowey, Somerset; Sheriff

Devon 1583; *m* Margaret, dau and heiress of John Walsh, of Cathanger, Somerset, Justice Common Pleas 1563–72, and *d* 6 May 1593, leaving:

(1) **Sir Edward Seymour, 1st Bt** (E), so *cr* 29 June 1611, of Berry Pomeroy; MP Devon 1590–1611, High Sheriff 1595 and 1605; *m* 19 Sept 1576 Elizabeth, dau of Sir Arthur Champernowne, of Dartington, Devon, and *d* 11 April 1613, leaving an est s:

1a **Sir Edward Seymour, 2nd Bt**; MP Penrhyn 1601, Newport 1603–11, Lyme Regis 1614, Devon 1621–22, Callington 1624–25 and Totnes; ktd 1603, envoy Denmark *temp* JAMES I; his castle at Berry Pomeroy was destroyed in the Civil War; *m* 15 Dec 1600 Dorothy (*bur* 30 June 1643), dau of Sir Henry Killegrew, of Laroch, and *d* 5 Oct 1659, having had, with other issue:

1b **Sir Edward Seymour, 3rd Bt**; *bapt* 10 Sept 1610; V-Adml Devon, MP Devon 1640–44 and 1660 and Totnes 1661–87, High Sheriff 1679; *m* 1630 Anne (*d* 1695), dau of Sir John Portman, 1st Bt (*see* PORTMAN, V), and *d* 7 Dec 1688, having had, with other issue:

1c **Sir Edward Seymour, 4th Bt**, PC (1673); *b* 1633; MP Hendon 1661–78, Devon 1678–79, Totnes 1679–81 and 1695–98, Exeter 1685–85 and 1698–1708, Speaker H of C 1672–79, Treas Navy 1673–81, Commr Treasury 1691–94, Comptroller Household 1702–04, mainly responsible for the Habeas Corpus Act of 1679; *m* 1st *c* 7 Sept 1661 Margaret, dau and coheir of Sir William Wale, of North Lappenham, Rutland, Alderman London, and *d* 17 Feb 1707/8, leaving:

1d **Sir Edward Seymour, 5th Bt**; *b* 1663; MP W Looe 1690–95, Totnes 1708–10 and Gt Bedwyn 1711–15; *m* Laetitia (*d* 1738), only dau of Sir Francis Popham, KB, of Littlecote, and had, with another s (*d* unm) and eight daus:

1e EDWARD (Sir), **6th Bt**, and **8th Duke**

2e Francis, of Sherborne, Dorset; MP Gt Bedwyn 1732 and Marlborough 1734; *m* 30 July 1728 Elizabeth (*d* 20 March 1761), widow of Edward Richard Montagu, Viscount Hinchingbrooke (*see* SANDWICH, E), and only dau of Alexander Popham, MP, of Littlecote, and *d* 23 Dec 1761, having had, with a dau:

1f Henry, of Redland Court, Glos, Trent, Somerset, and Northbrook, Devon; Groom Bedchamber to GEORGE III; *m* 1st 26 July 1753 Caroline (*d* 2 June 1773), only dau of 2nd Earl Cowper (*see* LUCAS OF CRUDWELL, B), and had:

1g Caroline; *m* Sept 1775 William Danby, of Swinton Park, Yorks, and *dsps* 20 March 1821

2g Georgina; *b* 31 Dec 1756; *m* 27 Sept 1794 Louis, Count de Durpret, French Amb Venice

1f (cont.) Henry Seymour *m* 2nd 5 Oct 1775 Louise, Countess de Ponthon, of Normandy (*d* 1805), and by her had:

1g Henry, of Knoyle House, Wilts, Trent, Somerset, and Northbrook, Devon, JP, DL Wilts; *b* 10 Nov 1776; MP Taunton 1826–30, High Sheriff Wilts 1835; *m* 12 Jan 1817 Jane (*d* 14 March 1869), dau of Benjamin Hopkinson, of Bath, and Blagdon Court, Somerset, and *d* 27 Nov 1849, having had:

1h Henry Danby, of Trent, JP, DL Wilts and Somerset; *b* 1 July 1820; MP Poole 1850–68, Jt Sec Bd Control 1855–58; *d* unm 4 Aug 1877

2h Alfred, of Knoyle and Trent, JP, DL; *b* 11 Nov 1824; MP Totnes 1863–69 and Salisbury 1869–74; *m* 18 Aug 1866 Isabella (*d* 7 April 1911), widow of Beriah Botfield, MP, of Hopton Court, Salop, and 2nd dau of Sir Baldwin Leighton, 7th Bt (*qv*), and *d* 15 March 1888, leaving:

1i Jane Margaret; *b* 14 March 1873; *d* unm 5 Aug 1943

1h Jane; *m* 21 Aug 1847 Philip Pleydell-Bouverie and *d* 18 Sept 1892, leaving issue (*see* RADNOR, E)

2h Sarah Ellen; *m* 14 May 1857 William Ayshford Sanford, of Nynehead Court, Somerset, and *d* 14 Aug 1867, leaving issue. He *d* 28 Oct 1902

3h Louisa Caroline Harcourt; *m* 2 Sept 1862 Maj-Gen Sir Henry Creswicke Rawlinson, 1st Bt (*qv*), and *d* 31 Oct 1889, leaving issue

3e William, of E Knoyle, Wilts; *b* 1713; *m* 1st 17 April 1737 Elizabeth (*d* 22 March 1741/2), only child of John Hippye, of Frome; *m* 2nd 2 Aug 1745 Mary (*d* 8 Nov 1753), dau of Samuel Hyde, of Bromley, Kent, and *dsp* 5 Jan 1746/7

2d William; Lt-Gen; *dsp* 9 Feb 1728

1c (cont.) **Sir Edward** *m* 2nd 1674 Laetitia (*d* 16 March 1714), dau of Alexander Popham, of Littlecote, Wilts, and by her had, with three other sons (*d* unm):

3d Popham SEYMOUR later SEYMOUR-CONWAY (on his inheriting estates of his maternal cousin the Earl of Conway); *b* 1675; *d* unm, *k* in a duel 18 June 1699

4d FRANCIS SEYMOUR CONWAY, 1st BARON CONWAY OF RAGLEY; had issue (*see* HERTFORD, M)

5d Charles, of Staston, Dorset; had an only surv child:

1e Jane; *m* Aug 1750 Adml Thomas Lynn and had issue

1d Anne; *m* 8 Jan 1707/8 William BERKELEY later PORTMAN and *d* 10 May 1752, leaving issue (*see* PORTMAN, V)

2c Henry SEYMOUR later PORTMAN, of Orchard Portman, Somerset, which he inherited from his unc Sir William Portman, 5th Bt, when he assumed latter's name and arms; *m* 1st Penelope, dau of Sir William Haslewood, of Maidwell, Northants; *m* 2nd Meliora (*m* 2nd Thomas Fownes), dau of William Fitch, of High Hall, Dorset, and *dsp* Feb 1727/8 (*see also* PORTMAN, V)

1c Elizabeth; *m* Sir Joseph Tredenham, of Tregony, Cornwall

2b Henry, of Langley, Bucks, royalist Civil War, Groom Bedchamber; *b* 1612; *m* 1st Elizabeth (*d* June 1671), widow of William Barrat and dau of Sir Joseph Killgrew, but by her had no issue; *m* 2nd Ursula, widow of George Stawale and dau of Sir Robert Austen, 1st Bt, and *d* 9 March 1686, having by her had, with a dau:

1c Sir HENRY SEYMOUR, 1st and last Bt (E), so *cr* 4 July 1681, of Langley; *b* 20 Oct 1674; MP E Looe 1699–1713; *d* unm April 1714, when the btcy expired

3b Thomas; *m* Anne, dau of Sir Richard Anderson, of Penley, Herts, and had two sons and three daus

4b Joseph (Sir); ktd 1643; *m* his er bro's sis-in-law Bridget, dau of Sir Richard Anderson, and had a s and dau

1b Elizabeth; *m* Francis Courtenay, *de jure* 4th Earl of Devon (*qv*), and had issue; *m* 2nd Sir Amos Meredith, 1st Bt, of Marston, Devon (*d* 3 Sept 1669)

2b Mary; *m* Sir Jonathan Trelawny, 2nd Bt (*see* SALUSBURY-TRELAWNY, Bt), and had issue

3b Margaret; *m* Francis Trelawny, s of Sir John Trelawny, 1st Bt (*see* SALUSBURY-TRELAWNY, Bt)

The **1st Duke** *m* 2nd by 9 March 1534/5 Anne (*m* 2nd Francis Newdigate, of Hanworth, her late husb's steward, and *d* 16 April 1587 aged 90), dau of Sir Edward Stanhope, of Rampton, Notts, by Elizabeth, sis of John Bourchier, Earl of Bath (*see* BATH, M, preliminary remarks), and was executed 22 Jan 1551/2 by beheading, having been found guilty of felony (seemingly fomenting a riot by the common people of London) rather than high treason, following which a posthumous act of attainder was nevertheless passed against him 12 April 1552 depriving him and his heirs of all his titles, having by her had, with an est s (*d* an infant):

3 EDWARD SEYMOUR, 1st EARL OF HERTFORD, so *cr* 13 Jan 1558/9, as also BARON BEAUCHAMP; *b* 12 Oct 1537; restored in blood by Act of Parl 1553–54; Ld Lt Somerset and Wilts 1602 and 1608; *m* 1st *c* Dec 1560 Lady Catherine Grey (*d* 27 Jan 1567/8), dau and heiress of Henry, Duke of Suffolk, sis of LADY JANE GREY and gdau maternally of Charles Brandon, Duke of Suffolk, by MARY TUDOR (QUEEN DOWAGER of France and sis of HENRY VIII), following which marriage both the EARL and his w were imprisoned, partly perhaps out of ELIZABETH I's jealousy but equally if not more so for the dynastic threat their children might represent, particularly as the marriage was later found to be valid at Common Law although pronounced invalid by the Archbp of Canterbury 1561, and had, with another s and a dau (*d* young):

(1) Edward, *Lord Beauchamp*; *b* Tower of London 21 Sept 1561 (it was one more cause of fury in ELIZABETH I that he and his immediate yr bro had been born as a result of what would in the 20th century be called a conjugal visit by his f to his mother, albeit an unauthorised one, for although both were imprisoned it was supposed to be in separate quarters); although the **1st Duke of Somerset**'s descendants by his 1st w had lodged a petition against the claims of those by the 2nd w to the titles (basing their claim on the supposedly invalid marriage of the 1st Earl of Hertford and Lady Catherine Grey), Edward *Lord Beauchamp* was the beneficiary of a ruling by letters patent 14 May 1608 to the effect that the Barony of Beauchamp and Earldom of Hertford should vest in him and the heirs male of his body (each of whom was specifically named in the recital of the letters patent because of the assertion by the opposite side that the descendants of the Hertford-Grey marriage were illegitimate); *m* by 1 July 1582 Honora, dau of Sir Richard Rogers, of Bryanston, Dorset, and *dvp*, *bur* 21 July 1612, having had:

1a Edward, *Lord Beauchamp*, KB (1616); *bapt* 12 June 1586; *educ* Magdalen Coll Oxford; *m* 1 June 1609 Lady Anne Sackville (*m* 2nd 7 Oct 1622 Sir Edward Lewes), dau of 2nd Earl of Dorset (*see* SACKVILLE, B), and *dsps* in the lifetime of his gf, being *bur* 15 Sept 1618

2a WILLIAM SEYMOUR, **2nd Duke of Somerset** (restored 13 Sept 1660 by Act of Parl, also as 2nd BARON SEYMOUR), also 2nd EARL OF HERTFORD (and 2nd BARON BEAUCHAMP), in addition *cr* 3 June 1641 MARQUESS OF HERTFORD (E), KB (1616), PC (Feb 1640/1 and 1660); *b* 1 Sept 1587; *educ* Magdalen Coll Oxford; MP Marlborough Dec 1620–Feb 1620/1, called up Feb 1620/1 to Ho Lds *vp* in his f's Barony of Beauchamp, Jt Ld Lt Somerset March 1638/9, pro-Parl on eve of Civil War but later fought for royalists, Govr and Master Household to PRINCE OF WALES (later CHARLES II) 1641–43, royalist Lt-Gen SW England and S Wales 1642, defeated Parliamentarians under Sir William Waller at Battle of Lansdown and captured Bristol 1643, Groom Stole Jan 1643/4, Gentleman Bedchamber 1660, Ld Lt Wilts and Somerset July-Oct 1660; *m* 1st secretly 22 June 1610 Lady Arabella Stuart, only dau and heiress of 1st and last Earl of Lennox of the 1572 *cr* (*see* MORAY, E) and cousin of JAMES I, following which he was obliged to flee to France, while Lady Arabella was imprisoned first at Lambeth and later in The Tower of London, where she *dsp* insane 27 Sept 1615; *m* 2nd 3 March 1616/7 Frances, est dau of 3rd Viscount Hereford (*qv*), and *d* 24 Oct 1660, having by her had, with another s (*d* an infant):

1b William, *Lord Beauchamp*; *b* 1621; *d* unm *vp* and was *bur* 16 June 1642

2b Robert, *Lord Beauchamp*; *b* 1622; *d* unm *vp*, *bur* 30 Jan 1645/6

3b Henry, *Lord Beauchamp*; *b* 1626; *m* 28 June 1648 Mary (*m* 2nd 17 Aug 1657 1st Duke of Beaufort (*qv*) and *d* 7 Jan 1714/15), sis of 1st Earl of Essex (*qv*), and *dvp* 30 March 1654, having by her had surv issue:

1c WILLIAM SEYMOUR, **3rd Duke of Somerset**; *b* 17 April 1652; *d* unm 12 Dec 1671, when the Tottenham Park and Savernake Forest, Wilts, estates, together with other landed property, passed to his sis the Countess of Ailesbury (and from her ultimately to the Brudenell-Bruce Marquesses of Ailesbury, *qv*)

1c Elizabeth; *m* 31 Aug 1676 2nd Earl of Ailesbury (*see* AILESBURY, M) and *d* 12 Jan 1696/7

4b JOHN SEYMOUR, **4th Duke of Somerset**; MP Marlborough 1661–71, Ld Lt Wilts and Somerset 1672–75; *m* 1661 Sarah (*m* 3rd *c* 17 July 1682 2nd Baron Coleraine and *dsp* 2 Nov 1692), widow of George Grimston (*see* VERULAM, E) and dau and heiress of Sir Edward Alston, MD, Pres Coll Physicians, and *dsp* 29 April 1675, when the Marquessate expired

1b Frances; *m* 1st 28 Oct 1652 2nd Viscount Molyneux (*dsp*, *bur* 2 July 1654; *see* 1970 edn SEFTON, E); *m* 2nd 4th Earl of Southampton (*d* 16 May 1667); *m* 3rd 1676 9th Lord (Baron) Darcy de Knayth (*qv*) and was *bur* 5 Jan 1680/1

2b Mary; *m* by 1649 3rd Earl of Winchilsea (*see* WINCHILSEA and NOTTINGHAM, E) and *d* by 10 April 1673, leaving issue (*see also* BATH, M)

3b Jane; m 7 May 1661 3rd Viscount of Dungarvan, est s of 2nd Earl of Corke and (1st Earl of) Burlington, and d 23 Nov 1679, leaving issue (see CORK and ORRERY, E)

3a FRANCIS SEYMOUR, 1st BARON SEYMOUR OF TROWBRIDGE, Co Wilts, so cr 19 Feb 1640/1, PC (1641); Chllr Duchy Lancaster 1660; b c 1590, ktd 23 Oct 1613; m 1st c 1620 Frances, dau and coheir of Sir Gilbert Prinne/Pryne, of Allington, Wilts, and had:

1b CHARLES SEYMOUR, 2nd BARON SEYMOUR OF TROWBRIDGE; b 1621; MP Gt Bedwyn 1640 and Wilts 1661–66; m 1st Mary, dau and sole heiress of Thomas Smith, of Soley, Wilts, and had a (d an infant) and two daus; m 2nd 1654 Elizabeth (m 2nd 16 Sept 1672 Sir John Ernle, of Whetham, Chllr Exchequer, and was bur 30 Oct 1691), est dau of 1st Baron Alington of Killard, and d 7 Aug 1665, having by her had, with other issue (d young):

1c FRANCIS SEYMOUR, **5th Duke of Somerset**; b 17 Jan 1657/8; educ Eton and Harrow; travelled in Italy and after a visit to a church at Lerici with some companions who insulted a lady was shot dead at the door of his inn 20 April 1678 by Horatio Botti, a Genoese nobleman and husband of the lady in question; d unm

2c CHARLES SEYMOUR, **6th Duke of Somerset** ('The Proud Duke'), KG (Jan 1683/4), PC (1701); b 13 Aug 1662; educ Harrow and Trin Coll Cambridge; Ld Lt E R Yorks 1682–87 and Somerset 1683–87, led Somerset Militia in suppressing Monmouth's Rebellion 1685, Speaker Ho Lds 1689, Ld Pres Cncl and a Ld of Trade Jan–July 1702, Master Horse 1702–Jan 1711/2 and 1714–15; through force of personality helped secure the Hanoverian succession 1714 by a timely though unsolicited appearance before the Privy Council, although neither a PC at that time nor an occupant of any office of importance; m 1st 30 May 1682, as her 3rd husb, Lady Elizabeth née Percy, only child of 5th Earl of Northumberland (see NORTHUMBERLAND, D), and had, with other issue:

1d ALGERNON SEYMOUR, **7th Duke of Somerset**, called up to Ho Lds as LORD (Baron) PERCY (see NORTHUMBERLAND, D), cr in addition 2 Oct 1749 BARON WARKWORTH OF WARKWORTH CASTLE, Co Northumberland, and EARL OF NORTHUMBERLAND, also cr 3 Oct 1749 BARON COCKERMOUTH, Co Cumberland, and EARL OF EGREMONT, Co Cumberland (all GB); b 11 Nov 1684; MP (Tory) Marlborough 1705–08 and Northumberland 1708–22, served War of Spanish Succession 1708–13 (present Battle of Oudenarde 1708, ADC to 1st Duke of Marlborough (qv) Battle of Malplaquet 1709), Col 15th Foot 1709, Govr Tynemouth Castle 1710–Feb 1749/50, Capt and Col 2nd Troop Horse Gds Feb 1714/5–40, Brig-Gen 1727, Maj-Gen 1735, Govr Minorca 1737–42, Lt Gen 1739, Col Roy Regt Horse Gds 1740–50, Govr Guernsey 1742–Feb 1749/50, Gen 1747; m shortly after 1 March 1714/5 Frances (d 7 July 1754), est dau and coheir of Henry Thynne (only s of 1st Viscount Weymouth; see BATH, M), and d 7 Feb 1750, when the Earldom of Hertford and Barony of Beauchamp (both 1559) and the Barony of Seymour of Trowbridge expired, the Earldom of Northumberland and Barony of Warkworth passed to his s-in-law and the Earldom of Egremont and Barony of Cockermouth passed to his n, having had:

1e George, Viscount Beauchamp; b 11 Sept 1725; dvp 11 Sept 1744

1e ELIZABETH, s f as BARONESS PERCY (of the cr effectively bestowed 1722); m 16 July 1740 Sir Hugh Smithson, 4th Bt, later 1st Duke of Northumberland (qv)

1d Elizabeth; m 4 June 1707 7th and last Earl of Thomond (see INCHIQUIN, B) and dsp 2 April 1734

2d Katherine; m 15 July 1708 Sir William Wyndham, 3rd Bt, of Orchard Wyndham, PC, MP (d 17 July 1740), and d 9 April 1731, having had, with a dau (d unm):

1e CHARLES WYNDHAM, 2nd EARL OF EGREMONT (see EGREMONT, LECONFIELD and, B, preliminary remarks), as which s unc

2e PERCY WYNDHAM later WYNDHAM-O'BRIEN (following death 20 Sept 1741 of his unc-by-marriage 7th Earl of Thomond (see above), whose estates he inherited), 1st and last EARL OF THOMOND, so cr 11 Dec 1756, as also BARON IBRACKAN (both I), PC (1757); b c 1723; educ St Mary Hall Oxford; MP (Tory) Taunton 1745–47, Minehead 1747–54 and 1761–68, Cockermouth 1754–61 and Winchelsea 1768–74, a Ld Treasury 1755–56, Treasurer Household 1757–61, Ld Lt Somerset 1764–76; d unm 21 July 1774, when the Earldom expired

1e Elizabeth; m 1749 George Grenville, PC, and d 5 Dec 1769, leaving issue (see TEMPLE OF STOWE, E)

3d Anne; m 17 Sept 1719 3rd Duke of Leeds (see 1963 edn) and dsps 27 Nov 1722. He d 9 March 1731

2c (cont.) The **6th Duke** m 2nd 4 Feb 1725/6 Lady Charlotte Finch (d 21 Jan 1773), dau of 7th Earl of Winchilsea and (2nd Earl of) Nottingham (qv), and d 2 Dec 1748, having by her had:

4d Frances; m 3 Sept 1750 John, Marquess of Granby (see RUTLAND, D), and d 25 Jan 1761, leaving issue

5d Charlotte; m 6 Oct 1750 3rd Earl of Aylesford (qv) and d 15 Feb 1805, leaving issue

1c Honora; m 9 Feb 1675/6 Sir Charles Gerard, 3rd Bt, and was bur 11 May 1731, leaving issue

1b Frances; m 23 June 1662 1st and last Viscount Downe of the 1675 cr and was bur 20 Sept 1679 (see DUCIE, E)

3a (cont.) The 1st BARON SEYMOUR OF TROWBRIDGE m 2nd by 1636 Catherine (dsp, bur 5 March 1700/01), dau of Sir Robert Lee, of Billesley, by Anne, dau of Sir Thomas Lowe, Ld Mayor London, and d 12 July 1664

1a Honora; m 9 July 1610 Sir Ferdinando Sutton, KB, s and heir of 5th Baron Dudley (qv), and was bur 23 March 1620, leaving issue

(3) Thomas; m Isabel, dau of Edward Onley, of Catesby, Northants, and dsp 20 Aug 1619

3 (cont.) The 1st EARL OF HERTFORD m 2nd by Nov 1595 Frances (dsp 14 May 1598), dau of 1st Baron Howard of Effingham (see EFFINGHAM, E); m 3rd

c 27 May 1601 Frances (m 3rd, as his 3rd w, 2nd Duke of Lennox and (1st Duke of) Richmond and (see MORAY, E), and dsp 8 Oct 1639), widow of Henry Pranell, of London, and dau of 1st Viscount Howard of Bindon, and d without further issue 6 April 1621

4 Henry; m Lady Jane Percy, dau of 1st Earl of Northumberland of the 1557 cr (see NORTHUMBERLAND, D), and dsp

1 Anne; m 1st 3 June 1550 John Dudley, Earl of Warwick (dsp executed for treason 21 Oct 1554), s of John Dudley, Duke of Northumberland (see NORTHUMBERLAND, D, preliminary remarks), the great rival of the Protector Somerset; m 2nd 29 April 1555 Sir Edward Unton, KB, of Wadley, Berks, and d by 17 Jan 1587/8

2 Mary; m 1st Andrew Rogers, of Branston, Dorset; m 2nd Sir Henry Peyton

3 Elizabeth; m Sir Richard Knightley, of Norton, Northants, and d 3 June 1602. He d 1 Sept 1615

The 5th Bt d 29 Dec 1740; his s,

Sir Edward Seymour, 6th Bt, and **8th Duke of Somerset,** as which s 5th cousin once-removed 7 Feb 1749/50; bapt 17 Jan 1694/5; educ Magdalen Coll Oxford; MP (Tory) Salisbury 1741–47, Ld Lt Wilts 1752–57; m 5 March 1716/7 Mary, only dau and heiress of Daniel Webb, of Monkton Farley and Melksham, Wilts, and heiress of her uncle, Edward Somner, of Seend, Wilts, and d 15 Dec 1757, leaving:

1 EDWARD SEYMOUR, **9th Duke of Somerset**; b 2 Jan 1717/8; educ Winchester and Oriel Coll Oxford; d unm 2 Jan 1792

2 WEBB SEYMOUR, **10th Duke of Somerset**; inherited his maternal gf's estate of Monkton Farley; b 3 Dec 1718; m 11 Dec 1769 Mary Ann (d 23 July 1802), dau and sole heiress of John Bonnell, of Stanton Harcourt, Oxon, and d 15 Dec 1793, leaving:

(1) EDWARD ADOLPHUS SEYMOUR later ST MAUR, **11th Duke of Somerset**, KG (1837); b 24 Feb 1775; educ Eton and Ch Ch Oxford; m 1st 24 June 1800 Lady Charlotte Douglas Hamilton (d 10 June 1827), dau of 9th Duke of Hamilton and (6th Duke of) Brandon (qv), and had, with two daus (d unm):

1a EDWARD ADOLPHUS SEYMOUR later ST MAUR, **12th Duke of Somerset**, also 1st and last EARL SAINT MAUR, of Berry Pomeroy, Co Devon (UK), so cr 19 June 1863, KG (1862), PC (1851); b 20 Dec 1804; educ Eton and Ch Ch Oxford; MP (Tory) Okehampton 1830–31 and (Lib) Totnes 1834–55, a Ld Treasury 1835–39, Sec E India Bd 1839–41, Parly U-Sec Home Dept June-Sept 1841, Ch Commr Woods and Forests 1850–51 and Works 1851–52, 1st Ld Admlty 1859–56, Ld Lt Devon and Er Bro Trin Ho 1861–85; m 10 June 1830 Jane Georgiana (d 14 Dec 1884), yst dau of Thomas Sheridan, s of Richard Brinsley Sheridan, the playwright, and dspms 28 Nov 1885, when the Earldom of St Maur expired, having had:

1b (Edward Adolphus) Ferdinand, Earl Saint Maur, called up 9 July 1863 to Ho Lds vp in f's Barony of Seymour; b 17 July 1835; dspl unm & vp 30 Sept 1869, having had by Rosa Elizabeth Swan, of Higham, nr Bury St Edmunds, Suffolk (m 14 Sept 1872 François Tournier):

1c (Richard) Harold, of Horton, Chipping Sodbury, Glos; b 6 June 1869; Maj; had:

1d Frederick Percy St Maur; m April 1923 Hope Wilhelmena Albermarle Blakeney and had:

1e Edward St Maur

2b Edward Percy; b 19 Aug 1841; Attaché Vienna, Madrid and Paris; dvp unm 20 Dec 1865

1b Jane Hermione; m 26 Oct 1852 Sir Frederick Ulric Graham, 3rd Bt, of Netherby (qv), and d 4 April 1909, leaving issue

2b Ulrica Frederica Jane; m 1 June 1858 Lord Henry Frederick Thynne, PC, 2nd s of 3rd Marquess of Bath (qv), and d 26 Jan 1916, leaving issue

3b Helen Guendolen; m 2 Aug 1865 Sir John William Ramsden, 5th Bt (qv), and d 14 Aug 1910, leaving issue

2a ARCHIBALD HENRY ALGERNON SEYMOUR later ST MAUR, **13th Duke of Somerset**, DL Leics; b 30 Dec 1810; d unm 12 Jan 1891

3a ALGERNON PERCY BANKS SEYMOUR later ST MAUR, **14th Duke of Somerset**; b 22 Dec 1813; Capt RHG; author: The Old Coaching Days; m 17 May 1845 Horatia Isabella Harriet (d 28 Oct 1915), 2nd dau of John Philip Morier, Br Min Dresden (see HERTFORD, M), and d 2 Oct 1894, leaving:

1b ALGERNON ST MAUR, **15th Duke of Somerset**, JP, TD; b 22 July 1846; Lt 60th Rifles, Hon Col 4th Bn Wilts Regt, KJStJ; m 5 Sept 1877 Susan Margaret, DStJ, Médaille de la Reconnaissance (France) and Serbian and Spanish Red Cross (d 20 Jan 1936), yr dau of Charles MacKinnon, and dsp 22 Oct 1923

2b Percy; b 11 Nov 1847; Maj 1st Bn Roy Fus; m 18 March 1899 Hon Violet White (d 2 July 1927), yst dau of 2nd Baron Annaly (qv), and d 16 July 1907, leaving:

1c Helen Violet; b 21 March 1900; m 1st 12 Nov 1924 Maj George Edward Gosling, MC, DL, 10th Roy Hus (d 20 Nov 1938), of Stratton Audley Park, Bicester, s of Col George Gosling, and had issue; m 2nd 21 July 1947 Maj-Gen John Frederick Boyce Combe, CB, DSO and bar, 11th Hus, s of Capt Christian Combe, and d 12 Aug 1975. He d 12 July 1967

2c Lettice; b 30 Oct 1902; m 18 April 1928 Gen Sir Richard London McCreery, GCB, KBE, DSO, MC, DL, 12th Roy Lancers, est s of Walter McCreery, of Bilton Park, Rugby, and had issue. He d 18 Oct 1967

3c Lucia Mary; b 19 March 1906; m 5 Jan 1938 Maj Edward Frederic Gosling, Roy Dragoons, 2nd s of Maj William Sullivan Gosling, JP, DL, of Hassobury, Essex, and d 6 July 1954

3b Ernest; b 11 Nov 1847; m 9 Nov 1907 Dora, dau of Rev John Constable, Rector Marston Biggott, Somerset, and d 21 May 1922

4b Edward; b 7 Feb 1849; Lt 60th Rifles; m 20 Aug 1879 Lilian (dsp 21 Sept 1910), dau of John Stanhope, and d 15 Sept 1920

1a Charlotte Jane; m 31 March 1839 William Blount, of Orleton, Herefs, and d 7 Oct 1889 aged 86, having had issue. He d 27 July 1885

2a Anna Maria Jane; m 13 Sept 1838 William Tollemache and d 23 Sept 1873, leaving issue (see DYSART, E)

(1) (cont.) The **11th Duke** m 2nd 28 July 1836 Margaret (dsp 18 July 1880), est dau of Sir Michael Shaw-Stewart, 5th Bt (qv), and d 15 Aug 1855

(2) Webb John; *b* 7 Feb 1777; FRS; *d* unm 15 April 1819

3 William; *b* 1724; barrister; *m* 5 June 1767 Hester (*d* May 1812), dau and sole heiress of John Maltravers, of Melksham, Wilts, and *d* 5 Nov 1800, having had two sons and a dau

4 Francis (Very Rev); *b* 1726; Dean Wells; *m* 1749 Catherine (*d* 24 Dec 1801), dau of Rev Thomas Payne, and *d* 16 Feb 1799, having had, with another s (*d* unm):

(1) Francis Compton; Col; *m* 3 Sept 1787 Leonora (*d* 27 June 1795), widow of John Hudson, seaman, and dau of George Perkins, publican, of Woolwich, and *d* 1822, leaving:

1a Francis Edward; *b* 21 Sept 1788; Capt RN; *m* 4 Feb 1815 Elizabeth (*d* 11 July 1851), 2nd dau of Charles Cooke, and *d* 26 July 1866, leaving:

1b Francis Payne (Rev); *b* 23 Dec 1815; Rector Havant; *m* 1st 13 Sept 1848 Jane Margaret (*d* 25 Oct 1860), yst dau of Rev Alexander Robert Charles Dallas, and had issue (the surv daus being granted by roy warrant Aug 1925 precedence as duke's daus):

1c Francis Alexander Dallas; *b* 23 Sept 1853; *d* unm 18 Jan 1883

2c EDWARD HAMILTON, **16th Duke**

1c Julia Margaret; *m* 9 April 1874 Rev Canon Charles Augustus Hulbert, Rector Castor, and *d* 22 Aug 1928, leaving issue. He *d* 1919

2c Emily Charlotte; *m* 14 Oct 1873 Charles Henry Dallas, Japanese CS, and *d* 11 Nov 1900, leaving issue. He *d* 1894

3c Evelyn Hamilton; *b* 4 Sept 1855; *d* 8 Aug 1859

4c Beatrice Jane; *m* 19 June 1883 Rev Charles Arthur Skelton, RD Woking, Hon Canon Winchester, and *d* 18 Nov 1944, leaving issue. He *d* 10 Jan 1913

1b (cont.) The Rev Francis Seymour *m* 2nd 4 Nov 1862 Blanche Catherine (*d* 14 March 1907), dau of H B Ward, and *d* 4 July 1870, having by her had:

5c Blanche Maud; *b* 14 Sept 1863; Sister Community Holy Name; *d* 7 Aug 1913

6c Gertrude Ward; *d* unm 10 Sept 1952

7c Agnes Mary; *d* unm 29 May 1956

1b Elizabeth Seymour; *m* 18 Aug 1836 John Lowdham Brett, of Ocle Court, Herefs, and had issue. He *d* 30 Nov 1881

2b Charlotte Hamilton Seymour; *m* 15 April 1837 Philip Penry Williams, DL, of Stoke Ho, Tenbury, Worcs, and had issue. He *d* 9 Feb 1873

2a Edward William, of Porthmawr, Breconshire; *b* 1791; Cdr RN; *m* 1st 27 Aug 1821 Charlotte Alice (*dsp* 10 Oct 1847), widow of Richard Wilkins and 3rd dau and coheir of James Greene, of Turton Tower and Clayton Hall, Lancs, and Llansantffraed, Mon, MP Arundel; *m* 2nd 19 April 1849 Elizabeth (*dsp* 14 Sept 1862), dau of Rev Charles Graham, Vicar Petham, Kent; *m* 3rd 5 Nov 1863 Louisa Frances, yst dau of William Macdowall Grant, of Arndilly, and *dsp* 6 July 1874

3a Henry John Hyde; *b* 1 May 1795; *m* 20 Nov 1821 Charlotte (*d* 20 Jan 1869), yst dau of Sir Samuel Whitcombe, and *d* 3 Nov 1860, leaving, with other issue:

1b Henry (Rev); *b* 4 July 1825; Rector Holme Pierrepont, Notts; *m* 1st 4 Nov 1851 Susannah Biscoe (*d* 8 May 1889), dau of Rev Robert Tritton (*see* TRITTON, Bt), and had:

1c Henry Sidney; *b* 15 Sept 1855; *m* 16 April 1896 Hon Helen Smith (*see* HAMBLEDEN, V) and *d* 26 March 1930, leaving:

1d Edward William, TD , JP (Dorset 1945), DL (1959); *b* 27 March 1897; *educ* Eton and New Coll Oxford; Lt Gren Gds (SR) WW I, Lt-Col RA (Devon Yeo) WW II, dir W H Smith 1924–44, High Sheriff Dorset 1957; *m* 18 Nov 1925 Barbara Judith, yr dau of Lt-Col George Reginald Lascelles, CVO, OBE (*see* HAREWOOD, E)

2c Edward Adolphus William (Rev); *b* 31 July 1858; *d* unm 28 Feb 1891

3c Evelyn Stuart; *b* 21 Sept 1864; Lt 4th Bn Sherwood Foresters; *m* 9 Nov 1897 Henrietta (*d* 1941), dau of Turner A Macan, of Elstow, Beds, and Cardiff, Co Armagh, and *d* 27 May 1935

1c Emily Gertrude; *b* 17 July 1852; *d* unm 5 Dec 1912

2c Julia Mary; *b* 31 Oct 1853; *d* unm 9 Dec 1943

3c Emmeline St Maur; *b* 23 Sept 1860; *m* 3 Feb 1885 8th Viscount Torrington (*qv*) and *d* 7 June 1912, leaving issue

4c Madeline St Maur; *b* 11 Nov 1862; *m* 11 Aug 1885 Francis Abel Smith, of Wilford Ho, Notts, and *d* 13 Sept 1951, leaving issue. He *d* 20 March 1908

5c Lilian Octavia; *b* 18 March 1868; *m* 29 Dec 1896 Rev Louis Herbert Wellesley, of Sandroyd Ho and Fairmile Court, Cobham, Vicar Daybrook, Notts, s of Alfred Wellesley Wesley, of Bryn Rhoddyn, N Wales, and *d* 5 July 1905, leaving issue

1b (cont.) The Rev Henry Seymour *m* 2nd 7 Jan 1892 Emmeline Millicent (*d* 12 Oct 1912), dau of James Walker, of Neville Park, Tunbridge Wells, and *d* 12 Aug 1911

1b Charlotte Payne; *m* 7 Aug 1845 Rev Hon Charles James Willoughby and *d* 13 Jan 1892, leaving issue (*see* MIDDLETON, B)

2b Jane Seymour Treherne; *m* 5 May 1846 Henry James Hoare, of Morden Lodge, Surrey, and *d* 14 Dec 1903, leaving issue. He *d* 16 Feb 1859

3b Frances; *m* 3 June 1856 Rev G F Coke, of Lemor Ho, Herefs, and *d* 14 July 1902, leaving issue. He *d* 13 Feb 1885

4b Mary Alice; *m* 20 July 1854 Rev Constantine Estlin Pritchard, Rector S Luffenham, and *d* 5 July 1918, leaving issue. He *d* 6 Oct 1869

(1) Mary; *m* 1st Sept 1773 John Hyde, DD, Judge Supreme Court Bengal, Dean Wells, Canon Windsor, Chaplain in Ordinary to GEORGE III; *m* 2nd 4 Feb 1798 Rev John Payne

(2) Catherine *m* 1st 6 June 1776 (*divorce* 1782) John Newton, of King's Bromley; *m* 2nd M Constant

(3) Frances; *m* 1st Nov 1784 Rev Thomas Bovet, DD; *m* 2nd 11 May 1803 Rev James Tuson

1 Mary; *m* 20 Oct 1759 Vincent John Biscoe (*d* 29 April 1770), of Hookwood, Surrey, and *d* 21 July 1762, leaving issue (*see* SAINT JOHN OF BLETSO, B)

The 15th DUKE's 3rd cousin once-removed,

EDWARD HAMILTON SEYMOUR, **16th Duke of Somerset**, KBE (1919), CB (1915), CMG (1918); *b* 19 May 1860; *educ* Blundell's and RMC Sandhurst; joined Roy Dublin Fus 1880, Capt 1888, tfd Army Ordnance Dept 1896, Maj 1898, Lt-Col 1903, Col 1907, served WW I, Hon Brig-Gen 1920, Hon Col Somerset Yeo (TA), Col RAOC, 3rd Cl Order White Eagle Serbia; *m* 28 July 1881 Rowena (*d* 13 Nov 1950), dau of George Wall, of Colombo, Ceylon, and *d* 5 May 1931, leaving:

EVELYN FRANCIS EDWARD SEYMOUR, **17th Duke of Somerset**, DSO (1918), OBE (1919), JP Wilts; *b* 1 May 1882; *educ* Blundell's and RMC Sandhurst; Lt-Col Roy Dublin Fus, Boer War 1901–02 (Queen's Medal, five clasps), Aden 1903, WW I (despatches), Lt-Col Devonshire Regt WW II 1939–41, Col Gen Staff 1941, Ld Lt Wilts 1942, Coronation Medal 1937; *m* 3 Jan 1906 Edith Mary (*d* 19 April 1962), only child of William Parker, JP, of Whittington Hall, Derbys, and *d* 26 April 1954, having had:

1 Francis William; *b* 28 Dec 1906; *d* 14 May 1907

2 Algernon Francis Edward; *b* 22 July 1908; *d* 14 Feb 1911

3 PERCY HAMILTON SEYMOUR, **18th Duke of Somerset**; DL (Wilts 1960); *b* 27 Sept 1910; *educ* Blundell's and Clare Coll Cambridge (BA 1933); Maj Wilts Regt; *m* 18 Dec 1951 *Gwendoline Collette (Jane), 2nd dau of Maj John Cyril Collette Thomas, of Burn Cottage, Bude, Cornwall, and *d* 1984, leaving:

(1) JOHN MICHAEL EDWARD SEYMOUR, **19th and present Duke of Somerset**

(2) +Francis Charles Edward [The Lord Francis Seymour, 27 Palliser Rd, London W14]; *b* 10 Aug 1956; *educ* Eton; slr; *m* 22 May 1982 *Paddy, yr dau of Col Anthony John Irvine Poynder, MC, RE, of Gassons, Slindon, Sussex, and has:

1a +Webb; *b* 1990

1a *Poppy Hermione Alexandra; *b* 1988

(1) *Anne Frances Mary; *b* 11 Nov 1954

1 *Susan Mary [The Lady Susan Seymour, Sunnyside, Maiden Bradley, Warminster, Wilts]; *b* 26 April 1913; served WW II, late divnl Pres BRCS

Seat: Berry Pomeroy, Totnes, Devon. A castle on the site was erected *c* 1300 by the Pomeroys (*see* HARBERTON, V) but is now in ruins. The manor house there dates from the mid-16th century and was built by Protector (the **1st Duke of**) **Somerset**, who used the walls of the castle as external shields.

SOPER

Creation: B. (LP, UK) 12 May 1965.

THE BARON SOPER, of Kingsway, London Borough of Camden (The Rev Donald Oliver Soper) [The Rev and Rt Hon The Lord Soper, 19 Thayer St, London W1M 5LJ]; *b* 31 Jan 1903; *educ* Aske's Sch Hatcham, St Catharine's Coll Cambridge (BA 1926, MA 1928, Hon Fell 1966, Hon DD 1988), Wesley Ho Cambridge and LSE (PhD 1929); ordained Methodist Ministry 1929, Min S London Mission 1926–29, Centl London Mission 1929–36 and W London Mission 1936–78, Ppres Methodist Conf 1953, Chm Shelter 1974–78; Life FTCL, Peace Award World Methodist Cncl 1981, author: *Christianity and Its Critics*, *Popular Fallacies about the Christian Faith*, *Will Christianity Work?*, *Christianity Today*, *Calling for Action* (1984); *m* 3 Aug 1929 Marie Gertrude (*d* Jan 1994), dau of Arthur Dean, of Norbury, and has:

1 *Ann Loveday Dean [The Hon Mrs Ann Horn, 54 St Barnabas Rd, Cambridge]; *b* 15 April 1931; BSc; *m* 29 Nov 1952 (*divorce* 1979) Gabriel Horn, MD, BSc, Fell King's Coll Cambridge, s of A Horn, of Lodz, Poland, and has two sons and two daus

2 *Bridget Mary Dean; *b* 17 Dec 1933; MCSP; *m* 15 Sept 1956 Owen Henry Kemmis (*d* 1985), only s of Hubert Beresford Kemmis, of London NW11, and has a s

3 *Judith Catharine Dean [The Hon Mrs Jenkins, 12 Brookland Hill, London NW11]; *b* 25 Oct 1942; BSc; *m* 1970 *Alan Jenkins, BEd

4 *Caroline Susan Dean [The Hon Mrs Blacker, 91 Wendell Rd, London W12]; *b* 11 Aug 1946; BA; *m* 1975 *Terence Blacker, er s of Gen Sir Cecil Hugh Blacker, KCB, OBE, MC (*see* BUXTON, Bt)

Lineage: JAMES FRIEND SOPER, of East Hill, Wandsworth; *m* Eliza (*d* 25 Nov 1930 aged 79) and *d* 17 Feb 1933 aged 84, leaving:

ERNEST FRANKHAM SOPER, of Wallington; *b* 5 Sept 1870; memb Average Adjusters' Assoc; *m* 1 Aug 1900 Caroline Amelia (*d* 22 Aug 1967), dau of Walter Chatfield Pilcher, of Wandsworth, and *d* 11 April 1962, leaving:

1 DONALD OLIVER, *cr* a **Baron**

2 Meredith Ross; *b* 6 Nov 1907; *educ* Aske's Sch Hatcham and St Catharine's Coll Cambridge (BA 1929, MA 1927); *m* 22 April 1933 Ruth (*d* 15 Nov 1966), dau of John Osborne Peed, of London, and *d* 26 Oct 1934, leaving:

(1) *Dinah Ross; *b* 21 April 1935; *m* 3 Sept 1960 Michael James Essex, s of Stanley James Essex, of Littlehampton, Sussex, and has a s and three daus

1 *Millicent Ellen; *b* 24 July 1905; *m* 22 Dec 1934 Eric Proom Lawrence, AICS, s of Joseph Edward Lawrence, BSc, of Wylam-on-Tyne, Northumberland, and has two sons and a dau

SOULBURY

Arms: Sa. on a chevron or between three plates, each charged with a cross patée gu., a ram's head per pale sa. and gu. **Crest:** A plate charged with a ram's head erased per pale gu. and sa. **Supporters:** Two ravens sa., each charged with a plate, thereon a cross patée gu. **Motto:** *Non vi sed virtute* ('Not by force but by virtue'). **Creations:** B. (UK) 6 Aug 1941, V. (UK) 16 July 1954.

THE 2ND VISCOUNT SOULBURY, of Soulbury, Co Buckingham, and **Baron Soulbury**, of Soulbury, Co Buckingham (James Herwald Ramsbotham) [The Rt Hon The Viscount Soulbury, House of Lords, London SW1A 0PW]; *b* 21 March 1915; *s f* 1971; *educ* Eton and Magdalen Coll Oxford; *m* 5 April 1949 Anthea Margaret (*d* 26 June 1950), only dau of David Wilton

Lineage: JOHN RAMSBOTHAM; among the King's tenants in Tottington, Lancs, May 1443; had:

OTTIWELL RAMSBOTHAM; had:

GEOFFREY RAMSBOTHAM, of Tottington; living 1524; unc of:

RICHARD RAMSBOTHAM, of Digfield and Carr House and Ramsbottom; had:

RICHARD RAMSBOTHAM, of Digfield and Carr Ho; had:

JOHN RAMSBOTHAM, of Old Hall, Stand, Lancs; living 1600; had:

RICHARD RAMSBOTHAM, of Old Hall; *d* 1675, leaving:

JOHN RAMSBOTHAM, of Old Hall; *m* Elizabeth Whitehead (*d* 1660) and had:

RICHARD RAMSBOTHAM, of Old Hall; *m* 1690 Joan, 3rd dau of Ferdinando Stanley, and had:

JOHN RAMSBOTHAM, of Old Hall; *m* Elizabeth, n of Very Rev Richard Wroe, of Manchester Collegiate Ch, and had:

JOHN RAMSBOTHAM, of Old Hall; *m* Rebecca, dau of James Bury, of Chamber Hall, Bury, and *d* 1794, having had, with two er sons (John, *b* 1770, *d* unm 1818; James, *b* 1773, *d* 1835):

THOMAS RAMSBOTHAM, of Centre Vale, Lancs; *b* 1775; *m* 26 May 1802 Esther (*d* Jan 1826), dau of James Openshaw, of Redvales, Bury, and *d* 22 April 1839, having had, with an est s (John, *dsp* 1833) and a yst s (Thomas, Rev Canon), *b* 1819, Rector Midelton, Lancs, Canon Manchester Cathedral, *m* Mary Wyatt Smith and *d* 1881, having had, with two sons, Agnes Mary, *m* 1869 her cousin Lt Thomas Ramsbotham, RN, and had issue; *see below*):

JAMES RAMSBOTHAM, of Old Hall, Stand, Centre Vale, Todmorden and Crowborough Warren, Sussex, JP; *b* 10 March 1814; *m* 20 April 1837 Jane (*d* 22 Dec 1897 aged 81), only dau of Joshua Fielden, of Waterside, Todmorden, and *d* 6 March 1888, leaving:

1 John, JP Sussex; *b* 26 Dec 1839; *educ* Winchester; Hon Maj 3rd Bn Roy Sussex Regt; *m* 1st 28 July 1864 Emilie Helen Leigh (*d* 18 April 1874), yst dau of William Clare, of The Hollies, Edge Lane, Liverpool, and had:

(1) James Hugh Fielden; *b* 8 June 1865; *d* 12 April 1874

(2) Ralph Leigh; *b* 17 Nov 1872; *educ* Lancing and Clare Coll Cambridge (MA); barrister Inner Temple 1897; *m* 8 July 1903 May Elizabeth, only dau of Alfred Thomas West, of S Kensington, and *d* Aug 1937, having had:

  1a Marjorie Helen Leigh; *b* 23 May 1905; *d* unm 1966

  2a Jocelyn Elizabeth Leigh; *b* 22 Oct 1908; *d* unm 1947

(1) Alice Mary; *b* 1, *d* 9 Aug 1868

(2) Hilda; *b* 28 Jan 1871; *m* 9 Oct 1895 Rev Henry Alfred Ransome, Vicar St Peter's, Field Broughton, est s of Rev J H Ransome, Vicar Kirkoswald, Hon Canon Carlisle, and *d* 1952, leaving issue. He *d* 4 July 1917

1 (cont.) John Ramsbotham *m* 2nd 1 Sept 1885 Sophia Borman Standaloft (*dsp* 1897) and *d* 23 Nov 1905

2 Thomas; *b* 10 Aug 1842; Lt RN; *m* 1st 26 Aug 1869 his cousin Agnes Mary Ramsbotham (*see above*) and had:

(1) Godfrey; *d* unm 1946

(1) Gertrude Alice; *m* 18 April 1906 William Holding, only s of William Holding, of Elm Grove, Kingsclere, and had issue

(2) Helen Margaret; *m* 29 Oct 1902 Capt Guy Elliott Harcourt, of Ankerwyke Priory, Bucks, and had issue

(3) Agnes Fielden; *m* 31 March 1918 Charles Lawrence Freeman, s of Robert Freeman, and *dsp* 1940

(4) Lucy Wyatt; *m* 28 Feb 1923 Lt-Col E A C Matthews, IMS, and *dsp*

2 (cont.) Thomas Ramsbotham *m* 2nd 22 June 1892 Emily Blanche Fatt, of Warminster, and *d* 28 Dec 1913, having by her had:

(5) Mildred Isabel Eleanor; *m* Capt William Bryan

3 Fielden; *b* 10 July 1846; *educ* Lancing; *m* 9 June 1874 Edith Henrietta Anne, dau of Rev Robert Walker, Prof Experimental Philosophy, Wadham Coll, Oxford, and *d* 29 May 1922, leaving:

(1) Edward Rishton; *b* 7 April 1875; *m* 20 Nov 1900 Hilda Jane, 2nd dau of William Birdseye, and *d* 26 Nov 1925, having had:

  1a James Fielden; *b* 23 Sept 1902; *m* 6 Feb 1929 Doris Julia, JP (Bucks 1959) (*m* 2nd Walker Phillips, of Bletchley, Bucks), only dau of William Reynolds, of Leighton Buzzard, and *d* 25 Nov 1966, leaving:

    1b *Michael John Fielden; *b* 4 March 1935; *m* 19 June 1962 *Gillian Diana Anne, er dau of A E W Henderson, of Wingrave, Bucks, and has:

      1c *Richard Fielden; *b* 26 March 1966

      1c *Sarah Anne; *b* 26 March 1963

    2b *Geoffrey Edward [Geoffrey Ramsbotham Esq, Solden Hill House, Byfield, Daventry, Northants]; *b* 19 Sept 1936

    1b *Lois Elizabeth; *b* 3 Feb 1930; *m* 23 April 1952 James Donald Meikle Howat, MB, BCh, MRCS, LRCP, and has:

      1c *Alexander James; *b* 24 July 1955; *educ* Sedbergh

      1c *Fiona Elizabeth; *b* 23 June 1953

  2a Harold Rishton; *b* 19 Nov 1903; *m* 2 June 1931 Mary Elizabeth Palmer and *d* 6 April 1961, leaving:

    1b *Edward George Rishton; *b* 28 April 1933; *m* 16 Nov 1962 *Cherrilyn Mary Hamilton and has:

      1c *Cherie Elizabeth; *b* 20 Feb 1965

      2c *Tania Ann; *b* 22 May 1966

    2b *James; *b* 3 Jan 1936; *educ* Mata Mata Coll, NZ; *m* *Olive Bridget Mary, 2nd dau of James Patrick Morrin, of Dublin, and has:

      1c *Stephen James; *b* 17 Aug 1975

      1c *Anita Morrin; *b* 11 Nov 1971; *m* 24 May 1969 *Olive Bridgette Mary, dau of E Morrin, of Dublin

    3b *Philip John; *b* 20 Dec 1944; *m* July 1967 *Nancy Miles

    1b *Heather Mary; *b* 19 Nov 1938; *m* 29 Aug 1964 Malcolm Joseph Beehre, s of Roy Malcolm Beehre, of NZ, and has:

      1c *Heather Jayne; *b* 8 Feb 1965

      2c *Susan Mary; *b* 25 March 1966

      3c *Kym Elizabeth; *b* 28 Nov 1967

    2b *Elizabeth Jane; *b* 26 Aug 1947; *m* Sept 1965 Bruce Dick and has:

      1c *Christopher Mark; *b* 11 Sept 1965

      2c *Andrew Neville; *b* 30 March 1967

  3a Philip Vincent; *b* 30 March 1906; *m* 27 June 1953 *Mary Grayling and *d* Aug 1953, leaving:

    1b *Elizabeth Jane; *b* March 1954

  4a Hugh; *b* 21 Sept 1910; *d* 10 July 1912

(2) James Humphrey; *b* 13 July 1876; *m* 14 Oct 1905 Ruth Elizabeth Clifford and *dsp* 11 Feb 1935

(1) Edith Holdsworth; *b* 29 Nov 1877; *d* unm 20 June 1961

(2) Mildred Frances; *b* 17 Jan 1879; *d* unm 5 Feb 1960

(3) Ruth Agnes Fielden; *b* 12 July 1884; *d* unm 10 April 1959

4 Richard Hugh; *b* 1 May 1848; *educ* Winchester and Queens' Coll Cambridge; *m* 8 Feb 1872 Agnes Geraldine (*d* 22 Dec 1924), dau of Henry Hoyle, of Little Harwood Hall, Blackburn, and *d* 8 May 1917, leaving:

(1) Henry; *b* 13 July 1876; *m* 12 July 1917 Mary Battle and *dsp* 25 Dec 1920

(2) Joshua Fielden; *b* 26 June 1878; MInstCE, Dir Lighthouses Australia 1913; *m* 9 Dec 1908 Ruth, yr dau of Harry Arnold, of Milnthorpe, Westmorland, and *d* 19 Oct 1951, leaving:

  1a Nicholas Arnold; *b* 1 May 1910; *dsp* 1966

  2a James Fielden; *b* 1 May, *d* 5 May 1910

  1a *Jane Fielden; *b* 30 Nov 1912

(1) Frances; *b* 10 Nov 1872; *d* unm 1943

(2) Jane Fielden; *b* 25 Feb 1874; *d* unm 22 Dec 1925

(3) Christina Agnes; *b* 26 June 1887; *m* 17 Nov 1915 John Douglas Nickels, er s of John Tetley Nickels, of The Day House, Shrewsbury, and *d* 21 Dec 1931, leaving issue

5 Philip Bury, JP Devon; *b* 4 March 1854; *educ* Lancing; *m* 19 Sept 1878 Florence Elizabeth (*d* 31 Aug 1937), 3rd dau of Rev Richard King, of Prestwich, Lancs, and *d* 16 July 1927, having had:

(1) Richard Bury, MBE; *b* 27 April 1880; *educ* Shrewsbury and Magdalen Coll Oxford (BA 1903, MA 1912, BLitt 1924); Maj Res Offrs IA WW I, NWF India and Mesopotamia, 2nd Oxon Bn HG 1940–44 WW II, Indian Educnl Serv, Pro-V-Chllr Moslem U Aligarh, UP, India, Hon Freeman Woodstock 1951; *m* 6 Nov 1910 Eveline Florence (*d* 27 Dec 1972), yr dau of George James Perram, CIE, and *d* 23 Sept 1970, leaving:

  1a *Richard Hugh Bury; *b* 12 Sept 1915; *educ* Beaumont and Corpus Christi Coll Oxford (MA); IA WW II; *m* 10 July 1946 *Helen, er dau of Victor John Gadban, of Blundens, Froyle, Hants, and has:

    1b *Catherine Mary; *b* 26 April 1947; *m* 18 July 1970 Peter James Jackson, yst s of H H Jackson, of Nottingham, and has:

      1c *Matthew Henry; *b* 9 Sept 1972

    2b *Lucy Helen [Mrs Matthew Murton, Glynfryn Farm, Penuwch, nr Tregaron, Dyfed]; *b* 26 March 1952; *m* *Matthew Murton and has:

      1c *Laurie; *b* 2 May 1982

      1c *Liv; *b* 2 May 1982

  1a *Elizabeth Bathurst; *b* 24 July 1912; *m* 6 Nov 1946 David Woodward, OBE, and has:

1b *Elizabeth Deodata; *b* 27 Sept 1947

(2) Phillip Bury; *b* 7 Nov 1890; *d* 22 Feb 1891

(3) Geoffrey Bury; *b* 14 June 1893; *educ* Wellington and Corpus Christi Coll Oxford; Lt 3rd Bn Roy Sussex Regt (attd 1st Bn S Staffs Regt); *ka* 16 May 1915

(1) Charlotte Louise, of Budleigh Salterton, S Devon; *m* 1st 26 Oct 1904 Capt James Herbert Lowry, IA, 6th s of Lt-Gen Robert William Lowry, CB (*dsp* 24 Aug 1911); *m* 2nd 20 Aug 1915 Capt H P V Hickman, RN (*das* at sea 9 Nov 1918), s of Maj R J Hickman, 60th Rifles, and had issue

6 Edward Geoffrey, JP Sussex; *b* 1 April 1856; *educ* Malvern; *m* 14 July 1881 Octavia Lucy Newbould (*d* 24 Aug 1913), 8th dau of Charles Chadwick, MD, of Leeds, and *d* 25 March 1929, having had:

(1) Dorothy Helen; *b* 5 Oct 1882; *d* unm 22 Jan 1967

(2) Sybil Margaret; *b* 4 Feb, *d* 12 April 1880

(3) Margaret; *b* 7 Oct 1886; *d* unm Dec 1952

7 Herwald, of Crowborough Warren, Sussex, JP Sussex; *b* 29 Oct 1859; *educ* Malvern and Magdalen Coll Oxford; *m* 25 Aug 1885 Ethel Margaret (*d* 20 Feb 1943), 3rd dau of Thomas Bevan, JP, DL, of Stone Park, Kent, and *d* 11 Aug 1941, leaving:

(1) HERWALD, 1st Viscount

(2) Wilfrid Hubert; *b* 20 Dec 1888; *educ* Uppingham and Clare Coll Cambridge; Brevet Col Artists' Rifles, Capt and Brevet Maj W Yorks Regt; *m* 5 Oct 1914 Phyllis Dorothy Roper-Curzon, dau of Philip Scott, of The Glen, Queenstown, and *d* 7 Nov 1978, leaving:

1a *Michael Philip; *b* 12 Nov 1919; *educ* King's Coll Cambridge (MA)

1a *Claire Patricia; *b* 7 Jan 1916; *m* 12 April 1939 Hugh William Shillito, 2nd s of Canon Shillito, of Blofield Rectory, Norwich, and has:

1b *Martin Lancelot; *b* 3 Sept 1943; *educ* City of London Sch

2b *Richard Arthur; *b* 13 March 1948; *educ* Westminster and Magdalen Coll Oxford

1b *Susan Margaret; *b* 26 July 1941; *m* 18 Dec 1965 Francis Martin Baillie Reynolds, 2nd s of Eustace Baillie Reynolds, of St Albans, Herts, and has:

1c *Barnabas William Baillie; *b* 5 Aug 1967

2c *Martin Alexander Baillie; *b* 5 June 1969

2b *Christina Mary; *b* 27 Feb 1950

(3) Reginald, OBE; *b* 1 May 1891; Capt RN, Inspr Coastguard 1938–51, Actg Lt-Col HG 1952; *m* 3 Oct 1932 Amabel Anne (*d* 27 Jan 1974), formerly w of Capt Charles Lexington Manners Sutton, MBE (*see* RUTLAND, D), and dau of Maj Ludlow Coape Ludlow, of Beach Green, Withyham, Sussex, and *dsp* 20 Nov 1969

(1) Eleanor Bevan; *b* 21 May 1892; *d* unm 9 Oct 1952

1 Alice Fielden; *m* 17 Feb 1874 Lt-Col John Bridges Walker, RA, 2nd s of Rev Robert Walker, of Wadham Coll, Oxford, and *d* 1938, leaving issue. He *d* 21 Oct 1925

2 Frances; *m* 14 Nov 1872 Capt Robert Watts Davies, RN, est s of B Davies, of Prince Edward's Island, and *d* 1944, leaving issue. He *d* 6 Sept 1903

JAMES RAMSBOTHAM's gs,

Sir HERWALD RAMSBOTHAM, 1st Viscount Soulbury, of Soulbury, Co Buckingham, so *cr* 16 July 1954, as also earlier 6 Aug 1941 BARON SOULBURY, of Soulbury, Co Buckingham (both UK), GCMG (1949), GCVO (1954), OBE (1919), MC`, PC (1939), DL (Beds 1944–54); *b* 6 March 1887; *educ* Uppingham and Univ Coll Oxford (BA 1910, MA 1949, Hon Fell); barrister Inner Temple 1912, MP (C) Lancaster 1929–41, Parly Sec: Bd Educn 1931–35 and Min Ag and Fisheries 1935–36, Min Pensions 1936–39, First Commr Works 1939–40, Pres Bd Educn 1940–41 Govr-Gen Ceylon 1949–54, Hon LLD Ceylon U, Chm: Assistance Bd 1941, Jt Ctee Teachers' Salaries, Govrs Dulwich Coll 1942–49, Co Cdr 7th Beds Regt, Staff Capt 53rd Inf Bde, DAAG 8th Div and Maj WW I (despatches three times), KGStJ 1952; *m* 1st 11 Nov 1911 Doris Violet (*d* 20 Feb 1954), dau of Sigmund de Stein, of Kensington, and gdau of Baron de Stein, of Antwerp, and had:

1 JAMES HERWALD RAMSBOTHAM, **2nd and present Viscount Soulbury**

2 +PETER EDWARD, GCMG (1978, KCMG 1972, CMG 1964), GCVO (1976), DL (Hants 1992) [The Hon Sir Peter Ramsbotham GCMG GCVO DL, East Lodge, Ovington, Alresford, Hants SO24 0RA]; *b* 8 Oct 1919; heir presumptive; *educ* Eton and Magdalen Coll Oxford (Hon Fell 1991); Lt-Col Intell Corps WW II (despatches, Croix de Guerre avec Palme), Br HC Cyprus 1969–71, Amb: Teheran 1971–73 and USA 1974–77, Govr and C-in-C Bermuda 1977–80; dir: Lloyds Bank 1981–91, Lloyds Bank Internat 1981–83, S Regnl Bd Lloyds Bank 1981–90 (chm 1983–90), Commercial Union Assur 1981–90; tstee Leonard Cheshire Fndn 1981–94, chm: Ryder-Cheshire Fndn for Relief of Suffering 1982–, World Memorial Fund for Disaster Relief 1992–96, govr King's Sch Canterbury 1981–90, Hon LLD: Akron U 1975, Coll of William and Mary 1975, Maryland U 1976, Yale 1977; KStJ 1976; *m* 1st 30 Aug 1941 Frances Marie Massie (*d* 2 Dec 1982), dau of Hugh Massie Blomfield, of the Bd of Trade; *m* 2nd 1985 *Dr Zaida Mary Hall, widow of Ruthven Hall, and by his 1st w has had:

(1) +Oliver Peter [Oliver Ramsbotham Esq, 4 Melbourne Terrace, Bradford, W Yorks BD5 0HV]; *b* 27 Oct 1943; *educ* Eton; *m* 4 Sept 1965 *Meredith Anne, only dau of Brian Jones, of The White Ho, Easton Royal, Wilts, and has:

1a +Edward Herwald; *b* 8 July 1966

2a +Benedict Oliver David; *b* 8 Oct 1967

3a *Alexander Meredith; *b* 7 June 1969

(2) +Simon Edward [Simon Ramsbotham Esq, 36 Bensham Lane, Croydon, Surrey]; *b* 23 Sept 1949; *educ* Eton; *m* 1976 *Sandra Cayley and has:

1a +David Peter; *b* 1981

1a *Elizabeth Sarah; *b* 1978

2a *Allison Frances; *b* 1983

(1) Mary Frances; *b* 23 Nov 1945; *m* 1st 1981 Charles Gray (*d* 1982); *m* 2nd 1993 *Christopher Coulston and *d* 1 Dec 1994

1 Enid Gladys; *b* 9 Sept 1912; *d* 12 Jan 1914

2 *Joan Eleanor [The Hon Mrs O'Grady, 32 Addison Ave, London W11 4QR]; Midford Place, Midford, Bath, Avon]; *b* 6 Sept 1917; *educ* LMH Oxford; *m* 16 Dec 1950 *Maj Robert Hardress Standish O'Grady, MC, Irish Gds, only s of Lt-Col P J Standish O'Grady, of Abingdon, Shankhill, Co Dublin, and has:

(1) *Jeremy Robert [Jeremy Standish O'Grady Esq, 32 Addison Ave, London W11 4QR]; *b* 12 July 1953; *educ* Ampleforth

(1) *Jane Elizabeth [Miss Jane Standish O'Grady, The Cottage, 141 St Mark's Rd, London W10]; *b* 20 Feb 1952

(2) *Selina Joan [Miss Selina Standish O'Grady, 29 Linden Gdns, London W2]; *b* 12 May 1956

The **1st Viscount** *m* 2nd 10 Nov 1962 Ursula (*d* 12 Nov 1964), widow of Frederick Wakeham and dau of Armand Jerome, and *d* 30 Jan 1971

SOULSBY OF SWAFFHAM PRIOR

Creation: B. (LP, UK) 1990.

THE BARON SOULSBY OF SWAFFHAM PRIOR, of Swaffham Prior, Co Cambridge ((Ernest Jackson) Lawson Soulsby) [The Rt Hon The Lord Soulsby of Swaffham Prior, Old Barn House, Swaffham Prior, Cambs CB5 0LD]; *b* 23 June 1926; *educ* Queen Elizabeth GS Penrith and Edinburgh U; PRCVS 1984 (Sr V-Pres 1985, memb cncl 1978–), DVSM, PhD, MA (Cantab), FRCVS, Fell Wolfson Coll Camb 1978–93; Veterinary Officer City of Edinburgh 1949–52, Lecturer Clinical Parasitology Bristol U 1952–54 and Animal Pathology Cambridge 1954–63, Prof Parasitology Pennsylvania U 1964–78, Prof Animal Pathology Cambridge 1978–93 (Emeritus 1993–), chm veterinary advsy ctee Horserace Betting Levy Bd 1985–96 (memb 1984–), Ford Fndn Visiting Prof Ibadan U 1964, Richard Merton Guest Prof Justus Liebig U 1974–75, Hon AM 1972, Hon DSc Pennsylvania 1984, Hon DVM Léon, Hon DSc Paradinya, Hon DVSM Edinburgh 1991, R N Chaudhury Gold Medal Calcutta Sch Tropical Medicine 1976, Behring-Bilharz Prize Cairo 1977, Ludwig-Schunk Prize Justus Liebig U 1979, author: *Textbook of Veterinary Clinical Parasitology* (1965), *Biology of Parasites* (1966), *Reaction of the Host to Parasitism* (1968), *Immunity to Animal Parasites* (1972), *Parasitic Zoonoses* (1974), *Pathophysiology of Parasitic Infections* (1976), *Epidemiology and Control of Nematodiasis in Cattle* (1981), *Immunology, Immunopathology and Immunoprophylaxis of Parasitic Infections*, vols I, II, III and IV (1986); *Zoonuses* (1998); *m* 1st 1950 Margaret Macdonald; *m* 2nd 1962 *Georgina Elizabeth Annette, dau of John Whitmore Williams, of Cambridge, and by his 1st w has:

1 *John Angus Lawson; *b* 1954

2 *Katrina Yvonne; *b* 1950; *m* 1990 *— Bulloch

Lineage: WILLIAM GEORGE LAWSON SOULSBY; *m* Agnes — and had:

(ERNEST JACKSON) LAWSON, *cr* a **Baron**

SOUTHAMPTON

Arms: Quarterly, 1st and 4th, France and England; 2nd, Scotland; 3rd Ireland; over all a sinister baton, company arg. and az., a crescent for difference. **Crest:** On a chapeau gu. doubled erm. a lion statant guardant or, crowned with a ducal coronet az. and gorged with a collar counter-compony arg. and of the 4th. **Supporters:** Dexter, a lion guardant or, crowned with a ducal coronet az. and gorged with a collar counter-compony erm. and of the 2nd; sinister, a greyhound arg., gorged as the dexter. **Motto:** *Et decus et pretium recti* ('The ornament and recompense of virtue'). **Creation:** B. (GB) 17 Oct 1780.

THE 6TH BARON SOUTHAMPTON, of Southampton, Hants (Charles James FitzRoy) [The Rt Hon The Lord Southampton, Stone Cross House, Chagford, Devon TQ13 8JU]; *b* 12 Aug 1928; *s f* 1989; *educ* Stowe; Master Easton Harriers 1968–69, MFH Blankney 1971–72; *m* 1st 29 May 1951 Pamela Anne (*d* Feb 1997), dau of Edward Percy Henniker, of Clematis, Yelverton, S Devon, and has had:

1 Charles; *b* 18 Jan 1954; *educ* Gresham's; *m* 7 Aug 1975 Joanna Dana (*m* 2nd 1977 Paul Farrant), er dau of Chandos Robert Henry Brudenell-Bruce (*see* AILESBURY, M), and was *k* in a car crash in NZ 15 Oct 1975

2 +EDWARD CHARLES [The Hon Edward FitzRoy, Venn Farm, Morchard Bishop, Devon EX17 6SQ]; *b* 8 July 1955; *educ* Gresham's and RAC Cirencester; *m* 30 March 1978 *Rachel Caroline Vincent, 2nd dau of Peter John Curnow Millett, of West Underdown, Drewsteignton, Nr Exeter, Devon, formerly of S India, and has:

  (1) +Charles Edward Millett; *b* 18 Jan 1983

  (1) *Fiona Joan Margaret; *b* 1979

  (2) *Sarah Barbara Sibell; *b* 1981

  (3) *Julia Rachel Caroline; *b* 1984

1 *Geraldine Anne [The Hon Mrs Fuller, Rose Cottage, Church Rd, Lympstone, Devon EX8 5JT]; *b* 31 Dec 1951; *m* 1st 1969 (*divorce* 19–) Gavin Prescott; *m* 2nd 14 April 1977 *Richard Gordon Fuller, s of Gordon Wallace Fuller, of Luton, and has:

  (1) *Joshua FitzRoy; *b* 1978

  (2) *Oliver; *b* 1981

  (1) *Victoria; *b* 1983

The 6th BARON *m* 2nd Oct 1997 *Alma Pasqual Perez, of Tarlac, nr Manila, The Philippines, formerly w of Bryan Slater, and by her has:

  3/2 +/*A child; *b* 5–12 June 1998

Southampton title: For older creations of an Earldom of Southampton, *see* WINCHESTER, M, preliminary remarks, since the name of the county town and county were considered interchangeable in the Middle Ages, at any rate where peerage titles were concerned.

By the 16th century this confusion had ceased and in 1537 William Fitzwilliam was created Earl of Southampton. He was a member of a Yorkshire family who are thought to have been Angles or Scandinavians in origin, despite their Norman-sounding name, and first prominent in the 12th century. The new Earl of Southampton descended from a younger brother of the 14th-century ancestor of the FitzWilliams created Earls FitzWilliam from 1716 (*see* 1970 edn). His mother was a Nevill(e) (*see* ABERGAVENNY, M), daughter of the 1st Marquess of Montagu of the 1470 creation (*see* also NORTHUMBERLAND, D, and MONTAGU OF BEAULIEU, B, preliminary remarks).

The new Earl of Southampton was a courtier, diplomat and fighting man (mostly naval) active in the early part of HENRY VIII's reign, rising to Treasurer of the Household 1525–37, Chancellor of the Duchy of Lancaster (he was also an MP) 1529–42, Lord Privy Seal 1540–42 and — his crowning achievement — High Admiral 1536–40. He helped suppress the Pilgrimage of Grace in 1536 and on being raised to the peerage the following year was granted large swathes of monastic lands. On his death in 1542 the Earldom expired.

Some five years later Thomas Wriothesley was promoted Earl of Southampton, having previously been created Baron Wriothesley. Thomas came of a family of heralds, his father having been York Herald and his grandfather Garter King of Arms (as was his uncle), while a cousin served as Windsor Herald more or less contemporaneously with Thomas's own career. He started as a civil servant before branching out into diplomacy and high political and legal office as Lord Keeper of the Great Seal and Lord Chancellor respectively. He was one of the executors of HENRY VIII's will and a governor to EDWARD VI. He sided with the Warwick faction against Protector Somerset but failed to profit from Warwick's ultimate triumph. He is generally considered to have been one of the least scrupulous time-servers in an admittedly dangerous era; certainly the story of his torturing a Protestant on the rack with his own hands while having amassed a fortune from the destruction of the monasteries and chantries, two props of the pre-Reformation system, rings particularly unpleasantly.

At least Thomas Wriothesley's son the 2nd Earl continued faithful to Catholicism, moreover at a time when it was increasingly impolitic to do so. He was thought to have connived at the attempt of the Duke of Norfolk to marry MARY QUEEN OF SCOTS around 1570 and was imprisoned in the Tower as a result. His son, the 3rd Earl, was involved in the failed Essex putsch of 1600/1 and accordingly attainted. The titles were restored to him by JAMES I, however, who also made him a Knight of the Garter, though late in the same reign he incurred the King's displeasure for opposing Buckingham (*see* JERSEY, E). It is this Earl of Southampton who was Shakespeare's acknowledged patron.

The 4th Wriothesley Earl of Southampton was a particularly staunch royalist during the Civil War and was one of only four peers who put in an appearance at CHARLES I's funeral. As might have been expected, he was showered with honours and offices at the Restoration, including the post of Lord High Treasurer. On his death in 1667 the Earldom expired.

The next person to hold a peerage of Southampton was CHARLES II's mistress Barbara Villiers (*see* JERSEY, E), whose Duchy of Cleveland was created simultaneously with a subsidiary Earldom of Southampton in 1670. Her son Charles, originally surnamed Palmer after his nominal father, Barbara's husband, but later FitzRoy in acknowledgement of his royal paternity, inherited the Earldom of Southampton, along with the Dukedom, in 1709, having long been known as Earl of Southampton by courtesy during his mother's lifetime. With his own son's death in 1774 this creation too became extinct. But it must have seemed only natural to revive the title when some six years later the ennoblement took place of a member of another family illegitimately descended from CHARLES II, the younger brother of the 3rd Duke of Grafton (*see* below).

Lineage: The 2nd DUKE OF GRAFTON (*qv*) had a 2nd s:

Lord AUGUSTUS FitzROY; *m* Elizabeth, dau of Col William Cosby, and had:

CHARLES FitzROY, **1st Baron Southampton**, of Co Southampton, so *cr* 17 Oct 1780; *b* 25 June 1737; Ensign 1st Foot (Gren) Gds 1752, Capt 1756, Lt-Col 1758, fought Battles of Minden 1759 and Kirchdenkern 1761 during Seven Years War, MP (Whig to 1770, Tory to *c* 1783, thereafter Whig again) Orford 1759–61, Bury St Edmunds 1761–74 and Thetford 1774–80, Groom Bedchamber 1760–62, Col 119th Foot 1762–63, 14th Dragoons 1765–72 and 3rd Dragoons 1772–97, V-Chamberlain to QUEEN CHARLOTTE 1768–82 and PRINCE OF WALES (later GEORGE IV) 1780–97; *m* 27 July 1758 Anne (*d* 13 July 1807), dau and coheir of Adml Sir Peter Warren, KB, and had, with other issue (*dsp*):

1 GEORGE FERDINAND, **2nd Baron**

2 Charles; *b* 5 Sept 1762; Gen; *m* 21 Sept 1816 Eliza, widow of Clavering Savage and dau of S F Barlow, and *dsp* 18 Oct 1831

3 William; *b* 21 July 1764; *d* 28 Aug 1786

4 Henry; *b* 13 Sept 1765; *m* 4 Jan 1790 Lady Anne Wellesley (*m* 2nd Aug 1799 Charles Culling Smith), est dau of 1st Earl of Mornington (*see* WELLINGTON, D), and *d* 19 March 1794, leaving, with another dau (*d* unm):

  (1) Georgiana Frederica; *m* 25 July 1814 7th Duke of Beaufort (*qv*) and *d* 11 May 1821, leaving issue

5 Warren; *b* 1 Sept 1768; *m* 11 Feb 1794 Maria Theresa Josepha, dau of Andrew d'Isaac, a German Chllr of State, and *d* 24 May 1806, leaving issue

6 Frederick; *b* 10 Oct 1769

7 William, of Kempston, Norfolk; *b* 12 Dec 1773; Lt-Gen; *m* 1st 20 May 1799 Catherine (*d* 16 May 1808), sis of Sir Simon Houghton Clarke, 9th Bt, and had:

  (1) William Simon Houghton, of Kempston, JP Norfolk; *b* 8 Dec 1802; Mil Offr; *m* 21 July 1829 Anne (*d* 15 May 1860), dau of Thomas Bagge (*see* BAGGE, Bt), and *d* 11 May 1882, having had, with a dau (*d* unm):

    1a William, of Northcote House, Rugby, JP Warwicks; *b* 29 Nov 1830; Maj-Gen, Lt-Col cmdg 31st Regtl Dist, formerly 47th Foot; *m* 3 Aug 1864 Gertrude Mary (*d* 1 Dec 1896), dau of Capt Samuel Henry Wentworth, RE, and *d* 7 Oct 1902, having had, with a dau (*d* unm):

      1b William Wentworth; *b* 25 April 1867; *d* 25 Jan 1884

      2b Philip FitzWilliam; *b* 24 Feb 1870; Capt RA; *d* 30 Sept 1923

      3b Frederick Henry, RD; *b* 22 Jan 1872; Capt RNR; *m* 4 Jan 1904 Eleanor (*d* 30 April 1969), dau of William Allan, of Avondale, Gosforth, and *d* 9 July 1937, having had, with a dau (*d* unm):

        1c William Wentworth FitzROY later STEWART-FitzROY (deed poll Sept 1958) [Mrs William Stewart-FitzRoy, 407 Russell Rd Apt 403, Gaithersburg, MA 20877-2854, USA]; *b* 28 Sept 1907; Capt RN, WW II and Korea, Cdre Supt HM Dockyard Singapore, Naval Attaché Belgrade, Naval ADC to HM THE QUEEN 1961–62, Admlty Regnl Offr Scotland 1962–72, Hon Sheriff Sutherland 1974; *m* 1st 26 April 1934 Margaret Patricia (*d* 1984), dau of Douglas Stewart Grant, of New York; *m* 2nd 1988 *Evelyn, widow of Col John Fogg Twombly III, US Army, and dau of James Wallace Nichol, of Washington, DC, and *d* 23 Oct 1998, leaving by his 1st w:

          1d +Allan Wentworth [Cdr Allan Stewart-FitzRoy RN, 12 St George's Ave, Warblington, Havant, Hants PO9 2RY]; *b* 3 Feb 1935; *educ* Nautical Coll Pangbourne and RNC Dartmouth; *m* 27 Sept 1960 *Susan Elizabeth, only dau of Capt Horace Gerald Southwood, CBE, DSC, RN, of Alverstoke, Hants, and has:

            1e *Louise; *b* 4 July 1962; *m* 6 Aug 1988 *Maj Michael John Stone, Duke of Wellington's Regt, and has:

              1f *Arthur Maxallan John; *b* 18 March 1994

              1f *Alexandra Susan Joy; *b* 1 Oct 1990

            2e *Jane; *b* 26 April 1964; *m* 20 June 1987 *Rupert John Eastell and has:

              1f *Tom Jonathan; *b* 24 Jan 1992

              1f *Georgina Jane; *b* 16 Jan 1994

            3e *Helen; *b* 23 Sept 1967; *m* 7 Sept 1996 *Jon Poley

          2d +Douglas James [Douglas Stewart-FitzRoy Esq, 51 Brondesbury Villas, London NW6 6AJ]; *b* 10 July 1943; *educ* Epsom Coll

          3d +Roderick Charles STEWART-FitzROY later FitzROY (deed poll 1976); *b* 24 Nov 1947; *educ* Sherborne, RMA Sandhurst and Scottish Police Coll, Tullialean Castle, Fife; *m* Sept 1972 *Susan, dau of H C Ruse, of Arbroath, and has:

            1e +James; *b* 1973

            1e *Amanda Jane; *b* 1976

          1d *Anne Patricia; *b* 10 Aug 1936; MBA, CPA

      4b George Francis; *b* 10 April 1873; *d* 17 July 1927

      5b Charles Edward (Sir); *b* 19 Jan 1876; *educ* Bedford Sch, slr 1898 and 1929–41, assist slr Customs and Excise 1917–29, ktd 1934; *m* 17 Aug 1915 Sarah Louise (*d* 1955), dau of Henry Limmer, of Bury St Edmunds, and *dsp* 4 April 1954

      6b Robert Hope FitzROY later FitzROY-KELLY (roy licence 4 Jan 1937) later still FitzROY again; *b* 10 Sept 1881; *educ* Rugby and Cooper's Hill Coll; Maj RGA; *m* 20 May 1915 Stella Agnes Piercy, yr dau and coheir of Brig-Gen Richard Makdougall Brisbane Francis Kelly, CB, DSO, and *d* 14 Sept 1952

    2a George Dartmouth; *b* 22 May 1832; Capt RN; *m* 11 Jan 1866 Caroline Catherine (*d* 8 Nov 1928), est dau of Cluny Macpherson, CB, of Cluny Castle, Inverness-shire, and *d* 7 Dec 1890, leaving:

      1b George Ewen Macpherson; *b* 26 Dec 1866; *d* 21 March 1936

      2b Gordon Duncan Seymour; *b* 15 Feb 1868; *m* 1st 25 July 1891 Marie (*d* 1894), widow of Howel Turner, MD, of Norwich; *m* 2nd Adalia Leasure, of Kansas City, and *d* 1936, leaving:

        1c Albert Loring; *b* 1900

        2c +Francis George; *b* 1903

      1b Emily Sarah Lucy; *b* 11 Feb 1871; *d* unm 3 June 1947

      2b Georgina Elizabeth Catherine; *b* 23 April 1872; *m* 3 Feb 1915 William Colin MacLeod, s of Capt Norman MacLeod, of Orbost, Isle of Skye, and *d* 16 May 1948

      3b Margaret Caroline Anne; *b* 27 Dec 1877; *d* unm 1 Dec 1934

    3a Ferdinand, Lt-Col RA; *b* 15 June 1833; *m* 18 Sept 1855 Mary Helena (*d* 1905), dau of Maj George Russell Cremelin, CB, and *d* 11 Sept 1907, leaving:

      1b Ferdinand Trevor, of Ard-Falen, Alexandria, Victoria, Australia; *b* 11 Jan 1857; *m* *c* 1904 Maud Harvey Hamilton and *d* 1928, leaving:

        1c +Eric Hamilton; *b* *c* 1906

        2c +Herbert Cromwell; *b* *c* 1907

        1c *Kathleen Mary; *b* *c* 1904

        2c *Elizabeth Lorraine; *b* *c* 1912

2b Reginald *b* 6 Aug 1858

3b George William; *b* 1 March 1861

4b Herbert; *b* 25 April 1867

5b Frederick Voyle; *b* 6 July 1869

1b Annie

2b Emilia Mary

4a Philip; *b* 8 March 1837; Col 1st Bn Northumberland Fus; *d* 19 Jan 1892

5a Frederick Keppel; *b* 1838; 81st Regt; *d* 1863

6a Edward Albert, JP Surrey; *b* 7 Feb 1840; Lt-Col RA; *m* 29 Oct 1874 Lucy Jannetta Julia (*d* 15 July 1932), yst dau of Cluny Macpherson, CB, and *d* 27 Dec 1915, leaving:

1b Eva Mary Lucy St John; *b* 7 Sept 1875; *m* 6 Jan 1903 Lt-Col Stewart Ward William Blacker, DSO, RFA, of Carrickblacker, Co Armagh, s of Rev Canon Robert Shapland Carew Blacker, of Carrickblacker and Woodbrook, and *d* 8 July 1952, leaving issue. He *d* 6 Sept 1935

1a Catherine; *b* 1841; *m* 1864 W F Arundell and *d* 7 Oct 1912, having had issue

(2) George William Howe; *b* 17 Dec 1803; Lt RN; *ka* Battle of Navarino 1827

(3) Arthur William Bagot; *b* 1805; Bombay Cav; *d* 1879

(4) Charles William Henry Gage; *b* 7 Jan 1807; Cdr RN; *m* 18 May 1837 Caroline Emily (*d* 10 Aug 1908), 3rd dau of Richard Phayre, of Claremont, Shrewsbury, and *d* 25 Jan 1886, having had, with a dau (*d* unm):

1a Gage Charles; *b* 19 April 1845; Lt 6th Dragoon Gds; *d* unm 5 March 1872

(5) Frederick Thomas William Coke (Rev); *b* 30 Jan 1808; Rector Gt Ringstead, Norfolk; *m* 31 May 1834 Emilia Le Strange, est dau of Henry Styleman, of Snettisham Hall, Norfolk, and *d* 20 Feb 1862, having had, with a dau (*d* unm):

1a Frederick Southampton Le Strange; *b* 7 July 1836; Capt 15th Foot; *m* 12 April 1877 Anne Woolsey (*d* 16 Feb 1927), 3rd dau of Edward Atkinson, of Seafield Hall, Donabate, and Carrick Brenna, Monkstown, Co Dublin, and *d* 23 May 1890, leaving:

1b Violet le Strange; *b* 21 March 1878; *m* 3 Sept 1903 Maj John Francis Giffard, N Staffs Regt, and *d* 21 May 1936, leaving:

2b Evelyn; *b* 1881; *m* 4 Dec 1913 Capt Harold Wilbraham Tollemache (*see* TOLLEMACHE, B) and *dsp* 25 May 1969

3b Lilian Kathleen; *b* 1884; *d* unm 16 Sept 1966

2a Henry William; *b* 27 June 1838; RN; had:

1b Hugh

3a Cecil Augustus, of Havelock North, NZ; *b* 10 Jan 1844 *m* 21 Feb 1878 Susanna, yst dau of William Betham, of Taita, Wellington, NZ, and had:

1b Gwendoline le Strange; *m* 4 Sept 1918 Lt Ronald W Williams, RFA, s of F W Williams, of Napier, NZ

1a Emily Katharine L'Estrange; *m* 21 June 1859 Frederick HOGGE later ARCHDALE (1866) and *d* 1871, leaving issue

2a Adela; *m* 14 Feb 1874 Arthur Blundell, yst s of William Blundell, and *d* 19 June 1887, leaving issue

7 (cont.) Lt-Gen The Hon William FitzRoy *m* 2nd 4 July 1811 his cousin Lady Elizabeth FitzRoy (*d* 3 March 1839), dau of 3rd Duke of Grafton (*qv*), and *d* 19 May 1837

1 Charlotte; *m* 30 July 1795 2nd Viscount of Dungannon of the 1766 *cr* (*see* DOWNSHIRE, M) and *d* 22 Nov 1828, leaving issue

2 Emily; *m* 3 May 1799 2nd Baron Bagot (*qv*) and *dsps* 8 June 1800

3 Louisa; *m* 18 Dec 1792 James Allen, of Bromsgrove, Worcs

4 Georgiana; *m* 26 Jan 1807 Maj-Gen Hon Sir William Ponsonby, KCB, and *d* 6 Feb 1835, leaving issue (*see* BESSBOROUGH, E)

The 1st BARON *d* 21 March 1797; his est s,

GEORGE FERDINAND FitzROY, **2nd Baron Southampton**; *b* 7 Aug 1761; *educ* Eton; Lt 3rd Dragoons 1778, Capt 14th Foot 1780 and 41st Foot 1787, Maj 51st Foot 1792, Lt-Col 2nd Foot Gds 1793, Brevet Col 1796, Col 34th Foot 1797–1810, Maj-Gen 1801, Lt-Gen 1808, Groom Bedchamber to PRINCE OF WALES (later GEORGE IV) 1783, MP (Whig) Bury St Edmunds 1784–87; *m* 1st 2 July 1784 Laura (*d* 29 June 1798), dau of Hon Frederick Keppel, Bp Exeter (*see* ALBEMARLE, E), and had two daus (Georgiana Maria, *m* 2 June 1814 John Horace Thomas Stapleton (*see* FALMOUTH, V); another dau, *d* unm); *m* 2nd 2 Dec 1802 Frances Isabella (*d* 3 June 1838), dau of Lord Robert Seymour (*see* HERTFORD, M), and by her had:

1 CHARLES, **3rd Baron**

2 Henry, PC; *b* 2 May 1807; MP; *m* 29 April 1839 Hannah Mayer (*d* 2 Dec 1864), sis of 1st Baron Rothschild (*qv*), and *d* 17 Dec 1859, having had:

(1) Arthur Frederick; *b* 15 Dec 1842; *d* 8 Nov 1858

(1) Caroline Blanche Elizabeth; *m* 30 June 1864 Sir Coutts Lindsay, 2nd and last Bt, and *d* 4 Aug 1912, leaving issue (*see* CRAWFORD and BALCARRES, E)

2 Anne Caroline; *m* Oct 1828 Rev Humphry Allen, incumbent Trin Chapel, Clifton, and *d* 3 Aug 1857. He *d* 6 June 1868

The 2nd BARON *d* 24 June 1810; his er s,

CHARLES FitzROY, **3rd Baron Southampton**; *b* 28 Sept 1804; Ld Lt Northants 1867–72; *m* 1st 23 Feb 1826 Harriet (*dsp* 23 Oct 1860), only dau of Hon Henry FitzRoy Stanhope (*see* HARRINGTON, E); *m* 2nd 25 Feb 1862 Ismania Catherine, VA (*d* 18 Aug 1918), Ldy Bedchamber-in-Ordinary to HM QUEEN VICTORIA 1878–1901, dau of Walter Nugent (*see* JENKINSON, Bt), and by her had:

1 CHARLES HENRY, **4th Baron**

2 Edward Algernon, PC (1924), JP, DL Northants; *b* 24 July 1869; Page of Honour to HM QUEEN VICTORIA, Capt 1st Life Gds, cmdg mtd troops Gds Div 1915–16 (wounded), memb Northants CC 1896–1921, MP S Northants 1900–06 and 1910–18 and Daventry 1918–43, Dep Chm Ways and Means 1923 and 1924–28, Speaker H of C 1928–43, Hon LLD Cantab 1931, Hon DCL Oxon 1934; *m* 19 Nov 1891 Muriel, CBE (1918), DGStJ, *cr* 1943 Viscountess Daventry (*qv*), and *d* 3 March 1943, leaving issue

1 Ismay Mary Helen Augusta; *m* 12 June 1883 Rev Lord Charles Edward FitzRoy, 4th s of 7th Duke of Grafton (*qv*), and *d* 22 April 1952, having had issue

2 Frederica Louisa; Maid of Honour to HM QUEEN VICTORIA; *m* 12 Feb 1890 Percy Edward Crutchley, est s of Gen Charles Crutchley, of Sunninghill Park, Berks, and *d* 9 April 1932, leaving issue. He *d* 16 Oct 1940

3 Blanche Georgiana; *m* 6 Dec 1887 3rd Baron Penrhyn (*qv*) and *d* 28 Nov 1944, leaving issue

The 3rd BARON *d* 16 July 1872; his er s,

CHARLES HENRY FitzROY, **4th Baron Southampton**, OBE (1919); *b* 11 May 1867; *educ* Eton and RMC Sandhurst; 2nd Lt 10th Hus 1887, Capt 1892–93, Maj 4th Bn Yorks Regt WW I, Lt-Col 1919; *m* 9 July 1892 Lady Hilda Mary Dundas, er dau of 1st Marquess of Zetland (*qv*), and had:

1 CHARLES, **5th Baron**

1 A dau; *d* an infant 1893

2 Dorothy; *b* 26 March 1895; *m* 6 July 1916 Capt John McKerrell McKerrell-Brown, Seaforth Highrs, only s of John William McKerrell-Brown, JP, of Sherwood, Colinton, Midlothian, and *d* 27 Nov 1957, leaving issue

3 Victoria Alexandrina Sibell; *b* 25 June 1898; *m* 21 Jan 1925 (*divorce* 1941) Maj William Vandeleur Beatty, of Phantom Ho, Newmarket, bro of 1st Earl Beatty (*qv*)

4 *Ismay Hilda Margaret [The Hon Mrs Sale, 15 St Paul's Mews, Ramsey, IOM]; *b* 3 Dec 1908; *m* 8 Feb 1928 Brig Walter Morley Sale, CVO, OBE (*d* 29 Aug 1976), RHG, Crown Equerry 1955–61, Extra Equerry to HM THE QUEEN 1961, 3rd s of Charles Vincent Sale, of Aston Rowant Ho, Oxon, and has:

(1) *Charles Richard Walter [Charles Sale Esq, Garey Manor, Lezayre, Ramsey, IOM]; *b* 5 Nov 1928; *educ* Eton and RMC Sandhurst; Capt RHG (ret 1954); *m* 9 Oct 1958 *Marian Eleanor, 2nd dau of Maj John Darling Young, Life Gds, of Thornton Hall, Bletchley, Bucks, and has:

1a *Nigel Richard; *b* 9 Oct 1962

1a *Lucinda Marian; *b* 3 Nov 1965

(1) *Caroline Ismay Maud [Miss Caroline Sale, Charlcot, Ripon, Yorks]; *b* 12 Dec 1934

The 4th BARON *d* 7 Dec 1958; his only s,

CHARLES FitzROY, **5th Baron Southampton**, disclaimed his peerage for life 16 March 1964; *b* 3 Jan 1904; *educ* Harrow; 2nd Lt RHG and Pioneer Corps, Jt MFH Grove 1930–32; *m* 1st 22 June 1927 Margaret (*d* 3 Feb 1931), dau of Preb Herbert Mackworth Drake, Vicar Berry Pomeroy, Devon, and had:

1 CHARLES JAMES FitzROY, **6th and present Baron Southampton**

The **5th Baron** *m* 2nd 12 Jan 1940 (*divorce* 1944) Phyllis Joan, formerly w of David H Leslie and dau of Francis Archibald Lloyd; *m* 3rd 3 Feb 1951 Rachel Christine (*d* 1985), dau of Charles Zaman, of Lille, France, and *d* 1989

SOUTHBY

Arms: Or, a chevron between three apples gu.
Crest: A demi-lion or, holding in the dexter paw an apple gu.
Creation: Bt. (UK) 12 June 1937.

SIR JOHN RICHARD BILBE SOUTHBY, 3RD BT, of Burford, Co Oxon [Sir John Southby Bt, Lomagundi, High St, Nash, Bucks MK17 0EP]; *b* 2 April 1948; *s* f 1988; *educ* Peterhouse Rhodesia and Loughborough U (BSc); CEng, MIEE, FIMgt, Freeman Grocers' Co 1969, (Liveryman 1996), joined E Midlands Electricity Bd 1971, network gen manager E Midlands Electricity 1996–; *m* 30 July 1971 *Victoria Jane, est dau of John Wilfred Sturrock, of Wolverhampton, and has:

1 +PETER JOHN; *b* 20 Aug 1973; *educ* Oundle and Magdalen Coll Oxford (BA); *m* 29 July 1995 *Katherine Margaret, dau of Dr R N Priestland, of Nottingham

2 +James William; *b* 1984

1 *Sarah Jane; *b* 10 Sept 1975

Lineage: RICHARD SOUTHBY, of Buckland, Berks; granted lands by HENRY VII 1501; had:

JOHN SOUTHBY, of Burford, Oxon; *d* 1554, leaving, with other issue:

JOHN SOUTHBY, of Carswell, Berks; *d* 1599, leaving:

RICHARD SOUTHBY, of Carswell; *m* Jane, est dau of Edward Keate, of Lockinge, Berks, and *d* 1606, leaving, with other issue:

ROBERT SOUTHBY, of Appleton, Berks; *m* Anne (*d* 26 Dec 1697), dau of John Mayott, of Abingdon, and *d* 25 Feb 1679, having had, with other issue:

RICHARD SOUTHBY; *bapt* 25 Dec 1647; *m* Elizabeth — and *d* 21 Oct 1701, leaving, with other issue:

RICHARD SOUTHBY, of Winterburn, Chieveley, Berks; *m* Naomi — and *d* 14 Jan 1746, leaving, with other issue:

RICHARD SOUTHBY, of Appleton, JP; *bapt* 16 Sept 1710; *m* Frances Elizabeth (*d* 7 May 1757), est dau of John Head, of Hodcott, Berks, and *d* 17 June 1762, leaving, with other issue:

RICHARD SOUTHBY, of Chieveley; *bapt* 26 July 1750; *m* Mary (*d* 20 April 1846), dau of John Hawkins, of Newbury, and *d* 30 Dec 1824, having had an er s:

RICHARD SOUTHBY, of Hodcott; *b* 4 June 1804; *m* 13 Jan 1834 Anna Maria (*d* 25 Sept 1882), only dau of James Judd, of Newton Toney, Wilts, and *d* 26 Jan 1854, leaving an est s:

RICHARD SOUTHBY, of Chieveley; *b* 19 June 1838; *m* 7 Jan 1879 Hon Isabella Hewitt (*d* 19 March 1924), 2nd dau of 4th Viscount Lifford (*qv*), and *d* 11 Dec 1921, having had:

1 Richard; *b* 1880; *d* in infancy at Darjeeling

2 Evelyn John James; *b* 6 Aug 1882; Lt-Cdr RN; *m* 1913 Vera (*m* 2nd 8 Dec 1938 Oliver St John Kneller, s of Col St John Kneller), dau of Henry St John Kneller, of Woodlands, Bournemouth, and *d* 27 March 1937, leaving:

(1) Helen Mary, of Holy Cross Abbey, Stapehill, Dorset; *d* 1973

3 ARCHIBALD RICHARD JAMES (Sir), **1st Bt**

1 Olivia Mary Ann; *b* 9 Sept 1881; *d* unm 20 Aug 1925

The yst s,

Sir Archibald Richard James Southby, 1st Bt (UK), so *cr* 12 June 1937, JP (Surrey 1927–38 and Oxon 1938–46), DL Surrey 1933–46; *b* 8 July 1886; *educ* Brandon House Sch Cheltenham and HMS *Britannia*; Cdr RN (ret 1920) WW I, Flag Lt and Flag Lt-Cdr Grand Fleet and N America and WI Station 1913–18, memb Allied Naval Armistice Commn 1918–19 and Naval Inter-Allied Commn of Control 1919–20; MP Epsom 1928–47, Assist Govt Whip 1931–35, a Ld Commr Treasury 1935–37, HG WW II, memb Parly Delegn to Buchenwald Concentration Camp April 1945, Yr Bro Trin House 1944, Chev Legn Hon; *m* 1st 20 July 1909 (*divorce* 1962) Phyllis Mary (*d* 25 April 1974 aged 87), er dau of Charles Henry Garton, of Banstead Wood, Surrey, and had:

1 (ARCHIBALD) RICHARD CHARLES (Sir), **2nd Bt**

2 +Patrick Henry James [Lt-Cdr Patrick Southby RN, Robins Mill, Overbury, Glos GL20 7NT]; *b* 29 Oct 1913; ADC to Viceroy India 1938–40, RN WW II; *m* 6 Nov 1939 *Lady Anne Adeline Hope, est dau of 2nd Marquess of Linlithgow (*qv*), and has:

(1) +Richard Henry Alexander [Richard Southby Esq, The Red House, Overbury, Glos GL20 7PB]; *b* 4 Aug 1941; *educ* Eton and Worcester Coll Oxford (MA); *m* 13 April 1985 *Nicola Claire Wallop, est dau of Jonathan Janson (*see* PORTSMOUTH, E), and has:

1a *Alexander Richard Janson; *b* 15 July 1987

1a *Henrietta Elizabeth; *b* 22 June 1989

(1) *Mary Anne [Mrs Martin Kenyon, 70 Stockwell Park Rd, London SW9]; *b* 1 Aug 1946; *educ* Benenden and Courtauld Inst London U; *m* 6 March 1975 *Martin Robert Kenyon (*see* KENYON, B) and has:

1a *Eliza

Sir Archibald *m* 2nd 28 March 1962 *Noreen Vera [Noreen Lady Southby, 18 Harbour View Rd, Parkstone, Dorset BH14 0PE], only dau of Bernard Compton Simm, of Ashbourne, Derbys, and *d* 30 Oct 1969.

His er s,

Sir (Archibald) Richard Charles Southby, 2nd Bt, OBE (1945); *b* 18 June 1910; *educ* Eton and Magdalen Coll Oxford (MA); ADC to Govr Madras 1934–37, WW II: Cmdt 170 OCTU (Italy) 1942–43, CO 10 RB (Italy) 1944, GSO1, 50 BLU (Italy) 1945; GSO(1) MMIA Rome 1946–47, RAF Staff Coll Bracknell 1947, RARO 1948, Hon Lt-Col Rifle Bde, US Medal Freedom; *m* 1st 18 Sept 1935 (*divorce* 1947) Joan Alice, only dau of Reginald M Balston, of S Kensington; *m* 2nd 22 May 1947 (*divorce* 1964) Olive Marion, formerly w of Gen Sir (James Newton) Rodney Moore, GCVO, KCB, CBE, DSO, and dau of Sir Thomas Bilbe-Robinson, GBE, KCMG, and by her had:

1 Sir JOHN RICHARD BILBE SOUTHBY, **3rd and present Bt**

Sir Richard *m* 3rd 5 Sept 1964 Hon Ethel Peggy (*d* 3 Aug 1978), widow of Brig Bernard Lorenzo de Robeck, MC and bar, DL, RA, and yst dau of 1st Baron Cunliffe (*qv*); *m* 4th 1979 *Iris MacKay Robertson [Iris Lady Southby, Greystone House, Stone, Tenterden, Kent], dau of Lt-Col Granville MacKay Heriot, DSO, RM, and widow of Brig Ian Charles Alexander Robertson, and *d* 1988

SOUTHWELL

Arms: Arg. three cinquefoils pierced gu., each charged with five annulets of the field. **Crest:** A demi-Indian goat arg., armed, eared and ducally gorged gu., charged on the body with three annulets in pale of the last. **Supporters:** Two Indian goats arg., armed, eared and ducally gorged and chained gu., and charged on the body with three annulets in pale of the last. **Motto:** *Nec male notus eques* ('A knight not badly known'). **Creations:** Bt. (I) 4 Aug 1662, B. (I) 4 Sept 1717, V. (I) 18 July 1776.

THE 7TH VISCOUNT SOUTHWELL OF CASTLE MATTRESS, Baron Southwell of Castle Mattress, Co Limerick, and a **Baronet** (Sir (Pyers) Anthony Joseph Southwell, Bt) [The Rt Hon The Viscount Southwell, PO Box 2211, 8062 Paphos, Cyprus; *b* 14 Sept 1930; *s* unc 1960; *educ* Beaumont and RMA Sandhurst; 8th King's Roy Irish Hus 1951–55 (Capt 1955), internat management and mktg consultant, dir Tobenoil 1975–; *m* 3 Dec 1955 *Barbara Jacqueline, yr dau of Andrew Raynes, of Harpenden, Herts, and has:

1 +RICHARD ANDREW PYERS; *b* 15 June 1956; *educ* Ampleforth

2 +Charles Anthony John; *b* 27 Sept 1962; *educ* Ampleforth

Lineage: JOHN SOUTHWELL, of Felix Hall, Essex; MP Lewes 1450; *m* — Samon alias Pryde, and had:

1 JOHN

2 Robert; *m* Isabella, dau of John Boys, of Norfolk, and had:

(1) Richard; *m* Amy, dau of Sir Edward Wychingham, who brought him Woodrising, Norfolk, and had an er s:

1a Robert (Sir)

2a Francis; Auditor Exchequer *temp* HENRY VIII; *m* Dorothy, dau and coheir of William Tendring, and had, with an est s and two yst sons:

1b Robert (Sir); Master of the Rolls; *m* Elizabeth, dau of 1st Earl of Nottingham of the 1596 *cr* (*see* EFFINGHAM, E), and had:

1c Richard (Sir); *m* 1st —; *m* 2nd Mary, dau of Thomas Darcy, of Danbury, and had an only s:

1d Richard, of Horsham St Faiths, Norwich; ancestor of:

1e Robert (Sir); Clerk PC to CHARLES II, Envoy Extrdy, Pncpl Sec Ireland 1690; *d* 1702, leaving:

1f Edward; Pncpl Sec Ireland; had:

1g Edward, of Kings Weston, Glos; Pncpl Sec State Ireland; *m* 1729 Catherine Watson (*d* April 1765), sis and coheir of 2nd and 3rd Earls Sondes (*see* 1970 edn), and had:

1h EDWARD SOUTHWELL, 20th BARON DE CLIFFORD (*qv*), inherited through his mother

1c Katherine; *b c* 1591; *m* 13 May 1618 Sir Coreville Verney, *de jure* 7th Lord (Baron) Willoughby de Broke (*qvv*) and *de jure* 14th/15th Lord (Baron) Latimer (of Corby), and *d* 13 April 1657

The er s,

JOHN SOUTHWELL; *m* Joan, dau of William Curzon, of Brightwell, Suffolk, and had:

ROBERT SOUTHWELL, of Barham Hall, Suffolk; High Sheriff Norfolk and Suffolk 1494; had an est s:

JOHN SOUTHWELL, of Barham; *m* Elizabeth, dau of Robert Foster, of Birch, Essex, and had, with two yr sons and six daus:

JOHN SOUTHWELL, of Barham, moved to Ireland *temp* JAMES I; had, with three er sons (Robert (Rev), SJ, executed Tyburn 4 Feb 1591; Sir Richard, of Singland, Co Limerick, memb Cncl to Pres Munster, Dep Govr Clare 1640, *dsp* 1640; John, had two daus, ws of Henry Clare and Edward Clare):

EDMUND SOUTHWELL, of Castle Mattress, Co Limerick; *m* Catherine, dau and heiress of Garret Herbert, of Rathkeale, and had, with four other sons and two daus:

Sir Thomas Southwell, 1st Bt (I), so *cr* 4 Aug 1662, of Castle Mattress; Sheriff Cos Limerick, Kerry and Clare; *m* Elizabeth (*d* 19 Sept 1705), dau of William Starkey, of Dromoland, Co Clare, and had:

1 Richard, of Callow; MP (I Parl) Askeaton, Co Limerick, 1661–66; *m* Lady Elizabeth O'Brien (*m* 2nd John MacNamara, of Cratloe, Co Clare), dau of 1st Earl of Inchiquin (*see* INCHIQUIN, B), and *dvp* by Feb 1679/80, having had:

(1) THOMAS, **1st Baron**

(2) John; *ka* Battle of Namur

(3) William; Capt Battleaxe Gds, MP (I Parl) Kinsale 1703–13, Castlemartyr 1713–15 and Baltimore 1715–19, fought for WILLIAM III in Ireland and Spain; *m* Lucy (*d* 25 Aug 1733), dau and coheir of William Bowen, of Ballyadams, Queen's Co, and *d* 21 Jan 1719, having had, with other issue:

1a Bowen; *b* 1712; MP (I Parl) Downpatrick 1755–60; *m* 1753 Lady Elizabeth Cornwallis, dau of 1st Earl Cornwallis (*see* CORNWALLIS, B)

1a Bridget; *m* 20 Sept 1737 5th Earl of Drogheda (*qv*) and *d* 27 July 1761, leaving issue

(4) Richard, of Enniscourt, Co Limerick; High Sheriff Co Limerick 1707, MP 1729; *m* Agnes (*d* Aug 1743), widow of Richard Lee and dau of George Rose, and *d* 17 Sept 1729, having had an only s:

1a Sarah (*m* 2nd 30 May 1739 William Talbot, of Mount Talbot), dau of Henry Rose, and *d* 1716, leaving:

1d Agnes Elizabeth; *m* 11 Aug 1750 1st and last Earl Wandesford and *d* 21 April 1781, leaving a dau

(1) Elizabeth; *m* — Morris

(2) Catharine; *m* Gen David Crichton and had issue (*see* ERNE, E)

1 Gertrude; *m* John Pigott (*d* 8 May 1717), of Kilkenny, Co Limerick, and had issue

2 Joan; *m* William Oughtred Courtenay

Sir THOMAS *d* between 7 Dec 1680 and 1681; his gs,

Sir Thomas Southwell, 2nd Bt, and **1st Baron Southwell of Castle Mattress**, Co Limerick (I), so *cr* 4 Sept 1717, PC (1710 and 1714); *b c* 1665; *educ* Ch Ch Oxford; Williamite in Ireland after Glorious Revlution of 1688 in England, attainted and sentenced to death by JAMES II's I Parl May 1689 but pardoned by JAMES 1690, MP (I Parl) Co Limerick 1695–99, 1703–13 and 1715–17; *m* April 1696 Lady Meliora Coningsby (*d* 1735), est dau of 1st Earl Coningsby, and had, with other issue (*d* young):

1 THOMAS, **2nd Baron**

2 Henry, of Stoneville, Co Limerick; MP 1729–58; *m* Dulcinea, dau of Rev Henry Royse, of Natinan, and *d* 20 Oct 1758, having had a s two daus

3 Robert; *k* in a duel 30 May 1724

4 Edmond; *b* 16 March 1705

5 Richard (Rev); *educ* Trin Coll Dublin (BA), MA Oxon; Rector Dungourney, Co Cork; *m* Jane Kenat and had an only dau Meliora (*m* Capt William Fulke Greville, RN, MP (*d* 1837) and had issue; *see* WARWICK, BROOKE and, E)

6 William; *b* 13 March 1715

The 1st BARON *d* 4 Aug 1720; his est s,

THOMAS SOUTHWELL, **2nd Baron Southwell of Castle Mattress**, PC (I 1726); *b* 7 Jan 1698; MP (I Parl) Leitrim 1717–20, FRS 1734, Govr Limerick to 1762; *m* March 1719 Mary (*d* 17 Aug 1766), est dau of Thomas Coke, of Melbourne, Derbys (gs of Sir John Coke, Sec of State *temp* CHARLES II; *see* also LOTHIAN, M, sub **Seat**), and *d* 19 Nov 1766, leaving:

THOMAS GEORGE SOUTHWELL, **3rd Baron** and **1st Viscount Southwell of Castle Mattress**, Co Limerick (I), so *cr* 18 July 1776; *b* 4 May 1721; *educ* Lincoln's Inn and Ch Ch Oxford; Offr 2nd Foot Gds 1738, Constable Limerick Castle 1749–80, MP (I Parl) Enniscorthy 1747–60 and Co Limerick 1761–66, Govr Co Limerick 1762 -80; *m* 18 June 1741 Margaret (*d* 18 July 1802), dau and coheir of Arthur Cecil Hamilton, of Castle Hamilton, Co Cavan, and had, with another s (*d* young) and dau (*d* unm):

1 THOMAS ARTHUR, **2nd Viscount**

2 Robert Henry, of Castle Hamilton; *b* Oct 1745; MP (I Parl) Downpatrick 1776–83, Lt-Col 8th Dragoons; *m* 1786 Fridiswede, dau of John Moore, of Tullyallen, Co Louth, MD, and *d* 29 Aug 1817, leaving:

(1) Robert Henry, of Castle Hamilton; *b* 9 July 1789; *m* 1st 20 July 1839 Charlotte, widow of Frederick Lumley Savile (*see* SCARBROUGH, E) and dau of Rt Rev G De la Poer Beresford, DD, Bp Kilmore (*see* WATERFORD, M); *m* 2nd — and *dsp*

The 1st VISCOUNT *d* 29 Aug 1780; his est s,

THOMAS ARTHUR SOUTHWELL, **2nd Viscount Southwell of Castle Mattress**; *b* 16 April 1742; *educ* Trin Coll Dublin; MP (I Parl) Co Limerick 1767–68; *m* 7 Nov 1774 Sophia Maria Josepha (*d* 6 Jan 1796), 3rd dau of Francis Joseph Walsh, Count de Serrant in France, and *d* 15 Feb 1796, leaving:

1 THOMAS ANTHONY SOUTHWELL, **3rd Viscount Southwell of Castle Mattress**, KP (1837); *b* 25 Feb 1777; *m* 14 May 1799 Jane (*d* 26 Oct 1853), 2nd dau of John Berkeley (*see* BERKELEY, B), and *d* 29 Feb 1860, having had, with two other daus (*d* unm):

(1) Thomas Arthur; *b* 22 Oct 1801; *d* 31 Dec 1829

(2) Charles Henry Robert; *b* 26 Nov 1807; *d* unm

(1) Sophia Catherina Maria; *m* 7 June 1830 Charles Auguste, Marquis de Choiseul Beaupré

(2) Matilda Maria; *m* 28 Sept 1839 Richard More O'Ferrall, PC, JP, DL, MP, of Ballina, Govr Malta, and *d* 25 May 1882, leaving issue. He *d* 27 Oct 1880

(3) Paulina Eliza Maria; *m* 17 June 1844 Count Henri (Carlevaris) di San Damiano, Offr Sardinian Roy Gd

2 Charles, KCH; *b* 17 March 1779; Army Offr; *d* 13 Dec 1851

3 Arthur Francis; *b* 6 Feb 1789; Lt-Col; *m* 9 April 1834 Mary Anne Agnes, dau of Thomas Dillon, of Mount Dillon, Co Dublin, and *d* 17 Feb 1849, leaving:

(1) THOMAS ARTHUR JOSEPH, **4th Viscount**

(2) Charles Francis Xavier; *b* 9 Dec 1839; granted with sisters by roy licence 25 Sept 1860 rank of viscount's daus/yr s; *d* unm 8 Aug 1875

(1) Marcella Maria Agnes; *d* unm 28 Jan 1901

(2) Jane Mary Matilda; *m* 3 May 1860, as his 2nd w, John David FitzGerald, Baron FitzGerald of Kilmarnock (a style rather than peerage title granted him, who was a Ld of Appeal in Ordinary, for life 1882), and *d* 26 Feb 1910, having had issue. He *d* 16 Oct 1889

(3) Mary Paulina; *m* 19 Sept 1867 FM Sir Evelyn Wood, VC, GCB, GCMG, and *d* 11 May 1891, leaving issue (*see* PAGE WOOD, Bt)

(4) Margaret Mary; *m* 5 Aug 1869 Charles Standish Barry, of Leamlara, Co Cork, and *d* 9 April 1916, leaving issue. He *d* 10 Nov 1897

1 Margaret; *m* 19 Dec 1794 12th Viscount Gormanston (*qv*) and *d* 26 Jan 1820, leaving issue

2 Paulina; *m* 1806 Richard O'Ferrall-Caddell, of Harbourstown, Co Meath, and *d* 5 May 1856, leaving issue (*see* STAFFORD, B)

The 3rd VISCOUNT's n,

THOMAS ARTHUR JOSEPH SOUTHWELL, **4th Viscount Southwell of Castle Mattress**, KP (1871); *b* 6 April 1836; Cornet 13th Hus 1855, Lt 1857, ret 1858, Ld Lt and custos rotulorum Co Leitrim 1872; *m* 24 Aug 1871 Charlotte Mary Barbara (*d* 4 Feb 1929), est dau of Sir Pyers Mostyn, 8th Bt (*qv*), and *d* 26 April 1878, leaving, with a dau (Frances Mary Winifred, *b* 4 April 1874, *m* 8 June 1898 Maj Herbert Marmaduke Joseph Stourton and *d* 7 March 1950, leaving issue; *see* MOWBRAY, SEGRAVE and STOURTON, B):

ARTHUR ROBERT PYERS SOUTHWELL, **5th Viscount Southwell of Castle Mattress**; *b* 16 Nov 1872; Capt RE, Maj Salop Yeo, Actg Lt-Col cmdg a Bn MGC; *m* 28 Oct 1897 Hon Dorothy Katharine Walrond (*d* 18 Sept 1952), 3rd dau of 1st Baron Waleran (*see* 1963 edn), and *d* 5 Oct 1944, leaving:

1 ROBERT ARTHUR WILLIAM JOSEPH SOUTHWELL, **6th Viscount Southwell of Castle Mattress**; *b* 5 Sept 1898; *educ* RNCs Osborne and Dartmouth; RN: served WW I, Lt-Cdr 1927, Cdr 1938; *m* 1st 19 Jan 1926 (*divorce* 1931) Violet Mary Weldon, only child of Paymaster-Cdr Francis Weldon Walshe, MVO, OBE, RN, and had:

(1) *Susan Mary; *b* 19 Dec 1926; *m* 24 March 1951 *Keith Francis MacRae and has:

1a *John Francis; *b* 1952

2a *Paul Finlay; *b* 1955

1 (cont.) The **6th Viscount** *m* 2nd 1943 Josephine (*d* 3 July 1973), formerly w of Capt Henry Marryat Hardy and dau of Dennis Joseph de la Mole, and *d* 18 Nov 1960

2 Francis Joseph; *b* 31 March 1900; *educ* Oratory Sch and RMC Sandhurst; Lt Roy Welch Fus; *m* 18 Nov 1924 Agnes Mary Annette, er dau of Charles William Clifford (*see* CLIFFORD, Bt), and *d* 7 Jan 1953, leaving:

(1) (PYERS) ANTHONY JOSEPH SOUTHWELL, **7th and present Viscount Southwell of Castle Mattress**

(1) *Evelyn Mary Elizabeth [Mrs Harold Hope, 19 Mortlake St, Islington, Christchurch, New Zealand]; *b* 14 Nov 1926; *m* 1952 *Harold Hope and has:

1a *Carol; *b* 1953

2a *Valerie; *b* 1956

(2) *Barbara Frances Magdalene [Mrs Peter Fowler, Beech Tree House, Market Drayton, Salop]; *b* 29 May 1928; *m* 27 Oct 1949 *Peter Frederick Fowler, s of Cyril Frederick Fowler, of Market Drayton, and has:

1a *Simon Peter; *b* 2 July 1965

1a *Vivienne Anne; *b* 3 Aug 1951

2a *Gillian Clare; *b* 3 April 1953

3a *Sarah Elizabeth; *b* 4 June 1959

3 John Michael; *b* 17 Dec 1901; Lt-Cdr RN WW II, AFRAeS; *m* 29 Sept 1932 *Daphne Lewin (*d* 28 Dec 1998) only child of Sir Geoffrey Lewin Watson, 3rd Bt (*see* 1959 edn), and was *kas* in a flying accident Dec 1944

1 Elizabeth Katherine Mary; *b* 2 June 1904; *m* 19 April 1930 Lt-Col Donald Robert Grant Cameron, MBE, Roy Scots (*d* 17 Oct 1961), s of Duncan George Cameron, of Surbiton, and had:

(1) *Angus Duncan John [Angus Cameron Esq, Shamrock Farm, Assington, Colchester, Essex]; *b* 14 Dec 1932; *educ* Stowe and RMC Sandhurst; late Capt QO Cameron Highrs; *m* 3 Dec 1960 *Gillian Jane, yr dau of Frederick Basil Tomkins, of Wimborne, Dorset, and has:

1a *Edward Richard Pyers; *b* 17 May 1963

1a *Catriona Louise; *b* 18 Sept 1961

(2) *Iain Donald Robert; *b* 22 Sept 1937; *educ* Nautical Coll Pangbourne; *m* 1963 *Margaret Victoria Williams and has:

1a *James; *b* 27 May 1965

2a *John; *b* 27 May 1965

1a *Susan Fiona; *b* 11 Feb 1964

2a *Elizabeth Clare; *b* 2 June 1966

2 Joan Evelyn Mary; *b* 24 Sept 1909

SPEARMAN

Arms: Az. on a chevron erm. between three tilting-spears arg., headed or, a red deer's head erased ppr. **Crest:** A lion rampant ppr., gorged with a collar gemelle or, supporting a tilting spear also ppr., enfiled with a mural crown or. **Motto:** *Dum spiro spero* ('While I breathe I hope'). **Creation:** Bt. (UK) 28 April 1840.

SIR ALEXANDER YOUNG RICHARD MAINWARING SPEARMAN, 5TH BT [Sir Alexander Spearman Bt, PO Box 10004, Vledekloof 7560, Cape, S Africa]; *b* 3 Feb 1969; *s* f 1977; *m* 1994 *Anne Stine, dau of Kaj Munch, of Hyllinge, Denmark

Lineage: CHARLES SPEARMAN, of Thornley, Co Durham; *m* 1st —; *m* 2nd Margaret, sis of William Young, Govr Grenada and Tobago, and had:

ALEXANDER YOUNG SPEARMAN; Maj RA; *m* Agnes, dau of James Morton, of Bonan Hill, and had, with other issue:

1 ALEXANDER YOUNG (Sir), **1st Bt**

2 John Robert; *b* 8 June 1795; *ka* aboard the *Amphion* 13 March 1811

3 James Morton, Capt RA; *b* 4 March 1797; *m* 27 Oct 1829 Harriet, dau of Algernon Frampton, MD

4 Ralph William, barrister; *b* 9 April 1803; *d* 24 April 1845

5 George Wasey; *b* 18 Feb 1808; Midshipman *Delight*, frigate, believed to have foundered at sea in a hurricane 23 Feb 1824 off Mauritius

The est s,

Sir Alexander Young Spearman, 1st Bt (UK), so *cr* 28 April 1840, PC; *b* 13 Sept 1793; Assist Sec Treasury, Controller-Gen and Sec to Commrs Reduction Nat Debt; *m* 29 Dec 1826 Jane (*d* 19 June 1877), dau of Duncan Campbell, of Inveraw, Argyll, and had, with two daus (*d* unm):

1 Alexander Young; *b* 7 July 1832; *m* 1st 31 May 1855 Mary Anne Bertha (*d* 14 Jan 1860), yst dau of Sir Joseph Bailey, 1st Bt (*see* GLANUSK, B), and had surv issue:

  (1) JOSEPH LAYTON ELMES (Sir), **2nd Bt**

1 (cont.) Alexander Spearman *m* 2nd 2 April 1861 Louisa Anne Caroline Amelia (*m* 2nd 5 July 1870 Henry Harlington Seel, Richmond Herald (*d* 1882), and *d* 15 Feb 1933), only dau of Edward Pellew Mainwaring, and *d* 14 Aug 1865, having by her had:

  (2) Alexander Young Crawshay Mainwaring; *b* 20 March 1862; Cdr RN, cmded Collingwood Bn RN Bde WW I; *m* 26 May 1892 Jessie Aubrey, MBE (*m* 2nd 6 June 1923 Lt-Col Edward Loch and *d* 17 Nov 1933), dau of Rev Cadwallader Coker, Rector Fringford, Oxon, and was *ka* Dardanelles 4 June 1915, leaving:

    1a Alexander Cadwallader Mainwaring (Sir); *b* 2 March 1901; *educ* Repton and Hertford Coll Oxford; memb Grieveson, Grant, stockbrokers, MP Scarborough and Whitby 1941–66, PPS to Pres BOT, ktd 1956; *m* 1st 11 Aug 1928 (*divorce* 1951) Diana Violet Edith Constance (*d* 1991), er dau of Sir Arthur Havelock James Doyle, 4th Bt (*see* 1970 edn); *m* 2nd 27 April 1951 *Diana Josephine [Lady Spearman, The Old Rectory, Sarratt, Herts; Fealar, Enochdhu, Blairgowrie, Perthshire; 32 Queen Anne's Gate, London SW1], only child of Col Sir Lambert Ward, 1st Bt (*see* 1956 edn), and *d* 1982, leaving by her:

      1b +Lochain Alexander; *b* 9 April 1952; *educ* Milton Abbey; *m* 25 March 1977 *Pilin de Garrigues and has:

        1c +Alexander James; *b* 27 March 1984

        2c +Jack; *b* 1986

        1c *A dau; *b* 1980

      2b +John Dominic; *b* 25 April 1954; *educ* Eton; *m* 7 Aug 1976 (*divorce* 1978) Rebecca, dau of Sir Alan Lewis Wigan, 8th Bt (*qv*)

      3b +Andrew Mark; *b* 4 June 1960; *m* 1994 *Elisa, dau of Tom Jeremy King, CH, PC, MP, and has:

        1c *A dau; *b* 21 Feb 1997

      4b +James; *b* 6 Nov 1964

     1b *Zara Ann Louise; *b* 27 May 1956; *m* 1979 *Iain A Milligan

    1a Marjorie Aubrey; *m* 30 Aug 1928 Maj Henry Percy Bagge, MC, 4th s of Sir Alfred Thomas Bagge, 3rd Bt (*qv*), and *d* 5 July 1951, leaving issue

  (3) Charles Edward; *b* 10 Sept 1863; PhD Leipzig, Hon LLD, FRS, hon memb: Br Psychological Soc, Kentucky Acad Sciences, Deutsche Gesellschaft für Psychologie, Psychotechnical Soc Prague and Deutsche Akademie, for memb Société Française de Psychologie, London U: Reader Experimental Psychology 1906, Emeritus Prof Psychology, Capt Roy Munster Fus and Northumberland Fus and GSO WW I; *m* 4 Sept 1901 Frances Henrietta Priaulx (*d* 22 Oct 1955), dau of John Aikman, MD, and *d* 17 Sept 1945, having had:

    1a Alexander Louis Charles John; *b* 15 March 1916; Lt RN WW II; *ka* 29 May 1941

    1a Fan Caroline; *b* 3 Sept 1902; *m* 1 March 1927 Capt Philip Charles Forman, RN (*d* 4 Nov 1965), 7th s of Rev A F E Forman, and had:

      1b *Roderick Philip Carey [Roderick Forman Esq, 1 Westons Yard, Eton, Windsor, Berks]; *b* 2 June 1936; *educ* Eton and Trin Coll Cambridge (MA); late Sub-Lt RNVR

      1b *Prudence Caroline; *b* 7 Jan 1928; *m* 29 July 1950 *John Henderson Bowles and has:

        1c *Brendon Philip; *b* 22 April 1953

        2c *Stafford John William; *b* 14 April 1957

        1c *Bridget Nancy; *b* 26 June 1951

      2b *Jennifer Mary Priaulx [Mrs Alastair Porter, High Oak, Savill Rd, Lindfield, Sussex]; *b* 7 Feb 1930; *educ* St Hilda's Coll Oxford (MA); *m* 28 Aug 1954 *Alastair Robert Wilson Porter, s of James Porter, and has:

        1c *Angus James; *b* 9 June 1957

        2c *Duncan Roderick; *b* 22 Oct 1961

        1c *Frances Jennifer; *b* 31 July 1955

      3b *Nancy Chevallier; *m* 1960 *Jeffrey James Cox and has:

        1c *John James; *b* 22 May 1962

        2c *Meyrick; *b* 2 March 1964

    2a *Alice Louisa Jean [Mrs Martin Strong, 35 Arterberry Rd, London SW20 8AG]; *b* 26 Oct 1903; *m* 12 Dec 1928 Martin William Strong (*d* 1978), s of William S Strong, of Cairo, and has:

      1b *Richard Martin [Richard Strong Esq, 25 Newstead Way, London SW19 5HR]; *b* 3 Oct 1929; *m* 1st 15 Sept 1956 (*divorce* 1969) Ann Georgina, dau of Richard P Sargent, of London; *m* 2nd 1971 *Venetia Mary, dau of Ian T Henderson, and by his 1st w has:

        1c *Simon Alexander; *b* 21 March 1959

      2b *Christopher John [Christopher Strong Esq, Summerbee Farm, Chapel Lane, Stoke, Hants SP11 0LZ]; *b* 3 Aug 1932; W/Cdr RAF (ret); *m* 31 July 1956 *Brenda Mary, dau of A Willbery, of Nottingham, and has:

        1c *Michael Alexander [Michael Strong Esq, Clements Meadow, Cross Lane, Marlborough, Wilts]; *b* 25 Dec 1957; *m* 1990 *Sarah Faughey and has:

          1d *Theodore Martin Arthur; *b* 1991

          2d *Magnus John Patrick; *b* 1993

          1d *Lucy Josephine; *b* 1987

        1c *Penelope Anne [Mrs Michael Stone, Hay House, Hay St, Braughing, Herts]; *b* 8 May 1959; *m* 1987 *Michael John Kenneth Stone and has:

          1d *Henry Michael Charles; *b* 1992

          1d *Phoebe Alice; *b* 1988

          2d *Bryony Elizabeth; *b* 1990

        2c *Helen Jean [Mrs Ross MacKay, 53 Hilltop Rd, Clareville, Sydney 2107 NSW, Australia]; *b* 24 Dec 1960; *m* 1987 *Dr Ross MacKay and has:

          1d *Samuel James James; *b* 1989

          1d *Kitty Alexandra Beatrice; *b* 1992

      3b *Michael Charles [Michael Strong, 2727 Windover Dve, Corona del Mar, CA 92625, USA]; *b* 12 Jan 1935; *m* 1st 6 July 1963 (*divorce* 1968) Lysbeth Joanna (*d* 2 Aug 1970), er dau of Dr Crispin Bullmore Lanyon, of Falmouth, and has:

        1c Crispin Alexander; *b* 26 April 1964; *d* 2 Aug 1970

        1c Morwenna Frances; *b* 2 Oct 1965; *d* 2 Aug 1970

      3b (cont.) Michael Strong *m* 2nd 1968 *Margaret Christine, dau of Edwin V Price, of Chester, and by her has:

        2c *Edward Charles; *b* 17 Dec 1970

        3c *James Alexander; *b* 16 June 1972

        4c *Christopher Edwin; *b* 23 Nov 1977

      1b *Patricia Anne [Mrs John Barrett, 5 Wickfield Close, Christchurch, Dorset]; *b* 9 July 1931; *m* 30 March 1957 John Barrett (*d* 19–), s of F Barrett, and has:

        1c *Hazel Jean; *b* 7 April 1963

    3a *Ivy Joy [Mrs Thomas Barnes, Beechfield Cottage, Upper High St, Castle Cary, Somerset BA7 7AT]; *b* 20 Oct 1912; *m* 26 Oct 1939 Lt-Col Thomas Harold Barnes, TD, Derbys Yeo (*d* 1971), s of Alfred Thomas Holland Barnes, and has:

      1b *Belinda Marion [Mrs Bill Martin, Billy Bee Ranch 3024 FM 1165, Kempnor, Tx, USA]; *b* 21 Feb 1941; *m* 1st 28 Dec 1963 (*divorce* 1994) John Part, BA Dublin, slr, s of Alexander Francis Part, of London; *m* 2nd 22 March 1997 *Bill Martin and by her 1st husb has:

        1c *Emma Josephine [Mrs Benjamin Robson, The Little House, Biddestone, Wilts]; *b* 7 Sept 1967; *m* 1993 *Benjamin Oliver Hugh Robson

        2c *Tracy Belinda; *b* 13 Jan 1970

        3c *Joanna Frances; *b* 1974

      2b *Susannah Mainwaring [Mrs Andrew Thomson, Ashgate Old Forge, Fivehead, Curry Rivel, Somerset]; *b* 17 March 1944; *m* 30 June 1966 *Andrew Wilson Thomson, s of Andrew Wilson Thomson, of Glasgow

    4a Anne Mainwaring; *b* 23 July 1918; *m* 26 Sept 1940 *Santiago Perez-Walker, s of Santiago Perez Pena, of Santiago, and *d* 10 March 1998, leaving:

      1b *Santiago Alexander [Sr Santiago Perez-Spearman, Fundo Betania, Mallarauco, Meli Pilla, Chile]; *b* 1941; *m* 1963 *Gladys Schuler and has:

1c *Santiago Gonzalo; *b* 1965

1c *Amaya Paulina; *b* 1967

2c *Carola Francisca; *b* 1972

2b *Patrick Charles; *b* 1945; *m* 1969 *Ana Maria Bulnes and has:

1c *Sebastian; *b* 1971

1c *Moira; *b* 1973

3b *Francis Anthony; *b* 1949; *m* 1973 *Maria Soledad Ramirez and has:

1c *Loreto Victoria; *b* 1974

2c *Constanza Sol; *b* 1980

3c *Paulina Eugenia; *b* 1982

1b *Maria Evelyn; *b* 1943; *m* 1964 *Arturo Mardones and has:

1c *Diego; *b* 1967

1c *Magdalena; *b* 1965

2c *Octavia; *b* 1968

2 Edmund Robert, CMG, JP Middx; *b* 10 May 1837; Capt Uxbridge Yeo Cav, Actg 1st Sec Dip Serv, V-Consul Chantilly 1901–18; *m* 16 Aug 1859 Lady Maria Louisa Fitzmaurice (*d* 6 Oct 1917), 3rd dau of 5th Earl of Orkney (*qv*), and *d* 6 Oct 1918, having had:

(1) Edmund Alexander Malcolm; *b* 17 May 1862; *d* 30 Nov 1896

(2) Robert Wickham Morant, JP; *b* 16 Dec 1867; Priv Sec to Govr Falkland Islands and Actg Clerk to Exec; *d* unm 15 Oct 1913

(1) Marie Jane Louise; *m* 12 July 1882 Rev Henry Washington, Vicar St Saviour's, Pimlico, and *d* 1937

(2) Cecil Augusta Margaret Isabella; *m* 8 June 1889 Rev Llewellyn Christopher Watson Bullock, Rector Gt and Little Wigborough Essex 1925–33, assist master Rugby, and *d* 31 Jan 1959, leaving issue. He *d* 10 Feb 1936

3 Horace Ralph; *b* 26 Dec 1840; Col IA; *m* 24 Aug 1867 Isabella (*d* 24 July 1927), est dau of Thomas Sutherland, and *d* 18 March 1908, leaving:

(1) Horace Ralph; *b* 7 May 1868; *m* 1890 Louisa, dau of James Parker, and had:

1a Horace Layton; *b* 1896

1a Lily Alexandrina Campbell; *b* 1892

2a Isabella Lucy; *b* 1893

(2) Alexander Young; *b* 27 Nov 1872, Capt and Brevet Maj Roy Warwicks Regt, Nile Expdn 1898, Boer War 1901–02 (despatches); *m* 8 Nov 1898 Mary Cramond, dau of Edward Etches, of Litchurch Grange, Derbys, and *d* 24 Oct 1911, leaving:

1a Horace Edward James; *b* 16 Sept 1899; *educ* Trin Coll Glenalmond and Uppingham; Maj RA; *m* 16 June 1934 *Mary, dau of Jon Constantinescu, of Romania

2a Alexander Young; *b* 8 Jan 1904; Lt-Cdr RN WW II; *d* 2 Oct 1942 in HMS *Curacao* in collision with RMS *Queen Mary*

(3) Iverach Ian Sutherland; *b* 1874; *d* 24 Jan 1920

4 Rudolph Herries, barrister, Recorder Bridgnorth; *b* 14 April 1845; *m* 17 Dec 1885 Dorothy Jane (*d* 1 Feb 1940), dau of Edward W Mantell, of Golden Manor, Hanwell, and *d* 2 Aug 1900, leaving:

(1) Jane; *m* 1st 26 Jan 1915 Rev David Jessopp Bethell (*d* 1924), Vicar Bodlestreet Green, Sussex; *m* 2nd 25 Nov 1937 Jack Borley (*d* 22 April 1959), est s of Robert William Borley, and *d* 18 July 1955

(2) Margaret Dorothy

1 Jane Alexandrina; *m* 24 Jan 1850 William Layton Lowndes and *d* 24 May 1897

2 Augusta Herries; *m* 4 April 1861 Rev Morris Edgar Stanbrough, Rector Creyke, Yorks, and *d* 1 May 1907, leaving issue. He *d* 9 April 1901

Sir ALEXANDER *d* 20 Nov 1874; his gs,

Sir Joseph Layton Elmes Spearman, 2nd Bt, JP, DL Glam, JP Salop; *b* 22 Sept 1857; *educ* Eton and BNC Oxford; Capt 2nd Bde Welsh Div RA, High Sheriff Glam 1882; *m* 1st 31 Oct 1878 Ethel (*d* 18 July 1909), dau of William Leask, and had:

1 Joseph William; *b* 22 Aug 1879; Lt 3rd Bn Suffolk Regt; *m* 1900 Evelyn Daisy Oram and *d* 1917, leaving:

(1) Gwendoline Daisy Elizabeth; *b* 1911; *m* 19– and *d* 1994, leaving:

1a *Valerie; *b* 19–; *m* 19– *Guy Godefroy and has issue

2 ALEXANDER YOUNG (Sir), **3rd Bt**

3 Robert Henry; *b* 15 Nov 1882; Lt RN; *d* unm 7 Sept 1952

1 Ethel Nest, OBE (1918); *b* 31 Oct 1884; *m* 12 April 1910 Maj Geoffrey Stirling Newall, OBE, JP, DL (*d* 16 July 1952), RASC (TA), est s of Frederick Stirling Newall, and *d* 13 June 1968, having had issue

2 Gwendolen Anne; *b* 7 June 1887; *m* 24 Nov 1910 Sir John Dixon, 2nd Bt (*qv*), and *d* 2 April 1974, leaving issue

3 Sybil Mary; *b* 2 March 1890; *m* 7 April 1920 Rev William Steele Dobson, Rector St Anne, Lewes, s of Ezekiel Dobson, and *d* 26 Jan 1949, leaving issue. He *d* 27 March 1950

4 Margaret Eileen; *b* 29 May 1892; *m* 4 Oct 1924 Edgar George Roberts (*d* 29 Dec 1951), s of G E Roberts

5 Constance Isobel; *b* 26 Nov 1895

Sir Joseph *m* 2nd 18 Feb 1914 Carrie (*d* 18 Jan 1944), widow of Richard Sykes, of Roundhay Grange, Yorks, and Denver, USA, and dau of Frederick Eastwood, of Huddersfield, and *d* 11 Feb 1922

His est surv s,

Sir Alexander Young Spearman, 3rd Bt; *b* 19 June 1881; *educ* Stubbington Sch and Tonbridge; consulting mining engr Min Munitions 1914–18, CD WW II; *m* 25 Oct 1909 Dorothy Catherine, dau of Capt Thomas Bowyer Bower, and *d* 11 Feb 1959, leaving:

1 **Sir Alexander Bowyer Spearman, 4th Bt**; *b* 15 Feb 1917; *educ* Westminster; Hon Capt 10th Bn 7th Rajputs WW II (Staff Capt Delhi 1941–43, Paiforce 1943–45); Fire, Accident and Marine Manager Union Guarantee and Insur Cape Town 1955–57, Tech Assist to Gen Manager 1957–58, dir: Jack Ginsburg (Pty) 1960–67, Delta Insur Brokers (Pty) Cape Town 1967–77, FCII; *m* 10 April

1950 Martha, dau of John Green, of Naauwpoort, S Africa, and *d* 17 May 1977, leaving:

(1) Sir ALEXANDER YOUNG RICHARD MAINWARING SPEARMAN, **5th and present Bt**

(1) *Catherine Wendy Nest; *b* 18 June 1959; *m* 1979 *Jonathan Mort and has:

1a *Rebecca Claire Spearman; *b* 1994

(2) *Lynne Dorothy Anne; *b* 18 Dec 1962; *m* 1982 *Gregory Lloyd and has:

1a *Nicola; *b* 1988

2a *Chelsea Anne; *b* 1991

(3) *Daphne Joan Constance Eileen; *b* 14 Oct 1965

2 +RICHARD IAN CAMPBELL [Dr Richard Spearman, 70 Hatherley Rd, Winchester, Hants SO22 6RR]; *b* 14 Aug 1926; heir presumptive; *educ* Clayesmore and Birkbeck Coll London U (BSc 1952, PhD 1962); FLS, FZS, Fell Inst Biology, DSc 1952, FRSM, memb Soc Experimental Biology and Br Ecological Soc, hon sr lecturer UCL

1 Joan Dorothy Ethel; *b* 29 May 1912; served WW II; *m* 6 Aug 1960 William Taunton Oliver (*d* 1983), s of Rev William James Robert Taunton Oliver, Vicar Brackenfield, Derbys, and *d* 30 Nov 1994

SPEELMAN

Creation: Bt. (E) 9 Sept 1686.

SIR CORNELIS JACOB SPEELMAN, 8TH BT [Jonkheer Sir Cornelis Speelman Bt, 29 Blackall Rd, Exeter, Devon]; *b* 17 March 1917; *s f* 1949; *educ* Perth U W Australia (BA 1958); late Educn Dept Roy Dutch Army, modern languages master Geelong GS and Clifton, tutor Exeter Tutorial Coll; is a Br subject; *m* 1st 1972 Julia Mona Le Besque (*d* 1978); *m* 2nd 1986 *Irene Agnes van Leeuwen

Lineage: CORNELIS SPEELMAN; Govr-Gen Dutch E India; *m* Petronella Maria Wonderaer and *d* 11 Jan 1684, leaving:

JOHN CORNELIS SPEELMAN, of Batavia; *b* 1 Feb 1659; *m* 1683 Debora (granted rank of Bt's widow 9 Sept 1686; *d* 25 Sept 1695 aged 40), dau of John Nicolaes Kievit, of Rotterdam, Attorney Fiscal Admlty of the Maes, and Alida, dau of Adml Maerton van Tromp, of Holland and W Friesland, and *d* 4 June 1686 before the roy warrant of his *cr* as a Bt had passed the Gt Seal, leaving an only s:

Sir Cornelis Speelman, 1st Bt (E), so *cr* 9 Sept 1686; *b* 19 Jan 1684; feudal Ld of Nieland Scabinus at Bois le Duc, The Netherlands, Alderman Bois le Duc; *m* 11 Jan 1716 Agatha, feudal Ldy of Heeswyk and Dinther, dau of Jacob van der Houven, and *d* 30 April 1746, leaving an est surv s:

Sir Cornelis Speelman, 2nd Bt; *b* 5 Oct 1722; Ld of Heeswyk and Dinther, Burgomaster Leiden; *m* 10 June 1745 Cornelia Clara (*d* 7 Aug 1764), dau of Jacob van der Meer, and *d* 19 Sept 1787, leaving an est s:

Sir Cornelis Jacob Speelman, 3rd Bt; *b* 26 May 1747; Ld of Heeswyk and Dinther, declared 1817 one of the Dutch nobility with title Jonkheer; *m* 18 May 1779 Catherina (*d* 20 Feb 1811), dau of Abraham Verster, and *d* 14 June 1825, leaving, with an est and yst s (*dsp*):

1 **Jonkheer Sir Abraham Florentius Speelman, 4th Bt**; *b* 3 Sept 1784; Ld of Wulverhorst, Burgomaster Boxtel, Noble of N Brabant; *m* 1 April 1818 Sophia Balthina (*d* 25 March 1863), dau of Anthony Balthasar Stoop, and *d* 25 Aug 1840, leaving:

(1) Jonkheer Sir Cornelis Jacob Abraham Speelman, **5th Bt**; *b* 5 Jan 1823; Gen Dutch Artillery; *m* 25 April 1856 Anna Judith, dau of Jonkheer Jean Herman Martens Hora-Siccema by Isabella Antoinette, Baroness van Imhoff, and *dspms* 18 Jan 1898, having had:

1a Cornelis Jacob; *b* 30 March 1863; *d* 20 Nov 1864

2 Helenus Marinus SPEELMAN-WOBMA; *b* 29 Oct 1787; Pres Court of Justice, a Noble of Friesland; *d* 20 March 1867, having had:

(1) Cornelis Jacob; *b* 17 Dec 1817; Pres Court of Justice, a Noble of Friesland; *m* Elizabeth Woltera Sandrina, dau of Jacobus Enschedé, and *d* 7 March 1891, having had:

1a **Jonkheer Sir Helenus Marinus Speelman, 6th Bt**; *b* 27 July 1852; Burgomaster Harlingen, Offr Dutch Navy; *m* 27 March 1884 Wendelina Cornera, dau of Jonkheer Johan Æmilius Abraham van Penhuys, Govr Groningen, V-Pres Cncl of State there, by Catharine Johanna van Sminia, and *dsp* 17 May 1907

2a Jacob; *b* 22 Jan 1855; *m* 30 Aug 1880 Emilie Françoise Wilhelmine (*d* 6 Feb 1885), dau of Jonkheer Vrijthoff, and *d* 22 Oct 1883, having had an only child:

1b **Jonkheer Sir Cornelis Jacob Speelman, 7th Bt**; *b* 22 Sept 1881; Collector Town Dues Zandvoort; *m* 25 Jan 1916 Maria Catharina Helena, dau of Boudewyn Frans Castendijk, Notary of Arnhem, and *d* 3 Feb 1949, leaving:

1c Sir CORNELIS JACOB SPEELMAN, **8th and present Bt**

SPENCER

DIEU · DEFEND · LE · DROIT

Arms: Quarterly, arg. and gu., in the 2nd and 3rd quarters a fret or, over all on a bend sa. three escallops of the 1st. **Crest:** Out of a ducal coronet or a griffin's head arg., gorged with a bar gemelle gu., between two wings expanded of the second. **Supporters:** Dexter, a griffin per fess erm. and erminois, gorged with a collar sa., the edges flory-counterflory and chained of the last, on the collar three escallops arg.; sinister, a wyvern, erect on his tail erm., collared and chained as the griffin. **Motto:** *Dieu defend le droit* ('God defend the right'). **Creations:** B. and V. (GB) 3 April 1761, V. (Althorp, Co Northampton) and E. (GB) 1 Nov 1765, V. (UK) 19 Dec 1905 (Althorp, of Great Brington, Co Northampton).

THE 9TH EARL SPENCER, *Viscount Althorp*, Co Northampton, **Viscount Spencer of Althorp**, Co Northampton, **Viscount Althorp**, of Great Brington, Co Northampton, and **Baron Spencer of Althorp**, Co Northampton (Charles Edward Maurice Spencer) [The Rt Hon The Earl Spencer, Althorp, Northants NN7 4HG]; *b* 20 May 1964 (HM THE QUEEN stood sponsor); *s f* 1992; *educ* Eton and Magdalen Coll Oxford; Page Honour to HM THE QUEEN 1977–79; correspondent NBC News 1987–91 and 1993–95, reporter: Granada TV 1991–93, NBC Super Channel 1995–96; Patron Lifeline and ChildLine charities 1997–, author *Althorp: The Story of an English House* (1998); *m* 1989 (*divorce* 3 Dec 1997) (Catherine) Victoria, only dau of John Lockwood, of London SW14, and has:

  1 +LOUIS FREDERICK, *Viscount Althorp*; *b* 14 March 1994

  1 *Kitty Eleanor; *b* 1990

  2 *Eliza Victoria; *b* 1992

  3 *Katya Amelia; *b* 1992 (twin)

Spencer previous creation: For the Barony of Spencer of Wormleighton *see* MARLBOROUGH, D.

Lineage: The 3rd EARL OF SUNDERLAND (*see* MARLBOROUGH, D) had a 3rd s:

JOHN SPENCER; *b* 13 May 1708; inherited 11 and 12 Jan 1733/4 his f's family's Spencer estates in Beds, Northants (including Althorp) and Warwicks, together with most of his grandmother Sarah Duchess of Marlborough's property, including the Manor of Wimbledon and the Duchess's recently constructed property of Wimbledon Park; MP Woodstock, Ranger Windsor Gt Pk; *m* 14 Feb 1733/4 Georgina Carolina (*m* 2nd 1 May 1750 2nd Earl Cowper (*see* LUCAS OF CRUDWELL, B) and *d* 21 Aug 1780), 3rd dau and coheir of John Carteret, 2nd Earl Granville of the Jan 1714/5 *cr* (*see* GRANVILLE, E, preliminary remarks), and *d* 20 June 1746, leaving:

JOHN SPENCER, **1st Earl Spencer**, so *cr* 1 Nov 1765, as also VISCOUNT ALTHORP, Co Northampton, and previously 3 April 1761 BARON SPENCER OF ALTHORP, Co Northampton, and VISCOUNT SPENCER OF ALTHORP, Co Northampton (all GB); *b* 19 Dec 1734; MP (Whig) Warwick 1756–61, St Albans: High Steward 1772, Mayor 1779; *m* 20 Dec 1755 Margaret Georgiana (*d* 18 March 1814), er dau of Stephen Poyntz (*see* MORDAUNT, Bt) and *d* 31 Oct 1783, leaving, with two daus (Georgiana, *m* 5 June 1774 5th Duke of Devonshire (*qv*) and *d* 30 March 1806, leaving issue; Henrietta Frances, *m* 27 Nov 1780 3rd Earl of Bessborough (*qv*) and *d* 11 Nov 1821, leaving issue):

GEORGE JOHN SPENCER, **2nd Earl Spencer**, KG (1799), PC (1794); *b* 1 Sept 1758; *educ* Harrow and Trin Coll Cambridge; MP (Whig) Northampton 1780–82 and Surrey 1782–83, a Ld Treasury March–July 1782, Ld Privy Seal July-Dec 1794, Special Amb Vienna 1794, First Ld Admlty 1794–1801 (under his administration the victories of St Vincent and Camperdown took place, the mutinies at Spithead and the Nore were quelled and Nelson was promoted), Home Sec 1806–07, St Albans: High Steward 1783–1807 and Mayor 1790, Govr Charter House 1800, Er Bro Trin House 1795–1834, FRS 1780, FSA 1785, bibliophile who built up at Althorp what was said to be Europe's most splendid library in private hands, 1st Pres Roxburghe Club 1812; *m* 6 March 1781 Lady Lavinia Bingham (*d* 8 June 1831), est dau of 1st Earl of Lucan (*qv*), and *d* 10 Nov 1834, having had:

  1 JOHN CHARLES SPENCER, **3rd Earl Spencer**, PC (1830); *b* 30 May 1782; *educ* Harrow and Trin Coll Cambridge; MP (Whig) Oakhampton 1804–06, Northants 1806–32 and S Northants 1832–34, a Ld Treasury 1806–07 and

1830–34, Chllr Exchequer, a Ld Trade and Commr Indian Affrs 1830–34, FRS 1820, MFH Pytchley; *m* 13 April 1814 Esther (*d* 11 June 1818), only dau and heiress of Richard Acklom, of Wiseton Hall, Notts, and *dsp* 1 Oct 1845

  2 Robert Cavendish (Sir), KCH; *b* 24 Oct 1791; Capt RN; *d* 4 Nov 1830

  3 FREDERICK, **4th Earl**

  4 George (Very Rev); *b* 21 Dec 1799; *educ* Eton and Trin Coll Cambridge; took Anglican orders 1824, Chaplain to Bp Chester, Rector Brington, Northants; turned RC 1830, ordained 1832, Priest W Bromwich 1832–39, Prof Oscott 1839–46, Superior (as Ignatius of St Paul) Order of Passionists, trans. *Life of Blessed Paul of the Cross*; *d* 1 Oct 1864

  1 Sarah; *m* 4 March 1813 3rd Baron Lyttelton and *d* 13 April 1870, leaving issue (*see* COBHAM, V)

  2 Georgiana Charlotte (GEORGE III and QUEEN CHARLOTTE stood sponsors); *m* 14 April 1814 Lord George Quin, 2nd s of 1st Marquess of Headfort (*qv*), and *d* 21 Feb 1823, leaving issue

The 3rd EARL's bro,

FREDERICK SPENCER, **4th Earl Spencer**, KG (1849), CB (1827), PC (1846); *b* 14 April 1798; *educ* Eton; RN: joined 1811, Midshipman 1811–15, Lt 1818, Cdr 1821, Capt 1825–28 (fought Battle of Navarino 1827), R-Adml 1852, V-Adml 1857, MP (Whig) Worcs 1831–32, and Midhurst 1832–34 and 1837–41, Kt St Louis France, St Anne Russia, Redeemer Greece, Ld Chamberlain 1846–48, Ld Steward Household 1854–57; *m* 1st 23 Feb 1830 his 2nd cousin Elizabeth Georgina (*d* 10 April 1851), 2nd dau and coheiress (*see* CLINTON, B, and EXETER, M) of William Stephen Poyntz, MP, of Cowdray, Sussex, and had, with two daus (*d* unm):

  1 JOHN POYNTZ SPENCER, **5th Earl Spencer**, KG (1865), PC (1859), VD; *b* 27 Oct 1835; *educ* Harrow and Trin Coll Cambridge; MP (Lib) S Northants April-Dec 1857, Ld Lt Northants 1872–1908, Hon Col Northants Yeo, Er Bro Trin House, Hon LLD Cantab, Dublin and Wales, Hon DCL Oxon, Chllr Victoria, Groom Stole to HRH THE PRINCE CONSORT 1859–61 and HM EDWARD VII when Prince of Wales 1862–66, Ld Lt Ireland 1868–74 and 1882–85, Ld Pres Cncl 1880–83 and Feb–Aug 1886, First Ld Admlty 1892–95, memb Prince of Wales's Cncl 1898–1901 and Cncl Duchy Cornwall 1901–07, Keeper Privy Seal, three times MFH Pytchley; *m* 8 July 1858 Charlotte Frances Frederica, VA (*d* 31 Oct 1903), 3rd dau of Frederick Charles William Seymour (*see* HERTFORD, M), and *dsp* 13 Aug 1910

The **4th Earl** *m* 2nd 9 Aug 1854 Adelaide Horatia Elizabeth (*d* 29 Oct 1877), dau of Sir Horace Beauchamp Seymour (*see* HERTFORD, M), and *d* 27 Dec 1857, having by her had, with a dau (Victoria Alexandrina, CI (HM QUEEN VICTORIA stood sponsor), *m* 20 July 1881 1st Viscount Sandhurst (*qv*) and *d* 13 March 1906, having had issue):

  2 CHARLES ROBERT SPENCER, **6th Earl Spencer**, KG (1913), GCVO (1911), VD, PC (1892); *b* 30 Oct 1857; *educ* Harrow and Trin Coll Cambridge (MA); Ld Lt Northants 1908, Hon Col 4th Bn Northants Regt, MP N Northants 1880–85 and Mid-Northants 1885–95 and 1900–05, Groom-in-Waiting to HM QUEEN VICTORIA Feb–July 1886, V-Chamberlain 1892–95, Ld Chamberlain 1905–12, being *cr* 19 Dec 1905 VISCOUNT ALTHORP, of Great Brington, Co Northampton (UK), to enable him to take up the post, Grand Cross: Dannebrog Denmark, St Olav Norway, Polar Star, Rising Sun Japan, White Eagle Serbia, Red Eagle, Charles III Spain and Philippe le Bon France; *m* 25 July 1887 Hon Margaret Baring (*d* 4 July 1906), dau of 1st Baron Revelstoke (*qv*), and had:

    (1) ALBERT EDWARD JOHN, **7th Earl**

    (2) Cecil Edward Robert, DSC and bar (1918); *b* 20 May 1894; Lt-Cdr RN WW I (despatches, Croix de Guerre); *d* 14 Feb 1928 following a riding accident

    (3) George Charles; *b* 15 Aug 1903; *educ* RNCs Osborne and Dartmouth; Capt RA, Lt Leicester Yeo (TA), Sub-Lt RN; *m* 1st 13 June 1931 (*divorce* 1962) Barbara (*d* 1978), only dau of Benjamin Blumenthal, of Paris, and had:

      1a +(George Cecil) Robert (Maurice) [Robert Spencer, 314 Crane's Nest Way, West Palm Beach, FL 33410, USA]; *b* 14 July 1932 (HRH the late DUKE OF KENT stood sponsor); *educ* Eton; late Capt Leics and Derbys Yeo (TAO), late Lt 11th Hus (PAO)

      1a (Maud) Catherine Hélène; *b* 19 June 1934 (HM THE late QUEEN MAUD OF NORWAY stood sponsor); *m* 24 Nov 1958 Gerald Weiler, only s of P M Weiler, of New York, and *d* 1993

    (3) (cont.) The Hon George Spencer *m* 2nd 9 Nov 1966 (Kathleen Elizabeth) Sheila (*d* 9 Nov 1968), formerly w of (a) William Geoffrey Lowndes and (b) Lt-Col Robert Fitzroy Hamilton Pascoe Stuart-French, and yr dau of J J Henderson, and *d* Oct 1982

    (1) Adelaide Margaret (Delia), DCVO (1950, CVO 1947); *b* 26 June 1889; Hon FRCM 1954, Extra Woman Bedchamber to HM QUEEN ELIZABETH THE QUEEN MOTHER; *m* 18 Feb 1914 Col Hon Sir Sidney Cornwallis Peel, 1st and last Bt (*see* PEEL, E)

    (2) Lavinia Emily; *b* 29 Sept 1899; Extra Lady-in-Waiting to HM QUEEN ELIZABETH THE QUEEN MOTHER when Duchess of York; *m* 9 April 1919 4th Baron Annaly (*qv*) and *d* 9 May 1955, leaving issue

    (3) (Alexandra) Margaret Elizabeth, GM (1941); *b* 4 July 1906 (HM QUEEN ALEXANDRA stood sponsor); author *A Spencer Childhood* (1994); *m* 7 July 1931 (*divorce* 1947) Hon Henry Montagu Douglas-Home, MBE (*d* 1980), 2nd s of 13th Earl of Home (*qv*), and *d* 26 May 1996, having had issue

The 6th EARL *d* 26 Sept 1922; his est s,

ALBERT EDWARD JOHN SPENCER, **7th Earl Spencer**, TD, JP (Northants 1916), DL (1935); *b* 23 May 1892 (HM EDWARD VII stood sponsor); *educ* Harrow and Trin Coll Cambridge (BA 1913, MA 1946); Capt 1st Life Gds WW I (wounded), ADC Personal Staff 1915–19, Hon Col: 4th Bn Northants Regt (TA) 1924–37, Northants AA Regt (RA) TA 1937–61, 4th/5th Northants Regt (TA) 1961–67, Northants: Ld Lt 1952–67, CA, Pres Hunts and Northants TFA, memb Church Assembly (Ho Laity) 1930–35, Tstee Wallace Collection 1945–66, memb Standing Commn Museums and Galleries 1948–66, chm Advsy Cncl V and A 1961–69, Chm Govrs Wellingborough Sch 1946, Grand Visitor and Chm Northampton Gen Hosp 1935–48, chm Management Ctee Northampton Area Hosps 1948 and Sulgrave Manor Bd, FRSA, Hon DLitt Leicester, KStJ; *m* 26 Feb 1919 Lady Cynthia Elinor Beatrix Hamilton, DCVO (1953), OBE (1943), Ldy Bedchamber to HM QUEEN ELIZABETH THE QUEEN MOTHER 1937–72 (*d* 4 Dec 1972), 2nd dau of 3rd Duke of Abercorn (*qv*), and had:

1 (EDWARD) JOHN, **8th Earl**
1 *Anne [The Lady Anne Wake-Walker, East Bergholt Lodge, Suffolk CO7 6QU]; *b* 4 Aug 1920; 3rd Offr WRNS WW II; *m* 10 Feb 1944 Capt Christopher Baldwin Hughes Wake-Walker, DL, RN (*d* 5 April 1998) (*see* WALKER, Bt, of Oakley House), and has issue

The 7th EARL *d* 9 June 1975; his only s,

(EDWARD) JOHN SPENCER, **8th Earl Spencer**, MVO (1954), JP (Norfolk 1970), DL (Northants 1961); *b* 24 Jan 1924 (HM QUEEN MARY and HRH THE DUKE OF WINDSOR stood sponsor); *educ* Eton, RMC Sandhurst and RAC Cirencester; Capt Roy Scots Greys WW II (despatches), ADC to Govr S Australia 1947–50, Equerry to TM GEORGE VI 1950–52 and THE QUEEN 1952–54, CC Northants 1952, High Sheriff Northants 1959, Hon Col Northants Regt (TA), T&AVR 1967–71, Dep Hon Col Roy Anglian Regt 1971, chm: Nat Assoc Boys' Clubs 1962–79, Northants Assoc Boys' Clubs 1962–80 (pres 1980–92), tstee: King George's Jubilee Tst, Queen's Silver Jubilee appeal, memb UK Cncl European Architectural Heritage year 1975; *m* 1 June 1954 (*divorce* 1969) Hon Frances Ruth Burke Roche (*m* 2nd 2 May 1969 (*divorce* 1990) Peter Shand Kydd), yr dau of 4th Baron Fermoy (*qv*), and had:

  1 John; *b* and *d* 12 Jan 1960
  2 CHARLES EDWARD MAURICE SPENCER, **9th and present Earl Spencer**
  1 *(Elizabeth) Sarah Lavinia [The Lady Sarah McCorquodale, Stoke Rochford, Grantham, Lincs]; *b* 19 March 1955 (HM QUEEN ELIZABETH THE QUEEN MOTHER stood sponsor); *educ* West Heath; Tstee Diana Princess of Wales Memorial Fund 1997–; *m* 17 May 1980 *Neil Edmund McCorquodale, High Sheriff Lincs 1987, only s of Alistair McCorquodale by Rosemary, er dau of Maj Herbert Broke Turnor, gs of 13th Earl of Westmorland (*qv*), and has:

    (1) *George; *b* 1984
    (1) *Emily; *b* 2 July 1983
    (2) *Celia; *b* 1989
  2 *(Cynthia) Jane [The Lady Jane Fellowes, 5a The Old Barracks, Kensington Palace, London W8]; *b* 11 Feb 1957 (HRH THE DUKE OF KENT stood sponsor); *educ* West Heath; *m* 1978 *Sir Robert Fellowes, GCB, KCVO, PC (*see* DACRE, B), and has:

    (1) *Alexander Robert; *b* 23 March 1983
    (1) *Laura Jane *b* 19 July 1980
    (2) *Eleanor Ruth; *b* 20 Aug 1985
  3 DIANA FRANCES; *b* 1 July 1961; *educ* West Heath; Col-in-Ch: Roy Hants Regt to 1996, Princess of Wales's Own Regt (Canada) to 1996, 13th/18th Roy Hus (Queen Mary's Own), W Nova Scotia Regt to 1996, Princess of Wales's Roy Regt to 1996, and Roy Australian Survey Corps to 1996, Hon Air Cdre RAF Wittering, Cambs, to 1996, Order Al Kamal Egypt 1982, Grand Cross Order House of Orange Netherlands 1982; *m* 29 July 1981 (*divorce* 28 Aug 1996) HRH THE PRINCE OF WALES (*see* ROYAL FAMILY) and *d* in a car crash in Paris 31 Aug 1997, leaving issue

The **8th Earl** *m* 2nd 14 July 1976 *Raine (*m* 3rd 8 July 1993 (*divorce* Jan 1995, reverted to 2nd husb's name) Count Jean-François de Chambrun) [Raine Countess Spencer, 24 Farm St, London W1X 7RE], only child of Alexander George McCorquodale, of The White Lodge, Speen, Berks, by Dame Barbara Cartland, DBE, of Camfield Place, Hatfield, Herts (*see* 1970 edn MCCORQUODALE OF NEWTON, B), and formerly w of 9th Earl of Dartmouth (*qv*), and *d* 1992

Seats: Althorp, Northants; Spencer House, St James's, London SW1.

The Sir John Spencer who bought the Althorp estate in 1508 (*see* MARLBOROUGH, D) built the first house there around the same time. It was a red-brick structure surrounded by a moat (filled in during the 1790s). Althorp was substantially altered in 1650 by the 1st Earl of Sunderland's Countess, Lady Dorothy Sydney (*see* DE LISLE, V), who converted the Tudor inner courtyard to a vast drawing room and added the main staircase. The present building is mostly late 18th-century work by Henry Holland, however. (The **9th** and present **Earl** has expressed his regret at this transformation of Tudor and Stuart gem but admits that it made maintenance much easier over the next 200 years.) Nevertheless the entrance hall in Palladian style, together with its fine plaster ceiling, survives from the 1730s, over half a century earlier, the design being by Roger Morris, who is also responsible for the stable block, and Colen Campbell. Known as the Wootton Hall after the massive painting on the walls by John Wootton (1678?–1765), it was considered by Sir Nikolaus Pevsner the noblest Georgian room in Britain. The former art collection, once among the most splendid in private hands anywhere, has suffered considerable depredations in recent years. The 18th-century stable block, a handsome structure with a central pediment punctured by an oculus and standing on four pillars, was designated as a memorial museum to DIANA PRINCESS OF WALES in autumn 1997 and opened in the summer of 1998. The architect responsible for the conversion is Rasshied Din.

Spencer House in London, currently leased out by the family, dates from the mid-18th century. John Vardy was the original architect but was summarily dismissed in 1758 by the **1st Earl** after completing the exterior and ground floor interior. He was replaced by James 'Athenian' Stuart, who designed the first-floor state apartments in neo-classical style. A restoration programme was completed by the mid-1990s.

SPENCER-NAIRN

Arms: Per fess arg. and sa. on a chaplet four escallops all counterchanged, in the chief point a crescent of the second for difference. **Crest:** A terrestrial sphere with semi-meridian and stand ppr. **Motto:** *Usque conabor* ('I will strive to the end'). **Creation:** Bt. (UK) 20 Jan 1933.

SIR ROBERT ARNOLD SPENCER-NAIRN, 3RD BT, of Monimail, Co Fife, DL Fife (1995) [Sir Robert Spencer-Nairn Bt DL, Barham, Cupar, Fife KY15 5RG]; *b* 11 Oct 1933; *s f* 1970; *educ* Eton and Trin Hall Cambridge; late Lt Scots Gds; V-Ld Lt Fife 1996; *m* 4 May 1963 *Joanna Elizabeth, only dau of Lt-Cdr George Stevenson Salt, RN (*see* SALT, Bt, of Weeping Cross), and has:

  1 +JAMES ROBERT; *b* 7 Dec 1966; *educ* Glenalmond and RAC Cirencester; *m* 23 July 1994 *Dominique Jane, only dau of Michael Williamson
  2 +Andrew George; *b* 1 July 1969; *educ* Glenalmond, Reading U and RAC Cirencester
  1 *Katharine Elizabeth; *b* 10 May 1964

Lineage: Sir MICHAEL BARKER NAIRN, 1st Bt (*qv*), had a 2nd s:

Sir ROBERT NAIRN later SPENCER-NAIRN (1928), **1st Bt** (UK), so *cr* 20 Jan 1933, TD JP Fife, DL; *b* 11 July 1880; *educ* Rugby and Trin Hall Cambridge; Maj Fife and Forfar Yeo WW I, ktd 1928, Pres Scottish U Assoc 1931–32, dir Michael Nairn & Co and Michael Nairn and Greenwich, MFH Fife 1932–47; *m* 13 Feb 1906 Clara Kathleen (*d* 26 Jan 1966), yst dau of C Chaloner Smith, of Cobham, Surrey, and had:

  1 DOUGLAS LESLIE SPENCER (Sir), **2nd Bt**
  2 +Michael Alastair Spencer, TD, JP (Fife 1951) [Maj Michael Spencer-Nairn TD JP, Baltilly House, Ceres, Fife KY15 5QG]; *b* 13 Jan 1909; *educ* Shrewsbury and Trin Hall Cambridge (BA 1931, MA 1935); Maj Fife and Forfar Yeo (TA) WW II; *m* 25 Oct 1935 *Ursula Helen, twin dau of Howson Foulger Devitt (*see* DEVITT, Bt), and has:

    (1) *Alastair Ian; *b* 26 July 1938; *d* following a car crash 19 June 1960
    (2) +Angus [Angus Spencer-Nairn Esq, La Fontaine, Rue du Pont, St John, Jersey, CI]; *b* 23 Jan 1947; *educ* Eton and RAC Cirencester (MRAC); CA, ptnr Rawlinson and Hunter; *m* 6 July 1968 *Christina Janet, er dau of Col Hugh Stewart Gillies, MC, of Kindar House, New Abbey, Dumfries, and has:

      1a +Michael Angus; *b* 1975
      1a *Fiona Louise; *b* 1974
    (1) *Sarah Ursula [Mrs John Scoular, Tonderghie, Whithorn, Wigtownshire]; *b* 13 June 1937; *m* 28 April 1967 *John Richard Scoular, s of Rev John Greenshields Scoular, and has:

      1a *Alastair John Greenshields; *b* 24 Dec 1972
      1a *Anys Helen; *b* 1978
    (2) *Catriona Jane [Mrs George Tremlett, River House, The Green, Elstead, Surrey GU8 6DA]; *b* 21 Feb 1945; *m* 1st 29 March 1969 (*divorce* 1980) Paul Hosegood Kirton, BSc, er s of Robert James Kirton, CBE, and has:

      1a *Ian Nigel; *b* 6 April 1970
      1a *Clare Helen; *b* 1972
      2a *Lena Harriet; *b* 11 Jan 1974
      3a *Mary Rose; *b* 11 Jan 1974
    (2) (cont.) Mrs Catriona Kirton *m* 2nd 1986 *George Edward Derrington Tremlett, s of Laurence Edward Paul Tremlett
  3 +(Robert) Frank [Frank Spencer-Nairn Esq, Castle Carey, St Peter Port, Guernsey, CI]; *b* 17 Nov 1910; *educ* Shrewsbury and Trin Hall Cambridge (BA, MA 1936); Capt Black Watch (TA) WW II; *m* 1st 16 Oct 1936 (*divorce* 1948) Caroline Isabel, only child of H A Chadwick, of Calgary, and has had:

    (1) Andrew Frank; *b* 8 Aug 1940; *d* 7 Oct 1941
    (1) *Isabel Susan; *b* 3 Sept 1937; *m* 25 June 1966 *Brig Nicholas John Ridley, OBE, QOH, er s of Col Charles William Ridley, OBE, by Heather Cameron, est dau of Gen Sir Philip Christison, 4th Bt (*see* 1970 edn), and has had:

      1a *Nicholas Charles Philip Christison; *b* 1973
      1a Alexia Kathleen; *b* 10 May 1967; *d* 1992
      2a *Susanna Mary; *b* 28 June 1969

3 (cont.) Frank Spencer-Nairn *m* 2nd 27 Feb 1954 *Mary Anna, dau of Walter E Hettmann, of San Francisco, and by her has:

(2) *Martha Ann; *b* 7 June 1955; *m* 1984 *Seth M Milliken II and has:

1a *Eliza Clark; *b* 1987

(3) *Charlotte Emily; *b* 28 Feb 1957; *m* 1989 *Duncan MacGuigan

(4) *Elspeth Margaret; *b* 11 June 1958; *m* 1981 (*divorce* 1988) Edgar W Swift and has:

1a *Clinton Spencer; *b* 19–

(5) *Margaret Cynthia; *b* 12 Feb 1965

1 *(Kathleen) Matilda, MBE [Mrs William Webb MBE, Mendlesham Manor, Brockford Rd, Mendlesham, Suffolk IP14 5SG]; *b* 12 July 1913; *m* 1st 21 May 1938 (*divorce* 1948) Maj Ronald Richards, RA, only s of Harold Richards; *m* 2nd 1948 William Webb (*d* 1991), s of William Webb, and by him has:

(1) *William Spencer; *b* 16 Sept 1948; *educ* Tonbridge and Trin Hall Cambridge

(2) *Alan Gordon; *b* 30 April 1951; *educ* Tonbridge

(3) *Michael Charles; *b* 6 July 1952; *educ* Milton Abbey

2 *(Helen) Clare [Mrs John Hume, Damside, Auchterarder, Perthshire]; *b* 30 April 1917; *m* 1st 4 April 1939 Maj John Henry Courthope Powell, 2nd Fife and Forfar Yeo (TA) (*ka* Normandy 19 July 1944), only s of Richard Henry Powell, and has:

(1) *Elizabeth Clare [Mrs Colin Scott-Dempster, Old Faskally House, Killiecrankie, Pitlochry, Perthshire PH16 5LG]; *b* 30 May 1942; *m* 1 Oct 1965 *Rev Canon Colin Thomas Scott-Dempster, s of Ronald Scott-Dempster, WS, and has:

1a *Robert Andrew; *b* 30 April 1967

2a *Harry Colin; *b* 1985

1a *Clare Ann; *b* 7 June 1969

(2) *Margaret Ann; *b* 9 July 1944; *m* 8 Jan 1966 *Capt Stephen James Lindsay (*see* CRAWFORD and BALCARRES, E), and has issue

2 (cont) Mrs John Powell *m* 2nd 23 Nov 1945 John William Gardner Hume (*d* 1976), s of John Kirkland Hume, and by him has had:

(1) John Robert; *b* 15 Oct 1949; *d* following a car crash 16 July 1969

(3) *Mary [Mrs John FitzGerald, The Old Rectory, Rodmarton, Glos GL7 6PE]; *b* 31 March 1947; *m* 1972 *John FitzGerald and has:

1a *John William Broun; *b* 1973

2a *Edward James Broun; *b* 1975

1a *Katherine Mary; *b* 3 July 1979

2a *Louisa Clare; *b* 1984

3 *(Adela) Margaret [The Rt Hon The Lady Colnbrook, 3 Ursula St, London SW11 3DW]; *b* 14 Nov 1924; *m* 21 Jan 1944 Baron Colnbrook (Sir Humphrey Atkins, KCMG (1983), PC (1973), *b* 12 Aug 1922 , MP (C) Merton and Morden 1955–70 and Spelthorne 1970–87, Govt Ch Whip 1973–74, NI Sec 1979–81, LP 1987, *d* 4 Oct 1996] and has:

(1) *Charles Edward Spencer; *b* 30 Oct 1952; *educ* Eton; barrister; *m* 1980 *Clare Margaret, dau of Henry Neville Hemsley, and has:

1a *Edward Oliver; *b* 1982

2a *Nicholas Charles; *b* 1985

3a *Matthew Spencer; *b* 1988

1a *Katherine Margaret Lucy; *b* 1992

(1) *Sheila Kathleen [Mrs Royston Schroeder, Ellimore Farm, Lustleigh, Devon]; *b* 26 Oct 1944; *m* 1st 15 Feb 1964 (*divorce* 1972) Peter Thornycroft Romer-Lee, er s of Charles Romer-Lee and Mrs P V Mackinnon, and has:

1a *Richard Peter; *b* 9 July 1965; *educ* Sherborne; *m* 1991 *Kirsten, dau of Col Richard Smith, and has:

1b *Max Humphrey; *b* 1997

2a *Anthony James; *b* 27 Feb 1967; *educ* Sherborne; *m* 1997 *Katherine Tully

(1) (cont.) Mrs Sheila Romer-Lee *m* 2nd 1975 (*divorce* 1978) Keith Allen Manners; *m* 3rd 1982 Royston Joseph Schroeder (*d* 1994)

(2) *Julia Margaret [Mrs John Keay, Succoth, Dalmally, Argyll]; *b* 16 Sept 1946; *m* 1st 5 March 1966 (*divorce* 1972) David Charles Roderick, er s of Rev Charles Roderick; *m* 2nd 1972 *John Stanley Melville Keay and by him has:

1a *Alexander John Melville; *b* 1973

2a *Samuel Michael Cosmo; *b* 1979

1a *Anna Julia; *b* 1974

2a *Nell Christina; *b* 1977

(3) *Sally Mary [Mrs William Clegg, Homer House, Ipsden, Oxford]; *b* 18 Feb 1948; *m* 16 Sep 1970 *William F Clegg, s of J N Clegg, and has:

1a *William Humphrey; *b* 1975

1a *Islay Mary; *b* 1973

The 1st Bt *d* 20 Oct 1960; his est s,

Sir Douglas Leslie Spencer Spencer-Nairn, 2nd Bt, TD, JP; *b* 24 Dec 1906; *educ* Shrewsbury and Trin Hall Cambridge (BA 1928, MA 1932); Lt-Col (Staff) Black Watch (TA) WW II, MP (C) Centl Ayrshire 1955–Sept 1959, PPS to Parly Sec BOT 1958–59, dir Nairn & Williamson Hldgs; *m* 1st 20 Jan 1931 (*divorce* 1946) Elizabeth Livingston (*d* 1985), only dau of Arnold James Henderson, and had:

1 Sir ROBERT ARNOLD SPENCER-NAIRN, **3rd and present Bt**

2 +John Chaloner [John Spencer-Nairn Esq, 2046 West 13th Ave, Vancouver V6J 2HJ, BC, Canada]; *b* 1 April 1938; *educ* Eton; late 2nd Lt RAC; *m* 1st 4 Nov 1966 (*divorce* 1970) *Barbara Lynn, er dau of Murray Kamichik, of Montreal; *m* 2nd 1971 *Lucie, dau of Pierre Belanger, and by her has:

(1) +John Henderson; *b* 1973

(1) *Kim Sheilagh; *b* 1975

(2) *Tara Lucie; *b* 1977

1 *Mary Elizabeth [Mrs Andrew Houstoun, Kirkhill, Lintrathen, Kirriemuir, Angus DD8 5JH]; *b* 22 Dec 1931; *m* 14 Aug 1953 *Maj Andrew Beatty Houstoun, OBE, MC, DL, Roy Dragoons, est s of William McAulay Houstoun, of Sachel Court, Alford, Surrey, and has:

(1) *William Robert [William Houstoun Esq, Cairnhall, Lintrathen, Kirriemuir, Angus DD8 5JJ]; *b* 20 Dec 1954; *educ* Harrow and Edinburgh U; *m* 1981 *Sarah Molly, dau of Col Charles Sivewright, CB, MC, DL, of Talland House, S Cerney, Glos, and has:

1a *Camilla Mary; *b* 15 May 1983

1a *Rosemary Sarah; *b* 5 Sept 1984

(2) *David Waldron [David Houstoun Esq, Glenkilrie, Blacklunans, Blairgowrie, Perthshire PH10 7LR]; *b* 20 May 1957; *educ* Harrow; *m* 1989 *Morag Lynne, dau of John Davidson, of Forter, Glenisla, Perthshire, and has:

1a *Andrew James; *b* 28 Oct 1990

1a *Claire Kathryn; *b* 21 Oct 1992

2a *Rachel Elizabeth; *b* 28 Nov 1995

(3) *Alexander Michael [Alexander Houstoun Esq, Kerbet House, Kinnettles, by Forfar, Angus DD8 1TQ]; *b* 27 July 1958; *educ* Harrow; *m* 1988 *Margaret Susan, dau of Duncan Kerr, of The Hillocks, Broughty Ferry, and has:

1a *Michael Paterson; *b* 1990

2a *Robert Duncan; *b* 1992

(4) *Andrew Neil [Andrew Houstoun Esq, Nether Gelvan, Fossoway, Kinross KY13 7PN]; *b* 23 Dec 1961; *educ* Harrow and RAC Cirencester; *m* Oct 1995 *Victoria Margaret, dau of David L Laird, of West Memus, Forfar, Angus

Sir Douglas *m* 2nd 22 Nov 1946 (Elizabeth) Louise (*d* 1992), dau of Frederick Vester, of the American Colony, Jerusalem, and *d* 8 Nov 1970, leaving:

3 +(Christopher) Frank [Frank Spencer-Nairn Esq, Culligran, Struy, Beauly, Inverness-shire IV4 7JX]; *b* 10 May 1949; *educ* Eton and Magdalene Coll Cambridge; FCA, MBA Cape Town; *m* 13 Sept 1975 *Juliet Constance, yr dau of Oswald Frank Baker Baker (*see* PERTH, E), and has:

(1) +Douglas Frederick; *b* 28 May 1986

(1) *Philippa Lucy; *b* 19 Sept 1980

(1) *Jenny Anne Helen; *b* 3 April 1983

2 *Teresa Leslie [Mrs John Ingleby, Malling Farm, Port of Menteith, Stirling]; *b* 17 Jan 1952; *m* 25 Oct 1975 *John Mungo Ingleby, est s of John A Ingleby, and has:

(1) *Mungo Henry; *b* 1981

(2) *(John) Frederick; *b* 1988

(1) *Kim Louise; *b* 24 Sept 1978

(2) *Rosie; *b* 1990

SPENCER-SMITH

Arms: Sa. on a fess cotised between three martlets or as many crescents az. **Crest:** A sword point upwards ppr., pommel and hilt or, and a pen point downwards in saltire arg. **Motto:** *Marte et ingenio* ('By war and wit'). **Creation:** Bt. (UK) 11 June 1804.

SIR JOHN HAMILTON SPENCER-SMITH, 7TH BT, of Tring Park, Co Hertford [Sir John Spencer-Smith Bt, Hazel House Quarantine Kennels, Elsted, W Sussex GU29 0JT]; *b* 18 March 1947; *s f* 1959; *educ* Milton Abbey and Lackham Coll Ag Wilts; *m* 1980 (*divorce* 1992) Mrs Christine Parris, dau of John Theodore Charles Osborne, of Durrington, W Sussex, and has:

1 *Jessica Kirsten; *b* 23 Jan 1985

Lineage: ADAM SMITH; Dundee burgess; granted land nearby by JAMES V 5 Dec 1535; *m* Matilda Anderson and *d* between 1542 and 1567, leaving:

HENRY SMITH; had:

JOHN SMITH; Recorder Forfar; bought the Glasswell estate, Angus; royalist Civil War; *m* Agnes, dau of Andrew Wylie, Dundee merchant, and *d* by 1660, leaving:

HENRY SMITH, of Glasswell; *m* Anne, dau of Sir Gilbert Ramsay of Banff, and had:

JAMES SMITH of Camno; *b* 1664; bought the Atherstone estate; *m* Grizel, dau of Alexander Watson of Wallace Craigie; his 4th s:

JOHN SMITH; *b* 1703; London merchant; *m* Mary (*d* 26 March 1787), dau of Griffin Ransom, of Lambeth, and *d* 27 July 1787, having had:

1 Joshua, of Eristoke Park, Wilts; *b* 1735; MP; *m* 1766 Sarah Gilbert and *d* 20 March 1819, having had:

(1) Maria; *m* 18 Aug 1787 1st Marquess of Northampton (*qv*) and *d* 14 March 1843, leaving issue

(2) Elizabeth; *m* William John Chute, MP, of The Vyne and Pickenham Hall, Hants, and *dsp*. He *d* 1824

(3) Augusta; *m* 1798 Charles Smith, of Suttons, Stapleford Tawney, Essex, MP Westbury (*see* SMITH-MARRIOTT, Bt), and *d* 1845, leaving:

1a **Sir Charles Joshua Smith, 2nd Bt**; *b* 31 May 1800; *m* 1st 28 Oct 1823 Belinda (*dsp* 22 Jan 1825), dau and heiress of George Colebrooke; *m* 2nd 2 July 1826 Mary (*d* 3 July 1842), 2nd dau of William Gosling, of Roehampton, and *d* 14 Jan 1831, leaving:

1b **Sir Charles Cunliffe Smith, 3rd Bt**, JP, DL Essex; *b* 15 Sept 1827; High Sheriff Essex 1852; *m* 15 Feb 1855 Agnes Frederica (*d* 4 March 1913), yst dau of Capel Cure, of Blake Hall, and *d* 31 July 1905, leaving:

1c **Sir Drummond Cunliffe Smith, 4th Bt**; *b* 23 Feb 1861; High Sheriff Essex 1915, Lt W Essex Militia; *d* unm 8 May 1947

2c Reginald Cunliffe, JP Sussex; *b* 5 Dec 1863; 2nd Life Gds; *m* 11 Nov 1892 Maud Eleanor (*d* 7 April 1932), 3rd dau of Robert Gosling, of Hassobury, Herts, and *dsp* 6 Feb 1917

1c Frederica Mary; *b* 25 Sept 1856; *d* unm 26 March 1908

2c Laura; *b* 23 Nov 1858; *m* 22 Jan 1891 Rev Charles George Beaumont Hotham (*see* HOTHAM, B) and *d* 9 Nov 1927

1b Mary Charlotte; *m* 13 May 1861 Lt-Gen Gaspard Le Marchant Tupper, CB, Col Cmdt RA, and *d* 22 April 1879, leaving issue. He *d* 2 July 1906

2b Augusta Elizabeth; *m* 17 Oct 1857 Rev Lawrence George Capel Cure, Rector Roding Abbess, Essex, s of Capel Cure, of Blake Hall Essex, and *d* 14 Nov 1915, having had issue. He *d* 27 June 1912

2a Spencer, of Brooklands, Hants, JP; *b* 8 March 1806; *m* 3 Sept 1835 Frances Anne (*d* 22 Feb 1897), dau of Sir Michael Seymour (*see* CULME-SEYMOUR, Bt), and *d* 2 May 1882, having had, with another s (*d* young) and two daus (*d* unm):

1b Drummond Spencer; *b* 13 Sept 1837; *d* unm 3 Nov 1874

2b Seymour Spencer; *b* 11 Feb 1841; Capt RN; *d* unm 1 Aug 1893

3b Spencer Compton SMITH later HAMILTON-SPENCER-SMITH (roy licence 1872) (Rev); *b* 22 June 1842; MA Oxon, Vicar Kingston, Dorset; *m* 18 July 1872 Mary (*d* 23 March 1923), dau of Adml Cospatric Baillie-Hamilton (*see* HADDINGTON, E), and *d* 11 May 1911, leaving:

1c DRUMMOND COSPATRIC (Sir) **5th Bt**

2c Michael Seymour, DSO (1919), MC; *b* 6 July 1881; Lt-Col Gen List, City London: Lt, High Sheriff 1926, Dir Bank England; *m* 25 July 1907 Evelyn Penelope (*m* 2nd 28 July 1934 Elliot Francis Montagu Butler and *d* 5 March 1974), dau of Rev Arthur Delmé-Radcliffe, and *d* 20 Jan 1928, leaving:

1d Peter Compton; *b* 12 Nov 1912; *educ* Eton and New Coll Oxford; Maj 79th Herts Yeo (HAA Regt) RA (TA); *m* 27 June 1950 *Philippa Mary [Mrs Peter Spencer-Smith, High Down House, Hitchin, Herts SG5 3BL], yr dau of Capt Richard Ford, Rifle Bde, and *d* 1993, leaving:

1e +MICHAEL PHILIP; *b* 2 April 1952; heir presumptive; *educ* Eton

2e +Gerald Peter Harry; *b* 22 Dec 1954; *educ* Eton

2d Jeremy Michael, CB (1971), OBE (1959), MC (1945); *b* 28 July 1917; *educ* Eton and New Coll Oxford; Maj-Gen, Welsh Gds WW II, cmded 3rd Bn KAR Kenya 1959–60, GOC Wales 1968–70, Dir Manning Army 1970–72

1d Beatrice Mary; *b* 27 March 1909; *m* 16 Sept 1939 W/Cdr Sir Richard Bellingham Graham, 10th Bt, of Norton Conyers (*qv*), and had issue

1c Margaret Cecily; *m* 26 July 1900 John Swinnerton Phillimore and *d* 6 Aug 1965 aged 90, leaving issue (*see* PHILLIMORE, B)

4b Orlando Spencer (Rev); *b* 17 Dec 1843; *educ* Oriel Coll Oxford (MA); Rector Swyre; *m* 27 April 1876 Theodosia (*d* 1 Oct 1890), dau of Gen Sir Richard England, GCB, and *d* 23 Nov 1920, leaving:

1c Gerald Montagu, DSO (1917); *b* 4 June 1881; *educ* Eton; Col RA WW I (wounded three times, despatches three times), GSO(1) and Perm Pres Selection Bd for Offrs War Office WW II; *m* 16 July 1912 Iris Mary (*d* 4 May 1967), dau of Richard Arthur Hamilton Seymour (*see* CULME-SEYMOUR, Bt), and *d* 9 Oct 1951, having had:

1d John Seymour; *b* 24 June 1913; *d* 17 Nov 1937

1d *Judith [Mrs Harry Lee, Popple Hill, Graffham, W Sussex GU28 0QF]; *b* 17 Oct 1917; *m* 9 March 1940 Harry Illtyd Lee (*d* 1985), only s of Charles Wilfred Lee, JP, and has:

1e *James Seymour [James Lee Esq, 71 Sumner Place Mews, London SW7 3EF]; *b* 20 Nov 1945; *educ* Down House Northiam; film director; *m* 1st 1967 (*divorce* 19—) Sally, dau of Edwin Hector Gordon Hill-Brookes, AFC, and has had:

1f Orlando Spencer Seymour; *b* 1968; *d* 1981

1e (cont.) James Lee *m* 2nd 1978 *Hannah Marion Teresa, dau of Patrick Joseph Lennon, and by her has:

2f *Edward Joseph Seymour; *b* 1985

3f *Jack Illtyd Seymour; *b* 1989

1f *Grace Olivia Seymour; *b* 1986

2f *Florence Daphne Seymour; *b* 1993

1e *Caroline Susan; *b* 17 June 1941

2e *Ann [Mrs Nicholas Carter, 60a Stanhope Gdns, London SW7]; *b* 25 Feb 1943; *m* 7 Dec 1963 *Nicholas Hugh Carter, only s of Archibald Louis Hugh Carter, and has:

1f *Maximilian Hugh; *b* 19 June 1965

2f *Adam James Louis; *b* 1977

1f *Emma Louise; *b* 17 Oct 1966

2f *Sophie Ann; *b* 1 March 1969

3e *Lindsey Victoria [Mrs Angel Andrews, 6 Grosvenor Ave, London SW14 8BX]; *b* 2 Dec 1954; *m* 1979 *Angel Peter Andrews and has:

1f *Nyah Zoe; *b* 1977

2f *Jasmine Judy; *b* 1994

1d (cont.) Mrs Harry Lee also adopted:

*Michael Gerald Harry; *b* 1957

2c Richard Osbaldeston; *b* 18 Feb 1885; *educ* Eton and St John's Coll Oxford (BA); Lt-Col and Brevet-Col Hants Regt WW I (wounded, despatches), cmded Princess Beatrice's IoW Rifles 1932–36; *m* 1st 20 June 1912 Murielle Alethe Victoria (*d* 12 July 1931), 3rd dau of Leonard Guise John Wingfield-Stratford (*see* POWERSCOURT, V), and had:

1d Roland Wingfield; *b* 13 April 1916; *educ* Chillon Coll Switzerland; Maj 79th Hants Regt; *m* 29 Oct 1948 *Helen Rosamund [Mrs Roland Spencer-Smith, Three Corners, Old Newton Rd, Kingskerswell, S Devon TQ12 5LB], 2nd dau of Lt-Col James Percy Earp, OBE, MC, and *d* 1988, leaving:

1e +Richard Mervyn [Richard Spencer-Smith Esq, 124 Hampstead Way, London NW11 7XY]; *b* 19 Aug 1954; *m* 1989 *Sotiria Dracopoulou and has:

1f +Roland Mikhail Alexander; *b* 1990

1e *Jennifer Murielle; *b* 18 July 1952; *m* 1st 1973 (*divorce* 1984) Peter Leslie Riley; *m* 2nd 1990 *Simon Andrew Cyprian Dunstan and by him has:

1f *Ysobel Sophie Helen; *b* 1991

2d +Drummond Mervyn [Drummond Spencer-Smith Esq, Jade Cottage, Bidford-on-Avon, Warwicks B50 4NL]; *b* 11 Jan 1920; *educ* Wellington; Capt RTR; *m* 1960 (*divorce* 1994) June Patrysha, dau of Bertram George Finn, and has:

1e +Christopher Rex; *b* 1962; *m* 1986 (*divorce* 1994) Serena Richwood and has:

1f *Naomi Kate; *b* 1987

2f *Danielle Eve; *b* 1990

1e *Rosalind Muriel; *b* 1960; *m* 1988 *Colin George Woodnutt and has:

1f *Simon Edward; *b* 1989

2c (cont.) Lt Col Richard Spencer-Smith *m* 2nd 7 Sept 1932 Christian Louisa (*d* 17 Aug 1962), dau of Lt-Col H E Passy, and *d* 24 March 1962, having by her had:

1d *Rosan Winifred; *b* 31 Oct 1934

1c Katherine Winifred; *b* 11 April 1877; *m* 7 June 1905 George Winn and *d* 8 Feb 1954, leaving issue. He *d* 27 March 1947

2c Theodosia Lettice; *b* 20 Jan 1879; *m* 19 Aug 1899 Cdr Edward Alexander Thomas, RN, and *d* 1943, leaving issue. He *d* 27 Dec 1913

3c Pamela; *b* 8 April 1883; *d* unm 30 Aug 1965

4c Olive Dorothea; *b* 27 April 1886; *d* unm 14 May 1929

5b Gilbert Joshua; *b* 17 Dec 1843; Capt 85th KLI and 3rd Bn Hants Regt; *m* 10 Aug 1875 Edith Charlotte (*d* 26 March 1936), dau of Hon Dudley Worsley Pelham (*see* YARBOROUGH, E), and *d* 4 Feb 1928, leaving:

1c Gilbert Seymour Worsley; *b* 22 May 1894; Lt 5th Bn Hants Regt; *ka* 9 April 1918

1c Madeline Charlotte; *d* unm 12 April 1970

2c Edith Frances; *m* 3 Sept 1907 John Connop Thirwall Llewelyn and *d* 21 Aug 1962, leaving issue. He *d* 11 April 1933

3c Grace Isabel; *m* 27 Dec 1911 Capt James Gordon Fraser, OBE, RN, yr s of Arthur M Fraser, of Winnipeg, and had:

1d *Jean Grace Mary; *b* 28 July 1914; *m* 10 April 1948 David Stewart, OBE, only s of Col David Brown Douglas Stewart of Banchory-Devenick and Leggart, VD, JP, DL

2d *Olive Iona Rachel; *b* 8 May 1919; *m* 1945 Thomas Blakiston O'Reilly, yr s of Francis Joseph O'Reilly by Jessie Carmichael, dau of Capt Thomas Wright Blakiston (*see* BLAKISTON, Bt), and has:

1e *James Blakiston; *b* 15 Oct 1954

1e *Andrea Frances; *b* 30 Nov 1949

4c Mary Elinor; *m* 29 Sept 1931 Langlois Benjamin Lefroy, 2nd s of Capt William Edward Lefroy, of Cardenton Ho, Athy, Co Kildare, and Bay View, Ladner, BC. He *d* 11 Nov 1959

5c Rachel; *m* 11 Aug 1921 John Laurence Westmacott, est s of Rev Canon Westmacott, and had:

1d Gilbert John; *b* 13 July 1929; *educ* Winchester; MICE; *m* 13 July 1963 *Gillian Mary, er dau of W/Cdr J G Llewelyn, RAF, and had:

1e *Andrew John; *b* 19 Aug 1964

1e *Lucinda Mary; *b* 25 April 1966

1d *Mary Elizabeth; *b* 26 May 1922; *m* 12 June 1943 Cdr Stephen Aubone Hammick, DSC, RN (*see* HAMMICK, Bt), and has issue

2d *Helen Amabel; *b* 28 Feb 1924; *m* 11 April 1953 Cyril Geoffrey Marmaduke Alington, 4th s of Col Arthur Cyril Marmaduke Alington, of Swinhope Hall, Lincs, and has:

1e *Rosemary Jane; *b* 17 Dec 1953

2e *Jill Amabel; *b* 4 Sept 1956

3d *Edith Rosemary; *b* 30 Jan 1926; *m* 15 Dec 1949 *Richard James Douglas McCulloch Kinsman, s of James Charles Patrick Kinsman, OBE, and has:

1e *Simon John Charles; *b* 18 Jan 1954

1e *Anne Edith; *b* 23 Sept 1950

2e *Lucy Rachel; *b* 19 Oct 1957

6c Frances Maude; *m* 8 April 1923 Henry Maxwell Armstrong, 3rd s of Henry Bruce Armstrong, PC (NI), Senator NI, HM Lt Co Armagh, and *d* 6 June 1962. He *d* 1972

7c Beatrice Evelyn

8c Octavia; *d* unm 7 Feb 1976

1b Eleanor Spencer; *m* 19 Sept 1861 Robert Gosling, DL, of Hassobury, Essex, and *d* 25 Sept 1932, having had issue. He *d* 23 Aug 1894

2b Dora Spencer; *m* 21 Sept 1876 Rev John Jenkyns, of Steeple Court, Botley, Hants, Rector Durley, Hants, and *d* 19 April 1915, leaving issue. He *d* 16 April 1915

3b Frances Adela Spencer; *b* 30 May 1857; *d* unm 23 Feb 1949

3a Drummond, BCL Cambridge; *b* 13 April 1812; *d* unm 5 Nov 1832

1a Augusta; *m* 8 April 1829 Rev Henry Watson Wilder and was drowned with him 2 July 1836, leaving issue

2a Emma; *m* Rev James Edward Austen Leigh and *d* 10 Nov 1876, leaving issue. He *d* 8 Sept 1874

3a Frances; *m* 30 Oct 1834 Rev Richard Seymour, Canon Worcester, and *d* 27 April 1871, leaving issue (*see* CULME-SEYMOUR, Bt)

4a Sarah Eliza; *m* 9 June 1835 Sir Denis le Marchant, 1st Bt (*qv*), and *d* 6 March 1894 aged 86

5a Charlotte Judith; *m* Feb 1833 Arthur Currie and *d* 20 March 1840, leaving issue (*see* CURRIE, Bt)

6a Maria Louisa; *m* 10 Feb 1844 Rev Sir John Hobart Culme-Seymour, 2nd Bt (*qv*), and *d* 24 July 1887, having had issue

(4) Emma; *d* unm 1860

2 Sir JOHN SMITH later SMITH-BURGES (roy licence 10 June 1790), 1st and last Bt (GB), so *cr* 4 May 1793, of Havering Bower, Thorpe Hall, and Eastham, Essex; Dir HEICS; *m* 1771 Margaret (*m* 2nd 23 July 1816 4th Earl Poulett (*see* 1970 edn) and *dsp* 28 May 1838), only dau of Ynyr Burges, HEICS, and *dsp* 24 April 1803, when the btcy expired

3 **Sir Drummond Smith, 1st Bt** (UK), so *cr* 11 June 1804, with remainder, in default of his own male issue, to the male descendants of his n-in-law Charles Smith, of Suttons, by the latter's w Augusta, dau of Sir Drummond's er bro Joshua; *b* 1740; *m* 1st Mary (*dsp* 27 Feb 1804), est dau and heiress of Sir Ellis Cuncliffe, 1st Bt (*qv*); *m* 2nd 16 April 1805 Elizabeth (*d* 2 July 1835), widow of Sir Francis Sykes, 1st Bt, of Basildon (*qv*), and est dau of 2nd Viscount Galway (*qv*), and *dsp* 22 Jan 1816

4 Thomas, of Fonthill, Jamaica, and Bersted Lodge, Bognor, Sussex; *m* Susannah (*d* 13 Oct 1856), 2nd dau of William Mackworth-Praed, MP, of Bitton Court, Devon, and *dsp* 1824

1 Elizabeth; *m* Andrew Jelfe, of Penhill, Surrey, and had issue

2 Emma Mary; *m* 7 Aug 1800 13th Baron of Dunsany (*qv*) and *dsp* June 1828

The 4th Bt's cousin,

Sir Drummond Cospatric Hamilton-Spencer-Smith, 5th Bt, OBE (1923); *b* 4 Nov 1876; *educ* Eton and New Coll Oxford; Lt-Col RA 1900–24, Staff Offr and Mil Sec to GOC NZ Forces 1910–13, WW I: Staff Offr RHA (despatches), Cmdt 4th Army Artillery Sch 1916–17, Cmdt RA Offrs Cadet Sch Exeter 1917–18, cmded 14th RHA Bde 1918, International Commn Control Berlin 1920–24; *m* 1st 6 Dec 1915 Roma (*d* 12 Nov 1918), dau of Arthur Hope, of Timaru, NZ; *m* 2nd 27 Sept 1923 Mary Aurora (*d* 20 July 1958), widow of Col Ridley Boileau, RE, and dau of Rev Canon Henry Tudor, and *d* 18 Dec 1955, leaving by his 1st w:

Sir Thomas Cospatric Hamilton-Spencer-Smith, 6th Bt; *b* 8 Dec 1917; *educ* Eton; Capt Oxon and Bucks LI WW II; *m* 15 June 1944 *Lucy Ashton [Lucy Lady Hamilton-Spencer-Smith, 2 Heathfield Gate, Bepton Rd, Midhurst, W Sussex GU29 9JB], only dau of Thomas Ashton Ingram, and *d* 14 Oct 1959, when the family seat of Suttons was sold, leaving:

Sir JOHN HAMILTON-SPENCER-SMITH later Sir JOHN SPENCER-SMITH, **7th and present Bt**

SPENS

Arms: Quarterly, 1st and 4th, or a lion rampant gu. within a bordure of the last charged with eight roses arg. (for SPENS of Lathallan), in the dexter chief point a heart ensigned with an Imperial crown, both ppr.; 2nd and 3rd, gyronny of eight or and sa., charged of a quarter in dexter chief per bend arg. and az. (for CAMPBELL of Glendouglas); over all on an inescutcheon or a lion rampant gu. surmounted by a bend sa. charged with three mascles arg., the inescutcheon ensigned with the circlet of a Lord-Baron's coronet (for SPENS). **Crest:** A hart's head erased ppr. **Supporters:** Dexter, an elephant; sinister, a mallard, wings closed, both ppr. **Motto:** *Si Deus quis contra* ('If God be with us, who can stand against us?').
Creation: B. (UK) 20 Aug 1959.

THE 3RD BARON SPENS, of Blairsanquhar, Co Fife (Patrick Michael Rex Spens) [The Rt Hon The Lord Spens, Gould, Frittenden, Kent TN17 2DT]; *b* 22 July 1942; *s f* 1984; *educ* Rugby and Corpus Christi Coll Cambridge (BA 1964); FCA 1967, dir Morgan Grenfell 1972–82, md Henry Ansbacher 1983–87, proprietor Patrick Spens & Co, Chartered Accountants; *m* 12 March 1966 *Barbara Janet Lindsay, dau of R-Adml Ralph Lindsay Fisher, CB, DSO, OBE, DSC, of Dalnacreoch, Gartmore, by Stirling, and has:

1 +PATRICK NATHANIEL GEORGE; *b* 14 Oct 1968; *educ* Rugby

1 *Sarah Helen; *b* 2 Aug 1970; *educ* Benenden and Bristol U (MA)

Lineage: HENRY de SPENS; *d* shortly after 1300, leaving:

THOMAS de SPENS; *d* 1322, leaving:

WILLIAM de SPENS, 1st of Lathallan, Fife, which he held from his kinsmen the Earls of Fife (*see* FIFE, D, preliminary remarks), though from 1425 the SPENSes held it direct from the Crown; *m* Isabel Campbell and *d* 1432, leaving:

JOHN de SPENS, 2nd of Lathallan; *m* Isabel, dau of Sir John Wemyss of Reres/Rires (*see* WEMYSS and MARCH, E), and had:

ALEXANDER de SPENS, 3rd of Lathallan; *m* Katharine, dau of Sir Andrew Wood of Largo, and *d* after 1460, leaving:

ROBERT SPENS, 4th of Lathallan; *d* by 1474, leaving:

JOHN SPENS, 5th of Lathallan; *m* Margaret, dau of Patrick Dunbar of Kilconquhar, s and heir of 10th and last Earl of Dunbar/March (*see* DUNBAR, Bt of Mochrum), and had:

JOHN SPENS, 6th of Lathallan; *m* Helen, dau of Sir John Arnot of that Ilk, and *d* 1520, leaving:

ALEXANDER SPENS, 7th of Lathallan; *m* a dau of Durie of that Ilk and *d* by 1548, leaving:

JAMES SPENS, 8th of Lathallan; *m* Elizabeth, dau of John Seton of Lathrisk, and *d* 1595, having had (with other issue, including ARTHUR, 9th of Lathallan, and the latter's s ALEXANDER, 10th of Lathallan, *dsp*):

ALEXANDER SPENS, 11th of Lathallan; *m* Catherine, dau of Alexander of Skeddoway, and *d* 1635, leaving:

THOMAS SPENS, 12th of Lathallan; *m* Margaret, dau of Nathaniel Moncrief of Randerston, and *d* by 1662, leaving:

NATHANIEL SPENS, 13th of Lathallan; *m* 1665 Margaret, dau of Sir Thomas Gourlay of Kincraig, and had:

THOMAS SPENS, 14th of Lathallan; *m* his 1st cousin Margaret Gourlay and *d* by 1700, leaving:

THOMAS SPENS, 15th of Lathallan; *m* Janet, dau of Sir Robert Douglas of Glenbervie, Bt (*see* 1949 edn), author *Scots Baronage* (1792), and had a 4th s:

NATHANIEL SPENS, 1st of Craig Sanquhar, which he bought 1792 though the estate had been a Spens property much earlier (from 1385 to 1524); *b* 17 April 1728; Pres Roy Coll Physicians Edin 1794–96, MD, memb Roy Co Archers 1750–1815; *m* Mary, dau of Milliken of Milliken, Renfrewshire, and *d* 21 June 1815, leaving a 2nd s:

THOMAS SPENS; *b* 1763; MD, FRCP Edin, Brig Roy Co Archers; *m* Bethia, dau of Andrew Wood, MD Edin, and *d* 1842, leaving a 4th s:

WILLIAM SPENS; *b* 1807; *m* Janet Hill (*d* 20 March 1901), dau of Walter Cook, WS, of Edinburgh, and *d* 1868, having had a 5th and yst s:

NATHANIEL SPENS, of Kensington, JP Surrey; *b* 1850; *educ* Glasgow Acad; memb Roy Co Archers; *m* 1882 Emily Jessie (*d* 24 March 1926), dau of William Connal, of Solsgirth, Perthshire, and Park Circus, Glasgow, by Emily Jessie, dau of Lt-Col Robert Nutter Campbell of Ormidale, and *d* 30 May 1933, having had:

 1 (WILLIAM) PATRICK (Sir), **1st Baron**

 2 Nathaniel; *b* 1885; *d* an infant

 3 Robert Francis Connal; *b* 11 Oct 1890; *educ* Rugby; *d* following an accident 11 April 1907

 1 Emily Jessie; *m* 15 Sept 1903 Lt-Col Edmund William Furse, RHA, s of Edmund Furse, and had issue. He was *ka* 19 May 1918

 2 Janet Dorothy; *d* umn 23 Dec 1972 aged 85

 3 Mary Helen; *m* 19 Dec 1922 G/Capt Robert Hugh Hanmer, OBE, MC, DL, RAF, est s of Rev Hugh Hammer (*see* HANMER, Bt), and *d* 19 Sept 1945, leaving issue

NATHANIEL SPENS's est s,

 (WILLIAM) PATRICK SPENS, **1st Baron Spens**, of Blairsanquhar, Co Fife (UK), so *cr* 20 Aug 1959, KBE (1947, OBE 1918), PC (1953), KC (1926); *b* 9 Aug 1885; *educ* Rugby and New Coll Oxford (BA 1907, MA 1942); barrister Inner Temple 1911, Bencher 1933, Treasurer 1958, MP (C) Ashford 1933–43 and S Kensington Feb 1950–59, ktd 1943, WW I: 5th Queen's Roy Regt (despatches three times), Capt and Adj India and Mesopotamia 1914–18, DAAG Meerut Div 1918–19, Capt 1st Bn Kent HG 1940–43, Ch Justice India 1943–47, Chm Arbitral Trbnl India 1947–48, Ch Commr St John's Ambulance Bde India 1944–47, memb Imp War Graves Commn 1931–43 and 1949–65, dir: SR 1938–43, Prudential Assur 1949–61, memb London Ctee Bank Scotland, KStJ 1945; *m* 1st 15 Sept 1913 Hilda Mary (*d* 5 March 1962), er dau of Lt-Col Wentworth Grenville Bowyer, JP, DL, RE, of Weston Manor, Olney, Bucks (*see* DENHAM, B), and had:

 1 WILLIAM GEORGE MICHAEL SPENS, **2nd Baron Spens**, QC; *b* 18 Sept 1914; *educ* Rugby and New Coll Oxford (BA 1935); RA and Indian Mounted Art WW II, ret as Maj 1948, barrister Inner Temple 1945, Br Control Commn Germany 1945–55, CA 1960, ptnr Fuller, Jenks, Beecroft & Co 1955–61, dir Fedn Br Carpet Mfrs; *m* 30 June 1941 Joan Elizabeth (*d* 3 Dec 1994), dau of Reginald Goodall, and *d* 19 Nov 1984, leaving:

  (1) PATRICK MICHAEL REX SPENS, **3rd and present Baron Spens**

  (2) +William David Ralph [The Hon William Spens, Marsh Mills Cottage, Over Stowey, Somerset]; *b* 23 Nov 1943; *educ* Rugby and Corpus Christi Coll Cambridge (BA 1966); barrister Inner Temple 1972; *m* 25 Nov 1967 *Gillian Mary, only dau of Albert Edwin Jowett, OBE, MD, FRCS, and has:

   1a +James Michael William; *b* 15 Dec 1969

   1a *Tamsin Caroline; *b* 4 June 1971

  (1) *Mallowry Ann; *b* 30 Sept 1949

 2 Robert Richard Patrick, MC (1940); *b* 1 Feb 1916; *educ* Rugby and Wye Coll; Capt Norfolk Yeo WW II France and N Africa; *m* 2 Sept 1939 Elizabeth Clare (*m* 2nd 7 June 1955 Francis David Corbin, TD; *d* 1990), dau of George Catterall Leach, and *das* 15 Feb 1942, leaving:

  (1) *Charmian Helen [Mrs William Scott, Meiklewood, Stirling FK8 3AF]; *b* 5 Oct 1940; *m* 23 July 1960 *William Thomas Scott, only s of Thomas Ian Scott and Mrs J D Bissett, and has:

   1a *Thomas Robert George; *b* 1973

   1a *Elisabeth Charlotte; *b* 11 Aug 1962

   2a *Alexandra Mary; *b* 30 April 1965; *m* 1987 *Hugh Colin Graham-Watson, yr s of Charles Fitzjames Graham-Watson, of Andorra, and has:

    1b *Archibald Edward; *b* 1990

    1b *Amber Isobel; *b* 1989

 3 David Francis; *b* 15 July 1921; *d* 10 April 1923

 1 *Patricia Mary [The Hon Mrs Grier, Mulberry House, Abbots Morton, Worcs WR7 4NA]; *b* 15 July 1919; *m* 5 Nov 1946 Anthony MacGregor Grier, CMG (*d* 1989), s of Very Rev Alexander Roy MacGregor Grier, and has:

  (1) *Anthony Richard MacGregor [Anthony Grier Esq, Oak Cottage, 5 Lewins Rd, Epsom Common, Surrey KT18 7TL]; *b* 4 Oct 1948; *educ* St Edward's Oxford and Exeter Coll Oxford; *m* 1976 *Sally, er dau of K H Ong, of Singapore, and has:

   1a *Alexander Anthony MacGregor; *b* 1978

   1a *Cristelle Patricia; *b* 1983

  (2) *Francis John Roy [Francis Grier Esq, 22 Rydal Gdns, Wembley, Middx HA9 8RZ]; *b* 29 July 1955; *educ* Eton; *m* 1st 1976 Shelagh Elizabeth, dau of Alec John Frederick Banks; *m* 2nd 1990 *Anjali, dau of Joseph D'Souza, and has:

   1a *Savitri Patricia; *b* 1992

   2a *Indira Cicely; *b* 1995

  (1) *Lynda Mary [Mrs John Payne, The Gable House, Abbots Morton, Worcs WR7 4NA]; *b* 16 July 1947; *educ* St Swithin's Winchester, LMH Oxford and King's Coll Hosp; *m* 1981 *John D Payne, s of Percy Jennings Payne, and has:

   1a *Robert John; *b* 1983

   2a *David Roy Christopher; *b* 1984

 2 *(Emily) Susan, MBE (1970) [The Hon Susan Spens MBE, Flat 6, 47 The Drive, Hove, Sussex BN3 3JE]; *b* 25 April 1924; *educ* Heathfield, Birkbeck Coll London (MA); WRNS WW II, FO 1956–72, IAEA 1972–82

The **1st Baron** *m* 2nd 25 May 1963 *Kathleen Annie Fedden [The Rt Hon The Dowager Lady Spens, Gould, Frittenden, Kent], dau of Roger Dodds, of Bath and Northumberland, and *d* 15 Nov 1973

SPICER

Arms: Per chevron or and sa. in chief two cinquefoils and in base a tower, all counterchanged. **Crest:** Out of the battlements of a tower a cubit arm in armour ppr., holding in the gauntlet an annulet or. **Motto:** *In Deo solo spes mea* ('My hope is in God alone'). **Creation:** Bt. (UK) 17 July 1906.

SIR NICHOLAS ADRIAN ALBERT SPICER, 5TH BT, of Lancaster Gate, Borough of Paddington [Sir Nicholas Spicer Bt, The Old Rectory, Stanford Bishop, Worcs WR6 5TT]; *b* 28 Oct 1953; *s f* 1993; *educ* Eton and Birmingham U (MB, ChB 1977); GP 1982–; *m* 1992 *Patricia Carol, 2nd dau of Warwick Dye, of Auckland, NZ, and has:

 1 +JAMES PETER WARWICK; *b* 12 June 1993

 2 +Andrew Nicholas Kingsley; *b* 1 Aug 1995

Lineage: JAMES SPICER, JP, DL, of Woodford Green, Essex; *m* Louisa (*d* 1892), 3rd dau of Evan Edwards, of Denmark Hill, and *d* 1888, leaving:

Sir Albert Spicer, 1st Bt (UK), so *cr* 17 July 1906, PC (1912), JP Essex; *b* 16 March 1847; Treas London Missionary Soc 1885–1910, MP (Lib) Monmouth 1892–1900 and Hackney Centl 1906–18, first lay Chm Congregl Union England and Wales 1893; *m* 6 March 1879 Jessie Stewart (*d* 21 May 1934), dau of David Stewart Dykes, of Grove Hill, Surrey, and *d* 20 Dec 1934, leaving:

 1 **Sir (Albert) Dykes Spicer, 2nd Bt**; *b* 27 Nov 1880; *educ* Mill Hill and Univ Coll Oxford (BA 1902, MA 1903); 3rd Warden Fishmongers' Co 1954; *m* 27 April 1910 Alice Frances Mary (*d* 1 Dec 1963), dau of Rev William Douglas Morrison, and had:

  (1) *Patricia Morrison [Mrs Tyrrell Young, 143 Cranmer Court, London SW3 3HE]; *b* 1911; *m* 24 May 1933 *Tyrrell Francis Young, est s of Maj Frank Young, RA, and has:

   1a *Michael Francis Dykes; *b* 19 May 1934; *educ* Charterhouse and Trin Coll Cambridge

   2a *David Tyrrell [David Young Esq, Green End Farm, Henham, Herts]; *b* 6 Jan 1938; *educ* Charterhouse; *m* 11 Sept 1965 *Madeline Helen Celia, only dau of Anthony Burton Capel Philips, and has:

    1b *Melanie Rosamund; *b* 11 March 1969

    2b *Annabel Katherine; *b* 19–

    3b *Corinna Helen; *b* 19–

   1a *Rosamond Alison; *b* 31 May 1944

  (2) *Pamela Rosamond [Mrs John Johnstone, Mole Hall, Widdington, Essex CB11 3SS]; *b* 1 April 1914; *m* 2 April 1936 *John Stuart Johnstone, only child of John Forsyth Johnstone, and has:

   1a *Douglas Stuart; *b* 17 March 1953; *educ* Harrow

   1a *Caroline Rosamond [Mrs Paul Mascaux, Godfrey's Farm, Cherry Green, Essex]; *b* 2 Feb 1938; *m* 2 Feb 1963 *Paul-Louis Mascaux and has:

    1b *Pascal René Stuart [Pascal Mascaux, 10405 Hollis Lane, Olathe, Kansas City 66061, USA]; *b* 12 Jan 1965; *m* 1987 *Anne Strickler and has:

     1c *Paul; *b* 1992

     2c *Henry; *b* 1994

  (3) *Althea Dykes [Mrs John Bankes, Mynachlog, Northop, Clwyd CH7 6AF]; *b* 1918; *m* 1st 16 Sept 1939 Lt Joseph Alwyn Francis Baxendale (*d* 2 June 1940 of wounds recd in action), Surrey and Sussex Yeo, est s of Capt Guy Vernon Baxendale, of Framfield Place, Uckfield, Sussex; *m* 2nd 12 Feb 1945 *John Wynne Bankes, er s of Robert Wynne Bankes, CBE, of Soughton Hall, Northop, and has had:

   1a *Nigel John Eldon; *b* 23 March 1946; *educ* Eton

   2a *Andrew Dykes Scott; *b* 28 Oct 1955; *educ* Eton; *m* 1984 *Ariane, dau of Arthur John Goodman (*see* ANGLESEY, M), and *d* 1987

   1a *Lavinia Althea [Mrs Andrew Gordon, The Steading, Blair Atholl, Perthshire]; *b* 31 Dec 1949; *m* 1972 *Capt Andrew Duncan Gordon, AAC

 2 STEWART DYKES (Sir), **3rd Bt**

 3 Lancelot Dykes, DSO (1919), MC and bar; *b* 22 March 1893; *educ* Rugby and Trin Coll Cambridge; Capt 9th Bn Yorks LI WW I (despatches), chm Spicers paper mfrs and stationers 1951–59; *m* 1st 6 Oct 1920 (*divorce* 1935) Iris Beverley, er dau of William Pallett Cox, and had:

(1) Roger Lancelot, MC; *b* 15 Jan 1922; Lt KOYLI WW II (despatches); *ka* 31 May 1944

3 (cont.) Lancelot Spicer *m* 2nd 1 Aug 1951 Dorothy, widow of Russell Beverley and dau of Frank Edwin Gwyther, CIE

1 Marion Dykes; *d unm* Nov 1949

2 Bertha Dykes; *d unm* 25 Jan 1968

3 Grace Dykes; *m* 26 March 1913 5th Baron Hampton (*qv*) and *d* 18 May 1959, leaving issue

4 Janet Dykes; *m* 11 Feb 1915 John Baldwyn Beresford, CBE, yr s of Rev John Jervis Beresford, and had issue. He *d* as a result of enemy action Oct 1940

5 Gwendolen Elaine Dykes; *m* 27 March 1918 Ronald McKinnon Wood, MA, MICE, FRAES (*d* 22 Oct 1967), 3rd s of Thomas McKinnon Wood, PC, and had:

(1) *David McKinnon; *b* 12 Feb 1919; *educ* Stowe, Bryanston and Cambridge (MA), London and Nottingham Us (MEd); *m* 16 May 1947 *Jocelyne, BA, dau of William Withycombe, and has issue

(2) Alastair McKinnon; *b* 27 April 1920; *educ* Bryanston and Cambridge; *d unm* 1 Dec 1949

(1) *Eva Jean McKinnon; *b* 9 May 1923; *m* 24 July 1947 Peter Trubshawe, s of Vyvian Trubshawe, of London, and has issue

6 Eva Dykes, MBE (1959); *b* 29 May 1898 *educ* Somerville Coll Oxford (MA 1926); Missionary China and Nigeria; *d umn* 28 May 1974

7 Olga Dykes; *b* 5 Oct 1901

8 Ursula Dykes; *m* 3 June 1927 Sydney Barnett Mackenzie Potter, only s of Sydney Barnett Potter, of Cranbrook Park, Essex, and had issue

Sir DYKES *d* 27 Oct 1966; his bro,

Sir Stewart Dykes Spicer, 3rd Bt; *b* 2 Nov 1888; *educ* Clifton; Capt RN WW I (despatches) and WW II, BBC 1935–51; *m* 11 Jan 1917 Margaret Grace, JP Sussex (*d* 7 March 1967), yr dau of Thomas Paterson Gillespie, and had:

1 PETER JAMES (Sir), **4th Bt**

1 Elizabeth Chalmers; *b* 13 Aug 1924; *m* 15 Aug 1953 Anthony Chenevix-Trench and had issue (*see* ASHTOWN, B)

2 *Janet Dykes [Miss Janet Spicer, Greencroft, Speke Close, Ilminster, Somerset TA19 9BJ]; *b* 7 Aug 1931; *educ* Reading U (BSc 1954), Toronto U (MSA 1957), LSE (Dip Soc Admin 1963) and Bristol U (Applied Soc Studies Cert 1967); Child Care Offr Herts CC

3 *Margaret Grace Gillespie [Mrs John Heap, 25 High St, Harston, Cambridge CB2 5PX]; *b* 18 March 1933; *m* 10 Sept 1960 *John Arnfield Heap, CMG, PhD, Dip Serv, only child of David Heap, of Shalford, Surrey, and has:

(1) *Thomas John Gillespie; *b* 1966; *m* 1992 *Tammany Robin Stone

(1) *Sarah James [Mrs Leonard Byatt, 5 South Rd, W Bridgford, Notts]; *b* 1961; *m* 1991 *Leonard Joseph Byatt

(2) *Alice Margaret; *b* 1964; *m* 1st 1988 (*divorce* 19–) Andrew Richard Ginger; *m* 2nd 1993 *Neil Michael Gough

Sir STEWART *d* 11 Jan 1968; his only s,

Sir Peter James Spicer, 4th Bt; did not use title; *b* 20 May 1921; *educ* Winchester, Trin Coll Cambridge and Ch Ch Oxford (MA 1947); T/Lt RNVR WW II (despatches), Assist Sec to Dels OUP 1970; *m* 27 Aug 1949 *Margaret [Mrs Peter Spicer, 15 Washington St, Chichester PO19 3BN], er dau of Sir (James) Steuart Wilson, of Fenn's, Petersfield, Hants, and Lady (Adrian) Boult, and *d* 1993, having had:

1 Sir NICHOLAS ADRIAN ALBERT SPICER, **5th and present Bt**

1 *Phyllida Margaret [Mrs David Worcester, Gillham's Croft, High Leigh Rd, Sidlesham, W Sussex PO20 7NR]; *b* 18 Sept 1950; *m* 1979 *David John Worcester

2 Celia Mary; *b* 19 Feb 1952; *d* 1 July 1953

3 *Alison Celia [Mrs Giles Mills, Brixey's Farmhouse, Sandford, Hants BH24 3BU]; *b* 16 Nov 1955; *m* 1980 *Giles Marshall Hallam Mills

4 A dau; *b* and *d* 21 Feb 1960

5 *Susanna Juliet [Miss Susanna Spicer, Flat 3, 12 Palace Rd, London SW2 3NG]; *b* 6 March 1963

STAFFORD

Arms: Arg. a chief vairée or and gu., over all a bend sa. **Crest:** A dexter cubit arm in armour erect, the hand appearing clenched within the gauntlet all ppr. **Supporters:** Dexter, a lion rampant arg.; sinister, a swan arg., beaked and legged sa., ducally gorged per pale gu. and of the second. **Motto:** *Ung je serviray* ('I will serve but one master'). **Creation:** B. (E) 12 Sept 1640.

THE 9TH BARON STAFFORD, of Co Stafford (Francis Melfort William Fitzherbert, DL (Staffs 1994)) [The Rt Hon The Lord Stafford DL, Swynnerton Park, Stone, Staffs ST15 0QE]; *b* 13 March 1954; *s f* 1986; *educ* Ampleforth, Reading U and RAC Cirencester; dir (non-exec): Tarmac Industl Products Div 1987–93, Mid-Staffs Mental Health Fndn 1990–, Hanley Ec B S 1992–; Pro-Chllr Keele U 1993–, Govr Harper Adams Ag Coll 1990–, patron one living (but as RC cannot present); *m* 28 June 1980 *Katherine Mary, 3rd dau of John Codrington, of London SW13, and has:

1 +BENJAMIN JOHN BASIL; *b* 8 Nov 1983

2 +Toby Francis; *b* 27 March 1985

1 *Teresa Emily; *b* 15 June 1987

2 *Camilla Rose Jane; *b* 19 Dec 1989

Stafford, other creation: For the Marquessate of Stafford, *see* SUTHERLAND, D.

Lineage (of Stafford): HUGH de CALVACAMP; *b* most likely *c* 890; of French rather than Norman extraction; had, with another (er?) s (Hugh, *b* probably by 915, monk at Abbey of St Denis, France, Archbp Rouen, Normandy, 942, had issue (probably illegitimate), made over that part of the archiepiscopal lands consisting of the feudal territory of Toeni (modern Tosny, on the Seine southeast of Rouen) to his bro Ralph and *d* 10 Nov 989 or 990):

RALPH/RODULF de TOENI; had:

RALPH/RODULF de TOENI; *b* probably by 970; feudal Ld also of Conches; custodian with his s of Castle of Tillières from 1013 or 1014; took part in Norman expdn to S Italy *c* 1015; had, with possibly two other sons (Ralph?; Robert?):

ROGER de TOENI, also called ROGER de CONCHES; *b* probably *c* 990; fought Muslims in Spain; *m*(?) 1st(?) Stephanie (*m* 2nd GARSIAS, KING OF SPAIN), sis of Raymond Berenger, Count of Barcelona; *m* (2nd?) Godeheut (*m* 2nd Richard, 3rd Count of Evreux), dau of —, and *d* 1038 or 1039 in battle against a neighbouring noble whose territory he had overrun in a revolt against the succession of WILLIAM I (THE CONQUEROR) to his f's Norman possessions on the grounds that WILLIAM was illegitimate, leaving, with possibly two other sons:

1 Ralph, usually called Ralph de Conches; *b* probably *c* 1025–30; participated in Norman invasion of England 1066, being accordingly granted lands in Berks, Essex, Glos, Herefs, Herts, Norfolk and Worcs; *m* Elizabeth/Isabel, dau of Simon de Montfort, Seigneur of Montfort l'Amaury, and *d* 24 March, probably 1101/2, leaving, with an er s (Roger, *dvp*):

(1) Ralph, called either de Toeni or de Conches; *m* 1103 Alice, yr dau of Waltheof, Earl of Northumberland (*see* NORTHUMBERLAND, D, preliminary remarks), Northampton and Huntingdon, and *d c* 1126, leaving:

1a Roger, called de Toeni or de Conches; *b* probably *c* 1104; *m* Ida, dau of Baldwin III, Count of Hainault, and *d* between autumn 1157 and the beginning of 1162, leaving:

1b Ralph, called de Toeni or de Conches; *m* Margaret, dau of Robert, 2nd Earl of Leicester of the post-Conquest creation made in favour of Robert's f Robert de Beaumont, and *d* 1162, leaving:

1c Roger, called de Toeni or de Conches; accompanied RICHARD I on Third Crusade; his remaining Norman fiefs captured from him by the King of France by 1204; *m* Constance, dau of Richard de Beaumont, Vicomte of Beaumont (*see* BEAUMONT, Bt), and *d c* Jan 1208/9, leaving:

1d Ralph, called de Toeni; *b* probably 1189 or 1190; *m c* 1233 Pernel, dau of Walter de Lacy, and *d c* autumn 1239, leaving, with an est s (presumably *dvp*) and a yst s (Ralph):

1e Roger; *b* autumn 1235; *m* by 1255 Isabel — and *d* by 12 May 1264, leaving:

1f Ralph; *b* 1255; *m* by 1276 Mary — and *d* 29 July 1295, leaving:

    1g ROBERT DE TONI/TONY, 1st and last LORD (Baron) TONY (E), so *cr* by writ of summons 6 Feb 1298/9 to Parl (according to later doctrine); *b* 4 April 1276; ktd by 22 July 1298, when took part in English victory over Scots at Falkirk, also present Siege Carlaverock 1300; *m c* 26 April 1293 Maud, dau of Malise, 6th Earl of Strathearn, and *dsp* by 28 Nov 1309, when his Barony expired

    1g Alice; *b c* 1283; *m* 1st Thomas de Leyburn; *m* 2nd Jan or Feb 1309/10, as his 2nd w, 10th Earl of Warwick of the 1808 *cr* (*see* WARWICK, BROOKE and, E); *m* 3rd by 25 Feb 1316/17, as his 1st w, 1st Lord (Baron) Zouche (*qv*) (of Richard's Castle, Mortimer or Ashby)

  2b Roger

  3b Baldwin; took up residence in Hainault; left issue

  4b Geoffrey; clerk, *i.e.*, in holy orders

2a? Ralph?

2a/3a Hugh

4a? Simon?

1a Godeheut; *m* Robert de Neubourg, yr s of Henry de Beaumont, 1st Earl of Warwick (*qv*) of the 1088 *cr*

(1) Godeheut; *m* Baldwin, s of Eustace, Count of Boulogne

2 Robert, called de Stafford; held by 1086 nearly 70 manors in Staffs, more than 25 in Warwicks, more than 20 in Lincs, 10 in Oxon one in Worcs and one in Northants; built what later became known as Belvoir Castle (*see* RUTLAND, D); allegedly *m* Avice de Clare, and *d* probably 1088, leaving:

(1) Nicholas; *m* Maud — and *d* in or after 1138, leaving:an est s:

  1a Robert; Sheriff Staffs 1155–60; *m* Avice — and *d* between 1177/8 and 1184/5, leaving:

    1b Robert; *m* Basilia — and *d* 1193 or 1194

    1b Millicent; *m* by 1193 Hervey BAGOT later DE STAFFORD (on acquiring the de Stafford inheritance through his w; *d* by 25 Aug 1214; *see* also BAGOT, B) and *d* by Jan 1224/5, leaving:

      1c Hervey; *m* by 1214 Pernell, dau of William de Ferrieres, 3rd Earl of Derby (*see* DERBY, E, preliminary remarks), and *d* by 12 May 1237, leaving:

        1d Hervey; *m* Mabel, dau of Richard de Mucegros, and *dsp* by 7 Oct 1241

        2d Robert; *m* 1st Alice, dau of Thomas Corbet, of Caus, Salop; *m* 2nd Joan — and *d* by 4 June 1261, leaving by his 1st w:

          1e Nicholas; *m* —, probably dau of Geoffrey de Langley, and *d c* 1 Aug 1287, leaving:

            1f EDMUND, 1st LORD

          2e Edmund

3 Gazon

1 Alice; *m* William fitz Osbern, 1st Earl of Hereford of the creation made shortly after the Conquest (*see* also HEREFORD, V, preliminary remarks)

NICHOLAS De STAFFORD's s,

EDMUND De STAFFORD, 1st LORD (Baron) STAFFORD (E), so *cr* by writ of summons 6 Feb 1298/8 to Parl (according to later doctrine); *b* 15 July 1273; *m* by 1298 Margaret, sis and ultimate coheir of Ralph Basset, (1st?) Lord (Baron) Basset (of Drayton), and *d* by 12 Aug 1308, leaving:

RALPH De STAFFORD, 2nd LORD (Baron) STAFFORD and 1st EARL OF STAFFORD (E), so *cr* 5 March 1350/1, KG (1348), KB (Jan 1326/7), JP (Staffs March 1331/2); *b* 24 Sept 1301; campaigned against Scots 1336, 1337 and 1343 and French at Battles of Sluys 1340 and Crécy 1346 and Siege of Calais 1346–47, also 1355–60; Steward Household Feb 1340/1, Seneschal Aquitaine or Gascony Feb 1344/5–March 1345/6 and Aquitaine Oct 1346–March 1346/7; *m* 1st probably *c* 1326–27 Katharine, dau of Sir John Hastang, of Chebsey, Staffs; *m* 2nd by 6 July 1336 Margaret, Baroness Audley in her own right according to later doctrine, dau of Hugh Audley, 1st and last Earl of Gloucester of the 1337 *cr* and 1st Lord (Baron) Audley of the 1317 *cr* (*see* 1970 edn), and *d* 31 Aug 1372, having by her had, with an er s (Ralph, *m* 1 Nov 1344 Maud (*m* 2nd 1352 WILLIAM V, DUKE OF BAVARIA, and *dsp* 10 April 1362), er dau of Henry, 4th Duke of Lancaster (ggs of HENRY III), and *dvp* by 1347) and four daus (including Beatrice, *m* 1st 1350 2nd Earl of Desmond of the 1329 *cr* (*see* DENBIGH and DESMOND, E, preliminary remarks), *m* 2nd *c* 1 Jan 1358/9 4th Lord (Baron) De Ros (*qv*) of Hamlake, *m* 3rd by 20 Aug 1385 Sir Richard de Burley (*dsp* 23 March 1387) and *d* April 1415):

HUGH De STAFFORD, 2nd EARL OF STAFFORD, KG (1375/6); *b* by 1342; served Hundred Years War in Aquitaine 1359 on and Spain 1367; *m* by 1 March 1350/1 Philippa, dau of 11th Earl of Warwick (*qv*) of the 1088 *cr*, and *d* 13 Oct 1386, having had:

1 Ralph; Kt of RICHARD II's Household; murdered in Yorks May 1385 by Sir John de Holand, RICHARD II's half-bro and later 1st and last Duke of Exeter of the 1397 *cr*, to avenge the killing by one of Ralph's retainers of his favourite Esq

2 THOMAS De STAFFORD, 3rd EARL OF STAFFORD; *b* by 1368; ktd 1390; *m* Anne (*m* 2nd her bro-in-law 5th EARL (*see* below); *m* 3rd Sir William Bourchier, Count of Eu (*see* BERNERS, B), and *d* 16 Oct 1438), dau and ultimately sole heir of Thomas of Woodstock, 1st and last Earl of Buckingham of the 1377 *cr* and 1st Duke of Gloucester of the 1385 *cr* (6th s of EDWARD III), and *dsp* 4 July 1392

3 WILLIAM De STAFFORD, 4th EARL OF STAFFORD; *b* 21 Sept 1375; *d* 6 April 1395 prior to his investiture as Earl

4 EDMUND De STAFFORD, 5th EARL OF STAFFORD, KG (1402), KB (1399); *b* 2 March 1377/8; Constable England 1403; *m* his er bro's widow Anne and was *ka* Battle of Shrewsbury 21 July 1403, leaving, with another dau (*d* young):

(1) HUMPHREY STAFFORD, 1st DUKE OF BUCKINGHAM (E), so *cr* 14 Sept 1444, as also earlier 1431 COUNT OF PERCHE, Normandy (part of HENRY VI's policy of conferring native fiefs on his leading supporters in English-occupied France), having apparently already been recognised as EARL OF BUCKINGHAM in right of his mother, KG (1429), PC (1424); *b* 15 Aug 1402; ktd 1421, Lt-Gen Normandy 1430–32, Seneschal Halton 1439, Capt Calais

and Lt the Marches 1442–51, Amb France 1446, Warden Cinque Ports and Constable Dover and Queenborough Castles 1450; *m* by 18 Oct 1424 Anne, dau of 1st Earl of Westmorland (*see* ABERGAVENNY, M), and was *ka* fighting on the Lancastrian side Battle of Northampton 10 July 1460, having had, with three other sons:

1a Humphrey, *Earl of Stafford*; *m* Margaret, dau of 1st Duke of Somerset of the 1448 *cr* (*see* BEAUFORT, D), and *dvp* on or after 17 Dec 1457 and possibly after 19 Jan 1457/8, leaving:

1b HENRY STAFFORD, 2nd DUKE OF BUCKINGHAM, KG (1474), KB (1465); *b* 4 Sept 1455; Constable Nottingham Castle 1460, Warden Cinque Ports 1483, recognised as hereditary Ld High Constable July 1483; *m* Katharine Woodville (*m* 2nd Jasper Tudor, 1st and last Duke of Bedford of the 1485 *cr* (*dspl* 1495) and 3rd Sir Richard Wingfield, KG; *see* POWERSCOURT, V), dau of 1st Earl Rivers and sis of EDWARD IV's w ELIZABETH, and was beheaded without trial and attainted 2 Nov 1483 for conspiring on behalf of the future HENRY VII, leaving:

1c EDWARD STAFFORD, 3rd DUKE OF BUCKINGHAM, as which restored (also to his other titles) Nov 1485, KG (c 1499), KB (1485), PC (1509); *b* 3 Feb 1477/8; Ld High Constable and Ld High Steward for HENRY VIII's Coronation 1509, cmded English army's right wing at victory of Thérouanne over French 1513; *m c* 14 Dec 1490 Eleanor, dau of 3rd Earl of Northumberland of the March 1415/6 *cr* (*see* NORTHUMBERLAND, D), and was beheaded for high treason 17 May 1521, having made an enemy of Wolsey and endangered his position by his vanity, especially his loquacity in reminding hearers of his descent from EDWARD III, following which his titles were forfeited by attainder (Parly ratification 31 July 1523), leaving:

1d HENRY STAFFORD, 1st BARON STAFFORD (E), so *cr* Nov-Dec 1547, also restored in blood (but not his f's titles) and by Ho Lds resolution 12 Feb 1557/8 had back the precedency of the original Barony of Stafford; *b* 18 Sept 1501; granted by HENRY VIII 1522 several of his f's forfeited lands in Staffs and other counties, also the Manor and Castle of Stafford 1531; Recorder Stafford 1532, Bencher Middle Temple by 1551, Chamberlain Exchequer Feb 1553/4, Ld Lt Staffs 1559, Ranger Cannock Forest 1560; *m c* Feb 1518/9 Ursula, dau of Sir Richard Pole, KG (*see* ABERGAVENNY, M), and *d* 30 April 1563, having had, with at least seven other children:

1e Henry; *dvp* an infant

2e HENRY STAFFORD, 2nd BARON STAFFORD; *b* by 1534; ktd 1553, MP Salop 1555; *m* by 25 Sept 1557 Elizabeth, sis of William Davy, of Holbeach, Lincs, and *dsp* 1 Jan 1565/6

3e Thomas; *b* by 1534; beheaded 28 May 1557 for high treason

4e EDWARD STAFFORD, 3rd BARON STAFFORD; *b* 17 Jan 1535/6; MP Stafford 1558 and 1559, V-Adml Glos 1587, Cncllr March of Wales 1601; *m* by 23 Nov 1566 Mary, dau of 3rd Earl of Derby (*qv*), and *d* 18 Oct 1603, having had:

1f Edward; *dvp* an infant 27 Jan 1568/9

2f EDWARD STAFFORD, 4th BARON STAFFORD; *bapt* 20 Sept 1572; *m* perhaps by 22 Nov 1595 Isabel, dau of Thomas Forster, of Tong, Salop, and *d* 25 Sept 1625, having had:

1g Edward; *bapt* 9 July 1601; *m* just prior to 15 May 1617 Anne, est dau of James Wilford, of Newman Hall, Quendon, Essex, and *dvp* 6 April 1621, leaving:

1h HENRY STAFFORD, 5th BARON STAFFORD; *b* 24 Sept 1621; *d* unm 4 Aug 1637

1h MARY Stafford, **Baroness Stafford**, Co Stafford (E), so *cr*, with her husb, 12 Sept 1640, as also 5 Oct 1688 COUNTESS OF STAFFORD (E) for life; *b c* 1620; *m* 12 Oct 1637 Sir William HOWARD, KB, **1st Baron Stafford**, so *cr* jointly with his w, and 1st and last Viscount Stafford (attainted 7 Dec 1680), 3rd s of 21st/14th Earl of Arundel, (3rd Earl of) Surrey and (1st Earl of) Norfolk (*see* NORFOLK, D), and *d* 13 Jan 1693/4, having had, with four other daus (three being nuns):

1i HENRY HOWARD later STAFFORD-HOWARD (1688), 1st EARL OF STAFFORD (E), so *cr* 5 Oct 1688, with remainder, in default of heirs male of his body, to his brothers and their male issue; *b c* 1648; Col of Foot 1688, Jacobite following Glorious Revolution; *m* 3 or 6 April 1694 Claude-Charlotte (*d* 14 May 1739), dau of Philibert, Count de Gramont (*see* ABERCORN, D), and *dsp* 27 April 1719

2i John HOWARD later STAFFORD-HOWARD, of Stafford Castle; JAMES II's Amb to LOUIS XIV when former exiled at St Germain March 1695/6, Controller and Commr JAMES II's Household in exile 1696, V-Chamberlain to QUEEN MARY OF MODENA (JAMES II's widow) 1701; *m* 1st Dec 1682 Mary, dau of Sir John Southcottt, of Merstham, Surrey, and by her had, with three other daus (Xaveria Beatrice, *bapt* 12 Feb 1696, nun; Louise Francoise, *bapt* 7 Dec 1698, nun; Marie Honorée, *bapt* 6 Feb 1701):

1j WILLIAM STAFFORD-HOWARD, 2nd EARL OF STAFFORD; *b c* 1690; *m c* 1718 his 1st cousin Anne (*d* 21 May 1725), dau of George Holman (*see* below), and *d* Jan 1733/4, leaving:

1k WILLIAM MATTHIAS STAFFORD-HOWARD, 3rd EARL OF STAFFORD; *b* 24 Feb probably 1718/9; FRS 1743; *m* 8 July 1743 Henrietta (*m* 2nd 11 Oct 1759 1st Earl of Farnham (*see* FARNHAM, B) and *d* 30 Aug 1761), dau and heiress of Richard Cantillon, Paris banker, and *dspsl* 28 Feb 1750/1

1k Mary Apollonia Scholastica; *b* 17 Feb 1721; *m* 25 May 1744, as his 2nd w, Guy Auguste, Count de Rohan Chabot, and *dsp* 16 May 1769

2k Anastasia; *b* 21 Oct 1722; nun Order Immaculate Conception, Paris; assumed title of Baroness Stafford; *d* 27 April 1807

3k Anne; *b* 15 May 1725; nun; *d* 16 May 1792

2j JOHN PAUL STAFFORD-HOWARD, 4th and last EARL OF STAFFORD; *b* 26 June 1700; *m* 1738 Elizabeth Mary Michael (*d* 16 Jan 1783), dau of Abraham Ewens, of Somerset, and *dsp* 1 April 1762, when the Earldom expired

1j MARY Stafford-Howard; *m* 1 Oct 1699 Francis PLOWDEN (*bur* 30 April 1712) (*see* PLOWDEN, B) and *d* 26 April 1765, leaving:

   1k Francis; *bapt* 9 Sept 1707; RC priest; *d* 5 Sept 1788

   1k Louise Anne; *bapt* 5 Dec 1705; *d* unm 1784

   2k Marie Françoise; *bapt* 17 May 1704; *m* 1733 Sir George Jerningham, 5th Bt (*d* 21 Jan 1774), and was *bur* 30 Sept 1785, leaving an est s:

      1l Sir WILLIAM JERNINGHAM, 6th Bt; *b* 7 March 1736; *m* 16 June 1767 Hon Frances Dillon (*d* 1 March 1825), est dau of 11th Viscount Dillon (*qv*) of Costello-Gallen, and *d* 14 Aug 1809, leaving:

         1m GEORGE WILLIAM, **2nd Baron**

         2m William Charles; *b* 13 Oct 1772; Offr in Austrian service; *m* 1st 5 Oct 1803 Anne (*d* 26 Aug 1814), est dau of Thomas Wright, of Fitzwalters, Essex, and had:

            1n Edmund William; *b* 5 Sept 1805; *m* 25 June 1829 Matilda (*d* 14 July 1865), dau of Christopher Waterton, of Woodlands, Doncaster, and *d* 2 Nov 1860, having had:

               1o Charlotte; *m* 11 Aug 1853 James Arthur Dease, of Turbotston, Co Westmeath, and *d* 30 March 1905, leaving issue. He *d* 5 Sept 1874

               2o Ida; *m* 3 Aug 1859 Myles William Patrick O'Reilly, of Knock Abbey, Co Louth, MP Co Longford, and *d* 20 April 1878, leaving issue. He *d* 6 Feb 1880

               3o Frances; *d* unm 5 May 1901

               4o Clementina; *m* 6 June 1861 William Mostyn, 7th s of Sir Edward Mostyn, 7th Bt (*qv*), and *d* 7 Dec 1925

               5o Madeline; *m* 8 Dec 1868 Baron Alfred Hainguerlot and had issue

               6o Clara; nun; *d* 3 Jan 1871

            2n Arthur William; *b* 26 Feb 1807; Adml; *m* 19 April 1836 Sophia Mary Margaret (*d* 18 Oct 1899), dau of Richard O'Ferrall-Caddell (*see* SOUTHWELL, V), and *d* 24 Nov 1889, having had:

               1o Paulina, a nun; *d* 4 Feb 1868

               2o Agnes Mary; *m* 3 Oct 1865 Stanley George Edward CARY later CARY-CADDELL (roy licence 5 May 1900; *d* 10 July 1902), of Follaton, Devon, and *d* 16 July 1921, leaving issue

               3o Cecilia Mary; *m* 30 April 1862 Capt Iltyd Thomas Mansel Nicholl, RN, 2nd s of John Nicholl, PC, MP, DCL (*d* 17 Dec 1885), of Merthyr Mawr, Glam, and *d* 15 Feb 1879, leaving issue

            3n William Charles; *b* 28 Nov, *d* 25 Dec 1809

            4n Frederick William; *b* 1 Aug 1813; served 29th Regt; *m* 14 Sept 1837 Georgiana Howe (*d* 5 Feb 1894), only child of Rev George Mangles, and *d* 11 Nov 1870, having had:

               1o Adolphus Frederick James; *b* 24 June 1842; *m* 7 April 1866 Matilda Georgiana (*d* 15 Jan 1900), 2nd dau of William Felix Riley, of Forest Hill, Windsor, and *d* 15 Sept 1904, leaving:

                  1p Sir (WILLIAM) HENRY STAFFORD JERNINGHAM, 11th Bt, JP Norfolk; *b* 28 Nov 1867; Lt RE WW I; *m* 1st 16 Jan 1896 Annette Mary Audley (*d* 29 Nov 1896), widow of Alfred Fellowes and dau of William Hinds, of King's Walden Bury, Herts; *m* 2nd 15 Jan 1902 Coralie (*d* 19 March 1949), dau of Benjamin Francis Hallowell-Carew, of Beddington Park, Surrey, and *dspm* 20 Dec 1935, when the btcy expired, leaving by his 1st w:

                     1q Cecilia Annette Mary; *m* 22 March 1920 John Challenger Murray, est s of Sir John Murray, KCB, and *d* 23 Jan 1955, leaving issue. He *d* 13 Jan 1939

                  1p Clementina Mary; *b* 13 April 1869; *d* unm 29 May 1944

                  2p Gertrude Maud; *b* 12 Aug 1871; *d* unm 7 July 1940

                  3p Emily Georgina; *b* 11 Feb 1873; *d* unm 8 May 1956

               1o Frances Agnes Mary Ann; *b* 27 Dec 1838; *m* 30 June 1866 Edward Moorat, yst s of J S Moorat, of Bush Hill Park, Edmonton, and had issue

               2o Constantia Lucretia; *b* 4 April 1840; *m* 21 July 1863 James Henry Corballis, of Ratoath Manor, Co Meath, and *d* 11 Oct 1914, having had issue. He *d* 10 Dec 1903

3o Isabella; *b* 1847; *m* 1879 Maj Charles Frederick Marriot, 6th Dragoon Gds, and *d* 4 Aug 1929, having had issue. He *d* 1905

1n Lucretia; *b* 10 Aug 1804; *m* 19 July 1836 13th Viscount Gormanston (*qv*) and *d* 5 Feb 1891, leaving issue

2n Louisa Mary; *b* 14 July 1808; Mother Superior Franciscan Convent, The Lodge, Taunton; *d* 25 April 1893

3n Gertrude Frances; *b* 31 July 1811; *m* 18 Nov 1834 Sir Edward Charles Blount, KCB, and *d* 9 Nov 1897, having had issue (*see* BLOUNT, Bt)

2m (cont.) William Jerningham *m* 2nd Aug 1816 Anne, dau of Edward Moore, and *d* 1 Oct 1820

3m Edward, of Painswick, Glos; *b* 14 July 1774; barrister; *m* 15 Oct 1804 Emily (*d* 24 June 1822), est surv dau of Nathaniel Middleton, of Townhill, Hants, and *d* 29 May 1822, having had, with other issue (*d* unm):

   1n Charles William Edward, of Painswick; *b* 27 Nov 1805; barrister; *m* 6 Sept 1841 Emma Mary Wynn (*d* 13 June 1888), dau of Evan Wynn Roberts, of Grove Ho, Surrey, and *d* 26 Feb 1854, having had:

      1o Hubert Edward Henry (Sir), KCMG, JP, DL Northumberland; *b* 18 Oct 1842; Dip Serv: joined 1866, Colonial Sec Br Honduras 1887–89 and Mauritius 1892–93 (Govr 1893–97), Govr Trinidad and Tobago 1897–1900, MP Berwick 1881–85, FGS, FSA; *m* 3 Dec 1874 Annie (*d* 9 Oct 1902), widow of Charles Mather, of Longridge, Northumberland, and dau of Edward Liddell, of Benton Park, Northumberland, and *dsp* 3 April 1914

      2o Fitzhugh D'Este; *b* 1843; Lt RN; *d* unm 19 Jan 1865

      3o Charles Edward Wynn, JP Co London; *b* 26 March 1854; *d* 7 Feb 1921

      1o Edith Mary; *b* 14 Dec 1845; *m* 13 April 1874 Charles Edward Harris Edmonstoune Cranstoun, of Corehouse, Lanarks, and *d* 19 Dec 1929, leaving issue. He *d* 19 June 1888

      2o Emily Beatrice; *b* 15 Nov 1846; *d* unm 13 April 1884

   2n James Edward; *b* 31 Jan 1817; Army Offr; *m* 19 May 1846 Sophia, 2nd dau of Rev Sir William Murray, 9th Bt, of Dunerne (*qv*), and *dsp* 22 Aug 1848

   1n Mary Clementina; *b* 6 Sept 1810; *m* 9 March 1838 Victor Amédée, Marquis de Ripert-Monclar, est s of Marquis de Ripert-Barret, and *d* 21 Aug 1864, leaving issue

   1m Charlotte Georgiana; Woman Bedchamber to QUEEN ADELAIDE, granted Oct 1831 rank of baron's dau; *m* 16 June 1795 Sir Richard Bedingfeld, 5th Bt (*see* (PASTON-)BEDINGFELD, Bt), and *d* 29 July 1854, leaving issue

2i (cont.) John STAFFORD-HOWARD *m* 2nd 15 Feb 1707/8 Theresa (*m* 2nd — O'Donnell), dau of Robert Strickland, of Sizergh, Westmorland, Treas to MARY OF MODENA, and *d* 11 Nov 1714, having by her had:

   3j Edward; *bapt* 7 Nov 1708; *d* unm 18 Oct 1746

   4j Charles; *bapt* 12 April 1713

   2j Marie Henriette; *b* 8 Dec 1711; *dsp* 5 Nov 1755

3i Francis; Groom Bedchamber to JAMES II; *m* Eleanor (*d* 1707), dau of Henry Stanford, of New Inn, Staffs, and *d* 1708, having had:

   1j Henry; *m* Mary, dau of Thomas Berkeley, of Spetchley (*see* BERKELEY, B), and *dsp* 1743

1i Isabella; *m* 1669 5th Marquess of Winchester (*qv*) and *dsp* 5 Sept 1691

2i Anastasia; *m* George Holman, of Warkworth, Northants, and had issue

1f Dorothy; royalist Civil War, defended Stafford Castle against Parly forces 1643; *m* — Jervis and *d* in or after 1646

5e Walter; *dsp* in or after 1571

6e Richard; *m* Mary, dau of John Corbet, of Lee, Salop, and had:

   1f ROGER STAFFORD, 6th and last BARON STAFFORD, to which, however, he was in irregular fashion denied any right (the Crown arguing he was too poor) on his preferring a claim 4 Aug 1637, being required to surrender the dignity, which he did 7 Dec 1639 (despite such surrenders being held illegal in the case of English peerages the very next year) in return for £800 (over £36,000 in late-1990s terms); *b c* 1572–75; *d* unm *c* 1640, when the Barony expired in any case

   1f Jane; *b c* 1581; allegedly *m* a joiner, of Newport, Salop, and *d* in or after 1637, leaving a s, who allegedly earned his living as a cobbler

1e Dorothy; *m* Sir William Stafford, of Grafton, and had issue

2c HENRY STAFFORD, 1st and last EARL OF WILTSHIRE (E), so *cr* 28 Jan 1509/10, KG (1505), PC (by 1520); *b c* 1479; *m* between 22 Nov 1503 and 18 Oct 1505 Cicely, Baroness Harington and Baroness Bonville in her own right according to later doctrine, dau of 1st Lord (Baron) Bonville and 6th Lord (Baron) Harington (*see* ABERGAVENNY, M) and widow of Thomas Grey, 1st Marquess of Dorset, and *dsp* March 1522/3, when the Earldom expired

2a Henry (Sir); *m* by 1464 Margaret (*m* 4th by Oct 1473 1st Earl of Derby; *qv*), widow of Edmund Tudor, 1st Earl of Richmond of the 1452 *cr* (by whom she was mother of HENRY VII), formerly w of John de la Pole, 2nd Duke of Suffolk of the 1448 *cr*, and dau of John Beaufort, 1st and last Duke of Somerset of the 1443 *cr* (*see* BEAUFORT, D), and *d* 4 Oct 1471

3a JOHN STAFFORD, 1st EARL OF WILTSHIRE (E), so *cr* 5 Jan 1469/70, KG (1472), KB (1461); *b* 24 Nov 1420; participated in Yorkist victory over Lancasrians of Hexham 15 May 1464, Steward Duchy Cornwall for life 1469, Ch Butler of England 1471; *m c* 1458 Constance, only dau and heiress of Henry Green, of Drayton, Northants, and *d* 8 May 1473, leaving:

1b EDWARD STAFFORD, 2nd and last EARL OF WILTSHIRE, KB (1475); *b* 7 April 1470; *m c* 3 July 1494 Margaret, dau of Edward Grey, Viscount Lisle, and *dsp* 24 March 1498/9, when the Earldom expired

1a Anne; *m* 1st *c* April 1460 Sir Aubrey de Vere, s of 12th Earl of Oxford (*see* SAINT ALBANS, D); *m* 2nd Sir Thomas Cobham (*dspml* 1471), s of 2nd Lord (Baron) Cobham (of Sterborough) (*see* COBHAM, V, preliminary remarks), and *d c* 14 April 1472, leaving issue

2a Joan; *m* 1st by 14 March 1461 (*annulled* by 1477), as his 1st w, 2nd Viscount Beaumont (*see* BEAUMONT, Bt); *m* 2nd Sir William Knyvett, of Buckenham, Norfolk

3a Katharine; *m* 3rd Earl of Shrewsbury and Waterford (*qv*)

(1) Anne; *m* 1st Edmund de Mortimer, 5th Earl of March (*dsp* of plague 18 Jan 1424/5); *m* 2nd by 6 March 1426/7, as his 1st w, John Holand, 1st Duke of Exeter of the Jan 1443/4 *cr*, and *d* 20 or 24 Sept 1432, leaving issue

5 Hugh (Sir), KG; *m* by Sept 1410, as her 1st husb, Elizabeth Bourchier, only dau and heiress of 3rd Lord (Baron) Bourchier (*see* BERNERS, B), and *dsp* 25 Oct 1420

1 Margaret; *m* 1st Earl of Westmorland (*see* ABERGAVENNY, M)

2 Katherine; *m* by 23 Nov 1383 Michael de la Pole, 2nd Earl of Suffolk (*d* 18 Sept 1415) of the 1385 *cr*, and *d* 8 April 1419, leaving issue

3 Joan; *m* a little while after 20 Oct 1392 1st and last Duke of Surrey (*see* WAKE, Bt), and *dsp* 30 Sept or 1 Oct 1442

The 1st BARON (and BARONESS)'s ggggs,

Sir GEORGE WILLIAM JERNINGHAM later STAFFORD-JERNINGHAM (roy licence 5 Oct 1826), 7th Bt, as which *s f* 1809, and **2nd Baron Stafford**, as which recognised on reversal 17 June 1824 of attainder of 1680, although an erroneous belief grew up that the reversal was retroactive, so that such persons who between 1680 and 1824 would have held the Barony but for the attainder were to be counted in the enumeration as actually having done so, hence the **2nd Baron** was **8th** etc.; *b* 27 April 1771; FSA 1829; *m* 1st 26 Dec 1799 Frances Henrietta (*d* 14 Nov 1832), yst dau and coheir of Edward Sulyarde, of Haughley Park, Suffolk; *m* 2nd 26 May 1836 Elizabeth (*dsp* 29 Oct 1862), dau of Richard Caton, of Md., USA, and *d* 4 Oct 1851, having by his 1st w had, with four other daus (*d* unm):

1 Sir HENRY VALENTINE STAFFORD-JERNINGHAM, 8th Bt, and **3rd Baron Stafford**; *b* 2 Jan 1802; MP (Whig) Pontefract 1830–35; *m* 1st 12 Feb 1829 Julia Barbara (*dsp* 19 Nov 1856), dau of Edward Charles Howard (*see* NORFOLK, D); *m* 2nd 13 Sept 1859 Emma Eliza (*m* 2nd 24 April 1887 her niece's widower Basil Thomas Fitzherbert; *see* below) and *d* 11 Nov 1912), dau of Frederic Sewallis Gerard (*see* GERARD, B), and *dsp* 30 Nov 1884

2 Edward; *b* 4 Aug 1804; Lt 6th Dragoon Gds; *m* 16 June 1828 Marianne (*d* 10 Aug 1859), dau of John Smythe, and *d* 22 July 1849, having had, with another s and dau (*d* young):

(1) Sir AUGUSTUS FREDERICK FITZHERBERT STAFFORD-JERNINGHAM, 9th Bt, and **4th Baron Stafford**; *b* 28 June 1830; *d* unm 12 Feb 1892, having been ajudged insane since 19 Feb 1862

(2) Sir FITZHERBERT EDWARD STAFFORD-JERNINGHAM, 10th Bt, and **5th Baron Stafford**; *b* 17 July 1833; *d* unm 12 June 1913, when the btcy passed to his cousin (*see* above)

(1) Emily Charlotte; *b* 31 March 1835; *m* 13 Oct 1858 Basil Thomas Fitzherbert, DL, of Norbury Manor, Derbys, and Swynnerton Park, Staffs (*see* above, also below **Lineage (of Fitzherbert)**), and *d* 9 Nov 1881, having had, with another s (*d* an infant):

1a FRANCIS EDWARD FITZHERBERT later FITZHERBERT-STAFFORD (roy licence, 22 Nov 1913), **6th Baron Stafford**, DSO (1900), JP, DL Staffs; *b* 28 Aug 1859; *educ* Beaumont; joined Lancs Militia 1877, Staffs Yeo 1882–98, Boer War 1900–02 (despatches),Capt and Hon Maj QO Staffs Imp Yeo, Maj and Hon Lt-Col 3rd Bn Roy Lancaster Regt, Lt-Col Staffs Vol Regt WW I, High Steward Stafford; *m* 20 April 1903 Dorothy Hilda (*d* 15 Dec 1958), dau of Albert Octavius Worthington, JP, DL, of Maple Hayes, Staffs, and *dsp* 18 Sept 1932

2a Basil John; *b* 28 Oct 1861; granted 21 Nov 1913 with surv siblings rank of baron's dau/yr s; served Boer War 1900–02, Lt RFC and RAF WW I 1917–19; *d* unm 10 May 1923

3a EDWARD STAFFORD FITZHERBERT, **7th Baron Stafford**, KCB (1920, CB 1918), JP, DL; *b* 17 April 1864; *educ* St Mary's Coll Oscott; RN: served HMS *Britannia* 1877, *Temeraire* 1879, *Minotaur* Egyptian Campaign 1882, Lt 1886, served E Indies Station, Torpedo Offr HMS *Edgar* 1893 Med and China, Cdr 1899, Capt 1904, Flag Capt to Adml cmdg Portsmouth Reserve 1905–07 and to C-in-C Plymouth 1907–08, Capt HMS *Bedford* China Station 1908, Capt Supt contract-built ships Clyde Dist 1911–14, Capt HMS *Colossus* Grand Fleet WW I, R-Adml 1915, Adml Minesweeping 1915–17, Dir Torpedoes and Mines 1917–18, C-in-C Cape 1918–20, V-Adml 1920, ret 1923, Adml 1925; Orders Rising Sun Japan, St Stanislas Russia, Tower and Sword Portugal and US DSM; *d* unm 28 Sept 1941

4a Thomas Charles; *b* 30 Aug 1869; Capt Lancs Hus, Boer War 1900–02, WW I, Albert Medal 1916; *m* 30 April 1925 Helen Beryl Frances, JP (Staffs 1942–52) (*d* 3 Dec 1959), widow of Maj Henry Brougham, RA, and 2nd dau of John Michael Waters, of Hill House, nr Farnham, Surrey, and *d* 20 Sept 1937, leaving:

1b BASIL FRANCIS NICHOLAS FITZHERBERT, **8th Baron Stafford**; *b* 7 April 1926; *educ* Ampleforth; Lt Scots Gds WW II 1944; dir Barclays Bank Birmingham, Pres N Staffs Inst Mktg, memb Staffs AEC, Show Dir

Staffs Ag Show; *m* 16 June 1952 *Morag Nada [The Rt Hon Morag Lady Stafford, Beech Farm House, Beech, Stoke-on-Trent, Staffs ST4 8SJ], yr dau of Lt-Col Alastair Campbell, Argyll and Sutherland Highrs, of Altries, Milltimber, Aberdeenshire, and *d* 1986, leaving:

1c FRANCIS MELFORT WILLIAM FITZHERBERT, **9th and present Baron Stafford**

2c +Thomas Alastair; *b* 9 Aug 1955; *educ* Ampleforth and RMA Sandhurst; late Capt Scots Gds; *m* 8 May 1982 *Deborah Susan, yr dau of Peter Alan Beak, of Brazil, and Mrs B S A Westley, of The Coach House, Englefield Green, and has:

1d +Rory; *b* 1989

1d *Tamara Frances; *b* 1986

2d *Perdita Aileen; *b* 1987

3c +Philip Basil [Philip Fitzherbert Esq, Beech Farm Cottage, Beech, Staffs ST4 8SJ]; *b* 7 Oct 1962; *educ* Ampleforth and Durham U (BA); *m* 1991 *Caroline T, yr dau of Michael Hadock, of Bodedern, Anglesey, and has:

1d +Basil Edward; *b* 17 Jan 1998

1d *Emily; *b* 10 Feb 1995

2d *Philippa; *b* 10 Feb 1995

1c *Aileen Mary [The Hon Mrs Littleton, Old Walls, Hannington, Hants]; *b* 29 March 1953; *m* 12 April 1980 *Antony Robin Walhouse Littleton (*see* HATHERTON, B) and has issue

2c *Caroline Fiona [The Hon Mrs Tellwright, The Sydnall farm, Woodseaves, Market Drayton, Salop]; *b* 13 Oct 1956; *m* 9 May 1981 *William Kirkland Tellwright, est s of William Tellwright, of Park Springs, Salop, and has:

1d *Turia Mary; *b* 1984

2d *Laura Caroline; *b* 1987

3c *Wendy Helen [The Hon Mrs Hill, The Hide, 6 Esterbrooke St, London SW1]; *b* 28 April 1961; *m* 5 Nov 1983 *Jeremy John Maurice Hill, est s of Lt-Col and Mrs Colin Hill, of Coley Court, E Harptree, Avon, and has:

1d *Thomas Colin Evelyn; *b* 1985

2d *Nicholas Jeremy John; *b* 1987

2b Evelyn Thomas Francis Ralph; *b* 7 Oct 1928; *educ* Ampleforth; granted March 1942 rank of baron's yr s; Lt 3rd Bn Gren Gds; accidentally drowned while sailing at Fayid 9 March 1952

1a Beatrice Mary Teresa; *b* 1862; *m* 24 July 1895 Sir Trevor John Chichele Chichele-Plowden , KCSI (*d* 5 Nov 1905), and *d* 22 Oct 1949, leaving:

1b Hester Mary Beatrice; *b* 1902; *m* 1922 Cdr Kenneth Gordon Poland, RNVR (*d* 1970), and *d* 1993, leaving:

1c *Trevor Peter Gordon [Lt-Cdr Trevor Poland RN, 3 Cheyne Gdns, London SW3]; *b* 1923; *m* 1st 1944 June Mary (*d* 1969) est dau of Henry Bowlby, and has:

1d *Peter Kenneth; *b* 1945

1d *Jill; *b* 1948

1c (cont.) Lt-Cdr Trevor Poland *m* 2nd 1969 *Lorette Elizabeth Johanna, dau of Dr Poland, J M Durr, of Cape Town, and by her has:

2d *Sophie Victoria; *b* 1982

2c *John Michael [John Poland Esq, Fermain, W Wittering, W Sussex]; *b* 1925; *educ* Downside and Trin Coll Cambridge; *m* 1952 (*divorce* 1983) Diana Mary Angela Forbes, dau of Leo Forbes O'Connor (*see* BYRON, B), and has:

1d *Simon John Joseph; *b* 1957

2d *Jonathan David; *b* 1958

3d *Matthew John; *b* 1963

1d *Sara Daphne Mary; *b* 1954

2d *Lucy Mary; *b* 1959; *m* 1987 *(Geoffrey Roger George) Chandos Elletson, yr s of Daniel Hope Elletson, of Parrox Hall, Lancs, and has:

1e *Frederick Chandos John; *b* 1990

3c *David Kenneth; *b* 1929; *educ* Downside; *m* 1st 1958 (*divorce* 1967) Joanna Mary, est dau of Capt J B Hall, RN, and had:

1d *Kevin John; *b* 1959

2d *Jeremy David; *b* 1961

3c (cont.) David Poland *m* 2nd 1967 *Isie Suzeti, only dau of Maj Louis Esselen, of S Africa, and *d* 1982, having by her had:

1d *Caroline Mary; *b* 1969

4c *Michael Desmond [Michael Poland Esq, Lower Preshaw House, Upham, Hants SO32 2HP]; *b* 1937; *educ* Downside; MFH; *m* 1st 1969 (*divorce* 1980) Elizabeth, dau of Philip Asprey, of Perry, Worplesdon, Surrey; *m* 2nd 1981 *Mrs Carolyn Mary Denison, 2nd dau of W/Cdr William James Maitland Longmore, CBE (*see* FORRES, B), and by his 1st w has:

1d *Lara Hester Mary; *b* 1969; *m* 1998 *William Sussmann, s of Peter Sussmann, of London NW11

2d *Emma Elizabeth; *b* 1970

3d *Liza Evelyne Theresa; *b* 1973

4d *Anna Louise; *b* 1974

1c *Daphne Elizabeth Beatrice [Mrs Edward Thorneycroft, Tigbourne Farm, Wormley, Surrey GU8 5TT]; *b* 1933; *m* 1960 *Edward Kendall Thorneycroft, MBE, TD, DL, and has:

1d *Tom Edward; *b* 22 April 1962

1d *Mary Louise [Mrs Jeremy Campbell-Lamerton, The Old Rectory, Rendlesham, Suffolk IP12 2QY]; *b* 18 March 1961; *m* 1985 *Jeremy Campbell-Lamerton, est s of Col Michael John Campbell-Lamerton, of Burmington House, Shipston-on-Stour, Warwicks, and has:

1e *Harry Alexander; *b* 10 Jan 1987

1e *Alice Louisa; *b* 24 Sept 1988

2e *Olivia Rose; *b* 12 July 1990

3e *Poppy Camilla; *b* 11 Feb 1993

2a Evelyne Mary Walburga; *d unm* 7 March 1950

3a Alice Mary Wilhelmina, JP Lancs; *m* 1 Feb 1894 Maj Richard Trappes-Lomax, JP (*d* 23 June 1936), of Allsprings, Great Harwood, Lancs, and *d* 29 July 1955, leaving, with other issue (all *dsp* including Michael Trappes-Lomax, Somerset Herald):

1b Basil Charles, MC; *b* 14 Aug 1896; Brig; *m* 25 June 1929 Diana Mary (*d* 1995), dau of Cdr A E Silvertop, RN, and *d* 8 Oct 1963, leaving:

1c David Edward; *b* 14 July 1930; *educ* Downside; Maj Scots Gds; *m* 12 April 1980 *Gillean, widow of S/Ldr David Hill [Mrs David Trappes-Lomax, 40 Amderley Drive, Eaton, Norwich, Norfolk] and *dsp* 24 Nov 1993

2c *John Michael [John Trappes-Lomax Esq, 131 Southgate St, Bury St Edmunds, Suffolk IP33 2AF]; *b* 23 April 1947; *educ* Downside and Gonville and Caius Coll Cambridge

1c *Alice Mary [Mrs John Wells, Creaber, Gidleigh, Devon]; *b* 27 March 1938; *m* 17 Jan 1959 *John Edward Benedict Wells and has:

1d *Benedict Swithin [Maj Benedict Wells, King's Royal Hussars, c/o BFPO 17]; *b* 19 Dec 1960; King's Roy Hus; *m* 1989 *Vicki Caroline, dau of Stanley Alexander Maitland, of Chipstead, Surrey, and has:

1e *James Edward Benedict; *b* 1994

1e *Sophie Louise Cameron; *b* 1990

2e *Georgia Rose; *b* 1991

3e *Juliet Katherine; *b* 1993

2d *Thomas Edward [Thomas Wells Esq, 133 Tilehurst Rd, London SW18]; *b* 12 Oct 1962; *m* 1990 *Katherine J Rich

1d *Katherine Mary Horatia [Mrs John Almond, Creaber, Gidleigh, Devon TQ13 8HS]; *b* 28 Oct 1959; *m* 1988 *John Collingwood Almond and has:

1e *Edward; *b* 5 Aug 1980

1e *Lucy Horatia; *b* 16 Sept 1991

2b Nicholas Hugh; *b* 1911; Col; *m* 1938 Gertrude Maisie (*d* 1994), dau of Lt-Col Hugh Charles Stockwell, OBE, and *d* 1969, leaving:

1c *Hugh Richard Nicholas [Hugh Trappes-Lomax Esq, 28 Blackford Ave, Edinburgh EH9 2PH]; *b* 1943; *m* 1968 *Jocelyn Ncekei, dau of Johnson Karandi, of Meru, Kenya, and has:

1d *Simon Mwenda; *b* 1968; *m* 1993 *Marie-Christine Michaela, dau of Michael Edward Skrutkowski, of Bromma, Sweden

2d *Robert Kimathi; *b* 1980

1d *Catherine Nkirote; *b* 1970

2d *Helen Kagendo; *b* 1977

2c *Mark Clement; *b* 1946

1c *Tessa Margaret; *b* 1941

2c *Nicola Frances [Mrs Anthony Eastwood, Foulscales House, Newton-in-Bowland, Clitheroe, Lancs]; *b* 1944; *m* 1964 *Anthony Miles Trevor Eastwood and has:

1d *Anthony Charles; *b* 1965

2d *Benjamin Miles; *b* 1966

3d *Carl Hugh; *b* 1968

3b Stephen Richard, MC, TD; *b* 1913; Maj WW II; *m* 1952 *Alison Marjorie Gundrede [Mrs Stephen Trappes-Lomax, The Farm House, Little London, N Walsham, Norfolk], only dau of George Algernon Perkins, of Bure House, Lamas, Norwich, and *d* 1982, leaving:

1c *Francis George [Francis Trappes-Lomax Esq, Croft Cottage, Cann's Lane, Hethersett, Norwich NR9 3JE]; *b* 1955; *m* 1986 *Annette Chalkley and has:

1d *Christopher Michael; *b* 1990

1d *Catherine Ruth; *b* 1988

2c *Richard Nicholas Henry; *b* 1960

1c *Mary Alison Catherine [Mrs Alexander Cockburn, Rosedene, Aylsham Rd, Swanton Abbott, Norwich NR10 5AH]; *b* 1953; *m* 1984 *Alexander Cockburn, er s of Denison Cockburn, of Chipping Campden, Glos, and has:

1d *George Stephen Denison; *b* 1986

2d *Alastair William Richard; *b* 1989

2c *Clare Gundrede [Mrs Brian Gibson, Longworth House, Great Wolford, Shipston-on-Stour, Warwicks CV36 5NQ]; *b* 1957; *m* 1983 *Brian Ronald Weir Gibson, s of Ronald Gibson, of Lowood, W Lothian, and has:

1d *Emma Clare; *b* 1987

4a Maud Mary Josephine; Franciscan nun

(2) Rosa; *b* Sept 1838; nun; *d* 25 Sept 1880

3 George Sulyarde, KCH, CB; *b* 17 Feb 1806; Envoy Extrdy and Min Plen Sweden 1859–72; *d* unm 18 May 1874

4 Charles William; *b* 22 Aug 1807; Lt 6th Dragoon Gds; *d* unm 4 April 1884

5 William George; *b* 15 July 1812; Min Resident Lima 1857–74; *m* 1 April 1860 Eglantina Narcissa, dau of Frederick Augustus Elmore, of Lima, and *dsp* 16 July 1874

6 Francis Hugh Joseph; *b* 20 March 1814; *d* unm 9 Oct 1874

1 Charlotte Georgina; *b* 8 Oct 1800; *m* 6 Aug 1823 12th Lord Lovat (*qv*) and *d* 28 May 1876, leaving issue

2 Laura Maria; *b* 15 Jan 1811; *m* 21 July 1829 Hon Robert Edward Petre, s of 9th Baron Petre (*qv*), and *d* a nun 24 June 1886

Lineage (of Fitzherbert): HERBERT; had, with two yr sons (Robert fitz Herbert, of Osmeston; Hugh fitz William fitz Herbert, of Derby):

WILLIAM fitz HERBERT; granted Manor of Norbury, Derbys, 1125 by William, Prior of Tutbury, Derbys; had, with a dau (Agnes):

WILLIAM fitz HERBERT, of Norbury; held a kt's fee of Robert de Ferrieres, 2nd Earl of Derby (*qv*) of the 1138 *cr*, and *d* in or after 1166, leaving:

JOHN FITZHERBERT, of Norbury; *m* Agnes, dau and heiress of Osbert de Stretton, of Etwall, Derbys, and had:

JOHN FITZHERBERT, of Norbury; living 1228; *m* Emmeline, dau of William de Grendon, of Ockbrook, Derbys, and had:

Sir WILLIAM FITZHERBERT, of Norbury; Sheriff Notts and Derbys 1272–74; *m* 1st —; *m* 2nd — and by her had two daus (Helen, *m* Walter de Ridware, of Staffs, and had issue; Jane); by his 1st w he had, with two yr sons (William, ancestor of the FITZHERBERTs of Somersal Herbert, Derbys (who died out in the male line 1803, following which their representation was continued by the JACSONs of Bebington, Cheshire, into whom a FITZHERBERT heiress married) and the FITZHERBERT Bts (*qv*); Richard, ancestor of the FITZHERBERTs of Twycross, Leics):

Sir HENRY FITZHERBERT, of Norbury; Sheriff Derbys and Notts 1263–64; *m* the dau of Ralph de Chaddesdon, of Chaddesdon, Derbys, and *d* after 24 April 1291, leaving, with a yr s (Roger, Rector Norbury 1306):

Sir JOHN FITZHERBERT, of Norbury; living 1350; *m* Margaret, dau of Sir Walter de Montgomery, of Marston Montgomery and Cubley, Derbys, and had, with two yr sons:

WILLIAM FITZHERBERT, of Norbury; *fl* 1348–77; *m* 1st Jane, dau of Sir Nicholas Kniveton, of Mercaston, Derbys; *m* 2nd Jane (*dsp*), dau of Sir Alured Selney, of Newton Solney, Derbys, and by his 1st w had:

WILLIAM FITZHERBERT, of Norbury; *fl* 1363–98; *m* Alice, dau of Nicholas Longford, of Longford, Derbys, and had:

HENRY FITZHERBERT, of Norbury; living 1411; *m* — Downes, of Oreton in Taxall, Cheshire, and had:

NICHOLAS FITZHERBERT, of Norbury; *b* 1400; MP Derbys 1446 and 1452, High Sheriff 1448 and 1466; *m* 1st Alice, dau of Henry Booth, of Arleston, Derbys; *m* 2nd Isabel Ludlow, of Stokesay, Salop, and *d* 19 Nov 1473, having by her had four daus and by his 1st w, with two yr sons (John, of Etwall, Derbys, King's Remembrancer Exchequer, a Teller Exchequer 1475, *m* 1st Margaret, dau and heiress of Robert Babington, and was ancestor of the FITZHERBERTs of Perry Hall, Staffs, *m* 2nd Joan and *d* between 31 Oct 1502 and 12 May 1503, having by her had four daus; Robert, of Uphall, Herts, *m* Elizabeth, dau of Ralph Jocelyn, of Sawbridgeworth, Herts, and was ancestor of the FITZHERBERTs of Kidlington and Begbroke, Oxon):

RALPH FITZHERBERT, of Norbury; *m* Elizabeth (*d* 1496), dau and heiress of John Marshall, of Upton, Leics, and Sedsall, Doveridge, Derbys, and *d* 2 March 1483/4, having had, with six daus:

1 John, of Norbury; *m* Benedicta, dau of John Bradburne, of The Hough, Derbys, and *d* 24 July 1531, having had, with an illegitimate dau (Jane, *m* Anthony Basford, of Broadlow Ash):

(1) Nicholas; *m* 1501 Dorothy, dau of Sir Ralph Longford, and *dsp* & *vp* 1517

(1) Elizabeth; *m* Sir Philip Draycote, of Painsley, Staffs, and had issue

(2) Anne; *m* John Wells, of Hoar Cross, Staffs, and had issue

(3) Edith

2 Henry; London mercer; *m* Elizabeth, dau of Robert Godwin, London draper, and had:

(1) Elizabeth; *m* William Whitt, of London

3 ANTHONY (Sir)

4 Thomas; DCL, Rector Norbury 1500–18, Preb Lichfield 1513; *d* unm 1532

5 William; Preb Hereford 1482, Rector Wrington, Somerset, 1476, and St Magnus London 1498, Preb Lincoln 1506

6 Richard

The 3rd s,

Sir ANTHONY FITZHERBERT, of Norbury; *b* 1470; Judge Common Pleas 1522, author: *La Graunde Abridgement* and other legal works; *m* 1st Dorothy (*dsp* 1497), dau of Sir Henry Willoughby, of Wollaton, Notts; *m* 2nd Mathilda (*d* 1521), dau and coheir of Richard Cotton, of Hamstall Ridware, and *d* 27 May 1538, having by her had:

1 Thomas (Sir), of Norbury; High Sheriff Staffs 1547 and 1555; *m* 1534 Anne, dau and heiress of Sir Arthur Eyre, of Padley, Hathersage, Derbys, and *dsp* Tower of London 1 Dec 1591

2 John, of Padley, Derbys; *m* Catherine, dau of Edward Restwolde, of The Vache, Bucks, and *d* 1590, having had, with other issue:

(1) Thomas, of Norbury; *m* Elizabeth, dau of John Westby, of Westby, Yorks, and Mowbrick, Lancs, and *dsp*

(2) Anthony , of Norbury; *m* Martha, widow of William Garton, of London, and dau of Thomas Austen, of Oxley, Staffs, and *d* 1613, leaving:

1a John (Sir), of Norbury; Sheriff Derbys 1626, Col Dragoons 1642; *m* c 1631 Dorothy, dau of John Harpur, of Breadsall, Derbys, and sis of Sir John Harpur, of Swarkestone, and *dsp* 13 Jan 1649

1a Helen

2a Mary; *m* Thomas Lewyn, of Norfolk

3a Catherine; *m* John Milward, s of Sir Thomas Milward, of Eaton Dovedale, Derbys

4a Anne; *m* Richard Congreve, of Congreve, Salop, and Stretton, Derbys

5a Elizabeth; *m* Sir John Fitzherbert, of Tissington, and *d* 17 Feb 1630, leaving issue (see FITZHERBERT, Bt)

(3) Nicholas; Sec to Cardinal Allen; *dsp* 1612

(1) Jane; *m* Thomas Eyre, of Dunston, Derbys

(2) Mathilda; *m* Thomas Barlow, of Barlow, Derbys

(3) Elizabeth; *m* Sir Robert Harcourt (see VERNON, B)

(4) Mary; *m* Thomas Draycote, of Sydnall

3 Richard, of Harlesmere, Staffs; *m* Mary Westcote and had:

(1) William

(2) Nicholas, of Blythebury, Staffs

4 William, of Swynnerton, Staffs; *m* Elizabeth (*m* 2nd John Gatacre, of Gatacre, Salop, and was *bur* 4 April 1616), yr dau and coheir of Humphrey Swynnerton, of Swynnerton, through whom he acquired that Manor, and had:

(1) Thomas, of Swynnerton and Bledlow, Bucks; *m* 1580 Dorothy, only dau and heiress of Edward East, of Bledlow and Frissills, Bucks, and after her death became a Jesuit; *d* 1640, having:

1a Edward, of Swynnerton and Bledlow; m Bridget (m 2nd Sir Edmund Windsor, of Knightley), dau of Sir John Caryll, of Angmering, Sussex, and dvp 25 Nov 1612, leaving:

    1b WILLIAM

1a Elizabeth; m Joseph Mayne, of Crestlow, Bucks

(2) Anthony

(1) Anne; m Walter Heveningham, of Aston and Pipe, Staffs

1 Elizabeth; m William Basset, of Langley, Derbys, and Blore, Staffs

2 Dorothy; m 1st Sir Ralph Longford, of Longford; m 2nd Sir John Port, of Etwall

3 Catherine; m John Sacheverel, of Morley, Derbys

Sir JOHN FITZHERBERT's 1st cousin once-removed,

WILLIAM FITZHERBERT, of Norbury and Swynnerton; one of the intended Kts of the Royal Oak 1660 (a chivalric order mooted by CHARLES II but never implemented); m 1st Anne, dau of Sir Basil Brooke, of Madeley, Salop; m 2nd Eleanor, widow of Sir Henry Pierce, of Shercock, and Richard Fitzwilliam (dvp, er s of 1st Viscount Fitzwilliam of Merrion; see 1833 edn) and dau of Sir Francis Stafford, of Portglenone, Co Antrim, and Bradfield, Berks and had, with other issue:

1 BASIL, his heir

2 Thomas, of Shercock, Co Cavan; m the only child of Henry Pierce, of Pierce Court (or Shercock), and had:

    (1) William; ancestor in the female line of the FITZHERBERTs of Black Castle, Co Meath

1 Mary; m John Gower, of Colmers, Worcs

2 Frances; m John Giffard, of Chillington, Staffs

3 Bridget; m Basil Bartlett, of Castle Morton, Worcs

The est s,

BASIL FITZHERBERT, of Norbury and Swynnerton; m Jane, dau and heiress of John Cotton, of Gedding Abbots, Hunts, and Boscobel and White Ladies, Salop, and had an est s:

WILLIAM FITZHERBERT, of Norbury and Swynnerton; m 1679 Elizabeth, only dau and heiress of Robert Owen, of Weppra, Flints, s of John Owen, Bp St Asaph, and had an est s:

THOMAS FITZHERBERT, of Norbury and Swynnerton; m 1713 Constantia, dau and coheir of Sir George Southcote, of Blytheborough, Lincs, and d 1765, having had, with four daus (including Mary, m Thomas Weld, yr s of Humphrey Weld (yr s of Humphrey Weld, of Lulworth Castle, Dorset), and d Bruges 1766; Catherine, m Robert Berkeley, of Spetchley, Worcs):

THOMAS FITZHERBERT, of Norbury and Swynnerton; m 1st 1737 Elizabeth, dau and coheir of Anthony Meaborne, of Pontop, Co Durham, but by her had no issue; m 2nd 1743 Mary Teresa (d 26 Feb 1791), dau of Sir Robert Throckmorton, 4th Bt (see 1970 edn), and d 3 Oct 1778, having by her had:

1 Thomas, of Norbury and Swynnerton; b 30 Aug 1746; m 1778 Mary Anne (went through a form of marriage 15 Dec 1785, in contravention of the Royal Marriage Act, with THE PRINCE OF WALES later GEORGE IV and d 29 March 1837), widow of Edward Weld, of Lulworth Castle, Dorset, and d 7 May 1781, having had a s (d an infant)

2 BASIL

3 Edward Cotton; d Manchester 1768

4 William FITZHERBERT later FITZHERBERT-BROCKHOLES (roy licence 3 June 1783), of Claughton, Lancs; m 1791 Mary, est dau and coheir of James Windsor Heneage, of Cadeby, Lincs, and Gatcombe, IOW, and d 1817, leaving issue, which failed in the male line on the death 11 Jan 1875 of his gs James Fitzherbert-Brockholes, of Claughton, when that estate passed to his cousin William Joseph Fitzherbert (see below)

1 Constantia; m 1st 8 Aug 1768 Joseph BROCKHOLES formerly HESKETH (d 1782), of Claughton, Lancs; m 2nd Philip Saltmarshe and dsp 1813

2 Barbara; m 1st George Tasburg, of Bodney, Norfolk; m 2nd George Crathorne, of Crathorne, and Ness, Yorks, and d 1808, leaving by him a dau

3 Charlotte; m 22 Nov 1779 Sir Thomas Gage, 6th Bt (d 1 Dec 1798), of Hengrave, Suffolk (for whose early ancestry see GAGE, V), and d 29 Aug 1790, leaving issue

4 Teresa; m Thomas Hornyold, of Blackmore Park and Hanley Castle, Worcs, and Knightly, Salop, and d 18 Dec 1815, leaving issue. He d 31 Dec 1814

5 Lucy; m 1792 James Dormer and d 1816, leaving issue (see DORMER, B)

The 2nd s,

BASIL FITZHERBERT, of Norbury and Swynnerton; b 1748; m 1786 Elizabeth (d 1797), yr dau and coheir of James Windsor Heneage, of Cadeby, Lincs, and Gatcombe, IOW, and d 23 May 1797, having had, with two other daus:

1 Thomas, of Norbury and Swynnerton, DL Staffs; b 21 Jan 1789; High Sheriff Staffs 1831; m 15 July 1809 Mary Anne Sophia (d 11 Aug 1858), dau of John Palmer Chichester, of Arlington Court, Devon (see 1888 edn CHICHESTER, Bt), and dsps 4 Feb 1857, having had:

    (1) Charles; b 21 June 1810; Cornet 10th Light Dragoons; m 1832 Mary, dau of Patrick Gibbons, of Dublin, and dvp 1834, having had:

        1a Thomasina; b 1833; m — Collins and dsp

    (2) Thomas Lewis; b 1811; d an infant

2 Basil; b 2 July 1790; d unm

3 John, of Norbury and Swynnerton; b 2 Sept 1792; Capt 80th Regt; d unm 13 Oct 1863

4 George; b 30 July 1793; Offr 14th Regt; d unm 1852

5 Francis; b 20 Nov 1796; m 28 July 1828 his cousin Maria Teresa (d 4 June 1876), dau of John Vincent Gandolfi, of E Sheen, Surrey, by Teresa, dau of Thomas Hornyold (see above), and d 29 May 1857, having had, with other issue (d young):

    (1) Basil Thomas, of Norbury and Swynnerton, JP, DL Staffs; b 29 March 1836; m 1st 13 Oct 1858 Emily Charlotte (d 9 Nov 1881), sis of 4th and 5th Barons Stafford, and had issue (see above); m 2nd 24 April 1887 Emma Eliza (dsp 11 Nov 1912), widow of 3rd Baron Stafford, and dau of Frederic Sewallis Gerard (see GERARD, B), and d 13 April 1919

(2) William Joseph FITZHERBERT later FITZHERBERT-BROCKHOLES (on inheriting 1875 the estates of his cousin James Fitzherbert-Brockholes; see above), of Claughton; d 21 Jan 1924

STAIR

Arms: Quarterly; 1st, or on a saltire azure nine lozenges of the field (for DALRYMPLE); 2nd, or a chevron chequy sable and argent, between three water bougets of the second (for ROSS); 3rd, grand quarter, quarterly 1st and 4th counterquartered, 1st and 4th, gules three cinquefoils ermine, 2nd and 3rd, argent a galley, sails furled, sable, the whole within a bordure compony argent and azure, the first charged with hearts gules, the second with mullets argent (for HAMILTON of Bargany); 2nd and 3rd, gules on a fess between three crescents or as many mullets azure (for DE FRANQUETOT); 4th, grand quarter, quarterly 1st and 4th, gules, on a chevron between three cinquefoils argent as many round buckles azure (for HAMILTON of Fala); 2nd and 3rd, gules three martlets argent (for MAKGILL). **Crest:** A rock proper. **Supporters:** Two storks, each holding in the beak a fish, all proper. **Motto:** Firm. **Creations:** E. (S) 8 April 1703, V. (of Stair) (S) 21 April 1690 and (of Dalrymple) (S) 8 April 1703, L. (Glenluce and Stranraer) (S) 21 April 1690 and (Newliston, Glenluce and Stranraer) (S) 8 April 1703, B. (UK) 1841, Bt. (of Stair) (NS) 2 June 1664 and (of Cousland) 28 April 1698.

THE 14TH EARL OF STAIR, Viscount (of) Stair, Viscount Dalrymple, **Lord Glenluce and Stranraer, Lord Newliston, Glenluce and Stranraer, Baron Oxenfoord of Cousland,** Co Midlothian, and a **Baronet** (Sir John David James Dalrymple, 15th Bt, of Stair, and 11th Bt, of Cousland) [The Rt Hon The Earl of Stair, Lochinch Castle, Stranraer, Wigtownshire DG9 8RT]; b 4 Sept 1961; s f 1996; educ Harrow and RMA Sandhurst

Lineage: The present DALRYMPLEs claim but cannot prove descent via the DALRYMPLEs of Camraggan from feudal Barons of Dalrymple, Ayrshire. The baronial lands there were in the period 1371–77 half held by Malcolm, s of Gillchrist, s of Adam de Dalrympill, and half by Hew, s of Roland de Dalrympill. Both Roland and Adam seem to have been of Scottish origin rather than, say, Norman or Flemish, as many other leading families now regarded as Scottish were in the Middle Ages.

WILLIAM de DALRYMPLE; m Agnes Kennedy and through her acquired the lands of Stair-Montgomery, Ayrshire, 1429; had:

WILLIAM DALRYMPLE, of Stair, in Kyle, Ayrshire; m Marion, dau of Sir John Chalmers of Gadgirth, Ayrshire, and a Lollard (subscriber to a series of beliefs regarded as heretical in the 14th century, when Lollardy first flourished, but in many ways a precursor of the Protestants of the Reformation some 150 years later); various Lollards of Kyle, of whom Marion was one, were interrogated as to their doctrines by JAMES IV's Cncl 1494 but were dismissed without punishment; had:

JOHN DALRYMPLE; m c 1507 Christine Crawfurd, allegedly dau of the Laird of Leifnories, and dvp, leaving:

WILLIAM DALRYMPLE; had a charter of Stair 1530; m Margaret Wallace and had:

JAMES DALRYMPLE of Stair; supported Reformation 1560, opposed marriage of MARY QUEEN OF SCOTS to Lord Darnley; m 1563 Isabel, dau of Thomas Kennedy of Bargany, and d 5 Aug 1586, leaving:

1 John; m Margaret (m 2nd 1614 Alexander Cuninghame of Portown), dau of William Dunbar of Blantyre, and had:

    (1) James, of Stair; made over the estate of Stair to his unc (see below); m 15 April 1613 Marjory, dau of Allan Cathcart of Waterside, and had:

        1a James

2 James, of Stair and Drummurchie, Ayrshire; took over the family estate from his nephew; m 9 Sept 1617 Janet (m 2nd Hugh Campbell of Balloch and d 1663), dau of Fergus Kennedy of Knockdaw, Ayrshire, and d 1625, leaving, with a yr s (see DALRYMPLE-HAY, Bt):

(1) **Sir James Dalrymple, 1st Bt** (NS), so *cr* 2 June 1664, and **1st Viscount (of) Stair**, so *cr* 21 April 1690, as also LORD GLENLUCE AND STRANRAER (both S); *b* 1619; Commr for Admin of Justice (Protectorate equivalent of Ld of Session) 1657 and Ld of Session as Lord Stair 13 Feb 1660/1, Pres Court of Session 1672 but removed 1681 and obliged to retire to Holland 1682 for refusing to take the Test (imposed in Scotland 1681 by an Act of Parl ordaining that officials must declare their adherence to Protestantism), returned with WILLIAM III 1688 and restored as Pres; *m* 21 Sept 1643 Margaret (*d* 1692), est dau of James Ross of Balneil and widow of Fergus Kennedy of Knockdaw, and *d* 20 Nov 1695, having had:

1a JOHN DALRYMPLE, **2nd Viscount** and **1st Earl of Stair**, so *cr* 8 April 1703, as also LORD NEWLISTON, GLENLUCE AND STRANRAER and VISCOUNT DALRYMPLE (all S), with remainder, failing his own male issue, to the heirs male of his f; styled *Master of Stair* 1690–95 under which appellation he is notorious as the man who authorised the Massacre of Glencoe 1692; Ld Justice Clerk, afterwards Ld Advocate and Sec of State; *m c* 18 Jan 1668/9 Elizabeth, dau and heiress of Sir John Dundas of Newliston, Linlithgowshire, and *d* 8 Jan 1707, having had (with other issue):

1b JOHN DALRYMPLE, **2nd Earl of Stair**, KT (1710); cmded a Bde Battle of Oudenarde 1708 and carried the despatches announcing the victory to England, later FM, Cdr forces on the Rhine, 2ic to GEORGE II Battle of Dettingen 1743, C-in-C S Britain, Amb Extrdy France after death of LOUIS XIV, rep S peer 1707–08, 1715–34 and 1744–47; *m* Eleanor, dau of 2nd Earl of Loudoun (*qv*) and widow of James, Viscount Primrose, but had no issue; when his next bro and heir presumptive *m* a peeress the **2nd Earl** surrendered all his honours to the Crown 1707, obtained a new charter containing, in default of male issue, a reversionary clause in favour of any one of the male descendants of the **1st Viscount** he cared to name, and drew up a deed just before his death without issue 9 May 1747 nominating his n John Dalrymple, s of his 2nd bro George; the nomination was contested by James Dalrymple, 2nd s of Col William Dalrymple, MP, of Glenmure, and the Countess of Dumfries, and the Ho of Lds decided in James's favour 2 May 1748

2b William of Glenmure; Col and MP Ayrshire in the last pre-Union Scottish Parl; *m* 1698 Penelope, Countess of Dumfries in her own right (*see* BUTE, M), and had, with other issue:

1c WILLIAM DALRYMPLE-CRICHTON, **4th Earl of Stair** and EARL OF DUMFRIES, as which *s* his mother Penelope 6 March 1741/2; *m* 1st Lady Anne Gordon, est dau of 2nd Earl of Aberdeen (*see* ABERDEEN AND TEMAIR, M); *m* 2nd Anne, dau of William Duff of Crombie, but *dsps* 27 July 1768, when the Earldom of Dumfries passed to his est sister's s and that of Stair to his cousin George

2c JAMES DALRYMPLE, **3rd Earl of Stair**; *dsp* 1760

3b George, of Dalmahoy, Co Edinburgh; Baron Exchequer Scotland; *m* Eupheme (*d* 8 July 1761), est dau of Sir Andrew Myreton, 1st Bt, of Gogar, Co Edinburgh, and *d* 29 July 1745, having had:

1c JOHN DALRYMPLE, **5th Earl of Stair**; styled himself Earl of Stair for a short while after his unc's death 9 May 1747 but the judgement of the Ho of Lds went against him 1748; nevertheless he inherited his unc's estates and in 1768 the Earldom itself; rep S peer 1771–74; *m* Margaret, dau of George Middleton, London banker, and *d* 13 Oct 1789, leaving:

1d JOHN DALRYMPLE, **6th Earl of Stair**; rep S peer 1790–1807 and 1820–21, Amb to Prussia; *dsp* 1 June 1821

2c William; Gen, Lt-Govr Chelsea Hosp; *m* 13 Sept 1783 Marianne Dorothy (*d* 28 Oct 1785), 2nd dau of Adml Sir Rober Harland, 1st Bt, and *d* 23 Feb 1807, leaving:

1d JOHN WILLIAM HENRY DALRYMPLE, **7th Earl of Stair**; *b* 16 Nov 1784; *m* 1st 28 May 1804 (*annulled* June 1820) Johanna, dau of Charles Gordon of Cluny; *m* 2nd 3 June 1808 (not considering the previous marriage valid, but *divorced* 1809 because of the prior contract of 1804) Laura (*dsp* 11 July 1834), yst dau of John Manners, of Grantham Grange, by Louisa, Countess of Dysart (*qv*), and *dsp* Paris 22 March 1840

2a Sir James Dalrymple, **1st Bt** (NS), so *cr* 28 April 1698, of Borthwick, Killock and Cousland; Pncpl Clerk Court of Session; *m* 1st 2 Jan 1679 Catherine (*bur* 17 Jan 1689), 3rd dau of Sir James Dundas of Arniston; *m* 2nd 4 Sept 1691 Esther (*bur* 7 April 1700), 3rd dau of John Cunningham of Enterkin and widow of James Fletcher of New Cranston; *m* 3rd 7 Sept 1701 Jane Halkett and *d* May 1719, leaving by his 1st w:

2b Sir John Dalrmple, **2nd Bt**, of Cousland; Pncpl Clerk of Session 1708; *m* 1st 7 Aug 1702 Elizabeth, dau of his step-mother by James Fletcher, and had two sons and two daus; *m* 2nd Sidney (*d* 20 Oct 1759), dau of John Sinclair of Ulbster (*see* SINCLAIR, Bt), and *d* 24 May 1743, having by her had several children; his est s:

1c **Sir William Dalrymple, 3rd Bt**, of Cousland; *b* 23 Sept 1704; *m* 1st 1726 Agnes (*d* 13 Oct 1750), dau of William Crawford, of Glasgow, and had, with other issue:

1d Sir JOHN DALRYMPLE later HAMILTON-DALRYMPLE-MAKGILL, **4th Bt**; *b* 1726; Baron Court of Exchequer Scotland, author: *Memoirs of Great Britain and Ireland*; *m* 7 Oct 1760 his cousin Elizabeth, only child and heiress of Thomas Hamilton Makgill of Fala and Oxenfoord Castle, Co Edinburgh (*see* OXFUIRD, V), and *d* 26 Feb 1810, having had, with other issue:

1e **Sir John Hamilton Dalrymple, 5th Bt**, and **8th Earl of Stair**, as which *s* cousin 1840, KT; *b* 15 June 1771; Gen, Col 46th Foot, Keeper Gt Seal Scotland, *cr* 11 Aug 1841 BARON OXENFOORD OF COUSLAND, Co Midlothian (UK), with remainder to his bro; *m* 1st 23 June 1795 Harriet (*d* 16 Oct 1823), dau of Rev Robert Augustus Johnson; *m* 2nd 8 June 1825 Adamina (*d* 1 Aug 1857), dau of 1st Viscount Duncan of Camperdown (*see* 1933 edn CAMPERDOWN, E), and *dsp* 10 Jan 1853

2e NORTH HAMILTON, **9th Earl**

1e Elizabeth; *m* Myles Sandys (*d* 28 Sept 1839), of Graythwaite Hall, Lancs, and *d* 1832, leaving issue

2e Jane; *m* William Horsman and *d* 1833, having had issue

3e Martha; *m* 1809 Lt Thoms Sampson, 59th Regt (*ka* capture of Java 1811), and *d* 1863

2d William; Army Offr; *m* Diana, dau of Rigby Molyneux, of Preston, Lancs, by Mary, dau of Oliver Marton, of Capernwray, and had, with other issue:

1e Marton; *m* 1798 Frances Ingram Spence, of Hanover Sq (*m* 2nd Rev John Thomson, Min Duddingstone), and *d* 21 Nov 1809, leaving:

1f Molyneux

1f Frances; *m* John Goldingham

2f Caroline Lucy; *m* Negaputnam, India, 7 July 1828 Thomas Prendergast, s of Gen Sir Jeffrey Prendergast, and *d* 1839, leaving issue

1c (cont.) **Sir William** *m* 2nd Anne Philip and was *bur* 20 March 1771, having by her had, with other issue:

3d James; Lt-Col; *d* unm 1800

4d Samuel; *b* 1760; Lt-Gen; *m* 1st 1791 Hannah (*d* 1829), dau of John Tweddell, of Inthank Hall, Northumberland, and had issue; *m* 2nd 10 May 1831 Mary Amelia, dau of Roper Head, and *d* 2 Oct 1832

1d Jane; *m* Maj-Gen Roberts and *d* 1826

2d Wemyss; *m* Hon Leveson Granville Keith Murray (*see* DUNMORE, E) and *d* 1804

3 Sir HEW DALRYMPLE, **1st Bt** (NS), so *cr* 29 April 1698; memb Faculty of Advocates, Pres Court Session June 1698, MP N Berwick; *m* 1st 12 March 1682 Marion, dau of Sir Robert Hamilton; *m* 2nd Elizabeth (*dsp* 21 March 1742), dau of John Hamilton and widow of James Hamilton, and *d* 1 Feb 1737, having had by his 1st w, with other issue (*see* HAMILTON-DALRYMPLE, Bt):

(1) Hew; *b* 30 Nov 1690; advocate 1710, Ld of Session as Lord Drummore 1726, Ld of Justiciary 1745; *m* Anne, dau and heiress of John Horn of Horn and Westhall, and *d* 18 June 1755, leaving, with other issue (*see* HAMILTON-DALRYMPLE, Bt), an est surv s:

1a Robert DALRYMPLE later DALRYMPLE-HORN-ELPHINSTONE of Horn and Westhall; Gen, Col 53rd Foot; *m* 9 July 1754 Mary (*d* 3 March 1774), dau and heir of Sir James Elphinstone, 3rd Bt, of Logie (*qv*), and *d* 1794, leaving, with other issue:

1b James; *b* 24 March 1762; *m* 30 March 1790 Margaret Davidson, heiress of Midmar, and *dsp* en route to Lisbon 21 April 1798

2b Sir ROBERT DALRYMPLE-HORN-ELPHINSTONE, **1st Bt** (UK), so *cr* 16 Jan 1828; *b* 27 Feb 1766; Lt-Col Scots Fus Gds; *m* 21 May 1800 Graeme (*d* 28 Jan 1870), dau of Col David Hepburn, 2nd s of James Congalton Hepburn of Congalton and Keith Marischal, and *d* 11 Oct 1848, having had, with other issue:

1c Sir JAMES DALRYMPLE-HORN-ELPHINSTONE, **2nd Bt**; *b* 20 Nov 1805; MP (C) Portsmouth, a Jr Ld Treasury 1874–80; *m* 27 April 1836 Mary (*d* 16 Nov 1876), 4th dau of Lt-Gen Sir John Shaw Heron Maxwell, 4th Bt (*qv*), and *d* 26 Dec 1886, having had, with other issue:

1d Sir ROBERT ELPHINSTONE DALRYMPLE-HORN-ELPHINSTONE, **3rd Bt**, DL; *b* 6 Sept 1841; Lt 60th Rifles; *m* 17 Nov 1875 Nina (*m* 2nd 16 July 1901 Lt-Gen Sir J Bevan Edwards, KCB, KCMG (*d* 8 July 1922), and *d* 31 Dec 1916), only child of John Balfour, of S Kensington, and *dsp* 11 Feb 1887

2d Sir GRAEME HEPBURN DALRYMPLE-HORN-ELPHINSTONE, **4th Bt**; *b* 12 Sept 1841; *m* 5 Jan 1875 Margaret Anne Alice (*d* 12 March 1932), yst dau of James Ogilvie Fairlie, JP, DL, of Coodham, Ayrshire, and *d* 22 May 1900, leaving:

1e Mary Constance; *d* 22 May 1910

2e Esther Winifred; *m* 8 Nov 1917 Lt-Col Thomas Alexander Headlam, E Yorks Regt, and *dsp* 15 Jan 1960. He *d* 19 Jan 1953

1d Margaret Burnet; *m* 11 Sept 1873 Rev John Maturin Warren, Rector Bawdrip, Somerset, and *d* 1 April 1914, leaving issue. He *d* 1901

2c Hew Drummond DALRYMPLE-HORN-ELPHINSTONE later ELPHINSTONE-DALRYMPLE; *b* 29 July 1807; *m* 6 Nov 1838 Helenora Catherine (*d* 2 Nov 1889), yst dau of Lt-Gen Sir John Shaw Heron-Maxwell, 4th Bt (*qv*), and *d* 28 April 1893, leaving:

1d Sir ROBERT GRAEME ELPHINSTONE-DALRYMPLE, **5th Bt**; *b* 17 Jan 1844; Col IA; *m* 27 April 1871 Flora Loudoun (*d* 23 Nov 1906), dau of James William Macleod, and *d* 16 April 1908, having had:

1e John Maxwell; *b* 20 Jan 1873; Lt Dorset Regt; *d* unm 4 March 1903

2e Sir EDWARD ARTHUR ELPHINSTONE-DALRYMPLE, **6th Bt**; *b* 3 Oct 1877; Capt IA; *m* 3 Sept 1909 Jane Muriel Gibbons (*d* 25 Jan 1937), er dau of John Gibbons Hawkes, of Surmount, Ovens, Co Cork, and *dsp* 22 April 1913

3e Sir FRANCIS NAPIER ELPHINSTONE-DALRYMPLE, **7th Bt**, CBE (1922), DSO (1918); *b* 17 July 1882; WW I (despatches, Order White Eagle Serbia 5th Cl with swords, Offr Crown Italy) France, Gallipoli, Palestine: Col RA, DAAG 1915–17, AAG and T/Lt-Col 1917–19, AA&QMG 1919–23, DAA&QMG 1923–24, Cmdt Roy Mil Sch Music Kneller Hall 1925–29, AA&QMG W Cmd Chester WW II; *m* 30 Sept 1909 Edith Ethel (*d* 3 May 1973), only dau of Lt-Col Edward Hemery Le Breton, Roy Irish Regt, and *dspm* 18 Dec 1956, when the btcy became dormant, leaving:

1f Penelope Eleanor; *b* 3 July 1911; *m* 1st 9 Sept 1939 F/O James Peter Henry Balston, AAF (*kas* 27 March 1940), 2nd s of F W Balston; *m* 2nd 2 March 1954 *Russell Alexander Lovell, Jr [Russell Lovell Jr, 9 Jonathan Lane, Sandwich, MA 02563, USA], er s of Russell Alexander Lovell, of Worcester, Mass., and *dsp* 24 Feb 1995

2f *Daphne Jean [Mrs David Meynell, 6 Elm Rd, Gt Stukeley, Hunts PE17 5AU]; *b* 1916; *m* 17 Dec 1938 Brig David Meynell, CBE, Roy Irish Fus (*d* 1986), s of Brig-Gen Godfrey Meynell, CMG, JP, of Meynell Langley, Derbys, and has:

1g *Timothy; *b* 1940

2g *Peter David; *b* 1945

1e Helenora Catherine; *d* unm 12 July 1909

1d Stuart Mary

3c Francis Anstruther DALRYMPLE-HORN-ELPHINSTONE later ELPHINSTONE-DALRYMPLE; *b* 18 Aug 1813; Bengal CS; *m* 3 Dec 1846 Mary Anne (*d* 9 July 1904), 3rd dau of Maj-Gen Herbert Bowen, CB, and *d* 5 July 1885, leaving:

1d Stair; *b* 3 May 1848; *m* 3 May 1876 Agnes Laura (*d* 28 March 1912), adopted dau of Arthur Southard, of Fern Lodge, Bracknell, Berks, and *dsp* 18 June 1886

2d Hew ELPHINSTONE-DALRYMPLE later DRUMMOND; *b* 27 Jan 1857

3d Ernest Charles; *b* 3 Dec 1859; Natal Mounted Police; *d* 20 Sept 1911

4d Francis Herbert; *b* 2 June 1862

1d Helen Frances; *m* 22 Jan 1873 Adam Hay Gordon of Avochie (*dsp* 12 July 1894)

4c Charles DALRYMPLE-HORN-ELPHINSTONE later ELPHINSTONE-DALRYMPLE; *b* 23 March 1817; *m* 1st 12 Sept 1849 Harriet Albinia Louisa (*d* 13 Feb 1854), est dau of Alexander Gordon of Ellon, Aberdeenshire, and had:

1d William Robert; *b* 1 Feb 1854; Capt 4th Bn Scots Fus; *d* 7 Dec 1890

4c (cont.) Charles ELPHINSTONE-DALRYMPLE *m* 2nd 24 April 1860 Christian (*d* 16 Oct 1919), est dau of William Gordon-Cuming-Skene of Pitlurg and Parkhill, Aberdeenshire, and *d* July 1891, having by her had:

1d Anne Alexandrina; *d* unm 11 Feb 1941

5c John Hamilton, CB; *b* 5 Jan 1819; Gen Scots Fus Gds, Col 1st Bn Highland LI; *m* 23 April 1851 Georgina Anne (*d* 15 April 1887), widow of F Garden Campbell of Troup and Glenlyon and est dau of William P Brigstocke, MP, of Birdcombe Court, Somerset, and *dsp* 28 June 1888

6c George Augustus Frederick, of West Hall; *b* 6 May 1826; Colonial Sec Qld; *d* unm 22 Jan 1876

1c Mary Frances; *m* 17 Aug 1830 Patrick Boyle (*see* GLASGOW, E) and *d* 15 Sept 1880

1b Jean; *m* Alexander Gordon Davidson, 2nd s of Gordon of Gight

2b Mary; *m* Sir Ernest Gordon, Bt, of Park (*see* 1835 edn) and *d* 24 Oct 1824

3b Margaret; *m* 16 Sept 1785 Sir Robert Burnett, 7th Bt, of Leys (*see* 1970 edn), and *d* 18 March 1849, leaving issue

4 Thomas; MD, Physician-in-Ordinary to the Sovereign in Scotland

5 Sir DAVID DALRYMPLE, 1st Bt (NS), so *cr* 8 May 1700, of Hailes, Haddingtonshire; advocate 1688, MP (S Parl) Culross 1697–1707 and (GB Parl) 1707–08 and Haddington 1708–21, Commr Union of E and S Parls 1707, Queen's Advocate Scotland 1709–20, Auditor Exchequer 1720–21; *m* 4 April 1691 Janet (*d* 26 Dec 1726), dau of Sir James Rochead of Inverleith and widow of Alexander Murray of Melgund, and *d* 3 Dec 1721, having had, with other issue:

(1) Sir JAMES DALRYMPLE, 2nd Bt, of Hailes; *b* 24 July 1692; MP Haddington 1722–34, Auditor Exchequer Scotland; *m c* 17 Dec 1725 Lady Christian Hamilton, dau of 6th Earl of Haddington (*qv*), and *d* 24 Feb 1751, having had, with 12 other children:

1a Sir DAVID DALRYMPLE, 3rd Bt, of Hailes; *b* 28 Oct 1726; LLD Edin, advocate 1748, Ld of Session as Lord Hailes 1766, a Ld Justiciary 1776; *m* 1st 12 Nov 1763 Anne (*d* 18 May 1768), dau of George Broun, Ld of Session as Lord Colstoun, and had:

1b Christian, of Hailes; *d* unm 9 Jan 1838

1a (cont.) Sir DAVID *m* 2nd 20 March 1770 Helen (*d* 10 Nov 1810), dau of Sir James Fergusson, 2nd Bt (*qv*), and *d* 29 Nov 1792

2a James; Lt-Col Roy Scots Regt; *m* 28 Sept 1773 Elizabeth, dau of Charles St Clair of Herdmanstoun (*see* SINCLAIR, L) and *dsp* 21 Nov 1791

3a Hugh; Capt RN; *m* 2 May 1754 Helen, dau of 5th Earl of Wemyss (*see* WEMYSS and MARCH, E), and *dsp* 11 Dec 1784

4a John; Ld Provost Edinburgh; *m* 28 June 1774 Anne Young, dau of Walter Pringle, of St Kitts, and *d* 8 Aug 1779, leaving, with a dau:

1b Sir JAMES DALRYMPLE, 4th Bt; *d* unm Dec 1800

2b Sir JOHN DALRYMPLE, 5th and last Bt; Col; *m* 28 Dec 1807 Mary, dau of Edward Rushworth, of Farringford Hill, IOW, and *dsp* 17 Oct 1829, when the btcy expired

(2) Hugh DALRYMPLE later DALRYMPLE-MURRAY-KYNYNMOUND of Melgund and Kynynmound; *d* 1741, leaving:

1a Agnes; *m* Sir Gilbert Elliot, 3rd Bt, and had issue (*see* MINTO, E)

(1) Janet; *m* 1st Sir John Baird, 2nd Bt, of Newbyth, of the Feb 1679/80 *cr* (*dsp* Sept 1745; *see* BAIRD, of Saughton Hall); *m* 2nd Gen Hon James St Clair of Dysart (*see* SINCLAIR, L) and *dsp* 8 Jan 1766

The 8th EARL OF STAIR's bro,

NORTH HAMILTON DALRYMPLE, **9th Earl of Stair**; *b* 1776; *m* 1st 27 May 1817 Margaret (*d* 22 April 1828), dau of James Penny, of Arrad, Lancs, and had, with a dau (*d* unm):

1 JOHN HAMILTON, **10th Earl**

1 Anne; *m* 22 May 1845 Sir John Dick-Lauder, 8th Bt (*qv*), and *d* 10 Aug 1919, leaving issue

2 Agnes; *m* 4 April 1848 John More Nisbett, of Cairnhill, Lanarks (*d* 29 Jan 1904), and *d* 17 July 1900, leaving issue

3 Margaret Penny; *m* 27 April 1859 Allan Alexander Maconochie Welwood, LLD (*d* 29 May 1885), of Meadowbank and Garvock, est s of Alexander M Welwood, Memb Court of Session as Lord Meadowbank, and *d* 1888

The **9th Earl** *m* 2nd 23 March 1831 Martha Willet (*d* 5 June 1869), dau of Col George Dalrymple, and *d* 9 Nov 1864, having by her had:

2 George Grey, of Elliston, St Boswell's, DL (Lanarks); *b* 22 May 1832; Lt Scots Gds; *m* 10 Nov 1853 Ellinor Alice (*d* 11 May 1903), dau of 9th Lord Napier and Ettrick (*qv*), and *d* 30 Nov 1900, leaving, with another s (*d* an infant):

(1) George North; *b* 14 Feb 1856; *m* 2 Aug 1894 Margaret Jane (*d* 25 Oct 1934), dau of David Vannett, and *d* Dec 1912, leaving, with another s (*d* unm):

1a Walter Grey North Hamilton; *b* 17 June 1896; Maj King's Own Hus, WWs I (despatches) and II; *m* 17 June 1929 (*divorce* 1945) Melisande Germaine Violet Craigie (*d* 28 April 1969), dau of Robert G Hunter, of London, and *d* 24 Dec 1969, leaving:

1b *Dawn Mary Kathleen; *b* 9 Jan 1930; *m* 12 April 1956 *Peter Humphrey Methuen, er s of Lt-Col Lionel Methuen, OBE, MC, and has:

1c *Piers Harry North; *b* 14 Sept 1966

(2) Walter Francis; *b* 27 July 1857; *m* 9 Jan 1886 Agnes Raney (*d* 1925), dau of William Charles Owen, and *d* 11 Jan 1892, leaving:

1a Donald Francis Napier; *b* 20 Nov 1888; *m* 1st (*divorce* 1913) Muriel M M Alger; *m* 2nd 23 June 1913 Blanche Annie Elphinstone (*d* 1952), dau of Sir John Humphreys, JP, DL, and *d* 1947

2a Basil Walter; *b* 26 Jan 1891; *m* 1st 17 Jan 1920 (*divorce* 1925) Aileen Eugenie, only dau of Maj Charles May Hayes-Newington, and had:

1b *Elizabeth Mary Wetherall [Mrs Elizabeth Phillips, 11 Rylston Road, Eastbourne, Sussex]; *b* 31 Oct 1920; Jr Cdr ATS WW II; *m* 4 Oct 1945 (*divorce* 1954) Sub-Lt Anthony Edward Home Phillips, RNVR, only s of Sir Herbert Phillips, KCMG, OBE, and has:

1c *Anthony Jeremy Herbert Home; *b* 1947

2a (cont.) Basil Dalrymple *m* 2nd 1930 Erica Isolde (*d* 1977), dau of Lt-Col P N G Reade, RA, and *d* 1977

1a Zelda Raney; *b* 18 Oct 1886; *m* 14 Jan 1913 Capt James Geoffrey Penrose Ingham, DSO, RN (*d* 11 Sept 1958), s of Judge Robert Wood Ingham, and *d* 17 Feb 1966, leaving issue

(1) Mary Adelaide Wilhelmina Elizabeth; *b* 25 Dec 1858; *d* unm 22 April 1943

The 9th EARL's est s,

JOHN HAMILTON DALRYMPLE, **10th Earl of Stair**, KT, JP and DL (Lanarks); *b* 1 April 1819; Capt Scots Gds; MP Wigtownshire 1841–56, Ld Lt Wigtownshire and Ayrshire, Capt Roy Co Archers, HC Gen Assembly Church Scotland 1869–71, Chllr Glasgow U, LLD; *m* 9 Dec 1846 Louisa Jane Henrietta Emily de Franquetot (*d* 30 June 1896), est dau of Augustin Louis Joseph Casimir Gustave, Duke de Coigny, by Henrietta Dundas Dalrymple Hamilton, and *d* 3 Dec 1903, having had, with three daus (*d* unm):

1 JOHN HEW NORTH GUSTAVE HENRY HAMILTON, **11th Earl**

2 North de Coigny DALRYMPLE later DALRYMPLE-HAMILTON (roy licence 1896), of Bargany, Dailly, Ayrshire, MVO, JP (Ayrshire and Wigtownshire), DL (Ayrshire); *b* 31 Oct 1853; Brevet Col cmdg 3rd Bn Scots Gds; *m* 7 Sept 1880 Marcia Kathleen Anne (*d* 1 July 1907), dau of Hon Sir Adolphus Frederick Octavius Liddell, KCB (*see* RAVENSWORTH, B), and *d* 4 Nov 1906, having had:

(1) North Victor Cecil (Sir), KCVO (1952, CVO 1937), CB (1949), JP (Ayrshire); *b* 19 March 1883 (HRH PRINCESS CHRISTIAN OF DENMARK stood sponsor); *educ* Eton and RMC Sandhurst; Maj and Brevet Lt-Col Scots Gds WW I; V-Lt Ayrshire, chm Ayrshire TA&AFA, Ensign and Adj Roy Co Archers; *m* 27 April 1910 Lady Marjorie Alice Coke (*d* 24 Dec 1946), er dau of 3rd Earl of Leicester (*qv*), and *dsp* 16 Feb 1919

(2) Frederick Hew George of Bargany (Sir), KCB (1945); *b* 27 March 1890 (HM GEORGE V stood sponsor); served RN WW I, cmded 4th Destroyer Flotilla Mediterranean Fleet 1933–36, RNC Dartmouth 1936–39, HMS *Rodney* 1939–41 (despatches), Adml cmdg Iceland 1941–42, Naval Sec to 1st Ld Admlty 1942–44, 2i/c Home Fleet 1944–45 (despatches), V-Adml Malta and Flag Offr Cent Mediterranean 1945–46, Flag Offr Scotland and NI 1946–48, Adml Br Jt-Servs Mission Washington, DC, 1948–50, Lt Roy Co Archers; *m* 28 Sept 1918 Gwendolen (*d* 8 Nov 1974), 3rd dau of Sir Cuthbert Edgar Peek, 2nd Bt (*qv*), and *d* 26 Dec 1974, leaving:

1a +North Edward Frederick, CVO (1961, MVO 1954), MBE (1953), DSC (1943), DL (Ayrshire 1973) [Capt North Dalrymple-Hamilton of Bargany CVO MBE DSC DL RN, Lovestone House, Bargany, Ayrshire KA26 9RF]; *b* 17 Feb 1922 (HRH THE DUKE OF WINDSOR stood sponsor); *educ* Eton; Capt RN, WW II, Korea 1952–53, HMS *Birmingham* and SS *Gothic* Roy Cwlth Tour 1953–54, Exec Offr HM Yacht *Britannia* 1958–60, cmded 17th Frigate Sqdn 1963–64, Dir Naval Sigs MOD 1965–66, Dir Weapon Equipment Surface MOD 1967–69, ret 1970, Lt Roy Co Archers; *m* 1st 23 July 1949 Hon Mary Helen Colville (*d* 26 Oct 1981), er dau of 1st Baron Clydesmuir (*qv*); *m* 2nd 1983 *Geraldine Inez Antoinette, dau of Maj Frank Harding and widow of Maj Rowland Beech, MC, and has by his 1st w:

1b +(North) John Frederick Dalrymple-Hamilton [John Dalrymple-Hamilton Esq. Houdston, Girvan, Ayrshire KA26 9PH]; *b* 7 May 1950; *educ* Eton and Aberdeen U; Page of Honour to HM QUEEN ELIZABETH THE QUEEN MOTHER 1964–66; *m* 1980 *Sally-Anne, dau of Robert Boothby How, of St Andrews, Fife, and has:

1c +Hew North Robert; *b* 1981

2c *Edward; *b* 1986

1c *Catherine Mary Anne; *b* 1982

2b +James Hew Ronald; *b* 4 Dec 1955; *educ* Eton; *m* 1986 *Pippa, only dau of Maj David Metcalfe, of Minchinhampton, Glos, and has:

1c +Frederick David George; *b* 1990

2c +Jack Louis Robert; *b* 1994

1c *Clementine Mary; *b* 1989

1a *Christian Margaret, MBE (1989), DL (Wigtownshire) [Miss Christian Dalrymple-Hamilton MBE, Cladyhouse, Cairnryan, Stranraer, Wigtownshire DG9 8OX]; *b* 20 Sept 1919

2a *Graeme Elizabeth [Mrs Alexander Laing, Relugas House, Forres, Moray IV36 OQL]; *b* 29 Oct 1926 (HM QUEEN ELIZABETH THE QUEEN MOTHER stood sponsor); *m* 3 June 1948 Alexander Grant Laing, MC (*d* 1988), 2nd s of Hector Stanley Laing, of E Lothian, by Margaret Norris, dau of Sir Alexander Grant, 1st Bt, and has:

1b *Alasdair North Grant [Alasdair Laing Esq, Logie House, Forres, Moray IV36 OQN]; *b* 30 Dec 1949; *educ* Eton; Lt Scots Gds; *m* 2 Feb 1979 *Hon Lucy Ann Anthea Low, yr dau of 1st Baron Aldington (*qv*), and has:

1c *Alexander William Grant; *b* 7 March 1982

2c *Frederick Charles Grant; *b* 17 Nov 1985

1c *Emma Mary Grant; *b* 19 April 1980

2b *Fergus Hew Grant [Fergus Laing Esq, Craggan, Grantown on Spey, Morayshire]; *b* 22 Feb 1951; *educ* Gordonstoun; *m* 28 July 1979 *Priscilla Mary, yr dau of Michael Keith (*see* MANN, Bt), and has:

1c *Michael Hew Grant; *b* 1 March 1984

1c *Iona Rose Grant; *b* 23 Jan 1982

2c *Henrietta Mary Grant; *b* 7 May 1986

3c *Elizabeth Ruby Grant; *b* 8 June 1988

1b *Carolyn Margaret Grant [Mrs James Balfour, Wintershill Hall, Durley, nr Southampton SO3 2AL]; *b* 26 July 1952; *m* 4 April 1981 *Capt James Melville John Balfour, RGJ, and has:

1c *Edward James Melville; *b* 9 March 1982

1c *Laura Elizabeth; *b* 31 March 1984

2c *Margaret Carolyn; *b* 10 Sept 1985

2b *Fiona Mary Grant [The Hon Mrs Jonathan Warrender, Minuntion, Pinmore, Girvan, Ayrshire KA26 0LA]; *b* 5 Sept 1954; *m* 1979 *Hon Jonathan James Warrender, yr s of 2nd Baron Bruntisfield (*qv*), and has issue

(1) Victoria Alexandra; *b* 5 Nov 1886 (TM QUEENs VICTORIA and ALEXANDRA stood sponsors); *d* 5 June 1890

3 Hew Hamilton (Sir), KCVO (1932), JP, DL (Wigtownshire); *b* 27 Sept 1857; Hon Lt-Col 3rd Bn Roy Scots Fus; MP Wigtownshire 1915–18, Chm Tstees Nat Galleries Scotland, V-Chm Nat Library Scotland, Capt Roy Co Archers; *d* unm 11 July 1945

4 Robert McGill (Rev); *b* 11 Oct 1862; MA Oxon; Vicar Sneinton, Notts, 1902–17; *d* unm 9 April 1938

1 Jane Georgina; *m* 10 March 1800 Sir Arthur Pencarves Vivian, KCB (*see* SWANSEA, B), and *d* 8 June 1914, leaving issue

2 Anne Henrietta; *m* 19 Nov 1881, as his 1st w, Maj-Gen William Vesey Brownlow, CB (*d* 15 March 1928), only surv s of William Brownlow, JP, DL, of Knapton House, Queen's Co (now Co Laois), and *dsp* 18 Feb 1898

The 10th EARL's est s,

JOHN HEW NORTH GUSTAVE HENRY HAMILTON DALRYMPLE, **11th Earl of Stair**, JP (Wigtownshire, Ayrshire and City of Glasgow); *b* 12 June 1848; BA Cantab; Maj RHG, Maj and Hon Lt-Col Ayrshire Imp Yeo; Provost Stranraer 1900, Ld HC Church Scotland 1910, Brig Roy Co Archers; *m* 10 April 1878 (*divorce* 1905) Susan Harriet (*d* 9 Feb 1946), dau of Sir James Grant-Suttie, 6th Bt (*qv*), and *d* 2 Dec 1914; having had:

1 JOHN JAMES, **12th Earl**

1 Beatrice Susan; *m* 1 June 1908 (*divorce* 1922) 16th Earl of Eglinton and (4th Earl of) Winton (*qv*) and *d* 10 May 1962, leaving issue

2 Marjorie Louise, OBE (1920); DGStJ 1920, headmistress Abbots Hill Sch, Hemel Hempstead; *d* unm 10 June 1971

The 11th EARL's only s,

JOHN JAMES DALRYMPLE, **12th Earl of Stair**, KT (1937), DSO (1919), JP, DL (Wigtownshire), DL (Midlothian 1931); *b* 1 Feb 1879; *educ* Harrow and RMC Sandhurst; Hon Col 5th Bn KOSB (TA), Hon A/Cdre City of Edinburgh (B) Sqdn AAF 1930–38, Lt-Col Scots Gds (Hon Col 1936), Boer War 1900–02 and WW I (despatches, prisoner); MP (C) Wigtownshire 1906–14, Ld Lt Wigtownshire 1935–61, Convener Wigtown CC, chm Ag Ctee Wigtownshire, Capt-Gen Roy Co Archers, Ld HC Gen Assembly Church Scotland 1927–29; *m* 20 Oct 1904 Violet Evelyn, JP Wigtownshire (*d* 22 Feb 1968), only dau of Col Frederick Henry Harford, Scots Gds, of Down Place, Windsor, and *d* 4 Nov 1961, having had:

1 JOHN AYMER, **13th Earl**

2 +Hew North, TD, DL (Ayrshire 1955) [The Hon Hew Dalrymple TD DL, Castlehill, Ballantrae, Girvan, Ayrshire KA26 0LA]; *b* 27 April 1910; *educ* Eton; Capt 2nd Bn Black Watch (TA) WW II N Africa and Burma (twice wounded); memb Roy Co Archers; *m* 1st 20 June 1938 Mildred Helen (*d* 1980), dau of Hon Thomas Henry Frederick Egerton (*see* SUTHERLAND, D) and formerly w of 4th Baron Oranmore and Browne (*qv*), and has:

(1) +Robert Hew; *b* 10 Nov 1946 (HRH THE DUCHESS OF GLOUCESTER stood sponsor); *educ* Fettes; *m* 22 April 1976 *Caroline Anne, yr dau of (Charles) Patrick Maule Hunting, CBE, TD, FCA, of The Old House, Birch Grove, Sussex, and has:

1a +Hamish Hew; *b* 1979

2a +Alastair North; *b* 1982

2 (cont.) The Hon Hew Dalrymple *m* 2nd 20 Jan 1983 *Helen M W Phillips

3 Andrew William Henry; *b* 10 May 1914; *educ* Eton and Peterhouse Cambridge (MA, BSc); *k* plane crash 25 Dec 1945

4 +Colin James, JP, DL (Midlothian 1961) [Maj The Hon Colin Dalrymple JP DL, Oxenfoord Mains, Dalkeith, Midlothian]; *b* 19 Feb 1920; *educ* Eton and Trin Coll Cambridge (BA 1941); Maj Scots Gds WW II Italy 1944–45, memb Roy Co Archers; *m* 1st 25 Aug 1945 (*divorce* 1954) Pamela Mary, formerly BRCS Welfare Offr, only dau of Maj John Lamplugh Wickham, CVO, of Basingstoke, and has:

(1) *Caroline Mary; *b* 24 July 1946; *m* 31 April 1973 *Michael Scott, ARICS, of Troloss, Elvanfoot, Lanarks, s of M M Scott, of Cakemuir Castle, Tynehead, Midlothian, and has:

1a *Alexander James Scott; *b* 1975

1a *Camilla Rose Scott; *b* 1978

4 (cont.) Maj The Hon Colin Dalrymple *m* 2nd 12 March 1956 *Fiona Jane, only dau of Adml Sir Ralph Alan Bevan Edwards, KCB, CBE, of Empshott, Hants, and by her has:

(1) +Andrew David; *b* 10 Oct 1959; *m* 1987 *Bryony, dau of W A Major, of Shilston Barton, Modbury, S Devon, and has:

1a +Hew William James; *b* 1993

1a *Louisa Alice Clare; *b* 1990

(2) *Serena Jane; *b* 20 Oct 1957; *m* 1979 *Maj James Peter Greenwell and has issue (*see* GREENWELL, Bt)

(3) *Rose Joanna; *b* 6 May 1962; *m* 1987 *Charles Leighton Dudgeon, s of John Dudgeon, of W Lothian, and has:

1a *Edward John Dudgeon; *b* 1993

1a *Sara Rose Dudgeon; *b* 1991

1 *Jean Margaret, DCVO (1969, CVO 1957); *b* 15 Aug 1905; Woman Bedchamber to HM QUEEN ELIZABETH THE QUEEN MOTHER 1946–; *m* 10 Oct 1931 Lt-Col Arthur Niall Talbot Rankin (*see* RANKIN, Bt) and has issue

2 Marion Violet ('Snowy'), JP (Pembs 1965); *b* 1 Feb 1908; Order of Mercy, FRAgS; *m* 10 June 1930 Maj Hon (Richard) Hanning Phillips, MBE, Welsh Gds, 2nd s of 1st Baron Milford (*qv*), and *d* 18 June 1995, leaving issue

The 12th EARL's est s,

JOHN AYMER DALRYMPLE, **13th Earl of Stair**, KCVO (1978, CVO 1964), MBE (1941), JP (1936), DL (Wilts 1953); *b* 9 Oct 1906; *educ* Eton and RMC Sandhurst; Col Scots Gds, Bde Maj 3rd (London) Inf Bde and Regtl Adj Scots Gds 1935–38, WW II Middle East 1941 Bde Maj 16th Inf Bde (despatches), Lt-Col cmdg 1st Bn Scots Gds 1942–43, AMA HQ AAI 1944, cmdg Trg Bn Scots Gds 1945, cmdg 2nd Bn Scots Gds 1946–49, Regtl Lt-Col cmdg Scots Gds 1949–52, ret 1953; Ld Lt Wigtown 1961–81, Capt-Gen Roy Co Archers and Gold Stick Scotland 1973–88; *m* 14 Jan 1960 *Davina Katherine, DL, MFH Wigtownshire, only dau of Hon Sir David Bowes Lyon, KCVO, JP, DL (*see* STRATHMORE and KINGHORNE, E), and *d* 26 Feb 1996, leaving:

1 JOHN DAVID JAMES DALRYMPLE, **14th and present Earl of Stair**

2 +(DAVID) HEW; *b* 30 March 1963; heir presumptive; *educ* Harrow

3 +Michael Colin; *b* 1 April 1965; *educ* Harrow; *m* 1991 *Harriet Lucy, er dau of Lt-Cdr Jocelyn Charles Roden Buxton, VRD, RNVR (*see* BUXTON, Bt), and has:

(1) +William Hew; *b* 1992

(2) +Angus; *b* 1993

(3) +Peter; *b* 26 April 1996

STALLARD

Creation: B. (LP, UK) 1983.

THE BARON STALLARD, of St Pancras, London Borough of Camden (Albert William Stallard) [The Rt Hon The Lord Stallard, Flat 2, 2 Belmont Street, London NW1 8HH]; *b* 5 Nov 1921; *educ* Low Waters and Hamilton Acad Scotland; engr 1937–65, tech trng offr 1965–70, memb: St Pancras Cncl 1953–59 (Alderman 1962–65), Camden Cncl 1965–70 (Alderman 1971), MP (Lab) St Pancras N 1970–74, Camden 1974–83, PPS to: Min Ag 1973–74, Min Housing and Construction 1974–76, Assist Govt Whip 1976–78, Ld Commr Treasury 1978–79; *m* 1944 *Julie, dau of William Cornelius Murphy, and has:

1 *Richard; *b* 1945; *educ* Richard Acland Sch London; *m* 1969 *Carol, dau of William Packman, and has issue

2 *Brenda; *b* 1949; *m* 1971 (*divorce* 1987) Colin Hills and has issue

Lineage: FREDERICK STALLARD; had:

ALBERT WILLIAM STALLARD, *cr* a **Baron**

STAMER

Arms: Quarterly, 1st and 4th, gu. on a fess indented arg. a lion passant az., armed and langued gu.; 2nd and 3rd, az. a civic cap between three castles inflamed ppr.; over all a cross erm., charged with the sword of state of the City of Dublin per pale ppr.

Crest: A stag's head erased ppr., gorged with a mural crown or.

Mottoes: 1 (over crest) Jubilee, 2 (under shield) *Virtute et valore* ('By valour and strength'). **Creation:** Bt. (UK) 15 Dec 1809.

SIR (LOVELACE) ANTHONY STAMER, 5TH BT [Sir Anthony Stamer Bt, 5 Windrush Court, 175 The Hill, Burford, Oxon OX18 4RE]; *b* 28 Feb 1917; *s* f 1941; *educ* Harrow, Trin Coll Cambridge (BA 1947, MA 1963) and RAC Cirencester; WW II: RAF 1939–41, Offr ATA 1941–45, AMIMI 1963, exec dir: Bentley Drivers Club 1969–73, Bugatti and Ferrari Owners Club 1973–75 (Hon Treas 1975–81); *m* 1st 1 Jan 1948 (*divorce* 1953) Stella Huguette, only dau of Paul Burnell Binnie, of Brussels, and Mrs Arthur Lascelles Hoyle, of Mouans-Sartoux, AM, France; *m* 2nd 15 Jan 1955 (*divorce* 1959) Margaret Lucy, dau of Maj T A Belben, IA, and

Mrs S M Stewart, of Zimbabwe; *m* 3rd 23 June 1960 (*divorce* 1968) Marjorie June, dau of T C Noakes, of Cape Province, S Africa; *m* 4th 1983 Mrs Elizabeth Graham Smith (*d* 1992), dau of C J R Magrath and widow of G P H Smith, of Colyton, Devon; *m* 5th 16 April 1997 *Pamela Grace, dau of E A Hawkins, of Solihull, and widow of P B Cheston, and by his 1st w has:

1 +PETER TOMLINSON; *b* 19 Nov 1951; *educ* Malvern and Southampton U; late S/Ldr RAF; *m* 1979 (*divorce* 1989) Dinah Louise, dau of Thomas Selwyn Berry, and has:

(1) +William Peter Alexander; *b* 20 Sept 1983

(1) *Antonia Louise; *b* 1981

1 *Lucinda Jane; *b* 14 Dec 1949

Lineage: THOMAS STAMER, of Ennis, Co Clare; *m* Catherine, dau of Paul Lovelace, of Ballybride, Co Roscommon, and *d* 1783, leaving, with an er s (Henry, *m* the dau and heiress of John Vincent, of Curryhills, Co Kildare, and was killed at Prosperous, Co Kildare, in the 1798 Uprising):

Sir William Stamer, 1st Bt (UK), so *cr* 15 Dec 1809; *b* 1765; Sheriff , Alderman and twice Ld Mayor Dublin (2nd time 1819), cmded a Dublin Yeo regt 1798–1831; *m* 25 Sept 1791 Martha (*d* 22 Oct 1837), dau of John Rawlins, of Finglas, Dublin, and had, with other issue:

1 LOVELACE (Sir), **2nd Bt**

2 William (Rev); *b* 3 Aug 1803; DD, Rector and Patron St Saviour's, Bath; *m* 1st 11 Nov 1826 Anne Margaret (*d* 13 April 1833), 2nd dau of Col Jeremy Lock, Bombay Service, and had, with another dau (*d* young):

(1) Charlotte Matilda; *m* 1st 12 July 1851 Richard Appleyard, barrister (*d* 29 May 1876); *m* 2nd 24 July 1877 Rev George Musgrave (*d* 1885), of Shillington Manor, Beds, and Borden Hall, Kent, and *d* 1893

2 (cont.) Dr William Stamer *m* 2nd 8 July 1841 Eleanor Louisa (*d* 16 Oct 1886), dau of R Houlditch, of Edenham Ho, Hampstead, and *d* 20 Nov 1866

1 Lucinda; *m* Nov 1818 Sir William Smith, Capt RHA, and *d* 28 Oct 1882, leaving issue. He *d* 3 April 1835

2 Louisa; *m* John Jackson, of Armagh, and had issue

3 Caroline; *m* 12 Nov 1830 Horatio Frederic Halpin, HEICS (*d* 1840), and had issue

4 Elizabeth; *m* 1840 William Edward Hughes (*dsp*), of Johnstown Ho, Co Meath, and *d* 15 Jan 1886

The 1st Bt *d* 14 Jan 1838; his er s,

Sir Lovelace Stamer, 2nd Bt; *b* 29 April 1797; RN (wounded Battle of Lissa, present capture of Graon, medal and two clasps), Capt 4th Dragoon Gds; *m* 25 Sept 1828 Caroline (*d* 10 Sept 1872), only dau of John Tomlinson, of Cliff Ville, Staffs, and *d* 5 March 1860, leaving, with a yr s (William John Alexander, *b* 19 July 1833, *d* 10 Feb 1908):

Rt Rev Sir Lovelace Tomlinson Stamer, 3rd Bt; *b* 18 Oct 1829; *educ* Rugby and Trin Coll Cambridge (MA, DD); Bp Suffragan Shrewsbury 1885–1905; *m* 16 April 1857 Ellen Isabel (*d* 8 Dec 1933), dau of Joseph Dent, of Ribston Hall, Yorks, and had:

1 LOVELACE (Sir), **4th Bt**

2 Frederick Charles (Rev); *b* 28 Aug 1860; *educ* Harrow and Trin Coll Cambridge (BA 1882, MA 1886); Rector Berrington Salop 1920–24 and Lathbury 1936–38; *m* 1st 1 July 1891 Ethel Emma (*d* 28 June 1931), dau of Alexander Donovan, of Framfield Place, Sussex, and had:

(1) William Donovan, CB (1948), CBE (1941), DSO (1938), MC (1918); *b* 14 June 1895; *educ* Rugby and RMC Sandhurst; Maj-Gen N Staffs Regt, WW I (wounded twice, despatches), Palestine 1937 and 1938 (despatches) and WW II (despatches), GOC Sudan and Eritrea 1945–48, Col N Staffs Regt 1945, US Legn Merit; *d* unm 21 Sept 1963

(2) Hugo Frederick Barnabas; *b* 25 Feb 1900; *educ* Haileybury; Capt Canadian Army, WWs I and II; *m* 10 June 1925 Kathleen Florence Louise, dau of James Whittome, of Duncan, Vancouver, and *d* 28 Oct 1980, leaving:

1a +James Alexander Donovan; *b* 1 Aug 1928; *m* June 1951 *Patricia Louise, dau of A J McNeil, of Duncan, and has:

1b +Gregory McNeil; *b* 9 March 1956

2a +Brian Lovelace; *b* 15 May 1939; *m* 6 May 1961 *Lillian, dau of John Kopec, of Kitchener, Ontario, and has:

1b *Brenda Lea; *b* 12 Aug 1962

2b *Carol Anne; *b* 15 Dec 1964

1a *Marion Joan [Mrs John Fox, 1147 Williams Rd, Richmond, Vancouver, BC, Canada]; *b* 28 May 1926; *m* Aug 1947 *John Ernest Fox, s of E S Fox, of Duncan, and has:

1b *John Patrick; *b* 24 June 1950

2b *Geoffrey Ernest; *b* 28 May 1951

1b *Kathleen Jennifer; *b* 26 Jan.1948

2b *Diane Joan; *b* 24 June 1950

2a *Kathleen Charmian; *b* Oct 1936

3a *Claire Judith; *b* Nov 1937; *m* Dec 1960 *John Harold Reginald Lee, s of S T Lee, of Qualicum Beach, BC, and has:

1b *Susan Anne; *b* 29 June 1961

2b *Jennifer Louise; *b* 29 Oct 1962

3b *Pamela Jane; *b* 10 Feb 1968

(1) Gladys Mabel; *b* 21 June 1892; *m* 29 July 1924 Maj Anthony James Bagot Chester, MC (*see* BAGOT, B), and had issue

(2) Marion Ethel; *b* 7 Aug 1893; *m* 19 July 1921 Geoffrey Dent, MC (*d* 3 Aug 1978), s of Francis Dent, of Hatfield, Loughton, Essex, and *d* 27 Sept 1971, leaving issue

2 (cont.) The Rev Frederick Stamer *m* 2nd 25 Oct 1932 Elizabeth Esther, widow of R J Croft, of Rotherfield, Sussex, and dau of J W Barnes, and *d* 14 May 1952

3 William Edward; *b* 25 Jan 1864; *m* 2 June 1894 Evelyn Cicely (*d* 12 March 1952), est dau of Edward Herbert Wood, of Newbold Revel, Warwicks, and *d* 16 Dec 1945, leaving:

(1) William Arthur John; *b* 14 July 1899; *educ* Eton; Capt Seaforth Highrs (Canada) WW II; *m* 1935 *Helen, dau of Dr Wilfrid Anthony Legh Jackson, of Bearwood, Lavington, BC, and *d* 1991, leaving:

1a +William John Derek [William Stamer Esq, PO Box 247, Barrière, BC, Canada V0E 1E0]; *b* 23 July 1940; *m* 1st 1961 (*divorce* 1964) Marcelle Blanche, dau of David Howrie, of Vernon, BC, and has:

1b +Rodney William; *b* 1961

1a (cont.) William Stamer *m* 2nd 25 Nov 1967 *Valerie Margaret, dau of Roy MacQuarrie, of Revelstoke, BC, and by her has:

2b *John Edward; *b* 1962; *m* 1990 *Carleen Gail, dau of Gordon Zerr, of Barrière, BC, and has:

1c *Brittany Marie; *b* 1993

2c *Nicole Alexandra; *b* 1994

3b *Cory Wayne; *b* 1963; *m* 1994 *Barbara Lynn, dau of Barry Ross, of Barrière, BC, and has:

1c *Tiana Leah; *b* 1995

2c *Trista Lynn; *b* 1998

4b William John David; *b* 20 Feb 1970; *d* 1989

1b *Patricia Leah; *b* 20 Feb 1970

1a *Judith Cecily [Mrs Arthur Jaik, 6909 Palfrey Dve, Vernon, BC, Canada VIB 1A7]; *b* 3 Jan 1939; *m* 1st 22 March 1957 (*divorce* 1960) Glen Fletcher, of Lavington, BC, and has:

1b *Rhondda Jane; *b* 1957; *m* 1981 *Christopher Oostlander and has:

1c *Adam Nickolas; *b* 1983

2c *Ryan Jeffrey; *b* 1985

1a (cont.) Mrs Judith Fletcher *m* 2nd Sept 1964 *Arthur G Jaik and by him has:

2b *Catherine Louise; *b* 1965; *m* 1994 *Paul Chabot and has:

1c *Jennifer Rose; *b* 1989

2c *Saleena Irene; *b* 1993

3c *Caitlyn Christine; *b* 1995

3b *Susan Christine; *b* 26 May 1968

2a *Rosemary Shane [Mrs Ronald Haywood, 1191 Crestwood Dve, Kamloops, BC V2C 5G8, Canada]; *b* 15 Oct 1943; *m* May 1964 *Ronald Edwin Haywood and has:

1b *John Christopher [John Haywood Esq, 321 Stevens Dve, Kamloops, BC V2H 1L5, Canada]; *b* 8 April 1968; *m* 6 Sept 1997 *Elaine Klein, dau of Doug Chambers, of Kamloops, and has:

1c *Julia Crystal Gail; *b* 11 Feb 1988

2c *Jillene Ann; *b* 4 Jan 1998

1b *Alison Jane [Mrs Brent Miller, 1953 Gardiner Rd, Kamloops, BC V2C 6V8, Canada] ; *b* 1 Dec 1966; *m* 1st 1989 (*divorce* 1994) Clayton Jay Paull; *m* 2nd 16 April 1995 *Brent Ernest Miller and by him has:

1c *Lauren Elizabeth; *b* 25 Sept 1995

2c *Sarah Kathleen; *b* 9 Aug 1997

4 Reginald Dent (Rev); *b* 2 Sept 1865; *educ* Rugby and Pembroke Coll Cambridge (BA 1887, MA 1894); Vicar Prees Salop 1913–29; *d* unm 4 Feb 1951

5 Arthur Cowie, CBE (1920); *b* 7 March 1869; MIME, MILE, Assist Ch Mech Engr LNER; *m* 18 July 1900 Everilda Mary (*d* 25 June 1954), dau of George Arthur Thompson, of Terrington Hall, York, and *d* 14 Feb 1944, having had:

(1) Joan Eleanor; *b* 26 Aug 1909; *m* 25 April 1933 William Howard Lawson (*see* HOWARD-LAWSON, Bt) and *d* 27 April 1989, leaving issue

1 Ellen Caroline; *b* 29 Jan 1858; *d* unm 27 March 1946

2 Mabel Frederica; *b* 12 July 1862; *m* 12 Sept 1895 Rev Preb Arthur Paice, Vicar St Mary, Lichfield, and *d* 16 April 1918. He *d* 3 July 1923

3 Evelyn Lucinda; *b* 9 April 1871; *d* unm 2 May 1958

The 3rd Bt *d* 29 Oct 1908; his est s,

Sir Lovelace Stamer, 4th Bt, JP Staffs and Salop; *b* 4 April 1859; Maj 16th Lancers Boer War, Lt-Col Staffs Yeo WW I (despatches), Adj Staffs and Warwicks Yeo Cav, ADC to Govr of Madras; *m* 29 Sept 1909 (Eva) Mary (*d* 8 June 1974 aged 92), est dau of Robert Charles Otter, of Royston Manor, Clayworth, Notts, and *d* 1 Oct 1941, having had:

1 Sir (LOVELACE) ANTHONY STAMER, **5th and present Bt**

1 Isabel Eva; *b* 11 Oct 1910; *m* 2 April 1936 Middleton Fitch Kemp (*d* 26 June 1989), est s of C W Middleton Kemp, of Copt Hall, Ightham, Kent, and *d* 11 April 1993, leaving:

(1) *Robin Middleton [Robin Kemp Esq, Broad Hayes Farm, Stockland, Devon EX14 9EL]; *b* 25 Jan 1939; *educ* Nautical Coll Pangbourne and RAC Cirencester; *m* 1st 29 July 1964 (*divorce* 1990) Marion Heather, dau of Robert Heather Edgett, of Vancouver; *m* 2nd 1990 *Carole Elizabeth, dau of J B Setter, of Bristol

2 Honora Mary; *b* 8 Feb 1912; *m* 23 July 1938 Lt-Col Derek Gordon Hughes, RE (*d* 13 April 1993), s of Rev Edward Watkin Hughes, Rector Upton St Leonard's, Glos, adopted a dau, and *d* 9 March 1973

STAMP

FIDEI · COMMISSA · TENEO

Arms: Gu. between two garbs or three bezants in bend, each charged with a horse passant sa. **Crest:** Issuant from a mount vert bezantée a demi-horse arg. **Supporters:** On either side a horse arg., resting the interior hind leg on a bezant. **Motto:** *Fidei commissa teneo* ('I hold in trust what is entrusted to me'). **Creation:** B. (UK) 28 June 1938.

THE 4TH BARON STAMP, of Shortlands, Co Kent (Trevor Charles Bosworth Stamp) [The Rt Hon The Lord Stamp, 15 Ceylon Rd, London W14 0PY]; *b* 18 Sept 1935; *s* f 1987; *educ* The Leys Sch Cambridge, Gonville and Caius Coll Cambridge (BA 1956), Yale (MSc 1957) and St Mary's Hosp (MB, BCh, MD 1972); FRCP 1978 London and Edinburgh; Consultant Physician and Dir Dept Bone and Mineral Metabolism Roy Nat Orthopaedic Hosp 1974–, Hon Consultant Physician and Sr Lecturer Middx Hosp and UCL Sch Medicine 1974–; *m* 1st 21 March 1963 (*divorce* 1971) Anne Carolynn, dau of John Kenneth Churchill, of Tunbridge Wells, and Mrs Eric Grey Dudley, of Greystone Cottage, Great Alne, Warwicks, and has:

1 *Catherine Anne Louise; *b* 22 Oct 1963

2 *Emma Caroline; *b* 22 April 1968

The 4th BARON *m* 2nd 18 July 1975 *Carol Anne, dau of Robert Keith Russell, of Lower Bourne, Farnham, Surrey, and by her has:

1 +NICHOLAS CHARLES TREVOR; *b* 27 Feb 1978

3 *Lucinda Jane; *b* 21 April 1976

Lineage: WILLIAM STAMP, of Merton, Surrey; *b* 1817; *m* 15 April 1844 Naomi, dau of Josiah Rees Harris, and *d* 7 July 1875, leaving:

CHARLES STAMP, of Bexley, Kent; *b* 26 Nov 1852; *m* 30 Sept 1875 Clara Jane, dau of Richard Evans, and had:

1 JOSIAH CHARLES, **1st Baron**

2 Charles Alfred; *b* 21 Nov 1890; FCS; *m* 29 Sept 1915 Edith Parsons and *d* 18 Oct 1963, leaving:

(1) *Barry Hartnell; *b* 23 Nov 1921; *educ* London U (BA); *m* 1943 *Norah Clare Rich and has:

  1a *Gavin Mark [Gavin Stamp Esq, 1 Moray Place, Strathbungo, Glasgow G41 2AQ]; *b* 15 March 1948; *educ* Dulwich and Gonville and Caius Coll Cambridge; Lecturer Mackintosh Sch Architecture Glasgow 1990–, architectural writer; Hon FRIAS, Hon FRIBA; *m* 12 Feb 1982 *Alexandra Frances Artley, jnlst, and has:

    1b *Agnes Mary; *b* 4 April 1984

    2b *Cecilia Jane; *b* 2 Feb 1986

  2a *Gerard Christopher; *b* 22 March 1955; *m* 21 Sept 1985 *Jacqui Newman and has:

    1b *Rupert Charles; *b* 11 July 1994

    1b *Eleanor Rose; *b* 1 April 1990

  1a *Jacqueline Clare; *b* 24 Oct 1951; *m* 10 Aug 1974 *David Riley and has:

    1b *Suzanne; *b* 14 Aug 1981

(2) *Walter Rosse; *b* 11 Aug 1925; *educ* London U (BSc); *m* 11 March 1950 *Alice Glanford

3 (Laurence) Dudley (Sir), CBE (1946); *b* 9 March 1898, Prof Social Geography LSE 1948–58 (Prof Emeritus 1958), Pres Internat Geographic Union 1952–56, memb Roy Commn Common Land 1955–58 and Nature Conservancy 1958, Ch Advsr Rural Land Use Min Ag 1942–55, ktd 1965, DLitt, DSc, Hon LLD Clark U 1955, Hon LLD Edinburgh, Hon DSc Nat U Warsaw 1963, Hon DSc Exeter 1965, Hon EkonD Stockholm; *m* 5 May 1923 Else Clara, BA (*d* 30 July 1962), dau of Arthur Unett Rea, of Bude, and *d* 8 Aug 1966, leaving:

(1) *Bryan Unett Dudley [Bryan Stamp Esq, Ebbingford Manor, Bude, Cornwall EX23 8LN]; *b* 13 April 1929; *educ* Marlborough and McGill (BA); late Lt RA, FRGS, dir Geographical Publicns 1955 on; *m* 30 June 1962 *Susan Hargrave, er dau of G Darnley-Smith, CBE, of Dame Lys, Watlington, Oxon, and has:

  1a *Jonathon James Whittington Dudley; *b* 13 Aug 1968

1 Addie Clara

2 Bertha Caroline

CHARLES STAMP *d* 10 June 1935; his est s,

JOSIAH CHARLES STAMP, **1st Baron Stamp**, of Shortlands, Co Kent (UK), so *cr* 28 June 1938, GCB (1935), GBE (1924, KBE 1920, CBE 1918), DL; *b* 21 June 1880; Clerk Inland Revenue 1896, Assist Sec Inland Revenue 1916–19, Br Rep: League Nations Double Taxation Ctee 1923, Dawes Ctee German Fin 1924 and Young Ctee Reparations 1929; memb: Roy Commn Income Tax 1920, NI Fin Arbitration Ctee 1923, Ctee on National Debt 1924, Coal Industry Enquiry 1925, Cncl Duchy Lancaster, Ec Advsy Cncl; Rede Lecturer Cambridge 1926, Lt City London, Dir Bank England, Govt Advsr Ec Co-ordination and Pres: Inter-deptl Ctee Ec Policy, Roy Statistical Soc, IPA 1937, NIESR, Genealogical Soc 1940–41 and Inst Tport; pres and chm LMSR, Charter Mayor Beckenham 1935, Hon Freeman: Beckenham 1936, Blackpool 1936, a Pilgrim Tstee, Col Engr and Rly Staff Corps RE (TA), Hon Col SR 1938, Newmarch Lecturer Statistics London U, Order Astaur 1st Cl Afghanistan, Grand Cross and Star Austrian Order Merit, KGStJ, DSc London, Hon DSc Oxon, Hon ScD Cantab, Hon LLD Edinburgh, Leeds, Dublin, St Andrews, Sydney, McGill, Toronto, W Ontario, Manchester, Harvard, Columbia, Johns Hopkins, North Western, Duke, California, South Western, Syracuse, Washington and Lee, Hon DEcon Lisbon, Hon DLaw Athens, FBA; *m* 17 Oct 1903 Olive Jessie, JP Kent, dau of Alfred Marsh, of Grove Park, and was *k* with his w and est s by enemy action 16 April 1941, leaving:

1 WILFRID CARLYLE, **2nd Baron Stamp**; *b* 28 Oct 1904; *educ* Leys Sch and King's Coll Cambridge (MA); ACA; *m* 10 Dec 1929 Katharine Mary (*d* 1985), er dau of Tom Wickett, of Redruth, and was *k* 16 April 1941, leaving:

(1) *(Nancy) Elizabeth [The Hon Elizabeth Stamp, 11 Harpes Rd, Oxford OX2 7QJ]; *b* 21 June 1931; *educ* St Andrews (MA 1953)

(2) *Veronica [The Hon Mrs McWatters, The Grove, Dundry, Bristol BS18 8JG]; *b* 25 May 1934; MRCS, LRCP 1960; *m* 15 July 1961 *Richard Alfred Hugh McWatters, yr s of Sir Arthur Cecil McWatters, CIE, of Oxford, and has:

  1a *Rupert Charles; *b* 31 July 1967

  1a *Philippa Mary; *b* 26 Feb 1964

  2a *Bridget Penelope; *b* 2 Aug 1965

(3) *Jessica Catherine [The Hon Mrs Dow, 30 Norfolk Farm Rd, Pyrford, Woking, Surrey GU22 8LH]; *b* 21 Sept 1936; *educ* London U (BA 1958); *m* 9 Sept 1961 *John Edward Chalmers Dow, only s of Donald James Dow, of Calcutta and Edinburgh, and has:

  1b *Charlotte Mary; *b* 19 Aug 1963; *m* 1990 *Kevin John Davis, est s of F J Davis, of Worcester Pk, Surrey, and has:

    1c *Emily Jessica Lycett; *b* 1992

    2c *Jemima Lucy Katharine; *b* 1996

  2b *Juliette Elizabeth Chalmers; *b* 23 March 1966; *m* 1995 *Daniel Hugh Chisholm, s of Dr Duncan Chishom (*see* WINDLESHAM, B)

2 TREVOR CHARLES STAMP, **3rd Baron Stamp**, as which deemed to have *s* bro rather than f direct under a Ho Lds decision 30 Sept 1941; *b* 13 Feb 1907; *educ* Leys Sch, Gonville and Caius Coll Cambridge (MA, MD 1936) and St Bart's Hosp (MB, BCh), MRCS Eng, LRCP London 1931, FRCPath 1963, Prof Bacteriology London U Roy Postgrad Med Sch 1947, US Medal Freedom with Silver Palm 1947; *m* 5 April 1932 Frances Dawes (*d* 29 Jan 1998), dau of Charles Henry Bosworth, of Evanston, Ill., and *d* 1987, leaving:

(1) TREVOR CHARLES BOSWORTH STAMP, **4th and present Baron Stamp**

(2) +Josiah Richard [The Hon Josiah Stamp, Flat B, 11 Lymington Rd, London NW6 1HX]; *b* 15 Dec 1943; *educ* Winchester and Queens' Coll Cambridge (BA 1965)

3 (Arthur) Maxwell; *b* 20 Sept 1915; *educ* Leys Sch and Clare Coll Cambridge (BA 1937, MA 1941); barrister Inner Temple 1939, Lt-Col Intell Corps WW II, Advsr Govrs Bank England 1954–57, alternative UK exec dir IMF 1951–52; dir: Philip Hill Higginson & Co 1958–65, De La Rue 1968, chm: Maxwell Stamp Assocs 1968, Maxeast Ltd 1968, Godfrey Bonsack (DFI) 1969, Triplex Hldgs 1963, Hill Samuel 1965; *m* 1st 24 Oct 1938 (*divorce* 1943) Janet Tyler, only dau of B Tyler Bryan, of Beaumont, Tex.; *m* 2nd 28 Jan 1944 *Alice Mary [The Hon Mrs Maxwell Stamp, 1 Holly Oaks, Wormingford, Essex], formerly w of John Hagon and er dau of Walter Richards, of Hereford, and *d* 1984, leaving:

(1) +Anthony Philip Josiah [Anthony Stamp Esq, Bonds Cottage, Wormingford, Essex]; *b* 1 Dec 1947; *educ* Winchester and Jesus Coll Cambridge (BA); *m* 1969 *Rosemary Ann, dau of Hume Boggis-Rolfe, CB, CBE, and adopted:

  *Joseph Anthony; *b* 23 April 1975

  *Marianna Rose; *b* 1977

  *Laura Dorothea; *b* 1982

(1) *Marian Ellina; *b* 13 Feb 1945; *educ* Somerville Coll Oxford (BA 1966; DPhil); Prof Animal Behaviour 1997; *m* 19 Aug 1967 (*divorce* 1984) (Clinton) Richard Dawkins, only s of Clinton John Dawkins, of Over Norton Park, Chipping Norton, Oxon

(2) *Alison Mary [Mrs Richard Cooke, 1 Holly Oaks, Wormingford, Essex CO6 3BD]; *b* 19 Aug 1950; *educ* Cranborne Chase and Somerville Coll Oxford (BA); *m* 1980 *Richard Cooke, of Sudbury House, Wrotham, Kent, er s of Canon Alfred Gordon Cooke, of The Rectory, St Columb Major, Cornwall, and has:

  1a *Maxwell Richard Gordon; *b* 1985

  1a *Florence Mary; *b* 1982

  2a *Hannah Marian; *b* 1984

4 +(Jos) Colin [The Hon Colin Stamp, 12 Ullswater Rd, London SW13 9PJ]; *b* 22 Dec 1917; *educ* Leys Sch and Queens' Coll Cambridge (MA); Lt RNVR WW II, local dir Barclays Bank Div Mktg Servs Europe of Travellers Cheque Div, American Express Internat Banking Corp 1972; author: *Abroad on Sunday Morning* (1954); *m* 1st 26 June 1940 (*divorce* 1956) Althea, dau of Mrs William M Dawes, of Evanston, Ill., and has:

(1) *Olive Judith; *b* 17 April 1941; *educ* Wellesley (BA 1962) and Boston U (MA 1965); *m* 15 June 1963 (*divorce* 1975) Eugene Farr Humphrey III, only s of Eugene Farr Humphrey, of Montclair, NJ, and has:

  1a *Eugene Jos; *b* 1971

  1a *Alison Dudley; *b* 1968

(2) *Althea Patricia Dawes; *b* 22 July 1943; *educ* Wellesley (BA 1965) and York U Toronto (PhD 1981); *m* 1981 *Stephen Katz, of Toronto

(3) *Ann Jocelyn; *b* 18 Aug 1945

(4) *Rowena Jane; *b* 16 June 1953; *m* 1977 *Patrick Olwell, of Nellysford, Va., and has:

    1a *Matthew; *b* 1978

    2a *Aaron; *b* 1981

4 (cont.) The Hon Colin Stamp *m* 2nd 27 Dec 1958 *Gillian Penelope, er dau of Guy St John Tatham, of Johannesburg, and by her has:

(1) +Robert Colin; *b* 28 Sept 1960; *educ* St Paul's and Corpus Christi Coll Cambridge (BA); *m* 1988 *Susan Caroline, dau of John F Lester, and has:

    1a +Samuel Robert Josiah; *b* 1990

    1a *Olivia Joscelyne Isabel; *b* 1993

(2) +Jonathan Guy; *b* 12 Sept 1963; *educ* St Paul's and Balliol Coll Oxford (BA)

STANIER

Arms: Or on a pile az. ten escallops, four, three, two and one of the field. **Crest:** In front of a griffin's head erased ppr. three escallops or.
Motto: *Pietate fortior* ('Stronger by piety').
Creation: Bt. (UK) 16 July 1917.

SIR BEVILLE DOUGLAS STANIER, 3RD BT, of Peplow Hall, Market Drayton, Co Salop [Sir Beville Stanier Bt, King's Close House, Whaddon, Bucks MK17 0NG]; *b* 20 April 1934; *s* f 1995; *educ* Eton; 2nd Lt Welsh Gds 1953 (ret as Capt 1960), ADC to Govr-Gen Australia 1959–60, stockbroker Kitcat & Aitken 1960–76 (ptnr 1968–76), farmer 1976–; *m* 23 Feb 1963 *(Violet) Shelagh, er dau of Maj James Stockley Sinnott, of Tetbury, Glos, and has:

1 +ALEXANDER JAMES SINNOTT; *b* 10 April 1970

1 *Henrietta Claire; *b* 16 May 1965

2 *Lucinda Katherine; *b* 16 June 1967; *m* 14 Sept 1996 *James Martin, yr s of John Martin and Mrs John Simpson, of Exeter

Lineage: JOHN STONHEWER, of The Hurst, Biddulph, Staffs; *d* in or after 1560, leaving, with two yr sons (Thomas, *d* 1590; John, of Cromborrow, Horton, Staffs):

WILLIAM STONHEWER; bought Oxehay and Gillow House, Biddulph, 1554–74, from the GER(R)ARDs; is stated to have settled the Barleyford estate 1576 (on his s?); *m* Ellen — and *d* by 1595, leaving four sons; the 3rd s:

RICHARD STONHEWER/STONYER, of The Hurst; *m* Anne (*bur* 5 Dec 1615 aged 80), dau of Francis Meate, of Gratton, Horton, and *d* between 12 July and 25 Aug 1597, having had, with other issue, including two er sons (Francis, of Biddulph, *m* 7 Nov 1588 Elizabeth (*d* between 28 Nov 1613 and 29 April 1614), widow of John Bolton, of Gillow Heath Head, and was *bur* 15 July 1601, leaving issue; Richard):

THOMAS STONYER/STONHEWING; *bapt* 20 June 1570; *m* 21 Oct 1610 Isabel, dau of John Bolton, of Gillow Heath Head, and *d* between 16 March 1644 and 1647, having had, with other issue, including a yr s (John, *bapt* 18 Dec 1619, *m* Rachel (*d* 29 Aug 1690), dau and heiress of Robert Allestrey, of Uppington, Co Salop, and *d* 7 April 1691, being ancestor of the STANIERs of Uppington and Wroxeter, Salop):

THOMAS STONYER, of The Hey Hill, Biddulph; *bapt* 13 Oct 1611; *m* 20 March 1636 Anne, dau of William Bolton, of Knipersley, Biddulph, and had, with three yr sons and a dau:

THOMAS STONYER, of The Hey Hill; *b* 7 Jan 1638; *m* Ursula — (*bur* 15 Dec 1716) and had:

FRANCIS STONYER; *bapt* 10 Feb 1667; *m* 6 Oct 1699 Elizabeth Rookery (*bur* 20 May 1739) and *d* 12 Dec 1721, leaving:

THOMAS STONYER, of Biddulph; *b* 14 Dec 1703; *m c* 25 Feb 1726 Anne Baddeley (*bur* 10 Oct 1783 aged 80) and *d* 30 April 1745, leaving, with two er sons:

FRANCIS STONYER later STANIER; *bapt* 10 Sept 1737; Mayor Newcastle-under-Lyme, Staffs, 1771; *m* 10 Nov 1768 Dorothy Pickstock (*d* 31 March 1803) and *d* 11 Oct 1805, leaving:

THOMAS STANIER, of Moor House, Biddulph; *b* Oct 1769; *m* 4 April 1805 Ann Halmarack (*bur* Aug 1861) and *d* 10 April 1856, leaving an s:

FRANCIS STANIER, of Moor House and Madeley Manor, Staffs; *b* 11 July 1808; attorney, Mayor Nwcastle-under-Lyme 1851; *m* 1836 Mary (*d* 14 Oct 1880), dau

of Thomas Sparrow Wilkinson, of Newcastle-under-Lyme, and *d* 13 Oct 1856, having had, with other issue, including two yr sons (Thomas, of Madeley Manor, JP Staffs, *b* 1841, 31st Regt, *m* 1882 Constance (*d* 3 April 1925), dau of Forbes Benignus Winslow, MD, and *d* 16 May 1904; Randle Baddeley, *m* Anne (*d* 27 Feb 1906), dau of R A Dallas) and two daus (Mary Jane, *m* 2 Aug 1882 George Henry Gordon (*d* 21 July 1928), of Wincombe Park, Wilts, and had issue; Alice, *m* Chester Master, of Sherborne, Dorset, and had two sons):

FRANCIS STANIER later FRANCIS PHILIP BROADE STANIER (on inheriting 12 Aug 1856 the estate of Philip Barnes Broade, JP, of Fenton Vivian and Fenton Manor Ho, Staffs) later still STANIER again (roy licence 1876), of The Moor House and Peplow Hall, Salop, JP, DL Salop, JP Staffs; *b* 30 Jan 1838; Capt 3rd King's Own Staffs Militia, High Sheriff Salop 1894; *m* 6 June 1860 Caroline Judith (*d* 29 Jan 1905), dau of Gen William Justice, of Green Park, Bath, and had:

1 Frank Justice, JP Staffs; *b* 20 Oct 1862; *m* 13 June 1894 Beatrice (*m* 2nd 17 June 1911 Arthur Bensley Gardner (*d* WW II) and *d c* 1947), yr dau of Dr Wharton P Hood, and *d* 2 Feb 1909, leaving:

(1) Frank Adolphus Hood, JP (Salop 1922); *b* 1895; *educ* Charterhouse; Lt-Col King's Shropshire LI; *m* 1st 9 Sept 1919 (*divorce* 1936) his cousin Dulce Constance (*d* 1986), only dau of **Sir Beville Stanier, 1st Bt**, and *d* 9 March 1949, having had:

    1a Frank Justice; *b* 18 May 1926; *educ* Canford and RAC Cirencester; *m* 25 Feb 1952 *Kathleen Gertrude Isobel, dau of F S Brettell, of Smethcote Manor, Hadnall, Salop, and *d* 19 Sept 1988, leaving:

        1b *Natasha Jane; *b* 19 Nov 1952; *m* 18 July 1975 (*divorce* 1984) Philip Harry Evans and has:

            1c *Philip Frank; *b* 29 June 1976

            2c *Mark Shane; *b* 20 May 1979

    1a June Bevilline; *b* 1923; *m* 19– Alfred Higgins and *d* 8 Dec 1984, leaving:

        1b *Redvern James; *b* 1944; *m* 1966 *Jacqueline Holden

        2b *Ian Beville; *b* 1946

        3b *John William *b* 1957; *m* 19– *Grace Winwood and has:

            1c *Alice; *b* 1982

            2c *Hannah; *b* 1985

        1b *Vanessa Constance; *b* 1951; *m* 19– *Derek Millington and has:

            1c *Sarah; *b* 1981

            1c *Richard; *b* 1985

(1) (cont.) Lt Col Frank Stanier *m* 2nd —; *m* 3rd 1938 *Dorothy, CStJ, dau of Lt-Col F J Courtenay Hood, DSO, and *d* 9 March 1949

2 BEVILLE (Sir), **1st Bt**

3 William Sneyd; *b* 5 May 1871; *d* unm 20 May 1903

1 Lucy Caroline; *m* 11 June 1896 Arthur Tyrwhitt-Drake, of Crendle Court, Sherborne, Dorset, and *d* 30 Dec 1937, having had issue. He *d* 12 Feb 1938

2 Eleanor Mary; *m* 10 Aug 1898 Capt John Francis Fisher, RA (*ka* 20 Nov 1901), est s of John Fisher, of Ham Common, Surrey, and *d* May 1958, leaving issue

3 Leila Dorothy; *m* 16 April 1903 Charles Gordon Darroch Farquhar, s of Adml Sir Arthur Farquhar, KCB, of Drumnagesk, Aberdeenshire and *d* 26 Feb 1961, leaving issue. He *d* 3 July 1946

FRANCIS STANIER *d* 7 Oct 1900; his 2nd s,

Sir Beville Stanier, 1st Bt (UK), so *cr* 16 July 1917, JP, DL Salop; *b* 12 June 1867; Ld Manors of Peplow and High Hatton, MP (C) Newport (Salop) 1908–18 and Ludlow 1918–21, Capt Salop LI (TF), Sec Salop TFA 1914–18; *m* 12 Dec 1894 Sarah Constance (*d* 13 June 1948), dau of Rev Benjamin Gibbons, of Waresley Ho, Worcs, and *d* 15 Dec 1921, leaving:

1 **Sir Alexander Beville Gibbons Stanier, 2nd Bt**, DSO (1940 and bar 1945), MC, JP (1949), DL (1951); *b* 31 Jan 1899; *educ* Eton and RMC Sandhurst; Welsh Gds WW I 1917–48, Mil Sec Gibraltar 1927–30, WW II: Bde Cdr 1940–45, cmded regt 1945–48, Brig (ret 1948) (despatches), Salop: CC 1950–58, High Sheriff 1951, Pres St John Ambulance Bde 1950–60; CStJ, Cdr Order Leopold II, Croix de Guerre Belgium with palms, US Silver Star; *m* 21 July 1927 Dorothy Gladys (*d* 1973) dau of Brig-Gen Alfred Douglas Miller, CBE, DSO, of Shotover Pk, Wheatley, Oxon, and *d* 1995, leaving:

(1) Sir BEVILLE DOUGLAS STANIER, **3rd and present Bt**

(1) *Sylvia Mary Finola; *b* 9 May 1928

2 Philip Francis; *b* 6 Sept 1901; *educ* Shrewsbury and Wye Ag Coll; *m* 6 April 1929 Kathleen Mary (*d* 1986), est dau of Edgar Turrall, JP, of Coundon Hall, Coventry, and *d* 28 Jan 1977, leaving:

(1) *Philippa Mary [Miss Philippa Stanier, 19 Townsend Park, Luston, Leominster, Herefs HR6 0DZ]; *b* 27 Sept 1930

(2) Constance Lutra Hope; *b* 14 Jan 1933; *m* 13 Sept 1969 *Halbert Peter Gray Glendinning, er s of Maj Halbert James Glendinning, DSO, MBE, RA, of Glen Ho, Merriott, Somerset, and had:

    1a *James Beville *b* 24 Oct 1970

    2a *Philip Peter *b* 27 April 1972

3 Edward; *b* 26 June 1905; P/O RAF; *d* unm 13 July 1926

1 Dulce Constance; *b* 18 Feb 1897; *m* 9 Sept 1919 (*divorce* 1936) her cousin Lt-Col Frank Adolphus Hood Stanier and had issue (*see above*)

STANLEY OF ALDERLEY, SHEFFIELD and

Arms: Arg. on a bend az. three stag's heads cabossed or, a crescent for difference. **Crest:** On a chapeau gu. doubled erm. an eagle, wings expanded or, preying upon an infant ppr., swaddled of the first, banded arg. **Supporters:** Dexter, a stag or, gorged with a ducal coronet, line reflexed over the back, and charged on the shoulder with a mullet az.; sinister, a lion regardant ppr., gorged with a plain collar arg., thereon three escallops gu. **Motto:** *Sans changer* ('Without changing'). **Creations:**, B. (I) 20 Sept 1783 (Sheffield), B. (GB) 9 May 1839 (Stanley of Alderley), B. (UK) 12 May 1848 (Eddisbury of Winnington), Bt. (E) 25 June 1660.

THE 8TH BARON STANLEY OF ALDERLEY, 8TH BARON SHEFFIELD OF ROSCOMMON, **Baron Eddisbury of Winnington** and a **Baronet** (Sir Thomas Henry Oliver Stanley, 14th Bt, DL (Gwynedd 1985)) [The Rt Hon The Lord Stanley of Alderley DL, Trysglwyn Fawr, Amlwch, Anglesey LL68 9RF; Rectory Farm, Stanton St John, Oxon OX9 1HF]; *b* 28 Sept 1927; *s* cousin 1971; *educ* Wellington and Northants Inst of Ag; Capt Coldstream Gds 1945–52 and Gds Para Co, tenant farmer New Coll Oxford 1954–, chm Thames Valley Cereals 1978–, govr St Edward's Sch Oxford 1979–, memb Ctee Management RNLI 1981– and chm fundraising 1985–94; *m* 30 April 1955 *Jane Barrett, dau of Ernest George Hartley, of Lower Farm, Milton-under-Wychwood, Oxon, and has:

1 +RICHARD OLIVER [The Hon Richard Stanley, Rectory Farm, Stanton St John, Oxon OX9 1HF]; *b* 24 April 1956; *educ* St Edward's Sch Oxford and UCL (BSc 1977); *m* 12 Feb 1983 *Carla Mary Angela, er dau of Dr Kenneth Thomas Clyde McKenzie, of Solihull, and has had:

  (1) Oliver Richard Hugh; *b* 1986; *d* 1989

  (1) *Maria Elizabeth Jane; *b* 1988

  (2) *Imogen Alexandra Ruth; *b* 1990

  (3) *Hermione Helena Rose; *b* 1992

2 +Charles Ernest [The Hon Charles Stanley, 34 Rosaline Rd, London SW6 7QT]; *b* 30 June 1960; *educ* St Edward's Sch Oxford and Nottingham U (BA); *m* 26 Aug 1989 *Beverley Ann, er dau of Michael Emmitt, of Swineshead, Lincs, and has:

  (1) *Venetia Jane; *b* 1992

  (2) *Olivia Marie; *b* 3 May 1995

3 +Harry John; *b* 20 Aug 1963; *educ* St Edward's Sch Oxford, UCL (LLB) and Cambridge (LLM); *m* 22 May 1998 *Shirin, er dau of Z Kassim-Lakha, of Brussels

1 *Lucinda Maria [The Hon Mrs Brazel, Lilly Pilly, Shepparton, Victoria 363, Australia]; *b* 21 Feb 1958; *educ* Headingley Sch Oxford; *m* 1 Oct 1983 *Peter Brazel, s of Benedict Brazel, of Lyndhurst, S Australia, and has:

  (1) *Thomas Owen; *b* 1984

  (2) *Harry Jack; *b* 1987

  (3) *Jack Alexander; *b* 1988

Lineage (of Holroyd): ISAAC HOLROYD; moved to Ireland from England; Sheriff Dublin 1686; *m* Mary Holroyd and was *bur* 17 Jan 1706/7, leaving, with a yr s (Isaac, *bapt* 16 April 1684, barrister) and a dau:

JOHN HOLROYD, of Dublin; *b* 1680; *m* Sarah, sis of John Elwood, LLD, V-Provost and MP U of Dublin, and was *bur* 29 Dec 1729, leaving, with a yr s (Rev William, *educ* Trin Coll Dublin (BA 1737, MA 140)) and a dau:

ISAAC HOLROYD, of Dunamore, Co Meath; *b* July 1708; BA Dublin 1728; barrister; *m* Dorothy (*d* 29 Aug 1777), dau of Daniel Baker, of Penn, Bucks, and *d* 11 July 1778, having had an only surv s:

JOHN HOLROYD later BAKER-HOLROYD (on inheriting 1768 his unc Rev Jones Baker's Bucks, Middx and Yorks estates), **1st Baron Sheffield of Roscommon**, Co Roscommon (I), so *cr* 20 Sept 1783, with remainder in default of male issue of his body to his two daus successively by his 1st w and the male issue of their bodies, as also 9 Jan 1781 BARON SHEFFIELD OF DUNAMORE, Co Meath (I), BARON

SHEFFIELD OF SHEFFIELD, Co York (UK) and 22 Jan 1816 VISCOUNT PEVENSEY and EARL OF SHEFFIELD (both I), with in all four last cases ordinary remainder to heirs male of his body, PC (1809), of Grave Hall, Ferrybridge, Yorks, and Sheffield Place (later Park), Sussex, which he bought 1769 from 2nd Earl De La Warr (*qv*) for £31,000 (over £1.5m in late-1990s terms); *b* 21 Dec 1735; Cornet 21st Dragoons 1760, Capt 1761, Maj 1777, Col and fndr 22nd or Sussex Regt 1779–1821; MP (Tory) Coventry Feb–July 1780 and Nov 1780–84 and Bristol (Whig, later Pittite) 1790–1802; took a leading part in suppressing the Gordon Riots; the friend and patron of the historian Edward Gibbon, some of whose miscellaneous writings he edited; FRS 1783, Pres Bd Ag 1803, Memb BOT 1809–21; *m* 1st 26 April 1767 Abigai (*dspms* 3 April 1793), only dau of Lewis Way, of Richmond, Surrey, and had, with a s (*d* young):

1 Maria Josepha; *m* 11 Oct 1796 **1st Baron Stanley of Alderley** and *d* 1 Nov 1863, leaving issue (*see* below **Lineage (of Stanley)**)

2 Louisa Dorothea; *m* 14 March 1797 Lt-Gen Sir William Henry Clinton, GCB, and *d* 14 May 1854, leaving issue (*see* LINCOLN, E)

The **1st Baron** *m* 2nd 26 Dec 1794 Lady Lucy Pelham (*dsp* 18 Jan 1797), dau of 1st Earl of Chichester (*qv*); *m* 3rd 20 Jan 1798 Lady Anne North (*d* 18 Jan 1832), 2nd dau of 2nd Earl of Guilford (*qv*), and *d* 30 May 1821, leaving by her:

  1 GEORGE AUGUSTUS FREDERICK CHARLES HOLROYD, **2nd Baron Sheffield of Roscommon** and 2nd EARL OF SHEFFIELD; *b* 16 March 1802; *educ* Eton and Ch Ch Oxford; a Ld Bechamber Jan-April 1835, a Ld in Waiting (Tory) 1858–59, FRS 1860; *m* 6 June 1825 Harriet (*d* 1 Jan 1889 aged 87), est dau of 2nd Earl of Harewood (*qv*), and *d* 5 April 1876, having had:

    (1) Frederic Henry Stuart, *Viscount Pevensey*; *b* 24 Oct 1827; *d* 21 March 1829

    (2) HENRY NORTH HOLROYD, **3rd Baron Sheffield of Roscommon** and 3rd and last EARL OF SHEFFIELD, JP, DL Sussex; *b* 18 Jan 1832; *educ* Eton; Attaché Constantinople 1851–52 and 1853–56 and Copenhagen 1852–53, MP (C) E Sussex 1857–65, Hon Col HQ Home Cos Divnl Engrg RE; *d* unm 21 April 1909, when all his titles expired bar the Barony of Sheffield of Roscommon

    (3) Douglas Edward; *b* 20 June 1834; barrister; *d* 9 Feb 1882

    (1) Susan Harriet; *m* 26 June 1849 Edward William Harcourt, of Stanton Harcourt, Oxon, and *d* 5 April 1894, leaving issue (*see* VERNON, B)

  3 Anne Frederica; *m* 14 June 1827 Hon Arthur Legge, s of 3rd Earl of Dartmouth (*qv*), and *d* 31 Aug 1829, leaving issue

Lineage (of Stanley): Sir JOHN STANLEY (3rd s of 1st Lord (Baron) Stanley; *see* DERBY, E); *m* Elizabeth, dau and heiress of Sir Thomas We(e)ver, of We(e)ver, Cheshire, and was ancestor of:

Sir THOMAS STANLEY, of We(e)ver and Alderley, Cheshire; High Sheriff Cheshire *c* 1632; *m* Elizabeth, dau and coheir of Sir Peter Warburton, of Grafton Hall, Tilston, Cheshire, Judge Common Pleas 1600–21, and *d* 21 Nov 1605, leaving an only surv s:

Sir THOMAS STANLEY, **1st Bt** (E), so *cr* 25 June 1660, of Alderley; *b* 31 May 1597; *educ* Oxford and Lincoln's Inn; Sheriff Cheshire 1630–31; *m* by 1625 Elizabeth, dau of Sir Thomas Pitt, of Kyrewyard, Worcs, and was *bur* 31 Aug 1672, leaving an est s:

Sir Peter Stanley, **2nd Bt**, of Alderley and We(e)ver; *b* 29 May 1626; *educ* Gray's Inn; Sheriff Cheshire 1677–78; *m* 1650 Elizabeth, dau of Sir John Leigh, of Northcourt, IoW, and was *bur* 4 Oct 1683, leaving an est s:

Sir Thomas Stanley, **3rd Bt**, of Alderley and We(e)ver, which latter, however, he sold *c* 1710; *b* 25 March 1652; *educ* Gray's Inn; *m* by 1682 Christian, dau of Sir Stephen Lennard, 1st Bt, of W Wickham, Kent, and *d* 1721, having had, with two daus (*d* unm):

  1 **Sir James Stanley, 4th Bt**, of Alderley; *m* Nov 1740 Frances, yst dau of George Butler (*see* VAUX OF HARROWDEN, B), and *dsp* and was *bur* 17 March 1746/7

  2 **Sir Edward Stanley, 5th Bt**, of Alderley; *m* by 1726 Mary, only dau of Thomas Ward, London banker, and *d* 28 Aug 1755, leaving:

    (1) **Sir John Thomas Stanley, 6th Bt**, of Alderley; *b* 26 March 1735; Gentleman Privy Chamber to GEORGE III; *m* 20 April 1763 Margaret (*d* 1 Feb 1816), dau and heiress of Hugh Owen, of Penrhôs, Anglesey, and *d* 29 Nov 1807, having had, with other issue:

      1a JOHN THOMAS, **1st Baron**

      2a Edward (Rt Rev); *b* 1 Jan 1779; DD; Bp Norwich; *m* 8 May 1810 Catherine (*d* 5 March 1892), dau of Rev Oswald Leycester, Rector Stoke, Salop, and *d* 6 Sept 1849, having had, with other issue:

        1b Arthur Penrhyn (Very Rev); *b* 13 Dec 1815; DD, Dean Westminster, Canon Ch Ch Oxford, Hon Chaplain to HM QUEEN VICTORIA, to HRH THE PRINCE OF WALES, FRS; *m* 22 Dec 1863 Lady Augusta Frederica Elizabeth Bruce, VA 3rd Cl, dau of 7th Earl of Elgin and (11th Earl of) Kincardine (*qv*), and *d* 18 July 1881

        2b Charles Edward; *b* 15 June 1819; Capt RE; *m* 30 April 1846 Eliza Dolby (*d* 10 Oct 1901), est dau of William Clayton, of Lostock Hall, Lancs, and *dsp* 13 Aug 1849

        1b Catherine Maria; *m* 2 April 1850 Very Rev Charles John Vaughan, DD, Dean Llandaff, Master The Temple, Headmaster Harrow, and *d* 2 Aug 1899

      1a Margaretta Louisa Anne; *m* 25 Nov 1802 Gen Sir Baldwin Leighton, 6th Bt (*qv*), and *d* 8 Jan 1842, leaving issue

The 6th Bt's er s,

  Sir John Thomas Stanley, 7th Bt, and **1st Baron Stanley of Alderley**, Co Chester (UK), so *cr* 9 May 1839; *b* 26 Nov 1766; *educ* Edinburgh U; MP (Whig) Wootton Basset 1790–96, Maj Roy Cheshire Militia 1767–98, Sheriff Anglesey 1809, Chm Cheshire QS, FRS, FSA 1788; *m* 11 Oct 1796 Lady Maria Josepha Holroyd (*d* aged 92), est dau of **1st Baron Sheffield of Roscommon** and 1st EARL OF SHEFFIELD (*see* above), and *d* 2 Oct 1850, having had, with other issue:

  1 EDWARD JOHN STANLEY, **2nd Baron Stanley of Alderley**, PC (1841); *b* 13 Nov 1802; *educ* Eton and Ch Ch Oxford; MP (Whig) Hindon 1831–32 and N Cheshire 1832–41 and 1847–48, U-Sec Colonies 1833–34 and Home Dept July-Nov 1834, Sec Treasury 1835–41, Paymaster-Gen June–Sept 1841, Feb 1852 and 1853–55, U-Sec For Affrs 1846–52; *cr vp* 12 May 1848 BARON EDDISBURY OF WINNINGTON, Co Chester (UK), V-Pres BOT Feb 1852 and 1853–55, Pres BOT 1855–58, PMG with Cabinet seat 1860–66; *m* 7 Oct 1826 in

Florence and 26 June 1833 at Alderley Henrietta Maria (d 16 Feb 1895), dau of 13th Viscount Dillon (qv) of Costello-Gallen, and d 16 June 1869, having had, with other issue:

(1) HENRY EDWARD JOHN STANLEY, **3rd Baron Stanley of Alderley**; b 11 July 1827; educ Eton and Trin Coll Cambridge; FO: joined 1847, Attaché Constantinople 1851, Sec Legation Athens 1854–59 and Special Mission Danubian Provinces 1856–58; underwent several forms of marriage (apparently twice according to Islamic rites (of which faith the 'groom' professed to be an adherent) in 1862, 6 Nov 1869 at the St George Hanover Sq registry office and 15 May 1874 at the RC Church of St Alban Macclesfield) with Fabia, dau of Santiago Federico San Roman, of Seville, who was apparently recd as his w in the UK, but who turned out to be identical with Serafina Fernandez y Funes, of Alcandete, Jaen, Spain, who had m 30 Sept 1851 Ramon Peres y Abril (d 16 May 1870), so that the ceremonies conducted in 1862, 1869 and 1874 were bigamous and he must on his death 10 Dec 1903 be considered as having been unm

(2) John Constantine; b 30 Sept 1837; Col Gren Gds; m 15 Aug 1871 Susan Mary Elizabeth, DBE (m 2nd 17 Aug 1881 1st and last Baron St Helier, GCB, PC (d 9 April 1905; see 1905 edn), and d 25 Jan 1931), dau of Keith William Stewart-Mackenzie of Seaforth (see GALLOWAY, E), and d 23 April 1878, leaving:

1a Madeline Cecilia Carlyle, JP Surrey; b 2 July 1876; Order Mercy; m 5 Jan 1903 1st Earl of Midleton (see MIDLETON, V) and d 2 June 1966, leaving issue

2a Osma Mary Dorothy; b 1877; m 21 July 1896 Augustus Henry Eden Allhusen, JP, DL, of Stoke Court, Bucks, and d 6 Oct 1965, leaving issue. He d 2 May 1925

(3) EDWARD LYULPH, **4th Baron**

(4) Algernon Charles (Rt Rev); b 16 Sept 1843; MA Cantab, Bp Emmaus 1903–28, Assist Pontifical Throne, Canon St Peter's Rome; d 23 April 1928

(1) Alice Margaret; m 3 Feb 1853 Lt-Gen Augustus Henry LANE-FOX later LANE-FOX-PITT-RIVERS (roy licence 1880), Gren Gds (d 4 May 1900), and d 19 May 1910, leaving issue

(2) Henrietta Blanche; m 23 Sept 1851 7th Earl of Airlie (qv) and d 5 Jan 1921, leaving issue

(3) Katherine Louisa; m 8 Nov 1864 John, Viscount Amberley, and d 28 June 1874, leaving issue (see RUSSELL, E)

(4) Rosalind Frances; m 4 Oct 1864 9th Earl of Carlisle (qv) and d 12 Aug 1921, leaving issue

2 William Owen, of Penrhôs; b 13 Nov 1802; Capt Gren Gds, Ld Lt and MP Anglesey 1837–47, Chester 1850–57 and Beaumaris 1857–74; m 14 Feb 1832 Ellen, dau of Sir John Williams, 1st Bt, of Bodelwyddan (qv), and d 24 Feb 1884

1 Lucy Anne; m 24 Sept 1833 Marcus Theodore Hare, RN, and d 15 March 1869, having had issue. He d 30 July 1845

2 Isabella Louisa; m 23 Oct 1826 Capt Sir William Edward Parry, RN, and d 13 May 1839, leaving issue

3 Matilda Abigail; m 6 Oct 1828 Henry John Adeane, of Babraham, Cambs, and d 28 July 1850, having had issue. He d 11 May 1847

4 Harriet Alethea; m 20 Aug 1835 Gen Thomas William Scott and d 24 April 1888, leaving issue. He d 1868

The 3rd BARON's bro,

EDWARD LYULPH STANLEY, **4th Baron of Stanley of Alderley** and **4th Baron Sheffield of Roscommon**, as which s 2nd cousin 1909, PC (1910); b 16 May 1839; educ Eton and Balliol Coll Oxford (Fell 1862–69); barrister Inner Temple 1865, MP (Lib) Oldham 1880–85, V-Chm London Sch Bd 1897–1904, author: *Our National Education* (1899); m 6 Feb 1873 Mary Katharine, CBE (1920) (d 4 Jan 1929), dau of Sir Lothian Bell, 1st Bt (qv), and d 18 March 1925, having had:

1 ARTHUR LYULPH STANLEY, **5th Baron Sheffield of Roscommon** (under which single title he was known in his lifetime) and **5th Baron Stanley of Alderley**, KCMG (1914), DL Anglesey and Cheshire; b 14 Sept 1875; educ Eton and Balliol Coll Oxford (MA); Capt Anglesey RE Militia Bower War 1899–1901 and Cheshire Yeo, barrister Inner Temple 1902, memb LCC Lewisham 1904, MP (Lib) Eddisbury (Cheshire) 1906–10, PPS to PMG 1906–10, Priv Sec Office Woods and Forests 1912, High Sheriff of Anglesey 1913, Govr Victoria 1914–19, Pres Br-Australian Soc, Hon Col 29th Inf Regt Cwlth Forces; m 29 Aug 1905 Margaret Evelyn, OStJ (d 12 April 1964), dau of Henry Gordon, of Prestons, Ightham, Kent, and d 22 Aug 1931, had:

(1) EDWARD JOHN STANLEY, **6th Baron Stanley of Alderley** (under which single title he was known in his lifetime) and **6th Baron Sheffield of Roscommon**; b 9 Oct 1907; educ Eton and Balliol Coll Oxford; Lt-Cdr RNVR WW II; m 1st 3 March 1932 (divorce 1936) Victoria Audrey Beatrice, 2nd dau of Viscount Ingestre (see SHREWSBURY and WATERFORD, E), and had:

1a *Edwina Maureen [The Hon Mrs Epstein, 146 Benhill Rd, London SE5 7LZ]; b 19 Jan 1933; m 1st 5 Jan 1953 (divorce 1965) John Dawnay Innes, 2nd son of Lt-Col James Archibald Innes, DSO (see DOWNE, V); m 2nd 25 Oct 1968 *(Joshua) Philip Epstein, s of Dr Samuel Hyman Epstein, of Boston, Mass., and by her 1st husb has:

1b *Thomas John Stanley [Thomas Innes Esq, 64 Monnow St, Monmouth, Gwent]; b 1954; educ Eton; m 1989 *Irma Fingal-Rock and has:

1a *Oliver Edward Zachariah FINGAL-ROCK INNES; b 1984

1a *Aphrodite Irma Emilie Clementine FINGAL-ROCK INNES; b 1987

2b *Richard James [Richard Innes Esq, Manor Hall, Moulton St Mary, Norfolk]; b 1955; m 1987 *Auriol I, yr dau of R H F Stanton, of Bungay, Suffolk, and has:

1c *Archibald John Stanton; b 1992

2c *Dominic Robert; b 1994

1b *Mary Clementine Adelaide [Mrs Alexander Drewchin, Box 920, RD1 Honesdale, PA 18431, USA]; b 1960; m 1986 *Alexander Nikolaevich Drewchin

(1) (cont.) The **6th Baron** m 2nd 18 Jan 1944 (divorce 1948) (Edith Louise) Sylvia, actress (d 30 June 1977), widow of Douglas Fairbanks, Sr, formerly w of Lord Ashley (er s of 9th Earl of Shaftesbury; qv) and dau of Arthur Hawkes; m 3rd 6 April 1951 (divorce 1957) Thérèse, dau of Gen Edouard Husson, of Toulon; m 4th 15 Sept 1961 Kathleen (Kitty) Margaret (d 1 April 1996),

widow of Sir Edmund Frank Crane and dau of Cecil Murray Wright, of Malden, Surrey, and d 3 March 1971

(2) LYULPH HENRY VICTOR OWEN STANLEY, **7th Baron Sheffield of Roscommon** (under which single title he was known in his lifetime) and **7th Baron Stanley of Alderley**; b 22 Oct 1915; educ Eton and Balliol Coll Oxford; Lt-Cdr RNVR, BBC Home Service Announcer 1945–47, Public Information Offr UN 1948–57; d unm 23 June 1971

(1) Mary Katharine Adelaide; b 30 May 1906; m 9 Jan 1926 Hon Maurice Fox Pitt Lubbock, yst s of 1st Baron Avebury (qv), and had issue

(2) Pamela Margaret; b 6 Sept 1909; actress as Pamela Stanley; m 7 Oct 1941 S/Ldr Sir (Henry) David Cunynghame, 11th Bt (qv), and had issue

(3) *Victoria Venetia; b 29 June 1917; m 20 Jan 1942 *Lt-Cdr James Douglas Woods, RCNVR, and has had:

1a *Virginia Louise [Mrs Finn Simmelhag, 31 Boswell Ave, Toronto, Ontario, Canada]; b 3 March 1943; educ Univ of Toronto (BA, MA 1968); m 13 June 1964 *Finn Simmelhag, s of Eigil Theodor Simmelhag

2a *Teresa Clare; b 9 Feb 1946

3a Angela; b 20 Dec, d 24 Dec 1958

2 Edward John; b 14 May 1878; Res Sokoto, W Nigeria; d unm 14 Nov 1908

3 Oliver Hugh, DSO (1918), JP, DL Anglesey; b 23 Oct 1879; educ Clifton; Lt-Col Res Offrs RA, Boer War 1899–1902, WW I (despatches thrice, Croix de Guerre); m 8 July 1919 Lady (Alice) Kathleen Violet Thynne (d 4 Oct 1977 aged 86), JP Anglesey, est dau of 5th Marquess of Bath (qv), and d 13 Feb 1952, having had:

(1) John Norman; b 24 Jan 1922; educ Stowe; d following an accident 21 Dec 1947

(2) Martin Oliver; b 9 Jan 1924; educ Winchester; d with er bro 21 Dec 1947

(3) THOMAS HENRY OLIVER STANLEY, **8th and present Baron Stanley of Alderley** and **8th Baron Sheffield of Roscommon**

(4) +Richard Morgan Oliver [The Hon Richard Stanley, Sandfield, Breach Lane, Shaftesbury, Dorset SP7 8LD]; b 30 April 1931; educ Winchester and New Coll Oxford; granted rank of baron's yr s 1973; m 27 July 1956 *Phyllida Mary Katherine, 3rd dau of Lt-Col Clive Grantham Austin (see SCARBROUGH, E), and has:

1a +Martin Thomas Oliver [Martin Stanley Esq, 1 Lavender Gdns, London SW11 1DH]; b 24 June 1957; educ Harrow; late 17th/21st Lancers; m 1982 *Georgina Mary Victoria, only dau of George Grimm, of Chelsea, and has:

1b +Oliver George; b 1984

2b +Hugh Richard Timothy; b 1992

1b *Clementine Masha; b 1986

2b *Isabella Kate; b 1988

2a +Oliver Hugh [Oliver Stanley Esq, Parsonage Farm, Bentworth, Hants GU34 5RB]; b 30 June 1959; educ Harrow; late Coldstream Gds; m 1985 *Sophie Elizabeth, dau of Nicholas Holmes, of Hook Norton Manor, Banbury, Oxon, and has:

1b *Arabella Anne; b 1989

2b *Sabrina Laura; b 1992

3b *Susannah Rose; b 1994

1a *Serena Emma Rose [Mrs Matthew Jebb, Airdsilla, Delgany, Co Wicklow, Ireland]; b 8 Aug 1961; m 1987 *Matthew Hilary Jebb (see POLLEN, Bt) and has:

1b *Edwin Grancis; b 1988

2b *A son; b 1990

3b *Theodore Philip; b 1992

2a *Laura Sylvia Kathleen; b 22 July 1968; m 20 Dec 1996 *David Barbour,, est s of Clive Barbour, of Croston, Lancs, and Mrs Valerie Barbour, of Cheltenham

(1) Mary; b 18 Feb; d 25 Feb 1921

1 Henrietta Margaret, OBE (1919); m 12 June 1901 Adm Sir William Edmund Goodenough, GCB, MVO, and d 21 Aug 1956, leaving issue (see GOODENOUGH, Bt)

2 Katharine Florence Clementine; d 10 April 1884

3 Sylvia Laura, MBE; m 24 April 1906 Brig-Gen Hon Anthony Morton Henley, CMG, DSO (see HENLEY, B), and had issue

4 Blanche Florence Daphne; m 15 July 1912 Brig-Gen Eric Pearce-Serocold, CMG, KRRC, 2nd s of Charles Pearce-Serocold, of Taplow Hill, Bucks, and d 17 July 1968, leaving issue. He d 26 June 1926

5 (Beatrice) Venetia; m 26 July 1915 Hon Edwin Samuel Montagu, PC, 2nd s of 1st Baron Swaything (qv), and d 3 Aug 1948, leaving issue

STANSGATE

Arms: See BENN, Bt. **Creation:** V. (UK) 12 Jan 1942.

(An)T(h)ony Neil Wedgwood Benn, PC (1964) [Tony Benn PC, 12 Holland Park Ave, London W11]; b 3 April 1925; s f as 2nd Viscount 1960 but disclaimed peerage for life 31 July 1963; educ Westminster and New Coll Oxford (Pres Union 1947, BA 1948, MA); P/O RAFVR and Sub-Lt (A) RNVR 1943–45, Talks Producer BBC Overseas Serv 1949–50, MP (Lab) Bristol SE Nov 1950–Nov 1960, petitioned Parl unsuccessfully for right to renounce Viscounty irrevocably 1955, disqualified from H of C 1960, re-elected in by-election May 1961, unseated by Election Court July 1961, re-elected MP Bristol SE 1963–83 and MP Chesterfield 1984–, PMG 1964–44, Min Tech 1966–70, Min Power 1969–70, chm Lab Party 1970–72, Industry Sec and Min Posts and Telecommunications 1974–75, Energy Sec 1975–79, Lab Party leadership candidate 1976, 1988 and dep leadership 1971 and 1981; author: *The Privy Council as a Second Chamber* (1957), *The Regeneration of Britain* (1964), *The New Politics* (1970), *Arguments for Socialism* (1979), *Arguments for Democracy* (1981), *Out of the Wilderness, Diaries 1963–67* (1987), *Fighting Back* (1988), *Office Without Power, Diaries 1968–72* (1988), *Against the Tide, Diaries 1973–76* (1989), *Conflicts of Interest, Diaries 1977–80*

(1990), *A Future for Socialism* (1991), *The End of an Era, Diaries 1980–90* (1992); CIEE, FRSA 1970, Hon LLD Strathclyde U 1969, Hon DTech Bradford U 1979, Hon DSc Aston; *m* 17 June 1949 *Caroline Middleton, est dau of James Milton de Camp, of Cincinnati, Ohio, and has:

1 +STEPHEN MICHAEL WEDGWOOD; *b* 21 Aug 1951; *educ* Holland Park Comprehensive and Keele U; *m* 1988 *Ashika Nita, dau of Stuart Ashley Bowes, of Tel Aviv U, and has:

(1) +Daniel; *b* 10 Dec 1991
(1) *Emily; *b* 1989

2 +Hilary James Wedgwood; *b* 26 Nov 1953; late Dep Leader Ealing Educn Ctee, Special Advsr to Sec State Educn and Employment 1997–; *m* 1st 1973 Rosalind Retey (*d* 1979); *m* 2nd 1982 *Sally Clark and has three sons and a dau

3 +Joshua William Wedgwood; *b* 9 May 1958; *m* 1984 *Elizabeth Feeney and has a s

1 *Melissa Anne Wedgwood; *b* 20 Feb 1957; author *Madonna and Child* (1997); has issue

Lineage: Sir JOHN WILLIAM BENN, 1st Bt (*qv*); had a 2nd s:

WILLIAM WEDGWOOD BENN, **1st Viscount Stansgate**, of Stansgate Co Essex (UK), so *cr* 12 June 1942, DSO (1917), DFC (1918), PC (1929); *b* 10 May 1877; *educ* Paris and UCL (BA 1903, Fell 1919); A/Cdre RAFVR, MP (Lib) St George Div Tower Hamlets 1906–18, Leith 1918–27, (Lab) N Aberdeen 1928–31 and Manchester Gorton 1937–41, Jr Ld Treasury 1910–15, Chm Nat Relief Fund 1914, Sec State India 1929–31, Air 1945–46, V-Pres Italian Mil Commn 1943–44, Pres Inter-Parly Union 1947–57, Capt Yeo and with RNAS and RFC WW I (despatches twice), Coastal Cmd RAF WW II (despatches), Croix de Guerre, Legn Hon, Bronze Medal for Valour and War Cross Italy; *m* 17 Nov 1920 Margaret Eadie, dau of Daniel Turner Holmes, MP Govan, and *d* 17 Nov 1960, having had:

1 Michael Julius Wedgwood, DFC; *b* 5 Sept 1921; *educ* Westminster; F/Lt RAFVR WW II; *d* of injuries recd on ops 23 June 1944

2 ANTHONY NEIL WEDGWOOD BENN, **briefly 2nd Viscount Stansgate**
3 +David Julian Wedgwood [The Hon David Benn, Stansgate Cottage, Southminster, Essex]; *b* 28 Dec 1928; *educ* Balliol Coll Oxford (BA Hons 1951, Sec Union 1951); *m* 28 Dec 1959 *June Mary, er dau of Ernest Charles Barraclough, of Lightcliffe, nr Halifax, Yorks, and has:

(1) +Piers Michael Wedgwood; *b* 4 Aug 1962
(1) *Cordelia Frances Margaret Wedgwood; *b* 26 June 1964

STAPLES

Arms: Arg. on a fess engrailed ermines, between three hurts, two dragon's heads erased or. **Crest:** A demi-negro affrontée ppr., holding a bolt-staple or. **Motto:** *Teneo* ('I retain').
Creation: Bt. (I) 18 July 1628.

SIR GERALD JAMES ARLAND STAPLES, 16TH BT, of Lissan, Co Tyrone [Sir Gerald Staples Bt, 5 Little Stodham House, Liss, Hants GU33 6LJ]; *b* 2 Dec 1909; *s* bro 1997; *m* 7 April 1951 *Henrietta Owen, dau of Arland Ussher, of Blackrock, Co Dublin, and has:

1 *Emily Ann [Mrs Kerry McDonald, 11 Rhoscolyn Drive, Tattenhoe, Milton Keynes MK4 3AE]; *b* 2 March 1952; *m* 1st 1974 (*divorce* 1984) Howard James Anthony Smith; *m* 2nd 1988 *Kerry William John McDonald and by her 1st husb has:

(1) *Juliet Clare; *b* 28 Aug 1980

2 *Jacqueline Mary [Mrs Timothy Pullen, 19 Willowdale Close, Petersfield, Hants]; *b* 8 Sept 1954; *m* 1985 *Timothy Pullen

Lineage: ALEXANDER STAPLES, of Yate Court, Glos; *m* 1st Avis, dau of Richard Browne, of Marlborough, Wilts; *m* 2nd Elizabeth — and *d* 22 Aug 1590, having had, with four er sons (George, bought the Manor of Fovant, Wilts, *m* Anne, dau of Henry Tutt, of W Meon, Hants; Richard, of Boreham, *m* Edith, dau of John Gifford; Alexander, of Nottingham; Edward, *d* unm 1602) and a 6th and yst s (William):

Sir Thomas Staples, 1st Bt (I), so *cr* 18 July 1628, of Lissan, Co Tyrone, and Faghanvale, Co Londonderry; High Sheriff Co Tyrone 1640; *m* by Sept 1623 Charity, only child of Sir Baptist Jones, of Vintnerstown, Co Londonderry, and *d* 31 May 1653, leaving:

1 **Sir Baptist Staples, 2nd Bt**, of Lissan and Faghanvale; *d* unm June 1672
2 **Sir Alexander Staples, 3rd Bt**, of Lissan and Faghanvale; High Sheriff Co Tyrone 1661, MP Strabane 1661–65; *m* Elizabeth — (*d* between 18 and 25 May 1681) and *dspm* between 26 May 1665 and 5 March 1672/3 having had two daus
3 **Sir Robert Staples 4th Bt**, of Lissan, Co Tyrone; High Sheriff 1703, MP Dungannon 1692 and Clogher 1695; *m* 13 March 1682 Mary, est dau of John Vesey, Archbp Tuam (*see* DE VESCI, B), and *d* 21 Nov 1714, having had, with other issue:

(1) **Sir John Staples, 5th Bt**; *b* 22 Sept 1684; *m* Mary *née* Goslin, widow of Josiah Haydock, and *dspm*, having had, with two other daus:

1a Isabella Elizabeth; *m* 26 June 1794, as his 1st w, Gerald Fitzgerald, of Coolamowle and Bath

(2) **Sir Alexander Staples, 6th Bt**; *b* 7 June 1693; *m* Abigail, dau and heiress of Thomas Townley, of Co Cavan, and had:

1a **Sir Robert Staples, 7t Bt**; *b* 1 Aug 1740; *m* 1761 Alicia, dau of Rev Thomas Staples, of Lissan, and had:

1b Sarah; *m* 1785 Samuel Jacob, of Mobarnane, Co Tipperary

1a (cont.) **Sir Robert** *m* 2nd Mary, widow of Chambré Brabazon Ponsonby (*see* BESSBOROUGH, E), and by her had:

1b **Sir Robert Staples, 8th Bt**; *b* 13 Feb 1772; *d* unm 24 June 1832
2b Anna Maria; *m* 1799 Ralph Smyth, of Gaybrook, Co Westmeath

1a (cont.) **Sir Robert** *m* 3rd 1776 Hon Jane Vesey (*d* 1822), yst dau of 1st Baron Knapton (*see* DE VESCI, V), and *d* 1816, having by her had, with another dau:

3b Elizabeth Selina; *m* 10 Jan 1807 Richard FitzHerbert, 2nd son of John Ruxton, of Black Castle, Co Meath
4b Isabella; *m* 1794 Gerald Fitzgerald, of Coolanowle, Queen's Co, and *d* 1803, leaving issue. He *d* 8 April 1845
5b Anne; *m* 1805 her cousin Rt Hon George Knox, DCL (*see* RANFURLY, E), and *d* 1811

(3) Thomas (Rev); *b* 22 June 1702; Rector Derryloran; *m* 15 May 1735 Grace (*d* 1791), dau of John Houston, of Castle Stewart, Co Tyrone, and *d* Aug 1762, leaving, with other issue:

1a John, PC; *b* 1 March 1736, MP Co Antrim; *m* 1st 14 June 1764 Ann (*d* 31 May 1771), dau of Rt Hon William Conolly, of Castletown, Co Kildare, and had, with other issue:

1b William Connolly; *m* July 1797 Anne (*m* 2nd Richard Napier and *d* 30 March 1867), est dau of Sir James Stewart, 7th Bt, of Ramelton (*qv*), and *d* 30 March 1798, having had a s (*d* young)
1b Louisa Anne; *m* 24 June 1785 Adml Hon Sir Thomas Pakenham, GCB, and had issue (*see* LONGFORD, E)
2b Henrietta Margaret; *m* 9 Feb 1796 2nd Earl of Clancarty (*qv*) and *d* 30 Dec 1847, leaving issue

1a (cont.) John Staples *m* 2nd 14 Oct 1774 Henrietta (*d* 1813), dau of 3rd Viscount Molesworth (*qv*), and *d* 22 Dec 1820, having by her had:

2b **Sir Thomas Staples, 9th Bt**, QC; *b* 31 July 1775; *m* 27 Oct 1813 Catherine (*d* 20 Jan 1872), dau of Rev John Hawkins, est s of Rt Rev James Hawkins, DD, Bp Raphoe, and *dsp* 14 May 1865
3b John Molesworth (Rev); *b* 1 Sept 1776; Rector Lissan and Upper Moville; *m* Sept 1813 Annie (*d* 23 July 1869), est dau of Nathaniel Alexander, DD, Bp Meath, and *d* 4 April 1859, having had, with other issue:

1c John; *b* 1816; Captain 7th Bengal Light Cav; *k* nr Cawnpore during Indian Mutiny 8 June 1857
2c **Sir Nathaniel Alexander Staples, 10th Bt**, JP, DL; *b* 1 May 1817; Capt Bengal Artillery; *m* 21 Oct 1844 Elizabeth Lindsay (*d* 4 Dec 1907), only dau of Capt James Head (*see* HEAD, Bt), and *d* 12 March 1899, leaving, with another dau (*d* unm):

1d **Sir John Molesworth Staples, 11th Bt**; *b* 29 Dec 1847; *dsp* 3 Feb 1933
2d James Head, JP, DL Co Tyrone; *b* 13 Oct 1849; barrister; *m* 4 Aug 1883 Mary Emma Radclife (*d* 15 Sept 1910), est dau of Robert Holbeche Dolling, DL, of Edenmore, and *dsp* 25 Aug 1917
3d **Sir Robert Ponsonby Staples, 12th Bt**; *b* 30 June 1853; *m* 25 April 1883 Ada Louise (*d* 3 March 1940), dau of H Stammers, of London, and *d* 18 Oct 1943, having had:

1e **Sir Robert George Alexander Staples, 13th Bt**; *b* 21 Sept 1894; *educ* Campbell Coll Belfast and Trin Coll Dublin; Lt RASC WW I, dir Peter Marsh & Sons (NI) 1961; *m* 26 July 1922 Vera Lilian, yst dau of John Jenkins, of Beckenham, Kent, and *dspm* Dec 1970, leaving:

1f *Hazel Marion [Mrs Henry Dolling, Lissan House, Cookstown, Co Tyrone BT80 9SW]; *b* 13 June 1923; *m* 1 Sept 1970 Harry Holbeche Radclyffe Dolling (*d* 1986)
2f Elizabeth Hope; *b* 26 Sept 1924; *m* 1 Sept 1951 (Charles) Cameron Gough, DSC, only s of Charles Gough, of Chilvester House, Calne, and *d* 6 Aug 1970, leaving:

1g *Jeremy Cameron Gough; *b* 4 June 1958
1g *Vivien Hazel; *b* 30 April 1953
2g *Philippa Jane; *b* 24 June 1956

1e Violet Hope, MBE; *b* 4 Feb 1896; *m* 1st 28 Feb 1922 Lt-Col William Magill Kennedy, CIE, IA (*k* India 22 Sept 1923), Dep Commr Assam, s of Charles George Blagrave Kennedy, JP, of Mullantean, Co Tyrone; *m* 2nd Dec 1927 Maj Arthur William Dobbin, DSO, RA (*d* 6 Nov 1951), s of Col Dobbin, of Dunmullagh, O'Heath, Co Louth
2e Beatrice Joyce Head; *b* 23 Sept 1900; *m* 27 April 1955 Joseph O'Neill and *d* 21 July 1960
3e Nora Lettice Mary; *b* 2 Oct 1902; *m* 8 Dec 1924 Capt Percy Clement William Tatton-Tatton, Roy Fus, s of John Tatton-Tatton, and *d* 2 Nov 1940
1d Cecilia; *m* 30 June 1874 Frederick Greer, JP, of Tullylagan, Co Tyrone, and *d* 13 July 1891, leaving issue

3c Thomas Staples; *b* Sept 1824; Maj-Gen, BSC; *m* 11 June 1868 Grace, dau of Ven William Hulbert Wolseley, Archdeacon Kilfenora (*see* WOLSELEY, Bt, of Mount Wolseley), and *d* 24 Oct 1886, leaving:

1d John Molesworth; *b* 2 May 1869; *m* 26 April 1905 Helen Lucy Johnstone, yr dau of Richard Williams Barrington (*see* BARRINGTON, Bt), and *d* 22 May 1948, leaving:

1e **Sir John Richard Staples, 14th Bt**; *b* 5 April 1906; *m* 7 Oct 1933 Sybell(a) (*d* 12 July 1995), dau of Dr Charles Henry Wade, of Effort Ho, Shere, Surrey, and *d* 1989, leaving:

1f *Eileen Sybell [Mrs Timothy Kilpatrick, Hale House, Churt, Farnham, Surrey GU10 2JQ]; *b* 4 May 1939; *m* 1968 *Timothy Geary Edward Kilpatrick and has:

1g *Amanda Charlotte *b* 1971

2g *Sarah Patricia *b* 1974

2f *Barbara Helen; *b* 24 Sept 1941; *m* 1st 1968 Alistair Hutchinson-Russell (*d* 1973); *m* 2nd 1974 Anthony Warren England; *m* 3rd 1988 *Keith Burton

1e *Alice Henrietta; *b* 12 Dec 1909

2e *Eileen Patience; *b* 24 Aug 1917

2d Thomas; *b* 1870; *m* 14 April 1903 Mary Ussher (*d* 23 Nov 1966), yr dau of Frederick Greer, JP, of Tullylagan, and *d* 4 April 1963, leaving:

1e **Sir Thomas Staples, 15th Bt**; *b* 9 Feb 1905; *m* 9 Feb 1952 Frances Ann Irvine (*d* 1981), of Toronto, and *dsp* 19 Dec 1997

2e GERALD JAMES ARLAND STAPLES, **16th and present Bt**

3e +RICHARD MOLESWORTH [Richard Staples Esq, 113 Huntsbury Ave, Christchurch 2, New Zealand]; *b* 11 June 1914; heir presumptive; *m* 1954 Marjorie Charlotte Thomsen (*d* Dec 1997), of Christchurch

1e Grace; *b* 15 July 1906; *m* 22 April 1932 Horace Roland Rambaut Dowd (*d* 1975), s of Charles William Dowd, of Roscrea, Co Tipperary, and *d* 23 June 1997, leaving:

1f *Peter [Peter Dowd Esq, The Manse, East Main St, Lismore, Co Waterford, Ireland]; *b* 16 Dec 1935; *m* 22 April 1961 *Constance Evelyn, dau of James Honnibrook, of Lismore, and has:

1g *Derek Roland James; *b* 4 Oct 1965

2g *Charles Peter Staples; *b* 8 Jan 1967

1g *Sandra Evelyn [Mrs Sean Willoughby, The Mall, Lismore, Co Waterford, Ireland]; *b* 2 May 1962; *m* 1992 *Sean Willoughby

2g *Sharon Jean Mary [Mrs David Warren, New Ross, Co Wexford, Ireland]; *b* 29 June 1964; *m* 19– *David Fergus Warren and has:

1h *Amy; *b* 1989

2f *Thomas Charles [Thomas Dowd Esq, Barton, Deerpark Rd, Lismore, Co Waterford, Ireland]; *b* 22 March 1944; *m* 19 Sept 1963 *Henrietta Elizabeth Frances, dau of Francis Sweetnam, of Ballydehob, Co Cork, and has:

1g *Richard William Romney; *b* 6 July 1967; *m* 1992 *Sile Cronin, of Killarney, Co Kerry

1g *Gillian Helen; *b* 30 Aug 1964; has by David William Murphy, of Lismore:

1h *Zach Jordan DOWD; *b* 19–

2g *Diana Joan; *b* 28 Aug 1965; *m* 1989 *Patrick Brendan Kiersey, of Kilmacthomas, Co Waterford, and has:

1h *Jack James; *b* 1992

2h *Max Thomas; *b* 1993

1h *Hazel Kate; *b* 1989

3f *Christopher Romney Rambaut [Christopher Dowd Esq, Doeville Deerpark, Lismore, Co Waterford, Ireland]; *b* 1948; *m* 1976 *Una Bridget Cotter, of Tallow, Co Waterford, and has:

1g *Robert James; *b* 1982

2g *Justin Edward; *b* 1986

1g *Louise Sarah; *b* 1979

2e *Elizabeth Lindsay [Mrs James Rawlence, 42 Ridgeway, off Horsecastles Lane, Sherborne, Dorset]; *b* 2 Dec 1911; *m* 1st 5 July 1933 Henry Eric St George Harpur (*d* 27 Nov 1947), s of Rev Henry Singleton de la Mazière Harpur, of Armagh; *m* 2nd 1961 John Frank Harris (*d* 1971); *m* 3rd 1972 James Victor Thomas Rawlence, MBE, RN (*d* 1993), and by her 1st husb had:

1f *Elizabeth Lindsay St George; *b* 1937; *m* 1961 *Trevor Arthur Lant and has:

1g *Myles Arthur; *b* 1963

1g *Philippa Lindsay; *b* 1969

3e *Pamela June [Miss Pamela Staples, 22 New St, Lismore, Co Waterford, Ireland]; *b* 3 June 1923

3d Noel Richard Ponsonby; *b* 25 Dec 1879; *m* 1905 Kathleen (*d* 1966), dau of Alexander Avis Hamilton, of Blackrock, Co Dublin, and *d* 1958, leaving:

1e Richard Nathaniel; *b* 19 June 1908; *m* 1939 *Isabel MacMillan and *d* 1975, leaving:

1f *Heather Anne; *b* 1941

2f *Sheila Elizabeth *b* 1944

2e Anthony; *b* 30 March 1920; *m* 1950 Margaret Eva Duffield (*d* 1970) and *d* 1975, leaving:

1f *Noel Leslie *b* 1954; *m* 1972 *Dwaine Grant van Eeuwen

1e *Anne Veronica; *b* 10 Sept 1910; *m* 1936 Lt-Col Richard McNaughton Lendrum, DSO (*d* 1976), and has:

1f *Richard Brian; *b* 1949; *m* 1970 *Gail Jeanette Robinson

1f *Jillian Anne; *b* 1944; *m* 1965 *Raymond Thomas Benwell

2e *Flora Hamilton; *b* 21 Jan 1912

3e *Kathleen; *b* 30 March 1920; *m* 19– (*divorce* 1972) Alexander Clarke Wilson, of Vancouver

1c Charlotte Melosina; *m* 23 April 1851 John McPherson, MD, and had issue. He *d* 1890

2c Catherine Mabella; *m* 14 March 1861 Thomas L Kennedy and *d* 28 March 1870, leaving issue

4b Richard; *m* Barbara (*m* 2nd Dec 1826 Sir Alexander McDonnell, 1st and last Bt, PC (*dsp* 1875), dau of Hugh Montgomery, of Benvarden, and *dsp* 1819

3b Grace Louisa; *m* 12 Oct 1807 1st Marquess of Ormonde (*qv* 1970 edn) and *d* 3 May 1860, having had issue

4b Frances; *m* 1804 her cousin Rt Rev Hon Richard Ponsonby (*see* BESSBOROUGH, E)

5b Charlotte Melosina; *m* 7 June 1819 William Lenox Conyngham, of Spring Hill, JP, DL, and *d* 1847, leaving issue

6b Catherine; *m* 21 Aug 1813 Rev Robert Alexander, est s of Alexander Nathaniel, Bp Meath, and *d* 12 March 1830, leaving issue

7b Elizabeth; *m* Rev Hugh Hamilton, of Innishmacsaint, Co Fermanagh (*d* 1865)

2a Alexander (Rev); *b* 11 Jan 1739; *m* Jane Wilson and had, with two daus:

1b Thomas (Rev); had a dau

2b Alexander (Rev); Rector Gowran, Co Kilkenny; *m* 1816 Dorothea (*d* 1859), only child of Rev Monsey Alexander, and *d* 1864, having had five sons and three daus

3b William; *m* Elizabeth Frances (*m* 2nd 25 May 1811 William O Wallis Ogle), dau of G P Monck, MP, and *dsp*

1b Jane; *m* 1792 Rev Thomas Monck, bro of 1st Viscount Monck (*qv*)

STARKEY

Arms: Arg. a bend engrailed vair between six storks sa.
Crest: A stork arg. semée of estoiles az.
Motto: *Homo proponit, Deus disponit* ('Man proposes, God disposes').
Creation: Bt. (UK) 9 July 1935.

SIR JOHN PHILIP STARKEY, 3RD BT, of Norwood Park, in the Parish of Southwell, Co Nottingham, JP (Newark 1981), DL Notts (1981) [Sir John Starkey Bt JP DL, Norwood Park, Southwell, Notts NG25 0PF]; *b* 8 May 1938; *s f* 1977; *educ* Eton and Ch Ch Oxford (MA); Sloan Fell London Business Sch, with Anthony Gibbs & Sons Ltd, High Sheriff Notts 1987–88, a Ch Commnr 1985–91, chm: Notts br CLA 1977–80, E Midlands Regnl Ctee Nat Tst 1986–; UK v-pres Confedn of European Agriculture 1989–, FRSA 1990; *m* 10 Jan 1966 *Victoria Henrietta Fleetwood, 2nd dau of Lt-Col Christopher Herbert Fleetwood Fuller, TD, of Jaggards, Corsham, Wilts (*see* FULLER, Bt), and has:

1 +HENRY JOHN *b* 13 Oct 1973

1 *Suzannah Clare; *b* 5 Oct 1966; *m* 1989 *Jonathan Beatson-Hird, yr s of Dr John Beatson-Hird, of Oldwell, Ashton-under-Hill, nr Evesham, Worcs, and has:

(1) *Hubert John; *b* 1992

(2) *Digby George; *b* 1994

2 *Elizabeth Victoria; *b* 1975

3 *Katherine Alexandra; *b* 12 Aug 1977

Lineage: JOHN STARKY, of Longwood House, in Huddersfield; *bapt* 23 Oct 1608, bought lands at Brockholes, in Ovendon 1671. He was *s* by his est *s*:

JOHN STARKEY, of Longwood Ho; *bapt* 16 Jan 1641; *m* Anne, and *d* 1702, leaving with other issue, an est *s* and heir:

JOHN STARKEY, of Longwood Ho, who, in conjunction with his bro sold the Brockholes estate; *bapt* 7 Feb 1675; *m* 7 May 1697 Alice Drake, and had an only *s*:

JOHN STARKEY, of Marsh, in Huddersfield; *bapt* 1 Dec 1701; *m* Martha, and *d* 10 June 1782, leaving several sons and daus, of whom the est *s*:

JOHN STARKEY, of Littletown, Liversedge, Yorks; *bapt* 12 June 1734; *m* 26 May 1760 Martha (who *m* 2nd — Bradley, of Huddersfield), dau of Joshua Collingwood, of Huddersfield, and *d* 1764, leaving issue, an only *s*:

JOHN STARKEY, of Wheat Ho, Huddersfield, and Heaton Lodge, Yorks; *bapt* 17 June 1762; *m* 26 March 1787 Abigail (*d* 1844), dau of William Dewhurst, of Warley, Yorks, and *d* 24 May 1813, leaving, with other issue, a 2nd *s*:

JOHN STARKEY, of Spring Lodge, Huddersfield, Yorks, DL and JP W Riding; *b* 7 April 1792; *m* 14 Jan 1835 Sarah Anne (*d* 30 Aug 1880), est dau of Joseph Armitage, DL, JP, of Huddersfield, and *d* 13 Dec 1856, leaving, with other issue:

1 LEWIS RANDLE, of whom presently

2 John Frederick, of Bodicote Ho, Banbury, DL, JP; *b* 11 April 1839; *m* Aug 1877 Mary Margaret (*d* 10 July 1908), dau of Rev Henry Snow, Vicar of Bibury, Glos, and *d* 15 June 1925, leaving:

(1) John Henry, DL, JP Warwicks, Lt-Col late The Rifle Bde, served in S African War and WW I, Land Tax Commr from 1927; *b* 18 Oct 1881; *educ* Wellington and RMC Sandhurst; *m* 29 May 1915 Phyllis Quayle, only child of Brig-Gen Morey Quayle Jones, CB, CMG, CBE, DL, JP, of Barton Mere, Suffolk, and *d* 16 Feb 1959, leaving:

1a Morey John Peter, JP (Warwicks 1959), Gen Commr of Income Tax 1970, Maj late 1st Roy Dragoons, served WW II (despatches, French Croix de Guerre), MFH Warwickshire 1958–61 *b* 17 July 1916; *educ* Eton and RMC Sandhurst; *m* 20 April 1949 *Ann Pauline, dau of Lt-Col Victor Jones, OBE, 14/20th Hus, of Broadway, Worcs, and *d* 30 Dec 1974, having had:

1b *Jane Victoria; *b* 27 July 1950; *educ* Tudor Hall

2b Sarah Ann; *b* 29 June, *d* 22 Oct 1956

1a *Diana Isabel Margaret; *b* 20 June 1919; *m* 1st 22 May 1940 (*divorce* 1961) Peter McBean, s of Atholl McBean, of San Francisco, USA, and has:

1b *Judith Diana; *b* 30 April 1941; *m* 30 April 1965 Harry-Selby Hunt, son of Harry C Hunt, of Pebble Beech, CA, USA, and has:

1c *Natasha; *b* 1 Jan 1970

2b *Sheila Margaret; *b* 22 July 1943; *m* 19 Dec 1966 Philip Howard

3b *Edith Starkey; *b* 3 Oct 1951

1a (cont.) Mrs Diana McBean *m* 2nd 14 Aug 1961 David Harry Weatherby, only s of Sir Francis Wetherby, MC, of Whatcote, Shipston-on-Stour, Warwicks

(1) Jane Margaret; *b* 1878; *m* 23 Aug 1905 Col Walter Goring (*see* GORING, Bt), and *d* 1 May 1956

(2) Emily Mary; *b* 1879; *m* 8 Nov 1910 Sir Lister Lister-Kaye, 6th Bt, JP (*qv*), and *d* 10 May 1944, leaving issue

(3) Rosamund Agnes; *b* 1880; *m* 7 Sept 1909 V-Adml Bernard St George Collard, CB, DSO, 3rd s of Rev Canon John Marshall Collard, MA, by his w Grace Jane Sarah, 3rd dau of Capt Anthony Oliver Molesworth (*see* MOLESWORTH, V), and *d* 16 Feb 1957, leaving issue. He *d* 12 April 1962

(4) Olive Grace; *b* 1883; *m* 6 March 1915 Lt-Col Arthur Guy Leslie Pepys, MC, 2nd son of Hon Henry Leslie Pepys, and *d* 1 Aug 1961, leaving issue (*see* COTTENHAM, E)

John Starkey's s,

LEWIS RANDLE STARKEY, of Norwood Park, Notts, DL, JP, High Sheriff 1891, MP S Div W Riding 1874–80, formerly Capt 2nd West York Yeo Cav; *b* 13 March 1836; *m* 5 May 1858, his cousin, Constance Margarette (*d* 6 April 1919), dau of Thomas Starkey, JP, and *d* 16 Sept 1910, leaving:

1 JOHN RALPH (Sir), **1st Bt**

2 Lewis Edward, Lt-Col 4th Hus, served in Egyptian Campaign, and S African War (despatches); *b* 23 Nov 1862; *educ* Eton; *m* 6 July 1906, his cousin, Mary Kathleen (*d* 18 Aug 1926), dau of Thomas Stanton Starkey, 9th Lancers, of Huttons Ambo Hall, York, and *d* 27 Dec 1943, leaving:

(1) (Lewis) Stanton, JP (1965–68), CC (1954), CA (1970), NR Yorks, Lt-Col late Gren Gds, joined Gren Gds 1927, served with 3rd Bn in Egypt 1934–35, served WW II 1939–45 (despatches), cmdg 1st Bn Gren Gds 1944–45, Lt-Col 1944, ret 1947, underwriting memb Lloyd's 1958; *b* 22 July 1906; *educ* privately, and RMC Sandhurst; *m* 1st 14 June 1944 Claire Desirée (*d* 3 March 1956), formerly w of Hon Phelim Robert Hugh O'Neill (*see* RATHCAVAN, B), and dau of Detmar Jellings Blow, of Hilles, Stroud, Glos, and had:

1a *Kathleen Mary; *b* 13 March 1946; *m* 2 Sept 1972 *John Fitzgerald Willcox Jenyns, yr s of (Roger) Soame Jenyns, JP, of Bottisham Hall, Cambridge

(1) (cont.) Lt Col Stanton Starkey *m* 2nd 1 Nov 1957 Lady Georgiana Mary (*d* 11 Jan 1976), formerly w of Lt Home Reginald Kidston, RN, and est dau of 5th Earl Howe, PC, CBE (*qv*), and *d* 5 Sept 1975

3 Thomas Randle, JP Notts, late Capt Notts YC; *b* 1 April 1864; *d* unm 13 Nov 1916

4 Arthur Henry; *b* 31 May 1865; *d* unm 18 Aug 1947

1 Constance Agnes; *m* 1st 23 April 1903 R H Warwick (*d* 19–), of Burgage Manor, Southwell, Notts; *m* 2nd 1 July 1916 Herbert George Armitage, s of Rev George Armitage, of Broughton Askey Rectory, Leics, and *d* 17 April 1948

2 Margarette Eveline; *m* 12 Sept 1895 Rev John Frederick Lord, MA, est s of John Pickup Lord, of Hallow Park, Worcester, and *d* 27 Dec 1943, leaving issue

3 Laura Beatrice; *d* unm 6 July 1920

The est son,

Sir John Ralph Starkey, 1st Bt, so *cr* 9 July 1935, JP, DL, Capt S Notts Yeo, MP Newark Div Notts 1906–22; *b* 1 March 1859; *m* 31 Oct 1888 Emily (*d* 24 Nov 1944), 2nd dau of Sir Charles Seely, 1st Bt (*see* SHERWOOD, B), and had:

1 WILLIAM RANDLE (Sir), **2nd Bt**

1 Hilda Margaret; *m* 28 Jan 1915 Capt Charles Edward Parker, MC, son of Rev Hon Archibald Parker (*see* MACCLESFIELD, E), and had issue

2 Phyllis Lilian; *d* unm 18 Aug 1918

3 Alice Barbara, formerly JP Notts

4 Florence Erica; *m* 20 April 1918 Maj-Gen Bevil Thomson Wilson, CB, DSO (*d* 1975) s of Alexander Wilson, FRCS, DL, of Manchester, and had:

(1) *Alexander James (Sir), KBE (1974, CBE 1966, MBE 1948), MC, Maj-Gen late Lancs Fus, formerly Lt-Col The Rifle Bde, served WW II (despatches), and Kenya 1955 (despatches), Ch of Staff UN Force in Cyprus from 1964, Acting Force Cdr 1965–66, Dir Army Recruiting 1967–70, GOC NW Dist from 1970; *b* 13 April 1921; *m* 3 Oct 1958 *Hon Jean Margaret, formerly wife of Capt Anthony Paul, and 2nd dau of 2nd Baron Rankeillour, GCIE, MC (*qv*), and has:

1a *William Robert Bevil; *b* 15 Aug 1959

2a *Rupert James; *b* 4 Jan 1961

(1) *Priscilla Florence; *b* 2 Oct 1923; *m* 3 July 1948 Julian Philip Gerard Wathen, yst s of Gerard Anstruther Wathen, CIE, of 2, Buckland Crescent, NW3, and has:

1a *Simon Walter Julian; *b* 20 Jan 1950; *educ* Harrow

1a *Penelope Lucy Priscilla; *b* 25 Feb 1952; *educ* St Paul's Girls Sch

2a *Henrietta Katharine Priscilla; *b* 20 June 1954; *educ* St James's, West Malvern

5 Helen Frances; *m* 23 May 1922 Humphrey Parker-Jervis (*see* ST VINCENT, V) and *d* 10 Jan 1998, leaving issue

6 Sylvia Augusta; *m* 1st 10 Sept 1925 Capt Eustace Ruffel Drake Long, CBE, RN (*d* 30 June 1941), s of Rev David Long; *m* 2nd 22 Nov 1951 Reginald Evelyn Welby-Pelham, JP (*d* 19 March 1965), 3rd son of Hon Evelyn Cornwallis Anderson-Pelham, DL, JP (*see* YARBOROUGH, E), and by 1st husb had:

(1) *David Andrew; *b* 1929

(1) *Phoebe Olivia; *b* 1926; *m* 1954 *Henry Martin Shone, and has:

1a *Jeremy Patrick Martin; *b* 1955

2a *Anthony Michael John; *b* 1957

3a *Patrick Douglas; *b* 1959

4a *Colin Henry Philip; *b* 1964

7 *Margaret Lucy; *m* 28 June 1927 Lt-Col James Aubrey Henry Bellingham Somerville, DSO, late RA, 2nd s of Bellingham Arthur Somerville (*see* SOMERVILLE, Bt)

Sir John *d* 13 Nov 1940, and was *s* by his only son,

Sir William Randle Starkey, 2nd Bt, JP (1934), DL (1942), CC (1937), CA (1949–58) Notts, High Sheriff 1954; *educ* Eton and RMC Sandhurst; Lt-Col (TA), late Capt Rifle Bde, served in Iraq 1919–20, and WW II 1939–45 with 2nd Bn London Irish Rifles and Reconnaissance Corps, barrister, Middle Temple 1937, v-chm Notts Quarter Sessions 1949–62, memb Trent River Bd 1946–64, Trent River Authority 1965–68; *b* 11 Dec 1899; *m* 25 April 1935 Irene Myrtle (*d* 11 Nov 1965), dau of Capt Philip Francklin, MVO, RN, and *d* 10 July 1977, leaving:

1 Sir JOHN PHILIP STARKEY, **3rd and present Bt**

2 +Michael William [Michael Starkey Esq, Cutlersforth Farm, Halam, nr Newark, Notts NG22 8AP]; *b* 20 Sept 1946; *educ* Eton, Newcastle U, Trent Business Sch and Nottingham U; BSc, MBA, MInstAM (Dip), MBIM; *m* 1974 *Gillian Mary, dau of E Treflyn Roberts of Shotton, Deeside, Clwyd and has:

(1) +Edward Thomas William; *b* 1978

(1) *Isabella Irené Marianne; *b* 1983

1 *Caroline Myrtle [Lady Hervey-Bathurst, Somborne Park, nr Stockbridge, Hants]; *b* 1 April 1936; *m* 7 Dec 1957 *(Frederick) John Charles Gordon Hervey-Bathurst, only son of Sir Frederick Peter Methuen Hervey-Bathurst, 6th Bt (*qv*), and has issue

STEEL OF AIKWOOD

Creation: B. (LP, UK) 19 April 1997.

THE BARON STEEL OF AIKWOOD, of Ettrick Forest in the Scottish Borders (Sir David Martin Scott Steel, KBE (1990), PC (1977), DL (Roxburgh, Ettrick and Lauderdale (1990)) [The Rt Hon The Lord Steel of Aikwood KBE PC DL, Aikwood Tower, Ettrick Bridge, Selkirkshire TD7 5HJ]; *b* 31 March 1938; *educ* Prince of Wales Sch Nairobi, George Watson's Coll and Edinburgh U; Assist Sec Scottish Lib Party 1962–64; TV interviewer BBC 1964–65; MP (Lib) Roxburgh Selkirk and Peebles 1965–83, Tweeddale Ettrick and Lauderdale 1983–88, (Lib Dem) 1988–97); memb Parly Delegn to UN Gen Assembly 1967; Lib Ch Whip 1970–75; Leader Lib Party 1976–88; TV presenter: STV 1966–67, Granada 1969, BBC 1971–76; Chm Shelter Scotland 1969–73 and Countryside Movement 1996–97; Pres: Anti-Apartheit Movement GB 1966–69, Lib Internat 1994–97; memb: Br Cncl Churches 1971–75, Management Cncl Centre Studies Social Policy 1971–76, Advsy Cncl European Discussion Centre 1971–76; Chubb Fell Yale U 1987; Rector Edinburgh U 1982–85; FRSA 1990; Freedom of: Tweeddale 1988, Ettrick and Lauderdale 1990; DUniv Stirling 1991; Hon DLitt Buckingham; Hon DUniv Heriot Watt, Hon LLD Edinburgh, Cdr's Cross Order Merit Germany 1992; author: *Boost for the Borders* (1964), *Out of Control* (1968), *No Entry* (1969), *The Liberal Way Forward* (1975), *A New Political Agenda* (1976), *Militant for the Reasonable Man* (1977), *New Majority for a New Parliament* (1978), *High Ground of Politics* (1979), *A House Divided* (1980), *Border Country* (with Judy Steel, 1985), *Mary Stuart's Scotland* (with Judy Steel, 1987), *Against Goliath: David Steel's story* (1989); *m* 1962 *Judith Mary, dau of W D MacGregor, CBE, of Dunblane, and has two sons and a dau

Lineage: The Very Rev Dr DAVID STEEL; *m* 1937 *Sheila Martin, of Aberdeen, and had:

DAVID MARTIN SCOTT, *cr* a **Baron**

STEPHENSON

Arms: Vair on a pale between two pallets gu. three leopard's faces or, two flaunches of the second. **Crest**: A rock thereon a falcon's head erased ppr., gorged with a collar vair, pendant therefrom an escutcheon vert charged with two arrows saltirewise, points downwards or. **Creation**: Bt. (UK) 16 July 1936.

SIR HENRY UPTON STEPHENSON, 3RD BT, of Hassop Hall, Co Derby, TD [Sir Henry Stephenson Bt TD, Tissington Cottage, Rowland, Bakewell, Derbys DE45 1NR]; *b* 26 Nov 1926; *s f* 1982; *educ* Eton; High Sheriff Derbys 1975, late Maj QO Yorks Dragoons, dir: Stephenson Blake (Holdings) Ltd, Thos Turton and Sons Ltd; *m* 19 May 1962 *Susan Diana Ruth, only child of Maj John Ernest Clowes, of Clifton, Ashbourne, Derbys, and has:

1 *Fiona Kathleen; *b* 2 April 1964
2 *Annabel Mary; *b* 9 Aug 1965
3 *Emma Frances; *b* 14 Feb 1968
4 *Lucy Clare; *b* 1970

Lineage: JOHN STEPHENSON, of Sheffield; *b* 1762; *m* Jane Green, and was father of:

JOHN STEPHENSON, of Endcliffe, Sheffield; *b* 1790; *m* 2 Feb 1821 Elizabeth (*d* 12 Dec 1826), dau of John Kirk, and *d* 29 Sept 1864, leaving:

SIR HENRY STEPHENSON, of The Glen, Endcliffe Vale, Sheffield, JP (WR Yorks and Sheffield), Mayor Sheffield 1887, ktd 1887; *b* 2 Dec 1826; *m* 19 June 1862 Emma (*d* 5 Aug 1921), dau of Thomas James Parker, of Sheffield, and *d* 24 Aug 1904, leaving:

1 John Parker; *d* young
2 HENRY KENYON (Sir), **1st Bt**
1 Catherine Mary; *m* 6 Jan 1891 George Ernest Branson, JP, Hon Col 4th (Hallamshire) Bn York and Lancaster Regt, and *d* 17 Jan 1956, leaving issue. He *d* 14 May 1940
2 Emma; *m* 11 June 1895 Lt-Col John Rodgers, of 14 Endcliffe Ave, Sheffield, and *d* 1960, leaving issue. He *d* 19 Jan 1919

The 2nd s,

Lt-Col Sir Henry Kenyon Stephenson, 1st Bt, (UK) so *cr* 16 July 1936, DSO (1918), VD, JP (WR Yorks and Sheffield), DL (Yorks); *b* 16 Aug 1865; Hon LLD and Pro-Chllr Sheffield Univ; Ld Mayor of Sheffield 1908–09 and 1910–11, High Sheriff of Derbyshire 1932; MP Sheffield (Park Div) 1918–23, chm Stephenson, Blake and Co Ltd, of Sheffield and London, had Diamond Jubilee Medal 1897 and Coronation Medals 1902 and 1911, Hon Freeman Sheffield 1929, Lt-Col RFA (TA), WW I (despatches three times, star, two medals); *m* 10 Jan 1894 Frances (*d* 29 Oct 1953), est dau of Maj William Greaves Blake, JP, DL, of Mylnhurst, Ecclesall, Sheffield, and had:

1 HENRY FRANCIS BLAKE (Sir), **2nd Bt**
2 William Raymond Shirecliffe; *b* 27 Aug 1898; *educ* Eton; served WW I 1917–18 as 2nd Lt 11th Hus (SR) (two medals), jt md Thos Turton and Sons, Ltd; *m* 11 April 1923 Madeleine Rose (*d* 1990), dau of George Montagu Butterworth, of Westward Ho!, Devon, and *d* 1977 leaving:

(1) +TIMOTHY HUGH, TD, JP (Sheffield) [Timothy Stephenson Esq TD JP, Lomberdale Hall, Bakewell, Derbys DE4 1LU]; *b* 5 Jan 1930; heir presumptive; *educ* Eton and Magdalene Coll Cambridge; *m* 7 July 1959 *Susan Lesley, yr dau of George Arthur Harris, of Sycamore Grange, Bradway, Sheffield, and has:

1a +Matthew Francis Timothy [Matthew Stephenson Esq. 3 Stoke Park Rd, Stoke Bishop, Bristol BS9 1LE]; *b* 24 Aug 1960; *m* 1984 *Philipa Delphine, dau of John Lincoln, of Aldersley Ho, Chester, and has:

1b +John Louis; *b* 1986
1b *Jessica Frances; *b* 1985
2b *Madeleine Clare; *b* 1990

2a +Oliver George [Oliver Stephenson Esq, The Estate House, Frinkley, nr Doncaster DN5 7BU]; *b* 6 Oct 1962; *m* 1992 *Fiona Alice Jane, dau of Maj Sir David Peter Michael Malcolm, 11th Bt (*qv*), and has:

1b *Augustus William Malcolm; *b* 1994

2b *Alfred Hugh Malcolm; *b* 1996

(1) *Susan Madeleine [Mrs Charles Murray, 3 Belgrave Dve, Sheffield S10 3LQ]; *b* 10 Jan 1924; *educ* Sheffield High Sch, Benenden and St Andrews (MA); *m* 26 Feb 1949 *Charles Graham Murray, MBE, JP, DL, s of Dr Charles Graham Murray, of Worksop, and has:

1a *Elizabeth Susan; *b* 27 March 1951
2a *Jane Madeleine; *b* 26 Feb 1953; *m* 1983 *John Ferretti, and has:
1b *Matthew Robert; *b* 1987
2b *James Alexander; *b* 1990
3a *Anne Catriona; *b* 21 Jan 1955; *m* 1982 *Frank W Womack and has:
1b *Alastair Edward; *b* 1984
2b *Thomas Martin; *b* 1986

(2) *Jocelyn Frances [Mrs David Wilson, 363 Fulwood Rd, Sheffield S10 3BS]; *b* 12 Oct 1926; *m* 10 July 1948 *David Clement Wilson, yr s of Preb Clement Eustace Macro Wilson (*see* HAMILTON OF DALZELL, B), and has:

1a *Christopher Michael Rockley; *b* 24 June 1957
1a *Olivia Frances; *b* 17 May 1952; *m* 1976 (*divorce* 1989) Christopher A Cooke
2a *Sarah Margaret; *b* 19 Oct 1954; *m* 1982 *Jaime Acosta and has:
1b *Simon; *b* 1985
2b *Nicolas; *b* 1988

3 Percival John Parker; *b* 18 May 1900; *educ* Eton; *m* 23 Sept 1930 (*divorce* 1948) Pamela Benton, er dau of Sir Walter Benton Jones, 2nd Bt (*qv*), and *d* 1973, leaving:

(1) *Jennifer Barbara [Mrs John Thornton, Alburgh House, Alburgh, Harleston, Norfolk]; *b* 8 Nov 1931; *m* 25 Oct 1958 *John Henry Thornton, yr s of Rev John Gordon Thornton, and has:

1a *Edward John; *b* 25 May 1963
2a *Robert Walter; *b* 18 March 1968
1a *Katherine Louise; *b* 27 April 1961; *m* 1986 *Timothy James Stapleton Harris and has:
1b *Georgina Rose; *b* 1991
2b *Annabel Louise; *b* 1994

4 Charles Eustace Kenyon; *b* 7 Sept 1903; *educ* Eton and Clare Coll Cambridge (BA 1926); Lt-Col QO Yorks Dragoons WW II, jt md Thos Turton and Sons Ltd, dir Lyon and Lyon Ltd, Knottingley; *m* 4 March 1930 *Nancy Barbara [Mrs Charles Stephenson, The Outrake, Bakewell, Derbys], er dau of Harry Limnell Lyon, JP, of Hillam Hall, Monk Fryston, Yorks, and *d* following an accident 10 Feb 1971, leaving:

(1) +Charles Lyon, TD [Maj Charles Stephenson TD, The Cottage, Great Longstone, Derbys DE45 1UA]; *b* 15 Aug 1935; *educ* Eton; Maj Roy Yeo Regt, md Stephenson Blake (Hldgs) Ltd and Thomas Turton and Sons; *m* 1st 1 March 1960 (*divorce* 1972) Margot Jane, dau of Tony Malcolm Tinker, and has:

1a +George Lyon [George Stephenson Esq, Hurdcott, Barford St Martin, Wilts SP3 4BA]; *b* 23 April 1962; *educ* Eton; *m* 1990 *Lucilla, dau of Jeremy Clay, of Fawley Court, nr Hereford, and has issue
2a +Rupert Nicholas; *b* 24 Dec 1964
1a *Belinda Jane; *b* 17 July 1963

(1) (cont.) Maj Charles Stephenson *m* 2nd 1974 *Hon Sarah Merryweather Norrie, GGSM, dau of 1st Baron Norrie (*qv*)

(1) *Harriet Ann [Mrs John Francis, Meadow Bank, Castle Eden, Co Durham]; *b* 12 Sept 1931; *m* 8 Nov 1951 (*divorce* 1973; *remarried* 1976) *John Bulkley Herbert Francis, s of Capt Mark Herbert Francis, MBE, of Wilton Lodge, Blyth, Notts, and has:

1a *Charles Mark; *b* 4 April 1952; *educ* Bradfield
2a *Timothy; *b* 24 Jan 1960
1a *Clare; *b* 8 May 1955
2a *Charlotte Ann; *b* 30 Oct 1963

1 Evelyn Mary; *m* 5 April 1923 Sir Anthony Henry Mather Jackson, DL, JP, 6th Bt (*see* JACKSON, Bt, of Birkenhead), and had issue
2 Helena Millicent Frances; *b* 25 May 1906; *d* 1996
3 *Cynthia Margaret, MBE (1948) [Miss Cynthia Stephenson MBE, 17 Sydney House, Woodstock Rd, London W4]; *b* 3 Sept 1910
4 *Emma Letitia Gertrude [Mrs Philip Lawton, Fenner House, Glebe Way, Wisborough Green, W Sussex]; *m* 25 Oct 1941 Gp/Capt Philip Charles Fenner Lawton, CBE, DFC, RAuxAF (*d* 1993), only s of Charles Studdart Lawton, of, 19, Hampstead Lane, Highgate, London N6, and has:

(1) *Charles Henry Huntly; *b* 17 April 1946; *educ* Westminster; *m* 1979 *Sarah Margaret, dau of Rev Christopher Hugo Lambert, of 26 Abingdon Villas, London W8, and has:

1a *Timothy Philip Hugo; *b* 1982
1a *Hermione Margaret Clare; *b* 1984

(1) *Philippa Rosemary; *b* 6 May 1943; *m* 1974 *Lt-Cdr Michael Henry White, RN, and has issue:

1a *Richard *b* 1978
1a *Serena *b* 1976
2a *Lucinda; *b* 1983

Sir Henry *d* 20 Sept 1947, and was *s* by his est *s*

Sir (Henry) Francis Blake Stephenson, 2nd Bt, OBE (1941), TD, JP (Sheffield 1931), DL (Derbys 1948); *b* 3 Dec 1895; *educ* Eton; High Sheriff 1948, sometime Pro-Chllr and Chm Cncl Sheffield U (Hon LLD 1955), and Hon Col Sheffield U OTC, Maj and Brevet Lt-Col QO Yorkshire Dragoons, WW I (star, two medals) and WW II 1939–43, dir Stephenson, Blake and Co and Thos Turton and Sons; *m* 25 Nov 1925 *Joan [Joan Lady Stephenson, Hassop Green, Bakewell, Derbys], est dau of Maj John Herbert Upton, JP, of Ingmire Hall, Sedbergh, and *d* 1982, leaving:

1 Sir HENRY UPTON STEPHENSON, **3rd and present Bt**

STERLING OF PLAISTOW

Arms: Chequy argent and sable, three lyres bendwise in bend gules.
Crest: A salamander statant upon its hind legs sable, enflamed proper, and holding between the forefeet the Hebrew letter 'Ehaim' argent. **Motto:** *Usque per ignem* ('All the way through fire').
Creation: B. (LP, UK) 1991

THE BARON STERLING OF PLAISTOW, of Pall Mall in the City of Westminster (Sir Jeffrey Maurice Sterling, CBE (1977), Ktd 1985) [The Rt Hon The Baron Sterling of Plaistow CBE, 17 Brompton Sq, London SW3]; *b* 27 Dec 1934; *educ* Reigate GS, Preston Manor County Sch and Guildhall Sch of Music; Advisor: Paul Schweder & Co 1955–57, G Eberstadt & Co 1957–62; Finance Dir Gen Guarantee Corp 1962–64; md Gula Investments Ltd 1964–69; Chm: Sterling Guarantee Trust plc 1969–85, P&O Steam Navigation Co 1983–; dir BA 1979–82; Special Advisor to: Sec State Industry 1982–83, Trade & Industry 1983–90; Chm: Organisation Ctee World ORT (Organisation for Rehabilitation by Training) Union 1969–73, ORT Technical Services 1974–, V-Pres British ORT 1978–; Pres: Gen Cncl British Shipping 1990–91, EC Shipowners Assocs 1992–94; Dep-Chm and Hon Treas London Celebrations Ctee Silver Jubilee 1975–83; Chm: Young Vic Co 1975–83, Govr Royal Ballet Sch 1983– and Royal Ballet 1986–; V-Chm and Chm Exec Motability 1977–; Hon FIME 1991, Hon FICS1992; Hon MRICS 1993; *m* 1985 *Dorothy Ann Smith and has a dau

Lineage: HARRY STERLING; had:

JEFFREY MAURICE STERLING, *cr* a **Baron**

STEVENS OF LUDGATE

Arms: Argent a bear rampant proper and a chief embattled azure.
Crest: A triple mount vert, thereon a crest coronet or, the lesser finials (two manifest) pearled proper statant, within the same a swan, wings displayed proper about the neck two ribands nowed and the ends flotant to the rear gules and argent.
Supporters: Dexter, a lion sejant erect and guardant or; sinister, a cairn terrier also sejant erect and guardant proper, the compartment comprising a grassy mount also proper. **Motto:** Perseverance.
Creation: B. (LP, UK) 1987.

THE BARON STEVENS OF LUDGATE, of Ludgate, City of London (David Robert Stevens) [The Rt Hon The Lord Stevens of Ludgate, 11 Devonshire Sq, London EC2M 4YR]; *b* 26 May 1936; *educ* Stowe and Sidney Sussex Coll Camb (MA); dir: Philip Hill Higginson Erlangers 1959–68, Hill Samuel Securities 1959–68, Drayton Gp 1968–74, Utd Newspapers 1974–; md Samuel Montagu 1974–78; chm: Drayton Far East 1976–93, English & Internat 1976–79, City & For 1976–, Consolidated Venture 1979–93, Drayton Consolidated 1980–92, Drayton Japan 1980–88, Mid States 1989–95, Oak Industs 1989–, EDC for Civil Engrs 1984–86, Utd Newspapers 1981–, Express Newspapers 1985–, Montagu Investment Management 1980–93 (ch exec 1980–87), Britannia Arrow Hldgs 1989–93 (dep-chm 1987–89), Invesco to 1997, Premier Asset Management 1997– and Personal Number Co 1998–; *m* 1st 1961 (*divorce* 1970) Patricia Ann, dau of George Warren Rose; *m* 2nd 1977 Mrs Melissa Sadoff (*d* 1989), dau of Milos Milicevic and Countess Andrassy; *m* 3rd 1990 *Mrs Meriza Giori and has by his 1st w:

  1 *Andrew David; *b* 1966
  2 *Judith Ann; *b* 1964

Lineage: (ARTHUR) EDWIN STEVENS, CBE; *m* Kathleen Alberta, dau of Charles James, and had:

DAVID ROBERT STEVENS, *cr* a **Baron**

STEWART of Athenree

Arms: Quarterly, 1st, or a lion rampant within a double-tressure flory counter-flory gules (for Scotland); 2nd, or a fess chequy azure and argent, in chief a portcullis sable (for STEWART); 3rd, argent a saltire between four roses gules, barbed vert (for LENNOX); 4th, or a lion rampant gules (for FIFE), the whole within a bordure company argent and azure charged with three thistles proper. **Crest:** A unicorn's head, couped argent, armed and crined or, between two olive branches proper. **Motto:** Forward. **Creation:** Bt. (UK) 21 June 1803.

SIR DAVID JOHN CHRISTOPHER STEWART, 7TH BT, of Athenree, Co Tyrone [Sir David Stewart Bt, Tower View, 8 Silver St, Wiveliscombe, Somerset TA4 2PA]; b 19 June 1935; s f 1994; educ Bradfield and RMA Sandhurst; Capt (ret 1965) Roy Inniskilling Fus, seconded to Trucial Oman Scouts 1957–58, Jebel Akhdar campaign 1957, Kuwait Op 1961, UN Peace-keeping Force Cyprus 1964, dir: Maurice James Hldgs, Coventry, 1969–77, Papropak 1977–79, owner George Inn, Middlezoy, Somerset, 1982–85, proprietor David Stewart Picture Framing and Restoration 1990–; memb Fine Art Trade Guild; m 7 Nov 1959 *Bridget Anne, er dau of Patrick Wood Sim, and has:

1 *Siobhan Amanda [Mrs Toby Holland, 21 Rockwell Green, Wellington, Somerset TA21 9BT]; b 6 Feb 1961; m 19 April 1986 *Toby Mark Andrew Holland, s of Bryant Holland, of London, and has:

  (1) *George David Bryant; b 28 Dec 1988

  (1) *Aimee Grace; b 9 Nov 1990

2 *Selina Godfray [Miss Selina Stewart, 49 Allfarthing Lane, London SW18]; b 30 October 1964

3 *Sophie Caroline [Mrs Jonathan A'Court-Wills, 2 Upper Holway Rd, Taunton, Somerset TA1 2HD]; b 3 Aug 1966; m 1 Sept 1990 *Jonathan A'Court-Wills, s of Anthony Wills, of Wellington, Somerset, and has:

  (1) *Patrick David Anthony; b 5 April 1992

  (1) *Alice Victoria Anne; b 13 Jan 1996

Lineage: ANDREW STEWART; migrated from Scotland to Gortigal, Co Tyrone, c 1620; m Sarah — and d by 6 Oct 1658, leaving, with an est s (Robert, had a dau (Janet, m 1684 R Bell), two yr sons (Andrew; James, Offr RN, m a dau of Adml Sir Cloudesley Shovel and was ka) and a dau (Annie), a 2nd s:

HUGH STEWART, of Gortigal; m Margaret, dau of Thomas Morris, of Mountjoy Castle, and had, with three yr sons:

JOHN STEWART, of Gortigal; b 1681; m 1710 Mary Kennedy, of Scotland, and had, with five daus and another s:

Rev HUGH STEWART; b 1711; Rector Termon, Co Tyrone; m 1755 Sarah (d 1764), sis and coheir of Sir Henry Hamilton, Bt, of Castle Conyngham, Co Donegal, and d Jan 1800, having had, with two yr sons (Andrew, Offr HEICS, ka India; Rev Henry, DD, Rector Loughgilly, Co Armagh, m 1st Sophia, dau of William Clossy, of Dublin, and had issue, m 2nd 20 Aug 1842 Harriet Anne, widow of George Scholes, of High Bank, Manchester) and three daus:

Sir John Stewart, 1st Bt (UK), so cr 21 June 1803, of Athenree; b 1757; Attorney-Gen Ireland 1799 (drafted Act of Union), MP Co Tyrone 1802–06 and 1812–25; m Mary (d 28 May 1795), est dau of Mervyn Archdale, JP, of Castle Archdale, Co Fermanagh, and had, with a dau (d unm):

1 HUGH (Sir), **2nd Bt**

2 Mervyn, of Martray Ho, Co Tyrone, JP; b 27 May 1794; High Sheriff 1830; m 17 June 1822 Frances (d 1895), dau of Rev George Vesey, DD, of Derrabard House, Co Tyrone, and d 1885, leaving, with a dau (d unm):

  (1) John Archdale; b 3 May 1824; d unm 25 June 1859

  (2) Mervyn; b 4 Jan 1826; Capt RA; d unm 31 Oct 1874

  (3) George Vesey, MBE, of Martray, Kati Kati, NZ, JP NZ and Co Tyrone; b 4 Oct 1832; educ Trin Coll Dublin; migrated to NZ, fndr there Stewart Special Settlements, Kati Kati and Te Puke (for emigrants from north of Ireland), 1st Mayor Tauranga; m 1st 17 April 1856 Margaret Torrens (d July 1914), dau of John Rowley Miller, of Moneymore, Co Derry, and had:

1a Mervyn Archdale; b 3 Jan 1859; m 1881 Phoebe Louisa (d 19 Oct 1951), dau of Robert Hornidge Gledstanes, and d 8 Dec 1951, having had:

  1b George Cecil; b 1883; NZ Expdny Force WW I; m Irene, dau of Dr John Ward, of Kati Kati, NZ, and was ka 1 Oct 1918

  1b Mary Sophia Ethel; m 1918 Robert Rutland Turner (d 23 Dec 1927), of NZ, and had:

    1c *Stewart Rutland; b 1919; m 1942 *Kathleen, dau of W O'Connor, of Ashburton, NZ, and has:

      1d *A son; b 1943

    1c *Phoebe Ethne; b 1923; m 1944 *Clifford Cedric Mountier

  2b *Evelyn Frances; m 1940 Alfred Edward Sheppard, of Wellsford, NZ. He d 1958

2a George Vesey; b March 1861; m 1890 Cecilia Isabella (d 1947), dau of Thomas Anderson, and d 1892, leaving:

  1b Erin Lucy Sophia

  2b Daisy Cecilia; d 23 May 1953

  3b Georgina Frances; m 6 July 1925 Norman Lawrence Wilson, s of Herbert Wilson, and had:

    1c *Lawrence Stewart; b 1928

    2c *George Archdale; b 1930

    1c *Kerry Robin [Miss Kerry Wilson, 5 Maungarei Rd, Remuera, Auckland 5, New Zealand]; b 1933

    2c *Patricia Cecilia; b 1934

3a John Rowley Miller; b 25 Nov 1862; m 1st 1886 Ellen Louisa (d 1912), dau of John Furniss, of Auckland, NZ, and had:

  1b Mervyn Oswald; b 1888; m 1915 Ivy Mona (d 19–), dau of Robert Ernest Lester, of Kohukohu, Auckland, NZ, and d 1946, leaving:

    1c +Mervyn Leslie Lester; b 1916; m 19– and has:

      1d +Trevor Rex [Trevor Stewart Esq, Takanini, Auckland, New Zealand]; b 1940

    2c +Donald Walton [Donald Stewart Esq, 1 Mainston Rd, Remuera, Auckland, New Zealand]; b 1919; m 1941 *Joan Eunice, yst dau of Harry John Brunsdon, of Christchurch, NZ, and has:

      1d +Roger Alan [Roger Stewart Esq, 106 Wheturangi Rd, Greenland, Auckland, New Zealand]; b 19–; gen manager L'Oreal; m 19– *Linda Denise Marsden and has:

        1e +Hamish; b 19–

        1e *Stephanie Gina; b 19–; m *Alistair Woodhead

        2e *Alexia; b 19–

        3e *Sarra-Jane; b 19–

      2d +Ian Murray [Ian Stewart Esq, Hopkins Crescent, Kohimarara, Auckland, New Zealand]; b 19–; m 19– *Jo Anne Mills and has:

        1e +Barnaby; b 19–

        1e *Felicity; b 19–

      3d +Evan Alistair; b 19–; m 19– *Avril Burberry and has:

        1e +Troy Anthony; b 19–

        2e +Andrew; b 19–

        1e *Lucinda; b 19–

      4d +Peter Mark; b 19–; m 1987 *Jennifer Dowling

    1d *Juliet Cynthia [Mrs Donald Worrall, 15 Awatea Rd, Parnell, Auckland, New Zealand]; b 1942; m 1969 *Donald Rex Worrall and has:

      1e *Allister Stewart; b 1971

      2e *Marcus James; b 1973

      3e *Elliot John; b 1974

      4e *Jonathan Charles; b 1978

    3c +Kenneth Archdale [Kenneth Stewart Esq, 70 Ray Small Dve, Papakura, New Zealand]; b 1922; sr clerk Min Works, Auckland; m 1951 *Elma Pearl, dau of Harold Kirtlan, of Kaitaia, NZ, and has:

      1d +Murray Kenneth; b 1952; m 19– *Barbara Lynn, dau of Hugh Douglas, of Wellington, NZ, and has:

        1e +Daniel Craig; b 1978

        1e *Kirsty Nicole; b 1981

      1d *Gael; b 1953; m 19– *David Alexander Spick and has:

        1e *Matthew David; b 1975

        2e *Allister Lee; b 1978

    2d *Jennifer Anne; b 1958; m 1983 *Peter George Neate and has:

      1e *Sam George; b 1988

      1e *Anna-Marie; b 1985

  2b George Leslie; b 1893; m 1927 *Lillian Alice, dau of William Henry Ridsdale, of Whangarei, NZ, and d 1938, leaving:

    1c +Ross Ridsdale [Ross Stewart Esq, 3/22 Mansels Rd, Tauranga, New Zealand]; b 18 March 1934; m 2 July 1966 *Jillian Michelle, dau of Robert Hamilton Bartie, of 532 Gladstone Rd, Gisborne, NZ, and has:

      1d +Jonathan Bruce [Jonathan Stewart Esq, 81 West Harbour Drive, Nth Harbour, Auckland, New Zealand]; b 14 Aug 1969; m 20 Nov 1994 *Vanessa Jayne, dau of Leonard Douglas Heal, of Inglewood, NZ, and has:

        1e +Benjamin Andrew; b 21 Dec 1997

  3b Trevor Rowley; b 1896; m 26 June 1920 Dora, dau of Edwin Hall, of Waihi, NZ, and had:

    1c Colin Trevor; b 16 Jan 1925; m 1948 *Bessie Rebie, dau of Frederick Clarke Shroff, of Te Puna, Tauranga, NZ, and d 1965, leaving:

      1d +Gary Colin [Gary Stewart Esq, Minden Rd, RD Te Puna, Tauranga, New Zealand]; b 1953

      2d +Peter Gregory; b 1958

      1d *Colette Marie; b 1950

    1c *Shirley Rita; b 29 March 1921; m 1st 1945 (divorce 1950) William Lloyd Stevens; m 2nd 1969 *Francis Victor Parker and by her 1st husb has:

1d *Kay Stewart; b 1947

1b Adela Louisa; b 1887; m 1st 1905 Richard George Mackay (d 1916) and had issue; m 2nd Hugh Gibb and d 1964

2b Florence Mabel; b 1889; m 1915 Stanley James Weston and d 1962, leaving issue

3b Elsie Hilda; b 1892; m 1913 Fred Norman Rhodes and had issue

4b Rita; d unm 25 Dec 1920

5b Doris; b 1895; m 1922 Kenneth Richard James and d 1955, leaving issue

3a (cont.) John Stewart m 2nd Jan 1913 Louise Beatrice, dau of Thomas Gorst Travis, of Dunedin, NZ, and d 1945, having by her had:

4b John Rowley Miller; b July 1914; F/O RAF; drowned NZ while swimming

6b *Lorraine Travis [Mrs Alfred Willan, Hastings Rd, Stratford, Taranaki, New Zealand]; b 1917; m 1937 *Alfred Shepherd Willan and has:

1c *Michael Frederick Stewart; b 7 Oct 1941

2c *Jock Stewart; b 27 Aug 1944

3c *Bruce Stewart; b 1 May 1946

1c *Pamela Stewart; b 10 Oct 1939

4a Hugh Alexander Montgomery Moore, JP (NZ); b 3 Nov 1867; m 1st 1891 Susan (d 15 Aug 1926), dau of William Tasman Clark, CE, of Hobart, and had:

1b James Edward Frederick Vesey Tasman; b 18–; m 19– and had:

1c +Noel Montgomery; b 19–

2b Frederick; b 189–

3b Alfred William Tasman; b 1894; m 1918 Elizabeth May Davies and had:

1c +John Hugh Vesey; b 1920; m *Joan Kipping and has:

1d +Roger

2d +Jeffery

3d +Rex

1d *Caroline

2c +Ronald James; b 1925; m and has:

1d +Robert

1d *Elizabeth

2d *Louise

3d *Katy

1c *Muriel Gertrude May; b 1918; m 1st 19– Harry Lauder and has:

1d *Allan

2d *Larry

1c (cont.) Mrs Lauder m 2nd *Mervyn Fisher and by him has:

1d *Sandra

2c *Doreen Phyliss Anzac; b 1928; m 19– *Harold Edward Collins and has:

1d *John Edward; b 1957

1d *Janet May; b 1956; m 19– *Christopher Stuart and has:

1e *Grant

1e *Kirsty May

2e *Stacey Louise

2d *Julie Jean; b 1966; has:

1e *Daniel Alexander COLLINS

4b Hugh (Peter) Alexander Murray; b 1897; m 1927 Veronica Carey and d 1978, leaving:

1c +Hugh Murray Robert; b 1928; m 1950 *Beryl Eileen Keen and has:

1d +Ronald Graham; b 1952; m 1980 *Noelene Erin North and has:

1e *Jarred Ronald; b 1985

2e *Aaron Hugh; b 1989

1e *Mellissa Noelene; b 1983

1d *Eileen Mary; m 1976 (divorce 1995) Graham Laut Frith and has:

1e *Paul Laut; b 1981

1e *Lisa Marie; b 1980

1d (cont.) Mrs Eileen Frith m 2nd *Ronald Jones had by him has:

2e *Andrew Stewart; b 1996

1c *Pamela Beatrice; b 1935; m 1955 *Robert Leslie Hines and has:

1d *Michael Robert; b 1956; m 1982 *Florence Ly Raitt and has:

1e *Benjamin Robert; b 1989

2e *Stuart Alan; b 1992

1e *Laura Veronica; b 1990

2d *Peter John; b 1959; m 1986 (divorce 1987) Joanne Bentley

1d *Judith Ann; b 1961; m 1982 *Stephen Douglas John Gibbons and has:

1e *Scott Robert John; b 1984

1e *Katrina Louise; b 1986

5b Ranfurly Henry Gilbert; b 1899; m 19– Emma Frances Newman (d 1967) and d 1972, leaving:

1c +William Henry Albert Harvey [William Stewart Esq, Ohauiti Rd 782, RD3, Tauranga, New Zealand]; b 1929; m 1951 *Joan Alison, dau of David Prestney, and has:

1d +Brian William; b 1966; m 1992 *Joy Pamela Dick and has:

1e *Amy Elizabeth; b 1991

2e *Casey Ann; b 1994

1d *Julie Frances; b 1953; m 19– *Peter Robert Gray, s of Jack Gray, of Te Puke, and has:

1e *Richard Bruce; b 1977

1e *Jennifer Louise; b 1975

2e *Alison Julie; b 1980

2d *Colleen Margaret; b 1955; m 19– *Philip Edward Watts, s of Thomas Watts, of Tauranga, and has:

1e *Andrew Thomas; b 1980

2e *Ryan Philip; b 1983

3e *Caleb John; b 1991

1e *Anna Liese; b 1987

3d *Janelle Beverley; b 1957; m 19– *John Anthony Arts, s of Bernhard J Arts, of Tauranga, and has:

1e *Anthony James; b 1989

1e *Renée Marise; b 1982

2e *Sarah Rochelle; b 1983

3e *Katie Monique; b 1985

4d *Debora Joy; b 1959; m 1st 19– (divorce 19–) Paul Anthony Hogg and has:

1e *Adam Stewart; b 1984

4d (cont.) Mrs Debora Hogg m 2nd 19– *Thomas William Smith and by him has:

2e *William Stewart; b 1990

3e *Hugh Stewart; b 1993

2c +Trevor Ernest; b 1931; m 1955 *Joan Alice, dau of Andrew Stanley Fisher, and has:

1d +Kevin Mark; b 1959; m 1984 *Vanessa Amiria Milner and has:

1e +Dion Mark; b 1984

2d +Steven Wayne; b 1962; m 19– *Megan Rose Jackson and has:

1e *Matthew Allan; b 1986

1e *Stacey Janna; b 1992

3d +David Ernest; b 1968; has:

1e *Jacob Mathew; b 1996

4d +Philip Trevor; b 1972; has:

1e *Jake Zane; b 1996

1d *Maureen Anne; b 1957; has:

1e *Philippa Joan; b 1988

2d *Shona Joy; b 1961; m 19– *William Francis Mortleman and has:

1e *Rory Shane; b 1988

2e *Hayley Maree; b 1991

3d *Sarah Lisa-Marie; b 1970

1c *Valerie Elizabeth Grace; b 1933; m 19– *Patrick John Jean

2c *Dawn Frances; b 21 Sept 1937; m 19– (divorce 1974) Ronald Leslie Nicholson and has had:

1d Robin Leslie; b 7 Dec 1956; d 8 Dec 1956

1d *Linda Dawn; b 29 Sept 1960; m 28 June 1982 (divorce 1987) Stephen John Clarke and has:

1e *Peter Joseph; b 25 Sept 1984

1e *Lena Helen; b 3 Sept 1983

2d *Christine Frances; b 12 May 1964

3d *Ronda Erin; b 4 Sept 1969

1b *Christina Martina Alice; m 1920 Robert Hynds, s of Robert Hynds Tauranga, and had:

1c *Robert Hugh Owen; b 1920; m 1950 *Emily Agnes Constance Hobbs and has:

1d *Derek Arthur Robert; b 1950; m 1976 *Jenny Peers and has:

1e *Jason; b 1980

1e *Rachael; b 1977

2d *Trevor Owen; b 1952; m 1972 *Pauleen Collins and has:

1e *Michael; b 1975

2e *Tristan; b 1978

1e *Maree; b 1971; m 1991 *Graham Armer and has:

1f *Adrian; b 1993

1f *Catherine; b 1992

1d *Pauline Faye; b 1955; m 1980 *David Meade and has:

1e *Glen; b 1986

1e *Jessica; b 1984

2d *Pamela Audrey; b 1955; m 1972 *Peter Grant and has:

1e *Tracey Lee; b 1972

2e *Nicola Ellen; b 1978

3e *Angela Rose; b 1982

1c *Oleen Rose; m William Hart

2b *Myrtle Ivy Jane; m Reginald Frederick Polley and had:

1c *Reginald Frederick Hugh; b 1927; m 1953 *Nancy Edmundson and has:

1d *David Reginald; b 1956; m Jan Diane Hillman and has:

1e *Jordan William Hugh; b 1985

2e *Reon William Segar; b 1989

1e *Camille Isabella; b 1994

2d *Ian Allen; b 1959; m 1984 *Briar Commons and has:

1e *Ben Jackson; b 1989

1e *Lara Charlotte; b 1986

3d *Bruce Steven; b 1962; m *Michelle Veronica Dumphy and has:

1e *Blair Vauhan; b 1989

2e *Zane Fraser; b 1995

2c *George Robert Hutson; b 1930; m 1956 *Shirley Doreen Work and has:

1d *Stuart Hutson; b 1963; m 1989 *Lynette Watkins and has:

1e *Grace Catherine; b 1992

2e *Scarlet Rose; b 1996

2d *Craig Robert; b 1963; m *Jaquiline Worsfold and has:

1e *Helena; b 1995

1d *Janine Linda; *b* 1958; *m* 1st Barry James Palmer and has:

    1e *Kaylie Jan; *b* 1977

    2e *Lauren; *b* 1980

1d (cont.) Mrs Janine Palmer *m* 2nd Murray Connor and by him has:

    1e *James; *b* 1988

    2e *Daniel; *b* 1989

    3e *Alicia; *b* 1985

1d (cont.) Mrs Janine Connor *m* 3rd *Wayne McLaren and by him has:

    4e *Kayla; *b* 1994

    5e *Teani; *b* 1995

2d *Michele Susan; *b* 1960; *m* 1991 *Loubo Raskovic and has:

    1e *Sarah Jean; *b* 1992

4a (cont.) Hugh Alexander Montgomery Stewart *m* 2nd 16 March 1932 Edith, est dau of Joseph Cantwell of Hawkes Bay, NZ, and *d* 21 Nov 1954, having by him had:

3b *Coral Elizabeth; *b* 19–

5a Andrew Charles Henry Arbuthnot; *b* 23 Sept 1870; *m* 1st 1935 Agnes (*d* 1944), dau of Luther Wright; *m* 2nd 1945 *Blanche Camilla D'Outhoorn, dau of William Shaw, of Kildare, Ireland, and *d* 3 Dec 1961

6a William Nassau; *b* 14 Dec 1873; served Otago Bn NZ Expdny Force France 1916; *m* 31 July 1920 May Eveline (*d* 1963), 3rd dau of Luther Wright, of Bradford, and *d* 10 March 1954

1a Emily Charlotte Sophia; *m* 12 June 1879 Richard Villiers Surtees and *d* leaving issue. He *d* 26 April 1938

2a Fanny Montgomery; *m* 1886 Michael Patrick Shaw-Stewart and *d* 1947, leaving issue (*see* SHAW-STEWART, Bt)

3a Mary Phoebe; *m* 1885 Arthur Roderick Dumbleton, of Grey Lynn, Auckland, NZ, and *d* 26 July 1962, leaving issue

(3) (cont.) George Stewart *m* 2nd Oct 1919 Alice Stein and *d* 1 March 1920

(4) Hugh, JP (NZ); *b* 5 Sept 1841; Capt RA; *m* 28 April 1870 Adela Blanche (*d* 12 Feb 1910), dau of Maj James Anderson, DL, of Havering Grange, and *d* 14 April 1909, leaving:

1a Mervyn James (Rev); *b* 17 March 1871; Capt DCLI WW I, Vicar Manuden Essex 1928–55, FSA Scot, FRGS; *m* 28 March 1910 Margaret Emma (*d* 2 Jan 1968), 2nd dau of Frederick Jeffray Steuart, of New Plymouth, NZ, and *d* 20 Feb 1961, leaving:

1b +Hugh St Clair, MBE (1945) [Lt-Col Hugh Stewart MBE, Oak Cottage, Cheapside Lane, Denham, Bucks UB9 5AD]; *b* 14 Dec 1910; *educ* St John's Coll Cambridge (BA 1932, MA 1948); Lt-Col cmdg Army Film and Photographic Unit WW II; *m* 31 July 1934 Frances Henley (*d* 1982), only child of Dr Henley Frank Curl, of Wokingham, Berks, and has:

1c +Andrew Mervyn; *b* 15 June 1943; *educ* Rugby; *m* 1st 3 Dec 1966 (*divorce* 1991) Carol-Anne, only dau of Stanley Burritt Featherstone, of Uitenhage, S Africa; *m* 2nd 1991 *Maaike, dau of Dr Ir Johan Joseph Breen, of Forinchem, Holland, and by his 1st w has:

1d *Zoe Abbygail *b* 1971

2c +Michael Henley [Michael Stewart Esq, Heathlands, Keepers Lane, Hyde Heath, Bucks HP6 5RJ]; *b* 1949; *educ* Rugby and Southampton U; *m* 1st 1971 Jillian Maureen (*d* 1980), dau of Stanley Gold, of Reigate, and has:

1d +Simon Mark Hugh; *b* 1977

2d +Paul Daniel *b* 1978

2c (cont.) Michael Stewart *m* 2nd 1985 *Ann Frances, dau of Frank Harris, of Feltham, and by her has:

1d *Sally Ann; *b* 1985

2d *Clare Henley June; *b* 1987

3d *Hannah Daisy; *b* 1989

1c *Penelope Agnes [Mrs Hugh Forsyth, Linden Lodge, Austen Way, Chalfont St Peter, Bucks]; *b* 19 April 1939; *educ* Somerville Coll Oxford (BA 1960, MA 1965); *m* 11 Aug 1962 *Hugh Macdonald Eales Forsyth, s of Hugh Forsyth, of Takeley, Essex, and has:

1d *Kevin Hugh; *b* 11 April 1969

2d *Angus Edward Eales *b* 1975

1d *Sophie Frances *b* 1971

2c *MARGARET later TROTTIE; *b* 24 June 1949; *educ* Girton Coll Cambridge (MD 1974); *m* 1971 *Anthony Kirwan and has:

1d *Jonathan Anthony; *b* 1987

1d *Eleanor Catherine; *b* 1979

2d *Frances Marguerite; *b* 1982

2b +David [David Stewart, 2425 153rd Avenue SE, Bellevue, Washington 98007, USA]; *b* 12 Feb 1912; AFRAeS, Boeing rep; *m* 1st 1942 Marjorie Susan Carroll (*d* 10 Dec 1961), yr dau of Rev Frederick Charles Costeloe, Vicar Staveley, Carlisle, and has:

1c +Gordon Archdale [Gordon Stewart, 9760 Barnett Valley Rd, Sebastopol, CA 95472, USA]; *b* 3 April 1944; *educ* St Columba's and Pacific Lutheran U (BS 1966); *m* 1982 *Cora Docken

2c Simon Jeffray; *b* 3 Aug 1945; *educ* St Columba's and Washington U (BA 1967, MBA 1969); *m* 14 Sept 1968 Carolyn Frances Sroufe (*d* 1992), yr dau of Eugene L Henderson, of Seattle, and *d* 1993, leaving:

1d +Patrick Jeffray; *b* 1979

1d *Rachel Elizabeth; *b* 1976

3c +David James [David Stewart, 7338 47th Avenue NE, Seattle, Washington 98115, USA]; *b* 2 May 1952; *educ* Washington U (MBA); *m* 1979 (*divorce* 1994) Carole Cummins; *m* 2nd 1997 *Vickie Davie and by his 1st w has:

1d +Michael Cameron; *b* 1985

1d *Susan Blake; *b* 1989

2b (cont.) David Stewart *m* 2nd 15 Nov 1963 *Grace Edman Cunningham, only dau of Paul Maxwell Edman, of Madison, Conn.

1b *Mary Jeffray [Mrs John Furness, Estone, Steeple Aston, Oxon]; *b* 14 July 1913; Sect Offr WAAF WW II ; *m* 3 Feb 1944 Dr John Edgar Furness (*d* 1974), late W/Cdr RAF, s of Tom Edgar Furness, and has:

1c *Diana Ruth [Mrs Ronald Gardner, Spring Vale, Steeple Aston, Oxon]; *b* 17 Dec 1944; *m* 1973 *Ronald Gardner and has:

1d *Samantha Kim; *b* 1975

2d *Karen Louise; *b* 1978

3d *Sally Marie; *b* 1984

2b *Audrey Mervyn; *b* 7 Nov 1914; F/O WAAF WW II; *m* 3 Oct 1946 William Herbert Allen, MBE, late F/Lt RAFVR, s of William Henry Allen, of Tunbridge Wells. He *d* 1972

1 Barbara; *m* 1856 Henry Moutray, of Killymoon Castle, Co Tyrone, and *d* 1876, leaving issue. He *d* Feb 1875

2 Mary; *m* 1857 Robert Hornidge Gledstanes and *d* Jan 1920 having had issue. He *d* 1876

3 Phoebe Julia; *m* 1857 Edward Hornidge, of Tulfarris, Co Wicklow, and *d* 1890, leaving issue. He *d* 29 March 1874

The 1st Bt *d* 22 June 1825; his er s,

Sir Hugh Stewart, 2nd Bt; *b* 14 May 1792; MP Co Tyrone 1830–35; *m* 1st 19 Jan 1826 Julia (*d* Nov 1830), dau of Marcus McCausland Gage, of Bellarena, Co Londonderry, and had:

1 JOHN MARCUS (Sir), **3rd Bt**

1 Julia; *m* 25 April 1857 Very Rev Thomas Olphert (*d* 1901), Dean Derry, and had issue

Sir Hugh *m* 2nd 28 Feb 1837 Elizabeth (*d* 2 Sept 1902), dau of Rev Henry Lucas St George, of Dromore, Co Tyrone, and by her had, with a dau (*d* unm):

2 Hugh; *b* 14 April 1840; Capt 39th and 22nd Foot, Govr Kilkenny Prison; *m* 11 June 1874 Harriet Emily (*d* 26 June 1934), dau of Rev Howard St George, and *d* 8 Feb 1909, leaving:

(1) Hugh, DSO, MC; *b* 15 April 1881; Maj/T/Lt-Col RAMC, MB, WW I (despatches twice); *m* 19 Jan 1907 Muriel Dalzell, 2nd dau of Hugh McKean, of Rathgar, Dublin, and was *kas* 12 April 1918, leaving:

1a Hugh Dalzell; *b* 16 Aug 1908; Maj W Yorks Regt WW II; *ka* 1 April 1941

2a Desmond St George ; *b* 28 June 1917; Lt RTR WW II (POW); *d* 1967

1a *Muriel Denise Evelyn; *b* 8 Nov 1912; *m* 14 Aug 1942 *John Gunn Murray-Matheson, MB, ChB, s of Rev Norman Matheson, of Beauly, Inverness-shire, and has:

1b *Desmond John; *b* 11 Jan 1950

2b *Nigel Hugh; *b* 4 April 1951

1b *Ann Christine; *b* 1 July 1943; *m* 10 June 1966 *Dr Richard John Purvis, only s of Findlay Purvis, of Edinburgh

2b *Rosemary Jean Denise; *b* 28 Jan 1947

(2) Herbert St George; *b* 20 Feb 1888; Lt 6th Bn Roy Inniskilling Fus WW I *m* 1922 Eileen Elizabeth, dau of Tom N Burberry, of The Shrubbery, Basingstoke, and *d* 20 June 1932

(1) May Elizabeth; RRC, QAIMNS, served WW I France and Italy (despatches)

(2) Agnes Grace

(3) Harriet Amy

3 Henry Lucas St George; *b* 24 Dec 1847; Lt-Col 3rd Bn HLI; *m* 14 Jan 1875 Margaret Smyth (*dsp* 28 Aug 1877), est dau of John Kerr, of Heathfield, Greenock, and *d* 3 June 1933

2 Elizabeth; *m* 23 Sept 1857 Capt Hugh Montgomery Archdall, 52nd LI, of Drumadravy, Co Fermanagh, 7th s of Edward Archdall, JP, DL, of Riversdale, Co Fermanagh, and *d* 10 June 1923, leaving issue. He *d* Sept 1880

3 Mary; *m* 24 Aug 1859 Capt Richard Weld Litton, 30th Regt, s of Edward Litton, PC, MP Coleraine, and *d* 1 Jan 1871, leaving issue. He *d* 27 Jan 1905

Sir HUGH *d* 19 Nov 1854; his est s,

Sir John Marcus Stewart, 3rd Bt, DL Co Tyrone; *b* 19 Nov 1830; High Sheriff 1858, 6th Dragoons, Gentleman Usher to Ld Lt Ireland; *m* 1 Dec 1856 Annie Coote (*d* 12 Oct 1913), est dau and coheir of George Powell Houghton, of Kilmannock, Co Wexford, and *d* 26 Feb 1905, having had, with two sons (*d* in infancy):

1 **Sir Hugh Houghton Stewart, 4th Bt**, JP, DL; *b* 15 Sept 1858; *educ* Wellington and RMC Sandhurst, High Sheriff 1903, Brig-Gen cmdg 77th Bde 1914–15, Hon Brig-Gen 1916, Lt-Col and Hon Col cmdg 4th Bn Roy Inniskilling Fus, Maj 2nd Bn Roy Irish Rifles, Boer War (medal 22nd Imp Yeo 1901 and 3rd Bn Essex Regt 1902 (medal with five clasps), WW I 1914–16; *m* 1st 28 Aug 1915 Amy (*d* 13 Sept 1924), widow of Frederick Charles Caldwell and sis of Walpole Eyre Greenwell (*see* GREENWELL, Bt); *m* 2nd 1 Aug 1925 Agnes Mary (Agatha) (*d* 5 April 1952), dau of Robert Rutherford Morton, of Halstead, Essex, and *dsp* 18 Jan 1942

2 GEORGE POWELL (Sir), **5th Bt**

3 John Marcus; *b* 21 April 1863; *m* 1888 Ada Loveday (*d* 1896) and *d* 9 Nov 1906, leaving:

(1) Gladys Edith Houghton

(2) Muriel Gage; *d* unm 12 Oct 1943

4 Charles Gage; *b* 28 July 1864; Capt S Lancs Regt; *d* unm 28 Sept 1898

5 Albert Fortescue, CMG (1918), OBE (1919); *b* 30 March 1868, Lt-Col Suffolk Regt, formerly Beds Regt, Boer War 1901–02 (despatches, medal with clasp), WW I (despatches, brevet), Order Leopold; *m* 3 July 1902 Marguerita Minnie Eva (*d* 15 April 1940), 3rd dau of Jonathan Whitby Christian, Ld Justice Appeal Ireland, and *d* 25 Nov 1925

6 Cosmo Gordon, CB (1921), CMG (1915), DSO (1895); *b* 21 Nov 1869; Col RA (ret 1925 as Brig-Gen), served Kurrem Force 1893, Chitral 1895, with Col Kelly's Gilgit Column (despatches, medal and clasp), Sudan 1897–1900, Egyptian Army (despatches, Medjidie medal and three clasps), Boer War 1901–02 (Queen's medal with four clasps), and WW I (despatches six times, wounded, Brev Lt-Col, Brev Col, Croix de Guerre), reward for distinguished service 1931, FRGS; *m* 22 Feb 1911 Gladys Berry (*d* 10 June 1973), yr dau of J H Honeyman, MD, of Auckland, NZ, and *d* 19 April 1948, leaving:

(1) Charles Cosmo Bruce, CMG (1962); *b* 29 July 1912; *educ* Eton and King's Coll Cambridge; barrister Middle Temple 1937, Counsellor For Serv, Lt-Col RE (TA) WW II (despatches); *d* unm 10 July 1988

7 Julian Leslie (Rev); *b* 3 Sept 1873; Vicar Cople, Beds, 1938–39, Rector Dogmersfield, Hants, 1939–40, CF 1902 and 1917–19; *m* 5 Oct 1904 Henrietta Georgina (*d* 21 Sept 1952), yst dau of Col Henry Lane, JP, DL, of Broadoak, Bexhill, and *d* 3 Dec 1951

1 Annie Coote Houghton; *d* unm 20 May 1945

2 Mary; *d* unm 19 May 1943

3 Madeleine Delamont; *d* unm 1 March 1960

The 4th Bt's bro,

Sir George Powell Stewart, 5th Bt; *b* 7 Oct 1861; Burma 1891–92, DAAG Roy Jersey Militia 1902–08, Lt-Col Roy Inniskilling Fus (cmdg Regtl Depot WW I), Boer War 1900–02 (Queen's medal with three clasps, King's medal with two clasps); *m* 14 Feb 1895 Florence Maria Georgina (*d* 2 March 1957 aged 92), dau of Col Sir James Godfray, ADC, of Grainville Manor, St Saviour's, Jersey, and had:

1 John Houghton; *b* 19 Nov 1895; Lt Roy Inniskilling Fus; *ka* 16 May 1915

2 HUGH CHARLIE GODFRAY (Sir), **6th Bt**

1 Mary; *b* 12 Dec 1899; *m* 29 April 1930 Guy Janvrin Robin, yr s of Charles Janvrin Robin, of Steephill, Jersey, and *d* 10 Jan 1989

Sir GEORGE *d* 16 July 1945; his only surv s,

Sir Hugh Charlie Godfray Stewart, 6th Bt, DL (Co Tyrone 1971); *b* 13 April 1897; *educ* Bradfield and RMC Sandhurst; Maj Roy Inniskilling Fus, WWs I (wounded) and II, High Sheriff Co Tyrone 1955; *m* 1st 24 April 1929 (*divorce* 1942) Rosemary Elinor Dorothy (*m* 2nd 1942 (*divorce* 1954) Roderick Ian Wade-Gery, of West End Farm, Stagsden, Beds, and *d* 4 Jan 1986), only dau of Maj George Peacocke, W India Regt, and Roy Inniskilling Fus, and had:

1 Sir DAVID JOHN CHRISTOPHER STEWART, **7th and present Bt**

1 *Elinor Godfray [Mrs John Macdonell, 10 North Rd, Hythe, Kent CT21 5UH]; *b* 5 March 1930; *m* 4 July 1953 *John Michael Macdonell, s of John Forbes Macdonell, of St Neots, and has:

(1) *Michael John Alistair [Michael Macdonell Esq, The Park, Weston Underwood, Bucks MK46 5JZ]; *b* 21 Dec 1960; *educ* Winchester; *m* 1987 *Sara Belinda Bleakley, of Rochdale, and has:

1a *Charles Michael; *b* 23 Feb 1995

1a *Lydia Rose; *b* 14 Dec 1996

(1) *Sarah Jane Elinor [Mrs Graham Shewell, Keymer, The Street, Plaxtol, Sevenoaks, Kent TN15 0QQ]; *b* 2 June 1959; *m* 1st 1981 (*divorce* 1985) Brian Cadogan and has:

1a *Jonathan Joseph; *b* 17 Aug 1981

2a *Patrick Michael; *b* 24 April 1983

(1) (cont.) Mrs Sarah Cadogan *m* 2nd 1988 *Graham Shewell, s of Hugh Shewell, of Sheringham, and has:

3a *Hugh Timothy; *b* 4 March 1989

1a *Teresa Elinor; *b* 15 April 1992

Sir Hugh *m* 2nd 14 July 1948 *Diana Margaret, dau of Capt James Edmond Hibbert, MC, DFC, and Mrs Raymond Blennerhassett Bannon, of Blanchard Ho, St Peter, Jersey, and *d* 31 July 1994, leaving by her:

2 +HUGH NICHOLAS [Hugh Stewart Esq, Lowlands, Tibberton, Glos]; *b* 20 April 1955; heir presumptive; *educ* Portora Roy Sch; *m* 1976 *Anna Leeke and has:

(1) +Kieran Andrew Liam; *b* 1979

(1) *Cherissma; *b* 1974

(2) *Tamsin Kerry *b* 1977

(3) *Lauren; *b* 1987

2 *Jane Diana; *b* 2 April 1949; *m* 1973 *John T Costelloe and has:

(1) *Hugh John; *b* 1974

(1) *Nicola; *b* 1977

(2) *Jessica; *b* 1981

STEWART
of Balgownie

Arms: Or a fess chequy az. and arg. between in chief a Roman charioteer driving a chariot with two horses and in base a demi-figure of St Kentigern bearing a crozier in his left hand, his right hand raised in benediction, all ppr. **Crest:** A dexter hand couped at the wrist holding a sword erect in pale ppr., hilted and pommelled or. **Motto:** *Metue nunquam* ('Never fear'). **Creation:** Bt. (UK) 10 Dec 1920.

SIR (JOHN) SIMON WATSON STEWART, 6TH BT, of Balgownie, Co Dunbarton [Sir Simon Stewart Bt, 38 Dukes Ave, London W4 2AE]; *b* 5 July 1955; *s* f 1990; *educ* Uppingham and Charing Cross Med Sch (BSc 1977, MB, BS London 1980); MD, FRCP, FRCR; *m* 3 June 1978 *Dr Catherine Stewart, dau of H Gordon Bond, of Heyeswood Ho, Shiplake, Oxon, and has:

1 +JOHN HAMISH WATSON; *b* 12 Dec 1983

1 *Anna Rebecca Watson; *b* 1 May 1987

Lineage: ALEXANDER STEWART, of Springhill, Muirkirk, Ayrshire, JP; *b* 11 June 1822; *m* 21 June 1847 Marian (*d* 26 Sept 1886), dau of James Watson, merchant, of Coatbridge, and *d* 31 Aug 1906, leaving:

Sir James Watson Stewart, 1st Bt (UK), so *cr* 10 Dec 1920, JP (Dunbartonshire and Glasgow), DL (Glasgow and Lanarks); *b* 12 Feb 1852; CA, LLD Glasgow U, Ld Provost Glasgow, Ld Lt Co of City of Glasgow 1917–20, Cdr Legn Hon, Order Crown Belgium,; *m* 6 Sept 1883 Marion Symington (*d* 23 Oct 1943), dau of Rev Alexander Young, of Darvel, Ayrshire, and *d* 3 Nov 1922, leaving:

1 **Sir Alexander Watson Stewart, 2nd Bt**; *b* 5 Nov 1886; *d* unm 4 Feb 1934

2 JAMES WATSON, **3rd Bt**

3 Malcolm Gilbert Watson, DFC; *b* 5 June 1898; Capt RFC, F/Lt RAFVR WW II; *m* 11 Sept 1923 Evelyn Maud (*d* 3 Nov 1981), yst dau of John Allan Stewart, of Glasgow, and *d* 1971, leaving:

(1) +John Allan [John Stewart Esq, Tepic 80 Col Roma, Mexico DF, Mexico]; *b* 11 July 1928; *m* 4 July 1959 *Maria del Ruffiggio Vargas, of Mexico City, and has:

1a +John Eric; *b* 26 Oct 1960

(1) *Edith Mary Hedley [Mrs Francis McCall, 5 Clyde Pk, Redland, Bristol BS6 6RR]; *b* 3 Sept 1924; *m* 11 Sept 1948 *Francis Lockhart McCall, yst s of Harold William Lockhart McCall, of Margate, Kent, and has:

1a *Peter Lockhart; *b* 3 Aug 1949

2a *Charles Michael Lockhart; *b* 9 April 1956

1a *Aline Mary Lockhart; *b* 12 Dec 1950

2a *Sara Elizabeth Lockhart; *b* 25 June 1954

3a *Louise Evelyn Lockhart; *b* 13 March 1963

1 Helen Reid Young; *b* 14 Dec 1890; *m* 2 June 1917 Kenneth Watson Rogers and *d* 1958, leaving issue. He *d* 1957

2 Marion Symington Young; *b* 15 Jan 1894; *m* 13 June 1918 John Blackwood and *d* 10 Feb 1970. He *d* 6 Aug 1969

3 Jemima Reid Fairley; *b* 1895; *d* unm 1978

4 Anna Young; *b* 1896; *m* 1927 Ian Crawford Findlay (*d* 22 Feb 1929) and *dsp* 1973

5 Evelyn Young Watson; *b* 1899; *m* 14 Dec 1923 Lt-Col James Smart Hardie, OBE (*d* 1974), s of H D Hardie, and *d* 1981, leaving:

(1) *Henry David Stewart, OBE (1967); *b* 15 April 1925; *m* 1955 *Shelagh, dau of J H Smyth, of Bombay, and has:

1a *James Henry Smythe; *b* 30 Jan 1957

1a *Clare Elizabeth

2a *Hilary Jane

(1) *Marion Evelyn Stewart; *b* 16 Feb 1928; *m* 1952 *Rev George Lewis Blackman and has:

1a *Henry David Stewart; *b* 28 Nov 1953

2a *Anthony George; *b* 30 Dec 1955

3a *Hamish Flint; *b* 13 Sept 1956

4a *Ian Arthur Floyd; *b* 6 Oct 1958

The 2nd Bt's bro,

Sir James Watson Stewart, 3rd Bt, JP Co and City Glasgow; *b* 6 Aug 1889; *educ* Kelvinside Acad and Uppingham; CA, RASC Motor Tport and Lt RGA (TF) WW I, Maj HG WW II; *m* 30 March 1921 Jane (*m* 2nd 14 Oct 1961 (*divorce* 1966, resumed 1st husb's name STEWART by deed poll 1967) Neil Charteris Riddell), dau of James Morton Sim, Glasgow merchant, and *d* 4 June 1955, leaving:

1 **Sir James Watson Stewart, 4th Bt**; *b* 8 Nov 1922; *educ* Uppingham and Aberdeen U; RA, 1st SAS Para Regt 1941–47; *m* 1st 30 Nov 1946 Anne Elizabeth (*d* 1979), est dau of Joseph Greer Glaister, of Carlisle; *m* 2nd 1980 *Avril Veronica Gibb [Avril Lady Watson Stewart, Undercliff Court, Wemyss Bay, Renfrewshire PA18 6AL], DStJ, FRSA, Hon FBID, Hon MASC, artist, calligrapher and lecturer, only dau of Andrew Adamson Gibb, of Glasgow, and *dsp* 1988

2 **Sir John Keith Watson Stewart, 5th Bt**; *b* 25 Feb 1929; *educ* Uppingham and RMA Sandhurst; Capt Scottish Horse (TA); *m* 7 May 1954 *Mary Elizabeth [Mary Lady Stewart, Flat O, 55 Hans Rd, London SW3 1RN], er dau of John Francis Moxon, of Horton Hall, nr Leek, Staffs, and *d* 1990, leaving:

(1) Sir JOHN SIMON WATSON STEWART, **6th and present Bt**

(2) +James Watson [James Stewart Esq, The Old Vicarage, Melchbourne, Beds MK44 1BQ]; *b* 7 March 1960; *educ* Winchester, Durham U and RMA Sandhurst; *m* 1987 *Judy Anne, dau of John George Bamford, of Uttoxeter, Staffs, and has:

1a +Thomas Murdoch Watson; *b* 1992

1a *Emma Victoria Watson; *b* 1990

2a *Alice Georgina Watson; *b* 1993

(1) *Caroline Felicity Watson; *b* 31 Jan 1958; *educ* Lycée Française de Londres; *m* 1982 *Neil Barry Solomons, FRCS (Ed), s of Dr Arthur Solomons, of Port Elizabeth, S Africa, and has:

1a *Lucy; *b* 1983

2a *Kate; *b* 1985

STEWART of Ramelton

Arms: Or a fess chequy az. and arg., surmounted of a bend engrailed and in chief a rose gu., all within a bordure of the third charged with three lions rampant of the fourth. **Crest:** A dexter arm erect, couped at the elbow, the hand holding a heart all ppr. and in an escrol over the same the motto: **Motto:** *Nil desperandum* ('Nothing is to be despaired of'). **Creation:** Bt. (I) 2 May 1623.

SIR ALAN D'ARCY STEWART, 13TH BT, of Ramelton, Co Donegal [Sir Alan Stewart Bt, One Acre House, Church St, Ramelton, Co Donegal, Ireland]; *b* 29 Nov 1932; *s* f 1982; *educ* All Saints Coll Bathurst, NSW; yacht-builder; *m* 31 March 1952 *Patricia, dau of Lawrence Turner, of Ramelton, and has:

1 +NICHOLAS COURTNEY D'ARCY; *b* 4 Aug 1953; *educ* New U of Ulster (BSc, HDipEd)

2 +Lindsay Stephen d'Arcy; *b* 22 Feb 1956; *m* 1983 *Jane Maria d'Arcy, dau of Albert Rossley, of The Haw Ho, Ray, Co Donegal, and has:

(1) *Emma Naomi d'Arcy; *b* 1983

1 *Constance Patricia; *b* 31 Aug 1954; *m* 1978 *Malcolm McMillan and has:

(1) *James; *b* 1980

(2) *Peter; *b* 1981

2 *Siobhan d'Arcy; *b* 15 Aug 1960

Lineage: Sir WILLIAM STEWART, 2nd of Garlies (*see* MORAY, E); had a 3rd s:

Sir THOMAS STEWART of Minto; *d* 1500, leaving a 3rd s:

ARCHIBALD STEWART, 1st of Fintalloch, Penningha, Wiftownshire; ancestor (gf?) of:

ARCHIBALD STEWART, 3rd of Fintalloch; *d c* 1596, leaving:

Sir William Stewart, 1st Bt (I), so *cr* 2 May 1623, of Newtownstewart, Co Tyrone, and Ramelton, Co Donegal, PC (I); migrated to Ireland 1608 as Capt of 100 foot soldiers, undertaker (*i.e.*, broker) of escheated lands in Co Wexford 1612; made a free denizen of Ireland and ktd 1613; granted large tracts of land in Cos Donegal anbd Tyrone; MP (I Parl) Co Donegal 1613–15 and 1634–35; *m* Frances, 2nd dau

of Sir Robert Newcomen, 1st Bt, of Mosstown, Co Longford, and *d* between 8 Oct 1646 and 28 July 1647, leaving:

1 **Sir Alexander Stewart, 2nd Bt**; Covenanter; *m c* 1648 his 1st cousin Catherine (*m* 2nd 1st Earl of Granard (*qv*) and *d* 8 Dec 1714), dau of Sir Robert Newcomen, 2nd Bt, by his 1st w Anne Boleyn, and was *k* Battle of Dunbar 3 Sept 1650 fighting for CHARLES II, leaving:

(1) **Sir William Stewart, 3rd Bt**, and 1st VISCOUNT MOUNTJOY, of Co Tyrone, so *cr* 19 March 1682/3, as also BARON STEWART OF RAMALTON [*sic*], Co Donegal (both I), of Mountjoy Castle (whence his choice of title name, he leasing it from the Crown (after his ennoblement, however) and which itself was so called from having been constructed by 8th Lord (Baron) Mountjoy of the 1465 *cr*, who was Ld Dep Ireland 1599–1605), PC (I 1672); *b* Oct 1650; Capt King's Co Regt of Gds Ireland 1677–84, custos rotulorum Co Donegal 1679, Commr Revenue Ireland 1682–87, Master Gen Ordnance 1684, Col of Viscount Mountjoy's Foot (raised by himself) March 1684/5, served Imp forces at taking of Buda 1686, where badly wounded, Brig-Gen 1686, Pres Roy Soc Ireland 1686; as the pncpl Protestant in NI at the time of JAMES II's flight from England he was inveigled by the Ld Dep Duke of Tyrconnel (*see* TALBOT OF MALAHIDE, B) into going to Paris, nominally to warn JAMES of the hopelessness of trying to prevent an Anglo-Dutch landing in Ireland, but in reality to procure his incarceration in the Bastille, where he remained till 1692, being meanwhile attainted by JAMES II's I Parl May 1689 for non-attendance; *m* Mary, est dau of 1st Baron Coote of Coloony (*see* COOTE, Bt), and was *ka* 3 Aug 1692 at the Battle of Steinkirk during the wars between England and Holland on the one side and France on the other, leaving:

1a **Sir William Stewart, 4th Bt**, and 2nd VISCOUNT MOUNTJOY, PC (I 1710); cmded a Foot regt 1694–98 and 1702–13, Brig-Gen 1703, Maj-Gen 1707, Lt-Gen 1709, Col of Dragoons 1715, Master Gen Ordnance Ireland 1714–Jan 1727/8, a Keeper Gt Seal Ireland 1715; *m* 23 Nov 1696 Anne (*m* 2nd John Farquharson and *d* 27 Oct 1741), yr dau and eventual heiress of 1st Viscount Blesington (*see* CORK and ORRERY, E), thus acquiring the Boyle estates in Cos Wicklow and Kildare and the manor of Silchester, Hants, and *d* 10 Jan 1727, leaving, with five other sons and four other daus (*d* young):

1b **Sir William Stewart, 5th Bt**, and 1st and last EARL OF BLESINGTON, Co Wicklow, so *cr* 7 Dec 1745, PC (I 1748); *b* 7 April 1709; Govr Tyrone; *m* 10 Jan 1733/4 Eleanor (*d* 1 Oct 1774), dau and heiress of Robert FitzGerald, of Castle Dod, Co Cork, and *dspms* 14 Aug 1769, when all his peerages expired, having had:

1c William, *Viscount Mountjoy*; *b* 14 March 1734/5; *dvp* unm 2 Feb 1754

2c Lionel Robert; *b* 12 April 1736; *d* young

1b Mary; *m* Nov 1724 2nd and last Baron Tyrawley (*dspl* 14 July 1773) and *d* 5 Feb 1769

2a Alexander; Capt of Foot; *m* Mary, est dau of William Tighe, of Dublin, and *d* 1701, leaving:

1b Anne; *m* 1711 Luke Gardiner, PC, V-Treasurer Ireland, and had:

1c Charles, PC, of Dublin; *m* Florinda, dau of Robert Norman, of Lagore, Co Meath, and had:

1d LUKE GARDINER, 1st VISCOUNT MOUNTJOY OF MOUNTJOY, Co Tyrone, so *cr* 30 Sept 1795, as also earlier 19 Sept 1789 BARON MOUNTJOY OF MOUNTJOY, Co Tyrone (both I), PC (I 1780); *b* 7 Feb 1745; *educ* Eton and St John's Coll Cambridge; MP (I Parl) Co Dublin 1773–89; *m* 1st 3 July 1773 Elizabeth (*b* 4 May 1751; *d* in childbirth 7 Nov 1783; known with her sisters Anne, Marchioness Townshend (*qv*), and Barbara, Hon Mrs John Beresford (*see* WATERFORD, M), as the 'Three Irish Graces' and generally considered the three most beautiful women in Europe), est dau of Sir William Montgomery, 1st Bt, of Magbiehill, Peeblesshire (*see* 1830 edn), by Hannah, dau of Alexander Tomkyns, of Prehen, Co Londonderry; *m* 2nd 20 Oct 1793 Margaret, milliner, est dau of Hector Wallis, of Spring Mount, Queen's Co, and was *k* at New Ross, Co Wexford, 5 June 1798 leading his regt in an attempt to suppress the Uprising of that year, leaving by his 1st w, with an er s (*d* young):

1e CHARLES JOHN GARDINER, 1st and last EARL OF BLESINGTON (I), so *cr* 12 Jan 1816; *b* 19 July 1782; *educ* Eton; Govr Co Tyrone, rep I peer 1809–29; *m* 1st 11 July 1812 Mary Campbell, dau of Alexander McDougall, surgn, and widow of Maj William Browne, and had an only surv child:

1f Harriet Anne Frances; *b* 5 Aug 1812; *m* 1st 1 Dec 1827 (separated a few months later) Alfred, Count D'Orsay (*d* 4 Aug 1852), the celebrated dandy; *m* 2nd 1 Sept 1852, as his 1st w, Hon Charles Spencer Cowper (*see* LUCAS OF CRUDWELL, B) and *dsp* 17 Dec 1869

1e (cont.) The 1st and last EARL *m* 2nd 16 Feb 1818 Margaret (*dsp* Paris 4 June 1849, having, as a hostess who over 20 years organised glittering entertainments in concert with her stepson-in-law Count D'Orsay (with whom she lived), staved off mounting debts, towards the liquidation of which she wrote books (including *The Idler in Italy* (3 vols 1839–40), *The Idler in France* (1841) and *Confessions of an Elderly Gentleman* (1836)) and edited an annual (*The Keepsake*), 2nd dau of Edward Power, of Curragheen and Clonea, Co Waterford, and widow of Maurice St Leger Farmer, Capt 47th Regt (*d* 21 Oct 1817 by falling from a window in the King's Bench Prison while intoxicated), and *dspm* 25 May 1829, when his titles expired

3a Charles; MP Co Tyrone and Portsmouth, V-Adml the White, cmdg a naval expdn against the Sallee pirates 1720 and signing a treaty with the Emperor of Morocco

1a Mary; *m* 1st John Preston, of Ardsallagh, Co Meath, and had:

1b Peter Ludlow; *m* (*d* 19 June 1750), and had:

1c PETER LUDLOW, 1st EARL LUDLOW, so *cr* 3 Oct 1760, as also VISCOUNT PRESTON OF ARDSALLAGH, Co Meath, and earlier 19 Dec 1755 BARON LUDLOW OF ARDSALLAGH (all I), of Ardsallagh and Gt Stoughton, Hunts, PC (1782); *b* 21 April 1730; MP (Whig) Hunts

1768–96, Comptroller Household 1782–84; m 26 June 1753 Frances, est dau of 3rd Earl of Scarbrough (qv), and d 26 Oct 1803, leaving:

1d AUGUSTUS LUDLOW, 2nd EARL LUDLOW; b 1 Jan 1755; educ Eton; d unm 7 Nov 1811

2d GEORGE JAMES LUDLOW, 3rd and last EARL LUDLOW, GCB (1815, KB 1804); b 12 Dec 1758; joined Army 1778, served War American Independence (having served in the army that capitulated at Yorktown 1781) also Flanders 1793, losing his left arm Battle of Roubaix 17 May 1794, Maj-Gen 1798, Lt-Gen 1805, Gen 1814, Col 96th Foot 1801–05, 38th Foot 1805–36 and Scots Fus Gds 1836–42, cmded 2nd Bde Gds Battle of Aboukir 1801, also served N Germany 1805 and Copenhagen expdn 1807, Equerry to PRINCE OF WALES (later GEORGE IV) 1784–95, Dep Govr Berwick 1795–1842; d 16 April 1842, when his titles expired, leaving his property to Lord John Russell (see RUSSELL, E)

1a (cont.) Mrs John Preston m 2nd 3rd Earl of Granard (qv) and d 4 Oct 1758, leaving issue

2a Catherine; m Arthur Davis, of Carrickfergus, and had, with other issue:

1b Mary; m 16 July 1736 4th Earl of Granard (qv)

2 Thomas, of Fort Stewart, Co Donegal; b 1630; m a dau of John Montgomery, of Croghan, Co Donegal, and had, with four daus:

(1) William, of Fort Stewart; Col 9th Regt, Sheriff Co Donegal 1697; m 1693 Mary Anne, dau of Rt Rev Ezekiel Hopkins, Bp Derry, by Lady Aramintha Robartes, dau of 1st Earl of Radnor of the 1679 cr (see RADNOR, E, preliminary remarks), and d July 1713, having had, with two other sons and a dau:

1a Ezekiel, of Fort Stewart; m Anne, dau of Rev Charles Ward (see BANGOR, V), and d Oct 1734, leaving an only surv s:

1b **Sir Annesley Stewart, 6th Bt**, of Fort Stewart; b 1725; MP (I Parl) Charlemont 1763–97, Dublin banker; m Sept 1755 Mary, dau of John Moore, of Drumbanagher, and d March 1801, having had, with a dau (m her cousin John Moore, of Drumbanagher, and d 1852):

1c **Sir James Stewart, 7th Bt**, of Fort Stewart; b c 1760; MP (I Parl) Enniskillen 1783–90 and (UK Parl) Co Donegal 1802–18, Sheriff Co Donegal 1799; m 19 Dec 1778 Mary Susanna, dau of Richard Chapell Whaley, of Whaley Abbey, Co Wicklow, and d 20 May 1827, having had:

1d **Sir James Annesley Stewart, 8th Bt**, of Fort Stewart; b 1788; Co Donegal: Sheriff 1830, Col Roy Artilletry Militia 1855, V-Lt 1856, Col Inniskilling Dragoons; m Oct 1830 Jane (dsp 15 Jan 1886), dau of Francis Mansfield, of Castle Wray, Co Donegal, and dsp 13 April 1879

2d William Henry; b 1793; Lt 11th Light Dragoons (later 11th Hus) Waterloo Campaign, Maj 19th Lancers; d unm 6 June 1820

1d Anne; m 1st July 1797 William Conolly Staples (see STAPLES, Bt) and had issue; m 2nd Richard Napier and d 30 March 1867

2d Elizabeth Susanna; m 24 June 1820 Ven Charles Abel Moysey, DD, Archdeacon Bath, and dsp 1844. He d 17 Sept 1859

3d Sophia Frances; m Andrew Rutherfurd, PC (1851), of Crosshill, Slr-Gen Scotland 1837, Ld Advocate 1839, Ld of Session as Lord Rutherfurd, and d 10 Oct 1852. He dsp 13 Dec 1854

2c William; Col 89th Regt; m Anne, est dau of John Hyde, of Castle Hyde, Co Cork, and dsp 1842

2a Robert (Rev); b 1699; DD, Preb Freshford, Co Kilkenny; m Rachel, dau of Abraham Nickson, of Coolattin, Co Wicklow, and d 1772, having had, with two daus (Sarah; Frances):

1b Abraham; Army Capt; m 4 May 1761 his 1st cousin Hester, dau of Abraham Nickson, of Munny, Co Wicklow, and had, with two yr sons:

1c Abraham Augustus Ewart (Rev); b 1762; DD, Rector Donabate, Co Dublin, Chaplain to Ld Lt Ireland; m 24 Jan 1793 Frances (d May 1857), dau of William O'Connor, of Mongavlin, Co Donegal, and d Jan 1812, having had, with two other daus (d young or unm):

1d William Augustus; b 4 March 1797; Capt 58th Foot; m Feb 1830 Anna (d 6 June 1864), dau of William Molloy, of Blackfort, Co Tipperary, and d 23 Aug 1867, having had, with two daus (d unm):

1e **Sir Augustus Abraham James Stewart, 9th Bt**, JP Co Donegal, DL, of Fort Stewart; b 29 April 1832; barrister; d unm 26 Aug 1889

2e William Molloy; b 19 Nov 1833; m May 1864 Ellen (d 17 Dec 1917), widow of Francis Berkeley Drummond (see PERTH, E) and dau of W H Urquhart, and d May 1889, having had:

1f **Sir William Augustus Annesley Stewart, 10th Bt**, of Fort Stewart; b 1865; d unm 4 Jan 1894

2f HARRY JOCELYN URQUHART (Sir), **11th Bt**

1f Marion Drummond; m 19 July 1896 David Wann Aikman, CIE, MLC Punjab, s of A Aikman, and d Jan 1948. He d 21 Aug 1931

2f Henrietta Florence; m 27 Dec 1892 Capt Sackville Hamilton Berkeley, Indian Police, 2nd s of Maj-Gen James Cavan Berkeley, CIE, IA, and d 3 May 1959, leaving issue. He d 24 Nov 1925

3f Annie Hester; m 1910 Henry Charles King, of Salisbury, Rhodesia (d 28 April 1935), and had:

1g *Enid Gwendolen; b 21 May 1912; m 12 Feb 1935 Lt-Col William Maurice Clapp, MBE, Roy Signals (d 20 May 1970), and has:

1h *John William Maurice; b 18 Dec 1939; educ Eastbourne Coll; m 14 Sept 1968 *Barbara Ann, dau of John Charles Clifford Davies, of Great Wigsell, nr Hawkhurst, Kent, and has:

1i *Zoe Alice Katherine; b 15 Feb 1970

3e James Augustus, of Sunny Side, Buncrana, Co Donegal, JP; b 7 March 1835; m 12 June 1884 Ann Wilhelmina Jean (d 9 Feb 1913), dau of William Wray, of Oakpark, Co Donegal, and d 8 Sept 1915, leaving:

1f James Augustus; b 17 Aug 1894; Lt 2nd Munster Fus WW I; ka 1 May 1915

1f Wilhelmina Augusta; d unm 30 Jan 1970

2f Mary Adeline Cecil; d unm

3f Edith Frances

4f Augusta Anna Blanche; d unm 1 Sept 1945

5f Hester Leonora Sophia; d unm 3 Feb 1965

6f Flora Euphemia; d 2 Nov 1958

4e Robert John Jocelyn; b 28 Aug 1838; Maj-Gen Roy Berks Regt, FRGS; m 20 Jan 1880 Adeline (d 11 Sept 1938), dau of Thomas Southey, of Caversham, and dsp 10 Nov 1908

5e Harry Hutchinson Augustus; JP Suffolk; b 5 Feb 1840; Capt 9th Regt, Col cmdg Donegal Artillery Militia; m 1st 13 Oct 1874 Lucy Sarah (d 26 July 1875), est dau of Lt-Gen Richard BURNABY, Col Cmdt RE, of Freeford, Lichfield; m 2nd 22 Nov 1879 Frederica Elizabeth (d 28 June 1912), dau of Frederic Somes, of Beech Hill, Park, Loughton, Essex, and d 24 May 1916, leaving:

1f Walter Annesley; b 1 March 1883; Counsellor Dip Serv; m 9 June 1920 Phyllis Lucie (d 1981, having m 2nd 22 Feb 1938 Benjamin Worthy Horne), only child of Edmund L Horne, of Earls Court, and d 10 April 1937, leaving:

1g Dorothy; b 20 Aug 1924

2g *Rosemary [Mrs John Haire, Somerville, Woodlands Rd, Bromley, Kent]; b 15 June 1928; m 29 April 1950 *Col John Arthur Haire, er s of Rev Arthur Haire, of The Hurst, Horam, Sussex, and has:

1h *John Stewart [John Haire Esq, 33 Radnor Walk, London SW3]; b 3 Aug 1957; BA

1h *Susan Mary [Mrs Frank Hinks, The Old Vicarage, Shoreham, Sevenoaks, Kent]; b 4 March 1952; educ Ravensbourne Coll of Art (BA), RAS Cert (PG); m 1982 *Frank Peter Hinks and has:

1i *Julius James; b 1984

2i *Alexander John; b 1985

3i *Benjamin Stewart; b 1987

2h *Anne Rosemary [Mrs Alan Groom, 65 Lee Rd, London SE3 9EN]; b 11 July 1954; educ Benenden; MRCGP, DROCG, DCH, MFFP; m 1981 *Alan Frederick Graeme Groom, FRCS, and has:

1i *William Douglas Ian; b 1985

2i *Frederick Thomas; b 1990

1i *Alice Suzanne; b 1987

2f Charles Frederic Somes, MC; b 31 Aug 1884; Lt 2nd Dragoon Gds (Queen's Bays), Maj Roy Munster Fus; ka 4 April 1918

3f William Mountjoy; b 20 Sept 1886; d 31 Dec 1967

4f Adrian Harry; b 25 Feb 1888; Lt Gloucestershire Regt; ka Cameroons 29 Aug 1914

1f Marjorie Augusta; b 6 Feb 1891; m 17 Oct 1914 Rev Owen Manby, Rector Rishangles, Norfolk, 1938–43, 2nd s of Thomas Manby, and d 26 Dec 1965, leaving two daus. He d 18 Jan 1951

1e Frances Augusta; m 1870 William Campbell and had issue

2d Henry Hutchinson; b 23 June 1798; MD Dublin, fndr Stewart Instn Palmerston; m 15 July 1830 Eliza (dsp 22 Feb 1880), dau of Rev J Going, and d 1879

3d Lorenzo Moore; b 1 April 1800; m Emily, dau of Richard Quinton, and d 1865, leaving:

1e Abraham Augustus; b 1838; Surgn 176th Foot; k by a fall from his horse in India 1876

2e Richard Quinton; b 1844; m 1874 Isabel Christiana, dau of Erasmus Wilson Williams, of Dublin, and had:

1f Richard Evans Augustus; b 24 May 1875; d unm

2f Lorenzo Moore; b 1 March 1882; Lt Donegal RGA; m 1906 Ivy Mercilla (d 1967), dau of Walter Edmond Pachaud Wordsworth, of Rampur Haut, India, and d 1926, leaving:

1g Trevor Eugene St Quinton; b 1907; m 1932 *Edna Maude and d 1980, leaving:

1h *Pamela Jean [Mrs Leon Kings, 18 Norton Dve, Dianella, Perth, W Australia]; b 1934; m 1962 *Leon Allan Kings

2g +Harold Vivian Moore [Harold Stewart Esq, 18 Nangkita Rd, Kalamunda, Perth, WA 6076, Australia]; b 1908; CEng, MIMechE; m 1st 1932 (divorce) Ella Marie (d 1986), dau of John Tracey Falconer, and has:

1h *Olga Deirdre Moore [Mrs Olga Malone, 6 Grey Place, Morpeth, Northumberland NE61 1TT]; b 1936; m 1964 (divorce 1991) Gordon Edward Malone and has:

1i *Amanda Jane; b 1966; BA London

2i *Catherine Ellen; b 1968; BA, PhD Oxford; m 1996 *Dr Nicholas Mark Henstridge and has:

1j *Jacob William; b 25 Feb 1998

2h *Roslyn Anne Moore [Mrs Alan Rutherford, 18 Murrayfield Gdns, Edinburgh EH12 6DF]; b 1944; m 1966 *Alan Gray Rutherford, OBE, BSc, PhD, CChem, CEng, FRSC, FInstE, FRSA, Hon Col Parachute Regt, and has:

1i *Simon Gray; b 1967

1i *Sarah Caroline; b 1971; educ Merton Coll Oxford (MA) and Edinburgh U (PhD); FRSA

1g (cont.) Harold Stewart m 2nd 1956 *Helen Elizabeth, dau of Archibald Ronald Robb, and by her has:

1h +Michael Ian Moore; b 1958; educ WA Univ (BCom); Maj RACT; m 1988 *Janelle Skehan, BPharm (Sydney), Dip Hosp Pharm and has:

1i +Callam Michael Moore; b 1994

1i *Ellenore Anne Moore; b 1991

2h +Richard Quinton Moore; b 1964; educ Curtain U WA (B(app)Sc)

1f Isabella Florence; *m* 1901 Godfrey Preece, of Westbury, Long Island, NY, and had issue. He *d* 18 Jan 1945

2f Emily Gertrude

1e Mary Florence; *m* 1870 Dr George Owens and had issue

2e Frances Adelaide; *m* 1st 1878 John Owens, MD (*d* 1883); *m* 2nd 1887 Rev William Stoney, of Castlebar. He *d* 1906

4d Annesley (Rev); *b* 27 April 1802; had:

1e Frances; *m* Adml Richard Brydges Beechey (*d* 1895) and *d* 1909

5d Robert; *b* 22 April 1803; MD; *m* 1833 Mary Frances (*d* 18 Aug 1875), er dau of Peter Abercrombie Le Clerc, and *d* 1875, leaving:

1e James; *b* 1 April 1839; FRCP Edin, Surgn RN; *m* 1st Matilda (*d* 21 Jan 1906), dau of Richard Connery, and had two sons and three daus; *m* 2nd 2 Feb 1909 Edith Alberta Mitchel and *d* 2 Dec 1928

1e Frances; *b* 19 Sept 1836; *m* 1861 Rev Canon Richard Irvine, BD, of Belfast, and *d* 6 Nov 1907, having had issue

2e Harriet Emily; *b* 27 Jan 1838; *d* unm 30 June 1912

3e Hester Perrin; *b* 1 Oct 1843; *d* unm 9 June 1928

6d Charles Lennox; *b* 12 June 1810; *m* 13 March 1849 Harriet Elizabeth, dau of Samuel Lomas, RN, of Kilrush, Co Clare, and *dsp*

1d Hester; *m* Rt Hon Louis Perrin, Judge Queen's Bench Ireland, and *d* 1873. He *d* 1864

1 Catherine; *m* 1631 Sir James Montgomery, of Rosemount, s of 1st Viscount Montgomery of the Great Ardes, and had:

(1) William; *b* 27 Oct 1633; author: *Montgomery MSS*.

2 Anne; *m* Sir William Sempill, of Letterkenny, Co Donegal (*see* SEMPILL, L), and had issue

The 10th Bt's bro,

Sir Harry Jocelyn Urquhart Stewart, 11th Bt, DL Co Donegal; *b* 1871; High Sheriff Co Donegal 1905, Maj Donegal Artillery; *m* 12 Aug 1896 Isabel Mary (*d* 23 March 1956), dau of Col Francis Stewart Mansfield, DL, of Castle Wray, Co Donegal, and had:

1 William Francis; *b* 6 Oct 1901; L/Sgt RCE WW II; *m* 21 Dec 1923 Lucy Dorothy, yst dau of Archibald Metcalfe-Smith, of London, and was *ka* Normandy 7 June 1944

2 JOCELYN HARRY (Sir), **12th Bt**

3 Walter Annesley; *b* 29 April 1907; *m* July 1929 Dora Longridge

4 Malcolm Geoffrey; *b* 7 Dec 1908; F/Lt RAF WW II; *m* 21 Dec 1946 Joan (*d* 28 Oct 1968), dau of Col Cox, of Camberley, Surrey, and *d* 28 April 1974, leaving:

(1) +Robin Gordon Alan [Robin Stewart Esq, 50 Parkholme Rd, London E8 3AQ]; *b* 1 Feb 1948; *educ* Reed's Sch; *m* 6 June 1973 *Barbara Anne, dau of Wilfred Miller, of Grasscroft, Yorks, and has:

1a +James Malcolm; *b* 1978

2a +Thomas Annesley; *b* 1979

3a +William Francis; *b* 1984

(2) +Jonathan Malcolm [Jonathan Stewart Esq, South View, Rectory Rd, Gt Haseley, Oxon]; *b* 2 Nov 1951; *educ* Reed's Sch; has:

1a *Sorrel; *b* 18 Aug 1984

5 Alan Robert; *b* 16 June 1910; *d* 10 Feb 1916

1 Isabel; *b* 2 June 1897; *d* unm 26 Dec 1974

2 Kathleen Mary; *m* 24 Feb 1925 Geoffrey Watt, MC, of Claragh, Ramelton, and *d* 24 Dec 1941

3 Hester Anna Lilian; *d* unm 20 July 1965

4 Violet May; *m* 14 April 1926 (*divorce*) Brig Allister Colvin Baillie, OBE, MC, RE (*d* 1971), of Hazels, Pyle Hill, Surrey, s of Sir Duncan Baillie, KCSI, ICS, and had issue

5 *Evelyn Frances; Sgt WAAF WW II; *m* 1958 *Louis Botha, of S Africa

The 11th Bt *d* 12 May 1945; his est surv s,

Sir Jocelyn Harry Stewart, 12th Bt; *b* 24 Jan 1903; Sgt AIF WW II; *m* 1st 20 July 1932 Constance Mary (*d* 2 April 1940), dau of D'Arcy Shillaber, of NSW, and *d* 1982, having had:

1 Sir ALAN D'ARCY STEWART, **13th and present Bt**

Sir Jocelyn *m* 2nd 16 Dec 1946 *Katherine Christina, dau of James Sweeney, of Tamney, Co Donegal, and by her had:

2 +Brian Jocelyn; *b* 20 Sept 1948

3 +Terence Annesley; *b* 29 Aug 1949

1 *Marie Jeanette [Mrs Harry Scott, Greenhill, Convoy, Co Donegal, Ireland]; *b* 22 Oct 1947; *m* 19– *Harry Scott and has issue

2 *Katherine Benedicta; *b* 14 Jan 1951

STEWART of Stewartby

Arms: Or a fess chequy az. and arg. between a portcullis with its chains in chief and in base a lymphad, sails furled, oars in action, sa., flagged gu. **Crest:** A lymphad as in the arms. **Motto:** There remaineth a rest. **Creation:** Bt. (UK) 4 March 1937.

SIR RONALD COMPTON STEWART, 2ND BT, of Stewartby, Co Bedford, DL (Beds 1974) [Sir Ronald Stewart Bt DL, Maulden Grange, Maulden, Beds MK45 2AU]; *b* 14 Aug 1903; s f 1951; *educ* Rugby and Jesus Coll Cambridge; High Sheriff Beds 1954, chm London Brick 1966–79; *m* 10 June 1936 Cynthia, OBE (1959), JP (Beds 1941) (*d* 1987), dau of Harold Farmiloe, of Purley Park, nr Reading

Lineage: Rev ALEXANDER STEWART; Min Congregational Church Barnet; *d* 3 Nov 1874, leaving, with other issue:

Sir HALLEY STEWART, of The Red House, Harpenden, Herts, JP Sussex; *b* 18 Jan 1838; MP Spalding 1887–95 and Greenock 1906–10, ptnr Stewart Bros and Spencer, Rochester, v-chm London Brick Co and Forders Ltd, Pres Soc Liberation Religion from State Patronage and Control; chm Sir Halley Stewart Tst, endowed Halley Stewart Laboratory Hampstead; ktd 1932; *m* 20 June 1865 Jane Elizabeth (*d* Dec 1924), dau of Joseph Atkinson, of Upper Norwood, Surrey, and *d* 26 Jan 1937, having had:

1 Reginald Halley; *b* 15 Oct 1868; *m* 1 June 1893 Kate Mildred Stevens (*d* 9 April 1961 aged 88) and *d* 22 April 1926, leaving issue

2 (PERCY) MALCOLM (Sir), **1st Bt**

3 (Bernard) Halley; *b* 6 May 1874; MD 1911, MB 1907, BCh 1904, FRS (Edin), FKC (Lond), pres Sir Halley Stewart Tst; *m* 11 April 1905 Mabel Florence Wyatt and *d* 30 July 1958, leaving issue (*see* STEWARTBY, B)

1 Bertie Jane Louise; *m* 11 Oct 1902 Ernest Cecil Haram and *d* 28 March 1961 aged 90, leaving issue. He *d* 30 Sept 1929

The 2nd s,

Sir (Percy) Malcolm Stewart, 1st Bt (UK), so *cr* 4 March 1937, OBE (1918), JP, DL Beds; *b* 9 May 1872; *educ* Roy High Sch Edinburgh and Univ Sch Hastings; Dir for Min Munitions Govt Rolling Mills Southampton 1917–19, Commr Special Areas (England and Wales) 1934–36, pres Assoc Portland Cement, Br Portland Cement, Cement Makers' Fedn, Roy Caledonian Schs, Nat Cncl Social Serv and Cement Statistical and Tech Bureau, chm London Brick and Sir Halley Stewart Tst, High Sheriff Beds 1941, Hon LLD Manchester 1937; *m* 1st 1896 Cordelia (*d* 28 Sept 1906), 2nd dau of Sir Joseph Compton Rickett, DL, PC, MP, and had:

1 Cyril Malcolm Halley; *b* 10 Nov 1900; *d* 31 July 1927

2 Sir RONALD COMPTON STEWART, **2nd and present Bt**

1 Cordelia Marguerite; *m* 1st 28 June 1927 (*divorce* 1934) Ernest Sadd Brown, s of Ernest Brown, and had a dau; *m* 2nd 11 Sept 1935 Thomas Tennant Baxter, er s of Frank Baxter, of Chelsea, and *d* 2 Jan 1964. He *d* 3 Nov 1947

Sir Malcolm *m* 2nd 25 April 1907 Beatrice Maud, OStJ (*d* 21 May 1960), 2nd dau of Joseph Bishop Pratt, mezzotint engraver, and *d* 27 Feb 1951, having by her had:

3 Malcolm; *b* 20 Dec 1909; *educ* Harrow and BNC Oxford (BA 1932, MA 1937); Lt RNVR WW II; *m* 14 Feb 1935 (*divorce* 1957) Mary Stephanie de Bertodano, dau of 8th Marquis del Moral, of Red Croft, Malmesbury, Wilts

2 *Yvonne Elizabeth Diana [Mrs Thomas Savory, Kings Head Cottage, Cley next the Sea, Norfolk]; *b* 4 July 1915; *educ* Somerville Coll Oxford (BA 1936, MA 1950); *m* 16 March 1948 Thomas Doggett Savory (*d* 1988), s of Lionel Savory, and has:

(1) *Thomas Stewart; *b* 23 Jan 1949; *m* 1975 *Susan Elizabeth Allen and has:

1a *Elizabeth Susan; *b* 1986

(2) *Malcolm Doggett; *b* 28 Sept 1950; *m* 1975 *Julia Mary Dring and has:

1a *Edward James Doggett; *b* 1980

1a *Hannah Caroline; *b* 1977; *educ* Marlborough

2a *Jessica Mary Alice; *b* 1987

STEWART of Strathgarry

Arms: Quarterly, 1st and 4th, or a fess chequy az. and arg. (for STEWART); 2nd and 3rd, arg. a galley sa., sails furled, oars in action ppr., flagged gu. (for LORN); the whole within a bordure per pale, dexter vert, sinister arg., charged with three roses gu., barbed and seeded vert; overall at the fess point an inescutcheon arg. charged with a sinister hand apaumée gu. (as a Bt of the UK).
Crest: A unicorn's head, couped arg., armed and crined or.
Motto: (over the shield) *Quhidder will zie* ('Whether will ye?').
Creation: Bt. (UK) 17 Aug 1960.

SIR ALASTAIR ROBIN STEWART, 3RD BT, of Strathgarry, Co Perth [Sir Alastair Stewart Bt, Walter's Cottage, Little Baddow, Essex CM3 4TQ]; *b* 26 Sept 1925; *s* bro 1992; *educ* Marlborough; Lt 1st Roy Glos Hus 1945–47, dir Neale and Wilkinson Ltd 1947–71, md Stewart and Harvey Ltd 1971–90; *m* 9 May 1953 *Patricia Helen, MBE, BA (Arch), ARIBA, dau of John Alfred Merrett, of Pondhead Farm, Forest Green, Surrey, and has:

1 +JOHN KENNETH ALEXANDER; *b* 15 Dec 1961; *educ* Marlborough and Pembroke Coll Cambridge (BA); *m* 1994 *Catherine Mary Wright and has:
  (1) *Jessica Ellen Janetta; *b* 1995
1 *Judith Patricia; *b* 9 June 1954; *educ* St Felix Co High Sch Chelmsford and Bristol Poly; *m* 1993 *David Usill, of London
2 *Lucy Janetta; *b* 3 July 1956; *educ* St Felix Co High Sch and Newcastle Poly (BA); *m* 1992 *Dennis John Van Liew, of Des Moines, Iowa, and has:
  (1) *Elizabeth Patricia; *b* 1997
3 *Catherine Helen; *b* 27 June 1958; *educ* St Felix Co High Sch, Marlborough and Trin Hall Cambridge (BA); *m* 1993 *Eric Leon Neven, of Brussels, and has:
  (1) *Guy Alastair; *b* 1995
  (1) *Helen Lucienne; *b* 1994

Lineage: ALAN STEWART, 3rd of Appin, had a 4th s:

DONALD STEWART, 5th of Invernahyle, Perths; had a 2nd surv s:

Rev DUNCAN STEWART, 1st of Strathgarry and Inverhadden; Min Blair Atholl; *m* Anne, dau of Rev Aeneas McLaine, Min Kilginan, and had an est s:

ALEXANDER STEWART, 2nd of Strathgarry; *m* Amelia, dau of Robertson of Kincraigie, and had an est s:

Rev ALEXANDER STEWART, 3rd of Strathgarry; Min Blair Atholl; *m* Isabel, dau of Rev John Robertson of Lude, and had an est s:

Rev DUNCAN STEWART, 4th of Strathgarry; Min Balquidder; *m* Arabella, dau of Duncan Campbell of Achtyre, and had an est s:

ALEXANDER STEWART, 5th of Strathgarry; *b* 1779; Col HEICS; *m* Janetta, dau of Ralph Allen Daniell, of Trelissick, Cornwall, and *d* 23 June 1835, leaving, with two er sons (Allan Duncan, had a s (Alexander, f of Alan Douglas); Alexander) and a dau (Janetta):

HINTON DANIELL STEWART, 6th of Strathgarry; *b* 9 Feb 1835; *m* 30 Sept 1869 Lucy (*d* 4 Nov 1926 aged 80), dau of Dr Donald Macfarlane, of Perth, and *d* 4 Nov 1926, leaving, with three er sons (Donald Alan, *b* 8 June 1871, *m* Maud McHardy and had two sons (Donald Ian, *b* 28 May 1897, *d* 12 Nov 1960; Eric Hinton, *b* 25 July 1899, had a s (Robin Hinton, *b* 9 May 1930); Hinton Arthur, *b* 1873, *d* 1958; Alastair Duncan, *d* 4 Oct 1917 aged 38) and six daus (Isabel Charlotte, *b* 1875, *d* 1948; Janetta, *b* 1875, *d* 1880; Harriet, *b* 1877, *d* 1947; Lucy Vere, *b* 1883; Beatrice Mary, *b* 1885, *d* 1925; Esmé Victoria, *b* 1887, *m* 1922 (*divorce* 1943) Hugh Eric Douglas Orr Ewing (see ORR EWING, Bt) and *d* 5 Dec 1967, leaving issue):

The 4th s,

Sir Kenneth Dugald Stewart, 1st Bt (UK), so *cr* 17 Aug 1960, GBE (1950, KBE 1927), JP (Manchester 1940); *b* 29 March 1882; *educ* Trin Coll Glenalmond; traded in China 1903–19, Br Del Peking Conf 1925–26, dir Manchester Ship Canal Co 1928, chm Lancs Cotton Corp 1928–32 and TSB 1946–66 (Pres 1966), V-Pres Nat Savings Ctee 1959; *m* 1 March 1913 Noel (*d* 1 March 1949), yst dau of Kenric Brodribb, of Melbourne, Australia, and *d* 19 May 1972, leaving:

1 **Sir David Brodribb Stewart, 2nd Bt**, TD; *b* 20 Dec 1913, *educ* Marlborough and Manchester Coll Tech (BSc); md Francis Price (Fabrics) Ltd, Brevet Col

Duke of Lancaster's Own Yeo (TA) WW II; *m* 14 Sept 1963 *Barbara Dykes [Dowager Lady Stewart, Sassella, 6048 Horwl St, Niklausen, Switzerland], widow of Donald Ian Stewart, MC, and dau of Harry Dykes Lloyd, of Daisy Lawn, Brough, Yorks, and *d* 17 Oct 1992

2 Sir ALASTAIR ROBIN STEWART, **3rd and present Bt**

1 *Janetta Kenric [Miss Janetta Stewart, 1 The Ridings, Links Rd, Ashtead, Surrey KT21 2HQ]; *b* 6 Oct 1918; *educ* LMH Oxford (BA 1942)
2 *Lesley Mary [Mrs John Berger, No 3 Collingwood-Blue Water Place, Beacon Bay 5241, S Africa]; *b* 9 March 1921; *educ* Malvern Girls' Coll; *m* 19 Sept 1942 John Berger (*d* 1982), MRCVS, s of Harry August Emil Berger, of Bickley, Kent, and has:
  (1) *David Kenneth; *b* 5 April 1964
  (1) *Jennifer; *b* 10 Sept 1944; *educ* Aberdeen U (BSc) and Berkeley U, Calif. (MSc)
  (2) *Vere; *b* 8 Jan 1946; *educ* Aberdeen U (BA) and Sussex U
  (3) *Elizabeth; *b* 27 July 1948; *educ* Nottingham U (BSc); *m* 1972 *Peter Moore and has:
    1a *Kathleen Lesley; *b* 1980
    2a *Carissa; *b* 1981

STEWART-CLARK

Arms: Sa. a fess chequy arg. and az. between a crescent or in chief and a boar's head couped of the last, armed and langued of the third, in base, a bordure erm. **Crest:** An anchor cabled gu.
Motto: Sure and steadfast. **Creation:** Bt. (UK) 12 Feb 1918.

SIR JOHN (JACK) STEWART-CLARK, 3RD BT, of Dundas Castle, in West Lothian [Sir Jack Stewart-Clark Bt MEP, Dundas Castle, S Queensferry, Edinburgh EH30 9SP; Puckstye House, Holtye Common, Kent TN8 7EL]; *b* 17 Sept 1929; *s* f 1971; *educ* Eton and Balliol Coll Oxford, Harvard Business Sch; 2nd Lt Coldstream Gds 1948–49, memb Roy Co Archers, with J & P Coats 1952–69, md: J & P Coats Pakistan Ltd 1961–67, J A Carp's Garenfabrieken Holland 1967–79, Philips Electrical Ltd London 1971–75 and Pye (Cambridge) 1974–79, dir: Pye Hldgs 1975–79, Low & Bonar plc 1982–95 and Oppenheimer Internat to 1984, TSB Scotland 1986–89, Pioneer Concrete Hldgs Plc 1989–, MEP (C): Sussex E 1979–94, E Sussex and Kent S 1994–, a V-Pres Euro Parl 1992–97; *m* 16 July 1958 *Jonkvrouwe Lydia Frederika Loudon, 3rd dau of Jonkheer James William Loudon, of Valkehorst, Valkensward, Holland, and has:

1 +ALEXANDER DUDLEY [Alexander Stewart-Clark Esq, 28 Fairfield St, London SW18 1DW]; *b* 21 Nov 1960; *educ* Worth Abbey
1 *Daphne Beatrix Felicia [Mrs Nicholas Stephenson, 68 Waldron Rd, London SW18]; *b* 17 July 1959; *m* 6 Sept 1997 *Nicholas Stephenson and has:
  (1) *Chiara; *b* 1986
2 *Nadia Marie Anne [Mrs Patrick Waterfield, The Dial House, Forton, Hants SP11 6NU]; *b* 4 Jan 1963; *m* 9 Jan 1990 *Patrick J Waterfield, yr s of Jolyon Waterfield, of Edge Grove, Aldenham, Herts, and has:
  (1) *Natasha Sophie; *b* 30 April 1993
  (2) *Elena Grace; *b* 30 April 1993
  (3) *Emily Rose; *b* 12 Aug 1998
3 *Zarina Gabrielle; *b* 29 June 1965
4 *Natalie Frederika Louise; *b* 30 Nov 1969

Lineage: JOHN CLARK, of Gateside, Paisley (see CLARK, Bt, of Dunlambert); *b* 1791; *m* 1819 Elizabeth Aitken (*d* 5 May 1880) and *d* 27 June 1864, leaving:

STEWART CLARK, of Dundas, Linlithglow, and Cairndhu, Co Antrim, JP Cos Linlithgow, Renfrew and Antrim, DL Renfrewshire; *b* 2 Jan 1830; MP Paisley 1884–85; *m* 25 April 1860 Annie (*d* 21 March 1910), 5th dau of John Smiley (see SMILEY, Bt), and had:

1 JOHN STEWART (Sir), **1st Bt**
1 Annie Smiley; *m* 28 April 1886 Bryce Allan, of The Cliff, Wemyss Bay, and *d* 2 Oct 1925
2 Robina Elizabeth
3 Norah Kathleen; *m* 25 April 1889 her cousin Lt-Col James Clark, CB, DL, KC (see CLARK, Bt, of Dunlambert) and *d* 14 July 1959

4 Edith Stewart, DBE (1921); *m* 7 Feb 1906 Sir Thomas James Dixon, 2nd Bt, PC (*see* GLENTORAN, B), and *d* 20 Jan 1964 aged 92

STEWART CLARK *d* 21 Nov 1907; his est s,

Sir JOHN CLARK later **STEWART-CLARK** (1909), **1st Bt** (UK), so *cr* 12 Feb 1918, JP, DL Linlithgow; *b* 14 Sept 1864; memb Roy Co Archers, dir: Clark and Co and Scottish Prov Inst; *m* 10 June 1903 Marie Gertrude (*d* 2 Jan 1937), 2nd dau of Maj Marcell Conran, of Brondyffryn, Denbighs, and had:

1 STEWART (Sir), **2nd Bt**

2 John Conran Tommy; *b* 6 July 1906; *d* unm 14 March 1977

3 Dudley; *b* 17 July 1911; F/Lt RAFVR WW II; *ka* Sept 1941

4 Alan; *b* 4 April 1914

1 *Elizabeth (Betty) Morna; *b* 4 April 1914; *d* 13 Oct 1998

2 *(Marie) Rona

Sir JOHN *d* 3 March 1924; his est s,

Sir Stewart Stewart-Clark, 2nd Bt, JP (Linlithgowshire 1936); *b* 4 July 1904; *educ* Eton; served Coldstream Gds, memb Roy Co Archers, played squash for Scotland 1937 and 1946; *m* 10 Feb 1927 Jane Pamela (*d* 1993), yr dau of Maj Arundell Clarke, of Fremington Ho, North Devon, and *d* 1 Dec 1971, having had:

1 Sir JOHN (JACK) STEWART-CLARK, **3rd and present Bt**

1 *(Sara) Norina Marie [Mrs Patrick Bowlby, Caythorpe Hall, Grantham, Lincs]; *b* 25 April 1932; *m* 23 Sept 1961 *Patrick Thomas Salvin Bowlby, TD, est s of Col Francis Edwin Salvin Bowlby, MC, JP, and has:

(1) *Anthony Francis Salvin; *b* 1962; *m* 1988 *Camilla Victoria, only dau of James Cookson, of Sticklepark, Yarlington, Wincanton, Somerset, and has:

1a *James; *b* 1993

(2) *Michael Stewart Salvin; *b* 1964; *m* 1987 *Amanda Jane Harvey and has:

1a *Thomas Edward Salvin; *b* 1988

(1) *Karina Jane Maria Minette Salvin; *b* 1968

STEWART-RICHARDSON

Arms: Quarterly of six, 1st and 6th, arg. on a fess az. between a bull's head or in chief and in base a lymphad sa, a saltire of the field (for RICHARDSON); 2nd, arg. a lion rampant az. within a bordure gu. (for STEWART); 3rd, az. three garbs or (for COMYN); 4th, arg. on a bend az. three buckles or (for LESLIE); 5th, gyronny of eight or and sa. (for CAMPBELL). *Crest:* A cubit arm in armour grasping a sword, all ppr. *Supporters:* Dexter, a wyvern; sinister, an eagle, wings erect, both ppr. *Motto: Virtute acquiritur honos* ('Honour is gained by valour'). *Creation:* Bt. (NS) 13 Nov 1630.

SIR SIMON ALAISDAIR IAN NEILE STEWART-RICHARDSON, 17TH BT, of Pitfour Castle, Co Perth [Sir Simon Stewart-Richardson Bt, Lynedale, Longcross, Surrey KT16 0DP]; *b* 9 June 1947, *s* f 1969; *educ* Trin Coll Glenalmond; *m* Nov 1990 *Marilene Cabal do Nascimento and has:

1 +JASON RORIE; *b* 5 Oct 1990

1 *Janaina; *b* 20 May 1988

Lineage: ROBERT RICHARDSON; Commendator (lay proprietor following Reformation) St Mary's Isle; had:

JAMES RICHARDSON, of Smeaton, Haddingtonshire; had:

1 James (Sir), of Smeaton; *d* 25 Dec 16–, leaving:

(1) James, of Smeaton; *m* Rachel Wardlaw and *d* 11 June 1634, leaving:

1a **Sir James Richardson, 3rd Bt**; only assumed btcy 1678; ktd 1651; *m* 1st by 1649 Anne McGill (*d* by 25 May 1672); *m* 2nd his cousin(?) Helen (*d* 1688), widow of Sir John Hamilton of Redhouse, Haddingtonshire, and probably sis of **2nd Bt** and *d* 1680, leaving by his 1st w:

1b **Sir James Richardson, 4th Bt**; sold Smeaton 1708; *m* 1666 Margaret, 6th dau of 1st Earl of Lothian (*see* LOTHIAN, M), and *d* 28 May 1717, leaving:

1c **Sir James Richardson, 5th Bt**; Capt Scots Foot Gds; *dsp* 13 April 1731

2c **Sir William Richardson, 6th Bt**; Lt Col Kerr's Dragoons; *m* Eleanor, est dau of Robert Hilton, of Bishop's Auckland, and *d* 4 April 1747, leaving:

1d **Sir Robert Richardson, 7th Bt**; Capt RA; *dsp* 1752, when the btcy once more became dormant, remaining so till 1782

2 Robert; living 1635; *m* Elizabeth — and had:

(1) James, of Forganderry, Perths, or Forgan, Fife (probably the latter); *m* Margaret Miller and had:

1a James; town clerk Perth; *m* Janet Duncan and *d* 1723, leaving:

1b George; WS Edinburgh; *m* Jean, dau of James Watson, of Woodend, Stirlingshire, and had:

1c **Sir James Richardson, 8th Bt**; of Belmont; *d* unm 24 Nov 1788

2c **Sir George Richardson, 9th Bt**, of Westminster; Capt HEIC naval serv; *m* Mary (*bur* 15 Jan 1828), dau of David Cooper, RN, and *d* 11 Dec 1792, having had, with six daus:

1d **Sir George Preston Richardson, 10th Bt**; *b* with his bros before their parents' marriage but legitimated by it; Maj 64th Foot; *d* unm 21 Oct 1803 of wounds recd at capture of St Lucia 22 June previously

2d **Sir James Preston Richardson, 11th Bt**; Lt 17th Native Inf; *d* unm 8 Nov 1804 of wounds recd in action

3d **Sir John Charles Richardson, 12th Bt**; *b c* 1785; Cdr RN; *dsp* 12 April 1821, when the btcy became dormant till 1837

3c John; barrister Middle Temple; denied nephews' legitimacy and assumed btcy 1791; *dsp* 1801

2a William, of Forgandenny/Forganderry; had:

1b Thomas, of Perth; *m* Beatrix Austin and had, with other issue:

1c James; baker in Perth; *m* Ann Wilson and *d* 1762, leaving a dau (Jean, *m* John Ross of Balgersho)

2c John, of Pitfour; *d* 1821, leaving, with a dau (Margaret, *m* James Hay, DL, of Seggieden, Perths, and *d* 14 March 1819, leaving issue:

1d James, of Pitfour; *m* Elizabeth, est dau and coheir of James Stewart of Urrard, Perths, and *d* 26 July 1823, leaving, with three daus (*d* unm):

1e JOHN (Sir), **13th Bt**

2e Thomas, of Ballathy; Capt 3rd Lt Dragoons; *d* unm 1840

3e Robert RICHARDSON later RICHARDSON-ROBERTSON, CB, of Tulliebelton, Ballathie and Kinnaird, JP, DL; *b* 14 Nov 1809; Lt-Gen, Col 3rd Dragoon Gds; *m* 1st 26 Sept 1850 Hon Martha Rollo (*dsp* 17 Sept 1857), dau of 8th Lord Rollo (*qv*); *m* 2nd 29 March 1869 Lady Julia Louisa (*d* 24 Oct 1870), dau of 11th Earl of Leven and 8th Earl of) Melville (*qv*), and *d* 1 Nov 1883

1e Elizabeth; *m* Maj-Gen Campbell, KH

2e Christina; *m* 12 Feb 1824 Robert Clerk-Rattray (*d* 27 Oct 1851) and had issue

3e Jemima; *m* 24 Sept 1834 Archibald Butter, of Faskally, Perths, and had issue

(2) **Sir Robert Richardson, 1st Bt** (NS), so *cr* 13 Nov 1630, of Pencaitland, Haddingtonshire; MP (S Parl) Haddingtonshire 1630; sold an estate (evidently not Pencaitland, however) 1634 to John Sinclair, being on bad terms with his s; *m* 4 Jan 1610 Euphan, dau of Sir John Skene of Curriehill, Ld Clerk Registrar 1594–1612, and *d* 1635, having had, with two daus (one of whom was probably Helen, w of **3rd Bt**) and another s (Alexander, *dspm* (it is thought) 1639):

1a **Sir Robert Richardson, 2nd Bt**; *b* 24 Jan 1613; sold Pencaitland to James Makgill of Cranstoun Riddell; *dsp* 1640 or 1642, following which the btcy was dormant till 1678

3 George; Capt Gen Handyside's Regt of Foot; *dsp* 1748

1 Helen; *m* Robert Dunbar, of Grange Hill

The 12th Bt's 3rd cousin once-removed,

Sir JOHN RICHARDSON later **STEWART-RICHARDSON** (on inheriting his gf's Urrard estate), **13th Bt**, of Pitfour, JP, DL Perths; *b* 1 Sept 1797; advocate 1820, Sec Order Thistle 1834–75, Maj-Gen Roy Co Archers; *m* 20 Dec 1826 Mary (*d* 31 July 1886), dau of James Hay, of Colliepriest, Devon, and *d* 1 Dec 1881, having had, with a dau (*d* unm):

1 JAMES THOMAS STEWART (Sir), **14th Bt**

2 Henry Gresham; *b* 28 Oct 1844; *m* 27 Aug 1868 Gertrude (*d* 19 Jan 1928), yst dau of Joseph Gabett Studdert, of Woodlawn, Co Clare, and *d* 26 April 1883, leaving:

(1) Charles Robert; *b* 23 Aug 1877; W Australian Police; *m* 1905 Edith, 2nd dau of Albert Berryman, of Bath, and *d* 26 Nov 1954, having had:

1a Alistair De Vere; *b* 16 Aug 1906; Dep Gen Man Bank NSW; *m* 30 April 1944 *Joan Wilson, 2nd dau of Edward Wilson Hunt, of NSW, and *d* 1983, leaving:

1b +Donald Bruce; *b* 6 March 1946; has a s and dau

2a Robert Bertram; *b* 11 July 1914; *d* 3 April 1919

3a +Dudley Austin [Dudley Stewart-Richardson Esq, 322 Hector St, Tuart Hill, W Australia]; *b* 20 Dec 1924; *m* 1948 *Barbara Jean Clark and has:

1b +Kenneth John; *b* 1950

2b +Peter Dudley; *b* 1953

1a *Beatrice Edith; *b* 15 Dec 1909; *m* 1948 *Clive Edwards

2a *Constance; *b* 4 Dec 1918; *m* 20 Sept 1941 *Harry Hatch, Richard Hatch, of Booragoon, W Australia, s of Henry Richard Hatch, and has:

1b *Geoffrey Neil; *b* 13 Jan 1943; electrician; *m* 19– *Sylvia Redford, dau of Alexander Mair, of Hilton Park, and has:

1c *Peter Geoffrey; *b* 20 Sept 1965

1c *Carolyn Alexandra; *b* 28 Dec 1967

2b *Brian Richard; *b* 13 Oct 1946

1b *Lorraine Elizabeth; *b* 22 May 1950; *m* 19 April 1969 *Neil Raymond Stanley, of W Australia

3a *Sadie Mary; *b* 18 April 1921; *m* 1963 *Frank Chinnock, of Mt Barker, W Australia

(2) John Henry; *b* 1879; Maj 9th Bn Roy Highrs (Black Watch) WW I (ret 1919); *m* 18 Dec 1924 Anne (*d* 1980), er dau of Thomas Jackson, of Carnforth, Lancs, and *d* 29 Nov 1952, leaving:

1a +Ian Douglas; *b* 19 Dec 1925

(1) Henrietta Gertrude; *b* 13 Aug 1871; *d* unm 14 Nov 1939

(2) Beatrice Helen; *b* 5 April 1874; *d* unm 29 April 1939

(3) Alice Lucy; *b* 20 Nov 1875; *d* unm 9 Feb 1951

(4) Violet Roberta, MVO (1941), OBE (1933); *b* 1882; Treasury 1917–22, Assist to Establishment Offr Roy Household 1922–36, Establishment Offr 1936–42; *d* unm 13 Feb 1967

3 John Ramsay; *b* 6 Sept 1846; *m* 1882 Florence (*d* 6 Feb 1944), dau of G H Clarke, of Auckland, NZ, and *d* 1 May 1927, leaving:

(1) Arthur James; *b* 3 April 1884; Yorks Dragoons Yeo WW I; *m* 1914 Kathleen Mary (*d* 31 Dec 1964), dau of Charles Hunter, of Cambridge, NZ, and *d* 3 Sept 1950, leaving:

1a +Edward James [Edward Stewart-Richardson Esq, PO Box 10038, Arataki, Mt Maunganui, NZ]; *b* 22 Sept 1915; RNZAF WW II; *m* 28 March 1948 Heather Gladys (*d* 1985), dau of Charles Edward Scott, of Auckland, NZ, and has:

1b +John Scott [John Stewart-Richardson Esq, 11c Birdwood Cres, Parnell, Auckland, New Zealand]; *b* 3 April 1950; *educ* King's Coll Auckland, NZ, and Auckland U; stockbroker

1b *Julia [Mrs Christopher Cornthwaite, 41 Dudley Rd, Mission Bay, Auckland, New Zealand]; *b* 25 July 1953; *educ* St Cuthbert's Coll Auckland and Otago U; *m* 1990 *Christopher William Cornthwaite and has:

1c *Guy Edward; *b* 1991

2c *James William; *b* 1994

2a +John Charles [John Stewart-Richardson Esq, 1 Haworth Ave, Cambridge, New Zealand]; *b* 14 Oct 1925; RNZAF WW II; *m* 1950 *Edith Margaret, dau of Percival McIver, of Wellington, NZ, and has:

1b +Ian; *b* 1954; *m* 1984 *Patricia, dau of Robert Searle, of Cambridge, NZ, and has:

1c +Kurt Jon; *b* 1984

1b *June; *b* 1950; *m* 1970 *Allan Ross Browne, s of Ivan Browne, of Cambridge, NZ, and has:

1c *Scott Michael; *b* 1973

2c *Glen Andrew; *b* 1977

3c *Aaron Paul; *b* 1978

1a *Kathleen Sheila [Mrs Derek Pocknall, 4A Oxford St, Masterton, New Zealand]; *b* 19 Oct 1921; *m* 15 July 1946 *Derek Pocknall, of Masterton, NZ, s of W Pocknall, of Auckland, and has:

1b *Robert Forrest; *b* 12 Dec 1949; *educ* Wairarapa Coll Masterton, NZ

2b *Graeme Forrest; *b* 12 Dec 1949; *educ* Wairarapa Coll

3b *David Thomas; *b* 18 Sept 1953

1b *Susan Mary; *b* 24 Nov 1948

2b *Helen Jean; *b* 8 Aug 1958

2a *Barbara Mary [Mrs Peter Wilson, 4 Oleander Lane, Mount Maunganui, New Zealand]; *b* 22 Oct 1930; *m* 1st 28 Dec 1949 Bernard Harold Vosper (*d* in car crash 14 Aug 1960) and has:

1b *Frank Stewart; *b* 14 June 1952; *educ* Wanganui Collegiate Sch, NZ; *m* 1979 (*divorce* 19–) Claire Jeanette, dau of Lionel Montague, of Matamata, NZ, and has:

1c *Kirk James; *b* 1981

1c *Lauren Jane; *b* 1980

2c *Brook Jade; *b* 1986

2b *Richard Arthur; *b* 31 May 1953; *educ* Wanganui Collegiate and Matamata Coll; *m* 1st 1979 (*divorce* 19–) Sue —; *m* 2nd 1984 (*divorce* 199–) Tina Noutsos, of Athens, and has:

1c *Nikolas Harold; *b* Nov 1984

1c *Sarah Elizabeth; *b* 1987

2b (cont.) Richard Wilson *m* 3rd 1997 *Dione Haswell

1b *Jennifer Kaye; *b* 25 May 1955; *m* 1981 *Neil Brooks, of Rotorua, and has:

1c *Mitchell Peter; *b* 1987

2c *Jackson Stewart; *b* March 1997

2a (cont.) Mrs Bernard Vosper *m* 2nd 2 Sept 1962 *Peter George Wilson and by him has:

3b *Stewart James; *b* 1968; *educ* Matamata Coll

2b *Robyn Jane; *b* 3 Oct 1963; *educ* Matamata Coll; *m* 1997 *Paul Kenna, of Wellington, NZ

(2) John Ramsay; *b* 29 Sept 1887; *m* 1914 Kathleen, 2nd dau of John Knight, of Whangerei, NZ, and *d* 29 Jan 1939

(1) Evelyn Mary; *m* 1911 Charles Willard McBride, 2nd s of William McBride, of Christchurch, NZ, and *d* Feb 1957, leaving issue

4 Edmund Robert, JP, DL Perths; *b* 13 July 1848; Lt-Col N Staff Regt, Lt-Col and Hon Col 4th Bn Sherwood Foresters; *m* 29 Nov 1879 Jessica Mary (*d* 1894), only dau of Montagu Stephen Williams, QC, and *d* 20 Dec 1917, having had:

(1) Robert Montagu, MC (1917) and two bars 1918; *b* 26 June 1886; *educ* Eton; Maj 11th Hus WW I (despatches), Hon Attaché Washington, DC; *m* 23 Oct 1929 Elizabeth Peabody Stewart Hall (*d* 13 Nov 1943), only dau of Alexander Main Stewart, of New York, and *dsp* 30 Oct 1949

(1) Louise Mary; *m* 15 Dec 1904 Albert Edward Cox (*d* 23 March 1937), of Dungarthill, Perths, and *d* 22 Dec 1960, leaving issue

(2) Edith Muriel; *m* 9 Nov 1921 Lt-Col Ranald Hume Macdonald (*d* 20 Jan 1935), s of Lord Kingsburgh, KCB, FRS, LLD, Ld Justice Clerk Scotland, and *d* 26 May 1960

(3) Olive Marguerite; *m* 16 Feb 1920 Maj Kenneth Douglas Lorne Maclaine, MC (*d* 20 May 1935), and *d* 5 April 1959, leaving issue

1 Mary Louisa; *m* 3 Oct 1865 Rt Rev George Forrest Browne, DD, DCL (*d* 1 June 1930), Bp Bristol, and *d* 22 June 1903, leaving issue

2 Elizabeth Charlotte; *m* 24 June 1869 Rev Henry Murray Oswald (*d* 18 Aug 1911), Rector Gt Hallingbury, Essex, and *d* 13 Feb 1930

Sir JOHN's est s,

Sir James Thomas Stewart-Richardson, 14th Bt, VD, DL Perths; *b* 24 Dec 1840; Capt 78th Highrs, Hon Col 3rd Vol Bn Black Watch, Sec Order Thistle 1875–93; *m* 20 Oct 1868 Harriett Georgina Alice (*d* 26 Oct 1924), 2nd surv dau of Rupert John Cochrane, of Halifax, Nova Scotia, and *d* 14 Feb 1895, having had, with a dau (*d* unm):

1 EDWARD AUSTIN (Sir), **15th Bt**

2 John Lauderdale; *b* 18 Jan 1878; Lt (SR) Coldstream Gds; *m* 6 May 1916 Nora Joyce (*d* 10 May 1966), yst dau of William Rigby, of Alderley Edge, Cheshire, and was *ka* 17 May 1916

3 Neil Graham, DSO (1918); *b* 23 Oct 1881; Lt-Col NI Horse, Capt Seaforth Highrs, Boer War, WW I, cmded 1st/4th Roy Scots Fus Palestine 1918 (despatches), ADC to Govr-Gen Australia; *m* 23 Oct 1924 Alexandra (*d* 2 Aug 1972), dau of Peter Ralli (*see* RALLI, Bt), and *d* 23 Feb 1934, leaving:

(1) +Peter Neil Ralli, MBE (1964) [Brig Peter Stewart-Richardson MBE, Creake Abbey Cottages, Fakenham, Norfolk NR21 9LF]; *b* 9 Feb 1926; *educ* Eton; Brig Coldstream Gds, Croix de Guerre (Bronze Star-Territoire d'Operacion Exterieur) 1950, High Sheriff Norfolk 1989; *m* 29 Sept 1954 *Patricia Ann, dau of Maj John Michael Evans Lombe, MC, RA, and has:

1a Neil Graham John; *b* 2 Sept 1955; *educ* Eton; 2nd Lt Coldstream Gds; *d* 15 June 1978

2a +Michael Peter Alastair; *b* 12 March 1957; *educ* Eton and RMA Sandhurst; 2nd Lt Coldstream Gds; *m* 23 Sept 1982 *Amanda, only dau of John Baker, of Higher Shortwood Farm, Litton, Bath, and has:

1b +Rory Neil John; *b* 1989

1b *Lucy Alexandra; *b* 1987

1a *Mary-Ann [Mrs Mary-Ann Gemmell, The Ship House, Burnham Overy Staithe, Norfolk PE31 8JB]; *b* 15 March 1961; *m* 1st 1981 (George) Dominic Mackintosh Warre, yst s of Maj John Antony Warre, MC, of Barrowden, Oakham, Leics; *m* 2nd 1987 (*divorce* 19–) David Stewart Gemmell, s of Lt-Col Arthur Stewart Gemmell, of Ingarsby Old Hall, Leics, and by him has:

1b *George Neil; *b* 1988

1b *Mary Rose; *b* 1990

2a *Katherine Jane; *b* 26 March 1966

(2) +Alastair Lucas Graham [Alastair Stewart-Richardson Esq, 120 Woodsford Sq, London W14 8DT; 7 King's Bench Walk, Temple, London EC4Y 7DS]; *b* 29 Nov 1927; *educ* Eton and Magdalene Coll Cambridge (MA); barrister Inner Temple 1952; *m* 29 May 1969 *(Diana) Claire, yr dau of Brig George Streynsham Rawstorne, CBE, MC, of Sutherland, and has:

1a +James George; *b* 2 March 1971

2a +Hugh Neil; *b* 18 March 1977

1a *Sarah Alexandra; *b* 20 Feb 1974

1 Mary Ramsay; *b* 1 Aug 1869; ARRC 1915, QAIMNS (Res) WW I (despatches), Queen Elisabeth of Belgium medal; *d* unm 23 May 1960

2 Alice Evelyn Isabella; *b* 12 July 1870; *m* 29 Jan 1903 Col James Adam Gordon Richardson-Drummond-Hay, Coldstream Gds (*d* 27 Dec 1928), of Seggieden, Perths, and *d* 13 Jan 1945, leaving issue

3 Christian Maule; *b* 23 Oct 1881; Sr Cmdt ATS (ret 1941); *m* 24 Nov 1908 Maj Hon Alexander David Murray (*see* MANSFIELD and MANSFIELD, E) and *d* 24 Sept 1964, leaving issue

4 Gladys Hermione; *b* 31 May 1883; *d* unm 15 Aug 1966

5 Esther Drummond; *b* 24 Jan 1887; *d* unm 30 Aug 1949

Sir JAMES's est s,

Sir Edward Austin Stewart-Richardson, 15th Bt; *b* 24 July 1872; Capt 3rd Bn Black Watch, ADC to Govr Qld 1899–1902, 2nd Bn Black Watch and Qld Inf Boer War, WW I; *m* 19 April 1904 Lady Constance Mackenzie (*m* 2nd 4 Aug 1921 Dennis Luckie Matthew and *d* 24 Nov 1932), yr dau of 2nd Earl of Cromartie (*qv*), and *das* 28 Nov 1914, leaving, with a yr s (Torquil Cathel Hugh, MC, *b* 22 Aug 1909, Capt RA (TA) WW II, *d* unm 17 Sept 1961):

Sir Ian Rorie Hay Stewart-Richardson, 16th Bt; *b* 25 Sept 1904; *educ* ISC Windsor; Maj Irish Gds WW II Africa and Italy (wounded, despatches twice); *m* 1st 14 June 1940 (*divorce* 1944) Katherine Kelly, yr dau of Ernest George Punchard; *m* 2nd 29 Nov 1944 *Audrey Meryl [Mrs Patrick Robertson, Lynedale, Longcross Rd, Longcross, Surrey KT16 0DP] (*m* 2nd 16 May 1975 *Patrick Pearson Robertson), est dau of Claude Odlum, of Naas, Co Kildare, and *d* 16 June 1969, having by her had:

1 Sir SIMON ALAISDAIR STEWART-RICHARDSON, **17th and present Bt**

2 +Ninian Rorie; *b* 25 Jan 1949; *educ* Rannoch Sch Perths; industrialist, commercial pilot; *m* 21 Oct 1983 *Joan Kristina, dau of Howard Smee, of Rio de Janeiro, and has:

(1) +Edward Rorie; *b* 22 July 1988

(2) +William Howard; *b* 1990

(1) *Olivia Joan; *b* 1987

1 *Claudia Mavis Philippa [Mrs Anthony Wainwright, 29 Stratford Rd, London W8 6RA]; *b* 28 May 1946; *m* 1970 *R Anthony Wainwright and has:

(1) *Guiam Edward; *b* 1985

(1) *Sarah; *b* 1987

2 *(Roslyn) Alison [Mrs Peter Wear, 33 Findon Rd, London W12 9PP]; *b* 26 June 1952; *m* 1984 *Peter Glennerster Wear and has:

(1) *Christopher Algernon; *b* 1988

(1) *Jessica; *b* 1986

STEWARTBY

Arms: Or a fess chequy azure and argent between a portcullis with chains in chief and a lymphad, sails furled, oars in action sable, flagged gules in base, all within a bordure azure, a label of three points gules. **Crest:** A lymphad as in the shield between two fleurs-de-lys or. **Supporters:** Dexter, a stag proper attired or, gorged with a collar engrailed gules; sinister, a lion proper gorged with a collar engrailed chequy argent and gules. **Motto:** There remaineth a rest. **Creation:** B. (LP, UK) 1992.

THE BARON STEWARTBY, of Portmoak in the District of Perth and Kinross (Sir (Bernard Harold) Ian Halley Stewart, RD (1972), PC (1989)) [The Rt Hon The Lord Stewartby RD PC, 2 Baldwin Crescent, London SE5 9LQ]; *b* 10 Aug 1935; *educ* Haileybury (Life Govr 1977) and Jesus Coll Camb (MA, DLitt 1978, Hon Fell 1994); RNVR 1954–56, Lt-Cdr RNR; dir: Brown Shipley & Co 1971–83, Brown Shipley Holdings 1980–83, Victory Insurance Co 1976–83, Seccombe Marshall & Campion Hldgs 1989–, Diploma plc 1990–, Standard Chartered plc 1990– (dep chm 1993–); MP (C) Hitchin 1974–83 and N Herts 1983–92, Memb Public Expenditure Ctee 1977–79, PPS to Chllr Exchequer 1979–83, Parly U-Sec MOD 1983, Ec Sec Treasury 1983–87, Min State: Armed Forces MOD 1987–88, NI Office 1988–89, Public Accounts Ctee 1991–92; ktd 1991; chm: Throgmorton Tst 1990–, Delian Lloyd's Investment Tst 1993–95, British Acad Ctee for Sylloge of Coins of Br Isles 1967–; V-Chm Westminster Ctee for Protection Children 1975–92; dep chm Angerstein Underwriting Tst 1995–, Tstee Sir Halley Stewart Tst 1978–, V-Pres St John's Ambulance Herts 1977–, KStJ 1992 (CStJ 1986); FBA 1981, FRSE 1986, FSA, FSA (Scot); author: *The Scottish Coinage* (1955), *Studies in Numismatic Method* (coauthor 1983), *Coinage in Tenth-Century England* (coauthor 1989), *New History of the Royal Mint* (1992); *m* 1966 *Hon Deborah Charlotte, dau of 3rd Baron Tweedsmuir (*qv*), and has:

1 *Henry Ernest Alexander Halley; *b* 15 July 1972; *educ* Haileybury and Jesus Coll Camb; late 2nd Lt Roy Scots, corporate fin exec analyst Schroders

2 *Lydia Barbara Rose Anna Phoebe; *b* 16 Jan 1969; *educ* Haileybury and St Andrew

3 *(Dorothy) Louisa Charlotte Amabel; *b* 11 Oct 1970; *educ* Haileybury and Jesus Coll Cambridge

Lineage: (BERNARD) HALLEY STEWART (*see* STEWART, Bt, of Stewartby); *d* 30 July 1958, leaving:

Prof HAROLD CHARLES STEWART, CBE; FRSE; *m* 1st Dorothy Irene Lowen (*d* 1969); *m* 2nd Audrey Patricia Nicolle and had by his 1st w:

BERNARD HAROLD IAN HALLEY, *cr* a **Baron**

STEYN

Creation: B. (LP, UK) 16 Dec 1994.

THE BARON STEYN, of Swafield, Co Norfolk (Sir Johan van Zyl Steyn, PC (1992)) [The Rt Hon The Lord Steyn PC, House of Lords, London SW1A 0PW]; *b* 15 Aug 1932; *educ* Jan van Riebeck Sch Cape Town, U of Stellenbosch and Univ Coll Oxford; barrister S Africa 1958, Sr Counsel Supreme Court S Africa 1970, barrister English bar from 1973 (Bencher Lincoln's Inn 1985), QC 1979, Presiding Judge N Circuit 1989–91, High Court Judge Queen's Bench 1985–91, a Ld Justice Appeal 1992–95, a Ld Appeal in Ordinary 1995–; Hon LLD QMW 1997; *m* 1st (divorce 19–) Jean; *m* 2nd *Susan Leonore, née Lewis, and by his 1st w has, with two sons:

1 *Linda; *m* 30 Sept 1995 *Robert Lewis, s of Mrs Kathleen Lewis, of Cheadle

2 *Karen; *m* 26 July 1997 *Alexander Glasebrook, s of David Glasebrook, of Harpenden, Herts

STIRLING-HAMILTON

Arms: Gu. three cinquefoils within a bordure arg. **Crest:** An armed man from the middle, brandishing a sword aloft, ppr. **Motto:** *Pro patria* ('For one's country'). **Creation:** Bt. (NS) 1673.

SIR MALCOLM BRUCE STIRLING-HAMILTON, 14TH BT, of Preston, Co Haddington [Sir Malcolm Stirling-Hamilton Bt, Narborough Hall, King's Lynn, Norfolk PE32 1TE]; *b* 6 Aug 1979; *s f* 1989; *educ* Stowe

Lineage: Sir JOHN HAMILTON of Fingalto(u)n (*see* ABERCORN, D); *m* 1st Jane, dau and heir of Sir James Lyddell, of Preston, Haddingtonshire; *m* 2nd Anna, dau of Sir William de Seton of Seton (*see* EGLINTON and WINTON, E), and was perhaps *k* at the defeat by English of Homildon Hill (at which he was certainly present) 14 Sep 1402; ancestor of:

Sir ROBERT HAMILTON, of Fingalton and Preston; *m* 1st Margaret, dau of Sir John Mowat of Stonehouse; *m* 2nd Marion, dau of Sir David Crighton of Cranstonriddell; *m* 3rd 1516 Helen, dau of Sir James Schaw of Sauchy, and had:

1 Robert, of Fingalton and Preston; *m* Katherine, dau of James Tweedie of Drummeizier, and had:

  (1) James; *k sp* & *vp* 30 April 1523 in Edinburgh High St in an encounter between feuding adherents of the Earls of Arran and Angus

  (2) David (Sir), of Fingalton and Preston; early Protestant but fought for MARY QUEEN OF SCOTS at Battle of Langside 1568; *m* Janet, dau of Sir William Baillie of Lamington, and had, with other sons (*d unm*):

    1a George, of Fingalton and Preston; *m* 1563 Barbara, dau of Sir John Cockburn of Ormiston, and *d* 1608, having had (with five married daus):

      1b John (Sir), of Fingalton and Preston; attainted for participating in Raid of Ruthven (*see* CARLISLE, E) but restored; Covenanter, MP (S Parl) E Lothian 1639–41, sat convention of estates 1643–44; *m* Johanna, dau of Sir Thomas Otterburn of Redhall, and *d* 1644, having had:

        1c James (Sir), of Fingalton and Preston; *b* 1589; ktd 1615; *m* 1609 Barbara, dau of Sir Robert Mure of Caldwell, and *d* Oct 1644, having had:

          1d Robert; *dsp* & *vp* 1632

          2d John; *m* 1st 1633 Anne, dau of 1st Earl of Carnwath (*see* 1940 edn); *m* 2nd 1641 Margaret, dau of Sir John Seton of St Germans, and *dsp* 1647

          1d Anne; *m* her cousin Sir Thomas Hamilton of Fingalton and Preston and had issue (*see below*)

      2b James; *m* Margaret Inglis and had several daus

      3b Robert, of Newhaven; *m* 1606 Janet, dau of Johnston of Elphinstone, and had:

        1c Thomas (Sir), of Fingalton and Preston; *m* 1st Margaret Murray; *m* 2nd his cousin Anne, dau of Sir James Hamilton of Fingalton and Preston, and by her had:

          1d **Sir William Hamilton, 1st Bt** (NS), so *cr* 5 Nov 1673, with remainder to heirs male whatsoever, of Preston and Fingalton; *b c* 1645; sold 1681 his estates to his dau's f-in-law Sir James Oswald and settled in Holland; *m* 1670 Rachel, dau of Sir Thomas Nicolson of Cockburnspath, and *dspm c* 1690, having had:

            1e Rachel; *d unm*

            2e Anne; *m* 1st 1697 Thomas, est s of Sir James Oswald; *m* 2nd 1705 Gilbert Burnet, s of Sir Thomas Burnet of Crimond

            3e Jane; *m* 1695 George Stirling of Letham

          2d **Sir Robert Hamilton, 2nd Bt**; *b* 1650; *d unm* 1701, when the btcy became dormant till 1816

        1c (cont.) Sir Thomas *m* 3rd Rachel, sis of Gilbert Burnet, Bp Salisbury, and widow of Sir Thomas Nicolson of Cockburnspath, and *d* 1672

     2a Patrick; *k sp* at Hamilton 2 April 1595 by Sir John Hamilton of Lettrich

      (1) Janet; *m* John Hamilton of Broomhill

      (2) Gilles; *m* John Stewart, Yr. of Hallcraig

2 John; leased Airdrie from the Abbot of Newbottle; *m* Ellen Crawford and was *ka* Flodden 9 Sep 1513, leaving:

  (1) Methusalem, of Airdrie; *m* Christian Bell and had:

1a Gavin, of Airdrie; *m* 1567 Isabella, dau of James Robertson of Earnock, and *d* 1591, leaving:

1b John, of Airdrie; *b* 1569; *m* Janet, dau of Robert Hamilton of Torrance, and had:

1c John; *m* Margaret, only dau of James Hamilton, and *dsp*

2c Gavin, of Airdrie; *m* Jane, dau of Robert Montgomery of Hazlehead, and *d* 29 Dec 1681, leaving:

1d Robert, *de jure* 3rd Bt, of Airdrie; did not use title; *m* by 1681 Elizabeth, dau of William Cochrane of Rochsoles, and had:

1e William, *de jure* 4th Bt, of Airdrie; *b* 6 March 1681; did not use title; Min Bothwell 1709; *m* by 1714 Margaret (*d* 2 April 1773), dau and heir of John Bogle of Sandyhills, and *d* 25 May 1749, having had:

1f Robert, *de jure* 5th Bt, of Airdrie, which he sold with the other remaining family property when his business ventures failed; *b* 1714; did not assume title; *m* by 1748 Mary dau of John Baird of Craigton, and *d* 1756, having had:

1g William, *de jure* 6th Bt; *b* 1748; did not assume title; *d* unm 1756

2g John, *de jure* 7th Bt; *b c* 1750; did not assume title; *d* unm 1778

3g Robert, *de jure* 8th Bt; *b* 1754; did not assume title; *d* unm at St Helena 8 June 1799

1g Grizel; *m* John Arnot

2g Mary; *m* Thomas Cochrane, MD

2f John; had two sons (*d* unm)

3f James

4f Thomas; *b* 1728; Prof Anatomy Glasgow U; *m* Isabel, dau of Dr William Anderson, and *d* 1781, having had:

1g William; *b c* 1760; MA Glasgow; surgn, Prof Anatomy Glasgow U 1781; *m* Elizabeth, dau of William Stirling of Drumpelier, and *d* 1793, leaving:

1h WILLIAM (Sir), **9th Bt**

2h Thomas; *b* 1789; Army Offr, author: *Cyril Thornton, Annals of the Peninsular Campaign* and other works; *m* 1st Annette, dau of Archibald Montgomery Campbell; *m* 2nd 15 Feb 1834 Maria Frances Geslip (*d* 27 Aug 1875), widow of Sir Robert Townsend Farquhar, 1st Bt (*qv*), and 4th dau of Joseph François Louis de Lautour, of Hexton House, Herts, and *dsp* 1842

1f Elizabeth; *m* Rev Daniel St Clair, Min Longformacus, and had issue

1e Louisa; *m* 10 Sept 1704 James Balfour, 1st of Pilrig, Midlothian, and had issue (*see* BALFOUR OF INCHRYE, B)

2d William; Pncpl Edinburgh U; *d* 1732, leaving issue

3 James

4 David, of Langton and Olivestob; *m* Margaret, dau of 2nd Lord Seton (*see* EGLINTON and WINTON, E)

1 Margaret; *m* Sir Robert Dalzell of that Ilk

The *de jure* 8th Bt's 1st cousin once-removed,

Sir William Stirling Hamilton, 9th Bt, which title he assumed 1834, having been declared heir male to the **2nd Bt** 1816; *b* 1788; *educ* Balliol Coll·Oxford (BA); advocate 1813; Professor Logic and Metaphysics Edinburgh U; *m* 1829 Janet (*d* 24 Dec 1877), dau of Hubert Marshall, and had:

1 WILLIAM (Sir), **10th Bt**

2 Hubert; *b* 1834; MA Oxon; advocate, Sheriff Substitute Edinburgh; *m* 17 June 1868 Louisa Wentworth (*d* 27 April 1904), dau of Laurence Davidson, and *d* 20 Dec 1901, leaving:

(1) William; *b* 7 July 1869; *m* 12 Oct 1898 Kathleen (Isabella Ruby) (*d* 12 June 1961), dau of George Robert Elsmie, CSI, LLD, of Drayton, Torquay, and *d* 4 Dec 1958, leaving:

1a Hubert, of Sunbury; *b* 31 Oct 1902; *m* Esmé Trigg and was *k* with her by enemy action 30 Nov 1940

2a Robert William; *b* 26 Nov 1905; *educ* Winchester and Magdalen Coll Oxford; Keeper Ashmolean Museum Oxford, FBA 1960; *m* 3 April 1935 *Eileen Hetty [Mrs Robert Hamilton, Haskers, Westleton, Suffolk], dau of Francis Goldworth Lowick, and had:

1b +ANDREW ROBERT (Rev) [The Rev Andrew Hamilton, 16 Cranston Close, Reigate, Surrey]; *b* 5 Sep 1937; heir presumptive; *educ* New Coll Oxford; FCA; *m* 1972 *Josephine Mary, dau of Reginald Sargant

2b +(William) Alexander Hubert [Alexander Hamilton Esq, 92 Woodwarde Rd, London SE22 8UT]; *b* 22 Feb 1941; *educ* Trin Coll Cambridge; *m* 31 July 1966 *Cecilia Louise Somerville, dau of Maj Charles Erling Bernard Catt (*see* 1970 edn SOMERVILLE, Bt), and has:

1c +Alexander James Erling; *b* 25 June 1967; *m* 19– *Angelika Ilse, dau of Wolfgang Klaus Oehrl, of Oldenburg, Germany

1c *Anna Cecilia Louise; *b* 16 May 1969

3b +Thomas; *b* 25 Jan 1952; *educ* Magdalen Coll Oxford; *m* 1st 1978 Cornelia, dau of Willy Brüllmann, of Zuben, Switzerland; *m* 2nd 1991 *Sally Lisa, dau of Donald Charles McArthur, and by her has:

1c +Robert Louis; *b* 1993

1b *Penelope Frances [Mrs Brereton Fairclough, Garden Cottage, Aldersey Park, Handley, Chester CH3 9ED]; *b* 4 July 1936; *m* 1st 17 Sept 1960 (*annulled* 1985) Maj Robert Alan Mountcastle Seeger, MC, RM; *m* 2nd 30 Sept 1989 *Lt-Col Brereton Robert Fairclough, MC, TD, S Lancs Regt, and by her 1st husb has:

1c *Frances Clare; *b* 10 June 1965; *m* 1994 (*annulled* 1998) Avard Warren Kaleoaloha Pereira and has:

1d *Kaela Kalawai Penelle; *b* 10 Oct 1994

2c *Katharine Anne; *b* 12 Oct 1966

2b *Katharine Jane Patricia; *b* 15 March 1955; *educ* Camberwell Coll Art; *m* 1987 *Bernard Francis Purcell and has:

1c *George Alexander; *b* 1992

1c *Stephanie Jane; *b* 1990

1a Kathleen Elizabeth; *m* 10 Jan 1934 Edward Reginald Pierssene (*d* 26 Dec 1954), s of Rev Rene Pierssene, Vicar Chandlers Ford, Hants, and had:

1b Anne Gillian; *b* 20 Feb 1936; *m* 30 April 1960 *Lancelot Maurice Heler, s of F W Heler, of Wootton Grange, Warwicks, *d* 199–

(2) Hubert; *b* 10 July 1878; *m* — (*m* 2nd A W Deller)

(3) Harry Austen; *b* 15 Feb 1880; Maj RFA; *m* 16 April 1907 Madeleine (*m* 2nd — Armstrong (*k* steeplechasing) and *d c* 1930), dau of Fernand Toucas Messillon, of Paris, and was *ka* 25 Jan 1916, leaving:

1a Anthony Edmund Hubert; *b* 12 Feb 1908; *m* — and was *kas* 1944 *sp*

2a Archibald George; *b* 12 Nov 1909; *k* in an air accident 1934

3 Thomas; *b* 1843; MB, FRCS Edin; *m* 6 Nov 1873 Helen (*d* 4 June 1932), dau of H W Nutt, and *d* 20 Dec 1918, leaving:

(1) William Gavin, *b* 4 Oct 1874; Supt Presidency of Jail, Calcutta, Lt-Col IMS; *m* 1st 23 Feb 1908 Louise (*d* 14 Oct 1914), dau of Alison Cunningham, of Peterborough; *m* 2nd 29 Dec 1916 Helen (*d* 18 March 1950), dau of Dugald Stewart Macphee, of Helensburgh, Dunbartonshire, and *d* 10 Dec 1937 following a train crash at Castle Cary, Somerset, leaving:

1a John William Stirling, MC; *b* 26 Sept 1919; BA Oxon 1946; Capt Argyll and Sutherland Highrs WW II; *m* 10 June 1945 *Kathleen Dorothea, dau of John Alexander Thomson, MBE, of Helensburgh, and *d* 1959, leaving:

1b +Alastair Colin Stirling [Alastair Hamilton Esq, Tillyfourie Farm, Monymusk, Aberdeenshire]; *b* 19 Dec 1954; *m* 1979 *Miranda Louise, dau of Jeffrey Watson Boughey, of Monymusk, and has:

1c *Rory Colin Stirling; *b* 1980

2c *James Alexander; *b* 1982

3c *Thomas Daniel; *b* 1986

1b *Alison Lesley [Mrs Nicholas Parsons, Ballindarroch House, Aldourie, Inverness-shire]; *b* 30 April 1947; *m* 1970 *Nicholas Parsons and has:

1c *Alexander; *b* 19–

1c *Claudia; *b* 19–

2b *Daphne Helen [Mrs Michael Murray, Kilmahumaig, Crinan, Lochgilphead, Argyll PA31 8SW]; *b* 11 Nov 1950; *m* 1977 *Michael Murray and has:

1c *William John Balfour; *b* 1985

1c *Nina Katharine; *b* 1982

2a +Alastair Gavin, DSC (1945) [Lt-Cdr Alastair Hamilton DSC, RN, Dunmar, Tighnabroaich, Argyll PA21 2AE]; *b* 7 Sept 1922; RN WW II and Korea; *m* 3 Nov 1956 *Gillian Bomford, of Sutton, Surrey, and has:

1b +Jock; *b* March 1962

1b Gail; *b* 25 Sept 1960; *m* 1986 *Patrick J Dempsey and *d* 1993, leaving:

1c *Harry John; *b* 1991

1c *Katharine Phoebe; *b* 1988

2b *Katharine; *b* March 1964; *m* 1989 *R Martin Pender and has:

1c *Patrick Iago; *b* 1992

1a *Margaret Audrey [Mrs Charles Turcan, Oxey Barn, Woodside, Lymington, Hants]; *b* 5 Feb 1918; 2nd Offr WRNS WW II; *m* 27 June 1946 *Charles Ian Turcan, CA, s of Charles Somerville Turcan, of Edinburgh, and has:

1b *Gavin Charles; *b* 1948

2b *Alan Ronald Hamilton; *b* 1952; *m* 1985 *Gillian Hart and has:

1c *Mathew; *b* 1987

1c *Sarah; *b* 1989

1b *Lydia Helen [Mrs Nicholas Clough, 159 Maldon Rd, Colchester, Essex]; *b* 1950; *m* 1978 *Nicholas Hampton Oldham Clough and has:

1c *Anthony Oldham; *b* 1984

2c *David James; *b* 1988

1c *Charlotte Emma; *b* 1981

(2) Hubert Stirling; *b* 1879; *d* unm 27 Sept 1963

(1) Helen Gladys; *m* 1921 John Watson Simpson, MB (*d* 11 Jan 1929), s of James Cowle Simpson, of Carfin Hall, Holytown, by Margaret, 6th dau of Sir John Watson, 1st Bt, JP, DL, and *d* 2 June 1984, leaving:

1a John Anthony; *b* 22 Jan 1923; *educ* Radley; *m* 18 May 1985 *Gweneth Mary, dau of Dr Kenneth Bates, of St Albans, Herts, and *d* 3 Feb 1994

1a *Moyra Anne Margaret [Mrs David Luther, Shaggs Flood, Wambrook, Chard, Somerset TA20 3EU]; *b* 1924; *m* Sept 1951 *David John Luther, only s of Maj Alan Charles Grenville Luther, MC (*see* GAINSBOROUGH E), and has:

1b *Charles Anthony; *b* 19 July 1952; *educ* Michaelhouse Natal

2b *Robert Guy; *b* 2 Nov 1955; *educ* Michaelhouse Natal

1b *Carola Mary; *b* 14 Sept 1959; *educ* Roedean (S Africa)

2a *Rosemary Hamilton [Mrs Sydney Garnar, Spicklewood, Coach Rd, Seal Chart, Kent TN15 0HD]; *b* 1926; *m* Sept 1954 *Sydney Anthony Holden Garnar, s of Sydney Robert Garnar, of The Old Place, Wrotham, Kent, and has:

1b *Clive Robert Sydney [Clive Garnar Esq, 57 Hartsland Rd, Sevenoaks TN13 3TW]; *b* 16 Jan 1963

1b *Yvonne Alison Lindsay; *b* 21 Nov 1960; *m* 25 Aug 1995 *Anthony Harvey Constant, s of Harvey Constant, of Hout Bay, CP, S Africa

1 Elizabeth; *d* unm 2 Mar 1882

The 9th Bt *d* 6 May 1856; his s,

Sir WILLIAM HAMILTON later STIRLING-HAMILTON (deed poll 1889), **10th Bt**, CB; *b* 17 Sept 1830; engr Peshawar Valley 1855–57, took part in suppression of Indian Mutiny 1857 (medal with clasp), Capt RA 1866, Maj RHA 1872, Lt-Col 1875, CO RA Western Dist 1881–85, Lt-Gen 1889, Gen and Col cmdt 1895; *m* 15 Oct 1856 Eliza Marcia (*d* 14 Feb 1922), est dau of Maj-Gen — Barr, RHA, and *d* 27 Sept 1913, having had, with a yr s (John, MBE (1920), *b* 2 Dec 1873, *educ* Jesus Coll Cambridge (MA), MRCS, LRCP London, *d* 4 Feb 1932) and five daus (Louisa, *d* 1863; Janet, *d* unm 26 Dec 1941; Elizabeth, *d* unm; Mary, *d* unm 31 Aug 1949; Eliza, *d* unm 2 June 1933):

Sir William Stirling-Hamilton, 11th Bt; *b* 4 Dec 1868; *educ* Jesus Coll Cambridge; *m* 24 May 1902 Mabel Mary (*d* 22 June 1959), dau of Maj-Gen Henry Tyndall, CB, and *d* 7 Oct 1946, leaving:

Sir Robert William Stirling-Hamilton, 12th Bt; *b* 5 April 1903; *educ* RNC Dartmouth; RN: WW II (despatches twice), Cdre RN Barracks Portsmouth 1952–54, ret as Capt 1954; *m* 4 Jan 1930 Eileen, only dau of Rt Rev Henry Kemble Southwell, CMG, DD, Bp Suffragan Lewes, and *d* 14 Feb 1982, having had:

1 Malcolm Kenneth William; *b* 25 July 1934; *d* 14 Nov 1936

2 **Sir Bruce Stirling-Hamilton, 13th Bt**, JP (W Sussex 1959); *b* 5 Aug 1940; *educ* Nautical Coll Pangbourne and RMA Sandhurst; Capt QO Highrs; *m* 4 Sept 1968 *Stephanie, est dau of Dr William Campbell, of Alloway, Ayr, and *d* 17 Sept 1989, leaving:

  (1) Sir MALCOLM BRUCE STIRLING-HAMILTON, **14th and present Bt**

    (1) *(Georgina) Claire; *b* 2 Sep 1970

    (2) *Iona Stephanie; *b* 1985

1 *Joanna Eileen; *b* 26 Oct 1930; *m* 1 Jan 1955 *Ian Kroyer MacKinnon, QO Highrs, yr s of William MacKinnon of MacKinnon, OBE, of Hollingbourne, Kent

2 *Eila Mary; *b* 22 Jan 1939; *m* 1st 19 Dec 1959 Lt Timothy Martin Woodford, RN (*k* in a Fleet Air Arm crash 8 July 1966), only s of Morris Milner Woodford, of Mayfair, and has:

  (1) *Charlotte Amanda; *b* 25 Sept 1960; m 1981 *Capt Charles Rodney Style, RN (*see* STYLE, Bt)

  (2) *Amanda Caroline; *b* 10 Sept 1962

2 (cont.) Mrs Timothy Woodford *m* 2nd 30 Dec 1967 *George Rudolf Wratislaw Walker, only s of Rev Richard Bickersteth Roscoe Walker, of The Vicarage, Northleach, Glos, and by him has:

  (3) *Harriet Nicola; *b* 1970

  (4) *Emily Mary; *b* 1972

STOCKDALE

Arms: Erm. on a bend sa. between two escallops gu. three pheons arg. **Crest:** Issuant from a crown vallary or a gryphon's head gu. **Motto:** *Omnia mei dona dei* ('All my things are gifts of God'). **Creation:** Bt. (UK) 5 Dec 1960.

SIR THOMAS MINSHULL STOCKDALE, 2ND BT, of Hoddington, Co Southampton [Sir Thomas Stockdale Bt, Manor Farm, Weston Patrick, Hants RG25 2NT; 73 Alderney St, London SW1V 4HH]; *b* 7 Jan 1940; *s f* 1989; *educ* Eton and Worcester Coll Oxford (MA); barrister Inner Temple 1966; *m* 5 June 1965 *Jacqueline Ha-Van-Vuong, of Saigon, and has:

1 +JOHN MINSHULL; *b* 13 Dec 1967

1 *Charlotte Fermor; *b* 27 May 1970

Lineage: WILLIAM STOCKDALE, of Scarborough, Yorks, had:

Rev ROBERT STOCKDALE; *b* 1 Aug 1728; MA Cantab, Fell Sidney Sussex Coll Cambridge, Canon York, Vicar Hayton, Yorks, and St Mary's Bishop Hill, York; *m* Katharine, dau and coheir of Peter Minshull, of Hutton Cranswick, Yorks, and *d* 19 Jan 1780, leaving, with an er s (Robert, *b* 9 Jan 1791, MA, Fell and Pres Pembroke Coll Cambridge, *d* unm 1 Sept 1831) and a dau (Catherine, *m* 17 Sept 1807 Rev Benjamin Parke, Preb Ely, Vicar Tylney All Saints, Norfolk, and *dsp* 28 May 1841):

Rev WILLIAM STOCKDALE, of Mears Ashby Hall, Northants, JP; *b* 5 April 1767; MA, Fell Jesus Coll Cambridge, Vicar Mears Ashby, Rector Wilby, Northants; *m* Honour, dau of Rev Godfrey Woolley, Rector Hawnby, Vicar Hutton Buscall, Yorks, and *d* 27 Feb 1858, having had, with four daus:

1 William Walter (Rev); *b* 6 March 1814; Rector Wyching, Kent; *m* 1st Mary Martha Margaret, dau of Capt James Douglas, 10th Hus, of Rhydyfran, Cards, and had:

  (1) Reginald Walter (Rev), of Grafton, NSW; *b* 9 Jan 1852; *m* 1st Adela Hilton Sophia Louisa, dau of Rev Canon James John Douglas, BD, Rector Kirriemuir, Forfarshire, and had:

    1a Reginald Walter Douglas; *b* 11 April 1892; *d* 1896

    2a William Walter Barnabas; *b* 10 Jan 1896; *ka* 1918

3a James Angus Minshull; *b* 3 Dec 1897; *m* 1st 15 July 1922 Elsie Eileen, dau of William Consett Proctor, slr, and had:

  1b *William John Douglas (Rev); *b* 12 Oct 1924; ThL; *m* *Jeanne, dau of Dr W Graham, of Eucha, Victoria, NSW

  2b *James Owen; *b* 30 Oct 1925; *m* *Gloria, dau of Maj W B Carter, and has:

    1c *Ian Philip; *b* 6 Nov 1952

    1c *Jane Maree; *b* 26 Nov 1955

  1b *Beatrice Mary; *b* 17 March 1927; *m* 22 Aug 1953 *Wiliam Goulder and has issue

  2b *Eileen Dell; *b* 17 March 1927; *m* 16 Jan 1948 *Hugh Wittleton and has issue

3a (cont.) James Stockdale *m* 2nd *Dorothea Madeline Beatrice, dau of Henry Nuttall, of Co Wicklow

4a Reginald Ian Henry (Ven); *b* 28 March 1899; ThL, Archdeacon Moree, Vicar Gen Armidale Diocese, NSW, 1961–64; *m* 28 Jan 1935 Catriona Mary Caulfield (*d* 23 Jan 1970, dau of Dr John Alexander Cameron and *d* 30 June 1971, leaving:

  1b *John Alexander Douglas; *b* 15 March 1936; MSc; *m* March 1957 *Helen, dau of Douglas Sutton, and has:

    1c *Alexander Michael; *b* 28 Dec 1959

    1c *Kim Helen; *b* 21 April 1958

    2c *Shane Victoria; *b* 26 June 1962

  2b *William Angus; *b* 29 Sept 1942; *m* 19 July 1969 *Ruth Kentish, of Newcastle, NSW

  1b *Sheila Mary; *b* 16 Feb 1939

1a Mary Louisa; *b* 11 Dec 1893; *m* 15 Aug 1914 Llewellyn George Irby and had issue (*see* BOSTON, B)

2a Adela Denton Sophia; *b* 4 Sept 1900; *m* 1st 1921 Joseph Thomas Webb, of Donnington, Tenterfield, NSW, and had issue; *m* 2nd 1962 Alexander MacRae, of Brisbane

(1) (cont.) The Rev Reginald Stockdale *m* 2nd Elizabeth Harriet Collard and *d* 23 Aug 1904

  (1) Mary Catherine Ellen; *b* 6 Oct 1853; *d* 1861

1 (cont.) The Rev William Stockdale *m* 2nd 16 April 1875 Emma (*d* 5 Feb 1886), dau of James Ashenden, and *d* 19 Feb 1893, having had further issue

2 Robert (Rev); *b* 26 Aug 1817; *educ* Durham U (BA); Rector Wilby, Northants; *d* unm 31 July 1853

3 HENRY MINSHULL

4 Septimus (Rev); *b* 25 Jan 1824; *educ* Jesus Coll Cambridge (BA); Rector Wilby; *m* 27 Feb 1849 Caroline (*m* 2nd 5 May 1859 Rev Robert Gibbings and *d* 20 Jan 1894), dau of Rev Hon Paul Anthony Irby (*see* BOSTON, B), and *dsp* 11 May 1849

5 Benjamin Parke; *b* 20 Oct 1827; *d* unm 22 Jan 1875

The 3rd s,

HENRY MINSHULL STOCKDALE, of Mears Ashby Hall, JP, DL Northants; *b* 30 Sept 1822; *educ* Jesus Coll Cambridge (MA); barrister Lincoln's Inn, Chm Northants QS, Capt Northants Militia; *m* 12 Aug 1858 Sarah Emily (*d* 15 May 1896), dau of Rev Robert Hervey Knight, Rector Weston Favell, Northants, and *d* 3 Oct 1913, having had:

1 HENRY MINSHULL

2 Robert William (Rev); *b* 31 Oct 1862; *educ* Winchester and Jesus Coll Cambridge (MA 1888); Vicar Burton Leonard, Yorks, 1926–33, Greenhow Hill 1920–26, St Silas, Hunslet, Yorks 1905–16; *m* 1 March 1905 Emily (*d* 6 March 1951), dau of Israel Fozard, of Armley, Leeds, and *d* 13 March 1946, leaving:

  (1) *Honor; *b* 28 Feb 1907

  (2) *Katharine Fozard; *b* 8 Sept 1908; *educ* Harrogate Coll and Leeds U (BA 1930); *m* 28 Oct 1940 James Harvey Sutcliff, yr s of Dr Edward Harvey Sutcliff, of Torrington, N Devon, and has:

    1a *John Robert Harvey; *b* 8 June 1942; *educ* Dulwich and St Bartholomew's Hosp (MB, BS 1966); *m* 24 Feb 1968 *Rosemary, dau of George Hughes Higginson, of Shrewsbury, and has:

      1b *Emma Rose Harvey; *b* 6 Jan 1969

      2b *Jane Katharine; *b* 17 Jan 1970

    2a *George Edward; *b* 17 March 1945; *educ* Dulwich and Nottingham U (BSc 1966, MSc)

  (3) *Isabel Anne; *b* 10 Jan 1911; *educ* Harrogate Coll

3 Eustace Hervey; *b* 27 Sept 1864; *educ* Winchester and RMC; Lt 68th Durham LI; *d* unm 19 Sept 1886

4 Herbert Edward, CB (1919), CMG (1916), DSO (1915); *b* 22 June 1867; *educ* Wellington and RMA Woolwich; joined RA 1886, Col Boer War 1899–1901 (despatches, Queen's Medal with six clasps), Brig-Gen WW I (despatches five times); *m* 4 Feb 1909 Margaret Frances (*d* 8 Nov 1973), er dau of Rev Canon J T Bartlet, of Little Houghton, Northants, and *d* 28 Dec 1953, leaving:

  (1) *Margaret Mary; *b* 6 Aug 1912

1 Emily Honour; *d* unm 5 Oct 1945

2 Ellice Katharine; *d* an inf 1865

3 Mabel Katharine Mary; *d* unm 18 Sept 1941

The est s,

HENRY MINSHULL STOCKDALE, of Mears Ashby Hall, JP Northants; *b* 8 Feb 1861; *educ* Winchester and Jesus Coll Cambridge (MA 1888); Patron livings of Wilby and (with co-tstees) Mears Ashby, barrister Inner Temple 1886, Maj 3rd Bn Northants Regt; *m* 7 July 1896 Florence Margaret Rose (*d* 20 Jan 1952), dau of Rev Charles Villiers (*see* CLARENDON, E), and *d* 20 Feb 1946, leaving:

1 *(Henry Charles) Minshull; *b* 5 April 1902; *educ* Winchester; Capt 1st Northants Yeo TA 1937, served WW II, Hon Lt-Col TARO, High Sheriff Northants 1952; *m* 10 May 1932 Hon Margaret Violet Henderson (*d* 25 Sept 1976), sis of 2nd Baron Faringdon (qv), and has:

  (1) *Henry Minshull [Henry Stockdale Esq, Hill Farm, Mears Ashby, Northants]; *b* 23 April 1933; *educ* Winchester; late 2nd Lt Northants Yeo; *m*

28 March 1957 *Caroline Frances, er dau of Cdr Lawrence St George Rich, DSO, RN, and has:

  1a *Henry Charles Minshull; *b* 16 Sept 1960

  1a *Charlotte Anne; *b* 31 March 1958

  2a *Alyson Catherine; *b* 31 Aug 1966

(2) Christopher Minshull; *b* 19 Nov 1936; *educ* Eton; *m* 20 Feb 1965 *Sylvia Mary Victoria, only dau of Brig Claude Nicholson, CB (*see* NICHOLSON OF WINTERBOURNE, B), and *d* 12 May 1970, leaving:

  1a *Mary; *b* 9 June 1968

(1) *Rosemary Violet; *b* 14 Oct 1934; *m* 12 July 1954 *Sir Anthony John Tennant (*see* GLENCONNER, B) and has issue

(2) *Margaret Jane; *b* 12 March 1940; *m* 23 June 1960 *Capt Richard Hugh Nicholson, 16th/5th Queen's Roy Lancers (*see* NICHOLSON OF WINTERBOURNE, B)

2 Sir Edmund Villiers Minshull Stockdale, 1st Bt (UK), so *cr* 5 Dec 1960, JP (City London 1948–63, Inner London 1968–69); *b* 16 April 1903; *educ* Wellington (later Govr); Bank of England: joined 1921, Assist Pncpl 1937, Dep Pncpl 1945, Assist to Govrs Reserve Bank India 1935, memb London Stock Exchange 1946–60, City London: memb Common Cncl 1946, Alderman Cornhill Ward 1948, Lt 1948, Sheriff 1953, Ld Mayor 1959–60; Govr: Roy Bethlem and Maudsley Hosps, Christ's and Bridewell Hosps 1948–63, ktd 1955, V-Pres King Edward's Sch Witley 1960–63, Utd Westminster Schs 1948–54, memb Advsy Bd and Visiting Ctee Holloway Prison 1948–61 (Chm 1951–53), Emergency Bed Service King Edward Hosp Fund 1961–69, dir Embankment Tst, a Church Commr 1962, memb Exec and Fin Ctee Winchester Diocesan Bd Finance 1963, Jr Grand Warden (Acting Rank) Grand Lodge England 1960–61, V-Pres The Griffins (formerly Holloway Discharged Prisoners Aid Soc) 1965, KStJ, Gd Offr Legn Hon, Gd Offr Orden de Mayo Argentina, Gd Cross Order Merit Peru, Order Triple Power Nepal, Kt Cdr Order Crown Thailand, Cdr Roy Order N Star Sweden, Gold Medal Madrid; *m* 24 July 1937 Hon Louise Fermor-Hesketh (*d* 19 Sept 1994), er dau of 1st Baron Hesketh (*qv*), and *d* 1989, having had:

  (1) Sir THOMAS MINSHULL STOCKDALE, **2nd and present Bt**

  (2) +Frederick (Freddie) Minshull [Frederick Stockdale Esq, Eastwood Farm, Chilsham Lane, Herstmonceux, Sussex BN27 4QH]; *b* 20 May 1947; *educ* Eton and Jesus Coll Cambridge (MA); proprietor Pavilion Opera, author; *m* 1st 25 Nov 1970 (*divorce* 1989) Joanna Lennox, 2nd dau of Capt Roger Edward Lennox Harvey, JP, DL, of Parliament Piece, Ramsbury, Wilts, and has:

    1a +Harry Tevis Minshull; *b* 1973

    2a +Alexander Breckenridge Minshull; *b* 5 Feb 1975

    3a +Valentine Frederick Minshull; *b* 15 Dec 1981

  (2) (cont.) Frederick Stockdale *m* 2nd 1992 *Adele Elizabeth Lavinia, dau of Lincoln Mason, of Swinton, Manchester, and by her has:

    4a +Charles Lincoln Minshull; *b* 1994

    1a *Louise Elizabeth Florence; *b* 1995

  (1) Anne-Louise; *b* 30 May 1938; *m* 24 Oct 1963 Charles Marcus Edwards, Dip Serv, s of John Basil Edwards, JP, of Birchwood Hall, Malvern, Worcs, and *d* Nov 1970

STOCKTON

Arms: Argent a chief or, overall, between three open books proper edged or and bound azure, those in chief inscribed respectively in letters sable '*Miseres*' and '*Discere*' and that in base also in letters sable inscribed '*Succo*', and as many mullets azure, a lion rampant sable. **Crests:** Upon a helm with a wreath or, azure and sable, within sprigs of oak fructed or, a dexter cubit arm and a sinister arm embowed, both proper, the dexter hand gauntletted or and with the other brandishing a two-handed sword proper, hilt, pommel and quillons sable. **Supporters:** Dexter, a lion rampant gules; sinister, an American bald-headed eagle proper, the compartment comprising a crenellated wall proper, in the portal thereof an anchor azure, and joined on either side by two bars wavy azure to a grassy mount, growing from that on the dexter a long branch and from that on the sinister a thistle both proper. **Creations:** E. and V. (UK) 1984.

THE 2ND EARL OF STOCKTON and **Viscount Macmillan of Ovenden**, of Chelwood Gate, Co E Sussex, and of Stockton-on-Tees, Co Cleveland (Alexander Daniel Alan Macmillan) [The Rt Hon The Earl of Stockton, Hayne Manor, Stowford, Devon EX20 4DB; 25 Eccleston Place, London SW1W 9NP]; *b* 10 Feb 1943; *s* gf 1986; *educ* Eton, U of Paris and Strathclyde U; chm Macmillan Publishing Ltd 1980–, Hon DLit DeMontfort U 1993, Hon D Univ Strathclyde U 1995, Hon Dr Laws Westminster U 1996, Upper Renter Warden Merchant Taylors' Co 1996–97; *m* 1st 1970 (*divorce* 1991) (Hélène) Birgitte (Bitta), dau of Alan Douglas Christie Hamilton, of Stable Green, Mitford, Northumberland, and has:

  1 +DANIEL MAURICE ALAN, *Viscount Macmillan*; *b* 9 Oct 1974; *educ* Eton and Parsons Art Sch New York City; male model

  1 *Rebecca Elizabeth; *b* 1980

  2 *Louisa Alexandra; *b* 1982

The 2nd EARL *m* 2nd 23 Dec 1995 *Miranda, dau of Richard Quarry and Diana Lady Mancroft (*qv*) and formerly w of Sir Nicholas Nuttall, 3rd Bt (*qv*)

Lineage: MALCOLM MACMILLAN; crofter, of The Cock, Arran island; *d* 1823, leaving 12 children, four of whom *d* young; the 10th:

DANIEL MACMILLAN; *b* 1813; bookseller's apprentice Irvine, Ayrshire, 1824–31; fndr with his bro Alexander Macmillan and Co, publishers, 1843; *m* 1850 Frances, dau of — Orridge, chemist, of Cambridge, and *d* 1857, leaving, with three other children:

MAURICE CRAWFORD MACMILLAN; *b* 1853; *educ* Uppingham and Christ's Coll Cambridge; classics master St Paul's; *m c* 1883, as her 2nd husb, Helen (Nellie) Artie Tarleton (*b* Spencer, Indiana, 1856; *m* 1st 1875 — Hill (*d* six months later); *d c* Sept 1937), dau of — Belles, doctor, of Kentucky, and *d* March 1936, leaving:

  1 Dan(iel); *b* 1886

  2 Arthur; *b* 1890

  3 (MAURICE) HAROLD MACMILLAN, **1st Earl of Stockton**, so *cr* 1984, as also VISCOUNT MACMILLAN OF OVENDEN, of Chelwood Gate, Co E Sussex, and Stockton-on-Tees, Co Cleveland (both UK), OM (1976), PC (1942); *b* 10 Feb 1894; *educ* Eton and Balliol Coll Oxford; Capt Gren Gds WW I (thrice wounded), MP (U) Stockton-on-Tees 1924–29 and 1931–45 and (C) Bromley 1945–64, Parly Sec Min Supply 1940–42, Parly U-Sec Colonies Feb–Dec 1942, Min Resident N Africa Dec 1942–May 1945, Sec State Air May–July 1945, Min Housing and Local Govt 1951–54, Min Defence 1954–55, For Sec April–Dec 1955, Chllr Exchequer 1955–57, PM and First Ld Treasury Jan 1957–Oct 1963; Chllr Oxford U 1960–86, pres Macmillan Ltd 1974–86, Hon Freeman City London 1961, FRS 1962; Hon DCL Oxon 1958, Hon LLD: Cantab 1961 and Sussex 1963; *m* 1920 Lady Dorothy Evelyn Cavendish, GBE (*d* 1966), 3rd dau of 9th Duke of Devonshire (*qv*), and *d* 1986, having had:

  (1) Maurice Victor, *Viscount Macmillan of Ovenden*, PC (1972); *b* 27 Jan 1921; *educ* Eton and Balliol Coll Oxford; WW II in Sussex Yeo, MP (C) Halifax 1955–64 and Farnham 1966–84, Ec Sec Treasury 1963–64, Ch Sec Treasury 1970–72, Sec State Employment 1972–73, PMG 1973–74; chm Macmillan and Co 1967–70 (later Gp Chm); *m* 1942 *Hon Katharine Margaret Alice Ormsby-Gore [Viscountess Macmillan of Ovenden, 9 Warwick Sq, London SW1], 2nd dau of 4th Baron Harlech (*qv*), and *dvp* 1984, having had:

    1a ALEXANDER DANIEL ALAN MACMILLAN, **2nd and present Earl of Stockton**

    2a Joshua Edward Andrew; *b* 1945; *educ* Eton and Balliol Oxford; *d unm* 1965

    3a +Adam Julian Robert [The Hon Adam Macmillan, 65 Cambridge St, London SW1V 4PS]; *b* 1948; *educ* Eton and U of Strasbourg; *m* 1982 *Sarah Anne Mhuire, yr dau of Dr Brian MacGreevy, of S Kensington, and has:

      1b +Frederick Maurice Brian; *b* 1990

      2b +A son; *b* 7 Sept 1995

      1b *Sophia Elizabeth Katherine; *b* 1985

      2b *Alice Charlotte Rose; *b* 1987

    4a +David Maurice Benjamin; *b* 1957; *educ* Harrow; *m* 19–, as her 2nd husb, *Arabella, dau of Peregrine Pollen (*see* POLLEN, Bt), and has:

      1b +Finn; *b* 19–

      2b *Mabel; *b* 30 March 1998

    1a Rachel Mary Georgina; *b* 1955; *m* 1982 (*divorce* 1986) Leith Corbett, only s of H M Corbett, of Sydney, NSW, and *dsp* 1987

  (1) *(Ann) Caroline [The Lady Caroline Faber, Fisher's Gate, Withyham, E Sussex TN7 4BB]; *b* 1923; *m* 1944 *Julian Tufnell Faber, s of Alfred Faber, and has had:

    1a *Michael David Tufnell [Michael Faber Esq, 2A Lyall Mews, London SW1]; *b* 1945; *educ* Eton and Trin Coll Cambridge; *m* 1968 *Catherine Suzanne, dau of Count Robert de Braine, of Cannes, France, and has:

      1b *Richard Julian Robert; *b* 1974

      1b *Elizabeth Anne Catherine; *b* 1971

    2a Mark James Julian; *b* 1950; *educ* Eton and Balliol Coll Oxford; *m* 1983 *Ann [Mrs Mark Faber, 12 Tite St, London SW3], dau of Christopher Griffith, of Natal, South Africa, and *d* 1991, leaving:

      1b *Alexander John Julian; *b* 1986

      2b *Luke Christopher Michael; *b* 1990

      3b *Thomas Mark Nicholas; *b* 1992

    3a *David James Christian [David James Faber Esq MP, House of Commons, London SW1]; *b* 1961; *educ* Eton and Balliol Coll Oxford; MP (C) Westbury 1992–, PPS to: Min State FCO 1994–96 and Sec State Health 1996–97, jr oppn For Affrs spokesman 1997–98, dir Sterling Mktg 1987– (chm 1991–); *m* 1st 1988 (*divorce* 1996 or 1997) Sally Elizabeth, er dau of Mrs Kenneth J Gilbert, of Yelverton, Devon; *m* 2nd 20 Nov 1998 *Sophie, dau of Martyn Hedley and has by his 1st w:

      1b *Henry Mark Tufnell; *b* 1992

    4a *James Edwin Charles [James Faber Esq, 30 Harcourt Terr, London SW10]; *b* 1964; *educ* Eton and Edinburgh U

    1a *Anne Christine Adriane, JP (Inner London 1994) [The Hon Mrs David Bernstein JP, 27 Tregunter Rd, London SW10 9LS]; *b* 1944; *m* 1st 1970 (*divorce* 1981) Michael Roger Lewis Cockerell and has:

1b *(William) Michael Victor Lewis; b 1973
1b *Sophia Charlotte Evelyn; b 1970
1a (cont.) Mrs Anne Cockerell m 2nd 1995 *Hon David Sidney Bernstein, s of Baron Bernstein (LP, d 1993)
(2) Catherine; m 1950 (Harold) Julian Amery, PC (cr BARON AMERY OF LUSTLEIGH (LP), of Preston, Co Lancs, and Brighton, Co E Sussex 1992; d 1996), s of Leopold Charles Maurice Stennett Amery, CH, PC, and d 1991, leaving:
    1a *Leopold Harold Hamar John; b 1956; educ Eton and Balliol Coll Oxford
    1a *(Caroline) Louise Michelle [The Hon Louise Amery, Cahamuckee, Kealkil, Bantry, Co Cork, Ireland]; b 1951
    2a *Theresa Catherine Roxanne [The Hon Mrs Boteler, 17 Colnbrook St, London SE1 6EZ]; b 1954; m 1984 *John Harvey Boteler, yr s of Lt-Cdr John Harvey Trevor Boteler, RN, of Frinton-on-Sea, Essex, and Mayfair, and has:
       1b *Jack Francis Clair; b 1987
       2b *Harry Julian Trevor; b 1993
       1b *Catherine Audrey Roxanne; b 1989
    3a *(Alexandra) Elizabeth Charmian (twin) [The Hon Mrs Hare, 11 Denbigh St, London SW1]; b 1956; m 1988 *(Alan Simon) Mercury Hare and has issue (see LISTOWEL, E)

STODART OF LEASTON

Creation: B (LP, UK) 1981.

THE BARON STODART OF LEASTON, of Humbie, District of E Lothian (James Anthony Stodart, PC (1974)) [The Rt Hon The Lord Stodart of Leaston PC, Lorimers, N Berwick, E Lothian EH39 4NG]; b 6 June 1916; educ Wellington; MP (C) Edinburgh West 1959–74, Jt Parly U-Sec Scottish Office 1966–69, Oppn Spokesman Ag and Scottish Affrs 1966–69, Parly Sec MAFF 1970–72, Min State MAFF 1972–74; Dir FMC 1980–82; Chm: Ag Credit Corp 1975–87, Ctee Inquiry Local Govt Scotland 1980, Manpower Review Veterinary Profession UK 1984–85; author: Land of Abundance (coauthor, 1962); m 1940 Hazel Jean (d 18 March 1995), dau of Lt Ronald James Usher (see USHER, Bt)

Lineage: Col THOMAS STODART, CIE, IMS; m Mary Alice Coullie and had a yr s:

JAMES ANTHONY, cr a **Baron**

STODDART OF SWINDON

Creation: B. (LP, UK) 1983.

THE BARON STODDART OF SWINDON, of Reading, Roy Co of Berks (David Leonard Stoddart) [The Rt Hon The Lord Stoddart of Swindon, Sintra, 37a Bath Rd, Reading, Berks RG1 6HL]; b 4 May 1926; educ St Clement Danes and Henley GSs; Memb Reading County Borough Cncl 1954–72; MP (Lab) Swindon 1970–83; PPS to Min Housing and Construction 1974–75, Assist Govt Whip 1975, Ld Commr Treasury 1976–77, Oppn Whip and Energy Spokesman Ho Lds 1983–88; Chm Campaign for Ind Britain 1985–; m 1st 1946 (divorce 1960) Doreen M Maynard and has:

    1 *Janet Victoria; b 1947; m 1967 (divorce 1996) Jack Pudney and has issue

BARON STODDART m 2nd 1961 *Jennifer, adopted dau of Mrs Lois Percival-Alwyn, and has:
    1 *Howard David; b 1966
    2 *Mathwyn Hugh; b 1969

Lineage: ARTHUR LEONARD STODDART; m Queenie Victoria Price and had:

DAVID LEONARD, cr a **Baron**

STOKES

Arms: Gyronny of eight or and sa. a lion rampant double queued erm., on a chief or an estoc erect between two speedwell flowers stalked and leaved ppr. **Crest:** A demi-lion queued erm., holding between the paws a piston with connecting rod arg., the crown enflamed ppr. **Motto:** Speed well. **Creation:** B. (LP, UK) 9 Jan 1969.

THE BARON STOKES, of Leyland, Co Palatine of Lancaster (Sir Donald Gresham Stokes, TD, DL (Lancs 1968)) [The Rt Hon The Lord Stokes TD DL, 2 Branksome Cliff, Westminster Rd, Poole, Dorset BH13 6JW]; b 22 March 1914; educ Blundell's and Harris Inst Tech Preston (DTech, FIMechE, CEng, MSAE, FIMI, FCIT, FICEE); Lt-Col REME WW II, Leyland Motors: student apprentice 1930, export manager 1946, gen sales and serv manager 1950, dir 1954, md and dep chm Leyland Motor Corp 1963, chm 1967, chm and md BLMC1968-75, pres BL 1975–79, consultant Leyland Vehicles 1979–81, chm: AEC Ltd, Scammell Lorries Ltd, Leyland Motors Ltd, Standard-Triumph Internat Ltd, Forshaw Motor Gp, Jack Barclay Ltd 1980–90, Ec Devpt Cncl Electronics Industry 1966–67, Br Arabian Advisry Co 1977–85, Two Counties Radio Ltd 1979–94, Dovercourt Motor Co 1982–90, dep-chm Internat Reorganisation Corp 1969, pres: Soc Motor Mfrs and Traders 1961–62 and Manchester U Inst Sci and Tech 1968–76 , v-pres Employers' Engrg Fedn, memb: NW Ec Planning Cncl 1965–70 and Cncl CBI, dir: Nat West Bank 1969–81, London Weekend TV 1967–71, KBH Communications 1985– (chm 1987–96), Scottish & Universal Investments 1980–92, GWR Gp 1990–94, Beherman Auto-Transports NV (Belgium); ktd 1965; Liveryman Carmen Co, Offr Crown Belgium, Cdr Order Leopold II Belgium, Hon Fell Keble Coll Oxford 1968, Hon LLD Lancaster 1967, Hon DTech Loughborough 1968, Hon DSc Southampton 1969 and Salford 1971; m 25 May 1939 Laura Elizabeth Courtenay (d 1 April 1995), dau of Frederick Lamb, and has:

    1 *Michael Donald Gresham [The Hon Michael Stokes, Longfield House, Mill Bank, Fladbury, Worcs WR10 2QA]; b 13 June 1947; educ Southampton U (BSc); m 1st 30 May 1970 (divorce 1980) Inger Anita, yr dau of Douglas Percy, of Hotspur Ho, Hythe, Hants; m 2nd 21 June 1985 *Theresa, dau of John Edgar Papworth, and by his 1st w has:
       (1) *Anthony Gresham; b 9 April 1976
       (1) *Sian Michele; b 29 Nov 1973
       (2) *Laura-Jean; b 30 April 1991

Lineage: HARRY POTTS STOKES, of Hannafore, Looe, Cornwall; had an er s:

DONALD GRESHAM, cr a **Baron**

STONE OF BLACKHEATH

Creation: B. (LP, UK) 2 Aug 1997.

THE BARON STONE OF BLACKHEATH, of Blackheath, London Borough of Greenwich (Andrew Zelig Stone) [The Rt Hon The Lord Stone of Blackheath, House of Lords, London SW1A 0PW]; b 7 Sept 1942; educ Cardiff High Sch; Marks and Spencer: management trainee 1966, merchandise manager 1973, PA to chm 1978–80, divnl dir 1986, dir Menswear, Children's Wear, Ladies' Wear 1990, jt md 1994–; dir: Thorn plc 1996–, Weizmann Inst Fndn; FRSA; m 1973 *Vivienne Wendy Lee and has a s and two daus

Lineage: SYDNEY STONE; m Louise Sophia Gould and had:

ANDREW ZELIG, cr a **Baron**

STONHOUSE

SUBLIMIORA·PETAMUS

Arms: Arg. on a fess sa., between three hawks volant az.. a leopard's face between two mullets or. **Crest:** A talbot's head, couped arg., collared sa., lined and catching a dove volant of the first. **Motto:** *Sublimiora petamus* ('Let us seek the sublime'). **Creations:** Bt. (E) 7 May 1628 and 5 May 1670 (but with precedence of 7 May 1628).

SIR MICHAEL PHILIP STONHOUSE, 15TH and 18TH BT, of Radley, Berks [The Rev Sir Michael Stonhouse Bt, 3413 Balfour St, Saskatoon, Saskatchewan, Canada S7H 3Z3]; *b* 4 Sept 1948; *s f* 1993; *educ* Medicine Hat Coll Alberta U (BA) and Wycliffe Coll (MDiv); Deacon 1977, Priest 1978, Assist Curate St Peter's Calgary 1977–80, Rector Parkland 1980–87, St Mark's Innisfail and St Matthew's Bowden 1987–92, St James Saskatoon 1992–; *m* 1977 *Colleen Eleanor, dau of James Albert Councill, of Toronto, and has:

  1 +ALLAN JAMES; *b* 20 March 1981
  2 +David Michael; *b* 1983
  3 +Philip; *b* 1987

Lineage: ROBERT STONHOUSE, of Milgate, Bearsted, Kent; *m* Rose Royden and had:

GEORGE STONHOUSE, of Little Peckham, Kent; Ld Manor Radley, Berks, merchant of the staple, a Clerk Green Cloth *temp* ELIZABETH I; *m* 1st Elizabeth (*dsp*), dau of Nicholas Gibson; *m* 2nd 1 Sept 1555 Elizabeth (*m* 2nd 13 Oct 1574 Richard Kingsmill), dau of David Woodroffe, Alderman and Sheriff London 1554–55, and *d* 20 July 1573, having by her had, with other issue:

  1 WILLIAM (Sir), **1st Bt**
  2 Nicholas, of Boxley, Kent; *bapt* 5 Jan 1563; *m* Joan, dau of Robert Duke, of Otherton, Devon, and was ancestor of the extinct STONEHOUSEs of Standen Hussey and Hungerford Park, Berks
  3 James (Sir), of Amerden Hall, Debden, Essex; *bapt* 30 Dec 1566; *m* 1st Joane, dau of William Baronsdale, MD; *m* 2nd Anne (*d* March 1651/52), widow of Richard Corbet, of Stoke, and dau of Sir Humphrey Weld, and *d* 1 Dec 1638, leaving:
    (1) Sir JAMES STONHOUSE, 1st Bt (E), so *cr* 10 June 1641, of Amerden Hall; had:
      1a Sir JAMES STONHOUSE, 2nd Bt, of Amerden Hall; *m* Mary Blewitt, of Holcombe, Devon, and *d* by 2 May 1654, leaving:
        1b Sir BLEWET STONHOUSE, 3rd Bt, of Amerden Hall; *b c* 1654; *educ* Ch Ch Oxford and Lincoln's Inn; *d* unm *c* 1670
        2b Sir GEORGE STONHOUSE, 4th Bt, of Amerden Hall; *m* (Margaret?) Hamilton and had:
          1c Sir JOHN STONHOUSE, 5th Bt, of Amerden Hall and Bishops Itchington, Warwicks; *m* Elizabeth, dau of George Cole, of Buckish, Devon, and Enstone, Oxon, and *d* between 31 July 1681 and 12 Jan 1681/2, leaving:
            1d Sir GEORGE STONHOUSE, 6th and last Bt, of Amerden Hall; *bapt* 14 Jan 1678/9; *educ* Gloucester Hall Oxford; *d* unm 13 April 1695, when the btcy expired
    1 Elizabeth; *m* Edward Chard, of Burleigh Park, Leics
    2 Dionysia; *m* Sir Edward Hext, of Ham, Somerset

The est s,

Sir William Stonhouse, 1st Bt (E), so *cr* 7 May 1628, of Radley, Berks; *b c* 1556; *educ* Merchant Taylors', Inner Temple and Univ Coll Oxford (MA 1583); High Sheriff Oxon 1606; *m* (licence 7 June 1592) Elizabeth, dau and heiress of John Powell, of Pengethley, Herefs, and *d* 5 Feb 1631/2, having had:

  1 **Sir John Stonhouse, 2nd Bt**; *b c* 1602; *educ* Trin Coll Oxford and Gray's Inn; MP Abingdon 1628–29, Gentleman Bedchamber to CHARLES I, ktd 1629; *d* unm 14 June 1632
  2 GEORGE (Sir), **3rd Bt**
  3 William of Cokethorpe, Oxon, BCL; *m* Elizabeth (*m* 2nd 13 Nov 1663 Nicholas Bowell, of Bentley, Hants), and was ancestor of the extinct STONHOUSEs of Cokethorpe
  1 Elizabeth; *m* Edward Perrot, of Northleigh, Oxon

---

  2 Mary; *m* Rev William Langton, DD, Rector Brightwell, Berks
  3 Ursula; *m* John Denton, of North Ashton, Oxon
  4 Anne; *m* George Windsor, of Bentley, Hants
  5 Dionysia; *m* Sir Cornelius Fairmeadow

The 2nd Bt's bro,

Sir George Stonhouse, 3rd Bt, and **1st Bt** (E), so *cr* 5 May 1670, with precedence of 7 May 1628 and remainder to his yr sons (he having disinherited the est, allegedly for marrying without paternal consent), following an attempt (ajudged illegal in English law) by him to surrender the original btcy for regrant; *b c* 1608; MP Abingdon April–May 1640, Nov 1640–Jan 1643/4 (disbarred for royalism), 1660 and 1661–75; *m* 22 April 1633 Margaret, dau of 1st Baron Lovelace of Hurley (see LOVELACE, E, preliminary remarks, and LYTTON, E), and *d c* 1675, leaving:

  1 **Sir George Stonhouse, 4th Bt**; *b c* 1638; *m* Anne, widow of — Scarlett, and had, with another dau:
    (1) **Sir George Stonhouse, 5th Bt**; *m* Anne, dau of James Ashton, of Lancs, and *d* 24 Feb 1736/7, having had, with 13 other children:
      1a George; Lt Price's Regt; *dsp* 1712
      2a **Sir John Stonhouse, 6th Bt**; *d* unm 12 July 1740
      1a Margaret
    (1) Mary; *m* 20 Aug 1691 Sir Robert Legard
  2 **Sir John Stonhouse**, **2nd Bt** (of the 1670 *cr*), of Radley; *b c* 1639; *educ* Queen's Coll Oxford and Gray's Inn; MP Abingdon 1675–81, 1685–87 and Jan–Feb 1690; *m* (licence 10 Oct 1668) Martha, widow of Richard Spencer, London merchant, and dau and heiress of Robert Brigges (yr s of Sir Moreton Brigges, 1st Bt), and *d c* 1700, leaving:
    (1) **Sir John Stonhouse, 3rd Bt**, of Radley, PC (1713); *b c* 1673; *educ* Queen's Coll Oxford and Inner Temple; MP Berks 1701–33, Comptroller Household 1713–14; *m* 1st 1695 Mary (*dspm* by 1706), dau and sole heiress of Henry Mellish, of Sanderstead, Surrey, and by her had, with a s (*d* young) and two other daus (*d* unm):
      1a Martha; *b* 28 Aug 1697; *m* 23 May 1723 Arthur Vansittart, of Shottesbroke, Berks
    (1) (cont.) **Sir John** *m* 2nd 29 Aug 1706 Penelope, dau of Sir Robert Dashwood, 1st Bt, of Kirtlington (*qv*), and *d* 10 Oct 1733, leaving by her:
      1a **Sir John Stonhouse, 4th Bt**, as which *s f* 1733, and **7th Bt**, as which *s* cousin 1740; *b* 30 May 1710; *educ* St John's Coll Oxford; *d* unm 22 Sept 1767
      2a **Sir William Stonhouse, 5th Bt**, and **8th Bt**; *b c* 1714; *educ* St John's Coll Oxford and Middle Temple; Sheriff Berks 1771–72; *d* unm by 1777
      3a **Rev Sir James Stonhouse, 6th Bt**, and **9th Bt**; *b* 1718; *educ* St John's Coll Oxford (BCL Jan 1742/3, DCL 1747); Rector Clapham 1753–92; *d* unm 13 April 1792
      2a Penelope; *m* 1st 29 Oct 1723 Sir Henry Atkins, 4th Bt; *m* 2nd 31 Oct 1733 1st Earl Gower (see SUTHERLAND, D) and *d* 19 Aug 1734, leaving issue by both husbs
      3a Catherine; *b* 25 May 1708; *m* 29 May 1745 Robert Lee, 4th and last Earl of Lichfield of the 1674 *cr* (*dsp* 4 Nov 1776; see LICHFIELD, E, preliminary remarks), and *d* 8 March 1754
      4a Anne; *m* 21 Aug 1733 Sir William Bowyer, 3rd Bt, and *d* 22 May 1785, leaving issue (see DENHAM, B)
      5a Susannah; *m* 1744 Peter Serle, of Testwood, Hants, and *d* 22 Nov 1753
      6a Dionysia; *b* 19 Oct 1715; *m* 11 July 1751 Rev — Bennett
  3 James; *b* 1641; *m* (licence 11 Dec 1673) Mary Heron, of Abingdon, Berks, and *d* 1729, leaving:
    (1) Richard, of Tubney, Berks; *m* Caroline — and *d* 1725, leaving, with a dau (*d* unm):
      1a **Rev Sir James Stonhouse, 7th Bt**, and **10th Bt**; *b* 9 July 1716; *educ* St John's Coll Oxford; physician Northampton Infirmary, Rector Gt and Little Cheverel, Wilts, 1763–95; *m* 1st 20 May 1742 Anne (*d* 1 Dec 1747), Maid of Honour to QUEEN CAROLINE, w of GEORGE II, dau of John Neale, of Allesley, Warwicks, and had:
        1b Neale; *b* 1743; Paymaster HEICS; *d* unm 1772
        2b **Sir Thomas Stonhouse, 8th Bt**, and **11th Bt**; *b* 1774; *d* unm 1810
        1b Sarah; *m* 24 Oct 1767 George Vansittart, of Bisham Abbey, MP Berks, and had issue
        2b Lucy; *m* 1772 Thomas Palk, HEICS, and *d* 1773
      1a (cont.) The **Rev Sir James** *m* 2nd 18 Nov 1754 Sarah (*d* 10 Dec 1788), only child and heiress of Thomas Ekins, of Chester-on-the-Water, Northants, and *d* 8 Dec 1795, having by her had, with two daus:
        3b John; *b* 1759; HEICS, Judge Court Appeal Calcutta; *m* Sarah (*d* 8 March 1855), dau of Capt Richard Stephens, and *d* Feb 1803, leaving, with a dau:
          1c **Sir John Brooke Stonhouse, 9th Bt**, and **12th Bt**; *b c* 1797; Bengal CS, Registrar Zilla Court Ghazepur; *d* unm 2 Dec 1848
          2c **Sir Timothy Vansittart Stonhouse, 10th Bt**, and **13th Bt**; *b* 26 Jan 1799; Madras CS; joined 1815, Accountant-Gen, memb Mint Ctee, provisional memb Cncl 1850, ret 1858; *m* 1825 Mary Diana (*d* 31 Dec 1873), est dau of Rev George William Milner Mordaunt Sturt, of Long Critchill, Dorset, and *d* 30 Jan 1866, leaving:
            1d Sir HENRY VANSITTART STONHOUSE later apparently VANSITTART (1866–76), **11th Bt**, and **14th Bt**; *b* 6 May 1827; Lt 74th Highrs, later Offr 94th Regt, 1848–54, ADC to Govr Madras 1850–55, Offr of a (presumably Union) Black Regt Charleston, SC, in American Civil War, jailed 1866 for defrauding a black of his pension; magistrate and teacher in a black sch St Stephen's, Berkley Co (SC?), clerk, bookkeeper and postmaster Trial, Berkley Co, till dismissed for inattention to duty; *m* 18 June 1851 Charlotte (*d* 21 Aug 1857), 4th dau of John Beatty West, MP Dublin, and *d* 13 Nov 1884, having had:
              1e Vansittart Henry Pottinger; *b* 6 May 1852; *d* Feb 1853
              2e Reginald Charles Dowdeswell; *b* 9 July 1853; barrister; *d* unm 6 May 1882

3e **Sir Ernest Hay Stonhouse, 12th Bt**, and **15th Bt**; *b* 27 June 1855; *educ* Cheltenham; *m* 4 Nov 1897 Louise Catherine (*d* 30 June 1930), dau of Ludowick William Rees, of Cheltenham (*see* 1970 edn REES, Bt), and *dsp* 18 Dec 1937

1d Diana; *m* 16 Jan 1851 Charles Norman Pochin, HEICS, and *d* 20 April 1857, leaving issue. He *d* 26 Aug 1870

2d Emily Mary; *m* 7 Dec 1843 George Pakenham Monckton (*see* GALWAY, V) and *d* 18 Dec 1911

3d Selina Ann Mary Charlotte; *m* 2 Jan 1854 Charles Philip Gostling, Madras CS, and *d* 3 May 1906, leaving issue. He *d* 2 April 1857

4d Evelina Caroline Neale; *m* 12 Jan 1869 William Stephen Mair Goodenough, of Savile Ho, Weston Park, Bath, only s of Rev Stephen Goodenough, and *d* 24 Nov 1926. He *d* 28 Jan 1913

5d Lydia Letitia Purvis; *m* 4 Jan 1881 Sir Robert Stickney Blaine, JP, of Summerhill, Bath, s of Benjamin Blaine, of Hull, and *d* 18 April 1922, leaving issue. He *d* 15 Dec 1897

3c Henry (Rev); *b* 20 March 1801; Fell New Coll Oxford; *m* 29 April 1835 Emily (*m* 2nd 5 Nov 1877 Rev Joseph Gosworth, DD), yst dau of Rev George William Sturt, of Long Critchill, Dorset, and *dsp* 31 May 1876

4b Timothy STONHOUSE later STONHOUSE-VIGOR (roy licence 1795 on death of his bro-in-law Henry Vigor) (Ven); *b* 18 Sept 1765; Vicar Sunninghill, Berks, Archdeacon Gloucester; *m* 6 July 1796 Charlotte (*d* 9 Feb 1851), dau of Rev Thomas Huntingford, and *d* 3 Jan 1831, having had, with seven daus:

1c Henry (Rev); *b* Nov 1802; Preb Ledbury, Rector Eaton Bishop, Herefs; *m* 24 March 1829 Louisa Burt (*d* 7 June 1890), er dau and coheir of John Taylor Gordon, MD, and *d* 7 May 1838, having had, with two daus:

1d George; *d* young

2d Alfred Henry Say; *b* 24 June 1832; barrister, Recorder Southampton; *m* 25 April 1867 Gertrude, dau of William Bird, of Crouch Hall, Middx, and *dsp* 24 June 1889

2c Charles STONHOUSE-VIGOR later STONHOUSE (Rev); *b* 28 Jan 1807; Rector Frimley, Surrey; *m* 16 Jan 1839 Anne Lucy (*d* 16 May 1864), dau of Frederick Christian Lewis, and *d* 8 Feb 1883, leaving:

1d Charles Frederick; *b* 18 March 1843; *dsp* 1898

2d Edward; *b* 24 Jan 1845; *m* Mary, dau of W Penton, of Australia, and *dsp* 20 June 1931

3d Gilbert Heathcote; *d* 28 June 1879, leaving:

1e A dau; *b* 3 June 1878; *d* young

1d Emily Mary; *m* 16 March 1876 John Viret Gooch and *d* 16 Aug 1921, leaving issue (*see* GOOCH, Bt, of Clewer)

2d Rosalie; *m* 6 Feb 1897 Arthur Cadlick Pain, JP, of St Catherine's, Frimley, Surrey, and *d* 22 May 1936, leaving issue. He *d* 29 Dec 1937

3c Arthur (Rev); *b* 1 April 1810; Vicar Walford, Herefs; *m* Nov 1832 Sophia (*d* 8 May 1868), dau of William Sheppard, of Clifton, and *d* 17 Oct 1883, having had, with four other daus:

1d James; *b* 2 Jan 1835; Lt Madras Army; *m* 6 May 1858 Corinne (*d* 7 Feb 1859), est dau of C Reade, Madras CS, and *d* 1 April 1872, leaving:

1e Charles Cecil Gordon; *b* 29 Jan 1859; *d* 6 April 1929

2d William Liscombe; *b* 15 Dec 1837; BA Oxon; *m* 28 July 1870 Mary Gorges Ponsonby (*d* 14 Dec 1930), dau of William Milton Bridger, of Halnaker Ho, Sussex, and *d* 15 Oct 1907, leaving:

1e Sybil Sophia; *b* 11 May 1871

3d George Arthur; *b* 8 June 1847; *m* 27 March 1880 Ada (*d* 6 April 1929), dau of John Innes Allan, and *d* 1 Jan 1907, leaving:

1e ARTHUR ALLAN (Sir), **13th/16th Bt**

1e Ella Maud; *b* 8 March 1883; *m* 1st 16 Dec 1909 (*divorce* 1922) Stanley Le Sage, s of Sir John M Le Sage, and had issue; *m* 2nd Clive Mills and *d* 8 April 1947

2e Dorothy Mabel; *b* 13 Dec 1887; *m* 29 April 1908 Samuel Robert Nightingale, only s of Samuel Nightingale, and had issue. He *d* 21 Feb 1955

4d Edward Huntingford; *b* 1851; *d* 1907

1d Rosalie; *m* 17 Jan 1861 Rev John Reddaway Luxmoore, Vicar Ashford, Derbys, and *d* 1921, leaving issue

2d Josephine Emily; *m* 1890 Rev Thomas Owen Rocke, Rector Clungunford, Salop, and *d* 1906. He *d* 11 May 1892

4c Edward; *b* 17 Sept 1813; *d* 15 June 1857

5c Frederick (Rev); *b* 7 Sept 1815; Rector Honiley, Warwicks; *d* 29 Sept 1889

2a Richard; *b* 1725; Lt Pawlett's Regt of Marines 1740–46; *d* 1775

1 Elizabeth; *m* 1st July 1658 Sir Richard Stydolph, Bt (*d* 13 Feb 1666/7), of Norbury; *m* 2nd 25 June 1685 3rd Baron Byron (*qv*) and *d* 28 Dec 1703

The 12th/15th Bt's cousin,

Sir Arthur Allan Stonhouse, 13th Bt, and **16th Bt**; *b* 24 Feb 1885; *educ* St Paul's; memb Cncl and Reeve Municipal Dist Pine Lake, life memb Alberta Assessors Assoc and Alberta Sch Tstees Assoc, memb and chm Red Deer Sch Div, dir and v-pres Alberta Sch Tstees Assoc; *m* 2 April 1914 Beatrice, dau of Thomas Feron, of Santa Monica, Calif., and *d* 22 Nov 1967, having had:

1 **Sir Philip Allan Stonhouse, 14th Bt**, and **17th Bt**; *b* 24 Oct 1916; *educ* Western Canada Coll and Queen's U Kingston, Ontario; *m* 19 June 1946 *Winifred Emily, est dau of John M Shield, of Lethbridge, Alberta, and *d* 1993, leaving:

(1) Sir MICHAEL PHILIP STONHOUSE, **15th/18th and present Bt**

(2) +Timothy Allan; *b* 19 July 1950; BA, Dip Ed; *m* 1976 *Marija, dau of George Baros, of Edmonton, Alberta, and has:

1a +Matthew Paul; *b* 1980

2a +Benjamin Judah; *b* 1983

1 Geraldine Dorothy; *b* 9 June 1921; *m* 29 May 1941 F/Lt Ross Patterson MacLean, MBE, RCAF, and had:

(1) *Dennis Jay; *b* 31 Aug 1942

(1) *Bonnie Dee; *b* 31 Aug 1942; registered nurse 1964; *m* June 1966 *Dr David M Anderson and has:

1a *Scott Paterson; *b* 3 May 1967

2a *David Norman; *b* 9 Oct 1968

2 *Margaret Eleanor; *b* 21 March 1924; *m* 1953 *Lt-Cdr William Mansfield La Nauze, CD, RCN, and has:

(1) *Patricia Joan; *b* 7 Nov 1954; *m* 1980 *Paul Williams

3 Marjorie Kathleen; *b* 21 March 1924; *m* 20 Feb 1947 S/Ldr R A L Mitchell, RAF, and *d* 20 Aug 1957, leaving issue

STOREY

Arms: Per fess arg. and sa. a pale counter-changed three storks, also sa. **Crest:** In front of an escallop or a stork's head erased sa., gorged with a mural crown gold. **Badge:** A stork sa., grasping in the dexter claw an escallop or. **Creation:** Bt. (UK) 30 Jan 1960.

SIR RICHARD STOREY, 2ND BT, of Settrington, E Riding, Co York, CBE [The Hon Sir Richard Storey Bt CBE, Settrington House, Malton, Yorks YO17 8NP; 7 Douro Place, London W8 5PH]; *b* 23 Jan 1937; *s* f 1978; *educ* Winchester and Trin Coll Cambridge (BA 1960, LLB 1961); barrister Inner Temple 1962, chm Portsmouth & Sunderland Newspapers plc 1973–, memb Yorks and Humberside CBI Regnl Cncl 1974–76, V-Pres: Newspaper Soc (memb cncl 1980–) and Press Cncl 1980–86, memb Nat Cncl and Exec CLA 1980–84 (chm Yorks exec 1974–76), cncl memb INCA-FIEJ Research Assoc 1983–88, memb CBI Employment Policy Ctee 1984–88, chm Hillier Arboretum Management Ctee 1989–, dir: Reuters Holdings plc 1986–92, The Press Assoc Ltd 1986–95 (chm 1991–95), Fleming Enterprise Investment Tst plc 1989– (chm 1996–), Sunderland plc 1996–), High Sheriff N Yorks 1992–93, Hon Fell Portsmouth U 1992, Hon DLitt Sunderland Poly 1989; *m* 30 Sept 1961 *Virginia Anne, 3rd dau of Sir Kenelm Henry Ernest Cayley, 10th Bt (*qv*), and has:

1 +KENELM [Kenelm Storey Esq, The Grange, Settrington, N Yorks YO17 8NP]; *b* 4 Jan 1963; *educ* Winchester and George Washington U, Washington, DC (BBA)

1 *Elisabeth; *b* 27 Dec 1964; *m* 1988 *Rowland Bruce Ranald Critchley, er s of Col I R Critchley, of Altina, by Crieff, Perthshire, and has:

(1) *Fergus Ranald; *b* 24 Dec 1990

(2) *Douglas Bruce; *b* 26 March 1994

(1) *Lucilla (twin); *b* 1990

2 *Melissa [Mrs Christopher Stourton, 37 Patience Rd, London SW11]; *b* 6 July 1968; *m* 1992 *Christopher Nigel Paul Stourton (*see* MOWBRAY, SEGRAVE and STOURTON, B)

Lineage: ROBERT STOREY, of Whitburn, Co Durham; had, with a dau (Mary, *m* William Barwick and *d* 1887, having had issue; *see* 1970 edn BARWICK, Bt):

SAMUEL STOREY, DL, JP Co Durham; *b* 13 Jan 1840; MP Sunderland 1881–95 and Jan-Dec 1910, Mayor Sunderland 1876–78 and 1880, chm Durham CC 1894–97 and 1898–1905; *m* 1st 1864 Mary Ann (*d* 26 May 1877), dau of John Addison, of Monkwearmouth; *m* 2nd 19 Dec 1898 Sarah (*d* 13 May 1908), widow of John Newton, and *d* 18 Jan 1925, having by his 1st w had, with another s and four daus:

FREDERICK GEORGE STOREY, JP Co Durham; *b* 17 Feb 1868; *educ* St John's Coll Cambridge; barrister Middle Temple; *m* 1892 Mary Dagmar (*d* 6 July 1949), dau of Thomas George Hutton, JP, of Sunderland, and *d* 24 Feb 1924, having had, with a yr s and four daus:

Sir Samuel Storey, 1st Bt, and BARON BUCKTON (LP), so *cr* 30 Jan 1960 and 16 June 1966 respectively (both UK); *b* 18 Jan 1896; *educ* Haileybury and Trin Coll Cambridge (BA 1916, MA 1920); barrister Inner Temple 1919, memb Sunderland Borough Cncl 1928–31, CC ER Yorks 1946–64, MP (C) Sunderland 1931–45 and Stretford 1950–66, chm Standing Ctees and T/Chm Ctees H of C 1957, Dep Chm Ways and Means 1964–65 (Chm 1965–66), pres The Newspaper Soc 1933–34; *m* 25 July 1929 Elisabeth, JP (*d* 20 July 1951), dau of Brig-Gen Wilfred James Woodcock, DSO, and *d* 1978, leaving:

1 Sir RICHARD STOREY, **2nd and present Bt**

1 *Jacquetta [The Hon Mrs Cator, The Old House, Ranworth, Norfolk; 12 Warwick Sq Mews, London SW1]; *b* 19 April 1930; *m* 13 Oct 1956 *Francis Cator, yr s of Lt-Col Henry John Cator, MC, of Woodbastwick Hall, Norfolk, and has:

  (1) *Charles Francis; *b* 21 April 1959; *m* 1987 *Jane, dau of Robert Culverwell, of Luckington, Wilts, and widow of William J Russell, and has:

    1a *Samuel Charles; *b* 1992

    1a *Rosanna; *b* 1988

    2a *Jessica Clare; *b* 1989

  (2) *Mark; *b* 30 Oct 1960; *m* 1991 *Hon Isabel Alicia Claire Crossley, est dau of 3rd Baron Somerleyton (*qv*), and has:

    1a *Benjamin Hugo; *b* 1988

    1a *Lara Louise; *b* 1992

  (3) *Harry; *b* 27 May 1964; *m* 1992 *Kathleen Jean, dau of Capt Alan Mackay, of Port Macquarrie, Australia, and has:

    1a *Frederick Francis; *b* 1993

  (l) *Elisabeth Anne; *b* 27 July 1957; *m* 1982 *Rupert Thomas Newton Thistlethwaite and has issue (*see* PORTSMOUTH, E)

STOTT

Arms: Gu. three pallets or, each charged with as many pellets, on a chief of the second a heart between two battle-axes of the first.
Crest: Upon a chaplet of roses fesswise gu. a martlet sa.
Motto: *Alta petit* ('He aims at the heights').
Creation: Bt. (UK) 3 July 1920.

SIR ADRIAN GEORGE ELLINGHAM STOTT, 4TH BT, of Stanton, Co Gloucester [Sir Adrian Stott Bt, The Downs, Little Amwell, Herts SG13 7SA]; *b* 7 Oct 1948; *s f* 1979; *educ* Br Columbia U (BSc (Maths) 1968, MSc (Town Planning) 1974) and Waterloo U Ontario (MMaths (Computer Sci) 1971); dir planning rural region BC 1974–77, town planning consultant 1977–80, real estate portfolio manager 1980–86, md marketing co 1986–88, management consultant 1989–; MCIP

Lineage: CHARLES STOTT, of Hundersfield, Rochdale, Lancs; *d* Oct 1623, leaving, with other issue:

JOHN STOTT, of Hundersfield; *m* Feb 1616 — and *d* April 1660; his 2nd s:

JOHN STOTT, of Hundersfield; *b* April 1622; had:

JOHN STOTT, of Rochdale; *m* 1st 3 Oct 1671 Mary (*d* April 1674), dau of Thomas Shore, of Rochdale, and *d* March 1723, leaving by his 2nd w (*d* May 1725):

ABRAHAM STOTT, of Rochdale; *b* Oct 1689; *m* 28 Oct 1724 Sarah Wilkin (*d* Feb 1745) and *d* Sept 1763; his 3rd s:

ABRAHAM STOTT, of Rochdale; *b* Feb 1742; *m* 21 Oct 1761 Sarah Butterworth, of Rochdale (*d* April 1800), and *d* Jan 1798; his 3rd s:

JOHN STOTT, of Rochdale; *b* Feb 1771; *m* Eliz abeth — and had, with an er s:

JAMES STOTT, of Oldham, Lancs; *b* July 1803; *m* 18 June 1821 Mary Heathorne, of Crompton, and had:

ABRAHAM HENTHORNE STOTT, of Oldham; *b* 25 April 1822; *m* 31 Dec 1851 Eliza (*d* 27 Oct 1906), 6th dau of Edward Ainsworth, of Wicken Hall, New Hey, nr Rochdale, and *d* 17 Feb 1904, having had, with other issue:

Sir Philip Sidney Stott, 1st Bt (UK), so *cr* 3 July 1920, JP Glos; *b* 20 Feb 1858; architect and engr, FSA, Hon ARIBA, High Sheriff Glos 1925; *m* 1st 29 Aug 1884 Hannah (*d* 23 April 1935), only child of James Nicholson, of Oldham, Lancs, and had:

  1 GEORGE EDWARD (Sir), **2nd Bt**

  2 Philip Nicholson; *b* 4 May 1896; 2nd Lt 10th Bn Manchester Regt (TA); *d* 21 March 1915

  1 Esther; *m* 7 Oct 1908 Edgar Wharton, MB, ChB, BSc, LMSSA, and *d* 14 Feb 1958, leaving issue. He *d* 9 May 1961

  2 Doris; *m* 19 Nov 1918 Maj Valentine Stevens Bland, MC, RFA, s of George Roxberry Bland, of Kilburn, and had issue. He *d* 9 Nov 1957

Sir Philip *m* 2nd 2 Jan 1936 Mary Bridges (May B Lee, RMS), portraitist and miniaturist, memb Roy Miniature Soc, Ridley Art Club, Soc Women Artists and

Soc Miniaturists, exhibitor RA and Salon des Artistes Français Paris, est dau of John Bridges Lee, barrister, and *d* 31 March 1937

His only surv s,

  Sir George Edward Stott, 2nd Bt; *b* 20 May 1887; *educ* Rossall; High Sheriff Glos 1947–48, P/O RAFVR, WWs I and II, 10th Bn Manchester Regt, registered architect, FIAA and S, LRIBA; *m* 12 June 1912 Kate (*d* 16 Feb 1955), only dau of George Swailes, JP, of Oldham, and had:

  1 PHILIP SIDNEY (Sir), **3rd Bt**

  2 +Christopher George Swailes; *b* 18 May 1924; *educ* Malvern; RAFVR, MRAC WW II 1943–47; *m* 1st 17 Nov 1953 (*divorce* 19–) Winifred Marshall, formerly w of — Mossford and dau of William Don, and has:

    (1) *Sarah Caroline; *b* 20 Aug 1956

  2 (cont.) Christopher Stott *m* 2nd 19– *Anne McMahon, of Lisdoonvarna, Co Clare, and by her has:

    (1) +Christopher John McMahon; *b* 19–

  3 +Derek Nicholson [Derek Stott Esq, 29 Birnagana Ave, Sandy Bay, Tasmania 7005 Australia]; *b* 1 May 1928; *educ* Malvern; MIEE; *m* 1993 *Eileen Bridget, dau of Dr D G Wilde, of Epsom, Surrey

  1 Marjorie; *b* 25 Aug 1916; *d* 6 Dec 1918

Sir GEORGE *d* 11 July 1957; his est s,

  Sir Philip Sydney Stott, 3rd Bt; *b* 23 Dec 1914; *educ* Rossall and Trin Hall Cambridge; ARIBA, AIAA; *m* 16 Aug 1947 *Cicely Florence, widow of P/O Vincent Charles William Trowbridge, RCAF, and only dau of Bertram Ellingham, of Ely Ho, Hertford, and *d* 9 Dec 1979, having had:

  1 Sir ADRIAN GEORGE ELLINGHAM STOTT, **4th and present Bt**

  2 A son; *b* and *d* 1 Dec 1950

  3 +VYVYAN PHILIP [Vyvyan Stott, 7 Dunbarton Dve, Kenmore, Qld 4069, Australia]; *b* 5 Aug 1952; heir presumptive

STRABOLGI

Arms: Quarterly, 1st and 4th, arg. an eagle displayed gu., surmounted by a bend vert, thereon three fleurs-de-lys or (for KENWORTHY); 2nd, per saltire arg. and sa., on a chief of the last two plates, each charged with a saltire gu. (for LEATHAM); 3rd, per chevron or and gu., in chief two lions passant of the last, in base a rose arg., barbed and seeded ppr. (for LUND). **Crest:** An eagle displayed arg., collared gu., holding in either claw a fleur-de-lys gold. **Motto:** *Sans bruit* ('Without noise'). **Creation:** B. (E) 20 Oct 1318 (but *see* below against 10th EARL OF ATHOLL).

THE 11TH BARON STRABOLGI (David Montague de Burgh Kenworthy) [The Rt Hon The Lord Strabolgi, House of Lords, London SW1A 0PW]; *b* 1 Nov 1914; *s f* 1953; *educ* Gresham's and Chelsea Sch of Art; Lt-Col RAOC WW II, PPS to Min State Home Office 1968–69 and Leader Ho Lds 1969–70, Assist Oppn Whip and Spokesman Arts 1970–74, Capt Yeomen Gd (Dep Govt Ch Whip) Ho Lds 1974–79, Dep Speaker and Dep Chm Ctees Ho Lds 1986–, memb Br Section Franco-Br Cncl 1981, dep chm Bolton Bldg Soc (chm 1986–87), Extra Ld-in-Waiting 1998, Freeman City London 1960, V-Pres Franco-Br Soc, Offr Legn Hon 1981; *m* 1st 22 July 1939 (*divorce* 1946) Denise, yr dau of Jocelyn William Godefroi, MVO; *m* 2nd 20 Sept 1947 (*divorce* 1951) Angela, only child of George Victor Street, of Barton Lawn, Herts; *m* 3rd 5 Nov 1955 (*divorce* 1961) Myra Sheila, dau of Jack Litewka; *m* 4th 3 June 1961 *Doreen Margaret, er dau of Alexander Morgan, of Ashton-under-Lyne, Lancs

Lineage: MELMARE (bro of MALCOLM III KING OF Scots in the late 11th century) had:

MADACH, 1st EARL OF ATHOLL/ATHOLE (S), so *cr* by 1115 (*see also* ATHOLL, D, preliminary remarks), at a time when the earlier Mormaers of Scotland (*see* BUCHAN, E, preliminary remarks) were beginning to be recognised as Earls, the territory of Atholl having comprised the northeast section of what later became Perthshire; *m* apparently 1st —; *m* (probably 2nd) *c* 1133 Margaret (*m* 2nd Erlend *Ugni*, Jarl of Orkney; *see* CAITHNESS, E), dau of Ha(a)akon, Jt Earl of Orkney and apparently Jt Earl of Caithness (*qv*), and *d c* 1152, having had issue by his 2nd w (*see* CAITHNESS, E) and specifically, apparently by his 1st w:

MALCOLM, 2nd EARL OF ATHOLL; *m* 1st —; *m* 2nd Hextilda, dau of Uchtred/Waltheof and widow of Richard Comyn, and *d* between 1186 and Aug 1198, leaving, apparently by his 1st w:

HENRY, 3rd EARL OF ATHOLL; *m* Margaret — and *dspms* just prior to Jan 1210/11, leaving:

1 ISABEL, COUNTESS OF ATHOLL in her own right; *m* (apparently 1st) by Jan 1210/11 Thomas OF GALLOWAY, known as EARL OF ATHOLL in right of his w (*d* 1231; bro of Alan of Galloway), who had grants of land in Herefs, Northumberland, Warwicks and Worcs, also Ireland, from KING JOHN OF ENGLAND; apparently *m* 2nd Alan de Lundin (who seems, from his temporary designation as Earl of Atholl 1233 and 1235, to have held the Earldom in trust for his w) and *d* by 25 Sept 1237, leaving apparently by Thomas:

(1) PATRICK OF GALLOWAY, 5th EARL OF ATHOLL; *d* unm 1242 at Haddington, murdered by burning at the hands of Walter Bisset, who he had overcome in a tournament

2 FERNELITH, COUNTESS OF ATHOLL in her own right; *m* by 1242 David HASTINGS, EARL OF ATHOLL in right of his w (living 1244), and had:

(1) ADA, COUNTESS OF ATHOLL in her own right; *m* John OF STRATHBOGIE, EARL OF ATHOLL in right of his w, s of David of Strathbogie (3rd s of, Duncan, Earl of Fife, Justiciar Scotland, who granted David the lands of Strathbogie, one of five districts of Aberdeenshire) and *d* (as did her husb) between 1254 and Christmas 1264, leaving:

1a DAVID OF STRATHBOGIE, 8th EARL OF ATHOLL; ktd 1264; *m* 1st Helen —; *m* 2nd by 1265 Isabel (*b* after 1245, *m* 2nd just after 7 Nov 1270 Alexander de Balliol of Cavers and *d* Feb 1292), dau of Richard of Dover/of Chilham (Kent) (s of Richard Fitzroy (*d* in or after 1232) by Rose, dau and heiress of Robert of Dover, illegitimate s of KING JOHN) by Maud, Countess of Angus in her own right, thus acquiring the Manor of Chilham, and *d* of plague at Carthage 6 Aug 1270, having joined the 7th Crusade under LOUIS IX OF FRANCE, leaving by her:

1b JOHN OF STRATHBOGIE, 9th EARL OF ATHOLL; one of the Scottish magnates who recognised MARGARET, THE MAID OF NORWAY, as heir to the Scottish Crown 5 Feb 1283/4; swore fealty to EDWARD I OF ENGLAND 1292; nevertheless fought in the Scottish army against the English at defeat by latter of Scots at Dunbar 28 April 1296 and was held prisoner in the Tower of London 1296–31 July 1297; *m* as her 1st husb Margaret, dau of 6th Earl of Mar (*qv*), and having been captured again by the English after the Battle of Methven 19 June 1306 was beheaded in London 7 Nov 1306 and stripped of his title and lands (including Chilham), leaving:

1c DAVID OF STRATHBOGIE, 10th EARL OF ATHOLL, as which restored by EDWARD II OF ENGLAND between 21 Aug 1307 and 20 May 1308, though stripped of such title 1314 by ROBERT I (THE BRUCE) KING OF SCOTS after rebelling against him, even though made Constable of Scotland earlier by ROBERT; despite the absence of any writ of summons for him to the English Parl of 20 Oct 1318 or genuine evidence of his sitting in it he is deemed by a Ho Lds resolution of 7 May 1914 to have been *cr* (**1st**) **Lord** (Baron) **Strabolgi** (E) in virtue of a supposed writ of summons to that body; even later writs of summons, however, were worded to "David (de) Strabolgi, *comiti* [*i.e.*, 'Earl of'] Athol" rather than "*domini* [*i.e.*, 'Lord'] Strabolgi"; granted by EDWARD II Feb 1312 Manors of Elton and Cave, Yorks (forfeited 3 May 1313), and 8 Oct 1314 Manors of Aylsham, Causton and Fakenham, Norfolk, but sided 1317 on with EDWARD II's rebellious cousin Thomas, Earl of Lancaster, for which pardoned 22 Oct 1318 and regranted Chilham 28 Nov 1321; Ch Warden Northumberland 1322; held a command in the English army in Gascony 1325; *m* Joan (*d* between 8 June and 24 July 1326), dau of John Comyn of Badenoch, and *d* 28 Dec 1326, leaving:

1d DAVID OF STRATHBOGIE, 11th EARL OF ATHOLL and supposedly **2nd Lord** (Baron) **Strabolgi**; *b* 1 Feb 1308/9; held land in Bucks, Herts, Lincs, Norfolk, Northumberland and Yorks; granted 1330 the Manor of Odogh, Ireland, part of the estate of his great-uncle Aymer de Valence, Earl of Pembroke (*see* PEMBROKE and MONTGOMERY, E, preliminary remarks); participated in English-organised defeat of Scots at Dupplin 12 Aug 1332 and was restored by the English candidate for the Scottish throne John Balliol to his Scottish honours and estates; *m* Catharine, dau of Henry de Beaumont, Earl of Buchan (*see* BUCHAN, E, preliminary remarks), and was *k* in an encounter at Kilblane 30 Nov 1335, leaving:

1e DAVID, 12th EARL and supposedly **3rd Lord**

2d Adomar (Sir), of Atholl; granted lands of Mitford and Marderfen, Northumberland, which had belonged to his mother; granted 1360 Manor of Filton by his n, 12th EARL OF ATHOLL; MP and Sheriff Northumberland; *m* Maria — and *d* 14 April 1402, having had two daus

The 11th EARL's s,
DAVID OF STRATHBOGIE, 12th EARL OF ATHOLL and supposedly **3rd Lord** (Baron) **Strabolgi**; *b c* 1332; participated on English side in Hundred Years War in France from 1355; *m* between 24 Sept 1342 and 1361 Elizabeth (*m* 2nd John Malewayn and *d* 22 or 23 Oct 1375), dau of Henry, 2nd Lord (Baron) Ferrers (of Groby), and *dspm* 10 Oct 1369, when the supposed Barony of Strabolgi is deemed by the Ho Lds 1914 resolution to have fallen into abeyance and the Earldom of Atholl, inasmuch as such an entity existed as an English peerage dignity at all, probably expired, having had:

1 Elizabeth; *m* 1st 1376 or 1377 Sir Thomas Percy, called of Atholl, 2nd s of 1st Earl of Northumberland of the 1377 *cr* (*see* NORTHUMBERLAND, D), and had:

(1) Henry (Sir), of Atholl; *m* as her 2nd husb Elizabeth (*d* 21 Jan 1440/1), widow of 5th Lord (Baron) Scales (*d* 7 Dec 1402; *see* ATHOLL, D) and dau of Matthew Braose/Bruce, of Gower, and *d* 25 Oct 1432, leaving:

1a Elizabeth; *m* 1st Thomas Burgh; *m* 2nd Sir William Lucy (*dsp*, *k* Battle of Northampton 1460) and *d* 28 Sept or 16 Oct 1455, leaving by her 1st husb:

1b Sir THOMAS BURGH, KG (*c* 1484), apparently 1st LORD (Baron) BURGH (*qv* throughout from now on in descent for further biographical details) of the notional 1487 *cr*; had, with other issue:

1c Sir EDWARD BURGH, (?)2nd LORD (Baron) BURGH(?) and *de jure* 4th LORD (Baron) STRABOLGI, which he is deemed to have become as sole heir on the death 8 April 1496 of 4th Lord (Baron) Grey (*qv*; *see* also below) (of Codnor), when any abeyance in the supposed Barony of Strabolgi naturally terminated; had, with other issue:

1d THOMAS BURGH, 1st LORD (Baron) BURGH and *de jure* 5th LORD (Baron) STRABOLGI; had, with other issue:

1e WILLIAM BURGH, 2nd LORD (Baron) BURGH and *de jure* 6th LORD (Baron) STRABOLGI; had, with other issue:

1f THOMAS BURGH, 3rd LORD (Baron) BURGH and *de jure* 7th LORD (Baron) STRABOLGI; had, with other issue:

1g ROBERT BURGH, 4th LORD (Baron) BURGH and *de jure* 8th LORD (Baron) STRABOLGI; *d* 26 Feb 1601/2, when both Baronies, inasmuch as the existence of both can be predicated, fell into abeyance between his sisters

1g ELIZABETH Burgh; *m* 1st after 17 Jan 1598/9 George BROOKE; *m* 2nd by 24 Oct 1605 Francis Reade and had by her 1st husb:

1h William (Sir), KB; *m* twice and *d* 20 Sept 1643, all his descendants becoming extinct 1747 bar those through his 2nd dau (by his 2nd w):

1i HILL Brooke; *m c* 27 Dec 1657 Sir William BOOTHBY, 1st Bt (*qv*), and *d* 14 May 1704, leaving, with other issue:

1j Sir WILLIAM BOOTHBY, 3rd Bt; had, with other issue:

1k FRANCES Boothby; *m c* 1 Sept 1715 William THORP and had:

1l MARY Thorp; *m* 20 May 1736 Gervase DISNEY and had, with other issue:

1m LUCY Disney; *m* 24 Feb 1784, as his 1st w, Rev Thomas LUND (*d* 24 Oct 1832) and was *bur* 10 Nov 1792, leaving:

1n Thomas; *b* 7 Dec 1786; *d* unm, *bur* 20 Jan 1829

1n Hariott; *bapt* 21 Dec 1787; *d* unm 2 Jan 1863

2n LUCY Lund; *bapt* 21 Dec 1787; *m* Capt William Henry Cockerell LEATHAM, of Kirkham Abbey, Yorks (*d* 6 Aug 1852), and *d* 18 Feb 1866, leaving:

1o HARRIET ELIZABETH Leatham; *m* 24 Jan 1849, as his 2nd w, Rev Joseph KENWORTHY (*d* 2 July 1875), Rector Ackworth, Yorks, MA Caius Coll Cambridge, s of Joshua Kenworthy, of Cragg Vale, Yorks, and *dvm* 2 March 1853, having had, with another s and a dau (both *d* young):

1p Henry Paul D'Isney; *b* 11 Nov 1849; *d* unm 2 April 1874

2p CUTHBERT MATTHIAS, **9th Lord**

2a Margaret/Margery; *m* 1st by 5 May 1434 3rd Lord (Baron) Grey (*qv*) (of Codnor) and had issue (4th Lord (Baron) Grey (of Codnor), *dspl* 1496); *m* 2nd Sir Richard de Vere (*dsp*), 4th s of 12th Earl of Oxford (*see* SAINT ALBANS, D), and *d* 28 Sept 1464

1 (cont.) Lady Percy *m* 2nd by May 1390 Sir John Scrope (*d* between 18 and 23 Dec 1405), 5th s of 1st Lord (Baron) Scrope (of Masham) (*see* YARBOROUGH, E), and by him had two daus; *m* 3rd Robert de Thorley and *d* in or after 1416

2 Philippa; *b c* 1362; *m* 1st by 20 March 1376/7 (*annulled*) Sir Ralph Percy (*dsp* 15 Sept 1397), 3rd s of 1st and last Earl of Northumberland of the 1377 *cr* (*see* NORTHUMBERLAND, D); *m* 2nd John Halsham (*d* 16 April 1415), of Coombs, Sussex, and *d* 1 or 2 Nov 1395, having by him had:

(1) John; *b c* 1389; *dsp* by 8 Feb 1404/5

(2) Hugh (Sir); *b c* 1390; *dsp* 28 Feb 1441/2

(3) Richard; *d* by 28 Feb 1441/2, leaving:

1a Joan; *m* John Lewkenor (*ka* Battle of Tewkesbury 1471) and *dsp* 12 May 1495

The 3rd s,
CUTHBERT MATTHIAS KENWORTHY, **9th Lord** (Baron) **Strabolgi**, as which recognised on termination of supposed abeyance in his favour 1916, being summoned to Parl by writ 9 May 1916; *b* 24 Feb 1853; *educ* Rossall Sch and Pembroke Coll Cambridge; *m* 15 Aug 1884 Elizabeth Florence (*d* 23 Oct 1951), 5th dau of George Buchanan Cooper, of Sacramento City, Calif., by Elizabeth, dau Jean de Beverley Mackenzie, of Braemar, Aberdeenshire, and had:

1 JOSEPH MONTAGUE, **10th Lord**

2 Cuthbert Reginald Leatham (Rev); *b* 20 April 1889; *educ* Oxford (MA); Midshipman RN, Rector W Winch, Norfolk, 1932–47; *m* 19 Aug 1913 Amy Catherine, 6th dau of Frederick Evitt, of Rook Hall, Maldon, Essex, and *d* 7 May 1963, leaving:

(1) Cuthbert Reginald D'Isney; *b* 12 May 1914; Maj Gordon Highrs WW II, Regtl Sec 1968; *m* 1st Jan 1941 (*divorce* 1947) Patricia Kathleen, only dau of Brig Sir Francis William Crewer Fetherston-Godfrey, OBE, DL, of Jersey, and had:

1a +David Patrick Francis KENWORTHY later MALCOLM (on adoption by Miss Malcolm 16 April 1947; *b* 17 Sept 1942; *educ* RAC Cirencester; *m* *Jennifer Shirley, dau of Albert Edward Willcox, of Rotorua, NZ, and has:

1b +Hamish Kenworthy; *b* 31 Oct 1971

2b +Angus Jonathan Kenworthy; *b* 20 Oct 1972

(1) (cont.) Maj Cuthbert Kenworthy *m* 2nd 9 Aug 1947 (*divorce* 1958) Joan Mary, er dau of Lt-Col Rupert Alexander Gaskion Stewart, RM, of Winthorpe Ho, nr Newark, Notts, and by her had:

2a +Duncan Alexander D'Isney [Duncan Kenworthy Esq, 3 Grasslees, Rickleton, Washington, Tyne and Wear NE38 9JA]; *b* 1950; *m* 1975 *Alwyn Jean Flack and has:

1b +Stewart Alexander D'Isney; *b* 1982

1b +Kirsten Jane; *b* 1979

1a +Sheena Mary [Mrs Allan de Jager, 8 Allambic St, The Gap, Brisbane, Qld 4061, Australia]; *b* 29 May 1948; *m* 1969 *Allan de Jager and has:
  1b +A son; *b* 1969
  1b +A dau; *b* 1972
(1) (cont.) Maj Cuthbert Kenworthy *m* 3rd 4 June 1960 *Mrs Peggy Owtram and *d* 1987

The 9th LORD *d* 1 Feb 1934; his est s,
JOSEPH MONTAGUE KENWORTHY, **10th Lord** (Baron) **Strabolgi**; *b* 7 March 1886; *educ* Eastman's Naval Acad Hants and HMS *Britannia*; Lt-Cdr RN WW I (cmdg HMS *Bullfinch*, on Admlty War Staff, Assist Ch Staff Gibraltar), HG WW II, MP (Lib later Lab) Kingston-on-Hull March 1919–Oct 1931, author: *Will Civilisation Crash?*; *The Freedom of the Seas* (with Sir George Young); *India — A Warning*; *Sailors, Statesmen and Others, an Autobiography*; *The Real Navy*; *New Wars, New Weapons*; *The Battle of the River Plate*; *Narvik and After*; *The Campaign in the Low Countries*; *From Gibraltar to Suez*; *Sea Power in the Second World War*; *m* 1st 4 Dec 1913 (*divorce* 1941) Doris Whitley (*d* 1988), only child of Sir Frederick Whitley Whitley-Thomson, JP, MP; *m* 2nd 1 Feb 1941 Mrs Geraldine Mary Hamilton (*d* 16 May 1970), only dau of Maurice Francis, of Kensington, and *d* 8 Oct 1953, leaving by his 1st w:

1 DAVID MONTAGUE DE BURGH KENWORTHY, **11th and present Lord Baron Strabolgi**

2 (Jonathan) Malcolm Atholl (Rev); *b* 16 Sept 1916; *educ* Oundle and Pembroke Coll and Ridley Hall Cambridge (BA 1938, MA 1947); Curate St Mary's, Hornsey Rise, 1941–43, CF NW Europe and India Cmd 1944–47, Rector St Clement's Oxford 1947–54, Vicar Hoddesdon Herts 1954–63, All Saints Burton-on-Trent 1963–65, Presbyter-in-Charge St John's Bangalore, India, 1965–66, Vicar Ch Ch with Holy Trinity Penge 1966–75, Rector Yelverton, Northants, 1975 on; *m* 1st 27 Nov 1943 Joan Marion (*d* 23 Jan 1963), dau of Claude Gilbert Gaster, of Tunbridge Wells, and had:
  (1) +Elizabeth Joan; *b* 19 Dec 1944; *m.*1stly 29 Aug 1964 (*divorce* 1977) Geoffrey Greetham, s of Thomas Greetham, of Harden, Yorks, and has:
    1a +Jonathan; *b* 11 Feb 1967
    2a +Matthew; *b* 2 Nov 1968
    3a +Alexander; *b* 17 June 1971
  (1) (cont.) Mrs Elizabeth Greetham *m* 2nd 1978 (*divorce* 1986) David Woodman and by him has:
    4a +Edward; *b* 1980
    1a +Katherine; *b* 1980 (twin)
  (2) +Brenda Marion [Mrs Geoffrey Collins, 3/4 Eyeworth, Sandy, Beds]; *b* 10 June 1946; *m* 1 June 1974 *Geoffrey Collins, s of Leonard George Collins, of Cowbridge, S Glam, and has:
    1a +Ian Gareth; *b* 1981
2 (cont.) The Rev Hon Malcolm Kenworthy *m* 2nd 14 Sept 1963 *Victoria Hewitt, dau of Mrs Ernest Budd, of Henley-on-Thames, Oxon, and *d* 1991, leaving by her:
  (1) +ANDREW DAVID WHITLEY; *b* 25 Jan 1967; heir presumptive; *educ* Monkton Combe
  (2) James Atholl; *b* 19 July 1971; *d* 1993
  (3) +Penelope Ruth; *b* 14 Sept 1964; *m* 1986 *Dr Samuel B P Bass, s of P A Bass, and has:
    1a +Oliver William; *b* 1993
    1a +Laura Charlotte; *b* 1992
    2a +Katrina; *b* 199–
3 Basil Frederick de la Pole, TD (1945); *b* 24 March 1920; *educ* Oundle and Lincoln Coll Oxford (BA 1948, MA 1952); Capt TARO WW II (POW); FInstPet, MInstT; *m* 18 March 1948 (*divorce* 1965) Chloë, yr dau of Gerard Walter Sandeman (*see* NEWTON, B), and *d* 15 Feb 1998, leaving:
  (1) +Forflissa Viola [Mrs William Healey, White Lodge, Whydown, Bexhill, E Sussex TN39 4RB]; *b* 23 Sept 1949; *m* 1970 *William John Healey, yst s of John Healey, and has:
    1a +Patrick Joseph; *b* 1975
    2a +Charlotte Eleanor; *b* 1977
    3a +Megan Jane Florence; *b* 1981
    4a +Rachel Lilian; *b* 1983
  (2) +Nicolette Elizabeth [Mrs John Vincent, 8 Charlotte St South, Bristol 1]; *b* 14 Aug 1950; *m* 1972 *Prof John Russell Vincent, only s of Prof John Joseph Vincent, MSc, MSc, FTI, of Wilmslow, Cheshire, and has:
    1a +Leo Jonathan; *b* 1984
  (3) +Emma ('Dizzy') Yseult [Mrs Sebastian Kent, The Old Rectory, Fonthill Gifford, Wilts SP3 6QH]; *b* 28 Feb 1958; *m* 1988 *P Sebastian Kent, only s of Maj Leonard Kent, of Amesbury, Wilts, and has:
    1a +Miranda Jacket; *b* 23 Aug 1992
    2a +Elfreda Helen; *b* 7 Aug 1994
    3a +Olivia Mercedes; *b* 12 July 1996
1 +Ferelith Rosemary Florence [The Hon Lady Hood, 31 Avenue Rd, London NW8 6BS]; *b* 31 May 1918; *m* 30 April 1946 *Sir Harold Joseph Hood, 2nd Bt (*qv*), and has had issue

STRACEY

Arms: Erm. on a cross engrailed between four eagles displayed gu. five cinquefoils or. **Crest:** A lion rampant erminois, ducally crowned gu., supporting a cross patée-fitchée of the last.
Creation: Bt. (UK) 15 Dec 1818.

SIR JOHN SIMON STRACEY, 9TH BT, of Rackheath, Norfolk [Sir John Stracey Bt, Holbeam Wood Cottage, Wallcrouch, Wadhurst, E Sussex TN5 7JT]; *b* 30 Nov 1938; *s* cousin 1971; *educ* Wellington and McGill; *m* 30 March 1968 *Martha Maria, dau of Johann Egger, of Innsbrück, Austria, and has:
  1 *Daniela; *b* 23 Sept 1968
  2 *Nadja; *b* 1973

Lineage: WILLIAM STRACYE, of Manewden, nr Saffron Walden; *m* Agnes — and had an est s:

HENRY STRACIE, of Latton, Essex; *m* Margaret — and *d* 1611, leaving, with two er sons:

HENRY STRACIE, of Stratford, Essex; *bapt* 9 Aug 1585; *m* Anne — and *d* in or after 1649, leaving, with other issue, including two er sons (Abraham, shipowner; William, of Hornchurch, Essex):

JOHN STRACEY, of London; had, with two er sons (Richard, *b* 29 Nov 1660; Randolph, of Woodford, Essex, *b* 28 Feb 1664, Comptroller Chamber and Town Clerk London):

EDWARD STRACEY, of London; *b* Aug 1669; *m* Mary, dau of Capel Loft, of St Albans, and *d* between 20 July 1706 and 1713, having had, with other issue:

Sir JOHN STRACEY; *b* 19 Oct 1698; Recorder City London, ktd 1748; *m* Mary, dau of Richard Hardinge (*see* HARDINGE, V), and *d* Feb 1748/9, leaving, with a dau (Anne, *m* 1st Rev John Freeman, Rector Caistor and Rackheath, and 2nd Rev Robert Parr, of Norwich):

Sir Edward Stracey, 1st Bt (UK), so *cr* 15 Dec 1818, of Rackheath Hall, Norfolk; *b* 4 June 1741; *m* 1st 1766 Elizabeth (*d* June 1775), widow of John Williamson and dau of Richard Lathom, of Whiston, Lancs, and had:

1 **Sir Edward Hardinge John Stracey, 2nd Bt**; *b* Sept 1768; *m* 17 July 1810 Anne (*d* 3 Dec 1832), dau and sole heiress of William Brooksbank, of The Beach, Cheshire, and *d* 14 July 1851

2 Hardinge Charles; *b* 1769; *d* 5 May 1816

3 **Rev Sir George Stracey, 3rd Bt**; *b* Dec 1770; Rector Rackheath; *m* March 1814 Sophia Anne, yst dau and heiress of Edmund Mapes, of Rollesby Hall, Norfolk, and *d* 27 Dec 1854, leaving:
  (1) Sophia; *m* 5 Dec 1839 Henry Brydges Clarke, 2nd s of T T Clarke, of Swakeleys, Middx, and *d* 2 June 1899, leaving issue
  (2) Charlotte Brooksbank; *m* 1851 Berkley Augustus Macdonald Macpherson (*d* 15 Feb 1902)

4 JOSIAS HENRY (Sir), **4th Bt**

5 John, of Sprowston Lodge, Norfolk; *b* 26 Nov 1772; *m* 1st 1 Feb 1814 Harriet, widow of Thomas Ainslie and dau of Thomas Comyn; *m* 2nd 3 Aug 1819 Emma Elizabeth (*d* 10 March 1863), yst dau of Christopher Clitherow, of Bird's Place, Herts, and *d* 15 Oct 1858, having by her had:
  (1) Edward John STRACEY later STRACEY-CLITHEROW (roy licence 20 July 1865 under terms of will of James Clitherow, of Boston House, Middx), of Boston House and Hotham Hall, Yorks, JP Middx, Norfolk, Glos and E R Yorks; *b* 4 June 1820; High Sheriff Middx 1889, Lt-Col Scots Fus Gds; *m* 20 Aug 1846 Harriot (*d* 22 July 1906), dau of Edward Marjoribanks, of Greenlands, near Henley-on-Thames (*see* 1935 edn TWEEDMOUTH, B), and *dsp* 20 Sept 1900
  (2) William James STRACEY later STRACEY-CLITHEROW (roy licence 27 Oct 1900) (Rev), of Boston House; *b* 8 Aug 1821; MA Cantab; Vicar Buxton, Rector Oxnead, Norfolk; *m* 8 Aug 1849 Maria Diana (*d* 9 Feb 1902), est dau of Lt-Gen James Claud Bourchier, of Lavant House, Chicester, and *d* 30 June 1912, having had:
    1a John Bourchier, CBE (1919), TD, of Hotham Hall, JP E R Yorks; *b* 31 May 1853; V-Lt E R Yorks (previously DL), Maj Scots Gds, Lt-Col cmdg E R Yeo and 2nd Bn Welsh Gds WW I, Hon Col 26th Armoured Car Co; *m* 1897

Alice (*d* 22 Nov 1919), widow of Charles Henry Gurney and dau of Hon Toby Henry Prinsep, and *dsp* 28 June 1931

2a Claud Edward; *b* 29 March 1855; Capt Scots Gds; *m* 1st 25 Oct 1897 Alice Maud (*d* 24 Dec 1925), 6th dau of Gen Lord Alfred Henry Paget, CB (*see* ANGLESEY, M); *m* 2nd 2 Sept 1930 Winifred (*d* 17 Dec 1952), formerly w of Capt William Farrell, RE, and dau of Dr James Elias, of Brentwood, Pendleton, Lancs, and *dsp* 3 Dec 1940

3a Eustace William Clitherow, JP Middx; *b* 29 March 1864; Lt-Cdr RN; *m* 7 Feb 1900 Frances Evelyn Veronica (*d* 7 April 1962), dau of John Birbeck Evelyn Stansfield, and *d* 1 March 1930, leaving:

  1b Christopher Bryan, DSC, Cdr RN ; *b* 22 July 1903; served WW II (despatches); *m* 26 Nov 1928 Maida Daughne Laurel, only dau of Hon Francis Almeric Butler (*see* LANESBOROUGH, E), and had:

    1c +Dominick Peter [Lt-Cdr Dominic Stracey Clitherow RN, 3 St Aubyn St, Devonport, Auckland 9, New Zealand]; *b* 13 Sept 1939; *educ* Harrow, Gonville and Caius Coll Cambridge (MA) and London U (BSc); DPSC, BSc, CEng, MIEE, attd RNZN; *m* 1971 *Penelope Bronwen, dau of L Griffiths, of Henley-in-Arden, Warwicks, and has:

      1d +Henry Dominic; *b* 1979

      2d +Simon Andrew (twin); *b* 1979 (twin)

      1d *Charlotte Emma; *b* 12 March 1972

      2d *Virginia Louise; *b* 12 March 1972

  1b Rhona; *b* 26 Aug 1901

  2b Monica; *b* 28 Aug 1905; *m* 26 Nov 1938 Hugh Morton Eden (*see* EDEN OF WINTERTON, B)

  3b *(Mary) Barbara; *b* 27 June 1909; *m* 27 Aug 1938 Francis Stanton Blake (*d* Feb 1947), only s of John Amory Lowel Blake, of Boston, Mass.

  4b Ursula Diana; *b* 17 May 1911

1a Emma Maria; *m* 8 April 1875 Col Charles Birch-Reynardson, Gren Gds, of Holywell, Lincs, and *m* 12 March 1944, leaving issue. He *d* 14 Nov 1919

2a Alice Harriott Argyll; *m* 17 Dec 1872 1st Baron Hothfield (*qv*) and *d* 29 June 1914, leaving issue

3a Evelyn; *m* 14 Aug 1879 3rd Baron Templemore (*see* DONEGALL, M) and *d* 3 Dec 1883, leaving issue

4a Margaret Susan; *m* 25 April 1889 Charles Somerville Orde, of Hopton, Norfolk, and *d* 26 Jan 1955 aged 93, leaving issue. He *d* 15 Feb 1937

5a Ida Marion; *m* 19 Jan 1914 Henry Booth Hohler, DL, JP, of Fawkham Manor, Kent, and *d* 6 July 1945. He *d* 14 Feb 1916

(1) Emma Anne; *m* 21 Oct 1845 Eustace Arkwright and *d* 6 June 1902, having had issue. He *d* 15 Sept 1846

1 Julia; *m* Rev Benjamin Ker Vaughan

2 Sophia; *m* Jonathan Micklethwait

Sir Edward *m* 2nd 24 Sept 1777 Elizabeth (*d* 1825), dau of Edward Bull, of Frome, Somerset, and *d* 16 Jan 1829, leaving by her two sons and a dau (all *d* unm)

The 3rd Bt's bro,

Sir Josias Henry Stracey, 4th Bt; *b* 13 Nov 1771; *m* 23 June 1800 Diana (*d* 13 June 1854) est dau of David Scott, of Dunninald, and had:

1 HENRY JOSIAS (Sir), **5th Bt**

2 Edward John; *b* 12 May 1808

3 Hardinge Robert; *b* 29 Sept 1814; HEICS; *m* 29 Aug 1839 Barbara Elizabeth (*d* 11 May 1910), dau of Capt James Balfour Robertson, RN, and *d* 31 March 1844, leaving:

  (1) Hardinge Richard; *b* 21 Aug 1840; Lt-Col 98th Regt; *m* 21 Dec 1883 Mary (*d* 1944), dau of Adml Frederick Byng Montrésor, and *d* 2 March 1924, having had:

    1a William Montrésor; *b* 29 Sept 1887; *d* 5 Dec 1890

    1a Constance Mary; *b* 18–

    2a Elizabeth Julia; *b* 18–; *m* 1 March 1909 Charles Henry Garner Richardson and had:

      1b *Richard Hearle; *b* 1914

      2b *Peter Tremayne; *b* 1916

      1b *Elizabeth Barbara; *b* 1911

      2b *José Antonia Doreen; *b* 1921

    3a Ruth; *m* 20 Feb 1930 J Wilfred Wickes, consulting engr, of Durban, Natal, and had:

      1b *A dau; *b* 1931

    4a Margaret Diana; *b* 1896

  (1) Julia Clifton; *d* unm 4 Sept 1928

1 Louisa *m* 30 Oct 1819 Charles Heaton Ellis, of Wyddial Hall, Herts (*d* 1865)

2 Emma; *m* 27 March 1820 Charles Struth and *d* 11 Aug 1861

3 Adelaide; *m* 1839 12th Baron Bentinck and *d* 19 Sept 1857, having had issue (*see* PORTLAND, E)

4 Diana Julia Wildbrat; *m* 31 Jan 1833 Sir Henry Durrant, 3rd Bt (*qv*), and *d* 9 Feb 1867, leaving issue

5 Ann Matilda Pauline; *m* 8 Jan 1838 Rev George Curteis Luxford, of Higham, Sussex, and *d* 18 March 1904. He *d* 1893

The 4th Bt *d* 6 Nov 1855; his est s,

Sir Henry Josias Stracey, 5th Bt; *b* 31 July 1802; Capt 1st Roy Dragoons, MP E Norfolk 1855–57, Gt Yarmouth 1859–65 and Norwich 1868–70, High Sheriff Norfolk 1871; *m* 5 March 1835 Charlotte (*d* 12 April 1884), only dau and heiress of George Denne, of The Paddock, Canterbury, and had:

1 EDWARD HENRY GERVASE (Sir), **6th Bt**

2 Henry Hardinge Denne; *b* 16 Dec 1839; Maj-Gen, Col Scots Gds: Adj Scots Gds 1877–79, Col, Maj-Gen, Cmdt Sch Instruction Aux Forces, London, 1879–80, Mil Sec Bombay 1880–82, cmded S London Dist, Sudan Expdn 1885 (despatches, medal and bronze star), Jubilee Medal; *d* 15 March 1930

3 Dudley Lyon Winder; *b* 25 May 1841; *d* 26 May 1878

4 Hardinge Arthur; *d* 4 Nov 1864

5 Gilbert Hardinge, JP, DL Norfolk; *b* 30 May 1844; Capt Norfolk Militia Artillery, CC Norfolk; *m* 10 Oct 1867 Louisa Anne (*d* 9 Feb 1933), only dau of Richard Groucock, and *d* 21 Feb 1907, leaving:

  (1) Gilbert Foard; *b* 29 July 1868; Lt 3rd Bn Durham LI; *d* 10 Dec 1937

  (2) Hardinge Graham; *b* 16 Jan 1870; *d* 1898

  (3) Ernest Henry Denne; *b* 13 April 1871; ADC to Govr UP India, Lt-Col cmdg 9th Bn Norfolk Regt; *m* 3 Dec 1907 Faith Dorothy Beatrice Mounteney (*d* 9 Aug 1965), only dau of Henry Downes Popham, and *d* 16 March 1948, having had:

    1a +HENRY MOUNTENEY [Henry Stracey Esq, White Barn, Walberswick, Suffolk IP18 6TS]; *b* 24 April 1920; heir presumptive; *m* 1st 1943 Susanna, dau of Adair Tracey, and has:

      1b *Amarilla; *b* 1943

    1a (cont.) HENRY STRACEY *m* 2nd 1950 Lysbeth, only dau of Charles Ashford, of New Zealand, and by her has:

      1b +Rupert; *b* 28 May 1951

      1b *Miranda Hinemoa; *b* 1955

    1a (cont.) HENRY STRACEY *m* 3rd 1961 *Jeltje, yst dau of Scholte de Boer, of Oppenhuizen, Friesland, Holland

    1a *Noel Margaret Jephson [Mrs Charles Purdon-Coote, Durham House, Balsham, Cambs]; *b* 25 Dec 1908; *m* 30 Sept 1933 Maj Charles Robert Purdon-Coote (*see* COOTE, Bt) and has issue

    2a Joan Cypria Mounteney; *b* 31 May 1910

    3a Rosamund Hardinge; *b* 30 July, *d* 7 Oct 1911

  (4) Reginald George; *b* 12 Sept 1881; Capt Scots Gds, Boer War, WW I (despatches); *ka* 1 Jan 1915

  (1) Hilda Marguerite; *m* 19 July 1910 Capt Leicester William Le Marchant Carey, Roy Fus, only s of Maj-Gen Constantine Phipps Carey, CB, RE, and *d* 3 Sept 1954. He was *ka* 17 Oct 1914

6 Gerald Hyde Charles; *b* 7 Nov 1846; Capt 2nd Bn Roy Warwicks Regt; *m* 17 Jan 1888 Ellen Edith (*d* 17 May 1937), only dau of J H Norgate, of Framingham Pigot, and *d* 24 Sept 1896, leaving:

  (1) Diana Gwendoline Edith Cecil; *m* Oswald Toynbee Falk, CBE, s of H John Falk, of West Kirby, Cheshire, and *d* 28 April 1963, leaving issue

7 Kingston; *b* 1848; *d* unm 9 April 1886

8 Randolph Harboard; *b* 12 April 1857; *d* unm 1 Aug 1906

1 Charlotte; *m* 25 Jan 1859 1st Earl Sondes (*see* MONSON, B) and *d* 23 June 1927, having had issue

2 Frances Julia; *m* 19 April 1871 John Bathurst Graver Browne, of Morley Hall, Norfolk, and had issue. He *d* 26 Oct 1880

3 Constance Adelaide; *m* 21 March 1857 Hon Harbord Harbord, bro of 5th Baron Suffield (*qv*), and *d* 22 Aug 1876, leaving issue

4 Anne Rosalie; *m* 3 Oct 1871 Alexander Richard Pemberton, only surv s of C R Pemberton, of Newton, Cambs, and *d* 29 Feb 1872

5 Isabel Geraldine; *m* 22 June 1875 2nd Earl of Kimberley (*qv*) and *d* 20 Jan 1927, leaving issue

6 Diana Madeleine; *d* unm 2 June 1908

The 5th Bt *d* 7 Aug 1885; his est s,

Sir Edward Henry Gervase Stracey, 6th Bt, JP, DL Norfolk; *b* 3 Dec 1838; Capt Norfolk Artillery Militia; *m* 28 April 1870 Mary Gertrude (*d* 26 Jan 1907), dau of Sir Charles Des Voeux, 2nd Bt (*see* 1940 edn), and *d* 6 June 1888, leaving:

1 **Sir Edward Paulet Stracey, 7th Bt**; *b* 5 July 1871; *educ* Wellington; Lt 2nd Life Gds, Hon Maj Household Cav (Res), High Sheriff Norfolk 1928; *m* 1st 17 Dec 1902 Mary Elizabeth Brinsley (*d* 10 April 1935), dau of Algernon Brinsley Sheridan, of Frampton Court, Dorset, and had:

  (1) Brinsley Hugh; *b* 28 Jan 1904; *d* 24 Sept 1919

  (2) **Sir Michael George Motley Stracey, 8th Bt**; *b* 7 July 1911; *educ* Harrow and Queen's Coll Oxford; *d* unm 25 Sept 1971

  (1) *Margaret Rosalind Linley [Mrs Peter Harris, 189 Cranmer Court, Sloane Ave, London SW3]; *b* 8 Oct 1907; *m* 6 April 1959 Peter Edward Clement Harris (*d* 1976), s of Sir Austin Edward Harris, KBE

1 (cont.) **Sir Edward** *m* 2nd 16 July 1935 Kathleen Emily, dau of Robert Alexander Robertson, of Old Castle, Collooney, Co Sligo, and *d* 23 Aug 1949, leaving by her:

  (2) *Dereen Elizabeth Paulette [Mrs James Bartlett, Paddocks Farm, Cranbrook, Kent]; *b* 23 Nov 1937; *m* 3 April 1965 *James Douglas Grove Bartlett, only s of Douglas Bartlett, of Kinta, Rustington, Sussex, and has:

    1a *Christopher James Edward Douglas; *b* 25 May 1966

    2a *Peter Sean Charles; *b* 24 Jan 1969

    3a *Richard Gerald Patrick; *b* 1971

2 Algernon Augustus Henry; *b* 5 April 1873; Capt 9th Bn Norfolk Regt WW I (wounded); *m* 27 March 1928 Olive Beryl (*m* 2nd 8 May 1943 Maj George Alastair Mounsey, Cairo Military Police (*das* 12 July 1945), and *d* 1972), 4th dau of Maj Charles Robert Eustace Radclyffe, of Hyde, Wareham, Dorset, and *d* 8 Dec 1941, leaving:

  (1) Sir JOHN SIMON STRACEY, **9th and present Baronet**

  (1) *Ramona Beryl [Mrs Theodore Darvas, Flat 1, 5 St George's Terrace, London NW1 8XH]; *b* 4 Feb 1930; *m* 21 March 1959 *Theodore Frederic Darvas, only s of Dr S Darvas, of Marylebone, and has:

    1a *Jane Caroline; *b* 1 Jan 1963

    2a *Anna Judith; *b* 27 Nov 1966

STRACHEY

Arms: Quarterly, 1st and 4th, arg. a cross between four eagles displayed gu. (for STRACHEY); 2nd and 3rd, or three crescents sa., on a canton of the second a ducal coronet gold (for HODGES). **Crest:** An eagle displayed gu., charged on the breast with a cross-crosslet fitchée arg. **Motto:** *Cœlum non animum* ('Circumstances change, but not the mind'). **Creation:** Bt. (UK) 15 June 1801.

Charles Strachey [Charles Strachey Esq, 31 Northchurch Terr, London NE1 4EB]; *b* 20 June 1934; *s* 1st cousin once-removed 1973 as 6th Bt but does not use title; *educ* Westminster and Magdalen Coll Oxford; late local govt offr; *m* 1973 *Janet Megan, dau of Alexander Miller, of Earls Barton, Northants, and has:

1 *Jane Alice; *b* 1975

Lineage: WILLIAM STRACHIE, of Saffron Walden, Essex; *b* 1493; *d* 1587, leaving:

WILLIAM STRACHEY, of Saffron Walden; *m* 1st Mary, dau of Henry Cooke, of Lysting, Kent; *m* 2nd Elizabeth Brockett and *d* between 8 Nov 1598 and 13 Feb 1598/9, leaving:

WILLIAM STRACHEY, of Saffron Walden and Wandsworth; *m* 1595 Frances, dau of William Fo(r)ster, of Crowhurst, Surrey, and had:

WILLIAM STRACHEY, of Camberwell, Surrey; *m* 1st 1620 Eleanor Read, of Presteigne, Radnorshire; *m* 2nd 1629 Anne Bourn, of Greenstead Hall, Essex; *m* 3rd 2 Dec 1632 Elizabeth (*d* 1672), widow of Samuel Jepp and dau of William Cross, of Blackmore in Cannington, Somerset, and *d* 1634, leaving by her:

JOHN STRACHEY, of Sutton Court, Somerset, which he inherited from his mother; *b* 1634; *educ* Lincoln Coll Oxford (BA 1653); barrister Lincoln's Inn 1660; *m* Dec 1662 Jane (*d* 30 Oct 1727), 2nd dau of George Hodges, of Wedmore, Elm, Buckland, and Streme, Somerset, and *d* 4 Feb 1674, leaving:

JOHN STRACHEY, of Sutton Court; *b* 10 May 1671; FRS, antiquary; *m* 1st 10 May 1692 Elizabeth (*d* 9 Dec 1722), dau of William Elletson; *m* 2nd Christiana (*d* 1743), dau of Richard Staveley, and *d* 11 June 1743, having by her had a s (Samuel, *k* Siege Minorca 1762) and by his 1st w, with other issue, including an est s (Hodges, of Sutton Court, *b* 11 Feb 1696, *dsp* 1746):

HENRY STRACHEY, of Sutton Court; *b* 22 Feb 1707; *m* 1st 19 Sept 1727 Helen (*d* 8 Feb 1745), dau of Robert Clerk, MD, of Listonfield, Midlothian; *m* 2nd Frances Quarme, of Truro, and *d* 23 May 1765, leaving by his 1st w, with a yr s (John (Ven), *b* 30 July 1738, LLD, FSA, Archdeacon Suffolk, Chaplain in Ordinary to GEORGE III, Preb Llandaff, *m* 14 Nov 1770 Anne (*d* 12 Feb 1824), only dau of George Wombwell, London merchant, Consul at Alicante, and *d* 17 Dec 1818, having had issue):

Sir Henry Strachey, 1st Bt (UK), so *cr* 15 June 1801, of Sutton Court; *b* 23 May 1737; Sec to 1st Baron Clive of Plassey (*see* POWIS, E) 1764, MP 1770–1810, Sec Commn for restoring peace in America 1774, Jt Sec Treasury 1782, U-Sec State 1782, Master Household; *m* 23 May 1770 Jane (*d* 12 Feb 1824), widow of Capt Latham, RN, and only dau of John Kelsall, of Greenwich, and *d* 3 Jan 1810, leaving:

1 **Sir Henry Strachey, 2nd Bt**; *b* 6 Dec 1772; *d* unm 11 April 1858

2 Edward; *b* 18 Dec 1774; Bengal CS; *m* 13 Oct 1808 Julia Woodburn, yst dau of Maj-Gen William Kirkpatrick, Bengal Army, and *d* 3 Jan 1832, leaving:

(1) EDWARD (Sir), **3rd Bt**

(2) Henry; *b* 24 Feb 1816; Lt-Col Bengal Army, explorer; *m* 6 Sept 1859 Joanna Catherine (*d* 9 May 1917), 2nd dau of Rudolph Cloeté, of Newlands, S Africa, and *d* 9 Feb 1912, leaving:

1a Julia Charlotte; *b* 14 April 1864; *m* 15 Oct 1884 Sir William Chance, 2nd Bt (*qv*), and *dsp* 30 Aug 1949

(3) Richard (Sir), GCSI; *b* 24 July 1817; Lt-Gen RE, memb Cncl of Sec State India 1875–89, LLD, FRS; *m* 1st 27 Dec 1854 Caroline (*dsp* 19 Sept 1855), dau of Rev George Bowles; *m* 2nd 4 Jan 1859 Jane Maria (*d* 14 Dec 1928), dau of Sir John Peter Grant of Rothiemurchus, GCMG, KCB, and *d* 12 Feb 1908, having had:

1a Richard John, CMG (1918); *b* 19 May 1861; Col Rifle Bde; *m* 30 Dec 1896 Grace Alice (*d* 10 June 1954), dau of FM Sir Henry Wylie Norman, GCB, GCMG, CIE, and *d* 23 Oct 1935

2a Ralph; *b* 28 Sept 1868; *m* 29 Oct 1901 Margaret Winifred (*d* 9 Aug 1972), dau of Albert Severs, and *d* 18 June 1923, leaving:

1b Richard Philip Farquhar; *b* 10 Aug 1902; novelist; *m* 1st 1927 (*divorce* 1940) Frances Esmé, dau of Charles John Rudd, and had:

1c *Philippa [Miss Philippa Hawtin, La Casita Vieja, Pt de El Collado, 03729 Lliber, Alicante, Spain]; *b* 19 Sept 1927; took name HAWTIN by deed poll 1961

2c *Victoria [Mrs Mark Holloway, 9 Dolforgan Court, Louisa Terrace, Exmouth, Devon EX8 2AQ]; *b* 14 Jan 1929; took name HUNTER by deed poll 1951; *m* 1952 *Mark Graham Holloway and has issue

1b (cont.) Richard Strachey *m* 2nd 23 Dec 1943 *Simonette Mary Reynolds [Mrs Richard Strachey, 25 Park Town, Oxford], formerly w of S John Woods and dau of Charles Foster Atchison, of IOW, and *d* 20 March 1976

2b John Ralph Severs; *b* 22 Oct 1905; *m* 1st 12 Oct 1933 (*divorce* 1941) Isobel Bertha (*d* 1987), dau of Ronald Leslie, and had:

1c Charlotte Augusta; *b* 2 Aug 1935; *m* 1st 1955 (*divorce* 1960), as his 1st w, Anthony Blond, publisher, er s of Neville Blond,CMG, OBE, of Gotwick Manor, East Grinstead, Sussex, by his 1st w Eileen Reba (who *m* 2nd Richard Morris-Marsham; *see* ROMNEY, E); *m* 2nd 1960, as his 1st w, *Peter Jenkins, jnlst, and *d* 1970, leaving by him:

1d *Amy; *b* 20 Oct 1963

2b (cont.) John Strachey *m* 2nd 16 June 1945 *Rosemary, dau of Douglas Mavor, and *d* 1983, leaving by her:

1c +HENRY LEOFFRIC BENVENUTO [Henry Strachey Esq, c/o Middleton & Upsall, solicitors, Eastgate House, 94 East St, Warminster, Wilts BA12 9BG]; *b* 17 April 1947; heir presumptive; *m* 1st 1971 (*divorce* 1982) Julie Margaret Hutchens; *m* 2nd 1983 *Susan Christine, dau of John Ernest Skinner, of Cosham, Hants

1b *Ursula Margaret [Mrs Cyril Wentzel, 1 Grange Lodge, The Grange, London SW19 4PR]; *b* 29 June 1911; late FCO; *m* 12 Dec 1939 *Cyril Charles Wentzel, barrister, s of Charles Augustus Wentzel, of Johannesburg

3a Oliver, CBE (1943); *b* 3 Nov 1874; *educ* Eton; *m* 1st 21 Jan 1901 (*divorce* 1908) Ruby Julia, dau of Julius Mayer, and had:

1b Julia Frances; *b* 14 Aug 1901; *m* 1st 22 July 1927 Hon Stephen Tomlin (*d* 5 Jan 1937), yr s of Baron Tomlin (LP; *see* 1935 edn); *m* 2nd 1952 (*divorce* 1967) Lawrence Burnett Gowing, CBE, s of Horace Burnett Gowing

3a (cont.) Oliver Strachey *m* 2nd 31 May 1911 Rachel Conn (*d* 16 July 1940), dau of Benjamin Francis Conn Costelloe, and *d* 14 May 1960, having by her had:

1b Christopher; *b* 16 Nov 1916; *educ* King's Coll Cambridge (MA); *d* 18 May 1975

2b *Barbara; *b* 17 July 1912; *educ* Oxford (BA); *m* 1st 16 Jan 1934 (*divorce* 1937) Olaf Hultin, s of Professor Arvid Hultin, of Helsingfors, and has:

1c *Roger Olavson [Roger Hultin Esq, 9 Bedford Gdns, London W8]; *b* 30 Oct 1934

2b (cont.) Mrs Barbara Hultin *m* 2nd Sept 1937 Wolf Halpern, RAFVR (*das* 1943), s of Dr Georg Halpern, of Jerusalem

4a (Giles) Lytton; *b* 1 March 1880; *educ* Abbotsholme, Leamington Coll, Liverpool U and Trin Coll Cambridge (LLD); biographer and essayist, author: *Landmarks in French Literature, Eminent Victorians, Queen Victoria, Elizabeth and Essex, Portraits in Miniature, Books and Characters, etc*; *d* unm 21 Jan 1932

5a James Beaumont; *b* 26 Sept 1887; *educ* St Paul's and Trin Coll Cambridge; translator and ed with his w of Sigmund Freud; *m* 4 June 1920 Alix, psycho-analyst (*d* 28 April 1973), dau of Harry Smythe Sargant-Florence, of Lord's Wood, Marlow, and *dsp* 25 April 1967

1a Elinor; *m* 16 Dec 1882 James Meadows Rendel, barrister, of Kensington and Acton, Wittersham, Kent, and *d* July 1944, leaving issue. He *d* 27 Aug 1937

2a Dorothea; *m* 18 April 1903 Simon Bussy, artist, of Roquebrune, France, and *d* 1 May 1960, leaving issue. He *d* 1954

3a Philippa, CBE (1951); Govr Bedford Coll London, Hon Sec Fawcett Soc; *d* unm 23 Aug 1968

4a (Joan) Pernel; MA, Fell and Tutor, later Pncpl Newnham Coll Cambridge 1923–41; *d* unm 19 Dec 1951

5a Marjorie Colvile; *d* unm 16 Jan 1964

(4) William, JP Somerset; *b* 22 June 1819; Bengal CS 1838–43, Colonial Office 1848–70; *d* unm 29 Nov 1904

(5) John (Sir), GCSI, CIE; *b* 5 June 1823; memb Cncl Govr-Gen India 1870–73 and 1876–80, Lt-Govr NW Provinces 1874–76, Hon DCL Oxon; *m* 8 Oct 1856 Katherine Jane, CI (*d* 10 April 1907), dau of George Batten, BCS, and *d* 19 Dec 1907, leaving:

1a John, MVO; *b* 5 Sept 1857; Lt-Col IA, Afghanistan 1880–81 (medal), Burma 1885–87 (despatches, medal) and Black Mountain Expdn 1891 (clasp, Hazara), Sec 1907–10 and Gen Manager 1910–13 Army and Navy Stores; *d* unm 30 Nov 1945

2a Arthur (Sir); *b* 5 Dec 1858; BA, LLB Cantab; barrister, Ch Justice High Court NW Provinces India, ktd 1899; *m* 22 Oct 1885 Ellen (*d* 14 July 1924), dau of John Conolly, and *dsp* 14 May 1901

3a Charles (Sir), KCMG, CB; *b* 17 Sept 1862; Assist U-Sec Colonial Office; *m* 26 July 1893 Ada Margaret (*d* 16 Jan 1925), dau of Rev Alexander Raleigh, DD, of Kensington, and *d* 15 March 1942, leaving:

1b John Francis; *b* 1894; *educ* Marlborough and Oxford; composer, Sub-Lt RN WW I (invalided); *m* Bridget — (*d* 21 May 1974) and *d* 27 May 1972

1a Katherine; *d* 5 Feb 1872

2a Winifred; *m* 12 June 1883 Sir Hugh Shakespear Barnes, KCSI, KCVO, BCS, and *d* 20 Aug 1892, leaving issue. He *d* 15 Feb 1940

3a Nina; *m* 1st 27 Dec 1894 William Edmund Marriott (*d* 1915), s of Rev Wharton Booth Marriott, and had issue; *m* 2nd 24 Oct 1916 (*divorce* 1927) Lindsay Millais Jopling, ICS, and *d* 28 July 1946

4a Mary Lawrence; *m* 25 April 1903 Capt Willoughby Baynes Huddleston, CMG, RIN, s of Maj Graham Egerton Huddleston, E Surrey Regt, and *d* 25 Oct 1955. He *d* 1 May 1953

5a Jane; *d* unm 22 June 1958

(6) George; *b* 8 Aug 1828; Min Resident Saxony 1890–97; *m* 1st 5 June 1857 his cousin Anne Maria Georgiana (*dsp* 25 Jan 1858), est dau of Richard Strachey, of Ashwick Grove (*see below*); *m* 2nd 1862 Catherine (*d* 9 Nov 1920), est dau of Rev John Bazett Doveton, Rector Burnett, Somerset, and *d* 25 Feb 1912, leaving:

1a Lionel; *b* 28 Jan 1864; *d* 31 Aug 1927

2a Bertram; *b* 29 Sept 1865; Capt IA; *d* unm 11 Feb 1954

3a William; *b* 3 June 1867; *m* 1 July 1904 Nina Alma Grosvenor, of New York, and *d* 3 July 1911, leaving:

  1b Reginald; *b* 1905; *d* 1973

  1b Ella Mary; *m* 1930 Lawrence Tarpley

1a Margaret; Roy Humane Society's Medal; *d* unm 5 April 1955

2a Edith Mary; *d* unm 26 Nov 1960

3a Georgiana; *d* unm 5 Dec 1917

(1) Jane; *m* 15 Oct 1842 John Hare, of Bristol, and *d* 13 July 1886, leaving issue
3 Richard, of Ashwick Grove, Oakhill, Bath; *b* 21 May 1781; *m* 1 June 1830 Anne Marie (*d* Dec 1845), dau of Alexander Powell, MP, of Hurdcott Ho, Wilts, and *d* 5 May 1847, leaving, with other issue:

(1) Richard Charles, of Ashwick Grove, JP; *b* 2 Nov 1835; *m* 25 March 1857 Charlotte Lindsay (*d* Nov 1919), 3rd dau of Ralph Barchard Hankin, of Bedford, and *d* 30 July 1901, leaving:

1a Richard Sholto, of Ashwick Grove, JP; *b* 12 March 1859; Engr State Rlwy Dept and Agent Assam-Bengal Rlwy India; *m* 28 Jan 1911 Hon Mildred Cunningham Davey, JP Somerset (*d* 2 May 1942), 2nd dau of Baron Davey of Fernhurst (LP, *see edn*), and *d* 30 Dec 1936

2a Theodore Edward; *b* 9 June 1860; barrister Inner Temple; *m* 1st 29 Jan 1913 Beatrice Catherine (*d* 25 April 1913), er dau of Rt Rev S E Marsden, DD, Bp Bathurst, NSW; *m* 2nd 20 Feb 1917 Ella de Burgh (*d* 1941), 6th dau of Maj-Gen Archibald Hammond Utterson, CB, and *d* 19 July 1921

3a Claude Mainwaring; *b* 1 Sept 1861; *m* 1887 Emily Chisholm (*d* 4 Aug 1922), dau of James Macpherson, of Ninde, Inverness-shire, and had:

  1b Claude Otto; *b* 1888; *ka* Gallipoli May 1915

  2b Ewen Macpherson; *b* 13 Sept 1892; NZ Expdny Force WW I Gallipoli and France; *m* 8 Aug 1923 Doris Isabel Grace, 3rd dau of W W Bicknell, of Greytown, NZ, and *d* 2 Nov 1970, having had:

    1c Grace Macpherson; *b* 26 May 1924; *d* unm 30 March 1944

    2c Judith Helen; *b* 18 Nov 1928; *d* 10 April 1932

  3b Richard Clive; *b* 1895; NZ Inf; *ka* 4 Aug 1917

  1b Aileen Marion; *m* 1920 Edwyn Grenville Temple, of Spree Farm, Geraldine, NZ, and had issue

  2b Olive Margaret, MBE; served WW II (despatches); *m* 28 March 1929 Robert Reginald Blackford and *d* 26 June 1962, leaving issue

4a Reginald Clive; *b* 28 Nov 1866; *m* 6 Nov 1893 Ann Ellen (*d* 18 Dec 1951), dau of Henry William Gibson, Dep Commr Bahraich, Oudh, and *d* 1 April 1903, leaving:

  1b Richard Clive, MC; *b* 8 July 1897; *educ* Repton and RMC Sandhurst; Maj 1st Bn Somerset LI WW I (despatches); *m* 1st 4 Jan 1928 (*divorce*) Olive Zöe, only dau of Hugh Carleton Formby, of The Manor Ho, Shipton-Bellinger, Hants, and had:

    1c *Anne Julia; *b* 30 July 1930; *m* 24 Jan 1953 John Branfoot Simpson Pedler, s of Tom Simpson Pedler, LLB, barrister, of Notting Hill, and has:

      1d *Dominic Julian; *b* 19 Dec 1959

      1d *Francesca Julia Teresa; *b* 6 June 1954

  1b (cont.) Maj Richard Strachey *m* 2nd 1951 *Florence Irene, dau of Philip William Rogers, of Burma

  1b Carlotta Marion; *b* 9 Sept 1895; *m* 17 April 1952 Rev James Reginald Stevens, s of James Stevens, of Farnham, Surrey

  2b Dorothea Helen; *m* 1930 Maj Charles Douglas St Leger, MC, FRIBA

5a Henry Cyril Gray; *b* 25 Sept 1873; *d* 18 Oct 1954

1a Mary Charlotte Georgiana; *m* 27 Sept 1881 Cyril Goodricke Hawdon, of NZ, and had issue

2a Constance Margaret; *m* 10 July 1884 Frederick Seymour Whalley and *d* 10 Dec 1935, leaving issue. He *d* 15 April 1903

3a Marion Lindsay; *d* unm 3 Sept 1889

4a Mildred; *m* Sept 1896 Walter Tudway Phipps, 2nd son of Arthur Constantine Phipps, of Whitstone Ho, Somerset, and *d* 27 Dec 1904, having had issue. He *d* 28 April 1902

5a Violet Helen; *d* unm 24 April 1961

(2) Alexander; *b* 20 Feb 1845; *m* 3 Nov 1875 Fanny Augusta (*d* 22 May 1907), only dau of Arthur Constantine Phipps, of Whitstone Ho, Somerset, and *dsp* 28 May 1900

(1) Anne Maria Georgiana; *b* 22 June 1831; *m* 5 June 1857 her 1st cousin George Strachey (*see above*) and *dsp* 25 Jan 1858

(2) Joanna; *b* 8 June 1832; *m* 5 July 1859 Rev George E F Masters and *d* 14 Nov 1906

(3) Mary Augusta; *b* 21 June 1838; *m* 6 Aug 1836 Charles Isaac Elton, QC, MP (*see* ELTON, Bt), and *d* 2 Feb 1914

(4) Charlotte Margaret; *b* 8 Dec 1839; *m* 2 Feb 1865 Capt John James Phillipps, 60th Rifles, and *d* 17 April 1893, leaving issue

(5) Harriet Octavia; *b* 27 Dec 1840; *m* Oct 1862 Capt George Vanburgh Law, Madras SC, and *d* 3 Dec 1865

(6) Katharine; *b* 28 Aug 1842; *m* Dec 1862 Lt-Col John Francis Mair Winterscale, JP, Rifle Bde and 3rd Bn Wilts Regt, and *d* 17 Aug 1870

(7) Isabel; *b* 20 Feb 1845; *m* 10 Dec 1875 John Holland Baker, Commr Crown Lands, Wellington, NZ, and *d* 1920, leaving issue
1 Charlotte Margaret; *d* 1801
2 Lucy; *m* 29 July 1817 Col Frederick William Wollaston, DL, JP, of Shenton Hall, Leics, and *dsp* his widow 10 March 1863

The 2nd Bt's n,

Sir Edward Strachey, 3rd Bt, JP, DL Somerset; *b* 12 Aug 1812; High Sheriff Somerset 1864; *m* 1st 27 Aug 1844 Elisabeth (*dsp* 11 April 1855), est dau of Rev W Wilkieson, of Woodbury Hall, Beds; *m* 2nd 3 Nov 1857 Mary Isabella (*d* 5 Oct 1883), 2nd dau of John Addington Symonds, MD, of Clifton, and *d* 24 Sept 1901, leaving by her:

1 **Sir Edward Strachey, 4th Bt**, and 1ST BARON STRACHIE, of Sutton Court, Co Somerset (UK), so *cr* 3 Nov 1911, PC (1912), JP, DL Somerset; *b* 30 Oct 1858; *educ* privately and Ch Ch Oxford;Lt 4th Bn Somerset LI 1877–82, MP (Lib) S Somerset 1892–1911, Treas Household 1905–10, Parly Sec Bd Ag and Fish 1909–11, Paymaster-Gen 1912–15, CA Somerset; *m* 17 Jan 1880 Constance (*d* 22 Dec 1936), dau of Charles Bampfylde Braham and n of Frances, w of 7th Earl Waldegrave (*qv*), and *d* 25 July 1936, leaving:

(1) **Sir Edward Strachey**, 2ND BARON STRACHIE, JP (Somerset 1903); *b* 13 Jan 1882; *educ* Harrow; 2nd Lt 4th Bn Oxon LI 1900, Lt Gren Gds 1902, Capt 4th Bn Somerset LI 1911, WW I in Mesopotamia, Persia and India 1914–20, Lt-Col 1919, Assist Priv Sec to 1st Ld Admlty 1909, Priv Sec to his f as Parly Sec Bd Ag and Fish 1910–11; *m* 14 March 1933 Violet Mary Yea (*d* 27 Feb 1962), widow of William Ethelred Jennings and dau of Walter Lacy Rogers, JP, and *dsp* 17 May 1973, when the Barony expired

(1) Frances Constance Maddalena; *m* 27 April 1911 3rd Baron O'Hagan (*qv*) and *d* 1 Aug 1931, leaving issue

2 (John) St Loe, JP, DL Surrey; *b* 9 Feb 1860; *educ* Balliol Coll Oxford (BA 1884); barrister Inner Temple 1885, High Sheriff Surrey 1914, Hon DLitt Bristol 1925, ed *Spectator*; *m* 13 July 1887 Henrietta Mary Amy, OBE, JP Surrey (*d* 22 Oct 1957 aged 91), dau of Charles Turner Simpson, and *d* 26 Aug 1927, having had:

(1) Thomas Clive; *b* 9 Sept 1888; Lt Surrey Imp Yeo; *d* 1 March 1907

(2) (Evelyn) John St Loe, PC (1946); *b* 21 Oct 1901; *educ* Eton and Magdalen Coll Oxford; W/Cdr RAFVR, MP (Lab) Aston 1929–31, Dundee 1945–50 and Dundee W 1950, Parly U-Sec Air 1945–46, Min Food 1946–50, Sec State War 1950–51, jnlst, author: *The Coming Struggle for Power, The Theory and Practice of Socialism, What are we to do, Contemporary Capitalism, The End of Empire, The Strangled Cry* and *On the Prevention of War*; *m* 1st 24 April 1929 (*divorce* 1933) Esther, only dau of Patrick Francis Murphy, of New York; *m* 2nd 13 Oct 1933 Celia, 3rd dau of Rev Arthur Hume Simpson, and *d* 15 July 1963, leaving:

1a CHARLES STRACHEY, **6th and present Bt**

1a *Elizabeth [Mrs Hamid Al Quadhi, 18 Southdean Gdns, London SW19 6NU]; *b* 13 May 1936; *m* 1958 Hamid Al Quadhi (*d* 1986) and has:

  1b *James; *b* 10 June 1959

  1b *Samia; *b* 15 July 1964

1a (cont.) Mrs Hamid Al Quadhi also adopted:

  *Hannah; *b* 1962

(1) (Mary) Amabel Nassau; *b* 10 May 1894; author and jnlst; *m* 31 July 1915 Maj Sir (Bertram) Clough Williams-Ellis, CBE, MC, JP, FRIBA, Welsh Gds, 2nd surv s of Rev John Clough Williams-Ellis, of Glasfryn, Caernarvs, and Brondanw, Merioneths, and had issue

3 Henry; *b* 21 Nov 1863; artist; *d* unm 28 Oct 1940

1 Frances; *b* 23 Oct 1874; *m* 6 Sept 1902 William Henry Cantrell Shaw, JP, MB, BC, s of John Shaw, of Normanton Ho, Derbys, and *d* 10 Feb 1960, leaving issue. He *d* 27 Nov 1938

Stradbroke

Arms: Sa. a fess dancettée or between three crescents arg.
Crest: A pyramid of bay-leaves in the form of a cone vert.
Supporters: Dexter, a lion arg., maned and tufted or; sinister, a sea-horse arg., maned and finned or, the tail round an anchor az., each supporter gorged with a wreath of bay vert. **Motto:** *Je vive en espoir* ('I live in hope'). **Creations:** Bt. (E) 17 Aug 1660, B. (GB) 14 June 1796, E. and V. (UK) 18 July 1821.

THE 6TH EARL OF STRADBROKE, Co Suffolk, **Viscount Dunwich**, Co Suffolk, **Baron Rous of Dennington**, Co Suffolk, and a **Baronet** (Sir Robert Keith Rous, Bt) [The Rt Hon The Earl of Stradbroke, Mount Fyans, RSD Darlington, Vic 3271, Australia]; *b* 25 March 1937; *s f* 1983; *educ* Harrow; *m* 1st 3 Sept 1960 (*divorce* 1976) Dawn Antoinette, dau of Thomas Edward Beverley, of Brisbane, Qld, and has:

1 +ROBERT KEITH, *Viscount Dunwich*; *b* 15 Nov 1961; *educ* Woolawere High Sch Sydney NSW

2 +Wesley Alexander; *b* 22 Oct 1972

1 *Ingrid Arnel; *b* 12 April 1963; has:

  (1) *Sam; *b* 1994

2 *(Sophia) Rayner; *b* 27 Sept 1964; has:

  (1) *Jake; *b* 1993

  (1) *Olivia; *b* 1990

  (2) *Kaylon; *b* 1991

  (3) *Cerana; *b* 1992

3 *Heidi Simone; *b* 27 March 1966; *m* 1991 *Timothy Crick and has:

  (1) *Joshua William; *b* 1992

  (2) *Thomas Oscar; *b* 1993

4 *Pamela Keri; *b* 15 May 1968

5 *Brigitte Aylena; *b* 13 June 1970

The 6th EARL *m* 2nd 2 March 1977 *Roseanna Mary Blanche, yr dau of Francis Reitman (*see* LYVEDEN, B), and by her has:

3 +Hektor Fraser; *b* 25 May 1978

4 +Maximilian Otho; *b* 1981

5 +Henham Mowbray; *b* 20 Sept 1983

6 +Winston Walberswick; *b* 1986

7 +Yoxford Ulysses Uluru; *b* 1989

8 +Ramsar Fyans; *b* 1992

6 *Zea Katherina *b* 18 Oct 1979

7 *Minsmere Mathilda; *b* 1988

Lineage: Sir ANTHONY ROUS, of Dennington, Suffolk; bought Henham Hall, Suffolk, from Sir Arthur Hopton 1544; *m* Agnes, dau of Thomas Blennerhasset of Friend's, Norfolk, and had an er s:

THOMAS ROUS, of Dennington and Henham Hall; *m* 1st Catherine (*dsp*), dau and heiress of Giles Hansard; *m* 2nd Anne, dau of Sir Nicholas Hare, of Bruisyard, Suffolk, and by her had:

Sir THOMAS ROUS, of Dennington and Henham Hall; *m* Pernell, dau of St John Goodwyn, of Winchington, Bucks, and had:

Sir JOHN ROUS, of Henham Hall; *m* Elizabeth, dau of Sir Christopher Yelverton, of Easton, Norfolk, and was *bur* 10 Sept 1653, having had, with other issue, including an er s (Christopher, *b* 1605, *m c* 5 May 1630 Elizabeth (*m* 2nd 1644 Sir Poynings More, 1st Bt, of Loseley, Surrey, and *d* 13 Sept 1666), dau of Sir William Fytche, of Ramsden, Essex, and *dsp* & *vp* 23 March 1635):

Sir John Rous, 1st Bt (E), so *cr* 17 Aug 1660, of Henham Hall; *b* 1608; High Sheriff Suffolk 1635, MP Dunwich 1660 and 1661 and Eye 1665; *m* 1st 23 June 1636 Anne (*dsp*), only dau of Nicholas Bacon, of Gillingham, Norfolk (*see* BACON, Bt); *m* 2nd 1656 Elizabeth (*d* 7 July 1670), dau of Thomas Knyvett, of Aswelthorpe, Norfolk, and *d* 27 Nov 1670, having by her had, with three other daus (including Catherine, *m* John Harbord, s of Sir Charles Harbord (*see* SUFFIELD, B), of Stanninghall, Norfolk; Mary, *m* Richard Coke; *see* LEICESTER, E):

Sir John Rous, 2nd Bt; *educ* Cambridge; High Sheriff Suffolk 1678, MP Eye 1685–87 and Suffolk 1689–90; *m* 1st 1676 Philippa, dau of Thomas Bedingfeld, of Darsham Hall, Suffolk, and had, with three daus:

Sir John Rous, 3rd Bt; MP Dunwich 1705–08; *d unm* 1 Feb 1730/1

Sir John *m* 2nd (licence 8 Sept 1686) Anne (*bur* 25 Feb 1735/6), dau and heiress of Robert Wood, of Kingston-on-Thames, and *d* 8 April 1730, having by her had, with other issue:

2 **Sir Robert Rous, 4th Bt**; *m* 1726 Lydia (*d* 13 Oct 1769), dau of John Smith, of Holton, Suffolk, and *d* 8 June 1735, leaving:

  (1) **Sir John Rous, 5th Bt**; Suffolk: High Sheriff 1759, MP 1768; *m* 5 June 1749 Judith (*m* 2nd Rev Edward Lockwood, of Lambourne, Essex, and *d* 10 Sept 1794), dau and heiress of John Bedingfeld, of Beeston St Andrew, Norfolk, and had, with two other daus:

    1a JOHN (Sir), **1st Earl**

    1a Frances; *m* Dec 1771 Sir Henry Dashwood Peyton, 1st Bt (*see* 1959 edn), and *d* 27 May 1808, leaving issue. He *d* May 1789

The 5th Bt *d* 31 Oct 1771; his only s,

Sir John Rous, 6th Bt, and **1st Earl of Stradbroke**, Co Suffolk, so *cr* 18 July 1821, as also VISCOUNT DUNWICH, Co Suffolk (both UK), and earlier 14 June 1796 BARON ROUS OF DENNINGTON, Co Suffolk (GB); *b* 30 May 1750; *educ* Westminster and Magdalen Coll Oxford; MP (Tory) Suffolk 1780–96; *m* 1st 26 Jan 1788 Frances Juliana (*d* 20 June 1790), only dau and heiress of Edward Warter-Wilson, of Bilboa, Co Limerick (*see* CARBERY, B), and had:

1 Frances Anne Juliana; *m* 6 July 1816 V-Adml Hon Sir Henry Hotham, KCB, and *d* 31 Jan 1859, leaving issue (*see* HOTHAM, B)

The **1st Earl** *m* 2nd 23 Feb 1792 Charlotte Maria (*d* 15 Jan 1856), dau of Abraham Whittaker, of Stratford, Essex, and Lyston House, Herfs, and by her had, with other issue:

1 JOHN EDWARD CORNWALLIS, **2nd Earl**

2 Henry John; *b* 23 Jan 1795; Adml RN, MP Westminster; the celebrated authority in racing circles; *m* 2 Jan 1836 Sophia (*d* 30 Jan 1871), only surv dau of James Ramsay Cuthbert, of Grosvenor Sq, and *d* 19 June 1877

3 William Rufus, of Worstead House, Norfolk, DL; *b* 1 Aug 1796; Capt Coldstream Gds; *m* 27 Dec 1822 Louisa (*d* 1 Oct 1876), yst dau of James Hatch, of Clabery Hall, Essex, and *d* 2 March 1875, having had, with a dau (*d* young):

  (1) William John, of Worstead Ho; *b* Oct 1833; Lt-Col Scots Gds; *d* 12 April 1914

  (1) Henrietta Diana; *m* 20 Jan 1876 Ernest Valentine Leon, Vicomte de Satgé de St Jean, est s of Vicomte de St Jean, of Castelnau, Pyrénées Orientales, France, and *d* March 1913

2 Charlotte Marianne Harriet; *m* 27 Dec 1810 Nathaniel Micklethwait, of Taverham and Beeston, Norfolk, and *d* 29 April 1830, leaving issue

3 Louisa Maria Judith; *m* 23 Feb 1824 Spencer Horsey de Horsey, MP (*d* 20 May 1860), and *d* 24 March 1843, leaving, with other issue:

  (1) Adeline Louisa Maria; *m* 1st 20 Sept 1858, as his 2nd w, 7th Earl of Cardigan (*see* AILESBURY, E); *m* 2nd 20 Aug 1873 Don Antonio Manuel de Lancastere Soldana, Count de Lancastere (*d* 1898), and *d* 25 May 1915

The 1st EARL *d* 27 Aug 1827; his est s,

JOHN EDWARD CORNWALLIS ROUS, **2nd Earl of Stradbroke**; *b* 13 Feb 1794; *educ* Westminster; Coldstream Gds: Ensign 1810, Lt and Capt 1814, Peninsular War (medal with five clasps) and Netherlands 1814–15, Capt 93rd Foot 1817 and Nova Scotia Fencibles 1818, ret 1821, Col E Suffolk Militia 1830–44, Ld Lt and V-Adml Suffolk 1844–86; *m* 26 May 1857 Augusta (*d* 11 Oct 1901), widow of Col H F Bonham, 10th Hus, and 2nd dau of Rev Sir Christopher John Musgrave, 9th Bt, of Hartley Castle (*qv*), and had:

1 GEORGE EDWARD JOHN MOWBRAY, **3rd Earl**

1 Augusta Fanny; *m* 8 May 1880 (*divorce* 1904) Cecil Francis William Fane and *d* 10 Feb 1950, leaving issue (*see* WESTMORLAND, E)

2 Sophia Evelyn; *m* 20 April 1888 Maj George Hamilton Heaviside, Inniskilling Dragoons, and *d* 5 Nov 1940. He *d* 27 Nov 1906

3 Adela Charlotte; *m* 19 Feb 1887 Thomas Belhaven Cochrane (*see* DUNDONALD, E) and *dsp* 18 May 1911

4 Hilda Maud; *m* 31 Jan 1891 Charles Fitzroy Ponsonby McNeill, 3rd s of Capt Duncan McNeill, Scots Greys, and was drowned 15 Aug 1904, leaving issue. He *d* 22 Nov 1955

5 Gwendoline Audrey Adeline Brudenell, CBE (1919); *m* 26 June 1895 Brig-Gen Sir Richard Beale Colvin, KCB, TD, of Monkhams, Waltham Abbey, Essex, and *d* 4 Aug 1952, leaving issue. He *d* 17 Jan 1936

The 2nd EARL *d* 27 Jan 1886; his only s,

GEORGE EDWARD JOHN MOWBRAY ROUS, **3rd Earl of Stradbroke**, KCMG (1920), CB (1904), CVO (1906), CBE (1919), VD, TD, JP Suffolk; *b* 19 Nov 1862; *educ* Harrow and Trin Coll Cambridge (BA 1884, MA 1890); Col 1st Norfolk RGA 1888–90, V-Adml Suffolk 1890–1947, ADC to TM EDWARD VII 1902–10 and GEORGE V 1910–30, Col 3rd E Anglian Bde RFA 1909–16, CA and CC (Chm 1911–24) E Suffolk, Col RFA WW I, Col cmdg Kantara Area 1919–20, Govr Victoria 1920–26, Parly Sec Ag and Fisheries 1928–29, Hon Col 660th Heavy AA Regt RA (TA), Chm Suffolk TAA, Pres: Nat Sea Fisheries Protection Assoc, Cncl Nat Artillery Assoc; Pro Grand Master Mark Masons, Provincial Grand Master Suffolk Freemasons, Pro Grand Master E Anglian Mark Masons, Cross Order Saviour Greece, KGStJ, Silver Jubilee Medal 1935, Coronation Medal 1937; *m* 23 July 1898 Helena Violet Alice, DBE (1927), DGStJ (*d* 14 April 1949), only dau of Lt-Gen James Keith Fraser, CMG (*see* 1967 edn FRASER, Bt, of Ledeclune), and *d* 20 Dec 1947, leaving:

1 JOHN ANTHONY ALEXANDER ROUS, **4th Earl of Stradbroke**, JP (Suffolk 1931); *b* 1 April 1903 (HM QUEEN ALEXANDRA stood sponsor); *educ* RNCs Osborne and Dartmouth and Ch Ch Oxford; Suffolk: CC 1931–46, Ld Lt and custos rotulorum 1948–78 (DL 1946–48), CA 1953–64, Alderman 1970; Cdr RN, Hon Col 660 HA Regt RA (TA) 1952–55, Pres TA&VRA E Anglia, V-Pres Assoc Drainage Authorities and Roy Br Legn, Pres Eastern Area Br Legn, chm Deejan Hldgs and Ipswich Bd Eagle Star Insur, Provincial Grand Master Suffolk Freemasons, Dep Grand Master Grand Lodge Mark Master Masons and E Anglia Mark Masons 1967, Grand Master 1973, KStJ; *m* 15 Jan 1929 Barbara (*d*

30 Aug 1977), yr dau of Lord Arthur Hugh Grosvenor (*see* WESTMINSTER, D), and *d* 14 July 1983, leaving:

(1) *Marye Violet Isolde [The Lady Marye Rous, Sacaba Beach, Malaga 29004, Spain]; *b* 16 March 1930

(2) *Penelope Anne [The Lady Penelope Gilbey, White Lion House, Wangford, Suffolk NR34 8RL]; *b* 31 July 1932; *m* 1st 19 June 1950 (*divorce* 1960) Cdr Ian Dudley Stewart Forbes, DSC, RN (*see* FORBES, Bt, of Newe), and has:

  1a *Charles Stewart; *b* 23 Jan 1956; *educ* Westminster, Trin Coll Oxford (BA), RAC Cirencester and Wye Ag Coll

  1a *Catriona; *b* 1 Aug 1951; *m* 18 July 1981 *Michael W C Bradley, s of Malcolm Bradley, of Albany Ho, Highfield, Lymington, Hants

  2a *Caroline Ianthe; *b* 23 Nov 1952; *educ* York U; *m* 11 May 1977 *Katsukisa Sakai, of Tokyo, and has:

    1b *Tyler Christopher Forbes; *b* 9 March 1978

(2) (cont.) Lady Penelope Forbes *m* 2nd 15 May 1961 (*divorce* 1969) John Cator, er son of Lt-Col Henry John Cator, MC (*see* CAYLEY, Bt); *m* 3rd 1984, as his 3rd w, *Anthony James Gilbey (*see* GILBEY, Bt)

2 (WILLIAM) KEITH, 5th Earl

3 George Nathaniel; *b* 5 April 1911; *educ* Harrow, Geelong GS Australia and Trin Coll Cambridge (BA 1932); Maj Life Gds, Trans-Jordan FF 1938–42, Palestine 1936–39 (despatches), WW II; *m* 1 Sept 1949 Joyce, JP (*d* 1985), yst dau of Col Charles Harpur, OBE, JP, of Benhall, Saxmundham, Suffolk, and *d* 9 Sept 1982, leaving:

(1) +Robert Charles, DL (Suffolk 1995) [Robert Rous Esq DL, Dennington Hall, Woodbridge, Suffolk]; *b* 30 July 1953; *educ* Harrow and Trin Coll Cambridge (MA); lay canon St Edmundsbury Cathedral; ARICS; *m* 1976 *Teresa Mary Mercedes, dau of David Keith Ford Heathcote, of Badlingham Manor, Chippenham, Cambs, and has:

  1a +Peter George; *b* 1984

  1a *Laura Frances; *b* 1982

(1) *Georgina Alice; *b* 22 Aug 1951; *educ* Heathfield; *m* 20 Sept 1975 *Charles H W Holloway, er s of A G W Holloway, of Minchinhampton, Glos, and has:

  1a *George Henry Rous; *b* 1983

  2a *Edward Charles; *b* 1986

  1a *Alice Victoria Pendrill; *b* 1978

  2a *Lucinda Rose; *b* 1980

(2) *Veronica Rose; *b* 7 Sept 1958; *educ* Heathfield; *m* 2 Sept 1989 *James Harry Astley Maberly, est s of Lt-Col J E A Maberly, of Zimbabwe, and has:

  1a *Edward George Astley; *b* 1991

  2a *Harry Robert Astley; *b* 1993

(3) *Frances Diana; *b* 13 May 1961; *educ* Heathfield; *m* 1985 *Hon Charles Richard Boscawen, 3rd s of 9th Viscount Falmouth (*qv*), and has issue

4 Peter James Mowbray; *b* 23 Jan 1914; *educ* Melbourne GS, Harrow and RMC Sandhurst; Maj 16th/5th Lancers WW II (Italy Star); *m* 24 June 1942 Elizabeth Alice Mary (*d* 8 Feb 1968), yr dau of Maj Hon Alastair Fraser (*see* LOVAT, L), and *d* 17 May 1997, having had:

(1) *Michael James Mowbray [Michael Rous Esq, 57 Parma Crescent, London SW11 1LU]; *b* 14 Aug 1945; *educ* Elston Hall and St George's Coll Rhodesia; *m* 1989 *Isabelle M B, est dau of François Le Chevallier, of Paris

(2) Peter George Anthony Mowbray; *b* 23 Oct 1948; *d* following an accident 29 Feb 1952

(3) +Simon Roderick [Simon Rous Esq, Burston, Dulverton, Somerset]; *b* 20 Feb 1950; *educ* St Ignatius Coll, St George's Coll Rhodesia and Trin Coll Cambridge (MA); *m* 1978 *Carol A, dau of Robert Dawson, of Bolton, Lancs, and has:

  1a +Oliver Mowbray Abdel Rahman; *b* 1981

  1a *Clare Elizabeth Khalida; *b* 1979

  2a *Rebecca Mary Alice; *b* 1987

  3a *Henrietta Florence; *b* 1988

(4) +(John) Sebastian [Sebastian Rous Esq, Kamusha, Box 25, Mvurwi, Zimbabwe]; *b* 4 Feb 1953; *educ* St George's Coll; *m* 1980 *Valda Louise, dau of Alastair Guy Waterhouse, of Middleton Hall, Youlgrave, Derbys, and has:

  1a +Justin Henry; *b* 1980

  2a +William James; *b* 1984

  1a *Julia Louise; *b* 1982

(5) +Edmund Felix; *b* 12 Oct 1954; *educ* St George's Coll; *m* 1982 *Jane N, er dau of Derek Willshaw, of Sussex, and has:

  1a +Sebastian James; *b* 1985

  1a *Emma Jade; *b* 1982

  2a *Elizabeth Frances; *b* 1988

(6) +Peter Joseph; *b* 3 June 1956; *educ* St George's Coll

(7) +Christopher Hugh [Christopher Rous, PO Box 432, Upperville, VA 22176, USA]; *b* 19 Oct 1958; *educ* St George's Coll; *m* 1987 *Elisabeth Christman, only dau of Dr Stokes Jerome Smith, of Spartanburg, SC, and has:

  1a +Simon Joseph; *b* 1990

  1a *Katherine Elisabeth; *b* 1988

(1) *Petronilla [Mrs John Cockin, 13 The Ferns, Carlton Rd, Tunbridge Wells TN1 2JT]; *b* 28 March 1943; *m* 18 June 1966 *(Thomas) John Peter Cockin, only s of S/Ldr J B Cockin, of Tunbridge Wells, and has had:

  1a *James Francis John; *b* 19 April 1968

  2a *John Joseph; *b* 1970

  3a Charles Hereward John; *b* and *d* 1974

  4a *Michael Hereward John; *b* 1975

  1a *Antonia Patricia Mary [Mrs Nicholas Osborne, 24 Fair Heath, 43 Putney Hill, London SW15]; *b* 10 May 1967; *m* 1993 *Nicholas Edward Osborne

(2) *Helena Sibyl [Mrs Michael Beasley, 83 Beaumont Rd, London W4]; *b* 1 Feb 1947; *m* 1972 *Michael Clive Rashleigh Beasley and has:

  1a *Thomas; *b* 1979

  2a *George; *b* 1983

  1a *Charlotte; *b* 1981

(3) *Elizabeth Anne [Mrs Bruce Powell, Broadhatch House, Bentley, Hants]; *b* 19 Aug 1951; *m* 1977 *Bruce Lewis Hamilton Powell and has:

  1a *Louis Edmund; *b* 1983

  1a *Jemima Anne; *b* 1978

  2a *Camilla (Millicent) Mary Augusta; *b* 1979

  3a *Harriet Elizabeth Maud; *b* 1980

(4) *Philippa Mary Catherine [Mrs Anthony Eyre, Poppy Cottage, Driffield, Glos GL7 5PY]; *b* 19 Dec 1962; *m* 1986 *Anthony John Stratford Eyre, yr s of Raymond John Eyre, of London, and has:

  1a *Edmund Anthony Bobo; *b* 1988

  2a *Giles Peter Dusmet; *b* 1989

  3a *Hew Raymond Bundu; *b* 1991

  4a *Elena Alice; *b* 1993

5 Christopher Simon; *b* 3 Jan 1916; *d* 22 Feb 1925

1 Pleasance Elizabeth; *b* 11 May 1899; *m* 12 May 1923 Owen McKenna, s of Patrick McKenna, of Shotts, Lanarks, and has:

(1) *Wilfrid Patrick John; *b* 30 March 1924; *m* 2 Aug 1951 *Moira Gowan, only dau of Hugh McFadden, and has:

  1a *Vivyan John Ian; *b* 18 May 1952

  1a *Sara Elizabeth Anne; *b* 30 April 1954

  2a *Marye Patricia; *b* 10 Aug 1956

  3a *Philippa Jane; *b* 11 May 1959

  4a *Adrienne Claire; *b* 14 April 1965

(1) *Maureen Sophia; *b* 11 March 1927

2 (Catherine) Charlotte, OBE (1972); *b* 5 May 1900; Sqdn Offr WAAF, BRCS Relief Org Italy WW II; *d* 19 Sept 1983

3 (Betty) Helena Joanna; *b* 24 April 1901; *m* 17 Sept 1930 Maj Douglas Beresford-Ash (*see* WATERFORD, M) and *d* 4 Nov 1969, leaving issue

The 4th EARL's bro,

 (WILLIAM) KEITH ROUS, **5th Earl of Stradbroke**; *b* 10 March 1907; *educ* Harrow and Geelong GS Australia; T/Lt RNVR, Lt RN, WW II; *m* 1st 7 Aug 1935 (*divorce* 1940) Pamela Catherine Mabell (*d* 15 Sept 1972), only dau of Capt Hon Edward Kay-Shuttleworth (*see* SHUTTLEWORTH, B), and had:

1 (ROBERT) KEITH ROUS, **6th and present Earl of Stradbroke**

2 +William Edward (Sir), KCB (1992), OBE (1980, MBE 1974) [Lt-Gen The Hon Sir William Rous KCB OBE, RHQ Coldstream Gds, Wellington Barracks, London SW1E 6HQ]; *b* 23 Feb 1939; *educ* Harrow and RMA Sandhurst; 2nd Lt Coldstream Gds 1959, cmded 2nd Bn 1979–81 and 1st Inf Bde 1983–84, Dir PR (Army) 1985–87, GOC 4 Armoured Div 1987–89, Comdt Staff Coll 1989–91, Mil Sec 1991–94, QMG and memb Army Bd 1994–96, 27th Col Coldstream Gds 1994; chm: Kingston Hosp NHS Tst 1996–, Br Greyhound Racing Bd 1998–; managing tstee BLESMA 1994–; *m* 20 June 1970 *Judith Rosemary, only child of Maj Jocelyn Arthur Persse, of Roxborough, Co Galway, and has:

  (1) +James Anthony Edward; *b* 22 Dec 1972

  (2) +Richard William Jocelyn; *b* 9 Nov 1975

The **5th Earl** *m* 2nd 19 July 1943 *(April) Mary [The Hon Mrs Keith Rous, Clovelly Court, Bideford, N Devon EX39 5SZ] (prefers former style), est dau of Brig-Gen Hon Arthur Asquith, DSO (*see* OXFORD AND ASQUITH, E), and *d* 18 July 1983 (four days after his er bro), having had by her:

3 +John [The Hon John Rous, Clovelly Court, Bideford, Devon EX39 5SZ; 94 Oakley St, London SW3 5NR]; *b* 31 July 1950; *educ* Gordonstoun and U of Kent; *m* 1984 *Zeenat, dau of Dr K Hameed, of Lucknow, and has:

  (1) *Maha Magdalene; *b* 18 Oct 1987

  (2) *Zoya Constance; *b* 23 Nov 1990

1 *(Christine) Caroline Catherine [The Lady Caroline Armstrong, Dalby, Terrington, N Yorks]; *b* 27 April 1946; *educ* Cranborne Chase, Zambia U and London U (BSc, PGCE, Dip Ed); *m* 4 Feb 1978 John Francis Burnett Armstrong (*d* 1992), s of George Burnett Armstrong, MC, and has:

  (1) *Henry Francis Arthur Rous; *b* 19 Oct 1978

  (2) *John George William Rous; *b* 1982

  (1) *Catherine Julia Cecily; *b* 1986

2 *Henrietta Elizabeth [The Lady Henrietta Rous, Clovelly Court, Bideford, N Devon; 6 Cadogan Mansions, Sloane Sq, London SW1]; *b* 17 Nov 1947; jnlst

3 Mary Anne; *b* 15 March 1949; *d* 5 Nov 1950

4 *Virginia [The Lady Virginia Gibbs, The Home Farm, Barrow Gurney, Bristol]; *b* 13 June 1950; *educ* Bristol U (BSc); *m* 12 Oct 1974 *Anthony William Hew Gibbs (*see* ALDENHAM and HUNSDON OF HUNSDON, B) and has issue

STRAFFORD

Arms: Quarterly, sa. and arg., in the 1st quarter a lion rampant of the second; over all in bend sinister a representation of the colours of the 31st Regt. **Crests:** 1 Out of a mural crown an arm embowed, grasping the colours of the 31st Regt of Foot, pendant from the wrist by a riband the gold cross awarded the 1st Earl for gallantry, all ppr., and on an escroll the word 'Mouguerre', 2 An heraldic antelope statant erm., attired or. **Supporters:** Dexter, a heraldic antelope erm., attired or; sinister, a lion or. **Motto:** *Tuebor* ('I will defend').
Creation: B. (UK) 12 May 1835, E. and V. (UK) 18 Sept 1847.

THE 8TH EARL OF STRAFFORD, *Viscount Enfield,* of Enfield, Co Middx, and **Baron Strafford of Harmondsworth,** Co Middx (Thomas Edmund Byng) [The Rt Hon The Earl of Strafford, Apple Tree Cottage, Easton, Hants SO21 1EF]; *b* 26 Sept 1936; *s f* 1984; *educ* Eton and Clare Coll Cambridge; late Lt Roy Sussex Regt; *m* 1st 2 Aug 1963 (*divorce* 1980) Jennifer Mary Denise, er dau of William Morrison May, PC, MP, FCA, of Mertoun Hall, Holywood, Co Down, and has:

1 +WILLIAM ROBERT, *Viscount Enfield; b* 10 May 1964; *educ* Winchester and Durham U; *m* 1994 *Karen Elizabeth, er dau of Graham Lord, of Leyland, Lancs, and has:

> (1) *Saskia Ruth Jessica; *b* 15 Oct 1996

2 +James Edmund; *b* 27 June 1969; *educ* Winchester and Edinburgh U; *m* 1994 *Whitney Osborn, er dau of Charles McVeigh III, of Donhead Hall, Shaftesbury, Dorset, and has:

> (1) *Leo Walter; *b* 20 March 1998
> (1) *Marley McVeigh; *b* 9 Sept 1996

1 *Georgia Mary Caroline; *b* 6 Sept 1965 *educ* Westonbirt and Centl Sch of Drama; *m* 1990 (*divorce* 1995) Daniel S Chadwick, yr s of Lynn Chadwick, of Lypiatt, Glos, and has:

> (1) *Tiger Rose; *b* 15 Oct 1990

2 *(Harriet Clare) Tara; *b* 6 April 1967; *educ* Westonbirt; *m* 1994 *T Christopher Wilbur, s of Richard Wilbur, of Hawaii, and Mrs Richard Anger, of California, and has:

> (1) *Grace Edith Lilivokalini; *b* 15 Feb 1995

The 8th EARL *m* 2nd 30 May 1981 *Julia Mary (Judy), yr dau of Sir Dennis Pilcher, CBE, of Pulborough, W Sussex, and formerly w of Derek Nicholas Howard

Strafford, Earldom of, previous creations. Sir Thomas Wentworth, 2nd Bt, of Wentworth Woodhouse, Yorks, was created Earl of Strafford in January 1639/40. He had started his public career as an opponent of the Court, delivering speeches while an MP in the 1620s on behalf of popular freedom and being jailed in the Marshalsea in 1627 for declining to pay a forced loan CHARLES I had tried to levy. The next year he underwent a dramatic conversion to the Court's point of view and was ennobled, initially as a Baron then as a Viscount. Thereafter he was Lord President of the Council of the North and Lord Deputy of Ireland.

The policy he called 'thorough' was in practice simply firm administration of CHARLES I's policies, but the unpopularity it brought him led to his impeachment by Parliament. He was thrown to the wolves by CHARLES I, despite the latter's pledge to stand by him, and beheaded in 1641, when his titles were forfeited by reason of his attainder. They were revived for his son William a little over six months later and after the Restoration the attainder was reversed. On William's death without issue in 1695 the titles all expired bar the Barony of Raby, which passed to a cousin, Thomas Wentworth.

Thomas was made Earl of Strafford of the third creation in 1711. His promotion arose from his prominence as a diplomat — he was one of the British plenipotentiaries negotiating the Treaty of Utrecht that ended the War of Spanish Succession. Like his predecessor he faced impeachment, this time by the first Parliament of GEORGE I's reign, and not for a policy of 'thorough' but for his part in the Treaty, which by 1715 was highly unpopular. The storm abated, however. He almost certainly professed Jacobite sympathies in secret since the titular James III created him Duke of Strafford in the Jacobite peerage in January 1721/2. The Earldom passed first to his son then to a cousin and expired on the latter's death in 1799. The 3rd and last Earl of Strafford of the 1711 creation attempted to

leave all his property (including his entailed Yorkshire estates) to his nephew-in-law George Byng (*see below*), but unwisely drafted the will himself. The ensuing litigation (Howe *v* Dartmouth) dragged on for years and went all the way up to the House of Lords before being settled in 1847, when it was held that George Byng could only inherit the 3rd Earl's personal property, chattels and house in St James's Square.

Lineage: The 1st VISCOUNT TORRINGTON (*qv*) had a 3rd s:

ROBERT BYNG; *bapt* 27 Nov 1703; Paymaster Navy, Govr Barbados; *m* 19 Dec 1734 Elizabeth (*bur* 16 Sept 1786), dau and coheir of Jonathan Forward, contractor of transport for the Admlty, and was *bur* 7 Oct 1740, leaving, with two yr sons (Robert, *d* Black Hole of Calcutta 20 June 1756; John, *b* 1739, *bur* 8 July 1764):

GEORGE BYNG, of Wrotham Park, Middx; *b* 1735; MP Middx; *m* 5 March 1761 Anne (*d* 1806), dau of William Conolly, PC, of Castletown, Co Kildare, by Anne, est dau of 2nd Earl of Strafford of the 1711 *cr* (*see above*), and *d* 27 Oct 1789, having had, with three er sons (George, of Wrotham Park, *b* 17 May 1764, MP Middx 56 years (Father H of C), *m* Harriet, dau of Sir William Montgomery, 1st Bt (*see* 1831 edn), and *dsp* 10 Jan 1847; William, *b* 5 Oct 1770, Maj 92nd Foot, *k* in a duel in Guernsey 1795; Robert, *b* 21 Dec 1773, *d* 1829) and three daus (Anne Elizabeth, *d* 1847; Caroline; Frances, *d* 1851):

JOHN BYNG, **1st Earl of Strafford,** so *cr* 18 Sept 1847, as also VISCOUNT ENFIELD, Co Middx, and earlier 12 May 1835 BARON STRAFFORD OF HARMONDSWORTH, Co Middx (all UK), GCB (1831), KCB 1815), GCH (1826), PC (I 1828); *b* 1772; *educ* Westminster; Ensign 33rd Foot 30 Sept 1793, Lt 1 Dec 1793, Capt 1794, served Flanders 1793–95, ADC to Gen Vyse Ireland (helped suppress 1798 Uprising), Maj 60th Foot 1799, Lt-Col 29th Foot 1800, Capt and Lt-Col 3rd Foot Gds 1804, Col 1810, Brig-Gen 1811, Maj-Gen 1813, served Peninsular War 1811–14, cmded 2nd Gds Bde Waterloo 1815, Maj-Gen Staff (N Dist) 1816–28, Col 2nd W India Regt 1822–28, 29th Foot 1828–50 and Coldstream Gds 1850–60, Lt-Gen 1825, C-in-C Ireland 1828–31, MP (Whig) Poole 1831–35, Govr Londonderry and Culmore 1832–60, FM 1855, Kt 2nd Cl St Vladimir Russia 1815, Kt Maria Theresa Austria 1815, twice thanked by Parl for servs; *m* 1st 14 June 1804 Mary Stevens (*d* 17 June 1806), est dau and coheir of Peter Mackenzie, of Grove Ho, Twickenham, Middx, and had:

1 GEORGE STEVENS, **2nd Earl**

The **1st Earl** *m* 2nd 9 May 1808 Marianne (*d* 26 Oct 1845), 2nd dau of Sir Walter James JAMES formerly HEAD, 1st Bt, and by her had:

2 William Frederick; Capt 13th Light Dragoons; *m* 17 Aug 1861 Flora Fox (*d* 18 Feb 1919), only dau of Maj Quintus Vivian, of Wellingborough, Northants, and *d* 12 Feb 1877, leaving:

> (1) Violet; *m* 10 April 1883 Maj Edmund Distin Maddick, CBE, FRCS, RAF, late RN, Chev Order Crown Italy, and *d* 1929, leaving issue. He *d* 6 July 1939

1 Harriet Frances; *m* 14 June 1828 Capt Charles Ramsden, 60th Regt, 4th s of Sir John Ramsden, 4th Bt (*qv*), and *d* 5 Nov 1873

2 Frances; *m* 24 Sept 1844 Henry Tufnell, MP, of Tufnell Park, and *d* 4 June 1846

3 Caroline Frances; *m* 18 Aug 1835 Sir Walter George Stirling, 2nd Bt (*see* 1934 edn), and *d* 27 May 1898. He *d* 1 Dec 1888

The 1st EARL *d* 3 June 1860; his er s,

GEORGE STEVENS BYNG, **2nd Earl of Strafford,** PC (1835); *b* 8 June 1806; *educ* Sandhurst; 2nd Lt 29th Foot, Lt 1825, Capt Rifle Bde 1826 and 47th Foot 1830, ret 1835, MP (Whig) Milborne Port 1830–32, Chatham 1834–35 and 1837–52 and Poole 1835–37, Comptroller Household to Ld Lt Ireland 1831–32, a Ld Treasury June–Nov 1834, Comptroller Household 1835–41, Lt-Col Roy W Middx Militia 1837 (Col 1844–49), Treas Household June–Sept 1841, Jt Sec India Bd Control 1846–47, called up to Ho Lds *vp* in f's Barony 8 April 1853, Hon Lt RNR 1870, FRS 1841; *m* 1st 7 March 1829 Lady Agnes Paget (*d* 9 Oct 1845), 5th dau of 1st Marquess of Anglesey (*qv*), and had:

1 GEORGE HENRY CHARLES BYNG, **3rd Earl of Strafford;** *b* 22 Feb 1830; *educ* Eton and Ch Ch Oxford (BA 1852, MA 1854); MP (Lib) Tavistock 1852–57 and Middx 1857–74, Lt-Col 2nd Middx Militia 1853–71 (Hon Col 1871–78), Lt-Col 17th Middx Rifle Vols 1860–62 (Hon Col 1862), Sec Poor Law Bd 1865–66, U-Sec For Affrs 1871–74, called up to Ho Lds *vp* in f's Barony 26 Feb 1847, a Ld in Waiting May–Sept 1880, U-Sec India 1880–83, 1st Civ Serv Commr 1880–88, Ld Lt Middx 1884–98; *m* 25 July 1854 Alice Harriet Frederica (*d* 22 Dec 1928), est dau of 1st Earl of Ellesmere (*see* SUTHERLAND, D), and *dsp* 28 March 1898

2 HENRY WILLIAM JOHN BYNG, **4th Earl of Strafford,** KCVO (1897), CB (1895); *b* 21 Aug 1831; *educ* Eton; Page Hon 1840–47, Groom-in-Waiting 1872–74 and Equerry in Ordinary 1874–99 to HM QUEEN VICTORIA, Lt-Col Coldstream Gds 1863, Hon Col 7th Bn KRRC; *m* 1st 15 Oct 1863 Henrietta (*d* 11 Jan 1880), est dau of HE Count Christian Danneskiold Samsoe, and had:

> (1) George Albert Edward Alexander; *b* 1 April 1867; Page-of-Honour to HM QUEEN VICTORIA, Lt 7th Bn KRRC, ADC to Govr Cape Good Hope; *d* unm (drowned en route between Naples and Gibraltar) 4 April 1893
> (2) John George Thomas Wentworth; *b* 8 March 1870; Attaché Paris; *d* unm 6 Jan 1894
> (1) Mary Elizabeth Agnes; Maid of Honour in Ordinary to HM QUEEN VICTORIA; *m* 23 June 1898 Count de Mauny Talvande, of Domaine du Bourg, Pontballain, Sarthe, France, and *d* 18 Feb 1946, leaving issue. He *d* Nov 1941
> (2) Amy Frederica Alice; Order Mercy; *m* 3 Nov 1894 4th Earl of Normanton (*qv*) and *d* 29 March 1961, leaving issue

2 (cont.) The **4th Earl** *m* 2nd 6 Dec 1898 Cora (*m* 3rd 9 Dec 1903 Martyn Thomas Kennard (*d* 12 May 1920) and *d* 11 Oct 1932), widow of Samuel Colgate, of Uplands, New Hamburg-on-Hudson, USA, and *dspms* 16 May 1899, *k* by a train at Potter's Bar, Middx

3 FRANCIS EDMUND CECIL, **5th Earl**

1 Agnes Mary Georgiana; *m* 30 Dec 1858 2nd Baron Hylton (*qv*) and *d* 8 April 1878, leaving issue

2 Mary Caroline Charlotte; *b* 1838; *m* 22 July 1862 Richard Arkwright, DL, MP Leominster, and *d* 13 Dec 1933. He *d* 14 Nov 1918

3 Victoria Alexandrina Anna Maria (HM QUEEN VICTORIA stood sponsor); *m* 18 June 1870 Arthur Clarges Loraine Fuller, s of George Arthur Fuller, of The Rookery, Dorking, and *dsp* 1 Feb 1899

The **2nd Earl** m 2nd 16 March 1848 Harriet Elizabeth (d 26 June 1892), yr dau of 1st Baron Chesham (qv), and d 29 Oct 1886, leaving by her:

4 Charles Cavendish George, JP (Cornwall, Devon and Hants); b 9 Feb 1849; Col 1st Life Gds, Nile Expdn 1884–85 (despatches, brevet); d unm 16 May 1918

5 Alfred John George; b 4 May 1851; Capt 7th Hus, ADC to Govr-Gen Canada; m 10 Jan 1887 Lady Winifred Anne Henrietta Christina Herbert (m 2nd 4th March 1890 1st and last Baron Burghclere (d 6 May 1921) and d 28 Sept 1933, leaving issue), dau of 4th Earl of Carnarvon (qv), and dsp 8 Nov 1887

6 Lionel Francis George; b 26 Sept 1858; Maj RHG Boer War 1899–1900; m 26 July 1902 Lady Eleanor Mabel Howard (m 2nd 11 Oct 1922 Henry Ernest Atkinson (d 3 Oct 1926), resumed maiden name and d 9 March 1945), est s of Rev Francis Home Atkinson, of Morland Hall, Penrith, dau of 18th Earl of Suffolk and (11th Earl of) Berkshire (qv), and d 27 May 1915, leaving:

    (1) (Eleanor) Myrtle Howard; b 6 Dec 1908; d March 1997

7 JULIAN HEDWORTH GEORGE BYNG, 1st and last VISCOUNT BYNG OF VIMY, so cr 12 Jan 1928, so also earlier 7 Oct 1919 (with thanks of Parl and £30,000 [over £540,000 in late-1990s terms]) BARON BYNG OF VIMY, of Thorpe-le-Soken, Co Essex (both UK), GCB (1919, KCB 1916, CB 1906), GCMG (1921, KCMG 1915), MVO (1902); b 11 Sept 1862; educ Eton and RMC Sandhurst; joined 10th Roy Hus 1883, Sudan Expdn 1884, Capt 1889, DAAG Aldershot 1897–99, cmded S African Light Horse Boer War 1900–01, Brevet Lt-Col 1900, Column Cdr 1901–02 (despatches), Brevet Col 1902, cmded 10th Roy Hus 1902–04, Cmdt Cav Sch 1904–05, cmded 2nd Cav Bde E Cmd 1905–07 and 1st Cav Bde Aldershot Cmd 1907–09, Maj-Gen 1909, GOC E Anglian Div 1910–12, GOC Br Troops Egypt 1912–14, WW I: cmded 3rd Cav Div 1914–15, Cav Corps 1915, Lt-Gen 1915, cmded 9th Army Corps Dardanelles 1915–16, 7th Army Corps Feb-April 1916, Canadian Expdny Force May 1916–June 1917, Gen 1917, Cdr 3rd Army 1917–19, Govr-Gen Canada 1921–26, Ch Commr Met Police 1928–31, FM 1932, V-Pres Roy Empire Soc, memb Clonial Inst, Hon Col 5th Bn Essex Regt and Suffolk Heavy Bde, RA (TA), LLD Toronto U, LLB Alberta U, Canada, Hon LLD Cantab, Hon DCL Oxon, KGStJ; m 30 April 1902 Marie Evelyn, DGStJ (d 20 June 1949), only child of Hon Sir Richard Charles Moreton, KCVO (see DUCIE, E), and dsp 6 June 1935, when his titles expired

4 Susan Catherine Harriet, OBE (1920), JP Bucks; OStJ; m 23 Dec 1905 Col Thomas Trueman, IA, of White Hill Ho, Chesham, Bucks, and d 7 Feb 1936. He d 1916

5 Elizabeth Henrietta Alice; d 30 Aug 1920

6 Margaret Florence Lucy; m 11 June 1890 Hon John Richard de Clare Boscawen, s of 6th Viscount Falmouth (qv), and d 6 March 1945, leaving issue

The 4th EARL's bro,

Rev FRANCIS EDMUND CECIL BYNG, **5th Earl of Strafford**; b 15 Jan 1835; educ Eton and Ch Ch Oxford (MA); Deacon 1858, Priest 1859, Curate Prestwich 1858–59, Rector Little Casterton, Rutland, 1859–62, Perpetual Curate Holy Trin Twickenham 1862–67, Chaplain Hampton Court Palace 1867, Vicar St Peter's Cranley Gdns 1867–69, Hon Chaplain 1867–72 and Chaplain-in-Ordinary 1872–79 to HM QUEEN VICTORIA and to Speaker H of C 1874–89; m 1st 8 June 1859 Florence Louisa (d 14 Feb 1862), dau of Sir William Miles, 1st Bt (qv), and had:

1 Arthur George; b 25 April 1860; d 17 Jan 1861

2 EDMUND HENRY BYNG **6th Earl of Strafford**, JP, DL Middx; b 27 Jan 1862; educ Eton; CA Middx 1901–46 and Herts 1901–48, AMICE; m 17 Dec 1894 Mary Elizabeth (d 2 Oct 1951), sis of 1st and last Baron Colebrooke (see 1939 edn), and d 24 Dec 1951, leaving:

    (1) (Florence) Elizabeth Mary Alice; b 12 Feb 1897; m 26 Jan 1928 (divorce 1931, resumed maiden name April 1952) Michael William Lafone, 19th Hus, only s of Maj Edgar Mortimore Lafone, OBE, and d 14 Jan 1987, leaving:

        1a *Julian Michael Edmund LAFONE later BYNG (April 1952, took by roy licence 5 Sept 1969 the Byng arms under terms of will of the **6th Earl**) [Julian Byng Esq, Wrotham Park, Barnet, Herts EN5 4SB]; b 20 Oct 1928; educ Eton, Lausanne U and King's Coll Cambridge; m 28 Oct 1960 *Eve Finola, dau of Capt Michael St Maur Wellesley-Wesley, and has:

            1b *Robert Michael Julian Wentworth; b 19 June 1962; educ Millfield

            2b *Patrick James John Wentworth; b 30 July 1965; educ Eton and Buckingham U; m 21 July 1995 *Anna, dau of Sir Kenneth Scott, KCVO, CMG

            3b *Thomas Francis Edmund Wentworth; b 7 Aug 1970; educ Eton and Brown U, RI

            1b *Georgiana Margaret Elizabeth; b 31 March 1964; m 16 April 1988 *Piers Alastair Carlos Monckton (see GALWAY, V) and has had:

                1c *Oliver George Carlos; b 29 Aug 1993

                1c Isobel Mary Elizabeth; b 19 Dec 1989; d 16 Dec 1991

                2c *Emily Louise; b 29 Aug 1991

    (2) Mary Millicent Rachel; b 22 Feb 1899; m 20 Oct 1927 Maj-Gen Robert Francis Naylor, CB, CBE, DSO, MC, Roy Signals, only surv s of Charles Topham Naylor, of Barton End Ho, Nailsworth, and had issue. He d 23 Dec 1971

The 5th Earl m 2nd 4 Aug 1866 Emily Georgina (d 27 Oct 1929), est dau of Adml Lord Frederic Kerr (see LOTHIAN, M), and d 18 Jan 1918, having by her had:

3 Algernon Kerr Hubert; b 5 Feb; d 28 Dec 1872

4 Ivo Francis, JP Northumberland; b 20 July 1874; educ Radley; m 12 March 1901 Agnes Constance (d 10 Nov 1950), dau of S Smith Travers, of Hobart, Tasmania, and d 11 June 1949, having had:

    (1) George Arthur Francis; b 5 April 1903; Naval Cadet; d Osborne 14 March 1917

    (2) ROBERT CECIL, **7th Earl**

    (1) Agnes Perpetua; b 7 March 1908; d unm 3 June 1936

5 Antony Schomberg, DSO (1918); b 31 March 1876; Lt-Col and W/Cdr RAF WW I (despatches, Legn Hon); m 2 July 1902 Lucy Margaret (d 13 Oct 1940), yst dau of Edward Howorth Greenly, of Titley Court, Herefs, and d 8 April 1934, leaving:

    (1) William Humphrey Schomberg; b 31 May 1906; educ Radley; T/Maj Intell Corps WW II (despatches); m 7 Dec 1935 Mona (d 1964), est dau of Capt Oswald Charles Merriman Barry, DSO, RN

    (1) Gillian Sarah b 15 July 1904; m 28 Oct 1924 Thomas Theodore Barnard, MC, PhD, er s of Thomas Henry Barnard, JP, of Kempston, Beds, and d 29 May 1961, leaving issue

1 Beatrice Agnes; d young 17 March 1868

2 Rachel Theodora; d unm 25 Sept 1932

3 Irene Hilare; d unm 24 March 1908

4 Anne Dorothy Frederica; m 24 Sept 1903 Capt James Harold Cuthbert, DSO, Scots Gds (ka 27 Sept 1915), of Beaufont Castle, Northumberland, and dsp 31 Jan 1907

5 (Hester) Joan, DBE (1927); Ldy-in-Waiting to HRH THE PRINCESS ROYAL 1918–22, Extra Ldy-in-Waiting 1922, Ldy-in-Waiting and Ch Staff to TRH THE DUKE AND DUCHESS OF YORK World Tour 1927; m 1st 10 June 1913 Capt Hon Andrew Edward Somerset Mulholland (ka 1 Nov 1914), est s of 2nd Baron Dunleath (qv), and had issue; m 2nd 27 Nov 1922 10th Earl of Cavan (qv) and d 31 Aug 1976, having had further issue

Then 6th EARL's n,

ROBERT CECIL BYNG, **7th Earl of Strafford**; b 20 July 1907; educ RNC Dartmouth and Clare Coll Cambridge (BA 1931, MA 1940); m 1st 1 Jan 1934 (divorce 1947) Maria Magdalena Elizabeth [Mrs James Royds, Orchard Close, Twyford, Hants] (m 2nd, as his 2nd w, James Henry Royds (d 1997); see PERTH, E), dau of Henry Cloete, CMG, of Alphen, Cape Town; m 2nd 19 June 1948 Clara Evelyn (d 1985), dau of Sir Nusserwanjee Nowrosjee Wadia, KBE, CIE, of Bombay, and d 4 May 1984, leaving by his 1st w:

1 THOMAS EDMUND BYNG, **8th and present Earl of Strafford**

2 +Julian Francis; b 3 May 1938; educ Eton; 2nd Lt KRRC, attd Ghana Mil Forces, Capt Queen's Roy Rifles (TA); m 1st 10 Sept 1966 (divorce 1983) Ingela Brita, dau of Axel Berglund, of Stockholm; m 2nd 18 Feb 1984 *Mrs Prudence Mary Kent, dau of Albert Edward Delany, of Qld, Australia, and by his 1st w has:

    (1) +Francis Gustaf; b 11 Nov 1968; educ Eton and UEA

    (2) +(George Michael) Alexander; b 11 Sept 1973; educ Eton and Warwick U

STRANG

Creation: B. (UK) 16 Jan 1954.

THE 2ND BARON STRANG, of Stonesfield, Co Oxford (Colin Strang) [The Rt Hon The Lord Strang, Stansfield Cottage West, Hole Bottom, Todmorden, W Yorks OL14 8DD]; b 12 June 1922; s f 1978; educ Merchant Taylors' and St John's Coll Oxford (MA, BPhil); Essex Yeo WW II, philosophy lecturer Queen's U Belfast 1951–53 and King's Coll Newcastle 1953, Prof Philosophy U of Newcastle 1975–82, Dean Faculty of Arts 1976–79, ret 1982; m 1st 3 July 1948 (divorce 1955) Patricia Marie, dau of Meiert Charles Avis, of Johannesburg; m 2nd 21 April 1955 Barbara Mary Hope (d 12 April 1982), Prof English Language Newcastle U, dau of Frederick Albert Carr, of Wimbledon; m 3rd 1984 *Mary Shewell, dau of Richard Miles, of Sheffield, and by his 2nd w has:

1 *Caroline Jane; b 30 June 1957; educ Westfield Sch, Newcastle U (BSc) and Northumberland U (MSc); m 8 April 1978 *Paul William Miller, s of Christopher Miller, of Ashington, Northumberland, and has:

    (1) *James William; b 15 Feb 1985

    (2) *Daniel John; b 16 Jan 1987

Lineage: CHRISTOPHER STRANG, of Lickprivick, E Kilbride; tenant farmer; possibly f of:

JAMES STRANG, of Craighall, E Kilbride, and Shawton, Glassford, Lanarks; farmer; m c 1780 Janet Baird and had, with three er sons (Christopher, b 11 April 1782, d in infancy; Christopher, of Picketlaw, Carmunnock, b 22 Feb 1786, farmer, m 12 March 1809 Lilias Wilson, of E Kilbride, and d 16 Dec 1861, leaving issue; George, of Crosslees, Eaglesham, Renfrewshire, b 2 May 1788, farmer, m April 1822 Ann Muir, of Eaglesham, and had issue) and two daus (Helen, b 24 March 1784, m William Shearer, farmer, of Highflatt, E Kilbride, and d 22 Feb 1860, leaving issue; Ann, b c 1800, m Allan Lindsay, of E High Craigs, Eaglesham, and d 27 Nov 1862, leaving issue):

JAMES STRANG, of Bonnyton, Eaglesham; b 22 March 1790; farmer; m 14 April 1818 Elizabeth (b 20 Oct 1799), dau of William Jamieson, farmer, of Netherton, Eaglesham, by Margaret Martinholm, and d 7 Dec 1860, leaving:

1 James, of Shaw, Newton Mearns, Renfrewshire, farmer; b 28 March 1820; m 14 July 1848 Ann Craig (b 1825), and had, with a yr s (William) and eight daus (Agnes, m — Carswell and had issue; Elizabeth, m John Morrison and had issue; Anne; Janet, m James Lambie and had issue; Jane; Margaret; Ellen; Marion):

    (1) James; m — Osborne, and had issue, three daus

2 WILLIAM

3 Christopher, of Redbog, Torrance, Dunbartonshire; b 5 Sept 1826; farmer; m 23 June 1854 Elizabeth Brown, of Carmunnock, and had:

    (1) James; m 1st Elizabeth Strang (see below) and had:

        1a May; m Frank Baumgartner and had issue

        2a Elizabeth; m David Strang (see below) and had:

    (1) (cont.) James Strang m 2nd Kathleen Bush and by her had:

        1a Christopher; m 24 Oct 1940 *Margaret Ann, dau of Thomas William Rees, and d 20 Dec 1965, leaving:

            1b *Michael James; b 24 Oct 1942; m 21 June 1963 *Janet Ann Frances Renouf and has:

                1c *Ruth Jane; b 25 June 1964

                2c *Rachael Anne; b 17 Aug 1966

        2a *Lionel; m *Nancy Wild and has:

            1b *James

            1b *Jennifer

            2b *Janet

            3b *Sally

3a *Gordon William; FCA; *m* 10 Sept 1949 *Elizabeth Piercy, er dau of Sir Dallas Bernard, 1st Bt (*qv*), and has:

 1b *Richard

 2b *Andrew

 3b *Malcolm

 1b *Caroline; *b* 12 Oct 1963

(2) Matthew; *m* Margaret Wallace and had:

 1a *James

 1a *Margaret

 2a *Elizabeth

 3a *Jessie

(1) Mary; *m* Joseph Morrison

4 John, of Crossvegate, Milngavie, Dunbartonshire, and Cardington, Beds; farmer; *m* Mary White and had, with a s (James), an est dau (Jessie) and three yst daus (Mary; Margaret; Ellen, *m* James Buchanan):

(1) Elizabeth; *m* her cousin James Strang (*see above*) and had issue

1 Janet; *b* 10 May 1828; *m* William Steven, farmer, of Mid Borland, Eaglesham, and had issue

2 Margaret; *b* 9 July 1831; *m* James Craig, farmer, of Floors, Eaglesham, and had issue

3 Elizabeth; *m* John McGregor, of Helensburgh, and had issue

4 Ellen; *m* John Johnston, farmer, of Chapelside, E Kilbride, and had issue

The 2nd s,

WILLIAM STRANG, of Bowhouse, Carmunnock; *b* 3 Aug 1822; farmer; *m* 7 Feb 1861 Jessie (*d* 29 May 1884 aged 42), dau of Robert Gibb, of Glebe St, Glasgow, and *d* 4 Jan 1906, having had, with a yr s (Robert, *d* young) and a dau (Jessie Pender, *b* 1880, *m* 16 Aug 1915 Dr Gavin Brown, of Hull, and *d* 21 March 1966, having had issue (*d* in infancy)):

JAMES STRANG, of Rainham Lodge, Upminster, Essex, Ham Farm, Beckenham, Kent, and Wickcroft, Theale, Berks; *b* 19 July 1864; *educ* Glasgow Acad; farmer; *m* 16 March 1892 Margaret (*b* 2 July 1870; *d* 6 Jan 1957), dau of William Steven, farmer, of Temples, Eaglesham, and *d* 7 Jan 1951, having had:

1 WILLIAM (Sir), **1st Baron**

2 James; *d* in infancy

3 John; *b* 4 Dec 1895; *educ* Palmer's Sch Grays, Essex; Capt 9th Black Watch WW I; *ka* 1918

4 James; *b* 11 Sept 1897; *educ* Palmer's Sch Grays and E Anglian Inst Ag; farmer and auctioneer; *m* 11 Sept 1924 Edna Kathleen, dau of Ernest Kirkman, of Hornchurch, Essex, and *d* 26 Nov 1956, leaving:

(1) *John Kirkman; *b* 19 Oct 1926; *educ* St Bartholomew's Sch Newbury and Reading U (BSc Ag); farmer; *m* 17 Dec 1955 *Elizabeth Mary, dau of Arthur Jeffery, and has:

 1a *Simon James; *b* 2 Nov 1961

 1a *Margaret Jane; *b* 1956

 2a *Clare Gillian; *b* 30 Aug 1958

(1) *Maureen; *b* 5 May 1931; *educ* Kendrick Sch, Reading; *m* 20 June 1959 *John Michael Heyes Dewhurst, s of John Dewhurst, of Preston, Lancs, and adopted:

 *Andrew John; *b* 22 Feb 1964

 *Matthew James; *b* 29 Jan 1966

 *Sarah Noelle; *b* 22 Oct 1968

5 David Steven, MBE (1954); *b* 24 May 1900; *educ* Palmer's Sch Grays; *m* 14 July 1927 Elizabeth (*d* Sept 1968), dau of James Strang, of Home Farm, Laleham, Middx (*see above*), and had:

(1) *Peter David; *b* 9 July 1928; *educ* Leighton Park and Northampton Inst Ag, Moulton; farmer; *m* 3 Nov 1954 *Una Margaret Baxter and has:

 1a *Nigel David Stephen; *b* 30 July 1955

 1a *Alison Una; *b* July 1958

(2) Gavin John; *d* 1953

6 Robert; *b* 30 Sept 1901; *educ* Whitgift Sch and Edinburgh U (MB, ChB 1925, ChM 1946, FRCS 1928); FRCS Eng 1935, surgn, Lt-Col RAMC, served WW II 1939–45 (despatches), Offr of Order of Orange-Nassau; *m* 30 Dec 1933 Dorothy (*d* 26 Dec 1967), dau of Robert Camm, of Collie, W Australia, and has:

(1) *John Robert; *b* April 1936; *educ* Merchant Taylor's and St John's Coll Oxford (BA 1960); *m* 19 May 1962 *Jennifer Katherine Mary, dau of William Penrose Nash, of Amersham, Bucks

(1) Joan Margaret; *b* 24 Sept 1934; *educ* Godolphin Sch, Salisbury; *m* 23 March 1963 Thomas Israel Newman, BSc, AInstP, s of David Neumann, of Nuremberg, Germany, and *dsp* 16 April 1968. He *d* Aug 1968

(2) Susan Clare; *b* 12 June 1939; *educ* Godolphin Sch, Salisbury; SRN; *m* 8 June 1963 John Eastcott Hayzelden, barrister, yr s of Allan Frederick George Hayzelden, of Pinner, Middx, and had:

 1a *Clare Margaret; *b* 11 Nov 1964

 2a *Gillian Susan; *b* 17 Sept 1966

7 George, farmer; *b* 26 Oct 1906; *educ* Whitgift Sch and Reading U; *m* 9 Nov 1935 *Elizabeth, dau of William John Cumber, CBE, of The Chestnuts, Theale, Berks, and had:

(1) *Elizabeth Ann; *b* 20 July 1937; *educ* Headington Sch, Oxford; *m* 7 Oct 1961 *Alec Rodwell Davey, er s of William Alexander Davey, MBE, of Slade Farm, Rogate, Sussex, and has:

 1a *Richard William; *b* 27 June 1963

 1a *Julia Elizabeth; *b* 8 May 1966

(2) *Margaret Jill; *b* 25 April 1939; *educ* Headington Sch, Oxford

8 Leslie Christopher; *b* 23 Jan 1910; *educ* Reading Sch, Reading U and UCL (BSc, PhD); AMIChemE, chemical engr; *m* 4 Feb 1942 *Kate Mary, dau of H H Sparvell, of Theale, and had:

(1) *David James; *b* 27 April 1944; *educ* King's Coll Sch Wimbledon and St Andrews (BSc)

(1) *Judith Mary; *b* 26 Nov 1948; *educ* Lady Eleanor Holles Sch Hampton and Southampton U

JAMES STRANG's est s,

WILLIAM STRANG, **1st Baron Strang**, of Stonesfield, Co Oxford (UK), so *cr* 16 Jan 1954, GCB (1953), KCB 1948, CB 1939), GCMG (1950, KCMG 1943, CMG 1932)), MBE (1918); *b* 2 Jan 1893; *educ* Palmer's Sch Grays, UCL (BA 1912, Fell 1946, Hon LLD 1954, memb Coll Ctee 1955 and Chm 1963) and Sorbonne; Univ of Paris; 4th Bn Worcs Regt and HQ 29th Div WW I, Dip Serv: 3rd Sec Belgrade 1919, 2nd Sec 1920, FO 1922, 1st Sec 1925, Counsellor Moscow 1930–33, FO 1933, Assist U-Sec 1939–43, UK Rep European Advsy Commn 1943–45, Political Adviser to C-in-C Br Forces Occupn Germany 1945–47, PUS FO (German Section) 1947–49, PUS For Affrs 1949–53 (ret 1953), Chm: Nat Pks Commn 1954–66, Food Hygiene Advsy Cncl 1955, Roy Inst Internat Affrs 1958–66, memb: Nature Conservancy 1954–66, Gen Advsy Cncl BBC 1957–64, Dep Speaker Ho Lds 1962, author: *The Foreign Office* (1955), *Home and Abroad* (1956), *Britain in World Affairs* (1961), *The Diplomatic Career* (1962); *m* 1 March 1920 Elsie Wynne (*d* 23 Sept 1974), dau of Josiah Edward Jones, of Addiscombe, and *d* 27 May 1978, leaving:

1 COLIN STRANG, **2nd and present Baron Strang**

1 Jean; *b* 17 April 1921; *educ* Manor House Godalming and Fribourg, Switzerland; *d* 21 Oct 1988

STRANGE

Arms: Parted per fess waved or and gu. **Crest:** Two arms ppr. drawing an arrow to the head in a bow or. **Supporters:** Dexter, a naked savage wreathed about the head and middle with oak leaves, holding over his dexter shoulder a club, all ppr.; sinister, a knight armed at all points, the visor of his helmet up, a spear resting on his sinister arm and a shield hanging thereon, also ppr. **Motto:** *Marte et arte* ('By valour and skill'). **Creation:** B. (E) 7 March 1627/8.

THE BARONESS STRANGE ((Jean) Cherry Drummond of Megginch) [The Rt Hon The Lady Strange, Megginch Castle, Errol, Perthshire PH2 7SW; 160 Kennington Rd, London SE11 6QR]; *b* 17 Dec 1928; *s f* as 16th holder of Barony 1986 on termination of abeyance, also as 11th of Megginch, Ch of Drummond of Concraig and Lennoch within the Clan Drummond and Feudal Baroness of Megginch; *educ* St Andrews (MA 1951) and Newnham Coll Cambridge; Pres War Widows' Assoc of GB 1990–, author: *Love from Belinda* (1960), *Lalage in Love* (1962), *Creatures Great and Small* (1968), *Love is for Ever* (1988), *The Remarkable Life of Victoria Drummond, Marine Engineer* (1994); FSA (Scot), Hon FIMarE; *m* 2 June 1952 *Capt Humphrey Ap EVANS later DRUMMOND of Megginch (Lord Lyon decree 14 March 1966), MC, late RA, only surv s of Maj James John Pugh Evans, MBE, MC, JP, DL, of Lovesgrove, Aberystwyth, Cards, and has:

1 +ADAM HUMPHREY; *b* 20 April 1953; *educ* Eton and RMA Sandhurst; Maj Gren Gds; *m* 1988 *Hon Mary Emma Jeronima Dewar, est dau of 4th Baron Forteviot (*qv*), and has:

(1) +John Adam Humphrey; *b* 3 Nov 1992

(1) *Sophia Frances; *b* 19 March 1991

2 +Humphrey John Jardine [The Hon Humphrey Drummond, 64 Comeragh Rd, London W14 9HR]; *b* 11 March 1961; *educ* Eton and Imp Coll London (BSc 1981), PhD 1988; DIC, MRSC, CChem, ARCS; *m* 20 Sept 1997 *Zara Daisy, only dau of Sir Ian Rankin, 4th Bt (*qv*)

3 +John Humphrey Hugo [The Hon John Drummond, 57 Icadiye Caddesi, Kuzguncuk, Iskudar, Istanbul, Turkey]; *b* 26 June 1966; *educ* Eton and St John's Coll Cambridge (MA); ACA 1993

1 +Charlotte Cherry [The Hon Charlotte Drummond, #222 2500 Q St NW, Washington, DC 20007, USA]; *b* 14 May 1955; *educ* Heathfield and Dundee Coll of Commerce

2 +Amélie Margaret Mary [Duchesse de Magenta, Château de Sully, 71360 Epinac, Saone-et-Loire, France]; *b* 2 July 1963; *educ* Heathfield, Dundee Coll of Commerce and London Poly; *m* 1990, as his 2nd w, *Philippe, 8th Marquis de MacMahon, 4th Duc de Magenta, and has:

(1) +Maurice Marie Patrick Bacchus Humphrey; *b* 30 March 1992

(1) +Pélagie Jeanne Marie Marguerite Charlotte Natalie; *b* 24 June 1990

3 +Catherine Star Violetta [Mrs Giles Herdman, 149 Cambridge St, London SW1]; *b* 15 Dec 1967; *educ* Heathfield, Dundee Coll of Commerce and Hertfords U; *m* 20 April 1996 *Giles Herdman

Lineage: The 7th EARL OF DERBY (*qv*) and **1st Lord** (Baron) **Strange** (E), so *cr* (effectively; *see* DERBY, E) 7 March 1627/8; had, with other issue:

1 CHARLES STANLEY, **2nd Lord** (Baron) **Strange** and 8th EARL OF DERBY; had:

  (1) WILLIAM GEORGE RICHARD STANLEY, **3rd Lord** (Baron) **Strange** and 9th EARL OF DERBY; *dspms* 5 Nov 1702, when the Barony fell into abeyance between his daus, devolving on the er with the death of the younger 1714, whereby the abeyance naturally terminated, having had, with a s (*dvp* unm) and the yr dau aforementioned (*d* unm 1714):

    1a HENRIETTA MARIA, *de jure* BARONESS STRANGE in her own right from 1714; *m* 1st 21 May 1706 4th Earl of Anglesey of the 1661 *cr* (*d* 18 Sept 1710; *see* VALENTIA, V) and had a dau (*dvm* unm); *m* 2nd 24 July 1714 1st Earl of Ashburnham (*see* 1924 edn) and *d* 26 June 1718, having by him had:

      1b HENRIETTA BRIDGET ASHBURNHAM, *de jure* BARONESS STRANGE in her own right; *d* unm 8 Aug 1732

  (2) JAMES STANLEY, **6th Lord** (Baron) **Strange** and 10th EARL OF DERBY; *b* 3 July 1664; *dspms* 1 Feb 1735/6, having had a s (*dvp* an infant)

1 AMELIA ANNE SOPHIA Stanley; *m* 5 May 1659 John MURRAY, 1st Marquess of Atholl and *d* 22 Feb 1702/3, leaving with other issue (*see* ATHOLL, D):

  (1) JOHN MURRAY, 1st DUKE OF ATHOLL; *m* 1st and had, with other issue:

    1a JAMES MURRAY, **7th Lord** (Baron) **Strange**, as which s cousin 1 Feb 1735/6, and 2nd DUKE OF ATHOLL; *m* 2nd 7 May 1749, as her 1st husb, Jean, dau of John Drummond, 10th of Lennoch and 3rd of Megginch, and by his 1st w had, with other issue:

      1b CHARLOTTE Murray, **Baroness Strange** in her own right; *m* her cousin John MURRAY, 3rd DUKE OF ATHOLL and had, with other issue (*see* ATHOLL, D):

        1c JOHN MURRAY, **9th Lord** (Baron) **Strange** and 4th DUKE OF ATHOLL; *m* 1st and had, with other issue:

          1d JOHN MURRAY, **10th Lord** (Baron) **Strange** and 5th DUKE OF ATHOLL; *d* unm

          2d JAMES MURRAY, 1st BARON GLENLYON; had, with other issue (*see* ATHOLL, D):

            1e GEORGE AUGUSTUS FREDERICK JOHN MURRAY, **11th Lord** (Baron) **Strange** and 6th DUKE OF ATHOLL; had:

              1f JOHN JAMES HUGH HENRY MURRAY, **12th Lord** (Baron) **Strange** and 7th DUKE OF ATHOLL; had, with other issue (*see* ATHOLL, D):

                1g JOHN GEORGE MURRAY, **13th Lord** (Baron) **Strange** and 8th DUKE OF ATHOLL; *dsp*

                2g JAMES THOMAS MURRAY, **14th Lord** (Baron) **Strange** and 9th DUKE OF ATHOLL; *d* unm 8 May 1957, when the Barony fell into abeyance

    1d Charlotte; *m* 1st Sir John Menzies, 4th Bt (*dsp* 1800; *see* 1911 edn); *m* 2nd 28 May 1801 Adml Sir Adam Drummond, KCH, 7th of Megginch, and *d* 31 May 1832, leaving, with other issue:

      1e John, 8th of Megginch, JP, DL Perths; *b* 10 April 1803; *educ* Eton and RMC Sandhurst; Capt Gren Gds; *m* 20 Nov 1835 Frances Jemima, MVO (*d* 22 Dec 1891), Woman Bedchamber to HM QUEEN VICTORIA, 4th dau of Gen Sir John Oswald of Dunnikier, Fifeshire, GCB, GCMG, and *d* 15 May 1889, leaving:

        1f Malcolm, 9th of Megginch and of Kilspindie, Perthshire, JP, DL; *b* 2 March 1856; *educ* Eton; Capt Gren Gds Sudan Expdn 1885, Groom Privy Chamber 1890–93, Groom in Waiting in Ordinary 1893–1901 to HM QUEEN VICTORIA; *m* 30 April 1890 Hon Geraldine Margaret Amherst (*d* 24 Aug 1956), 6th dau of 1st Baron Amherst of Hackney (*qv*), and *d* 29 May 1924, leaving:

          1g JOHN DRUMMOND, 10th of Megginch, **15th Lord** (Baron) **Strange**, so recognised on termination of abeyance 18 Dec 1964; *b* 6 May 1900; *educ* Eton; Lt Gren Gds WW I, Black Watch WW II; author of 10 books; *m* 8 Feb 1928 Violet Margaret Florence (*d* 16 Oct 1975), formerly w of Capt Edmund Owen Ethelston Peel, MC, and only dau of Sir Robert William Buchanan-Jardine, 2nd Bt (*qv*), and *d* 13 April 1982, when the Barony fell into abeyance (terminated 1986) between his three daus:

            1h (JEAN) CHERRY, **present Baroness Strange**

            2h +Heather Mary [The Hon Mrs Currey, The Mill House, Santon, IoM]; *b* 9 Nov 1931; *m* 11 Aug 1954 *Lt-Cdr Andrew Christian Currey, RN, only s of R-Adml Harry Philip Currey, CB, OBE, of Pond Cottage, Newton Valence, Hants, and has:

              1i +Robert James Drummond [Robert Currey Esq, 99 Ritherdon Rd, London SW17]; *b* 24 Sept 1955; *educ* Eton and South Bank Poly (BSc 1977); *m* 5 Nov 1983 *Diana Jane, dau of Kenneth Garrod, of Aldeburgh, Suffolk, and has:

                1j +Cosmo Charles Drummond; *b* 1985

                1j +Francesca Rose; *b* 1989

              2i +John Andrew Fairbridge; *b* 1 Aug 1959; *educ* Stowe

              1i +Arabella Mary Christian; *b* 25 July 1958; *educ* Hampden House; *m* 1st 1987 Reiner Friedhelm Gustav Gerland, s of Karl Heinz Gerland, of Kassel, Germany, and has:

                1j +Oskar Gustav Christian; *b* 1987

              1i (cont.) Mrs Arabella Gerland *m* 2nd 1993 *Nicholas Buckworth and by him has:

                2j +Titus; *b* 1994

            3h +(Margaret) April Irene [The Hon Lady Agnew-Somerville, Mount Auldyn, Jurby Rd, Ramsey, IoM]; *b* 3 April 1939; *m* 14 Dec 1963 *Sir Quentin Charles Somerville Agnew-Somerville, 2nd Bt (*qv*), and has issue

        1g Jean; *d* unm 11 Nov 1974

        2g Victoria Alexandrina, MBE (1941); *d* unm 25 Dec 1978

        3g Frances Ada; *d* unm 9 Nov 1974

    1f Mary, JP Perthshire; *d* unm 6 June 1934

1c (cont.) The **9th Lord** *m* 2nd and had further issue (*see* ATHOLL, D)

(1) (cont.) The 1st DUKE *m* 2nd and had further issue (*see* ATHOLL, D)

STRANG STEEL

Arms: Arg. a bend chequy sa. and erm. between two lion's heads erased gu., on a chief az. two billets or, a crescent of the first for difference. **Crest:** A lion's head erased gu. **Motto:** (over the crest) *Prudentia et animis* ('With prudence yet spirit'). **Creation:** Bt. (UK) 2 July 1938.

SIR (FIENNES) MICHAEL STRANG STEEL, 3RD BT, of Philiphaugh, Selkirk, DL (Borders Region 1990) [Maj Sir Michael Strang Steel Bt DL, Philiphaugh, Selkirk TD7 5LX]; *b* 22 Feb 1943; *s* f 1992; *educ* Eton; Maj 17th/21st Lancers 1962–80, forestry commr 1988–, memb Roy Co Archers; *m* 14 April 1977 *Sarah (Sal) Jane, er dau of J A S Russell, of Mayfield, Lochmaben, Dumfriesshire, and has:

1 +(FIENNES) EDWARD; *b* 8 Nov 1978; *educ* Glenalmond

2 +Sam Arthur; *b* 1983

1 *Tara Diana; *b* 1980

Lineage: JAMES STEEL, of High Side and The Hall of Carnduff, Lanarks; *b* 1743; *m* 1768 Anne Greenshields, of Kerse, and *d* 1775, leaving, with an er s (Thomas):

JAMES STEEL; *b* 1771; *m* 1795 Janet, only dau of John Alison, of The Hall, Carnduff, and had a 2nd s:

JOHN STEEL; *b* 1801; *m* 1830 Grace (*d* 1888), dau of James Strang, of Westhouse, E Kilbride, Lanarks, and *d* 1872, having had four sons, the 2nd s:

WILLIAM STRANG STEEL, of Philiphaugh, Selkirk, JP, DL; *b* 6 Oct 1832; *m* 1st 25 Oct 1881 —; *m* 2nd 28 April 1908 Florence Elphinstone (*d* 24 April 1936), yst dau of Maj-Gen Burnett Ford, Madras Army, and *d* 2 Jan 1911, leaving by his 1st w, with a dau (Grace Strang, *b* 25 Nov 1884, DGStJ, *m* 5 Dec 1905 Lt-Gen Sir Aylmer Hunter-Weston of Hunterston, KCB, DSO (*d* following an accident 18 March 1940), and *dsp* 28 Feb 1954):

Sir Samuel Strang Steel, 1st Bt, so *cr* 2 July 1938, TD, JP Selkirk; *b* 1 Aug 1882; *educ* Eton and Trin Coll Cambridge (MA); Maj Lothians and Border Horse Yeo WW I, MP (U) Ashford (Kent) 1918–29, PPS to Min Ag 1923–24 and Fin Sec Treasury 1925, Pres Scottish U Assoc 1937–38 and 1942–43, memb Forestry Commn 1932, Selkirk: Convener CC 1946, Ld Lt 1948–58 (previously DL), Lt Roy Co Archers, dir: LNER to 1948 and Bank Scotland; *m* 3 Aug 1910 Hon Vere Mabel Cornwallis (*d* 8 Oct 1964), 2nd dau of 1st Baron Cornwallis (*qv*), and had:

1 FIENNES WILLIAM STRANG (Sir), **2nd Bt**

2 Jock Wykeham Strang; *b* 23 April 1914; *educ* Eton; *m* 14 Nov 1945 *Lesley [Mrs Jock Strang Steel, Haydean, Haddington, E Lothian EH41 4HN], only dau of Lt-Col Sir John Reginald Noble Graham, 3rd Bt, VC, OBE, of Larbert (*qv*), and *d* 1991, leaving:

  (1) +Malcolm Graham Strang, WS [Malcolm Strang Steel Esq WS, Barrowmore, Mawcarse, Kinross KY13 7SL]; *b* 24 Nov 1946; *educ* Eton, Trin Coll Cambridge (BA) and Edinburgh U (LLB); slr, sec Standing Cncl Scottish Chiefs 1973–83, memb Roy Co Archers, FRSA; *m* 21 Oct 1972 *Margaret Philippa, yst dau of William Patrick Scott, OBE, TD, DL, of Kierfold, Sandwick, Stromness, Orkney, and has:

    1a +Patrick Reginald Strang; *b* 15 Dec 1975; *educ* Eton

    1a *Laura Strang; *b* 18 Oct 1977

  (1) *Celia Jane Strang, LVO (1989); *b* 17 Dec 1948; Ldy-in-waiting to HRH THE PRINCESS ROYAL 1977–; *m* 11 Sept 1976 *Malcolm Alastair Innes (*see* INNES, Bt, of Balvenie), and has issue

  (2) *Susan Rachel Strang; *b* 13 April 1952; *m* 1980 *Sir Crispin Hamlyn Agnew of Lochnaw, 11th Bt (*qv*), and has issue

3 James Malcolm Strang; *b* 4 Nov 1919; *educ* Eton and Trin Coll Cambridge; Lt Gren Gds WW II; *ka* 17 March 1943

4 +Robert Stanley Strang [Robert Strang Steel Esq, Sluie, by Banchory, Kincardineshire AB31 4BA]; *b* 1 June 1934; *educ* Eton and RAC Cirencester; *m* 26 April 1958 *Caroline Angela Elaine, only dau of Lt-Col William Hugh Carter, of Rosslyn, Tain, Ross-shire, and has:

(1) +David William Strang; *b* 24 Oct 1961; *educ* Glenalmond and RAC Cirencester; chartered surveyor; *m* 1991 *Fiona Louise, yr dau of Dr Richard Legge, of Edinburgh, and has:

    1a +Charles William Brooke; *b* 18 Sept 1995

    1a *Alice Charlotte Strang; *b* 1993

    2a *Olivia Rose; *b* 17 April 1997

(2) +Richard James Strang; *b* 28 Aug 1963; *educ* Eton; *m* 20 July 1996 *Sophia Juliet, dau of Rodney Shirley, of The Manor House, Buckingham

1 *Grizel Mabel Strang [Miss Grizel Strang Steel, Beechwood, Selkirk TD7 5LU]; *b* 24 Dec 1921

The 1st Bt *d* 14 Aug 1961; his est s,

Sir (Fiennes) William Strang Steel, 2nd Bt, JP (Selkirkshire 1965), DL (1955); *b* 24 July 1912; *educ* Eton and RMC Sandhurst; Maj 17th/21st Lancers WW II, memb Forestry Commn 1958, Convener Selkirk CC 1967; *m* 7 Aug 1941 Joan (*d* 5 June 1982), only dau of Brig-Gen Sir Brodie Haldane Henderson, KCMG, CB, of Upp Hall, Braughing, Herts, and *d* 1992, having had:

1 Sir (FIENNES) MICHAEL STRANG STEEL, **3rd and present Bt**

2 +Colin Brodie Strang [Colin Strang Steel Esq, Threepwood, Blainslie, Galashiels, Selkirkshire TD1 2PY]; *b* 2 June 1945; *educ* Eton and RAC Cirencester; FRICS; *m* 24 Oct 1970 *April Eileen, only dau of Aubrey Fairfax Studd, of Cahoo Ho, Regaby West, Ramsey, IoM, and has:

    (1) +James William; *b* 3 Aug 1973

    (2) +Alistair Fairfax; *b* Nov 1975

    (3) +Peter Brodie; *b* 1977

1 Diana Joan Strang; *b* 7 Dec 1947; *m* 20 June 1970 *Maj (Anthony) Francis Gradidge, 17th/21st Lancers [Maj Francis Gradidge, The Old Brewery Cottage, Netheravon, Wilts SP4 9PQ], s of Brig J H Gradidge, of Cocks Ho, Ashton Keynes, Wilts, and was *k* in a car crash 1975, leaving:

    (1) *Richard; *b* 14 Dec 1971

    (1) *Clare; *b* 12 May 1973

STRATHALMOND

Arms: Tierce in pairle, az., gu. and sa., three cinquefoils or.
Crest: In front of a bezant gutté d'huile a stag's head erased ppr.
Supporters: Dexter, a pheasant; sinister, a grouse ppr.
Creation: B. (UK) 18 Feb 1955.

THE 3RD BARON STRATHALMOND, of Pumpherston, Midlothian (William Roberton Fraser) [The Rt Hon The Lord Strathalmond, House of Lords, London SW1A 0PW]; *b* 22 July 1947; *s f* 1976; *educ* Loretto; CA, md London Wall Membs Agy 1986–91, dir London Wall Hldgs 1986–91, chm R W Sturge Ltd 1991–94; *m* 9 June 1973 *Amanda Rose, yr dau of Rev Gordon Clifford Taylor, and has:

1 +WILLIAM GORDON; *b* 24 Sept 1976

2 +George Edward; *b* 10 March 1979

1 *Virginia Audrey Hart; *b* 22 Dec 1982

Lineage: WILLIAM FRASER, of Glasgow; had:

WILLIAM FRASER, **1st Baron Strathalmond**, of Pumpherson, Co Midlothian (UK), so *cr* 18 Feb 1955, CBE (1918); *b* 3 Nov 1888; *educ* Glasgow Acad; chm BP, ktd 1939, KStJ, Offr Legn Hon, Hon LLD Birmingham U 1951; *m* 7 Oct 1913 Mary Roberton (*d* 17 Oct 1963), dau of Thomson McLintock (*see* McLINTOCK, Bt), and *d* 1 April 1970, leaving:

1 WILLIAM FRASER, **2nd Baron Strathalmond**, CMG, OBE (1944), TD (1955); *b* 8 May 1916; *educ* Loretto and Clare Coll Cambridge; Lt-Col RASC WW II, barrister Inner Temple and Lincoln's Inn 1946, md BP 1962, dir: Prudential Assur 1973–76 and Nervarthill 1976, chm Govan Shipbuilders, US Bronze Star, KStJ; *m* 31 March 1945 *Letitia [The Rt Hon Letitia Lady Strathalmond, 155 Fawn Lane, Portola Valley, CA 94025, USA], only dau of Walter Martin Krementz, of Morristown, NJ, and *d* 27 Oct 1976, leaving:

    (1) WILLIAM ROBERTON FRASER, **3rd and present Baron Strathalmond**

    (1) *Cordelia [The Hon Mrs Cordelia Brown, 75 Carthew Rd, London W6 0DU]; *b* 12 Dec 1949; *m* 1981 (*divorce* 1986) Ralph Lyman Brown

    (2) *Christina [The Hon Mrs Lebus, 70 Ellerby St, London SW6 6EZ]; *b* 5 Nov 1954; *m* 1974 *Timothy Andrew Lebus and has:

        1a *David Oliver; *b* 1983

---

1 *Mary Joan [The Hon Lady Westbrook, White Gables, Prestbury, Cheshire]; *b* 29 Oct 1922; *m* 15 Feb 1945 *Sir Neil Gowanloch Westbrook, s of F Westbrook, of Wilmslow, Cheshire, and has:

    (1) *Fraser Gowanloch; *b* 5 March 1946; *educ* Oundle; *m* 1971 (*divorce* 1993) Jane Bray

    (1) *Mary Joan; *b* 1 Feb 1950; *m* 1 June 1974 *Robert Michael John Keene, yr s of Brig T P Keene, of The Gables, Bideford, Devon

STRATHCARRON

Arms: Per fess or and az. a galley of the first, masts, oars and tackling ppr., flagged gu., in the dexter chief point a hand couped fessways holding a dagger paleways, in the sinister a cross crosslet fitchée of the last, over all a fess chequy of the second and arg.
Crest: A cat-a-mountain sejant guardant, having its dexter paw raised ppr. **Supporters:** Dexter, a private soldier of the Cameron Highlanders in full service dress of the period 1916–18; sinister, a Macpherson clansman of the period of 1745. **Motto:** *Le cridhe's le cliu* ('With heart and head'). **Creations:** Bt. (UK) 26 April 1933, B. (UK) 11 Jan 1936.

THE 2ND BARON STRATHCARRON, of Banchor, Co Inverness, and a **Baronet** (Sir David William Anthony Blyth Macpherson, Bt) [The Rt Hon The Lord Strathcarron, 22 Rutland Gate, London SW7 1BB]; *b* 23 Jan 1924; *s f* 1937; *educ* Eton and Jesus Coll Cambridge; F/Lt RAFVR WW II 1942–47, memb Br Parly Delegn Austria 1964, dir: Kirchhoff Ltd (London), Seabourne World Express Gp, Kent Internat Airport plc, sr ptnr Strathcarron & Co, motoring correspondent *The Field* 1954–, Pres: Guild Motoring Writers 1971–, Vehicle Builders & Repairers Assoc 1983–, Driving Instrs Assoc 1982–, IRTE 1990–; Chm: All Party Parly Motorcycle Gp and The Order of the Road; author: *Motoring for Pleasure* (1963); FIMI 1989, FCIT 1991, Fell Inst Advanced Motorists 1993, Pres Fellowship Motor Industry 1995; *m* 1st 10 Feb 1947 (*annulled* July 1947) Valerie, est dau of T Norman Cole, of Mayfair; *m* 2nd 18 May 1948 Diana Hawtrey (*d* 23 April 1973), only dau of Cdr Ralph Hawtrey Deane, RN, and formerly w of John Noel Ormiston Curle (*see* KINGSDOWN, B); *m* 3rd 1974 *Mrs Eve Samuel, only dau of John Comyn Higgins, CIE, ICS, of Alford, Lincs, and formerly w of Hon Anthony Gerald Samuel (*see* BEARSTED, V), and by his 2nd w has:

1 +IAN DAVID PATRICK [The Hon Ian Macpherson, 1 Leinster Mews, London W2 3EY]; *b* 31 March 1949; *educ* Horris Hill Newbury and Grenoble U; *m* 13 July 1974 *Gillian Rosamund, dau of Frank Allison, of Cheltenham, Glos

2 +Andrew Charles James; *b* 5 Jan 1959; *educ* Stanbridge Earls

Lineage: JAMES MACPHERSON; *b* 1650; had:

ALEXANDER MACPHERSON; *b* 1683; had:

JAMES MACPHERSON; *b* 1715; had:

SOMHAIRLID *Mor* ('Big', 'The Great' or perhaps just 'The Elder') MACPHERSON; *b* 1745; *m* Jessie Kennedy and had:

JAMES MACPHERSON; *b* 1788; *m* Anne Campbell and had:

IAN *Dubh* ('The Dark') MACPHERSON; *b* 1825; *m* Isabella Cattancach and had:

JAMES MACPHERSON, JP, of Newtonmore, Kingussie, Inverness-shire; *b* 19 Sept 1848; merchant; *m* Jan 1876 Anne (*d* 23 Jan 1924), dau of James Stewart, of Strone, Kingussie, and *d* 17 July 1922, leaving:

1 Thomas Stewart (Sir), CIE (1922), JP Inverness-shire; *b* 21 Aug 1876; *educ* George Watson's Coll, Edinburgh U (MA 1897) and Trin Coll Oxford (LLD); joined ICS 1899, Dist and Sessions Judge Bihar and Orissa 1913, Judicial Commr Chota Nagpur 1916, Superintendent and Remembrancer Legal Affrs and Sec Legislative Cncl 1917, Registrar High Court Judicature Patna 1920, barrister Middle Temple 1920, Judge Patna High Court 1921, 1923 and 1924, Additional Judge 1925, Judge 1927, V-Chllr Patna U 1930–33, ktd 1933, CC Inverness-shire; *m* 20 June 1902 Helen, est dau of Rev Archibald Borland Cameron, DD, of Edinburgh, and *d* 6 Aug 1949, leaving:

    (1) James Archibald Stewart; *b* 19 Oct 1902; *educ* Edinburgh Acad and Edinburgh U (MB, ChB); *m* 10 Sept 1934 Elsie Margaret (*d* 26 March 1962), dau of Dr Alexander Bruce Giles, of Palmerston Place, Edinburgh, and *d* 15 Jan 1959, leaving:

1a *Thomas Alexander Stewart [Thomas Macpherson Esq, Caerketton, 39 Swanston Ave, Edinburgh EH10 7BX]; *b* 3 Dec 1935; *educ* Edinburgh Acad; chartered surveyor; FRICS, FSAScot; *m* 28 July 1962 *Catherine, dau of William James Moyes, of Edinburgh, and has:

  1b *Bruce James Stewart; *b* 13 March 1966; MA (Hons) Edinburgh U, MA Durham U

  1b *Helen Margaret Stewart; *b* 25 April 1964; RGN, MW; *m* 9 April 1988 *Derek Alexander McCabe, yr s of A H B McCabe, of Edinburgh, and has:

    1c *Christopher Alexander; *b* 8 Dec 1991

    1c *Sarah Catherine; *b* 10 Sept 1994

  1b *Alison Catriona Stewart; *b* 5 May 1970; SRCh, DPodM, MAR; *m* 28 Aug 1997 *Stephen Robert Simpson, yr s of Brian Simpson

(2) *George Philip Stewart, OBE (1943), TD (1945) [Brig George Macpherson OBE TD, 18 Duke's Lodge, Holland Park, London W11; The Old Rectory, Aston Sandford, Bucks]; *b* 14 Dec 1903; *educ* Edinburgh Acad, Fettes, Oriel Coll Oxford (BA 1925, MA 1944), Yale and Edinburgh U; CA Edin 1930, 7th/9th Bn Roy Scots 1927–36, 1st Bn London Scottish 1939, Brig 1945, Dir: Fin Div Allied Control Commn Austria 1945–46, Kleinwort, Benson, Lonsdale, Standard Life Assur; Scottish Rugby Football and Athletic International; *m* 1 Oct 1939 *Elizabeth Margaret Cameron, dau of James Cameron Smail, CBE, LLD, of Edinburgh, and has:

  1a *Ewen Cameron Stewart; *b* 19 Jan 1942; *educ* Fettes, Queens' Coll Cambridge and London Graduate Business Sch

  2a *Roderick James Stewart [Rodrick Macpherson Esq, 3 Holland Park Mews, London W11]; *b* 19 Sept 1945; *educ* Fettes, Edinburgh U and RAC Cirencester

  3a *(Philip) Strone Stewart [Strone Macpherson Esq, 8 Holland Park Mews, London W11]; *b* 21 July 1948; *educ* Fettes and Oriel Coll Oxford

(3) NIALL MALCOLM STEWART MACPHERSON, 1st and last BARON DRUMALBYN, of Whitesands, Co Dumfries (UK), so cr 9 Nov 1963, KBE (1974), PC (1962); *b* 3 Aug 1908; *educ* Edinburgh Acad, Fettes and Trin Coll Oxford (BA 1929, MA 1932); WW II: Queen's Own Cameron Highrs, Staff Coll 1942, T/Maj 1942; MP (C) Dumfries 1945–63, Jt U-Sec Scotland 1955–60, Parly Sec BOT 1960–62, Min Pensions and NI 1962–63, Min State BOT 1963–64, Min without Portfolio 1970–74, Dep Pres Assoc Br Chambers Commerce 1970, Pres Highland Soc London 1971–76; *m* 27 July 1937 Margaret Phyllis (*d* 13 Aug 1979), dau of Julius Joseph Runge, of Kippington Court, Sevenoaks, Kent, and *d* 11 Oct 1987, when the Barony expired, having had:

  1a *Jean Stewart [The Hon Lady Weatherall, Craig House, Bishop's Waltham, Hants SO32 1FS]; *b* 14 Nov 1938; *m* 12 May 1962 *V-Adml Sir James Lamb Weatherall, KBE, RN, Marshal Dip Corps, only s of Lt-Cdr Alwyne Thomas Hirst Weatherall, RNR, and has:

    1b *Ian James Stewart; *b* 19 March 1976

    1b *Annie Norah; *b* 17 Jan 1974

    2b *Elizabeth Alwynne; *b* 19 March 1976

  1a Sir James and Lady Weatherall also adopted:

    *Niall Anthony Stewart; *b* 23 April 1967; *educ* Wellington

    *Sarah Margaret; *b* 26 Sept 1968

  2a *Mary Stewart [The Hon Mrs Rees, 62 Prospect Quay, Point Pleasant, London SW18 1PR]; *b* 2 Aug 1942; *educ* Ancaster House and Edinburgh U; *m* 1st 15 July 1967 (*divorce* 1991) Philip Dudley Wilson, s of Dudley Wilson, of Claremont, Penrith Cumberland; *m* 2nd 30 April 1994 *Howard Alvine Rees, s of Alvine Edwin Rees, of Highbury

  3a (Helen) Norah Stewart; *b* 12 Feb 1947; *d* unm 9 Oct 1969

(4) *Archibald Ian Stewart; *b* 10 Aug 1913; *educ* Edinburgh Acad, Fettes, Edinburgh U and Columbia U Coll of Physicians and Surgeons (Gunning Victoria Jubilee Prizeman 1940, MB, ChB 1936); ChM 1953, FRCS (E) 1940, FRSE, Lt-Col RAMC, Consultant Surgn Roy Infirmary Edinburgh, Roy Edinburgh Hosp and Leith Hosp, Sr Lecturer Surgery Edinburgh U

(5) *Ronald Thomas Stewart, CBE (1968), MC (1941) and two bars (1944, 1945), TD (1945) [Col Ronald Macpherson CBE MC TD, 4 Somers Crescent, London W2]; *b* 14 Jan 1920; *educ* Edinburgh Acad, Fettes and Trin Coll Oxford (BA 1947); QO Cameron Highrs WW II, OC 1st London Scottish 1961–64, Col 56 Bde 1964–67, Territorial Col Lond Dist 1967–69, Chm Achilles Club, dep chm and md William Mallinson & Sons, Chev Legn Hon, Croix de Guerre with Palms, Resistance Medal, Kt's Cross St Mary Bethlehem, Medal of St Just of Trieste; *m* 19 Dec 1953 *Jean Henrietta, dau of David Butler-Wilson, of Burlington House, Alderley Edge, Cheshire, and has:

  1a *Angus Cameron Stewart; *b* 19 Dec 1958

  1a *Ishbel Jean Stewart; *b* 16 July 1960

(1) *Sheila Ann Margaret Stewart [Mrs Harold Kittermaster, Penvalla, Broughton, by Biggar, Lanarks]; *b* 7 April 1906; *m* 3 Sept 1929 Harold James Kittermaster (*d* 1967), 2nd s of Frederick James Kittermaster, of Rugby, and has a s and two daus

(2) *Helen Catriona Stewart (Rhona), OBE (1961); *b* 18 Sept 1914; MA Edin; *m* 24 Oct 1938 James Asher Mackintosh, barrister, only s of Prof James Mackintosh, KC, LLD, Sheriff Ross, Cromarty and Sutherland, Dean Law Faculty Edin U, and has three sons

2 JAMES IAN, **1st Baron**

3 John Donald; *b* 25 July 1883; *educ* Newtonmore and Kingussie Schs; Capt QO Cameron Highrs (TA) WW I (despatches, wounded three times, invalided 1917); *m* 15 March 1922 Mary Kininmonth, dau of John Simpson, of Newtonmore, and *dsp* 2 Jan 1960

The 2nd s,

Sir James Ian Macpherson, 1st Bt, and **1st Baron Strathcarron**, of Banchor, Co Inverness (both UK), so cr 26 April 1933 and 11 Jan 1936 respectively, PC (GB 1918, I 1919), JP; *b* 14 May 1880; *educ* Edinburgh U (LLB, Hon LLD); barrister Middle Temple 1906, KC 1919, Bencher 1930, MP (Lib) Ross and Cromarty 1911–36, Parly Sec to U-Sec War 1914–16, U-Sec War 1916–18, V-Pres Army Cncl and Dep Sec State War 1918–19, Ch Sec Ireland 1913–20, Min Pensions 1920–22, Recorder Southend-on-Sea 1931, Freeman Roy Burgh Dingwall 1936, Lt Col City London Vol Regt; *m* 24 Sept 1915 Jill (*d* 4 Aug 1956, having *m* 2nd 22 June 1938 Hedley Ernest Le Bas (*d* 4 Dec 1942), only s of Sir Hedley Francis Le

Bas), only dau of Sir George Wood Rhodes, 1st Bt (*qv*), and *d* 14 Aug 1937, having had:

1 DAVID WILLIAM ANTHONY BLYTH MACPHERSON, **2nd and present Baron Strathcarron**

1 Fiona Margaret; *b* 9 Feb 1917; *m* 29 Oct 1935 Sir Peter Francis Runge (*d* 1970), 2nd s of Julius Joseph Runge, of Kippington Court, Sevenoaks, Kent, and *d* 12 June 1998, leaving:

  (1) *Anthony Peter; *b* 1937; *educ* Eton and Trin Coll Oxford; *b* 1970 *Mrs Susan Grievson, dau of Denis Cooil, of IoM, and has:

    1a *Lucy Victoria; *b* 1971

  (2) *Charles David; *b* 1944; *educ* Eton and Ch Ch Oxford; *m* 1st 1967 (*divorce* 1980) Harriet, dau of John Bradshaw, of Inkpen, Berks, and has:

    1a *Thomas Peter; *b* 1971

    1a *Louise Dele; *b* 1973

  (2) (cont.) Charles Runge *m* 2nd 1981 *Jil, only dau of John Liddell, of Greenock, and by her has:

    2a *Emma Virginia; *b* 1986

  (3) *Michael Robert; *b* 1947; *m* 1986 *Misae Yeggie and has:

    1a *Robert Andrew; *b* 1987

  (1) *Julia Norah; *b* 1939; *m* 1st 1958 (*divorce* 1973) Michael D'Arcy Stephens (*see* McGOWAN, B); *m* 2nd 1982 *James Connell and by her 1st husb has:

    1a *D'Arcy Mark; *b* 1965

    1a *Katherine Alison; *b* 1960

2 *Ann Patricia [The Hon Lady Lowson, Oratory Cottage, 33 Ennismore Gdns Mews, London SW7 1HZ]; *b* 14 Feb 1919; OStJ; *m* 17 July 1936 Sir Denys Colquhoun Flowerdew Lowson, 1st Bt (*qv*), and has issue

STRATHCLYDE

Arms: Gu. three bear's heads erased arg., muzzled az., within a bordure indented or, charged with three mullets of the third, a crescent of the second for difference. **Crest:** A bear's head erased gu., muzzled arg. **Supporters:** Two bears gu., muzzled arg.
Motto: *Ab obice suavior* ('A leader of men').
Creation: B. (UK) 4 May 1955.

THE 2ND BARON STRATHCLYDE, of Barskimming, Mauchline, Ayrshire (Thomas Galloway Dunlop Du Roy De Blicquy Galbraith, PC (1995)) [The Rt Hon The Lord Strathclyde PC, House of Lords, London SW1A 0PW]; *b* 22 Feb 1960; *s* gf 1985; *educ* Wellington, UEA and U of Aix-en-Provence; Ld in Waiting 1988–89, Parly U-Sec Employment and Min Tourism 1989–90, Environment July-Sept 1990, Scottish Office (Ag and Fisheries) 1990–92, Environment 1992–93, DTI 1993–94, Min State DTI 1994, Govt Ch Whip Ho Lds 1994–97, C Ch Whip 1997–98, C Leader Ho Lds 1998–; *m* 1992 *Jane, er dau of John Skinner, of Chenies, Herts, and has:

1 *Elizabeth Ida Skinner; *b* 1993

2 *Annabel; *b* 15 May 1996

3 *A dau; *b* 27 Jan 1999

Lineage: GILCHRIST *Bretnach* ('The Briton'), 1st recorded Ch of the GALBRAITHs or *Clann-'a-Bhreatannich* ('Children of the Britons', from their occupying territory in the Lennox, an area north of Dumbarton, which in turn was called 'the Fortress of the Britons' and was former capital of the Kingdom of Strathclyde; the latter had been established as a kingdom of the Ancient Britons after the Roman evacuation of Britain in the 5th century and was not united with the kingdom of the Scots till 1124; the Galbraith chiefs may well have been remote cadets of the old royal house of Strathclyde); had a stronghold on the island of Inchgalbraith in Loch Lomond; living 1193; *m* a dau of Alwyn *Og* ('The Younger') Mac Mureadhach, allegedly 1st Earl of Lennox (*see* RICHMOND and GORDON, D, preliminary remarks), and had, with a yr s (Ridderch/Rodarcus):

GILLESPIC GALBRAITH, 2nd Chief; living 1200; had, with a yst s (Malcolm):

1 Arthur, 3rd Chief; had:

  (1) William (Sir), of Buthernock (later Baldernock), of which with Kincaid he had charter from his cousin Maldouen, 3rd Earl of Lennox, *c* 1238; 4th Chief; Co-Regent of Scotland 1255; *m* a dau of Sir John 'The Red' Comyn, 2nd Lord

of Badenoch (for whose family *see* BUCHAN, E, preliminary remarks), and *d* after 1278, leaving:

1a William, 2nd of Buthernock and 5th Chief; *m* Willelma (*m* 2nd Gilbert, known as of Buthernock (in right of his w) and probably the same person as the Gilbert de Hamilton who was ancestor of the Dukes of Abercorn; *qv*), dau of Sir William Douglas, 3rd of Douglas (*see* QUEENSBERRY, M), and *d* by 1296, leaving:

1b Joan, heiress of the lands of Dalserf; *m* — de Keith, probably yr s of the hereditary Marshal of Scotland (*see* KINTORE, E), and had issue

2 Maurice, 1st of Gartconnel; Steward of the Lennox 1263; *m c* 1240 Catherine, dau of Gillepatrick Mac Maelbride, and had:

(1) Arthur (Sir), 2nd of Gartconnel and 6th Chief; obtained Mains jointly with his f in exchange for other lands *c* 1260; granted a charter of Bannachra in Luss and other lands by Malcolm, 4th Earl of Lennox, by 1268; supported ROBERT I (THE BRUCE) against the English and *d* after 1314, having had:

1a Donald; did homage for the lands of Kilbride in Glenfruin 1296; *dvp* after 1310

2a Patrick, 7th Chief; Steward of the Lennox 1313; got charters of Cammoquhil and Balcarrage; *d* in or after 1330, leaving:

1b William, 8th Chief; acquired Arlehaven after 1342; *m* a dau of Kincaid of that Ilk, who brought him Balmore and a quarter of Kincaid, and *d c* 1393, having had:

1c James, of Balmore and Kincaid; held Easter and Wester Buthernock; *dvp* after 1381, leaving:

1d Margaret; probably the Galbraith heiress said to have *m* Walter Buchanan of that Ilk, 13th Ch of the Buchanans (*m* 2nd Isabel, dau of 2nd Duke of Albany; *see* MORAY, E)

1c A dau; heiress of Gartconnel; *m* Alexander Logan, yr bro of Sir Robert Logan, 1st of Restalrig, and was ancestor of the LOGANs of Gartconnel

2c Janet, heiress of Mains; *m* (contract Sept 1373) Nicholas Douglas (*see* MORTON, E) and had issue

3a Maurice, 1st of Culcreuch in Strathendrick; living 1320; had:

1b Arthur, 2nd of Culcreuch; inherited Bannachra and the Kilbride lands; living 1342; had:

1c James, 3rd of Culcreuch and 9th Chief, in whose time many GALBRAITHs allegedly rose to help the ex-Regent's s Sir James *Mor* Stewart sack Dumbarton in support of the overthrown Albany and Lennox families, then to have fled with their families (traditionally 600 in all) to Kintyre and the Isle of Gigha, where they adopted the surname MacBhreatnaich/Bretny ('Son of the Briton') and had descendants there as late as the 19th century; *m* a sister of Robert, *de jure* 12th Earl of Mar (*qv*) and 1st Lord Erskine, and *d* in or after 1425, leaving:

1d JAMES, 10th Chief

2d Thomas, of Millig (site of the present Helensburgh)

3d Patrick, 1st of Garscadden; Esquire to his cousin the Master of Erskine, whose f exchanged Dumbarton Castle for Kildrummy Castle but was cheated by the government, whereupon Patrick Galbraith took the former 1443 and *k* its new keeper, Sir Robert Sempill of Fulwood, being rewarded by his uncle 1st Lord Erskine with Garscadden; living 1456; ancestor of the GALBRAITHs of Garscadden

2c Alexander; had:

1d Mary; *m* Robert Colquhoun, 2nd of Camstradden (*see* COLQUHOUN, Bt)

2b William, 1st of Portnellan; ancestor of the GALBRAITHs of Portnellan

The 9th Chief's est s,

JAMES GALBRAITH, 4th of Culcreuch and 10th Chief; *d* by 27 July 1455, leaving:

ANDREW GALBRAITH, 5th of Culcreuch and 11th Chief; feudal Baron of Over Johnstone; held also Bannachra and Millig; regranted *c* 1474 the Kilbride lands to John Galbraith, 3rd of Portnellan, in exchange for a red rose on St John's Day in summer if demanded; *d* 1476, leaving:

1 Thomas, 6th of Culcreuch and 12th Chief; rebelled against JAMES IV and was hanged 16 Oct 1489

2 James, 7th of Culcreuch and 13th Chief; rebelled with his bro but escaped and in 1490 had restored him his bro's forfeited estates (which as well as the lands of Bannachra, Colcreuch, Millig and the feudal Barony of Over Johnstone comprised Calyegat, Culyownane and Thomdarroch); *m* Agnes (*m* 2nd 3rd Lord Somerville (*see* 1868 edn) and *d* in or after 1528), dau of Humphrey Colquhoun, 12th of Luss (*see* COLQUHOUN, Bt), and *d c* 1512, leaving:

(1) Andrew, 8th of Culcreuch and 14th Chief; took part in attempt by 12th Earl of Lennox (*see* MORAY, E) to rescue JAMES V from the Douglases and was the most important leader to escape alive from the battlefield of Manuel near Linlithgow 1526; pardoned for his part in the attempt 1527; *m* Margaret, dau of John Stirling of Craigbernard (*see* SALTOUN, L), and *d c* 1530, leaving, with a dau (Christian, *m* Edward Buchanan, 2nd of Spittal):

1a James, 9th of Culcreuch and 15th Chief; pardoned for unspecified crimes 1547; was by 1560 a supporter of the Reformation; *m* Feb 1547/8 Catherine, dau of David Barclay, 5th of Ladyland), and *d* by Oct 1575, leaving:

1b James, 10th of Culcreuch and 16th Chief; Sheriff-Depute Dunbartonshire 1578 on; *m* his cousin Margaret (Im 2nd by 24 April 1593 Sir Aulay Macaulay, 12th of Ardencaple, Chief of his Clan, who *d* 1617), dau of Hugh Craufurd, 11th of Kilbirnie, and *d c* 1592, having had, with three daus:

1c Robert, 11th of Culcreuch and 17th Chief; Sheriff-Depute Dunbartonshire 1597; sold Over Johnstone 1621; alienated Culcreuch 1624 and allegedly migrated to Ireland, where he *d* by 5 Feb 1642, having *m c* 1586 Margaret, dau of James Seton, 10th of Touch (*see* SETON, Bt, of Abercorn), and had, with seven yr sons (Robert; Harry; Andrew; Adam; Patrick; John; William) and two daus:

1d James, 18th Chief; lost his remaining lands through his f's debts; had:

1e James, 19th Chief; last of the sr line of the Chiefs of the Galbraiths to have been traced

2b John; outlawed for robbery with violence 1584

3b Andrew; outlawed 1583; *m c* 1577 Elizabeth Galbraith and had:

1c James, 3rd in Ballocharne; *m* (contract 31 Dec 1599) Margaret, dau of Constantine Walkinshaw

2c John; had his property forfeited for complicity in murdering the Laird of Bonhill's bro 1593

(2) Humphrey; Tutor (guardian) of Culcreuch *c* 1530–34 during the 15th Chief's minority; outlawed and stripped of guradianship by PC, for unlawful killing 1534; had illegitimately:

1a James; legitimated; had illegitimately:

1b James; Paniter (household official responsible for pantry) to JAMES VI; had:

1c Francis; also Paniter to JAMES VI; living 1588

(3) Walter; living 1542/3

(4) Robert, 1st of Blairquhois; *m* 1548 Janet, dau of Sir Ninian Seton, 3rd of Touch (*see* SETON, Bt, of Abercorn), and was ancestor of, among others, Robert Galbraith (Edinburgh burgess prosecuted for trafficking in tobacco 1617), George Galbraith (privateer during Third Dutch War 1672–74), Maj Hugh Galbraith, 1st of Cappahard, Co Galway, Orangeman 1689), James Galbraith, 1st of Balgair (which he entailed 1705, naming as 8th in line his kinsman George Galbraith (*see* below)), R-Adml James Galbraith (involved in taking Havana 1762), James Galbraith, 3rd of Cappahard, High Sheriff Co Galway 1778, Gen Sir William Galbraith, KCB (fought Afghan War 1878–80, Hazara Expedn 1888) and James Gailbraith, 10th of Balgair, which he sold 1914

(1) Janet; acquired Garshake 1536

(2) Margaret; *m* William Cockburn, s of Christopher Cockburn of Chouslie and gs of Sir William Cockburn of that Ilk

3 Humphrey; pardoned 1490 for participation in Lennox's rising 1489; had, with other issue:

(1) John; leased Balgair, next to Culcreuch; *m* a sister of George Buchanan, historian and childhood mentor of JAMES VI, and *d* after 1566, having had, with two daus:

1a Humphrey, in Balgair; *m* Isobel Cunningham and *d* 1578, leaving:

1b James; *m* Mary Buchanan of Ibert and settled in Ireland

2b John; Glasgow merchant; settled in Ireland

2a WILLIAM

3a George; sec to his uncle George Buchanan

The 2nd s,

WILLIAM GALBRAITH, in Wester Balgair; had, with four yr sons (James; Robert; William; Humphrey):

JOHN GALBRAITH, in the Hill of/Middle Balgair; had:

WILLIAM GALBRAITH, in the Hill of Balgair; *m* 1st Jean Buchanan (*d* 1660); *m* 2nd — and was *k* by robbers 1686, leaving by his 1st w, with other issue, including an er s (John, in Hill of Balgair, living 1706):

GEORGE GALBRAITH, in the Hill of Balgair; *m* Janet Harvie and *d c* 1735, having had, with four daus and five other sons (including William, of Blackhouse, Stirlingshire, *b* 1678, *m* 1706 Agnes Harvie, of Blackhouse, and *d* 1757, having had issue; Robert, of Wester Edinbellie, Stirlingshire, *m* 1715 Helen Key and had issue), a 2nd s:

WALTER GALBRAITH, in Williamston in Easter Glins, Balfron, Stirlingshire; *b c* 1680; *m* 1st —; *m* 2nd 22 Oct 1715 Isobel Harvie and by her had issue, as also, by his 1st w, with an er s (George, *m* 5 May 1737 Helen Christal and had issue):

JAMES GALBRAITH; *bapt* 16 Feb 1710; *m* 18 March 1736 Margaret Galbraith and had, with four other sons (including an est Walter, *bapt* 1737, *m* 16 Dec 1766 Jane Garland and had issue; a 3rd s, Robert, *bapt* 5 May 1751, *m* Henrietta Aird and had six sons), a 2nd s:

JOHN GALBRAITH, of Wyndford, Glasgow, and Milngavie, Dunbartonshire; *bapt* 7 May 1749; miller; *m* Agnes Brodie (*d* 1825) and had, with an er s:

WILLIAM GALBRAITH; *b* 7 Sept 1783; miller, Cncllr Dumbarton, shipowner Dumbarton and Port Dundas, Glasgow; *m* 10 March 1805 Jean (*d* 5 April 1856), dau of John Weir of Hillfoot, of Kilmardinny, Dunbartonshire (2nd s of Gilbert Weir of Barrochan, nr Milngavie), and *d* 11 Nov 1869, having had, with seven daus and three yr sons:

WALTER GALBRAITH, of Glasgow; *b* 1 Dec 1827; CA; *m* 26 Dec 1854 Helen (*d* 22 Feb 1895), dau of John Sands, of Kinross, and *d* 14 Dec 1913, having had issue:

1 WILLIAM BRODIE, of whom presently

2 John Sands, JP, Solicitor of Glasgow; *b* 15 May 1857; *m* 25 April 1895 Jeanie (*d* 11 Sept 1958), dau of Samuel Alexander, of London, and *d* 30 May 1923, having had issue

3 Walter Murray; *b* 12 Feb 1859; *m* 28 June 1905 Margaret Isobel (*d* 21 March 1944), dau of James Hardie, of Auckland, NZ, and *d* 25 March 1928, having had:

(1) Walter James Murray; *b* 9 June 1909; CA Glasgow; *m* 1st 1937 (*divorce*) Constance Campbell, dau of Prof Orr, of Edinburgh; *m* 2nd 27 Aug 1957 *Lesley, formerly w of Malcolm Steel Purvis and dau of Alexander Gray McIntyre, and *d* 17 May 1965

(2) Percy Hardie Murray; *b* 17 June 1912; 2nd Lt IA 1934, WW II India and Burma, cmded 1st Bn Burma Regt 1944 and 2nd Bn Karen Rifles 1946–48, ret as Lt-Col 1948, Attorney-General's Dept Australia 1951 on; *m* 14 April 1938 *Lynley Mary Margot, dau of Henry Jackson, of NZ, and had:

1a *Henrietta Margaret Alison; *b* 3 June 1943; *m* *J Andrew Edgley and has:

1b *Geraldine Alison; *b* 25 Feb 1964

2b *Jennifer Margaret; *b* 26 July 1965

2a *Eleanor Lynley; *b* 4 Jan 1947; *educ* Melbourne U; *m* 4 Dec 1971 *Alan Quick

(1) Margaret Isobel Hardie Murray; *b* 10 July 1910; *m* 20 March 1935 Geoffrey T Upton, Hon Col Fiji Regt, and *d* 1951, leaving a dau

4 David Sands; *b* 30 May 1864; *d* young

5 Joseph Hardie; *b* 25 Oct 1866; *d* young

6 James Hardie, TD, JP, DL; *b* 9 Feb 1871; Lt-Col cmdg 1st/7th HLI WW I; *m* 16 Nov 1899 Susan, dau of John White, of Kames, Argyllshire, and *d* 1954, leaving issue

1 Isabella Sands; *b* 4 Oct 1861; *d* young

The est s,

WILLIAM BRODIE GALBRAITH, of Overton, Kilmacolm, Renfrewshire, JP; *b* 18 Oct 1855; *educ* Glasgow Acad; CA in Glasgow; *m* 9 Oct 1888 Annie Jack (*d* 12July 1942), 2nd dau of Thomas Dunlop (*see* DUNLOP, Bt), and *d* 23 Sept 1945, having had:

1 Walter Weir; *b* 28 July 1889; MB, ChB, FRFPS (G), FRCSE, Capt RAMC WW I; *m* 30 April 1918 Lucy, dau of Alexander Peter Anderson, JP, of Red Hall, Glasgow, and *d* 25 Nov 1960, leaving:

(1) +Walter Anderson; *b* 19 Aug 1922; *educ* Harrow and St John's Coll Cambridge (BA 1946, MA); engr, AMIME; *m* 19 Oct 1968 *Katharine Mary Rosamund, dau of Capt C C Clark, RA and RAF, of Smiley Knowes, N Berwick

(1) *Alix Margaret Gray; *b* 28 Oct 1919; *m* 1st 14 May 1949 (*divorce* 1964) Angus Cameron Smith, s of James Robert Fyfe Smith, of Etchingham, Sussex; *m* 2nd 4 Nov 1967 *Arthur Leonard Jayne, FSVA, s of Col Arthur Alfred Jayne, DSO and bar, OBE, MC, of Peters Court, Moseley, Warwicks

(2) *Cynthia Graeme Dunlop; *b* 6 April 1926; *educ* Sherborne and Glasgow U (MA); *m* 11 Oct 1952 *Eric Osborne Gibson, MB, ChB, DRCOG, and has:

1a *Eric Nicholas Galbraith; *b* 11 April 1954

2a *Walter Alexander; *b* 16 July 1960

1a *Victoria Lucy Galbraith; *b* 20 June 1955

2a *Sharon Graeme Anderson; *b* 8 June 1958

2 THOMAS DUNLOP, **1st Baron**

3 William Brodie; *b* 26 July 1892; Capt 1st/7th HLI WW I; *ka* 12 July 1915

4 David Boyd; *b* 28 July 1894; Lt 1st/7th HLI WW I; *ka* 20 Aug 1915

5 Norman Dunlop; *b* 25 March 1896; Lt 1st/7th HLI WW I; *ka* Sept 1918

6 Robert Jack; *b* 15 Oct 1898; Lt RGA WW I; *m* 3 Nov 1925 Hope, dau of Thomas Russell, JP, of Bearsden, Dunbartonshire, and had:

(1) *Hamish Galbraith Russell [Hamish Galbraith Esq, Kinnettas, Strathpeffer, Highlands]; *b* 18 Sept 1926; *educ* Ch Ch Oxford (MA); Headmaster Loretto Jr Sch; *m* 31 Aug 1954 *Sheila Mary Wyllie Guild and has:

1a *Robert Hamish Wyllie; *b* 21 June 1955; *m* 13 Dec 1997 *Gillian, yr dau of Capt John Edington, of Gladsmuir, E Lothian

1a *Susan Margaret Guild; *b* 31 May 1957

2a *Frances Mary Hope; *b* 9 May 1962

(2) *David Hope [David Galbraith Esq, West Garth, Craigmillar Ave, Milngavie, Dunbartonshire]; *b* 18 Sept 1926; *m* 5 April 1956 *Valerie Greta Scott and has:

1a *Angus James Scott; *b* 29 July 1966

1a *Rosalind Hope; *b* 7 March 1957

2a *Catherine Scott; *b* 7 March 1957

3a *Alison Margaret; *b* 18 May 1961

4a *Jane Valerie; *b* 11 March 1964

7 *Alexander Henderson; *b* 29 Dec 1904; *educ* Harrow and St John's Coll Cambridge (BA); Maj Argyll and Sutherland Highrs WW II; *m* 28 Nov 1934 Eleanor (*d* 31 Oct 1974), dau of William Lorimer, of Glasgow, and has:

(1) *(Alexander) William Lorimer; *b* 9 Dec 1935; *educ* Loretto; 2nd Lt The Cameronians (Scottish Rifles) 1954–56, travel exec with Wm Martin & Co, Glasgow

(1) *Margaret Anne Lorimer; *b* 12 Oct 1938; *m* William James Kessler, s of Charles Kessler, of Manchester

(2) *Eleanor (Nora) Lorimer; *b* 5 June 1946; *m* 28 April 1967 Donald M White, s of M R White, of Gatehouse of Caprington, Ayrshire, and has issue

1 Annie Dunlop; *b* 28 March 1900; *m* 12 April 1923 Lt-Col Douglas McCrone Martin, s of James Martin, of Kilmacolm, and has:

(1) *Anne Galbraith; *b* 25 Jan 1924; WRNS WW II 1942–45; *m* 25 Sept 1947 *Dennis Williams, DSC, late Lt RNVR, s of H B Williams, of Glasgow, and has issue

(2) *Agnes Mary Galbraith; *b* 22 Nov 1926; WRNS WW II 1942–45; *m* 13 July 1951 *Arthur John Russell Yencken, s of Arthur Yencken, For Serv, and has issue

(3) *Alison Douglas; *b* 6 May 1936; *m* 8 April 1958 *Jeremy Herbert Gibbs (*see* ALDENHAM and HUNSDON OF HUNSDON, B) and has issue

WILLIAM GALBRAITH's 2nd s,

THOMAS DUNLOP GALBRAITH, **1st Baron Strathclyde**, of Barskimming, Co Ayr (UK), so *cr* 4 May 1955, PC (1953); *b* 20 March 1891; *educ* Glasgow Acad (Hon Govr), RNCs Osborne and Dartmouth and RN Staff Coll; RN 1903–22, WW I in HMS *Audacious* and *Queen Elizabeth*, ret as Cdr RN, CA 1925, ptnr Galbraith, Dunlop & Co, of Glasgow, memb Glasgow Town Cncl 1933–40, on Staff of C-in-C Coast Scotland 1939–40, Dep Br Admiralty Supply Rep Washington 1940–42, MP (C) Pollok 1940–55, Jt Parly U-Sec Scotland May–July 1945 and 1951–55, Min State Scottish Office 1955–58, chm N of Scotland Hydro-Electric Bd 1959–67, Govr Wellington 1947–61, Freedom Dingwall 1965 and Aberdeen 1966, Hon FRCP (Edin) and RCPS (Glasgow); *m* 2 Dec 1915 Ida Jean (*d* 1985), est dau of Thomas Galloway, JP, of Auchendrane, Ayrshire, and *d* 1985, having had:

1 Thomas Galloway Dunlop (Sir); *b* 10 March 1917; *educ* Wellington (Govr), Ch Ch Oxford (BA 1938, MA 1947) and Glasgow U (LLB 1946); Lt RNVR WW II, MP (U) Hillhead 1948, Assist C Whip 1950, Scottish U Whip 1950–57, a Ld Commr Treasury 1951–54, Civil Ld Admlty 1957–59, Jt Parly U-Sec Scotland 1959–62 and Tport 1963–64, memb Roy Co Archers, Oppn Tport Spokesman 964–65, V-Chm C Tport Ctee 1966–69, Hon Pres Scottish Georgian Soc, Chm: Ctee Nuclear Propulsion for Merchant Ships 1957–59, Scottish U Members' Ctee; *m* 11 April 1956 (*divorce* 1974) Simone Clotilde Fernande Marie Ghislaine, est dau of Jean du Roy de Blicquy, of Bois d'Hautmont, Brabant, Belgium, and *dvp* 2 Jan 1982, leaving:

(1) THOMAS GALLOWAY DUNLOP DU ROY DE BLICQUY GALBRAITH, **2nd and present Baron Strathclyde**

(2) +CHARLES WILLIAM DU ROY DE BLICQUY [The Hon Charles Galbraith, 59 Cleaver Sq, London SE11 4EA]; *b* 20 May 1962; heir presumptive; *educ* Wellington and St Andrews; granted with sis rank of baron's dau/yr s 1987; *m* 1992 *Bridget Anne, dau of Brian Reeve, of Marford, Clwyd, and has:

1a +Humphrey Eldred Galloway; *b* 2 Nov 1994

2a +Alexander Charles Geoffrey; *b* 15 Jan 1997

(1) *(Anne Marie) Ghislaine du Roy [The Hon Mrs Kennerley, 112 Streathbourne Rd, London SW17 8QY]; *b* 14 Dec 1957; *m* 1989 *Peter Dilworth Kennerley, TD, s of John Dilworth Kennerley, of Whitchurch Canonicorum, Dorset, and has:

1a *Samuel John Maximillian; *b* 1992

1a *Sarah Marie Louise; *b* 1991

2 William Brodie Galloway; *b* 20 Sept 1918; *educ* Wellington; Lt RN WW II; *ka* 12 Oct 1940

3 +James Muir Galloway, CBE (1984) [The Hon James Galbraith CBE, Rawflat, Ancrum, Roxburghshire TD8 6UW]; *b* 27 Sept 1920; *educ* RNC Dartmouth, Ch Ch Oxford (MA) and RAC Cirencester; Lt RN WW II, FRICS, CC Dumfriesshire 1952, JP Inverness-shire 1953–54, dir Buccleuch Estates Ltd 1964–, memb Home Grown Timber Advsy Ctee 1978–90, chm: Timber Growers UK 1980–83, Forestry Industry Ctee of GB 1987–90 and Scottish Forestry Tst 1990–95; *m* 27 Sept 1945 *Anne, er dau of Maj Kenneth Paget, of Old Rectory Ho, Itchen Abbas, Hants, and has:

(1) +Brodie Thomas Paget [Brodie Galbraith Esq, 13 Trowlock Ave, Teddington, Middx]; *b* 20 Nov 1948; *educ* Wellington and Besançon U; late Capt Queen's Own Hussars; *m* 1983 *Fauziah Mohammad and has:

1a +Alexander; *b* 1988

1a +Diana; *b* 1984

2a *Selina; *b* 1986

(2) +James Muir Paget [James Galbraith Esq, 7 Saxe-Coburg Place, Edinburgh EH3]; *b* 12 May 1955; *educ* Eton and RAC Cirencester; ARICS; memb Roy Co Archers; *m* 1990 *Mrs Antoinette C Hudson, dau of Brig Peter Robert Ashburner, CBE, MC, of Wamil Hall, Mildenhall, Suffolk

(3) +John Kenneth Paget [John Galbraith Esq, Belses Muir, Ancrum, Roxburghshire]; *b* 30 Dec 1956; *educ* Eton; *m* 7 May 1983 *Dorothy, dau of John P S Hunter, JP, of Torbeag, Banavie, Inverness-shire and has:

1a +Donald; *b* 1983

2a +Jock; *b* 1993

1a *Anna; *b* 1985

2a *Emily; *b* 1987

3a *Flora; *b* 1991

(1) *Sara Caroline Paget [Mrs John McCorkell, Clanmurry House, Dromore, Co Down BT25 1NL]; *b* 16 July 1950; *m* 3 Sept 1977 *John Barry Ernest McCorkell, er s of Col Sir Michael William McCorkell, KCVO, OBE, TD, of Ballyarnett, Co Derry, and has:

1a *Harry James Michael; *b* 2 July 1988

1a *Rosanna Helen Jane; *b* 3 July 1985

4 +Norman Dunlop Galloway [The Hon Norman Galbraith, Newton Hall, Gifford, by Haddington, E Lothian SH41 4JN]; *b* 25 Jan 1925; *educ* Wellington; Sub-Lt RNVR WW II, dir Ben Line Steamers 1968–86; *m* 9 Sept 1950 *Susan Patricia, er dau of Cdr Jan Herbert Farquharson Kent, RN, of Jersey, and has:

(1) +Norman Thomas Galloway [Norman Galbraith Esq, Over Newton, Gifford, by Hoddington, E Lothian EH41 4JN]; *b* 23 Aug 1955; *educ* Wellington and Newcastle U; FRICS; *m* 1987 *Quona Rose, dau of Maj Cecil Geoffrey Braithwaite, of Lochmalony, Cupar, and has:

1a +Jake Geoffrey Kent; *b* 1989

2a +James Jan Kent; *b* 1991

1a *Ann Rose Braithwaite; *b* 1990

(1) *Patricia Jane [Mrs Christopher Rowe, Withy Shaw House, Goring Heath, Oxon RG8 7RT]; *b* 3 June 1951; *m* 1981 *Christopher John Rowe and has:

1a *John Edward; *b* 1983

2a *Hamish Patrick Rowe; *b* 1990

(2) *Diana Susan [Mrs Andrew Windham, Shobdan Farm, St Margarets, Vowchurch, Herefs HR2 0LW]; *b* 29 March 1954; *m* 4 Dec 1976 *Andrew Guy Windham (*see* BOWYER-SMYTH, Bt) and has issue

5 +David Muir Galloway [The Hon David Galbraith, Burnbrae Lodge, Mauchline, Ayrshire]; *b* 8 March 1928; *educ* Wellingon and RAC Cirencester; *m* 5 Aug 1967 *Marion Bingham, only dau of Maj Bruce Bingham Kennedy, TD, of Doonholm, Ayr, and has:

(1) +William James Kennedy; *b* 15 June 1970; *educ* Glenalmond, Newcastle U (BSc) and RMA Sandhurst; Capt Roy Scots Dragoon Gds

(1) *Fiona Jane Kennedy; *b* 21 Nov 1968; *m* 1991 *Andrew P Robinson, s of R L Robinson, of Top Cottage, Thornyflat Farm, Ayr

(2) *Mary Ida Galloway; *b* 17 Sept 1973

(3) *Alice Sylvia Kennedy; *b* 18 Feb 1976

1 *Ida Jean Galloway; *b* 21 Jan 1922; *educ* Queen Ethelburga's; 3rd Offr WRNS WW II

2 *Heather Margaret Anne Galloway; *b* 27 Feb 1930

STRATHCONA AND MOUNT ROYAL

Arms: Quarterly: 1st and 4th, arg. on a bend indented between four cross crosslets gu. three maple leaves or; 2nd and 3rd, gu. on a fess arg. between a demi-lion rampant or in chief and a canoe of the last with four men rowing ppr., in the stern a flag of the second flowing towards the dexter inscribed with the letters NW sa., a hammer surmounted of a nail in saltire of the last. **Crest:** On a mount vert a beaver eating into a maple tree ppr.
Supporters: Dexter, a trooper of the Regiment of Strathcona's Horse ppr.; sinister, a navvy standing on a railway sleeper, chaired and railed all ppr. **Mottoes:** 1 (over) Perseverance, 2 (below) *Agmina ducens* ('Leading the armies'). **Creation:** B. (UK) 26 June 1900.

THE 4TH BARON STRATHCONA AND MOUNT ROYAL, of Mount Royal, Quebec, and Glencoe, Co Argyll ((Donald) Euan Palmer Howard, DL (Angus)) [The Rt Hon The Lord Strathcona and Mount Royal DL, 16 Henning St, London SW11 3DR; Kiloran, Isle of Colonsay, Argyll PA61 7YU]; *b* 26 Nov 1923; *s f* 1959; *educ* Eton, Trin Coll Cambridge and McGill; Lt RNVR WW II 1942–47; with Urwick, Orr & ptnrs, industl consultants, 1950–56, Govt Whip 1973–74, Parly U-Sec MOD Jan–March 1974, Jt Dep Leader Oppn Ho Lds 1976–79, Min State MOD 1979–81, chm: Bath Festival Soc 1966–70, Tallon Ltd and Bristol Repetition Ltd, dep chm SS *Great Britain* project (tporting Brunel's ship from Falkland Isles to UK), v-chm Maritime Tst, fndr chm Coastal Forces Heritage Tst 1995–, Pres UK Pilots Assoc, Falkland Is Tst 1982– and Steamboat Assoc of GB 1972–, dir: Dundonian 1976–, Computing Devices Hastings 1981–92; memb Cncl Nat Fedn Housing Socs; Fishmongers' Co: 2nd Warden 1995–96, 3rd Warden 1996–97; *m* 1st 20 Feb 1954 (*divorce* 1977) Lady Jane Mary Waldegrave, 2nd dau of 12th Earl Waldegrave (*qv*); *m* 2nd 14 Feb 1978 *Patricia, dau of Harvey Evelyn Thomas and widow of John Middleton, and has by his 1st w:

1 +(DONALD) ALEXANDER SMITH; *b* 24 June 1961; *educ* Gordonstoun and London Business Sch (MBA); *m* 1992 *Jane Maree, dau of R Shaun Gibb, of Sydney, NSW, and has:

  (1) +(Donald) Angus Ruaridh; *b* 1994
  (1) *Amelia Alexandra; *b* 1996

2 +Andrew Barnaby (twin); *b* 17 Aug 1963; *educ* Gordonstoun and Fettes; *m* 1994 *Katharine E, est dau of C Oldfield, of Uplyme, Devon

1 *Jane Elizabeth Sterling [The Hon Mrs Morris-Jones, Eardisley Park, Eardisley, Herefs HR3 6NT]; *b* 23 Jan 1955; *educ* Sherborne and Somerville Coll Oxford; *m* 1987 *Nigel MORRIS later MORRIS-JONES (deed poll), only s of M H Morris Jones, of Tarvin, Cheshire, and has:

  (1) *Sophia Venetia; *b* 1989
  (2) *Lydia Iona; *b* 1991
  (3) *Kiloran Imogen; *b* 1993
  (4) *Eloïse Georgia (twin); *b* 1993

2 *Katharine Mary [The Hon Mrs Joll, 17 Durand Gdns, London SW9 0PS]; *b* 11 Sept 1956; *m* 1st 16 Aug 1975 (*divorce* 1982) Gavin Michael Jasper Strachan, yr s of M F Strachan, of Edinburgh; *m* 2nd 30 March 1982 *(William) Evelyn Hinton Joll, s of Evelyn Joll, of S Kensington, and has:

  (1) *Harry Augustus; *b* 1983
  (1) *Flora Katharine Kiloran; *b* 1985
  (2) *Hannah Olympia; *b* 1988

3 *Caroline Anne; *b* 30 March 1959

4 *Emma Laura Louise [The Hon Mrs Zwill, 34 Merehaye, Wooloowin, Brisbane, Qld 4030, Australia]; *b* 17 Aug 1963; *m* 18 May 1996 *David Zwill, s of William Zwill, of Adelaide, and has:

  (1) *Joshua; *b* 1997

Lineage: ALEXANDER SMITH, of Archiestown, Elgin; *b* 1780; *m* 1813 Barbara (*d* 18 April 1874 aged 90), dau of Donald Stuart, of Leanchoil, Abernethy, Inverness-shire, and *d* 3 March 1847, having had, with an est s (John Stuart, *b* 1815, MA Aberdeen, MD Edin, LRCS 1839, Staff Surgn-Maj Army Medical Dept, India, first Chinese and Maori wars, *m* Elizabeth Cousins, of Surrey, and *d* 1

March 1899, leaving two daus), a yst s (James McGrigor, *b* 1822, *d* 29 Oct 1826) and three daus (*d* unm):

DONALD ALEXANDER SMITH, **1st Baron Strathcona and Mount Royal**, of Mount Royal, Quebec, Canada, and Glencoe, Argyll, so *cr* 26 June 1900, with special remainder, in default of male issue, to his dau and her heirs male (in recognition of his raising and fitting out Strathcona's Horse for service in the Boer War), also earlier 23 Aug 1897 BARON STRATHCONA (a Gaelic approximation to Glencoe, land in the vicinity of which he had acquired just prior to his ennoblement) AND MOUNT ROYAL (*i.e.*, Montreal), of Glencoe, Argyll, and Mount Royal, Quebec, Canada, with remainder to heirs male of his body, GCMG (1896), GCVO (1908), PC (Canada 1896), DL Argyllshire; *b* 6 Aug 1820; *educ* Anderson Inst Forres; Hudson's Bay Co: apprentice clerk 1838, Ch Trader 1852, Ch Factor 1862, last Resident Govr 1869, Dep Govr 1888–96, Govr 1896–1914, Special Commr throughout Riel Rebellion Red River Settlements 1869–70, Ch Commr Fur Trade 1870–74, Land Commr 1874–79, MEC NW Territories 1870, memb Winnipeg and St John Manitoba Legislature 1871–84, MP (Canadian Parl) Selkirk 1871–79 (unseated on petition) and Montreal W 1887–96; promoted construction of Canadian-Pacific Rlway; Hon Pres Bank of Montreal, V-Pres Dominion Rifle Assoc, Hon Col 10th (Scottish) Bn Liverpool Regt, Roy Canadians, 79th Cameron Highrs Canada and Victoria Rifles Montreal, Canadian HC UK 1896–1914, memb Roy Commn War S Africa 1902, Chllr McGill 1903–14, Rector Aberdeen U 1899–1902 and Chllr 1903–14, Hon LLD Cantab, Glasgow, Aberdeen, Victoria (Manchester), Birmingham, St Andrews, Dublin, Yale, Alberta, Toronto, Queen's, Laval and Ottawa, Hon DCL Oxon and Durham, Hon Freeman Aberdeen, Bath, Bristol, Edinburgh and Forres, Hon Cdre Roy St Lawrence Yacht Club, FRS 1904, KGStJ; *m* 9 March 1853 Isabella Sophia (*d* 12 Nov 1913 aged 89), dau of Richard Hardisty, Ch Trader Hudson's Bay Co, and formerly w of — Grant, and *dspm* 21 Jan 1914, when the 1897 Barony expired, leaving:

1 MARGARET CHARLOTTE Smith, **Baroness Strathcona and Mount Royal**; *b* 17 Jan 1854; LGStJ; *m* 8 March 1888 Robert Jared Bliss HOWARD, OBE, MD, FRCS (*d* 9 Jan 1921), s of Robert Palmer Howard, MD, LLD (*d* 1889), of Montreal, and *d* 18 Aug 1926, leaving:

  (1) DONALD STERLING PALMER HOWARD, **3rd Baron Strathcona and Mount Royal**; *b* 14 June 1891; *educ* Eton and Trin Coll Cambridge (BA 1913); Capt 3rd Hus WW I (Belgian Croix de Guerre), MP (C) N Cumberland 1922–26, PPS to 1st Ld Admlty 1925–27, memb Indian Statutory Commn 1927–30, Chllr Primrose League 1930–31, Capt Yeomen Gd 1931–34, Parly U-Sec War and V-Pres Army Cncl 1934–39, Lt-Col London Scottish (Gordons) TA, Hon Col Artists Rifles (TA) 1938, WW II: Mil Liaison Offr Combined Munitions Assignment Bd Washington 1943–44, Liaison with US Army London and France 1944–45, CC Argyll 1952, US Legn Merit and Bronze Star; *m* 25 Oct 1922 Hon Diana Evelyn Loder (*d* 1985), 3rd dau of 1st Baron Wakehurst (*qv*), and *d* 22 Feb 1959, having had:

    1a (DONALD) EUAN PALMER HOWARD, **4th and present Baron Strathcona and Mount Royal**

    2a +Barnaby John [The Hon Barnaby Howard, 1224 River Rd, Orange Pk, FL 32073, USA; St Ann's Bay, RR4 , Baddeck, NS B0E 1B0, Canada]; *b* 23 Nov 1925; *educ* Eton and Trin Coll Cambridge (BA 1948, MA 1954); Sub-Lt (A) RNVR WW II, Commr S Rhodesia Forestry Commn 1957; *m* 1st 19 Jan 1952 (*divorce* 1967) Elizabeth, yr dau of Frank McConnell Mayfield, of St Louis, Mo., and has had:

      1b Alan Sterling; *b* 15 April 1956; *d* 1992
      1b *Elizabeth Kiloran [Vicomtesse Philippe de Lapérouse, 2 White Gate Lane, St Louis, MO 63124, USA]; *b* 20 May 1957; *m* 1982 *Vicomte Philippe de Lapérouse, est s of Count Bertrand de Lapérouse, of Fairhaven, NJ, and has:

        1c *Patrick Henri Louis Léon Marie; *b* 1985
        1c *Kiloran Elizabeth Diana Marie; *b* 1986
        2c *Isabelle Marthe Jeanne Marie; *b* 1990

      2b *Sarah Anne Catriona; *b* 11 Sept 1962; *m* 1983 (*divorce* 1992) Dr Jeffrey Lee Thomasson, MD, and has:

        1c *Robert Howard; *b* 1987
        2c *Alan Mayfield; *b* 1988
        1c *Patricia Delzell; *b* 1991

    2a (cont.) The Hon Barnaby Howard *m* 2nd 4 Oct 1970 Mrs Mary-Jane Bishop (*d* 1994), dau of Ambrose Chambers; *m* 3rd 1996 his cousin *Linda Frances Kitson

    3a +Jonathan Alan; *b* 15 Nov 1933; *educ* Eton, Trin Coll Cambridge, Roy Inst Tech Stockholm and Stockholm U; late Lt Coldstream Gds and Argyll and Sutherland Highrs (TA); *m* 1st 16 Aug 1956 (*divorce* 1969) Hon Brigid Mary Westenra, only dau of 6th Baron Rossmore (*qv*), and has:

      1b *Nicola Charlotte; *b* 13 June 1958

    3a (cont.) The Hon Jonathan Howard *m* 2nd 1970 (*divorce* 1981) Cecilia Philipson and has by her:

      1b Olof Philipson; *b* 1970

    1a A dau; *b* 31 Oct, *d* 3 Nov 1927

    2a *Diana Catriona [The Hon Mrs Faber, Rodmell, Mill Lane, Lewes, E Sussex BN7 3HS]; *b* 13 March 1935; *m* 7 June 1956 *Prof Michael Leslie Ogilvie Faber, er s of George Valdemar Faber, of W Kensington, and has:

      1b *Rory Valdemar; *b* 1956; *m* 1997 *Julie Ann, only dau of Dr Robert Johnson, DVM, of Los Altos, Calif.
      2b *Guy Donald George; *b* 1959
      1b *Laura Diana; *b* 1958; *m* 1993 *John R Percival, s of Michael Percival, of London SW1
      2b *Charlotte Victoria (twin); *b* 1958; *m* 1990 *John Marais and has:

        1c *Edward John; *b* 1991
        1c *Maria-del-Mar; *b* 1989

  (2) Robert Henry Palmer; *b* 1893; 2nd Lt 4th Bn E Surrey Regt; *ka* 8 May 1915
  (3) Arthur Jared Palmer (Sir), KBE (1953), CVO (1937), DL (Co London 1937), JP (Sussex 1939); *b* 30 May 1896; *educ* Eton; Capt Scots Gds WW I (wounded, Croix de Guerre), memb Westminster City Cncl 1925, Mayor Westminster 1936–37, Tstee Imp Rels Tst 1937, Pncpl Air Raid Warden London CD WW II 1939–42, Jt Treas St Thomas's Hosp 1943–64, MP (Lab) St George's Westmin-

ster 1945–50, Fell King's Coll London 1947, chm Delegacey 1951; *m* 20 June 1922 Lady Leonora Stanley Baldwin (*d* 1989), dau of 1st Earl Baldwin of Bewdley (*qv*), and *d* 26 April 1971, leaving:

1a Robin Jared Stanley; *b* 17 May 1924; *educ* Eton and Trin Coll Cambridge (MA); Scots Gds WW II 1942–45; *d* 1989

2a +Alexander [Alexander Howard Esq, Poronui Station, RD3, Taupo, New Zealand]; *b* 24 Nov 1930; *educ* Eton and Trin Coll Cambridge (MA); Scots Gds 1949–51; *m* 24 June 1959 *Penelope Joanna, only child of Gershom Radcliffe Layton Warren, of Saanichton, Vancouver Is, and has:

1b +Shamus Alexander; *b* 9 Oct 1962

2b +Harry Alexander; *b* 3 March 1967

3b +Rory Jared; *b* 1973

1a *Kiloran Margaret; *b* 21 July 1926; *m* 13 June 1951 Hon Langley Gordon Haslingden Russell, MC (*d* 16 Sept 1975), only s of 2nd Baron Russell of Liverpool (*qv*), and has issue

2a *Jill [Mrs Peter Lumsden, 24 Holland Villas Rd, London W14]; *b* 17 March 1934; *m* 3 Oct 1958 *Peter James Scott Lumsden, yr s of Lt-Gen Herbert Lumsden, CB, DSO, MC, and has:

1b *James Herbert; *b* 17 Oct 1962

1b *Alice Margaret; *b* 25 Aug 1961

2b *Susanna Helen; *b* 26 Nov 1965

(1) Frances Margaret Palmer; *b* 13 Feb 1889; *m* 24 May 1913 Capt James Buller Kitson, DSO, RN, s of Rev John Buller Kitson, Rector Lanreath, Cornwall, and *d* 5 Oct 1958, leaving issue

(2) Edith Mary Palmer, MBE (1941); *b* 7 April 1895; Order Mercy and bar; *m* 1st 6 April 1918 6th Baron Congleton (*qv*) and had issue; *m* 2nd 5 July 1946 F/Lt Alfred Eric Rowland Aldridge, RAF (*d* 11 June 1950), s of Alfred Frank Aldridge, of Caterham, Surrey, and resumed name Congleton by deed poll 17 Jan 1951

(2) *Kiloran Emma; *b* 14 Sept 1959

STRATHEDEN and CAMPBELL

Arms: Gyronny of eight or and sa. within a bordure engrailed quarterly or and az., charged with eight buckles, counterchanged. **Crest:** A boar's head erased gyronny of eight or and sa. **Supporters:** 1 On either side a buck arg., attired and hoofed or, the dexter gorged with a collar compony gu. and of the second, therefrom pendant an escutcheon gyronny of eight or and sa.; the sinister gorged with a collar, therefrom pendant an escutcheon gold charged with three chaplets of laurel, two and one ppr. (for STRATHEDEN) (illustrated), 2 On either side a lion guardant gu., the dexter gorged with a collar or, pendant therefrom an escutcheon az. charged with a saltire arg., the sinister gorged with a wreath of shamrocks ppr., pendant therefrom an escutcheon or and gu. (for CAMPBELL, not illustrated). **Motto:** *Audacter et aperte* ('Boldly and openly'). **Creation:** B. (UK) 22 Jan 1836 (Stratheden) and 30 June 1841 (Campbell).

THE 6TH BARON STRATHEDEN OF CUPAR, Co Fife and **6TH BARON CAMPBELL OF ST ANDREWS**, Fife (Donald Campbell) [The Rt Hon The Lord Stratheden and Campbell, Yalara, MS 401, Cooroy, Qld 4563, Australia]; *b* 4 April 1934; *s* f 1987; *educ* Eton; *m* 8 Nov 1957 Hilary Ann Holland (*d* 1991), dau of Lt-Col William D Turner, of Simonstown, S Africa, and has:

1 +DAVID ANTHONY [The Hon David Campbell, 6 Lawnville Rd, Cooroy, Qld 4563, Australia]; *b* 13 Feb 1963; *m* 1993 *Jennifer Margaret Owens and has:

(1) *A dau; *b* 199–

1 *Tania Ann [The Hon Tania Campbell, 36 Charles Kurz Dve, Mudgeeraba, Qld 4213, Australia]; *b* 19 Sept 1960; *m* 1984 *Paul Hamment, of Melbourne, has resumed maiden name and has:

(1) *Jenna Cherie CAMPBELL; *b* 9 Nov 1985

2 *Wendy Meriel; *b* 27 Jan 1969

3 *Joyce Margaret *b* 1971

Campbell, previous creations: For the Scottish Lordship of Parliament of Campbell *cr* 1445 and Earldom of Campbell and Cowall *cr* 1701, see ARGYLL, D. For the Scottish Lordship of Parliament of Campbell of Loudoun *cr* 1601, see LOUDOUN, E.

Lineage: GEORGE CAMPBELL, descended from the CAMPBELLs of Keithock, a branch of the CAMPBELLs of Argyll; supported 1st Marquess of Argyll (*qv*) in latter's tergiversations to the detriment of his own finances; settled 1662 at St Andrews, acquiring the estate of Baltullo, parish of Ceres; his est s:

JOHN CAMPBELL; *educ* St Andrews (MA 1677); had:

GEORGE CAMPBELL; sold Baltullo; had:

Rev GEORGE CAMPBELL; DD, Min Cupar; *m* 1776 Magdalene, only dau of John Hallyburton of Fodderance, a branch of the HALLYBURTONs of Pitcur, and *d* 1825, having had, with an er s (Sir George, of Edenwood, Fife, *m* Margaret (*d* 1873), dau of Andrew Christie of Ferrybank, and *d* 20 May 1854, leaving issue; see LEVINGE, Bt) and five daus (Janet, *m* Rev Dr Gillespie, LLD, of St Andrews; Jane, *m* James Greig of Balbardie; Eliza, *d* 13 March 1874; Lindsay, *m* David Johnston of Overton; Magdalene, *m* Charles Grace, MD):

JOHN CAMPBELL, **1st Baron Campbell of St Andrews**, Co Fife (UK), so *cr* 30 June 1841, PC (GB 22 June 1841, I 5 July 1841); *b* 15 Sept 1779; *educ* Cupar GS and St Andrews (MA); barrister Lincoln's inn 1806, Bencher 1827, KC 1827, MP (Whig) Stafford 1830–32, Dudley 1832–34 and Edinburgh 1834–41, Slr-Gen 1832–34, ktd 1832, Attorney-Gen March-Dec 1834 and 1835–41, Ld Chllr Ireland June-Aug 1841, Chllr Duchy Lancaster 1846–50, Ch Justice Queen's Bench 1850–59, Ld Chllr 1859–61, author: *Lives of the Lord Chancellors* (1845–57); *m* 8 Sept 1821 MARY ELIZABETH SCARLETT (*d* 25 March 1860), *cr* 22 Jan 1836 (at a time when her husb had twice missed being appointed Master of the Rolls and in consequence resigned as Attorney-Gen; he thereafter swiftly took the post up again) **Baroness Stratheden of Cupar**, Co Fife (UK), with remainder to the heirs male of her body, er dau of 1st Baron Abinger (*qv*), and *d* 23 June 1861, leaving:

1 WILLIAM FREDERICK CAMPBELL, **2nd Baron Stratheden of Cupar** and **2nd Baron Campbell of St Andrews**, DL Roxburghshire; *b* 15 Oct 1824; *educ* Eton, Balliol Coll Oxford and Trin Coll Cambridge (Pres Union 1847); MP (Lib) Cambridge 1847–52 and Harwich 1859–60, Hon Col 7th Vol Bn KRRC; *d* unm 21 Jan 1893

2 HALLYBURTON GEORGE, **3rd Baron**

3 Dudley; *b* 24 Dec 1833; MA Cantab; barrister; *d* unm 24 Jan 1900

1 Louise Madeline; *m* 13 Sept 1850 Rev W S White (*d* 8 July 1893), Preb Lincoln, Rector Potter Hanworth, Lincs

2 Mary Scarlett; *m* 8 July 1869 Joseph Alfred Hardcastle, of Holt, Norfolk, MP Bury St Edmunds. He *d* 8 Aug 1899

3 Cecilia Mina; *m* 29 July 1862 Henry Robert Vaughan Johnson, barrister, 3rd s of Rev John Johnson, LLD, Rector Yaxham-cum-Welborne, Norfolk, and *d* 12 June 1928, leaving issue. He *d* 23 Feb 1899

4 Edina; *m* 4 Oct 1859 Rev William Arthur Duckworth, of Orchard Leigh Park, Frome, and *d* 21 Dec 1916, leaving issue. He *d* 6 Dec 1917

The 2nd BARON's bro,

HALLYBURTON GEORGE CAMPBELL, **3rd Baron Stratheden of Cupar** and **3rd Baron Campbell of St Andrews**, JP, DL Roxburghs, JP Co Galway; *b* 18 Oct 1829; *educ* Eton, Haileybury, Trin Coll Cambridge (MA) and Lincoln's Inn; HEICS 1849–55, Assoc Queen's Bench 1853, Sec Commissions Court Chancery 1860–73, Lt-Col 40th Middx Rifles 1866–72, Master Supreme Court Judicature; *m* 24 Aug 1865 Louisa Mary (*d* 20 June 1923), est dau of Alexander James Beresford Beresford-Hope, PC, MP (*see* SALISBURY, M), and *d* 26 Dec 1918, having had:

1 John Beresford, DSO, JP, DL Roxburghs and Co Galway; *b* 20 June 1866; High Sheriff Co Galway 1907, Capt 1st Bn Coldstream Gds and Roy Gds (Res) Regt WW I (despatches); *m* 15 Jan 1895 Hon Alice Susan, JP Roxburghs (granted 7 Feb 1921 rank of baron's widow; *d* 25 Jan 1949), 2nd dau of 1st Baron Hamilton of Dalzell (*qv*), and was *ka* 25 Jan 1915, leaving:

(1) Donald; *b* 16 April 1896; Lt 3rd Bn Coldstream Gds; *ka* 19 July 1916

(2) ALISTAIR CAMPBELL, **4th Baron Stratheden of Cupar** and **4th Baron Campbell of St Andrews**, CBE (1964), JP (Roxburghs 1945); *b* 21 Nov 1899; *educ* Eton and RMC Sandhurst; Coldstream Gds: Regtl Adj 1931–34, Staff Offr Local Forces Kenya and Uganda 1936–39, Lt-Col cmdg 5th Bn WW II 1941–44 (wounded, despatches), Regtl Lt-Col cmdg 1945–46, Brig cmdg 32nd Gds Bde and 4th Inf Bde 1946–49, DDPS War Office 1949–50, Roxburghs: Chm Educn Ctee 1955–58, Convener CC 1960–68, V-Lt 1962–81 (DL 1945–62); Chm: Edin and E of Scotland Ag Coll 1956–81, Hill Farming Research Org 1958–69, Historic Bldgs Cncl Scotland 1969–81; Pres Assoc CCs Scotland 1966–68; Capt Roy Co Archers; Hon LLD Edin; *m* 1st 6 Feb 1923 Jean Helen St Clair, CBE (1954) (*d* 9 Aug 1956), dau of Col William Anstruther-Gray (*see* ANSTRUTHER, Bt); *m* 2nd 21 Dec 1964 *Mrs Noël Christabel Vincent, dau of Capt Conrad Viner, and *dspm* 1981, leaving by his 1st w:

1a *Moyra Jean [The Hon Moyra Campbell, Scraesburgh, Jedburgh, Roxburghs]; *b* 14 July 1924

2a *Clayre [The Lady Richard Percy, 212 Lambeth Rd, London SE1 7JY]; *b* 28 May 1927; *m* 1st 17 Aug 1950 (*divorce* 1974) Baron Ridley of Liddesdale (LP, *d* 1993; *see* RIDLEY, V) and has issue; *m* 2nd 18 Dec 1979, as his 2nd w, Lord Richard Charles Percy (*d* 1989), s of 8th Duke of Northumberland (*qv*)

3a *Fiona [The Hon Fiona Campbell, 158 Lambeth Rd, London SE1 7DF]; *b* 4 Feb 1932

(3) GAVIN CAMPBELL, **5th Baron Stratheden of Cupar** and **5th Baron Campbell of St Andrews**; *b* 28 Aug 1901; *educ* Eton and RMC Sandhurst; Maj KRRC, Lt-Col 19th (Kenya) Bn KAR WW II (released due ill health 1944); *m* 26 April 1933 Evelyn Mary (*d* 1989), yr dau of Col Herbert Austen Smith, CIE, IMS, of Hawkhurst, Kent, and *d* 1987, leaving:

1a DONALD CAMPBELL, **6th and present Baron Stratheden of Cupar and Baron Campbell of St Andrews**

(1) Jean; granted rank of baron's dau 12 Jan 1921; *m* 5 April 1939 Alexander George Seton, er s of George Seton, of Stonehall, Wolf's Castle, Pembs, and *d* 10 Feb 1952, leaving issue

2 Cecil Arthur; *b* 3 April 1869; *m* 3 Sept 1915 Josephine Theodora (Dixon) (*d* 10 Aug 1932), dau of Richard Henry Williams, of New York and Madison, NJ, and *d* 6 April 1932, leaving:

   (1) Richard Cecil Hallyburton; *b* 1 June 1916; *d* 25 Nov 1936

3 Kenneth Hallyburton; *b* 21 May 1871; *m* 22 May 1905 Rosalinda Emily (*d* 20 July 1960), only dau of Henry Maurice William Oppenheim, and *d* 6 April 1947, having had:

   (1) Hamish Lionel; *b* 15 June 1906; *d* 8 Dec 1923

   (2) Ian George Hallyburton, TD, QC (1957); *b* 19 July 1909; *educ* Charterhouse and Trin Coll Cambridge (MA); barrister Inner Temple and Lincoln's Inn 1932, Ld Chllr's Legal Visitor 1963, WW II: Artists Rifles, Rifle Bde, Allied Commn Italy and Allied Mil Govt Austria, Hon Col; *m* April 1949 *Betty Yolande, widow of Lt-Col Hugh Allan Bruno, MBE, and yr dau of Somerset Maclean, and adopted:

      *James Ian Somerset; *b* 15 July 1955

      *Camilla Rose; *b* 6 Dec 1956

4 Douglas Hallyburton; *b* 3 May, *d* 6 Aug 1876

1 Mildred Louisa; *b* 29 Nov 1867; *d* unm 7 March 1951

STRATHMORE AND KINGHORNE

Arms: Quarterly, 1st and 4th, argent a lion rampant azure, armed and langued gules, within a double tressure flory-counterflory of the second (for LYON); 2nd and 3rd, ermine three bows stringed palewise proper (for BOWES); Royal Augmentation (granted to the holder of the Earldom only): en surtout an inescutcheon azure, thereon a rose argent, barbed vert and seeded or, ensigned with the Imperial Crown proper, within a double tressure flory-counterflory of the second, the said inescutcheon ensigned with an Earl's coronet proper. **Crest:** Between two slips of laurel a lady to the girdle, habited and holding in her dexter hand a thistle all proper. **Supporters:** Dexter, a unicorn argent, armed, unguled, maned and tufted or; sinister, a lion per fess or and gules. **Motto:** *In te Domine speravi* ('In Thee Lord have I put my trust'). **Creations:** L. (S) 28 June 1445 (Glamis), E. (Kinghorne, from 1 July 1677 Strathmore and Kinghorne) and L. (Lyon and Glamis, from 1 July 1677 subsumed in full designation of Earldom of Strathmore and Kinghorne) (S) 10 July 1606, B. (UK) 1 July 1887, E. (UK) 1 June 1937 (Strathmore and Kinghorne).

THE 18TH EARL OF STRATHMORE AND KINGHORNE, Viscount Lyon, **Lord Glamis, Tannadyce, Sidlaw and Strathdichtie,** Baron Bowes of Streatlam Castle, Co Durham, **and of Lunedale,** Co York, and **Earl of Strathmore and Kinghorne** (Michael Fergus Bowes-Lyon, DL (Angus 1994)) [The Rt Hon The Earl of Strathmore and Kinghorne DL, Glamis Castle, Forfar, Angus DD8 1QJ]; *b* 7 June 1957; *s* f 1987; *educ* Eton, Aberdeen U (BLE 1979) and RMA Sandhurst; Page of Hon to HM QUEEN ELIZABETH, THE QUEEN MOTHER 1971–73, Capt Scots Gds 1980, Govt Whip 1989–91, Dep Govt Ch Whip 1991–94, dir Polypipe plc 1994–, Lancaster plc 1994–, Pres Boys' Bde 1994–; *m* 1984 *Isobel Charlotte, yr dau of Capt Anthony E Weatherall, of Cowhill, Dumfriesshire, and has:

1 +SIMON PATRICK, *Lord Glamis; b* 18 June 1986

2 +John Fergus; *b* 1988

3 +George Norman; *b* 1991

Lineage: Sir JOHN LYON of Forteviot and later Glamis, Forfarshire, which granted by ROBERT II 1372; an Auditor of the Chamberlain Jan 1368/69, Keeper Privy Seal 1371, Chamberlain Scotland 1377–82, ktd by 20 Oct 1377; *m* by 4 Oct 1376 Jean (*m* 3rd Sir James Sandilands of Calder; *see* TORPHICHEN, L), dau of ROBERT II by his 1st w Elizabeth Mure and widow of John Keith (*see* KINTORE, E), thereby acquiring the feudal Barony of Kinghorne and thanedom of Tanna-

dyce, and was *k* 4 Nov 1382 by Sir James Lindsay of Crawford (*see* CRAWFORD and BALCARRES, E), leaving:

Sir JOHN LYON, 2nd of Glamis; ktd 1404; *m* his cousin Elizabeth, sis of 1st Earl of Menteith (*see* MONTROSE, D), and *d c* 1435, leaving, with two yr sons:

PATRICK LYON, **1st Lord Glamis** (S), so *cr* 28 June 1445, PC (S 1445); a hostage to the English for ransom of JAMES I 28 March 1424–9 June 1427; a Ld Auditor Treasury 1450–51, Master Household 1450–52, Amb England 1451 and 1455, Keeper Balveny, Kildrummy and Kindrocht Castles 1456–59, a Ld Session 1457; *m* shortly after 1427 Isabel (*m* 2nd 1st Lord Kennedy (*see* AILSA, M) and *d* 1484), dau of Sir Walter Ogilvy of Lintrathen (*see* AIRLIE, E), and *d* 21 March 1459, having:

1 ALEXANDER LYON, **2nd Lord Glamis**; a Ld Auditor of Parl and a Ld of Cncl; *m* just prior to 17 Feb 1449/50 Agnes (*m* 2nd 20 Oct 1487 Walter Ker of Cessford; *see* LOTHIAN, M), dau of 1st Lord Crichton (*see* ERNE, E), and *dsp* 1486

2 JOHN, **3rd Lord**

3 William, 1st of Easter Ogil (to which vindicated his right 20 June 1498 after a dispute with his n, **4th Lord**), Pettanys and Tannadyce, Forfarshire; had:

   (1) William, 2nd of Easter Ogil; had:

      1a William, 3rd of Easter Ogil; living 9 Aug 1547; *d* 1567, leaving:

         1b John, 4th of Easter Ogil; had:

            1c James, 5th of Easter Ogil; living 1591; ancestor of:

               1d William, 10th of Easter Ogil, which he made over to trustees 1718, it being 1740 settled on John Lyon of Balgillo

            2c Alexander, of Auchmudy; *m* Isabel Lindsey and had:

               1d David, of Hookehill; *m* Susanna Wood and had:

                  1e Patrick, 1st of Carse, in the territorial Barony of Rescobie, Angus, which he acquired through his w; *b* 1637; *educ* St Andrews; advocate 1671, Burgess Dundee 1671 and Edinburgh 1681, Ld of Session as Lord Carse 1683, Adml Depute and Ld of Justiciary 1684; *m* Elizabeth, sis of William Gray of Invereightie and widow of Patrick Lyon of Brigton (*see* below), and *d* 4 Jan 1694, leaving:

                     1f Patrick, 2nd of Carse; *b* 30 Nov 1672; *m* 8 Aug 1699 Mary Borthwick, widow of Sir Alexander Livingstone of Glentirren, Angus, and *d* March 1707, leaving:

                        1g Patrick, 3rd of Carse; *bapt* 3 Oct 1701; *d* unm Dec 1732

                        2g John, 4th of Carse, which he sold to Capt Charles Gray, of Dundee; *b c* 1701; Surveyor Customs Dunbar; *m* Janet Brand (*d* by 11 Jan 1775) and *d* May 1747, leaving:

                           1h James; Capt 35th Regt; *m* Mary (*m* 2nd Rev George Coxe, Rector Twyford, Hants), only child and heiress of James Hamilton of Ballencreiff (12th in descent from Alexander Hamilton of Innerwick; *see* HADDINGTON, E), Keeper Stores Chatham and Woolwich, and gdau of Alexander Hamilton of Ballencreiff, MP, PMG for Scotland, by Mary, 4th dau of 2nd Marquess of Lothian (*qv*), and was *ka* Battle of Bunker Hill June 1775 at start of War of American Independence, leaving:

                              1i James (Sir), KCB (1815), GCH (1817); *b* posthumously 1775; *educ* Göttingen U at the expense of QUEEN CHARLOTTE, w of GEORGE III; Hon Col KOSB, cmdg Hanoverian Bde at Waterloo, Govr Barbados 1828–33, Lt-Gen 1830, Equerry to HRH DUKE OF CAMBRIDGE, Kt Cdr Maximilian Joseph (Bavaria), Order Sword Sweden, Kt Cross Order Willem Netherlands; *m* Anne (*d* 1850), dau of Edward Coxe, of Hampstead, and *d* 16 Oct 1842, leaving:

                                 1j Mary; *m* Maj William Reader, of Castlebar, Co Mayo, and Oxford, and had two sons

                                 2j Eleanor Elizabeth; *b* 1825; *m* 17 Feb 1855, as his 1st w, Rev Richard Bryans, of Roden Ho, Sussex, est s of James Bryans, JP, DL, of Belfield, Windermere, and *d* 1876, leaving issue

                  1c Barbara; *m c* 1580 Thomas Ogilvy of Inshewan and had issue

4 Patrick; living 1481

1 Elizabeth; *m* Alexander Robertson of Strowan

The 2nd LORD's bro,

JOHN LYON, **3rd Lord Glamis**, PC (S 1489); a Ld Auditor of Parl and a Ld of Cncl 1484–94; a Gt Justice south of the River Forth 1487/8, Jt Justiciar Scotland 1489–94, Amb England 1491; *m* probably by 1450 Elizabeth, dau of Sir John Scrymgeour of Dudhope (*see* DUNDEE, E), and *d* 1 April 1497, having had:

1 JOHN, **4th Lord**

2 David, of Baky and Cossins and Haltoun of Erse; *m c* Sept 1505 Elizabeth, dau of 5th Earl of Crawford (*see* CRAWFORD and BALCARRES, E), and was *ka* Flodden 9 Sept 1513, leaving:

   (1) John, 2nd of Cossins, also of Craigmillar Castle; *m* Margery, dau of 3rd Lord Ogilvy (*see* AIRLIE, E), and had:

      1a John, 3rd of Cossins; *m* Margaret, dau of William Drummond of Balloch and widow of (a) John Campbell of Murthlie and (b) Robert Spittell, and had:

         1b John, 4th of Cossins; *b* 1587; *m* Jean Campbell and *d c* 22 May 1637, leaving:

            1c Thomas, 5th of Cossins; *b* 1607; *m* Jean, dau of Sir Peter Young of Seytoun, Almoner to JAMES VI and I, and *d* 1659, leaving:

               1d Peter, 6th of Cossins, JP (Forfarshire 1663); Commr War Forfarshire 1648; *m* Margaret, dau of Sir John Ogilvy, 1st Bt (*qv*), and *d* 1663, leaving:

                  1e John, 7th of Cossins; Commr Supply Forfarshire 1678, *dsp c* 1684

                  2e David; living 1665

            2b George, of Balmuchtie, Forfarshire; *m* Catherine Wishart of Balgarroch (*d c* 1635) and *d c* 1640, leaving:

               1c John, 1st of Wester Ogil, Forfarshire, which he acquired 1652; *m* Catherine Ogilvy of Balfour and had:

1d George, 2nd of Wester Ogil; Commr Supply Forfarshire 1686; *m* 1673 Jean (living 1704), dau of Sir William Nisbet of Dean, W Lothian, and *d c* 21 Jan 1703, leaving:

1e William (Rev), 3rd of Wester Ogil; *b* 9 Oct 1675; Min Airlie 1700; *m* 1st Jean, dau of David Melville of Pitgarvie, and had:

1f George (Rev), 4th of Wester Ogil; *b* 26 Aug 1711; *educ* St Andrews; Min Longforgan 1738; *m* 1st Aug 1739 Katherine, dau of Rev John Hodge of Bothkenna, Min Longforgan, and had a dau (*dsp*); *m* 2nd 14 June 1744 Margaret (*d* 9 April 1793), dau of Hugh Rodger, Provost Glasgow 1732, and *d* 12 Feb 1793, leaving by her:

1g William, 5th of Wester Ogil; *b* 22 May 1748; *dsp* 12 Aug 1795

2g Hugh, 6th of Wester Ogil; *b* 29 Jan 1749; Capt Bengal Artillery; *m* 1787 Janet, est dau of Charles Jobson, Dundee merchant, and *d* 12 Oct 1797, leaving:

1h George, 7th of Wester Ogil (later called Glenogil), WS; *b* 18 Nov 1787; *m* 28 March 1810 Catherine Menzies, 3rd dau of Rev Dr Thomas Fleming, of Edinburgh, and *d* 14 Nov 1866, leaving:

1i Hugh, 8th of Glenogil, WS 1849, JP Forfarshire; *b* 1812; *educ* Edinburgh High Sch, Edinburgh Acad and Glasgow U; Commr Supply, genealogist; *d* unm 8 July 1891

2i George, JP; *b* 8 Oct 1815; Hon Sheriff Substitute Forfarshire; *m* 29 June 1853 Christian, dau of Rev Dr Andrew Thomson, of Edinburgh, and *d* 1888, leaving:

1j Andrew Thomson, 9th of Glenogil; *b* 1856; *educ* Forfar Acad; *m* 6 Sept 1881 Julia, dau of William Shepherd, of Skedbuth, Haddingtonshire

2h Charles Jobson (Rev); *b* 9 Feb 1789; *educ* Trin Coll Cambridge (MA); episcopal Min St Andrews, CF; *m* 1st — English and had issue; *m* 2nd 1831 Margaret, 6th dau of Patrick Playfair of Dalmarnock, and *d* 26 May 1859, leaving further issue

3g George; *b* 20 Feb 1755; *m* June 1800 Margaret (*m* 2nd Sir Alan Fergusson, Dep Keeper Scottish Regalia), dau of Capt John Stewart of Stanton, and *d* 7 Sept 1812, leaving:

1h George, of Kirkmichael, which he sold to his bro John, and Dubrusean, Dumfriesshire; *b* 15 July 1804; Lt-Col 2nd Life Gds; *m* Phoebe (*d* 1893), dau of Adml Johnston of Cowhill, Dumfriesshire, and *d* 1879, leaving:

1i Charles James; *b* 22 Dec 1828; Lt, AQMG, HEICS; *m* Maud, dau of William Crauford, of Bombay, barrister, and *d* 7 April 1856, leaving issue

2i John Elliott; *b* 14 June 1835; Lt RN; *k* Australia 1858

3i Cecil Edward Leny; *b* 5 Aug 1842; Capt 77th Regt; *m* 30 April 1872 (Frances) Maude Hind, 3rd dau of Charles Palmer-Morewood, JP, DL, of Alfreton Pk, Derbys, and Ladbroke Hall, Warwicks, and *dsp*

4i Walter Fitzgerald Knox; *b* 29 Feb 1844; *m* 20 June 1883 Isabella Romanes, dau of William Towers-Clarke, JP, of Wester Moffat, Lanarks, and *d* 28 May 1894, leaving issue (*dsp*)

1i Margaret; *m* Robert Begbie, est s of James Begbie, MD, of Edinburgh, and had issue

2j Phoebe; *m* 1860 M Hyslop Maxwell, of Glangaber, Kirkcudbrightshire, and *d* 12 April 1923, leaving issue

2h John Stewart, 2nd of Kirkmichael; *b* 1 Dec 1808; Capt 4th Dragoons; *m* 1836 Mary Theresa, only dau of Thomas Dickson, of Queenstown, Ontario, and *d* 23 Dec 1862, leaving:

1i George Francis, 3rd of Kirkmichael; *b* 6 Sept 1837; RN: joined 1851, served Crimean War, ret as Cdr; *m* 1867 Emma Ramsay, dau of James Stark, MD, FRS, of Huntfield, Lanarks, and *d* 22 March 1881, leaving:

1j John Stewart, 4th of Kirkmichael, JP Dumfriesshire; *b* 11 June 1868; *educ* Wellington; *m* 9 Aug 1899 Esme Agnes Mary Helen (*d* 25 June 1930), only dau of Colin Dunlop, JP, of Lockerbie Ho, Dumfriesshire, and *d* 24 March 1934, leaving:

1k John George; *b* 13 Jan 1901; *educ* Wellington; Maj RA 1939; *m* 1st 23 Feb 1928 (*divorce* 1943) Laura, dau of John Bryce Duncan, of Newlands, Dumfries, and had:

1l +John Francis Stewart; *b* 9 Oct 1929; *educ* Charterhouse

1l *Adeline Mary; *b* 17 Feb 1931; *m* 11 Jan 1958 *James Henry Wilson Walker, s of William James Pettigrew Wilson Walker, and has:

1m *Peter; *b* 27 Nov 1968

1m *Rosemary; *b* 7 Jan 1959

2l *Lois Christine [Mrs John McConnel, The Old Manor House, Whichford, Warwicks]; *b* 9 Dec 1933; *m* 6 Aug 1955 *John William McConnel, s of Frederick Whigham McConnel, and has:

1m *James Archibald Roberts; *b* 25 Oct 1958

2m *John Andrew Douglas; *b* 9 July 1961

3m *William Kennedy; *b* 26 July 1962

1m *Fiona Mary; *b* 6 Oct 1957

1k (cont.) Maj John Lyon *m* 2nd 14 April 1943 *Mary, 2nd dau of 11th Earl of Wemyss and (3rd Earl of) March (*qv*) and widow of Algernon Walter Strickland (*see* STRICKLAND-CONSTABLE, Bt)

2k +Colin Arthur, 5th of Kirkmichael; *b* 11 July 1907; *educ* Wellington

2j Adam Walter Scott; *b* 14 Nov 1870; *educ* Haileybury; *m* Sept 1897 Elizabeth Jemima, 4th dau of Michael Bal-

main, of Woodland, Dumfriesshire, and *d* 8 Jan 1929, leaving:

1k Francis Thomas Balmain; *b* 2 Sept 1898

3j Francis Howard, DSO; *b* 4 Jan 1875; Cdr (E) RN WW I; *m* 9 April 1908 Evelyn Bayard (*d* 2 April 1928), only dau of Maj Henry Hall, 15th Hus

1j Isabella Alice; *m* 28 July 1903 Maj Andrew Coats, DSO (*d* 17 Feb 1930), bro of 1st Baron Glentanar (*see* 1970 edn), and *dsp*

2j Mary Theresa; *m* 28 Jan 1902 Col William Scott-Elliott, DSO (*d* 11 Feb 1943), yst s of James Scott-Elliott, of Newton, Dumfriesshire, and had issue

4g James (Rev); *b* 29 March 1759; Min Glamis 1780, DD Aberdeen U 1823; *m* 25 Jan 1786 Agnes (*d* 14 Sept 1840), est dau of John Ramsay L'Amy of Dunkenny, Angus, and *d* 3 April 1830, leaving:

1h George, of Snowdoun Ho, Co Stirling; *b* 30 March 1789; had issue

2h William (Rev); *educ* Aberdeen U (MA 1812); Min Old Machar 1823; *dsp* 1828

1h Agnes Hamilton; *b* 13 March 1787; *m* 18 Aug 1812 Rev William Rogers, Min Rescobie, Angus, and *d* 30 July 1816

1g Margaret; *b* 6 April 1751; *m* 30 Sept 1773 Rev John Playfair, DD, FRS, Pncpl St Andrews (1799) and Historiographer Roy Scotland, and had issue (*see* 1939 edn PLAYFAIR, B)

1f Jean; *m* 19 Sept 1728, as his 2nd w, Rev Alexander Moncrieff of Culfargie (*d* 7 Oct 1761), Min Abernethy, a Fndr Seccession Ch, Prof Divinity Associated Presbytery 1742, and *d* 1791, leaving issue

1e (cont.) The Rev William Lyon *m* 2nd 16 Dec 1719 Agnes, dau of Rev Alexander Glas, Min Kinclaven, and by her had:

2f William; *b* 2 June 1722; Writer (law practitioner) Dundee, Er Glasite Community 1758; *d* unm 1803

3f Robert, of Logyrait, Perths, later Old Buckenham, Norfolk; Glasite Elder 1764; *m* 18 Aug 1755 Mary Miller, of Perth, and *d* 14 Sept 1801, leaving:

1g George, of Old Buckenham and Campden Grove, London; *b* 13 Jan 1770; merchant; *m* 7 Aug 1797 Anne (*d* 11 March 1836), dau of John Thomas, of Llangadock, Carmarths, and *d* 15 July 1850, leaving, with other issue:

1h George, of Valparaiso; *b* 25 Jan 1803; *m* 4 Aug 1830 Carmen Santa Maria (*b* 1813) and *d* 21 Nov 1866, leaving issue

2h William, JP; *b* 30 Sept 1813; *m* 29 Oct 1851 Louisa Charlotte (*d* 18 April 1872), dau of William Norton, of Epsom, Surrey, and *d* 16 Jan 1892, leaving:

1i William Rawson; *b* 10 Feb 1854; *educ* Winchester; Lt Roy Surrey Militia; *m* 19 April 1883 Louisa Sophia, dau of Rev Matthew Harvey Buckland, of Laleham, Middx, and had:

1j Francis Hamilton; *b* 22 Nov 1885; *educ* Winchester

2i George Kenneth; *b* 14 July 1855; Bengal CS, Dep Commr Darjeeling; *m* 16 Dec 18– Etta Ellen, 3rd dau of Warren Hastings D'Oyly, Bengal CS, and *d* 30 May 1888, leaving issue

3i Percy Comyn; *b* 9 Aug 1862; *educ* King's Sch Bruton and Oriel Coll Oxford; Bengal CS, Dir Ag Lower Bengal 1898; *m* 17 Feb 1890 Adeline Eliza, dau of Hon Henry Beverley, Puisne Judge Calcutta

4i Herbert; *b* 29 April 1867; *educ* Winchester and Corpus Christi Coll Oxford (MA 1898); schoolmaster

2e Robert (Rev); *b* 17 Feb 1685; *educ* St Andrews; Min Kilfauns 1712; *m* 8 Dec 1714 Jean Dalgleish and had issue

3e George, of the Overgate of Dundee; *b* 28 July 1688; Burgess and Guild Brother 1717, Bailie 1725, five times Dean of Guild 1738–48, merchant and shipowner; *m* 1st 21 Nov 1716 Elizabeth, sis of Andrew Wardroper, Provost Dundee, and had:

1f George; *bapt* 24 June 1718

3e (cont.) George Lyon *m* 2nd 16 Jan 1738 Janet, est dau of Rev Alexander Duncan, of Strathmartine, and had further issue; *m* 3rd 18 Feb 1747 Jean Chapeman, widow of John Auld, surgn, of Aucherarder, Perths, and had further issue

4e James (Rev); *b* 1694; Min Blairgowrie 1723; *m* Allison, dau of Rev George Gillespie, Min Strathmilgo, Fifeshire, and had:

1f George (Rev); *b* 17 Feb 1729; *educ* Dundee; Min Strathmilgo 1754; *m* 11 Nov 1757 Sophia (*d* 5 Feb 1822), dau of Rev David Marshall, Min Kirkcaldy, and had:

1g Thomas; surgn HEICS; *k* unm 1805 in the Baltic

2g Jasper; merchant in W Indies; *m* Rebecca Boyle and had issue (*dsp*)

1g Allison; *m* 2 Nov 1788 William Walker (*d* 21 March 1804), of Demperston, Fifeshire, s of James Walker, of Falfield, and *d* 2 Oct 1833, leaving issue

1e Margaret; *b* 30 May 1681; *m* Rev John Ramsay, Min Bendochy 1700–47

2d John (Rev); *educ* St Andrews; Min Airlie 1663 and Glamis 1681

3d Sylvester (Rev); *b c* 1641; *educ* St Andrews; Min Kinnettles 1667 and Kirriemuir 1669; *d* 1 May 1713, leaving a dau (*m* Rt Rev James Rait, Bp Brechin 1742–77)

4d Frederick, of Auchinlaigh; *b c* 1652; *educ* St Andrews; Min Airlie 1682; *m* Isobel Gramond and *d* Sept 1699, leaving issue

3 William; *k* Flodden 9 Sept 1513

4 George; *k* Flodden 9 Sept 1513

1 Violet; *m* 1st Lord (Fraser of) Lovat (*qv*)

2 Janet; *m* Gilbert Hay

3 Christian; *m c* 24 April 1492 4th Earl of Erroll (*qv*)

4 Agnes; *m* 1st 5th Lord Forbes (*qv*); *m* 2nd John Ross of Craigy

5 Margaret; *m* James Rynd, Yr. of Broxmouth

6 Mariota; *m* William Ochterlony

7 Elizabeth; *m* William Forbes and *dsp*

The 3rd LORD's est s,

JOHN LYON, **4th Lord Glamis**; *m c* 18 May 1487 Elizabeth (*m* 2nd by 27 July 1511 3rd Earl of Huntly (*see* HUNTLY, M); *m* 3rd by 5 June 1525 4th Earl of Rothes, *qv*), dau of 2nd Lord Gray (*qv*), and *d* 1500, leaving:

1 GEORGE LYON, **5th Lord Glamis**; *d* a minor Feb/March 1504/5

2 JOHN, **6th Lord**

3 Alexander; Precentor Moray; *d* 1541

The 5th LORD's bro,

JOHN LYON, **6th Lord Glamis**; *b c* 1491; *m* by 12 Dec 1527 Janet (*m* 2nd by 1535, as his 2nd w, Alexander Campbell of Skippinch/Skipness, 2nd s of 2nd Earl of Argyll (*see* ARGYLL, D), and was burnt at the stake on the Castle Hill of Edinburgh 17 July 1537 by order of JAMES V), sis of 6th Earl of Angus (*see* HAMILTON and BRANDON, D), and *d* 8 April 1528, having had, with a yr s (George, imprisoned with his bro (*see* below) 1537, released on death of JAMES V 1542, *d* unm soon after) and two daus (Margaret, *d* unm 15 June 1610; Elizabeth, *m* 1st John, Master of Forbes (*see* FORBES, L), *m* 2nd Thomas Craig of Balmely, *m* 3rd John Tullock of Montcoffes, *m* 4th John Abernethy of Balcors; *see* SALTOUN, L):

JOHN LYON, **7th Lord Glamis**, PC (S Feb 1543/4); found guilty of treason 18 July 1537 (the day following his mother's execution), his honours and lands forfeited and he sentenced to death when he should be of age as part of JAMES V's campaign of extirpation against the DOUGLASes but restored 15 March 1542/3 following JAMES's death; *m* 6 Feb 1542/3 Janet Keith, sis of 4th Earl Marischal (*see* KINTORE, E), and *d* 1558, leaving:

1 JOHN, **8th Lord**

2 Thomas (Sir), of Auldbar; at one time styled *Master of Glamis* as heir presumptive to the title; Ld of Session 1585–93, Treas Scotland 1585–96, Capt King's Gd Scotland; *m* 1st Agnes, sis of 5th Lord Gray (*qv*) and widow of (a) Robert Logan of Restalrig and (b) 5th Lord Home (*see* HOME, E), and had two daus; *m* 2nd 1586 Euphame, dau of 6th Earl of Morton (*qv*), and *d* 18 Feb 1607/8, having by her had, with another s and a dau:

(1) John, of Auldbar; *m* a dau of George Gladstones, DD, Archbp St Andrews, and had issue

1 Margaret; *m* 1st (contract 30 Sept 1566) 4th Earl of Cassillis (*see* AILSA, M); *m* 2nd (contract 30 Dec 1577) 1st Marquess of Hamilton (*see* HAMILTON and BRANDON, D) and *d* 1626

The 7th LORD's er s,

JOHN LYON, **8th Lord Glamis**, PC (S 1567); *b c* 1544; Extrdy Ld of Session 1570–73, Ld Chllr Scotland 1573–March 1577/8; *m* 11 April 1561 Elizabeth, dau of 5th Lord Saltoun (*qv*) of Abernethy and widow of William Meldrum of Fyvie, and was shot in the head 17 March 1577/8 in an encounter between his followers and those of the 11th Earl of Crawford, leaving, with three daus (Elizabeth, *m* 1st (contract 18 May 1575, *divorce* 21 May 1585) 6th Lord Gray (*qv*), *m* 2nd (contract 14 Feb 1586/87) William KERR later KIRKALDY of Grange and by him had issue (*see* LOTHIAN, M); Jean, *m* 1st (contract 19 March 1582/83) Robert Douglas, Yr., Master of Morton (*see* MORTON, E), *m* 2nd (contract 29 July 1587) 8th Earl of Angus (*see* HAMILTON and BRANDON, D), *m* 3rd 1st Lord Spynie (*see* CRAWFORD and BALCARRES, E); Sibilla; living 1579):

PATRICK LYON, **1st Earl of Kinghorne**, so *cr* 10 July 1606, as also LORD LYON AND GLAMIS (both S), PC (S by 1606); *b* 1575; *m* June 1595 Anne (*d* 27 Feb 1618), dau of 1st Earl of Tullibardine (*see* ATHOLL, D), and *d* 19 Dec 1615, having had:

1 JOHN, **2nd Earl**

2 James, of Auldbar; MP Angus, Covenanter; *dsp* by 13 Aug 1641

3 Patrick; *d* young

4 Frederick, of Brigton, of which had charter 1622; MP Forfarshire, Burgess and Guild Brother Dundee 1620; Covenanter; *m* 1st Margaret of Auchmartine, dau of Sir Patrick Ogilvy of Inchmartins (*see* SEAFIELD, E), and had:

(1) Patrick, of Brigton (sold 1743 by his descendant Charles Lyon of Brigton); living 1666; *m* Elizabeth (*m* 2nd Sir Patrick Lyon, Ld of Session as Ld Carse (*see* above), and had issue), sis of William Grey of Invereightie, and had issue

4 (cont.) Frederick Lyon of Brigton *m* 2nd Jean Stewart, widow of George Crichton of Arbeckie, but *d* 1660 leaving by her no issue

1 Anne; *m* 1618 10th Earl of Erroll (*qv*) and *d* 8 Feb 1837

2 Jean; *d* by 2 Oct 1618

The 1st EARL's est s,

JOHN LYON, **2nd Earl of Kinghorne**, PC (S 1641); *b* 13 Aug 1596; Burgess and Guild Brother Dundee 1620; *m* 1st (contracted 19 June 1618) Lady Margaret Erskine, 3rd dau of 18th/2nd Earl of Mar (*qv*), by whom he had no surv issue; *m* 2nd Lady Elizabeth Maule (*m* 2nd 30 July 1650 3rd Earl of Linlithgow (*see* LINLITHGOW, M, preliminary remarks) and *d* Oct 1559), only dau of 1st Earl of Panmure, and *d* 12 May 1646, leaving by her, with a dau (Elizabeth, *m* (contract 28 Aug 1665) 1st Earl of Aboyne; *see* HUNTLY, M):

PATRICK LYON, **3rd Earl of Kinghorne** later **3rd Earl of Strathmore and Kinghorne**; *b* 29 May 1643, PC (S 1674–89 and March 1691/2); *educ* St Andrews; Burgess and Guild Brother Dundee 1660; got 30 May 1672 a regrant of the 1606 creations with limitation to him and the heirs male of his body, in default of which to any person nominated by him, in default of which to his heirs male whatsoever, in default of which to his heirs and assigns whatsoever; got another charter 1 July 1677 changing his full title of 1606 to EARL OF STRATHMORE AND KINGHORNE, VISCOUNT LYON, LORD GLAMIS, TANNADYCE, SIDLAW AND STRADICHTIE with original precedence; Lt King's Life Gd of Honour 1672–80, a Ld Treasury and Commr Exchequer 1680, Extrdy Ld of Session 1686–89, Sheriff Forfarshire 1694; *m* 23 Aug 1662 Lady Helen Middleton (*d* May 1708), dau of 1st Earl of Middleton (*see* MIDDLETON, B, preliminary remarks), and *d* 15 May 1695, having had:

1 JOHN, **4th Earl**

2 Patrick, of Auchterhouse; MP Angus 1702–15; *m* Margaret (*d* 14 April 1742), n of 3rd Earl of Northesk (*qv*), and *dsp*, *ka* Battle of Sheriffmuir 13 Nov 1715 (presumably fighting against the Jacobites rather than for them)

3 Charles; *d* 1692

1 Grizel; *m* 8 May 1696 3rd Earl of Airlie (*qv*)

2 Elizabeth; *m* 1st 2nd Earl of Aboyne; *m* 2nd 3rd Lord Kinnaird (*see* 1970 edn); *m* 3rd Capt Alexander Grant of Grantsfield and *d* Jan 1739

The 3rd EARL's est s,

JOHN LYON, **4th Earl of Strathmore and Kinghorne**, PC (S 1695 and Feb 1702/3); *b* 8 May 1663; *educ* St Andrews; Sheriff Forfarshire 1696; avoided imprisonment for suspected complicity in the abortive French invasion of Scotland 1708 on behalf of the Jacobites by obtaining a medical certificate testifying to his infirmity; *m* (contract 21 Sept 1691) Lady Elizabeth Stanhope (*d* 24 April 1723), dau of 2nd Earl of Chesterfield (*see* 1967 edn CHESTERFIELD and STANHOPE, E), and *d* 10 May 1712, having had:

1 Patrick, *Lord Glamis*; *b* 1692; *dvp* by 10 Sept 1709

2 Philip, *Lord Glamis*; *bapt* 29 Oct 1693; *dvp* 18 March 1711/2

3 JOHN LYON, **5th Earl of Strathmore and Kinghorne**; *bapt* 27 April 1696; *ka* Battle of Sheriffmuir 13 Nov 1715 while taking part in the Jacobite Uprising of that year

4 CHARLES LYON, **6th Earl of Strathmore and Kinghorne**; *bapt* 12 July 1699; *educ* Oxford; *m* 25 July 1725 Lady Susan Cochrane (*m* 2nd 2 April 1745 George Forbes, her factor, later Master of The Horse to Bonnie Prince Charlie, and *d* 23 June 1754), 2nd dau of 4th Earl of Dundonald (*qv*), and *dsp* 11 May 1728 after being wounded in a street scuffle 9 May

5 Hendrie; *bapt* 1 July 1700; *d* young

6 JAMES LYON, **7th Earl of Strathmore and Kinghorne**; *bapt* 24 Dec 1702; *m* 6 March 1731 Mary (*d* 7 Sept 1731), dau of George Oliphant, MD, and *dsp* 4 Jan 1735

7 THOMAS, **8th Earl**

1 Helen; *m* 1714 7th Lord Blantyre (*see* 1900 edn) and *dsp* 19 Dec 1723

2 Mary; *d* unm 26 May 1780

3 Catherine; *d* young

The 7th EARL's bro,

THOMAS LYON, **8th Earl of Strathmore and Kinghorne**; *bapt* 6 July 1704; MP Forfarshire 1734–34/5; *m* 20 July 1736 Jean (*d* 13 May 1778), dau and heiress of James Nicholson, of W Rainton, Co Durham, and *d* 18 Jan 1753, leaving:

1 JOHN, **9th Earl**

2 James Philip; *b* 2 July 1738; HEICS; murdered on orders of Mir Cossim, Nabob of Bengal, 1763

3 Thomas, of Hetton Ho, Durham; *b* 1741; MP Montrose 1768–74 and Forfarshire 1774–79; *m* 13 June 1774 Mary Elizabeth (*d* 13 May 1811), dau of Farren Wren, of Binchester, Co Durham, and *d* 13 Sept 1796, having had surv issue:

(1) John, of Hetton Ho, Durham; *m* 3 Feb 1812 Anne (*m* 2nd 1830 Lt John William Oldmixon, RN), dau of Barrington Price, and *d* 20 June 1829, leaving:

1a Maria; *m* 1832 Hon Russell Barrington (*d* 15 Feb 1835) and *d* 20 July 1871, leaving issue (*see* 1970 edn BARRINGTON, V)

(2) Charles; *b* 1792; *m* — Gibson and *d* 14 Aug 1859

(1) Mary; *m* 1 Jan 1799 Thomas Wilkinson and *d* 22 June 1803

(2) Anne

(3) Frances; *m* 24 June 1811 Rev Thomas Thurlow, bro of 2nd Baron Thurlow (*qv*), and *d* 5 Jan 1863

(4) Charlotte; *m* 20 Nov 1809 Rev Henry George Liddell (*see* RAVENSWORTH, B) and *d* 30 Jan 1871

(5) Susan; *m* 20 May 1811 Rev John Fellowes, 4th s of Robert Fellowes, JP, DL (*d* 20 Feb 1838), of Shottisham Pk, Norwich, and *d* 14 Oct 1864, having had issue

(6) Mary Anne; *m* 31 Oct 1821 John Clutterbuck, of Warkworth, Northumberland

1 Susan; *m* 5 Sept 1763 Gen John Lambton (*see* DURHAM, E) and *d* 26 Feb 1769, leaving issue

2 Anne; *m* 15 July 1768 John Simpson, of Bradley, Co Durham, and had issue (*see* RAVENSWORTH, B)

3 Mary; *d* unm 22 May 1767 aged 18

4 Jane; *d* unm 22 Aug 1836 aged 60

The 8th EARL's est s,

JOHN LYON later BOWES (Act of Parl 1767), **9th Earl of Strathmore and Kinghorne**; *b* 17 July 1737; *educ* Pembroke Coll Cambridge; rep S Peer 1767–76; *m* 24 Feb 1767 Mary Eleanor (*m* 2nd 17 Jan 1777 (*divorce* 1789) Andrew Robinson STONEY later BOWES, MP Newcastle-on-Tyne 1780–84, High Sheriff Co Durham 1780, er s of George Stoney, of Greyfort, Co Tipperary, and *d* 28 April 1800), only dau and heiress of George Bowes, of Streatlam Castle and Gibside, Co Durham, and *d* 7 March 1776, leaving:

1 JOHN BOWES, **10th Earl of Strathmore and Kinghorne**; *b* 14 April 1769; *educ* Pembroke Coll Cambridge; Cornet RHG 1786, Capt 65th Foot 1789, ret 1791; rep S peer 1796–1806 and 1807–12, *cr* 18 July 1815 BARON BOWES OF STREATLAM CASTLE, Co Durham, AND OF LUNEDALE, Co York (UK); *m* 2 July 1820 Mary (*m* 2nd 16 March 1831 Sir William Hutt, KCB, PC, and *d* 5 May 1860), dau of J Milner, of Staindrop, Co Durham, and *dspl* the following day, when the UK Barony expired, leaving by his w:

(1) John; *b* before his parents' marriage; claimed f's peerages but declared illegitimate because his parents had no Scottish domicile; had they done so he would under Scottish law have been legitimated by their marriage; *d* 1885, bequeathing the English estates he had inherited to his legitimate cousin the **13th Earl**

2 George, of St Paul's Walden, Herts; *b* 17 Nov 1771; *m* 14 June 1805 Mary (*m* 2nd 1811 Barrington Price), dau of Edward Thornhill, of Kingston Lisle, Berks, and *dsp* 26 Dec 1806

3 THOMAS, **11th Earl**

1 Mary; *m* 11 May 1789 Col Barrington Price, of Becket, Glos and *d* 22 April 1806

2 Anna Maria; *m* 22 Jan 1778 Henry James Jessop and *d* 29 March 1832

The 10th EARL's bro,

THOMAS BOWES later LYON-BOWES, **11th Earl of Strathmore and Kinghorne**; *b* 3 May 1773; *educ* Eton and Pembroke Coll Cambridge; High Sheriff Leics 1810; *m* 1st 25 March 1800 Mary Elizabeth Louisa Rodney (*d* 1 June 1811), only dau and heiress of George Carpenter, of Redbourn, Herts, and had:

  1 Thomas George, *Lord Glamis*; *b* 6 Feb 1801; *m* 21 Dec 1820 Charlotte (*d* 19 Jan 1881), dau of Joseph Valentine Grinstead, and *dvp* 27 Jan 1834, having had:

    (1) A son, *b* and *d* 18 Oct 1821

    (2) THOMAS GEORGE LYON-BOWES, **12th Earl of Strathmore and Kinghorne**; *b* 28 Sept 1822; Cornet 1st Life Gds 1839, ret 1846, Capt S Herts Yeo Cav, rep S peer 1852–65, Lt-Col Forfar Yeo 1856–62; *m* 30 April 1850 Charlotte Maria (*dsp* 3 Nov 1854), est dau of 6th Viscount Barrington (*see* 1970 edn), and *dsp* 13 Sept 1865

    (3) CLAUDE, **13th Earl**

    (1) Charlotte; *d* 22 Oct 1844 aged 18

    (2) Frances; granted 8 Feb 1847 with her er bro (later **13th Earl**) rank of earl's yr s/dau; *m* 2 Feb 1858 Hugh Charles Trevanion (*d* 20 May 1901) and *d* 27 Jan 1903, leaving issue

  1 Mary Isabella; *m* 8 Aug 1824 (*divorce* 1833) John Walpole Willis, DL (*d* 10 Sept 1877), and had issue

The **11th Earl** *m* 2nd 1812 Eliza, dau of Col Northcote, and by her had:

  2 Sarah; *m* 1st 2 Nov 1834 George Augustus Campbell (*dsp* 7 Nov 1841), HEICS, 2nd s of Robert Campbell of Skipness (for whose early ancestry *see* ARGYLL, D); *m* 2nd 13 July 1843 Maj Charles Philip Ainslie, 14th Light Dragoons, and *d* 6 June 1847

The **11th Earl** *m* 3rd 8 Dec 1817 Marianne (*d* 23 Oct 1849), dau of John Cheape of Sauchie and widow of Sir Alexander Campbell, 4th Bt, of Ardkinglass, and *d* 27 Aug 1846

The 12th EARL's bro,

CLAUDE LYON-BOWES later BOWES-LYON, **13th Earl of Strathmore and Kinghorne**, JP (Sussex), DL (Dundee); *b* 21 July 1824; *educ* Winchester and Ch Ch Oxford; Cornet 2nd Life Gds 1848, Lt 1852, ret 1854, Hon Freeman Forfar 1868, Hon Burgess Dundee 1874, rep S peer 1870–87, Ld Lt Forfarshire 1874–1904, Pres Highland Ag Soc 1885–86 and 1890–95; *cr* 1 July 1887 BARON BOWES OF STREATLAM CASTLE, Co Durham, AND OF LUNEDALE, Co York (UK); *m* 28 Sept 1853 Frances Dora (*d* 5 Feb 1922), dau of Oswald Smith, of Blendon Hall, Kent, and *d* 16 Feb 1904, having had:

  1 CLAUDE GEORGE, **14th Earl**

  2 Francis, JP and DL Forfarshire and Northumberland, of Ridley Hall, Bardon Mill, Northumberland; *b* 23 Feb 1856; *educ* Eton; Col cmdg 2nd Vol Bn Black Watch (Roy Highrs); *m* 22 Nov 1883 Lady Anne Catherine Sybil Lindsay (*d* 15 Dec 1936), 4th dau of 25th Earl of Crawford and (8th Earl of) Balcarres (*qv*), and *d* 18 Feb 1948, having had:

    (1) Charles Lindsay Claude; *b* 15 Sept 1885; MICE, Lt 3rd Bn Black Watch (Roy Highrs); *ka* 23 Oct 1914

    (2) Geoffrey Francis; *b* 30 Sept 1886; *educ* Eton; Capt Black Watch (Roy Highrs) WW I 1914–16 (wounded); *m* 31 Oct 1914 Edith Katherine (*d* 19 Sept 1971), dau of Sir Lewis Amherst Selby-Bigge, 1st Bt, KCB (*see* 1970 edn), and *d* 30 Aug 1951, leaving:

      1a (Francis) James Cecil (Sir), KCVO, CB, OBE (1962), MC and bar; *b* 19 Sept 1917; *educ* Eton; Maj-Gen 1955–57, cmded 2nd Bn Gren Gds 1957–59 and 157th Lowland Bde Scotland 1963, GOC 52nd Lowland Div/Dist 1966–68, GOC Berlin (Br Sector); *m* 22 April 1941 *Mary [Lady Bowes Lyon, Beltingham House, Bardon Mill, Northumberland], 2nd dau and coheiress of Sir Humphrey Edmund de Trafford, 4th Bt (*qv*), and *d* 1977, leaving:

        1b +John Francis [John Bowes Lyon Esq, D5 Albany, Piccadilly, London W1V 9RG]; *b* 13 June 1942; *educ* Ampleforth

        2b +David James, DL (Midlothian 1992) [David Bowes Lyon Esq DL, Heriot Water, Heriot, Midlothian EH38 5YE]; *b* 21 July 1947; *educ* Ampleforth; *m* 17 Nov 1976 *(Elizabeth) Harriet, only dau of Sir John Rupert Colville, CB, CVO (*see* COLVILLE of CULROSS, V), and has:

          1c +James Francis John; *b* 1979; Page of Hon to HM THE QUEEN 1991–

          2c +Charles David; *b* 1989

          1c *Georgina Alice; *b* 6 Feb 1978

          2c *Alexandra Violet; *b* 1986

        1b *Fiona Ann [Mrs Joseph Goodhart, Great Givendale, Pocklington, Yorks YO4 2TT]; *b* 3 July 1944; *m* 4 Jan 1966 *Joseph Henry Goodhart, TD, DL, s of Lt-Col Joseph Henry Goodhart, MC, of Kirkbymoorside, Yorks, and has:

          1c *James Henry; *b* 27 March 1970

          2c *David Andrew; *b* 20 Oct 1971

          1c *Camilla Bridget; *b* 11 Feb 1968; *m* 1994 *(David) Benjamin Ridgwell, yr s of Dr Stanley Ridgwell, of London

      1a *Caroline Anne Lindsay [Mrs Llewellyn Ross Llewellyn, Casa Al Ghaba, Alfeição, 8100 Loulé, Algarve, Portugal]; *b* 7 May 1916; *m* 1 Aug 1939 Lt Llewellyn Ross Llewellyn, RNVR (*d* 1988), er s of Brig-Gen Evan Henry Llewellyn, DSO, JP, of Nethway Ho, S Devon, and has:

        1b *Llewellyn Charles [Llewellyn Llewellyn Esq, 44 Drayton Gdns, London SW10 9SA]; *b* 1943; *m* 1966 *Kathleen Mary, dau of John Charles Roche, of Nairobi, and has:

          1c *Sophie Anita; *b* 1971

          2c *Eleanor Loveday Caroline (Daisy); *b* 1976

        2b *Simon Lindsay; *b* 1945; *m* 1970 (*divorce* 1992) Stella Willis and has:

          1c *Fergus John; *b* 1975

          1c *Emma; *b* 1977

      2a *Sarah Susannah [Mrs Peter Ryder, Ardmore, Riverbank Rd, Ramsey, IoM]; *b* 20 May 1920; *m* 29 May 1940 Lt-Col Peter Hugh Dudley Ryder, MBE (*d* 1993; *see* HARROWBY, E), and has issue

    (3) Ronald George, MVO (1925); *b* 22 June 1893; RN; joined 1906, ret as Capt, Equerry to HRH PRINCE GEORGE 1923–25, Capt Dockyard, King's

Harbour-Master and Dep Supt Malta 1936–39, served WWs I and II (despatches both), Dir Navigation Admlty 1940–42, Dir Welfare Admlty 1945–47; *m* 1st 24 Jan 1925 (*divorce* 1947) Mary Claire, only dau of James Russell; *m* 2nd 30 June 1947 *Cecilia, dau of Isaac Goldinger and formerly w of (a) Joseph Mordechai Marks and (b) Capt John Cyril French, S African Scottish Regt, and *dsp* 17 April 1960

    (1) Muriel Frances Margaret; Nurse WW I France 1918 (despatches); *d* unm 31 Oct 1968

    (2) Doris Cicely; *b* 16 Dec 1887; *d* unm 27 Oct 1918

    (3) Winifred Geraldine; *b* 18 Dec 1889; *d* unm 9 Jan 1968

    (4) Lilian Helen; *b* 22 Dec 1895; poetess; *d* unm 25 July 1949

  3 Ernest; *b* 4 Aug 1858; 2nd Sec Dip Serv; *m* 23 Nov 1882 Issobel Hester (*d* 15 July 1945), dau of Harvey Drummond (*see* PERTH, E) and *d* 27 Dec 1891, having had:

    (1) Hubert Ernest; *b* 6 Oct 1883; *educ* Haileybury and RMC Sandhurst; Capt Serv Bn Roy Fus WW I (wounded); *m* 1st 14 Jan 1905 Mary Agnes (*d* 5 March 1914), dau of James Hay Smeaton, and had:

      1a +Hubert Ernest Malcolm; *b* 17 May 1907; F/Lt RAFO; *m* 12 July 1943 (*divorce* 1964) Fanny Rose (*d* 27 July 1969), dau of Simon Jacobs, of S Africa, and has:

        1b *Jennifer Merrill; *b* 12 April 1944; *educ* Tel Aviv U (BA); *m* *Stephen Byk and has:

          1c *A dau; *b* 1977

      2a Douglas Ian Gordon; *b* 30 June 1912; Lt CAC WW II; *m* 20 June 1942 Charlotte (*d* 11 March 1988), dau of Norman Herbert Gardner, and *d* 6 Sept 1997, leaving:

        1b +Douglas Malcolm [Douglas Bowes-Lyon Esq, 1474 Lloyd George, Verdun, PQ H4H 2P5, Canada]; *b* 7 Aug 1946; *m* 1975 *Diane Fréchette and has:

          1c +Douglas Cedric; *b* 3 Sept 1981

          2c +Derric Fergus; *b* 13 Oct 1985

          3c +Darrel Lucien; *b* 6 April 1990

          1c *Léa-Marie; *b* 10 Feb 1979

        2b +David Gordon [David Bowes-Lyon Esq, 780 Edgewood Rd, Pickering, Ontario L1V 2Z9, Canada]; *b* 7 Aug 1949; *educ* Concordia U (B Comm); *m* 1974 *Elizabeth, dau of Donald Allan Rodier, and has:

          1c *Marianne Elizabeth; *b* 1978

          2c *Andrea Lynn; *b* 1980

        1b *Charlotte Mary Diane [Mrs Jean Wagner, 6508 Vineyard Dr, Orleans, ONT K1C 2M5, Canada]; *b* 19 April 1943; *m* 1965 *Jean D Wagner and has:

          1c *Richard Steven; *b* 1968

          2c *Ian Gordon; *b* 1982

          3c *Andrew James; *b* 1983

          1c *Heidi; *b* 1970

        2b *Deborah Jane [Miss Deborah Bowes-Lyon, PO Box 4500, Sydney, Nova Scotia B1P 6L1, Canada]; *b* 9 June 1958

      1a Constance Mary; *b* 24 Dec 1904; won decree of legitimation by Ct of Session Edinburgh June 1924; *m* 29 July 1933 George Clark Dow (*d* 5 April 1967), tobacco planter, s of William Dow, of Kilmarnock

    (1) (cont.) Hubert Bowes-Lyon *m* 2nd 13 Aug 1919 Margaret May (*d* 25 May 1966), only dau of Frank Nuttall, of Belfast, and widow of James Graham, and *d* 28 April 1959, having by her had:

      2a *Sonia Gabrielle [Mrs Stephen Murphy, Higher Polgrain, St Wenn, Bodmin, Cornwall]; *b* 1 Oct 1922; late ATS; *m* 15 May 1948 *Lt-Col Stephen Otteran Murphy, MBE, Devonshire Regt, s of Maj Frank D'Assisi Murphy, of Dunsland Ct, Exbourne, Devon

    (1) Susan Frances; *b* 25 Oct 1884; drowned in wreck of SS *Sidon* off Coruna Spain 28 Oct 1885

    (2) Dorothea Marion; *b* 12 April, *d* 10 July 1886

    (3) Joan Isobel Margaret; *b* 30 April 1888; *m* 1st 24 June 1909 Capt Alfred Ernest Parker (*ka* 7 Nov 1914), 3rd Bn Black Watch, late 10th Roy Hus, yst s of Alfred Traill Parker, of Aigburth, and had issue; *m* 2nd Aug 1915 (*divorce* 1926) Capt Frank Ashton Bellville (*d* 22 July 1937), 3rd s of William John Bellville, and *d* 6 July 1954

    (4) Marjorie Effie; *b* 6 July 1889; *m* 1st 20 April 1909 Capt Douglas Walkden Roberts, RA (*d* 20 Jan 1920), s of John M Roberts, of Bath, and had issue; *m* 2nd 16 Jan 1924 Richmond Campbell Pinder (*d* 16 Jan 1926), s of Walter Pinder, of Bishops Stortford, Herts, and had further issue; *m* 3rd 3 Aug 1927 Brig-Gen Sir Ormonde de l'Epee Winter, KBE, CB, CMG, DSO (*d* 13 Feb 1962), s of William Henry Winter, of Sutton Ct Lodge, Chiswick

    (5) Ernestine Hester Maud; *b* 19 Dec 1891; *m* 1st 23 Nov 1910 (*divorce* 1918) Francis Winstone Scott (*d* 14 May 1948), s of Walter Scott, of Mostyn, Tadworth, and had two sons; *m* 2nd 4 Oct 1918 10th Baron de Longüeil and had two more sons

  4 Herbert, DL Forfarshire; *b* 15 Aug 1860; barrister; *d* unm 14 April 1897

  5 Patrick, JP Kent, DL Angus; *b* 5 March 1863; *educ* Cambridge (BA); Lt RN, Maj Essex Regt, barrister; *m* 9 Aug 1893 Alice Wiltshire (*d* 1 March 1953), ward of Capt Arthur Lister-Kaye, of Manor Ho, Stretton-on-Dunsmore, and *d* 5 Oct 1946, having had:

    (1) Gavin Patrick; *b* 13 Dec 1895; Lt Gren Gds; *ka* Nov 1917

    (2) Angus Patrick; *b* 22 Oct 1899; *d* 10 July 1923

    (1) Jean Barbara; *b* 9 Oct 1904; *d* unm 7 Jan 1963

    (2) *Margaret Ann [Mrs Francis d'Abreu, 36 Cumberland Terrace, London NW1 4HP]; *b* 19 June 1907; *m* 2 June 1945 Lt-Col Francis Arthur Philip d'Abreu, ERD, ChM, FRCS (*d* 16 Nov 1995), s of John Francis d'Abreu, LRCP, LRCS, DPH, of Handsworth, Staffs, and has:

      1a *Anthony Patrick John; *b* 1946; *educ* Stonyhurst and London U (BA 1970); *m* 1967 (*divorce* 1976) Rachel Jane, dau of Maj W Green, and has:

        1b *James Simon Francis; *b* 21 July 1969

        1b *Catherine Jane Ann; *b* 1966

1a *Francesca Ann; *b* 1948; *m* 1970 *Kieran Patrick Fogarty

2a Anna Teresa; *b* 1950; *m* 1977 (*divorce* 1990) Nicholas Robin Le Fowne Hurt and *d* 17 April 1995, leaving:

  1b *(Cassandra) Isobel Ann; *b* 1980

6 Kenneth; *b* 26 April 1867; *d* unm 9 Jan 1911

7 Malcolm; *b* 23 April 1874; *educ* Eton and Trin Hall Cambridge; Capt 2nd Life Gds Boer War 1899–1900 and 1902, Lt-Col 5th Bn Black Watch (TF) WW I (wounded); *m* 28 Sept 1907 Winifred (*d* 30 May 1957), only dau of Hector John Gurdon-Rebow, DL, of Wyvenhoe Park, Essex, and formerly w of Charles Eustace Hutton, and *d* 23 Aug 1957, leaving:

  (1) *(Clodagh) Pamela [Pamela Lady Lever, Lessudden Cottage, St Boswells, Melrose, Roxburghs TD6 0BH]; *b* 15 July 1908; *m* 1st 18 April 1931 (*divorce* 1952) W/Cdr Lord Malcolm Avendale Douglas-Hamilton, OBE, DFC, MP (*d* 21 July 1964), 3rd s of 13th Duke of Hamilton and Brandon (qv), and has issue; *m* 2nd 5 March 1962 Sir Tresham Joseph Philip Lever, 2nd Bt (qv)

1 Constance Frances; *m* 21 Dec 1893 Robert Francis Leslie Blackburn (Ld of Session as Lord Blackburn 1918–35, *d* 21 March 1944), s of Robert Blackburn, and *d* 19 Nov 1951, leaving issue

2 Mildred Marion; *m* 1 July 1890 Augustus Edward Jessup, of Torquay, and *d* 9 June 1897, having had issue

3 Maud Agnes; *d* unm 28 Feb 1941

4 Evelyn Mary; *d* 15 March 1876

The 13th EARL's est s,

CLAUDE GEORGE BOWES-LYON, **14th Earl of Strathmore and Kinghorne**, KG (1937), KT (1928), GCVO (1923), TD, JP, DL Dundee; *b* 14 March 1855; *educ* Eton; Lt 2nd Life Gds 1876–82, Ld Lt Forfarshire 1904–36, Pres Angus TAA, Hon Col 4th/5th Bn Black Watch, KStJ; CC Herts, Hon LLD St Andrews, Freedom Arbroath 1932; *cr* 1 June 1937 EARL OF STRATHMORE AND KINGHORNE (UK); *m* 16 July 1881 Nina Cecilia, GCVO, DStJ (*d* 23 June 1938), dau of Rev Charles William Frederick Cavendish- Bentinck (*see* PORTLAND, E), and *d* 7 Nov 1944, having had:

1 PATRICK BOWES-LYON, **15th Earl of Strathmore and Kinghorne**; JP (Co Durham) and DL (Angus); *b* 22 Sept 1884; Capt Scots Gds, Maj 5th Bn Black Watch (TA) WW I (wounded); *m* 21 Nov 1908 Lady Dorothy Beatrice Godolphin Osborne (*d* 18 June 1946), 3rd dau of 10th Duke of Leeds (*see* 1963 edn), and *d* 25 May 1949, having had:

  (1) John Patrick, *Master of Glamis*; *b* 1 Jan 1910; Lt Scots Gds WW II 1939–41; *ka* Halfaya Pass 19 Sept 1941

  (2) TIMOTHY PATRICK BOWES-LYON, **16th Earl of Strathmore and Kinghorne**; *b* 18 March 1918; *educ* Stowe; 2nd Lt Black Watch Res Offrs (ret ill health 1944 as Hon Lt), Dep Govr-Gen Roy Stuart Soc 1959–72; *m* 18 June 1958 Mary Bridget (*d* 8 Sept 1967), dau of Peter Brennan, of Clonaslee, Co Laois, and *dsps* 13 Sept 1972, having had:

    1a Caroline Frances; *b* 8 Dec 1959; *d* 1 Jan 1960

  (1) Cecilia; *b* 28 Feb 1912; *m* 8 March 1939 *Maj Kenneth Douglas Evelyn Herbert Harington (*see* HARINGTON, Bt) and *dsp* 20 March 1947

  (2) Nancy Moira; *b* 18 March 1918; *m* 1st 25 April 1940 (*divorce* 1950) Lance Amigo Percy Burra Robinson, RAFVR, only s of Capt P D Robinson, 9th Northumberland Fus, and Mrs E L Dimond, of Ladywood Seal, Chart, Kent, and had issue; *m* 2nd 1954 John Michael Matheson Blair (*d* 16 Dec 1955), 2nd s of Ribton Gore Blair, MC, of St Mary's, New Buckenham, Norfolk, and *d* 11 Feb 1959

2 John Herbert, DL (Forfar); *b* 1 April 1886; *educ* Eton and New Coll Oxford; Lt 5th Bn Black Watch WW I (wounded); *m* 29 Sept 1914 Hon Fenella Hepburn-Stuart-Forbes-Trefusis (*d* 19 Sept 1966), yr dau of 21st Baron Clinton (qv), and *d* 7 Feb 1930, having had:

  (1) Patricia; *b* 6 July 1916; *d* 18 June 1917

  (2) Anne Ferelith Fenella; *b* 5 Dec 1917; *m* 1st 28 April 1938 (*divorce* 1948) Viscount Anson (*d* 18 March 1958), er s of 4th Earl of Lichfield (qv), and had issue; *m* 2nd 6 Sept 1950 *HH PRINCE GEORG OF DENMARK, CVO (*see* 1967 edn ROYAL LINEAGE) and *d* 1980

  (3) Nerissa Jane Irene; *b* 18 Feb 1919

  (4) Diana Cinderella Mildred; *b* 14 Dec 1923; bridesmaid to HRH THE PRINCESS ELIZABETH (later HM THE QUEEN) 20 Nov 1947; *m* 24 Feb 1960 Peter Gordon Colin Somervell (*d* 1993), only surv s of Maj Sir Arnold Colin Somervell, OBE, JP, DL, of High Borrams, Windermere, Westmorland, and *d* 1986, leaving:

    1a *Katherine Elizabeth; *b* 23 Aug 1961 (HM THE QUEEN stood sponsor); *m* 1991 *Robert W P Lagneau, s of Michel Lagneau

  (5) *Katherine; *b* 4 July 1926

3 Alexander Francis; *b* 14 April 1887; *d* unm 19 Oct 1911

4 Fergus; *b* 18 April 1889; Capt 8th Bn Black Watch; *m* 17 Sept 1914 Lady Christian Norah Dawson-Damer (*d* 29 March 1959, having *m* 2nd 4 June 1919 Capt William Frederick Martin, MGC (*d* 6 Oct 1947), 3rd s of Charles William Wall Martin, LLD, of Killenshandra, Co Cavan), dau of 5th Earl of Portarlington (qv), and was *ka* 27 Sept 1915, leaving:

  (1) Rosemary Lusia; *b* 18 July 1915; Coronation Medal 1937; *m* 28 April 1945 Edward Wilfrid George Joicey-Cecil (*see* EXETER, M) and *d* 1989, leaving issue

5 Michael Claude Hamilton, JP Beds; *b* 1 Oct 1893; *educ* Eton and Magdalen Coll Oxford; Capt 3rd Bn Roy Scots WW I (POW), Lt-Col HG WW II, V-Lt Beds 1945–53 (formerly DL); *m* 2 Feb 1928 Elizabeth Margaret, MBE (1945) (*d* 19 Jan 1959), only dau of John Cator, of Woodbastwick Hall, Norfolk, and *d* 1 May 1953, leaving:

  (1) FERGUS MICHAEL CLAUDE BOWES-LYON, **17th Earl of Strathmore and Kinghorne**; *b* 31 Dec 1928; *educ* Eton and RMA Sandhurst; 2nd Lt Scots Gds 1949, Capt 1953 (ret 1961), memb Roy Co Archers and Edinburgh Stock Exchange 1963, dir T Cowie plc 1979–87, V-Lt Co Angus 1979–87 (DL 1973–79); *m* 10 April 1956 *Mary Pamela, DL (Angus 1989) [The Rt Hon Mary Countess of Strathmore and Kinghorne DL, Glamis House, Glamis, Forfar, Co Angus DD8 1SA], yr dau of Brig Norman Duncan McCorquodale, MC, of Maxton Ho, St Boswells, Roxburghshire, and Winslow, Bucks (*see* 1970 edn McCORQUODALE OF NEWTON, B), and *d* 1987, leaving:

1a MICHAEL FERGUS BOWES-LYON, **18th and present Earl of Strathmore and Kinghorne**

1a *Elizabeth Mary Cecilia [The Lady Elizabeth Leeming, Skirsgill Park, Penrith, Cumbria]; *b* 23 Dec 1959; *educ* St Hilda's Coll Oxford; *m* 1990 *Antony Richard Leeming, est s of Richard Leeming, and has:

  1b *Richard Fergus; *b* 1992

  2b *Andrew Michael; *b* 1996

  1b *Teresa Mary; *b* 1994

2a *Diana Evelyn; *b* 29 Dec 1966; *m* 8 April 1995 *Christopher Godfrey-Faussett, er s of Richard Godfrey-Faussett, of Badlesmere, Kent, and has:

  1b *Laura Christian Elizabeth; *b* 1997

(2) +(Michael) Albemarle [The Hon Albemarle Bowes-Lyon, 6 Pembroke House, 7 Chesham St, London SW1]; *b* 29 May 1940; granted with sisters rank of earl's dau/yr s 1974; *educ* Eton and Magdalen Coll Oxford; dir Coutts & Co 1969–93, Govr Peabody Tst 1982–, Hon Treas Family Serv Units 1976–

(1) *Mary Cecilia [The Lady Mary Colman, Bixley Manor, Norwich, Norfolk NR14 8SJ]; *b* 30 Jan 1932; Extra Lady-in-Waiting to HRH PRINCESS ALEXANDRA 1970–; *m* 10 Nov 1951 *Sir Timothy James Alan Colman, KG (1996), JP, Ld Lt Norfolk 1978–, er surv s of Geoffrey Colman, of Framingham Chase, Norfolk, and has:

  1a *James Russell; *b* 12 Jan 1962; *m* 1994 *Sasha L, dau of Robert Cotterell, of Upper Norton, Herefs

  2a *Matthew Geoffrey; *b* 10 July 1966; *m* 4 April 1997 *Jane, yr dau of James Johnston, of Sydney, NSW

  1a *Sarah Rose [Mrs Peter Troughton, The Lynch House, Upper Wanborough, Wilts SN4 0BZ]; *b* 3 May 1953; Lady-in-Waiting to HRH THE DUCHESS OF KENT 1990–; *m* 1977 *Peter J C Troughton, est s of Sir Charles Hugh Willis Troughton, CBE, MC, TD, of Ullapool, Ross-shire, and has:

    1b *Michael; *b* 1981

    1b *Rose; *b* 1979

    2b *Lucy; *b* 1984

  2a *Sabrina Mary; *b* 4 Feb 1955; *m* 1976 *Christopher Arthur Penn, s of Lt-Col Sir Eric Charles William MacKenzie Penn, GCVO, OBE, MC, and has:

    1b *Rory; *b* 1980

    1b *Louisa; *b* 1983

  3a *Emma Elizabeth; *b* 10 Feb 1958; *m* 1986 (*divorce* 1994) Richard Henry Ramsbotham, yst s of Gen Sir David Ramsbotham, GCB, CBE, and has:

    1b *Sophie; *b* 1987

(2) Patricia Maud; *b* 30 Jan 1932; *m* 10 June 1964 (*divorce* 1970) Oliver Robin Tetley, er s of Geoffrey Tetley, and *d* 1 April 1995, leaving:

  1a *Alexander; *b* 4 March 1965; *educ* Eton, U of Wales and RMA Sandhurst; Capt Scots Gds; Equerry to HRH THE DUKE OF KENT 1993–

6 David (Sir), KCVO (1959), JP (Herts); *b* 2 May 1902; *educ* Eton and Magdalen Coll Oxford (MA); Min Ec Warfare 1940, Br Emb Washington 1942–44, Herts: High Sheriff 1950, Ld Lt 1952–61, Capt Herts Regt (TA), dir: Roy Exchange Assur, Times Publishing Co, Martins Bank, Dunlop Rubber; *m* 6 Feb 1929 Rachel Pauline (*d* 21 Jan 1996), yr dau of Lt-Col Herbert Henry Spender Clay, CMG, MC, PC, MP (*see* ASTOR, V), and *d* 13 Sept 1961, leaving:

  (1) +Simon Alexander [Simon Bowes-Lyon Esq, St Paul's Walden, Bury, Herts SG4 8BP]; *b* 17 June 1932; *educ* Eton and Magdalen Coll Oxford; FCA, co dir, Ld Lt Herts 1986–; *m* 11 April 1966 *Caroline Mary Victoria, er dau of Rt Rev Victor Joseph Pike, CB, CBE, Bp Sherborne, and has:

    1a +Fergus Alexander; *b* 27 April 1970; *educ* Eton and Newcastle U

    2a +David Victor; *b* 19 Oct 1973; *educ* Eton, BNC Oxford and York U

    3a +Andrew Simon; *b* 1979; *educ* Eton

    1a *Rosemary Pema; *b* 1 Dec 1968; *m* 7 Sept 1996 *David Glazebrook, er s of Ben Glazebrook

  (1) *Davina Katharine [The Rt Hon The Countess of Stair, Lochinch Castle, Stranraer, Wigtownshire]; *b* 2 May 1930; *m* 14 Jan 1960 *13th Earl of Stair (qv) and has issue

1 Violet Hyacinth; *b* 17 April 1882; *d* 17 Oct 1893

2 Mary Frances, DCVO (1939); *b* 30 Aug 1883; *m* 14 July 1910 16th Lord Elphinstone (qv) and *d* 8 Feb 1961, leaving issue

3 Rose Constance, GCVO (1953, DCVO 1945); *b* 6 May 1890; Hon LLD Queen's U Belfast (1951), CStJ; *m* 24 May 1916 4th Earl Granville (qv) and *d* 17 Nov 1967, leaving issue

4 +ELIZABETH ANGELA MARGUERITE [HM Queen Elizabeth The Queen Mother, Clarence House, London SW1; Royal Lodge, Windsor Great Park, Berks; Castle of Mey, Caithness]; *b* 4 Aug 1900; *m* 26 April 1923 HM GEORGE VI (*d* 6 Feb 1952) and has issue (*see* ROYAL FAMILY)

Seat: Glamis Castle, Forfar, Angus. The oldest part of Glamis is the east wing, dating from the early 15th century, though a royal hunting lodge is thought to have stood on the same site as far back as the first half of the 11th century, when MALCOLM II supposedly died in it. The **1st Lord Glamis** extended the original building to form an L-shape, adding a two-floor wing to the old four-storey tower keep that had stood there before. Well before the beginning of the 17th century there were two towers, though it seems only to have been in the 17th century that they were linked. The **2nd** and **3rd Earls** undertook the greatest remodelling programme of all, extending wings to form inner courtyards and building a completely new westerly wing to render the original southeast tower block less obtrusive. The old tower was built up and roofed over as well as having its steps widened. In addition a series of 'witch's hat' conical coverings were scattered elsewhere about the structure. Internally the great hall was transformed into a sitting room; its magnificent fireplace is particularly noteworthy. The vaulted ceiling there was retained but covered in decorative plaster work. The west wing was destroyed by fire in 1800 but rebuilt. Just before the end of the 19th century the **13th Earl** laid out a Dutch garden. Twentieth-century additions include the billiard room ceiling and fireplace, which was taken from the family's Gibside property in Co Durham. The chapel contains a striking ceiling of paintings in panel-form by Jacob de Wet.

STRATHSPEY

Arms: Gules three antique crowns or. **Crest:** A burning hill proper. **Supporters:** Two savages wreathed about the head and middle with laurel proper. **Mottoes:** 1 (over crest) *Craig elachie* ('The rock of alarm'), 2 (under arms) Stand fast. **Creations:** Bt. (NS) 30 Aug 1625, B. (UK) 17 June 1884.

THE 6TH BARON STRATHSPEY OF STRATHSPEY, Cos Inverness and Moray, and a **Baronet** (Sir James Patrick Trevor Grant of Grant, Bt) [The Rt Hon The Lord Strathspey, The School House, Lochbuie, Isle of Mull, Argyllshire PA62 6AA]; *b* 9 Sept 1943; *s f* 1992, also as 33rd Ch of Clan Grant; *educ* Edinburgh, New York and RAC Cirencester; *m* 6 Aug 1966 (*divorce* 1984) Linda, yr dau of David Piggott, of Forfar, and has:

1 *Carolyn Anne Maclean; *b* 4 March 1967

2 *Philippa Jane; *b* 2 June 1971

3 *Victoria Louise; *b* 30 March 1976

The 6th BARON *m* 2nd 1985 (*divorce* 1993) Margaret, dau of Robert Drummond, of Fife

Lineage: Sir(?) JOHN/IAN *Ruadh* ('Red-haired') GRANT; Sheriff Inverness 1434, allegedly also ktd; *m* probably Matilda (*d* by 31 Jan 1434), dau of Gilbert of Glencarnie, and had, with apparently a yr s (Patrick Mac Ian Roy, allegedly *m* Janet, 3rd dau of Malcolm, 10th Ch of Mackintosh):

Sir DUNCAN GRANT, 1st of Freuchie (later called Castle Grant); *b* by 1413; *d* 1495, having had, with two daus (Catherine, *m* as his 3rd w Lachlan Mackintosh and with him was ancestor of the Chs of the MACKINTOSHes; she may also have *m* Alexander Baillie of Dunain and Sheuglie; Muriel, *m* Patrick Leslie of Balquhain and *d c* 1472, leaving issue):

JOHN (probably that JOHN GRANT called *Mor* ('The Elder')) GRANT, Yr. of Freuchie; held the lands of Inverallan from 9 May 1482; probably the member of the Grant clan who *m* Muriel, dau of Malcolm Mackintosh, 10th Ch of his clan, and *dvp* by 16 Sept 1482, leaving, with two yr sons (Patrick, of Ballindalloch, thought to have been his er bro's twin, *d* on or after 8 June 1555, leaving issue, from whom the GRANTs of Ballindalloch and GRANTs of Dalvey, later Dunlugas, claimed descent; William, allegedly ancestor of the GRANTs of Blairfindy):

JOHN *Am Bard Ruadh* ('The Red Bard') GRANT, 2nd of Freuchie; *m* (contract 16 Sept 1484) Margaret, dau of Sir James Ogilvy of Deskford (*see* SEAFIELD, E), and *d* 1 May 1528, having had, with three other daus and an illegitimate s (John/Ian *Mor*, of Glenmoriston), *m* 1st (*divorce*) Elizabeth/Isabella, dau of Walter Innes of Innermarkie (*see* INNES, Bt, of Balvenie), *m* 2nd *c* 1544 Agnes, dau of William Fraser of Teachers; *see* LOVAT, L):

1 JAMES

2 John; *m* a dau of Strachan of Culloden and *d* 1553, leaving issue, from whom stem the GRANTs of Corriemony and GRANTs of Sheuglie

1 Margaret; *m c* 10 May and 8 Nov 1508 Thomas Cumming, s of John Cumming of Erneside

2 Anne; *m* 1st John Hallyburton of Pitcur; *m* 2nd *c* 1512 3rd Lord (Fraser of) Lovat (*qv*) and *d* by 1536

3 Agnes; *m c* 22 Oct 1520 Donald Cameron, Yr. of Lochiel

4 Elizabeth; *m* John Mackenzie of Kintail (*see* CROMARTIE, E)

The er legitimate s,

JAMES *Sheumas nan Creach* ('James of the Forays') GRANT, 3rd of Freuchie; *m* 1st Elizabeth, dau of 6th Lord Forbes (*qv*), and had:

1 JOHN

2 William, of Finlarg; *dsp* by 22 Dec 1560

3 Duncan, of Easter Elchies; *m* Marjory, 3rd dau of Robert Leslie, 5th s of William Leslie of Aikenway, and *d* Oct 1580, leaving issue

1 Isobel; *m* by 1543 Archibald Campbell, est s of Sir John Campbell of Cawdor (*see* CAWDOR, E), and had issue

2 Margaret; *m c* 15 Sept 1552 Thomas Cumming of Altyre

3 Janet; *m* 1st *c* 26 Jan 1552/3 Alexander Sutherland of Duffus; *m* 2nd *c* 26 Sept 1577 James Dempster of Auchterless (*d* by 7 Jan 1591/2) and *d* after 17 but by 31 Oct 1600

4 Agnes; *m c* 24 Aug 1558 David Ross, s of Alexander Ross of the Holm

JAMES GRANT, 3rd of Freuchie, *m* 2nd Christian Barclay (*m* 2nd Arthur Forbes of Balfour) and *d* 26 Aug 1553, leaving apparently by her:

4 Archibald, of Ballentomb; *m c* 1599 Isabella, dau of Cumming of Erneside, and *d* by 15 June 1619, leaving issue(*see* GRANT, Bt, of Monymusk and Cullen)

The est s,

JOHN ('The Gentle') GRANT, 4th of Freuchie; Baillie Kinloss Abbey; granted by charter the Parkhill estate, Fifeshire, following its forfeiture by John Leslie 25 Oct 1577; *m* 1st by 19 Feb 1539/40 Lady Margaret Stewart (*d* 1555), dau of 3rd Earl of Atholl of the 1457 *cr* (*see* MORAY, E); *m* 2nd by 8 March 1557/8 Lady Janet Leslie (*m* 3rd 1589 James Elphinstone (*see* ELPHINSTONE, L) and *d* 17 Dec 1591), dau of 4th Earl of Rothes (*qv*) and widow of David Crichton of Waughton, and *d* 3 June 1585, having by her had, with seven daus (including Barbara, *m* Colin *Cam* Mackenzie of Kintail and had issue; *see* CROMARTIE, E):

1 Duncan, Yr. of Freuchie; *m* 20 Feb 1568/9 Margaret (*m* 2nd Alexander Forbes of Pitsligo (*see* FORBES, Bt, of Newe); *m* 3rd Alexander Gordon of Abergeldie (for whose early ancestry *see* HUNTLY, M); *m* 4th 1604 William Sutherland of Duffus, for whose early ancestry *see* SUTHERLAND, D), dau of William Mackintosh of Mackintosh, and *dvp* after 19 Feb but by 25 March 1581/2, having by her had:

(1) JOHN

(2) James, of Ardneidlie, Edinvillie and Logie; *m* 1st *c* 2 Dec 1560 Grizel, sis of Alexander Menzies of that Ilk; *m* 2nd 8 June 1602 Catherine (*d* 19 Sept 1658 aged 77), dau of William Rose, 11th of Kilravock, and *d* by 8 July 1623, being ancestor of the GRANTs of Moyness

(3) Patrick *Og* ('The Younger'); ancestor of the second line of GRANTs of Easter Elchies

(4) Robert; ancestor of the GRANTs of Lurg

(5) Duncan, of Dandaleith; had issue

2 Patrick; ancestor of the GRANTs of Rothiemurchus

JOHN GRANT, 4th of Freuchie's gs,

JOHN GRANT, 5th of Freuchie; *m* (contract 15 April 1591) Lady Lilias Murray, dau of 1st Earl of Tullibardine of the 1606 *cr* (*see* ATHOLL, D), and *d* 2 Sept 1622, having had, with four daus (including Katherine, *m* Alexander Ogilvy of Kempcairn, yrs of 1st Lord Ogilvy of Deskford; *see* SEAFIELD, E):

Sir JOHN GRANT, 6th of Freuchie; *b* 17 Aug 1596; *m* (contract 11 Dec 1613) Mary, dau of 1st Lord Ogilvy of Deskford (*see* SEAFIELD, E), and *d* 1 April 1637, having had, with six sons (Patrick, of Cluniemoir, tutor (guardian) of Grant, had three daus; Alexander, had two daus; George, Maj, Govr Dumbarton Castle, *dsp*; Robert, gf of Robert *Og* ('The Younger'), of Milton; Mungo, ancestor of the GRANTs of Kinchirdie; Thomas, of Balmacaan, had issue):

JAMES GRANT, 7th of Freuchie; *b* 24 June 1616; *m* 24 April 1640 Lady Mary Stewart (*d* 18 Dec 1662), dau of 3rd Earl of Moray (*qv*), and was *bur* 10 Oct 1663, having had, with a yr s (Patrick, ancestor of the GRANTs of Wester Elchies) and three daus:

LUDOVIC GRANT, 8th of Freuchie and 1st of Grant, of which had charter 28 Feb 1694; *m* 1st (contract 20 Dec 1671) Janet (*d* 1697), only child of Alexander Brodie of Lethen; *m* 2nd (contract 1 March 1701) Jean (*d* 31 Jan 1734), dau of Sir Patrick Houstoun, Bt, of Houstoun, and widow of (a) Walter, 3rd s of Walter Dundas of Dundas, and (b) Richard Lockhart of Lee, and was *bur* 19 Nov 1714, having by his 1st w had, with two other sons and another dau:

1 Alexander, 2nd of Grant; Brig-Gen; Ld Lt Inverness-shire and Banffshire, MP Inverness-shire 1702–07 and in first five GB Parls; *m* 1st 3 Dec 1698 Elizabeth (*d* 22 April 1708), dau of James, Lord Doune, est s of 5th Earl of Moray (*qv*); *m* 2nd 7 April 1709 Anne (Maid of Hon to QUEEN ANNE *d* 10 June 1717), dau of John Smith, Speaker H of C (*see* STRICKLAND-CONSTABLE, Bt), and *dsps* 14 Aug 1719

2 JAMES (Sir)

3 George, of Culbin; Maj, Govr Inverness Castle; *d* unm Dec 1755

4 Lewis, of Dunphail; Col; settled Jamaica; *d* 11 March 1742, leaving:

(1) Anne; *m* Patrick Grant, Min Logie Easter

1 Elizabeth; *m* (contract 15 Jan 1704) Hugh Rose, 16th of Kilravock, and *d* 1714, leaving issue

2 Anne; *m* (contract 30 Oct 1711) Col William Grant of Ballindalloch and had issue (*see* 1970 edn MACPHERSON-GRANT, Bt)

3 Janet; *m* 1710 Sir Roderick Mackenzie, 2nd Bt, of Scatwell (*qv*), and had issue

4 Margaret; *m* Dec 1716 11th Lord Lovat (*qv*)

LUDOVIC GRANT's yr s,

Sir JAMES GRANT later COLQUHOUN (on inheriting 1718 f-in-law's btcy (NS, *cr* 30 Aug 1625) under terms of a regrant to the latter of 1704; *see* COLQUHOUN, Bt) later still GRANT again (on inheriting his er bro's estates 1719), **6th Bt**, of Luss then of Grant; *b* 28 July 1679; *m* 29 Jan 1702 Anne (*d* 25 June 1724), only dau and sole heiress of **Sir Humphrey Colquhoun of Luss, 5th Bt**, and had, with two other sons and eight daus:

1 LUDOVIC (Sir), **7th Bt**

2 Sir JAMES COLQUHOUN of Luss, 1st Bt (*qv*)

3 Francis, of Dunphail, Elgin; *b* 10 Aug 1717; Lt-Gen, MP Elgin 1768–74; *m* 17 March 1763 Catherine Sophia, dau of Joseph Cox, of Stanford-in-the-Vale, Berks, and *d* 30 Dec 1781, leaving:

(1) James Ludovic; *b* 7 Feb 1765; Lt RN, Cdr HEICS, chm Mr Winsor's Ctee for Gas Lighting 1807, Govr Gas Light and Coke Co 1812, Master Attendant HEICS Madras 1821–27, inherited from his f the estate of Windmill Hill, Farnborough, Hants; *m* Ann Bazett and *d* 1827, having had:

1a Francis Bazett (Rev); *b* 13 Oct 1795; *educ* Eton and Ch Ch Oxford (MA); Vicar Dartford 1830–45, Shelton Staffs 1845–64, Cullompton Devon 1864–72; *m* 6 Nov 1821 Margaret, yr dau of Rev George William Auriol Hay Drummond (*see* KINNOULL, E), and *d* 13 Aug 1872, leaving:

1b Francis Ludovick Hay; *b* 27 Feb 1823

2b Alexander; *b* 10 Feb 1827; Hon Lt-Col Madras Light Cav; *m* 16 Oct 1852 Emma Catherine Sophia Wedikind, dau of Gen Charles Wedikind Nepean, 7th Madras Native Inf, and *d* 11 Jan 1872

3b Augustus Drummond; *b* 25 Jan 1838; Col 17th Madras Native Inf; *m* 1st Annie Baldwin, dau of Capt Charles Shaw, RN, and had:

    1c Annie; *b* 1877; *m* Edward Coombe and *d* 1938

3b (cont.) Col Augustus Grant *m* 2nd 1 June 1880 Anna Laura (*d* 30 June 1916), dau of Thomas William Lanchester, surgn, of Yoxford, and *d* 12 Sept 1886, having by her had:

    1c Charles Drummond Hay; *b* 1 Dec 1881; *d* 13 Dec 1887

    2c Evelyn Drummond Hay; *b* 16 Jan 1883; *m* 27 Nov 1918 Canon Herbert Victor Williams, TD (*d* 26 Sept 1960), of Buckminster Vicarage, Leics, and *d* 12 May 1948, leaving two sons and a dau

    3c Auriol Gertrude Drummond; *b* 3 June 1885; *m* 26 Nov 1913 Col Charles John Tanner (*d* 1964) and *d* 1964, leaving issue

1b Maria Jane; *b* 30 Sept 1829; *m* Robert Wallace Hamilton and had issue

2b Margaret Louisa; *b* 2 March 1833

3b Alice Hay; *b* 14 Oct 1842; *m* Wilberforce Heelas, slr, of Stroud, Glos, and had issue

2a James Ludovic; *b* 1 Oct 1797; *d* 11 June 1798

(2) Charles Thomas; *b* 1769; Capt Nizam's Army 1823, Paymaster Roy Scots; *m* 1st Hannah —; *m* 2nd 24 April 1798 Emilia Sophia, gdau of 7th Viscount Falkland (*qv*), and *d c* 1831, leaving issue

(3) Francis Alexander; *b* 28 July 1771; Puisne Judge Madras; *m* Charlotte Eliza Wills and *d* 20 March 1843

(1) Sophia Jane

(2) Ann Charlotte; *b* 1764; Ldy-in-Waiting to QUEEN CHARLOTTE; *m* 18 Dec 1780 Rt Rev Lord George Murray, Bp St David's, and *d* 27 April 1844, leaving issue (see ATHOLL, D)

(3) Charlotte Frances; *b* 1769; *d* unm 26 Sept 1852

4 Charles Cathcart, of Cardeny; *b* 3 April 1723; Capt RN; *d* unm 11 Feb 1772

1 Anne Drummonda; *m* 1727 Sir Henry Innes, 5th Bt, of Innes (see ROX-BURGHE, D) and *d* 15 Feb 1771, having had issue

2 Jean; *m* 1723, as his 2nd w, 1st Earl of Fife (see FIFE, D)

3 Clementina; *m* 1737, as his 1st w, Sir William Dunbar, 3rd Bt, of Durn (*qv*)

Sir JAMES *d* 16 Jan 1746/7; his est surv s,

Sir LUDOVIC GRANT later COLQUHOUN (1729 on inheriting Luss) later still GRANT again (1739, after becoming heir to the Grant estates on his er bro's death 1732 and eventually yielding to the necessity of making over the Colquhoun ones to his yr bro James), **7th Bt**; *b* 13 Jan 1707; MP Moray 1741–61; *m* 1st 6 July 1727 Marion (*dspm* 17 Jan 1735), dau of Sir Hew Dalrymple, 1st Bt, of N Berwick (see HAMILTON-DALRYMPLE, Bt); *m* 2nd 31 Oct 1735 Lady Margaret Ogilvy (*d* 20 Feb 1757), er dau of 2nd Earl of Seafield (*qv*), and *d* 18 March 1773, leaving an est s:

Sir James Grant of Grant, **8th Bt**; *b* 19 May 1738; MP Elgin and Forres 1761–68 and Banffshire 1790–95, Gen Cashier Excise Scotland 1795–1811, Ld Lt Inverness-shire 1794–1809; *m* 4 Jan 1763 Jean, only child of Alexander Duff, of Hatton, and *d* 18 Feb 1811, leaving, with other issue:

1 Sir LEWIS ALEXANDER GRANT later GRANT-OGILVY, **9th Bt**, and 5th EARL OF SEAFIELD (*qv*); *d* unm 26 Oct 1840

2 Sir FRANCIS WILLIAM GRANT later OGILVY-GRANT, **10th Bt**, and 6th EARL OF SEAFIELD; *m* twice and by his 1st w had, with other issue (see SEAFIELD, E):

    (1) **Sir John Charles Ogilvy-Grant of Grant, 11th Bt**, 7th EARL OF SEAFIELD and 1st BARON STRATHSPEY OF STRATHSPEY in the counties of Inverness and Moray (UK), so cr 14 Aug 1858, KT (1879); *b* 4 Sept 1815; *d* 18 Feb 1881, leaving:

        1a **Sir Ian Charles Ogilvie-Grant of Grant, 12th Bt**, 8th EARL OF SEAFIELD and 2nd and last BARON STRATHSPEY OF STRATHSPEY; *d* unm 31 March 1884, when the Barony expired

    (2) **Sir James Ogilvy-Grant of Grant, 13th Bt**, 9th EARL OF SEAFIELD and **1st BARON STRATHSPEY** of Strathspey, Cos Inverness and Moray (UK), so cr 17 June 1884; *b* 27 Dec 1817; *m* twice and *d* 5 June 1888, leaving by his 1st w:

        1a **Sir Francis William Ogilvy-Grant of Grant, 14th Bt**, 10th EARL OF SEAFIELD and **2nd Baron Strathspey**; *d* 3 Dec 1888, leaving, with other issue (see SEAFIELD, E):

        1b Sir JAMES OGILVY-GRANT OF GRANT later OGILVIE-GRANT OF GRANT, **15th Bt**, 11th EARL OF SEAFIELD and **3rd Baron Strathspey**; *d* 12 Nov 1915, leaving an only dau (see SEAFIELD, E), who *s* to the Scottish peerages

        2b **Sir Trevor Ogilvie-Grant of Grant, 15th Bt**, and **4th Baron Strathspey**; *b* 2 March 1879; *educ* Waitaki High Sch and St John's Coll NZ; NZ Civ Serv; *m* 1st 19 Dec 1905 Alice Louisa (*d* 18 Nov 1945), 3rd dau of Thomas Masterman Hardy-Johnston, MInstCE (London), of Christchurch, NZ; *m* 2nd March 1947 Effie (*d* 19 July 1949), dau of Gordon Cloete, JP, of CP, S Africa, and widow of Col Capron, York and Lancs Regt, and *d* 11 Nov 1948, leaving by his 1st w:

            1c Sir (DONALD) PATRICK TREVOR OGILVIE-GRANT OF GRANT later GRANT OF GRANT (*c* 1948), **16th Bt**, and **5th Baron Strathspey**; *b* 18 March 1912; *educ* Stowe and S Eastern Ag Coll; Lt-Col Gen List and MOD Land Agent 1972, FRICS, Assoc Land Agent's Soc; *m* 1st 24 Sept 1938 (*divorce* 1951) Alice (*m* 2nd 1953 Brig Alasdair Gillean Lorne Maclean, of Pennycross CBE, (*d* 1973)) [Mrs Alasdair Maclean of Pennycross, The School House, Lochbuie, Isle of Mull, Argyll PA62 6AA], only child of Francis Bowe, of Timaru, NZ, and had:

                1d JAMES PATRICK TREVOR GRANT OF GRANT, **6th and present Baron Strathspey**

                1d *(Geraldine) Janet [The Hon Janet Grant of Grant, 24 Denbigh Rd, London W11 2SN]; *b* 10 June 1940; ed *Dictionary of British Arms–Medieval Ordinary*; *m* 27 April 1963 (*divorce* 1972, resumed maiden surname 1972) Neil Hamish Cantlie, of Edinburgh, yr s of Adml Sir Colin Cantlie, KBE, CB, DSC, of Kirklands of Coull, Aboyne

                2d *Jacqueline Patricia [The Hon Mrs Hutton, Borrowstone House, Kincardine O'Neil, Aboyne, Aberdeenshire AB34 5AP]; *b* 19 Jan

1942; *m* 30 April 1966 *Malcolm Usheen Lingen Hutton, only s of Capt Ronald Stamford Lingen Hutton, MC, of Garvocklea, Laurencekirk, Kincardineshire

1c (cont.)The **5th Baron** *m* 2nd 1 Sept 1951 *Olive, Maj WRAC, ret [The Rt Hon The Dowager Lady Strathspey, Elms Cottage, Elms Ride, W Wittering, Sussex PO20 8LP], only dau of Wallace Henry Grant, of Norwich and Northampton, and *d* 27 Jan 1992, leaving by her:

    2d +MICHAEL PATRICK FRANCIS [The Hon Michael Grant of Grant, Elms Cottage, Elms Ride, West Wittering, Sussex PO20 8LP]; *b* 22 April 1953; heir presumptive; *educ* Harrow and Oriel Coll Oxford (BA 1974); ARICS

    3d *Amanda Caroline [The Hon Amanda Grant of Grant, 10 Nevern Pl, London SW5 9PR]; *b* 16 Feb 1955; *educ* St Margaret's Sch Bushey and Centl Sch of Art London (BA 1977)

1c Lena Barbara Joan; *b* 2 July 1907; *m* 5 April 1934 Herbert Frank Onslow (see ONSLOW, Bt) and *d* 1981, leaving issue

STRICKLAND-CONSTABLE

Arms: Quarterly, 1st and 4th, gules and vair, a bend or (for CONSTABLE); 2nd and 3rd, gules a chevron or, between three crosses-pattée argent on a canton ermine a buck's head erased and attired sable (for STRICKLAND). **Crests:** 1 A ship, sails furled, all or (for CONSTABLE), 2 A turkey cock in his pride proper (for STRICKLAND). **Motto:** *A la volonté de Dieu* ('By the will of God'). **Creation:** Bt. (E) 30 July 1641.

SIR FREDERIC STRICKLAND-CONSTABLE, 12TH BT, of Boynton, Co York [Sir Frederic Strickland-Constable Bt, The Estate Office, Old Maltongate, Malton YO17 0EG]; *b* 21 Oct 1944; *s* f 1994; *educ* Westminster, Corpus Christi Coll Cambridge (BA) and London Business Sch (MSc); *m* 1982 *Pauline Margaret Harding and has:

    1 +CHARLES; *b* 10 Oct 1985

    1 *Rose; *b* 1983

Lineage: ROGER STRICKLAND, of Marske, Yorks; *m* Mary Appleton and had:

WILLIAM STRICKLAND/STRYKELAND; allegedly accompanied Sebastian Cabot in voyages of discovery to the New World; bought the Boynton estate; granted arms 1550; probably the person of that name who was MP Scarborough 1558–85; *m* Elizabeth, est dau of Sir Walter Strickland, of Sizergh, by his 2nd w Catherine, sole dau and heir of Sir Ralph Nevill(e), of Thornton Bridge (see ABERGAVENNY, M), and *d* 1598, leaving, with a yr s (William, of Easton, *m* 1585 Catherine Carteill, of Sower):

WALTER STRICKLAND, of Boynton on the Wold, Yorks; *m* Frances, dau of Peter Wentworth, of Lillingston Dayrell, Bucks, and *d* 1635, having had, with a yr s (Walter, memb CROMWELL's 'Other House') and four daus:

Sir William Strickland, 1st Bt (E), so cr 30 July 1641, of Boynton; MP Hedon 1640–53 and E R Yorks 1654–6; memb the 'Other House' during Interregnum; *m* 1st 18 June 1622 Margaret (*d* 1629), dau of Sir Richard Cholmley, of Whitby, Yorks, and had four daus (including Margaret, *m* Sir John Cochrane of Ochiltree; see DUNDONALD, E); *m* 2nd 3 May 1631 Lady Frances Finch, est dau of 1st Earl of Winchilsea (see WINCHILSEA and NOTTINGHAM, E), and *d* 1673, having by her had:

Sir Thomas Strickland, 2nd Bt; MP Beverley 1659; *m* 19 Nov 1659 Elizabeth, dau and heiress of Sir Francis Pile, 2nd Bt, and had, with other issue:

1 WILLIAM (Sir), **3rd Bt**

2 Walter; *b* 1667; *m* and had, with other issue:

    (1)William; *m* 1st a dau and coheiress of Edward Charles Henshaw, of Eltham, by whom he had no issue; *m* 2nd Diana Moyser, of Beverley, and *d* 1788, having by her had:

        1a Walter; *m* Dorothy, only dau of Edmund Rolfe, of Heacham, by whom he had no issue

3 Charles; *b* 1672; Adml, cmded HMS *Southampton* capture of Vigo 1703; *d* 1724

1 Frances; *m* 1679 Sir Richard Osbaldeston

2 Anne; *m* Rt Hon John Smith, Speaker H of C (*d* 1720), and had issue (*see* STRATHSPEY, B)

Sir THOMAS *d* 20 Nov l684; his est s,

Sir William Strickland, 3rd Bt; *b* March 1665; MP Yorks 1689–1724; *m* 28 Aug 1684 Elizabeth, dau and eventually sole heiress of William Palmes, of Lindley, by Mary, dau and coheir of 6th Lord (Baron) Eure, and *d* 12 May 1724, having had an est s:

Sir William Strickland, 4th Bt; MP 1708–35, a Ld Treasury, Sec of War; *m* Catherine, dau of Sir Jeremy Sambroke, of Gubbins, Herts, and *d* 1 Sept 1735, having had, with a dau (Elizabeth, *m* John Freeman, of Chute Lodge, Wilts):

Sir George Strickland, 5th Bt; *b* March 1729; *m* 25 Nov 1751 Elizabeth Letitia (*d* 1813), 3rd dau of Sir Roland Winn, 4th Bt, of Nostell (*see* ST OSWALD, B), and had, with other issue:

1 WILLIAM (Sir), **6th Bt**

2 George, of Newton and Chestnut Grove, Yorks; *b* 30 Nov 1760; *m* 25 Sept 1792 Jane Eleanor, dau and coheir of Christopher Craggs, of Houghton-le-Spring, Co Durham, and *d* 5 June 1832, leaving, with other issue:

(1) Walter; *b* 15 Aug 1793; *m* 27 Dec 1839 Charlotte Augusta (*d* 25 May 1885), dau of John Carroll, of Merville, Co Clare, and *d* 31 July 1875, having had, with other issue:

1a Robert; *b* 10 April 1848; *m* 19 Oct 1876 Mary Katharine (*d* 11 March 1938), dau of Rev Lancelot Arthur Sharpe, Rector Tackley, Oxon, and *d* 15 Nov 1925, leaving:

1b Walter Robert; *b* 10 Dec 1879; Salt Revenue Admin Peking; *d* 29 Aug 1922

2b Claude Francis, CIE (1931), ICS; *b* 19 Dec 1881; *educ* Winchester and New Coll Oxford (BA 1904); *m* 1 Sept 1915 Dorothy Lisa (*d* 1972), dau of George A Branson, MA, of Riddell, Victoria, Australia, and *d* 30 Jan 1962, leaving:

1c *Patricia Elizabeth Mary [Mrs Arthur Denton, The Dial House, Lower Bourne, Farnham, Surrey]; *b* 24 Dec 1916; *m* 29 March 1941 *Col Arthur Vyvyan Denton, The Loyal Regt, er s of Henry Vyvyan Denton, of Llanbedr Hall, Denbighs, and has:

1d *Amanda Elizabeth Ann Vyvyan; *b* 6 Sept 1943; *m* 27 July 1968 *David Frederick James Leathers (*see* LEATHERS, V)

2d *Joanna Mary Vyvyan; *b* 3 April 1946; *m* 1974 *Martyn Laurence

2c *Frances Pamela Ann [Mrs Anthony Parr, Old Dove House, Kingbourne Green, Herts]; *b* 12 Feb 1919; *m* 1st 10 Jan 1942 Sgt (N) Anthony William Vivian, RAFVR (*ka* on air ops from Malta 8 Sept 1942), er s of Capt Hugh Vivian, of Chantry Acre, Bishopston, Glam; *m* 2nd 26 Sept 1946 *Capt Anthony James Parr, er s of Raymond Parr, For Serv, of The Old Dove Ho, Harpenden, Herts, and by him has:

1d *Francis Nicholas; *b* 18 Dec 1949; *educ* Eton and Magdalene Coll Cambridge; *m* 1974 *Sakiko Fukuda

1d *Laetitia Mary; *b* 30 June 1948; *educ* St Mary's Convent Ascot and Newnham Coll Cambridge; *m* 1970 *William Logan Jack, of Huntington Court, Kington, Herefs, and has:

1e *Robert Logan; *b* 1977

1e *Rosemary Ann; *b* 1979

3b Arthur George René; *b* 27 Sept 1885; *m*

4b Cecil Eustace, BSc; *b* 16 Feb 1889; *m* 1st 9 Aug 1924 (*divorce* 1942) Dorothy Enid, 2nd dau of Edward Stocker, of Blackheath, and had:

lc +Martin Robert Cecil [Martin Strickland Esq, 4 Irene Rd, Rondesbosch, CP, S Africa]; *b* 16 Sept 1927; BSc, AMIEE; *m* 7 March 1952 *Judith Melvia, dau of Cecil Kerr, and has:

1d +Walter Robert Cecil; *b* 8 June 1953; *m* 1980 *Christine Clark and has:

1e +James Robert; *b* 1984

1e *Natalie Judith; *b* 1982

2e *Kyle Rhoana; *b* 1989

2d +Hugh Edward; *b* 25 Nov 1964; *m* 1984 *Bridget Newmarch and has:

1e +Charles Robert; *b* 1987

1e *Evelyn Judith; *b* 1985

3d +Kenneth William; *b* 8 Oct 1959

4d +Alexander David; *b* 24 Nov 1965

2c +Walter Nicholas; *b* 15 Feb 1930; PhD; *m* 1st 1956 (*divorce* 1963) Margaret, dau of — Brown, of Dunoon, Argyll, and has:

1d *Gina Elizabeth; *b* 1963

2c (cont.) Dr Strickland *m* 2nd 1968 *Marie, dau of Lynn Shields, of Salt Lake City, and by her has:

1d +Robert Nicholas; *b* 1971

4b (cont.) Cecil Strickland *m* 2nd 29 Aug 1949 *Galatia, dau of Costa Patzatzis, of Cairo, and *d* 1981, leaving by her:

1c *Jessica Helen; *b* 1951; *m* 19– *Philip Lissaman, of Marlborough, NZ, and has:

1d *Bridget; *b* 1979

2d *Claire; *b* 1982

3d *Sandra; *b* 1983

5b Alban Reginald; *b* 18 March 1891; *ka* 20 Oct 1917

6b Clement Cyprian; *b* 26 Sept 1892; *educ* St John's Coll Oxford (BA); *m* 11 Sept 1920 Violet Isabel, 2nd dau of Meyrick Selby Lowndes, JP, and *d* June 1943, leaving:

1c +Paul Clement Lowndes (Rev); *b* 9 Aug 1921; Curate Oatlands Weybridge 1949–52, St John's Huddersfield 1952–54, Vicar Carlton Yorks 1954–58, Offton Suffolk 1958–61 and Debenham 1961; *m* 2 Feb 1950 *Emily, dau of Richard Herbert Hartley, of Pontefract, Yorks, and has:

1d Walter Francis Lowndes; *b* 29 May 1953; *educ* St John's Leatherhead; *d* 1970

1d *Janet Elizabeth; *b* 2 Nov 1951; *m* 1979 *Allan James Miller

2d *Mary Isobel; *b* 14 March 1961

2c +Robert Lowndes; *b* 9 March 1924

1b Mary Aimée; *m* 22 Nov 1913 Horace Graham Wyatt, Indian Educnl Serv, and had issue

2b Elsie Margarette; *m* 9 Aug 1910 Ronald William Hopkins, yst s of Harry Percy Hopkins, War Office, and *d* 12 April 1942, leaving issue

2a Henry Eustatius; *b* 4 Nov 1864; *d* 12 April 1934

1a Margaret; *m* 20 June 1871 Rev Henry T Wardroper, of Northmoor, Oxon, and *d* 1883, leaving issue

2a Agnes; *m* 12 Jan 1875 Reginald Foster Ward, yst s of Rev Charles Ward, and *d* 22 May 1916

3a Alice; *m* 28 Nov 1878 Thomas Henry Cheatle, MRCS (*d* 15 Dec 1906), of Burford, Oxon, and *d* 21 July 1935, leaving issue

4a Frances Anne; *m* 25 Jan 1876 Ferdinand Beamish (*d* 27 Dec 1920), of Dennisworth, Pucklechurch, Glos, and *d* 7 March 1929, leaving issue

5a Mary

6a Caroline; *m* 5 Oct 1876 William Gifford Scott, MB, of Lismore, Newton Abbot, Devon, and had issue

(2) Charles, of Sans Souci, Posilippo, Italy; *m* 23 April 1832 Elizabeth Mary (*d* 23 Dec 1870), er dau of Henry Deacon, of Longcross Ho, Glam, and *d* 11 April l862, leaving:

1a Walter Kennedy, of Sans Souci; *b* 1 March 1833; *m* 8 April 1872 Alice Christian (*d* 31 Dec 1906), only dau of Capt Matthew Campbell, HEICS, and *d* 3 Feb 1907, leaving:

1b Charles Walter Campbell; *b* 27 Feb 1873; Cdr RN; *m* 8 June 1909 Constance Margaret Lorn Campbell (*m* 2nd 27 Sept 1928 Benjamin Charles Apps, of Guildford, and *d* 10 April 1959), only dau of Maj F W Campbell, RHA, and was accidentally *k* 14 Sept 1918, leaving:

1c Constance Alice Lorn Campbell; *b* 2 July 1912

2c *Katarin Jarrard Campbell [Mrs John Privett, Priory Cottage, Naish, E Coker, Somerset BA22 9HQ]; *b* 5 Aug 1914; *m* 2 April 1938 *John Evan Privett, s of Edward Privett, and has:

1d *John Hugh Charles; *b* 1939; *m* 1971 *Jane Dilys Rowland Macqueen and has:

1e *Jonathan Edward Macqueen; *b* 1972

2e *Rowland Alexander Charles; *b* 1978

3e *Guy Frederick Andrew; *b* 1981

1e *Philada Jane; *b* 1974

2d *Robin Jarrard Campbell; *b* 1940; *m* 1964 *Penelope Lisbeth Bate and has:

1e *James Jarrard Campbell; *b* 1966

2e *Edward Tobias; *b* 1970

1e *Kathryn Louise; *b* 1968

3d *Alan Frederick; *b* 1943; *m* 1st 1975 (*divorce* 19–) Carolin Graham Fawcett; *m* 2nd 1981 *Jenny Maria Miller and by her has:

1e *Imogen Frances; *b* 1981

2e *Alice Rose; *b* 1987

1d *Christina Katarin; *b* 1946; *m* 1984 *Cedric Thomas Sandford and has:

1e *Anna Elizabeth; *b* 1990

1a Rosalie St Quentin; *m* 12 May 1863 Capt Thomas Charles Cholmeley, RN (*d* 11 April 1890), of Brandsby Hall, Yorks, and *d* 23 Sept 1923, leaving issue

(3) Thomas Alfred (Rev); *b* 6 Jan 1802; Rector Bredon, Worcs; *m* 19 Dec 1840 Anne Catherine (*m* 2nd 22 Jan 1856 Colin Campbell Baillie), only child of Rev Henry Fitzgerald, and *d* 7 Nov 1852, leaving:

1a George (Rev), of Chaceley, Worcs; *b* 29 Sept 1841; *m* 28 June 1870 Emily (*d* 28 April 1908), dau of Gerald Dillon, of Lacken, Co Westmeath, and *d* 6 Jan 1883, leaving:

1b Thomas Alfred Gerald; *b* 28 March 1871; *educ* Sidney Sussex Coll Cambridge (MA); *m* 25 Jan 1910 Gertrude Nesta (*d* 1 Oct 1960), dau of Edwin Corbett, Min Stockholm, and *dsp* 21 March 1957

2a Thomas Henry Forster; Lt 73rd Regt; *d* 19 June 1875

1a Alice Geraldine; *d unm* 30 Oct 1933

(4) Augustine Edmund Christopher, of Oaklands, Devon; *b* 1808; *m* Aug 1835 Susan Caroline (*d* 20 Oct 1882), yr dau of Henry Deacon, of Longcross Ho, Glam, and *d* 1892, leaving:

1a Algernon Augustine de Lille, of Apperley Court, Glos, JP Devon; *b* 26 Jan 1837; *educ* Merton Coll Oxford (MA); *m* 28 Jan 1863 Charlotte Anne (*d* 1890), yr dau of Peter Richard Hoare (*see* HOARE, Bt, of Luscombe), and *d* 18 Jan 1914, leaving:

1b Algernon Henry Peter; *b* 19 Dec 1863; *educ* Ch Ch Oxford (BA); *m* 25 Jan 1890 Mary Selina (*d* 13 Dec 1949), yst dau of Walter Drummond (*see* PERTH, E), and *d* 22 Feb 1928. leaving:

1c Algernon Walter; *b* 5 March 1891; Capt Glos Yeo; *m* Dec 1915 Lady Mary Charteris (*m* 2nd 14 April 1943 John George Lyon, s of John Stewart Lyon, of Kirkmichael, Dumfriesshire, and *d* 1991), dau of 11th Earl of Wemyss (and 7th Earl of) March (*qv*), and *d* 2 Aug 1938, leaving:

1d Algernon Guy; *b* 22 Sept 1916; Sgt RAF WW II; *ka* 9 May 1942

1d *Pamela Sabina [Mrs Henry van der Gucht, Apperley Court, Glos]; *b* 12 Nov 1921; *m* 17 Dec 1947 *Maj Henry Benjamin van der Gucht, MC, Roy Northumberland Fus, s of Maj George Tristram van der Gucht, IA, of Stoney Cross, Heathway, Camberley, and has:

1e *Guy Tristram; *b* 29 June 1951; *educ* Stowe

2e *Hugo Charles; *b* 6 Jan 1956; *educ* Eton

1e *(Juliet) Clare; *b* 21 Sept 1948

2d *Sara Ann Mary [Lady Carr, Burch, N Molton, S Molton, Devon EX 36 3JU]; *b* 3 March 1926; *m* 6 Sept 1950 *Prof Sir (Albert) Raymond Maillard Carr, MA, Warden St Antony's Coll Oxford 1968–87, only s of Reginald Henry Maillard Carr, of Winfrith, Dorset, and has:

1e *Adam Henry Maillard; *b* 1 July 1951; *educ* Eton

2e *Matthew Xavier Maillard [Matthew Carr Esq, 4 Perham Rd, London W14]; *b* 5 Feb 1953; *educ* Eton; portrait painter; *m* 1988

*Lady Anne Mary Somerset, only dau of 11th Duke of Beaufort (qv), and has:

  1f *Eleanor; b 1992

3e *Alexander Rallion Charles; b 8 Nov 1958

1e *Laura Selina Madeline [Mrs Richard Barrowclough, Burch, N Molton, S Molton, Devon EX36 3JU]; b 18 Nov 1954; m 1978 *Richard Edmond Barrowclough (see LIMERICK, E)

1c Barbara Mary; m 1st 3 Jan 1916 Martin Chicheley Albright, Worcs Yeo (ka 8 Nov 1917), only s of George Stacey Albright, CBE, JP, of Bromesberrow Place, Ledbury, Herefs; m 2nd 20 Oct 1926 Lt-Col George Henry Anson, MC, TD, DL, Staffs Yeo (d 21 Sept 1957), s of Henry Anson-Horton, JP, of Catton Hall, and d 18 Jan 1939

2b Augustine Cecil; b 31 Dec 1864; d 20 May 1925

3b Hubert Arthur; b 2 March 1867; m 16 Jan 1890 Rose Cecil (d 30 Sept 1939), est dau of Cecil Henry Russell (see RUSSELL, Bt, of Swallowfield), and d 16 April 1928

4b Claud Hugh; b 15 April 1871; m 1st 1895 (divorce 1904) Maud Mary, yst dau of Patrick Gordon-Canning, of Hartpury, and had:

  1c Walter Claud; b 1896; m 1st 3 March 1932 (divorce 1946) Charmian Louise, only child of Lt-Col Harold Cazenove Hessey, of Bethersden, Kent; m 2nd 26 Jan 1954 *Mary Julianne, er dau of Wilfred Henry Kellam-Harris, of Putney, and d 1982, leaving by her:

    1d +Walter Hugh Jeremy; b 25 Dec 1960

  2c Hugh Baring; b 1899; m 26 Feb 1955 *Pauline [Mrs Hugh Strickland, Ventonvaise, Callestick, Truro, Cornwall], dau of Percival Wood, of Shaldon, Devon, and d 1971, leaving:

    1d +Christopher Claud Hugh; b 1955

    1d *Sarah Janet; b 1962

4b (cont.) Claud Strickland m 2nd 12 Feb 1908 Una Clara Margaret (d 5 Feb 1959), dau of Charles Bell, of Langbraugh Hall, Cleveland, and d 16 Sept 1938, leaving by her:

  3c Claud Dobree; b 29 March 1909; F/O AAF WW II; m 3 Aug 1934 (divorce 1941) Lady Marguerite Bligh, dau of 9th Earl of Darnley (qv), and was ka Oct 1941

1b Hilda Rachel; m 23 Nov 1893 Capt Arthur Charles Stanley Clarke, Roy W Surrey Regt, and d 8 Sept 1933, leaving issue

2b Gwendolen Mary; d unm 2 Feb 1953

2a Walter Cecil, JP (Devon); b 25 May 1839; Capt 83rd Regt; m 31 July 1867 Mary Blanche (d 1 July 1917), 2nd dau of Maj-Gen John Polglase James, HEICS, and d 24 April 1913, leaving:

  1b Dudley Herbert Cecil; b 14 Nov 1869; m April 1901 Margaret (d 19–), 2nd dau of Edwin J Gilbert, of San Bernardino, USA, and d 1953, leaving:

    1c Arthur Cecil; b 3 Feb 1902

    1c Violet St Leger; b April 1903; m Frederick Sigrist

    2c Muriel Estelle; b Sept 1904

  2b Cecil St Leger; b 26 May 1876; m 4 June 1903 Lucy Estess (d 10 Nov 1968), yr dau of Henry Edward Smithes, of Mount Pleasant, Kansas, USA, and d 25 Jan 1929, leaving:

    1c Cecil Alexander; b 26 April 1913; educ Sherborne; Sgt Pilot RAF WW II (POW); m Oct 1858 Peggy Vyvyan Madeleine, dau of John Clement Carpenter Gatley, DCL, LLD, and dsp 2 Jan 1967

    1c *Cecile Daphne; m 14 April 1939 *Cdr Stuart Erskine Crewe-Read, RN, est s of Col Randolph Offley Crewe-Read, DSO, of Pennant, Abermule, Montgomeryshire, and has issue

    2c *Joan; m 28 Sept 1933 *Maj George Vilett Rolleston, ERD, JP, CC, only s of Maj George Reginald Aubrey Rolleston, of Bath, and has:

      1d *George Lancelot St Leger, MBE (1969) [George Rolleston Esq MBE, Holetown House, Sampford Spiney, S Devon]; b 8 May 1939; educ Marlborough; Capt Coldstream Gds (ret 1969), Dip Corps 1969; m 1976 *Claude-Annie, dau of N J Cointet, of Paris and Beirut, and has:

        1e *James Andrew St Leger; b 1981

        1e *Natalie Lucy; b 1980

1b Ethel Beatrice; m 1st 2 May 1893 (divorce 1901) Capt Ernest Edward Robinson and had issue; m 2nd June 1901 (divorce 1909) Lt-Col Roger Monck-Mason, DSO, Roy Munster Fus (d 1941), s of Thomas Monck-Mason, ICS, and d 1956

2b Augusta Blanche; m 14 Oct 1897 Lt-Gen Sir Louis Jean Bols, KCB, KCMG, DSO, Govr and C-in-C Bermuda (d 13 Sept 1930), and d 13 Feb 1949, leaving issue

3b Lilian Grace; m 5 June 1902 Thomas James LONGWORTH formerly BALLER (roy licence 1888) (d 1936), er s of G F H Baller, of Kimbolton, Hunts, and d Aug 1955

(1) Elizabeth Lætitia

(2) Catherine Charlotte; m 1837 Rev Henry FitzGerald, bro of Sir William FitzGerald, 2nd Bt (see 1902 edn), and dsp 9 Sept 1866

(3) Eleanor Sabina; m 1st April 1833 Rev Edward Cookson (d 4 Dec 1879), 3rd s of Isaac Cookson, of Meldon, and d 31 May 1891, leaving issue

(4) Georgiana; m 5 Sept 1837 Marchese Teodoro Carlo Strozzi, of Lavacchio, Tuscany, and d 27 Aug 1880, leaving issue

3 Walter, of Flamborough, Yorks; b 6 Dec 1771; m 1st 31 Aug 1803 Frances (d 23 April 1836), 2nd dau and coheir of Maximilian Western, of Cokethorpe Park, Oxon; m 2nd 29 June 1837 Sarah (d 11 Oct 1877), widow of Sir Francis Boynton, 8th Bt (qv), and by his 1st w had, with other issue:

  (1) Louisa; m 2 Nov 1833 Sir Henry Boynton, 10th Bt (qv), and d 1841

4 Henry Eustatius; b 31 Aug 1777; m 21 Dec 1802 Mary, est dau of Rev Edmund Cartwright, DD, FRS, of Woburn, Beds, and d 29 May 1865, having had four sons and two daus

1 Elizabeth; m 1781 her cousin Strickland Freeman; both d 1821

Sir GEORGE d 13 Jan 1808; his est s,

  Sir William Strickland, 6th Bt; b 12 March 1753; m 15 April 1778 Henrietta (d 26 March 1827), 3rd dau and coheir of Nathaniel Cholmley, of Whitby and Howsham, Yorks, and had, with other issue:

1 GEORGE (Sir), **7th Bt**

2 Nathaniel Constantine (Rev); b 7 Sept 1792; Vicar Reighton; m 1st 22 Oct 1835 Charlotte Danvers (dsp 3 Dec 1850), dau of S H T La Touche Hecker, of The Grove, New Radnor; m 2nd 28 March 1854 Harriet (d 21 Dec 1877), dau of Richard Hennings, and d 12 Jan 1886, leaving, with other issue:

(1) Walter Richard STRICKLAND later CHOLMLEY (1886) later still STRICKLAND again; b 25 April 1859; Boer War 1899–1902; m 20 Jan 1880 Julia Maud (d 13 Dec 1907), dau of Edward S Jenkyns, of the India Office, and d 26 Oct 1940, leaving:

  1a Walter Edward; b 24 Nov 1880; RE WW I; m 15 Aug 1931 Edith Fanny, dau of William George Goodall, and d 14 June 1914

  2a Gerald Constantine, MM; b 5 June 1888; Lt 3rd S African Inf WW I (wounded); m 1st March 1910 (divorce 1921) Mary, dau of John Hampton, and had:

    1b Gerald John; b 13 July 1911; MCQS Johannesburg; m 30 Nov 1940 Patricia (d 1988), dau of Archibald Edward Benson, of Pretoria, and d 1993, leaving:

      1c +John; b 6 July 1950

      1c *Margaret Julia Patricia [Mrs Hubert Malherbe, 12105 S Hidden Valley, Club Drive, Sandy, UT 84092, USA]; b 19 Jan 1942; m 1978 *Hubert Henri Malherbe

    1b Julia Mary; b March 1913; d May 1916

  2a (cont.) Gerald Strickland m 2nd 1 March 1922 Magdalene, dau of Peter Hunten, and d 1962, having by her had:

    2b Peter; b 8 Aug 1927; d Nov 1928

  3a Arthur William; b 16 March 1890; Roy Fus WW I (five times wounded); m 16 Dec 1916 Violet May (d 1 Jan 1956), dau of Edward S Margerum, of Merrylands, W Australia, and had:

    1b +Stanley Arthur [Stanley Strickland Esq, 28 Cavendish Rd, New Malden, Surrey KT3 6DH]; b 1 Jan 1920; RE WW II (Bomb Disposal); m 19 July 1952 *Eileen Mary, dau of Patrick Henry Keeley, of Surbiton, Surrey, and has:

      1c *Janet Frances [Miss Janet Strickland, 8 Spencer House, 8 Spencer Rd, Eastbourne, E Sussex BN21 4PA]; b 24 May 1960

    2b Robert Basil; b 12 Dec 1921; d 9 Jan 1922

    3b +John Edward [John Strickland Esq, 56 Chertsey Drive, N Cheam, Surrey]; b 17 April 1923; Queen's (Roy W Surrey) Regt WW II; m 31 Oct 1953 *Rose Ena, dau of George Thomas William Greenfield, of N Cheam, and has:

      1c +Christopher Graham; b 24 March 1962; m 1986 *Tracey Susan, dau of Charles Alec Lang, of Abbey Wood, London, and has:

        1d +Charlie; b 1990

        1d *Lauren; b 1986

      1c *Susan Carol; b 13 Jan 1960; m 1977 *Trevor Fisher, of Carshalton, Surrey, and has:

        1d *Alan David; b 1977

        2d *Liam Steven; b 1991

        1d *Natalie Alison; b 1979

      2c *Alison Ruth; b 1 Dec 1966; m 1989 *Frederick Charles Wakelin, of Shepperton, Middx, and has:

        1d *Charlotte Rose; b 1990

        2d *Rachel Louise; b 1992

    1b Barbara; b 14 June 1918; d 6 Oct 1931

  4a Cecil; b 16 Aug 1892; 3rd S African Inf WW I; d 8 Feb 1919 from effects of gas recd in action

  5a Stanley Martin; b 29 Jan 1895

  1a Frances Ethel; b 26 Dec 1882; m 23 Dec 1903 Harold Lionel Ainslie Sinclair, s of Duncan Sinclair, of Palmerston N, NZ, and had issue

  2a Julia; b 29 Oct 1884; m 1907 Alfred Gordon Harold Geale, of Somerset Strand, CP, S Africa, and had issue

  3a Harriet Maud; b 1 Sept 1886; m 1st 1909 George May (ka 1916), of Pretoria, and had issue; m 2nd 1920 Robert Francis Gilson (d 17 April 1946) and had further issue

  4a Muriel Winifred; b 21 Sept 1901; d 17 March 1917

(2) Hugh Strickland; b 21 Aug 1861; m 18 Oct 1898 Susannah Sophia (d 2 Feb 1941), dau of Nathaniel Nottage, of Hampstead, and d 2 Jan 1911, leaving:

  1a Nathaniel Lewis Hugh; b 14 Sept 1899; served WW I (POW); m 12 Aug 1923 Unity Margaret (d 1975), dau of Arthur Birch, of Watford, and d 6 Nov 1954, leaving:

    1b *Mavis Rae [Mrs Eric Earl, 7 Lombardy Drive, Berkhamsted, Herts]; b 13 Sept 1929; m 21 June 1952 *Eric Richard Earl and has:

      1c *Richard Lewis; b 25 Oct 1956

      2c *Graham Hugh; b 9 June 1961

    2b *Mary Joy [Mrs George Jones, Hayley House, Main St, Brancaster, N Norfolk]; b 13 Sept 1929; m 21 June 1952 *George Arthur Jones and has:

      1c *Bryan Howard; b 6 April 1953

      1c *Natalie Carolyn; b 13 Sept 1960

    3b *Margaret Anne [Mrs Israel Kessel, The Stables, Little Common, Stanmore, Middx]; b 1 Oct 1932; m 1st 6 June 1953 (divorce 1977) Lionel William Wood (d 1985) and by her 2nd m 1977 Dr Israel Kessel (d 1985) and by her 1st husb has:

      1c *Martin Lionel; b 2 Oct 1954

      1c *Jacqueline Margaret; b 25 Dec 1959

  1a Mavis Grace; b 18 Aug 1901

(3) George William; b 16 Feb 1863

(4) Nathaniel Henry; b 5 Nov 1866; m Maud Morris, of London

(5) Charles; b 29 Sept 1870; m 3 March 1904 Annie Grace, only dau of John Abram, of Cecil Ho, Hastings, MusD Oxon

(1) Henrietta Annie; b 11 March 1856; m 26 Jan 1879 Thomas Singleton Griesbach and d 25 Nov 1926, leaving issue

(2) Charlotte; b 12 May 1857

(3) May: *b* 10 May 1860; *m* 14 Aug 1879 Rev William Rowley, Vicar Reighton, Yorks, and had a dau

1 Caroline; *m* 9 Oct 1811 W F Lowndes-Stone, of Brightwell Park, Oxon, and *d* 11 April 1867, leaving issue

2 Anne; *m* 12 April 1814 Rev Francis Simpson, Vicar Carnaby and Boynton, Yorks, and *d* 7 Sept 1868 1eaving issue

3 Priscilla; *m* 16 June 1819 Charles Winn (*see* SAINT OSWALD, B) and *d* 19 Nov 1884 aged 88, leaving issue

Sir WILLIAM *d* 8 Jan 1834; his s,

Sir GEORGE STRICKLAND later CHOLMLEY (roy licence 17 March 1865), **7th Bt**; *b* 20 Nov 1782; MP W R Yorks 1831–41 and Preston 1841–67; *m* 1st 8 March 1818 Mary (*d* 10 Jan 1865), only child of Rev Charles Constable, of Wassand, Yorks; *m* 2nd 26 May 1867 Jane (*dsp* l 9 Oct 1898), est dau of Thomas Leavens, and *d* 23 Dec 1874, having by his 1st w had:

1 **Sir Charles William Strickland, 8th Bt**, DL, JP (E and N Rs Yorks); *b* 6 Feb 1819; *educ* Rugby and Trin Coll Cambridge; barrister, High Sheriff N R Yorks 1880; *m* 1st 19 Feb 1850 Georgina Selina Septima (*d* 13 June 1864), dau of Sir William Milner, 4th Bt (*qv*), and had:

(1) WALTER WILLIAM STRICKLAND, *de jure* 9th Bt; became a Czechoslovakian citizen and did not use title; *b* 26 May 1851; *educ* Trin Coll Cambridge (BA); *m* 1888 Eliza (*d* 22 Jan 1946), dau of W Vokes, and *dsp* 9 Aug 1938

1 (cont.) **Sir Charles** *m* 2nd 22 May 1866 Anne Elizabeth (*d* 7 April 1886), yst dau of Rev Christopher Nevile, of Thorney, Notts, and *d* 31 Dec 1909, having by her had:

(2) Frederic, JP (N R Yorks); *b* 7 Nov 1867; Maj RASC WW I (despatches twice); *m* 21 July 1903 Mary Beatrix (*d* 24 Sept 1965), 3rd dau of Sir John Thornycroft, FRS, LLD, and *d* 12 June 1934, leaving:

1a Elizabeth; *b* 5 June 1904; *m* 20 June 1929 Rev John Hargreaves Ashworth Cobham, est s of Rev George Cobham, and had issue

2a Diana Blanche; *b* 26 April 1911; *m* 8 Aug 1933 Rev Edward Denzil Chetwood Wright, est s of Maj Philip Wright, of Brattleby Hall, Lincs, and had issue

3a Lettice; *b* 9 Feb 1913; *m* 5 Aug 1936, as his 2nd w, **Sir Robert Frederick Strickland-Constable, 11th Bt**, *see* below) and had issue

(3) Eustace Edward; *b* 27 Nov 1870: *d* 9 April 1898

(4) Henry, OBE (1919); *b* 6 Oct 1873; Capt RN WW I; *m* 31 Aug 1910 Hon Ida Mary Hazel Willoughby (*d* 12 July 1966), dau of 10th Baron Middleton (*qv*), and *d* 2 Sept 1934, leaving:

1a *Monica Lucy Ann [Miss Monica Strickland, Barton Hill House, Whitwell, York YO6 7JY]; *b* 1 Sept 1916; *educ* London U (BSc 1938)

(1) Esther Anne, OBE (1920), JP (E R Yorks); *m* 18 June 1898 Col Hon Tatton Lane Fox Willoughby, JP, DL (*d* 10 July 1947), 6th son of 8th Baron Middleton (*qv*), and *d* 23 May 1940

2 Frederick; *b* 1820; *d* 13 Oct 1849

3 Henry STRICKLAND later STRICKLAND-CONSTABLE (roy licence 1803), of Wassand, Yorks, JP; *b* 18 March 1821; BA Cantab; *m* 28 April 1859 Cornelia Charlotte Anne (*d* 11 Feb 1911), yst dau of Col Henry Dumaresq, and *d* 20 March 1909, having had:

(1) Frederick Charles, of Wassand, JP (Yorks); *b* 16 March 1860; Lt-Col 3rd Bn E Yorks Regt, Capt RHG; *m* 3 Aug 1898 Margaret Elizabeth (*d* 17 June 1961), dau of R-Adml Hon Thomas Alexander Pakenhan (*see* LONGFORD, E), and *das* 20 Dec 1917, leaving:

1a **Sir Henry Marmaduke Strickland-Constable, 10th Bt**; *b* 4 Dec 1900; *educ* Eton and Magdalen Coll Oxford (BA); *m* 24 July 1929 Countess Ernestine Rex (*d* 1995), dau of Count Rex, late Saxon Min Vienna, and *d* 1975

2a ROBERT FREDERICK (Sir), **11th Bt**

1a Hilary Margaret; *b* 19 Sept 1935 (Henry John) Ralph Bankes, JP, of Kingston Lacy and Corfe Castle, Dorset, and *d* 11 Sept 1966, leaving issue

(2) Marmaduke; *b* 4 March 1862; *d* 29 Dec 1898

(1) Ethel; *m* 23 Sept 1880 2nd Baron Derwent (*qv*) and *d* 2 Oct 1891, leaving issue

(2) Rosamond; *d* unm 23 Nov 1931

(3) Mary Sophia; *m* 7 April 1897 John George Bulteel (*d* 8 May 1920), of Pamflete, and *d* 27 March 1959 aged 89, leaving issue

(4) Lucy Winifred; *m* 17 April 1907, as his 2nd w, Robert MacNeil Ker (*d* 15 Oct 1963), est s of Thomas Ripley Ker, of Dougalston, NB, and *d* 7 Dec 1942, leaving issue

1 Lucy Henrietta; *b* Feb 1822; *m* 19 Dec 1844 Rev James Powell MARRIOTT later COULTON CONSTABLE (*d* 10 Oct 1871), of Cotesbach, and *d* 8 July 1871, leaving issue

The 10th Bt's bro,

Sir Robert Frederick Strickland-Constable, 11th Bt; *b* 22 Oct 1903; *educ* Magdalen Coll Oxford (BA 1925, MA 1936, PhD 1940); Reader Thermodynanics London U, Lt-Cdr RNVR WW II; *m* 1st 21 Sept 1929 (*annulled* 1931) Rosalind Mary, yr dau of Arthur Webster, of Chelsea; *m* 2nd 5 Aug 1936 his cousin Lettice, yst dau of Maj Frederic Strickland (*see above*), and *d* 11 Dec 1994, leaving by her:

1 Sir FREDERIC STRICKLAND-CONSTABLE, **12th and present Bt**

2 +(John) Robert Francis [John Strickland-Constable Esq, Combe Wood, Brasted, Westerham, Kent]; *b* 26 April 1949; *educ* Bryanston, Slade Sch of Fine Art and London U (Higher Dip Fine Art); *m* 1971 *Christine, dau of D W Roberts, of St Paul's Cray, Kent, and has:

(1) +Thomas Robert; *b* 1975

(1) *Louisa Emma: *b* 1979

1 *Miranda; *b* 4 April 1938; *educ* London U (BA 1959)

2 *Elizabeth Diana; *b* 26 April 1940; *educ* RCM and Staatliche Hochschüle für Musik Cologne; LRAM; *m* 1972 *John Maxwell Fairley, BSc, and has:

(1) *Lucy Fiona; *b* 1974

(2) *Alice Susannah; *b* 1977

STRONGE

Arms: Arg. a chevron undée sa. between three lozenges az., in chief point an estoile gu. (for STRONGE). **Crests:** 1 An eagle with two heads displayed sa., beaked and legged az., langued gu., 2 A cluster of wine grapes ppr. **Mottoes:** 1 *Tentanda via est* ('A way is to be attempted'), 2 *Dulce quod utile* ('What is useful is agreeable'). **Creation:** Bt. (UK) 22 June 1803.

SIR JAMES ANSELAN MAXWELL STRONGE, 10TH BT, of Tynan Abbey, Co Armagh [Sir James Stronge Bt, Camphill Community Clanabogan, 15 Drudgeon Rd, Clanabogan, Omagh, Co Tyrone BT78 1TJ]; *b* 17 July 1946; *s* 2nd cousin 1981; *educ* privately

Lineage: MATTHEW STRONGE, of a branch of the STRANGs of Balcaskie; attainted by JAMES II's I Parl May 1689; leased land in Co Derry from the Golsmiths Corp of London; bought up more land in Cos Tyrone and Donegal; Warden Lifford, Co Donegal, 1713; *m* Anne — and *d* 1716, leaving:

JAMES STRONGE, of Croghan, Co Donegal, and Clonleigh; Sheriff Derry 1682–83; attainted by JAMES II's I Parl May 1689; *m* 1675 Margaret, dau of John Douglas, of Waterside, and had, with a dau (Isabella, *m* Thomas Babington):

Rev JOHN STRONGE; Rector Tynan, Co Armagh; *m* 19 Oct 1711 Ellinor, dau and coheir of Capt James Manson, of Tynan, and had four sons and a dau; the 2nd s:

MATTHEW STRONGE; Mayor Liverpool 1768–69; *m* Elizabeth, dau of Samuel Powell, of Stanedge Park, Radnorshire, by Elizabeth, dau of 3rd and last Barom Folliott of Ballyshannon, and had, with a dau (Elinor, *m* John Blackburne, of Wavertree Hall, Lancs, and *d* July 1842):

Rev Sir James Stronge, 1st Bt (UK), so *cr* 22 July 1803; *b* 1750; *m* 27 May 1785 Helen (*m* 2nd William Holmes, Treas Ordnance), dau and coheir of John Tew, Dublin Alderman (*see* FARNHAM, B), and *d* 1 Dec 1804, having had, with another s (*d* young) and a dau:

Sir James Matthew Stronge, 2nd Bt, DL (Armagh and Tyrone); *b* 6 April 1786; Gentleman Privy Chamber, DCL; *m* 5 Sept 1810 Isabella (*d* 12 April 1862), est dau of Nicolson Calvert, MP (*see* LIMERICK, E), and *d* 2 Dec 1864, leaving:

1 **Sir James Matthew Stronge, 3rd Bt**, JP, DL; *b* 25 Nov 1811; Lt 5th Dragoon Gds, High Sheriff Cos Armagh 1844 and Tyrone 1845, MP Co Armagh 1864; *m* 17 June 1836 Selina Elizabeth (*d* 23 July 1903), est dau of Andrew Nugent, JP, DL, of Portaferry, Co Down, and *dsp* 11 March 1885

2 **Sir John Calvert Stronge, 4th Bt**, JP (Armagh and Tyrone), DL; *b* 21 Feb 1813; barrister; *m* 14 Sept 1848 Margaret Zoë (*d* 14 Sept 1903), sis of 6th Viscount Charlemont (*qv*), and *d* 20 Dec 1899, having had, with two other daus (*d* unm):

(1) **Sir James Henry Stronge, 5th Bt**, PC (NI 1924); *b* 8 Dec 1849; *educ* Eton and BNC Oxford (MA), barrister Lincoln's Inn 1874, Maj 4th Bn Roy Inniskilling Fus, Imp Grand Master Loyal Orange Instn, High Sheriff Cos Tyrone 1880 and Armagh 1885; *m* 7 Oct 1885 Ethel Margaret (*d* 12 March 1926), dau of Col Ynyr Henry Burges, JP, of Parkanaur, Co Tyrone, and *dspms* 20 May 1928, having had:

1a James Matthew; *b* 10 Jan 1891; Lt Roy Irish Fus; *m* 10 July 1917 Winifred Elizabeth Charlotte (*d* 18 Oct 1968, having *m* 2nd 5 Jan 1920 Lt-Col Clarence Ivor Alistair Dubs, TD, Ayrshire Yeo (*d* 18 Aug 1943), s of Charles Ralph Dubs, of Glasgow), dau of Lt-Col Henry George Samuel Alexander, JP, 4th Bn Roy Inskilling Fus, of Carrickmore Ho, Co Tyrone, and was *ka* Aug 1917

1a Zoë Edith; *b* 22 Nov 1886; ARRC; *d* unm 14 June 1949

2a Daphne Helen; *b* 6 April 1889; *m* 14 April 1920 Gen Sir Walter William Pitt-Taylor, KCB, CMG, DSO, Rifle Bde, s of Charles Pitt-Taylor, and *dsp* 22 Dec 1945. He *d* 22 Nov 1950

3a Rose Ethel; *b* 21 Jan 1894; *m* 18 Aug 1920 Edmond St John Richardson (*d* 13 June 1953), est s of Capt Arthur Percy Richardson, of S Kensington, and has:

1b *Robert Edmond; *b* 8 March 1930; *educ* Bootham Sch York; *m* 15 July 1961 *Isabella Mary Catherine, dau of Col John Oliver Hopkinson, DSO, MC, Seaforth Highrs, of The Hill, Forres, Morayshire, and has:

1c *John; *b* 13 Feb 1965

1c *Fiona Rosalind; *b* 12 July 1963

2c *Ann Mary; *b* 18 April 1968

1b *Brenda [Mrs Ian Fletcher, Raheenduff, Foulksmills, Co Wexford, Ireland]; *b* 28 Dec 1926; *m* 26 Sept 1953 *Ian Cecil Forbes Fletcher, s of James Willoughby Fletcher, of Raheenduff, and has:

  1c *John Robert; *b* 2 Dec 1958

  2c *Richard Edmond; *b* 10 Sept 1961

  1c *Susan Joy; *b* 19 May 1957

  2c *Margaret Claire; *b* 2 Sept 1965

4a Jessy, MBE; *b* 21 Sept 1896; *d* 12 Oct 1984

5a Joy Winifred; *b* 26 April 1901; *m* 27 Nov 1929 Maj James C Fillery, JP, RA (*d* 21 Sept 1955), and *d* Jan 1972, leaving:

  1b Margaret Zoë; *b* 12 June 1932; *m* 3 Aug 1957 Ernest Barry Creese, s of E Creese, of Shooter's Hill, London, and *d* 9 May 1988, leaving:

    1c *Charles Edward; *b* 22 April 1962

    1c *Susan Joy; *b* 20 Oct 1959

  2b *Rose-Ann Marie; *b* 28 April 1935

(2) Francis William (Sir), KCMG; *b* 22 Nov 1856; Envoy Extrdy and Min Plen Chile 1913–19; *m* 10 Nov 1909 Maria Elizabeth Florence (*d* 13 Sept 1924), dau of Gen Hon Sir David Macdowall Fraser, GCB (*see* SALTOUN, L), and *d* 20 Aug 1924

(1) Alice Isabella; *d* unm 1 Dec 1941

3 Charles Walter, CB; *b* 29 June 1816; with Treasury; *m* 12 Sept 1860 Harriet (*d* 22 Nov 1893), dau of William Eades, and *d* 30 Jan 1898, leaving, with other issue:

(1) Walter Cecil; *b* 15 May 1860; *m* 10 Oct 1888 Violet Ada (*d* 11 Sept 1958), dau of Maj-Gen Sir Benjamin Travell Phillips, and *d* 11 Nov 1930, leaving:

  1a Humphrey Cecil Travell, CBE (1945), DSO (1919), MC; *b* 24 Feb 1891; Brig The Buffs, FRGS; *m* 26 Sept 1923 Elsie Margaret, est dau of Rev Canon Walter Fletcher Burnside, and *d* 27 March 1977, leaving:

    1b (Jane) Bridget; *b* 12 Oct 1927; *m* 4 Oct 1952 Henry Russell Stilwell, yst s of William M F Stilwell, of Lisbon, and had:

      1c *James Henry Cecil; *b* 28 Jan 1955

      2c *Matthew William; *b* 19 Oct 1956

      3c *Timothy Russel; *b* 3 April 1958

      4c *Hugh Crispin; *b* 14 June 1959

      5c *Alexander Charles; *b* 19 Feb 1961

      1c *Celia Anne; *b* 14 July 1953

      2c *Elizabeth; *b* 25 May 1967

  2a Rupert Maxwell, JP S Rhodesia; *b* 12 Oct 1892; Assist Native Commr; *m* 23 Sept 1918 Leonora Gertrude (*d* 21 Sept 1957), dau of Robert Charles Coffin, of Grahamstown, S Africa, and *d* 19 June 1964, leaving:

    1b *Rupert Humphrey Cecil, MM; *b* 20 July 1919; Sgt Roy W African Frontier Force (Nigerian Regt) WW II, Lands Dept Rhodesian CS; *m* *Vera Biggs and has:

      1c *David Maxwell Arthur; *b* 4 June 1945

      2c *Christopher Francis; *b* 13 Feb 1949

      3c *Anthony Travell; *b* 27 March 1951

    2b *Michael Travell; *b* 11 Aug 1931; *m* 12 July 1952 *Annetta Ruth Ashmead, of Salisbury, Rhodesia, and has:

      1c *Cherryl Zoë; *b* 25 June 1953

    1b *Violet Cecily; *b* 12 Dec 1921; *m* 1941 Henry Gordon Bluett Cumings, Sub-Accountant Native Affrs Rhodesia, and has had:

      1c Anthony Roy Frank; *b* 12 Jan 1944; *d* 20 April 1963

      2c *Beverley Cecil Gordon; *b* 21 May 1947

      3c *Charles Robert Maxwell; *b* 5 Dec 1949

      4c *Donald Henry Robin; *b* 28 April 1952

4 Edmond Robert Francis, JP Derry; *b* 17 July 1882; BA Dublin; Capt Roy Tyrone Fus; *m* 10 Feb 1859 Charlotte Newman (*d* 1 Aug 1900), 2nd dau of John Piercy Henderson, of Foswell Bank, Perths, and *d* 28 Feb 1911, having had:

(1) **Sir Walter Lockhart Stronge, 6th Bt**, JP (Down), DL (Co Armagh); *b* 5 Sept 1860; Capt 4th Bn Roy Inniskilling Fus; *dsp* 5 June 1933

(2) **Sir Charles Edmond Sinclair Stronge, 7th Bt**, JP (Down and Co Londonderry), DL (Co Londonderry); *b* 5 Feb 1862; Lt 4th Bn Roy Inniskilling Fus, High Sheriff Co Londonderry 1910, Recruiting Offr WW I (despatches); *m* 15 Nov 1892 Marian Iliff (*d* 28 Jan 1948), dau of Samuel Bostock, of The Hermitage, Walton Heath, nr Epsom, and *d* 5 Dec 1939, having had:

  1a **Sir (Charles) Norman Lockhart Stronge, 8th Bt**, PC (NI 1946), MC, JP (Cos Londonderry 1923 and Armagh 1928); *b* 23 July 1894; *educ* Eton; Capt Roy Inniskilling Fus and Roy Irish Rifles (36th Ulster Div) WW I (despatches twice, Croix de Guerre Belgium), NI Horse (RAC) WW II 1939–40 (invalided), High Sheriff Co Londonderry 1934, MP (NI Parl) Mid-Armagh 1938–69, Assist Parly Sec Min Fin 1940, Ch Whip 1941–44, Speaker NI H of C 1945–69, HM's Lt Co Armagh 1939 and 1975 (previously DL), KStJ, Chev Order Leopold Belgium 1946; *m* 15 Sept 1921 Gladys Olive, OBE (1943), OStJ (1949), Silver Medal American Red Cross 1946, chm WVS NI, only dau of Maj Henry Thomas Hall, of Knockbrack, Co Galway, and was murdered 1981 with his est s by terrorists at his home, Tynan Abbey, Co Armagh, having had:

    1b **Sir James Matthew Stronge, 9th Bt**; *b* 21 June 1932; *educ* Eton and Ch Ch Oxford (BA 1956, MA 1960); Capt Gren Gds (RARO), MP (NI Parl) Mid-Armagh 1969, memb Ulster Assembly 1973; murdered with f 1981

    1b *Daphne Marian [Mrs Thomas Kingan, Glenganagh 39 Bangor Rd, Groomsport, Bangor, Co Down BT19 6JF]; *b* 27 June 1922; WRNS WW II; *m* 11 Dec 1954 *Thomas John Anthony Kingan, er s of William Sinclair Kingan, DL, of Glenganagh, Bangor, and has:

      1c *James Anthony John; *b* 4 Jan 1957

    2b *Evelyn Elizabeth [Mrs Charles Olivier, Rosemary Cottage, Amport, Hants]; *b* 12 Feb 1925; WRNS WW II; *m* 17 Sept 1960 Brig Charles Harold Arthur Olivier, CBE, RA (*d* 1992), Dep Comdt Bramshill Police Coll, er s of Capt Robert Harold Olivier, DCLI, of Wilton, Wilts

    3b Rosemary Diana; *b* 16 Feb 1928; *d* 2 July 1929

  1a Pauline Marian; *b* 5 June 1898; *d* 24 June 1922

(3) Harry William, JP (Cos Down and Louth); *b* 17 Aug 1869; BA Dublin; *m* 18 June 1902 Elinor Louisa (*m* 2nd 5 Dec 1911 Sir William Smith-Marriott, 8th

Bt; *qv*), dau of Ludlow Eustace Maude (*see* HAWARDEN, V), and *dsp* 21 Feb 1907

(4) Edward Owen Fortescue; *b* 22 March 1871; *m* 22 Aug 1903 Maude Elizabeth Mary, dau of Edward William Bailey, of Glenluce, Ballycastle, Co Antrim, and *d* 11 Nov 1949, leaving:

  1a Maxwell Du Pré James; *b* 12 July 1904; *educ* Eton; *m* 25 April 1945 Eileen Mary (Eila) (*d* 2 Sept 1976), yr dau of Maurice Marcus McCausland, PC, of Drenagh, Limavady, Co Londonderry, and had:

    1b Sir JAMES ANSELAN MAXWELL STRONGE, **10th and present Bt**

    1b *Helen Mary Eileen; *b* 23 July 1948; *m* 1971 *Philip Rodney Allen-Morgan and has:

      1c *William Frederick Stronge; *b* 1975

      1c *Allanah Mary; *b* 1974

      2c *Laura Myfanwy; *b* 1978

(1) Ethel Mary Emily; *m* 14 Sept 1887 Capt Arthur Percy Richardson, Roy Irish Rifles and 10th Suffolk Regt, and *d* 13 June 1938, leaving issue

(2) Evelyn Frances Charlotte; *m* 10 Dec 1890 Hon Edward Hewitt (*see* LIFFORD, V) and *d* 19 June 1956 aged 90

(3) Edith Mary Beatrice; *d* unm 16 Feb 1948

5 Maxwell Du Pré, of Raheenduff Ho, Foulks Mill, Co Wexford, JP; *b* 4 Dec 1824; Capt 52nd LI, Lt-Col cmdg Sligo Rifles, Col cmdg DCO Sligo Artillery; *m* 13 Dec 1852 Jane Colclough (*d* 27 Feb 1904), only dau and heiress of Joseph Fade Goff, of Raheenduff, Co Wexford, and *dsp* 31 Dec 1916

1 Frances Helen; *m* 1835 Thomas Vesey Nugent, 2nd s of Andrew Nugent, JP, DL, of Portaferry, Co Down, and *d* 8 July 1908, leaving issue. He *d* 3 Feb 1890

2 Pauline Caroline; *m* 3 Nov 1842 Capt William Bunbury McClintock-Bunbury, RN, and *d* 1 Jan 1876, leaving issue (*see* RATHDONNELL, B)

3 Catharine Brownlow; *m* April 1850 Lt-Col George Augustus Jocelyn McClintock, Sligo Rifles, of Fellows Hall, Co Armagh, and *d* 26 Nov 1914, leaving issue. He *d* 24 Dec 1873

STUART

Arms: Or a fess checky az. and arg., an inescutcheon arg. charged with the lion of Scotland debruised with a bendlet raguly or.
Crest: A roebuck statant arg., ducally gorged gu. **Motto:** *Avito viret honore* ('He flourishes by the honour of his ancestors').
Creation: Bt. (E) 27 June 1660.

SIR PHILLIP LUTTRELL STUART, **9TH BT**, of Hartley Mauduit, Co Southampton [Sir Phillip Stuart Bt, Apt 50, 10980 Westdowne Rd, RR2 Ladysmith, BC V0R 2E0, Canada]; *b* 7 Sept 1937; *s unc* 1959; late F/O RCAF, pres Agassiz Industries Ltd; *m* 17 Feb 1st 1962 (*divorce* 1968) Marlene Rose, dau of Otto Muth, of Winnipeg, and has:

1 *Cynthia Louise [Miss Cynthia Stuart, 42 Arthur St N, Guelph, ON N1E 4T8, Canada]; *b* 27 Jan 1963

Sir PHILLIP *m* 2nd 1969 *Beverley Claire Pieri and by her has:

1 +GEOFFREY PHILLIP; *b* 5 July 1973 [Geoffrey Stuart Esq, 1000 Waller St, Winnipeg, Manitoba R3T 1P2, Canada]

2 *Brenda Claire [Miss Brenda Stuart, 7-74 Carlton St, Winnipeg, Manitoba R3C 1N9, Canada]; *b* 1969

Lineage: ANDREW STUART, yr s of Alexander Stuart, 2nd s of Walter Stuart, Seneschal of Scotland, ggs of Walter, 1st High Steward of Scotland; *m* the dau of James Bethe and had an only s:

ALEXANDER STUART, to whom CHARLES VI of France granted an honourable augmentation to his arms; had:

JOHN STUART; first of the family to settle in England; *m* Mary Talmache and had an er s:,

Sir JOHN STUART; *m* the dau of Sir Thomas Keyriell, Kt and had:

THOMAS STUART; *m* the dau of John Humerston and had:

RICHARD STUART; *m* the dau and heiress of John Boreley and had:

NICHOLAS STUART, of Well, Norfolk; *m* Cecilia Baskerville, and had (with a 2nd s, Nicholas, gf of Elizabeth Cromwell, mother of OLIVER):

SIMEON STUART, of Lakenheath; *m* Johanna, dau and heiress of Edward Bestney, of Sone, and had a yst s:

NICHOLAS STUART; bought the Hartley Mauduit estate and had:

SIMEON STUART, of Hartley Mauduit; *m* Dorothy, widow of Sir Christopher Paget, of Doddershall, and dau of Sir Richard Ingoldsby, of Lithenborough, Bucks, and had:

Sir Nicholas Stuart, 1st Bt (E), so *cr* 27 June 1660, of Hartley Mauduit, Hants; *b* 1616; a Chamberlain Exchequer *c* 1660; *m* 29 April 1641 Mary, only dau of Sir Miles Sandys, of Missenden, and *d* 15 Feb 1709/10, having had, with two er sons (Nicholas, *b* 26 March 1642, *d* unm Nov 1664; Miles, *b* 10 Jan 1646, *m* Jane, dau of Nicholas Johnson, of London, and *dsp* 31 Dec 1670) and six daus (including Mary, *m* Sir James Worsley, of Pilewell):

CHARLES STUART; *b* 1657; *m* 12 Aug 1678 Clemence, est dau and coheir of Sir William Hovell, of Hillington, Nofolk, and *dvp* by 1709, leaving:

Sir Simeon Stuart, 2nd Bt; MP Hants, a Chamberlain Exchequer 1712–61; *m* Elizabeth, only dau of Sir Richard Dereham, 3rd Bt, and *d* 11 Aug 1761, having had, with other issue (all *d* unm bar Elizabeth, *m* Hewer Edgely Hewer, and Anne, *m* George Bourne):

Sir Simeon Stuart, 3rd Bt; MP Hants, a Chamberlain Exchequer 1761–79; *m* a dau of Lt-Col Hooke, Govr Minorca, and *d* 19 Nov 1799, leaving:

Sir Simeon Stuart, 4th Bt; *m* 20 May 1789 Frances Maria (*d* 4 Jan 1848), only surv child of 3rd Earl of Carhampton (*see* 1828 edn), and *d* 14 Jan 1816, having had, with two yr sons (William Frederick, *b* 30 May 1794, Capt 5th Dragoon Gds, *d* 6 Dec 1878; Barclay John, *b* 26 June 1796, *d* 1813) and a dau (Ann Luttrell, *d* 9 March 1813):

Sir Simeon Henry Stuart, 5th Bt; *b* 23 Oct 1790; Capt 10th Hus Peninsular War (medal with four clasps), Comptroller to GEORGE IV; *m* 1st 25 Oct 1815 Georgiana Frances (*d* 16 Jan 1840), dau of George Gun-Cuninghame, and had:

1 **Sir Simeon Henry Stuart, 6th Bt**; *b* 15 June 1823; Lt 71st HLI; *m* 1st 15 April 1846 Julia Maria (*dsps* 10 Jan 1848), dau of Hon James Cuthbert, 60th Regt, of Berthier Manor, Canada East; *m* 2nd 15 Oct 1850 Catherine Henrietta (*d* 14 Dec 1897), dau of Gen Henry Lechmere Worrall (*see* LECHMERE, Bt), and *d* 21 Aug 1891, having by her had:

(1) **Sir Simeon Henry Lechmere Stuart, 7th Bt**; *b* 15 May 1864; Lt 5th Dragoon Gds, Capt Suffolk Imp Yeo, Maj and DAAG Imp Yeo Boer War 1900–01 (despatches, medal with three clasps), Lt-Col 2nd Co London Yeo 1909–13, cmded 2nd Entrenching Bn BEF 1916–17 (despatches, Col 1918); *m* 31 March 1891 Florence Louise, MBE (*d* 28 June 1936), only dau of Henry Harmond Gudge, Sec Austrian Legation, and *dsp* 25 Nov 1939

(1) Mabel Frances Luttrell; *d* 12 Dec 1886 aged 35

(2) Catherine Eva; *m* 6 April 1875 Rev Thomas Lane Coulson Bridges, Rector Warkton, Northants, and *d* 1 June 1897. He *d* 11 Oct 1932

2 Robert Charles William; *b* 27 Oct 1826; Lt-Col 72nd and 2nd Regts; *m* 22 Sept 1859 Madeline Torriano Maurice (*m* 2nd 1889 John Wessely Shillington, Army Surgn, of Ottawa, and *d* 1 May 1920), dau of Thomas Cooper, and *d* 21 Jan 1883, leaving:

(1) **Sir Houlton John Stuart, 8th Bt**; *b* 21 Dec 1862; *d* unm 3 May 1959

(2) Fitzmaurice Edward; *b* 11 July 1864; *m* 1887 Jane, dau of Dr William Bell, and *dsp* 24 April 1897

(3) Denny Macdougall; *b* 6 Jan 1868; *m* 1909 Georgina Frances Mary (*d* 5 Feb 1941), dau of John B Vezina, of Quebec, and *dsp* Jan 1949

(4) Luttrell Hamilton; *b* 4 Nov 1869; *m* 1st 1895 Clara Ida (*dsp* March 1935), dau of John Kerr, of St Joseph, Mo., USA; *m* 2nd 1936 Irene Ethel (*m* 2nd 1959 Jack Victor Hoskins), dau of Philip Jackman, of Saperton, BC, and *d* 1 Nov 1953, leaving:

1a **Sir PHILIP LUTTRELL STUART, 9th and present Bt**

(1) Lillian Mary Madeline; *b* 1861; *m* A T Phillips, of Ottawa, and *d* 1891, leaving issue

(2) Ethel Madeline; *b* Feb 1866; *m* 1886 Hugh Grant and had issue

(3) Dora Georgina; *b* 1872; *d* unm 10 Dec 1891

(4) Amy Madeline; *b* 1874; *m* 1899 Francis H Bacon and had issue

(5) Harriot Adelaide; *b* 1878; *m* 1906 Archibald Victor Mason and had issue

(6) Gwendoline Evelyn Macpherson *b* 1882; *m* 1907 William Frederick Carter and had issue

3 Arthur John; *b* 10 Nov 1828; Maj RM; *m* 7 April 1858 Frances Emily (*d* Jan 1873), 2nd dau of John C Kennedy, of Ballyrainey Ho, Co Down, and *d* 14 Sept 1868, having had:

(1) Arthur Kennedy; *b* 16 March 1859; *m* 1892 Luise Franziska, dau of Carl Joseph Pfeifer, of Freiberg-in-Baden, and had:

1a Arthur Ernest; *b* 1896

2a Charles Edwin; *b* 1897

(1) Frances Rether

1 Georgina Frances; *m* 14 July 1842 John Long, of Marwell Hall, and *d* 20 Oct 1890, leaving issue. He *d* 1894

2 Maria Henrietta; *m* 20 Oct 1845 Edward John Morant Gale, of Upham Ho, Hants, and had issue. He *d* 1894

3 Selina Jane Elizabeth; *m* 7 Feb 1857 Rev James Fletcher (*dsp* 8 May 1904)

Sir Simeon *m* 2nd 20 July 1857 Eliza, dau of John Fewings, and *d* 23 Oct 1868, leaving by her:

4 Frederick William; *b* 3 Sept 1858; *m* 1st 28 May 1888 Mildred Florence (*d* 31 July 1927), dau of William Grover Ashby; *m* 2nd 25 March 1931 Madeline-May (*d* 15 March 1939), est dau of P J Trouncer, of Preston, Sussex, and *d* 11 April 1949, having by his 1st w had:

(1) Lesley Mildred; *b* 24 Aug 1892; *m* 1st 5 May 1920 (*divorce* 1925) Lt-Cdr Basil Ashby Taylor, RN, 2nd s of A B Taylor, of Burgess Hill; *m* 2nd 17 May 1938 (*divorce* 1942) Maj Austin Gardner, MC, Essex Regt, est s of Maj Harry Gardner, Roy Scots

(2) Mary Joyce; *b* 14 July 1895; *m* 16 Aug 1933 Harold Asa Thomas, of Bineham, Chailey, Sussex, and *dsp* 12 Oct 1949. He *d* 11 April 1953

STUART OF FINDHORN

Arms: Quarterly: 1st, or a lion rampant within a double tressure flory counterflory gu., all within a bordure compony az. and arg. (for STUART); 2nd, or a fess chequy az. and arg. (for STEWART of Doune); 3rd, or three cushions within a double tressure flory counterflory gu. (for RANDOLPH); 4th, gu. a lion rampant within a bordure engrailed arg. (for GRAY); all within a bordure or for difference. **Crest:** In a nest vert a pelican feeding her young or, about her neck a collar engrailed gu. **Supporters:** Two capercailzie ppr., their wings closed. **Motto:** *Salus per Christum redemptorem* ('Salvation through Christ the Redeemer'). **Creation:** V. (UK) 20 Nov 1959.

THE 2ND VISCOUNT STUART OF FINDHORN, of Findhorn, Co Moray (David Randolph Moray Stuart) [The Rt Hon The Viscount Stuart of Findhorn, 38 Findhorn, Findhorn, Moray IV36 0YE]; *b* 20 June 1924; *s f* 1971; *educ* Eton and RAC Cirencester; FLAS, FRICS, ptnr Bernard Thorpe and ptnrs, Page of Hon to HM GEORGE VI 1937–39, Lt KRRC WW II 1942–47, Maj 6th7th Bn Roy Welch Fus (TA), DL Caernarvs 1963–68; *m* 1st 1945 Grizel Mary Wilfreda (*d* 24 April 1948), dau of David Theodore Fyfe and widow of Michael Gillilan, and has:

1 +(JAMES) DOMINIC [The Hon Dominic Stuart, 15 Stowe Rd, London W12]; *b* 25 March 1948; *educ* Eton; *m* 18 Aug 1979 *Yvonne Lucienne, dau of Edgar Després, of Ottawa

The 2nd VISCOUNT *m* 2nd 31 May 1951 (*divorce* 1979) Marian Emilia, dau of Gerald H Wilson, of Kintbury, Berks, and by her has:

2 +Andrew Moray; *b* 20 Oct 1957; *educ* Stowe

1 *Chloë Ann-Marie; *b* 15 April 1952

2 *Rosalie Jane; *b* 16 March 1954

3 *Vanessa Mary; *b* 25 Dec 1960

The 2nd VISCOUNT *m* 3rd 25 Sept 1979 *Margaret Anne, yr dau of Cdr Peter Du Cane, CBE, RN (*see* POLE, Bt, of Shute House)

Lineage: The 17th EARL OF MORAY (*qv*); had a 3rd s:

JAMES GRAY STUART, **1st Viscount Stuart of Findhorn**, of Findhorn, Co Moray (UK), so *cr* 20 Nov 1959, CH (1957), MVO (1921), MC and bar 1917, PC (1939); *b* 9 Feb 1897; *educ* Eton; Capt 3rd Bn Roy Scots and Bde Maj 15th Inf Bde (despatches) WW I, Equerry-in-Waiting to HRH THE DUKE OF YORK 1920–21, MP (C) Moray and Nairn 1923–59, Jr Ld Treasury 1935, memb MRC 1940, Jt Parly Sec Treasury 1941–45, Ch C Whip 1941–48, Sec State Scotland 1951–57, Chm U Party Scotland 1950–62, Hon LLD St Andrews 1957; *m* 4 Aug 1923 Lady Rachel Cavendish, OBE (1946) (*d* 2 Oct 1977 aged 75), 4th dau of 9th Duke of Devonshire, and *d* 20 Feb 1971, leaving:

1 DAVID RANDOLPH MORAY STUART, **2nd and present Viscount Stuart of Findhorn**

2 John Douglas; *b* 11 June 1925; *educ* RNC Dartmouth; Lt RN; *m* 1st 4 May 1957 (*divorce* 1958) Cecile Margaret, formerly w of George Maurice Tonge and dau of Gerald Harrison Barr; *m* 2nd 23 Sept 1969 *Caroline (*m* 3rd *Hon James Ogilvy; *see* AIRLIE, E), formerly w of Viscount Melgund (*see* MINTO, E) and er dau of 9th Earl of Jersey (*qv*), and *dsp* 1990

1 *Jean Davina [The Hon Mrs Ritchie, Tannachie, Findhorn, Moray IV36 0JY]; *b* 7 Jan 1932; *m* 1st 27 July 1951 Lt John Reedham Erskine Berney (*ka*) and has issue (*see* BERNEY, Bt); *m* 2nd 20 Jan 1954 Lt Percy William Jesson, RA, only s of Lt-Col Harold Jesson; *m* 3rd 1985 *Michael Denison Ritchie and by her 2nd husb has had:

(1) *Rayner Charles Percy [Rayner Jesson Esq, 13 Basing St, London W11]; *b* 15 Nov 1954; *m* 1987 *Gordana, dau of Veljko Simakovic, of Sarajevo, Yugoslavia

(2) *James Gray [James Jesson Esq, 6 Bishop's Ave, London E13]; *b* 16 Dec 1959

(1) Belinda Clare; *b* 9 March 1957; *d* 28 March 1959

(2) *Arabella Clare Lucy [Mrs Barry Ball, 8 Evening Court, Newmarket Rd, Cambridge CB5 8EA]; *b* 9 June 1962; *m* 1983 *Barry Ball

STUART-FORBES

Arms: Quarterly, 1st and 4th, az. on a chevron arg., between three bear's heads couped of the last muzzled gules, a man's heart ppr. (for FORBES of Monymusk); 2nd counterquartered, 1st and 4th, az. three bear's heads couped arg., muzzled gules (for FORBES of Pitsligo); 2nd and 3rd, az. three frases arg ., (for FRASER); 3rd, or, a bend gu. surmounted by a fess chequy az. and arg., in chief a crescent of the third (for STUART of Fettercairn). **Crest:** Issuing out of a baron's coronet a hand holding a scimitar proper. **Supporters:** Two bears proper. **Mottoes:** 1 (over crest) *Nec temere nec timide* ('Neither rashly, nor timidly') (for FORBES), 2 (under shield) *Lux mentis honestæ gloria* ('Glory is the light of a noble mind'). **Creation:** Bt. (NS) 30 March 1626.

SIR WILLIAM DANIEL STUART-FORBES, 13TH BT, of Pitsligo and Monymusk, Aberdeenshire [Sir William Stuart-Forbes Bt, 9 Churchill St, Blenheim, Marlborough, New Zealand]; *b* 21 Aug 1935; *s* unc 1985; *m* 1956 *Jannette MacDonald, dau of Hori Toki George MacDonald, of Marlborough, NZ, and has:

1 +KENNETH CHARLES [Kenneth Stuart-Forbes Esq, Nukuhau, Taupo, New Zealand]; *b* 26 Dec 1956; *m* 1981 *Susan, dau of Len Murray, of Taupo, NZ, and has:

(1) +Samuel Alexander Murray; *b* 21 Jan 1989

(1) *Amy Dawn; *b* 1982

(2) *Haylee Rachel; *b* 1985

2 +Daniel Dawson; *b* 1962

3 +Reginald MacDonald [Reginald Stuart-Forbes Esq, 26 Epping Pl, Taupo, New Zealand]; *b* 1964; *m* 1986 *Heather, dau of Philip Jones, of Riverton, Invercargill, NZ

1 *Catherine Florence [Mrs William Paraha, 6a Arihia St, Taupo, New Zealand]; *b* 1958; *m* 1975 *William Paraha and has:

(1) *William Bayden; *b* 1977

(1) *Jayde Rebekah; *b* 1980

2 *Eileen Jane [Mrs Neil Brown, 57 North Rd, Kaitaia, New Zealand]; *b* 1960; *m* 1981 *Neil Bertram Brown and has:

(1) *Jessica Charlotte; *b* 1985

(1) *Charlene Rachelle; *b* 1987

Lineage: The 2nd LORD FORBES (*qv*); had a 2nd s:

DUNCAN FORBES of Corsindae; *m* Christian Mercer, dau of the Laird of Balliol, Provost Perth, and widow of Gilbert Skene of that Ilk, and had:

WILLIAM FORBES of Corsindae; *m* Margaret Lumsden and had, with another s (James, of Corsindae, who continued his line):

DUNCAN FORBES; obtained the Priory lands of Monymusk, Aberdeenshire, at the Reformation; *m* Agnes Gray and *d* 1587, having had, with other issue:

WILLIAM FORBES of Monymusk; *m* (contract 5 Jan 1567/8) Lady Margaret Douglas, dau of 9th Earl of Angus (*see* HAMILTON and BRANDON, D), and *d c* 1618, having had, with other issue:

Sir William Forbes, 1st Bt (NS), so *cr* 30 March 1626, of Monymusk; *m* Elizabeth, dau of Wishart of Pittarow, and *d c* 22 July 1661, having had, with other issue:

Sir William Forbes, 2nd Bt; *m* 1632 Jean, dau of Sir Thomas Burnett, 1st Bt, of Leys (*see* 1970 edn), and had, with a dau (*m* George Rickart of Auchnacant):

Sir John Forbes, 3rd Bt; *m* 1st (contract 22 April 1659) Margaret, dau of 1st Viscount of Arbuthnott (*qv*); *m* 2nd 21 Feb 1673 Barbara, dau of John Dalmahoy, and *d c* 1713, having by her had, with other issue a s (John, ancestor of the OGILVIE-FORBESes of Boyndlie), and by his 1st w, with a dau (Jean, *m* — Maitland of Pittrichie):

Sir William Forbes, 4th Bt; sold Monymusk 1713 to Sir Francis Grant, 1st Bt, of Monymusk (*qv*); *m* Lady Jean Keith, dau of 1st Earl of Kintore (*qv*), and had, with other issue, including a dau (Mary, *m* William Urquhart of Meldrum):

JOHN FORBES; *m* (contract 4 Feb 1706) Mary (*m* 2nd 16th Lord Forbes, *qv*), dau of 3rd Lord Forbes of Pitsligo (*see* FORBES, Bt, of Newe), and *dvp* 13 Jan 1715, having had, with other issue:

Sir William Forbes, 5th Bt; *m* 1730 Christian (*d* 1789), dau of John Forbes of Boyndlie, and *d* 12 May 1743, leaving, with other issue:

Sir William Forbes, 6th Bt; *b* 5 April 1739; *educ* Edinburgh High Sch; banker; *m* 20 Sept 1770 Elizabeth (*d* 1802), dau of Sir James Hay, 4th Bt, of Haystoun (*see* 1949 edn HAY, Bt, of Smithfield), and *d* 12 Nov 1806, having had, with other issue:

1 WILLIAM (Sir), **7th Bt**

2 John Hay, of Medwyn, Peeblesshire; *b* Sept 1776; Ld of Session as Lord Medwyn; *m* 5 Aug 1802 Louisa (*d* 11 July 1845), dau of Sir Alexander Gordon-Cumming, 1st Bt (*qv*), and *d* 1854, leaving, with other issue:

(1) William, of Medwyn, DL Peeblesshire; *b* 25 May 1803; *m* 21 Dec 1841 Mary Anne (*d* 1896), dau of John Archer Houblon, MP, of Hallingbury, and *d* 1891, having had, with other issue:

1a John Houblon, JP; *b* 22 Aug 1852; *educ* Exeter Coll Oxford (BA); barrister; *m* 29 March 1883 Hon Alexandra Katherine May Fraser (*d* Nov 1939), dau of 18th Lord Saltoun (*qv*) of Abernethy, and *d* 5 June 1935, leaving:

1b Dorothy Charlotte Mary Eleanor; *b* 7 Jan 1884; *d* unm 21 Feb 1936

1a Mary Anne; *m* 14 Oct 1863 11th Earl of Mar and (13th Earl of) Kellie (*qv*), and *d* 22 May 1927, having had issue

2a Louisa; *m* 17 Oct 1877 Sir James Fergusson, 2nd Bt (*see* COLYER-FERGUSSON, Bt), and *d* 12 Sept 1878, leaving issue

3a Harriet; *m* 18 April 1871 Hon Augustus William Erskine (*d* 17 July 1914) and *d* 24 Feb 1884, leaving issue (*see* MAR and KELLIE, E)

(2) Alexander Penrose; *b* 6 June 1817; Bp Brechin 1847–75; *d* unm 8 Oct 1875

(3) George Hay (Rev); *b* 4 Aug 1821; *m* 14 April 1853 Eleanor Maria Irby (*d* 14 Aug 1878), dau of James Wemyss of Carlston, and *dsp* 7 Nov 1875

(1) Louisa Penuel; *m* 3 April 1832 3rd Baron Abercromby of Aboukir and Tullibody (*see* 1924 edn) and *d* 21 April 1882, leaving issue

3 George, of West Coates, Edinburgh; *b* 5 Sept 1790; *m* 8 Feb 1819 Mary (*d* 3 March 1877), dau of Sir John Hay, 5th Bt, of Smithfield (*see* 1949 edn), and *d* 26 Sept 1857, leaving, with other issue:

(1) Charles William, of Sandicotes, Dorset; *b* 1 Oct 1820; *m* 28 Aug 1860 Jane Agnes, dau of Walter Long, MP (*see* LONG, V), and *dsp* 1887

(2) George Edward; *b* 8 Aug 1828; *m* 11 June 1868 Louisa Lillias (*d* 18 Aug 1916), 2nd dau of Archibald Trotter, JP, of Dreghorn, and *d* 2 July 1881, leaving:

1a Edward Archibald (Rev); *b* 2 June 1869; *educ* Trin Coll Cambridge (MA); rector St Congan's, Turriff, Aberdeenshire, Canon St Mary's Cathedral Glasgow, CF 1915–16; *m* 18 Jan 1922 Enid Blackburn (MA) (*d* 1971), dau of Rev Canon Garden Llanoe Duff, Rector Turriff (*see* DUNBAR, Bt, of Hempriggs), and *d* 11 March 1929, leaving:

1b +Andrew Garden Duff [Andrew Forbes Esq, Overskibo House, Clashmore, Dornoch, Sutherland IV25 3RQ]; *b* 21 June 1925; *educ* Trin Coll Glenalmond, Trin Coll Cambridge (MA 1954) and Wellington Coll NZ; RNZAF 1943–45, RNZNVR 1945–47; *m* 1st 4 April 1953 (*divorce* 1980) Alison, dau of E St Clair Wilson, of Wellington, NZ; *m* 2nd 1989 Natalie Marion (*d* 1991), dau of Lt-Col John Duguid Milne, OBE, of Turriff, and by his 1st w has:

1c +Alexander Duff [Alexander Forbes Esq, Druminnor Castle, Rhynie, Aberdeenshire]; *b* 31 May 1955; *educ* Eton and Trin Coll Cambridge (MA)

1c *Barbara Elizabeth [Lady Grant, House of Monymusk, Monymusk, Aberdeenshire]; *b* 1 Feb 1954; *m* 31 Dec 1982 *Sir Archibald Grant, 13th Bt, of Monymusk (*qv*)

2c *Christian Margaret; *b* 8 Sept 1957; *m* 1985 *Edward Maurice O'Morchoe, of Ashford, Co Wicklow, and has:

1d *Frances Eileen; *b* 1989

2d *Patricia Christian; *b* 1991

3c *Louisa Mary; *b* 8 Nov 1961; *m* 1985 *Richard William Corbet Turnor, yr s of Maj Anthony Richard Turnor, CBE, of Malmesbury, Wilts (*see* LONDESBOROUGH, B), and has:

1d *William Michael Francis; *b* 1988

1d *Elizabeth; *b* 1990

2d *Rosalind Mary; *b* 1993

2b Edward Spencer Dundas; *b* 14 June 1928; Sub-Lt RN; *d* in an accident 9 Dec 1951

1b Elizabeth Helen; *b* 5 July 1923; WRNS 1942–46, BSc (Engr) London 1950; *m* 24 March 1951 Cdr Ralph Crichton Rupert Brooke, VRD, CEng, FIEE, RNR (*d* 1985), s of Rupert Woolby Brooke, FCS, FPS, of Sudbury, Suffolk, and *d* 1997, leaving:

1c *John Ralph; *b* 14 Sept 1953; *educ* Mill Hill

2c *Peter William; *b* 8 June 1957; *m* 1979 *Jennifer Margaret, yst dau of Walter Sidney Hobin, and has:

1d *Georgina Ellen Florence; *b* 1990

1c *Jane Elizabeth; *b* 16 June 1955; *m* 1st 1979 (*divorce* 1983) Graeme Tulley; *m* 2nd 1990 *Alistair Anderson Donald and by him has:

1d *Benjamin Alexander Samuel; *b* 1990

1d *Rebekah Jane Deborah; *b* 1992

2a Spencer Dundas; *b* 29 May 1874; Cdr RN; *m* 21 Feb 1913 Ethel, yst dau of Lt-Col James Selby Walker, Roy Highrs, Black Watch, and *das* aboard HMS *Monmouth* 1 Nov 1914, leaving:

1b Spencer Malcolm Edward; *b* posthumously 17 Nov 1914; *m* 1st 23 Dec 1940 (*divorce* 1948) Marie Terese, dau of Boleshaw Sulikowski, of Warsaw, Poland; *m* 2nd 27 April 1954 (*divorce* 1980) Elizabeth Lechmere, er dau of Sandys Stuart Macaskie by Mrs Raymond Windham de la Poer Beresford-Peirse (*see* BERESFORD-PEIRSE, Bt), and *d* 1995, leaving by her:

1c +James Fergus Spencer; *b* 8 Jan 1956; *educ* Eton

1c *Camilla Elizabeth Stuart; *b* 8 March 1958; *m* 1986 *Ian E Stewart, of Warninglid, Sussex

1a Marion Theodora; *d* unm 4 May 1946

2a Mabel Christian, JP (Edinburgh 1933); *m* 10 March 1922 Sir Thomas Barnby Whitson, DL, LLD (Edin), CA, FRSE, Ld Provost Edinburgh 1929–32 (*d* 1 Oct 1948), er s of Thomas Whitson, CA, of Edinburgh, and *d* 1971

(3) Louis; *b* 13 Jan 1830; Madras CS; *m* 30 April 1853 Emma Frances (*d* 16 Feb 1900), dau of Lt-Col — Colbeck, and *d* 2 Oct 1909, leaving:

1a Florence Mary Emma; *d* unm 13 Nov 1926

(4) James Arthur, JP Berwicks; *b* 25 Feb 1831; CA Northumberland, Capt RN Burmese War 1852, Baltic Campaign 1854–56; *m* 10 July 1867 Fearne Jemima (*d* 25 Jan 1904), dau of James Kinnear and widow of W E Aytoun, DCL, and *d* 24 June 1905, leaving:

1a Arthur George, MC; *b* Dec 1871; Capt 1st/4th Hants Regt (TF) WW I (despatches); *m* 31 July 1895 Kate (*d* Sept 1942), dau of Adam Wilkinson, JP, MD, and *d* 2 Dec 1922, having had:

1b James Arthur Charles; *b* 5 July 1897; Midshipman RN; *ka* Battle of Jutland 31 May 1916

2a Charles Hay, CBE (1919); *b* Sept 1873; Capt RN; *m* 19 Oct 1901 Emily Fawcus (*d* 7 Dec 1964), dau of James Carrall, Commr Customs China, and *d* 7 Nov 1919, leaving:

1b Reginald Arthur; *b* 30 June 1905; Lt-Cdr RN; *m* 1st 16 April 1930 (*divorce* 1944) Margaret Evelyn (*d* 1984), dau of Gideon Macpherson Rutherford (*see* WILLOUGHBY DE ERESBY, B), and had:

1c +James Hay; *b* 12 Feb 1931; *m* 7 July 1958 *Helen Reddy, of Montreal, and has:

1d +Peter Jonathan; *b* 30 Sept 1960

2d +Michael Todd; *b* 1 July 1963

1d *Susan Catherine; *b* 1 July 1959

1c *Margaret Christine [Mrs John Bankes, Tempus House, Hinton Ampner, Hants]; *b* 26 Aug 1933; *m* 19 Dec 1959 *John Jervis Murray Bankes, slr, est s of Capt Edward William Jervis Bankes, RN, of Winstanley Hall, Wigan, Lancs, and has:

1d *Henry Francis John; *b* 19 March 1966

1d *Caroline Margaret; *b* 10 March 1964; *m* 1993 *Jonathan Piers Young and has:

1e *Henrietta Margaret Evelyn; *b* 1994

1b (cont.) Reginald Forbes *m* 2nd 1944 *Joyce Charlotte Newton, of Quebec, and *d* 26 Dec 1975, leaving by her:

2c +William Henry; *b* 3 Dec 1944

2b John Hay, DSO; *b* 28 Aug 1906; Lt-Cdr RN WW II; *m* 7 June 1930 Edith Sheilah (*d* 7 Jan 1951, having *m* 2nd 4 Sept 1943 Lt-Col Hon Richard Martin Preston, DSO (*d* 20 May 1965), 2nd s of 14th Viscount Gormanston, *qv*), er dau of Reginald de Crecy Steel, of Weybridge, and *das* 2 Aug 1940, leaving:

1c Charles Hay; *b* 30 March 1931; tea planter, Inspr Kenya Police Reserve 1952–54, Dist Offr 1954–56; *m* 1 Aug 1959 *Juliet Rosalind, dau of Kenneth George Murray, and *d* 28 Jan 1998, leaving:

1d +John Hay; *b* 21 May 1960

2d +George Louis; *b* 7 May 1961

3d +Drostan Gerard; *b* 28 March 1962

1d *Sheilah Emily; *b* 18 June 1963

2c +Angus John Reginald [Angus Forbes, 2967 Routt Circle, Lakewood, CO 80215, USA]; *b* posthumously 19 April 1941; *m* 1st 1963 Victoria Seward, of California, and has:

1d +Richard Leland John; *b* 21 July 1965

1d *Caroline Lilah Jo; *b* 30 Dec 1963

2c (cont.) Angus Forbes *m* 2nd 19 Dec 1989 *Michelle de Witt and by her has:

2d +Ian Michael; *b* 25 Oct 1996

2d *Collette Barbara; *b* 25 Sept 1995

3d *Phoebe Fiona; *b* 5 Feb 1998

1c *Fiona Eileen [Mrs K Ruddle, Spring House, Bull Lane, Ketton, Rutland PE9 3TB]; *b* 23 Sept 1937; *m* 1st 9 Feb 1961 (*divorce* 1976) Anthony Haig Morse, yr twin s of Sydney Arthur Morse, of Bergh Apton Manor, Norfolk; *m* 2nd 1977 *K Anthony Ruddle and by her 1st husb has:

1d *Claire Emma [Mrs Martin Wilson, Chater Cottage, Aldgate, Rutland]; *b* 5 May 1962; *m* 1985 *Martin George Wilson and has:

1e *George Anthony; *b* 1986

1e *Harriet Claire; *b* 1988

2e *Mariella Victoria; *b* 1992

2d *Rachel Elizabeth; *b* 27 May 1965; *m* 1992 *Nicholas John Curran and has:

1e *Charlotte Amanda; *b* 12 April 1996

3b Cyril Louis later Dom James Forbes, OSB; *b* 9 Feb 1913; *educ* Oxford (MA); Benedictine monk Ampleforth 1931, Kt SMO Malta, Master St Benet's Hall Oxford 1964; *d* 18 Oct 1979

3a William Samuel; *b* Sept 1877; *m* 3 April 1898 Andrina Mabel Vesta Vallance and had, with other issue:

1b William Arthur Ian; *b* 2 Jan 1899; Lt Roy Scots (Res); *d* unm 1945

4a James Louis, OBE (1919); *b* 26 Jan 1880; Cdr RN, A/Cdre RAF; *m* 28 Jan 1919 Marjorie, 3rd dau of Sir Thomas Putnam and widow of Capt Philip Picot, and *d* 1965, leaving:

1b +James Alexander [Maj James Forbes, Mill Cottage, Fulmer, Bucks]; *b* 23 Nov 1919; Maj Gordon Highrs WW II; *m* 15 May 1946 *Susan Elizabeth, dau of Maj-Gen Alan Hugh Hornby, CB, CBE, MC, and has:

1c +Michael James; *b* 18 Feb 1949

1c *Caroline Susan; *b* 1953

5a Reginald Michael Norman, MC; *b* 29 Sept 1881; Col RA WW I (despatches, wounded), Hon Brig 1938, Order White Eagle Serbia; *d* unm 23 Jan 1969

1a Mary Constance, MBE (1918); *d* unm 11 March 1959

2a Emily Fearne Anne; *m* 4 Oct 1900 Capt John Elphinston Ryrie Oldfield, RA (*d* 16 May 1946), of Cantray House, Gollanfield, Inverness-shire, and *d* 14 April 1941, leaving issue

(1) Mary; *m* 19 Sept 1854 Rev Canon Thomas Dundas Harford Battersby, Vicar St John's, Keswick, and *d* 1885, leaving issue

1 Christian; *m* Sir Alexander Wood, KCMG, and *dsp* 1863

2 Rebecca; *m* Alexander Ranaldson Macdonell of Glengarry, Inverness-shire, and *d* 1840, leaving issue

3 Elizabeth; *m* 1803 Colin Mackenzie, of Portmore, Peeblesshire, and had issue

4 Jane; *m* James Skene of Rubislaw and had issue

Sir WILLIAM's est s,

Sir William Forbes, 7th Bt, of Cannan Park, Edinburgh; *b* 21 Dec 1773; *m* 19 Jan 1797 Williamina Wishart (*d* 5 Dec 1810), only child of Sir John Wishart BELSHES-WISHART later STUART, 4th Bt, of Fettercairn, and *d* 24 Oct 1828, having had, with other issue:

1 Sir JOHN STUART FORBES later HEPBURN-FORBES (added as heir to Alexander Hepburn Murray Belshes's territorial Barony of Invermay and the Balmanno estate, Perths), **8th Bt**; *b* 25 Sept 1804; *m* 14 June 1834 Lady Harriet Louisa Anne Kerr (*d* 26 April 1884), 3rd dau of 6th Marquess of Lothian (*qv*), and *d* 27 May 1866, leaving:

(1) Harriet Williamina; *m* 29 July 1859 20th Lord (Baron) Clinton (*qv*) and *d* 4 July 1869, leaving issue

2 Charles Hay, of Canaan Park; *b* 15 Oct 1806; *m* 5 July 1833 Jemima Rebecca (*d* 5 April 1905), 3rd dau of Alexander Ranaldson MacDonell of Glengarry, and *d* 5 Nov 1859, leaving, with other issue:

(1) WILLIAM STUART (Sir), **9th Bt**

(2) Alexander Charles (Rev); *b* 15 April 1837; *m* 2 April 1862 Williamina Joanna, dau of Roderick Cochrane, and *d* 1902, leaving, with other issue:

1a Charlotte Hay Stuart; *m* 1890 Thomas William Dewar, MD, FRCP (*d* 1931), of Kincairn, Dunblane, and *d* 22 Oct 1953, leaving issue

2a Ethel Macdonell; *m* 1892 Thomas Denton Stanger-Leathes and had issue

(1) Elizabeth Jane; *m* 7 Sept 1880 Rev George Digby (*d* 1883), Vicar Low, Harrogate, and *d* 1901

(2) Henrietta Jemima; *m* 1 Sept 1863 Rev Walter Hiley (*d* 14 Aug 1896), of Thorpe Arch, Yorks, and *d* 10 June 1883, leaving issue

(3) Adelaide Louisa; *m* 4 Aug 1868 Rev Francis Robert Traill (*d* 1883), Vicar Stanway, Glos, and *d* 29 July 1933, having had issue

3 James David; *b* 20 April 1809; Pncpl Utd Coll St Salvator and St Leonard, DCL, LLD; *m* 4 July 1843 Alicia (*d* 1885), dau of George Wauchope, and *d* 31 Dec 1868, leaving, with other issue:

(1) Edmund Batten; *b* 25 Dec 1847; *m* 2 July 1885 Charlotte Agnes (*d* 18 July 1958), dau of Maj-Gen Robert Adam Wauchope, and *d* 17 Feb 1924, having had, with other issue:

1a James Stuart, MC; *b* 13 Feb 1888; Capt RE WW I (despatches); *m* 29 July 1920 Merion Josephine, dau of Alexander Knight, of Dorset, and *d* 29 April 1935

1a Christian Alicia Hersey; *b* 9 Feb 1893; memb Chelsea BC; *m* 5 May 1917 Hon Gerald Hayne Guthrie Williamson (*d* 9 June 1966), 2nd s of 1st Baron Forres (*qv*), and *d* 26 Jan 1958, leaving issue

2a Katherine Jane Trefusis, DBE (1944); *b* 21 March 1899; Air Ch Cmdt WAAF, Dir WAAF 1939–43, CCG 1946–48; *m* 10 March 1966, as his 3rd w, Sir Robert Alexander Watson-Watt, CB, FRS, LLD, DSC (*d* 5 Dec 1973), s of Patrick Watson Watt, of Brechin, Angus, and *dsp* 18 June 1971

(2) George; *b* 5 April 1849; electrical engr, inventor, astronomer, Prof Nat Philosophy Anderson's Coll Glasgow, FRS, Hon LLD St Andrews; *d* 22 Oct 1936

Sir JOHN's n,

Sir William Stuart Forbes, 9th Bt; *b* 16 June 1835; *m* 1 July 1865 Marion (*d* 1889), 3rd dau of J Watts, of Bridgend, Nelson, NZ, and *d* 5 July 1906, having had, with other issue:

1 CHARLES HAY (Sir), **10th Bt**

2 William; *b* 1 April 1876; *m* 1906 Lillian Marian (*d* 1959), dau of James Moore, and *d* 14 Nov 1938, leaving:

(1) William John; *b* 1908; *d* 19–

(1) *Gwendolyn Mary [Miss Gwendolyn Forbes, 21 Elm Tree Ct, 123 Russell St, Palmerston North, New Zealand]; *b* 25 Sept 1911

(2) *Moya Gertrude *b* 28 Aug 1915; *m* 15 April 1942 Owen Alfred Wiley (*d* 1989), of Palmerston South, NZ, and has:

1a *Andrew Owen; *b* 1943

2a *Kevin Francis; *b* 1944

3a *Paul Royson; *b* 1948

4a *Gordon John; *b* 1956

3 Hugh; *b* 20 June 1882; *m* 1919 Kitty Ada (*d* 25 Aug 1951), dau of Archibald Brown, of Henley-on-Thames, and *d* 6 April 1938

1 Emma Louisa; *d* unm 4 April 1939

2 Marion Elizabeth; *m* 1917 Thomas Renwick (*d* 1927) and *d* 11 March 1940, leaving issue

3 Adelaide Amy; *m* 1903 William Miller and had issue

4 Beatrice Fullarton; *m* 8 July 1914 James Royston Callender, of Lower Hutt, NZ, and had:

(1) *William Stuart [William Callender Esq, 42 Renfrew Ave, Mount Albert, Auckland, New Zealand]; *b* 1915; *m* 1952 *Ella Jean Skuse and has:

1a *David Gordon; *b* 1953

2a *Robert Andrew; *b* 1956

1a *Linda Margaret; *b* 1955

(2) *Hugh Royston; *b* 1919; *m* 1949 *Mary Lorna Elliot, of Sydney, NSW, and has:

1a *Warwick Elliot; *b* 1951
1a *Vivien Elliot; *b* 1953
5 Georgina Gordon; *m* 1914 Edgar Crawford Stow, of Christchurch, NZ, and had issue
6 Mildred Gwendolen

Sir WILLIAM's est s,
Sir CHARLES HAY HEPBURN FORBES later STUART-FORBES, **10th Bt**; *b* 3 June 1871; *m* Jan 1896 Ellen (*m* 2nd R H Thompson), dau of Capt — Huntley, of Picton, Marlborough, NZ, and *d* Aug 1927, having had:

1 **Sir Hugh Stuart-Forbes, 11th Bt**; *b* 9 Nov 1896; *m* 6 June 1929 Ann Wallace Scott and *dsp* 26 June 1937
2 **Sir Charles Edward Stuart-Forbes, 12th Bt**; *b* 6 Aug 1903; *educ* Ocean Bay Coll NZ; *m* 10 Jan 1966 Ijah Leah MacCabe, of Wellington, NZ, and *d* 1985
3 William Kenneth; *b* 1906; *m* 16 March 1932 *Marjory Gilchrist (*m* 2nd 1951 Rayner Clifford Connolly) [Mrs Rayner Connolly, 60 Hutcheson St, Blenheim, Marlborough, New Zealand], and *d* 22 June 1946, leaving:

(1) Sir WILLIAM DANIEL STUART-FORBES, **13th and present Bt**
(1) *Avis Ilene [Mrs William Russell, 149 West St, S Hurstville, NSW 2221, Australia]; *b* 24 Dec 1932; *m* 1954 *William Charles Russell and has:
1a *Stuart William; *b* 1961; *m* 1983 *Laurette Dawn, dau of John Cooper, of Newcastle, NSW, and has:
1b *Gareth Stuart; *b* 1986
2b *Bryce Adrian; *b* 1992
1b *Lauren Renée; *b* 1984
1a *Janice Kathryn [Mrs Christopher Groube, 20 St James Parade, Elsternwick, Victoria, Australia]; *b* 1955; *m* 1981 *Christopher Wayne Groube and has:
1b *Nicolas James; *b* 1986
2b *Joshua Scott; *b* 1989
2a *Diane Avis [Mrs Allan Procter, 5 Charlotte Close, Poole, Dorset BH12 5HR]; *b* 1956; *m* 1987 *(Norman) Allan Procter and has:
1b *Daniel William; *b* 1989
2b *Michael Forbes; *b* 1992
3a *Susan Margaret [Mrs Alberto Gutierrez, 149 West St, S Hurstville, NSW 2221, Australia] ; *b* 1958; *m* 1981 *Alberto Juan Gutierrez and has:
1b *Andrew Ryan; *b* 1983
2b *Kameron Blair; *b* 1991
3b *Bryoni Kate; *b* 1989
4 James Albert; *b* 1907; *m* 1943 Ivy Kuhtz, of Masterton, NZ
5 Reginald Alexander; *b* 1909; *m* 2 Oct 1940 *Florence Anne Gilchrist (*m* 2nd 1986 Ross Sharpe), of Mahakipawa, NZ, and *d* 1974, having had:
(1) *Dorothy Anne; *b* 6 July 1947; *m* *Rex Smith and has:
1a *Todd; *b* 1974
(2) *Marilyn [Mrs Alister McAlpine, Wairau Valley, RD1, Marlborough, New Zealand]; *b* 1951; *m* 1972 *Alister James McAlpine and has:
1a *Sarah; *b* 1978
2a *; *b* 1981
3a *Katey; *b* 1985
1 *Lilian May; *m* 1st — Everett (*d* 1957) and has issue; *m* 2nd 19– E Waddington (*d* 1974)
2 Annie Elizabeth; *m* 20 April 1920 O'Hara Ray Hebberd, of Picton, NZ, and had issue
3 Ilene Myntle; *m* 1926 William Hounslow (*d* 1937) and had:
(1) *Kenneth Charles Patrick [Kenneth Hounslow Esq, Milton Terr, Picton, New Zealand]; *b* 1929
4 *Gertrude Ellen [Mrs Jack Jennings, 57 Ross St, Kilbernie, Wellington, New Zealand]; *m* 1939 Jack Jennings and has:
(1) *John David; *b* 1944; *m* 1968 *Beryl Margaret, yst dau of Eric Weightman, of Notts, and has:
1a *Richard David; *b* 1968
2a *Stuart Craig; *b* 1970
5 *Merlin [Mrs Ernest Williams, 134a Muller Rd, Blenheim, Marlborough, New Zealand]; *m* 1936 Ernest Edward Williams (*d* 1974), of Marlborough, NZ, and has:
(1) *Hugh Edward; *b* 1937; *m* 19– *Yvonne Carole, dau of Williams Nott, of Marlborough, NZ, and has:
1a *Daniel Isaac; *b* 1965
2a *Dale Lincoln; *b* 1980
1a *Carole Ann; *b* 1965
(1) *Lillian June [Mrs Anthony Ryan, Lochinvar, RD4, Blenheim, New Zealand]; *b* 1938; *m* 1959 *Anthony Laurence Roche Ryan and has:
1a *Christopher Michael; *b* 1963
2a *Edward Leo; *b* 1965
3a *Anthony John; *b* 1974
1a *Julia Felicia; *b* 1960
2a *Teresa Joan; *b* 1961
3a *Kathleen Patricia; *b* 1962
4a *Lucy Martha; *b* 1969
5a *Bernadette Maria; *b* 1971
6a *Michelle Joanne; *b* 1972
(2) *Barbara Joan (twin) [Mrs James Adams, 62 Howick Rd, Blenheim, Marlborough, New Zealand]; *b* 1938; *m* 1957 James Laurence Williams Adams (*d* 1982) and has:
1a *Michael James David; *b* 1962
1a *Karen Anne [Mrs Philip McNabb, 17 Fyfe St, Blenheim, New Zealand]; *b* 1957; *m* 1979 *Philip Walter McNabb
2a *Cheralee Merlin; *b* 1958
3a *Rose June; *b* 1960
6 *Gwendoline Rose; *m* 1952 Leonard Lowe (*d* 1965) and has:

(1) *Peter Morris; *b* Jan 1956
(1) *Barbara Theresa; *b* Nov 1956
(2) *Yvonne Maria; *b* 1959

STUART-MENTETH

Arms: Quarterly, 1st and 4th, or a bend chequy argent and sable; 2nd and 3rd, azure three buckles or, all within a bordure gules.
Crest: A lymphad, sails furled sable with flags gules, thereon a canton argent charged with the cross of St Andrew azure.
Mottoes: 1 (over the crest) *Dum vivo spero* ('Whilst I live I hope'), 2 (below arms) *Sub sole nihil* ('Nothing under the sun').
Creation: Bt. (UK) 11 August 1838.

SIR JAMES WALLACE STUART-MENTETH, 6TH BT, of Closeburn, Co Dumfries, and Mansfield, Co Ayr [Sir James Stuart-Menteth Bt, Nutwood, Auchencairn, Kirkcudbrightshire DG7 1QZ]; *b* 13 Nov 1922; *s* f 1952; *educ* Fettes, St Andrews and Trin Coll Oxford (MA); Lt Scots Gds WW II 1939–44 (wounded), with Paints Div ICI; *m* 23 April 1949 *(Dorothy) Patricia, yst dau of Frank Greaves Warburton, of Thorrington, Stirling, and has:

1 +CHARLES GREAVES [Charles Stuart-Menteth Esq, Monkcastle House, Kilwinning, Ayrshire KA13 6PN]; *b* 25 Nov 1950; *educ* Radley and Trin Coll Oxford; *m* 1976 *Nicola Mary Jane, er dau of V C R St Lawrence, of Salisbury, Wilts, and has:
(1) *Alice Clare; *b* 16 Feb 1977
(2) *Célia Jane; *b* 16 Sep 1978; *educ* Woldingham
(3) *Sarah Harriet; *b* 26 June 1982
(4) *Sophie Emily Flora; *b* 12 Nov 1995
2 +William Jeremy; *b* 31 Jan 1953; *m* 19– *Rosalind, est dau of J Lane, of Ruislip, Middx, and has:
(1) +James William; *b* 1987
(1) *Lucy Ann; *b* 1985

Lineage: Sir WILLIAM MENTETH of W Kerse, Stirlingshire (descended from Menteth of Ruskey); *m* Agnes, dau of *de jure* 14th Earl of Mar (*qv*), and had:

Sir WILLIAM MENTETH of W Kerse and Alva, Clackmannanshire; Hereditary Sheriff Clackmannanshire; *m* Helen Bruce, dau of the Laird of Airth, and had, with an er s (Sir William, of W Kerse, had issue):

JAMES MENTETH of Randifoord, Stirlingshire; *m* 1501 Janet, dau of Simpson, Laird of Aichintire, and widow of Archibald Crawford of Brecroft, and was *ka* Battle of Flodden 9 Sept 1513, having had, with other issue, including an er s (Patrick, of Randifoord, whose line died out with one Charles Menteth):

ANDREW MENTEH of Coalheughburn, Stirlingshire; *m* Margaret, dau of John Kinkead of Warriston, Midlothian, by Euphemia St Clair of Rosslyn (for whose earlier ancestry see CAITHNESS, E), and had:

ROBERT MENTETH of Coalheughburn; *m* Janet, dau of David Kinkead of that Ilk by Elizabeth, dau of Thomas Livingston of Mangerston, and had:

ALEXANDER MENTETH of Salmonet, Stirlingshire; *m* Rachel, dau of Gavin Sandilands of Lumford by Mary, dau of Robert Wauchope of Niddrie, and *d* 1638, leaving, with other issue:
1 Robert; Prof Philosophy Saumur, Min Dudingston, Canon Notre Dame, author: *Histoire des Troubles de la Grande Bretagne*
2 Alexander; merchant Edinburgh; *m* 1638 Agnes, dau of James Primrose, Clerk PC (see ROSEBERY, E)
3 WILLIAM
4 Andrew, of Newlands; moved abroad 1646
5 Patrick (Sir); ktd by CHARLES II; Lt-Col Dumbarton's Regt; *k* Siege of Dachstein 1675

ALEXANDER MENTETH's 3rd s,
WILLIAM MENTETH of Caribber, Linlithgow, which he acquired from James Gibb 1640; *m* 1st Christian, dau and coheir of Robert Boyd, of Kipps, Linlithgow; *m* 2nd Anne Elphinstone and by his 1st w had:
1 Robert, of Caribber, which he sold 1687; *m* 1680 Elizabeth, dau of Sir George Mowat, Bt, of Inglestoun (see 1829 edn), and had, with other issue (*d* unm):

(2) Charles; squandered most of his inheritance; *k* War of Spanish Succession

2 Robert; *k* Dettingen 1743

3 Alexander, whose only child *dsp*

4 James, of Burrowine, Perths; *m* (contract dated 10 Dec 1684) Gyles, dau of James Durie of Craigluscar, Fife, and *d* between 1712 and 1715, having had:

(1) William, of Burrowine; *m* 1st Anna Morrison and had a dau Anna, heiress to Robert Morrison; *m* 2nd Janet, dau of James Murray of East Grange, Culross, Fife, lawyer Edinburgh, by Janet, dau and coheir of James Stevenson, Provost Stirling, and *d c* 1747, having had:

1a James MENTETH later STUART-MENTETH (sign manual 12 March 1770) (Rev), of Closeburn, Dumfriesshire, Rector Barrowby, Lincs; *m* 15 April 1765 Catherine Maria, 4th dau of Rev Granville Wheler, of Otterden Place, Kent, by Lady Catherine Maria, dau of 7th Earl of Huntingdon (*qv*), and *d* 15 July 1802, leaving:

1b **Sir Charles Granville Stuart-Menteth, 1st Bt** (UK), so *cr* 11 Aug 1838, of Closeburn and Mansfield, Ayrshire; *b* 15 May 1769; *m* 13 Sept 1791 Ludivina (*d* 6 Feb 1852), dau of Thomas Loughnan by Philadelphia, dau of Robert Fergusson of Craigdarroch (*see* QUEENSBERRY, M), and *d* 3 Dec 1847, having had, with two other daus:

1c **Sir James Stuart-Menteth, 2nd Bt**; *b* 19 Aug 1792; *m* 17 Dec 1846 Jane (*d* 14 Oct 1905), dau of Sir Joseph Bailey, 1st Bt, MP, of Glanusk Park (*see* GLANUSK, B), and *dsp* 27 Feb 1870

2c Thomas Loughnan; *b* 31 Aug 1796; Capt 16th Lancers; *m* 7 Sept 1832 Isabella Maria (*d* 26 Jan 1868), 2nd dau of James Tobin, of Dublin, and *d* 22 Feb 1854, having had, with other issue:

1d **Sir James Stuart-Menteth, 3rd Bt**; *b* 29 July 1841; *m* 10 Dec 1872 Helen Gertrude (*d* 14 July 1928), dau of Darwin E Fay, of Fulton, NY, and *dspm* 28 Oct 1918, leaving:

1e Philadelphia Anna; *b* 14 Feb 1874; *m* 22 Feb 1906 Thomas Humfrey Vines (*d* 14 July 1922), Pncpl Sind Madrasah, Karachi, s of Rev T H Vines, Rector Fiskerton, Lincs, and *d* 31 Oct 1967

2e Helen Isabel; *b* 9 May 1875; *d* 17 April 1919

1d Philadelphia; *b* 17 May 1834; *m* 10 May 1852 Cornelius Collins Beard, MD (*d* 15 May 1906), of New Orleans, and *d* 29 March 1881, leaving two sons and two daus

3c Charles Granville, of Entry Hill Ho, Bath; *b* 1 Dec 1800; MA Cantab; barrister; *m* 19 Sept 1826 Cecilia Louisa (*d* 23 March 1874), dau of Walter Cecil, of Moreton Jeffries, Herefs, n of Sir William Drummond of Logie Almond and gdau of Lady Catherine Drummond, dau of 3rd Earl of Dunmore (*qv*), and *d* 8 May 1880, leaving:

1d Charles Granville, JP Hants; *b* 8 Sept 1828; *m* 16 June 1868 Cecil (*d* 1896), dau and coheir of Hutches Trower, of Unsted Wood, Surrey, and *dsp* 10 April 1907

4c William; *b* 31 July 1805; Col Bengal Army; *m* Sept 1826 Sarah (*m* 2nd Capt A B Chalmers), dau of Col Hamilton, and *d* India July 1857, having had, with other issue:

1d **JAMES FREDERICK** (Sir), **4th Bt**

1d Ludivina; *m* Brevet Lt-Col J F Nembhard, 50th Bengal NI, and *d* 1856

2d Sarah Selina Hamilton; *m* 1857 Col Gerard Noel Money, CB, and *d* 1895

3d Harriet Rose Amy; *m* 2 April 1872 Col George F O Boughey, CSI, RE (*d* 17 Jan 1918), and *d* 23 Feb 1925, leaving issue (*see* BOUGHEY, Bt)

4d Alice Annie Campbell; *m* 6 Oct 1874 Lt-Gen Henry Doveton Hutchinson, CSI, IA (*d* 21 Nov 1924), and *d* 11 Jan 1924, leaving issue

5d Emily Edith Ada; *m* 1st 11 Oct 1873 Capt Harry Harris Burland, 85th Regt (*d* 1876), and had issue; *m* 2nd 1885 James Edward Whiting (*d* 1917), Ch Engr Irrigation Br PWD, India, and had further issue

5c Francis Hastings (Rev); *b* 6 Oct 1807; Vicar Thorpe Arch, Yorks; *m* 11 March 1834 Cora (*d* 11 Feb 1876), dau of Rupert Chawner, MD, and *d* 8 March 1875, having had:

1d Rosa Mary; *m* 1856 Rev George William Coopland (*d* 1857) and had issue

2d Ludivina Sophia; *m* 5 May 1857 Rev W H Jackson, Rector Thorpe Arch, and had issue

3d Catherine Maria; *m* 15 July 1862 Rev Preb Thomas Hotchkin Vines, Rector Fiskerton, and *d* 19 June 1921, leaving issue

6c Alexander; *b* 10 March 1809; *m* 1841 Harriet, dau of Gen Patrick Alexander Agnew, HEICS, and *d* 11 Aug 1885, having had:

1d Charles Alexander; *d* 19 Nov 1876 aged 34

2d Patrick William; *b* 1845; *m* 1871; *d* 1925

3d Andrew Agnew; *b* 7 Feb 1853; barrister; *m* 1st 6 Oct 1885 Mary (*d* 5 May 1896), yst dau of Robert Vans Agnew, JP, DL, of Sheuchan and Barnbarroch, Wigtownshire, and had:

1e Charles Bruce; Lt NZ Forces; *b* 1892; *ka* Gallipoli 8 May 1915

1e Lois Elaine; *m* 1908 (*divorce*) Charles Sutherland Allan, s of Judge Alexander Sunderland Allan, Registrar Supreme Court, Wellington, NZ, and *d* 1965, leaving issue

2e Valerie Harriet; *b* 1888; *m* 14 Aug 1918 E B Solano (*d* 1918) and *d* 7 April 1920

3d (cont.) Andrew Stuart-Menteth *m* 2nd 1897 Margaret Antoinette, dau of Alexander Sutherland Allan, and *d* 25 Sept 1916, having by her had:

2e Thomas Alexander, MBE (1942); *b* 1901; *educ* Queen's Coll Oxford (MA, BSc (1938); Maj Roy Berks Regt (TA) WW II 1939–42; *m* 30 April 1931 Kathleen Frances, JP Salop (*d* 31 July 1966), dau of Frank John Constable Curtis, of Well Cottage, Goodrich, Herts, and Georgia Estate, Jamaica, and widow of Capt Arthur Taylor, of Cruckton Hall, Salop, and had:

1f Robert Andrew; *b* 2 Feb 1932; *d* Nov 1946

3e Jean Antoinette; *b* 1898

4e Elizabeth Mary; *b* 16 Nov 1903; *m* 1 June 1933 Daniel Maclelland Laird, FRICS, s of John Laird, of Lynton, Kilmacolm, Renfrewshire, and had:

1f *Michael Andrew; *b* 25 Jan 1936; *educ* Hertford Coll Oxford (MA)

7c Granville Wheler (Rev); *b* 27 March 1811; MA Oxon; Rector Morcott; *m* 29 Aug 1837 Jane (*d* 10 Feb 1899), 2nd dau of Rev Edward Thorold (*see* THOROLD, Bt), and *d* 1 Sept 1887, leaving:

1d Granville Thorold (Rev); *b* 6 June 1838; *educ* Univ Coll Oxford (BA); *m* 1st 13 July 1865 Susan Ogilvy (*d* 8 Jan 1881), only dau of Thomas Oliver, and had:

1e Charles Granville; *b* 26 Nov 1868; *educ* St John's Coll Oxford (MA); *d* unm 25 March 1943

2e Edward Thorold (Rev); *b* 23 Oct 1871; Curate St Paul's Leicester 1909–12; *d* unm 29 Nov 1948

1e Evelyn Ogilvy, *d* unm 9 Aug 1950

2e Mary Oliver

1d (cont.) The Rev Granville Stuart-Menteth *m* 2nd 1887 Annie (*d* 1942), 2nd dau of Henry Lakeman, of Cornwall, and *d* 27 July, 1934, having by her had:

3e Ludivina Granville

1c Philadelphia Stuart; *m* 24 April 1827 9th Earl of Mar and (11th Earl of) Kellie (*qv*) and *dsp* 15 Dec 1853

The 3rd Bt's cousin,

Sir James Frederick Stuart-Menteth, 4th Bt; *b* 26 Feb 1846; Lt-Col 2nd Dragoon Gds; *m* 1st 12 Aug 1868 Frances Octavia Moore (*d* 12 Aug 1887), dau of Gen Sir James Wallace Sleigh, KCB, and had:

1 James Wallace; *b* 2 March 1871; *d* unm Sept 1904

2 Charles Granville; *b* 4 Sept 1872; *d* 1 Oct 1882

3 **WILLIAM FREDERICK** (Sir), **5th Bt**

4 Walter Erskine; *b* 30 March 1877; *m* 13 July 1905 Violet Grace (*d* 15 Oct 1970), yst dau of Henry Lafone, and *d* 22 Sept 1956, leaving:

(1) Walter Granville; *b* 24 April 1906; *educ* Rugby and Hertford Coll Oxford; ACA, Maj Queen's Roy (W Surrey) Regt WW II (despatches); *m* 1st 5 June 1937 (*divorce* 1950) Marianne Marguerite (*d* 14 April 1975), est dau of Jules Cuenod, of Burier, La Tour de Peilz, Switzerland; *m* 2nd 2 Nov 1957 *Edith Pauline, est dau of James Harold Wadsworth, of Bletchingley, Surrey, and *d* 25 Nov 1970, leaving by his 1st w:

1a +Charles Henry; *b* 15 April 1938; *educ* Rugby

2a +James Sleigh; *b* 29 Sept 1940; *m* 24 Feb 1968 *Barbara Richardson

1a *Marie Octavia; *b* 10 July 1939

(2) +Henry Alexander, DSC [Cdr Henry Stuart-Menteth DSC RN, The Little House, 16 Inverleith Terrace, Edinburgh EH3 5NS]; *b* 26 Aug 1912; Cdr RN WW II (despatches); *m* 19 July 1952 *Penelope, only dau of Digby Giles, of Toorak, S Australia, and has:

1a +Andrew Alexander [Andrew Stuart-Menteth Esq, 18 Marion St, Brighton, Melbourne, Vic 3186, Australia]; *b* 7 Sept 1954; *m* 1988 *Pamela, dau of Capt J C Chapman, of Melbourne, and has:

1b +James Alexander; *b* 1989

1b *Lucy Linda; *b* 1990

2a +Walter Henry; *b* 2 March 1957

1a *Harriet Lucy; *b* 13 Dec 1959; *m* 1991 *James H Brennan, 2nd s of Lt-Col M W Brennan, of Painswick, Glos, and has:

1b *Thomas Michael; *b* 1992

1b *Kate Florence; *b* 1994

2b *Zoe Alice; *b* 1997

(1) Frances Beryl; *b* 10 June 1907; *m* 27 Sept 1930 2nd Baron Hankey (*qv*) and *d* 31 Dec 1957, leaving issue

(2) *Lucy Violet [Mrs Donald Brain, Crossways, Godstone, Surrey]; *b* 3 Sept 1911; *m* 28 Feb 1942 Maj Donald Brain, Canadian Army (*ka* Italy Dec 1943), 3rd s of G H Brain, of Montreal W, and has:

1a *Donald Rowan; *b* 24 June 1943; *educ* Fettes and Chelsea Coll of Art; film director/producer

5 Arthur Hastings; *b* 13 Feb 1882; Maj IA; *m* 20 Dec 1913 Mabel Frances (*d* 1956), dau of Surgn-Maj E Morton, IMS, and widow of R C Hickie, of Abbey Wood, Kent, and *dsp* 1956

1 Lillian Frances; *b* 24 Feb 1884; *m* 18 April 1928 Rev Gilbert Biscoe Ramsay (*see* RAMSAY, Bt), and *d* 7 Jan 1958

Sir James *m* 2nd 5 Sept 1888 Elizabeth Alyson (*d* 30 Nov 1915), dau of Capt Edward Algernon Blackett, RN, of Wylam, and by her had:

6 Montagu, MC; *b* 14 June 1893; Capt Lincs Regt and RAF, WW I (wounded) and WW II

2 Margaret Alice; *b* 18 June 1889; *m* 9 March 1910 Angus Edward Ogilvy and *d* 20 Sept 1956, leaving issue (*see* OGILVY, Bt)

3 Katherine Olive; *b* 23 Aug 1890; *m* 14 Feb 1933 Edward Algernon Blackett Prior (*d* 16 March 1962), est s of Charles Matthew Prior, of Adstock Manor, Bucks

4 Alyson Mona; *b* 15 April 1895; *m* 18 Aug 1921 Charles Kaisin, MD, and had issue

Sir JAMES *d* 7 Sept 1926; his est surv s,

Sir William Frederick Stuart-Menteth, 5th Bt; *b* 18 June 1874; memb Roy Co Archers; *m* 14 Nov 1921 Winifred Melville (*d* 9 June 1968), dau of Daniel Francis and widow of Capt Rupert George Raw, DSO, Northumberland Fus, and *d* 20 Feb 1952, leaving:

1 Sir JAMES WALLACE STUART-MENTETH, **6th and present Bt**

2 +Charles Granville [Charles Stuart-Menteth Esq, Woodchester House, Stroud, Glos GL5 5NY]; *b* 6 July 1928; *educ* Glenalmond and Worcester Coll, Oxford (BA); late 2nd Lt Scots Gds; *m* 12 June 1963 *Priscilla Helen, er dau of Thomas Newman (*see* NEWMAN, Bt, of Mamhead), and has:

(1) +James William Francis; *b* 11 Oct 1965

(2) +Alexander Granville; *b* 18 May 1971

(1) *Alice Caroline; *b* 16 July 1969

1 *Ludivina Frances; *b* 9 Jan 1927; *m* 23 Sept 1947 Capt William Sawbridge How, BA (*d* 1990), est s of Capt William Fitzherbert How, of Balnacarron House, St Andrews, Fife, and has:

  (1) *Stuart Sawbridge; *b* 1950
  (2) *Anthony Edward; *b* 1951
  (1) *Helen Frances; *b* 9 July 1955; *educ* Cranborne Chase

1 Lesley Evelyn Stuart; *b* 26 Aug 1922; *educ* Cheltenham Ladies' Coll and Girton Coll Cambridge (BA 1944, MA 1948); *d unm* 1 July 1998

Sir Eric *m* 2nd 9 July 1949 Lilian Rosamond (*d* 27 Aug 1958), widow of Percy Alan Farrer Manby, Supreme Ct Judge Straits Settlements and Fedn Malay States, and est dau of Ernest Holtham Leeder, of Swansea; *m* 3rd 9 July 1959 Ada Hope (*d* 1990), widow of Norman Alfred Yarrow (*see* YARROW, Bt) and dau of Forrest Bertram Leeder, MRCS, LRCP, of Victoria, BC, and *d* 25 Oct 1977

STUART TAYLOR

Arms: Per pale gu. and az. a fox's brush erect or between two bezants in fess. **Crest:** A demi-fox gu., brush or, supporting a banner also gu., charged with a seax gold. **Motto:** *Docere sed discere* ('Teaching but also learning'). **Creation:** Bt. (UK) 11 July 1917.

SIR NICHOLAS RICHARD STUART TAYLOR, 4TH BT, of Kennington, Co London [Sir Nicholas Stuart Taylor Bt, White Lodge, Hambrook, W Sussex PO18 8RG]; *b* 14 Jan 1952; *s f* 1978; *educ* Bradfield; slr 1977; *m* 1984 *Malvena Elizabeth, BSc, MB, BS, FRCA, only dau of Daniel David Charles Sullivan, of E Finchley, and has:

  1 *Virginia Caterina; *b* 1989
  2 *Olivia Malvena; *b* 1991

Lineage: SAMUEL TAYLOR, of Heybridge, Essex; *d* 1839 aged 62, leaving:

DAVID TAYLOR, of Kennington; *b* 23 March 1809; MRCS; *m* 23 June 1842 Maria (*d* 26 Jan 1902), dau of Edward Churton, of London, and had:

  1 Arthur, of Marton, NZ; *b* 7 Aug 1843; MB Lond, MRCS; *d* July 1881
  2 FREDERICK (Sir), **1st Bt**
  3 Herbert, of Kennington; *b* 4 Aug 1850; MB Lond, MRCS; *m* 28 Oct 1884 Gertrude, dau of C H Carter, MD, of Pewsey, Wilts, and *d* 2 Dec 1914, leaving four sons
  4 Leonard; *b* 30 Jan 1853; Assist Commr Indian CS; *bur* landslide at Naini Tal 20 Sept 1880
  5 Charles; *b* 22 July 1854; *d* March 1883
  6 David Churton; *b* 4 Sept 1856; *educ* London U (BA); slr; *m* Frances Edith, dau of James Turner Powell, of S Lambeth, and *d* 12 Jan 1938, leaving three sons and two daus
  1 Clara; *m* 6 June 1891 Edmund Savory, of The Grange, W Rudham, Norfolk, and *d* 4 Feb 1935. He *d* 16 Aug 1903

DAVID TAYLOR *d* 16 March 1894; his est surv s,

Sir Frederick Taylor, 1st Bt (UK), so cr 11 July 1917; *b* 6 April 1847; MD Lond 1870, FRCP 1872, MRCS 1868, Pres Roy Coll Physicians 1915–18, Consultant Physician Guy's Hosp, memb Senate London U; *m* 31 Oct 1884 Helen Mary (*d* 25 May 1917), dau of Frederic Manby, of E Rudham, Norfolk, and had:

  1 ERIC STUART (Sir), **2nd Bt**
  2 Harold Charles Norman; *b* 26 Oct 1892; *educ* Charterhouse and St John's Coll Cambridge (BA); Capt 20th London Regt; *ka* 21 May 1916
  1 Norah Helen; *b* 10 Sept 1885; memb Roy Miniature Soc, exhibitor RA, Paris Salon (Silver Medal 1932, Gold Medal 1952)

The 1st Bt *d* 2 Dec 1920; his er s,

Sir Eric Stuart Taylor, 2nd Bt, OBE (1919); *b* 28 June 1889; *educ* Clifton, King's Coll Cambridge (MA 1927, MD 1919, BCh) and Guy's Hosp (MRCP London); took STUART as surname rather than forename; Capt RAMC (TF) WW I (despatches twice), memb Cncl Cheltenham Ladies' Coll, Médaille des Epidémies; *m* 1st 23 Nov 1920 Evelyn Thérèse, JP Glos, MA Oxon (*d* 14 March 1946), dau of Lt-Col James Calvert, CBE, MD, FRCP, of Harley St, W1, and had:

  1 **Sir Richard Laurence Stuart Taylor, 3rd Bt**; *b* 27 Sept 1925; *educ* Winchester and King's Coll Cambridge (BA 1949, MA 1959); Roy Glos Hus WW II; *m* 9 Sept 1950 *Iris Mary [Iris Lady Stuart Taylor, White Lodge, Hambrook, W Sussex PO18 8RG], est dau of Rev Edwin John Gargery, Vicar Ivinghoe, Bucks, and *d* 10 Sept 1978, leaving:

    (1) Sir NICHOLAS RICHARD STUART TAYLOR, **4th and present Bt**
    1 *(Anne) Caroline [Miss Caroline Stuat Taylor, 1 Franche Court Rd, London SW17 0JX]; *b* 28 Oct 1955; *educ* St Michael's Sch Petworth and Grenoble U; md SKGB 1996–

STUCLEY

Arms: Quarterly, 1st and 4th, az. three pears or (for STUCLEY); 2nd and 3rd, per fess embattled arg. and sa. three buck's attires, each fixed to the scalp, counterchanged (for BUCK). **Crest:** Between a buck's attires as in the arms sa. a lion rampant or, the sinister paw holding a battle-axe, resting on the shoulder, ppr. (for BUCK). **Motto:** *Bellement et hardiment* ('Handsomely and hardily'). **Creation:** Bt. (UK) 26 April 1859.

SIR HUGH GEORGE COPLESTONE BAMPFYLDE STUCLEY, 6TH BT, of Affeton Castle, Co Devon [Sir Hugh Stucley Bt, Affeton Castle, Worlington, Devon EX17 4TU]; *b* 8 Jan 1945; *s f* 1983; *educ* Milton Abbey and RAC Cirencester; late Lt Blues and Royals, formerly RHG (Blues), chm Devon br CLA 1995–97; *m* 22 Jan 1969 *Angela Caroline, er dau of Maj Richard Charles Robertson Toller, MC, of Orchard Ho, Kingston Lisle, Berks, by his w Diana Valerie, MBE, yst dau of Maj Anthony Chaworth-Musters, of Rowans, Lee-on-Solent, Hants, and has:

  1 +GEORGE DENNIS BAMPFYLDE; *b* 26 Dec 1970; *m* 6 Sept 1997 *Amber Camilla, yr dau of Thomas Gage (*see* GAGE, V)
  2 +Peter Richard; *b* 29 June 1972
  1 *Charlotte Catherine; *b* 4 May 1975
  2 *Lucinda Sarah; *b* 13 Nov 1977

Lineage: JOHN STYEUCLE, of Great and Little Stukeley, Hunts; *m* Agnes — and was probably f of:

RICHARD ST(Y)UCLE(Y); living July 1388, Esq to RICHARD II; *m* as her 2nd husb Elizabeth (*d* 18 April 1414), widow of John Bonville (by whom she was mother of 1st Lord (Baron) Bonville, so *cr* (according to later doctrine) by writ of summons to Parl 10 March 1448/9) and dau and heiress of John Fitz Roger, of Chewton, Somerset, by which marriage he acquired the Manor of Mershton, nr Chichester, Sussex, and *d* by Nov 1441, leaving, with an er s (Roger):

HUGH STUCLEY; Sheriff Devon 1448–49; *m* Katherine (*m* 2nd by 9 Jan 1458/9 William Bour(g)chier, called to Parl 2 Jan 1448/9 as 9th Lord (Baron) FitzWarin in right of his 1st w Thomasine Hankeford, and *d* 26 March 1467), dau and heiress of John Affeton, of Affeton, Devon (whose ancestors had held that manor since EDWARD I's time), by Elizabeth, coheir of Sir Roger Manningford, of Dorset, and had:

NICHOLAS STUCLE(Y); *m* Thomasine (*d* 29 Nov 1477), widow of Robert Chuddelegh and est dau of John Kokeworthy, of Yarnescombe, Devon, and had:

Sir THOMAS STUCLEY, of Affeton; *m* Anne, dau and heiress of Sir Thomas Wood, of Clyffe, Devon, Ch Justice Common Pleas, and *d* 30 Jan 1542, leaving:

Sir HUGH STUCLEY, of Affeton; *m* Jane, 2nd dau of Sir Lewis Pollard, of Gt Grilleston, Devon, and *d* 6 Jan 1559, leaving:

Sir LEWIS STUCLEY, of Affeton; *m* Dorothy, dau of Sir Giles Hill, and *d* 1 Dec 1581, leaving:

JOHN STUCLEY, of Affeton; *m* Frances, 2nd dau of John St Leger, of Annersley, Devon, by Catherine, dau of 3rd Lord (Baron) Bergavenny (*see* ABERGAVENNY, M), and *d* 15 Jan 1610, leaving:

Sir LEWIS STUCLEY, of Affeton; *m* Frances, est dau of Thomas Monck or Le Moine, of Potheridge, Devon (*see* MONCK, V), and *d* 1620, leaving:

JOHN STUCLEY, of Affeton and W Worlington; *d* 31 Jan 1637, leaving, with an er s (Sir Thomas, of Affeton and W Worlington, *dspms* 20 Sept 1663):

Rev LEWIS STUCLEY, of Affeton and Bideford, Devon; Chaplain to OLIVER CROMWELL; *m* Susanna (*d* 1692), dau and coheir of Robert Dennis, Bideford merchant, and *d* July 1687, leaving:

  1 Dennis, of Affeton and Bideford; *d unm* 1741

2 Thomas; *d* by 10 Sept 1742, leaving:

(1) Dennis; *s* to the Affeton estates; *d unm* 1755

3 Lewis; barrister Middle Temple, Master Bench Soc Middle Temple; *dsp* 1748

1 Sarah; *m* George Buck, JP Devon (*d* 9 Nov 1743), seven times Mayor Bideford, 3rd *s* of Hartwell Buck by Sibella Ford, and *d* 4 Feb 1742, leaving, with three other sons (*dsp*), a 3rd *s*:

(1) John; thrice Mayor Bideford, MP Taunton; *m* 1st Judith (*d* 1739), only child of William Pawley, of Bideford; *m* 2nd Grace (apparently *dsp*), only child of Roger Melhuish, and *d* 3 April 1745, having by his 1st w had, with two yr sons:

1a George, of Affeton (which he inherited from his cousin Dennis Stucley 1755) and Daddon, JP Bideford and Devon; *b* 7 July 1731; *m* Anne (*d* 11 Feb 1820 aged 90), dau of Paul Orchard, of Hartland Abbey, and *d* 26 Jan 1794, having had:

1b George Stucley, of Affeton; *bapt* 8 March 1754; *m* 8 April 1780 Martha (*m* 2nd 1801 Lt-Col James Kirkman and *d* 30 Nov 1833 aged 80), est dau of Rev Richard Keats, Rector Bideford and King's Nympton, and sis of Adml Sir Richard Goodwin Keats, KB, and *dvp* 30 Nov 1791 leaving a 3rd *s*:

1c Lewis William, of Affeton; MP Exeter 1826–32 and N Devon 1839–57; *m* 18 April 1808 Anne (*d* 12 April 1879), dau of Thomas Robbins, of Roundham, Berks, and *d* 25 April 1858 , havng had, with a dau (*d unm*):

1d GEORGE STUCLEY (Sir), **1st Bt**

1d Louisa; *m* 9 June 1840, as his 2nd w, Samuel Trehawke Kekewich, JP, DL, of Peamore, Devon, and *d* 11 April 1880, leaving issue. He *d* 1 June 1873

2c Richard Buck, of Bideford, Capt RN; *b* 23 Oct 1785; *m* Angelica McDonald, and *d* 12 Aug 1830, leaving issue:

1d Richard Hugh Keats (Rev); Rector St Dominick, Cornwall

1d Martha; *m* Maj Oliver D'Arcy, 18th Regt (*d* 3 Feb 1880)

The only *s*,

Sir GEORGE STUCLEY BUCK later STUCLEY (roy licence 27 July 1858), **1st Bt** (UK), so *cr* 26 April 1859, of Affeton Castle and Hartland Abbey, Devon, JP, DL Devon; *b* 17 Aug 1812; MP Barnstaple 1855–59 and 1865–68, High Sheriff Devon 1863, Col Cmdt Devonshire Artillery; *m* 1st 22 Dec 1835 Lady Elisabeth O'Brien (*d* 9 May 1870), dau and coheir of 11th Baron of Inchiquin (*qv*), and had, with a dau (*d unm*):

1 **Sir (William) Lewis Stucley, 2nd Bt**, JP, DL Devon; *b* 27 Aug 1836; CA Devon, Lt-Col Gren Gds Crimea; *m* 1st 15 April 1869 Rosamund Head (*d* 29 Sept 1877), only dau of Henry Pottinger Best, of Doddington Grove, Berks; *m* 2nd 5 Feb 1879 Marion Elizabeth (*d* 3 Aug 1934), est dau of Lt-Col Henry Edward Hamlyn Fane (*see* WESTMORLAND, E), and *dsp* 19 Feb 1911

2 Lewis George Orchard; *b* 25 April 1843; Lt 36th Foot; *d* 11 Oct 1870

3 **Sir Edward Arthur George Stucley, 3rd Bt**; *b* 12 Feb 1852; Maj 1st S Australian Regt; *m* 29 Dec 1892 May (*d* 15 Nov 1922), est dau of Hon Thomas King, Min Educn S Australia, and *dsp* 7 Dec 1927

Sir GEORGE *m* 2nd 31 Jan 1872 Louisa (*d* 18 Nov 1913), 4th dau of Bernard Granville, of Wellesbourne Hall, Warwicks, and *d* 13 March 1900, leaving by her:

4 HUGH NICHOLAS GRANVILLE (Sir), **4th Bt**

5 Humphrey St Leger; *b* 7 June 1877; Maj Gren Gds, Nile Campaign (fought Battle of Omdurman), Boer War 1900–02, WW I; *m* 22 Oct 1908 Dorothy Beatrix Rose (*d* 29 Jan 1954), only child of Francis Henry Carew (*see* CAREW, Bt), and was *ka* 29 Oct 1914, leaving:

(1) Peter Francis Carew; *b* 10 Aug 1909; *educ* Eton and Magdalene Coll Cambridge (MA 1943); Capt Gren Gds WW II; *d unm* 7 March 1964

(2) Lewis Robert Carew; *b* 14 Dec 1910; Maj Gren Gds WW II; *das* Italy 16 Sept 1943

The 3rd Bt's half-bro,

Sir Hugh Nicholas Granville Stucley, 4th Bt, JP, DL Devon; *b* 22 June 1873; Lt-Cdr RN; *m* 6 Feb 1902 Gladys (*d* 21 March 1950), dau of Wynne Albert Bankes, JP, DL, of Wolfeton Ho, Dorchester, and had:

1 DENNIS FREDERICK BANKES (Sir), **5th Bt**

2 Anthony; *b* and *d* Dec 1912

3 John Humphrey Albert, DSC; *b* 12 July 1916; *educ* RNCs Dartmouth and Greenwich; Lt-Cdr RN WW II, barrister Middle Temple 1957, Circuit Judge 1974; *m* 2 July 1941 Natalia, dau of Don Alberto Jiménez Fraud, CBE, of Oxford

4 Bernard Thomas Fane; *b* 10 May 1918

1 Elizabeth Florence; *b* 9 Feb 1906; vol with French Army 1939 (despatches), author: *Life is for Living* and *Magnolia Street*, etc; *m* 16 Feb 1955 (*divorce* 1959) John Grant Lawrence Northmore, only *s* of John Northmore, of Pen Tor, Ipplepen, Newton Abbot, Devon, and *d* 26 July 1974

2 *Priscilla [Countess Priscilla Zamoyski, 143 Bowerhinton, Martock, Somerset]; *b* 1 Feb 1911; *m* 29 Aug 1936 (*divorce* 1956) Count Andrzej Zygmunt Zamoyski (*d* 1 Aug 1964), *s* of Count Wladislaw Zdzislaw Zamoyski, and has:

(1) *Zygmunt Ignacy Stukeley; *b* 23 Nov 1937; *educ* Stowe and Ch Ch Oxford

(1) *Betka Marya [Mrs Betka Zamoyska, 47 Parkview Court, Fulham High St, London SW6 3LL]; *b* 13 March 1948; *educ* Cranborne Chase and LMH Oxford (BA 1969); *m* 1988 (*divorce* 1993) Benjamin Hargreaves

Sir HUGH *d* 25 Oct 1956; his est surv *s*,

Sir Dennis Frederick Bankes Stucley, 5th Bt, JP (Devon 1937), DL (1955); *b* 29 Oct 1907; *educ* Harrow and RMC Sandhurst; Lt Gren Gds, Mayor Bideford 1954–56, Devon: CA 1955, High Sheriff 1956, Maj Roy Devon Yeo Artillery (142nd Field Regt) RA (TA), chm SW Advsy Ctee Forestry Commn 1958 and Timber Growers Orgn 1965–68; *m* 5 Jan 1932 Hon Sheila Margaret Warwick Bampfylde (*d* 12 July 1996), only dau of 4th Baron Poltimore (*qv*), and *d* 17 Sept 1983, having had:

1 John; *b* and *d* 30 July 1933

2 Sir HUGH GEORGE COPLESTONE BAMPFYLDE STUCLEY, **6th and present Bt**

1 *Margaret Cynthia [Mrs Gerald Hohler, Trent Manor, Sherborne, Dorset DT9 4SL]; *b* 3 Sept 1934; *m* 29 July 1953 *Gerald Arthur Hohler, only *s* of Sir Thomas Beaumont Hohler, KCMG, CB, JP, of Fawkham Manor, Kent, and has:

(1) *Thomas Edward; *b* 23 Dec 1958

(1) *Henrietta Margaret Cynthia; *b* 11 Dec 1955; *m* 1994 *Charles Richard Seymour (*see* HERTFORD, M)

(2) *Lucinda Jane Astell; *b* 22 Dec 1960; *m* 1982 *Richard Clephane Compton (*see* NORTHAMPTON, M)

2 *Rosemary Anne [The Rt Hon Rosemary Viscountess Boyne, Burwarton, Bridgnorth, Salop WV16 6QH]; *b* 8 Jan 1936; *m* 11 April 1956 10th Viscount Boyne (*qv*) and has issue

3 *Christine Elizabeth [The Rt Hon The Lady Cobbold, Knebworth House, Knebworth, Herts; 2d Park Place Villas, London W2]; *b* 25 April 1940; *m* 7 Jan 1961 *2nd Baron Cobbold (*qv*) and has issue

4 *Sara Susan [Mrs Charles Worthington, Court Hall, N Molton, N Devon]; *b* 6 Aug 1942; *m* 1st 24 Oct 1963 (*divorce*) Sir Michael Peto, 4th Bt, of Barnstaple (*qv*), and has issue; *m* 2nd 18 March 1971 *Charles William David Worthington and by him has:

(1) *Anna; *b* 1972

STUDD

Arms: Gu. a lion rampant between three crescents arg., on a chief masoned two tilting-spears in saltire, all ppr. **Crest:** Out of a mural crown two arms embowed in armour, the hands in gauntlets holding two tilting spears saltirewise, all ppr. **Motto:** *Nous tenons le droit* ('We hold the right'). **Creation:** Bt. (UK) 16 Oct 1929.

SIR EDWARD FAIRFAX STUDD, 4TH BT, of Netheravon, Wilts [Sir Edward Studd Bt, Kingsbury House, Kingsbury Episcopi, Martock, Somerset TA12 6AU]; *b* 3 May 1929; *s* bro 1977; *educ* Winchester; late Lt Coldstream Gds, chm Gray Dawes Travel 1988–96, dir Inchcape & Co 1974–86, memb Ct Assistants Merchant Taylors' Co 1977 (Master 1987–88 and 1993–94); *m* 30 Sept 1960 *Prudence Janet, only child of Alastair Douglas Fyfe, OBE, of Grey Court, Riding Mill, Northumberland, and has:

1 +PHILLIP ALASTAIR FAIRFAX; *b* 27 Oct 1961; *m* 1987 *Georgina A G, dau of Sir Roger Albert Gartside Neville, VRD, of Possingworth Manor, Blackboys, E Sussex, and has:

(1) +Kynaston Roger Fairfax; *b* 31 Dec 1993

(1) *Imogen Mary Henrietta; *b* 31 July 1991

2 +Christopher Andrew Eric; *b* 27 Oct 1968

1 *Alexandra Mary; *b* 27 March 1965

Lineage: WILLIAM STODDE, of Stonham Aspall, Suffolk; *m* Joan — and *d* 1491, leaving, with four other sons (including an est, John, to whom he left Stonham Aspall and whose only *s* John *d* by 21 May 1559, dividing his lands between his six daus) and two daus, a 2nd *s*:

THOMAS STUDDE, of Gosbeck; living 1511; ancestor in the 8th degree of:

JOHN STUDD, of Battisford and Coddenham; *m* March 1750/51 Anne (*d* 1790), 2nd dau of Edward Lynch, of Bilford Hall, Suffolk, and had, with a dau Elizabeth and four yr sons:

JOHN LYNCH STUDD, of Swatisfield Hall, Suffolk; *m* 22 March 1779 Susan (*d* 1844), dau of Lionel Mayhew, of Wetheringsett, and *d* 24 June 1820, leaving:

EDWARD STUDD, of Swatisfield Hall; *b* 4 Aug 1794; *m* 4 Sept 1817 Mary Anne Murphy (*d* 1 June 1859) and *d* 28 Feb 1822, having had:

EDWARD STUDD, of Tidworth Ho, Marlborough, Wilts; *b* 25 Dec 1819; *m* 1st 31 Jan 1846 Henrietta Margaret Hudson and had two sons and two daus; *m* 2nd 6 Nov 1856 Dorothy Sophia (*d* 20 March 1923), dau of John Thomas, of Bletsoe Castle, Beds, and *d* 27 July 1877, leaving by her:

1 (JOHN EDWARD) KYNASTON (Sir), **1st Bt**

2 George Brown; *b* 20 Oct 1859; *m* Mabel Preston and *d* 13 Feb 1945, leaving issue

3 Charles Thomas; *b* 2 Dec 1860; fndr Heart of Africa Mission, Pres World-Wide Evangelization Crusade; *m* 7 April 1888 Priscilla Livingstone Stewart (*d* 1930) and *d* 16 July 1931, leaving, with two other daus:

(1) Dorothy Catherine Topsy; *m* 14 Feb 1912 Rev Gilbert Arthur Barclay, yst s of Robert Barclay, JP, of High Leigh, Hoddesdon, Herts, and The Grove, Cromer, Norfolk, and had issue

(2) Pauline Evangeline Priscilla; *m* 24 Nov 1919 Norman Percy Grubb, 2nd s of Rev Harry Percy Grubb, and had issue

4 Arthur Haythorne; *b* 19 Nov 1863; *d* 26 Jan 1919

5 Herbert William, CB, CMG, DSO; *b* 26 Dec 1870; *educ* Eton and Trin Coll Cambridge; Boer War 1899–1902 (Queen's medal, six clasps, King's medal, two clasps, Brevet-Col), Ch Staff Supreme War Cncl 1917–19 WW I (wounded, despatches), Brig-Gen cmdg Coldstream Gds, Cdr Legn Hon, Order Crown Italy, Order Aviz Portugal, Offr Order Leopold Belgium, Italian Croix de Guerre, US DSM; *m* 1st 19 April 1894 Mary (*d* 14 May 1930), widow of Maj William Utting Cole and dau of Maj Horace de Vere, of Curragh Chase, Co Limerick; *m* 2nd 20 Dec 1930 Alice Maude (*d* 13 Sept 1950), dau of David Tullis, of Rutherglen, and *d* 8 Aug 1947, leaving by his 1st w:

(1) Mary de Vere; *m* 29 June 1915 Sir (Charles) Michael Palairet, KCMG, 2nd s of Capt Charles Harvey Palairet, of Westhill, Ledbury, Herefs, and *d* 2 Feb 1977, leaving issue. He *d* 5 Aug 1956

(2) Dorothy Mary Fairfax; *m* 2 Sept 1919 Thomas Folliott Powell, JP, of Sharow Hall, Ripon, Yorks, and had issue

6 Reginald Augustus; *b* 18 Dec 1873; *d* unm 3 Feb 1948

1 Dora Sophia; *b* 13 Oct 1867; *m* 2 Dec 1890 William Graham Bradshaw, CBE, of Down Park, Crawley Down, Sussex, s of Richard Bradshaw, and *d* Dec 1959, leaving issue. He *d* 16 March 1941

The est s,

Sir (John Edward) Kynaston Studd, 1st Bt (UK), so *cr* 16 Oct 1929, OBE (1919); *b* 26 July 1858; *educ* Eton and Trin Coll Cambridge (MA, LLD, Capt Cricket XI 1884); City London: Lt, Alderman Farringdon-Without Ward, Sheriff 1922–23, ktd 1923, Ld Mayor 1928–29, Dep Cmdt Co London Cadets, Maj cmdg Vol Force, Pres MCC 1930; *m* 1st 10 Dec 1884 Hilda (*d* 22 April 1921), dau of Sir Thomas William Brograve Proctor-Beauchamp, 4th Bt (*qv*), and had:

1 ERIC (Sir), **2nd Bt**

2 Ronald Granville, DSO (1919); *b* 6 Sept 1889; Cdr RN WW I (despatches, Croix de Guerre Belgium); *m* 2 April 1919 Kathleen (*d* 22 Dec 1975), widow of Granville Keith Falconer Smith, Coldstream Gds, and dau of 4th Earl of Leitrim (*see* 1953 edn), and *dsp* 9 Jan 1956

3 Lionel Fairfax (Rev); *b* 16 May 1891; *educ* Winchester; Army Capt; *ka* Ypres 15 Feb 1915

4 Bernard Cyril; *b* 24 Aug 1892; *educ* Winchester; Pres The Polytechnic, Chm Cncl Mission to Lepers; *m* 14 Oct 1925 Caryl Theodora (*d* 14 April 1977), er dau of Brig-Gen Charles de Winton, CMG, and *d* 30 March 1962, leaving:

(1) *Diana Caryl [Mrs Anthony Cavalier, 1213 Shady Ave, Pittsburgh, PA, USA]; *b* 14 Aug 1928; *m* 1st 17 Nov 1954 (*divorce* 1976) Anthony Ross Pope, only s of Walter Ross Pope by Colette, only dau of Sir Charles Doughty, QC; *m* 2nd 1976 Anthony Carroll Cavalier (*d* 1986) and by her 1st husb has:

1a *David Bernard Anthony Edward Beauchamp; *b* 4 Feb 1961; *m* 1991 *Janice Ann Woolheater and has:

1b *Nicholas Anthony; *b* 16 May 1993

2b *Jonathan Robert; *b* 9 March 1996

2a *Simon Charles Kynaston Beauchamp; *b* 9 March 1964; *m* 1989 *Felicia Anna Maria Campano and has:

1b *Desiree Jeanene; *b* 12 April 1993

1a *Sara Caryl Beauchamp [Mrs Colin Chase, Meadow Cottage, Wineham, Sussex BN5 9AY]; *b* 28 Sept 1955; *m* 1978 *Colin Weston Patrick Chase and has:

1b *David Weston; *b* 1982

1b *Kathryn Diana; *b* 1986

2a *Caroline Diana Beauchamp [Mrs Michael Thorne, Crane's Farm, Sibford Rd, Epwell, Oxon OX15 6LH]; *b* 30 Aug 1957; *m* 1988 *Michael Joseph Mackenzie Thorne and has:

1b *Joseph William Ross; *b* 1992

1b *Pia Sophie Elizabeth; *b* 1991

(2) *Joanell Vera [Mrs Robert Chappell, Arndown, 7 Elm Hill, Warminster, Wilts BA12 0AU]; *b* 17 Dec 1933; *m* 1 April 1959 *Lt-Col Robert Henville Chappell, OBE, Queen's Regt, only s of Lt-Col Hereward Chappell, OBE, IA, of Ditchling, Sussex, and has:

1a Bruce Hereward; *b* 22 Feb 1961; *d* 19 Oct 1976

2a *Gavin Bernard [Gavin Chappell Esq, Brook House, 27 Newport Mews, Portway, Warminster, Wilts]; *b* 27 March 1963; *m* 1988 *Jessica Lynn Holm

1a *Kathryn Joanell; *b* 2 June 1966; *m* 1992 *Capt Simon William Daniel Butt, Capt RRW, s of Lt-Col William Butt, of Cirencester, Glos, and has:

1b *Tobias Simon Benjamin; *b* 1 Aug 1997

1b *Imogen Hannah Joanell; *b* 20 March 1995

1 Vera Constance Victoria; *b* 14 June 1897; missionary nurse India, Kaisar-i-Hind Silver Medal; *d* 13 April 1984

Sir Kynaston *m* 2nd 18 June 1924 HSH Princess Alexandra Lieven, Red Cross Nurse WW I (Russian Imperial St George's Medal) (*d* 14 Nov 1974), dau of Prince Paul Lieven, Grand Master Ceremonies Russian Imperial Court, and *d* 14 Jan 1944

His est s,

Sir Eric Studd, 2nd Bt, OBE (1946); *b* 10 June 1887; *educ* Winchester; V-Pres Poly Regent St, MLA India, MLC and MLA Bengal, Capt IA WW I, Intell Offr HQ Staff 12th (CD) Regn and AFFC (NFS) WW II; *m* 8 June 1923 (Kathleen) Stephana (*d* 21 Sept 1976), only dau of Lydstone Joseph Langmead, and *d* June 1975, leaving:

1 **Sir (Robert) Kynaston Studd, 3rd Bt**; *b* 9 July 1926; *educ* Winchester; Capt Coldstream Gds, v-chm Poly Travel Ltd, dir Sir Henry Lunn Ltd; *m* 19 April 1958 *Anastasia [Anastasia Lady Studd, Manor Farm, Rockbourne, Fordingbridge, Hants], dau of Lt-Col Harold Boscawen Leveson-Gower (*see* SUTHERLAND, D), and *d* 27 May 1977, leaving:

(1) *Sara Alexandra; *b* 22 Feb 1959

(2) *Jane Anastasia; *b* 14 March 1961; *m* 1988 *Christopher John Hall, er s of Sir Peter Hall, KBE, of S Chailey, Sussex, and Leslie Caron, actress, of Paris, and has:

1a *Frederick Amery Kynaston; *b* 1989

2a *Benjamin Charles Edward; *b* 1992

(3) *Anne Elizabeth; *b* 1 July 1964

2 Sir EDWARD FAIRFAX STUDD **4th and present Bt**

3 +John Eric (Rev) [The Rev John Studd, Albion Lodge, Halterworth Lane, Romsey, Hants]; *b* 4 Dec 1934; *educ* Winchester and Clare Coll Cambridge (MA 1962); *m* 27 Sept 1969 *Nea Mildred, dau of Gordon Penn Kennett, of Balwyn, Vic, Australia

1 *Elizabeth Stephana [Mrs Victor Spindel, Court Barn, Pond Meadow, West Wickham, Cambs CB1 6RY]; *b* 24 June 1924; *m* 25 Oct 1954 Victor Erwin Spindel (*d* 6 Aug 1996), er s of Jona Spindel, of Israel, and has:

(1) *Daniel Jonas Arthur; *b* 26 Sept 1962

STUDHOLME

Arms: Vert a horse statant arg., caparisoned or, on a chief of the second three mullets of six points pierced gu. **Crest:** A horse's head arg., bridled and charged on the neck with a spur or. **Motto:** *Semper paratus* ('Always prepared'). **Creation:** Bt. (UK), 3 July 1956.

SIR HENRY WILLIAM STUDHOLME, 3RD BT, of Perridge, Co Devon [Sir Henry Studholme Bt, Halscombe Farm, Ide, Devon EX2 9TQ]; *b* 31 Jan 1958; *s f* 1990; *educ* Eton and Trin Hall Cambridge (MA); ACA, ATII; *m* 1988 *(Sarah) Lucy Rosita Deans-Chrystall, only dau of Richard S Deans, of Christchurch, NZ, and has:

1 +JOSHUA HENRY PAUL; *b* 2 Feb 1992

2 +Jacob William Richard; *b* 1993

1 Lorna Jane; *b* 1990

Lineage: JOHN STUDHOLME, of Thursby, Cumberland; *b c* 1515; *m* Marion — and *d* 1564, having had, with other issue:

THOMAS STUDHOLME, of Thursby; *m* Isobel — and *d* 1601, leaving:

JOHN STUDHOLME, of Thursby; *d* 1657, leaving:

JOHN STUDHOLME, of Eveninghill, Thursby; *m* 14 June 1652 Agnes Ritson and *d* July 1673, having had an only surv s:

JOHN STUDHOLME, of Studholme and Steps, Thursby, later of Eveninghill; *m* Isobel Huntingdon (*d* Nov 1751), of E Cuthwaite, and had, with other issue:

JOSEPH STUDHOLME, of Mainsfold, Gt Orton, later of Hole Ho, Thursby; *b* 1682; *m* 16 Oct 1707 Elizabeth (*d* 9 Nov 1745), dau of John Moore, of Midtown Orton, and *d* 6 Feb 1755, leaving an est s:

JOHN STUDHOLME, of Hole Ho and Moore End, Thursby; *b* Aug 1708; *m* Elizabeth (*d* 30 Nov 1793), dau of Joseph Jefferson, of W Cuthwaite, and *d* 17 Oct 1796, leaving:

JOSEPH STUDHOLME, of St Nicholas, Carlisle; *b* 1744; *m* 26 Oct 1786 Mary (*d* 23 July 1795), dau of John Moore, of Gt Orton, and *d* 2 July 1825, leaving an est s:

JOHN STUDHOLME, of Studholme, Abbey Holme, later St Nicholas and Morton Head, Cumberland; *b* 1787; *m* 6 April 1824 Elizabeth (*d* 1874), dau of Paul Nixson, of Carlisle and Dent, Yorks, and *d* 1847, leaving:

1 Joseph, JP King's Co; sold the last of the family estates and settled in Ireland, where he bought Kilmaine and Ballyeighan, King's Co, High Sheriff King's Co 1891; *m* 11 July 1878 Mary Hastings (*d* 26 May 1933), dau of James Robert Davis, of Dublin, and *d* 12 April 1904, having had:

(1) John; *b* and *d* 5 July 1882

(2) Lancelot Joseph Moore, MC, of Ballyeighan and Kilmaine; *b* 21 Sept 1884; High Sheriff King's Co 1909, Capt 7th Leinsters WW I; *ka* Somme 9 Sept 1916

(1) Elizabeth Charlotte Anne; *m* 10 Oct 1904 Maj Ambrose William Newbold, 67th Punjabis, s of Rev J J Newbold, Rector Clonbroney, Co Longford, and *dsp* 13 Dec 1905

(2) Mary Hastings; *m* 30 Aug 1906 Capt Charles Augustus Vivian (*ka* Ypres 27 April 1915), 15th Ludhiana Sikhs, s of Col Aylmer MacIver Campbell of Asknish, and *d* 21 Nov 1930, leaving two sons (both *ka* WW II) and a dau

(3) Rosalind; *b* 28 Oct 1887

2 JOHN

3 Paul; *b* 1831; *d* unm 1899

4 Michael, of Te Waimate, NZ, where settled 1854; *b* 31 Jan 1833; *m* 18 April 1860 Iphigenia Maria Louisa (*d* 4 Feb 1917), dau of Henry Channon, of Mayfair, and *d* 25 Sept 1886, leaving:

  (1) Michael Cuthbert; *b* 3 Aug 1864; *d* unm 14 April 1895

  (2) Edgar Channon, of Te Waimate; *b* 29 July 1866; *educ* Christ's Coll, NZ; *m* 20 April 1909 Nancy, est dau of Charles Wells, of Amberley, NZ, and *d* 2 June 1949, leaving:

    1a *Michael David; *b* 1 July 1913; *educ* Christ's Coll, NZ; *m* 15 April 1944 *Barbara, dau of J W K Lawrence, of Christchurch, NZ, and has:

      1b *Michael Carlisle; *b* 22 Jan 1951

      1b *Katherine Jane; *b* 5 Oct 1945; *m* 15 Nov 1969 *John Field Hazlewood, s of R Hazelwood, of Victoria

      2b *Nichola Louise; *b* 28 Jan 1948

    2a *Joseph Channon; *b* 6 Jan 1915; *educ* Christ's Coll, NZ; Capt NZ Div Cav Regt WW II; *m* 31 March 1940 *Jeanetta, dau of H B S Johnstone, of Springbank, Otaio, and has:

      1b *Paul Joseph; *b* 15 Nov 1943; *educ* Christ's Coll, NZ; *m* 15 March 1968 *Beverley Jane, only dau of John Henry Arkwright, DFC, of Overton, Marton, NZ

      2b *Henry Channon; *b* 17 March 1950; *educ* Christ's Coll and Lincoln Ag Coll Canterbury, NZ

      1b *Emily Rose; *b* 26 Aug 1941; *m* 19– *Robert Ashley George Johnson and has:

        1c *Rosalind Emily; *b* 24 Nov 1966

        2c *Sarah Elizabeth; *b* 15 June 1968

    3a *Daniel Lindsay [Maj Daniel Studholme, Tawhero, Eketahuna, New Zealand]; *b* 5 March 1920; *educ* Christ's Coll, NZ; Maj NZ Div Cav Regt WW II, with UN Truce Orgn Palestine 1963–64 as NZ Govt rep, chm Eketahuna CC; *m* 15 April 1950 *Diana Mary, dau of L V Lawrence, of Christchurch, NZ, and adopted:

      *Edgar Lynn; *b* 2 June 1952; *educ* Christ's Coll, Christchurch

      *Annabel Louise; *b* 25 April 1955

    1a *Janet Helen; *b* 23 Aug 1910; MEF WW II (despatches), Dir NZ Jr Red Cross

    2a *Rosalind Carlisle; *m* Dec 1940 James Michael Hennessy, MC, s of Maj G T Hennessy, of Garry Owen, Waimate, NZ, and has issue

  (3) Carlisle, of Pentland Hills, NZ; *b* 23 July 1870; *d* unm 16 Nov 1916

  (4) Paul, of Fraser St, Tauranga, NZ; *b* 2 May 1872; *m* 27 Feb 1900 Ida Gertrude (*d* 16 Aug 1950), dau of Thomas Masterman Hardy-Johnson, AMICE, of Christchurch, NZ, and *d* 13 Feb 1965, leaving:

    1a Michael Paul; *b* 3 May 1903; Lt NZ Div Cav Regt; *ka* Crete 20 May 1941

    1a Ida Ruth; *b* 21 Nov 1900; *m* 27 April 1921 Douglas Deans and had issue

    2a Audley Lena; *b* 2 June 1902; *m* 9 May 1927 Frank Douglas Mill and had issue

    3a *Effie Diana; *b* 19 Oct 1915; *m* 17 Jan 1940 Charlton Edward Dawson, s of Charlton Greenway Dawson, of Auckland, and has:

      1b *Charlton Michael; *b* 10 Feb 1942

      1b *Annabel Louise; *b* 28 March 1946; *m* 13 Nov 1969 *David Henry Haddrell, of Auckland

  (5) Harold; *b* 21 Oct 1876; *m* Charlotte, dau of M McCulloch, of Melbourne, Australia, and *d* 5 July 1950, leaving:

    1a *Harold McCulloch; *b* 19– *Beth, dau of Sir Thomas Hunter, of Wellington, NZ, and has three sons

    2a Geoffrey; RNR; lost at sea 1943

    1a *Marjorie; *m* Donald Meyers, of Christchurch, NZ

  (6) Geoffrey; *b* 15 Nov 1878; *d* unm 30 June 1883

  (1) Fanny, OBE; *b* 30 June 1861; *m* 5 July 1883 Alexander Boyle (*see* GLASGOW, E) and *d* 13 May 1930, leaving issue

  (2) Emily; *b* 4 Jan 1864; *m* 5 Oct 1882 John Mathias Barker, of Waihi, Woodbury, NZ, and *d* 22 July 1938, having had issue

  (3) Ruth; *b* 4 July 1875; *m* 1896 Norton Francis, of Waimate, NZ, and *dsp* 17 Sept 1902

  (4) Mabel; *b* 1 Sept 1879; *m* 1903 Mostyn Innes-Jones, Maj NZ Forces Boer War, and had issue

1 Frances; *d* unm 1906

2 Elizabeth; *d* unm 1914

3 Ada; *m* Charles Baker Stoney, MD, s of Robert Johnson Stoney, of Parsonstown, King's Co, and *d* 14 Feb 1921, leaving issue. He *d* 1904

The 2nd s,

JOHN STUDHOLME, of Merevale and Coldstream, NZ; *b* 29 May 1829; settled Waimate 1854, memb Provincial Cncl Canterbury and Ho of Reps; *m* 10 Feb 1862 Lucy Ellen Sykes (*d* 1 Dec 1926), dau of William Moorhouse, JP, of Knottingley, Yorks, and *d* 7 March 1903, leaving:

1 John, CBE, DSO, of Coldstream and Middleton Riccarton, NZ; *b* 10 Feb 1863; *educ* Christ's Coll, NZ, and Ch Ch Oxford (MA 1891); Lt-Col NZ Forces; *m* 1st 23 June 1897 Alexandra (*d* 15 Oct 1907), 4th dau of Most Rev William Thomson, Archbp York (*see* THOMSON, Bt, of Old Nunthorpe, Bt), and had:

  (1) John Morton Rangabé; *b* 11 July 1898; *educ* Christ's Coll NZ, RMC Sandhurst and Magdalen Coll Oxford; Lt NZEF WW I; *m* 1925 Lucienne, dau of Marc Aubé, of Aubervilliers, Seine, France, and *d* 24 Jan 1951

  (2) Richard Home (Sir), OBE (1945); *b* 7 Nov 1901; *educ* Eton and Trin Coll Cambridge (MA 1927); slr, Col RA WW II, City London: Alderman 1954, Lt 1955, Sheriff 1960–61, ktd 1962, Cdr Order Lion Finland, Grand Offr Order Republic Tunisia, Order Tri Shakti Patta Nepal, OStJ; *m* 6 Jan 1927 Alice Rosemary, 4th dau of Rt Rev Cecil Wilson, Bp Bunbury, W Australia, and *d* 2 May 1963, leaving:

    1a *John Richard Julius [John Studholme Esq, 32 Heath Drive, Brookwood, Surrey]; *b* 4 July 1929; *educ* Eton and St Andrews (MA 1953); *m* 18 Nov

1969 *Sheana Margaret MacDougall, yr dau of Stephen John Hadfield, of Edinburgh, by Jean Louisa Moray, 2nd dau of Col Alexander James MacDougall of MacDougall, CMG, JP, DL, of Dunollie, Oban, Argyllshire

    1a *(Rosemary) Ann Home; *b* 20 April 1928; *m* 1958 Joseph Los Chovanec, only s of Andrew Los Chovanec, of Toronto

  (3) Derek Skene, MBE; *b* 27 April 1904; *educ* RNC Dartmouth and Corpus Christi Coll Cambridge (BA 1925); Lt-Col RA WW II; *m* 14 July 1931 Elizabeth Janet, est dau of Charles John Crawford, of St Andrews, Fife, and *d* 22 Oct 1973, leaving:

    1a *Joseph John Anson; *b* 21 Aug 1935; *educ* Christ's Coll, NZ, and RAC Cirencester; *m* 12 Dec 1962 *Pamela Susan, dau of Dr Peter C S Unwin, of Christchurch, NZ, and has:

      1b *John Peter Rangabé; *b* 3 Jan 1964

      2b *Alistair William Anson; *b* 4 June 1965

      3b *Hamish Andrew Howard; *b* 12 Dec 1967

    2a *Richard Crawford; *b* 26 May 1937; *educ* Christ's Coll, NZ, and Corpus Christi Coll Cambridge; master at Christ's Coll, NZ; *m* 13 Dec 1967 *Philippa Mary, dau of Hugh Beaufoy Foster, of Christchurch, and has:

      1b *Belinda Jane; *b* 25 Sept 1969

      2b * Elizabeth Rachel; *b* 28 July 1971

      3b *Alexandra Mary Rose; *b* 5 Dec 1972

    1a Aline Janet; *b* 29 Dec 1933; *m* 22 March 1958 *Capt David Belfield Nolan, CBE, RN [Capt David Nolan CBE RN, Grove House, Baltonsborough, Somerset BA6 8QP], s of J G Nolan, of Gisborne, NZ, and *d* 11 June 1993, leaving issue

  (4) Humphrey Francis; *b* and *d* 1905

1 (cont.) Lt-Col John Studholme *m* 2nd 1910 Katharine Georgiana (*d* 14 May 1946), 2nd dau of Sir Charles Bowen, KCMG, of Middleton Grange, Canterbury, NZ, and *d* 26 May 1934

2 WILLIAM PAUL

3 Joseph Francis, of Ruanui, NZ; *b* 10 March 1866; *m* 1902 Eliza Hersey (*d* 21 Sept 1948), 2nd dau of Maj-Gen Robert Adam Wauchope, and *dsp* 12 July 1930

1 Lucy Ellen; *m* 1894 William Barton, of White Rock, and Fareham, NZ, and *d* 2 April 1945, leaving issue

2 Florence Mary; *d* unm 14 Feb 1946

The 2nd s,

WILLIAM PAUL STUDHOLME, of Perridge Ho, Devon, JP NZ; *b* 23 April 1864; *educ* Christ's Coll, NZ, and Magdalen Coll Oxford (MA); barrister Inner Temple 1887, High Sheriff Devon 1936; *m* 11 Aug 1897 Mabel (*d* 12 Feb 1953), dau of Henry F Gray, of Waiora, Canterbury, NZ, and *d* 23 Feb 1941, having had:

1 Paul Francis William; *b* 31 May 1898; *educ* Eton and RMC Sandhurst; 2nd Lt 1st Bn Devonshire Regt WW I; *ka* Paschendale 4 Oct 1917

2 HENRY GRAY, 1st Bt

3 John Wyndham, DSC; *b* 2 Feb 1903; *educ* RNCs Osborne and Dartmouth; Cdr RN; *m* 28 April 1942 *Elsie Margery, 3rd dau of Douglas Oliver, of Hassendean Bank, Hawick, and *d* 5 Feb 1968, leaving:

  (1) *Geoffrey William John; *b* 12 May 1947; *educ* Trin Coll Glenalmond

  (1) *Heather; *b* 12 March 1943

  (2) *Rosemary Elizabeth; *b* 18 Feb 1946

1 Eleanor Elizabeth; *b* 2 Jan 1902; *m* 16 April 1925 Cdr (S) Alan Robert Percy Brown, RN, er s of Col Henry Brown, DSO, of Houndwood Ho, Reston, Berwicks, and *d* 31 July 1975, leaving two sons and a dau. He *d* 30 Nov 1973

The 2nd s,

Sir Henry Gray Studholme, 1st Bt (UK), so cr 3 July 1956, CVO (1953), DL (Devon 1969); *b* 13 June 1899; *educ* Eton and Magdalen Coll Oxford (BA 1921, MA 1931); Lt Scots Gds (SR) WW I, memb LCC 1931–45, served WW II 1940–44, MP (C) Tavistock 1942–66, C Whip 1945–56, Jt Hon Treas C Party 1956–62; *m* 10 April 1929 *Judith Joan Mary [Judith Lady Studholme, 30 Abbey Mews, Amesbury Abbey, Wilts SP4 7EX], only dau of Henry William Whitbread, of Norton Bavant Manor, Warminster, Wilts, and *d* 1987, leaving:

1 **Sir Paul Henry William Studholme, 2nd Bt**; *b* 16 Jan 1930; *educ* Eton and RMA; Capt Coldstream Gds (ret 1959); *m* 2 March 1957 Virginia Katherine (*d* 1990), yr dau of Sir (Herbert) Richmond Palmer, KCMG, CBE, of Knightsbridge, and *d* 1990, leaving:

  (1) **Sir HENRY WILLIAM STUDHOLME, 3rd and present Bt**

  (2) +James Paul Gilfred; *b* 10 Feb 1960; *educ* Eton and Reading U (BSc); *m* 1992 *Charlotte Serena, twin dau of Jeremy Gwynne Pilcher (*see* LAWSON, Bt, of Weetwood), and has:

    1a +Arthur James Gilfred; *b* 22 July 1996

  (1) *Anna Katherine; *b* 23 Feb 1965; *educ* St Mary's Calne and York U (BSc); *m* 1992 *Duncan M Watts, yr s of T C Watts, of Rottingdean, E Sussex

2 +Joseph Gilfred [Joseph Studholme Esq, The Court House, Lower Woodford, Wilts SP4 6NQ]; *b* 14 Jan 1936; *educ* Eton and Magdalen Coll Oxford (BA 1959); 2nd Lt KRRC 1954–56, chm and md Editions Alecto Gp 1963–; *m* 5 Sept 1959 *Rachel, yr dau of Capt Sir William Albemarle Fellowes, KCVO (*see* DACRE, B), and has:

  (1) +Andrew Gilfred; *b* 20 Aug 1962; *educ* UEA (BA); *m* 1988 *Joanna, yr dau of Eric D Thompson, of Shamley Green, Surrey, and has had:

    1a Edward William Gilfred; *b* and *d* 1992

    2a +Cosmo Edward Gilfred; *b* 1993

    1a Nancy Elisabeth Rachel; *b* 2 June 1998

  (2) +Henry Alexander; *b* 6 Jan 1967; *educ* Magdalen Coll Oxford (BA)

  (3) +Hugo William Robert; *b* 10 Nov 1968; *educ* Bristol U (BSc)

1 *Henrietta Mary [Mrs Thomas St Aubyn, Dairy House Farm, Ashford Hill, Berks RG15 8BL]; *b* 24 Dec 1931; *m* 21 Nov 1953 *Maj Thomas Edward St Aubyn (*see* SAINT LEVAN, B) and has issue

STYLE

Arms: Sa. a fess or fretty of the field between three fleurs-de-lys gold, a bordure of the second. **Crest:** A wolf's head couped sa., collared or, the lower part of the neck fretty of the last. **Creation:** Bt. (E) 21 April 1627.

SIR WILLIAM FREDERICK STYLE, 13TH BT, of Wateringbury, Kent [Sir William Style Bt, 2430 N, 3rd Lane, Oconomowoc, WI 53066, USA]; *b* 13 May 1945; *s* f 1981; *m* 1st 1968 (*divorce* 1971) Wendy Gay, dau of Gene Wittenberger, of Hartford, Wis., and has:

1 *Shannon Gay; *b* 1969

2 *Erin Kay; *b* 1972

Sir WILLIAM *m* 2nd 1986 *Linnea Lorna, dau of Donn Erickson, of Sussex, Wis., and by her has:

1 +WILLIAM COLIN; *b* 1995

3 *McKenna Ashleigh; *b* 1987

4 *McKayla; *b* 1990

Lineage: WILLIAM STYLE, of Ipswich; had:

Sir JOHN STYLE; London Alderman *temp* HENRY VII; had:

Sir HUMPHREY STYLE, of Langley; Sheriff Kent c 1544, Esq of the Body to HENRY VIII; *m* Bridget, dau of Sir Thomas Baldrey, and had:

1 Edmund; had:

(1) William; had:

1a Sir THOMAS STYLE, 1st and last Bt (E), so *cr* 20 May 1627, of Langley; Gentleman Privy Chamber to JAMES I, Cupbearer to CHARLES I, ktd; *m* Elizabeth, widow of Sir Robert Bosvill, of Eynsford, and dau and heiress of Robert Pershall, of Lincoln's Inn, and *dsp* 10 Nov 1659, when the btcy expired

2 OLIVER

3 Nicholas; London Alderman; *d* 1615

The 2nd s,

OLIVER STYLE, of Wateringbury, Kent; London Alderman, Sheriff 1605; *m* Susanna, dau of John Bull, and *d* 4 March 1621/2, leaving an only surv s:

Sir Thomas Style, 1st Bt (E), so *cr* 21 April 1627, of Wateringbury; *m* 1615 Elizabeth (*d* 20 May 1650), only dau and heiress of Robert Foulkes, of Montesning, Essex, and had:

1 THOMAS (Sir), **2nd Bt**

1 Elizabeth; *m* Sir Edward Monins, 2nd Bt, of Waldershare, and *d* 1703

2 Susan; *m* Sir John Read, 1st Bt, and *d* 1657, leaving issue

3 Anne; *m* Sir John Buck, 1st Bt

The 1st Bt *d* 18 Oct 1637; his only s,

Sir Thomas Style, 2nd Bt; *b* 1624; *m* 1st Elizabeth (*d* 10 Dec 1679), dau of Sir William Armine, Bt, of Osgodby, Lincs, and had, with four daus:

1 Thomas; *m* Mary (*m* 2nd Sir Thomas Middleton), dau of Sir Stephen Langham, and *dsp* & *vp* 30 Aug 1672

2 **Sir Oliver Style, 3rd Bt**; *dsp* 12 Feb 1702/3

Sir Thomas *m* 2nd Margaret (*d* 5 Dec 1718), dau of Sir Thomas Twisden, Bt, of Bradbourne, Kent (see 1937 edn), Judge King's Bench, and *d* 19 Nov 1702, having by her had, with other issue:

3 **Sir Thomas Style, 4th Bt**; *m* Elizabeth (*d* 25 Oct 1737), dau of Sir Charles Hotham, 4th Bt (see HOTHAM, B), and *d* 11 Jan 1769, leaving:

(1) **Sir Charles Style, 5th Bt**; *m* 7 March 1770 Hon Isabella Wingfield (*d* 24 Sept 1808), dau of 1st Viscount Powerscourt (*qv*), and *d* 18 April 1774, leaving, with a dau:

1a **Sir Charles Style, 6th Bt**; *m* 29 March 1794 Camilla (*d* 17 Sept 1829), est dau of James Whatman, of Vinters, Kent, and *d* 5 Sept 1804, having had, with two daus:

1b **Sir Thomas Style, 7th Bt**; Army Offr; *d* unm Spain 5 Nov 1813

2b **Sir Thomas Charles Style, 8th Bt**, JP, DL Co Donegal; *b* 21 Aug 1797; MP Scarborough 1837–41; *m* 28 Oct 1822 Isabella (*d* 27 Dec 1881 aged 84), dau of Sir George Cayley, 6th Bt (*qv*), and *d* 23 July 1879, having had:

1c Emma; *d* Aug 1834

(2) Robert (Rev); Vicar Wateringbury, Rector Mereworth; *m* Priscilla (*d* 18 June 1832), dau of Rev John Davis, and had, with a dau (*d* unm):

1a Charles, of Glenmore, Stranorlar, Co Donegal; *b* 1777; *m* April 1812 Frances (*d* 20 Jan 1875), est dau of John Cochrane, of Edenmore, Stranorlar, and *d* 21 Dec 1853, having had, with other issue:

1b Charles; *b* 19 March 1816; *m* 22 Feb 1841 Emma (*d* 15 Oct 1898), dau of John Francis Norris, and *d* 21 Oct 1845, leaving:

1c Emma Frances; *d* unm 4 Feb 1890

1b Anna Maria; *m* 1838 Lt-Col John Pitt Kennedy and *d* 3 Dec 1902, leaving issue. He *d* 28 June 1879

2b Elizabeth; *m* 24 Sept 1850 John James Hamilton Humphreys, barrister, and *d* 28 April 1918 aged 87, leaving issue. He *d* 1890

3b Isabella; *m* Sept 1858 John Henry Kincaid, of Dublin, and *d* Aug 1867

2a William, of Bicester Ho, Oxon; *b* 26 April 1785; Capt RN; *m* 22 Dec 1814 Louisa Charlotte (*d* 25 Oct 1866), dau of Rev Hon Jacob Marsham (see ROMNEY, E), and *d* 24 Feb 1868, having had, with a dau (*d* unm):

1b WILLIAM HENRY MARSHAM (Sir), **9th Bt**

2b Charles Montague (Rev); *b* 21 Aug 1830; DD, MA Oxon; Fell St John's Coll Oxford, Rector S Warnborough, Hants; *m* 24 Sept 1867 his cousin Jessie Elizabeth (*d* 1922), dau of Robert Bullock Marsham (see ROMNEY, E), and *d* 7 Dec 1916, leaving:

1c Richard Charles Montague; *b* 20 Sept 1870; *m* 22 Oct 1892 Esther Lavinia, dau of Edwin Potter, and *d* 1946

3b Albert Frederick; *b* 20 May 1837; *m* 30 April 1868 Eliza (*d* 30 April 1898), dau of Henry Tubb, of Bicester, Oxon, and *d* Dec 1895, having had, with another dau (*d* an infant):

1c George Montague; *b* 7 March 1869; *educ* New Coll Oxford (BA); Maj W Kent Yeo; *m* 1st 7 April 1896 (*divorce* 1921) Eleanora Morrison, dau of James Morrison Kirkwood, of Yeo Vale, Bideford, Devon, and had:

1d Oliver George; *b* 1 Feb 1897; *educ* Eton; *m* 19 Jan 1923 Guinevere (*d* 1975), dau of Rev Walter Matthew Parker, and *d* 1973, leaving:

1e +George Michael Oliver; *b* 5 Aug 1927; *m* 18 July 1951 *Mary Jeans and has:

1f *Elizabeth Mary; *b* 18 July 1952

2f *Sarah Jane; *b* 1955

3f *Caroline Ann; *b* 1956

1e *Patricia Norah; *b* 1924; *m* 11 May 1946 (*divorce* 1970) G/Capt Deryck Hugo Cross, RAF, s of Solomon Cross, and has:

1f *Robert Humphrey Hugo; *b* 21 July 1951

1f *Alison Guinevere Hugo; *b* 30 June 1947; *m* 1972 *Gerald Bunyan and has:

1g *Kathleen Jill; *b* 1973

2f *Frances Jane Hugo; *b* 25 Jan 1949; *m* 1969 *Richard Charles Mortimore

1d Priscilla; *b* 9 Dec 1899; *m* 3 March 1923 Eric Wilson Pardoe, of Ol Magogo, Gilgil, Kenya, 4th s of Rev John Pardoe, of Leyton Manor, Essex, and *d* 23 April 1946, leaving issue. He *d* 11 April 1965

2d Patience Paulina; *b* 24 July 1901; *m* 6 Oct 1928 Col Claude Ernest Torin Erskine, CIE, DSO, MC, QVO Corps of Guides (*d* 24 Aug 1964), s of Claude Francis Erskine, and had:

1e *Claude Anthony; *b* 19 July 1932; *educ* Charterhouse; *m* 9 May 1959 *Diana Margery, 2nd dau of Harold Kanaar, of Kokstad, Cape Province, and has:

1f *Claude Mark; *b* 2 Aug 1961

2f *Timothy Harold; *b* 3 Oct 1962

3f *Paul Anthony; *b* 25 Feb 1965

4f *Jonathon Montague; *b* 7 May 1968

1e *Elizabeth Constance; *b* 31 Oct 1930; *m* 17 Dec 1955 *James Allan Howard, BA, LLB, Sr Counsel S Africa, son of George Valentine Howard, of Pietermaritzburg, and has:

1f *George Allan; *b* 17 Sept 1956

2f *Robert James; *b* 23 May 1962

1f *Jane Pauline; *b* 20 May 1958

1c (cont.) Maj George Style *m* 2nd 10 Dec 1921 Mary Burwood (*d* July 1941), formerly w of Cherry Kearton and dau of William Coates, and *d* 21 Oct 1942

2c Charles Humphrey; *b* 8 May 1877; Capt Roy E Kent Yeo; *m* 15 Nov 1899 Annie Maude Harriet (*d* 8 March 1942), 3rd dau of Gen Sir Hugh Henry Gough, VC, GCB, and *d* 11 June 1936, leaving:

1d Charles Richard; *b* 13 April 1901; *educ* Marlborough; Lt 14th Hus; *m* 29 Nov 1938 (*divorce* 1950) Gabrielle Muriel Currie, dau of James Wadsworth Ritchie, of Texas, and *dsp* 3 March 1960

2d Humphrey Bloomfield; *b* 12 Nov 1902; *educ* Marlborough and Pemboke Coll Cambridge; *m* 23 Dec 1935 Anita Dolores (*d* 19–), dau of Charles Brunson, and had:

1e +Charles Humphrey; *b* 7 March 1944; *educ* Osgoode Law Sch; *m* 1971 *Elizabeth Ann Hoskin, of London, Ontario

1e *Ursula Anne [Mrs William Carter, 49 Sagebrush Lane, Don Mills, Ontario, Canada]; *b* 18 Oct 1936; *m* 1959 *William Swaisland Carter and has:

1f *William Alarik; *b* 1963

1f *Roberta Jean; *b* 1960

2f *Jacqueline Anne; *b* 1966

3f *Adrienne Julia; *b* 1971

2e *Ingrid Priscilla; *b* 8 Nov 1939; *m* 1960 *Henry Evan Cockshutt Schulman and has:

1f *Charles Eric; *b* 1965

1f *Frances Yvonne; b 1961

2f *Audrey Alexis; b 1963

3e *Diana Maria [Mrs Robert Tweedy, 7 Royal Oak, Don Mills, Toronto, Canada]; b 28 Nov 1941; m 27 Aug 1965 *Robert Tweedy, s of James Donald Tweedy, of Toronto, and has:

1f *Laura Anne; b 1968

2f *Lisa Diana; b 1973

3d Hubert Anthony; b 9 Jan 1910; educ Marlborough; Capt IA; m 14 Feb 1942 *Enid Margaret [Mrs Hubert Style, Broomscroft Cottage, 144 Canon Lane, Wateringbury, Kent ME18 5PQ], only dau of Leonard Frederick Leonard, of Reigate, Surrey, and d 1992, leaving:

1e +John Richard [John Style Esq, Broomscroft Cottage, Canon Lane, Wateringbury, Kent ME18 5PQ]; b 22 Dec 1943; educ Marlborough and Coll of Law; slr 1970; m 1990 (divorce 1994)Caroline A M, only dau of Anthony Sparrow, of Abinger Hammer, Surrey, and has:

1f +Alexander Nicholas Hubert; b 1991

2e +(Robert) Nicholas Humphrey; b 19 March 1949; educ Marlborough; m 1982 *Mrs Diana Schoeller, dau of J Leal, of Johannesburg, and has:

1f +Jonathan Rupert Anthony; b 1982

2f +Freddy; b 1984

1f *Sophy (twin); b 1984

1d Barbara Anne; b 6 June 1904

2d Camilla; b 9 Sept 1906; m 11 July 1935 Antony Cuthbert Morris-Marsham (see ROMNEY, E) and had issue

3c Robert Henry, JP Kent; b 20 Oct 1881; Lt 6th Dragoon Gds, Capt Roy E Kent Yeo, High Sheriff Kent 1924; m 15 Feb 1905 Grace Winifred (d 1977), 3rd dau of John Bazley-White (see ROTHES, E), and d 17 June 1945, having had:

1d Ralph Montague; b 5 Jan 1906; d 5 Oct 1907

2d John Peter; b 15 Oct 1908; d 25 Feb 1918

3d +David Leslie [David Style Esq, Plaxtole, Bowling Green Rd, Castletown, IoM]; b 1913; educ Radley; RN WW II

1d Betty Winifred; b 6 Sept 1907; m 23 Feb 1938 Henry Cuthbert Hatfeild, yst s of Capt Charles Taddy Hatfeild, and had issue. He d 11 June 1951

2d *Gabrielle Ursula; b 28 Feb 1911; m 2 Sept 1936 *Capt Richard Taylor White, DSO, RN, and has issue (see WHITE, Bt, of Wallingwells)

1c Florence Louisa; m 1st 22 Nov 1898 Charles Stratton (d 28 May 1907), of Heathfield, Bletchington, Oxon, s of John Locke Stratton, and had issue; m 2nd 21 June 1910 William Henry Allen, of Evenley Hall, Brackley, and had further issue. He d 13 Dec 1936

1b Frances Isabella Anne; m 1 Sept 1856 Henry Stewart, of Corcam, Stanorlar, and d 1865

3a Thomas; Capt RN; d unm 1820

1a Margaretta; m John Johnston and d Sept 1863, leaving issue. He d July 1859

2a Henrietta; m June 1808 John Francis Norris and had issue. He d 2 Nov 1854

3a Elizabeth; m Adml John Drake and d 4 Dec 1854. He d 6 Aug 1864

4a Clara; m July 1845 Col — Wilson and d 31 Dec 1861

(3) William; Lt-Gen; m Catherine, sis and coheir of John Long Bateman, and dsp 1786

The 8th Bt's cousin,

Sir William Henry Marsham Style, 9th Bt, JP (Donegal and Mon); b 3 Sept 1826; MA Oxon; High Sheriff Co Donegal 1856; m 1st 18 Dec 1848 Rosamond Marion (d 15 Jan 1883), dau of 1st Baron Tredegar (see 1963 edn), and had:

1 William Charles Marsham; b 5 Oct 1849; dvp unm 2 Sept 1887

2 FREDERICK MONTAGUE (Sir), **10th Bt**

3 Henry Albert Glenmore; b 11 June 1862; m 5 May 1886 Annie Lydia (d 1951), dau of Samuel Fletcher Goldsmith, and d 1916, leaving:

(1) Glenmore Rodney; b 29 June 1887; m 5 July 1912 Mary Margaret, dau of John Maurice Tobin, and had:

1a +Rodney Henry [Mr Rodney Style, 3645 3rd Ave South, Minneapolis, MN, USA]; b 3 March 1914; m 1st 17 June 1943 Kathleen Quillin (d 7 April 1952); m 2nd 24 Jan 1959 *Lorretta Goodyear and has by his 1st w:

1b *Mary Kathryn; b 8 Feb 1947

2a James Glenmore; b 2 Aug 1916; m 30 Dec 1943 *Le Etta Smith and dsp, ka Belgium 29 Dec 1944

3a Robert George; b 26 Nov 1920; ka France 6 June 1944

4a Gerald Eugene; b 24 Jan 1922; m 18 June 1945 *Marguerite Keogan and d 9 May 1966, leaving:

1b +James Robert; b 15 Sept 1948

1b *Ann Marie; b 17 March 1951

5a +William Hugh; b 3 Oct 1924; m 1956 *Mary Ann Ferrell and has:

1b +Robert George; b 1959

2b +William Edward; b 24 Sept 1961

1b *Susan Marie; b 1957

2b *Margaret Mary; b 2 March 1965

6a +Charles Albert; b 1 Oct 1926; m 15 March 1950 *Delores Jaqua and has:

1b +Gregory Charles; b 19 Sept 1951

2b +Gary Kevin; b 26 Oct 1952

7a +Jerome Everett, b 28 Feb 1932; m 1955 *Margaret Ryan and has:

1b +David Ryan; b 2 Nov 1963

1b *Kathleen Michelle; b 1956

2b *Maureen Anne; b 1956

3b *Barbara Jo; b 20 June 1959

8a +Vincent Joseph; b 19 April 1934; m 1956 *Jane Sizer and has had:

1b Matthew Vincent; b 15 June 1958; d 26 June 1961

2b +Stephen Joseph; b 23 Oct 1959

1b *Nona Marie; b 6 Feb 1962

2b *Chad Patrick; b 27 Oct 1963

1a *Margaret Clare; b 5 June 1918; Franciscan nun from 1937

2a *Mary Crescent; b 18 May 1923; m 14 March 1944 *Maurice Finney

3a *Elizabeth Ann; b 2 June 1928; m 1955 *Gene Sullivan and has:

1b *Joseph Donald; b 25 July 1956

2b *Thomas Michael; b 11 Nov 1958

4a *Catherine Theresa; b 1 Oct 1929; m 1951 *Robert E Olson and has:

1b *Mark Joseph; b 6 Aug 1952

2b *Stephen George; b 28 Sept 1953

3b *Jonathan Robert; b 4 Oct 1954

4b *Eric James; b 3 Sept 1961

5b *Christopher; b 25 Oct 1966

1b *Julie Ann; b 12 Feb 1951

2b *Jenifer; b 4 Oct 1954

3b *Maybeth; b 9 April 1957

4b *Lisa Marie; b 25 April 1959

5b *Ella; b 4 May 1962

6b *Theresa; b 23 Sept 1965

(1) Rosamund Lydia; b 1891

(2) Brenda Helen; b 31 Aug 1897

(3) Viola; b 31 Aug 1897; m 14 June 1921 Merton Crandall Dayton and had issue

4 Rodney Charles; b 4 May 1863; Nile Expdn 1885–86, NWF India 1897–98, WW I (Comdt lines communication France 1914–15), Lt-Col cmdg QO Roy W Kent Regt, Hon Brig-Gen; m 19 Oct 1911 Helène Pauline (d 1975), dau of Herman Greverus Kleinwort (see KLEINWORT, Bt), and d 30 Oct 1957, leaving:

(1) +Godfrey William (Sir), CBE (1961), DSC (1942) [Lt-Cdr Sir Godfrey Style CBE DSC RN, 30 Carlyle Court, Chelsea Harbour, London SW10 0UQ]; b 3 April 1915; educ Eton; RN: served Roy Yacht Victoria and Albert 1938, Flag Lt to C-in-C Home Fleet 1939–41, WW II (despatches twice, wounded), invalided from RN 1945; underwriting memb Lloyd's, dep chm Northern Star Insur, dir: Europa Private Insur, Europe Assistance Ltd, chm Nat Advsy Cncl Employment Disabled 1963 (memb Cncl 1944 and chm Sheltered Employment Ctee 1954–63), memb Advsy Panel Disabled Living Fndn 1966, Dir Star Centre for Youth 1967, memb: Cncl Croquet Assoc 1957–67 (Hon Treas 1962–67), Soc Sciences Adv Panel, Nat Fund Research Polio and other Crippling Diseases 1969; Govr Sir Oswald Stoll Fndn 1975–84 and Queen Elizabeth Fndn for Disabled 1975–, ktd 1973; m 1st 30 Oct 1942 (divorce 1951) Jill Elizabeth, 2nd dau of George Bellis Caruth, of Drumard Cottage, Ballymena, Co Antrim, and has:

1a +Montague William [Montague Style Esq, 27 rue des Romains, 68480 Bettlach, France]; b 9 Oct 1943; educ Eton, HEC Paris and INSEAD (MBA); m 18 July 1970 *Susan Jennifer Wrightson (see WRIGHTSON, Bt), and has:

1b +Oliver Rodney; b 6 May 1976

1b *Sophie Elizabeth; b 20 June 1974

1a *Helen Anne; b 9 March 1946; m 3 Aug 1971 *Lt Col Charles Frederick Byng Stephens, Welsh Gds, s of Maj Frederick Stephens, CBE, DSO, of Orchard Hill, Ampney Crucis, Glos, and has:

1b *Alexandra Claire; b 1973

2b *Georgina Kate; b 1976

2a *Marieka Louise; b 12 Dec 1947; m 18 April 1969 *Charles John Hamilton Fisher, only s of John Oswald Hamilton Fisher, of Fulham, and has:

1b *Hugo Hamilton; b 27 Oct 1970

1b *Louise Hamilton; b 1973

(1) (cont.) Lt-Cdr Sir Godfrey Style m 2nd 31 March 1951 Sigrid Elisabeth (d 1985), formerly w of Bengt Julin, of Stockholm, and dau of Per Stellan Carlberg, of Jönköping, Sweden; m 3rd 1984 *Valerie Beauclerk, dau of Lt Cdr Cecil Hulton-Sams, RN (see HAWARDEN, V), and widow of Duncan McClure, and by his 2nd w has:

2a *Charles Rodney [Capt Charles Style RN, Wood Cottage, Cornwood, Ivybridge, Devon]; b 15 Jan 1954; educ Eton and Cambridge; m 1981 *Charlotte Amanda, er dau of Lt Timothy Martin Woodford, RN (see STIRLING-HAMILTON, Bt), and has:

1b *Amanda Clare; b 1981

2b *Annabel Daisy; b 1983

3b *Elizabeth Sigrid; b 1990

(2) +(Rodney) Gerald [Col Gerald Style, Fairmont, Sands Rd, Seale, Farnham, Surrey GU10 1LW]; b 28 Oct 1920; educ Eton; Coldstream Gds 1940–46, Col Northumberland Fus, cmded 1st Bn 1962–65, MOD 1970, Comdt RMSM Kneller Hall 1973–75, licentiate Br Inst Professional Photography; m 1st 8 Jan 1944 (divorce 1952) Melloney, yr dau of Maj-Gen Sir (Sanford) John Palairet Scobell, KBE, CB, CMG, DSO; m 2nd 18 Oct 1952 *Barbara, 3rd dau of John Austin Hill, of Natick, Mass., and has:

1a +William Bryant [Maj William Style, c/o RHQ Coldstream Gds, Wellington Barracks, Birdcage Walk, London SW1]; b 21 March 1954; educ Eton; m 1977 *Celia Maria, yr dau of Hon Robert Latham Baillieu, MBE, TD (see BAILLIEU, B), and has:

1b +Edward Rodney; b 1980

2b +Robert William; b 1982

1b *Jennifer Hélène; b 1988

2a +Rodney Hill [Rodney Style Esq, Greenacre, Steeple Aston, Oxon OX5 3RT]; b 25 March 1956; educ Eton; ACA, ATII; m 1982 *Georgina Eve, yr dau of John Kinlock Kerr (see LOTHIAN, M), and has:

1b +George Oliver; b 1985

2b +Hugo Gerald (twin); b 1985

1b *Elizabeth Daisy; b 1989

3a +John Glenmore [John Style Esq, Calle Rafel Ripolles 13, La Selva del Camp, Tarragona, Spain]; *b* 28 Oct 1957; *educ* Eton and London U (BA); *m* 1988 *Concepción, only dau of José Muñoz Sainz, of Corral de Calatrava, Ciudad Real, Spain, and has:

  1b *Hélèna Barbara; *b* 1995

1a *Caroline Mary [Mrs Adam Southwell, Prince Hall Hotel, Two Bridges, Yelverton, Devon]; *b* 19 Jan 1964; *m* 1988 *Adam Francis Southwell, 2nd s of Kenneth Southwell, of Tavistock, Devon

(1) *Rosamond Marguerite [Mrs Antony Allen, The Garden House, Mordington, Northumberland]; *b* 14 Aug 1912; *m* 1st 19 Oct 1934 R-Adml John Harvey Forbes Crombie, CB, DSO (*d* 31 Aug 1972), s of James Forbes Crombie; *m* 2nd 1980 *Antony William Allen and by her 1st husb has:

  1a *James Rodney Forbes; *b* 1935; Capt late Queen's Own Highrs; *m* 1961 (*divorce* 1977) Lee Adrienne Chavet

  1a *Rosanna Mary [Mrs Malcolm Shennan, Ash House, Rimpton, Yeovil, Somerset BA22 8AN]; *b* 1937; *m* 1964 *Maj Malcolm Kenneth Shennan, late RSG, and has:

    1b *Mark Douglas; *b* 1970

    1b *Melissa; *b* 1967; *m* 15 June 1996 *Hugh Alexander Stewart

  2a *Annabel Jean [Mrs Simon Younger, Baro, Haddington, E Lothian EH41 4PF]; *b* 1944; *m* 1964 *Simon Gerard Younger and has:

    1b *James Henry; *b* 1965; *m* 1997 *Gillian Ellis

    2b *Jonathan Simon; *b* 1979

    1b *Mary-Claire; *b* 1967

    2b *Eugenie Hope; *b* 1968; *m* 1996 *Simon Thomasson

    3b *Sophie Rosamond; *b* 1973

  3a *Julia Rosamond; *b* 1947; *m* 19– *John Henry Trotter

(2) *Mary Dorothy [Mrs Neil Campbell, Chennell Park, Tenterden, Kent TN30 6XA]; *b* 5 Feb 1918; *m* 19 Sept 1939 *Maj Neil Arthur Campbell, TD, RA, s of Ronald George Campbell, of Great Hollenden, Underriver, Kent (*see* 1970 edn CAMPBELL OF ESKAN, B), and has:

  1a *Alistair Neil [Alistair Campbell Esq, Tunstall Green, Tunstall, Suffolk]; *b* 1941; *m* 1970 (*divorce* 1975) Jane, dau of Michael Gatehouse

  2a *Jeremy George [Jeremy Campbell Esq, The Mount, Corby Glen, nr Grantham, Lincs]; *b* 1948; *m* 1973 *Penelope Hudson and has:

    1b *Toby George Mungo; *b* 1975

    2b *Angus Neil Morgan; *b* 1977

    1b *Camilla Mary; *b* 1981

  3a *Gerald Angus [Gerald Campbell Esq, Keepers Cottage, Chennell Park, Tenterden, Kent TN30 6XA]; *b* 1951; *m* 1976 (*divorce* 1992) Dorian Isobel, dau of Maj Anthony Peter Howorth Greenly (*see* GIBSON, Bt, of Great Warley), and has:

    1b *George Richard Angus; *b* 1979

    2b *Henry Neil Edward; *b* 1980

  1a *Joanna Mary; *b* 1946; *m* 1972 *Philip Thompson and has:

    1b *James Courtney; *b* 1974

    2b *Charles Neil; *b* 1976

1 Rosamond Louisa; *m* 8 April 1872 Henry Price Holford, 10th Hus, and *d* 21 June 1899, leaving issue

2 Selina Isabella; *d* unm 5 Nov 1934

3 Lydia Francis; *m* 12 Jan 1875 Benjamin Francis Meynell Bloomfield, DL, of Castle Caldwell, Co Fermanagh, and *d* 23 June 1900, leaving issue. He *d* 1886

4 Mary Louisa; *m* 24 April 1884 Rev Thomas Thornhill Peyton and *d* 21 July 1909, leaving issue (*see* PEYTON, B).

Sir William *m* 2nd 2 June 1885 Ellen Catherine (*d* 1 Sept 1922), widow of Henry Hyde Nugent Bankes and est dau of Edward Taylor Massy (*see* MASSY, B), and *d* 31 Jan 1904

His est surv s,

  Sir Frederick Montague Style, 10th Bt; *b* 16 May 1857; *m* 14 Oct 1886 Caroline (*d* 27 Sept 1933), dau of Frederick G Schultz, and *d* 22 July 1930, leaving, with a dau (Louisa Violet, *b* 18 Jan 1894, *m* Ewald H Muehlmeier and *d* 9 Jan 1960):

Sir William Frederick Style, 11th Bt; *b* 11 July 1887; *m* 1st 26 Feb 1912 Florence (*d* 1918), dau of J Timm, and had:

  1 **Sir William Montague Style, 12th Bt**; *b* 21 July 1916; *m* 20 Nov 1941 *La Verne [La Verne Lady Style, 334B Riverview Dve, Delafield, WI 53018, USA], dau of T M Comstock, and *d* 1981, leaving,

    (1) Sir WILLIAM FREDERICK STYLE, **13th and present Bt**

    (2) +Frederick Montague [Frederick Style Esq, N5866 Rockland Beach, Hilbert, WI 54129, USA]; *b* 5 Nov 1947; *m* 1971 (*divorce* 1988) Sharon, dau of William H Kurz, of Menomonee Falls, Wis., and has:

      1a *Jennifer K; *b* 1977

      2a *Christina S; *b* 1979

  1 *Helen [Mrs Gilbert Schiltz, 943 Jacinto West Indies Bay, Venice, FL, USA]; *b* 27 July 1913; *m* 19– *Gilbert L Schiltz and has:

    (1) *Susan; *b* 19–; *m* 19– *Dennis Grosse

    (2) *Mary Lou; *b* 19–; *m* 19– *Michael Duell

Sir William *m* 2nd 10 Feb 1923 Genevieve, dau of Peter L'Estrange, and *d* 27 June 1943, leaving by her:

  2 *Dorothy Jean; *b* 30 Nov 1923

SUDELEY

Arms: Quarterly, 1st and 4th, or an escallop in the chief point sa. between two bendlets gu. (for TRACY); 2nd and 3rd, or a bend engrailed vert, plain cotised sa. (for HANBURY). **Crests:** 1 On a chapeau gu., doubled erm., an escallop sa. between two wings or (for TRACY), 2 Out of a mural crown sa. a demi-lion rampant or, holding in the paws a battle-axe sa., helved gold (for HANBURY). **Supporters:** On either side a falcon, wings elevated ppr., beaked and belled or. **Motto:** *Memoria pii æterna* ('The pious are held in everlasting remembrance'). **Creation:** B. (UK) 12 July 1838.

THE 7TH BARON SUDELEY OF TODDINGTON, Co Gloucester (Merlin Charles Sainthill Hanbury-Tracy) [The Rt Hon The Lord Sudeley, 25 Melcombe Court, Dorset Sq, London NW1 6EP]; *b* 17 June 1939; *s* cousin 1941; *educ* Eton and Worcester Coll Oxford (BA 1963); Pres Montgomeryshire Soc 1972–73, V-Pres Prayer Book Soc, Chm: Monday Club, Human Rights Soc and Constitutional Monarchy Assoc, V-Chllr Monarchist League, FSA, co-author *The Sudeleys, Lords of Toddington* (1987); *m* 18 Jan 1980 (*divorce* 1988) Hon Elizabeth Mairi, er dau of Viscount Bury (*see* ALBEMARLE, E) and formerly w of Alastair Michael Hyde Villiers (*see* CLARENDON, E)

Lineage (of Hanbury): GUY de HANBURI, of Hanbury, Worcs; living *temp* HENRY II; had:

GEOFFREY de HANBURY, of Hanbury; had, with an er s (Henry; living 1238):

GUY de HANBURY; held land in Hanbury; had:

GEOFFREY de HANBURY; Bailiff to successive Bps Worcester; *d* by 1319, leaving:

  1 Henry; *b* *c* 1285; said to have rebelled against EDWARD II 1319; MP Worcs 1320; the first-known bearer of the Hanbury arms; ancestor of the sr line of HANBURYs, extinct 17th century

  2 Philip; Verderer Forest of Feckenham; owed £600 (some £145,000 in late-1990s terms) by Roger de Mortimer 1318

  3 Nicholas; living 1317; Verderer Forest of Feckenham *temp* Edward II; *m* Elizabeth — and *d* 1331, leaving:

    (1) Reginald; held a quarter of a kt's fee in Hanbury, Verderer Forest of Feckenham, MP Worcs 1363 and 1382/3; *dspm* after 1390

  4 Robert; *m* Ellen de Newent and had:

    (1) Robert; in Holy Orders; Chamberlain N Wales 1330 on; *d* after 1348

    (2) JOHN

    (3) Geoffrey; living 1352–88; *m* Joan —

The 2nd s,

JOHN de HANBURY, of Middle Beanhall; living 1324; had:

EDWARD de HANBURY, of Middle Beanhall; Collector Kts' fees for Worcs 1428; *d* in or after 1451, leaving, with two er sons (Humphrey, *d* 1501, ancestor of the HANBURYs of Beanhall later BATEMAN-HANBURYs, whose rep William Hanbury was *cr* Baron Bateman of Shobdon 1837 (*see* 1931 edn); Edward, of Bromsgrove, *fl* 1449–1503):

JOHN HANBURY, of Feckenham, where held a quarter of a kt's fee; *fl* 1440–1505; had:

RICHARD HANBURY, of Elmley Lovett, Worcs; *fl* 1457–82; *m* 1st Catherine Smyth and had a s; *m* 2nd Margery Tynter and had, with three yr sons (Henry, of Buriton, Hants, *m* Bridget Webb and had a s (Thomas, Auditor Exchequer, bought Manors of Corhampton, Mapledurham and Petersfield); John, of Walton, *d* 1559; Thomas, Vicar Catheridge, *d* unm 1565):

RICHARD HANBURY; *b* 1480; was leasing Crown estate of Elmley Lovett by 1524; *m* a dau of Philip Bassett and had, with two yr sons (Thomas, of Berinton, *m* Joan Poole and *d* 1557; William, *d* 1577):

JOHN HANBURY, of Elmley Lovett; *b* 1516; *m* 1st a dau of John Brode, of Dunclent, Glos, and had:

  1 Richard; *b* 1533; goldsmith and pioneer ironmaster S Wales, acquiring extensive property around Pont-y-Pool, Mon, 1570 on; *m* 28 April 1560 Alice, dau

and heir of Jasper Fisher, thrice Prime Warden Goldsmiths' Co and Crown Jeweller to QUEEN MARY, and d 20 May 1608, having had:

(1) Alice; b 1572; m William Coombs, MP, of Warwick, and d by 1608

(2) Elizabeth; b 1570; m Sir Edmund Wheeler, of Riding Court, Bucks, and d 1633, leaving issue

JOHN HANBURY m 2nd Elizabeth, dau of Francis Bradley, of Swynford, Worcs, and by her had:

2 Philip; b 1545; dsp 1628

3 RICHARD

4 Robert; b 1549; d 1601; ancestor of the HANBURYs of Ilam Hall, Staffs

1 Joyce; b 1549; m 22 May 1576 William Wilde, of Upton Warren

2 Fortune; b 1533; m 13 Oct 1578 Thomas Best, of Kinver

The er s by the 2nd w,

RICHARD HANBURY, of Elmley Lovett; b 1548; m his cousin Margery, dau of Francis Bradley Jr, of Swynford, and d 1590, leaving, with a yr s (Philip, of Panteg, Mon, ancestor of the HANBURYs of Holdfield Grange) and two daus (Rose, m Richard Budd, Auditor to JAMES I; Elizabeth, m 21 Aug 1580 Rev John Cole, Rector Elmley Lovett):

JOHN HANBURY, of Pont-y-Pool, Mon, and Hoarstone, Worcs; b 1575; memb Goldsmiths' Co; inherited Monmouthshire propert from his uncle Richard Hanbury 1608; MP Glos 1629, High Sheriff Worcs 1649; m 1616 Anne (d 18 Feb 1668/9), dau of Christopher Capel, MP, of Gloucester, and d 16 July 1658, having had:

1 Richard, of Pont-y-Pool; b 1618; educ Magdalen Coll Oxford; m 1650 Mary, widow of Sir Edward Morgan, Bt and dau of Sir John Bridgeman, 1st Bt (see BRADFORD, E), and dsp

2 CAPEL

3 Christopher; b 1622; d unm by 1658

3 John; b 1631; living 1658

1 Bridget; m Gregory Wiltshire, of St John's, Middx

The 3rd s,

CAPEL HANBURY, of Pont-y-Pool and Hoarstone; b 1625; High Sheriff Worcs 1689; m 1st his cousin Elizabeth (d by 1675), dau of William Capel, of Gloucester; m 2nd Honor (d 1681), dau of Edward Salwey, MP, of Stanford, Worcs; m 3rd Elizabeth, niece of Brian Duppa, Bp Winchester, and widow of Robert Foley, of Stourbridge (see FOLEY, B), and d 14 Jan 1704, leaving by his 1st w, with a dau (Mary, m John Hoo, of the Middle Temple):

JOHN HANBURY, of Pont-y-Pool Park and Coldbrook Park, Mon; b 1664; educ Pembroke Coll Oxford; Maj, MP Gloucester 1701–15 and Mon 1720–34; m 1st Albinia (dsp 1702), dau of Maj-Gen William Selwyn, of Matson, Glos; m 2nd Bridget (d 1741), only dau and eventual heir of Sir Edward Ayscough, of Stallingborough and S Kelsey, Lincs, and d 14 June 1734, having by her had:

1 John, of Caerleon, Mon; b 1705; m 1733 Anne, dau and heir of Thomas Price, of Llanfoist Ho, Mon, and dsp 1737

2 CAPEL

3 Charles HANBURY later HANBURY-WILLIAMS (Sir), KB (1744), of Coldbrook Park; b 8 Dec 1708; educ Eton; MP Mon 1734–47 and Leominster 1754–69, Ld Lt Herefs, High Steward Leominster, Paymaster Marines 1739–46, Min Dresden 1746, Amb Berlin and St Petersburg 1749–57; m July 1732 Lady Frances Coningsby (d 1781), yr dau and coheir of 1st Earl of Coningsby of the 1719 cr, and had:

(1) Frances; m 4th Earl of Essex (qv) and d 19 July 1759, leaving issue

(2) Charlotte; m Cdr Hon Robert Boyle-Walsingham, RN, MP, and d 12 April 1790, leaving issue (see SHANNON, E)

4 George HANBURY later HANBURY-WILLIAMS, of Coldbrook Park, which he inherited from his bro; b 23 Sept 1715; educ Eton; m 1748 Margaret, dau of Maj John Chambré, and d 11 Dec 1764, leaving issue

5 Thomas; b 1722; Capt RN; d unm 1778

The 2nd s,

CAPEL HANBURY, of Pont-y-Pool Park; b 1707; educ Ch Ch Oxford; MP Leominster 1741–47 and Mon 1747–65; refused a peerage; m 7 Oct 1743 Hon Jane Tracy, only dau of 5th VISCOUNT TRACY OF RATHCOOLE (see below **Lineage (of Tracy)**), and d 7 Oct 1765, leaving, with two daus (Henrietta, Frances, d unm):

JOHN HANBURY, of Pont-y-Pool Park; b 6 Aug 1744; educ Eton and Magdalen Coll Oxford; MP Mon 1765–85; m 12 Feb 1774 Jane, dau of Morgan Lewis, of St Pierre Park, Mon, and d 4 April 1784, leaving:

1 John Capel, of Pont-y-Pool Park; b 27 Jan 1775; d unm 21 Dec 1796

2 Capel HANBURY later HANBURY-LEIGH (added 1797 under terms of will of cousin, 5th and last Baron Leigh (qv) of Stoneleigh of the 1643 cr), of Pont-y-Pool Park; b 6 Oct 1776; High Sheriff 1799 Mon and 1827 Brecon, Ld Lt Mon 1836–61; m 1st Molly Anne (dsp 1846), widow of Sir Robert Humphrey Mackworth, 2nd Bt (qv); m 2nd 20 Aug 1847 Emma Elizabeth (d 1888), 4th dau and eventual sole heiress of Thomas Rous, of Court-y-rala, Glam, and Llanwern Ho, Mon, and d 28 Sept 1861, leaving:

(1) John Capel, of Pont-y-Pool Park, JP (Mon, Herefs), DL (Mon); b 14 May 1853; educ Eton and Trin Coll Cambridge; High Sheriff Mon 1878, Hon Col 3rd Bn S Wales Borderers; m 1885 Louisa Charlotte (d 1927), dau of Col Edward Hungerford Eagar, and d 8 May 1921, having had:

1a Capel Lionel Charles; b 1 Oct 1893; educ Winchester; d 9 Aug 1908

1a Ruth Julia Margarette; b 16 Feb 1903; m 18 Dec 1923 Maj Gerald Evan Farquhar Tenison, 3rd Dragoon Gds (d 21 Aug 1954), of Lough Bawn, Co Monaghan, and Overbury Hall, Suffolk, and had:

1b *Richard Hanbury Tenison later HANBURY-TENISON (roy licence 28 Sept 1951) (Sir), KCVO (1995), JP (Gwent 1979) [Sir Richard Hanbury-Tenison KCVO JP, Clytha Park, Abergavenny, Gwent NP7 9BW]; b 3 Jan 1925; educ Eton and Magdalen Coll Oxford; Capt Irish Gds WW II 1943–45 (wounded), Counsellor For Serv (ret 1975), High Sheriff Gwent 1977, Ld Lt Gwent 1979– (DL 1973–79), S Wales regnl dir Lloyds Bank 1980–91 (chm 1987–91), Hon Col 3rd Bn Roy Regt Wales 1982–90, Pres TA&VRA Wales 1985–90, KStJ 1990 (CStJ 1980); m 12 May 1955

*Euphan Mary, er dau of Maj Arthur Balcarres Wardlaw-Ramsay (see SALTOUN, L), and has issue

2b Patrick John, of Good Hope, Jamaica; b 1 March 1928; educ St Columba's Ireland; m 11 Nov 1949 *Frances Eleanor, yr dau of Alan Jackman, of Evanston, Ill., and d 3 Sept 1989, having had:

1c *)John Alan; b 25 Oct 1950; educ Eton; m *Peggy Jo Goodman and has:

1d *Caitlin

2c Richard Leigh; b 13 Oct 1953; d 4 Sept 1975

1c *Susan Marina; b 24 Jan 1955

2c *Ruth Emily; b 7 Sept 1957; m *Wayne Webb

3b *(Airling) Robin TENISON later HANBURY-TENISON (roy licence 28 Sept 1951), OBE (1981) [Robin Hanbury-Tenison Esq OBE, Cabilla Manor, Cardinham, Bodmin, Cornwall PL30 4DW]; b 7 May 1936; educ Eton and Magdalen Coll Oxford (MA); farmer, explorer and author, pres: Survival Internat (chm 1969–81), Cornwall Tst for Nature Conservation 1988–95, FLS, FRGS; m 1st 14 Jan 1959 Marika (d 1982), only dau of John Montgomerie Hopkinson, TD, of Garwyn's Farm, Plummers Plain, Horsham, Sussex; m 2nd 1983 *Mrs Louella Edwards, dau of Lt-Col G T G Williams, DL, and has by his 1st w:

1c *Rupert Thomas Treveddoe; b 28 Aug 1970; m 2 Sept 1995 *Francesca Anne Hall

1c *Lucy Antonia; b 20 Jan 1960; m 29 Sept 1990 *Peter John Boutwood and has:

1d *Daisy May; b 24 March 1991

2d *Hetty Silverstone; b 8 July 1994

1b *(Marguerite) Anne; b 28 Nov 1925; WRNS WW II; m 7 June 1952 Maj Harry Kerr Aitken, MC, Argyll and Sutherland Highrs (d 2 Jan 1997), s of Reginald Aitken, of Ivor, Kingston, Jamaica, and has:

1c *Robert Hanbury Tenison; b 19 May 1955; educ Eton and Queen's Coll Oxford; Col Roy Regt Wales; m *Joanna, dau of Maj-Gen Lennox Napier, CB, OBE, MC, and has:

1d *Robert Frederick Harry; b 3 Aug 1994

1c *Clarissa Julia; b 23 March 1953; m *Julian Francis Fonseca, of White House, Llanvetherine, and has issue

2c *Cherry Anne; b 26 July 1958; m *Richard Hope-Simpson, of Laundry Cottage, Llanvapley

2b *(Ruth) Hilaria; b 4 Feb 1932; m 10 Aug 1953 Christopher John Frederick Kunhardt (d 25 May 1990), only s of Col John Conrad Gie Kunhardt, IMS, and Mrs Marian Campbell Howison, of Ardmoy, Perth, and has issue

(1) Emma Charlotte; m 4 March 1878 Cdr Lord Robert Brudenell-Bruce, RN, 4th s of 3rd Marquess of Ailesbury (qv), and d 30 March 1921, leaving issue

(2) Frances Elizabeth; m 12 Dec 1868 Hon Lionel George Ashley, s of 7th Earl of Shaftesbury (qv), and dsp 2 Aug 1875

3 CHARLES HANBURY later HANBURY-TRACY (roy licence 19 Dec 1798), **1st Baron Sudeley of Toddington**, Co Gloucester (UK), so cr 12 July 1838; b 28 Dec 1777; educ Rugby and Ch Ch Oxford; High Sheriff Glos 1800–01 and Montgomeryshire 1804–05, helped raise 1803 the Montgomeryshire Legion, of which Lt-Col, MP (Whig) Tewkesbury 1807–12 and 1832–37, chm judges designs for new Houses of Parl 1835 in wake of fire which had destroyed the old ones; Ld Lt Montgomeryshire 1848–58; m 29 Dec 1798 Hon Henrietta Susanna Tracy (d 5 June 1839), only child and heiress of 8th and last VISCOUNT TRACY OF RATHCOOLE (see below **Lineage (of Tracy)**), and had:

(1) THOMAS CHARLES, **2nd Baron**

(2) Henry, DL; b 11 April 1802; MP Bridgnorth 1837–38; m 19 June 1841 Rosamond Anne Myrtle (d 2 April 1865), sis of 9th Earl Ferrers (qv), and d 6 April 1889, having had:

1a Charles Henry Tamworth; b 14 Jan 1842; d 3 Sept 1923

2a Arthur; b 30 June 1843; d 4 Sept 1856

1a Rosa Mary; b 21 June 1844; d unm 12 Sept 1913

2a Henrietta Susanna; b 28 March 1847; m 5 Aug 1891 Thurlow Augustus Astley, of Eastlea Court, Frimley, Surrey (see 1970 edn ASTLEY, Bt), and dsp 19 June 1926. He d 17 Aug 1918

(3) John Capel; b 19 Aug 1803; educ Oriel Coll Oxford (BA 1829); d unm 4 May 1852

(4) Capel Arthur; b 5 Jan 1809; HEICS; m 18 Sept 1833 Eliza Anne (m 2nd Capt Graham and d 1837), dau of Lt-Col John Tyler, RA, and dsp 28 July 1834

(5) William; b 18 Jan 1810; educ Exeter Coll Oxford; Madras CS, Assist Judge and Jt Criminal Judge Cochin 1841, ret 1846; d unm 27 Feb 1887

(6) Edward (Rev); b 6 Feb 1812; educ Exeter Coll Oxford (BA 1835, MA 1847); Rector Sully Glam 1838–48, Chaplain Embassy Vienna 1848–56; d unm 12 Sept 1887

(1) Henrietta; d unm 28 Jan 1890 aged 90

(2) Frances; d unm 23 Dec 1867

(3) Laura Susanna; d unm 30 June 1881

The 1st BARON d 10 Feb 1858; his est s,

THOMAS CHARLES HANBURY-TRACY later LEIGH (roy licence 11 April 1806) later still HANBURY-TRACY again (roy licence 30 March 1839), **2nd Baron Sudeley of Toddington**; b 5 Feb 1801; educ Ch Ch Oxford; MP (Whig) Wallingford 1831–32, Ld Lt Montgomeryshire 1858–63; m 25 Aug 1831 Emma Elizabeth Alicia (d 14 July 1888), dau of George Hay DAWKINS-PENNANT formerly DAWKINS (see PENRHYN, B), and d 19 Feb 1863, having had:

1 SUDELEY CHARLES GEORGE LEIGH later HANBURY-TRACY (roy licence 30 March 1839), **3rd Baron Sudeley of Toddington**; b 9 April 1837; educ Harrow; Capt Gren Gds 1857–63, Ld Lt Montgomeryshire 1863–77; d unm 28 April 1877

2 CHARLES DOUGLAS RICHARD, **4th Baron**

3 Algernon Cornwallis Henry; b 21 March 1844; d 8 Feb 1845

4 Alfred Francis Algernon (Rev); b 13 Oct 1846; educ Eton and Ch Ch Oxford (BA 1867, MA 1870); Vicar St Barnabas, Pimlico; m 1st 21 April 1868 Agnes Jane (d 12 Dec 1926), est dau of Henry James Hoare, of Morden Lodge, Surrey;

m 2nd 16 Feb 1928 Evelyn Margaret (*d* 18 April 1948), dau of Frederick K H Haselfoot, barrister, and *d* 31 Jan 1929, having had by his 1st w:

(1) Bertram Henry Algernon; *b* 21 July 1875; *educ* Winchester, Trin Coll Oxford and Durham U (BA 1898); *m* 1921 Caroline Rowland (*d* 18 Jan 1954), widow of Walter Winans and dau of Henry Belcher, MD, of Hove, and *dsp* 7 Nov 1952

(1) Una Theodora Alicia; *b* 12 Jan 1870; *m* 12 Aug 1901 Bertram Miles and *d* 13 Jan 1959

(2) Sybil Mary Agnes; *b* 22 June 1873; *m* 27 April 1898 Ambrose Bartholomew Tunnard and *d* 26 April 1905, leaving issue. He *d* 6 Aug 1941

5 Frederick Stephen Archibald; *b* 15 Sept 1848; *educ* Trin Coll Cambridge (BA); MP Montgomery 1877–85 and 1886–92, Lt-Col Worcester Yeo Cav; *m* 8 Sept 1870 Helena Caroline (*d* 13 Sept 1916), dau of Sir Thomas Winnington, 4th Bt (*qv*), and *d* 9 Aug 1906, having had:

(1) Eric Thomas Henry, OBE (1919), JP Dorset; *b* 4 July 1871; *educ* Eton; Maj Coldstream Gds, Boer War 1809–1902 (Queen's medal with three clasps, King's medal with two clasps) and WW I; *m* 6 Nov 1902 Dorothy Louisa (*d* 16 April 1951), yst dau of Sir Edward Harris Greathed, KCB, of Uddens Ho, Dorset, and *d* 24 May 1953, leaving:

1a Claud Edward Frederick HANBURY-TRACY later HANBURY-TRACY-DOMVILE (deed poll 1961 under terms of will of Sir Compton Domvile), TD; *b* 11 Jan 1904; *educ* Eton and Trin Coll Cambridge (BA 1925); Maj RA (TA) WW II; *m* 1st 6 July 1927 (*divorce* 1948) Veronica May (*d* 1985), dau of Cyril Grant Cunard, JP (*see* 1970 edn CUNARD, Bt), and had:

1b +(DESMOND) ANDREW JOHN HANBURY-TRACY [Andrew Hanbury-Tracy Esq, 7 Gainsborough Drive, Sherborne, Dorset DT9 6DS]; *b* 30 Nov 1928; heir presumptive; *educ* Sherborne and RAC Cirencester; ARICS 1965; *m* 1st 22 June 1957 (*divorce* 1966) Jennifer Lynn, only dau of Dr Richard Christie Hodges, of Elizabethan Ho, Westgate, Warwick, and has:

1c +Nicholas Edward John; *b* 13 Jan 1959; *educ* Milton Abbey

1b (cont.) ANDREW HANBURY-TRACY *m* 2nd 4 April 1967 Lillian, dau of Nathaniel Laurie; *m* 3rd 1988 *Mrs Margaret Cecilia White, dau of Alfred Henry Marmaduke Purse, and by his 2nd w has:

2c +Timothy Christopher Claud; *b* 25 March 1968; *m* 1 June 1996 *Anneliese M Arthur

2b +Charles William Justin HANBURY-TRACY; *b* 14 April 1938; *educ* Sherborne; *m* 8 March 1969 (*divorce* 1983) Sarah Jane, yr dau of Lt-Col George Ashley, The Cameronians (Scottish Rifles), of Rosamondford Lodge, Aylesbeare, Devon, and has:

1c +Justin; *b* 28 June 1971

2c +Edward Claud; *b* 1976

1c *Emily; *b* 5 Jan 1970

1b *Mary Claudia Elizabeth [Mrs Robert Cross, West End House, 1 Step Terrace, Winchester SO22 5BW]; *b* 19 May 1931; *m* 25 April 1953 *Robert Singlehurst Cross, only s of Lt-Col Charles Norman Cross, MC, of Park Ho, Market Drayton, Salop, and has:

1c *Edward Robert; *b* 7 Oct 1956; *educ* Charterhouse and Peterhouse Cambridge (BA 1978)

1c *Lucy Cunard (retains maiden name); *b* 1 July 1954; *m* 31 May 1980 *Richard Walter Emanuel, s of Walter Braithwaite Emanuel, of Fulham

2c *Sylvia Mary; *b* 21 March 1961

3c *Anna Elizabeth; *b* 31 March 1964

1a (cont.) Maj Claud HANBURY-TRACY-DOMVILE *m* 2nd 30 April 1954 Marcella Elizabeth Willis (*d* 26 Sept 1983), er dau of Canon John Willis Price, Rector Croughton, Northants, and *d* 22 Feb 1987

(2) Claud Sudeley Francis; *b* 3 Nov 1873; *d* 12 May 1874

(1) Edith Julia Helena; *m* 25 July 1916 Maj Ramsay Robert Feilden, Loyal Regt, s of Rev Canon George Ramsay Feilden, and *dsp* 24 Oct 1954. He *d* 1 April 1956

(2) Cyprienne Emma Madeleine, OBE (1919); *d unm* 16 April 1954

(3) Violet Mary Claudia; *m* 14 Aug 1900 Sir Wyndham Rowland Dunstan, KCMG, FRS, LLD Aberdeen, s of John Dunstan, Constable and Govr Chester Castle, and *d* 6 May 1963, leaving issue. He *d* 20 April 1949

(4) Hilda Adelaide Eleanor; *m* 1919 Edward James Heron-Maxwell (*see* HERON-MAXWELL, Bt) and *d* 7 June 1962

(5) Gwyneth Rose Goda; *d unm* 30 Oct 1903

6 Hubert George Edward, DL Bristol; *b* 14 Aug 1855; *educ* Eton and Ch Ch Oxford (BA 1877); barrister Inner Temple 1880; *d unm* 2 Nov 1940

1 Juliana Sophia Elizabeth; *d unm* 8 June 1899

2 Georgiana Henrietta Emma; *m* 6 Oct 1859 Capt Charles Henry Maude and *d* 8 March 1921, leaving issue (*see* HAWARDEN, V)

3 Adelaide Francis Isabella; *m* 17 May 1859 Rev Frederick Peel and *d* 18 Dec 1917, leaving issue (*see* PEEL, E)

4 Alice Augusta Gertrude; *m* 28 May 1861 Maj-Gen Charles F Webber, CB, RE, 3rd s of Rev Thomas Webber, of Leckfield, Co Sligo, and *d* 25 Feb 1877, leaving issue

5 Gertrude Emily Rosamund; *b* 24 Jan 1842

6 Madeline Emily Augusta; *m* 30 Dec 1875 4th Baron de Mauley (*qv*) and *d* 28 Jan 1938, leaving issue

The 3rd BARON's bro,

CHARLES DOUGLAS RICHARD HANBURY-TRACY, **4th Baron Sudeley of Toddington**, PC (1886), JP (Montgomeryshire, Glos), DL (Montgomeryshire); *b* 3 July 1840; RN 1854–63 (Baltic in Crimean War and China and Pacific Stations, Lt 1860, Gunnery Lt 1862); MP (Lib) Montgomery 1863–77, barrister 1866, Ld-in-Waiting 1880–85, Chm Br Commn to Vienna Electrical Exhibition 1883, Capt Gentlemen-at-Arms 1886, FRS 1888, dir P&O Steamship Co and Sir William Armstrong & Co; *m* 9 May 1868 Ada Maria Katherine (*d* 6 Jan 1928), dau of Hon Frederick James Tollemache (*see* DYSART, E), and *d* 9 Dec 1922, leaving:

1 WILLIAM CHARLES FREDERICK HANBURY-TRACY, **5th Baron Sudeley of Toddington**, JP (Glos and Warwicks); *b* 19 April 1870; *educ* Harrow and Trin Coll Cambridge; Capt Irish Gds SR WW I, Roy Humane Soc's Medal; *m* 24 Aug

1905 (*divorce* 1922) Edith Celandine Cecil (*see* EXETER, M) and *dsp* 5 Sept 1932

2 Algernon Henry Charles, CMG; *b* 11 April 1871; Brevet Maj Res Regt RHG, Uganda Expdn 1897–99 (despatches, medal and clasp), Boer War 1899–1900 (despatches, medal with three clasps) and Abyssinia 1901 (despatches, medal and clasp), Star Ethiopia, Star Zanzibar; *m* 2 Dec 1905 Sylvia (*d* 5 Sept 1958), widow of Sir Windham Robert Carmichael-Anstruther, 9th and 6th Bt (*see* 1970 edn), and dau of Sir Frederick Darley, GCMG, PC, and *d* 3 Dec 1915, leaving:

(1) RICHARD ALGERNON FREDERICK HANBURY-TRACY, **6th Baron Sudeley of Toddington**; *b* 20 April 1911; Maj RHG WW II; *m* 30 Nov 1940 *Elizabeth Mary [Lady Collins, Kirkham Bank, Knaresborough, N Yorks HG5 9BT] (*m* 2nd 27 Oct 1965 Maj Sir Arthur James Robert Collins, KCVO, only s of Col William Fellowes Collins, DSO, JP, DL, of Knaresborough), 3rd dau of R-Adml Sir Arthur Bromley, 8th Bt (*qv*), and *das* & *sp* at sea 26 Aug 1941

(1) Ursula Katharine, JP (Hants 1944); *b* 11 April 1909; granted rank of baron's dau 23 Feb 1933; *m* 1st 31 Dec 1935 Brig Claude Nicholson, CB (*d* as POW Germany 26/27 June 1943; *see* NICHOLSON OF WINTERBOURNE, B), and had issue; *m* 2nd 4 July 1946 G/Capt Archibald Hugh Herbert MacDonald, AFC, RAF (*d* 10 Nov 1947), ADC to Viceroy India, s of Archibald MacDonald and Countess Paul Desfontaines de Preux, of Rabat, Morocco

3 Felix Charles Hubert, Lt Scots Gds; *b* 27 July 1882; *m* 11 June 1908 Madeleine Llewellyn (*m* 2nd 6 June 1929 Capt Caryl Liddell Hargreaves, Scots Gds (*d* 26 Nov 1955), s of Reginald Gervis Hargreaves, of Cuffnells, and *d* 5 Aug 1958, leaving further issue), only dau of Brig-Gen George Llewellen Palmer, CB, of Lackham, Lacock, Wilts, and was *ka* 19 Dec 1914, leaving:

(1) (Michael) David Charles; *b* 29 March 1909; Capt Scots Gds WW II; *m* 3 Nov 1937 Colline Amabel, widow of Lt-Col Frank King, DSO, OBE, 4th Hus, and only dau of Lt-Col Collis George Herbert St Hill, Roy Devon Yeo, and *d* 22 Aug 1940 of wounds recd at Dunkirk, leaving:

1a MERLIN CHARLES SAINTHILL HANBURY-TRACY, **7th and present Baron Sudeley of Toddington**

(2) (Ninian) John Frederick; *b* 7 Dec 1910; *educ* Eton and Trin Coll Cambridge (MA); explorer, Sudan Political Serv 1933–34, Scots Gds 1939–41 (invalided) and IA Special Forces 1944–46, FRGS; *m* 1st 11 Jan 1935 (*divorce* 1954) Hon Blanche Mary Arundell (*d* 1993), er dau of 15th Baron Arundell of Wardour (*see* 1940 edn), and had:

1a *Jennifer Avril Mary [Mrs Martin Morland, 50 Britannia Rd, London SW6 2JP]; *b* 24 May 1941; *m* 6 June 1964 *Martin Robert Morland, CMG, Amb Burma 1986–90, est s of Sir Oscar Charles Morland, GBE, KCMG, of The High Hall, Thornton-le-Dale, Yorks, and has:

1b *William; *b* 1965

2b *Anthony; *b* 1967

1b *Catherine Mary; *b* 1966

(2) (cont.) John Hanbury-Tracy *m* 2nd 10 Aug 1954 Daphne Mary Christian (*d* 27 May 1983), widow of Maj Charles Scott, MC, of Little Place, Pool Hill, Newent, Glos, formerly w of Guy William John Farquhar (*see* FARQUHAR, Bt) and 2nd dau of Col Vivian Henry, CB (*see* MILBANK, Bt), and *d* 25 June 1971

1 Eva Isabella Henrietta, DBE (1918); *b* 25 Jan 1869; *m* 24 Aug 1889 Henry Torrens Anstruther and *d* 19 June 1935, leaving issue (*see* ANSTRUTHER, Bt)

2 Florence Emma Louisa; *b* 11 Feb 1873; *m* 24 June 1891 Capt Charles Warden Sergison, DL, Scots Gds, of Cuckfield Park, Sussex, and *d* 4 Nov 1911, leaving issue. He *d* 20 Jan 1911

3 Ida Madeleine Agnes; *b* 20 Jan 1875; *m* 20 Feb 1894 Francis Pelham Whitbread, of Knightsbridge and Burford Ho, Tenbury Wells, 3rd s of Samuel Whitbread, of Southill and Cardington, Beds, and *d* 29 April 1959, leaving issue. He *d* 29 Oct 1941

4 Alice Evelyn Agatha; *b* 12 Aug 1877; *m* 4 Oct 1898 Maj Bertram William Arnold Keppel and *d* 5 Nov 1955, leaving issue (*see* ALBEMARLE, E)

5 Rhona Margaret Ada; *b* 13 July 1879; *m* 17 Aug 1905 Col Bertram Abel Smith, DSO, MC, of Cossington, Leics, and 45 Montagu Sq, W, yst s of Robert Smith, of Goldings, Herts, and *d* 22 May 1926, leaving issue. He *d* 21 Sept 1947

Lineage (of Tracy): Count RALPH (de Gouy?), probably of Valois but possibly of Amiens, and very possibly of Carolingian male ancestry further back; *m* Eldegarde and *d* 926 or 943, leaving:

WALTER I, Count of Amiens and probably also of Vexin and Valois; *m* Adela, probably dau of Fulk I, Count of Anjou, and *d* 992–98, leaving, with other issue:

WALTER II, 'The White', Count of Vexin, Valois and Amiens; built the Castle of Crespy in Valois, fndr Monastery of St Arnulf, Valois, 1008; *m* Adela and *d* 1017–24, leaving, with other issue:

DREUX/DROGO, Count of Vexin and Amiens; *m* Godgifu (*m* 2nd Eustace II, Count of Boulogne), sis of EDWARD THE CONFESSOR OF ENGLAND and dau of ETHELRED II THE REDELESS by his 2nd w Emma (dau of RICHARD I, DUKE OF NORMANDY), and *d* on a pilgrimage to the Holy Land 1035, having had a 2nd s:

RALPH, described by contemporaries as *Comes* (possibly a courtier of comital rank but without a territorial earldom, at any rate in England, for he was French), to support the dignity; (*see* NORTHUMBERLAND, D, for a discussion of earldoms at this time), but also possibly Earl of Worcester or conceivably Hereford (he was employed at a high level against a Welsh incursion into England and revolts by various earls throughout the 1050s, though on one occasion he and his soldiers ran away before fighting even began); and/or even the E Midlands; held Sudeley and Toddington, Glos, and Chilvers Cotton, Warwicks; *m* Getha and *d* 21 Dec 1057, leaving:

HAROLD de SUDELEY; in the Domesday Survey 1086 is recorded as holding Burton Dasset, Warwicks, and land in Droitwich, Worcs, as well as his patrimony; granted land in Sudeley to Winchcombe Abbey; had:

JOHN de SUDELEY; living 1130; *m* Grace, dau of William de Tracy (*d c* 1136), illegitimate s of HENRY I, late in whose reign he *d*, leaving:

1 Ralph, *m* Emma and *d* by autumn 1192, leaving:

(1) Otuel; *m* Margaret and *d* 1198

(2) Ralph; *m* Isabel and *d* by 26 Feb 1221/2, leaving:

  1a Ralph; *m* Imenia and *d* by 19 March 1241/2; probably *f* of:

    1b Bartholomew (Sir); ktd by 1269, Sheriff Herefs 1272; *m* Joan and *d* by 29 June 1280, leaving:

      1c JOHN De SUDELEY, 1st LORD (Baron) SU(DE)LEY(E) in the English peerage, deemed by later doctrine to have been so *cr* by writ of summons to Parl 29 Dec 1299; *b c* 1275; served against Scots and Welsh on land and the French at sea 1282–1336; Chamberlain Household 1306; pardoned 1321 for having opposed EDWARD II's favourites the Despensers (*see* FALMOUTH, V); *d* by 18 April 1336, having had:

        1d Bartholomew; *m* Maud, dau of John, s of Piers de Montfort, and *dvp*, leaving:

          1e JOHN De SUDELEY, 2nd LORD (Baron) SU(DE)LEY(E); *b c* 1304/5; not called to Parl; *m* Eleanor de Scales, thought to have been dau of Robert, 2nd Lord (Baron) Scales, and *d* by 19 Feb 1339/40, leaving an only s:

            1f JOHN De SUDELEY, 3rd LORD (Baron) SU(DE)LEY(E); *b c* 1337/8; not called to Parl; served in Gascony 1364 during Hundred Years War; ktd by 1367; *d* 11 Aug 1367, apparently *sp*, when according to later doctrine the Barony of Sudeley would have fallen into abeyance between his sisters

            1f Joan; *m* Sir William Boteler/le Botiler, possibly s or gs of William Boteler, of Wem, Salop, leaving:

              1g THOMAS BOTELER, notional 4th LORD (Baron) SU(DE)LEY(E); *b c* 1354; not called to Parl; *m* by 18 July 1385 Alice, just conceivably dau of Sir John Beauchamp, of Powick, and *d* 21 Sept 1398, leaving:

                1h JOHN BOTELER, notional 5th LORD (Baron) SU(DE)LEY(E); *dsp* and apparently unm by 1410

                2h WILLIAM BOTELER, notional 6th LORD (Baron) SU(DE)LEY(E); *m* Alice and *d* by 20 Dec 1417

                3h RALPH BOTELER, notional 7th LORD (Baron) SU(DE)LEY(E) of the 1299, but the impossibility of his holding any such status in contemporary eyes is shown by his being *cr* by patent 10 Sept 1441 BARON SUDELEY, Co Gloucester (E), KG (1440); apparently ktd by 1418 (though in 1419 called esquire) but certainly by Jan 1434/5; granted land in France 1420/1, Capt Arques and Crotoy in France 1423, Ch Butler to HENRY VI Jan 1434/5, memb King's Council France and Normandy 1440, Treasurer Exchequer 1443–46; *m* 1st by 6 July 1419 Elizabeth, widow of John Hende; *m* 2nd *c* 8 Jan 1462/3 Alice, dau of 5th Lord (Baron) Deincourt and widow of 7th Lord (Baron) Lovel (of Titchmarsh) and *de jure* 4th Lord (Baron) Holand, and *dspms* 2 May 1473, when the Barony of 1441 expired but the notional one of 1299 would by later doctrine have been deemed to have fallen into abeyance between his sisters' issue, having had:

                  1i Thomas; *m* Eleanor, sis of 1st Earl of Shrewsbury and Waterford (*qv*), and *dsp* & *vp* between 1450 and 1468

                1h Elizabeth; *m* — Norbury and had:

                  1i Henry (Sir); had:

                    2j John; coheir in 1473 to the 1299 Barony of Su(de)ley(e)

                  2i Joan; *m* Hamon Belknap and had:

                    1j William; coheir in 1473 to the 1299 Barony of Su(de)ley(e)

    2f Margery; *b c* 1337; *m* after 11 Aug 1367 Sir Robert Massey and *dsp* by 14 May 1379, when the abeyance of 1367 was naturally terminated

2 William, had the manor of Toddington, Glos, made over to him by his bro, also lands there in exchange for Burton Dassett, Warwicks, *c* 1139–48; presented the manor of Thaneworth, another gift of his bro, to the Abbey of Gloucester; held one (kt's?) fee of his bro 1166; had, with a yr s (Alard, Rector Toddington):

  (1) Henry; *m* Hawise and had:

    1a Oliver; living 1201–04; had:

      1b Henry; living 1230

    2a William; Escheator Glos 1247–52; had land in N Piddle, Worcs, granted him and his w *c* 1250; Constable Gloucester 1264; pardoned as follower of the late Simon de Montfort (*see* LEICESTER, E, preliminary remarks) and his lands restored him 20 June 1268; *m* Margery and had:

      1b John, of Toddington; of age by 26 June 1275; *m* Margery and *d* by 1287, leaving, with an er s (John):

        1c William, of Toddington; feudal Ld of Doynton, Glos, and Burgate with Ford Hundred, Hants, 1316; *m* Joan and *d* in or after 1338, leaving, with a yr s (William, Rector Toddington 1351):

        1d John (Sir), of Studeley and Toddington, Glos; feudal Ld of Doynton; Sheriff Glos 1363, 1365, 1369, 1370 and 1378; *d* on or after 16 Nov 1388, leaving:

          1e William (Sir); feudal Ld Toddington, Sheriff Glos 1394 and 1417, Collector Subsidy (a tax) Glos 1404 and 1420; *m* Alice (*m* 2nd Edmund Giffard) and had, with two yst sons (Thomas, living 4 April 1408; Robert, living 4 April 1408):

            1f WILLIAM

          2f John, of N Piddle, where land leased him by his f 1424; bought further land there 1444–49; *m* Agnes and *d* in or after 1458, leaving three sons (William; John; Roger) and two daus (Florence; Joyce)

Sir WILLIAM's est s,

  WILLIAM TRACY; Glos: Sheriff 1420 and 1443, MP 1442; *m* Margaret (living 1446) and *d* by 4 Oct 1477, leaving:

HENRY (HARRY) TRACY; of age by 4 Oct 1477; *m* Alice, dau and coheir of Thomas Baldington, of Adderbury, Oxon, and *d* by 5 Feb 1506, leaving:

Sir WILLIAM TRACY, of Toddington; Sheriff Glos 1512; *m* Margaret, dau of Sir Thomas Throckmorton, of Corse Court, Glos, and *d* in or after 1530 (by which time he was a Protestant, though it is possible he did not die till after the major Dissolution of the Monasteries in 1536 since he is described in some sources as having acquired several former church estates), having had, with other issue:

1 WILLIAM, for whom *see* futher below

2 Richard, of Stanway, Glos; *m* Barbara, dau of Thomas Lucy (*see* RAMSAY-FAIRFAX-LUCY, Bt), and *d* 1569, leaving:

  (1) Sir PAUL TRACY(E), 1st Bt (E), so *cr* 9 June 1611, of Stanway; *b c* 1550; Sheriff Glos 1586–87; *m* 1st *c* 1580 Anne, dau of Ralph Shakerley, of Aynho, Northants, and had 10 sons and 10 daus; *m* 2nd 19 Aug 1619 Anne, dau of Sir Ambrose Nicholas, Ld Mayor London 1575, and widow of William Dutton, and *d* 4 March 1625/6, having had no issue by her; his est surv s by his 1st w:

    1a Sir RICHARD TRACY, 2nd Bt; *b c* 1581; *educ* Queen's Coll Oxford and Middle Temple; ktd 1603, Sheriff Glos 1628–29; *m c* 20 July 1603 Anne, 3rd dau of Sir Thomas Coningsby, of Hampton Court, Herefs, and was *bur* 25 Aug 1637, leaving:

      1b Sir HUMPHREY TRACY, 3rd Bt; *b c* 1611; *educ* Queen's Coll Oxford and Middle Temple; Sheriff Glos 1639–40, royalist Civil War, when estate sequestrated; *m* Elizabeth — and was *bur* 15 Jan 1657/8, leaving:

        1c Sir RICHARD TRACY, 4th Bt; *dsp* unm and was *bur* 6 July 1666

      2b Sir JOHN TRACY, 5th and last Bt; *bapt* 3 Aug 1612(?); *m* by 10 Sept 1663 Juliana, dau of Sir Erasmus de la Fontaine, and *dsp* 28 Feb 1677/8, when the btcy expired, leaving the Stanway estate to Ferdinando, s of 3rd Viscount Tracy of Rathcoole (*see* below)

  (2) Samuel, of Clifford Priory, Herefs; *m* and left issue; his ggs Samuel Tracy was living unmarried aged 29 in 1683

3 Robert, *dsp*

The est s,

WILLIAM TRACY, of Toddington; *m* Agnes, dau of Sir Simon Digby, of Col(e)shill, Warwicks (*see* DIGBY, B), and had:

JOHN TRACY, of Toddington; *m* Elizabeth, dau of 1st Baron Chandos of Sudeley (*see* CHANDOS, V, preliminary remarks), and *d* 1551, leaving, with other issue:

Sir JOHN TRACY, of Toddington; *m* Anne, dau of Sir Thomas Throckmorton, of Tortworth, Glos, and *d* 25 Sept 1591, leaving:

JOHN TRACY, 1st BARON and VISCOUNT TRACY OF RATHCOOLE, Co Dublin (I), so *cr* 12 Jan 1642/3; *b c* 1570; served in an expdn to Normandy 1591, where ktd 8 Oct; MP Glos 1597–98, Sheriff Glos 1609, royalist Civil War, hence estate sequestrated 1644; *m c* 1590 Anne, 5th dau of Sir Thomas Shirley, of Wiston, Sussex, and *d* between 7 May 1647 and 14 Feb 1647/48, leaving:

ROBERT TRACY, 2nd BARON and VISCOUNT TRACY OF RATHCOOLE; *b c* 1592; *educ* Queen's Coll Oxford and Middle Temple; ktd 1616, MP Glos 1620–22, 1626 and March-May 1640, royalist Civil War; *m* 1st by 1617 Bridget, sis of Sir Thomas Lyttelton, 1st Bt (*see* COBHAM, V), and had, with other issue:

1 JOHN TRACY, 3rd BARON and VISCOUNT TRACY OF RATHCOOLE; *b* 1617; *educ* Queen's Coll Oxford and Middle Temple; *m c* 1655 Elizabeth, 3rd dau of 1st Baron Leigh (*qv*) of Stonleigh of the 1643 *cr*, and *d* 8 March 1686/7, having had, with other issue:

  (1) WILLIAM TRACY, 4th BARON and VISCOUNT TRACY OF RATHCOOLE; *m* 1st *c* 12 July 1679 Frances Devereux, dau of 6th Viscount Hereford (*qv*), and had:

    1a Elizabeth; *m* 1st Robert Burdett, of Foremark, Derbys, and had issue (*see* LATYMER, B); *m* 2nd 1716 Robert Holden, of Aston, Derbys, and had further issue. He *d* 7 June 1746

  (1) (cont.) The 4th VISCOUNT *m* 2nd *c* 30 Aug 1688 his cousin Jane, dau of Sir Thomas Leigh (*see* LEIGH, B), and *d* 18 April 1712, leaving:

    1a THOMAS CHARLES TRACY, 5th BARON and VISCOUNT TRACY OF RATHCOOLE; *b* 27 July 1690; *m* 1st 27 Dec 1712 Elizabeth, sis of Sir William Keyt, 3rd Bt, and had:

      1b William; *b* 25 Aug 1715; *educ* Univ Coll Oxford; *dvp* unm and was *bur* 15 April 1752

      1b THOMAS CHARLES TRACY, 6th BARON and VISCOUNT TRACY OF RATHCOOLE; *b* 15 June 1719; *m* 10 Feb 1755 Harriet (*bur* 8 Aug 1795), dau of Peter Bathurst, of Clarendon Park, Wilts (*see* FERRERS, E), and *dsp* 10 Aug 1792

      1b Jane; *m* 7 Oct 1743 Capel Hanbury and had issue (*see* above **Lineage (of Hanbury)**)

    1a (cont.) The 5th VISCOUNT *m* 2nd Frances, 1st dau of Sir John Pakington, 4th Bt (*see* HAMPTON, B), and *d* 4 June 1756, leaving:

      3b JOHN TRACY, 7th BARON and VISCOUNT TRACY OF RATHCOOLE; *b* 18 Aug 1722; *educ* Abingdon GS and Univ Coll Oxford 1741, BA 1745, Fell All Souls and MA there 1749, U Proctor 1755, BD 1757, DD 1761, Warden All Souls 1766–93, Rector Didbrook; *d* unm 2 Feb 1793

      4b Robert Pakington; *b* 28 Aug 1725; *d* unm Aug 1748

      5b HENRY LEIGH TRACY, 8th and last BARON and VISCOUNT TRACY OF RATHCOOLE; *b* 25 Jan 1732/3; *educ* Abingdon GS; Lt 7th Foot (Roy Fus) 1757, Capt 98th Foot 1760–63; *m* 12 Dec 1767 Susannah (*bur* 25 Nov 1783), dau of Anthony Weaver, of Morville, Salop, and n of Anne Weaver (*m* 1707 John Blayney, of Gregynog, nr Newtown, Montgomeryshire, whose s by her Arthur Blayney *dsp* 1795, leaving his Welsh estates to the 8th VISCOUNT), and *dspm* 29 April 1797, when his titles expired, leaving:

        1d HENRIETTA SUSANNA Tracy; inherited the Welsh property (*see* above) and property in Salop which her husb sold to increase the size of his Montgomeryshire estate; *m* 29 Dec 1798 **1st Baron Sudeley of Toddington** (*see* above) and *d* 5 June 1839

  (2) Ferdinando; *b* 1659; inherited Stanway from his cousin Sir JOHN TRACY, 5th and last Bt (*see* above); *m* 1680 Katherine, dau of Sir Anthony Keck, and *d* 1682, leaving:

    1a John; *m* Anne, only dau of Sir Robert Atkins, of Saperton, Ch Baron Exchequer, and *d* 1735, leaving, with other issue:

1b Anthony TRACY later TRACY-KECK; *m* Lady Susan Hamilton, dau of 4th Duke of Hamilton (*see* HAMILTON and BRANDON, D) and *d* 30 May 1769, leaving:

   1c Henrietta Charlotte; *m* 12th Viscount Hereford (*qv*; *dsp*)

   2c Susan; *m* Francis Charteris, Lord Elcho (*see* WEMYSS and MARCH, E, in whose family Stanway remains)

2 Horace; *bapt* 28 June 1618

The 2nd VISCOUNT ,*m* 2nd Dorothy (*d* 1685), dau of Thomas Cocks, of Castleditch, Herefs, and was *bur* 11 May 1662, having by her had:

3 Robert; *b c* 1655; Judge Common Pleas; *d* 11 Sept 1735, having had issue

SUFFIELD

Arms: Quarterly, 1st and 4th, quarterly az. and gu., an imperial crown or between four lions rampant arg. (for HARBORD); 2nd and 3rd, arg. a fleur-de-lys gu. (for MORDEN). **Crest:** On a chapeau gu., doubled erm., a lion couchant arg. **Supporters:** Dexter, a lion rampant or, charged on the shoulder with a fleur-de-lys gu., gorged with a crown flory az. and chained of the last; sinister, a leopard guardant ppr., gorged with a similar crown and chained or. **Motto:** *Æquanimiter* ('Even-mindedly'). **Creations:** Bt. (GB) 22 March 1745/6, B. (GB) 21 Aug 1786.

THE 11TH BARON SUFFIELD, of Suffield, Norfolk, and a **Baronet** (Sir Anthony Philip Harbord-Hamond, Bt, MC (1950)) [Maj The Rt Hon The Lord Suffield MC, Gardeners Cottage, Gunton Park, Hanworth, Norfolk NR11 7HL]; *b* 19 June 1922; *s f* 1951; *educ* Eton; Maj Coldstream Gds (ret 1961), WW II 1942–45 N Africa and Italy, Malaya 1948–50, Offr Order Orange-Nassau with swords 1950, memb Gentlemen-at-Arms 1973–92 (Harbinger 1990–92); *m* 16 Jan 1952 Elizabeth Eve (*d* 1995), er dau of His Hon Judge Richard Edgedale (*see* ALDENHAM and HUNSDON OF HUNSDON, B), and has:

1 +CHARLES ANTHONY ASSHETON [The Hon Charles Harbord-Hamond, 12B Albert Bridge Rd, London SW11 4PY]; *b* 3 Dec 1953; *educ* Eton; Capt Coldstream Gds 1972–79, Equerry to HM THE QUEEN 1977; *m* 10 Sept 1983 (*divorce* 1990) Lucy Lennox Scrope, yr dau of Cdr A S Hutchinson, of Langford Grange, Lechlade, Glos

2 +John Edward Richard [The Hon John Harbord-Hamond, 28 Swanage Rd, London SW18 2DY]; *b* 10 July 1956; *educ* Eton and RMA Sandhurst; barrister; *m* 16 July 1983 *Katy (Katherine Margaret Lucy), dau of Maj Raymond Seymour (*see* HERTFORD, M), and has:

   (1) +Sam Charles Antony; *b* 1989

   (2) +George Edward Seymour; *b* 1991

   (3) +A son; *b* 19 March 1996

   (1) *Alice Mary; *b* 1986

3 +Robert Philip Morden [The Hon Robert Harbord-Hamond, Harbord House, Cromer, Norfolk]; *b* 10 March 1964; *educ* Harrow; *m* 1st 12 March 1994 (*divorce* 1998) Sarah Jane, only dau of Derek Stevens; *m* 2nd 29 April 1998 *Anita Ferruzi

1 *Caroline Mary Elaine [The Hon Mrs Twiston-Davies, The Mynd, Much Dewchurch, Herefs HR2 8DN]; *b* 15 Dec 1960; *m* 1985 *Audley William Twiston-Davies and has issue (*see* ARCHDALE, Bt)

Lineage: JOHN MORDEN, of Gt Bradley, Suffolk, and Suffield, Norfolk; *b c* 1657; *m* Judith, sis and coheir of Harbord CROPLEY later HARBORD, of Gunton Hall, Norfolk (which he inherited 1710 from his maternal uncle John Harbord), and est dau of William Cropley, of Hawley, Suffolk (by Catherine, dau of Sir Charles Harbord, Surveyor-Gen to CHARLES I), and *d* 27 Oct 1726, having had an est s:

Sir WILLIAM MORDEN later HARBORD (Act of Parl 1742 on inheriting Gunton from his maternal uncle), **1st Bt** (GB), so *cr* 22 March 1745/6, KB; *m* 25 April 1732 Elizabeth (*d* 8 Aug 1777), dau and coheir of Robert Britiffe, of Baconsthorpe, Norfolk, and *d* 17 Feb 1770, leaving:

Sir Harbord Harbord, 2nd Bt, and **1st Baron Suffield**, of Suffield, Co Norfolk (GB), so *cr* 21 Aug 1786; *b* 15/26 Jan 1734; MP (Whig) Norwich 1756–86, Groom Bedchamber 1763; *m* 7 Oct 1760 Mary (*d* 1 June 1823), dau and coheir (with her sis Elizabeth, *m* 1st Earl of Wilton, *qv*) of Sir Ralph Assheton, 3rd Bt, of Middle-

ton, Lancs (for whose earlier ancestry *see* CLITHEROE, B), and *d* 4 Feb 1810, having had, with other issue:

1 WILLIAM ASSHETON HARBORD, **2nd Baron Suffield**; *b* 21 Aug 1766; MP Ludgershall 1790–96 and Plympton 1807–10, Ld Lt Norfolk 1808–21, V-Adml Suffolk; *m* 4 June 1792 Lady Caroline Hobart (*d* 27 Oct 1850), dau of 2nd Earl of Buckinghamshire (*qv*), and *dsp* 1 Aug 1821

2 EDWARD, **3rd Baron**

1 Mary; *m* 1783 Sir George Armytage, 4th Bt (*qv*)

2 Louisa; *d* 2 March 1838

3 Catherine; *m* 1802 J Petre

The 2nd BARON's bro,

EDWARD HARBORD, **3rd Baron Suffield**; *b* 10 Nov 1781; *educ* Eton and Ch Ch Oxford; MP (Whig, later (from *c* 1819) self-professed 'Liberal' at a time when the term was not in general use as a party label, being in favour of abolishing the slave trade and relaxing both the penal regime and the game laws) Yarmouth (Norfolk) 1806–12 and Shaftesbury 1820–21; *m* 1st 19 Sept 1809 Georgiana (*d* 30 Sept 1824), dau and heiress of 2nd Baron Vernon (*qv*) of Kinderton, and had:

1 EDWARD VERNON HARBORD, **4th Baron Suffield**; *b* 19 June 1813; *educ* Eton and Ch Ch Oxford; MFH Quorn 1838; *m* 1 Sept 1835 Charlotte Susannah (*dsp* 15 Aug 1859), only dau of 2nd Baron Gardner (*see* 1970 edn) of Uttoxeter, and *dsp* 22 Aug 1853

2 Alfred Assheton; *b* 29 Jan 1819; Army Offr; *d* 1841

1 Georgiana Mary; *m* 1st 2 Oct 1837 George Edward Anson, CB (*d* 1849); *m* 2nd 24 Oct 1855 Charles Edward Boothby and *d* 13 Nov 1903, having had issue (*see* BOOTHBY, Bt)

The **3rd Baron** *m* 2nd 12 Sept 1826 Emily Harriett (*d* 3 Jan 1881), yst dau of Evelyn Shirley (*see* FERRERS, E), and was *k* in a fall from his horse 6 July 1835, having by her had:

3 CHARLES HARBORD, **5th Baron Suffield**, GCVO (1901), KCB (1876), PC (1886), JP, DL Norfolk; *b* 2 Jan 1830; Lt 7th Hussars 1848, Hon Col 3rd Vol Bn Norfolk Regt, Col 2nd Bde E Div RA, formerly 7th Hus, Ld-in-Waiting, ADC to HM QUEEN VICTORIA 1868–72, Ld Bedchamber to HRH THE PRINCE OF WALES later HM EDWARD VII 1872–1901, Master Buckhounds 1886, Ld-in-Waiting 1901–10; *m* 1st 4 May 1854 Cecilia Annetta (*d* 16 Feb 1911), Ldy Bedchamber to HM QUEEN ALEXANDRA, sis of 1st Baron Revelstoke (*qv*); *m* 2nd 15 July 1911 Frances Amelia Jessie Eliot (*d* 2 April 1934), widow of Col Charles C Rich, RHA, and dau of Maj Robert Poole Gabbett, RHA, and *d* 9 April 1914, having by his 1st w had, with another dau (*d* an infant):

  (1) CHARLES HARBORD, **6th Baron Suffield**, CB (1900), MVO (1902); *b* 14 June 1855; *educ* Eton; served Boer War 1900, Lt-Col and Brevet Col Scots Gds, Groom-in-Waiting in Ordinary to HM QUEEN VICTORIA 1895–1901, Capt Yeomen Gds 1916–18; *m* 26 Nov 1896 Evelyn Louisa, JP Norfolk (*d* 6 Feb 1951), dau of Capt Eustace John Wilson-Patten, er surv son of 1st and last Baron Winmarleigh (*see* 1891 edn), and *d* 10 Feb 1924, having had:

    1a VICTOR ALEXANDER CHARLES HARBORD, **7th Baron Suffield**; *b* 12 Sept 1897 (HM QUEEN VICTORIA stood sponsor); Capt Scots Gds, Page of Honour to HM GEORGE V 1910–14, served WW I 1915–18 (wounded); *m* 21 Feb 1925 (*divorce* 1937) Hon Olwen Philipps, 2nd dau of 1st and last Baron Kylsant (*see* SAINT DAVIDS, V), and *dsp* 11 June 1943

    2a JOHN HARBORD, **8th Baron Suffield**; *b* 1 July 1907; 2nd Lt 108th Suffolk and Norfolk Yeo Field Bde (RA); *d unm* 23 June 1945

    1a Doris Cecilia; *b* 12 March 1900

    2a Lettice Evelyn; *b* 12 May 1904

  (2) Assheton Edward; *b* 20 Jan 1861; Capt and Hon Maj 2nd Bde, E Div RA; *m* 3 April 1905 May Constance (*d* 7 Feb 1928), widow of Arthur Blackwood, of Melbourne, and yst dau of Surg-Gen James Macnabb Cuningham, CSI (*see* FAIRLIE-CUNINGHAME, Bt), and *d* 18 July 1929

  (1) Cecilia Margaret; *b* 15 June 1856; Ldy Bedchamber to HM QUEEN ALEXANDRA 1901–25; *m* 15 July 1878 1st Marquess of Lincolnshire, KG, and *d* 6 Oct 1934, leaving issue (*see* CARRINGTON, B)

  (2) Alice Marion, OBE (1920); *b* 23 June 1857; *m* 15 April 1886 2nd Baron Hillingdon (*see* 1970 edn) and *d* 13 Sept 1940, leaving issue. He *d* 6 April 1919

  (3) Elizabeth Evelyn; *b* 23 Feb 1860; *m* 17 April 1880 20th Baron Hastings (*qv*) and *d* 19 Feb 1956, leaving issue

  (4) Judith; *b* 12 June 1862; Maid of Honour to HM QUEEN VICTORIA; *m* 13 June 1901 Rev Sir Frederick Sullivan, 7th Bt (*qv*), and *dsp* 4 Feb 1942

  (5) Winifred; *b* 31 Dec 1864; *m* 20 July 1889 Col Geoffrey Carr Glyn, CMG, DSO, MVO, and *d* 6 Jan 1949, leaving issue (*see* WOLVERTON, B)

  (6) Eleanor; *m* 9 Feb 1895 Sir Richard George Musgrave, 12th Bt, of Hartley Castle (*qv*), and *d* 12 July 1936, leaving issue

  (7) Bridget Louisa; *m* 20 June 1898 Hon Sir Derek Keppel, GCVO, KCB, CMG, CIE, and *d* 24 Sept 1951, leaving issue (*see* ALBEMARLE, E)

4 William; *b* 22 Jan 1831; Lt Scots Gds, Capt 90th Regt; *m* 1st 17 Nov 1855 Gertrude Hyde (*d* 8 April 1881), 2nd dau of Charles Dennis, and had, with another dau (*d unm*):

  (1) Morden Charles; *b* 30 July 1858; *m* 17 March 1885 Emilia, dau of Cornelius Kleinschmidt, of Bahia, and *dsp* 10 April 1911

  (2) Alfred Cropley; *b* 15 March 1860; *m* 25 July 1903 Marta Alexandrine Wilhelmina Lundmann and *dsp* 2 April 1916

  (3) Geoffrey Walter Harbord, **9th Baron Suffield**; *b* 12 Nov 1861; *m* 19 March 1902 Eliza Jane (*d* 10 May 1933), widow of A R Beaumont and dau of John Mills, and *dsp* 23 May 1946

  (1) Theresa Mary; *m* 1 Jan 1887 Philip Edward Ripley and *d* 5 June 1924

4 (*cont.*) Capt The Hon William Harbord *m* 2nd 3 Nov 1886 Edith Mary Augusta (*d* 4 Aug 1924), yst dau of Shadwell M Boulderson, Bengal CS, and *d* 25 July 1900

5 John (Rev); *b* 21 Feb 1832; MA Cantab, Rector S Repps, Norfolk; *m* 14 April 1857 Caroline Penelope (*d* 8 Jan 1933), 4th dau of Anthony Hamond, of Westacre, Norfolk, and *d* 23 Nov 1900, leaving, with another *s* (*d* an infant):

  (1) Ralph Assheton; *b* 10 Sept 1859; Capt 1st Vol Bn Norfolk Regt; *m* 7 June 1899 Mary Ada Portman (*d* 13 May 1900), only dau of Maj Francis Hastings

Toone Gordon-Cumming (*see* GORDON CUMMING, Bt), and *d* 18 May 1913, leaving:

1a Judith Mary; *b* 5 March 1900

(2) Philip, of Northwold Lodge, Brandon, and Morden Ho, Cromer, JP Norfolk; *b* 6 Sept 1861; Lt 1st Vol Bn Norfolk Regt; *m* 26 Oct 1892 Elinor Julia (*d* 1 Jan 1932), dau of Henry William Forester (*see* FORESTER, B), and *d* 19 April 1928, having had:

1a John, MC (1918); *b* 12 Aug 1893; Capt 1st Norfolk Yeo WW I (despatches); *d* 10 July 1918 of wounds recd in action

2a Philip Anthony Assheton, MC; *b* 1 Aug 1897; Lt Gren Gds WW I (despatches); *d* 1 Dec 1917 of wounds recd in action

(3) RICHARD MORDEN, **10th Baron**

(4) Arthur Morden (Rev); *b* 11 Sept 1866; BA Cantab, Rector Chilton Foliat, Wilts 1907–16; *d* 21 May 1929

(5) Lionel Anthony; *b* 19 Feb 1870; Capt RFC (later RAF), formerly Beds Militia, Egyptian Mounted Police (ADC to Lord Kitchener) and Roy Norfolk Regt, WW I; *m* 30 Aug 1893 Mary Sophy Theresa (*d* 19 Feb 1956), yst dau of Henry Sydenham Singleton, of Melland Hazely, Winchfield, and *d* 21 Aug 1919, leaving:

1a Phyllis Mary; *b* 20 Sept 1895; *m* 17 Sept 1919 George Henry Pryce (*d* 19 Aug 1950), yst s of Lt-Col John Pryce, of Gunley, Montgomeryshire, and had:

1b *Richard Anthony Seyssyllt Mostyn; *b* 2 July 1921; *educ* Radley; Maj 12th FF Regt IA WW II

1b *Mary Rosamond; *b* 19–; WRNS WW II

2a Patience; *b* 31 July 1900; *d* unm 27 Aug 1965

3a Sophy Almina; *b* 1902; *m* 16 Nov 1921 (*divorce* 1938) Gerald Howard Wilson, of Belcombe, Saxlingham, Norfolk, only surv s of Cecil Wilson, of High Ho, Thorpe, Norwich, and had:

1b *Gillian Mary; *b* 17 Sept 1923

2b *April Geraldine; *b* 10 April 1925; *educ* Kingdon Ward Sch of Speech Therapy, SW1 (LCST 1962)

(6) Cecil Edward; *b* 31 Jan 1871; *d* unm 7 July 1893

(7) Maurice Assheton, JP Witwatersrand; *b* 24 Oct 1874; *educ* Haileybury; Inspr Johannesburg Town Police 1902–08, Capt Res Offrs, Capt 1st Imp Light Horse Boer War 1899–1902; *m* 1st 27 Sept 1905 (*divorce* 1918) Isabel Jessie Lowth, widow of Richard Hedley Robinson, of Kirkby Mallory Hall, Leics, and 4th dau of Baron Frederic von Wurtzburg-Schade, of Wurtzburg, Prussia; *m* 2nd 30 April 1929 Ethel Florence (*d* 1992), widow of Francis Tugwell Cowley and dau of George William Goldsmith, of Hastings, and *d* 9 Jan 1954, leaving:

1a +Patrick Rupert Shirley [Patrick Harbord Esq, 16 Clarence Rd, Bohemia, St Leonards-on-Sea, Sussex]; *b* 2 Aug 1930; *m* 15 Jan 1955 *Jean Shirley, dau of Reginald George Webb, of Pebsham Farm Cottage, Bexhill-on-Sea, and has:

1b +Alan Anthony [Alan Harbord Esq, Brookwood, 44 Wadhurst Close, St Leonards-on-Sea, E Sussex TN37 7AZ]; *b* 20 May 1956; *m* 1977 (*divorce* 1997) Nicola, only dau of R Greenhalf, of Hastings, and has:

1c +Matthew Aaron; *b* 1984

1c *Stacey Jane; *b* 1977

1b *Shirley Ann [Mrs Roy Jennings, Owls Roost, 9 Aviemore Dve, Oakley, Hants]; *b* 28 June 1958; *m* 1984 *Roy Anthony Jennings, only s of Lawrence Hamilton Jennings, of Gt Yarmouth, Norfolk

2a +Ralph Assheton Edward [Ralph Harbord Esq, Scotsford Cottage, 12 New Town, Uckfield, E Sussex]; *b* 16 March 1932; *m* 1 Aug 1959 *Angela, only dau of Stanley Walter D'Eath, of St Leonards-on-Sea, Sussex, and has had:

1b +Richard; *b* 23 Nov 1964

1b A dau; *b* 16 Feb 1970

(1) Mary; *b* 28 Jan 1858; *m* 3 Sept 1878 Geoffrey Fowell Buxton, CB (*see* BUXTON, Bt), and *d* 18 Nov 1940, leaving issue

(2) Rachael; *b* 6 April 1864; *m* 2 June 1908 Rev Andrew Robert Vaughan Daubeney, Vicar Croxton, Norfolk, and *dsp* 26 Feb 1947

(3) Dorothy; *b* 21 Jan 1868; *d* unm 14 Sept 1940

(4) Katharine *b* 13 Jan 1869; *d* unm 2 Jan 1953

(5) Margaret; *b* 6 Dec 1872; *d* unm 22 May 1956

(6) Maud; *b* 1 July 1877; *m* 1 July 1897 Col Alexander Graham Shortt, RA, and *d* 3 Jan 1952, leaving issue. He *d* 1951

(7) Hilda; *b* 31 Jan 1881; *d* unm 29 Dec 1964

6 Ralph; *b* 17 May 1833; Capt 71st Regt, memb Household of Ld Lt Ireland; *m* 5 Sept 1865 Elizabeth Pole (*d* 6 March 1915), 2nd dau of Edward W H Schenley, of Prince's Gate, and *d* 6 Jan 1878, having had, with another dau (*d* unm):

(1) Edward Ralph, DSO (1900), MC (1919); *b* 7 April 1870; *educ* Clifton; Capt 3rd Bn Cheshire Regt, Boer War 1900 and WW I (wounded, POW); *m* 17 Oct 1906 Annie Evelyn (*d* 1980), est dau of Henry Herbert Riley-Smith, of Toulston, Tadcaster, and *d* 29 May 1950, leaving:

1a William Edward; *b* 15 Dec 1908; *educ* Eton and Worcester Coll Oxford; dep chm John Smith's Tadcaster Brewery; *m* 1st 9 June 1938 (*divorce* 1949) Vivien Sylvia, dau of Lt-Col Foster Newton Thorne, Roy Sussex Regt, and Lady Aykroyd, and *d* 28 July 1992, leaving:

1b +Charles Francis [Charles Harbord Esq, Torres do Colegio, Monte Judeu, 8600 Lagos, Portugal]; *b* 2 Oct 1943; *educ* Harrow; *m* 1st 1 May 1972 Honor Lois, yr dau of Thomas Saul, of Seacroft, Lincs; *m* 2nd 1980 *Sarah Juliet, dau of Peter Blandy, of Chelsea, and has:

1c *Astrid Anne Sylvia; *b* 1981

2c *Davina Auriol Bridget; *b* 1986

2b David Ralph Foster; *b* 18 Sept 1947; *educ* Worksop Coll; Capt 15th/19th King's Roy Hus; *m* 10 May 1974 *Lauretta Chinty (*m* 2nd 1978 Nicholas Charles Wetherill Ridley), only dau of Sir Henry John William Bruce, 6th Bt, of Downhill (*qv*), and *d* following an accident 22 July 1974

1a (cont.) William Harbord *m* 2nd 5 Dec 1950 (*divorce* 1959) Christine Winifred, dau, of Alan Higham, of Richmond, Surrey, and by her had:

3b +Christopher Evelyn; *b* 25 March 1953; *educ* Albury, NSW

1b *Gay Diana; *b* 15 Nov 1951

2a +Ralph Evelyn; *b* 2 Feb 1915; *educ* Eton; Lt RNVR WW II, Flag Lt to C-in-C Plymouth, Freeman City London; *m* 10 April 1950 Madeleine Betty Kezia (*d* 23 Oct 1993), only dau of Robert Finlay-Greig, of Buenos Aires, and *d* 9 May 1993, leaving:

1b +Robert Ralph; *b* 9 Dec 1950; *educ* Eton; Lt RGJ 1970; *m* 1984 *Clare Mary Petre, dau of Capt Thomas Hornsby (*see* PETRE, B), and has:

1c +Harry Robert Thomas; *b* 1991

2c +Charles Edward Ralph; *b* 1994

2b +Jeremy Julian; *b* 22 May 1953; *educ* Eton and RMC Sandhurst; Lt TAVR, late Capt Life Gds; *m* 1984 *Monique Katherine Marie, er dau of Maj Theobald Henry Robert Fetherstonhaugh, and has:

1c +James Henry Sebastian Charles; *b* 1988

1c *Sophie India Charlotte; *b* 1986

1a *Bridget [Mrs Noel Nickols, 2 Beech Court, Harrogate, N Yorks HG2 0EU]; *b* 23 Aug 1907; *m* 21 Oct 1931 Noel Fraser Nickols (*d* 25 April 1966), s of Harold Nickols, of Sandford Ho, Kirkstall, Leeds

2a *Elizabeth Mary [Mrs John Hodges, 31 Marlborough Court, Pembroke Rd, London W8 6DE]; *b* 22 Aug 1912; Ch Offr WRNS WW II, CStJ; *m* 9 Nov 1946 Capt John Michael Hodges, DSO, CStJ, RN (*d* 1987), s of Adml Sir Michael Hodges, KCB, CMG, MVO, of The White Ho, Thatcham, Berks, and has:

1b *Patrick Michael [Patrick Hodges Esq, Bentworth Place, Bentworth, Hants GU34 5JP]; *b* 16 March 1948; *educ* Eton; *m* 1974 *Alison Mary, dau of W/Cdr Roy Dossetter, RAF, of Andover, and has:

1c *Rupert Henry; *b* 1982

1c *Katherine Mary; *b* 1978

1b *Judith Evelyn [Mrs William Heal, Burgh Parva Hall, Melton Constable, Norfolk NR24 2PU]; *b* 16 Dec 1952; *m* 1982 *Maj William F A Heal, Roy Anglian Regt, s of Lt Col W A Heal, OBE, of Denston, Suffolk, and has:

1c *Jeremy William Austin; *b* 1984

1c *Olivia Claire Evelyn; *b* 1983

3a *(Dorothy) Primrose [Mrs Edward d'Abo, 18 White Rock Ho, White Rock Rd, Hastings, E Sussex TN34 1LE]; *b* 26 March 1919; *m* 29 June 1939 *Maj Edward Nassau Nicolai d'Abo, KOYLI (RARO), yr s of Gerard Louis d'Abo (*see* KINDERSLEY, B), and has:

1b *Philip Edward [Philip d'Abo Esq, The Old Squash Ct, Leigh Court Close, Cobham, Surrey KT11 2HT]; *b* 19 June 1941; *educ* Harrow; *m* 1972 *Fay Mary St Claire, dau of William Barbour, and has:

1c *Camilla Sophie Louise; *b* 1973

2c *Lucy Dorothy; *b* 1977

2b *Michael David [Michael d'Abo Esq, Hillcrest House, St George's Ave, Kings Stanley, Glos GL10 3HJ]; *b* 1 March 1944; *educ* Harrow; composer and musician; *m* 1st 23 Dec 1966 (*divorce* 1982) Margaret Evelyn, dau of George Lyndon, of Chelmsford, Essex, and has:

1c *Benjamin Byron; *b* 6 Nov 1967

1c *Olivia Jane; *b* 22 Jan 1969

2b (cont.) Michael d'Abo *m* 2nd 1982 (*divorce* 1993) Karen Sue, dau of William Gilbert, of Michigan, USA; *m* 3rd 6 April 1996 *Lisa Nicola Jane, dau of Arthur Weaver, of Twyning, Glos, and by his 2nd w has:

2c *Bruno George; *b* 18 July 1984

3b *(Andrew Gerard) Noel [Noel d'Abo Esq, 187 Amesbury Ave, London SW2 3BJ]; *b* 5 Jan 1948; *educ* Harrow; *m* 1980 *Caroline Lydia Susan, yr dau of Edward Burnham, of Chelwood Beacon Cottage, Haywards Heath, W Sussex, and had:

1c Robert Edward Louis; *b* 24 Aug, *d* 14 Sept 1980

1c *Polly Primrose; *b* 1983

2c *Phoebe Rose; *b* 1989

1b *(Penelope) Carol [Lady Baker, The Old Vicarage, Damerham, Fordingbridge, Hants SP6 3HU]; *b* 5 Jan 1948; *m* 1970 Sir Nicholas Brian Baker, MP (C) N Dorset 1979–95 (*d* 25 April 1997), s of Col Harold Stanley Baker, OBE, and has:

1c *Matthew Ronald Nicholas; *b* 1976

1c *Annabel Dorothy Clementine; *b* 1980

4a *Molly [Mrs John Atkinson-Clark, 1c Edificio El Chambel, Calle Miguel Caño 15, Marbella 29600, Spain]; *b* 28 March 1921; *m* 1st 3 June 1941 (*divorce* 1946) Lt Roy Laird-MacGregor, RA, only s of E G Laird-MacGregor, ICS, of Crawley Hill Ho, Camberley; *m* 2nd 26 Dec 1953 John Cecil Atkinson-Clark (*d* 2 Oct 1969), only s of Henry George Atkinson-Clark (*see* MEYRICK, Bt), and has:

1b *George Evelyn [George Atkinson-Clark Esq, Manor House Farm, Beckerings Park, Lidlington, Beds MK43 0RA]; *b* 18 July 1960; *educ* Eton and RAC Cirencester; Maj Scottish Yeo (TA), memb Roy Co Archers; *m* 1986 *Hon Sarah Anne Elliott, twin dau of Baron Elliott of Morpeth (LP, *qv*), and has:

1c *Edward George; *b* 25 Aug 1988

2c *Henry William; *b* 20 Feb 1993

1c *Sophie Catherine; *b* 7 April 1990

(2) Horatio; *b* 10 Feb 1875; Lt 3rd Bn S Wales Borderers; *ka* Elandslaagtye, S Africa, 25 Feb 1902

(1) Florence Mary; *m* 1916 Vere Finch, 2nd s of Henry Finch, of The Croft, Manton, Oakham (and n of Sir Arthur Fludyer, 5th Bt; see 1922 edn), and *d* 7 Aug 1937

(2) Emily Fanny; *m* 3 March 1904 Capt A J E Des Barres, Roy Irish Rifles, and *d* 24 Feb 1909, leaving issue. He *d* 11 Feb 1908

(3) Ida; *m* 9 Oct 1909 Harry Atherton Brown, est s of Charles Atherton Brown, of Grendon Hall, Atherstone, Warwicks, and *d* 26 Aug 1956, leaving issue. He *d* 18 May 1961

7 Walter; *b* 1 July 1834; Maj 7th Hus; *m* 1st 5 May 1875 (*divorce* 1900) Lady Eleanor (*d* 15 Sept 1905), widow of Herbert Fitzroy Eaton, of Stetchworth Park,

Cambs, and only dau of 7th Duke of Grafton (*qv*), and had, with another s (*d* an infant):

(1) Eric Walter, DSO (1917); *b* 14 March 1879; Capt RN WW I (despatches), WW II on staff of C-in-C Portsmouth; *m* 26 Sept 1911 Rose Mary Adeline Dagmar Amelia (*d* 28 Nov 1952), dau of Lt-Col George Charles Keppel Johnstone, Gren Gds (*see* JOHNSTONE, Bt), and *dsp* 18 March 1952

(1) Sybil Charlotte Eleanor, OBE (1920); *b* 27 Feb 1876; *m* 15 Feb 1896 Sir Herbert Walter Samuelson, KBE (*see* SAMUELSON, Bt), and *d* 20 Jan 1961, leaving issue

7 (cont.) Maj The Hon Walter Harbord *m* 2nd 1901 Mary (*d* 1939), dau of W Reid, of Moyvalley, Co Kildare, and *d* 28 Jan 1913

8 Harbord; *b* posthumously 14 Feb 1836; Hon Lt-Col Norfolk Artillery Militia; *m* 1st 21 March 1857 Constance Adelaide, 3rd dau of Sir Henry Stracey, 5th Bt (*qv*), and had:

(1) Harbord; *b* 1869; Imp Yeo Boer War 1900–01; *d* unm 8 April 1907

(1) (Constance) Nina; *m* Andrew Smith

(2) Beatrice Geraldine; *m* 14 Feb 1888 Geoffrey Frederick Pilkington Bennet, of East Barton Farm, Bury St Edmunds, 2nd s of Maj Philip Bennet, of Rougham Hall, Bury St Edmunds, Suffolk

8 (cont.) Lt-Col The Hon Harbord Harbord *m* 2nd 4 Dec 1878 Barbara Sophia Harriot (*d* 15 March 1929), widow of his niece's f-in-law Maj Philip Bennet and est dau of Edgar Disney, of The Hyde, and *d* 11 Feb 1894, having by her had:

(3) Ruth

1 Emily; *m* 19 Oct 1852 Rev Randall Burroughes, of Hoveton Hall and Burlingham Hall, Norfolk, er surv s of Henry Negus Burroughes, MP, of Burlingham Hall, and *d* 21 March 1912, leaving issue. He *d* 26 Dec 1872

The 9th BARON's cousin,

RICHARD MORDEN HARBORD later HARBORD-HAMOND (roy licence 6 Nov 1917), **10th Baron Suffield**, DL (Norfolk); *b* 24 Aug 1865, Adml, served Egyptian War 1882 (medal with clasp, bronze star) and WW I 1914–17 (Legn Hon); *m* 11 Sept 1913 Nina Annette Mary Crawfuird (*d* 8 Nov 1955), dau of John William Hutchison, of Lauriston Hall, and Edlingham, Kirkcudbrightshire, and *d* 2 Feb 1951, having had:

1 ANTHONY PHILIP HARBORD-HAMOND, **11th and present Baron Suffield**

1 Penelope Mary; VAD and American Ambulance WW II

2 *Charity Patricia; VAD and BRCS WW II

SUFFOLK and BERKSHIRE

NOUS MAINTIENDRONS

Arms: Quarterly, 1st, gu. a bend between six cross crosslets fitchées arg., on the bend an escutcheon or charged with a demi-lion rampant, pierced through the mouth with an arrow, within a double tressure flory counterflory gu. (for HOWARD); 2nd, gu. three lions passant-guardant in pale or and a label of three points arg. (for THOMAS of Brotherton, s of EDWARD I); 3rd, chequy or and az. (for WARREN); 4th, gu. a lion rampant arg. (for MOWBRAY); in the centre of the shield a crescent for difference. **Crest:** On a chapeau gu. doubled erm. a lion statant guardant, tail extended or, ducally gorged gu., and charged on the body with a crescent for difference. **Supporters:** Two lions arg., each charged on the breast with a crescent sa. **Mottoes:** *Nous maintiendrons* ('We will maintain') and *Non quid, sed quo modo* ('Not what but how'). **Creations:** E. (E) 21 July 1603 (Suffolk) and (E) 7 Feb 1625/6 (Berkshire), V. and B. (E) 22 Jan 1621/2.

THE 21ST EARL OF SUFFOLK and 14TH EARL OF BERKSHIRE, Viscount Andover, Co Southampton, and **Baron Howard of Charleton**, Wilts (Michael John James George Robert Howard) [The Rt Hon The Earl of Suffolk and Berkshire, House of Lords, London SW1A 0PW]; *b* 27 March 1935; *s* f 1941; *educ* Winchester and Le Rosey; late Sub-Lt RNVR; *m* 1st 1 Oct 1960 (*divorce* 1967) Simone, PR consultant, dau of Georges Litman, of Paris, and formerly w of Michel Paulmier, and has had:

1 Lucinda; *b* 26 March 1961; *d* 21 Dec 1962

The 21st/14th EARL *m* 2nd 22 Sept 1973 (*divorce* 1980) Anita Robsahm, yst dau of Robin Fuglesang, of Cuckfield, Sussex, and by her has:

1 +ALEXANDER CHARLES MICHAEL WINSTON ROBSAHM, *Viscount Andover*; *b* 17 Sept 1974

2 *Katherine Emma Frances Anita Robsahm; *b* 9 April 1976

The 21st/14th EARL *m* 3rd 15 Dec 1983 *Linda Jacqueline, dau of Lt-Col Vincent Rudolph Paravicini, of Nutley Manor, Basingstoke, and formerly w of 4th Viscount Bridport (*qv*), and by her has:

3 *Philippa Mimi Jacqueline Henrietta; *b* 1985

4 *Natasha Rose Catherine Linda; *b* 1987

Suffolk, other creations: Shortly after the Norman Conquest an Earldom combining Norfolk and Suffolk was conferred on one Ralph the Staller. At that time, and seemingly for nearly three centuries afterwards, no distinction was made between Norfolk and Suffolk for the purpose of conferring titles based on county names, the two areas being conflated as the land of the East Angles. In any case, with Ralph's death a few years after he was created Earl the title apparently passed back into the possession of the Crown, though within another year it seems to have been conferred on Ralph's son, called Ralph de Gael from a fief he held in Britanny. The second Ralph, Earl of this somewhat shadowy creation, rebelled against WILLIAM I (THE CONQUEROR) in 1075 and was stripped of his titles and lands.

It was not till March 1336/7 that there was another Earl of Suffolk. This time the grantee was Robert de Ufford, later also a Knight of the Garter. He was one of EDWARD III's leading associates in the early phases of the Hundred Years War. His son William de Ufford, 2nd Earl of Suffolk, was also made a KG. William's first wife was a granddaughter of Thomas of Brotherton, Earl of Norfolk and a younger son of EDWARD I. The label in the present Earls of Suffolk and Berkshire's arms derived from the Brotherton line is perhaps the clue to why the name Suffolk was chosen when Lord Thomas Howard was created an Earl in 1603.

Following William de Ufford's death, when the Earldom of Suffolk of the second creation is deemed to have expired, the title was conferred in 1385, barely three and a half years later, on Michael de la Pole, of a prosperous but bourgeois family from Hull. His career as diplomat and official flourished (he was Lord Chancellor in the mid-1380s) but his being a favourite of RICHARD II made him unpopular with the more established nobility and he was tried *in absentia* for high treason and on being found guilty forfeited his titles. Shortly before RICHARD II's own fall the son, another Michael, was restored to his father's honours but this restoration was itself annulled on HENRY IV's coming to the throne. Michael managed to make his peace with the new King, however, and had the Earldom restored to him a second time.

The 3rd Earl of Suffolk of the de la Pole family, yet another Michael, married Elizabeth Mowbray, daughter of the Duke of Norfolk of the creation prior to the Howard one (though the two families were connected by marriage anyway). Here again is a possible source of choice of Suffolk as a name title in the case of Lord Thomas Howard some two centuries later. The 4th de la Pole Earl of Suffolk played an important part in national and international affairs during HENRY V's and HENRY VI's reigns and was promoted first Marquess then Duke of Suffolk. The new Duke of Suffolk became a scapegoat for the increasing failure of English arms in France towards the end of the Hundred Years War and was first imprisoned in the Tower, then banished and finally done to death shortly after he had taken ship from English shores to go into exile.

The Duke, for all his disgrace, had never been attainted and his son John de la Pole succeeded him in the titles. John married Elizabeth of York, sister of EDWARD IV and RICHARD III, with the result that his son the 3rd Duke (and 6th Earl) of Suffolk became after the TUDORs had ascended the throne a potential claimant to it and a very real embarrassment to the new dynasty. The de la Poles, at any rate such of them who had not gone abroad or were content to live in obscurity, were accordingly liquidated by the usual Tudor methods of trumped up attainders and beheadings.

The Dukedom of Suffolk was revived for Charles Brandon, an amiable and athletic man whose grandfather, though himself of relatively obscure antecedents in East Anglia, was connected by marriage with the WINGFIELDs (*see* POWERSCOURT, V) and through them with the MOWBRAYs, hence with the 3rd Earl of Suffolk of the 1385 creation. Charles Brandon was either extraordinarily lucky or extraordinarily adroit in that his aspirations never seemed to arouse HENRY VIII's febrile suspicions. He was said at the time of his ennoblement — having started as a commoner he was a Duke by the age of thirty — to be angling for the hand of the EMPEROR MAXIMILIAN's daughter MARGARET OF SAVOY, Regent of the Netherlands, but in the end had to content himself with a trio of Kings for in-laws when he won the hand of HENRY VII's daughter Mary, Queen Dowager of LOUIS XII of France and sister of HENRY VIII of England. The Brandon-held Dukedom of Suffolk, created in February 1513/4, expired with the death in 1551 of Charles's younger son, who had held it only thirty minutes. Another Dukedom of Suffolk was conferred in a matter of weeks on Charles Brandon's son-in-law, Henry Grey, Marquess of Dorset, the father in his turn of LADY JANE GREY. With Henry's death, following in any case an act of attainder, this last ducal creation involving Suffolk also disappeared.

Berkshire, other creations: The Lord Norris (of Rycote) whose granddaughter married the 2nd Earl of Lindsey (and whose descendant is the current Earl of Lindsey and Abingdon; *qv*) was promoted Earl of Berkshire in January 1620/1 but the title did not survive him, although the Barony of Norris, being created by writ of summons, did and is a subsidiary peerage of the Earl of Lindsey and Abingdon.

Lineage: The 4th DUKE OF NORFOLK (*qv*) had by his 2nd w an est s:

THOMAS HOWARD, **1st Earl of Suffolk** (E), so *cr* 21 July 1603, and 1st BARON HOWARD DE WALDEN (*qv*), so *cr* by writ of summons to Parl 24 Oct 1597, KG (1597), PC (1603); *b* 24 Aug 1561; *educ* (?)St John's Coll Cambridge(?); Capt *Golden Lion* during defence of England against Spanish Armada 1588, ktd July 1588, cmded the sqdn in the Azores in which Sir Richard Grenville was lost aboard the *Revenge* 1591, V-Adml Cadiz Expdn 1596 and Azores Expdn 1597; Ld Lt: Cambs and Isle Ely 1598–1626, Suffolk 1605, Dorset (Jt 1611) 1613; Capt-Gen and Adml the Fleet in the Downs 1599, Constable Tower London Feb–March

1600/1, High Steward Cambridge U 1601–14, Ld Chamberlain 1603–14, frequently Jt Commr for office of Earl Marshal (*see* NORFOLK, D); played leading role in revealing the Gunpowder Plot 1605 and was apptd a Commr to interrogate the conspirators and preside at their trial (*see* also NORTHUMBERLAND, D); Capt Gent Pensioners 1605–14, a Commr Treasury 1612–14, Ld High Treasurer England 1614–18 (when relieved of his post for peculation — the evidence for which included the huge expenditure he incurred in erecting Audley End, of which JAMES I observed that it was too large for a king though it might do for a Lord Treasurer — and fined with his 2nd w (whose avarice has been blamed for his dishonesty) £30,000 (well over £1.5m in late-1990s terms), later scaled down to £7,000 and a term of imprisonment in the Tower of London); High Steward Essex 1615–25; *m* 1st by 9 May 1577 Mary (*dsp* 7 April 1578), sis and coheir of 5th Lord (Baron) Dacre (*qv*) (of Gilsland); *m* 2nd by 1583 his cousin Catherine (*d* Sept 1633), widow of Richard Rich (est s of 2nd Baron Rich; *see* WARWICK, BROOKE and, E, also 1970 edn RICH, Bt), est dau and heir of Sir Henry Knyvet(t), of Charleton, Wilts, through whom that estate came to the HOWARDs, and n of 1st and last Lord (Baron) Knyvet (of Escrick), and *d* 28 May 1626, having by her had, with other issue:

1 THEOPHILUS HOWARD, **2nd Earl of Suffolk**, KG (1627), PC (1628); *bapt* 13 Aug 1584; *educ* Magdalene Coll Cambridge; MP Maldon 1605–10, Gent Pensioners: Lt 1605–14 and Capt 1614–19, Cncllr Colony of Virginia 1609, called up to Ho Lds *vp* in f's Barony of HOWARD DE WALDEN 8 Feb 1609/10, Govr Guernsey March 1609/10, Jt Ld Lt Cumberland, Northumberland and Westmorland 1614–39 and Cambs, Suffolk and Dorset 1626–40, Ld Warden Cinque Ports and Constable Dover Castle 1628–40; *m* March 1611/2 Lady Elizabeth Home (*d* 19 Aug 1633), dau and heiress of 1st (and *de facto* last) Earl of Dunbar, of the 1605 *cr*, and *d* 3 June 1640, leaving:

(1) JAMES HOWARD, **3rd Earl of Suffolk**, KB (Feb 1625/6); *bapt* 10 Feb 1619/20; Jt Ld Lt Suffolk 1640 and Ld Lt (Parly appointment) March 1641/2 and (post-Restoration, this time with Cambs) 1660–80/1, parliamentarian Civil War, Earl Marshal for Coronation CHARLES II 1661, Jt Commr for that office 1673; *m* 1st 1 Dec 1640 Lady Susan Rich (*d* 1649), 3rd dau of 1st Earl Holland of the 1624 *cr* (for whose earlier ancestry *see* 1970 edn RICH, Bt), and had:

1a Essex; *m* 4 March 1666/7 1st Baron Griffin of Braybrooke and *d* on or after 31 Jan 1704/5, leaving issue (*see* BRAYBROOKE, B)

(1) (cont.) The **3rd Earl** *m* 2nd just after 19 Feb 1650/1 Barbara, widow of (a) Richard Wenman (s of 2nd Viscount Wenman of Tuam) and (b) Sir Richard Wentworth and dau of Sir Edward Villiers (*see* JERSEY, E), and by her had, with another dau:

2a Elizabeth; *m* Sir Thomas Felton, Bt, of Playford, Suffolk, and had issue (*see* HOWARD DE WALDEN, B)

(1) The **3rd Earl** *m* 3rd *c* 10 June 1682 Lady Anne Montagu, est dau of 3rd Earl of Manchester (*see* MANCHESTER, D), and *dspm* 7 Jan 1688, when the Barony of Howard de Walden fell into abeyance

(2) Thomas; had:

1a James; *m* Charlotte Jemima Henrietta Maria Boyle (*m* 2nd William, Earl of Yarmouth; *see* HERTFORD, M), illegitimate dau of CHARLES II by Viscountess Shannon, and *d* 1669, leaving:

1b Stuarta; Maid of Honour to QUEEN MARY II; *d* unm 1706

(3) GEORGE HOWARD, **4th Earl of Suffolk**; *b* 1625; *m* 1st Catharine, dau of John Alleyne, of Moggerhanger, Beds, and had, with other issue:

1a Mary; *m* Lt-Gen Percy Kirke, MP Looe and Keeper Whitehall Palace

2a Anne; *m* William Jephson, MP Mallow, Co Cork

(3) (cont.) The **4th Earl** *m* 2nd by 1686 Anne (*d* July 1710), widow of James Cowper and dau of John Wroth, of Loughton, Essex (by Elizabeth, dau of 1st Baron Maynard of Wicklow; *see* 1865 edn MAYNARD, V), and *dspm* 21 April 1691

(4) HENRY HOWARD, **5th Earl of Suffolk**; *bapt* 18 July 1627; *m* 1st between 30 Nov 1660 and 1670 Mary, only dau and heiress of 3rd Baron Castle Stuart (*see* CASTLE STEWART, E), and had:

1a HENRY HOWARD, **6th Earl of Suffolk**, also 1st EARL OF BINDON, Co Dorset, and BARON CHESTERFORD, Co Essex (both E), so *cr vp* 30 Dec 1706, PC (1708 and 1714); *b* 1670; *educ* Magdalene Coll Cambridge; MP (Whig) Arundel 1695–98 and Essex 1705–06, Dep Earl Marshal 1706–18, Ld Lt Essex 1714–18; *m* 1st 6 Aug 1691 Lady Auberie Anne Penelope O'Brien (*d* 2 Dec 1703), 4th dau of 6th Earl of Thomond (*see* INCHIQUIN, B), and had:

1a CHARLES WILLIAM HOWARD, **7th Earl of Suffolk** and 2nd and last EARL OF BINDON; *b* 9 May 1693; *m* 9 July 1715 Arabella, dau and coheir of Sir Samuel Astry, of Henbury, Glos, and *dsp* 9 Feb 1721/2, when the Earldom of Bindon and Barony of Chesterford expired

1a (cont.) The **6th Earl** *m* 2nd April 1705 Henrietta (*dsp* 2 Aug 1715), widow of his 1st w's bro Henry Horatio O'Brien, Lord Ibrackan, and 3rd dau of 1st Duke of Beaufort (*qv*), and *d* 19 Sept 1718

2a EDWARD HOWARD, **8th Earl of Suffolk**; *b* 1672; imprisoned Tower London 1725 for trafficking in documents protecting the bearer from arrest; poetaster; *d* unm 22 June 1731

3a CHARLES HOWARD, **9th Earl of Suffolk**; *b* 1675; *m* 2 March 1705/6 Henrietta (GEORGE II's mistress; *m* 2nd 26 June 1735 Hon George Berkeley (*see* BERKELEY, B) and *d* aged *c* 79 26 July 1767), sis of 1st Earl of Buckinghamshire (*qv*), and *d* 28 Sept 1733, leaving:

1b HENRY HOWARD, **10th Earl of Suffolk**; *b* 1 Jan 1706/7; MP (Whig but anti-Walpole) Beeralston 1728–33; *m* 13 May 1735 Sarah (*m* 2nd 10 Oct 1752 7th Viscount Falkland (*qv*) and *d* 27 May 1776), only dau and heiress of Thomas Inwen, of Southwark, and *dsp* 22 April 1745

(4) (cont.) The **5th Earl** *m* 2nd 22 Nov 1691 Mary (*d* Jan 1720/1), widow of (a) Charles Vermuyden, MD, and (b) Sir John Maynard, Serjeant-at-law, and est dau of Rev Ambrose Upton, Canon Ch Ch Oxford, and *d* 10 Dec 1709

(1) Catherine; *m* 1st George Stewart, Lord D'Aubigny (*ka* Edgehill 23 Oct 1642), 2nd s of 3rd Duke of Lennox (*see* MORAY, E); *m* 2nd *c* 1649 1st Earl of Newburgh (*qv*) and *d* 1650

(2) Elizabeth; *m* 1 Oct 1642, as his 2nd w, 4th Earl of Northumberland of the 1557 *cr* (*see* NORTHUMBERLAND, D), and *d* 11 March 1704/5, having had issue

(3) Margaret; *m* 1st Earl of Orrery (*see* CORK and ORRERY, E) and had issue

(4) Anne; *m* Thomas Walsingham, of Scadbury, Kent, and had issue (*see* ROSSE, E)

(5) Frances; *m* Sir Edward Villiers (*see* JERSEY, E)

2 THOMAS HOWARD, **1st Earl of Berkshire**, so *cr vp* 7 Feb 1625/6, as also earlier 22 Jan 1621/2 BARON HOWARD OF CHARLETON, Wilts, and VISCOUNT ANDOVER, Co Southampton (all E), KG (1625), KB (Jan 1604/5); *b c* 1590; *educ* Cambridge; MP Lancaster 1605–11, Wilts 1614 and Cricklade 1620–22; royalist Civil War; *m* 26 May 1614 Lady Elizabeth Cecil, dau of 2nd Earl of Exeter (*see* EXETER, M), and *d* 16 July 1669, having had, with another s and dau (*dsp*):

(1) CHARLES HOWARD, **2nd Earl of Berkshire**, KB (Feb 1625/6); called up to Ho Lds *vp* 3 Nov 1640 in f's Barony; *m* 10 April 1637 Dorothy, 2nd dau of Thomas, Viscount Savage, and gdau of Countess Rivers in her own right, and *d* 1679, having had three sons (*dvp*) and two daus (both of whom *dsp*, one having *m* Sir Henry Bedingfeld, 2nd Bt, *qv*)

(2) THOMAS HOWARD, **3rd Earl of Berkshire**; *bapt* 14 Nov 1619; MP Wallingford 1641–44, royalist Civil War; *m* 1st Frances, dau of Sir Richard Harrison, of Hurst, Berks, and had:

1a Frances; *m* Sir Henry Winchcombe and with him was ancestor of the HOWARD-HARTLEYs of Bucklebury, Berks

2a Mary; *d* unm

(2) (cont.) The **3rd Earl** *m* 2nd Margaret (*dsp*), dau of Sir Thomas Parker, of Ratton, Sussex, and *dspm* 12 April 1706

(3) Henry; inherited the Rivensby estate from his gf, 2nd Earl of Exeter; *m* Elizabeth (*m* 3rd as his 2nd w 1st and last Baron Crofts of Saxham), widow of 1st and last Baron Craven (*qv*) of Ryton and dau of 2nd Baron Spencer of Wormleighton (*see* MARLBOROUGH, D), and *dsp* 1663, when Rivensby passed to the **11th/4th Earl**

(4) William; *bapt* 27 June 1622; *m* Elizabeth, dau of a Lord of Session in Scotland, and had, with a dau (Dorothy, *m* Col James Graham, of Levens, Westmorland, and had Catherine, w of her cousin **11th/4th Earl**):

1a Craven; *m* 1st 29 July 1673 Anne Ogle; *m* 2nd (licence 30 May 1683) Mary, dau and heiress of Col George Bowes, of Elford Hall, Staffs, and *d* 7 June 1700, leaving by her:

1b HENRY BOWES HOWARD, **4th Earl of Berkshire** and **11th Earl of Suffolk**, as which *s* cousin 22 April 1745; *b* 4 Nov 1687; Dep Earl Marshal 1718–25; *m* 5 March 1708/9 his cousin Catherine (*d* 13 March 1762), dau of Col James Graham, and *d* 21 March 1757, having had:

1c William, *Viscount Andover*; *b* 23 Dec 1714; *m* 6 Nov 1736 Lady Mary Finch (*d* 16 March 1803), 2nd dau of 2nd Earl of Aylesford (*qv*), and *d* 18 July 1756, leaving:

1d HENRY HOWARD, **12th Earl of Suffolk** and **5th Earl of Berkshire**, KG (1778), PC (1771); *b* 10 or 16 May 1739; *educ* Eton and Magdalen Coll Oxford; Ld Privy Seal Jan–June 1771, Sec State for North 1771–79; *m* 1st 25 May 1764 Mary Constantia (*dsps* 8 Feb 1767), dau of 1st Viscount Hampden (*qv*); *m* 2nd 14 Aug 1777 Lady Charlotte Finch (*d* 7 July 1808), dau of 3rd Earl of Aylesford (*qv*) and *d* 6 March 1779, leaving:

1e HENRY HOWARD, **13th Earl of Suffolk** and **6th Earl of Berkshire**; *b* posthumously 8 Aug, *d* 10 Aug 1779

2d Frances; *m* Richard BAGOT later HOWARD, bro of 1st Baron Bagot (*qv*), and had:

1e Mary, of Elford, Castle Rising, Norfolk, and Ashtead, Surrey; *m* 1807 Col Hon Fulke Greville UPTON later HOWARD (*d* 4 March 1846) and *dsp* 19 Oct 1877 in her 93rd year

2c Charles; *m* 1st Susannah Lane, widow (*d* Aug 1761); *m* 2nd Mary, widow of Henry Collins, and *dsp* 28 Sept 1773

3c THOMAS HOWARD, **14th Earl of Suffolk** and **7th Earl of Berkshire**; *b* 11 June 1721; *educ* Eton(?) and St John's Coll Oxford; barrister Inner Temple 1774, Bencher 1779, MP (Whig) Castle Rising 1747–68, Malmesbury 1768–74 and St Michael 1774–79; *m* 13 Aug 1747 Elizabeth (*d* 22 June 1769), dau of William Kingscote, of Kingscote, Glos, and *dspm* 3 Feb 1783, leaving:

1d Diana; *m* 23 Nov 1782 Sir Michael Le Fleming, 4th Bt (*qv*)

(5) Robert (Sir), of Vasterne, Wilts, KB; Auditor Exchequer; Restoration wit and minor poet; his male line ceased 1702 with his gs Thomas, the female with his gdau Diana, w of 8th Lord (Baron) Dudley (*qv*), when the estates reverted to the **5th Earl of Suffolk**

(6) Philip; *bapt* 5 March 1629; Col Gds *temp* CHARLES II; *m* Mary Jennings and was *bur* Sept 1717, having had, with a dau (*d* unm):

1a James, of Boughton, Cheshire; *b* 1 March 1679, Capt Army; *m* 1698 Katherine (*d* 1765 aged 93), dau of George Booth and gdau of Sir J Booth, of Dunham Massey, and *d* 13 June 1722, leaving, with two sons (*d* in infancy):

1b Catherine Elizabeth; *b* 1700; *m* 1734 Narcissus C Proby, of Damastown, Dublin, and Chester, and *d* 1775, leaving:

1c N— C— (Rev); Rector Stratford St Mary, Suffolk

2b Martha Maria; *b* 1705; *m* 1738 Rev Hon Charles Hervey (*see* BRISTOL, M) and *dsp* 1797

2a Charles; *b* 13 May 1681; Capt RN; *m* Elizabeth, dau of Edward Batten, and had:

1b Philip; *m* Margaret, dau and heiress of Francis Screen, of Edinburgh, and *d* 1741, having had, with two er sons:

1c JOHN, **15th/8th Earl**

2c Philip; *b* 1741; RN

1c Mary; *b* 1735; Woman of Bedchamber to PRINCESS AMELIA (2nd dau of GEORGE II)

1a Mary; *m* 1st 14 March 1726 1st Earl of Delorain (*see* BUCCLEUCH and QUEENSBERRY, D) and had issue; *m* 2nd April 1734 William Windham, of Earsham, Norfolk, and *d* 12 Nov 1744

(1) Elizabeth; *m* John Dryden, the poet

(2) Frances; *m* 8 Feb 1649/50, as his 2nd w, 9th Lord (Baron) Darcy de Knayth (*qv*)

(3) Mary; imprisoned 1650 for royalism; *d* unm

3 Henry; *m* Elizabeth (*m* 2nd *c* 1618, as his 1st w, 1st Duke of Newcastle-upon-Tyne; *see* DEVONSHIRE, D), only dau and heiress of William Bassett, of Blore, Staffs, and had:

(1) Elizabeth; *m* Sir John Harpur, of Swarkston

4 Charles (Sir); *m* Mary (*m* 4th Sir Richard Grenville, Bt, of Kilkhampton, Cornwall), widow of (a) Sir Allen Percy, KB, and (b) Thomas Darcy, s of Earl Rivers, and dau and heiress of Sir John Fitz, of Fitzford, and had:

(1) Elizabeth

5 Robert (Sir), KB

6 William (Sir), KB

7 EDWARD HOWARD, 1st BARON HOWARD OF ESCRICK, Co York (E), so *cr* 12 April 1628, KB (1616), of Escrick, Yorks, an estate he inherited through his mother; MP Calne 1624–25, Hertford March–April 1628 and Carlisle (during Interregnum) 1649–51, when unseated for peculation (bribes by royalists) and subject to imprisonment in the Tower London and a fine of £10,000 (over £400,000 in late-1990s terms); *m* 30 Nov 1623 Mary, 5th dau of 1st Baron Boteler of Brantfield (*see* JERSEY, E), and *d* 24 April 1675, leaving:

(1) THOMAS HOWARD, 2nd BARON HOWARD OF ESCRICK; *bapt* 24 Oct 1625; Offr 1st Ft Gds in Flanders fighting with Spanish against French; *m* 1st 21 July 1646 Elizabeth, dau of 1st Earl of Peterborough (*see* MORDAUNT, Bt); *m* 2nd June 1677 Jane Drake, of Somerset, and *dsps* 24 Aug 1678

(2) WILLIAM HOWARD, 3rd BARON HOWARD OF ESCRICK; *educ* Corpus Christi Coll Cambridge; Anabaptist preacher, Trooper OLIVER CROMWELL's Life Gds; nevertheless plotted to restore monarchy and accordingly sent to prison 1658; MP (Whig) Winchelsea 1660, sided with Titus Oates, whose baseless accusations he gave currency to, at time of 'Popish Plot', and later was involved in the Rye House Plot but informed against his co-conspirators, thus procuring their execution; *m* Frances, dau of Sir James Bridgeman (*see* BRADFORD, E), and was bur 24 April 1694, leaving:

1a CHARLES HOWARD, 4th and last BARON HOWARD OF ESCRICK; *m* Aug 1694 Elizabeth, dau of 6th Baron Chandos of Sudeley (*see* TEMPLE OF STOWE, E) and widow of (a) 3rd Baron Herbert of Chirbury (*see* POWIS, E) and (b) 2nd Earl of Inchiquin (*see* INCHIQUIN, B) and *dspl* 29 April 1715, when the Barony expired, leaving by a Mrs Pyke:

1b Charlotte

1 Elizabeth; *m* 1st 1st Earl of Banbury (*see* KNOLLYS, V); *m* 2nd 4th Baron Vaux of Harrowden (*qv*)

2 Frances; *m* 1st (*divorce*) 4th Viscount Hereford (*qv*); *m* 2nd 26 Dec 1613 1st and last Earl of Somerset of the 1613 *cr* (*see* LOTHIAN, M)

3 Catherine; *m* 1 Dec 1608 2nd Earl of Salisbury (*see* SALISBURY, M) and was bur 27 Jan 1672/3, having had issue

The 14th/7th EARL's cousin,

JOHN HOWARD, **15th Earl of Suffolk** and **8th Earl of Berkshire**; *b* 7 March 1738/9, served War American Independence, Gen 1802; *m* 2 July 1774 Julia (*d* 19 Oct 1819), dau of John Gaskarth, of Penrith, and *d* 23 Jan 1820, having had:

1 Charles Nevison, *Viscount Andover*; *b* 13 May 1775; *m* 21 June 1796 Jane Elizabeth (*m* 2nd 17 April 1806 Adml Sir Henry Digby, KCB (*d* Aug 1842), and *d* 29 April 1863), dau of 1st Earl of Leicester (*qv*), and was *k* by the accidental discharge of his fowling-piece 11 Jan 1800

2 THOMAS, **16th/9th Earl**

1 Catherine; *m* Rev George Bisset and *d* 1850. He *d* Nov 1828

The 15th/8th EARLs' yr s,

THOMAS HOWARD, **16th Earl of Suffolk** and **9th Earl of Berkshire**; *b* 18 Aug 1776; *m* 14 Jan 1803 Hon Elizabeth Jane Dutton (*d* 18 April 1836), est dau of 1st Baron Sherborne (*see* 1970 edn), and had, with three other daus (*d* unm):

1 CHARLES JOHN, **17th/10th Earl**

2 Henry Thomas; *b* 16 Jan 1808; MP, Capt; *m* 24 April 1845 Georgiana Maria (*d* 23 Nov 1859), est dau of Gen Sir John Wright Guise, 3rd Bt (*qv*), and *d* 29 Jan 1851, leaving, with two sons (*d* unm):

(1) Elizabeth Frances; *m* 18 Dec 1872 Richard William Selby Lowndes, of Elmers, Bletchley, and *d* 2 March 1898, leaving issue. He *d* 18 May 1914

3 Richard Edward; *b* 1812; LLD, DCL; *d* 1873

4 James Kenneth; *b* 5 March 1814; Cmmr Woods and Forests; *m* 10 Feb 1845 Lady Louisa FitzMaurice (*d* 12 June 1906), only dau of 3rd Marquess of Lansdowne (*qv*), and *d* 7 Jan 1882, leaving, with two other sons (*d* unm):

(1) Kenneth HOWARD later HOWARD-BURY (roy licence 14 Dec 1881), JP, DL; *b* 27 Nov 1845; Capt RA, High Sheriff King's Co 1884; *m* 30 Sept 1881 Lady Emily Alfreda Julia Bury, of Charleville Forest, King's Co (*d* 28 Feb 1931), yst dau of 3rd Earl of Charleville (*see* 1875 edn), and *d* 24 Aug 1885, leaving:

1a Charles Kenneth, DSO (1918), DL Co Westmeath; *b* 15 Aug 1883; *educ* Eton and RMC Sandhurst; Lt-Col 60th Rifles, Hon Col 85th E Anglian Field Bde, RA (TA) 1927, served WW I (despatches six times), headed Mt Everest Expdn 1921, MP Bilston Nov 1922–Oct 1924 and Chelmsford Nov 1926–Oct 1931, PPS to Sec State War Dec 1922–Jan 1924; *d* unm 20 Sept 1963

1a Marjorie Alfreda Beaujolais; *b* 16 July 1885; *d* unm 8 Dec 1907

(1) Winifrede; *m* 7 Sept 1886 Maj-Gen Cyril Hugh Pennycuick Ducat, Roy Canadians, and *d* 11 Sept 1933, leaving issue. He *d* 19 Feb 1932

1 Elizabeth; *m* 22 June 1826 3rd Baron Sherborne (*see* 1970 edn) and *d* 29 July 1845, leaving issue. He *d* 8 March 1883

2 Jane Elizabeth; *m* 5 April 1836 Sir John Ogilvy, 9th Bt (*qv*), and *d* 28 July 1861, leaving issue

The 16th/9th EARL *d* 4 Dec 1851; his est s,

CHARLES JOHN HOWARD, **17th Earl of Suffolk** and **10th Earl of Berkshire**; *b* 7 Nov 1804; *m* 2 Sept 1829 his distant cousin Isabella (*d* 20 June 1891), 2nd dau of Lord Henry Molyneux Howard (*see* NORFOLK, D), and had, with two other daus (*d* unm):

1 HENRY CHARLES, **18th/11th Earl**

2 Greville Theophilus, of Castle Rising Norfolk; *b* 22 Dec 1836; barrister, Commr in Lunacy; *m* 18 Sept 1873 Lady Audrey Jane Charlotte Townshend (*d* 20 Feb 1926), having *m* 2nd 10 Aug 1882 Gen Sir Redvers Buller, VC, GCB,

GCMG, PC (*d* 2 June 1908), of Downes, Devon, and had further issue), yst dau of 4th Marquess Townshend (*qv*), and *d* 28 July 1880, leaving:

(1) Henry Greville; *b* 25 June 1877; Lt KRRC; *d* unm 20 July 1899

(2) Charles Alfred (Sir), GCVO (1956, KCVO 1944), DSO (1917) and bar (1918), of Castle Rising, DL Norfolk; *b* 29 July 1878; *educ* Eton and RMC Sandhurst; Lt-Col KRRC, Boer War 1900–01 and WW I (despatches, Legn Hon), cmded 162nd Inf Bde 1929–32, Brig cmdg 12th Inf Bde at Dover and Dep Constable Dover Castle 1932–35, Hon Brig 1935, Serjeant-at-Arms H of C 1935–56, Hon Freeman Dover 1935; *m* 21 Dec 1908 Miriam Eleanore (*d* 14 Feb 1959), est dau of Lt-Col Edward Mashiter Dansey, OBE, 1st Life Gds, and *d* 5 Jan 1958, having had:

1a Henry Redvers Greville; *b* 31 Oct 1911; Lt-Col KRRC WW II; *m* 1st 13 July 1940 (*divorce* 1946) Patience, yst dau of Lt-Col Charles Rice Iltyd Nicholl, TD, of S Kensington, and had:

1b +Greville Patrick Charles [Greville Howard Esq, Castle Rising, King's Lynn, Norfolk]; *b* 22 April 1941; *educ* Eton; *m* 1st 17 Dec 1968 (*divorce* 1972) Zoë Rosaleen, yst dau of Douglas Walker, of Knightsbridge and Paris; *m* 2nd 1978 Mary Rose (*d* 1980), yst dau of Sir (Edward) John Chichester, 11th Bt (*qv*); *m* 3rd 1981 *Mary Cortland, dau of Robert Culverwell, of Bridges Ct, Luckington, Wilts, and by her has:

1c +Thomas Henry Greville; *b* 1983

2c +Charles Edward John; *b* 1986

1c *Annabel Rosemary Diana; *b* 1984

1b *Amanda Susan Diana; *b* 8 July 1943; *m* 4 April 1968 (Alexander) Simon James Montague Burton (*d* 1972), s of A J Burton, of Carlshead Ho, Yorks, and has:

1c *Michael Alexander Greville James; *b* 1971

1c *Sophie Amelia Sarah; *b* 14 March 1970

1a (cont.) Lt-Col Henry Howard *m* 2nd 2 June 1948 *Odette [Mrs Henry Howard, Castle Rising, King's Lynn, Norfolk], widow of F/Lt Gordon Crosby, RAF, and dau of Henry Clark, of Ventnor, IoW, and *d* 11 Feb 1978, having by her had:

2b *Katharine Venetia [Mrs Katharine Howard, Calle Sol 21, Jimena de la Frontera, 11330 Cadiz, Spain]; *b* 29 Nov 1948; *m* 19 Dec 1980 *Alvaro Alvarez and has:

1c *Samara ALVAREZ HOWARD; *b* 18 Oct 1982

2c *Marta ALVAREZ HOWARD; *b* 21 Sept 1984

3c *Lucia ALVAREZ HOWARD; *b* 4 Oct 1985

2b (cont.) Mrs Katharine Howard also has by *Miguel Mateo:

1c *Henry Greville Michael FITZ-HOWARD; *b* 12 May 1978

1a Diana Mary; *b* 5 Dec 1909; *d* 25 Dec 1918

(1) Dorothy Elizabeth; *b* 1 March 1875; *m* 4 Feb 1907 Ralph E Macan, yst s of Turner Arthur Macan, of Elstow Lodge, Bedford, and *d* 2 Sept 1952. He *d* 18 April 1945

(2) Joyce Etheldreda; *b* 11 May 1876; *m* 31 Oct 1903 Col Sir Arthur Havelock James Doyle, 4th Bt (*see* 1970 edn), and *d* 5 Oct 1961, leaving issue. He *d* 19 Feb 1948

3 Bernard Thomas; *b* 27 Aug 1841; Lt Rifle Bde; *d* unm 25 Sept 1868

4 Cecil Molyneux; *b* 30 March 1849; *m* 1877 Amy (*d* 31 Jan 1915), dau of Leo Schuster, and *dsp* 28 April 1903

1 Isabella Julia Elizabeth; *m* 18 June 1863 Francis Henry Atherley, Rifle Bde, of Landguard Manor, IoW, and *d* 8 Nov 1910, leaving issue. He *d* 31 March 1897

The 17th/10th EARL *d* 14 Aug 1876; his est s,

HENRY CHARLES HOWARD, **18th Earl of Suffolk** and **11th Earl of Berkshire**; *b* 10 Sept 1833; MP Malmesbury 1859–68; *m* 2 Dec 1868 Mary Eleanor Lauderdale (*d* 31 Oct 1928), dau of Hon Henry Coventry (*see* COVENTRY, E), and had:

1 HENRY MOLYNEUX PAGET, **19th/12th Earl**

2 James Knyvett Estcourt; *b* 1 May 1886; *educ* Winchester; Maj RHG (Spec Res), WWs I and II; *m* 9 July 1925 Nancy Induna Frances Caroline (*d* 13 Dec 1972), er dau of Edgar Lubbock (*see* AVEBURY, B), and *d* 5 Dec 1964, leaving:

(1) *Virginia Mary Eloïse; *b* 13 Nov 1926; *m* 3 July 1948 *Capt David John Richard Ker, MC, DL, JP, Coldstream Gds, only s of Maj Alfred William Ker, OBE, DL, of Portavo, and has:

1a *David Peter James [David Ker Esq, 85 Bourne St, London SW1W 8HF]; *b* 23 July 1951; *educ* Eton; fndr and proprietor David Ker Fine Art 1980; *m* 1974 *Alexandra Mary, dau of V-Adml Sir Dymock Watson, KCB, CBE, DL, of Trebinshwyn, Brecon, and has had:

1b David Edward Richard; *b* 1979; *d* 1980

2b *David Humphry Rivers; *b* 1982

1b *Clare Rose; *b* 1977

1a *Caroline Moira; *b* 17 July 1949; *m* 6 Sept 1968 (*divorce* 1972) Thomas William Fellowes (*see* HAMPDEN, V)

2a *Camilla Rosanna Gian; *b* 1 June 1959

(2) *Priscilla Margaret; *b* 11 March 1930; *m* 9 July 1954 *Jeremy Porter, s of AVM Cedric Ernest Victor Porter, CBE, of Pigeons Farm, Greenham, Berks, and adopted:

*Mary-Ann Elizabeth; *b* 11 Jan 1960

*Katharine Frances Jane; *b* 27 Oct 1961

1 Mary Muriel Sophie, JP Wilts; *b* 1 March 1870; *m* 18 July 1893 Henry Robert Beauclerk Coventry and *d* 19 Feb 1938, leaving issue (*see* COVENTRY, E)

2 Eleanor Mabel; *b* 11 Feb 1873; *m* 1st 26 July 1902 Maj Hon Lionel Francis George Byng, s of 2nd Earl of Strafford (*qv*), and had issue; *m* 2nd 11 Oct 1922 Henry Ernest Atkinson (*d* 3 Oct 1926), est s of Rev Francis Home Atkinson, of Morland Hall, Penrith, resumed by deed poll 14 Dec 1927 her 1st husb's name and *d* 9 March 1945

3 Agnes Isabel; *b* 30 June 1874; *m* 23 Jan 1917 Maj Arthur Vernon Poynter, DSO, Scots Gds, only s of Lt-Col James Poynter, and *dsp* 16 Oct 1970. He *d* 1 March 1955

4 Katharine Millicent; *b* 10 Sept 1883; *d* unm 1 April 1961

The 18th/11th EARL *d* 31 March 1898; his er s,

HENRY MOLYNEUX PAGET HOWARD, **19th Earl of Suffolk** and **12th Earl of Berkshire**; *b* 13 Sept 1877; Extra ADC to Viceroy India, Capt 4th Bn Glos Regt,

Maj Wiltshire Bn 3rd Wessex Bde RFA; *m* 26 Dec 1904 Marguerite Hyde (*d* 5 March 1968), yst dau of Levi Zeigler Leiter, of Dupont Circle, Washington, DC, and sis of Marchioness Curzon of Kedleston (*see* SCARSDALE, V), and had:

1 CHARLES HENRY GEORGE, **20th/13th Earl**

2 Cecil John Arthur, Lt RTC; *b* 24 June 1908; *educ* Eton; *m* 12 Feb 1939 *Frances Drake [The Hon Mrs Cecil Howard, 1511 Summit Ridge Dve, Beverly Hills, CA, USA], dau of Edwin Morgan Dean, of Newcastle, Northumberland, and Toronto, Canada, and *d* 1985

3 Greville Reginald; *b* 7 Sept 1909; *educ* Eton and RMC Sandhurst; Lt KSLI, Lt-Cdr RNR, WW II, memb Westminster Cncl 1937–50 (Mayor 1946–47), MP St Ives Feb 1950–66; *m* 24 Nov 1945 Mary (*d* 1994), yr dau of William Smith Ridehalgh, of Broughton Lodge, Cartmel, Lancs, and *d* 1987, leaving:

  (1) *Caroline Margaret [Mrs Robert Godden, Polkanugga Farm, St Martin, Helston, Cornwall]; *b* 18 May 1947; *m* 1st 1 Nov 1965 Nigel Stacey, s of William Percival Stacey, of Lelant, Cornwall; *m* 2nd 1970 *Robert Mark Godden

The 19th/12th EARL was *ka* 21 April 1917; his est s,

CHARLES HENRY GEORGE HOWARD, **20th Earl of Suffolk** and **13th Earl of Berkshire**, GC (1941); *b* 2 March 1906; Ch Field Res and Experimental Offr Directorate Sci Research Min Supply WW II, bomb disposal pioneer, model for the BBC TV series *The Dragon's Opponent*, BSc Edin, FRSE, FRSSA, FZS; *m* 7 March 1934 Mimi, actress (*d* 22 Feb 1966), dau of Alfred George Forde-Pigott, and was *k* by enemy action 12 May 1941, having had:

1 MICHAEL JOHN JAMES GEORGE ROBERT HOWARD, **21st and present Earl of Suffolk and 14th and present Earl of Berkshire**

2 +Maurice David Henry [The Hon Maurice Howard, 3 Walpole St, London SW3]; *b* 3 Nov 1936; *educ* Eton and Sorbonne; served RN 1955–57 Suez; *m* 18 Feb 1978 *Vicky, er dau of G B Summers, of Newcastle-upon-Tyne, and has:

  (1) *Annabel Frances Victoria; *b* 1979

3 +Patrick Greville [The Hon Patrick Howard, Far Upton Wold, Moreton-in-Marsh, Glos GL56 9TG]; *b* 18 Aug 1940; *educ* Eton, Grenoble, Heidelberg and Peterhouse Cambridge (BA); Lt Roy Wilts Yeo; *m* 22 Sept 1966 *Mary Elizabeth, er dau of Dr Clarence Laverne Johnson, of Mayfair, and Mrs Neil Perrins, 4th dau of Sir Ernest Bland Royden, 3rd Bt (*qv*), and has:

  (1) +Jason Patrick; *b* 10 April 1968; *m* 1991 *Amanda Jane, dau of Sir (James) Gerard Waterlow, 4th Bt, of Harrow (*qv*), and has:

    1a *Ava Suzanne; *b* 10 June 1997

  (2) +Rory Alexander; *b* 18 Sept 1970

  (3) +Timothy Charles; *b* 1973

  (4) +Charles Edward; *b* 1974

SULLIVAN

Arms: Per fess, the base per pale, in chief or a dexter hand, couped at the wrist, holding a sword erect ppr., hilted gu., the blade entwined with a serpent ppr., between two lions rampant respectant of the second, the dexter base vert charged with a buck trippant or, on the sinister base per pale arg. and sa. a boar passant, counter-changed. **Crest:** On a ducal coronet or a robin, holding in the beak a sprig of laurel ppr. **Motto:** *Lamh foisdineach an uachtar* ('What we gain by conquest we secure by clemency'). **Creation:** Bt. (UK) 22 May 1804.

Richard Arthur Sullivan [Richard Sullivan, 2460 North Park Blvd, Santa Ana, CA 92706, USA]; *b* 9 Aug 1931; *s* *f* 1977 but does not use title; *educ* Cape Town U (BSc (Eng)) and MIT (SM); MASCE, MICE; geo-environmental consultant; *m* 17 Feb 1962 *Elenor Mary, est dau of Kenneth Merson Thorpe, of Somerset West, CP, S Africa, and has:

1 +CHARLES MERSON [Charles Sullivan Esq, The Old Chapel, Alswear, S Molton, Devon EX36 4LH]; *b* 15 Dec 1962; *educ* Cambridge (MA, VetMB); MRCVS; *m* 19 June 1993 *Helen Mary, er dau of Dr Alun Garbett Alexander, of Neath, W Glam, and has:

  (1) *Hannah Robyn; *b* 10 Dec 1996

1 *Katherine Anne; *b* 13 Dec 1963; *educ* Houston U (BSc)

2 *Sarah Elizabeth; *b* 24 April 1965; Texas (BA) and Calif U (MA)

3 *Margaret Mary; *b* 21 Jan 1969; e George washington U (BA)

Lineage: PHILIP O'SULLIVAN, of Dromeragh, Co Cork; *d* 1737, leaving:

BENJAMIN O'SULLIVAN later SULLIVAN, of Dromeragh; *b* 15 June 1720; Clerk of the Crown for Cos Cork and Waterford 1752; *m* 3 Jan 1742 Bridget (*d* 8 July 1802), dau of Rev Paul Limric, DD, and had:

1 Benjamin (Sir); *b* 23 April 1747; Puisne Judge Madras, ktd 1801; *m* Eliza, dau of Adml Sir Digby Dent, and *d* 12 Oct 1810, leaving issue

2 John, PC (1805); *b* 21 July 1749; U-Sec War 1801–05; *m* 24 May 1789 Henrietta Anne Barbara (*d* 12 Dec 1828), dau of 3rd Earl of Buckinghamshire (*qv*), and *d* 31 Oct 1839, having had issue

3 RICHARD JOSEPH (Sir), **1st Bt**

4 Henry Boyle; *d* unm 1783

1 Margaret; *m* 1770 Gen Gordon Forbes, Col 29th Foot, and had issue

2 Elizabeth; *m* Patrick Lawson

3 Sabinia; *m* John Otto Bayer and *d* 1784, leaving issue

4 Henrietta; *m* 1st Col Alexander Maclellan; *m* 2nd John Balfour, of Trenaby, Orkney, MP Orkney

5 Ann; *m* 1781 Lt-Col George Hallam, of White Barns, Herts, and *d* 1840

The 3rd s,

Sir Richard Joseph Sullivan, 1st Bt (UK), so *cr* 22 May 1804, of Thames Ditton, Surrey; *b* 10 Dec 1752; *m* 3 Dec 1778 Mary (*d* 24 Dec 1832), only surv dau of Thomas Lodge, of Leeds, and *d* 17 July 1806, having had:

1 **Sir Henry Sullivan, 2nd Bt**; *b* 13 March 1785; Lt-Col Coldstream Gds; *ka* (unm) in a sortie from the garrison of Bayonne 14 April 1814

2 **Sir Charles Sullivan, 3rd Bt**; *b* 28 Feb 1789; Adml the Blue; *m* 21 Nov 1818 Jean Anne (*d* 9 July 1863), only dau of Robert Taylor, of Ember Court, Surrey, and *d* 21 Nov 1862, having had, with a dau (*d* unm):

  (1) **Sir Charles Sullivan, 4th Bt**; *b* 13 Jan 1820; *d* unm 3 Dec 1865

  (2) **Sir Edward Robert Sullivan, 5th Bt**, JP, DL Lancs; *b* 29 Oct 1826; *m* 29 Sept 1859 Mary (*d* 4 Oct 1907), yst dau of Henry Currie, of W Horsley Place, Surrey, MP Guildford, and *d* 22 July 1899, having had, with another dau (*d* unm):

    1a Maud Ann; *m* 22 Aug 1905 Arthur Remington Robert and *dsp* 11 Jan 1939

  (1) Mary Margaret; *m* 20 Feb 1869 her cousin Henry Currie, of W Horsley Place, Surrey, and *d* 10 April 1905. He *dsp* 1873

  (2) Jean; *m* 5 Dec 1863 Rev Henry Nele Loring, Min Boarhunt-with-Southwick, Hants, est s of Adml Sir John Wentworth Loring, KCB, KCH, and *d* 3 Feb 1865

3 Edward Richard; *b* 8 June 1791; Madras CS; *m* 1815 Eliza Maria, dau of Gen Sir James Lillyman Caldwell, GCB, and *d* 6 Oct 1824, leaving:

  (1) Richard James; *b* 15 Aug 1816; *m* 15 Aug 1850 Hessie, dau of Laurence Cloete, of Zandvliete, Cape of Good Hope, and *dsp* 6 Feb 1858

  (2) Frederick Henry Frederick; *d* 31 March 1840

  (1) Maria Charlotte; *m* 29 May 1839 Sir John Lees, 3rd Bt (*see* LEES, Bt, of Blackrock), and *d* 3 Jan 1881, leaving issue

4 Frederick (Rev); *b* 1 Feb 1797; Vicar Kimpton, Herts; *m* 1st 3 Jan 1821 Arabella Jane (*d* 27 Jan 1839), dau of Valentine H Wilmot, of Farnborough, Hants, by Barbarina, later Baroness Dacre (*qv*), dau of Adml Sir Chaloner Ogle, 1st Bt (*see* 1940 edn), and had, with other issue:

  (1) FRANCIS WILLIAM (Sir), **6th Bt**

  (2) Henry Eden; *b* 14 Nov 1835; *m* 2 June 1859 Margaret Louisa (*d* 5 Aug 1910), dau of James Peirce, of Llanelly, Brecon, and *d* 12 April 1903, having had, with other issue:

    1a Charles Wilmot; *b* March 1865; *d* April 1924

    2a William; *b* 1871; PWD India; *d* 1907

    1a Agnes Vernon, OBE (1918); *m* 31 March 1885 Sir Henry Francis Wigram (*see* WIGRAM, Bt) and *dsp* 23 Sept 1957

    2a Mary Augusta; *m* 1893 John Lea Walton Kitching and *d* 6 July 1943. He *d* 18 Jan 1937

    3a Rhoda; *m* 14 Aug 1901 Rev George Henry Croasdaile Bowen, Rector Thrybergh, Yorks, Hon Canon Sheffield, and *d* Nov 1954. He *d* 1956

  (1) Barbarina Charlotte; *m* 20 July 1846 Adml Hon Sir Frederick William Grey, GCB (*see* GREY, E), and *d* 23 March 1902

4 (cont.) The Rev Frederick Sullivan *m* 2nd 1843 Emily (*dsp* 25 April 1856), est dau of Levi Ames, and *d* 28 July 1873

5 Arthur; *b* 1801; Maj; *d* 7 June 1832

6 William, CB; *b* 10 Oct 1804; Col 58th Regt, Maj-Gen; *m* Euphemia Caulfield (*d* 25 Aug 1877), widow of Capt Dalton, RE, and dau of Thomas Knox Hannington, and *d* 6 Jan 1870

1 Charlotte; *m* 1824 William Hale, of King's Walden, Herts, and *d* 28 March 1873

2 Eliza; *m* 1814 Rev Hon Frederick Pleydell-Bouverie and *d* 2 July 1846, leaving issue (*see* RADNOR, E)

The 5th Bt's cousin,

Sir Francis William Sullivan, 6th Bt, KCB, CMG, JP Beds and Herts; *b* 31 May 1834; Adml, ADC to HM QUEEN VICTORIA 1877–78, Sr Offr Cape of Good Hope Station, Kt Medjidie 2nd Cl; *m* 17 Aug 1861 Agnes (*d* 1 Jan 1917), 2nd dau of Hon Sir Sydney Bell, Ch Justice Cape of Good Hope, and *d* 13 May 1906, leaving:

1 **Rev Sir Frederick Sullivan, 7th Bt**; *b* 28 April 1865; *educ* Wellington and Exeter Coll Oxford (MA); Rector Southrepps Norfolk 1900–21; *m* 1st 13 June 1901 Hon Judith Harbord (*dsp* 4 Feb 1942), dau of 5th Baron Suffield (*qv*); *m* 2nd 4 Dec 1943 Mary Mildred (*d* 25 Dec 1952), widow of Lt-Col Ferdinand Cospatrick Logan-Home and dau of Col Hon Augustus Cathcart (*see* CATHCART, E), and *dsp* 24 July 1954

2 Richard; *b* 17 Aug 1866; Capt RN; *m* 25 Nov 1905 Beatrix Evelyn (*d* 17 Dec 1936), est dau of Arthur Magniac, of The Hermitage, Ascot, and *d* 4 June 1928, leaving:

  (1) RICHARD BENJAMIN MAGNIAC (Sir), **8th Bt**

(2) Valentine Arthur; *b* 1 Dec 1907; *educ* St Andrew's Grahamstown, S Africa; 5th Field Regt SAA WW II; *m* 3 Aug 1937 Mollie-Maureen Madge (*d* 1985), dau of William Nicholas Craig, of Sale, Cheshire, and *d* 29 April 1965, leaving:

   1a +Peter Craig Valentine [Peter Sullivan Esq, Mercury House, Riebeck St, Wynberg 7800, Cape Town, S Africa]; *b* 23 Jan 1941; *educ* Cape Town U (BA)

   1a Elizabeth Bridget Patricia; *b* 20 May 1947; *d* 22 June 1993

(3) Dermot Ogle; *b* 10 Feb 1909; *d* July 1941

1 Gertrude Agnes; *m* 20 Dec 1892 John Lionel Lyster and *d* 3 Dec 1937, leaving issue. He *d* 12 Dec 1908

Sir FREDERICK's n,

Sir Richard Benjamin Magniac Sullivan, 8th Bt; *b* 26 Oct 1906; *educ* St Andrew's Grahamstown; Colonial Admin Serv (ret 1957); *m* 10 April 1928 Muriel Mary Paget (*d* 1988), yst dau of Francis Charles Trayler Pineo, and *d* Aug 1977, leaving:

1 Sir RICHARD ARTHUR SULLIVAN, **9th and present Bt**

2 +Michael Francis [Michael Sullivan Esq, 12 Gloucester Cres, London NW1 7DS]; *b* 4 April 1936; *educ* Cambridge U (BA, MB, BChir 1958), MRCS, LRCP, FRCS 1966; *m* 1st 24 Aug 1957 (*divorce* 1978) Inger, only dau of Arne Mathieson, of Oslo, and has:

   (1) +Richard Alexander Dermot [Richard Sullivan Esq, Stephens Farm, Bloxworth, Wareham, Dorset BH20 7EB]; *b* 9 Jan 1961; *educ* Reading U (BA); *m* 27 Oct 1993 *Julia Elizabeth, est dau of Peter Graham Macdonald-Smith, of Bloxworth, Dorset

   (1) *Vivienne Nicola; *b* 9 Jan 1965

2 (cont.) Michael Sullivan *m* 2nd *Caroline Mary, er dau of Maj Christopher John Griffin, of Hall Farmhouse, Oxborough, Norfolk, and by her has:

   (2) *(Emma) Lucy Mary; *b* 22 Nov 1980

SUTHERLAND, Duke of

Arms: Arg. a lion rampant gu. between three pheons sa. **Crest:** On a chapeau gu., doubled erm., a lion rampant of the first supporting an arrow or, feathered and headed arg. **Supporters:** Dexter, a horse arg., ducally gorged or; sinister, a griffin or, ducally gorged az. **Motto:** *Sic donec* ('Thus so far'). **Creations:** Bt. (E) 2 June 1620, B. (E) 16 March 1702/3 (Gower of Stittenham), E. and V. (GB) 8 July 1746 (Gower, Trentham, respectively), M. (GB) 1 March 1786, D. (UK) 28 Jan 1833, E. and V. (UK) 6 July 1846 (Ellesmere and Brackley respectively).

THE 6TH DUKE OF SUTHERLAND, Marquess of Stafford, Earl Gower, **Earl of Ellesmere**, Viscount Trentham, Co Stafford, **Viscount Brackley**, of Brackley, Co Northampton, **Baron Gower of Stittenham**, Co York, and a **Baronet** (Sir John Sutherland Egerton, Bt, DL (Berwicks 1955)) [His Grace The Duke of Sutherland DL, Mertoun, St Boswell's, Roxburghshire TD6 0EA; Lingay Cottage, Hall Farm, Newmarket, Suffolk CB8 0TX]; *b* 10 May 1915; *s* f in Earldom of Ellesmere and Viscountcy of Brackley 1944 and cousin in all other titles 1963; *educ* Eton and Trin Coll Cambridge; Capt RAC (TA) WW II (POW); *m* 1st 29 April 1939 Lady Diana Evelyn Percy (*d* 16 June 1978), yr dau of 8th Duke of Northumberland (*qv*); *m* 2nd 16 August 1979 *Evelyn Mary, est dau of Maj Robert Moubray, JP, DL (*see* MORRISON-BELL, Bt)

Lineage: WILLIAM *filius* (i.e., son of) GUH(I)ER (the latter seemingly a Breton), held Stittenham, Yorks, 1167; presumably kin to:

ALAN GO(I)HER; had *s* to Stittenham by 1176; presumably kin to:

Sir JOHN GOWER; did mil service under EDWARD I; presumably kin to:

LAWRENCE GOWER; participated in Piers Gaveston's muder 1312, for which pardoned by EDWARD II *c* 1314; presumably f of:

Sir NICHOLAS GOWER; MP Yorks 1339; *d* in or after 1351, leaving:

Sir THOMAS GOWER, of Stittenham, Yorks; *m* Agnes, dau of Thomas Thwaites, of Lovetofts, Yorks, and had, with a yr *s* (Sir Thomas, served France under HENRY V, Govr Castle of Mans, *m* Joan, a Frenchwoman of Alençon, and had issue, who were naturalized *c* 1433) and four daus (Anne, *m* Sir Ralph Ellerker,

of Risby; Margaret, *m* James Aislaby, of S Dalton; Alice, *m* William Hungate, of Saxton; Joan, *m* Robert Constable):

Sir JOHN GOWER, of Stittenham; standard-bearer to PRINCE EDWARD, s of HENRY VI; *m* Elizabeth, dau of Edward Goldsborough, a Baron Exchequer *temp* RICHARD III and HENRY VII, and was beheaded after the Lancastrian defeat of Tewkesbury 4 May 1471, leaving, with four yr sons (Robert, of London; John (Sir); George; Walter) and two daus (Elizabeth, *m* Christopher Fenton, of Creake; Jane, *m* Hugh Clitherow, of Bradingham):

Sir EDWARD GOWER, of Stittenham; *m* Margery, widow of John St Quintin of Harpham and dau of Sir Robert Constable, of Flamborough, Yorks, and had, with a yr *s* (Richard, *m* Agnes, dau and coheir of William Leving, of Acklam, Yorks, and had four sons (Edward; Thomas; Francis; Ralph)) and three daus (Katherine, *m* Walter de la River, of Bransby, Yorks; Agnes, *m* as his 2nd w Sir John Widdrington, of Widdrington, Northumberland; Barbara, *m* Sir Henry Widdrington, s of the aforementioned Sir John by his 1st w):

THOMAS GOWER, of Stittenham; Capt light horse in Scottish campaign 1547, Master Ordnance against Scots 1560; *m* 1st Anne, dau of James Mauleverer and coheir of her gf Sir William Mauleverer, of Arncliffe, but had no issue by her; *m* 2nd Barbara, dau of John Baxter, and had:

THOMAS GOWER, of Stittenham; *m* Mary, dau of Gabriel Fairfax (*see* FAIRFAX OF CAMERON, V), and had:

Sir Thomas Gower, 1st Bt (E), so *cr* 2 June 1620, of Stittenham; *b* July/Aug 1584; Sheriff Yorks 1620–21, ktd, royalist Civil War; *m* 28 May 1604 Anne (*d* 28 Oct 1633), dau and coheir of John D'Oyley, of Merton, Oxon, and *d* by 12 June 1655, having had, with other issue, including a yr *s* (D'Oyley, royalist Col Dragoons Civil War, had a dau Faith, who *m* Gabriel Brooke, of Burton, and was ancestor of the BROOKE-FIRMANs of Gateforth, Yorks):

Sir Thomas Gower, 2nd Bt; *b c* 1605; MP Malton 1661–72, twice Sheriff Yorks, ktd 1630, royalist Civil War; *m* 1st Elizabeth (*dsp*), sis of 1st Earl of Carlisle (*qv*); *m* 2nd Frances, dau and coheir of Sir John Leveson, of Malling, Kent, and Lilleshall, Staffs (*see* ST JOHN-MILDMAY, Bt), and was *bur* 3 Sept 1672, having had, with three daus:

1 Thomas; *b* 25 Oct, *bur* 5 Nov 1632

2 Edward; *m* Dorothy, dau of Thomas Wentworth, of Elmsall, Yorks, and *dvp*, *bur* 24 Jan 1662, leaving, with another child (*bur* 31 Jan 1666):

   (1) **Sir Thomas Gower, 3rd Bt**; *bapt* 2 Oct 1665; Col of Foot; *d* unm 28 Oct 1689

   (1) Frances; *m* Sir James Wood, Col Battle of the Boyne, and *dsp* 1690

   (2) Dorothy; *bapt* 18 Feb 1668

3 Sir WILLIAM GOWER later LEVESON-GOWER (added *c* 1668 on inheriting his great-uncle Sir Richard Leveson's huge Trentham estate, Staffs), **4th Bt**; MP Merton Feb-March 1673, Newcastle-under-Lyme 1675–81 and 1689–91 and Salop 1681; *m* Lady Jane Granville (*d* 27 Feb 1696), est dau of 1st Earl of Bath of the 1661 *cr* (*see* BATH, M, preliminary remarks) and heiress of her n, 3rd and last Earl of Bath, and had, with two yr sons (Richard; William; both *d* unm):

   (1) JOHN, **1st Baron**

   (1) Katherine; *b* 31 Jan 1670; *m* 16 May or possibly June 1687 Sir Edward Wyndham, 2nd Bt (*see* EGREMONT, LECONFIELD and, B), and had issue

   (2) Jane; *m* 2 May 1692 4th Earl of Clarendon of the 1661 *cr* (*see* CLARENDON, E) and *d* 24 May 1725

Sir WILLIAM *d* Dec 1691; his est s,

Sir John Leveson-Gower, 5th Bt, and **1st Baron Gower of Stittenham**, Co York (E), so *cr* 16 March 1702/3, PC (1702–07); *b* 7 Jan 1674/5; MP (Tory) Newcastle-under-Lyme 1692–1703, Commr for Union of Scottish and English Parls 1706; *m* Sept 1692 Lady Catherine Manners (*d* 7 March 1722), dau of 1st Duke of Rutland (*qv*), and had, with another dau (*d* young):

1 JOHN, **1st Earl**

2 William, MP Staffs 1720–56; *m* 26 May 1730 Anne, dau of Sir Thomas Grosvenor, 3rd Bt (*see* WESTMINSTER, D), and *d* 13 Dec 1756, leaving a dau, Catherine

3 Thomas; MP Newcastle-under-Lyme 1722; *d* unm 12 Aug 1727

4 Baptist; MP Newcastle-under-Lyme 1727; *d* unm 4 Aug 1782

1 Jane; *m* 5 Jan 1718/20 John Proby (*see* PROBY, Bt) and *d* 10 June 1726, leaving issue

The 1st BARON *d* 31 Aug 1709; his est s,

JOHN LEVESON-GOWER, **1st Earl Gower**, so *cr* 8 July 1746 as also VISCOUNT TRENTHAM, Co Stafford (both GB), PC (1742); *b* 10 Aug 1694; DCL Oxon, Ld Privy Seal 1742–43 and 1744–54, Ld Lt Staffs 1742–54, Col 1745; *m* 1st 13 March 1711/2 Lady Evelyn Pierrepont (*d* 26 June 1727), 3rd dau of 1st Duke of Kingston-upon-Hull (*see* KINGSTON, E, preliminary remarks), and had, with two other sons and two other daus:

1 GRANVILLE, **1st Marquess**

1 Mary; *b* 30 Oct 1717; *m c* 1739 Very Rev Sir Richard Wrottesley, 7th Bt, and *d* 30 April 1778, leaving issue (*see* WROTTESLEY, B)

2 Gertrude; *b* 15 Feb 1714/5; *m* 2 April 1737 4th Duke of Bedford (*qv*) and *d* 1 July 1794, leaving issue

3 Frances; *b* 12 Aug 1720; *m* 1744 Lord John Philip Sackville (*see* SACKVILLE, B) and *d* 1788

4 Elizabeth; *b* 20 Jan 1723/4; *m* 7 May 1751 3rd Earl Waldegrave (*qv*) and *d* 28 April 1784, having had issue

5 Evelyn; *b* 26 Jan 1724/5; *m* 1st 29 June 1744 1st Earl of Upper Ossory; *m* 2nd 6 Feb 1759 Richard Vernon, of Hilton, Staffs, and *d* 14 April 1763, leaving issue

The 1st Earl *m* 2nd 31 Oct 1733 Penelope (*d* 19 Aug 1734), widow of Sir Henry Atkins, Bt, and dau of Sir John Stonhouse, 7th Bt (*qv*), and by her had a dau (*d* young); *m* 3rd 16 May 1736 Mary (*d* 12 Feb 1785), widow of 3rd Baron Lucas of Crudwell (*qv*) and dau and coheir of 18th Lord (Baron) Clifford (*see* DE CLIFFORD, B), and by her had, with an er s:

2 John; *b* 11 July 1740; Adml; *m* 5 July 1773 Frances (*d* 14 July 1813), est dau of Adml Hon Edward Boscawen (*see* FALMOUTH, V), and *d* 28 Aug 1792, leaving:

(1) John; *b* 25 June 1774; Gen, MP; *m* 27 Dec 1796 Isabella Mary (*d* 28 May 1817), dau of Philip Bowes Broke, of Broke Hall, Suffolk, and *d* Sept 1816, leaving, with two other daus (*d* unm):

1a John, of Bill Hill, Wokingham, Berks, JP, DL Berks; *b* 5 April 1802; *m* 18 April 1825 Charlotte Gertrude Elizabeth (*d* 4 Aug 1876), dau of Col Henry Hugh Mitchel and gdau of 5th Duke of Beaufort (*qv*), and *d* 18 Nov 1883, leaving, with two daus (*d* unm):

1b John Edward, of Bill Hill, JP; *b* 20 March 1826; Capt 68th Foot; *m* 1st 7 March 1850 Harriet Jane (*dsp* 25 April 1878), 2nd dau of Capt John Hunter; *m* 2nd 1 May 1879 Katherine Elizabeth (*d* 20 April 1928), est dau of Basil Cochrane (*see* DUNDONALD, E), and *d* 21 Jan 1892, leaving:

1c John Henry, of Bill Hill; *b* 20 Sept 1880; *educ* Eton and Ch Ch Oxford; Lt Gren Gds, DC Baringo 1907; *d* unm 3 Nov 1912

1c Idonea Gertrude; *m* 22 July 1907 Henry Michael Hodgson, OBE, only s of Charles Hodgson, and had issue. He *d* 12 Oct 1955

2b Hugh Broke Boscawen; *b* 12 Aug 1836; Capt 65th Regt; *m* 20 June 1865 Janet Elizabeth (*d* 6 June 1904), dau of Rev Henry Curtis Cherry, and *d* 25 May 1890, leaving:

1c Charles Cameron, CMG (1916), OBE (1919); *b* 30 June 1866; Col RFA (TF), Maj Indian Cav, WW I (despatches); *m* 17 Aug 1892 Beatrice (*d* 2 Nov 1952), est dau of Henry Francis Makins (*see* MAKINS, Bt), and *d* 26 May 1951, leaving:

1d Harold Boscawen; *b* 2 July 1905; *educ* Harrow; Lt-Col Res Offrs and 7th Hus WW II; *m* 11 June 1930 Kathleen May, OBE (*d* 1984) 2nd dau of Sir Murrough John Wilson, KBE, of Cliffe Hall, Co Durham (*see* INCHIQUIN, B), and *d* 17 Oct 1973, leaving:

1e Charles Murrough; *b* 13 April 1933; *educ* Eton; Maj Yorks Yeo; *m* 11 June 1960 *Rosemary Anne (*m* 2nd 1987 Ronald Patrick Thorburn, FRICS), yr dau of Maj Charles John Frederick Platt, 3rd KOH, of Barnby Manor, Newark, Notts, and *d* 24 Nov 1985, leaving:

1f +Mark Broke [Mark Leveson-Gower Esq, 54 Brocklebank Rd, London SW18 3AT]; *b* 6 Aug 1961; *m* 1987 *Emma Joy, er dau of Desmond O'Connor Cameron, of Horsegrove Ho, Rotherfield, Sussex, and has:

1g +Hugh Charles; *b* 1993

1g *Jemima Anastasia; *b* 1996

2f +Henry Boscawen Boddington; *b* 1 Sept 1962; added w's maiden name as forename; *m* 1992 *Paula Ruth, DPhil, yr dau of David Boddington, of Poole, Dorset, and has:

1f +Reuben Boddington; *b* 1993

1f *Alice Victoria; *b* 5 Jan 1966; *m* *Mark W V Mathewson, yr s of Neil Mathewson, of Cullaloe, Fife

1e *Anastasia; *b* 25 Nov 1931; *m* 19 April 1958 Sir (Robert) Kynaston Studd, 3rd Bt (*qv*), and has issue

1d Janet, JP Inner London; *b* 19 May 1893; VAD WW I; *d* 30 April 1974

2c Philip, CMG (1918), DSO (1917), DL Hants; *b* 6 Feb 1871; NWF India 1897–98 (medal with two clasps), Boer War 1899–1902, WW I (wounded, despatches, Belgian Croix de Guerre): Col Notts and Derbys Regt, Bde Cdr 1915, Hon Brig-Gen 1919; *m* 2 Oct 1899 Eleanor Marcia (Norah) (*d* 21 March 1975), dau of Christopher Robert Nugent, JP, of The Hall, Pinner, and *d* 17 June 1939, leaving:

1d Hugh Nugent; *b* 1 July 1900; *educ* Haileybury and RMA Woolwich; Lt RFA, Capt and ADC to GOC-in-C Allied Forces Constantinople 1919–22, Brig RA, Burma Campaign WW II 1941–45 (despatches); *m* 1st 28 March 1934 (*divorce* 1948) Avril Joy (*k* car crash Mexico 1978), formerly w of Prince George Imeritinsky and dau of Sir John Ashley Mullens, and had:

1e *Lucinda Gaye; *b* 12 Nov 1935; *m* 5 May 1955 Sir Spencer Le Marchant, MP (*see* LE MARCHANT, B), and has issue

1d (cont.) Brig Hugh Leveson-Gower *m* 2nd 8 June 1949 Rachel (*d* 18 Dec 1981), formerly w of Michael Humphrey Wilkins and yst dau of Maj Harold Hunter Grotrian (*see* GROTRIAN, Bt), and *d* May 1979

1d *Elizabeth Ellen [Mrs Mark Harford, 8 Court St, Sherston, Wilts SN16 0LL]; *b* 11 Jan 1915; *m* 5 Dec 1945 Mark William Harford (*d* 13 Jan 1969), s of Hugh Wyndham Luttrell Harford, of Horton Hall, Chipping Sodbury, Glos, and has:

1e *Philip Hugh [Philip Harford Esq, Horton Hall Farm, Horton, Avon BS17 6QN]; *b* 14 Aug 1946; *educ* Switzerland; *m* 1982 *Willa, yr dau of William Joseph Franklin, of St Mary's Mead, Witney, Oxon, and has:

1f *William Scandrett; *b* 1984

1f *Harriet Kate Isabel; *b* 1987

2e *Gerald Mark [Gerald Harford Esq, Trewyn, Abergavenny, Gwent NP7 7PG]; *b* 8 June 1948; *educ* Eton; *m* 1985 *Camilla Margaret, est dau of Alistair Allan Horne, and has:

1f *Auriol Louise; *b* 1987

2f *Elizabeth Mida; *b* 1989

1c Edith; *d* unm 20 July 1953

2c Mabel; *d* unm 6 March 1967

3c Gertrude; *m* 24 June 1909 Robert Henry Whitworth, only s of James Whitworth, of Earl's Barton, Northants, and *d* 29 Dec 1963, leaving issue. He *d* 30 March 1948

3b Sackville; *b* 27 Aug 1839; *d* unm 3 May 1874

2a Edward; *b* Feb 1807; Army Offr; *m* 23 March 1839 Frances Cecilia (*d* 29 July 1861), dau of Dr William Powell, of Waterlooville, Hants, and *d* 6 Dec 1853

1a Isabella; *m* 8 Sept 1825 Sir John Thomas Ibbetson Selwyn, 6th Bt (*see* 1902 edn ROOKWOOD, B), and *d* 24 Sept 1858, leaving issue. He *d* 20 March 1869

(2) Edward; *b* 8 May 1776; R-Adml the Blue; *m* 13 Nov 1822 Charlotte Elizabeth (*d* 18 July 1826), 2nd dau of Harry Mount, of Wasing Place, Reading, and *d* 6 Dec 1853, leaving:

1a Elizabeth; *b* 13 April 1824; *m* 28 Aug 1854 Charles Patton Keele, of Southampton, and *d* 4 April 1875, leaving issue. He *d* 29 Aug 1914

2a Frances Charlotte; *b* 13 Dec 1825; *m* 7 Nov 1854 Vicomte Papillon de la Ferté, of Versailles, and *d* 18 March 1915, having had issue. He *d* 7 Jan 1883

(3) William, of Titsey Place, Oxted, Surrey; *b* 6 Aug 1779; Ld Manor and Patron Living Titsey, Ld Manor of Foyle, Oxted; *m* 20 Aug 1804 Katherine Maria (*d* 7 Oct 1808), dau and heiress of Sir John Gresham, 6th Bt, of Titsey, and *d* 3 Oct 1851, leaving:

1a William, of Titsey Place; *b* 23 Nov 1806; *m* 17 June 1834 Emily Josephine Eliza (*d* 16 April 1872), dau of Sir Francis Hastinge Doyle, 1st Bt (*see* 1970 edn), and *d* 15 Dec 1860, having had:

1b Granville William Gresham, of Titsey Place, JP, DL Surrey; *b* 25 Feb 1838; MA, FSA, MP Reigate 1863–66; *m* 21 May 1861 Hon Sophia Leigh, LJStJ (*d* 12 July 1926), yst dau of 1st Baron Leigh (*qv*), and *d* 30 May 1895, having had, with five other sons (*d* young):

1c Ronald William Gresham; *b* 22 Sept 1863; *d* unm 21 July 1889

2c Granville Charles Gresham, of Titsey Place, JP, DL Surrey; *b* 25 Sept 1865; *educ* Eton and Balliol Coll Oxford (BA 1888, MA 1894); TFR, Lt Hants Yeo Cav 1892–96, Maj Sussex Yeo 1914–15, Maj W Kent Yeo 1915–16; *m* 3 Feb 1894 Evelyn Mildred (*d* 18 April 1957), 2nd dau of Henry Arthur Brassey (*see* BRASSEY OF APETHORPE, B), and *d* 4 Dec 1948, having had:

1d Richard Henry Gresham, of Titsey Place; *b* 27 Nov 1894; *educ* Eton; Maj Gren Gds (SR) WW I, DAQMG (Movements) London Dist WW II 1944–47; *d* unm 7 Feb 1982

2d Ronald Charles Granville Gresham; *b* 23 May 1896; *educ* Eton; Lt Coldstream Gds (SR); *d* 1 Aug 1917 of wounds recd in action

3d Thomas Christopher Gresham; *b* 19 June 1903; *educ* Eton and Trin Coll Cambridge

4d Alan John Gresham; *b* 22 Sept 1909; *educ* Eton and Magdalene Coll Cambridge (BA 1931); Maj Coldstream Gds SR; *d* unm 14 Aug 1974

3c Frederick Archibald Gresham (Rev); *b* 20 Feb 1871; MA Oxon, Rector Singleton Sussex 1913–28, Hon CF 1917–18; *m* 1st 14 June 1897 Cecil Eyre (*d* 6 July 1939), dau of Sir Walpole Lloyd Greenwell, 1st Bt (*qv*); *m* 2nd 1940 Elizabeth (*d* 1964), dau of George Dodds, of Newcastle-on-Tyne, and *d* 3 Oct 1946, having by his 1st w had, with another s and dau (*d* young):

1d +Humphrey Leigh Gresham; *b* 29 May 1908; *m* 1st 20 Dec 1929 (*divorce* 1941) Tracy, dau of Robert Hughes; *m* 2nd 1942 Cecily Marion (*d* 1980), dau of Henry Saxe-Wyndham

1d Judith Elyn Gresham; *b* 24 July 1905; *m* 1st 19 July 1928 (*divorce* 1939) Malcolm Septimus Vaughan, MBE, est s of Ernest Vaughan, of The Field Ho, Clent, Worcs, and had issue; *m* 2nd 5 July 1939 Maj Errol Reginald Thorold Holmes, RA, cricketer, est s of Arthur Charles Smithson Holmes, of Tandridge Hall, nr Oxted, Surrey, and had further issue. He *d* 16 Aug 1960

4c Evelyn Marmaduke Gresham; *b* 18 March 1872; *m* 1 Feb 1906 Elo Janet Catherine (*d* 20 March 1963 aged 92), yst dau of Lt-Col James Ross Farquharson of Invercauld, and *d* 25 Jan 1938, leaving:

1d Alastair Marmaduke Gresham; *b* 14 June 1907; *educ* Bradfield; *m* 1st 5 April 1934 Marjorie Blackburn (*d* 1936), dau of Herbert Cawtheray, and had:

1e +Anthony Gresham [Anthony Leveson-Gower Esq, 24A Oak Tree Rd, Whitehill, Bordon, Hants GU35 9DF]; *b* 1934

1d (cont.) Alastair Leveson-Gower *m* 2nd Sept 1939 Barbara (*d* 17 Jan 1997), dau of William George Higgins, and *d* 14 Oct 1990, having by her had:

2e +Robert Alastair [Robert Leveson-Gower Esq, 3 Briarwood Rd, St Johns, Woking, Surrey, GU21 1XD]; *b* 31 Aug 1946

2d Rupert Evelyn Gresham; *b* 25 April 1911; *educ* Bradfield; Capt King's Own Royal Regt; *m* 28 July 1956 *May [Mrs Rupert Leveson-Gower, Manor Farm, Standlake, Oxon], dau of William Clinkard, and *d* 1985, leaving:

1e +Charles William Gresham; *b* 6 Oct 1959

1e *Catherine Anne Gresham; *b* 1957

5c Henry Dudley Gresham (Sir); *b* 8 May 1873; *educ* Winchester and Magdalen Coll Oxford (Cricket Blue 1893–96, Capt 1896); cricketer, played for Surrey 1895–1920 (Capt 1908–10) and England in S Africa 1909–10 (Capt), selector 1909, 1924 (chm) and 1928–30 (chm); Maj RASC WW I (despatches); Pres Surrey CCC 1929–39, Hon Freedom Scarborough (where organised annual cricket festival) 1950, ktd 1953; *m* 23 April 1908 Enid Mary (*d* 7 Aug 1975 aged 94), er dau of Robert Sharp Borgnis Hammond Chambers, KC, and *dsp* 1 Feb 1954

6c Cecil Octavius Gresham, MBE (1919); *b* 2 Jan 1875; T/Capt RASC; *m* 11 Dec 1899 Emma Mary (*d* 29 Jan 1964 aged 89), dau of Philip de Clermont, of Ivy Ho, Godstone, Surrey, and *d* 6 July 1937, leaving:

1d Granville Howard Roderick Gresham; *b* 20 Oct 1900; *m* 2 June 1938 Anne, dau of Maj Francis Hawley, RSG, and *dsp* 14 Sept 1958

1d Constance Violet Gresham; *b* 10 March 1913

7c Clement Edward Gresham; *b* 28 Dec 1876; Lt 3rd Bn Sussex Regt and Prince Albert's Somerset LI, Boer War 1901–02 (medal with five clasps) and WW I, Capt, Legn Hon, Chev Order Redeemer Greece and St Sava Serbia, Comptroller Household to Govr-Gen Canada 1905–09; *d* unm 20 June 1939

1c Margaret Emily Gresham; *b* 10 Feb 1862; *m* 2 April 1891 Charles Lyon Liddell (*see* RAVENSWORTH, B) and *d* 24 April 1948, leaving issue

2c Ethel Sophia Gresham; *b* 6 Oct 1866; *m* 6 Feb 1907 Edward Henry Liddell (*see* RAVENSWORTH, B) and *d* 5 June 1950

3c Katherine Ursula Gresham; *b* 19 April 1878; *m* 15 Sept 1908 Rev Richard Busk Paterson Wells, RD, Hon CF, of Waterleet, Uplyme, Dorset, est s of Rev Harry Morland Wells, of Scarletts, Twyford, Berks, and *d* 1 Jan 1963, leaving issue. He *d* 6 Feb 1963 aged 89

2b Arthur Francis Gresham; *b* 25 April 1851; *educ* Eton and Ch Ch Oxford (BA 1874, MA 1877); Dip Serv 1876–1905: 3rd Sec 1879, 2nd Sec 1881, Sec Legation 1895–1905, T/Clerk FO 1917, KJStJ, Special Constable HQ Control Dept Section XI WW I, Freedom City London 1913, FSA, FRHS; *m* 4 Aug 1881 Caroline Frederica (*d* 20 Oct 1895), yst dau of George Savile Foljambe (*see* LIVERPOOL, E), and *d* 26 Dec 1922, having had:

1c William George Gresham; *b* 12 March 1883; *educ* Eton and Ch Ch Oxford; Clerk Ho Lds, barrister Inner Temple, Lt (T/Capt) Inns of Court OTC 1907–19, Lt Coldstream Gds (R) 1918; *ka* 9 Oct 1918

2c Osbert Charles Gresham; *b* 3 Nov 1888; *educ* Eton and HMS *Britannia*; CA Wilts, Cdr RN WW I Mediterranean Fleet and Dardanelles, WW II at Admlty Compass Observatory; *m* 4 Aug 1931 Winifred van Allen Phillips, est dau of Robert Young, of Ottawa, and *dsp* 14 April 1968

1c Emily Selina Augusta Gresham; *b* 29 Oct 1885; SRN, SR Mental Nurse, CMB, Diploma Roy Sch Art Needlework with gold seal 1912, DGStJ; *d* unm 9 Nov 1957

2c Victoria Sibell Ermyntrude Gresham; *b* 27 March 1887 (HIM THE EMPRESS FREDERICK OF GERMANY stood sponsor); *d* 27 Nov 1977

1b Emily Katharine Mary; *b* 11 June 1835; *m* 22 May 1866 Rev James Haldane Stewart, Rector Brightwell, Oxon, and *d* 6 Nov 1912, leaving issue. He *d* 24 Feb 1879

2b Mary Elizabeth; *b* 10 Nov 1836; *d* unm 6 Sept 1908

3b Selina Frances Diana; *b* 29 Feb 1840; *m* 23 Aug 1864 Rev William Champion Streatfeild, of Chart's Edge, Kent, Rector Frant, Sussex, and *d* 27 Oct 1916, having had issue. He *d* 8 Aug 1912

4b Caroline Susan Gresham; *b* 2 Sept 1842; *d* unm 3 Jan 1911

5b Frances Albinia Gresham; *b* 7 March 1846; *m* 30 July 1868 Arthur Wyatt-Edgell, DL, of Cowley Place, Devon, and *d* 28 Nov 1930, leaving issue. He *d* 26 June 1911

1a Katharine Frances; *m* 23 April 1845 Capt George Hope, RN, and *d* 26 Feb 1880, leaving issue (*see* LINLITHGOW, M)

2a Frances Elizabeth; *b* 25 Sept 1808; *d* unm 7 Dec 1869

(4) Augustus; *b* 21 June 1781; RN; *d* 2 Sept 1802

(5) Granville (Rev); *b* 14 May 1787; Rector Titsey and Tatsfield, Surrey, and St Mabyn, Cornwall; *d* unm 28 Sept 1841

(1) Frances; *b* 12 Oct 1782; *m* 1813 John Ward, of Durham, and *d* 29 Aug 1894, leaving issue

(2) Elizabeth; *b* 19 Nov 1784; *m* 1803 John Tillie Coryton, of Pentillie Castle, Cornwall, and *d* 1824, leaving issue

The 1st EARL *d* 25 Dec 1754; his est surv s,

GRANVILLE LEVESON-GOWER, **1st Marquess of Stafford**, so *cr* 1 March 1786, KG (1771), PC (1755); *b* 4 Aug 1721; *educ* Westminster and Ch Ch Oxford; MP (Tory to 1749, Whig thereafter) Bishops Castle 1744–47, Westminster 1747–54 and Lichfield April–Dec 1754, a Ld Admlty 1749–51, Ld Lt Staffs 1755–1800, Ld Privy Seal 1755–57 and 1784–94, Ld Chamberlain 1763–65, Ld Pres Cncl 1767–79; *m* 1st 23 Dec 1744 Elizabeth (*dsps* in May 1746), dau of Nicholas Fazakerly, MP Preston, of Penwortham, Lancs; *m* 2nd 28 March 1748 Lady Louisa Egerton (*d* 14 March 1761), dau and eventual coheir of 1st Duke of Bridgwater (*see* GREY EGERTON, Bt), and had:

1 GEORGE GRANVILLE, **1st Duke**

1 Louisa; *m* 26 Dec 1777 Sir Archibald Macdonald, 1st Bt, of East Sheen (*see* BOSVILLE-MACDONALD, Bt), and *d* 29 Jan 1827, leaving issue

2 Caroline; *m* 22 March 1770 5th Earl of Carlisle (*qv*) and *d* 27 Jan 1824, leaving issue

3 Anne; *m* 5 Feb 1784 Most Rev and Rt Hon Edward Venables Vernon Harcourt, PC, Archbp York (*see* VERNON, B), and *d* 16 Nov 1832, leaving issue

The **1st Marquess** *m* 3rd 23 May 1768 Susannah (*d* 15 Aug 1805), dau of 6th Earl of Galloway (*qv*), and by her had:

2 GRANVILLE LEVESON-GOWER, *cr* EARL GRANVILLE (*qv*)

4 Georgiana Augusta; *m* Nov 1797 2nd Earl of St Germans (*qv*) and *d* 24 March 1806, leaving issue

5 Charlotte Sophia; *m* 16 May 1791 6th Duke of Beaufort (*qv*) and *d* 12 Aug 1854, leaving issue

6 Susan; *m* 30 July 1795 1st Earl of Harrowby (*qv*) and *d* 26 May 1838, leaving issue

The 1st MARQUESS *d* 26 Oct 1803; his est s,

GEORGE GRANVILLE LEVESON-GOWER later SUTHERLAND-LEVESON-GOWER, **1st Duke of Sutherland** (UK), so *cr* 28 Jan 1833, KG (1806), PC (1790); *b* 9 Jan 1758; *educ* Westminster and Ch Ch Oxford; MP (Tory) Newcastle-under-Lyme 1779–84 and Staffs 1787–99, Amb Paris 1790–92, Ld Lt: Sutherland 1794–1813 and Staffs 1800–01, Col Staffs Vol Cav 1794–1800; called up to Ho Lds *vp* 25 Feb 1799 in f's Barony; Jt PMG 1799–1801; *m* 4 Sept 1785 Elizabeth, Countess of Sutherland (*qv*) in her own right (*d* 29 Jan 1839) and *d* 19 July 1833, having had:

1 GEORGE GRANVILLE LEVESON-GOWER later SUTHERLAND-LEVESON-GOWER (roy licence 12 May 1841), **2nd Duke of Sutherland** and 20th EARL OF SUTHERLAND (*qv*; as which s mother), KG (1841); *b* 8 Aug 1786; *educ* Harrow and Ch Ch Oxford; MP (Whig) St Mawes 1808–12, Newcastle-under-Lyme 1812–15 and Staffs 1815–20, called up to Ho Lds *vp* 25 Nov 1826 in f's Barony; Ld Lt: Sutherland 1831–61 and Salop 1839–45, High Steward Stafford 1833, Pres Highland Ag Soc 1837–41; *m* 28 May 1823 Lady Harriet Elizabeth Georgiana Howard, VA (2nd Cl) (*d* 27 Oct 1868), 3rd dau of 6th Earl of Carlisle (*qv*), Mistress of the Robes to HM QUEEN VICTORIA, and *d* 22 Feb 1861, having had, with three other daus (*d* in infancy):

(1) GEORGE GRANVILLE WILLIAM SUTHERLAND-LEVESON-GOWER, **3rd Duke of Sutherland**, KG (1864); *b* 19 Dec 1828; *educ* Eton and King's Coll London; MP (Lib) Sutherland 1852–61, Ld Lt Cromarty 1853–92 and Sutherland 1861–92, Lt-Col 1st Sutherland Rifle Vols; *m* 1st 20 June 1849 Anne, VA, only child of John Hay-Mackenzie, of Newhall and Cromarty, *cr* Countess of Cromartie (*qv*) in her own right, and *d* 25 Nov 1888, having had:

1a George Granville, *Earl Gower*; *b* 27 July 1850; *d* 5 July 1858

2a CROMARTIE SUTHERLAND-LEVESON-GOWER, **4th Duke of Sutherland**, KG (1902); *b* 20 July 1851; *educ* Eton; Cornet 2nd Life Gds 1870, Lt 1875; MP (Lib) Sutherland 1874–86, Ld Lt Sutherland 1892–1913, CA Staffs, Hon Col sometime cmdg Staffs Yeo, Hon Col 5th Bn Seaforth Highrs, Mayor Longton 1895; *m* 20 Oct 1884 Lady Millicent Fanny St Clair-Erskine (*d* 20 Aug 1955, having *m* 2nd 17 Oct 1914 (*divorce* 1919) Brig-Gen Percy Desmond FitzGerald, DSO, 11th Hus (*d* 17 Aug 1933) and 3rd 27 Oct 1919 (*divorce* 1925) Lt-Col George Ernest Hawes, DSO, MC, Roy Fus (*d* 1945)), dau of 4th Earl of Rosslyn (*qv*), and *d* 27 June 1913, having had:

1b GEORGE GRANVILLE SUTHERLAND-LEVESON-GOWER, **5th Duke of Sutherland**, KT (1929), PC (1936), JP Sutherland; *b* 29 Aug 1888; *educ* Eton; Cdr RNR, Hon Col 4th/5th Seaforth Highrs (TA), Lt 2nd Dragoons and Lovat Scouts Yeo WW I, Pres: TAA, Air League, Br Olympic Assoc, Navy League 1922–24; Grand Prior Primrose League (Chllr 1925), V-Pres Roy Aero Club, FRGS, Ld High Commr Gen Assembly Ch Scotland 1921–23, U-Sec: Colonies 1922, Air Min 1922–24, Paymaster-Gen 1925–28, Parly U-Sec War and V-Pres Army Cncl 1928–29, Ld Steward Household 1936–37, Ld Lt Sutherland, Order Crown Italy; *m* 1st 11 April 1912 Lady Eileen Gwladys Butler, DGStJ, JP, Mistress Robes to HM QUEEN MARY 1916–21 (*d* 24 Aug 1943), er dau of 7th Earl of Lanesborough (*qv*); *m* 2nd 1 July 1944 Clare Josephine (*d* 17 Feb 1998), formerly w of (a) Alexander Blake Shakespear, CIE, of Cawnpore, and (b) Col Vincent Ashforth Blundell Dunkerly, DSO, JP, of Knightsbridge, and 2nd dau of Herbert O'Brien, of Calcutta, and *d* 1 Feb 1963

2b Alastair St Clair, MC, DL Sutherland; *b* 24 Jan 1890; Lt Lovat Scouts Yeo, Maj RHG (Blues) and Gds MGR, ADC Personal Staff 1918 WW I (despatches, wounded); *m* 27 April 1918 Elizabeth Hélène (*m* 3rd 14 June 1931 Baron George Osten Driesen and *d* 26 Sept 1931), formerly w of John Leishman and dau of Warren Gardener Demarest, of New York, and *d* 28 April 1921, leaving:

1c ELIZABETH MILLICENT, COUNTESS OF SUTHERLAND (*qv*) in her own right

1b Victoria Elizabeth; *b* 5 Aug 1885; *d* 28 Jan 1888

2b Rosemary Millicent; *b* 9 Aug 1893; *m* 8 March 1919 3rd Earl of Dudley (*qv*) and *d* 21 July 1930 following a plane crash, leaving issue

3a FRANCIS SUTHERLAND-LEVESON-GOWER; *s* mother as 2nd EARL OF CROMARTIE (*qv*)

1a Florence; *m* 15 Nov 1876 Henry Chaplin, MP, later 1st Viscount Chaplin (*see* 1970 edn) and *d* 10 Oct 1881, leaving issue. He *d* 29 May 1923

2a Alexandra (HM QUEEN ALEXANDRA stood sponsor); *d* unm 16 April 1891

(1) (cont.) The **3rd Duke** *m* 2nd 4 March 1889 Mary Caroline (*m* 3rd 12 Nov 1896 Sir Albert Kaye Rollit (*d* 12 Aug 1922), MP Islington, and *d* 25 May 1912), widow of Arthur Kindersley Blair, 71st HLI, and yr dau of Rev Richard Michell, DD, Pncpl Hertford Coll Oxford, and *d* 22 Sept 1892

(2) Frederick George; *b* 11 Nov 1832; Offr Rifle Bde; *d* of fever off Sebastopol 6 Oct 1854

(3) Albert; *b* 21 Nov 1843; Capt 2nd Life Gds; *m* 19 March 1872 Grace Emma Townshend (*d* Dec 1923), only dau of Sir Thomas Abdy, 1st Bt (*qv*), and *d* 23 Dec 1874, leaving:

1a Frederic Neville; *b* 31 May 1874; *educ* Eton and Ch Ch Oxford; MP Sutherland 1900–06; *m* 19 Aug 1916 Blanche Lucie Gillard and *dsp* 9 April 1959

(4) Ronald Charles SUTHERLAND-GOWER; *b* 2 Aug 1845; MP Sutherland 1867–74, Tstee Nat Portrait Gallery and Shakespeare Memorial Building Stratford-on-Avon; *d* unm 9 March 1916

(1) Elizabeth Georgiana; *m* 31 July 1844 8th Duke of Argyll (*qv*) and *d* 25 May 1878, leaving issue (*see* BAIRD, Bt, of Newbyth)

(2) Evelyn; *m* 4 Oct 1843 12th and last Lord Blantyre (*d* 15 Dec 1900) and *d* 24 Nov 1869, leaving issue

(3) Caroline; *m* 30 Sept 1847 4th Duke of Leinster (*qv*) and *d* 8 May 1887, leaving issue

(4) Constance Gertrude; *m* 28 April 1852 1st Duke of Westminster (*qv*) and *d* 19 Dec 1880, leaving issue

2 FRANCIS LEVESON-GOWER later EGERTON (roy licence 24 Aug 1833), **1st Earl of Ellesmere**, of Ellesmere, Co Salop, so *cr* 6 July 1846, as also VISCOUNT BRACKLEY of Brackley, Northants (both UK), KG (1855), PC (GB and I 1828); *b* 1 Jan 1800; *educ* Eton and Ch Ch Oxford; Cornet 10th Hus 1821–23, MP (Lib C or Canningite) Bletchingley 1822–26, Sutherland 1826–31, S Lancs 1835–46, a Ld Treasury April–Sept 1827, U-Sec Colonies Jan–May 1828, Ch Sec to Ld Lt Ireland 1828–30, Sec at War July–Nov 1830; Ld Lt Lancs 1856–57, Tstee Nat Portrait Gallery 1856–57, versifier and author; *m* 18 June 1822 Harriet Catherine (*d* 17 April 1866), er dau of Charles Greville by Charlotte, dau of 3rd Duke of Portland (*see* PORTLAND, E), and *d* 18 Feb 1857, having had:

(1) GEORGE GRANVILLE FRANCIS EGERTON, **2nd Earl of Ellesmere**; *b* 15 June 1823; *educ* Ch Ch Oxford; MP (Lib C) N Staffs 1847–51; *m* 29 April 1846 Lady Mary Louisa Campbell (*d* 24 Nov 1916 aged 91), dau of 1st Earl Cawdor (*qv*), and *d* 19 Sept 1862, leaving:

1a FRANCIS CHARLES GRANVILLE EGERTON, **3rd Earl of Ellesmere**, JP, DL (Lancs and Northants); *b* 5 April 1847; *educ* Eton and Trin Coll Cambridge; Hon Col Duke of Lancaster's Own Yeo and 7th Bn Manchester Regt (VD), KJStJ; *m* 9 Dec 1868 Lady Katherine Louisa Phipps, LGStJ (*d* 23 Sept 1926), 2nd dau of 2nd Marquess of Normanby (*qv*), and *d* 13 July 1914, leaving:

1b JOHN FRANCIS GRANVILLE SCROPE EGERTON, **4th Earl of Ellesmere**, MVO (1909), DL (Lancs); *b* 14 Nov 1872; Hon Col RASC (T), Lt-Col and Brevet-Col 3rd Bn Roy Scots, Boer War 1900 and WW I (despatches), ADC to HM GEORGE V, KJStJ; *m* 28 Oct 1905 Lady Violet Lambton, DGStJ (*d* 22 Feb 1976), est dau of 4th Earl of Durham (*qv*), and *d* 24 Aug 1944, leaving:

1c JOHN SUTHERLAND EGERTON, **5th and present Earl of Ellesmere and 6th and present Duke of Sutherland**

1c Anne Katherine; *m* 8 April 1931 Lt-Col Geoffrey Babington, 16th/15th Lancers, only s of Lt-Gen Sir James Melville Babington, KCB,

KCMG, 16th Lancers, and *d* 15 July 1964, leaving issue. He *d* 8 Dec 1856

2c Jane Mary; *m* 7 Feb 1934 Richard Ladislas Scrope, est s of Henry Scrope, of Danby, and had:

    1d *Simon Egerton; *b* 23 Dec 1934; *educ* Ampleforth and Trin Coll Cambridge; late 2nd Lt Coldstream Gds

    1d *Elizabeth Jane; *b* 5 June 1937

3c Mary; *m* 12 Jan 1945 *Lt-Col Conyers Stephen Scrope, MC, The Green Howards, est s of Stephen Scrope, of Middleham, Yorks, and had:

    1d *Annabel Margaret Diana; *b* 13 Nov 1945

    2d *Rosemary; *b* 10 July 1947

    3d *Diana Theresa Violet; *b* 2 Feb 1951

4c *Susan Alice [The Lady Susan Askew, Stone House, Sprouston, Kelso, Roxburghshire]; *b* 1913; *m* 4 Oct 1933 (*divorce* 1966) Maj John Marjoribanks Askew, CBE, Gren Gds, only s of William Haggerston Askew, JP, of Ladykirk, Berwicks, and has:

    1d *Henry John [Henry Askew Esq, Ladykirk House, Berwick-upon-Tweed, TD15 1SU; 77 Chester Row, London SW1W 8JL]; *b* 5 April 1940; *educ* Eton; late Gren Gds, dir Gerrard & Reid Ltd 1967; *m* 1978 *Rosemary Eileen, dau of Dr (Charles) Edmunds Darby Taylor, of Alnwick Ho, Little Shelford, Cambs, and has:

        1e *Jack; *b* 1984

        2e *George; *b* 1986

        3e *William; *b* 1992

    1d *Sarah Caroline [The Rt Hon The Lady Faringdon, Buscot Park, Faringdon, Oxon SN7 8BU; 28 Brompton Sq, London SW3 2AD]; *b* 1 June 1936; *m* 30 June 1959 *3rd Baron Faringdon (*qv*) and has issue

5c *Margaret, CVO (1994) [The Lady Margaret Colville CVO, The Close, Broughton, Hants SO20 8AA]; *b* 1918; Jr Cdr ATS WW II, Lady-in-Waiting to HRH PRINCESS ELIZABETH 1946–49, Extra Woman Bedchamber to HM QUEEN ELIZABETH THE QUEEN MOTHER 1990–; *m* 20 Oct 1948 Sir John Rupert Colville, CB, CVO (*see* COLVILLE OF CULROSS, V), and has issue

6c Alice, CVO (1957); *b c* 1923; T/Ldy-in-Waiting to HRH PRINCESS ELIZABETH 1949–52, Woman Bedchamber to HM THE QUEEN 1953; *d* by her own hand 1977

2b Francis William George; *b* 4 Dec 1874; Maj Duke of Lancaster's Own Yeo; *m* 2 Nov 1897 Hilda Margaret (*d* 22 Dec 1958), dau of Rev Canon Curteis, and *d* 4 April 1948, having had:

1c Roger Francis; *b* 7 Feb 1899; *d* 26 Dec 1905

2c Cyril Reginald; *b* 7 Sept 1905; *educ* Lancing and Trin Coll Cambridge; Capt Hants Regt WW II, Prime Warden Dyers' Co 1954; *m* 1st 18 Dec 1934 Mary (*d* 23 Sept 1949), only dau of Sir Ronald Hugh Campbell, GCMG, PC, and had:

    1d +FRANCIS RONALD [Francis Egerton Esq, Ley Farm, Stetchworth, Suffolk CB8 9GX]; *b* 18 Feb 1940; heir presumptive; *educ* Eton and RAC Cirencester; *m* 11th May 1974 *Victoria Mary, twin dau of Maj-Gen Edward Alexander Wilmot Williams, CB, CBE, MC (*see* ADDINGTON, B), and has:

        1e +James Granville; *b* 12th Aug 1975

        2e +Henry Alexander; *b* 28th Feb 1977

    1d *Lucy Helen [Mrs Michael Pelham, Old Way House, Beaulieu, Hants SO42 7YL]; *b* 5 Dec 1937; *m* 25 Oct 1958 *Michael Alan Pelham, JP, s of Harry Alan Pelham, and has:

        1e *Charles Peregrine [Charles Pelham Esq, Apt 5b, Mountain Lodge, 44 Mt Kellett Rd, The Peak, Hong Kong; 12A Charleville Mansions, Charleville Rd, London W14 6JB]; *b* 27 July 1959; *m* 10 Aug 1990 *Clare Johanna Marina, dau of Wallace Earl Britton, of Aptos, Calif., and has:

            1f *Henry Cyril; *b* 29 Sept 1992

            2f *George Marcus; *b* 9 April 1994

            1f *Avanete Johanna; *b* 4 March 1998

        1e *Laura Mary [Mrs Ronald Slade, 10 Hollywood Court, Hollywood Rd, London SW10 9HR; Rimska, 12147 Praha 2, Czech Republic]; *b* 15 May 1962; *m* 1996 *Ronald John Slade, s of Ronald Slade, of Dulwich

    2d *Katharine Mary [Mrs Franklin Watts, 42 Chiddingstone St, London SW6 3TG]; *b* 6 Sept 1942; *m* 1979 *Franklin Watts and has:

        1e *Angus William; *b* 17 Feb 1982

        1e *Camilla Mary; *b* 19 March 1984

    3d *Alice Marian [Mrs Thomas Fremantle, Wayside Cottage, E Markham, Newark, Notts NG22 0RE]; *b* 17 Oct 1946; *m* 26 June 1971 *Lt Thomas David Fremantle, RN (*see* COTTESLOE, B), and has issue

2c (cont.) Cyril Egerton *m* 2nd 29 Jan 1954 Mary Truda (*d* 1982), only dau of Sir Thomas Sydney Lea, 2nd Bt (*qv*), and *d* 1992

1c Phyllis Mary; *b* 15 Oct 1900; *m* 1st 14 Feb 1920 (*divorce* 1934) Guy Coltman-Rogers, DL (*d* 22 Feb 1976), est s of Charles Coltman-Rogers, JP, of Strange Park, Radnorshire, and had:

    1d David Alan; *b* 13 Feb 1924; Welsh Gds WW II; *m* 22 April 1952 *Jane (*m* 2nd 20 July 1961 Col Charles Hamilton Mitchell, DSO, OBE (*d* 23 July 1964), s of Maj Charles Mitchell DSO, OBE; *m* 3rd 11 Feb 1967 Alastair Hew Roderick Lyell, s of Angus Chambers Lyell, of Chippenham, Cambs), dau of Brig-Gen Charles Richard Woodroffe, CMG, CVO, CBE, of Bembridge, IoW, by his 2nd w Islay Mary Cecil, yst dau of Lt-Col Augustus Henry Macdonald-Moreton (*see* DUCIE, E), and *d* 22 Dec 1957, leaving:

        1e *Jonathan Guy Coltman; *b* 2 Aug 1953; *educ* Eton

        2e *Timothy Charles; *b* 20 May 1956; *educ* Stowe

        3e *David James Julian; *b* 22 Oct 1957

    1d *Helen Muriel Coltman; *b* 12 Nov 1920; ATS WW II

2d *Penelope Elizabeth; *b* 15 June 1922; WRNS WW II; *m* 26 April 1947 Lt-Cdr Charles St Clair Cameron, RN, er s of V-Adml Cyril St Clair Cameron, CBE, of Park Cottage, Hook Green, Kent, and has:

    1e *Alan Gordon; *b* 16 Nov 1949; *educ* Canford

    1e *Belinda Jane; *b* 6 Feb 1948

    2e *Stella Mary; *b* 22 March 1954

    3e *Penelope Ann; *b* 22 March 1954

3d *Gillian Margaret; *b* 25 Sept 1927; *m* 14 March 1964 (*divorce* 1969) Francesco Aprea, s of Luca Aprea, of Rome, and has:

    1e *Elizabeth Ann; *b* 5 Oct 1964

1c (cont.) Mrs Phyllis Coltman-Rogers *m* 2nd 10 Oct 1934 (*divorce* 1946) Anthony Richards, s of Rev George Gurney Richards

3b Thomas Henry Frederick; *b* 10 Sept 1876; Assist Priv Sec to Chllr Exchequer 1902; *m* 23 Oct 1902 Lady Bertha Anson (*d* 30 Aug 1959), est dau of 3rd Earl of Lichfield (*qv*), and *d* 1 Oct 1953, leaving:

1c Mildred Helen; *b* 15 Nov 1903; *m* 1st 5 Feb 1925 (*divorce* 1936) 4th Baron Oranmore and Browne (*qv*) and had issue; *m* 2nd 20 June 1938 Hon Hew North Dalrymple, TD, 2nd s of 12th Earl of Stair (*qv*), and *d* 1980, leaving further issue

2c *Pamela Katharine [Mrs Ralph Stockley, Owls, Middle Hill, Englefield Green, Surrey]; *b* 12 May 1918; *m* 27 Aug 1940 Lt-Col Ralph Capel Stockley, Roy Northumberland Fus (*ka* Nov 1944), only s of Brig-Gen Hugh Roderick Stockley, CIE, of Tudor Ho, Oaksey, Wilts, and has:

    1d *Jane Margaret [Mrs Gerard Chichester, Llangoed, Erwood, Builth Wells, Powys LD2 3TJ]; *b* 22 Oct 1942; *m* 1974 *Gerard Balfour Chichester and has:

        1e *Henry Ralph; *b* 11 Jan 1977 *educ* Eton and Worcester Coll Oxford

        2e *Charles Edmond; *b* 20 Sept 1978; *educ* Eton

    2d *Sally Elizabeth [Mrs Christopher Lewis, Malt Office Farm, Metfield, Harleston, Norfolk]; *b* 6 Sept 1944; *educ* London U (BA 1968); *m* 1978 *Dr Christopher John Tudor Lewis and has:

        1e *Beatrice Emily Frances; *b* 1979

    2d (cont.) Dr and Mrs Lewis also adopted 1983:

        *John Claude; *b* 1976

4b Wilfred Charles William; *b* 21 Sept 1879; Lt 1st Dragoons Boer War 1900–02 (wounded), Lt-Col RAF WW I (despatches); *m* 21 Dec 1914 Florence Maletha Capell (*d* 21 Jan 1951), only dau of Francis Henry Horatio Capell Reade, and *dsp* 27 Dec 1939

5b Reginald Arthur; *b* 6 July 1886; *d* unm 13 Sept 1904

1b Mabel Laura; *b* 16 Dec 1869; *d* unm 25 Nov 1946

2b Alice Constance; *b* 12 Nov 1870; *d* unm 6 Nov 1932

3b Beatrice Mary, MBE (1920); *b* 5 Nov 1871; *m* 5 Aug 1896 1st Baron Rochdale (*see* ROCHDALE, V) and *d* 7 Sept 1966, leaving issue

4b Katharine Augusta Victoria; *b* 2 Dec 1877; DGStJ; *m* 3 June 1905 Charles Hardy, JP, of Odsal House, Harbledown, Canterbury, est s of Charles Stewart Hardy, of Chilham Castle, and *dsp* 27 Oct 1960. He *d* 11 Nov 1940

5b Leila Georgina; *b* 23 Dec 1881; nun; *d* 22 Aug 1964

6b Helen Constance; *b* 24 Sept 1884; *d* unm 3 April 1901

2a Alfred John Francis; *b* 6 Feb 1854; Lt Gren Gds, MP Eccles; *m* 28 April 1881 Isabella Corisande Gertrude (*d* 22 April 1910), dau of Hamilton Gorges, of Kilbrew, Co Meath, and *dsp* 25 Sept 1890

(2) Francis; *b* 15 Sept 1824; Adml, Ld Lt Surrey, MP E Derbys 1868–86; *m* 26 Sept 1865 Louisa Caroline (*d* 21 Sept 1907), only dau of 7th Duke of Devonshire (*qv*), and *d* 15 Dec 1895, leaving:

1a William Francis, DL Surrey; *b* 1 March 1868; Lt 17th Lancers, Capt W Kent Yeo and 1st Vol Bn Roy Lancaster Regt; *m* 8 Aug 1894 Lady Alice Susan Godolphin Osborne (*d* 16 March 1951), 2nd dau of 9th Duke of Leeds (*see* 1963 edn), and *d* 21 March 1949, leaving:

1b Francis; *b* 17 Jan 1896; Capt 17th Lancers and RAF; *m* 7 Feb 1921 Hon Doris Mary Pottinger Meysey-Thompson (*d* 27 March 1953, having *m* 2nd 1 March 1938 Maj John Humphrey Allison Seed, TD, DL, JP, only s of Benjamin Shaw Seed, of Everthorpe Hall, Brough, E Yorks), 3rd dau of 1st Baron Knaresborough (*see* MEYSEY-THOMPSON, Bt), and *d* 8 June 1935, leaving:

    1c Anthony Francis; *b* 2 Nov 1921; *educ* Eton; Lt 60th Rifles and F/Lt RAF; *m* 17 Aug 1946 Pauline Clodagh Seaton (*d* 12 Jan 1997), only dau of Trevor Toulmin Seaton Leadam, of Colebrooke, Watersfield, Sussex, and *d* 1985, having had:

        1d A son; *b* 8 April, *d* 9 April 1947

        2d +Simon Francis Cavendish [Simon Egerton Esq, Old Hoyle, Heyshott, W Sussex GU29 0DX]; *b* 13 Dec 1949; *educ* Milton Abbey; *m* 25 April 1990 *Juliet Susannah, only dau of Robert Assheton Barrett (*see* CLITHEROE, B), and has:

            1e *Isabella Louise Greville; *b* 1994

        3d +Fulke Charles Granville; *b* 2 Aug 1952; *educ* Stanbridge Earls

    2c Michael Godolphin; *b* 20 Sept 1926; *educ* Eton; Lt 17th/21st Lancers; *m* 1st 2 Nov 1951 Pamela Nicolette, formerly w of Patrick William Meade-Newman and yr dau of Giulio Giorgio de Gardiol, of La Fontana and Luserna San Giovanni, Turin, Italy; *m* 2nd 22 May 1957 Elizabeth Anne Bowring (*d* 1994), only dau of Leslie Bowring Wimble, of Romany Ridge, N Chailey, Sussex, and *d* 1979, leaving:

        1d +Mark William Godolphin; *b* 14 Jan 1958; *m* 1st 1979 (*divorce* 1983) Nicola J Hawkes and has:

            1e *Sophia Annabel Godolphin; *b* 1983

        1d (cont.) Mark Egerton *m* 2nd 1991 *Mercedes Abadia Gomez, of Fuengirola, Spain, and by her has:

            2e *Sacha Louise; *b* 1993

    2d Robin Michael Bowring; *b* 11 March 1962; *m* 1985 *Suzanne, dau of John Edward Liversidge, of Birdham, Sussex, and *d* 1988 following a car crash, leaving:

1e *Kathryn Rebecca; *b* 1986

2e *Charlotte Louise; *b* 1987

3d +Nicholas; *b* 19 Sept 1967

3c +David William; *b* 22 Jan 1930; *educ* Stowe; late Capt 17th/21st Lancers; *m* 27 Sept 1956 *Patricia Mary Treharne, formerly *w* of William Rippon Bissill and only dau of Archibald Allan Treharne Thomas and Mrs Dorothy Nelson, of Mayfair, and has:

1d +Francis David; *b* 21 Sept 1959; *educ* Stowe, RAC Cirencester (ARICS) and Keble Coll Oxford (BA)

2a Frederick Greville; *b* 15 April 1869; Cdr RN; *d* of wounds recd in action Ladysmith 3 Nov 1899

1a Blanche Harriet; *b* 27 June 1871; *d* unm 14 May 1943

2a Dorothy Charlotte, OBE (1920), JP Surrey; *b* 6 Oct 1874; *d* unm 2 Aug 1959

3a Christian Mary, MBE (1918); *b* 17 June 1876; *d* umn 26 Nov 1970

(3) Algernon Fulke, of Worsley Old Hall, DL; *b* 31 Dec 1825; DCL, Hon Col Duke of Lancaster's Own Yeo Cav, MP SE Lancs 1868–80 and Wigan 1882–85, Sec Admlty 1874–80; *m* 22 Jan 1863 Alice Louisa (*d* 28 March 1905), est dau of Lord George Cavendish (*see* DEVONSHIRE, D), and *d* 14 July 1891, leaving:

1a George Algernon; *b* 1 Dec 1870; Maj 19th Hus; *d* unm 13 May 1915 of wounds recd in action

2a Ralph Greville; *b* 27 Nov 1876; *d* 9 Jan 1877

1a Margaret Louise; *m* 10 Oct 1901 George Chichester May, KC, 2nd s of George Augustus Chichester May, PC, Ld Ch Justice Ireland 1877–87, and *d* Oct 1950, leaving issue. He *d* 3 Nov 1924

2a Blanche Susan; *d* unm 1 Nov 1940

3a Katherine Alice; *d* 13 Dec 1962 aged 95

4a Sybil Mary; *d* 27 Aug 1873

5a Violet Ellinor; *m* 27 Jan 1914 Frederick Walter Stephenson, of Melbury Abbas, Shaftesbury, 2nd s of Sir Augustus Frederick William Keppel Stephenson, KBE, and *d* 6 March 1968 aged 95. He *d* 19 May 1944

6a Mary Florence

7a Evelyn Harriet; *d* unm 3 Nov 1964

(4) Arthur Frederick; *b* 6 Feb 1829; Lt-Col; *m* 2 June 1858 Helen (*m* 2nd 15 July 1875 Maj-Gen Sir William Julius Gascoigne, KCMG (*d* 9 Sept 1926), and *d* 15 June 1928), yst dau of Martin Tucker Smith, MP, and *d* 25 Feb 1866, leaving:

1a Granville George Algernon, CB (1905); *b* 10 May 1859; Seaforth Highrs and Yorks Regt Afganistan 1879–80, Egyptian Expdn 1882, Nile Expdn 1898 and WW I (despatches), cmded Lowland Div TF 1914–15, Base Cmdt MEF 1915–16, Col HLI 1921–29, Maj-Gen; *d* unm 3 May 1951

2a Cecil Martin; *b* 4 Dec 1860; *m* 16 Aug 1906 Gladys Mary, dau of Alfred Ingram Sharpe, and *d* 10 Jan 1931

3a Claude Francis Arthur, JP Suffolk; *b* 23 Jan 1864; Maj TFR, MICE; *m* 28 June 1900 Alexandra Elizabeth (*d* 30 July 1938), widow of William Charles Bellairs and dau of Henry Nattras Ritchie, of Thorpe, Surrey, and *d* 8 May 1957, leaving:

1b Scrope Arthur Francis Sutherland, JP (Wilts 1955); *b* 12 June 1902; *educ* Wellington and Trin Coll Cambridge (BA); Lt-Col HLI WW II (despatches, POW); *m* 16 Jan 1933 Marjorie (*d* 1992), only dau of Hugh Morrison (*see* MARGADALE, B), and *d* 1986, leaving:

1c *Sarah Jane Mary; *b* 13 May 1934

2c *Susan Alexandra [Mrs David Yorke, Hall Foot, Worston, Clitheroe, Lancs BB7 1QA]; *b* 5 June 1936; *m* 29 July 1957 *David John Yorke (*see* CLITHEROE, B) and has:

1d *John Alexander; *b* 21 Jan 1959; *m* 25 April 1988 *Alexandra Hall Hall

2d *Charles Scrope Edward; *b* 3 Feb 1965

1d *Sophia Caroline Annabel; *b* 7 Jan 1961; *m* 8 Sept 1984 *Nicholas Antony Bevil Acland (*see* ACLAND, Bt, of Oxford)

3c *Katharine Rose [Mrs Peter Sanguinetti, Sand Hall, Wedmore, Somerset BS28 4XF]; *b* 25 Sept 1946; *m* 15 Nov 1973 *Peter John Sanguinetti, s of Jack Sanguinetti, of Sand Hall, and has:

1d *Edward Francis; *b* 1979

1d *Charlotte Emma Georgiana; *b* 1983

4a Arthur Frederick, DSO (1900); *b* 15 Jan 1866; Capt 1st Bn Cameron Highrs, Nile Expdn 1898 (two medals, two clasps), Boer War 1900–02 (despatches, two medals, six clasps) and WW I, Hon Lt-Col 2nd/9th Roy Scots; *m* 19 Oct 1939 Helen Louisa, widow of Capt Francis Dykes Walker, of Dalny Ho, Midlothian, and dau of James Hodson, and *dsp* 19 Feb 1942

1a Louisa Blanche; *m* 14 Aug 1888 John A Jameson, of Glen Lodge, Co Sligo, and Chelsea, and *d* 30 March 1937, leaving issue

(5) Granville; *b* 1834; RN; *k* at sea 27 Jan 1851

(1) Alice Harriet Frederica; *m* 25 July 1854 3rd Earl of Strafford (*qv*) and *d* 22 Dec 1928

(2) Blanche; *m* 27 Dec 1865 7th Earl of Sandwich (*qv*) and *dsp* 20 March 1894

1 Charlotte Sophia; *m* 27 Dec 1814 13th Duke of Norfolk (*qv*) and *d* 7 July 1870, leaving issue

2 Elizabeth Mary; *m* 16 Sept 1819 2nd Marquess of Westminster (*see* WESTMINSTER, D) and *d* 11 Nov 1891 aged 94, leaving issue

SUTHERLAND, Countess of

Arms: Gules three mullets or (arms of SUTHERLAND of that Ilk), on a bordure of the second a double tressure flory-counterflory of the first (honourable augmentation). **Crest:** A cat-a-mountain sejant rampant proper. **Supporters:** Dexter, a savage man wreathed about the head and loins with laurel proper, holding in his exterior hand a club gules resting upon his shoulder; sinister, another like savage, sustaining in his sinister hand and against his shoulder, upon a staff ensigned by the coronet of an earl, a banneret gules charged with three mullets or. **Motto:** *Sans peur* ('Fearless'). **Creation:** E. (S) *c* 1235.

THE COUNTESS OF SUTHERLAND (Elizabeth Millicent Sutherland) [The Rt Hon The Countess of Sutherland, Dunrobin Castle, Golspie, Sutherland; House of Tongue, By Lairg, Sutherland; 39 Edwardes Sq, London W8 6HJ]; *b* 30 March 1921; *s* unc 1963 as 24th holder of what is the premier earldom of Scotland, also as Chief of Clan Sutherland; chm Dunrobin Castle Ltd; *m* 5 Jan 1946 *Charles Noel Janson, DL, late Welsh Gds, est s of Charles Wilfrid Janson, of Belgravia (*see* below, **Lineage (of Janson)**), changed her name to SUTHERLAND 1963 and has had:

1 +ALISTAIR CHARLES ST CLAIR, *Lord Strathnaver, Master of Sutherland* [Lord Strathnaver, Sutherland Estates Office, Golspie, Sutherland KW10 6RP]; *b* 7 Jan 1947; *educ* Eton and Ch Ch Oxford (BA); Met Police 1969–74, IBM (UK) Ltd 1974–79; *m* 1st 29 Nov 1968 (*divorce* 1980) Eileen Elizabeth, only dau of Richard Wheeler Baker, Jr, of Princeton, NJ, and has:

(1) +Rachel Elizabeth; *b* 10 Aug 1970

(2) +Rosemary Millicent; *b* 10 Sept 1972

1 (cont.) *Lord Strathnaver m* 2nd 21 March 1980 *Gillian, er dau of Robert Murray, of Gourock, Renfrewshire, and by her has:

(1) +Alexander Charles Robert, *Master of Strathnaver*; *b* 1 Oct 1981

(3) +Elizabeth; *b* 24 April 1984

2 +Martin Dearman; *b* 7 Jan 1947; *educ* Eton; RHG (Blues) 1967–68; *m* 14 Feb 1974 *Hon Mary Ann Balfour, only dau of 1st Baron Balfour of Inchrye (*qv*), and has:

(1) +James Charles Harold; *b* 6 Sept 1975

(2) +Nicholas George; *b* 9 Feb 1977

(3) +Benjamin Edward; *b* 22 June 1979

(4) +Alexander Martin; *b* 14 April 1981

(5) +Christopher David; *b* 28 Sept 1984

3 Matthew Peter Demarest; *b* 8 April 1955; *educ* Eton; *d* 5 Dec 1969

1 *Annabel Elizabeth Hélène; *b* 16 May 1952; *m* 29 Oct 1982 *John Vernon Bainton, of Darling Pt, Sydney, NSW, only s of Richard Bainton, of Point Piper, Sydney

Lineage (of Sutherland): FRESKIN, allegedly of Flemish origins, granted large estates by DAVID I, including Strabrock, W Lothian, and Duffus, Moray; confirmed in these by roy charter 1166–71; *d* by 1172, leaving:

WILLIAM; of age by 1160; seems to have *d* in or after 1204, having had, with two yr sons (William de Moravia i.e., 'of Moray') living 1195, *d* by 1226, alleged ancestor of the MORAYs of Bothwell; Andrew, Parson Duffus 1203):

HUGH FRESKIN or MORAY, feudal Ld of Duffus; had large estates in Sutherland by 1211; granted Skelbo and other lands to St Gilbert Moray (possibly his nephew), Archdeacon Moray and from 1223 Bp Caithness; *d* between 1214 and 1222, having had, with two yr sons (Walter, feudal Ld of Duffus, *m* Eupheme, dau of Ferquhard Mac Taggart, 1st Earl of Ross, and *d* 1263, having had issue; Andrew, Bp Moray 1222, *d* 1242):

WILLIAM MORAY later (between 1229 and 1232) SUTHERLAND, **1st Earl of Sutherland**, so *cr c* 1235; *d* allegedly 1248, leaving:

WILLIAM SUTHERLAND, **2nd Earl of Sutherland**; supporter of EDWARD I's overlordship of Scotland; *d* probably by 7 July 1307, leaving:

1 WILLIAM SUTHERLAND, **3rd Earl of Sutherland**; supported ROBERT I (THE BRUCE) against the English attempt at maintaining overlordship; *d* by Dec 1330

2 KENNETH SUTHERLAND, **4th Earl of Sutherland**; allegedly *m* Marjory/Mary, widow of John de Strathbogie, 9th Earl of Atholl of the *cr* deemed to have been effected by 1115, and dau of 6th Earl of Mar (*qv*), and was *k* at the Scottish defeat by the English of Halidon Hill 19 July 1333, leaving:

(1) WILLIAM, **5th Earl**

(2) Nicholas; ancestor of the SUTHERLANDs of Duffus (*see* DUNBAR, Bt, of Hempriggs)

(1) Eustachia; *m* 1330 Gilbert Moray of Culbin and had issue

The er s,

WILLIAM SUTHERLAND, **5th Earl of Sutherland**; fought at Scottish defeat by English of Neville's Cross 17 Oct 1346; *m* 1st between 3 Aug and 28 Sept 1345 Margaret (*d c* 1346), sis of DAVID II (who by charter 1345 raised the Earldom of Sutherland to a regality (jurisidiction with quasi-regal powers), though this lapsed on the **5th Earl**'s death), and had:

1 John, *Master of Sutherland*; *b c* 1346; *dvp* of the plague *c* 8 Sept 1361 while a hostage in England for DAVID II

The **5th Earl** *m* 2nd by 9 Nov 1347 Joanna, widow of (a) Malise, 7th Earl of Strathe(a)rn of the *cr* deemed to have been effected by *c* 1128, (b) John Campbell, 1st and last Earl of Atholl of the *c* 1320 *cr* (*see* ARGYLL, D), and (c) Maurice Moray, 1st Earl of Strathearn of the Feb 1343/4 *cr*, and dau of Sir John Menteith of Rusky, and by her had:

2 ROBERT, **6th Earl**

3 Kenneth, of Drummoy, ancestor of the SUTHERLANDs of Forse

The 5th EARL *d* by 19 June 1371; his er surv s,

ROBERT SUTHERLAND, **6th Earl of Sutherland**; *b c* 1347; *m* 1389 Margaret, illegitimate dau of Sir Alexander Stewart ('The Wolf of Badenoch'), 1st Earl of Buchan of the *c* 1382 *cr* (and 4th s of ROBERT II), apparently by Mariot Athyn, and *d* by 1427, leaving:

JOHN SUTHERLAND, **7th Earl of Sutherland**; *b c* 1390; ktd 1408; *m* by 1342 Margaret (*d* 1510), a famous beauty, dau of Sir William Baillie of Lamington, and had:

1 Alexander, *Master of Sutherland*; *dvp* by 22 Feb 1455/6

2 JOHN, **8th Earl**

3 Nicholas, living 1448

4 Thomas *Beg* ('The Little'); allegedly ancestor of the SUTHERLANDs of Strathallie

5 Robert, living 1487

1 Janet; *m* Alexander Dunbar, 3rd s of Sir Alexander Dunbar of Westfield (*see* DUNBAR, Bt, of Mochrum), and had issue

The 7th EARL *d c* 1460; his est surv s,

JOHN SUTHERLAND, **8th Earl of Sutherland**, in whose favour his father resigned the Earldom 22 Feb 1455/6, but who was found incapable of managing his own affairs 1494; *m* 1st 1467 Finvola (allegedly killed in a robbery just after a narrow escape from drowning while crossing the River Unes by ferry), dau or gdau of Archibald/Celestine Macdonald (*see* BOSVILLE MACDONALD, Bt), and had:

1 JOHN SUTHERLAND, **9th Earl of Sutherland**; like his father was found incapable of managing his affairs; *d* unm July 1514

1 ELIZABETH Sutherland, **Countess of Sutherland** in her own right; *m c* 1500 Adam Gordon of Aboyne (*d* 17 March 1537/8), 2nd s of 2nd Earl of Huntly (*see* HUNTLY, M), who accordingly was styled Earl of Sutherland; she resigned the Earldom 10 Nov 1527 to their est s, though reserving the life-rent to herself and her husb, and *d* Sept 1535, having had, with four daus:

(1) Alexander, *Master of Sutherland*; *b c* 1501; *m c* 16 June 1520 Lady Janet Stewart (*m* 2nd by 13 May 1532 Sir Hew Kennedy of Girvanmains, Ayrshire; *m* 3rd by 4 Nov 1544 1st Lord Methven (*see* MORAY, E); *m* 4th 3rd Lord Ruthven, *see* CARLISLE, E), est dau of 2nd Earl of Atholl of the 1457 *cr* (*see* MORAY, E), and *dvp* & *vm* 15 Jan 1529/30, having had:

1a JOHN, **11th Earl**

2a Alexander, *k* by a fall from his horse at Elgin 1552

1a Janet; *m* 1537 Sir Patrick Dunbar of Cumnock and Westfield in Moray

2a Beatrice; *m* William Sinclair of Dunbeath and *d* 1529

(2) John, whose only child *m* George Gordon of Cochlarachie

(3) Adam; *k* Battle of Pinkie 10 Sept 1547

(4) Gilbert, of Garty; *m* Isabel (persuaded by her cousin the 4th Earl of Caithness (*qv*), long an enemy of the Earls of Sutherland, to poison her nephew-in-law the **11th Earl**, his w and son when they were her guests at her house of Helmsdale; supposedly committed sucide in prison while awaiting trial for their murder), dau of Alexander Sinclair of Dunbeath, and had issue

The **8th Earl** *m* 2nd Margaret, seemingly widow of John Munro, 11th of Foulis (*see* MUNRO, Bt, of Foulis-Obsdale), and allegedly dau of Sir William Calder of Calder, and (?)by her(?) had:

2 Alexander (possibly an illegitimate s); initially disputed right to the Earldom with his half-bro, claiming an entail existed by which the title passed to him, but waived his claim July 1509 (he never produced the entail, so its very existence must remain doubtful); *b* 1498; *m* the dau of Iye Roy Mackay of Strathnaver and was *k* in a skirmish *c* 1520, leaving issue

The **8th Earl** *m* 3rd Catherine (living 1512) and *d c* 1508

The COUNTESS's gs,

JOHN GORDON, **11th Earl of Sutherland**, called 'The Good Earl John'; *b* 1525; fought Battle of Pinkie 1547; having earlier supported the pro-French party in Scotland, he became a Ld of the Articles 1558 and one of the Lds of the Congregation by Jan 1559/60 and engaged in a skirmish against the French about then, when he was wounded; implicated in his cousin the Earl of Huntly's rebellion 1562; his titles and estates accordingly forfeited; he was pardoned 1565 and the forfeiture reversed 19 April 1567; *m* 1st between 21 Nov 1545 and 12 June 1546 Elizabeth (*dsp* by 18 May 1548), widow of James Stewart, 1st and last Earl of Moray of the 1500 *cr* and illegitimate s of JAMES IV, and only dau of 3rd Earl of Argyll (*see* ARGYLL, D); *m* 2nd *c* 6 Aug 1548 Helen (*d* by 25 Nov 1564), widow of 6th Earl of Erroll (*qv*), dau of 12th Earl of Lennox (*see* MORAY, E) and former mistress of JAMES V, by whom she had a s, and by her had, with another s (*d* young) and two daus (*d* unm):

1 ALEXANDER, **12th Earl**

1 Margaret; designated according to the alleged plot of the 4th Earl of Caithness (*see* above) as his 2nd son's bride, since on the death of her bro the Earldom of Sutherland would pass to her and her husband

2 Jean; *m* 1st Alexander Innes of that Ilk (*see* ROXBURGHE, D); *m* 2nd Thomas, s of 4th Earl of Huntly (*see* HUNTLY, M), and *d* Jan 1584

The **11th Earl** *m* 3rd Marion, widow of 4th Earl of Menteith (*see* MONTROSE, D) and dau of 4th Lord Seton (*see* EGLINTON and WINTON, E) and *d* with her 23 June 1567, both of them poisoned by his aunt (*see* above), although his son escaped through having been out of the house when the fatal dose was administered (apparently in mugs of ale)

His only surv s,

ALEXANDER GORDON, **12th Earl of Sutherland**; *b c* late June 1552; made over the Earldom to his est s 18 March 1580/1, obtaining a regrant of the dignity from the Crown 23 March 1580/1; swapped 1583 his Aboyne estate with the Earl of Huntly for that of Strathnaver, as Lords of which succeeding est sons of the Earls of Sutherland were henceforth called by courtesy; Hereditary Sheriff Inverness within Sutherland 1589; *m* 1st *c* 1567 (*divorce* 30 June 1572 for her adultery with Iye Mackay of Farr; *see* REAY, L) Lady Barbara Sinclair (*m* 2nd after 10 Sept 1574 Alexander Innes, 16th of that Ilk (*see* ROXBURGHE, D), and *d* 1573), dau of 4th Earl of Caithness (*qv*), his guardian during his minority (having purchased the post), the instigator of his parents' murder and author of at least one attempt on his (the **12th Earl**'s) life; *m* 2nd 13 Dec 1573 Jean (*m* 3rd Alexander Ogilvie of Boyne and *d* 14 May 1629), divorced w of 4th and last Earl of Bothwell (*see* BUCHAN-HEPBURN, Bt), and dau of 4th Earl of Huntly (*see* HUNTLY, M), and by her had, with two sons (*d* in infancy):

1 John, **13th Earl**

2 Sir ROBERT GORDON, 1st Bt, so *cr* 28 May 1625 (the first such ever in the Baronetage of Nova Scotia), of Letterfourie, Sutherland, also of Gordonstoun, Morayshire; *b* 14 May 1580; author: *The History of the Earldom of Sutherland*; *m* 16 Feb 1613 Louisa (*d* Sept 1680), dau and heiress of John Gordon of Glenluce, and *d* March 1654, having had issue (*see* 1902 edn)

3 Alexander (Sir); *b* 5 March 1585; *m* Margaret Mcleod, of Assynt, and had issue

1 Jane; *b* 1 Nov 1574; *m* Dec 1589, as his 2nd w, Huistean/Hugh Mackay of Farr (*see* REAY, L) and had issue

2 Mary; *b* 14 Aug 1582; *m* (contract 21 Feb 1597/8) David Ross of Balnagown but *dsp* 1605

The 12th EARL *d* 6 Dec 1594; his est s,

JOHN GORDON, **13th Earl of Sutherland**; *b* 20 July 1576; having surrended the Hereditary Shrievalty and Earldom of Sutherland, was regranted them 29 April 1601 with remainder, failing heirs male of his body, to his bros Robert and Alexander and the heirs male of their bodies, whom failing, to Adam, 3rd s of 1st Marquess of Huntly (*qv*) and his heirs male whatsoever, obtaining simultaneously a charter once more erecting the Earldom into a regality (*see* above against **5th Earl**); *m* 5 Feb 1599/1600 Agnes (*d* 18 Sept 1617), dau of 4th Lord Elphinstone (*qv*), and had, with three er sons (*d* young):

1 JOHN, **14th Earl**

2 Adam; *b* 15 May 1613; Lt-Col Swedish Army; *ka* Battle of Nordlingen in Thirty Years War 27 Aug 1634

3 George; *b* posthumuously 9 Feb 1616; *m* Rose, dau of 1st Earl of Antrim (*qv*)

1 Elizabeth; *m* 25 Feb 1619 James Crichton of Frendraught and had issue

2 Anne; *m* Dec 1623 Sir Gilbert Menzies of Pitfodels and *d* in a shipwreck off the coast of Holland July 1648

The 13th EARL *d* 11 Sept 1615; his est s,

JOHN GORDON, **14th Earl of Sutherland**, PC (S 1641); *b* 9 March 1608/9; *educ* Dornoch Sch and Edinburgh and St Andrews Us; granted new charter of Hereditary Shrievalty of Sutherland 1631; leading Covenanter (first to sign) Feb 1637/8, and maintained his Covenanting zeal throughout Civil War, Ld Privy Seal Scotland March 1648/9–51; obtained a regrant of the Earldom 21 Feb 1661/2 with remainder to his est s and the latter's heirs male; *m* 1st 14 Feb 1631/2 Lady Jean Drummond (*d* 29 Dec 1637), only child of 1st Earl of Perth (*qv*), and had:

1 John, *Lord Strathnaver*; *b* 21 Nov 1632; *d* 14 Oct 1637

2 GEORGE, **15th Earl**

3 Robert; *b* 31 Dec 1635; *m* (contract 14 Nov 1665) Jane (*m* 2nd March 1676 Hugh Mackay of Strathy), dau of 2nd Lord Reay (*qv*), and *dsp* 1671

1 Jean; *b* 10 Oct 1634; *m* (contract 11 July 1657) Capt Robert Stewart of Eday and had issue

2 Anne; *m* 3 May 1683 3rd Viscount of Arbuthnott (*qv*)

The **14th Earl** *m* 2nd 24 Jan 1638/9 Anne (*dsp* 29 July 1658), 2nd dau of 7th Lord (Fraser of) Lovat (*qv*), and *d* 14 Oct 1679

His s,

GEORGE GORDON, **15th Earl of Sutherland**, PC (S 1689); *b* 2 Nov 1633; Ld Privy Seal Scotland 1656; obtained a regrant of the Earldom 24 June 1681 with remainder to his est s and himself and the heirs male of both his and his est son's bodies, in default of which, to the heirs female of his est son's body without division and their heirs male; Commr Gt Seal Scotland 1689; *m* 11 Aug 1659 Jean (*d* 5 Jan 1715), widow of Archibald, Earl of Angus (*see* HAMILTON and BRANDON, D), and est dau of 2nd Earl of Wemyss (*see* WEMYSS and MARCH, E), and *d* 4 March 1702/3, leaving:

JOHN GORDON later SUTHERLAND (1690), **16th Earl of Sutherland**, KT (1716), PC (S 1687, Feb 1689/90 and Feb 1702/3, GB Jan 1720/1); *bapt* 2 March 1660/1; Col Foot Regt Flanders 1694–97, Commr for Union of S and E parls Feb 1705/6; regranted Earldom 29 March 1706 with remainder to his only s and himself and his heirs male of the body, then to his son's heirs male of the body, in default of which to the heirs female of the body of his son without division and their issue male, in default of which to his own heirs female; rep S peer 1707–08 and 1715–33; Ld Lt: Caithness, Elgin, Nairn, Ross and Cromarty and Sutherland 1715–25, as which did much to quell the 1715 Uprising; Lt-Gen 1715; *m* 1st 28

April 1680 Helen, gdau of 1st Earl of Dundonald (*qv*), and had issue, with a dau (*d* unm):

1 William, *Lord Strathnaver*; *b* just before 19 Dec 1683; Col of Foot 1702–10, MP (Whig) Wick Burghs 1708–09 (election annulled since he was est s of a Scottish peer), helped f suppress 1715 Uprising; *m* (contract 9 Oct 1705) Katharine (*d* 21 March 1765), dau of William Morison, MP, of Preston Grange, Haddingtonshire, and *dvp* 19 July 1720, having had:

(1) John, *Lord Strathnaver*; *b* Nov 1706; *bur* 12 Dec 1720

(2) WILLIAM, **17th Earl**

(3) George; *d* unm 13 March 1736

(1) Helen; *m* 12 April 1740 Sir James Colquhoun of Luss, 1st Bt (*qv*) and *d* 7 Jan 1791, leaving issue

(2) Janet; *m* 24 Oct 1740 George Sinclair of Ulbster (*see* THURSO, V) and *d* 9 June 1795, leaving issue

1 Jean; *m* (contract 31 Aug 1702) James, Lord Maitland, est s of 5th Earl of Lauderdale (*qv*), and *d* 11 Feb 1747

The **16th Earl** *m* 2nd Katherine (*dsp* 1703), widow of Lord Doune (*see* MORAY, E) and 2nd dau of Sir Lionel Tollemache, 3rd Bt, by Elizabeth, Countess of Dysart in her own right (*qv*); *m* 3rd (contract 11 Aug 1727) Frances (*dsp* 20 Dec 1732), widow of Sir John Travel, MP, and *d* 27 June 1733

His gs,

WILLIAM SUTHERLAND, **17th Earl of Sutherland**; *b* 2 Oct 1708; MP (Whig) Sutherland 1727–32, rep S peer 1734–47; opposed 1745 Uprising, though barely escaping being taken prisoner when Jacobites occupied Dunrobin (*see* below against **Seat**), fought at Culloden 1746, compensated with £1,000 (over £60,000 in late–1990s terms) for the Hereditary Shrievalty of Sutherland when such jurisdictions were abolished by Parl 1747; *m c* 17 April 1734 Lady Elizabeth Wemyss (*d* 20 Feb 1747), est dau of 4th Earl of Wemyss (*see* WEMYSS and MARCH, E), and *d* 7 Dec 1750, having had, with a dau (Elizabeth, *m* 29 Aug 1757 her cousin James Wemyss of Wemyss and *d* 24 Jan 1803):

WILLIAM SUTHERLAND, **18th Earl of Sutherland**; *b* 28 May 1735; *educ* Winchester, Harrow, Enfield and U of Göttingen; Lt Roy Scots Regt, Capt 58th/56th Foot 1775, Lt-Col 1759, Lt-Col cmdg a Highland Bn 1759–63, ADC to GEORGE III with Col's rank 1763–66; rep S peer 1763–66; *m* 14 April 1761 Mary (*m* 1 June 1766), dau and coheir of William Maxwell of Preston, Kirkcudbrightshire, by Elizabeth, dau of William Hairstanes of Craigs, Dumfriesshire, and *d* 16 June 1766, just over two weeks after his w (they were *bur* in one grave at Holyrood Abbey 9 Aug 1766), having had, with an er dau (Catherine, *b* 24 May 1764, *d* 3 Jan 1766):

ELIZABETH Sutherland, **Countess of Sutherland** in her own right, as which recognised by Crown 21 March 1771, notwithstanding counterclaims to the title by two cousins; *b* 24 May 1765; *m* 4 Sept 1785 George Granville LEVESON-GOWER, 1st DUKE OF SUTHERLAND (*qv*), and *d* 29 Jan 1839, leaving, with other issue:

GEORGE GRANVILLE LEVESON-GOWER later SUTHERLAND-LEVESON-GOWER (roy licence 12 May 1841), **20th Earl of Sutherland** and 2nd DUKE OF SUTHERLAND; had, with other issue:

GEORGE GRANVILLE WILLIAM SUTHERLAND-LEVESON-GOWER, **21st Earl of Sutherland** and 3rd DUKE OF SUTHERLAND; had, with other issue:

CROMARTIE SUTHERLAND-LEVESON-GOWER, **22nd Earl of Sutherland** and 4th DUKE OF SUTHERLAND; had:

1 GEORGE GRANVILLE SUTHERLAND-LEVESON-GOWER, **23rd Earl of Sutherland** and 5th DUKE OF SUTHERLAND; *dsp* 1 Feb 1963, when the Dukedom passed to his cousin

2 Alastair St Clair, MC, DL (Sutherland); *b* 24 Jan 1890; Maj RHG (Blues) and Gds MG Regt, Lt Lovat Scouts Yeo, ADC Personal Staff 1918, WW I (despatches, wounded); *m* 27 April 1918 Elizabeth Hélène (*m* 3rd 14 June 1931 Baron George Osten Driesen and *d* 26 Sept 1931), dau of Warren Gardener Demarest, of New York, and formerly w of John Leishman, and *d* 28 April 1921, leaving:

(1) ELIZABETH MILLICENT, **present Countess of Sutherland in her own right**

1 Victoria Elizabeth; *b* 5 Aug 1885; *d* 28 Jan 1888

2 Rosemary Millicent; *b* 9 Aug 1893; *m* 8 March 1919 3rd Earl of Dudley (*qv*) and *d* 21 July 1930 following a plane crash, leaving issue

Lineage (of Janson): JOHN I'ANSON, probably of Hauxwell, Yorks; Capt of a man-of-war *temp* HENRY VIII; *d* in the KING's serv, leaving, with a yr s (James, *b* 1503):

CHRISTOPHER I'ANSON, of Hauxwell; *m* Isabel, dau of Robert Moore, and *d* between 18 Sept and 18 Nov 1577, leaving:

RALPH I'ANSON, of Hauxwell; *m* Anne — (*bur* 5 Sept 1613) and was *bur* 19 May 1623, having had:

JAMES I'ANSON; *m* Janet Edin (*bur* 2 Dec 1657) and *dvp* 1615, leaving:

WILLIAM I'ANSON; *bapt* 23 Nov 1604; *m* 6 May 1634 Margaret (*bur* 30 Jan 1659), dau of Owen Dent, of Leyburn, Yorks, and had:

JAMES I'ANSON, of Woodhall, Coverdale; *b* 27 Sept 1638; Quaker; *m* 19 Dec 1664 Jane (*d* 6 Feb 1700), dau of William Horner, of Woodhall, and *d c* 1702, leaving:

JOHN I'ANSON, of Leyburn; *b* 30 Jan 1666; linen-weaver; *m* 23 Feb 1698 Anne, dau of Arthur Hudson, of Helme in Kildewicke, Yorks, and had:

JOSHUA I'ANSON; *b* 9 May 1700; *m* 22 Feb 1730 Beatrice (*bur* 31 Dec 1770), dau of Thomas Headley, of High Moss, Yorks, and was *bur* 28 March 1786, leaving:

JOSHUA I'ANSON; *b* 1740; *m* Hannah, dau of Thomas Moses, of Raby, Co Durham, and had:

WILLIAM I'ANSON later JANSON, of Darlington; *b c* 1772; Quaker by 1792, linen-draper in London, Lloyd's underwriter 1803; *m* 15 Nov 1796 Mary (*b* 1769), dau of Andrew Hill, of Holborn, by Mary (*m* 2nd Robert Sargeant), dau of John Dearman, of Braithwaite, and *d* 4 April 1848, having had:

1 Edmund; *b* 24 Oct 1797; *m* 24 Aug 1820 Elizabeth, dau of Richard Lowe, of Worcester, and *dvp* 2 Sept 1826, leaving:

(1) William Edmund; *b* 26 Oct 1823; *d* 1841

(1) Elizabeth; *b* 8 Sept 1826; *m* 3 Aug 1848 James Hack Tuke, banker, of Hitchin, Herts, s of Samuel Tuke, of Lawrence House, York, and *d* 22 Jan 1869

2 Richard; *b* 18 April 1799; *m* 1st Mary, dau of James Backhouse, of Darlington, and had:

(1) Mary Jane; *b* 1824; *d* 1838

2 (cont.) Richard Janson *m* 2nd 1 Jan 1828 Anne, dau of Joseph Foster, of Bromley, and *dvp* 18 July 1830, leaving by her:

(1) Richard; *b* 1829; *d* 1880, leaving issue

3 Alfred; *b* 6 Dec 1800; *m* 1st Sarah Musgrave Dillwyn and had issue; *m* 2nd Eliza, dau of John Masterman, MP

4 Frederick, of Stoke Newington; *b* 1 Aug 1803; *m* 1 Aug 1827 Sarah Tindall (*d* 31 Dec 1864), of Scarborough, and *dvp* 23 July 1832, leaving issue

5 WILLIAM

6 John; *b* 3 April 1807; *d* 16 Sept 1833

1 Mary (twin with William); *b* 6 June 1805; *d* unm 9 March 1888

2 Eliza; *b* 17 June 1810; *d* unm 1 June 1896

3 Caroline; *b* 11 Feb 1813; *d* unm 24 March 1903

WILLIAM JANSON's 5th s,

WILLIAM JANSON, of Tottenham, Middx; *b* 6 June 1805; Lloyd's underwriter 1837; *m* 31 March 1829 Eliza Jane (*d c* 1873), dau of John Petty Dearman, of Birmingham, and *d* 1 Jan 1868, having had:

1 John William; *b* 13 Dec 1831; memb Lloyd's; *m* 1st 4 June 1856 Louisa, dau of Lewis Burnand; *m* 2nd 14 April 1904 Ellen Charlotte, est dau of Frederick James Chester, of Poyle Park, Surrey, and widow of G O Mellick Herron, of Newdigate Place, Surrey, and *dsp* 25 Jan 1906

2 A son; *b* 20 Sept, *d* 7 Oct 1835

3 Frederick William; *b* 26 May 1842; *d* 15 Oct 1863

4 DEARMAN

5 Charles Albert; *b* 19 Dec 1849; *m*, and *d* 21 Feb 1882

1 Mary; *b* 27 Aug 1830; *m* 30 Aug 1850 George Stacey (*d* 22 May 1858), of Bruce Grove, Tottenham, and *d* 26 Dec 1866, leaving issue

2 Caroline; *b* 11 June 1833; *d* unm 27 Jan 1864

3 Louisa

4 Jane Eliza; *b* 28 May 1839; *m* 29 July 1858 Samuel Lloyd, JP, of Warwicks, and had issue

5 Ellen Sophia

6 Margaret; *b* 27 July 1843; *m* Rev John Nathaniel Smith and had issue

7 Isabella

WILLIAM JANSON's 4th s,

DEARMAN JANSON, of Chislehurst, Kent; *b* 6 July 1847; memb Lloyd's; *m* 29 Sept 1874 Rachel Louisa (*d* 2 March 1939), 3rd dau of Sampson Samuel Lloyd, JP, MP, of Dolobran, Mongomeryshire, and aunt of 1st Baron Lloyd (*see* 1970 edn), and *d* 1907, leaving:

1 CHARLES WILFRID

2 Arthur Dearman; *b* 1881; WW I in French Army with Br Ambulance Ctee (Croix de Guerre); *d* unm 31 Oct 1919

1 Caroline; *m* 21 Dec 1912 Prof Sir Keith Grahame Feiling, OBE, MA, DLitt, and had issue

DEARMAN JANSON's er s,

CHARLES WILFRID JANSON; *b* 1897; Capt Coldstream Gds WW I; *m* 28 Nov 1916 Nora, dau of Arthur Cook, of Aigburth, Lancs, and *d* April 1966, leaving, with other issue:

1 *Charles Noel, DL (Sutherland 1959–93); *b* 25 Dec 1917; *educ* Eton and Ch Ch Oxford (MA); T/Capt Welsh Gds; jnlst, Paris corresp *Economist* 1949–53, *Sunday Times* 1950–51, fndr *Africa Confidential* 1960 and *Soviet Analyst* 1972; *m* 5 Jan 1946 *Countess of Sutherland (*see* above)

2 *Hugh Dearman; *m* 1st 9 June 1948 (*divorce* 1955) Cornelia Rowena (Cara), er dau of Maj Hon Oscar Montague Guest (*see* WIMBORNE, V), and has:

(1) *Charles James; *b* 29 May 1952

(1) *Sarah; *b* 9 April 1950

2 (cont.) Hugh Janson *m* 2nd 25 Oct 1960 *Olwen Marcia Blanche, dau of Cotterell Boughton Mordaunt-Smith (*see* SMITH-GORDON, Bt) and widow of Wayne Ewing Harriss

Seat: Dunrobin Castle, Golspie, Sutherland. For once the cliché 'fairy-tale' is apt. But as with many fairy tales there is a grim side. Much of Dunrobin is built, as it were, on the ruins of crofter homesteads. For the 1st Duke of Sutherland evicted some 5,000 Highland tenants to accommodate sheep. It was his son, however, who commissioned Sir Charles Barry in 1840 to extend the old castle of the Earls of Sutherland.

A fortress stood on the site of the present building in medieval times. A tower dating from the late 13th century, only a generation after the creation of the Earldom although rebuilt about the turn of the 14th and 15th centuries, still forms the heart of the present-day mansion. The southeastern flank (what is visible on the left of the trilateral view from the seaward side — the best-known vantage point) is late 16th century. The central block on this side is late 18th-century and the right-hand flank is Barry's work. During World War I Dunrobin became a hospital and a fire in 1915 did much damage, although only a relatively small part of the castle was destroyed. After the Armistice Sir Robert Lorimer, who in recent years has begun to receive recognition outside specialist architectural circles, was engaged to carry out restoration.

SUTHERLAND, Bt

SANS PEVR

Arms: Gu. a chevron flory counter-flory between in chief three mullets and in base a lymphad, all or. **Crest:** Upon the trunk of a tree a cat salient ppr. **Motto:** *Sans peur* ('Without fear').
Creation: Bt. (UK) 16 June 1921.

John Brewer Sutherland [John Sutherland Esq, Ross, Belford, Northumberland]; *b* 19 Oct 1931; *s f* 1980 but does not use title; *educ* Sedbergh and St Catharine's Coll Cambridge; *m* 1st 20 Nov 1958 Alice Muireall, JP (*d* 21 Sept 1984), dau of William Stamford Henderson, of Kelso, Roxburghs; *m* 2nd 20 Jan 1988 *(Ailsa) Heather, dau of David Alexander Gray, of Chester-le-Street, and by his 1st w has:

1 +PETER WILLIAM [Peter Sutherland Esq, Swarland East House Farm, Swarland, Northumberland]; *b* 18 May 1963; *m* 1988 *Suzanna Mary, dau of R Michael Gledson, of Newlands Mill Lane, Little Shrewley, Warwicks, and has:

    (1) *Kate Alice; *b* 2 Aug 1993

    (2) *Lucy Suzanna; *b* 2 Nov 1995

2 +Christopher John; *b* 28 Dec 1965

3 +Robert Brewer; *b* 19 Nov 1970

1 *Susan Muireall [Mrs Alastair Jollans, Southfield House, Painswick, Glos]; *b* 22 Dec 1960; *m* 1992 *Alastair Peter Jollans and has:

    (1) *Daniel John Peter; *b* 3 Jan 1994

    (1) *Alice Jane; *b* 2 Oct 1995

Lineage: BENJAMIN SUTHERLAND, of Thurso; *b* 1 Dec 1799; *m* Allison Johnson (*d* 2 Feb 1875), dau of Donald Munro, and *d* 10 July 1879, leaving:

BENJAMIN JOHN SUTHERLAND, of Thurso Ho, Newcastle; *b* 26 July 1833; *m* 16 Sept 1859 Mary Ann (*d* 24 Dec 1901), dau of Joseph Proud, of Carrs Hill, Co Durham, and *d* 4 Feb 1901, leaving:

1 Benjamin John; *b* 2 April 1863; *d* 7 Jan 1909

2 Joseph William; *b* 2 April 1863; *d* 21 April 1896

3 ARTHUR MUNRO (Sir), **1st Bt**

4 Herbert Stanley; *b* 13 Nov 1869; *m* 19 June 1901 Mary (*d* 27 Aug 1943), dau of James Lamb, and *d* 20 May 1953, leaving issue

1 Elizabeth; *d* unm 1 Sept 1935

2 Florence Jane; *d* unm 27 April 1949 aged 79

3 Helena Alice; *m* 17 April 1913 Irving Livingston Roe, of Lindisfarne, Princeton, NJ, USA, and had issue

The 3rd s,

Sir Arthur Munro Sutherland, 1st Bt (UK), so *cr* 16 June 1921, KBE (1920), DL Northumberland, High Sheriff 1943, JP Newcastle; *b* 2 Oct 1867; *educ* Newcastle GS; shipowner and coal exporter, Governing Dir B J Sutherland & Co and Newcastle Commercial Exchange, Sheriff Newcastle-upon-Tyne 1916–17, Ld Mayor 1918–19, Pres: Chamber of Shipping 1930, Shipping Fedn 1937 and Newcastle and Gateshead Chamber Commerce; dir: John Bowes and Ptnrs, Barnett Bros, London Donkin & Co and N of England Protecting & Indemnity Assoc, Hon Freeman Newcastle 1936, DCL Durham 1932, Cdr Order St Olav Norway, KGStJ; *m* 1st 7 June 1893 Fanny Linda (*d* 28 Oct 1937), 2nd dau of Robert Hood Haggie, of Newcastle, and had:

1 Arthur Munro; *b* 13 Aug 1894; *educ* Mill Hill; *m* 2 Nov 1921 Nina Marguerite Crawshay (*d* 10 Aug 1985), only dau of Arthur Skelton Wimble, of Whitley Bay and St Helier, Jersey, and *d* 1 Nov 1941, leaving:

    (1) Peter Munro; *b* 17 Aug 1924; *educ* Stowe; F/O RAF WW II; *kas* 31 July 1944

    (1) *Nina Marguerite Munro [Mrs James Slater, The Mill Cottage, Eglingham, Northumberland NE66 2TX]; *b* 19 May 1923; *m* 9 July 1949 James Keith Whittenbury Slater, MSc (*d* 20 July 1968), est s of Sir William Kershaw Slater, KBE, DSc, FRS, and has:

        1a *Bill Munro; *b* 25 Dec 1953; *educ* Sibford Sch

        2a *Peter Munro; *b* 28 March 1956; *educ* Stowe

        1a *Gail Munro; *b* 22 May 1950

        2a *Kim Munro; *b* 4 April 1952

    (2) *Ann Munro; *b* 2 July 1928

2 (BENJAMIN) IVAN (Sir), **2nd Bt**

3 +(Robert) Gordon [Gordon Sutherland Esq, Piper's Hill, Castle Terrace, Berwick-upon-Tweed]; *b* 10 Jan 1908; *m* 1st 17 Dec 1934 (*divorce* 1958) Helen Wallace, dau of Edward Farish, of Wigton, Cumberland, and has:

    (1) +Arthur Ian; *b* 19 Feb 1936; *educ* The Leys Sch Cambridge and Bristol U

    (2) +David Wallace; *b* 16 Aug 1938; *educ* Malvern and Trin Coll Dublin

3 (cont.) Gordon Sutherland *m* 2nd 1958 *Emily Hayes, of Hanwell, Middx

1 Linda Kathleen; *m* 19 March 1928 Henry Armstrong (*d* 17 Nov 1955), est s of Henry Armstrong, of Newcastle, and *d* 6 June 1988

Sir Arthur *m* 2nd 19 Oct 1938 Ella Bertha Louise (*d* Jan 1940), widow of William Robertson Heatley, OBE, Br Consul Odense, Denmark, and dau of — Christensen, of Copenhagen, and *d* 30 March 1953

His er surv s,

Sir (Benjamin) Ivan Sutherland, 2nd Bt; *b* 16 May 1901; *educ* Uppingham; *m* 1st 23 April 1927 (*divorce* 1944) Marjorie Constance Daniel (*d* 3 May 1980), yr dau of Frederic William Brewer, OBE, of Newcastle, and had:

1 JOHN BREWER SUTHERLAND, **3rd and present Bt**

2 +(David) Michael [Michael Sutherland Esq, Northfield, Lowick, Northumberland]; *b* 14 June 1940; *educ* Sedbergh and St Catharine's Coll Cambridge; *m* 11 Aug 1966 *Caroline Mary, dau of Robert Simon Hogan, of Blackrock, Co Dublin, and has:

    (1) *Julia Ruth; *b* 29 May 1967

    (2) *Serena Louise; *b* 1971

    (3) *Polly Anne; *b* 1975

Sir Ivan *m* 2nd 12 Dec 1944 *Margaret, JP (1966) [Margaret Lady Sutherland JP, The Smithy, Embleton, Northumberland], CC Northumberland, dau of Albert Owen, of Fairways, Chalfont St Giles, Bucks, and *d* 6 Nov 1980, leaving by her:

3 +William; *b* 20 Sept 1945; *educ* Leys Sch Cambridge and St Catharine's Coll Cambridge; *m* 24 Nov 1966 (*divorce* 19–) Sarah Lucy, dau of Dr Cecil Gilbert, of Benton, Newcastle, and has:

    (1) +Mark Rupert; *b* 25 April 1967

    (2) +Dylan Paul; *b* 1970

    (3) +Hal; *b* 1988

    (1) *Ceri Jane; *b* 3 June 1968

    (2) *Amy Gail; *b* 30 May 1969

4 +Owen [Owen Sutherland Esq, The Farmhouse, Low Newton-by-the-sea, Northumberland]; *b* 21 March 1947; *educ* Leys Sch Cambridge and St Catharine's Coll Cambridge; *m* 1971 *Margaret Ann, dau of Daniel Herbert Williams, of Rainhill, Liverpool, and has:

    (1) +Jonathan Ben; *b* 1976

    (1) *Victoria Jane; *b* 1974

5 +Ben; *b* 3 May 1949; *educ* Leys Sch Cambridge and Essex U; *m* 1986 *Bonna Howell and has:

    (1) *Lesley Ann; *b* 1986

SUTTON

TOUT·JOURS·PREST

Arms: Quarterly, 1st and 4th, arg. a canton sa. (for SUTTON); 2nd and 3rd, arg. a cross fleury az. (for LEXINGTON). **Crest:** A wolf's head erased gu. **Motto:** *Tout jours prest* ('Always ready').
Creation: Bt. (GB) 14 Oct 1772.

SIR RICHARD LEXINGTON SUTTON, 9TH BT, of Norwood Park, Co Nottingham [Sir Richard Sutton Bt, Moor Hill, Langham, Dorset SP8 5NY]; *b* 27 April 1937; *s f* 1981; *educ* Stowe; farmer; *m* 1959 *Fiamma, only dau of Giuseppe Marzio Ferrari, of Rome, and has:

1 +DAVID ROBERT; *b* 26 Feb 1960; *educ* Milton Abbey; *m* 1992 *Annette, only dau of B David, of Aller, Langport, Somerset, and has:

    (1) *Charlotte Emily; *b* 1994

1 *Caroline Victoria; *b* 10 April 1965; *m* 1989 *Alexander C Gibbs, s of C E Gibbs, of Bourton, Dorset, and has:

    (1) *Charles Toby; *b* 1991

    (2) *Robert Alexander; *b* 1993

Lineage: SEWARD; feudal Ld of Sutton, Holderness, Yorks, allegedly living 1066, more probably at the time of the Domesday Survey 21 years later; alleged ancestor of:

ROLAND, of Sutton-on-Trent; living c 1220; m Alice, dau of Richard de Lexington/Laxton (later Tuxford), Notts, sis and coheir of Robert de Lexington, Ld Manors Averham and Tuxford, Notts, and had, with a yr s (William, m Matilda and was ancestor of the Barons Dudley, qv):

Sir ROBERT de SUTTON, of Averham; m 2nd Isabella, dau and coheir of Sir Hugh Pigott, of Dodington, and d c 1281, leaving by her:

Sir JAMES SUTTON, of Averham; m Agnes (d c 1326), dau of Sir John Barry, of Torlaton, Notts, and d 1304, leaving:

RICHARD SUTTON, of Averham; b c 1306; m Alice, dau and coheir of Sir Richard Bingham, of Bingham, and d 1339, leaving:

JOHN SUTTON, of Averham; m Johanna, dau and heir of Henry Musters, of Syrston, and d 1369, leaving:

Sir ROWLAND SUTTON, of Averham; b c 1348; m Catherine, dau of Sir Henry Hasty, and d 1397, leaving:

HENRY SUTTON, of Averham; m Margaret, dau of Sir Hugo Hussy, of Flintham, Notts, and d 1416, leaving:

RICHARD SUTTON, of Averham; m Catherine, dau of Edmund FitzWilliams, of Aldwark (Wadworth), and d 1468, leaving:

ROBERT SUTTON, of Averham; m Elizabeth, dau of Thomas Stanley, of Pipe, and d 1500, having had:

HENRY SUTTON; m Alice, dau of Sir Nicholas Byron, of Colwick, and dvp 1492, leaving:

Sir THOMAS SUTTON, of Averham; m Catherine, dau of Sir Thomas Basset, of Fledburgh, and d 1520, leaving:

Sir HENRY SUTTON, of Averham; m Alice, dau of Francis Hall, of Grantham, Lincs, and d 1559, leaving, with an er s (Edward, dsp):

WILLIAM SUTTON, of Aram/Aversham; m Anna, dau of John Rodney, of Buckwell, Somerset, and had:

Sir WILLIAM SUTTON, of Aram; b c 1559; ktd 1603; m 1584 Susan, dau of Thomas Cony, of Bassingthorpe, Lincs, and d 1611, having had:

1 ROBERT SUTTON, 1st BARON LEXINTON OF ARAM, Co Nottingham (E), so cr 21 Nov 1645; educ Trin Coll Cambridge; MP Notts 1624–25, April–May 1640 and 1640–43 (deprived of seat as royalist); m 1st 14 April 1616 Elizabeth (dsp), sis of 8th Earl of Rutland (see RUTLAND, D); m 2nd after 16 April 1635 Anne, dau of Sir Guy Palmes, of Lindley, Yorks, and widow of Sir Thomas Browne, Bt; m 3rd 21 Feb 1660/1 Mary, dau of Sir Anthony St Leger, and d 13 Oct 1668, leaving by her an only s:

  (1) ROBERT SUTTON, 2nd and last BARON LEXINTON OF ARAM, PC (March 1691/2–1714); b 6 Jan 1661/2; Gent Bedchamber 1692–1702, a Ld Trade 1699–1702, Amb Spain 1712–13 and Southern Peace Congress 1718; m c 14 Sept 1691 Margaret, dau of Sir Giles Hungerford, of Coulston, Wilts, and dspms, having had, with a s (d young):

    1a Bridget; m 27 Aug 1717 3rd Duke of Rutland (qv) and was ancestress through her yst s of the MANNERS-SUTTONs, who inherited the Sutton estates

2 Richard

3 HENRY, of whom presently

4 Gervas

The 3rd s,

HENRY SUTTON; m Mabel, dau of Henry Faunt, and had:

ROBERT SUTTON; had:

1 ROBERT (Sir)

2 Richard, of Scofton, Notts; b 1674; Lt-Gen, Govr Bruges; m Catherine de Tolmer and d July 1737, leaving, with other issue:

  (1) Robert, of Scofton; m Anne, dau of C Throckmorton, and d 13 Nov 1776, leaving:

    1a Robert, of Scofton and later Bath; had:

      1b Robert William Evelyn Sutton, of West Retford

    1a Ann Sutton; m 1767 Sir Robert Gunning, 1st Bt (qv), and had issue

The er s,

Sir ROBERT SUTTON, KB, PC; b 1671; Amb: Holland, Constantinople and Paris, MP Notts; m 10 Dec 1724 Judith (d 17 May 1749), widow of 3rd Earl of Sunderland (see MARLBOROUGH, D) and dau and coheir of Benjamin Tichborne, and d 13 Aug 1746, having had, with an er surv s (John, bought Norwood Park, Notts, and dsp 1772):

Sir Richard Sutton, 1st Bt (GB), so cr 14 Oct 1772, of Norwood Park; b 31 July 1733; educ Trin Coll Cambridge (MA); MP St Albans 1768–80, Sandwich 1780–84 and Boroughbridge 1784–96, U-Sec 1766–72; m 1st Susan (dsp 12 June 1766), sis of Sir Claude Champion de Crespigny, 1st Bt (see 1953 edn); m 2nd Ann (d 2 Dec 1787), yr dau and coheir of William Peere Williams, of Cadleigh, Devon, and had, with other issue:

1 John; b 1770; m Sophia Frances (m 2nd 4 Oct 1804 Thomas Wright, of Bramcote, Notts, and d 9 Feb 1844), dau of Charles Chaplin, of Tathwell, Lincs (see 1970 edn CHAPLIN, V), and dvp 15 Sept 1801, leaving:

  (1) RICHARD (Sir), **2nd Bt**

2 Robert Nassau; b 1 Aug 1776; Capt 7th Fus, ADC to Sir R Abercrombie Egypt 1801; m 20 May 1812 his cousin Mary Georgiana (d 10 Nov 1846), dau of John Manners-Sutton (see RUTLAND, D), and d 7 April 1833, leaving, with other issue:

  (1) Robert (Rev), of Scawby, Lincs, JP Parts of Lindsey; b 1 March 1813; m 4 May 1847 Charlotte (d 11 Nov 1872), only sis and heiress of Sir John Nelthorpe, 8th and last Bt (see 1865 edn), and d 10 March 1885, leaving:

    1a Robert Nassau SUTTON later SUTTON NELTHORPE (roy licence 1884), OBE (1918), of Scawby Hall, JP; Maj 8th Hus; b 13 May 1850; m 1 Jan

1885 Hon Dulcibella Eden (d 6 April 1925), est da of 4th Baron Auckland (qv), and d 17 Nov 1937, having had:

      1b Oliver, CBE (1942), DSO (1919), MC, JP Lincs; b 5 June 1888; educ Eton and RMA Woolwich; Col Rifle Bde and 5th Bn Lincs Regt WW I (despatches), WW II on staff, V-Lt Lincs 1946 (previously DL), Croix de Guerre; m 29 July 1914 Marjorie Elspeth Constable (d 1976), only dau of Charles Constable Curtis, DL (see ONSLOW, E), and d 25 May 1963, leaving:

        1c +Roger, MBE (1945), TD, JP (Parts of Lindsey 1946), DL (Lincs 1950) [Lt-Col Roger Sutton Nelthorpe MBE TD JP DL, Scawby Hall, Brigg, Lincs]; b 5 March 1918; educ Eton; Lt-Col Sherwood Rangers Yeo (TA) WW II, High Sheriff Lincs 1970

        2c John Richard; b 26 Jan 1923; educ Eton; Lt RNVR WW II; m 15 July 1946 *Mary Elizabeth, only dau of Tom Cunningham Brown, of The Cottage, Scawby, and d 1994, leaving:

          1d +Anthony Julian; b 3 May 1948; educ Charterhouse; m 29 Dec 1973 *Margaret V, yst dau of R F Schumacher, of Blue Cottage, Upton, Didcot, Berks, and has:

            1e +Thomas Max; b 3 July 1977

            1e *Clare Lydia; b 1979

        1c *Ann; b 5 Sept 1919

      2b Christopher, MC; b 14 Jan 1890; Maj Coldstream Gds (SR) WW I (despatches); d unm 27 Feb 1951

      3b Griffith, JP Lincs; b 21 Aug 1892; BA Oxon, barrister Inner Temple 1919; m 19 Dec 1922 Constance Adine Maud (d 10 Dec 1923), dau of Allan Harvey Drummond (see PERTH, E), and d 23 Nov 1947, leaving:

        1c +Jan William; b 7 Dec 1923; Warrant Offr RAF

      1b Ursula; d unm 25 April 1936

    2a Henry John; b 9 Dec 1851; Lt 87th Roy Irish Fus; d 1910

    3a Francis Richard; b 27 March 1853; m 1881 Edith Louisa (d 7 Aug 1931), 3rd dau of Arthur Pryor, JP, DL, of Hylands, Essex, and d 20 Aug 1923, leaving:

      1b Richard Coningsby; b 12 May 1882; m 9 March 1904 Katharine Helen (d 28 Oct 1925), dau and coheir of Francis Foljambe Anderson, of Lea, Lincs, and gdau of Sir Charles Henry John Anderson, 9th Bt (see 1891 edn), and d 12 Sept 1905, leaving:

        1c Francis Richard Heywood, MC; b 10 Feb 1905; educ Eton; T/Capt RAC (TA) WW II; m 1st 5 Sept 1929 (divorce 1937) Barbara Jean, dau of A D Tait; m 2nd 1939 (divorce 1961) Vera Kathleen, dau of John Waldock, and had:

          1d +(Richard) Oliver, AFC (1970); b 22 Aug 1940; educ Eton; Roy Rhodesian Air Force, Lt RN; m March 1967 *Hélène, only dau of Ministro Carlo de Franchis, of Rome, and has:

            1e +Francesco Charles; b 27 Dec 1967

        1c (cont.) Francis Sutton m 3rd 1960 Mrs Audrey Theodosia Madeleine Davis (d 1974), dau of Lancelot Squarey (see GOSFORD, E), and d 25 June 1970

        1c *Olinda Margaret [Mrs Donald Gawne, The Wash, West Coker, Yeovil, Somerset]; b posthumously 4 March 1906; m 12 July 1934 Maj Donald Hammick Gawne, King's Own Roy Regt, s of Col John Moore Gawne, and has:

          1d *Robert Atholl [Robert Gawne Esq, c/o Royal Bank of Canada, Keweaitin, Ontario, Canada]; b 10 Sept 1936; m 9 April 1966 *Kae, yst dau of K Fraser, of Harrisota, Manitoba, and has:

            1e *Kelly Robert; b 1967

            2e *Kevin Donald; b 1971

          2d *John Francis; b 9 March 1939; m 31 Oct 1964 *Hilary Ann, er dau of R Medforth, of Nairobi, and has:

            1e *Nicola Caroline; b 1967

            2e *Amanda Louise; b 1971

        2c Olivia Katherine (twin); b 5 March 1906; m 12 July 1934 Capt Edward Hugh Vaux, ARIBA, Roy Sussex Regt, 7th s of Rev George Bowyer Vaux, of The Yews, Odiham, Hants, and dsp 23 Oct 1965

      2b Francis Arthur; b 15 Feb 1884; d a POW 1944

      1b Olinda Emily; m 12 July 1909 Lt-Col Arthur Campbell Watson, DSO, 7th Hus, s of William Farnell, of Henfold, Capel, Surrey, and d 14 Jan 1969, leaving issue. He d 16 Jan 1952

      2b Sylvia Katherine; m 20 April 1909 Maj Sir John St Vigor Fox, JP, DL, s of Capt John Wilson Fox, 12th Lancers, of Girsby Manor, Lincs, and Stanham, Cheshire and d 2 June 1974, leaving issue. He d 2 July 1968

    4a Hugh Nelthorpe; b 3 May 1857; d 16 July 1914

    1a Mary Georgiana; m 8 Feb 1876 Coningsby Charles Sibthorp, of Canwick Hall, Lincs, and dsp 19 Feb 1902. He d 9 May 1932

    2a Evelyn Charlotte; m 16 Dec 1884 Maj Paul Swinburne (see 1949 edn SWINBURNE, Bt), and d 8 Oct 1927. He dsp 19 Jan 1905

    3a Mabel Albinia; m 29 June 1876 Montagu Richard Waldo Sibthorp, of Cranwick Hall, Lincs, yr bro of the above, and d 14 June 1937, leaving issue. He d 19 March 1929

    4a Janetta Nina; m 10 Feb 1886 Rev Geoffrey Barrington Simeon (see SIMEON, Bt), and d Oct 1931, leaving issue

  (2) Frederick; b 26 Feb 1817; Capt 11th Hus; m 1st 12 May 1841 Eliza (d 1844), dau of Rev W M Jones, Vicar Ospringe, Kent, and had, with two sons (d unm):

    1a Ruth Isabella; m 2 April 1866 Col Frederick Lockwood Edridge, CB, Lancashire Fus, s of Rev C C Edridge, of Malverleys, E Woodhay, Hants, and d 22 April 1903, leaving issue. He d 12 Feb 1913

  (2) (cont.) Capt Frederick Sutton m 2nd 19 Oct 1847 Georgina (d 20 March 1898), dau of Ven Archdeacon Croft, and d 2 June 1900, having by her had, with another s and dau (d young):

    1a Algernon Charles; b 6 Feb 1852; m 20 Oct 1886 Winifred Alice (d 23 Oct 1956), yr dau of William Edwin Cotton Fell, of Lochrin, Edinburgh, and d 23 Nov 1932, having had:

1b Frederick Nassau; *b* 18 April 1888; *educ* Charterhouse; *m* 1st 8 Nov 1922 Ethel Rose (*d* 12 March 1955), dau of Thomas Bernard Paxton, of Williams Lake, BC; *m* 2nd 26 Nov 1955 *Christine Isabel, widow of H H Spencer and dau of Thomas Bernard Paxton, of Williams Lake

2b Campbell Percy; *b* 26, *d* 27 June 1890

3b Fergus Algernon; *b* 23 Aug 1891; Lt S Lancs Regt; *ka* 26 Feb 1915

4b John Henry Patrick; *b* 15 March 1896; Capt S Lancs Regt (SR) and RAF WW I (despatches); accidentally *k* whilst flying 16 Aug 1921

1b Irene Winifred; *b* 18 Oct 1892; *m* 28 July 1926 Maj Henry Edmund Barkworth, RA (*das* 10 March 1940), s of Edmund Barkworth, of Seaton, Devon, and had:

  1c *Susan Althea; *b* 26 July 1927

  2c *Rosemary Anne; *b* 15 Dec 1928; *m* 23 Oct 1948 Maj Charles Ronald Croker Elverson and has:

    1d *Ronald Peter Charles; *b* 14 March 1950; *educ* Cheltenham and St Edmund Hall Oxford

    2d *John Henry Patrick; *b* 8 Sept 1951; *educ* Cheltenham

    3d *Christopher William; *b* 23 May 1955; *educ* Cheltenham

  3c *Verbena Clarice; *b* 9 April 1932; *m* 19 June 1954 *William Brian Evans and has:

    1d *Camilla Jane; *b* 11 Aug 1960

    2d *Julian; *b* 5 June 1963

    3d *Rosamund; *b* 5 June 1963

2a Herbert Arthur; *b* 4 April 1853; *m* 8 Sept 1893 Josephine Constance Stanley (*d* 1 June 1905), dau of Joshua Verney Lovett Lace, of Christleton Old Hall, Cheshire, and *d* 31 May 1924, leaving:

  1b Roland Manners Verney; *b* 9 Dec 1895; *m* 27 Dec 1927 Dora (*d* 1984), dau of Elijah Whitehurst, of Overdale, Brinnington, Stockport, and *d* 29 June 1957, leaving:

    1c *Ursula Constance [Mrs Norman Yearsley, Windbrow, 307 Cromwell Lane, Burton Green, Kenilworth, Warwicks]; *b* 24 Sept 1929; *m* 14 Sept 1963 *Norman Yearsley and has:

      1d *Jonathan Manners; *b* 18 Sept 1968

3a Charles Nassau (Rev); *b* 9 Feb 1859; Rector Withyham Sussex 1892–1916; *m* 27 Sept 1883 Edith Mary (*d* 9 Feb 1918), dau of Lt-Col Haydon Lloyd Cafe, 94th Regt, and *d* 23 Nov 1916, leaving:

  1b Charles Lexington Manners, MBE (1946); *b* 26 April 1891; *educ* Eton; Capt Roy Fus, Bde Maj 1917; *m* 1st 12 Sept 1917 (*divorce* 1932) Amabel Anne (*d* 22 Jan 1974), dau of Maj Ludlow Couper Ludlow, of Beech Green, Withyham, Sussex, and had:

    1c John Manners; *b* 8, *d* 11 July 1918

    2c John Charles Ludlow Manners [John Sutton Esq, Willerby Lodge, Staxton, N Yorks]; *b* 7 April 1921; *educ* Charterhouse; Capt Roy Fus WW II; *m* 5 Feb 1946 Daphne Agnes (*d* 4 Aug 1961), only dau of William Francis Wormald, JP, of Willerby Wold, Scarborough, Yorks, and had:

      1d +Richard Manners; *b* 5 May 1947; *educ* Charterhouse; *m* 1st 1972 (*divorce* 1979) Mary de Witt, dau of Charles Diebold, of Buffalo, NY; *m* 2nd 1979 *Penelope Jane, dau of Anthony Gray Quinlan, of Scarborough, and has:

        1e +William Lexington Manners; *b* 1980

        2e +Thomas Anthony Manners; *b* 1982

      2d +William Reginald Manners; *b* 6 Oct 1949; *educ* Charterhouse; *m* 1982 *Janet Risa, dau of Benjamin Chubac, of NJ, USA, and has:

        1e *Emily Anne; *b* 1983

        2e *Lydia Beth; *b* 1985

      3d +Oliver Ludlow Manners; *b* 6 Dec 1950; *educ* Charterhouse; *m* 1980 *Virginia Sarah, dau of Paul Lipscombe Marriott, of Welshpool, and has:

        1e +Philip Ludlow Manners; *b* 1984

        1e *Anna Lucy; *b* 1983

    2c (cont.) John Sutton *m* 2nd 1962 *Gillian [Mrs John Sutton, Willerby Lodge, Staxton, N Yorks], dau of Edwin Stanley Harris, of Newcastle-upon-Tyne, and *d* 1992, leaving by her:

      1d *Virginia Anne; *b* 1964; *m* 1989 *Sebastian J T Foster, of Harrogate, s of Lt-Cdr J R Foster, RN, of Godalming, Surrey, and Mrs N Ward, of Cleckheaton, W Yorks

  1b (cont.) Maj Charles Sutton *m* 2nd 11 June 1932 Gladys Louise (*d* 19–), formerly w of Edward Clarence Redvers Richardson and dau of Percy Gubb, of Lowestoft, and *d* 8 Oct 1962, leaving by her:

    1c *Philippa Mary [Mrs John Selby-Green, Pashley Farm, Ticehurst, Sussex]; *b* 24 April 1936; *m* 1st 1956 Derek Walter Pryke; *m* 2nd 1982 *John Selby-Green and by 1st husb has:

      1d *Kelham Charles Manners; *b* 1959

      2d *Timothy John Manners; *b* 1961

      1d *Flavia Anne [Mrs Andrew Jackson, 26 Bassingham Rd, London SW18 3AG]; *b* 1957; *m* 1986 *(Leslie) Andrew Jackson, est s of Ralph Jackson, of Hopehay, Cartmel, Cumbria

2a Amy Georgina; *m* 9 June 1875 Capt Frank Hay Chapman, RN, of Alverstoke, s of William Greenwood Chapman by Elizabeth Drummond-Hay (*see* KINNOULL, E), and *d* 17 April 1923, leaving issue. He *d* 12 April 1943

3a Eva Pulteney Marguerite; *m* 2 June 1881 Col John Warre Sill, RE, s of Rev John Parkinson Sill, of Wetheringsett Rectory, Suffolk, and *d* Sept 1903, leaving issue. He *d* 3 Nov 1921

(2) Mary Isabella; *m* 2 June 1840 Sir George Baker, 3rd Bt, of Loventor, Devon, and *d* 6 May 1855, leaving issue (*see* BAKER WILBRAHAM, Bt)

(3) Anna Maria; *m* 12 Dec 1853 Baron van Aerssen Beÿeren van Voshol (*d* 20 Aug 1857)

1 Anne Georgiana; *m* Rev Robert Chaplin and had issue (*see* 1970 edn CHAPLIN, V)

2 Isabella Frances; *m* 1799 Rev William Chaplin, JP, and had issue (*see* 1970 edn CHAPLIN, V)

Sir Richard *m* 3rd 8 April 1793 Margaret (*dsp* 3 Jan 1824), dau of John Porter, of Wandsworth, Surrey, and *d* 10 Jan 1802

His gs,

Sir Richard Sutton, 2nd Bt; *b* 16 Dec 1799; *m* 19 Dec 1819 Mary Elizabeth (*d* 1 Jan 1842), dau of Benjamin Burton, of Burton Hall, Co Carlow, and *d* 13 Nov 1855, having had, with another s (*d* young) and dau (*d* unm):

1 **Sir John Sutton, 3rd Bt**; *b* 18 Oct 1820; High Sheriff Notts 1867; *m* 23 Aug 1844 Emma Helena (*d* Jan 1845), est dau of Col Francis Sherlock, KH, of Southwell, Notts, and *d* 5 June 1873

2 RICHARD (Sir), **4th Bt**

3 Francis; *b* 2 Sept 1822; Capt RHG; *m* 19 April 1855 Lady Evelyn Mary Stuart (*d* 27 Oct 1899), sis of 4th Earl of Portarlington (*qv*), and *d* 26 Nov 1906, having had, with another s (*d* young):

  (1) Francis Richard Hugh Seymour; *b* 22 July 1858; *educ* Eton; Capt and Hon Maj Yorks Hus (Imp Yeo), Sheriff of Hants 1918; *m* 21 July 1881 Lady Susan Lascelles (*d* 22 Jan 1925), dau of 4th Earl of Harewood (*qv*), and *d* 28 March 1926, having had:

    1a Francis Henry, MC (1918); *b* 4 Dec 1882; *educ* Eton; Lt-Col 11th Hus (cmdg 1924–28) WW I (despatches), MFH S Dorset 1928–36 and Cowdray 1936–44; *m* 22 July 1914 Aileen, dau of Richard Henry Gosling, of Hawthorn Hill, Berks, by Kathleen, dau of Sir Swinnerton Dyer, 10th Bt (*qv*), and *d* 15 May 1957, having had:

      1b Francis John; *b* 20, *d* 22 July 1915

      2b Richard David; *b* 29 Aug 1923; *educ* Eton; Lt-Col 11th Hus (PAO) WW II; *m* 23 April 1965 *Sally Christine [Mrs Ian Mitchell, Evergreen Cottage, Cherington, Glos GL8 8SH] (*m* 2nd 2 June 1994 *Ian Mitchell), er dau of James Douglas Graeme Reid, of Cruivie, Wormit-on-Tay, Fife, and *d* following a car crash 13 Aug 1965, leaving:

        1c *Frances Elizabeth; *b* posthumously 27 April 1966

      1b Beryl Susan; *b* 21 March 1919; *m* 18 Jan 1945 Maj Victor Harry Hugh McCalmont, Roy Dragoons, (*d* 27 March 1993), only s of Maj Dermot Hugh McCalmont, of Mount Juliet, Thomastown, Co Kilkennyand *d* 9 Dec 1987, leaving:

        1c *Peter Victor; *b* 11 Nov 1946; *educ* Milton Abbey; *m* 1st 19– (*divorce* 19–) Annabel FitzJohn; *m* 2nd 20 March 1993 *Penelope Brown

        2c *Harry Richard Dermot; *b* 7 June 1955; *educ* Harrow; *m* 11 June 1988 *Elizabeth, dau of H R T FitzJohn, of Dereen Lodge, Costello, Co Galway

        1c *Diana Emily Helen; *b* 19 April 1948; *m* 24 April 1968 (*divorce* 19–) Robert Morton, only s of Robert Morton, of Carnagh Ho, New Ross, Co Wexford

    2a Lionel Tatton; *b* 23 Sept 1894; Lt ASC (Mech Transport) WW I; *d* 27 April 1920

    1a Violet Eveleen; *b* 7 Dec 1883; *m* 1st 1 Sept 1903 (*divorce* 1920) Maj-Gen Albemarle Bertie Edward Cator, CB, DSO, Scots Gds (*d* 18 Nov 1932), s of Albemarle Cator, of Woodbastwick Hall, Norfolk, and had issue; *m* 2nd Aug 1920 Capt Esme Francis Wigsell Arkwright, MC (*d* 10 Nov 1934), and *d* 7 May 1948

    2a Angela Désirée; *b* 5 March 1889; *m* 10 Jan 1910 Lt-Col Francis Alexander Umfreville Pickering, DSO, RSG, s of H Umfreville Pickering, of Kincardine, Aberdeenshire, and *d* 7 Nov 1955, leaving issue. He was *ka* 23 Dec 1917

4 Charles; *b* 16 Aug 1823; Capt 12th Lancers; *m* 10 July 1861 Alicia Frances Anna (*m* 2nd 18 May 1893 Hon Robert Needham (*dsp* 11 Nov 1899), s of 2nd Earl of Kilmorey (*qv*), and *d* 17 June 1903), est dau of Sir Willoughby Wolstan Dixie, 8th Bt (*see* 1970 edn) and *d* 21 Jan 1892, having had:

  (1) Charles Wolstan; *b* May 1862; Lt RN; *d* unm Oct 1895

  (2) Algernon Trevor; *b* 1863; *d* 15 Aug 1914

  (3) Evelyn Willoughby; *b* 1868; Lt 7th Hus; *d* unm, drowned India 25 June 1893

5 Augustus (Rev); *b* 13 Jan 1825; Preb Lincoln, Rector W Toft, Norfolk; *m* 2 Oct 1851 Charlotte Robina (*d* 10 Oct 1888), dau of John Carter, of Northwold, and *d* 10 June 1885, having had:

  (1) Arthur Frederick (Rev); *b* 5 July 1852; Vicar Earl's Colne, Essex, 1924, Preb Lincoln, RD Loveden 1915–24; *d* unm 18 Nov 1925

  (2) Richard; *b* 23 Dec 1856; *d* 1885

  (3) Gilbert William; *b* 15 May 1858; *m* 14 Oct 1890 Mabel Affleck (*d* 13 Nov 1930), dau of Rev John Peacock, and *d* 23 Nov 1929, leaving:

    1a John Gilbert, DSC; *b* 13 Jan 1892; Cdr RN (ret 1933) WW I in Submarine Service, WW II 1939–44; *m* 1st 12 Sept 1918 Eva Maud (*d* 2 July 1919), only child of Thomas Cook, of Hobland, Bradwell, Gt Yarmouth, and had:

      1b Roger; *b* 17 June 1919; *educ* Oundle; F/Lt RAF WW II; *ka* 1942

    1a (cont.) Cdr John Sutton *m* 2nd 7 Aug 1920 (*divorce* 1940) Ida Margaret, dau of Charles Halls, and by her had:

      2b +Richard John Beverley [Lt-Cdr Richard Sutton RN, Foxfield, Ansty, Dorset DT2 7PJ]; *b* 26 April 1922; *educ* Imp Service Coll Windsor; *m* 29 Dec 1949 *Ann Stella, dau of Brig Charles Hall Woodhouse, OBE, MC, of Higher Melcombe, Dorset, and has:

        1c +Richard Charles; *b* 6 Feb 1955; *educ* Milton Abbey and RMA Sandhurst; Maj 4th/7th Roy Dragoon Gds; *m* 1985 *Jane Elizabeth, only dau of Lt Cdr John Alan Bird, RN, of The Cottage, Nottington, Dorset, and has:

          1d +Hugo George Richard; *b* 1990

          1d *Sophie Georgina Elizabeth; *b* 1988

        1c *Amanda Clare; *b* 15 Nov 1952; *m* 1973 *Robert Stephen MacKenzie, QRIH

      1b *Felicity Ruth [Mrs Denis Atkinson, Home Cottage, Orford St, Puddletown, Dorset DT2 8TL]; *b* 7 Oct 1926; *m* 12 April 1951 Maj Denis Cary Atkinson, JP, 4th/7th Roy Dragoon Gds (*d* 1985), only s of Col Eric Garnet Atkinson, MVO, and has:

        1c *Timothy Charles Garnet; *b* 17 Aug 1960; *educ* Milton Abbey and RAC Cirencester

1c *Tessa Margaret [Mrs Michael Malyon,Yew Tree Cottage, Barton Stacey, Hants SO21 3RT]; *b* 13 Feb 1951; *m* 1977 (*divorce* 1988) Maj Michael John Herbert Malyon, Roy Hus, and has:

1d *Giles William Herbert; *b* 1989

1d *Mary Louise; *b* 1980

2d *Isobel Alice; *b* 1982

1a (cont.) Cdr John Sutton *m* 3rd 16 Nov 1940 (*divorce* 1950) Katherine (*d* 1977), 2nd dau of George Balfour-Kinnear, WS (*see* MONTGOMERY, Bt), and by her had:

3b +Henry Richard; *b* 22 Sept 1945; *educ* Sch of Navigation, Portsmouth

2b *Judith [Mrs J Langley, 14B Merdra Place, Padbury 6025, W Australia]; *b* 23 Feb 1942; *m* 1st 24 July 1961 *Michael William Cox, s of William Frank Cox; *m* 2nd 19– * —Langley, and by her 1st husb has:

1c *Anthony William; *b* 24 Oct 1961

2c *Nicholas Michael; *b* 4 Aug 1963

1a (cont.) Cdr John Sutton *m* 4th 2 Dec 1950 *Violet [Mrs John Sutton, Manor House, Portesham, Dorset], dau of Herbert James Godwin, OBE, of Greatham, Petersfield, Hants, and *d* 1982

(4) Rowland; *b* 1859; *m* 1889 Augusta Margaret (*d* 12 Feb 1924), dau of Rev Edmund Thomas Daubeney, Rector Swaffham, Norfolk and *d* 1927, leaving:

1a Lawrence Seymour; *b* 6 Jan 1905; Lt E African Forces WW II; *m* 1st 20 June 1936 Muriel Geraldine (*d* 14 Feb 1940), dau of Maj L A Sherrard, and had:

1b *Rosemary Margaret; *b* 10 July 1937; WRNS 1956–62 (3rd Offr 1958); *m* 7 Sept 1962 (*divorce* 1974) Jack Anthony Eden, s of Jack Eden, of Bransgore, Hants, and has:

1c *Sally Jane; *b* 29 July 1963

2c *Susan Rosemary; *b* 30 Dec 1964

2b *Molly [Mrs Graham Waterman, Greensmiths, Butts Green, Essex]; *b* 10 Feb 1940; *m* 22 July 1966 *Graham John Waterman, only s of Alfred George Waterman, of The Old Hall, Brooke, Norfolk, and has:

1c *Matthew Charles; *b* 28 April 1967

2c *Julian Rupert; *b* 24 June 1969

3c *Charlotte Lucy; *b* 1973

1a (cont.) Lawrence Sutton *m* 2nd 11 Aug 1942 *Martha Joyce, dau of W L Williams, of Cefn-y-dre, S Wales, and *d* 28 April 1967

1a Dorothy Mary Charlotte; *b* 1893; *m* 29 May 1917 John Selwyn Browning, s of Rev Canon Charles William Browning, Vicar Bromham, Beds

2a Robina Margaret Hill; *b* 1898; *m* 1st 3 Dec 1919 (*annulled* 1927) Capt Denis Menezes Miller, 14th Hus, of Blandford Lodge, White Knights, Reading, s of Thomas Miller, Br Consul; *m* 2nd 14 July 1927 Lt-Col Geoffrey Benedict Clifton-Brown (*see* BROWN, Bt) and had issue

(5) Lawrence Herbert; *b* 20 March 1865; *m* 1st 23 July 1919 Eleanor Godfrey Sealey (*d* 13 Sept 1919); *m* 2nd 26 Feb 1921 Eleanor Margaret, est dau of Alfred Marshall, FRIBA, of Burras Ho, Otley, and *dsp* 15 Feb 1954

(1) Augusta Mary; *d unm* 12 March 1899

(2) Catherine Mabel; *m* 1 Aug 1888 William Henry Ryder and *d* 21 Sept 1900, leaving issue (*see* HARROWBY, E)

6 Henry George; *b* 21 July 1826; 12th Lancers; *m* 1st 6 Feb 1849 Matilda Harriet (*d* 25 Nov 1885), est dau of G H Walker Heneage, of Compton Bassett, Wilts; *m* 2nd 16 Oct 1895 Evelyn (*d* 1 March 1938), dau of Rev George Sloane-Stanley, and *d* 10 May 1905, having by his 1st w had:

(1) Edward (Rev); *b* 24 Feb 1850; Rector Emley, Yorks; *d unm* 29 Nov 1900

(2) George Francis; *b* 31 Dec 1858; Lt Coldstream Gds; *d unm* Sudan Campaign 1885

(3) Hugh Clement, CB (1916), CMG (1919); *b* 20 Jan 1867; Adj Coldstream Gds 1894–98, Boer War 1899–1902 (despatches, brevet, two medals, seven clasps), Dep Assist Dir Rlwys S Africa 1900–02, DAAG Cape Colony 1903–06, cmdg 1st Bn Coldstream Gds 1910–13, WW I: AAG War Office 1913–16, DA&QMG BEF 1916–17, Dep IGC Mesopotamia 1917 and IGC 1919 (despatches four times), Col i/c Admin London Dist 1920, Dep Dir Personal Servs War Office 1921, Maj-Gen, Lt-Govr and Sec Roy Hosp Chelsea 1923–28, Orders St Anne Russia 2nd Cl with Swords and Rising Sun Japan 3rd Cl; *m* 1st 25 July 1891 Mabel Ida (*d* 29 March 1896), 4th dau of Sir Campbell Munro, 3rd Bt, of Lindertis (*qv*), and had:

1a Nigel Eustace Philip; *b* 29 March 1896; *educ* Eton and Ch Ch Oxford; Lt-Col Coldstream Gds, WWs I and II, Sec-Gen Inter-Allied Reparation Agency 1946–51, Exec Sec NATO 1951–52, Chev Legn Hon; *m* 1st 6 April 1921 Stella Clementina (*d* 8 June 1945), dau of Montagu Whittingham Price by Clementina, dau of Col Ernest Villiers (*see* CLARENDON, E), and had:

1b +John Hugh Torquil [Maj John Sutton, Bayfield Brecks, Holt, Norfolk]; *b* 3 Nov 1923; *educ* Eton and Ch Ch Oxford; Maj (ret) Coldstream Gds; *m* 11 Sept 1952 *Carola Mariette, yr dau of Maj Ulick Otway Vortigen Verney, OBE (*see* VERNEY, Bt, of Claydon House), and has:

1c +Hugh Nigel John [Hugh Sutton Esq, St Margarets House, Mapledurham, Berks]; *b* 1 Oct 1954; *m* 1987 *Miranda F, only dau of John Goldsmid, of Copyhold Farm, Goring Heath, Oxon, and has:

1d *Emma Frances Juliet; *b* 1989

2d *Olivia Henrietta Jonquille; *b* 1991

3d *Rebecca Virginia Jonquille; *b* 1991

2c +Mark Richard [Mark Sutton Esq, 42 Clarendon Dve, London SW15 1AE]; *b* 29 July 1956; *m* 1985 *Rose, yst dau of Samuel Carr, Chelsea, and has:

1d +Thomas Samuel; *b* 1991

1d *Phoebe Esmé; *b* 1988

1c *Catherine Stella Louise; *b* 14 March 1959

1b *Elizabeth Ann; *b* 27 Oct 1927

2b *Juliet Carmen [Mrs Ian Grant-Suttie, Mountain Ave, Woodstock, Vermont 05091, USA]; *b* 3 May 1930; *m* 1 Oct 1951 *(Robert) Ian Grant-Suttie (*see* GRANT-SUTTIE, Bt) and has issue

1a (cont.) Lt-Col Nigel Sutton *m* 2nd 21 March 1951 *Elisabeth Clothilde Hedwige (Zita), formerly w of Lt-Col Lewis Evelyn Gielgud, MBE, and dau of Zoltan Gruszner, of Budapest, and *d* 18 March 1956

(3) (cont.) Maj-Gen Hugh Sutton *m* 2nd 15 Sept 1898 Hon Alexandra Mary Elizabeth Wood, est dau of 2nd Viscount Halifax (*see* HALIFAX, E), and *d* 15 April 1928, having by her had:

1a Margaret Agnes; *b* 26 Sept 1899; *m* 6 April 1937 Hon John Julian Chetwynd, yr s of 8th Viscount Chetwynd (*qv*), and had issue

2a Mary Frances; *b* 12 June 1904; *d* 2 April 1975

3a *Elizabeth Mary [Mrs Elizabeth Tindall-Lister, Luccas Farm, Powerstock, Dorset]; *b* 17 April 1910; *m* 1st 29 Jan 1931 (*divorce* 1936) Sir (Ronald) Mark Cunliffe Turner (*d* 1980), only s of Christopher Rede Turner, of Greenhedges, Sheringham, Norfolk, and has issue; *m* 2nd 21 May 1936 (*divorce* 1976) John Tindall-Lister, yst s of Sir William Tindall Lister, KCMG, KCVO, MD, FRCS, of London, and by him has:

1b *Francis Hugh William Bernard; *b* 1937

2b *Charles John Alexander; *b* 1945

1b *Mary Nerissa Anna; *b* 1941

2b *Sarah Janet Consuelo; *b* 1947

7 Frederick Heathcote; *b* 30 Sept 1833; Rector Brant Broughton, Lincs; *d* 2 March 1888

1 Emily Mary; *m* 27 June 1848 1st Baron Trevor (*qv*) and *d* 24 Jan 1855, leaving issue

2 Sophia Louisa; *m* 6 May 1852 Col Samuel William Clowes, of Broughton Old Hall, Lancs, and *d* 18 Feb 1853, having had issue. He *d* 31 Dec 1898

3 Frances Amelia Victoria; *m* 23 Oct 1861 Ambrose Charles Lisle March Phillipps de Lisle, of Garendon Park and Grace Dieu Manor, Leics, and *d* 28 April 1871, leaving issue. He *d* 27 Nov 1883

The 3rd Bt's bro,

Sir Richard Sutton, 4th Bt, DL Notts; *b* 21 Oct 1821; 1st Life Gds; *m* 1st 18 May 1845 Anna (*d* 8 July 1846), dau of Rev H Houson, Rector Brant Broughton, Lincs; *m* 2nd 29 July 1851 his cousin Harriet Anne (*d* 22 March 1901), dau of William Fitzwilliam Burton, of Burton Hall, Co Carlow, and *d* 2 Oct 1878, having by her had:

1 **Sir Richard Francis Sutton, 5th Bt**; *b* 20 Dec 1853; High Sheriff Berks 1887; *m* 5 April 1888 Constance Edith (*m* 2nd 30 July 1895 Hubert Delaval Astley (*see* HASTINGS, B) and *d* 1 Sept 1940), dau of Sir Vincent Corbet, 3rd Bt (*see* 1970 edn), and *d* 25 Feb 1891, leaving:

(1) **Sir Richard Vincent Sutton, 6th Bt**, MC; *b* 26 April 1891; Capt and Adj 1st Life Gds and Gds MG Regt WW I (wounded twice, despatches twice); *das unm* 29 Nov 1918

2 ARTHUR EDWIN (Sir), **7th Bt**

3 Alexander George; *b* 19 Aug 1862; Lt Roy Wilts Yeo Cav; *m* 12 June 1885 Eugenia Kathleen (*m* 2nd 1 June 1895 Maj FitzRoy Pleydell Goddard (*d* 12 Aug 1927), and *d* 8 June 1947), dau of Thomas Richard Merry, and *d* 25 July 1893, having had:

(1) Thomas Alexander; *b* 1 June 1888; *m* 3 Sept 1913 (*divorce* 1943) Gwendoline (*d* 5 Nov 1968), dau of Thomas Forsyth-Forrest, and *d* 24 July 1945, leaving:

1a John Alexander; *b* 23 July 1915; *educ* Charterhouse; *m* 5 Jan 1950 Violet Deirdre [Mrs John Sutton, Badbury Wick House, Chiseldon, Wilts], er dau of James Sheringham Shepherd, of Killerack, Doneraile, Co Cork, and *d* 1981, leaving:

1b +Charles Alexander; *b* 30 Sept 1950; *educ* Millfield; *m* 1979 *Susan Nita, yr dau of Brian Richard Notton, of The Old Malthouse, Wanborough, Wilts

1b *Grania Jane; *b* 31 Jan 1952; *m* 1985 *(Robert) Nicholas Bovill Whitehead, of Badbury Wick Farmhouse, Chiseldon, Wilts, est s of T B Whitehead, of Chisbury, Wilts, and has:

1c *Hugh Alexander Bovill; *b* 1989

2c *Thomas James Bovill; *b* 1989 (twin)

1c *Eleanor Amanda Deirdre; *b* 1987

1a *(Margaret) Pamela [Pamela Lady Bunbury, 9 Lee Rd, Aldeburgh, Suffolk IP15 5HG]; *b* 22 April 1919; *m* 28 Nov 1940 Sir John William Napier Bunbury, 12th Bt (*qv*), and has issue

2a *Gillian; *b* 9 Dec 1921; *m* 3 July 1946 Robert Clarkson Crosbie Dawson, MC, only s of George Crosbie Dawson, FSI, of Little Woodcote, Kenilworth, Warwicks, and has:

1b *James; *b* 1 July 1948; *educ* Radley

2b *William George; *b* 24 April 1950; *educ* Radley and RMA Sandhurst

3b *Richard; *b* 3 Feb 1952; *educ* Radley

4b *Thomas; *b* 20 Sept 1956; *educ* Radley

(1) Naomi; *d unm*

4 Henry Cecil; *b* 26 Sept 1868; Lt Hants Yeo Cav; *m* 6 Nov 1913 Constance Diana (*d* 14 March 1960), est dau of Hon Herbert Welbore Ellis Agar (*see* NORMANTON, E), and *d* 24 May 1936, leaving:

(1) +Cecil Roland; *b* 24 Feb 1918; late 2nd Lt 99th (Bucks and Berks Yeo) Field Bde, RA (TA); inherited estates of his cousin the **6th Bt**; *m* 26 June 1943 *Lilian Elizabeth, dau of T W Gore, of Knighton, Ramsbury

1 Anna Harriet; *m* 25 July 1874 Col Augustus Henry Macdonald-Moreton, Coldstream Gds, and *d* 9 May 1924, leaving issue (*see* DUCIE, E)

2 Emily Judith; *m* 2 Nov 1876 Sir William Henry Levinge, 9th Bt (*qv*), and *d* 12 Jan 1921, leaving issue

3 Helen Mary; *m* 17 April 1884 Capt Ernest de Vismes du Boulay, RHA, of Swains Lodge, Bembridge, IoW, and *d* 17 April 1928, leaving issue. He *d* 22 Dec 1930

4 Mary Evelyn; *m* 9 May 1881 Capt Blair Onslow Cochrane, OBE (1919), RHA, and *d* 6 Feb 1934, leaving issue (*see* DUNDONALD, E)

5 Maud Ethelreda; *d unm* 26 May 1946

6 Georgina Mary; *m* 11 July 1889 4th Baron Langford (*qv*) and *d* 16 Dec 1901, leaving issue

7 Winifred Aline; *m* 1st 21 Feb 1893 Algernon Seymour Bernard Oakley, CE, s of Rev Charles Edward Oakley; *m* 2nd 30 Jan 1906 Maj Cecil William Wilson, DSO, 4th s of James Wilson, DL, JP, of Currygrane, Co Longford, and *d* 5 May 1945. He *d* 7 April 1937

8 Beatrice Zoë; *m* 18 Feb 1897 Lt-Col John Edward Rhodes, 60th Rifles, of Apley Rise, Ryde, IoW, est s of John William Rhodes, JP, DL, of Hennerton, Berks, by Marie Ada, dau of Edward Mackenzie, of Fawley Court, Oxon, and *d* 7 Nov 1921, leaving issue

The 6th Bt's uncle,

Sir Arthur Edwin Sutton, 7th Bt; *b* 24 Sept 1857; *m* 11 Sept 1885 Cecil Blanche (*d* 7 Jan 1948), est dau of Walter Douglas Dumbleton, of Oakhurst, Cape Colony, and *d* 4 Feb 1948, leaving, with a dau (Esmé, *m* 23 May 1912 Brig-Gen William Denman Croft, CB, CMG, DSO, Cameronians, 4th s of Sir Herbert George Denman Croft, 9th Bt (*see* CROFT, Bt, of Croft Castle), and had issue:

Sir Robert Lexington Sutton, 8th Bt; *b* 18 Jan 1897; *educ* Wellington and RMC Sandhurst; Lt 1st Life Gds WW I; *m* 23 July 1936 *Gwynneth Gwladys (Daphne) [Daphne Lady Sutton, Clinger Farm, Wincanton, Somerset], only dau of Maj Arnold Charles Gover, MC, of Pilton, and *d* 1981, leaving:

1 Sir RICHARD LEXINGTON SUTTON, **9th and present Bt**

2 +James Anthony [James Sutton Esq, Marsh Cottage, Penselwood, nr Wincanton, Somerset BA9 8LP]; *b* 11 March 1940; *educ* Stowe, Millfield and Loughborough Coll of Advanced Technology; DLC, GMIMechE; *m* 24 Oct 1964 *Dale, only dau of Capt Cecil William Stevens, of Windrush Mill, Burford, Glos, and has:

  (1) +Tristan Antony; *b* 26 Feb 1966; *m* 29 July 1995 *Catherine Louise, dau of David Masters, of Bagmore Farm, Silton, Dorset, and has:

   1a +William Oliver; *b* 31 March 1998

  (1) *Chloë Emma; *b* 3 Jan 1968

SWANN

Arms: Az. a swan rousant ppr. within an orle of lymphads, sails furled, flags flying to the dexter or. **Crest:** A demi-swan, wings expanded, between two buffalo's horns ppr. **Motto:** Ever forward. **Creation:** Bt. (UK) 16 July 1906.

SIR MICHAEL CHRISTOPHER SWANN, 4TH BT, of Prince's Gardens, Kensington, TD [Sir Michael Swann Bt TD, 38 Hurlingham Rd, London SW6 3RQ]; *b* 25 Sept 1941; *s* f 1991; *educ* Eton; late Lt 2nd Greenjackets (KRRC), 4th Bn RGJ (T&AVR) 1964–79 (Brevet Lt-Col 1979), dir GVG Fin Servs 1988–, ptnr Smith Swann & Co 1992–, v-chm Gabbitas Truman and Thring 1987–, Gen Commr Income Tax 1988–; APMI 1971; *m* 1st 24 April 1965 (*divorce* 1985) Hon Lydia Mary Hewitt, est dau of 8th Viscount Lifford (*qv*); *m* 2nd 1988 *Marilyn Ann Morse, dau of Leslie Charles Tobitt, of Montevideo, Uruguay, and by his 1st w has:

1 +JONATHAN CHRISTOPHER; *b* 17 Nov 1966; *educ* Eton; *m* 1994 *Polly, dau of Cdr David Baston

2 +Toby Charles; *b* 17 Jan 1971; *educ* Stowe

1 *Tessa Margaret; *b* 11 April 1968; *educ* Sacred Heart Convent Tunbridge Wells

Lineage: JOHN FREDERICK SCHWANN, of London; *m* Henrietta, dau of Rev Robert Kell, of Birmingham, and had, with other issue:

Sir CHARLES ERNEST SCHWANN later SWANN (roy licence 11 Dec 1913), **1st Bt** (UK), so *cr* 16 July 1906, PC (1911); *b* 25 Jan 1844; MP (Lib) N Manchester 1886–1918; *m* 20 Sept 1877 Elizabeth (*d* 13 April 1914), dau of David Duncan, of Manchester, and had:

1 (CHARLES) DUNCAN (Sir), **2nd Bt**

2 Harold, JP Herts; *b* 29 Jan 1880; *educ* Eton; Capt TAR; *m* 14 May 1907 Dorothea Alma (*d* 27 Feb 1969), er dau of Henry de Courcy Agnew, JP (*see* AGNEW, Bt, of Lochnaw), and *d* 7 Nov 1953, having had:

  (1) Charles Brian; *b* 21 July 1913; *educ* Eton; P/O RAFVR; *m* 1st 9 Sept 1939 (*divorce* 1955) Vanessa Fiaschi Dalrymple, er dau of Ernest William Dalrymple Tennant, OBE (*see* GLENCONNER, B), and had:

   1a *Julia Vanessa [Mrs Blyth Thompson, Applecross, 150 Empire Place, Sandhurst, Johannesburg, S Africa]; *b* 30 Aug 1940; *m* 22 Oct 1960 *Blyth

Metcalf Thompson, late Capt E Surrey Regt (TA), 2nd s of Frederik Rowland Blyth Thompson, of Transkei, and has:

   1b *William Rowland Blyth; *b* 14 Nov 1962
   2b *Dendy Martin Blyth; *b* 1972
   1b *Vanessa Eirene; *b* 17 Sept 1961
   2b *Moya Ann; *b* 16 Oct 1965
   3b *Hannah Yvonne; *b* 5 July 1967
   4b *Sonya Suzanne; *b* 5 June 1969
   2a *Karin Clarissa; *b* 8 June 1942
   3a *Virginia Caroline [Mrs David Hughes, Mid Lambrook Manor, S Petherton, Somerset]; *b* 13 Oct 1948; *m* 28 April 1971 *David Winkfield Hughes, only s of Dr William Gerald Hugh Hughes, of The Manor Cottage, Compton Pauncefote, Somerset, and has:

   1b *Thomas Percy Winkfield; *b* 1974
   1b *Harriet Elfreda; *b* 1972

  (1) (cont.) Charles Swann *m* 2nd 8 Aug 1955 *Anne Corben [Mrs John MacKinnon, The Old Rectory, Houghton, Huntingdonshire] (*m* 2nd 17 Oct 1967 Maj John Farquhar MacKinnon, MC, JP, yst s of Donald De Burgh D'Arcy MacKinnon), yr dau of Cyril Alwyn Harrison, and *d* 7 Jan 1966

  (1) Helen; *b* 6 Oct, *d* 8 Dec 1911

3 Laurence Averil; *b* 30 May 1881; *educ* Eton and Merton Coll Oxford; *m* 26 Feb 1913 (*divorce* 1925) Emeline Elexina, est dau of John E Prégent, of Boston, Mass., and *dsp* 13 Nov 1953

4 Geoffrey, JP Herts; *b* 25 July 1883; *educ* Westminster and Ch Ch Oxford; RASC WW I, dir London Produce Clearing House Ltd, memb: No 1 (NE) Hosp Gp 1948–57, Management Cttee Herts Trg Sch, Home Office Approved Sch Ware 1950 (chm 1961); *m* 29 July 1911 Florence Mildred (*d* 8 Jan 1964), 2nd dau of John Henry Brodie, of Hamsell Manor, Eridge, and *d* 28 Aug 1965, having had:

  (1) Kenneth Geoffrey, MC; *b* 19 Oct 1915; *educ* Eton and Ch Ch Oxford; Maj 86th (E Anglian) (Herts Yeo) Field Bde RA (TA) WW II; *m* 9 Jan 1942 Delmira Marion (*m* 2nd 4 Jan 1947 Peter Richard Hampton, MC, only s of Robert Hampton, of Moffat Cottage, Ashtead, and *d* 25 Aug 1947), yr dau of Sir (Ferdinand) Michael Kroyer-Kielberg, KBE, of Stockgrove Park, Leighton Buzzard, and was *ka* France 20 June 1944, leaving:

   1a +Christopher Kenneth, of Santa Barbara, Calif.; *b* 1 Nov 1942; *educ* Eton and Internat Sch Geneva; *m* 1968 *Kathleen Harriet Brodarick

   1a *Penelope Ann; *b* posthumously 25 Dec 1944

  (1) *Janet Elizabeth, JP Herts [Mrs Charles Bardswell JP, The Grange, Walkern, Herts]; *b* 23 Dec 1913; *m* 24 Jan 1939 *Charles Gifford Bardswell, S/Ldr RAFVR, AE, s of Noel Dean Bardswell, MVO, MD, FRCP, of The Chase, Chigwell, Essex, and has had:

   1a *Charles Nicholas; *b* 10 May 1941; *educ* Eton and Lincoln Coll Oxford (BA); *m* 24 Sept 1969 *Sarah Josephine, BSc, dau of Sir (Thomas) Leslie Rowan, KCB, CVO, of Chelsea, and has:

    1b *Charles Leslie Geoffrey; *b* 1981
    1b *Catherine Jane Elizabeth; *b* 1971
    2b *Alice Victoria Josephine; *b* 1974
    3b *Isabella Louise Clementine; *b* 1979

   2a *Philip Geoffrey; *b* 8 Sept 1948; *educ* Eton and Univ Coll Oxford (BA); *m* 1973 *Alexandra Augusta, only child of Iver Lunn, of Towersley, Oxon, and has:

    1b *Josephine Elizabeth; *b* 1977
    2b *Sonya Caroline; *b* 1979

   1a *Veronica Elizabeth; *b* 30 Aug 1945; *educ* St Andrews (BSc 1967) and Linacre Coll Oxford (Dip Advanced Maths 1968); *m* 1974 *Roger Gaymer BROADIE formerly BROADIE-GRIFFITH and has:

    1b *Helen Elizabeth; *b* 1978
    2b *Charlotte Anne; *b* 1981

  (2) *Phyllis Mildred [Mrs John Fegen, Porta-beg, Ballykeeran, Co Westmeath, Ireland]; *b* 26 Jan 1919; *m* 26 Jan 1946 *John Charles Fegen, DSC, Lt RNVR, yr s of Francis Harry Fegen, of Guildford, and has:

   1a *Richard Kenneth; *b* 30 June 1947; *educ* Eton and Trin Coll Dublin; *m* 1982 *Charmian Sadgrove and has:

    1b *Robin; *b* 1985
    1b *Polly Lucinda; *b* 1983
   1a *Frances Lynette; *b* 3 June 1950
   2a *Lucy Mildred; *b* 24 March 1953; *m* 1976 *Simon Burdett and has:

    1b *Jonathan; *b* 1983
    1b *Chloë; *b* 1979

  (3) *Kathleen Mary Prudence [Mrs Allan Thomson, 8 Nicholson Rd, Wellington 4, New Zealand]; *b* 2 April 1921; *m* 20 March 1945 *Capt Allan Priestley Thomson, NZ Forest Service, s of James Allan Thomson, of Dominion Museum, Wellington, and has had:

   1a David Allan; *b* 20 Jan 1948; *d* 1965
   2a *Michael Kenneth; *b* 1 Sept 1951
   3a *Peter Geoffrey; *b* 16 Nov 1955
   4a *Andrew Brodie; *b* 29 July 1958; *m* 1987 *Razimah Ishmail
   1a *Celia Margaret; *b* 22 June 1946; *m* 1970 *Brian Herbert Bockett and has:

    1b *David; *b* 1972
    2b *Nicholas; *b* 1977
    1b *Kirsten Margaret; *b* 1974

1 Elizabeth Kathleen Mildred; *b* 21 March 1887; *m* 16 Sept 1913 Eliot Albert Cross Druce, s of Albert Druce, of Thornhill, Sevenoaks, and *d* 23 Feb 1962. He *d* 24 Oct 1934

Sir CHARLES *d* 13 July 1929; his est s,

Sir (Charles) Duncan Swann, 2nd Bt; *b* 27 Jan 1879; *educ* Eton and Balliol Coll Oxford (BA 1901, MA 1904); barrister Inner Temple 1904, MP Hyde 1906–10; author: *The Book of a Bachelor*, etc; *m* 28 Oct 1909 Dorothy Margaret (*d* 30 April

1971), dau of Capt Robert Harry Johnson, 64th Regt, and *d* 10 March 1962, having had:

1 Guy Charles; *b* 3 Nov 1910; *d* 5 Jan 1911

2 **Sir Anthony Charles Christopher Swann, 3rd Bt**, CMG (1958), OBE (1950); *b* 29 June 1913; *educ* Eton and New Coll Oxford (BA 1936, MA 1938); Min Defence and Internal Security Kenya, Maj KAR WW II; *m* 28 Nov 1940 *Jean Margaret [Dowager Lady Swann, 25 Hurlingham Sq, London SW6 3DZ], yr dau of John Herbert Niblock-Stuart, of Nairobi, and *d* 1991, leaving:

(1) Sir MICHAEL CHRISTOPHER SWANN, **4th and present Bt**

SWANSEA

Arms: Or on a chevron az., between three lion's heads erased ppr., as many annulets of the field, a chief embattled gu., thereon a wreath of oak of the 1st between two martlets arg. **Crests:** 1 A lion's head erased ppr., charged with two bezants palewise and gorged with a collar gu., thereon three annulets or with a chain of the last; 2 Issuant from a bridge of one arch, embattled at each end, a tower ppr., a demi-hussar of Her Majesty's 18th Regt of Dragoons (Hussars), habited, armed and accoutred, holding in his dexter hand a sabre, all ppr., and in his sinister a pennon flying to the sinister, gu. **Supporters:** Dexter, a dragon, wings elevated gu., gorged with a collar or charged with three torteaux; sinister, a horse arg., saddle and bridle ppr., trappings gu., gorged with a collar sa., charged with three bezants. **Motto:** *Vive anima Dei* ('Live by the Spirit of God'). **Creation:** Bt. (UK) 13 May 1882, B. (UK) 9 June 1893.

THE 4TH BARON SWANSEA OF SINGLETON, Co Glamorgan, and a **Baronet** (Sir John Hussey Hamilton Vivian, Bt, DL (Powys 1962)) [The Rt Hon The Lord Swansea DL, 16 Cheyne Gdns, London SW3 5QT]; *b* 1 Jan 1925; *s f* 1934; *educ* Eton and Trin Coll Cambridge; Freeman Gunmakers' Co, memb Cncl Nat Rifle Assoc 1975–, Pres: Welsh Rifle Assoc, Cwlth Shooting Fedn, Shooting Sports Tst; Dato Serilaila Jasa (Brunei) 1971, CStJ 1994]; *m* 1st 19 April 1956 (*divorce* 1973) Miriam Antoinette (*d* Jan 1975), 2nd dau of Anthony William Fabio Caccia-Birch, MC, of Guernsey Lodge, Marton, NZ (*see* 1970 edn CACCIA, B); *m* 2nd 29 Dec 1982 *Mrs Lucy Temple Richards, dau of Rt Rev Hugh Rowlands Gough, CMG, OBE, TD, DD (*see* 1970 edn KINNAIRD, L), and has by his 1st w:

1 +RICHARD ANTHONY HUSSEY; *b* 24 Jan 1957; *educ* Eton and Durham U; *m* 24 Aug 1996 *Mrs Anna Brooking, dau of Michael Austin, of Victoria, Australia, and Mrs Lynette Austin, of Hong Kong

1 *Amanda Ursula Georgina [The Hon Mrs Lowther, Nortoft Grange, Guilsborough, Northants NN6 8QB]; *b* 22 Nov 1958; *m* 1985 *Hugh William Lowther and has issue (*see* LOWTHER, Bt)

2 *Louisa Caroline Sarah; *b* 13 Feb 1963; *m* 1990 *Paul David Vincent, only s of Peter Vincent, of Bowdon, Cheshire

Lineage: JOHN HENRY VIVIAN, JP, DL Glam, of Singleton, Glam; *b* 9 Aug 1785 (bro of 1st Baron Vivian, *qv*); MP Swansea 1832–55, Maj Roy Stannary Artillery, FRS, FGS; *m* 30 Oct 1816 Sarah (*d* 8 Sept 1886), est dau of Arthur Jones, of The Priory, Reigate, and had, with a dau (*d* unm):

1 HENRY HUSSEY, **1st Baron**

2 William Graham, of Clyne Castle and Parc le Breos, Glam, JP, DL Glam; *b* 25 Nov 1827; High Sheriff Glam 1866; *d* unm 21 Aug 1912

3 Arthur Pendarves (Sir), KCB, JP, DL Glam, JP Cornwall; *b* 4 June 1834; Hon Col 6th Bn Welch Regt, Brig-Gen cmdg S Wales Vol and Border Bde, MP W Cornwall 1868–85, High Sheriff Cornwall 1889, CC Glam 1889–98, CA Cornwall 1898–1926; *m* 1st 3 March 1867 Lady Augusta Emily Wyndham-Quin (*d* 11 Feb 1877), est dau of 3rd Earl of Dunraven and Mount-Earl (*qv*), and had:

(1) Henry Wyndham, JP; *b* 3 Feb 1868; BA Cantab; Maj 2nd Vol Bn Welch Regt; *m* 19 Jan 1899 Lady Maude Clements (*m* 2nd 15 Sept 1910 Christopher Foulis Roundell, CBE, and *d* 19 Jan 1932), dau of 4th Earl of Leitrim (*see* 1953 edn), and *d* 17 Nov 1901, having had:

1a Audrey Emily; *b* 24 Sept 1899; *m* 7 Dec 1921 Richard Preston GRAHAM later GRAHAM-VIVIAN (roy licence 21 Aug 1929), MVO, MC, Norroy and Ulster King of Arms, 2nd s of Sir Richard Graham, 4th Bt, of Netherby (*qv*), and had issue

(2) Gerald William, CMG (1918); *b* 10 June 1869; Capt RN; *d* 14 Aug 1921

(1) Caroline Mabel; *b* 26 June 1873; *m* 21 June 1904 4th Baron Seaton (*d* 12 March 1955; *see* 1953 edn) and *dsp* 3 June 1948

(2) Clarice Gertrude; *b* 3 March 1875; *d* unm 21 Nov 1961

3 (cont.) Brig-Gen Sir Arthur Vivian *m* 2nd 10 March 1880 Lady Jane Dalrymple (*d* 8 July 1914), dau of 10th Earl of Stair (*qv*), and *d* 18 Aug 1926, having by her had:

(2) Edith Evelyn; *b* 22 Dec 1880; *m* 1st 8 Nov 1911 Lt-Col Algernon Bingham Anstruther Stewart, DSO (*see* GALLOWAY, E), and had issue; *m* 2nd 19 June 1922 Henry de Grey Lennox (*see* RICHMOND and GORDON, D) and *d* 17 Feb 1932

(3) Lilian Ursula; *b* 18 July 1888; OStJ; *m* 1st 7 Feb 1912 Capt William Mackworth Parker, Rifle Bde (*see* PARKER, Bt, of Shenstone Lodge); *m* 2nd 4 April 1921 V-Adml Everard John Hardman-Jones, CB, OBE, s of R J Hardman-Jones, of Woodlands, Binfield, Berks, and *d* 6 Nov 1966. He *d* 28 June 1962

4 Richard Glynn, DL, of Sketty Hall, Swansea; *b* 31 Aug 1835; MA Cantab; FRGS, Burgess Swansea; *m* 11 March 1885 (*divorce* 1891) Laura Hermione Beatrice, only dau of Henry Craigie Halkett, Bengal CS, and *dsp* 7 June 1910

1 Betsy Sarah; *m* 29 Aug 1840 Sir William Gibson Craig, 2nd Bt, PC (*see* 1933 edn), and *d* 15 Feb 1895, leaving issue. He *d* 12 March 1878

2 Caroline Gertrude Walker; *m* 21 June 1848 William Jones Loyd, of Langleybury, Watford, and *d* 1893, having had issue. He *d* 28 Aug 1885

3 Henrietta Letitia Victoria; *m* 7 Dec 1865 Maj Clement Walker Heneage, VC, DL, 8th Hus, of Compton, Wilts, and *d* 16 March 1919, leaving issue. He *d* 9 Dec 1901

Maj JOHN VIVIAN *d* 10 Feb 1855; his est s,

Sir Henry Hussey Vivian, 1st Bt, and **1st Baron Swansea of Singleton**, Co Glamorgan (both UK), so *cr* 13 May 1882 and 9 June 1893 respectively; *b* 6 July 1821; Col 4th Glamorgan RV, MP (Lib) Truro 1852–57, Glamorgan 1857–85 and Swansea 1885–93; *m* 1st 15 April 1847 Jessie Dalrymple (*d* 28 Feb 1848), dau of Ambrose Goddard, MP, of The Lawn, Swindon, Wilts, and had:

1 ERNEST AMBROSE VIVIAN, **2nd Baron Swansea of Singleton**, JP, DL Glam; *b* 11 Feb 1848; *d* unm 17 July 1922

The **1st Baron** *m* 2nd 14 July 1853 Caroline Elizabeth (*d* 25 Jan 1868), only dau of Sir Montague John Cholmeley, 2nd Bt (*qv*), and by her had:

2 John Aubrey, JP, DL Glam; *b* 23 July 1854; *d* 1 March 1898

The **1st Baron** *m* 3rd 10 Nov 1870 Averil (*d* 14 Jan 1934), dau of Capt Richard Beaumont, RN (*see* ALLENDALE, V), and *d* 28 Nov 1894, having by her had:

3 Henry Hussey; *b* 5 Feb 1873; *d* 11 Dec 1898

4 ODO RICHARD, **3rd Baron**

1 Violet Averil Margaret, formerly of Sketty Hall, Swansea; *b* 3 Dec 1871; *m* 11 Oct 1899 Brig-Gen Douglas CAMPBELL later DOUGLAS (on inheriting estate of Mains, Dunbartonshire, 23 June 1925 from his unc Archibald Campbell Douglas of Mains), CB, Seaforth Highrs, and *d* 30 March 1943, having had issue. He *d* 17 June 1927

2 Averil; *b* 4 Dec 1876; *m* 28 Feb 1905 1st Baron Tryon (*qv*) and *d* 1 Feb 1959, leaving issue

3 Alberta Diana; *b* 10 Feb 1883 (TM EDWARD VII and QUEEN ALEXANDRA stood sponsor); *m* 18 April 1906 Sir William Henry Ingilby, 4th Bt (*qv*), and *d* 11 Dec 1968, leaving issue

4 Alexandra Gladys; *b* 10 Feb 1883 (HM QUEEN ALEXANDRA stood sponsor); *m* 7 Jan 1905 Maj Alexander Robert Leith, OBE, JP, DL, KRRC, er s of Maj Thomas Leith (*see* BURGH, B), and *d* 17 July 1966, leaving issue

The 2nd BARON's half-bro,

ODO RICHARD VIVIAN, **3rd Baron Swansea of Singleton**, DSO, MVO, TD (1916), JP, DL (Glam); *b* 22 April 1875; Hon Col 6th Bn Welsh Regt, Glamorgan Yeo 1901–19; *m* 25 Oct 1906 Hon Winifred Hamilton (*d* 3 Sept 1944), 4th dau of 1st Baron Holm Patrick (*qv*), and *d* 16 Nov 1934, having had:

1 JOHN HUSSEY HAMILTON VIVIAN, **4th and present Baron Swansea of Singleton**

1 Ursula Margaret; *b* 13 May 1910; *m* 13 July 1937 Hon Charles Brodrick Amyas Bernard, CBE, yr s of Lt-Col Ronald Percy Hamilton Bernard (*see* 1970 edn BANDON, E), and *dsp* 2 Aug 1963

2 Rosemary Winifred; *b* 4 June 1927; *m* 25 Jan 1947 (*divorce* 1969) Capt Robert John Pulleine Eden (*see* EDEN OF WINTON, B) and *d* 1981, leaving issue

3 *Averil, JP (Herts) [The Hon Mrs Houston JP, Paynters House, Datchworth, Herts SG3 6ST]; *b* 8 Jan 1930; *m* 27 June 1953 *Alexander William Houston, only s of Archibald Houston, and has:

(1) *Peter Richard Vivian [Peter Houston Esq, Fair Dawn, Packhorse Lane, S Stoke, Bath BA2 7DL]; *b* 11 July 1954; *educ* Oundle; *m* 1979 *Susan Caroline, yr dau of Maj Robert Evelyn Russell Smallwood (*see* BIRKMYRE, Bt)

(2) *Charles Robson Hamilton [Charles Houston Esq, Neen Sollars House, nr Cleobury Mortimer, Worcs DY14 0AH]; *b* 16 Oct 1959; *m* 1987 *Emma Woodbine, yst dau of Michael Woodbine Parish, MC, and has:

1a *Michael Charles Woodbine; *b* 3 July 1991

1a *Florence Rose Woodbine; *b* 25 June 1989

2a *Roselle Azalea Woodbine; *b* 9 Dec 1992

3a *Elsie Lily Woodbine; *b* 15 Dec 1994

(1) *Claire Mary [Mrs Patrick Mansel Lewis, Capel Isaf, Manordeilo, Llandeilo, Carm]; *b* 26 Aug 1956; *m* 1985 *Patrick Charles Archibald Mansel Lewis and has issue (*see* WHARNCLIFFE, E)

SWAYTHLING

Arms: Or on a mount vert a tent arg., between on the dexter a staff ppr., flowing therefrom a pennon az. charged with a lion rampant of the field, and on the sinister a palm tree, also ppr. **Crest:** A stag statant, holding in the mouth a sprig of palm ppr., in front of a flagstaff erect, also ppr., therefrom flowing to the dexter a banner az. charged with a lion rampant or. **Supporters:** On either side a figure representing a soldier of ancient Judea ppr. **Motto:** Swift yet sure. **Creations:** Bt. (UK) 23 June 1894, B. (UK) 18 July 1907.

THE 5TH BARON SWAYTHLING, of Swaythling, Co Southampton, and a **Baronet** (Sir Charles Edgar Samuel Montagu, Bt) [The Rt Hon The Lord Swaythling, House of Lords, London SW1A 0PW]; *b* 20 Feb 1954; *s* f 1998; *educ* Milton Abbey; *m* 24 Feb 1996, as her 2nd husb, *Hon Angela, dau of Baron Rawlinson of Ewell (*qv*), and has:

1 *Delilah Elaine; *b* 9 Jan 1998

Lineage: LOUIS SAMUEL, of Hunter St, Brunswick Sq, London, formerly of Liverpool; *b* 1794; *m* 17 Nov 1819 Henrietta, dau of Israel Israel, of Bury St, St Mary Axe, London, and *d* 27 Aug 1859, leaving, with other issue (*see* SAMUEL, V):

Sir MOSES SAMUEL later MONTAGU SAMUEL (roy licence 1894), **1st Bt**, and **1st Baron Swaythling**, of Swaythling, Co Southampton (both UK), so *cr* 23 June 1894 and 18 July 1907 respectively, JP, DL London, JP Hants; *b* 21 Dec 1832; MP (Lib) Whitechapel 1885–1900; *m* 5 March 1862 Ellen (*d* 15 March 1919), dau of Louis Cohen (*see* 1967 edn COHEN, Bt), and had:

1 LOUIS SAMUEL, **2nd Baron**

2 Edwin Samuel, PC; *b* 6 Feb 1879; *educ* Clifton, City of London Sch and Trin Coll Cambridge (MA); MP (Lib) Chesterton 1906–22, Parly U-Sec India 1910–14, Fin Sec Treasury 1914–15 and 1915–16, Chllr Duchy Lancaster 1915 and 1916, Min Munitions 1916, Sec State India 1917–22; *m* 26 July 1915 Hon (Beatrice) Venetia Stanley (*d* 3 Aug 1948), yst dau of 4th Baron Sheffield (*see* STANLEY OF ALDERLEY, SHEFFIELD and, B), and *d* 15 Nov 1924, leaving:

(1) Judith Venetia; *b* 6 Feb 1923; *m* 16 April 1962 *Milton Gendel and *d* 8 Nov 1972, leaving:

1a *Anna Venetia *b* 1963

3 Gerald Samuel; *b* 29 Sept 1880; *educ* Clifton; *m* 2 Feb 1909 Florence (*d* 20 Feb 1961), only dau of Percy M Castello, of York Terr, NW, and *d* 14 Aug 1956, leaving:

(1) Bryan de Castro Samuel; *b* 3 Aug 1916; *educ* Stowe; Capt RA WW II; *m* 21 Feb 1950 *Elcie [Mrs Bryan Montagu, 9 Hesper Mews, London SW5 0HH], only dau of John Weiser, and *d* 11 Dec 1997, leaving:

1a +Robert de Castro Samuel [Robert Montagu Esq, Mayfield House, The Grange, Ingham, Lincs LN1 2UY]; *b* 1956; *m* 1983 *Claire Strettell and has:

1b +James de Castro Samuel; *b* 1990

1b *Charlotte Claire; *b* 1992

1a *Lydia [Mrs Ian Coltman, 44 Normanton Ave, London SW19 8BB]; *b* 1959; *m* 1989 *Ian Leonard Coltman, er s of William A Coltman, of Catterick, N Yorks, and has:

1b *Zoe; *b* 1994

(1) Ina; *b* 12 Oct 1913; *m* 12 Oct 1937 *Alexander Poliakoff, only s of Joseph Poliakoff, of W Kensington, and had:

1a *Martyn; *b* 16 Dec 1947; *educ* Westminster and King's Coll Cambridge

2a *Stephen [Stephen Poliakoff Esq, 33 Devonia Rd, London N1 8JQ]; *b* 1 Dec 1952; *educ* Westminster and Cambridge U; playwright (won *Evening Standard* award for best playwright 1976 for *City Sugar*), film director; *m* 1983 *Sandy Welch and has issue

1a *Lucinda Jane; *b* 16 March 1957

2a *Miranda Ann; *b* 26 Aug 1959

4 Lionel Samuel, DSO (1917); *b* 8 Sept 1883; *educ* Clifton and New Coll Oxford (BA 1905, MA 1911); Hon Maj RM WW I (despatches, wounded), ptnr Samuel Montagu & Co; *m* 4 Oct 1944 *Sybil, formerly w of Edward Arthur Vesey Stanley (*see* DERBY, E) and dau of Maj Heathfield Butler Dodgson, DSO, RHA, of Handborough, Oxon, and *dsp* 26 April 1948

1 Henrietta, CBE (1950); *m* 7 Oct 1885 Ernest Louis Franklin, JP, of 50 Porchester Terr, W2, and Glenalla, Ray, Letterkenny, Co Donegal, s of Ellis A Franklin, of 35 Porchester Terr, W, and *d* 7 Jan 1964, leaving issue. He *d* 8 April 1950

2 Florence; *m* 15 July 1889 Montefiore Simon Waley and *d* 5 Jan 1944, leaving issue. He *d* 15 Oct 1910

3 Marian; *d* unm 7 July 1965 aged 96

4 Ethel; *m* 12 April 1893 Henry D'Arcy Hart, barrister, of 18 Pembridge Gdns, W, and *d* 29 Jan 1947, leaving issue. He *d* 25 Nov 1938

5 Lilian Helen, CBE (1955, OBE 1937), JP Co London; *b* 22 Dec 1873; *d* unm 22 Jan 1963

6 Elsie; *m* 31 Oct 1905 Reginald Abraham Simmons Myer, est s of Grenville David Myer, and *d* 26 July 1964, leaving issue. He *d* 11 April 1959

The 1st BARON *d* 12 Jan 1911; his est s,

LOUIS SAMUEL later SAMUEL-MONTAGU, **2nd Baron Swaythling**, JP Hants; *b* 10 Dec 1869; Orders Crown Belgium, St Sava Serbia, Crown Romania, Sacred Treasure Japan 2nd Cl; *m* 9 Feb 1898 Gladys Helen Rachel, OBE (1953), FRGS, FRPS, Assoc DStJ, Order Merit Japan, Order Precious Crown Japan, 1st Cl Japanese Red Cross, Cdr St Sava Yugoslavia, Offr Public Instruction France, Medal Queen Elisabeth Belgium (*d* 8 Jan 1965), er dau of Col Albert Edward Williamson Goldsmid, MVO, and had:

1 STUART ALBERT SAMUEL, **3rd Baron**

2 Ewen Edward Samuel, CBE (1951, OBE 1944), KC (1939), JP (Hants 1947), DL (1953); *b* 29 March 1901; *educ* Westminster, Harvard and Trin Coll Cambridge (BA and LLB 1923, MA 1948); barrister Middle Temple 1924, Bencher 1948, Treas 1968, Recorder: Devizes 1944–51 and Southampton 1951–61, Judge Advocate Fleet 1945–73, Dep Chm Hants QS 1948 (Chm 1951–61) and 1969 and Middx QS 1954 (Chm 1956–65), Chm Middx Area Gtr London QS 1965–69, V-Chm Centl Cncl Magistrates' Courts Ctees 1954–63 (Chm 1963), Pres Utd Synagogue 1954–62, Chm Gen Purposes Ctee RYA 1960–68, Lt-Cdr RNVR WW II, 3rd Cl Order Crown Yugoslavia, author: *The Man Who Never Was* (1953), *The Archer-Shee Case* (1974); *m* 14 June 1923 *Iris Rachel [The Hon Mrs Ewen Montagu, 24 Montrose Court, Exhibition Rd, London SW7 2QQ], dau of Solomon Joseph Solomon, RA, PRBA, and *d* 1985, leaving:

(1) +Jeremy Peter Samuel [Jeremy Montagu Esq, 171 Iffley Rd, Oxford OX4 1EL]; *b* 27 Dec 1927; *educ* Hotchkiss Sch USA, Gordonstoun, Trin Coll Cambridge and Guildhall Sch Music; museum curator; *m* 29 July 1955 *Gwen Ellen, dau of Jack Ingledew, of Westhouses, Derby, and has:

1a +Simon Joseph Samuel; *b* 18 June 1959; *m* 1st (*divorce* 1989) Judith, dau of Charles Lowy, of 14 Edgware Ct, High St, Edgware, and has:

1b *Avital Rose; *b* 1986

1a (cont.) Simon Montagu *m* 2nd 19– *Hepzibah, dau of Mordecai Cohen, of Jerusalem, and by her has:

1b *Aviad Mordecai Samuel; *b* 1992

2b *Ahinoam Rachel Samuel; *b* 1993

1a *Rachel Mary; *b* 13 March 1956; rabbi; *m* 1990 *Francis Samuel, s of Werner Treuherz, of Rochdale, and has:

1b *Eliezer Michael; *b* 1993

2a *Sarah Ruth; *b* 29 April 1958; *m* 1980 *Mark Roseman and has:

1b *Jacob Edward James Samuel; *b* 1981

1b *Abigail Shoshana; *b* 1984

2b *Kate Nechama; *b* 1987

(1) *Jennifer Iris Rachel [Miss Jennifer Montagu, 10 Roland Way, London SW7 3RE]; *b* 20 March 1931; *educ* LMH Oxford (BA 1952) and London U (PhD 1960); art historian

3 +Ivor Goldsmid Samuel; *b* 23 April 1904; *educ* Westminster, Roy Coll Science and King's Coll Cambridge (BA 1924, MA 1930); V-Pres Br Peace Ctee, memb Presidential Ctee World Cncl Peace, fndr-pres Internat Table Tennis Fedn, 1st Cl Order Liberation Bulgaria, Lenin Peace Prize, Order Pole Star Mongolia, author: *The Traitor Class*, *Plot Against Peace*, *Land of Blue Sky*, *Film World*, *With Eisenstein in Hollywood*, *The Youngest Son*; *m* 10 Jan 1927 Eileen, 5th dau of Francis Anton Hellstern

1 Joyce Ida Jessie, JP (Wilts 1966); *b* 10 Jan 1909; *m* 15 Aug 1941 Oliver Harry Frost, MBE, MC, s of Robert Frost, and has:

(1) *Timothy Oliver; *b* 6 May 1943; *educ* Marlborough and King's Coll Cambridge (BA 1964, MA 1968); *m* 28 Sept 1968 *Charlotte Birgitta Baskerville, yr dau of Thomas Halliday Baskerville Mynors (*see* MYNORS, Bt)

The 2nd BARON *d* 11 June 1927; his est s,

STUART ALBERT SAMUEL MONTAGU, **3rd Baron Swaythling**, OBE (1947), JP (Hants 1928–48) and (Surrey 1948); *b* 19 Dec 1898; *educ* Clifton, Westminster and Trin Coll Cambridge (BA 1921, MA 1926); Lt Res Offrs Gren Gds 1917–30, dir Samuel Montagu, V-Chm Price Regulation Ctee London Area 1943–46, Chm Retail Licensing Ctee London 1943, Master Farmers' Co 1962, Pres: Roy Assoc Br Dairy Farmers 1973–74 and English Guernsey Cattle Soc 1950 and 1951 and 1971–72; *m* 1st 21 April 1925 (*divorce* 1942) Mary Violet (*m* 2nd 1945 Henry Elliott-Blake, TD, FRCS (*d* 1983)), est dau of Maj Walter Henry Levy, DSO, and Hon Mrs Ionides, dau of 1st Viscount Bearsted (*qv*); *m* 2nd 13 Aug 1945 Jean Marcia, CBE (1943) (*d* 1993), Ch Controller and Dir ATS 1941–43, formerly w of S/Ldr G R M Knox, RAF, and dau of G G Leith-Marshall, and *d* 1990, having had by his 1st w:

1 DAVID CHARLES SAMUEL MONTAGU, **4th Baron Swaythling**; *b* 6 Aug 1928; *educ* Eton and Trin Coll Cambridge (BA); chm: Samuel Montagu 1970–73, Rothman Internat Ltd 1988–98, Orion Bank (and ch exec) 1974–79, Derby Tst Ltd and tstees Heather Tst for Arts; dir or former dir: J Rothschild Hldgs plc 1983–89, The Telegraph plc 1985–96, Montagu Tst Ltd, Carreras Ltd, Bovis Holdings Ltd, LWT, Union Commercial, Utd Br Securities Tst, Woodhall Tst; memb Bd Banking Supervision Bank of England 1990–96, Pres Assoc for Jewish Youth, Hon Prof European Business Sch 1997–; *m* 14 Dec 1951 *Christiane Françoise (Ninette), yr dau of Edgar Dreyfus, of Paris, and *d* 1 July 1998, leaving:

(1) CHARLES EDGAR SAMUEL MONTAGU, **5th and present Baron Swaythling**

(1) Fiona Yvonne; *b* 11 Nov 1952; *m* 1976 *Jonathan Leave and *dsp* 8 Feb 1982

(2) *Nicole Mary [The Hon Mrs Campbell, 33 Parkers Rd, Sheffield, Yorks S10 1BN]; *b* 8 Nov 1956; *m* 1987 *Nicholas C W Campbell, barrister, yst s of Prof Wilson Campbell, of Warkworth, Campbell, Northumberland

2 +ANTHONY TREVOR SAMUEL [The Hon Anthony Montagu, 78 Chelsea Park Gdns, London SW3 6AE]; *b* 3 Aug 1931; heir presumptive; *educ* Eton; late 2nd Lt Queen's Roy Regt, ptnr J Sebag & Co, chm Abingworth Ltd; *m* 26 June 1962 *Deirdre Bridget, yr dau of Brig Ronald Henry Senior, DSO, TD, of 2 Egerton Place, SW3, by Hon Norah Marguerite, est dau of 2nd Baron Joicey (*qv*), and has:

(1) +Rupert Anthony Samuel; *b* 5 Aug 1965; *educ* Eton

(2) +Damian William Samuel; *b* 21 Jan 1970; *educ* Eton

(1) *Georgina Mary [Mrs William Petty, 90 West Center St, Moab, Utah 84532, USA]; *b* 15 April 1963; *m* 16 Dec 1995 *William D Petty, est s of William Petty, of Littleton, Colorado, and has:

1a *Willa Mary; *b* 1 Nov 1997

1 *Jean Mary [The Hon Mrs Highett, 2A Gore St, London SW7 5PS]; *b* 8 Aug 1927; *m* 28 Nov 1951 *Lintorn Trevor Highett, MC, s of Maj Cecil Trevor Highett, of Wainsford Ho, Lymington, Hants, and has:

(1) *Paul Lintorn; *b* 11 May 1958; *educ* Eton

(1) *Clare Joanna; *b* 9 Aug 1956; *m* 9 July 1977 *Nigel Godfrey Powell Day, er s of R Day, of Woking, Surrey, and has:

1a *Peter; *b* 1986

1a *Emma Louise; *b* 1984

(2) *Stephanie Jane; *b* 20 Nov 1963

SWINFEN

PER · ARDUA · AD · ALTA

Arms: Per pale arg. and vert on a chevron between three battle-axes as many ermine spots, all counterchanged. **Crest:** A demi-lion rampant vert, charged on the body with a battle-axe erect and holding a like axe in bend arg. **Supporters:** Dexter, a lion guardant vert charged with a battle-axe arg.; sinister, a lion guardant arg., charged with a battle-axe vert. **Motto:** *Per ardua ad alta* ('Through hardships to the heights'). **Creation:** B. (UK) 1 Nov 1919.

THE 3RD BARON SWINFEN, of Chertsey, Surrey (Roger Mynors Swinfen Eady) [The Rt Hon The Lord Swinfen, House of Lords, London SW1A 0PW]; *b* 14 Dec 1938; *s f* 1977; *educ* Westminster and RMA Sandhurst; late Lt Roy Scots (The Roy Regt), ARICS 1970; *m* 24 Oct 1962 *Patricia Anne, only dau of Frank D Blackmore, of Dundrum, Co Dublin, and has:

1 +CHARLES ROGER PEREGRINE SWINFEN; *b* 8 March 1971

1 *Georgina Mary Rose Swinfen; *b* 1 Feb 1964; *m* 1990 *Capt Robin Edgar Douglas Liley, 2nd s of Capt Robert Liley, of Deal, Kent, and has:

(1) *Sophie Anne Clare; *b* 31 March 1994

(2) *Emily Alice Mary; *b* 30 Dec 1996

2 *Katherine Anne Dorothy Swinfen; *b* 18 May 1966; *m* 1993 *Capt Gareth Huw Davies, RTR, s of Dr Cyril Davies, of Bath

3 *Arabella Victoria Eleanor Swinfen; *b* 10 March 1969; *m* 1994 *Capt Charles E A Mayo, Light Dragoons, s of Col John Mayo, and has:

(1) *Elizabeth Rose Anne; *b* 10 Nov 1996

Lineage: GEORGE EADY, of Rugeley, Staffs, and St Albans, Herts; *b c* 1750; *m* 23 Dec 1777 Dorothy, dau of Joseph Marsh, of Colton, Staffs, and *d* 27 Aug 1790, leaving:

GEORGE JOHN EADY, of Sutton Coldfield, Warwicks; *bapt* 22 Sept 1783; Lt 50th Regt; *m* 15 Oct 1814 Jane, dau of Thomas Fletcher, of Haselour Hall, Staffs, and *d* 21 Sept 1826, leaving:

GEORGE JOHN EADY, of Chertsey, Surrey; *b* 12 Dec 1816; *m* 10 Sept 1846 Laura Maria (*d* 15 March 1894), dau of Richard Smith, of Chertsey, and *d* 13 May 1892; his 2nd s:

CHARLES SWINFEN EADY, **1st Baron Swinfen**, of Chertsey, Co Surrey, so *cr* 1 Nov 1919, PC (1913); *b* 31 July 1851; barrister Inner Temple 1879, QC 1893, Bencher 1901, Judge High Court Chancery 1901–13, ktd 1901, Ld Justice Appeal 1913–18, Master Rolls 1918–19, LLD Lond, memb Senate London U; *m* 6 Sept

1894 Blanche Maude (*d* 8 June 1946), yr dau of Sydney Williams Lee, of Putney, and had:

1 CHARLES SWINFEN, **2nd Baron**

1 Dorothy Blanche Swinfen; *b* 1896; *d unm* 1 April 1964

2 Muriel Letitia Swinfen; *b* 1906; *m* 1st 30 March 1925 (*divorce* 1938) Harold Hawthorn Myers, s of Frederic William Hawthorn Myers, of St James's, and had issue; *m* 2nd 7 Feb 1940 Sir Geoffrey Cuthbert Allchin, KBE, CMG, MC, only s of Thomas Cuthbert Allchin, and *d* 7 Dec 1957. He *d* 10 Jan 1968

The 1ST BARON *d* 15 Nov 1919; his only s,

CHARLES (CAROL) SWINFEN EADY, **2nd Baron Swinfen**; *b* 2 Feb 1904; *educ* Eton and Ch Ch Oxford; barrister Inner Temple 1931; *m* 1st 23 Jan 1937 (*divorce* 1945) Mary, yr dau of Col Harold Mynors Farmar, CMG, DSO, of Orchards, Bicknoller, Somerset, author as Mary Wesley (*m* 2nd 1952 Eric Otton Siepmann (*d* 1970), jnlst); *m* 2nd 10 Nov 1950 *Averil Kathleen Suzanne [Averil Lady Swinfen, Bureneskeet, Friars Hill, Thomastown, Co Kilkenny, Ireland], formerly w of Lt-Col Andrew Knowles, TD, and er dau of Maj William Marshall Hickman Humphreys, of Broomfield Ho, Midleton, Co Cork, and *d* 19 March 1977, having by his 1st w had:

1 ROGER MYNORS SWINFEN EADY, **3rd and present Baron Swinfen**

2 +(Hugh) Toby Swinfen; *b* 28 Feb 1941; *educ* Bryanston and Wadham Coll Oxford

SWINTON

LA · VERTU · SEUL · QUI · DONNE · LA · NOBLE

Arms: Quarterly, 1st and 4th, erm. on a fess sa. three mullets or, and (for distinction) a cross-crosslet of the second (for LISTER); 2nd, sa. three conies courant arg., and (for distinction) a cross-crosslet of the last (for CUNLIFFE); 3rd, or two chevronels sa., on a chief of the last three escallops of the field (for GREAME). **Crests:** 1 A stag's head ppr., erased or, attired sa., charged on the neck (for distinction) with a cross-crosslet sa. (for LISTER), 2 A greyhound sejant arg., collared with a ring attached sa., charged on the shoulder (for distinction) with a cross-crosslet sa. (for CUNLIFFE), 3 On a mount vert a pair of wings addorsed or, semé of escallops sa. (for GREAME). **Supporters:** On either side a stag ppr., collared with a chain or, suspended therefrom to the dexter a rose arg. and to the sinister an escallop arg. **Mottoes:** 1 *Retinens vestigia famae* ('Maintaining the tradition of fame') (for LISTER), 2 *Fideliter* ('Faithfully') (for CUNLIFFE), 3 *C'est la vertu seul qui donne la noblesse* ('Virtue alone confers nobility') (for GREAME). **Creations:** V. (UK) 29 Nov 1935, E. (UK) 5 May 1955.

THE 2ND EARL OF SWINTON, Viscount Swinton, of Masham, Co York, and Baron Masham of Ellington, Co York (David Yarburgh Cunliffe-Lister JP (N Yorks 1971), DL (N Yorks 1978)) [The Rt Hon The Earl of Swinton JP DL, Dykes Hill House, Masham, Yorks HG4 4NS]; *b* 21 March 1937; *s gf* 1972; *educ* Winchester and RAC Cirencester; CC N R Yorks 1961–74 and N Yorks 1974–77, Capt Yeomen Gd (Dep Govt Ch Whip Ho Lds) 1982–86, dir Leeds Perm Bldg Soc 1987–; *m* 8 Dec 1959 *Susan Lillian Primrose, BARONESS MASHAM OF ILTON (*qv*) and adopted (respectively Nov 1967 and Nov 1965):

*John Charles Yarburgh; *b* 10 May 1967; *educ* Belmont Abbey Herefs

*Clare Caroline; *b* 30 June 1965

Lineage (of Cunliffe): ROBERT CUNLIFFE, living at Hollins, Lancs, 1559–60, had an est s:

HENRY CUNLIFFE, of Hollins; *m* — Wood, of Woodhead, an heiress, and had:

NICHOLAS CUNLIFFE; *m* Christobell Hyndle and had, with four yr sons (Charles; Henry; Nicholas; Robert) and several daus:

ELLIS CUNLIFFE, of Hollins, Woodhead, and Baxenden, Lancs; *m* Janett, dau of John Crombrocke, of Whalley, Lancs, and *d* 1603/4, having had, with a yr s (Robert) and a dau (Mrgaret):

JOHN CUNLIFFE, of Hollins, and Woodhead; *m* Isabel, dau and heir of James Robinson, of Pendle, Lancs, and had:

1 Nicholas, of Hollins; *m* — Hartley, of Wycollar, and *d* by 7 Nov 1669, leaving:

(1) John, of Hollins; at first supported Parl, later opposed CROMWELL; his estates sequestrated and a garrison placed in his house at Hollins; pardoned by CHARLES II; *m* 1st — Hartley, of Winewall; *m* 2nd Mary, dau of Ralph Cheatham, of Castleton, and by her had, with other issue:

   1a Nicholas; *m* —, yr dau and coheir of — Foster, of Airton, and was ancestor of the CUNLIFFEs of Wycollar

   2a Ellis; Rector Newmarket and Etwall; *m* —, er dau and coheiress of — Foster, of Airton, and had issue (*see* CUNLIFFE, Bt)

2 Ellis; London merchant and Alderman; *m* Margaret, dau of Francis King, and *d* 3 Aug 1672, leaving issue

3 JOHN

4 Robert, of Whitefriars, London; *d* by 29 Oct 1647

5 Henry, of Brownbeck, Lancs; *d* 1663, leaving issue

The 3rd s,

JOHN CUNLIFFE, of Iconhurst, Accrington, Lancs; *m* Margaret — and was *bur* 19 Aug 1649, having had, with other issue:

ELLIS CUNLIFFE, of Wakefield, Yorks; *bapt* 12 May 1642; *m* Mary Stocks and *d* 1681, leaving:

NICHOLAS CUNLIFFE, of Ilkley, Yorks; *bapt* 8 Jan 1677; *m* 12 Feb 1701/2 Anne, dau of David Hodgson, of Bradford, and was *bur* 29 Oct 1724, leaving, with other issue:

ELLIS CUNLIFFE, of Ilkley and High Ho, Addingham, Yorks; *bapt* 7 June 1705; *m* 22 Oct 1738 Elizabeth, est dau and coheir of Rev Thomas Lister, Vicar Ilkley, by Mary, dau of Henry Bowling, and had, with other issue, including a yr s (Lister, *b* 1747, *d* 1778, ancestor of the CUNLIFFEs of Esholt):

JOHN CUNLIFFE, of High House; *bapt* 16 May 1724; *m* 22 Nov 1772 Mary (*d* 13 June 1834), only dau of Rev William Thompson, Rector Addingham, and *d* 19 March 1813, having had an est s:

ELLIS CUNLIFFE later CUNLIFFE-LISTER (added 1809 under terms of will of his 1st f-in-law Samuel Lister, of Manningham) later still LISTER KAY (added 1842 on death of his 2nd f-in-law William Kay, of Cottingham), of Manningham and Farfield, JP, DL; MP Bradford 1832–41; *m* 1st 1 April 1795 his cousin Ruth Myers (*dsp* July 1797), n and heir of Samuel Lister, of Manningham Hall; *m* 2nd Feb 1809 Mary (*d* 6 March 1844), dau of William Kay, of Cottingham; *m* 3rd 11 Nov 1844 Hon Eliza Mellifont (*d* 13 July 1855), dau of Richard Talbot, of Malahide, by Margaret, Baroness Talbot de Malahide (*qv*) and widow of George Waters Mellifont, of Ballenclea, Co Dublin, and *d* 24 Nov 1853, having had no issue by her but leaving by his 2nd w:

1 William CUNLIFFE-LISTER; *b* 3 Dec 1809; barrister, MP Bradford 1841; *d* unm 12 Aug 1841

2 John CUNLIFFE-LISTER later CUNLIFFE-KAY (roy licence 1844); *b* 17 Dec 1810; *m* 8 Dec 1846 Anne, dau of James Fenton, of Bamford Hall, Lancs, and *d* 27 Nov 1902, having had:

   (1) Ellis Cunliffe Lister CUNLIFFE-KAY later LISTER-KAY, of Godmersham Park, Canterbury, and Farfield Hall, Addingham, Yorks; *b* 18 Dec 1847; *m* 22 July 1869 his cousin Annie Clementina (*see* below) and *d* 13 March 1917, having had:

      1a Cunliffe Lister; *b* 2 May 1870; *d* 12 July 1911

      2a Foster Cunliffe; *b* 23 July 1871; *d* 21 Sept 1921

      1a Ruth; *b* 4 Dec 1881; *d* 22 Aug 1895

   (2) James Cunliffe LISTER-KAY, Lt 15th (The King's) Hus; *b* 12 March 1849; *d* 10 Sept 1875

   (3) Thomas Cunliffe LISTER-KAY; *b* 10 Dec 1850; *d* 8 Dec 1891

   (4) Foster Cunliffe LISTER-KAY, of Cladich and Auchlian, Argyllshire, JP; *b* 30 June 1852; Lt-Col 2nd Dragoon Gds; *d* 24 Oct 1913

   (1) Annie

3 Ellis CUNLIFFE-LISTER; *b* 11 April 1813; *d* 20 May 1833

4 SAMUEL CUNLIFFE-LISTER, 1st BARON MASHAM OF SWINTON, Co York, so *cr* 15 July 1891, JP, DL W and N R Yorks; *b* 1 Jan 1815; Hon LLD Leeds, Col W R Rifle Vols, bought the Swinton estate 1882 from George Danby Affleck, heir of Mrs Danby-Vernon-Harcourt, of Swinton Park (*see* VERNON, B), also the Jervaulx estate, High Sheriff N R Yorks 1887; *m* 6 Sept 1854 Annie (*d* 1875), dau of John Dearden, of Hollins Hall, Halifax, and *d* 2 Feb 1906, having had:

   (1) SAMUEL CUNLIFFE LISTER, 2nd BARON MASHAM OF SWINTON, JP N R Yorks; *b* 2 Aug 1857; *educ* Harrow and St John's Coll Oxford (BA 1878); *d* unm 24 Jan 1917

   (2) JOHN CUNLIFFE LISTER, 3rd and last BARON MASHAM OF SWINTON; *b* 9 Aug 1867; *m* 7 April 1906 Elizabeth Alice (*d* 28 May 1924), 2nd dau of William Rippon Brockton, of Farndon, Newark-on-Trent, and *dsp* 4 Jan 1924, when the Barony expired

   (1) Anne; *d* unm 28 July 1929

   (2) Mary Ewbank; *m* 1886 Rev Charles Ingram Boynton (*d* 18 May 1928), Rector Barmston, Yorks, yr s of Rev Griffith Boynton, Rector Barmston (*see* 1967 edn BOYNTON, Bt), and *d* 31 Dec 1896, having had:

      1a Ingram Cunliffe Griffith; *b* 22 Sept 1886; *d* 23 Nov 1889

      1a Mary Constance, JP (N R Yorks 1948); *m* 5 Sept 1912 **1st Earl of Swinton** (*see* **Lineage (of Lloyd)** below) and *d* 27 Sept 1974, leaving issue

   (3) Ada; *d* 23 May 1936

   (4) Edith; *d* unm 11 May 1962

   (5) Evelyn; *d* unm 6 Jan 1956

5 Thomas Thompson CUNLIFFE-LISTER, of Beamsley Hall, Yorks, JP W R Yorks; *b* 30 April 1821; *m* 22 April 1857 his er bro's sis-in-law Margaret (*d* 29 July 1907), dau of John Dearden, and *dsp* 1891

6 Henry CUNLIFFE-LISTER; *b* 13 May 1823; *d* 9 Feb 1829

1 Mary; *m* 28 Dec 1831 Joshua Ingham, of Blake Hall, Yorks, and *d* 17 Sept 1899, having had issue. He *d* 16 May 1866

2 Anne Elizabeth; *d* 15 Feb 1817

3 Harriet; *m* 27 Aug 1846 William Clement Drake Esdaile (*d* 6 Dec 1899), of Burley Manor, Hants, and *d* 1892, leaving:

   (1) Annie Clementina; *m* 22 July 1869 her cousin Ellis Cunliffe Lister Lister-Kay and had issue (*see* above)

4 Annie; *m* 12 Oct 1847 Hon Richard Gilbert Talbot, of Ballinclea, Co Dublin, 2nd s of 3rd Baron Talbot de Malahide (*qv*), and *d* 5 July 1902, having had issue

5 Elizabeth; *m* 1st Vavasour Carter, of Weston Hall, Yorks; *m* 2nd Maj Lee, 15th Hus

Lineage (of Lloyd): GAMALIEL LLOYD, of Mattersey, Notts; *m* Anne Briggs, of Wigan, Lancs, and *d* 1 Nov 1661, leaving, with three yr sons (Gamaliel; William; John) and a dau (Anne, *m* Joseph Smethurst and had issue):

GEORGE LLOYD, of Manchester; *b* 1650; *m* Martha Whittaker, of Newton Heath, Lancs, and *d* 1728, leaving an only surv child:

GAMALIEL LLOYD; Manchester merchant and mfr; *m* Elizabeth (*d* 30 Sept 1763), dau and coheir of John Carte, MB, of Manchester, and *d* 1749, leaving an only child:

GEORGE LLOYD, of Hulme Hall, nr Manchester, DL W R Yorks; MA Cantab, MB, FRS; *m* 1st Eleanor, dau of Henry Wright, of Offerton, Cheshire, and had, with other issue:

1 John, of Snitterfield, Warwicks, FRS; *m* Anne, dau and heiress of James Hibbins, MD, and had:

   (1) George, of Welcome Ho, Warwicks; *b* 7 March 1768; High Sheriff Warwicks 1806; *d* unm 11 July 1831

   (2) John Gamaliel; Bencher Middle Temple, High Sheriff 1832; *d* unm 1837

   (1) Charlotte; *m* 4 May 1802 Rev Thomas Warde

   (2) Purefoy; *d* unm

GEORGE LLOYD *m* 2nd 24 March 1742 Susannah, 4th dau of Thomas Horton, of Chadderton, Lancs, and sis of Sir William Horton, 1st Bt, of Chadderton, and *d* 4 Dec 1783, having by her had:

2 Gamaliel, of Bury St Edmunds; *b* 26 May 1744; Alderman Leeds (Mayor 1799); *m c* 1780 Elizabeth, dau of James Attwood, and had issue

3 GEORGE, of whom presently

4 Thomas, of Horsforth Hall

1 Susannah; *m* Rev Henry Wray and had two sons and a dau

The 3rd s,

GEORGE LLOYD, barrister; *m* Elizabeth, dau of Jeremiah Naylor, merchant, of Wakefield, and had:

1 GEORGE

2 Edward Jeremiah, of Oldfield Hall, Cheshire; *b* 22 June 1790; barrister; *m* 1822 Elizabeth, 2nd dau and coheir of William Rigby, of Oldfield Hall, and had no surv issue

1 Elizabeth; *m* 1st William Butler Laird (*d* 1810), of Strathmartin, nr Dundee; *m* 2nd Robert Alison, of Dundee

2 Susannah Georgiana

3 Mary Anne; *m* 1831 her cousin Rev Cecil Daniel Wray, Canon Collegiate Ch Manchester

The er s,

GEORGE LLOYD, of Stockton Hall, Yorks; *b* 21 May 1787; Capt 2nd Lancs Militia; *m* 17 May 1810 Alicia Maria, dau and coheir of John Greame, of Sewerby Ho, Yorks, and had:

1 George John LLOYD later YARBURGH (on inheriting the Heslington estate), of Heslington Hall, Yorks; *m* 1840 Mary Antonia, dau of Samuel Cheetham Hilton, of Pennington, Lancs, and *d* 1875, leaving:

   (1) Mary Elizabeth; *m* 8 May 1862 2nd Baron Deramore (*qv*) and *d* 22 Oct 1884, leaving issue

   (2) Susan Anne; *m* 25 Jan 1865 Charles Lethbridge, JP, and *d* 21 May 1908, having had issue (*see* LETHBRIDGE, Bt)

2 Yarburgh Gamaliel (Rev) LLOYD later LLOYD-GREAME (on inheriting the Sewerby estate, Yorks), JP E R Yorks; *b* 1813; *educ* Rugby and Trin Coll Cambridge (MA 1841); Vicar Dunston, Lincs; *m* 1839 Editha Christiania, 6th dau of William Augustus Le Hunte, of Artramount, Co Wexford, and *d* 1890, having had:

   (1) Yarburgh George LLOYD later LLOYD-GREAME (added 1867), of Sewerby Hall, Yorks, JP E and N R Yorks; *b* 1840; *educ* Trin Coll Cambridge (MA); Maj Yorks Artillery Militia; *m* 1867 Dora Letitia, 2nd dau of Rt Rev James Thomas O'Brien, Bp Ossory, and had:

      1a Yarburgh; *b* 1872; Lt Yorks Dragoons Yeo; *m* 11 Jan 1898 Alice Mary (*d* 13 Jan 1957), 3rd dau of Maj George Mark Leycester Egerton, of The Mount, York (*see* 1956 edn EGERTON OF TATTON, B), and *d* 29 Aug 1965, leaving:

         1b Nancy Helen; *m* 1930 Lt-Col Charles Henry Turner, JP, DL, of Turnerhall and Tipperty, Aberdeenshire (*d* 29 May 1963)

      2a Francis; *d* 1896

      3a PHILIP, **1st Earl**

      1a Editha

      2a Dora; *m* 1904 Lt-Col George Hannay, KOSB, and *d* 27 Jan 1967. He *d* 9 Oct 1932

   (1) Patty Warburton; *d* 1870

   (2) Editha; *d* 1859

   (3) Maria; *d* 1908

3 Henry LLOYD (Rev); *b* 1815; Rector Yarborough, Lincs; *m* 1858 Anne Eliza (*d* 27 May 1903), dau of Rev W Roy, DD, Rector Skerbeck, Lincs, and *d* 17 Nov 1862, leaving:

   (1) George William, of Stockton Hall, nr York, JP Lincs and N R Yorks; *b* 4 March 1861; *educ* Eton and Trin Coll Cambridge (MA 1886); High Sheriff N R Yorks 1909; *m* 26 Jan 1922 Mabel Jane (*d* 15 Oct 1947), 2nd dau of Rev Dawson Campbell, and *d* 4 Jan 1934

   (2) Henry John Greame; *b* 6 June 1862; Maj DCLI, Hon Col cmdg 3rd Bn DCLI; *m* 9 Dec 1886 Caroline Emily (*d* 24 Jan 1916), 2nd dau of John Harris Peter-Hoblyn, of Colquite, Bodmin, Cornwall, and *d* 13 April 1919, leaving:

      1a Cyril Gascoigne; *b* 11 Sept 1887; *educ* Eton and Trin Coll Cambridge; F/O RAF and ROC, Capt E R Yorks Yeo, WW I (despatches), WW II; *m* 12

April 1928 Violet Madge, yr dau of William Thomas Preston (*see* PRE-STON, Bt), and *d* 13 Jan 1965, leaving:

1b *Rosemary Joan Caroline; *b* 8 Feb 1929; *m* 17 Dec 1959 *Carleton John Richard Tufnell, only s of Lt-Cdr Richard Lionel Tufnell, RN, of The Manor Ho, Calmsden, Glos, and has had:

1c *Mark Henry; *b* 23 Nov 1964

2c *Richard LLoyd; *b* 30 Dec 1965

1c Emma Caroline; *b* 7, *d* 9 Sept 1961

2b *Barbara Anne; *b* 2 June 1932; *m* 30 March 1967 *Andrew Edward Buxton (*see* BUXTON, Bt) and has issue

2a John Rodney; *b* 21 June 1890; *educ* Eton and Merton Coll Oxford; Maj Cyprus Regt Pioneer Corps, E R Yorks Yeo, WWs I and II

3a Henry Greame, MC (1916); *b* 2 Dec 1892; *educ* Eton and Trin Coll Cambridge (MA); Capt DCLI, served WWs I and II

1a Caroline Doris

2a Kathleen Anne; *m* 26 April 1949, as his 3rd w, Col Cecil Neville Custance, er s of Capt Sydney Custance, DCLI. He *d* 25 Nov 1965

(1) Alicia Margaret; *d* 3 Oct 1937

4 Edward, of Lingcroft, nr York; *b* 1823; *m* 21 Sept 1854 Rosabelle Susan (*d* 20 July 1909), 4th dau of George Lloyd, of Cowesby Hall, and was drowned, 4 Feb 1869, leaving:

(1) Georgina Rosabelle, of Lingcroft and Crosscliff, Hackness, Scarborough; *m* 15 July 1879 Guy St Maur Palmes, 14th Hus, 3rd s of Rev William Lindsay Palmes, of Naburn Hall, and *d* 1936, having had issue. He *d* 29 Sept 1945

(2) Edith Maria Greame; *m* 22 April 1879 Frederick Reynard, of Sunderland-wick, Driffield, and Hobgreen, Ripon, Yorks, and *d* June 1934, leaving issue. He *d* 7 Feb 1926

(3) Cecil Mary; *m* 9 Nov 1887 Henry Charles Talbot Rice and *d* 10 Jan 1940, having had issue (*see* DYNEVOR, B)

Maj YARBURGH GEORGE LLOYD-GREAME's 3rd s,

PHILIP LLOYD-GREAME later CUNLIFFE-LISTER (roy licence 27 Nov 1924 on his w's inheriting the Swinton estates), **1st Earl of Swinton** and BARON MASHAM, of Ellington, Co York, so *cr* 5 May 1955, as also earlier 29 Nov 1935 VISCOUNT SWINTON, of Masham, Co York (all UK), GBE (1929, KBE 1920), CH (1943), MC, DL (N R Yorks 1948), PC (1922); *b* 1 May 1884; *educ* Winchester and Univ Coll Oxford (BA 1905, Hon Fell); barrister Inner Temple 1908, Maj WW I (despatches), Hon Air Cdre No 608 (NR) (B) Squadron RAuxAF 1936, Jt-Sec Min Nat Serv 1917–18, chm Perm Labour Sub-Ctee War Cabinet 1918, MP (C) Hendon 1918–35, memb Select Ctee Nat Expenditure 1919, Parly Sec BOT 1920–21, Addnl U-Sec For Affrs and Addnl Parly Sec BOT (Sec Dept Overseas Trade) 1921–22, Pres BOT 1922–Nov 1924–June 1929 and Aug–Nov 1931, Sec State Colonies Nov 1931–June 1935, Sec State Air June 1935–May 1938, Min Resident W Africa 1942–44, Min Civ Aviation 1944–45, Chllr Duchy Lancaster, Min Materials 1951–52, Dep Leader Ho Lds, Sec State Cwlth Rels Nov 1952–55, Chm: Imp Ec Conf 1923 and UK Commercial Corp 1940, Hon Freeman Shipwrights' and Wyredrawers' Cos, Grand Offr Order Leopold Belgium 1963, Hon LLD Liverpool U; *m* 5 Sept 1912 Mary Constance Boynton (*see* **Lineage (of Cunliffe)** above), and *d* 27 July 1972, having had:

1 John Yarburgh; *b* 10 June 1913; *educ* Winchester and Trin Coll Oxford; Maj Staffs Yeo WW II; *m* 28 May 1936 Anne Irvine (*d* 28 May 1961, having *m* 2nd 3 April 1944 Donald Phillott Chapple-Gill, of Brynderwen, Bwlch-y-Cibau, Montgomeryshire), yr dau of Rev Canon Robert Sumner Medlicott, Rector Burghclere, Berks, and *d* of wounds recd in action 14 April 1943, leaving:

(1) DAVID YARBURGH CUNLIFFE-LISTER, **2nd and present Earl of Swinton**

(2) +NICHOLAS JOHN [The Hon Nicholas Cunliffe-Lister, Glebe House, Masham, Ripon, Yorks]; *b* 4 Sept 1939; heir presumptive; *educ* Winchester and Worcester Coll Oxford; late 2nd Lt Welsh Gds; slr 1966, granted by roy warrant 1974 rank of earl's yr s; *m* 1st 19 Feb 1966 (*divorce* 19–) Hon (Elizabeth) Susan, est dau of 1st Viscount Whitelaw (*qv*), and has:

1a +Mark William Philip; *b* 15 Sept 1970

2a +Simon Charles; *b* 7 Nov 1977

1a *Lorna Mary; *b* 27 April 1968

(2) (cont.) The Hon NICHOLAS CUNLIFFE-LISTER *m* 2nd July 1996 *Pamela Sykes

2 Philip Ingram, DSO (1943); *b* 11 Feb 1918; *educ* Winchester and Magdalene Coll Cambridge; S/Ldr RAuxAF WW II (POW); *m* 1st 5 June 1940 (*divorce* 1947) Rosina Gladys, yr dau of Arthur George Emburey, of Cambridge, and had:

(1) Philip Algernon Guy; *b* 1 July 1941; *educ* Stowe and Sorbonne

(1) *Simone Philippa Judith Clare [Mrs Keith Howell, Mole Corner, Summer Gdns, E Molesey, Surrey KT8 9LT]; *b* 3 Jan 1943; *m* 1st 5 June 1965 (*divorce* 1980, having resumed maiden name 1976) Jack Frederick Deakin, s of J Deakin, of Manchester; *m* 2nd 1986 *Keith Howell and by her 1st husb has:

1a *Lorna-Jane CUNLIFFE-LISTER; *b* 1970

2a *Deborah Simone Jackeline CUNLIFFE-LISTER; *b* 1971

2 (cont.) S/Ldr The Hon Philip Cunliffe-Lister *m* 2nd 20 Sept 1947 Mary (*d* 1978, having *m* 3rd 27 June 1958 (*divorce* 1969) Robert Alexander Pleasant Craigie, only s of Sir Robert Leslie Craigie, GCMG, CB, PC, of Possingworth Manor, Uckfield, Sussex, and *m* 4th 1977 Maj Patrick Robert Reid, MBE, MC, who *d* 1990), formerly w of Robert Noel Stewart-Humphries and dau of Robert John Leggatt, of Hamilton, Lanarks, and *d* 14 June 1956, leaving by her:

(2) +(Julian) Michael [Michael Cunliffe-Lister Esq, 64 Hill Rd, Eastbourne, E Sussex BN20 8SN]; *b* 20 July 1949; *educ* Uppingham and Exeter U; *m* 1976 (*divorce* 1989) Penelope Susan, only dau of Lt Col David A Pinner, of White Cottage, Sandhurst Lane, Little Common, Bexhill, E Sussex, and has:

1a *Constance Alexandra Elise; *b* 1979

(2) *Madeline Frances Anne [Miss Madeline Cunliffe-Lister, 76 South St, Lewes, E Sussex]; *b* 7 Dec 1950; *educ* Cobham Hall

SYKES of Basildon

Arms: Arg., an eagle rising between three sykes (fountains) ppr., on a canton gu. a caduceus or, wings of the first. **Crest:** A demi-lady of Bengal in the complete dress of that country, holding in her dexter hand a rose gu. **Motto:** *Sapiens qui assiduus* ('He is wise who is assiduous'). **Creation:** Bt. (GB) 8 June 1781.

SIR (FRANCIS) JOHN BADCOCK SYKES, 10TH BT, of Basildon, Berks [Sir John Sykes Bt, Kingsbury Croft, Kingsbury St, Marlborough, Wilts SN8 1HU]; *b* 7 June 1942; *s* 1990; *educ* Shrewsbury and Worcester Coll Oxford (MA); slr 1968, ptnr Townsends of Swindon and Newbury, 1972–; *m* 30 April 1966 *Susan Alexandra, er dau of Adml of the Fleet Sir Edward Beckwith Ashmore, GCB, DSC, by Elizabeth Mary Doveton, only dau of R-Adml Sir Lionel Arthur Doveton Sturdee, 2nd Bt, CBE (*see* 1970 edn), and has:

1 +FRANCIS CHARLES; *b* 18 June 1968; *educ* Malvern and Worcester Coll Oxford (BA)

2 +Edward William; *b* 14 Aug 1970; *educ* Winchester and Manchester U (BA)

3 +Alexander Henry Ashmore; *b* 25 Feb 1974; *educ* Marlborough and Newcastle U

Lineage: WILLIAM SYKE, of Sandal Magna, Yorks; *d* by 14 Oct 1531, leaving, with three er sons (George, *d* in or after 1546; Richard; Robert, of Thornhill, *m* Jane, gn of Sir Thomas Wentworth):

WILLIAM SYKE(S), of Bootliffe; *m* by 1531 Joane — and *d* 1578, leaving, with two yr sons (Thomas, of Ossett; William, of Sandal):

ROBERT SYKES, of Flockton; *bur* 1614, leaving:

HENRY SYKES, of Flockton; *bur* 1617, leaving, with other issue, including an er s (Thomas, *bur* 1631) and a dau (Elizabeth, *bapt* 1581):

EDMOND SYKES, of Thornhill; *bapt* 1599; *m* 1642 Mary Beaumont and was *bur* 1645, leaving, with a dau (Mary, *bapt* 1645, *m* 11 June 1674 Francis Clegg and was *bur* 1686):

WILLIAM SYKES, of Thornhill; *bapt* 1643; *m* 1671 Elizabeth Stephenson and was *bur* 1686, having had, with three yr sons (Thomas, *bapt* 1675, *m* Ann Heaton and was *bur* 1720; William, *bur* 1682; John, *bapt* 1677, *m* 1718 Ellen Willcock and was *bur* 1739) and two daus (Mary, *bapt* 1672, *m* Abraham Ward; Ann, *bapt* 1674, *m* William Chappel):

FRANCIS SYKES, of Thornhill; *bapt* 16 Sept 1682; *m* 25 Sept 1707 Martha Fearnley and *d* 5 April 1766, having had, with four er sons (William, of Ackworth Park, *bapt* 1708, *m* Susannah, dau of Rev H Jenkin, and was *bur* 1777; John, of Strand-on-the-Green, Middx, *bapt* 1712, *d* 1792; Richard, of Chichester, Sussex, *bapt* 1727, *d* 1808; Francis, *b* and *d* 1730) and three daus (Elizabeth, *b* and *d* 1710; Frances, *bapt* 1718, *m* Thomas Wilson; Ruth, *bapt* 1724, *m* William Redfearn and *d* 1794):

Sir Francis Sykes, 1st Bt (GB), so *cr* 8 June 1781, of Ackworth Park; *bapt* 25 Feb 1732; MP Shaftesbury 1771–75 and 1780–84 and Wallingford 1784–1804; nabob, Ch Govr Cossimbazaar, Bengal; bought the Manor of Basildon, Berks, from the Countesses de Salis and of Sandwich (*qv*); *m* 1st 7 Feb 1766 Catherine (*d* 30 Dec 1768), dau of John Ridley; *m* 2nd 2 Sept 1774 Hon Elizabeth Monckton (*m* 2nd 16 Feb 1805 Sir Drummond Smith, 1st Bt (*see* SPENCER-SMITH), and *d* 2 July 1835), est dau of 2nd Viscount Galway (*qv*), and *d* 11 Jan 1804, having by her had a dau (Elizabeth, *m* 27 Sept 1797 Richard BENYON later DE BEAUVOIR and *d* 29 Oct 1822) and by his 1st w, with a yr s (John, RN, *d* aboard the *Grampus* 14 Jan 1781):

Sir Francis William Sykes, 2nd Bt; *b* 1767; MP Wallingford 1794–96, Col Berks Militia; *m* 10 Nov 1798 Mary Anne (*d* 27 Feb 1804), gdau of 1st Baron Henniker (*qv*), and *d* 7 March 1804, having had, with another s (*d* an infant) and dau (*d* unm):

1 **Sir Francis William Sykes, 3rd Bt**; *b* 8 Aug 1799; MA; *m* 8 Aug 1821 Henrietta (Disraeli's mistress; *d* 15 May 1846), dau of Henry Villebois, of Marham Hall, Norfolk, and *d* 6 April 1843, having had, with a dau (*d* unm):

(1) **Sir Francis William Sykes, 4th Bt**; *b* 18 June 1822; Offr 97th Regt and 2nd Life Gds; *d* unm 1 Jan 1866

(2) **Sir Frederick Henry Sykes, 5th Bt**; b 12 Feb 1826; Capt 11th Hus and RHG (Blues); m 5 Jan 1867 Caroline (d 29 Oct 1929), dau of M J Bettesworth, of Hayling, Hants, and d 20 Jan 1899, leaving:

1a Caroline Eva Henrietta; b 30 April 1872; m 7 Dec 1901 Capt Herbert Powley, RN, and d 1951. He d 7 Dec 1936

2a Violet Anne May; b 5 Aug 1880; m 23 Aug 1905 Ambrose Petrocokino, FRGS, of Flower Hill, Pangbourne, Berks, 2nd s of Themistocles Petrocokino, of Prestwich, Lancs, and d 4 Dec 1924, leaving issue. He d 10 Oct 1926

(3) **Sir Henry Sykes, 6th Bt**; b 9 Dec 1828; RN, Capt 1st Roy Dragoons Crimean War (medal); m Mary Winifred (d 30 Aug 1935), dau of Henry Tuck, and dsp 10 April 1916

2 William (Rev), of The Grotto, Basildon, Berks; b 25 Sept 1800; Vicar Cullompton, Devon, Rector Thornham, Suffolk; m 7 Dec 1821 Anna Maria Heath (d 14 Oct 1871), only dau of Edward Gattey, of Harefield Ho, Devon, and d 3 June 1875, having had, with two other sons (dsp):

(1) William Benyon; b 1823; d 1873

(2) Francis Henniker; b 1824; commnd 56th Regt

(3) Edward John (Rev); b 1827; Vicar Basildon, Berks; m 21 June 1866 Constance Mary (d 15 Nov 1919), dau of Edward Brown, and d 24 Dec 1891, having had:

1a Brian; b 25 March 1870; d young

2a **Sir Arthur Sykes, 7th Bt**; b 2 Sept 1871; d unm 5 Sept 1934

3a **Rev Sir Frederick John Sykes, 8th Bt**; b 10 Nov 1876; Rector Butterleigh Devon 1927–36, Vicar Stoke Canon, nr Exeter, 1936–46; d unm 17 March 1956

1a Edna; m 21 Oct 1902 Henry Jordan, s of Maj-Gen Jordan, CB, and d 5 Jan 1938, leaving issue

2a Muriel; b 17 Sept, d 1 Oct 1883

(4) Augustus Joseph; b 12 April 1831; Lt-Col 4th KOR; d 28 April 1884

(5) John Heath (Rev); b 22 April 1834; BA Oxon; Rector Billesley, Vicar Haselor, Warwicks; m 12 Aug 1862 Frances Amelia (d 27 Nov 1919), 4th dau of Rev Phillip Henry Nind, and d 26 March 1912, having had:

1a Francis William; b 21 May 1864; Commr under Br S Africa Co at Livingstone, NW Rhodesia, 1901–06, Matabele War 1896 (medal) and Boer War 1900 (medal, two clasps); m 25 April 1905 Beatrice Agnes (d 7 Aug 1953), yr dau of Edward Webb, of Durrington House, Harlow, and d 14 March 1945, leaving:

1b FRANCIS GODFREY (Sir), **9th Bt**

2b +John Patrick [John Sykes Esq, Craigview Grove, 41/143 Stock Rd, Bicton, W Australia 6157]; b 17 March 1909; educ Blundell's and Nelson Coll, NZ; m 31 Oct 1955 Patricia Cecily (d 1979), dau of E P Graham Little, of Adelaide, S Australia

3b Edward Heath; b 6 April 1912; FCA; m 1st 12 Oct 1957 Joan Margaret (d 22 July 1963), est dau of Harold Boston, of Hoylake, Cheshire; m 2nd 12 Dec 1964 *Doris, dau of William Henry Cowsill, of Hale, Cheshire

4b +Paul Lionel [Paul Sykes Esq, Unit 53, Retirement Village, Charlotte St, Burradoo, NSW 2576, Australia]; b 25 Jan 1915; m 1946 *Mrs Ann Stewart, of Sydney, NSW

1b *Beatrice Honora [Mrs Frederick Nind, 17 Holloway Dve, Pershore, Worcs]; b 31 March 1910; m 21 June 1949 Cdr Frederick D'Oyly Nind, RN, s of Frederick William Nind. He d 6 Feb 1962

2b *Mary Agatha [Mrs William Gilbert, Flat 14, St Nicholas Hospital, Salisbury, Wilts]; b 2 Aug 1913; m 21 Oct 1944 William Thomas Moran Gilbert, LRCPI, LRCSI, LM (d 1970), Colonial Med Serv, Assist Dir Med Servs Ghana, s of William Reilley Starkie Gilbert

3b *Janet Edith [Miss Janet Sykes, Flat 18, St Nicholas Hospital, Salisbury, Wilts]; b 16 May 1916

2a John Heath; b 23 April 1866; d 1 March 1892

3a William; b 27 Sept 1867; Lt-Col, Riding Master 3rd Dragoon Gds 1895–1912, Equitation Offr RMC Sandhurst 1912–21; m 14 Jan 1896 Eleanor Mary (d 5 June 1958), dau of Capt Henry Naylor, and d 3 March 1950, leaving:

1b John Henry; b 15 Oct 1896; educ Christ's Hosp and RMC Sandhurst; Brig IA, formerly 3rd Dragoon Gds, WW I, Palestine 1918–20, NW Frontier 1930–31 (despatches), WW II Egypt and N Africa 1941–43 (despatches), NW Army 1943–46; m 1st 30 Jan 1919 Leila Flowerdew (d 1970), dau of D S Macphee, of Glasgow; m 2nd 1971 Florence Cathleen (d 1983), dau of William Turner and widow of (a) James Mackay and (b) Sir (Stanley) Herbert Howard, and d 10 April 1975, having had:

1c John Lowson; b 25, d 27 July 1922

2c William Alan Flowerdew; b 22 Feb 1924; Sub-Lt RNVR WW II; ka 23 June 1944

1c *Margery Hope; b 7 July 1921; m 1941 Geoffrey Philip Eliot, s of Rev W F Eliot, and has three sons and a dau

2b Hugh William; b 25 March 1901; d 2 Nov 1940

3b Paul Carton (Rev); b 5 Oct 1903; Vicar Aymestrey with Leinthall Earles and Wigmore with Leinthall Starkes; m 20 June 1943 *Hendrika Pierternella [Mrs Paul Sykes, 25 Sydney St, Cheltenham, Glos GL52 6DJ], dau of G C van Vlaanderen and has two adopted children

4b Richard Alexander; b 5 Sept 1912; educ Sevenoaks Sch; Glos Hus WW II; m 15 Aug 1942 *Freda Serita [Mrs Richard Sykes, 20 Ashdale Ave, Pershore, Worcs WR10 1PL], dau of Lewis Field, and d 30 March 1981, leaving:

1c +William David [William Sykes Esq, 18 Markby Close, Duxford, Cambs CB2 4RS]; b 4 Nov 1946; educ St Edward's Sch Oxford; m 1978 *Josephine Helen White and has:

1d +Archie Frederick William; b 1984

1d *Chloë Alexandra; b 1981

2c +Anthony Richard John [Anthony Sykes Esq, Willoughby House, High St, Dorchester-on-Thames, Oxon]; b 29 April 1950; educ St Edward's Sch Oxford; m 1982 *Tessa Cox and has:

1d +Thomas Neill Alexander; b 1984

1d *Amanda Marie; b 1986

1b Alice Margery; b 3 Dec 1904; m 27 Sept 1966 Ewart Gladstone Morrison (d 1985), s of William Hay Morrison, of Kotagala, Ceylon and d 1997

4a Frederick; b 28 Sept 1868; had:

1b Frederick Heath Cyril; b 1897; m 1934 Judith Helen (d 1982), dau of Wyndham Henry Stubbs, of The Leasowes, Cressage, Salop, and d 1959, having had:

1c +Harry Wyndham; b 1936; m 1956 *Magdalena (Lena) Amelia, dau of Edward Julius Schulze, of Grand Prairie, Alberta, and has:

1d +Ronald Frederick; b 1963

1d *Dianne Lea; b 1957; m 1978 (divorce 1986) Martin Lavoie and has issue

2d *Patricia Lynn; b 1960

5a Alfred; b 6 July 1872; 1st Canadian Pioneers WW I 1916–18 (two medals); m 1902 Scènie Marguerite Genelle (d 19–) and d 2 July 1954, leaving:

1b *Marcedèsse Frances Doyley; b 1904; m 1st 1932 R Alston Jones; m 2nd 1947 *Brock R Darling and by her 1st husb has:

1c *George Sykes; b 1935

2b *Scènie Gwendoline Doyley; b 1906; m 1932 *George Michael Holley

6a Hugh Percival; b 10 June 1875; d unm 1892

7a Edward Ernest; b 24 Sept 1876; Boer War 1900–01 (Queen's medal, four clasps); m 1910 Rosalind (d 3 March 1948), widow of R Fitzstubbs and dau of Engr Cdr J Clements, RN, and d 1950, leaving:

1b Clement Edward Heath; b 27 Sept 1911; Engr Offr Br and Canadian Merchant Navies 1932–41, Engr Capt US Army S Pacific 1942–46; m 1951 *Isabel L [Mrs Clement Sykes, Pt Atkinson Light Station, Beacon Lane, W Vancouver, BC, Canada], dau of Robert Parry, and had:

1c +Sean Edward Heath; b 1953

2c +David Robert Heath; b 1954

1c *Sheila Anne Heath; b 1952

1b *Dorothy Heath; b 29 May 1914; m Lt Richard D Pepler, RNVR, and has issue

8a Charles Henry, DSO; b 16 Nov 1877; Lt Warwicks Yeo Boer War 1900–01 (Queen's medal), Capt 6th Bn Roy Fus (SR) WW I (despatches); m 16 Nov 1932 Gladys Mary (Betty), dau of George B Hogg, of Northumberland

1a Frances Emily; m 11 April 1890 George Malcolm, s of Lt-Gen Sir George Malcolm, GCB, and d 1955. He d 22 Oct 1938

2a Catherine Mary; d 1955

3a Agnes; m 1900 Edward Elwell and d 26 July 1954, leaving issue

4a Alice Heath; m 1910 William Heath Smith and d 31 Oct 1959, leaving issue. He d 1916

5a Mary Seymour; m 14 April 1909 Rev John Columbine Paterson-Morgan, Vicar Stoke Ferry, King's Lynn, s of Rev Richard James Morgan, and d 1957, leaving issue. He d 25 Nov 1965

6a Margaret; d unm 9 Sept 1958

(1) Anna Maria; m 21 Jan 1863 Rev Henry Willmott, Rector Kirkley, Lowestoft, and d 28 Nov 1930, leaving issue. He d 1873

(2) Katherine; m 21 Jan 1863 Col Percival Ashley Brown, 102nd Fus, and d 12 Oct 1914. He dsp 21 May 1904

The 8th Bt's cousin,

Sir Francis Godfrey Sykes, 9th Bt; b 27 Aug 1907; educ Blundell's and Nelson Coll NZ; regnl sec CLA 1956–71; m 1st 25 July 1934 Eira Betty (d 6 Sept 1970), only dau of George Wallace Badcock, of Hove and Nether Maudlin, Steyning, Sussex, and had:

1 Sir (FRANCIS) JOHN BADCOCK SYKES, **10th and present Bt**

1 *Elizabeth Ann Bowen [Dr Elizabeth Sykes, 19 Torriano Cottages, off Leighton Rd, London NW5]; b 17 Sept 1936; educ Howell's Sch, Denbigh, Bedford Coll London (BSc 1959, MSc 1962) and Edinburgh U (PhD); lecturer U of Wales, AFBPsS, CPsychol, ScFZS, Prof and Head Sch of Psychology Middx U, Hon Research Fell UCL

Sir Francis m 2nd 16 Sept 1972 Nesta Mabel Sykes (d 4 Jan 1982); m 3rd 9 Feb 1984 *Ethel Florence [Ethel Lady Sykes, 3 Hockey's Mill, Temeside, Salop SY8 1PD], dau of Lt-Col John Sinclair Liddell and widow of (a) Brian G Macartney-Filgate and (b) Cdr W Graeme Ogden, DSC, RNVR, and d 19 April 1990

SYKES of Kingsknowes

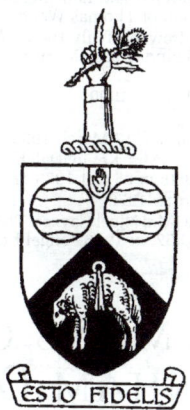

ESTO FIDELIS

SYKES of Sledmere

Arms: Per chevron gu. and sa. in chief two sykes (fountains) ppr. and in base a fleece or. **Crest:** A cubit arm, habited in a khaki sleeve and holding in the hand a teazle, slipped and leaved ppr. **Motto:** *Esto fidelis* ('Be faithful'). **Creation:** Bt. (UK) 17 June 1921.

SIR JOHN CHARLES ANTHONY LE GALLAIS SYKES, 3RD BT, of Kingsknowes, Co Selkirk; *b* 19 April 1928; *s* unc 1974; *educ* Churchers Coll; export merchant (ret); *m* 16 Oct 1954 (*divorce* 1969) Aitha Isobel, yr dau of Lionel Dean, of Hazeldene, New Mill, Huddersfield

Lineage: JOHN SYKES, of Almondbury, Yorks; *m* 14 June 1705 Mary Bray (*d* 1747), of Kirkheaton, and had, with other issue:

JOHN SYKES, of Honley, Almondbury; *m* Jan 1760 Hannah Womersley, of Holmfirth, and *d* 1768, leaving:

JOSEPH SYKES, of Kirkburton; *b* 1760; *m* 26 Dec 1793 Sarah Ibberson, of Kirkburton, and *d* 10 Oct 1816, leaving a 2nd s:

BENJAMIN SYKES, of Burton Dean, Kirkburton; *b* 27 Sept 1799; *m* July 1821 Harriet Wood, of Kirkburton, and *d* 9 Jan 1852, leaving, with other issue:

BENJAMIN SYKES, of Kirkburton; *b* 28 June 1830; *m* 7 March 1852 Rachel (*d* 28 Jan 1903), dau of George Carter, of Kirkburton, and *d* 21 Sept 1902, leaving other issue:

Sir Charles Sykes, 1st Bt (UK), so *cr* 17 June 1921, KBE (1918), JP Huddersfield; *b* 31 Dec 1867; *educ* National Sch Kirkheaton; woollen mfr, chm John Crowther and Sons, Dir Wool Textile Prodn, Chm Bd of Control Worsted Woollen Trade WW I, MP (C Lib) Huddersfield 1918–22; Cdr Order Leopold II Belgium; *m* 1 Sept 1892 Mary (*d* 17 July 1944), yst dau of Benjamin Newsome, of Huddersfield, and *d* 16 Nov 1950, leaving:

1 **Sir (Benjamin) Hugh Sykes, 2nd Bt**; *b* 8 June 1893; *educ* Leys Sch Cambridge; *m* 6 June 1935 *Audrey Winifred [Audrey Lady Sykes, Kestrel Grove, Hive Rd, Bushey Heath, Herts WD2 1JQ], only dau of Frederick Charles Thompson, of Cricklewood, and *dsp* 22 Dec 1974

2 Stanley Edgar; *b* 22 July 1895; Capt 5th Bn Duke of Wellington's W R Regt; *m* 16 March 1921 Florence Anaise (*d* 3 July 1955), dau of François Marie Le Gallais, of Jersey, and *d* 1 Dec 1963, leaving:

(1) Sir JOHN CHARLES ANTHONY LE GALLAIS SYKES, **3rd and present Bt**

(2) Michael Le Gallais; *b* 4 Jan 1932; *educ* Trent Coll; 2nd Lt 1st Duke of Wellington's Regt and Lt Sherwood Foresters; *m* 1st 15 Aug 1953 Joan, only dau of Cecil Groom, of Nuthall, Notts; *m* 2nd 1976 *Jacqueline Susan, only dau of Capt C Melia, and *d* 1981, leaving by his 1st w:

1a +DAVID MICHAEL [David Sykes Esq, The Chestnuts, Middle Lane, Nether Broughton, Leics]; *b* 10 June 1954; heir presumptive; *educ* Purbrook Park County GS; *m* 1st 1974 (*divorce* 1987) Susan Elizabeth, 3rd dau of G W Hall, and has:

1b +Stephen David; *b* 14 Dec 1978

1a (cont.) DAVID SYKES *m* 2nd 1987 *Margaret Lynne, only dau of John Thomas McGreavy, and by her has:

1b *Joanna Lauren; *b* 1986

2a + Christopher Cary; *b* 4 April 1959; *m* 1st 1978 (*divorce* 1984) Tina —; *m* 2nd 1989 *Anne Marie — and by his 1st w has:

1b *Lisa Tina; *b* 1979

2b *Kelly; *b* 1981

(1) *Mary Le Gallais; *b* 20 March 1926; *m* 3 April 1948 *Douglas Gordon Price, s of Lewis Gordon Price, of Charlton King's, Cheltenham, and has:

1a *Michael Charles Gordon; *b* 1 May 1951; *educ* Cheltenham GS

2a *Richard John Douglas; *b* 17 Jan 1955; *educ* Cleeve Comprehensive Sch

3 Charles Newsome; *b* 13 Nov 1899; *educ* Trin Coll Cambridge (BA 1921, MA 1927)

1 Mary Margaret; *m* 1 Sept 1920 Capt Guy Clifford, 7th Bn Duke of Wellington's W R Regt, and had:

(1) *Hugh Sykes; *b* 29 Sept 1921; *educ* Rossall

Arms: Arg. a chevron sa. between three sykes (fountains) ppr. **Crest:** A demi-triton, issuant from flags (or reeds), blowing a shell and wreathed about the temples with like flags, all ppr. **Creation:** Bt. (GB) 28 March 1783.

SIR TATTON CHRISTOPHER MARK SYKES, 8TH BT, of Sledmore, Co York [Sir Tatton Sykes Bt, Sledmere, Driffield, E Yorks YO25 0XG]; *b* 24 Dec 1943; *s f* 1978; *educ* Eton, d'Aix-Marseilles U and RAC Cirencester; landowner

Lineage: RICHARD SYKES, of Sykes-Dyke, nr Carlisle, had:

WILLIAM SYKES; living 1576; prosperous Leeds merchant; had, with two er sons (James, of Leeds; Edmund, of Leeds) and two yr sons (William, of The Kirkgate, Leeds; George, of Drightlington, nr Leeds, ancestor of Lt-Col Sykes, FRS, and John Sykes, of Highbury), a 3rd s:

RICHARD SYKES; Leeds merchant; *m* 10 June 1561 Sybil Reme and had, with other issue:

RICHARD SYKES; Ch Alderman and Mayor Leeds, Ld Manor Leeds (bought from the Crown 1625); *m* 30 Jan 1635 Elizabeth Mawson and *d* 29 March 1645, leaving, with four daus (who allegedly inherited £10,000 (over £430,000 in late-1990s terms) each):

1 John, of Leeds; *b* 1593; *m* Dorothy, dau of Edward Binns, of Horbury

2 Henry, of Hunslett Hall, Yorks; *b* 1601; *m* Mary, dau of Sir John Wood, of Beeston, and *dsp* 1656

3 Richard (Rev); *b* 1603; Rector Kirkheaton; *m* Grace, dau of Rev Richard Stooks, Rector Kirkheaton, and had, with other issue:

(1) John, of Dort, merchant; *m* Anne, of Delft, Holland, dau of Banney Reymes, of Overstrand, and *d* 2 June 1686, leaving:

1a Adriana; *m* 1712 Sir Griffith Boynton, 3rd Bt (*see* 1967 edn), of Burton Agnes, Yorks, and *dsp* 19 Nov 1724. He *d* 22 Dec 1731

4 William; *b* 1605; Ld Manor Leeds (*d* 25 Sept 1685), dau and coheir of Josias Jenkinson, of Leeds, and *d* 1652, leaving, with other issue:

(1) Richard, of Ledsham Hall, Yorks; imprisoned *temp* JAMES II for alleged participation Monmouth's Rebellion; *m* Elizabeth, dau of Thomas Scott, of Westthorpe, Bucks, one of CHARLES I's regicides, and left, with three other daus:

1a Anna, *m* Ralph Thoresby, FRS, historian of Leeds

(2) John; *m* Mary Casse, of Scotland, and *d* 1658, leaving two sons

(3) Daniel; *b* 1632; Mayor and merchant Hull; *m* Deborah, dau of William Oates, Mayor Pontefract, and *d* 1 Sept 1693, leaving a surv s:

1a Richard; *b* 1678; Hull merchant; *m* 1st 22 June 1704 Mary (*d* 4 April 1714), dau and coheir of Mark Kirkby, of Sledmere, Yorks (descended from Sir Robert Kirkby, who settled at Cottingham, nr Hull, 1540, also of the KIRKBYs of Kirkby Irelanth, Cumberland), and had, with three daus (*d* unm):

1b Richard; High Sheriff Yorks 1752, Capt Hull Volunteers; *dsp*

2b MARK (Sir), **1st Bt**

1a (cont.) Richard Sykes *m* 2nd 3 Aug 1721 Martha, dau of William Donkin, and by her had a surv s:

3b Joseph, DL E R Yorks; *b* 1723; twice Mayor Hull; *m* June 1754 Dorothy (*d* 1796), dau of Nicholas Twigg, and *d* 26 Nov 1805, leaving issue

(4) Joseph, of Leeds; *m* Bathiah Pickering, n of 7th and last Lord (Baron) Eure, and *d* 1709

The 2nd s,

Rev Sir Mark Sykes, 1st Bt (GB), so *cr* 28 March 1783; *bapt* 9 May 1711; DD Cantab, Rector Roos, Yorks; *m* 14 Feb 1735 Decima (*d* 9 March 1793), dau of Twyford Woodham, of Ely, and *d* 14 Sept 1783, leaving, with a dau (Mary, *m* John de Ponthieu):

Sir Christopher Sykes, 2nd Bt; *b* 23 May 1749; MA Oxon, DCL, MP Beverley 1784–90, fndr ag devpt Yorks Wolds; *m* 23 Oct 1770 Elizabeth (*d* 27 July 1803), dau of William Tatton, of Wythenshawe, Cheshire, and *d* 17 Sept 1801, having had:

1 Sir MARK SYKES later MASTERMAN-SYKES (added 1795), **3rd Bt**; *b* 20 Aug 1771; MP York 1807–20, High Sheriff Yorks; *m* 1st 11 Nov 1795 Henrietta (*dsp* July 1813), dau and heiress of Henry Masterman, of Settrington Hall, Yorks; *m* 2nd 2 Aug 1814 his 1st cousin Mary Elizabeth (*m* 2nd 16 Sept 1834 Dugdale Stratford Dugdale (*see* DUGDALE, Bt) and *d* 26 Oct 1846) only dau of William EGERTON formerly TATTON, of Tatton Park and Wythenshawe, Cheshire, and *dsp* 16 Feb 1823

2 TATTON (Sir), **4th Bt**

3 Christopher (Rev); *b* 18 Oct 1774; Rector Roos; *m* 14 May 1799 Lucy Dorothea (*d* 17 Dec 1828), dau and coheir of Henry Langford, of Stockport, and *d* 9 Nov 1857, leaving:

   (1) Lucy Elizabeth; *m* 1st 27 Sept 1827 Rev Hon Henry Duncombe (*see* FEVERSHAM, B); *m* 2nd 5 Jan 1837 Rev Charles Hotham (*d* 11 Feb 1866) and *dsp* 10 Dec 1877

   (2) Penelope; *m* 25 Nov 1837 Edward York, of Wighill Park, Yorks

1 Beatrice Hester Decima; *m* 16 Nov 1795 John Robinson Foulis and *d* April 1843, leaving issue

2 Elizabeth; *m* 11 Jan 1806 her 1st cousin Wilbraham Egerton, DL, JP, of Tatton Park, Cheshire, and *d* 28 Feb 1853, leaving issue (*see* 1956 edn EGERTON OF TATTON, B). He *d* 25 April 1856

The 3rd Bt's bro,

   Sir Tatton Sykes, 4th Bt; *b* 22 Aug 1772; *m* 19 Jan 1822 Mary Anne (*d* 1 Feb 1861), 2nd dau of Sir William Foulis, 7th Bt (*qv*), of Ingleby Manor, Yorks, and had, with two daus (*d* unm):

1 TATTON (Sir), **5th Bt**

2 Christopher, of Brantingham Thorpe, Yorks, JP, DL E R Yorks; *b* 10 Jan 1831; MP Beverley 1865–68, E R Yorks 1868–85 and Buckrose 1885–92; *d* unm 15 Dec 1898

1 Katherine Lucy; *m* 8 Aug 1850 Hon Thomas Grenville Cholmondeley, 2nd s of 1st Baron Delamere (*qv*), and *d* 6 March 1921, leaving issue

2 Sophia Frances; *m* 21 Sept 1853 R-Adml Hon Thomas Alexander Pakenham, s of 2nd Earl of Longford (*qv*), and *d* 15 Nov 1898, having had issue

3 Elizabeth Beatrice; *m* 15 Oct 1869 Very Rev Hon George Herbert, 3rd s of 2nd Earl of Powis (*qv*), and *d* 4 July 1883, leaving issue

4 Emma Julia; *m* 17 July 1862 Philip Bryan Davies-Cooke and *d* 7 Oct 1907, leaving issue (*see* COOKE, Bt)

Sir TATTON *d* 21 March 1863; his er s,

   Sir Tatton Sykes, 5th Bt, JP, DL E R Yorks; *b* 13 March 1826; High Sheriff E R Yorks 1869; *m* 3 Aug 1874 Christina Anne Jessica (*d* 2 June 1912), est dau of George Augustus Cavendish-Bentinck, PC, MP (*see* PORTLAND, E), and *d* 4 May 1913, leaving:

Sir Mark Sykes, 6th Bt, JP E R Yorks; *b* 16 March 1879; Capt 3rd Bn Yorks Regt Boer War 1902 (despatches), CC E R Yorks, Priv Sec to Ch Sec Ireland 1904–05, Hon Attaché Constantinople 1905–07, MP (C) Kingston-upon-Hull 1911–19, WW I: Lt-Col 5th Bn Yorks Regt, T/Col specially employed 1916–19, Hon Col 4th Bn E Yorks Regt, fndr memb Arab Bureau 1916 set up to reorganise the Arab Revolt under T E Lawrence, signatory Sykes-Picot Agreement 1916, author: *The Caliph's Last Heritage*, *Through Five Turkish Provinces*, *Dar-ul-Islam* and *Five Mansions of Othman*, memb E and N R TFA, 2nd Cl Order St Stanislas Russia, Cdr Star Romania with swords; *m* 28 Oct 1903 Edith Violet (*d* 21 July 1930), 3rd dau of Sir John Gorst, PC, MP, and had:

1 MARK TATTON RICHARD (Sir), **7th Bt**

2 Christopher Hugh; *b* 17 Nov 1907; *educ* Downside and Ch Ch Oxford; SAS Bde WW II (despatches, Croix de Guerre), Hon Attaché Berlin 1928–29 and Teheran 1930–31, 2nd Sec Teheran 1941–43, FRLS, author: *Wassmuss, Innocence and Design* (with Robert Byron), *Stranger Wonders*, *High Minded Murder*, *Four Studies in Loyalty*, *The Answer to Question 33*, *Character and Situation*, *Two Studies in Virtue*, *A Song for a Shirt*, *Dates and Parties*, *Orde Wingate*, *Cross Roads to Israel*, *Troubled Loyalty*, *Nancy—The Life of Lady Astor*, *Evelyn Waugh*, script-writer and producer BBC; *m* 25 Oct 1936 Camilla Georgiana (*d* 1983), only dau of Maj-Gen Sir Thomas Wentworth Russell, KBE, CMG (*see* BEDFORD, D), and *d* 1986, leaving:

   (1) +Mark Richard [Mark Sykes Esq, Great Norman Street Farm, Ide Hill, Kent]; *b* 9 June 1937; *educ* Downside and Ch Ch Oxford; *m* 1st 21 Feb 1962 (*divorce* 1965) Helen, only dau of Dr Arthur Norman Homewood, of Melbourne, Australia; *m* 2nd 19 Aug 1968 *Valerie, dau of Robert Goad, of Ide Hill, Sevenoaks, Kent, and by her has:

     1a +Thomas; *b* 1974

     2a +Frederick; *b* 1983

     3a +Joshua; *b* 1988

     1a *Lucy; *b* 4 Dec 1969; fashion ed *Town and Country*

     2a *Victoria ('Plum'); *b* 4 Dec 1969; *educ* Oxford; columnist with American *Vogue*

     3a *Alice; *b* 1972

3 Daniel Henry George; *b* 15 Oct 1916; *m* 24 July 1964 *Bridget, formerly w of Maj Wentworth Randolph Chetwynd, MBE (*see* CHETWYND, V), and only child of Col Theobald Alfred Walsh, DSO, and *dsp* 3 Sept 1968

1 Mary Freya; *b* 31 Aug 1904; *m* 17 Nov 1926 Sir Richard Everard Augustine Elwes, OBE, TD, High Court Judge, Lt-Col Northants Yeo, 5th s of Gervase Elwes, JP, DL, of Roxby, Lincs, and Billing Hall, Northants, and had issue. He *d* 4 Sept 1968

2 Everilda, twin; *b* 17 Nov 1907; *m* 28 Nov 1928 Lt-Col Adrian Cuthbert Scrope, The Green Howards, 3rd s of Henry Aloysius Scrope, of Danby Hall, Yorks, and had issue

3 Angela Christina; *b* 6 Sept 1911; *m* 11 May 1934 8th Earl of Antrim (*qv*) and *d* 1984, having had issue

Sir MARK *d* 16 Feb 1919; his est s,

   Sir (MARK TATTON) RICHARD SYKES later TATTON-SYKES (deed poll 13 July 1977), **7th Bt**, JP (E R Yorks1945), DL (1953); *b* 24 Aug 1905; *educ* Downside and Trin Coll Cambridge; Jt MFH Middleton East 1932–33 and 1938–39, WW II: Lt Green Howards (TA), Capt 1941, Lt-Col 1952, Pres: Bridlington C Assoc 1948, E R Georgian Soc 1961, E Yorks Local History Soc, N Counties Concerts; E R

Yorks: CA 1946, High Sheriff 1948, chm Driffield Magistrates; *m* 29 Sept 1942 Virginia (*d* 29 April 1970), only dau of John Francis Grey Gilliat by Lilian, widow of 5th Marquess of Anglesey (*qv*) and er dau of Sir George Chetwynd, 4th Bt (*qv*), and *d* 24 July 1978, having had:

1 Sir TATTON CHRISTOPHER MARK SYKES, **8th and present Bt**

2 +JEREMY JOHN; *b* 8 March 1946; heir presumptive; *educ* Ampleforth; *m* 1982 *Pamela June, only dau of Thomas Wood

3 +Christopher Simon Andrew; *b* 23 July 1948; *educ* Eton; photographer; *m* 25 Sept 1983 (divorce 1997) Belinda Susan Mary, yr dau of Frank Giles (*see* DE LA WARR, E), and has:

   (1) +Joseph Francis Richard; *b* 1990

   (1) *Lily; *b* 1984

4 +Richard Nicholas Bernard; *b* 17 March 1953; *educ* Ampleforth

1 *Arabella-Lilian Virginia [Mrs Kevin Delahunty, Scotts Farm, Stockley, Calne, Wilts]; *b* 28 May 1950; *m* 25 Oct 1975 *Kevin Delahunty and has:

   (1) *Damian John Richard; *b* 1976

2 *Henrietta Caroline Rose [Mrs Nigel Cayzer, Thriepley House, Lundie, Dundee DD2 5PA]; *b* 12 May 1957; *m* 1986 *Nigel Kenneth Cayzer and has issue (*see* CAYZER, Bt)

SYMONS OF VERNHAM DEAN

Creation: B. (LP, UK) Aug 1996.

THE BARONESS SYMONS OF VERNHAM DEAN, of Vernham Dean in the County of Hampshire (Elizabeth (Liz) Conway Symons) [The Rt Hon The Baroness Symons of Vernham Dean, House of Lords, London SW1A 0PW]; *b* 14 April 1951; *educ* Putney HS for Girls and Girton Coll Cambridge; Gen Sec Assoc First Div Civ Servs 1989–97 (admin tnee DOE 1974–77, dep gen sec Inland Revenue Staff Fedn 1988–89), memb gen cncl TUC, govr London Business Sch 1993–97, Parly U-Sec FCO 1997–, FRSA; has by *Philip Alan Bassett:

1 *A son

Lineage: ERNEST VIZE SYMONS, CB; *m* Elizabeth Megan Jenkins and had:

ELIZABETH CONWAY, *cr* a **Baroness**

SYNGE

Arms: Quarterly, 1st and 4th, az. three millstones ppr.; 2nd and 3rd, arg. an eagle displayed with two heads sa., beaked and legged gu.
Crest: Out of a ducal coronet or an eagle's claw ppr. **Motto:** *Cœlestia canimus* ('We sing of heavenly things'). **Creation:** Bt. (UK) 12 Aug 1801.

SIR ROBERT CARSON SYNGE, 8TH BT, of Kiltrough [Sir Robert Synge, 19364 Fraser Valley Highway, RR4, Langley, BC, Canada]; *b* 4 May 1922; *s* unc 1942; manager and owner Rob's Furniture; *m* 17 June 1944 *Dorothy Jean, dau of Theodore Johnson, of Cloverdale, Canada, and has:

1 *Donna Joan; *b* 8 May 1946; *m* 1967 *Richard David Harvey

2 *Wendy Marlene; *b* 8 July 1949

Lineage: RICHARD SYNGE, of Bridgnorth, Salop, Bailiff Bridgnorth 1598, 1605, 1617, 1623 and 1630; *m* 1 Jan 1593 Alice, dau of Roger Rowley, of Rowley, Salop, and was *bur* 7 March 1630/1, leaving, with other issue:

1 George (Rt Rev); *b* 1594; *educ* Balliol Coll Oxford (MA, DD); Burgess Bridgnorth 1628, Bp Cloyne 1638; *m* 1st Anne (drowned 1641 when fleeing to England), dau of Francis Edgeworth, of Dublin, and had issue, five of whom were drowned with their mother; *m* 2nd Elizabeth Stevens and *d* Aug 1652, having by her had issue (*see* CORK and ORRERY, E)

2 Edward (Rt Rev); *bapt* 14 Aug 1614; *educ* Trin Coll Dublin (MA, DD); Bp Ardfert 1661 and Cork, Cloyne and Ross 1663; *m* Barbara, dau and coheir of William Latham, of New Place, Co Londonderry, and *d* 22 Dec 1677, having had:

(1) Samuel (Very Rev); Dean Kildare; *m* 1678 Margaret, dau of Most Rev Michael Boyle, Archbp Armagh, and *d* 30 Nov 1708, having had issue

(2) EDWARD

(1) Mary; *m* 1680 Cdr Bryon Townsend, RN, MP, of Castle Townsend, and had issue

(2) Johanna; *m* John ffolliot, of Holybrook, Co Sligo

The yr s,

Most Rev EDWARD SYNGE; *b* 1659; *educ* Cork GS, Ch Ch Oxford (BA) and Trin Coll Dublin (MA); Bp Raphoe 1714, Archbp Tuam 1716; *m* Jane, dau of Rev Nicholas Proud, Dean Clonfert, and *d* 23 July 1741, leaving:

1 Edward (Rt Rev); *b* 1691; *educ* Trin Coll Dublin (Fell 1710); Bp Clonfert 1730, Cloyne 1731, Ferns 1733 and Elphin 1740; *m* Jane, dau of Robert Curtis, of Roscrea, Co Tipperary, and *d* 29 Jan 1762, having had, with two sons (*d* young):

(1) Alicia; *b* Dec 1726; *m* 1758 Joshua Cooper, of Markree

2 NICHOLAS

1 A dau; *m* — Hungerford, of Cahirmore

The yr s,

Rt Rev NICHOLAS SYNGE; DD, Archdeacon Dublin, Bp Killaloe 1745; *m* Elizabeth, dau of Frederick Richard Trench (*see* CLANCARTY, E), and *d* 1 Feb 1771, leaving, with several daus (the est Elizabeth *d* unm & the 2nd Mary *m* 3 June 1764 William Paisley Vaughan, of Golden Grove, Co Tipperary):

Ven EDWARD SYNGE, DD, of Syngefield, King's Co; Archdeacon Killala; *m* Feb 1753 Sophia Helena Maria (*d* 24 Jan 1799), dau of Rt Rev Samuel Hutchinson, Bp Killala, and *d* 9 Oct 1792, leaving:

1 Edward (Rev), of Lislee, Co Cork; *b* 8 Dec 1753; DD; *d* unm 1818

2 Sir SAMUEL SYNGE later HUTCHINSON SYNGE (roy licence 3 April 1813), 3rd Bt, as which *s* 1813 under special remainder, the btcy having been *cr* 11 Dec 1782 in favour of his maternal uncle, Sir Francis Hutchinson, 1st Bt (*dsp* 18 Dec 1807), of Castle Sallah, Co Wicklow; *b* 22 April 1756; MA, Archdeacon Killala; *m* 1st 12 June 1787 Frances (*d* 12 June 1788), dau of Hans Wood, of Rosmead, Co Westmeath, and had:

(1) Frances; *b* 28 May 1788; *d* unm 4 Dec 1869

2 (cont.) Sir SAMUEL *m* 2nd 3 March 1801 Dorothy (*bur* 15 Feb 1836), dau and coheir of John Hatch, and *d* 1 March 1846, having by her had:

(1) Francis, of Faney, Co Dublin; *b* 18 Jan 1802; *m* 17 June 1824 Louisa Frances (*d* 13 Jan 1876), dau of Hon Francis Hely-Hutchinson (*see* DONOUGHMORE, E)), and *dvp* 3 April 1833, leaving:

1a Sir EDWARD HUTCHINSON SYNGE, 4th and last Bt; *b* 31 Aug 1830; 6th and 5th Dragoon Gds, 48th Regt (Crimean medal and clasp); *d* unm 3rd Nov 1906, when the btcy expired

2a Coote; *b* 7 Aug 1832; Lt-Gen 2nd Dragoon Gds (Indian medal and clasp), Col 19th Hus; *m* 4 Aug 1888 Emily Charlotte (*d* 24 Feb 1929), widow of W Wright-Broughton and yst dau of Charles James Jecks, and *dsp* 13 Feb 1902

1a Frances Dorothy; *m* 1st 24 Sept 1846 James Hewitt (*see* LIFFORD, V) and had issue; *m* 2nd 1 Aug 1853 Maj David Philip Brown, 7th Hus, and *d* 21 Jan 1900, leaving further issue

(2) Sophia; *m* 26 Aug 1834 Capt Hon Coote Hely-Hutchinson, RN, and *d* 30 April 1896, leaving issue (*see* DONOUGHMORE, E)

3 George, of Rathmore, King's Co; *b* 24 June 1757; *m* 7 June 1787 Mary (*d* 1840), dau of Charles Macdonell, of New Hall, Co Clare, and *d* 1837 having had issue

4 ROBERT (Sir), **1st Bt**

5 Francis, of Glanmore Castle, Co Wicklow; *b* 15 April 1761; MP Swords; *m* 1st Barbara, dau and coheir of John Hatch, of Dublin, and had issue; *m* 2nd Elizabeth, widow of Col George Stewart and dau of Walter Taylor, of Castle Taylor, and *d* 17 Dec 1831, having by her had issue

1 Elizabeth; *b* 1755; *m* 1794 John Richard Ormesby, Army Capt, and *d* 1801

The 4th s,

Sir Robert Synge, 1st Bt (UK), so *cr* 12 Aug 1801; *m* 7 May 1784 Margaret (*d* 1 April 1838), dau of Theobald Wolfe, of Newtown, Co Dublin, and had, with two daus (*d* unm):

1 EDWARD (Sir), **2nd Bt**

2 Francis Hutchinson; *b* 30 April 1788; *m* 25 May 1819 Mary Anne (*d* 5 Nov 1871), 2nd dau of John Paget (*see* PAGET, Bt, of Cranmore Hall), and *dsp* 24 Aug 1854

3 Robert (Rev); *b* 31 Oct 1791; *m* 1st Aug 1820 Anne (*d* 2 Sept 1844), dau of Benjamin Follett, of Topsham, Devon, and had, with another s (*d* young):

(1) Robert Follett; *b* 12 June 1821; Maj 1st West India Regt; *m* 12 March 1855 Catherine Waddell Boyd (*d* 1892), yst dau of David Miller, barrister, of Kirkcudbrightshire, and *d* 22 Sept 1860, having had, with another s (*d* an infant):

1a Robert Follett Muter Foster Millington; *b* 5 Jan 1857; Lt-Col HLI, Egyptian Expdn 1882, Burma Expdn 1887–89 and Garrison Bn Northumberland Fus WW I; *m* Sept 1884 Charlotte Granville (*judicial separation* 1900; *d* July 1942), dau of Maj-Gen William James Stuart, RE, and *d* 31 March 1941, leaving:

1b Alan Hamilton Stuart; *b* 14 Feb 1886; *educ* Wellington; 2nd Lt Gen List and RFC WW I; *m* 1920 Alice May Bradley, of Washington, USA

(2) Francis Hutchinson; *b* 24 March 1823; Maj-Gen; *m* 1872 Lucy Frances, widow of Capt E T Dowbiggin, 7th Dragoon Gds, and dau of Maj-Gen Pole, and *d* 5 Sept 1881

(3) William Webb Follett; *b* 25 Aug 1826; Consul-Gen Cuba; *m* 27 Jan 1853 Henrietta Mary (*d* 15 Nov 1921), yst dau of Col Robert Dewar Wrainwright, US Marine Corps, and *d* 29 May 1891, leaving, with another s (*d* young) and a dau (*d* unm):

1a Robert Follett (Sir), KCMG (1919), MVO (1911); *b* 8 Dec 1853; Treaty Dept FO 1884–1901, Dep Marshal Ceremonies 1902, Offr Legn Hon, Cdr Orders Queen Isabella Spain, Rising Sun and Sacred Treasure Japan and Star Ethiopia; *m* 16 Feb 1881 Laura Mary (*d* 30 Nov 1937), dau of John Charles Fletcher, of Dale Park, Sussex, and *d* 22 Jan 1920

2a Francis Julian; *b* 2 July 1856; Registrar Supreme Court; *m* 11 Oct 1890 Mary Auchmuty (*d* 2 July 1920), dau of R Sands Tucker, of New York and Lenox, USA, and *d* 14 Sept 1938, leaving, with a dau (*d* an infant):

1b Robert Millington; *b* 26 Feb 1894; *educ* Eton and Trin Coll Oxford; Capt Coldstream Gds WW I (twice wounded), Order Rising Sun Japan; *m* 25 July 1922 Christabel Etienne (*d* 1988), dau of Charles Lyon Liddell (*see* RAVENSWORTH, B), and *d* 2 May 1964, leaving:

1c +Allen John Millington [Allen Synge Esq, 2 Diamond Terrace, London SE10 8QN]; *b* 15 Feb 1930; *educ* Millfield and Trin Coll Dublin; *m* 21 July 1955 *Olive Rachel, yr dau of Thomas Weir, of Ballymena, Co Antrim, and has:

1d +Daniel Thomas Millington; *b* 30 May 1963; *educ* Dulwich

2d +Timothy Auchmuty; *b* 10 Oct 1968

1d *Frances Clare [Mrs Frances Clark, Goose Cottage, 14 Fearon St, London SE10 0RS]; *b* 26 Nov 1959; *m* 1986 (*divorce* 1996) Bernard Fitzgerald Clark, yr s of Richard Clark, of Dibden Purlieu, Southampton

1c Pamela Mary; *b* 16 May 1923; served WW II (despatches, Middle East 1945); *m* 29 July 1966 Charles William Fane (*see* WESTMORLAND, E) and *d* Sept 1987, leaving

2c *Gillian Frances [Mrs George Ames, 305 Old Pickard Rd, Concord, MA, USA]; *b* 1 July 1933; *m* 28 June 1952 *Col George Stanley Ames, US Marine Corps, yr s of Oakes I Ames, of Cambridge, Mass., and has:

1d *Richard Millington; *b* 2 Nov 1955; *educ* Gordonstoun, Duke U and Georgia U; *m* 1982 *Laura Mahone, dau of Thomas Mahone Tolleson, of Atlanta, Ga., and has:

1e *Alexander Millington; *b* 1985

2e *Ian Mahone; *b* 1988

1e *Hannah Suzanne; *b* 1987

2d *John Bruton; *b* 28 Jan 1960; *m* 1989 *Donna Jean, dau of Mario Chiaravelotti, of N Conway, NH, and has:

1e *Evan George; *b* 1991

1e *Shanna Mae; *b* 1993

3d *Robert Oakes; *b* 1969; *educ* Gordonstoun and Rice U; *m* 1996 *Rachel Margaret, dau of Isamu Tsuchitani, of Arlington, Va.

1d *Elizabeth Whiting; *b* 1 April 1953; *educ* Concord Acad and Duke U; *m* 1984 *Alan Thomas Macdonald, s of Thomas Hugh Macdonald, of Canton, Mass., and has:

1e *Hugh Oakes Ames; *b* 1986

2e *Adrian Synge; *b* 1988

2b Allen Francis; *b* 6 Oct 1898;, Lt Irish Gds (SR); *ka* 27 Nov 1917

1b Violet Montresor; *b* 15 May 1896; *d* unm 13 April 1976

3a William Makepeace Thackeray; *b* 5 Aug 1860; T/Capt as Recruiting Offr 1916, Capt RA, Govr Walton Prison Liverpool; *m* 1st 12 May 1892 Ethel Elais (*d* 20 Feb 1895), er dau of Alfred Wilkinson, of Peterborough Ho, Harrow, and had, with another s (*d* young):

1b William Alfred Thackeray; *b* 16 Feb 1893; *educ* Charterhouse; Capt Res of Offrs King's Liverpool Regt, F/Lt RAFO WW I; *m* 5 Feb 1920 Hilda Marjorie (*d* 8 May 1967), yr dau of Ebenezer Pike, of Kilcrenagh, Co Cork, and *d* 27 Jan 1968, leaving:

1c +Brian Thackeray [Brian Synge Esq, 4 Pembroke Close, Grosvenor Cres, London SW1]; *b* 28 Nov 1920; *educ* Winchester; Hon Maj late Irish Gds, SBStJ; *m* 1st 14 April 1945 (*divorce* 1970) Alison Patricia, only dau of Brig Victor Frances Staples Hawkins, DSO, MC, and has:

1d +Barry Edward Thackeray [Barry Synge Esq, c/o 4 Pembroke Close, Grosvenor Cres, London SW1]; *b* 6 Feb 1949; *educ* Winchester; *m* 1986 (*divorce* 1990) Moira French, dau of Thomas Macdonald, of Ancrum, Roxburghs

2d +Mark Millington; *b* 8 July 1953; *m* 1984 *Clare Victoria, er dau of John Bulkley Herbert Francis, of Cowley, nr Cheltenham, Glos, and has:

1e *Annabel; *b* 1987

2e *Georgina Rose; *b* 1989

1d *(Norah) Melanie [Mrs Charles Birkett, 29 Rozel Rd, London SW4 0EY]; *b* 18 Jan 1947; *m* 1st 12 April 1969 (*divorce* 1976) Anthony Michael Elliott, s of Ernest Elliott, of Horsham, Sussex, and has:

1e *Rupert Francis William; *b* 1970

1e *Francesca Elisabeth; *b* 1972

1d (cont.) Mrs Melanie Elliott *m* 2nd 1984 *Charles Ross Birkett and by him has:

2e *(Charles) John Ross; *b* 1987

2e *Alice Emily Rose; *b* 1984

1c (cont.) Brian Synge *m* 2nd Nov 1970 *Mrs Pamela Columbine de Meo

2c +John Millington [John Synge Esq, 903 Drake Ho, Dolphin Sq, London SW1V 3NW]; *b* 27 May 1923; *educ* Winchester and Ch Ch Oxford (MA)

3a (cont.) William Synge *m* 2nd 12 Oct 1898 Ethel Rose (*d* 11 Nov 1957), dau of Henry Bramwell, of Crown East Court, Worcs, and *d* 13 April 1929, having by her had, with a s (*d* young):

1b Ethel Mary; *b* 2 Sept 1899; *m* 15 Jan 1931 Brig Norman MacLeod, OBE, Roy Scots Fus, yr s of Harold Hay Brodie MacLeod, MBE, of Milford Lodge, Salop, and *d* 8 Dec 1961. He *d* 17 June 1966

3 (cont.) The Rev Robert Synge *m* 2nd 1847 Katherine Eliza (*d* Sept 1850), est dau of Capt John Vincent, 16th Lancers, and *d* 8 Sept 1862, having by her had, with another s and a dau (both *d* young):

(4) Arthur Wolfe; *b* 1848; *d* 1870

1 Charlotte; *m* Lt-Col Sir John Maxwell Tylden, 52nd Regt, of Milstead, Kent, and *d* 8 March 1858

2 Anne Sophia; *m* 1829 James Greenwood

Sir ROBERT *d* 1804; his est s,

Sir Edward Synge, 2nd Bt; *b* 6 April 1786; *m* 19 Jan 1809 Mary Helena (*d* 20 Sept 1857), est dau of Robert Welsh, barrister, and *d* 22 July 1843, leaving:

1 **Sir Edward Synge, 3rd Bt**, JP, DL Co Cork; *b* 19 Nov 1809; High Sheriff Co Cork 1844; *m* 1st 16 Feb 1836 Margaret Jemima (*d* 14 Nov 1845), yst dau of Owen Saunders, of Largay, Co Cavan, and had, with two other daus:

(1) Charlotte Lydia; *m* 6 Oct 1870 Rev Patrick O'Rourke, AM, of Ardgroom, Co Cork, and *d* 28 Nov 1898, leaving issue

(2) Frances Patricia; *m* 3 May 1873 Francis Prittie Sadleir, of Oakwood, King's Co, and *d* 20 April 1885, leaving issue. He *d* 31 Jan 1887

1 (cont.) Sir Edward *m* 2nd 18 Aug 1846 Anne (*d* 23 Sept 1901), only dau of Henry Irwin, of Streamstown, Co Sligo, and Ray, Co Donegal, and *d* 1884, having by her had:

(3) Isabel Elizabeth; *d* 11 Aug 1859

2 **Sir Noah Hill Neale Synge, 4th Bt**; *b* 5 Feb 1811; *m* 18 May 1846 Catherine (*d* 30 Sept 1917 aged 98), dau of Stephen Vincent, and *dsp* 16 July 1886

3 ROBERT (Sir), **5th Bt**

4 Francis Hutchinson; *b* 2 July 1820; *d* 17 Sept 1871

5 Millington Henry, of Dysart, Co Clare; *b* 1 Sept 1823; Maj-Gen RE; *m* 22 Aug 1855 Jane (*d* 13 Jan 1915), dau of Thomas Bannerman (*see* BANNERMAN, Bt), and *d* 10 Sept 1907, having had a dau (*d* unm 2 Nov 1859)

1 Helen; *m* 30 Dec 1845 J W Warre Tyndale, barrister, and *d* 12 Dec 1881, leaving issue

The 4th Bt's bro,

Sir Robert Synge, 5th Bt; *b* 8 July 1812; Cdr RN; *m* 1st Jessie, dau of G Robyns, and had:

1 Jessie Maria; *d* unm 16 April 1869

Sir Robert *m* 2nd 21 Aug 1846 Laura (*d* 24 March 1882), dau of John Hart, and by her had, with a dau (*d* unm):

1 FRANCIS ROBERT MILLINGTON (Sir), **6th Bt**

2 Edward John Hutchinson; *b* 5 March 1854; *m* 4 Sept 1883 Leila Camilla (*d* 19 Dec 1935), dau of Charles Pemberton, of Grove Ho, Hampton, Middx, and Bayswater, and *d* 2 Oct 1886, having had, with a s (*d* an infant):

(1) Evelyn Mary; *b* 3 Aug 1884; *m* 23 Oct 1911 Brig-Gen Alick Gurdon Kemball, IA, 3rd s of Charles Gurdon Kemball, and *d* 8 Sept 1965, leaving issue. He *d* 11 Nov 1949

(2) Olive Marguerite; *b* 12 Jan 1886; *m* 20 June 1908 Claud Barton, Egyptian CS (*d* 25 Feb 1962), s of Dr Samuel Josiah Barton, of Norwich, and had:

1a *Andrew Synge; *b* 25 March 1909; *educ* Winchester, Magdalene Coll Cambridge (BA 1931) and RMA Woolwich; FICE, Maj RE WW II; *m* 23 Sept 1939 *Gertrude Ursula Désirée, dau of Maj Gordon Bluett Winch, DSO, and has:

1b *Christopher Synge; *b* 1 June 1942; *educ* Stowe; *m* 14 July 1965 *Catherine Anne, er dau of Sir John Ledward Royden, 4th Bt (*qv*), and has:

1c *Melissa; *b* 28 Nov 1970

2b *Geoffrey Bluett; *b* 25 July 1946; *educ* Berkhamsted

1a *Diana Synge; *b* 25 May 1914; *m* 18 Jan 1961 *Jacques Alois Hervé

2a *Judith Camilla Synge; *b* 12 Aug 1916

2 Laura Maria; *m* 15 Oct 1867 Capt Henry Pomeroy Gilbert, RN, and *dsp* 12 Sept 1927. He *d* 1891

3 Helen; *m* 8 Jan 1891 Rev Noel Platt, Rector Gt Parndon, Essex, and *d* 19 April 1925. He *d* 26 June 1908

Sir Robert *m* 3rd 1884 Jane Mary (*d* 10 Oct 1897), dau of Lewis Noel Boyer, and *d* 11 Sept 1894

His s,

Sir Francis Robert Millington Synge, 6th Bt; *b* 27 May 1851; Maj S Lancs Regt; *m* 1st 23 Feb 1876 Frances Elizabeth (*d* 16 June 1911), dau of Robert Evans, of Rock Ferry, Cheshire, and had:

1 **Sir Robert Millington Synge, 7th Bt**; *b* 17 Nov 1877; *d* unm 21 Dec 1942

2 Neale Hutchinson; *b* 22 Oct 1880; *m* 15 Oct 1910 Edith Elizabeth, dau of William Addy Thurlow, of Epping, and *d* 23 May 1929, leaving:

(1) Sir ROBERT CARSON SYNGE, **8th and present Bt**

(1) *Patricia Neale [Mrs Emerson Barden, 14227, 110th Ave, N Surrey, BC, Canada]; *b* 1924; Women's Div RCAF 1942–46; *m* 19 March 1948 *Emerson Edgar Barden, s of Emerson Porter Barden, of Yarrow, BC, Canada, and has:

1a *Neale Emerson; *b* 6 July 1953

1a *Linda Mae; *b* 29 Sept 1949

2a *Sherry Ann; *b* 31 Aug 1951

3 Edward; *b* 2 March 1882; *m* 1901 Agnes Emily, dau of James Jelley, and *d* 1966, having had:

(1) Edward; *b* 1902; *m* 1925 Alma, dau of Martin Hansen, and *d* 1928, leaving:

1a *Marjorie Irene; *b* 1926; *m* 14 Sept 1946 *William Thomas Kidner, late RCAF, s of William Henry Kidner, of Bristol, and has:

1b *Jacquelyn Ann; *b* 12 Jan 1951

2b *Patricia Lynn; *b* 25 Nov 1952

(2) +NEALE FRANCIS; *b* 28 Feb 1917; heir presumptive; Canadian Scottish WW II; *m* 30 Sept 1939 *Kathleen Caroline Bowes, of Kelowna, BC, and has:

1a +Allen James Edward; *b* 15 Jan 1942

1a *Sharon Eileen; *b* 28 May 1943

(1) *Molly Eileen; *b* 1908; *m* 1929 *Raymond Augustus McCarthy and has:

1a *Raymond Edward; *b* 14 April 1930; *m* 27 Jan 1950 *Helen, dau of Roy Dagg, of Prince George, BC, and has:

1b *Sharon Patricia; *b* 16 April 1951; *m* 1973 *Gerhard Mueller and has:

1c *Marcus Raymond George; *b* 1978

1c *Christa; *b* 1974

2a *Harold Douglas; *b* 31 March 1934

3a *Stanley Norman [Stanley McCarthy Esq, 1075 Lamar Place, Kamloops, BC, Canada]; *b* 25 Sept 1941; *m* 1961 *Karen Maureen, dau of Maurice Gregoire, of Penticton, BC, and has:

1b *Gregory Douglas; *b* 1967

2b *Edward Morris; *b* 1970

1b *Judith Maureen; *b* 1962

1 Frances Helen Millicent; *m* 1911 Archie Christie, slr, and has issue. He *d* 1921

2 Laura Eileen; *m* 1913 Octavius Studdert Maunsell, OBE, LRCP, LRCS, and *d* 12 Oct 1936

3 Lilian; *m* 19 Aug 1908 James Daniel Mitchell, slr, of Walcot, Birr, King's Co, and had issue. He *d* 1945

Sir Francis *m* 2nd 20 June 1912 Fanny Cecil (*d* 25 Jan 1961, having *m* 2nd 19 April 1940 Capt Robert Sandeman Peisley MacIvor, IA, of Golden Grove, Roscrea, Co Tipperary, who *d* 25 May 1941), yst dau of Charles Robert Wade-Gery, JP, of Wornditch Hall, Kimbolton, Hunts, and *d* 1 March 1924, leaving by her:

4 *Jessica Helen; *b* 18 Aug 1914; *m* 26 March 1940 (*divorce* 1949) F/Lt Alfred Davidson Colin Cleugh Fair, RAF, s of William John Fair, of Kingston, Ontario

SYSONBY

Arms: Gu. a chevron between three combs arg. **Crest:** Out of a ducal coronet az. three arrows, one in pale and two in saltire, points downwards, entwined by a snake ppr. **Supporters:** On either side a lion guardant crowned with a Saxon crown or and charged on the shoulder with a key, wards downwards and inwards az.
Motto: *Pro rege, lege, grege* ('For king, law and people').
Creation: B. (UK) 24 June 1935.

THE 3RD BARON SYSONBY, of Wonersh, Surrey (John Frederick Ponsonby) [The Rt Hon The Lord Sysonby, c/o Messrs Birch Cullimore Solicitors, Friars, White Friars, Chester CH1 1XS]; *b* 5 Aug 1945; *s f* 1956; *educ* privately

Lineage: Gen Sir HENRY FREDERICK PONSONBY, PC, GCB (*see* BESSBOROUGH, E); had:

FREDERICK EDWARD GREY PONSONBY, **1st Baron Sysonby**, of Wonersh, Co Surrey (UK), so *cr* 24 June 1935, GCB (1926, KCB 1918, CB 1906), GCVO (1921, KCVO 1910, CVO 1901, MVO 1897), PC (1914); *b* 16 Sept 1867; Lt-Col Gren Gds Boer War 1901–02 and WW I (despatches), Assist Priv Sec and Equerry to TM QUEEN VICTORIA 1895–1901, EDWARD VII 1901–10 and GEORGE V 1910–14, Keeper Privy Purse and Extra Equerry to HM GEORGE V 1914, Treasurer and Keeper Privy Purse 1920, Lt-Govr Windsor Castle and Constable Round Tower 1928, Receiver-Gen Duchy Lancaster; *m* 17 May 1899 Victoria Lily Hegan (Ria) (*d* 2 June 1955), er dau of Col Edmund Hegan Kennard (*see* KENNARD, Bt), and had:

1 Victor Alexander Henry Desmond; *b* 19 June (HM QUEEN VICTORIA stood sponsor), *d* 24 Nov 1900

2 EDWARD GASPARD, **2nd Baron**

1 Loelia Mary; *m* 1st 20 Feb 1930 (*divorce* 1947), as his 3rd w, 2nd Duke of Westminster (*qv*); *m* 2nd 1 Aug 1969 Sir Martin Alexander Lindsay, 1st Bt (*qv*), and *d* 1993

The 1st BARON *d* Oct 1935; his only surv s,

EDWARD GASPARD PONSONBY, **2nd Baron Sysonby**, DSO (1940); *b* 7 June 1903 (HM EDWARD VII stood sponsor); *educ* Eton; Page of Honour to HM GEORGE V 1916–19, Lt-Col 5th Bn The Queen's Roy Regt (TA) WW II (despatches); *m* 2 Oct 1936 Sallie Whitney (*d* 1977, having *m* 3rd 15 Feb 1958, as his 3rd w, Capt Edward Robert Francis Compton; *see* NORTHAMPTON, M), formerly w of George Edward Monkland and dau of Dr Leonard Cutler Sanford, of New York, and *d* 21 Jan 1956, leaving:

1 JOHN FREDERICK PONSONBY, **3rd and present Baron Sysonby**

1 *Carolyn Mary; *b* 9 Nov 1938

TALBOT OF MALAHIDE

· DEO · DATA ·

Arms: Quarterly, 1st and 4th, sable six martlets three two and one argent (for ARUNDELL); 2nd and 3rd, gules a lion rampant or within a bordure engrailed erminois (for TALBOT). **Crests:** 1 A wolf passant argent (for ARUNDELL), 2 On a chapeau gules doubled ermine a lion passant erminois (for TALBOT). **Supporters:** Dexter, a talbot or; sinister, a lion gules. **Mottoes:** 1 *Forte et fidele* ('Strong and faithful'), 2 *Deo data* ('God provides'). **Creation:** B. (I) 28 May 1831.

THE 10TH BARON TALBOT OF MALAHIDE and LORD MALAHIDE OF MALA-HIDE, Co Dublin ((Reginald) John Richard Arundell) [The Rt Hon The Lord Talbot of Malahide, Park Gate, Donhead St Andrew, Dorset SP7 9EU]; *b* 9 Jan 1931; *s* 1st cousin once-removed 1987; *educ* Stonyhurst and RMA Sandhurst; Kt SMO Malta 1977, KStJ 1988 (chm Cncl Wilts 1976–97, Chapter General 1993–); V-Ld Lt Wilts 1996 (DL 1983–96); *m* 1st 24 Sept 1955 Laura Duff (*d* 1989), yr dau of G/Capt Edward John Tennant, DSO, MC, JP (*see* GLENCONNER, B); *m* 2nd 1992 *Patricia Mary, est dau of John Cuthbert Widdrington Riddell, OBE, of Felton Pk, and Swinburne Castle, Northumberland, and formerly w of Maj Geoffrey Thomas Blundell-Brown, MBE, and by his 1st w has:

1 +RICHARD JOHN TENNANT, JP (Wilts 1991) [The Hon Richard Arundell JP, Hook Manor, Donhead, Dorset SP7 9EV]; *b* 28 March 1957; *educ* Stonyhurst and RAC Cirencester; cmded Roy Wessex Yeo (TA) 1979; *m* 29 Sept 1984 *Jane Catherine, dau of Timothy Heathcote Unwin, MFH, and has:

  (1) +John Richard; *b* 25 June 1998
  (1) *Isabel Mary; *b* 8 Sept 1986
  (2) *Emily Rose; *b* 1 Feb 1988
  (3) *Frances Laura; *b* 20 Jan 1990
  (4) *Lucinda Jane; *b* 18 Aug 1991

1 *Juliet Anne Tennant; *b* 22 Feb 1959; *m* 1987 *Simon James Teakle, s of John Anthony Teakle, MRCVS, of Southover Old Ho, Lewes, Sussex, and has:

  (1) *Humphrey; *b* 1990
  (2) *George; *b* 1991
  (1) *Sophie; *b* 1988
  (2) *Laura; *b* 1993

2 *Catherine Mary Tennant; *b* 16 April 1960; *m* 1993 *Andrew G Allwood, only s of C M Allwood, of Ferndown, Dorset, and has:

  (1) *Otto; *b* 30 May 1996
  (2) *Edward; *b* 6 Nov 1997
  (1) *Mary; *b* 22 Sept 1994

3 *Caroline Rose Tennant; *b* 13 June 1962

4 *Lucy Veronica Tennant; *b* 5 April 1965; *m* 1991 *Christopher S Daniel, only s of Lt-Cdr J J S Daniel, of W Meon, Hants, and has:

  (1) *Jack; *b* 26 Sept 1995
  (1) *Poppy; *b* 10 June 1997

Talbot, other creations: See SHREWSBURY and WATERFORD, E.

Lineage: Sir RICHARD TALBOT; granted Malahide, Co Dublin, *temp* HENRY II, also Castletown-Dalkey (now Rochestown), Co Dublin; *d* in or after *c* 1193, leaving:

REGINALD TALBOT or de WASUNVILLE; confirmed grants by his f to St Mary's Abbey, Dublin, *c* 1211; recovered Castletown-Dalkey 1223 following litigation; probably f (but possibly er bro) of:

ADAM TALBOT, of Malahide; living 1251; *m* Amice — and had:

Sir RICHARD TALBOT, of Malahide; *m* 1st Elizabeth Tuite, heiress to lands in Meath and Co Cork, and had:

 1 Richard fitz Richard Talbot, of Feltrim; *m* Cecilia — and had:
  (1) Richard fitz Richard Talbot; ancestor of the TALBOTs of Feltrim, later of Belgard, Co Dublin

Sir RICHARD *m* 2nd Juliane, probanbly dau of Sir James Keating, of Slievecoiltia, Co Wexford, and *d* 1288, leaving by her:

 2 Milo, to whom his f granted Malahide 1286; *m* Alianore — and *d* 1291, leaving:

---

(1) Richard fitz Milo (Sir); *b* 1287; feudal Ld of Malahide; *m* Margery de Ashebourne and *d* 1334, leaving:

1a Thomas (Sir); *b* 1328; feudal Ld of Malahide; summoned to Parl 1375; *m* Agnes, sis and heiress of William Kenewrick, and had:

 1b Richard (Sir); Sheriff Co Dublin, *m* Cecilia — (*m* 2nd Robert Gallane) and had:

  1c Thomas; minor at his f's death; had:

   1d Christopher; *dsp* a minor on or after 1 March 1399/1400

2b Thomas fitz Thomas; *s* his great-nephew as feudal Ld of Malahide; *d* between 12 Nov 1430 and 8 Nov 1432, leaving:

 1c Richard; feudal Ld of Malahide; *m* Matilda/Maud (*m* 3rd Jenico Darfas and 4th John Cornwallis, Ch Baron Exchequer Ireland *temp* HENRY VI, and *d* 12 July 1482), dau of Sir Christopher Plunket, of Killeen (*see* 1970 edn FINGALL, E), and *d c* 1442, leaving:

  1d Thomas; feudal Ld of Malahide; *m* 1st — Sommerton and had:
   1e PETER (Sir), for whom *see* further below
  1d (cont.) Thomas Talbbot *m* 2nd Elizabeth Buckley (living 29 Feb 1513/4) and *d* 23 July 1487, having by her had:
   2e John; ancestor of the TALBOTs of Dardistown, Co Meath
   3e Richard; *dsp*
   4e Thomas; *dsp*
   5e William, of Robertstown, Co Meath; *m* Genet Tew and had, with a 2nd or 3rd s (William, *b* 1486, living 1526):
    1f Patrick, of Belan, Co Kildare; *m* Genet, dau of Thomas FitzGerald, and had:
     1g Thomas
     2g Sir WILLIAM TALBOT, 1st Bt (I), so *cr* a 4 Feb 1622/3, of Carton, Co Kildare; MP (I Parl) Co Kildare 1613–15; *m* Alison, dau of John Netterville, of Castleton, Co Meath, and *d* 16 March 1633/4, having had, with eight daus:
      1h Sir ROBERT TALBOT, 2nd Bt, of Carton; *b c* 1610; MP (I Parl) Co Wicklow June-Oct 1634; *m* Grace Calvert, dau of 1st Baron Baltimore, and *dspm* 21 Oct 1670, having had:
       1i Sir WILLIAM TALBOT, 3rd Bt; Master Rolls 1689–90; *m* 1683 Anne, widow of 6th Viscount Dillon (*qv*) and dau of 2nd Earl of Westmeath (*qv*), and *dsp* 18 May 1691
       1i Frances; *m* her cousin Richard Talbot and was grandmother-in-law of **Baroness Talbot of Malahide** and **Lady Malahide of Malahide** (*see* below)
      2h John; *dsp* apparently by June 1685
      3h Garrett; *m* by 12 March 1633/4 Margaret, dau of Henry Gaydon, of Co Louth, and *d* by June 1685, leaving:
       1i William (self-styled 'Earl of Tyrconnel' and later 'Comte/Conde [Count] de Tyrconnel', having assumed his unc's attainted Earldom and taken up residence in France and Spain), of Haggardstown, PC (I); *b c* 1643; MP (I Parl called by JAMES II) Co Louth 1689; attainted and stripped of honours 1691, hence disabled from assuming either his cousin's btcy or his unc's peerage titles; *m* Mary, dau of Nicholas White, Alderman of and MP (JAMES II's I Parl May 1689) Clonmel, Co Tipperary, and allegedly *d* 26 Dec 1724, having had:
        1j Richard, self-styled *Lord Talbot*; *m* 19 Dec 1702 Lady Charlotte Talbot, dau of 1st and last Duke of Tyrconnel, and *dvp* 8 May 1716 while at sea departing from Scotland following the 1715 Uprising, in which he had supported the titular James III, leaving:
         1k Richard Francis, self-styled *Earl of Tyrconnel*; *bapt* 26 Dec 1710; Capt Fitz James's Regt of Irish Horse in French service Feb 1728/9, campaigning in Germany and Italy, also later in Flanders; captured at sea by British while sailing to join the 1745 Uprising in Scotland; Maj-Gen Jan 1747/8; French Min Plen Prussia 1748–52, Chev Order St Louis; *m* after 22 Nov 1745 Madeleine de Lys (*d* 2 Nov 1759) and *dsp* apparently 11/12 March 1752, when all his titles expired
         1k Maxie
      4h James
      5h Thomas; Franciscan friar
      6h Peter, SJ; *b* 1620; RC Archbp Dublin 1669–80; imprisoned Oct 1678 for supposed complicity in the 'Popish Plot'; *d* in prison just after 23 Oct 1680
      7h Gilbert; reportedly Col of a troop of 'rebels' (probably Confederate Irish in 1641 Uprising); *m* 1st — and had a dau (Jane); *m* 2nd Dorothy, 6th dau of 1st Earl of the County of Corke (*see* CORK and ORRERY, E) and widow of Sir Adam Loftus, and *d c* 1674
      8h RICHARD TALBOT, 1st and last EARL OF TYRCONNEL, so *cr* 20 June 1685, as also BARON OF TALBOTSTOWN, Co Wicklow, and VISCOUNT BALTINGLASS, Co Wicklow (all I), with remainder to his nephews, and in addition by JAMES II 30 March 1688/9 (nearly four months after the latter had been deemed to have vacated the throne of England but while he was still *de facto* King of Ireland) (1st and last) MARQUESS and DUKE OF TYRCONNEL (I), PC (I 9 June, E 8 Oct 1686), called 'Lying Dick Talbot'; *b* 1630; royalist during Wars in Ireland in 1640s and a royalist agent in England during Interregnum; in French service against Spaniards 1650s; Groom Bedchamber to DUKE OF YORK (later JAMES II) and Lt-Col Duke of York's Regt of Foot; served RN 3rd Dutch War; Capt Lord Berkeley's Regt of Horse 1672–73; as RC fell victim to and was imprisoned on suspicion of complicity in the 'Popish Plot' 1678–79; Col of Horse *c* Jan 1684/5, Lt-Gen Army Ireland March 1685/6, Ld Lt Ireland Feb 1686/7, Commr

Treasury Ireland 1689; fought Battle of the Boyne 1 July 1690 and continued the struggle in the South and West of Ireland against Williamite forces after JAMES II's departure to France, hence attainted and stripped of his honours 11 May 1691; *m* 1st Catherine, Maid of Honour to MARY OF MODENA (JAMES II's w), dau of Lt-Col Matthew Boynton, of Burton Agnes House, Yorks, and had, with a yr dau:

    1i Charlotte; *m* her cousin Richard, self-styled *Lord Talbot*, and *d* 14 Feb 1722 aged 46, leaving issue (*see above*)

    8h (cont.) The 1st and last DUKE *m* 2nd *c* Nov 1681 Frances, widow of Sir George Hamilton (*see* ABERCORN, D), and *dspm* 14 Aug 1691, when the Dukedom and Marquessate would have expired even if not already forfeited

THOMAS TALBOT *d* 23 July 1487; his est s,

Sir PETER TALBOT; *m* 1st Catherine, illegitimate dau of 8th Earl of Kildare (*see* LEINSTER, D); *m* 2nd Janet Eustace and *d* 10 July 1528, having had:

1 THOMAS (Sir)

2 John, to whom his f left his Cos Waterford and Kilkenny estates; *dspm*

3 Walter, of Trim, Co Meath; *dspm*

1 Margaret; *m* 1st Viscount Baltinglass of the 1541 *cr*

2 Eleanor; *d* unm 1526

3 Amy; *d* unm 1529

The est s,

Sir THOMAS TALBOT; *b c* 1503; *m* Katherine, dau of David Betagh, of Moynalty, Co Meath, and had, with two yr sons (Peter, *m* Elizabeth, dau of Robert Preston, of Ballymado, and *d* by 1595, leaving several sons; Robert, living 1595):

WILLIAM TALBOT; *m* Mary, dau of Peter Bermingham, Ld Ch Justice Ireland, and *d* 4 Feb 1595, having had:

1 PATRICK

2 John (Sir), of Castlering, Co Louth; ktd 1599; *m* his distant cousin Bridget (*d* 1619), dau of Sir John Talbot, of Grafton and Albrighton (*see* SHREWSBURY and WATERFORD, E), and *d* 7 Nov 1613, having had two sons (John; William) and two daus (Mary; Bridget), who all *dsp* & *vp*

3 Walter; *dsp*

1 Alice; *m* John Finglas, of Tobersool, Co Dublin

2 Mary; *d* unm

3 Anne; *m* William Wogan, of Rathcoffy, Co Kildare

4 Jane; *m* Robert Barnewall, of Dunbroe, Co Dublin

5 Elizabeth; *m* Christopher Russell, of Seatown, Co Dublin

The est s,

PATRICK TALBOT; *m* Katherine (*d* 6 Feb 1620), dau of Sir Christopher Cheevers, of Macetown, and *dvp* on or after 8 May 1581, leaving:

RICHARD TALBOT; *b* Feb 1569/70; *m* Elizabeth, dau of Sir Germain Kempe, and *d* 29 July 1640, leaving:

1 JOHN

2 George, of Dublin; *m* Mary — and *d* 1689/90, leaving:

    (1) Henry; Alderman Dublin under JAMES II's charter 1688–89; inherited the Mornington estate following death of his cousin Patrick Draycott 1702; *d* 1706, leaving:

        1a Draycott, of Mornington; *m* Jane Plunkett, dau of 8th Baron Louth (*qv*), and had:

            1b Plunket Henry; *m* his cousin Elizabeth (*d* 1792), dau of 9th Baron Louth, and *d* 1778

3 William, of Rudder, Co Meath; *d* 1683

1 Elizabeth; *m c* 1 March 1639/40 John Draycott, of Mornington, Co Meath

2 Jane

The est s,

JOHN TALBOT; *m* 1637 Lady Catherine Plunkett, dau of 1st Earl of Fingall (*see* 1970 edn), and *d* 1672, leaving:

RICHARD TALBOT; *b* 1638; Auditor-Gen Ireland 1688; *m* his cousin Frances (*d* 1718), dau and heiress of Sir ROBERT TALBOT, 2nd Bt (*see above*), and *d* 1703, having had, with other issue, including two er sons (Richard, *b* 1668, *dsp*; Robert, *dsp*), a 4th s (Valentine, *m* Mary, dau of James Tobin, of Ballaghtobin, Co Tipperary, and *d* 29 April 1749) and two daus (Mary, *m* 1706 Robert Dillon, Dublin barrister, and had an only dau (Frances, *m* James Butler, of Ballyragget, Co Kilkenny (*see* VAUX OF HARROWDEN, B); Susanna, *m* Nicholas Morres (*d* 1742), of Seafield, Co Dublin (*d* 1742; *see* MONTMORENCY, Bt), and had issue), a 3rd s:

JOHN TALBOT; *m* Frances, dau and heiress of Col Nicholas Wogan, of Rathcoffy (heir male and descendant of Sir John Wogan, Ch Govr Ireland 1295 and 1310), and had, with a yr s (Nicholas, Offr in Austrian service, *d* unm, *ka* Battle of Collin 1757):

RICHARD TALBOT; *m* by 1766 Margaret (*d* 27 Sept 1834), **Baroness Talbot of Malahide** and **Lady Malahide of Malahide**, Co Dublin (I), so *cr* 28 May 1831, with remainder to the heirs male of her body by her late husb, est dau of James O'Reilly (*see* NUGENT, Bt, of Ballinlough), and *d* 24 Oct 1788, leaving:

1 RICHARD WOGAN TALBOT, **2nd Baron Talbot of Malahide** and **Lord Malahide of Malahide**, PC (I 1836); *b c* 1766; MP (I Parl) Co Dublin 1790–91 (election annulled) and (UK Parl, Whig) 1807–30; Col; *cr* 8 May 1839 BARON FURNIVAL OF MALAHIDE, Co Dublin (UK); *m* 1st (licence 28 Nov 1789) Catherine (*d c* 1800), dau and heiress of John Malpas, of Chapel Izod and Rochestown, Co Dublin, and had:

    (1) John Malpas; *dvp* unm 1828

    (1) Catherine Frances; *m* 9 May 1809, as his 1st w, Lt-Gen Sir William Cornwallis Eustace, CB, KCH, and *d* 10 Dec 1816, leaving issue. He *d d* 9 Feb 1855

1 (cont.) The **2nd Baron** *m* 2nd 15 March 1806 Margaret (*dsp* 26 Nov 1861), dau of Andrew Sayers, timber merchant, and *dspms* 29 Oct 1849, when the 1839 Barony expired

2 JAMES TALBOT, **3rd Baron Talbot of Malahide** and **Lord Malahide of Malahide**; *b c* 1768; *educ* Trin Coll Dublin and Gray's Inn; *m* 26 Dec 1804 Anne

Sarah (*d* 13 March 1857), 2nd dau and coheir of Samuel Rodbard, of Evercreech Ho, Somerset, and *d* 20 Dec 1850, having had, with other issue:

(1) JAMES TALBOT, **4th Baron Talbot of Malahide** and **Lord Malahide of Malahide**, also 1st BARON TALBOT DE MALAHIDE, Co Dublin (UK), so *cr* 19 Nov 1856; *b* 22 Nov 1805; *educ* Trin Coll Cambridge (LLD, memb Senate Roy U of Ireland); MP (Lib) Athlone 1832–35, FSA 1854, FRS 1858, a Ld-inwaiting 1863–66, Pres: Archaeological Inst 1851–63 and 1867–83, RA (I) 1866–69 and Roy Ag Soc Ireland; *m* 9 Aug 1842 Maria Margaretta (*d* 9 Aug 1873), yst dau of Patrick Murray, of Simprim, Forfar, and *d* 14 April 1883, having had, with another s and two daus (*d* young or unm):

    1a RICHARD WOGAN TALBOT, **5th Baron Talbot of Malahide** and **Lord Malahide of Malahide**, JP, DL Co Dublin; *b* 28 Feb 1846; *educ* Eton; Lt 9th Lancers; *m* 1st 25 June 1873 Emily Harriette (*d* 24 Jan 1898), yst dau of Sir James Boswell, 2nd and last Bt, of Auchinleck, Ayrshire (*see* 1857 edn); *m* 2nd 10 Dec 1901 Isabel Charlotte, DBE, DGStJ (*d* 22 Feb 1932), widow of John Gurney, JP, of Sprowston Hall, Norfolk and Ham Ho, Essex, and dau of Robert Blake Humfrey, of Wroxham Ho, Norwich and *d* 4 March 1921, leaving by his 1st w:

        1b JAMES BOSWELL TALBOT, **6th Baron Talbot of Malahide** and **Lord Malahide of Malahide**, JP Ayrshire; *b* 18 May 1874; *m* 19 Sept 1924 (Lucy) Joyce Gunning (*m* 2nd 3 Oct 1951 Brig John Smith McCombe, DSO, MB (*d* 19 Oct 1959), s of R McCombe, and resumed her former married name 1960), er dau of Frederick Kerr, and *dsp* 22 Aug 1948

    2a Reginald Gilbert Murray, CBE (1918); *b* 30 Jan 1849; *educ* Trin Coll Cambridge (LLB); barrister; *m* 1st 28 April 1885 Edith Lucy Murray (*dsp* 10 Feb 1901), dau of Rev Jermyn Pratt, of Ryston Hall, Norfolk; *m* 2nd 3 Jan 1907 Richenda, 3rd dau of Charles Buxton, MP (*see* BUXTON, Bt), and *dsp* 7 May 1930

    3a Milo George, CB; *b* 14 Sept 1854; Jowaki Expdn 1877–78 (medal with clasp), Afghan War 1879–80 (despatches, medal with four clasps, bronze star), Nile Expdn 1897–99 (despatches, brevet, Egyptian medal with three clasps) and WW I (despatches), Lt-Col and Brevet Col RE, Dir Surveys Anglo-Egyptian Sudan; 2nd Cl Medjidie, 3rd Cl Osmanieh; *m* 25 April 1911 Eva (*d* 20 Feb 1951), yst dau of Col John Joicey, MP, of Newton Hall, Northumberland, and *d* 3 Sept 1931, leaving:

        1b MILO JOHN REGINALD **7th Baron Talbot of Malahide** and **Lord Malahide of Malahide**, CMG (1957); *b* 1 Dec 1912; *educ* Winchester and Trin Coll Cambridge (MA 1948); Dip Serv: FO 1937–39, Min Ec Warfare 1939–40, Ankara 1943–45, Beirut 1945–47, Amb Laos 1955–56, resigned 1958, dir Irish Investment Co Ltd; *d* unm at sea 14 April 1973, when the UK Barony expired

        1b *Rose Maud [The Hon Rose Talbot, Malahide, Fingal, Tasmania 7214, Australia]; *b* 14 Sept 1915; granted rank of baron's dau 2 Feb 1949

    1a Susan Ann; *m* 7 April 1864 Maj-Gen Cecil Robert St John Ives, of Moyns Park, Essex, and *d* 27 April 1918, leaving issue. He *d* 11 July 1896

(2) Richard Gilbert, of Ballinclea, Co Dublin; *b* 1810; *m* 12 Oct 1847 Anne Cunliffe (*d* 5 July 1902), dau of Ellis Cunliffe Lister-Kay (*see* SWINTON, E), and *d* 19 Aug 1879, leaving, with a dau (*d* unm):

    1a Richard Gilbert; *b* 4 Aug 1856; *m* 7 Oct 1891 Maud (*d* 12 Dec 1938), dau of Rev Edward Lovel, and *dsp* 12 July 1900

    2a Edward Lister-Kaye; *b* 10 Feb 1858; Lt Durham LI; *d* unm 15 Jan 1917

(3) George (Rt Rev Mgr); *b* 1816; Canon St Peter's, Chamberlain to HH POPE PIUS IX; *d* 16 Oct 1886

(4) Edward Plantagenet Airey (Rev); *b* 13 March 1817; *educ* Trin Coll Dublin (BA); Vicar Evercreech-cum-Chesterblade, Capt 34th Regt; *m* 1st 16 Oct 1850 Katherine Elinor (*dsp* 19 March 1879), dau and heiress of Francis Hoey, of Dunganstown Castle, Co Wicklow; *m* 2nd 2 Nov 1880 Anne Theodosia (*d* 10 Jan 1905), dau of Richard Beamish, FRS, and *dsp* 16 March 1904

(5) William Leopold Porsenna, JP, DL Sussex; *b* 24 April 1824; Lt-Col; *m* 26 June 1852 Mary Louisa (*d* 1 Feb 1918), dau of Anthony Lefroy (*see* KINGSTON, E), and *dsp* 12 Aug 1881

(1) Margaret Nugent; *m* 5 Sept 1835 Thomas Jones, of Stapleton and Hinton Charter Ho, nr Bath, and *d* 16 April 1887, leaving issue. He *d* 8 May 1848

(2) Harriett Mary Everard; *m* 31 Jan 1838 her cousin 1st and last Baron Airey, GCB (*d* 14 Sept 1881), and *d* 28 July 1881, having had issue

(3) Marianne Flora Etruria; *m* 16 Sept 1845 Rev Charles Walter Albyn Napier, Preb Chichester, and *d* 20 Dec 1878, having had issue. He *d* 23 Dec 1908

(4) Charlotte Etruria; *m* 7 April 1853 Henry Hobhouse, of Hadspen Ho, Somerset, and *d* 16 April 1855, leaving issue. He *d* 11 Feb 1862

3 John (Sir), GCB; *b* 1768; Adml; *m* 17 Oct 1815 Hon Juliana Arundell (*d* 18 Dec 1843), 3rd dau of 9th Baron Arundell of Wardour (*see* 1940 edn), and *d* 7 July 1851, leaving:

(1) John Reginald Francis George, of Rhode Hill, nr Lyme Regis, JP Devon and Dorset; *b* 25 March 1826; *m* 24 June 1858 Sarah Eliza (*d* 23 May 1878), dau of Rev David Jones, Rector Panteague and Tredunnock, Mon, and *d* 17 Jan 1906, having had:

    1a John Reginald Charles, of Rhode Hill, JP Devon and Dorset; *b* 15 Nov 1861; Lt 3rd Bn Yorks Regt, Mayor Lyme Regis 1901–03; *m* 2 Aug 1887 Maria Josephine (*d* 14 June 1939), only dau of 3rd Duke de Stacpoole, and *d* 5 Feb 1909, having had:

        1b Francis John Reginald; *b* 9 Jan 1889; *m* 8 Nov 1913 Violet Mallock (*d* 13 April 1927), dau of Arthur Thomas Mallock Bond, of Pyne Ho, Lyme Regis, and *dsp* 6 June 1957

        2b REGINALD STANISLAUS VICTOR TALBOT, **8th Baron Talbot of Malahide** and **Lord Malahide of Malahide**, MC (1918); *b* 7 May 1897; T/Capt Roy Berkshire Regt WW I, P/O RAFVR; *m* 24 April 1924 Cecily Elizabeth (*d* 10 Oct 1976), est dau of Maj Garstang Hodgson, of Clevedon, Somerset, and *dspm* 2 April 1975, leaving:

            1c *Ann Cecily Mary [The Hon Mrs Edwards, Malahide, Whiteway, Litton Cheney, Dorset DT2 9AG]; *b* 22 Dec 1931; *m* 1 Oct 1955 *Maj Edward Reginald Edwards, s of Edward John Edwards, of Pontypridd, Glam, and has:

                1d *Edward David; *b* 1956

                2d *John Llewellyn; *b* 1958

3d *Richard Reginald; *b* 1973

3b JOSEPH HUBERT GEORGE TALBOT, **9th Baron Talbot of Malahide** and **Lord Malahide of Malahide**; *b* 22 April 1899; T/Lt Coldstream Gds 1918; *m* 1st 5 July 1924 Hélène (*d* 1961), only dau of M Gouley, of Bessancourt, Seine-et-Oise, France; *m* 2nd 1962 (*divorce* 1970) Beatrice Bros, of Nice, and *d* 1987

1b Cecily Mary Gertrude; *b* 26 April 1891; *m* 8 Sept 1916 Capt Edmund Erconvald Garman, RASC, s of Cornelius Edward Garman, of Woodford, and had issue

2b Katherine Mary Josephine; *b* 22 March 1893; *d* 12 June 1897

2a Edward Reginald John; *b* 27 Oct 1868; Maj 3rd Bn Somerset LI; *m* 15 May 1909 Gladys Marie (*m* 2nd 25 Jan 1912 Capt Nigel William Francis Baynes; *see* BAYNES, Bt), est dau of T W Shortridge, MD, of Honiton, Devon, and *d* 16 May 1909

3a Reginald Aloysius; *b* July 1870; *m* 23 June 1898 Mabile Mary (*d* 20 Sept 1942), dau of Hon Robert Arthur Arundell, 4th s of 9th Baron Arundell of Wardour (*see* 1940 edn), and *d* 19 May 1922, having had:

1b Reginald John Arthur TALBOT later ARUNDELL (roy licence 1945); *b* 14 Dec 1900; *educ* St Benedict's; *m* 27 July 1929 Winifred (*d* 16 Aug 1954), dau of Richard Barrett Stanswick Castle, of Prestatyn, Flint, and *d* 24 Nov 1953, leaving:

1c (REGINALD) JOHN RICHARD ARUNDELL, **10th and present Baron Talbot de Malahide**

2c +Edward Renfric [Maj The Hon Edward Arundell, 82 Edith Grove, London SW10 0NH]; *b* 2 Nov 1933; *educ* Oratory Sch and RMA Sandhurst; granted 1991 rank of baron's yr s, Maj DCLI; *m* 27 Sept 1961 *Margaret Ann Honoria Merry, only dau of Brig John Francis Macnab, CBE, DSO, Queen's Own Cameron Highrs, and has:

1d *Lucinda Margaret Beatrice [Mrs Steven Nash, Lanescot House, Lanescot Par, Cornwall PL24 2RS]; *b* 17 Oct 1962; *m* 1987 *Dr Steven Roy Nash, MB, BS, MRCGP, s of Roy Nash, of Liskeard, Cornwall, and has:

1e *(Edward) Mungo Steven; *b* 1990

1e *Emma Margaret Alice; *b* 1988

2e *Tertia Mary; *b* 1993

3e *Flora May; *b* 1995

2d *Camilla Edwina Clare; *b* 2 March 1965

3d *Nicola Marina Merry [Mrs Dominic Chambers, Trafalgar Houseboat, 106 Cheyne Walk, London SW10]; *b* 31 Sept 1967; *m* 1992 *Dominic Peter Craven Chambers (*see* HERRIES, L)

2b Joseph Hubert Edward Pius; *b* 6 Aug 1903; *educ* St Benedict's; *m* 5 Jan 1943 *Mercia Cecelia, dau of Capt H C Cowell, of Southsea, and *d* 1975, leaving:

1c Clive Richard; *b* 5 Dec 1943; *educ* Oratory Sch; *m* 27 Nov 1965 *Pamela Maureen [Mrs Clive Talbot, 41 Headland Ave, Seaford, E Sussex], dau of Basil Coxwell, of Bahia, Brazil, and *d* 24 Oct 1994, leaving:

1d +Richard Paul [Lt-Cdr Richard Talbot, RN, c/o MOD (Navy), Whitehall, London SW1A]; *b* 5 June 1966; *educ* RNC Dartmouth; cmded HMS *Kingfisher* (1994) and *Arun* (1994–95); *m* 13 July 1996 *Emma Katherine, dau of Derek Harrison, of Guersney, and has:

1e *Camilla Isabel Katherine; *b* 8 Sept 1997

2d +Anthony John [The Rev Anthony Talbot, St Patrick's Church, Walsall, Staffs]; *b* 22 April 1967; *educ* Reading U (BSc) and Oscott Seminary (Louvain U STB); ordained 8 July 1995

3d +Michael Hugh Arnold [Michael Talbot Esq, 41 Headland Ave, Seaford, E Sussex BN25 4PZ]; *b* 23 March 1977; *educ* Newlands Sch and Southampton U

4d +Stephen Edward; *b* 5 May 1981; *educ* Oratory Sch

1d *Nicola Louise Cecilia [Mrs Gavin Cawley, 8 Lindley St, Lakenham, Norfolk]; *b* 3 June 1970; *educ* Micklefield Sch and Essex U (GIMA, PhD); *m* 4 Jan 1997 *Gavin Cawley

2d *Frances Mary; *b* 18 May 1984; *educ* St Teresa's Dorking

3b Francis Humphrey Nicholas; *b* 27, *d* 29 July 1904

4b Gilbert Aloysius Reginald; *b* 12, *d* 14 June 1905

5b Joseph Francis John; *b* 29 Feb 1908; *ka* 1 June 1940

6b Leonard Francis; *b* 6, *d* 8 March 1910

7b +Robert Peter Frederick Gerard [Robert Talbot Esq, 602 Hanworth Rd, Hounslow, Middx]; *b* 11 Nov 1916; *educ* Oratory Sch; *m* 1944 (*divorce* 1983) Blanche Edna Caseley, dau of Herbert Albert Caseley, and has:

1c +Anthony Robert John [Anthony Talbot Esq, 59 Vandyke, Great Hollands, Bracknell, Berks]; *b* 1946; *m* 1970 *Patricia Ayliffe Doris, dau of Arthur Edward Davis, and has:

1d +Christopher Anthony Matthew; *b* 1979

1d *Claire Elizabeth Patricia; *b* 1976

1c *Catherine Blanche Mary; *b* 1944

1b Mabile Katherine Mary; *b* 3, *d* 5 Oct 1899

2b Magdalen Mary Barbara; *b* 23, *d* 25 May 1902

3b *Lucy Geraldine Mary [Miss Lucy Talbot, Mayfield Residential Home, Hook, Hants]; *b* 10 Jan 1907

4b (Hilda Mary) Clare; *b* 23 Feb 1913; *m* 1972 Lt-Col Peter Coventry Grant, RE (*d* 1973), yr s of Maj-Gen Sir Philip Gordon-Grant, KCB, CMG, RE (*see* COVENTRY, E), and *d* 28 Nov 1995

4a Hubert George; *b* 15 Dec 1872; *d* 5 Nov 1874

1a Mary Julia Isabel; *m* 20 July 1887 Lt-Col Frederick Milbank Bland, RA, yst s of Rev Philip Bland, of Draycott, Staffs, and *d* 30 Oct 1927

2a Mary Katherine; *m* 1 Feb 1881 Sir Joseph Edward Radcliffe, 4th Bt (*qv*), and *d* 3 Jan 1943, leaving issue

3a Clara Mary Lucy; *m* 25 Nov 1896 Capt John Murray, 14th Hus, of Henwick, Berks, and *d* 8 June 1951

4a Mary Cecily; *m* 21 July 1886 Lt-Col Edward Henry Joseph Mostyn (*see* MOSTYN, Bt), and *d* 22 Nov 1916, leaving issue

5a Annette Mary Laura; *m* 9 June 1903 Alban James Woodroffe, MBE, JP, 3rd s of James Tisdall Woodroffe, Advocate-Gen Bengal, and had issue. He *d* 1 June 1964

(2) Nugent James Neill (Very Rev); *b* 2 Feb 1830; RC Canon; *d* Jan 1878

(1) Mary Juliana Charlotte; *m* 10 Oct 1849 George Thomas Whitgreave, of Moseley Court, Staffs, and *dsp* Oct 1854. He *d* 18 Feb 1863

(2) Margarita Victoriosa; *m* 26 April 1841 Sir William Edmund Pole, 9th Bt, of Shute Ho (*qv*), and *d* 23 Nov 1886

(3) Mary Laura; *m* 13 Aug 1857 Lewin Bentham Bowring, CSI, BCS, 3rd s of Sir John Bowring, and *d* 17 April 1866, leaving issue. He *d* 14 Jan 1910

(4) Christina Julia; *m* 3 Feb 1852 Edward Walford

(5) Mary Katherine; *m* 10 Sept 1856 Lucius Henry Fitzgerald, of Binfield, Berks, and *d* 27 Feb 1897 leaving issue. He *d* 9 Dec 1891

4 Thomas; Col, MLA Upper Canada; *d* 5 Feb 1853

5 Robert; *b* 1776; barrister; *m* 7 Oct 1828 Arabella (*d* 28 Oct 1855), widow of Hon Edward Bouverie, MP (*see* RADNOR, E), and dau of Adml Sir Chaloner Ogle, 1st Bt (*see* 1902 edn), and *d* 17 March 1843

6 Neil; Lt-Col 14th Light Dragons; *ka* Ciudad Rodrigo 1810

7 William; *d* 22 Dec 1845

1 Barbara; *m* 22 April 1792 Sir William Young, 2nd Bt, of Dominica (*qv*), and *dsp* 1 Feb 1830

2 Frances Gabriella; Countess (Austria), Canoness Roy Order St Anne Bavaria; *d* 28 April 1850

3 Catherine; *m* Oct 1797 Lt-Gen Sir George Airey, KCB, and *d* 13 May 1852, leaving issue. He *d* 18 Feb 1833

4 Ellza; *m* 1st George Waters Mellifont, of Ballenclea, Co Dublin; *m* 2nd 11 Nov 1844 Ellis Cunliffe Lister-Kay (*see* SWINTON, E) and *d* 13 July 1855

5 Charlotte; *m* 1st Lt-Col John Mervyn Cutcliffe, 23rd Dragoons, of Marwood Hill, Devon; *m* 2nd 1827 , as his 1st w, Gerald Fitzerald, JP, DL, of Coolanowle, Queen's Co, and Binfield, and *d* 9 Nov 1863, leaving issue. He *d* 15 Dec 1873

TANKERVILLE

Arms: Gu. a bezant between three demi-lions rampant arg. **Crests:** 1 Out of a mural coronet or a lion's head gu., charged on the neck with a bezant (for BENNET), 2 A double scaling-ladder or (for GREY). **Supporters:** Two lions arg., ducally crowned or, each charged on the shoulder with a torteau. **Motto:** *De bon vouloir servir le roy* ('To serve the king with goodwill'). **Creations:** B. (E) 24 Nov 1682, E. (GB) 19 Oct 1714.

THE 10TH EARL OF TANKERVILLE and **Baron Ossulston**, of Ossulston, Co Middx (Peter Grey Bennet) [The Rt Hon The Earl of Tankerville, 139 Olympia Way, San Francisco, CA 94131, USA]; *b* 18 Oct 1956; *s* f 1980; *educ* Grace Cathedral Sch San Francisco (chorister), Oberlin Conservatory, Ohio (BMus), and San Francisco State U (MA Mus)

Tankerville, previous creations: For the Anglo-Norman Countship of Tancarville, otherwise Tankerville or Tanquerville, *see* GREY, E, which also *see* for mention of the Barony of Grey of Warke, the 3rd and penultimate holder of which was promoted Earl of Tankerville in 1695 and was father-in-law of the **1st Earl** of the present creation (*see* below).

Lineage: ROGER BENNET, of Newbury, Berks; had:

THOMAS BENNET, of Newbury; had:

THOMAS BENNET, of London; had:

JOHN BENNET, of London and Newbury; *d c* 1559, leaving:

THOMAS BENNET, of Clapcot, nr Wallingford, Berks; *m* Anne, dau of Sir Michael Molines, of Mackney, Berks, and had:

1 RICHARD

2 Thomas (Sir); London: Sheriff 1594, Ld Mayor 1603–04, ktd 1603; bought 1609 Manor of Beachampton, Berks; *m* Mary, dau of Robert Taylor, Sheriff London *temp* ELIZABETH I, and *d* 16 Feb 1626/7, having had:

(1) Ambrose; *d* 22 March 1630/1

(2) Sir SIMON BENNET, 1st and last Bt (E), so *cr* 17 July 1627, of Beachampton; *m* 1624 Elizabeth (*d* 13 June 1636), dau of Sir Arthur Ingram, and *dsp* 21 Aug 1631, when the btcy expired

(3) Richard, of London; *m* Elizabeth (*m* 2nd Sir Heneage Finch; *see* WINCHILSEA and NOTTINGHAM, E), dau of William Cradock, and had:

1a Simon, of Beachampton, which inherited from his uncle the 1st and last Bt; *m* Grace, dau of Gilbert Moorwood, and *d* 1682, leaving:

1b Elizabeth; *m* Edward Osborne, Viscount Latimer, est s of 1st Duke of Leeds (*see* 1963 edn), and *dsps* 1 May 1680, having had two sons (*d* in infancy)

2b Grace; *m* John Bennet, of Abington, Cambs

3b Frances; *m* 13 July 1683 4th Earl of Salisbury (*see* SALISBURY, M) and *d* 7 or 8 July 1713, leaving issue

3 John; *dsp*

1 Anna; *m* William Duncombe, of Brickhill, Bucks

2 Margaret; *m* Sir George Croke, Judge Common Pleas

The er s,

RICHARD BENNET, of Clapcot; *m* Elizabeth, dau of Thomas Tisdale, of Sandford, Berks, and had:

1 Ralph; ancestor of the BENNETs of Morden, Surrey

2 JOHN (Sir)

3 Thomas; London: Alderman, Sheriff 1613–14; *m* Dorothy, dau of Richard May, of Rawmers, Sussex, and *d* 19 April 1620, having had issue

(1) Richard; had:

1a Jane; *m* 14 Sept 1648 James Scudamore (*dvp* 18 June 1668), s of 1st Viscount Scudamore of Sligo, and *d* 21 Feb 1699/1700, leaving issue (*see* BEAUFORT, D)

(2) Sir THOMAS BENNET, 1st Bt (E), so *cr* 22 Nov 1660, of Babraham, Cambs; *b c* 1597; *educ* Inner Temple; *m c* 1630 Mary, dau of Levinus Monke, and was *bur* 30 June 1667, leaving:

1a Sir LEVINUS BENNET, 2nd Bt; *b c* 1631; *educ* Gray's Inn; Sheriff Cambs 1652–53, MP Cambs 1679–93; *m* 6 July 1653 Judith, dau of William Boevey, of Flaxley Abbey, Glos (*see* CRAWLEY-BOEVEY, Bt), and *d* 5 Dec 1693, leaving, with eight daus:

1b Sir RICHARD BENNET, 3rd and last Bt; *bapt* 15 July 1673; *m* 27 June 1695 Elizabeth, dau of Sir Charles Caesar *alias* Adelmare, of Bennington, Herts, and *dspm* 23 May 1701, when the btcy expired, leaving a dau (Judith, *d* a child)

(1) Rebecca; *m* Sir Bulstrode Whitelock, Kt, *cr* Lord Whitelock by CROMWELL

The 2nd s,

Sir JOHN BENNET, of Dawley, Harlington, Middx; LLD, MP *temp* ELIZABETH, Commr to suppress heresy *c* 1600; Chllr to ANNE OF DENMARK, w of JAMES I; Judge Prerogative Court Canterbury, Chllr to Archbp York, Amb Spanish Netherlands 1617; *m* Anne, dau of Christopher Weeks, of Salisbury, Wilts, and *d* 1627, having had, with other issue, including a yr s (Sir Thomas, LLD, Master in Chancery, *m* 1st Charlotte, dau of William Harrison, of London, *m* 2nd Thomasine, dau and coheir of G Dethick, barrister, s of Sir William Dethick, Garter King of Arms, and by her had a s, Thomas Bennet, of Salthorp, Wilts):

Sir JOHN BENNET, of Dawley; *m* Dorothy, dau of Sir John Crofts, of Saxham, Suffolk, and *d* Nov 1658, having had, with other issue, including a yr s (HENRY BENNET, 1st EARL OF ARLINGTON; *see* GRAFTON, D):

JOHN BENNET, **1st Baron Ossulston**, of Ossulston, Co Middx (E), so *cr* 24 Nov 1682, KB (1661); *bapt* 5 July 1616; *educ* Pembroke Coll Oxford and Gray's Inn; Lt Gentlemen Pensioners *c* 1662–76, MP Wallingford 1663–79, Dep Post Master 1666–72; *m* 1st 28 Oct 1661 Elizabeth, widow of 2nd Earl of Musgrave of the Feb 1625/6 *cr* (*see* NORMANBY, M, preliminary remarks, and SHEFFIELD, Bt) and dau of Lionel Cranfield, 1st Earl of Middlesex, but by her had no issue; *m* 2nd *c* 1 May 1673 Bridget, sis of 1st Viscount Howe (*see* HOWE, E), and *d* 11 Feb 1694/, leaving:

CHARLES BENNET, **1st Earl of Tankerville** (GB), so *cr* 19 Oct 1714, KT (Feb 1720/1), PC (1716); *b c* 1674; *m* 3 July 1695 Lady Mary Grey, only dau and heiress of 3rd Baron Grey of Warke and 1st and last Earl of Tankerville of the 11 June 1695 *cr*, and *d* 21 May 1722, leaving:

1 CHARLES, **2nd Earl**

1 Bridget; *m* 20 May 1716 1st Earl of Portsmouth (*qv*) and *d* 12 Oct 1738, leaving issue

2 Annabella; *m* 10 Feb 1721 William Paulet and *d* 18 Nov 1769, leaving issue (*see* WINCHESTER, M)

3 Mary; *m* 1720 William Willmer, MP, of Sywel, Notts, and *d* 1729

The 1st EARL's s,

CHARLES BENNET, **2nd Earl of Tankerville**, KT (1730); *bapt* 21 Dec 1697; *educ* Eton and Winchester; Capt 8th Dragoons 1716, a Ld Bedchamber to PRINCE OF WALES 1729–33, Master Buckhounds 1733–37, a Ld Bedchamber 1737–38, Ld Lt Northumberland 1740–53; *m c* 1715 Camilla, Ldy Bedchamber to GEORGE II's QUEEN CAROLINE, dau of Edward Colville, butcher, of Whitehouse, Co Durham, and *d* 14 March 1753, having had, with a dau and a yr s (George, *b* 1727, *d* 1799):

CHARLES BENNET, **3rd Earl of Tankerville**; *b* 6 Sept 1716; *educ* Winchester; Ensign 3rd Foot Gds 1734, Capt 24th Foot 1739, Maj Cotterell's Regt of Foot 1741, Lt-Col 1st Foot Gds 1743–49, MP (Whig) Northumberland 1748–49; *m* 22 Sept 1742 Alicia (*d* 1755), 4th dau of Sir John Astley, 2nd and last Bt, of Patshull, Staffs, and *d* 27 Oct 1767, having had, with another s (*d* young):

1 CHARLES, **4th Earl**

2 Henry Astley; Gen; *d* 1815

1 Camilla Elizabeth; *m* 1st 5 Sept 1764 Count Donhoff (*d* 25 Sept 1764), of Poland; *m* 2nd 1778 Robert Robinson and *d* 2 Sept 1821

2 Frances Alicia; *m* 1st William Aslong; *m* 2nd Rev Richard Sandys, est s of Richard Sandys, of Northborne Court, Kent; *m* 3rd Rev Edward Beckingham Benson, Rector Deal

The 3rd EARL's est s,

CHARLES BENNET, **4th Earl of Tankerville**, PC (1782); *b* 15 Nov 1743; *educ* Eton; Jt PMG 1782–83 and 1784–86; *m* 7 Oct 1771 Emma (*d* 20 Nov 1836), yr dau and coheir of Sir James Colebrook, 1st Bt (*see* 1939 edn COLEBROOKE, B), and had:

1 CHARLES AUGUSTUS, **5th Earl**

2 Henry Grey; *b* 2 Dec 1777; *m* 15 May 1816 Gertrude Frances (*d* 23 Jan 1841), est dau of Lord William Russell (*see* BEDFORD, D), and *d* 29 May 1836, leaving:

(1) Charlotte Emma Georgiana; *b* 24 Jan 1818; *m* 24 Nov 1839 Rt Hon Fitzstephen (Patrick) French, MP, bro of 1st Baron de Freyne (*qv*), and had issue

(2) Gertrude Frances; *m* 1 Aug 1839 Hamilton Gorges, of Kilbrew, Co Meath. He *d* 1860

3 John Astley; *b* 21 Dec 1778; Capt RN; *m* 27 Aug 1811 Julia (*m* 2nd 19 May 1819 her former sis-in-law's widower 1st Baron Wrottesley (*qv*) and *d* 29 Sept 1860), dau of John Conyers, of Copthall, Essex, and *d* 14 Sept 1812

1 Caroline; *b* 22 Oct 1772; *m* 23 June 1795 1st Baron Wrottesley and *d* 7 March 1818, leaving issue

2 Anna; *b* 28 April 1774; *m* 19 July 1804 Rev Hon William Beresford, 3rd s of 1st Baron Decies (*qv*), and *d* Sept 1836, leaving issue

3 Margaret Alicia Emma; *b* 8 Aug 1780; *d* unm 27 March 1813

4 Mary Elizabeth; *b* 21 May 1785; *m* 26 July 1831 Sir Charles Miles Lambert Monck, 6th Bt (*see* MIDDLETON, Bt), and *d* 27 Feb 1861

5 Augusta; *b* 11 Nov 1786; *m* as his 1st w William Fanning, of Finchley, Middx, and Hendrick Ho, Oxon, and *dspm* 10 Feb 1809

6 Harriet; *b* 2 Dec 1788; *d* unm 6 March 1801

The 4th EARL *d* 10 Dec 1822; his est s,

CHARLES AUGUSTUS BENNET, **5th Earl of Tankerville**, PC (1806); *b* 28 April 1776; *educ* Eton and Trin Coll Cambridge; MP (Whig) Steyning 1803–06, Knaresborough 1806–18 and Berwick 1820–22, Treas Household 1806–07; *m* 28 July 1806 Corisande Armandine Sophie Leonice Hélène (*d* 23 Jan 1865), dau of Antoine Louis Marie Duc de Gramont, and *d* 25 June 1859, leaving, with two daus (including Corisande Emma, *m* 13 April 1830 3rd Earl of Malmesbury (*qv*) and *dsp* 17 May 1876):

CHARLES AUGUSTUS BENNET, **6th Earl of Tankerville**, PC (1866), JP, DL Northumberland; *b* 10 Jan 1810; *educ* Harrow and Ch Ch Oxford; MP (C) N Northumberland 1832–59, called up to Ho Lds *vp* in f's Barony 1859, Capt Gentlemen at Arms 1866–67, Ld Steward Household 1867–68; *m* 29 Jan 1850 Lady Olivia Montagu (*d* 15 Feb 1922), est dau of 6th Duke of Manchester (*qv*), and had:

1 Charles, *Lord Ossulston*; *b* 31 Dec 1850; *educ* Harrow; Lt Coldstream Gds 1870, Rifle Bde 1873, Afghan War 1878–79; *dvp* unm of cholera in India 29 June 1879

2 GEORGE MONTAGU, **7th Earl**

3 Frederick Augustus; *b* 30 May 1853; MA, barrister; *dvp* unm 5 Sept 1891

1 Corisande Olivia; *d* unm 11 Jan 1941

2 Ida Louise; *m* 6 Dec 1877 13th Earl of Dalhousie (*qv*) and *d* 24 Nov 1887, leaving issue

The 6th EARL *d* 18 Dec 1899; his only surv s,

GEORGE MONTAGU BENNET, **7th Earl of Tankerville**, JP, DL Northumberland; *b* 30 March 1852; *educ* Radley; RN: joined 1865, Midshipman 1867–69, Lt Rifle Bde 1872–80, ADC to Ld Lt Ireland 1876–80; *m* 23 Oct 1895 Leonora Sophia, VAD (*d* 15 Feb 1949), dau of James G van Marter, of New York, and had:

1 CHARLES AUGUSTER KER, **8th Earl**

2 George William; *b* 21 Nov 1903; *educ* Winchester and Trin Coll Cambridge (BA 1925, MA 1933); FBHI; *m* 12 Feb 1929 Constance Clare (*d* 26 Nov 1986), er dau of Cyril Wace, of Victoria, BC, and *dsp* 12 Feb 1981

1 Georgina; *b* 16, *d* 17 July 1896

2 Ida Olivia Sophie; *b* 10 Nov 1898; *d* May 1900

The 7th EARL *d* 9 July 1931; his er s,

CHARLES AUGUSTUS KER BENNET, **8th Earl of Tankerville**, JP (Northumberland 1939); *b* 16 Aug 1897; *educ* Eton; Lt RNAS and Capt RAF WW I, F/Lt RAFVR, Life Pres and Fndr Chillingham Wild Cattle Assoc, ARAeS; *m* 1st 20 Oct 1920 (*divorce* 1930) Roberta (*d* 23 Nov 1992), dau of John Nolan, of Chicago, and step-dau of Percy Mitchell, and had:

1 CHARLES AUGUSTUS GREY BENNET, **9th Earl of Tankerville**; *b* 28 July 1921; *educ* Radley; F/Lt RAFVR WW II; *m* 1st 15 May 1943 (*divorce* 1950) Virginia, formerly w of — Morris and dau of Louis M Diether, of Vancouver, BC, and had:

(1) Corisande Elizabeth; *b* 21 March 1947

1 (cont.) The **9th Earl** *m* 2nd 22 June 1954 Georgiana Lilian Maude, dau of Gilbert Wilson, DD, of Regina, Saskatchewan, and *d* 27 April 1980, leaving by her:

(1) PETER GREY BENNET, **10th and present Earl of Tankerville**

(2) Alexandra Katherine; *b* 5 May 1955; *d* 1993

(3) *Anne Thérèse; *b* 18 Oct 1956; *m* 1981 *Timothy Michael Poirier

2 +GEORGE ARTHUR GREY [The Rev The Hon George Bennet, 112 Norwich Rd, Wymondham, Norfolk NR18 0SZ]; *b* 12 March 1925; heir presumptive; *educ* Radley and Corpus Christi Coll Cambridge (BA 1946, MA 1951); C of E Deacon 1969, Priest 1970, Curate Radipole, Dorset, Vicar Shaston Team Ministry 1973–80, Rector Redenhall, Harleston, Wortwell and Needham 1980–90, turned RC 1994, Priest 1997, Assist Priest Wymondham Catholic Parish, late sr physics master Clifton, author: *Electricity and Modern Physics* (1965), *Progress through Lent* (1993) and *One Fold, One Shepherd* (1996); *m* 27 July 1957 *Hazel (Jane) Glyddon, only dau of Ernest William George Judson, of Bishopswood, Chard, Somerset, and has:

(1) +Adrian George; *b* 5 July 1958; *m* 1st 1984 (*divorce* 1991) Lucinda Mary, est dau of Ashley Bell, of Weetwood Hall, Wooler, Northumberland; *m* 2nd 1991 *Karel Ingrid Juliet Wensby-Scott

(2) +Neil Robert; *b* 23 March 1961

(1) *Helen Jane; *b* 31 May 1964

The **8th Earl** *m* 2nd 1 July 1930 *Violet, JP (Northumberland 1941) [The Rt Hon The Dowager Countess of Tankerville JP, Estate House, Chillingham, Northumberland], Order Vasa Sweden, dau of Erik Pallin, of Stockholm, and *d* 1 Dec 1971, leaving by her:

3 Ian; *b* 16 April 1935; *educ* Radley and Corpus Christi Coll Cambridge (BA Ag 1958, MA 1962); late Lt RNR; *d* unm 2 Nov 1998

1 *Corisande [The Lady Corisande Bain Smith, Wickens Manor, Charing, Kent]; *b* 10 April 1938; *m* 6 April 1963 *Lt-Cdr Timothy Bain Smith, RN, yr s of Lt-Col George Stewart Bain Smith, AM, of Ventonwyn, Cartmel, Lancs, and has:

(1) *James; *b* 16 Nov 1964; *educ* Winchester
(2) *Charles; *b* 1 Sept 1966; *educ* Winchester; *m* 4 Sept 1993 *Rebecca, dau of John Murphy, of St Anne's-on-Sea

TANLAW

Arms: Parted per chevron azure and argent, in chief two lymphads of the 2nd and in base a tiger's face affrontée proper, on a chief or a cross engrailed per cross indented azure and sable. **Crest:** A falcon proper, hooded gules, issuant out of a five-pointed Eastern crown or. **Supporters:** Dexter, a Prejevalski's mare proper; sinister, a roe deer also proper. **Motto:** *Pro vita vivo* ('I live for life').
Creation: B. (LP, UK) 1971.

THE BARON TANLAW, of Tanlawhill, Co Dumfries (Simon Brooke Mackay) [The Rt Hon The Lord Tanlaw, Tanlawhill, by Langholm, Dumfriesshire DG13 0PQ; 31 Brompton Sq, London SW3 2AE]; *b* 30 March 1934; *educ* Eton and Trin Coll Cambridge (MA 1966); late 2nd Lt 12th Roy Lancers Malaya; with Inchcape Gp 1960–66, md Inchcape & Co 1967–71 (dir 1971–92); Jt Treas Scottish Lib Party 1971–72 (Dep Chm 1972); chm: Thwaites & Reed 1971–74, Fandstan Gp 1973– (md 1973–), Building Ctee Buckingham U 1973–78, Parly Liaison Gp for Alternative Energy Strategies 1981–83; memb: Ld Chllr's Inner London Advsy Ctee on JPs 1972–83, Cncl Management Buckingham U 1973–, EC Sub Ctee F 1980–83, Ct Govrs LSE 1980–97; Pres: Sarawak Assoc 1972–75, Nat Appeal Elizabeth Fitzroy Homes 1985–; Fell Br Horological Inst 1997–; Hon Treas Scottish Peers Assoc 1979–85; Hon Fell Buckingham U 1981, DU 1983; *m* 1st 1959 *Joanna Susan, only dau of Maj John Henry Hirsch, of Sungrove Lodge, Newbury, and has had:

1 *James Brooke; *b* 1961; *m* *Anne-Marie, yr dau of Michael Barrett, of Midsomer Norton, Somerset
2 Joshua Alexander Brooke; *b* 1964; *d* 1967
1 *Iona Hélöise; *b* 1960; *m* 1978 (*divorce* 1988, resumed maiden name) Stephen P Hudson
2 *Rebecca Alexandra; *b* 1967; *m* 28 Jan 1995 *Mark Ayre-Smith, only s of Dr Robert Ayre-Smith, of Sydney, NSW

THE BARON TANLAW *m* 2nd 1976 *Rina Siew Yong, yst dau of Tiong Cha Tan, of Kuala Lumpur, Malaysia, and by her has:

3 *Asia Brooke; *b* 1980
3 *Brooke Brooke; *b* 1982

Lineage: The 2nd EARL OF INCHCAPE (*qv*) had (by his 2nd w) a 4th s:

SIMON BROOKE, *cr* a **Baron**

TAPPS GERVIS MEYRICK

Arms: Quarterly, 1st and 4th, sable on a chevron argent between three brands erect raguly or inflamed proper a fleur-de-lys gules between two Cornish choughs respecting each other, also proper (for MEYRICK); 2nd, argent between six ostrich feathers sable a cannon-ball of the last (for GERVIS); 3rd, azure on a fess or between three rhinoceroses argent as many escallops gules (for TAPPS).
Crests: 1 A tower argent, thereon, upon a mount vert, a Cornish chough proper, holding in the dexter claw a fleur-de-lys gules (for MEYRICK), 2 A greyhound couchant per pale argent and sable, charged on the body with two escallops fessways counterchanged (for TAPPS), 3 A plume of three ostrich feathers gules and sable bound by a wreath of laurel or, standing upon a mound proper (for GERVIS). **Mottoes:** *Heb Dduw, heb ddim, Duw a digon* ('Without God is to be without anything; God is enough').
Creation: Bt. (GB) 28 July 1791.

SIR GEORGE CHRISTOPHER CADAFAEL TAPPS GERVIS MEYRICK, 7TH BT, of Hinton Admiral, Co Southampton [Sir George Tapps Gervis Meyrick Bt, Hinton Admiral, nr Christchurch, Dorset BH23 7DY; Bodorgan, Anglesey]; *b* 10 March 1941; *s f* 1988; *educ* Eton and Trin Coll Cambridge; *m* 14 March 1968 *Jean Louise, yst dau of Lord William Walter Montagu Douglas Scott, MC (*see* BUCCLEUCH and QUEENSBERRY, D), and has:

1 +GEORGE WILLIAM OWEN; *b* 3 April 1970
2 +Charles Valentine Llewelyn; *b* 1972
1 *Suzannah Daisy; *b* 1978

Lineage (of Meyrick): EINION SAIS (*i.e.*, 'Saxon', from his being so much in England) Ap DAFYDD Ab IORWERTH, of Bodorgan, Llangadwaladr, Anglesey; Chamberlain at Richmond Palace to HENRY VI; *m* Efa, dau and heir of Maredudd ap Cadwgon, of Bodorgan, and had:

HEILIN; living 1465; appears to have *m* twice but it is uncertain by which w he had:

LLYWELYN Ap HEILIN; fought for HENRY VII Bosworth (his two-handed sword and salt-cellar being long preserved at Bodorgan); *m* Angharad, dau of Gwilym ap Gruffudd, of Llanfigel, and had:

MEURIG Ap LLYWELYN, of Bodorgan; *m* Margaret, dau of Syr Roland ap Hywel, incumbent Aberffraw, and had numerous issue, including, with a 2nd s (Roland, *b* 1505, first Protestant Bp Bangor, *d* 1566, ancestor of the MEYRICKs of Goodrich Court, Herefs) and a 3rd s (Edmund, Archdeacon Bangor, *d* 1605), an est s:

RICHARD MEYRICK; living 1559; *m* Jane, dau of Llywelyn ap Rhys ap Llywelyn, of Bodfeddan, and had:

RICHARD MEYRICK, of Bodorgan; *m* Margaret, dau of Rhys Wynn ap John, of Bodychen, Llandrgarn, Anglesey, and *d* by 1597, leaving:

RICHARD MEYRICK, of Bodorgan; *b c* 1567; High Sheriff Anglesey 1641; *m* Jane, dau of John Wyn ap Rhys, of Bodfeddan, and *d* between 18 Aug 1644 and 16 Jan 1644/5, leaving:

RICHARD MEYRICK; High Sheriff Anglesey 1647–48; *m* 1st Catherine, dau of Thomas Glyn, of Glynllifon, Llandwrog, Caernarvs; *m* 2nd Jane, dau of Owen Wood, of Llangwyfen, Anglesey; *m* 3rd Gaenor, dau of Hugh Gwyn Bodwrda, and *d* Nov 1669, leaving by his 2nd w:

WILLIAM MEYRICK; High Sheriff Anglesey 1675; had an est surv s:

OWEN MEYRICK; Anglesey: High Sheriff 1706, MP 1715–21; his 4th s:

RICHARD MEYRICK; *m* 25 July 1732 Jane, est dau of Charles Cholmondeley (*see* DELAMERE, B); his est s:

OWEN MEYRICK; *b* 1705; MP Anglesey 1761–68; *m* Esther, dau of J Putland, and had an est s:

OWEN PUTLAND MEYRICK; *m* Clara, dau and heiress of Richard Garth, of Morden, Surrey, and had:

CLARA Meyrick; *m* Augustus Eliott FULLER, of Rosehill Park, Sussex, and had:

1 Owen John Augustus FULLER later FULLER-MEYRICK (roy licence 6 May 1825); *d* unm 12 Feb 1876

2 Clara Fuller; *m* **Sir George William Tapps Gervis, 2nd Bt** (*see* below), and had:

  ?(1) Sir GEORGE ELIOTT TAPPS GERVIS later TAPPS GERVIS MEYRICK (added with arms under terms of his ggf OWEN's will), **3rd Bt**

Lineage (of Tapps Gervis): GEORGE GERVIS/JARVIS; *b* 1635; *d* 1718, leaving:

1 Lydia; *m* Sir Peter Mews, MP Christchurch, s of Rt Rev Peter Mews, DD, Bp Winchester, and *dsp* 6 April 1751

2 Agnes Maria; *m* William Clerke, of Buckland and Cromer Hall, Herts, and *d* 6 Jan 1726, leaving:

  (1) Benjamin; *m* Elizabeth, dau of J Hill, of Knavistock, and *d* 11 Feb 1758, having had:

    1a Joseph Gervis/Jarvis; *dsp*

3 Catherine; *m* Richard Tapps and had:

  (1) George Gervis; *m* Mary, dau of T Buck, and *d* 1735, leaving:

    1a George Gervis, of Hinton Admiral; barrister Lincoln's Inn; *m* Jane, dau of J Ivison, of Carlisle, and *d* 10 May 1774, leaving:

      1b GEORGE IVISON (Sir), **1st Bt**

      1b Jane; *m* Sir George Buggin (*m* 2nd Lady Cecilia Letitia Underwood, dau of 2nd Earl of Arran (*qv*); she *m* 2nd HRH AUGUSTUS FREDERICK, DUKE OF SUSSEX, and was *cr* Duchess of Inverness 1840), s of Barrington Buggin, and had issue

GEORGE TAPPS's only s,

Sir George Ivison Tapps, 1st Bt (GB), so *cr* 28 July 1791; *b* 5 Jan 1753; *m* 29 July 1790 Sarah (*d* 11 July 1813), dau of the above Barrington Buggin, and *d* 15 March 1835, leaving an only s:

Sir GEORGE WILLIAM TAPPS later TAPPS GERVIS, **2nd Bt**; *b* 24 May 1795; MP Christchurch; *m* 26 Sept 1825 Clara (*d* Dec 1831), est dau of Augustus Eliott Fuller, of Rosehill and Ashdown Ho, Sussex, and *d* 26 Aug 1842, having had:

1 GEORGE ELIOTT MEYRICK (Sir), **3rd Bt**

2 John Owen; *b* 19 July 1829; *d* 21 March 1844

3 Augustus; *b* 10 Dec 1831; *m* 1860 Maria Catherina Hortencia (*m* 2nd 1865 H R C Litchfield, LRCP) and *d* 17 April 1864, leaving:

  (1) Augusta Maria; *m* 2 Jan 1884 John Alexander Tynedale Powell (*m* 2nd 19 June 1900 Elizabeth Laura, dau of Rev Arthur Kemble, and *d* 2 June 1910, having had further issue), s of Alexander Pitts Elliott Powell, JP, DL, of Hurdcott Ho, Wilts, and *d* 2 Dec 1898, having had issue

1 Clara; *d* unm 10 April 1910

Sir GEORGE's est s,

Sir GEORGE ELIOTT MEYRICK TAPPS GERVIS later TAPPS GERVIS MEYRICK (roy licence 16 March 1876), **3rd Bt**; *b* 1 Sept 1827; High Sheriff Anglesey 1878; *m* 4 Dec 1849 Fanny (*d* 24 June 1892), 4th dau of Christopher Harland, of Ashbourne, Derbys, and *d* 7 April 1896, leaving:

1 GEORGE AUGUSTUS ELIOTT (Sir), **4th Bt**

1 Emma Douglas; *m* 20 Aug 1878 Maj Gerald Robert Spencer, RHA (*dsp* 13 May 1918), of Delves House, Ringmer, Sussex (*see* CHURCHILL, V), and *d* 29 May 1934

2 Clara; *m* 13 Aug 1895 Algernon John Fitzroy Nugent (*d* 15 March 1922), of Gally Hill, Winchfield, Hants, and *d* 20 April 1937

3 Fanny Augusta; *m* 2 Sept 1891 Francis John Douglas (*d* Jan 1934), of Nunwick, Simonburn, Northumberland, and *d* 5 April 1910, leaving issue (*see* 1970 edn DOUGLAS, Bt, of Springwood)

The 3rd Bt's s,

Sir George Augustus Eliott Tapps Gervis Meyrick, 4th Bt, of Hinton Admiral, JP, DL (Anglesey), JP (Hants); *b* 9 March 1855; High Sheriff Hants 1900; *m* 1 Oct 1884 Jacintha (*d* 21 April 1938), yst dau of Charles Paul Phipps, MP, of Chalcot, Wilts, and *d* 12 May 1928, leaving:

1 GEORGE LLEWELYN (Sir), **5th Bt**

2 Richard Owen, of Buckland Abbey, Nutwell Court and Yarcombe, Devon (estates inherited under the will of Lady Seaton); *b* 20 Oct 1892; *educ* Eton, Balliol Coll Oxford and RMC Sandhurst; Capt KRRC WW I; *m* 1st 21 March 1918 (*divorce* 1940) Evelyn Mabel, dau of Herbert James Harris, of Bowden, Lacock, Wilts, and had:

  (1) Richard Anthony; *b* 27 July 1920; *educ* Eton and Trin Coll Cambridge; Capt Gren Gds WW II (despatches); *m* 6 Jan 1949 *Alexandra Adele (Zandra) [Mrs Antony Baxter, Sheafhayne Manor, Yarcombe, nr Honiton, Devon] (*m* 2nd 20 June 1968 Antony Rising Baxter, s of Col D Baxter, of Longburton Ho, Sherborne, Dorset), dau of Brig Rupert Brett, DSO, of Langsmead House, Milton Common, Oxon, and *d* 14 April 1964, leaving:

    1a +James David; *b* 15 April 1950; *educ* Bredon Sch, Tewkesbury; *m* 1988 *Nicola Jane, dau of H M Williams, of White Ho, Llantilio Crossenny, Abergavenny, Gwent

    1a *Sarah Jacintha Barbara; *b* 14 Sept 1952; *m* 1989 *Walter John Dowe Taylor

  (2) Peter James Owen; *b* 16 May 1923; *educ* Eton; Lt Gren Gds WW II; *ka* 9 Sept 1944

2 (cont.) Richard Tapps Gervis Meyrick *m* 2nd 24 May 1940 *Bridget Mary, dau of John McLoughlin, of Dublin, and formerly w of Francis Samuel Nurse, and *d* 2 March 1948

1 Mary Jacintha; *m* 5 Jan 1929 Robert Weir Irving (*d* 11 Nov 1965), of NZ, and *dsp* 3 Oct 1973

2 Eva Clara

The 4th Bt's er s,

Sir George Llewelyn Tapps Gervis Meyrick, 5th Bt, JP (Hants), DL (Anglesey); *b* 23 Sept 1885; *educ* Eton and RMC Sandhurst; High Sheriff Anglesey 1939, Maj 7th Hus, RHG WW I (wounded, despatches), MFH New Forest 1919–60; *m* 28 Jan 1914 Marjorie (*d* 13 Jan 1972 aged 85), dau of Edward Hamlin, of Ceylon, and *d* 22 April 1960, leaving:

1 GEORGE DAVID ELIOTT (Sir), **6th Bt**

1 *Susan Hermione [Mrs Peter Green, Minstead Manor, Minstead, Lyndhurst, Hants]; *b* 29 Dec 1919; *m* 20 Sept 1945 *Peter John Green, MC, Roy Scots Fus, s of Capt Cecil Green, Coldstream Gds, and has issue

The 5th Bt's only s,

Sir George David Eliott Tapps Gervis Meyrick, 6th Bt, MC (1943), of Hinton Admiral; *b* 15 April 1915; *educ* Eton and Trin Coll Camb (BA 1937); High Sheriff Anglesey 1962, Lt-Col 9th Queen's Roy Lancers WW II (wounded, ret 1952); *m* 20 March 1940 *Ann [Dowager Lady Tapps Gervis Meyrick, Waterditch House, Bransgore, Christchurch, Dorset], yr dau of Edward Clive Miller, of Melbourne, Australia, and *d* 1988, leaving:

1 Sir GEORGE CHRISTOPHER CADAFAEL TAPPS GERVIS MEYRICK, **7th and present Bt**

1 *Caroline Susan Joan; *b* 30 April 1942; *m* 14 Nov 1963 *Richard Arthur Samuel Hulse, yr s of Sir (Hamilton) John Westrow Hulse, 9th Bt (*qv*), and has issue

TATE

THINCKE AND THANCKE

Arms: Erm. on a pale invected az. between four Cornish choughs ppr. two roses arg. **Crest:** A dexter arm embowed, vested az., cuffed or, the arm charged with two roses arg., the hand holding a pineapple erect slipped and two ears of wheat saltirewise, all ppr. **Motto:** *Thincke and thancke.* **Creation:** Bt. (UK) 27 June 1898.

SIR (HENRY) SAXON TATE, **5TH BT**, of Park Hill, Streatham Common, London, CBE (1991) [Sir Saxon Tate Bt CBE, 26 Cleaver Sq, London SE11 4EA]; *b* 28 Nov 1931; *s f* 1994; *educ* Eton and Ch Ch Oxford; Lt Life Gds 1949–51, dir Tate & Lyle plc 1956– (chm exec ctee 1973–78, md 1978–80, v chm 1980–82), chm London Futures and Options Exchange 1985–91, CEO Redpath Industries Ltd Canada 1965–73, ch exec Industrial Devpt Bd NI 1982–85, dir Tate Appointments Ltd 1982– (chm 1991–); FIMgt 1975; *m* 1st 5 Sept 1953 (*divorce* 1975) Sheila Ann (*d* 1987), est dau of Duncan Robertson (*see* WILLIAMS-WYNN, Bt); *m* 2nd 1975 *Virginia Joan Sturm and by his 1st w has:

1 +EDWARD NICHOLAS; *b* 2 July 1966

2 +Duncan Saxon; *b* 30 April 1968

3 +John William; *b* 8 Dec 1969

4 +Paul Henry; *b* 8 Dec 1969

Lineage: Rev WILLIAM TATE, of Chorley, Lancs; *b* 13 Oct 1773; *m* 13 Oct 1797 Agnes, dau of Nathaniel Booth, of Gildersome, Yorks, and *d* 9 May 1836, having had, with other issue:

Sir Henry Tate, 1st Bt (UK), so *cr* 27 June 1898, of Park Hill, Streatham Common, London, JP Surrey, London and Denbighs; *b* 11 March 1819; Tstee Nat Gallery, funded Tate Gallery; *m* 1st 1 March 1841 Jane (*d* 29 Nov 1883), dau of John Wignall, of Aughton, Lancs; *m* 2nd 8 Oct 1885 Amy Fanny, LGStJ (*d* 18 Oct 1919), only dau of Charles Hislop, of Brixton Hill, London, and *d* 5 Dec 1899, leaving by his 1st w, with another s (*d* an infant) and dau (*d* unm):

1 WILLIAM HENRY (Sir), **2nd Bt**

2 Alfred; *b* 12 Nov 1845; *m* 30 Sept 1874 Blanche (*d* 16 Aug 1939), dau of John Robert Hutton, of Liverpool, and *d* 30 Jan 1913, having had:

  (1) Reginald Henry; *b* 1 April 1877; *d* 11 June 1900

  (2) Alfred Leonard; *b* 26 May 1881; Maj 16th Lancers and Remounts; *m* 25 Feb 1909 Edith (*d* 6 Jan 1964 aged 90), dau of Henry Pooler, of Tibberton Manor, Newport, Salop

  (3) Eric Dean; *b* 29 Oct 1889; *d* unm 8 May 1962

  (1) Eveline; *m* 7 Dec 1912 Perceval Brodrick, s of Rev Alan Brodrick, Rector Brougham Gifford, Wilts, and *d* 19 March 1925

  (2) Pauline Blanche; *b* 13 Nov 1878; *m* 22 June 1899 John Thoburn McGaw, RI, RBA, of St Leonard's Forest, Horsham, s of Joseph McGaw, and *d* 24 April 1967, leaving issue. He *d* 21 April 1952

3 Edwin; *b* 22 March 1847; *m* 12 Aug 1874 Mary Edward (*d* 6 April 1935), dau of Alexander Guild, of Belfast, and *d* 14 Feb 1928, having had, with two other daus (*d* in infancy):

  (1) Edith Marguerite, MBE (1918); *b* 17 July 1878; *m* 5 Sept 1901 Frederick William Wignall, JP, DL, of The Rookery, Tattenhall, Cheshire, and Cambusmore, Sutherland, and *d* 3 April 1958, leaving issue. He *d* 6 May 1939

4 Caleb Ashworth; *b* 25 Oct 1850; *d* unm 5 April 1908

5 Henry; *b* 8 Dec 1853; *m* 26 Oct 1882 Grace (*d* 9 April 1945), dau of John Burton, of Streatham, and *d* 12 Feb 1902, leaving:

(1) Henry Burton; *b* 4 Oct 1883; *educ* Eton; Capt Warwicks Yeo WW I; *m* 1st 22 July 1909 (*divorce* 1925) Ida Guendolen (*d* 1969), only child of Robin Legge, of Chelsea, and had:

1a Anthony Henry; *b* 31 May 1910; *d* 26 Dec 1931

2a Robin David; *b* 21 March 1913; *d* 26 Dec 1931

1a *Julia Elizabeth Mary [Mme Paul Bernard, 22 Rue des Réservoirs, Versailles, France]; *b* 1 May 1919; *m* 7 July 1959 *Paul Georges Bernard, s of Charles Bernard, of Soisy-sur-Seine

(1) (cont.) Henry Tate *m* 2nd 22 Aug 1925 (*divorce* 1944) Maybird (later Mavis) Constance, JP (*d* 5 June 1947), formerly w of Capt Gerald Ewart Gott, MC, and only dau of Guy Weir Hogg (*see* HOGG, Bt); *m* 3rd 17 March 1944 Gwen (*d* 12 Oct 1957), yst dau of Herbert Edwards, of The Old Hall, Findern, Derbys, and *d* 29 Jan 1962

(2) Arthur Wignall, DSO (1919); *b* 14 April 1888; Lt Scottish Rifles, Lt-Col 3rd Bn Black Watch WW I (despatches twice, Croix de Guerre); *m* 20 Oct 1910 (Violet) Elaine (*d* 7 Nov 1973), only child of F W Few, and *d* 8 March 1939, leaving:

1a *Monica [Mrs Douglas Pelly, Swaynes Hall, Widdington, nr Newport, Essex]; *b* 1912; *m* 14 May 1935 *Douglas Gurney Pelly (*see* PELLY, Bt) and has issue

6 George Booth; *b* 15 Jan 1857; *m* 24 July 1884 Edith Katherine (*d* 31 Dec 1937), dau of James Walker Yates, of Ashton-on-Mersey, Cheshire, and *d* 30 April 1936, leaving:

(1) Kenneth Wylie; *b* 30 May 1885; *d* Feb 1968

(2) Gerald Ainslie; *b* 7 Jan 1889; *educ* Winchester and Univ Coll Oxford; *m* 15 Nov 1934 Audrey Barbara, widow of Henry David Cooper and 2nd dau of Capt Charles Norman Lacy, of Hove, Sussex, and *dsp* 22 May 1960

(3) (George) Vernon, MC (1919); *b* 21 April 1890; *educ* Winchester and Oxford; Capt 1st Bn Middx Regt WW I; *m* 22 Sept 1922 Evelyn Victoria (*d* 1979), widow of (a) 25th Baron de Clifford (*qv*) and (b) Arthur Roy Stock and dau of Walter Robert Chandler, and *d* 30 Sept 1955, leaving:

1a *Pamela Aloysia [Mrs Henry Forbes, 5 Lyne Place Manor, Bridge Lane, Virginia Water, Surrey GU25 4ED]; *b* 1923; *m* 5 July 1946 *Henry Forbes, yr s of Adml of the Fleet Sir Charles Morton Forbes, GCB, DSO, of Cawsand Place, Wentworth, Surrey, and has:

1b *Timothy John [Timothy Forbes Esq, Madrid Ho, 88 Bromfelde Rd, London SW4 6PS]; *b* 18 May 1947; *educ* Stowe; *m* 1973 *Rosemary Elisabeth Balliol, dau of Humphrey Salmon, and has:

1c *Charles Morton; *b* 1975

2c *Edward (Ned) Alexander; *b* 1983

1b *Amanda Aloysia Nicolette [Mrs Peter Woodroffe, 13 Cadogan St, London SW3 2PP]; *b* 4 April 1950; *m* 1973 *Peter Mackelean Woodroffe and has:

1c *Justin Mackelean; *b* 1977

2c *Clifford Derry; *b* 1979

2b *Vanessa Christina [Mrs John Kelly, Glenwood, 5 King Edward Rise, Ascot, Berks SL5 8JZ]; *b* 12 Jan 1955; *m* 19– *John Kelly

2a Virginia Ann; *b* 1931; *m* 27 May 1953 *Michael Jeremy Kindersley Belmont, est s of Capt Algernon Spencer Belmont, RA (*see* KINDERSLEY, B), and *d* 199–, leaving:

1b *Piers Anthony Robert; *b* 11 Sept 1954; *m* 1982 *Sally Anne Treweeke and has:

1c *Edward Algernon Spencer; *b* 1987

2c *Oliver Jeremy Thomas; *b* 1990

2b *Anthony Vernon Spencer; *b* 29 July 1956

1b *Elisa Ann; *b* 28 Jan 1959; *m* 1986 *Richard George Ford, s of Sir Edward Ford, KCB, KCVO, ERD (*see* SHREWSBURY and WATERFORD, E), and has issue

(1) Jane Marjorie; *b* 5 Oct 1895; *m* 17 Nov 1920 Redvers Arthur Oldham (*d* 1960), est s of Arthur Combermere Oldham, of Headley, Surrey, and has issue. He *d* 25 Sept 1960

1 Isolina; *m* 10 Sept 1879 Col Thomas Gee, JP, and *d* 5 March 1935. He *d* 5 Dec 1923

2 Agnes Esther; *m* 25 Oct 1876 Col Herbert John Robinson, s of John Robinson, of Ludlow, Salop, and *d* 26 Aug 1929, leaving issue. He *d* 25 Dec 1906

The 1st Bt's est s,

Sir William Henry Tate, 2nd Bt, JP, DL Lancs; *b* 23 Jan 1842; High Sheriff 1907; *m* 18 Nov 1863 Caroline Hill Rigby Glasgow (*d* 14 Dec 1927), adopted dau of John Glasgow, of Old Trafford, Manchester, and had:

1 Arthur Glasgow; *b* 23 Dec 1864; *d* 16 May 1866

2 ERNEST WILLIAM (Sir), **3rd Bt**

3 Alfred Herbert; *b* 3 May 1872; *m* 31 March 1910 Elsie Louise Vincent (*d* July 1957), only dau of Louis William Jelf-Petit, of Bodhyfrid, Llanrwst, N Wales, and *d* 25 May 1930, leaving:

(1) Louis William; *b* 16 March 1911; *educ* Stowe; *m* 28 July 1934 *Mary Christine [Mrs Louis Tate, Little Sadlers, Grayswood Rd, Haslemere, Surrey], only dau of Robert Charles Bolton, of Hill Ho, Alton, Hants, and *d* 1986, leaving:

1a +Jeremy Louis [Jeremy Tate Esq, Old Quarry Rise, Hargate Hill, Glossop, Derbys]; *b* 7 May 1937; *educ* Stowe; *m* 16 Sept 1961 *Rosemary Helen, dau of Charles David Collins, of Sawbridgeworth, Herts, and has:

1b +William James Louis; *b* 3 July 1965

1b *Julia Rosemary; *b* 11 April 1963

2b *Emma Margaret Rebecca; *b* 1976

(2) Francis Herbert; *b* 3 April 1913; *educ* privately and Ch Ch Oxford; *m* 4 Sept 1937 *Esther Frances [Mrs Francis Tate, Little Wissett, Hook Heath Gdns, Woking, Surrey GU22 0QG], only dau of Sir John Bromhead Matthews, KC, and *d* 12 Jan 1998, leaving:

1a +David Anthony [David Tate Esq, Stone Cross House, Crowborough, E Sussex TN6 3SH]; *b* 1 March 1941; *educ* Uppingham and Ch Ch Oxford; *m*

31 July 1969 *Jennifer Anne, only dau of John MacAndrews, of Harley St, W1, and has:

1b +Rupert David; *b* 1974

2b +Matthew Francis; *b* 1976

1a *Caroline Frances [Mrs Caroline Brisbane, 14 Balaclava Rd, Surbiton, Surrey KT6 5PN]; *b* 2 June 1946; *m* 1st 1973 (*divorce* 1984) Bruce Jerrit and has:

1b *Benedict Sinclair; *b* 1976

2b *Giles Zachary; *b* 1978

1a (cont.) Mrs Caroline Jerrit *m* 2nd 1984 (*divorce* 1991) Guy William Brisbane and by him has:

1b *Tessa Jennifer; *b* 1986

2a *Marianne Esther; *b* 10 June 1949

(3) John Frederick Peter; *b* 31 Jan 1923; *educ* Stowe; *m* 24 June 1949 *Celia Judith [Mrs John Tate, 7 Fisherton Island, Salisbury, Wilts SP2 7TG], dau of Adrian Corbett, and *d* 1989, leaving:

1a +Christopher John [Christopher Tate Esq, 22 Kings Court South, Chelsea Manor Gdns, London SW3 5EG]; *b* 1 May 1953; *educ* Stowe; *m* 1978 (*divorce* 1991) Jane, est dau of Capt A Bickett, of Derwas, Dolwen, Abergele, Clwyd, and has:

1b +Alexander John; *b* 1984

1b *Daisy Virginia; *b* 1981

1a *(Anne) Teresa [Mrs Rodney Reznek, 15 Park Ave North, London N8 7RU]; *b* 30 April 1951; FRCP, FRCR; *m* 1982 *Prof Rodney Reznek FRCP, FRCR

2a *Nicola Helen [Mrs Michael van der Gucht, Plume House, Up Nately, Hants RG27 9PR]; *b* 30 March 1955; *m* 1976 *Michael van der Gucht and has:

1b *Charles Graham; *b* 1980

2b *Benjamin Michael; *b* 1985

1b *Sarah Celia; *b* 1982

2b *Victoria Anthea; *b* 1992

3a *Sophia Louise [Mrs Thomas Wright, c/o John Swire & Sons (HK) Ltd, PO Box 1, GPO Hong Kong]; *b* 1 Aug 1958; *m* 1986 *Thomas Wright, and has:

1b *Matthew Adam Christopher; *b* 1988

1b *Katherine Elizabeth; *b* 1992

1 Ethel Caroline; *m* 11 June 1896 Col William Winwood Gossage, JP, RFA, and *d* 4 Jan 1948, leaving issue. He *d* 28 Aug 1934

2 Helen Frances; *m* 11 June 1896 Major Guy Winwood Gossage, RA (TF), and *d* 11 July 1944. He *d* 1917

3 Agnes Mary; *m* 29 April 1908 Lt-Col John Clements Waterhouse Madden, JP, DL, of Hilton Park, Co Monaghan, and *d* 3 May 1962, leaving issue. He *d* 22 Dec 1935

4 Isabel Marion; *m* 20 July 1905 Trevor Eyton, JP, DL, 2nd s of Adam Eyton, of Llanerch-y-Mohr, Flint, and *d* 23 Aug 1961, leaving issue. He *d* 26 June 1939

5 Caroline Beatrice; *b* 4 Oct 1877; *m* 22 Aug 1905 Maj Frederick Winwood Robinson, DSO, RFA, est s of Herbert John Robinson, of Moor Wood, Cirencester, and *d* 27 Feb 1965 aged 87. He *d* 18 April 1917 of wounds recd in action

6 Winifred; *m* 1st 23 Jan 1902 (*divorce* 1928) Alfred Hood (*d* 6 March 1940), of Strathalyn, Rosset, Denbighs, s of William Hood, of Chapelton, Kirkcudbrightshire, and had issue; *m* 2nd 14 June 1928 Frank Moffatt Smith, JP, and *d* May 1969. He *d* 6 March 1940

7 Beatrice; *m* 5 June 1907 Robert Holme Storey, JP, yst s of Sir Thomas Storey, and had issue. He *d* 15 Jan 1956

The 2nd Bt *d* 31 Dec 1921; his est surv s,

Sir Ernest William Tate, 3rd Bt, JP, DL Denbighs; *b* 7 Jan 1867; Denbighs: Maj Yeo, High Sheriff 1919; *m* 20 April 1892 Mildred Mary (*d* 3 Jan 1942), 2nd dau of Frederick Herbert Gossage, JP, of Camp Hill, Woolton, Liverpool, and had:

1 HENRY (Sir), **4th Bt**

1 Mildred Clara; *b* 20 July 1894; *m* 1st 24 Feb 1922 her aunt's bro-in-law Henry Winwood Robinson (*d* 31 March 1937), of Moor Wood, Cirencester, 3rd son of Col Herbert John Robinson of Upton Manor, Cheshire; *m* 2nd 1942 S/Ldr John Francis Mead, RAFVR. He *d* 28 April 1937

2 Joan; *b* 26 Dec 1896; *m* 29 April 1924 Lt-Col Roderick Croil Lloyd, DSO, MC, TD, JP, Roy Welch Fus, s of Lt-Col Edward Lloyd, of Hafod, Mold, and had issue

The 3rd Bt *d* 25 April 1939; his only s,

Sir Henry Tate, 4th Bt, TD, DL (Rutland 1964); *b* 29 June 1902; *educ* Uppingham and RMC Sandhurst; Lt Gren Gds, Hon Lt-Col Roy Welch Fus, Lt-Col Rutland HG 1954–57, CC Rutland 1958, High Sheriff 1949, Jt MFH Cottesmore 1946–58, chm: Rutland Ag Soc 1948–68, Melton C Assoc 1965–69; *m* 1st 1 Oct 1927 Nairne (*d* 1984), dau of Saxon Gregson-Ellis, JP, of Plas Clough, Trefnant, Denbighs; *m* 2nd 1988 *Edna Stokes [Dowager Lady Tate, Preston Lodge, Withcote, Leics LE15 8DP; The Cottage, Galltfaenan, Trefnant, Clwyd], and *d* 1994, leaving by his 1st w:

1 Sir (HENRY) SAXON TATE, **5th and present Bt**

2 +(William) Nicolas [Nicolas Tate Esq, 58 Guildford Grove, London SE10 8JT]; *b* 19 Nov 1934; *educ* Eton and Ch Ch Oxford; late 2nd Lt Gren Gds; *m* 7 Dec 1960 *Sarah Rose, er dau of Lt-Col Angus John Campbell Rose by Mrs Robert James Stephen, of Jersey, and has had:

(1) +Rupert Sebastian; *b* 13 Nov 1962

(2) A son; *b* 27, *d* 29 July 1966

(1) Melissa Nairne; *b* 4 July 1964; *d* 27 Dec 1969

(2) *Georgina Nairne; *b* 8 March 1969

TAVERNE

Creation: B. (LP, UK) 31 Dec 1995.

THE BARON TAVERNE, of Pimlico, City of Westminster, (Dick Taverne, QC (1965)) [The Rt Hon The Lord Taverne QC, 60 Cambridge St, London SW1V 4QQ]; *b* 18 Oct 1928; *educ* Charterhouse and Balliol Coll Oxford; barrister 1954, MP (Lab) Lincoln 1962–Oct 1972, (Dem Lab) March 1973–Sept 1974, Parly U-Sec Home Office 1966–68, Treasury: Min State 1968–69, Fin Sec 1969–70; Dir Inst Fiscal Studies 1970 (Dir-Gen 1979–81, Chm 1981–82), Chm Public Policy Centre 1984–87, OLIM Investment Tst 1989–, dir Axa Equity and Law 1972–, chm Axa Equity and Law Life Assur Soc 1997–, dep chm Centl European Growth Fund 1994–, memb Nat Ctee SDP 1981–87 (SDP Parly candidate Peckham 1982 and Dulwich 1983), Lib Dem Fedl Policy Ctee 1989–90, Pres PRIMA Europe 1993–98 (dir 1987–, chm 1991–93)); author: *The Future of the Left: Lincoln and after* (1973); *m* 1955 *Janice Hennessey and has:
  1 *Suzanne; *b* 1960; formerly with S6 Warburg, with FT Finance (publishers) June–Oct 1998
  2 *Caroline; *b* 1963

Lineage: Dr N J M TAVERNE; *m* L V — and had:

DICK, *cr* a **Baron**

TAYLOR OF BLACKBURN

Arms: Argent a bar wavy cotised wavy sable between three roses gules, barbed and seeded proper, all within a bordure vert, thereon eight bees volant proper. **Crest:** Statant on a grassy mount proper a lion or, supporting with the dexter forepaw at its base, growing from the front of the mount, a rose branch proper, reflexed over the lion's back and ending in three roses gules, barbed and seeded proper, on the mid-most a bee, also proper. **Supporters:** Dexter, a dragon statant erect gules, eyed, langued, clawed and the barb of its tail or, gorged with a bar wavy sable, fimbriated argent, and in its jaws an olive branch proper; sinister, a bull statant erect in trian aspect gules, armed and unguled and the tuft of its tail or, also gorged with a bar wavy sable fimbriated argent and also holding in its mouth an olive branch proper. **Motto:** *Labore et arte ad finem* ('By hard work and skill to the end'). **Creation:** B. (LP, UK) 1978.

THE BARON TAYLOR OF BLACKBURN, of Blackburn, Co Lancashire (Thomas Taylor, CBE (1974, OBE 1969), JP (Blackburn 1960), DL (Lancs 1994)) [The Rt Hon The Lord Taylor of Blackburn CBE JP DL, 9 Woodview, Cherry Tree, Blackburn, Lancs BB2 5LL]; *b* 10 June 1929; *educ* Blakey Moor Elementary Sch; Supt Sunday Sch 1947–59; Treas Blackburn Lab Party 1964–76; Memb: Blackburn Town Cncl 1954–76 (Leader 1972–76, Chm Policy and Resources Ctee 1972–76), NW Ec Planning Cncl, NW AHA, Cncl for Educnl Technology UK, Nat Fndn Educnl Research England and Wales, Schs Cncl, Bd Norweb 1977–80, Regnl Rent Tbnl, Public Schools Commn; Dep Dir Central Lancs Family and Community Project; Dir: Cncls and Educnl Press, EDS (Consultant 1994–); Chm: Govt Ctee Enquiry Management and Govt Schs, Nat Fndn Visual Aids, NW Electricity Consumer Cncl 1977–1980, Juvenile Bench; Pres: Free Church Cncl 1962–68, Assoc Educnl Ctees; Memb Cncl and Fndr Memb Lancaster U (Dep Pro-Chllr 1974–95); Elder URC; consultant Shorrock Security Systems; Freeman Blackburn 1992; author: *Taylor Report* (1973), Hon LLD Lancaster U 1996; *m* 1950 *Kathleen, dau of John Edward Nurton, and has:
  1 *Paul Nurton [The Hon Paul Taylor, 1 Risdale Grove, Blackburn]; *b* 1953; *m* 1978 *Diane Brindle

Lineage: JAMES TAYLOR; *m* Edith Gladys — and had:

THOMAS, *cr* a **Baron**

TAYLOR OF GRYFE

Creation: B. (LP, UK) 1968.

THE BARON TAYLOR OF GRYFE, of Bridge of Weir, Renfrewshire (Thomas Johnston Taylor, DL (Renfrewshire 1970)) [The Rt Hon The Lord Taylor of Gryfe DL, 33 Seagate, Kingsbarns, Fife KY16 8SR]; *b* 27 April 1912; *educ* Bellahouston Acad Glasgow; Pres Scottish CWS 1965–70; Memb: Exec Ctee Scottish Cncl (Devpt and Industry) 1964, BR Bd 1968–80, Bd Scottish TV 1968–82, Scottish Ec Cncl 1971–74, Internat Advsy Cncl Morgan Grenfell (Scotland); Chm: Forestry Commn 1970–76, Scottish Rlwys Bd 1971–80, Morgan Grenfell (Scotland) 1973–85, Ec Forestry Gp 1976–81, Isaac and Edith Wolfson Tst, Scottish Peers Assoc, Scottish Action on Dementia 1989–95; Dir: Whiteaway Laidlaw & Co 1971–89; Scottish Metropolitan Property Co Ltd 1972–88, BR Property Bd 1972–82, Friends Provident 1972–82; Tstee Dulverton Tst; FRSE 1977, Order Merit Germany 1992; Hon LLD Strathclyde 1974; *m* 1943 *Isobel, dau of Williams Wands, and has:
  1 *Jill; *b* 1945; *m* 1st 1969 Dr Thomas Egli; *m* 2nd 1976 *Hans Waber
  2 *Joyce [The Hon Mrs Richards, 1 Woodland Rise, London N10 3UP]; *b* 1948; *m* 1st 1969 (*divorce* 1980) Alan Begbie and has issue; *m* 2nd 1982 *John Huw Lloyd Richards

Lineage: JOHN SHARP TAYLOR; had:

THOMAS JOHNSTON, *cr* a **Baron**

TAYLOR OF WARWICK

Creation: B. (LP, UK) 21 Aug 1996.

THE BARON TAYLOR OF WARWICK, of Warwick, Co Warwick (John David Beckett Taylor) [The Rt Hon The Lord Taylor of Warwick, House of Lords, London SW1A 0PW]; *b* 21 Sept 1952; *educ* Keele U; barrister Gray's Inn 1978, memb (C) Solihull Dist Cncl 1986–90, C Parly candidate Perry Bar 1987, Cheltenham 1992, Special Advsr Home Sec 1990–91, consultant Lowe Bell Communications 1991–92, dir NW Thames RHA 1992–93, BBC radio and TV presenter/producer 1994–, v-pres Small Business Bureau 1997–, and Br Bd Film Classification 1998–, memb IOD 1997; *m* 15 Aug 1981 *Dr Jean Katherine, dau of Dr Harry Binysh, and has:
  1 *Mark; *b* 31 Oct 1997
  1 *Laura; *b* 29 Oct 1987
  2 *Alexandra; *b* 16 Feb 1995

Lineage: DERIEF DAVID SAMUEL TAYLOR; accountant, prof cricketer (Warwicks); *m* Enid Maud Beckett and *d* 1989, leaving:

JOHN DAVID BECKETT, *cr* a **Baron**

TEBBIT

Creation: B. (LP, UK) 1992.

THE BARON TEBBIT, of Chingford, London Borough of Waltham Forest (Norman Beresford Tebbit, CH (1987), PC (1981)) [The Rt Hon The Lord Tebbit PC CH, House of Lords, London SW1A 0PW]; *b* 29 March 1931; *educ* Edmonton Co GS; RAF 1949–51, RAuxAF 1952–55, airline pilot 1953–70, MP (C) Epping 1970–74, Chingford 1974–92, PPS to Min State Employment 1972–73, Memb Select Ctee Sci and Tech, Chm C Aviation Ctee, V-Chm and Sec C Housing and Construction Ctee; Sec H of C New Town Members Ctee; Parly U-Sec Trade 1979–81, Min State Industry 1981, Sec State: Employment 1981–83, DTI 1983–85, Cncllr Duchy Lancaster 1985–87, Chm C Party 1985–87; dir: J C Bamford Excavators 1987–91, Sears Hldgs 1987–, BT 1987–, BET 1987–, Spectator (1828) Ltd 1989–; presenter Sky TV 1989–; columnist *The Sun* 1995–; author: *Upwardly Mobile* (1988), *Unfinished Business* (1991); *m* 1956 *Margaret Elizabeth, dau of Stanley Daines, of Chatteris, Isle of Ely, and has:
  1 *John Beresford; *b* 1958; *m* 1984 *Penelope Robinson and has a s and two daus
  2 *William Mark; *b* 1965; with Robert Fleming to 1995, Butterfield Securities 1995–98, Rea Bros 1998–; *m* 1992 *Vanessa Hurrell
  1 *Alison Mary; *b* 1960; *m* 1981 *Raymond Shakespeare Smith and has a s and a dau

Lineage: LEONARD ALBERT TEBBIT, of Enfield; *m* Edith — and had a 2nd s:

NORMAN BERESFORD, *cr* a **Baron**

TEDDER

Arms: Sable a sword enflamed palewise all proper, in chief an eagle affronty volant, head to sinister or. **Crest:** Issuant from an astral crown or a lion sejant guardant sable, armed and langued or, holding in the sinister fore-paw a sword enflamed as in the Arms. **Supporters:** Two representations of the God Horus, all proper. **Motto:** For Freedom. **Creation:** B. (UK) 23 Jan 1946.

THE 3RD BARON TEDDER, of Glenguin, Co Stirling (Robin John Tedder) [The Rt Hon The Lord Tedder, 11 Kardinia Rd, Mosman, NSW 2088, Australia]; *b* 6 April 1955; *s* f 1994; dir The Glenguin Wine Co, CTM Australia Ltd and Koonta Pty Ltd; *m* 1st 1977 Jennifer Peggy (*d* 1978), dau of John Mangan, of NZ; *m* 2nd 1980 *Rita Aristea, yr dau of John Frangidis, of Sydney, and by her has:

  1 +BENJAMIN JOHN; *b* 1985

  2 +Christopher Arthur; *b* 1986

  1 *Jacqueline Christina; *b* 1988

Lineage: WILLIAM HENRY TEDDER, of Hampstead; *m* Elizabeth (*d* 1907), 3rd dau of Richard Ferris, of Kensington, and *d* 1909, leaving, with an est s (Sir Henry Richard, *b* 25 June 1850, FSA, Sec and Librarian Athenaeum, *m* 1st Alice (*d* 1915), dau of D Callan, and had two daus, *m* 2nd 1916 Violet, dau of Frederick H Anns, and *d* 1 Aug 1924) and a yst s (Owen Hugh, *d* 1956 aged 83), a 2nd s:

Sir ARTHUR JOHN TEDDER, CB (1918), of Hemyock, Devon; *b* 26 Dec 1851; Inland Revenue 1871–1918, Ch Inspr Customs 1910–1911 (Commr Bd 1911–18), ktd 1909; *m* 29 Aug 1878 Emily Charlotte (*d* 1941), est dau of William Henry Bryson, of Earlswood, and *d* 11 Aug 1931, leaving, with a dau (Margaret Elizabeth, *d* unm 4 May 1951):

ARTHUR WILLIAM TEDDER, **1st Baron Tedder**, of Glenguin, Co Stirling (UK), so *cr* 23 Jan 1946, GCB (1942, KCB 1942, CB 1937); *b* 11 July 1890; *educ* Whitgift Sch Croydon and Magdalene Coll Cambridge (Hon Fell 1943, U Chllr 1950); Colonial Serv Fiji 1914, Dorset Regt, RFC and RAF WW I, Constantinople Expdny Force 1922–23, CO Air Armament Sch Eastchurch 1932–34, Dir Trg Air Min 1934–36, A/Cdre 1934, AOC RAF Far East 1936–38, AVM 1937, Dir-Gen R & D 1938–40, Dep C-in-C RAF Middle East 1940, AM 1941, AOC-in-C Middle East 1941–42 (despatches), C-in C Mediterranean Allied Air Forces 1943, Dep Supreme Cdr Br and US Expdny Force 1944, ACM 1945, Ch Air Staff 1946–49, Chm Br Jt Servs Mission Washington 1950–51, Marshal RAF 1954; Hon Col RA 1938, a Govr BBC 1950 (V-Chm 1951), Chm Standard Motor Co 1954, Hon DCL Oxfon 1945, Hon LLD Leeds, Glasgow and Cantab 1946, Hon LLD Edin 1953, DLitt Birmingham 1951, Hon MICE, Chm: Roy Commn U Educn Dundee 1951, NRA 1952, Govrs Dauntsey's Sch 1951, Pres RAF Assoc 1952; Freedom Manchester 1945, London and Edinburgh 1946; Hon Freeman: Painters and Stainers', Mercers', Haberdashers' and Goldsmiths' Cos; Grand Cross Legn Hon and Croix de Guerre (with palm), Grand Cross Order Crown Belgium (with palm), Belgian Croix de Guerre (with palm), 1st Cl Order Kutuzov USSR, Grand Cross Order George I Greece, Order Polonia Restituta, Grand Offr Order Ouissam Alaouite Morocco, Ch Cdr US Legn Merit, US DSM, Grand Cordon Order Nichan Iftikhar Tunis, Silver Jubilee Medal 1935, Coronation Medal 1937; *m* 1st 1915 Rosalinde (*k* air crash nr Cairo 4 Jan 1943), dau of William McIntyre Maclardy, of Sydney, NSW, and had:

  1 Arthur Richard Brian; *b* 21 July 1916; F/O RAF WW II; *ka* over France 3 Aug 1940

  2 JOHN MICHAEL TEDDER, **2nd Baron Tedder**; *b* 4 July 1926; *educ* Dauntsey's Sch, Magdalene Coll Cambridge (MA, ScD) and Birmingham U (PhD 1951, DSc 1961); FRSE, Purdie Prof Chemistry St Andrew; *m* 17 April 1952 *Peggy Eileen [The Rt Hon The Dowager Lady Tedder, Little Rathmore, Kennedy Gdns, St Andrews, Fife KY16 9DJ], yr dau of Samuel George Growcott, of Birmingham, and *d* 1994, leaving:

    (1) ROBIN JOHN TEDDER, **3rd and present Baron Tedder**

    (2) +Andrew Jonathan, of Sydney, NSW; *b* 22 Aug 1958

    (1) *Anne Rosalinde; *b* 16 July 1963; *m* 1989 *Euan Angus Johnston, s of David Johnston, of Leuchars, Fife, and has:

      1a *Rory Alexander; *b* 1996

      1a *Jade; *b* 1991

  1 *Mina Una Margaret [The Hon Mina Tedder, Openfields, Barnyards, Kilconquhar, Fife]; *b* 1920; WAAF 1939–47, Assist Librarian Br Emb Washington, BBC TV 1954–57, Scottish TV Glasgow 1957–65, Dist Commr Nat Savings Alnwick, Northumberland

The **1st Baron** *m* 2nd 26 Oct 1943 Marie de Seton (*d* 3 Jan 1965), formerly w of Capt Ian Reddie Hamilton Black, CBE, RN, and yr dau of Col Sir Bruce Gordon Seton, 9th Bt, of Abercorn (*qv*), and *d* 3 June 1967, leaving by her:

  3 +Richard Seton [The Hon Richard Tedder, W Buckland, Luddesdown, nr Meopham, Kent]; *b* 23 May 1946; *educ* Dauntsey's Sch and Magdalene Coll Cambridge; *m* 1st 1975 (*divorce* 1987) Ann-Marie Adams; *m* 2nd 1989 *Lesley Anne, yr dau of John Coster, of Luddesdown

TEMPLE

Arms: Quarterly, 1st and 4th, or an eagle displayed sa.; 2nd and 3rd, arg. two bars sa., each charged with three martlets or. **Crest:** On a ducal coronet a martlet or. **Motto:** *Templa quam dilecta* ('How delightful are temples'). **Creation:** Bt. (UK) 16 Aug 1876.

SIR RICHARD ANTHONY PURBECK TEMPLE, 4TH BT, of The Nash, Kempsey, Co Worcester, MC (1941) [Sir Richard Temple Bt MC, c/o NatWest Bank, 55 Kensington High St, London W8 5ZG]; *b* 19 Jan 1913; *s* f 1962; *educ* Stowe, Trin Hall Cambridge and Lausanne U; Maj KRRC WW II (wounded); *m* 1st 24 Sept 1936 (*divorce* 1946) Lucy Geils (*d* air crash Brazil April 1952), 2nd dau of Alain Joly de Lotbinière, 8th Seigneur Pointe Platon, Quebec, and has:

  1 +RICHARD [Richard Temple Esq, 6 Clarendon Cross, London W11 4AP]; *b* 17 Aug 1937; *educ* Stowe; Lt RHG Cyprus 1958; *m* 25 July 1964 *Emma Rose, 2nd dau of Maj-Gen Sir Robert Edward Laycock, KCMG, CB, DSO, JP (*see* DUDLEY, E), and has:

    (1) *Lucy Martha; *b* 18 June 1965; *m* July 1993 *Julian Brookhouse and has:

      1a *Aaron Temple; *b* 20 June 1994

    (2) *Alice Frances; *b* 28 May 1967

    (3) *Daisy Louise; *b* 17 Jan 1971

  2 +Anthony St George [Anthony Temple Esq, 8A Rondu Rd, London NW2 3HA]; *b* 23 Feb 1941; *m* 1986 *Angelika Reda and has:

    (1) *Nicholas Christopher Lee; *b* 3 Nov 1986

Sir RICHARD *m* 2nd 25 March 1950 *Jean, yr dau of James Thompson Finnie, of Pollockshields, Glasgow, and widow of P/O Oliver Powell Croom-Johnson, and by her has:

  1 *Anne Sophia [Mrs Jeremy Amos, 24 Holland Park Ave, London W11]; *b* 12 Oct 1951; *m* 29 June 1974 *Jeremy Christopher Peter Amos, barrister, yr s of Hugh E Amos, of Geneva, and has:

    (1) *Alexander Rudolph; *b* 11 Nov 1978

    (2) *Benjamin Christopher; *b* 18 Oct 1980

Lineage: Rev WILLIAM DICKEN; Rector Shenton, Salop; *m* Elizabeth, dau of Dr — Hook, and had:

WILLIAM DICKEN, of Shenton; *m* 18 Nov 1740 Henrietta (*d* April 1797), only dau by his 1st w of Sir William Temple, 5th Bt (*see* TEMPLE OF STOWE, E), and *d* March 1784, leaving an est surv s:

JOHN DICKEN later TEMPLE (roy licence 23 Sept 1796), of The Nash and Stonehouse, Devon; *m* 19 April 1799 Elizabeth, dau of Capt Richard Boger, RN, and *d* 10 May 1831, leaving surv issue, with a dau (Elizabeth, *m* 19 April 1823 William Butt (*d* 1878), of Cornybury, Herts, and had issue):

RICHARD TEMPLE, of The Nash, JP, DL Worcs; sometime of Balliol Coll Oxford; *b* 28 Feb 1800; *m* 1st 25 March 1825 Louisa Anne (*d* 13 April 1837), dau of James Rivett-Carnac, BCS (*see* RIVETT-CARNAC, Bt), and had, with two other daus (*d* unm):

  1 RICHARD (Sir), **1st Bt**

  2 William Henry (Rev); *b* 19 Sept 1830; *m* 19 May 1863 Maria, widow of Francis Robert Neilson, of Bayswater, and 3rd dau of Sir Henry Willock, KLS, and had issue

  1 Anne Sophia; *m* 21 May 1850 Capt Charles Edmund Tennant, RN, of Needwood Ho, Burton-on-Trent, and *d* 8 May 1857, leaving issue. He *d* 2 Jan 1862

2 Louisa Maria; *m* 26 April 1853 Capt Grey Skipwith, RN, 4th s of Sir Grey Skipwith, 8th Bt (*qv*), and *d* 2 March 1864, leaving issue

3 Elizabeth Emma; *m* 16 Oct 1877 Rev John Walcot, of Bitterley Court, Ludlow, Salop, and *d* 10 March 1880

RICHARD TEMPLE *m* 2nd 28 Aug 1840 Penelope (*d* 12 Sept 1892), only child and heiress of Rev Alexander Luders, hereditary Kt HRE, Rector Woolstone, Glos, and *d* 20 Dec 1874, having by her had, with a dau (*d* unm):

3 John Alexander; *b* 4 April 1842; Col IA; *m* 21 Nov 1876 Elizabeth (*d* 6 Feb 1936), yr dau of Rev J D Mathias, and *d* 13 Dec 1928, leaving issue

4 Edward; *b* 4 July 1843; *d* 2 Nov 1911

5 George Theodore; *b* 24 Oct 1847; Lt-Cdr RN, Kt 1st Cl Order St Olaf, FRGS; *m* 26 Oct 1880 Philippa Desirée (*d* 30 April 1924), dau of Philip H Schwensen, of Hasvig, Norway, and *d* 21 Feb 1935, leaving issue

6 Henry Francis, JP; *b* 27 Nov 1850; *m* 1883 Louisa Smith and *d* 3 May 1930

4 Harriette Penelope; *m* 3 April 1872 John William Bund Willis Bund, CBE, DL, JP, of Wick Episcopi, Worcs, and *d* 26 March 1895, leaving issue. He *d* 7 Jan 1928

The est s,

Sir Richard Temple, 1st Bt (UK), so *cr* 16 Aug 1876, of The Nash, Kempsey, GCSI (1877, KCSI 1867), CIE, PC (1896), JP Worcs; *b* 8 March 1826; joined Bengal CS 1846, For Sec and Fin memb Cncil Govr-Gen India 1868–74, Lt-Govr Bengal 1874–76, Govr Bombay 1877–80, MP Evesham 1885–92 and Kingston Surrey 1892–95, V-Chm London Sch Bd 1885–88 (memb to 1894), FRS, DCL Oxon, LLD Cantab and Montreal; *m* 1st 27 Dec 1849 Charlotte Frances (*d* 2 March 1855), dau of Benjamin Martindale, and had, with two daus (*d* unm):

1 RICHARD CARNAC (Sir), **2nd Bt**

2 Henry Martindale; *b* 27 Feb 1853; Lt-Col IA, Agent of Govr-Gen India Khorasan and Seistan; *m* 15 March 1898 Florence Elizabeth (*d* 23 Sept 1899), est dau of Preston Karslake, of White Knights, Berks, and *d* 11 April 1905, leaving:

(1) Dorothea Lora Mary; *m* 15 Jan 1919 Brig Harold Temple-Richards, RM, CE, BSc, MInstCE, MIME, yst s of Capt John Cummins Richards, RN, and had issue. He *d* 2 Jan 1949

Sir Richard *m* 2nd 28 Jan 1871 Mary Augusta, CI (*d* 9 March 1924), dau of Charles Robert Lindsay (*see* CRAWFORD and BALCARRES, E), and by her had, with another s (*d* an infant):

3 Charles Lindsay, CMG; *b* 20 Nov 1871; V-Consul Manaus Brazil 1899–1901, N Nigeria: Resident 1901–10, Ch Sec 1910–13, Lt-Govr 1913–17, FRGS, FGS; *m* 28 April 1912 Olive Susan Miranda (*d* 16 May 1936), yr dau of Sir Reginald Macleod of Macleod, KCB, 27th Chief, and *dsp* 9 Jan 1929

Sir RICHARD *d* 15 March 1902; his est s,

Sir Richard Carnac Temple, 2nd Bt, CB, CIE, JP, DL; *b* 15 Oct 1850; IA Afghan War 1878–79 (medal, despatches), Burma War 1887–90 (medal with two clasps), Lt-Col, raised and cmded Vol Corps Burma 1887–94, Ch Commr Andaman and Nicobar Islands 1895–1904, FBA, FSA, FASB, FRGS, Hon V-Pres RAS, Hon Fell Trin Hall Cambridge, GCStJ; *m* 18 March 1880 Agnes Fanny, DGStJ (*d* 10 Sept 1943), dau of Maj-Gen George Archimedes Searle, Madras SC, and had:

1 RICHARD DURAND (Sir), **3rd Bt**

1 Ethel Godiva; *m* 6 Aug 1910 Lt-Cdr Martin Robertson-Glasgow, RN, of Salthaven, Kennel Ride, Ascot, 2nd s of Col John Campbell Robertson-Glasgow, of Westbury, Wilts, and *d* 7 April 1957, leaving issue. He was *ka* 27 July 1916

2 Mildred Hester; *m* 13 Feb 1909 John Stanley Wise, s of Charles Stanley Wise, of Chestnut Hill, Cumberland. He *d* 1961

The 2nd Bt *d* 3 March 1931; his only s,

Sir Richard Durand Temple, 3rd Bt, DSO (1918); *b* 27 Dec 1880; *educ* Harrow; Lt KRRC S Boer War 1901–02 (medal with four clasps), Lt-Col 5th Bn Worcs Regt, formerly cmdg 27th Bn Northumberland Fus, Col cmdg Labour Corps 1st Army BEF WW I (despatches six times, brevet, Croix de Guerre), FRGS; *m* 1st 25 March 1912 Katherine Marjorie (*d* 11 May 1932), widow of Francis Swithin Braithwait Anderton, of Bolton Royd, Bradford, Yorks, and dau of Frederic de la Fontaine Williams, and had:

1 Sir RICHARD ANTHONY PURBECK TEMPLE, **4th and present Bt**

Sir Richard *m* 2nd 31 Aug 1939 Marie Wanda (*d* 11 Feb 1997), dau of John Frederic Christian Henderson, of Bombay, and *d* 15 Sept 1962, leaving by her:

2 +Peter Paul Grenville [Peter Temple Esq, 2 Kellerton Rd, London SE13 5RD]; *b* 10 Jan 1941; *educ* Stowe; sales dir Encyclopaedia Britannica Internat; *m* 1st 1975 (*divorce* 1980) Heather Joy, dau of Duncan Alistair McKellar (*see* CAYZER, Bt) and formerly w of Kenneth Leonard Hyman; *m* 2nd 1983 *Veronica Margaret, 2nd dau of Geoffrey Trigg, of Southrepps, Norfolk, and has:

(1) +Richard John Geoffrey; *b* 1984

3 +John Anthony [John Temple Esq, 25 square du Val de la Cambre, 1050 Brussels, Belgium]; *b* 24 Sept 1942; *educ* Blundell's; *m* 1967 *Dominique Francine Paule Ghislaine Maire, dau of Jean-Maurice Vaes, and has:

(1) +Jean-Marc Peter Grenville; *b* 3 Feb 1968; *m* 21 Sept 1996 *Odile, dau of Jean-Jacques Matthieu de Wynendaele and Baroness Marie-Claire van der Elst

(1) *Sophie Anne Jacqueline; *b* 28 Nov 1970

(2) *Vanessa Chantal Marie; *b* 29 Jan 1973

TEMPLE OF STOWE

Arms: Quarterly, 1st and 4th grand quarters, quarterly sa. and or a bend arg. (for LANGTON); 2nd, gu. a fess between three cross-crosslets fitchée or (for GORE); 3rd, quarterly 1st and 4th, or an eagle displayed sa., 2nd and 3rd, arg. two bars sa., each charged with three martlets or (for TEMPLE). **Crests:** 1 An eagle or and a wyvern vert, their necks entwined regardant (for LANGTON), 2 On a mount vert a heraldic tiger salient arg., collared gu. (for GORE), 3 On a ducal coronet a martlet or (for TEMPLE). **Supporters:** Dexter, a lion rampant per fess nebuly or and gu., suspended from a ribbon round the neck gu. a shield of the arms of LANGTON; sinister, a horse arg. semée of eagles displayed sa., suspended from a ribbon round the neck gu., a shield of the arms of GORE. **Mottoes:** 1 *Templa quam dilecta* ('How delightful are temples') (for TEMPLE), 2 *Frangas non flectes* ('You may break but will not bend me') (for GORE), 3 *In hoc signo vinces* ('In this sign thou shalt conquer') (for LANGTON). **Creation:** E. (UK) 4 Feb 1822.

THE 8TH EARL TEMPLE OF STOWE, Co Buckingham ((Walter) Grenville Algernon Temple-Gore-Langton) [The Rt Hon The Earl Temple of Stowe, The Cottage, Easton, Hants SO21 1BH; Garth, Outertown, Stromness, Orkney]; *b* 2 Oct 1924; *s* cousin 1988; *educ* Nautical Coll Pangbourne; *m* 1st 24 July 1954 Zillah Ray (*d* 12 Oct 1966), dau of James Boxall, of Fir Grove, Tillington, W Sussex; *m* 2nd 1 June 1968 *(Margaret) Elizabeth Graham, only dau of Col Henry William Scarth, of Breckness, Orkney, and has by his 1st w:

1 +JAMES GRENVILLE, *Lord Langton*; *b* 11 Sept 1955; *educ* Winchester

2 +Robert Chandos [The Hon Robert Gore-Langton, 33 Horsford Rd, London SW2 5BW]; *b* 22 Nov 1957; *educ* Eton; jnlst; *m* 1985 *Susan Penelope, er dau of David Cavender, of The Manor Ho, Dowlish Wake, Somerset, and Mrs Jennifer Neubauer, of Smallcombe Ho, Bath, and has:

(1) +Louis Grenville; *b* 1990

(2) +Christopher Chandos; *b* 1993

(1) *Georgia Ray; *b* 1989

1 *Anna Clare GORE-LANGTON; *b* 19 May 1960; with BBC TV Bristol

Lineage (of Temple): ROBERT TEMPLE; feudal Ld of Temple, Leics, *temp* HENRY III; ancestor of:

PETER TEMPLE; granted Manor of Marston Boteler, Warwicks, and became *temp* EDWARD VI Ld Manor of Stowe, Bucks, where he built a mansion; *m* Millicent, dau of William Kekyll, of Newington, Middx, and had:

1 JOHN

2 Anthony; allegedly f of:

(1) William (Sir); *b* by 1555; *educ* Eton and King's Coll Cambridge (Fell 1576); MP Tamworth 1597, Provost Trin Coll Dublin 1609–Jan 1626/7, Master in Chancery Dublin Jan 1609/10, MP (I Parl) 1613–Jan 1626/7, ktd 1622; *m* Martha, dau of Robert Harrison, of Derbys, and *d* 15 Jan 1626/7, leaving:

1a John (Sir); Master Rolls Ireland; *m* Mary, dau of John Hammond, of Chertsey, Surrey, and *d* 14 Nov 1677, leaving, with two daus:

1b Sir WILLIAM TEMPLE, 1st and last Bt (E), so *cr* 31 Jan 1665/6, PC (1679–Jan 1680/1); *bapt* 20 April 1626; *educ* Bishops Stortford Sch and Emmanuel Coll Cambridge; MP (I Parl) Carlow 1660 and Co Carlow 1661–63, Envoy Brussels 1665 to negotiate Triple Alliance of England, The United Provinces and Sweden (1668), Amb The Hague 1668–70 and 1674 on (when negotiated marriage of Princess MARY and the future WILLIAM III), MP Northampton 1678 and Cambridge U 1679–81, Master Rolls Ireland 1677–96; settled at Moor Park, Farnham, Surrey, where he wrote his *Memoirs* and employed Jonathan Swift as secretary; *m* 31 Jan 1654/5 Dorothy, sis of Sir John Osborn, 1st Bt (*qv*), and *dspms* 27 Jan 1698/9, when the btcy expired, having had:

1c John; Paymaster Gen, Sec State for War 1689; died by his own hand, leaving:

1d Elizabeth; *m* her cousin John Temple (*dspms* Feb 1742) and had four daus

2d Dorothy; *m* Nicholas Bacon, of Shrubland, Suffolk, a cadet of the BACON Bts (*qv*)

2b John (Sir); Slr-Gen and Attorney-Gen Ireland, Speaker H of C Ireland; granted 1666 land near Phoenix Pk, Dublin, known as Palmerston; *m* 4 Aug 1663 Jane, dau of Sir Abraham Yarner, of Dublin, and *d* 1704, having had, with other issue:

1c HENRY TEMPLE, 1st VISCOUNT PALMERSTON, of Palmerston, Co Dublin, so *cr* 12 March 1722/3, as also BARON TEMPLE of Mount Temple, Co Sligo (both I); *b c* 1673; *educ* Eton; MP (Whig) E Grinstead 1727–34, Bossiney 1734–41 and Weobley 1741–47; *m* 1st Anne, dau of Abraham Houblon, Govr Bank of England; *m* 2nd 11 May 1738 Isabella, dau of Sir Francis Gerard, 2nd Bt, and widow of Sir John Fryer, Bt, and *d* 10 June 1757, having had by his 1st w:

1d Henry; *educ* Eton; *m* 1st 18 June 1735 Elizabeth (*dsp*), dau of Col Francis Lee by Lady Elizabeth Lee, dau of 1st Earl of Lichfield (*see* LICHFIELD, E, preliminary remarks); *m* 2nd 12 Sept 1738 Jane, dau of Sir John Barnard, Ld Mayor London 1737–38, and *dvp* 18 Aug 1740, leaving by her:

1e HENRY TEMPLE, 2nd VISCOUNT PALMERSTON; *b* 4 Dec 1739; *educ* Clare Hall Cambridge; MP E Looe 1762–68, Southampton 1768–74, Hastings 1774–84, Boroughbridge 1784–90, Newport (IoW) 1790–96 and Winchester 1796–1802, a Ld of Trade 1765–66, Admlty 1766–77 and Treasury 1777–82; *m* 1st 6 Oct 1676 Frances (*dsp*), dau of Sir Francis Poole, 2nd Bt, of Poole, Cheshire; *m* 2nd 5 Jan 1783 Mary, dau of Benjamin Mee, and *d* 16 April 1802, leaving by her:

1f HENRY JOHN TEMPLE, 3rd and last VISCOUNT PALMERSTON, KG (1856), GCB (1832), PC (1809); *b* 20 Oct 1784; *educ* Harrow, Edinburgh U and St John's Coll Cambridge; MP (Tory) Newport (IoW) 1807–11, Cambridge U (Whig from 1829, later still Lib) 1811–31, Bletchingley 1831–32, S Hants 1832–34 and Tiverton 1835–65, a Ld Admlty 1807–09, Sec at War 1809–28, For Sec 1830–34, 1835–41 and 1846–51, Home Sec 1852–55, PM and 1st Ld Treasury 1855–58 and June 1859–65; *m* 16 Dec 1839 his long-time mistress Emily Mary, dau of 1st Viscount Melbourne and widow of 5th Earl Cowper (*see* LUCAS OF CRUDWELL, B), and *dsp* in office 18 Oct 1865, when his peerages expired

2c John; *m* his cousin Elizabeth, dau of John Temple (*see above*)

1c Catharine; *bapt* 4 Sept 1664; *m* 1st 15 Dec 1681 Charles Ward, s of Sir Robert Ward, 1st and last Bt (*see* BANGOR, V); *m* 2nd Charles King, of Dublin, and *d* between 4 and 20 Aug 1694

2c Jane Martha; *m* 1st 8 March 1691/2 3rd Baron Berkeley of Stratton, of a cadet branch of the BERKELEYs of Berkeley (*see* BERKELEY, B); *m* 2nd, as his 2nd w, 1st Earl of Portland (*qv*)

3c Frances; *m* her bro-in-law 4th Baron Berkeley of Stratton and had, with other issue:

1d Charles; had:

1e Sophia; *m* 1st Baron Wodehouse and had issue (*see* KIMBERLEY, E)

2a Thomas (Rev); DD, Vicar Battersea, Surrey; had:

1b William, of Temple Sowerby, Westmorland, and Howgett Ho, Yorks; had:

1c Mary; *m* 1681, as his 2nd w, William Chapman, of Whitby, Yorks, and *d* 19 March 1739 aged 79, having had issue. He *d* 12 Feb 1720

PETER TEMPLE *d* 28 May 1577; his er son,

JOHN TEMPLE, of Stowe; *m* Susan, dau and heiress of Thomas Spencer, of Everton, Northants, and *d* 9 May 1603, leaving, with at least one dau (Elizabeth, *m* 2nd Baron Saye and Sele, *qv*) an est s:

Sir THOMAS TEMPLE, 1st Bt (E), so *cr* 24 Sept 1611, of Stowe; MP Andover 1588–89; *bapt* 9 Jan 1566/7; *m* 1595 Hester (*d* 1656), dau of Miles Sandys, of Latimer, Bucks, and *d* 1637, having had 13 children (Fuller, in his *Worthies*, claims Lady Temple lived to see 700 descendants), including:

1 Sir PETER TEMPLE, 2nd Bt; MP Bucks 1640–53; *bapt* 10 Oct 1592; *m* 1st 5 July 1614 Anne (*bur* 23 Jan 1619/20), dau and coheir of Sir Arthur Throckmorton, of Paulersbury, Northants, and had:

(1) Anne; *m* Thomas Roper, 2nd Viscount Baltinglass of the 1627 *cr*

(2) Frances; *m* Weston Ridgeway, 3rd Earl of Londonderry (*see* LONDONDERRY, M, preliminary remarks)

1 (cont.) Sir PETER *m* 2nd 20 May 1630 Christiana (*bur* 3 April 1655), dau and coheir of Sir John Leveson, of Halling, Kent, and was *bur* 12 Sept 1653, having by her had, with two other daus (Christiana; Martha):

(1) Sir RICHARD TEMPLE, 3rd Bt, KB (1661); *b* 1634; MP Warwicks 1654–55, Buckingham 1659 and Bucks 1660–97; rebuilt Stowe; *m* 1675 Mary (*bur* 15 May 1726), dau and coheir of Henry Knapp, of Weston, Oxon, and was *bur* 12 May 1697, having had, with two yr sons (Purbeck, *d* unm March 1698; Henry, *d* 1703):

1a Sir RICHARD TEMPLE, 4th Bt, 1st VISCOUNT COBHAM (*see* separate article COBHAM, V), so *cr* 23 May 1718, as also BARON COBHAM, of Cobham, Co Kent (GB), with special remainder, failing heirs male of his body, to his sis HESTER and the heirs male of her body, failing which to his sis Christian in like manner, having earlier 19 Oct 1714 been *cr* BARON COBHAM, of Cobham, Co Kent (GB), with ordinary remainder to heirs male of his body, PC (1716); *b* 24 Oct 1675; MP (Whig) Buckingham 1697–1702 and 1708–13 and Bucks 1704–08, served War of Spanish Succession in Low Countries, Col: 4th Dragoons 1710–13, 1st Roy Dragoons 1715–21, King's Own Horse 1721–33, 1st Horse Gren Gds 1742–44, 6th Horse 1744–45 and 10th Dragoons 1745–49, Envoy Vienna 1714–15, Constable Windsor Castle 1716–23, Govr Jersey 1723, Ld Lt Bucks 1728–38, Gen 1735, FM 1742; added the front and wings to Stowe; *m* Anne (*d* 20 March 1760), dau of Edmund Halsey, brewer, of Stoke Poges, Bucks, and *dsp* 13 Sept 1749, when the 1714 Barony expired

1a HESTER Temple, VISCOUNTESS COBHAM and BARONESS COBHAM in her own right (as which *s* er bro 1749) and COUNTESS TEMPLE in

her own right, so *cr* 18 Oct 1749, with remainder to heirs male of her body; *b c* 1690; *m c* 1710 Richard GRENVILLE (*see* KINLOSS, L, Lineage (of Grenville)) and *d* 6 Oct 1752, having had:

1b RICHARD GRENVILLE later GRENVILLE-TEMPLE (1752), 2nd EARL TEMPLE, KG (1760), PC (1756); *b* 26 Sept 1711; *educ* Eton; MP (Whig) Buckingham 1734–41 and 1747–52 and Bucks 1741–47, First Ld Admlty 1756–57, Ld Privy Seal 1757–61, Ld Lt Bucks 1758–63; remodelled Stowe in the grandiose style familiar today; *m* 9 May 1737 Anne (*d* May 1777), dau and coheir of Thomas Chambers, of Hanworth, Middx, by Mary, est dau of 2nd Earl of Berkeley (*see* BERKELEY, B) and *dsps* 11 Sept 1779, having had:

1c Elizabeth; *b* 1 Sept 1738; *d* 14 July 1742

2b George, PC (1762); *b* 14 Oct 1712; MP Buckingham 1741–70, a Ld Admlty 1744, 1st Ld Treasury 1747, Treasurer Navy 1754 and 1756, Sec State 1762, PM and First Ld Treasury 1763–65; *m* 1749 Elizabeth (*d* 5 Dec 1769), dau of Sir William Wyndham, Bt (*see* EGREMONT, LECONFIELD and, B), and *d* 13 Nov 1770, leaving:

1c GEORGE GRENVILLE later NUGENT-TEMPLE-GRENVILLE (roy licence 2 Dec 1779), 3rd EARL TEMPLE and 1st MARQUESS OF BUCKINGHAM, Co Buckingham (GB), so *cr* 4 Dec 1784, also 2nd EARL NUGENT (as which *s* f-in-law 1788), KG (1786), PC (1782); *b* 18 June 1753; MP (Whig) Bucks 1774–79, Ld Lt: Bucks 1782–1813 and Ireland 1782–83 and 1787–89 (during first term as which allegedly suggested the institution of the Order of St Patrick, of which he became the Grand Master), Sec State for four days in Dec 1783; *m* 16 April 1775 Lady Mary Elizabeth Nugent (*cr* BARONESS NUGENT OF CARLANSTOWN, Co Westmeath (I) 29 Dec 1800, with special remainder to her 2nd s, and *d* 16 March 1812), dau of Robert Craggs Nugent, 1st Earl Nugent (*d* 13 Oct 1788), and *d* 11 Feb 1813, having had:

1d RICHARD, 1st Earl

2d GEORGE GRENVILLE, 2nd and last BARON NUGENT OF CARLANSTOWN, GCMG (1832); *b* 31 Dec 1789; MP 1810–50, DCL, a Ld Treasury, Ld High Commr Ionian Islands 1832–35; *m* 6 Sept 1813 Anne Lucy (*d* 18 April 1848), dau of Hon Vero Poulett (*see* 1970 edn POULETT, E), and *dsp* 26 Nov 1850, when the Barony expired

1d Mary Anne; *b* 8 July 1787; *m* 26 Feb 1811 10th Baron Arundell of Wardour (*dsp* 21 June 1834; *see* 1940 edn) and *d* 1 June 1845

2c Thomas; *b* 31 Dec 1755; MP, First Ld Admlty 1806–07; *d* unm 17 Dec 1846

3c WILLIAM WYNDHAM GRENVILLE, 1st and last BARON GRENVILLE OF WOTTON-UNDER-BERNEWOOD, Co Buckingham (GB), so *cr* 25 Nov 1790, PC (I 1782, GB 1783); *b* 25 Oct 1759; *educ* Eton and Ch Ch Oxford; MP Buckingham 1782–84 and Bucks (1784–90), Ch Sec to bro as Ld Lt Ireland 1782–83, Paymaster-Gen 1783–84, Jt Paymaster-Gen 1784–89, V-Pres BOT 1786–89, Speaker H of C Jan-June 1789, Home Sec 1789–91, Pres Bd Control 1790–93, For Sec 1791–1801, PM and First Ld Treasury 1806–07; *m* 18 July 1792 Anne Pitt (*d* 13 June 1864), sis and heir of 2nd and last Baron Camelford and great-niece of 1st Earl of Chatham (*see* JERSEY, E), and *dsp* 12 Jan 1834, when the Barony expired

1c Charlotte; *m* 21 Dec 1771 Sir Watkin Williams Wynn, 4th Bt (*qv*), and *d* 29 Sept 1832, leaving issue

2c Elizabeth; *m* 12 April 1787 1st Earl of Carysfort and *d* 2 Dec 1842, leaving issue (*see* PROBY, Bt)

3c Hester; *m* 10 May 1782 1st Earl Fortescue (*qv*) and *d* 13 Nov 1847, leaving issue

4c Catherine; *m* 19 June 1780 2nd Baron Braybrooke (*qv*) and *d* 6 Nov 1796, leaving issue

3b James, PC; *b* 12 Feb 1715; MP, Dep Paymaster Forces, a Ld Treasury 1755–61; *m* 1740 Mary (*d* 15 Dec 1757), dau of James Smith, of Annables, Herts, and *d* Sept 1783, having had:

1c JAMES GRENVILLE, 1st and last BARON GLASTONBURY OF BUTLEIGH, Co Somerset (GB), so *cr* 20 Oct 1797, PC (1783); *b* 6 July 1742; *educ* Eton and Ch Ch Oxford; MP (Whig) Thirsk 1765–68, Buckingham 1770–90 and Bucks 1790–97, a Ld Treasury 1782–83; *d* unm 26 April 1825, when the Barony expired

2c Richard; Gen, MP Buckingham; *d* unm 27 April 1823

4b Henry; *b* 15 Sept 1717; Govr Barbados 1746–56, MP Bishop's Castle 1759 and Thirsk 1761, Amb Constantinople 1761, Commr Customs 1765–66; *m* 11 Oct 1757 Margaret Eleanor (*d* 19 June 1793), dau of Joseph Banks, of Revesby Abbey, Lincs, and *d* 22 April 1784, leaving:

1c Louisa; *b* 10 Aug 1758; *m* 10 March 1781 3rd Earl Stanhope (*d* 15 Dec 1816; *see* 1967 edn CHESTERFIELD and STANHOPE, E) and *d* 7 March 1829, leaving issue

5b Thomas Henry; *b* 3 April 1719; Capt RN; *ka* at sea 3 May 1747

1b Hester; *m* 16 Oct 1754 William Pitt the Elder, 1st Earl of Chatham (*see* JERSEY, E), and *d* 3 April 1803, leaving issue

2a Christian; *m* 8 May 1708 Sir Thomas Lyttelton, 4th Bt, and had issue (*see* COBHAM, V)

3a Mary; *m* 1st Rev Richard West, DD, Preb Winchester, and had issue (*see* BRIDPORT, V); *m* 2nd Sir John Langham, 4th Bt (*qv*), and *d* 16 Nov 1763, leaving issue

4a Penelope; *m* Moses Berenger

2 John (Sir); *b* 10 Nov 1593; *m* Dorothy, dau and coheir of Edmund Lee, of Stanton Bury, and *d* 1632, leaving:

(1) Peter (Sir); *b* 1613; *ktd* 1641; *m* Eleanor (*m* 2nd Richard Grenville; *see* KINLOSS, L, Lineage (of Grenville)), dau of Sir Timothy Tyrrell, of Okeley, and was *bur* 14 Jan 1659/60, leaving, with four er sons (*dsp*) and at least one dau (*m* her cousin Richard Grenville; *see* KINLOSS, L):

1a William, of Lillingstone Dayrell; *m* Mary Green, of Kent, and *d* Aug 1706, leaving:

1b Sir WILLIAM TEMPLE, 5th Bt, of Nash Ho, Worcs; *b* April 1694; *m* 1st May 1718 Elizabeth (*d* 1729), dau and heiress of Peter Paxton, MD, and had:

1c Paxton; *b* April 1720; *dvp* unm 1745

1c Henrietta; *m* 18 Nov 1740 William Dicken, of Shenton, and *d* April 1797, leaving issue (*see* TEMPLE Bt)

1b (cont.) Sir WILLIAM *m* 2nd Nov 1731 Elizabeth (*d* 2 Dec 1762), dau of Hugh Ethersey, of Leckhampstead, Bucks, and *dspms* 10 April 1760, having by her had:

2c Anna Sophia; *m* 24 June 1758 her cousin Sir RICHARD TEMPLE, 7th Bt (*see* below)

2b Sir PETER TEMPLE, 6th Bt; *m* 1st 1719 Elizabeth Broughton (*d* 1726), of Longdon, and had:

1c Peter; *b* 1721; *d* unm 1748

1c Elizabeth; *b* 1720; *d* unm 1742

2b (cont.) Sir PETER *m* 2nd 1729 Elizabeth (*d* June 1759), dau of John Mold, of Charlton, Oxon, and *d* 15 Nov 1761, having by her had:

2c Sir RICHARD TEMPLE, 7th Bt; Comptroller Excise; *b* 1 June 1731; *m* 24 June 1758 his cousin Anna Sophia (*d* 4 Oct 1805), dau and coheir of Sir WILLIAM TEMPLE, 5th Bt, and *dsp* 15 Nov 1786, when the btcy became dormant, though irregularly assumed thereafter (*see* below)

(2) Sir THOMAS TEMPLE (NS), 1st and last Bt, so *cr* 7 July 1662; Govr Nova Scotia 1656–70; *bapt* 10 Jan 1614; *d* unm 27 March 1674, when the btcy expired

(3) Edmund, of Sulby Priory, Northants; *bapt* 6 June 1622; Col Parly armies Civil War; *m* 1647 Eleanor, dau and coheir of Sir Stephen Harvey, of Hardingstone, Northants, and was *bur* 9 March 1667/8, leaving:

1a Stephen, of Sulby; *dsp, bur* 26 Oct 1672

2a John, of Sibbertoft; *m* Martha — (*d* 1723) and was *bur* 22 Feb 1702, leaving, with three daus:

1b Richard; *b* 1683

2b Purbeck, of Sibbertoft; *b* 1689; *m* Mary — (*d* 1771) and *d* 16 May 1763, leaving a s (Edward, *d* unm 15 Sept 1796) and three daus

3a Edmund, of Leicester; *m* Ellen — and *d* soon after 1690, having had three sons, one or all of whom may well have had issue that was extant as late as the mid–19th century:

1b Purbeck; living 14 July 1693

2b Richard

3b Edmund

(4) Purbeck (Sir), of Edgcombe Place, Surrey; ktd 1660, Govr Henley; *m* Sarah, dau of Robert Draper, and *dsp* Aug 1695

(1) Dorothy; *m* John Alston, of the Inner Temple

(2) Hester; *m* Edward Paschal, of Essex

(3) Mary; *b* 1623; *m* Robert Nelson, of Gray's Inn, and had:

1a John; settled Boston, Mass.; *m* Elizabeth, dau of William Taller, of Dorchester, Mass., and *d* 1734, leaving:

1b Mehetabel; *d* 1775; *m* 11 Aug 1721 Robert Temple, of Boston, and had:

1c Robert, of Ten Hills, nr Boston; *b c* 1728; *dspm* 1781, leaving, with an est and yst dau:

1d Mehetabel Hester; *m* 3rd Baron Dufferin and Claneboye (*qv*)

2d John; *bapt* 16 April 1732; Surveyor-Gen Customs N Dist America 1761–67, Commr Revenue 1767–74, Lt-Govr New Hampshire 1768–74, 1st post-Independence Br Consul-Gen America 1786–98; assumed the btcy 1786 as 8th holder of the title; *m* 20 Jan 1767 Elizabeth, dau of James Bowdoin, Govr Mass., and *d* New York 17 Nov 1798, leaving issue

3 Thomas (Rev), LLD; *b* 1604; Rector Bourton-on-the-Water, Glos, 1622–49; had issue

4 Miles; had issue

The 1st MARQUESS OF BUCKINGHAM's est s,

RICHARD TEMPLE-NUGENT-GRENVILLE later TEMPLE-NUGENT-BRYDGES-CHANDOS-GRENVILLE (roy licence 15 Nov 1799), **1st Earl Temple of Stowe**, Co Buckingham (UK), so *cr* 4 Feb 1822, with special remainder, failing heirs male of his body, to the heirs male of the body of HESTER, COUNTESS TEMPLE, his great-grandmother, with further remainder to Anna Eliza Mary, the only dau of his only son, and her male issue, and in default of such male issue to the 2nd, 3rd, and 4th and every other dau of his only son, and to their male issue, also on the same day (1st) DUKE OF BUCKINGHAM AND CHANDOS, being in addition 2nd MARQUESS OF BUCKINGHAM, 4th EARL TEMPLE, 3rd EARL NUGENT, 5th VISCOUNT COBHAM and 5th BARON COBHAM, KG (1820), PC (1806); *b* 20 March 1776; *educ* BNC Oxford and Magdalene Coll Cambridge; MP (Tory) Bucks 1797–1813, Commr India Bd 1800–01, V-Pres BOT and Jt Paymaster-Gen 1806–07, Ld Lt Bucks 1813–39, Ld Steward Household July–Nov 1830; *m* 16 April 1796 Lady Anne Eliza Brydges (*d* 15 May 1836), *de jure* Lady Kinloss (*qv*) in her own right according to a Ho Lds ruling of 21 July 1868 and dau and sole heiress of James, 3rd and last Duke of Chandos, and *d* 17 Jan 1839, leaving:

RICHARD PLANTAGENET TEMPLE-NUGENT-BRYDGES-CHANDOS-GRENVILLE, **2nd Earl Temple of Stowe** and 2nd DUKE OF BUCKINGHAM AND CHANDOS, also *de jure* 9th LORD KINLOSS (as which s mother 1836), KG (1842), GCH (1835), PC (1841); *b* 11 Feb 1797; *educ* Eton and Oriel Coll Oxford; MP (Tory) Bucks 1818–39, Ld Privy Seal 1841–42, author: *Courts and Cabinets of George III* and memoirs of the reigns of the last two Hanoverian Kings and QUEEN VICTORIA; *m* 13 May 1819 Lady Mary Campbell (*d* 28 June 1862), dau of 1st Marquess of Breadalbane (*see* 1970 edn BREADALBANE AND HOLLAND, E), and *d* 29 July 1861, leaving property amounting to less than £200 in value (so great had been his extravagance and lack of business sense) and issue:

1 RICHARD PLANTAGENET CAMPBELL TEMPLE-NUGENT-BRYDGES-CHANDOS-GRENVILLE, **3rd Earl Temple of Stowe**, 3rd and last DUKE OF BUCKINGHAM AND CHANDOS and 10th LORD KINLOSS, GCSI (1876), PC (1866); *b* 10 Sept 1823; *educ* Eton and Ch Ch Oxford; MP (C) Buckingham 1846–57, a Ld Treasury Feb-Dec 1852, chm LNWR 1852–61, Ld Pres Cncl 1866–67, Sec Colonies 1867–68, Ld Lt Bucks 1868–89; *m* 1st 2 Oct 1851 Caroline (*d* 28 Feb 1874), only dau of Robert Harvey, of Langley Park, Bucks, and had:

(1) MARY, LADY KINLOSS (*qv*) in her own right, as which *s f*

(2) Anne; *b* 25 Oct 1853; *m* 3 Aug 1882 Lt-Col George Rowley Hadaway, RA (*d* 1926), only s of Inspr-Gen S M Hadaway, of Mayfair, and *d* 18 March 1890, leaving:

1a Anne Mary; *b* 11 Nov 1884; *d* unm 23 April 1897

2a Caroline Adelaide; *b* 11 Nov 1884; *d* unm 20 Nov 1963

3a Alice Eva; *b* 1 Sept 1888

(3) Caroline Jemima Elizabeth; *b* 11 April 1858; *d* unm 25 May 1946

1 (cont.) The **3rd Earl** *m* 2nd 17 Feb 1885 Alice Anne (*m* 2nd 8 Aug 1894 1st and last Earl Egerton of Tatton (*see* 1956 edn EGERTON OF TATTON, B) and *d* 15 Sept 1931), dau of Sir Graham Graham-Montgomery, 3rd Bt, and *dspm* 26 March 1889, when the Dukedom, Marquessate and Earldoms of Temple and Nugent expired, while the Viscountcy and Barony of Cobham passed to his cousin Lord Lyttelton (*see* COBHAM, V) and the Lordship of Kinloss passed to his est dau (*see* above)

1 Anna Eliza Mary; *m* 9 June 1846 William Henry Powell Gore-Langton, DL, MP (*d* 11 Dec 1873), of Newton Park and Hatch Beauchamp (*see* below), and *d* 3 Feb 1879, leaving:

(1) WILLIAM STEPHEN, **4th Earl**

(2) Henry Powell, of Hatch Park, nr Taunton, Somerset, JP; *b* 14 Dec 1854; Col 3rd Bn Somerset LI, Lt 72nd Highrs; granted with yr bro and sisters rank of earl's daus/yr sons 1890; *m* 5 Sept 1878 Marguerite Lucy (*d* 8 Oct 1915), dau of Maj R Guthrie MacGregor, and *d* 13 Aug 1913, having had:

1a John Henry Cyril; *b* 19 June, *d* 31 Aug 1879

2a William Alec Grenville; *b* 3 Nov 1881; *d* 27 May 1893

3a Hubert Edwin, DSO (1918), DL Somerset; *b* 18 Aug 1883; Cdr RN, served WWs I (despatches, Croix de Guerre) and II; *m* 2 Sept 1909 his cousin Lady Alice Mary Temple-Gore-Langton (*d* 2 Jan 1961), 3rd dau of **4th Earl Temple of Stowe** (*see* below), and *d* 6 March 1968, having had:

1b Hubert Alastair Grenville; *b* 26 Dec 1910; *d* 27 March 1914

2b Alaric Hubert St George; *b* 14 Nov 1918; Lt-Cdr RN WW II; *m* 14 Dec 1946 *Margaret Edwina [Mrs Alaric Gore-Langton, Hatch Park, Hatch Beauchamp, Somerset], er dau of Lt-Col Donald McLeod Douglas, MC, of Sanderstead, Surrey, and *d* 1987, leaving:

1c +Chandos Alaric Graham; *b* 9 Dec 1949; *educ* Taunton Sch and St Catherine's Coll Oxford; *m* 1 Sept 1978 *Fiona, dau of Bernard Collins, of Pitsham Place, Midhurst, Sussex, and has:

1d +Chandos James Brydges; *b* 1987

1d *Emma Lucilla Clare; *b* 19 March 1983

2d *Lucy Fiona Alice; *b* 1985

2c +Grenville Julian Brydges; *b* 18 June 1954; *educ* Millfield

1c *Clare Margaret; *b* 18 June 1954; *m* 1984 *Peter E Jordan, yr s of Maj H J Godfrey Jordan, of Thornhill, Kiltimagh, Co Mayo, and has:

1d *Henry James Bourke; *b* 1987

2d *Oliver Charles d'Exeter (twin); *b* 1987

4a Robert Lancelot; *b* 30 March 1885; Lt West Somerset Yeo; *m* 22 Dec 1914 Winifreda Lillian Margaret (*d* 1987), er dau of Capt Arthur G Nixon, Rifle Bde, and *d* 26 Jan 1948, leaving:

1b Montagu Grenville; *b* 28 Jan 1919; *m* 10 May 1944 *Wilda Handlen (*m* 2nd 1971 D Smiley) and *d* 21 March 1968, leaving:

1c +Robert Edward [Dr Robert Gore-Langton, 650 Grandview, London, Ont, Canada N6K 3G6]; *b* 9 May 1950; *educ* Victoria U BC (BSc) and Trin Hall Cambridge (PhD); *m* 1989 *Dr Susan Anne Jennifer Daniel and has:

1d +Jonathan Kent; *b* 1990

1d *Jena Anne Catherine; *b* 1992

1c *Dixie Gillian [Mrs Dixie Gore-Langton, 588A 4678 Elk Dve, Victoria, BC V8Z 5MI, Canada]; *b* 11 Feb 1945; *m* 1st 1963 (*divorce* 1968) George Clifford Madill and has:

1d *Michael George; *b* 1964

2d *Lance Maurice; *b* 1967

1d *Susan Lorraine; *b* 1965

1c (cont.) Mrs Dixie Madill *m* 2nd 1971 (*divorce* 1978) John Molloy; *m* 3rd 1985 (*divorce* 19–, resumed maiden name) Stanley Moritz and by her 2nd husb had:

2d *Shannon Marie; *b* 1973

1b *Margaret Coeline [Mrs Andrew Stewart, 2326 Lincoln Rd, Victoria, BC V8R 6A4, Canada]; *b* 16 June 1920; *m* 16 June 1944 *F/Lt Andrew William Stewart, RCAF, and has:

1c David Andrew; *b* 10 Oct 1945; *d* 26 March 1958

2c *Ronald David; *b* 24 Dec 1961

1c *Heather Margaret; *b* 8 July 1948; *m* 8 July 1969 (*divorce* 1988) Peter John Lund, RCMP, of Ottawa, and has had:

1d David Alexander; *b* 1974; *d* 27 Feb 1998

1d *Wendy Anne; *b* 1969

2c *Victoria Ann; *b* 1 Sept 1953; *m* 1976 *Michael Reginald Ziegler, of Victoria, BC, and has:

1d *Tristan Brooks; *b* 1983

2b *Gillian Mary [Mrs George Barr, 7442 E Saanich Rd, Saanichton, BC V8M 1W2, Canada; 7 Killams Crescent, Taunton, Somerset]; *b* 8 Sept 1925; *m* 1st 3 Aug 1950 Hugo Wuerzer (*d* 1984); *m* 2nd 1986 *George Arthur Barr and by her 1st husb has:

1c *Nigel John; *b* 25 June 1955; *educ* St Edward's Sch, Oxford, Bath U and Birmingham U; *m* 1984 *Sheila Marion, dau of E F Thorpe, of Taunton, Somerset, and has:

1d *James Lewis; *b* 1985

1d *Laura Jane; *b* 1988

2c *Robert Guy; *b* 1959; *educ* Wellington Sch Somerset

1c *Wendy Margaret; *b* 27 May 1951; *m* 1976 *Lt Col David H Keenan and has:

1d *Nicholas Edward; *b* 1983

1d *Rosalind Jane (twin); *b* 1983

2c *Jane Felicity; *b* 14 Nov 1956

5a Norman Eric; *b* 22 July 1886; Lt 6th Dragoon Gds, WW I with Canadians (despatches); *m* 18 Aug 1914 Irene Monica, dau of Maj A G Greaves-Banning, and *d* 1971

6a Richard Gerald; *b* 16 March 1892; Capt Berks RGA, S/Lt RN, Lt-Cdr RCN WW II; *m* 1st 1925 (*divorce* 1936) Laura Edith Pryor, dau of Herbert W Bevan, and *d* 18 May 1978, leaving:

1b +Richard Eric Bevan [Richard Gore-Langton Esq, 5465 Alderley Rd, Victoria, BC, Canada]; *b* 1933; *m* 1957 *Marjorie Joyce, dau of Thomas A Boag, and has:

1c +Richard Thomas; *b* 1959

2c +Robert Bevan Joseph; *b* 27 May 1995

1c *Laura Gay; *b* 1961; *m* 1993 *Mark Joseph Ahern

6a (cont.) Lt-Cdr Richard Gore-Langton *m* 2nd 1936 *Doreen Audrey, dau of Aubrey H Davies, MB, MRCS, LRCP, and *d* 1978, leaving by her:

2b +Gerald Hugh; *b* 1947

3b +Norman Guy; *b* 1950

1b *Dorothy Veronica; *b* 1952

(3) Edward Grenville; *b* 16 May 1858; *m* 23 June 1888 Hon Florence Emily Murray (*d* 24 Dec 1902), dau of 9th Lord Elibank (*qv*), and *d* 16 March 1936, leaving:

1a Grenville Edward Murray; *b* 17 Oct 1891; *educ* Malvern; Lt Roy Scots (SR) WW I (despatches), Inter-Allied Plebiscite Commn Upper Silesia 1921–22, Capt Roy Warwicks Regt attd Intell Corps WW II; *d* unm 12 Aug 1967

1a Anna Dorothea Florence; *b* 8 July 1894; *m* 27 July 1926 George Ernest Gordon Hope-Johnstone (*see* ANNANDALE AND HARTFELL, E) and *d* 2 Jan 1959

(1) Mary Jane; *m* 1 Oct 1872 Henry Mills Skrine, DL, of Warleigh Manor, Somerset, and *d* 9 May 1923, having had issue. He *d* 7 March 1915

(2) Frances Anne; *m* 18 Dec 1879 Henry Gribble Turner, MCS, of Staplegrove Manor, Taunton, and *d* 5 July 1907. He *dsp* 15 Feb 1920

The 3rd EARL's n,

WILLIAM STEPHEN GORE-LANGTON later TEMPLE-GORE-LANGTON (roy licence 12 March 1892), **4th Earl Temple of Stowe**, JP, DL; *b* 11 May 1847; *educ* Eton and Ch Ch Oxford (BA); CA Somerset, Maj Somerset Yeo Cav, MP (C) Mid-Somerset 1878–85; *m* 29 Dec 1870 Helen Mabel (*d* 21 Nov 1919), 2nd dau of Sir Graham Montgomery, 3rd Bt (*qv*), and *d* 28 April 1902, leaving:

1 ALGERNON WILLIAM STEPHEN TEMPLE-GORE-LANGTON, **5th Earl Temple of Stowe**, JP Somerset; *b* 9 Nov 1871; *educ* Ch Ch Oxford (BA); Capt and Hon Maj 3rd Bn Somerset LI, Lt Coldstream Gds, Attaché Dip Serv, ADC and Priv Sec to Govr Cyprus, Staff Lt, attd Min Munitions and Nat Serv WW I; *m* 25 Jan 1913 Agnes (*d* 3 March 1941), widow of Alfred Burrows and dau of Charles de Laporte, and *dsp* 19 Feb 1940

2 Chandos Graham; *b* 8 Sept 1873; Capt N Somerset Imp Yeo and 1st Dragoon Gds (Gen Res); *m* 10 June 1907 Frances Ethel (*d* 25 May 1953), yst dau of Rev Arthur L Gore, and *d* 19 Aug 1921, leaving:

(1) CHANDOS GRANVILLE TEMPLE-GORE-LANGTON, **6th Earl Temple of Stowe**; *b* 13 July 1909; Lt-Col Roy Wilts Yeo, formerly N Som Yeo; *m* 1st 3 July 1934 (*divorce* 1940) Frances Vauriel Fenton (*m* 2nd 23 July 1979 Ronald James Scully), only dau of Maj Francis Vivian Lister, OBE, of Chisenbury Priory, Wilts; *m* 2nd 7 July 1943 Joan Helen (*d* 28 April 1977), only dau of Charles Abbott, of Penn, Bucks, and *dsp* 14 April 1966

(2) (RONALD) STEPHEN BRYDGES TEMPLE-GORE-LANGTON, **7th Earl Temple of Stowe**; *b* 5 Nov 1910; did not use title; travelling salesman Australia; *d* unm 1988

(1) *(Elizabeth) Ann [The Lady Ann Bathurst, 12A Northanger Court, Grove St, Bath BA2 6PE]; *b* 3 April 1908; granted rank of earl's dau 1941; *m* 7 July 1927 G/Capt Peter Bathurst and has issue (*see* BATHURST, E)

3 Evelyn Arthur Grenville, DSO (1918); *b* 5 April 1884; Cdr RN, served WWs I (despatches) and II; *m* 1922 Irene (*d* 30 Sept 1967), dau of Brig-Gen Cavendish Walter Gartside-Spaight, of Derry Castle, Killaloe, Ireland, and *d* 7 June 1972, leaving:

(1) (WALTER) GRENVILLE ALGERNON TEMPLE-GORE-LANGTON, **8th and present Earl Temple of Stowe**

(1) *Elspeth Dorina [Mrs Thomas Carlyon, The Glebe, Colan, Cornwall TR8 4NB]; *b* 21 Jan 1926; *m* 20 July 1950 *Thomas Alfred Spry Carlyon, yr s of Maj Alfred Spry Carlyon, of Cornwall, and has:

1a *William Thomas Alfred; *b* 1951; *educ* Stowe; *m* 1988 *Mrs Alison Jean Humphreys, dau of C H J Bellingham, of Cornworthy, Devon, and has:

1b *Sam; *b* 1991

2b *Thomas (triplet); *b* 1991

1b *Sophie (triplet); *b* 1991

1a *Nicola Elspeth; *b* 1954

1 Gertrude Alice; *m* 15 Dec 1904 Maj William Maurice Copland du Quesne Caillard, 7th Dragoon Gds, s of Camille Felix Désiré Calliard, JP, DL, County Court Judge, of Wingfield Ho, Wilts, and *d* 23 Nov 1919, leaving issue. He *d* 18 Nov 1955

2 Mabel Evelyn; *d* unm 11 Jan 1966 aged 92

3 Alice Mary, twin with Mabel Evelyn; *m* 2 Sept 1909 her cousin Cdr Hubert Edwin Gore-Langton and *d* 2 Jan 1961, leaving issue (*see* above)

4 Frances Aline; *m* 4 April 1908 Brig-Gen John Harington, CB, CMG, DSO, yst s of Sir Richard Harington, 11th Bt (*qv*), and *d* following an accident 20 March 1951, leaving issue

5 Clare Violet; *m* 20 Jan 1903 Thomas Francis Egerton, of Parkham, Binfield, Bracknell, Berks, only s of Maj George Mark Leycester Egerton, of The Mount, York, and *d* 29 March 1966, leaving issue (*see* 1956 edn EGERTON OF TATTON, B). He *d* 25 March 1951

Lineage (of Gore-Langton): GERARD GORE, Alderman London (*see* ARRAN, E); had a 4th s:

Sir JOHN GORE, Ld Mayor London 1624–25; *m* Hester, dau of Sir Thomas Campbell, and *d* 1636, leaving, with other issue, including three er sons (the est, Sir

John, of Gilstone, Herts, *m* Bridget, dau of Sir Edward Harington, 2nd Bt (*qv*), and *d* 1659):

WILLIAM GORE, of Morden, Surrey, later of Barrow Court, Barrow Gournay, Somerset, which he bought; *m* Jane, dau of Thomas Smith, of Tedworth, Wilts, and *d* 1662, leaving:

Sir THOMAS GORE; *m* Philippa, sis and coheir of Sir Giles Tooker, of Maddington, Wilts, and *d* 1675, leaving, with two er sons (William, *d* 1718, leaving issue; Thomas, *d* by 1725, leaving issue) and two daus (Jane, *m* Richard Baskerville, of Richardston; Anne, *m* — Stear):

EDWARD GORE; *m* Arabella, sis and coheir of Sir John Smyth, 3rd Bt, of Long Ashton, Somerset, and *d* 1742, leaving a 2nd s:

EDWARD GORE; *m* Barbara, widow of Sir Edward Mostyn, 5th Bt (*qv*), and dau and sole heiress of Sir George Browne, of Kiddington Park, Oxon, by Lady Barbara Lee, dau of 1st Earl of Lichfield (*see* LICHFIELD, E, preliminary remarks)), and *d* 1801, leaving:

1 William GORE later GORE-LANGTON (added on marriage), of Newton Park, Somerset; *b* Dec 1760; Col Oxford Militia; *m* 1st 1783 Bridget, only child and heiress of Joseph Langton, of Newton Park, and *d* 1847, having had:

(1) William, of Combe Hay; *b* 27 Sept 1787; *m* 21 Feb 1822 Jacintha Frances Dorothea, only child of Henry Powell Collins, of Hatch Beauchamp, and *dvp* 3 Oct 1828, leaving:

1a William Henry Powell, of Newton Park and Hatch Beauchamp, JP, DL; *b* 25 July 1824; MA, MP W Somerset 1851–59 and 1863–68; *m* 9 June 1846 Lady Anne Eliza Mary (*d* 3 Feb 1879), only dau of **2nd Earl Temple of Stowe**, and *d* 11 Dec 1873, leaving issue (*see* above)

(2) Edward; *b* 1789; Capt 52nd Regt Peninsular War and Waterloo Campaign; *m* — and *d* 3 March 1860

(3) John; Army Offr; *d* Ceylon

(1) Frances Matilda

1 (cont.) Col William Gore-Langton *m* 2nd Mary, only dau of John Browne, of Salperton, Glos, and by her had:

(4) William Henry, of Clifton, JP, DL Somerset; *b* 1802; MP Bristol 1852–65; *m* 1st 1824 Maria (*d* 7 Jan 1864), dau of John Lewis, and had issue; *m* 2nd 19 April 1865 Mary Ann, only dau of William Williams, of Pwll-y-Pant, Glam, and *d* 16 May 1875

(5) John Frederick; Capt Gren Gds; *d* 27 Oct 1834

(2) Mary Henrietta; *m* 20 Dec 1831 Sir John Montagu Burgoyne, 9th Bt, and *d* 1 April 1890, leaving issue. He *d* 17 March 1858

(3) Caroline Maria; *m* 5 July 1836 Col D'Oyly, Gren Gds

2 Charles (Rev), of Barrow Court, Somerset; Vicar Henbury; *m* 9 May 1798 Harriet, dau of Richard Little, of Grosvenor Place, and *d* 21 April 1841 aged 76, leaving:

(1) Montagu, of Barrow Court; *b* 1800; MP Barnstaple, High Sheriff Somerset 1852; *d* unm 8 Sept 1864

(2) William Charles (Rev); Rector Barrow; *d* unm 17 Feb 1842

(3) George (Rev); *b* 1 Jan 1807; Rector Newton St Loe; *m* 21 April 1841 Frances Anne, dau of Thomas Bates Rous, of Courtyrala, Glam, and *d* 1887, leaving:

1a Francis William George, TD, JP (Glam and Mon), DL (Glam), of Court-y-rala, Glam, and Westminster; *b* 22 June 1855; Lt-Col TFR, Maj City London Rough Riders Imp Yeo; *m* 1 Oct 1885 Lady Constance Grace Milles (*d* 28 Feb 1941), 3rd dau of 1st Earl Sondes (*see* MONSON, B), and *d* 17 July 1938, having had:

1b George Rous Temple; *b* 28 Dec 1889; 2nd Lt Coldstream Gds; *d* 1913

2b Christopher Gerald; *b* 25 Dec 1903; *educ* Eton; Capt; *m* 4 Feb 1930 Lady Barbara Susan Montgomerie, dau of 16th Earl of Eglinton and (4th Earl of) Winton (*qv*), and *d* 11 June 1954, leaving:

1c *John Temple; *b* 30 March 1931; *educ* Eton; late Capt Coldstream Gds; *m* 1st 29 April 1957 (*divorce* 1969) Serena Margaret, dau of Charles Francis Ewart Mounsey, of Yaxley Hall, Eye, Suffolk, and has:

1d *Christopher Charles; *b* 19 Dec 1959

1d *Charlotte Sara Jane; *b* 29 Oct 1958

2d *Georgina Susan; *b* 30 Jan 1962

1c (cont.) John Gore *m* 2nd 15 Oct 1969 *Antonia, formerly w of Alan Brodie Henderson (*see* FARINGDON, B) and only dau of Osmond James George McMullen, of Belgravia

1c *Susan Sara; *b* 26 Oct 1935; *m* 1st 17 Dec 1956 (*divorce* 1962) Basil Ziani de Ferranti, MP, yr s of Sir Vincent Ziani de Ferranti, MC, of Rose Hill, Over Alderley Edge, Cheshire, and has:

1d *Jonathan Christopher Vincent Ziani; *b* 7 Oct 1957

2d *Adrian Sebastian Ziani; *b* 24 Dec 1958

3d *Marcus Basil Ziani; *b* 25 July 1961 (HRH THE DUCHESS OF KENT stood sponsor); *m* 1990 *Alexandra, er dau of Hon Thomas Lindsay (*see* CRAWFORD and BALCARRES, E), and has issue

1c (cont.) Mrs Susan de Ferranti *m* 2nd 17 Aug 1963 *Peter Quixano Henriques, s of George Henriques, of Park Hall, Buxton, Derbys, and by him has:

4d *David Quixano; *b* 11 Dec 1964

5d *Benedict James Quixano; *b* 14 Oct 1967

1b Violet Gladys; *d* unm 11 May 1970

2b Crystal Gloria; *m* 14 April 1931 2nd Baron Brassey of Apethorpe (*qv*) and *d* 15 March 1962, leaving issue

TEMPLEMAN

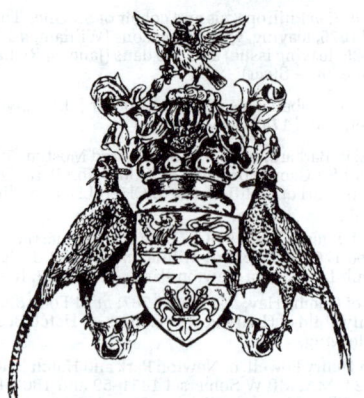

Arms: Per pale azure and gules a fess raguly between a lion passant in chief and in base a fleur-de-lys bourgeonny gold. **Crest:** An eagle or, beaked and legged and wings displayed gules, gorged with a coronet, its finials of roses also gules, and supporting by the dexter claw a kukri erect with the point of the blade outwards proper. **Supporters:** Dexter, a cock pheasant; sinister, a hen pheasant, both guardant and in the beak of each a grain of wheat proper. **Creation:** B. (LP, UK) 1982.

THE BARON TEMPLEMAN, of White Lackington, Co Somerset (Sir Sydney William Templeman, MBE (1946), PC (1978)) [The Rt Hon The Lord Templeman MBE PC, Mellowstone, 1 Rosebank Cres, Exeter EX4 6EJ]; *b* 3 March 1920; *educ* Southall GS and St John's Coll Cambridge (Hon Fell 1982); 2nd Lt 4th/1st Gurkha Rifles India and Burma WW II (despatches, Hon Maj); barrister Middle Temple and Lincoln's Inn 1947, QC 1964, Bencher Middle Temple 1969 (Treas 1987), Memb: Bar Cncl 1961–65 and 1970–72, Tbnl re Vehicle & Gen Insur Co 1971–72, Advsy Ctee Legal Educn 1972–74, Roy Commn Legal Servs 1976–79; Attorney-Gen Duchy Lancaster 1970–72, ktd 1972, High Court Judge Chancery Div 1972–78, Treas Senate Four Inns 1972–74, Ld Justice Appeal 1978–82, Ld Appeal in Ordinary 1982–94; Pres: Senate Inns of Court and the Bar 1974–76, Bar Assoc Commerce Fin and Industry 1982–85, Bar European Gp 1987–96; V-Pres Corp Sons of Clergy to 1996, Chm Bp London's Commn City Churches 1992–94; Hon Memb: Canadian Bar Assoc 1976, ABA 1976, Newfoundland Law Soc 1984; Hon DLitt Reading 1980, Hon LLD: Birmingham 1986, CNAA 1990, Exeter 1991, W of England 1993, Nat Law Sch India 1994; *m* 1st 1946 Margaret Joan (*d* 1988), dau of Morton Rowles; *m* 2nd 12 Dec 1996 *Sheila Barton, widow of Dr John Edworthy and dau of Frank Templeman, and by his 1st w has:

   1 *Peter Morton (Rev); *b* 1949; *m* 1973 *Ann Joyce, dau of Peter Williams, and has issue

   2 *Michael Richard; *b* 1951; *m* 1974 *Lesley Frances, dau of Henry Davis, and has issue

Lineage: HERBERT WILLIAM TEMPLEMAN; *m* Lilian — and had:

SYDNEY WILLIAM, *cr* a **Baron**

TENBY

Arms: Az. over water barry wavy in base a bridge of one arch ppr., on a chief arg. a portcullis sa. between two daffodils stalked and leaved, also ppr. **Crest:** A demi-dragon gu., holding between the claws a portcullis sa. **Supporters:** Dexter, a dragon gu.; sinister, a lion or; each gorged with a collar compony arg. and vert, pendant from the dexter an escutcheon gu. charged with a fort between two towers also arg. **Motto:** *Y gwir yn erbyn y byd* ('The truth against the world'). **Creation:** V. (UK) 12 Feb 1957.

THE 3RD VISCOUNT TENBY, of Bulford, Co Pembroke (William Lloyd-George, JP (Hants)) [The Rt Hon The Viscount Tenby JP, Triggs, Crondall, nr Farnham, Surrey]; *b* 7 Nov 1927; *s* bro 1983; *educ* Eastbourne Coll and St Catharine's Coll Cambridge (BA 1949); Capt Roy Welch Fus (TA); dir Williams Lea and Co 1988–, chm St James Public Relations 1990–; *m* 23 April 1955 *Ursula Diana Ethel, yst dau of Lt-Col Henry Edward Medlicott, DSO, and has:

   1 +TIMOTHY HENRY GWILYM; *b* 19 Oct 1962; *educ* Downside and U Coll of Wales Aberystwyth

   1 *Sara Gwenfron; *b* 10 Sept 1957

   2 *Clare Mair; *b* 2 March 1961

Lineage: The 1st EARL LLOYD-GEORGE OF DWYFOR (*qv*); had a 2nd s:

GWILYM LLOYD-GEORGE, **1st Viscount Tenby**, of Bulford, Co Pembroke (UK), so *cr* 12 Feb 1957, TD, PC (1941), JP; *b* 4 Dec 1894; *educ* Eastbourne Coll and Jesus Coll Cambridge (Hon Fell 1953): Maj RA WW I (despatches), MP (Lib) Pembs 1922–24 and 1929–50 and (Lib then C) Newcastle-upon-Tyne N 1951–57, Jr Whip 1924, Parly U-Sec BOT 1931 and 1939–41, Min Food 1941–42 and 1951–54, Min Fuel and Power 1942–45, Home Sec and Min Welsh Affrs 1954–57, Hon LLD Wales, Freeman City London, Hon Freeman: Haverfordwest, Cardiff, Pembroke and Tenby, chm Cncl on Tbnls 1961 and Govrs Eastbourne Coll; *m* 14 June 1921 Edna Gwenfron (*d* 1971), dau of David Jones, of Denbigh, and *d* 14 Feb 1967, leaving:

   1 DAVID LLOYD-GEORGE, **2nd Viscount Tenby**; *b* 4 Nov 1922; *educ* Eastbourne Coll and Jesus Coll Cambridge (BA 1947, MA 1949); WW II 1942–45 as Capt RA; *d* unm 1983

   2 WILLIAM LLOYD-GEORGE, **3rd and present Viscount Tenby**

TENNYSON

Arms: Gu. on a bend nebuly between three leopard's faces jessant-de-lys or a chaplet vert. **Crest:** A dexter arm in armour embowed, the hand gauntleted or, grasping a broken tilting spear, enfiled with a garland of laurel ppr. **Supporters:** Two leopards guardant gu., ducally crowned and semée of fleurs-de-lys or. **Motto:** *Respiciens prospiciens* ('Looking backwards and forwards'). **Creation:** B. (UK) 24 Jan 1884.

THE 5TH BARON TENNYSON OF ALDWORTH, Co Sussex, **AND OF FRESHWATER** in the Isle of Wight (Cdr Mark Aubrey Tennyson, DSC (1943), RN) [Cdr The Rt Hon The Lord Tennyson DSC RN, 304 Grosvenor Sq, Duke Rd, Rondebosch, Cape Town 7700, S Africa]; *b* 28 March 1920; *s* bro 1991; *educ* RNC Dartmouth; RN 1937–60 (ret as Cdr), served WW II (despatches); production manager Rowntree-Mackintosh (S Africa) 1960–67, export sales dir Joseph Terry and Sons (UK) 1968–82, skied for RN 1947–51, Capt RN Cresta Run team 1951–54; *m* 1964 Deline Celeste (*d* 1995), dau of Arthur Harold Budler, of Cradock, S Africa

Lineage: RALPH TENNYSON; *m* Dorothy, dau of John Chapman, and *d* 1735, leaving:

MICHAEL TENNYSON, of Preston, Yorks, and Stainton, Lincs; *m* Elizabeth, dau of George Clayton, of Grimsby, Lincs, by Dorothy, dau and coheir of Christopher Hildyard (gs and heir of Henry Hildyard, of Winestead, Yorks, by Lady Anne Leke, est dau of 1st Earl of Scarsdale of the 1645 *cr*; *see* SCARSDALE, V, preliminary remarks), and *d* Oct 1776, leaving, with a dau (Anne, *m* William Raines, of Wyton, Yorks):

GEORGE TENNYSON, of Bayons Manor and Usselby Ho, Lincs, JP, DL; MP; inherited 1794 the Clayton estate from his maternal uncle Christopher; *m* 1775 Mary (*d* 20 Aug 1825), dau and heiress of John Turner, of Caistor, Lincs, and *d* 4 July 1835, having had, with a yr s (*see* TENNYSON D'EYNCOURT, Bt) and two daus (Elizabeth, *m* Matthew Russell, MP, of Brancepeth Castle, Co Durham, and had issue; Mary, *m* John Bourne, JP, DL (*d* 15 Dec 1850), of Dalby, Lincs, and *d* 26 April 1864):

Rev GEORGE CLAYTON TENNYSON, LLD; *b* 1781; Vicar Somersby, Lincs; *m* 1805 Elizabeth (*d* 1865), dau of Rev Stephen Fytche, Vicar Louth, Lincs, and *dvp* 1832, leaving, with other issue:

1 Charles TENNYSON later TENNYSON-TURNER; also wrote poetry, as did his next yr bro, being co-author with the future Poet Laureate 1827 of *Poems by two brothers*

2 Frederick; *m* Maria Giuliotti, dau of a Ch Magistrate of Tuscany, and *d* 26 Feb 1898, leaving issue

3 ALFRED, **1st Baron**

4 Horatio; *m* Charlotte Maria (*d* 31 Oct 1868), yst dau of Dudley Christopher Cary Elwes, and *d* 2 Oct 1899, leaving issue

5 Arthur; *m* 1st 22 May 1860 Harriet, dau of Rev John West; *m* 2nd Emma Louisa (*d* 31 Aug 1919), dau of Rev Forster Maynard, and *d* 27 June 1899

1 Mary; *m* Alan Ker, Judge High Court Jamaica, Nevis and Dominica, and *d* 4 April 1884, leaving issue. He *d* 20 March 1885

2 Emily; *m* Capt Jesse, RN, and *d* 24 Jan 1887, leaving issue

3 Cecilia; *m* 14 Oct 1842 Edmund Law Lushington, of Park Ho, Kent, and *d* 18 March 1909, having had issue. He *d* 13 July 1893

The 3rd s,

ALFRED TENNYSON, **1st Baron Tennyson of Aldworth**, Co Sussex, **and of Freshwater** in the Isle of Wight (UK), so *cr* 24 Jan 1884; *b* 6 Aug 1809; *educ* Louth GS and Trin Coll Cambridge (Chllr's Medal 1829 with poem *Timbuctoo*); poet; works include: *Poems* (1842, including in Vol 1 *The Lady of Shalott* and *The Lotos-Eaters* and in Vol 2 *Locksley Hall* and *Ulysses*), *The Princess* (1847), *In Memoriam* (1850), *Maud* (1855), *The Idylls of the King* (1859, complete edn 1872–73), *Enoch Arden* (1864), *Crossing the Bar* (1889) and of course *The Charge of the Light Brigade*, Poet Laureate 1850, DCL 1855, FRS 1865; *m* 13 June 1850 Emily (*d* 10 Aug 1896), dau of Henry Sellwood, of Berkshire, and had:

1 HALLAM, **2nd Baron**

2 Lionel; *b* 16 March 1854; *m* 25 Feb 1878 Eleanor Mary Bertha (*m* 2nd 5 May 1888 Augustine Birrell, PC, KC (*d* 20 Nov 1933), and *d* 10 March 1915), dau of

---

Frederick Locker (later Locker-Lampson) by his 1st w Lady Charlotte Bruce, dau of 7th Earl of Elgin and (11th Earl of) Kincardine (*qv*), and *d* 20 April 1886, having had:

(1) Alfred Browning Stanley; *b* 20 Nov 1878; *educ* Eton and Trin Coll Oxford; Lt Leics Yeo WW I, Inspr Irish Local Govt Bd; *m* 17 Dec 1912 Hon Margaret Cicely Drummond (*d* 9 June 1963), er surv dau of 10th Viscount Strathallan (*see* PERTH, E), and *d* 28 Feb 1952, leaving:

1a +JAMES ALFRED, DSC [Lt-Cdr James Tennyson DSC RN, 222A Karori Rd, Wellington 6005, New Zealand]; *b* 26 Nov 1913; heir presumptive; served WW II (despatches), in NZ Govt Serv, Specialist in Navigation, on loan to RNZN 1953–56; *m* 11 Dec 1954 *Beatrice Aventon, BSc Victoria U, Wellington 1951, est dau of Alexander Tolhurst Young, barrister and slr, of Wellington, and has:

1b +David Harold Alexander; *b* 4 June 1960; *educ* Scot's Coll and Canterbury U, NZ (ME)

2b +Alan James Drummond; *b* 28 Jan 1965; *educ* Scot's Coll and Otago and Auckland Us NZ (MSc); has by *Susanna Ruth Brow:

1c *Andrew Barnard (Barney Brow) TENNYSON; *b* 1992

2a +Aubrey Drummond [Aubrey Tennyson Esq, Urb el Salze No 3, Escas, La Massana, Andorra]; *b* 26 March 1920; Capt late Essex Regt and Sudan Defence Force, formerly in Sudan CS; *m* 24 June 1966 *Mai Chin Yau, of Hong Kong, and has:

1b *Davina Mary; *b* 1969; *educ* Edgehill Coll Devon and Liverpool U (Bsc)

2b *Georgina Cicely; *b* 1979; *educ* Culford Sch, Bury St Edmunds

1a *Eleanor Rachel [Mrs Eleanor Tennyson-Moore, 41 Alver Quay, Gosport, Hants PO12 1SR]; *b* 1915; late sr art teacher Atherley Sch, Southampton, and Prof Art Baylor U, Waco, Texas; *m* 1st 11 Sept 1945 (*divorce* 1955) Maj David Rainsford Moore, Essex Regt, yr s of Canon Thomas Cumming Rainsford Moore; *m* 2nd 29 March 1967 (*divorce* 19–) William Charles Bigg, RAF, est s of Capt William Charles Bigg, OBE, RASC

(2) Charles Bruce Locker (Sir), CMG (1915); *b* 8 Nov 1879; *educ* Eton and King's Coll Cambridge (BA 1902, Hon Fell 1955); barrister Gray's Inn 1905, Sec Dunlop Rubber Co Ltd 1928–48, Legal Assist to Colonial Office 1911–19, Dep Dir FBI 1919–28, ktd 1945, DCL Cantab 1955, author: *Cambridge from Within*, *Life's all a Fragment*, *Stars and Markets* and various books on his gf; *m* 29 July 1909 Ivy Gladys, OBE (1918) (*d* 27 April 1958), dau of Walter J Pretious, and *d* 22 June 1977, having had:

1a Frederick Penrose; *b* 26 Aug 1912; Lt RNVR WW II, film director; *m* 19 Oct 1939 *Nova (*m* 2nd 27 Nov 1950 Alexander Hamilton Whyte, s of Sir Alexander Frederick Whyte, of Bayswater, and has issue), only dau of Arnold William Pilbeam, of Datchet, Bucks, and was *kas* in an air crash 7 July 1941

2a Charles Julian; *b* 7 Feb 1915; Capt 6th Oxon and Bucks LI WW II, author: *Rough Shooting* and *Suffolk Scene*; *m* 29 Sept 1937 *Yvonne (*m* 2nd 3 Oct 1947 Michael Jeans, s of Ronald Jeans, and has further issue), dau of Col R B le Cornu, and was *ka* Burma 7 March 1945, leaving:

1b +Simon; *b* 4 Dec 1939

1b *Penelope [Miss Penelope Tennyson, 40 Kent Gdns, London W14]; *b* 4 Dec 1939

3a +Hallam Augustine [Hallam Tennyson Esq, 1 Berkeley Rd, London N8 8RU]; *b* 10 Dec 1920; *educ* Eton and Balliol Coll Oxford; Head Rural Devpt Prog W Bengal 1946–49, Sec Cncl of Citizens of East London 1948–51, free-lance author and broadcaster 1951–55, features writer *News Chronicle* 1955–56, Producer BBC External Serv 1956–61, Staff Training Attachments Offr BBC 1964–68, Assist Head Drama (Sound) 1968–79, author: *Minds in Movement*, *Tito Lifts the Curtain*, *Saint on the March*, *The Wall of Dust*, *The Goddess*, *The Haunted Mind*, *It's Not Unusual* and TV and radio plays; *m* 16 Oct 1945 (*divorce* 1971) Margot, dau of Gustav Wallach, of Giesenkirchen, Germany, and has:

1b +Charles Jonathan Penrose; *b* 11 May 1955; *educ* Bootham Sch, York; physics Prof London U; *m* 1985 *Janice Hopson and has:

1c +Alexander Hallam Hopson; *b* 1986

2c +Matthew James; *b* 1988

3c +Frederick Penrose; *b* 1991

1c *Eleanor Edith; *b* 1998

1b *(Sita) Rosalind Joanna; *b* 28 April 1950; Dir Prince of Wales Tst 1989–91; *m* 1980 *Richard Grover

(3) Michael Sellwood; *b* 10 Dec 1883; *d* 1954

The 1st BARON *d* 6 Oct 1892; his er s,

HALLAM TENNYSON, **2nd Baron Tennyson of Aldworth and of Freshwater**, GCMG (1903, KCMG 1899), PC (1905), JP (Hants), DL (IoW); *b* 11 Aug 1852; *educ* Marlborough and Trin Coll Cambridge; barrister Inner Temple, Dep Govr IOW, Hon Col 20th Australian Light Horse and 13th Bde Australian Field Artillery, Govr S Australia 1899–1902, first Actg Govr-Gen Australia 1902, Govr-Gen 1902–04, Grand Cross Order Rising Sun Japan, Hon Litt D Cantab, Hon DCL Oxon, Hon LLD Melbourne and Adelaide; *m* 1st 25 June 1884 Audrey Georgiana Florence (*d* 7 Dec 1916), dau of Charles John Boyle (*see* CORK and ORRERY, E); *m* 2nd 27 July 1918 Mary Emily (*d* 20 July 1931), widow of Andrew Kinsman Hichens, of Monk's Hatch, Compton, Guildford, and dau of Charles Robert Prinsep, Advocate-Gen Calcutta, and had by his 1st w:

1 LIONEL HALLAM, **3rd Baron**

2 Alfred Aubrey; *b* 2 May 1891; *educ* Eton and Trin Coll Cambridge; Capt Rifle Bde WW I; *ka* March 1918

3 Harold Courtenay; *b* 27 April 1896; Sub-Lt RN WW I 1914–16; *ka* 29 Jan 1916

The 2nd BARON *d* 2 Dec 1928; his est s,

LIONEL HALLAM TENNYSON, **3rd Baron Tennyson of Aldworth and of Freshwater**; *b* 7 Nov 1889; *educ* Eton and Trin Coll Cambridge; Maj Rifle Bde, formerly Coldstream Gds, Staff Capt BEF 1915 WW I (wounded three times, despatches twice), Hon Col 51st London AA Bde RA (TA) 1932–47, also served WW II; played cricket for England *v* S Africa in five Test Matches 1913–14, captained and played for England *v* Australia in England in four Test Matches 1921, played for England *v* W Indies in three Test Matches 1926–27, author: *From Verse to Worse* and *Sticky Wickets*, Silver Jubilee Medal 1935 and Coronation Medal 1937; *m* 1st 27 March 1918 (*divorce* 1928) Hon Clarissa Madeline Georgiana Felicité (*d* 3 Sept 1960), formerly w of Capt William Adrain Vincent Bethell and only dau of 1st Baron Glenconner (*qv*); *m* 2nd 14 April 1934 (*divorce* 1943) Carroll, widow of Joseph William Donner, of Buffalo, NY, and dau of Howard Elting, of Chicago, and *d* 6 June 1951, having had by his 1st w:

1 HAROLD CHRISTOPHER TENNYSON, **4th Baron Tennyson of Aldworth and of Freshwater**; *b* 25 March 1919; *educ* Eton and Trin Coll Cambridge (BA 1940); War Office 1939–46, Hon Freeman Lincoln 1964, co fndr with Sir Charles Tennyson of Tennyson Research Centre, Lincoln; *d* 1991

2 MARK AUBREY TENNYSON, **5th and present Baron Tennyson of Aldworth and of Freshwaer**

3 Lionel; *b* 1 Aug, *d* 15 Aug 1925

TENNYSON-D'EYNCOURT

Arms: Quarterly, 1st and 4th, az. a fess dancettée between ten billets, four and six or (for D'EYNCOURT); 2nd and 3rd, gu. three leopard's faces or, jessant-de-lys az., over all a bend of the last (for TENNYSON). **Crests:** 1 A lion passant guardant arg., on the head a crown of fleur-de-lys or, the dexter forepaw supporting a shield charged with the arms of D'Eyncourt (for D'EYNCOURT), 2 A dexter arm in armour, the hand in a gauntlet or, grasping a broken tilting-spear enfiled with a garland of laurel ppr. (for TENNYSON). **Mottoes:** 1 *En avant* ('Forward') (for D'EYNCOURT), 2 *Nil temere* ('Nothing rashly') (for TENNYSON). **Creation:** Bt. (UK) 3 Feb 1930.

SIR MARK GERVAIS TENNYSON-D'EYNCOURT, 5TH BT, of Carter's Corner Farm, in the parish of Hurstmonceux, Co Sussex; *b* 12 March 1967; *s f* 1989; *educ* Charterhouse and Kingston Poly (BA); fashion designer; Freeman City London 1989

Lineage: GEORGE TENNYSON (*see* TENNYSON, B); *m* 1775 Mary Turner and *d* 1835; his yr s:

CHARLES TENNYSON later TENNYSON-D'EYNCOURT (roy licence 27 July 1835, thus augmenting his name because of a remote descent from the Earls of Scarsdale (*see* TENNYSON, B), whose subsidiary title was the Barony of D'Eyncourt), PC, of Bayons Manor and Usselby Ho, Lincs, JP, DL; *b* 20 July 1784; MA Cantab; MP Grimsby 1818–26, Bletchingley 1826–31, Stamford 1831–32 and Lambeth 1832–53, FRS, FSA, High Steward Louth; *m* 1 Jan 1808 Frances Mary (*d* 26 Jan 1878), only child and heiress of Rev John Hutton, of Morton, Lincs, and had, with other issue:

LOUIS CHARLES TENNYSON-D'EYNCOURT, of Bayons Manor, JP Parts of Lindsey; *b* 23 July 1814; barrister, Metropolitan Police Magistrate 1851–90; *m* 31 Aug 1852 Sophia (*d* 3 June 1900), yst dau and coheir of John Ashton Yates, of Dinglehead, Lancs, MP Carlow, by Frances Mary, dau of Very Rev Verney Lovett, DD, Dean Lismore, Co Waterford, and *d* 11 Dec 1896, having had:

1 Edmund Charles, of Bayons Manor; *b* 11 Feb 1855; *m* 20 July 1892 Charlotte Ruth, only child of Sir Augustus Frederick Godson, MP, and *d* 29 Oct 1924, leaving issue

2 Ashton Lovett; *b* 14 Dec 1860; Maj Roy Berks Regt; *m* 26 Oct 1922 Edith (*d* Sept 1943), 2nd dau of Sir Francis Houlton Hartwell, 3rd Bt (*qv*), and *dsp* 30 Aug 1926

3 EUSTACE HENRY WILLIAM (Sir), **1st Bt**

1 Alice Julia; *d* unm Oct 1873

2 Emma Frances Mary; *d* unm 7 Feb 1949

3 Henrietta Clara Eliza; *m* 28 July 1891 Herbert Edward Phillips and *d* 8 Dec 1948, leaving issue. He *d* Nov 1904

The yst s,

Sir Eustace Henry William Tennyson-d'Eyncourt, 1st Bt (UK), so *cr* 3 Feb 1930, KCB (1917, CB 1915); *b* 1 April 1868; V-Pres Inst Naval Architects; Dir Naval Construction Admlty 1912–23, Head Admlty Ctee producing first tank in 1916, V-Pres Tank Bd 1918; dir: Armstrong Whitworth 1924–27, Parsons Marine Turbine Co 1925; FRS, Hon DSc Durham, Hon LLD Cambridge, MICE, Order Medjidie 3rd Cl, US DSM, Cdr Legn Hon, for assoc memb French Académie de Marine; *m* 20 July 1898 Janet Watson (*d* 18 Dec 1909), widow of John Burns and dau of Matthew Watson Finlay, of Langside, nr Glasgow, and *d* 1 Feb 1951, leav-

ing, with a dau (Cecily Lovett, *b* 21 Aug 1899, *m* 17 Nov 1920 Percy George MAYER later MEIGHAR-LOVETT (deed poll 25 April 1938), OBE, est surv s of Max Mayer, and *d* 20 March 1971, leaving issue):

Sir (Eustace) Gervais Tennyson-d'Eyncourt, 2nd Bt; *b* 19 Jan 1902; *educ* Charterhouse; FRSA 1956, Prime Warden Fishmongers' Co 1960–61, memb Roy Inst, Pilgrims, Hon memb Smeatonian Soc Civ Engrs; *m* 1st 1 June 1926 Pamela (*d* 29 Dec 1962), yr dau of William Buckley Gladstone, of Moor Town Ho, Ringwood, Hants, and S Kensington, and had:

1 **Sir (John) Jeremy Eustace Tennyson-d'Eyncourt, 3rd Bt**; *b* 8 July 1927; *educ* Eton and Glasgow U; Sub-Lt RNVR 1945–48; *m* 1st 31 Dec 1964 (*divorce*) Sally June, formerly w of Colin Fyfe-Jamieson and est dau of Robin Stratford, QC, of Fernhill, Kilmacrennan, Co Donegal; *m* 2nd 20 Dec 1972 (*divorce* 1976) Brenda Mary Veronica, dau of Dr Austin Stafford; *m* 3rd 1977 *Norah [Norah Lady Tennyson-d'Eyncourt, Bayons House, Hinton St George, Somerset TA17 8RX], dau of Thomas Gill, of Sheffield, and *d* 1988

2 **Sir Giles Gervais Tennyson-d'Eyncourt, 4th Bt**; *b* 16 April 1935; *educ* Eton, Millfield and RMA Sandhurst; Capt Coldstream Gds; *m* 1966 *Juanita [Lady Tennyson-d'Eyncourt, c/o Hyde Mahon Bridges, 52 Bedford Row, London WC1R 4UH], dau of Fortunato Borromeo, and *d* 1989, leaving:

(1) Sir MARK GERVAIS TENNYSON-D'EYNCOURT, **5th and present Bt**

1 Philippa Janet; *b* 20 Dec 1928; *m* 30 July 1953 (*divorce* 1970) Nigel Nicolson, MBE (*see* CARNOCK, B) and had issue; *m* 2nd 20 March 1970 Sir Robin McAlpine (*see* McALPINE, Bt) and *d* 1987

Sir Gervais *m* 2nd 18 Feb 1964 *Vinnie Lorraine [Vinnie Lady Tennyson-d'Eyncourt, Catalino Pueblo, 2556 Avenida Maria, Tucson, AZ 85718, USA], widow of Robert J O'Donnell and yr dau of Andrew Pearson, of Minneapolis, and *d* 21 Nov 1971

TERRINGTON

Arms: Per fess or and az. a hurst of oak trees issuant in chief ppr. and two bars wavy in base arg. **Crest:** Issuant out of a wreath of roses arg., barbed and seeded ppr., a demi-woodman, also ppr., supporting in the dexter hand an axe or. **Supporters:** On either side an Airedale terrier ppr., gorged with a ducal coronet or. **Motto:** *Labor omnia vincit* ('Labour conquers all things'). **Creation:** B. (UK) 19 Jan 1918.

THE 5TH BARON TERRINGTON, of Huddersfield, Co York (Christopher Montague Woodhouse), DSO (1943), OBE (1944) [The Rt Hon The Lord Terrington DSO OBE, 59 Pegasus Grange, Whitehouse Rd, Oxford OX1 4QQ]; *b* 11 May 1917; *s* bro 1998; *educ* Winchester and New Coll Oxford (BA 1939, MA 1947); T/Col Intell Corps WW II (despatches twice), cmded Allied Mil Mission Greece 1943–44, Dir-Gen RIIA 1955–59, MP (C) Oxford 1959–66 and 1970–74, Parly Sec Min Aviation 1961–62, Jt Parly U-Sec Home Office 1962–64, Dir Educn and Training CBI 1966–70, dir IDC Gp, chm Cncl RSL 1977, US Legn Merit, Order Phoenix Greece with swords, FRSL 1951, Fell Trin Hall Cambridge 1950 and Visiting Fell Nuffield Coll Oxford 1956–64, Visiting Prof King's Coll London 1964–, special memb Academy Athens 1980, author: *Apple of Discord* (1948), *One Omen* (1950), *Dostoievsky* (1951), *The Greek War of Independence* (1952), *Britain and the Middle East* (1959), *British Foreign Policy since the Second World War* (1961), *Rhodes* (with J G Lockhart, 1963), *The New Concert of Nations* (1964), *The Battle of Navarino* (1965), *Post-War Britain* (1966), *The Story of Modern Greece* (1968), *The Philhellenes* (1969), *Capodistria: the founder of Greek Independence* (1973), *The Struggle for Greece (1941–1949)* (1976), *Something Ventured* (1982), *Karamanlis: the restorer of Greek democracy* (1982), *The Rise and Fall of the Greek Colonels* (1985), *Gemistos Plethon: the last of the Hellenes* (1986), *Rhigas Velestinlis* (1995); *m* 28 Aug 1945 Lady Davidema (Davina) Katharine Cynthia Mary Millicent (*d* 10 Sept 1995), widow of 5th Earl of Erne (*qv*) and yr dau of 2nd Earl of Lytton (*qv*), and has:

1 +CHRISTOPHER RICHARD JAMES [The Hon Christopher Woodhouse, 14 Crescent Grove, London SW4 7AH]; *b* 20 Sept 1946; *educ* Winchester and Guy's Hosp Med Sch, MB, FRCS, FEBU, Reader Urology UCL; *m* 27 Feb 1975 *Hon Anna Margaret, yr dau of 3rd Baron Milford (*qv*), and has:

(1) +Jack Henry Lehmann; *b* 1978

(1) *Constance Margaret Davina; *b* 1982

2 +Nicholas Michael John [The Hon Nicholas Woodhouse, 72 Kingston Rd, Oxford]; *b* 27 Feb 1949; *educ* Winchester and Ch Ch Oxford; *m* 29 June 1973 *Mary Jane Stormont, only dau of D M Stormont Mowat, of Long Crendon, Bucks, and has:

(1) +Thomas Duncan; *b* 1987

1 *Emma Davina Mary [The Hon Mrs Johnson-Gilbert, 79 Thurleigh Rd, London SW12 8TY]; *b* 19 April 1954; *m* 1981 *Christopher Ian Johnson-Gilbert, s of T I Johnson-Gilbert, of St John's Wood, and has:

(1) *Hugh Christopher Ian; *b* 1991

(1) *Cordelia Mary; *b* 1983

(2) *Jemima Catherine; *b* 1985

(3) *Imogen Alice; *b* 1990

Lineage: JAMES WOODHOUSE, of Flamborough, E R Yorks; *b* 1791; *m* Jane Carter (*d* 28 Nov 1876) and *d* 20 Nov 1830, leaving:

JAMES THOMAS WOODHOUSE, of Manchester; *b* 30 Aug 1817; *m* 28 March 1848 Dorothy (*d* 1868), yst dau of Thomas Marton, of Terrington, Yorks, and *d* 2 Feb 1878, having had an est s:

JAMES THOMAS WOODHOUSE, **1st Baron Terrington**, of Huddersfield, Co York (UK), so cr 19 Jan 1918, JP, DL E R Yorks, JP Bucks; *b* 16 July 1852; *educ* Hull Coll and UCL (LLB 1871); slr 1873, twice Pres Hull Law Soc, Pres Yorks Law Soc, memb Cncl Incorporated Law Soc UK, Alderman Hull, CC E R Yorks 1888–96, Mayor Hull 1890–91, ktd 1895, MP (Lib) Huddersfield 1895–1906 (Lib Parly candidate Howdenshire 1892), Railway Commr 1906–1921, Pres Assoc Municipal Corps, dir: Hull and Barnsley Rlwy Co, Law Debenture Corp, London City and Midland Bank and Nat Telephone Co, chm Govrs Hymer's Coll, Chm Roy Commn Losses under Defence of Realm Acts 1915, Maj 1st Vol Bn E Yorks Regt; *m* 9 Aug 1876 Jessie (*d* 25 May 1942), 3rd dau of Walter James Reed, of Skidby, Yorks, and *d* 8 Feb 1921, leaving:

1 HAROLD JAMES SELBORNE WOODHOUSE, **2nd Baron Terrington**, OBE (1919), JP Bucks; *b* 8 May 1877; *educ* Marlborough; slr 1899, Assist Slr Gt Northern Rlwy 1899–1902, recruiting duties as Lt 1916, dir Earle's Shipbuilding and Engrg Co and Eastern Morning and Hull News Co; imprisoned 1928–32 for fraudulent conversion; *m* 1st 8 May 1918 (*divorce* 1926) Vera Florence Annie, MP (Lib) Wycombe 1923–24, widow of Guy Ivo Sebright (*see* SEBRIGHT, Bt) and dau of Henry George Bousher, of London; *m* 2nd 28 July 1927 Rena De Vere Humphrey (*d* 19 May 1973), only child of Capt William Molyneux Shapland-Swiny, 42nd Roy Highrs, of Ballymurrogh and Cloghamon, Co Wexford, and *dsp* 19 Nov 1940

2 HORACE MARTON, **3rd Baron**

1 Gladys; *m* 27 May 1914 Charles Fitzgerald Blood, of Ballykilty, Quin, Co Clare, est s of John Blood, of Ballykilty, and *d* 20 Aug 1970 aged 89, leaving issue. He *d* 4 Sept 1953

2 Kathleen Jessie; *m* 24 May 1911 Eugene Monier Wason, 3rd s of Eugene Wason, PC, of Blair Dailly, Ayrshire, and had issue. He *d* 22 Dec 1966

The 2nd BARON's bro,

HORACE MARTON WOODHOUSE, **3rd Baron Terrington**, KBE (1952, CBE 1919); *b* 27 Oct 1887; *educ* Winchester and New Coll Oxford; barrister Inner Temple 1911, Pncpl Assist Sec Min Labour 1941–44, Chm: Nat Arbitration Tbnl 1947, Industl Court 1947, Air Tport Advsy Cncl 1947, Dep Speaker and Dep Chm Ctees Ho Lds 1948; *m* 1st 28 May 1914 Valerie (*d* 16 Nov 1958), dau of George Allen Phillips, of Leydens Ho, Edenbridge; *m* 2nd 22 Oct 1959 Phyllis Mary (*d* 28 Nov 1971), formerly w of Maj Charles Haggard, The Buffs, and yr dau of William Wilson Drew, ICS, and *d* 7 Jan 1961, leaving by his 1st w:

1 (JAMES ALLEN) DAVID WOODHOUSE, **4th Baron Terrington**; *b* 30 Dec 1915; *educ* Winchester and RMC Sandhurst; Maj (ret 1948) Roy Norfolk Regt and Queen's Westminster Rifles (KRRC) TA WW II (wounded), ADC to GOC Madras 1940; memb London Stock Exchange, ptnr Messrs Sheppards and Chse 1952–80, dir S J Carr and Co (Gunmakers) Ltd, dep chm: Wider Share Ownership Cncl, London Ctee Oxfam, Ctees Ho Lds 1961–63, memb Ecclesiastical Ctee 1979–98, V-Pres Small Farmers' Assoc, Dep Chm Nat Listening Library, Talking Books for Disabled (memb Bd), memb Internat Advsy Bd American U Washington, DC; *m* 7 Nov 1942 *Suzanne [The Rt Hon The Lady Terrington, The Mill House, Braemore, Hants], yst dau of Col Thomas Strutt Irwin, JP, DL, Roy Dragoons, of Justicetown, Carlisle, and Mill Ho, Holton, Suffolk, and *d* 6 May 1998, leaving:

(1) *Lavinia Valerie [The Hon Mrs Bolton, 24 Harcourt Terr, London SW10]; *b* 29 Aug 1943; *m* 23 July 1974 (*divorce* 1989), as his 2nd w, Nicholas George Bolton, only s of Sir George Lewis French Bolton, KCMG, (*d* April 1998) and has:

1a *Carina Suzanne; *b* 1976

2a *Sophie Davina; *b* 1979

(2) *(Georgina) Caroline [The Hon Mrs Leatham, The Little House, Quenington, Glos GL7 5BW]; *b* 1 July 1946; interior designer; *m* 16 Jan 1996 *Philip William Leatham, s of Maj Patrick Magor Leatham, MC, by Hon Cecily Berry, 5th dau of 1st and last Baron Buckland (*see* HARTWELL, B)

(3) *Davina Mary, LVO (1991); *b* 12 April 1955; Pres SOS, memb Gen Cncl Friends Elderly and Gentlefolks' Help, Ldy-in-Waiting to HRH THE PRINCESS MARGARET, COUNTESS OF SNOWDON 1975–79, then Extra Ldy-in-Waiting; *m* 22 July 1981, as his 2nd w, *2nd Earl Alexander of Tunis (*qv*) and has issue

2 +(CHRISTOPHER) MONTAGUE WOODHOUSE, **5th and present Baron Terrington**

TEVIOT

Arms: Quarterly, 1st and 4th, gu. on a chevron arg. three mullets of the field (for KERR of Ferniehurst); 2nd and 3rd, per fess gu. and vert on a chevron arg. between three mascles in chief or and a unicorn's head in base of the third, horned of the fourth, three mullets of the first (for KERR of Cessford); in the centre of the quarters a rose or. **Crest:** A stag's head erased ppr. **Supporters:** Two border terriers ppr. **Motto:** *Sero sed serio* ('Late, but in earnest'). **Creation:** B. (UK) 27 June 1940.

THE 2ND BARON TEVIOT, of Burghclere, Co Southampton (Charles John Kerr) [The Rt Hon The Lord Teviot, 28 Hazel Grove, Burgess Hill, W Sussex RH15 0B7]; *b* 16 Dec 1934; *s* f 1968; *educ* Eton; genealogist, dir Debrett's Peerage Ltd 1977–83, Burke's Peerage Research 1983–85, Burke's Peerage Ltd 1984–85, memb Advsy Cncl Public Records 1974–83, Fell Soc Genealogists 1975, Pres Assoc Genealogists and Record Agents 1997–; *m* 25 Sept 1965 *Patricia Mary, dau of Alexander Harris, and has:

1 +CHARLES ROBERT; *b* 19 Sept 1971

1 *Catherine Harriet; *b* 17 Jan 1976

Lineage: Lord CHARLES WYNDHAM KERR (*see* LOTHIAN, M); had:

CHARLES IAN KERR, **1st Baron Teviot**, of Burghclere, Co Southampton (UK), so cr 27 June 1940, DSO (1919), MC; *b* 3 May 1874; Lt-Col RHG and MGC WW I (despatches), MP (Lib) Montrose 1932–40, Jr Ld Treasury 1937–39, Comptroller Household 1939–40, Chm Nat Lib Org 1940, Ch Whip Nat Lib Party Ho Lds 1945, Ensign Roy Co Archers 1945, dir: Lloyds Bank, Nat Bank Scotland, Gen Accident Fire and Life Assur and G D Peters of Slough, memb: Bd Management St Dunstan's Hostel for Blinded Soldiers; *m* 1st 24 Jan 1911 (*divorce* 1930) Muriel Constance, only dau of William Gordon Canning, of Hartpury, Glos; *m* 2nd 31 July 1930 (Florence) Angela (*d* 1979), er dau of Lt-Col Charles Walter Villiers (*see* CLARENDON, E), and *d* 7 Jan 1968, leaving:

CHARLES JOHN KERR, **2nd and present Baron Teviot**

TEYNHAM

SPES · MEA · IN · DEO

Arms: Quarterly, 1st and 4th, arg. on a bend sa. three popinjays or, collared gu. (for CURZON); 2nd and 3rd, per fess az. and or a pale countercharged, three buck's heads erased of the 2nd (for ROPER). **Crests:** 1 A popinjay rising or, collared gu. (for CURZON), 2 A lion rampant sa., upholding in the dexter paw a ducal coronet or (for ROPER). **Supporters:** Dexter, a buck or; sinister, a heraldic tiger regardant arg. **Motto:** *Spes mea in Deo* ('My hope is in God'). **Creation:** B. (E) 9 July 1616.

THE 20TH BARON TEYNHAM, of Teynham, Kent (John Christopher Ingham Roper-Curzon) [The Rt Hon The Lord Teynham, Pylewell Park, Lymington, Hants SO41 5SJ]; *b* 25 Dec 1928; *s f* 1972; *educ* Eton; land agent; 2nd Lt Coldstream Gds, Capt The Buffs (TA), Palestine 1948, ADC to Govr and C-in-C Bermuda 1953–54 and 1955, Priv Sec and ADC to Govr and C-in-C Leeward Islands 1956, ADC to Capt-Gen and Govr Jamaica 1962, memb Cncl Sail Training Assoc 1964–, Pres Inst Commerce 1972–, V-Pres Inst of Export; OStJ; *m* 31 Oct 1964 *Elizabeth, yr dau of Lt-Col Hon David Scrymgeour-Wedderburn (*see* DUNDEE, E), and has:

1 +DAVID JOHN HENRY INGHAM; *b* 5 Oct 1965; *m* 1985 *Lydia Lucinda, est dau of Maj-Gen Sir Christopher John Airy, KCVO, CBE, and has had:

  (1) +Henry Christopher John Ingham; *b* 5 Feb 1986
  (2) Jack; *b* and *d* 1990
  (3) +Tommy; *b* 1992
  (1) *(Elizabeth) Poppy; *b* 1989

2 +Jonathan Christopher James; *b* 27 April 1973
3 +Peter Michael Alexander; *b* 1977
4 +William Thomas; *b* 1980
5 +Benjamin Alexander; *b* 1982
1 *Emma Elizabeth; *b* 19 Sept 1966; *m* 1988 *Robert A Murphy, yr s of Christopher Murphy, of Fulham, and has:

  (1) *Doone; *b* 1989
  (1) *Wilhelmina; *b* 1990
  (2) *Jemima; *b* 1992

2 *Sophie Patricia; *b* 30 Nov 1967; *m* 1995 *Rupert van den Bogaerde and has:

  (1) *Jake; *b* 1997
  (1) *Jasmine; *b* 1996

3 *Lucy Elspeth; *b* 23 July 1969; *m* 1991 *Benjamin Hugh Fraser (*see* LOVAT, L) and has issue
4 *Hermione Marie Hilda Edith; *b* 27 April 1973
5 *Alice Penelope Rachael; *b* 1983

Lineage: WILLIAM ROPER/ROUJPERE; *m* Elnith, dau and heiress of Edward Apeldore, of Appledore, Kent (Dean Court, Appledore, was still owned by the family 1779); presumably kin to:

JOHN ROPER, of Wellhall and St Dunstan's, Kent; High Sheriff 1521, Prothonotary King's Bench, Attorney-Gen; *m* Jane, dau of Sir John Fineux, of Swingfield, Ch Justice King's Bench, and coheir of her mother, Elizabeth, dau and heiress of William Apulderfeld, and *d* 1524, having had:

1 William; Clerk King's Bench; *m* Margaret (*d* 1564 and was *bur* according to her dying request with her f's head in her arms), dau of Sir and St Thomas More, Ld Chllr, and *d* 4 Jan 1577, having had, with other issue:

  (1) Thomas; Ch Clerk King's Bench; *m* Lucia, dau of Sir Anthony Browne and sis of Anthony Browne, Viscount Montagu, and *d* 1567; his est s:

    1a William (Sir), of Eltham and St Dunstan's; *m* Catherine, dau and coheir of Sir Anthony Browne, of Ridley Hall, Ch Justice Common Pleas, and had an est s:

      1b Anthony; had an only s:

        1c Edward; had:

          1d Elizabeth; *m* Edward Henshaw, of Hampshire, and was ancestor of the families of Sir Edward Dering, Bt, of Surrenden, and Sir Rowland Wynne, Bt, of Nostell (*see* SAINT OSWALD, B)

  (1) Elizabeth; *m* Sir Edward Bray

  (2) Margaret; *m* Sir William Dawtrey, of Moor House

2 CHRISTOPHER

1 Eleanor; *m* 1st John Moreton; *m* 2nd Sir Edmund Montang, Ld Ch Justice King's Bench; *m* 3rd Sir John Digby
2 Elizabeth; *m* 1st John Pilborrow, a Baron Exchequer; *m* 2nd Leonard Saunders
3 Margaret; *m* Henry Appleton, of Dartford, Kent
4 Anne; *m* Sir Edward Maddison
5 Elizabeth; *m* Sir John Dawnay
6 Agnes; nun at Dartford

The 2nd s,

CHRISTOPHER ROPER, of Badmangore, Kent; *m* Elizabeth, dau of Christopher Blore, of Teynham, and had an est s:

Sir JOHN ROPER, **1st Baron Teynham**, of Teynham, Kent (E), so *cr* 9 July 1616; *m* 1st 1560 Elizabeth (*d* 15 Sept 1567), dau and heiress of John Parke, of Malmaine, Kent; *m* 2nd Elizabeth, widow of Robert Monson and dau and heiress of John Dyon, of Tathwell, Lincs, and *d* 30 Aug 1618, leaving, with at least one dau (Elizabeth, who harboured at her husb's house of Harrowden the Jesuit Robert Gerard and was a suspect in the investigations into the Gunpowder Plot, hence imprisoned 1611–13, *m* 25 July 1585 George Vaux (*see* VAUX OF HARROW-DEN, B) and *d* in or after Nov 1625), an est s:

CHRISTOPHER ROPER, **2nd Baron Teynham**; *m* 20 June 1590 Catherine (*d* 2 Oct 1625), dau of John Seborne, of Sutton St Michael, Herefs, and *d* 16 April 1622, leaving, with at least one dau (Katharine, *m c* 1630, as his 2nd w, Sir Robert Thorold, 1st Bt (*qv*), of the 1644 *cr*), an est s:

JOHN ROPER, **3rd Baron Teynham**, KB (1616); *m* 20 Nov 1616 Mary (*d* 14 Dec 1640), dau of 2nd Baron Petre (*qv*), and *d* 27 Feb 1627, leaving, with two yr sons and four daus:

CHRISTOPHER ROPER, **4th Baron Teynham**; *m* 1st 1640 Mary (*d* 21 Dec 1647), dau of Sir Francis Englefield, of Wootton Bassett, Wilts, and had issue; *m* 2nd Philadelphia (*bur* 10 Nov 1655), widow of Sir John Mill, Bt, and dau of Sir Henry Knollys, of Grove Park, Hants, and by her had issue; *m* 3rd 29 March 1660 Margaret, dau of 17th Baron of Kerry and Lixnaw (*see* LANSDOWNE, M), and *d* 23 Oct 1673; his est s:

CHRISTOPHER ROPER, **5th Baron Teynham**; Ld Lt and custos rotulorum Kent; *m* 1674 Elizabeth, dau of 3rd Viscount Montagu, and *d* by 24 July 1689, having had, with other issue:

1 JOHN ROPER, **6th Baron Teynham**; *d unm* by 1697
2 CHRISTOPHER ROPER, **7th Baron Teynham**; *d unm* by 23 Sept 1699
3 HENRY ROPER, **8th Baron Teynham**; *b c* 1676; conformed to C of E; *m* 1st 25 Jan 1703/4 Catherine (*d* 26 April 1711), dau of 2nd Viscount Strangford (*see* 1869 edn), and had:

  (1) PHILIP ROPER, **9th Baron Teynham**; *b* 28 Feb 1707; *d unm* 13 June 1727
  (2) HENRY, **10th Baron**
  (1) Anne; *m* John Webb (*dvp*), er s of Sir John Webb, 3rd Bt, and *dsp*

3 (cont.) The **8th Baron** *m* 2nd 22 Jan 1715/6 Mary (*dsp, bur* 10 Jan 1716/7), dau of Sir John Gage, 4th Bt (*see* GAGE, V); *m* 3rd March 1717/8 Baroness Dacre in her own right (*qv*; she *m* 3rd 16 Oct 1725 Hon Robert Moore (*see* DROGHEDA, E) and *d* 26 June 1755), widow of Richard Barrett-Lennard and dau of 15th Lord (Baron) Dacre (*qv*), and shot himself while the balance of his mind was disturbed 16 May 1723, having by her had, with other issue (*see* DACRE, B):

  (3) Richard Henry (Rev); *b* Nov 1723; Rector Clones, Co Monaghan; *m* 1st 20 May 1755 Mary (*dsp* Jan 1758), dau of 3rd Viscount Chetwynd (*qv*); *m* 2nd 1760 Mary (*d* 16 Feb 1795), dau of Capt Thomas Tenison, of Finglas, Co Dublin, and *d* Nov 1810, leaving:

    1a Henry (Very Rev); *b* 19 March 1761; DD, Dean Clonmacnoise; *m* 29 Dec 1796 Mary (*d* 25 Oct 1843), dau of Rev Thomas Chamberlayne, and *d* 18 April 1847, leaving, with two daus:

      1b William Lennard (Rev); Rector Monaghan; *m* 21 Sept 1824 Charlotte, dau of John Paine Garnett, of Arch Hall, Co Meath, and *d* 13 Aug 1849, leaving:

        1c Mary Charlotte; *m* 24 Sept 1850 Matthew Henry Sankey, of Lurganbrae, Co Fermanagh, and *d* 7 Oct 1851, leaving issue

      2b John Henry; *b* 8 Nov 1803; *m* 27 Nov 1845 Annie Boxwell, dau of Henry Blanc, and *d* 15 July 1890, leaving:

        1c William Henry (Rev); *b* 5 Oct 1849; BA Dublin; Incumbent Clonard, Co Meath; *d* 14 Oct 1917

        1c Mary; *m* 3 Aug 1865 James Roper Whitestone and *d* 7 Oct 1891, leaving issue

      3b Henry Welladvice; *b* 25 Oct 1806; Maj 8th Regt; *m* 10 July 1851 Rosetta (*d* Aug 1856), dau of Maj Edward Butler, and *d* Oct 1883, leaving a dau (*d unm*)

      4b Blayney Tenison; *b* 10 Feb 1811; *m* 20 May 1848 Emily Jane, only child of William Kilpatrick, and *d* 30 March 1886, leaving:

        1c Blayney Tenison; *b* 31 Dec 1853; *m* June 1892 Emily Elizabeth (*d* 23 Jan 1937), dau of James Campbell Christian, of Sligo, and *d* 7 March 1938, leaving:

          1d Richard Blayney; *b* 21 Dec 1897; Lt-Col IA WW I Egypt and Mesopotamia, Waziristan 1919–21, WW II in India with Bengal Sappers and Miners; *m* 3 Sept 1930 Elmslie (*d* 5 Oct 1962), only dau of William Forbes-Garden, and *d* 12 Oct 1964, leaving:

            1e +Christopher Blayney [Christopher Roper Esq, 40 Northumberland Ave, Craighall Pk, Johannesburg 2196, S Africa]; *b* 28 July 1932; mining engr, ASCM, 2nd Lt RE 1953–55; *m* 28 Sept 1963 *Elizabeth Garthorne, 2nd dau of Andrew Ian Dalglish Brown, of Johannesburg, and has:

              1f *Katherine Elizabeth [Mrs Ian Burman, 22D Guildford Rd, Tunbridge Wells, Kent TN1 1LS]; *b* 22 March 1966; *educ* Witwatersrand U (BSc); *m* 1989 *Ian Frederick Burman

              2f *Margaret Jennifer; *b* 20 Dec 1967; *educ* Witwatersrand U (BPrimEd, BEd)

3f *Philippa Garthorne; *b* 28 Oct 1969; *educ* Inscape Coll (DipID)

1e *Margaret Elizabeth [Mrs John Cousins, 65 Harvey St, Taupo, New Zealand]; *b* 8 July 1935; *m* 21 Nov 1959 *Maj John David Cousins, 10th Princess Mary's Own Gurkha Rifles, s of Lt-Col Cyril Walter Cousins, of Orchard Leigh, Broadhempston, Devon, and has:

　1f *Terence David; *b* 21 Sept 1969; MB, ChB

　1f *Elizabeth Mary; *b* 1972

1d *Aileen Emily; *m* 14 Nov 1939 Gerald Richard Butler (*d* 9 June 1953), s of Gerald Walter Butler, of Ballyadams, Athy, Co Kildare, and *d* 29 July 1985

2d Margaret Noel; *m* 23 Aug 1923 Capt Robert Peverell Rogers, Wilts Regt, yr s of Capt John Peverell Rogers, of Penrose, and *d* 4 Nov 1925, leaving issue

2c Henry William; *b* 6 Feb 1858; *m* 1889 Margaret Jane (*d* 14 Jan 1950), est dau of William Aiken, MD, and *d* 1 July 1945, leaving:

　1d Blayney Trevor; *b* 2 Nov 1894; *educ* Campbell Coll Belfast; Northumberland Hus and 6th Dragoon Gds WW I; *m* 1925 Doris, dau of D S Kennaway, of Cramlington, and *dsp* 17 Feb 1969

1c Elizabeth Emily; *d* 1924

2c Caroline Fannie; *m* 27 Oct 1891 William Anthony Atthill, of Ramsgate, and *d* 1916, leaving issue

3c Mary Edith; *d* unm 5 May 1951

2a Cadwallader Blayney ROPER later TREVOR-ROPER (roy licence 14 Jan 1809 on inheriting Plas-Teg, Flints, from his cousin Mary Jane, Dowager Lady Dacre); *b* 8 Feb 1765; *m* 1st 22 Jan 1796 Elizabeth Anne (*d* 14 June 1816), dau of Henry Reveley, and had:

1b Charles Blayney, of Plas-Teg; *b* 22 Sept 1799; *m* 5 Dec 1821 Mary (*d* 19 Oct 1878), only dau of Samuel Knight, and *d* 9 Feb 1871, having had:

　1c Charles James, of Plas-Teg, JP, DL Flints; *b* 29 Oct 1823; MA Oxon; High Sheriff Flints 1878, Hon Col 6th Bn KRRC; *m* 1st 30 Nov 1854 Lucy Anne (*d* 1 March 1871), yst dau of Samuel Aldersey, of Cheshire; *m* 2nd 8 July 1873 Julia Maria (*d* 26 Sept 1943), est dau of Sir Cornelius Hendricksen Kortright, KCMG, and *dsp* 20 Sept 1901

　2c William; *b* 30 Dec 1827; *m* 1st 27 July 1864 Rose Myra (*d* 15 Nov 1874), dau of Rev John R N Kinchant, JP, Incumbent Llanvair Waterdene, and Bettws, Salop, and had:

　　1d Ethel Maud; *m* 28 June 1888 George Henry Philott, CE, of Plas Trevor, Cheltenham, and had issue. He *d* 1926

　2c (cont.) William Trevor-Roper *m* 2nd 23 Oct 1877 Elizabeth Cunninghame (*dsp* 12 Dec 1898), dau and coheir of Rev John Luxmore, of Kerslake, Devon, and *d* 1890

　3c George Edward; *b* 16 April 1831; *m* 21 Nov 1868 his cousin Harriette (*d* 1920), est dau of Richard Trevor-Roper (*see below*), and *d* 30 Sept 1893, leaving:

　　1d Charles Cadwaladr, of Plas-Teg; *b* 9 Feb 1884; Lt 5th Bn RWF, Capt 4th Bn Hants Regt; *m* 8 April 1913 Gertrude Alice (*d* 28 Feb 1962, having *m* 2nd 24 Feb 1925 Maj Robert Hugh Poyntz, MC, KSLI, who *d* 11 Oct 1931), only dau of William George Clabby, Indian Police, and *d* 3 Aug 1917 of wounds recd in action, leaving:

　　　1e Richard Dacre, DFC, DFM; *b* 19 May 1915; F/Lt RAF WW II; *m* 5 Sept 1942 *Patricia Audrey [Mrs John Straight, 292 Reading Rd, Winnersh, Berks] (*m* 2nd 1949 Frank Marvin; *m* 3rd 1955 John Derick Straight), dau of Richard Barrie Edwards, of Nottingham, and was *k* on air operations over Germany 31 March 1944, leaving:

　　　　1f +Charles Anthony [Charles Roper Esq, Brookdale House, N Huish, nr Totnes, S Devon]; *b* 15 June 1943; *educ* Wellington and Reading U (BSc, PhD); *m* 1967 *Carol Elizabeth, dau of Charles James Pape, and has:

　　　　　1g +Dacre Gabriel; *b* 1969

　　　　　2g +Mathew Blayney; *b* 1977

　　　　1e *Elizabeth Alice; *b* 7 Jan 1914; *m* 1 June 1935 Harry Hyde Parker (*see* PARKER, Bt, of Melford Hall)

　　　　2e *Anne; *b* 10 Sept 1916; *m* 22 Feb 1941 *Josiah Maddocks, s of James Maddocks, and has:

　　　　　1f *Richard James; *b* 1943; *m* 1st 1965 (*divorce* 1988) Dorothy Suzanne Pallett; *m* 2nd 1992 *Gillian Lillie Lovelock, formerly w of — Garner, and by his 1st w has:

　　　　　　1g *John Charles James; *b* 1967; *m* 1994 *Rachael Lorna Chamberlain

　　　　　　1g *(Valerie) Suzanne; *b* 1966

　　　　　2f *David Hugh; *b* 1950; *m* 1974 *Irene Alexandra Porteous and has:

　　　　　　1g *Alexander David; *b* 1983

　2d Geoffrey; *b* 1885; Roy Fus WW I; *ka* 1917

　　1d Alice Marian; *m* 27 Dec 1902 her yr sister's bro-in-law William Reginald Howard, barrister, s of John Howard, of Aberfeldy, and *d* 1944, leaving issue. He *d* 17 Feb 1966

　　2d Mabel; *m* 1899 Capt Frank Muncaster Howard, RAF, s of John Howard, of Aberfeldy, and *d* 22 March 1932

　　3d Helen; *m* 6 Nov 1901 Frank Arthur Money Hampe Vincent, CIE, CBE, MVO, of Moor Park, Herts, Commr Police Bombay, s of Robert William Edward Hampe Vincent, CIE, and *d* 24 Feb 1930. He *d* 21 Oct 1950

　　4d Norah, DGStJ; *m* 5 March 1902 Maj George Coventry Alletson, DSO, s of G H Alletson, of Northop, Flints, and had issue. He *d* 14 May 1928

　　5d Winifred; *d* unm Nov 1958

　　6d Violet; *m* 20 Nov 1907 William George Clabby, Indian Police, and *d* Sept 1936, leaving issue. He *d* 20 Oct 1924

　　7d Eveleen; *d* unm 27 Nov 1927

　　8d Florence; *m* 1 March 1927 Marsom Buttfield, of Jersey. He *d* 1939

9d Gwendoline; *m* 11 June 1914 Hugh Cecil Maynard Lousada and had issue

4c Richard Henry; *b* 28 Sept 1834; *m* 16 Sept 1864 Grace Carr (*m* 2nd 3 April 1901 Hugh William Trevor-Roper (*see below*) and *d* 1909), dau of Henry Messeena, MD, and *d* 9 March 1889, having had:

　1d Claude Henry; *b* 26 July 1869; *d* unm 12 Dec 1946

　2d Charles Harold; *b* 17 March 1872; *d* unm 1922

　3d Richard Harry; *b* 1, 7 Sept 1873

　4d Ernest Messeena; *b* 28 March 1875; *m* 14 May 1904 Claire (*d* 22 June 1942), only dau of John Dobson, of Altrincham and Buxton, and *d* 26 Aug 1956, leaving:

　　1e *Irene Dorothy; *b* 2 June 1906; *m* 1st 9 June 1934 (*annulled* 1941) Clifford Frank Humphries, est s of Frank Humphries, of Royston, Herts; *m* 2nd 14 July 1962 John Ernest Llewellyn Poulson

　5d Arthur Messeena; *b* 4 July 1876; T/Capt Devonshire Regt, Imp Yeo Boer War 1900–01; *m* 8 Oct 1902 Mary Winifred (*d* 1958), dau of James Keel, of Cheddar, Somerset, and *d* 7 May 1966, leaving:

　　1e Richard Teynham; *b* 25 July 1903; *m* 1928 Lilian M Prestwood (*d* 1978) and *d* 3 Jan 1968, leaving:

　　　1f +Richard Eric [Richard Trevor-Roper Esq, 14 Groby Rd, Glenfield, Leics]; *b* 1928; *m* 1st 17 April 1954 (*divorce* 1959) Patricia Anne McClintock and has:

　　　　1g +Richard Patrick [Richard Trevor-Roper Esq, 64 Hinau St, Wanganui, New Zealand]; *b* 19 Aug 1955; *m* 1977 *Michelle Anne Lhonneux and has:

　　　　　1h +Michael Patrick; *b* 1980

　　　　　2h +Jason Charles; *b* 1982

　　　　　3h +Ryan Paul; *b* 1986

　　　1f (cont.) Richard Trevor-Roper *m* 2nd 17 Oct 1964 *Marilyn Elizabeth Fox

　　　1f *Kathleen Edith [Mrs Kenneth Jones, 139 Leicester Rd, Thurcaston, Liecs]; *b* 16 Jan 1931; *m* 14 July 1951 *Kenneth Leslie Jones, s of Benjamin Jones, of Redmarley, Glos, and has:

　　　　1g *Nigel Kenneth; *b* 22 April 1952; *m* 1972 *Gillian Ann Hardy and has:

　　　　　1h *Nicola Marie; *b* 1976

　　　　　2h *Abbie Eileen; *b* 1978

　　2e Cyril Peter; *b* 31 May 1916; *m* 1940 *Lorna Eileen, dau of Harry J Smith, of Hillside Terrace, Dorchester, and *d* April 1995, leaving:

　　　1f *Virginia Yvonne; *b* 6 Jan 1943; *m* — Mahalski

　　　2f *Sandra Victoria; *b* 2 Oct 1946; *m* — Williams

　　　3f Susan Brenda; *b* 7 May 1952; *m* — Wallace and *d* 19–

　　1e Kathleen Victoria; *b* 16 May 1911; *m* 1940 *George Stanley White and *d* 4 April 1996

　　2e *Margaret Elizabeth [Mrs Niels Nielson, 23 Hampshire Rd, Aylestone, Leicester LE2 8HF]; *b* 25 Dec 1923; *m* 1946 *Niels Peter Nielson

6d Bertie William Edward; *b* 25 June 1885; *educ* Victoria U Manchester (MB and ChB 1908); MRCS and LRCP (Lond) 1908; *m* 15 Sept 1910 Kathleen Elizabeth (*d* 13 Dec 1964), dau of William R Davison, and *d* 3 Jan 1978, leaving:

　1e +HUGH REDWALD TREVOR-ROPER, BARON DACRE OF GLANTON (*qv*)

　2e +Patrick Dacre [Patrick Trevor-Roper Esq, 3 Park Sq West, London NW1 4LJ]; *b* 1916; *educ* Charterhouse and Clare Coll Cambridge; MRCS and LRCP Lond 1940, FRCS Eng 1947, MD Cantab 1959, DOMS Eng, FZS, Ophthalmic Surgn Westminster and Moorfields Hosps, late Capt NZ Med Corps

　1e Sheila Grace; *b* 1912; *m* 1st 25 March 1942 Keith Maelor Price, TD, s of D A Price, of Moorgate, Rotherham; *m* 2nd 10 May 1972 A Colin Kingham, MC, s of Arthur Kingham, JP, of Watford, Herts, (*d* 5 March 1975); *m* 3rd 2 Jan 1979 Sir Oliver Simmonds (*d* 25 Jan 1985) and *d* 15 Nov 1992, leaving by her 1st husb:

　　1f *Martin Trevor; *b* 15 Nov 1946; *educ* Brickwall

　　2f *Nicholas David [Nicholas Price Esq, Jackamasts Bottom Farm, Tetbury Rd, Cirencester, Glos]; *b* 22 Feb 1948; *educ* Charterhouse; *m* 13 June 1990 *Serena Ann Rosamund Helps and has:

　　　1g *Hugo; *b* 22 Aug 1991

1d Edith Grace; *m* 1896 Godrey Melland, BSc, ARSM, and *d* 30 April 1947

2d Lilian Blanche; *d* an infant 6 June 1870

3d Maud Mary; *m* 1899 John Howarth Tweedie, of Eltham, Kent, and *d* 14 Dec 1945, leaving issue

4d Grace Messeena; *m* 1902 Edward Barker Thornber, BA, and had issue

5d Naomi Messeena; *m* 27 Dec 1919 Hugh Robert Wallace Anderson and *d* 10 March 1962

6d Gladys; *m* George Earle and *d* April 1919, leaving issue

5c Dacre, of Pyleigh, Somerset; *b* 12 Jan 1839; *m* 25 Aug 1875 Louisa (*d* 29 April 1931), dau of William Wanklyn, of Manchester, and *d* 18 July 1922, leaving:

　1d Lennard Carew; *b* 22 July 1876; *m* 1st 15 Feb 1898 Margaret Helen (*d* 9 May 1901), dau of James Laffan, and had:

　　1e Arthur Teynham; *b* 3 May 1901; *d* 19 June 1920

　　1e *Kathleen Mary; *b* 2 Feb 1900; *m* 19 Nov 1924 Maj Robert Henry Bolton, MM, TD, Sherwood Foresters, s of William Henry Bolton, of Edinwinstowe

　1d (cont.) Lennard Trevor-Roper *m* 2nd 15 April 1909 Lisbeth Rankin (*d* 28 July 1970), dau of Alexander Knight Stein, and *d* 24 June 1948, having by her had:

2e +Lennard Dacre; *b* 8 Feb 1910; *m* March 1935 *Constance Mary, dau of R Barr, of Coventry

3e Ranulf, DFC; *b* 15 June 1915; F/Lt RAF WW II; *ka* Norway 31 March 1945

4e John Cadwaladr; *b* 18 Nov 1918; 4th Co London Yeo WW II; *ka* 13 June 1944

2e Amber Hazel; *b* 21 June 1906

3e *Janet Rankin; *b* 8 July 1911; 3rd Offr WRNS WW II; *m* 1942 Maj Vivian Malcolm Edward Bateson, King's Liverpool Regt (*d* 1958), and has:

1f *Simon Vivian Ranulf; *b* 7 Aug 1946; *educ* Imp Coll London U

1f *Julia Janet; *b* 7 Nov 1948; *m* 1965 (*divorce*) John Read, son of James Gregory Read, of 5, Loring Rd, Sharnbrook, and has issue:

1g *Sean Richard Malcolm; *b* 19 April 1965

2g *Conway Luke; *b* 22 April 1968

3g *Heathcliffe John; *b* 21 Jan 1970

1g *Amber Ruth; *b* 1966

4e *Elsie; *b* 26 Aug 1913; WRNS WW II; *m* 5 Dec 1942 Humphrey Barton Henderson, LDS (*d* Nov 1955), s of George Edward Walker Henderson, LRCP, LRCS, of St Andrews, and has:

1f *John Trevor Howard; *b* 23 May 1947; *m* 1 Nov 1969 *Jennifer Kinanne, dau of Wallace Stuart Mackay, of Chesham Bois, Bucks

1f *Stella Marian; *b* 25 Sept 1947; *m* 23 July 1966 *Dennis James Aris, s of C C Aris, of Leighton Buzzard

2d Hubert; *b* 5 Dec 1877; *ka* 13 June 1918

3d Henry Blayney; *b* 24 Sept 1881; *d* 1 April 1882

4d Ranulph Dacre (Rev); *b* 13 April 1893; Lt Sherwood Foresters, Maj RE, WW I (wounded twice), WW II, ordained 1959; *m* 23 Nov 1916 Joan Fraser (*d* 1976), only child of Robert Fraser Woodcock, MRCS, of Wigan, and *d* 1975, leaving:

1e +Robert ffarington; *b* 29 Aug 1917; *educ* U Coll Sch; Maj Lancs Fus WW II (wounded); *m* 19 Oct 1941 *Dorothy Davina, yst dau of James Mackay, of Edinburgh

2e Anthony Dacre, MC; *b* 1 Jan 1921; *educ* U Coll Sch; Capt IA, Hon Capt Lancs Fus, WW II (wounded), Korea 1950–51; *m* 16 Jan 1954 *Amy Frances [Mrs Anthony Trevor-Roper, The Flat, Great Oakley Hall, Great Oakley, Northants], yst dau of Capt John Douglas Collins, of Ingram Ho, Burton Bradstock, Dorset, and *d* 1986, leaving:

1f +Julian Dacre; *b* 25 Oct 1956

2f +Christopher Charles ffarington; *b* 26 Feb 1964

1f *Mary Anne; *b* 15 Dec 1954; *m* 1982 *Michael John Frederick Charles Buswell and has:

1g *Jonathan Charles; *b* 1982

2f *Susan Elizabeth; *b* 17 June 1958; *educ* Imp Coll Sci (BSc); ARCS 1980; *m* 1982 *Nicholas Mark Palmer, 2nd s of B E Palmer, of Hadley Green, Herts

1e *Helen Bennetta [Mrs Terence Summers, 15 Pigeon House Lane, Freeland, Oxford]; *b* 12 Aug 1919; *m* 1st 5 Jan 1940 Richard Stoate, s of John Stoate, of Bristol; *m* 2nd 13 July 1957 *Terence H Summers

2e *Joan Everilda [Mrs Joan Howell, 4 Wetherell Place, Bristol B58 1AR]; *b* 3 March 1923; *m* 19 June 1940 (*divorce* 1968) Owen John Howell, ARIBA (*d* 1982), est s of John Lloyd Howell, of London N20, and has:

1f *Robin John [Robin Howell Esq, Burtle Farm, Robins Lane, Burtle, Somerset TA7 8NT]; *b* 14 April 1941; *m* 1st 18 July 1963 (*divorce* 1984) Pamela Ann, dau of Alfred Raymond Reader, of Northampton; *m* 2nd 1984 *Claire, 2nd dau of Cyril Hunter, and by his 1st w has:

1g *Jonathan Raef; *b* 1964

2g *Nicholas Dacre; *b* 16 Dec 1966

3g *Christopher Noel; *b* 1 July 1969

4g *Benjamin James; *b* 1970

2f Trevor Owen; *b* 14 April 1944; *m* 24 April 1965 *Gillian, est dau of Roland Poole, of Croydon, Surrey, and *d* 1976

1f *Jennifer Eve [Mrs Anthony Duval, Burtle Farm, Robins Lane, Burtle, Somerset TA7 8NT]; *b* 11 Sept 1949; *m* 1970 *Anthony Stephen Duval and has:

1g *Simon Joseph; *b* 1975

2g *Timothy James; *b* 1978

1d Mary; *d* unm 19 May 1955

2d Margaret Roper; *b* 9 Jan 1884; *m* 25 Aug 1913 Vincent Daniel, BSc, and *d* 9 Oct 1965, leaving issue. He *d* 15 Nov 1952

1c Elizabeth Mary; *m* 26 Aug 1846 Capt Pellew Matson Briggs, Bombay Army, and *d* 2 June 1857, leaving issue. He *d* 13 April 1866

2c Anne; *m* 24 June 1847 Rev John Watson, of Lutterworth, and 21 April 1915, leaving issue. He *d* 3 April 1867

3c Gertrude; *m* 8 Nov 1860 Lt-Col Edmund G Maynard and had issue

4c Charlotte Blanche; *m* 26 Sept 1861 Rt Hon Henry Cecil Raikes, MP, of Llwynegrin Hall, Flints, and *d* 18 Dec 1922, leaving issue. He *d* 24 Aug 1891

5c Emily Constance; *m* 15 March 1865 Holland T Birkett and *dsp* 14 Nov 1865

2b Richard; *b* 7 Dec 1810; *m* 17 Aug 1841 Marian (*d* 12 Dec 1900), only dau of John Rigby, and had:

1c Henry Pellew; *b* 12 Aug 1846; *m* 27 Oct 1875 Amy Juliet (*d* 1889), yst dau of Rev George Preston, and *d* 5 Sept 1877, leaving:

1d Cyril Henry; *b* 13 May 1877

2c Hugh William; *b* 23 Oct 1858; *m* 3 April 1901 Grace Carr (*d* 1909), widow of Richard Henry Trevor-Roper (*see above*) and dau of Henry Messeena, MD, and *dsp* 1903

1c Harriette; *m* 21 Nov 1867 her cousin George Edward Trevor-Roper and *d* 1920 leaving issue (*see above*)

2c Marian Blanche; *m* 16 June 1874 V-Adml Oswald Peploe Tudor, CVO, s of Capt John Tudor, RN, and had issue. He *d* 5 Aug 1908

3c Florence; *m* 16 Sept 1890 Brian Melland, MD, of The Bower, Bowdon, Manchester, and *d* 12 Jan 1924, leaving issue

4c Eleanor; *m* 26 Sept 1893 Frederick Duncan Wills (*see* WILLS, Bt, of Blagdon) and *d* 26 Nov 1921

1b Mary Jane; *m* Honoratus Leigh Rigby and *d* 11 Nov 1863, leaving issue. He *d* 22 Oct 1851

2b Anna Maria; *m* 23 Dec 1827 James Boydell and had issue. He *d* 22 Dec 1862

2a (cont.) Cadwallader Trevor-Roper *m* 2nd 24 Sept 1817 Elizabeth (*d* 3 June 1820), dau of Rev Clark Gayton, and *d* 20 Oct 1832, having by her had:

3b George, of Fern Bank, Rock Ferry, Cheshire; *b* 14 May 1820; MD; *m* 24 April 1850 Amelia (*m* 2nd John Williams, of Moate Ho, Co Galway, and *d* 13 Jan 1902), 3rd dau of Capt Archibald Macdonald, RN, and *d* 14 Nov 1870, having had:

1c Cadwallader Blayney; *b* 10 Nov 1856; *d* unm 1877

2c George Dacre; *b* 17 Sept 1862; LRCP Edin, Surgn RN; *d* 7 Feb 1915

1c Amelia Elizabeth; *m* 1 Oct 1877 Philip Arthur Scott, of Queenstown, and had issue

2c Harriet Agnes; *m* 1st 7 April 1875 J W Langlands, of Merr Cottage, Oxton, Cheshire, *m* 2nd 12 July 1921 Maj Charles Beville

3c Clementina Hadow; *m* 19 Aug 1876 George Ward Cook and had issue. He *d* July 1931

4c Flora; *m* 8 June 1887 Col George McDonald, RE, of Carrol, Inverness-shire, and had issue

5c Caroline Fanny; *m* 27 Dec 1877 Edward Matthew Price, of The Philbreds, Maidenhead, and had issue

3b Agnes; *m* Henry Boydell and had issue

4b Caroline; *d* unm

3a William Roper, of Rathfarnham Castle; *b* 7 Jan 1768; barrister; *m* Elizabeth (*d* 1845), dau of R Fish, and *d* 16 July 1832, leaving:

1b Charles, of Fairfield, Co Dublin, JP; *m* 13 Sept 1831 Eleanor Catherine (*d* 1841), only dau of Maj William Hore, 67th Regt, 2nd s of William Hore, of Harperstown, and *d* 9 May 1861, having had, with a dau (*d* unm):

1c William, JP, of Fairfield, Artane, Co Dublin; *b* 1837; MA Dublin; *m* 6 Dec 1871 Helena Sophia (*d* 23 Feb 1926), 2nd dau of Samuel Strangman, of Summerland, Waterford, and *d* 6 April 1901, leaving:

1d Charles; *b* 23 Feb 1874; *m* 30 Sept 1913 Josephine Marita (*d* 18 Aug 1953), er dau of Adam Cook Newell, RM, of Kilgorrive, Ballinasloe, and *d* 1955, leaving:

1e +William Richard Charles; *b* 1920; NI Horse WW II 1940–42; *m* 1957 *Therese Margaret, dau of Henry Lewis Norman D'Arcy, of Glenageary, Co Dublin

2d Samuel Strangman; *b* 19 May 1876

3d William Trevor; *b* 20 Oct 1880; Lt RASC attd RGA WW I (despatches); *m* 1st 3 Sept 1913 Elsie Beatrice (*d* 1934), only dau of Thomas Holt, of Oxton, Cheshire, and had:

1e Trevor Holt; *b* 1914; *m* 2 July 1938 *Hylda Florence [Mrs Trevor Roper, 203 Rosses Court, Dun Laoghaire, Co Dublin, Ireland], dau of Charles T Marks, and *d* 1988, leaving:

1f *Penelope Margaret [Mrs David Proger, Crowe Abbey House, Killincarrig, Delgany, Co Wicklow, Ireland]; *b* 13 April 1944; *m* 22 June 1968 *David Allengame Proger, s of Glyndwr Waldron Proger, of Higher Bowden, Bovey Tracey, Devon, and has:

1g *Lizanne Margaret; *b* 7 Oct 1969; *m* 19– *David Molind and has:

1h *Owen Proger; *b* 8 Nov 1997

2g *Philippa Jane [Mrs Anthony McGuinness, 24 Millgrove, Killincarrig, Delgany, Co Wicklow, Ireland]; *b* 16 Nov 1972; *m* 19– *Anthony McGuinness

3g *Nicola Kate; *b* 28 Dec 1980

2e +Dacre Alexander [Dacre Roper Esq, Kings Shade, 70 The Street, Capel, Surrey RH5 5LA]; *b* 1921; Lt (L) RNVR WW II, AMIEE; *m* 1st 21 March 1945 Sylvia Mary, dau of Thomas H Jameson, of Dublin; *m* 2nd 1987 *Joan Hodges, of Beare Green, Surrey, and by his 1st w has:

1f *Lynda Susan; *b* 18 Feb 1948

3d (cont.) William Roper *m* 2nd 1938 *Janet Pegman and *d* 1956, having by her had:

3e +Anthony Arthur Trevor; *b* 1948

1d Florence Muriel; *b* 27 June 1879; *d* unm 23 April 1936

2c Henry; *b* 1841

3c Samuel Bradstreet; *b* 1845; *d* unm March 1900

1c Eleanor Catherine; *m* 29 April 1862 S P Lindsay

2c Emily; *m* 16 Aug 1871 Edward Doherty, of Glen Ho, Co Donegal, and *d* 25 Jan 1907, leaving issue

3c Charlotte; *m* 1st 25 April 1872 Walter B Woodward, MD (*d* 1905), of San Diego, Calif., s of Henry T Woodward, of Drumbarrow, Kells, Co Meath, and had issue; *m* 2nd 1907 Joseph W Coyner, MD (*d* 1914), of Los Angeles; *m* 3rd 1915 William Darby Coburn, of San Diego, and *d* 20 May 1931

2b Henry (Sir); *b* 16 April 1800; ktd 1839, Ch Justice Bombay; *m* 2 Sept 1847 Charlotte Lydia (*d* 16 Feb 1892), dau of Rev Hon Frederick Pleydell-Bouverie (*see* RADNOR, E), and *d* 20 March 1863, having had:

1c Henry Charles; *b* 6 April 1850; *educ* Eton and Merton Coll Oxford; barrister; *m* 14 Aug 1912 Hilda Kate Marguerite Collen (*d* 23 Feb 1966), dau of Alfred John Stearn, of Bythe Church, Cambridge, and *d* 12 Dec 1916, leaving:

1d +Alexander John Henry, TD; b 6 Aug 1913; educ Tonbridge and King's Coll London (BSc 1934); Capt RA, Fell Roy Empire Soc; m 1st 10 Sept 1947 Marjorie Edith (d 1981), dau of Henry Broom Vines, of Lower Field, Bourton, Berks; m 2nd 1983 *Evelyn Joan, dau of Herbert Vines, of Petwick Farm, Challow, Berks, and by his 1st w has:

1e +Richard Henry; b 29 Nov 1948; educ Abingdon Sch

1e *Margaret Hilda Jane; b 29 Aug 1950

2c Alexander William, CB (1914), CBE (1919); b 3 July 1862; Col RE, Hon Brig-Gen, Nile Expdn 1884–85 (medal with clasp and bronze star), Boer War 1899–1902 (Queen's medal with three clasps, King's medal with two clasps, brevet), WW I (1915 star and two medals); d unm 6 March 1940

1c Charlotte; b 31 Oct 1848; d unm 11 Aug 1930

2c Margaret Emma; d unm 13 Nov 1869

3c Alice; d young, 7 Jan 1862

4c Elizabeth Catherine; b 12 Nov 1857; m 14 Aug 1912 Carew Hervey St John-Mildmay, 3rd s of Sir Henry Bouverie Paulet St John-Mildmay, 5th Bt (qv), and d 18 Jan 1942

1b Jane Anne; m 21 Sept 1843 Thomas Joseph Fitzgerald, of Ballinaparka, Co Waterford, and d 9 Feb 1849. He d 23 Dec 1853

2b Eliza; m 26 Nov 1818 Hon Peter Boyle De Blaquiere (see 1920 edn DE BLAQUIERE, B) and d 18 Feb 1881. He d 23 Oct 1860

3b Isabella; m 12 March 1833 I L Lavit and d 5 April 1876

1a Anna Maria; m 1st 15 June 1788 Valentine Blake (d 1798), of Lehinch, Co Mayo; m 2nd James Shuttleworth, of Barton Lodge, Cheshire, and d 1810

2a Caroline; m 1802 Rev Richard Walwyn, s of James Walwyn, MP

(2) Anna Maria; b 20 Aug 1719; m Capt Peter Tyler, 52nd Regt, and d 1782, leaving issue

The 9th BARON's bro,

HENRY ROPER, **10th Baron Teynham**; m 1st 17 July 1733 Catherine (d 22 Sept 1765), dau of John Powell, of Sandford, Oxon, and had issue; m 2nd 28 Feb 1766 Anne (dsp 16 Jan 1771), dau of John Brinkhurst; m 3rd 7 Sept 1772 Elizabeth Newport, widow of Thomas Davis, and d 21 April 1781, leaving by his 1st w:

1 HENRY ROPER, **11th Baron Teynham**; b 7 May 1733; m 1st 2 June 1753 Wilhelmina (dsp Nov 1758), est dau and coheir of Sir Francis Head, 4th Bt (qv); m 2nd 1 Oct 1760 Elizabeth (d 4 Nov 1793), widow of John Mills, of Woodford Bridge, Essex, and dau of Joseph Webber, and d 10 Dec 1786, having had:

(1) HENRY, **12th Baron Teynham**; b 3 May 1764; d unm 10 Jan 1800

(2) JOHN ROPER, **13th Baron Teynham**; b 27 March 1767; d unm 6 Sept 1824

(1) Betty Maria; m 6 Jan 1785 her cousin Francis Henry Tyler, of Linsted Lodge, Kent, and d 1 March 1788, leaving issue

(2) Catherine; m 9 Aug 1793 her cousin and bro-in-law Francis Henry Tyler and d 1 Jan 1829, leaving issue. He d 9 April 1815

2 John; b 20 June 1734; m 21 March 1760 Anna Gabriella (d 1771), widow of Moses Mendes, of London, and 2nd dau of Sir Francis Head, 4th Bt (qv), and dsp 1780

3 Francis; b 25 Jan 1738; m 27 June 1765 his er bro's sis-in-law Mary (d 15 July 1834 aged 100), est dau and coheir of Launcelot Lyttelton, of Lichfield, and d 13 Aug 1793, leaving, with other issue:

(1) HENRY FRANCIS, **14th Baron**

4 Philip Roper; b 13 Oct 1739; m 21 March 1766 his er bro's sis-in-law Barbara (d 10 April 1805), 2nd dau of Launcelot Lyttelton, and d 1 Jan 1831, leaving, with five daus:

(1) Philip Henry; b 3 Nov 1771; Col; m 30 Jan 1806 Harriet (d 31 Jan 1854), widow of Capt John Bentham and dau of Thomas Banister, and d 2 June 1837, leaving, with other issue (d unm):

1a Edward Dacre; b 1 Feb 1813; Capt HEICS; m 17 Jan 1842 Louisa Sophia (d 27 Jan 1879), yst dau of William Dance, and d 19 Nov 1852, leaving:

1b Edward Frederick; b 6 Dec 1846; m 14 Jan 1882 Lina (d 27 Nov 1908), est dau of F Sievers, and dsp 5 Dec 1887

2b Frank Dacre; b 6 Nov 1848; m 24 March 1874 Caroline Amy Louisa (d 1913), dau of John Belgrave Guazzaroni Franklin, and d 1929, having had:

1c Bernard Dacre; b 16 Oct 1886; d 25 Nov 1918

1c Edith Florence

2c Lilian Mabel; m 1907 Rowland Newling Allport and had issue. He d 1942

3c Eva Muriel; d unm 28 Sept 1968

2a Augustus Frederick; b 19 Dec 1819; CE; m 23 Oct 1847 Lydia Mary Anne (d 1904), only child of John Henley, and d 16 Sept 1889, leaving:

1b Philip Henry; b 21 Sept 1849; d 20 May 1868

2b Charles Louis; b 31 Aug 1856; d 29 Dec 1935

1b Gertrude Tilson Glennie; b 24 Sept 1848; m William Evan Buxton and d his widow 13 Sept 1934

2b Harriet Mary Ann; b 12 May 1855; m William Thomas Wyatt and d 21 Jan 1941, leaving issue

3b Annie; b 30 Nov 1859; m 18– Albert Carter and d 9 Jan 1939, leaving issue

4b Caroline Florence; b 13 Dec 1863; m 1892 Ernest Tod Codrington. He d 1949

The 13th BARON's first cousin,

HENRY FRANCIS ROPER later CURSON (roy licence 22 Feb 1788 on inheriting cousin John Barnewall-Curson's Water Perry estate, Northants; see SCARSDALE, V) later still ROPER-CURZON (roy licence 2 June 1813), **14th Baron Teynham**; b 9 May 1767; m 1st 21 May 1788 Bridget (d 29 Nov 1826), dau and coheir of Thomas Hawkins, of Nash Court; m 2nd 16 July 1828 Sarah (dsp 28 June 1854), dau of Sir Anthony Brabazon, 1st Bt, of Brabazon Park, Co Mayo, and d 8 March 1842, leaving by his 1st w, with another dau (d unm):

1 HENRY ROPER-CURZON, **15th Baron Teynham**; b 20 March 1789; m 1st 30 Dec 1815 Susan Harriet (dsp 7 June 1839), widow of John Joseph Talbot (see SHREWSBURY and WATERFORD, E) and dau of Rev Bacon Bedingfeld; m

2nd 12 Dec 1839 Sarah (d 18 Aug 1855), dau and sole heiress of Stephen Rudd, of Merrion Lodge, Dublin, and dsp 23 Sept 1842

2 Thomas; b 25 Nov 1790; Capt RN; m 17 May 1823 Charlotte Caroline, widow of Robert Brown, and dsp 15 June 1833

3 GEORGE HENRY, **16th Baron**

4 John Henry; b 13 Feb 1802; m 1st 7 April 1829 Isabella (d 18 Sept 1858), dau and coheir of Col James Hodgson, and had, with other issue:

(1) James Gerald; b 10 Jan 1837; d 27 Jan 1881

(2) Richard Henry; b 26 Jan 1840; m 17 Jan 1863 Emily Cottam (d 26 May 1964), est dau of Joseph Milner Atkinson, of St Kitts, Yorks, and d 20 April 1924, having had:

1a Gerald Milner; d an infant

1a Mary Isabella; m 1891 Rev Albert James Skinner and dsp 8 Aug 1947

2a Kate Emily; d unm 22 May 1918

3a Laura Sybil; m 8 May 1886 Rev Arthur Wentworth Jones, Rector Buckland Ripers, Dorset, and d 4 April 1958, leaving issue. He d 1917

4a Gertrude Harriette Vaughan; d unm 23 July 1953

(1) Henrietta Maria; m 11 Dec 1851 M H Donald, of Braithwaite Ho, Cumberland, and d 27 April 1876

(2) Margaret Sidney; m 13 Oct 1859 Rev Canon T Trafford Shipman, Rector Lydiard Tregoze, Wilts, and d 1887, leaving issue. He d 1884

4 (cont.) John Roper-Curzon m 2nd 24 July 1860 Harriet Anne (m 2nd 11 Feb 1892 Rev Thomas Charles Griffith and d 26 March 1907), est dau of Maj John Harman Brown, 90th Regt, DL, and d 2 April 1886

5 Edward Henry, CB; b 25 Jan 1803; Capt RN, Kt Legn Hon and Redeemer Greece; m 1836 Lydia Bullock (d 13 Aug 1885) and d 16 April 1862, leaving:

(1) Edward; b 1837; d unm 24 March 1874

6 Algernon Henry; d 5 May 1860

7 Sidney Campbell Henry; b 12 Dec 1810; m 14 Nov 1837 Frances (d 8 Jan 1892), dau of Richardson Purves, of Sunbury Place, Middx, and d 13 July 1882, leaving:

(1) Edwin Purves; b 26 March 1848; barrister; m 6 Oct 1869 Ethel Anne (d 8 Aug 1876), yst dau of Rev Edward Doddridge Knight, of Nottage Court, Glam, and d 1893, leaving:

1a Sidney Doddridge Henry; b 22 Sept 1870; dsp 17 May 1932

2a Arthur Chichley Henry; b 28 Jan 1872

1a Mabel Frances Maud; b 18 June 1876; d unm 14 Oct 1895

(1) Alice Jane; m 14 Sept 1871 Capt Henry Richard Beattie, est s of Alexander Beattie, of Summerhill, Chislehurst, Kent, and d 21 Aug 1925. He dsp 13 Dec 1883

1 Julia; m 16 Aug 1832 Chevalier Bressand de Chevigny and d 30 Sept 1886 aged 90. He d 1848

2 Caroline; m 1821 Jean Marie Ange, Chevalier Martin des Pallières, and d 23 June 1869

The 15th BARON's bro,

GEORGE HENRY ROPER-CURZON, **16th Baron Teynham**; b 27 May 1798; m 1st 10 Feb 1822 Eliza Joynes (d 5 Nov 1871); m 2nd 21 Jan 1873 Elizabeth (dsp) 12 March 1895), only dau of William Jay, and d 26 Oct 1889, leaving by his 1st w:

HENRY GEORGE ROPER-CURZON, **17th Baron Teynham**; b 27 Dec 1822; m 19 April 1860 Harriet Anne Lovell (d 15 Sept 1916), dau of Rev Thomas Heathcote (see HEATHCOTE, Bt, of Hursley), and had:

1 HENRY JOHN PHILIP SIDNEY, **18th Baron**

2 Wyndham Henry Heathcote; b 12 Nov 1868; m 1st 27 Feb 1890 Grey (d 21 Oct 1901), only dau of David Bayne, of Adelaide, S Australia, and had:

(1) George Henry; b 10 March, d 24 Oct 1891

2 (cont.) The Hon Wyndham Roper m 2nd 15 Oct 1906 Laura (d 1913), dau of Henry Dewdney, of Haredon, Devon, and d 8 Oct 1927

1 Elnith Georgina Isabelle Beauchamp; m 25 Sept 1888 Lt-Col Solomon Watson, DL, RFA, of Ballingarrane, Co Tipperary, and Little Lypiatt, Corsham, Wilts, and d 12 Nov 1923, leaving issue. He d 29 May 1917

2 Harriet Anne Lovell; d unm 1958

The 17th BARON d 22 July 1892; his est s,

HENRY JOHN PHILIP SIDNEY ROPER-CURZON, **18th Baron Teynham**, JP, DL Kent; b 27 May 1867; Maj 6th Bn The Buffs (E Kent Regt), formerly Roy E Kent Imp Yeo, WW I, Chev Legn Hon; m 26 June 1895 Mabel (d 26 Nov 1937), 2nd dau of Col Henry Green Wilkinson, Scots Gds, of Pannington Hall, Ipswich, and had:

1 CHRISTOPHER JOHN HENRY, **19th Baron**

2 Ralph Henry; b 6 Aug 1899; educ Eton; E Kent Regt WW I (wounded), Capt and Actg Lt-Col Scots Gds WW II, For Serv 1948–56: Chargé d'Affaires Yemen 1953–55, Consul Skopjie 1955–56; m 12 Jan 1960 (Dorothy) Margaret (d 8 April 1967), er dau of William Dixon Campbell, of Notting Hill

The 18th BARON d 19 Dec 1936; his er s,

CHRISTOPHER JOHN HENRY ROPER-CURZON, **19th Baron Teynham**, DSO, DSC; b 6 May 1896; educ RNCs Osborne and Dartmouth; Lt City London, Capt RN WW I Grand Fleet as Staff Signal Offr HMS Minotaur, WW II (despatches) as Naval Control Serv Offr Port of London, later cmdg destroyers, cmded from HMS Ambitious minesweeping force in invasion area off N France 1944, cmded Naval Liberation Force at Kristiansand 1945, Cross of Liberty Norway, Dep Chm Ctees and Dep Speaker Ho Lds 1946–59, Chllr Primrose League 1948, Yr Bro Trin Ho, Govr and memb Managing Ctee RNLI, Dir Br Sailors' Soc, Chm Prince of Wales's Sea Training Sch Dover, Pres Nat Rd Tport Fedn, dir: Mitchell Cotts Gp, Southdown Motor Servs, chm AA 1952–57, memb Ctee Hosp St John of Jerusalem, KStJ, Chev Legn Hon; m 1st 19 Oct 1927 (divorce 1955) Elspeth Grace (m 2nd 1958 6th Marquess of Northampton (qv) and d 14 May 1976), est dau of William Ingham Whitaker, JP, DL, CA, of Pylewell Park, Lymington, Hants, and had:

1 JOHN CHRISTOPHER INGHAM ROPER-CURZON, **20th and present Baron Teynham**

2 +Michael Henry [The Hon Michael Roper-Curzon, Barton House, Ashurstwood, E Grinstead, W Sussex RH19 3FL]; b 19 April 1931; educ RNCs Dartmouth and Greenwich; Lt RN (ret), OStJ; m 30 Sept 1964 (divorce 1967) (Sybil) Maria, only child of Maj Robert Vickris Taylor, 16th/5th Queen's Roy Lancers

The **19th Baron** *m* 2nd 11 Feb 1955 *Anne Rita [Mrs Ian Edwards, Inwood House, Sarisbury Green, Hants] (*m* 2nd 25 April 1975 Dr Ian T Edwards (*d* 1988)), only child of Capt Leicester Charles Assheton St John Curzon-Howe, MVO, RN (*see* HOWE, E), and *d* 5 May 1972, leaving by her:
  1 *Henrietta Margaret Fleur [The Hon Mrs Green, 165 Walmer Rd, London W11 4EW]; *b* 25 Aug 1955; *m* 19– *Kevin Green and has:
    (1) *Eleanor Savannah; *b* 20 Dec 1996
  2 *Holly Anne-Marie [The Hon Holly Roper-Curzon, 19 Breer St, London SW6 3HE]; *b* 27 April 1963

THATCHER, Baroness

Arms: Per chevron azure and gules in chief two lions rampant guardant, the dexter contourny, supporting between them a double-warded key, wards upward or, and in base a tower also or, its portal sable, therein a portcullis gold. **Supporters:** Dexter, on a mount of tussocks of grass proper a male figure representing an Admiral of the Fleet on active service holding in his exterior hand a pair of binoculars, all proper; sinister, on a grassy mount vert a male figure representing Sir Isaac Newton, holding in his exterior hand a pair of scales all proper. **Motto:** Cherish freedom. **Creation:** B. (LP, UK) 1992.

THE BARONESS THATCHER, of Kesteven, Co Lincoln (Margaret Hilda Roberts, LG (1995), OM (1990), PC (1970)) [The Rt Hon The Baroness Thatcher LG OM PC, PO Box 1466, London SW1X 9HY]; *b* 13 Oct 1925; *educ* Grantham Girls' Sch and Somerville Coll Oxford (MA, BSc, Hon Fell 1970); barrister Lincoln's Inn 1954 (Hon Bencher 1975); MP (C) Finchley 1959–92, Jt Parly Sec Min Pensions and NI 1961–64, Memb Shadow Cabinet 1967–70, Chief Oppn Spokesman Educn 1969–70, Sec State Educn and Sci 1969–70, Co-Chm Women's Nat Commn 1970–74, Ch Oppn Spokesman Environment 1974–75, Leader Oppn 1975–79, PM and First Ld Treasury 1979–90, Min Civ Serv 1981–90; Chllr: Buckingham U 1992–, William and Mary Coll Williamsburg, Va., 1994–; Pres Grantham Town FC to 1998 and Bruges Gp, V-pres Roy Soc St George 1999–, memb bd Tiger Management, of Wall St, NYC, 1998–; Donovan Award USA 1981, FRS 1983, US Medal Freedom 1991; author: *In Defence of Freedom* (1986), *The Downing Street Years 1979–90* (1993), *The Path to Power* (1995); *m* 1951 *Sir Denis Thatcher, 1st Bt (qv), and has issue

Lineage: ALFRED ROBERTS; *m* 1917 Beatrice Ethel Stephenson and had:

MARGARET HILDA, *cr* a **Baroness**

THATCHER, Bt

Arms: Gules two chevrons or between three crosses moline argent, on a chief azure, between two fleur-de-lys also argent, a mural crown or masoned gules. **Crest:** A demi-lion rampant or within a circlet of New Zealand ferns argent, holding between the fore-paws a pair of shears proper. **Creation:** Bt. (UK) 1991.

SIR DENIS THATCHER, 1ST BT, of Scotney, Co Kent, MBE (1944), TD (1946) [Sir Denis Thatcher Bt MBE TD, 73 Chester Sq, London SW1W 9DU]; *b* 10 May 1915; *educ* Mill Hill; Maj RA 1938–46, served WW II ; dir Burmah Oil Trading 1969–, chm Atlas Preservative Co, v-chm Attwoods plc 1983–93, dir Quinton Hazell plc 1968–, consultant Amec plc and CSX Corp 1988–, Treas London Soc RFU Referees; *m* 1st 1942 (*divorce* 1946) Margaret Doris (*m* 2nd Sir Howard Hickman, 3rd Bt, *qv*), only dau of Leonard Kempson, of Potters Bar, Middx; *m* 2nd 1951 *Margaret Hilda Roberts (Baroness Thatcher; *qv*) and by her has:
  1 +MARK; *b* 15 Aug 1953; *educ* Harrow; *m* 1987 *Diane, only dau of T C Bergdorf, of Dallas, Texas, and has:
    (1) +Michael; *b* 1 Feb 1988
    (1) *Amanda Margaret; *b* 1993
  1 *Carol; *b* 15 Aug 1953; jnlst; author: *Below The Parapet* (biog of f, 1996)

Lineage: THOMAS HERBERT THATCHER, of Uffington, Oxon; had:

Sir Denis Thatcher, 1st Bt (UK), so *cr* 1991

THOMAS
of Garreglwyd

Arms: Per pale gu. and az. on a chevron arg. between in dexter chief a sower scattering seed and in sinister chief an eagle displayed, both or, and in base a garb of the last, three fleurs-de-lys sa. **Crest:** On the waves of the sea ppr., between two anchors sa., a ship in full sail, also ppr. **Motto:** *Fac recte et nil time* ('Do right and fear nothing'). **Creation:** Bt. (UK) 5 July 1918.

SIR (WILLIAM) MICHAEL MARSH THOMAS, 3RD BT, of Garreglwyd, Co Anglesey; *b* 4 Dec 1930; *s* f 1957; *educ* Oundle; former md Gors Nurseries Ltd; *m* 5

Dec 1953 (*divorce* 1969) Geraldine Mary, dau of Robert Duncan Henry Drysdale, of Trearddur Bay, Anglesey, and has:

  1 *Geraldine Dawn; *b* 29 May 1955

  2 *Elizabeth Penelope Kim; *b* 18 Dec 1959

  3 *Pippa-Jane; *b* 8 Sept 1963

Lineage: WILLIAM THOMAS, of Bootle, Lancs; had:

Sir Robert John Thomas, 1st Bt (UK), so *cr* 5 July 1918; *b* 23 April 1873; ship and insur broker, Treas Anglesey Eisteddfod Assoc 1903–18, High Sheriff Anglesey 1918, fndr Welsh Heroes Memorial Fund, MP Wrexham Dec 1918–Oct 1922 and Anglesey April 1923–May 1929; *m* 18 Feb 1908 Marie Rose (*d* 2 June 1948), dau of Arthur Burrows, of Shanghai, and had:

  1 WILLIAM EUSTACE RHYDDLAD (Sir), **2nd Bt**

  2 Robert Freeman; *b* 8 Jan 1911; Col; *m* 1st June 1947 (*divorce* 195–) Marcia (*m* 2nd 1955 Anthony Melville-Ross (*d* 1993), of Lewes, Sussex, and *d* 1992), dau of Maurice Sandberg, and had:

    (1) *Sarah Anne [Mrs Alexander Smith, 3 Wallands Crescent, Lewes, E Sussex BN7 2QT]; *b* 1948; *m* 1981 *Alexander James Smith and has:

      1a *Luke Alastair Robert; *b* 1982

  2 (cont.) Col Robert Thomas *m* 2nd 195– Gil —, of Belgium; *m* 3rd 1967 Rebe Firminger and *d* 1972, leaving by his 2nd w:

    (2) *Carinne; *b* 1958

  1 Audrey; *m* 3 Dec 1929 Cecil Owen, of Anglesey and Antwerp, s of O W Owen, of Liverpool, and *d* 19–, leaving:

    (1) John Garry; *m* Romaine L MacIver (*d* 1976) and *d* 1981

    (1) *Deirdre; nun

    (2) *Daphne [Mrs Frank Hopper, Ty Mel, Rhosneigr, Anglesey, Gwynedd LL64 5QU]; *b* 1934; *m* 19– C Frank Hopper (*d* 24 Nov 1997)

    (3) *Delphine [Miss Delphine Owen, Ty Mel, Rhosneigr, Anglesey, Gwynedd LL64 5QU]; *b* 1934

  2 Margaret Rosemary; *d unm* 12 Oct 1947 following an accident

Sir ROBERT *d* 27 Sept 1951; his er s,

Sir William Eustace Rhyddlad Thomas, 2nd Bt, MBE (1945); *b* 19 June 1909; Maj RA WW II; *m* 1st 1929 (*divorce* 1946) Enid Helena, of Harrogate, Yorks, est dau of Ernest Marsh, of Rawdon, Leeds; *m* 2nd 6 Dec 1947 (*divorce* 1951) Molly, yst dau of John McGeachin, of Eastbourne; *m* 3rd 1957 *Patricia Larkins and *d* 26 Dec 1957, leaving by his 1st w:

Sir WILLIAM MICHAEL MARSH THOMAS, **3rd and present Bt**

THOMAS of Wenvoe

Arms: Sa. a chevron and canton erm. **Crest:** A demi-unicorn erm., armed, crined and unguled or, supporting a shield sa. **Motto:** *Virtus invicta gloriosa* ('Invincible virtue is glorious'). **Creation:** Bt. (E) 24 Dec 1694.

SIR (GODFREY) MICHAEL DAVID THOMAS, 11TH BT, of Wenvoe, Glamorgan [Sir Michael Thomas Bt, 2 Napier Ave, London SW6 3PT]; *b* 10 Oct 1925; *s f* 1968; *educ* Harrow; Capt Rifle Bde 1944–56, ADC to GOC Br Troops Egypt and Mediterranean 1949–50, memb London Stock Exchange 1959–88; *m* 8 Sept 1956 *Margaret Greta, yr dau of John Cleland, of Stormont Ct, Godden Green, Sevenoaks, and has:

  1 +DAVID JOHN GODFREY; *b* 11 June 1961

  1 *Anne Margaret; *b* 25 Oct 1957; *m* 1987 *Robert Hutchison, er s of Sir Peter Hutchison, 2nd Bt (*qv*)

  2 *Diana Elizabeth; *b* 11 June 1961; *m* 1985 *Richard Allan Halford Brooks (*see* CRAWSHAW, B)

Lineage: EDMOND THOMAS, of Wenvoe, Glam; High Sheriff 1626–7; *m* 1st — and had a dau (Maria, *m* Jan 1614 George Kemeys); *m* 2nd by 1611 Frances (living a widow 1655), dau of George Catchmay, of Bigswear in St Briavel's, Mon, and by her had, with other issue:

  1 William; *bapt* 4 Aug 1611; *m* Jane (*m* 2nd Michael Oldisworth and was *bur* 14 April 1668), dau of Sir John Stradling, 1st Bt, of St Donats Castle, Glam, and *dvp* 9 June 1636, having had, with another dau:

    (1) Edmond, of Wenvoe; *bapt* 22 Nov 1638; MP Glam 1656; summoned to CROMWELL's 'Other House' by writ 10 Dec 1657; *m* 1st *c* 17 June 1652 Elizabeth, dau of Sir Lewis Morgan, of Ruperra, Glam; *m* 2nd 1 Aug 1671 Mary Lewis (*dsp, bur* 3 March 1721), of Penmark, Glam, and was *bur* 22 May 1677, having by his 1st w had:

      1a William; *m* (settlement 14 Feb 1672/3) Hon Mary Wharton (*m* 2nd 1678 Sir Charles Kemeys, 3rd Bt, of Cefn Mably), dau and eventual coheir of 4th Baron Wharton (*qv*), and *dvp* 28 April 1677, leaving:

        1b Edmond (Sir), of Wenvoe and Ruperra; *bapt* 26 Aug 1674; ktd 1686; *d unm, bur* 24 Jan 1692/3

        1b Anne, of Wenvoe and Ruperra; *b* 10 Aug 1675; *d unm* 1694

      1a Elizabeth; *m* 16 Dec 1675, as his 1st w, William Cheyne, 2nd and last Viscount Newhaven (whose ownership of an estate at Chelsea, Middx, is commemorated in Cheyne Row, Cheyne Walk etc), and *dsp, bur* 10 Aug 1677

      2a Frances; *d unm* by 1690/1

    (1) Elizabeth, of Wenvoe; *b c* 1630; *m* 1st Edward Ludlow, the Parly Gen (*dsp* 26 Nov 1692); *m* 2nd 1 Dec 1694 **Sir John Thomas, 1st Bt**, er s of William Thomas by Sarah, dau and heiress of John Powell, of Flemington, Glam, and putative gs of James Thomas, s of Edmond Thomas, of Wenvoe (*see below*), and *d* 8 Feb 1701/2

  2 James; allegedly f of:

    (1) William; had:

      1a **Sir John Thomas, 1st Bt** (E), so *cr* 24 Dec 1694, with remainder failing heirs male of his body to his bros; Sheriff Glos 1699–1700; *m* 1 Dec 1694, as her 2nd husb, Elizabeth Thomas (*see above*) and *dsp* 17 Jan 1702/3

      2a **Sir Edmond Thomas, 2nd Bt**; *b* 1667; *m* 28 March 1711 Mary (*m* 2nd Anthony Powell, of Coytrehen, Glam, and *d* 26 April 1745), dau of John Grubham Howe, PC (*see* HOWE, E), and had:

        1b EDMOND (Sir), **3rd Bt**

        2b John; Gen; *m* Sophia (*d* 25 May 1773), dau of 1st Earl of Albemarle (*qv*), and had, with other issue:

          1c Charles Nassau; Col, V-Chamberlain to THE PRINCE REGENT; *d unm* 3 April 1820

        3b William; *b* 1718

The 2nd Bt *d* 1723; his est s,

Sir Edmond Thomas, 3rd Bt; *bapt* 9 April 1712; MP Wilts; sold Wenvoe Castle to Peter Birt 1765; *m* June 1740 Abigail (*d* 9 May 1777), widow of William Northey, of Compton Basset, Wilts, and dau of Sir Thomas Webster, 1st Bt (*see* 1923 edn), and *d* 10 Oct 1767, leaving:

  1 **Sir Edmond Thomas, 4th Bt**; *d unm* 1789

  2 Frederick; Gds Offr; *k* in duel 5 Sept 1783

  3 **Sir John Thomas, 5th Bt**; *b* 6 July 1749; *m* 1782 Mary (*d* May 1845), dau of John Parker, of Hasfield Court, Glos, and had:

    (1) JOHN GODFREY (Sir), **6th Bt**

    (2) Frederick Jennings; *b* 19 April 1786; R-Adml; *m* 7 Aug 1816 Susannah (*d* 23 July 1828), only dau of Arthur Atherley, of Southampton, and *d* 19 Dec 1855, leaving, with another dau (*d unm*):

      1a Frederick; *b* July 1817; Lt RN; *d* 1834

      2a John Wellesley (Sir), KCB; *b* 22 May 1822; Lt-Gen, Col Hants Regt; *d unm* 6 Feb 1908

      3a Barclay; *b* 1 April 1827; Lt-Col 27th Regt; *m* 10 Aug 1853 Catherine, dau of William Guild, of Dablair Ho, Ayr, and *d* 12 Dec 1866, leaving:

        1b Frederick William; *b* 24 Oct 1856; Capt 2nd Bn Manchester Regt; *d* 17 Nov 1925

        1a Mary; *m* 10 Feb 1846 Rev Gilbert Heathcote and *d* 2 April 1854, leaving issue (*see* HEATHCOTE, Bt, of Hursley)

The 5th Bt *d* 14 Dec 1828; his er s,

Rev Sir John Godfrey Thomas, 6th Bt; *b* 1 Sept 1784; Vicar Wartling and Bodiam, Sussex; *m* 1st 1 April 1808 Frances (*d* Jan 1816), dau of Stephen Ram, of Ramsfort, Co Wexford, and had, with three daus (*d unm*):

  1 **Sir Edmond Stephen Thomas, 7th Bt**; *b* 6 Feb 1810; Maj; *d unm* 6 Feb 1852

Sir John *m* 2nd 10 March 1817 Elizabeth Anne, widow of Lt-Col Grey and est dau of Rev John Vignoles, of Cornahir, Co Westmeath, and *d* 7 May 1841, leaving by her:

  2 GODFREY JOHN (Sir), **8th Bt**

  3 John; *b* 25 Feb 1826; *m* 22 April 1847 Katherine Elizabeth (*d* 25 May 1886), yst dau of Capt Edmund C Bacon, RN (*see* BACON, Bt), and *d* 15 March 1861

  4 Charles; *b* 16 Aug 1828; Lt 54th Bengal Inf; *m* 16 July 1855 (*divorce* 1865) Mary Olive, only dau of Henry Welch, of Hailsham, Sussex, and *d* 17 Jan 1871, having had, with another dau (*d unm*):

    (1) Mary Amy; *m* 1878 Thomas Breeds and *d* 21 Sept 1919, leaving issue. He *d* 31 March 1931

    (2) Julia Fanny; *m* 13 Jan 1886 Thomas Rudolphus Dallmeyer, FRAS, 2nd s of J H Dallmeyer, and *d* 26 Sept 1936, leaving issue. He *d* 25 Dec 1906

  1 Eliza Julia; *m* 6 Dec 1855 Rev Gilbert Heathcote and *d* 30 March 1908, leaving issue (*see* HEATHCOTE, Bt, of Hursley)

  2 Julia; *m* 1st 1 Sept 1843 Rev Henry Berens Pratt; *m* 2nd 26 Nov 1848 William Kersteman and *d* 3 Nov 1895, leaving issue

  3 Caroline Margaret; *m* 17 March 1846 Ormus Biddulph and *d* 6 Sept 1896, leaving issue. He *d* 1887

  4 Paulina; *m* 15 June 1848 Herbert Mascall Curteis, of Windmill Hill and Peasmarsh, Sussex, MP Rye, and *d* 19 Oct 1914, leaving issue. He *d* 16 June 1895

The 7th Bt's half-bro,

Sir Godfrey John Thomas, 8th Bt; *b* 16 June 1824; *m* 25 Oct 1853 Emily (*d* 28 Feb 1917), est dau of William Chambers, of Bicknor, Kent, and Hafod, Cards, and *d* 13 July 1861, having had, with a yr s (Edmond Herbert, *b* 10 Feb 1861, *m* 28 Sept 1893 Agnes Marion (*d* Sept 1890), dau of Elias Pitts Squarey, of The Moot, Downton, and *dsp* 13 March 1894), another s (*d* an infant), and two daus (*d unm*):

Sir Godfrey Vignoles Thomas, 9th Bt, CB, CBE (1916), DSO (1901), DL Essex; *b* 27 March 1856; Afghan War 1878–80 (medal), Egypt 1882 (medal with two clasps), Sudan 1884 (medal with two claps, 4th Cl Medjidie), Col RA, formerly RHA, Boer War 1899–1901 (despatches twice, medal with seven clasps), Brig-Gen cmdg 3rd Div Artillery 1909–11, Brig-Gen cmdg 24th Div Artillery 1914–15 and No 2 Res Bde FRA (TF) 1916–17 WW I (despatches); *m* 30 April 1887 Mary Frances Isabelle (*d* 22 June 1946), est dau of Charles Oppenheim, of 40 Gt Cumberland Place, London W1, and *das* 17 Feb 1919, leaving:

Sir Godfrey John Vignoles Thomas, 10th Bt, GCVO (1947), KCB (1937), CSI (1922), PC (1958); *b* 14 April 1889; *educ* Harrow; Dip Serv: Attaché 1912, 3rd Sec 1914, 2nd Sec 1919, re-employed FO 1939–44; Priv Sec to TRH THE PRINCE OF WALES 1919–35 and DUKE OF GLOUCESTER 1937–57, Assist Priv Sec to HM EDWARD VIII 1936, Offr Legn Hon, CStJ; *m* 11 Sept 1924 Diana Mary Katherine, only dau of Ven Benedict George Hoskyns (*see* HOSKYNS, Bt), and *d* 4 March 1968, leaving:

Sir (GODFREY) MICHAEL DAVID THOMAS, **11th and present Bt**

THOMAS of Ynyshir

Arms: Arg. a bend gu. between in chief a pick sa. and in base a rose of the second, barbed and seeded ppr., all within a bordure also of the second. **Crest:** Upon a branch of olive fesswise an owl affrontée ppr. **Motto:** *Duw ein hymddiffynfa* ('God is our refuge'). **Creation:** Bt. (UK) 10 May 1919.

SIR WILLIAM JAMES COOPER THOMAS, 2ND BT, of Ynyshir, Co Glamorgan, TD, JP (Gwent 1958), DL (Gwent 1973) [Sir William Thomas Bt TD JP DL, Tump House, Llanrothal, Gwent NP5 3QL]; *b* 7 May 1919; *s* *f* 1945; *educ* Harrow and Downing Coll Cambridge; RA WW II, barrister Inner Temple 1948, High Sheriff Mon 1973–74; *m* 10 Dec 1947 Freida Dunbar (*d* 1990), yr dau of Frederick Alexander Whyte, of Montcoffer Ho, Banff, and has:

1 +WILLIAM MICHAEL; *b* 5 Dec 1948; *educ* Harrow and Ch Ch Oxford (BA 1971)
2 +Stephen Francis [Stephen Thomas Esq, Flat 6, 31 Dorset Sq, London NW1 6QJ]; *b* 13 April 1951; *educ* Harrow and Oriel Coll Oxford; *m* 1986 *Hon Jane Ridley, est dau of Baron Ridley of Liddesdale (*see* RIDLEY, V), and has:
    (1) +Toby James; *b* 1988
    (2) +Humphrey William; *b* 1991
1 *Sara Roberta Mary; *b* 12 March 1954; *m* 1988 *Ian W Jones, yr s of G V Jones, of Walton-on-the-Hill, Surrey, and has:
    (1) *Nicholas David Richard; *b* 1991
    (1) *Katherine Louise; *b* 1989

Lineage: THOMAS JAMES THOMAS; had:

Sir William James Thomas, 1st Bt (UK), so *cr* 10 May 1919, of Ynyshir, Glam, JP, DL Glam; *b* 10 March 1867; built and equipped Welsh U Medical Sch at King Edward VII's Hosp Cardiff, ktd 1914, Hon LLD U of Wales 1921, High Sheriff Glam 1936; *m* 11 April 1917 Maud Mary (*d* 10 Nov 1952), dau of George Cooper, of Hessle Ho, Bexhill-on-Sea, and *d* 3 Jan 1945, leaving:

1 Sir WILLIAM JAMES COOPER THOMAS, **2nd and present Bt**
2 Geoffrey George Mansel; *b* 7 March 1926; *educ* Harrow; *m* 10 Nov 1951 *Mrs Mary Wentworth Thomson, only dau of Capt H J Harries, of Llanelly, Glam
1 *Maureen Elizabeth Jane, JP (Cardiff 1964) [Mrs Joseph Gaskell JP, Park Mount, Park Rd, Dinas Powis, S Glam]; *m* 12 Feb 1942 *Joseph Gerald Gaskell, TD, only s of Col Joseph Gerald Gaskell, CB, TD, DL, of Cwrt Cefn, Lisvane, Glam, and has:
    (1) *Joseph William; *b* 5 June 1947; *educ* Harrow; barrister Inner Temple 197–
    (2) *Charles Peter; *b* 16 Oct 1950; *educ* Harrow

THOMAS OF GRESFORD

Creation: B. (LP, UK) 21 Aug 1996.

THE BARON THOMAS OF GRESFORD, of Gresford, Co Borough of Wrexham (Donald Martin Thomas, OBE (1982), QC (1979)) [The Rt Hon The Lord Thomas of Gresford OBE QC, Glasfryn, Gresford, Clwyd LL12 8RG]; *b* 13 March 1937; *educ* Grove Pk GS Wrexham and Peterhouse Cambridge; slr 1961, law lecturer 1966–68, barrister Gray's Inn 1967, Bencher 1989, Dep Circuit Judge 1974–76, Crown Court Recorder 1976–, Dep High Court Judge 1985–, Lib Parly candidate: W Flints 1964, 1966, 1970, Wrexham Feb 1974, Oct 1974, 1979, 1983, 1987, V-Chm Welsh Lib Pty 1967–69, Chm 1969–74, Pres Wrexham Lib Assoc and Welsh Lib Pty 1977, 1978 and 1979, also Welsh Lib Dems 1993–, chm Marcher Sound 1991–; *m* 1961 *Nan Kerr and has three sons and a dau

Lineage: HYWEL THOMAS; *m* Olwen — and had:

DONALD MARTIN, *cr* a **Baron**

THOMAS OF GWYDIR

Arms: Per pale vert and gules, in pale a sword, point upwards, hilt argent, pommel and quillons or, between in chief two portcullisses also or, all within a bordure engrailed of the last, thereon eight pellets. **Crest:** A grassy mount proper, statant thereon a stag, armed and unguled or, resting the dexter foreleg upon a staff raguly also or, and between the attires a cross engrailed gold. **Supporters:** Dexter, a dragon statant erect, tail nowed gules, gorged with a crown rayonny gold; sinister, a lamb statant erect or, gorged with a crown rayonny gules. **Motto:** *Nac anobeithier* ('Never despair'). **Creation:** B. (LP, UK) 1987.

THE BARON THOMAS OF GWYDIR, of Llanrwst, Co Gwynedd (Peter John Mitchell Thomas, PC (1964), QC (1965)) [The Rt Hon The Lord Thomas of Gwydir PC QC, 37 Chester Way, London SE11 4UR; Millicent Cottage, Elstead, Surrey GU8 6HD]; *b* 31 July 1920; *educ* Epworth Coll Rhyl and Jesus Coll Oxford (MA); Pilot Bomber Command RAF WW II (POW 1941–45); barrister Middle Temple 1947, Bencher 1971, Memb Wales and Chester Circuit; Dep-Chm: Cheshire QS 1966–70, Denbighs QS 1968–70, Recorder Crown Court 1974–88, MP (C) Conway 1951–66, Hendon S 1970–87, PPS to Slr-Gen 1955–59, Parly Sec Min Lab 1959–61, Parly U-Sec For Affrs 1961–63, Min State For Affrs 1963–64, Sec State Wales 1970–74, Chm C Party Orgn 1970–72, Pres Nat Union C Assocs 1973–75; Emeritus Master Bench 1991; *m* 1947 Frances Elizabeth Tessa (*d* 1985), only dau of Basil Dean, CBE (*see* WARWICK, BROOKE and, E), and has:

1 *David Nigel Mitchell [The Hon David Thomas, 72 Jerningham Rd, London SE14]; *b* 1950
2 *Huw Basil Maynard Mitchell [The Hon Huw Thomas, 1 Regent St, Oxford]; *b* 1953
1 *Frances Jane Mitchell [The Hon Mrs Clargo, 33 Oxford Rd, London SW15]; *b* 1954; *m* 1982 *Jeffrey Alex Clargo and has two sons and a dau
2 *Catherine Clare Mitchell [The Hon Dr Howe, 39 Culver Rd, St Albans, Herts AL1 4EB]; *b* 1958; PhD (Cantab); *m* 1989 *Martin Brian Howe and has:
    (1) *Eleanor; *b* 1990
    (2) *Dulcie; *b* 1994

Lineage: DAVID THOMAS; *m* Anne Gwendoline Mitchell and had:

PETER JOHN MITCHELL, *cr* a **Baron**

THOMAS OF MACCLESFIELD

Creation: B. (LP, UK) 2 Aug 1997.

THE BARON THOMAS OF MACCLESFIELD, of Prestbury, Co Chester (Terence James Thomas, CBE (1997)) [The Rt Hon The Lord Thomas of Macclesfield, 51 Willowmead Dve, Prestbury, Cheshire SK10 4DD]; *b* 19 Oct 1937; *educ* Queen Elizabeth GS Carmarthen, Bath U, INSEAD; with Nat Provincial then Nat West Bank 1962–71, Jt Credit Card Co 1971–73, The Cooperative Bank: mktg manager 1973–77, assist gen manager and jt gen manager 1977–83, dir 1984, exec dir gp devpt 1987, md 1988–97; dir: Stanley Leisure Orgn 1994–, One World Action Ltd 1997–, Nicaragua Health Fund 1997–, CDA; memb: Gen Cncl CIB, Ct Govrs UMIST 1996–, FCIB, FCIM, FRSA, CIMgt; *m* 1963 *Lynda, dau of William John Stevens, and has:

1 *Justin; *b* 12 July 1965
2 *Neil; *b* 2 May 1967
3 *Brendan; *b* 9 Jan 1969

Lineage: WILLIAM EMRYS THOMAS; *m* Mildred Evelyn — and had:
1 TERENCE JAMES, *cr* a **Baron**
1 *Joan [Mrs Joan Brannigan, 1A Warren Rd, Filton, Bristol]; *b* 2 Jan 1941; *m* 19– *— Brannigan

THOMAS OF SWYNNERTON

Arms: Quarterly argent and or a cross formy flory sable surmounted of a dragon's head erased gules. **Crest:** Upon a helm with chapeau gules doubled ermine, issuant from the top of a representation of the Torre d'Arnolfo on the Palazzo Vicariale at Scarperia in Italy argent, a bull's head sable, armed or. **Supporters:** Upon a compartment composed of a grassy mound proper thereon a bar embowed proper or, charged with a like barrulet wavy azure, a pair of falcons, wings expanded and addorsed argent, beaked, armed and belled or, legged gules, gorged with a torse or and gules and holding in the beak a quill argent penned or. **Motto:** Late but in time.
Creation: B. (LP, UK) 1981.

THE BARON THOMAS OF SWYNNERTON, of Notting Hill, Gtr London (Hugh Swynnerton Thomas) [The Rt Hon The Lord Thomas of Swynnerton, 29 Ladbroke Grove, London W11 3BB]; *b* 21 Oct 1931; *educ* Sherborne, Queens' Coll Cambridge and Sorbonne; FO 1954–57: Sec UK Delegn UN Disarmament Sub-Ctee 1955–56; lecturer RMA Sandhurst 1957; Reading U: Prof History 1966–76, Prof History Boston U, Chm Grad Sch Contemporary European Studies 1973–76; Chm CPS 1979–90; King Juan Carlos I Prof New York U 1995; Cdr Order Isabel la Católica Spain 1986, Order Aztec Eagle Mexico 1994; a fndr memb Passports for Pets; author: *The World's Game* (1957), *The Spanish Civil War* (1961), *The Suez Affair* (1967), *Cuba, or the Pursuit of Freedom* (1971), *The selected writing of José Antonio Primo de Rivera* (ed 1972), *Goya and the Third of May 1808* (1972), *Europe, the Radical Challenge* (1973), *John Strachey* (1973), *The Cuban Revolution* (1977), *An Unfinished History of the World* (1979), *The Case for the Round Reading Room* (1983), *Havannah* (1984), *Armed Truce* (1986), *A Traveller's Companion to Madrid* (1988), *Klara* (1988), *Even Closer Union: Britain's Destiny in Europe* (1991), *The Conquest of Mexico* (1993), *The Slave Trade* (1997) and *The Future of Europe* (1997); *m* 5 May 1962 *Hon Vanessa Mary Jebb, er dau of 1st Baron Gladwyn (*qv*), and has:

1 *(Charles) Inigo Gladwyn [The Hon Inigo Thomas, 10B, 85 First Ave, New York, NY 10003, USA]; *b* 1962; *educ* Latymer Upper Sch and UEA; *m* 28 June 1997 *Horatia Holly, dau of Baron Lawson of Blaby (*qv*)

2 *(Henry) Isambard Tobias [The Hon Isambard Thomas, 30 Hamilton Terrace, London NW8]; *b* 1964; *educ* Latymer Upper Sch, London Coll Printing and St Martin's Sch of Art
1 *Isabella Pandora [The Hon Isabella Thomas, 29 Ladbroke Grove, London W11 3BB]; *b* 1966; *educ* St Paul's Girls' Sch and Newnham Coll Cambridge

Lineage: Rev THOMAS THOMAS; *b c* 1805; Curate of Mothvey, Llanddansant and Dowlais, Rector Cwamman (Garnant) 1853–76; *m* Theophila (*d* 1898), dau of Theophilus Shenton, Rector Cwmamman and *d* 20 April 1896, leaving with other issue:

Rev THOMAS WILLIAM THOMAS; *b* 1850; Curate Widnes and St Bride's Fleet St, Rector Wicken and Newton-in-the-Isle; *m* Charlotte Susannah (*d* 21 April 1936), dau of Rev William Whitelegge, Rector Syderstone, Norfolk and *d* 27 Jan 1929, leaving:

1 Thomas Shenton (Sir), GCMG, OBE; *b* 13 Oct 1879; Govr Nyasaland 1929–32, Gold Coast 1932–34 and Straits Settlements Malaysia 1934–41; Japanese POW 1941–45; KStJ; *m* Lucy Marguerite (*d* 1978), dau of Col J A L Montgomery and had:
  (1) Bridget; *m* 1st Col Jack Lotinga, MC, and had issue; *m* 2nd 9th Earl of Saint Germans (*qv*)
2 William; had, with another s:
  (1) Harford; ed *Oxford Mail*, dep ed *The Guardian*
3 Cecil; ed *Daily Mirror*
4 HUGH
5 Basil; monk The Community Resurrection, Mirfield and Johannesburg
1 Gwendolen

The Rev THOMAS THOMAS's 4th s,

HUGH WHITELEGGE THOMAS, CMG; *b* 27 March 1887; joined Colonial Serv 1913, Sec Native Affrs Gold Coast; *m* 1929 Margery Augusta Angelo Swynnerton and *d* 1961, leaving:

HUGH SWYNNERTON, *cr* a **Baron**

THOMAS OF WALLISWOOD

Creation: B. (LP, UK) 20 Aug 1994.

THE BARONESS THOMAS OF WALLISWOOD, of Dorking, Co Surrey (Susan Petronella Arrow, OBE (1989), DL (1996) [The Rt Hon The Baroness Thomas of Walliswood OBE DL, Weathertop, Tower Hill, Dorking, Surrey RH4 2AP]; *b* 20 Dec 1935; *educ* Cranborne Chase and LMH Oxford; ch exec Br Clothing Industs Cncl for Europe 1974–78, chm and treas Richmond Lib Assoc 1974–77, Surrey CC 1985–97: chm 1996–97 (Highways and Tport Ctee 1993–96), memb Surrey Probation Ctee 1997–, non exec dir E Surrey Hosp and Community Tst 1992–96, Lib Alliance Parly candidate Mole Valley 1983 and 1987, Lib Dem Euro candidate 1994, Lib Dem Spokesperson Tport 1994–; *m* 1958 *David Churchill Thomas, CMG, Assist U-Sec FCO 1984–86, and has, with two daus:

1 *David William Penrose [The Hon David Thomas, c/o Christopher Little Literary Agency, 48 Walham Grove, London SW6 1QR]; *b* 17 Jan 1959; *educ* Eton and King's Coll Cambridge; ed *The Magazine* 1984–85, *Extra Magazine*, *Sunday Today* 1986, *Punch* 1989–92, author: *Bilko: the Fort Baxter Story* (with Ian Irvine, 1985), *Fame and Fortune* (1988), *Sex and Shopping* (1988), *Great Sporting Moments* (1990), *Not Guilty: in defence of the modern man* (1993), *Girl* (1995); *m* 1986 *Clare Jeremy and has two daus

THOMPSON of
Hartsbourne Manor

Arms: Per fess arg. and sa. a fess counter-embattled between three falcons jessed and belled or, all within a bordure engrailed and all counterchanged; in the chief point also within the bordure an anchor erect az., cable ppr. **Crest:** Out of a naval crown or an arm in armour, embowed ppr., garnished gold, the hand supporting a lance erect, also ppr. **Motto:** *Non quo sed quomodo* ('Not who by but how'). **Creation:** Bt. (UK) 11 Dec 1806.

SIR (THOMAS) LIONEL TENNYSON THOMPSON, 5TH BT, of Hartsbourne Manor, Co Hertford [Sir Lionel Thompson Bt, 16 Old Buildings, Lincoln's Inn, London WC2A 3UP]; *b* 19 June 1921; *s* f 1964; *educ* Eton; F/O RAFVR WW II (invalided 1944), AB Roy Fleet Auxiliary 1944–1946 (1939–45 and Aircrew (Europe) stars, Defence and Victory medals), barrister Lincoln's Inn 1952; *m* 11 March 1955 (*divorce* 1962) Margaret, only dau of Walter Herbert Browne by Mrs Cole, of Old Rectory Cottage, Woodmansterne, Surrey, and formerly w of Engr Capt Pieter van Beers, KPM, and has:

1 +THOMAS D'EYNCOURT JOHN [Thomas Thompson Esq, c/o King Sturge & Co, 7 Stratford Place, London W1N 9AE]; *b* 22 Dec 1956; *educ* Eton; BA, MSc, ARICS

1 *Sarah Catherine Elizabeth [Ms Sarah Thompson, 2330 Larkin St, San Francisco, CA 94109, USA]; *b* 20 Oct 1955

Lineage: Sir Thomas Boulden Thompson, 1st Bt (UK), so *cr* 11 Dec 1806, GCB (1822, KCB 1815); *b* 28 Feb 1766 (adopted s of Cdre Edward Thompson, RN, who *d* 17 Jan 1786); RN: served under Nelson at Tenerife 1797 (wounded), cmded 50-gun brig HMS *Leander* Battle of the Nile and while carrying despatches to UK was forced after a six-hour resistance against a French battleship *Le Généreux*, 74 guns, to surrender; ktd 1799 on his return to England; cmded HMS *Bellona* Battle of Copenhagen, when lost a leg; Comptroller Navy 1802–06, MP Rochester 1807–16, Treas Greenwich Hosp 1811, V-Adml the Red; *m* 25 Feb 1799 Anne (*d* 9 Sept 1846), est dau of Robert Raikes, of Gloucester, and *d* 3 March 1828; having had, with three daus (including Anne, *m* 18 Aug 1847 Daniel Prince, of Hendon, and *dsp* his widow 23 Jan 1874; Mary, *m* 10 July 1845 Rev Anderton Smith (*d* 27 Oct 1870), of Bath, and had issue):

Sir Thomas Raikes Trigge Thompson, 2nd Bt; *b* 1 April 1804; V-Adml; *m* 20 Oct 1847 Gertrude (*d* 3 Aug 1921), dau of Rev Robert Napier Raikes, Vicar Longhope, Glos, and *d* 26 Sept 1865, leaving, with a yr s (Edward, *b* 19 Sept 1853, *d* Feb 1883) and two daus (Gertrude Anne, *d* unm 1 March 1929; Emily Caroline, *d* unm 3 June 1941):

Sir Thomas Raikes Thompson, 3rd Bt; *b* 1 Jan 1852; *m* 7 July 1880 Alice Maude Lovett (*d* 18 April 1934), 4th dau of William Lochiel Cameron, HEICS, and had:

1 THOMAS RAIKES LOVETT (Sir), **4th Bt**

2 William Probyn; *b* 5 July 1882; *m* 24 April 1929 Kathleen Emma, 4th dau of George Radcliff, JP, of Wilmount, Kells, Co Meath, and was *k* in a train crash 12 April 1947

3 Lionel Graham Cameron; *b* 24 April 1895; Sub-Lt RN; *kas* North Sea 21 March 1916

1 Gladys Maude Gertrude; *m* 15 Dec 1919 Charles Fernand Cremer and had issue

The 3rd Bt *d* 4 Sept 1904; his est s,

Sir Thomas Raikes Lovett Thompson, 4th Bt, MC (1918); *b* 12 May 1881; *educ* Rugby and RMA Woolwich; RE and 7th, 18th and 3rd Hus WW I, Bde Maj 1915–16, GSO(2) 1916–17, cmded Light Armoured Motor Bde MEF 1918 (despatches twice, Brevet Maj), Lt-Col, re-employed 1940–41; *m* 1st 17 March 1914 (*divorce* 1936) Millicent Ellen Jean, 2nd dau of Edmund Charles Tennyson-D'Eyncourt (*see* TENNYSON-D'EYNCOURT, Bt); *m* 2nd 7 Jan 1943 Ellinor Mary, only dau of Maj Herbert Owain Pugh, DSO, DL, of Cymmerau, Glandyfi, Cards, and *d* 17 Sept 1964, having by his 1st w had:

1 Sir (THOMAS) LIONEL TENNYSON THOMPSON, **5th and present Bt**

2 John Edmunds Cameron, DSC; *b* 15 April 1923; Lt RN (Pilot, FAA) WW II; *k* in an air accident at sea off Scotland 18 June 1945

1 *Jane Olivia Marion [Mrs Derek Hague, Stud House, Chilton Foliat, Berks RG17 0TE]; *b* 6 Jan 1918; *m* 1st 19 July 1938 (*divorce* 1946) Maj David Owen Nares, RA, s of Owen Nares, of Maida Vale, and has:

(1) *(Caroline) Harriette; *b* 11 April 1940; *m* 22 July 1961 *Robert Jerram Belmont, yr s of Capt Algernon Spencer Belmont, RA (*see* KINDERSLEY, B), and has:

1a *Jason Robert; *b* 16 Nov 1969

1a *Sophia; *b* 18 April 1964

2a *Teresa Caterina; *b* 4 Feb 1967

1 (cont.) Mrs Jane Nares *m* 2nd 13 Feb 1948 Maj (John) Derek Kenyon Hague, MC, Scots Gds (*k* car crash 5 April 1966), only s of Sir Harry Hague, of The Chantry, Barnet Lane, Elstree, Herts, and by him has:

(2) *Melanie Clare; *b* 12 July 1957; *m* 1980 *Andrew John Melsom (*see* PASLEY, Bt)

THOMPSON of
Park Gate

Arms: Azure a bridge of three arches embattled proper, in chief the sun in his glory between two mullets of six points pierced or and in base an eagle displayed with two heads argent. **Crest:** In front of the battlements of a tower proper a cubit arm erect vested azure charged with a mullet as in the arms, the cuff argent, the hand proper holding five ears of wheat slipped or. **Motto:** Wheare vertue lys, love never dys. **Creation:** Bt. (UK) 18 April 1890.

SIR CHRISTOPHER PEILE THOMPSON, 6th Bt, of Park Gate, Guiseley, Yorks [Lt-Col Sir Christopher Thompson Bt, c/o Barclays Bank plc, PO Box 8, 13 Library Place, St Helier, Jersey CI]; *b* 21 Dec 1944; *s* f 1985; *educ* Marlborough and RMA Sandhurst; commnd 11th Hus (PAO) 1965, Lt-Col cmdg Roy Hus (PWO) 1985–87, ret 1990, Equerry to HRH PRINCE MICHAEL OF KENT 1989– (Priv Sec 1990–92), dir Logical Security Ltd 1996–, non-exec chm Nuclear Decommissioning Ltd 1995–; *m* 22 Nov 1969 *Anna Elizabeth, dau of Maj Arthur George Callander, of Avebury, Wilts, and has:

1 +PEILE RICHARD; *b* 3 March 1975; *educ* Harrow and Bristol U

1 *Alexandra Lucy; *b* 1973; *m* 17 June 1995 *Hon Piers Portman, 3rd s of 9th Viscount Portman (*qv*)

Lineage: WILLIAM THOMSON [*sic*]; *m* Oct 1622 Jane Smith, of Thrimble, Westmorland, and had:

JOHN THOMPSON, of Thrimble; *m* Margaret Holmes (*d* 1715), of Butterwick Cragg, and had:

MATTHEW THOMPSON, of Bampton Grange; *b* 1672; *m* 1702 Dorothy Noble (*bur* 4 Jan 1746), of Roughill, and *d* 1756, leaving:

MATTHEW THOMPSON, of Walmgate, Bampton, Westmorland; *b* 1707; *m* 1731 Elizabeth (*d* 1785), dau of Richard Wright, of Drybarrows, and *d* 1760, leaving, with other issue:

Rev JOHN THOMPSON; *b* 1740; MA, Vicar Knottingley, Yorks; *m* Mary, dau of Benjamin Peile, of Cockermouth, Cumberland, and Bradford, Yorks, and *d* 7 April 1792, leaving:

1 MATTHEW

2 Benjamin, of Park Gate, Guiseley, Yorks; *b* 4 Feb 1783; *m* 4 May 1812 Elizabeth (*d* 1 May 1866), dau of William Whitaker, of Milnhouse, Halifax, Yorks, and *d* 16 Feb 1857, leaving an only surv child:

(1) Mary Ann; *m* 10 May 1843 her cousin **Sir Matthew William Thompson, 1st Bt**, and *d* 5 Nov 1903, leaving issue

The Rev JOHN THOMPSON's er s,

MATTHEW THOMPSON, of Manningham Lodge, Bradford, Yorks, JP, DL; *b* 12 Feb 1781; *m* 30 April 1819 Elizabeth Sarah (*d* 20 June 1859), dau of Rev William Atkinson, of Thorpe Arch, Yorks, Fell Jesus Coll Cambridge, and *d* 23 Sept 1847, leaving:

1 MATTHEW WILLIAM (Sir), **1st Bt**

2 Benjamin Peile (Rev); *b* 3 Feb 1828; *educ* St Catharine's Hall Cambridge (MA); *m* 14 June 1854 Rosa Grevis, dau of Col Grevisse James, of Ightham Court, Kent, and had a s and two daus (one of whom *d* an infant)

1 Mary Elizabeth; *m* William James Lumsden, JP (*d* 27 Aug 1875), of Balmedie, Aberdeenshire, and had issue

2 Harriet Agnes; *m* Adml James Stoddart and *d* 1896, having had issue

MATTHEW THOMPSON's er s,

Sir Matthew William Thompson, 1st Bt (UK), so *cr* 18 April 1890, of Park Gate; *b* 1 Feb 1820; *educ* Trin Coll Cambridge (MA); barrister, Mayor Bradford 1862–63 and 1872–73, MP (Lib) Bradford 1867–68, chm Forth Bdge and Midland Rlwy Cos; *m* 10 May 1843 his cousin Mary Ann (*see above*) and *d* 1 Dec 1891, leaving:

1 PEILE (Sir), **2nd Bt**

2 Reginald, VD; *b* 17 April 1846; *educ* Trin Coll Cambridge (MA); Col 2nd Vol Bn W Yorks Regt; *m* 14 Oct 1874 Frances Harriet (*d* 4 Jan 1936), 4th dau of Rev Charles Smith Royds, JP, of Haughton, Staffs, and Heysham, Lancs, and *d* 19 Feb 1932, having had:

(1) Clement; *b* 8 Oct 1875; *educ* Charterhouse and Trin Coll Cambridge (BA); *d* unm 12 Nov 1929

(2) Gilbert; *b* 22 June 1877; Capt Connaught Rangers WW I (despatches twice); *m* 7 June 1906 Ethel Isabella (*d* 20 April 1959), dau of Marmaduke D'Arcy Wyvill, DL, of Constable Burton and Denton Park, Yorks, and was *ka* 24 Feb 1915, leaving:

1a Christopher Smith Byrom THOMPSON later THOMPSON-ROYDS (roy licence 1936); *b* 19 April 1907; *educ* Eton; Maj Roy Scots Fus; *m* 17 Oct 1936 *Yolande Anne [Mrs Christopher Thompson-Royds, Walton House, Walton, Wetherby, Yorks S23 7DQ], yr dau of Arthur Thomas Hodgson, JP, of Tatchbury Manor House, New Forest, and *d* 29 Aug 1967, leaving:

1b +Gilbert [Gilbert Thompson-Royds Esq, Seymour House, Market St, Charlbury, Oxon OX7 3PJ]; *b* 31 July 1939; *educ* Eton; *m* 1976 *Vanessa Maxine, dau of Mark Leslie Brandon (*see* SELBY, V), and has:

1c +Christopher Oliver; *b* 1 Dec 1978; *educ* Eton

2b +Matthew [Matthew Thompson-Royds Esq, The Glebe House, Somerleyton, Suffolk]; *b* 23 April 1942; *educ* Eton; *m* 31 Aug 1969 *Susan Damaris, er dau of Arthur Robert Jarrett, of Chedgrove Manor, Loddon, Norwich

3b +Timothy Christopher [Timothy Thompson-Royds Esq, North Lodge, Guilsborough, Northants NN6 8QE]; *b* 8 Jan 1950; *educ* Stowe; *m* 1983 *Anne, yr dau of Gordon Shafto Hedley (*see* WALDEGRAVE, E), and has:

1c +Mark Christopher; *b* 1989

1c *Katherine Louise; *b* 1985

1b *Laura Yolanda; *b* 26 Nov 1947

1a *Laura Barbara Frances [Lady Inglefield, 6 Rutland House, Marloes Rd, London W8 5LE]; *b* 1908; *m* 20 Dec 1933 Sir Gilbert Samuel Inglefield, GBE, TD, ARIBA, FRSA (*d* 1991), Ld Mayor London 1967–68, yr s of Adml Sir Frederick Inglefield, KCB, and has:

1b *David Gilbert Charles, [David Inglefield Esq, The Old Rectory, Staunton-in-the Vale, Orston, Notts NG13 9PE]; *b* 19 Nov 1934; *educ* Eton and Trin Coll Cambridge (BA 1958); *m* 1970 *Jean Mary MBE, only dau of Col Sir Alan Gomme-Duncan, MC, and has:

1c *Charles Nicholas David; *b* 1977

1c *Mary Victoria; *b* 1974

2b *(Christopher) Samuel [Samuel Inglefield Esq, Bryngwyn Manor, Bryngwyn, Raglan, Gwent NP5 2JH]; *b* 30 Oct 1936; *educ* Eton and Trin Coll Cambridge (BA 1960); *m* 1971 *Susan Lilias, dau of Henry Turcan, of Lindores House, Newburgh, Fife, and has:

1c *Edward Henry Samuel; *b* 1973; *educ* Eton

2c *Frederick Thomas Christopher; *b* 1982

1c *Olivia Barbara Jane; *b* 1972

2c *Katherine Lilias Cecilia; *b* 1977

1b *Elizabeth Isabel Albinia [Mrs Christopher Diggle, Orchard Grange, Old Warden, Biggleswade, Beds SG18 9HB]; *b* 30 July 1942; *m* 16 June 1962 Maj Christopher Wyndham Diggle (*d* 1986), 2nd s of Lt-Col Leonard Wyndham Diggle, of Orchard Grange, and has:

1c *Robert Dominic Charles [Robert Diggle Esq, 27 Langton St, London SW10 0JL]; *b* 2 Feb 1969; *educ* Eton

2c *Jonathan Benjamin Christopher [Jonathan Diggle Esq, 27 Langton St, London SW10 0JL]; *b* 1973; *educ* Eton

1c *Albinia Julia; *b* 8 July 1964; *m* 1988 *Richard Malcolm Jannion Trustram Eve (*see* SILSOE, B) and has issue

2c *Louise Georgina; *b* 30 Aug 1966

2a *Naomi Isabella [Mrs D'Arcy Dawes, Forge Cottage, Warehorne, Ashford, Kent]; *b* 1912; *m* 5 Oct 1935 Maj D'Arcy Armytage Dawes, 15th/19th King's Roy Hus (*d* 30 Jan 1967), only s of Col Henry Halford Dawes, OBE (*see* ARMYTAGE, Bt), and has:

1b *Charles Lancelot [Charles Dawes Esq, Leacon Hall, Warehorne, Ashford, Kent TN26 2JX]; *b* 23 Jan 1938; *educ* Eton and RMA Sandhurst; Capt 15th/19th King's Roy Hus; *m* 22 Aug 1964 *Valerie Ann, er dau of Col Edward Townsend and Mrs George Parkinson, of Fencote Hall, Northallerton, Yorks, and has:

1c *Nicholas Halford; *b* 21 Jan 1967; *m* 1994 *Katharine Lucy Penrose and has issue

2c *James Christopher; *b* 11 July 1968; *m* 1996 *Victoria Mary Clough and has issue

1c *Isla Caroline; *b* 9 June 1971

2b *Hermione Anne [Mrs John Birkbeck, Litcham Hall, King's Lynn, Norfolk PE32 2QQ]; *b* 5 Dec 1941; *m* 2 May 1964 *John Oliver Birkbeck, yr s of Col Oliver Birkbeck, DL (*see* MUNSTER, E), and has issue

(3) Whately; *b* 11 May 1881; *educ* Marlborough; Maj RFA WW I (despatches three times); *m* 11 Feb 1920 Violet Marian, only dau of Arthur Parkyns Smith, of Bedford, and *dsp* 7 Nov 1964

(4) Reginald, DSO (1919), TD (1920), JP, DL (Notts); *b* 12 May 1884; Lt-Col and Brevet-Col QO Yorks Dragoons WW I (despatches twice, Legn Hon,

Croix de Guerre), Jt MFH Rufford 1931–48; *m* 1st 2 Aug 1922 Marjorie Olive (*d* 24 Oct 1929), dau of James Arthur (*see* GLENARTHUR, B), and had:

1a *Elizabeth Olive [Mrs George Graham, Failford House, Mauchline, Ayrshire KA5 5TA]; *b* 15 June 1923; *m* 3 April 1948 Maj George Malcolm Graham (*d* 1980), only s of Maj John Malcolm Graham, of Woodhay Chase, Newbury, Berks, and has:

1b *James Anthony [James Graham Esq, La Hille, Fanjeaux 11270, France]; *b* 3 Nov 1952; *educ* Tabley House and the Sorbonne; *m* 1978 (*divorce* 1993) Hayat Lebbar

1b *Alexandra Mary [Mrs Adrian Speir, The Old Rectory, Melsonby, N Yorks DL10 5NF]; *b* 27 Dec 1949; *m* 1974 *Adrian John Speir, s of Michael Adrian Speir, of N Yorks, and has:

1c *Edward Francis; *b* 1976

2c *Harry James; *b* 1979

2a *Judith Mary [Miss Judith Thompson, Day Ash, Darley, Harrogate, Yorks]; *b* 23 March 1927

(4) (cont.) Col Reginald Thompson *m* 2nd 16 Nov 1932 Ruth Eleanor (*d* 1986), yr dau of Rev John Henry Hodgson, of Crowthorne, Berks, and widow of John Charles Bradley Firth, MC, of Blyth, Notts, and *d* 5 Nov 1965

(1) Mary Anastasia; *m* 11 Nov 1920 Evelyn Longley (*d* 4 March 1956), s of John Longley, of Eton House, Horley, and *d* 13 April 1962, leaving issue

(2) Agnes Theodosia; *m* 26 Jan 1928 Albert Arthur Magnall Isherwood, CMG, OBE (*d* 19 Aug 1957), Dir Educn Tanganyika Territory, s of Rev Arthur Isherwood, of Saverton, Trowbridge, Wilts, and *d* 16 Feb 1930

3 William Whitaker, VD, JP (London); *b* 27 Feb 1857; *educ* Trin Coll Cambridge (MA, LLB); barrister Inner Temple, Chm LCC 1910–11, Mayor Kensington 1911–12, memb Metropolitan Water Bd, Lt-Col 2nd Bn London Regt WW I (Malta, Egypt and Gallipoli); *m* 5 June 1889 Isabella Blanche Spencer (*d* 8 March 1945), dau of Spencer Robert Lewin, of The Bourne, Widford, Herts, and *d* 2 March 1920, leaving:

(1) Philip; *b* 30 March 1898; Capt 22nd Sqdn RAF; *ka* 23 March 1918

(1) Marion Jessie; *b* 1890; *m* 25 Jan 1930 her bro-in-law Dows Dunham (*d* 1984), Curator Egyptian Dept Museum of Fine Arts, Boston, Mass

(2) Eveline Spencer; *m* 1st 15 Dec 1914 Lt Geoffrey Harrington Sainsbury, RN; *m* 2nd 22 May 1920 Dows Dunham, s of Carroll Dunham, MD, of Irvington, New York, and *d* 12 Sept 1928, leaving issue

1 Eliza; *m* 12 July 1871 Rev John Vowler Tanner (*d* 15 April 1903), of King's Nympton, Devon, Rector Chawleigh, Devon, and *d* 29 Jan 1909, leaving issue

2 Bertha Mary; *m* 10 May 1894 Charles James Atkinson, of Bathwick Hill House, Bath, and *d* 12 July 1915

The 1st Bt's est s,

Rev Sir Peile Thompson, 2nd Bt; *b* 19 July 1844; *educ* Trin Coll Cambridge (MA); barrister Inner Temple 1869, ordained 1877; *m* 17 May 1871 Jessie Clare (*d* 25 Jan 1927), dau of Joseph Beaumont, of Greenhead Park, Huddersfield, Yorks, and *d* 8 April 1918, leaving:

1 **Sir Matthew William Thompson, 3rd Bt**; *b* 28 June 1872; *educ* Trin Coll Cambridge; artist, FRSA; *m* 3 Nov 1909 Harriet Kathleen (*d* 9 Jan 1969), only dau of Col Sheffield Hamilton-Grace (*see* GRACE, Bt), and *dsp* 25 Nov 1956

2 PEILE BEAUMONT (Sir), **4th Bt**

3 Miles Atkinson; *b* 7 July 1888; Lt Lincs Yeo WW I

1 Dorothy Noble; *b* 1 July 1884; *d* 5 Nov 1935

The 3rd Bt's yr bro,

Sir Peile Beaumont Thompson, 4th Bt; *b* 4 Feb 1874; *educ* Sedbergh and Trin Coll Cambridge (BA); mkt gdnr Guernsey; *m* 8 Oct 1908 Stella (*d* 26 Dec 1972 aged 93), dau of Arthur Harris, of Heaton Grove, Bradford, and *d* 8 Aug 1972, leaving:

1 **Sir Peile Thompson, 5th Bt**, OBE (1959, MBE 1950); *b* 28 Feb 1911; *educ* Canford and St Catharine's Coll Cambridge (BA 1933, MA 1959); Lt-Col Manchester Regt WW II, cmded 26th Bn KAR Kenya Emergency 1954–56 (despatches 1955); *m* 28 July 1937 Barbara Johnson (*d* 199–), only dau of Horace Johnson Rampling, of The Old Manor House, Harston, Cambs, and *d* 1985, leaving:

(1) Sir CHRISTOPHER PEILE THOMPSON, **6th and present Bt**

(1) *Ann Mary [Mrs Raymond Cheetham, Hillbrook House, Dipford Rd, Trull, Somerset]; *b* 10 May 1939; *m* 1st 2 April 1965 (*divorce* 1973) Arturo Cesare Pilato, s of Gino Pilato, of Naples, and has:

1a *Roberto Arturo Kenneth; *b* 4 July 1966; *educ* King's Coll Taunton and Cardiff U; *m* 30 July 1994 *Sarah Diana, dau of David Downs Larmuth, and has:

1b *Nicholas Robert; *b* 1 Jan 1998

2a *Leonardo Cesare; *b* 1970; *educ* King's Coll Taunton and De Montfort U

(1) (cont.) Mrs Ann Pilato *m* 2nd 1973 *Raymond Benjamin Cheetham, late Roy Hong Kong Police

1 *Mary Winifred Thompson [Mrs Hugh Kenyon, 9 Frobisher Gdns, Boxgrove, Guildford, Surrey]; *b* 14 July 1909; *m* 23 April 1941 *Hugh Kenyon, s of Rev Thomas Kenyon, of Malham, Skipton, Yorks, and has:

(1) *(Hugh) Matthew; *b* 18 May 1944; *educ* Rugby

(1) *Elizabeth Katharine; *b* 12 March 1942; *m* 1977 *Francis Pasco Grenfell (*see* GRENFELL, B)

THOMPSON
of Reculver

THOMPSON
of Walton-on-the-Hill

Arms: Az. a bend arg. between two ship's wheels or.
Crest: A demi-figure representing a Moorish Prince ppr., wreathed about the temples with a torse arg. and az., vested of a tunic paly arg. and az., fringed and garnished or, at his back supported by a guige gu. baldrickwise across the dexter shoulder a quiver az., replenished with arrows arg., flighted or, from the dexter hand a martlet rising az. and in the other a bow palewise stringed gu.
Motto: *Sapiens qui prospicit* ('He is wise who looks forward').
Creation: Bt. (UK) 28 Jan 1963.

SIR RICHARD HILTON MARLER THOMPSON, 1ST BT (UK), so *cr* 28 Jan 1963, of Reculver, Kent [Sir Richard Thompson Bt, Rhodes House, Sellindge, Kent TN25 6JA]; *b* 5 Oct 1912; *educ* Malvern; publisher India, Burma and Ceylon 1930–39, RN WW II 1940–46 (despatches, commissioned 1941, Lt-Cdr RNVR 1944), MP (C) Croydon W 1950–55, Croydon S 1955–66 and 1970–Feb 1974, Assist Govt Whip 1952, Ld Commr Treasury 1954, V-Chamberlain Household 1956, Parly Sec Min Health 1957–59, Parly U-Sec CRO 1959–60, Parly Sec Min Works 1960–62, Tstee Br Museum (Cottonian family tstee 1951–63, PM's tstee 1963–84), dir Rediffusion TV and Rediffusion Hldgs 1966–83, chm Capital and Counties Property Co 1971–77, Pres Br Property Fedn 1976–77, chm Br Museum Soc 1970–74, memb cncl Nat Tst 1978–84; *m* 9 Aug 1939 *Anne Christabel de Vere, only dau of Philip de Vere Annesley (*see* VALENTIA, V), and has:
1 +NICHOLAS ANNESLEY MARLER [Nicholas Thompson Esq, Maxgate, George Rd, Kingston-upon-Thames, Surrey KT2 7NR]; *b* 19 March 1947; *educ* King's Canterbury and Kent U (BA 1969); slr 1973, memb Westminster City Cncl 1978–86, Dep Ld Mayor Westminster 1983–84; *m* 1982 *Venetia Catherine, yst dau of John Horace Broke Heathcote (*see* HEATHCOTE, Bt, of London), and has:
  (1) +Simon William; *b* 10 June 1985
  (2) +Charles Frederick; *b* 25 Nov 1986
  (3) +David Jonathan; *b* 20 April 1990
  (1) *Emma Louise; *b* 24 July 1991
Lineage: RICHARD SMITH THOMPSON, of Low Abbey, Ellel, Lancs; *m* Elizabeth Smith (*d* 12 Nov 1886) and *d* 24 March 1886, leaving, with another s and six daus:

RICHARD SMITH THOMPSON; *b* 11 Nov 1868; *m* 3 Oct 1911 Kathleen Hilda (*d* 19 Oct 1916), yst dau of Sidney Marler, of Woolborough Ho, Barnes, Surrey, and *d* 16 March 1952, leaving:

Sir RICHARD HILTON MARLER THOMPSON, **1st and present Bt**

Arms: Per fess dancetty arg. and sa. of two upward and one downward points, each ending in a cross potent, three swans, one in chief and two in base counterchanged. **Crest:** A demi-figure affronté representing Neptune, wreathed about the middle with laver ppr., the mantle gu., clasped and crowned with an antique crown or, supporting in the dexter hand a trident sa. and in the sinister a spear ppr. **Motto:** Loyalty. **Creation:** Bt. (UK) 29 Jan 1963.

SIR PAUL ANTHONY THOMPSON, 2ND BT, of Walton-on-the-Hill, City of Liverpool [Sir Paul Thompson Bt, The Old Vicarage, Church Rd, Bickerstaffe, Lancs L39 0EB]; *b* 6 Oct 1939; *s f* 1984; *educ* Aldenham; co dir; *m* 14 Aug 1971 *Pauline Dorothy, dau of Robert Orrell Spencer, of Tippett Ho, Smithills, Lancs, and has:
  1 +RICHARD KENNETH SPENCER; *b* 27 Jan 1976
  2 +David Paul Charles; *b* 1978
  1 *Karena Melanie; *b* 1973
  2 *Nicola Robyn; *b* 1974
Lineage: WILLIAM THOMPSON, of Liverpool; *m* Elizabeth Simpson, of Liverpool, and *d* 1934, leaving:

ERNEST SIMPSON THOMPSON, of St Hilary, Deneshey Rd, Meols, Cheshire; *b* 3 Aug 1880; *m* 14 June 1905 Annie (*d* 4 April 1964), dau of Edwin Pugh, of Liverpool, and had, with an er s (Harold, *b* 29 April 1907) and a dau (Dorothy, *b* 30 Nov 1911, *m* 15 April 1936 William Griffith Williams, of Waterloo, Lancs):

Sir Kenneth Pugh Thompson, 1st Bt (UK), so *cr* 29 Jan 1963; *b* 24 Dec 1909; *educ* Arnot St Cncl Sch Liverpool and Bootle Secondary Sch; memb Liverpool City Cncl 1938–58, Regnl Offr Min Info 1939–45, MP (C) Walton 1950–64, chm Nat Advsy Ctee Local Govt 1956–57, Assist PMG 1957–59, Parly Sec Min Educn 1959–62, author: *Member's Lobby* and *Pattern of Conquest*; *m* 15 April 1936 Nanne, JP (Liverpool) (*d* 1994), dau of Charles Broome, of Liverpool, and *d* 1984, leaving:
1 Sir PAUL ANTHONY THOMPSON, **2nd and present Bt**
1 *Nanne Patricia; *b* 3 April 1942; *educ* Penrhos Coll Colwyn Bay; *m* 1st 3 Nov 1966 Tredinnick Michael Johns, s of Joseph Tredinnick Johns, of Ottery St Mary, Devon; *m* 2nd 1989 *Neil Charles Bedford and by her 1st husb has:
  (1) *Anna Melinda; *b* 4 April 1969

THOMSON of
Glendarroch

Arms: Arg. a stag's head cabossed gu., between the attires a shakefork sa., on a chief engrailed of the second a galley, sail furled, oars in saltire, between two towers triple-towered of the field. **Crest:** A dexter hand couped ppr., holding a cross crosslet fitchée az. **Motto:** *Deus providebit* ('God will provide'). **Creation:** Bt. (UK) 28 March 1929.

SIR (FREDERICK DOUGLAS) DAVID THOMSON, 3RD BT, of Glendarroch, Midlothian [Sir David Thomson Bt, Holylee, Walkerburn, Peeblesshire EH43 6BD]; *b* 14 Feb 1940; *s f* 1972; *educ* Eton and Univ Coll Oxford (BA 1961); shipowner, jt md Ben Line Steamers, dir Britannia Steam Ship Insur Assoc 1965– (chm 1986–), dir Through Tport Mutual Insur Assoc Ltd 1973– (chm 1983–); chm: Jove Investment Tst 1983–, Aberdeen European Index Investment Tst plc 1990–, Ptarmigan Internat Capital Tst plc 1990–, Laurence J Smith Ltd 1994–, S A Meacock & Co Ltd 1996–, dir: Cairn Energy plc 1971–, Danae Investment Tst plc 1979–, Martin Currie Pacific Tst plc 1985–, Kynoch Gp plc 1990–, Asset Management Investment Co plc 1994–, memb Roy Co Archers; *m* 29 April 1967 (*divorce* 1994) Caroline Anne, dau of Maj Timothy Stuart Lewis (*see* DAVENTRY, V), and has:

  1 +SIMON DOUGLAS CHARLES; *b* 16 June 1969
  2 +Christopher Michael David; *b* 1970
  1 *Sarah Anne Vanessa; *b* 1974

Lineage: WILLIAM THOMSON, of Craigbinning, Linlithgow, and Edinburgh; *d* 28 March 1889, leaving:

JAMES WISHART THOMSON, of Glenpark, Balerno, Midlothian; *b* 12 July 1841; *m* Dec 1865 Barbara Gray (*d* 6 Nov 1921), dau of Hugh Cunningham, and *d* 20 Aug 1907, having had, with other issue:

Sir Frederick Charles Thomson, 1st Bt (UK), so *cr* 28 March 1929, KC (Scotland 1923); *b* 27 May 1875; advocate 1901, barrister 1904, Lt Lovat Scouts and Scottish Horse WW I Egypt and Salonika, MP (U) S Aberdeen, PPS to Sir Robert Horne, GBE, PC, 1919–22, a Ld Commr Treasury 1923 and 1924–28, Slr-Gen Scotland 1923–24, V-Chamberlain Household 1928–29 and 1931, Treasurer 1931; *m* 7 April 1904 Constance Margaret (*d* 22 May 1970), yr dau of Hamilton Andrew Hotson, gen man Br Linen Bank, Edinburgh, and *d* 21 April 1935, leaving:

Sir (James) Douglas Wishart Thomson, 2nd Bt; *b* 30 Oct 1905; *educ* Eton and Univ Coll Oxford (BA 1928); shipowner, dir Ben Line Steamers (chm 1964–70), Bank Scotland and Life Assoc Scotland, MP S Aberdeen 1935–46, PPS to Min Shipping 1940; *m* 25 Sept 1935 *Evelyn Margaret Isabel (Bettina) [Bettina Lady Thomson, Old Caberston, Walkerburn, Peeblesshire], er dau of Lt-Cdr David William Sholto Douglas, RN, and *d* 3 Jan 1972, leaving:

  1 Sir (FREDERICK DOUGLAS) DAVID THOMSON, **3rd and present Bt**
  2 +William Andrew Charles [William Thomson Esq, 24 Hermitage Dve, Edinburgh]; *b* 20 Jan 1948; *educ* Gordonstoun; *m* 1976 *Cecilia Bernadette Gill and has:
    (1) +Douglas Charles; *b* 1978
    (2) +William Frederick; *b* 1981
    (3) +Charles David; *b* 1988
    (1) *Julia Margaret Clare; *b* 1983
  1 *Susan Evelyn Margaret [Mrs John Cavenagh, Withcote Hall, Oakham, Rutland]; *b* 7 Oct 1936; *m* 8 July 1961 *Capt John Michael Cavenagh, GM, s of Brig Thomas Francis Cavenagh, OBE, MC, of Withcote Hall, and has:
    (1) *Thomas Douglas; *b* 28 July 1966
    (1) *Sarah Louise; *b* 5 Oct 1964
    (2) *Bettina Susan Margaret; *b* 1971
  2 *Vanessa Jean Wishart [Mrs Anthony Roberts, Mossdale, Conistone with Kilnsey, N Yorks]; *b* 27 Feb 1942; *m* 6 June 1964 *Anthony Fenwick Denby Roberts (*see* ROBERTS, Bt, of Milner Field)
  3 *Jennifer Constance Anne [Mrs Howard Pighills, Conistone Fold, Conistone with Kilnsey, N Yorks]; *b* 6 Jan 1945; *m* 1989 *Howard Pighills

THOMSON of
Old Nunthorpe

Arms: Erm. a lion passant guardant or, on a chief az. two keys, wards inwards of the second. **Crest:** A lion rampant or gorged with an antique crown gu. between two roses arg., barbed, seeded, leaved and slipped ppr. **Motto:** *Semper fidelis* ('Always faithful'). **Creation:** Bt. (UK) 3 July 1925.

SIR MARK WILFRED HOME THOMSON, 3RD BT, of Old Nunthorpe, Co York [Sir Mark Thomson Bt, 48 Hay's Mews, London W1X 7RT]; *b* 29 Dec 1939; *s f* 1991; Lt RN (FAA) 1957–65, chm Moorgate Investment Management; *m* 26 June 1976 (*divorce* 1997) Lady Jacqueline Rosemary Margaret Rufus Isaacs, only dau of 3rd Marquess of Reading (*qv*), and has:

  1 +ALBERT MARK HOME; *b* 3 Aug 1979
  2 +Jake Michael Alfred; *b* 1983
  3 +Luke Ivo Charles (twin); *b* 1983
  1 *Daisy Jacqueline Carol; *b* 1977

Lineage: JOHN THOMSON, JP, of Kelswick Ho, Whitehaven; had:

Most Rev WILLIAM THOMSON, PC; *b* 11 Feb 1819; DD, MA Oxon; Provost Queen's Coll Oxford, Bp Gloucester and Bath and Wells, Archbp York, FRS; *m* 1855 Zoë, dau of James Henry Skene, Br Consul Aleppo, of Rubislaw Ho, Skene, nr Aberdeen, and Frewin Court, Oxon, and *d* 25 Dec 1890, leaving:

1 WILFRID FORBES HOME (Sir), **1st Bt**

2 Jocelyn Home, CB; Capt RA

3 Basil Home (Sir), KCB, JP London; *b* 21 April 1861; barrister Inner Temple, Stipendiary Magistrate Fiji 1884, Acting Native Commr Fiji 1889, Govr Dartmoor and Wormwood Scrubs Prisons 1896–1908, Sec Prison Commn 1908–13, Assist Commr Met Police 1913–21, Orders Crown Italy, Crown Belgium, Rising Sun Japan, Humane Soc's silver medal; author: *The Story of Scotland Yard*, *The Scene Changes*, etc; *m* 31 Oct 1889 Grace Indja (*d* 4 Feb 1950), dau of Felix Stanley Webber, of Shroton Ho, Dorset and *d* 26 March 1939, having had:

  (1) Vivian Home THOMSON later SEYMER (roy licence 3 Nov 1919), DSO (1918), MC and bar; *b* 17 Oct 1894; *educ* Radley and RMA Woolwich; Lt-Col RA WW I (despatches thrice), FRIBA, Hon Steward Westminster Abbey; *m* 29 April 1922 Lucy Ridgley (*d* 8 June 1971), er dau of Dr William Hepburn Buckler, of Baltimore, Md., by Georgina Grenfell, CBE, yst dau of Theodore Walrond, CB, of Calder Lodge, Maidenhead, and *d* 7 Jan 1967, leaving:
    1a *Nigel Victor Evelyn; *b* 23 Sept 1925; *educ* Rugby and Trin Coll Cambridge (MA); *m* 1st 4 Aug 1956 (*divorce* 1964) Evelyn Maude, dau of Charles Thomas Houghton, CB, CBE, and has:
      1b *Catherine Lucy Anne; *b* 23 Sept 1957
    1a (cont.) Nigel Seymer *m* 2nd 10 Sept 1964 *Anne Rosemary, only dau of John Richard Topping of Wimbledon, and by her has:
      1b *Henry Vivian John; *b* 16 July 1965
      2b *Robert Thomas William; *b* 29 March 1967
    1a *Alethea Penelope; *b* 1 Oct 1923; *m* 24 Aug 1946 (*divorce* 1961) Maj Peter James Sidney Hamilton, MBE, s of Maj Frank Carr Hamilton, RA, of Bishops Stortford, Herts, and has:
      1b *Andrew Nigel; *b* 8 Aug 1947; *educ* Rannoch; 2nd Lt Black Watch
      2b *David Hamish; *b* 17 Nov 1948; *educ* Wellington and Trin Coll Cambridge
      1b *Rosamond Jean; *b* 8 Aug 1947
      2b *Penelope Christa; *b* 29 Jan 1951; *educ* Sherborne Sch for Girls and Girton Coll Cambridge
    2a *Helen Mary; *b* 26 May 1927
  (2) *Amherst Felix Basil Home; *b* 1911; *educ* Radley and Ch Ch Oxford; scientist with Min of Supply then MOD RN Sci Serv, US Medal Freedom; *m* 16 Sept 1937 *Ruth, only dau of James Nathaniel Bartlett, of Grove Ho, Oxon, and has:
    1a *Julian Pittis Amherst; *b* 3 July 1938; *educ* St Christopher's Letchworth, Magdalen Coll Oxford (MA) and RAF Coll Henlow; F/Lt RAF; *m* 5 April 1963 *Margaret Ann, BM, BCh, dau of Arnold Rodgers, of Penzance

(1) *Enid Zaina; *m* 1942 Felix Wise

4 Bernard Henry Home; *b* 9 Jan 1874; *m* 1st 27 April 1905 Helen Margaret (*d* 17 Dec 1924), 2nd dau of Robert Stanley Scholfied, and had:

(1) *Keith Home, MBE (1952); *b* 16 Aug 1912; *m* 1st 1937 (*divorce*) Viola Mabel, dau of Roland Dudley, of Linkenholt Manor, Andover, Hants, and has issue; *m* 2nd 1957 *Virginia Parker and has further issue

(1) *Juliet; *b* 4 June 1909; *m* 1st 1936 (*divorce* 1944) John Stuart Daniel, s of Walter Daniel, of The Red House, St Peter's-in-Thanet, Kent, and has issue; *m* 2nd 6 Oct 1945 Sir Richard Hugh Stanley Allen, KCMG, only s of Sir Hugh Percy Allen, GCVO, and has further issue

4 (cont.) Bernard Thomson *m* 2nd 12 Feb 1938 Dorothea Elizabeth (*d* 1961) est dau of Lt-Col Charles Robert Sandford Woods, and *d* 13 June 1953, leaving by her:

(2) *Alexa Catherine Home; *b* 13 Dec 1940

(3) *Zoë Felicia Home; *b* 13 Dec 1940

(4) Jacqueline Ita Home; *b* 13 Dec 1940; *d* unm 25 Jan 1965

1 Ethel Zoë; *m* 1887 Canon Frederick Wildman Goodwyn and *d* 1 Jan 1941, leaving issue. He *d* 23 April 1931

2 Zoë Jane; *m* 1891 Rev Joshua Fielding Hoyle and *d* 7 June 1940, leaving issue

3 Beatrice Mary; *m* April 1886 Henry Edward Preston, of Moreby Park, Yorks, and *d* 22 Jan 1927, leaving issue. He *d* 5 June 1924

4 Alexandra; *m* 23 June 1897 Lt-Col John Studholme, CBE, DSO (*see* STUD-HOLME, Bt), and *d* 15 Oct 1907, leaving issue

5 Madeline Ita Mary; *m* 1902 John Assheton Rennie, s of George Banks Rennie, and *d* 10 April 1962. He *d* 15 Feb 1949

The est s,

Sir Wilfrid Forbes Home Thomson, 1st Bt (UK), so *cr* 3 July 1925, of Old Nunthorpe, York, JP E and W R Yorks; *b* 29 March 1858; ptnr Beckett and Co, bankers, of York; *m* 1 June 1899 Ethel Henrietta (*d* 24 Jan 1968), 2nd dau of Hon Reginald Parker (*see* MACCLESFIELD, E), and had:

1 IVO WILFRID HOME (Sir), **2nd Bt**

1 Sibell Doreen; *b* 20 March 1900; *m* 10 July 1928 Brig William George Harriott, OBE, MC, RA, s of George Moss Harriott, CSI, CIE, of Micklehithe, Stevenage, Herts, and *d* 8 May 1951

The 1st Bt *d* 29 Jan 1939; his only s,

Sir Ivo Wilfrid Home Thomson, 2nd Bt; *b* 14 Oct 1902; *educ* Eton; RAF WW II (despatches); *m* 1st 1 Nov 1933 (*divorce* 1954) Sybil Marguerite, yr dau of Claude William George Hugh Thompson, of the Red Ho, Escrick; *m* 2nd 13 Oct 1954 *Viola Mabel, dau of Roland Dudley and formerly w of Keith Home Thomson (*see* above), and *d* 1991, having had:

1 Sir MARK WILFRED HOME THOMSON, **3rd and present Bt**

1 Carol Serena; *b* 4 June 1935; *m* 8 Dec 1962 Lt-Cdr Michael Avison Parker, CVO, RN, 2nd s of Capt Charles Avison Parker, CBE, RAN, of Melbourne, Australia, and *d* 26 Jan 1977, leaving:

(1) *Kate Avison; *b* 29 Nov 1963

1 (cont.) Lt-Cdr and Mrs Michael Parker adopted:

*Charles Avison; *b* 1 Sept 1966

THOMSON OF FLEET

Arms: Arg. a stag's head cabossed ppr., on a chief az. between two mullets a hunting horn of the first stringed gu. **Crest:** A beaver sejant erect ppr., blowing on a hunting horn arg. slung over his dexter shoulder by a riband of the dress tartan ppr. to THOMSON of that Ilk and his dependers. **Supporters:** Dexter, a Mississauga Indian habited in the proper costume of his tribe, holding in his dexter hand a bow all ppr.; sinister, a shepherd bearing in the sinister hand a shepherd's crook, on his head a bonnet, all ppr., and wearing a kilt of the usual tartan ppr. to THOMSON of that Ilk and his dependers. **Motto:** Never a backward step. **Creation:** B. (UK) 10 March 1964.

THE 2ND BARON THOMSON OF FLEET, of Northbridge, City of Edinburgh (Kenneth Roy Thomson) [The Rt Hon The Lord Thomson of Fleet, 8 Kensington Palace Gdns, London W8; 8 Castle Frank Rd, Toronto, Ont M4W 2Z4, Canada]; *b*

1 Sept 1923; *s* f 1976; *educ* Upper Canada Coll Toronto and Cambridge U (MA); newspaper proprietor, PR Dept RCAF WW II, chm: The Thomson Corp and Thomson Corp plc, The Woodbridge Co, Thomson US Inc; dir: Hudson's Bay Co, IBM Canada; co-pres Times Newspapers Ltd 1971–81; *m* 13 June 1956 *Nora Marilyn, dau of Albert Vernard Lavis, of Toronto, and has:

1 +DAVID KENNETH ROY; *b* 12 June 1957

2 +Peter John; *b* 25 April 1965

1 *Lesley Lynne; *b* 2 Feb 1959

Lineage: ANDREW THOMSON; small tenant farmer on the Buccleuch estates 1679; had:

ARCHIBALD THOMSON; *b* May 1749; master mason, migrated to Canada 1773; *m* Elizabeth McKay, of Quebec City, and had, with 10 other children:

GEORGE THOMSON, of Scarborough, Ontario; *b* 1801; *m* Lydia Terry and had, with nine other children:

HUGH THOMSON; *b* 21 Sept 1834; leather and harness worker; *m* 1857 Mary Sylvester and had, with two other sons:

HERBERT THOMSON, of Toronto; *b* 5 Feb 1867; barber; *m* 1893 Alice, dau of William Coombs, of Dunkerton, Somerset, and had:

1 ROY HERBERT, **1st Baron**

2 Carl Norman; *b* 18 April 1896; *educ* Jarvis St Collegiate Sch Toronto; *m* 16 Sept 1925 Mabel Dorothy, dau of William Soul, of Toronto, and *d* 13 Nov 1957, leaving:

(1) *Gregory Bruce; *b* 21 June 1926; *educ* Corpus Christi Grade Sch and St Patrick's Coll Ottawa U (BCom); *m* 18 July 1953 *Mary Mildred, dau of Freeman Brownlee, of Ottawa, and has:

1a *Craig Ross; *b* 6 May 1954

2a *Carey Bruce; *b* 15 June 1955

3a *Michael Garry; *b* 31 March 1957

1a *Karen Lynne; *b* 15 March 1960

2a *Pamela Rae; *b* 23 April 1962

(2) *Murray Paul; *b* 5 March 1928; *educ* Corpus Christi Grade Sch and St Patrick's Coll Ottawa U (BCom); *m* 2 June 1951 *Marion Gertrude Ann, dau of George Kealey, of Ottawa, and has:

1a *Mark Carl; *b* 5 Jan 1954

2a *Scott Drew Paul; *b* 18 Jan 1961

1a *Brenda Lynne; *b* 9 March 1955

(3) *Herbert Garrett; *b* 29 Aug 1930; *educ* Corpus Christi Grade Sch, St Patrick's Coll High Sch and High Sch of Commerce; *m* 13 May 1961 *Dawn Marlene, dau of George Archibald Pethick, of Ottawa, and has:

1a *Ross Carl; *b* 21 April 1962

2a *Ronald George; *b* 25 June 1963

3a *Roy Colin; *b* 26 April 1968

(4) *Stanley Wallace; *b* 1 Jan 1932; *educ* Corpus Christi Grade Sch, St Patrick's Coll High Sch and High Sch of Commerce; *m* 26 Nov 1960 *Muriel Edna, dau of Ernest Gates, of Ottawa

(5) Ross Clark; *b* 1 Jan 1932; *educ* Corpus Christi Grade Sch and St Patrick's Coll High Sch; *d* 5 May 1949

(6) *Carl Norman; *b* 19 June 1933; *educ* Corpus Christi Grade Sch, St Patrick's Coll High Sch and High Sch of Commerce; *m* 16 Oct 1954 *Lorraine Gail, dau of Frederic Farmer, of Ottawa, and has:

1a *Carl Norman; *b* 7 Feb 1961

1a *Sherry Gail; *b* 9 Sept 1955

2a *Julie Lynn; *b* 14 Feb 1958

(1) *Barbara Ann; *b* 11 Feb 1936; *m* 6 Dec 1958 George Brancato, s of Jerome Brancato, of Brooklyn, NYC, and has:

1a *George; *b* 8 March 1962

1a *Cynthia Ann; *b* 27 Oct 1959

2a *Wendy Louise; *b* 2 Oct 1960

3a *Alicia Mabel; *b* 7 July 1964

(2) *Gloria Alicia; *b* 11 Feb 1936

The est s,

ROY HERBERT THOMSON, **1st Baron Thomson of Fleet**, of Northbridge, City of Edinburgh (UK), so *cr* 10 March 1964, GBE (1970); *b* 5 June 1894; *educ* Jarvis St Collegiate Sch Toronto; chm Thomson Organisation (owned *The Times* and *Sunday Times*), fndr Thomson Fndn, Chllr Memorial U Newfoundland, V-Chm Cwlth Press Union 1964, Liveryman Stationers' and Newspaper Makers' Cos, V-Pres Periodical Proprietors Assoc, Tstee Reuters, dir: Security Tst Co of Birmingham, Roy Bank Canada Tst Corp and Imp Life Assur Co Canada; FBIM, Hon DCL, Hon DLitt St John's Memorial U Newfoundland, Hon LLD Northern Michigan U, Hon LHD Long Island U, FRSA, Hon Col Toronto Scottish Regt 1961, Cdr Roy Order Phoenix Greece; *m* 22 Feb 1916 Edna Alice (*d* 22 Feb 1951), dau of John Irvine, of Drayton, Ontario, and *d* 4 Aug 1976, having had:

1 KENNETH ROY THOMSON, **2nd and present Baron Thomson of Fleet**

1 *Phyllis Audrey [The Hon Mrs Campbell, c/o Thomson Organisation Ltd, PO Box 4YG, 4 Stratford Place, London S1A 4YG]; *b* 6 July 1917; *m* 29 April 1947 *Clarence Elwood Campbell, s of George Brown Campbell, and has:

(1) *Linda Christine; *b* 13 March 1949

(2) *Patricia Faye; *b* 19 Sept 1951

(3) *Susan Elaine; *b* 13 May 1954

2 Irma Jacqueline; *b* 20 Oct 1918; *m* 9 Sept 1945 Glenn Brydson, s of David Brydson, of Toronto, and *d* 2 May 1966, leaving a dau

(3) *Nicholas Anthony; *b* 4 Jan 1969
2 *Diana Jocelyn [Miss Diana Thorold, 21 Gerrard Rd, London N1 8AY]; *b* 4 Oct 1942; *educ* Edinburgh U (MA) and London U (MA); sr lecturer Westminster U

Lineage: Sir RICHARD THOROLD, of Selby, Yorks; living 1369; *m* Joan, dau and heiress of Robert de Hough, of Marston, Lincs, and had:

JOHN THOROLD, of Selby and Marston; living 1379; *m* —, dau of William Mirfield, and had:

RICHARD THOROLD, of Marston; living 1438; *m* Isabel, dau of Ralph Birnaud, of Knaresborough, and had:

WILLIAM THOROLD; living 1473; *m* Joan (*m* 2nd 1482 Ralph Malhome), dau and heir of William Brerehaugh, of Selby, and had:

JOHN THOROLD, of Marston and Westburgh; living 1497; *m* Alice, dau of Thomas Staunton, of Staunton, Notts, and had:

WILLIAM THOROLD; feudal Ld of Marston and Blankney, Lincs; High Sheriff Lincs 1557–58; *m* 1st Dorothy, dau of Thomas Leeke, of Hallam, Notts, and had, with a dau:

1 ANTHONY (Sir)
2 William, of Harmston, Lincs; *m* Margaret, dau and heiress of — Baldock, of the City of London, and had:
  (1) William, of Harmston; *m* Rose, dau of Rowland Sherrard, of Lobthorpe, Lincs, and *dsp*
  (2) Thomas, of Harmston; *m* 1st Rebecca, dau of Thomas Green, of London; *m* 2nd Prudence, dau of Matthew Bedell, of London, and by her had a s (Matthew) and a dau (Elizabeth); his s by his 1st w:
    1a Charles, of Harmston; Sheriff and Alderman City London; *m* 1st Anne, dau of William Wheat, of Glympton, Oxon, and had a s (Thomas, *d* unm); *m* 2nd Anne, dau of George Clarke, of London, and by her had:
      1b Charles (Sir), of Harmston; ktd 1704, Sheriff City London 1706, Alderman Cordwainers' Ward; *d* unm 1 April 1709
      2b Sir GEORGE THOROLD, 1st Bt (GB), so *cr* 9 Sept 1709, with remainder to his yr bro, of Harmston; ktd 1708, City London: Alderman, Sheriff 1710, Ld Mayor 1720; *m* Elizabeth, dau of Sir James Rushout, Bt, of Northwick, Worcs (*see* 1887 edn NORTHWICK, B), and *dsp* 20 Oct 1722
      3b Sir SAMUEL THOROLD, 2nd and last Bt, of Harmston; *dsp* 1 Jan 1738, when the btcy expired
3 Richard, of Morton, Lincs; Capt English forces Low Countries; *m* 1st June, dau of Robert Coney, of Morton; *m* 2nd Elizabeth, dau of Richard Coney, of Bassingthorpe, Lincs, and *d* 1600, having had by his 1st w, with three yr sons:
  (1) John, of Morton; *m* 1st Elizabeth, dau of John Burgh, of Saltfleetby, Lincs; *m* 2nd Jane, dau of Edward Ellis, of Chesterton, Cambs, and by her had a s (Edmund, of Friston, Lincs) and several daus, and by his 1st w, with two yr sons (*dsp*) and a yr dau (Anne):
    1a Nathaniel, of Grantham and Gray's Inn; *m* Anne, dau of George Lascels, of Elston, Notts, and had, with an er s:
      1b Eubulus; *m* 1st Elizabeth, dau of Dr — Barbor, of Lincoln, but by her had no issue; *m* 2nd Mary Hodgkin, of Barston, Lincs, and had:
        1c John; *m* Anne, dau of John Alcock, of Lincs, and had:
          1d Sir NATHANIEL THOROLD, 1st and last Bt (GB), so *cr* 24 March 1741; apparently inherited the Harmston estate from his cousin the 2nd Bt of the 1709 *cr*; *d* unm Aug 1764, when the btcy expired
    1a Elizabeth; *m* Walter Brockett, of Brockett Hall, Herts

WILLIAM THOROLD *m* 2nd Margaret, widow of Henry Sutton, of Wellingore, Lincs, and dau of Sir Robert Hussey, and by her had:
  4 Edmund (Sir), of High Hall; ancestor of Sir William Thorold, last of his line (*d* 1666)
  5 Robert, of Low Hall, Lincs; *m* Agnes (*m* 2nd Augustine Earle, of Straglethorpe, Lincs), 2nd dau and heiress of William Audley, of the Haugh, by Jane (dau and heiress of Alexander Haugh, of the Haugh), and had:
    (1) Anthony, of the Haugh; *m* Catherine, dau of Edward Haselwood, of Maidwell, Northants, and had:
      1a Sir ROBERT THOROLD, 1st Bt (E), so *cr* 14 June 1644, of the Haugh; royalist Civil War; *m* 1st Anne (*dsp*), sis of Sir Henry Carvil, of St Mary's in Marshland, Norfolk; *m* 2nd *c* 1630 Katharine, dau of 2nd Baron Teynham (*qv*), and *d* by 1662, leaving:
        1b Sir ROBERT THOROLD, 2nd Bt, of the Haugh; imprisoned Tower London 1692 for high treason; *m* by 1653 Catherine, dau of Sir Henry Knollys, of Grove Place, Hants, and *d* by 1695, leaving:
          1c Sir ROBERT THOROLD, 3rd and last Bt, of the Haugh; *dsp* 30 Nov 1706, when the btcy expired
      (1) Sir ROBERT THOROLD, 1sr Bt (E), so *cr* 14 June 1644, of The Haugh (btcy expired with his gs Sir ROBERT THOROLD 1706)

WILLIAM THOROLD *d* 1569; his est s,
Sir ANTHONY THOROLD, of Marston; High Sheriff Lincs 1576; *m* 1st Margaret, dau of Henry Sutton, of Wellingore, Lincs, and had:
1 Thomas; *m* Anne, dau of Sir George Pierrepont, of Holme Pierrepont, Notts, and *dvp*, having had two daus
2 William; *m* Frances, dau of Sir Robert Tyrwhitt, of Kettleby, and *dvp*, leaving:
  (1) Anthony (Sir), of Marston; Sheriff Lincs 1617; *m* Elizabeth, dau of Thomas Molyneux, of Haughton, Notts, and had, with a yr dau (*d* unm):
    1a Mary, *m* 10 Jan 1629/30 1st Baron Widdrington of Blankney and was *bur* 20 Jan 1675/6, having had eight sons and two daus
    (2) WILLIAM (Sir), **1st Bt**
3 Antony, *dsp*
4 John (Sir), of Corrington, Lincs; Sheriff 1616
1 Mary; *m* John Markham, of Sedgebrooke, Lincs
2 Martha; *m* Sir Philip Tyrwhitt, of Stainfield

Sir ANTHONY *m* 2nd Anne, widow of George Babington and dau and coheir of Sir John Constable, of Kinoulton, and *d* 26 June 1594, having by her had:
3 Winifred; *m* 1st George Clifton, of Clifton; *m* 2nd Henry Kervill, of Wiggenhall, Norfolk; *m* 3rd Sir Edward Gawsell

---

THOMSON OF MONIFIETH

Creation: B. (LP, UK) 1977.

THE BARON THOMSON OF MONIFIETH, of Monifieth, Dundee (Sir George Morgan Thomson, PC (1966), DL (Kent 1992)) [The Rt Hon The Lord Thomson of Monifieth PC DL, Leeds Castle, Maidstone, Kent ME17 1PL]; *b* 16 Jan 1921; *educ* Grove Acad Dundee; RAF 1940–46; assist ed *Forward* 1946 (ed 1948–53), sometime ed *The Dandy*; MP (Lab) E Dundee 1952–72; Jt Chm Cncl Educn Cwlth 1959–64; Advsr Educn Inst Scotland 1960–64; Min State FO 1964–66, Chllr Duchy Lancaster 1966–67 and 1969–70, Jt Min State FO 1967, Sec State Cwlth Affrs 1967–68, Min without Portfolio 1968–69, Shadow Defence Min 1970–72; Chm Lab Ctee for Europe 1972–73; Commr EEC 1973–77; First Crown Estate Commr 1978–80, ktd 1981; dir: Roy Bank Scotland 1977–90, ICI 1977–89, ENO 1987–93; Dep-Chm: Ditchley Fndn 1978–, Pilgrims Tst 1977–, Woolwich Bldg Soc 1988–91 (dir 1979–91); Chm: IBA 1981–88 (Dep-Chm 1980), Value and Income Tst 1988–, Lib Dem Party 1989– (Lib Dem spokesman Ho Lds), Grant Leisure 1990–94, Woolwich Europe 1990–92, Suzy Lamplugh Tst 1990–93, Leeds Castle Fndn 1994– (Tstee 1987–); Pres: History of Advertising Tst 1985–, Prix Italia 1989–93; Tstee Thomson Fndn 1977–; Chllr Heriot Watt U 1977–91; V-Pres FRTS 1982–89; Hon LLD Dundee 1967; Hon DLitt: Heriot Watt 1973, New U Ulster 1984; Hon DSc Aston 1976; Hon DCL Kent; FRSE 1985; FRTS 1990; *m* 1948 *Grace, dau of Cunningham Jenkins, of Glasgow, and has:
1 *Caroline Agnes Morgan; *b* 1954; *m* 1st 1977 (*divorce* 1981) Ian Bradley; *m* 2nd 1981 *Roger Liddle and by him has:
  (1) *Andrew; *b* 1988
2 *Ailsa Ballantyne; *b* 1956; *m* 1978 *Baron Newby of Rothwell (*qv*) and has:
  (1) *Mark; *b* 1985
  (2) *Roger; *b* 1987

Lineage: JAMES THOMSON, of Monifieth; had:

GEORGE MORGAN, *cr* a **Baron**

THOROLD

Arms: Sa. three goats salient arg. **Crest:** A roebuck passant arg., attired or. **Motto:** *Cervus non servus* ('The stag is not a slave'). **Creation:** Bt. (E) 24 Aug 1642.

SIR ANTHONY HENRY THOROLD, 15TH BT, of Marston, Lincoln, OBE (1942), DSC (1942) and bar (1945), JP (Kesteven 1961), DL (Lincs 1959) [Capt Sir Anthony Thorold Bt OBE DSC JP DL RN, Syston Old Hall, Grantham, Lincs NG32 2BX]; *b* 7 Sept 1903, *s* f 1965; *educ* RNCs Osborne and Dartmouth; High Sheriff Lincs 1968, Alderman Kesteven CC 1958–74, leader Lincs CC 1973–81; served RN 1917–56 (ret as Capt 1956), served WW II, Cdre-in-Charge Hong Kong 1953–55, Naval ADC to HM THE QUEEN 1955–56; chm: Grantham Hosp Management Ctee 1963–74 and Lincoln Diocesan Tst and Bd of Finance 1966–71; *m* 28 Aug 1939 Jocelyn Elaine Laura (*d* 1993), er dau of Sir Clifford Edward Heathcote-Smith, KBE, CMG (*see* SMITH-MARRIOTT, Bt), and has:
1 +(ANTHONY) OLIVER [Oliver Thorold Esq, 8 Richmond Crescent, London N1 0LZ]; *b* 15 April 1945; *educ* Winchester and Lincoln Coll Oxford (BA); barrister Inner Temple 1971; *m* 12 April 1977 *Genevra M, yst dau of John Richardson, of Broadshaw, W Calder, Midlothian, and has:
  (1) +Henry Lowry; *b* 6 Aug 1981
  (1) *Lydia; *b* 31 Jan 1984
1 *Celia [Mrs Bryan Salwey, 5 West Hill Rd, London SW18 1LH]; *b* 30 Nov 1940; *m* 11 Aug 1962 *Capt Bryan David Salwey, RN, yst (twin) s of Humphrey John Salwey, OBE, JP, of St Lawrence Cottage, Barnes Close, Winchester, and has:
  (1) *Roger Penruddocke; *b* 4 Sept 1964; *m* 6 Jan 1996 *Julie Randall and has:
    1a *Saskia Alice Bauwina; *b* 18 April 1997
  (2) *David Guy; *b* 14 May 1966; airline pilot

The yr s,

Sir William Thorold, 1st Bt (E), so *cr* 24 Aug 1642, of Marston; *b* 1591; Sheriff Lincs 1632, MP Grantham 1661–77, royalist Civil War; *m* Anne (*d* by 1683), dau of John Blythe, of Stroxton, nr Grantham, and *d* 1677, having had:

1 William; *m* Elizabeth (*m* 2nd Sir William Trollope, 2nd Bt, *qv*), dau of Sir Robert Carr, Bt, but *dsp vp*

2 Anthony; *m* 19 Dec 1654 Grisilla, dau of Sir John Wray, 2nd Bt, of Glentworth, and *dvp*, leaving, with other issue:

(1) **Sir William Thorold, 2nd Bt**; *b* 1659; *m* 11 March 1679/80 Rebecca Garrett and *dsp* 1681

(2) **Sir Anthony Thorold, 3rd Bt**; *b* 1663; *m* 20 Aug 1683 Anna Maria (*m* 2nd John Lewis Mordaunt and *d* 1689), only dau of Thomas Harrington, of Boothby, and *dsp* 1685

(3) **Sir John Thorold, 4th Bt**; MP Grantham 1685–87, 1697–1700 and 1711–15 and Lincs 1701–08; *m* 7 Aug 1701 Margaret (*d* 23 Jan 1732/3), widow of Hon Francis Coventry (*see* COVENTRY, E) and dau of John Waterer, and *dsp* 14 Jan 1716/7

(1) Anne; *m* Sir Thomas Hodgson, of Bramwith, Yorks

3 John; *m* 1st 3 Aug 1665 Elizabeth, dau of Sir William Tredway, and had:

(1) **Sir William Thorold, 5th Bt**; *m* — Harrington and had:

1a **Sir Anthony Thorold, 6th Bt**; *d* under age 25 Aug 1721

3 (cont.) John Thorold *m* 2nd 8 Oct 1674 Elizabeth, widow of Thomas Sanderson, and by her had:

(2) JOHN (Sir), **7th Bt**

1 Elizabeth; *m* Sir Richard Wingfield, of Tickencote Ho, Rutland

2 Margaret; *m* William Beresford, of Leadenham, Lincs

3 Anne; *m* 1st Robert Bateman, of London; *m* 2nd — Cutts

4 Frances; *m* Sir Francis Leeke, Bt, of Sandyacre

5 Mary; *m* Thomas Pechell, of Normanton

6 Penelope; *m* George Lucas, of Fenton

The 6th Bt's uncle,

Sir John Thorold, 7th Bt; *bapt* 8 Dec 1675; High Sheriff Lincs 1723; *m* 1st 1703 Alice, only dau and heiress of William Sampson, of Gainsborough, Lincs, and had:

1 JOHN (Sir), **8th Bt**

2 William

1 Elizabeth

Sir John *m* 2nd Shortclift (*d* 1789), dau of William Langley, and *d* Jan 1748, having by her had:

3 Charles

His est s,

Sir John Thorold, 8th Bt; *b* 1703; High Sheriff Lincs 1751, Fell Lincoln Coll Oxford; *m* 6 Aug 1730 Elizabeth (*d* by May 1779), dau and coheir of Samuel Ayton, of W Herrington, Co Durham, and had, with other issue:

1 JOHN (Sir), **9th Bt**

2 Samuel, of Welham, Notts; *m* 13 Sept 1776 Susan (*d* 9 Feb 1839), dau of Samuel Goodacre, of Barkstone, Lancs, and *d* 18 Jan 1825, leaving:

(1) Michael (Rev); *b* 28 March 1776; *m* Elizabeth, dau of Rev — Richardson, and had:

1a Michael Wynne, of Harworth, Notts, and Bridlington Quay, Yorks; *b* 21 March 1803; *m* 22 Oct 1828 Eliza (*d* 28 June 1876), dau of Rev Richard Morton, and *d* 6 May 1872, leaving, with a dau (*d* unm):

1b Michael Richard, of The Park, Sutton Bridge, Lincs; *b* 25 Sept 1830; *m* 21 Dec 1853 Ann (*d* 10 Oct 1904), dau of Edward Gillbee, of Western Bank, Sheffield, and *d* 21 Feb 1916, leaving, with three daus (*d* unm):

1c Michael Edward (Rev); *b* 17 Oct 1855; *educ* Gonville and Caius Coll Cambridge (MA); Vicar St Philip and St Jacob Bristol; *m* 17 April 1884 Ada Jane (*d* 2 Aug 1938), er dau of Joseph Bairstow, of Halifax, Yorks, and *d* 3 Dec 1934

2c Richard Gillbee; *b* 24 Dec 1859; *m* 15 Aug 1900 Ellen Irene (*d* 26 Sept 1958), dau of Edward Hogg, of Pinner, Middx, and *d* 11 Jan 1940, having had:

1d Cecil Richard; *b* 3 Sept 1901; *d* Argentina Oct 1944

2d +(Edward) Lionel [Lionel Thorold Esq, Potterspury Lodge School, Towcester, Northants NN12 7LL]; *b* 26 Nov 1905; *educ* King's Canterbury and London U (BA); served WW II; late master Pangbourne Nautical Coll

1d *Irene Gillbee; *b* 3 Sept 1901; *m* 1st 25 June 1931 Clifford Hackney, MRCS, LRCP (*d* 12 Jan 1956); *m* 2nd 25 Nov 1958, as his 2nd w, Brig Charles Walter Massy, CBE, DSO, MC, DL (*see* MASSY, B)

2d Dorothy Mary; *b* 4 Sept 1907; FLA; *d* unm 8 Sept 1976

3d Sylvia Marianne; *b* 24 April 1911; *m* 1931 Noel Cecil Blomfield, s of E C Blomfield, and *d* 24 July 1933

1c Ethel Ann Louisa; *b* 9 June 1861; *m* 14 July 1891 Rev Harold James Blathwayt, Rector Eastwell, Leics, and Vicar Eaton, nr Grantham, and *d* 8 June 1930, leaving *d* 5 Feb 1915

2b Edmund; *b* 8 Sept 1832; Fell Magdalen Coll Oxford 1859; *m* 2 Aug 1859 Louisa (*d* 16 March 1876), 2nd dau of Edward Gillbee, and *dsp* 19 June 1899

3b William (Rev); *b* 15 Sept 1833; Vicar Weeton Lancs 1865–82; *m* 24 April 1862 Fanny, dau of George Nelson, and *dsp* 23 Aug 1900

(2) Samuel; *b* 27 April 1779; *m* Charlotte Lawrence (*d* 15 May 1837), dau of Robert Mowar, of Woodseats and Unstone Manor, Derbys, and *d* 16 Feb 1848, leaving:

1a Samuel George; *b* 1816; *dsp* 1837

2a Charles, of Welham, Notts, The Woodseats, and Unstone Manor, JP Notts; *b* 28 June 1821; Sherwood Rangers Yeo Cav; *m* 1 May 1845 Mary Bettina Georgina (*d* 18 Dec 1899), 7th dau of John Kirke, of Markham and Retford, Notts, and *d* 27 May 1891, leaving, with another s (*d* an infant) and dau (*d* unm):

1b Charles Edmund de More, of Welham, Notts; *b* 30 Oct 1848; *educ* Emmanuel Coll Cambridge (BA 1874, MA 1878); *d* 28 June 1922

2b Arthur Leonard Percy; *b* 1 Feb 1851; *d* unm 20 Dec 1882

3b William Henry Fanshawe, JP Derbys; *b* 28 Dec 1859; *d* unm 30 March 1942

4b Octavius Reginald; *b* 17 Nov 1864; *d* 23 March 1937

1b Agnes Selioke; *m* 24 March 1875 William Craven Rockliffe, MD, of Hessle, E R Yorks, and Hull, and *d* 29 July 1930. He *d* 23 June 1930

2b Gertrude Steuart; *m* 20 April 1880 Henry Walter Oliphant Collingwood, of Clayworth, Notts, and had issue

1a Susannah Harriet; *m* 1844 Rev J Harrison and *d* 1845

(3) Charles; *b* 2 Oct 1787; *m* 6 June 1814 Jane (*d* 30 Jan 1850), dau of John Gilby, and *d* 9 May 1820, leaving:

1a John; *b* 8 March 1817; *d* unm

1a Susannah; *m* 15 May 1856 John Cutts (*d* 5 March 1875)

1 Isabella; *m* 14 Aug 1759 Thomas Middleton Trollope, est s of Sir Thomas Trollope, 4th Bt (*qv*), and *d* 19 March 1803, leaving issue

Sir JOHN *d* 5 June 1775; his est s,

Sir John Thorold, 9th Bt; *b* 18 Dec 1734; MP Lincs 1779–96; *m* 18 March 1771 Jane (*d* March 1807), only dau and heiress of Millington Hayford, of Oxton Hall, Notts, and Millington, Cheshire, and had, with other issue:

1 JOHN HAYFORD (Sir), **10th Bt**

2 George (Rev); *b* May 1776; Rector Hougham-cum-Marston, Lincs; *m* 1 May 1804 Elizabeth (*d* 2 April 1856), only dau of Benjamin Baugh, and *d* 27 Sept 1823, leaving:

(1) Henry Baugh (Rev); *b* April 1805; BA Oxon, Rector Hougham-cum-Marston; *m* 1 July 1829 Julia (*d* 27 Jan 1871), only dau of John Thomas Ellis, of Wyddial Hall, Herts, and *d* 1885, having had:

1a Ellis Frederick; *b* 10 Oct 1830; MD; *m* 21 July 1868 Ellen Clara (*m* 2nd 20 Aug 1888 Edward Serle Thorold (*see* below) and *d* 7 April 1923), dau of Adml Sir John Kingcome, KCB, and *dsp* 24 Feb 1881

2a Reginald Henry; *b* 12 Oct 1831; 92nd Highrs; *m* 18 Aug 1868 Sarah Catherine (*d* 5 April 1922), dau of Adml Edward Philips Charlewood, and *d* 24 Aug 1910, leaving:

1b Reginald Charles; *b* 5 May 1871; *m* 30 March 1906 Elizabeth (*d* Aug 1965), dau of Nicolas Moncrieff Howitt, of Tawonga, Victoria, Australia, and *d* 1956, leaving:

1c +Reginald Moncrieff; *b* 1914; *m* 10 Sept 1942 Sheila Frances (*d* 1968), dau of Hugh Sinclair Mackay, of Tasmania, and has:

1d +Reginald David; *b* 12 Nov 1945

1d *Elizabeth Helen; *b* 17 Sept 1948

2c John Charles Nicholas; *b* 1916; *m* 7 Oct 1948 *Barbara Marian Nicolson [Mrs Tulloch Roberts, Brambletye, Conara 7211, Tasmania, Australia] (*m* 2nd Feb 1969 Tulloch Roberts), dau of John Nicolson Archer, of Brambletye, and *d* 22 Feb 1961, having had:

1d +Barry John; *b* 27 Oct 1949; *m* 1975 *Joanna, only dau of Keith Ian Benson, of Launceston, Tasmania, and has:

1e +John Charles Nicholas; *b* 1988

1e *Lydia Jane; *b* 1979

2e *Sabina Lucy; *b* 1980

3e *Emma Elizabeth; *b* 1985

2d David Nicholas; *b* 1 Feb 1951; accidentally drowned 13 Nov 1952

3d Simon Charles; *b* 1953; *d* 1970

4d +Marcus Jonathan; *b* 1958

1c *Florence Katharine; *b* 1907

2c *Elizabeth; *b* 1909

3c *Bertha Edith; *b* 27 April 1911; *m* 30 Aug 1941 *Christo Albertyn Smith, of Transvaal, and has:

1d *Christopher John; *b* 11 June 1945

1d *Lillemor Elizabeth; *b* 21 Dec 1942

4c *Margaret; *b* 1918

1b Lucy Charlewood; *m* 4 April 1893 Lt-Col Claud George Cole-Hamilton, CMG, DSO (*see* ENNISKILLEN, E), and *d* 14 Nov 1951, leaving issue

2b Katharine Rochfort; *d* unm 7 Oct 1950

3b Bertha Ruthven; *d* unm 20 July 1950

3a Arthur William; *d* unm 9 Feb 1854

1a Bertha Julia; *m* 19 Sept 1855 Rev J A Gould and *dsp* 31 Aug 1871

2a Lucy Elizabeth; *m* 1st 19 Feb 1862 W R Keats (*d* 1 Sept 1872) and had issue; *m* 2nd 9 July 1874 Adml Edward Philips Charlewood and *d* 19 May 1881, having had further issue

(2) George Edward; *b* 11 Feb 1806; Col 42nd Highrs; *m* 5 Nov 1835 Alice Alicia Anne (*d* 1893), dau of Maj-Gen Mann, RE, and *d* 4 April 1874, leaving, with a dau (*d* unm):

1a Reginald Gother; *b* 7 Aug 1837; Maj-Gen RE; *m* 1st 27 Oct 1858 Fanny (*d* 29 Nov 1869), dau of Lionel Lukin, and had, with a dau (*d* unm):

1b Hayford Douglas, CBE (1919); *b* 20 July 1861; Lt-Col and Brevet Col W R Regt; *m* 1883 Mary (*d* 11 Aug 1940), dau of Alexander R Kirkpatrick, of Donacomper, Co Kildare, and *d* 28 April 1934, having had:

1c Ivone Hayford; *b* 3 Oct 1884; *educ* Trin Coll Dublin (BA); Lt Hants Regt; *d* 30 Oct 1913

2c Rupert Alexander; *b* Feb 1886; *d* 3 Nov 1951

1c Evelyn Mabel; *m* 3 Aug 1880 Lt-Col Charles Henry Brookes, RE, and *d* 18 Aug 1948, having had issue. He *d* 1894

2c Hilda Maud; *d* unm 16 Feb 1952

3c Gertrude Beaujolois; *m* 1895 George William Wetton Ashdown, MD, of East View, Ripley, Derbys, and *d* 12 Aug 1913, leaving issue. He *d* 1920

1a (cont.) Maj-Gen Reginald Thorold *m* 2nd 19 Dec 1871 Charlotte Sophia (*dsp* 29 Dec 1910), dau of Capt James Frederick Elton, 40th Regt, of Widcombe, Bath; *m* 3rd 19 Feb 1913 Frederica Mary (*d* 13 Nov 1947), widow of

W Cecil Elton Hunt and dau of Sir James Cockle, FRS, Ch Justice Qld, and *d* 29 April 1928

1a Edith Rhoda; *m* 28 Jan 1873 Rev Edward Pattin Cole, Hon Canon Bristol, and *d* 10 Feb 1925, leaving issue. He *d* 26 Oct 1926

(3) Charles *b* 1807; *m* 25 May 1830 Sophia (*d* 19 March 1892), dau of Rev E Thorold (*see* below), and *d* 3 Feb 1868, leaving:

1a Algernon Charles Edward (Rev); *b* 8 March 1850; *educ* Clare Coll Cambridge (MA); Rector Hougham-cum Marston, Lincs; *m* 23 March 1871 Edith Mary (*d* 18 Feb 1909), dau of W Clay, and *d* 6 Jan 1922, leaving:

1b Algernon Herbert (Rev); *b* 28 Jan 1872; *educ* Lancing and Keble Coll Oxford (BA); Vicar Gwennap, Redruth, Cornwall, Hon Priest-Vicar Truro Cathedral; *m* 8 Oct 1901 Inez Theodora (*d* 12 March 1959 aged 84), dau of Alfred Beer, and *d* 25 Dec 1931, leaving:

1c Michael Herbert (Rev); *b* 15 July 1904; *educ* St Michael's Coll Tenbury, Truro Cathedral Sch and Sidney Sussex Coll Cambridge (BA 1925, MA 1929); Vicar All Souls' Brighton 1937–51 and St John the Baptist, Bathwick, Bath, 1951; *m* 14 Jan 1931 *Dorothy, yst dau of George Patrick Henfrey, of The Dower Ho, Beckenham, and Chesham Place, Brighton, and *d* 18 Oct 1956, leaving:

1d +Anthony Patrick de Buckenhold [Maj Anthony Thorold, c/o Barclays Bank, Marble Arch, London W1]; *b* 10 March 1938; *educ* Brighton Coll and Sidney Sussex Coll Cambridge; Maj RCT (ret 1974); *m* 28 April 1962 (*divorce*) Jane Antoinette, only dau of William Francis Paul Corbould, of Purley, Surrey, and has:

1e *Emma Jane [Mrs Andrew Tomalin, 8 Beech Close Court, Cobham KT11 2HA]; *b* 23 Feb 1963; *m* 1988 *Andrew Michael Tomalin, er s of David A Tomalin, of Crowborough, Sussex, and has, with two other children:

1f *Oliver Robert; *b* 21 May 1991

1f *Victoria Alice; *b* 31 May 1989

2f *Sophia Helen; *b* 17 May 1996

2e *Antonia Cecilia; *b* 10 June 1966; *m* 19– *Robert Goodman and has:

1f *Alexander William; *b* 16 Feb 1998

2d (Michael) Bernard; *b* 8 Oct 1942; *educ* St Edward's Sch Oxford and RMA Sandhurst; AMInstPet, Scots Gds 1961–64; *m* 1st 8 April 1967 (*divorce* 1971) Carolyn Alice, er dau of Martin James Pollock (*see* POLLOCK, Bt), and had:

1e +Rupert Michael James de Buckenhold; *b* 29 Jan 1969

2d (cont.) Bernard Thorold *m* 2nd 1971 *Mary Nihan [Mrs Bernard Thorold, 20 Silsoe Ho, Park Village E, London NW1 4AS], dau of James Mackenzie-Mair, of Beachborough Pk E, Folkestone, and *d* 1979, leaving by her:

2e +Crispin Crispian James Leofric; *b* 1973

1d *Ia Cecilia [Prof Ia McIlwaine, 10 Cromwell Close, London N2 0LL; 32 Morston Rd, Blakeney, Norfolk NR25 7BG]; *b* 20 April 1935; *educ* London U (BA 1956, PhD 1984); FLA; Dir Sch of Library, Archive and Info Studies, UCL; *m* 31 Dec 1966 *John Hamish St John McIlwaine, s of William Arthur St John McIlwaine, of Kingston, Jamaica, and has:

1e *(Katherine) Anne [Miss Anne McIlwaine, 3 Vanbern House, 83–85 Prince of Wales Rd, London NW5]; *b* 11 Feb 1969; *educ* Magdalen Coll Oxford and London U (BA 1990, MPhil 1992, MA 1997)

1c Mary; *b* 27 June 1908; *d* 31 Dec 1995

2b Arthur Charles Campbell; *b* 13 Sept 1873; *educ* Worcester Coll Oxford (MA); Headmaster Mentone GS nr Melbourne 1933–39; *m* 1st 15 Jan 1913 Kathleen May (*d* Jan 1922), only dau of Frederick Jeffrey, of Kensington, and had:

1c John Jeffrey de Buckenhold; *b* 4 Oct 1913; Headmaster Mentone GS; *m* 16 Dec 1953 *Nancy, only dau of Leslie O Thomas, of Toorak, Melbourne, and *d* 5 Nov 1982

2c +Patrick Hayford [Patrick Thorold Esq, 7 Broadbeach Blvd, Broadbeach, Qld 4218, Australia]; *b* 12 March 1916; *m* 1st 1940 (*divorce* 1949) Dorrit Wilhelmina, dau of J H Charles, of Melbourne, and has:

1d *Ruth Patricia [Mrs Roger Dunn, 109 Wellington St, Kew, Melbourne, Victoria, Australia]; *b* 1942; *m* 1966 *Roger MacLeod Dunn and has:

1e *Lachlan Thorold MacLeod; *b* 1968

2e *Tarquin Charles MacLeod; *b* 1972

1e *Phoebe Rebecca; *b* 1969

2c (cont.) Patrick Thorold *m* 2nd 3 Sept 1949 *Maureen Margaret, only dau of William George Mason, of Armadale, Melbourne, and by her has:

1d +Jeffery Michael; *b* 23 July 1955

2d *Joan Michele [Mrs Andrew Wilson, 12 Seymour Ave, Armadale, VIC 3143, Australia]; *b* 20 Dec 1952; *m* 1974 *Andrew Howard Knox Wilson and has:

1e *Benjamin Thorold Knox; *b* 1983

2e *Nicholas Andrew Jeffery; *b* 1985

3e *Patrick Howard Knox; *b* 1999

2b (cont.) Arthur Thorold *m* 2nd 1925 Jessie Isobel Marjory (*d* 31 Jan 1954), dau of Francis Wellington Were, of Melbourne, and *d* 16 Oct 1939

3b Ernest Hayford (Rev), CB (1934), CBE (1929, OBE (1919); *b* 17 Feb 1870; *educ* Highgate Sch and Queen's Coll Oxford (MA); DD, CF BEF 1914–16 (despatches twice) and Staff Offr to Chaplain-Gen 1916–21, Chaplain Roy Mil Chapel Bde Gds 1921–23, with Army of the Rhine 1923–24, Assist Chaplain-Gen Western Cmd 1924–26 and Southern Cmd 1926–30, Hon Chaplain to HM GEORGE V 1926 and Chaplain 1935–36, Assist Chaplain-Gen Aldershot Cmd 1930–31, Chaplain Tower of London 1931–38, Chaplain-Gen Forces 1931–39, Chaplain to TM EDWARD VIII 1936 and GEORGE VI 1937–40, Chaplain OStJ; *m* 23 Aug 1913 Dorothy Frances (*d* 14 March 1969), dau of Edward Herbert, of Croydon, and *d* 6 Feb 1940, leaving:

1c +John Robert Hayford (Rev) [The Rev John Thorold, St Deiniol's Library, Hawarden, Chester CH5 3DF]; *b* 2 Nov 1916; *educ* Westminster and King's Coll Cambridge (BA 1943, MA 1945); Sub-Lt (Sp) RNVR 1943–44, assist master Eton 1945–46, tutor Ripon Hall Oxford 1947–52, Vicar Mitcham 1952–86, Priest Oratory of the Good Shepherd and co-patron of five livings

2c +Henry Croyland (Rev) [The Rev Henry Thorold, Marston Hall, Grantham, Lincs]; *b* 4 June 1921; *educ* Eton and Ch Ch Oxford; Chaplain to Bp Brechin 1944–46, Chaplain RNVR 1946–49, assist master and chaplain Lancing 1949, housemaster 1954, co-patron five livings, author *Shell Guides to*: *Derbyshire, Staffordshire, County Durham, Nottinghamshire* and jt-author *Shell Guide to Lincolnshire*, also *Collins Guide to Cathedrals, Abbeys and Priories of England and Wales*, *Lincolnshire Churches Revisited* (with foreword by HRH THE PRINCE OF WALES), and *Collins Guide to the Ruined Abbeys of England, Wales and Scotland*

1b Gertrude Muriel Edith; *d* unm 29 March 1967

2a Wilfred Augustus Holden (Rev); *b* 22 Aug 1852; *educ* Clare Coll Cambridge (MA); Midshipman RN, Rector Stainby Lincs 1887–1905; *m* 11 April 1872 Harriott Vickary (*d* Jan 1933), only child of John Chase, of Kippences, W Liss, and *d* 3 June 1933, leaving:

1b Wilfred Lionel de Buckenhold (Rev); *b* 21 Feb 1873; *educ* Trin Coll Cambridge (BA 1894); Rector Stainby 1905–39; *m* 15 Oct 1902 Caroline Muriel (*d* 1 Aug 1947), er dau of Edward Greaves, of Weldon, Northants, and *d* 19 May 1975, having had:

1c Dorothy Muriel; *b* 20 Jan 1904; *d* 29 May 1910

1a Constance Cecilia May; *m* 1st 3 March 1868 Charles Cromwell Hockley (*d* 1874); *m* 2nd 1876 Rev William Chippendall, Vicar Tilton-on-the-Hill, Leics, and *d* 1891, leaving issue

(4) Arthur William; *b* 1808; *m* Anne Laura, dau of Maj Octavius Temple, and *d* 1888, leaving, with a dau (*d* unm):

1a Harry Octavius; *b* 15 July 1828; MRCS (Eng), Bde Surg IMS; *m* Amelia Laura Barrington and *d* 29 April 1912, leaving:

1b William Grant; *b* 1864; Maj IMS; *m* 1898 Annie Elizabeth (*d* 1951), dau of James Holden

2b Frederick Temple; Capt KOYLI; *ka* Boer War 1902

1a Laura Elizabeth; *m* April 1866 Rev Edmund John Hitchings, Chaplain RN

2a Anne Katherine; *m* 18 June 1868 Richard Brinsley Hooper and had issue

(5) Frederick Arthur; *dsp*

(6) William (Rev); *b* 20 Oct 1810; MA Oxon, Rector Warkleigh; *m* 29 May 1839 Frances Elizabeth (*d* 16 Nov 1904), dau of James Gould, and *d* 1888, leaving, with two daus (*d* unm):

1a George Aubrey William; *b* 15 Sept 1846; *educ* Exeter Coll Oxford (MA); *m* 7 June 1883 Elizabeth (*d* Jan 1930), widow of John B Short and dau of William Norton Barry, of Castlecor, and *d* 9 Feb 1932

2a Hubert Gould William; *b* 8 May 1854; Cdr RN; *m* 24 April 1889 Lora Marsh (*d* 28 March 1946), dau of Preston Karslake, of White Knights, Reading, and *d* 14 April 1906, having had, with a dau (*d* unm):

1b William George Preston; *b* 25 Sept 1892; *educ* Winchester and New Coll Oxford (MA); MInstCE, Capt Berks Yeo, Dep Ch Engr Met Water Bd; *m* 4 April 1940 (*annulled* 1942) Hon Phyllis Margaret Russell, OBE (1946), only dau of 2nd Baron Ampthill, GCSI, GCIE (*qv*), and *dsp* 23 April 1943

2b Guy Frederick (Sir), KCMG (1959, CMG 1945); *b* 21 July 1898; *educ* Winchester and New Coll Oxford (BA 1921); Lt RFA WW I 1917–18, Assist Sec Min Ec Warfare 1944–45, attd UK Delegn OEEC Paris Sept 1948, UK Fin Advsr and Ec Min Washington 1957–59, Dir Ag Mortgage Corp 1963–67, pres Corp Insur Brokers 1963–68; *m* 18 June 1928 Mary Wilder (*d* 6 June 1963), dau of Henry Wynnatt-Hussey, and *d* 16 Jan 1970, leaving:

1c +Peter Guy Henry [Peter Thorold Esq, 25 Stanley Crescent, London W11 2NA]; *b* 20 April 1930; *educ* Eton and New Coll Oxford (MA 1953]; *m* 1st 21 Dec 1954 (*divorce* 1963) Merilyn Mary, yr dau of Lt-Col Sir John Francis Roskell Reynolds, 2nd Bt, MBE (*qv*), and has:

1d +Marcus Guy Francis; *b* 8 Sept 1955; *educ* Millfield; *m* 1992 *Georgina C, er dau of Peter Armitage, of Tarporley, Cheshire, and has:

1e +Jack Guy Peter; *b* 3 March 1995

1e *Iona Sophie; *b* 2 May 1997

2d +Daniel Edward; *b* 9 July 1960

1d *Caroline Emelia; *b* 18 Nov 1956

1c (cont.) Peter Thorold *m* 2nd 26 June 1964 *Anne, yr dau of Robert Evelyn Herbert Fender, AFC, of The Manor Ho, Withington, Glos, and by her has:

2d *Nicola Anne; *b* 11 May 1965

2c +Julian Hubert; *b* 28 Jan 1933; *educ* Eton and New Coll Oxford (BA 1955, MA 1959); barrister Inner Temple 1959

3a John Leofric de Buckenhold (Rev); *b* 13 July 1864; *educ* New Coll Oxford (MA 1890); Rector Bromham, Wilts; *m* 6 Feb 1895 Jane Preston (*d* 23 May 1956), dau of Preston Karslake, of White Knights, Reading, and *d* 29 Jan 1940, leaving, with a dau (*d* an infant):

1b Henry Karslake, CB (1945), CBE (1942), DSC (1916), DFC (1921), AFC (1918); *b* 11 May 1896; *educ* Marlborough; joined RNAS 1915, WW I 1915–18, Mesopotamia 1920, WW II AOC 92 Gp 1943–45, SASO Flying Training Cmd 1946–47, ret 1947 as AVM, 3rd Cl Order Polonia Restituta 1942; *d* unm 10 April 1966

2b George Preston; *b* 11 May 1896; *educ* Marlborough and Trin Coll Oxford (MA, BM, and BCh 1926); Capt RM WW I, MRCS Eng, LRCP Lond 1926; *m* 6 July 1940 Madeleine Beatrice (*d* 1988), dau of Aubrey Carteret de Carteret, of Jersey, and *d* 27 Dec 1963, leaving:

1c *Laelia Karslake [Mrs Julian Hartnoll, 8 Etherden Rd, London W12]; *b* 21 April 1942; *m* 26 Sept 1964 *Julian Rodney Hartnoll, 2nd s of

James Rodney Blackett Hartnoll, of Bovingdon Ash, Bovingdon, Herts, and has:

    1d *Emma de Carteret; b 14 Oct 1965; m 2 Feb 1998 *Adam Donovan

    2d *Jenny Moulton; b 26 July 1967

3b Edward Leofric; b 9 June 1898; educ Marlborough and New Coll Oxford; Lt RGA WW I; m 1st 27 April 1928 (divorce 1942) Phyllis Frances, dau of Albert Charles Hills, of Biggleswade, and had:

    1c *Brenda Frances [Mrs Roy Hillier, The Granary, Roundway Farmhouse, Devizes, Wilts]; b 13 Aug 1929; m 1 Nov 1947 *Roy Hillier, s of Arthur Charles Hillier, and has:

        1d *Anthony Edward; b 1949; m 19– *Harriet Elvins and has issue

        2d *Nicholas Leofric; b 1952; m 19– *Jane Blower and has issue

3b (cont.) Edward Thorold m 2nd 20 June 1942 *Agnes Phyllis [Mrs Edward Thorold, St Agnes, Balcombe, Sussex], dau of Albert Humphrey Johnson, of London, and d 16 Sept 1965, having by her had:

    2c *Judith Rose [Mrs Michael Thorold-Palmer, Walkleigh House, S Holmwood, Dorking, Surrey]; b 1 Dec 1947; m 6 Sept 1969 *Michael Adrian PALMER later THOROLD-PALMER (deed poll), only s of Herbert James Palmer, of The White Hart Hotel, St Austell, Cornwall, and has:

        1d *Edward James; b 1972

        1d *Alexandra Louise; b 1974

4b Arthur John; b 30 Dec 1900; educ Marlborough; d unm 8 Aug 1970

5b Charles Aubrey; b 9 Nov 1906; educ Marlborough and Trin Coll Oxford (BA 1928, MA 1934); MD, Pncpl Research Offr Nigeria (ret 1957), Offr i/c Woburn Experimental Station (ret 1968); m 25 June 1949 *Katharine Mary [Mrs Charles Thorold, 99 Strawberry Vale, Twickenham, Middx TW1 4SJ], 3rd dau of Rt Rev Algernon Augustus Markham, Bp Suffragan Grantham 1937–49, and d 2 March 1998, having had:

    1c *Philippa Markham [Mrs Nicholas Killin, 50 Samdon St, Hamilton, NSW 2303, Australia]; b 28 April 1951; educ Oxford (DSc 1975); m 1981 *Nicholas Killin, MBA, and has:

        1d *Thomas William; b 1983

        2d *Samuel Charles; b 1989

        1d *Emily Katharine; b 1991

    2c A dau; b 4, d 7 Oct 1953

    3c *Joanna Mary [Mrs Paul Clifford, 14 Lakeside, Oxford OX2 8JG]; b 15 June 1955; MA Oxon and London; m 1977 *Paul Clifford, MA (Oxon) and has:

        1d *Sarah Katharine; b 1981

        2d *Elizabeth Rose; b 1984

1b Muriel Evelyn; b 12 June 1903; d Nov 1987

1a Godiva Marion; Lady Supt Middlesex Hosp 1876–1905; d 5 Jan 1918

2a Emily Elizabeth Paulina; m 18 May 1871 Edward Stewart-Jones, 2nd s of William Jones, of Fulwood Lodge, Liverpool, and d 7 Jan 1934, leaving issue. He d 14 Aug 1900

3a Alice Fanny Isabella; m 2 July 1868 Rev John Argylle Welsh Colling, Vicar Newton St Cyres, nr Exeter, and d 27 May 1921, leaving issue. He d 9 May 1911

3 Edward (Rev); b 6 Jan 1779; Rector Hougham-cum-Marston; m 20 June 1809 Mary (d 7 Jan 1874), only dau of Thomas Wilson, of Grantham, MD, and heiress of Thomas Bartholomew, of Bardney, and d 22 April 1836, having had, with a dau (d unm):

    (1) Edward Serle; b 29 July 1813; m 1st 14 Dec 1843 Amelia Jane (d 1887), dau of Rev J Hinde; m 2nd 20 Aug 1888 Ellen Clara (d 7 April 1923), widow of Ellis F Thorold (see above) and dau of Sir J Kingcome, KCB, and d 8 May 1899

    (2) Anthony Wilson (Rt Rev); b 13 June 1825; DD, Bp Rochester 1877–90 and Winchester 1890–95; m 1st 10 Jan 1850 Henrietta (d 18 Oct 1859), dau of Thomas Greene, and had:

        1a Edward Hayford; d young

    (2) (cont.) The Rt Rev Anthony Thorold m 2nd 19 Sept 1865 Emily (d 30 Dec 1877), est dau of John Labouchere, of Broome Hall, Surrey, and d 25 July 1895, having by her had:

    2a Algar Labouchere; b 9 Aug 1866; m 17 April 1894 Theresa Mary (d 15 March 1944), dau of Rev Owen Luttrell Mansel (see MANSEL, Bt), and d 30 May 1936, having had:

        1b Anthony Herbert Gerard (Rev); b 13 Aug 1896; Lt RN WW I (despatches), RC priest; d 1 Feb 1969

        2b Francis John Anselm; b 21 April 1901; educ Westminster; m 1 Dec 1932 Ann Amelia (d 6 July 1979), dau of William Somers, of Wick, Somerset, and d 4 June 1958, having had:

            1c Edward Anthony John; b 24 Jan 1937; d 7 Sept 1938

            2c +John Christopher; b 16 July 1940; m 23 Dec 1966 *Elizabeth Ann, dau of Noel John Colborne, of Chippenham, Wilts, and has:

                1d +Justin Algar; b 5 July 1967

                1d *Rebecca

            1c *Catherine Ann [Mrs Catherine Blaker, Woodcote Farm, Nutley, nr Uckfield, Sussex]; b 11 Sept 1933; m 3 Sept 1960 (divorce 1965) John Blaker, only s of Maj Sir Reginald Blaker, 2nd Bt (qv)

    3b Owen Edward Aloysius; b 1, d 3 April 1906

    1b Wilhemina Benedicta Mary Du Pré; b 22 Aug 1895; m 7 Aug 1920 Charles John Swainston-Goodger, s of Charles William Swainston-Goodger, of Newcastle, and d 22 Nov 1963, leaving issue. He d 20 March 1940

    2b Mary Catherine Ann; b 26 July 1899; m 8 Sept 1930 Count Maurice Anthony Michael de la Bedoyère, ed Catholic Herald, only s of Vicomte de la Bedoyère (see below), and d 4 Sept 1959, leaving issue

1a Dorothy Margaret; b 1872; Sister of Charity of St Vincent de Paul; d unm 15 Jan 1961

2a Sybil Emily; b 1873; m 31 July 1899 Vicomte Yvon de la Bédoyère, s of Marquis de la Bedoyère, and d 17 Nov 1914, leaving issue. He d 21 Jan 1948

(1) Mary; m 1834 Rev Robert Hustwick and had issue. He d 1868

    (2) Jane; m 29 Aug 1837 Rev Granville Wheler Menteth, yst s of Sir Charles Granville Stuart Menteth, 1st Bt (qv), and d 10 Feb 1899

    (3) Sophia; m 25 May 1830 Charles Thorold and d 19 March 1892, leaving issue (see above)

    (4) Ellen; m 28 March 1843 Rev Alexander Paton and had issue

1 Jane; m 1812 Capt Charles Thorold Wood, RHG, of Thoresby, Lincs, and d his widow 26 Feb 1861 aged 77

Sir JOHN d 25 Feb 1815; his est s,

Sir John Hayford Thorold, 10th Bt; b 30 March 1773; m 1st 1 Oct 1811 Mary (d Dec 1829), est dau and heir of Sir Charles Kent, 1st Bt, and had issue; m 2nd 12 July 1830 Mary Anne (m 3rd 10 April 1834 Adml Sir Charles Ogle, 2nd Bt, and dsp 4 Feb 1842), widow of John Dalton, Jr, of Turnham Hall, Lancs, and dau of George Cary, of Tor Abbey, Devon, and d 7 July 1831, leaving by his 1st w:

Sir John Charles Thorold, 11th Bt; b 26 June 1816; m 17 March 1841 Elizabeth Frances (d 3 April 1894), 3rd dau of Col Thomas Blackborne Thoroton-Hildyard, of Flintham Hall, Notts, and had, with two daus (d unm):

    1 JOHN HENRY (Sir), **12th Bt**

    2 Montague George; b 22 Aug 1844; RN; m 2 July 1881 Emmeline Laura (dsp 1 Oct 1918), widow of 6th and last Baron Rivers (see 1880 edn) and dau of Capt John Pownall William Bastard, and d 18 Dec 1920

    3 Cecil, of Boothby, Lincs, JP, DL; b 5 Oct 1847; Capt 1st Life Gds; m 2 Sept 1875 Annie Charlotte (m 2nd 25 Sept 1902 Ralph Henry Seymour Hall (see HALL, Bt, of Dunglass); m 3rd John Felix Riley and d 8 Feb 1913), dau of Gen E S Claremont, CB, and d 26 Feb 1895, leaving:

        (1) Marguerite; b 16 Aug 1876; m 1st 21 Sept 1897 Hon Maurice Raymond Gifford, CMG, and had issue (see GIFFORD, B); m 2nd 20 April 1920 Lt George Hugh Rayner, Roy Warwicks Regt, and d 9 Jan 1958. He d 19 Feb 1941

    4 Charles Cecil Hayford; b 26 Dec 1852; Lt-Col 2nd Bn RWF; m 22 Sept 1883 Mary Gertrude (m 2nd 28 Feb 1908 Brig-Gen Arthur Willoughby George Lowry Cole, CB, DSO (see ENNISKILLEN, E), and d 26 Dec 1941), dau of Thomas Browning, of Sale, Cheshire, and dsp, ka Boer War 24 Feb 1900

The 11th Bt d 26 April 1866; his est s,

Sir John Henry Thorold, 12th Bt, JP, DL Lincs; b 9 March 1842; Lt 17th Regt, MP Grantham 1865–68, Lt-Col 2nd Vol Bn Lincs Regt, Hon LLD Cantab, High Sheriff Lincs 1876; m 3 Feb 1869 Hon Alexandrina Henrietta Matilda (d 11 Dec 1931), est dau of 8th Baron Middleton (qv), and d 4 Oct 1922, having had:

    1 **Sir John George Thorold, 13th Bt**, JP, DL (Lincs 1926–45); b 2 Oct 1870; educ Eton; Maj 3rd Bn Lincs Regt Boer War (Queen's medal with two clasps), HQ Recruiting Offr Lincoln WW I; d unm 25 Dec 1951

    2 Henry Cecil; b 17 Nov 1871; Capt 2nd Bn Leics Regt Boer War; ka 18 Feb 1902

    3 JAMES ERNEST (Sir), **14th Bt**

    1 Aline, OBE (1918); m 8 Aug 1894 Ernest James Wythes, CBE, DL, of The Wood Ho, Epping, and d 27 Oct 1951, leaving issue. He d 13 Dec 1949

    2 Dorothy Marion; m 5 Sept 1912 Capt Hubert Edward Peter Dyke Acland and d 7 April 1958, having had issue (see ACLAND, Bt, of Columb John)

The 13th Bt's bro,

Sir James Ernest Thorold, 14th Bt; b 27 Jan 1877; educ Winchester; m 16 Dec 1902 Katharine (d 23 June 1959), est dau of Rev William Rolfe Tindal-Atkinson, and d 27 July 1965, leaving:

    1 Sir ANTHONY HENRY THOROLD, **15th and present Bt**

    2 Montague; b 27 March 1906; educ Lancing and St John's Coll Cambridge (BA); Lt-Col Leics Regt WW II (despatches), Offr Crown Belgium; m 23 Nov 1946 *Helen Moye [Mrs Montague Thorold, The Old Rectory, Stainby, Lincs NG33 5QX], late Jr Cdr ATS, yr dau of Capt Barnard Moye Stone, of Dovercourt, Essex, and d 11 March 1974, leaving:

        (1) +John Richard [John Thorold Esq, 52 Danemere St, London SW15]; b 6 Sept 1947; educ Kelly Coll, Tavistock; late 2nd Lt 9th/12th Roy Lancers, ARICS, land agent; m 1991 *Elizabeth A, dau of Lt-Col A J E Cruickshank, of Coxbridge, Somerset, and has:

            1a +Guy; b 1992

            1a *Alexandra (twin); b 1992

        (1) *(Rosemary) Julia [Miss Julia Thorold, 203A Castelnau, London SW13]; b 18 Jan 1950

    1 *Dorothy Aline [Miss Dorothy Thorold, 24 Bowling Green Court, Hospital Rd, Moreton-in-Marsh, Glos GL56 0BX]; b 15 Aug 1908

    2 *Mary Jocelyn [Mrs Walter Meyrick, Sawmill Close, Sharperton, Morpeth, Northumberland]; b 27 May 1914; m 1935 Walter Thomas Meyrick, JP, 5th s of Sir Thomas Meyrick, 1st Bt, KCB (qv), and has issue

THURLOW

Arms: Quarterly, 1st, or a saltire gu., on a chief of the last in sinister canton a mullet of the first, charged with a crescent of the second and for distinction a cross crosslet of the first (for BRUCE); 2nd, az. three garbs or and for distinction a cross crosslet of the second in the centre chief point (for CUMMIMG); 3rd, arg. on a chevron cotised sa. three portcullises with chains and rings of the first (for THURLOW); 4th, or a cross sa. (for HOVELL). **Crests:** 1 On a cap of maintenance ppr. a dexter arm in armour from the shoulder, resting on the elbow, also ppr., the hand holding a sceptre erect or (for BRUCE). 2 A lion rampant or, holding in the dexter forepaw a dagger ppr. (for CUMMING). 3 A raven ppr. gorged with a chain, and pendant therefrom a portcullis arg.(for THURLOW), 4 A greyhound couchant or, collared and line reflexed over the back sa. (for HOVELL). **Mottoes:** (over 1st crest) *Fuimus* ('We have been'), (over 2nd crest) *Courage*, (over 3rd crest) *Justitiæ soror fides* ('Faith is the sister of Justice'), (over 4th crest) *Quo fata vocant* ('Wherever fate may call'). **Supporters:** On either side a greyhound or, collared and line reflexed over the back sa. **Creation:** B. (GB) 12 June 1792.

THE 8TH BARON THURLOW OF THURLOW, Co Suffolk (Sir Francis Edward Hovell-Thurlow-Cumming-Bruce, KCMG (1961, CMG (1957)) [The Rt Hon The Lord Thurlow KCMG, 102 Leith Mansions, Grantully Rd, London W9 1LJ; Philham Water, Hartland, Bideford, N Devon EX39 6EZ]; *b* 9 March 1912; *s* bro 1971; *educ* Shrewsbury and Trin Coll Cambridge (BA, MA 1966); Assist Pncpl Dept of Ag Scotland 1935–37, tfd to Dominions Office 1937, Assist Priv Sec to Sec of State 1939, Assist Sec Office HC NZ 1939–44, Assist Sec Office HC Canada 1944–45, Secretariat Meeting Cwlth PMs London 1946, with UK Delegn Paris Peace Conf 1946 and UN Gen Assemblies 1946 and 1948, Pncpl Priv Sec to Sec State 1946, Assist Sec CRO 1948, Head Political Div Office HC New Delhi 1949–55, Establishment Offr CRO 1952, Head Commodities Dept CRO 1954, Advsr External Affrs to Govr Gold Coast 1955–56, Dep HC Ghana 1957 and Canada 1958–59, HC NZ 1959–63 and Nigeria 1963–67, Govr and C-in-C Bahamas 1968–72, KStJ 1969; *m* 11 Aug 1949 Yvonne Diana, CStJ (1969) (*d* 1990), dau of Aubyn Harold Raymond Wilson, of Westerlee, St Andrews, Fife, and formerly w of Mandell Creighton Dormehl, and has had:

1 +ROUALEYN ROBERT [The Hon Roualeyn Hovell-Thurlow-Cumming-Bruce, New Farm, Compton, Berks RG20 6RQ]; *b* 13 April 1952; *educ* Milton Abbey, ARICS; *m* 5 May 1980 *Bridget Anne Julia, only dau of (Hugh) Bruce Ismay Cheape, TD, of S Lodge, Isle of Mull, and has:
   (1) +Nicholas Edward; *b* 16 Feb 1986
   (2) +George Patrick Roualeyn; *b* 19 March 1990
   (1) *Tessa Iona; *b* 19 Oct 1987
   (2) *Lorna Belinda; *b* 27 Dec 1991
2 Peter Torquil Francis; *b* 21 April 1962; *educ* Shrewsbury; *d* 1985
1 *(Diana) Miranda [The Hon Mrs Bostroem, 345 San Luis Way, Novato, CA 94945, USA]; *b* 6 July 1954; *educ* Westonbirt; *m* 1st 14 Feb 1981 (*divorce* 1997) Michael J Gurney (*see* ERROLL, E); *m* 2nd 2 July 1997 *Vanya Bostroem and by her 1st husb has:
   (1) *Mungo; *b* 1982
   (1) *Rowan; *b* 1984
2 *Aubyn Cecilia [The Hon Mrs de Lisle, Cold Newton Lodge, Billesden, Leics LE7 9GL]; *b* 1 June 1958; *educ* Westonbirt and Exeter U; *m* 1986 *Frederick March Phillipps de Lisle, er s of Gerard March Phillipps de Lisle, of Quenby Hall, Leics, and has:
   (1) *James Gerard; *b* 1987
   (2) *Ralph Francis; *b* 1989
   (1) *Rosalie; *b* 1991

Lineage: WILLIAM THURLOW, of Burnham Ulp, Norfolk; had:

HUGH THURLOW, of Burnham Ulp; *m* Elizabeth, dau of Oliver Reymes, of Burnham, and had:

RICHARD THURLOW; *m* last Cecilia, sis of Sir Robert Houghton, Judge King's Bench, and *d* 1590, leaving, with other issue:
  1 EDWARD

2 Nicholas; had:
  (1) John; traveller in Europe, Asia and America; granted arms 1664; *d* 1665, leaving his estates to his cousin, Rev Thomas Thurlow

The er s,
  EDWARD THURLOW, of Burnham Ulp; *m* Katherine — and *d* 1623, leaving an only s:

WILLIAM THURLOW; *m* Mary, dau of Henry Violet, of Lynn, and *d* 1652, leaving, with two other sons and a dau:

Rev THOMAS THURLOW, Rector Wortham, Suffolk; *m* Elizabeth — (*d* 1744) and had:

Rev THOMAS THURLOW; *bapt* 21 Aug 1695; Rector Ashfield, Suffolk, later Knapton and Worden, Norfolk; *m* 10 Dec 1730 Elizabeth, dau and ultimately heiress of Robert Smith, of Ashfield, Suffolk (descended through his paternal gf, who was called Hovell rather than Smith, from Richard Hovell, Esq Body to HENRY V), by Anne, dau and coheir of Robert Torkington, of Brettenham, and *d* June 1762, having had:

1 EDWARD THURLOW, 1st BARON THURLOW OF ASHFIELD, Suffolk (GB), so *cr* 3 June 1778, with remainder to the heirs male of his body, and **1st Baron Thurlow of Thurlow**, Co Suffolk (GB), so *cr* 12 June 1792 (with remainder, failing male issue, to his nephews, Edward and Thomas Thurlow, and Edward South Thurlow, Preb Norwich), PC (1778), KC (1762); *b* 9 Dec 1731; *educ* King's Canterbury and Caius College Cambridge; barrister Inner Temple 1754, Bencher 1762, MP (Tory) Tamworth 1768–78, Slr-Gen 1770–71, Attorney-Gen 1771–78, Ld Chllr 1778–92, presided trial of Warren Hastings 1788; *dspl* unm 12 Sept 1806, when the 1778 Barony expired, having had by his mistress Mrs Hervey three daus (one of whom *m* Sir David Cunynghame, 5th Bt (*qv*) and another, Catherine, *m* 17th Lord Saltoun (*qv*) of Abernethy) and by —, dau of — Lynch, Dean of Canterbury, who he was rumoured to have married:
  (1) Charles; *d* while still a Cambridge undergraduate
2 Thomas (Rt Rev); DD, Dean Rochester 1779, Bp Lincoln 1779–87 and Durham 1787–91; *m* Anne (*d* 17 Aug 1791), dau of William Beere, of Lymington, and *d* 27 May 1791, leaving:
  (1) EDWARD, **2nd Baron**
  (2) Thomas (Rev), of Baynard's Park, Surrey, JP; *b* 6 Oct 1788; Prothonotary Common Pleas Co Durham; *m* 4 June 1811 Maria Frances (*d* 5 Jan 1863), 6th dau of Hon Thomas Lyon (*see* STRATHMORE AND KINGHORNE, E), and *d* 26 Sept 1874, leaving:
    1a Thomas Lyon, of Baynard's Park, DL; *b* 19 Nov 1814; *m* 22 Oct 1879 Emily (*d* 4 April 1890), yst dau of Richard Sumner, of Puttenham Priory, Surrey, and *dsp* 8 Sept 1894
  (1) Amelia Anne; *m* 1799 Lt-Gen Sir Edward Howarth, KCB, and *d* 8 Dec 1809. He *d* 5 March 1827
  (2) Elizabeth
  (3) Anne Elizabeth; *m* 12 April 1804 Charles Godfrey, of Wetherden Hall, Suffolk
3 John; Alderman and merchant Norwich; *m* Josepha (*d* 10 Dec 1786), dau of John Morse, of Norwich, and *d* 11 March 1782, leaving, with a dau:
  (1) Edward South (Rev); Preb Norwich; *m* 1st 17 July 1786 Elizabeth Mary (*d* 12 July 1808), dau of James Thompson, and had:
    1a Edward John (Rev); *b* 1788; LLB, Rector Lound, Suffolk; *d* 14 Dec 1883
    2a Frederick Charles; *b* 11 Sept 1798; *d* 1822
    3a Charles Augustus (Rev); *b* 9 July 1802; Chllr diocese and Hon Canon Chester, Rector Malpas, Cheshire; *m* 3 March 1836 Fanny Margaret (*d* 12 April 1861), yst dau of Sir Thomas Buckler Lethbridge, 2nd Bt (*qv*), and *d* 5 July 1873, having had:
      1b Charles Augustus Lethbridge; *b* 22 Nov 1836; *m* 1878 Agnes Rose (*d* 3 Sept 1930), dau of Rev R Morey, Rector Snitterby, Lincs, and *d* 18 Jan 1909, having had a dau (*d* unm)
      2b Edward Hovell; *b* 24 Jan 1839; Maj RA, Capt Berks Yeo Cav; *m* 16 Oct 1875 Georgina Violet (*d* 13 March 1931), only dau of George Dodd, DL, MP, and *d* 9 March 1925, leaving:
        1c Editha Aceituna; *b* 12 July 1876; *m* 20 July 1905 Maj Robert Chaloner Griffin, Roy Sussex Regt, of Barrymore, Wargrave, Berks, and Kensington, 2nd s of Robert Griffin, of Marlow, and *d* 10 June 1949, leaving issue. He *d* 13 July 1954
      3b Henry Frederick; *b* 11 July 1843; barrister; *d* unm 8 Oct 1878
      4b Ernest Hovell; *b* 14 Sept 1846; Lt-Col KRRC, Zulu War 1879, 1st Boer War 1881; *m* 29 Aug 1874 Celia (*d* 2 Feb 1922), est dau of Frederick T Turner, of The Cedars, Clapham Common, and *d* 22 July 1936, having had:
        1c Godfrey Hovell; *b* 12 Dec 1883; MT RASC WW I; *m* 26 Dec 1910 Amy (*d* 10 Sept 1931), dau of John Wellington Tippett, and *d* 6 Jan 1935
        1c Edith Helen; *b* 13 April 1875; *m* 16 Aug 1900 Capt Herbert Taylor, 16th Bn KRRC, and *d* 30 May 1952, leaving issue. He *d* 11 Oct 1915
      5b Reginald Heber; *b* 3 Jan 1848; Lt-Col 1st Bn Northumberland Fus; *m* 23 April 1881 Mary (*m* 2nd 15 Dec 1898 Lt-Col Henry Kilgour, 5th Fus (*das* 1915), and *d* 3 Nov 1945), dau of Henry Smyth, of Cairnburn, Co Down, and *d* 16 April 1891, leaving:
        1c Charles Edward Clarges; *b* 20 March 1882; Lt Northumberland Fus; *d* unm 6 Oct 1909
        1c Sydney Vera; *m* 25 Jan 1911 Brig Edward Frederick William Lees, DSO, RE, only s of George Frederick Lees, of Whyke, Chichester, and *d* 24 Jan 1952, leaving issue. He *d* 8 Feb 1969
        2c Dorothy Sybil Gertrude; *m* 10 Feb 1915 Lt-Col Victor Leopold Spencer Cowley, DSO, MC, Roy Ulster Rifles, and *d* 20 April 1970, leaving issue
      6b Hugh Hovell, JP Hants; *b* 3 Jan 1848; Lt-Col Prince Albert's Somerset LI, Sekukuni Expdn 1878, Zulu War 1879; *m* 10 Feb 1881 Winifred Beatrice (*d* 3 June 1945), yst dau of Rev John Hall Parlby, of Manadon, Devon, and *d* 24 Sept 1919, leaving:
        1c (Edward) Guy Lethbridge, CBE (1946), DSO (1915), DL (Berks 1946); *b* 6 Nov 1881; *educ* Wellington and RMC Sandhurst; Boer War

1899–1902, N Nigeria with W African Frontier Force 1904–06, WW I (despatches seven times: Col Somerset LI, GSO(1) War Office 1921–23 and Scottish Cmd 1923–27, AA & QMG 4th Div 1927–31, Brig 11th Ahmednagar Bde India 1931, ret 1932, Sec Berks TAA 1934–46; GSO(1) War Office WW II; Govr Roy Sch Bath (Chm 1952–60), Star Romania with Swords; m 28 Dec 1912 Margaret Merry, Médaille de la Reine Elisabeth de Belgique (d 18 June 1952), only dau of Lt-Col Edward Hensman Vaughan, of Penhayes, Kenton, Devon, and d 25 March 1966, leaving:

1d *Nancy Katharine [Mrs Henry Willis, Ellesboro, Brushford, Dulverton, Somerset TA22 9AW]; b 16 May 1914; m 11 May 1940 *Henry George Willis, 2nd s of David Willis, and has:

  1e *Nicholas Michael Thurlow [Nicholas Willis Esq, Via Cantonale 31, CH-6537 Grono, Switzerland]; b 5 Oct 1942; educ Harrow and London U (BA); m 1972 *Ann Catherine, dau of Harvey Roy (Jack) Callaway, of Mount Hope, W Va., and has:

    1f *Caroline Fiona; b 1973

    2f *Rebecca Margaret; b 1977

  2e *Ian Henry [Ian Willis Esq, Chapel Barn, Goodworth Clatford, Hants SP11 7QY]; b 9 July 1946; educ Harrow, RMC Sandhurst and Ch Ch Oxford (BA, BPhil); late Capt 4th/7th Dragoon Gds (despatches NI); m 1978 *Mary Catherine Ileana Camilla, er dau of Radu Tilea (see CARNARVON, E), and has:

    1f *Nicholas Henry David; b 21 June 1984

    2f *Edward Tilea; b 14 May 1986

    1f *Sophie Catherine Glory; b 18 Sept 1989

2d *Rosemary Margaret [Mrs James de Courcy Hughes, The Old Rectory, Hinton St George, Somerset TA17 8SP]; b 19 June 1919; Jr Cdr ATS WW II, Territorial Efficiency Medal; m 1st 14 Feb 1947 Maj Jasper John Ogilvie, MBE, Somerset LI (d 1974), s of Charles Struthers White Ogilvie, of Delvine, Perthshire and Lady Clifford of Chudleigh (qv), and has:

  1e *Philip John [Philip Ogilvie Esq, The Old Rectory, Hinton St George, Somerset TA17 8SP; Paseo del Parque 100, 11310 Sotogrande, Cadiz, Spain]; b 12 Nov 1948; educ Ampleforth; FCA; Kt SMOMalta; m 1981 *Loreto, dau of Col Eduardo Vega de Seoane y Barroso, of Madrid, and has:

    1f *Ian Alexander; b 14 May 1985

    2f *William Jasper Charles; b 1 April 1988

    3f *James Edward George; b 23 April 1990

  2e *David Jasper [David Ogilvie Esq, Keepers Piece, Chedington, Dorset DT8 3HX]; b 6 Dec 1952; educ Millfield

2d (cont.) Mrs Jasper Ogilvie m 2nd June 1976 *Lt-Cdr James Henry de Courcy Hughes, RN (ret)

1c Eva Winifred Hilda (Freda); b 18 Nov 1883; m 3 Feb 1907 Maj Claude Frederick Thornton, Wilts Regt, 2nd s of Capt Edward Brooke Thornton, of Moggerhanger, Beds, and d 22 May 1959, leaving issue. He d 23 Feb 1949

1b Edith Emma; d 28 Oct 1861

2b Fanny Evelyn; m 11 Sept 1876 Georges le Cornez, 3rd s of Henri le Cornez, and d his widow 12 April 1894, leaving issue

4a Henry Robert; b 1804; Maj; d 14 Aug 1850

(1) (cont.) The Rev Edward Thurlow m 2nd 10 April 1810 Susanna (d 26 Oct 1851), yst dau of Rev John Love, and d 17 Feb 1847, having by her had four sons and two daus (dsp)

The 1st BARON's n,

EDWARD THURLOW later HOVELL-THURLOW (roy licence 8 July 1814), **2nd Baron Thurlow of Thurlow**; b 10 June 1781; educ Charterhouse and Magdalen Coll Oxford; Clerk of Lunacy and Custody of Idiots 1786–1829, Clerk Presentation Petty Bag Office 1793–1829, Patentee Bankruptcy Office 1802–29, Clerk Hanaper 1802–29; poetaster; m 13 Nov 1813 Mary Katherine (d 28 Sept 1830), actress (notably as Polly Peachum in The Beggar's Opera), est dau of James Richard Bolton, attorney, of Long Acre, Covent Garden, and d 4 June 1829, leaving, with two yr sons (Thomas Hugh Hovell, b 13 May 1816, Capt 7th Foot; John Edmund Hovell, b 15 July 1817, Capt 85th Foot and E Kent Militia, d 31 Aug 1871):

EDWARD THOMAS HOVELL-THURLOW, **3rd Baron Thurlow of Thurlow**; b 12 Nov 1814; educ Eton; m 8 Nov 1836 Sarah (d 13 March 1840), only dau of Peter Hodgson, and d 2 March 1857, leaving:

1 EDWARD THOMAS HOVELL-THURLOW, **4th Baron Thurlow of Thurlow**; b 25 Oct 1837; d unm 22 April 1874

2 THOMAS JOHN HOVELL-THURLOW later HOVELL-THURLOW-CUMMING-BRUCE (roy licence 6 Aug 1874), **5th Baron Thurlow of Thurlow**, PC (1886), JP, DL Suffolk, Elgin and Nairn, DL Stirlingshire; b 5 Dec 1838; Dip Serv 1858–70, Ld-in-Waiting 1880–85 and 1886, Paymaster-Gen 1886, Ld HC to Gen Assembly Ch Scotland 1886, bankrupt 1894 and 1910; FRS; m 18 Oct 1864 Lady Elma Bruce (d 27 Nov 1923), only dau of 8th Earl of Elgin and (12th Earl of) Kincardine (qv) by his 1st w Elizabeth Mary, only child of Maj Charles Lennox Cumming-Bruce of Roseisle, Dunphail and Kinnaird, and had:

(1) James Frederick, DL Nairn; b 24 July 1867; Capt Black Watch; m 8 Dec 1891 Constance Gertrude Cecily (m 2nd 1 Jan 1910 Brig-Gen Edward Boustead Cuthbertson, CMG, MVO, Argyll and Sutherland Highrs, of Jermyns, Romsey, Hants (d 13 May 1942), and d 29 March 1954), Woman Bedchamber to HRH PRINCESS CHRISTIAN and 2nd dau of Thomas Henry Clifton, of Lytham Hall, Lancs, and dsp, ka Boer War 11 Dec 1899

(2) CHARLES EDWARD, **6th Baron**

(3) Henry Nigel; b 20 June 1875; d 18 Aug 1916

(4) Edmund Sigurd; b 17 Aug 1878; Lt Seaforth Highrs; d unm 11 Nov 1899

(1) Mary Elma; m 26 April 1893 Arthur Wellesley Anstruther, CB (see ANSTRUTHER, Bt), and dsp 11 Feb 1894

(2) Alice Margaret; d unm 28 Oct 1901

The 5th BARON d 12 March 1916; his est surv s,

Rev CHARLES EDWARD HOVELL-THURLOW-CUMMING-BRUCE, **6th Baron Thurlow of Thurlow**; b 6 Oct 1869; educ Eton and Trin Coll Cambridge

(BA 1891, MA 1905); Curate St Ignatius, Hendon, Sunderland 1898–1900, Chaplain to Mission to Seamen at Portland, Oregon, USA, 1900–05, for Valparaiso and W Coast of S America 1905–07, Assist Supt of Mission 1908–13, Vicar St Andrew with St Anne and St Philip, Auckland, Co Durham, RD Auckland 1913–22 and Liverpool N 1926, Chaplain Supt Mersey Mission to Seamen 1922–30, Chaplain to Master Mariners' Company 1920–30, Commissary of Bps of Falkland Islands 1919 and Johannesburg 1922, Rector Sedgefield Co Durham 1930–39; m 2 Feb 1909 Grace Catherine (d 16 Jan 1959), only child of Rev Canon Henry Trotter, of Barnet, and d 23 April 1952, leaving:

1 HENRY CHARLES HOVELL-THURLOW-CUMMING-BRUCE, **7th Baron Thurlow of Thurlow**, CB (1961), CBE (1956, OBE 1956), DSO (1944) and bar (1945); b 29 May 1910; educ Eton and RMC Sandhurst; Maj-Gen Seaforth Highrs, memb Roy Co Archers, ADC to HC and C-in-C Palestine 1936–39, Assist Mil Sec Palestine 1939–40, WW II: attd QO Cameron Highrs 1940–41, Libyan Arab Force 1941–42, Bde Maj 152 Inf Bde, Instr Sr Offrs' Sch 1943, served Middle East (despatches) and NW Europe, Lt-Col 1st Bn Gordon Highrs, Brig 44 (L) Inf Bde 1944, Cmdt BAOR Training Centre 1945–47, cmdg Highland Bde Training Centre 1947–48, AA and QMG 1st Inf Div 1950–52, Brig 39th Inf Bde 1954–58, Dep Dir Info War Office 1956–59, GOC Northumbrian Dist and 50th Div TA 1959–62, GOC Troops Malta 1962–63, ret 1964, Pres Missions to Seamen 1966, Co Pres SSAFA, Chm St Christopher's Hospice 1966, V-Chm Jerusalem and the East Mission 1967, CStJ; d unm 29 May 1971

2 FRANCIS EDWARD HOVELL-THURLOW-CUMMING-BRUCE, **8th and present Baron Thurlow of Thurlow**

3 +(James) Roualeyn (Sir), PC (1977) [The Rt Hon Sir Roualeyn Cumming-Bruce, Selaby, Gainford, Darlington DL2 3HF]; b 9 March 1912; educ Shrewsbury and Magdalene Coll Cambridge (MA, Hon Fell 1977); barrister Middle Temple 1937, Lt-Col RA WW II, Bencher 1959, Dep Treas 1974, Treas 1975, Chllr Diocese of Ripon 1954–58, Recorder Doncaster 1957–58 and York 1958–61, Jr Counsel Treasury (Common Law) 1959–64 , ktd 1964, High Court Judge (Probate, Admlty and Divorce) 1964–76, Ld Justice Appeal 1977–85; m 4 Aug 1955 Lady (Anne) Sarah Savile (d 1991), yst dau of 6th Earl of Mexborough (qv), and has:

(1) +Edward Simon [Edward Hovell-Thurlow-Cumming-Bruce, 33 Malward Rd, London SW12 8EN]; b 7 June 1958; m 1984 *Antonia Mary, er dau of Christopher Stephen Gaisford-St Lawrence (see MOSTYN, Bt), and has:

  1a +Michael Alastair; b 1985

  2a +William James Christopher; b 1987

  1a *Isabelle; b 1990

(2) +Richard Henry; b 19 May 1963

(1) *Jane Mary; b 11 Aug 1956; m 1980 *Josslyn Henry Robert Gore-Booth, only s of Sir Angus Gore-Booth, 8th Bt (qv), and has issue

4 +Alexander (Alec) Pascoe, OBE (1960); b 28 Oct 1917; educ Shrewsbury and Trin Coll Cambridge (BA 1939); Colonial Admin Serv 1946–61, Palestine, Zanzibar, Aden, Home CS 1961, Colonial (later FCO) Office, MOD 1968; m 21 Feb 1942 Catherine Agnes (d 17 Feb 1995), dau of Rev Hamilton Blackwood, of Scalby, Yorks, and has:

(1) +Charles Hamilton [Charles Hovell-Thurlow-Cumming-Bruce, Leazes Cottage, Leazes Place, Claypath, Co Durham]; b 8 June 1947; educ Gordonstoun and Exeter U (BA Hons); Clerk Ho Lds; m 9 July 1982 *Dr Vimala Valencia Herman, dau of Nicholas Herman

(2) +Nicholas Christian; b 22 June 1949; educ Gordonstoun

(1) *(Catherine) Veronica [Mrs George Yannoulopoulos, 2 Auckland Cottages, Auckland Rd, Cambridge CB5 8DP]; b 28 Nov 1943; m 4 April 1970 *George Nikolaou Yannoulopoulos, yst s of Nicholas E Yannoulopoulos, of Athens, and has:

  1a *Nicholas Alexis; b 27 Nov 1970

THURSO

Arms: Quarterly, 1st, az. a ship at anchor, her oars erected in saltire within the royal tressure or; 2nd and 3rd, or a lion rampant gu.; 4th, az. a ship under sail or; over all, dividing the quarters, a cross engrailed quarterly arg. and sa., all within a bordure quartered or and gu., the last charged with three stars of the first. **Crest:** A star of six rays waved arg. **Supporters:** Two red deer ppr. **Mottoes:** 1 (above the crest) *Ad astra virtus* ('The sky's the limit where virtue is concerned'), 2 (below the shield) *J'aime le meilleur* ('I love the best'). **Creations:** Bt. (GB) 14 Feb 1786, V. (UK) 10 April 1952.

THE 3RD VISCOUNT THURSO, of Ulbster, Caithness, and a **Baronet** (Sir John Archibald Sinclair, Bt) [The Rt Hon The Viscount Thurso, Orchard Cottage, Champneys, Herts HP23 6NY]; *b* 10 Sept 1953; *s* f 1995; *educ* Eton; FHCIMA 1991, Master Innholder 1991, dir: Lancaster Hotel 1981–85, Cliveden House Ltd 1987–93, Grenfell Hldgs 1992–95, Savoy Hotel plc 1993–, Fitness & Leisure Holdings 1995– and Walker Greenbank 1997–, md Champneys 1995–, Lib Dem spokesman tourism Ho Lds 1998–; *m* 12 June 1976 *Marion Ticknor, 2nd dau of Louis Davidson Sage, of Connecticut, and has:

1 +JAMES ALEXANDER ROBIN; *b* 14 Jan 1984

2 +George Henry MacDonald; *b* 1989

1 *Louisa Ticknor Beaumont; *b* 15 March 1980

Lineage: The 4th EARL OF CAITHNESS (*qv*); had a 2nd s :

WILLIAM SINCLAIR of Mey; *m* Margaret, dau of Magnus Mowat, of Balquhollie, and had, with another s (Patrick, acquired Ulbster 1596 from his cousin 5th Earl of Caithness, *d* unm):

JOHN SINCLAIR of Ulbster; *m* 1st Jean Chisholm (*d* 1614) and had, with other issue (possibly including the Elizabeth who *m* as his 1st w William Sinclair of Ratter; *see* CAITHNESS, E):

1 Patrick, of Ulbster; *m* 1647 Elizabeth, dau of John Mackay of Strathy, and had:

(1) John, of Ulbster; *m* Janet (*dsp*), dau of William Sinclair of Rattar, and entailed 1709 his estates on his cousin John Sinclair of Brims

(2) George (Sir), of Bilbster and Clyth; *m* Jean, dau of William Sinclair of Dunbeath, and *dsp*

(1) Mary; *m* 1675 Sir Robert Dunbar, 2nd Bt, of Northfield (*qv*), and had issue

(2) Elizabeth; *m* John Sinclair of Brabster (*see* SINCLAIR, Bt)

JOHN SINCLAIR *m* 2nd Katherine Stewart, illegitimate dau of Robert, Earl of Orkney, s of JAMES V, and by her had:

2 John, of Tannach; bought Brims 1660; *m* Margaret, widow of William Oliphant, Clerk of Wardrobe to CHARLES I, and dau of Charles Goldman, merchant burgess of Dundee, and had, with other issue:

(1) John, of Brims, later also of Ulbster; *m* Jean, dau of Sir George Munro of Newmore (*see* MUNRO, Bt, of Foulis Obsdale), and had, with other issue:

1a JOHN

1a Jean; *m* 1st Benjamin Dunbar, s of Sir William Dunbar, 1st Bt, of Hempriggs (*qv*); *m* 2nd 3rd Lord Reay (*qv*) and by him had issue

The son,

JOHN SINCLAIR of Ulbster; Heritable Sheriff Caithness; *m* 9 April 1714 Henrietta, dau of George Brodie of Brodie by Emilia, dau of James Brodie of Brodie and Mary, dau of 1st Earl of Lothian of the 1631 *cr* (*see* LOTHIAN, M), and had:

1 GEORGE

2 James, of Harpsdale; *m* 1st Margery, dau of David Sinclair of Southdun, and had:

(1) Henrietta, of Southdun; *m* Col Wemyss and had issue

(2) Janet; *m* Col Benjamin Williamson of Banniskirk

2 (cont.) James Sinclair *m* 2nd Mary Sutherland, of Clyne, and had by her a s (*d* young); *m* 3rd Catherine, dau of John Sinclair of Lybster, and by her had:

(3) Catherine; *m* Maj George Williamson

(4) Helen; *m* David Brodie of Hopeville

3 John; Maj; *m* Elizabeth, widow of John Wilmer, and *d* at York 1787

---

1 Emilia; *m* John Sutherland of Forse and had:

(1) George; claimed Earldom of Sutherland in competition with the Countess (later Duchess) of Sutherland (*see* SUTHERLAND, D)

JOHN SINCLAIR *d* 1736; his est s,

GEORGE SINCLAIR of Ulbster; *m* 24 Oct 1740 Janet (*d* 9 June 1795), sis of 17th Earl of Sutherland (*qv*), and had:

1 JOHN (Sir), **1st Bt**

1 Helen; *m* 1 Aug 1765 Alexander Campbell of Barcaldine (*see* CAMPBELL, Bt, of Barcaldine), and had, with other issue:

(1) Jane, *m* 1784 12th Earl of Caithness (*qv*)

2 Mary; *m* 1770 James Homerigg of Gamalshiels

3 Janet; *m* 15 April 1803 William Baillie of Polkemmet, later a Ld of Session

GEORGE SINCLAIR *d* 1776; his only s,

Sir John Sinclair, 1st Bt (GB), so *cr* 14 Feb 1786, with remainder, in default of his own male issue, to the male issue of his daus by primogeniture, of Ulbster, PC; *b* 1754; fndr and Pres Bd of Ag, MP, Cashier Excise Scotland, Col Caithness and Rothesay Fencibles, which he raised; agricultural innovator; author: *Statistical Account of Scotland*; DCL, FRS, FRAS; *m* 1st 26 March 1776 Sarah, dau of Alexander Maitland, of Stoke Newington, and had:

1 Hannah; *b* 1 Feb 1780; authoress; *d* unm 27 May 1818

2 Janet; *b* 17 April 1781; *m* (contract 11 June 1799) Sir James Colquhoun of Luss, 3rd Bt (*qv*), and *d* 21 Oct 1846, leaving issue

Sir John *m* 2nd 6 March 1788 Diana (*d* 22 April 1845), dau of 1st Lord Macdonald (*qv*), and by her had, with other issue:

1 GEORGE (Sir), **2nd Bt**

2 Alexander; *b* 17 June 1794; with HEICS, genealogist; *d* unm 9 Aug 1877

3 John (Ven); *b* 20 Aug 1797; Archdeacon Middx, Vicar Kensington, Treas Nat Soc Educn; *d* unm 22 May 1875

4 Archibald; *b* 20 Sept 1801; Capt RN, fndr Naval and Mil Club Scotland, author naval reminiscences; *d* 1 June 1859

5 William (Rev); *b* 4 Sept 1804; *educ* St Mary's Hall Oxford (MA); Capt Madras Cav; incumbent St George's, Leeds 1838, Rector Pulborough Sussex 1857, Preb Chichester 1874; *m* 1st 28 Dec 1837 Helen (*d* Oct 1842), dau of William Ellice and n of Rt Hon Edward ('Bear') Ellice, MP, of Invergarry, and had:

(1) Alexander Edward; *b* 30 May 1839; *dsp* 24 Sept 1887

(2) Walter; *b* 15 April 1841; Lt-Col 1st Bn S Staffs Regt; *m* 4 Feb 1874 Kathleen (*d* 19 Nov 1944, having *m* 2nd 8 Nov 1893 Maj-Gen George Upton Prior), dau of Henry B F Dickinson, of Ashton Keynes, Wilts, and *d* 1887, leaving:

1a Gladys Muriel; *m* 5 July 1921 Frank Hird, OBE, s of James Hird, RN, of Lowmoor, and *d* 6 May 1943. He *d* 21 Nov 1937

5 (cont.) The Rev William Sinclair *m* 2nd 15 April 1846 Sophia Mary Georgiana (*d* 22 July 1885), dau of Rev James Tripp, Rector Spofforth, and *d* 8 July 1878, having by her had:

(3) William Macdonald (Ven); *b* 3 June 1850; *educ* Balliol Coll Oxford (MA); DD, Vicar St Stephen's Westminster 1880–89, Canon Residentiary St Paul's, Archdeacon London 1889–1911, Rector Shermanbury 1911–16, Chaplain to OStJ, Chaplain to HM QUEEN VICTORIA 1883–1901, Hon Chaplain to TM EDWARD VII 1901–10 and GEORGE V 1910–17 Hon DD Glasgow, FRSL, FRGS; *d* unm 4 Dec 1917

(4) John Stewart (Ven), JP Co London; *b* 15 May 1853; *educ* Oriel Coll Oxford (MA); Archdeacon Cirencester, Hon Canon Gloucester; *m* 9 Aug 1893 Clara Sophia (*d* 16 May 1948), dau of John Dearman Birchall, JP, of Bowden Hall, Glos, and *d* 30 April 1919, leaving:

1a Ronald Sutherland Brook (Very Rev), MC (1917) and bar (1918); *b* 5 Sept 1894; *educ* Oriel Coll Oxford (BA 1919, MA 1920); Capt Glos Regt WW I, Vicar Ashford Kent 1931–37 and St Peter's Maidstone, Canon Residentiary Chester Cathedral 1937–44, Provost Guildford Cathedral 1944, Hon Canon Canterbury Cathedral 1952–53; *m* 13 Sept 1924 Patience Penelope (*d* 1988), yr dau of Herbert Chitty, FSA, of Hampstead, and *d* 13 May 1953, having had:

1b +Christopher Ronald [Christopher Sinclair Esq, 5 Fentiman Rd, London SW8]; *b* 1 May 1936; *educ* King's Canterbury and Exeter Coll Oxford; jnlst, dir Adcomm Ltd; *m* 5 Sept 1969 *Penelope Ann, dau of Edwin Alfred Springett, of Hampstead, and has:

1c *Sophie Letitia; *b* 1971

1b Patience Mary; *b* 12, *d* 13 May 1932

2a John Alexander (Sir), KCMG (1953), CB (1945), OBE (1940); *b* 29 May 1897; *educ* RNCs Osborne and Dartmouth and RMA Woolwich; WW I: Midshipman RN 1914–16, commnd RFA 1918, Maj RA 1935–37, GSO(3) War Office 1937, WW II GHQ Home Forces 1943–44, DMI War Office 1944–45, ret May 1952 as Maj-Gen, Cdr US Legn Merit 1945, Cdr Order Crown Belgium 1945; *m* 6 July 1927 Esmé Beatrice (*d* 1983), yr dau of Ven Thomas Karl Sopwith, Archdeacon Canterbury, and *d* 22 March 1977, leaving:

1b +Ian Alexander Charles [Prof Ian Sinclair, The Garth, 60 Marygate, York YO30 7BH]; *b* 14 Feb 1938; *educ* Eton and Worcester Coll Oxford (BA 1961, PhD); Prof Social Work York U; *m* 1 Nov 1969 *Elma Elizabeth, dau of Charles Henry Williams, of Braunton, Devon, and has:

1c +Andrew George; *b* 1970

2c +John Charles; *b* 1972

1c *Elizabeth Beatrice; *b* 1974

2b +Roderick John [Roderick Sinclair Esq, Downgate Farm, Petersfield, Hants]; *b* 10 July 1944; *educ* Gordonstoun; late 2nd Lt Scots Gds (Res); *m* 1st 1970 (*divorce* 1976) Lucinda Mary, dau of Eric Martin Smith, MP; *m* 2nd 14 May 1977 *Sarah Margaret, only dau of Brig Cyril Edwin Harold Dolphin, CBE, of Petersfield, Hants, and has:

1c +James Alexander; *b* 1984

1c *Natasha Esmé; *b* 1981

1b *Jean Esme [Mrs Christopher Seagrim, Hill Farm, Pulborough, W Sussex RH20 1BW]; *b* 8 April 1929; *m* 6 May 1961 *Christopher Bruce Seagrim, only s of Capt Cyril Bruce Seagrim, Napier's Rifles, of Meade Ho, Lavant, Sussex, and has:

1c *John Christopher; *b* 22 Feb 1965; *m* 1994 *Georgina Gay Hood, dau of Maj David Hood, MC, and has:

　1d *Ochre Georgina; *b* 25 Feb 1997

1c *Victoria Esmé; *b* 18 June 1962; *m* 1995 *Timothy Peter Townsend, s of Ian Townsend, and has:

　1d *Christopher Ian; *b* 13 Nov 1997

2b *Iona; *b* 12 Jan 1931; *m* 1 Oct 1955 *Lt-Gen Sir Robin Macdonald Carnegie, KCB, OBE, DL, late Queen's Own Hus, yr s of Sir Francis Carnegie, CBE, and has:

1c *Rupert Alexander; *b* 25 Aug 1959

1c *Catriona Jean; *b* 12 April 1957; *m* 1982 *Simon J N Heale, s of James Heale, and has:

　1d *James Newton; *b* 1985

　1d *Charlotte Esmé Serena; *b* 1987

　2d *Anna Frances; *b* 1989

2c *Rachel Clare; *b* 20 April 1962; *m* 1989 *Mark Goldring and has:

　1d *Rory Alexander Carnegie; *b* 15 Feb 1995

　1d *Natasha Kate; *b* 3 Oct 1992

1a Diana Clara; *b* 19 Oct 1899; *m* 14 Nov 1923 Thomas Elcho Vardon Ross-Ross (*d* 18 Dec 1960), est surv s of Donald Ross-Ross, of Lancaster, Ontario, and *d* 14 Sept 1994, leaving:

1b *John Durnford Sinclair [John Ross-Ross Esq, 23 Little London, Chichester, W Sussex PO19 1PB]; *b* 24 July 1927

1b Diana Meredith; *b* 11 Nov 1924; *m* 25 March 1953 Cyril Millar Goddard, s of James Pembroke Goddard, of Teignmouth, and *d* 6 April 1973, leaving:

1c *David Jonathan Sinclair; *b* 31 Jan 1957; *m* April 1987 *Janine Metcalf and has:

　1d *Emma Jane; *b* 24 Sept 1988

　2d *Alison Mary; *b* 7 April 1991

2c *Robin Andrew Durnford; *b* 3 Nov 1960; *m* June 1985 *Yvonne Kimpton and has:

　1d *Amy Fiona; *b* 6 July 1988

　2d *Hannah; *b* 14 Jan 1992

2a Margaret; *b* 5 Feb 1903; *m* 30 June 1926 Lt-Gen Sir Maurice Somerville Chilton, KBE, CB (*d* 21 Aug 1956), yr s of Thomas Chilton, of Liverpool, and had:

1b *Richard Thomas Sutherland; *b* 4 July 1931; *educ* Winchester and Magdalen Coll Oxford; *m* 27 Jan 1962 *Ann, dau of Arthur Trevor Gough, of S Kensington

1b *April Elizabeth; *b* 11 April 1928

2b *Jane Margaret [Mrs John Catt, The Old Forge, Gt Glemham, Suffolk IP17 2DA]; *b* 8 Nov 1934; *m* 1st 9 Feb 1957 Brig Richard John Bishop, MBE, MC, RA (*d* 3 May 1981), only s of Richard Mason Bishop, of Southport, Lancs; *m* 2nd 21 Oct 1983 John Catt (*d* 2 Jan 1998), and by her 1st husb has:

1c *Charles Richard Maurice; *b* 3 Aug 1960; *m* 2 Aug 1986 *Rosalind Jane Nelmes and has:

　1d *Thomas Richard Chilton; *b* 29 March 1993

　1d *Rosanna Emily Margaret; *b* 1 Nov 1990

　2d *Victoria Oenone; *b* 1 Sept 1994

1c *Katharine Margaret; *b* 28 Feb 1958; *m* 23 June 1979 *Samuel Guy Ruggles-Brise, Bt) and has issue (*see* RUGGLES-BRISE, Bt)

(5) Hugh Montgomerie, CB (1910), CMG (1917), CBE (1919); *b* 23 Feb 1855; Col RE, Cmdt Railway Tps 1915–19, Ch Engr Scottish Cmd; *m* 4 July 1905 Rosalie Sybil (*d* 20 Sept 1969), dau of Sir John Jackson, CVO, MP, LLD, of Henley Park, Henley, and *d* 10 July 1924, leaving:

1a John Montgomerie, DSO (1945); *b* 7 May 1906; *educ* Winchester and RMA Woolwich; Col RE, T/Brig, local Capt Transjordan FF 1930–35, WW II on Staff and cmdg 64th Field Regt RA (despatches), Palestine 1947–48 cmdg 41st Field Regt RA (despatches), Ch Sec Allied Commn for Austria 1945–47; *d* unm 5 Dec 1954

2a Hugh Macdonald; *b* 4 Feb 1910; *educ* Winchester and Oriel Coll Oxford (BSc 1933, BM and MA 1936, DM 1939); FRCP, FCS, LMSSA; Dir Int Inst of Human Nutrition 1972, Hon DSc, Fell and Tutor Magdalen Coll Oxford 1937–80 (V-Pres 1956–58), lecturer physiology and biochemistry 1937–76, Reader Human Nutrition and Dir Lab of Human Nutrition Oxford 1951–58, Visiting Prof Food Science Reading U 1970–80, editor-in-ch *International Encyclopedia of Food and Nutrition* (24 vols) 1969; Offr Orange Nassau Netherlands, US Medal Freedom with Silver Palm; *d* unm 22 June 1990

1a Rosalie Helen; *b* 18 Feb 1908; *m* 20 Feb 1941 Capt Royston O'Neil Haddock, RASC, s of John Daniel Haddock, of Dublin, and *d* 14 Dec 1986, leaving:

1b *Rogan Shane [Rogan Haddock Esq, Higher Hannaford, Landkey, Barnstaple, N Devon EX32 0NY]; *b* 11 Jan 1942; *educ* Barnstaple GS

1b *Janet Rosalie; *b* 23 July 1943; *m* 3 Jan 1970 (*divorce* 1973) Ernest Lewis Vine, only s of Maj E A Vine, of Cardigan, and has:

1c *Catherine Rose; *b* 16 Sept 1964;

2b *Bridget Helen; *b* 13 March 1948; *m* 21 Sept 1968 Dennis Ivor Maddocks and has:

1c *Robin Hugh; *b* 5 June 1970

2c *Nicholas *b* 1972

2a Catherine Julia, TD, JP (Berks 1951); *b* 23 Feb 1913; ATS WW II; *k* car crash 6 April 1961

(1) Helen; *m* 27 Oct 1880 Rev George Edmund Hasell, Hon Canon Carlisle, and *d* 21 Jan 1919, leaving issue. He *d* 20 Feb 1932

(2) Janet Mary; *d* unm 30 Nov 1936

1 Julia; *m* 13 Nov 1824 4th Earl of Glasgow (*qv*) and *d* 19 Feb 1868, leaving issue

2 Catherine; author: *Modern Accomplishments*, *Modern Society* and *Holiday House*; *d* 6 Aug 1864

3 Helen; *m* 10 Aug 1826 Stair Stewart, of Glasserton and Physgill, Wigtownshire, and *d* 25 April 1845

Sir JOHN *d* 21 Dec 1835; his est s,

Sir George Sinclair, 2nd Bt; *b* 23 Aug 1790; *m* 1 May 1816 Lady Catherine Camilla Tollemache (*d* 17 March 1863), sis of 8th Earl of Dysart (*qv*), and had, with other issue:

1 JOHN GEORGE TOLLEMACHE (Sir), **3rd Bt**

1 Emilia Magdalen Louisa; *m* 1st 12 Aug 1837 (*divorce*) Henry Bertie Tollemache and had issue (*see* DYSART, E); *m* 2nd 5 July 1841 Maj John Power, 29th Regt, s of Patrick Power, of Bellevue, Co Waterford, and *d* 19 Jan 1864, leaving further issue (*see* ELTON, Bt)

2 Adelaide Mary Wentworth; *m* 18 Aug 1845 George Hope-Johnstone and *d* 7 Sept 1873, leaving issue (*see* LINLITHGOW, M)

Sir GEORGE *d* 9 Oct 1868; his only surv s,

Sir John George Tollemache Sinclair, 3rd Bt; *b* 8 Nov 1824; Scots Fus Gds, V-Lt and DL Caithness, MP Caithness 1869–85, Page of Honour to QUEEN ADELAIDE; *m* 22 Nov 1853 (*divorce* 4 July 1878) Emma Isabella Harriet (*d* 1889), dau of William Standish Standish, of Duxbury Park, Lancs, and had, with a dau (*d* young):

1 Clarence Granville, DL; *b* 3 April 1858; Lt Scots Gds, Lt-Col 2nd Vol Bn Seaforth Highrs; *m* 18 Dec 1889 Mabel (*d* Nov 1890), dau of Mahlon Sands, of New York, and *dvp* 16 Nov 1895, leaving:

(1) ARCHIBALD HENRY MACDONALD, **1st Viscount**

2 George Felix Standish, JP Caithness; *b* 11 Jan 1861; Capt 2nd Vol Bn Seaforth Highrs; *m* 4 Nov 1884 Margaret (*d* 2 July 1932), sis of Sir John Rose George Sinclair, 7th Bt, of Dunbeath (*qv*), and *d* 10 June 1943, having had:

(1) Algernon Ronald Tollemache; *b* 22 Oct 1887; Capt 17th Bn Durham LI; *m* 27 March 1915 Brenda Stella, dau of Alfred Perry, and *d* 12 Dec 1934

(1) Dorothy Emma Olivia; *m* 16 April 1907 Cdr Llewellyn Edmund Traherne, RN, JP, of Coedarhydyglyn, nr Cardiff, and *d* 9 Oct 1957, leaving issue. He *d* of pneumonia contracted on active service 14 Oct 1914

(2) Olive Margaret Camilla; *m* 15 July 1914 Maj William Adam Sedgwick Rough, RAF, s of Col William Edward Morrison Rough, 7th Dragoon Gds, and had issue. He *d* 17 Nov 1969

1 Amy Camilla; *m* 8 July 1874 John Henry Fullarton Udny, of Udny Castle, Aberdeenshire (*see* BELHAVEN AND STENTON, L), and *d* 27 Feb 1925

2 Nina Mary Adelaide; *m* 22 July 1882 Lt-Gen Owen Lewis Cope Williams, of Temple Ho, Berks, MP Great Marlow, and *d* 13 Feb 1924. He *d* 20 Oct 1904

Sir JOHN *d* 29 Sept 1912; his gs,

Sir Archibald Henry Macdonald Sinclair, 4th Bt, and **1st Viscount Thurso**, of Ulbster, Co Caithness (UK), so cr 10 April 1952, KT (1941), CMG (1922), PC (1931), JP; *b* 22 Oct 1890; *educ* Eton and RMC Sandhurst; Maj Life Gds WW I, Personal Mil Sec to Sec State War 1919–21, Ld Lt Caithness 1919–64, Priv Sec to Sec State Colonies 1921–22, MP (Lib) Caithness and Sutherland 1922–45, Chm Ctees H of C 1925–30, memb Empire Mktg Bd 1927–30, Ch Liberal Whip 1930–31, Sec State Scotland 1931–32 and Air 1940–45, Leader Lib Pty 1935–45, Ld Rector Glasgow U 1938–46, Hon A/Cdre 600 (City of London) Sqdn RAuxAF 1942–49, Chev Legn Hon, Hon LLD Edin 1932 and Glasgow 1939; *m* 18 May 1918 Marigold (*d* 11 Feb 1975), dau of Lt-Col James Stewart Forbes (*see* FORBES, Bt, of Newe), and had:

1 ROBIN MACDONALD, **2nd Viscount**

2 +Angus John [The Hon Angus Sinclair, 19 The Chase, London SW4 0NP]; *b* 21 April 1925; *educ* Eton and New Coll Oxford; late Lt Scots Gds, with: BBC 1950–54, Nigerian Broadcasting Serv 1954–58, COI London 1959–74, COI Bristol 1974–85, Brit Cncl 1985–90, md Universal Aunts Ltd 1991–; *m* 1st 26 Feb 1955 (*divorce* 1967) Pamela Karen, er dau of Dallas Bower, of 69 Brook St, W1; *m* 2nd 27 Feb 1968 (*divorce* 1992) Judith Anne Percy; *m* 3rd 1992 *Kate, dau of William Fry and widow of Leonard Hunting, and by his 2nd w has:

(1) +Isaiah William Columba Stroma; *b* 10 June 1971

1 *Catherine [The Hon Mrs Zielenkiewicz, The Mill House, Isle Brewers, Taunton, Somerset]; *b* 25 Oct 1919; artist, memb Soc Scottish Women Artists; *m* 18 June 1957 Kazimierz Zielenkiewicz (*d* 1988), s of Josef Zielenkiewicz, of Sosnowiec, Poland, and has:

(1) *Clementina Stewart; *b* 23 April 1958; *m* 1st 1981 (*divorce* 1984) Roberto Lucarini, only s of Alvaro Lucarini, of Prato, Tuscany; *m* 2nd 1990 *Alain Stiegler, s of Mme Colette Stiegler, of Le Grand Pressigny, Touraine, and has:

1a *Max Casimir; *b* 1990

2 Elizabeth; *b* 5 June 1921; *m* 18 July 1942 *Lt-Col Archibald Michael Lyle, Scottish Horse (ret), yst s of Sir Archibald Lyle, 2nd Bt (*qv*), and *d* 1994, having had issue

The 1st VISCOUNT *d* 15 June 1970; his er s,

ROBIN MACDONALD SINCLAIR, **2nd Viscount Thurso**, JP Caithness 1959; *b* 24 Dec 1922; *educ* Eton, New Coll Oxford and Edinburgh U; F/Lt RAF WW II 1941–45, cmded Edin U Air Sqdn 1946, Capt Boats Edin U Boat Club 1946–47 (Green 1946, Blue 1947), memb Caithness CC 1949–61 and 1965–95, town cncllr Thurso 1957–61 and 1965–95, Dean of Guild 1968, Baillie 1960 and 1969, Police Judge 1971, Caithness: Ld Lt 1973–95 (V-Lt 1964–73, DL 1952–64), chm: Lochdhu Hotels Ltd, Thurso Fisheries Ltd; dir Caithness Glass Ltd, Stephens (Plastics) Ltd; pres North Country Cheviot Sheep Soc 1951–54, Highland Soc of London 1980–95; chm Caithness and Sutherland Youth Employment Ctee 1957–75, memb Red Deer Commn 1965–74; *m* 14 Feb 1952 *Margaret Beaumont, widow of Lt Guy Warwick Brokensha, DSC, FAA, and er dau of Col Josiah James Robertson, DSO, MBE, TD, JP, DL, of Norwood, Wick, Caithness and *d* June 1995, leaving:

1 JOHN ARCHIBALD SINCLAIR, **3rd and present Viscount Thurso**

2 +Patrick James [The Hon Patrick Sinclair, Woodford, Eel Pie Island, Twickenham, Middx]; *b* 21 Dec 1954; *educ* Fettes; *m* 1974 (*divorce* 1984) Carol North and has:

(1) +Jody Peter Fergus North; *b* 6 May 1975

(2) +Luke Robin; *b* 19 March 1979

2 (cont.) The Hon Patrick Sinclair also has:

(1) *Celeste Jennifer; *b* 1981

1 *Camilla Janet [The Hon Mrs Sanson, Puketotara Rd, RD3, Whangarei, New Zealand]; *b* 2 Aug 1957; *m* 1983 *Robert Bruce Sanson and has:

(1) *Mevagh Janet; *b* 21 Aug 1989

(2) *Nina Elizabeth; *b* 17 Oct 1992

TOLLEMACHE, Baron

Arms: Arg. a fret sa. **Crest:** A horse's head erased gu. between two wings or pellettée. **Supporters:** On either side a stag guardant ppr., gorged with a collar flory counterflory or. **Motto:** *Confido, conquiesco* ('I trust and am content'). **Creation:** B. (UK) 17 Jan 1876.

THE 5TH BARON TOLLEMACHE OF HELMINGHAM, Co Suffolk (Tim(othy) John Edward Tollemache [The Rt Hon The Lord Tollemache, Helmingham Hall, Stowmarket, Suffolk IP14 6EF]; *b* 13 Dec 1939; *s* f 1975; *educ* Eton; Lt Coldstream Gds 1959–62 (Kenya and Persian Gulf 1960–62), estate management Sandringham 1962–64, trainee Barings Bank Ltd 1964–65, joined Tollemache and Cobbold Breweries Ltd 1965, dir 1973–, jt md Barwell and Sons (Norwich) Ltd; chm: HHA E Anglia Regn 1979–83, St John's Cncl Suffolk 1982–89, St Edmundsbury Cathedral Appeal 1986–90 and CLA Suffolk 1990–93; dir: Fortis (UK) Ltd, pres: Suffolk Assoc of Local Cncls 1978–, Friends of Ipswich Museums 1980–96, Cheshire Cereal Soc 1983–, Suffolk Ag Assoc 1988 and Suffolk Family History Soc 1988–, The Milk Gp 1994–; v-pres: Cheshire Red Cross 1980– and Suffolk Preservation Soc 1992–, patron: Suffolk Accident Rescue Serv 1983– and Suffolk Assoc for the Blind 1992–, patron of four livings, V-Ld Lt Suffolk 1994– (DL Suffolk 1984–94), CStJ 1988; *m* 24 Feb 1970 *Alexandra Dorothy Jean, yr dau of Col Hugo Meynell, MC (*see* HALIFAX, E), and has:

  1 +EDWARD JOHN HUGO; *b* 12 May 1976 (HRH THE PRINCE OF WALES stood sponsor); Page of Hon to HM THE QUEEN 1988–90

  2 +James Henry Timothy; *b* 28 Aug 1980

  1 *Selina Karen; *b* 3 Oct 1973

Lineage: The 4th EARL OF DYSART (*qv*); had a yr dau and in her issue eventual coheir:

JANE Tollemache; *m* 1st 23 Oct 1771 Maj John Delap HALLIDAY (*d* 24 Oct 1794), of The Leasowes, Salop; *m* 2nd 4 March 1802 George David Ferry and *d* 28 Aug 1802, leaving by her 1st husb an est s:

JOHN RICHARD DELAP HOLLIDAY later TOLLEMACHE (roy licence 4 July 1821); *b* 1772; Adml; *m* 28 Feb 1797 Lady Elizabeth Stratford (*d* 13 May 1861), dau and coheir of 3rd Earl of Aldborough (*see* 1875 edn), and had, with a dau (*d* unm):

1 JOHN, **1st Baron**

2 Wilbraham Spencer, of Dorfold Hall, Cheshire, JP, DL Cheshire; *b* 3 Oct 1807; Rifle Bde and Coldstream Gds, High Sheriff Cheshire 1865; *m* 25 June 1844 Anne, est dau and heiress of Rev James Tomkinson, of Dorfold Hall, and *d* 15 Feb 1890, leaving, with a dau (*d* unm):

  (1) Henry James, of Dorfold Hall, JP Cheshire; *b* 5 July 1846; *educ* Ch Ch Oxford (BA); V-Lt Cheshire, MP W Cheshire 1881–85 and Eddisbury 1885–1906, Maj Earl of Chester's Yeo Cav; *m* 20 Jan 1904 Katharine Mary Frances (*d* 18 June 1916), widow of Thomas Edward Champion Streatfeild and dau of Rev Henry Arkwright, of Bodenham, Herefs, and *d* 2 April 1939

  (2) Algernon Edward (Rev); *b* 25 Jan 1851; BA Cantab; Vicar Hill Farrance, Somerset; *m* 14 Sept 1875 Agnes Mary (*d* 26 Oct 1915), dau of Metcalfe Larken, and *d* 6 April 1930

  (1) Julia Elizabeth Anne; *m* 10 May 1873 Charles Savile Roundell, JP, DL, yst s of Rev Danson Richardson Roundell, JP, DL, of Gledstone, Yorks, and *d* 28 Dec 1931, leaving issue. He *d* 3 March 1906

3 William Augustus; *b* 23 Nov 1817; Capt 2nd Life Gds; *m* 3 June 1846 Marguerite (*dsp* 1896), dau of John Home Purves (and step-dau of 1st Viscount Canterbury; *see* RUTLAND, D), and *d* 4 Feb 1911

1 Elizabeth Jane Henrietta; *m* 1st 5 Aug 1817 Lt-Col Christian Frederick Charles Alexander James Johnston, of Hilton; *m* 2nd 19 June 1826 7th Earl of Cardigan (*see* AILESBURY, M) and *d* 15 July 1858

2 Emily; *m* 28 Nov 1819 Charles Tyrwhitt Jones (*d* July 1876), 2nd s of Sir Thomas TYRWHITT later JONES, 1st Bt (*see* BERNERS, B), and *d* 3 Dec 1821, leaving issue

3 Jane; *m* 1819 George Finch, MP, of Burley-on-the-Hill, Rutland, and *dsp* 1821. He *d* 29 June 1870

4 Marcia; *m* 1829 Adml Frederick Edward Vernon Harcourt and *d* 27 Dec 1868, leaving issue (*see* VERNON, B)

---

5 Marianne; *m* 6 Sept 1827 Hubert De Burgh, of W Drayton, and *d* 24 July 1880, leaving issue. He *d* 1875

6 Selina; *m* 8 Dec 1829 Capt William Locke, 1st Life Gds (drowned Lake Como Oct 1832) and *d* 15 Dec 1893

7 Charlotte; *m* 2 Jan 1833 Capt George Hope, RN, and *d* 14 April 1837, leaving issue (*see* LINLITHGOW, M)

8 Georgina; *m* 21 Nov 1848, as his 2nd w, 1st and last Baron Mount-Temple of Mount-Temple and *d* 17 Oct 1901. He *dsp* 17 Oct 1888

JOHN TOLLEMACHE *d* 16 July 1837; his est s,

JOHN HALLIDAY later TOLLEMACHE, **1st Baron Tollemache of Helmingham**, Co Suffolk (UK), so *cr* 17 Jan 1876; *b* 7 Dec 1805; MP (C) S Cheshire 1841–68 and W Cheshire 1868–72; *m* 1st 2 Aug 1826 his cousin Georgina Louisa (*d* 18 July 1846), dau of Thomas Best by Lady Emily Stratford (*see* 1875 edn ALDBOROUGH, E), and had:

1 WILBRAHAM FREDERIC TOLLEMACHE, **2nd Baron Tollemache of Helmingham**, JP, DL Cheshire; *b* 4 July 1832; CA Cheshire 1887–1900, MP (C) W Cheshire 1872–85; *m* 1st 2 Dec 1858 Lady Emma Georgiana Stewart (*d* 24 Jan 1869), 2nd dau of 9th Earl of Galloway (*qv*), and had, with two daus (*d* unm):

  (1) Lyonel Plantagenet; *b* 28 Oct 1869; *m* 13 April 1883 Lady Blanche Sybil King (*m* 2nd 11 Nov 1903 Granville Landesborough Findlay, MB, ChB, and *d* 28 May 1923), only dau and heiress of 7th Earl of Kingston (*qv*), and *dvp* 28 Aug 1902, leaving:

    1a BENTLEY LYONEL JOHN TOLLEMACHE, **3rd Baron Tollemache of Helmingham**, JP, DL Cheshire; *b* 7 March 1883; *educ* Eton; T/Lt-Cdr RNVR, Capt 3rd Bn Cheshire Regt and 3rd Bn KOSB, Boer War 1902 and WW I (wounded); *m* 1st 17 Jan 1902 Wynford Rose (*d* 16 May 1926), only child of Gen Sir Arnold Burrowes Kemball, KCB, KCSI, and had:

      1b Dorothy Cecily; *b* 11 Feb 1907; *m* 28 Nov 1942 A/Cdre Reynell Henry Verney, CBE, DL (*see* WILLOUGHBY DE BROKE, B), and *d* 16 Dec 1994

      2b Frances Patricia; *b* 24 Nov 1908; WAAF WW II; *m* 10 Feb 1949 (*divorce* 1965) Charles Edward Lloyd-Worth, 2nd s of John Francis Lloyd-Worth

    1a (cont.) The **3rd Baron** *m* 2nd 23 Oct 1928 Lynette, MBE (1944), OStJ, dau of Alfred Vincent Pawson, of Nynehead Court, Somerset, and *d* 13 Jan 1955, leaving by her:

      3b *Sybil Diana; *b* 1 May 1930; *m* 24 Nov 1966 *Harold Diehl

    2a Denis Plantagenet, DSO (1919); *b* 12 Jan 1884; granted rank of baron's yr s 6 May 1905; High Sheriff Rutland 1933, Lt-Col 7th Hus, WW I (despatches, brevet, POW 1917–18); GSO(3) 1914, Bde-Maj 1914–15, cmded 1st Bn Northants Regt 1916–17 (and 7th Hus 1923–27, ret 1928); *d* unm 1 May 1942

  (2) Wilbraham John; *b* 5 Feb 1865; *d* unm 3 June 1914

  (3) Randolph Stewart; *b* 5 April 1866; Lt RN; *d* 13 May 1923

  (4) Arthur Wilbraham; *b* 9 Sept 1867; *d* 12 Aug 1932

1 (cont.) The **2nd Baron** *m* 2nd 2 Oct 1878 Mary Stuart (*d* 6 Jan 1939), dau of Lord Claud Hamilton (*see* ABERCORN, D), and *d* 17 Dec 1904

2 Lionel Arthur; *b* 28 May 1838; *educ* Balliol Coll Oxford; author; *m* 25 Jan 1870 Hon Beatrix Lucia Catherine (*d* 24 Dec 1926), yst dau of 1st Baron Egerton of Tatton (*see* 1956 edn), and *dsp* 29 Jan 1919

The **1st Baron** *m* 2nd 17 Jan 1850 Eliza Georgiana (*d* 4 Aug 1918 aged 90), dau of James Duff and step-dau of 4th Baron Rendlesham (*qv*), and *d* 9 Dec 1890, leaving by her:

3 John Richard Delap; *b* 22 Oct 1850; Lt RN; *m* 1st 26 Dec 1872 (*divorce* 1880) Eleanore, CA (*d* 23 Oct 1930), 4th dau of Hon Henry Starnes, Pres Cncl Quebec; *m* 2nd 1883 Margaret Ann, dau of F W Answorth, and *d* 6 Feb 1914

4 Hamilton James; *b* 22 Jan 1852; Durham LI; *m* 21 Oct 1879 Mabel (*d* 9 Feb 1941), 2nd dau of Robert Culling Hanbury, MP, of Bedwell Park, Herts, and *d* 16 June 1893, leaving:

  (1) Edward Devereux Hamilton, DSO (1919), MC (1918); *b* 1 June 1885; *educ* Eton and RMC Sandhurst; Maj-Gen; Col Coldstream Gds; WW I (wounded, despatches three times, Brevet Maj): GSO(3) 1915–16, Bde-Maj 1916–17, GSO(2) 1917–18; War Office 1919, Bde-Maj Aldershot 1923, cmded 1st Bn Coldstream Gds 1924–28, Assist Cmdt RMC 1929–32, GSO(1) 1st Div Aldershot 1932–36, Brig cmdg 128th Inf Bde (TA) 1936, ADC to HM GEORGE VI 1938, Brig cmdg Southampton Garrison 1939, later Portsmouth area; Order White Eagle Serbia 5th Cl with swords; *m* 9 Feb 1909 Violet Aline (*d* 8 May 1970), only child of Sir Joseph West Ridgeway, GCB, GCMG, KCSI, PC, and *d* 27 Aug 1947, leaving:

    1a JOHN EDWARD HAMILTON, **4th Baron**

  (2) Henry Robert Hamilton; *b* 11 Oct 1888; T/Lt Cameron Highrs 1914–15, Capt MT ASC 1915–19; *m* 10 Oct 1912 Ethel Maud (*d* 12 Oct 1953), only child of John Irwin, of Belmont, Mullingar, Co Westmeath, and *d* 15 Nov 1931, leaving:

    1a Anthony Henry Hamilton, GC; *b* 3 Aug 1913; S/Ldr RAuxAF WW II (wounded), ADC to Govr-Gen Canada 1945–47; *m* 1st 26 July 1947 (*divorce* 1960) Françoise, dau of Count Jean de Hauteclocque, Resident Gen Tunisia, and had:

      1b +Richard Lionel [Richard Tollemache Esq, 41 Lochaline St, London W6]; *b* 9 April 1950; *m* 1978 *Caroline, dau of Capt Edward Maxwell Cunningham Walker, OBE, RN, and has:

        1c +Max Philip Anthony; *b* 1987

        1c *Stephanie Elizabeth Louise; *b* 1985

      1b +Gregory Marmaduke Anthony [Gregory Tollemache Esq, 6 Elm Walk, Totnes, Devon TQ9 5YQ]; *b* 9 Jan 1954; *m* 1976 *Karin — and has:

        1c +Eugene Anthony; *b* 1976

      1b *Catherine [Mrs Malcolm Woolff, The Old Granary, Malton Rd, Orwell, Herts SG8 5QN]; *b* 9 May 1948; *m* 26 June 1970 *Malcolm Woolff and has:

        1c *Nicholas Elliot; *b* 1974

        1c *Georgina Juliet; *b* 1975

      2b *Juliette [Mrs Jonathan Cottam, 35 Kingsley Ave, London W13 0EQ]; *b* 17 Sept 1956; *m* 1979 *Jonathan Brian Cottam and has:

        1c *Alexie Juliette Daisie; *b* 1982

2c *Harriet Rosie Madeleine; b 1986

1a (cont.) S/Ldr Anthony Tollemache m 2nd Cecilia Vernon Mary (d 1993), dau of Bryce Cochrane, of Edinburgh, and d Paris 20 Feb 1977 following a car crash, leaving by her:

1b +Alexander Anthony; b 1958; educ Stowe and Exeter U; m 1987 *Nobuko Kida

1a Karin Irene Elizabeth; b 1916; m 13 Oct 1945 Cdr (S) William Gordon Jack, RN (d 1992), only s of Gordon Jack, of Berkhamsted, Herts, and d 1981, leaving:

1b *Michael Anthony Gordon; b 28 June 1946; educ Charterhouse and Lincoln Coll Oxford (BA); m 1980 *Anne, dau of Hugh Fletcher, of CP, S Africa, and has:

1c *Julia; b 1981

2c *Diana; b 1984

2b David Lionel; b 24 Feb 1954; educ Eton and Bristol U; d Bermuda 1985 following an accident

1b Vanessa Bettine; b 14 June 1948; educ UEA (BA); m 1978 *Michael Manassei di Collestatte and d 1985, leaving issue (see PERTH, E)

(1) Marguerite Emily; b 1880; m 27 Sept 1906 Lt-Col George Cecil Minett Sorel-Cameron, CBE (d 28 June 1947), Cameron Highrs, and d 12 Feb 1968 aged 87, leaving:

1a John, CBE, DSO; b 1907; m 1937 Catherine Nancy (Sally) (d 1984), yr dau of Frank Lee, of Well Heak, Halifax, and d 1986, leaving:

1b *Catriona [Mrs Maurice Cleary, 4 Holbein Mews, London SW1]; b 1940; m 1st 1963 (divorce 1967) Allan Carruthers and has:

1c *Rupert Harry Edgell; b 1963

1b (cont.) Mrs Catriona Carruthers m 2nd 1968 *Maurice Cleary and by him has:

2c *Angus Peter; b 1968

2a *Robert, CBE, AFC [Air Cdre Robert Sorel-Cameron CBE AFC, The White House, Whitwell, Norfolk, NR10 4RF]; b 1911; educ Wellington and Edinburgh U; Air Cdre RAF, Air Attaché Athens 1960–62; m 1939 Henrietta Grace (d 1997), dau of Capt John Radford-Norcop, of The Brand Hall, Market Drayton, Salop, and has:

1b *Alistair [Alistair Sorel-Cameron Esq, 49 Montgomery Rd, London W4 5LZ]; b 1940; m 1981 *Ann Kristine, dau of Kenneth Cole Harkess, MBE, of Kemsing, Kent, and has:

1c *George Jack; b 1988

1c *Henrietta Eve; b 1986

2b *James Sorel-Cameron Esq, 49 Evesham Rd, Stratford-on-Avon]; b 1948; m 1972 *Bridget Susan, est dau of Alan Henry Dring, of Tinkley Lodge, Nympsfield, Glos, and has:

1c *Robert James; b 1975

2c *Peter Alan; b 1982

3c *Matthew George; b 1984

1c *Catriona Jane; b 1973

2c *Joanna Helen; b 1979

1b *Victoria [Mrs Sayyid Rifaat, 27A Crawford Place, Newbury, Berks RG14 1XG]; b 1943; m 1968 *Sayyid Rifaat and has:

1c *Tariq Sayyid; b 1971

2c *Rashid Ali; b 1973

3c *Samir; b 1975

1c *Sasha Amy; b 1979

1a Agnes; b 1909; m 1933 Lt Col Cyril Hugh Kerr-Smiley and d 1986, leaving issue (see SMILEY, Bt)

2a *Hester Marguerite; b 1920; m 1945 Maj Sir George Andrew Dick-Lauder, 12th Bt (qv)

(2) Winifred Gertrude; b 1882; m 5 Nov 1910 Detmar Jellings Blow, JP, FRIBA (d 7 Feb 1939), 3rd s of Jellings Blow, JP, of Hiles, Painswick, Glos, and d 28 May 1954, leaving:

1a Richard Purcell; b 1915; m 1st 1939 (divorce 1956) Diana Hermione (m 2nd 1961 (divorce 1963) Marco Blow and d 1967), dau of Capt William Adrian Vincent Bethell (see GLENCONNER, B), and had:

1b *(Richard) David Detmar [David Blow Esq, 20 Kyrle Rd, London SW11 6AZ]; b 29 Jan 1942; m 1988 *Laurence Marie, dau of George Lécallier, of Neuilly, Paris, and has:

1c *John; b 27 Aug 1989

1c *Lucy; b 27 Aug 1995

2b *(Adrian) Simon [Simon Blow Esq, 35 Great Queen St, London WC2B 5AA]; b 23 July 1943; writer

1a (cont.) Richard Blow m 2nd 1957 *Catherine (d 1992), dau of Donald MacAskill, of Berneray, Inverness-shire, and d 1963, leaving by her:

1b *Catherine Anne [Miss Catherine Blow, 138 Wellington Bldgs, Ebury Bridge Rd, London SW1]; b 1960

2a Jonathan Oliver Tollemache; b 1919; m 1962 *(Elaine) Helga [Mrs Jonathan Blow, The Chalet Hotel, Kandy, Sri Lanka; Hilles Edge, Stroud, Glos GL6 6NW], dau of Edmund Frederick Lorenz de Silva, MBE, of Kandy, MP Kandy, Singhalese Amb France and memb Exec Bd UNESCO, and d 1977, leaving:

1b *Detmar Hamilton Lorenz Arthur [Detmar Blow Esq, 199 Strand, London WC2R 1DR; 67 Elizabeth St, London SW1W 9JP]; b 1963; educ Harrow and LSE (BA); barrister Middle Temple 1989; m 1989 *Isabella Delves, est dau of Sir Evelyn Delves Broughton, 12th Bt (qv)

2b *Amaury Hugh John Jellings [Amaury Blow Esq, Edge Farm, Edge, Stroud, Glos]; b 1965; educ Millfield

1b *Selina Jane [Miss Selina Blow, 42 Elizabeth St, London SW1W 9NI; Cherry Hill Cottage, Spoonbed Vale, Edge, Stroud, Glos]; b 1966; educ Hatherop Castle and Queen's Coll; fashion designer

1a Clare Desirée; b 1914; m 1st 1934 (divorce 1944) 2nd Baron Rathcavan (qv) and had issue; m 2nd 1944 *Lt-Col Lewis Stanton Starkey [Lt-Col Lewis Starkey, Huttons Ambo Hall, York] and d 1956, leaving by him:

1b Kathleen Mary; b 1946; m 1972 *John Fitzgerald Willcox Jenyns, yr s of Roger Soame Jenyns, of Bottisham Hall, Cambs, and d 1994, leaving:

1c *Clare Eulalia Starkey; b 1974

2a *Lucilla [Mrs Philip Warre-Cornish, The Tower, Woolstone, Faringdon, Oxon SN7 7QL]; b 1923; m 1948 Philip Warre-Cornish (d 1998) and has:

1b *Alexander Philip Hubert Detmar [Alexander Warre-Cornish Esq, le Sage, ten Broeklaan 81, Eindhoven, The Netherlands]; b 1949; educ Eton; m 1983 *Penelope Ann, dau of Dr Philip Canning Farrant, of Sidcup, Kent, and has:

1c *Katherine Mary; b 1985

2c *Harriet Jane; b 1988

3c *Anna Belinda; b 1991

2b *James Damian; b 1952

5 Murray Arthur; b 21 May 1853; m 13 July 1892 Margaret, dau of Henry Witter, of Tilstone, and Peckforton, Cheshire, and d 16 Oct 1913, leaving:

(1) Cecil Herbert, Capt; had:

1a *Betty Cecil; has:

1b *Murray

1b *Clare; m Peter Kennedy

2b *A dau

(2) Philip

(1) Amy Florence; d unm 13 April 1959

(2) Elsa Margaret; d unm 13 Jan 1965

(3) Winifred

6 Stanhope Alfred, of Bentley Manor, Suffolk, JP Suffolk; b 26 Aug 1855; BA Cantab, High Sheriff 1903; m 27 Sept 1905 Elizabeth (d 25 June 1958), dau of William Monks, and d 18 Dec 1934, having had:

(1) John Stanhope; b 15, d 20 June 1909

(1) *Rhona Elizabeth [Mrs John Monks, Bentley Cottage, St Just-in-Roseland, nr Truro, Cornwall]; b 1906; m 1st 1935 George Harrison, of Johannesburg (d 1935); m 2nd 4 Sept 1944 Wlodzimierz Jan Zbrowski (took 1950 name John Vladimir Moreton Monks; d 1981), only s of Marian Zbrowski, of Warsaw

(2) *Sheila Joyce; m 1st 22 April 1936 (divorce 1946) Francis William Frederick Otter-Barry (d 20 Feb 1967), est s of William Whitmore Otter-Barry, of Horkesley Hall, Essex; m 2nd 17 Jan 1947 Capt John Claude Smiley, Middx Yeo (TAR), 2nd s of Sir John Smiley, 2nd Bt (qv)

(3) *Ina Elaine [Miss Ina Tollemache, Hanby, 94A High Rd West, Felixstowe, Suffolk IP11 9JE]; b 1916

7 Duff; b 5 Jan 1859; m 1898 Emily (d 17 Feb 1939), dau of H Russell, and d 18 April 1936

8 Douglas Alfred; b 27 June 1862; BA Cantab; Maj Suffolk Imp Yeo, md Tollemache's Breweries; m 17 Aug 1887 Alice Mary (d 5 Oct 1959 aged 94), dau of John Head (see HEAD, V), and d 31 Dec 1944, leaving:

(1) Bevil Douglas; b 11 April 1889; Lt (SR) Coldstream Gds; ka 22 Dec 1914

(2) Humphrey Douglas; b 6 Dec 1893; Capt RN, WWs I and II; m 31 July 1924 Elsie Violet (d 1981), dau of William George Raphael, and d 24 Oct 1970, leaving:

1a +Michael Humphrey [Michael Tollemache Esq, Tollemache Hall, Offton, Suffolk IP8 4RT]; b 19 March 1930; educ Eton and London U (BSc Hort); m 29 Aug 1968 *Gay Rosemary Denise O'Grady, est dau of Hugh Edward O'Grady Thompson, of Castle Garde, Co Limerick, and has:

1b *Rosamond Sybil; b 9 Nov 1969; m 1993 *Ashley P de Laroque, only s of Charles de Laroque, of Lyndale Cottage, Chalfont St Peter, Bucks, and has:

1c *Rebecca; b 28 April 1997

2b *Juliet Elsie; b 1 June 1974

1a *Jean Margherita; b 20 Nov 1927; m 1st 29 June 1953 Sir Francis Cullen Grant, 12th Bt, of Monymusk and Cullen (qv), and has issue; m 2nd 1980, as his 2nd w, 2nd Baron Tweedsmuir (qv)

(3) Rupert Douglas; b 29 Aug 1903; m 22 Oct 1931 *Patricia Margaret (m 2nd 27 March 1941 Col Charles Dalby, CBE, 60th Rifles, yr s of Maj John Dalby, of Castle Donington, Leics, and has issue), only dau of Sir John Smiley, 2nd Bt (qv), and d 1 Aug 1933

(1) Cynthia Mary; b 18 Oct 1890; m 26 Aug 1916 Lt-Col Guy Rattray Dubs, MC, KRRC, only s of F E Dubs, of The Priory, St Andrews, Fife, and had issue. He d 23 Oct 1930

(2) Angela Mariota; b 10 June 1900; Hon Col 307 (N Cmd) Bn WRAC (TA) 1956, Sr Cmdt ATS; m 1st 12 July 1923 3rd Baron Belper (qv) and d 11 Feb 1995; m 2nd 2 Oct 1958 Rev (Harry) Norman WRIGLEY later TOLLEMACHE, Rector Binstead IoW 1953–58, s of Joseph Henry Wrigley, and d 11 Feb 1995

9 Stratford Haliday Robert Louis; b 25 June 1864; Lt KRRC; m 1st 14 Feb 1912 Ethel Julia (d 11 Jan 1928), 2nd dau of Henry Cavendish Cavendish, DL, of Chyknell, Salop; m 2nd 17 July 1930 Emma (d 2 April 1972), widow of Edward Cairn and dau of Silas Manasseh, of Singapore, and d 30 Aug 1937

10 Ranulph Carteret; b 1 Jan 1866; educ Harrow and Trin Coll Camb; m 1889 Annie Mary (d 25 April 1923), dau of William Smith, of Hampstead, and d 4 March 1960, having had:

(1) Cyril; b 1889; Capt RAF; m 7 Aug 1918 Nancy, 2nd dau of W Barnett, of Dublin, and d 5 Aug 1940

(2) Murray Carteret; b 1890; m 3 Feb 1917 Mrs Sheila Stanyon, dau of Col Arthur Hills Gleadowe-Newcomen, CIE, and d 1968

(3) Devereux John Rex; b 1891; m 25 April 1914 Gladys Victoria (d 17 March 1960), yr dau of John Waddington, of Waddington Old Hall, Yorks

(4) Eric Algernon; b 1892; m 12 March 1925 Kathleen (d 24 March 1952), yst dau of Verney Smith, of Melbourne, and dsp 17 Feb 1961

(5) Lawrence Lionel; b 1894; Cdr RN, WWs I and II (Japanese POW 1941–45); m 6 Jan 1926 Violet Mary (m 2nd 1956 Laurence Reid), dau of John Bayly A'deane, and d 14 June 1954, leaving:

1a *Margaret Ngaire Yoskyl A'deane [Mrs Antony Jackson, The White Pines, Takapau, Hawkes Bay, New Zealand]; b 10 Sept 1928; m 1955 *Antony Percy Jackson, s of L P Jackson, of Old Rectory Farm, Belstone, Devon, and has:

1b *Peter Lawrence; *b* 1956

2b *Timothy; *b* 1959

3b *Ashley; *b* 1961

1b *Alison; *b* 1958

2b *Ngaianne; *b* 1962

2a *Annette A'Deane [Mrs Bryan Philpott, Ashcott Station, RD Takapau, Hawkes Bay, New Zealand]; *b* 6 Feb 1950; *m* 1st 1974 (*divorce* 1981) Andrew Berne Vallence, of Pinawai, NZ and has:

   1b *Natasha A'Deane; *b* 1978

2a (cont.) Mrs Annette Vallaence *m* 2nd 1984 *Bryan Chesney Philpott and by him has:

   2b *Tamarin Mary A'Deane; *b* 1983

(6) Harold Vincent; *b* 1896; Capt Res Offrs Indian Cav; *m* 28 Oct 1937 Marjorie Violet (*d* 1990), dau of W H Lonsdale, of Rangoon, and *d* 1989, leaving:

   1a +Laurence Ranulph [Laurence Tollemache Esq, 46 Preston Grove, Faversham, Kent] *b* 26 July 1938; *m* 24 Sept 1960 *Maureen Elizabeth, dau of Harold Hex, of Taunton, Somerset, and has:

      1b +Paul Laurence; *b* 8 Jan 1965

      1b *Clare Elizabeth; *b* 1968

(1) Hilda; *b* 1895

(2) Elfreyda; *b* 1900; *m* 29 Jan 1938 Noel Sedgwick, s of Rev Mostyn Sedgwick

(3) Sybil; *b* 1901; *m* 24 Dec 1921 Henry Richard Clarke, s of Henry Richard Clarke, of Cotham, Bristol, and had issue

11 Mortimer Granville; *b* 12 April 1872; *educ* Eton and Trin Coll Cambridge; Capt TAR and Suffolk Regt WW I ; *m* July 1894 Margaret (*d* 1945), dau of Arthur Gorst, and *d* 27 March 1950, leaving:

(1) Dorothy Margaret; *b* 25 Aug 1895

(2) Leila Mary; *b* 13 Oct 1896; *m* 1st 6 Oct 1919 Capt Charles Ivor Phipson Smith-Ryland, Coldstream Gds (*d* 27 Dec 1929), s of William Charles Henry Alston Smith-Ryland, JP, of Barford Hill, Warwicks, and had:

   1a Charles Mortimer Tollemache (Sir), KCVO; *b* 1927; *m* 1952 *Hon Jeryl Marcia Sarah [The Hon Lady Smith-Ryland, Old Hall, Medbourne, Mkt Harborough, Leics LE16 8DZ], dau of Hon Robert Brampton Gurdon (*see* CRANWORTH, B), and *d* 1989, leaving:

      1b *Robin Charles; *b* 1953; *m* 1st 1982 (*divorce* 1985) Eliza S, dau of Cdr James George Greville Dugdale, RN; *m* 2nd 1985 *Baroness Hélène von Ludinghausen

      2b *David James; *b* 1961

      1b *Sarah Yoskyl; *b* 1955; *m* 1983 *(Luke Edward) Timothy Hue Williams and has:

         1c *Charles Luke; *b* 1991

         1c *Sophie; *b* 1984

         2c *Laura; *b* 1987

      2b *Joanna; *b* 1959

      3b *Petra Louisa; *b* 1970

   1a *June [Mrs Robert Bensley, Kahdena Rd, Morristown, NJ, USA]; *b* 1924; *m* 1946 *Robert W Bensley and has:

      1b *Robert Ward; *b* 1954

      2b *Charles Ivor; *b* 1958

      1b *Leila Hannah; *b* 1947

(2) (cont.) Mrs Charles Smith-Ryland *m* 2nd 20 April 1933 Victor Hamilton Aubrey Cartwright, 3rd s of Aubrey Cartwright, of Edgcote, Northants, and *d* 30 Oct 1971

1 Rhona Cecilia Emily; *b* 25 Sept 1857; *m* 17 April 1883 Col Thomas Wood, Gren Gds, of Gwernyfed, Breconshire, and *d* 10 Oct 1940, having had issue. He *d* 26 Sept 1933

The 3rd BARON's cousin,

JOHN EDWARD HAMILTON TOLLEMACHE, **4th Baron Tollemache of Helmingham**, MC (1940), DL (Suffolk 1958, Cheshire 1970); *b* 24 April 1910; *educ* Eton and RMC Sandhurst; Maj Res of Offrs Coldstream Gds WW II (wounded), chm: Tollemache's Breweries Ltd, Star Brewery, Cambridge, G T Jones (Oxford) Ltd and Barwell and Sons (Norwich) Ltd, dir: Tollemache's and Cobbold Breweries Ltd, Gen Reinsurance Co, NRG Reinsurance Co Ltd and New London Reinsurance Co; *m* 16 Feb 1939 Dinah Susan (*d* 10 Jan 1998), dau of Sir Archibald Auldjo Jamieson, KBE, MC, of The Drove Ho, Thornham, Norfolk, and *d* 27 May 1975, having had:

1 TIMOTHY JOHN EDWARD TOLLEMACHE, **5th and present Baron Tollemache of Helmingham**

2 +(John) Nicholas Lionel [The Hon Nicholas Tollemache, 1114 San Ysidro Dve, Beverly Hills, CA 90210, USA]; *b* 13 June 1941; *educ* Eton, Trin Coll Cambridge (MA) and Harvard (MBA); *m* 1st 17 Sept 1971 (*divorce* 1974) Heide Eva, dau of Gunther Wiedeck, of Bonn; *m* 2nd 1982 *Dietlinde Hannelore, dau of Hannelore Riegel, of Munich

3 +Michael David Douglas [The Hon Michael Tollemache, Framsden Hall, Stowmarket, Suffolk IP14 6HI]; *b* 23 Aug 1944; *educ* Eton and Trin Coll Cambridge (MA); dir Michael Tollemache Ltd 1967–, David Carritt Ltd 1983– and Artemis Fine Art (UK) Ltd 1983–; *m* 5 Feb 1969 *Theresa, dau of Peter Bowring, of Kensington, and has:

   (1) +Lyonel John Peter; *b* 24 Dec 1973

   (2) +Archibald Robert Bowring (twin); *b* 24 Dec 1973

   (1) *Melissa Natasha; *b* 1971; *m* 2 Aug 1997 *Dennis Kiley, s of Dennis Kiley, of London, and Dr Marthe Kiley-Worthington, of Devon

4 +Hugh John Hamilton [The Hon Hugh Tollemache, Sandbourne House, Earl's Croome, Worcs WR8 9DG]; *b* 17 Feb 1946; *educ* Eton; md Beshara Press Ltd; *m* 1986 *Rosanne, 2nd dau of Hon (Michael) Anthony (Rathbone) Cayzer (*see* ROTHERWICK, B), and has:

   (1) +Thomas Anthony Hamilton; *b* 1987

   (2) +David Charles John; *b* 1989

   (3) +John Edward Hugh; *b* 1992

Seat: Helmingham Hall, nr Stowmarket, Suffolk. The TOLLEMACHEs have owned Helmingham since early Tudor times, from when the earliest parts of the

present structure, chiefly the coutyard layout, the north and south fronts and the gateway, date. The main house was only finished in 1510, however. Other features, such as the gables, were added towards the end of the Tudor period. A hundred and fifty years later the interior was remodelled: the Boudoir and Library date from then. In the early 19th century Nash was brought in to work on the house's southerly facade, which he embellished with crenellation and mullions, also the bridge over the moat (which being a draw-bridge is raised every night). Shortly after his death the west front was altered too. The dining-room dates from this time as well, the designer being Anthony Salvin, who used architectural antiques taken from other houses. The original Tollemache Baronets died out in 1821 and the Helmingham property passed through females to the present owners. The current Lady Tollemache has restored Helmingham's gardens, which are open to the public, to such a high standard that they rated two stars in the *Good Gardens Guide* 1995, the highest level possible. The house, however, is not open to visitors.

TOLLEMACHE, Bt

Arms: Arg. a fret sa. **Crest:** A horse's head erased gu. between two wings pelletée or. **Motto:** *Confido conquiesco* ('I trust and am content'). **Creation:** Bt. (GB) 12 Jan 1793.

SIR LYONEL HUMPHRY JOHN TOLLEMACHE, 7TH BT, of Hanby Hall, Co Lincoln, JP (Leics 1978), DL (Leics 1980) [Maj Sir Lyonel Tollemache Bt JP DL, Buckminster Park, Grantham, Lincs NG33 5RU]; *b* 10 July 1931; *s* f 1990; *educ* Uppingham and RAC Cirencester; Maj Coldstream Gds (ret 1963), QALAS (1969), FRICS, High Sheriff Leics 1978–79, CC 1985–97; Govr Royal Star and Garter Home Richmond 1985–; *m* 6 Feb 1960 *Mary Joscelyne, est dau of Col William Henry Whitbread, TD, of Warren Mere, Godalming, Surrey, and has had:

1 Lyonel Thomas; *b* 23 Jan 1963; *educ* Stanbridge Earls; *d* 22 Aug 1996

2 +RICHARD JOHN; *b* 4 May 1966; *educ* Uppingham; *m* 24 Oct 1992 *Amanda Louise, est dau of Gordon Thomas Phillips, of Brickhill Pastures, Maulden, Beds, and has:

   (1) *Alice Mary; *b* 11 Sept 1997

1 *Katheryne Mary; *b* 18 Dec 1960; *educ* Benenden and Cambridge Coll of Arts and Tech (BA 1982); slr 1992

2 *Henrietta Joscelyne [Mrs David Chubb, Mill Farm, Coston, Leics LE14 2RP]; *b* 15 May 1970; *educ* St Mary's Wantage; BSc (Hons); *m* 1993 *Capt David J Chubb, Light Dragoons, s of Cdr Edwin Chubb, of Pennaton, S Brent, Devon

Lineage: JOHN MANNERS, of Grantham Grange, Lincs; MP Newark 1754–74; *m* 4 Sept 1765 Lady Louisa Tollemache, Countess of Dysart in her own right (*qv*), and *d* 23 Sept 1792 aged 62, having had:

Sir WILLIAM MANNERS later TALMASH (roy licence 6 April 1821), **1st Bt** (GB), so *cr* 12 Jan 1793 (with special remainder, failing heirs male of his body, to his bro), of Hanby Hall, Lincs, and Buckminster, Leics, styled *Lord Huntingtower* 1821–33; *b* 1766; MP Ilchester 1803–04 and 1806–07; *m* 12 Jan 1790 Catherine Rebecca (*d* 21 March 1852), 3rd dau of Francis Gray, of Lehenna, Co Cork, and *d* 11 March 1833, having had, with three daus:

1 Sir LIONEL WILLIAM JOHN MANNERS later TOLLEMACHE, **2nd Bt**, and 8th EARL OF DYSART (as which *s* grandmother 1840); *b* 18 Nov 1794; *m* 23 Sept 1819 Maria Elizabeth Toone and *d* 23 Sept 1878, having had:

   (1) William Lionel Felix, *Lord Huntingtower*; *b* 4 July 1820; *m* 26 Sept 1851 Katherine Elizabeth Camilla Burke and *dvp* 21 Dec 1872, having had, with other issue (*see* DYSART, E):

      1a **Sir William John Manners Tollemache, 3rd Bt**, and 9th EARL OF DYSART; *b* 8 March 1859; *m* 19 Nov 1885 Cecilia Florence Newton and *dsp* 22 Nov 1935

2 Felix Thomas; *b* 16 Feb 1796; *m* 1st 1 Oct 1825 Sarah (*d* 1831), only child of James Gray, of Ballincor, King's Co, and had:

   (1) William James Felix; *b* 12 Jan 1827; *d* 3 Nov 1859

   (1) Caroline *m* 15 Feb 1853 her cousin Rev R W L Tollemache and *d* 6 June 1867, leaving issue (*see* below)

2 (cont.) The Hon Felix Talmash *m* 2nd 27 April 1833 Frances Julia (*m* 2nd 8 May 1845 Adml John Pakenham (*see* LONGFORD, E) and *d* 26 July 1894), yst dau of Henry Peters, of Betchworth Castle, Surrey, and *d* 5 Oct 1843

3 Arthur Caesar; *b* 1 Sept 1797; *m* 17 Aug 1820 Catherine (*d* 23 July 1868), dau of Alberic Joseph Scheppers, and *d* 1 April 1848, having had, with another *s* (*d* young) and three daus (*d* unm):

(1) Arthur Lionel; *b* 29 Aug 1825; *m* 14 May 1857 Emily Susan (*d* 30 Sept 1915), est surv dau of Maj-Gen Sir Jeremiah Bryant, CB, Bengal Army, and *d* 3 Jan 1874, leaving:

1a Arthur Frederick Churchill, JP King's Co; *b* 1 Aug 1860; *educ* Ch Ch Oxford (BA); High Sheriff King's Co 1888; *m* 11 Jan 1888 Susan Eleanor (*d* 9 Dec 1918), est dau of Capt James Carter Campbell, RN, of Ardpatrick, Argyll, and *d* 18 Aug 1923, having had:

1b Arthur Henry William; *b* 5 April 1894; 2nd Lt RE and RFC; *ka* 19 July 1916

1b Eleanor Louisa Cornelia; *m* 5 Feb 1914 Capt Ernest Reginald Hayes Sadler, 8th Gurkha Rifles, IA, 2nd *s* of Lt-Col Sir James Hayes Sadler, KCMG, CB, and *d* 1 Dec 1934, leaving issue. He was *ka* 1 Nov 1914

2b Hermione Edith Agnes; *m* 30 July 1918 Capt Guy Edward Pelham-Clinton, MC, and had issue (*see* LINCOLN, E)

1a Emily Katherine; *m* 8 Nov 1888 George Ralph FitzRoy Cole, of Heatham Ho, Twickenham, and *d* 4 Nov 1940, leaving issue. He *d* 1 March 1910

2a Mary Rowena; *d* unm 25 March 1934

(2) Albert; *b* 17 Dec 1832; Bengal Artillery; *d* 28 April 1854

(1) Melanie Sophia; *m* 29 June 1849 Raymond Louis Abrial, est *s* of Raymond Benjamin Abrial, of Montauban, and *d* 19 July 1894

(2) Laura; *m* 7 Nov 1859 Albert, Count de Lastic St Jal, of Pomponna, France, and *d* his widow 8 Dec 1908, leaving issue

4 Hugh Francis (Rev); *b* 19 Sept 1802; Rector Harrington, Northants; *m* 22 June 1824 Matilda (*d* 29 Nov 1873), 5th dau of Joseph Hume, of Notting Hill, and *d* 2 March 1890, leaving, with two daus (*d* unm):

(1) Ralph William Lyonel TALMASH later TOLLEMACHE-TOLLEMACHE (Rev), JP; *b* 19 Oct 1826; MA Cantab; Rector S Witham, Lincs; *m* 1st 15 Feb 1853 his cousin Caroline (*d* 6 June 1867), only dau of Hon Felix Thomas Talmash (*see* above), and had, with a dau (Evelyne Clementina Wentworth Cornelia Maude, *d* unm):

1a LYONEL FELIX CARTERET EUGENE (Sir), **4th Bt**

2a Granville Gray Marchmont Manners Plantagenet; *b* 8 June 1858; *dsp* 20 April 1891

3a Marchmont Murray Grasett Reginald Stanhope Plantagenet; *b* 24 Dec 1860; *dsp* 10 April 1898

1a Florence Caroline Artemisia Hume; *m* 1st 4 Aug 1884 Maj William Pink Lonsdale. He *d* 11 Sept 1899. She *m* 2nd 1 Nov 1900 Col Thomas Hale, Connaught Rangers, and *d* 24 May 1915. He *d* 8 Feb 1907

(1) (cont.) The Rev Ralph Tollemache-Tollemache *m* 2nd 22 Feb 1869 Dora Cleopatra Maria Lorenza (*d* 8 Aug 1929), dau of Col Ignacio Antonio de Orellana y Revest, of the Spanish Army, and *d* 5 Oct 1895, having by her had:

4a Lyulph Ydwallo Odin Nestor Egbert Lyonel Toedmag Hugh Erchenwyne Saxon Esa Cromwell Orma Nevill Dysart Plantagenet; *b* 21 Aug 1876; *m* 1st 15 July 1897 Winifred Frances (*d* 1955), dau of Thomas Goldsbrough Anderson, of Tauranga, NZ; *m* 2nd 1957 *Kathleen, widow of Robert William Alexander Godfrey Gordon, of Huia, NZ, and dau of Michael Hinge, of Northolt, Middx, and *d* 1961, having by his 1st w had:

1b Lyulph Thomas; *b* 24 May 1899; *m* 1st 1924 (*divorce* 1943) Mavis, dau of Rev Charles Tuke, of Ellerslie, NZ; *m* 2nd 29 July 1946 his cousin *Phyllis Agnes Barham, yr dau of Maj Frederick Pitcairn Nunneley, OBE, MD, of Derrymore, Llandrindod Wells, Radnorshire, and *d* 17 Feb 1977, having by his 1st w had:

1c +Lyulph Hugh Tuke, MCSP London; *b* 1933; *m* 13 Aug 1960 his cousin *Nadja, er dau of U Victor Benziger, of Kappelmatt, Switzerland, by Eva, only dau of Capt Leo de Orellana Tollemache, FRGS (*see* below), and has:

1d +Ralph Victor Thomas; *b* 1968

2d +Damon Leo; *b* 1969

1d *Rachel Eva; *b* 27 Aug 1961

2d *Amanda Beatrice; *b* 6 July 1963

3d *Melanie Ruth *b* 24 Aug 1964

4d *Vanessa Mavis; *b* 24 Aug 1964

5d *Althea Phyllis Jessica; *b* 13 Jan 1967

1c *Diana Rosemary, JP (Croydon 1969); *b* 1928; *educ* U of NZ (BA 1949); *m* 1949 Saiyad Zarbaft Shah and has:

1d *Saiyad Mubarak; *b* 1959

1d *Layla Irene Zarbaft; *b* Dec 1949

2d *Shireen Haseena; *b* 1952

2b +Adrian Francis; *b* 1903; *m* 21 Jan 1938 *Una Florence, dau of Lionel Edward Mackenzie, of Perth, W Australia, and has:

1c +John Jeffrey; *b* 2 Jan 1941

2c +Peter Clive; *b* 7 April 1948

1c *Joan; *b* 27 Dec 1945

3b +Saxon George; *b* 1904; *m* 23 Aug 1933 *Ruth Bell, dau of Frederick George Wayne, and has:

1c +John Saxon Manners; *b* 13 Oct 1943

1c *Elizabeth Mary; *b* 27 Sept 1936; *educ* U of Otago, NZ; *m* 13 Aug 1966 *Maurice John Arthur Fuller, MSc, *s* of Arthur Ernest Fuller, of Auckland, NZ, and has:

1d *Michael Arthur; *b* 3 Sept 1968

1d *Katherine Ruth; *b* 3 Nov 1969

2c *Suzannah Jane; *b* 1 Jan 1940; *m* 13 Jan 1962 John Brian Miller, ME (NZ), PhD (Auckland), er *s* of Eric John Miller, of Whangarei, NZ, and has:

1d *Hugh Benjamin Tollemache; *b* 30 June 1965

1d *Jane Elizabeth; *b* 10 June 1963

4b +Archibald Douglas; *b* 21 June 1910; NZ Forces WW II; *m* 26 Oct 1935 *Edna May, only dau of Frederick Charles Willis, of Napier, NZ, and has:

1c *Janet Winifrid; *b* 6 Aug 1936; *m* 5 Oct 1957 *William Winston Lewins, *s* of William Lewins, of Auckland, NZ, and has:

1d *Robyn Ann; *b* 8 Aug 1963

2d *Denise Gay; *b* 1 Aug 1965

2c *Yvonne Dorothy; *b* 6 May 1938; *m* 11 Feb 1961 *John Walker Robinson, *s* of John Walker Robinson, of St Heliers, Auckland, and has:

1d *Tania Anne; *b* 14 Oct 1962

2d *Vicki Jan; *b* 24 March 1964

3d *Angela Patricia; *b* 6 Nov 1967

5b +James de Orellana; *b* 1916

1b *Winifred Dora; *m* 1926 Lawrence Galwey Walker and has had:

1c *Peter Robert Tollemache; *b* 24 Jan 1928; BA, LLM; *m* 30 Dec 1961 *Yvonne Isabella, dau of John James Fleming, of Pearoa, NZ, and has:

1d *Robert James Tollemache; *b* 24 March 1963

1d *Elizabeth Jane Stewart; *b* 26 Jan 1965

2d *Catherine Frances Tollemache; *b* 25 May 1966

2c *Richard Henry Tollemache; *b* 13 Jan 1935; BCivEng 1958; *m* May 1965 *Yvonne, dau of Percy Lawrence le Marquand, of Timaru, NZ, and has:

1d *Caroline Mary; *b* April 1966

3c *Michael Lawrence Galwey; *b* Dec 1939; *m* Feb 1961 *Kathleen Rosemary, dau of John Norris Buckland, of Little River, Christchurch, NZ, and has:

1d *Peter Lawrence Galwey; *b* 14 Nov 1962

2d *Andrew John Norris; *b* 23 April 1964

3d *Christopher Michael Tollemache; *b* 17 Aug 1966

1d *Michelle Kathleen; *b* 28 Sept 1961

1c Madeleine Frances Galwey; *b* 7 Dec 1930; *d* 14 May 1964

2c *Lyonella Marie Tollemache; *b* 13 May 1933; *m* 1963 *Henry Lynn Thetford and has:

1d *John Henry; *b* 2 Dec 1966

3c *Helen Dora Tollemache; *b* 19 Feb 1937; *m* 1959 *Colin Pringle Robertson, *s* of Robert Robertson, and has:

1d *Colin Lawrence; *b* 30 Nov 1961

1d *Maryann Madeleine; *b* 25 April 1960

2d *Sarah Jane; *b* 19 Aug 1964

3d *Jayne Winifred; *b* 12 Sept 1966

2b *Celia Kathrine Mabel; *m* 1927 Charles Tennant Smith and has:

1c *Guthrie Tennant; *b* 1933; *m* 1955 *Louise Florence, dau of Col Le Lievre, and has:

1d *Denys Guthrie; *b* 1957

2d *Gregory Tennant; *b* 27 July 1963

1d *Tressa Rawhiti; *b* 1955

2d *Julie Louise; *b* 1956

3b *Ethel Mary

4b *Vivien Rosamund; *m* 12 Nov 1934 Rev Harold Graham Titterton, LTh, Vicar St John's, Otumoetai, Tauranga, NZ, only *s* of Ernest Patrick Titterton, LRCP, LRCS, and has:

1c *Graham Richard; *b* 22 Sept 1947

1c *Jennifer Graham; *b* 16 July 1937; *m* 11 Jan 1964 *John Yeates and has:

1d *Christopher John; *b* 10 Oct 1964

2d *Peter Graham; *b* 8 July 1967

5b *Ruth Loraine; *m* 1944 *Ivan Edward Salter Bartlett and has:

1c *Timothy John; *b* 18 Jan 1951

1c *Jacqueline Jane; *b* 23 June 1949

5a Leo de Orellana TOLLEMACHE-TOLLEMACHE later TOLLEMACHE (roy licence 1908); *b* 19 Nov 1879; FRGS, Capt Lincs Regt; *m* 10 Sept 1906 Jessie Winifred (*d* 12 Jan 1967), dau of Charles Bryant, and *d* 1 Nov 1914, having had:

1b Gerald; *b* 25 Aug 1909; *d* 13 Aug 1911

2b +Frederick (Rev); *b* 28 Nov 1910; *educ* Keble Coll Oxford (BA 1931); RC priest

3b +Robert (Rev), TD; *b* 16 June 1914; *educ* Charterhouse and St Edmund's Coll Ware; RC priest, Chaplain WW II, Sr Chaplain Scottish Cmd

1b *Eva; *b* 13 Aug 1908; *m* 1935 U Victor Benziger (*d* Nov 1962) and has:

1c *Roderick Rupert Victor Leo; *b* 6 Feb 1938; *educ* Queen's Coll Oxford (BA 1959, MA 1963)

2c *Carl Dietrich Nicolaus Meinrad; *b* 29 March 1939; GIMechE 1960

3c *Stanislaus Quintus Rudolf; *b* 15 Nov 1945; *educ* RAM (GRSM, ARCO 1966)

1c *Nadja; *b* 15 July 1936; *educ* Somerville Coll Oxford (BA 1957, MA 1961); barrister Middle Temple 1960; *m* 13 Aug 1960 her cousin Lyulph Hugh Tuke Tollemache (*see* above) and has issue

2c *Dorothea Rosemary; *b* 16 Nov 1941; *m* 1968 *Nirmal Kumar Mazumdar, MS, FRCS (Edin), and has:

1d *Abhigit Victor; *b* 1 Nov 1969

1d *Anita Nadja; *b* 23 Sept 1968

6a Leone Sextus; *b* 10 June 1884; Capt Leics Regt, Bde Maj 1916; *m* 23 April 1914 Kathleen Mary (*d* 4 March 1915), yr dau of Capt J Mills, 3rd Dragoon Gds, and *das* 20 Feb 1917, leaving:

1b +Denys Herbert George; *b* 12 Jan 1915; *educ* Magdalene Coll Cambridge (BA 1936); F/Lt RAF Res WW II; *m* 14 April 1939 (*divorce* 1948) Eileen Frances Mary, dau of Owen Phelim O'Connor, The O'Conor Don, and has:

1c +Peter Denys; *b* 28 Oct 1940

2c +Nicholas Jon; *b* 20 Dec 1943

3c +Stephen Patrick; *b* 30 Jan 1946

1c *Susan Frances; *b* 2 Oct 1939

2c *Linda Mary; *b* 26 Jan 1945

7a Lyonulph Cospatrick Bruce Berkeley Jermyn Tullibardine Petersham de Orellana Dysart Plantagenet; *b* 11 Jan 1892; *educ* Winchester and New Coll Oxford (BA 1915, MA 1920); Maj TARO, Headmaster ISC Windsor 1935–41; *m* 22 Sept 1914 Lilian May (*d* 17 March 1969 aged 80), dau of Ernest T W Pearse, of Kamloops, BC, and *d* 30 Nov 1960, leaving:

1b +Miles de Orellana; *b* 4 April 1918; Lt RNVR; *m* 1st 18 April 1942 (*divorce*) Diana Muriel, dau of C C Hatry; *m* 2nd (*divorce*) Margaret, dau of Henry Williams, of Llwyn Gwern, Pontardulais; *m* 3rd 1949 *Joan Doreen, dau of G Saxon, and by her has:

1c +Timothy Miles Saxon; *b* 1950

2c +Bruce Robert Saxon; *b* 1951

3c +(Alastair) Murray Saxon; *b* 1953; *m* 19– *Ali Bluck and has:

1d +Duff Edward Yorke; *b* Oct 1989

4c +Iain Stuart William Saxon; *b* 1961

1c *Elspeth Mary Joan; *b* 1956

2a Dora Viola; *d* 4 July 1874

3a Mabel Helmingham; *b* 11 March 1872; *m* 1st 1 Sept 1896 Rev William Bryant, Vicar Clanfield, Oxon. He *d* 4 March 1927. She *m* 2nd 1950 Morgan Bletsoe and *d* 5 Jan 1955. He *d* 5 Jan 1955

4a Lyonesse Matilda Dora; *b* 9 Nov 1874; *m* 4 May 1897 Francis William Astley Cooper and *d* 26 Aug 1944, leaving issue (*see* COOPER, Bt, of Gadebridge)

5a Lyona Decima Veronica; *b* 19 April 1878; *m* 21 Jan 1909 Maj Charles Cecil Stone (*d* 1951) and *d* 17 Nov 1962, leaving:

1b *Lyonel Francis Tollemache; *b* 18 Oct 1909; Capt Coldstream Gds WW II; *m* 1st 5 Aug 1943 (*divorce* 1951) Mathilde Baldwin, dau of G Henry A Thomas, of New Orleans, and has:

1c *Michael Tollemache; *b* 12 Sept 1949

1c *Mathilde Thomas; *b* 1 Nov 1945; *educ* U of Madrid; *m* 29 July 1967 *Prieur James Leary, Jr, s of Prieur James Leary, of New Orleans, and has:

1d *Prieur James; *b* 23 Dec 1968

1b (cont.) Lyonel Tollemache *m* 2nd 19 Jan 1952 (*divorce* 1966) Marie Elodie, dau of Francis Marion Attaway, of New Orleans; *m* 3rd 17 Jan 1972 Wistane Claire, dau of Perus Marthond, of Paris

6a Lyonella Fredegunda; *b* 14 Jan 1882; *m* 17 May 1906 Frederick Pitcairn Nunneley, OBE, MD, of Derrymore, Llandrindod Wells (*d* 17 Dec 1922), est s of Rev Frederick Barham Nunneley, and *d* 3 Oct 1952, leaving:

1b Lyonella Joan Tollemache; *b* 2 Sept 1907; *m* 12 Dec 1935 Ernest Robin Vladimir Kindersley, s of Robin Kindersley, and *d* 14 March 1998, leaving:

1c *Patricia Dora Maria; *b* 29 Aug 1936

2b *Phyllis Agnes Barham; *b* 28 Feb 1909; *m* 29 July 1946 her cousin Lyulph Thomas Tollemache (*see above*)

7a Lyonetta Edith Valentine; *b* 14 Feb 1887; *m* 25 Feb 1909 Adolph Paul Oppé, CB, FBA (*d* 29 March 1957), 3rd s of S A Oppé, and *d* 7 Jan 1951, leaving:

1b Denys Lyonel Tollemache, MBE (1945); *b* 30 Jan 1913; *educ* Winchester and Trin Coll Cambridge; Maj Roy Berks Regt (TA) WW II; *m* 28 May 1949 *Jean Mary, dau of Charles Struthers White Ogilvie, of Delvine, Murthly, Perthshire, and Lady Clifford of Chudleigh (*qv*), and had:

1c *John Simon Tollemache; *b* 23 May 1951; *educ* Ampleforth

1c *Lucy Valentine Mary; *b* 14 Feb 1950

2c *Charlotte Mary Clare; *b* 26 May 1954

3c *Mary Josephine; *b* 2 Jan 1956

1b Armide Lyonesse Tollemache; *b* 25 March 1910; *d* unm 9 Oct 1995

(2) Clement Reginald (Rev); *b* 11 March 1835; *educ* BNC Oxford (MA); *m* 19 Jan 1869 Frances Josephine (*d* 26 Dec 1925), 3rd dau of Henry Simpson, of Seville, Portobello, and *d* 12 Nov 1895, leaving:

1a Mary; *m* 23 July 1903 Rev Bernard Charles Spencer Everett, MVO, Minor Canon St George's Chapel, Windsor, Chaplain Br Legation Copenhagen, 8th s of Rev A J Everett, and *d* 2 Aug 1955. He *d* 28 Aug 1943

2a Grace; *d* unm 19 March 1952

3a Æthel; *d* unm 26 May 1955

(3) Ernest Celestine (Rev); *b* 7 Jan 1838; *educ* Pembroke Coll Oxford (BA); Vicar of Well, Bedale, Yorks; *m* 8 Nov 1870 Henrietta Maria (*d* 16 Dec 1907), yr dau of Col Henry Dixon, of The Woodlands, Birkenhead, and *d* 16 Dec 1880, leaving:

1a Hugh Ernest; *b* 15 Aug 1871; *m* 27 Jan 1898 Caroline Mary (*d* 7 July 1957), dau of John Payne, and *d* 30 Jan 1936, leaving:

1b John Ernest; *b* 19 Nov 1898; *educ* RMC Sandhurst; Maj Gordon Highrs, WW I 1917–18 and WW II; *m* 19 Sept 1921 Violet Edith Gertrude, dau of W Rae Sands, and *d* 7 April 1969, leaving:

1c *Lyona Violet Anne Tollemache; *b* 17 Dec 1929; *m* 3 Aug 1950 Lt-Cdr Richard Milford Power Carne, RN, est s of Capt William Power Carne, RN, of Tresahor, Constantine, Cornwall, and has:

1d *William Lyonel Power; *b* 28 March 1957

1d *Caroline Julia Tollemache; *b* 5 May 1951

2d *Karenza Lyona Tollemache; *b* 6 May 1953

2a Henry Gilbert; *b* 7 March 1874; *m* 6 Jan 1895 Mary Elizabeth (*d* 17 June 1902), dau of William Morris, and *d* 3 Nov 1940, leaving:

1b Douglas Hugh; *b* 24 June 1898; Cdr (E) RN WW II; *m* 14 April 1931 *Alys Kynaston (*m* 2nd 1943 Cdr Richard Tolson, DSC, RN), dau of Rev John Henry Bebbington, Canon Chichester, Rector Slinfold, Sussex, and *das* in HMS *Bonaventure* 31 March 1941, leaving:

1c +Ian Henry Douglas [Ian Tollemache Esq, 265 Kings Road, London SW3 5EL]; *b* 1 Oct 1936; *educ* Lancing; *m* 1 Dec 1973 *Priscilla Anne, dau of Lt-Col D E Coker, of Friars Farm, Aldham, Essex

1c *Sheila Rosemary Edith; *b* 19 March 1939; *m* 20 April 1963 *Thomas Barry Nightingale, FCA, s of Thomas Nightingale, of Glandwr Hall, Barmouth, Merioneth, and has:

1d *Lucy Frances; *b* 9 March 1964

2d *Kate Elizabeth; *b* 23 Oct 1965

3d *Anna Ruth; *b* 2 Dec 1967

1b Dorothy Clare; *m* 1921 Arthur Edward Durling and *d* 1949, leaving:

1c *John Alfred Osborne; *b* 1929

1c *Pauline Mary Tollemache; *b* 1924; *m* 1954 *John Ingham Brooke and has issue

3a *Ralph Charles; *b* 14 Nov 1875

4a Reginald Douglas; *b* 24 March 1877; *d* 30 June 1916

1a Gwendoline Anna; *m* 3 Dec 1907 Gilbert Henderson Philips, er s of Rev Canon Gilbert Henderson Philips, and *d* 23 Aug 1945, leaving issue. He *d* 1 July 1936

(4) Augustus Francis (Rev); *b* 6 Sept 1839; *educ* Exeter Coll Oxford (MA); Vicar Whitwick Leics 1874–94; *d* 10 March 1923

(5) Anastasius Eugene; *b* 22 July 1842; Capt and Musketry Instr 22nd Foot; *m* 1 March 1870 Alice Elizabeth (*d* 11 March 1936), only surv child of Rev Curzon Cursham, of Hartwell, Northants, and *d* 16 March 1912, leaving:

1a Eugene Saxon Hengist Curzon Stewart; *b* 10 Nov 1875; Roy Fus; *d* unm 23 Sept 1944

2a Harold Wilbraham Molyneux; *b* 7 April 1881; Capt 1st Bn Beds and Herts Regt WW I (wounded), HG WW II; *m* 4 Dec 1913 Evelyn (*d* 25 May 1969), 2nd dau of Capt Frederick Southampton Le Strange FitzRoy, 15th Foot (*see* SOUTHAMPTON, B), and *dsp* 7 Aug 1966

3a Lyonel Alexander Arthur; *b* 29 July 1887; Capt 9th (Serv) Bn Rifle Bde WW I 1914–15 (wounded); *d* unm 20 Feb 1940

1a Alice Dysart Evelyn Stewart; *d* unm 21 Sept 1941

2a Matilda Amy Jane Ellen Louisa Manners; *d* unm 9 Aug 1926

3a Eugenia Saxonia Valeria Cornelia; *d* unm 22 July 1970

4a Louisa Ethelgiva Rowena; *m* 5 April 1910 Lt-Col Walter Francis Courtenay Chichele Plowden, IA, and *d* 19 March 1962, leaving issue. He *d* 28 Dec 1918

5a Dorothy Agnes Catherine

(1) Matilda Anne Frances; *m* 30 March 1869 Rev George Edmond Maunsell, Rector Thorpe Malsor, Kettering, and *d* 6 Feb 1899. He *d* 29 Oct 1875

(2) Louisa Harrington; *m* 11 Nov 1862 Col Rt Hon Thomas Edward Taylour (*see* HEADFORT, M) and *d* 9 April 1928, leaving issue

5 Frederick James; *b* 16 April 1804; MP Grantham; *m* 1st 26 Aug 1831 Sarah (*d* 3 Jan 1845), dau of Robert Bomford, of Rahinstown, Co Meath, and had a dau (*d* unm); *m* 2nd 4 Sept 1847 Isabella Anne (*d* 30 Aug 1850), est dau of George Gordon Forbes, and *d* 2 July 1888, leaving by her had:

(1) Ada Maria Katherine; *m* 9 May 1868 4th Baron Sudeley (*qv*) and *d* 6 Jan 1928, leaving issue

6 Algernon Gray; *b* 24 Sept 1805; MP Grantham 1832–37; *m* 28 Sept 1857 his cousin Frances Louisa (*d* 15 April 1893), widow of Lt George Richard Halliday, RN, and est dau of Hon Charles Tollemache (*see* DYSART, E), and *d* 16 Jan 1892

1 Louisa; *m* 9 Aug 1816 Sir Joseph Burke, 11th Bt, of Glinsk (*qv*), and *d* 18 April 1830, leaving issue

2 Catherine Camilla; *m* 1 May 1816 Sir George Sinclair, 2nd Bt, and *d* 17 March 1863, leaving issue (*see* THURSO, V)

3 Laura Maria; *m* 7 Aug 1847 Rt Hon James Grattan, of Tinnehinch, Co Wicklow, and *d* 12 July 1888 aged 81. He *d* 24 Oct 1854

The 3rd Bt's cousin,

Sir Lyonel Felix Carteret Eugene Tollemache, 4th Bt; *b* 15 Jan 1854; *educ* Jesus Coll Cambridge (BA 1876); Govr Star and Garter Home Richmond; *m* 22 June 1881 Hersilia Henrietta Diana (*d* 10 May 1953), dau of Henry Richard Oliphant, and *d* 4 March 1952, leaving:

1 **Sir (Cecil) Lyonel Newcomen Tollemache, 5th Bt**; *b* 14 March 1886; *d* unm 31 March 1969

2 John Eadred; *b* 28 July 1892; *educ* Magdalene Coll Cambridge (BA); Lt 8th Serv Bn Roy W Surrey Regt; *ka* 21 Aug 1916

3 HUMPHRY THOMAS (Sir), **6th Bt**

1 Beryl Hersilia; *d* unm 8 June 1944

2 Cynthia Joan Caroline; *m* 16 July 1918 Harry Scott Judd (*d* 1 June 1948), of Maces Place, Rickling, Essex, and *d* 31 Jan 1988, having had:

(1) *Anthony Hubert Scott; *b* 13 Aug 1919; FRAM; *m* 25 Feb 1956 Gloria Michelle (*d* 26 Dec 1997), dau of Harry Solloway of Los Angeles, and has had:

1a Terence Dominic; *b* 3 Oct 1957; pianist; *d* Dec 1979

1a *Diana Caroline; *b* 27 April 1963; LRAM

(2) John Harry Manners; *b* 8 July 1924; *m* 1 July 1954 *Sarah, yr dau of Gerald Millar, of Temes, Little Sampford, Essex and *d* 4 Oct 1958, leaving:

1a *Christopher John Henry; *b* 5 Oct 1957; *m* 19 Jan 1980 *Emma Mary Powell, est dau of Paul Williams, of Elmbridge Mill, Little Easton, Essex, and has:

1b *Thomas Jack Francis; *b* 21 Feb 1984

2b *Harry Mark Christopher; *b* 23 Dec 1985

1b *Katherine Mary; *b* 16 Nov 1981

1a *Isabella Sarah Veronica; *b* 2 April 1955

(1) *Barbara Hersilia; *b* 17 April 1926

3 Sibell Agnes; *m* 11 Feb 1933 Keith Guy Mayhewe, only s of Arthur Mayhewe, JP, DL, of Wyfolds, Eastbourne, and *dsp* 7 June 1954. He *d* 13 Feb 1954

The 5th Bt's bro,

Sir Humphry Thomas Tollemache, 6th Bt, CB (1952), CBE (1950), DL (Hants 1965); *b* 10 Aug 1897; *educ* Eastbourne Coll; served WW I 1916–18, Adj Depot RM 1929–31, Bde Maj 1936–39, WW II as CO 12th Bn RM 1941 and Landing Unit Middle East 1942, Col cmdg Small Ops Gp Far East 1944–45, A/Col cmdg RM depot 1946–47, CO Pay and Records Office RM 1947–49, Maj-Gen cmdg Portsmouth Gp RM 1949–52, ret 1952, Hon Col Cmdt Portsmouth Gp RM 1958–60, Col Cmdt RM 1961–62, Rep Col Cmdt 1962, memb Petersfield UDC 1954–59, Hants: CC 1957, CA 1969; *m* 6 Feb 1926 Nora Priscilla (*d* 1990), 2nd dau of John Taylor, of Broomhill, Eastbourne, and *d* 1990, leaving:

1 Sir LYONEL HUMPHRY JOHN TOLLEMACHE, **7th and present Bt**
2 +Robert Hugh Thomas [Robert Tollemache Esq, 27 Aubert Pk, London N5 1TP]; *b* 22 Feb 1937; *educ* Uppingham and Magdalene Coll Cambridge (BA 1960); *m* 25 Aug 1962 *Lorraine Frances Lougheed, est dau of Brig Frederick Joshua Allen, OBE, of Hambledon Cottage, Farnham, Surrey, and has adopted:
  *William Benjamin; *b* 20 May 1966; *educ* City of London Sch and UCL
  *Rosa Frances Laila; *b* 1970
1 *Priscilla Joan [Mrs John Gillett, Gulworthy Farm, Tavistock, Devon]; *b* 28 March 1927; *m* 19 April 1952 *John Chetwynd Gillett, yst s of Sir Alan Gillett, TD, DL (*see* CHETWYND, V), and has:
  (1) *Robert John Chetwynd [Robert Gillett Esq, Rock Pk, Gulworthy Farm, Tavistock, Devon]; *b* 31 Dec 1954; *educ* Blundell's; *m* 1977 *Clara Elizabeth, dau of Gordon William Heath, PhD, of Paignton, Devon, and has:
    1a *Ella Clare; *b* 1980
    2a *Sophie Louise; *b* 1982
  (2) *Andrew William Tollemache [Andrew Gillett Esq, 72 Heavitree Rd, Exeter, Devon]; *b* 22 June 1958; *m* 1979 *Rosemary McMahon and has:
    1a *David; *b* 1983
    2a *Edward; *b* 1989
    1a *Esther; *b* 1980
  (1) *(Diana) Mary; *b* 21 May 1953; *m* 1983 *Hugh Davies [Hugh Davies Esq, Cherry Brook House, Tavistock, Devon] and *d* 27 April 1996, leaving:
    1a *Peter; *b* 1987
    2a *Thomas (twin); *b* 1987
  (2) *Sara Jane [Mrs Michael Woolley, Roundabarrow Farm, St Anne's Chapel, Cornwall]; *b* 18 March 1962; *m* 1989 *Michael Woolley and has:
    1a *Daniel; *b* 1991
    1a *Alice; *b* 1990
2 Diana Margaret; *b* 20 April 1929; *m* 18 July 1953 *Daniel Johannes Haak, s of Daniel Haak, of Groede, Netherlands, and *d* 27 April 1996, leaving:
  (1) *Jonathan Daniel; *b* 8 Sept 1955; *educ* Millfield; *m* 1978 *Annabella Edith, dau of John Wickin, of Eastergate, Chichester, and has:
    1a *Jochen Daniel; *b* 1981
    1a *Anoushka Lara; *b* 1979
    2a *Naomi Tara; *b* 1985
  (2) *Roderick Johannes; *b* 3 Aug 1957; *m* 1980 *Nicola Jane, dau of Michael Cameron, MD, FRCS, FRCOG, and has:
    1a *Sam Michael; *b* 1984
    2a *Toby Daniel (twin); *b* 1984
    3a *Charlie; *b* 1985
    1a *Poppy Anna; *b* 1990
  (1) *Venetia Priscilla; *b* 6 June 1959; *m* 1988 *Phillip Robinson, of Southampton, and has:
    1a *Tristan Joshua; *b* 1994
  (2) *Felicity Nora; *b* 16 April 1961; *m* 1987 *Colin Rodger, of Petersfield, and has:
    1a *Megan Diana; *b* 1988
    2a *Hannah Margaret; *b* 1990
    3a *Tamsin Janna; *b* 1994

TOMBS

Arms: Azure on a saltire azure fimbriated argent a sun, its four rays in saltire extended and tipped with flame, all gold. **Crest:** Out of a crown rayonny or, each straight ray ending in a mullet or, a dexter arm embowed vested azure, the hand proper holding two keys in saltire, bows upwards gold. **Supporters:** Dexter, a unicorn argent, armed, unguled, bearded, maned and tufted or, sejant erect upon a grassy mount proper between two double roses, growing therefrom argent on gules and both barbed and seeded, stalked and leaved proper; sinister; a bear proper, clawed and muzzled or, sejant erect upon a like mount between two thistles growing therefrom also proper. **Motto:** Work and pray. **Creation:** B. (LP, UK) 1990.

THE BARON TOMBS, of Brailes, Co Warwick (Sir Francis Leonard Tombs) [The Rt Hon The Lord Tombs, Honington Lodge, Honington, Warwicks CV36 5AA]; *b* 17 May 1924; *educ* Elmore Green Sch Walsall, Birmingham Tech and London U (BSc); GEC 1939–45; Birmingham Corp 1946–47, Br Elec Authority and Centl Electricity Authority 1948–57; gen manager GEC Erith 1958–67; dir and gen manager James Howden & Co 1967–68; Scotland Electricity Bd: dir engrg, dep-chm, chm 1969–77; Chm: Electricity Cncl 1977–80, Weir Gp 1981–83, Turner & Newall 1982–89, Rolls-Royce 1985–92 (Dir 1982–92), Advsy Cncl Applied R&D 1985–87 (memb 1984–87), Engrg Cncl 1985–88, Advsy Cncl Sci and Tech 1987–90, Assoc Br Orchestras 1982–86, Ho Lds Select Ctee Sustainable Devpt 1994–, Old Mutual S Africa Tst 1994–, ktd 1978; dir: N M Rothschild & Sons 1981–94, Shell UK 1983–94; Pres: IEE 1982–82, Molecule Theatre Co 1993 (Chm 1985–92); V-Pres: FEng, Engrs for Disaster Relief 1985–94; memb: Nature Conservancy Cncl 1978–82, Standing Commn Energy and Environment 1978–, SERC 1982–85; Pro-Chllr and Chm Cncl Cranfield Inst Tech 1985–91; Chllr Strathclyde U 1991–98; Liveryman and Assist Warden Goldsmiths' Co; Freeman City London; Hon LLD Strathclyde U 1976; Hon DSc: Aston U 1979, Lodz U Poland 1980, Cranfield 1985, City U 1986, Bradford U 1986, Queen's U Belfast 1986, Surrey U 1988, Nottingham U 1989, Warwick 1990, Cambridge 1990; Hon DTech Loughborough U 1979; Hon DEd CNAA 1989; DU Strathclyde 1991; FEng 1977; Hon Fell: IEE 1991, IMechE 1989, ICE 1986, IChemE 1985, IProdE 1986; FRAeS 1994; Hon Memb Br Nuclear Energy Soc; *m* 1949 *Marjorie, dau of Albert Evans, of Walsall, and has:
  1 *Catherine Barbara; *b* 1950
  2 *Elisabeth Jane; *b* 1952
  3 *Margaret Clare; *b* 1958

Lineage: JOSEPH TOMBS; *m* Jane — and had:

FRANCIS LEONARD, *cr* a **Baron**

TOPE

Creation: B. (LP, UK) 20 Aug 1994.

THE BARON TOPE, of Sutton, London Borough of Sutton (Graham Norman Tope, CBE (1991)) [The Rt Hon The Lord Tope CBE, 88 The Gallop, Sutton, Surrey SM2 5SA]; *b* 30 Nov 1943; *educ* Whitgift Sch Croydon; company sec 1965–72, Insce manager 1970–72, Dep Gen Sec Vol Action Camden 1975–90, Pres Nat League Young Libs 1973–75 (V-Chm 1971–73), memb Lib Pty Nat Cncl 1970–76, exec ctee London Lib Pty 1981–84 and Pres London Lib Dems 1991–, Sutton Cncl: memb 1974–, leader Lib Dem Gp 1988–, leader oppn 1984–86, leader 1986–; MP (Lib) Sutton and Cheam 1972–Feb 1974 (Lib parly candidate Oct 1974), Lib spokesman environment Dec 1972–74, Lib Dem spokesman educn Ho Lds 1994–; Assist Whip 1998–; author: *Liberals and the Community* (1974); *m* 1972 *Margaret East and has:
  1 *Andrew; *b* 1974
  2 *David; *b* 1976

Lineage: LESLIE TOPE, of Plymouth; *m* Winifred Merrick, of Bermuda, and had:

GRAHAM NORMAN, *cr* a **Baron**

TORDOFF

Creation: B. (LP, UK) 1981.

THE BARON TORDOFF, of Knutsford, Co Chester (Geoffrey Johnson Tordoff) [The Rt Hon The Lord Tordoff, House of Lords, London SW1A 0PW]; *b* 11 Oct 1928; *educ* Manchester GS and Manchester U; Lib Party: Chm Assembly Ctee 1974–76, memb Nat Exec 1975–84, Chm Party 1976–79, Pres 1983–84; Ho Lds: Lib Ch Whip 1984–88 (Dep 1983–84), Lib Dem Ch Whip 1988–94, Chm Select Ctee EC 1994–, Pncpl Dep Chm Ctees 1994–; Chm Middle East Ctee Refugee Cncl 1990–95; Memb Press Complaints Commn 1995–; *m* 1953 *Mary Patricia, dau of Thomas Swarbrick, of Leeds, and has:
  1 *Nicholas Gregory; *b* 1958
  2 *Mark Edmund; *b* 1962
  1 *Mary Catherine; *b* 1954
  2 *Frances Jane; *b* 1956
  3 *Paula Mary; *b* 1960

Lineage: STANLEY ACOMB TORDOFF; *m* Annie Johnson and had:

GEOFFREY JOHNSON, *cr* a **Baron**

TORPHICHEN

SPERO · MELIORA

Arms: Quarterly, 1st and 4th, argent on a chief azure an Imperial crown or, in base a thistle vert, flowered gules; 2nd and 3rd, grand quarters, 1st and 4th argent, a bend azure (for SANDILANDS); 2nd and 3rd, argent a human heart proper, ensigned by an Imperial crown gules, on a chief azure three mullets of the field (for DOUGLAS). **Crest:** An eagle displayed proper. **Supporters:** Two savages wreathed round the loins and temples with oak leaves, each holding on the exterior shoulder a club proper. **Motto:** *Spero meliora* ('I hope for better things'). **Creation:** L. (S) 24 Jan 1564.

THE 15TH LORD TORPHICHEN, of Saint John of Torphichen, W Lothian (James Andrew Douglas Sandilands) [The Rt Hon The Lord Torphichen, Calder House, Mid-Calder, W Lothian EH53 0HN]; *b* 27 Aug 1946; *s* f 1975; *m* 3 July 1976 *Margaret Elizabeth, only dau of William A Beale, of Peterborough, NH, and has:

1 *Margaret Elizabeth Grizel; *b* 1979
2 *Mary Christian Sarah; *b* 1981
3 *Anne; *b* 19–
4 *Alison; *b* 19–

Lineage: JAMES SANDILANDS, of Sandilands, Clydesdale, confirmed to him 18 Dec 1348 by his bro-in-law William, Lord Douglas, as also by the same person the lands of Calder; *m* by 1349, as her 2nd husb of five, Eleanor, only sis of 1st Earl of Douglas (*see* QUEENSBERRY, M) and widow of Alexander Bruce, 1st and last Earl of Carrick (*qv*, preliminary remarks) of the *c* 1330 *cr*, and *d* by 1358, leaving an er s:

Sir JAMES SANDILANDS, 2nd of Calder; Margaret, Countess of Angus and Mar (*see* MORAY, E), engineered his renunciation (roy confirmation 1397) of any succession to the unentailed Douglas estates in favour of George Douglas, 1st Earl of Angus of the 1389 *cr* (*see* HAMILTON and BRANDON, D), her illegitimate s by 1st Earl of Douglas; *m* 1384 JOAN, dau of ROBERT II, and widow (a) of Sir John Keith (*see* KINTORE, E) and (b) Sir John Lyon of Glamis (*see* STRATHMORE AND KINGHORNE, E), and had:

Sir JAMES SANDILANDS, 3rd of Calder; a hostage in England for JAMES I 1421; heir of line of the DOUGLASes by death of 2nd Earl of Douglas and Isabel, Countess of Mar, 1407, hence the SANDILANDS' quartering the DOUGLAS arms; *d* by Dec 1426, leaving, with a yr s (James, assassinated with his n John):

Sir JOHN SANDILANDS, 4th of Calder; *m* Christian, 2nd dau of James Dundas of Dundas, and *d* 1439, having had, with an er s (John, *b c* 1431, assassinated 21 Aug 1451 for loyalty to JAMES II by Patrick Thornton, an adherent of the DOUGLASes):

Sir JAMES SANDILANDS, 5th of Calder; *m* 1st (dispensation 25 July 1463) Margaret, dau and heiress of John Kinloch of Curvie; *m* 2nd Margaret (*m* 2nd *c* 17 May 1509, as his 2nd w, 4th Earl of Erroll, *qv*), dau of Andrew Kerr of Aultountburn and Cessford (*see* LOTHIAN, M), and *d* by 1505, having had three sons (James, of Cravie, ancestor of Sir James Sandilands *cr* Lord Abercombie (S) 12 Dec 1647, the title expiring with the death 1681 of the latter's s James; John, of Gartcarron in Lennox, *d* by 10 May 1521; Peter, Rector Calder 1526, *d c* 4 May 1549) and two daus (Margaret, *m* 1st Robert Bruce of Auchinbowie of Stirling, *m* 2nd 3rd Lord Oliphant; the other dau *m* William Dishington of Ardross and had issue) and by his 1st w, with a dau (Christian, *m* 1st by 1498 David Hepburn of Waughton (*see* BUCHAN-HEPBURN, Bt), *m* 2nd Andrew Anstruther of that Ilk; *see* ANSTRUTHER, Bt):

JOHN SANDILANDS, 6th of Calder; *m c* 15 Oct 1481 Elizabeth, dau of Sir James Scrymgeour of Dudhope (*see* DUNDEE, E), and *dvp* by 13 Feb 1493/4, leaving, with a dau (Alison, *m* by 28 April 1508 Sir Alexander Boswell of Balmuto (*ka* Flodden)):

Sir JAMES SANDILANDS, 7th of Calder; *b* 1482; supported Reformation; *m* by Feb 1507/8 Mariot/Marjorie (*d* March 1562), only dau of Archibald Forrester of Corstorphine and widow of William, Master of Drummond (*see* PERTH, E), and *d* Dec 1559, leaving:

1 John, 8th of Calder; *m* 1st (contract 17 Oct 1524) Margaret, dau of Sir Robert Bartoun of Over Barnton, High Treasurer Scotland, and had:

(1) James, 9th of Calder; *m* Jean (*m* 2nd 1580 Harry Stewart of Craigiehall), dau of 4th Lord Ross, and *d* 17 Feb 1576/7, leaving:

1a JAMES, **2nd Lord**
1a Elizabeth; *m* John Mowbray, s of John Mowbray, of Barnbough
(1) Margaret; *m* (contract 27 March 1574) Henry Drummond of Riccartoun
(2) Eupheme; living 1567

1 (cont) John Sandilands *m* 2nd (contract 24 May 1560) Johanna (*m* 3rd David Crawfurd of Kerse), dau of 2nd Lord Fleming and widow of John, Master of Livingston, and *d c* 1565, having by her had:

(2) James (Sir), of Slamannan; Capt Blackness Castle 1592; *m* 1st Jean Crawfurd; *m* 2nd Barbara Napier and had issue by both
(3) Mary; *m* (contract 15 July 1586) Joseph Douglas of Pumpherston and had issue

2 JAMES SANDILANDS, **1st Lord Torphichen** (S) or perhaps **Lord Saint John/Saint John of Torphichen**, so *cr* effectively 24 Jan 1563/4 by a regrant to himself and his heirs and assignees of the lands, (territorial) baronies, estates and offices previously attaching to the office of Prior of the Knights of St John of Jerusalem in Scotland, he having held that post from 1546, just as Scotland was being transformed by the Reformation, of which he was a supporter (the Priors of the Knights of St John had previously been entitled to a seat in Parl among both the prelates and, through holding the feudal Barony of Torphichen, the greater Barons); Kt Order St John 1530; *m* a short while before 12 Sept 1560 Janet (*m* 2nd by 9 June 1584 John Grahame of Hallyards, *m* 3rd 6 May 1596 Sir Peter Young of Seaton and *d* 29 Nov 1596), dau of William Murray of Polmaise and Touchadam, and *dsp* 29 Sept 1579

1 Alison; *m* John Cockburn of Ormiston and *d* 21 Oct 1584
2 Margaret; *m* 1st Sir James Dundas of Dundas; *m* 2nd 1560 William Wauchope of Niddry Marischal
3 Agnes; *m* James Drummond

The 1st LORD's great-nephew,
JAMES SANDILANDS, **2nd Lord Torphichen**; *b c* 1574; *m* 1st (contract 1 Aug 1595) Elizabeth, dau of James Heriot of Trabroun, and had, with three other sons:
1 JAMES SANDILANDS, **3rd Lord Torphichen**; *b* 1596–97; *d unm* Jan 1621/2
2 JOHN, **4th Lord**
3 William, of Hilderstown; *educ* Edinburgh U (MA); *m* 1st 1626 Grizel Bannatyne and had two sons and three daus; *m* 2nd 1 Jan 1641 Elizabeth, widow of Col Sir George Cunningham, and by her had a s and four daus
1 Isabel; *bapt* 28 Oct 1607; *m* Hugh Wallace of Elderslie and had issue

The **2nd Lord** *m* 2nd Mary (*m* 2nd William Douglas of Pumpherston and *d* 15 May 1620), est dau of 7th Lord Somerville, and *d* Aug 1617 without further issue

The 3rd LORD's bro,
JOHN SANDILANDS, **4th Lord Torphichen**; *b* by 1600; *educ* Edinburgh U (MA); *m* (contract 28 Feb 1623/4) Isabel, dau of Sir Walter Dundas of Dundas, and *d* 1637, having had, with other issue (*d* unm):
1 JOHN SANDILANDS, **5th Lord Torphichen**; *bapt* 11 Feb 1625; *d unm* July 1649
2 WALTER, **6th Lord**
3 William, of Couston; *bapt* 13 May 1630; *m* Mary Eastoun and had issue
1 Isabel; *m* (contract 25 April 1666) Sir Thomas Kirkpatrick, 1st Bt (*qv*)
2 Margaret; *m* Thomas Marjoribanks of that Ilk and had issue

The 5th LORD's bro,
WALTER SANDILANDS, **6th Lord Torphichen**; *bapt* 12 May 1629; Burgess Edinburgh 1660; *m* 1st shortly after 27 May 1651 Jean (*dspms* on or after 13 June 1655), only child of Alexander Lindsay, Yr. of Edzell (*see* CRAWFORD and BALCARRES, E); *m* 2nd 28 April 1657 Catherine, dau of William, Lord Alexander, and gdau of 1st Earl of Stirling, and had by her:
1 Anne; *m* Robert Menzies, est s and heir-apparent of Sir Alexander Menzies, 1st Bt, and had issue
2 Catherine; *m* 29 April 1689 David Drummond of Cultmalindie

The **6th Lord** *m* 3rd 11 April 1671 Anne, only dau of 6th Lord Elphinstone (*qv*), and by her had:
3 Lilias; *b* 20 Feb 1672

The **6th Lord** *m* 4th 1672 Christian, only dau and heiress of James Primrose (*see* ROSEBERY, E), and *d* May 1696, having by her had, with other issue:
1 JAMES, **7th Lord**
4 Christian; *m* 22 June 1704 Robert Pringle, of London

The 6th LORD's only surv son,
JAMES SANDILANDS, **7th Lord Torphichen**; Capt Earl of Mar's Regt of Foot 1702 and 7th Hus 1709, Maj Feb 1711/2, Lt-Col 1713–22 (fought Battle of Sheriffmuir 1715), Burgess Edinburgh 1717, Commr Police; *m* 1703 Lady Jean Hume (*d* 10 Dec 1751), dau of 1st Earl of Marchmont, and *d* 10 Aug 1753, having had, with three daus (*d* unm):
1 James; Ensign 25th Foot, Lt 44th Foot; *d unm* 20 April 1749 from effect of wounds recd Battle of Prestonpans 21 Sept 1745, where also taken prisoner by Jacobites
2 WALTER SANDILANDS, **8th Lord Torphichen**; *b* 16 Aug 1707; advocate 1727, Burgess Edinburgh 1742, Sheriff Depute Co Edinburgh 1748; *m* 9 June 1757 Elizabeth (*d* 27 Sept 1779), only dau and heiress of Alexander Sandilands, MD, and *d* 9 Nov 1765, leaving an est s:
(1) JAMES SANDILANDS, **9th Lord Torphichen**; *b* 15 Nov 1759; 2nd Lt 21st Foot 1776, served War American Independence, capitulating Saratoga 17 Oct 1777, Capt 24th Foot 1781 and Coldstream Gds 1787, Lt-Col 1793, ret 1795, rep S peer 1790–1802,; *m* 6 April 1795 Anne, only surv child of Sir John Inglis, 4th Bt, of Cramond, and *dsp* 7 June 1815
3 Patrick; *b* 1 Nov 1708; Cdr of an E Indiaman; *dsp* in a storm
4 Alexander; *bapt* 25 Sept 1711; *d* young
5 Andrew; Maj 21st Regt Battles of Dettingen and Fontenoy 1745 (wounded); *d* unm 27 June 1776
6 George; *b* 9 March 1717; *d* young
7 Charles; *bapt* 20 June 1720; Lt RN; *d unm* on the Cartagena Expdn 1741

8 Robert; Offr Scottish Bde in Dutch serv and Lord Aberdour's Light Dragoons; *m* Grisel (*d* 10 Feb 1776), dau of Sir Thomas Kirkpatrick, 3rd Bt (*qv*), and *d* 18 May 1791, having had, with three daus:

  (1) JAMES SANDILANDS, **10th Lord Torphichen**; *b* 21 July 1770; Capt HEINS; *m* 3 Nov 1806 Margaret Douglas (*d* 13 Dec 1836), 2nd dau of John Stirling of Kippendavie, and *d* 22 March 1862, leaving:

    1a ROBERT SANDILANDS, **11th Lord Torphichen**; *b* 3 Aug 1807; Offr Scots Fus Gds 1825–31, ret as Capt; *m* 25 July 1865 Helen (*d* 23 July 1885), yst dau of Thomas Maitland, a Ld of Session as Lord Dundrennan, and *dsp* 24 Dec 1869

    2a John (Rev); *b* 1 Nov 1813; Rector Coston, Leics; *m* 24 July 1845 Helen (*d* 29 Jan 1887), dau of James Hope, Clerk Signet, and *d* 18 March 1865, leaving:

      1b JAMES WALTER, **12th Lord**

      2b John Hope; *b* 24 July 1847; granted 7 June 1870 with surv siblings rank of Ld of Parl's dau/yr s; *m* 1 Aug 1877 Helen Mary Anne (*d* 27 Feb 1909), only dau of Thomas Tourle, of Waratah, NSW, and *d* 2 May 1903, leaving:

        1c James Bruce; *b* 9 April 1883; *m* 26 Feb 1909 Aline (*d* 1972), dau of F G Taylor, of Uralla, NSW, and *d* 5 Aug 1951, having had:

          1d James Walter, DFC; *b* 12 June 1912; RAAF WW II; *das* India 13 April 1944

          2d John Douglas; *b* 7 Dec 1915; RAAF WW II; *das* Tunis 16 Feb 1942

          3d Geoffrey Bruce Hope; *b* 10 June 1922; RAAF WW II; *m* 31 May 1944 *Dorothy Mary [Mrs Henry Carlson, 3000 Quadra St, Victoria, BC, Canada] (*m* 2nd 8 Nov 1952 Henry Myron Carlson, s of Wilfred Carlson, of Saskatchewan, and has further issue), only dau of George Nelson Joyce, of Victoria, BC, and was *ka* 16 Oct 1944, leaving:

            1e *Joyce Hope [Miss Joyce Sandilands, 4444 Tremblay Dve, Victoria, BC V8N 4W5, Canada]; *b* posthumously 13 March 1945; *m* 11 July 1964 (*divorce* 1979, resumed maiden name) Duncan Leslie Atchison, CA, and has:

              1f *James Geoffrey; *b* 14 Jan 1965

              1f *Christine Anne; *b* 19 Feb 1967; *m* 1990 *Steven Falconer, of Victoria, BC, and has:

                1g *Shayla Christine; *b* 1994

          1d *Helen Lucy [Mrs Richard Trevitt, Braeside, Uralla, NSW, Australia]; *b* 11 Dec 1909; *m* 9 Dec 1936 *Richard Riley Trevitt and has:

            1e *Richard John [Richard Trevitt Esq, Sandon, Uralla, NSW, Australia]; *b* 11 Sept 1938; *m* 5 Sept 1961 *Mollie Juanita, dau of A L Blomfield, of Quirindi, NSW, and has:

              1f *Marcus John; *b* 8 July 1964

              2f *Justin James; *b* 28 Nov 1966

              1f *Annette Juanita; *b* 16 May 1963

            2e *Simon Bruce; *b* 20 Aug 1942; *m* 11 Dec 1965 *Robyn Anne Brown and has:

              1f *Shaun Richard; *b* 1967

              1f *Fiona Jane; *b* 1969

            1e *Robin Ann Lucy; *b* 28 Oct 1939; *m* 24 June 1965 *David Edward Moore, PhD, and has:

              1f *Richard Edward; *b* 12 Aug 1966

              2f *Andrew Geoffrey; *b* 1968

              1f *Amanda Gillian; *b* 1969

          2d *Aline Dorothy [Mrs Harold Roberts, 8 Ocean View Dve, Alstonville, NSW 2477, Australia]; *b* 6 Jan 1920; *m* 1st 3 Feb 1941 Godfrey Rees-Jones, RAAF (*ka* over Germany 16 Aug 1942); *m* 2nd 29 Oct 1955, as his 2nd w (Arthur) Harold Roberts (*d* 26 Aug 1996) and has by him:

            1e *Marc Bruce [Marc Roberts Esq, Down House, 90 Down Rd, Guildford, Surrey GU1 2PZ]; *b* 19 Aug 1959; *m* 1991 *Deborah Lee Scott and has:

              1f *Brendan Marc; *b* 31 July 1997

            2e *Ian Geoffrey; *b* 1964

            1e *Julie Aline [Mrs Glenn Johns, 5 Robyn Ave, French's Forest, Sydney, NSW 2086, Australia]; *b* 27 July 1957; *m* 1979 *Glenn Raymond Johns and has:

              1f *Lee Michael; *b* 1981

              2f *Matthew Marc; *b* 1982

              3f *Adam Glenn; *b* 1984

        1c Helen Caroline; *b* 1880; *d* 1898

    3b Francis Robert; *b* 12 Jan 1849; Cdr RN, 4th Cl Osmanieh; *m* 4 June 1885 Maude Bayard (*d* 13 Sept 1936), dau of Frederick Augustus Wiggins, and *d* 30 July 1887, having had:

      1c Robert Walter; *b* 12, *d* 28 Jan 1886

    4b Douglas; *b* 23 Oct 1851; Lt 43rd Regt; *d* 23 Dec 1882

    1b Helen Jane; *m* 7 Feb 1891 Charles Woodbine Parish (*d* 7 Sept 1922), s of Sir Woodbine Parish, KCH, and *d* 13 Oct 1935, leaving issue

    3a James; *b* 2 Oct 1821; Capt 8th Hus; *d unm* 29 April 1902

    1a Mary; *m* 4 Aug 1828 William Ramsay Ramsay (*d* 14 March 1850), of Edinburgh, and *dsps* 21 Jan 1891

The 11th LORD's est n,

JAMES WALTER SANDILANDS, **12th Lord Torphichen**; *b* 4 May 1846; *educ* Eton; Capt Rifle Bde 1877, rep S peer 1894–Jan 1910 and Dec 1910–15; *m* 25 May 1881 (*divorce* 1890) Ellen Frances (*d* 1943), dau of Lt-Gen Charles Edward Parke Gordon, CB, and *d* 20 July 1915, having had:

1 James Archibald Douglas, *Master of Torphichen*; *b* 6 Oct 1884; *educ* Eton and Balliol Coll Oxford; Assist Resident Nyasaland Protectorate 1909; *dvp unm* 29 Sept 1909

2 JOHN GORDON SANDILANDS, **13th Lord Torphichen**; *b* 8 June 1886; *educ* Eton and Birmingham U; *m* 1st 3 June 1916 Grace Douglass (*d* 4 Jan 1948), 2nd dau of Winslow Pierce, of Long Island, NY; *m* 2nd 19 Sept 1950 Isabel Fernandez (*d* car crash 7 Oct 1976), dau of Richard Bowden Daniel, of Jacksonville,

Fla., and widow of Youel Richard Phillips, of Kenya, and *d* 1 July 1973, leaving by his 1st w:

  (1) JAMES BRUCE SANDILANDS, **14th Lord Torphichen**; *b* 26 Oct 1917; *educ* Eton and Balliol Coll Oxford; *m* 1st 15 Oct 1943 (*divorce* 1952) Mary Thurstan, only dau of Randle Henry Neville Vaudrey, of Edgbaston, Birmingham; *m* 2nd Aug 1955 (*divorce* 1967) Margaret Jane, dau of George Dawson, of New York; *m* 3rd 23 April 1973 *Pamela Mary [Pamela Lady Torpichen, 16 Moore St, London SW3], dau of John Howard Snow and widow of Thomas Hodson-Pressinger, and *d* 12 July 1975, leaving by his 1st w:

    1a (JAMES) ANDREW DOUGLAS SANDILANDS, **15th and present Lord Torphichen**

    1a *Alison Mary [The Hon Mrs Baldwin, 9 Alwyne Ave, Shenfield, Essex CM15 8QT]; *b* 18 July 1944; *m* 2 April 1966 *David Maurice Baldwin, s of Maurice Baldwin, of Rolton Pk, Birmingham, and has:

      1b *Emma Alison; *b* 5 April 1968; *m* 1989 *Dr Iain Coldham and has:

        1c *Peter James; *b* 27 June 1992

        2c *Andrew Thomas; *b* 29 March 1998

        1c *Jennifer Emma; *b* 28 Dec 1994

      2b *Petra Josephine; *b* 1972

3 Walter Alexander; *b* 26 April 1888; Lt RFA; *m* 25 June 1918 (*divorce* 1930) Nancy Margaret, yst dau of Hubert Powell, of Lewes, and *d* 9 Feb 1966, leaving:

  (1) Bruce Walter, OBE (1970); *b* 14 July 1921; RM WW II, surveyor Malayan CS; having been lost in Sabah Jungle for two months, his death was announced 20 Feb 1974

  (2) +DOUGLAS ROBERT ALEXANDER; *Master of Torphichen* [The Master of Torphichen, 109 Royal George Rd, Burgess Hill, W Sussex]; *b* 31 Aug 1926; heir presumptive; RASC 1945–48; driving instructor; *m* 1st 1949 Ethel Louise Burkitt and has:

    1a +Robert Powell; *b* 1950; *m* 1974 *Cheryl Lin Watson, of Eastbourne

  (2) (cont) The *Master of Torphichen* *m* 2nd *Suzette Vera (*née* Pernet) and by her has:

    2a +Bruno Charles; *b* 1977

    3a +Edward Louis; *b* 1979

  (1) *Jean Eleanor; *b* 25 Jan 1920; ATS WW II; *m* 1st 26 March 1947 (*divorce* 1951) Edward Cecil Doudney (*d* 1 March 1956); *m* 2nd 3 June 1955 Col (Richard) Greville Acton Steel, TD (*d* 1981), yr s of Col Richard Alexander Steel, CMG, CIE, and has by him:

    1a *James Alexander Drummond; *b* 12 April 1958

  (2) *Jonet Christian; *b* 6 June 1924; nurse WW II; *m* 1st 22 April 1944 Capt John Osborne Wigg, RN (*d* 1981); *m* 2nd John Hine (*d* 19–), of Houston, Texas, and has by her 1st husb:

    1a *Anthony John Osborne; *b* 4 March 1955

    1a *Coralie Ann Osborne; *b* 14 Nov 1945; *m* 6 Nov 1965 *Keith Clement

    2a *Nina Jonet Osborne; *b* 9 Oct 1947; *m* 9 April 1966 (*divorce* 1983) Roderic Erskine Swift and has:

      1b *Damien John Erskine; *b* 22 April 1968

      2b *Julian James Sheridan; *b* 1971

    1b *Amanda Jane Osborne; *b* 25 Sept 1966; *m* 1986 *Peter Dyke

1 Alison Margaret; *b* 29 July 1883

TORRINGTON

Arms: Quarterly, sa. and arg, in the 1st quarter a lion rampant of the second. **Crest:** An heraldic antelope statant erm., horned, tusked, maned and hoofed or. **Supporters:** Dexter, an heraldic antelope erm., horned, tusked, maned and hoofed or, standing on a ship's gun ppr.; sinister, a sea-horse ppr. on a like gun. **Motto:** *Tuebor* ('I will guard'). **Creations:** Bt. (GB) 19 Nov 1715,
V. and B. (GB) 21 Sept 1721.

THE 11TH VISCOUNT TORRINGTON, Co Devon, **Baron Byng of Southill**, Co Bedford, and a **Baronet** (Sir Timothy Howard St George Byng, Bt) [The Rt Hon The Viscount Torrington, Great Hunts Place, Owslebury, Hants SO21 1JL]; *b* 13 July 1943; *s gf* 1961; *educ* Harrow and St Edmund Hall Oxford; memb Ho Lds

Select Ctee EEC 1984–87; md Anvil Petroleum plc 1977–86; dir: Flextech 1988–93, Alliance Resources 1993–95, Conrad 1993–96; md Heritage Oil & Gas 1996– ; *m* 7 Nov 1973 *Susan Honour, twin dau of Michael George Thomas Webster, of The Vale, Windsor Forest, Berks, and has:

1 *Henrietta Rose; *b* 19 Aug 1977
2 *Georgina Isabel; *b* 23 Sept 1980
3 *Malaika Anne; *b* 13 April 1982

Torrington, other creations: One of the titles showered in 1660 on General George Monck, architect of the Restoration, was the Earldom of Torrington. It expired with his son, the 2nd Earl (and 2nd Duke of Albemarle), in 1688. The title was resurrected the following year for Arthur Herbert, a scion of the Herberts Barons Herbert of Chirbury (*see* POWIS, E). Unlike Monck, the new Earl of Torrington was predominantly a naval man (though he did hold Army appointments). He had served in the Second Dutch War, in the Mediterranean against Algerian pirates (when like Nelson he was blinded in one eye), as beneficiary of the 'Protestant Wind' when he escorted WILLIAM III to Torbay in 1688 and against the French off Bantry Bay in 1689. After his defeat by a superior French force in the action off Beachy Head a year after his ennoblement he was court-martialled and never given a command again. The title expired with him in 1716. A Barony of Torrington was conferred just over two months after his death on Thomas Newport, youngest son of the 1st Earl of Bradford (*qv*) of the 1694 creation. On the grantee's death without issue in 1719 this title also expired.

Lineage: THOMAS BING, of Wrotham, Kent, *temp* HENRY VIII; *m* Joan, dau and heir of Thomas Hikke, and had, with eight other sons, an est surv one:

JOHN BING; *m* 1535 Agnes, dau of Robert Spencer, of Essex, and had, with two other sons:

1 ROBERT
2 Thomas; Fell Peterhouse Cambridge, Master Clare Hall 1571, Regius Prof Law 1574, V-Chllr 1572 and 1578, a Master of Chancery and Dean of the Arches 1595; *m* April 1571 Katherine Randall and was *bur* 23 Dec 1599, leaving, with other issue:

(1) Henry; of Grantchester, Cambs; *bapt* 26 July 1573; Serjeant-at-Law and Counsel to Cambridge U, MP Sudbury 1614; *m* Katherine, dau of Thomas Clench, of Holbrook, Suffolk, and *d* 3 March 1634
(2) Andrew, Fell Peterhouse 1592, Regius Prof Hebrew 1608, one of the translators of the Authorised Version of the Bible, Archdeacon Norwich 1618 and Rector Winterton; *d* March 1652
(3) Humphrey; *educ* Eton and King's Coll Cambridge, V-Provost 1634; *d* Nov 1677

The est s,
ROBERT BING; MP Steyning 1555 and Abingdon 1559, High Sheriff Kent 1593; *m* 1st Frances, dau and heir of Richard Hill, and had:

1 GEORGE
2 John; *dsp*
3 Francis; memb Gray's Inn 1574; *d* unm

ROBERT BING *m* 2nd Mary (*bur* 6 Nov 1586), dau of William Maynard, and *d* 2 Sept 1595, having by her had, with two other sons:

4 William; *bapt* 18 Aug 1586; Capt Deal Castle

The est s,
GEORGE BING; *b* 1556; MP Rochester 1584 and Dover 1604–14; *m* Jane, dau of William Crowmer, of Tunstall, Kent, and was *bur* 20 July 1616, having had, with other issue, including a dau (Elizabeth, *bapt* 14 Feb 1591, *m* Sir Thomas Polhill, of Shoreham):

GEORGE BING; *bapt* 13 Oct 1594; *educ* Gray's Inn; *m* 1617 Catherine (*d* 18 March 1656/7), dau of John Hewitt, of Headley Hall, Yorks, and was *bur* 2 June 1659, having had:

1 Robert; *bapt* 7 April, *bur* 10 May 1625
2 JOHN
1 Hester; *bapt* 26 July 1621; *m* Benjamin Man, 4th s of Thomas Man, of St Mary's, Bothaw, and Master Haberdashers' Co

The est surv s,
JOHN BING; *b c* 1628; apprentice draper June 1646, Freeman 1653, traded abroad till 1658; *m* 14 April 1662 Philadelphia (*d* Feb 1688), dau of George Johnson, of Loans, Surrey, and had:

1 GEORGE, **1st Viscount**
2 John; *b c* 1665; Army Capt; *bur* 1705
3 Robert; in Ireland; Offr RM; *m* Charlotte, illegitimate dau of 4th Baron Howard of Escrick (*see* SUFFOLK and BERKSHIRE, E), and was *bur* 28 July 1726, having had:

(1) Philadelphia; *d* unm

4 Francis; Lt-Col RHG (Blues and Royals); *m* Helen Smith (*bur* 1753) and was *bur* 31 Jan 1734

JOHN BING *d* 1683; his est s,
Sir George Byng, 1st Bt, so *cr* 19 Nov 1715 (for servs in defending Br coasts against the Jacobites during the Uprising that year), as also 21 Sept 1721 **1st Viscount Torrington**, Co Devon, and BARON BYNG OF SOUTHILL, Co Bedford (all GB), KB (1725); *b* 27 Jan 1663/4; served RN from 1678 (also KORL Regt and RHG Army), R-Adml March 1702/3, ktd 1704 for his part in the attack on Gibraltar and Battle of Malaga earlier the same year, V-Adml Jan 1704/5, MP (Whig) Plymouth 1705–21, Adml the Blue Jan 1707/8, helped defeat the French-assisted Jacobite attempt at an invasion of Scotland March 1707/8, C-in-C Channel May 1708 and Mediterranean 1709, a Ld Admlty 1709–Jan 1713/4 and Oct 1714–21, Adml the White and C-in-C Channel again July-Sept 1711, C-in-C Baltic 1717, Adml of the Fleet March 1717/8–Jan 1732/3, C-in-C Mediterranean again 1718–20 (when he completely overwhelmed a Spanish fleet of 18 sail laying siege to Messina), Envoy Plen to Fez, Morocco and Italian States 1718–20, Treas Navy 1720–24, R-Adml of GB 1720–Jan 1732/3, First Ld Admlty 1727–Jan 1732/3; *m* 5 March 1690/1 Margaret (*d* 30 March 1755), dau of James Master, of E Langdon, Kent, and *d* 17 Jan 1732/3, having had, with other issue:

1 PATTEE BYNG, **2nd Viscount Torrington**, PC (GB 1732, I 1734); *bapt* 25 May 1699; MP (Whig) Plymouth 1721–27 and Beds 1727–33, Treas Navy 1724–34;

m 11 June 1724 Lady Charlotte Montagu, yst dau of 1st Duke of Manchester (*qv*), but *dsps* 23 Jan 1746/7
2 Matthew; *b* 13 Sept 1700; *d* Florence Dec 1714
3 GEORGE, **3rd Viscount**
4 ROBERT; had issue (*see* STRAFFORD, E)
5 John; *b* 28 Oct 1704; Adml the Blue; bought an estate at S Mymms, Middx, where he built Wrotham Park; *d* unm 14 March 1757, executed by firing squad aboard HMS *Monarque* at Portsmouth, as Voltaire said, 'pour encourager les autres' after a Court Martial had found him guilty of bad judgement but cleared him of cowardice and recommended him to mercy, leaving Wrotham to his n by his bro Robert
6 Edward; *b* 30 Nov 1706; Col; *m* Mary, dau and heiress of John Bramston, of Screens, Essex, and was *bur* 5 Aug 1756
1 Sarah; *b* 2 Oct 1695; *m* 8 Aug 1710 John Osborn (*bur* 14 Jan 1718/9), est s of Sir John Osborn, 2nd Bt, of Chicksands, Beds (*qv*), and *d* Nov 1775, leaving issue

The 2nd VISCOUNT's bro,
GEORGE BYNG, **3rd Viscount Torrington**; *bapt* 21 Sept 1701; Col 4th Marines 1744–48 and 48th Foot 1749–50, Maj-Gen 1747; *m* 21 Aug 1736 Elizabeth Daniel, gdau of Sir Peter Daniel, and *d* 7 April 1750, leaving:

1 GEORGE BYNG, **4th Viscount Torrington**; *b* 11 Oct 1740; *educ* Westminster and Trin Coll Cambridge; Min Plen Brussels 1783–92; *m* 10 July 1765 Lady Lucy Boyle (*d* 18 March 1792), only dau of 5th Earl of Cork and Orrery (*qv*), and *dspm* 14 Dec 1812, having had:

(1) Lucy Elizabeth; *m* 1st Earl of Bradford (*qv*)
(2) Georgiana Elizabeth; *m* 21 March 1786 6th Duke of Bedford (*qv*) and *d* 10 Oct 1801, leaving issue
(3) Isabella Elizabeth; *m* 24 April 1794 2nd Marquess of Bath (*qv*) and *d* 1 May 1830
(4) Emily; *m* 1 July 1800 Henry Seymour (*see* HERTFORD, M) and *d* 3 Sept 1824

2 JOHN BYNG, **5th Viscount Torrington**; *b* 18 Feb 1742/3; *educ* Westminster; Lt-Col Gren Gds 1776; author: *The Torrington Diaries* (ed C Bruyn Andrews, 1934–38); *m* 3 March 1767 Bridget (*d* 1823), dau of Cdre Arthur Forrest, RN, and had:

(1) GEORGE, **6th Viscount**
(2) Edmund; *b* 1774; Commr Colonial Audit Office; *d* 1854
(3) John; HEICS; *m* 5 Nov 1806 Amelia, dau of J Mayne, and *d* 23 Nov 1811, leaving:

1a George Percy; Cdr RN; *d* 14 Sept 1840
2a John (Rev); *b* 16 Aug 1811; Rector Boxford, Suffolk, Vicar Langford, Beds; *m* 1 Sept 1840 Williamina Hebe (*d* 26 May 1889), dau of Rev Henry Morice, Vicar Ashwell, Herts, and *d* 25 March 1884, leaving, with two other daus (*d* unm):

1b John Morice (Rev); *b* 30 Oct 1846; Rector Wymondham, Oakham; *m* 15 Dec 1875 Emily Eden (*d* 25 Aug 1885), 3rd dau of Rev Anthony Singleton Atcheson, Rector Teigh, Rutland, and *d* 24 Nov 1885, leaving:

1c Vincent Gerard Eden Morice; *b* 1876; *dsp* 12 Oct 1895

1b Frederica Amelia; *m* 7 Oct 1875 Bertram Fulke Hartshorne, barrister, of Manor Ho, Water Eaton, Oxon, and *d* 15 Jan 1934, leaving issue. He *d* 1921
2b Matilda Clara Beatrice; *m* 14 Jan 1880 Col Arthur Henry Wavell and *d* 19 June 1918, leaving issue. He *d* 16 Jan 1891
1a Amelia; *m* 20 April 1836 Maj-Gen Lawrence Fyler, CB, and had issue. He *d* 21 Sept 1873
(4) Henry Dilkes; V-Adml; *m* Maria Jane (*d* 17 May 1874), dau of J B Clerke, and *d* 24 Sept 1860, having had:

1a Henry; *b* 11 Sept 1811; Capt RN; *m* 1st 10 June 1839 Mary Anne (*d* 25 Nov 1852), only child of William Webb, of The Views, Essex, and a descendant of John Cranmer, bro of Thomas, Archbishop Cranmer, and had, with two other sons (*d* young):

1b Alfred Molyneux BYNG later CRANMER-BYNG (roy licence 1 Feb 1882 for him and his issue), of Quendon Hall, Essex, JP, DL; *b* 19 March 1840; Lt-Col Gren Gds; *m* 1st 20 June 1870 Caroline Mary (*d* 31 Jan 1887), dau of Rt Hon Henry Tufnell, MP, and had:

1c Launcelot Alfred Cranmer, of Folly Mill, Thaxted, Essex, JP; *b* 23 Nov 1872; CA Essex, FRSA, Capt TFR, Cmdt POW Camp 1917; *m* 1st 4 March 1894 Harriet (*d* 13 April 1913), dau of Isaac Hammersley; *m* 2nd 30 March 1916 Daisy Elaine (*d* 1981), dau of N B Beach, of Chelmsford, and *d* 15 Jan 1945, leaving:

1d +JOHN LAUNCELOT, MC (1944) [Maj John Cranmer-Byng MC, 190 Glengrove Ave, Toronto, Canada]; *b* 18 March 1919; heir presumptive; *educ* Haileybury and King's Coll Cambridge (MA 1944); Maj Airborne Forces WW II 1940–45, history lecturer Hong Kong U, Prof History Toronto U; *m* 19 Jan 1955 *Margaret Ellen, only dau of R H Hardy, of Sevenoaks, Kent, and has:

1e +Colin Hugh, of Toronto; *b* 10 Sept 1960; *m* 19 Oct 1984 *Lisa Anne, dau of I A Dallimore, of Toronto, Canada, and has:

1f +John Nicholas; *b* 10 Nov 1990
2f +Peter Joseph; *b* 11 April 1994
1f *Leslea Anne; *b* 27 Oct 1986
2f *Mary Margaret; *b* 21 Oct 1988
3f *Sarah Jaine; *b* 21 May 1992

1e *Alison Caroline; *b* 12 Oct 1956; *m* 2 July 1985 *Howard Lan, s of Tse Wing Lan, of Toronto
2e *Sheila Margaret; *b* 23 Dec 1962

2c Hugh Edward Cranmer; *b* 12 Dec 1873; Lt RGA; *m* 24 Oct 1916 Kathleen, dau of George Edward West, of Little Easton, Dunmow, Essex, and *d* 20 Sept 1949, leaving:

1d Rosaleen Sheila; *b* 8 Oct 1917; *m* 7 Oct 1939 John Edward Nicholls, s of Francis Joseph Nicholls, of The Park, Dunmow, Essex, and *d* 19 March 1955, leaving two sons

1c Harriet Beatrice Cranmer; *b* 1 Dec 1874; *m* 1st 21 June 1900 John Charles Potter, of Earnsdale, Darwen, and had issue. He *d* 1920. She *m* 2nd 18 July 1925 Sir Robert Rodney Wilmot, 6th Bt (*see* 1931 edn), and *d* 16 April 1967. He *d* 16 Aug 1931

1b (cont.) Col Cranmer-Byng *m* 2nd 14 Feb 1888 Emma Evangeline (*d* 7 April 1924), yst dau of Ker Baillie-Hamilton, CB (*see* HADDINGTON, E), and *d* 20 May 1906

2b Henry Webb; *b* 8 March 1841; Lt 99th Foot; *dsp* July 1896

3b Arthur Hervey; *b* 13 Oct 1845; Maj 3rd Bn Prince of Wales's Leinster Regt, Lt-Cdr RN; *m* 8 June 1869 Florence (*d* 1914), est dau of William Fuller-Maitland, of Stansted, Essex, and *d* 19 May 1923, leaving:

   1c Arthur Maitland; *b* 26 Sept 1872; Capt Roy Fus, Boer War 1902 and WW I; *ka* France Sept 1914

   2c Harold Robert; *b* 2 Nov 1874; *m* 1930 Madeleine, dau of Francis George West, and *d* 13 Feb 1938

   3c John Anstruther; *b* 15 Sept 1877; Boer War 1901–02; *m* 1915 Rachel Wyllie, dau of William Hampden Brodie, of Glenbucket, Scotland, and *d* 1960, leaving:

      1d Arthur Maitland; *b* 1917; S African Artillery WW II; *m* 1965 *Joan Stuart Marr [Mrs Arthur Byng, Glenbucket, Box 1146, Rustenburg 0300, Transvaal, S Africa], and *d* 1983, leaving:

         1e *Joanne Rachel; *b* 1969

         2e *Ann Maitland; *b* 1970

      1d *Julienne Wyllie; *b* 1919; *m* 1st 1941 John Duncan (*d* 19–), of Durban, Natal; *m* 2nd 1965 Courtice Jocelyn Leigh-Hunt (*d* 1976) and by her 1st husb has:

         1e *Annette Jenifer; *b* 1943

         2e *Patricia Jane; *b* 1945

         3e *Julienne Rachel; *b* 1947

      2d *Norah Cranmer; *b* 1921; *m* 1949 John Winnall Franklin Hampton (*d* 19–)

      3d *Mary Maitland; *b* 1923; *m* 1946 *Arthur Harold Hampshire Davison and has:

         1e *Ian Hampshire; *b* 1948

         2e *Neil Torrington; *b* 1953

         3e *Bruce Dale; *b* 1958

   4c Ralph Edmund; *b* 31 May 1880; *d* unm 8 Sept 1958

   1c Kathleen Mary; *b* 9 June 1870; *m* 30 April 1901 Alexander Stillingfleet Gordon, s of Rev Cosmo Spencer Gordon, and *d* 11 Dec 1959, leaving issue. He *d* 26 Jan 1955

   2c Beatrice Margaret Florence; *b* 16 Oct 1875; *d* unm 9 Aug 1960

   3c Norah Wilhelmina; *b* 17 March 1879; *d* unm 23 June 1962

4b Edward Francis; *b* 4 April 1847; *m* 24 April 1896 Edith Jessie, 3rd dau of Capt Edward Croker, Carabiniers, and *dsp* 5 Jan 1907

5b Harold Edmund, of Wicken, Essex, JP; *b* April 1851; CC Essex; *d* unm 27 Nov 1902

1b Cecilia Mary; *m* 13 Jan 1869 Capt Frederick Stephens, 2nd Life Gds, of Bentworth Lodge, Alton, Hants, s of John Stephens, of Caversham Place, Oxon, and *d* 11 May 1915, leaving issue. He *d* 1 April 1909

2b Edith Mary; *m* 16 Sept 1873 Cecil James Stephens, 12th Lancers, and *d* 2 Jan 1900, leaving issue

3b Anne Mary; *m* 26 June 1873 Col Edward Frewen, CB, of Brickwall, Sussex, and *d* 11 May 1922, having had issue. He *d* 13 Jan 1919

1a (cont.) Capt Henry Byng *m* 2nd 9 June 1857 Mary (*d* 1895), est dau of Lt-Col Gubbins, CB, of Belmont, Hants, and *d* 2 June 1881, having by her had, with a dau (*d* unm):

6b Frederick John; *b* 11 July 1861; *d* 1895

4b Frances Mary; *m* 1st 13 Oct 1887 Lt-Col Charles Borton, 14th Regt, Adj HAC (*d* 1890); *m* 2nd 30 June 1892 John Augustin Davis (*d* 1892), of Swindon, Wilts; *m* 3rd 7 Jan 1895 James Cornwallis Gubbins and *d* 9 April 1899

2a Edmund Disney;, Capt 1st Bengal Fus; *m* 16 April 1852 Elizabeth Egbertha, dau of John Horsley, Madras CS, and *d* 18 April 1853, leaving:

   1b Ella Napier; *d* unm 8 March 1906

3a John Clarke; *b* 21 March 1824; V-Adml, Chev Legn Hon and Medjidie; *m* 1st 25 Aug 1863 Penelope Margaret (*dsp* 31 Dec 1889), 3rd dau of Capt Thomas Garth, RN, of Haines Hill, Berks; *m* 2nd 16 July 1891 Ethel Frances (*m* 2nd 27 June 1899 Col George Ralph Collier Westropp, CB, IA (*d* 18 Aug 1934), s of Maj-Gen George Ralph Collier Westropp, IA), dau of Maj-Gen J Á Tytler, VC, CB, and *d* 2 July 1896, leaving:

      1b Beatrice Eva Tytler; *b* 10 Jan 1893; *m* 10 Jan 1914 (*divorce* 1922) Gambier Baptist Edward Noel and has issue (*see* GAINSBOROUGH, E)

   1a Cecilia; *m* 22 Nov 1837 Maj-Gen M R S Whitmore (*d* 1884) and had issue

   2a Beatrice; Maid-of-Honour to HM QUEEN VICTORIA; *m* 14 Aug 1863 Col Henry Blundell-Hollinshead-Blundell, CB, of Deysbrook, MP SW Lancs, and *dsp* 3 Oct 1884. He *d* 28 Sept 1906

(5) Frederick Gerald; FO, Gentleman Usher Privy Chamber; *m* Catherine Neville (*d* 8 Dec 1871) and *d* 5 June 1871

(1) Elizabeth Lucy; *m* 1st 26 Sept 1797 R-Adml Percy Frazer (*d* 9 Dec 1827); *m* 2nd 1836 Rev George Goodenough Lynn and *d* 18 Jan 1846

(2) Cecilia; *m* 31 Oct 1805 J Robert Gregge Hopwood, of Hopwood Hall, Lancs, and had issue. He *d* 1854

(3) Anna Maria Bridget; *m* 29 Aug 1794 Very Rev Charles Henry Hall, Dean Durham, and *d* 30 Oct 1852. He *d* 1827

(4) Bridget Augusta Forrest; *m* 9 July 1806 Capt Hon Charles Herbert, RN, and *d* 4 March 1876, leaving issue (*see* CARNARVON, E)

(5) Georgiana; *m* Rev Geoffrey Hornby and *d* 23 July 1856, leaving issue. He *d* 4 March 1850

(6) Beatrice Charlotte; *m* 30 Nov 1820 Rev Colin Alexander Campbell, Rector Widdington, Essex, bro of Sir Guy Campbell, 1st Bt (*qv*), and *d* 12 March 1848

(7) Lucy Juliana; *m* 5 Oct 1809 Sir John Morris, 2nd Bt (*qv*), and *d* 27 Nov 1881, leaving issue

The 5th VISCOUNT *d* 8 Jan 1813; his est s,

GEORGE BYNG, **6th Viscount Torrington**; *b* 5 Jan 1768; V-Adml the Blue 1825 and the White 1830; *m* 1st 8 Feb 1793 Elizabeth (*d* 20 Aug 1810), dau of Philip Langmead, MP Plymouth, and had:

1 Lucy Elizabeth; *m* 28 July 1836 Rev John Lukin and *d* 2 April 1875

The **6th Viscount** *m* 2nd 5 Oct 1811 Frances Harriet (*d* 7 Feb 1868), dau of Adml Sir Robert Barlow, GCB (*see* BARLOW, Bt, of Fort William), and *d* 18 June 1831, having by her had, with a dau (*d* unm):

1 GEORGE BYNG, **7th Viscount Torrington**; *b* 9 Sept 1812; *educ* Eton; DCL, Hon Col 3rd and 4th Bns QOR W Kent Regt, Ld-in-Waiting 1837–41 and 1859–84, Govr and C-in-C Ceylon 1847–50; *m* 18 March 1833 Mary Anne (*d* 26 Jan 1885 aged 80), only dau of Sir John Dugdale Astley, 1st Bt, of Everley (*see* 1970 edn), and *d* 27 April 1884, having had:

   (1) Frances Elizabeth; *d* 2 Sept 1853

2 Robert Barlow Palmer; *b* 30 Nov 1816; Maj Bengal NI; *m* 11 Feb 1839 Elizabeth Maria Lowther (*m* 2nd 1 Feb 1861 Rev William Winchester, Chaplain Bengal, and *d* 5 Nov 1868), est dau of Col Gwatkin, Bengal Army, and was *k* during Indian Mutiny 18 Dec 1857, leaving:

   (1) GEORGE STANLEY BYNG, **8th Viscount Torrington**; *b* 29 April 1841; Lt-Col The Rifle Bde (Indian medal and clasp), ADC and a Priv Sec to Ld Lt Ireland, Ld-in-Waiting March–Oct 1889; *m* 1st 19 Jan 1882 Alice Arabella (*d* 18 Dec 1883), dau of James Jameson, of Airfield, Dublin, and had:

      1a Bridget Vera; *b* 11 Nov 1882; *m* 1st 9 Nov 1909 Maj Frank Peyton Skipwith (*ka*) and had issue (*see* SKIPWITH, Bt); *m* 2nd 22 Feb 1919 William Gordon Cardew, Army Cyclist Corps, s of Lt-Col George Masters Cardew, Hants Regt, of Exeter, and *d* 23 Nov 1962, leaving further issue

   (1) (cont.) The **8th Viscount** *m* 2nd 3 Feb 1885 Emmeline St Maur (*d* 7 June 1912), dau of Rev Henry Seymour (*see* SOMERSET, D), and *d* 20 Oct 1889, having by her had:

      1a GEORGE MASTER BYNG, **9th Viscount Torrington** I; *b* 10 Sept 1886; *educ* Eton and RMC Sandhurst; Lt RNVR 1914, Capt RAF, 2nd Lt Rifle Bde 1906–09, Page of Honour to TM QUEEN VICTORIA 1899–1901 and EDWARD VII 1901–03, served WW I; *m* 1st 23 Sept 1910 (*divorce* 1921) Eleanor (committed suicide by coal-gas poisoning while of unsound mind 8 Dec 1931), actress (a Gaiety Girl), er dau of Edwin Souray, of Long Ditton, Surrey; *m* 2nd 1 Sept 1923 Norah Elizabeth Ursula (*d* 29 Jan 1968), formerly w of Harold Ferens and dau of Capt Robert Wood-Pottle, 5th Roy Irish Lancers, and *dsp* 24 May 1944

   (2) Robert Lowther; *b* 29 July 1842; Capt RN; granted 1884 with his siblings rank of viscount's dau/yr s; *d* 15 Oct 1886

   (3) Sydney; *b* 9 April 1844; Lt 104th Foot; *m* 21 June 1871 Annie Sebright (*d* 4 Feb 1926), 3rd dau of Henry Chellingworth, of Park Attwood, Worcs, and *d* 27 Feb 1920, leaving:

      1a ARTHUR STANLEY, **10th Viscount**

      2a Robert Nelson; *b* 26 May 1878; *d* unm 31 March 1944

      3a Francis Dacres; *b* 7 July 1880; Capt Rifle Bde WW I; *m* 1915 Kate (*d* 1965), dau of Charles Arthur Russell, of Teddington, and was *ka* 3 Sept 1916, leaving:

         1b Francis Russell Dacres; *b* 1916; Lt RA WW II; *ka* Normandy 5 July 1944

      4a Cecil Eustace; *b* 11 Oct 1884; *d* unm 11 June 1925

      1a Sydney Lilian Sebright; *m* 1894 Leonard Cecil Freeman, s of James Henry Freeman, of Enfield, Middx, and had issue. He *d* 1952

      2a Ada Geraldine Maude; *m* 21 March 1903 John Portsmouth, of E Sheen, er s of John Portsmouth, of Basingstoke, and *d* 4 Feb 1922

      3a Evelyn Beatrice; granted Jan 1946 with surv sisters rank of viscount's daus; *d* unm 8 Jan 1968

      4a Gladys Irene; *m* 23 July 1910 her er sister's bro-in-law Henry Portsmouth and had issue. He *d* 27 May 1933

   (4) Nelson; *b* 3 April 1845; Cdr RN; *m* 1st 28 June 1870 Louisa Ann (*d* 1 April 1897), widow of Rev T R Brownrigg and dau of T E Owen; *m* 2nd 28 Sept 1897 Sarah Florinda (*d* 28 Nov 1946), dau of Rev John Gage Ball, Rector Killybegs, Co Donegal, and *d* 2 Feb 1931

   (5) Francis Russell; *b* 2 July 1853; *m* 10 June 1880 Emily Mary (*d* 16 June 1938), dau of James Lambe, and *d* 24 Aug 1903, leaving:

      1a George Cyril; *b* 1881; *d* unm 14 Dec 1904

      1a Mabel Frances; *b* 1884; *m* 1st 9 Feb 1904 Capt Alfred Brankston Pembroke, yst s of Edward Pembroke, of Blackheath, and has issue. He *d* 1916. She *m* 2nd 1919 Francis Joseph Binning, est s of Col Joseph Binning, CIE

   (1) Sophie; *m* 19 April 1871 George Marshall, of Hardres Court, Canterbury, est s of George Marshall, of St Leonards-on-Sea, and *d* 7 Jan 1910, leaving issue

3 James Master Owen, DL (Kent); *b* 20 July 1818; barrister; *m* 5 Aug 1856 Caroline Louisa (*d* 2 April 1906), dau of William Cook (*see* COOK, Bt), and *dsp* 21 May 1897

4 Russell John Morris; *b* 4 Aug 1823; Lt RN; *d* 27 April 1850

2 Hilare Caroline; *m* 30 April 1845 Adml Sir William Hutcheon Hall, KCB, FRS (*d* 25 June 1878), and *d* 16 Jan 1889, leaving issue

The 9th VISCOUNT's cousin,

ARTHUR STANLEY BYNG, **10th Viscount Torrington**; *b* 23 July 1876; Lt-Col RASC, formerly E Kent Yeo, Boer War 1900–02 (despatches), India 1904–08 and WW I (despatches, Legn Hon); cmded RASC Bedford and Belfast Dists 1917–20; *m* 1st 14 Jan 1909 (*divorce* 1936) Louise Annette (*d* 11 Oct 1961), only dau of Joseph Rawlins, of Cirencester, by Annette, dau of Rev Francis de Montmorency St George (*see* ST GEORGE, Bt), and had:

1 George; *b* 18 Feb 1918; Paymaster-Lt RN, on staff of R-Adml Naval Air Stations May 1939; *m* 3 Sept 1942 *Anne Yvonne [Mrs Michael Bostock, 12 Southgate Villas, St James Lane, Winchester, Hants SO23 9SG] (*m* 2nd 27 Jan 1951 Howard Henry Masterton Carpenter (*d* 1976), FAI, s of William Henry Howard Carpenter, FAI, of 34, Orchard Court, W1; *m* 3rd 1991 Michael Ingram Bostock), only dau of Capt Ronald Guy Pearson Wood, MC, 7th Dragoon Gds, of Durban, and *das* 15 July 1944, leaving:

(1) TIMOTHY HOWARD ST GEORGE BYNG, **11th and present Viscount Torrington**

1 *Joan; *b* 6 Jan 1910; *m* 1st 5 June 1941 (*divorce* 1950) Maj William Mackreth Peter Osborne, RA, s of Alan Fell Osborne, of Reigate; *m* 2nd Sept 1951 Thomas James Reynolds, MRCVS

2 Betty; *b* 21 March 1911; WW II with VAD (RN); *d* unm 25 Feb 1964

3 *Honor [The Hon Mrs Honor Humphreys, 26 Swan Court, London SW3]; *b* 29 Aug 1912; *m* 27 Feb 1937 (*divorce* 1951) Lisle Marles Humphreys

The **10th Viscount** *m* 2nd 17 March 1936 (*divorce* 1952) Rosamond Ella, dau of V-Adml Alexander Percy Davidson, DSO, and *d* 28 Nov 1961, having by her had:

4 *(Rosamond Stella) Frances [The Hon Mrs Cross, 2 St Boniface Rd, Ventnor, Isle of Wight]; *b* 23 Jan 1937; *m* 1st 10 Sept 1960 (*divorce* 1985) Anthony Brockington Cobb, est s of Basil Brockington Cobb, of E Wellow, Hants; *m* 2nd 1991 *Frank Stephen Cross and by her 1st husb has:

(1) *Dorian Byng; *b* 12 Sept 1965

(1) *Michelle Pandora; *b* 2 Nov 1961

TOUCHE of Dorking

Arms: Vert a lion rampant arg., holding between the forepaws a portcullis chained or, between two fleurs-de-lys, one in sinister chief, the other in dexter base arg. **Crest:** Between two fleurs-de-lys or a Dorking cock ppr. **Motto:** *Vigilate* ('Be watchful'). **Creation:** Bt. (UK) 3 July 1962.

SIR RODNEY GORDON TOUCHE, 2ND BT, of Dorking, Surrey [Sir Rodney Touche Bt, 2403 Westmount Pl, 1100 8th Ave SW, Calgary, Alberta T2P 3T9, Canada]; *b* 5 Dec 1928; *s* f 1972; *educ* Marlborough and Univ Coll Oxford; jnlst; emigrated to Canada 1956; pres: Touche Vintcent INV Cons 1965–69; TTY Inv Cons 1969–80 and Village Lake Louise Ltd, Alberta, Canada 1972–85; *m* 30 April 1955 *Ouida Ann, er dau of Frederick Gerald MacLellan, of Moncton, NB, Canada, and has:

1 +ERIC MacLELLAN; *b* 22 Feb 1960; *m* 1990 *Leeanne Marie, dau of Arthur Stringer, of Pontiex, Saskatchewan, and has:

(1) *Braden Stringer; *b* 2 Oct 1990

(1) *Danielle Erica; *b* 9 Feb 1992

1 *Amanda Ann; *b* 23 Jan 1956; *m* 1978 *Peter M Bowler and has:

(1) *Samuel McNamara; *b* 7 Sept 1987

(1) *Sarah Jane; *b* 17 March 1983

(2) *Anne MacLellan; *b* 8 July 1985

2 *Susan Ruth; *b* 26 July 1957; *m* 1st 1983 Pasquale Tartaglia and has:

(1) *Cosmo Alexander Touche; *b* 4 Dec 1990

2 (cont.) Mrs Susan Tartaglia *m* 2nd 1992 *Trevor B Arends, s of Kaj Arends, of USA, and by him has:

(2) *Sebastian Valdimar Touche; *b* 30 Oct 1992

(1) *Islah Valerie Touche; *b* 1 Oct 1993

(2) *Siri Ouida Elizabeth Touche; *b* 17 July 1995

3 *Karen Marie; *b* 9 Aug 1961; *m* 1986 *Michael Lightstone and has:

(1) *Jesse Lyon; *b* 10 July 1990

(1) *Samantha Touche; *b* 26 July 1988

(2) *Kate Annie; *b* 6 Sept 1992

Lineage: Sir GEORGE ALEXANDER TOUCHE, 1st Bt, of Westcott (*qv*) had a 3rd s:

Sir Gordon Touche, 1st Bt (UK), so cr 3 July 1962, PC (1959); *b* 8 July 1895; *educ* Marlborough and Univ Coll Oxford (BA 1921, MA 1923); barrister Inner Temple 1922, MP (C) Reigate 1931–50 and Dorking 1950–64, Dep Chm Ways and Means 1956–59, Dep Speaker H of C and Chm Ways and Means 1959–62, Hon Freeman Reigate 1942, dir Tstees Corp, ktd 1952; *m* 7 April 1926 Ruby Anne Hume-Purvis (*d* 1989), er dau of Sir Duncan James Macpherson, CIE, and *d* 19 May 1972, leaving:

1 Sir RODNEY GORDON TOUCHE, **2nd and present Bt**

1 *Daphne Margaret [Mrs Patrick Wells, Snells, Great Henny, Sudbury, Suffolk CO10 7LT]; *b* 28 Feb 1927; *m* 18 Jan 1952 *Patrick Wilfred Wells, 3rd s of William Wells, OBE, MICE, MIME, of Santiago, Chile, and has:

(1) *Derrick Gordon; *b* 12 March 1956; *educ* The Leys Sch; *m* 1st 1984 (*divorce* 1991) Katherine Ann, yr dau of Guy Simpson, of Earl Soham, Suffolk, and has:

1a *George Patrick Charles; *b* 1985

1a *Elizabeth Florence; *b* 1987

(1) (cont.) Derrick Wells *m* 2nd 1997 *Diana, yst dau of Robert Long, of Bishops Waltham, Hants, and by her has:

2a *James Rodney Mitchell; *b* 5 Oct 1997

(2) *William Patrick; *b* 26 Jan 1960; *m* 1985 (*divorce* 1996) Jane Elizabeth, dau of John Alexander, of Ufford, Suffolk, and has:

1a *Thomas Alexander; *b* 1987

2a *Robert William; *b* 1990

(1) *Jennifer Margaret; *b* 8 Jan 1953

TOUCHE of Westcott

Arms: Arg. a lion salient between a fleur-de-lys in the sinister chief and a like fleur-de-lys in the dexter base vert. **Crest:** Two fleurs-de-lys gu., resting thereon a mullet of six points or. **Motto:** *Vigilate* ('Be watchful'). **Creation:** Bt. (UK) 5 July 1920.

SIR ANTHONY GEORGE TOUCHE, 3RD BT, of Westcott, Surrey [Sir Anthony Touche Bt, Stane House, Ockley, Surrey RH5 5TQ]; *b* 31 Jan 1927; *s* uncle 1977; *educ* Eton; FCA, ptnr George A Touche & Co (later Touche Ross), ret 1968, dir Touche Remnant & Co 1965–89 (chm 1971–81), dir: Nat West Bank Plc 1968–90 (dep chm 1977–87), Friends' Provident (dep chm 1983–93) Life Office; Prime Warden Goldsmiths' Co 1987; *m* 5 April 1961 *Hester Christina, er dau of Dr August Friedrich Werner Pleuger, of Birchington, Kent, and has had:

1 +WILLIAM GEORGE; *b* 26 June 1962; *m* 1987 *Elizabeth Louise, yst dau of Allen Bridges, of Lyford Cay, Bahamas, and has:

(1) +Harry George; *b* 3 June 1992

(2) +James Alexander; *b* 1994

(1) *Lucy Madeleine; *b* 1996

2 Andrew James; *b* 11 March 1964; *d* 1984

3 +Peter Francis; *b* 21 Oct 1968; *m* 1996 *Laura Jefferson, dau of Thomas Coolidge, of Connecticut

1 *Helen Mary; *b* 25 Jan 1966; *m* 1989 *Heinrich Hofmann, s of Leonard Hofmann, of Baden-Württemberg, and has:

(1) *Michael Leonhard; *b* 22 May 1997

Lineage: Rev JOHN TOUCHE, AM, DD, of Aberlour and Mortlach; *b* 1700; *m* 29 Aug 1739 Elizabeth, dau of Rev John Scrogie, of Huntly, and *d* 23 Oct 1780, leaving:

WILLIAM TOUCHE; *b* 8 March 1747; RN; *m* Margaret Hay and *d* 1800, leaving:

Rev JOHN EDWARD TOUCHE, of Maderty and Kinnoull; *m* 16 May 1818 Penelope, 3rd dau of John Gray, and *d* 11 June 1852, leaving:

ANTHONY MURRAY TOUCHE, of Edinburgh; *b* 29 Nov 1829; banker; *m* 23 June 1854 Margaret (*d* 28 April 1899), dau of Alexander Guild, of Edinburgh, and *d* 30 March 1897, leaving, with two daus (*d* unm):

1 John Edward; *b* 5 May 1855; FRSE, MIMechE; *m* 30 June 1909 Sarah Minns (*d* 12 March 1952), dau of Thomas Minns Ware, of Hingham, Mass., and *d* 9 June 1938, leaving:

(1) *John Edgeworth David [John Touche Esq, 1/4 Wyvern Park, Edinburgh 9]; *b* 9 Dec 1913; *educ* St John's Coll Cambridge (MA); AFRAeS; *m* 26 Sept 1942 *Joan Beryl, only dau of Gilbert Waterhouse, of Sheffield, and has:

1a *Murray Lincoln David; *b* 13 July 1951

2 William, of Calcutta; *b* 13 June 1858; *m* 15 Aug 1889 Edith Brereton (*d* 5 May 1959), dau of Henry Louis Wright, of Bombay, and *d* 29 Sept 1914, leaving:

(1) Edith Margaret; *m* 9 Nov 1915 Stephen Leonard Sale, 2nd s of Sir Stephen George Sale, KCIE

(2) Constance; *m* 25 Feb 1920 Capt Hugh Carswell Findlay, MC

3 GEORGE ALEXANDER (Sir), **1st Bt**

4 James Wyllie Guild; *b* 11 Dec 1866; *d* 18 Jan 1912

1 Grace Ramsay; *m* 13 July 1886 William Pollock and *d* 7 Oct 1933

The 3rd s,

Sir George Alexander Touche, 1st Bt (UK), so cr 5 July 1920; b 24 May 1861; MP N Islington 1910–18, Lt City London, Sheriff 1915–16, Alderman 1915–21, sr ptnr George A Touche & Co, of London, Birmingham, Montreal, Toronto, Winnipeg, and Touche, Niven & Co, of New York and Chicago; Order of St Sava Serbia 2nd Cl; ktd 1917; m 4 June 1887 Jessie (d 15 Dec 1917), yst dau of Isaac Brown, and d 7 July 1935, leaving:

1 **Sir Norman George Touche, 2nd Bt**; b 11 May 1888; educ Marlborough and Univ Coll Oxford (BA 1910, MA 1921, BCL 1921); barrister Lincoln's Inn 1914, WW I with ASC; m 22 Dec 1923 Eva Maitland, est dau of Patrick Euan Cameron, of Salachan, Ardgour, Argyll, and d 18 May 1977, leaving:

(1) *Penelope Maitland, MBE [Mrs Joseph Mason MBE, Crabtree Meadow, Hope, Hope Valley, Derbys S33 6SA]; b 25 July 1930; educ Edin U (BSc 1952); m 19 April 1954 *Joseph Edwin Mason, PhD, BSc, er s of Edwin Mason, of Acocks Green, Birmingham, and has:

1a *Donald George; b 15 Feb 1955; educ Marlborough

2a *Brian Richard; b 23 Nov 1960

1a *Barbara Jane; b 16 Dec 1956

(2) *Brenda Margaret; b 6 June 1932; educ Newnham Coll Cambridge (BA 1954); m 24 March 1956 (divorce) Ronald Edward Artus, s of Ernest Edward Artus, of Hucclecote, Glos, and has:

1a *Colin Edward; b 25 Nov 1957

2a *Alan Norman; b 14 Sept 1959

3a *Philip Matthew; b 22 Jan 1964

1a *Lucy Katharine; b 22 July 1961

2 Donovan Meredith; b 13 Dec 1891; educ Marlborough; FCA; m 25 July 1925 Muriel Amy Frances (d 1983), est dau of Rev Charles R Thorold Winckley, of Lillington, Warwicks, and d 25 March 1952, leaving:

(1) Sir ANTHONY GEORGE TOUCHE, **3rd and present Bt**

(1) *Isabel Amy [Mrs David Reid, The Folly, Tetbury, Glos]; b 20 Jan 1930; m 23 Oct 1962 *David Murray Arthur Reid, est s of Edmund Lewis Reid, MC, FRCS, of the White Cottage, Blackthorne, Oxon

3 Sir GORDON COSMO, 1st Bt, so cr 1962 (see TOUCHE, Bt, of Dorking)

4 George Lawrence Capel; b 23 Jan 1903; educ Marlborough and Univ Coll Oxford (BA 1925); FCA, ptnr Touche Ross, Bailey and Smart; m 1st 17 Nov 1928 Ursula Grace D'Oyly (d car crash 18 July 1968; see D'OYLY, Bt); m 2nd 20 March 1969 *Elizabeth [Mrs George Touche, Holmbush House, Ashington, W Sussex RH20 3AT], formerly w of Paolo Treves and dau of Henry Kunzer, of London, and d 1 Feb 1995

TOWNSHEND

HÆC·GENERI·INCREMENTA·FIDES

Arms: Quarterly, 1st and 4th, az. a chevron erm. between three escallops arg. (for TOWNSHEND); 2nd and 3rd, quarterly gu. and or, in the first quarter a mullet arg., in the centre a crescent sa. (for VERE). **Crest:** A stag statant ppr., attired and unguled or. **Supporters:** Dexter, a stag sa., attired and unguled or; sinister, a greyhound arg. **Motto:** Hæc generi incrementa fides ('Faith obtained these honours for our race'). **Creations:** Bt. (E) 16 April 1617, B. (E) 20 April 1661, V. (E) 2 Dec 1682, M. (GB) 31 Oct 1787.

THE 7TH MARQUESS TOWNSHEND OF RAYNHAM, Co Norfolk, **Viscount Townshend of Raynham**, Co Norfolk, **Baron Townshend of Lynn Regis**, Co Norfolk, and a **Baronet** (Sir George John Patrick Dominic Townshend, Bt, DL (Norfolk 1951)) [The Most Hon The Marquess Townshend DL, Raynham Hall, Fakenham, Norfolk NR21 7EP]; b 13 May 1916; s f 1921; educ Harrow; 2nd Lt RA (TA), Capt Scots Gds, ADC to GOC Eastern Cmd 1936–39, PA to CIGS 1939–40, chm: Raynham Farm Co Ltd 1957–, Anglia TV 1958–86, Anglia Television Group plc 1971–86, Anchor Enterprises Ltd 1967–88, Survival Anglia Ltd 1971–86, Norfolk Ag Station 1974–87, Roy Norfolk Ag Assoc 1978–85, AP Bank Ltd 1975–87; v chm: Norwich Union Life Insur Soc 1973–86 and Norwich Union Fire Insur Soc 1975–86; dir: D E Longe and Co 1962–90 (chm 1982–90), E Coast Grain Ltd 1962–90 (chm 1982–90), London Merchant Securities plc 1964–95, Scottish Union and Nat Insur Co 1968–86, Maritime Insur Co Ltd 1968–86, Napak Ltd 1968–90 (chm 1982–90), Norwich Union Hldgs 1981–86, Anglia Radio Ltd, Invergordon Distillers (Holdings) Ltd; Tstee E Anglian Savings Bank, Govr Roy

Ag Soc; Hon DCL UEA, FRSA; m 1st 2 Sept 1939 (divorce 1960) Elizabeth Pamela Audrey, JP (Norfolk 1950) (m 2nd 1960 Brig Sir James Gault, KCMG, and d 1989), only dau of Lt-Col Thomas Luby, ICS, and has:

1 +CHARLES GEORGE, Viscount Raynham [Viscount Raynham, Pattesley House, Fakenham, Norfolk; 22 Ebury St, London SW1]; b 26 Sept 1945; educ Eton; m 8 Oct 1975 Hermione (d 1985 in a motor accident), only child of Lt-Cdr Robert Martin Dominic Ponsonby, RN (see BESSBOROUGH, B), and formerly w of Anthony J C Evans; m 2nd 1990 *Mrs Alison Marshall, yr dau of Sir Willis Ide Combs, KCVO, CMG, of Wadhurst Pk, E Sussex, and by his 1st w has:

(1) +Thomas Charles; b 2 Nov 1977

(1) *Louise Elizabeth; b 23 July 1979

1 *Carolyn Elizabeth Ann [The Lady Carolyn Townshend, 89 Elizabeth St, London SW1W 9PG]; b 27 Sept 1940; m 1st 13 Oct 1962 (divorce 1971, resumed maiden name) Il Patrizio Genovese Antonio Capellini, s of Vincenzo Capellini and Donna Anna Candeo Vanzetti, of Genoa; m 2nd Jan 1973 (annulled Nov 1974) Edgar Miles Bronfman, of NY, s of Samuel Bronfman, of Montreal, and by her 1st husb has:

(1) *Vincenzo Charles TOWNSHEND; b 1963; educ Milton Abbey

2 *Joanna Agnes [The Lady Joanna Boegnor, 120 East 87th St, New York, NY 10128, USA]; b 19 Aug 1943; m 1st 27 Sept 1962 (divorce 1968) Jeremy George Courtenay Bradford, s of Cdr George Francis Norton Bradford, RN; m 2nd 1 Jan 1978 (divorce 1984) James Barry Morrissey, of Boston, Mass.; m 3rd 1991 *Christian Marc Boegnor, s of Etienne Boegnor, and by her 1st husb has:

(1) *Francis James Patrick; b 28 Oct 1963 (HRH PRINCESS BENEDIKTE OF DENMARK stood sponsor); educ Dartington

The 7th MARQUESS m 2nd 22 Dec 1960 Ann Frances (d 1988), only dau of Arthur Pellew Darlow, of Portugal, and by her has:

2 +John Patrick [The Lord John Townshend, 31 Coleherne Rd, London SW10 9BS]; b 17 June 1962; educ Eton and London U; m 1987 (divorce 1991) Rachel Lucy, dau of FM Sir John Chapple, GCB, KBE

3 *Katherine Ann; b 29 Sept 1963; m 1991 *Piers W Dent, yst s of Robin Dent, of Olivers, Painswick, Glos, and has:

(1) *Lucia; b 1992

(2) *Mollie; b 1995

Lineage: JOHN TOWNSHEND, of Raynham, Norfolk; d 1465, leaving:

Sir ROGER TOWNSHEND; MP Calne, Wilts; Serjeant-at-law 1478, King's Serjeant 1483, Judge Court Common Pleas 1484, ktd 1484; m Eleanor, dau of William Lunsford, of Battle, Sussex, by Thomasine Barrington (who m 2nd Philip Sidney, of Penshurst (see DE LISLE, V) and 3rd John Hopton), and d on or after 14 Aug 1493, having had, with two yr sons and three daus (m respectively Philip Cressner, Ralph Castell, of Raveningham (see BACON, Bt), and Sir Thomas Wodehouse; see KIMBERLEY, E):

Sir ROGER TOWNSHEND, of Raynham; MP Calne; m Anne (d 25 July 1551), dau and coheir of William de Brewse, of Wenham Hall, Suffolk, and Stinton Hall, Salle, Norfolk, and had, with three other sons:

1 John, of Brampton, Suffolk; m Eleanor, dau of Sir John Heydon, KB, of Baconsthorpe, Norfolk, and dvp, leaving an est s:

(1) Richard, of Brampton; m Catherine (m 2nd Sir William Roper), dau and coheir of Sir Humphrey Brown, of Ridley Hall, Terling, Essex, Judge Common Pleas, and d by 12 Feb 1544/5, having had an only s:

1a ROGER (Sir)

2 Robert (Sir); Ld Ch Justice Chester; m 1516 Alice, dau and heiress of Robert Poppy, of Twyford, Norfolk, and dvp 8 Feb 1556/6, leaving an est s:

(1) Thomas, of Mergate Hall, Bracon Ash, Norfolk; m Elizabeth Periante, widow of Sir Humphrey Styles, and was ancestor of the TOWNSHENDs of Salop

3 Thomas, of Testerton, Norfolk; m 1st Anne, dau of Richard Southwell, of St Faith, Norfolk; m 2nd Elizabeth, dau of John Calybut (see WALPOLE, B) and d by 21 Nov 1573

1 Katherine; m Sir Henry Bedingf(i)eld (see PASTON-BEDINGFELD, Bt)

2 Susan; m Sir Edmund Windham and had issue

Sir ROGER d 25 Nov 1551; his ggs,

Sir ROGER TOWNSHEND, of Raynham; ktd 1588 following service against the Armada; m Jane (m 2nd 9 March 1597/8 7th Lord (Baron) Berkeley; qv), yst dau of Sir Michael Stanhope (see 1967 edn CHESTERFIELD and STANHOPE, E), and was bur 30 June 1590, leaving an est s:

Sir JOHN TOWNSHEND; MP Norfolk; ktd at Siege of Cadiz 1596; m Anne, est dau and coheir of Sir Nathaniel Bacon, KB (see BACON, Bt), and was k in a duel with Sir Matthew Browne 2 Aug 1603, leaving an er s:

Sir Roger Townshend, 1st Bt (E), so cr 16 April 1617; MP Oxford 1621–22 and Norfolk 1628–29; m 1628 Mary (m 2nd 21 June 1638 2nd Earl of Westmorland; qv), 2nd dau and coheir of 1st and last Baron Vere of Tilbury (see SAINT ALBANS, D), and d 1 Jan 1636/7, having had:

1 **Sir Roger Townshend, 2nd Bt**; b 21 Dec 1628; d Geneva 1647/8

2 HORATIO, **1st Viscount**

1 Mary; m May 1650, as his 1st w, 2nd Baron Crewe of Stene

2 Jane; m John Windham

3 Anna; m William Cartwright, of Aynho Park, Northants, and d 1 Feb 1667

4 Edith; d unm

5 Vere; m 30 Aug 1660 Sir Ralph Hare, of Stowe, Norfolk, and dsp

The 1st Bt's bro,

Sir Horatio Townshend, 2nd Bt, and **1st Viscount Townshend of Raynham**, Co Norfolk, so cr 11 Dec 1682, as also earlier 20 April 1661 BARON TOWNSHEND OF LYNN REGIS, Co Norfolk (both E); bapt 16 Dec 1630; MP Norfolk 1656–58 and 1660, Cncllr of State May–Dec 1659, Ld Lt Norfolk 1661–Feb 1675/6; m 1st by 13 April 1659 Mary (dsp), dau and sole heiress of Sir Edward Lewkenor, of Denham, Suffolk; m 2nd 27 Nov 1673 Mary (d Dec 1685), dau of Sir Joseph Ashe, of Twickenham, Middx, and had:

1 CHARLES, **2nd Viscount**

2 Roger; MP Norfolk, later Yarmouth; d unm 22 May 1709

3 Horatio; MP Yarmouth, later Heytesbury; Commr Excise; *m* Alice Starkey and *d* Oct 1751, leaving:

(1) Laetitia; *m* 24 July 1749 9th Earl of Exeter (*see* EXETER, M)

The 1st VISCOUNT was *bur* 10 Dec 1687; his est s,

CHARLES TOWNSHEND, **2nd Viscount Townshend of Raynham**, KG (1724), PC (1707); *b* 18 April 1675; *educ* Eton and King's Coll Cambridge; FRS 1706, Ld Lt Norfolk 1701–13 and 1714–30, Capt Yeomen Gd 1707–11, Jt Amb The Hague Congress 1709–11, Sec State for the North 1714–16 and Feb 1720/1–30, Ld Pres Cncl 1720–21; agricultural improver, hence the sobriquet 'Turnip Townshend'; *m* 1st 3 July 1698 Elizabeth (*d* 11 May 1711), only dau and heiress of 1st Baron Pelham of Laughton (*see* CHICHESTER, E) by his 1st w, and had, with other sons (*d* unm):

1 CHARLES, **3rd Viscount**

2 Thomas; *b* 2 June 1701; a Teller Exchequer, MP Cambridge U; *m* 2 May 1730 Albinia (*d* 7 Sept 1739), dau of Col John Selwyn, of Matson, Glos, and *d* 21 Apr 1780, having had an est s:

(1) THOMAS TOWNSHEND, 1st VISCOUNT SYDNEY OF ST LEONARDS, Co Gloucester, so *cr* 11 June 1789, as also earlier 6 March 1783 BARON SYDNEY OF CHISLEHURST, Co Kent (both GB); *b* 24 Feb 1732/3; Home Sec; *m* 19 May 1760 Elizabeth (*d* 1 May 1826), est dau and coheir of Richard Powys, of Hintlesham Suffolk, and *d* 30 June 1800, having had:

1a JOHN THOMAS TOWNSHEND, 2nd VISCOUNT SYDNEY OF ST LEONARDS; *b* 21 Feb 1764; *m* 1st 12 April 1790 Hon Sophia Southwell (*d* 9 Nov 1795), dau of 20th Baron de Clifford (*qv*), and had:

1b Sophia Mary; *m* 15 Jan 1833 Hon Peregrine Francis Cust (*see* BROWN-LOW, B),and *dsp* 6 Dec 1852

2b Mary Elizabeth; *m* 1st 4 Oct 1825 George James Cholmondeley (*see* CHOLMONDELEY, M) and had issue; *m* 2nd 9 Feb 1832 2nd Earl of Romney (*qv*) and *d* 25 Dec 1847, having had further issue

1a (cont.) The 2nd VISCOUNT *m* 2nd 27 May 1802 Lady Caroline Clements (*d* 9 Aug 1805), 3rd dau of 1st Earl of Leitrim (*see* 1953 edn), and *d* 20 Jan 1831, having by her had an only s:

1b JOHN ROBERT TOWNSHEND, 1st and last EARL SYDNEY OF SCADBURY, Co Kent, so *cr* 27 Feb 1874, and 3rd and last VISCOUNT SYDNEY OF ST LEONARDS, GCB (1863), PC (1853); *b* 9 Aug 1805; MA Cantab; Capt Deal Castle, Ld Lt Kent, Ld Chamberlain, Ld Steward Household; *m* 4 Aug 1832 Lady Emily Caroline Paget (*d* 9 March 1893), dau of 1st Marquess of Anglesey (*qv*), and *dsp* 14 Feb 1890, when his titles expired

2a William Augustus; *b* 10 March 1776; *d* unm 3 July 1816

3a Horatio George Powys (Sir), KCH; *b* 6 Feb 1780; Col, Lt-Govr Round Tower Windsor Castle; *d* unm 25 May 1843

1a Georgiana; *b* 1 June 1761; State Housekeeper Windsor Castle; *d* unm 12 Sept 1835

2a Mary Elizabeth; *b* 2 Sept 1762; *m* 10 July 1783 2nd and last Earl of Chatham (*see* JERSEY, E) and *dsp* 20 May 1821

3a Frances; *b* 20 Feb 1772; *m* 20 Oct 1794 3rd Baron Dynevor (*qv*) and *d* 13 Aug 1854, leaving issue

4a Harriet Katherine; *b* 29 Nov 1773; *m* 24 March 1795 4th Duke of Buccleuch and (6th Duke of) Queensberry (*qv*) and *d* 24 Aug 1814, leaving issue

3 William; *b* 9 June 1702; ADC to GEORGE II, Groom Bedchamber and Privy Purse to FREDERICK, PRINCE OF WALES; *m* 29 May 1725 Henrietta (*d* 1755), dau of Lord William Powlett (*see* WINCHESTER, M), and *d* 29 Jan 1738, leaving, with three daus:

(1) CHARLES TOWNSHEND, 1st BARON BAYNING OF FOXLEY, Co Berks (GB), so *cr* 20 Oct 1797, PC (1777); *b* 27 Aug 1728; *educ* Eton and Clare Hall Cambridge; MP (Whig to 1770, then Tory) Yarmouth 1756–84 and 1790–96, a Ld Admlty 1765–70 and Treasury 1770–77; *m* 21 Aug 1777 his cousin Annabella Powlett (*d* 3 Jan 1825), dau of Rev Richard Smyth and gdau and heiress of William Powlett, s of Lord William Powlett (*see* WINCHESTER, M), and *d* 19 May 1810, leaving, with five daus (*d* unm):

1a CHARLES FREDERICK POWLETT TOWNSHEND later POWLETT, 2nd BARON BAYNING OF FOXLEY; *b* 26 Sept 1785; MP (Tory) Truro 1808–10; *d* unm 2 Aug 1823

2a HENRY WILLIAM POWLETT TOWNSHEND later WILLIAM-POWLETT (roy licence 8 Sept 1823), 3rd and last BARON BAYNING OF FOXLEY; *b* 8 June 1797; *educ* Eton and St John's Coll Cambridge; Vicar Honingham, Norfolk; *m* 9 Aug 1842 Emma (*d* 10 Nov 1887), dau of William H Fellowes (*see* DE RAMSEY, B), and *dsps* 5 Aug 1866, when the Barony expired

1 Elizabeth; *m* 1st Earl Cornwallis (*see* CORNWALLIS, B) and *d* 1 Dec 1785, leaving issue

The **2nd Viscount** *m* 2nd by 25 July 1713 Dorothy (*d* 29 March 1726), sis of 1st Earl of Orford (*see* WALPOLE, B), and *d* 21 June 1738, having had, with other issue:

4 Edward (Very Rev); *b* 25 Oct 1719; DD, Dean Norwich; *m* 11 May 1747 Mary (*d* 21 Feb 1816), dau of Gen Price, and *d* 27 Jan 1765, leaving, with three other daus (*d* unm):

(1) Edward (Rev); *m* 23 March 1789 Louisa Sarah (*d* 7 March 1853), dau of Sir William Milner, 1st Bt (*qv*)

(1) Elizabeth; *m* Rev Walter Wren Driffield, Rector Eswarton, Suffolk, and Southchurch, Essex

(2) Charlotte; *m* 1st 12 May 1773 John Norris; *m* 2nd 1779 Thomas Fauquier

2 Dorothy; *m* May 1743 Very Rev Spencer Cowper, Dean Durham

3 Mary; *m* Lt-Gen Edward Cornwallis (*see* CORNWALLIS, B)

The est s,

CHARLES TOWNSHEND, **3rd Viscount Townshend of Raynham**; *b* 11 July 1700; *educ* Eton and King's Coll Cambridge; MP (Whig) Gt Yarmouth; called up to Ho Lds *vp* 22 May 1723 in f's barony; Ld Bedchamber, Ld Lt Norfolk 1730–38; *m* 29 May 1723 Audrey (*d* 9 March 1788), only dau and heiress of Edward Harrison, of Ball's Park, Herts, and had, with other issue:

1 GEORGE, **1st Marquess**

2 Charles, PC; Chllr Exchequer Aug 1766; *m* 18 Sept 1755 Caroline, Baroness Greenwich in her own right (*d* 11 Jan 1794), dau and coheir of 2nd Duke of Argyll (*qv*) and widow of Earl of Dalkeith (*see* BUCCLEUCH and QUEENSBERRY, D), and *d* 4 Sept 1767, having had, with two sons (*d* unm):

(1) Anne; *m* 1st 22 March 1779 Richard Wilson, of Co Tyrone; *m* 2nd John Tempest

The 3rd VISCOUNT *d* 12 March 1764; his est s,

GEORGE TOWNSHEND, **1st Marquess Townshend of Raynham**, Co Norfolk (GB), so *cr* 31 Oct 1787, PC; *b* 28 Feb 1723/4 (GEORGE I stood sponsor); *educ* Eton and St John's Coll Cambridge; Col 64th Foot June–Dec 1759 and 28th Foot 1759–73, Maj-Gen 1761, Lt-Gen Ordnance 1763–67, Ld Lt Ireland 1767–72 and Norfolk, Col 2nd Dragoon Gds, High Steward Tamworth, Yarmouth and Norwich, Govr Jersey, Master-Gen Ordnance; fought Battles of Dettingen, Fontenoy, Culloden and Laffeldt; Quebec surrendered to him as C-in-C after the death of General Wolfe, Gen 1782, FM 1796; *m* 1st 19 Dec 1751 Lady Charlotte Compton, Baroness Ferrers and Baroness Compton, both in her own right (*d* 14 Sept 1770; *see* FERRERS, E), only surv child of 5th Earl of Northampton (*see* NORTHAMPTON, M), and had, with another s and two more daus:

1 GEORGE TOWNSHEND, **2nd Marquess Townshend of Raynham**, also 4th BARON FERRERS and 8th BARON COMPTON (as both of which *s* mother 1770), also 1st EARL OF LEICESTER (GB), so *cr* 18 May 1784; *b* 18 April 1753; *educ* Eton and St John's Coll Cambridge; Jt PMG 1794–99, Ld Steward Household 1799–1802; *m* 24 Dec 1777 Charlotte (*d* 2 Feb 1802), dau of Eaton MAINWARING later ELLERKER, of Risby Park, Yorks, and coheir of her uncle, Roger Mainwaring Ellerker, and *d* 27 July 1811, having had, with other issue:

(1) GEORGE FERRARS [*sic*, a spelling insisted on by his f] TOWNSHEND, **3rd Marquess Townshend of Raynham**; *b* 13 Dec 1778; *educ* Eton and Trin Coll Cambridge; *m* 12 May 1807 Sarah (left her husb 8 May 1808 and filed suit against him for non-consummation; she went through a form of marriage 24 Oct 1809 with John Margetts (*d* 24 June 1842), a brewer of St Ives, Hunts (by whom she had numerous issue, the est surv s of which union styled himself Earl of Leicester till declared illegitimate by Act of Parl 1843, having sat as MP (C) Bodmin from 1841 till 1843 under the style Earl of Leicester); *m* 2nd (*i.e.*, after her legal husb's death) 10 Jan 1856 James Laidler, of Fenton, Northumberland, and *dspl* 11 Sept 1858), dau of William DUNN later DUNN-GARDNER, and *dsp* 31 Dec 1855 in Italy, where he had been obliged to live after what was presumably rather too openly homosexual activity, having been disinherited by his f, when the Earldom of Leicester expired and the Baronies of Ferrers of Chartley and Compton fell into abeyance among his sisters and their issue

(2) Charles Vere Ferrers; *b* 16 Sept 1785; *m* 24 March 1812 his cousin Charlotte (*d* 21 March 1866), est dau of Gen William Loftus by Lady Elizabeth Townshend, and *dsp* 5 Nov 1853

(1) Charlotte Barbara; *m* 6 April 1805 Lt-Col Cecil Bisshopp, s of 12th Lord (Baron) Zouche (*qv*), and *dsp* 3 Oct 1807. He *d* of wounds received in action in Upper Canada 11 July 1813

(2) Harriet Anne; *m* 11 March 1813 Edward Ferrers, of Baddesley Clinton, Warwicks, and *d* 1 June 1845, leaving issue. He *d* 11 Aug 1830

(3) Elizabeth Margaret; *m* 5 Aug 1815 Joseph Moore Boultbee, of Springfield Ho, Warwicks, and *d* 18 Dec 1868, having had issue. He *d* 24 May 1860

2 John, PC, of Ball's Park, Herts; *b* 19 Jan 1757; MP Cambridge U, Westminster and Knaresborough; *m* 10 April 1787 Georgiana Anne (*d* 4 May 1851), dau of William Poyntz, of Midgham, Berks, and *d* 25 Feb 1833, having had:

(1) Charles Fox; *b* 28 June 1795; fndr Pop (the Eton Soc); *d* unm *vp* 2 April 1817

(2) JOHN, **4th Marquess**

(3) George Osborne (Rev); *b* 13 Nov 1801; granted with sisters rank of marquess's dau/yr s; *m* 1839 Jessie Victoria (*d* 16 April 1897), 2nd dau of V-Adml John MacKellar, and *d* 7 Sept 1876, leaving:

1a Charles Thornton; *b* 29 Jan 1840; *m* 1st 2 July 1859 Louise (*d* Jan 1878), est dau of John Graham, of Melbourne, Australia; *m* 2nd 23 Dec 1880 Caroline, est dau of George Seear, of London, and *d* 13 May 1889, having by his 1st w had:

1b Charles Vere Ferrers (Sir), KCB, DSO; *b* 21 Feb 1861; Shropshire LI, Roy Fus, Sudan Expdn 1884–85, Hunza Nayar Expdn 1891–92, Chitral 1895, Dongola 1896, Nile Expdn 1897–98, Boer War 1899–1900, Maj-Gen cmdg Orange Free State Dist 1909–11, a Div TF 1912–13, Jubbulpore Bde India 1913–15 and Indian Expdny Force Mesopotamia (defence of Kut-el-Amara 1915–16) WW I (despatches, Croix de Guerre), MP Wrekin 1920–24; *m* 22 Nov 1898 Alice (*d* 9 Dec 1965), Br War Medal, Victory medal, Croix de Guerre, Médaille d'or de la Reconnaissance Française, dau of Count Louis Cahen d'Anvers, of Château de Champs, Seine-et-Marne, France, and *d* 18 May 1924, leaving:

1c Audrey Dorothy Louise; *b* 21 Jan 1900; Médaille de la Resistance, Médaille de la Guerre 1940–45 Belgium; *m* 22 Nov 1922 (*divorce* 1936) Count Baudouin de Borchgrave d'Altena, s of Comte Paulo Borchgrave d'Altena, and had:

1d *Arnaud Charles Paul Marie Philippe; *b* 26 Oct 1926; *educ* King's Canterbury; RN 1942–46, Médaille Maritime; *m* 1st 1950 (*divorce* 1959) Dorothy Solon and has:

1e *Arnaud; *b* 1952

1d (cont.) Arnaud de Borchgrave d'Altena *m* 2nd 1959 *Eileen Ritschel and by her has:

1e *Trisha Theresa; *b* 1961

1d Diane Marie Madeleine Louise; *b* 1 Jan 1924; *d* 5 April 1940

2d *Marina Audrey Felicité; *b* 24 March 1932; *m* 1 Sept 1955 Charles Winton Browne Rankin, MBE, s of John Tennant Rankin, and has:

1e *Gavin Philippe Baudouin; *b* 1957

2e *James Rowland Evelyn; *b* 21 Jan 1959

2b George Augustus; *b* 1 Nov 1865; merchant navy offr; *k* at sea 30 Aug 1883

2a George Ferrars; *b* 28 March 1854; Govt Land Transfer Office; *m* 1st Elizabeth Brenda Baillie (*d* 1891) and had:

1b Ferrars Ernest Osborne; *b* 1882; *m* 13 April 1910 Isabel Dorothy Ferrers (*d* 22 July 1971), dau of William Henry Nicholson, of Rama Rama, Auckland, NZ, and *d* 20 Aug 1953, leaving:

  1c Henry George; *b* 3 June 1911; *m* 13 March 1943 *Elaine Florence, dau of T E Frith, of Melbourne, Australia, and *d* 1979, having had:

    1d +Ferrars Edwin [Ferrars Townshend, Pitua Rd, Tauranga, New Zealand]; *b* 2 Nov 1944; *m* 1980 *Gillian Adams

    2d Richard Lance; *b* 30 March 1947; *d* 8 July 1953

    3d +Anthony Stuart; *b* 22 July 1956

2b Stuart Villiers; *b* 22 July 1884; *m* 1936 Edith Myrtle, dau of W Ernest Potts, of Invercargill, NZ, and *d* 20 Aug 1954

3b Geoffrey Keith; *b* 1888; painter; *m* 19– Dorothy Reynolds, of Melbourne, and *dsp* Sept 1969

1b Audrey Brenda; *m* 1st 30 June 1903 William John Greenbank and had issue; *m* 2nd 13 Feb 1913 William Henry Rossiter and had further issue

2b Doris; *m* 4 April 1909 (*divorce* 1928, resumed maiden name) Carl August Nienholdt, of Hamburg, and had:

  1c (Elisabeth) Brenda Clifford; *b* May 1913; *m* Oct 1937 Paul Altstadt, s of Heinrich Altstadt, of Flensburg, and *d* July 1945, leaving:

    1d *Detlef; *b* July 1944; *m* 1969 *Gabriel, dau of A Gentiman, of Hamburg

    1d *Karin; *b* Nov 1940; *m* March 1964 *Joachim Schonoor, of Hamburg, and has issue

    2d *(Anna) Doris; *b* June 1942; *m* April 1967 *Detlef Harber, of Berlin, and has issue

  2c Maja; *b* Dec 1920; *d* July 1927

2a (cont.) George Townshend; *m* 2nd Clara Jenkins (*d* 17 May 1958) and *d* 26 Sept 1942, having by her had:

4b George Ferrers Vere; *b* 1897; *m* 1921 Fanny Elizabeth (*d* 30 March 1965), dau of James Matthew Brassington, of Staffs, and *d* 1957, leaving:

  1c *Diana Vere [Mrs Noel Gedye, 1/19 Selwyn Ave, Mission Bay, Auckland 5, New Zealand]; *b* 1927; *m* 1949 *Noel Trevor Gedye, AMIStructE, and has:

    1d *Christopher John; *b* 1950; *m* 1973 *Ranee Joy Murphy and has:

      1e *Shari Justin; *b* 1980

      1e *Nichole Jade; *b* 1984

    2d *Stephen Warren; *b* 1953; *m* 1977 *Roseann Hare

    3d *Michael Jonathan; *b* 1957; *m* 1984 *Victoria Ruth Ohms

  3b *Rua Hildyard Bute [Mrs Robert Hanna, 18 Tautari St, Orakei, Auckland 5, New Zealand]; *b* April 1902; *m* 1st 1927 (*divorce* 1934) Vivian Herbert Judd; *m* 2nd 24 May 1934 Robert Hanna (*d* 1975) and by her 1st husb has:

    1c *Raynham George HANNA; *b* 1928 (took step-f's name by deed poll)

    2c *Ross Townshend HANNA; *b* 1930

    3c *Mason Townshend HANNA (twin); *b* 1930

  4b *Rere Fortescue [Mrs Digby McGarry, 201 Victoria Ave, Remuera, Auckland 5, New Zealand]; *b* 7 Aug 1904; *m* 1924 *Digby Felix McGarry and has:

    1c *Digby Rochefort Dillon; *b* 18 April 1925; *m* April 1954 *Kathrine Mary Palmer and has:

      1d *William Digby; *b* 15 May 1955

      2d *Roger Michael; *b* 15 Oct 1959

      1d *Penelope Jane; *b* 15 Feb 1957

      2d *Joanna Mary; *b* 26 Oct 1967

  5b *Rata Victoria; *b* 1912; *m* 1934 *Jack Mason Norling and has:

    1c *Michael Holmden Mason; *b* 1935

3a Ernest Edwin; *b* 4 Feb 1858; *m* 1882 Rosa Harriet (*d* 30 Nov 1937), dau of E A Plumley, of Auckland, and *d* 1945, having had:

  1b Clifford Edwin; *b* 1884; *m* 17 Aug 1915 Rose Evelyn, MBE (1967), dau of John Abraham Greensill, of Picton, NZ, and *d* 1958, leaving:

    1c John Edwin; *b* 17 April 1918; RNZAF WW II; *m* 4 Nov 1943 *Mary [Mrs John Townshend, 9A Waterhouse St, Taradale, Napier 4001, New Zealand], dau of William Joseph Curran Sharp, Supt P&T Dept Straits Settlements and FMS, and *d* 9 Febv 1990, leaving:

      1d +Keith Edwin [Keith Townshend Esq, 9A Waterhouse St, Taradale, Napier 4001, New Zealand]; *b* 19 April 1948; *m* 20 Dec 1981 *Margaret Johanna, dau of Joseph Boldero, of Kawhia, NZ, and has:

        1e +David John Edwin; *b* 12 Nov 1982

        2e +James Raynham; *b* 29 Dec 1983

      1d *Margaret Ann [Mrs Ian Bambry, 21 Whiting Cres, Greenmeadows, Taradale, New Zealand]; *b* 12 Sept 1944; *m* 1st 1963 (*divorce* 1972) Earl Dudley Gee, RNZAF; *m* 2nd 1974 (*divorce* 1982) John Leslie Taylor; *m* 3rd 24 Oct 1998 *Ian Bambry and by her 1st husb has:

        1e *Richard John Earl GEE later TOWNSHEND (deed poll); *b* 13 Feb 1969; *m* 6 May 1989 *Joanna McKinley and has issue

        1e *Michelle Margaret; *b* 7 Oct 1963; *m* Ist 1984 (*divorce* 1991) Neville McAlister; *m* 2nd 11 Nov 1995 *Brendan Quinn

        2e *Lisa Ann; *b* 24 Dec 1966

    2c +George Maling, JP [George Townshend Esq JP, 2/26 Rothesay Bay Rd, Auckland, New Zealand]; *b* 25 May 1921; *educ* Marlborough Coll, NZ; RNZAF WW II, City Cncllr; *m* 1st 23 March 1944 Alice Joyce (*d* 1986), est dau of Alfred Wilfred Nye, of Coromandel, NZ; *m* 2nd 1987 *Heather Joan Pallesen, 3rd dau of Douglas Brown, of Hastings, NZ, and by his 1st w has:

      1d +Colin David [Colin Townshend Esq, 7 Edgecumbe St, Hamilton, New Zealand]; *b* 3 May 1948; *m* 1969 *Jennifer Pearl, est dau of Ian Alfred Madsen, of Napier, NZ, and has:

        1e +Glen David; *b* 1971

        2e +Zane Colin; *b* 1972

        1e *Tara Jean; *b* 1974

1d *Yvonne Joy [Mrs Brett Denize, 27 Haseler Cres, Howick, Auckland, New Zealand]; *b* 21 Aug 1946; *m* 1971 *Brett Denize and has:

  1e *Donna Joy; *b* 1972

  2e *Rowena Helen; *b* 1975

3c Charles Roberts; *b* 4 July 1926; *educ* Marlborough Coll, NZ; *m* 15 March 1952 *Dorothy Winifred [Mrs Charles Townshend, 11 Whakarire Ave, Westshore, Napier, New Zealand], dau of Frederick Leo Luks, of Auckland, NZ, and *d* 1987, leaving:

  1d +Robert Paul; *b* 7 Oct 1965

  1d *Denise Kaye [Mrs Stephen Greer, 10 Matai Place, Tametea, Napier, New Zealand]; *b* 25 Dec 1955; *m* 1980 *Stephen Alexander Greer, slr, and has:

    1e *Alexander Townshend; *b* 1982

    2e *Charles Townshend; *b* 1989

    1e *Rebecca Ellen; *b* 1984

  3c (cont.) Mr and Mrs Charles Townshend also adopted:

    *Mark Richard; *b* 19 June 1962

2b Charles Ernest Osborne; *b* 1888 ; *d* 5 Aug 1927

1b Tiria Vere Ferrars; *b* 1901; *m* 1926, as his 1st w, Thomas Stewart Raymond White, and *d* 2 May 1956, leaving a s and two daus

4a Henry; *b* 8 Aug 1859; *m* 14 Jan 1885 Emily Jane (*d* 1942), dau of E A Plumley, of Auckland, NZ, and *d* 1945, leaving:

  1b Henry Brooke Villiers; *b* 8 July 1888; slr Supreme Court NZ 1917, barrister 1920, NZ Expdny Force 1917–19; *d* unm 1968

  1a Augusta Mary; *m* 16 Aug 1865 Col George Brooke Meares, Roy Fus, of Dol-Lys Hall, Montgomerys, Cdr Kneller Hall, and *d* 25 Jan 1919, leaving issue. He *d* 4 Aug 1894

  (1) Audrey Harriet; *m* 11 Oct 1826 Rev Robert Ridsdale, Preb Chichester, and *d* 24 March 1873. He *d* 1876

  (2) Elizabeth Frances; *m* 20 Oct 1813 Adml Sir Augustus Clifford, 1st Bt, CB, Gentleman Usher of the Black Rod, and *d* 10 April 1862, leaving issue. He *d* 8 Feb 1877

  (3) Jane; *m* 6 Nov 1824 John Hildyard and *d* 7 March 1878. He *d* 1855

1 Elizabeth; *m* 7 May 1790 Gen William Loftus (*see* ELY, M) and *d* 21 March 1811, leaving issue

The **1st Marquess** *m* 2nd 19 May 1773 Anne (*d* 29 March 1819), dau and coheir of Sir William Montgomery, Bt, of Magbie Hill, Peeblesshire, by his w Hannah, dau and coheir of Alexander Tomkyns, of Prehen, Co Londonderry, and *d* 14 Sept 1807, having by her had:

3 Frederick (Rev); Rector Stiffkey 1792–1836; *d* unm and insane 18 Jan 1836, having murdered his next yr bro during a long coach trip they took together 40 years previously

4 Charles; MP Yarmouth; murdered by his er bro 27 May 1796

5 James Nugent Boyle Bernardo, KCH; *b* 11 Sept 1785; Capt RN; *m* 8 May 1813 Elizabeth (*m* 2nd 4 Sept 1844 Capt W H Henderson, CB, RN, and *d* 15 July 1873), dau of P Wallis, and *d* 28 June 1842

2 Charlotte; *m* 17 Aug 1797 6th Duke of Leeds and *d* 30 July 1856, having had issue (*see* 1963 edn). He *d* 10 July 1838

3 Harriet; *m* 16 Sept 1811 Lt-Gen 3rd Baron de Blaquiere and *d* 9 Nov 1848, leaving issue (*see* 1920 edn). He *d* 2 Nov 1851

The 3rd MARQUESS's cousin,

JOHN TOWNSHEND, **4th Marquess Townshend of Raynham**; *b* 28 March 1798; R-Adml; *m* 18 Aug 1825 Elizabeth Jane (*d* 27 Jan 1877), est dau of R-Adml Lord George Stuart, CB, and gdau of 1st Marquess of Bute (*qv*), and had, with another s (*d* an infant):

1 JOHN VILLIERS STUART, **5th Marquess**

2 James Dudley Brownlow Stuart; *b* 14 Dec 1832; RN; *d* 11 Aug 1846

1 Anne Maria; *m* 9 Feb 1854 Capt Alexander Nowell Sherson and *d* 14 Feb 1899, leaving issue. He *d* 10 Feb 1882

2 Elizabeth Clementina; *m* 15 July 1856 1st Baron Saint Levan (*qv*) and *d* 18 Nov 1910, leaving issue

3 Audrey Jane Charlotte; *m* 1st 18 Sept 1873 Hon Greville Theophilus Howard, 2nd s of 17th Earl of Suffolk and (10th Earl of) Berkshire (*qv*), and had issue; *m* 2nd 10 Aug 1882 Gen Rt Hon Sir Redvers Buller, VC, GCB, GCMG, PC, of Downes, Devon, and *d* 20 Feb 1926, having had further issue. He *d* 2 June 1908

The 5th MARQUESS *d* 10 Sept 1863; his s,

JOHN VILLIERS STUART TOWNSHEND, **5th Marquess Townshend of Raynham**, JP, DL Norfolk and Middx; *b* 10 April 1831; High Steward Tamworth, MP Tamworth 1856–63; *m* 17 Oct 1865 Lady Anne Elizabeth Clementina Duff (*d* 31 Dec 1925), est dau of 5th Earl of Fife (*see* FIFE, D), and had:

1 JOHN JAMES DUDLEY STUART, **6th Marquess**

1 Agnes Elizabeth Audrey; *b* 12 Dec 1870; *m* 2 Sept 1903 James Andrew Cuninghame Durham, FSA, of Cromer Grange and E Raynham Ho, Norfolk, Hon Attaché Dip Serv, s of Rev James Samuel William Durham, DD, Rector Ladbroke, Warwicks, and *d* 15 March 1955, leaving issue. He *d* 30 Sept 1954

The 5th MARQUESS *d* 26 Oct 1899; his s,

JOHN JAMES DUDLEY STUART TOWNSHEND, **6th Marquess Townshend of Raynham**, DL Norfolk; *b* 17 Oct 1866; *m* 9 Aug 1905 Gwladys Ethel Gwendolen Eugénie, Mayor King's Lynn 1928, Pres Roy Norfolk Ag Assoc 1929, Pres and Fndr Officers' Sunday Club 1914–18 and 1940–46 (*m* 2nd 29 Oct 1946 Bernard le Strange (*d* 13 March 1958), yr s of Capt Roland le Strange, JP, DL, of Hunstanton Hall, Norfolk, and *d* 10 Oct 1959), er dau of Thomas Sutherst, barrister, and *d* 17 Nov 1921, having had:

1 GEORGE JOHN PATRICK DOMINIC TOWNSHEND, **7th and present Marquess Townshend of Raynham**

1 Elizabeth Mary Gladys; *b* 16 Oct 1917; *m* 1st 20 Oct 1939 (*divorce* 1947) Sir (Eric) Richard Meadows White, 2nd Bt, of Boulge Hall, Suffolk (*qv*), and had issue; *m* 2nd 15 March 1949 John Clifford Roberts, s of John Joseph Roberts, and *d* 31 Dec 1950

Seat: Raynham Hall, Fakenham, Norfolk. The true architect of this highly original house is unknown, for though Inigo Jones has been suggested expert opinion is divided. The actual sponsor of the undertaking was **Sir Roger Townshend, 1st Bt**, but his first effort fell down after being started in 1619 with stone from a priory which had been first dissolved and then demolished. Jones would not have designed anything so slipshod. On the whole it looks as if Raynham owes its appearance to Venetian influences absorbed by **Sir Roger** on a Grand Tour he made to Italy around the time of the second attempt at a building programme, that is to say the early 1620s, plus Inigonian notions translated into Norfolk actuality by Sir Roger's chief mason, one William Edge.

The chief features are the Dutch gables at either end of both the east and west fronts. These rise almost as high again as the two-floored supporting structure beneath them and although curved at the side are surmounted by classical rectilinear pediments and punctured by an oculus window. The main entrance on the east facade also is surmounted by a classical pediment, but this time it rises on ionic columns in between which is a tall curved-topped window. It seems that the east facade made much more use of Venetian features originally but either in the late 17th century or the first third of the 18th, when William Kent was called in to modernise the inside, a more homely Anglo-Saxon note was struck, with standard Georgian sash windows replacing the more generously proportioned ones of a hundred years before.

TREFGARNE

RATIONE ET CONCILIO

Arms: Or a dragon rampant gu., over all on a bend az. a leek of the first between two thistles ppr. **Crest:** On a mount vert a palm tree ppr., suspended therefrom an escutcheon or, charged with a portcullis gu. **Supporters:** On either side a Herefordshire bull charged on the shoulder with an escutcheon or, thereon a portcullis az. **Motto:** *Ratione et concilio* ('By reason and counsel').
Creation: B. (UK) 21 Jan 1947.

THE 2ND BARON TREFGARNE, of Cleddau, Co Pembroke (David Garro Trefgarne, PC (1989)) [The Rt Hon The Lord Trefgarne PC, The Old Barn, Kettlewell Close, Horsell, Surrey GU21 4HZ]; *b* 31 March 1941; *s f* 1960; *educ* Haileybury (Life Govr 1992–) and Princeton; Roy Aero Club Bronze Medal (jointly) 1963 for flight UK to Australia and back in light aircraft; Oppn Whip Ho Lds 1977–79, Govt Whip 1979–81, Parly U-Sec: Tport 1981, FCO 1981–82, DHSS 1982–83, MOD 1983–85, Min State: MOD (Def Support 1985–86, Def Procurement 1986–89), DTI 1989–90; co dir and pres Metcom, chm Engrg Training Authority 1992–; *m* 9 Nov 1968 *Hon Rosalie, dau of Baron Lane of Horsell (LP), and has:

  1 +GEORGE GARRO; *b* 4 Jan 1970; jnlst with *Daily Telegraph*
  2 +Justin Peter Garro; *b* 5 Jan 1973; *educ* LAMDA
  1 *Rebecca Rosalie; *b* 28 Jan 1976

Lineage: The Rev DAVID GARRO-JONES, of Milford Haven, Pembs; *b* 12 May 1864; *m* 12 May 1892 Sarah (*d* 4 Feb 1928), dau of Morgan Griffiths, of Tan-y-Cefn, Breconshire, and *d* 1 March 1935, leaving:

GEORGE MORGAN GARRO-JONES later TREFGARNE (deed poll 21 Jan 1954), **1st Baron Trefgarne**, of Cleddau, Co Pembroke (UK), so *cr* 21 Jan 1947; *b* 14 Sept 1894; *educ* Caterham Sch; barrister Gray's Inn 1923, Hon Capt RAF, served Denbighs Yeo 1913, WW I with S Wales Borderers and RFC, Advsy Offr US Air Serv 1918, MP (Lib) S Hackney Oct 1924–May 1929 and N Aberdeen Nov 1935–June 1945, Priv Sec to Lord Greenwood at Home Office, Dept Overseas Trade and while Ch Sec Ireland 1919–21, Parly Sec Min Production 1942, chm: Radio Production Ctee 1942–45, Centl Priority Ctee and Raw Materials Ctee 1944–45, TV Advsy Ctee 1945–47; memb Empire Parly Mission W Africa 1928 and Electoral Machinery Ctee 1941, fndr and chm Colonial Devpt Corp 1947–50, chm W E Sykes Ltd; *m* 9 May 1940 Elizabeth (*m* 2nd 3 March 1962 (*divorce* 1966) Cdr Anthony Tosswill Courtney, OBE, RN, s of Basil Tosswill Courtney, of Ben Rhydding, Yorks; *m* 3rd 25 Feb 1971 Hugh Cecil Ker (*d* 1987), of St Michel, Cannes, France, and *d* 1987), yr dau of Charles Edward Churchill, of Ashton Keynes, Wilts, and *d* 27 Sept 1960, having had:

  1 DAVID GARRO TREFGARNE, **2nd and present Baron Trefgarne**
  2 +Trevor Garro; *b* 18 Jan 1944; *educ* Cheltenham and Cranfield Inst Tech (postgraduate course industl management 1967–69); chm Nesco Investments plc 1979–87; *m* 1st 16 Feb 1967 (*divorce* 1979) Diana Elizabeth, 2nd dau of Michael Edward Gibb, of Forge Ho, Taynton, Oxon, and has:

    (1) +Rupert Michael Garro; *b* 1972
    (2) +Oliver Edward Garro; *b* 1974

    (1) *Susannah Julia; *b* 1976
2 (cont.) The Hon Trevor Trefgarne *m* 2nd 1979 *Caroline France, dau of Michael Gosschalk, of Monte Carlo, and by her has:

    (3) +Mark Michael Garro; *b* 1982
    (2) *Camilla Amélie; *b* 1988
3 +Gwion George Garro [The Hon Gwion Trefgarne, Cherry Croft, Hewelsfield, Lydney, Glos]; *b* 2 April 1953; *educ* Milton Abbey and Merrist Wood and Usk Ag Coll; tree surgn; *m* 1986 *Jacqueline Louise, dau of Alan Rees, of Brockwier, Gwent, and has:

    (1) +Samuel Ivor Garro; *b* 1987
    (1) *Hannah Elizabeth; *b* 1989
1 *Mary Elizabeth; *b* 12 July 1940; barrister Gray's Inn 1971

TRENCHARD

NOSCE·TEIPSUM

Arms: Per pale arg. and az., in the first three pallets sa., all within a bordure of the last. **Crest:** A cubit arm erect, vested az., cuffed arg., holding in the hand a cinqueda sword, both ppr. **Supporters:** On either side an eagle gu., the dexter charged with a thistle leaved and slipped, the sinister with a truncheon or. **Motto:** *Nosce teipsum* ('Know thyself'). **Creations:** Bt. (UK) 9 Oct 1919, B. (UK) 23 Jan 1930, V. (UK) 31 Jan 1936.

THE 3RD VISCOUNT TRENCHARD, Baron Trenchard, of Wolfeton, Co Dorset, and a **Baronet** (Sir Hugh Trenchard, Bt) [The Rt Hon The Viscount Trenchard, 25 Copthall Ave, London EC2R 7DR]; *b* 12 March 1951; *s f* 1987; *educ* Eton and Trin Coll Cambridge (BA 1973); Capt 4th RGJ, TA 1973–80, memb Gen Affairs Ctee Japan Securities Dealers Assoc 1987–88 (dir 1994–95), Japan Assoc Corporate Execs 1987–95 and Exec Ctee Br Chamber Commerce in Japan 1993–95, chm Securities Ctee European Business Community Japan 1993–95, dir Dover Japan KK 1985–87, Kleinwort Benson Ltd 1986–96, Robt Fleming & Co Ltd 1996–; memb cncl RAF Benevolent Fund 1991–; *m* 9 April 1975 *Fiona Elizabeth, only dau of 2nd Baron Margadale (qv), and has:

  1 +ALEXANDER THOMAS; *b* 26 July 1978; *educ* Eton and St Hugh's Coll Oxford; Page of Hon to HM THE QUEEN 1990–93
  2 +William James; *b* 14 May 1986
  1 *Katherine Clare; *b* 2 Nov 1980
  2 *Laura Mary; *b* 20 Dec 1987

Lineage: SIMON TRENCHARD, of Cricket St Thomas, Somerset; *m* Edith — (*d* March 1601) and *d* June 1600, leaving, with other issue:

HUGH TRENCHARD, of Cricket St Thomas; *b* 1571; *m* 2nd — and had, with other issue:

JOHN TRENCHARD, of Maudlin in Thorncombe; *b* Oct 1618; *m* 1st Mary —; *m* 2nd Barbara Hooper and *d* 1667, leaving by his 1st w, with an er s (John, of Maudlin, *b* June 1658, *d* c 1741, leaving issue):

OLIVER TRENCHARD, of Laymore in Thorncombe; *b* Sept 1662; *m* 19 Oct 1682 Mary Hooper and *d* 1746, having had, with other issue:

GEORGE TRENCHARD, of Laymore; *b* Dec 1706; *m* Elizabeth, dau of James Horder, of Rampisham, Dorset, and had, with a yr s and a dau:

JOHN TRENCHARD, of Laymore; *b* 1738; *m* Anne, only dau of John Stuckey, of Winsham, Somerset, and *d* 1782, leaving, with an er s (John, of Exmouth, Devon, *b* Dec 1765, *d* unm 25 April 1840) and two daus (Anne, *m* William Newberry and had issue; Elizabeth, *m* Robert Smith, of Southcombe, Devon):

WILLIAM TRENCHARD, of Taunton and Oathill, Somerset; *b* 1771; *m* 11 April 1803 Lucy (*d* 23 June 1843), dau of Nehemiah Upcott, of Colhampton, Devon, and *d* 1 July 1828, having had, with two er sons (William, *b* 24 Dec 1803, *d* 10 April 1804; John, of Exmouth, *b* 31 Oct 1807, *m* 17 Jan 1838 Margaret (*d* 13 April 1871), er dau of Joshua Gottreux, of Neufchatel, Switzerland, and had issue) and two yst sons (Francis Frederick, MRCS, of Bayswater, *b* 26 April 1816, *d* 1844; Frederick Alfred, of Exmouth, *b* 1818) a 3rd s:

HENRY CHARLES TRENCHARD, of Taunton; *b* 19 Feb 1813; *m* 1st 6 Jan 1836 Elizabeth (*d* 1840), dau and coheir of Matthew Montague, of Clifton, Glos; *m* 2nd Nov 1841 Mary Bush, dau of Rev Samuel Alford, and *d* Sept 1881, leaving issue by her and by his 1st w, with a dau (Elizabeth Montague, *b* 1837):

HENRY MONTAGUE TRENCHARD; *b* 29 July 1838; Capt KOYLI; *m* 3 June 1869 Georgina Louisa Catherine Tower, dau of Capt John Skene, RN, by Georgina, dau of Henry Lumsden of Auchindoir and Clova, Aberdeenshire, and *d* 1914, having had, with other issue:

Sir Hugh Montague Trenchard, 1st Bt, so *cr* 9 Oct 1919, as also 31 Jan 1936 **1st Viscount Trenchard**, and earlier 23 Jan 1930 BARON TRENCHARD, of Wolfeton, Co Dorset (all UK), GCB (1924, KCB 1918, CB 1914), OM (1951), GCVO (1935), DSO (1906); *b* 3 Feb 1873; Roy Scots Fus 1893–1912: Boer War 1899–1902 with Imp Yeo, Bushmen's Corps and Canadian Scouts and Mounted Inf (severely wounded, Queen's medal with three clasps, King's medal with two clasps), Capt 1900, W Africa Frontier Force 1904–10, cmded operations in Owerri Dist 1904, cmded two operations 1905, cmded Bende-Onitsha Hinterland Expdn 1905–06 (despatches twice), T/Lt-Col while Cmdt Southern Nigerian Regt 1908, seconded to RFC 1912, Assist Cmdt Centl Flying Sch 1913–14, cmded Mil Wing 1914, W/Cdr France 1914–15, Col 1915, T/Brig 1915, Maj-Gen 1916, cmded RFC France 1915–17, Cdr Independent Air Force 1918, C-in-C Inter-Allied Independent Air Force 1918 (thanks of Parl and £10,000 (over £194,000 in late-1990s terms) for servs in WW I), Ch Air Staff 1918–30, AM 1919, Pncpl Air ADC to HM GEORGE V 1921–25, ACM 1922, Marshal RAF 1927, Commr Met Police 1931–35, Pres Comrades of RAF 1933, Tstee Imp War Museum 1937–45, Pres American and Br Cwlth Assoc 1942, Chm Govrs London Sch Hygiene and Tropical Medicine 1947; Cdr Legn Hon, Croix de Guerre, Cdr Order Leopold Belgium and Crown Italy, 3rd Cl St Anne Russia, US DSM, Order Sacred Treasure Japan 1st Cl; Hon LLD Cantab 1919, Hon DCL Oxon 1926; *m* 17 June 1920 Katherine Isabel Salvin (Ch Comdt ATS 1938–41) (*d* 5 March 1960), widow of Capt Hon James Boyle, Roy Scots Fus (*see* GLASGOW, E), and 2nd dau of Edward Salvin Bowlby, of Gilston Park, Herts, and Knoydart, Inverness-shire, and *d* 10 Feb 1956, having had:

1 Hugh; *b* 6 June 1921; *educ* Eton; Lt Gren Gds WW II; *ka* March 1943

2 THOMAS TRENCHARD, **2nd Viscount Trenchard**, MC (1945); *b* 15 Dec 1923; *educ* Eton; Capt KRRC WW II; Min State: DTI 1979–81, MOD 1981–1983; dir: T Wall and Sons Ltd 1953–66, Unilever & Unilever NV 1967–77, Carpets Internat 1977–79; chm: Walls Meat Co Ltd 1960–66, Sausage and Meat Pie Mfrs Assoc 1959–73; Pres: Inst of Grocery Distribution, Bacon and Meat Mfrs Assoc 1974–79, Roy Inst Public Health and Hygiene 1970–79; memb ARC 1970–79; *m* 19 June 1948 *Patricia [The Rt Hon Patricia Viscountess Trenchard, Abdale House, N Mymms, Herts AL9 7TX], only dau of Adml Sir Sidney Robert Bailey, KBE, CB, DSO, and *d* 1987, leaving:

(1) HUGH TRENCHARD, **3rd and present Viscount Trenchard**

2 +John [The Hon John Trenchard, Lower Abbotts Wootten, Whitchurch Canonicorum, Dorset DT6 6NL]; *b* 13 March 1953; *educ* Eton; *m* 1983 *Clare, yst dau of Edward Chandos de Burgh Marsh, of The Old Rectory, Salcott, Essex, and has:

1a +Thomas Edward; *b* 13 May 1988

1a *Emma Clare; *b* 31 Jan 1991

(3) +Thomas Henry; *b* 16 July 1966; *educ* Haileybury; *m* 1997 *Sarah Saunders and has:

1a *Katherine Elizabeth; *b* 1997

TREVELYAN of Nettlecombe

Arms: Gu. a demi-horse arg., hoofed and maned or, issuing out of water in base ppr. **Crest:** Two arms counter-embowed ppr., habited az., holding in the hands a bezant surmounted by a sea parrot. **Motto:** Tyme tryeth troth. **Creation:** Bt. (E) 24 Jan 1661/2.

SIR EDWARD NORMAN TREVELYAN, 11TH, of Nettlecombe, Somerset [Sir Edward Trevelyan Bt, 3180 Via Real, Carpinteria, CA 93013, USA]; *b* 14 Aug 1955; *s* f 1996; *educ* U of Calif San Diego (BA History 1981), U of Calif Santa Barbara (MA Pol Sci 1986); Olympic gold medallist Soling C1 Yachting event 1984; administrator U of Calif 1990–; *m* 1993 *Debbie J Mullin and has:

1 +REED EDWARD; *b* 6 Oct 1996

Lineage: HENRY TREVELYAN, feudal Ld of Trevillion, Cornwall; *m* Alice, dau and heiress of Sir John Botreaux, and was gf of:

Sir JOHN TREVELYAN; High Sheriff Cornwall 1449–50, MP Cornwall 1453; *m* Elizabeth, dau and heiress of Thomas Whalesborough, of Whalesborough, Cornwall (s of John Whalesborough, by Joan, sis of Sir Simon de Ralegh), and *d* 1494, having had, with other issue, including two yr sons (George, Chaplain to HENRY VIII; Humphrey, *m* Margaret, dau of Sir Rice ap Thomas, KG):

Sir JOHN TREVELYAN, KB (1501), of Trevillion and Nettlecombe, Somerset; *m* the dau of Sir John Halywell, of Devon, and *d* 1522, leaving:

JOHN TREVELYAN, of Nettlecombe; *m* Avice, dau and heiress of Nicholas Cockworthy, of Yarnscombe, Devon, and *d* 1558, leaving an est s:

JOHN TREVELYAN, of Trevelyan and Nettlecombe; *m* Maud, dau of Giles Hill, of Honiton, and *d* 1563, leaving:

JOHN TREVELYAN, of Trevelyan; *m* Wilmot, dau of John Harris, of Hayne, Serjeant-at-law, and *d* 1577, leaving:

JOHN TREVELYAN; High Sheriff Somerset 1619; rebuilt the mansion house of Nettlecombe; *m* Urith, dau of Sir John Chichester, MP (*see* DONEGALL, M), and *d* 1623, leaving:

JOHN TREVELYAN; *m* Margaret, dau of George Luttrell, of Dunster Castle, Somerset, and had an est s:

GEORGE TREVELYAN; royalist Civil War; *m* Margaret, dau of Sir Robert Strode, of Parnham, Dorset, and *d* 1653, leaving an est s:

Sir George Trevelyan, 1st Bt (E), so *cr* 24 Jan 1661/2; *educ* Wadham Coll Oxford; *m* 8 Jan 1655/6 (*d* by 28 Nov 1689), only dau and heiress of John Willoughby, of Leahill, Devon, and *d* 1671, having had, with other issue, including a dau (Margaret, *m* Sir Thomas Putt, 2nd and last Bt (*dsp* 5 May 1721)):

Sir John Trevelyan, 2nd Bt; *b c* 1670; *educ* Wadham Coll Oxford; MP Somerset 1695–98 and 1700 and Minehead 1708–16 and 1718–22; *m* 1st 1693 Urith (*d* 1697), dau of Sir John Pole, 3rd Bt, of Shute (*qv*), and had a dau (*d* young); *m* 2nd 1700 Susanna (*d* 1718), dau and heiress of William Warren, of Stallensthorne, Devon, and *d* 25 Sept 1755, having by her had, with other issue:

Sir George Trevelyan, 3rd Bt; *bapt* 18 Nov 1707; *m* 1733 Julia (*d* 28 Dec 1787), only dau of Sir Walter Calverley, 1st Bt, of Calverley, Yorks, and eventual heir of her bro, Sir Walter Calverley Blacket, 2nd and last Bt (*d* 1777, having taken the name BLACKET under terms of will of his cousin, Sir William Blacket, 2nd and last Bt), and had, with three other daus:

1 JOHN (Sir), **4th Bt**

2 Walter; *m* 1st 14 July 1772 Margaret, er dau and coheir of James Thornton, of Netherwitton, Northumberland, and had:

(1) Walter Blacket; *d* unm 3 April 1818

(2) Raleigh, of Netherwitton; *b* 6 Aug 1781; *m* 14 June 1819 Elizabeth (*d* 16 Sept 1885), 2nd dau of Robert Grey, of Shorestone Hall, Northumberland, and *d* 12 May 1865, having had, with a dau (*d* young):

1a Thornton Raleigh; *b* 18 April 1820; *m* 11 April 1842 Dorothy, dau of Matthew Henderson, of Galashiels, and *d* 14 Feb 1845, leaving:

1b Thornton Roger, of Netherwitton, JP (Northumberland); *b* 1 Jan 1843; *m* 1 Jan 1864 Dobrée Wilkinson (*d* 11 Jan 1904), dau of J W Fraser, of Bath, and *d* 16 Jan 1904, leaving:

1c John Spencer, of Netherwitton; *b* 8 Dec 1864; *m* 1897 Eleanor Margaret (*d* 1961), yr dau of W Brook Mortimer, of Hay Carr, Lancs, and *d* 3 Nov 1943, having had:

1d John Thornton; *b* 9 March 1898; *m* 19 June 1928 Anne Georgina (*d* 1989), dau of Prof John Dobson Wardale, of Newcastle, and *d* 12 Aug 1970, leaving:

1e +John Cecil Raleigh [John Trevelyan Esq, Netherwitton Hall, Morpeth, Northumberland NE61 4NW]; *b* 13 July 1933; *educ* Marlborough; High Sheriff 1982; *m* 25 Jan 1962 *Jane, dau of Brig Roger Peake, DSO, OBE, of Chelsea, and has:

1f +John Henry Thornton; *b* 4 Oct 1968

1f *Caroline Georgina; *b* 28 Nov 1962

2f *Tessa Margaret Thornton; *b* 5 April 1966; *m* 17 June 1995 *Jonathan Luke Henry Goodhart, s of Lt-Col M H Goodhart

2e +Edward Calverley Thornton [Edward Trevelyan Esq, Dalton House, Dalton, Northumberland]; *b* 26 Aug 1935; *educ* Marlborough; *m* 27 April 1962 *Elizabeth Anne, er dau of O Geoffrey Blayney, MC, of High Shield, Hexham, Northumberland, and has:

1f +Julian Blackett Thornton; *b* 8 March 1963

2f +Hugh Robert Thornton; *b* 1973

1f *Rosemary Joy; *b* 30 March 1965

2f *Amanda Fay; *b* 22 Aug 1967

1e *Anne Margaret Thornton [Mrs John Usborne, Glan-Nant, Crickhowell, Breconshire]; *b* 5 Feb 1930; *m* 29 Aug 1953 *John Humphrey Usborne, er s of Lt-Col John Usborne, of Writtle, Essex, and has:

1f *Richard Thomas; *b* 18 July 1954; *educ* Malvern; *m* 198– *Henrietta E M, 6th dau of B C White-Spunner, of Brookes Hall, Horsington, Somerset, and has:

1g *Thomas Masters; *b* 1983

1g *Alice; *b* 1985

2f *John Edward; *b* 18 July 1954; *educ* Malvern; *m* 1980 *Diana, dau of A Glynne-Percy, of Tomatin, Inverness-shire, and has:

1g *Joanna Susan; *b* 1983

2g *Sarah Margaret; *b* 1985

3f *Andrew Thornton [Andrew Usborne Esq, George House, 21 High St, Colsterworth, Lincs NG33 5NE]; *b* 16 Sept 1956; CEng, MICE; *m* 1983 *Lamorna, yr dau of K J Hammond Forder, of Fulham, and has:

1g *Harriet Georgina; *b* 1991

2g *Eleanor Victoria Thornton; *b* 1995

1f *Joan Mary Thornton; *b* 13 Feb 1932; *m* 23 Nov 1963 *George Campbell Wilkinson, TD, er s of Col George Edward Wilkinson, MC, TD, DL, of Wylam Cottage, Northumberland, and has had:

     1g A son; *b* 14, *d* 21 March 1967

     1g *Anne Margaret; *b* 16 March 1965

2d Roger de Thornton; *b* 3 June 1901; Lt RN; *d* 1928

1d Caroline Nora Constantia; *b* 3 June 1902; *m* 22 May 1931 William Eric Davis, 3rd s of Sir Robert Henry Davis, of Ashtead, Surrey, and had:

    1e *Patrick Brian Trevelyan; *b* 5 Nov 1935

    1e *Margaret Trevelyan; *b* 20 Aug 1932

    2e *Caroline Trevelyan; *b* 28 June 1939; *m* 25 Jan 1969 *Richard Charles Patterson, s of Robert Henry Brice Patterson, of Congresbury, Somerset, and has:

      1f *James Edward; *b* 1 April 1970

2c Walter Raleigh; *b* 10 Dec 1865; *d* 1904

3c Roger de Thornton; *b* 8 Nov 1867; *m* in USA and *d* there

4c George Alfred Thornton; *b* 21 March 1871; *m* in USA and *d* there

5c Freeman Blackett Thornton; *b* 5 Jan 1874; *m* 5 Jan 1898 Louise (*d* 22 April 1944), 2nd dau of Col Sir Philip Watts, KCB, FRS, LLD, DSc, and *d* 1943, having had:

    1d Dora Humphrys Thornton; *b* 12 Feb 1900; *d unm* 23 June 1936

    2d Lillian Agnes Thornton; *b* 22 March 1901; *m* 7 July 1926 Lt-Col Robert Hunter Smith, OBE, RASC, s of William James Smith, of Algeciras, Spain, and had issue. He *d* 27 Sept 1935

1c Lilian Elizabeth Margaret Thornton; *m* 12 June 1897 Ralph Spencer, of Walbottle Hall, and *d* 1944, having had issue. He *d* 23 Aug 1926

1b Constance Mary; *m* 1st 7 Jan 1864 James Jodel Mackie and had issue; *m* 2nd 10 Aug 1869 Robert Benn and *d* 1921

2a Walter Blackett; *b* 17 March 1821; BA Cantab; barrister; *m* Helena Caroline (*d* 14 March 1898), widow of Rev Bryan Faussett and dau of **Sir John Trevelyan, 5th Bt** (*see below*), and *d* 10 Oct 1894, leaving:

    1b Herbert; *b* 6 July 1847; Maj Royal Inniskilling Fus; *d* 28 Jan 1912

    2b Walter Blackett; *d* 21 Dec 1920

    3b Willoughby Fenwick; *b* 1 Aug 1856; Staff Paymaster APD, Lt-Col 2nd Bn N Staffs Regt; *d* 16 July 1919

    1b Constance Helena; *m* 27 Dec 1877 Sir Arthur Moseley Channell, PC, High Court Judge, and *d* 14 Sept 1929, leaving issue

3a Raleigh; *b* 15 Aug 1833; *m* 16 Oct 1844 Sarah Flora, 2nd dau of Capt Macdonald, 36th Regt, and *d* 25 Aug 1882

1a Constance; *m* 7 Aug 1850 Robert Hawdon and *d* 23 Dec 1867. He *d* Nov 1855

2a Helena; *m* 3 Nov 1852 her cousin Lt-Col James Harrington Trevelyan and *d* 18 Dec 1905, leaving issue (*see below*)

2 (cont.) Walter Trevelyan *m* 2nd Margaret (*d* 26 March 1838), dau of Richard Hitchens, of Poltair, Cornwall, and *d* 1819, having by her had:

  (3) Walter Calverley; *b* 1807; *m* 1828 Isabella (*d* 10 April 1872), dau of C Tait, and *d* 3 Dec 1849, leaving:

    1a Walter Raleigh; *b* 11 April 1842; *m* 29 Sept 1863 Marion Adelaide (*d* 30 Dec 1928), only dau of Rev John Charles William Leslie, of Ballibay, and *d* 11 July 1898, leaving:

      1b Walter Raleigh; *b* 26 Aug 1865; T/Capt ASC, Capt 4th Bn Leinster Regt; *m* 25 June 1891 (*divorce* 1903) Georgina Alice (*d* 16 Sept 1923), only child of Edmund Whitney Fetherston-Whitney, 3rd s of Rev Sir Thomas Francis Fetherson, 4th Bt (*see* 1923 edn), and *das* 19 April 1916, having had:

        1c Walter Raleigh Fetherstonhaugh, JP Essex; *b* 16 Oct 1893; *educ* RMC Sandhurst; Col IA, WWs I (despatches) and II (despatches, invalided 1943); *m* 6 April 1921 Olive Beatrice, Kaisar-i-Hind Silver medal (*m* 2nd June 1953 Col William Henry Ralston, DSO, OBE, MC (*d* 1962), and *d* 28 June 1976), 2nd dau of Thomas Gibbons Frost, of Mollington Hall, Chester, and *d* 12 Jan 1953, leaving:

          1d +(Walter) Raleigh [Raleigh Trevelyan Esq, 18 Hertford St, London W1Y 7DB; St Cadix, St Veep, Cornwall PL22 0PB]; *b* 6 July 1923; *educ* Winchester; Capt Rifle Bde WW II Italy (despatches); author, publisher 1948–88

          2d +John Amyas [John Trevelyan Esq, 1 Roseacre, Church Lane, Alpheton, Suffolk CO10 9BL]; *b* 30 June 1928; *educ* Winchester; Rifle Bde; *m* 12 June 1954 *Patricia Mary, yr dau of Stuart Tuffield Moore, of Eastbourne, Sussex, and has:

            1e +Amyas John Stuart; *b* 14 Sept 1957; *m* 1988 *Claire Diane, dau of Harry Whittle, and has:

              1f +Philip John Amyas; *b* 1991

              1f *Alice Margaret; *b* 1989

            2e +Oliver Willoughby; *b* 3 Jan 1961; *m* 1990 *Louise Elizabeth, dau of Alan Thompson, and has:

              1f *Mary Elizabeth; *b* 1991

              2f *Katherine Louise; *b* 1993

              3f *Esme Olivia; *b* Oct 1996

            3e +Rupert Patrick; *b* 20 July 1963; *m* 1987 *Sara Jane, dau of Richard Glanville, and has:

              1f *Grace Kathryn; *b* 1989

              2f *Olilvia Jane; *b* 1991

              3f *Anna Florence; *b* 1993

            1e *Elizabeth Virginia [Mrs Anthony Webb-Martin, Bishopslea Sch, PO Belvedere, Harare, Zimbabwe]; *b* 18 June 1955; *m* 1984 *Anthony Terrell Webb-Martin, est s of J J Webb-Martin, of Marondera, Zimbabwe, and has:

              1f *Stuart John; *b* 1987

              2f *Matthew Trevelyan; *b* 1990

    1c Armorel Avice Kate; *d unm* on service in France 27 Feb 1917

    2b (Charles) Leslie Calverley; *b* 25 March 1874; *m* 14 Feb 1911 Esmé Gwladys (*d* 9 June 1970 aged 89), yst dau of William Jones Menzies, of Empshott Grange, Hants, and *d* 19 Aug 1947, leaving:

1c Leslie Calverley; *b* 25 Sept 1912; *educ* Westminster and Pembroke Coll Oxford (MA); *m* 1 April 1939 Prudence Mary (*d* 1986), yst dau of Alfred Stanley Fawcett, of Standhills, Dore Moor, Derbys, and *d* 1982, leaving:

    1d +Anthony Leslie Calverley [Anthony Trevelyan Esq, Three Gables, Kemerton, Glos GL20 7HR]; *b* 28 April 1941; *educ* Seaford Coll; *m* 1 April 1972 *(Jean) Victoria, yr dau of Lt-Col G K Barker, DSO, of Bourton-on-the-Water, and has:

      1e *Charlotte Louise; *b* 1973; *educ* St Mary's Wantage and London Coll of Fashion (BA Hons)

      2e *Esmé Gwendolen; *b* 17 Aug 1975; *educ* St Mary's Wantage and Bath U (BSc)

      3e *Alexandra Mary; *b* 6 June 1979; *educ* St James's and The Abbey Malvern

    2d +(Amyas) Charles [Charles Trevelyan Esq, Wood Stanway, nr Cheltenham, Glos]; *b* 25 Jan 1946; *educ* Harrow and RMA Sandhurst; Maj Scots Dragoon Gds (3rd Carabiniers); *m* 1989 *Angela Joan, SRN, RSCN, dau of Cecil Pike, of The Wagon Ho, Higher Langham, Somerset, and has had:

      1e +Piers Calverley Charles; *b* 1990

      1e Prudence; *b* and *d* 1993

      2e *Henrietta Prudence Angela; *b* 1994

    1c Audrey Esmé Rollo; *b* 28 Oct 1915; *m* 18 Nov 1940 Michael Marie Arsène Thiébaut, s of Col Jules Thiébaut, and *d* Rome 25 Nov 1975 following an accident

1b Adelaide Isabella; *m* 1899 Frederick Richard Minchin, 4th s of William Minchin, of Eversham, Co Dublin, and *d* 4 Aug 1927

2b Florence Emmeline; *m* 1899 Walter W T Chapman and *d* 17 Sept 1938, leaving issue

3b Nora Kathleen; *m* 29 Oct 1901 Bertram Charles Elliot (*see* MINTO, E) and *d* 23 Dec 1937

1a Frances Isabella; *m* 24 Nov 1860 Albrecht Bischof

2a Margaret Lydia; *m* 2 Sept 1862 John Pearson Cresswell, MRCS, and had issue

3a Harriet Julia Emmeline; *m* 15 June 1865 Robert William Head and *d* Jan 1923, leaving issue

(1) Julia Anne; *m* George Dennis John, of Penzance

(2) Frances Susanna; *m* 31 Aug 1839 John Dangerfield, of Hampstead, and had issue

1 Julia; *m* Sir William Yea, Bt (*see* 1864 edn)

The 3rd Bt *d* 11 Sept 1768; his er s,

Sir John Trevelyan, 4th Bt; *b* 6 Feb 1735; *m* 20 April 1757 Louisa Marianne (*d* 29 Feb 1772), dau and coheir (with her sis Susannah Louisa, w of 11th Baron Saint John of Bletso; *qv*) of Peter Simond, and *d* 18 April 1828, having had, with other issue:

1 **Sir John Trevelyan, 5th Bt**; *b* 1 Jan 1761; *m* Aug 1791 Maria (*d* 1852), dau of Sir Thomas Spencer Wilson, 6th Bt (*see* 1970 edn MARYON-WILSON, Bt), and *d* 23 May 1846, having had, with another s (*d young*) and a dau (*d unm*):

  (1) **Sir Walter Calverley Trevelyan, 6th Bt**; *b* 31 March 1797; *m* 1st 21 May 1835 Paulina (*d* 13 May 1866), dau of Rev W Jermyn, DD; *m* 2nd 11 July 1867 Laura Capel (*d* 2 April 1879), dau of Capel Loft, of Troston Hall, Suffolk, and *d* 23 March 1879

  (2) Arthur; *b* 1802; *m* 1835 Elizabeth, dau of A Mackay, of Aberdeen, and *dsp* 6 Feb 1878

  (3) Edward Spencer; *b* 1805; *m* 1833 Catherine Anne (*d* 22 Nov 1877), dau of John Forster, and *d* 23 Aug 1854, leaving:

    1a Florence; *m* 5 July 1890 Prof Salvatore Cacciola, MD

  (4) Alfred Wilson; *b* 1807; *m* 1830 Matilda Margaret, dau of John Royce, of Limerick, and *d* 1830, leaving:

    1a **Sir Alfred Wilson Trevelyan, 7th Bt**; *b* posthumously 26 April 1831; *m* 15 Feb 1860 Frances (*d* 4 Dec 1907), dau of Rt Hon James H Monahan, Ld Ch Justice Common Pleas Ireland, and *d* 18 April 1891, having had:

      1b Pauline; *m* 15 Oct 1891 Lt-Col Sir Gilbert Redvers Heathcote, 8th Bt, of Hursley (*qv*), and *dsp* 3 June 1897

      2b Beatrice; *m* 26 Nov 1894 Arnold Alers Hankey, s of John Alers Hankey, and *d* 30 Sept 1946

      3b Madeline; *m* 22 Sept 1909 Joseph Monteith, DL, of Cranley, Carstairs, Lanarks, and *d* 5 Jan 1944, leaving issue. He *d* 10 Oct 1911

      4b Etheldreda; *d unm* 16 March 1949

      5b Hildegarde; *d unm* 18 July 1948

      6b Evangeline Mary Frances; *b* 1875; *d* 1881

(1) Maria Jane; *m* 7 June 1828 Rev Noel Thomas Ellison, Rector Nettlecombe and Huntspill, Somerset, and *d* a widow 20 Dec 1860

(2) Emma; *m* 22 June 1830 Capt Alexander Wadham Wyndham, Scots Greys, 2nd s of William Wyndham, of Dinton, and *d* 17 May 1857

(3) Beatrice; *m* 13 May 1830 Ernest Augustus Perceval and *d* 19 March 1898, having had issue (*see* EGMONT, E)

(4) Laura Agnes; *m* 15 March 1836 Rev John Woodhouse, Rector Huish Champflower, Somerset, and *d* 12 May 1899, leaving issue

(5) Helena Caroline; *m* 1st 4 Oct 1837 Rev Bryan Faussett (*d* 30 June 1855) and had issue; *m* 2nd her cousin Walter Blackett Trevelyan (*see above*) and *d* 14 March 1898

2 Walter (Rev); *b* 19 Jan 1763; Vicar Henbury, Rector Nettlecombe; *m* 1787 Charlotte (*m* 2nd 19 Jan 1836 1st Baron Carrington (*qv*) and *d* 22 April 1849), 3rd dau of John Hudson, of Bessingby, Yorks, and *d* 3 Nov 1830, having had, with other issue:

(1) John; *m* 25 Oct 1838 Jane Caroline (*m* 2nd 29 Oct 1860 Thomas Cuffe Adams, of Charlcombe, and Sydney Place, Bath, and *d* Sept 1877), yst dau of Rev John W Astley, Rector Quenington, Glos, and *d* 20 July 1852, having had, with two daus (*d unm*):

1a Willoughby John, of St Perranuthnoe, Cornwall; *b* 28 July 1839; *m* 31 Dec 1863 Eliza (*d* 6 April 1912), only dau of Rev Charles Saunders Skelton Dupuis, and *d* 25 Aug 1867, leaving:

  1b **Sir Walter John Trevelyan, 8th Bt**; *b* 28 Jan 1866; High Sheriff Cornwall 1906, Ld Manor St Perranuthnoe, Marazion, Cornwall; *m* 16 July 1901 Alice Edith (*d* 1 Feb 1964), yst dau of William James Money, CSI, and *d* 23 Dec 1931, having had:

    1c **Sir Willoughby John Trevelyan, 9th Bt**; *b* 16 April 1902; *educ* Eton and RMC Sandhurst; *d unm* 23 Dec 1976

    1c Joan Alice Trevelyan; *m* 14 April 1937 Garnet Ruskin Wolseley (*see* WOLSELEY, Bt, of Mount Wolseley), and *d* 10 April 1943, leaving issue. The Nettlecombe estate passed to her son on the death of the **9th Bt**

    2c Urith; *d unm* 27 March 1929

  1b Eliza Caroline; *m* 27 Oct 1906 Edward Maurice Greenway, of Basil, Nettlecombe, Taunton, and *d* 21 Jan 1926

  2a Walter Raleigh; *b* 29 Aug 1840; Lt-Col Bombay SC Afghan War 1879–80; *d* 12 May 1920

  1a Julia Henrietta; *m* 8 Aug 1863 Col Edwin B Bond and *d* 29 Aug 1876, leaving issue

  2a Fanny Rosalind

  3a Florence Beatrice; *m* Thomas Richard Peareth, 12th Lancers, 3rd s of William Peareth, of Usworth, Thorpe Mandeville, Northants, and had issue. He *d* 13 Aug 1878

  4a Helena Mary

(2) George (Rev); *b* 1803; Rector Malden-cum-Chessington, Surrey; *m* 14 May 1835 Anne (*d* 29 March 1867), dau of Henry Goss, and *d* 3 June 1850, leaving issue, with two daus (*d unm*):

  1a Walter (Rev); *b* 8 March 1840; *dsp* 1884

  2a George Edward, of Riverside, Calif.; *b* 1 April 1848; *m* Evelyn Sophia and *d* a widower 6 Nov 1915, leaving:

    1b George Hamilton; *d* 1918

    2b Edward Walter; *b* 1881; *m* 1911 Kathleen E H, dau of William Irving, and *d* 1947, leaving:

      1c **Sir Norman Irving Trevelyan, 10th Bt**; *b* 29 Jan 1915; *educ* The Cate Sch, Carpinteria, Calif., and Harvard; *m* 11 July 1951 *Jennifer Mary [Jennifer Lady Trevelyan, 1041 Adella Ave, Coronado, CA 92118, USA], dau of Arthur Elliott Riddett, of Burgh Heath, Surrey, by Gwendolen Francis, and *d* 1996, having had:

        1d Sir EDWARD NORMAN TREVELYAN, **11th and present Bt**

        2d +George Arthur; *b* 27 June 1958

        1d A dau; *b* and *d* 20 April 1952

        2d *Jane; *b* 25 May 1953; *m* 1978 *David Floyd Lewis

      1c *Eva; *b* 1919; *m* 1951 (*divorce* 1970) Lt-Cdr Alexander Benedict Yakutis, USNR, and has issue

    1b Evelyn Helena; *m* 1912 Robert Irving and *d* 13 Dec 1957

  1a Charlotte Anne; *m* 14 Sept 1858 Andrew Johnston, DL, MP, of Woodford Green, Essex, est s of Andrew Johnston, MP, of Renny Hill, Fife, and *d* 29 July 1921. He *d* 28 Feb 1922

(3) Willoughby; *b* 15 Dec 1805; Lt-Gen EICS; *m* 1st Ann Mary Astley (*d* 31 Dec 1855) sis of his est bro's w; *m* 2nd 20 Sept 1859 Elizabeth (*m* 2nd 1880 Very Rev John Burton, Provost St Ninian's, Perth), 3rd dau of of Rev Henry Addington Simcoe, of Penheale, Cornwall, and Walford Lodge, Devon, and *d* 1871, having by his 1st w had:

  1a Harrington Astley; *b* 16 March 1835; Lt-Col 7th Hus, served 11th Hus in Charge of Light Brigade at Balaclava; *m* 20 May 1858 Henrietta Louisa, dau of John Ambrose Harrison, of Brighton, and *d* Oct 1900, leaving:

    1a Alice Mary; *m* 10 April 1891 Henry Finlay Morier, of Glasgow, and *dsp* 8 March 1949

(4) James Harrington; *b* 9 Nov 1811; Lt-Col 60th Rifles; *m* 3 Nov 1852 his cousin Helena (*d* 18 Dec 1905), dau of Raleigh Trevelyan, of Netherwitton (*see* above), and *d* 5 Nov 1875, leaving:

  1a Charles Edgar Harrington; *b* 27 April 1856

  2a Edmund James Willoughby; *b* 7 Aug 1859; *educ* Radley; *d* 29 Jan 1956

  1a Eugenie Arabella Mary

  2a Pauline Eulalia Louisa; *d unm* 13 Nov 1923

  3a Ada Bibiannah Emma

3 George (Ven); *b* 23 Nov 1764; Archdeacon Taunton, Canon Wells, Rector Nettlecombe; *m* 9 Feb 1795 Harriet (*d* 15 Feb 1854), dau of Sir Richard Neave, 1st Bt (*qv*), and *d* 13 Oct 1827, leaving, with two other daus (*d unm*):

  (1) George (Rev); *b* 29 Nov 1796; *m* 2 April 1833 Frances Anne (*d* 22 July 1877), only dau of Lt-Col Lumsden, and *dsp* 26 April 1871

  (2) John (Rev); *b* 26 Feb 1799; RN, Vicar Milverton, Somerset; *d unm* 16 Aug 1844

  (3) Henry Willoughby, CB; *b* 26 Jan 1803; Maj-Gen RA; *m* Nov 1837 Emilia Anne (*d* 7 Oct 1894), dau of S H Greig, and *d* 31 Aug 1876, leaving:

    1a Henry Willoughby, JP Somerset; *b* 4 Jan 1847; Col 4th Bn Duke of Wellington's W R Regt, formerly 3rd Hus; *m* 17 July 1879 Charlotte Emily (*d* 27 June 1931), yst dau of Lt-Col Joseph Walker Pease, of Hesslewood Ho, Yorks, and *d* 27 Aug 1929

    2a Ernest John (Sir); *b* 7 Dec 1850; barrister, DCL, Fell and Sub-Warden All Souls, Assessor Court of Chllr Oxford U, High Court Judge Calcutta 1885–98, Reader Indian Law Oxford 1900–23; *m* 1st 27 Nov 1880 Mary Katharine (*d* 22 March 1885), yst dau of Patrick Black, MD, and had:

      1b Henry; *b* 22 Nov 1881; *educ* RMA Woolwich; Lt-Col RE; *m* 20 Aug 1906 Josephine Marie (*d* 12 July 1968), 2nd dau of Dr Louis Ferdinand Antelme, of Port Louis, Mauritius, and *d* 1971, having had:

        1c Peggy; *b* 16 June 1912; *m* 19 June 1947 John Syme Whyte, of Fleet, Hants, and *d* 26 Oct 1947 following a train accident

        2c *Mary Katharine [Mrs Harold Proudlock, Heath Cottage, 16 Fields Rd, Alsager, Cheshire]; *b* 28 Sept 1926; *m* 20 Dec 1947 *Harold Stewart Proudlock, s of R Proudlock, of Fleet, Hants, and has:

    1d *Michael Trevelyan; *b* 16 March 1949; *educ* Sandbach Sch and Reading U; *m* 1976 *Guyonne Christine, dau of Dr W G Davies, of Paris, and has:

      1e *Eleanor Claire; *b* 1977

      2e *Karen Aude; *b* 1980

    2d *David Seymour; *b* 3 Feb 1951; *educ* Sandbach Sch and Manchester U

    3d *John Stewart; *b* 14 Feb 1956; *m* 1988 *Christina Louise, dau of G W Abbott, of Black Bourton, Oxon

    1d *Susan Marie; *b* 2 Feb 1959; *m* 1989 *Ian Nimmo

  1b Phyllis; *b* 27 May 1883; *d* April 1885

  2a (cont.) Sir Ernest Trevelyan *m* 2nd 21 Aug 1890 Julia Isabel (*d* 18 Oct 1903), yr dau of Edward Wallhouse Mark, Br Consul Marseilles, and by her had:

    2b Wilfred; *b* 10 Oct 1893; 2nd Lt 5th Bn Rifle Bde; *ka* 4 May 1915

    3b Percy; *b* 16 Jan 1900; Sub-Lt RN; *d* 10 March 1919

    2b Hilda; *b* 28 July 1892; *m* 28 July 1913 Marmaduke Theakstone Hancock, FCCA, s of Preb Frederick Hancock, and *d* 31 Dec 1973. He *d* 21 Feb 1923

    3b Doris; *b* 23 Aug 1895; *m* 25 Nov 1925 William Henry Joshua Walker, s of Henry Walker, of Sheffield, and *d* 18 Jan 1968, leaving issue. He *d* 4 June 1955

    4b Sylvia; *b* 21 Aug 1898; *m* 7 Feb 1924 Lt-Col Geoffrey Ronald Hawtrey Deane, OBE, RE (*d* 29 June 1961), yr s of Ralph Hawtrey Deane, of Eastcote, and *d* 11 Dec 1982, leaving:

      1c *Barbara; *b* 9 Dec 1924

      2c *Elisabeth; *b* 9 Nov 1926; *m* 5 Nov 1959 John Charles William Napier-Munn, s of Rev William Edward Napier-Munn, of Worthing, Sussex, and has:

        1d *Simon Deane; *b* 7 Aug 1961

        1d *Nicola Tamsin; *b* 25 Nov 1963

      3c *Janet Anne; *b* 7 May 1929; *m* 19 June 1954 Roderick William Chisholm, s of William Andrew Chisholm, of London SE9, and has:

        1d *Alastair James; *b* 24 May 1959

        2d *John Angus; *b* 22 Aug 1962

        1d *Jane Catherine; *b* 7 April 1955

        2d *Teresa Mary; *b* 14 April 1957

      4c *Charlotte; *b* 5 Sept 1933; *educ* St Andrews (BSc 1956)

    5b *Joan; *b* 21 Feb 1901; *m* 1 Oct 1929 Charles Chichele Oman, s of Sir Charles William Chadwick Oman, KBE, DCL, LLD, of Oxford, and has:

      1c *Charles Trevelyan; *b* 7 May 1934

      1c *Julia Trevelyan, CBE (1986) [Lady Strong, The Laskett, Much Birch, Herefs HR2 8HZ]; *b* 11 July 1930; designer, dir Oman Productions Ltd; *m* 1971 *Sir Roy Colin Strong, PhD, FSA, writer and historian, Dir V&A 1974–87, s of G E C Strong, of N London

  2a (cont.) Sir Ernest Trevelyan *m* 3rd 7 Dec 1909 Winifred Helen (*d* 25 Oct 1962), dau of Sir Charles Umpherston Aitchison, KCSI, CIE, LLD, and *d* 29 July 1924

  1a Emily Frances; *m* 28 July 1864 Col E D Vibart, ISC, and *d* 1889

  2a Julia Agnes; *d unm* 1944

(4) Sir CHARLES EDWARD TREVELYAN, 1st Bt, of Wallington (*qv*)

(5) Edward Otto (Rev); *b* 19 June 1810; *m* 27 Aug 1844 Emma (*d* 11 Nov 1890), dau of Charles Horsfall Bill, of Storthes Hall, Huddersfield, and *d* 9 July 1880, having had:

  1a Edward; *b* 11 Nov 1857; *m* 27 Dec 1893 Eleanor, dau of William Pearse, and *d* 15 June 1945, having had:

    1b John Otto; *b* 4 April 1907; *d* 25 Jan 1908

    1b Gertrude Eileen; *educ* LMH Oxford (BA, Newdigate Prize for English Verse 1927); *d unm* 17 Feb 1941

  1a Emma Theresa; *m* 4 Aug 1869 Rev Octavius Pechell Greenstreet and *d* 1 April 1872

  2a Mary Caroline; *b* 5 Sept 1846; *d unm* 11 Oct 1870

  3a Edith; *b* 1849; *d* 1850

  4a Etheldreda; *m* 1 Aug 1882 Rev James Murray Murray-Dixon, of Aston Hill, Aylesbury, Rector Swithland, Loughborough 1884–1925, and *d* 1943, leaving issue

(6) William Pitt (Rev); *b* 31 March 1812; MA Oxon, Rector Calverton, Bucks; *m* 1 June 1852 Maria (*d* 9 Oct 1903), 3rd dau of Hon Philip Pleydell-Bouverie (*see* RADNOR, E), and *d* 22 Dec 1905, leaving:

  1a William Bouverie (Rev); *b* 25 June 1853; *educ* Trin Coll Cambridge (MA); Warden The Retreat Ho, Beaconsfield, Vicar St Matthew's, Westminster; *d unm* 10 April 1929

  2a John Charles (Rev); *b* 1 Jan 1857; Rector of Yaxham Norfolk 1915–27; *m* 16 June 1881 Elizabeth Wood (*d* 22 June 1935), dau of Thomas Irvine, of Liverpool, and *d* 29 Oct 1944, leaving:

    1b Charles William (Rev), MC; *b* 3 Aug 1887; *educ* Wellington and Magdalen Coll Oxford (MA 1919); Maj London Rifle Bde WW I (despatches), APM 1916; assist master Wellington 1920–42 and Chichester Theological Coll 1943; Deacon 1943, Priest 1944, Assist Curate Ilfracombe 1943–46, Preb Wells 1957, Vicar Trull, Taunton, 1946–58; *m* 30 Dec 1930 Maud Dorothe (*d* 1986), dau of Frederick Augustus Dixey, MA, MD, FRS, Hon Fell Wadham Coll Oxford, and *d* 24 March 1974, leaving:

      1c John Francis; *b* 5 Feb 1934; *educ* Wellington and Aberdeen U (BSc Forestry 1958); late 2nd Lt RM; *m* 1 Nov 1958 *Elizabeth Mary [Mrs John Trevelyan, RD2 Te Puke, New Zealand], dau of Harvey Brockenshaw, of Weston-super-Mare, and *d* 13 Dec 1996, leaving:

        1d +Andrew John [Andrew Trevelyan Esq, 6 Watea Rd, Mount Albert, Auckland, New Zealand]; *b* 25 March 1961; *m* 1991 *Jenny Elizabeth, dau of Michael James Grainger, of Bramhall, Cheshire

        2d +James Edward; *b* 8 Nov 1962; BE; *m* 1994 *Vicki Kathryn, dau of Anthony Wilfred Long, of Rotorua, NZ

        1d Sarah Jane; *b* 13 Nov 1959; *d* 25 July 1964

2d *Fiona Catherine; *b* 9 April 1965

3d *Katrin Elizabeth; *b* 30 Nov 1966

2c +James Willam Irvine (Rev) [The Rev Preb James Trevelyan, The Rectory, Rookwood Close, Honiton, Devon EX14 8BH]; *b* 9 Oct 1937; *educ* Wellington, Selwyn Coll Cambridge (BA 1964, MA 1967) and Cuddesdon Theological Coll Oxford; Deacon 1965, Priest 1966, Assist Curate St Saviour's Folkestone, Vicar Lenham with Boughton Malherbe Kent 1972–78, Rector Honiton 1978–, Preb Exeter 1995–; *m* 23 Aug 1969 *Felicity Jane, dau of Joseph Gibson, of Burnside, Barbon, Westmorland, and Blackburn, and has:

1d +Robert William Dixey; *b* 28 Nov 1970

1d *Lucy Catherine; *b* 1974

1c *Janet Isabel [Miss Janet Trevelyan, 5 Holcombe Lane, Bathampton, Bath]; *b* 14 April 1932

2c *Elizabeth Margaret [Mrs Robert Franklin, Verno House S, Lyndhurst Rd, Christchurch, Dorset BH23 4SG]; *b* 26 Oct 1939; *m* 4 April 1964 *Robert Adrian Franklin, MA, MB, BChir, LRCP, MRCS, yr s of Rev Edward C Franklin, of Devizes, and has:

1d *Nicholas Robert; *b* 5 Aug 1969

1d *Clare Elizabeth; *b* 3 July 1965

2d *Susan Dorothe; *b* 16 April 1967

1b Elizabeth Bouverie; *b* 5 March 1885; *d* unm 24 Nov 1964

2b Ruth; *b* 21 July 1894; *m* 2 Jan 1924 Rev Robert Elliott Monro (*d* 18 Nov 1948), son of Rev Robert Douglas Monro, of Little Munden, Herts, and has:

1c *Mary Joan; *b* 18 Sept 1925; V-Pres Coll of the Ascension Selly Oak

2c *Elizabeth Trevelyan; *b* 23 Aug 1928; *educ* St Hugh's Coll Oxford (BA 1950, MA 1956); *m* 11 April 1956 Rev Ronald Oliver Bowlby, Vicar Croydon, Canon Canterbury, s of Oliver Bowlby, of Beaufort Ho, Bath, and has:

1d *Richard Monro; *b* 22 Dec 1958

2d *Christopher Maunsell; *b* 26 June 1961

3d *Thomas Tevelyan; *b* 24 Nov 1966

1d *Rachel Helena; *b* 29 Jan 1957

2d *Anna Elizabeth; *b* 18 June 1963

3c *Anne Ruth; *b* 6 Oct 1932; *educ* RCM (ARCM 1953)

3b Joan Mary; *b* 3 March 1897; Sister Community of Sisters of Love of God Oxford; *d* 2 Sept 1961

3a George Philip (Rev); *b* 14 Sept 1858; *educ* Trin Coll Cambridge (MA); Vicar St Albans Hindhead 1908–11 and St Stephen's Bournemouth 1912–28; *m* 15 April 1896 Monica Evelyn Juliet (*d* 17 March 1962), dau of Rev Sidney Philips, and *d* 5 Feb 1937, leaving:

1b John, CBE (1971, OBE 1949); *b* 11 July 1903; *educ* Lancing and Trin Coll Cambridge (BA 1925, MA 1930); Dir Br Families' Educn Service Germany and Educn Westmorland 1938–46, Sec Br Bd Film Censors 1958–71; *m* 1st 18 Sept 1928 (*divorce* 1949) Kathleen Margaret, dau of Charles Hallé Pass, of Barrow-in-Furness, and had:

1c Nicholas; *b* and *d* 23 Oct 1932

1b (cont.) John Trevelyan *m* 2nd 1 June 1949 (*divorce* 1959) Joan Frieda, BM, BCh, dau of Francis Clayton Scott (*see* SCOTT, Bt, of Yews), and by her had:

2c +James Philip [James Trevelyan Esq, 33 Brockman Ave, Dalkeith, W Australia]; *b* 11 Nov 1948; *educ* W Australia U (BEng, MEngSc); MIEAust; *m* 1971 (*divorce* 1994) Jolin, dau of Frank Edmondson, of Floreat Pk, W Australia, and has:

1d +Charles Francis; *b* 1974

2d +Nicholas James; *b* 1976

1d *Clare Rose; *b* 1983

1c *Sarah Juliet [Mrs Jimmy Boyle, 5a Abbey Mount, Edinburgh]; *b* 1950; *m* 1980 *James (Jimmy) Boyle, writer and sculptor, and has:

1d *Suzannah Angela; *b* 1984

2d *Kydd; *b* 1987

1b (cont.) John Trevelyan *m* 3rd 1959 Jean (*d* 1972), dau of Robert Mutch, and by her had:

3c +Jonathan [Jonathan Trevelyan Esq, 15 The Rowans, Marchwood, Southampton SO4 4YW]; *b* 1959; *educ* Bristol U (BSc, PhD); *m* 1980 *Karen Elizabeth, dau of Kenneth Frank Ireland, and has:

1d +David John; *b* 1988

4c +Simon (twin) [Simon Trevelyan Esq, 5 Beverley Place, Springfield, Milton Keynes MK6 3LJ]; *b* 1959; *educ* Birmingham U (BS); *m* 1982 *Isobel Catherine, dau of Dr Oliver Watt, OBE, of Glasgow, and has:

1d +James Oliver; *b* 1988

1d *Anna Joëlle; *b* 1985

1b (cont.) John Trevelyan *m* 4th 1974 Rosalie Evelyn (*d* 1979), dau of Joseph Lopez-Salzedo, and *d* 1986

2b HUMPHREY TREVELYAN, BARON TREVELYAN, of Saint Veep, Co Cornwall (UK, LP), so *cr* 12 Feb 1968, KG (1974), GCMG (1965, KCMG 1955, CMG 1951), CIE (1948), OBE (1941); *b* 27 Nov 1905; *educ* Lancing and Jesus Coll Cambridge (BA 1927, Hon Fell); ICS and Indian political serv, FO 1947–67: Counsellor Baghdad 1948–50, ec advsr UK HC Germany 1951–53, Chargé d'Affaires Peking 1953–55, Amb Cairo 1955–56, U-Sec UN 1958, Amb Baghdad 1958–61, Dep U-Sec FO 1962, Amb Moscow 1962–65, HC Aden 1967, Pres Cncl Foreign Bondholders 1965–, dir Matheson and Co, BP Co, Electric and English Electric Cos, and Br Bank of Middle East; Chm Tstees Br Museum 1970–79, Hon LLD Cantab 1970, Hon DCL Durham 1973, Hon DLitt Leeds 1975; *m* 10 Nov 1937 *Violet Margaret [The Rt Hon The Lady Trevelyan, 24 Duchess of Bedford Ho, London W8 7QN], only dau of Gen Sir William Henry Bartholomew, GCB, CMG, DSO, and *d* 1985, having had:

1c *Susan Anne [The Hon Mrs Busse, c/o Ministry of Foreign Affairs, Bonn, Germany]; *b* 10 Jan 1941; *m* 26 April 1961 *Harald Busse, s of Gerhard Busse, of Cologne, and has:

1d *Allan Georg; *b* 29 May 1962

2d *Jan Michail; *b* 4 June 1963

1d *Nicola Andrea; *b* 20 May 1967

2c *Catherine Mary, OBE (1977); *b* 23 Sept 1943; *m* 1990, as his 3rd w, *Robert Kee

1b Mary, CBE (1968, OBE 1956); *b* 22 Jan 1897; *educ* Grovely Coll Boscombe and RCM (ARCM); ARCO; fndr and govr Internat Students' House, London, Warden Student Movement Ho 1932–46, first Advsr to Overseas Students London U 1949–65; *d* unm 10 Jan 1983

2b Avice; *b* 6 March 1898

3b Beryl; *b* 29 Nov 1899; *educ* Girton Coll Cambridge (MA 1925); *m* 21 June 1927 Philip John Durrant, PhD, Fell and V-Master Selwyn Coll Cambridge, s of Louis Durrant, and has:

1c *John Paul; *b* 20 Sept 1928; *educ* Gordonstoun and RMA Sandhurst; Maj Roy Signals; *m* 1959 *Vivienne, dau of Alfred Trenerry, and has:

1d *Jeremy Mark; *b* 1960

2d *Jonathan Humphrey; *b* 1963

1c *Clare Elizabeth; *b* 29 Nov 1932; *educ* Girton Coll Cambridge (MA 1960, MB 1959, BChir 1958); *m* 1961 *Rev Burton Jones Whitehead and has:

1d *Philip Trevelyan; *b* 1964

2d *Nicholas Bruce Trevelyan; *b* 5 Feb 1966

1d *Mary Louise; *b* 1962

4b *Urith Monica [Mrs Harry Carpenter, St John's Home, St Mary's Rd, Oxford OX4 1QE]; *b* 11 May 1909; *educ* Somerville Coll Oxford (BA 1937, MA 1941); *m* 21 June 1940 Rt Rev Harry James Carpenter, DD (*d* 1993), Bp Oxford 1955–70, s of William Carpenter, of Liss, Hants, and has:

1c *Humphrey William Bouverie [Humphrey Carpenter Esq, 6 Farndon Rd, Oxford OX2 6RS]; *b* 29 April 1946; *educ* Marlborough and Keble Coll Oxford; *m* 1973 *Mari Christina, dau of Caradog Prichard, and has:

1d *Clare Nia; *b* 1978

2d *Katherine Sioned; *b* 1981

4a Francis; *b* 21 Oct 1862; *m* 8 Feb 1888 Annie Mahony (*d* 16 Sept 1908) and *dsp* 24 Jan 1908

(1) Frances Agnes; *m* 13 Sept 1842 Rev Hon Charles George Perceval, bro of 6th Earl of Egmont (*qv*), and *d* 16 Oct 1873, leaving issue

TREVELYAN of Wallington

Arms: Gu. a demi-horse arg., hoofed and maned or, issuing out of water in base ppr. **Crest:** Two arms counter-embowed ppr., habited az., holding in the hands a bezant. **Motto:** Tyme tryeth troth.
Creation: Bt. (UK) 13 March 1874.

SIR GEOFFREY WASHINGTON TREVELYAN, 5TH BT, of Wallington, Northumberland [Sir Geoffrey Trevelyan Bt, Lower Silkstead, 3 Abbey Mill End, St Albans, Herts AL3 4HN]; *b* 4 July 1920; *s* bro 1996; *educ* Oundle and Trin Coll Cambridge (MA); dir: Chatto and Windus Ltd, Chatto and Windus (Educnl) Ltd, The Hogarth Press Ltd, Chatto and Jonathan Cape Ltd, Consolidated Scientific Instruments Ltd; *m* 3 May 1947 *Gillian Isabel, est dau of Alexander Louis Sandison Wood, OBE, of Spencer's Farm, Whelpley Hill, Bucks, and has:

1 +PETER JOHN; *b* 11 Sept 1948; *educ* Oundle and Trin Coll Cambridge; *m* 1996 *Diane Terry

1 *Sandra Mary; *b* 5 Aug 1951; *educ* Badminton and Newcastle U; *m* 1974 *David Bradley and has:

(1) *Robert; *b* 1980

(2) *James; *b* 1982

Lineage: Sir Charles Edward Trevelyan, 1st Bt (UK), so *cr* 13 March 1874, KCB (1848), of Wallington, Northumberland (*see* TREVELYAN, Bt, of Nettlecombe); *b* 2 April 1807; Assist Sec Treasury 1840–59, Govr Madras 1850–60, fin memb

Govr-Gen of India's Cncl 1862–65; *m* 1st 23 Dec 1834 Hannah More (*d* 5 Aug 1873), dau of Zachary Macaulay and sis of Lord Macaulay, and had:

1 GEORGE OTTO (Sir), **2nd Bt**

1 Margaret Jean; *m* 25 Nov 1858 1st Viscount Knutsford (*qv*) and *d* 26 Aug 1906, having had issue

2 Alice Frances; *m* 14 Dec 1871 William Stratford Dugdale (*see* DUGDALE, Bt) and *d* 2 Jan 1902, leaving issue

Sir Charles *m* 2nd 14 Oct 1875 Eleonora Ann (*d* 1 March 1919), yr dau of Walter Campbell, 4th s of Walter Campbell of Islay and Shawfield, and *d* 19 June 1886

His s,

Sir George Otto Trevelyan, 2nd Bt, OM, PC, DL; *b* 20 July 1838; *educ* Harrow and Trin Coll Cambridge (BA 1861, MA 1864, Hon Fell, Hon LittD 1868); MP (Lib) Tynemouth 1865–68, Border Burghs 1868–86 and Glasgow 1887–97, a Ld Admlty 1869–70, Parly Sec Admlty 1880–82, Ch Sec Ireland 1882–84, Chllr Duchy Lancaster with seat in Cabinet 1884–85, Sec for Scotland 1886 and 1892–95, High Steward Stratford-on-Avon 1912–17; author *Life and Letters of Lord Macaulay*; Hon LLD Edin, Hon DCL and Hon Fell Oriel Coll Oxford; *m* 29 Sept 1869 Caroline (*d* 26 Jan 1928), dau of Robert Needham Philips, MP, of The Park, Manchester, and Welcombe, Stratford-on-Avon, and had:

1 CHARLES PHILIPS (Sir), **3rd Bt**

2 Robert Calverley, poet; *b* 28 June 1872; *educ* Harrow and Trin Coll Cambridge (BA and LLB 1894); *m* 7 June 1900 Elizabeth (*d* 16 Oct 1957), dau of Jan des Amorie van der Hoeven, of The Hague, and *d* 21 March 1951, having had:

(1) Paul; *b* 20 Dec 1906; *d* 22 March 1909

(2) Julian Otto; *b* 20 Feb 1910; *educ* Bedales and Trin Coll Cambridge; painter and etcher, tutor RCA 1955–63, Capt RE (Camouflage) WW II 1940–43; *m* 1st 30 July 1934 (*divorce* 1949) Ursula Frances Elinor, est dau of Bernard Richard Meirion Darwin, CBE, of Gorringes, Downe, Kent; *m* 2nd 20 March 1951 *Mary OBE, RA, DLitt [Miss Mary Fedden OBE, Durham Wharf, Hammersmith Terr, London W6 9TS], dau of Vincent Fedden, and *d* 1988, leaving by his 1st w:

1a +Philip Erasmus [Philip Trevelyan Esq, Hilltop Farm, Appleton-le-Moors, Kirkbymoorside, N Yorks]; *b* 22 Aug 1943; *educ* Bryanston, Dept Fine Art King's Coll Newcastle and RCA; *m* 1975 *Eleanor, dau of Matthew Prior, of Cambridge, and has:

1b +Jack Elisha; *b* 1977

2b +Matthew Robert; *b* 1978

1b *Susannah; *b* 1987

(1) Susan Caroline; *b* 13 Sept, *d* 16 Sept 1908

3 George Macaulay, CBE (1920), OM (1930); *b* 16 Feb 1876; *educ* Harrow and Trin Coll Cambridge (BA 1806, MA 1900, Fell 1898); Cmdt BRC Unit Italy WW I, Regius Prof Modern History Cambridge 1927–43, Master Trin Coll Cambridge 1940–51, High Steward Cambridge 1946, Tstee Br Museum and Nat Portrait Gallery, Gd Cross Chev Order St Maurice and St Lazarus of Italy, Italian Silver Medal for military valour; author: *English Social History, England in the Age of Wycliffe, England under the Stuarts, The English Revolution 1688, England under Queen Anne, British History of the Nineteenth Century, History of England, Garibaldi and the Making of Italy, Lord Grey of the Reform Bill, Grey of Falloden*; Hon LLD St Andrews and Hon DCL Oxon 1929, Hon LittD Cantab, Manchester, London, Harvard, Yale, Durham, Nottingham; *m* 19 March 1904 Janet Penrose, CH (1936) (*d* 1956), 2nd dau of Humphry Ward, and *d* 20 July 1962, having had:

(1) Theodore Macaulay; *b* 5 July 1906; *d* 19 April 1911

(2) Charles Humphry; *b* 6 March 1909; *educ* Trin Coll Cambridge (MA); Fell King's Coll Cambridge 1947; *m* 11 June 1936 *Mary Trumbull [Mrs Charles Trevelyan, Gazely, Trumpington, Cambridge], yst dau of Winchester Bennett, of New Haven, Conn., and *d* 1 April 1964, leaving:

1a +Thomas Arnold [Thomas Trevelyan Esq, 31 Orbel St, London SW11 3NX]; *b* 27 Dec 1942; *educ* Bryanston, King's Coll Cambridge (MB, BChir) and St Thomas's Hosp; MRCGP; *m* 1st 26 Feb 1965 (*divorce* 1974) Anne Margaret, dau of James Jones, of Sanderstead, Surrey, and has:

1b +Harry; *b* 29 Feb 1968

1b *Emma Susan; *b* 12 Oct 1966

2b *Selina Rose; *b* 9 July 1969

1a (cont.) Thomas Trevelyan *m* 2nd 1974 *Anita, dau of Reginald Martyn Smith, of Chaddesley Corbett, Worcs, and by her has had:

2b Jack Humphry; *b* and *d* 13 Nov 1984

3b *Clare Molly; *b* 11 Sept 1981

4b *Victoria Rossanna; *b* 26 Sept 1986

2a +George Macaulay [George Trevelyan Esq, 76a St Mark's Rd, Henley-on-Thames, Oxon]; *b* 1 April 1944; *educ* Bryanston, Queen's Coll Oxford, and LSE; *m* 1st 17 Sept 1966 Susan, 2nd dau of Mark Pearson, of Bulcote, Notts, and has:

1b +Will Mark; *b* 1971

1b *Sasha France; *b* 1969

2b *Laura Kate; *b* 1968

2a (cont.) George Trevelyan *m* 2nd 19– *Valerie Elizabeth, dau of Tom Preston, of Dewsbury, W Yorks, and by her has:

2b +Thomas Trumbull; *b* 1988

3a +Humphry Bennett [Humphry Trevelyan Esq, Diamond Cottage, Keyhaven, Hants SO41 0TP]; *b* 1 April 1944; *educ* Bryanston and Trin Coll Cambridge

1a *Jane Winchester [Mrs Jane Armstrong, 188 Peckham Rye, London SE22]; *b* 29 Aug 1938; *educ* Perse Sch for Girls and Dartington Hall; *m* 8 Oct 1960 (*divorce* 1984) David Armstrong and has:

1b *Richard Michael Boris; *b* 10 Sept 1961

1b *Sarah Jane; *b* 9 Feb 1965

2b *Rachel Susan; *b* Sept 1966

2a *Mary Harriet; *b* 11 Dec 1939; *educ* Bedales and St Thomas's Hosp (MB, BS 1963); *m* 1971 *James Barton

(1) *Mary Caroline; *b* 19 Feb 1905; *educ* Somerville Coll Oxford (MA 1951); author: *William Wordsworth: a Biography* (1957); Hon LittD Leeds 1967 and

Durham 1968; *m* 29 Sept 1930 Rt Rev John Richard Humpidge Moorman, DD, Bp Ripon, 2nd s of Prof Frederic William Moorman, BA, PhD, of Leeds

The 2nd Bt *d* 17 Aug 1928; his est s,

Sir Charles Philips Trevelyan, 3rd Bt, PC (1924), JP Northumberland; *b* 28 Oct 1870; *educ* Harrow and Trin Coll Cambridge (BA 1892, MA 1896), MP (Lib) Yorks Elland 1899–1918 and Newcastle-upon-Tyne Centl 1922–31, Priv Sec to Ld Lt Ireland 1892–95, Parly Charity Commr 1906–08, Parly Sec Bd Educn 1908–14, Pres Bd Educn Jan–Nov 1924 and June 1929–March 1931, CC, Ld Lt Northumberland and Newcastle 1930–49 (resigned); Pres Northumberland and Durham Assoc in London 1936, Hon DCL Durham 1929; *m* 6 Jan 1904 Mary Katharine, OBE (1963), JP (Northumberland 1932) (*d* 8 Oct 1966), yst dau of Sir Hugh Bell, 2nd Bt (*qv*), and *d* 24 Jan 1958, having had:

1 **Sir George Lowthian Trevelyan, 4th Bt**; *b* 5 Nov 1906; *educ* Sidcot Sch and Trin Coll Cambridge; artist craftsman with Peter Waals Workshops, fine furniture, 1930–31, trained and worked in F M Alexander re-education method 1932–36, taught at Gordonstoun and Abinger Hill Sch 1936–41; Capt Rifle Bde WW II, warden Salop Adult Coll 1947–71; fndr, pres and dir Wrekin Tst 1971–92; author: *A Vision of the Aquarian Age, The Active Eye in Architecture, Magic Casements, Operation Redemption*; *m* 14 Aug 1940 Éditha Helen (*d* 26 Oct 1994), dau of Col John Lindsay Smith, CBE, and *d* 7 Feb 1996, having adopted:

*Catriona [Mrs Richard Tyson, The Old Vicarage, Hawkesbury, Badminton, S Glos GL9 1BN]; *b* 1944; *educ* Moreton Hall Sch and Sussex U (BA); *m* 1st 13 Jan 1968 (*divorce* 1984) Matthew Tomalin, s of Roger Tomalin, ARIBA, of Highgate; *m* 2nd 1986 *Richard T Tyson, est s of Cdr A Tyson, RN, of S Harting, W Sussex, and by her 1st husb has had:

1a Oliver Robert; *b* 9 Jan 1971; *d* 1990

2a *Jack Lindsay; *b* 1972

2 Hugh Patrick; *b* 17 March 1915; *d* 17 April 1916

3 Sir GEOFFREY WASHINGTON TREVELYAN, **5th and present Bt**

1 Pauline, CBE (1967, OBE 1954), JP (1948); *b* 9 Oct 1905; Dep Chm Nat Pks Commn 1956–66, memb Br Waterways Bd 1963–68; *m* 3 Sept 1929 John Gordon Dower, ARIBA, AMTPI (*d* 3 Oct 1947), er s of Robert Shillito Dower, of Ilkley, Yorks, and had:

(1) *Michael Shillito Trevelyan; *b* 15 Nov 1933; *educ* The Leys Sch, St John's Coll Cambridge (BA) and UCL (Dip Town Planning), Sports Cncl 1965–67, Dir Dartington Amenity Research Tst 1967, memb English Tourist Bd 1969; *m* 1 Sept 1960 *Agnes (Nan), er dau of Allan Done, of Pontefract, Yorks, and has:

1a *John; *b* 27 Nov 1961

2a *Daniel Guy; *b* 19 March 1964

3a *Alexander Michael; *b* 28 Feb 1968

(2) *Robert Charles Philips; *b* 27 Oct 1938; *educ* The Leys Sch, St John's Coll Cambridge (MA) and Edinburgh U (BArch); ARIBA; *m* 4 Nov 1967 *Frances Helen, MB, BS, LRCP, MRCS, only dau of Henry Edmeades Baker, of Cobham, Kent, and gdau of Sir Herbert Baker, KCIE, DCL

(1) *Susan Florence; *b* 5 Jan 1931; BA London; *m* 21 Dec 1954 Trevor Casbay Handoll, only s of George Edward Handoll, and has:

1a *John Trevelyan Casbay; *b* 6 Feb 1957

1a *Helen Hanora Georgina; *b* 6 Feb 1957

2 Katharine; *b* 7 May 1908; *m* 29 March 1932 (*divorce* 1939, resumed maiden name by deed poll 19 June 1939) Johann Gottfried Georg Götsch (*d* 1956), 2nd s of Georg Götsch, of Berlin, and had:

(1) *Erika Karla Trevelyan; *b* 17 Feb 1933; *m* 29 June 1957 (*divorce*) Robin Murray Lees, only s of Dr G M Lees, MC, DFC, FRS, of Matching Green, Essex, and has:

1a *Nicholas Martin; *b* 14 May 1960

2a *Dominic Charles Jacob; *b* 24 Aug 1964

1a *Henrietta Frances; *b* 30 April 1963

(2) *Elisabeth Trevelyan; *b* 10 Nov 1935; *m* 1967 *Stephen Greenfield

(3) *Katharine Mary Trevelyan; *b* 22 June 1940; *m* 17 Aug 1963 Jeremy Norman Chapple, BSc, only s of L Norman Chapple, of Toehill, Membury, Devon, and has:

1a *Penelope Jane; *b* 18 May 1966

3 *Marjorie [Lady Weaver, 14 Marston Close, London NW6 4EU]; *b* 5 April 1913; *m* 11 Sept 1941 *Sir Tobias Rushton Weaver, CB, s of Sir Lawrence Weaver, KBE, and has:

(1) *Lawrence Trevelyan [Prof Lawrence Weaver, 4 Huntley Gdns, Dowanhill, Glasgow G12 9AS]; *b* 13 Oct 1948; *educ* Clifton and Corpus Christi Coll Cambridge; Prof Child Health; *m* 2 Nov 1991 *Camilla Rohini Simmons and has:

1a *Robin Lintorn; *b* 29 Oct 1993

1a *Marion Sophia; *b* 24 Dec 1995

(1) *Kathleen JP (Essex) [Mrs Nicholas Abbott JP, Crouches, The Broadway, Great Dunmow, Essex CM6 3BQ]; *b* 15 March 1943; Chm Dunmow and Saffron Walden PSD; *m* 22 Jan 1966 *Nicholas John Milford Abbott, er s of Cyril John Milford Abbott, of Crouches, and has:

1a *Simon Milford; *b* 1971

2a *Benjamin Tobias; *b* 1973

1a *Rachel Mary BATES; *b* 22 Aug 1967; by *Jonathan David Miles has:

1b *Stan Jean MILES ABBOTT; *b* 28 Nov 1995

2b *Louis Pascal MILES ABBOTT; *b* 28 Nov 1995

2a *Judith Caroline; *b* 17 Feb 1969

(2) *Caroline [Mrs Michael Baker, 24 Wellington Pk, Clifton, Bristol BS8 2UT]; *b* 14 Oct 1945; *m* 1986 *Michael Herbert Baker, est s of Henry Baker

(3) *Rachel [Mrs Charles Munn, Hodore, Hartfield, Sussex]; *b* 26 Nov 1950; *m* 1974 *Charles David Munn and has:

1a *George Patrick; *b* 1976

2a *Toby Charles; *b* 1984

1a *Louise Caroline; *b* 1978

2a *Emily Claire; *b* 1980

4 *(Florence) Patricia, JP (Northumberland) [Mrs Patricia Jennings JP, Wallington, Cambo, Northumberland NE61 4AR]; *b* 17 March 1915; *m* 1st 3 Jan 1942 Lt Frederick Philip Cheswright, RNVR (*d* 28 Aug 1946), only s of Mrs Elsie Cheswright; *m* 2nd 25 Sept 1950 (*divorce* 1975) S/Ldr Reginald Joseph Jennings, MC, RAFVR, 3rd s of Charles John Jennings, of Margaretting, Essex, and by her 1st husb has:

  (1) *Hugh Weedon Nicholas [Hugh Cheswright Esq, The Two Queens, Cambo, Northumberland NE61 4BA]; *b* 3 Oct 1942; *educ* Gordonstoun; advtsg dir; *m* 1st 18 May 1968 (*divorce* 1979) Rosemary Frances, dau of Norman Walduck, hotelier, of Lower Woodside, Hatfield, Herts; *m* 2nd 1980 *Jean Moya, dau of David William Barratt, and by his 1st w has:

    1a *Sebastian Charles Philip; *b* 1 Jan 1971

    2a *Rupert James Macaulay; *b* 1972

  (1) *Janet Vanessa; *b* 12 Dec 1943; *m* 1st 2 May 1964 (*divorce* 1985) (Geoffrey) Brian Parker, yst s of Donald Parker, JP, of Mill Ho, Mildenhall, Suffolk; *m* 2nd 1988 *David G Hall and by her 1st husb has:

    1a *Philip Christopher Liam; *b* 20 April 1967; has:

      1b *George; *b* 9 April 1998

    2a *Jonathan Hugh; *b* 30 Oct 1968; has:

      1b *Thea Dora Christy; *b* 6 Feb 1996

TREVOR

Arms: Quarterly, 1st and 4th, per bend sinister erm. and ermines a lion rampant or (for TREVOR); 2nd and 3rd, sa. on a fess arg. between three leopards passant guardant or, spotted of the field, as many escallops gu. (for HILL). **Crests:** 1 A wyvern sa. (for TREVOR), 2 A reindeer's head couped gu., attired and collared or (for HILL). **Supporters:** Dexter, a lion ermines, ducally gorged and chained, chain reflexed over the back or, pendant from the collar an escutcheon arg. charged with a wyvern sa.; sinister, a leopard or, spotted sa., ducally gorged and chained as the dexter, pendant from the collar an escutcheon erm. charged with a reindeer's head couped gu., attired or. **Motto:** *Per Deum et ferrum obtinui* ('By God and my sword I have prevailed'). **Creation:** B. (UK) 5 May 1880.

THE 5TH BARON TREVOR OF BRYNKINALT, Co Denbigh (Marke Charles Hill-Trevor) [The Rt Hon The Lord Trevor, Brynkinalt, Chirk, Clwyd LL14 5NS; Auch, Bridge of Orchy, Argyllshire]; *b* 8 Jan 1970; *s* f 1997; *educ* Shrewsbury

Lineage: JOHN Ap DAVID later TREVOR, of Brynkinalt, Denbighs; *m* Agnes, dau and heiress of Peter Cambre, and had, with other issue, including a yr s (Richard, probable ancestor of the extinct Barons Trevor of Bromham, from 1776 also Viscounts Hampden; *see* HAMPDEN, V, preliminary remarks):

ROBERT TREVOR, of Brynkinalt; *m* Katherine, dau and heiress of Llewellyn ap Ithel, of Mold and Plasteg, Flints, and was ancestor of:

Sir EDWARD TREVOR, of Brynkinalt; living *temp* ELIZABETH I; *m* 1st Anne Balle; *m* 2nd Rose, dau of Henry Usher, DD, Archbp Armagh, and by his 1st w had an est s:

JOHN TREVOR, of Brynkinalt; *m* Margaret, dau of John Jeffreys, of Acton, Denbighs, and had, with an er s (Edward, *dsp*):

Sir JOHN TREVOR, PC, of Brynkinalt; Speaker H of C, ktd 1670, Master Rolls, Commr Gt Seal; *m* Jane (*d* Aug 1704), widow of Roger Puleston, of Emrall, and dau of Sir Roger Mostyn, 1st Bt (*see* MOSTYN, B), and *d* 20 May 1717, having had, with four sons (Edward, of Brynkinalt, *dsp*; Arthur, Usher Rolls Chapel, *dsp*; John, Master Examiner's Office in Chancery, *dsp*; Tudor, ship's capt, *dsp*):

ANNE Trevor; *m* 1st 1690 Michael HILL, PC, MP (*d* 1699), of Hillsborough, Co Down; *m* 2nd 1 Dec 1716 1st Viscount Midleton (*qv*) and *d* 5 Jan 1747, leaving by her 1st husb, with other issue (*see* DOWNSHIRE, M):

TREVOR HILL, 1st VISCOUNT HILLSBOROUGH; *b* 1693; had:

WILLS HILL, 1st MARQUESS OF DOWNSHIRE; had by his 1st w:

ARTHUR HILL, 2nd MARQUESS OF DOWNSHIRE; had:

ARTHUR HILL, 3rd MARQUESS OF DOWNSHIRE; had, with two er sons:

ARTHUR EDWIN HILL later HILL-TREVOR, **1st Baron Trevor of Brynkinalt**, Co Denbigh (UK), so *cr* 5 May 1880, JP, DL (Denbighs, Co Down, Notts and Salop); *b* 4 Nov 1819; inherited 1862 the Trevor estates of Brynkinalt, Flintshire, and other property from his third cousin once-removed 3rd and last Viscount of Dungannon (*see* DOWNSHIRE, M); *educ* Eton and Balliol Coll Oxford; Gentleman Bedchamber to Ld Lt Ireland 1844–45, MP (C) Co Down 1845–80, Lt-Col S Down Militia 1845, Maj N Salop Yeo Cav 1863; *m* 1st 27 June 1848 Mary Emily (*d* 24 Jan 1855), est dau of Sir Richard Sutton, 2nd Bt (*qv*), and had:

  1 ARTHUR WILLIAM HILL-TREVOR, **2nd Baron Trevor**, JP; *b* 19 Nov 1852; *educ* Eton; V-Lt Denbighs, Lt-Col 1st Life Gds, Cmdt Denbighs Vol Regt 1917–20 (Hon Col); *m* 1st 30 Aug 1893 Annie Mary Eleanor (*dsp* 10 May 1895), dau of 17th Lord Saltoun (*qv*) of Abernethy; *m* 2nd 7 Dec 1897 Rosamond, MBE (1918) (*d* 5 Feb 1942), widow of 4th Earl of Bantry (*see* 1891 edn) and dau of Hon Edmund Petre (*see* PETRE, B), and *dsps* 19 May 1923, having had:

    (1) Mary Rosamond; *b* 22 Feb 1899; *d* 11 Dec 1904

  1 Gertrude Mary; *d* 13 Feb 1870

The **1st Baron** *m* 2nd 15 April 1858 Hon Mary Catherine Curzon (*d* 20 Aug 1911), sister of 4th Baron Scarsdale (*see* SCARSDALE, V), and *d* 25 Dec 1894, having by her had:

  2 George Edwyn; *b* 15 Nov 1859; Lt Salop Yeo Cav, Maj TFR, Maj cmdg 4th/8th Bn DCO Middx Regt; *m* 1st 26 April 1893 (*divorce* 1910) Ethel Georgina Mary (*d* 16 Oct 1960 aged 88), est dau of Hillyar Chapman, of Kilhendre, Ellesmere; *m* 2nd 22 Oct 1910 Helen (*d* 23 May 1919), dau of Thomas Stuart, of Edinburgh, and *d* 21 July 1922, having by 1st w had:

    (1) Hillyar George Edwin; *b* 31 Dec 1895; Lt Scots Gds; *ka* 21 Dec 1914

  3 CHARLES EDWARD, **3rd Baron**

  4 Michael Rowland; *b* 16 March 1866; *d* 7 Dec 1877

  5 Nevill Windsor; *b* 23 Jan 1869; Lt Salop Yeo Cav, Thorneycroft's Mounted Inf and 2nd Life Gds; *ka* Boer War 24 Jan 1900

  6 Marcus Richard; *b* 25 Sept 1872; Lt Thorneycroft's Mounted Inf and E Lancs Regt, ADC and Priv Sec to Lt-Govr Pretoria, served Boer War and WW I; *d* unm 6 Jan 1918

  7 Arthur Eustace; *b* 15 July 1876; Hon Presidency Magistrate and JP Bombay; Lt-Col Cmdt Bombay Vol Artillery; Assist Provost-Marshal Belfast WW I; *d* unm 20 March 1916

  2 Edith Maria, OBE (1918); *b* 30 March 1861; *m* 31 July 1890 Augustus William West, s of Sir Algernon West, GCB, PC, and *d* 14 Nov 1940. He *d* 2 Aug 1929

  3 Nina Emily; *b* 22 Nov 1862; *d* 26 July 1894

  4 Mary Alice; *d* young 20 Aug 1867

  5 Leila Sophy; *b* 18 Sept 1870; *d* 6 March 1937

  6 Mary; *b* 12 Sept 1878; *m* 1st 2 Jan 1901 (*divorce* 1913) Maj James Archibald Morrison, DSO, MP (*see* MARGADALE, B), and had issue; *m* 2nd 9 Oct 1915 (*divorce* 1948) Douglas Alexander Mitchell Carruthers, explorer, s of Rev William Mitchell Carruthers, and *d* 3 Sept 1962. He *d* 23 May 1962

  7 Anne; *b* 18 May, *d* 21 May 1881

The 2nd BARON's half-bro,

CHARLES EDWARD HILL-TREVOR, **3rd Baron Trevor**, JP Denbighs; *b* 22 Dec 1863; *educ* Eton; Capt 3rd Bn RWF, Assist Priv Sec to Govr NZ 1897–1904, BRC Corps attd French Army WW I 1917–18, Croix de Guerre with Silver Star; *m* 27 July 1927 Phyllis May, OStJ (*d* 1990), 2nd dau of James Arthur Sims, of Ings Ho, Kirton in Lindsey, Lincs, and had:

  1 CHARLES EDWIN, **4th Baron**

  2 +Nevill Edward, DL (Denbighshire 1965) [The Hon Nevill Hill-Trevor DL, Plas Lledrod, Llansilin, Salop SY10 7PU]; *b* 25 April 1931; *educ* Shrewsbury; F/O RAF Regt, ADC to C-in-C Fighter Command 1958–59, ADC to Ch of Air Staff 1959–60, Jt Master Border Cos (NW) Otter Hounds 1950–59, High Sheriff Denbighs 1965–66, Jt Master Sir W W Wynn's Hounds 1970–78; *m* 18 July 1963 *Deborah Helen Benson, only dau of William Thomas Benson Jowitt, of Crag Hill, Killinghall, Yorks, and has:

    (1) *Caroline Anne; *b* 1 April 1965

    (2) *Diana Rosemary; *b* 10 April 1967

The 3rd BARON *d* 22 Dec 1950; his er s,

CHARLES EDWIN HILL-TREVOR, **4th Baron Trevor**, JP (Denbighs 1959); *b* 13 Aug 1928; *educ* Shrewsbury; Chm Berwyn PSD, Tstee and Memb Cncl Roy Forestry Soc of England, Wales and NI, CStJ; *m* 4 Jan 1967 *Susan Janet Elizabeth, only dau of Ronald Ivor Bence, DSC, VRD, BM, BCh, of Selly Oak, Birmingham, and *d* 1 Jan 1997, leaving:

  1 MARKE CHARLES HILL-TREVOR, **5th and present Baron Trevor**

  2 +IAIN ROBERT; *b* 1971; heir presumptive

TRIMLESTOWN

MALO · MORI · QUAM · FOEDARI

Arms: Erm. a bordure engrailed gu. **Crest:** From a plume of five ostrich feathers or, gu., az., vert and arg., a falcon rising of the last. **Supporters:** Dexter, a griffin arg.; sinister, a lion gu. **Motto:** *Malo mori quam foedari* ('Death before dishonour'). **Creation:** B. (I) 4 March 1461.

THE 21ST BARON TRIMLESTOWN, of Trimlestown, Co Meath (Raymond Charles Barnewall) [The Rt Hon The Lord Trimlestown, Autumn Cottage, Chiddingfold, Surrey GU8 4TP]; *b* 29 Dec 1930; *s* bro 1997; *educ* Ampleforth

Lineage: Sir CHRISTOPHER BARNEWALL; Ch Justice King's Bench Ireland; *d* just before 12 Oct 1446, leaving, with an er s (*see* BARNEWALL, Bt):

Sir ROBERT BARNEWALL, **1st Baron Trimlestown**, of Trimlestown, Co Meath (I), so *cr* 4 March 1461; *ktd* by 8 Aug 1455; *m* 1st Anne/Elizabeth, dau and heiress of Christopher Browne/le Brun, of Roebuck, Co Dublin; *m* 2nd — and *d* by 1471/2, leaving by his 1st w an er s:

CHRISTOPHER BARNEWALL, **2nd Baron Trimlestown**; involved in Lambert Simnel's impersonation but pardoned; *m* Elizabeth, dau of Sir Thomas Plunkett, of Rathmore, and *d* by June 1513, leaving an est s:

JOHN BARNEWALL, **3rd Baron Trimlestown**, PC (I by 21 Dec 1521); Second Judge King's Bench Ireland Jan 1513/4, *ktd* by Jan 1513/4, V-Treasurer Ireland 1522, High-Treasurer 1524–30; granted 1532 136 acres in Dunleer to hold as the Manor of Trim; Ld Chllr Ireland 1534–38; *m* 1st Genet/Janet, dau of John Bellew, of Bellewstown; *m* 2nd Margaret, dau of Patrick FitzLeons; *m* allegedly twice more and *d* 25 July 1538, leaving an only s by his 1st w:

PATRICK BARNEWALL, **4th Baron Trimlestown**, PC (I by Oct 1539); *m* Catherine, widow of Christopher Delahyde, Recorder Drogheda, and dau of Richard Taylor, of Swords, Co Dublin, and *d* between 28 Aug 1561 and 6 March 1562/3, leaving:

1 ROBERT BARNEWALL, **5th Baron Trimlestown**, PC (I by March 1563/4); *ktd* 1566; *m* 1559 Amy, only dau of Richard Fyan, Mayor Dublin 1564, and *dsp* 27 Oct 1573

2 PETER BARNEWALL, **6th Baron Trimlestown**; *ktd* 1583; *m* Katherine Nugent, sis of 4th Baron Delvin (*see* WESTMEATH, E) and *d* 14 April 1598, leaving an only s:

(1) ROBERT BARNEWALL, **7th Baron Trimlestown**; his dispute with 9th Baron of Dunsany (*qv*) over precedence settled in his favour 1634; *m* by 1594 Genet, dau of Thomas Talbot, of Dardistown, Co Meath, and *d* 13 Dec 1639, having had, with other issue:

1a Christopher; *b c* 1595; *m* 1st by 1614 Elizabeth, dau of Sir Edward FitzGerald, of Tecroghan, Co Meath; *m* 2nd July 1621 Jane, dau of Andrew Brereton and widow of Sir Richard Nugent, and *dvp* 8 May 1622, having by his 2nd w had no issue but by his 1st an est s:

1b MATTHIAS BARNEWALL, **8th Baron Trimlestown**; *b c* 1614; a leader of the 1641 Uprising, accordingly outlawed 1642; *m* by 13 Dec 1639 Jane, yst dau of 1st Viscount Netterville of Dowth, and *d* 17 Sept 1667, having had, with two yr sons (*d* unm) and two daus:

1c ROBERT BARNEWALL, **9th Baron Trimlestown**; *m* 20 July 1668 Margaret (*d* 5 Nov 1678), dau of Sir William Dungan, 2nd Bt, and sis of William, 1st Earl of Limerick of the Jan 1685/6 *cr* (*see* LIMERICK, E, preliminary remarks), and *d* June 1689, leaving:

1d MATTHIAS BARNEWALL, **10th Baron Trimlestown**; sat in JAMES II's I Parl May 1689, Capt Viscount Galmoye's Cavalry 1689 and Col of a Jacobite Foot Regt after the Battle of the Boyne 1690, being accordingly attainted 16 April 1691 and his title and estates forfeited; Lt Duke of Berwick's 1st Horse Gds in French service Jan 1691/2; *d* unm, *ka* in a victorious charge against a German formation at the Battle of Roumont 8 Sept 1692

2d John, usually known as 11th Baron Trimlestown despite the title's being under attainder; *b* 1672; managed to get back his estates but his plea to be restored to the title turned down 1697; *m* 1703 Mary, dau

and heiress of Sir John Barnewall, of Ballybrittan, King's Co, and *d* 7 April 1746, having had:

1e Robert, usually known as 12th Baron Trimlestown despite the attainder; doctor in France; *m* 1st Margaret, dau of James Rochfort, of Laragh, Co Kildare; *m* 2nd by 1757 Elizabeth (*d* 1781), dau of John Colt, of Brightlingsea, Essex, by whom he had a s (Joseph, *b c* 1757, *d* unm 1782); *m* 3rd Anne, allegedly n of Rev James Hervey, of Weston Favell, Northants, and 5th dau of William Hervey, a London merchant, and *d* 6 Dec 1779, having by his 1st w had, with three er sons (*d* young):

1f THOMAS BARNEWALL, **13th Baron Trimlestown** (attainder reversed 1795); *b c* 1739; Kt SMO Malta as RC but later conformed to C of I; *m* Anna — (*d* 24 June 1831) and *d* unm 24 Dec 1796

2e John; *m* in France 1740 Lady Waters and *dsp*

3e Richard; *m* his distant cousin Frances, dau of 3rd Viscount Barnewall of Kingsland, and had:

1f NICHOLAS BARNEWALL, **14th Baron Trimlestown**; *b* 29 June 1726; *m* 1st 1 Nov 1768 Martha Henrietta (*d* May 1782), only dau of Joseph d'Auguin, Pres Parlement of Toulouse, and had, with an er s (*d* young):

1g JOHN THOMAS BARNEWALL, **15th Baron Trimlestown**; *b* 29 Jan 1773; *m* 16 Jan 1793 Maria Theresa (*d* 12 Oct 1824), dau of Richard Kirwan, of Cregg, Co Galway, and *d* 7 Oct 1839, having had, with a dau (*d* unm):

1h THOMAS BARNEWALL, **16th Baron Trimlestown**; *b* 14 April 1796; Sheriff Co Dublin 1830; *m* 3 Nov 1836 Margaret Randalina (*d* 4 Sept 1872), dau of Philip Roche (*see* DUNSANY, B), and *dspms* 4 Aug 1879, having had, with a s (*d* an infant):

1i Anna Maria Louisa; *m* 4 June 1868 Robert Henry Elliot, DL, of Clifton Park, Roxburghs, and Ballybrittas, King's Co, and *d* 16 April 1914, leaving issue. He *d* 19 Aug 1914

1g Rosalie; *m* 3 Dec 1795 Peter, Count D'Alton, and *d* Florence 2 Feb 1864, leaving issue

1f (cont.) The **14th Baron** *m* 2nd 8 Aug 1797 Alicia (*m* 2nd Lt-Gen Sir Evan Lloyd, of Ferney Hall, Salop (*d* 1846), and *d* 25 Nov 1860 aged 87), 2nd dau of Lt-Gen Charles Eustace, of Robertstown, Co Kildare, and *d* 17 April 1813

4e Thomas; Offr in French serv

5e James; *d* in Spain

6e Anthony; *b* 1721; *k* Battle of Krotzka 22 July 1739

1e Thomasine; *m* 9 Feb 1729 10th Viscount Gormanston (*qv*) and *d* 10 Jan 1788

2e Margaret; *m* Jan 1736 8th Viscount Mountgarret (*qv*) and *d* June 1764

3e Bridget; *m* 6 April 1753 Robert Martin, of Dangan and Ballinahinch Castle

2a Patrick; *m* 1st Katherine, dau of Robert Barnewall, of Bremore, Co Dublin; *m* 2nd Katherine, dau of Mathew King, of Co Kildare, and by his 1st w had:

1b Christopher, of Woodtown, Co Meath; *m* —, dau of Gerald Nangle, of Kildalkey, Co Meath, and had:

1c Richard, of Clonylogan; *m* 1st Aminett, widow of James Caddell and sis of James Barnewell, of Bremore, and had an only dau:

1d Elizabeth; *m* Henry Plunkett

1c (cont.) Richard Barnewall *m* 2nd 3 March 1712 Bridget, dau of Henry Piers, of Ballydrimney, Co Meath, and *d* Feb 1718, leaving:

1d Christopher, of Fyanstown; *b* 1715; *m* Cecilia, dau of Mathew Dowdall, of Clone, Co Meath, and had, with a dau (Anne, *m* 13 Oct 1777 Columbus Drake, of Roristown):

1e Richard, of Fyanstown, on whom as heir to the title the **14th Baron Trimlestown** entailed his estates; *m* Katherine, dau of George Byrne, of Seatown, Dundalk, Co Louth, and *d* 1827, leaving:

1f Christopher, of Meadstown; *m* Nov 1793 Anne, dau of Charles Aylmer, of Painstown, and *d* 14 Aug 1849, having had, with other issue, including a dau (Esmay Mary, *m* 29 Sept 1836 Sir Aylmer John Barnewall, 9th Bt, (*qv*), and *d* 5 March 1879, leaving issue):

1g Charles, JP Co Meath; *m* 1st Katherine (*dsp*), dau of John Connolly, of New Haggard, Co Meath; *m* 2nd 9 Oct 1844 Letitia (*d* 3 March 1886), dau of Gerald Aylmer, of Lyons, and *d* 2 May 1873, leaving:

1h CHRISTOPHER PATRICK MARY BARNEWALL, **17th Baron Trimlestown**; *b* 6 Oct 1846; *d* unm 10 Sept 1891

2h Gerald Aylmer; *b* 8 May 1856; *d* unm 2 July 1871

3h CHARLES, **18th Baron**

1h Katherine; nun

2h Anne; granted with her sisters rank of baron's dau 2 Aug 1893

3h Esmay; *m* 1883 Nicholas Francis Coppinger and had issue

4h Mary Jane; nun

5h Helena

6h Letitia; nun

7h Angelina; nun

8h Cecilia; *m* 5 Oct 1907 Maj Henry Chamney, CMG, s of Rev Joseph Chamney, DD, of Ard Ronan, Co Louth, and *dsp* 11 July 1908

9h Marcella

10h Margaret; *m* 19 Jan 1899, as his 1st w, Bertrand Lambert and *dsp*

2f Joseph, of Bloomsbury, Co Meath; *b* 1781; *m* 1817 Margaret, est dau of Thomas Everard, of Randalstown, Co Meath, and had, with three daus (Barbara; Charlotte; Katherine):

1g Richard, of Bloomsbury, JP, DL; *b* Feb 1821; *m* 1845, as her 1st husb, Helena Maria (*m* 2nd —), yst dau of Charles Whyte Roche, of Limerick, and *dsp* 3 Feb 1866

2g Thomas, of Bloomsbury; *b* 25 March 1825; among his male line descendants, if any, is the heir presumptive to the Barony

3f Patrick, of Causestown; *m* Barbara, dau of Thomas Everard, of Randlastown, and *dsp* Aug 1854

1f Cecilia; *m* 1st John Connolly, of New Haggard, Co Meath; *m* 2nd Charles Nangle (*d* 5 Sept 1847)

1a Mary; *m* Robert Barnewall, of Shankhill, Co Dublin

The 17th BARON's bro,

CHARLES ALOYSIUS BARNEWALL, **18th Baron Trimlestown**, DL; *b* 14 May 1861; *m* 1st 26 Oct 1889 Margaret Theresa (*d* 9 Jan 1901), dau of Richard John Stephens, of Brisbane, Qld; *m* 2nd 10 Dec 1907 Mabel Florence (*d* 16 March 1914), dau of William Robert Shuff, of Torquay, Devon; *m* 3rd 12 Aug 1930 Josephine Francesca (*d* 15 June 1945), 2nd surv dau of Sir Christopher John Nixon, 1st Bt (*qv*), and by his 1st w had:

1 Reginald Nicholas Francis; *b* 24 Sept 1897; Capt Leinster Regt WW I; *d* 24 March 1918 of wounds recd in action

2 CHARLES ALOYSIUS, **19th Baron**

1 Ivy Esmay Myee; *b* 14 Sept 1890; *m* 1st 30 April 1917 John Radcliff, Nigerian CS (*d* 1953), est s of George Edward Radcliff, JP, of Wilmount, Kells, Co Meath, and had issue; *m* 2nd 30 April 1956 John Kidd, s of Thomas Kidd, of Linares, Spain. He *d* 13 Sept 1958

2 Marcella Hilda Charlotte; *b* 29 June 1893; *m* 4 July 1917 Maj Charles Bathurst, MC, Duke of Wellington's W R Regt, s of Lancelot Bathurst, and *dsp* 11 Sept 1965. He *d* 25 Aug 1942

3 Letitia Anne Margaret; *b* 23 Sept 1895; *m* 11 June 1919 Lt-Col Cuthbert Hanson Townsend, E Surrey Regt, of Ewell, Surrey, s of V-Adml Samuel Philip Townsend, and *d* 2 May 1938, leaving issue. He *d* 27 Jan 1956

4 Geraldine Christina Marjory; *b* 14 June 1900; *d* 23 June 1902

The 18th BARON *d* 26 Jan 1937; his only surv s,

CHARLES ALOYSIUS BARNEWALL, **19th Baron Trimlestown**; *b* 2 June 1899; *educ* Ampleforth; Lt Irish Gds WW I; *m* 1st 16 June 1926 Muriel (*d* 22 June 1937), only child of Edward Oskar Schneider, of Mansfield Lodge, Whalley Range, Manchester; *m* 2nd 7 May 1952 Freda Kathleen (*d* 1987), dau of Alfred Allen Watkins, of Ross-on-Wye, Herefs, and *d* 1990, having by his 1st w had:

1 ANTHONY EDWARD BARNEWALL, **20th Trimlestown**; *b* 2 Feb 1928; *educ* Ampleforth; Irish Gds 1946–48, naval architect 1949–53, European Sales exec P&O Shipping Co 1965–74; *m* 1st 30 Sept 1963 (*divorce* 1973) Lorna Margaret Marion (*d* 1988), dau of Charles Douglas Ramsay; *m* 2nd 14 May 1977 *Mary Wonderly [The Rt Hon The Lady Trimlestown, PO Box 215, Ada, MI 49301, USA], er dau of Judge Thomas Francis McAllister, of Grand Rapids, Michigan, and *dsp* 21 Aug 1997

2 RAYMOND CHARLES, **21st and present Baron Trimlestown**

1 *Diana [The Hon Mrs Birtwistle, Rogate, W Sussex]; *b* 13 Oct 1929; *m* 30 Oct 1954 *Anthony Gerard Astley Birtwistle, yst s of James Astley Birtwistle, of Hoghton, Lancs, and Wroxton, Oxon, and has:

(1) *Caroline Muriel Mary [Mrs Stewart Oliver, Creek Farm, Brancaster, Norfolk]; *b* 24 July 1955; *m* 1982 *Stewart Oliver, s of S/Ldr H W Oliver, OBE, RAF, of Staithe Ho, Brancaster Staithe, Norfolk, and has:

1a *Alexander Charles James; *b* 1985

2a *George Anthony Andrew; *b* 1989

1a *Charlotte Mary Rose; *b* 1983

(2) *Emma Francis Mary [Mrs Oliver Pawle, 33 Blenkarne Rd, London SW11 6HZ]; *b* 6 Nov 1957; *m* 1982 *Oliver John Woodforde Pawle, s of Roger Pawle, OBE, of Parkstone, Dorset, and has:

1a *James Roger Woodforde; *b* 1985

1a *Lucy Diana Mary; *b* 1988

2a *Victoria Louise Maria; *b* 1992

(3) *Lucinda Jane Mary [Mrs Malcolm Reid, 30 Melody Rd, London SW18 2QF]; *b* 28 Aug 1960; *m* 1986 *P Malcolm G Reid, yst s of Dr Kenneth Reid, of Rest Harrow, Cooden, Sussex, and has:

1a *Charles Anthony Gilmore; *b* 1991

1a *Emily Louise Mary; *b* 1988

2a *Olivia Charlotte Mary; *b* 1997

(4) *Sophia Louise Mary [Mrs Julian Lynn, New Cottage, Lower High St, Wadhurst, E Sussex]; *b* 3 March 1964; *m* 4 Oct 1996 *Julian Stirling Emmet Lynn, s of Mrs Graeme Hamilton and stepson of Graeme Hamilton, of Eastling, Kent, and has:

1a *Frederick Graeme Stirling; *b* 1997

TRITTON

Arms: Arg. on a bend cotised gu. a bezant between two helmets or.
Crest: A horse statant arg., resting the dexter forefoot upon a bezant.
Motto: *En avant* ('Forward'). **Creation:** Bt. (UK) 1 Aug 1905.

SIR ANTHONY JOHN ERNEST TRITTON, 4TH BT, of Bloomfield, Lambeth, London [Major Sir Anthony Tritton Bt, River House, Heytesbury, Wilts BA12 0EE]; *b* 4 March 1927; *s f* 1976; *educ* Eton; Maj (ret) QOH; *m* 12 Oct 1957 *Diana, only dau of R-Adml St John Aldrich Micklethwait, CB, DSO (*see* WELBY, Bt), and has:

1 +JEREMY ERNEST [Jeremy Tritton Esq, 6 St Stephen's Terrace, London SW8 1DH]; *b* 6 Oct 1961

1 *Clarissa Mary Penelope [Mrs John Delamere, The Old Rectory, Avening, Glos GL8 8NF]; *b* 21 June 1959; *m* 1988 *John Charles Joseph Delamere, yr s of F A Delamere, of Rathgowan, Mullingar, Co Westmeath, and has:

(1) *Hugo Fitzherbert; *b* 1989

(1) *Camilla Sophia; *b* 1991

Lineage: ROBERT TRITTON, of Charing, Kent; *m* Joan — (*bur* 14 Dec 1598) and was *bur* 17 Nov 1610, leaving:

ROBERT TRITTON; living at Kennington 1630; held land there and at Boughton Aluph, Kent, 1632; had, with two yr sons (Robert, *bapt* 11 May 1613, *bur* 20 May 1639; Samuel, of Aldington, *bapt* 21 Oct 1617, *m* Anne — (*m* 2nd 3 July 1666 Edward Goddard, of Mersham) and *d* by 17 Feb 1663, leaving a s (Robert, under age in 1666) and two daus (Elizabeth; Jane)) and two daus (Jane, *bapt* 9 May 1610, *m* (licence 3 Aug 1632) John Ferne, of Godmersham; Marye, *bapt* 7 Oct 1921):

JOHN TRITTON, of Kennington, nr Ashford, Kent; held land there and at Boughton Aluph, Hinxhill, Bilsington and Eastwell; *m* 1st 23 June 1629 Elizabeth Starker; *m* 2nd Grace (*bur* 5 Feb 1675), widow of William Tucker, of Goodnestone, and was *bur* 2 May 1676, having by his 1st w had, with a yr s (Robert, inherited lands at Ashford from his f, had a s (John, under age in 1673)) and four daus (Elizabeth, *b* 1635, *m* (licence 8 Jan 1665) John Crouch, of Kennington; Mary, *bapt* 10 July 1636; Sarah, *bapt* 30 Jan 1638/9; Martha, *bapt* 16 May, *bur* 6 Sept 1641):

JOHN TRITTON; held land at Kennington and Hinxhill, Bilsington, Eastwell, Walland Marsh and Newchurch, Kent; *m* 1st Nov 1682 Margaret (*bur* 4 Jan 1688/9), dau of Nicholas Ladd, of Swingfield; *m* 2nd 1691 Susan Bates (*bur* 9 March 1709) and was *bur* 13 Aug 1716, having had, with two yr sons (Samuel, *b* 16 May 1685, inherited land at Willsborough, Ashford, Bilsington, Rucking and Walland Marsh, Kent, *m* (licence 21 July 1713) Sarah Pilcher, of St Mary in Dove, and *d* 21 Jan 1742/3, having had a s (Samuel, *d* young) and three daus (Sarah, *b* 1719, *m* James Flint, of Ashford, and *d* 18 May 1786; Hannah, *m* Richard Sackett and had issue; Mary, *m* Thomas Thurston); Robert, *b* 28 Dec 1688, *d* July 1689) and two daus (Mary, *b* 26 Oct 1686, *bur* 8 Nov 1686; Margaret, *b* 28 Dec 1688, *d* 12 June 1691):

JOHN TRITTON; held land at Kennington, Eastwell, Hinxhill, Newchurch and Ashford; *b* 16 Oct 1683; *m* 1st 3 March 1705 Hannah (*d* 13 Sept 1717), dau of John Shaw, of W Chiltington, Sussex, and had:

1 John, of Kennington and Ashford; *b* 11 Oct 1707; *m* 23 July 1738 Anne (*d* 14 Aug 1777 aged 75), dau of John Futcher, of Romsey, Hants, and *d* 26 May 1742, leaving:

(1) John, of Kennington; *b* 31 Dec 1739; *m* 1772 Catherine Blunden, of Ashford, and *dsp* 21 June 1795

(2) Thomas, of Ashford; *b* April 1742; *d* unm by 25 Jan 1771

2 Samuel; *b* and *d* 1710

3 THOMAS

1 Margaret; *b* 1713; *d* 1727

JOHN TRITTON *m* 2nd 20 Sept 1720 Sarah (*d* 5 Dec 1761), dau of John Futcher, of Romsey, apparently his est son's w's sister, and *d* 1 May 1739, having by her had:

4 Robert, of Ashford; *b* 17 Oct 1732; *m* Anne (*d* 1794), dau of Thomas Vaxham, and *d* 8 Jan 1795, having had:

(1) Ewell; *b* 25 Jan 1774; Capt RN; *d* 28 Sept 1819

(1) Sarah; *b* 1772; *m* 1st John Billington, of Kennington, and had issue; *m* 2nd Rev Moyle Breton, DD, of Boughton Aluph. He *d* 1821

(2) Elizabeth; *d* young

(3) Anne; *d* young

1 Rebecca; *b* 30 July 1723; *m* 29 Oct 1745 Robert Courthope Sims, MD, of Dunmow, and *d* 1781, leaving issue. He *d* 1812

2 Hannah; *b* 13 April 1725; *d* 22 May 1730

3 Anne; *b* 3 Dec 1726; *m* 4 April 1752 John Pay, of Tenterden

The est s,

THOMAS TRITTON, of Kennington, Ashford and Battersea; *b* 28 July 1717; *m* 1 Aug 1754 Anna Maria (*d* 20 July 1793), dau of Henton Brown, of Lombard St and Clapham Common, and *d* 11 Nov 1786, having had:

1 JOHN HENTON

2 James; *b* 4 April, *d* 6 Dec 1759

3 George, of W Hill, Wandsworth; *b* 18 Aug 1761; *m* 1st 1790 Louisa (*d* 1801), dau of Matthew Howard, of Bow Church Yard, and had:

(1) George; *b* 1795; *d* 1803

(2) William, of The Grove, Wrington, Somerset; *b* 1800; *m* 1826 Jane Dennistoun, dau of James and Lady Janet Buchanan, of Blairvadock, Ardinconnal, Dunbartonshire, and *d* 19 June 1851, leaving:

1a George Sinclair; *b* 23 June 1828; *d* Nov 1892

1a Margaret; *m* 21 Feb 1856 Alexander James Dennistoun-Brown, of Balloch Castle, Loch Lomond, Dunbartonshire

(1) Anna Maria; *b* 1793; *m* Rev Thomas Linwood Strong, Rector Sedgefield, Co Durham, and *d* 1807, leaving issue

(2) Elizabeth; *b* 1798; *m* 1819 Lt-Col Hon James Sinclair, 3rd s of 12th Earl of Caithness (*qv*), and *dsp* 7 Jan 1856

(3) Louisa; *b* 1797; *d* 1866

3 (cont.) George Tritton *m* 2nd 13 April 1808 Margaret (*d* 1843), widow of Colquhoun Grant and dau of Alexander Abernethie, MD, and *d* 16 March 1831

4 James Brown; *b* 25 June 1763; *d* 1 March 1764

1 Sarah Shaw; *b* 19 Feb 1765; *m* 10 Dec 1783 Edward Fawkes, of Waddon, and *d* 6 Aug 1818, leaving issue. He *d* 1829

The est s,

JOHN HENTON TRITTON, of Lombard St and Gloucester Pl, London, and Beddington, Kent; *b* 29 April 1755; banker; *m* 6 Aug 1783 Mary (*d* 25 Feb 1827 aged 73), dau of John Barclay, of Lombard St and Cambridge Heath, and *d* 20 May 1833, leaving:

1 John, of Lombard St and Gloucester Pl; *b* 23 Dec 1788; *m* 29 May 1820 Elizabeth Mary (*d* 26 Jan 1834), dau of Edmund Hammond Biscoe, of Limpsfield, and *dsp* 19 Jan 1832

2 HENRY

3 Robert (Rev); *b* 1 May 1792; Rector Morden, Surrey; *m* 1 May 1818 Mary (*d* 20 Oct 1835), est dau of Vincent Hilton Biscoe, of Hookwood, Surrey, and *d* 27 Nov 1877, having had:

(1) Robert (Rev); *b* 24 Jan 1819; Rector Otford and Bognor; *m* 24 May 1849 Charlotte (*d* 7 May 1893), dau of Rev Henry Lindsay, of Sundridge, Kent, and *d* 1 April 1898, leaving:

1a Robert Lindsay; *b* 9 Dec 1850; *m* Aug 1875 Helen Temple (*d* 6 Sept 1925), formerly w of — Spears and dau of Temple Craig, of Philadelphia, USA, and *d* Nov 1927, leaving:

1b Robert Craig, of Richmond, Va.; *b* 27 June 1880; *m* 1908 Helen, dau of William Parrish, of Richmond, Va, and had:

1c *Grace; *b* 19 Dec 1912

2c *Helen; *b* 21 March 1914

3c *Katherine; *b* 19 Jan 1917

1b Mary Josephine; *b* 7 May 1877; *m* 1900 Lucian White Ryland, of Richmond, Va, and *d* July 1940

2b Charlotte Lindsay; *b* Feb 1879; *m* 1st 2 March 1902 Alexander Fleet Ryland, of Richmond, Va, and had issue; *m* 2nd Herman Devenney and *d* 25 Aug 1960

3b Marie Constance; *b c* 1883; *m c* 1905 Blythe Moore

2a Arthur Henry, of The Priory, Leatherhead, Surrey, JP (Surrey 1904); *b* 28 May 1855; CC Surrey, MFH Surrey Union 1910–18; *m* 1st 8 Nov 1878 Louisa (*d* 10 July 1917), widow of David Woolf and dau of David Davis, of Glasgow; *m* 2nd 1918 Mabel, dau of William Holloway, of Thames Ditton, and *d* 3 April 1936, having by his 1st w had:

1b Arthur Robert, of Godmersham Park, Kent; *b* 26 Aug 1884; *educ* Eton; *m* 4 Nov 1935 Elsie (*d* 23 Feb 1983), widow of Sir Louis Bernard Baron, 1st and last Bt (*see* 1934 edn), and dau of Bruno Richter, of New York, and *dsp* 26 Jan 1957

2b Nigel Charles; *b* 29 May 1891; *educ* Eton; Queen's Roy W Surrey Regt WW I, memb London Stock Exchange, MFH Surrey Union 1945–50, Chm St Luke's Hostel 1945–58, High Sheriff Surrey 1958; *m* 2 June 1914 Ruth Borradaile (*d* 14 June 1965), dau of Edward George Coles, of Pebblecoombe, Headley, Surrey, and *dsp* 9 July 1971

1b Winifred Louie; *b* 3 Oct 1879; *m* 7 June 1905 Arthur Gerard Miller and *d* 14 Sept 1949, having had issue. He *d* 195–

1a Mary Charlotte; *b c* 1852; *m* 8 Aug 1872 R M Hennell, of Hastings, and had issue. He *d c* 1894

2a Alice Maria; *b* 27 Feb 1854; *m* 11 Jan 1877 Clement Godson, MD, of Sharsted Court, Westgate-on-Sea, Kent, and *d* 8 April 1931, leaving issue. He *d* 26 Nov 1913

3a Minna Elizabeth; *d* 11 May 1893

(2) William Biscoe (Rev); *b* 26 Sept 1820; *m* Eleanor Willet, widow of Rev William Ayling and est dau of Osgood Hanbury, DL, of Holfield Grange, Essex

(3) Frederick Biscoe; *b* 1825; Col RWF; *m* 1st 27 Oct 1859 Selina Charlotte (*d* 17 April 1863), dau of Charles Maryatt, of Potters Bar; *m* 2nd Augusta Fox, dau of — Young, and *d* 23 Jan 1904, having by his 1st w had:

1a Seymour Biscoe (Sir), KBE (1918); *b* 30 July 1860; *educ* Haileybury and UCL; MInstCE, MIMechE, MINA, MILocoE, ptnr Rendel, Palmer and Tritton, consulting engrs to Govt of India; *m* 14 June 1888 Alice May (*d* 28 Jan 1933), dau of Louis Jullion, PhD, of Low Fell, Co Durham, and *d* 21 Nov 1937, leaving:

1b Julian Seymour; *b* 31 Oct 1889; *educ* Rugby and King's Coll London; RE WW I, Pres: Institution of Locomotive Engrs 1947 and 1951, FIDIC 1958–63, Chm Assoc Consulting Engrs 1953 and 1955, MICE, MIMechE, PPILocoE, MConsE; *m* 21 Jan 1918 Effie Theodora Eleanor, er dau of Rev Canon W G Kerr, of Truro, and had:

1c *Trevor Lindsey Julian; *b* 5 July 1921; *educ* Uppingham; *m* 13 Dec 1947 *Eveline Noël, dau of Norman Bellerby, of Dorking, Surrey, and has:

1d *Ian Gordon; *b* 9 Feb 1953

1d *Alison Lindsey; *b* 26 June 1950

1c *Theodora Kerr Julian; *b* 31 Dec 1918; *m* 30 Nov 1945 *John Mavin Beazley

2b Frederick Seymour; *b* 1 Sept 1892; *m* 21 March 1929 Monica (*m* 2nd 21 Dec 1952 Richard Canning Brown, yr s of William Brown, of The Manor, Aldbourne, Wilts), dau of Francis Despard, of Co Tipperary, and *dsp* 30 Dec 1949

1b May Seymour; *b* 20 Nov 1898; *m* 17 Sept 1925 Lancelot Richard Stephen Monckton (*see* MONCKTON OF BRENCHLEY, V) and had issue

(4) Charles Biscoe; *b* 1828; *d* 1833

(5) John Biscoe; *b* 1829; *d* 1831

(6) Vincent Biscoe; *b* 8 Oct 1835; *m* 28 July 1859 Helen Catherine (*d* 17 Jan 1924), dau of Charles Kelson, of Devon, and *d* 19 May 1915, having had:

1a Vincent Biscoe; *b* 8 Nov 1862; *m* 8 Nov 1890 Linda (*d* 3 July 1952), only dau of Maj-Gen Reginald Curtis (*see* CURTIS, Bt), and *d* 27 July 1931, having had:

1b Reginald Hilton Biscoe; *b* 12 April 1896; *d* 7 Oct 1909

1b Marianne Helen; *b* 5 Dec 1892; *m* 15 April 1915 Rev Canon Francis Rochfort Bonsey and *d* 9 April 1967, having had issue

2b Dorothy Winifred; *b* 17 Jan 1894

3b Joan; *b* 24 Dec 1901

2a Hilton Biscoe; *b* 19 March, *d* 15 May 1864

3a Charles Biscoe; *b* 10 Dec 1865; *d* 10 Oct 1924

4a Hubert Biscoe; *b* 27 June 1868; *d* 7 Nov 1915

5a Cecil Biscoe; *b* 10 May 1877; *m c* 1919 Alice Euphemia Thompson (*m* 2nd Dr Richards) and *d* 30 Nov 1935

1a Florence Helen; *b* 12 Aug 1860; *d* 14 Sept 1938

(1) Mary Biscoe; *b* 1822; *d* 1834

(2) Anna Maria Biscoe; *b* 1823; *m* 1865, as his 2nd w, FM Sir Daniel Lysons, GCB, s of Rev D Lysons, of Hempstead Court, Glos. He *d* 29 Jan 1898

(3) Caroline Biscoe; *b* 1825; *d* 1832

(4) Susanah Biscoe; *b* 1826; *m* 4 Nov 1851 Rev Henry Seymour (*see* SOMERSET, D) and *d* 8 May 1889, leaving issue

(5) Elizabeth Biscoe; *b* 1832; *m* 26 Oct 1852 Rev Canon William Chetwynd-Stapylton (*see* CHETWYND, V) and *d* 18 Sept 1893, leaving issue

1 Mary; *b* 27 July 1794; *d* unm 3 Sept 1852

The 2nd s,

HENRY TRITTON, of Lombard St, Battersea, Beddington and Lyons Hall, Essex; *b* 26 Feb 1790; banker; *m* 8 March 1814 Amelia (*d* 28 March 1855), dau of Joseph Benwell, of Battersea and Henley, and *d* 20 April 1838, having had:

1 Henry, of Lombard St, Portland Pl and Beddington; *b* 7 July 1815; *m* 23 April 1839 Elizabeth Ann (*d* 3 June 1901), dau of Rev Patrick Maxwell, and *d* 2 Jan 1877, leaving:

(1) Henry John, JP Surrey; *b* 22 Nov 1842; Capt KOLI Militia, Maj Middx Yeo, High Sheriff Surrey 1882; *m* 31 May 1866 Anna Isabella (*d* 21 Oct 1914), 4th dau of Rev Richard Buller, Rector Lanreath, Cornwall, and *d* 17 Feb 1922, having had:

1a Henry Maxwell Buller; *b* 8 April 1867; Lt 14th Hus; *d* 15 Jan 1890

2a Richard Buller; *b* 1868; *d* 29 March 1868

1a Mildred Isabella; *b* 23 March 1869; *m* 15 July 1908 her cousin Thomas Buller Bradshaw, of Lifton Park, Devon, and *dsp* 16 Nov 1942. He *d* 27 Oct 1927

2a Blanche Georgina Hornby; *b* 10 Aug 1870; *m* 24 Oct 1923 John Granger Mudge, 2nd s of Arthur Thomas Mudge, JP, of Sydney, Plympton, Devon, and *dsp* 18 May 1932. He *d* 8 July 1948

3a Emmeline Caroline Alexandra; *b* 19 Oct 1871; *m* 20 April 1892 Walter John Deacon Radcliffe, JP, of Warleigh, Tamerton Foliot, Devon, and *d* 22 May 1953, leaving issue. He *d* 28 Nov 1930

(2) Edward William; *b* 3 Aug 1844; *m* 30 Sept 1874 Hon Alice Jane Verney (*d* 8 Jan 1882), dau of 17th Baron Willoughby de Broke (*qv*), and *d* 1 Jan 1901, leaving:

1a Oswald; *b* 28 July 1875; *educ* Charterhouse and RMA Woolwich; Maj RA WW I, Observer Corps WW II; *m* 5 Aug 1914 Violet Margaret (*d* 28 Feb 1968), dau of Rev Canon Gordon Sedgwick, of Sherbourne, Warwicks, and *d* 1 March 1963

2a Louis John; *b* 11 March 1879; *m* 24 Dec 1924 Kathleen Vere (*d* 22 May 1964), dau of Maj Thomas Gough, and *dsp* 29 April 1927

3a John Cecil, ICS; *b* 8 Feb 1880; *d* unm Aug 1905

1a Claude; *b* 18 Sept 1881

(3) Wilfred Francis; *b* 9 March 1849; *m* 1st 9 Feb 1872 Marion Amelia Churcher, formerly w of James Joseph McDonald, of Birmingham, and dau of Mrs Harvey, of Birmingham; *m* 2nd Daisy Barton, of Mayfair, and *d* 2 Oct 1930, having by 1st w had:

1a Winifred

(1) Emily Mary; *b* 20 July 1840; *m* 3 Feb 1870 her bro's bro-in-law Adml Sir Alexander Buller, GCB, s of Rev Richard Buller, and *d* 6 April 1920, leaving issue. He *d* 3 Oct 1903

(2) Caroline Elizabeth; *b* 1 Jan 1846; *m* 27 April 1865 Charles Alexander Hall Hall, of Watergate, W Sussex, and *d* 28 Jan 1887, leaving issue. He *d* 14 Jan 1927

(3) Anna Henrietta; *b* 7 May 1847; *m* 10 June 1885 Charles Duberly, s of Rev Charles Duberly, Rector Wolsingham, Co Durham, and *d* 27 Feb 1920, leaving issue. He *d* 18 Sept 1918

(4) Catherine Louisa; *b* 6 Aug 1850; *m* Rev Clement René Sharpe and *d* 12 March 1912, leaving issue. He *d* 26 Sept 1905

(5) Mary Eleanor; *b* 3 March 1852; *d* unm 18 March 1927

(6) Elizabeth Anne; *b* 13 March 1853; *d* unm 11 April 1917

(7) Edith Isabella; *b* 4 May 1855; *m* 15 Jan 1879 John Henry Bridges, JP, of Beddington, Surrey, and *d* 12 May 1907, leaving issue. He *d* 12 Feb 1925

2 JOSEPH

1 Amelia; *m* 5 May 1841 Rev Israel May Soule (*d* 1866)

2 Harriet; *m* 29 Aug 1843 Joseph Gurney

3 Anna Maria; *b* 11 Sept 1825; *d* 28 Jan 1828

The yr s,

JOSEPH TRITTON, of Lombard St, Bloomfield, Norwood, and Lyons Hall, Essex; *b* 21 Sept 1819; *m* 8 Nov 1843 Amelia (*d* 12 Feb 1908), dau of Joseph Hanson, of Brixton Hill, and *d* 1 May 1887, having had:

1 Joseph Herbert, of Lyons Hall and Lombard St; *b* 5 Sept 1844; Lt City London, dir Barclays Bank; *m* 17 June 1869 Lucy Jane (*d* 4 Jan 1919), dau of Henry Abel Smith, of Wilford, Notts, and *d* 11 Sept 1823, having had:

(1) Herbert Leslie Melville, DL Essex; *b* 20 Dec 1870; *educ* Eton and Trin Coll Cambridge; Maj Essex Yeo, High Sheriff Essex 1933, pres Equitable Life Assur Soc, dir Barclays Bank, chm: Barclays DCO, London Bd of Bank of NSW; *m* 11 July 1894 Gertrude Susan (*d* 8 June 1955), dau of M John A Gosset, Ch Clerk Inland Revenue, and *d* 21 Nov 1940, having had:

1a Ralph Leslie; *b* 5 March 1900; *m* Alys, MBE (1946) (*m* 2nd Patrick Dyke Dennis; *m* 3rd June 1947 Peter Gordon Colin Somervell, er s of Sir Arnold Colin Somervell, OBE), dau of A D S Duncan, of Wellington, NZ, and *d* 15 Jan 1929

2a George Henton; *b* 23 May 1905; *m* 9 Feb 1928 Iris Mary (*d* 16 Feb 1967, having *m* 2nd 20 Aug 1937 Robin Arthur Barnes-Gorell (*d* 17 June 1966), yr s of Maj Arthur Gorell Barnes-Gorell, JP, of Glapwell Hall, Derbys), dau of Sheriff Ronald Hugh Baillie, OBE, DL, of Jedbank, Jedburgh, Roxburghs, and *d* 6 March 1934, leaving:

1b *Alan George, DL (Essex 1993) [Alan Tritton Esq DL, Lyons Hall, Great Leighs, Essex]; *b* 2 Oct 1931; dir Barclays Bank Ltd 1974–91 (India Advsr 1992–), chm: Plantation and Gen Investments 1994–, University Life Assur Soc 1994–; dir Equitable Life Assur Soc 1976– (v-pres 1983–), memb cncl Int Ch of Commerce 1975–90; v-pres RGS 1983–, High Sheriff Essex 1992; *m* 1st 22 March 1958 (*divorce* 1970) (Elizabeth) Clare (*m* 2nd 1973 Andrew McLaren and 1991 changed her name by deed poll to McLaren-Throckmorton; *see* 1970 edn THROCKMORTON, Bt), est dau of Prof Alphonsus Ligouri D'Abreu, OBE, MCh, FRCS, of The Leys, Alvechurch, Worcs; *m* 2nd 1972 *Diana Marion Spencer and by his 1st w has:

1c *(Robert) Guy Henton; *b* 18 Nov 1963; *m* Sept 1995 *Jane Pyecraft and has:

1d *Lara Ursula; *b* 6 Sept 1996

2c *Charles Courtenay; *b* 12 May 1965; *m* May 1993 *Anneli Clare Pougatch and has:

1d *Felix Michael Courtenay; *b* 30 May 1996

1c *Christina Margaret; *b* 24 Sept 1960; *m* 1st 28 April 1984 (*divorce* 1990) Rupert Birch and has:

1d *Magnus Courtenay; *b* 12 Aug 1987

1c (cont.) Mrs Christina Birch *m* 2nd *(Adam) Benedict Williams and has:

2d *Merlin Anthony Baillie; *b* 27 March 1994

3d *Jasper Ambrose George; *b* 18 Aug 1997

1d *Flavia Elizabeth Ruth; *b* 15 Dec 1995

1b *Margold Elizabeth; *b* 15 Nov 1928; *m* 4 March 1950 John Duncan Hervey MacRae, only surv s of Capt John Duncan George MacRae, JP, DL, of Ballimore, Argyllshire, and has:

1c *Miranda Mary; *b* 21 Jan 1951

2c *Mairi Jean; *b* 14 Aug 1952

3c *Rosalind Clare; *b* 3 Jan 1955

4c *Valerie Anne; *b* 14 Feb 1960

5c *Georgina; *b* 28 Nov 1963

1a Lucy Constance; *b* 18 June 1895; *m* 12 July 1920 Reginald James Johnstone Bevan, est s of Maj Reginald Johnstone Bevan, RA, and had issue. He *d* 1 Dec 1942

2a Marjorie Gertrude; *b* 14 April 1897; *m* 9 Jan 1928 Cecil Garnett. He *dsp* 26 Sept 1948

(2) Charles Robert; *b* 29 Nov 1871; *m* 1929 Gwladys Ellen (*d* 1944), formerly w of David Cecil Fowler Burton, of Cherry Burton, Yorks, and dau of R W Parry, and *dsp* 1944

(3) Arthur Francis; *b* 24 Feb 1873; *m* 3 Oct 1905 Beatrice May, dau of Percy Edward Laurence, of The Grove, Witham, Essex, and *d* 8 Aug 1930, leaving:

1a *Patrick Arthur; *b* 3 Aug 1906; *educ* Eton; ptnr Hoseltine Powell & Co to 1972; *m* 1st 3 Jan 1931 (*divorce* 1948) Judith Alice Mabel, est dau of Capt Henry Albert Le Fowne Hurt, CMG, RN, of Castern Hall, Derbys; *m* 2nd 19 Sept 1950 *Veronica Mary, widow of Albert Marcus Rueff and est dau of Hon Clive Pearson (*see* COWDRAY, V), and by his 1st w has:

1b *Nicholas Arthur [Nicholas Tritton Esq, Mount Temple House, Moneygold, Co Sligo, Ireland]; *b* 11 Nov 1931; *educ* Eton; *m* 2 May 1960 *Jill, dau, of O S Hooper, and has:

1c *Joanna Frances; *b* 31 March 1961

2b Patrick Claude Henry; *b* 18 May 1934; *educ* Eton and Trin Coll Cambridge; KAR Mauritius, Master Mr Tritton's Hounds Mexico City; *m* 1st 1 March 1962 (*divorce* 1973) Nancy, formerly w of (a) Alfred de Marigny

and (b) Baron Ernst Lyssardt von Hoyningen-Huene and dau of Sir Harry Oakes, 1st Bt (*qv*); *m* 2nd 1978 *Hon Georgina Ward [The Hon Mrs Tritton, Marsella 44, Mexico 6, DF Mexico], dau of 1st Viscount Ward of Witley (*see* DUDLEY, E), and *dsp* 1 Feb 1998

2a *Alan Michael, DSC; *b* 6 July 1919; *educ* Eton; *m* 10 Oct 1942 (*divorce* 1965) Joanna Sylvia, only dau of Charles James Round, JP, DL, of Birch Hall, Essex, and has:

1b *Oliver Michael; *b* 24 Aug 1943; *educ* Gordonstoun; *m* 27 July 1973 *Beatriz, dau of Alberto de la Vega and Countess de Sancedilla, of Mexico, and has:

1c *Neil Andrew; *b* 3 April 1975

1a *Brigit Mary; *b* 3 Nov 1907; *m* 18 May 1935 Lt-Col William Arthur Roger Ames, OBE, of Flaxford, Dorney, Windsor, and has issue. He *d* 10 Nov 1962

2a Anne; *b* 29 Jan 1912; *m* 7 Feb 1938 Sir Nigel John Mordaunt, 13th Bt (*qv*), and *d* 1980, having had issue

3a *Susan; *b* 13 Nov 1913; *m* 16 Dec 1946 James Gray Round, JP, DL, of Birch Hall, Essex, and has:

1b *Claire; *b* 2 Sept 1947; *m* 19 Oct 1968 *Patrick Rupert HICKMAN later COTTRELL (*see* HICKMAN, Bt)

2b *Brigit Olivia; *b* 2 Aug 1949

3b *Anne Sybil; *b* 11 July 1953

(4) Claude Henry, OBE (1918), DL (Essex 1940–57); *b* 12 Oct 1874; *educ* Winchester and New Coll Oxford; Maj RASC WW I; *m* 17 July 1906 Evelyn Mary (*d* 10 Dec 1965), dau of Hon Edward Gerald Strutt, CH (*see* RAYLEIGH, B), and *d* 8 Feb 1959, leaving:

1a Ronald Edward; *b* 29 April 1907; *educ* Winchester; High Sheriff Essex; *m* 30 April 1934 Andrina (Anne) Frances (*d* 12 Feb 1998), dau of Ronald Paul Schweder, of Chelsea, and has:

1b *Paul Sebastian [Paul Tritton Esq, Haslers Farm, Leighs Rd, Little Waltham, Essex CM3 3NH]; *b* 23 Feb 1939; *educ* Eton, Tours U France and Philadelphia U USA; late 5th Roy Inniskilling Dragoon Gds

1b *Andrina Jane; *b* 21 July 1944; *m* 21 June 1963 David Roger Montgomery Zambra, only s of Lt-Col Warren Zambra, MBE, RA

2a John Hedley, MBE (1945); *b* 18 March 1913; *educ* Winchester; Lt-Col RA WW II (despatches); *m* 28 Feb 1942 *(Susette) Pamela, dau of Maj Thomas Edmund Skewes-Cox, of Providence Cottage, S Green, Southwold, Suffolk, and had:

1b *Adrian John; *b* 5 May 1946; *educ* Charterhouse; *m* *Linda Evelyn, dau of Herbert Latham, of Adelaide, S Australia, and *d* 26 May 1998, leaving:

1c *Thomas John; *b* 27 Nov 1975

2c *Barnaby; *b* 19–

2b *Peter Robert Jolliffe; *b* 22 May 1951; *educ* Charterhouse

2a (cont.) Lt-Col and Mrs John Tritton also adopted:

*Annabel Catherine; *b* 5 Jan 1956

*Claire Susette; *b* 5 Jan 1956

(5) Alan George; *b* 28 Nov 1882; *ka* 28 Dec 1914

(1) Elizabeth Mary, JP (Essex 1934); *b* 13 Sept 1876; *d* unm 16 Dec 1959

(2) Annette Lucy Amelia; *b* 4 Oct 1880; *d* unm 7 Jan 1948

(3) Violet Alice; *b* 23 June 1883; *d* unm 17 Sept 1956

(4) Olive Marguerite Beatrice; *b* 3 April 1886; *d* unm 23 April 1964

2 (CHARLES) ERNEST (Sir), **1st Bt**

1 Annette Amelia; *b* 16 Jan 1847; *m* 20 June 1872 William Leatham Barclay, of Reigate, Surrey, and *d* 6 April 1873, leaving issue. He *d* 6 Jan 1893

2 Jessie Margaret; *b* 16 June 1857; *d* unm 11 Aug 1943

3 Ethel Harriett; *b* 2 Sept 1859; *d* unm 19 May 1885

The yr s,

Sir (Charles) Ernest Tritton, 1st Bt (UK), so *cr* 1 Aug 1905, of Bloomfield, Lambeth, London; *b* 4 Sept 1845; *educ* Trin Hall Cambridge (BA); MP (C) Lambeth Norwood 1892–1906; *m* 30 May 1872 Edith (*d* 18 Feb 1921), 2nd dau of Frederick Green, of S Kensington, and had:

1 ALFRED ERNEST (Sir), **2nd Bt**

1 Florence Annette; *b* 6 Sept 1874; *m* 2 July 1899 John Liebenrood, s of Capt John Liebenrood, RN, of Prospect Park, Reading, and *d* 10 Dec 1961, leaving issue. He *d* 26 Aug 1945

2 Laura Edith; *b* 15 April 1876; *d* unm 26 May 1968

Sir ERNEST *d* 28 Dec 1918; his only s,

Sir Alfred Ernest Tritton, 2nd Bt; *b* 8 June 1873; *educ* Trin Coll Cambridge (BA, LLB); *m* 22 June 1898 Agneta Elspeth (*d* 17 March 1960), only dau of William Middleton Campbell, of Camis Eskan, Helensburgh, Dunbartonshire, and Fen Place, Turner's Hill, Sussex, and had:

1 GEOFFREY ERNEST (Sir), **3rd Bt**

1 Edith Gwendolin; *b* 23 Sept 1902; *m* 23 Oct 1924 Sir Jeremiah Colman, 2nd Bt (*qv*), and had issue

2 Elspeth Muriel; *b* 27 May 1907; *m* 11 Aug 1927 Sir Robert Annesley Wilkinson Dent, CB, s of Robert Wilkinson Dent, JP, of Flass, Westmoreland, and had issue

3 Anstice Marion; *b* 17 July 1909; *m* 9 April 1931 Lt-Col Sir George Arthur Harford, 2nd Bt (*qv*), and *d* 1993, having had issue

Sir ALFRED *d* 2 Sept 1939; his only s,

Sir Geoffrey Ernest Tritton, 3rd Bt, CBE (1958, MBE 1945), DL (1956); *b* 3 Nov 1900; *educ* Eton and Trin Coll Cambridge (BA); T/Maj Rifle Bde (TA) WW II, Croix de Guerre, US Bronze Star, Medal of Merit 1st Cl; Wilts: CC 1955, High Sheriff 1958; *m* 2 July 1925 Mary Patience Winifred (*d* 28 Jan 1960), yst dau of John Kenneth Foster, of Coombe Park, Oxon, and Egton Manor, Cleveland, Yorks, and *d* 15 Nov 1976, leaving:

1 Sir ANTHONY JOHN ERNEST TRITTON, **4th and present Bt**

1 *Julia Mary [Mrs Richard Kingzett, 18 Sloane Ave, London SW3 3JE]; *b* 2 March 1930; *m* 20 Sept 1952 *Richard Norman Kingzett, only s of Norman Froggatt Kingzett, MBE (*see* AGNEW, Bt, of Great Stanhope Street), and has:

(1) *Jan Anthony; *b* 25 Oct 1955; *educ* Eton

(2) *Christopher Richard Colin [Christopher Kingzett Esq, 68 Camberwell Grove, London SE5 8RF]; *b* 17 Oct 1958; *m* 1989 *Madeleine Anne, dau of Theodore Peter Donahue, of Litchfield, Conn., and has:

    1a *Emily Rose Julia; *b* 1990

    2a *Catherine Augusta Mary; *b* 1992

TROLLOPE

Arms: Vert three stags courant arg., attired or, within a bordure of the second. **Crest:** On a mount vert a stag courant arg., attired or, holding in the mouth an oak-leaf ppr. **Motto:** *Audio sed taceo* ('I hear but am silent'). **Creation:** Bt. (E) 5 Feb 1641/2.

SIR ANTHONY SIMON TROLLOPE, 17TH BT, of Casewick, Co Lincoln [Sir Anthony Trollope Bt, Churinga Lodge, 28 Midson Rd, Oakville, NSW 2765, Australia]; *b* 31 Aug 1945; *s* f 1987; *educ* Sydney U (BA); mktg exec with Ricegrowers Co-op Ltd, memb Australian Mktg Inst 1988–, breeds Rhodesian Ridgebacks and Anglo-Arab horses; *m* 1969 *Denise, dau of Trevern Thompson, of N Sydney, NSW, and has:

  1 *Kellie Yvette; *b* 1970

  2 *Analese Christine; *b* 1972

Lineage: JOHN TROLOP, of Thornlaw/Thornley, Co Durham, which he acquired from the Bp of Durham *c* 1300; ancestor of:

JOHN TROLOPE/TROWLOPE, of Thornlaw; held by 1390 the Manor of Morden, Co Durham, through his w, dau and coheir of Thomas Lumley; presumably kin to:

JOHN TROLLOPE; *m* Margaret, dau and heir of Roger Lumley, 4th s of Thomas Lumley (*see* SCARBROUGH, E) by Elizabeth, illegitimate dau of EDWARD IV, and through her came into further lands at Seaton and Hartlepool, Co Durham; presumably kin to:

Sir ANDREW TROLOP/TROWLOP; a cdr Battle of Wakefield

The TROLLOPEs of Thornlaw took part in the Rebellion of the Northern Earls 1569 (*see* NORTHUMBERLAND, D, and ABERGAVENNY, M) and suffered accordingly; their impoverishment was completed in the Civil War.

JOHN TROLLOPE, of a yr branch, settled at Thurlby and Bourne, Lincs, *c* 1560; had:

WILLIAM TROLLOPE, of Thurlby and Bourne; bought the Manor of Casewick, Uffington, Lincs (nr Stamford, Rutland), from Sir James Evington 1621; *m* Alice, dau of William Sharpe, of Bourne, and *d* 8 June 1638, leaving:

Sir Thomas Trollope, 1st Bt (E), so *cr* 5 Feb 1641/42, of Casewick; *b* 1595; Sheriff Lincs 1641–42; *m* 1st 1620 Hester, dau of Nicholas Street/Sturt, of Hadleigh, Suffolk, and had:

  1 **Sir William Trollope, 2nd Bt**; High Sheriff Lincs 1659–60; *b* 3 Jan 1621; *m* Elizabeth (*bur* 27 Feb 1661), widow of William Thorold (*see* THOROLD, Bt) and dau of Sir Robert Carr, 3rd Bt, and *dspm* 16 May 1678, leaving:

    (1) Elizabeth Carr; *b* 1661; *m* Charles Fox, est s of Sir Stephen Fox (*see* ILCHESTER, E), and *dsp* 1702/3

Sir Thomas *m* 2nd 16 Nov 1635 Mary (*bur* 16 June 1688), dau of Sir Christopher Clitheroe, Ld Mayor London 1634, and *d* between 20 March 1651/2 and 7 March 1654/5, having by her had:

  2 Thomas, of Barham, Lincs; *m* Anne, dau of Anthony Collins, of Whitton, Middx, and had:

    (1) THOMAS (Sir), **3rd Bt**

  3 Anthony, barrister; *d* unm

  4 Matthew; *m* 1676 Elizabeth Dowse and *d* 1691, leaving:

    (1) Thomas; *m* Anne Browne and had:

      1a Jane; *b* 1729; *d* unm 1827, leaving her property to her cousin Rev Thomas Daniel Trollope (*see* below)

  1 Bridget; *m* 29 July 1679 Edward Mainwaring, of Whitmore, Staffs, and was *bur* 27 May 1723, leaving issue

The 2nd Bt's n,

Sir Thomas Trollope, 3rd Bt; Sheriff Lincs 1703–04; *m* 1690 Susannah (*d* 2 June 1724/25), dau and coheir of Sir John Clobery, of Bradstone, Devon, by his

---

2nd w Anne, sis and coheir of Sir William Cranmer, descendant of Archdeacon Cranmer, bro of Archbp Cranmer, and had, with other issue:

  1 THOMAS (Sir), **4th Bt**

  2 Henry, *b* 1693; London merchant; *m* 1717 Elizabeth (*d* 1761), dau of John Barne, London merchant, and *d* 7 Dec 1763, leaving, with two other daus:

    (1) Thomas; *b* 5 Aug 1718; London merchant; *m* 1750 Amelia, dau of J Page, and *d* 21 Feb 1761, leaving:

      1a Thomas Daniel (Rev); *b* 1760; Rector Abbots Ripton and Hartford, Hunts, 1794–1814, and Down Frome, Dorset, 1814–28; *m* 6 Aug 1793 his cousin Anne, dau of Rev John Trollope (*see* below), and *d* 27 Aug 1828, leaving:

        1b Thomas, of Wethersfield, Essex; *b* 1797; surgn; *m* 1st Mary Canning; *m* 2nd Anne (*d* 13 March 1862), dau of John Sewell, and *d* 8 Oct 1854, leaving:

          1c Thomas; *b* 12 Aug 1830; MD Cantab, MRCP London; *m* 13 Feb 1858 Esther Sarah (*dsp* 26 Feb 1880), dau of Capt J A Huffam, RN, and *d* 21 April 1905

        2b William; *b* 1798; *d* unm 8 Oct 1867

        3b John J (Rev); *b* 10 May 1800; Rector Crowmarsh Gifford, Oxon; *m* 10 May 1831 Elizabeth Bunce, dau of Rev William Hazel, of Wallingford, Berks, and *d* 5 Feb 1878, leaving, with six other daus (*d* unm):

          1c John Herbert; *b* 25 Feb 1832; *d* unm

          2c Edward Hazel; *b* 5 May 1833; *m* Mary, dau of W Mitchell, of Wickham, Hants, and *d* 1897, leaving:

            1d Herbert Edward; *b* 3 July 1859; *m* 1901 Sarah Ann (*d* 6 Oct 1958), dau of John Wall, of Wedmore, Somerset, and *d* 1930, leaving:

              1e John Herbert Hazel; *b* 1908; *m* 21 Aug 1939 Ruth (*d* 1987), dau of Frederic Warry, of Freshford, and *d* 1991, leaving:

                1f *Beatrice Mary; *b* 13 May 1942; *m* 2 Nov 1963 *Peter Old, s of William Charles Old, of Cheselbourne, Dorset, and has:

                  1g *Andrew; *b* 29 June 1967

                  1g *Rachel [Mrs Mervyn Bate, Splatt Farm, Tresmeer, Cornwall]; *b* 4 Nov 1964; *m* 1986 *Mervyn William Bate and has:

                    1h *Verity Ruth; *b* 1989

                    2h *Hannah Rachel; *b* 1992

                2g *Sarah; *b* 1971; *m* 1993 *Wagner Rangel, Jr, of Curitiba, Brazil

              2f *Maureen Hazel [Mrs Ian Kampel, 25 Holmfield Ave, Iford, Bournemouth]; *b* 15 Feb 1945; *m* 1973 *Ian Joseph Kampel, CEng, MIEE, MBIM, and has:

                1g *Timothy Ian; *b* 1978

                1g *Alison Jane; *b* 1975

              3f *Susan Bridget [Mrs Elemér Fejér, 97 Goldcroft Rd, Westham, Weymouth, Dorset DT4 0EA]; *b* 20 Oct 1947; *m* 27 Sept 1969 *Elemér László Géza Fejér, est s of Dr E A I Fejér, of Taunton, and has:

                1g *Karen Lisa; *b* 1974

                2g *Trudy Lynne; *b* 1977

              1d Catherine Ada Mary; *d* unm 13 Aug 1942

              2d Gertrude Alice Mary; *d* unm 10 March 1945

              3d Lillian Agnes Mary; *d* unm 14 Nov 1945

           3c Henry; *b* 17 Nov 1847; barrister

           4c Thomas William; *b* 21 June 1855; *d* unm

          1c Catherine; *m* 1st 1864 William Payne (*dsp* 1864); *m* 2nd 1894 Edward Fairthorne, of Slade End, Wallingford

          2c Lucy; *d* unm 29 April 1947

          3c Susan Wilgress

      2a Arthur William (Rev); *b* 1768; *educ* Christ's Hospital and Cambridge (DD); Vicar Ugley, Essex, Perpetual Curate Berden, Essex, 1796; Headmaster Christ's Hospital 1797; FSA; *m* 25 Aug 1797 Sarah (*d* 28 Aug 1849), dau of W Wale, and *d* 24 May 1827, leaving:

        1b William (Rev); *b* 1798; assist classics master Christ's Hospital 182?–32, Vicar Wigston Magna, Leics, 1834; migrated to Tasmania, where Incumbent St Mary's Chirch, Green Ponds; author of biblical commentaries, Homeric criticism and a history of Christ's Hospital; *m* Sarah, dau of William Clarke, of E Bergholt, Suffolk, and *d* 23 March 1862, leaving:

        2b Arthur (Rev); *b* 1799; Curate St Mary-le-Bow, Cheapside; *d* 12 Sept 1848

        3b George; *b* 11 April 1802; Ch Clerk Christ's Hospital; *m* 11 July 1838 his yr bro's sis-in-law Alicia (*d* 1887), dau of Walter William Welby, and *d* 8 Jan 1864, leaving:

          1c Alice Jane; *d* 20 Jan 1924

          2c Mary Ann Sybil; *m* 15 June 1864 Rev William Mayou Daniel and *d* 16 July 1932, leaving issue

        4b Edward; *m* 1st 11 Sept 1833 Mary Ann, dau of W W Welby; *m* 2nd Catherine, dau of — Daniel, and *d* 7 Oct 1847, having had issue

    (2) William Arthur; Army Capt; *ka* 1800

    (3) John (Rev); *b* 1 Aug 1729; Rector Sawtry St Andrew and Hartford, Hunts; *m* 1st Anne (*d* 1759), dau of — Guyon, and had:

      1a Henry (Sir), GCB; *b* 20 April 1756; Adml of the Fleet; *m* Fanny Burt (*d* 3 April 1816) and *dsp* 2 Nov 1839

      2a Thomas, Col RM; *b* 21 April 1757; *m* 1789 Anne Steele (*d* 16 Sept 1845) and *d* 17 July 1805, leaving issue

    (3) (cont.) The Rev John Trollope *m* 2nd Jan 1761 Catherine (*d* 22 April 1828), dau of Rev W Martin Annesley, DD, Preb Sarum, Vicar Bucklebury and Rector Frilsham, Berks, and *d* 10 July 1794, having by her had, with three other daus:

      3a Arthur William; *b* 15 Dec 1771; Capt 40th Regt; *m* 26 Dec 1797 Mary (*d* 19 July 1822), dau of Barnard Foord, and *d* 20 Sept 1799, leaving:

1b Barnard TROLLOPE later FOORD-BOWES (roy licence 30 Oct 1861), of Cowlam, Yorks; *b* 25 Oct 1798; *m* 27 July 1818 Mary (*d* 7 Jan 1861), dau of S Greathead, and *d* 10 June 1870, leaving:

    1c Emily Mary Worsop; *m* John Harwood

2b William Henry; *b* 4 April 1800; Capt HEICS; *m* 30 July 1834 Mary Arthur (*d* 1891), dau of J A Worsop, of Langford Ho, Wilts, and *d* 24 Sept 1873, leaving:

    1c Arthur Barnard (Rev); *b* 31 July 1836; Rector Cowlam, Yorks; *m* 18 April 1864 Isabella (*d* 27 March 1875), dau of David Fowler Burton, DL, of Cherry Burton Hall, Yorks, and *dsp* 22 April 1872

    2c Henry Anthony; *b* 30 Sept 1837; R-Adml; *m* 26 Oct 1870 Harriet (*d* 22 March 1912), widow of G T Gordon, DL, of Cuckney, Notts, and dau of Rev T Harrison, of Firby Hall, Yorks, and *dsp* March 1894

    3c Richard Brunton; *b* 21 Jan 1844; RN; *d* 8 May 1865

    4c Edward Charles; *b* 20 Aug 1849; Maj RA; *m* 1st 5 Oct 1871 Louisa Sarah (*d* 19 Aug 1882), dau of Robert Pipon, and had:

        1d Mary Emily Arthur; *m* 19 Sept 1917 Frederick William Cape, Divl Inspr Bd Educn, and *d* 1 March 1951. He *d* 14 March 1749

    4c (cont.) Maj Edward Trollope *m* 2nd 27 May 1886 Eva Annie Noel (*d* 14 July 1924), dau of Capt Frederick Dampier Rich, RN (*see* 1970 edn RICH, Bt), and *d* 23 Feb 1904, having her had:

        2d Constance Zara; *m* 20 Feb 1917 Capt Reginald Gilbert Vernon, Dorsetshire Regt, and *d* 9 May 1960, leaving issue. He *d* 21 Oct 1956

    1c Mary Ann; *m* 19 Aug 1862 F A Bradburne and *d* 15 Sept 1897, leaving issue

    2c Eliza Maria; *m* 19 Aug 1862 Rev G G P Glossop and *d* 14 Feb 1929, leaving issue. He *d* 23 April 1874

4a George Barne, CB; *b* 17 April 1779; R-Adml; *m* 18 March 1813 Barbara (*d* 11 July 1874), dau of Joseph Goble, and *d* 31 May 1850, leaving:

    1b Henry; *b* 3 Aug 1815; R-Adml; *m* 10 Oct 1861 Mary, dau of Rev J Hopton, and *dsp* 22 April 1879

    2b John Joseph (Rev); *b* 15 Nov 1817; MA Oxon, Preb Hereford; *m* 7 Dec 1850 Anne Mary Theresa (*d* 22 Nov 1905), widow of Capt H F Alston, 99th Regt, and dau of John Walsh, of Anne Mount, Co Kilkenny, and *d* 8 Jan 1893, having had:

        1c Helen Lucy; *b* 21 Feb 1852; *d* unm 29 April 1947

        2c Catherine Annesley; *m* 22 July 1902 Rev James Albert A Owen, of Ch Ch Oxford, and *d* 23 June 1939. He *d* 18 July 1907

    3b Charles (Rev); *b* 4 Feb 1819; Rector Stibbington, Wansford, Hon Canon Ely 1868; *m* 30 Oct 1872 Eleanor (*d* 5 July 1929), dau of Rev William Hiley Bathurst (*see* BLEDISLOE, V), and *d* 8 Sept 1907, having had:

        1c Charles Henry Bathurst (Rev); *b* 27 April 1876; *educ* Trin Coll Cambridge (BA 1898, MA 1902); Rector Escrick, Yorks; *d* unm 11 Jan 1962

        1c Eleanor Mary; *b* 1 March 1875; *d* unm 27 July 1965

    4b Frederick; *b* 20 July 1820; Capt Bengal SC; *m* 24 Oct 1844 Mary Victoria (*d* March 1912), dau of Charles Francis, and *d* 11 Sept 1857, having had:

        1c George Frederick; *b* 31 July 1845; *m* 18 Jan 1870 Clara Sophia (*d* 1892), dau of Robert William Hudswell, and *d* 21 June 1871, leaving:

            1d Frederick William; *b* 14 Feb 1871; AMIMechE; *m* 1906 Florence Anne (*d* 1941), dau of Edmund Potter, of Kidderminster

        2c Francis Henry; *b* 1 April 1847; *m* 14 Dec 1874 Florence Maria Lyttelton, dau of C F Chubb, and *dsp* 9 June 1875

        3c Charles William Annesley, ISO; *b* 20 Jan 1850; Pncpl Clerk Exchequer & Audit Dept; *m* 23 Aug 1877 Marian Eirene (*d* 8 May 1930), dau of Rev William Watson, and *d* 15 March 1935, leaving:

            1d George Henry Annesley (Very Rev); *b* 12 Dec 1879; CSSR, Rector St Mary's Clapham; *d* unm 21 Nov 1933

            2d Leonard Edward Annesley; *b* 13 March 1892; *educ* Westminster; RGA WW I; *m* 3 April 1922 Cecily Aimée, dau of Albert Derrick, of Fishbourne, IOW

            1d Mary Gertrude Annesley; *b* 22 May 1878; *d* 2 April 1892

            2d Dorothy Marian Annesley; *m* 29 April 1920 Vincent Groom, of E Worlington, Devon, and *d* 16 Sept 1937. He *d* 27 May 1932

        4c Edward Pearson; *b* 24 Dec 1852; *dsp*

    1b Barbara *m* 21 Feb 1878 Rev W Watson and *dsp*

1a Anne; *b* 1765; *m* her cousin Rev Thomas Daniel Trollope (*see* above) and *d* 1802, leaving issue

1 Anne; *m* Samuel Clarke, of W Bromwich, Staffs

2 Elizabeth; *m* William Noel, Judge Court Common Pleas

Sir THOMAS *d* 22 Nov 1729; his est s,

Sir Thomas Trollope, 4th Bt, *bapt* 21 Dec 1691; *m* 1721 Diana (*d* 1783), dau and coheir of Thomas Middleton, of Stansted, Essex, and *d* 7 Oct 1784, having had, with three other sons and two daus:

1 Thomas Middleton; *b* 31 July 1721; *m* 14 Aug 1759 Isabella (*d* 19 March 1803), est dau of Sir John Thorold, 8th Bt (*qv*), and *dvp* 27 April 1779, leaving, with other issue:

    (1) **Sir Thomas William Trollope, 5th Bt**; *b* 1762; MA Cantab; *d* unm 13 May 1789

    (2) **Sir John Trollope, 6th Bt**; *b* 1766; *m* 24 March 1798 Anne (*d* 23 Dec 1855), dau of Henry Thorold, of Cuxwold, Lincs and *d* 28 April 1820, having had, with a dau (*d* unm):

    1a **Sir John Trollope, 7th Bt**, and 1st BARON KESTEVEN OF CASEWICK, Co Lincoln, so *cr* 15 April 1868; *b* 5 May 1800; *educ* Eton; Capt 10th Hus, MP (C) S Lincoln 1841–68, Pres Poor Law Bd 1852, Custos Rotulorum Soke of Peterborough; *m* 26 Oct 1847 Julia Maria (*d* 2 Nov 1876), est dau of Sir Robert Sheffield, 4th Bt (*qv*), and *d* 17 Dec 1874, having had, with another dau (*d* unm):

        1b **Sir John Henry Trollope, 8th Bt**, and 2nd BARON KESTEVEN OF CASEWICK; *b* 22 Sept 1851; *educ* Eton and Magdalene Coll Cambridge; *chm* Lincs TFA, Lt-Col cmdg Lincs Yeo Boer War 1900; *m* 25 March 1914 Amy Myddleton (*d* 13 April 1941), widow of Edgar Lubbock (*see* AVE-

BURY, B) and only dau of Christopher Gilbert Peacock, of Greatford Hall, Stamford, and *dsp* 26 July 1915

        2b Robert Cranmer, JP, DL Somerset; *b* 7 Nov 1852; Maj 3rd Bn Northants Regt; *m* 22 Oct 1885 Ethel Mary (*d* 25 March 1934), dau of Col George Henry Warrington Carew, of Crowcombe Court, Somerset, and *d* 25 Nov 1908, leaving:

            1c **Sir Thomas Carew Trollope, 9th Bt**, and 3rd and last BARON KESTEVEN OF CASEWICK; *b* 1 May 1891; Capt Lincs Yeo WW I; *d* unm 5 Nov 1915 of wounds recd in action on a Transport off the Algerian coast, when the Barony expired

            1c Dorothy Nesta, of Casewick, JP (Lincs 1939), inherited the family estates; granted by roy warrant 30 Oct 1916 rank of baron's dau; *m* 17 Oct 1918 Col Froude Dillon BELLEW later TROLLOPE (roy licence 1920), DSO, OBE, MC, DL, Somerset LI, of Okehampton Manor, Somerset, and *d* 6 March 1975, leaving issue. He *d* 18 Dec 1959

        3b Charles William; *b* 24 Sept 1855; *d* 5 July 1897

        1b Julia; *m* 13 May 1869 Sir Robert Henry Hobart, 1st Bt, KCVO, CB (*qv*), and *d* 11 Aug 1931, leaving issue

2a Thomas; *d* 29 Oct 1822

3a Charles (Sir), KCB; *b* 21 Oct 1808; Col 53rd Foot, Gen; *m* 1st 25 March 1840 Frances (*d* 29 Sept 1862), only child of John Lord, and had, with a dau (*d* an infant):

    1b Francis Charles; *b* 7 June 1857; Lt-Col Gren Gds; *d* 28 Jan 1913

    2b **Sir William Henry Trollope, 10th Bt**; *b* 14 Sept 1858; *educ* Eton and Trin Coll Cambridge (MA 1884); barrister Inner Temple 1883; *m* 12 Dec 1894 Louisa Charlotte Campbell (*d* 6 May 1930), only dau of Capt Frederick Erskine Johnston, RN, and *dspms* 24 Aug 1921, having had:

        1c Angela Erskine; *m* 6 Feb 1918 Thomas Arthur Walter Giffard, MBE, JP, DL, of Chillington Hall, Wolverhampton, and *d* 4 May 1965, leaving issue

        2c Sylvia

    3b **Sir Thomas Ernest Trollope, 11th Bt**; *b* 14 Sept 1858; *educ* Eton and Magdalene Coll Cambridge (MA); barrister Inner Temple 1885; *d* unm 23 Sept 1927

3a (cont.) Gen Sir Charles Trollope *m* 2nd 31 March 1864 Cordelia Maria (*d* 3 Dec 1909), yst dau of Maj-Gen James Patrick Murray, CB (*see* ELIBANK, L), and *d* 5 July 1888, having by her had:

    1b Elizabeth William Mina; *m* 23 Aug 1892 Capt Edmund Thomas Chivers Bower, Oxon LI, and *d* 24 Nov 1950, leaving issue. He *d* 3 Oct 1937

4a Arthur; *b* 11 July 1810; Capt 36th Regt; *m* 22 July 1845 Elizabeth (*d* 4 Oct 1877), dau of Rev Richard Lucas, of Edith Weston, Rutland, and *d* 19 Jan 1880, leaving:

    1b Edgar; *b* 19 April 1849; *d* 26 Aug 1894

    2b Andrew (Rev); *b* Feb 1851; Rector Edith Weston; *d* 24 March 1896

    3b Alfred; *b* 4 Oct 1857; *d* 10 Aug 1927

    4b **Sir Henry Cracroft Trollope, 12th Bt**; *b* 5 June 1860; AMICE, MISE; *m* 1st 1891 Louisa Jane (*d* 1920), dau of C C Bawden; *m* 2nd 26 June 1926 Evelyn Elizabeth (*m* 2nd 1 July 1942 Hubert Thornhill Back, of Cape Town, and *d* June 1950), 2nd dau of Edward Francis Felix Cesari, Lt 43rd Inf, Italian Army, gs of Col Joseph Cesari, of Napoleon's Army, and *dsp* 29 May 1935

    5b **Sir Arthur Grant Trollope, 13th Bt**, JP; *b* 10 June 1866; Orange Free State Civ Serv, Lt-Col The Buffs; Chitral Relief Force 1895, Boer War 1902 (despatches), WW I (despatches twice); *m* 1889 Anna Georgina (*d* 15 July 1956), dau of Franklin Prestage, of Darjeeling, India, and *d* 14 Feb 1937, leaving:

        1c Laura Harriet; *b* 3 Jan 1899; song- and hymn-writer as 'Pax Lady'; *m* 3 Aug 1920 Charles Wreford, of Newton St Cyres, Devon (*d* 11 Feb 1937), and had:

            1d *Aurelia Cary Roslyn; *b* 20 Aug 1921; *m* 29 July 1950 William Macintosh Ball, FRICS, Agent to the Church Commissioners, er s of Herbert Frederick Ball, ARICS, of Covington Way, Norbury, and has:

                1e *John Trollope Macintosh; *b* 10 June 1954

                1e *Aurelia Cary Rennie; *b* 26 Sept 1958

        2c Iona Rebecca; *b* 1907; *m* 1st 29 Nov 1927 Lt-Col Cleveland Mervyn Keble, OBE, Wiltshire Regt (*d* 18 Jan 1948), s of Col Alfred Ernest Conquer Keble, of Moortown House, Ringwood, Hants; *m* 2nd 10 Oct 1953 *Stephen Philp [Stephen Philp Esq, Wellbrook, Peterchurch, Herefs HR2 0SS], er s of Robert Charles Penny Philp, MC, of Clarke's Farm, Darby Green, Camberley, and *d* 14 April 1994, leaving by her 1st husb:

            1d *Elizabeth Felicia [Mrs Philip Armes, Howard Lodge, Hurstpierpoint, Sussex]; *b* 1928; *m* 1st 1949 (*divorce* 1967) Lt-Col Peter Lawrence de Carteret Martin, Cheshire Regt; *m* 2nd 1967 *Philip Arthur Harcourt Armes and by her 1st husb has:

                1e *David Peter de Carteret; *b* 1950

                1e *Fiona Elizabeth; *b* 1953; *m* 1977 *Paul Jamieson Beesley

            2d *Heather Fiona; *b* 1933; *m* 1958 (*divorce* 1964) Maj Anthony Frederick Walker, Cheshire Regt

1b Anne Elizabeth; *b* 11 May 1846; *m* 8 Jan 1873 Rev Charles Edwin Jarvis and *d* 14 May 1915

2b Mary Matilda; *b* 24 Oct 1847 *m* 1873 W H Broadley Smith, of Friar Gate, and *d* 7 April 1905, having had issue. He *d* 1912

3b Constance Lucas; *b* 22 Dec 1851; *d* unm 11 Sept 1872

4b Julia Emily; *b* 1 Jan 1855; *d* unm 28 Oct 1928

5b Harriet Augusta; *b* 4 Aug 1856; *d* unm 21 Dec 1937

6b Beatrice; *b* 7 March 1859; *d* unm 21 Dec 1937

7b Laura; *b* 27 Dec 1861; *d* unm 13 Nov 1953

5a Frederick; *d* unm 1821

6a Edward (Rt Rev); *b* 15 April 1817; DD, Rector Leasingham, Lincs, Archdeacon Stowe, Suffragan Bp Nottingham 1877; author: *The Family of Trollope* (1875); *m* 1st 30 Sept 1846 Grace (*d* 21 Oct 1890), dau of Sir John Henry Palmer, 7th Bt, of Carlton (*qv*); *m* 2nd 13 Jan 1892 Louisa Helen (*dsp*

25 May 1904), dau of Rev H B S Harris, and *d* 11 Dec 1893, having by his 1st w had:

  1b Mary Grace; *m* 10 Oct 1867 Sir Richard Lewis De Capell Brooke, 4th Bt (*see* 1940 edn), and *d* 16 July 1924, leaving issue. He *d* 3 Feb 1892

  2b Caroline Julia; *m* 27 June 1871 Wyrley Peregrine Birch, of Cranford, Northants, and had issue

  1a Anne; *m* 1827 Thomas Tryon, of Bulwick Park, Northants, and *d* 12 Feb 1877, leaving issue (*see* TRYON, B)

  2a Matilda; *m* 18 June 1838, as his 2nd w, Charles Wykeham Martin, JP, DL, of Leeds Castle, Kent, and *d* 5 June 1876, having had issue. He *d* 30 Oct 1870

  3a Laura; *m* 11 Nov 1852 Joseph Sidney Tharp, of Chippenham Park, Cambs, and *d* 1877. He *d* 4 March 1875

  4a Julia; *m* 30 April 1846 Rev George Birch Reynardson, Rector Eastling, Kent, 2nd s of Gen Thomas Birch Reynardson, and *d* 16 Feb 1855, leaving issue. He *d* Nov 1892

(3) Henry (Rev); Rector Harrington; *m* 1803 his cousin Diana (*d* 17 Feb 1854), dau of Rev Anthony Trollope, and *dsp* 24 July 1839

(1) Isabella; *m* John Linton, of Frieston, Lincs, and *d* 18 Feb 1842

2 Anthony (Rev); *b* 1737; Rector Cotterhead, Herts; *m* Penelope (*d* 30 June 1788), 2nd dau of Adolphus Meetkirk, and *d* 3 June 1806, leaving, with other issue:

(1) Thomas Anthony; *b* 1774; barrister Lincoln's Inn; *m* 1809 Frances (*d* 6 Oct 1863), author: *Domestic Manners of the Americans* (1832), *The Vicar of Wrexhill* (1837), *The Life and Adventures of Michael Armstrong, the Factory Boy* (1840) and 38 other works, yst dau of Rev William Milton, Vicar Heckfield, Hants, and *d* 26 Oct 1835, having had:

  1a Thomas Adolphus; *b* 29 April 1810; historian; *m* 1st 1848 Theodosia (*d* Florence 14 April 1865), dau of Joseph Garrow; *m* 2nd 29 Oct 1866 Frances Eleanor (*d* 14 Aug 1913), dau of Thomas Ternan, and *d* 11 Nov 1892, having by his 1st w had:

    1b Beatrice; *m* 16 Aug 1880 1st and last Baron Stuart of Wortley (*see* WHARNCLIFFE, E) and *d* 26 July 1881, leaving issue

  2a Anthony; *b* 24 April 1815; *educ* Harrow and Winchester; with GPO, ed *St Paul's Magazine* 1867–70, Lib Parly candidate Beverley 1868, author: *The Macdermots of Ballycloran* (1847), *The Kellys and the O'Kellys* (1848), *The Warden* (1855), *Barchester Towers* (1857), *The Three Clerks* (1858), *Doctor Thorne* (1858), *Framley Parsonage* (1860), *Orley Farm* (1861–62), *The Small House at Allington* (1862–64), *Can You Forgive Her?* (1864–65), *The Last Chronicle of Barset* (1866–67), *The Claverings* (1866–67), *Phineas Finn* (1867–69), *He Knew He Was Right* (1868–69), *Sir Harry Hotspur of Humblethwaite* (1870), *Ralph the Heir* (1870–71), *The Eustace Diamonds* (1871–73), *Phineas Redux* (1873–74), *The Way We Live Now* (1874–75), *The Prime Minister* (1875–76), *The Duke's Children* (1879–80), *Dr Wortle's School* (1880), *Mr Scarborough's Family* (1882–83) and other works, including the *Autobiography* (1883), travel books and biographies of Cicero, Palmerston and Thackeray; *m* 11 June 1844 Rose (*d* 25 May 1917), dau of Edward Heseltine, of Rotherham, Yorks, and *d* 6 Dec 1882, having had:

    1b Henry Merivale; *b* 13 March 1846; barrister; *m* 1884 Ada (*d* 16 Nov 1935), dau of John Joseph Strickland, and *d* 24 March 1926, leaving:

      1c Thomas Anthony; *b* 26 Dec 1893; Lt RASC, attd Rifle Bde; *d* unm 16 Feb 1931

      1c Muriel Rose; *b* 30 March 1885; *d* unm 17 Dec 1953

    2b Frederic James Anthony; *b* 27 Sept 1847; *m* 14 Dec 1971 Susanna (*d* 1910), dau of William Farrand, of Forbes, NSW, and *d* 31 May 1910, having had:

      1c Frank Anthony; *b* 27 Sept 1872; *d* unm 25 July 1936

      2c Harry Reginald; *b* 7 Dec 1873; *d* 17 July 1924

      3c **Sir Frederic Farrand Trollope, 14th Bt**, JP (NSW); *b* 20 Sept 1875; manager Legal and Security Dept Commercial Banking Co Sydney; *d* unm 9 Nov 1957

      4c John Arthur; *b* 1881; *d* 28 March 1936

      5c Clive Heseltine; *b* 14 Nov 1883; with Bank of NSW, 9th Australian Field Ambulance WW I; *d* unm 1952

      6c GORDON CLAVERING (Sir), **15th Bt**

      1c Frances Kathleen; *m* 1907 Wilfred Meillon and *d* 1951, leaving issue. He *d* 1931

      2c Effie Madeline; *d* unm 1951

  1a Cecilia Frances; *m* 11 Feb 1839 Sir John Tilley, KCB, and *d* 1845

The 14th Bt's bro,
Sir Gordon Clavering Trollope, 15th Bt; *b* 29 Oct 1885; *m* 16 Aug 1913 Mary Isabel, yst dau of Owen Blacket, of Lindfield, Sydney, and had:

1 ANTHONY OWEN CLAVERING (Sir), **16th Bt**

2 +Gordon Paul Clavering [Gordon Trollope Esq, Dougherty Apartments, 1 Victor St, Chatswood, NSW 2067, Australia]; *b* 3 July 1918

1 Barbara Mary Clavering; *b* 10 May 1914; *d* unm 7 Nov 1960

Sir GORDON *d* 18 Oct 1958; his er s,
Sir Anthony Owen Clavering Trollope, 16th Bt, JP (NSW); *b* 15 Jan 1917; dir Thomas C Denton and Co Pty Ltd, of Sydney, 2nd/5th Field Regt Roy Australian Artillery Middle East and New Guinea WW II; *m* 2 May 1942 *Joan Mary Alexis [Dowager Lady Trollope, 31 Pacific Highway, Wahroonga, NSW 2076, Australia], dau of Alexis Robert Gibbes, of Balgowlay, NSW, and *d* 1987, leaving:

1 Sir ANTHONY SIMON TROLLOPE, **17th and present Bt**

2 +HUGH IRWIN [Hugh Trollope Esq, Casewick Cottage, 26 Bayswater Rd, Lindfield, NSW 2070, Australia]; *b* 31 March 1947; heir presumptive; *m* 1971 *Barbara Anne, dau of William Ian Jamieson, of Lawley Crescent, Pymble, NSW, and has:

  (1) +Andrew Ian; *b* 1978

  (1) *Edwina Anne; *b* 1976

  (2) *Jennifer Kate; *b* 1980

TROUBRIDGE

NE · CEDE · ARDUIS

Arms: Or on a bridge embattled of three arches, through which water is flowing towards the base ppr., a tower of the second, thereon hoisted a broad pennant flying towards the sinister, on a canton az. two keys in saltire the wards upwards or. **Crest:** A dexter arm embowed, habited az., holding a flagstaff, thereon a flag az. charged with two keys in saltire or. **Motto:** *Ne cede arduis* ('Do not give in to difficulties'). **Creation:** Bt. (GB) 30 Nov 1799.

SIR THOMAS RICHARD TROUBRIDGE, 7TH BT, of Plymouth, Devon [Sir Thomas Troubridge Bt, The Manor House, Elsted, W Sussex GU29 0JY; 96 Napier Ct, Ranelagh Gdns, London SW6 3XA]; *b* 23 Jan 1955; *s f* 1988; *educ* Eton and U Coll Durham (BSc Eng); ACA 1980, FCA 1991, ptnr Price Waterhouse 1989–; *m* 9 June 1984 *Hon Rosemary Douglas-Pennant, yr dau of 6th Baron Penrhyn (*qv*), and has:

1 +EDWARD PETER; *b* 10 Aug 1989

2 +Nicholas Douglas St Vincent; *b* 27 April 1993

1 *Emily Rose; *b* 4 June 1987

Lineage: RICHARD TROUBRIDGE, of Cavendish St, London; had:

Sir Thomas Troubridge, 1st Bt (GB), so *cr* 30 Nov 1799; Adml; fought Battles of the Nile and Cape St Vincent; blockaded Civita Vecchia and took Rome late summer 1799; MP Gt Yarmouth 1801–05; *m* Frances (*d* 13 June 1798, widow of Govr Richardson and dau of Capt John Northall, and was lost at sea Feb 1807 in the *Blenheim* returning from the East Indies, leaving, with a dau (Charlotte, *m* 29 Nov 1809 Gen Sir Charles Bulkeley Egerton, GCMG, KCH, bro of Sir John Grey Egerton, 8th Bt (*qv*), and *d* 1 Jan 1849, leaving issue):

Sir Edward Thomas Troubridge, 2nd Bt, CB; fought Battle of Copenhagen 1801, R-Adml the Red, MP Sandwich 1831–47; *m* 18 Oct 1810 Anna Maria (*d* 14 May 1873), dau of Adml Hon Sir Alexander Forrester Inglis Cochrane, GCB (*see* DUNDONALD, E), and *d* 7 Oct 1852, having had, with a yr s (Edward Norwich, Capt RN, *d* 1850) and two daus (Maria Louisa, *m* 1856 Rev T A Walrond (*d* Oct 1873) and *d* 1867; Charlotte Frances, *d* unm 25 March 1900):

Sir Thomas St Vincent Hope Cochrane Troubridge, 3rd Bt, CB; *b* 25 May 1815; Maj 7th Roy Fus, Col Crimean War (lost right leg and left foot Battle of Inkerman), Chev Legn Hon, Kt Medjidie, ADC to HM QUEEN VICTORIA, DAG Clothing Dept; *m* 1 Nov 1855 Louisa Jane (*d* 29 Aug 1867), dau of Daniel Gurney (*see* ERROLL, E), and *d* 2 Oct 1867, having had:

1 Thomas Hay; *d* young

2 **Sir Thomas Herbert Cochrane Troubridge, 4th Bt**; *b* 13 Sept 1860; *educ* Wellington and RMC Sandhurst; T/Capt Staff, Capt 1st Bn KRRC, FSA; *m* 13 July 1893 Laura (*d* 8 July 1946), author *The Book of Etiquette* (1926), dau of Charles Henry Gurney, and *d* 5 Dec 1938, having had:

(1) **Sir (Thomas) St Vincent Wallace Troubridge, 5th Bt**, MBE (1919); *b* 15 Nov 1895; *educ* Wellington and RMC Sandhurst; Hon Lt-Col KRRC, WWs I (wounded, Croce di Guerra, Order Crown Italy) and II on Gen Staff (despatches); Examiner Plays Ld Chamberlain's Office 1952; *m* 2 Sept 1939 Pamela, 2nd dau of Percy Clough, of The Knowle, Keighley, Yorks, and *dsp* 16 Dec 1963

(1) Louise Rachel; *b* 30 May 1894; *m* 28 Sept 1918 (*divorce* 1928) Capt Kenneth Gordon Woodbine Shennan, RHG, only surv s of David Shennan, of Belgravia, and *d* 11 Nov 1961

(2) Rosemary Blanche; *b* 6 April 1905; *m* 1st 28 Oct 1925 Capt Roderick Kilgour MACKENZIE formerly MARTINEAU (roy licence 1915), Seaforth Highrs (*d* 10 Jan 1937), est s of Sir William Martineau, of Kincraig, Invergordon, Ross-shire, and had issue; *m* 2nd 9 March 1940 Michael Clifford Wentworth Dilke, 2nd s of Sir Fisher Wentworth Dilke, 4th Bt (*qv*), and *d* 25 June 1974, having had further issue

3 Ernest Charles Thomas (Sir), KCMG, CB, MVO; *b* 15 July 1862; Naval Attaché Vienna 1901, Madrid 1902 and Tokyo 1902–04, Flag Capt to C-in-C Mediterranean 1907–08, Cdre Chatham 1908–10, ADC to TM EDWARD VII and GEORGE V 1909–11, Priv Sec to First Ld Admlty 1910–12, R-Adml 1911, Ch War Staff 1912–13, cmded Cruiser Sqdn Mediterranean 1913–14 and Br Naval Contingent Serbia 1915–16, V-Adml 1916, Adml 1919, silver medal of Roy

Humane Soc; *m* 1st 29 Dec 1891 Edith Mary (*d* 10 Jan 1900), yr dau of William Duffus, of Halifax, NS, and had:

(1) Thomas Hope (Sir), KCB (1946), DSO (1942) and bar (1943); *b* 1 Feb 1895; *educ* RNC Dartmouth; V-Adml, Naval Attaché Berlin 1936–39, served WWs I and II (despatches four times, American DSM), Fifth Sea Ld (Air) 1945–46, Adml (Air) 1946–47, Flag Offr (Air) Home and 2nd-in-Cmd Mediterranean Station 1948–49, Legn Hon; *m* 5 Aug 1925 Lily (*d* 17 April 1983), dau of Herman Greverus Kleinwort (*see* KLEINWORT, Bt), and *d* 29 Sept 1949, leaving:

1a PETER (Sir), **6th Bt**

2a Edward St Vincent; *b* 16 March 1930; Maj RM, ret 1974; *m* 1st 24 Aug 1955 (*divorce* 1974) Jennifer Ann, dau of Edward Billing-Lewis, of Maidstone, Kent, and had:

1b +Rodney St Vincent [Rodney Troubridge Esq, 19 Richbourne Terrace, London SW8 1AS]; *b* 10 Oct 1957

1b *Charlotte Louise; *b* 18 Sept 1960; *m* 1987 *Timothy Smith and has:

1c *Titus Oliver; *b* 25 Feb 1998

1c *Lucy Jennifer; *b* 8 Aug 1989

2b *Emma Marguerite; *b* 29 Sept 1963; has:

1c *Joshua Jovian Edward HEALEY; *b* 2 April 1996

2a (cont.) Maj Edward Troubridge *m* 2nd 1974 *Patricia Barbara [Mrs Edward Troubridge, 90 Troy Court, High St Kensington, London W8 7RE], dau of Maj Chevalier Hannibal Alexander Scicluna, OBE, of Malta, and formerly w of Cdr P G Nelson, of Oslo, and *d* 1992, leaving by her:

3b *Amelia Clare; *b* 1974

3a +Thomas [Thomas Troubridge Esq, 1B Gertrude St, London SW10]; *b* 26 Dec 1939; *educ* Eton; *m* 1st 15 Sept 1971 (*divorce* 1977, *annulled* by RC Church 1978) Baroness Marie-Christine (*m* 2nd HRH PRINCE MICHAEL OF KENT; *see* ROYAL FAMILY), dau of Baron Gunter von Reibnitz; *m* 2nd 1981 *Mrs Petronella Forgan (*née* von Woyrsch), formerly w of James Russell Forgan

1a *(Elizabeth) June [Mrs Alan Baxter, 46 South St, St Andrews, Fife KY16 9JT]; *b* 13 Aug 1933; *m* 6 Sept 1956 Alan George Laurie Baxter (*d* 1988), er surv s of Lt-Col Noel Edward Baxter, JP, DL, of Gilston, Leven, Fife, and has:

1b *Edward Thomas; *b* 2 March 1960

1b *Elizabeth Anne; *b* 2 Jan 1958

2b *Sarah Evelyn; *b* 31 Aug 1962

3b *Mary Emma; *b* 28 Nov 1965

4b *Louisa Jane; *b* 14 Aug 1969; *m* 19– *Mihai Cocris and has:

1c *Oliver

2c *Sholto

(1) Mary Laura; *b* Feb 1894; *m* 26 Feb 1916 Lt-Col Robin Otter, MC, JP, DL, Norfolk Regt (*d* 20 May 1965), son of Col Robert Charles Otter, VD, JP, DL, of Royston Manor, Retford, Notts, and had:

1a *Ann Eva; *b* 13 Dec 1916; *m* 1 June 1939 Arnold Massey Gamble, s of Arnold Gamble, of Gamston, Retford, Notts, and has:

1b *Timothy Massey; *b* 24 July 1941; *educ* Charterhouse

2b *Rodney Michael; *b* 14 July 1944; *educ* Charterhouse and Mons Offr Cadet Sch; investment consultant, late 16th/5th The Queen's Roy Lancers

2a *Barbara Mary; *b* 4 Nov 1919; *m* 27 July 1946 Maj Frederick Edlmann de Bohun Boone, MC, s of Maj Henry Griffiths Boone, DSO, RFA, of Amwellbury, Herts, and has:

1b *Christopher Henry; *b* 20 Dec 1947; *educ* Eton; late Lt Blues and Royals

2b *William Robin; *b* 14 July 1950; *educ* Eton

3b *Edward Arthur; *b* 15 May 1958

1b *Elizabeth Mary; *b* 16 May 1955

3a *Susan Elizabeth; *b* 7 Aug 1922; *m* 1st 18 Aug 1943 Maj Marmaduke John Matthews, 17th Lancers (*d* 6 May 1966), s of Marmaduke Humphrey Matthews, of Croford Mills, Somerset; *m* 2nd 7 March 1969 *Norman Dudley Hart, s of A H Hart, of Enfield, and by her 1st husb has:

1b *David Marmaduke; *b* 13 March 1945; *educ* King's Sch Bruton; *m* 6 March 1968 *Felicity, dau of S Shapland, and has:

1c *Rebecca Jane; *b* 6 May 1969

2b *Jeremy John; *b* 31 May 1947; *educ* King's Sch Bruton

4a *Lucy Jane; *b* 20 Dec 1932; *m* 1 Oct 1955 Francis Denzil Newton, er s of Maj-Gen Thomas Cochrane Newton, CB, DSO, OBE, of The Downs, Croxton, Hunts, and has:

1b *Thomas Robin; *b* 29 April 1958

1b *Charlotte Mary; *b* 25 Oct 1956

2b *Sarah Lucy; *b* 20 Dec 1959

(2) Charlotte Edith Annette; *b* 28 Aug 1896; *m* 1st 3 Oct 1916 Lt Ernest Alfred Collyer Lloyd, Scots Gds (*ka* 31 July 1917), s of Ernest Octavius Lloyd, and had issue; *m* 2nd 14 July 1920 Daniel Walter Thomas Gurney, MC, KRRC, only s of Walter Somerville Gurney, of N Runcton Hall, Norfolk, and *d* 6 Sept 1976, leaving further issue

3 (cont.) Adml Sir Ernest Troubridge *m* 2nd 10 Oct 1908 Margot Elena Gertrude (Una Vincenzo), 4th Cl Serbian Order of St Sava (*d* 25 Sept 1963), dau of Capt Harry Ashworth Taylor, MVO (*see* MONTEAGLE OF BRANDON), and *d* 28 Jan 1926, having by her had:

(3) Andrea Theodosia; BBC Home Service announcer; *m* 1st 15 Nov 1933 (*divorce* 1941) Theodore Egerton Nicholson Warren, s of Sir Norcott Hastings Yeeles Warren, KCIE, and had issue; *m* 2nd 4 Oct 1948 Brig Douglas John Tulloch Turnbull, CBE, DSO, 2nd s of Lt-Col Walter James Turnbull, VD, MICE, and was *k* in a car crash Oct 1966

1 Amy Louisa Harriet; *d* 7 July 1932

2 Laura Elizabeth Rachel; *m* 2 Aug 1888 Adrian Charles Francis Hope and *d* 15 March 1929, leaving issue (*see* LINLITHGOW, M)

3 Violet Elizabeth Emily; *m* 22 Nov 1893 Walter Somerville Gurney, est s of Sir Somerville A Gurney, KCVO, of N Runcton Hall, and *d* 14 Aug 1931, leaving issue. He *d* 1 July 1942

---

4 Helen Cecil Margaret; *m* 21 June 1917 Maj John Brabant Bate, RAMC (TA), s of Robert Bate, of Bridgwater, Somerset, and *d* 27 July 1958, aged 82. He *d* 11 April 1937

The 5th Bt's cousin,

Sir Peter Troubridge, 6th Bt; *b* 6 June 1927; *educ* Eton; Lt-Cdr RN, ret 1967; chm Standing Cncl Btage 1981 (dep chm 1979–81); *m* 10 April 1954 *Hon Venetia Daphne Weeks [The Hon Mrs Forbes, Earlstoun Lodge, Dalry, Castle Douglas DG7 3TY], yr dau of Lt-Gen 1st and last Baron Weeks, KCB, CBE, DSO, MC, TD (*see* 1959 edn); *m* 2nd 18 April 1995 *William Frederick Eustace Forbes, er s of Lt-Col William Forbes, CBE, DL, of Callendar and *d* 1988, leaving:

1 Sir THOMAS RICHARD TROUBRIDGE, **7th and present Bt**

1 *Amanda Marguerite; *b* 26 May 1957; *m* 1991 *Timothy M H Payne, yst s of Anthony D Payne, of Marnhull, Dorset, and has:

(1) *Daisy; *b* 28 May 1997

2 *Camilla June; *b* 14 Sept 1961

TRUMPINGTON

Arms: Gyronny of eight ermine and azure, three hedgehogs two and one, gold. **Supporters:** Dexter, a boxer bitch; sinister, a bay colt, both proper. **Motto:** *Gagne tout sans atouts* ('Win all with no trumps'). **Creation:** B. (LP, UK) 1980.

THE BARONESS TRUMPINGTON, of Sandwich, Co Kent (Jean Alys Campbell-Harris, PC (1992)) [The Rt Hon The Baroness Trumpington PC, 36 Cyril Mansions, Prince of Wales Dve, London SW11 4HP]; *b* Oct 23 1922; *educ* privately in England and France; Cncllr (C) Cambridge City 1963–73, Cambs 1973–75, Mayor Cambridge 1971–72; JP (Cambridge 1972–75, S Westminster 1976–82); memb: Air Tport Users Ctee 1972–80 (Chm 1979-80), Bd Visitors Pentonville Prison 1975–83, Mental Health Review Tbnl 1975–81; Gen Commr Taxes 1976–83; UK Rep UN Commn Status of Women 1979–82; Baroness-in-Waiting 1983–85 and 1991–92, Parly U-Sec: DHSS 1985–87, MAFF 1987–89; Min State MAFF 1989–92, Extra Baroness-in-Waiting 1998–; Hon FRCPath 1992, Hon ARCVS 1994, hon memb Br Veterinary Assoc 1995–; *m* 1954 (William) Alan Barker (*d* 1988) and has:

1 *Adam Campbell [The Hon Adam Barker, October Cottage, Town Croft, Hartfield, E Sussex TN7 4AD]; *b* 1 Aug 1955; *m* 1985 *Elizabeth M, er dau of Eric Marsden, of Stourpaine Manor, Blandford, Dorset, and has:

(1) *Christopher; *b* 1989

(1) *Virginia Giverny; *b* 1987

Lineage: ARTHUR EDWARD CAMPBELL-HARRIS, MC; *m* Doris Marie Robson and had:

JEAN ALYS, *cr* a **Baroness**

TRUSCOTT

Arms: Arg. three chevronels gu. between two mullets in chief of the last, pierced of the field, and a knight's helmet in base ppr., a chief chequy of the second and first. **Crest:** A fasces erect surmounted by a palm branch slipped and an arrow saltireways, all ppr.
Mottoes: 1 *Gwir yn erbyn y byd* ('Truth against all the world'),
2 (over the crest) *In utrumque paratus* ('Prepared for either').
Creation: Bt. (UK) 16 July 1909.

SIR GEORGE JAMES IRVING TRUSCOTT, 3RD BT, of Oakleigh, East Grinstead, Sussex [Sir George Truscott Bt, BM QUILL, London WC1N 3XX]; *b* 24 Oct 1929; *s* f 1973; *educ* Sherborne; *m* 1st 9 Oct 1954 (annulled 1958) Irene Marion Craig Barr Brown; *m* 2nd 8 Sept 1962 *Yvonne Dora, yst dau of Frank Edward Nicholson, of Carshalton, Surrey, and by her has:

1 +RALPH ERIC NICHOLSON; *b* 21 Feb 1966

1 *Ruth Emma; *b* 22 Feb 1967

Lineage: THOMAS TRUSCOTT, of Truro; *b* 1777; *d* 1847, leaving:

JAMES TRUSCOTT, of Essex Lodge, Norwood; *b* 1805; memb Common Cncl City London; *d* 1858, leaving:

Sir FRANCIS WYATT TRUSCOTT, of Park Crescent, London, and later Oakleigh, E Grinstead, Sussex; *b* 23 Nov 1824; Lt City London, Ld Mayor London 1879–80; *m* 5 Jan 1847 Eliza (*d* 2 May 1899), yst dau of James Freeman, of Turnham Green, Middx, and *d* 3 March 1895, leaving, with other issue:

1 James Freeman; *b* 11 Sept 1849; *m* Emily Matilda (*m* 2nd R Rugeley Bury and *d* 23 Oct 1922), dau of Henry Greene, of Greville Lodge, Kilburn, and *d* 10 March 1892, having had:

(1) James Ralph; *b* 22 April 1876; Lt City London, Lt-Col Labour Corps WW I; *m* 1st Isobel Minna, dau of Rev John Bury; *m* 2nd Hilda (*d* 2 Dec 1922), widow of Maj Colin Napier Buchanan Dunlop, DSO, and 2nd dau of Harrison Benn; *m* 3rd 22 Dec 1923 Winifred Mary (*d* 1 April 1961), est dau of Charles Beadell, and *d* 5 March 1924, leaving issue

(2) Wyatt Henry; *b* 11 June 1877; *d* 1882

(3) Roy Francis, OBE (1919); *b* 4 Sept 1881; *educ* King's Coll Cambridge (MA); barrister Inner Temple; Lt City London, memb Court Common Cncl City London, Capt 16th Bn Sherwood Foresters, Lt-Col GHQ Staff France WW I, Order Aviz Portugal; *m* 3 May 1913 Ruth Meda Angerstein (*d* 1 Feb 1948), dau of Rev Canon J F Kendall, Vicar Richmond, Surrey, and *d* 12 April 1938

(4) Cyril Alfred; *b* 16 July 1883; Lt RNVR; *d* 23 April 1917 of wounds recd in action

(1) Doris Hope; *b* 16 Sept 1888; *m* 3 Oct 1911 Gerald Vyvian Greenall, MC, only s of Peter Greenall, of Warborough, Wallingford, and *d* 19 Aug 1977, having had a s and dau. He *d* 1936

2 GEORGE WYATT (Sir), **1st Bt**

3 Henry Dexter, JP; *b* 22 June 1861; Lt City London, Master Vintners' 1922, Musicians' 1925 and Stationers' Cos 1938; *m* 23 Oct 1894 Eveline Metcalf (*d* 8 Nov 1945), 2nd dau of Wyndham Gibbes, of Notting Hill, and *d* 31 March 1950, having had:

(1) Ronald Wyndham; *b* 24 July 1903; *d* 12 June 1920

(2) Denis Henry (Sir), GBE (1958), TD (1950), JP; *b* 9 July 1908; *educ* Rugby and Magdalene Coll Cambridge; pres Brown Knight and Truscott Ltd (printers and stationers), of London EC, memb Court Common Cncl City of London 1938, 33rd St Pancras AA Bn RE (TA) 1938, Lt RA (AA) WW II, Grand Offr Order Merit Italy, Grand Cross Merit Order Merit Germany, Alderman Dowgate Ward 1947, Sheriff City London 1951–52 , ktd 1953, Master Vintners' 1955–56, Musicians' 1956–57 and Stationers' Cos 1959–60, chm Squash Rackets Assoc, Ld Mayor London 1957–58, Lt City London 1977; *m* 4 June 1932 *Ethel Margaret, yst dau of Alexander Lyell, of Gardyne Castle, Guthrie, Angus, and had:

1a *Rosemary; *b* 11 Aug 1934; *m* 4 April 1959 Hugh Richard Lines, 2nd s of Arthur Edwin Lines, of Putney, and has:

1b *William Richard Truscott; *b* 26 Sept 1960

2b *Edward Robert; *b* 6 March 1962

1b *Susan Rosemary; *b* 24 Aug 1963

2b *Catherine Rosalind; *b* 1 May 1965

3b *Elizabeth Rosamund; *b* 1 May 1965

2a *Elspeth [Mrs John Whitmore, Perryhill Farmhouse, Edenbridge Rd, Hartfield, E Sussex]; *b* 4 Feb 1936; *m* 17 Jan 1959 John Whitmore, est s of Paul Whitmore, of Wimbledon, and has:

1b *James Nicholas; *b* 25 Dec 1961

2b *David John; *b* 6 Dec 1963

3b *Charles; *b* 13 Nov 1966

1b *Alexandra Jane; *b* 5 Feb 1960

2b *Georgina Mary; *b* 13 Aug 1970

3a *Jane; *b* 14 Sept 1937; *m* 30 May 1964 John Anthony Fairbank (*d* following an accident 14 Feb 1966), s of Lt-Col Harry Nevill Fairbank, DSO, MC, DL, of Clifton, Bristol, and has:

1b *Simon Nevill; *b* 6 July 1965

1b *Alison Johanna; *b* posthumously 11 Oct 1966

4a Anne [Mrs George Preston, Patchfield, Corfe Castle, Dorset BH20 5HU]; *b* 20 Oct 1943; *m* 1 April 1967 Maj George Edward Preston, 2nd RTR, yr s of Phillip A Preston, TD, of Stoke Trister, Somerset, and has:

1b *Nicholas Oliver; *b* 5 Feb 1968

2b *Richard Timothy; *b* 18 Sept 1969

1b *Susanna Jane; *b* 9 Oct 1970

2b *Sarah Lucy; *b* 3 June 1974

(1) Kathleen Phyllis; *b* 19 Sept 1897

1 Louisa Edith; *m* 26 March 1874 Sir Homewood Crawford, CVO, s of John Crawford, JP, of Margate, and *dsp* 12 July 1933. He *d* 17 Nov 1936

The 2nd s,

Sir George Wyatt Truscott, 1st Bt (UK), so *cr* 16 July 1909, JP; *b* 9 Oct 1857; chm Brown, Knight and Truscott Ltd, Lt City London, Alderman Dowgate Ward 1895–1941, Sheriff 1902–03, Ld Mayor 1908–09, Master Stationers', Haberdashers', Vintners' and Musicians' Cos, Hon Freedom City London 1937, Grand Cross Order St Stanislas Russia and Order Vasa Sweden; Kt Cdr Order Rising Sun Japan; Offr Order Leopold Belgium and Legn Hon, Coronation Medal 1902, ktd 1902; *m* 26 Oct 1889 Jessie Guthrie, DGStJ (*d* 3 Aug 1921), est dau of George Gordon Stanham, of Grove Park, Chiswick, and had:

1 Francis George, MC; *b* 12 Aug 1894; *educ* Trin Coll Cambridge (BA); Lt 6th Bn Suffolk Regt and 47th (London) Div Cyclist Co Div Mounted Troops (TF), attd RFC, WW I (despatches); *k* in aerial battle 6 April 1917

2 ERIC HOMEWOOD STANHAM (Sir), **2nd Bt**

1 Mary Guthrie; *b* 1st 2 March 1890; *m* 1st 2 March 1915 (*divorce* 1923) Arthur Sydney Waller, of Salisbury, S Rhodesia, s of H Sydney Waller, of Farmington, Glos, and had issue; *m* 2nd 15 May 1929 Francis Wigglesworth, 4th s of Alfred Wigglesworth, of Aberdeen. He *d* 27 July 1945

2 Nancy Wyatt; *b* 27 March 1892; *m* 23 May 1918 Harold Percy Gabb, MC, TD, MRCS, LRCP, Lt-Col RAMC (TAR), 2nd s of James Percy Alwyne Gabb, MD, of Guildford, and *d* 30 March 1966, having had issue. He *d* 18 March 1964

Sir GEORGE *d* 16 April 1941; his only surv s,

Sir Eric Homewood Stanham Truscott, 2nd Bt; *b* 16 Feb 1898; *educ* Rugby and Trin Coll Cambridge (BA 1920, MA 1925); 2nd Lt 15th Bn Suffolk Regt WW I 1916–18, Gunner 26th (Searchlight) Regt RA (TA) WW II; *m* 1st 1 May 1924 Mary Dorcas (*d* following an accident 1 Dec 1948), only dau of Rev Canon Thomas Henry Irving, Vicar Hawkshead, Ambleside, and had:

1 Sir GEORGE JAMES IRVING TRUSCOTT, **3rd and present Bt**

1 *Jennifer Margaret Anne [Mrs Edward Segar, Stanton Hill, Priorsfield Rd, Godalming, Surrey GU7 2RQ]; *b* 22 July 1932; *m* 26 July 1958 *Lt-Cdr Edward Martyn Theodore Segar, RN, only s of Maj Edward Segar, of Totland Bay, IOW, and has:

(1) *John Edward; *b* 27 Oct 1965

(1) *Jane Margaret; *b* 14 Aug 1959

(2) *Anne Mary; *b* 18 Sept 1962

Sir Eric *m* 2nd 23 Sept 1950 Marjorie Berta (*d* 25 Aug 1951), widow of Alfred William Sutton and yr dau of Prof Leonard Trelawny Hobhouse, LittD; *m* 3rd 7 March 1953 Renée Franklin, formerly w of William Archibald Redgrave and yr dau of John William Marshall, of Endsleigh, Highfield Hill, Norwood, and *d* 11 May 1973

TRYON

Arms: Az. a fess embattled, between in chief three estoiles and in base a portcullis chained or. **Crest:** Issuant from a crown composed of four roses set upon a rim or a bear's head sa., charged with seven stars in the form of the constellation Ursa Major gold.
Supporters: Dexter, an army pensioner in hospital uniform; sinister, a postman holding with the exterior hand a letter-sack over his shoulder, ppr. **Motto:** Do right and fear not.
Creation: B. (UK) 18 April 1940.

THE 3RD BARON TRYON, of Durnford, Wilts (Anthony George Merrick Tryon, DL (Wilts 1992)) [The Rt Hon The Lord Tryon DL, The Manor House, Great Durnford, Wilts SP4 6BB]; *b* 26 May 1940; *s f* 1976; *educ* Eton; Page of Hon to HM THE QUEEN 1954–56, Capt Roy Wilts Yeo and Wessex Yeo, dir Lazard Bros and Co Ltd 1976–83, chm: English & Scottish Investors Ltd 1977–88, Swaine Adeney Briggs 1991–93, Salisbury Cathedral Spire Tst 1985–; pres Anglers Conservation Assoc 1985–; *m* 13 April 1973 (*divorce* 5 Nov 1997) Dale Elizabeth (*d* 15 Nov 1997), est dau of H P D (Barry) Harper, of Melbourne, Australia, and has:

1 +CHARLES GEORGE BARRINGTON; *b* 15 May 1976; Page of Hon to HM THE QUEEN 1988–; *educ* Edinburgh U

2 +Edward Henry; *b* 18 Dec 1979; *educ* Marlborough

1 *Zoë Elizabeth; *b* 1 May 1974

2 *Victoria Clementine; *b* 18 Dec 1979; *educ* Marlborough

Lineage: PETER TRIEON; migrated from the Spanish Netherlands *c* 1562; naturalized Englishman; *d* 1611, leaving:

MOYSES TRYON; bought Harringworth, adjoining Bulwick, Northants; High Sheriff Northants 1624; presumably kin to:

THOMAS TRYON, of Bulwick; *m* 1st — Weston (*dsp*); *m* 2nd Harriet, dau of Very Rev Dr Brereton, Dean Lichfield, and by her had:

1 THOMAS

2 Charles William; *d* unm

3 Samuel; Maj-Gen; *m* a dau of Sir John Harvey, KCB, and had six children

4 Robert, of Heathfield Ho, Fareham; R-Adml; *m* 1st 9 Dec 1840 Henrietta (*d* 1848), dau of Adml James Prevost; *m* 2nd 3 Jan 1855 Lelia Sophia (*d* 25 Aug 1889), 6th dau of Sir Grey Skipwith, 8th Bt (*qv*), and by her had:

(1) Henry William, JP Wilts; *b* 1855; Gordon Highrs; *m* 1881 Fanny (*d* 11 July 1926), dau of Richard Turnor, of Kingsworthy Ho, Winchester, and *d* 3 March 1929, leaving:

1a Edith Augusta Muriel; *b* 11 Aug 1882; *m* 27 June 1907 (*divorce* 1918) Ronald Louis Charteris (*see* WEMYSS and MARCH, E) and *d* 22 June 1960

(2) Charles Robert; *b* 1857; *m* 9 May 1905 Esther (*d* 21 July 1958), only dau of Sir Henry Bromley, 5th Bt (*qv*), and *d* 21 Oct 1916, leaving:

1a Henry Robert; *b* 29 Oct 1907; *d* 21 Aug 1913

2a *Charles Edward TRYON later TRYON-WILSON (roy warrant 28 Dec 1951), CBE (1945, MBE 1943), DSO (1944), DL (Westmorland 1971–74, Cumbria 1974 [Brig Charles Tryon-Wilson CBE DSO DL, Dallam Tower, Milnthorpe, Cumbria LA7 7AG]; *b* 20 Sept 1909; *educ* Shawnigan Lake Sch, BC, Canada, and Trin Coll Glenalmond; 60th Rifles 1927–30, Roy Fus 1930–36 and 1938–46, WW II (despatches twice), Brig; *m* 1st 5 June 1937 Cicely Joan (*d* 14 March 1969), yst dau of Capt Henry Whitworth, of Kilnwick Percy, Pocklington; *m* 2nd *Rosemary Lucas and by his 1st w has:

1b *Cicely Susan Esther; *b* 23 Nov 1938; *m* 1st 25 Jan 1961 (*divorce* 1969) Timothy Francis Villiers-Smith (*see* NORTHBOURNE, B) and has issue; *m* 2nd 1970 *John M W Newman, only s of A C Newman, of Farnham Royal, Bucks

2b Sarah Gay; *b* 12 Feb 1940; *d* 26 Nov 1941

3a John; *b* 10 July 1914; *m* 26 April 1944 *Ethel (*m* 2nd 19 Jan 1963 Francis Woodowes Henstock, s of C P Henstock, of Argentina and Canada), dau of H J Cunliffe, and *d* 17 Feb 1958, leaving:

1b *David John; *b* 1 Jan 1947

2b *Robert Hugh Cunliff; *b* 6 July 1950

1b *Heather Ethel Margaret; *b* 18 Feb 1954

4a *Thomas Charles; *b* 1 Oct 1916; *m* 1949 *Josta, dau of — Visschers, of Deventer, Holland, and has:

1b *Thomas Jan *b* 1951

2b *Peter Willem; *b* 1954

3b *John Hendrik; *b* 10 April 1961

1a *Ruth Esther; *b* 15 June 1906; *m* 18 Oct 1934 Harold Williams, s of L Miles Williams, of Montreal, and has:

2a *June; *b* 5 June 1912; *m* 12 June 1937 C D Osborn, s of Col G Osborn, RA, of Lavington, BC, Canada, and has issue

1 Harriet; *m* 26 June 1832 Rev Christopher Whichcote, Rector Aswarby, Vicar Swarby, Lincs, 5th s of Sir Thomas Whichcote, 5th Bt (*see* 1940 edn), and *d* 28 Sept 1872. He *d* 4 Jan 1885

The est s,

THOMAS TRYON, of Bulwick Park, Northants, JP, DL Northants; *b* 22 May 1802; High Sheriff 1833; *m* 1827 Anne (*d* 12 Feb 1877), dau of Sir John Trollope, 6th Bt (*qv*), and *d* 21 Aug 1872, leaving:

1 Thomas, of Bulwick Park, JP Northants; *b* 1830; High Sheriff 1875, Lt-Col 7th Roy Fus; *m* 15 July 1873 Alice (*d* 2 May 1932), 6th dau of Rev Samuel Vere Dashwood, of Stanford Hall, Notts, and *d* 19 Dec 1888, having had:

(1) Guy Thomas Lewes; *b* 22 Oct 1878; 2nd Lt 2nd Bn Gren Gds; *das* unm 24 April 1901 Boer War

(1) Eva Mildred, of Bulwick Park; *m* 12 July 1898 Ernest William Proby Conant, of Lyndon Hall, Rutland, and *d* 6 Sept 1957, leaving issue. He *d* 14 Aug 1920

(2) Ouida Mary; *m* 12 Aug 1908 Capt Francis Alexander Chetwode Hamilton, Scottish Rifles, er s of Rev Charles Chetwode Hamilton, and *d* 4 June 1953, leaving issue. He *d* 10 Oct 1956

(3) Violet Alice Grace; *m* 18 Sept 1912 Maj Egerton Augustus Stafford-O'Brien, of Blatherwycke Park, Northants, est s of Horace Stafford Stafford-O'Brien, of Blatherwycke Park, and *d* 4 Feb 1939, leaving issue. He *d* 6 June 1963

2 Henry; Lt Rifle Bde; *ka* Siege of Sebastopol 20 Nov 1854

3 GEORGE

4 Richard, of The Lodge, Oakham, Rutland, JP; *b* 31 Aug 1837; High Sheriff Rutland 1881, Capt Rifle Bde; *m* 11 June 1867 Jane Anna Lucy (*d* 14 May 1928), widow of John William Cheney Ewart and est dau of Gen William Augustus Johnson, MP, of Witham-on-the-Hill, and *d* 12 Dec 1905, leaving:

(1) Richard; *b* 17 May 1868; Capt Rifle Bde; *m* 18 July 1894 Edith Campbell (*d* 12 May 1931), est dau of William Clarence Watson, of 39 Gloucester Sq, W, and Colworth, Beds, and was *ka* 10 Jan 1915, leaving:

1a *Richard George Laurence; *b* 19 Aug 1902; *educ* RMC Sandhurst; Maj Rifle Bde; *m* 1st 30 July 1929 (*divorce* 1962) Lucinda, dau of Thomas Frame-Thomson; *m* 2nd 27 July 1962 *Gertrude Lilian, only dau of Benjamin Forces, of Fairfield, Broughty Ferry, Angus, and by his 1st w has:

1b *Richard Thomas; *b* 16 Feb 1940; *educ* Nautical Coll Pangbourne; *m* 24 April 1965 *Clare, only dau of Richard Peter Hammond-Chambers-Borgnis, of Little Hill Cottage, Hurst, Berks, and has:

1c *Nicola; *b* 25 March 1968

1b *Rosemary Margaret; *b* 16 July 1930; *m* 11 Oct 1952 W/Cdr John Martin Baskerville Edwards, RAF, only s of Geoffrey Richard Edwards, OBE (*see* SIMON, V), and has:

1c *Richard John Simon; *b* 21 Dec 1953; *educ* Ampleforth

2c *Benedict John Martin; *b* 25 June 1960

1c *Caroline Lucy; *b* 23 Jan 1955

2c *Anne Elizabeth; *b* 7 Jan 1959

2b *Anne; *b* 9 June 1932; *m* 28 May 1953 *Walter Desmond McGredy Johnston, MB, BCh, er s of Walter Irwin Johnston, of Drumlyn Hill, Portadown, Co Armagh, and has:

1c *Desmond Peter; *b* 14 Jan 1961

1c *Margaret Anne; *b* 14 May 1954

2c *Kathleen Louise; *b* 2 Feb 1957

2a Julian Guy; *b* 5 Nov 1907; Capt NZ Forces; *m* 8 March 1944 Marjorie (*m* 2nd 3 Oct 1957 Sir Ronald Montague Joseph Harris, KCVO, CB), est dau of Sir Harry Calver Williams Verney, 4th Bt, of Claydon (*qv*), and *d* 11 Dec 1950, leaving:

1b Martin Verney; *b* 5 Jan 1945; *d* unm 30 April 1968

1b *Edith Catherine; *b* 13 Oct 1948; *m* 17 April 1971 Rev Colin Bruce Slee, 2nd s of H S Slee, of Acton

(2) Henry; *b* 24 Aug 1874; Capt 8th Bn Rifle Bde; *ka* 15 Sept 1916

(3) Julian; *b* 2 Oct 1876; *d* unm 5 Nov 1907

(1) Mary Lucy; *b* 7 May 1870; *d* unm 10 March 1956

(2) Jane Matilda; *b* 27 Aug 1872; *d* unm 9 March 1955

(3) Georgina Catherine; *b* 2 Sept 1875; *d* unm 14 Feb 1956

(4) Margaret Constance; *b* 12 June 1878; *m* 8 Aug 1906 Charles Alexander Muntz, of Whissenthorpe, Rutland, and *d* 15 Feb 1939

The 3rd s,

Sir GEORGE TRYON, KCB; *b* 1832; V-Adml; *m* 5 April 1869 Hon Clementina Heathcote (*d* 8 Nov 1922), dau of Baroness Willoughby de Eresby (*qv*) in her own right, and went down with his flagship HMS *Victoria* whilst cmdg the Mediterranean Fleet 22 June 1893, having ordered her and HMS *Camperdown*, only 1,200 yds away, to turn in on each other, resulting in their collision and the death of 422 other men, an extraordinary manoeuvre for which no satisfactory explanation has ever been given, leaving:

GEORGE CLEMENT TRYON, **1st Baron Tryon**, of Durnford, Co Wilts (UK), so *cr* 18 April 1940, PC (1922); *b* 15 May 1871; *educ* Eton and RMC Sandhurst; Gren Gds: joined 1890, Capt 1899, Boer War 1899–1900 (medal, two clasps), ret 1903, rejoined 1914, Maj; MP (C) Brighton 1910–40, Parly U-Sec Air 1919–20, Parly Sec Min Pensions 1920–22, Min Pensions Oct 1922–Jan 1924, Nov 1924–June 1929 and Sept 1931–June 1935, PMG June 1935–April 1940; Chllr Duchy Lancaster April–May 1940, First Commr Works May–Oct 1940, Parly Sec Min Pensions Oct–Nov 1940; *m* 28 Feb 1905 Hon Averil Vivian (*d* 1 Feb 1959), 2nd dau of 1st Baron Swansea (*qv*), and *d* 24 Nov 1940, leaving, with a yr s (Aylmer Douglas, *b* 16 July 1909, *educ* Eton and Trin Coll Cambridge (BA 1931), Capt Gren Gds, *d* unm 25 Jan 1996):

CHARLES GEORGE VIVIAN TRYON, **2nd Baron Tryon**, GCVO (1969, KCVO 1953), KCB (1962), DSO (1945), DL (1972); *b* 24 May 1906; *educ* Eton and RMC Sandhurst; Lt-Col (Hon Brig) Gren Gds, formerly cmdg 5 Gds Bde, ADC to Govr-Gen Canada 1933–34, Adj Gren Gds 1934–37, ADC London Dist 1937–39, served WW II (despatches), Assist Keeper Privy Purse to HM GEORGE VI 1949–52, Keeper Privy Purse and Treasurer to HM THE QUEEN Oct 1952–71, regnl dir Lloyds Bank 1972, Tstee Ascot Authority 1952, Dep Sr Steward Jockey Club 1972; Cdr Legn Hon 1960, Chev Order Leopold II Belgium, Belgian Croix de Guerre avec palme, OStJ 1972; *m* 3 Aug 1939 *Etheldreda Josephine [The Rt Hon Dreda Lady Tryon, Church Farm, Great Durnford, Wilts], dau of Lt-Col Sir Merrik Raymond Burrell, 7th Bt, CBE (*qv*), and *d* 9 Nov 1976, leaving:

1 ANTHONY GEORGE MERRICK TRYON, **3rd and present Baron Tryon**

1 *Patricia Joan Kathleen [The Hon Mrs Macdonald, 103 Caroline St, S Yarra, Vic 3141, Australia]; *b* 9 Jan 1942; *m* 11 Aug 1973 *(Chesborough) Ranald Macdonald, s of H C H Macdonald, and has:

    (1) *Hamish Aylmer Syme; *b* 27 April 1977

    (1) *Laura Christina; *b* 30 Dec 1974

TUCK

CUM · DEO

Arms: Or an antique lamp flaming az., in base a hurt charged with four Fs in cross of the field, on a chief of the second two hands in the act of blessing of the first. **Crest:** A lion sejant sa., supporting with the paws an artist's palette ppr., inscribed thereon the word 'Thorough' sa. **Motto:** *Cum Deo* ('With God').
Creation: Bt. (UK) 19 July 1910.

SIR BRUCE ADOLPH REGINALD TUCK, 3RD BT, of Park Crescent, St Marylebone [Sir Bruce Tuck Bt, PO Box 274, Montego Bay, Jamaica]; *b* 29 June 1926; *s f* 1954; *educ* Canford; Lt Scots Gds 1945–47; *m* 1st 26 April 1949 (*divorce* 1964) Louise, dau of John C Renfro, of San Angelo, Texas, and has:

1 +RICHARD BRUCE; *b* 7 Oct 1952; *educ* Millfield

2 +Christopher John; *b* 20 July 1954

Sir BRUCE *m* 2nd 22 Feb 1968 *Pamela Dorothy (Nicky) Allen, dau of Alfred Michael Nicholson, of London, and by her has:

1 *Charlotte Emily Pamela; *b* 1974; *m* 26 Sept 1988 *Baron Ottavio Serena di Lapigio, er s of Baron Serena di Lapigio, of Rome, Italy

Lineage: RAPHAEL TUCK, of Highbury; *b* 7 Aug 1821; fndr Raphael Tuck and Sons, fine art publishers; *m* March 1848 Ernestine (*d* 4 March 1895), dau of David Lissner, and *d* 16 March 1900, leaving:

1 Herman; *b* 8 Jan 1849; *m* 12 Sept 1883 Mathilda, dau of Lion Lion, and *d* 13 Sept 1909

2 ADOLPH (Sir), **1st Bt**

3 Gustave; *b* 7 Nov 1857; *m* 2 July 1884 Esther, dau of Morris Lyons

4 Hugo; *b* 8 Feb 1861; *m* 24 Dec 1896 Louisa, dau of Herman Gosschalk

1 Julia; *b* 16 Dec 1850; *m* 1875 Joseph Broady and *d* 26 Dec 1903

2 Rose; *b* 13 March 1855; *m* 10 Oct 1877 Barnet Goodman

3 Minnie; *b* 21 Aug 1859; *m* 7 March 1883 Sigmund Birn

The 2nd s,

    Sir Adolph Tuck, 1st Bt (UK), so *cr* 19 July 1910; *b* 30 Jan 1854; chm and md Raphael Tuck and Sons; *m* 11 Oct 1882 Jeanette (*d* 15 March 1948), dau of William Flatau, of Lusan Ho, Highbury, and had:

1 WILLIAM REGINALD (Sir), **2nd Bt**

2 Desmond Adolph; *b* 27 March 1889; *educ* Clifton and King's Coll Cambridge; chm and jt md Raphael Tuck and Sons, Capt 3rd Co of London Yeo, F/Cdr RAF, WW I, Croix de Guerre

1 Gladys Evelyn; *b* 30 Jan 1885; *m* 25 Jan 1910 Joseph Henry Jacobs, of 73 Portland Place, W1, and Woodland Court, Chesham Bois, Bucks, s of Chapman Jacobs, of Swansea, and *d* 26 June 1967, leaving issue. He *d* 8 Aug 1949

2 Sybil Grace; *b* 16 Aug 1887; *m* 30 Dec 1925 Sir Edward David Stern, 1st and last Bt (*d* 17 April 1933)

---

3 Muriel Jenetta; *b* 9 June 1892; *m* 15 July 1924 Leonard Goldsmid-Montefiore, s of Claud Joseph Goldsmid-Montefiore, and had issue. He *d* 23 Dec 1961

Sir ADOLPH *d* 3 July 1926; his er s,

    Sir (William) Reginald Tuck, 2nd Bt; *b* 8 July 1883; *educ* Clifton; Maj 3rd Co of London Yeo WW I, jt md Raphael Tuck and Sons, Roy Humane Soc's Silver Medal (Auckland, NZ) for life-saving; *m* 20 Dec 1916 Gladys (*d* 23 Feb 1966), widow of Desmond Fosberry Kettle, Auckland Mounted Rifles, and 2nd dau of Nathan Alfred Nathan, of Wickford, Auckland, NZ, and *d* 12 May 1954, leaving:

1 Sir BRUCE ADOLPH REGINALD TUCK, **3rd and present Bt**

1 Joan Annette; *m* 1st 8 Jan 1936 (*divorce* 1942) Alwyn Eric Bolton, only s of Eugene Bolton, of Gill Wood End, Wadhurst, Sussex; *m* 2nd 8 June 1944 (*divorce* 1960) Maj Edwin Franklin Morgenthau, US Army, er s of Max Morgenthau, of Los Angeles, and *d* 9 Aug 1961, leaving issue

2 *Moyra Grace; *b* 1920; WAAF WW II; *m* 1st 16 Jan 1947 Lee David Greif (*d* 23 Aug 1950), yr s of David Greif, of Baltimore, Md.; *m* 2nd 14 Sept 1951 Alvin Greif, Jr, Maj USAAF (*d* 5 Jan 1958), s of Alvin Greif, of Florida; *m* 3rd 12 Feb 1959 *Capt Nigel Digby Pemberton, 13th/18th Roy Hus (QMO), yr s of Roland Thomas Pemberton, of London

TUGENDHAT

Creation: B. (LP, UK) 1993.

THE BARON TUGENDHAT, of Widdington, Co Essex (Sir Christopher Samuel Tugendhat) [The Rt Hon The Lord Tugendhat, 35 Westbourne Park Rd, London W2 5QD]; *b* 23 Feb 1937; *educ* Ampleforth and Gonville and Caius Coll Cambridge; leader and feature writer *Financial Times* 1960–70; MP (C) Cities of London and Westminster 1970–74, City of London and Westminster S 1974–76; Memb EEC Commn 1977–81 (V-Pres 1981–85); dir: Sunningdale Oils 1971–76, Phillips Petroleum 1972–76, NatWest Bank 1985–91 (dep chm 1990–91), BOC Gp 1985–, Commercial Union Assur 1988–91, LWT Hldgs 1991–94, Eurotunnel 1991–; Chm: CAA 1986–91, RIIA Chatham Hse 1986–95, Abbey Nat 1991–, non-exec chm Blue Circle 1996–; V-Pres Cncl Br Lung Fndn 1986–, Govr Cncl Ditchley Fndn 1986–, ktd 1990, Chllr Bath U 1998–; author: *Oil: the biggest business* (1968), *The Multinationals* (1971), *Making Sense of Europe* (with William Wallace, 1986), *Options for British Foreign Policy in the 1990s* (1988); *m* 1967 *Julia Lissant, dau of Kenneth D Dobson, of Keston, Kent, and has:

1 *James Walter; *b* 1971

2 *Angus George Harrry; *b* 1974

Lineage: GEORG TUGENDHAT; Dr; *m* Maire Littledale and had an er s:

CHRISTOPHER SAMUEL, *cr* a **Baron**

TUITE

ALLELUIAH

Arms: Quarterly arg. and gu. **Crest:** An angel vested arg. holding in the dexter hand a flaming sword ppr., the sinister resting on a shield of the arms, **Motto:** *Alleluiah* ('Praise ye the Lord').
Creation: Bt. (I) 16 June 1622.

SIR CHRISTOPHER HUGH TUITE, 14TH BT, of Sonagh, Co Westmeath [Sir Christopher Tuite Bt, c/o The Midland Bank, 33 The Borough, Farnham, Surrey GU9 7NJ]; *b* 3 Nov 1949; *s f* 1981; *educ* Wellington, Liverpool U (BSc) and Bristol U (PhD); Controller Nature Conservancy; research offr Wildfowl Tst 1978–81; *m* 1976 *Deborah Anne, dau of A E Martz, of Pittsburgh, Pa., and has:

1 +THOMAS LIVINGSTON; *b* 24 July 1977

2 +Jonathan Christopher Hannington; *b* 1981

Lineage: Sir RICHARD de TUITE; accompanied Strongbow (*see* PEMBROKE and MONTGOMERY, E, preliminary remarks) to Ireland 1172; *d* 1211, leaving, with another s (Sir Richard 'the Black'):

MAURICE TUITE; ancestor of:

JOHN TUITE, of Sonagh, Co Westmeath; *m* Margaret, dau of Edward Nugent, of Dysart, and *d* 1597, leaving:

Sir Oliver Tuite, 1st Bt (I), so cr 16 June 1622, of Sonagh; *b c* 1588; *m* Mabel, dau of Sir Gerald Aylmer, 1st Bt (*qv*), and *d* 1642, having had:

THOMAS TUITE; *m* Martha, dau of Thomas Luttrell, of Luttrellstown, and *dvp* Oct 1624, leaving:

1 **Sir Oliver Tuite, 2nd Bt**; *m* Elinor (*m* 2nd Maj Owen O'Connor), dau of Roger O'Ferrall, of Mornine, Co Longford, and *d* Aug 1661, having had an only *s*:

    (1) **Sir James Tuite, 3rd Bt**; *d unm* Feb 1664

2 **Sir Henry Tuite, 4th Bt**; *m* Diana (*m* 2nd Rev John Twells), dau of Kympton Mabbott by Susan Hyde, sis of 1st Earl of Clarendon of the 1661 *cr* (*see* CLARENDON, E, preliminary remarks), and *d* May 1679, having had, with a dau (Jane, *m* Thomas Candler, of Callan Castle, Co Kilkenny), an only *s*:

    (1) **Sir Joseph Tuite, 5th Bt**; *b* 1677; *m* May 1706 Mary (*d* May 1749), dau of John Perceval, of Knightbrook, and *d* 1727, leaving:

        1a **Sir Henry Tuite, 6th Bt**; *m* 1st 1728 Mary (*d* 25 Feb 1729), dau of George Rochford and sis of 1st Earl of Belvedere, and had:

            1b **Sir George Tuite, 7th Bt**; *b* 20 Feb 1729; murdered Sonagh 12 Feb 1783

        1a (cont.) **Sir Henry** *m* 2nd 6 July 1741 Mary, dau of Marcus Anthony Morgan, of Cottlestown, Co Sligo, and *d* 9 April 1765, having by her had:

            2b **Sir Henry Tuite, 8th Bt**; *b* 1742; Offr RN; *m* Nov 1784 Elizabeth Dorothea (*d* 1850 aged 85), 2nd dau of Thomas Cobbe, of Newbridge, Co Dublin, and gdau of Charles Cobbe, Archbp Dublin, and *dsp* Aug 1805

            3b Mark Anthony; *b* Dec 1745; Capt 9th Dragoons; *m* 10 Dec 1774 Patience (*d* 1 Jan 1803), 2nd dau of Marlborough Stirling, Prothonotary Court Common Pleas Ireland, and had:

                1c GEORGE (Sir), **9th Bt**

                1c Lucinda; *m* Rev James W Stirling, Rector Athlone, Co Westmeath

                2c Maria; *m* 1st Richard Anderson Rose, of Fox Hall, Co Tipperary; *m* 2nd Capt William White, 61st Regt; *m* 3rd Henry Melville, MD, and *d* his widow 18 Jan 1860 aged 79

            4b Hugh, of Sonagh, which he inherited from **8th Bt**; *b* July 1747; Army Capt Siege Gibraltar; *m* 1792 Sarah Elizabeth, dau of Lt-Col Daniel Chenevix, of Ballycommon, King's Co, and *d* 1843, having had:

                1c Henry; *b* 1794; *d* 1811

                2c Hugh Morgan, of Sonagh, JP, DL Co Westmeath; *b* 1795; High Sheriff 1822 and Co Longford 1837, MP Co Westmeath 1826–30 and 1842–47; *m* 1st 6 Feb 1826 Mary (*d* 14 March 1863), 2nd dau of Maurice O'Connor, of Mount Pleasant, King's Co, and had:

                    1a Joseph, of Sonagh, JP, DL Co Longford, JP Co Westmeath; *b* 15 Oct 1828; Lt 15th Regt, High Sheriff Co Longford 1868; *m* 1st 8 Jan 1852 Ellen Mary (*d* 2 Dec 1863), dau of Rev Charles Fox Chawner, Rector Bletchingley, and had:

                        1b Henry Maurice, of Sonagh, JP Co Westmeath; *b* 15 Oct 1856; High Sheriff 1915; *m* 8 March 1886 Constance Edith, dau of Henry Murray Campbell, of Halston, Co Westmeath

                        1b Marion Charlotte Mary; *m* 1879 Brook Pakenham Bridges Taylor, only *s* of Bridges Taylor, of Bifrons, Kent, and *d* 28 Feb 1922. He *d* 17 Jan 1923

                    1a (cont.) Joseph Tuite *m* 2nd 4 June 1868 Ellen (*dsp* 26 April 1898), yst dau of James Brownell Boothby, of Twyford Abbey (*see* 1970 edn BOOTHBY, B), and *d* 21 Feb 1910

                    1a Sarah Elizabeth; *m* 12 Aug 1852 Henry L Falret, Conseiller de Préfecture de Melum, Seine et Marne (authorised by Imperial Sign Manual to take name DE TUITE in France), and had issue. She *d* July 1905

                (2) (cont.) Hugh Tuite *m* 2nd 8 Oct 1863 Hester Maria (*dsp* Jan 1875), dau of John Hogan, of Auburn, Co Westmeath, and *d* 16 Aug 1868

                (3) George Gustavus; RN, Lt-Col 3rd Light Dragoons; *m* Dora, dau of Thomas Wood, of Littleton, Middx, and *dsp* 7 Oct 1849

                (1) Penelope Melesina; *m* 1820 John Charles Lyons, of Ledestown, Co Westmeath

The 8th Bt's n,

    Sir George Tuite, 9th Bt; *b* 8 June 1778; *m* 8 June 1807 Janet (*d* 21 Feb 1845), widow of Maj Thomas Woodall, 12th Foot, and *d* 15 June 1841, having had, with a dau (*d unm*):

1 **Sir Mark Anthony Henry Tuite, 10th Bt**; *b* 24 March 1808; Capt 19 Regt; *m* 18 Nov 1854 Charlotte (*d* 9 April 1878), dau of Richard Hugh Levinge, of Levington Park, Co Westmeath, and *dsp* 18 March 1898

2 Hugh Manley; *b* 7 Oct 1811; Maj-Gen RA; *m* 21 Aug 1854 Frances Maria (*d* 1901), dau of Lt-Col Richard Williams, 68th Foot, and *d* 4 Jan 1889, leaving:

    (1) **Sir Morgan Harry Paulet Tuite, 11th Bt**; *b* 27 Oct 1861; Lt 9th Bn Rifle Bde; *d unm* 16 Nov 1946

    (2) Hugh George Spencer; *b* 17 April 1863; Lt 2nd Bn Northumberland Fus, Capt Indian Labour Corps, Hazara Campaign 1888 (medal with clasp), Indian Labour Corps WW I, memb History of War Ctee War Office 1919–22; *m* 14 Feb 1893 Eva Geraldine (*d* 25 Jan 1951), dau of Peter Valentine Hatton, of Co Wicklow, and *d* 6 Jan 1933, leaving:

        1a **Sir Brian Hugh Morgan Tuite, 12th Bt**; *b* 1 May 1897; *educ* Kelvinside Acad and Highgate Sch; Lt Roy Northumberland Fus and Queen Victoria's Rifles WW I (wounded), Maj Roy Pioneer Corps WW II; *d unm* 26 Aug 1970

        2a DENNIS GEORGE HARMSWORTH , **13th Bt**

        1a Joan Frances Valentine; *b* 12 Nov 1894; Women's Legion, WVS and CD WW II; *d unm* 8 Aug 1956

        2a Moira Gwendolen Hatton; *b* 19 Dec 1899; *m* 19 July 1922 S/Ldr Henry John Hunter, RAF, 3rd *s* of William Hunter, of Reigate, and had issue. He *d* 2 Jan 1958

    (1) Hester Gwendolen Rose; *b* 20 June 1868; *m* 22 Dec 1896 George S Eckford, 5th Bn Roy Munster Fus, *s* of T Porteous Eckford, of Drumarten, Co Dublin, and *d* 5 March 1949

3 George James Hanover; Capt 19th Regt; *d* 1 Sept 1853

4 Thomas Basil; *b* 1816; Maj 11th Foot; *m* 25 Oct 1853 Mary Caroline (*d* 14 Aug 1914), dau of Henry Hegart Breen, Govr St Lucia, and *d* 23 July 1871, leaving:

---

    (1) Mark Anthony; *b* 2 May 1857; Col IA; *m* 15 Aug 1883 Madeline Rachel (*d* 18 Oct 1921), dau of Surgn-Gen J M Joseph, MD, LLD, IMS, and *d* 4 Jan 1944, having had:

        1a Henry Mark; *b* 24 Sept 1885; Lt-Col 26th Bn Roy Fus, formerly Border Regt; *d* 24 March 1918 of wounds recd in action

    (2) Henry Hugh; *b* 1 April 1861; *m* 2 April 1891 Marion Hewett Alberta (*d* 6 Dec 1948), dau of Rev Allan Wallace, and *d* 31 Jan 1937, having had:

        1a Mark Alan Wallace; *b* 1 Feb 1892; Lt Tank Corps; *d* 2 Dec 1917 of wounds recd in action

        1a Honor Kathleen; *b* 1898; *d unm* 24 Nov 1967

    (3) Thomas Hugh; *b* 22 July 1868; *m* 1927 Frances Emily Frisby (*d* 28 Aug 1963 aged 94), dau of John Roberts, and *dsp* 15 March 1952

    (4) Edwin Walter; *b* 21 Feb 1872; *d unm* 2 Feb 1961

    (1) Lizzie; *m* 25 April 1901 W Beardmore and *d* 31 Aug 1915

    (2) Jessie Ellen; *d unm* 24 Oct 1952

1 Eliza Dorothea; *m* 1838 Count Giovanni Salamos, of Patras, Greece, and *d* 19 Aug 1861

The 12th Bt's bro,

Sir Dennis George Harmsworth Tuite, 13th Bt, MBE (1946); *b* 26 Jan 1904; *educ* St Paul's; Maj RE WW II; *m* 15 Feb 1947 *Margaret Essie [Margaret Lady Tuite, 7 Vicarage Gdns, Grayshott, Surrey GU26 6NH], only dau of Col Walter Leslie Dundas, DSO, IA, of Farnham, Surrey, and *d* 1981, leaving:

1 Sir CHRISTOPHER HUGH TUITE, **14th and present Bt**

2 +Jeremy Denis [Jeremy Tuite Esq, Haye Farm, Fingringhoe, Essex]; *b* 8 Dec 1951; *educ* Wellington and Leeds U (MB, FRCS); *m* 1978 (*divorce* 1997) Anne, dau of J Ebdon-Robinson, and has:

    (1) +Anthony; *b* 1982

    (2) +Edward Jeremy; *b* 1984

    (3) +James Carey John; *b* 1987

    (1) *Sally Anne; *b* 1990

3 +Patrick Leslie; *b* 10 Feb 1954; *educ* Wellington and Leeds U (BSc); *m* 1992 *Gillie M, dau of Dr K Martin McNicol, of Grayshott, Surrey

TUPPER

Arms: Per fess az. and or on a fess erm. between two boars passant in chief or and a sprig of mayflower slipped and leaved in base ppr. three escallops gu. **Crest:** Upon a mount vert a greyhound statant sa., charged on the body with two escallops or, holding in the mouth a sprig of mayflower as in the arms. **Motto:** *L'Espoir est ma force* ('Hope is my strength'). **Creation:** Bt. (UK) 13 Sept 1888.

SIR CHARLES HIBBERT TUPPER, 5TH BT, of Armdale, Halifax, Nova Scotia [Sir Charles Tupper Bt, Suite 1101, 955 Marine Dve, W Vancouver, BC V7T 1A9, Canada]; *b* 4 July 1930; *s* 1967; *m* 13 June 1959 (*divorce* 1976) Bernice Yvonne Quinn and has:

    1 +CHARLES HIBBERT [Charles Tupper Esq, 5164 Sam's Way, Nanaimo, BC V9T 6C4, Canada]; *b* 10 July 1964; *m* 1987 *(Elizabeth) Ann Heaslip and has:

        (1) *Cara-Lyn Ann; *b* 1991

Lineage: At some point prior to 1522 two brothers fled persecution, presumably religious (for example because they were followers of Martin Luther), in their native Hesse Cassel, Upper Saxony, and settled in Holland. The descendant of one, Daniel Tupper, was in 1813 Burgomaster of Rotterdam. Another member of the family settled at Sandwich, Kent, and was ancestor of:

THOMAS TUPPER; migrated to Sangus (subsequently Lynn), Mass., 1635; moved elsewhere in the colony in 1637 and with nine companions founded and incorporated the town of Sandwich, Mass.; had:

THOMAS TUPPER; *b* 1637; *m* Martha, dau of Govr Mayhew, of Martha's Vineyard, and had:

ELIAKIM TUPPER; had:

ELIAKIM TUPPER; had:

CHARLES TUPPER, of Cornwallis, Nova Scotia, where he moved from Lebanon, Conn., 1760; *m* 24 Oct 1762 Elizabeth West and *d* aged 72, leaving, with 10en other sons and four daus:

Rev CHARLES TUPPER, of Kingston, Nova Scotia; *b* 6 Aug 1794; DD; *m* Miriam (*d* 4 July 1851), widow of John Lowe and dau of James Lockhart, of Parrsboro, Cumberland, NS, and *d* 19 Jan 1881, leaving, with other issue:

Sir Charles Tupper, 1st Bt (UK), so *cr* 13 Sept 1888, PC (Canada 1870 (Pres 1870–72), UK 1907), GCMG (1886, KCMG 1879), CB (1867), of Armdale, Halifax, *b* 2 July 1821; MP (NS and Canadian Parls) 36 years, PM Nova Scotia 1864–67, Dominion Min of: Inland Revenue 1872–73, Customs 1873, Public Works 1878–79 and Railwys and Canals 1879–84, Canadian HC London 1883–87 and 1888–96, Min Finance 1887–88, Plenipotentiary Fishery Commn Washington, DC, 1887–88 and negotiation of Treaty on Franco-Canadian Trade 1893, memb Exec Cncl Imp Inst and Br Empire League, Sec State Canada 1896, PM 1896, Leader Oppn 1896–1900; Hon LLD Cambridge, Edinburgh, Acadia NS and Queen's U Canada; LRCS and MD Edin, FRGS; *m* 8 Oct 1846 Frances Amelia (*d* 11 May 1912), dau of Silas Hibbert Morse, of Amherst, Cumberland, NS, and *d* 30 Oct 1915, having had, with two other daus (*d* young):

1 James Stewart, QC (Canada 1890); *b* 29 Oct 1851; *educ* McGill (BA); barrister Canada 1875, Bencher Law Soc of Manitoba 1900, Treas 1906–10, Pres 1910–13; *m* 1st 8 Sept 1875 Mary Wilson (*d* 7 Aug 1876), dau of Andrew Robertson, of Elmbank, Montreal, and had:

  (1) Marie Stewart

1 (cont.) James Tupper *m* 2nd 9 June 1880 Ada Campbell (*d* 26 Sept 1921), dau of Hon Sir Thomas Galt, and *dvp* 29 April 1915, leaving by her:

  (1) **Sir Charles Stewart Tupper, 2nd Bt**, KC (1928); *b* 8 Aug 1884; *educ* McGill (BA 1905); barrister Manitoba 1908, Lt 43rd Bn Cameron Highrs Canada WW I; *m* 17 Dec 1910 Margaret Peters, only dau of Charles Morse, DCL, QC, of Ottawa, and *d* 16 July 1960, leaving:

    1a *Margot Stewart [Miss Margot Tupper, Portage Sch, Portage La Prairie, Manitoba, Canada]; *b* 8 Jan 1928

  (2) Jessie Campbell

  (3) Frances

2 Charles Hibbert (Hon Sir), KCMG, of Parkside, Vancouver, BC, PC Canada, KC; *b* 3 Aug 1855; *educ* Harvard (LLB); MP Picton NS 1882, 1887, 1888, 1891, 1896 and 1900, Min Marine and Fisheries 1888–94, Min Justice 1894–96, Bencher Law Soc of BC; *m* 9 Sept 1879 Janet, DGStJ (*d* 1 June 1935), dau of Hon James Macdonald, of Blink Bonnie, Halifax, Ch Justice Nova Scotia, and *d* 30 March 1927, leaving:

  (1) **Sir Charles Tupper, 3rd Bt**; *b* 10 Dec 1880; *educ* McGill (BSc 1901); civ engr, Lt 72nd Bn Seaforths of Canada and 11th Canadian MR (despatches), Maj 11th Canadian Rlwy Troops WW I; *m* 12 April 1910 Mary Mira Douglas, dau of Hon Arthur R Dickey, QC, of Amherst, NS, and *d* 19 June 1962, leaving:

    1a *Janet Macdonald [Mrs Philip Underwood, PO Box 117, Grafton, Ont, Canada]; *b* 21 July 1920; *m* 22 Dec 1944 *Capt Philip Lionel Underwood, late RCA, s of Harry Lionel Underwood, of Toronto, and has:

      1b *Harry Charles Gordon; *b* 20 June 1951; *m* 1984 *Denise Ireland

      1b *Mary Fielding; *b* 4 Dec 1946; *m* 6 June 1969 *Claude Frédéric de Kerckhove Varent, s of André de Kerckhove Varent, and has:

        1c *Charles André Philippe; *b* 1976

        2c *Derrick Tupper Daniel; *b* 1978

      2b *Nora Frances; *b* 18 April 1958; *m* 1984 *Gary Jay Tenenbaum

    2a *Dorothy Joyce [Mrs Edward Dunlop, 6 Meredith Crescent, Toronto M4W 3B6, Canada]; *b* 29 Nov 1922; *m* 12 Aug 1944 *Maj Edward Arunah Dunlop, OBE, GM, late QO Rifles Canada, s of Hon Edward Arunah Dunlop, and has:

      1b *Edward Arunah; *b* 1946; *m* 1976 *Valerine Glen Hardacre

      1b *Charlotte Mary Ferguson; *b* 1949

  (2) JAMES MACDONALD (Sir), **4th Bt**

  (3) Reginald Hibbert, QC; *b* 25 Oct 1893; LLD BC, Maj 2nd Res Bn Seaforth Highrs Canada, Midshipman RN, WW I (wounded); *m* 27 Sept 1915 Isabel Marion Wilson (*d* 1969) and had:

    1a +Charles Gordon Hibbert (Victor); *b* 30 Oct 1918; Lt Seaforth Highrs Canada WW II; *m* 8 June 1946 *Margaret Ada (BA McGill), dau of James Albert Campbell, QC, of Vancouver, and has:

      1b +Charles Reginald Hibbert; *b* 20 Dec 1947

    2a +David Wilson Hibbert; *b* 18 June 1921; LLB, RCAF WW II 1942–45; *m* 1st 31 May 1947 Joan Margot (*d* 19–), dau of Col Austin Gillies, VD, of Ottawa; *m* 2nd — and by his 1st w has:

      1b +Sidney Victor Hibbert; *b* 24 May 1948

      2b +Charles Austin Hibbert; *b* 28 Sept 1951

      1b *Julie Isabel; *b* 7 April 1953

  (4) Victor Gordon, MC; *b* 4 Feb 1896; Capt (A/Maj) 16th Canadian Inf Bn Canadian Expdny Force WW I (despatches, wounded twice); *ka* 9 April 1917

  (1) Sophie Almon; *m* 4 Dec 1905 Capt Cecil Mark Merritt, 16th Bn Canadian Scottish (*ka* Ypres 26 April 1915), and had issue

  (2) Frances Lillian; *m* Sept 1920 Lt-Col G H Kirkpatrick, DSO, and *d* 28 July 1940, having had issue

  (3) Janet Miriam Grace; *m* 30 Dec 1915 Maj Walter Glen Cuyler Holland, Canadian Scottish Regt, and had issue

3 William Johnston, KC 1914; *b* 29 June 1862; barrister 1886, Lt-Govr Manitoba 1934, KGStJ; *m* 6 July 1887 Margaret (*d* 28 Feb 1950), dau of Hon James Macdonald, of Blink Bonnie, and *d* 16 Dec 1947, having had:

  (1) Charles William; *b* 26 Sept 1898; Lt Canadian Artillery WW I; *m* 1st 1929 Rae Macdonald and had:

    1a *Margaret Ray [Mrs William Price, 700 Cardinal St, St Laurent, Quebec, Canada]; *b* 1931; BA, BLS; *m* 1956 *William Macdonald Price and had:

    1b *Charles Macdonald [Charles Price Esq, 1354 Gatehouse Dve, Mississauga, Ont L5H 1A5, Canada]; *b* 1958; MD, CM; *m* 1983 *Mary Shanahan, BEng, and has:

      1c *Rae Francis; *b* 1989

    2c *Thomas McMurray; *b* 1990

    3c *Joseph Charles; *b* 1992

  2b *Scott William; *b* 1960; ARCT; *m* 1988 *Martine Chevrier

(1) (cont.) Charles Tupper *m* 2nd 1941 Winifred Lillian Craske (*d* 24 May 1956) and *d* 31 Oct 1960, leaving by her:

  1a +Charles James; *b* 28 Sept 1942; BScE

(2) Stewart Macdonald; *b* 4 June 1902; 2nd Lt Winnipeg Rifles; *d* 4 March 1960

(1) Katherine Gladys

(2) Frances Amelia; *d* 4 Oct 1902

(3) Emma Lilian; *m* Bertram Stanley Harris and *d* 7 Feb 1942, leaving issue

(4) Edith Margaret; *d* unm 9 Feb 1962

1 Emma; *m* 22 July 1869 Maj-Gen Donald Roderick Cameron, CMG, of The Mount, Bexley Heath, Kent, and *d* 5 Nov 1925, leaving issue. He *d* 23 Dec 1921

The 3rd Bt's bro,

Sir James Macdonald Tupper, 4th Bt; *b* 22 Dec 1887; Assist Commr RCMP, ret 1941, Hon Lt-Col; *m* 26 March 1928 (Mary) Agnes Jean Collins and *d* 23 June 1967, leaving:

1 Sir CHARLES HIBBERT TUPPER, **5th and present Bt**

1 *Janet Mary [Mrs William Couldwell, 50-5880 Hampton Place, Vancouver, BC V6T 2E9, Canada]; *b* 28 Feb 1929; trained Vancouver Gen Hosp Sch of Nursing 1951; *m* 17 March 1951 *William John Couldwell, CM, MD, W/Cdr RCAF Res (ret), s of William Blythe Couldwell, of S Burnaby, BC, and has:

  (1) *William Tupper [Dr William Couldwell, 16 Tarryabit Dve, Waccabuc, NY 10597, USA]; *b* 15 Dec 1955; BSc, MDCM, PhD; has:

    1a *Mitchell William Galen; *b* 1991

    1a *Sandrine Marie Camille; *b* 1991

    2a *Genevieve Christine; *b* 1993

  (1) *Susan Janice [Mrs John McCormack, 4666 West 3rd Ave, Vancouver, BC V6R 1N4, Canada]; *b* 18 Feb 1953; BA, BArch; *m* 1977 *John Joseph McCormack, Dip Arch, MRAIC, and has:

    1a *John Paget; *b* 1981

    2a *Brendan William; *b* 1984

    3a *Liam James Couldwell; *b* 1988

  (2) *Sandra Lee [Mrs Sandra Hegedus, 204 3641 West 28th Ave, Vancouver, BC V6S 7S3, Canada]; *b* 15 Sept 1954; BA; *m* 1982 (*divorce* 1987) Gabor Hegedus (*d* 1990) and has:

    1a *Andras Zoltan Couldwell; *b* 1983

TURING

Arms: Arg. on a bend sa. three boar's heads couped or.
Crest: A hand holding a helmet ppr. **Supporters:** Two stags ppr.
Motto: *Audentes fortuna juvat* ('Fortune aids the daring').
Creation: Bt. (NS) *c* 1638.

SIR JOHN DERMOT TURING, 12TH BT, of Foveran, Aberdeenshire [Sir John Turing Bt, 68 Marshalswick Lane, St Albans, Herts AL1 4XF]; *b* 26 Feb 1961; *s* 3rd cousin once-removed 1987; *educ* Sherborne, King's Coll Cambridge and New Coll Oxford; *m* 26 July 1986 *Nicola Jane, dau of Malcolm Douglas Simmonds, of Wimborne, Dorset, and has:

1 +JOHN MALCOLM FERRIER; *b* 5 Sept 1988

2 +James Robert Edward; *b* 6 Jan 1991

Lineage: WILLIAM de TURIN (possibly kinsman of Adam Turin, concerned in matters relating to the park of Fyvie 1323) had a charter of Foveran, Aberdeenshire, from DAVID II on its recognition from Henry de Steabroke; probably f of:

ANDREW TURIN of Foveran; *fl* 1388–1424; had:

JOHN TURIN of Foveran, of which had a (presumably confirmatory) charter 1441; *m* Janet Hay and had:

WILLIAM TURIN of Foveran; *d c* 1482; putative f of:

JOHN TURIN of Foveran; *m* Catherine Vaux and *d c* 1503, leaving:

WILLIAM TURIN of Foveran; living 1508; had:

GILBERT TURIN; *m c* 1505 Helen Cheyne and *d c* 29 March 1527, leaving:

WILLIAM TURIN of Foveran; *d c* 9 Feb 1555/6, leaving:

ROBERT TURIN of Foveran; *m c* 31 May 1556 Helen Carnegie (*see* FIFE, D) and *d c* 1580, leaving:

Sir WILLIAM TURING of Foveran; *d c* 1613, leaving, with other issue:

1 **Sir John Turing, 1st Bt** (NS), so *cr c* 1638, supposedly with remainder to heirs male whatsoever, of Foveran; served heir to an er bro (his f's est s) 1616; supported CHARLES I in Bishops' Wars; *m* 25 May 1624 Barbara (*d* Feb 1639), dau of George Gordon of Gight, and *d* 1662, having had:

(1) George; *m* (contract 18 June 1652) Margaret, dau of John Forbes of Leslie, and *dvp c* 27 Feb 1657, leaving:

1a **Sir John Turing, 2nd Bt**, though not recorded as having publicly assumed the title; sold the family estate; *d* unm Feb 1682

2 Henry, of Savock in Foveran; *d c* 27 Feb 1657, leaving:

(1) John; living 1657; *m* Janet Seaton (*m* 2nd Robert Harvey of Mamulay) and had, with other issue:

1a **Rev Sir John Turing, 3rd Bt**; *b* 1680; Min Drumblade 1703–33; *m* 24 Dec 1700 Jean, dau of Rev John Dunbar of Forglen, and *d* 5 Feb 1733, having had, with other issue:

1b **Rev Sir Alexander Turing, 4th Bt**; *bapt* 9 Aug 1702; Min Oyne 1729–82; *m* 11 April 1740 Anna Brown and *d* 24 Aug 1782, having had, with other issue:

1c John; *bapt* 19 May 1742; *d* young

2c **Rev Sir Inglis Turing, 5th Bt**; *b* 1743; Rector St Thomas-in-the-Vale Jamaica; *d* unm Jamaica 15 Nov 1791

3c **Sir Robert Turing, 6th Bt**, of Banff; *bapt* 25 Feb 1745; *m* 12 Oct 1797 Anne (*d* 7 Dec 1809), dau of Col Donald Campbell of Glendsaddel, and *dspm* 21 Oct 1831, leaving:

1d Anna Amelia

2d Mary; *m* Maj-Gen Francis Aiskell, HEICS

4c Arthur James; *bapt* 19 March 1756; Capt 4th Bn Madras NI; *d* between 2 July and 1 Oct 1793

2b Robert, of Fort St George; *bapt* 11 Oct 1711; surgn; *m* 14 Jan 1755 Mary de Morgan (*bur* 17 Jan 1800), widow of Thomas Taylor, and *d* 26 Dec 1764, leaving:

1c Robert; *b* 17 April 1760; *dsp* 5 June 1801

1c Mary; *b* 5 April 1757; *m* 30 Aug 1773 her cousin John Turing (*see* below)

2c Helen; *b* 14 Oct 1758; *m* 30 Aug 1773 Edward Saunders and had issue

1b Helen; *bapt* 13 May 1716; *m* her cousin Henry Turing (*see* below) and was *bur* 19 Nov 1776

2a Henry, of Coupar, Fife; merchant; living 1706; *m* Margaret Lasone and had, with other issue:

1b Henry, of London; *bapt* 28 Sept 1708; *m* his cousin Helen (*see* above) and was *bur* 3 Oct 1777, having had, with other issue:

1c John, of London and Knowlton, Kent; memb Cncl Madras; *m* 30 Aug 1773 his cousin Mary (*see* above) and *d* 19 Dec 1808, having had issue

3a Walter (Rev); Min Rayne; *m* 1 March 1709 Anne (*d* 1746), dau of James Ogilvie of Bodentowl, and *d* 3 Jan 1743, having had, with other issue:

1b James; factor Campvere, merchant in Holland; *m* (contract dated 17 Dec 1748) Martha Colnet and *d* 19 Dec 1788, having had, with other issue:

1c John, of Middleburg; *b* 13 Jan 1751; factor Campvere; *m* 10 Dec 1787 Margaret, dau of William Tennent, of Musselburgh, and *d* 4 July 1798, leaving:

1d **Sir James Henry Turing, 7th Bt**; *b* 10 Dec 1791; Br Consul Rotterdam; *m* 20 Sept 1821 Antoinette (*d* 19 April 1884), dau of Sir Alexander Ferrier, KH, and *d* 13 Feb 1860, having had:

1e John Alexander; *b* 1823; *d* 1824

2e James Henry; *b* 1824; *d* 1836

3e **Sir Robert Fraser Turing, 8th Bt**, as which confirmed by Lyon King of Arms 1882 and ratified by a PC Special Ctee 1912 following a challenge to his right to bear the title; *b* 29 Aug 1827; Br Consul Rotterdam; *m* 1st 29 June 1853 Catherine Georgiana (*d* 6 Aug 1905), dau of Walter Stevenson Davidson, of Lowndes Sq, London, and Saxonbury, Kent; *m* 2nd 22 Aug 1906 Ethel Sophia (*d* 26 Sept 1927), 2nd dau of Rev George B Perry-Ayscough (*see* CONGLETON, B) and widow of Rev Herbert Meade Ramus, and *d* 4 Jan 1913, leaving by his 1st w:

1f **Sir James Walter Turing, 9th Bt**; *b* 3 Jan 1862; Lt 2nd Vol Bn Roy Sussex Regt; *m* 5 Feb 1891 Mabel Rose (*d* 26 Oct 1952), dau of Andrew Caldecott, of Pishiobury, Herts, and *d* 21 Feb 1928, leaving:

1g **Sir Robert Andrew Henry Turing, 10th Bt**; *b* 13 Sept 1895; *educ* Eton and RMC Sandhurst; Capt Res Offrs Rifle Bde WW I (despatches, wounded); *d* unm 6 Jan 1970

2g **Sir John Leslie Turing, 11th Bt**, MC; *b* 13 Sept 1895; *educ* Wellington; Lt Seaforth Highrs WW I (wounded); *m* 1975 Irene Nina (*d* 15 Feb 1997), dau of Trevor John Tatham and widow of Capt W W P Shirley-Rollison, RN, and *dsp* 1987

1f Catherine Antoinette; *b* 28 March 1854; *m* 22 June 1895 Rev William Frederick Shaw (*d* 2 Feb 1931), Rector W Stoke, Preb Chichester, and *d* 11 March 1936, leaving issue

2f Blanche Amelia; *b* 5 Jan 1857; *m* 14 July 1886 Robert Walter Wordsworth (*d* 27 April 1914), s of Rt Rev Charles Wordsworth, Bp St Andrews, and *d* 12 Dec 1944, leaving issue

3f Florence Ellen; *b* 28 Oct 1859; *d* unm 3 Oct 1947

4f Julia; *b* March 1869; *d* unm 8 May 1948

4e Alexander; *b* 1835; *d* unm 1882

5e Henry, ISO; *b* 1 Aug 1843; Br Consul S Holland 1882–1913; *m* 8 Oct 1868 Jeanne Marie Catherina (*d* 2 Dec 1917), dau of Sebastian Abraham Chabot, of Rotterdam, and *d* 22 March 1922, leaving:

1f Louis; *b* 24 Sept 1870; *d* unm 28 May 1945

1f Antoinette; *d* unm 25 Dec 1960

2f Emily; *d* unm 12 Oct 1936

3f Agnes Nancy; *m* 31 March 1898 Karl Staib (*d* 13 March 1930), s of Michael Staib, of Ulm, Württemberg, and *d* 20 Feb 1966

6e Edward; *b* 1 Aug 1843; accidentally drowned in Lake Neuchâtel 1862

1e Antoinette Margaret Campbell; *m* 10 Aug 1842 Rt Rev Henry Mackenzie, DD, Bp Suffragan Nottingham, and *d* 20 Dec 1907, leaving issue (*see* MACKENZIE, Bt, of Coul)

2d John Robert; *b* 1793; *m* Jane Fraser and *d* 1828, leaving:

1e John Robert (Rev); *b* 1826; Vicar Edwinstowe, Notts; *m* Fanny Boyd and *d* 1883, leaving:

1f Arthur; *ka* unm NW Frontier India 1899

2f Julius Mathison; *b* 9 Nov 1873; ICS; *m* 1 Oct 1907 Ethel Sara (*d* 6 March 1976), dau of Edward Waller Stoney, CIE, MInstCE, and *d* 3 Aug 1947, leaving:

1g John Ferrier; *b* 1 Sept 1908; slr 1931, Queen's Roy Regt WW II, with Claims Commn established by Lord Lyon King of Arms 1960; *m* 1st 1934 (*divorce* 1960) Joan, dau of Robert Humphreys, ICS, of Cork, and *d* 21 Feb 1983, having had:

1h Brian John; *b* 17 April 1943; *d* an infant

1h *Inagh Jean [Mrs Herbert Aspinall, 21 Hoyles Rd, Wellington, Somerset TA21 9AH]; *b* 25 Jan 1936; *m* 1st 1960 (*divorce* 1980) Warren Gray, slr, of Taunton, Somerset; *m* 2nd 1980 Herbert Aspinall (*d* 23 Oct 1997) and by her 1st husb has:

1i *Mark Warren; *b* 1961; *m* 1994 *Rita Paula Keller and has:

1j *Natalie Lisa; *b* 1995

2i *Stephen Paul; *b* 20 Oct 1969

1i *Rachel Mary; *b* 1963; *m* 1990 *Mark Richard Barnes, and has:

1j *Thomas David; *b* 1993

2j *George Christopher; *b* 1997

1j *Anna Clare; *b* 1997

2i *Deborah Jean; *b* 1964; *m* 1995 *Jason Wright and has:

1j *Kiah Callula; *b* 1996

2h *Shuna [Mrs Shuna Hunt, 3 The High St, Small Dole, Henfield, Sussex]; *b* 11 May 1940; *m* 1968 (*divorce* 1983) Albert Hunt and has:

1i *Nevil; *b* 1970

3h *Janet Ferrier [Mrs Alan Robinson, 137 Westfields, St Albans, Herts AL3 4JR]; *b* 1 Feb 1947; *m* 1981 *Alan John Robinson, ARICS, and has:

1i *Lisa Ferrier; *b* 1982

2i *Clare Elizabeth; *b* 1985

1g (cont.) John Turing *m* 2nd 1960 *Beryl Mary Ada [Mrs John Turing, 72 Chirgwin Rd, Truro, Cornwall TR1 1TT], dau of Herbert Vaughan Hann, and by her had:

2h **Sir JOHN DERMOT TURING, 12th and present Bt**

2g Alan Mathison, OBE; *b* 23 June 1912; *educ* Sherborne and King's Coll Cambridge (Fell 1935); FRS, Reader Mathematics Manchester U 1948–51; *d* unm 7 June 1954

3f Harvey Doria; *b* 1 May 1877; *m* 20 July 1918 Violet Ethel (*d* 17 Jan 1961), dau of Rev Harry Alsager Sheringham, and *d* 7 Sept 1950, leaving:

1g *Penelope Anne Tryon [Miss Penelope Turing, 411 Beatty House, Dolphin Sq, London SW1 3PL]; *b* 5 April 1925; author and lecturer

1f Fanny Jane; *m* 6 April 1893 Sir Herbert Trustram Eve, KBE, and *d* 1 Feb 1934, leaving issue (*see* SILSOE, B)

2f Charlotte Jessie; *d* unm *c* 1942

3f Helen Margaret; *d* unm *c* 1942

4f Sybil Montague; Deaconess; *d* 6 Jan 1952

3d Charles Edward; *b* 1794; *d* 1802

TURNER OF CAMDEN

Creation: B. (LP, UK) 1985.

THE BARONESS TURNER OF CAMDEN, of Camden, Greater London (Muriel Winifred Price) [The Rt Hon The Baroness Turner of Camden, 87 Canfield Gdns, London NW6]; *b* 18 Sept 1927; Assist Gen Sec ASTMS 1970–87; Memb: Occupational Pensions Bd 1978–93, Central Arbitration Ctee Brokers' Registration Cncl 1980–90, TUC General Cncl 1981–87, Equal Opportunities Commn 1982–88, dir Ian Greer Assocs 1991–97; Jr Spokesperson Social Security 1986–96, Pncpl Oppn Spokesperson Employment 1988–96, Ho of Lds Chm Ombudsman Cncl, PIA 1994–; Hon LLD Leicester U 1992; *m* 1955 *Reginald Thomas Frederick Turner, MC, DFC, DFC (USA), W/Cdr RAF.

Lineage: EDWARD PRICE had:

MURIEL WINIFRED, *cr* a **Baroness**

TWEEDDALE

Arms: Quarterly,1st and 4th, argent three escutcheons gules (for HAY); 2nd, gules three bars ermine (for GIFFORD); 3rd, azure three cinquefoils argent (for FRASER). **Crest:** A goat's head erased argent, horned or. **Supporters:** Two bucks proper, attired or, collared azure, charged with three cinquefoils argent. **Motto:** *Spair noucht* ('Spare nought'). **Creations:** L. (S) 29 Jan 1487/8, E. (S) 1 Dec 1646 (Tweeddale), M., E. (Gifford) and V. (S) 17 Dec 1694, B. (UK) 6 Oct 1881.

THE 13TH MARQUESS OF TWEEDDALE, Earl of Tweeddale, Earl of Gifford, Viscount of Walden, Lord Hay of Yester and Baron Tweeddale of Yester (Edward Douglas John Hay) [The Most Hon The Marquess of Tweeddale, House of Lords, London SW1A 0PW]; *b* 6 Aug 1947; *s* f 1979, also as hereditary Chamberlain of Dunfermline and presumed heir to the btcy of Hay of Smithfield; *educ* Milton Abbey and Trin Coll Oxford (BA Hons PPE).

Lineage: Sir JOHN de HAYA; probably kin to the HAYs later Earls of Erroll (*qv*); *m* the dau and heiress of Robert de Lyne, of Locherwort, Co Edinburgh, and had:

Sir WILLIAM de HAYA of Locherwort; living 1263; swore fealty to EDWARD I 17 July 1291 and 28 Aug 1296 after the Battle of Dunbar, at which he was captured by the English; *d* on or after 31 Oct 1308, leaving:

Sir GILBERT de HAYA of Locherwort; *fl temp* ROBERT I; *m* Margaret, dau and coheir of Sir Simon Fraser, of Oliver Castle and Neidpath (*see* SALTOUN, L), and had:

Sir THOMAS de HAYA of Locherwort; *m* Lora, dau and heiress of Sir William de Cuningesburgh and widow of Richard de Bykretone, thus acquiring Tullybody, Clackmannanshire, and *d* by 15 Oct 1335, leaving:

Sir WILLIAM de HAYA of Locherwort; Sheriff Peebles 1387; *d* by 29 Aug 1392, leaving:

Sir THOMAS de HAYA of Locherwort; *b* by 1357; Sheriff Peebles; *m* Janet/Jean, er dau and coheir of Hugh Gifford of Yester, Haddingtonshire, thus acquiring the castle and a quarter of the lands of Yester, and *d* after 1397, leaving:

Sir WILLIAM HAY of Locherwort and Yester; *m* his putative cousin Alice, allegedly dau of Sir Thomas de la Haye, 7th of Erroll (*see* ERROLL, E), and *d* 1421, leaving:

1 Thomas (Sir), of Locherwort and Yester; *d* unm Feb 1433/4
2 DAVID (Sir)
3 Edmund; had issue (*see* HAY, Bt, of Alderston)
1 Margaret, *m* 2nd Earl of Angus (*see* HAMILTON and BRANDON, D)
2 Janet/Jean; *m* Sir Alexander Home of Home (*see* HOME, E)
3 Alice; *m* her cousin Gilbert of the Haye and was mother by him of 1st Earl of Erroll (*qv*)

4 Elizabeth; *m* Duncan Macdowal of Makerstown

The 2nd s,
Sir DAVID HAY of Yester, of which he acquired 1452 a further half in addition to the quarter share he already possessed, and Locherwort; *m* Elizabeth, only dau of 1st Earl of Angus (*see* HAMILTON and BRANDON, D) and widow of 1st Lord Forbes (*qv*), and *d* by 2 Sept 1478, leaving an est s:

JOHN HAY, **1st Lord Hay of Yester** (S), so *cr* 29 Jan 1487/8, of Wester Hoprew, Peeblesshire, which his f settled on him; Sheriff Peebles; *m* 1st by 7 July 1462 Mariot, dau of 1st Lord Lindsay of the Byres (*see* LINDSAY, E), and had:
1 Thomas, *Master of Yester*, of Hoprew; *m* probably by 1483 Elizabeth, possibly dau of 2nd Lord Borthwick (*qv*), and *dvp* probably between 29 Sept 1502 and 8 Nov 1504, leaving:
(1) Thomas (Sir), *Master of Yester*, of Hoprew; *b c* 1483; ktd by 7 July 1508; *dsp* by 23 Oct 1508 and if he survived his gf, which is by no means certain, would have briefly been **2nd Lord Hay of Yester**

The **1st Lord** *m* 2nd *c* 1468 Elizabeth, dau and eventual heiress of George Cunningham of Belton, and *d* it is thought Sept 1508 and definitely by 23 Oct 1508, having by her had:
2 JOHN, **2nd (3rd?) Lord**
3 William, of Nether Menzion, of which had a charter from his f 9 Oct 1495; *d* by 12 July 1512
4 George, of Oliver Castle, which his f made over to him 21 Feb 1502/3, and of Menzion following his er bro's death; *m* Euphemia Wauchope and was ancestor of the HAYs of Menzion
5 Nicholas; Preb Bothans; *d* 1498
1 Margaret; *m* 1491 4th Lord Borthwick (*qv*) and had issue
2 Isobel; *m* by 1496 Robert Lauder of The Bass

The 1st LORD's est surv son,
JOHN HAY, **2nd (3rd?) Lord Hay of Yester**; *b c* 1470; had 4 May 1482 charter of the (territorial) Barony of Snaid, Dumfriesshire, ktd by 15 Feb 1503/4; Sheriff Depute Peebles; acquired 1512 the remnant of the Yester lands; *m* Elizabeth Crichton and was *ka* Battle of Flodden 9 Sept 1513, having had:
1 JOHN, **3rd (4th?) Lord**
2 Thomas; Preceptor Hosp of St Leonard's Peebles 1521, Provost Bothan 1539, Archpriest Dunbar 1542
3 John, of Smithfield; living 27 May 1528; had issue (*see* 1949 edn HAY, Bt, of Smithfield)
1 Elizabeth; *m* James Tweedie of Drumelzier and had issue
2 Christian; *m* William Stewart of Traquair and had issue (*see* MORAY, E)
3 Jean/Marion; *m* George Broun of Colstoun (*d* by 15 Feb 1519/20) and *d* June 1564, leaving issue (*see* BROUN, Bt)

The 2nd (3rd?) LORD's est s,
JOHN HAY, **3rd (4th?) Lord Hay of Yester**; had a charter of the lands of Hoprew, Peebles 7 Oct 1509, ktd by 10 June 1510; *m* by 17 Sept 1509 Elizabeth, sis of 6th Earl of Angus (*see* HAMILTON and BRANDON, D), and *d* 12 May–19 July 1543, leaving:
1 JOHN, **4th (5th?) Lord**
2 Thomas; Provost Bothans; *d* between 30 Jan 1555/6 and 2 May 1558
1 Elizabeth; *m c* 15 June 1527 4th Lord Seton (*see* EGLINTON and WINTON, E)
2 Beatrice; *m* William Wauchope, Yr. of Niddrie (for whose family in later generations *see* DON-WAUCHOPE, Bt)

The 3rd (4th?) LORD's est s,
JOHN HAY, **4th (5th?) Lord Hay of Yester**, PC (by 25 June 1545); *b c* 1510; captured by English at their victory over Scots of Pinkie 10 Sept 1547 and sent to the Tower of London, where he remained till peace was made; Provost Peebles 1555; *m* just prior to 18 Oct 1533 Margaret, est dau of 4th Lord Livingston, and *d* by 30 Jan 1555/6, having had, with two yr sons (Thomas, Min of the Cross Kirk of Peebles 1566–84, *d* by 11 June 1584; James, living 28 March 1573) and two daus (Margaret, *m* (contract 11 Feb 1566/7) Sir Robert Lauder of Poppill; Christian, *m* Henry Lauder):

WILLIAM HAY, **5th (6th?) Lord Hay of Yester**, PC (S by 1565); *b* 1538; Sheriff Peebles Jan 1555/6, Provost Peebles 1562; fought for MARY QUEEN OF SCOTS Battle of Langside 1568 but a Protestant certainly by 1570; involved in Raid of Ruthven (*see* CARLISLE, E); *m* (contract 28 Oct 1559) Margaret, dau of Sir John Kerr of Ferniehirst (*see* LOTHIAN, M), and *d* Aug 1586, having had:
1 WILLIAM, **6th (7th?) Lord Hay of Yester**, PC (S 1589); *b c* 1561; got regrant of lands and honours 21 Feb 1590/1 with limitation to heirs male but *d* before being reinfeoffed in them; *m* Mary, dau of John Maxwell, 5th Lord Herries of Terregles (*qv*) in right of his w, and *d c* 29 May 1591, having had:
(1) Margaret; living unm 1627
(2) Jean; *m* Alexander Horsburgh, of Peeblesshire, and had:
1a John
(3) Agnes; living unm 1627
(4) Christian; *m* (contract 26 Feb 1603) Archibald Newton of Newton, Haddingtonshire
(5) Elizabeth; *m* by 23 June 1617 James Tweedie of Drumelzier, Peeblesshire
(6) Grizel; *m* (contract 12 Feb 1620) George Hepburn of Alderston
2 JAMES, **7th (8th?) Lord**
1 Margaret; *m* 1582 7th Lord Borthwick (*qv*) and had issue
2 Catherine; *m* (contract 15 Feb 1587/88) Robert Swinton of Swinton and had issue
3 Jean; *m* Sir James Hay of Barra
4 Elizabeth; *m* William Ker of Broomland
5 Grizel; *m* 7 June 1576 (*annulled* 18 Aug 1585) Robert Home, Yr. of Heuch
6 Beatrix; *m* by 23 March 1640 William Congilton, Yr. of Congilton

The 6th (7th?) LORD's bro,
JAMES HAY, **7th (8th?) Lord Hay of Yester**, KB (1603); *b c* 1564; Sheriff Peebles; his er bro's regrant confirmed 29 May 1591; *m* by 6 Aug 1591 Margaret, dau

of 1st Earl of Lothian of the 1606 *cr* (*see* LOTHIAN, M), and *d* 3 Feb 1608/9, having had issue:

1 JOHN, **1st Earl**

2 William (Sir), of Linplum; had a charter of his lands 14 Sept 1611; *m* (contract 18 Nov 1618) Anne (*bur* Oct 1658), dau of William Murray of Dunearn, and *d* by 18 April 1648, having had, with other issue:

(1) Sir JAMES HAY, 1st Bt (NS), so *cr* 26 March 1667, of Linplum; MP Haddington 1669–74; *m* 1st (contract 4 Feb 1661) Jean, sis of Sir Francis Scott, 1st Bt, of Thirlestane (*see* NAPIER and ETTRICK, L); *m* 2nd 27 April 1682 Anna Livingston and *d* 1704, having by his 1st w had, with three daus (*d* unm):

1a John, Yr. of Linplum; *m* 4 July 1685 Jean, dau of Sir John Foulis, 1st Bt, of Ravelston (*see* FOULIS, Bt), and *dvp* by 16 April 1687, leaving:

1b Margaret; *b* 30 June 1686; *m* her cousin Lord William Hay (*see* below) and *d* 3 Oct 1753, leaving issue

2a Sir ROBERT HAY, 2nd and last Bt, of Linplum; Lt-Col Scots Greys; *d* unm 20 Dec 1751, when the btcy expired

(1) Margaret; *m* Sir John Baird of Newbyth (*see* BAIRD, Bt, of Saughton), and had issue

3 Robert; *dsp*

1 Margaret; *m* 1st (contract 15 Nov 1607), as his 3rd w, 1st Earl of Dunfermline (*see* EGLINTON and WINTON, E) and had issue; *m* 2nd *c* 1633 1st Earl of Callendar (*dsp* 25 March 1674) and *d* 30 Dec 1659

The 7th (8th?) LORD's est s,

JOHN HAY, **1st Earl of Tweeddale** (S), so *cr* 1 Dec 1646, with remainder to heirs male forever, PC (S 1641); *b* 1595–96; Sheriff Peeblesshire Feb 1608/9, Burgess Edinburgh 1616 and Glasgow 1638, Auditor Exchequer Feb 1633/4; Covenanter, hence opposed to CHARLES I's attempts to impose episcopalian church govt, cmdg troops in the two Bishops' Wars; Col of Foot for Co Edinburgh, Haddingtonshire and Peeblesshire Civil War, Commr of Estates 1643–51, but supported CHARLES II 1651; *m* 1st (contract 24 March and 5 April 1624) Jean (*d* 21 Aug 1625), dau of 1st Earl of Dunfermline (*see* EGLINTON and WINTON, E), and had:

1 JOHN, **1st Marquess**

The **1st Earl** *m* 2nd (contract 22 and 25 Dec 1641) Margaret (*m* 2nd 9th Earl of Glencairn (*see* CUNINGHAME, Bt) and *d* 27 Jan 1664/5), est dau of 6th Earl of Eglinto(u)n (*see* EGLINTON and WINTON, E), and *d* 25 May 1653, leaving by her:

2 William, of Drumelzier; *b* Dec 1649; *m* 23 Nov 1695 Elizabeth, only surv dau of 1st Viscount of Kingston (*see* EGLINTON and WINTON, E), and *d* 1726, having had:

(1) Alexander, of Drumelzier and Whittinghame; *m* 1st Anne (*d* 1743), 4th dau of 5th Lord Blantyre (*see* 1900 edn), and had, with other issue:

1a Alexander; Offr in E Indiaman *Norfolk*; *d* 6 Dec 1758

2a Robert, of Drumelzier, Whittinghame and Linplum; *b* 18 April 1731; HEICS; *m* 7 Feb 1786 Janet (*d* 29 Aug 1808), est dau of James Erskine of Cardross, and *d* 21 Aug 1807, leaving, with three other daus (*d* unm):

1b William, of Duns Castle, Berwicks, JP, DL; *b* 29 Feb 1788; Col Militia, Convenor Berwicks; *m* 13 May 1816 Mary (*d* 10 June 1863), er dau of Maj John Bradstreet Garstin, 65th Regt, only s of Lt-Col Robert Garstin, DL, of Harrold Ho, Beds, and *d* 16 May 1876, leaving, with two other daus (*d* unm):

1c William James, of Duns Castle, JP, DL; *b* 26 May 1827; *m* 12 Jan 1865 Margaret Caroline (*d* 29 March 1894), 2nd dau of William Hay, of Hopes, Haddington, and *dsp* 18 Dec 1893

2c Alexander Charles; *b* 24 Feb 1829; Gen Madras Army; *m* 18 April 1860 Annie (*d* 15 March 1923), dau of Maj-Gen Richard Stewart Dobbs, and *d* 8 May 1893, leaving:

1d William Hope; *b* 8 June 1862; *m* 16 Sept 1891 Emma Elizabeth (*d* 13 June 1970), dau of William Bates, of Shoal Lake, Manitoba, and *d* April 1920, leaving:

1e William Frank; *b* 22 July 1892; *m* 21 Aug 1923 Una Constance (*m* 2nd E Marshall, of Michigan), dau of James Clerk, of Valcartier, Quebec, and *dsp* 17 Jan 1940

2e George Harold, DSO (1917), DL Berwicks (1948); *b* 30 Aug 1893; *educ* Highfield Sch Hamilton Ontario and RMC Canada; Lt-Col Roy Scots WW I (despatches); *m* 20 July 1935 *Patricia Mary [Mrs George Hay, 106 Polwarth Terrace, Edinburgh], only dau of Maj Etienne Hugonin, of Edinburgh, and *d* 13 Dec 1967, leaving:

1f +Alexander Douglas [Alexander Hay Esq, Duns Castle, Berwickshire TD11 3NW]; *b* 2 Aug 1948; *educ* Rugby; *m* 20 Jan 1973 *Aline Mary, yr dau of Robert R Macdougall, of Edinburgh, and has:

1g +Robert Alexander; *b* 29 July 1976

1g *Caroline Laura; *b* 1978

2f +Philip Antony; *b* 13 Sept 1950; *educ* Rugby; *m* 1975 *Helena Anne, dau of Frank Sim, of Alloa, and has:

1g +George Francis; *b* 1979

1g *Felicity Patricia; *b* 1977

1f *Caroline Mary; *b* 11 Aug 1944; *m* 3 June 1967 *George Michael Mackinnon Thomson, s of George Reid Thomson, of Kinellar Ho, Kinellar, Aberdeenshire, and has:

1g *George Jolyon Hay; *b* 7 Oct 1970

1g *Mary Emma Julia; *b* 7 Oct 1970

2f *Barbara Elizabeth; *b* 5 Jan 1947; *m* 1979 *Dr Michael John Chevalier Asher

2d Francis Stuart, of Duns Castle; *b* 22 July 1863; V-Lt Berwicks; *m* 17 Oct 1903 Laura Elizabeth (*d* 21 Nov 1940), dau of Col G Fordyce-Buchan, of Kelloe, Berwicks, and *d* 27 Nov 1928

3d Charles Alfred; *b* 15 Dec 1867; *m* 31 Oct 1898 Florence Olga (*d* 1951), dau of J H Dickinson, and *d* 29 June 1930, leaving:

1e Aileen Anne; *b* 31 Aug 1899; *m* 24 Aug 1933 William John Carless

4d Alexander Graham; *b* 9 June 1871; *m* 1st Jan 1896 Antonietta Sylvester; *m* 2nd 1934 Stella Dalrymple (*d* Nov 1957), dau of Gen Sir John Ross, GCB, and *dsp* 29 Nov 1942

5d Edward George; *b* 21 Oct 1879; Capt Devonshire Regt; *m* 13 Nov 1917 Ascelin Frances Collett, 2nd dau of James Collett Mason, JP, of Ashurst Place, Langton Green, Kent, and *d* 8 Oct 1945, leaving:

1e *Nora Margaret; *b* 24 July 1922; *m* 15 Aug 1942 *John Robertson Campbell, s of William Campbell, of Perth, and has had:

1f *David Michael Hay; *b* 4 Oct, 1944

2f *Christopher William John; *b* 4 Oct 1949

3f *Stuart Calvin; *b* 23 May 1953

1f Ruth Jeannie; *b* 13 June 1943; *m* 19– *— Phillmore, of Australia

2f *Tessa Margaret [Mrs David Joyce, 89 Northway, Woose Hill, Wokingham, Berks RG11 9PQ]; *b* 4 Sept 1946; *m* *Maj David Joyce and has issue

3f *Lynn Nora Mary; *b* 25 May 1952

4f *Sally Anne Frances; *b* 1956

1d Mary Henrietta; *m* 1 Sept 1886 Col Sir Neville Francis Chamberlain, KCB, KCVO, CB (*d* 28 May 1944) and *d* 26 July 1936, leaving issue (*see* 1970 edn CHAMBERLAIN, Bt)

2d Helen Cordelia; *m* 4 Jan 1905 Edwin Robert John Sandys-Lumsdaine, JP (*d* 24 May 1933), of Lumsdaine, Berwicks, and *d* 13 July 1946, leaving issue

3c Robert Mordaunt; *b* 4 Oct 1833; *d* unm 29 May 1910

1c Mary; *m* 11 Aug 1840 George Stirling Home Drummond of Blair-Drummond and Ardoch, JP, DL (*d* 3 June 1876), and *d* 4 April 1855

2c Anne Elizabeth; *m* 19 Feb 1855 Robert Graham Moir (*d* 3 March 1864), of Leckie, Stirling, and *d* 21 Aug 1919, having had issue

3c Cordelia; *m* 28 June 1848 J B Yonge, JP, of Puslinch, Devon (*dsp* 12 Nov 1863)

4c Janet Matilda; *m* 8 Oct 1856 Charles Thomas Constantine Grant (*d* 8 May 1891), of Kilgraston, and *d* 15 March 1908, leaving issue

2b James, of Linplum; *b* 2 May 1790; *d* 2 Dec 1819

3b Alexander, of Nunraw; *b* 6 Sept 1796; *ka* Waterloo 18 June 1815

4b Robert, of Linplum and Nunraw, JP; *b* 6 Jan 1799; Eastern traveller, Egyptologist, author: *Hay's Illustrations of Cairo*; *m* 1828 Kalitza (*d* 5 June 1885), dau of Capt Alexandros Psaraki, Proestós (Chief Magistrate) of Apodhúlo, Crete, and *d* 4 Nov 1863, having had, with a dau (*d* unm):

1c Robert James Alexander, of Linplum, JP; *b* 14 May 1840; *educ* Magdalene Coll Cambridge (MA); *m* 5 April 1875 Caterina Maria Teresa (*d* 6 Oct 1897), 3rd dau of Giuseppe de Frescobaldi, Marchese di Monte Castello, of Tuscany, and *d* 28 Aug 1928, having had:

1d Robert William Seton; *b* 24 July 1878; *m* 15 April 1900 Maria (*d* 6 May 1961), dau of Antonio Baratti, and *d* 19 March 1965, having had, with another dau (*d* an infant):

1e Robert Dino James; *b* 15 June 1901; *m* 15 April 1942 Laura (*d* 1984), dau of Gen N Fochetti, and *d* 1977, having had:

1f +William Robert Alexander; *b* 3 June 1947

1f *Patricia Caterina Maria [Miss Patricia Hay, via di Trasone 5, 00199 Rome, Italy]; *b* 11 Nov 1944

2e +Alexander Giuseppe [Alexander Hay Esq, 4 S Lorenzo di Rabatta, 06070 Perugia, Cenerente, Italy]; *b* 20 Nov 1906; Cdr Crown Italy; *m* 11 Oct 1937 *Giovanna Bice, dau of Cdr Mario Dasso, and has:

1f +Andrew Alexander Mario [Andrew Hay Esq, 6 Favorita Rubbiano, 06070 Perugia, Cenerente, Italy]; *b* 16 July 1941; *m* 1966 *Maria Pia Antoinetta Mancini and has:

1g +Alexander; *b* 1966

2g +Massimo; *b* 1971

3g +Maurizio; *b* 1973

1f *Mary Grace Alexandra; *b* 8 March 1939; *m* 1965 *Manfredo Manfredi

2f *Roberta Alexandra; *b* 4 Nov 1942; *m* 1965 *Alberto Bonotti

3f *Jane Alexandra; *b* 23 July 1948

4f *Daniela Alexandra; *b* 15 March 1953

1e Caterina Mary Elisa; *b* 18 Dec 1904; *d* unm 1 Feb 1938

2d Charles; *b* and *d* 11 June 1879

3d Alexander James Dino; *b* 11 June 1879; Lt-Col 3rd Bn E Surrey Regt; *m* 2 Aug 1902 Edith May, only dau of Judge Young, Recorder Gloucester, and widow of Frederick W Barff, barrister Inner Temple, and *dsp* 24 Aug 1956

2c James William; *b* 5 Aug 1841; *m* 12 Jan 1874 Josephine Maria Ruth Alvarez-Molyneux (*d* 21 May 1886) and *d* 30 April 1917, leaving, with a s (*d* young):

1d Daisy Maria Kalitza

2d Madeline Christian

1c Kalitza Janet Erskine Christian; *m* 7 May 1863 her cousin Mary's widower George Stirling Home Drummond of Blair Drummond and Ardoch and *d* 6 Aug 1914

5b Charles Erskine, of Nunraw; *b* 20 Oct 1801; *d* 5 May 1827

1b Henrietta; *m* 29 Jan 1882 Charles Alexander Moir of Leckie (*d* 18 Aug 1845) and *d* 6 Aug 1854, leaving issue

1a Anne; *m* 1st 14 Nov 1751 Sir Patrick Hepburn-Murray, 4th Bt, of Balmanno (*d* 5 April 1756); *m* 2nd 7 Oct 1762 Archibald Stirling of Keir (*dsp* 1783) and *d* 14 Oct 1807

2a Margaret; *m* 1770 Sir Henry Seton, 4th Bt, of Culbeg and *d* 2 March 1809, leaving issue (*see* SETON, Bt, of Abercorn)

(1) (cont.) Alexander Hay *m* 2nd 21 March 1752 his cousin Jean (*dsp* 9 Oct 1764), dau of Lord David Hay (*see* below), and *d* 13 March 1789

(2) William; *dsp*

(1) Margaret; *m* 7th Lord Blantyre (*d* 17 Nov 1743; *see* 1900 edn) and *d* 13 Dec 1782, leaving issue

The 1st EARL's er s,

JOHN HAY, **1st Marquess of Tweeddale**, so *cr* 17 Dec 1694, as also EARL OF GIFFORD, VISCOUNT OF WALDEN and LORD HAY OF YESTER (all S), with remainder to his heirs male whatsoever, PC (S Feb 1660/1–74, 1682 and 1689, E 1669–74); *b* 13 Aug 1625; *educ* Edinburgh U; Sheriff Peebles to 1686; royalist Civil War in England 1641–43, Col Linlithgow and Tweeddale Regt Covenanter Army Scotland 1643–47, as which fought on the Parly side Battle of Marston Moor 2 July 1644; supported CHARLES II and participated in royalist camapign in England 1648 (fought Battle of Preston 17 Aug) and again 1651; MP E Lothian in CROMWELL's Parl 1656–58 and 1659–60, Commr for Security of Ld Protector CROMWELL 1656, Burgess Edinburgh Jan 1659/60, Extrdy Ld of Session 1664–74, a Ld Treasury Scotland 1667–74, Burgess Glasgow 1670, Commr Exchequer 1682 and Treasury 1687–89 and 1689–96, Ld High Chllr Scotland Jan 1691/2–96, Commr Admlty 1695–96, High Commr to S Parl 1695–96; *m* (contract 24 Sept 1644) Jean (*d* Nov 1688), dau of 1st Earl of Buccleuch (*see* BUCCLEUCH and QUEENSBERRY, D), and *d* 11 Aug 1697, having had, with other issue:

1 JOHN, **2nd Marquess**

2 David, of Belton, E Lothian, of which he had a charter 9 Dec 1687; *bapt* June 1656; Commr Supply Haddington; *m* Rachel (*d* 14 Jan 1760), dau of Sir James Hayes, of Gt Bedgbury, Kent, and *d* 1726, having had, with other issue:

(1) James, of Belton; *bapt* 31 July 1710; Maj; *m* 20 June 1780 his cousin Dorothea (*d* 29 Jan 1814), sis of **7th Marquess of Tweeddale**, and *d* 6 Feb 1798, leaving:

1a David, of Belton; *b* 21 May 1781; Capt 91st Highrs; *d* unm 23 Nov 1819

2a George; *b* 10 Jan 1784; *d* 16 Dec 1798

3a James, of Belton; *b* 6 March 1786; R-Adml; *m* 10 Nov 1824 Mary (*d* 26 April 1880), 2nd dau of Robert Hathorn Stewart of Physgill by Isabella, dau of Sir Stair Agnew, 6th Bt, of Lochnaw (*qv*), and *d* 3 Feb 1857, having had, with other issue:

1b James George HAY later BAIRD-HAY of Belton, JP, DL; *b* 12 Sept 1826; Capt 92nd Highrs; *m* 17 June 1862 Jane (*d* 26 June 1916), est dau of William Baird, DL, of Elie, and *d* 3 March 1913

2b Robert John (Sir), KCB; *b* 21 April 1828; Lt-Gen, Col Cmdt RA, Govr RMA Woolwich 1887–89, Pres Ordnance Commn 1889–91 and Dir of Artillery 1891–95; *m* 20 April 1861 Georgina Harvey, dau of Sir Alexander Ramsay, 2nd Bt (*qv*), and *d* 25 Nov 1910, having had:

1c David; *b* 2 March 1862; *d* 9 July 1912

2c Edward; *b* 6 Jan 1865; Midshipman RN; *das* 5 March 1884

3c James, of Belton, JP E Lothian; *b* 11 May 1870; *educ* Wellington and RMA Woolwich; Maj RA Boer War, WW I; *m* 23 April 1914 Grace Elinor Horatio (*d* 5 Nov 1952), yst dau of John Gilchrist-Clark of Speddoch, and *dsp* 3 Jan 1954

4c Archibald; *b* 9 Aug 1872; Lt-Col RWF, China 1900 (medal and clasp), Boer War (despatches, medal, five clasps), WW I; *ka* 3 Feb 1917

3b Lauderdale; *b* 31 Oct 1829; Ensign Madras Inf; *d* 21 Sept 1851

4b David; *b* 26 May 1833; Lt Bengal Inf; *d* 6 June 1858

5b Edward; *b* 11 Feb 1835; Cdr RN; *ka* 30 April 1864

1b Isabella Agnew; *m* 8 Dec 1859, as his 2nd w, James Baird of Auchmedden, JP, DL (*dsp* 20 June 1876), and *d* 7 Dec 1904

2b Mary Stewart; *m* 4 July 1860 Maj Henry Leslie Hunt and *d* 3 Feb 1903, leaving issue

3b Agnes Morgan; *m* 20 Nov 1865 Gen Edward Herbert Maxwell, CB (*see* MAXWELL, Bt), and *d* 23 Feb 1926

4b Adelaide Louisa; *m* 19 Jan 1869 Francis Maxwell of Gribton (*d* 1892) and *d* 21 Jan 1900, leaving issue

5b Laura Buchan; *m* 22 April 1885 William Weir (*d* 1913), of Kildonan, and *d* 2 Oct 1926

(1) Jean; *m* 21 March 1752 her distant cousin Alexander Hay of Drumelzier (*d* 13 March 1789) and *dsp* Oct 1764

3 Alexander, of Spott; *b* July 1663; Commr Supply Haddington; *m* 22 April 1697 Catherine, dau of Laurence Charters, and *d* 31 July 1737, leaving:

(1) John, of Lawfield; *b* 24 March 1698; *dsp* Dec 1758

(2) William, of Lawfield and Spott; *b* 30 Dec 1699; *m* 11 May 1759 Elizabeth, dau of Sir Robert Sinclair, 5th Bt, of Stevenston, and had:

1a Robert, of Lawfield and Spott; *m* 1791 Catherine, only dau of Humphrey Babington, and *d* 1844, leaving:

1b William, CB; *b* 14 Oct 1792; Army Capt, Commr Met Police; *m* 1829 Sarah, dau of Richard Sparkes, and *d* 29 Aug 1855, leaving issue

1b Sarah Catherine Isabella; *m* 3 Oct 1865 Frederick Henry Wood, DL (*d* 26 July 1886), of Hollin Hall and Copmanthorpe, Yorks, and *d* 3 May 1909

2a William; Capt 83rd Regt; *d* 15 March 1795

3a John; *d* 28 Sept 1783

(1) Catherine; *m* (settlements 21 Aug 1738) Sir Phillip Anstruther, 2nd Bt, of Balcaskie (*see* ANSTRUTHER, Bt, of that Ilk), and *d* 11 Feb 1759, leaving issue

1 Margaret; *m* 10 Oct 1675 3rd Earl of Roxburghe (*see* ROXBURGHE, D) and *d* 22 Jan 1753, leaving issue

2 Jean; *m* (contract 12 Oct 1693) 1st Earl of March (*see* WEMYSS and MARCH, E) and *d* July 1729, leaving issue

The 1st MARQUESS's est s,

JOHN HAY, **2nd Marquess of Tweeddale**, PC (S 1670–74 and 1684); *b* 1645; Col Militia Regt of Foot Haddingtonshire 1668–Jan 1674/5 and Linlithgowshire and Peeblesshire 1682, Burgess Edinburgh 1668, Capt Militia Regt of Horse Berwicks and Haddingtonshire 1689, Sheriff Haddingtonshire 1694–1713, Commr Admlty 1695, High Treas Scotland 1695, and High Commr S Parl 1704, Ld Chllr Scotland Oct 1704–March 1704/5, rep S peer 1707–08, FRS 1666; *m* 11 Dec 1666 Mary (*d* 20 March 1702), only child of 1st and last Duke of Lauderdale (*see* LAUDERDALE, E), and *d* 20 April 1713, having had:

1 CHARLES HAY, **3rd Marquess of Tweeddale**, PC (S March 1697/8); *b* just prior to 11 Nov 1667; Burgess Edinburgh 1694, Sheriff Haddingtonshire 1714–15, rep S peer March 1714/5–Dec 1715, Ld Lt Haddingtonshire Aug-Dec 1715 ; *m* 1693 Susan (*d* 7 Feb 1736/7), widow of 2nd Earl of Dundonald (*qv*) and dau of Anne, Duchess of Hamilton in her own right (*see* HAMILTON and BRANDON, D), by 1st Earl of Selkirk (*qv*), and *d* 17 Dec 1715, having had, with three other issue:

(1) JOHN HAY, **4th Marquess of Tweeddale**, PC (Feb 1741/2); *b c* 1695; Extrdy Ld of Session March 1720/1–62, Burgess Glasgow 1721 and Edinburgh 1753, rep S peer 1722–34 and 1742–62, Pncpl Sec State Scotland 1742–46, Govr Bank Scotland 1742, Ld Justice-Gen 1761–62; *m* 24 May 1748 Lady Frances Carteret (*d* 25 Dec 1788), dau of 2nd Earl Granville of the Jan 1714/5 *cr* (*see* GRANVILLE, preliminary remarks), and *d* 9 Dec 1762, having had, with other issue:

1a GEORGE HAY, **5th Marquess of Tweeddale**; *b* 12 July 1758; *d* 4 Oct 1770

1a Catherine; *b* 7 June 1753; *m* 23 April 1774 her cousin Maj William Hay of Newhall and *d* 11 July 1776, leaving issue (*see* below)

(2) Charles, of Linplum; MP Haddington 1741, Maj-Gen, led the English Gds at Fontenoy 30 April 1745; *d* unm 1 May 1760

(3) GEORGE HAY, **6th Marquess of Tweeddale**; *b c* 1700; one of the Gentlemen Bd of Police 1755–71; *d* unm 16 Nov 1787

2 John; Brig-Gen War Spanish Succession, present Battles of Schellenberg 1704 and Ramillies 1706; *m* 1st Lady Elizabeth Dalzell, only child of 4th Earl of Carnwath (*see* 1940 edn); *m* 2nd Elizabeth (*m* 2nd Gen Robert Hunter, Govr Jamaica (*d* 31 March 1734), and had issue), dau of Sir Thomas Orby, Bt, and *dsp* 25 Aug 1706

3 William, of Newhall; Brig-Gen, Lt-Col 3rd Foot Gds; *m* his cousin Margaret, only child of John Hay of Linplum (*see* above), and *d* 31 Oct 1723, leaving, with other issue:

(1) John, from whose creditors the **6th Marquess** bought the Newhall estate, willing it to John HAY-MACKENZIE (*see* below); *m* Dorothy (*d* 23 Sept 1808), dau of John Hayhurst, a labourer, of Quernmore, Lancs, and *d* 10 Dec 1765, leaving:

1a William; Offr 3rd Foot Gds, Maj S Fencible Regt; *m* 1st 23 April 1774 his cousin Catherine, only surv child of **4th Marquess of Tweeddale**, and had:

1b Frances; *m* 4 Aug 1797, as his 1st w, Hon Charles Manners Tollemache and *d* 29 March 1801, leaving issue (*see* DYSART, E)

1a (cont.) William Hay *m* 2nd 6 March 1779 Mary (*m* 2nd Walter Campbell of Shawfield), only dau of William Nisbet of Dirleton, Haddington, and *d* 23 July 1781, having by her had a s (*d* an infant)

2a GEORGE, **7th Marquess**

3a Edward; *m* 3 May 1790 Maria, er dau of 6th Lord Elibank (*qv*), and *d* 5 Dec 1814, leaving:

1b John HAY later HAY-MACKENZIE; *m* 23 April 1828 Anne (*d* Sept 1869), 3rd dau of Sir James Gibson Craig, 1st Bt (*see* GIBSON-CRAIG-CARMICHAEL, Bt), and *d* 9 July 1949, leaving issue (*see* CROMARTIE, E)

1a Dorothea; *m* 20 June 1780 James Hay of Belton and *d* 29 Jan 1814, leaving issue (*see* above)

2a Margaret; *m* Alan Makdougal (*d* 24 Dec 1807) and *d* 1838, leaving issue

(2) James, WS; *m* Oct 1744 Jane, dau of John Henderson, of Liston, Haddington, and *d* 31 May 1779, leaving issue

(3) Richard HAY later HAY-NEWTON of Newton, Haddington; *m* Anne, sis of Lt-Col John Stuart, of the Gds, and *d* 18 June 1776, leaving:

1a John, of Newton; *dsp* 1789

2a Richard, of Newton; *d* unm 19 Oct 1793

3a William, of Newton; *b* 1747; *m* 1791 Alicia (*d* 1841), dau of Anthony Foster of Jardinefield, and *d* 12 Feb 1829, having had:

1b Richard, of Newton; *d* unm 23 Dec 1848

2b William Waring, of Newton, DL; *b* 20 Sept 1795; *m* 1st 19 June 1821 Jane Frances (*dsp* 5 July 1833), only child of Thomas Gregson, of Blackburn, by Elizabeth, est dau of Anthony Foster of Jardinefield; *m* 2nd 15 Feb 1844 Jane, dau of James Clerk Rattray of Bonnington and Craighall Rattray, a Baron Court Exchequer Scotland and *dsp* 15 May 1860

3b George Foster HAY later PRIMROSE-HAY; HEICS; *m* Jane, 2nd dau of James Primrose of Burnbrae and *dsp* 1856

4b John Stuart, of Newton; *m* 4 Aug 1829 Margaret Eliza (*m* 2nd 12 May 1866 Maj Robert Duncan Fergusson of Cassillis (*see* FERGUSSON, Bt) and *d* 21 Jan 1888), yst dau of William Fairlie, and *d* 19 Nov 1863, leaving:

1c William Drummond Ogilvy HAY later HAY-NEWTON, of Newton, JP, DL; *b* 12 Jan 1832; Capt 72nd Highrs Indian Mutiny 1858–59; *m* 10 Aug 1871 Adeline Charlotte (*d* April 1929), est dau of Lt-Col Robert Gordon, and *d* 14 June 1916, leaving:

1d George, of Newton; *b* 5 Aug 1872; *d* unm 25 April 1968

2d Stuart HAY-NEWTON later HAY, DSO (1916); *b* 28 March 1876; Boer War (two medals, five clasps), Bde Maj BEF and Brevet Lt-Col Cameron Highrs WW I (despatches); *m* 27 Feb 1908 Inna Vera Evelyn (*d* 28 July 1971), only child of Hon Louis Guy Scott, bro of 8th Earl of Clonmell (*see* 1935 edn), and *d* 10 May 1960, leaving:

1e *(Inna) Veronica Adeline; *b* 16 Feb 1909; *m* 5 Aug 1966 *Brig Stanley Oswald Jones, OBE, MC, late RWF, s of John Jones, of Pontypool

2e *Vera Jean [Miss Vera Hay, Woodhouse Farm, Marsh, Aylesbury, Bucks]; *b* 26 June 1910

3e *Evelyn Sheelagh; *b* 26 June 1910

1d Albreda Julia; *d* unm 14 March 1950

2c Francis John Stuart, MVO; *b* 19 April 1843; Capt 14th Hus; Br Consul Ajaccio 1888, Stockholm 1889, Oporto 1891, Consul-Gen Algiers 1897, Queen's Messenger, Dep Govr IoW and Carisbrooke Castle 1910–13, Offr Legn Hon; *m* 25 April 1887 Lucy Jane (*d* 10 March 1939), dau of Maj Robert Fergusson (see FERGUSSON, Bt) and widow of Hon Arthur Hay Fraser (see SALTOUN, L), and d 2 March 1913

  1c Margaret; m 14 Feb 1871 Gustavus Irwin Knight, of Dorking

  2c Alice Wilhelmina Mary; m 17 Oct 1871 Frederic William Gustave Fergusson, yst s of Sir James Fergusson, 4th Bt (qv), and dsp 1896

  3c Ernestine; m 15 June 1871 Evan Allen Hunter and dsp 16 Dec 1874

  4c Ida Mary; m 1 Jan 1891 Thomas Colcott Fox, MB, FRCP (d 1916), and d 13 Nov 1930

 5b Anthony James

 1a Jean; m 13 July 1780 James Walker of Dalry, WS (d 1817), a Pncpl Clerk of Session, and had issue (see 1970 edn WILLIAMS-DRUMMOND, Bt)

  (1) Susan; m 22 Aug 1742 John Scott of Malleny and had issue

  (2) Jane; m Archibald Murray of Murrayfield (see MURRAY, Bt, of Blackbarony) and had issue

 1 Anne; m 12th Lord Ross (d 15 March 1738) and had issue

 2 Jean; m 29 April 1697 9th Earl of Rothes (qv) and d 4 Sept 1731, leaving issue

The 6th MARQUESS's 1st cousin once-removed,

  GEORGE HAY, **7th Marquess of Tweeddale**; b 1753; Offr HEICN, Burgess Edinburgh 1788, Ld Lt Haddingtonshire 1794–1804, rep S peer 1796–1804; m 18 April 1785 Hannah Charlotte, dau of 7th Earl of Lauderdale (qv), was imprisoned with her in the fortress of Verdun by NAPOLEON and d there 9 Aug 1804, leaving, with two other daus (d unm):

1 GEORGE, 8th Marquess

2 James; b 23 March 1788; Gen, Col 36th Foot; m 18 Aug 1813 Elizabeth (d 30 Sept 1861), dau and heiress of James Forbes of Seaton, Aberdeenshire, and d 18 Aug 1862, having had, with other issue:

  (1) James Gordon, of Seaton and Mapis Hill House, Middx, JP; b 15 Oct 1815; barrister; m 13 Nov 1878 Mary Catherine (m 2nd Edward Magee and d 11 Feb 1892), est dau of Henry Hill Cox, of Kemerton, Glos, and d 8 Feb 1883, leaving:

   1a Gilbert James; b 6 Dec 1879; d 30 July 1883

   2a Malcolm Vivian, of Seaton, JP, DL; b 21 Jan 1881; educ Beaumont; LLD Aberdeen 1950, Maj 3rd Bn Gordon Highrs WW I (wounded), memb Roy Co Archers, KStJ; m 1st 13 May 1902 Florence (d 3 Jan 1943), dau of George Erlington, of Paris, and had:

    1b James Malcolm, DL Aberdeenshire; b 30 June 1907; educ Ampleforth; Maj Gordon Highrs WW II (wounded); m 19 April 1941 *Mary Eleanora Basset, dau of Charles Ernest Basset Lothian Curzon (see HOWE, E), and d 1987, leaving:

     1c +Malcolm Charles [Malcolm Hay of Seaton, Eddinglassie, Glass, nr Huntly, Aberdeenshire]; b 4 March 1956; educ Ampleforth and Magdalene Coll Cambridge; m 1983 *Deborah Louise, dau of Lt-Cdr Derek Malcolm Rouse, MBE, RN, of Bonchurch, IoW, and has:

      1d +James Malcolm Douglas; b 1985

      2d +Oliver Charles Quintin; b 1987

      1d *Georgina Eileen; b 1990

      2d *Isabel Jane; b 1993

      3d *Katherine Louise; b 1993 (twin)

     1c *Elizabeth Mary [Mrs David Gillespie, The Lodge, St Mary's Abbey, Woolmer Hill, Haslemere, Surrey GU27 1QA]; b 3 Oct 1942; m 20 June 1977 *David Buchanan Gillespie and has:

      1d *Hamish Peregrine Curzon; b 10 Sept 1979

     2c *Joanna Margaret; b 31 July 1945; m 29 Dec 1973 *Brig Ewen Duncan Cameron, OBE (see RUGGE-PRICE, Bt), and has:

      1d *Louisa Mary; b 1976

      2d *Clare Elizabeth; b 1977

     3c *Nicola Anne; b 17 Oct 1958; m 1983 *Andrew Lachlan Rattray, yst s of Capt James Silvester Rattray, 28th of Rattray, and has:

      1d *Thomas Alexander; b 1987

      2d *Hew Lachlan; b 1989

      1d *Flora May; b 1992

    2b +Peter Brian [Maj Peter Hay, Titford Hold, Awliscombe, Devon]; b 29 June 1918; educ Ampleforth; Maj Gordon Highrs WW II (despatches, POW); m 27 July 1946 *Marigold Armatrude, only dau of Lt-Col Alan George Eden, of Culver, Devon, and has:

     1c +Angus Malcolm; b 22 Sept 1947; educ Ampleforth; Capt RSG 1970 and Abu Dhabi Def Force; m 1978 (divorce 1984) Miranda Mary, dau of Anthony Seymour Bellville, of Bembridge, IoW

     2c +James Andrew [James Hay Esq, 112 Farm Lane, London SW6]; b 1 Dec 1949; educ Ampleforth; m 1975 (divorce 1979) Emma, dau of (Rondle) Owen Charles Stable, QC, of Much Hadham, Herts

      1c *Charlotte Jeradine; b 12 Feb 1959; m 1988 *John Paul Deacon and has:

      1d *Maximillian James; b 1989

      1d *Georgia Florence; b 1991

      2d *Jessica Charlotte; b 1991 (twin)

    1b *Elizabeth Charlotte Sarah [Lady Hodson, Middle Farm, Dinder, Wells, Somerset]; m 15 Nov 1928 Sir Arnold Wienholt Hodson, KCMG (d 26 May 1944), Govr and C-in-C Gold Coast, s of Algernon Hodson, of Hove, Sussex, and has had:

     1c Arnold; b and d 4 Aug 1929

     1c *Jean Rosemary Hay [Mrs John Nutt, Filbert House, E Ilsley, Berks]; b 16 Dec 1930; m 1st 21 June 1958 (divorce 1972) John Wilfrid Gillams, only s of R T Gillams, of Solihull, Warwicks, and has:

      1d *Judith Elizabeth [Mrs Luc Mella, 45 Potter St, Melbourne, Derbys]; b 31 July 1960; FRCS; m 1987 *Luc Mella, airline pilot, and has:

       1e *Sophie Louise; b 1988

       2e *Stephanie Laurie; b 1990

       3e *Florence Emily; b 1992

      2d *Charlotte Louise; b 8 April 1963; MB; m 1993 *Francis Owen Boyd, MB

1c (cont.) Mrs Jean Gillams m 2nd 1977 *John Allister Nutt

  2c *Elisabeth Anne Hay [Mrs Francis Floyd, Middle Farm, Dinder, Wells, Somerset]; b 4 Aug 1934; m 1st 6 July 1963 (divorce 1983) Anthony Arthur Verrier, only s of Albert Willis Verrier; m 2nd *Francis Floyd and has by her 1st husb:

   1d *Charles Simpson; b 1966

   1d *Frances Joan; b 1968

  2b Georgiana Catherine; b 23 June 1910; m 23 Sept 1941 George Richard Williams (d 1993), s of Edward George Williams, of Ballymena, Co Antrim, and d 1989, having had:

   1c Malcolm George; b 3 Feb 1948; d 13 Dec 1956

   1c *Olga Georgiana [Ms Olga Williams, 53 Nipigon Ave, Willowdale, Ont M2M 2V9, Canada]; b 14 June 1942; has:

    1d *Sarah Georgiana; b 1978

   2c *Maureen Elizabeth; b 25 Aug 1943

   3c *Ann Catherine [Mrs Ronald Thorne, 708 Gilbert St W, Whitby, Ont L1N 1S2, Canada]; b 29 April 1945; m 1970 *Ronald Thorne and has:

    1d *Christopher Malcolm; b 1970

    2d *Jaimie Ronald George; b 1974

    3d *Robin Francis; b 1978

  3b Frances Mary; b 3 Aug 1914; m 28 Nov 1941 *Arthur Ernest Parker, s of Arthur Parker, of Cambridge, and d 22 Oct 1994, leaving:

   1c *John Frances; b 17 Nov 1944

   2c *Anthony David; b 21 April 1947

   3c *Gerald Stephen [Gerald Parker Esq, 40 Bedford Rd, Hitchin, Herts SG5 2TY]; b 17 Jan 1953

   4c *Robert Charles; b 1 Sept 1955

   1c *Sara Laura; b 31 Oct 1942; m 25 July 1964 *Nicholas McConochie

2a (cont.) Maj Malcolm Hay of Seaton m 2nd 23 May 1956 Alice Ivy, DStJ, ARCM (d 1974), dau of Herbert John Wigmore, of Perth, W Australia, and widow of Walter Moncrieff Paterson, of Tilliefoure, and d 27 Dec 1962

  3a Cuthbert Joseph; b 30 March 1882; educ Beaumont; Capt 2nd Bn Gordon Highrs WW I (wounded); m 7 July 1908 Letitia Griffith (d 1982), dau of Frederick Heylighter Fausset, of Willsborough, Co Sligo, and d 1970, having had:

   1b +Ronald Cuthbert, DSO (1945), DSC and bar [Cdr Ronald Hay DSO DSC RN, South Mill, Amesbury, Wilts]; b 4 Oct 1916; educ Ampleforth; Lt-Col RM WW II; m 24 Oct 1944 Barbara (d 28 Nov 1997), dau of Lt-Col George Rochfort Grange, of Strathblane, Stirlingshire, and has:

    1c +Charles Edward Ronald [Charles Hay Esq, Letton House, Blandford, Dorset DT11 7ST]; b 15 May 1948; educ Ampleforth; m 1975 *Susan Rodica, dau of Terence Prendergast, of Steeple Claydon, Bucks, and has:

     1d +Jeremy Charles; b 1976

     1d *Hannah Rodica Barbara; b 1980

    2c +James Philip Burness; b 28 Aug 1957; BSc; m 1996 *Jacqueline Elizabeth, dau of Peter Gallery, and has:

     1d *Rebecca Elizabeth Barbara; b 31 Jan 1997

    1c *Penelope Rochfort; b 22 May 1946; m 1977 *Maj John Julius Rogers, Roy Hus (PWO), and has:

     1d *Katherine Philippa; b 1978

     2d *Vanessa Victoria; b 1981

     3d *Olivia Hilary; b 1983

    2c *Sarah Elizabeth; b 27 Nov 1951; m 1st 1980 (divorce 1990) Alistair Macrae; m 2nd 1997 *Christopher James Allan and by her 1st husb has:

     1d *Calum Andrew; b 1980

     1d *Athene Hope; b 1983

  2b +John Malcolm [Lt-Cdr John Hay RN, Mirrabooka, 56 Mugga Way, Red Hill, Canberra, ACT, Australia]; b 9 Jan 1918; educ Ampleforth; Lt-Cdr RN WW II; m 3 Jan 1952 *Alicia Gertrude Maria, only dau of Herbert Moore, of Sydney, NSW, and has:

   1c +Richard Malcolm [Richard Hay Esq, Characene Pk, RMB 117, Summer Hill Rd, Bungendore, NSW 2621, Australia]; b 22 Jan 1953; m 1972 *Maureen Loretta, dau of Walter Larkin, of San Fransisco, and has:

    1d +David Richard; b 1983

    1d *Katie Elizabeth; b 1985

  1b *Mary Vivien [Mrs Samuel Jerome, Fiveways, Terry's Lanc, Cookham, Berks SL6 9RR]; b 13 Aug 1909; m 1st 1937 John Ohlsson Ripley (d 1947); m 2nd 1960 Samuel K Jerome (d 1966) and has by her 1st husb:

   1c *Michael; b 1939

  2b Margaret Patricia; b 14 June 1911; d Oct 1987

  3b *Mary Charlotte [Mrs Neil Smith, Box 1317, Esperance 6450, W Australia]; b 25 March 1915; m 1947 Lt-Col Neil Sylvester Smith, RAF Signals (d 1981), and has:

   1c *Stephen Neil; b 1948; m 1984 his cousin *Jacqueline Mary, yr dau of Sqdn/Ldr W D K Franklin by Margaret Patricia, 2nd dau of Capt Cuthbert Joseph Hay, and has:

    1d *Ashley Christopher; b 1984

    2d *Simon Matthew; b 1987

    1d *Sophia Gilliam; b 1990

   2c *Graham John; b 1957

   1c *Diana Mary [Mrs Brian Campbell, 139 Orange Valley Rd, Lesmurdie 6076, W Australia]; b 1949; m 1st 1969 (divorce 1976) Peter John Thompson and has:

    1d *Bentley Warrick James; b 1972

    2d *Grant Peter; b 1974

   1c (cont.) Mrs Diana Thompson m 2nd 1978 *Brian Barbrec Campbell and by him has:

    3d *Reuben Gregory Barbrec; b 1980

    1d *Zoe Louise; b 1983

(1) Louise Margaret Gordon; *b* 8 May 1820; *m* 26 Oct 1844 Baron Theodore Gudin (*d* April 1880) and *d* 1890, leaving issue

3 John, CB, KCH; *b* 1 April 1793; R-Adml, MP Haddington 1826–30 and Windsor 1847, Kt Grand Cross Order Charles III Spain; *m* 2 Sept 1946 Mary Anne (*d* 30 Nov 1850), er dau of Donald Cameron of Locheil, 22nd Ch Clan Cameron, and *dsp* 26 Aug 1851

4 Edward George; *b* 7 May 1799; Col; *d* unm 12 Nov 1862

5 Thomas (Rev); *b* 25 Aug 1800; Rector Rendlesham Suffolk 1830–73; *m* 29 Aug 1833 Harriet (*d* 24 Jan 1891), dau of Sir Alexander Kinloch, 8th Bt, of Gilmerton (*qv*), and *d* 1890, having had two sons and three daus (*dsp*)

1 Dorothea Frances; *m* 23 Oct 1809 John Henry Ley (*d* 21 Aug 1950), Clerk H of C, and *d* 12 Oct 1875, having had issue

2 Hannah Charlotte; *m* 1 June 1815 John Tharp (*see* DUNMORE, E) and *dsp* 3 May 1876

3 Elizabeth; *m* 7 Sept 1813 James Joseph Hope-Vere and *d* 19 Dec 1868, leaving issue (*see* LINLITHGOW, M)

4 Julia Tomasina; *m* 28 July 1828 1st and last Baron Broughton of Broughton-de-Gyfford and *d* 3 April 1835, leaving issue (*see* HOBHOUSE, Bt)

The 7th MARQUESS's est s,

GEORGE HAY, **8th Marquess of Tweeddale**, KT (1820), GCB (1867, KCB 1862, CB 1815); *b* 1 Feb 1787; Ensign 88th Foot June 1804, Lt 52nd Foot Oct 1804, served Sicily and (as ADC to 1st Duke of Wellington; *qv*) Peninsular War 1806 on, Capt 10th Foot 1807, Lt and Capt 1st Foot (Gren) Gds 1808, badly wounded as DAQMG Battle of Busaco 27 Sept 1810, Capt 15th Light Dragoons 1811, Maj 41st Foot 1812, Lt-Col (present as AQMG Battle of Vittoria) 21 June 1813, Lt-Col 100th Foot (as which badly wounded nr Niagara 5 July) 1814 during War of 1812, rep S peer 1818–76, Ld Lt Haddingtonshire 1823–76, Col 1825, ADC to GEORGE IV and WILLIAM IV 1825–37, Burgess Glasgow 1826, Maj-Gen 1837, Govr and C-in-C Madras 1842–48, Lt-Gen 1846, Col 30th Foot 1846–62, 42nd Foot 1862–63 and 2nd Life Gds 1863–76, Gen 1854, Lt-Gen Roy Co Archers and Gold Stick in Waiting 1863, Pres Highland Ag Soc 1869–73, FM 1875; *m* 28 March 1816 Susan, 3rd dau of 5th Duke of Manchester (*qv*), and *d* 10 Oct 1876, having had, with other issue:

1 George, *Earl of Gifford*; *b* 26 April 1822; *educ* Trin Coll and Trin Hall Cambridge (MA); Capt E Lothian Yeo Cav 1850, Priv Sec to Sec for War 1854–55, MP (Lib) Totnes 1855–62; *m* 13 Oct 1862 Helen Selina (*d* 13 June 1867), dau of Thomas Sheridan and widow of 4th Baron Dufferin and Claneboye (*qv*), and *dsp* & *vp* 22 Dec 1862

2 ARTHUR HAY, **9th Marquess of Tweeddale**, DL (Haddington); *b* 9 Nov 1824; *educ* Leipsig and Geneva; Ensign and Lt Gren Gds 1841, Lt and Capt 1846, Capt and Lt-Col 1854, ADC to Viceroy India Sutlej Campaign 1845–46 and AAG 1st Div Crimean War, Col 1860, ret 1863; Fell Linnaean Soc 1865, Pres RZS 1868–78, FRS 1871; author: *Ornithological Works* (1881); *m* 1st 18 Feb 1857 Helena Eleanora Charlotte Augusta (*d* 30 Sept 1871), Ldy Bedchamber to HRH THE PRINCESS OF WALES, only child of Count Adolphus Augustus Frederic Kielmansegge, Hanoverian Min UK; *m* 2nd 8 Oct 1873 Julia Charlotte Sophia (*d* 17 May 1937, having *m* 2nd 24 Jan 1887 Sir John Rose, 1st Bt, of Montreal (*qv*) and 3rd 3 Feb 1892 Maj Sir William Eden Evans Gordon, MP (*d* 31 Oct 1913)), sis of 1st and last Baron Seaforth (*see* CROMARTIE, E), and *dsp* 29 Dec 1878

3 WILLIAM MONTAGU, **10th Marquess**

4 John, GCB; *b* 23 Aug 1827; Crimean and China Wars, MP Wick 1857–59, Ripon 1866–71, a Ld Admlty 1866, 1868–71, 1880–83 and 1886, cmded Channel Sqdn 1877–79, C-in-C Mediterranean 1883–86 and Devonport 1887–88, Adml the Fleet, Chev Legn Hon, Grand Cross Medjidie; *m* 8 June 1876 Annie Christina (*d* 24 Oct 1932), dau of Nathaniel Grace Lambert, MP, of Denham Ct, Bucks, and *d* 4 May 1916, leaving:

(1) John Arthur Lambert; *b* 28 Aug 1877; Cdr RN; *d* unm 1 May 1944

(2) Thomas William; *b* 25 Aug 1882; *educ* Clifton; S/Ldr RAFVR, Lt-Col cmdg Leics Yeo WW I (despatches), MP S Norfolk Nov 1922–Nov 1923; *d* unm 10 July 1956

(1) Minnie Christina Brenda; *b* 31 May 1880; *m* 5 June 1905 Sholto Charles, Lord Aberdour, est s of 19th Earl of Morton (*qv*), and *d* 27 Aug 1954, leaving issue

(2) Annie Norma; *b* 26 Aug 1885; *d* 30 March 1886

1 Susan Georgiana; *m* 21 Jan 1836 10th Earl of Dalhousie (*qv*) and *d* 6 May 1853, leaving issue

2 Hannah Charlotte; *m* 30 June 1843 Simon Watson Taylor (*d* 25 Dec 1902), of Erlestoke Park, Wilts, and *d* 10 Nov 1887, leaving issue

3 Louisa Jane; *m* 4 June 1841 Robert Balfour Wardlaw Ramsay (*d* 26 June 1882), of Whitehill, Edinburgh, and Tillicoultry, Clackmannanshire, and *d* 9 Sept 1882, having had issue

4 Elizabeth; Ldy Roy Order Victoria and Albert; *m* 18 April 1839 2nd Duke of Wellington (*qv*) and *dsp* 13 Aug 1904

5 Jane; *m* 9 June 1863 Lt-Gen Sir Richard Chambré Hayes Taylo(u)r, GCB, and *d* 13 Dec 1920, leaving issue (*see* HEADFORT, M)

6 Emily; *m* 17 Jan 1856 Sir Robert Peel, 3rd Bt (*see* PEEL, E), and *d* 4 April 1924, having had issue

The 9th MARQUESS's bro,

WILLIAM MONTAGU HAY, **10th Marquess of Tweeddale**, KT (1898), DL Berwicks; *b* 29 Jan 1826; *educ* Haileybury; Bengal CS 1845–62 (DC Simla and Supt Hill States N India), MP (Lib) Taunton 1865–68 and Haddington Burghs Aug-Dec 1878; *cr* 6 Oct 1881 BARON TWEEDDALE OF YESTER, Co Haddington (UK), Ld HC Ch Scotland 1890–92 and 1896–97, chm: N Br Rlwy Co to 1899, Direct Spanish, Europe and Azores and W African Telegraph Cos, Globe Telegraph and Tst Co and Stock Conversion and Investment Tst, Govr Commercial Bank Scotland, Pres Scottish Widows' Fund; *m* 18 May 1878 Candida Louise, CBE (1920), Pres Ladies' Emergency Ctee Navy League, Order Merit Italian Red Cross (*d* 14 Feb 1925), 3rd dau of Vincenzo Bartolucci, of Cantiano Marche, Italy, and Greenville Park, Co Kilkenny, and *d* 25 Nov 1911, having had:

1 WILLIAM GEORGE MONTAGU HAY, **11th Marquess of Tweeddale**, JP East Lothian; *b* 4 Nov 1884; *educ* Eton and Ch Ch Oxford; Capt SR 1st Life Gds, Maj RFA (TF), WW I (wounded); Ld Lt E Lothian 1945, Ensign Roy Co Archers 1952; *m* 1st 7 Dec 1912 Marguerite Christine (*d* 15 Oct 1944), dau of Alexander Ralli (*see* RALLI, Bt), and step-dau of Lewis Einstein, and had, with a s (*b* and *d* 16 July 1928):

(1) *Hélène Candida [The Rt Hon The Viscountess Kemsley, Field House, Lubenham, Leics LE16 9TR]; *b* 5 Sept 1913; DStJ; *m* 21 June 1933 *2nd Viscount Kemsley (*qv*) and has issue

(2) *(Marguerite) Georgina Christine [The Lady Georgina Coleridge, 33 Peel St, London W8 7PA]; *b* 19 March 1916; ed Homes and Gardens 1949–63, , dir Country Life Ltd 1962–74, George Newnes 1963–69, Special Projects IPC Women's Magazines 1971–74, V-Pres Gtr London Fund for Blind 1981–, Freeman Stationers' and Newspapermakers' Co 1973, author: *Grand Smashional Pointers* (cartoons, 1934), *I Know What I Like* (1959), *That's Racing* (1978); *m* 20 Sept 1941 Capt Arthur Nicholas Coleridge (*see* COLERIDGE, B) and has issue

(3) *(Christine) Daphne [The Lady Daphne Stewart, Middle Blainglie, Galashiels TD1 2PF]; *b* 29 March 1919; *m* 1st 12 June 1939 (*divorce* 1947), as his 1st w, Lt-Col David Morley-Fletcher, OBE, TD, Rifle Bde (*d* 15 April 1971), yr s of Bernard Morley Morley-Fletcher, and has:

1a *Hugo David Montagu [Hugo Morley-Fletcher Esq, The Old Vicarage, Padbury, Bucks]; *b* Sept 1940; *educ* Stowe and Trin Coll Cambridge (MA); FSA; dir Christie's 1969–; *m* 1st 14 Jan 1967 (*divorce* 19–) Josceline Mary, yr dau of Sir (Henry) Josceline Phillimore (*see* PHILLIMORE, B), and has:

1b *Gifford Henry Montagu; *b* 13 June 1969

1b *Hester Mary Victoria; *b* 1972

1a (cont.) Hugo Morley-Fletcher *m* 2nd 1980 *Belinda Mary, dau of William Miles David, of Pontefract, Yorks, and by her has:

2b *Isabella Frances; *b* 1981

1a *Victoria Catherine Margaret [Miss Victoria Fletcher, 5 Brewery Ct, Haddington, E Lothian EH41 4DG]; *b* 8 Feb 1942; memb Chartered Soc Physiotherapy

(3) (cont.) Lady Daphne Morley-Fletcher *m* 2nd 22 July 1957 Lt-Col Francis Robert Cameron Stewart, late IA (*d* Oct 1996), s of Sir Francis Hugh Stewart, CIE, MA

(4) *Frances Elizabeth Ann [The Lady Frances Pearson, Coedsaithpren, Nantgaredig, Carmarthen, Dyfed]; *b* 1926; *m* 27 Oct 1956 Nigel Arthur Pearson (*d* 8 Dec 1975), only s of Sir Neville Arthur Pearson, 2nd Bt, of St Dunstan's (*d* 1975, *see* 1970 edn)

1 (cont.) The **11th Marquess** *m* 2nd 24 March 1945 Marjorie Helen (*d* 24 Nov 1977), dau of Henry John Wagg, OBE, and formerly w of Lt-Col Joseph Henry Nettlefold, and *d* 30 March 1967

2 Arthur Vincent; *b* 16 March 1886; Capt Irish Gds; *m* 27 May 1911 Menda (*d* 5 Jan 1959, having *m* 2nd 3 Jan 1916 Col Robert Edward Kennard Leatham, DSO, who *d* 11 May 1948), dau of Ambrose Ralli (*see* RALLI, Bt), and was *ka* 14 Sept 1914, leaving:

(1) Jean; *b* 27 Aug 1912; *m* 4 April 1932 Lt-Col Sir William Vivian Makins, 3rd Bt (*qv*), and *d* 1993, leaving issue

3 Edward Douglas John, DL; *b* 2 Nov 1888; Lt-Col Essex Regt, Maj Gen Gds, WW I Gallipoli, Egypt and France; CC Sussex; *m* 1st 18 Oct 1917 Violet Florence Catherine (Bridget) (*d* 17 March 1926), only dau of Maj Cameron Barclay, 10th Hus, of York, and had:

(1) DAVID GEORGE MONTAGU, **12th Marquess**

(1) *Marioth Christina [The Lady Marioth Hay, Forbes Lodge, Gifford, East Lothian EH41 4JE]; *b* 1 Sept 1918; granted 1970 with half-sis rank of marquess's dau; *m* 1st 18 Dec 1940 (*divorce* 1954, resumed maiden name by deed poll 1971) Lt-Col George Richard Trotter, RSG (*d* 24 Sept 1970), 2nd s of Col Algernon Trotter (*see* EGLINTON and WINTON, E), and has:

1a *Richard Reginald [Richard Trotter Esq, 52 Leander Ave, Hillside, Bulawayo, Zimbabwe]; *b* 12 Oct 1941; *educ* Eton; *m* 1974 *Marion, er dau of Lt-Col Ralph Maxwell Campbell, of Chasehayes, Stockland, Devon, and has:

1b *Georgina Maryoth Maxwell; *b* 24 Aug 1978

2a *Edward George [Edward Trotter Esq, The Cottage, Bohunt Manor, Liphook, Hants GU30 7DL]; *b* 1943; *m* 1973 *Jemima Rachel McLay, er dau of Niel Mills, of Upton Grey Ho, Hants, and has:

1b *George; *b* 1977

1b *Joanna; *b* 1975

1a *Bridget Mary [Mrs John Ellwood, 2 McLaren Rd, Edinburgh EH9 2BH]; *b* 1944; *m* 1981 *John Ellwood, s of Capt Victor Ellwood, RFC, and has:

1b *Sophy Catherine; *b* 1982

(1) (cont.) Lady Maryoth Trotter *m* 2nd 2 March 1954, as his 2nd w, Sir Gifford Wheaton Grey Fox, 2nd and last Bt (*d* 11 Feb 1959; *see* 1959 edn); *m* 3rd 2 April 1963 (*divorce* 1971) Sir Jack (John Hastings) James, KCVO, CB (*d* 1980), Dep Master and Comptroller Roy Mint, s of Clement Fletcher James

3 (cont.) Lt-Col Lord Edward Hay *m* 2nd 5 July 1928 Audrey Clara Lilian (*m* 3rd 28 Feb 1948 (*divorce* 1952) Hon Niall Greville Chaplin (*d* 8 Feb 1963), 2nd s of 2nd Viscount Chaplin (*see* 1970 edn); *m* 4th 12 Dec 1952 Maj-Gen Sir Stewart Graham Menzies, KCB, KCMG, DSO, MC (*d* 29 May 1968), s of John Graham Menzies), yr dau of Sir Thomas Paul Latham, 1st Bt (*qv*), and formerly w of Sir Henry Ralph Stanley Birkin, 3rd Bt, *qv*), and was *k* by enemy action at the Gds Chapel, Wellington Barracks, 18 June 1944, leaving by her:

(2) *Caroline Susan Elizabeth; *b* 16 April 1930; *m* 1st 20 Oct 1953 (*divorce* 1970) Richard Noel Marshall Armitage (*d* 1986), only s of Reginald Moxon Armitage, MusB, FRCO, ARCM, and has:

1a *Charles Edward Marshall; *b* 6 Aug 1954; *educ* Eton; *m* 1987 *Judith, only dau of F Reed, of Hampton, Middx

2a *Alexander James [Alexander Armitage Esq, 81 Lonsdale Rd, London SW13]; *b* 17 May 1958; *educ* Eton; *m* 1987 *Carolyn Margery, dau of Peter Allen, of Portsmouth, and has:

1b *Sophie Clare; *b* 1987

2b *Daisy Elizabeth Collette; *b* 1990

(2) (cont.) Lady Caroline Armitage *m* 2nd 1970 *Reginald Charles Tyrrell

1 (Susan Elizabeth) Clementine, CBE (1918); *b* 9 Aug 1879; Queen Elisabeth of Belgium medal; *m* 4 Nov 1901 Capt Walter Waring, DL, MP, 1st Life Gds (*d* 16 Nov 1930), s of Charles Waring, MP Poole, and *d* 15 Feb 1964, leaving issue

2 Candida Louisa; *b* 25 Aug 1882

The 11th MARQUESS's n,
DAVID GEORGE MONTAGU HAY, **12th Marquess of Tweeddale**, GC, AM (1941); *b* 25 Oct 1921; *educ* Eton; RLSM, Lt RNR WW II (Lloyd's War Medal); *m* 1st 26 Oct 1946 (*divorce* 1958) *Hon Sonia Mary Peake (*m* 2nd 1966 Maj Michael William Vernon Hammond-Maude, JP, late WRNS, 2nd dau of 1st Viscount Ingleby (*qv*), and had:

1 EDWARD DOUGLAS JOHN HAY, **13th and present Marquess**
2 +CHARLES DAVID MONTAGU [The Lord Charles Hay, 336a Gilmerton Rd, Edinburgh EH17 7PA]; *b* 6 Aug 1947 (twin); heir presumptive; *educ* Milton Abbey and Trin Coll Oxford
3 +Alistair James Montagu [Alistair Hay Esq, 26 Swanson St, Erskineville, NSW 2043, Australia] (does not use courtesy title); *b* 4 Nov 1955; *educ* Eton and Univ Coll Oxford (MA, DPhil); botanist; has taken Australian citizenship

The **12th Marquess** *m* 2nd 14 Jan 1959 Nella Doreen (*d* 1979), late Sgt WRAF, dau of M Dutton, and *d* 23 Jan 1979, leaving by her:
4 +Andrew Arthur George [The Lord Andrew Hay, Eastridge House, Binley, Hants SP11 6HA]; *b* 24 Oct 1959; *educ* Fettes and RAC Cirencester; ARICS; ptnr Knight, Frank and Rutley, estate agents; *m* 1986 *Rosanna Meryl, 2nd dau of John Brabazon Booth, of Darver Castle, Dundalk, Co Louth, and has:

  (1) +Angus; *b* 1991
  (2) +Rory; *b* 1993
5 +Hamish David Montague; *b* 24 Oct 1959; *educ* Fettes, Wadham Coll Oxford (BA) and King's Coll Hosp (MB, BS, DA)

TWEEDSMUIR

Arms: Az. a fess between three lion's heads erased arg. **Crest:** A sunflower ppr. **Supporters:** Dexter, a stag ppr., attired or, collared gu.; sinister, a falcon ppr., jessed, belled and beaked or, armed and collared gu. **Motto:** *Non inferiora secutus* ('Not following meaner things'). **Creation:** B. (UK) 1 June 1935.

THE 3RD BARON TWEEDSMUIR, of Elsfield, Oxford (William de l'Aigle Buchan) [The Rt Hon The Lord Tweedsmuir, West End House, Hornton, Oxon OX15 6DAJ; *b* 10 Jan 1916; *s* bro 1996; *educ* Eton and New Coll Oxford; S/Ldr RAFVR WW II; *m* 1st 25 Oct 1939 (*divorce* 1946) Nesta Irene, only dau of Lt-Col C D Crozier, RA, and has:

1 *Perdita Caroline; *b* 16 Dec 1940; *m* Nov 1968 (*divorce* 1977) Edward Connolly, of Concord Academy, Concord, Mass., and has:

  (1) *Cressida; *b* 1969

The 3rd BARON *m* 2nd 5 Dec 1946 (*divorce* 1960) Barbara Howard (*d* 17 Feb 1969), dau of Ernest Nash Ensor, of Wimbledon, and by her has:
1 +JOHN WILLIAM HOWARD De L'AIGLE (TOBY) [The Hon Toby Buchan, c/o Lloyds Bank, Wallingford, Oxon]; *b* 25 May 1950; *educ* Magdalen Coll Sch Oxford; *m* 22 Oct 1977 *Amanda Jocelyn, 2nd dau of Sir Gawain Westray Bell, KCMG, OBE, of Hidcote Manor, Glos, and has:

  (1) +John Alasdair Gawain; *b* 20 Nov 1986
  (2) +Christopher Charles Westray; *b* 1988
2 +(Charles Walter) Edward Ralph [The Hon Edward Buchan, 53 Lilleshall Rd, London SW4 0LW]; *b* 5 Aug 1951; *educ* Magdalen Coll Sch and Southampton U; *m* 1982 *Fiona J, yr dau of Paul Carlisle, of Penyrwrlodd, Llanigon, Hay-on-Wye, Herefs, and has:

  (1) +William Edward Francis Ewelme; *b* 1984
  (1) *Annabel; *b* 1986
  (2) *Laura; *b* 1988
  (3) *Amilia Katherine; *b* 1992
3 +James Ernest [The Hon James Buchan, 37 Gloucester Crescent, London NW1 7DL]; *b* 11 June 1954; *educ* Eton; jnlst with Financial Times, author: *Frozen Desire: an inquiry into the meaning of money* (1997); *m* 1986 *Lady Evelyn Rose Phipps, 2nd dau of 4th Marquess of Normanby (*qv*), and has:

  (1) +Nicholas Adam; *b* 10 Feb 1992
  (1) *Elizabeth Blanche; *b* 27 May 1989
  (2) *Barbara Rose Averil; *b* 18 Oct 1995
2 *Deborah Charlotte, JP; *b* 19 Oct 1947; *m* 8 Oct 1966 *Baron Stewartby (LP; *qv*) and has issue

3 *Laura Mary Clare [The Hon Mrs Chanter, Maison Bacchus, Gajan, 37030 St Mamert du Gard, France]; *b* 25 June 1953; *m* 1980 *Robin Chanter and has:

  (1) *Bacchante Pallas-Athene; *b* 1981
  (2) *Artemis Helen Bacchante; *b* 1982
  (3) *Aphrodite Barbara Bacchante; *b* 1984
  (4) *Demeter Violetta Bacchante; *b* 1988
4 *Ursula Margaret Bridget [The Hon Mrs Wide, Church Cottage, Main St, Glapthorn, Northants PE8 5BE]; *b* 25 June 1953; *m* 1979 *Charles Thomas Wide, QC, yr s of Nicholas Wide, and has:

  (1) *Thomas Nicholas Buchan; *b* 1984
  (1) *Emily Susan; *b* 1982

The 3rd BARON *m* 3rd 20 July 1960 *Sauré Cynthia Mary, dau of Maj Gerald Edward Tatchell, Roy Lincs Regt, and by her has:
4 +Alexander Edward; *b* 10 March 1961; *m* 1993 *Sarah, dau of George Pickles, and has:

  (1) +Patrick; *b* 1994
  (1) +Roland; *b* 1997

Lineage: JOHN BUCHAN, of Stellknowe, Midlothian; *b* 3 June 1811; slr and banker Peebles; *m* 10 July 1844 Violet (*d* 15 April 1876), dau of William Henderson, of Peebles, and *d* 24 Sept 1883, leaving, with other issue:

Rev JOHN BUCHAN; *b* 23 April 1847; Min John Knox Church Glasgow; *m* 2 Dec 1874 Helen (*d* 19 Dec 1937), dau of John Masterton, of Broughton Green, Peebles, and *d* 19 Nov 1911, having had:

1 JOHN, **1st Baron**
2 William; *b* 18 Feb 1880; *educ* BNC Oxford (BA); Registrar Land Banks Bengal, ICS; *dsp* 11 Nov 1912
3 James Walter; *b* 27 May 1882; MA, LLB, Town Clerk Peebles, gen ed and part author: *The History of Peebles-shire*; *d* unm 4 May 1954
4 Alastair Ebenezer; *b* 12 June 1894; Lt Roy Scots Fus; *ka* Arras 9 April 1917
1 Violet Katherine; *b* 20 Nov 1888; *d* 16 June 1893
2 Anna, JP (Peeblesshire); author: *Unforgettable, Unforgotten; Olivia in India; The Setons* and other books; *d* unm 24 Nov 1948

The est s,
JOHN BUCHAN, **1st Baron Tweedsmuir**, of Elsfield, Co Oxford (UK), so *cr* 1 June 1935, GCMG (1935), GCVO (1939), CH, PC (1937), JP, DL Oxon and Peeblesshire; *b* 26 Aug 1875; *educ* Glasgow U and BNC Oxford (MA, Hon Fell, Hon DCL); barrister Middle Temple 1901, Hon Bencher; Priv Sec to HC S Africa 1901–03, WW I Br HQ France 1916–17 (T/Lt-Col), Dir Info 1917–18, MP (C) Scottish Us 1927–35, Ld HC Gen Assembly Ch Scotland 1933 and 1934, Govr-Gen Canada 1935–40, Pres Scottish History Soc 1929–33, Tstee: Nat Library Scotland and Pilgrim Tst; Chllr Edinburgh U 1937, author of 100 books, including: *Prester John* (1910), *The Thirty-Nine Steps* (1915), *Greenmantle* (1916), *Mr Standfast* (1919), *Huntingtower* (1922), *The Three Hostages* (1924), *John Macnab* (1925), *Castle Gay* (1930), *Sir Walter Scott* (1932), *The Island of Sheep* (1936), *Memory Hold-the-Door* (autobiography, 1940) and *Sick Heart River* (1941), KGStJ, Orders Crown Italy and Crown Belgium; Hon LLD Edin, Glasgow, St Andrews, Harvard, Yale, McGill, Toronto and Queen's, Manitoba, Hon DLitt Columbia, Hon DD Victoria U Toronto, Hon FRCP and Roy Coll Surgns Canada; *m* 15 July 1907 Susan Charlotte, DGStJ, author of biography, fiction and children's stories (*d* 21 March 1977), est dau of Hon Norman de l'Aigle Grosvenor (see EBURY, B), and *d* 11 Feb 1940, leaving:

1 JOHN NORMAN STUART BUCHAN, **2nd Baron Tweedsmuir**, CBE (1964, OBE 1945), CD (1964); *b* 25 Nov 1911; *educ* Eton and BNC Oxford (BA 1933); Assist Dist Offr Uganda 1934–36, Hudson Bay Co's serv 1937–39, Canadian Army WW II CMF and NW Europe (wounded, despatches twice), Lt-Col cmdg Hastings and Prince Edward Regt 1943 (Hon Col 1955–60), Pres Fedn Cwlth and Br Empire Chambers Commerce 1954–57, memb BOAC Bd 1955–64, Govr Cwlth Inst 1958–77 (Tstee 1977–), Pres Inst Exports 1963–67, Chm: Advertising Standards Authority, Cncl on Tbnls 1973–80; Order Orange Nassau with swords Netherlands, Rector Aberdeen U 1948–51, Hon LLD Aberdeen 1948 and Queen's U Canada 1955; FRSE, FRGS, FRSA, FZS; author: *Hudson's Bay Trader* (1951), *Always a Countryman* (1953) and *One Man's Happiness* (memoirs); *m* 1st 27 July 1948 Priscilla Jean Fortescue, PC (*d* 1978), MP Aberdeen S 1946–66, Parly U-Sec Scottish Office 1962–64, *cr* a LP 1970 as Baroness Tweedsmuir of Belhelvie, yr dau of Brig Alan Fortescue Thomson, DSO, of Craighall, Kennethmont, Aberdeenshire, and widow of Maj Sir Arthur Lindsay Grant, 11th Bt, of Monymusk and Cullen (*qv*); *m* 2nd 1987 *Jean Margherita [The Rt Hon Jean Lady Tweedsmuir, Flat 2, The White House, 24 Dirleton Ave, N Berwick, E Lothian EH39 4BQ], dau of Capt Humphrey Douglas Tollemache, RN (see TOLLEMACHE, B), and widow of Sir Francis Grant, 12th Bt, of Monymusk and Cullen (*qv*), and *d* 20 June 1996, having by his 1st w had:

  (1) *(Priscilla) Susan (Susie); *b* 22 Aug 1949; *m* 24 Aug 1974 *Baron Selkirk of Douglas (*qv*) and has issue
2 WILLIAM De L'AIGLE BUCHAN, **3rd and present Baron Tweedsmuir**
3 Alastair Francis, CBE (1968, MBE 1945); *b* 9 Sept 1918; *educ* Eton and Ch Ch Oxford; Maj 14th Canadian Hus (Res) WW II; assist ed *Economist* 1948–51, Washington correspondent *Observer* 1951–55, dip and def correspondent 1955–58, Dir Inst Strategic Studies 1958–69, Cmdt IDC 1970–76, Prof Internat Rels Oxford 1974–76; *m* 11 April 1942 Hope (*d* 2 June 1997), dau of David Gordon Gilmour, of Ottawa, and *d* 4 Feb 1976, leaving:

  (1) +David John Brian Washington, OBE (1993); *b* 11 Feb 1947; *educ* Eton and Ch Ch Oxford; *m* 9 March 1st 1974 (*divorce* 1980) Sarah, dau of G L Cawkwell, of Oxford; *m* 2nd 1981 *Eugenie Elisabeth, dau of Prof Charles Maechling, Jr, of Washington, DC, and has:

    1a +Charles; *b* 1986
    1a *Susannah Janet; *b* 1983
  (2) +Benjamin William Alastair [Benjamin Buchan Esq, 6 Franconia Rd, London SW4]; *b* 23 April 1948; *educ* Eton and Univ Coll Oxford; *m* 20 April 1974 *Elizabeth, dau of Maj Peter Oakleigh-Walker, of The Meade, Crondall, Surrey, and has:

    1a *Adam Peter Alastair; *b* 1980
    1a *Eleanor Rose; *b* 1983

(1) *(Anna) Virginia Pauline [Mrs Kenneth Peake, 103 The Bowery, New York City, NY 10002, USA]; *b* 9 Sept 1953; *m* 1983 *Kenneth David Peake, s of Kenneth Peake, of Penyffordd, N Wales, and has:

1a *Ella Hope Dongqiong Buchan; *b* China 15 June 1995

1 Alice Caroline Helen; *m* 29 July 1933 Maj Sir Brian Fulke Ramsay-Fairfax-Lucy, 5th Bt (*qv*), and *d* 1993, having had issue

TWISLETON-WYKEHAM-FIENNES

Arms: Quarterly, 1st and 4th, azure three lions rampant or (for FIENNES); 2nd and 3rd, argent a chevron between three moles sable (for TWISLETON). **Crests:** 1 A wolf sejant proper, ducally gorged and chained or (for FIENNES), 2 An arm embowed and vested sable, cuffed argent, hand proper, holding a molespade or, headed and armed of the second. **Motto:** *Fortem posce animum* ('Look for a brave spirit'). **Creation:** Bt. (UK) 30 June 1916.

SIR RANULPH (TWISLETON-WYKEHAM-)FIENNES, 3RD BT, of Banbury, Co Oxon, OBE (1993) [Sir Ranulph Fiennes Bt OBE, Greenlands, Exford, Somerset TA24 7NU]; *b* posthumously 7 March 1944; *s f* 1944; *educ* Eton; Capt RSG, attd 22 SAS Regt 1966 and Sultan's Armed Forces Muscat 1968–69 (Dhofar Service Medal 1968), ret 1970; led Br Expdn: White Nile 1969, Jostedalsbre Glacier 1970, Headless Valley, BC, 1971, N Pole 1977, Transglobe 1979–823, Trans-Antarctic 1992–93, Polar Medal 1987 (clasp 1995), author: *A Talent for Trouble* (1970), *Ice Fall in Norway* (1972), *The Headless Valley* (1973), *Where Soldiers Fear to Tread* (1975), *Hell on Ice* (1979), *To the Ends of the Earth* (1973), *Bothie, the Polar Dog* (with Virginia Fiennes, 1984), *Living Dangerously* (autobiography, 1987), *The Feather Men* (1991), *Atlantis of the Sands* (1992), *Mind Over Matter* (1993), *The Sett* (1996); TV reporter and film maker, Liveryman Vintners' Co 1960; *m* 9 Sept 1970 *Virginia F Pepper, Polar medal (1987)

Lineage: The 11th BARON SAYE AND SELE (*qv*) had a 2nd s:

Sir Eustace Edward Twisleton-Wykeham-Fiennes, 1st Bt (UK), so *cr* 30 June 1916, JP (Berks and Dorset); *b* 29 Feb 1864; Lt-Col Oxon Hus, Riel Rebellion NW Canada 1885 (medal with clasp) and Egypt 1888–89 (despatches, medal with clasp, bronze star), Pioneer Expdn Mashonaland 1890 (medal and clasp), Boer War 1900–02 (despatches twice, Queen's medal and King's medal with three clasps), WW I Flanders and Dardanelles, DAQMG Plymouth Garrison (despatchs, two medals, Mons Star), MP (Lib) Banbury 1906–10 and 1910–18, PPS to 1st Ld Admlty 1912–14; Govr and C-in-C Seychelles 1918–21 and Leeward Islands 1921–29, memb Ctee Brompton Consumptive Hosp and Dep Chm Roy Albert Orphanage Bagshot, V-Pres W London Hosp, memb Ctee Roy Cancer Hosp; *m* 6 Nov 1894 Florence Agnes, OBE (1918) (*d* 31 Oct 1950), dau of John Rathfelder, of Constantia, S Africa, and widow of Arthur Woodward Fletcher, and *d* 9 Feb 1946, having had:

1 John Eustace; *b* 22 Aug 1895; Capt 2nd Bn Gordon Highrs; *ka* Arras 18 June 1917

2 **Sir Ranulph (Twisleton-Wykeham-)Fiennes, 2nd Bt**, DSO (1943); *b* 12 Nov 1902; ADC to Govr-Gen Canada 1928–30, Coronation Medal 1937, Palestine Medal 1938–39, Lt-Col cmdg RSG (RAC) WW II (Adj 1930–33); *m* 7 Aug 1931 Audrey Joan (*d* 1995), 2nd dau of Sir Percy Wilson Newson, 1st and last Bt (*see* 1949 edn), and *d* 1943, leaving:

1 Sir **RANULPH (TWISLETON-WYKEHAM-)FIENNES, 3rd and present Bt**

1 *Susan Valerie; *b* 15 Jan 1933; *educ* Capetown U (BA 1951); *m* 24 April 1957 *Maj John Jervoise FitzGerald Scott, Roy Dragoons, er s of Cdr Geoffrey Thomas Archibald Scott (*see* SCOTT, Bt, of Rotherfield), and has:

(1) *Arabella Caroline; *b* 1959; *m* 1986 *Francis D Williams

(2) *Venetia Lucy; *b* 1963

2 *Celia Florence [Mrs Robert Brown, Charles Johnson Memorial Hospital, Nqutu, Zululand, via Dundee, S Africa]; *b* 29 Feb 1936; *educ* Trin Coll Dublin (MD 1960); *m* 20 June 1964 *Capt Robert Savage Brown, MC, yst s of Dr Milton Brown, of St Paul, Minn., and has:

(1) *Anthony Newson Savage; *b* 26 July 1966; *m* 1993 *Sarah Halcyon, dau of William Frantzich

(1) *Deirdre Ann Savage; *b* 26 March 1965; *m* 1987 *James Evans Brabenec and has:

1a *James Jordan; *b* 1993

(2) *Nicola Lois Savage; *b* 24 Jan 1969; *m* 1991 *Keith Eric Schlechte and has:

1a *Alexandra Rose; *b* 1993

3 *Gillian Audrey [Mrs Timothy Hoult, Lower Octon Grange, Foxholes, Driffield, North Humberside]; *b* 6 Dec 1938; *m* 18 June 1960 *Timothy George Hoult, yr s of Lt-Col Joseph Murray Hoult, of Norton Place, Lincoln, and has:

(1) *Andrew George; *b* 16 May 1966

(1) *Rosalind Amy Elfrida; *b* 3 July 1961

(2) *Rachel Celia; *b* 3 Jan 1963

TYRWHITT

Arms: Gu. three lapwings or. **Crest:** A savage ppr., wreathed and cinctured vert, holding with both hands a club, also ppr. **Supporters:** Dexter, a savage wreathed about the loins and head with oak ppr. and holding over the shoulder in the exterior hand a club or; sinister, a sailor in the Royal Navy, holding in the exterior hand a coil of rope ppr. **Motto:** Tyme tryeth truth. **Creation:** Bt. (UK) 13 Dec 1919.

SIR REGINALD THOMAS NEWMAN TYRWHITT, 3RD BT, of Terschelling and of the City of Oxford [Sir Reginald Tyrwhitt, 51 Whitecross St, Barton-on-Humber, S Humberside]; *b* 21 Feb 1947; *s f* 1961; *educ* Downside; late Lt RA; *m* 16 Sept 1972 (*divorce* 1980, *annulled* 1984) (Sheila) Gail, dau of William A Clinton Crawford Nicoll, of Kingsham Old Farm, Liphook, Hants; *m* 2nd 1984 *Charlotte, only dau of Capt Angus Jeremy Christopher Hildyard, DL, RA (*see* MORRIS, B), and has:

1 +ROBERT ST JOHN HILDYARD; *b* 15 Feb 1987

1 *Letitia Mary Hildyard; *b* 1988

Lineage: Capt JOHN TYRWHITT, RN (*see* BERNERS, B); had, with two er sons (Sir Thomas, 1st Bt; John, *b* 2 Aug 1768):

RICHARD TYRWHITT, of Nantyr Hall, Denbighs; *b* 25 Aug 1772; barrister Inner Temple, Recorder Chester 1822–36; *m* 4 Aug 1797 Elizabeth (*d* 18 Aug 1846), dau of Rev Jonathan Lipyeatt, Rector Gt Hallingbury, Essex, and *d* 30 Jan 1836, having had, with other issue:

ROBERT PHILIP TYRWHITT; *b* 15 July 1798; barrister Middle Temple, Met Police Magistrate 1847–71; *m* 30 Sept 1824 Catharine Wigley (*d* 14 Nov 1863), er dau of Henry St John, of Crouch Hill, Middx, and had, with other issue:

Rev RICHARD ST JOHN TYRWHITT; *b* 19 March 1827; Vicar St Mary Magdalen Oxford; *m* 1st 28 June 1858 Eliza Anne (*d* 8 Sept 1859), dau of John Spencer Stanhope, of Canon Hall, Yorks, and had:

1 Walter Spencer Stanhope; *b* 6 Sept 1859; RBA, MA; *m* 14 Oct 1913 Ursula (*d* 9 Feb 1966), dau of Rev Henry Mervyn Tyrwhitt, and *d* 17 Jan 1932

The Rev RICHARD TYRWHITT *m* 2nd 2 Jan 1861 Caroline (*d* 6 Dec 1883), yr dau of John Yorke, of Bewerley Hall, Yorks, and by her had:

2 Cecil Robert (Rev); *b* 25 Dec 1862; Rector Whichford, Warwicks; *m* 28 Oct 1908 Alexandra Caroline, dau of Rev Henry Newport, Rector Tarrant Hinton, Somerset, and *d* 26 March 1924

3 Hugh St John; *b* 21 May 1865; *m* 16 Nov 1898 Alice Noel (*d* 8 April 1958), dau of Joseph Carter, of Roma, Qld, and *d* 4 Jan 1935, leaving:

(1) *Richard Yorke; *b* 7 March 1905; *m* 10 May 1939 *Ketha Lomax Willis and has:

1a *Richard Norman St John; *b* 1 Sept 1943

1a *Helen Frances; *b* 28 April 1940

(1) Noel Frances St John; *b* 30 March 1901; *m* 27 April 1927 Guy Stuart L'Estrange, er s of Henry L'Estrange, LRCP, LRCS, of Brisbane, Qld, and had:

1a *Richard Guy Tyrwhitt; *b* 18 Sept 1929; *m* 17 Aug 1963 *Janis, 2nd dau of Arthur Edward Ilott, of Tambo, Qld, and has:

1b *Andrew Richard; *b* 26 Dec 1965

2b *Guy Owen; *b* 15 April 1969

2a *Henry Tyrwhitt; *b* 4 Oct 1938; *m* 19 Oct 1962 *Sue Sheila Ann, dau of Samuel Owen Cowlishaw, of Yandilla Homestead, Yandilla, Qld, and has:

1b *Ross Owen; b 25 July 1964

2b *Peter Harry; b 27 July 1966

1a *Dodie Elfreda Noel; b 12 June 1928; m 3 June 1968 *Stephen Henry Steiger and has:

    1b *Robert Stephen; b 17 Dec 1968

2a *Mildred Alice; b 28 June 1932; m 3 June 1959 John Lahey Gardner, only s of Rev Alfred Robert Gardner, CF, of E Malvern, Victoria, Australia, and has:

    1b *Bruce John; b 11 April 1967

    1b *Margaret Frances; b 25 May 1961

    2b *Robyn Anne; b 13 Oct 1963

4 Beauchamp Edward; b 15 Aug 1867; m 1 Nov 1892 Eva Elizabeth (d 20 Aug 1929), dau of Robert Bentley Shaw Yates, of Rotherham, Yorks, and d 17 Jan 1929, leaving:

(1) Eva Frances St John; m 17 July 1915 Douglas Allix Wilkinson and had issue

(2) Margaret Caroline Barbara; m 10 Jan 1928 Maj Elwin Charles Hamilton Evered, Somerset LI, est s of Rev (Ranulph) Hamilton Evered, Rector Shenley, Bucks, and d 3 Jan 1945

5 REGINALD YORKE (Sir), **1st Bt**

6 Roland; b 15 Aug, d 24 Sept 1872

1 Alice Catherine; b 1864; nun at St Mary's Priory, Princethorpe, Rugby; d 15 Nov 1943

2 Frances Mary; d unm 4 Nov 1959

The Rev RICHARD TYRWHITT m 3rd 16 June 1885 Eliza Jane (d 20 Dec 1886), dau of Charles Waddell, HEICS, and d 6 Dec 1895

His 5th s,

Sir Reginald Yorke Tyrwhitt, 1st Bt (UK), so cr 13 Dec 1919 with thanks of Parl and a grant of £10,000 (over £180,000 in late-1990s terms), GCB (1929, KCB 1917, CB 1914), DSO (1916); b 10 May 1870; RN 1883–1934: Lt 1892, Cdre 1st Cl 1914, R-Adml 1919, V-Adml 1925, Adml 1929, Adml the Fleet 1934, served HMS *Cleopatra* in landing party for protection of inhabitants at Bluefields, Nicaragua, 1894, cmded 2nd Destroyer Flotilla 1912–13, Destroyer Flotillas of 1st Fleet 1913–14, WW I: cmded 1st and 3rd Flotillas and the Harwich Force, including Battles of Heligoland 28 Aug 1914 (despatches) and Dogger Bank 24 Jan 1915, SNO Gibraltar 1919–20, cmded 3rd Light Cruiser Sqdn 1921–22, CO Coast of Scotland and Adml Supt HM Dockyard Rosyth 1923–25, C-in-C China Station 1927–29, C-in-C The Nore 1930–33, First and Pncpl Naval ADC to HM GEORGE V 1932–34, Freedom Oxford and Ipswich 1919, Cdr Legn Hon, Croix de Guerre, Mil Order Savoy, Order Sacred Treasure Japan 1st Cl; Hon DCL Oxford 1919; m 24 Feb 1903 Angela Mary (d 8 June 1953), dau of Matthew Corbally, JP, DL, of Rathbeale Hall, Co Dublin, and had:

1 ST JOHN REGINALD JOSEPH (Sir), **2nd Bt**

1 Mary Joan Caroline, DBE (1949, OBE 1946), TD; b 27 Dec 1903; Brig WRAC WW II, Sr Controller and Dir ATS 1946–49, Dir WRAC 1949–50, Brig 1950, Hon ADC to HM GEORGE VI 1949–50; d unm 13 Feb 1997

2 Patricia Angela Mary; b 27 Feb 1913; Sr Cdr ATS WW II; m 31 Aug 1945 Capt Anthony John Alfred Lacy, Suffolk Regt (see LACY, Bt), and d 8 July 1998, leaving:

(1) *David Anthony (Rev Fr); b 1947; RC priest for Birmingham Archdiocese 1972, commnd Naval Chaplain 1981

(2) *John Reginald [John Lacy Esq, Gellfachreth, Llanfachreth, Dolgellau, Gwynedd LL40 2EH]; b 1948; m 1970 *Johneen Florence, dau of Michael Whitfield, of Wellesbourne, Warwicks, and has:

    1a *Mark Logan Tyrwhitt; b 1973; m 1998 *Lois Ann, dau of Alan Clingo, of S Wootton, Norfolk

    2a *Michael John; b 1981

    1a *Olivia Johneen; b 1976

(3) *Richard Patrick James [Richard Lacy Esq, Moat Farmhouse, Mill Green, Edwardstone, Suffolk CO10 5PY]; b 1950; m 1973 *Penelope Anne, JP, dau of Hon Simon Chelmsford Loader Maffey (see RUGBY, B), and has:

    1a *Timothy James; b 1985

    1a *Laura Penelope; b 1980

    2a *Diana Louise; b 1984

(1) *Anne Mary [Mrs Anthony Poulter, Four Winds, Woodbine, Cumbria LA13 0NF]; b 20 Jan 1953; m 9 April 1994 *Capt Anthony Mervyn Poulter, OBE, RN, s of Mervyn Brian Poulter

Sir REGINALD d 30 May 1951; his only s,

Sir St John Reginald Joseph Tyrwhitt, 2nd Bt, KCB (1961, CB 1957), DSO (1943), DSC (1942) and bar (1944); b 18 April 1905; educ RNCs Osborne and Dartmouth; Lt 1928, Lt-Cdr 1936, Cdr 1940, Capt 1945, R-Adml 1955, V-Adml 1958, Naval ADC to Govr-Gen S Africa 1932–34, Flag Offr Flotillas Indian Navy 1955–56, Ch Allied Staff Mediterranean 1958–59, a Ld Commr Admlty, 2nd Sea Ld and Ch Naval Personnel 1959–61, Yr Bro Trinity House; m 22 Jan 1944 *Nancy Veronica [Lady Agnew, Pinehurst, Friary Rd, S Ascot, Berks] (m 2nd 27 Sept 1965, as his 2nd w, Sir (William) Godfrey Agnew, KCVO, CB (d Dec 1995), only s of Lennox Edelsten Agnew, of Tunbridge Wells, Kent), only child of Charles Newman Gilbey (see GILBEY, Bt), and d 10 Oct 1961, leaving:

1 Sir REGINALD THOMAS NEWMAN TYRWHITT, **3rd and present Bt**

2 +John Edward Charles; b 27 July 1953; MA Cantab 1975; ACA 1979; m 1978 *Melinda Ngaire, only dau of Anthony Towell, MC, of Long Island, NY, and has:

(1) +St John Thomas Anthony; b 1980

(2) +Oliver Edward John; b 1982

(3) +Alexander William James; b 1984

1 *Veronica Mary [Mrs Christopher Boast, 11 Turner St, Gawler, SA 5118, Australia]; b 2 Dec 1944; educ St Mary's Convent, Ascot; m 1979 *Christopher Miles Boast and has:

(1) *Charles St John; b 1980

(2) *Timothy William; b 1982

ULLSWATER

Arms: Or six annulets sable, three, two and one, a crescent for difference. **Crest:** A dragon passant argent. **Supporters:** On either side a horse argent, gorged with a wreath of laurel vert and charged on the shoulder with a portcullis chained or. **Motto:** *Magistratus indicat virum* ('The office indicates the man').
Creations: V. (UK) 8 July 1921.

THE 2ND VISCOUNT ULLSWATER, of Campsea Ashe, Suffolk (Nicholas James Christopher Lowther, PC (1994), JP (Wilts)) [The Rt Hon The Viscount Ullswater PC JP, The Old Rectory, Docking, Norfolk PE31 8LJ]; b 9 Jan 1942; s ggf 1949; educ Eton and Trin Coll Cambridge; late Capt Wessex Yeo, amateur jockey, Pres Wilts: Assoc Boys' Clubs, and T&AVR 1973; Ld in Waiting (Govt Whip) 1989–90, Parly U-Sec Employment 1990–93, Capt Gentlemen at Arms (Govt Ch Whip) 1993–94, Min State Environment 1994–95, Priv Sec to HRH PRINCESS MARGARET, COUNTESS OF SNOWDON 1998–; m 10 June 1967 *Susan, only dau of James Howard Weatherby, of Lemington Grange, Moreton-in-Marsh, Glos, by Mary, yst dau of Maj-Gen Sir Hereward Wake, 13th Bt (qv), and has:

1 +BENJAMIN JAMES [The Hon Benjamin Lowther, The Old Rectory, Docking, Norfolk PE31 8LJ]; b 26 Nov 1975; educ Eton and Bristol U

2 +Edward John; b 8 Oct 1981; educ Eton; Page of Honour to HM THE QUEEN to 1996

1 *Emma Mary; b 2 Aug 1968; plays alto saxophone with The Reverend James Taste band

2 *Clare Priscilla; b 17 July 1970; m 31 Oct 1996, as his 2nd w, *Mark Flawn-Thomas, s of Peter Flawn-Thomas

Lineage: The Hon WILLIAM LOWTHER, of Campsea Ashe, Wickham Market, Suffolk, bro of 3rd Earl of Lonsdale (qv); m Hon Charlotte Alice Parke (d 5 Jan 1908), dau of 1st and last Baron Wensleydale of Walton (see 1868 edn), and d 23 Jan 1912, leaving:

JAMES WILLIAM LOWTHER, **1st Viscount Ullswater**, of Campsea Ashe, Co Suffolk (UK), so cr 8 July 1921, GCB (1921), PC (18 July 1898), JP (Cumberland and Suffolk); b 1 April 1855; educ Eton, King's Coll London (Fell) and Trin Coll Cambridge (LLM); barrister Inner Temple 1879 (bencher 1906), MP (C) Rutland 1883–85 and Mid-Cumberland (which fought unsuccessfully 1885) 1886–1921, Parly U-Sec For Affrs 1891–92, Chm Ways and Means Ctee and Dep Speaker H of C 1895–1905 (Speaker 1905–21), Speaker's Electoral Reform Conf 1916–17, 4th Charity Commr 1887, CA E Suffolk 1914 and 1928, Lt-Col 5th Bn Suffolk Vol Regt 1917, Tstee: Br Museum 1922–31 and Nat Portrait Gallery 1924, Chm: Cumberland QS 1900–06, Roy Commission Proportional Representation 1918, Fedl Devolution Conference 1919, Roy Commn London Govt 1921–23, Review Ctee Political Honours Commn 1923–24, Ag Wages Bd 1928, Lds and Commons Ctee on Electoral reform 1929–30 and BBC Investigation Ctee 1935, Freeman City London 1924, Hon DCL Oxon, Hon LLD Cantab and Leeds; author: *A Speaker's Commentaries* (1925); m 1 March 1886 Mary Frances (d 16 May 1944), dau of Alexander James Beresford-Hope (see SALISBURY, M), and d 27 March 1949, having had :

1 Christopher William; b 18 Jan 1887; educ Eton and Trin Coll Cambridge; Hon Attaché Morocco 1907 and Mexico 1907–09, with Pearson & Sons and Griffiths & Sons to 1912, Maj Westmorland and Cumberland Yeo WW I (wounded), MP (C to Jan 1921, Ind following Horatio Bottomley from Jan 1921) Cumberland N 1918–22, unsuccessfully fought Wallsend 1922 and 1923 and Workington 1931, chm Br Dominions Land Corp, dir: Bolsom Bros, Cumberland News and Yorkshire Insur; m 1st 17 June 1910 (divorce 1921) Ina Marjorie Gwendoline, OBE (1934) (m 2nd Lord George Cholmondeley (see CHOLMONDELEY, M) and d 9 July 1969), yst dau of Canon Raymond Pelly (see PELLY, Bt), and had:

(1) John Arthur, MVO (1937); b 13 Oct 1910; educ Eton; Sec to HRH THE late DUKE OF KENT 1935; Lt RNVR WW II; m 22 July 1937 Priscilla (d 10 Nov 1945), yr dau of Reginald Everitt Lambert, of Pensbury Ho, Shaftesbury, Dorset, and was k in a flying accident 25 Aug 1942, leaving:

1a NICHOLAS JAMES CHRISTOPHER, **2nd and present Viscount Ullswater**

1a *Kirstin Elizabeth [The Hon Mrs Welton, Willowbrook House, Lower Dean, Northleach, Glos]; b 8 June 1939; granted Feb 1951 rank of viscount's dau; *m* 1st 6 Jan 1966 (*divorce* 19–) Capt Caledon Alexander, late 7th QOH, er s of Capt Francis John Alexander, RN, of S Kensington, and has:

  1b *James Caledon; *b* 24 Sept 1969

  2b *Charlotte Jane; *b* 22 Jan 1968

1a (cont.) The Hon Mrs Kirstin Alexander *m* 2nd 9 April 1976 *Anthony Edward Ord Welton

1 (cont.) The Hon Christopher Lowther *m* 2nd 16 Feb 1921 Dorothy (*m* 3rd 21 July 1936 Capt Hugh Cullen, MC), dau of Arthur Henry Bromley-Davenport and formerly w of Capt Samuel Guy Loveridge, and *d* 7 Jan 1935, having by her had:

  (1) *Rosemary [The Hon Mrs Goolden, Forge Cottage, Withyham, Sussex]; *b* 25 Feb 1922; 2nd Offr WRNS WW II, granted Oct 1950 with her surv sis rank of viscount's dau; *m* 7 July 1945 *Lt (S) Douglas Cyril Aubrey Goolden, RNVR, s of Cdr Cyril Goolden, DSO, RN, of Colombo, Ceylon, and has:

    1a *Michael Cyril Christopher [Michael Goolden Esq, Foxes Bank Farm, Washwell Lane, Wadhurst, E Sussex TN5 6LN]; *b* 7 Sept 1947; *educ* Lancing and Oriel Coll Oxford; *m* 1977 *Siegrith, yr twin dau of Basil Vickers, of Skelmore, Ayrshire, and has:

      1b *Freya Polly Tamsin; *b* 22 Oct 1980

      2b *Camilla Sophia Marique; *b* 8 Sept 1984

      3b *Chloë Florence Basilia; *b* 24 Feb 1988

    2a *Alastair Richard Lowther; *b* 14 Aug 1954; *educ* Lancing and Bristol U

    1a *Jill Priscilla; *b* 28 Sept 1949; *m* 19 May 1984 *Paul Douglas Marshall, s of Frank Marshall, of Hampton and has:

      1b *Philip Guy Douglas; *b* 2 Sept 1991

      1b *Oriel Rosalie Tess; *b* 4 Nov 1984

      2b *Verity Frances Marina; *b* 16 May 1986

  (2) Christine; *b* 16 Jan, *d* 4 Aug 1927

  (3) *Jennifer [The Hon Mrs Sullivan, 19 Minster Yard, Lincoln LN2 1PY]; *b* 11 June 1932; *m* 1st 9 Sept 1954 (*divorce* 1962), as his 2nd w, 7th Earl of Lonsdale (*qv*) and has issue; *m* 2nd 15 Dec 1962 (*divorce* 1972) F/Lt William Edward Clayfield, DFC, RAF, s of Walter H Clayfield, of Nuneaton; *m* 3rd 29 March 1976 (*divorce* 1980) Rev Oswald Dickin Carter (*d* 1986); *m* 4th 1981 *James Cornelius Sullivan

2 Arthur James Beresford; *b* 28 Oct 1888; *educ* Eton; barrister Inner Temple 1911, Capt 3rd Bn Suffolk Regt WW I (wounded), Assist Commr Kenya Colony 1918–20, ADC to Govr S Rhodesia 1923; *d* unm 2 March 1967

1 Mildred, OBE (1917); Assist Pay Offr Cmd Pay Office 1915–19 WW I, in CD, MOI and BOT WW II, borough cncllr St Marylebone 1944, Long Service Medal for 22 years service with CD 1962; *d* unm 2 July 1973

USHER

Arms: Gules a saltire between four batons argent garnished azure. **Crest:** A dexter arm couped below the elbow, vested azure, cuffed argent, holding in the hand a baton proper. **Motto:** *Ne vile velis* ('Wish nothing base'). **Creation:** Bt. (UK) 29 Aug 1899.

SIR (WILLIAM) JOHN TEVENAR USHER, 7TH BT, of Norton, Ratho, Co Midlothian, and of Wells, Hobkirk, Co Roxburgh [Sir John Usher Bt, 7 Thorngate Rd, Hayfields, Pietermaritzburg 3201, S Africa]; *b* 18 April 1940; *s* cousin 1994; *educ* Uppingham; *m* 1st 6 Jan 1962 (*divorce* 1990) Rosemary Margaret, yr dau of Col Sir Reginald Douglas Henry Houldsworth, 4th Bt (*qv*); *m* 2nd 1992 *Georgina Elizabeth, dau of Charles Manclark, and by his 1st w has:

  1 +ANDREW JOHN [Andrew Usher Esq, 61 Waldron Rd, London SW18 3TA]; *b* 8 Feb 1963; *educ* Hilton Coll S Africa; *m* 3 Oct 1987 *Charlotte Louise Alexandra, only dau of Robert Barry Eldridge, and has:

    (1) +Rory James Andrew; *b* 11 June 1991

    (2) +Callum William Edward; *b* 2 June 1994

  2 +Michael William Reginald; *b* 1967; *educ* Maritzburg Coll

  1 *Caroline Rosemary; *b* 16 March 1966

Lineage: GEORGE USHER, of Darnick, Melrose, Roxburghshire; *b* 14 Dec 1626; *m* Bessie Tait and had, with other issue:

JOHN USHER; *b* 26 Dec 1651; *m* Margaret Turnbull and had, with other issue:

JAMES USHER; *b* 1672; *m* Isabella Mercer and had, with other issue:

JOHN USHER; *b* 12 March 1710; acquired land in Darnick, nr Melrose, Roxburghshire, including Toftfield; *m* Janet White, of Ancrum, and had:

JAMES USHER, of Toftfield; *b* 17 July 1738; *m* 25 May 1765 Margaret Greive, of Melrose, and *d* 15 Nov 1816, leaving, with other issue:

ANDREW USHER, of Edinburgh; *b* 7 April 1782; whisky merchant, fnder Andrew Usher & Co 1813; *m* 31 Dec 1806 Margaret (*d* 24 Feb 1860), dau of Thomas Balmer, of Ettrickbrae, Roxburghs, and *d* 17 Aug 1855, leaving, with eight daus:

  1 James; *b* 21 March 1811; *d* 24 May 1862, leaving issue

  2 Thomas; *b* 27 Oct 1821; *m* Caroline Henderson and *d* 30 June 1896, leaving, with other issue:

    (1) Harry Lawrence, of Summerfield, Dunbar; had:

      1a Alice Margaret; *m* 1917 her cousin Ronald James Usher (*see below*) and *d* 1975, leaving issue

      2a Jean Elspeth; *m* 11 June 1918 her cousin **Sir John Turnbull Usher, 3rd Bt**, and *d* 6 Jan 1950, leaving issue

  3 Andrew, DL, of Northfield, St Abbs, Hall Manor, Peebles, and Johnstounburn, E Lothian; *b* 5 Jan 1826; gave The Usher Hall to city of Edinburgh; *m* 1st 14 Aug 1850 Elizabeth Langmuir Miller (*d* 14 June 1876) and had:

    (1) Howard Graham; *b* 22 Dec 1866; *dsp* 10 Nov 1890

    (1) Jane Binning; *b* 6 April 1859; *m* 14 July 1897 William Gordon Burn-Murdoch, JP (*d* 19 July 1939), and *dsp* 12 June 1927

    (2) Elizabeth Stewart; *b* 12 Nov 1862; *m* 30 April 1885 — St Clair Cunningham (*d* 19 April 1906) and *d* 30 March 1951, leaving issue

  3 (cont.) Andrew Usher *m* 2nd 23 Dec 1879 Marion Blackwood Murray (*d* 28 Jan 1925) and *d* 1 Nov 1898, leaving by her:

    (3) Mary Murray; *b* 19 Nov 1884; OStJ; *m* 31 March 1910 Col Chichester de Windt Crookshank, JP (E Lothian), DL, MP (U) Berwick and Haddington 1924–29 and Bootle 1931–35 (*d* 23 Oct 1958), and *d* 2 July 1960, leaving issue

4 Sir John Usher, 1st Bt (UK), so cr 29 Aug 1899, JP (Midlothian), DL (Caithness); *b* 18 Jan 1828; distiller and sr ptnr Andrew Usher & Co, fndr chair public health Edinburgh U 1898, built a public health inst 1902, LLD Edinburgh 1903; *m* 18 Aug 1853 Mary Anne (*d* 15 March 1902), dau of Thomas Balmer, commr to Duke of Richmond, and *d* 24 March 1904, having had:

  (1) John Andrew; *b* 23 Jan 1856; *d* unm 20 April 1878

  (2) Thomas Balmer; *b* 7 Sept 1857; *d* unm 20 Dec 1878

  (3) ROBERT (Sir), **2nd Bt**

  (4) Frederick; *b* 12 Dec 1862; *m* 26 Nov 1901 Rose Emil (*m* 2nd 8 July 1911 Colin Mackenzie Black, CVO, WS (*d* 5 Oct 1943), only s of A D M Black, WS, of Edinburgh, and *d* 1958), est dau of Rev William John Knox-Little, Canon Worcester, and *d* 27 Oct 1909, leaving:

    1a Neil John William Heriot USHER later MURRAY-USHER (added on marriage) later still USHER again, JP (Kirkcudbrightshire); *b* 16 July 1903; *educ* Eton and Trin Coll Oxford; Lt 7th Bn KOSB; *m* 1st 14 Dec 1929 (*divorce* 1937) Elizabeth Evelyn (*d* 1990), only child of Lt-Col Frederick Murray-Baillie, of Cally, and had:

      1b +James Neil [James Usher Esq, Murrayton, Gatehouse of Fleet, Kircudbrightshire]; *b* 8 July 1931; *educ* King's Canterbury and RAC Cirencester; *m* 22 April 1957 (*divorce* 1977) Sara Winefred, dau of Lt-Col Laurence Richardson Younger, Ayrshire Yeo, and Mrs Ian R Pitman, of Langlands, Kircudbright, and has:

        1c +Peter James; *b* 17 Oct 1961

        1c *Rosanne Helen; *b* 18 Jan 1960

        2c *Diana Katherine; *b* 12 Nov 1968

    1a (cont) Neil Usher *m* 2nd 15 Nov 1938 *Dorothy Margaret, est dau of Rev Colin William Scott-Moncrieff, of Winchester, and *d* 8 Oct 1989

    2a Derick Oliver Heriot; *b* 7 Oct 1907; Lt Black Watch; *d* 8 Oct 1935

    1a Annette May Heriot; *b* 27 July 1905; *d* unm 25 Sept 1954

  (5) Francis James; *b* 4 July 1864; *m* 12 Aug 1896 Catherine Edwards (*d* 18 Feb 1930), dau of Simeon Jones, of St John, NB, and *d* 5 Sept 1938, leaving:

    1a Francis Simeon Caverhill; *b* 26 Dec 1902; Lt Res Offrs Scots Gds; *m* 9 Dec 1935 Jean Lindsay (*d* 13 Dec 1954), dau of William Edmonstone Kitson, of Blanerne, Berwicks, and *d* 23 Oct 1954, leaving:

      1b +Francis John [Francis Usher Esq, Dunglass, Cockburnspath, Berwickshire TD13 5XF]; *b* 21 March 1937; *educ* Clifton Hall Edinburgh and Ecole de Roches France; *m* 15 April 1967 *Merilyn Haswell, only dau of William Lyle Brown, DSO, TD, MD, of White Ridge, Bamburgh, Northumberland, and adopted:

        *Simon Francis; *b* 1975

        *Katharine Caverhill; *b* 1972

  (1) Agnes Stuart; *b* 28 July 1867; *m* 5 Dec 1895 (*divorce* 1921) John Little (*d* 6 July 1931) and *d* 26 Sept 1948, leaving issue

  (2) Mary Anne; *b* 6 Nov 1868; *m* 28 Aug 1890 Thomas Greenshields Leadbetter, of Spital Tower, Denholm, Roxburghs, and *d* 11 Nov 1955, leaving issue

Sir John's 3rd s,

Sir Robert Usher, 2nd Bt, JP (Roxburghshire and Midlothian), DL (Caithness); *b* 25 May 1860; Jt MFH Linlithgowshire and Stirlingshire with his two yr bros *c* 1904; *m* 26 Aug 1890 Katherine Scott (*d* 2 June 1948), dau of James Turnbull, of Edinburgh, and *d* 21 Feb 1933, leaving:

  1 **Sir John Turnbull Usher, 3rd Bt**, OBE (1945), JP; *b* 2 June 1891; *educ* Uppingham; Capt Inniskilling Dragoons, Maj Res Offrs 9th Lancers, Lt-Col and Brevet-Col cmdg Lanarks Yeo WW I, Roy Pioneer Corps WW II, memb Roy Co Archers, Silver Jubilee 1935 and Coronation 1937 Medals; *m* 11 June 1918 his cousin Jean Elspeth, 2nd dau of Harry Lawrence Usher (*see above*), and *d* 5 May 1951, leaving:

    (1) Katharine Alice; *b* 28 Jan 1920; *m* 10 April 1943 George Simpson MacKnight, WS (*d* 18 Dec 1952), s of George Simpson MacKnight, of Linlithgow, and *d* 1978, leaving:

      1a *Neil John; *b* 27 Dec 1946; *educ* Tabley Ho Knutsford

1a *Elspeth Anne; *b* 4 Aug 1949

(2) *Jacqueline [Mrs William Faulkner, Rosybank House, Coldstream, Berwicks TD12 4AZ]; *b* 7 July 1931; *m* 1st 11 Oct 1955 (*divorce* 1980) Capt Christopher Michael Wolfe Murray, Gordon Highrs (*see* MURRAY, Bt, of Blackbarony); *m* 2nd 18 April 1998 *Cdr William John Macnamara Faulkner, RN, of Petersfield, Hants, and by her 1st husb has issue

2 Ronald James, DSC, of Aravriagh, Oban, Argyll, and Pulteneytown, Caithness; *b* 24 Sept 1892; Lt RN WW I, Maj HG WW II; *m* 28 April 1917 his cousin Alice Margaret (*see* above), dau of Harry Lawrence Usher, and *d* 29 Sept 1948, having had:

(1) (Robert) Ronald Harry; *b* 15 May 1924; Lt RN WW II (despatches); *m* 3 Sept 1945 Jane (*m* 2nd 3 July 1954 James Murray Gregory-Jones, of Penarth, Glam and had further issue), dau of James Hall, of Ryton-on-Tyne, and *d* 29 April 1947, leaving:

1a *Elizabeth Margaret [Mrs Elizabeth Richards, Wild Thyme Cottage, Dinas Powis, S Glam, Wales]; *b* 9 Sept 1946; *m* 5 Sept 1969 (*divorce* 1982) David Patrick Richards and has:

1b *Peter James; *b* 1970

2b *Oswain David; *b* 1973

1 Hazel Jean; *b* 3 July 1918; SSStJ 1977; *m* 9 Sept 1940 *Baron Stodart of Leaston (*qv*) and *d* 18 March 1995

2 Margaret Daphne; *b* 14 Oct 1920; *m* 5 June 1946 William Kirkpatrick (*d* 1967), s of James Kirkpatrick, of Newbie Mains, Annan, Dumfriesshire, and *d* 1996, leaving:

(1) *Ronald James; *b* 31 March 1948

(1) *Susan Woodrow; *b* 4 Sept 1949

(2) *Margaret Anne; *b* 12 Aug 1953

3 **Sir (Robert) Stuart Usher, 4th Bt**; *b* 19 April 1898; *educ* Uppingham and RMC Sandhurst; Lt Inniskilling Dragoons, Roy Humane Soc's Bronze Medal 1927; *m* 12 Dec 1930 Gertrude Martha (*d* 1984), 2nd dau of Lionel Barnard Sampson, of Argentina, and *d* 10 Nov 1962, leaving:

(1) **Sir Peter Lionel Usher, 5th Bt**; *b* Oct 1931; *d* unm 1 June 1990

(2) **Sir Robert Edward Usher, 6th Bt**; *b* 18 April 1934; *educ* privately; *d* unm 26 Sept 1994

4 Alexander Balmer; *b* 8 March 1902; Maj Lothian and Border Horse Yeo WW II; *ka* France June 1940

5 William Dove; *b* 10 March 1904; *educ* Uppingham and Clare Coll Cambridge; *m* 26 April 1939 Christa Elizabeth (*d* 6 Feb 1996), dau of Bruno von Tevenar, of Tanganyika, and *d* 2 May 1969, leaving:

(1) **Sir (WILLIAM) JOHN TEVENAR USHER, 7th and present Bt**

(2) +Stuart Alexander [Stuart Usher Esq, Under Langlee, Jedburgh TD8 6PB]; *b* 12 July 1941; *educ* Uppingham; *m* 12 Dec 1981 *Gillian Anne, dau of Herbert Anthony Creeke, MRCS, and has:

1a +Richard William; *b* 16 Oct 1986

1a *Katherine Anne; *b* 19 Dec 1983

6 Thomas Clive, CBE (1945), DSO and bar (1943); *b* 21 June 1907; *educ* Uppingham; Brig RA WW II, ADC to HM THE QUEEN 1957–58; *m* 8 Sept 1939 *Valentine [Mrs Thomas Usher, Wells Stables, Hawick, Roxburghs], dau of Brig Cecil Valentine Stockwell, DSO, of Victoria, BC, and *d* 17 Nov 1982, leaving:

(1) *Margaret Anne [Mrs Alan Mactaggart, West Nisbet, Jedbugh, Roxburghs]; *b* 23 June 1941; *m* 1964 *Alan Harry Mactaggart, yr s of William Alexander Mactaggart, CBE, JP, of Bewlie, Melrose, and has:

1a *David Clive; *b* 25 Dec 1966

2a *William Jeremy; *b* 8 Jan 1970

1 Jean Scott; *b* 18 Sept 1893; *d* 5 March 1902

2 Grizel Mary; *b* 25 Nov 1895; *d* 14 Jan 1896

VALENTIA

Arms: Paly of six argent and azure, over all a bend gules. **Crest:** A Moor's head in profile, couped proper, wreathed about the temples argent and azure. **Supporters:** Dexter, a Roman soldier in armour or, short sleeves and apron gules, face, arms and legs bare, the latter sandalled argent, on his head a helmet gold, on the top three feathers of the second, holding in his exterior hand a shield, thereon a female's head; sinister, a Moorish prince proper in armour or, wreathed round the temples argent and azure, short sleeves and apron gules, boots gold, behind him a sheaf of arrows proper fastened by a pink ribbon, in his exterior hand a bow proper. **Motto:** *Virtutis amore* ('By the love of virtue'). **Creations:** Bt. (I) 7 Aug 1620, V. (I) 11 March 1621/2, B. (I) 8 Feb 1628/9.

THE 15TH VISCOUNT OF VALENTIA, Baron Mountnorris, of Mountnorris, Co Armagh, and a **Baronet** (Premier Bt of Ireland) (Sir Richard John Dighton Annesley, Bt); *b* 15 Aug 1929; *s f* 1983; *educ* Marlborough and RMA Sandhurst; Capt RA, ret 1957, farmer Zimbabwe 1957–, sch master Ruzawi Prep Sch Marondera 1977–83; *m* 10 Aug 1957 *Anita Phyllis, only dau of William Arthur Joy, of Bristol, and has had:

1 +FRANCIS WILLIAM DIGHTON; *b* 29 Dec 1959; *educ* Falcon Coll Bulawayo; *m* 1982 *Shaneen Hobbs and has:

(1) *Kirsten; *b* 1986

(2) *Sarah Ashleigh; *b* 1989

2 Richard Dighton; *b* 1 April 1962; *educ* Falcon Coll; *d* 1989

3 +Peter John; *b* 18 Dec 1967; *educ* Falcon Coll; *m* 1987 *Deborah Coetes

1 *Sarah Joy [The Hon Mrs Frewen, Hillside Farm, N Bergersdorp, NE Cape, S Africa]; *b* 3 Aug 1958; *m* 1980 *Mark K Frewen and has:

(1) *Matthew; *b* 1991

(1) *Samantha Joy; *b* 1987

Valentia, previous creations: Sir Donald Maccarty *Mor* ('The Great' or 'The Elder'), Chief of his name in Ireland, was in 1565 created Earl of Clancare and Baron of Valentia as part of the Tudor policy (only intermittently successful) of trying to win over the leading Irish families by a judicious distribution of titles. In 1597 the new Earl renounced not only his titles but his allegiance to the English Crown. On his death without male issue soon after, the titles expired in any case.

In March 1620/1 Henry Power, born of a Denbighshire family but newly settled in Ireland, was created Viscount of Valentia. On his death without issue in 1642 the Viscountcy expired. Even before his death the reversion of the title (strictly speaking the title name) was settled on Francis Annesley, who it has been alleged was in some way related to Power, though this is not proven and in any case Power had at the time two living brothers, each with issue, in whose favour the revival of the title might more appropriately have been effected.

Lineage: GEORGE ANNESLEY, of Newport Pagnell, Bucks, allegedly descended from the ANNESLEYs of Ruddington, Notts, themselves a cadet branch of the ANNESLEYs of Annesley, Notts; had, with a yr s (Thomas):

ROBERT ANNESLEY; naval offr and Capt in the forces sent by ELIZABETH I to suppress the Earl of Desmond's rising in Ireland; later took part in the plantation of Munster; *m* Beatrix, dau of John Cornwall, of Moor Park, Herts; his (or perhaps his bro Thomas's) est s:

Sir Francis Annesley, 1st Bt (I), and **1st Viscount of Valentia**, Co Kerry, so *cr* 7 Aug 1620 and 11 March 1621/2 respectively (though in the latter case with the expectancy of becoming a Viscount only on the death of the Viscount Valentia *cr* on 1 March 1620/1 (*see* **previous creations** above), an event which did not occur till 26 May 1642), as also between whiles 8 Feb 1628/9 BARON MOUNTNORRIS, of Mountnorris, Co Armagh (all I), PC (I 1616–Feb 1635/6); *b* by 1 Feb 1583/4; in service of Sir Arthur Chichester, 1st and last Baron Chichester of Belfast (*see* DONEGALL, M) and Ld Dep Ireland, possibly at first in a relatively menial capacity such as that of butler but latterly on terms of close friendship (if not quite equality) such that he was put in the way of acquiring large tracts of Irish land during the Plantation of Ulster and the granting by the Crown of estates further south confiscated from native Irish families; Comptroller Works Ireland

1606, Jt Clerk Cncl Munster 1607–11, Clerk Tallies and Pells Ireland 1612–25, MP (I Parl) Lismore 1613–14 and Co Armagh 1614–15, MP (E Parl) Carmarthen 1625 and Newton in Makerfield 1628–29, ktd 1616, Commr for reformation of Ireland March 1621/2 and Plantation of Ulster 1622, V-Treas and Receiver-Gen Revenue Ireland 1625, Treas at Wars Ireland 1632; sentenced to death for supposed insubordination during Ld Deputyship of Lord Wentworth, who had been given cause to look on him with disfavour, but sentence commuted to house arrest 1635–37, though relieved of all his posts on grounds of corruption, for which there seems to have been some justification; *m* 1st *c* 1608 Dorothy (*d* 3 May 1624), dau of Sir John Philipps, 1st Bt (*see* SAINT DAVIDS, V), and had issue (extinct in the male line, presumably by 1844, otherwise the **10th Viscount**, who was of a junior branch to this one, could not have inherited the title):

1 ARTHUR ANNESLEY, **2nd Viscount of Valentia** and 1st EARL OF ANGLESEY, so *cr* 20 April 1661, as also BARON ANNESLEY, of Newport Pagnell, Co Buckingham (both E), PC (1661); *b* 10 July 1614; *educ* (allegedly) Magdalen Coll Oxford and (definitely) Lincoln's Inn; MP Radnorshire 1647–53, Dublin (E Parl) 1659–60 and Carmarthen 1660, Pres Cncl of State 1660, V-Treas Ireland 1660–67, Treas Navy 1667–68, Ld Privy Seal 1673–82; *m* 24 April 1638 Elizabeth (*bur* 20 Jan 1697/8), dau and coheir of Sir James Altham, a Baron Exchequer, of Oxhey, Herts, and *d* 6 April 1686, having had, with other issue:

(1) JAMES ANNESLEY, **3rd Viscount of Valentia** and 2nd EARL OF ANGLESEY; *b c* 1645; *educ* Ch Ch Oxford; *m c* 17 Sept 1669 Elizabeth (*d* 7 Dec 1700), dau of 8th Earl of Rutland (*see* RUTLAND, D), and *d* 1 April 1690, leaving:

1a JAMES ANNESLEY, **4th Viscount of Valentia** and 3rd EARL OF ANGLESEY; *bapt* 13 July 1674; *educ* Ch Ch Oxford; *m* 28 Oct 1699 Lady Catherine Darnley (*m* 2nd 16 March 1705/6 1st Duke of the County of Buckingham and of Normanby (*see* SHEFFIELD, Bt) and *d* 14 March 1743), illegitimate dau of Catherine Sedley (*see* MEXBOROUGH, E), Countess of Dorchester in her own right, by JAMES II, and *dspm* 21 Jan 1701/2, leaving:

1b Catherine; *m* 1st Sept 1718 William Phipps and had issue (*see* NORMANBY, M); *m* 2nd John Sheldon, of Croydon, and *d* 18 Jan 1735

2a JOHN ANNESLEY, **5th Viscount of Valentia** and 4th EARL OF ANGLESEY, PC (1710); *bapt* 18 Jan 1676; V-Treas, Receiver-Gen and Paymaster Forces, all in Ireland, 1710; *m* 21 May 1706 Henrietta, *de jure* Baroness Strange in her own right (*m* 2nd 24 July 1714 1st Earl of Ashburnham (*see* 1924 edn) and *d* 26 June 1718), est dau and coheir of 9th Earl of Derby (*qv*), and *dsps* 18 Sept 1710

3a ARTHUR ANNESLEY, **6th Viscount of Valentia** and 5th EARL OF ANGLESEY, PC (E and I 1710); *educ* Cambridge (MA 1699); Gentleman Privy Chamber 1691, Fell Magdalene Coll Cambridge, MP (Tory) Cambridge U 1702–10 (and High Steward Feb 1721/2–37) and (I Parl) New Roll 1703–10, Govr Co Wexford 1727; *m* the Saturday preceding 27 July 1701/2 his cousin Mary (*d* 22 Jan 1718), dau of 1st Baron Haversham (*see* below), and *dsp* 1 April 1737

1a Elizabeth; *m* Robert Gayer, of Stoke Poges, Bucks, and *d* Dec 1725, leaving issue

(2) ALTHAM ANNESLEY, 1st BARON ALTHAM, of Altham, Co Cork (I), so *cr* 14 Feb 1680/1, with remainder, failing his own male issue, to his yr bros and their issue male; MA Oxon; attainted by JAMES II's Irish Parl May 1689; *m* 1st 3 Sept 1678 Alicia (*dsp* 4 June 1684), dau of Hon Charles Leigh, s of 1st Baron Leigh (*qv*) of Stoneleigh of the 1643 *cr*; *m* 2nd July 1697 Ursula (*m* 2nd 1701 Samuel Ogle, MP (*d* 10 March 1718); *m* 3rd 29 Dec 1720 William Vesey, MP, and was *bur* 16 May 1725), dau of Sir Robert Markham, 2nd Bt, of Sedgebroke, Lincs, and *d* 26 April 1699, leaving by her:

1a JAMES GEORGE ANNESLEY, 2nd BARON ALTHAM, *d* an infant 1699 or 1700

(3) RICHARD ANNESLEY, 3rd BARON ALTHAM; *b c* 1655; *educ* Magdalen Coll Oxford (BD 1677, DD 1689); Preb Westminster 1679 and Exeter March 1680/1, Dean Exeter 1681; *m* by 1689 Dorothy (*d* between 30 June 1715 and 18 Feb 1717/8), dau of John Davey, of Ruxford, Devon, and *d* 19 Nov 1701, leaving:

1a ARTHUR ANNESLEY, 4th BARON ALTHAM; *b c* 1689; *m* 1st 8 April 1703 his cousin Phillips [*sic*], dau of 1st Baron Haversham (*see* below); *m* 2nd 22 July 1707 (separation 1717, after which he took one Joan Landy (*see* below) under his protection and declared her to be Lady Altham) Mary Sheffield, illegitimate dau of 1st Duke of the County of Buckingham and of Normanby (*see* SHEFFIELD, Bt), and *d* 16 Nov 1727, leaving by her:

1b JAMES ANNESLEY, apparently *de jure* 5th BARON ALTHAM and *de jure* 7th VISCOUNT OF VALENTIA and 6th EARL OF ANGLESEY (as which would normally have *s* his f's 1st cousin on latter's death 1737); *b* 1715; opposed his f's raising money to fund a spendthrift way of life, hence apparently spirited away to a remote place of education, it being shortly afterwards claimed that he had died; on his f's death his uncle assumed the title and sold him into slavery to an American plantation owner but he managed to get away to Jamaica and from there sailed to England, arriving in 1740 and suing his uncle for ejectment; at the hearing, which started 11 Nov 1743, the defendant argued that JAMES was illegitimate, being s of the 4th BARON by Joan Landy; the jury disagreed and found 26 Nov 1743 for the plaintiff, who got back the family estates; yet he apparently never assumed the titles; his uncle was in addition found guilty 3 Aug 1744 of assault on his nephew (*i.e.*, presumably the selling into slavery); *m* 1st — Chester (*d* 22 Dec 1749), of Staines, Middx, and had:

1c JAMES ANNESLEY, apparently *de jure* 6th BARON ALTHAM, 8th VISCOUNT OF VALENTIA and 7th EARL OF ANGLESEY; *dsp* 6 Nov 1763

1b (cont.) The apparently *de jure* 5th BARON/7th VISCOUNT/6th EARL *m* 2nd 14 Sept 1751 Margaret, 2nd dau of Thomas I'Anson, of New Bounds, Tunbridge (Wells?), and *d* 5 Jan 1760, leaving by her:

2c — ANNESLEY, apparently *de jure* 7th BARON ALTHAM, 9th VISCOUNT OF VALENTIA and 8th EARL OF ANGLESEY; *b c* 1759; *d* unm 1764

2a RICHARD ANNESLEY, **7th Viscount of Valentia** and 6th and last EARL OF ANGLESEY, as which as a matter of historical fact he is deemed to have *s* cousin 1 April 1737, taking his seat in the English Ho Lds as an Earl 10 May 1737 and in the Irish Ho Lds as a Viscount 4 Oct 1737 and continuing to sit in those legislatures, notwithstanding the legal decision of 26 Nov 1743 (*see* above), to say nothing of the conviction pronounced upon him 3 Aug 1744, neither of which, however, were competent to decide on the rightful holder of the titles of honour but only, respectively, as to the estates or whether an assault had taken place, also 5th BARON ALTHAM, as which as a matter of historical fact is deemed to have *s* er bro 16 Nov 1727 and as which took seat in Irish Ho Lds 28 Nov 1727; *b* 1694; Govr Co Wexford by 1745; *m* 1st 25 Jan 1715 (separated 1719) Ann (*dsp* and was bur 13 Aug 1741), dau of Capt John Prust, of Monkleigh, N Devon; allegedly *m* 2nd 1715, apparently bigamously, Anna (*d* 1765), dau of John Simpson, a rich clothier, of Meath St, Dublin, and by her had three daus; *m* 3rd(?) 15 Sept 1741, again apparently bigamously but according to a decision of 1 June 1772 by the Irish courts validly, Juliana (*m* 2nd, as his 1st w, Matthew Talbot, of Castle Talbot, Co Wexford), dau of Richard Donovan, merchant, of Co Wexford, and *d* 14 Feb 1761, when the Barony of Annesley and Earldom of Anglesey, both being English peerages, were deemed to have expired, leaving by her:

1b ARTHUR ANNESLEY, **8th Viscount of Valentia** (as which deemed by Irish Ho Lds decisions of 5 Dec 1765 and 5 Nov 1771 to have legitimately *s* his f, but by the GB Ho Lds was found 22 April 1771 not to be entitled to the honours in the peerage of England) and 1st EARL OF MOUNTNORRIS (I), so *cr* 3 Dec 1793, PC (I 1776); *b* 7 Aug 1744; *educ* Ch Ch Oxford; Govr Co Wexford 1776–78, FSA 1799, FRS 1800; *m* 1st 10 May 1767 Lucy Fortescue (*d* 20 May 1783), only dau and eventual heiress of 1st Baron Lyttelton of Frankley (*see* COBHAM, V), and had:

1c Arthur; *b* 2 Nov 1769; *dvp* and was *bur* 26 March 1771

2c GEORGE ANNESLEY, **9th Viscount of Valentia** and 2nd and last EARL OF MOUNTNORRIS, as which (in addition to being the holder of the two Baronies of Altham and Mountnorris) was recognised by the UK Ho Lds 6 March 1817, which thus contradicted its own ruling as to the petitioner's legitimacy of 22 April 1771 (when, however, it was only the GB Ho Lds not the UK one); also claimed 30 Jan 1819 the Earldom of Anglesey but although the Ctee for Privileges began to examine the claim no decision was reached; *b* 4 Dec 1770; *educ* Rugby and BNC Oxford; MP Yarmouth (IoW) 1808–10, Govr Co Wexford, FRS 1796, FSA, FLS, author: *Voyages and Travels to India, Ceylon, the Red Sea, Abyssinia, and Egypt* (4 vols 1809); *m* 3 Sept 1790 Anne (*d* 6 Jan 1835), 8th dau of *de jure* 8th Earl of Devon (*qv*), and *dspms* 23 July 1844, when the Earldom and Barony of Altham expired, having had:

1d George Arthur, *Viscount Valentia*; *b* 20 Oct 1793; *educ* Harrow and Ch Ch Oxford; MP (Tory) Co Wexford 1830–31; *m* 21 Oct 1837 Frances Cockburn (*d* 27 Jan 1856), only dau of Charles James Sims, of Jamaica, and *dsp* & *vp* 16 March 1841

2d William; *b* 1796; *d* unm 1830

3c Charles

4c Mathew

1c Juliana Lucy; *m* 4 July 1789 5th Baron Farnham (*qv*) and *dsp* 10 Oct 1833

2c Hester Annabella; *m* 14 Dec 1801 Maj-Gen Norman Macleod (*d* 16 March 1830) and *d* 14 Aug 1844, leaving:

1d Arthur Lyttelton MACLEOD later ANNESLEY (roy licence 31 Oct 1844), of Arley Castle, Staffs, and Camolin Park, Co Wexford; *b* 30 Nov 1802; *m* 18 March 1835 Mary (*d* 22 Feb 1886), dau of John Bradley, of Colborne Hall, Staffs, and *d* 24 Oct 1882, leaving:

1e Arthur Lyttelton ANNESLEY later LYTTELTON-ANNESLEY (Sir), KCB, KCVO; *b* 2 Sept 1837; Crimea 1855, Col 11th Hus 1902–20, Lt-Gen, Kt Cdr Order Christ Portugal, FRGS; *d* unm 16 Feb 1926

2e John George; *b* 8 Aug 1839; Capt 11th Hus; *m* 7 March 1877 Emily Margaret, dau of Sir Thomas Bernard Dancer, 6th Bt (*see* 1933 edn), and *d* 2 Oct 1892, leaving three daus

1e Georgina Lyttelton; *m* 28 June 1859 Richard Tanfield Vachell (*d* 12 March 1868), of Coptford Hall, Essex, and had issue

2e Annabella Lucy; *m* 7 July 1868 Capt William Montagu Gent-Thorp (*d* 12 Nov 1899), of Chippenham Park, Cambs, and *dsp* 7 Dec 1929

3e Augusta Mary; *m* 14 Sept 1865 Horace Neville Tharp (*d* 21 Feb 1902) and had issue

1b (cont.) The **8th Viscount** *m* 2nd 20 Dec 1783 Sarah (*d* 2 Jan 1849), 3rd dau of Sir Henry Cavendish, 2nd Bt (*see* WATERPARK, B), and *d* 4 July 1816, having by her had:

5c Henry Arthur; *b* 24 March 1792; *m* 14 Aug 1818 Sarah (*d* 23 March 1861), est dau of B Ainsworth, of Hallowell, Lancs, and *dsp* 20 Aug 1818

6c Richard

3c Catherine; *m* 4 Dec 1814 Lord John Somerset and *d* 25 June 1865, leaving issue (*see* BEAUFORT, D)

4c Frances Caroline; *m* 10 Oct 1810 Sir James Webster-Wedderburn (*see* OGILVY-WEDDERBURN, Bt) and *d* 22 Jan 1837, leaving issue

2b Richard; *m* 1761 Robert Phaire, of Temple Shannon, Co Wexford

1b Juliana; *m* 31 May 1765 Sir Frederick Flood, 1st and last Bt (*d* 1 Feb 1824), and *dsp* April 1768

2b Katherine; *m* Lt-Col John O'Toole (Count O'Toole, of the Irish Bde in France), of Ballyfad, Co Wexford

1a Elizabeth; *b c* 1699; *m* 1st William Green; *m* 2nd her cousin 2nd and last BARON HAVERSHAM (*see* below); *m* 3rd 15 Feb 1746/7, as his 2nd w, Fitzwilliam White, of Louth, Lincs; *m* 4th 12 March 1750/1 Samuel Ashurst, of Gray's Inn, and *d* 5 Nov 1772

(1) Frances; *b c* 1648; *m* 1st John Wyndham; *m* 2nd 14 July 1668, as his 1st w, 1st Baron Haversham (*m* 2nd 10 May 1709 Martha Graham, a widow, and *d* 1 Nov 1710) and *d* 3 March 1704/5, leaving:

1a MAURICE THOMPSON, 2nd and last BARON HAVERSHAM; *b* 1675; Page to SOPHIA, ELECTRESS OF HANOVER, MP (Whig) Bletchingley 1695–98 and Gatton 1698–1705, Treas Excise 1717–18; *m* 1st Elizabeth, dau of John Smith, of Herts; *m* 2nd 16 Aug 1737 his cousin Elizabeth (*see above*) and *dspm* 11 April 1745, when the Barony expired

1a Phillips [*sic*]; *m* 8 April 1703, as his 1st w, her cousin 4th BARON ALTHAM (*see above*) and *dsp* May 1704

2 Robert; *d* at Rome

3 John, of Ballysonan Castle, Co Kildare; *b* 11 Sept 1616; *m* Charity, dau of Henry Warren, of Grangebeg, and *d* 1695, leaving, with two yst sons (Robert; George) and three daus:

(1) Francis, of Ballysonan; MP New Ross 1695; *m* Deborah, sis of Jeffrey Paul, MP, and *d* 1707, leaving four daus

(2) Maurice, of Little Rath, Co Kildare; MP Clonmines 1695; *m* Sarah (*d* 5 July 1705), 2nd dau of 4th Lord Blayney, Baron of Monaghan (*see* 1874 edn), and *dspms* 17 Feb 1718

(3) John, of Ballysax; *m* Eleanor Bishop and *d* 13 April 1720, having had four sons (Francis; Richard, himself f of two sons, John and Charles; John, allegedly *dspm*; Maurice, f of two sons, John and Francis) and three daus

The **1st Viscount** *m* 2nd by 1629 Jane (*d* 12 March 1683), dau of Sir John Stanhope , of Elvaston, Derbys (*see* 1967 edn CHESTERFIELD and STANHOPE, E), and widow of Sir Peter Courten(e), 1st and last Bt, of Addington/Aunton, Worcs, and was *bur* 23 Nov 1660, having by her had an est s:

4 Francis, of Castlewellan, Co Down; *b* 23 Jan 1628/9; *m* 29 Dec 1662 Deborah (*d* 4 Sept 1672), dau of Henry Jones, Bp Meath, and widow of John Bowdler, and had, with two other sons (*dsp*):

(1) Francis, of Thorganby, Yorks; *bapt* 24 Oct 1663; MP GB and I Parls; *m* 1st 5 July 1695 Elizabeth, dau of Sir Joseph Martin; *m* 2nd July 1732 Elizabeth (*dsp* 20 May 1736), dau of John Cropley, of Rochester, and widow of William Gomeldon, of Sommerfield Hall, Kent; *m* 3rd 31 Aug 1737 Sarah, dau of W Sloane, of Portsmouth, and widow of Sir Richard Fowler, and *d* 7 April 1750, having had by his 1st w, with three other sons (*d* young) and two daus:

1a Francis (Rev); LLD, Rector Winwick, Lancs; *m* Anne, dau and coheir of Sir Robert Gayer by Elizabeth, dau and eventual heiress of 2nd Earl of Anglesey, and *dvp* 1 May 1740, leaving:

1b Arthur, of Bletchington Park, Oxon; *b* 1733; *m* Elizabeth, dau of Charles Baldwin, of Aqualate, and *d* Feb 1773, leaving, with other issue:

1c Arthur, of Bletchington Park; *b* 1760; *m* 1 Feb 1785 Catharine, dau and heiress of Adml Sir Charles Hardy, and *d* 20 Jan 1841, having had, with three other sons and two daus (*d* unm):

1d ARTHUR ANNESLEY, **10th Viscount of Valentia**, which title he assumed 1844 but made no effort to establish his right to; *b* 30 Nov 1785; *educ* Harrow; *m* 12 Aug 1808 Eleanor (*d* 10 June 1843), yst dau of Henry O'BRIEN later STAFFORD-O'BRIEN, of Blatherwycke Pk, Northants, and Stone Hall, Co Clare, and *d* 30 Dec 1863, having had, with two other sons and three daus (*d* unm):

1e Arthur; *b* 14 Sept 1809; *educ* Eton; *m* 18 Jan 1836 Flora Mary (*m* 2nd 3 March 1847 Hon George Talbot Devereux (*see* HEREFORD, V) and *d* 5 Nov 1884), dau of Lt-Col James Macdonald, yr bro of John Macdonald, 18th Ch of Clanranald, and *dvp* 27 Oct 1844, leaving:

1f ARTHUR ANNESLEY, **11th Viscount of Valentia**, KCVO (1923), MVO 1901), CB (1900), TD, JP Oxon; *b* 23 Aug 1843; *educ* RMA Woolwich; Lt 10th Hus (served 1864–72), MFH Bicester 1872–74, High Sheriff Oxon 1874, MP (C) Oxford 1895–1917, Hon Col QO Oxon Hus, Comptroller Household 1898–1905, CSO and AAG Imp Yeo Boer War 1900 (despatches, medal), Ld-in-Waiting 1915–24, Chm Oxon CC, High Steward City of Oxford 1924; *cr* 7 May 1917 BARON ANNESLEY, of Bletchington, Co Oxon (UK); *m* 30 Jan 1878 Laura Sarah (*d* 16 Nov 1933), yst dau of Daniel Hale Webb, of Wykham Park, Oxon, and widow of Sir Algernon William Peyton, 4th Bt (*see* 1959 edn), and *d* 20 Jan 1927, having had:

1g Arthur; *b* 24 Aug 1880; *educ* Eton; 2nd Lt 10th Hus 1900, Boer War 1900–02 (Queen's and King's medals), Lt 1901, Capt 1907, Adj 1907–09, WW I; *ka* 16 Nov 1914

2g CARYL ARTHUR JAMES ANNESLEY, **12th Viscount of Valentia**, CVO (1924), JP, DL Oxon; *b* 3 July 1883; *educ* Eton and RMC Sandhurst; joined Oxon LI 1903, Lt 1905, Capt 1st Roy Dragoons 1913 (Maj 1923), ADC to Govrs Madras 1907–12 and Bengal 1912–13 and to HRH PRINCE ARTHUR OF CONNAUGHT 1920–21 (Priv Sec and Comptroller 1922–38), High Steward Banbury 1932–47; *d* unm 6 Oct 1949, when the UK Barony expired

1g Vere; *b* March 1879; *m* 23 July 1901 Rev Guy Ronald Campbell and *d* 18 May 1975, leaving issue (*see* CAWDOR, E)

2g Violet Kathleen; *b* 18 March 1882; *m* 15 April 1920 Charles Henry Gore (*see* ARRAN, E) and *d* 4 Sept 1963, leaving issue

3g Helen; *b* 30 July 1884; *m* 3 Oct 1905 Col John Pemberton Heywood-Lonsdale, DSO, Salop Yeo (*d* 12 Aug 1944), of Poundon, Bicester, and Drumgoon, Co Fermanagh, and *d* 21 July 1965, leaving issue (*see* ROLLO, L)

4g Lettice, CVO (1937); *b* 24 Sept 1885; Cmdt Aux Hosp 1916–19 (despatches twice), Ldy-in-Waiting to HM QUEEN ELIZABETH THE QUEEN MOTHER when DUCHESS OF YORK 1932–36, Woman Bedchamber to HM THE QUEEN when PRINCESS ELIZABETH 1937–44, Extra Woman of the Bedchamber 1944, OStJ; *m* 18 Oct 1911 Capt Geoffrey Vaux Salvin Bowlby, RHG (*ka* 13 May 1915), 4th s of Edward Salvin Bowlby, of Gilston Pk, Herts, and had issue

5g Hilda Cecil; *b* 19 April 1889; *d* unm 20 Sept 1972

6g Dorothy; *b* 11 May 1892; *m* 27 July 1921 Joseph Francis Vaughan Gibbs (*see* ALDENHAM and HUNSDON OF HUNSDON, B) and had issue

1f Mary; *m* 24 Feb 1855 Lt-Col Walter Chideoke Nangle, RA (*d* Sept 1902), yst s of George Nangle, of Kildalkey, Co Meath, and *d* 27 Sept 1879, leaving issue

2f Flora; *m* 23 June 1863 Col Francis Lyon, RA (*k* 26 Feb 1885), and *d* 4 Aug 1924, having had issue

2e Algernon Arthur Sydney, JP Middx; *b* 25 May 1829; Lt 16th Lancers, Hon Col 4th Bn Oxon LI, Sec to Govr Hong Kong 1860; *m* 11 Oct 1864 Helen Sydney (*d* 31 Oct 1925), yr dau of Griffith Richards, QC, and *d* 6 Sept 1908 leaving:

1h Arthur Sydney Evelyn; *b* 16 July 1865; Capt Rifle Bde Boer War 1901–02 (medal with four clasps); *d* unm 6 Aug 1914

1h Helen Sydney Martha; *b* 14 Nov 1867; *d* unm 12 March 1953

2h Mabel Sydney Augusta Katherine; *b* 12 May 1869; *m* 20 April 1893 William James Yorke Scarlett, JP (*d* 30 Oct 1954), and *d* 15 March 1950, leaving issue

1e Frances Arthur Charlotte; *m* 17 Oct 1852 Capt William Linkskill (*d* 1900), of Tynemouth Lodge, Northumberland, and *d* 13 May 1904, having had issue

2e Matilda Arthur Marianne; *m* 18 July 1845 John Kent Egerton Holmes (*d* 16 June 1848) and *d* 23 May 1894, leaving issue

3e Eva Arthur Henry Medora; *m* 12 Jan 1853 Sir Henry Robinson, KCB, and *d* 1894, leaving issue (*see* LYNCH-ROBINSON, Bt)

4e Nea Arthur Ada Rose d'Amour; *m* 24 April 1846 1st Baron Rosmead, GCMG, PC (*d* 28 Oct 1897; *see* 1933 edn), and *d* 13 Jan 1904, leaving issue

2d Charles Annesley Francis (Rev), of Eydon Hall, Northants; *b* 26 Dec 1787; *d* 26 Sept 1863

1d Catherine Elizabeth; *m* 1814 Rev Hon John Evelyn Boscawen (*see* FALMOUTH, V) and *d* 30 July 1859, leaving issue

2d Barbara Caroline; *m* Oct 1814 Thomas Tyrwhitt-Drake (*d* 21 March 1852), of Shardeloes, and *d* 5 Nov 1883, leaving issue

3d Mary; *m* Rev John Tyrwhitt-Drake (*d* 26 June 1860), Rector Amersham, and *d* 19 Nov 1827

2a Martin (Rev); *bapt* 12 Oct 1701; DD; *m* 12 Dec 1732 Mary, dau and coheir of William Hanbury, of Little Marcle, Herefs, by Frances, sis and heiress of Sir John Cotton, 4th Bt, of Connington, Hants, and *d* June 1749, having had, with other issue:

1b Arthur Henry (Rev); DD; had:

1c Arthur (Rev), of Clifford Chambers, Glos; *b* 30 Oct 1769; *m* 14 Jan 1800 Elizabeth Vere (*d* 15 June 1865), dau of George Booth Tyndale, and *d* 9 Feb 1845, leaving, with two daus (*d* unm):

1d Francis (Rev); *b* 8 Dec 1800; MA Oxon; Rector Clifford Chambers, hereditary Cottonian family Tstee Br Museum; *m* 3 May 1836 Charlotte (*d* 27 June 1837), dau of Rev Henry Hodges Mogg, and *d* 2 Aug 1882, leaving:

1e Maria Charlotte; *b* 1837; *m* 21 Aug 1862 her cousin Rev Francis Hanbury Annesley and *d* 22 Feb 1915, leaving issue (*see* below)

2d Arthur; *b* 1 May 1803; *m* 2 June 1838 Elizabeth Vere (*d* 10 Feb 1902), dau of Rev Thomas G Tyndale, and *d* 11 Aug 1883, leaving, with two daus (*d* unm):

1e Henry Arthur (Rev); *b* 22 July 1841; Vicar Shepton Montague, Somerset, Theological Associate King's Coll London, civil servant, hereditary Cottonian family Tstee Br Museum; *m* 17 March 1874 Anna Maria (*d* 13 Dec 1927), 5th dau of William Monckton (*see* GALWAY, V), and *d* 1 Sept 1924, leaving:

1f Rev WILLIAM MONCKTON ANNESLEY, *de jure* 13th VISCOUNT OF VALENTIA, though never proved claim; *b* 23 Jan 1875; *educ* Peterhouse Cambridge (BA 1903, MA 1909); Vicar Brewham-cum-Redlynch, Somerset, Cottonian Tstee Br Museum, CF WW I 1916–18; *m* 14 June 1938 *Gladys May Kathleen [The Rt Hon Gladys Viscountess Annesley, Wassall House, Wincanton, Somerset], dau of Uriah Fowler, and *dsp* 26 Feb 1951

2f Arthur Henry; *b* 16 Jan 1876; *d* unm 1947

3f Philip de Vere; *b* 23 Feb 1879; *educ* Wadham Coll Oxford (BA 1903); slr 1907, Cottonian family Tstee Br Museum, 2nd Lt W R Regt and Area Comdt attd 2nd Army France WW I 1916–18; *m* 20 April 1907 Christabel Charlotte, BEM (*d* 6 Oct 1955), 3rd dau of John Christopher Tomson, and *d* 8 Aug 1949, having had:

1g Christopher; *b* 11 April 1913; *d* 2 Nov 1914

1g *Anne Christabel de Vere [Lady Thompson, Rhodes House, Sellindge, Ashford, Kent TN25 6JA]; *b* 2 Jan 1909; *m* 9 Aug 1939 *Sir Richard Hilton Marler Thompson, 1st Bt, of Reculver (*qv*), and has issue

1f Sophia Mary; *b* 26 Jan 1877; *d* unm 31 Jan 1954

2f Eleanor Catherine; *b* 18 Aug 1881; *m* 5 Oct 1909 Edwin Jesse Septimus Molyneux and *d* 14 Sept 1969, leaving issue

2e William Oliver Tyndale; *b* 10 Nov 1849; LSA London, FRCS; *m* 1892 Mary (*d* 16 Sept 1917), dau of D J Bostel, and *dsp* 1922

3e Arthur Francis Biscoe; *b* 10 Nov 1849; with Bd of Educn; *m* 19 Sept 1891 Kate (*d* 19 March 1922), dau of Richard Gillespie, and *d* 3 Feb 1915, leaving:

1f Caroline Vere; *b* 17 Feb 1893; *m* 1st 22 Jan 1918 Lt Richard Vincent Sturt, RGA (*d* 6 Jan 1923), s of Richard Sturt, of Ascot, Berks, and had:

1g *Margaret Vere; *b* 27 Nov 1918; *m* 5 June 1946 *Cuthbert Graham Pile, s of Cuthbert Pile, of Horley, Surrey, and has:

1h *Hugh Richard Graham [Hugh Pile Esq, Highfield, 100 Osborne Rd, Newcastle-upon-Tyne, Northumberland]; *b* 30 March 1948; *educ* Ardingly and King's Coll Cambridge

1h *Verity Catherine; *b* 4 July 1952

1f (cont.) Mrs Richard Sturt *m* 2nd 4 Feb 1926 Arthur Cyril Wallis (*d* 1977), s of Arthur Wallis, of Springfield Rd, NW, and by him had:

1g *Christopher Arthur Annesley; *b* 18 Dec 1928; *m* 13 Aug 1955 *Jeanne Marie, dau of James Brady, of S Holmwood, Surrey, and has:

1h *Julia Caroline Annesley; *b* 9 May 1957

2h *Nicola Jane Annesley; *b* 23 April 1959

3h *Anna Marie Annesley; *b* 14 April 1965

2f Cicely Prout Tyndale; *b* 10 Sept 1895; *m* 27 Oct 1921 Robert Willsher Hilder and *d* 17 Sept 1926, having had issue

4e George Dighton; *b* 18 June 1853; *m* 24 July 1883 Elizabeth Sophia (*d* 19 March 1928), dau of John Watson, of Linden Ho, Lee, Kent, and *d* 14 July 1931, leaving:

1f FRANCIS DIGHTON ANNESLEY, **14th Viscount of Valentia**, as which recognised 9 June 1959, MC; *b* 12 Aug 1888; *educ* St Lawrence Coll Ramsgate and Guy's Hosp; MRC, LRCP 1914, Brig RAMC WW I (Croix de Guerre Belgium), Afghanistan 1919, Waziristan and NWFP 1922–23 and WW II; *m* 8 Aug 1925 Joan Elizabeth (*d* 1986), 2nd dau of John Joseph Curtis, of Sandhurst, Berks, and *d* 16 March 1983 leaving:

1g RICHARD JOHN DIGHTON ANNESLEY, **15th and present Viscount of Valentia**

1g *Elizabeth Mary Jean [The Hon Mrs Sylvester Bradley, Knighton Manor, Durweston, Dorset DT11 0QA]; *b* 6 May 1926; *m* 12 June 1948 Maj James Terence Ralph Sylvester Bradley, MA, CEng, MIERE, Roy Signals (*d* 1987), s of Lt-Col Charles Reginald Sylvester Bradley, of The Manor Ho, Langton Herring, Dorset, and has:

1h *Charles Robin [Charles Sylvester Bradley Esq, 9 Pembroke Rd, Westbourne, Bournemouth BH4 8HE]; *b* 7 April 1959; *educ* Bryanston; *m* 1985 *Jennifer Roberts and has:

1i *Jolyon Robin; *b* 1986

1i *Christabel Morwenna; *b* 1990

1h *Fiona Elizabeth [Miss Fiona Sylvester Bradley, 195A Quemerford, Calne, Wilts SN11 8JX]; *b* 5 Oct 1949

2h *Heather Mary [Mrs Michael Dias do Nascimento, Quinta dos Sobreiros, Faxelhas, PO Box 75, 8300 Silves, Algarve, Portugal]; *b* 30 June 1951; *m* 1978 *Dr Michael Dias do Nascimento, BVMS, MRCVS, and has:

1i *Charles James; *b* 1979

2i *Edward Michael; *b* 1980

3i *Jorge Norman; *b* 1988

3h *Catherine Alison [Mrs Toby Goddard, 2 Ham Lane, Marnhull, Dorset DT10 1JN]; *b* 26 June 1957; *m* 1984 *Toby C Goddard, s of Keith Goddard, FRICS, FSVA, and has:

1i *Hamish Toby; *b* 1989

1i *Alexandra Catherine; *b* 1987

2g *Susan Margaret [The Hon Mrs Milln, Nanterrow, Tregongeeves Lane, Polgooth, Cornwall PL26 7AX]; *b* 18 Feb 1931; *m* 8 May 1954 *Peter Lindsay Milln, only s of Alexander Lindsay Milln, of Bibury, Glos, and has:

1h *Jeremy James; *b* 20 April 1956; *educ* Bryanston

1h *Teresa Clare; *b* 2 April 1958; *m* 1983 *John Joseph Doran, of Mullingar, Co Westmeath, and has:

1i *Fabian James; *b* 18 Jan 1985

2i *Jonathan Lindsay; *b* 31 July 1988

2h *Eleanor Eve [Mrs John Channon, Herons Lake, Polbrook, Bodmin, Cornwall]; *b* 6 March 1961; *m* 1987 (*divorce* 1994) John Courtnay Channon, est s of George H Channon

3h *Jessica Rose; *b* 4 April 1964; *m* 6 May 1995 *Mark Thomas Fisher and has:

1i *Mungo James; *b* 19 Sept 1996

3g *Helen Jennifer Frances [The Hon Mrs Casswell, The Limes Barn Farm, Smarden, Kent]; *b* 13 Oct 1935; *m* 19 Jan 1957 *Simon FitzRoy Casswell, yst s of His Hon Joshua David Casswell, QC, of Wimbledon, and has had:

1h Hugh FitzRoy; *b* 18 April 1958; *d* 1976

2h *Edward FitzRoy; *b* 18 April 1958; *m* 19– *Rosemary Tassel and has:

1i *James FitzRoy; *b* 1987

2i *Mark; *b* 1989

1h *Jane Elizabeth; *b* 12 June 1962

2h *Karen Ray; *b* 15 Jan 1969

1f Muriel Mary Grace; *b* 1 July 1884; *d* 1974

5e Edward Dallas; *b* 15 Feb 1855; MA Oxon; *m* 1893 Mary Jane (*d* 15 Aug 1928), dau of Edward Bate, of Kelsterton, Flints, and *d* 22 Feb 1927

1e Catherine Vere; *b* 21 March 1843; *m* 31 Aug 1869 Rev Charles Dunlop Smith (*d* 1923), of Westbury Ho, Westbury Pk, Bristol, and *d* 16 Oct 1877, leaving issue

3d William (Rev); *b* 17 June 1804; Vicar Abbot's Leigh, nr Bristol; *m* 17 June 1835 Laura Anne (*d* 18 Nov 1888 aged 84), dau of Maj-Gen Oliver Jones, of Fonmon Castle, Glam, and *d* 3 April 1884, leaving, with two daus (*d* unm):

1e Charles Henry (Rev); *b* 23 July 1840; *d* 1922

2e Oliver Francis Theodore; *b* 2 Jan 1842; Maj RHA; *m* 18 Aug 1885 Isabel (*d* 9 Aug 1935), 3rd dau of Charles Addington Hanbury, JP, DL, of Belmont Ho, E Barnet, Herts, and Strathgrave, Dingwall, Ross-shire, and *d* 17 Sept 1905, leaving:

1f Laura Daphne Theodora; *m* 20 April 1912 Col Lenox Arthur Dutton Naper, DSO, RA (*d* 8 Oct 1965), est s of Col William Dutton Naper, JP, and *d* 31 Jan 1974, leaving:

1g Merrik Oliver Lennox; *b* 13 Feb 1913; *educ* Wellington and New Coll Oxford; P/O RAF WW II, *ka* N Africa 2 April 1943

2g Nigel William Ivo, MC (1944); *b* 12 Aug 1922; *educ* Wellington; Capt Rifle Bde WW II; *m* 3 Nov 1945 *Carola Elisabeth, yr

dau of Lt-Col Denis George Farr Darley, of Prospect, Sallins, Co Kildare, and *d* 28 April 1978, leaving:

1h *James Denis Merrik; *b* 25 June 1949

2h *Charles William Lenox; *b* 17 Jan 1951

3h *Francis Graham Dutton; *b* 17 Sept 1953

1h *Audrey Carola; *b* 20 Sept 1947

1g *Meriel Daphne Selina [Mrs Peter Staveley, Knowle Cottage, Newton Poppleford, Devon EX10 0BN]; *b* 8 April 1920; *m* 24 March 1951 *Lt-Cdr Peter Minet Staveley, RN, yr s of Maj Arthur Godfrey Staveley, RA, and has:

1h *Anthony Arthur Merrik; *b* 23 March 1952; *m* 25 Sept 1980 *Julia Caroline Morgan and has:

1i *Michael Peter; *b* 23 Feb 1983

2i *Benjamin Richard; *b* 25 July 1985

3i *Thomas Anthony; *b* 31 March 1990

2h *Clive Lenox; *b* 8 March 1955

1h *Claire Susan Meriel; *b* 11 March 1960

2f Isabel Myrtle; *m* 15 Nov 1921 Lt-Col Edward Shirley Godman, OBE, Dorset Regt (*d* 25 Jan 1951), est surv s of Percy Sanden Godman, JP, and *d* 25 Feb 1978, leaving issue

3e William Martin, Capt RN; *b* 16 Feb 1846; *d* unm 10 April 1899

4d George; *b* 13 Sept 1808; *m* 3 Aug 1833 Emily, dau of Albert Forster, and *d* 8 April 1872, having had, with a dau (*d* unm):

1e Francis Hanbury (Rev); *b* 19 Dec 1837; MA Oxon; Rector Greete and Hope Bagot, Salop, Tstee Br Museum; *m* 21 Aug 1862 Maria Charlotte (*d* 22 Feb 1915), only dau of Rev Francis Annesley (*see* above), and *d* 21 May 1914, having had:

1f Reginald Cecil; *b* 15 April 1865; *dsp* 1882

2f Arthur Dighton; *b* 20 Oct 1866; *educ* Marlborough and Trin Coll Oxford (MA 1894), *d* unm 8 July 1943

3f Francis Cotton; *b* 12 April 1871; slr 1895; *m* 15 Jan 1914 Charlotte Cassandra (*d* 24 Dec 1924), yst dau of Charles Barclay, of Bayford, Herts, and *d* 11 July 1951, leaving:

1g Mary Cassandra; *b* 5 Feb 1916; *d* unm 11 Jan 1964

1f Edith Vere, OBE (1920); *b* 25 Sept 1863; *m* 2 Aug 1893 Robert Wilkinson Dent, JP (*d* 3 Nov 1940), s of Thomas Wilkinson John Dent, of Flass, Maulds Meaburn, Penrith, and *d* 12 Oct 1948, having had issue

2f Isabel Charlotte; *b* 17 Dec 1868; *m* 19 Feb 1901 Rev George William Tyndale Tyndale-Biscoe, Rector Shalstone, Bucks, and *d* 17 Feb 1930, leaving issue

3f Alice Tyndale; *b* 25 April 1873; *m* 1 Sept 1914 Thomas Henry Gillam (*d* 27 March 1939), JP, of The Woodlands, Bathwick Hill, Bath, 2nd s of Rev T H Gillam, Vicar Weaverham, Cheshire, and *d* 17 April, 1953

2e Reginald Carey; *b* 26 March 1844; Lt-Col 1st Bn QO Cameron Highrs; *m* 14 Jan 1875 Mary Frances Burnard (*d* 25 Aug 1920), est dau of William Baron Mew, and *d* 7 Feb 1922, having had:

1f George William; *b* 5 Nov 1875; S Rhodesian Vols; *d* unm 9 June 1904

2f Clifford Reginald Templeman, DSO (1916); *b* 4 Jan 1877; *educ* Haileybury; Lt-Col RASC WW I (despatches); *m* 3 Oct 1907 Clara Mabel (*d* 20 April 1954), est dau of Col Samuel Martin Gully, Norfolk Regt, of Bracondale, Norfolk, and *d* 12 April 1971, leaving:

1g Reginald Clifford Martin; *b* 8 March 1909; *educ* Stowe; Br S Africa Police; *m* 4 Nov 1940 Ann Isabella (*d* 1986), est dau of John Robert Strachan, of Firthview, Tain, Ross-shire, and *d* 1994, leaving:

1h *Kathleen Elaine Vere; *b* 19 Dec 1941; *m* 29 Jan 1966 *Beverley Aldington Bird, s of Frank Bird, of Bulawayo, Zimbabwe, and has:

1i *Clive Robert; *b* 1982

1i *Glynnis Ann; *b* 1970; *m* 1989 *Henry Kevin Botes and has:

1j *Dean Stephen; *b* 1989

2j *Matthew Ryan; *b* 1992

2i *Jane Claire; *b* 1972

2h *Sheila Rosalind; *b* 18 Oct 1945; *m* 3 July 1965 *Michael Stuart Allen, Br S Africa Police, est s of Cyril Raymond Allen, of Mulberry Cottage, Dumbleton, Worcs, and has:

1i *Stuart David; *b* 1969

2i *Christopher Michael; *b* 1985

1i *Deborah Michelle; *b* 3 April 1966; *m* 1989 *Paul Whitechurch and has:

1j *Gary Paul; *b* 1990

1j *Ashleigh Lara; *b* 1994

2j *Kirsten Michelle; *b* 1994 (twin)

2i *Nicole Paula; *b* 1983

1g *Vere Bessie Mabel [Miss Vere Annesley, 18 Wykeham Pl, Lymington, Hants]; *b* 16 March 1910

3f Martin Tyndale; *b* 11 Nov 1896; *educ* Cheltenham; 2nd Lt 3rd Bn Cameron Highrs WW I 1917–18 (despatches, two medals), Capt Res Offrs RA, T/Capt KAR 1926–27, WW II 1939–41 (POW); *m* 3 April 1935 Marjorie Jex Blake (*d* 1980), er dau of Lt-Col Bertram Everard Winter, Wilts Regt and APD, and *d* 17 April 1965, leaving:

1g +Richard Bruce; *b* 28 Dec 1937; *educ* Gresham's; ACA; *m* 9 Sept 1972 *Elizabeth Mary Emily, dau of T F Doyle, of Armanagh, Glenbrook, Co Cork, and has:

1h *Charlotte Mary; *b* 19 July, 1973

2h *Philippa Vere; *b* 1975

3h *Sophie Elizabeth; *b* 19 June 1977
1f Mary Emily Vere; *b* 11 Dec 1878; *m* 9 Oct 1902 Maj Wilbraham Taylor, ASC and 7th Dragoon Gds (*d* 2 March 1924), est s of Lt-Col Wilbraham Taylor, Rifle Bde, and *dsp* 30 Sept 1957
1e Georgina Cecilia; *b* 10 Sept 1841; *m* 31 July 1869 Col Charles Ball-Acton, CB, 51st KOYLI (*d* 3 Feb 1897), yst s of Col William Acton, MP, of W Acton, Rathdrum, and *d* 21 Nov 1912, leaving issue
5d Martin
1d Elizabeth Vere; *m* 16 Oct 1838 Rev Arthur Mogg (*d* 25 March 1840) and *d* 24 March 1887, leaving issue
3a WILLIAM ANNESLEY, *cr* VISCOUNT GLERAWLEY (*see* ANNESLEY, E)

VARLEY

Creation: B. (LP, UK) 1990.

THE BARON VARLEY, of Chesterfield, Co Derbys (Eric Graham Varley, PC (1974), DL (Derbys 1989)) [The Rt Hon The Lord Varley PC DL, 189 Middlecroft Rd, Staveley, Derbys]; *b* 11 Aug 1932; *educ* Ruskin Coll Oxford; engr's turner 1952–55, coal miner 1955–64, NUM: branch sec 1955–64, memb Area Exec Ctee Derbys 1956–64, MP (Lab) Chesterfield 1964–84, Assist Govt Whip 1967–68, PPS to PM 1968–69, Min State Min Tech 1969–70, Chm TU Gp Lab MPs 1971–74, Sec State: Energy 1974–75, Industry 1975–79, Ch Oppn Spokesman Employment 1979–83, Treas Lab Party 1981–83 Memb Ho Lds Select Ctee ECs 1991–, chm and ch exec Coalite Gp 1984–89; regnl dir Lloyds Bank N & E Midlands 1987–89, Midlands and N Wales 1989–91; Visiting Fell Nuffield Coll 1977–81; Steward and Bailiff Manor Northstead 1984–; dir: Ashgate Hospice Ltd 1987–96, Cathelco Ltd 1989–, Laxgate Ltd 1991–; *m* 1955 *Marjorie, dau of Alfred Turner, of Duckmanton, Derbys, and has a s

Lineage: FRANK VARLEY; *m* Eva — and had:

ERIC GRAHAM, *cr* a **Baron**

VASSAR-SMITH

Arms: Quarterly, 1st and 4th, per bend embattled az. and or, in the sinister chief point a cuirass with tasces attached, in the dexter base point a well-head, all counterchanged (for SMITH); 2nd and 3rd, arg. an Etruscan vase gu., in chief two fusils az., each charged with a fleur-de-lys or (for VASSAR). **Crests:** 1 A dexter arm embowed in armour ppr., bound above the elbow with a scarf gu. and holding in the hand an arrow in bend, point downwards or, and a pair of pincers in fess sa. (for SMITH), 2 An Etruscan vase or between two branches of oak fructed ppr. (for VASSAR). **Motto:** *Labor et veritas* ('Labour and truth'). **Creation:** Bt. (UK) 10 July 1917.

SIR JOHN RATHBORNE VASSAR-SMITH, 4TH BT, of Charlton Park, Charlton Kings, Co Gloucester [Sir John Vassar-Smith Bt, St Ronan's School, Hawkhurst, Kent TN18 5DJ]; *b* 23 July 1936; *s f* 1995; *educ* Eton; Headmaster St Ronan's Sch 1972–; *m* 1971 *Roberta Elaine, dau of W/Cdr Norman Williamson, and has:

1 +RICHARD RATHBORNE; *b* 29 Dec 1975
2 +David Rathborne; *b* 1978

Lineage: EDWARD SMITH, of London; *b* 17 March 1792; slr; had:

RICHARD TEW SMITH, of Wotton Hill Ho, Glos; *b* 1815; *m* Emily (*d* 1852), dau of Jabez Vassar, of Shipdam, Norfolk, whose ancestors included the fndr of Vassar Coll in the US, and *d* 1870, leaving:

Sir RICHARD VASSAR SMITH later VASSAR-SMITH (roy licence 1883), **1st Bt** (UK), so *cr* 10 July 1917, JP, DL Glos and Gloucester, DL Bristol; *b* 11 July 1843; CA Glos, Dep Grand Master and Provincial Grand Master Masons Glos and Herefs, chm Lloyds Bank and Nat Provincial For Bank, dir: London and Rio Plate

Bank, P&O For Banking Corp and Yorks Penny Bank, Pres: Ctee London Clearing Bankers and Bankers' Inst, Cdr Order Redeemer Greece; *m* 30 Aug 1866 Mary (*d* 9 Oct 1930), dau of John Partridge, of Malvern, Worcs, and *d* 2 Aug 1922, leaving:

1 **Sir John George Lawley Vassar-Smith, 2nd Bt**; *b* 10 Dec 1868; *educ* Cheltenham and Trin Coll Cambridge (BA 1890); *d unm* 2 May 1942
2 Charles Martin; *b* 5 June 1881; Maj KSLI, Boer War 1901–02 (medal with four clasps), WW I (despatches); *m* 29 Dec 1908 Gladys Emmeline (*d* 24 Nov 1970 aged 88), dau of Col William Hans Rathborne, RE, and *d* 25 Nov 1920, leaving:
(1) **Sir Richard Rathborne Vassar-Smith, 3rd Bt**, TD (1950); *b* 24 Nov 1909; *educ* Lancing and Pembroke Coll Cambridge (BA 1931); Maj RA WW II, Headmaster St Ronan's 1957–72; *m* 27 July 1932 *Mary Dawn, dau of Sir Raymond Wybrow Woods, CBE, and *d* 12 Aug 1995, having had:
1 Charles Richard Raymond; *b* 13 June 1934; *d* 26 June 1937
2a Sir JOHN RATHBORNE VASSAR-SMITH, **4th and present Bt**
1a *Juliet Rathborne; *b* 10 May 1941
1 Beatrice Helena; *d unm* 20 Feb 1965 aged 89
2 Margaret Katharine; *m* 15 Aug 1910 Col Fairlie Russell Ozzard, IMS, s of James William Ozzard, and *d* 22 Sept 1960
3 Dorothy Millicent; *m* 10 June 1913 Rev Reginald Guy Langley Marriott, Vicar Twyning Glos 1927–42, and *d* 26 Feb 1962. He *d* 17 Jan 1951

VAUX OF HARROWDEN

Arms: Quarterly, 1st and 4th, gu. a fess nebuly or, in chief a horse rampant between two estoiles and the like in base, all of the last (for GILBEY); 2nd and 3rd, per bend sinister erm. and erminois a lion rampant or (for MOSTYN). **Crest:** In front of a tower ppr. issuant from the battlements thereof a dragon's head gu. charged with a fleur-de-lys or, all between two ostrich feathers arg. **Supporters:** Dexter, a griffin sa., beaked or, the four legs gold; sinister, a buck or, each gorged with a torse arg. and gu., pendant therefrom by a ring gold an escutcheon of the arms of VAUX. **Motto:** *Hodie non cras* ('Today, not tomorrow'). **Creation:** B. (E) 27 April 1523.

THE 10TH BARON VAUX OF HARROWDEN, Co Northampton (John Hugh Philip Gilbey) [The Rt Hon The Lord Vaux of Harrowden, Cholmondeley Cottage, 2 Cholmondeley Walk, Richmond, Surrey TW9 1NS]; *b* 4 Aug 1915; *s* bro 1977; *educ* Ampleforth and Ch Ch Oxford (BA 1937); Maj Duke of Wellington's Regt WW II; *m* 5 July 1939 his cousin *Maureen Pamela, est dau of Hugh Gilbey (*see* GILBEY, Bt), and has:

1 +ANTHONY WILLIAM [The Hon Anthony Gilbey, Rusko, Gatehouse of Fleet, Kirkcudbrightshire]; *b* 25 May 1940; *educ* Ampleforth; FCA; *m* 4 July 1964 *Beverley Anne, only dau of Charles Alexander Walton, of Cooden, Sussex, and has:
(1) +Richard Hubert Gordon; *b* 16 March 1965; *educ* Ampleforth
(2) +Philip Alexander Charles; *b* 30 March 1967; *educ* Ampleforth; *m* 15 Oct 1994 *Charlotte, dau of Timothy Britton, of Hatfield Broad Oak, Essex
(1) +Victoria Caroline; *b* 4 Jan 1969
(2) +Elizabeth Muriel Emma; *b* 1989
2 +William John [The Hon William Gilbey, The Grange, Waltham St Lawrence, Berks]; *b* 24 Feb 1944; *educ* Ampleforth; *m* 24 April 1971 *Caroline, dau of Alan H Ball, and has:
(1) +Thomas Edward; *b* 16 March 1972; *m* 13 July 1996 *Beth, yst dau of Peter Martin, of Kingston, Surrey
(2) +James William; *b* 24 Jan 1978
(1) +Charlotte Katharine; *b* 4 March 1974
3 +Michael Christopher [The Hon Michael Gilbey, Pheasants Ridge, Hambleden, Oxon RG9 6SD]; *b* 29 Dec 1949; *educ* Ampleforth and St Andrews U (MA 1971); ARICS (1974); *m* 21 Aug 1971 his cousin *Linda, yr dau of Arthur Sebastian Gilbey (*see* GILBEY, Bt), and has:
(1) +Henry John; *b* 7 Feb 1973
(2) +Julian Sebastian; *b* 1 May 1975
(3) +William Michael Arthur; *b* 18 July 1979

1 +Penelope Margaret; *b* 22 Aug 1942; *m* 25 Jan 1965 *John Charles Haynes, est s of Joseph Gladstone Haynes, of Castlecroft, Wolverhampton, and has:

  (1) +Charles Thomas Francis; *b* 17 Aug 1967

  (2) +Edward Hugh Gordon; *b* 10 April 1976

  (1) +Alexandra Louise [Mrs Christopher Courage, Edgcote, Banbury, Oxon]; *b* 17 March 1966; *m* 1991 *Christopher John Courage

  (2) +Bridget Clare; *b* 21 July 1969

Lineage: HUBERT de VALLIBUS or VAUX; *fl* 1149; held extensive lands, notably the seigneurie from which he took his name nr Falaise, Normandy, and various feudal Ldships in the N of England; ancestor of the VAUXes of Gilsland, an estate which passed through an heiress *temp* HENRY III to Thomas de Moulton, and the VAUXes of Tryermayne, Cumberland, the heiress of which *temp* EDWARD I *m* William le Vaux, of Catterlen, ancestor in the female line of the Barons Brougham and Vaux (*qv*)

His yr bro,

ROBERT de VALLIBUS/VAUX; living *temp* STEPHEN; held Ldships in Suffolk and Norfolk; fndr Pentney Priory, Norfolk; *d temp* HENRY II, leaving:

WILLIAM de VAUX; living *temp* HENRY II; had:

ROBERT de VAUX; had, with an er s (Robert, *dsp c* 1211):

OLIVER de VAUX; accompanied KING JOHN to Ireland 1203; later opposed JOHN, hence his lands forfeited, though they were restored him by HENRY III *c* 1218; Justice itinerant *c* 1234; *m* Petronilla, widow of Henry de Mara and William de Longchamps, and *d* after 1244, having had, with an est s (Robert; *dsp*) and a dau (Eleanore):

2 William, of Tharston and Wisset; *m* Alianore (*d* 26 Oct 1274, having *m* 2nd, as his 3rd w, Roger de Quency, Earl of Winchester (*see* WINCHESTER, M, preliminary remarks) and 3rd, as his 2nd w, Roger de Leyburne, of Elham), 7th and yst dau of William de Ferrers, 5th Earl of Derby (*qv*, preliminary remarks) of the 1138 *cr*, and *dsp* 5 Dec 1252

3 John; High Sheriff Norfolk and Suffolk 1263–65; fought Battle of Evesham 1265, presumably for the King against Simon de Montfort, Earl of Leicester (*qv*, preliminary remarks); was granted house property in London *c* 1265; Justice itinerant *c* 1278; Steward Duchy of Aquitaine *c* 1283; *m* Sibilla — (*d* by 1261) and *d c* 1288, leaving:

  (1) Petronillia; *m* William de Nerford

  (2) Maud; *m* 1st Lord (Baron) De Ros (*qv*) of Helmsley

4 Roger; presumably ancestor (f?) of:

  (1) Elias; *m temp* EDWARD II Elizabeth, widow of Sir John Joce, and was probably f of:

    1a William, of Bottisham, Cambs; *d* by 1373, leaving:

      1b William, of Bottisham; *m* Joan, sis and in her issue heiress of Sir William Thirning, Ld Ch Justice (*d* 1413), from whom the Gt and Little Harrowden estate, Northants, ultimately passed, presumably by inheritance, to his gs William (*see* below), and had:

        1c William, of Bottisham and Northampton; *m* by 1399, Eleanor (*m* 2nd Thomas Chambre, of Sprotton, Northants), dau and heiress of Sir Thomas Drakelowe, of Wileby, Northants, and *d* 1405, having had, with two daus (Eleanor, *m* Thomas Gifford, of Twyford, Bucks, and had issue; Isabel, *m* Sir William Tresham and had issue):

          1d William, of Gt and Little Harrowden; High Sheriff Northants 1436–37; *m* Maud, sis and coheir of Sir William Lucy, and *d c* 1460, leaving:

            1e William (Sir), of Harrowden; on the triumph of the Yorkists 1461 was attainted 1461 and deprived of his vast possessions, including feudal Ldships in Beds, Berks, Bucks, Cambs, Herefs, Leics, Northants and Warwicks; fled to Italy then France but returned to England on restoration of HENRY VI, fighting on the Lancastrian side Battle of Barnet 14 April 1471 and being *k* Battle of Tewkesbury 4 May 1471; *m* by 22 Dec 1456 Katharine (Ldy-in-Waiting to HENRY VI's w MARGARET OF ANJOU), dau of George Penis(t)on, of Courtesello, Piedmont, an English refugee, and had:

              1f NICHOLAS VAUX, **1st Baron Vaux of Harrowden** (E), so *cr* 27 April 1523, KB (1497); *b c* 1460; allegedly *educ* Oxford; procured nullification of his f's attainder on HENRY VII's coming to the throne, also restoration of his estates Nov 1485; Steward Olney and Newport Pagnell, Bucks, Nov 1485; fought Battle of Stoke 1487, following which he was *ktd*; High Sheriff Northants 1495–96, 1501–02 and 1516–17; Constable Rockingham Castle 1502, Lt Guisnes Castle in English-held Picardy 1502 and 1509 on, Kt for the Body to HENRY's VII and VIII; *m* 1st Elizabeth, dau and heiress of 5th Lord (Baron) FitzHugh (*see* ABERGAVENNY, M) and widow of Sir William Parr, KG (hence grandfather of QUEEN KATHARINE PARR), and had three daus; *m* 2nd between 17 Nov 1507 and 29 Jan 1507/8 Anne, dau and coheir of Sir Thomas Green, of Boughton and Green's Norton, Northants, and *d* 14 May 1523, leaving by her:

                1g THOMAS VAUX, **2nd Baron Vaux of Harrowden**, KB (1533); *b* 25 April 1509; allegedly *educ* Cambridge; Govr Jersey Jan 1525/6–July 1536, composed poetry, notably 'The Assault of Cupide' and 'The Aged Louer [Lover]', which were published in a collection amassed by Tottel, of *Tottel's Miscellany* fame, in 1557; *m* between 25 April and 10 Nov 1523 Elizabeth (*d* 20 Nov 1556), dau and heiress of Sir Thomas Cheyne, of Fen Ditton, Cambs, and Thenford and Irthlingborough, Northants, by his 2nd w Anne, dau of Sir William Parr, KG, and *d* 1556, having had an er s:

                  1h WILLIAM VAUX, **3rd Baron Vaux of Harrowden**; *b* just prior to 14 Aug 1535; recusant, hence often imprisoned and fined, his most celebrated role in this regard being the harbourer of Edmund Campion; *m* 1st by 1 June 1557 Elizabeth (*d* 1562), dau of John Beaumont, of Gracedieu, Leics (*see* BEAUMONT, Bt), and had, with other issue:

1i Henry; *b* 1558–59; intended to become a priest; arrested as a recusant and imprisoned Marshalsea 1586–87; *d unm* Nov 1587

1i Anne; well known in the history of English Catholicism in penal times as Mrs Perkins, the recusant; *d unm* 1635

1h (cont.) The **3rd Baron** *m* 2nd 1563–64 Mary, dau of John Tresham, of Rushton, Northants, and *d* 20 Aug 1595, having by her had, with other issue:

  2i George; *bapt* 27 Sept 1564; *educ* English Coll Douai; *m* 25 July 1585 Elizabeth, dau of 1st Baron Teynham (*qv*), and *dvp* 13 July 1594, leaving:

    1j EDWARD VAUX, **4th Baron Vaux of Harrowden**; *b* 13 Sept 1588; suspected (like his mother; *see* TEYNHAM, B) of involvement in the Gunpowder Plot; imprisoned March 1611/2–14 for refusing to take the Oath of Allegiance and 13–25 Nov 1625 for resisting a search of his house for concealed weapons; Col of an English regt in Spanish serv in Flanders 1622–24; *m* by 2 July 1632 Elizabeth, dau of 1st Earl of Suffolk (*see* SUFFOLK and BERKSHIRE, E) and widow of 1st Earl of Banbury, and *dsp*(*l*? *See* KNOLLYS, V) 8 Sept 1661

    2j William; *d* a child

    3j HENRY VAUX, **5th Baron Vaux of Harrowden**; Capt in Spanish serv in Flanders 1625–28; *d unm* 20 Sept 1663, when the Barony fell into abeyance between his sisters or their issue

  1j MARY, for whom *see* further below

  2j Joyce; nun at Eye, Suffolk; *bur* 16 May 1667

  3j Catherine; *m* as his 2nd w 7th Lord (Baron) Bergavenny (*see* ABERGAVENNY, M) and had issue

The 5th BARON's est sis,

MARY Vaux; *m* as his 1st w Sir George SIMEON, of Baldwin Brightwell, Oxon, and *d c* 1622, having had an only surv dau:

ELIZABETH Simeon; *m* 1st Sir John Conyers, of Sockburn, Co Durham, and had three daus, the two yr of whom *d* unm while the est *m* 11th Earl of Shrewsbury and Waterford (*qv*); *m* 2nd, as his 2nd w, Edmund Roe BUTLER, 4th Viscount Mountgarret (*qv*) and *d* 18 Feb 1674, leaving by him, with a dau:

EDWARD BUTLER, on whom his f settled the Manor of Ballyraggett and other estates in Co Kilkenny; *m* Elizabeth, dau of George Mathew, of Thomastown, Co Tipperary, and *d* 1691, having had, with two other sons (including an er, Edmund, of Ballyraggett, *m* Rose O'Neill, of Dublin, and *dsp* 13 Oct 1694):

GEORGE BUTLER, of Ballyraggett; *m* Catherine, dau of 3rd Baron Kingston of the 1660 *cr* (*see* KINGSTON, E), and *d* Sept 1752, having had, with two yr sons (Edmund, Dean Cathedral Ch of Douai, Flanders; Gerald Alexander, *dsp*) and three daus (including Mary, *m* Ralph Standish, of Standish, Lancs, and *dsps*; Frances, *m* Nov 1740 Sir James Stanley, 4th Bt (*see* STANLEY OF ALDERLEY, SHEFFIELD and, B), and *dsp*):

JAMES BUTLER; *m* Frances, dau and heiress of Robert Dillon (*see* TALBOT OF MALAHIDE, B), and *dvp* 1746, leaving, with an est s (Robert, of Ballyraggett, *m* 1st Mary, dau of 4th and last Baron Bellew (*qv*) of Duleek, *m* 2nd Elizabeth, est dau of 5th and last Baron Langdale of Holme, and *dsp* June 1788, having settled his estates on his next bro's bro-in-law Walter Kavanagh, of Borris(-in-Ossory?) in the event, ultimately fulfilled, of neither he nor his next bro's having sons) and a yst s (James, RC Archbp Cashel), a 2nd s:

GEORGE BUTLER, of Ballyraggett; *m* 1st Mary Norris; *m* 2nd Mary, sis of Walter Kavanagh (*see* above), and *d* 30 Jan 1813, leaving by her no issue, but by his 1st w:

MARY LUCINDA Butler; *m* 17 May 1801 Charles MOSTYN (*see* MOSTYN, Bt) and *d* 2 Dec 1831, leaving, with a dau (*see* SLADE, Bt):

GEORGE CHARLES MOSTYN, **6th Baron Vaux of Harrowden**, as which recognised on termination of abeyance in his favour 12 March 1838; *b* 7 March 1804; *m* 9 July 1828 Caroline (*d* 30 Sept 188, aged 75), est dau of Arthur Vansittart, of Shottesbrook, Berks, by Caroline, dau of 1st Baron Auckland (*qv*), and *d* 28 Jan 1883, having had:

1 George Charles; *b* 3 April 1830; Maj 3rd Roy Surrey Militia; *m* 9 Aug 1859 Mary (*d* 17 Feb 1917), 2nd dau of Rt Rev James Henry Monk, DD, Bp Gloucester and Bristol, and *dvp* 1 June 1879, having had, with another s (*d* young):

  (1) HUBERT GEORGE CHARLES, **7th Baron**

  (2) Ranulph Edward Montague; *b* 16 June 1861; Capt RA; *m* 3 April 1888 Caroline Blanche (*d* 1943, having *m* 2nd Jack Stanley Whitestone, of Long Island, NY (*d* 1940)), est dau of Maj William Fiske Melbourne, and *d* 31 Aug 1898, leaving:

    1a Montague Albert; *b* 11 Oct 1893; *d* 14 Oct 1951

  (3) Harold Plantagenet; *b* 26 Dec 1865; *educ* Oscott; *m* 4 July 1894 Elena (*d* 9 Feb 1953), dau of Antonio Zammit, Spanish Consul-Gen Rome, and *d* 13 Aug 1951, having had, with another s (*d* young):

    1a George Anthony; *b* 11 April 1898; *educ* Downside and Balliol Coll Oxford; Lt 60th Rifles WW I, Maj Intell Corps WW II; *m* 18 Sept 1924 Catherine Sibylla (*d* 1983), dau of Bernard Henry Holland, CB (*see* KNUTSFORD, V), and *d* 26 May 1972, having had:

      1b +Richard Anthony [Richard Mostyn Esq, 3 Flamingo Drive, Greenside, Mutare, Zimbabwe]; *b* 22 June 1927; *educ* RNC Dartmouth; Lt RN (ret), FIAC S Africa, LIMTA S Africa; *m* 14 Feb 1961 *Mary, dau of James Joseph Michie, of Marian Hill, Natal, and has:

        1c +Anthony Damian; *b* 12 Nov 1964; CA Zimbabwe; *m* 14 Feb 1997 *Deborah Lawrenson, of Gillingham, Kent, and has:

          1d +Harriet Christine; *b* 1997

        2c +Christopher Francis Joseph; *b* 1 May 1966; *m* 23 March 1996 *Jody Kim, dau of Henry Kasprow, of Prince George, BC

        1c +Nicola Mary; *b* 23 Dec 1961; *m* 1981 *Grant Taylor, of Redcliffe, Qld, and has:

          1d +Grant Alexander; *b* 1994

1d +Alana Clare; *b* 1986

2c +Clare Sibylla; *b* 13 June 1963; *m* 1983 *Morgan Hore, of Dagenham, Essex, and has:

1d +Mark Patrick; *b* 1983

2d +Kevin Anthony; *b* 1987

2b Christopher Harold; *b* 2 Oct 1930; *educ* Lycée d'Antibes and HMS *Worcester; Lt RN; k* plane crash 25 July 1958

3b +Valentine Francis Damian [Valentine Mostyn Esq, 50 Cranley Mews, London SW7]; *b* 23 Feb 1943; *educ* Lycée d'Antibes, St Josephs' Coll Ipswich, Oxford Sch of Architecture and Canterbury Sch of Architecture (Dip Arch); ARIBA; *m* 1974 *Gay, dau of H Field, of Malibu, Calif., and has:

1c +Amy Clare; *b* 1974

2c +Sarah Jane; *b* 1977

1b +Juliet Veronica [Mrs Anthony Lightfoot, Valley Farm Cottage, Brundish, Suffolk IP13 8BP]; *b* 9 July 1925; *m* 15 May 1952 *Anthony Lightfoot, only adopted s of Kenneth Lightfoot, and has:

1c +Edward Jude; *b* 28 Sept 1953; *educ* Framlingham Coll and UCL; *m* 1st 1977 (*divorce* 1982) Hilary Diane Carver; *m* 2nd 1983 *Gaynor Alison Clark and by her has:

1d +Alexander Richard; *b* 16 July 1985

1d +Jessica Louise; *b* 7 Feb 1984

2c +Dominic Anthony; *b* 7 April 1955; *educ* Stradbroke Sch and Colchester Art Coll

3c +Paul Jerome; *b* 29 April 1956; *m* 31 May 1982 (*divorce* 1992) Claudia Miéville

1c +Mary Victoria; *b* 20 May 1959; *m* 1998 *Robert Pendered and has:

1d *Matilda Mary; *b* 25 July 1996

2d +Emily Rachel; *b* 31 Jan 1998

2c +Catherine Lucy; *b* 30 Dec 1966; *m* 20 June 1992 (*divorce* 1993) James Hartley Berwick

2b +Joan Elizabeth Verena [Ms Joan Mostyn, No 8 Cockington Rd, Mandara, Harare, Zimbabwe]; *b* 3 June 1948; *educ* RCA (MA); *m* 17 April 1970 (*divorce* 1977) Anthony John Dyson; has by *Douglas Jones, of San Francisco:

1c *Santiago Alexis Kanjuchi Sadiq; *b* 1981

(1) Beatrice Violet Mary; *b* 27 July 1862; *m* 9 Nov 1895 Sir Charles Rivers Wilson, GCMG, CB (*d* 9 Feb 1916), of Mayfair, s of Melvil Wilson, and *d* 17 April 1925

(2) Gwendolina Hyacinth Roma; *b* 10 July 1864; *m* 21 Dec 1898 Sir John Home, 12th Bt (*qv*), and *d* 22 March 1960, leaving issue

(3) Myrtle Mabel Muriel; *b* 14 April 1869; *m* 8 Feb 1902 Sir Henry Herbert Wombwell, 5th Bt (*qv*), and *d* 26 March 1960

2 Montagu Henry; *b* 25 April 1838; Lt 1st Dragoons; *m* 5 Aug 1869 Frances Mary (*d* 23 Aug 1918), est dau of Patrick J Kearney, DL, of Miltown House, Co Meath, and *d* 13 Dec 1904, leaving:

(1) Montagu John; *b* 15 Nov 1870; *m* 1 Sept 1921 Hannah Cohen (*d* 19–), est dau of Simon Sacke, of Johannesburg, and *d* 17 Aug 1939

(1) Muriel Mary Monica; *b* 27 June 1876; *m* 12 April 1904 Cdr Charles Henry Cecil Kerr-Pearse, RN, and *d* 1933, leaving issue

1 Mary Caroline; *m* 28 Nov 1868 Roger Eykyn, JP, DL, of Gayton House, Northants, MP Windsor 1866–74, and *d* 20 Sept 1895

2 Georgina Louisa; *b* 23 April 1846; *d* unm 29 Jan 1942

The 6th BARON's gs,

HUBERT GEORGE CHARLES MOSTYN, **7th Baron Vaux of Harrowden**, JP, DL; *b* 4 June 1860; *educ* Oscott and Trin Coll Cambridge (MA); Dip Serv: joined 1883, 3rd Sec 1886, 2nd Sec 1891–99, posted to Cairo, Stuttgart, Darmstadt, Belgrade and Berne; bought back Gt Harrowden Hall 1895 from George Wentworth-FitzWilliam, whose ancestor had acquired the property exactly 300 years before from Charles Knollys, self-styled Earl of Banbury, s of the Nicholas KNOLLYS previously VAUX bequeathed the place by the **4th Baron**; *see* above), his step-f or possibly his real f (*see* KNOLLYS, V); *m* 1st 25 Aug 1886 Eleanor Margaret (*d* 18 Sept 1896), dau of Sir Alexander Matheson, 1st Bt (*qv*); *m* 2nd 15 May 1902 Margaret Annette Jane (*d* 8 April 1922), only child of Sir William Chichele Plowden, KCSI; *m* 3rd 5 June 1924 Mary Winefride Teresa (*d* 14 Dec 1944), only dau of Sir Joseph Radcliffe, 4th Bt (*qv*), and widow of Capt Thomas Cecil de Trafford (*see* DE TRAFFORD, Bt), and *d* 25 Oct 1935, when the Barony again fell into abeyance, leaving by his 1st w:

1 GRACE MARY ELEANOR Mostyn, **Baroness Vaux of Harrowden** in her own right, as recognised on termination of abeyance in her favour 8 July 1938; *b* 22 May 1887; *educ* Hillside Convent Farnborough; *m* 15 July 1911 William Gordon GILBEY (*see* GILBEY, Bt) and *d* 11 May 1958, leaving:

(1) PETER HUBERT GORDON GILBEY, **9th Baron Vaux of Harrowden**; *b* 28 June 1914; *educ* Ampleforth and St Benet's Hall Oxford (BA 1939, MA 1943); OSB 1932, Priest 1940; *d* 1 Nov 1977

(2) JOHN HUGH PHILIP GILBEY, **10th and present Baron Vaux of Harrowden**

(1) +Mary Agnes Margaret [The Hon Mary Gilbey, Dolphins, Gt Harrowden, Wellingborough, Northants]; *b* 13 April 1928

2 Gladys Flora Matheson; *b* 14 July 1889; *m* 5 Aug 1911 George Victor Bellasis Charlton (*d* 25 June 1943), 5th s of Edward Charlton, MD, DCL, of Newcastle, and *d* 1975, leaving:

(1) +Eleanor Margaret Mary; *b* 1912

(2) Anne Mary Georgina; *b* 1913; *m* 22 July 1948 Hugh Dougal Fyfe Baird (*d* 1979), only s of Lt-Col Hugh Baird, OBE, of Harborne, Birmingham, and *d* 1994, leaving:

1a +(Rosemary) Gillian [Mrs Charles King, Hillhead of Dens, Blackhills, Peterhead, Aberdeen AB42 3LT]; *b* 8 May 1950; *m* 1st 1974 (*divorce* 1980) Barry Lambert; *m* 2nd 1981 *Charles Davies King and by him has:

1b +Patrick Charles; *b* 1987

(3) +Joan Mary Winefride [Mrs Harry Ripper, 1A Recreation Ground, Sible Hedingham, Essex CO9 3JD]; *b* 1915; *m* 1st 4 Oct 1941 P/O Ian Alexander Bruce Johnstone, RAF (*ka* 12 March 1942), s of Alexander Johnstone, of Forest Lodge, King's Gate, Aberdeen; *m* 2nd 27 Nov 1945 *F/O Harry James Hubert Ripper, RAF, er s of Harry Joseph Edward Ripper, of The Bays, Sible Hedingham, and by him has:

1a +Christopher James [Christopher Ripper Esq, 12 Manor Rd, Grimscote, Towcester, Northants NN12 8LN]; *b* 29 Aug 1946; *educ* Blackfairs Sch, Laxton, Northants; *m* 1974 (*divorce* 1997) Julie Margaret Long, of Sydney, NSW, and has:

1b +Georgina Louise; *b* 1977

2b +Annabel Merry; *b* 1979

3b +Holly Charlton; *b* 1981

1a +Judith Caroline [Mrs Judith Ford, 51 Begbroke Crescent, Begbroke, Oxon OX5 1RW]; *b* 10 July 1949; *m* 1 May 1971 (*divorce* 1993) Philip William Ford and has:

1b +Adam George; *b* 1975

1b +Samantha Anne; *b* 1973

(4) +Dorothy Mary Amy [Mrs Digby Auden, Dolphin House, 2 Back Lane, Hardingstone, Northants NN4 6BX]; *b* 16 April 1919; *m* 30 April 1958 *Digby Michael Auden, yr s of Lt-Col Edward Humphrey Auden, MBE, of Repton, Derbys, and has had:

1a Julian Michael; *b* 12 Sept 1961; *k* in an accident 1973

1a +Penelope Clare Auden [Mrs Paul Radford, 8 Darwin Cl, Porterswood, St Albans, Herts AL3 6LH]; *b* 9 April 1960; *m* 1986 *Paul Radford and has:

1b +Michael Julian Auden; *b* 1988

2b +Dominic Peter Auden; *b* 1990

3b +Sebastian Thomas Auden; *b* 1992

4b +Oliver Lawrence Auden; *b* 1996

1b +Catriona Helen Margaret Auden; *b* 1987

(5) +Frances Mary Elizabeth [Mrs Stephen Ripper, Orchard House, High St Green, Sible Hedingham, Essex CO9 3LG]; *m* 6 June 1947 her er sis's bro-in-law *Stephen Louis Dudley Ripper and has had:

1a +Anne Mary Frances [Mrs Anton Shellim, 12 Moreton Ave, Harpenden, Herts AL5 2ET]; *b* 1 July 1948; *m* 1983 *Anton Brooke Shellim and has:

1b +Alexander Brooke; *b* 1985

1b +Rebecca Frances; *b* 1987

2a Susan Mary Margaret; *b* 2 April 1951; *d* unm 1990

3a +Catherine Mary Alison [Mrs John Malone, 8 Greenbank Crescent, Edinburgh EH10 5SG]; *b* 6 April 1955; *m* 1st 1974 (*divorce* 1980) George Hales; *m* 2nd 1980 *John Alexander Malone and by him has:

1b +Martin John; *b* 1988

1b +Amy Frances; *b* 1984

3 Dorothy Alice; *b* 27 Jan 1893; *educ* Bedford Coll London (BA 1922); religious of Congregation of Christian Education; *d* 19–

VAVASOUR

Arms: Quarterly, 1st and 4th, or a fess dancettée sable, in the dexter chief point a cross-crosslet for difference of the second (for VAVASOUR); 2nd and 3rd, sable a bend or between six fountains (for STOURTON). **Crests:** 1 A cock gules, combed and wattled or, charged with a fountain for difference (for VAVASOUR), 2 A demi-monk habited in russet proper, girdle or, wielding in his dexter hand a scourge or of five knotted lashes of the last (for STOURTON). **Creation:** Bt. (UK) 14 Feb 1828.

SIR ERIC MICHEL JOSEPH MARMADUKE VAVASOUR, 6TH BT, of Hazlewood, Yorks [Sir Eric Vavasour Bt, 15 Mill Lane, Earl Shilton, Leics LE9 7AW]; *b* 3 Jan 1953; *s* cousin 1997; *educ* St Joseph's Coll Stoke-on-Trent and Manchester U (BSc); AMIEE; *m* 1976 *Isabelle Baudouin Françoise Alain Cécile Cornelie Ghislaine, dau of André van Hille, of Brussels, and has:

1 +JOSEPH IAN HUGH ANDRE; *b* 22 Jan 1978

2 +Thomas Bernard André Hugh; *b* 1984

1 *Emilie Isabelle Marguerite Monique; *b* 1980

Lineage: MAUGER (I?); tenant in Yorks 1086 of among others William de Percy (*see* NORTHUMBERLAND, D; either this MAUGER (I?) or another person of the same name (MAUGER (II?)), possibly MAUGER (I?))'s s, witnessed a charter of Alan de Percy temp HENRY I); had, with an er s (Robert):

A son or dau; had, with a yr s (Robert):

WILLIAM Le VAVASOUR (*i.e.*, 'the vassal' or 'the sub-tenant'); witness to a charter *c* 1158–63; *d* after Michaelmas 1189 but before 29 June 1191, leaving:

1 Robert; Deputy for Sheriff Lancs 1197; allowed York Minster a right of way to transport quarried stone across his land at Hazlewood, Yorks, *c* 1225; *m* 1st — and had:

 (1) Maud; *m* 1st *c* 1199 Theobald Fitz Walter (*see* MOUNTGARRET, V) and had issue; *m* 2nd 1207 Fulk Fitz Warin

1 (cont.) Robert le Vavasour *m* 2nd 1208 Juliane, dau of Thomas de Multon and widow of Thomas de Rie, and *d* by 1227, having by her had (with perhaps another s, Henry):

 (1) JOHN

2 Mauger; ancestor of the VAVASOURs of Denton and Weston

1 Agnes; had:

 (1) Nicholas —

2(?) Mabel(?); had:

 (1) Adam de Criding

ROBERT Le VAVASOUR's s,

JOHN Le VAVASOUR; *b c* 1212–13; *m c* 1242–44 Alice (*d* just before 22 June 1295), dau of Robert de Cockfield, and *d* after autumn 1283 but by 1284–85, leaving, with two other sons (Mauger; John) and two daus (Amanda; Margaret):

WILLIAM Le VAVASOUR, 1st LORD (Baron) VAVASOUR (E), so *cr* by writ of summons to Parl (according to later doctrine) 6 Feb 1297/8; *b c* 1265; granted leave to crenellate his house at Hazlewood 1290, fought in vanguard at Battle of Falkirk (EDWARD I's victory over Scots under William Wallace) 1298; at Siege of Carlaverock in Scottish wars 1300, Keeper Pontefract Castle to May 1311; *m* by 1280 Nichole — and *d* just before 22 March 1312/3, having had, with other issue:

1 WALTER Le VAVSOUR, 2nd LORD (Baron) VAVASOUR; *b c* 1280; called to Parl 26 July 1313; *m* by(?) 18 March 1310/1 Eleanor — and *dsp* by 7 Dec 1315

2 Robert; never called to Parl (nor were any of his successors); *dsp* just before 24 July 1322

3 Henry; *b c* 1290; *m* Constance — and *d* 1 Dec 1342, leaving:

 (1) Henry; *m c* 1326 Amabel FitzHugh, dau of 1st Lord (Baron) FitzHugh and *d* just before 27 Nov 1349, leaving:

 1a Henry; *b* 1328–29; *dsp* just before 25 May 1355

 2a William; *b* after 25 May but before 1 Aug 1334; *m* by 16 Oct 1361 Elizabeth, dau of Sir Hugh de Cressy, and *d c* 15 Aug–8 Sept 1369, leaving:

  1b William; *b c* 1358; *dsp c* 1386–87

  2b Henry (Sir); *m* Margaret, dau of Sir William Skipwith (*see* SKIPWITH, Bt), and *d* 27 March 1413, leaving:

   1c Henry; *b c* 1402; *m* Joan, dau of John Langton, and *d* just before 15 Jan 1452/3, leaving:

    1d Henry (Sir); *m* Joan, dau of Sir William Gascoigne, and *d* 22 Dec 1499, leaving:

     1e William; *dsp* 26 March or 24 May 1500

    2e Henry; *b c* 1456; *m* Elizabeth, dau of Sir John Everingham, and *d* 31 Oct or 1 Nov 1515, leaving:

     1f John; *m* Anne Scrope, dau of 6th Lord (Baron) Scrope (of Bolton), and *d* 11 Aug 1524, leaving:

      1g William (Sir); *b* 20 Nov 1514; *m* Elizabeth, dau of Anthony 'Cavalay', and *d* 9 May 1566, leaving:

       1h John; *b* 1538; *m* Eleanor, dau of Sir Nicholas Fairfax, and *dsp* 1609

       2h Ralph; *m* 1st Ursula, dau of Sir William Fairfax; *m* 2nd Elizabeth, dau of Richard Peck, and *d* by(?) Easter 1611, leaving by her:

        1i William, of Hazlewood, Yorks; *b* 1569; *m* Anne, dau of Sir Thomas Manners (*see* RUTLAND, D), and *d* by 1626, having had:

         1j Sir THOMAS VAVASOUR, 1st Bt (E), so *cr* 24 Oct 1628, of Hazlewood; Kt Marshal CHARLES I's Household; *m* Ursula, dau of Walter Giffard, of Chillington, Staffs, and *d* by March 1635/6, having had:

          1k Sir WALTER VAVASOUR, 2nd Bt; *b c* 1612; raised a cavalry regt for CHARLES I Civil War, nominated a Kt of Royal Oak 1660 (order of chivalry planned by CHARLES II but never instituted); *m c* 8 March 1635/6 Ursula Belasyse (*b c* 1617), dau of 1st Viscount Fauconberg of Henknowle, and *d* on or after 13 Aug 1666, leaving:

           1l Sir WALTER VAVASOUR, 3rd Bt; *b c* 1644; *m* Jane, dau of Sir Jordan Crossland, of Newby, Yorks, and *dsp* 16 Feb 1712/3

          2k William; Maj Royalist Army Civil War; *d* unm

          3k Thomas; *k* Battle of Marston Moor (Parliamentarian victory) 1644

          4k John; *d* unm

          5k Peter, of York; MD; *m* Elizabeth, dau of Philip Langdale, of Langthorpe, and was *bur* 26 Nov 1659, having had:

           1l Sir WALTER VAVASOUR, 4th Bt; *b c* 1659; *d* unm 1740

           2l Peter; *b c* 1667; *d* 6 June 1735, leaving:

            1m Sir WALTER VAVASOUR, 5th Bt; *m* 1st Elizabeth (*dsps*), dau of Peter Vavasour, of Willitoft, E R Yorks; *m* 2nd April 1741 Dorothy Langdale (*d* 25 April 1751), dau of 4th Baron Langdale of Holme and aunt through her bro 5th Baron Langdale of

Holme of Mary (w of 17th Baron Stourton; *see* MOWBRAY, SEGRAVE and STOURTON, B), and *d* 13 April 1766, leaving:

            1n Sir WALTER VAVASOUR, 6th Bt; *b* 16 Jan 1744; *m* Sept 1797 Jane, only dau of William Langdale, and *dsp* 3 Nov 1802

            2n Sir THOMAS VAVASOUR, 7th and last Bt; *d* unm 20 Jan 1826, when the btcy expired

            3n Peter; Gen in Austrian service; *m* Countess von Paisburg and *dsp* 1818

           1k Mary; nun; *d* 24 Dec 1631

           2k Frances; *m* Alphonso Thweng(e), of Kilton Castle, Yorks

The 7th and last Bt's 1st cousin once-removed (17th Baron Stourton's 2nd s),

Sir EDWARD MARMADUKE JOSEPH STOURTON later VAVASOUR (roy licence 27 Feb 1826 on inheriting the 7th Bt's estates), **1st Bt** (UK), so *cr* 14 Feb 1828; *b* 6 May 1786; Capt Yorks Hus 1817–24; *m* 6 Aug 1813 Marcia Bridget (*d* 10 June 1826), only dau of James Lane Fox, MP, of Bramham Park, Yorks, and *d* 16 March 1847, having had, with three other daus:

1 **Sir Edward Marmaduke Joseph Vavasour, 2nd Bt**; *b* 17 Jan 1815; *d* unm 23 Aug 1885

2 Charles Joseph; *b* 15 April 1817; *d* unm 21 April 1846

3 William Joseph; *b* 26 Feb 1822; *m* 12 Jan 1846, as her 1st husb, Hon Mary Constantia Clifford, dau of 7th Baron Clifford of Chudleigh (*qv*), and *d* 11 Jan 1860, having had, with four other daus:

 (1) **Sir William Edward Joseph Vavasour, 3rd Bt**, JP (W R Yorks); *b* 28 Nov 1846; Maj Yorks Hus, served Papal Zouaves; *m* 5 Oct 1870 Mary Teresa (*d* 20 March 1927), 2nd dau of Edward Joseph Weld, of Lulworth Castle, Dorset, and *d* 18 Nov 1915, leaving:

  1a **Sir Leonard Pius Vavasour, 4th Bt**; *b* 23 Sept 1881; *educ* Downside; Capt RN, WWs I and II; *m* 18 Aug 1913 Ellice Margaret (*d* 8 Jan 1965 aged 84), er dau of Henry Ellis Hay Nelson and formerly w of Lt Arthur Bisset Streynsham Hoskins Master, RN, and *d* 14 Sept 1961, leaving:

   1b **Sir Geoffrey William Vavasour, 5th Bt**, DSC (1943); *b* 5 Sept 1914; *educ* RNC Dartmouth; Cdr RN WW II, dir W M Still & Sons (kitchen equipment mfrs) 1962–80; *m* 1st 23 Jan 1940 (*divorce* 1947) Joan Millicent Kirkland, dau of Arthur John Robb, of Rowland's Castle, Hants, and had:

    1c *Jacqueline Mary; *b* 1 Feb 1941; *m* 17 Sept 1966 *Capt Peter John Whittington (ret), 14th/20th King's Hus, of Barns Oak, Waldron, E Sussex, yst s of Theodore Whittington, of Danehill, Sussex, and has:

     1d *Edward James; *b* 1977

     1d *Anna Catherine; *b* 1974

    2c *Elizabeth Anne [Mrs Calvin P Winn, 11109 SW 113 Place, Miami, FL 33176, USA]; *b* 30 March 1943; *m* 1st 30 June 1965 (*divorce* 1968) Terence Hickman, only s of Alan Hickman, of The Shard, Minchinhampton, Glos; *m* 2nd 26 July 1968 James Monroe Woodman III, s of James Monroe Woodman II, of Key Biscayne, Fla., and has:

     1d *Elizabeth Anne; *b* 7 March 1969

     2d *Lara; *b* 6 March 1970

    2c (cont.) Mrs Woodman *m* 3rd 1989 *Calvin Palme Winn

   1b (cont.) **Sir Geoffrey** *m* 2nd 1971 (*divorce* 1980) (Marcia) Christine, dau of Marshall Shaw Lodge, of Batley, Yorks, and formerly w of Maj Dennis Wieler, of Feathercombe, Hambledon, Surrey, and *d* 28 July 1997

   1b *Elizabeth Mary [Mrs Garth Bird, The Oast House, Great Broadhurst Farm, Broad Oak, nr Heathfield, Sussex]; *b* 13 Aug 1917; *m* 1st 6 April 1940 Lt Michael John Priaulx Walters, RN (*ka* April 1941), yr s of Lt-Col Hubert de Lancey Walters, of Guernsey, and has:

    1c *Simon de Lancey [Simon Walters Esq, Tundry House, Dogmersfield, Hants]; *b* (posthumously) 1941; *m* 1966 *Sarah, dau of Brig Thomas Gwythr Charles, and has:

     1d *Mark; *b* 1967

     2d *Barnaby; *b* 1974

     1d *Gemma; *b* 1969

     2d *Abigail; *b* 1976

   1b (cont.) Mrs Michael Walters *m* 2nd 19 Sept 1942 *Brig Garth Raymond Godfrey Bird, s of Herbert William Bird, of Cranleigh, Surrey, and by him has:

    2c *Christopher John Godfrey [Christopher Bird Esq, 78 Masbro Rd, London W14]; *b* 1946; *m* 1972 (*divorce* 1989) Hon Catherine Mary Dormer, yr dau of 15th Baron Dormer (*qv*)

    3c *Anthony Nigel Godfrey [Anthony Bird Esq, 47 Buckingham Place, Brighton, Sussex]; *b* 1953

    1c *Fiona Mary [Mrs Robin Nicholson, 7 Highbury Pl, London N5 1QZ]; *b* 1943; *m* 1969 *Robin Alaster Nicholson and has:

     1d *Zachary Luke; *b* 1971

     2d *Solomon Rufus; *b* 1974

     3d *Caspian Ned; *b* 1978

  2b *Josephine Mary; *b* 4 Sept 1921; 3rd Offr WRNS WW II; *m* 7 Oct 1942 R-Adml Derick Henry Fellowes Hetherington, CB, DSC (*d* 1992), of South Lodge, Rose Lane, Oxford, Domestic Bursar Merton Coll, Oxford, er s of Cdr Henry Reginald Hetherington, RD, RNR, of Haslemere, Surrey, and has had:

   1c Andrew Vavasour; *b* 13 July 1943; *d* 29 Jan 1952

   2c *Mark; *b* 23 March 1950

   1c *Virginia Mary; *b* 9 June 1947

   2c *Teresa; *b* 30 Dec 1951

   3c *Dinah Mary; *b* 22 July 1957

  2a Bernard Joseph; *b* 24 Oct 1886; Lt MGC, formerly RGA; *m* 28 Sept 1925 Mildred Rowena Atherstone, yr dau of Lt-Col Herbert M A Hales, Govr Parkhurst Prison, and *d* 1946

  1a Ellen Mary; *b* 9 Aug 1871; *d* 15 Oct 1922

2a Annette Mary; *b* 1 Oct 1872; *m* 1st 24 Feb 1897 Henry Marmaduke Salvin (*d* 2 Nov 1924), 2nd s of Marmaduke Charles Salvin, JP, DL, of Burn Hall, Co Durham; *m* 2nd 8 Dec 1926 Lt-Col Herman Charles Joseph Salvin, JP, DL, RA (*d* 20 Feb 1943), of Croxdale Hall, Co Durham, 2nd s of Henry T T Salvin, of Croxdale, and *dsp* 3 Jan 1941

3a Evelyn Mary Theresa; *b* 14 Oct 1873; nun; *d* 1953

4a Mary Josephine, OBE (1920); *b* 12 Dec 1874; *m* 30 Nov 1907 Maj John Frederick Loder-Symonds (*ka* Ypres 31 Oct 1914), 1st Bn S Staffs Regt, est s of Capt Frederick Cleave Loder-Symonds, of Hinton Manor, Berks, and *d* 15 July 1958

5a Maude Mary; *b* 23 Aug 1883; nun

(2) Oswald Hugh Stanislaus; *b* 3 June 1848; served Papal Zouaves in unsuccessful defence of Rome against forces of Italian nationalism 1870; *m* 8 Aug 1877 Sarah Anne (*d* 12 April 1937), dau of James Smith, of Draycott, Staffs, and *d* 10 Jan 1925, having had:

1a Oswald Joseph Stanislaus; *b* 7 Feb 1883; *educ* Stonyhurst; *m* 24 June 1915 Mary Dorothy (*d* 25 Aug 1952), dau of Bernard Moore, of The Grange, Draycott, and *d* 1973, leaving:

1b Hugh Bernard Moore; *b* 4 July 1918; *educ* Stonyhurst; Capt RA WW II; *m* 9 Dec 1950 Monique Pauline Marie Madeleine (*d* 1982), dau of Maurice Erick Beck, of St Aubin-sur-Scie, Seine Maritime, France, and *d* 1989, leaving:

1c Sir ERIC MICHEL JOSEPH MARMADUKE VAVASOUR, **6th and present Bt**

1c *Anne Pauline Mary Draycott; *b* 4 April 1969

2b Bede Joseph Stourton; *b* 9 Dec 1922; PO RAFVR WW II; *kas* 12 June 1942

1b *Dorothy Constance [Sister Dorothy Vavasour, Provincial House, The Ridgeway, Mill Hill, London NW7 1EH]; *b* 17 April 1916; Sister of Charity of St Vincent de Paul

2a Edward James Marmaduke; *b* 30 Jan 1886; *d* unm 15 July 1957

3a George Francis Aloysius; *b* 10 April 1890; *d* 24 Sept 1897

4a John Wilfrid Leonard; *b* 23 Nov 1891; served Canadian Artillery WW I; *m* 25 Jan 1940 Joyce (*m* 2nd 13 Oct 1961 Robert William Ellett), dau of George Frederic Mayer, of Louth, Lincs, and *d* 27 Nov 1955, leaving:

1b *Margaret Anne; *b* 2 Oct 1940

2b *Angela Mary; *b* 11 Aug 1943; *m* 3 April 1963 *Ronald James Edgington, of Farningham, Kent, est s of Henry James Edgington, of Bexleyheath, and has:

1c *Alexander James; *b* 19 Jan 1968

1c *Fiona Anne; *b* 6 Jan 1966

3b *Frances Joyce Sarah; *b* 2 March 1949

5a Hubert Philip Anthony; *b* 12 Jan 1895; Lt KOYLI WW I; *d* unm 1 Feb 1963

6a George Raphael Tobias; *b* 6 Aug 1898; *d* 1 Oct 1899

7a Joseph Everard Dunstan; *b* 16 Jan 1902

1a Constantia Mary Josephine; *b* 13 Feb 1881; *d* unm 31 Jan 1953

2a Edith Mary Gertrude; *b* 11 Feb 1882; *d* unm 30 Sept 1955

3a Cecilia Monica Mary; *b* 22 Nov 1884

4a Winifred Mary Lucy; *b* 28 Feb 1888; nun of the Convent of the Sisters of Charity; *d* 3 Dec 1968

5a Lucy Mary Gwendoline (Sister Mary Yolande); *b* 20 Feb 1893; Franciscan nun; *d* 10 May 1967

6a Elizabeth Mary Veronica; *b* 20 Feb 1897

7a Angela Mary Clara; *b* 14, *d* 24 Feb 1900

(3) Henry Dunstan; *b* 10 Jan 1850; *m* 1 Sept 1887 Bertha Eleanor Mary (*d* 31 May 1959), est dau of Thomas Peter Redwood, of Burleigh, Blenheim, NZ, and *d* 22 Jan 1927, having had, a dau, Betty (*d* unm):

1a George Marmaduke; *b* 13 Sept 1891; Lt NZ Rifle Bde; *ka* 12 Oct 1918

2a Rudolph Dunstan; *b* 4 Jan 1894; T/Lt RFA and F/O RFC; *d* 16 Jan 1917

3a Edward Joseph Henry; *b* 21 Sept 1888; *m* 12 Oct 1927 Mary (*d* 14 Nov 1975), 3rd dau of Duncan Leslie, of Perth, and *d* 3 May 1978, leaving:

1b +Paul [Paul Vavasour Esq, 41 Serpentine Rd, Sevenoaks, Kent TN13 3XS]; *b* 3 Jan 1929; *educ* Stonyhurst and London U (BSc); FICE, FIHT; *m* 26 July 1952 *Pauline Mary, only dau of Charles John Cable, of Sevenoaks, and has:

1c +Dunstan Edward [Dunstan Vavasour Esq, 16 Oak St, Rugby CV22 5EA]; *b* 9 May 1963; *educ* Stonyhurst and Oxford (MA); MIEE; *m* 1988 *Jill, dau of John Edward Fellows, of Stonebroom, Derbys, and has:

1d +Oliver James; *b* 21 Nov 1991

2d +William Alastair John; *b* 4 Jan 1995

1c *Catriona Mary; *b* 6 May 1955; *educ* Durham U (BSc); *m* 1992 *Maj Nigel D Wylie Carrick, 2nd King Edward VII's Own Goorkhas (Sirmoor Rifles), er s of Maj N Wylie Carrick, of Duntisbourne Abbots, Glos, and has:

1d *Harry Norbert Paul; *b* 8 July 1994

1d *Lucy Elizabeth Mary; *b* 31 May 1993

2c *Elspeth Anne [Mrs Paul Fox, Yeoman Oast, Manor Farm, Laddingford, Kent]; *b* 13 May 1956; *m* 1979 *Paul Julian Fox, only s of Paul Maurice Fox, of W Kirby, The Wirral and has:

1d *Miles Edward; *b* 14 Jan 1983

1d *Oriana Mary; *b* 3 Nov 1980

2d *Miranda Jane; *b* 14 May 1985

3c *Matilda Alice; *b* 14 Feb 1961; *educ* Oxford (MA); *m* 1988 *Maj Nicholas Keith Cooper, RAMC, er s of Basil Keith Cooper, of Croyde, Devon, and has:

1d *Hugh Edward Keith; *b* 6 Sept 1990

2b +Christopher Edward [Christopher Vavasour Esq, 14 Tipper Ave, Bronte, NSW 3024, Australia]; *b* 28 April 1938; *educ* King's Sch Canterbury and RAC Cirencester; *m* 1st 29 June 1963 (*divorce* 14 Nov 1986) Cecilie May, yr dau of Cecil Dudley Morris, of Brede, Sussex, and has:

1c +Philip James Edward [Philip Vavasour Esq, c/o Magpie House, Stubbs Cross, Ashford, Kent TN26 1HF]; *b* 11 Nov 1964; *educ* Kelly Coll; *m* 1990 *Joanna Marjorie, dau of Alan George Smith, of Burwash, Sussex, and has:

1d +Edward Dominic George; *b* 10 Nov 1995

1d *Fenella Molly May; *b* 19 Aug 1993

2c +Simon Mark Andrew [Simon Vavasour Esq, 9 Wood St, Norwich, Norfolk NR4 7QY]; *b* 12 May 1966; *educ* King's Sch Canterbury and London U (MB, BS); *m* 1992 *Sara Lucy, er dau of Geoffrey Jacques, and has:

1d +Harry Geoffrey George; *b* 1 July 1997

1d *Rosie Charlotte May; *b* 5 Aug 1993

2d *Kate Victoria Alice; *b* 8 Jan 1995

3c +Charles William Alexander [Charles Vavasour Esq, Magpie House, Stubbs Cross, Ashford, Kent TN26 1HF]; *b* 26 March 1971; *educ* King's Sch Canterbury and Oxford Brookes U (BA)

2b (cont.) Christopher Edward Vavasour *m* 2nd 1987 *Penelope Joanne, dau of H David S Luetchford, of Noosa, Qld, and has:

1c *Susannah Mary-Jane; *b* 1989

4a Francis Noel (Rev), SJ; *b* 4 Dec 1900; Chaplain Magistral Obedience SMO Malta 1956; *d* 18 Oct 1981

5a Harold Hugh; *b* 23 Dec 1902; *m* 20 April 1939 *Margery Constance, est dau of Harold Oakley Goulter, of Sevenoaks, Blenheim, NZ, and *d* 1989, leaving:

1b +Hugh Gerald [Hugh Vavasour Esq, Hazlewood, 34 Brook St, Blenheim, New Zealand]; *b* 7 Sept 1940; *m* 24 Sept 1966 *Belinda Mary, only dau of Leonard George Clarke, of Wellington, and has:

1c +Andrew Philip Henry; *b* 22 July 1968; *educ* Massey U (BAg)

1c *Sarah Mary Constance; *b* 19 May 1967; *m* 1988 *James Haddon Barr, s of Henry John Haddon Barr, of Invercargill, NZ, and has:

1d *Angus Haddon Dunstan; *b* 1991

2d *Jock Henry Hugh; *b* 1993

2c *Rachel Isolda Mary; *b* 1972

3c *Alice Francesca Mary; *b* 1977

2b +Philip Joseph [Philip Vavasour Esq, 112 Karori Rd, Wellington, New Zealand]; *b* 13 Sept 1943; *m* 1973 *Elizabeth Robyn, dau of Robert Barnett, of Nelson, NZ, and has:

1c +Jonathan Charles; *b* 1982

1c *Carolyn Elizabeth; *b* 1980

1b *Nicola Mary Clare; *b* 9 June 1947; *m* 1972 *Kerry Gould Louis Nolan, of Kaiapoi RD, NZ, and has:

1c *David; *b* 1976

1c *Rosamond Mary Hope; *b* 1974

2c *Abigail; *b* 1978

6a Gerard Aloysius; *b* 12 April 1904; *m* 22 April 1930 Lilian Frances (*d* 1997), 3rd dau of Francis Campbell, of Blenheim, NZ, and *d* 1983, having had:

1b Peter Francis; *b* 22 Feb 1931; *d* 11 Nov 1932

2b +Michael Philip; *b* 30 May 1932; *m* 1st 26 Nov 1955 Margaret Anne (*d* 25 Nov 1963), twin dau of Frederick Herbert Baldwin Redward, of New Plymouth, NZ, and has:

1c +Gerard Joseph [Gerard Vavasour Esq, 19 Powell Dve, Queanbeyan, NSW, Australia]; *b* 15 April 1956; *m* 1st 1978 (*divorce* 1983) Colleen Bishop, of Sydney, and has:

1d +Daniel; *b* 1980

1c (cont.) Gerard Vavasour *m* 2nd 1984 *Sonja Westerburg, of Queanbeyan, and has:

2d +Alexander; *b* 1990

1d *Tamara; *b* 1987

2c +Philip Charles Dunstan [Philip Vavasour Esq, 21 Alice Jackson Crescent, Gilmore, ACT, Australia]; *b* 22 April 1960; apprentice RAA; *m* 1987 *Katherine Lions, of Sydney, and has:

1d *Nicola Frances; *b* 1993

1c *Angela Margaret; *b* 20 May 1959; *m* 1979 *Gary Smith, of Terrigal, NSW, and has:

1d *Scott Aaron; *b* 1983

2d *Shaun Thomas; *b* 1986

1d *Jessica Leanne; *b* 1989

2c *Rose Lilian Mary; *b* 14 Aug 1962

2b (cont.) Michael Vavasour *m* 2nd 9 Oct 1965 *Pamela Anne, yr dau of Reginald Benedict Marston, of Long Jetty, NSW, and has:

3c +Christopher Paul; *b* 6 Sept 1966

3b +Bernard John [Bernard Vavasour Esq, Toi Downs, RD4, Blenheim, New Zealand]; *b* 28 Nov 1933; *educ* Canterbury Ag Coll (DipAg); *m* 16 May 1964 *Susan Ferrier, 2nd dau of Bruce Colville Morton, of Takapau, NZ, and has had:

1c Dominic John; *b* 6 Nov, *d* 7 Nov 1964

2c +Joseph Murray; *b* 28 Sept 1970

3c +Matthew Colville; *b* 19 Aug 1971

4c +Dominic Gerard; *b* 1974

5c +Gerard Bruce; *b* 1977

1c *Maria; *b* 22 May 1966

2c *Katherine Mary; *b* 2 May 1968; *m* 1987 *Andrew Keith Boniface and has:

1d *Karl Andrew; *b* 1989

2d *Christopher Ryan; *b* 1994

1d *Stacey Marie; *b* 1986

3b (cont.) Mr and Mrs Bernard Vavasour adopted:

*Thomas William; *b* 14 Dec 1964; *m* 1992 *Kris Mills and has:

1d *Dayle Marshall; *b* 1996

1d *Kelsey May; *b* 1993

4b Murray Gilbert; *b* 25 Jan 1938; *d* 6 July 1941

1b *Priscilla [Mrs Marian Adamski, Highlands, Kahui Rd, RD 34, Rahotu, Taranaki, New Zealand]; *b* 31 Jan 1936; *m* 27 June 1959 *Marian Josef Adamski and has:

2 1c *Peter Bernard; *b* 12 Oct 1961

2c *Anthony John; *b* 6 Jan 1968; *m* 1988 (*divorce* 1996) Leanne, dau of Peter Tanner, and has:

1d *Haiden James; *b* 1989

2d *Kyle Jozef; *b* 15 Nov 1989

3d *Jordon Jessie; *b* 31 Jan 1991

3c *Damian Joseph; *b* 25 Oct 1969

1c *Maria Ann; *b* 29 June 1963

2c *Frances Mary; *b* 2 Nov 1964

3c *Theresa; *b* 6 April 1966; *m* 22 Feb 1997 *Simon Donald Wilcox

2b *Bertha Eleanor Mary [Mrs Michael Newman, PO Box 257, Midland, Perth, W Australia]; *b* 30 June 1942; *m* 1st 19 Aug 1967 (*divorce* 1987) Michael John Baldwin, s of Jack Henry Patrick Baldwin, of Middle Green Farm, Baulking, Berks, and has:

1c *Bruce Phillip; *b* 11 March 1970

1c *Anita Jane; *b* 10 Oct 1968

2c *Penelope Debra; *b* 1975

2b (cont.) Mrs Bertha Baldwin *m* 2nd 19– Michael Newman, of Cowslip Valley, Marlborough, NZ

3b *Colleen Mary; *b* 4 Oct 1943; *m* 1973 *Don Alan Robertson and has:

1c *Gilbert Alan; *b* 1974

2c *James Wallace; *b* 1977

3c *Philip Duncan; *b* 1981

1c *Colette Marie; *b* 1976

2c *Sophie Anne; *b* 1979

7a John Louis; *b* 28 Oct 1905; *m* 22 June 1937 *Madeleine Hope (*m* 2nd 1988 her bro-in-law Henry Philip Bede Vavasour), yr dau of Ernest John Brammall, of Blenheim, NZ, and *d* 1987, leaving:

1b +Jeremy Dunstan Trevor [Jeremy Vavasour Esq, Koitaki Plantation, PO Box 133, Port Moresby, Papua New Guinea]; *b* 28 Oct 1942; *m* 15 July 1966 *Joan Reilly, only dau of George Robert Moss, of Melbourne, and has:

1c +Simon John; *b* 1974

1c *Peta; *b* 1 Dec 1967

2c *Kimble; *b* 1971

1b *Anne [Mrs David Adams, 23 Mulara St, Alice Springs 0870, NT, Australia]; *b* 28 Feb 1938; *m* 5 Jan 1963 *David Eric Stewart Adams, 2nd s of Ronald Stanley Adams, of Harare, Zimbabwe, and has:

1c *Jacqueline Anne; *b* 6 Nov 1968

2c *Gillian Merle; *b* 1970

3c *Sandra Claire; *b* 1972

2b *Teresa Virginia [Mrs Brian Cowan, 15 Harrier Crescent, Umhlanga Rocks 4320, Natal, S Africa]; *b* 4 Nov 1939; *m* 6 Jan 1962 *Brian John Cowan, s of John P Cowan, of Pietermaritzburg, and has:

1c *John Michael; *b* 1964

1c *Anne Juliet; *b* 1967

2c *Sara Jill; *b* 1971

3b *Marcia Jane [Mrs Owen Finger, Mowla Bluff Station, PO Box 356, Broome 6725, W Australia]; *b* 31 March 1952; *m* 1979 *Owen William Finger

8a Henry Philip Bede; *b* 9 June 1907; *m* 1st 4 May 1949 Rosamond Mary (*d* 1973), dau of Daniel Riddiford, of Featherston, NZ, and had:

1b +Peter Dunstan [Peter Vavasour Esq, The Favourite, Blenheim, New Zealand]; *b* 1950; *m* 1978 Anna Caroline (*d* 1985), dau of David Churchill Gould, of Sunsfield, Christchurch, NZ, and has:

1c +Louis Dunstan; *b* 1980

2c +Felix William; *b* 1982

1c *Claudia Annabelle; *b* 1984

2b +Francis William Joseph; *b* 1951

3b +Rollo Charles Joseph (twin); *b* 1951

4b +Charles Edward; *b* 1954

1b *Mary Rosamond (twin); *b* 1954

2b *Aletha Thérèse; *b* 1955

8a (cont.) Henry Vavasour *m* 2nd 1988 *Madeleine Hope [Mrs Henry Vavasour, Harford, 72 Murphy's Rd, Blenheim, New Zealand], widow of his bro John Louis Vavasour, and *d* 1997

1a Gwendolen Mary; *b* 25 Aug 1888; *m* 1st 5 Feb 1910 (*divorce* 1935) Ian Featherstone Johnston, 7th s of Hon Charles Johnston, of Wellington, NZ; *m* 2nd 1936 William Sellars Bennett and had issue

2a Blanche Eleanor Mary; *b* 9 Feb 1890; nun

3a Pearl Constantia; *b* 25 June 1895; *m* 5 Feb 1924 Francis Felix Reid, CBE (*d* 1966), s of Leonard Greenwell Reid, of Blenheim, NZ, and had:

1b *Christopher Robin James [Christopher Reid Esq, Redwood, Blenheim, New Zealand]; *b* 26 Sept 1925; *m* 26 April 1958 *Clare, widow of Peter Goulter

1b *Angela; *b* 31 July 1929; *m* Feb 1956 *Richard Fawcett, of Boston Spa, Yorks, and has:

1c *Thomas Francis; *b* 31 Jan 1957; *educ* Ampleforth and RAC Cirencester

2c *Anthony James; *b* 4 Nov 1961, *educ* Ampleforth

3c *Peter Edward; *b* 26 Oct 1963; *educ* Ampleforth

1c *Teresa Mary; *b* 16 May 1958

2c *Sarah Jane; *b* 5 July 1959

(4) Edward Joseph Everard; *b* 12 Sept 1855; *d* unm Antigua 25 Sept 1895

(1) Angela Mary Galdina; *b* 18 April 1854; *m* 17 June 1880 Francis Thomas Eyston (*dsp* 8 Dec 1888), of Charnwood Towers, Whitwick, Leics, and *d* 12 Aug 1930

4 George Joseph; *b* 18 July 1824; *m* 1st 5 Oct 1850 Amalia Ernestina Elizabatha (*d* 21 Dec 1861), dau of Carl Theodor Bell, of Mannheim, Baden; *m* 2nd 29 April 1880 (*annulled* 1889) Anne (*d* 29 Jan 1928), dau of John Heppenstall, of Bentley, Yorks, and *dsp* 25 March 1895

5 Philip Joseph (Rev); *b* 26 Feb 1826; RC priest, Canon Chapter Diocese of Leeds; *d* 19 April 1887

1 Marcia Mary; *b* 2 Feb 1816; *m* 12 Nov 1835 10th Lord Herries of Terregles (*qv*) and *d* 13 Nov 1883, leaving issue

VENTRY

Arms: Quarterly, 1st and 4th, sable on a chief ermine three fusils gules (for DE MOLEYNS); 2nd and 3rd, per pale or and sable two chevronels between three griffins passant counterchanged (for EVELEIGH). **Crests:** 1 A savage's head, couped at the shoulders and affrontée proper (for DE MOLEYNS), 2 A goat's head erased per chevron or and sable, attired of the 2nd, in the mouth a branch of laurel proper. **Supporters:** Two lions or, ducally collared and chained azure. **Motto:** *Vivere sat vincere* ('To conquer is to live enough'). **Creations:** Bt. (I) 7 Dec 1797, B. (I) 31 July 1800.

The device on the 1st and fourth quarters, less the ermine, was used by Sir John de Moleyns, of Stoke Poges, Bucks, who was granted the advowson (right to appoint to church benefice) of Burnham Abbey, Bucks, 1328 and *d* 1360. But no link between the Mullinses and the earlier de Moleynses has been proved, despite the assumption of the latter name in 1841.

THE 8TH BARON VENTRY, of Ventry, Co Kerry, and a **Baronet** (Sir Andrew Wesley Daubeny de Moleyns, Bt) [The Right Hon The Lord Ventry, Hill of Errol House, Errol, Perthshire PH2 7TQ]; *b* 28 May 1943; *s* unc 1987; *educ* Aldenham; farmer 1961–, dir Burgie Lodge Farms Ltd 1970–, mktg manager Unico (UK) Ltd; *m* 1st 26 Feb 1963 (*divorce* 1979) Nelly Edouard Renée, dau of Abel Chaumillon, of Loma de los Riseos, Torremolinos, Spain, and has:

1 +FRANCIS WESLEY; *b* 1 May 1965; *educ* Gordonstoun

1 *Elizabeth-Anne Stuart; *b* 11 March 1964; *m* 1990 *Justin D Byford, only s of T J Byford, of Belgrade, by Mrs J D Campane, of Barnes, Surrey

2 *Brigitte Catherine; *b* 15 May 1967

The 8th BARON *m* 2nd 1983 *Jill Rosemary, dau of Cecil Walter Oram, and by her has:

3 *Lisa; *b* 1985

Lineage: FREDERICK WILLIAM MULLINS; Col; settled Ireland *c* 1666 and bought land in Co Kerry, renaming the town Ballingolin as Burnham (where he established his seat) after his Norfolk birthplace; MP (I Parl) Dingle 1692–95 and Tralee 1695–96; *m* Jane, dau and coheir of Very Rev John Eveleigh, Dean Ross, of Blackhall and Coplands Meade, St Giles's, Oxford, and *d* 3 Nov 1712, having had:

FREDERICK MULLINS; *m* 1685 Martha (*m* 2nd Henry Parr, of Dingle), est dau of Thomas Blennerhassett, of Littur, Co Kerry (*see* INCHIQUIN, B), and *dvp* 3 Oct 1695, leaving:

WILLIAM MULLINS, of Burnham; *b* 1691; *m* 1716 Mary, dau of George Rowan, of Maghera, Co Derry, by Mary, only dau of Thomas Blennerhassett, and *d* 3 May 1761, leaving an est s:

Sir Thomas Mullins, 1st Bt, and **1st Baron Ventry**, of Ventry, Co Kerry (both I), so cr 7 Dec 1797 and 31 July 1800 respectively; *b* 25 Oct 1736; *educ* Trin Coll Dublin; *m* 5 Oct 1757 Elizabeth (*d* 16 Jan 1823), dau of Townsend Gunn, of Rattoo, and *d* 11 Jan 1824, having had:

1 WILLIAM TOWNSEND MULLINS, **2nd Baron Ventry**; *b* 25 Sept 1761; *educ* Trin Coll Dublin; MP (I Parl) Dingle Jan–Dec 1800; *m* 1st 12 July 1784 Sarah Anne (*dspm* Nov 1788), dau of Sir Riggs Falkiner, 1st Bt (*see* 1949 edn), and had:

(1) Anna; *m* 1811 Richard Orpen Townsend, of Ardtully, Co Kerry, s of Richard Orpen

(2) Elizabeth; *m* 17 Dec 1810 Nicholas de la Cherois Crommelin, of Carrowdore Castle, Co Down, and *d* 1820, leaving issue

1 (cont.) The **2nd Baron** *m* 2nd 12 May 1790 (*divorce by Act of (I) Parl 1796*) Frances Elizabeth, only dau of Isaac Sage; *m* 3rd 10 Sept 1797 Clara (*m* 2nd 1832 Peter FitzGibbon Henchy and *d* 1837), dau of Benjamin Jones, and *dspms* 5 Oct 1827, having by her had:

(1) Thomas; *b* 12 Aug 1798; *d* unm & *vp* 31 May 1817

2 Townsend; *b* 19 March 1763; *m* 1784 Christabella, dau of Solomon Dayrolles, of Henry Park, Surrey, Gentleman Privy Chamber to GEORGEs II and III and Br Resident Brussels, and *d* 1799, leaving:

(1) THOMAS TOWNSEND AREMBERG, **3rd Baron**

3 Thomas; Lt-Col; *m* 15 July 1810, dau of William Reader and widow of Maj-Gen Archer, and *dsp* Feb 1823

4 Richard; *b* 1766; Capt 31st Regt, W Indies and Walcheren Expdn 1809 (disastrous Br invasion of Low Countries during Napoleonic Wars); *m* 2 Oct 1798 Jane Guyon Grey and had, with other issue:

(1) Richard Townsend; *m* Sept 1837 Charity (*d* 5 Nov 1847), dau of William Collis, of Lismore, Co Kerry, and *d* 1850, having had a s (*d* young)

(1) Jane; *m* 1st 9 June 1823 Richard John Sutcliffe Mellin, of Wakefield, and had issue; *m* 2nd 17 March 1840 James Henley, 5th Dragoon Gds, and *d* 5 Jan 1866

(2) Sarah; *m* Nov 1829 Thomas Arthur Blennerhassett and *d* 18 Dec 1881

(3) Madeline Rhoda; *m* 10 April 1867 Archibald S Chartres and *d* 25 May 1885

5 Edward; *b* 1777; Maj; *m* 11 Feb 1805 Elizabeth (*d* 10 Feb 1871), dau of Robert Hilliard, of Listrim, Co Kerry, and *d* 31 July 1841, leaving:

(1) Thomas, QC; *b* 24 Jan 1807; barrister, Co Court Judge Co Kilkenny; *m* 11 Jan 1827 Jemima (*d* 7 April 1883), dau of Capt William Robert Broughton, CB, RN (*see* BROUGHTON, Bt), and *d* 5 March 1900, leaving:

1a Edward Charles; *b* 28 Jan 1828; Maj RE; *d* 17 Aug 1856

2a Townsend Aremberg; *b* 20 June 1838; Maj-Gen RA, Inspecting Offr Aux Artillery SE Div; *m* 5 June 1866 Selina Harriet (*d* 12 April 1927), only dau of Henry Sneyd French, and *d* 13 Nov 1926, leaving:

1b Richard Philip Aremberg; *b* 13 Dec 1881; Maj and Brevet Lt-Col Rifle Bde WW I (twice wounded); *m* 21 May 1919 Muriel Stoughton (*d* 12 July 1955), 3rd dau of Charles Stoughton Collison, of E Bilney, Norfolk, and widow of Percy Athelstan Nightingale (*see* NIGHTINGALE, Bt), and *d* 8 Jan 1939

1b Vera May Theodora; *b* 30 May 1880; *m* 23 April 1908 John Wilkinson (*d* 18 Aug 1939), of W Park, Skelmorlie, Ayrshire, and had issue

1a Rose Gertrude Mullins; *m* 24 Nov 1864 Lt-Col George Eyre Massy (*see* MASSY, B) and *d* 1 Feb 1869

2a Emmeline Theodora; *m* 5 Dec 1872 Maj Loftus Corbet Singleton (*d* 1 May 1881), 92nd Highrs, and *d* 7 Dec 1930, leaving issue

(2) William Bishop (Rev); *b* 4 March 1821; Preb Wells, Vicar Burrington, Somerset, 1871–1901; *m* 1st 6 Oct 1846 Sarah Anne (*d* 3 July 1872), est dau of Thomas Clark, of Bellefield Ho, Trowbridge, Wilts; *m* 2nd 4 Aug 1873 Clara Louisa Elizabeth (*d* 19 Oct 1912), est dau of George Thomas Pollard, JP, of Hundhill, Yorks, and Ashfield, Cheltenham, and *d* 15 Jan 1908, having by his 1st w had, with four daus (*d* unm):

1a Thomas Edward; *b* 20 Oct 1847; BA Oxon; *m* 16 May 1877 Kathleen Gwendoline, dau of James Pike, JP, and *dsp* 21 June 1914

2a Alured Bayfield (Rev); *b* 5 Nov 1851; MA Oxon; Rector Chester-le-Street, Co Durham, 1895–1919; *m* 1st 5 June 1888 Mary Louisa (*d* 26 Jan 1908), dau of Fleet Paymr John Lyon, RN, and had:

1b Alice Louisa Eveleigh; *b* 5 March 1889

2a (cont.) The Rev Alured Mullins *m* 2nd 27 April 1922 Florence Randolph, dau of Rev G L Harvey, Rector Yate, Glos, and *d* 8 Jan 1925

(3) Edward Henry Guyon; *b* 1 Jan 1823; *m* 10 Aug 1858 Maria Louisa (*d* 15 March 1862), er dau of Edward Day Stokes, of Tralee, and *d* 24 July 1911, leaving:

1a Edward Henry; *b* 17 Sept 1859; *m* 3 Sept 1879 Florence Evelyn, dau of Francis Pierson, of Egerton Lodge, Cheshire, and *dsp* 21 May 1898

1a Edith Anne; *b* 8 Nov 1860; *d* unm 26 Jan 1941

2a Maria Louisa; *b* 8 March 1862; *m* Feb 1888 Thomas Creswick Oliver (*d* 19 April 1939), of Netherlea, Altrincham, Cheshire, est s of William Creswick Lomas Oliver, of Hollin Old Hall, Bollington, Cheshire, and had issue

(1) Elizabeth Jemima; *m* 8 Aug 1842 John Pennefather

(2) Clara Maria; *m* 1st Oct 1837 Robert James Berkeley, QC (*d* 31 Oct 1873); *m* 2nd 21 June 1876, as his 2nd w, Andrew Carden, JP, DL (*d* 27 Nov 1876), of Barnane, Co Tipperary

6 Frederick Ferriter (Rev); *b* 1778; *m* 6 Dec 1800 Elizabeth, only dau and heiress of William Croker, of Johnstown, and *d* 30 Dec 1832, leaving:

(1) Frederick William; of Beaufort Castle, Co Kerry, and Raby Ho, Leamington; *b* 29 June 1804; MP Kerry; *m* 1826 Lucia (*d* 1 Feb 1889), est dau and coheir of Adml William Robert Broughton, CB (*see* BROUGHTON, Bt), and *dsp* 17 March 1874

(2) William (Rev); *b* 15 July 1806; *m* 30 Aug 1848 Kate Maria Rochfort (*d* 1896), yst dau of Maj John Rochfort Rae, 72nd Highrs, and *d* 5 March 1863, leaving:

1a William Townsend; *b* 16 July 1850; 50th Regt; *m* 16 July 1872 Evelyn Florence, yst dau of Thomas Arthur Blennerhassett, of Tralee, and *d* 28 May 1900, leaving:

1b William Frederick; *b* 1 Dec 1874

1b Evelyn Florence; *b* 3 Dec 1877

2a Alured Aremberg; *b* 3 March 1854; *d* 25 March 1886

1a Rose Blanche; *m* 2 Jan 1873 Lt-Col William Phibbs (*d* Aug 1894), 1st Bn Dorset Regt, and had issue

2a Kate Clara; *m* 11 April 1874 Lt-Col Harry d'Arch Breton, RE, and had issue

3a Edith Agnes; *m* 1885 William G Miles and had issue

(3) Alured; *b* 1 July 1807; *d* 3 Aug 1859

---

1 Theodora; *m* 1772 Edward Brice, of Kilroot

2 Elizabeth; *m* 1780 Richard Blennerhassett, of Ballymacprior, and *d* 1844

3 Arabella; *m* 1780 Richard McGillycuddy, The McGillycuddy of the Reeks (*d* 1826), and *dsp* 1821

4 Charlotte; *m* 2 May 1792 Richard Pierse Mahony and *d* 29 April 1816

5 Catherine; *m* 1792 James Hozier

6 Helena Jane; *m* 1799 Arthur Blennerhassett, of Blennerville, and *d* 1846

The 2nd BARON's n,

THOMAS TOWNSEND AREMBERG MULLINS later De MOLEYNS (roy licence 16 Feb 1841), **3rd Baron Ventry**; *b* Jan 1786; Lt 7th Regt of Foot (Roy Fus) 1807, Capt 1811, served Peninsula War (wounded Albuera) and War of 1812 (wounded New Orleans), ret 1817; *m* 18 Aug 1821 his cousin Eliza Theodora (*d* 25 Oct 1879), 2nd dau of Sir John Blake, 10th Bt, of Menlough (*qv*), by Sir John's 2nd w Rose, dau of Edward Brice and Hon Theodora Mullins (*see* above), dau of 1st Baron Ventry, and *d* 18 Jan 1868, having had:

1 DAYROLLES BLAKENEY, **4th Baron**

2 Frederick William; *b* 24 July 1835; *d* 2 April 1882

3 Edward Alured; *b* 25 Nov 1836; Capt Kerry Militia; *d* unm 16 Feb 1908

4 Denis John; *b* 12 May 1844; Lt Roy Welch Fus; *d* Oct 1886

1 Christabella; *m* 9 June 1844 Cdr Charles Hawkey, RN (*d* 1889), and *dsp* 8 Aug 1900

2 Rose; *m* 3 March 1847 Richard Chute (*d* Sept 1862), of Chute Hall, Co Kerry, and *d* 21 April 1898, leaving issue

3 Eliza; *m* 1850 Rev Henry Joy Tombe, BD, Canon Christ Church, Dublin, and *d* 30 Oct 1888, leaving issue

4 Helena Emily; *m* 22 June 1865 Edward James Saunderson, PC, MP (*d* 21 Oct 1906), of Castle Saunderson, Co Cavan, and *d* 17 Jan 1926, leaving issue

The 3rd BARON VENTRY's est s,

DAYROLLES BLAKENEY MULLINS later De MOLEYNS later still EVELEIGH-De MOLEYNS (roy licence 3 Nov 1874), **4th Baron Ventry**, DL (Co Kerry); *b* 22 Jan 1828; Lt-Col 4th Bn Roy Munster Fus 1854–85, rep I peer 1871; *m* 12 Sept 1860 Harriet Elizabeth Frances (*d* 13 Dec 1906), er dau of Andrew Wauchope of Niddrie Marischal, Midlothian (for whose early ancestry *see* DON-WAUCHOPE, Bt), and *d* 8 Feb 1914, having had:

1 FREDERICK ROSSMORE WAUCHOPE De MOLEYNS later EVELEIGH-DE MOLEYNS, **5th Baron Ventry**, DSO (1897), DL (Co Kerry); *b* 11 Dec 1861; *educ* Harrow; Maj and Brevet Lt-Col 4th Hus Boer War 1896–97 (despatches twice); *d* unm 22 Sept 1923

2 ARTHUR WILLIAM, **6th Baron**

3 Edward Dayrolles; *b* 31 May 1871; *d* 7 July 1930

4 Richard Andrew; *b* 13 June 1874; Lt 4th Roy Munster Fus; *d* unm July 1917

5 John Gilbert; *b* 27 May 1878; Lt 4th Bn Roy Munster Fus; *m* 20 Sept 1899 Marguerite (*d* 18 Feb 1982 aged 103), dau of George Edward Noon, and *d* 4 Jan 1928, leaving:

(1) John Andrew EVELEIGH-De MOLEYNS later WAUCHOPE of Niddrie Marischal (deed poll 1945); *b* 24 Sept 1900, Lt RN; *m* 11 April 1923 Rosemary Eve (*d* 1975), dau of R-Adml John Arthur Tuke, and *d* 26 Jan 1956, having had:

1a Patrick Frederick John; *b* 27 April 1924; *d* 30 March 1927

2a +Andrew Dermod [Andrew Wauchope Esq, The Cottage, Lochtower, Kelso, Roxburghshire TD5 8PD]; *b* 11 Feb 1932; *educ* Ampleforth and RMC Sandhurst; *m* 10 Oct 1957 *Jennifer, dau of William Siggers, and has:

1b +James Andrew; *b* 7 Aug 1963; *m* 1992 *Victoria Neil and has:

1c +Angus; *b* 10 March 1995

2c +Robin; *b* 27 April 1998

1c *Emma Catherine; *b* 5 Aug 1993

2b +Ian Simon; *b* 7 Aug 1963; *m* 1989 *Sarah Barlow and has:

1c *Lara; *b* 13 Jan 1990

2c *Katie; *b* 20 Aug 1991

1b *Fiona Jane; *b* 14 May 1958; *m* 1980 *William Elliot and has:

1c *Christopher; *b* 15 June 1982

1c *Nicola; *b* 3 May 1984

2b *Nicola Ann; *b* 1 Sept 1959; *m* 1990 *Douglas Dale and has:

1c *Alexander William; *b* 16 Jan 1994

1c *Constance Jennifer; *b* 2 June 1995

3a Brian Murray Xavier; *b* 1 Sept 1936; *d* 1993

1a *Oenone Eileen Frances [Mrs Timothy Willis, Meadowcroft, Station Rd, Gt Ayton, Middlesbrough, N Yorks TS9 6HB]; *b* 12 Feb 1931; *m* 23 Aug 1952 *Timothy Robert Crum Willis, DL (N Yorks), s of Robert Lewis Willis, of Glasgow, and has:

1b *Robert Nigel Crum; *b* 5 July 1954; *m* 1984 *Paula Carol Hamilton and has:

1c *Simon Robert Crum; *b* 1987

1c *Deborah Carol Jane; *b* 1988

2b *Andrew James Scott; *b* 2 June 1956; *m* 1992 *Linda Marinaro and has:

1c *Robin Christopher Scott; *b* 1994

2c *James Michael Billop; *b* 17 Jan 1998

3b *John Douglas Charles; *b* 9 Feb 1960

4b *Michael Philip Bruce; *b* 31 Aug 1966; *m* 1993 *Karen Edwick and has:

1c *Stephanie Megan Edwick; *b* 6 March 1995

2c *Georgina Chloe Edwick; *b* 6 March 1995

(2) Frederick Arthur; *b* 8 March 1907; *educ* Repton; Dip Serv, Col RA WW II, US Legn Merit; *m* 27 Oct 1936 Sheila Marie, dau of Adml Sir Ernest Frederic Augustus Gaunt, KCB, CMG, and *dsp* 6 May 1962

(1) *Eileen Mildred Alice; *b* 13 May 1912; *m* 21 Dec 1939 *Harold Alan Coldham, LLB, DipEd, AICA, of Osterley, Middx, s of Francis Russell Coldham, of Ballarat, Victoria, and has:

1a *Simon Frederick Russell [Simon Coldham, La Bastia, Propriano, France]; *b* 4 Oct 1940; *educ* Charterhouse and Corpus Christi Coll Oxford (MA, PhD)

2a *Christopher Alan; *b* 17 March 1943; *educ* Lancing

1a *Marie Audrey Stephanie; *b* 17 March 1943

1 Frances Elizabeth Sarah; *b* 30 Dec 1862; DJStJ; *m* 1st 21 March 1882 4th Marquess Conyngham (*qv*) and had issue; *m* 2nd 27 April 1899 John Russell Bedford Cameron and *d* 8 July 1939, having had further issue

2 Mildred Rose; *m* 26 July 1888 1st Baron Saint Audries (*see* 1970 edn) and *d* 11 Oct 1949, leaving issue

3 Hersey Alice; *b* 31 March 1867; *m* 18 Oct 1886 1st Marquess of Linlithgow (*qv*) and *d* 3 April 1937, leaving issue

4 Maud Helen; *m* 24 April 1900 1st Baron Gretton (*qv*) and *d* 29 July 1934, leaving issue

The 5th BARON VENTRY's bro,

ARTHUR WILLIAM De MOLEYNS later EVELEIGH-De MOLEYNS, **6th Baron Ventry**; *b* 6 April 1864; *educ* Uppingham; *m* 2 June 1897 Evelyn Muriel Stuart (*d* 29 March 1966 aged 89), yst dau of Lansdowne Daubeney, JP, of Norton Court, Norton Malreward, Pensford, Somerset, and *d* 6 July 1936, leaving:

1 ARTHUR FREDERICK DAUBENEY EVELEIGH-De MOLEYNS later ARTHUR FREDERICK DAUBENEY OLAV EVELEIGH-De MOLEYNS, **7th Baron Ventry**; *b* 28 July 1898; *educ* Wellington; Lt Irish Gds and Airship Branch RAF WW I (wounded), Hon A/Cdre No 902 (Co of London) Balloon Sqdn AAF 1938, F/Lt RAFVR Balloon Command and Intell WW II, King Haakon VII's Freedom Medal; *d* unm 1987

2 Francis Alexander Innys; *b* 15 Nov 1901; *educ* Repton; F/Lt RAFVR WW II; *m* 1st 25 March 1925 Norah Caroline (*d* 26 Aug 1937), dau of Robert Hudson, of Beck Hall, Norfolk, and had:

(1) *Valentia [Mrs Nathaniel Grant-Dalton, Place House, St Anthony-in-Roseland, Cornwall TR2 5EZ]; *b* 16 Dec 1928; *m* 19 Sept 1950 *Maj Nathaniel Duncan Spry Grant-Dalton, RHA, High Sheriff Cornwall 1986 and underwriting memb Lloyd's, only s of Lt-Col Duncan Grant-Dalton, CMG, DSO, JP, of Place House, and had:

1a *Kevin Duncan Spry; *b* 23 Dec 1952; *educ* Radley; *m* 1980 *Amanda Charlton, dau of F E de Smitt, of Wimbledon, and has:

1b *Samuel Duncan Spry; *b* 1985

2b *Jolyon; *b* 1991

1b *Pippa Charlton; *b* 1988

1a *Miranda Jane; *b* 14 Jan 1955; *m* 1983 *Simon James Forrester, er s of Maj-Gen Michael Forrester, CB, CBE, DSO, MC, of W Worldham, Hants, and has:

1b *Nicholas Francis; *b* 1985

2b *Frederick Richard George; *b* 1990

2a *Nicola Frances [Mrs Ian Campbell, 11 Burcote Rd, London SW18]; *b* 15 Feb 1957; *m* 1979 *Ian Adair Campbell, 2nd s of Lt-Col Robert Adair Campbell, of Altries, Maryculter, Aberdeenshire, and has:

1b *Hamish Adair; *b* 1982

2b *Oliver Alistair; *b* 1985

3b *Robert Francis; *b* 1988

2 (cont.) The Hon Francis Eveleigh-de Moleyns *m* 2nd 8 Dec 1938 (*divorce* 1952) Joan (*m* 3rd Nigel Eric Springett), est dau of Harold Wesley, of The Wilderness, E Molesey, Surrey, and widow of F/Lt H G Adams, RAF, and by her had:

(1) ANDREW WESLEY EVELEIGH-De MOLEYNS later DAUBENEY De MOLEYNS (deed poll 1966), **8th and present Baron Ventry**

(2) *Sally Joan [Mrs Robin Hart, Hillside House, The Square, Portscatho, Cornwall TR2 5HW]; *b* 9 May 1940; *m* 17 Aug 1963 *Robin Edmead Hart, s of George Edmead Hart, of Beaulieu, Mitton Grove, Shrewsbury, and has:

1a *Christopher Wesley; *b* 17 Aug 1964; *educ* Truro Sch

1a *Penelope-Jayne; *b* 26 Oct 1965; *m* 18 Dec 1991 *Timothy Michael O'Brien, s of James O'Brien, of Derby, and has:

1b *Thomas George; *b* 14 March 1992

1b *Connie Alexandra; *b* 6 April 1994

2a *Carol-Ann; *b* 25 Jan 1967; *m* 4 April 1998 *Paul Alexander Fraser, s of Ronnie Fraser, of Edinbrugh

3a *Rachel-Elizabeth; *b* 9 Aug 1970

2 (cont.) The Hon Francis Eveleigh-de Moleyns *m* 3rd 18 Feb 1954 Dorothy Mercado (*d* 1957), dau of Samuel Harvey, of London, and widow of Sir Charles Henry Augustus Frederick Lockhart Ross, 9th and last Bt, of Carstairs (*see* 1940 edn); *m* 4th 4 Aug 1963 *Olivia Phoebe [Lady John Conyngham, Windmill Cottage, Yapton Rd, Barnham, W Sussex], only dau of Capt Percy Neave Leathers, of Robertsbridge, Sussex, and widow of his cousin Lord John Victor Albert Blosse Conyngham (*see* CONYNGHAM M), and *d* 29 April 1964

1 Mary Helen; *b* 27 June 1900; *m* 12 July 1923 Theodore Arthur Richard Barnes-Gorell (*d* 14 Oct 1950), er s of Arthur Barnes-Gorell, and *d* 18 Jan 1970, leaving issue

VERNEY of Claydon House

Arms: Quarterly, 1st and 4th, azure on a cross argent fimbriated or five mullets gules (for VERNEY); 2nd and 3rd, paly of six, erminois and pean, a bend engrailed counter-changed (for CALVERT).
Crests: 1 A phoenix in flames looking at rays of the sun proper and charged with five mullets in cross or (for VERNEY), 2 Out of a mural coronet argent two spears erect, therefrom two pennons flowing towards the dexter, one erminois the other pean (for CALVERT).
Mottoes: 1 *Ung sent, ung sol* ('One faith, one sun') (for VERNEY), 2 *Servata fides cineri* ('Faith kept with my ancestor') (for CALVERT).
Creation: Bt. (UK) 3 Dec 1818.

SIR RALPH BRUCE VERNEY, 5TH BT, of Claydon House, Bucks, KBE (1974), JP (Bucks 1954) [Sir Ralph Verney Bt KBE JP, Ballams, Middle Claydon, Bucks MK18 2ET]; *b* 18 Jan 1915; *s* f 1974; *educ* Canford and Balliol Coll Oxford (BA 1937); WW II: Maj Berks Yeo 1945 and Bucks Yeo 1946 (2nd Lt 1940), Bucks: CC 1952–73 (Chm Fin Ctee 1957, Planning Ctee 1967), High Sheriff 1957, CA 1961, V-Ld Lt (late V-Lt) 1965–84 (DL 1960–65), Pres CLA 1961–63, High Steward Buckingham 1966, Chm: Chilterns Standing Conf, Forestry Commn Nat Ctee (England) 1968–80, Nature Conservancy Cncl 1980–83, memb: Milton Keynes Devpt Corp and Roy Commn Environmental Pollution 1973–79, V-Pres GB European Confedn Ag, Tstee Radcliffe, Ernest Cook and Chequers Tsts; *m* 7 July 1948 *Mary, JP, yr dau of Percy Charles Vestey (*see* VESTEY, Bt), and has:

1 +EDMUND RALPH [Edmund Verney Esq, Claydon House, Bucks MK18 2EX]; *b* 28 June 1950; *educ* Harrow and York U; FRICS, High Sheriff Bucks 1998–99; *m* 1982 *Daphne Primrose, dau of Col Hamilton Farquhar Fausset-Farquhar, DSO, TD, JP (*see* 1970 edn MACPHERSON-GRANT, Bt), of Lovelocks Ho, Shefford Woodlands, Berks, and has:

(1) +Andrew Nicholas; *b* 9 July 1983

(1) *Ella; *b* 1985

1 *Sarah Dorothy [Mrs George Caird, 15 Chad Rd, Birmingham B15 3ER]; *b* 11 Aug 1953; *m* 1974 *George Caird, yst s of Rev Dr G B Caird, Principal's Lodgings, Mansfield Coll, Oxford, and has:

(1) *Adam Benjamin; *b* 1977

(2) *Oliver Ralph; *b* 1978

(3) *Edmund George; *b* 1989

(1) *Iona Katherine Mary; *b* 1991

2 *Mary Jane; *b* 24 Oct 1957

3 *Francesca Marjorie; *b* 14 May 1963; *m* 1987 *Peter Kershaw, of Halifax

Lineage: Rev — CALVERD; *b* 1555; Min Andover, Hants; *d* 1624, leaving:

FELIX CALVERD/CALVERT, of Little Hadham, Herts; *b* 18 Aug 1596; *m* Elizabeth/Susan Betts, of Colchester, and was *bur* 18 May 1674, having had, with an est s (*d* young) and six daus:

1 Felix, of Furneaux Pelham, Herts; *b* 15 Feb 1623; *m* Joane Day, of Hadham, and *d* 22 March 1698, having had, with other issue:

(1) William; *bapt* 4 Nov 1667; *m* 1689 his cousin Honor (*see* below) and was ancestor of the CALVERTs of Ockley Court

2 THOMAS

3 Peter, of Nine Ashes, Herts; *bapt* 10 May 1630; *m* by licence 3 April 1669 Honor (*bur* 25 Nov 1711), dau of Honor Bates, of Hertford, and was *bur* 27 Jan 1675/6, leaving:

(1) Peter; Army Offr; *k* in a duel at Chester, *bur* 23 Sept 1689, aged 20

(2) Felix, of Nine Ashes; *b* posthumously, *bapt* 26 March 1676; *m* Elizabeth (*d* 29 Aug 1722 aged 48), only dau and heiress of Joshua White, Citizen of London, and *d* 8 April 1713, having had, with other issue:

1a Richard, of Hall Place, Bexley, Kent; *m* 9 Dec 1741 Mary (*d* 6 Jan 1789), widow of Hon John Verney, est s of 1st Earl Verney (*see* BRAYE, B), and 3rd dau and coheir of Josiah Nicholson, of Clapham, and *d* 31 Jan 1782, leaving:

1b Richard, of Fulmer, Bucks; *m* — Freeman, widow of — Edsall, of Boreham, Essex and *dsp* 13 Nov 1814

2b George; Offr Coldstream Gds; m 9 Aug 1789 Mary, only dau of Richard Haddock and dsp 7 Jan 1821

1b Catherine; inherited the Verney estates on the death unm 15 Nov 1810 of her half-sis Baroness Fermanagh (see BRAYE, B) and assumed with her husband the name of VERNEY; m 5 April 1785 Rev Robert WRIGHT later VERNEY, Rector Middle Claydon, Bucks (d 24 April 1820), and dsp 9 Jan 1827, leaving the Verney estates to her cousin Sir HARRY CALVERT later VERNEY, **2nd Bt** (see below)

2a Peter, of Nine Ashes and St George's, Hanover Sq; m 14 Feb 1723 his cousin Honor Calvert (see below) and was bur 27 Jan 1772, leaving issue, now extinct in the male line, but including a dau Mary, who m her 3rd cousin Thomas Calvert, of Hutton, Essex (see below), and a dau Frances (m 7 Aug 1774 Hon Charles Hamilton (d 1781) and d 1787)

1a Mary; m her 2nd cousin Felix Calvert (see below) and was bur 26 May 1757

2a Susannah; bapt 24 May 1712; m John Peyton (d 1741) and had issue (see 1959 edn PEYTON, Bt)

(1) Honor; b 1671; m her cousin William Calvert (see above) and d 31 Jan 1724

(2) Jane; dvp; bur 9 April 1676

(3) Susan; m 6 Feb 1690 Sir Alexander Rigby (d 20 April 1717)

4 John; bapt 25 March 1636/7; dsp & vp

The 2nd s,

THOMAS CALVERT, of London; b 1625; m Anne (d 8 Feb 1710) dau of William Ambrose, of Reading, Berks, and was bur 25 Sept 1668, having had, with two daus and another s:

FELIX CALVERT, of Albury Hall, Herts, and Marcham, Berks; MP Reading 1713–16; m (licence 28 July 1689) Mary (d 1729), dau of Sir Francis Winnington, (see WINNINGTON, Bt), and d 28 Dec 1736, having had, with other issue, including a dau (Honor, m 14 Feb 1723 her 2nd cousin Peter Calvert (see above) and was bur 2 April 1756), an est s:

FELIX CALVERT, of Albury Hall; b 5 Sept 1699 or perhaps 1693; m 6 Feb 1723 his cousin Mary Calvert (see above) and d 29 April 1755, having had:

1 Felix; bapt 25 Oct 1723; bur April 1724

2 John, of Albury Hall; b May 1726; MP Wendover, Herts twice and Tamworth; m 8 Aug 1757 Elizabeth (d 20 Feb 1807 aged 75), dau of Sir Edward Hulse, 1st Bt (qv), and d 22 Feb 1804, leaving issue, now extinct in the male line

3 Thomas, of Hutton, Essex; b 1727; m 27 May 1773 his 3rd cousin Mary (d 1 Sept 1828 aged 102), dau of Peter Calvert (see above), and dsp Dec 1792

4 Felix, of London; b 20 Jan 1729; m 9 Feb 1758 Rebecca (m 2nd 19 March 1773 Sir Yelverton Peyton, 8th and last Bt (dsp 18 Oct 1815), and d 12 Sept 1812), dau of Thomas Bayley, of Allesley, Warwicks, and d 18 Oct 1764, leaving issue

5 PETER

6 Richard; b 1742; d 19 April 1743

1 Honora; bur 24 June 1741, unm

2 Mary; bapt 6 May 1725; d unm April 1775

3 Elizabeth; bapt 28 June 1730; m 3 Jan 1767 James Burnett

4 Anne; b 7 May 1732; m 20 Dec 1756 Christopher Anstey (d 3 Jan 1812, aged 80), of Trumpington, Cambs, and d 31 Jan 1812

5 Jane; m 7 May 1759 Thomas Western, of Abingdon Hall, Cambs

The 5th s,

PETER CALVERT, of Hampton Court Palace; b 3 Sept 1733; m 8 July 1762 Mary (bur 7 June 1800), dau of Dr Thomas Reeve, MD, and d 6 Dec 1810, having had, with a dau (Maria, d unm 17 March 1838) an only surv s:

Sir Harry Calvert, 1st Bt (UK), so cr 3 Dec 1818, GCB, GCH; bapt March 1763; Col 14th Foot, Buckingham Regt, Govr Chelsea Hosp, Adj-Gen Forces, Gen; m 8 June 1799 Caroline (d 17 June 1806), 2nd dau of Thomas Hammersley, of Pall Mall, and d 3 Sept 1826, leaving:

1 HARRY (Sir), **2nd Bt**

2 Frederick, QC, DL Bucks; b 9 June 1806; MP Aylesbury 1850–51; m 14 Sept 1865 Lucy Caroline (d 3 May 1884), est dau of 2nd Earl of Powis (qv), and dsp 6 June 1891

1 Mary; b 1800; m 24 July 1827 Rev John William Cunningham (d 30 Sept 1861), Vicar Harrow, and d 11 Feb 1849, leaving issue

2 Emily Caroline; b 30 June 1803; m 4 Nov 1835 Rev William Robert Fremantle (see COTTESLOE, B) and d 14 July 1877

3 Frances Anne; b Sept 1804; m 26 July 1826 Abel Smith (d 3 Feb 1859), of Woodhall Park, Herts, MP (n of 1st Baron Carrington, qv), and d 18 Nov 1885, leaving at least eight children

The 1st Bt's er s,

Sir HARRY CALVERT later VERNEY (roy licence 9 Feb 1827 on inheriting the Verney estates), **2nd Bt**, PC, DL; b 8 Dec 1801; Maj 1st Gren Gds, MP (Lib) Buckingham 1832–41, 1857–74 and 1880–85 and Bedford 1847–52; m 1st 30 June 1835 Eliza (d 2 Jan 1857), dau of Adml Sir George Hope-Vere, KCB (see LINLITHGOW, M); m 2nd 24 June 1858 Frances Parthenope (dsp 12 May 1890), er dau of William Edward Nightingale, of Embly, Hants, and Lea Hurst, Derbys, and sis of Florence Nightingale, OM, and d 12 Feb 1894, having had, with three daus (d unm):

1 EDMUND HOPE (Sir), **3rd Bt**

2 Harry Calvert; b 7 Aug 1840; d 10 Oct 1851

3 George Hope VERNEY later LLOYD-VERNEY (roy licence 11 Feb 1888 on inheriting Clochfaen from his w's unc, who had inherited it from his maternal grandmother Sarah, dau and heiress of Jenkin Lloyd, of Clochfaen), of The Cedars, Esher, Surrey; b 5 March 1842; Capt Rifle Bde, Col 3rd Bn Hants Regt; m 23 Oct 1866 Harriet Julia Morforwyn (d 31 July 1913), dau of Maj-Gen Charles Thomas Edward Hinde, Bengal Army, and d 14 June 1896, having had:

(1) James Hope, of Carriden Ho, Boness; b 5 Feb 1869; d unm 13 Nov 1909

(2) Harry (Sir), GCVO (1936 KCVO 1927, CVO 1917, MVO 4th Cl 1909), of The Clochfaen, Llanidloes; b 23 Jan 1872; educ Eton; Gentlemen Usher and Dep Master Household to HM EDWARD VII 1907–10, Groom-in-Waiting to HM GEORGE V 1911–31, Priv Sec to HM QUEEN MARY 1919–35 (Treas HM

1932–36), Extra Groom-in-Waiting 1931–36 to HRH THE PRINCE OF WALES later HM EDWARD VIII 1936 and HM GEORGE V 1937–50, 2nd Cl Order Crown Prussia, Offr Legn Hon; m 6 June 1889 Lady Joan Elizabeth Mary Cuffe (d 27 Feb 1951), Extra Woman Bedchamber to HM QUEEN MARY, est dau of 5th and last Earl of Desart, KP (see 1935 edn), and d 28 Feb 1950, having had:

1a HARRY GEORGE later GERALD (deed poll 1941), DSO (1945), MVO (1937); b 10 July 1900; educ Eton; Page of Honour to HM GEORGE V 1914–17, started in Gren Gds, WW II: Instr Staff Coll 1940, cmded 2nd Bn Irish Gds, 1st Gds Bde Italy, 6th Gds Tank Bde and 7th Armoured Div Normandy and NW Europe (despatches twice), also 56th London Armoured Div 1947–48, ret 1948 as Maj-Gen, OStJ; m 26 Feb 1926 Hon Joyce Sybil Vivian Smith, 3rd dau of 1st Baron Bicester (qv), and d 3 April 1957, leaving:

1b +Peter Vivian [Maj Peter Lloyd-Verney, Skiveralls Ho, Chalford, Stroud, Glos]; b 13 Nov 1930; educ Eton and Trin Coll Dublin (MA, BAg); Maj Irish Gds, ret 1970, author; m 1st 14 July 1959 (divorce 1982) Caroline Evelyn, est dau of George Anthony Harford, of Widden Hill Ho, Horton, Glos; m 2nd 1983 *Elizabeth Anne, dau of W/Cdr Harry St George Burke, RAF, of Auberies, Bulmer, Essex, and widow of Christopher George James Oldridge de la Hey, and has by his 1st w:

1c +Harry George Vivian [Harry Lloyd-Verney Esq, Kimsbury Farmhouse, Upton Hill, Glos]; b 5 Oct 1960; m 1st 1985 (divorce 1989) Sarah Mary Cotterill, dau of R P Voelcker, of Stanton St Quintin, Wilts; m 2nd 1992 *Lavinia Mary Delves, yst dau of Sir Evelyn Delves Broughton, 12th Bt (qv), and widow of Douglas D Dawes, and by her has:

1d *Harriet Charity; b 11 Nov 1992

1c *Louisa Margaret; b 12 July 1962; m 1993 *Matthew Jeremy Higgs and has:

1d *Florence Nettle; b 1994

2c *Henrietta Nell; b 3 July 1965; m 1987 *Thomas Richard William Lapage-Norris, est s of Capt T E Lapage-Norris, of Worton, Wilts

1b *Bridget Mary [Mrs Michael Sarson, Hansteads, E Hanney, Oxon]; b 31 Dec 1926; m 20 Oct 1951 *Michael Barry Sarson, FCA, yr s of Capt Maurice John Sarson, of Woodgreen, Fordingbridge, Hants, and has:

1c *Michael Vivian; b 16 Feb 1953; educ Eton

2c *David Peter; b 22 Feb 1955; educ Eton

1c *Mary Anne; b 26 Aug 1959

2c *Jane Elizabeth; b 13 Dec 1962

2a Ulick Otway Vortigern, OBE (1946); b 30 June 1902; educ Eton; T/Lt-Col Rifle Bde WW II Italy, France and Burma, FO 1946–47 and 1955–60 (Paris 1947–51, Beirut 1951–53); m 6 Nov 1929 Esmé Louise (d 2 Sept 1978), 3rd dau of Charles Austin Smith-Ryland, of Barford Hill, Warwicks, and d 19 July 1979, leaving:

1b +Harry Ulick Dennis [Harry Lloyd-Verney Esq, The Garden House, Cheriton, Hants]; b 6 Oct 1940; educ Eton; ACA 1965; m 1976 *Sarah Fane, yr dau of Maj A P P Ricketts, of The Old Manse, Nigg, Ross and Cromarty, and has:

1c *Louisa Florence; b 5 Nov 1977

2c *Alice Sarah; b 5 July 1979

3c *Camilla Anne; b 1981

1b *Anne Margaret, JP Shrewsbury; DL Salop 1986; b 7 Aug 1930; m 5 Jan 1951 *Col John Montagu Flint, MBE, late RE, of The Dower House, Gt Ness, Salop, er s of Maj Eric Charles Montagu Flint, DSO, of Hembury Castle, nr Torrington, Devon, and has:

1c *Charles John Raffles; b 7 May 1952; educ Eton; barrister; m 1978 *Diana Rosemary, er dau of Maj Robert Topham, of Plasyn Grove, Ellesmere, Salop, and has:

1d *William Charles Raffles; b 1982

1d *Julia; b 1984

2c *Michael Edward Stamford; b 24 Sept 1956; educ Eton; m 1981 *Fiona, 2nd dau of Prof Alasdair Steele-Bodger, of The Old Rectory, Hale, Hants, and has:

1d *Alasdair Stamford; b 1987

2d *Oliver John Montagu; b 1989

1c *Sarah Esme; b 13 Jan 1955; m 1976 *Maj Christopher Thomas Stanton Prestwich, 15th/19th King's Roy Hus, and has:

1d *Edward Joseph Stanton; b 1985

1d *Emma Charlotte Esmé; b 1983

2c *Elizabeth Anne; b 23 June 1958; m 1983 *Colin Michael Wood and has:

1d *Christopher James; b 1987

1d *Helen Sarah; b 1990

2b *Carola Mariette; b 4 July 1932; m 11 Sept 1952 *Maj John Hugh Torquil Sutton (see SUTTON, Bt) and has issue

3a Desmond Ralph; b 21 Jan 1905; educ Eton; T/Maj Intell Corps WW II; m 5 July 1940 (divorce 1948) Lady Kathleen Irene Cole (d 2 July 1976), yst dau of 5th Earl of Enniskillen (qv), and d 25 June 1957

1a Joan Verena; b 25 Jan 1908; m 20 Jan 1931 Hon Gustavus Hamilton-Russell, est s of 9th Viscount Boyne (qv), and d 1 April 1938, having had issue

(3) Edward Vortigern; b 8 March 1874; Lt 3rd Bn Hants Regt; d unm 12 Nov 1893

(1) Catherine Morforwyn; m 1 Nov 1888 Edwin Philip Abel Smith (d 31 Dec 1936), est s of Rev Albert Smith, of Wendover, and dsp 28 May 1890

(2) Morfowyn Mary Levison; b 6 Aug 1880; m 30 Aug 1904 Rev Gerald Charles Fanshawe (d 15 April 1924), Hon Canon Winchester, Rector St Maurice and St Lawrence Winchester, and d 10 May 1957, having had issue

4 Frederick William, JP Bucks, Derbys; b 26 Feb 1846; educ Ch Ch Oxford (MA); barrister Inner Temple, Lt Bucks Yeo Cav, MP N Bucks 1906–10, Counsellor Siamese Legation, CC London and Bucks, Order White Elephant Siam 3rd Cl; m 8 June 1870 his er bro's sis-in-law Maude Sarah (d 28 Aug 1937), yr

dau and coheir of Sir John Hay Williams, 2nd Bt, of Bodelwyddan (*qv*), and *d* 26 April 1913, leaving:

  (1) Sir RALPH VERNEY, 1st Bt, of Eaton Sq (*qv*)

  (1) Gwendolen; *b* 4 Jan 1881; *d* unm 6 Aug 1932

  (2) Kathleen; *b* 9 Sept 1883; *m* 10 April 1912 Lt-Col Frank Graham Newton, CBE, DSO, VD, s of Richard Newton, of Brisbane, and *d* 12 March 1966, leaving issue

The 2nd Bt's est s,

Sir Edmund Hope Verney, 3rd Bt; *b* 6 April 1838; RN: Crimean War 1854–55 (medal, Sebastopol Clasp, Turkish Medal), Indian Mutiny 1857–58 (medal, Lucknow Clasp, despatches, promoted Lt), ret as Capt, Chm Anglesey QS 1877–90, MP (Lib) N Bucks 1885–86 and 1889–91, CC Brixton LCC, FRGS; *m* 14 Jan 1868 Margaret Maria, Hon LLD (*d* 7 Oct 1930), er dau and coheir of Sir John Hay Williams, 2nd Bt, of Bodelwyddan (*qv*), and *d* 8 May 1910, leaving:

1 **Sir Harry Calvert Williams Verney, 4th Bt**, DSO (1918); *b* 7 June 1881; *educ* Harrow and Balliol Coll Oxford (BA 1905, MA 1907); MP (Lib) N Bucks 1910–18, Assist Priv Sec to Colonial Secs 1907–10, PPS to Ch Sec Ireland 1911–14, Parly Sec Bd Ag 1914–15, CC Bucks 1910–30, WW I: Capt ASC 1916–17, Lt-Col Gen List 1917–20, AAG 1918, CC Anglesey 1937–55, dir Metro Rlwy Co, author: *The Verneys of Claydon* and *Florence Nightingale at Harley Street*; *m* 7 Dec 1911 Lady Rachel Catherine Bruce (*d* 17 Dec 1964), dau of 9th Earl of Elgin and (13th Earl of) Kincardine (*qv*), and had:

  (1) Sir RALPH BRUCE VERNEY, **5th and present Bt**

  (2) +Stephen Edmund (Rt Rev), MBE (1945) [The Rt Rev Stephen Verney MBE, Charity Sch Ho, Church Rd, Blewbury, Oxon OX11 9PY]; *b* 17 April 1919; *educ* Harrow and Balliol Coll Oxford (MA 1948); Capt Intell Corps WW II; Curate-in-Charge Conventional Dist New Clifton 1952, Vicar St Francis Clifton 1957–58, Leamington Hastings, also Diocesan Missioner Coventry 1958, Canon Coventry 1965–70 and St George's Chapel Windsor 1970–77, Bp Repton; *m* 1st 13 Dec 1947 Priscilla Avice Sophie (*d* 26 Feb 1974), only dau of George Francis Ignatius Schwerdt, of Alresford, Hants and has:

    1a +Robert Francis [Robert Verney Esq, Lower Camelot, S Cadbury, Somerset BA22 7HA]; *b* 3 April 1949; *educ* Harrow; *m* 16 April 1974 *Marianne Juliet, yr dau of Francis Henry Haine, FRCS, LRCP, LRCS, and has:

      1b +Alistair Francis; *b* 15 April 1976

      2b +Nicholas Stephen; *b* 12 Dec 1978

      3b +Christopher Felix; *b* 25 Sept 1982

    1a *Rachel Penelope [Mrs Nicholas Wheeeler-Robinson, Pigotts, N Dean, Bucks HP14 4NF]; *b* 22 Oct 1952; ARCM 1972; *m* 1982 *Nicholas Wheeler-Robinson and has:

      1b *Charles Ralph; *b* 1988

      2b *Caleb John; *b* 1992

      1a *Olivia Alice; *b* 1989

    2a *Helen Mary [Mrs Jonathan Impett, 14a Liverpool Rd, Kingston-on-Thames KT2 7SZ]; *b* 1 March 1955; *m* 1986 *Jonathan Impett and has:

      1b *Thomas Gabriel; *b* 1986

      1b *Lara Priscilla; *b* 1989

    3a *Katharine Priscilla [Mrs Michael Berman, 14 Caroline Terrace, London SW1W 8JS]; *b* 2 June 1958; *m* 1985 *Michael Berman and has:

      1b *Jonathan Stephen; *b* 1986

      2b *Adam Michael; *b* 1993

      1b *Imogen Emily; *b* 1989

  (2) (cont.) The Rt Rev Stephen Verney *m* 2nd 1981 *Mrs Sandra Bailey of Llandeilo Fawr, and has by her has had:

    2a Harry Stephen; *b* and *d* March 1982

  (3) +Hugh Alexander [Hugh Verney Esq, The Mill, Snowshill Rd, Broadway, Worcs]; *b* 14 April 1920; *educ* Harrow and Oriel Coll Oxford (BA 1946, MA 1957); Lt Gren Gds WW II (wounded); *m* 18 Nov 1950 *Ann Mary, er dau of Samuel Ernest Chesterman, of The Old Hall, Wing, Rutland, and has had:

    1a A son; *b* and *d* 31 Dec 1951

    2a Thomas Harry; *b* 17 Oct 1958; *educ* Harrow; *d* 1988 following a road accident

    3a +Mark; *b* 2 Feb 1962; *educ* Harrow

    4a +Jonathan; *b* 2 Feb 1962; *educ* Harrow

    1a *Fiona Ann [Mrs Mark Hope, Sunninghill, Banchory, Kincardineshire AB31 3TR]; *b* 30 Nov 1952; *m* 1975 *Mark Hope, yst s of Capt P H Hope of Ham, Wilts, and has:

      1b *Harry Alexander; *b* 1988

      2b *Jonathan Mark; *b* 1990

    2a *Teresa Joan; *b* 30 Nov 1954; *m* 1975 (*divorce* 1980) Robin Hales, of Malvern Link, Worcs

    3a *Julia Mary; *b* 16 April 1956; *m* 1992 *Iain Smith

  (4) +Andrew Felix [Andrew Verney Esq, The White House, Pewsey, Wilts SN9 5DW]; *b* 4 June 1921; *educ* Harrow and Balliol Coll Oxford; MRCS and LRCP 1948, DORCOG 1953; *m* 10 March 1955 *Theodosia Olive, widow of Frank Barrington Craig and 3rd dau of James Winstanley Cropper, of Ellergreen, Kendal, and has:

    1a +Caspar Charles Andrew [Caspar Verney Esq, Ashfield House, 56 Kirk Lane, Yeadon, Leeds LS19 7ET]; *b* 1 Feb 1961; *m* 17 July 1986 *Wilma Birnie, 4th dau of William Hutchinson Thomson, GM, of Fraserburgh and has:

      1b +Joseph Alexander [Joseph Verney Esq, Ashfield House, 56 Kirk Lane, Yeadon, Leeds]; *b* 25 Dec 1984

      2b +George Andrew; *b* 4 Nov 1987

      3b +Edward Jonathan; *b* 24 July 1991

    1a *Caroline Rachel [Mrs Guy Dagul, Britwell Lodge, Benson, Oxon OX10 6SD]; *b* 10 April 1956; *m* 1 Nov 1985 *Guy Robert Dagul, s of Harvey Dagul, of St Albans, Herts, and has:

      1b *Samuel Matthew; *b* 25 Jan 1990

      2b *William Arthur; *b* 1 April 1993

      1b *Rose Elizabeth; *b* 6 Feb 1988

  (5) +Lawrence John (Sir),TD (1955), DL (Bucks 1967) [His Honour Sir Lawrence Verney TD DL, Windmill House, Church Lane, Oving, Bucks HP22 4HL]; *b* 19 July 1924; *educ* Harrow (Govr 1972–87, ed *Harrow School Register* 1948–) and Oriel Coll Oxford (BA 1950, MA 1953); Capt Gren Gds WW II, barrister Inner Temple 1952 (Bencher 1990), Hon-Col 1 (Roy Bucks Yeo) Signal Sqdn (SC) 1997–, Dep Chm QS: Bucks 1962–71 and Middx 1971, Circuit Judge 1972–90, Recorder London 1990–98; OStJ 1992; ktd 1993; *m* 9 Sept 1922 *Zoë Auriel, yr dau of Lt-Col P G Goodeve-Docker, of Maughanaclea, Kealkil, Bantry, Co Cork

  (1) Marjorie; *b* 21 June 1913; *m* 1st 8 March 1944 Capt Julian Guy Tryon (*see* TRYON, B); *m* 2nd 3 Oct 1957 Sir Ronald Montague Joseph Harris, KCVO, CB (*d* 22 Jan 1995), First Church Estates Commr, only s of Rev Joseph Montague Harris, of Blue Bridge Ho, Halstead, Essex, and *d* Dec 1986

  (2) *Mary Rachel [Mrs Geoffrey Roberts, W Flat Riding Sch, Grimsthorpe, Lincs PE10 0LY]; *b* 21 June 1916; *m* 2 Sept 1947 *Rev Geoffrey Thomas Roberts, s of Thomas Andrew Roberts, of Yelvertoft, Warwicks, and has:

    1a *(Gillian) Marjorie; *b* 5 Oct 1950

    2a *Susan Jane; *b* 23 Oct 1953; *m* 1982 *Paul Morgan and has:

      1b *Benjamin Andrew; *b* 1992

      1b *Claire Susan; *b* 1983

      2b *Anna Mary; *b* 1983 (twin)

      3b *Lucy Rachel; *b* 1987

  (3) *Catherine [Mrs Richard Hare, Bywater, The Street, Ewelme, Oxon OX10 6HQ]; *b* 23 Dec 1925; *m* 7 Dec 1947 Richard Mervyn Hare, FBA, Fell Corpus Christi Oxford, White's Prof Emeritus Moral Philosophy, s of Charles Francis Aubone Hare, and has:

    1a *John Edmund [John Hare Esq, 144 Benjamin St SE, Grand Rapids, MI 49506, USA]; *b* 26 July 1949; *educ* Rugby, Balliol Coll Oxford and Princeton; Prof; *m* 1976 *Theresa, dau of William Forsyth, of Princeton, NJ, and has:

      1b *Andrew Forsyth; *b* 1983

      1b *Catherine Elizabeth; *b* 1980

    1a *Bridget Rachel [Mrs William T George, Little Pond, 92 Penn Dixie Rd, Nazareth, PA 18064, USA]; *b* 15 Dec 1950; *m* *William Toy George, Jr, and has:

      1b *Samuel Benton; *b* 1980

      1b *Anisa Louise; *b* 1982

    2a *(Amy) Louise [Mrs Philip Knight, 92 Hamilton Rd, Reading, Berks RG1 5RD]; *b* 5 June 1953; *m* 1984 *Philip Gerald Knight and has:

      1b *Hannah Ellin; *b* 1987

    3a *Ellin Catherine; *b* 1 Sept 1955; has:

      1b *Matt Martin; *b* 1991

1 Ellin; *b* 9 Sept 1873; *m* 20 Oct 1879 Lt-Col William Henry Salmon, KRRC (*d* 25 Dec 1927), and *d* 8 Jan 1947, leaving issue

2 Lettice Sarah; *b* 14 Feb 1875; *d* unm 7 June 1908

3 Ruth Florence; *b* 8 Dec 1879; Life Govr Church Missionary Soc and U Coll N Wales; *d* unm 9 June 1968

Seat: Claydon House, Bucks. The present structure was erected in the mid–1750s by the 2nd Earl Verney (*see* against Mrs Catherine Verney above, also BRAYE, B), who ruined himself trying to outshine his fellow Buckinghamshire magnates the Earls Temples of Stowe (*qv*). He had a more purely public-spirited side to his character in that he was responsible for finding Edmund Burke a seat in Parliament. He intended his creation to be a westerly extension to an earlier house, but today the westerly extension is all that survives. What is left is astounding enough, though the outside, faced with stone and set amidst the north Buckinghamshire flatlands, while perfectly agreeable, gives no hint of the interior. Here unique wood carvings by Luke Lightfoot in a splendidly uninhibited high rococo style climax in a hugely ornate Chinese Room of unparalleled ornateness, though not everything is curvilinear: the doors have conventional rectangular panels and the ceiling cornice is in a standard dentitulated pattern. The parquet flooring and stairs in wrought iron are highly noteworthy, however. The Florence Nightingale museum, which includes a bedroom and dressing room used by the great nursing philanthropist, commemorates the family connection covered in detail in the **Lineage** section above.

VERNEY of Eaton Square

Arms: Quarterly, 1st and 4th, azure on a cross argent, fimbriated or, five mullets gules (for VERNEY); 2nd and 3rd, paly of six erminois and pean, a bend engrailed counterchanged (for CALVERT).
Crests: 1 A demi-phoenix in flames proper, charged with five mullets in cross or and looking at the rays of the sun (for VERNEY), 2 Out of a mural crown argent two flag staffs erect, therefrom two pennons flowing towards the dexter, one erminois, the other pean (for CALVERT). **Mottoes:** 1 *Ung sent ung soleil* ('One faith, one sun'), 2 *Servata fides cineri* ('Faith kept with one's ancestor').
Creation: Bt. (UK) 16 July 1946.

(John) Sebastian Verney [Sebastian Verney Esq, 34 Gladstone St, London SE1 6EY]; *b* 30 Aug 1945; *s* f 1993 but does not use title; *educ* Eton

Lineage: Sir HARRY VERNEY, 2nd Bt, of Claydon House (*qv*); had:

FREDERICK WILLIAM VERNEY; MP; had:

Sir Ralph Verney, 1st Bt (UK), so *cr* 16 July 1946, of Eaton Square, City of Westminster, CB (1934), CIE (1920), CVO (1921); *b* 25 May 1879; *educ* Harrow and Ch Ch Oxford; Lt-Col Rifle Bde Boer War 1900–02 (two medals with four clasps), Egypt, India and WW I (wounded), ADC to Govr Qld 1907–09, Priv Sec Govr NSW 1909–12, Mil Sec Viceroy India 1916–21, Sec to Speaker H of C 1921–1955, Examiner Private Bills and Taxing Offr 1927–46, ktd 1928, Order Sacred Treasure Japan 3rd Cl, Order White Elephant Siam 3rd Cl, Cdr Order Star Romania; *m* 11 Nov 1909 Janette Cheveria Hamilton, yr dau of Sen Hon James Thomas Walker, of Sydney, NSW, and *d* 23 Feb 1959, leaving:

1 **Sir John Verney, 2nd Bt**, MC (1944), TD (1970); *b* 30 Sept 1913; *educ* Eton and Ch Ch Oxford; Maj RAC WW II (despatches twice), memb Legn Hon (France); painter, illustrator and author: *Verney Abroad* (1954), *Going to the Wars* (1955), *Friday's Tunnel* (1959), *Look at Houses* (1959), *February's Road* (1961), *Every Advantage* (1961), *The Mad King of Chichiboo* (1963), *A Dinner of Herbs* (1966), *Fine Day for a Picnic* (1968), *Seven Sunflower Seeds* (1968) and *Samson's Hoard* (1973); *m* 29 March 1939 *(Jeanie) Lucinda [Lady Verney, 21 Chalcot Rd, London NW1], dau of Maj Herbert Musgrave, DSO, RE, and *d* 2 Feb 1993, having had:
   (1) Julian Comus Ralph; *b* 3 July 1940; *d* 19 Nov 1948
   (2) Sir (JOHN) SEBASTIAN VERNEY, **3rd and present Bt**
   (1) *Sabrina Anne; *b* 14 Feb 1947
   (2) *Juliet Rose; *b* 13 Feb 1949; *m* 1st 25 Sept 1970 (*divorce* 19–) Michael Benjamin, only s of — Benjamin and Mrs R Washtell, of London N11, and has:
      1a *Thomas Michael; *b* 1971
      2a *Julian; *b* 1973
   (2) (cont.) Mrs Juliet Benjamin *m* 2nd 1979 *Simon Hugh Arden Acworth, only s of Maj G W Acworth, MVO, of Woodeaton, Oxon, and by him has:
      3a *Robin; *b* 1983
      1a *Florence Mary; *b* 1980
   (3) *Rose Lucinda; *b* 17 Aug 1950; *m* 15 April 1978 *Peter Zinovieff, er s of Maj Leo Zinovieff, and has:
      1a *Olga; *b* 1978
      2a *Katarina; *b* 1981
      3a *Iliena; *b* 1983
   (4) *Candida Harriet; *b* 10 March 1953; *m* 1980 *Timothy C Molloy, s of Maj T R Molloy, MC, of Wincanton, Somerset, and has:
      1a *Henry; *b* 1981
      2a *Ned; *b* 1984
      3a *Theo; *b* 1986
   (5) *(Alice) Angelica; *b* 9 Feb 1956; *m* 1984 *David James Risk Kennard, yr s of Maj Robert William Kennard, MC, TD, of Barton Farm, Guiting Power, Glos, and has:
      1a *Paris Timothy; *b* 1986
      2a *Hector; *b* 1988

3a *Edgar Robert; *b* 1991
2 David; *b* 31 May 1918; *educ* Eton; Lt-Cdr RN WW II, High Sheriff Cornwall 1964; *m* 17 Jan 1948 *Hon Mary Kathleen Boscawen [The Hon Mrs Verney, Trevella, St Erme, nr Truro, Cornwall TR4 9BS], only dau of 8th Viscount Falmouth (*qv*), and *d* 1992, leaving:
   (1) +CHRISTOPHER RALPH EVELYN VERNEY; *b* 4 Oct 1948; heir presumptive; *educ* Eton and Trin Coll Cambridge; *m* 1976 *Madeliene Lindberg
   (1) *Margaret Mary; *b* 13 Nov 1950; *m* 15 May 1971 *Peter Michael Bickford-Smith, only s of Michael George Bickford-Smith, of Trevarno, Helston, Cornwall, and has:
      1a *Michael Rupert David; *b* 1984
      1a *Sacha Ann Mary; *b* 21 March 1975
      2a *Charlotte Ann Bertha; *b* 1977
      3a *Stephanie May; *b* 1989
   (2) *Rosemary Janette; *b* 1 July 1958; *m* 24 April 1982 (*divorce* 1991) John Kenna, yst s of Raymond Kenna, of Foxrock, Dublin, and has:
      1a *Justin; *b* 1987
      2a *Nicholas Harry; *b* 1990
      1a *Lamorna Daisy; *b* 1985
1 *Joscelyne [Mrs Andrew Thorne, Cottage 32, Headbourne Worthy House, Winchester SO23 7JG]; *b* 23 Feb 1915; *m* 5 April 1941 Capt Andrew Thorne, Gren Gds (*d* 1991), est s of Gen Sir (Augustus Francis) Andrew Nicol Thorne, KCB, CMG, DSO and two bars, DL, of Knowl Hill Ho, nr Reading, Berks (*see* PENRHYN, B), and has had:
   (1) Nicholas Andrew; *b* 11 Jan 1942; *educ* Eton and RMA Sandhurst; Capt Gren Gds; *m* 11 Sept 1969 *Diana Lesley Kathryn (*m* 2nd 1977 Ian Mitchell Thomas, of Floriston Hall, Wixoe, Suffolk), only dau of Donald Leslie, of Horley Place, Horley, Surrey, and *d* 1976, leaving:
      1a *Alexander Francis Andrew Nicholas; *b* 1972
      1a *Camilla Claire Louise; *b* 1976
   (1) *Joanna Mary [Mrs John Friedberger, North Woolding Cottage, The Harrow Way, Whitchurch, Hants RG28 7QT]; *b* 24 March 1945; *m* 13 Aug 1966 *Maj-Gen John Peter William Friedberger, CB, CBE, Roy Hus (PWO), only s of Brig John Cameron Friedberger, DSO, DL, of Southsea, Hants, and has:
      1a *Richard Mark; *b* 1973
      1a *Rosanna Catharine; *b* 15 June 1967; *m* 1991 *James Robert Perceval Armitage, s of Jeremy Armitage, and has:
         1b *Luke Robert; *b* 14 April 1993
         2b *William John; *b* 9 March 1995
         3b *Oliver James; *b* 4 June 1997
      2a *Lucinda Jane; *b* 5 April 1970
   (2) *Carola Joscelyne [Mrs Nigel Symington, Parsonage Farm Ho, Fletching, E Sussex]; *b* 21 June 1948; *m* 1978 *Nigel Howard Symington, of Bolney, Sussex, and has:
      1a *Lucy Elizabeth Joscelyne; *b* 1980
      2a *Fiona Juliet; *b* 1982
      3a *Victoria Carola; *b* 1984

VERNON, Baron

Arms: Quarterly, 1st and 4th quarterly of four, 1st and 4th, argent a fret sable, 2nd and 3rd, or on a fess azure three garbs of the field (both for VERNON); 2nd and 3rd, azure two bars argent (for VENABLES). **Crests** 1 A boar's head erased sable, ducally gorged or (for VERNON), 2 A wyvern argent, standing on a weir of the last banded azure, pierced through the body in fess by an arrow and devouring a child proper. **Supporters:** Dexter, a lion gules, gorged with a collar and chain reflexed over the back or; sinister, a boar sable, gorged with a ducal coronet and chain reflexed over the back or. **Motto:** *Ver non semper viret* ('Vernon always flourishes'/'The spring does not always flourish'). **Creation:** B. (GB) 12 May 1762.

THE 10TH LORD VERNON, BARON OF KINDERTON, Co Chester (John Lawrance Venables-Vernon) [The Rt Hon The Lord Vernon, Sudbury House, Sudbury, Derbys DE6 5HT]; *b* 1 Feb 1923; *s* f 1963; *educ* Eton and Magdalen Coll Oxford; Capt Scots Gds WW II 1942–46, barrister Lincoln's Inn 1949, Cabinet Office 1953–57, Colonial Office (attd Kenya Govt) 1957–58, FO 1959–61, JP Derbys 1965–77, co-proprietor Africa Confidential, memb Peak Park Planning Bd 1974–76, Chm Population Concern 1984–89; *m* 1st 7 July 1955 (*divorce* 1982) Sheila Jean, yr dau of W Marshall Clark, OBE, BSc, MICE, of Johannesburg; *m* 2nd 14 July 1982 *Sally June, est dau of Robin Stratford, QC, of Fernhill, Kilmacrennay, and formerly w of (a) Colin Fyfe-Jamieson and (b) Sir (John) Jeremy Eustace Tennyson-d'Eyncourt, 3rd Bt (*qv*), and has had by his 1st w:

1 (Georgina) Frances; *b* 1 Dec 1963; *educ* Cranborne Chase and Cambridge; author: *Privileged Children* (1982), *Gentlemen and Players* (1984), *A Desirable Husband* (1987), *The Bohemian Girl* (1988), *The Marquis of Westmarch* (1989) and *The Fall of Dr Onslow* (1991); *d* 1991

2 *Joanna Elizabeth; *b* 30 Sept 1965; *m* 1992 *Alexander Rupert Fitzalan Howard and has issue (*see* NORFOLK, D)

Lineage (of Vernon): RICHARD; feudal Ld of Vernon and holder of many manors at the time of the Domesday Survey 1086; enjoyed a local prominence in the County Palatine of Chester as Baron of Shipbrooke (a subinfeudatory rank but not a peerage title) conferred by Hugh d'Avranches or *Lupus* (*i.e.*, 'Wolf', so-called from his ferocity and acquisitiveness), Earl of Chester with quasi-regal powers, so *cr* 1071 in the reign of his great-uncle of the half-blood WILLIAM I (THE CONQUEROR)); had a 2nd s:

WILLIAM de VERNON; ggf of:

RICHARD de VERNON; *m* 1171 Avice, dau and coheir of William de Avenell, of Haddon, Derbys, and *dvp*, leaving, with two other sons:

1 Warine; *s* gf as Baron of Shipbrooke; *m* Auda, dau and coheir of William Malbank, Baron of Wich-Malbank (later Nantwich), Co Palatine of Chester (holder of a similar dignity to that of the Barons of Shipbrooke), and had, with a yr s (Ralph):

(1) Warine, Baron of Shipbrooke; *m* Margaret, dau of Ralph de Andeville and widow of Hugh de Altaribus, and had, with a s (Warine, *dsp*), three daus (who after prolonged litigation with their maternal unc Ralph were obliged to give up to him half their patrimony):

1a Margery; *m* Richard de Wilburgham and has issue (*see* SKELMERSDALE, B)

2a Edith; *m* Sir William Stafford

3a Rohesia; *m* John Littlebury

2 William (Sir); Ch Justice Chester *c* 1231; *m* 1230 Margery (*d* 1239), dau of Sir Robert de Stockport, thus acquiring Appleby Parva, Leics, and had:

(1) Richard; granted 1252 by HENRY III the Castle of the Peak, Derbys

(2) Robert; exiled by HENRY III with his bro Richard for oposing the King in the Barons' Wars of the 1260s

3 Robert, of Nether Haddon; had a dau and heiress:

(1) Hawise; *m* 1231 Gilbert le Franceys, s of Adam le Franceys, s of John le Franceys, of Meaburn, Cumberland, and had:

1a Richard (Sir); took name VERNON by 1252; *m* Margaret de Vipont and had:

1b Richard (Sir), of Haddon; *m* 1st Alianore (*dsp*), dau of Giles de Frenes; *m* 2nd Juliana, dau of William de Vescy, of Alnwick, Northumberland, and Malton, Yorks, by Agnes, dau of William de Ferrers, 5th Earl of Derby (*qv*, preliminary remarks) of the 1138 *cr*, thus acquiring Arleston, Derbys, and by her had:

1c Richard (Sir); *m* Maud, dau and coheir of William de Camville, 2nd Lord (Baron) Camville/Canville of the notional 24 June 1295 *cr*, and *dvp* by 3 Feb 1322/3, leaving, with a dau (Isabella, *m* 1337 Sir Richard Stafford, of Pype, Staffs):

1d William (Sir); *b* 1312/3; *m* Margaret, dau of Robert de Stopford, and had:

1e Richard (Sir), of Haddon and Arleston; *m* Juliana, sis and heiress of Fulco de Pembruge and dau of Robert/Roger de Pembruge by Juliana Zouche, and *d* 1377, leaving:

1f Richard (Sir), of Haddon and Arleston; *b* 1370; *m* Jane, dau and heiress of Rhys ap Griffith, of Wichnor, Staffs, and *d* 1401, leaving, with a yr s and two daus:

1g Richard (Sir), JP Staffs 1417, Derbys 1422; *b* 1390; High Sheriff Staffs 1416–17 and Derbys and Notts 1424, MP Staffs 1419 and 1421 and Derbys 1422 and 1426–143– also Speaker of the Parl at Leicester 1426, Steward Duchy of Lancaster estates and Constable Castle of the Peak 1424–44, Treas Calais 1445–51; *m* Benedicta (*d* 1444), dau of Sir John Ludlow, of Tong, Salop (which he inherited 1446 from Isabella, widow of Fulco de Pembruge), and *d* Sept 1451, leaving an est surv s:

1h William (Sir), Kt; *b* 1416; MP Derbys 1442–51 and 1467 and Staffs 1455–56, Kt Constable of England; *m* Margaret, dau and heiress of Sir William Swynfen by Jocosa, yst dau of William Durvassal *alias* Spernore and heiress also of Robert Pype, and *d* 1467, leaving, with two yr sons and four daus:

1i Henry (Sir), KB, PC, feudal Ld of Haddon; Govr and Treasurer to PRINCE ARTHUR, est s of HENRY VII; *m* Anne, dau of 2nd Earl of Shrewsbury and Waterford (*qv*), and *d* 1511, having had, with six daus and four yr sons:

1j Richard (Sir), of Haddon; *m* Margaret, dau of Sir Robert Dymoke, and *d* 1517, leaving:

1k George (Sir) called 'King of the Peak', for his extensive possessions, which included Haddon and 29 other manors; *m* Margaret, dau by his 2nd w of Sir George Talboys, of Kyme, Lincs, *de jure* 9th Lord (Baron) Kyme (notional *cr* 24 June 1295) according to later doctrine, and sis of 1st Lord (Baron) Tailboys, and *d* 1567, leaving:

1l Dorothy; *m* Sir John Manners, yr s of 1st Earl of Rutland (*see* RUTLAND, D), taking Haddon to her husb's family

2l Margaret; *m* Thomas Stanley, 2nd s of 2nd Earl of Derby (*qv*), taking Tong Castle to her husb's family

1k Agnes; *m* (Sir?) John Cokayne, of Ashbourne Hall (*see* CULLEN OF ASHBOURNE, B)

2i Thomas; *m* Anne, er dau and coheir of Sir John Ludlow, of Stokesay and Hodnet, Salop, by Elizabeth, alleged by her ggs Henry (*see* below) to be dau of Margaret Audley/Tuchet (dau of 5th Lord (Baron) Audley; *see* WAKE, Bt) by Richard Grey, 1st Lord Grey (of Powis) (*see* GREY, B), but quite possibly Margaret's dau by her 1st husb Sir Roger Vaughan, and had:

1j Thomas, of Stokesay, Salop; *d* 1561, leaving, with other issue (extinct in the male line 1666):

1k Henry; advanced 1584 a claim (alleged 1731 by John Kynaston, another much later claimant, to rest on forged documentation) to the Barony of Grey (of Powis) through his paternal gf's mother, styling himself Lord Powis; *dsp* 1606

2j HUMPHREY

3j John (Sir); memb Cncl of Wales and the Marches, custos rotulorum Derbys; *m* Ellen, dau and coheir of Sir John de Montgomerie, thus acquiring Sudbury, Derbys, and *d* 1545, leaving:

1k Henry (Sir), of Sudbury; *m* 1547 Margaret, dau and coheir of Humphrey Swinnerton, of Swinnerton and Hilton (*see* DYER, Bt), and *d* 1569, leaving with two daus:

1l John; *m* Mary, widow of his cousin Walter Vernon (*see* below) and dau of Sir Edward Littleton (*see* HATHERTON, B), and *dsp* 1600

2l Henry, of Hilton and Essington, Staffs; *m* Dorothy, dau of Sir Anthony Heveningham, and *d* 21 June 1592, leaving:

1m Margaret; *b* posthumously; *m* her 3rd cousin Sir Edward Vernon (*see* below)

1j Eleanor; *m* Francis Curzon (*see* SCARSDALE, V)

The 2nd s,

HUMPHREY VERNON; *m* Alice, yr dau of Sir John Ludlow (*see* above), and *d* 1542, leaving, with other issues:

1 George, of Hodnet; *m* Elizabeth, dau of Thomas Pigot, of Chetwynd, Salop, and was *bur* 1553, leaving, with an er s (Richard, *d* young):

(1) John, of Hodnet; *b c* 1546; *m* 1564 Elizabeth, dau of Sir Richard Devereux (*see* HEREFORD, V), and *d* 1592, having had, with 13 other children:

1a Robert (Sir), KB; *b* 1577; Comptroller Household to ELIZABETH I; *m* Mary, sis of 1st Viscount Kilmorey (*see* KILMOREY, E), and *d* 1625, leaving:

1b Sir HENRY VERNON, 1st Bt (E), so cr 23 July 1660; b c 1605; royalist Civil War, MP Salop 1660 and W Looe 1661–76; m 1636 Elizabeth, dau of Sir Richard White, of The Friars, Anglesey, and d April 1676, leaving:

1c Sir THOMAS VERNON, 2nd Bt, of Hodnet; a Teller Exchequer; m 1st 9 Sept 1675 Elizabeth (dsp, bur 19 June 1676), dau of Thomas Cholmondeley (see DELAMERE, B) and sis of his bro-in-law (see below); m 2nd 30 June 1677 Mary, dau of George Kirke and sis of Diana, Countess of Oxford (see SAINT ALBANS, D), and d 5 Feb 1682/3, leaving by her, with two daus (d unm):

1d Sir RICHARD VERNON, 3rd and last Bt, of Hodnet; b 22 June 1678; educ Ch Ch Oxford; Envoy to AUGUSTUS, KING OF POLAND; d unm 1 Oct 1725, when the btcy expired

1c Elizabeth; m 1675 Robert Cholmondeley and d 1685, leaving:

1d Elizabeth; m John Atherton, of Atherton and Bewsey, Lancs, and had:

1e Elizabeth; m 1722 Thomas Heber, of Marton, Yorks, and had, with an er s (Richard, dsp 1766):

1f Reginald; had, with two other sons and a dau:

1g Reginald (Rt Rev); Bp Calcutta; had:

1f Emily; m Algernon Charles PERCY later HEBER-PERCY (see NORTHUMBERLAND, D), whereby the Hodnet estate ultimately passed to the HEBER-PERCYs

2 Thomas; m Helena, dau of Ralph Shirley, and d 1556, leaving:

(1) Walter, of Houndshill; b 1552; m: as her 1st husb Mary Littleton (see above) and d 1592, leaving an only surv s:

1a Edward (Sir); b 1584; m 1613 his cousin Margaret (see above) and d 1657, leaving, with seven daus:

1b HENRY (Sir)

2b Edward, of N Aston, Staffs; Col; granted Clontarf Castle, Co Dublin; dspm

3b John; QMG English forces Ireland; ancestor of the VERNONs of Clontarf Castle

4b Walter; d unm

The est s,

Sir HENRY VERNON; b 1615; m Muriel, dau and heiress of Sir George Vernon, of Haslington, Judge Common Pleas, and d 9 March 1657/8, having had, with four other sons (including two who dsp and Henry, of Hilton, Staffs, b 1637, ancestor of the VERNONs of Hilton Park, VERNONs of Harefield Park and VERNON-WENTWORTHs of Wentworth Castle; also John, whose dau Penelope m 1st Sir William Dukinfield and 2nd John Astley):

GEORGE VERNON, of Sudbury; b 1635; MP Derby 1679–81 and 1698–1700; m 1st Margaret, dau of Edwin Onely, of Catesby, Northants, and had a s (dsp) and five daus; m 2nd Dorothy, sis of 1st Earl Ferrers (qv), and by her had two daus; m 3rd Catherine, dau of Sir Thomas Vernon, of Twickenham Park, Middx, London merchant, and sis of 3rd w of 1st VISCOUNT HARCOURT OF STANTON HARCOURT (see **Lineage (of Harcourt)** below), and d 1702, leaving by her:

HENRY VERNON, of Sudbury; b c 1686; MP Co Stafford; m 1st Anne (d April 1714), only dau and heiress of Thomas Pigot, of Chetwynd, Salop (by Mary, sis of Peter Venables, the last Baron of Kinderton, another of the Co Palatine of Chester dignities already mentioned (see Shipbrooke and Wich-Malbank above), though following the annexation of the Earldom of Chester to the Crown by HENRY III in 1265 their significance was purely vestigial), and had issue; m 2nd Matilda (dsp), dau of Thomas Wright, of Longstone, Derbys, and d 25 Feb 1718/9, leaving an only s:

GEORGE VERNON later VENABLES-VERNON (on inheriting the Venables estate in Cheshire on the death 28 April 1715 without issue of his cousin Anne, w of 2nd Earl of Abingdon (see LINDSEY and ABINGDON, E), Peter Venables's dau), **1st Lord Vernon, Baron of Kinderton**, Co Chester (GB), so cr 12 May 1762; b 9 Feb 1709/10; MP (anti-Walpole Whig) Lichfield 1731–47 and Derby 1754–62; m 1st 21 June 1733 Mary (d 23 Feb 1739/40), dau and coheir of 6th Baron Howard of Effingham (see EFFINGHAM, E), and had surv issue:

1 GEORGE VENABLES-VERNON, **2nd Lord Vernon, Baron of Kinderton**; b 9 May 1735; educ Westminster and Trin Hall Cambridge (MA); MP (Whig) Weobley 1757–61, Bramber 1762–68 and Glam 1768–80; m 1st 16 July 1757 Louisa Barbara (dsps 16 Feb 1786), dau of 4th and last Baron Mansell of Margam (see MANSEL, Bt); m 2nd 25 May 1786 Jane Georgiana (d 31 May 1823), dau of William Fauquier, of Hanover, and d 18 June 1813, leaving by her:

(1) Georgiana; m 19 Sept 1809 3rd Baron Suffield (qv) and d 13 Sept 1824, leaving issue

1 Mary; m 5 Jan 1763 George ADAMS later ANSON (see LICHFIELD, E)

The **1st Baron** m 2nd 22 Dec 1741 Anne (dsp 22 Sept 1742), dau of Sir Thomas Lee, 3rd Bt, of Hartwell, Bucks (see 1826 edn); m 3rd 10 April 1744 Martha (d 8 April 1794), sis of 1st EARL HARCOURT OF STANTON HARCOURT (see **Lineage (of Harcourt)** below), and d 21 Aug 1780, having by her had surv issue:

2 HENRY, **3rd Baron**

3 Edward (Most Rev) VENABLES-VERNON later VERNON-HARCOURT (roy licence 15 Jan 1831 on inheriting Harcourt estates 1830; offered a revived peerage (presumably embodying the name Harcourt) by the former PM the 2nd Earl Grey (qv) 1838), PC; b 10 Oct 1757; DD, DCL, Preb Gloucester 1785–91, Bp Carlisle 1791–1807, Archbp York 1807–47; m 5 Feb 1784 Lady Anne Leveson-Gower (d 16 Nov 1832), 3rd dau of 1st Marquess of Stafford (see SUTHERLAND, D), and d 5 Feb 1847, having had, with another s (d young) and two daus (d unm):

(1) George Granville VERNON-HARCOURT later HARCOURT, of Nuneham Courtenay, Oxon; b 6 Aug 1785; MP Lichfield 1806–31 and Oxon 1831–61; m 1st 27 March 1815 Elizabeth (d 9 Sept 1838), est dau of 2nd Earl of Lucan (qv), and had:

1a Elizabeth Lavinia; m 7 Jan 1835 6th Earl of Abingdon (see LINDSEY and ABINGDON, E) and d 16 Oct 1858, having had issue

(1) (cont.) George HARCOURT m 2nd 30 Sept 1847 Frances Elizabeth Anne (m 3rd 20 Jan 1863 1st and last Baron Carlingford (see 1898 edn) and d 5 July 1879), widow of 7th Earl Waldegrave (qv) and dau of John Braham, a noted tenor), and d 19 Dec 1861 without further issue

(2) Leveson (Rev); b 1788; Chllr York; m 19 Aug 1815 Hon Caroline Mary Peachey (d 16 July 1871), dau of 2nd Baron Selsey (see 1838 edn), and d 26 July 1860

(3) William (Rev) VERNON-HARCOURT later HARCOURT; b June 1789; Canon York, first Sec then Pres Br Assoc; m 11 July 1824 Matilda Mary (d 19 Nov 1876), dau of Col William Gooch, and d 1 April 1871, leaving, with another dau (d unm):

1a Edward William, DL, of Nuneham Courtenay and Stanton Harcourt, Oxon; b 26 June 1825; MP Oxon 1878–86; m 26 June 1849 Lady Harriet Holroyd (d 5 April 1894), only dau of 2nd Earl of Sheffield (see STANLEY OF ALDERLEY, SHEFFIELD and, B), and d 19 Dec 1891, leaving:

1b Aubrey, JP, DL (Oxon), of Nuneham Park and Stanton Harcourt; b 16 Aug 1852; High Sheriff Oxon 1894 and 1897; d unm 22 March 1904

1b Edith; m 27 Oct 1875 12th Earl of Winchilsea and (7th Earl of) Nottingham (qv) and d 6 Jan 1944, leaving issue

2a William George Granville (Sir), PC (1880), DL (Hants), of Nuneham Courtenay, Stanton Harcourt and Malwood, Lyndhurst, Hants; b 14 Oct 1827; MA Cantab; LLD, KC, MP Oxford 1868–80, Derby 1880–95 and Mon W 1895–1904, Slr-Gen 1873–74, ktd 1873, Home Sec 1880–85, Chllr Exchequer 1886 and 1892–95; m 1st 5 Nov 1859 Maria Theresa (d 1 Feb 1863), dau of Thomas Henry Lister (see CLARENDON, E), and had, with an er s (d an infant):

1b LEWIS HARCOURT, 1st VISCOUNT HARCOURT, of Stanton Harcourt, Co Oxon, so cr 3 Jan 1917, as also BARON NUNEHAM, of Nuneham-Courtenay, Co Oxon (both UK) PC (1905); b 31 Jan 1863; educ Eton; Priv Sec to his f when Home Sec and Chllr, MP (Lib) Rossendale 1904–16, First Commr Works 1905–10 and 1915–16, Sec State Colonies 1910–15; Ttstee Br Museum, Nat Portrait Gallery, Wallace Collection and London Museum; Hon DCL Oxon; m 1 July 1899 Mary Ethel, GBE (1918), JP (Oxon), DGStJ, dau of Walter Hayes Burns, of New York and N Mymms Park, Herts, and d 24 Feb 1922, having had:

1c WILLIAM EDWARD HARCOURT, 2nd VISCOUNT HARCOURT, KCMG (1957), OBE (1945, MBE 1943), DL (Oxon 1952); b 5 Oct 1908 (HM EDWARD VII stood sponsor); educ Eton and Ch Ch Oxford (BA 1930, MA 1954); 63rd (Oxon Yeo) Anti-Tank Regt RA and Staff WW II; Min (Ec) Br Embassy Washington and Head UK Treasury Delegn US 1954–57, UK Exec Dir IBRD and IMF 1954–57, md Morgan Grenfell, chm: Legal and Gen Assur, Gresham Fire and Accident Insur Soc, Gresham Life Assur and Br Cwlth Insur; Chm Tstees London Museum 1961–; Hon Fell St Antony's Coll Oxford; m 1st 1 June 1931 (divorce 1942) Hon Maud Elizabeth Grosvenor, dau of 4th Baron Ebury (qv), and had:

1d *(Elizabeth) Ann [The Hon Mrs Gascoigne, The Manor House, Stanton Harcourt, Oxon]; b 17 Feb 1932; m 19 Jan 1954 *Crispin Gascoigne, only s of Maj-Gen Sir Julian Alvery Gascoigne, KCMG, KCVO, CB, DSO (see NEWMAN, Bt, of Mamhead), and has:

1e *William Harcourt Crisp; b 22 Nov 1955; m 1980 *Susan Alexandra, dau of Aubrey Greville Williams, of E Grimstead, Wilts, and has:

1f *Julian Aubrey Harcourt; b 1984

2f *Frederick William; b 1986

3f *Ralph Edward; b 1989

1e *Elizabeth Laura; b 31 July 1958; m *Peter Nicholas Offord, est s of L R Offord, of London N21, and has:

1f *Nicholas Alvery Harcourt; b 1990

1f *Venetia Vernon; b 1988

2f *Cecily Katherine; b 1992

2e *Mary Ann; b 20 March 1961; m 1986 *Matthew Charles Louis Crosby, only s of Dr Jack Lionel Crosby, of Stanhope, Co Durham, and has:

1f *Miles William Southe; b 1989

2f *George Crispin Ivo; b 1992

2d *Penelope Mary; b 17 May 1933; m 14 Aug 1954 *Maj Anthony David Motion, late 9th Queen's Roy Lancers, s of Maj Malcolm Davie Motion, and has:

1e *Stephen Anthony; b 1 Aug 1967

2d (cont.) Maj and The Hon Mrs Motion also adopted:

*Georgina; bapt 24 Oct 1965

3d Virginia; b 16 Jan 1937; m 14 June 1958 *Julian Francis Wells, s of Dr Arthur Quinton Wells, of Shipton Manor, Oxon, and d 19–, leaving:

1e *Philip Vernon; b 29 Dec 1962

1e *Sonia Clare; b 21 July 1960

2e *A dau; b 11 Sept 1966

1c (cont.) The 2nd VISCOUNT m 2nd 23 Jan 1946 Elizabeth Sonia (d 30 Oct 1959), widow of Lionel Cyril Gibbs (see ALDENHAM and HUNSDON OF HUNSDON, B) and 2nd dau of Sir Harold Edward Snagge, KBE, and d 1979, when his peerages expired

1c Doris Mary Thérèse; b 30 March 1900; m 17 Nov 1924 6th Baron Ashburton (qv) and d 1981, leaving issue

2c Olivia Vernon; b 5 April 1902; educ LMH Oxford; Woman Bedchamber to HM QUEEN ELIZABETH THE QUEEN MOTHER 1951–61; V-Chm Govrs Roy Free Hosp 1951–61, Chm Elizabeth Garrett Anderson Hosp 1945–84; m 29 Oct 1923 Hon Godfrey John Arthur Murray Lyle Mulholland, MC, yst s of 2nd Baron Dunleath (qv), and d 1984, leaving issue

3c Barbara Vernon, OBE (1944); b 28 April 1905; Regnl Adminr WVS N Midland region WW II; m 1st 25 July 1925 (divorce 1936) Robert Charles Horace Jenkinson (see JENKINSON, Bt); m 2nd 26 Jan 1937 William James Baird (d 2 Feb 1961), of Elie, Fife, and d 19 May 1961

2a (cont.) Sir William Harcourt m 2nd 2 Dec 1876 Elizabeth Cabot (d 1 April 1928), dau of Hon John Lothrop Motley, US Amb UK, and widow of Thomas Poynton Ives, of RI, USA, and d 1 Oct 1904, leaving by her:

2b Robert; b 7 May 1878; educ Eton and Trin Coll Cambridge; MP (Lib) Montrose Burghs 1908–18, PPS to Home Sec 1908, Lt RNVR WW I, F/Lt RAFVR WW II; m 26 July 1911 Margorie Laura (d 4 Nov 1977), only dau of William Samuel Cunard (see 1970 edn CUNARD, Bt), and d 8 Sept 1962, leaving:

1c *Mary Elizabeth [Mrs Ian Johnston, Malwood Walk, Minstead, Hants SO43 7GF]; b 1922; late Flt Offr WAAF; m 17 June 1950 *Cdr Ian Rochfort Johnston, RN, s of Capt Basil Lyall Johnston, RN, of Shawford, Hants, and has:

1d *Sarah Elizabeth [Mrs William Ziegler, Lords Oak Cottage, Landford, Wilts SP5 2DW]; b 6 Dec 1956; m 1979 *William James Archer Ziegler (see BROWNLOW, B) and has issue

2d *Laura Catherine [Miss Laura Johnston, 8 Pembroke Gdns Cl, London W8 6HR]; b 16 March 1960

1a Cecilia Caroline; m 18 Feb 1864 Adml Sir Edward Bridges Rice, KCB (d 30 Oct 1902), of Dane Court, Kent, and d 17 Feb 1912, leaving issue

2a Selina Anne; m 8 June 1854 Sir Warwick Charles Morshead, 3rd and last Bt, of Trenant (d 17 March 1905), and dsp 14 Sept 1883

3a Mary Annabella; m 24 April 1860 George de la Poer Beresford and d 11 July 1917, leaving issue (see WATERFORD, M)

(4) Frederick Edward; b 15 June 1790; Adml; m 1829 Marcia (d 27 Dec 1808), dau of Adml J R Delap Tollemache (see TOLLEMACHE, B), and d 1 May 1883, leaving, with two daus (d unm):

1a Augustus George, of Ryde, IoW; b 24 Dec 1834; educ Balliol Coll Oxford (MA); DSc Oxford, DCL Durham, LLD McGill U; FRS; m 10 Sept 1872 Rachel Mary (d 24 June 1927), 2nd dau of 1st Baron Aberdare (qv), and d 23 Aug 1919, leaving:

1b Bernard Francis; b 23 Dec 1877; Maj Welsh Regt WW I; m 1st 23 April 1912 Irene Margaret (d 19–), only child of Sydney Nicholls, of Bayswater; m 2nd 11 June 1931 Mrs Elizabeth Sommerhoff (d 19–) and dsp 19 May 1959

2b Simon Evelyn; b 19 Jan 1882; m 3 Aug 1916 Dorothy Margaret, MBE (1948) (d 1987), only child of Sir Robert Arundell Hudson, and d 21 Feb 1966, having had:

1c Simon; b 2 July 1917; d car crash 9 Oct 1941

2c Robert; b 26 Dec 1918; educ Marlborough and Ch Ch Oxford (BA 1938, MA 1968); Capt RTR WW II; m 25 Sept 1948 *Sylvia Jeannette (Jane), only dau of Lt-Col Charles Henry Kitching, DSO, of Fairhaze Cottage, Piltdown, Sussex, and d 19–

1c *Anne [Miss Vernon-Harcourt, 60 Burton Court, London SW3]; b 11 July 1925

1b Mildred Edith; b 26 Sept 1874; educ Cambridge (MA); nurse ARRC France and Italy WW I (despatches); d unm 14 Oct 1965

2b Mabel Frances; b 26 Sept 1874; educ Oxford High Sch and Girton Coll Cambridge (MA); Headmistress Co High Sch for Girls Chelmsford; m 28 Dec 1910 William Arthur Price (d 13 May 1954), s of Rev Bartholomew Price, Master Pembroke Coll Oxford, and d Oct 1965, leaving issue

3b Cecil Violet; b 17 Nov 1875; m 25 June 1901 Nowell Charles Smith (d 21 Jan 1961), Headmaster Sherborne 1909–27, er s of Horace Smith, of Beckenham, and d 24 Jan 1961, leaving issue

4b Helen Dorothea; b 19 Nov 1876; m 17 April 1900 Sir William Beach Thomas, KBE (d 12 May 1957), 2nd s of Rev Daniel George Thomas, and d 4 Aug 1969, leaving issue

5b Janet Isabel; b 3 June 1879; MA Dublin; Headmistress Runton Hill Sch W Runton, Norfolk; d unm 18 Feb 1966

6b Doris Margaret; b 21 Aug 1883; d unm 15 Sept 1953

7b Winifred Rachel; b 17 Jan 1886; m 4 Dec 1913 Herbert John Schiele (d 1919), s of Edward C Schiele, of Argentina, and d 19–, having had issue

8b Isabel Marcia; b 12 Aug 1887; m 23 July 1919 (Cornelius) Jan Olivier (d 24 March 1955)

2a Leveson Francis; b 25 Jan 1839; MA Oxon; MInstCE, Prof Civil Eng UCL 1882–1905, Emeritus Prof 1906, Cdr Imp Franz Josef Order Austria-Hungary 1904; m 2 Aug 1870 Alice (d 28 Aug 1919), yr dau of Lt-Col Henry Rowland Brandreth, RE, FRS, and d 14 Sept 1907, having had, with another s (d young):

1b Leveson William; b 15 Oct 1871; educ Oxford (BA); barrister; m 18 May 1899 Rose Adelaide (d 25 Sept 1959, having m 2nd 31Oct 1914 Matthew Liddell, of Stillington Hall, Easingwold, who d 18 Jan 1934), est dau of Frederic Lawrence, of Caerleon, Mon, and d 30 April 1909, leaving:

1c +WILLIAM RONALD DENIS, OBE (1947) [Col William Vernon-Harcourt OBE, Quoin Cottage, Southwick Rd, Denmead, Portsmouth, Hants PO7 6LA]; b posthumously 4 May 1909; heir presumptive; educ Eton and Magdalene Coll Cambridge (BA 1930, MA); Col S Wales Borderers (24th Regt) Burma WW II 1941–42 (despatches), CD Offr SE Hants, 1957–68; m 29 May 1937 *Nancy Everil, only child of Lt-Col Bertram Henry Leatham, DSO, Green Howards, and has:

1d +Anthony William [Anthony Vernon-Harcourt Esq, Monks Farm, Debden Green, Saffron Walden, Essex CB11 3LX]; b 29 Oct 1939; educ Eton and Magdalene Coll Cambridge (BA 1960, MA 1966); m 3 Dec 1966 *Cherry Stanhope, er dau of Thomas James Corbin, of Lime Tree House, Spaldwick, Hunts, and has:

1e +Simon Anthony; b 24 Aug 1969

2e +Edward William; b 21 May 1973

3e +Oliver Thomas; b 15 Aug 1977

1e *Charlotte Lucy [Miss Charlotte Vernon-Harcourt, 115 Howard Rd, Leicester LE2 1Xt]; b 12 Jan 1968; has by *Paul Kaye:

1f *Hector Thomas Vernon KAYE; b 20 April 1998

1d *Anne Dorothy [Mrs Peter Cobb, The Old School, Clanfield, Hants]; b 23 Sept 1945; m 1st 30 Sept 1967 (divorce 1974) Nicholas Guy William Bloxam, only s of Lt-Col Guy Cholmley Bloxam, OBE, of Berwick Cottage, Lympne, Kent; m 2nd *Peter George Cobb and has by her 1st husb:

1e *Richard William; b 27 June 1971

2e *David Vernon; b 3 March 1974

1c (Rose Mary) Dorothy; b 2 March 1900; m 1st 5 Sept 1922 Hon Frederick Somerset Gough-Calthorpe (d 19 Nov 1935), only s of 8th Baron Calthorpe (see 1970 edn), and had issue; m 2nd 12 Aug 1949 Lt-Col Guy Alexander Ingram Dury, MC, Gren Gds, s of Theodore Seton Dury, of London SW1, and d 19–

1b Evelyn Alice; b 30 Dec 1876; m 6 Aug 1903 Arthur Clutton-Brock (d 8 Jan 1924), barrister, s of J A Clutton-Brock, of Weybridge, and d 28 July 1964, leaving issue

2b Violet Mary; b 22 March 1883; m 28 Jan 1911 John Pascoe Elsden (d 14 April 1950), barrister, s of Charles William Elsden, and had issue

1a Jane; m 18 April 1872 Rev Francis Digby Legard and d 22 March 1875, leaving issue (see LEGARD, Bt)

(5) Henry; b 1791; Lt-Col; m 20 April 1835 Frances (d 15 Oct 1872), dau of 5th Earl of Oxford and (Earl) Mortimer (see OXFORD AND ASQUITH, preliminary remarks, also 1853 edn), and dsp 26 Feb1853

(6) Granville VERNON-HARCOURT later HARCOURT VERNON, of Grove Hall, E Retford, Notts; b 26 July 1792; barrister, Chllr York Diocese; m 1st 22 Feb 1814 Frances Julia (d 5 Feb 1844), dau and coheir of Anthony Hardolph Eyre, of Grove, Notts; m 2nd 22 Nov 1845 Pyne Jesse Brand Trevor (d 3 March 1872), dau of 21st Lord (Baron) Dacre (qv) and widow of John Henry Cottrell, and d 8 Dec 1879, having by his 1st w had, with another s (d young):

1a Granville Edward; b 23 Nov 1816; MP Newark; m 23 Nov 1854 Lady Selina Catherine Meade (m 2nd 8 July 1862 John Bidwell (d 22 Aug 1873) and 3rd 14 Aug 1880 Henry Arthur William Hervey, CB (d 11 May 1908), and d 20 Nov 1911), only dau of 3rd Earl of Clanwilliam (qv), and dsp 1 Feb 1861

2a Evelyn Hardolph (Rev), of Grove Hall; b 30 Aug 1821; Preb Lincoln; m 19 April 1849 Jane Catherine (d 15 May 1891), yst dau of Edward St John-Mildmay (see ST JOHN-MILDMAY, Bt), and d 26 Jan 1890, having had, with another dau (d unm):

1b Edward Evelyn, JP, DL, of Grove Hall; b 19 Jan 1853; CC, High Sheriff Notts 1894, Capt Notts Yeo Cav; m 1st 9 Sept 1879 Grace (d 9 March 1881), dau of Rev Alleyne FitzHerbert (see FitzHERBERT, Bt), and had:

1c Hardolph Venables; b 3 March, d 11 March 1881

1b (cont.) Edward Harcourt Vernon m 2nd 22 Aug 1883 Frances Theresa (d 20 Feb 1937), dau of Sir William FitzHerbert, 4th Bt (qv), and d 16 May 1932, having by her had:

2c Granville Charles FitzHerbert, DSO (1916), OBE (1945), MC (1919), JP (Notts 1932 and Brecon 1939); b 30 May 1891; educ Eton; Lt-Col Gren Gds WW I (wounded three times, despatches), WW II; m 17 Oct 1925 Celine (d 12 April 1949), dau of M Van Hecke, of Brussels, and dsp 21 Feb 1974

3c (Egerton) Gervase Edward, MC (1919); b 13 July 1899; educ Eton; Capt Gren Gds (SR), WWs I and II; m 29 June 1932 *Norma [Mrs Gervase Harcourt-Vernon, Little Tudor, Cranbrook, Kent], dau of George William Hatherley, and d 14 Feb 1976, leaving:

1d *Anne Letitia; b 23 Nov 1933; SRN, SCM

2d *Pamela Teresa Marigold [Mrs Antony Cox, Wensley Hall, nr Matlock, Derbys DE4 2LL]; b 30 June 1938; educ Bedgebury Park, London U (BSc 1958) and Newnham Coll Cambridge (MA 1965); m 1 July 1961 *Antony Dawson Cox, FRCP, FRCPsych, FRCPCH, Emeritus Prof UMDS London U, s of William Ronald Cox, of Canterbury, and has:

1e *Simon; b 10 Oct 1962; m 24 June 1989 *Antonia, dau of Dr Edgar Feuchtwanger, of Dean, Hants, and has:

1f *George Leo Vernon; b 6 Jan 1994

2f *Thomas Gerrard Kennedy; b 31 Oct 1996

2e *Nicholas; b 19 Jan 1964; m 15 June 1996 *Kitty, dau of Adrian Secker, of Iver, Bucks

3e *Hugo Francis; b 14 June 1967

3d *Rosalind Elizabeth Ida [Mrs Christopher Howell, 36 Guards Club Rd, Maidenhead, Berkshire SL6 8BN]; b 29 July 1942; educ Bedgebury Park and Bp Otter Coll Chichester; m 6 Aug 1966 *Christopher Howell, s of Albert Howell, of Highcliffe, Hants, and has:

1e *Candida Justine; b 1969

2e *Madeleine Theresa; b 1977

1c Sybil Ida; b 6 June 1884; d unm 17 Jan 1954

2c Ida Beatrice; b 26 Sept 1885; MSc, AIC; d unm 6 April 1973

3c Muriel Theresa; b 13 June 1887; m 5 April 1921 Walter Gordon Duncan (d 10 Sept 1930), 2nd s of Walter Duncan, and d 22 Feb 1975

4c Evelyn Hermione; b 27 May 1889; d unm 23 Aug 1943

2b Algernon Hardolph (Rev); b 7 July 1858; Vicar Clocolan, S Africa, Canon Bloemfontein Cathedral; m 1st 1881 Kate (d 5 April 1883), dau of J Candler, and had:

1c Janet Kate; b 27 March 1883; m 7 Feb 1906 Capt Dugald Stewart Gilkison, Scottish Rifles (ka 1914), and d 21 Aug 1969, leaving issue

2b (cont.) The Rev Algernon Harcourt Vernon m 2nd 5 May 1886 Georgiana Marguerite (d 27 July 1951), dau of John Martin, and d 15 Dec 1936, having had by her:

1c Granville Arthur; b 1888; Natal Roy Carabiniers, RAF WW I, Special Serv WW II; m 21 Feb 1928 Mrs Mary Muriel Champion (née Sutherland), of Larne, NI, and d 19 May 1964

2c Hardolph Evelyn; b 1889; 2nd Rhodesians WW I; ka E Africa May 1915

2c Dorothy Margaret; b 1887; d 19–

3c Marjorie Frances; b 1891; m 1924 Capt Ritchie Francis Henry Moffet (d 16 Jan 1957), RAF and SAAF; d 19–

3b Walter Granville; b 31 Oct 1860; Lt 4th Bn Sherwood Foresters; m 1884 Helen Rebecca (d 1926), dau of J W Traer, and d Nov 1937, leaving:

1c Evelyn Maude; b 5 Nov 1882; d unm 26 March 1943

4b Herbert Evelyn; b 12 Jan 1863; Lt 4th Bn Sherwood Foresters; m 14 Nov 1885 Mary Adelaide (d 13 July 1936), dau of Hon George W Allan, Senator Canada, and d 17 Dec 1943, having had:

1c Humphrey Bingham; *b* 24 March 1889; *d* 3 May 1909

2c Arthur Arundell; *b* 12 Oct 1895; E Surrey Regt, RFC and RAF WW I, RCAF WW II; *m* 12 Sept 1925 (Alice) Margaret (*d* 1977), est dau of Rev Edward Cartwright Cayley (*see* CAYLEY, Bt), and *d* June 1971, leaving:

  1d +Granville Patrick [Granville Harcourt Vernon Esq, 57 Glengowan Rd, Toronto, Ont M4N IG3, Canada]; *b* 15 Nov 1926; *educ* U of Toronto (BA); LLB, QC; *m* 11 Sept 1954 *Deborah Perry Smith, dau of Walter Dent Smith, of Toronto and Wilmington, Del., and has:

    1e +Geoffrey William [Geoffrey Harcourt Vernon Esq, 20 Elmer Ave, Toronto, Ont, Canada]; *b* 7 April 1958; BA Toronto, BLA Guelph; *m* 1980 (*divorce* 1994) Cynthia Jane Gunn and has:

      1f *Caitlin Elizabeth; *b* 1988

      2f *Julia Robin; *b* 1991

    1e *Catherine [Mrs Robert Martin, 71 Rosedale Heights Drive, Toronto, Ont, Canada]; *b* 6 March 1956; BA Queen's, MBA Western Ontario; *m* 1987 *Robert Bruce McFarran Martin and has:

      1f *Richard; *b* 1988

      2f *Stephen Taylor; *b* 1990

      3f *Scott Edward; *b* 1993

    2e *Susan Elizabeth [Mme Denis Pellerin, 22 bis rue de Sevres, 92150 Suresnes, France]; *b* 13 Nov 1961; BSc Queen's, MBA INSEAD; *m* 1992 *Denis Pellerin and has:

      1f *Sarah Caroline; *b* 26 Feb 1996

  2d +Hugh [Hugh Harcourt Vernon Esq, 176 Melrose Ave, Toronto M5M 1Z1, Canada]; *b* 27 Sept 1930; *educ* Toronto U (BA); *m* 1st 27 June 1953 Elizabeth Virginia Richardson, dau of Harold Richard Forbes Richardson, DDS, of Toronto; *m* 2nd 1978 *Shirley Rose Archer, dau of Cecil Ernest Woodford, of Prestatyn, Clwyd, and formerly w of — Archer, and has by his 1st w:

    1e +Christopher Hugh; *b* 24 July 1956

    1e *Nancy Margaret; *b* 7 May 1960

    1e *Tannis Elizabeth; *b* 21 Feb 1964

  3d +John Anthony [John Harcourt Vernon Esq, 1565 Bigbay Point Rd, RR#4 Barrie, Ont L4M 4S6, Canada]; *b* 6 April 1938; *educ* York U (BA); *m* 1975 *Susan Elaine dau of Thomas Tinniswood Vaulkhard, of Victoria, BC, and has:

    1e +Mark Nicholas; *b* 1984

    2e +Stephen Andrew; *b* 1984

    1e *Marin Georgina; *b* 1982

  1d *Joy [Ms Joy Harcourt Vernon, 977 Highview Terrace, Nanaimo, BC V9R 6K5, Canada]; *b* 5 Aug 1934; *educ* U of BC (BA, MSW)

  2d *Rosemary [Mrs John Moorhead, Sussex Corner, New Brunswick E0E 1R0, Canada]; *b* 29 Dec 1935; *educ* U of Toronto (BA); *m* 4 June 1960 *Rev John Francis Moorhead, Rector St Paul's, Dauphin, Manitoba, s of Rt Rev William Henry Moorhead, and has:

    1e *Margaret Patricia; *b* 17 March 1961

    2e *Nancy Catherine; *b* 22 July 1967

    3e *Cynthia Mabel; *b* 1970

1c Marjorie Catherine; *b* 24 March 1892; *d* 10 Dec 1893

1b Mary Frances; *m* 24 April 1879 Rev Algernon Frederick Ebsworth (*d* 22 Feb 1918), Rector W Tofts, Vicar Stanford, Norfolk, and *d* 7 Oct 1940, leaving issue

2b Frances Jessie; Mother Superior St Michael's House, Bloemfontein, SA; *d* 5 Sept 1938

3b Selina Jane; *m* 6 Sept 1893 Paulet Bertram St John-Mildmay (*see* ST JOHN-MILDMAY, Bt) and *d* July 1925

3a Henry Arthur; *b* July 1825; Maj RA; *d* unm 12 Nov 1862

4a Charles Egerton; *b* 13 June 1827; Capt RN; *m* 25 July 1865 Louisa Anne, yst dau of Capt Garth, RN, of Haines Hill, Berks, and *d* 14 May 1872, having had a dau (*d* an infant)

1a Marianne Frances; *m* 20 Sept 1843 Humphrey St John-Mildmay, MP, 6th s of Sir Henry St John-Mildmay, 3rd Bt (*qv*), and *d* 13 Feb 1873, leaving issue

(7) Octavius Henry; *b* 26 Dec 1793; V-Adml; *m* 22 Feb 1838 Anne Holwell (*d* 26 June 1879), dau of William Gater and widow of William Danby, of Swinton Park, Yorks, and *d* 14 Aug 1863

(8) Charles (Rev); *b* 14 Nov 1798; Preb Carlisle; *d* unm 10 Dec 1870

(9) Francis, JP (Sussex), of St Clare, IoW, and Buxted Park, Sussex; *b* 6 Jan 1801; Col, Equerry to HRH THE DUCHESS OF KENT; *m* 20 Nov 1837 Catherine Julia (*d* 5 Dec 1877), est dau of 3rd Earl of Liverpool (*see* JENKINSON, Bt), and *dsp* 23 April 1880

(10) Egerton, JP, DL, of St Clare and Whitwell; *b* 1803; *m* 8 Dec 1859 Laura (*d* 5 Feb 1889), dau of Sir William Milner, 4th Bt (*qv*), and *d* 19 Oct 1883

(1) Louisa Augusta; *m* 14 June 1825 Sir John Vanden-Bempdé-Johnstone, 2nd Bt, and *d* 4 Aug 1869, leaving issue (*see* DERWENT, B)

(2) Georgiana; *m* 4 Dec 1846 Gen George A Malcolm, CB (*d* 2 June 1888), and *dsp* 29 Oct 1886

2 Elizabeth; *m* 26 Sept 1765 her cousin 2nd EARL HARCOURT OF STANTON HARCOURT (*see* **Lineage (of Harcourt)** below) and *dsp* 25 Jan 1826

The 2nd BARON's half-bro,

  HENRY VENABLES-VERNON later SEDLEY (roy licence 19 March 1779) later VENABLES-VERNON again (on inheriting the title 18 June 1813), **3rd Lord Vernon, Baron of Kinderton**; *b* 17 April 1747; *educ* Westminster; Groom Bedchamber 1770–1809; *m* 1st 14 Feb 1779 Elizabeth Rebecca Anne Nash *alias* Sedley (*d* 16 Aug 1793), illegitimate dau and heiress of Sir Charles Sedley, 2nd and last Bt, of Nuthall, Notts, and had:

1 GEORGE CHARLES, **4th Baron**

1 Catherine; *d* 29 April 1867 aged 85

2 Louisa Henrietta; *m* 4 Nov 1816 Rev Brooke Boothby (*see* BOOTHBY, Bt) and *d* 6 March 1861, leaving issue

The **3rd Baron** *m* 2nd 29 Nov 1795 Alice Lucy (*d* 1 Aug 1827), dau of Sir John Whiteford, 3rd Bt, and *d* 27 March 1829, leaving by her:

2 Henry; *b* 1796; Lt-Col Gren Gds; *m* 29 Aug 1822 Eliza Grace, dau of Edward Coke, of Longford Court, Derbys (*see* LEICESTER, E), and *d* 12 Dec 1845, leaving, with a dau (*d* unm):

  (1) Edward Henry; *b* 5 July 1823; Lt RN; *m* 21 Jan 1851 Louisa Sophia Charlotte (*d* 1895), dau of Ven J G de Joux, Archdeacon Mauritius, and *d* 7 Jan 1856, leaving:

    1a William Henry (Sir), KBE (1921); *b* 1 Jan 1852; Slr-Gen Jersey 1880, Attorney-Gen 1884, Cdre Roy CI Yacht Club, Balliff and Pres Roy Court and States of Jersey 1899–1931, ktd 1903, Hon LLD U of Caen 1923; *m* 18 Dec 1880 Julia Matilda (*d* 5 March 1954), only child of Philip Gosset, of Bagot Manor, Jersey, and *d* 23 Jan 1934

3 John (Rev); *b* 8 March 1798; Rector Nuthall and Kirkby-in-Ashfield, Notts; *m* 1st 24 Nov 1830 Frances Barbara (*d* 7 Dec 1848), 2nd dau of Thomas Duncombe (*see* FEVERSHAM, B); *m* 2nd 15 Dec 1853 Caroline (*d* 17 July 1894), yr dau of Gen Hon Sir Edward Paget, GCB (*see* ANGLESEY, M), and *d* 11 Dec 1875, having by his 1st w had:

  (1) Frederick; *b* 8 Oct 1834; *d* 20 March 1835

The 3rd BARON's est s,

  GEORGE CHARLES SEDLEY later VENABLES-VERNON, **4th Lord Vernon, Baron of Kinderton**; *b* 4 Dec 1779; *educ* Westminster; Capt 2nd Foot Gds (Coldstream Gds); *m* 5 Aug 1802 Frances Maria (took by roy licence 26 June 1826 the name WARREN only under terms of will of Dowager Viscountess Bulkeley of Cashel (*née* Warren) and *s* to the Poynton estate, Cheshire; *d* 17 Sept 1837), only dau and heiress of Adml Sir John Borlase Warren, Bt, GCB, PC, and *d* 18 Nov 1835, leaving:

  GEORGE JOHN VENABLES-VERNON later WARREN (roy licence 14 Oct 1837), **5th Lord Vernon, Baron of Kinderton**; *b* 22 June 1803; *educ* Eton and Ch Ch Oxford; MP (Whig) Derbys 1831–32 and S Derbys 1832–34; *m* 1st 30 Oct 1824 Isabella Caroline (*d* 14 Oct 1853), est dau of Cuthbert Ellison, JP, DL of Hebburn, Co Durham; *m* 2nd 14 Dec 1859 his cousin Frances Maria Emma (*m* 2nd 19 July 1881 Rev Charles Martyn Reed and *d* 29 May 1907), only dau of Rev Brooke Boothby (*see* above), and *d* 31 May 1866, having by his 1st w had, with another s (*d* an infant):

1 AUGUSTUS HENRY, **6th Baron**

2 William John VENABLES-VERNON later BORLASE-WARREN-VENABLES-VERNON, JP (Derbys and Staffs), DL (Staffs); *b* 1 April 1834; Accademico Corrispondente della Crusca Florence, Socio Corrispondente del Reale Instituto Lombardo di Scienza e Letteratura Milan, Commendatore Order Crown Italy, Cav Order SS. Maurice and Lazarus Italy, Kt Roy Order St Olaf Norway; *m* 1st 8 May 1855 Agnes Lucy (*d* 30 Sept 1881), 3rd dau of Sir John Peter Boileau,1st Bt (*qv*), and had:

  (1) Reginald William; *b* 27 Jan 1856; *m* 20 May 1879 Edith Georgiana Cowper (*m* 2nd 7 March 1918 D J Dewar-Murray), est dau of William Smith Cowper Cooper, of Toddington Manor, Beds, and *d* 26 April 1912, leaving:

    1a Agnes Ida; *b* 16 Jan 1882; *d* unm 19–

    2a Mabel Eveline; *b* 17 Feb 1883; *m* 17 Feb 1909 Frank Southby Walker

2 (cont.) William Borlase-Warren-Venables-Vernon *m* 2nd 25 Feb 1884 Annie Georgiana (*d* 6 Aug 1933), dau of Charles Eyre, of Welford, Berks, and *d* 12 Nov 1919, having by her had:

  (2) Arnold; *b* 18 Oct 1887; Lt-Cdr Gren Gds; *m* 3 Dec 1909 (*divorce* 1935) Col Frederic Ernest Wilson, IMS, s of Maj Wilson, Scots Greys, and *d* 23 May 1957, leaving issue

  (1) Mary Anne Alice; *b* 23 March 1885; Midshipman RN; *d* 19 June 1906

1 Caroline Maria; *m* 7 May 1845 Rev Frederick Anson (*see* LICHFIELD, E) and *d* 20 Aug 1918 aged 92, leaving issue

2 Adelaide Louisa; *m* 12 June 1855 Adm Sir Reginald John Macdonald, KCB, KCSI, 20th of Clanranald (*d* 15 Dec 1899), and *d* 27 April 1913, leaving issue

3 Louisa Warren; *m* 16 April 1873 Rev Thomas Parry Garnier (*d* 18 March 1898), Rector Cranworth with Letton and Southburgh, Norfolk, Hon Canon Norwich, and *d* 1894, leaving issue

The 5th BARON's est s,

  AUGUSTUS HENRY VENABLES-VERNON, **6th Lord Vernon, Baron of Kinderton**; *b* 1 Feb 1829; *educ* Magdalene Coll Cambridge; Capt Scots Fus Gds; Pres Roy Ag Soc; *m* 7 June 1851 Lady Harriet Anson (*d* 15 Feb 1898), 3rd dau of 1st Earl of Lichfield (*qv*), and *d* 1 May 1883, having had, with two other sons and another dau (*d* in infancy):

1 GEORGE WILLIAM HENRY, **7th Baron**

2 William Frederick Cuthbert; *b* 18 July 1856; *m* 17 April 1884 Louisa, 3rd dau of Brig-Gen D M Frost, US Army, of St Louis, Mo., and *d* 2 Aug 1913, having had, with two daus (*d* in infancy):

  (1) Richard Henry; *b* 27 Jan 1885; *d* 9 April 1921

  (2) William Walter; *b* 22 April 1890; 2nd Lt RE, S Staffs Regt; *ka* 11 Oct 1916

1 Diana; *b* 22 Feb 1852; *m* 4 May 1896 Charles Edmund Newton, DL (*d* 2 July 1908), of Mickleover Manor, Derbys, and *d* 22 July 1920

2 Mildred; *b* 8 Feb 1853; *m* 2 Nov 1878 Hon Henry Augustus Stanhope, of Ashe Warren, Overton, Hants, 3rd s of 5th Earl Stanhope (*see* 1967 edn CHESTERFIELD and STANHOPE, E), and *d* 18 March 1915, leaving issue

3 Margaret; *b* 15 May 1865; *m* 4 Aug 1887 Rev Frederick Tufnell (*d* 28 Feb 1920), 3rd s of Edward Carleton Tufnell, barrister, and *d* 27 Dec 1888, leaving issue

4 Alice; *b* 13 Feb 1868; *m* 1 Feb 1896 Rev Somerset Corry Lowry (*d* 29 Jan 1932) and *d* 2 Oct 1933, leaving issue

5 Adela; *b* 12 Oct 1870; *m* 9 April 1896 R-Adml Algernon Horatio Anson and *d* 1 Jan 1931, leaving issue (*see* ANSON, Bt)

The 6th BARON's est s,

  GEORGE WILLIAM HENRY VENABLES-VERNON, **7th Lord Vernon, Baron of Kinderton**, PC (1892); *b* 25 Feb 1854; *educ* Eton; Lt Scots Gds, Capt 12th Lancers and Hon Corps Gentlemen-at-Arms 1892–94, memb Roy Commn Ag 1893–94, V-Chm Assoc Chambers Commerce; *m* 14 July 1885 Frances Margaret (*d* 23 June 1940), dau of Francis C Lawrance, of New York, and *d* 15 Dec 1898, having had:

1 GEORGE FRANCIS AUGUSTUS VENABLES-VERNON, **8th Lord Vernon, Baron of Kinderton**; *b* 28 Sept 1888; *educ* Eton and Ch Ch Oxford; Capt Derbys Yeo 1914, Dip Serv: Hon Attaché Constantinople 1908, Munich 1909; Capt Derbys Yeo WW I; *d* unm 10 Nov 1915 of illness contracted on active serv at Gallipoli

2 FRANCIS LAWRANCE WILLIAM, **9th Baron**

1 Fanny Lawrance; *b* 8 July 1886; *m* 1st 15 June 1910 Maurice Raoul Duval (*ka* 18 May 1916), of the Château de Marolles, and had issue; *m* 2nd 1918 Lt Jean de Kermaignant

The 8th BARON's bro,

FRANCIS LAWRANCE WILLIAM VENABLES-VERNON, **9th Lord Vernon, Baron of Kinderton**, DL (Derbys); *b* 6 Nov 1889; *educ* Eton and Ch Ch Oxford; Lt-Cdr RN WW I N Sea and Mediterranean; *m* 9 Feb 1915 Violet Miriam Nightingale (*d* 28 Sept 1978 aged 83), dau of Col Charles Herbert Clay, and *d* 18 March 1963, leaving:

1 JOHN LAWRANCE VENABLES-VERNON, **10th and present Lord Vernon, Baron of Kinderton**

1 Avice Irene; *b* 28 June 1919; *m* 16 March 1940 *Francis William Marten, CMG, MC, late Dip Serv, Hon Lt-Col Rifle Bde, er s of V-Adml Sir Francis Arthur Marten, KBE, CMG, of Whittington, Glos, and *d* 7 Aug 1964, leaving a s and dau

Lineage (of Harcourt): TURCHETIL, Sire de Harcourt, Normandy; *fl* 1024; presumably kin to:

WILLIAM de HARCOURT; had, with an er s (Robert, ancestor of the Ducs d' Harcourt in France):

IVO de HARCOURT; inherited his f's English lands; had:

Sir ROBERT de HARCOURT; Sheriff Leics and Warwicks 1199, 1201 and 1202; *m* Millicent, only child of Richard de Camville (possibly the Richard de Camville who was half-bro of William de Camville, f of the 1st Lord (Baron) Camville/Canville of the notional 24 Jan 1295 *cr*; *see* also above against the Sir Richard Vernon who *d* Feb 1322/3), of Stanton, Oxon, thus acquiring that Manor, which became known subsequently as Stanton Harcourt, and *d* 1202, leaving:

Sir WILLIAM de HARCOURT, of Stanton Harcourt; *m* Alice, est dau of Sir Thomas Noel (*see* GAINSBOROUGH, E), of Ronton and Ellenhall, Staffs, which latter manor he thus acquired, and had an er s:

Sir RICHARD de HARCOURT, of Stanton Harcourt and Ellenhall; *m* Arabella, dau of 1st Earl of Winchester of the *cr* made *c* Feb 1206/7 (*see* WINCHESTER, M, preliminary remarks), thus acquiring the Manor of Bosworth, and *d* 1258, leaving an er s:

Sir WILLIAM de HARCOURT, of Stanton Harcourt, Ellenhall and Bosworth; *m* 1st Alice, dau of Roger la Zouche (*see* ZOUCHE, B) and had two daus (Margaret, *m* Sir John Cantelupe (cognate with Cauntelo?) and *dsp*; Arabella, *m* Fulco de Pembruge; *see* above against the Sir Richard Vernon who *d* 1377); *m* 2nd Eleanor/Hillaria, dau of Sir Henry de Hastings by Ada, dau of David, Earl of Huntingdon (*see* HASTINGS, B), and by her had:

Sir RICHARD de HARCOURT, of Stanton Harcourt; *m* Margaret, 2nd dau of 1st and last Lord (Baron) Beke of the notional 1295 *cr* (*see* WILLOUGHBY DE ERESBY, B), and *d* 1293, leaving an er s:

Sir JOHN de HARCOURT, of Stanton Harcourt; ktd 1306; *m* 1st Eleanor, dau of Eudo la Zouche (possibly the same person as the Eon (Eon being an alternative form of Eudo) la Zouche who was f of the 1st Lord (Baron) (La) Zouche (*qv*) (of Haryngworth)); *m* 2nd Alice, dau of Peter Corbet, of Caus Castle, Salop (quite possibly that Piers or Peter Corbet who was called to Parl by writ of summons 24 June 1295, thus according to later doctrine becoming 1st Lord (Baron) Corbet; *see* also 1970 edn CORBET, Bt), and *d* 1330, leaving by his 1st w:

Sir WILLIAM de HARCOURT, of Stanton Harcourt; *m* Jane (*m* 2nd Ralph de Ferrers), possibly dau of Sir Richard de Grey (*see* GREY, B), and *d* 6 June 1349, having had, with an er s (Sir Richard, *m* Joan, dau of Sir William de Shareshull, of Sharehull, Staffs, and *dvp*, leaving a dau Elizabeth):

Sir THOMAS HARCOURT, of Stanton Harcourt; MP Oxon 1376; *m* Alice/Eleanor/Maud, dau of John, (probably Lord (Baron) Grey (of Rotherfield), and widow of Sir John Botetourt, and *d* 12 April 1417, leaving an est s:

Sir THOMAS HARCOURT, of Stanton Harcourt; *m* Joan, dau of Sir Robert Francis, of Foremark, Derbys, and had, with other issue:

1 Robert (Sir), KG, of Stanton Harcourt; Commr to negotiate peace with France 1476; *m* Margaret, dau of Sir John Byron, of Clayton, Lancs (*see* BYRON, B), and was *k* 14 Nov 1470, leaving, with three other sons (*dsp*):

   (1) John (Sir), of Stanton Harcourt; *m* Anne, dau of Sir John Norreys, of Bray, Berks (*see* LINDSEY and ABINGDON, E), and *d* 26 June 1485, leaving an only surv s:

      1a Robert (Sir), KB, of Stanton Harcourt; Standard Bearer to HENRY VII at Battle of Bosworth; *m* Agnes, dau of Thomas Lymbrake, and had five surv daus

2 Richard (Sir), of Wytham, Berks; *m* 1st Edith, dau of Thomas St Clere; *m* 2nd Eleanor, dau of Sir Roger Lewknor, of Raunton, Staffs, and by her had issue; *m* 3rd Katherine, widow of Sir Miles Stapleton, of Bedale, Yorks, and heir of Thomas de la Pole, and had by his 1st w, with at least one dau (Anne, *m de jure* 3rd Lord (Baron) Saye and Sele; *qv*), an est s:

   (1) Christopher (Sir); *m* Jane, dau of Sir Miles Stapleton, and *dvp*, leaving, with two other sons (*dsp*):

      1a Simon (Sir); inherited Stanton Harcourt; ktd 1513; *m* 1st Agnes, dau of Thomas Dayrell, of Scotney; *m* 2nd Elizabeth, widow of Sir Richard Yorke and dau of 1st Baron Darcy (of Aston), and *d* 1547, leaving by his 1st w an er s:

         1b John (Sir), of Stanton Harcourt; *m* Margaret, dau and ultimate heiress of Sir William Barentyne, of Hasley, Oxon, and *d* 19 Feb 1564/5, leaving, with five yr sons and eight daus:

            1c Simon (Sir), of Stanton Harcourt; *m* 1st Mary, dau of Sir Edward Aston, of Tixall, Staffs; *m* 2nd Grace, widow of William Robinson, of

Drayton Vassett, Staffs, and dau of Humphrey Fitzherbert, of Upsal, Herefs; *m* 3rd Jane, dau of Sir William Spencer, of Wormleighton, Warwicks (*see* MARLBOROUGH, D), and widow of Sir Richard Bruges, of Shefford, Berks; his est s, presumably by his 1st w:

   1d Walter (Sir), of Stanton Harcourt and Ellenhall; ktd 1591; *m* Dorothy, dau of William Robinson, of Drayton Bassett, and had an er s:

      1e Robert (Sir), of Stanton Harcourt; explored Guyana 1609; *m* 1st Frances, dau of Geoffrey de Vere (*see* SAINT ALBANS, D); *m* 2nd Elizabeth, dau of John Fitzherbert, of Padley, Derbys (*see* STAFFORD, B), and *d* 1631, leaving (presumably by his 1st w) an est s:

         1f Simon (Sir), of Stanton Harcourt; ktd 1627, cmded a regt against Scots 1639–40, Govr Dublin 1641; *m* Anne (*m* 2nd Sir William Waller, of Osterley Park, Middx), dau of (5th?) Baron Paget (*see* ANGLESEY, M), and was *k* 1642 at Kilgobbin Castle, Co Wicklow, by adherents of the Irish Uprising that had broken out the year before, leaving an est s:

            1g Philip (Sir), of Stanton Harcourt; ktd 1660, MP Oxon 1680–88; *m* 1st Anne (*d* 23 Aug 1664), dau of Sir William Waller, of Osterley Park, and had:

               1h SIMON, 1st VISCOUNT

            1g (cont.) Sir Philip *m* 2nd Elizabeth, dau of John Lee, of Ankerwycke, Wraysbury, Bucks, and *d* 20 March 1687/8, leaving further issue, being by her ancestor of the HARCOURTs of Ankerwycke

Sir PHILIP's s,

SIMON HARCOURT, 1st VISCOUNT HARCOURT OF STANTON HARCOURT, Co Oxford, so *cr* 11 Sept 1721, as also earlier 3 Sept 1711 BARON HARCOURT OF STANTON HARCOURT, Co Oxford (both GB), PC (1710–154 and 1722); *b* Dec 1661; *educ* Pembroke Coll Oxford (DCL 1702); barrister Inner Temple 1683 (Treas 1702–03), Recorder Abingdon 1686, MP (Tory) Abingdon 1690–1705, 1708–09 and 1710, Bossiney 1705–08 and Cardigan Feb–Sept 1710, Slr-Gen 1702–07, ktd 1703, Commr for Union of S and E Parls 1706, Attorney Gen April 1707–Feb 1707/8 and Sept–Oct 1710, Ld Keeper 1710, Ld Chllr 1713–14, Tory to *c* 1720, Whig thereafter; *m* 1st 18 Oct 1680 Rebecca, dau of Rev Thomas Clark; *m* 2nd Elizabeth (*dsp* 16 June 1724), dau of Richard Spencer, of Derbys and London, and widow of Richard Anderson, of Penley, Herts; *m* 3rd 30 Sept 1724 Elizabeth, dau of Sir Thomas Vernon (*see* above) and widow of Sir John Walter, 3rd Bt, and *d* 28 July 1727, having by his 1st w had an only surv s:

SIMON HARCOURT; *b c* 1685; bought the Nuneham Courtney estate 1719 from 4th Earl of Wemyss (*see* WEMYSS and MARCH, E) for £17,000 (just over £1,000,000 in late-1990s terms); *m* Elizabeth, dau of John Evelyn, of Wotton, Surrey, and *dvp* 1 July 1720, leaving, with two other daus (*d* young):

1 SIMON HARCOURT, 1st EARL HARCOURT OF STANTON HARCOURT, Co Oxford, so *cr* 1 Dec 1749, as also VISCOUNT NUNEHAM OF NUNEHAM COURTNEY [*sic*], Co Oxford (both GB), PC (1751); *b* 1714; *educ* Westminster; a Ld Bedchamber 1735–51, Col 1745, Maj-Gen 1755, Lt Gen 1759, Gen 1772, Govr to PRINCE OF WALES (later GEORGE IV) 1751–52, Master Horse and Ld Chamberlain to QUEEN CHARLOTTE 1761–63 and 1763–68 respectively, Amb Paris 1768–72, Ld Lt Ireland 1772–77; *m* 16 Oct 1735 Rebecca, only dau of Charles Samborne Le Bas, of Pipewell Abbey, Northants, and *d* 16 Sept 1777, apparently by drowning in a well at Nuneham Park while trying to rescue his dog, which had fallen into the well too, leaving:

   (1) GEORGE SIMON HARCOURT, 2nd EARL HARCOURT OF STANTON HARCOURT; *b* 1 Aug 1736; *educ* Westminster; MP (Whig) St Albans 1761–68, DCL Oxon 1786, Master Horse to QUEEN CHARLOTTE 1790–1809; played host to his distant cousin the Duc d'Harcourt when the latter was a refugee in England from the French Revolution; *m* 26 Sept 1765 his cousin Hon Elizabeth Venables-Vernon (*see* **Lineage (of Vernon)** above) and *dsp* 20 April 1809

   (2) WILLIAM HARCOURT, 3rd and last EARL HARCOURT OF STANTON HARCOURT, GCB (1820); *b* 20 March 1742/3; Ensign 1759, Lt-Col 31st Foot 1764, Light Dragoons 1765 and 16th Light Dragoons 1768 (Col 1779–1830), served War American Independence, Col 1777, Maj-Gen 1782, Lt Gen 1793, Gen 1798, Equerry to QUEEN CHARLOTTE 1761–67, ADC to GEORGE III 1777–80, Extra Groom Bedchamber 1766, MP (Tory) Oxford 1768–74, Govr Fort William 1794–95, Hull 1795–1801, Portsmouth 1811–26 and Plymouth 1826–30, Govr RMC 1801–11, Master Robes 1808–09, Master Horse to QUEEN CHARLOTTE 1809–18, Dep Ranger Windsor Gt Pk 1806–30, FM 1821; *m* 3 Sept 1778 Mary, est dau of Rev William Danby, of Swinton, Yorks, and widow of Thomas Lockhart, of Craighouse, and *dsp* 17 June 1830, when his titles expired

1 Martha; *b* 15 July 1715; *m* 10 April 1744, as his 3rd w, **1st Lord Vernon, Baron of Kinderton** (*see* **Lineage (of Vernon)** above), and *d* 8 April 1794, leaving issue, who became the representatives of the HARCOURTs

VERNON, Bt

Arms: Or on a fess azure between two crosses moline in pale gules three garbs of the field. **Crest:** In front of a demi-female figure affrontée proper vested azure, around the temples an oak wreath vert, holding in the dexter hand a sickle and in the sinister two ears of wheat slipped also proper, a garb fesswise or. **Motto:** *Vernon semper viret* ('Vernon ever flourishes/Spring does not last forever').
Creation: Bt. (UK) 24 Jan 1914.

SIR NIGEL JOHN DOUGLAS VERNON, 4TH BT, of Shotwick Park, Co Chester [Sir Nigel Vernon Bt, Top-y-Fron Hall, Kelsterton, Clwyd CH6 5TF]; *b* 2 May 1924; *s f* 1967; *educ* Charterhouse; Lt RNVR WW II 1942–45, with Spillers 1945–65, dir: Castle Brick Co 1965–71, Deeside Merchants 1971–74 and Travel Finance 1971–87, late chm Joseph Heap & Sons (rice millers), dir Hogg Insur Brokers 1986–96 and AON Risk Services Ltd 1996–; *m* 29 Nov 1947 *Margaret Ellen, est dau of Robert Lyle Dobell, of The Mount, Waverton, nr Chester, and has had:

1 +JAMES WILLIAM [James Vernon Esq, The Hall, Lygan-y-Wern, Pentre Halkyn, Clwyd CH8 8BD]; *b* 2 April 1949; *educ* Shrewsbury; FCA, ptnr Grant Thornton; *m* 30 May 1981 *Davinia Elizabeth, er dau of Christopher David Howard (*see* PORTMAN, V), and has:

  (1) +George William Howard; *b* 25 July 1987

  (2) +Guy Alexander Howard; *b* 26 April 1993

  (1) *Harriet Lucy Howard; *b* 29 May 1985

2 John Alan; *b* 18 Sept 1956; *educ* Shrewsbury; *d* 1987

1 *Caroline Margaret; *b* 29 July 1953; *m* 5 Sept 1974 (*divorce* 1978) Simon Jonathan Salusbury-Trelawny (*see* SALUSBURY-TRELAWNY, Bt)

Lineage: WILLIAM VERNON, of Cogshull, Gt Budworth, Cheshire; *b c* 1434; held land in the Manor of Halton 1460; *m* Emma — and *d* by 1507, leaving:

RICHARD VERNON, of Cogshull; features in Halton manorial court rolls 1494–1513; had:

RICHARD VERNON, of Cogshull; *m* Alice — and *d* by 1546, leaving:

THOMAS VERNON, of Barnton, Gt Budworth; *bur* 10 March 1592, leaving:

THOMAS VERNON, of Barnton; *m* Margaret — and was *bur* 8 March 1610, leaving, with two er sons:

RICHARD VERNON, of Aston, Gt Budworth; *m* 1st — and had issue; *m* 2nd 1619 Jane Forest and *d* April 1634; his 3rd s by his 1st w:

JOHN VERNON, of Aston; *bur* 21 July 1659, having had, with two yr sons and a dau:

THOMAS VERNON, of Aston, later of Allostock, Gt Budworth; *bapt* 28 Feb 1639/40; *m* Mary — (*bur* 17 April 1687) and was *bur* 9 Nov 1695, having had, with an er s and two daus:

THOMAS VERNON, of Somerford Booths, Cheshire; *bapt* 14 Aug 1675; *m* 30 Dec 1704 Hannah Winkle, of Blackdon, and was *bur* 10 June 1744, having had, with an er s and three daus:

RICHARD VERNON, of Mutlow, Gawsworth, Cheshire; *b* 1715; *m* 20 Jan 1737 Ann Wood (*bur* 12 Feb 1795), of Astbury, Cheshire, and *d* 16 Jan 1790, having had, with two er sons and a yst s:

JOHN VERNON, of Mutlow; *bapt* 26 Sept 1748; *m* 14 Oct 1770 Nancy Thornycroft (*d* 24 Dec 1812), of Gawsworth, and *d* 4 Dec 1809, having had, with two yr sons:

WILLIAM VERNON, of Mutlow; *b* 6 May 1773; *m* 2 Sept 1799 Elizabeth (*d* 5 Feb 1853), dau of William Mather, of Ipstones, Staffs, and widow of — Berrisford, and *d* 22 Aug 1823, having had, with two yr sons and two daus:

JOHN VERNON, of Fole, Checkley and Rudyard Horton, Staffs; *b* 24 May 1803; *m* 1st 26 Feb 1835 Elizabeth (*d* 8 Jan 1850), dau of John Allen, of Lazenby, Cumberland; *m* 2nd 26 Feb 1857 Margaret (*dsp* 20 April 1889), dau of Timothy Berrisford, of Reapsmoor, Staffs, and widow of Thomas Edge, and *d* 4 Aug 1887, having by his 1st w had, with a yr s (John, *b* 17 Nov 1837, *d* 17 Dec 1838) and a dau (Elizabeth Allen, *b* 18 Aug 1842; *m* 29 March 1875 Arthur Corden Manley, of Barrowash, Derbys, and *dsp* 15 July 1888):

Sir William Vernon, 1st Bt (UK), so *cr* 24 Jan 1914, of Shotwick Park, Cheshire; *b* 13 Dec 1835; head W Vernon & Sons (millers) of London and Liverpool; *m* 30 July 1857 Jane Margaret (*d* 4 June 1910), dau of Thomas Cooper, of Fulford, Staffs, and *d* 24 June 1919, having had, with another s (*d* an infant):

1 (JOHN) HERBERT (Sir), **2nd Bt**

2 William Allen; *b* 10 Nov 1860; *m* 9 Aug 1888 Elizabeth (*d* 9 Feb 1952), dau of Herbert Marson, of Marsh Ho, Blyth Bridge, Staffs, and *d* 16 Feb 1939, having had:

  (1) Herbert Wallace; *b* 14 Sept 1890; *educ* Sedbergh; served RAF; *m* 10 Jan 1924 Gertrude Mary (*d* 15 Jan 1959), er dau of Tom Jackson, JP, of Waterfoot, Heaton, Bolton, and *d* 1974, leaving:

    1a +Bryan Tom Jackson [Bryan Vernon Esq, The Deacons, High St, Yarmouth, IoW PO41 0PN]; *b* 15 Nov 1925; *educ* Loretto; Sub-Lt RNVR; *m* 29 Jan 1955 *Anne Cecilia, est dau of Harry S Burgess, of Beck Hall, Thornton Dale, Yorks, and has:

      1b +Andrew Bryan; *b* 11 Dec 1955; *educ* Oundle; *m* 1982 *Patricia May Gorecki and has:

        1c +Thomas Andrew; *b* 1983

        1c *Alexandra Mary; *b* 1985

      2b +Charles Harry; *b* 29 June 1960

      3b +Timothy William; *b* 26 Sept 1962; *m* 1988 *Tessa Hodgson

      1b *Belinda Anne; *b* 16 July 1957; *m* 1980 (*divorce* 1987) Timothy John Hughes-Williams, of Valbonne, Provence, France, and has:

        1c *Mark Alan; *b* 1983

        1c *Victoria Anne; *b* 1981

    2a +Richard Wallace [Richard Vernon Esq, Park Lodge, 46 Park Rd, Aldeburgh, Suffolk IP15 5EU]; *b* 18 Oct 1927; *educ* Loretto and Clare Coll Cambridge (MA); 2nd Lt RA, dir R K Harris, J I Jacobs (Insur) Ltd 1967–82, Harrison Horncastle Insur Brokers Ltd 1982–84, md Towry Law (Internat) Ltd 1984–88; *m* 8 Jan 1955 *Pamela Violet, only dau of Lt-Col Alexander George William Grierson (*see* GRIERSON, Bt), and has:

      1b +David Grierson [David Vernon Esq, 77 Brodrick Rd, London SW17 7DX]; *b* 31 May 1956; *educ* Radley; *m* 1988 *Rosemary Nicola Myer and has:

        1c +William Grierson; *b* 1990

        1c *Hannah Emily; *b* 1992

        2c *Lucy Nicola; *b* 1994

      2b +Simon Richard [Simon Vernon Esq, 135 Crane Dve, San Anselmo, CA 94960, USA]; *b* 28 March 1958; *m* 1985 *Vanessa Anne Hudson and has:

        1c +James Richard Alexander; *b* 1988

        2c +Tobias Edward; *b* 1990

        1c *Melissa Anne; *b* 1992

      1b *Sally Pamela Clare [Mrs Robert Daniell, 8 Arminger Rd, London W12 7BB]; *b* 22 April 1960; *m* 1986 *Robert William Blackburn Daniell and has:

        1c *Thomas Christopher Hebden; *b* 1988

        2c *Patrick Richard; *b* 1990

        1c *Natasha Annette; *b* 1993

      2b *Joanna Caroline [Mrs Charles Bennett, The Old Forge, Elmdon, nr Saffron Walden, Essex CB11 4NL]; *b* 26 March 1963; *m* 1986 *Charles Albury George Bennett and has:

        1c *George Albury Richard; *b* 1992

        2c *Edward Charles; *b* 1994

  (2) Reginald Thornycroft; *b* 13 May 1892; *educ* Bradfield; Capt RAF; *m* 15 July 1920 Margarita Grace (*d* 17 Sept 1989), yr dau of Joseph Constantine, of Harlsey Hall, Northallerton, Yorks, and *d* 1977, leaving:

    1a William Hamo Constantine; *b* 12 July 1928; *educ* Eton; drowned off the coast of Spain 4 Jan 1953

    2a +George Thornycroft [George Vernon Esq, 2539 Benvenue Ave, Berkeley, CA 94704, USA]; *b* 9 June 1935; *educ* Eton and Trin Coll Cambridge (BA 1958); 2nd Lt 14th/20th Hus

    3a +James Loudon; *b* 27 Oct 1940; *educ* Eton and Trin Coll Dublin (BA); dir Constantine Hldgs 1977, underwriting memb Lloyd's 1980, Liveryman Skinners' Co 1979; *m* 1971 *Elspeth Mary Stewart, dau of Rev Cyril Raby Thomson, of Holy Trinity Vicarage, Southwell, Notts, and has:

      1b +Alexander James Constantine; *b* 1971

      2b +Eliot Antony Stewart; *b* 1975

      1b *Rossanna Mary Anderson; *b* 1976

      2b *Tara Katharine Loudon; *b* 1979

    1a Dorothy; *m* 6 Sept 1941 Capt Robert Arnold Frank Johnston, Queen's Roy Regt, s of Ernest Johnston, of Cockshut, Reigate, Surrey, and *d* 20 July 1958, leaving issue

    2a Pamela Margaret; *b* 1924; *d* 198–

    3a *Jean Winifred [Mrs John Prescot, Fairlight House, E Grinstead, Sussex]; *b* 1926; *m* 27 Feb 1954 *John Stewart Prescot, s of Brig Cynric Puleston Prescot, CBE, MA, MICE, ACGI, and has:

      1b *Charles Stewart; *b* 15 April 1957

      2b *Alastair John Vernon; *b* 8 Jan 1960

      3b *Nigel Kenrick Grosvenor; *b* 26 April 1962

      1b *Margaret Louise; *b* 5 Feb 1955

    4a *Margaret Elizabeth; *b* 1933; *educ* LMH Oxford (BA 1955); *m* 1972 *Rev Jeremy Peake, s of Sir Charles Brinsley Pemberton Peake

  (3) William Hamo; *b* 16 July 1895; *educ* Sedbergh; Lt 4th Bn London Regt WW I; reported *ka* Oct 1916

  (4) Wilfred Douglas (Sir), JP (Surrey 1952); *b* 27 April 1897; *educ* Sedbergh and Trin Coll Cambridge (MA); Lt RAF, pres (formerly chm) Spillers Ltd (ret 1969), ktd 1960, High Sheriff Surrey 1960, Fell IOD; *m* 12 April 1923 Nancy Elizabeth, yr dau of Tom Jackson, JP, of Waterfoot, Heaton, Bolton, and *d* 17 July 1973, having had:

    1a John Hamo Jackson; *b* 14 March 1924; *educ* RNC Dartmouth; Lt RN WW II; *kas* Nov 1944

2a +(William) Michael (Sir) [Sir Michael Vernon, Fyfield Manor, Fyfield, Andover, Hants SP11 8EN]; *b* 17 April 1926; *educ* Marlborough and Trin Coll Cambridge (MA); Lt RM, chm: Spillers Ltd 1968–80, RNLI 1989–96; ktd 1996; *m* 1st 25 April 1952 (*divorce* 1977) Rosheen Elizabeth Mary, dau of George O'Meara, of Johannesburg; *m* 2nd 1977 Jane Olivia Colston (*d* Jan 1998), dau of Dennis Kilham-Roberts, and by his 1st w has had:

  1b John Patrick; *b* 12 July 1956; *d* 13 March 1957

  2b +Mark Thornycroft; *b* 7 March 1958; *m* 1986 *Harriet Laura, est dau of John Bertrand Worsley (*see* NAPIER OF MAGDALA, B), and has:

    1c +Wilfred Allan; *b* 1996

    1c *Jessica Rosheen; *b* 1988

    2c *Phoebe Rose; *b* 1991

(1) Daisy Hilda; *b* 19 Nov 1893; *m* 21 July 1917 Reginald Charles Dickins (*d* 14 Sept 1961), Capt 4th Bn London Regt, est s of Charles Thomas Dickins, of Chestnuts, Putney Hill, and *d* 199–, leaving issue

(2) Helen Dorothy Winifred; *b* 17 June 1899; *m* 6 April 1922 Robert John Sayer Read, of Hapton Hall, Norwich, est s of Robert John Read, of Rivington, Eaton, Norwich, and *d* 26 June 1942, leaving issue

(3) *Nanny Uarda Elsie; *b* 20 June 1901; *m* 5 May 1927 Prof Victor Wilkinson Dix, FRCS (*d* 1992), of Tunbridge Wells, s of Wilkinson Dix, of Tunbridge Wells, and has:

  1a *Peter Vernon [Peter Dix Esq, Birchdale, Mount Park Rd, Harrow, Middx HA1 3JP]; *b* 3 April 1932; *m* 11 April 1964 *Kristina Mary, dau of John Charles Sidley, OBE, and has:

    1b *Caroline Joanna; *b* 19 Nov 1964

    2b *Philippa Mary; *b* 11 Jan 1968

    3b *Rosemary Helen; *b* 11 Oct 1973

  1a *Ursula Winifred [Mrs John Ozanne, 19 Trinity Close, Tunbridge Wells, Kent TN2 3QP]; *b* 6 July 1928; *m* 13 May 1950 John Michael Ozanne (*d* 19 Oct 1958), s of Maj E H B Ozanne, of Crowborough, Sussex, and has:

    1b *Julian Victor; *b* 15 Feb 1958

    1b *Rosalind Sylvia; *b* 24 April 1952

    2b *Nicola Rachel; *b* 30 April 1955

  2a *Elsie Bettina [Mrs Ian Farrow, The New Vicarage, Bisley, Glos GL6 7BJ]; *b* 28 Feb 1936; *m* 11 March 1961 *Ian Edmund Dennett Farrow and has:

    1b *John Stephen; *b* 29 March 1969

    2b *David Peter Vernon; *b* 19 Jan 1972

    1b *Chantalle Louise; *b* 19 July 1964

    2b *Jacqueline Sheelagh; *b* 7 June 1966

3 Thomas Thornycroft; *b* 17 Dec 1862; Lt-Col 7th Bn Liverpool Regt TFR; *d* unm 24 Jan 1919

4 Henry Richard Cooper (Rev); *b* 12 Oct 1865; *educ* Queens' Coll Cambridge (MA); Vicar Rothersthorpe, Northants; *m* 20 July 1893 Jessie Georgina (*d* 4 Feb 1952), dau of Rev George Woodfield Paul, MA Oxon, Hon Canon Peterborough, and *d* 8 Sept 1935, leaving:

(1) Gerald Richard (Rt Rev); *b* 13 Feb 1899; *educ* Winchester, Magdalen Coll Oxford (BA 1921, MA 1927) and Cuddesdon Theological Coll; Bp in Madagascar 1940–50, Vicar Finedon, Northants, and Assist Bp Peterborough 1952–57, Dean Belize, Br Honduras, 1952–63; *d* unm 12 May 1963

(2) John Digby Thornycroft; *b* 30 June 1901; *m* 7 April 1932 *Hilda Alice Maud, SRN [Mrs John Vernon, Bemzells, Hurstmonceux, E Sussex], er dau of Herbert Edward Rollings, of Norwich, and *dsp* 7 May 1945

1 Elizabeth Cooper; *d* unm 20 Aug 1956

The 1st Bt's est s,

Sir (John) Herbert Vernon, 2nd Bt; *b* 12 July 1858; High Sheriff Cheshire 1926, Ld Manors of Shotwick and Gt Sanghall; *m* 1 June 1889 Elizabeth (*d* 11 March 1947), dau of John Bagnall, of Tean Leys, Staffs, and *d* 13 June 1933, having had:

1 (WILLIAM) NORMAN (Sir), **3rd Bt**

2 Herbert Douglas; *b* 4 Jan 1893; Lt Gren Gds; *ka* 15 Sept 1916

3 Humphrey Bagnall, MC; *b* 5 July 1895; *educ* Charterhouse and Magdalen Coll Oxford (BA and MA 1921); Lt Gren Gds WW I, High Sheriff Cheshire 1951–52; *m* 6 Sept 1938 *Sibyl Mason [Mrs Humphrey Vernon, Beechdale Ho, Stonecross, Exford, Somerset], yst dau of Samuel Mason Hutchinson, of The Marfords, Bromborough, Cheshire, and *d* 1979, leaving:

(1) +John Humphrey [John Vernon Esq, 26 Pembroke Place, Bampton, Oxon OX18 2EZ]; *b* 7 Dec 1940; *educ* Charterhouse and Magdalen Coll Oxford; *m* 1st 1973 (*divorce* 1996) Alison Margaret, only dau of William Warnock Watt, of Sheriffhales, Salop; *m* 2nd April 1997 *Tina Jeanette, est dau of James Oscar Carlson, of St Mary's, Pennsylvania, and by his 1st w has had:

  1a +Andrew William; *b* 1981

  1a *Nicola Jane; *b* 1978

(2) +Richard Bagnall [Richard Vernon Esq, Little Tranby, Seven Corners Lane, Beverley, E Yorks]; *b* 10 June 1944; *educ* Charterhouse; *m* 14 June 1969 *Deborah Florence, er dau of Dr Geoffrey Oswald Atyeo Briggs, of The Kennels, Thoresby Park, Notts, and has:

  1a +Toby Richard; *b* 1971

4 John Stafford; *b* 4 March 1900; *educ* Charterhouse and Magdalen Coll Oxford; 2nd Lt Gren Gds; *m* 23 Feb 1933 *Beryl Eileen, only dau of William Turner, of St Arvans, Hampton Wick, and *dsp* 6 March 1970

1 Nina Elizabeth Margaret

The 2nd Bt's est s,

Sir (William) Norman Vernon, 3rd Bt; *b* 19 April 1890; *educ* Charterhouse and Magdalen Coll Oxford (BA 1912, MA 1919); md Spillers Ltd 1929–49, dir Allied Bakeries 1952–57, pres Nat Assoc British and Irish Millers 1931–32, memb Tithe Redemption Commn 1936–55, Dir Flour Milling Min Food 1939–41, memb Flour Advsry Ctee 1929–44, dir Baltic Exchange 1944 and chm 1946–47, chm Food Mission to Occupied Germany 1945, FISMA, Kt Order White Rose Finland, Coronation Medal 1937; *m* 3 June 1921 (Caroline) Janet (*d* 3 Nov 1973), dau of David Macdonald Roberts-Macdonald, of Kinlochmoidart, and *d* 12 April 1967, leaving:

  1 Sir NIGEL JOHN DOUGLAS VERNON, **4th and present Bt**

1 *Diana Elizabeth [Mrs Joseph de Grondines de Landry, 20 Tarrant Wharf, Tarrant St, Arundel, W Sussex BN18 9NY]; *b* 21 April 1922; Section Offr WAAF WW II; *m* 1st 3 July 1943 (*divorce* 1949, *annulment* 1951) Bohuslav F Kovarik, DFM (*d* 1969), Czechoslovak Air Force, s of Karel Kovarik, of Prestezov, Czechoslovakia; *m* 2nd 14 July 1951 *Joseph Olivier Patrick Hamelin de Grondines de Landry, yr s of Edmond Hamelin de Grondines de Landry, of Ottawa

VERULAM

MEDIOCRIA FIRMA

Arms: Quarterly, 1st and 4th, argent on a fess sable three rowels of six points or pierced gules; in the dexter chief an ermine spot sable (for GRIMSTON); 2nd, sable a fess dancettée between two leopard's faces or (for LUCKYN); 3rd, argent three bugle horns sable, stringed gules (for FORRESTER). **Crest:** A stag's head erased proper, attired or. **Supporters:** Dexter, a stag regardant proper, attired or; sinister, a griffin regardant or. **Motto:** *Mediocria firma* ('Moderate things are stable'). **Creations:** Bt. (E) 2 March 1628/9, V. (Grimston) and B. (Dunboyne) (I) 29 May 1719, L. (S) 22 July 1633 (Forrester), B. (GB) 6 July 1790 (Verulam of Gorhambury), E. and V. (Grimston) (UK) 24 Nov 1815.

THE 7TH EARL OF VERULAM, Lord Forrester, Baron Dunboyne, Viscount **Grimston, Baron Verulam of Gorhambury, Viscount Grimston** and a **Baronet** (Sir John Duncan Grimston, Bt) [The Rt Hon The Earl of Verulam, Gorhambury, St Albans, Herts AL3 6AH]; *b* 21 April 1951; *s* f 1973; *educ* Eton and Ch Ch Oxford (MA 1976); dir Baring Bros 1987–96, md ABN-AMRO Bank NV 1996–; *m* 12 Sept 1976 *Dione Angela, er dau of Jeremy Fox Eric Smith, DL (*see* BURRELL, Bt), and has:

1 +JAMES WALTER, *Viscount Grimston*; *b* 6 Jan 1978

2 +Hugo Guy Sylvester; *b* 5 Nov 1979

3 +Sam George; *b* 18 Oct 1983

1 *Flora; *b* 28 Sept 1981

Verulam, previous creation: See BACON, Bt.

Lineage (of Grimston): WILLIAM de GRYMSTON; had:

THOMAS GRYMSTON; had 2nd s:

ROBERT de GRIMSTON, of Ipswich, Suffolk; *m* —, dau of Sir Anthony Spelman, thus acquiring lands at Risehungles and Ipswich, and had:

EDWARD GRIMSTON; Amb to DUKE OF BURGUNDY 1449 (his portrait by Peter Christus 1446, said to be the earliest surviving fully documented painting of an Englishman, hangs in the Nat Gallery); *m* 1st Alice, allegedly a lady of the Court of MARGARET OF ANJOU; *m* 2nd Mary, dau of William Drury, of Rougham, Suffolk; *m* 3rd 26 Aug 1471, as her 3rd husb, Philippa, sis of 1st Earl of Worcester of the 1449 *cr* (*see* BEAUFORT, D, preliminary remarks) and widow of (a) 9th Lord (Baron) De Ros (*qv*) of Helmsley and (b) Sir Thomas Wingfield (*see* POWERSCOURT, V), and by his 2nd w had, with four yr sons and three daus:

EDWARD GRIMSTON; gf of:

Sir EDWARD GRIMSTON, PC; Comptroller Calais 1552–58, following taking of which by French was held in the Bastille 19 months till he escaped by sawing through the window-bars with a file and knotting sheets to reach the ground; MP Ipswich *temp* ELIZABETH I; *d* aged 92, leaving:

EDWARD GRIMSTON, of Bradfield, Essex; MP Eye; *m* Joan, dau of Thomas Risby, of Lavenham, Suffolk, and maternal gdau of John Harbottle, of Crossfield, Suffolk, and *d* 15 Aug 1610, leaving, with a yr s:

Sir HARBOTTLE GRIMSTON, 1st Bt (E), so *cr* 25 Nov 1611, of Bradfield, ktd March 1603/4, Sheriff Essex 1614–15, MP Harwich 1614 April–May 1640 and Nov 1640–Feb 1647/8 and Essex 1626 and 1628–29; imprisoned 1627 for refusing to pay the forced loan demanded by CHARLES I; *m* Elizabeth, dau of Ralph Coppinger, of Stoke, Kent, and *d* 19 Feb1647/8, having had, with an est s (*dvp*) and three yr sons:

Sir HARBOTTLE GRIMSTON, 2nd Bt, PC (1660); *b* 27 Jan 1602/3; *educ* Emmanuel Coll Cambridge; barrister Lincoln's Inn, MP Harwich 1628, Colchester April–May 1640, Nov 1640–48 (when deprived of seat) and 1660–81 and

Essex 1656–58, Recorder Harwich 1634, Parliamentarian early stages of Civil War but later royalist, Speaker H of C 1660, Master Rolls 1660–85, High Steward St Albans 1664; *m* 1st 16 April 1629 Mary, dau of Sir George Croke, Judge Common Pleas, of Waterstoke, Oxon; *m* 2nd by 1652 Anne (*bur* 20 Sept 1680), est dau and eventual heiress of Sir Nathaniel Bacon, KB, of Culford Hall, Suffolk (*see* BACON, Bt), n of Sir Francis Bacon, *cr* 12 July 1618 Baron of Verulam (and later Viscount St Albans), and widow of Sir Thomas Meautys, and *d* 2 Jan 1684/5, having by his 1st w had, with other issue:

1 George; *educ* BNC Oxford and Lincoln's Inn; *m* Sarah (*m* 2nd 1656 4th Duke of Somerset (*qv*); *m* 3rd 1682 2nd Baron Coleraine and *dsp* 2 Nov 1692), dau and coheir of Sir Edward Alston, MD, Pres Coll Physicians, and *dvp* 5 June 1655

2 Sir SAMUEL GRIMSTON, 3rd and last Bt; *b* 7 Jan 1643; MP St Albans 1668–81 and 1689–1700; *m* 1st Elizabeth, est dau of 1st Earl of Nottingham (*see* WINCHILSEA and NOTTINGHAM, E), and had:

(1) Elizabeth; *m* (licence 24 Nov 1687), as his 1st w, William Savile, 2nd Marquess of Halifax (*see* HALIFAX, E, preliminary remarks), and had issue

2 (cont.) Sir SAMUEL *m* 2nd by 1674 Anne (*d* 22 Nov 1713), yst dau of 2nd Earl of Thanet (*see* DE CLIFFORD, B), and *dspm* Oct 1700, when the btcy expired

1 Mary; *m* 20 Jan 1647/8 **Sir Capell Luckyn, 2nd Bt** (*d* 1680), of Messing Hall, Essex, er s of **Sir William Luckyn, 1st Bt** (E), so *cr* 2 March 1628/9, of Little Waltham, Essex, High Sheriff Essex 1637–38 (*b* 1594 (s of William Luckyn (*d* 13 Dec 1610), of Mascalls, Gt Haddow, Essex, by Margaret, dau of Thomas Jenny, of Bury St Edmunds), *m* 2nd 1 Dec 1634 Elizabeth (*d* 7 July 1667), dau of Sir Edward Pynchon, of Writtle, Essex, and *d* by 28 Feb 1660/1), by his 1st w (*m c* 1620) Mildred, dau of Sir Gamaliel Capell, of Raines or Rayne, Essex, and *d* 18 March 1719, having had, with other issue:

(1) **Sir William Luckyn, 3rd Bt**; *m* 1 Dec 1681 Mary (*d* 1749), dau of William Sherington, London Alderman, and *d* 1708, having had, with other issue:

1a **Sir Harbottle Luckyn, 4th Bt**; *d* unm 4 Feb 1736/7

2a Sir WILLIAM LUCKYN later GRIMSTON (on inheriting his great-uncle's Gorhambury and other estates), **5th Bt**, and **1st Viscount Grimston**, so *cr* 29 May 1719, as also BARON DUNBOYNE, of Co Meath (both I); *b c* 1683; MP (Whig) St Albans 1711–22 and 1727–34; *m* 14 Aug 1706 Jean, dau of James Cooke, of London, and *d* 15 Oct 1756, having had, with 16 other children:

1b Samuel; *b* 28 Dec 1707; *m* 5 Nov 1730 Mary (*m* 2nd 1740 2nd Viscount Barrington; *see* 1970 edn), dau and heiress of Henry Lovel, merchant, and *dsp* 19 June 1737

2b JAMES, **2nd Viscount**

3b Harbottle GRIMSTON later LUCKYN (roy licence 1750)

(1) Sarah; *m* as his 3rd w Dacre Barrett (*see* DACRE, B)

2 Elizabeth; *m* 1650 Sir George Grubham Howe, 1st Bt (*d* 26 Sept 1678), of Cold Barwick, Wilts, and had issue

The 1st VISCOUNT's est surv s,

JAMES GRIMSTON, **2nd Viscount Grimston**; *b* 9 Oct 1711; MP (Whig) St Albans 1754–61; *m* 19 June 1746 Mary, dau of William Bucknall, of Oxhey Place, Herts, and *d* 15 Dec 1773, having had, with two other daus (*d* unm):

1 JAMES BUCKNALL, **3rd Viscount**

2 William GRIMSTON later BUCKNALL (under terms of will of maternal unc); *b* 23 June 1750; *m* Sophia (*d* 4 March 1836), dau and coheir of Richard Hoare, of Boreham, Essex, and *d* 25 April 1814, leaving an only surv dau:

(1) Sophia Askell; *m* 22 Nov 1804 Hon Berkeley Paget (*see* ANGLESEY, M)

3 Harbottle GRIMSTON later BUCKNALL (Rev); DD; *d* unm 30 Jan 1823

1 Jane; *m* 6 Oct 1774 Thomas Estcourt and *d* 1829, leaving issue

2 Mary; *m* 3 April 1777 William Hale, of King's Walden, and *d* 9 April 1846, leaving issue

3 Susannah Askell; *m* 15 July 1781 John Warde (*d* 9 Dec 1838), of Squerryes Court, Westerham, Kent, and *dsp* 29 May 1842

The 2nd VISCOUNT's est s,

JAMES BUCKNALL GRIMSTON, **3rd Viscount Grimston**; *b* 9 May 1747; *educ* Eton and Trin Hall Cambridge; *cr* 6 July 1790 BARON VERULAM OF GORHAMBURY, Co Hertford (GB), DCL Oxon 1793, High Steward St Albans 1807–08; *m* 28 July 1774 Harriot, only dau and eventual heiress of Edward Walter, MP, of Stalbridge, Dorset, by Harriot (*d* 7 Nov 1786), 2nd dau of **5th Lord Forrester of Corstorphine** (*see* **Lineage (of Forrester)** below), and *d* 30 Dec 1808, having had, with two daus:

JAMES WALTER GRIMSTON, **1st Earl of Verulam**, so *cr* 24 Nov 1815, as also VISCOUNT GRIMSTON (both UK), in addition **4th Viscount Grimston** etc, as which *s* f, and **10th Lord Forrester of Corstorphine**, as which *s* mother's 1st cousin 1808 (*see* **Lineage (of Forrester)** below); *b* 26 Sept 1775; *educ* Harrow and Ch Ch Oxford; MP (Tory) St Albans 1802–08, Lt-Col Herts Militia 1808–09, High Steward St Albans 1809–45, Ld Lt Herts 1823–45, a Ld Bedchamber Jan–April 1835; *m* 11 Aug 1807 Lady Charlotte Jenkinson (*d* 16 April 1863), dau of 1st Earl of Liverpool of the 1796 *cr* (*see* JENKINSON, Bt), and *d* 17 Nov 1845, leaving:

1 JAMES WALTER, **2nd Earl**

2 Edward Harbottle (Rev); *b* 2 April 1812; Rector Pebmarsh, Essex; *m* 15 June 1842 Frances Horatia (*d* 14 July 1906), est dau of John Philip Morier, and *d* 4 May 1881, leaving:

(1) Walter Edward; *b* 16 May 1844; *m* 1st 19 June 1872 Emily (*d* 1 Feb 1884), 3rd dau of Arthur Pryor, of Hylands, Essex; *m* 2nd 8 July 1885 Ellen Jane (*d* 13 March 1938), dau of Robert Woodhouse, of Writtle, Essex, and *d* 28 July 1932, having by his 1st w had:

1a Francis Walter; *b* 1 July 1873; *d* 1 May 1876

1a Susan Edith; *m* 14 June 1899 Lt-Col Arthur Faulconer Poulton, CVO, CBE, Suffolk Regt (*d* 15 Nov 1935), Ch Constable Berks, s of Dep Surgn-Gen Charles Walter Poulton, MD, and *d* 12 Jan 1968, leaving issue

2a Cecilia; *m* 11 June 1904 Lt-Col Forrester Colvin Watson, OBE, MC, JP, DL, 3rd Hus (*d* 8 Feb 1951), s of William Farnell Watson, of Henfold, Dorking, Surrey, and *d* 23 Dec 1960, leaving issue

3a Mary Noel; *m* 11 Jan 1905 Capt Henry Hamilton Gepp, Essex Yeo (*d* 15 July 1945), est s of Rev Henry John Gepp, and *d* 4 March 1937, leaving issue

4a Eleanor Vera; *m* 25 Nov 1908 Lt-Col Arthur Mervyn Toulmin, RM (*d* 24 Oct 1960), s of Rev Fredrick Bransby Toulmin, and *d* 26 March 1937

(1) Charlotte Mary; *m* 23 June 1869 Cecil Frederick Reid (*d* 1898), est surv s of William Reid, of The Node, Herts, and *d* 24 Sept 1932, leaving issue

(2) Eleanor; *m* 1st 17 Aug 1870 Capt William John Wauchope of Niddrie Marischal, Midlothian, 6th Inniskilling Dragoons (*d* 26 Nov 1882; *see* also DON-WAUCHOPE, Bt, and VENTRY, B); *m* 2nd 3 Aug 1887 Lt-Col Henry C S Goldfrap, Lincs Regt, of Farnborough, and *d* 13 May 1933

3 Robert; *b* 18 Sept 1816; *d* unm 7 April 1884

4 Charles; *b* 3 Oct 1818; Capt Coldstream Gds; *dsp* 8 Oct 1856

5 Francis Sylvester (Rev); *b* 8 Dec 1822; Rector Wakes Colne, Essex; *m* 1 Feb 1847 his er bro's sis-in-law Katherine Georgiana (*d* 2 March 1879), 4th dau of John Philip Morier, and *d* 28 Oct 1865, leaving, with another s (*d* young):

(1) George Sylvester; *b* 31 Dec 1847; *m* 29 May 1874 Margaret (*d* 3 Dec 1924), dau of William Bush, and *d* 7 Dec 1926, leaving, with another s (*d* an infant):

1a Francis Sylvester, CIE (1917); *b* 26 Dec 1876; ch engrg advsr Dir Ordnance Factories India 1906, Supt Rifle Factory Ishapore 1914 and Metal and Steel Factory Ishapore 1920, Dir Ordnance Factories and Mfre India 1929, MInst CE; *m* 19 Oct 1907 Eleanor Vincent (*d* 22 June 1960), dau of Arthur William Lawrence Reddie, and *d* 5 Jan 1969, leaving:

1b +Francis Brian Sylvester; *b* 22 Sept 1908; *educ* Cheltenham; S/Ldr RAFVR WW II; *m* 20 April 1940 (*divorce* 1954) Monica Katherine (*d* 1978), yr dau of Col Hon Sir Maurice Charles Andrew Drummond, KBE, CMG, DSO (*see* PERTH, E)

(2) Edward John; *b* 24 July 1851; *m* 1st 11 Dec 1876 Annie Kate (*d* 23 Nov 1887), yst dau of Sir Arthur Buller, MP Liskeard, and had, with a dau (*d* unm):

1a Arthur; *b* 11 Oct 1877; RN; *d* 19 Aug 1895

2 (cont.) Edward Grimston *m* 2nd 29 Dec 1888 Toonie Clara, er dau of Lionel L Woodhouse, and *d* 9 April 1913, leaving by her:

2a Horace Sylvester; *b* 28 Oct 1891; Lt Wilts Regt; *ka* Oct 1914

(3) Hugh Francis; *b* 11 Feb 1856; *d* 4 July 1932

(1) Mary; *b* 17 June 1849; *m* 15 Nov 1890 Horace Egerton Green, DL, of King's Ford, Essex (*dsp* 17 Sept 1905), s of Henry Egerton Green, of Colchester and *d* 23 Feb 1937

(2) Evelyn Horatia; *m* 28 Feb 1876 her cousin's bro-in-law Edmund Pryor (*d* Feb 1888), 2nd s of Arthur Pryor, and *d* April 1928, leaving issue

(3) Margaret Katharine, MBE; *m* 13 April 1882 her 1st cousin Col Hon Walter Philip Alexander and *d* 12 Sept 1929, leaving issue (*see* CALEDON, E)

1 Katherine; *m* 1st 14 Jan 1834 John Foster Barham, MP (*d* 22 May 1838), of Stockbridge, Hants; *m* 2nd 4 June 1839 4th Earl of Clarendon (*qv*) and *d* 4 July 1874, leaving issue

2 Emily Mary; *m* 5 Sept 1835 2nd Earl of Craven (*qv*) and *d* 21 May 1901, leaving issue

3 Mary Augusta Frederica; *m* 3 Oct 1840 4th Earl of Radnor (*qv*) and *d* 5 April 1879, leaving issue

4 Jane Frederica Harriot Mary, VA; Ldy Bedchamber to HM QUEEN VICTORIA; *m* 4 Sept 1845 3rd Earl of Caledon (*qv*) and *d* 30 March 1888, leaving issue

The 1st EARL's est s,

JAMES WALTER GRIMSTON, **2nd Earl of Verulam**; *b* 22 Feb 1809; *educ* Harrow (Govr 1862–92) and Ch Ch Oxford; MP (Tory) St Albans 1830–31, Newport Cornwall 1831–32 and Herts 1832–45, Ld Lt Herts 1846–92, Lt-Col S Herts Yeo Cav 1847–64, a Ld-in-Waiting 1852–53 and 1858–59, Pres Camden Soc 1873; *m* 12 Sept 1844 Elizabeth Joanna (*d* 5 July 1886), dau of Maj Richard Weyland, of Woodeaton, Oxon, and *d* 27 July 1895, having had:

1 JAMES WALTER, **3rd Earl**

2 William; *b* 7 Jan 1855; Cdr RN; *d* unm 10 May 1900

3 Robert (Rev); *b* 18 April 1860; *educ* Cambridge (MA); Canon St Albans; *m* 20 Aug 1896 Gertrude Mary Amelia (*d* 30 Aug 1949), est dau of Rev Charles Villiers (*see* CLARENDON, E), and *d* 8 July 1928, leaving:

(1) ROBERT VILLIERS GRIMSTON, 1st BARON GRIMSTON OF WESTBURY (*qv*)

(2) Edward Harbottle (Rev); *b* 22 May 1901; Curate St Nicholas Newport, Lincs, 1936–39 and Brighton with W Blatchington 1939–43, Vicar Isleworth 1943–59 and Arundel 1959–65; *d* unm 22 Feb 1965

(1) Joan Florence Mary, CBE (1964); *m* 31 Jan 1922 Sir Cecil Gustavus Jacques Newman, 2nd Bt, of Cecil Lodge (*qv*) and *d* 15 Sept 1969, leaving issue

(2) Violet Gwendolen; *m* 16 Dec 1926 Lt-Col Arthur William Acland and had issue (*see* ACLAND, Bt, of St Mary Magdalen Oxford)

1 Harriot Elizabeth; Ldy-in-Waiting to HI and RH THE DUCHESS OF EDINBURGH; *m* 24 March 1885 Maj-Gen Francis Harwood Poore, RMA (*d* 19 Feb 1928), Equerry to HRH The DUKE OF EDINBURGH, and *d* 15 Aug 1888, leaving issue

2 Jane; *b* 12 Dec 1848; *m* 25 Feb 1897 Sir Alfred Jodrell, 4th and last Bt (*d* 15 March 1929; *see* 1929 edn), and *d* 2 Nov 1920

3 Maud; *m* 20 Dec 1881 Hon Paulyn Francis Cuthbert Rawdon-Hastings, bro of 11th Earl of Loudoun (*qv*), and *d* 3 Sept 1929, leaving issue

The 2nd EARL's est s,

JAMES WALTER GRIMSTON, **3rd Earl of Verulam**, JP Herts; *b* 11 May 1852; *educ* Harrow; Lt 1st Life Gds 1870–78, Hon Maj Herts Yeo Cav, MP (C) St Albans 1885–92, CA Herts 1912, Chm St Albans QS to 1923; *m* 30 April 1878 Margaret Frances (*d* 4 Oct 1927), est dau of Sir Frederick Ulric Graham, 3rd Bt, of Netherby (*qv*), and *d* 11 Nov 1924, having had:

1 JAMES WALTER, **4th Earl**

1 Helen; *m* 18 Nov 1908 Rt Hon Sir Felix Cassel, 1st Bt (*qv*), and *d* 7 Oct 1947, leaving issue

2 Hermione; *b* 1881; *m* 28 Sept 1904 Cdr Bernard Buxton and *d* 3 April 1924, leaving issue (*see* BUXTON, Bt)

3 Aline; *m* 24 July 1907 Maj Geoffrey Arthur Barnett, MBE, Herts Yeo (*d* in an accident 12 Aug 1957), s of Charles Edward Barnett, and *d* 12 July 1970, leaving:

(1) (Peter) Cedric; *b* 1910; *m* 1941 *Sylvia Irina [Mrs Cedric Barnett OBE, 7 Upper Belgrave St, London SW1], dau of Lt-Col William David Kenny, OBE, of Dun Laoghaire, Co Dublin, and *d* 1980, leaving:

1a *Ulric David [Ulric Barnett Esq, Towersley Manor, Thame, Oxon OX9 3QR]; *b* 1942; *educ* Eton and Magdalen Coll Oxford; *m* 1969 *Marie-Jane, dau of Capt de Frégate Jean Levasseur, and has:

  1b *Rory Nicholas; *b* 1971

  2b *Oliver Louis; *b* 1979

  1b *Natalie Aline; *b* 1974

1a *Patricia [Mrs Samuel Goodenough, 26 Stanhope Gdns, London SW7]; *b* 1945; *m* 1st 1968 (*divorce* 1975) Oscar Jorge Potier and has:

  1b *Rupert Alexander; *b* 1969

1a (cont.) Mrs Patricia Potier *m* 2nd 1975 (*divorce* 1979) Dennis Nagle; *m* 3rd 1979 Samuel Henry Kenneth Goodenough (*d* 1983), yst s of Sir William Macnamara Goodenough, 1st Bt (*qv*), and by her 2nd husb has:

  1b *Patricia; *b* 1975

2a *Susan [Mrs Charles Blackwood, Brickworth Park, Whiteparish, Wilts]; *b* 1947; *m* 1967 *Capt Charles Temple Blackwood, late Gren Gds, and has:

  1b *James Temple; *b* 1969

  2b *Jonathan Charles; *b* 1971

4 Elizabeth; *b* 1885; Woman Bedchamber to HM QUEEN MARY 1924–36, Extra Woman Bedchamber 1936–53; *m* 1st 1 June 1908 Maj Hesketh Vernon Hesketh-Prichard, DSO, MC (*d* 14 June 1922), of Praewood, St Albans, s of Hesketh Brodrick Prichard, 25th KO Bdrs, and had:

(1) Michael; *b* 19 Feb 1909; *educ* Fettes; Maj RA; *m* 7 July 1938 Venetia Alice (*d* 1992), dau of Sir Frederick Daniel Green, and *d* 1988, leaving:

1a *Richard Michael [Richard Hesketh-Prichard Esq, 1703 Calveryman Lane, Katy, TX 77449, USA]; *b* 22 March 1939; *educ* Fettes; *m* 2 Oct 1965 (*divorce* 1981) Elizabeth Susan, yst dau of John Cuthbert Ottaway, MBE, TD, of St Albans, and has:

  1b *James Michael; *b* 7 Nov 1966; *educ* Pembroke Coll Cambridge

  2b *Thomas Richard Edward; *b* 5 Oct 1969

  1b *Rebecca Sophie Venetia; *b* 25 April 1971; *educ* Exeter U

1a *Cicely Elizabeth Theodosia [Mrs Cicely Jacoby, Cross Farm, Drewsteignton, Devon EX6 6PA]; *b* 29 May 1942; *m* 17 Dec 1966 (*divorce* 1980) Martin Charles Jacoby, FLS, s of John Martin Jacoby, and has:

  1b *Charles John; *b* 13 Sept 1967

  1b *Katherine Venetia; *b* 29 April 1970

2a *Venetia [Mrs David Lascelles, Meadle Cottage, Meadle, Bucks HP27 9UD]; *b* 6 March 1948; *educ* Trin Coll Dublin; *m* 1972 *David Richard Lascelles and has:

  1b *Harry Francis; *b* 1978

  1b *Alice Virginia; *b* 1976

(2) Alfgar Cecil Giles, DSO, MC; *b* 9 May 1916; *educ* Stowe and Queens' Coll Cambridge; Roy Fus WW II (despatches); presumed *ka* Austria 3 Dec 1944

(1) Diana; *b* 26 March 1912; Jr Cdr ATS; *d* unm 12 July 1970

4 (cont.) Lady Elizabeth Hesketh-Prichard *m* 2nd 12 July 1927 Maj Thomas Augustus Motion, JP, MFH (*d* 20 Feb 1942), yr s of Richard William Motion, of Carlisle Ho, Clapton, and *d* 1975, leaving by him:

(2) *Joan Elizabeth Mary, JP, DL Herts [Lady Stuart-Smith JP DL, Serge Hill, Abbots Langley, Herts WD5 0RY]; *b* 1929; *educ* St Anne's Coll Oxford (BA 1951); High Sheriff, Herts 1983; *m* 28 March 1953 *Rt Hon Sir Murray Stuart-Smith, PC, Ld Justice of Appeal, and has:

1a *Jeremy Hugh [Jeremy Stuart-Smith Esq, Pie Corner, Abbots Langley, Herts WD5 0SG]; *b* 18 Jan 1955; *educ* Radley and Corpus Christi Coll Cambridge; QC; *m* 1982 *Hon Arabella Clare Montgomery, dau of 2nd Viscount Montgomery of Alamein (*qv*), and has had issue

2a *Mark; *b* 24 Oct 1958; *educ* Radley and Cambridge

3a *Thomas Richard Steven Peregrine [Thomas Stuart-Smith Esq, The Barn, Serge Hill, Abbots Langley, Herts]; *b* 14 Feb 1960; *educ* Radley and Corpus Christi Coll Cambridge; *m* 1986 *Dr Susan Jane Evans, of Ardnadam Ho, Ardnadam, by Dunoon, Strathclyde, and has:

  1b *Benjamin; *b* 1989

  2b *Harry Horatio; *b* 1992

  1b *Rose; *b* 1987

1a *Katherine [Mrs David Docherty, Serge Hill, Abbots Langley, Herts WD5 0RY]; *b* 11 Jan 1957; *m* 1992 *Dr David Docherty and has:

  1b *Flora Olivia Annie; *b* 1993

  2b *Polly; *b* 1996

2a *Jane [Mrs Hugh Raven, 14 Avondale Park Gdns, London W11]; *b* 3 Oct 1961; *m* 1992 *Hugh Jonathon Earle Raven and has:

  1b *Katherine Sarah Faith; *b* 1996

  2b *Madelaine Emma Beatrice; *b* 1998

3a *Elizabeth; *b* 3 Oct 1961; *m* 1990 *Adam Beck, er s of Sir Philip Beck, and has:

  1b *Sam; *b* 1994

  1b *Isabella; *b* 1996

5 Sibyl; *m* 16 March 1915 Maj Hon Alastair Thomas Joseph Fraser (*see* LOVAT, L) and *d* 1 Aug 1968, leaving issue

6 Vera; SRN, SCM; *m* 21 Jan 1922 Maurice Francis Headlam, CB, CMG (*d* 2 Nov 1956), Comptroller Gen Nat Debt Office 1927–38, Treas Remembrancer and Dep Paymaster Ireland 1912–20, s of Francis John Headlam, and *d* 29 June 1970, leaving:

(1) *Anthony Francis [Anthony Headlam Esq, c/o Child and Co, 1 Fleet St, London EC4]; *b* 20 June 1923; *educ* Eton and King's Coll Cambridge (MA); KRRC WW II; *m* 14 Sept 1956 (*divorce* 1977) Jill Caroline, dau of Bruce R Campbell, of Sydney, NSW, and has:

1a *Hugh Francis [Hugh Headlam Esq, 17 Harbut Rd, London SW11 2RA]; *b* 25 Jan 1960; *educ* Eton; *m* 2 July 1994 *Romany Mary, dau of V Adml Sir Philip Alexander Watson, KBE, LVO, of Bodicote, Oxon, and has:

  1b *Jemima Florence Mary; *b* 7 May 1996

1a *Caroline Ann [Mrs Crispin Black, 95 St George's Sq, London SW1V 3QW]; *b* 16 Sept 1963; *m* 25 Oct 1996 *Maj Crispin Nicholas Black, MBE, Welsh Gds, s of John Black

(2) Christopher Grimston; *b* 1 Feb 1925; *educ* Eton and King's Coll Cambridge (MA); RNVR WW II; *m* 5 Feb 1959 *Sarah, dau of Sir John Richard Hobhouse, MC, JP, of Taunton, Somerset, and *d* 1989, leaving:

1a *Thomas Walter; *b* 22 Feb 1962

1a *Catherine Sophia; *b* 4 Jan 1960

(3) *(James) Nicholas [Nicholas Headlam Esq, The Old Rectory, Brampton Abbotts, Herefs HR4 7JE]; *b* 2 Oct 1926; *educ* Eton and New Coll Oxford; *m* 22 Jan 1966 *Elisabeth Jane, est dau of Sir Peter William Shelley Yorke Scarlett, KCMG, KCVO, and has:

1a *Anthony John Nicholas; *b* 24 Dec 1969

1a *Fenella Jane; *b* 20 Nov 1967

2a *Mary Amelia; *b* 1972

The 3rd EARL's only s,

JAMES WALTER GRIMSTON, **4th Earl of Verulam**, JP Herts; *b* 17 April 1880; *educ* Eton and Ch Ch Oxford (BA 1905, MA 1909, memb U boat crew 1900); electrical engr, fndr and chm Enfield Cables Ltd; *m* 27 Oct 1909 Lady Violet Constance Maitland Brabazon, yr dau of 12th Earl of Meath (*qv*), and *d* in a car crash 29 Nov 1949, having had:

1 JAMES BRABAZON GRIMSTON, **5th Earl of Verulam**, JP (Herts 1949); *b* 11 Oct 1910; *educ* Eton and Ch Ch Oxford (BA 1932, MA 1937); FRGS, FSA, FBIM, CIEE, chm Enfield Rolling Mills Ltd; *d* unm 19 Oct 1960

2 JOHN, **6th Earl**

3 Brian, DFC; *b* 19 March 1914; *educ* Rugby and Trin Coll Cambridge (BA 1935); S/Ldr RAFVR WW II; *ka* 4 April 1943

4 Bruce David, DFC; *b* 8 Dec 1915; *educ* Stowe and Trin Coll Cambridge (BA 1938); F/Lt RAFVR WW II; *ka* 12 July 1944

The 5th EARL's bro,

JOHN GRIMSTON, **6th Earl of Verulam**, DL (Herts 1963); *b* 17 July 1912; *educ* Oundle and Ch Ch Oxford; F/Lt RAuxAF (Res) WW II, Hon A/Cdre No 1 (Co of Hertford) Maritime HQ Unit, RAuxAF; MP St Albans 1943–45 and 1950–59; gp md Delta Metal Co Ltd, chm Enfield Rolling Mills Ltd, Pres London Chamber Commerce 1963–66, Pres Inst of Metals 1962; *m* 2 June 1938 Marjorie Ray (*d* 21 Dec 1994), est dau of Walter Atholl Duncan, and *d* 15 April 1973, leaving:

1 JOHN DUNCAN GRIMSTON, **7th and present Earl of Verulam**

1 Elisabeth Harriot; *b* 31 Aug 1939; *m* 30 May 1958 (*divorce* 1972) John Christopher George, *Viscount Pollington*, er s of 7th Earl of Mexborough (*qv*), and *d* 1987, leaving issue

2 *Hermione Frances [The Lady Hermione Grimston, Old Pondyards, Redbourn Rd, St Albans, Herts]; *b* 27 Sept 1941; *m* 1st 5 June 1965 (*divorce* 1971) Richard John Perronet Thompson, er s of R-Adml John Yelverton Thompson, CB; *m* 2nd 15 June 1971 (*divorce* 1982, resumed maiden name) James Darell Dickson Thompson-Schwab

3 *Romayne Bryony [The Lady Romayne Bockstoce, 1 Hill St, S Dartmouth, MA 02748, USA]; *b* 18 Aug 1946; *m* 11 Jan 1973 *John Roberts Bockstoce, s of Clifton Bockstoce, of Connecticut, and has:

(1) *John Grimston; *b* 27 June 1976

4 *Iona Charlotte [Countess of Mount Charles, Slane Castle, Co Meath, Ireland]; *b* 25 Oct 1953; *m* 1985, as his 2nd w, *Henry Vivian Pierpoint, Earl of Mount Charles, est s of 7th Marquess Conyngham (*qv*)

Lineage (of Forrester): HENRY FORRESTER of Corstorphine, Co Edinburgh (bro and heir of Sir James Forrester of Corstorphine); *m* Helen Preston of Craigmillar and *d* between 21 Aug 1612 and 30 July 1618, leaving:

Sir George Forrester, 1st Bt (NS), and **1st Lord Forrester of Corstorphine** (S), so *cr* 17 Nov 1625 and 22 July 1633 respectively, with remainder of the latter to his heirs male whatever; after his s's death got a regrant of the peerage 5 July 1651 with remainder to (a) his 3rd dau Joanna's husb JAMES and their issue in tail male, (b) JAMES's yr bro WILLIAM, husb of his 4th and yst dau Lilias, and their issue in tail male, (c) issue of the bros by their said wives in tail general (*i.e.*, including females) according to primogeniture and (d) JAMES and his heirs male or of entail to be made by him; *m* (contract between 27 Nov and 1 Dec 1606) Christian, dau of Sir William Livingstone of Kilsyth, and *dspms* by 10 Aug 1652, having had, with two er daus:

1 John, *Master of Corstorphine*; *m* 1634 Agnes, dau of Sir Alexander Falconer of Halkerto(u)n and widow of Alexander Keith of Benholm, and *dsp* & *vp*

1 JOANNA Forrester; *m* (contract 15 Dec 1649), as his 1st w, JAMES BAILLIE later FORRESTER, **2nd Lord Forrester of Corstorphine**, as which *s* f-in-law under special remainder (*b* 29 Oct 1629, s of Maj-Gen William Baillie of Letham and Torwoodhead, Stirlingshire), and *d* on or after 8 Feb 1652; he *m* 2nd by July 1661 Jean, dau of 1st and last Earl of Forth and Brentford (*see* CARLISLE, E), and *d* 26 Aug 1679, having by his 1st w had an only child (*b* 8 Feb 1652, *d* an infant) and by his 2nd w further issue (who all took the name RUTHVEN), but being *s* without the special remainder by his bro (*and* the bro), leaving:

2 Lilias; *b* 18 Sept 1634; *m* by 1 March 1650 WILLIAM BAILLIE, *de jure* 3rd LORD FORRESTER OF CORSTORPHINE (*b* 12 Dec 1632; did not assume the title; *d* May 1681) and *d* 1681, leaving:

(1) WILLIAM BAILLIE later FORRESTER, **4th Lord Forrester of Corstorphine**; *m* by 1684 Margaret, dau of Sir Andrew Birnie of Saline, and *d* 1705, having had, with three other sons:

1a Andrew; *b* 11 May 1686; *d* an infant

2a GEORGE FORRESTER, **5th Lord Forrester of Corstorphine**; *b* 23 March 1688; Lt-Col 26th Foot at victory over Jacobites of Preston 13 Nov 1715 (wounded), Col 30th Foot 1716–17, 2nd Horse Gren Gds 1717–19 and 4th Horse Gren Gds 1719–27; *m* by 1724 Charlotte, dau and coheir of Anthony Rowe, of Oxon, and *d* Feb 1742/3, leaving:

  1b GEORGE FORRESTER, **6th Lord Forrester of Corstorphine**; *b* 14 July 1724; RN: Lt 1735, Capt 1740, Cdr 1744; *d* unm 26 June 1748

  1b CAROLINE Forrester, **Lady Forrester of Corstorphine** in her own right, 8th holder of title, as which *s* her cousin **7th Lord**; *m* her cousin Capt George COCKBURN of Ormistoun, RN (*d* 23 July 1770), Comptroller Navy 1756–70, and *d* 25 Feb 1784, having had an est and only surv dau:

  1c ANNA MARIA COCKBURN, **Lady Forrester of Corstorphine** in her own right, 9th holder of title; *d* unm 3 Dec 1808
  2b Harriot; *m* Edward Walter, MP, of Stalbridge, Dorset, and *d* 7 Nov 1786, leaving:

    1c Harriot; *m* 28 July 1774 **3rd Viscount Grimston** (*see* Lineage (of Grimston) above) and *d* 7 Nov 1786, leaving:

      1d JAMES WALTER GRIMSTON, **10th Lord Forrester of Corstorphine**, as which *s* mother's 1st cousin, also **1st Earl of Verulam** etc (UK), so *cr* 24 Nov 1815, and **4th Viscount Grimston** etc, as which *s* f (*see* **Lineage (of Grimston)** above)

  3a John; Capt RN; *m* Elizabeth, sis of Sir Charles Tyrrel, and *d* 12 Jan 1737, leaving:

  1b WILLIAM FORRESTER, **7th Lord Forrester of Corstorphine**; *m* Hannah — and *dsp* Nov 1763

Seat: Gorhambury, St Albans, Herts. Sir Nicholas Bacon, father of the 1st Bt (*qv*), bought Gorhambury in 1561. Before the dissolution of the religious houses in the 1530s it had formed part of the estates of St Alban's Abbey. An even more venerable link with the past is the Roman theatre of Verulamium, the remains of which are abutted by one of the lodges to the present park. Sir Nicholas was doubtless prompted to enlarge his new home to a conspicuous degree following a jocular remark about its pokiness by ELIZABETH I. He bequeathed it to his younger son by his second wife, the celebrated Sir Francis, some of whose books have been preserved to this day in the current house's library. Sir Francis died without issue and in 1652 Sir HARBOTTLE GRIMSTON, 2nd Bt (*see* above), bought the estate from a cousin of his 2nd wife, Sir Thomas Meautys, who had a life interest in it. The price, £10,000 (just over £400,000 in late-1990s terms), was a remarkable bargain, perhaps occasioned by the prevailing bear market in gentleman's seats following Cromwellian fines and sequestrations in the wake of the Civil War. The remains of what might be called the Baconian Gorhambury survive dilapidated in the park, though two stained glass windows from it of *c* 1620 have been put on display in the hall of the present house.

The latter was built by the **3rd Viscount** between 1777 and 1784 in the Palladian style to the designs of Sir Robert Taylor. The central block, of two and a half storeys of nine bays, surmounted by a balustrade and steps to a *piano nobile* climaxing in a pediment supported by six Corinthian columns, the two outer ones at each end bunched together, was originally flanked by two wings. In 1816 one was demolished, the other extended. In the 20th century the main block was refaced in gleaming Portland stone. The internal decorations include two important Roman chimney pieces by Piranesi, one in the Yellow Drawing Room, the other in the Library.

VESTEY, Baron

Arms: Azure in base barry wavy of four argent and of the first an iceberg issuant proper, on a chief of the second three eggs, also proper. **Crest:** In front of a springbok's head couped at the neck proper three mullets fesswise azure. **Supporters:** Dexter, a sheep proper; Sinister, a bull argent. **Motto:** *E labore stabilitas* ('From work comes stability'). **Creations:** B. (UK) 20 June 1922, Bt. (UK) 21 June 1913.

THE 3RD BARON VESTEY, of Kingswood, Co Surrey, and a **Baronet** (Sir Samuel George Armstrong Vestey, Bt, DL (Glos 1982)) [The Rt Hon The Lord Vestey DL, Stowell Park, Northleach, Glos GL54 3LE]; *b* 19 March 1941; *s* gf 1954; *educ* Eton; Lt Scots Gds 1960–63, dir Union Internat Co, Pres: London Meat Trade and Drovers Benevolent Assoc 1973, St John's Ambulance Bde Glos, Glos Assoc Boys Clubs, Br Inst Meat 1978–83 and Steeplechase Co Cheltenham, Master of the Horse 1998–, Liveryman Butchers' Co, OStJ: Chllr 1988–91, Ld Prior 1991–; *m* 1st 11 Sept 1970 (*divorce* 1981) Kathryn Mary, er dau of John Eccles, of Moor Park, Herts, and has:

  1 *Saffron Alexandra; *b* 27 Aug 1971; *m* 18 May 1996 *Matthew Charles Idiens, only *s* of Cdr Simon Idiens, RN

  2 *Flora Grace; *b* 22 Sept 1978

The 3rd BARON *m* 2nd 22 Dec 1981 *Celia Elizabeth, dau of Maj Guy Knight, MC, of Lockinge Manor, Wantage, Oxon, and by her has:

  1 +WILLIAM GUY; *b* 27 Aug 1983; Page of Honour to HM THE QUEEN to 1998
  2 +Arthur George; *b* 1985
  3 *Mary Henrietta; *b* 1992

Lineage: WILLIAM VESTEY, of Leeds; had:

SAMUEL VESTEY, of Liverpool; *b* 9 March 1832; *m* 14 April 1858 Hannah (*d* 19 Jan 1884), dau of William Uttley, of Westbar-in-Stansfield, Yorks, and *d* 14 May 1902, having had, with two daus (*d* unm):

1 WILLIAM, **1st Baron**
2 John Uttley; *b* 15 Feb 1863; *dsp* 18 April 1880
3 Sir EDMUND HOYLE VESTEY, 1st Bt, of the 1921 *cr*, of Shirley, Surrey (*qv*)
4 Percy; *b* 5 June 1867; *m* 26 Sept 1895 Mary Elizabeth (*d* 5 Jan 1956), dau of Thomas Poulson, of Chicago, and *d* 22 Oct 1897, leaving a s
5 Sydney Stead; *b* 19 March 1871; *m* 1st 26 Aug 1896 his sis-in-law Alice, dau of George Ellis, of Tranmere, Birkenhead; *m* 2nd Eliza (*d* 13 Feb 1960), dau of John Worrall, and *d* 1 Nov 1923, having by her had two sons and a dau
6 Francis Joseph; *b* 6 May 1875; *m* 9 June 1890 Cissy Mildred (*d* USA 28 Aug 1972), dau of James Miller, of London, and *d* 19 May 1962, leaving three sons and a dau
1 Annie; *b* 12 May 1861; *d* unm 14 Jan 1891
2 Beatrice Sarah; *b* 7 Aug 1864; *d* unm 19 July 1940
3 Florence Martha; *b* 31 Oct 1872; *m* 20 June 1894 David Daniel Jones (*d* 3 Feb 1933), had issue, added by deed poll 21 Nov 1938 the name VESTEY and *d* 28 Nov 1961

SAMUEL VESTEY's est s,
  Sir William Vestey, 1st Bt, and **1st Baron Vestey**, of Kingswood, Co Surrey (both UK), so *cr* 21 June 1913 and 20 June 1922 respectively; *b* 21 Jan 1859; *educ* Liverpool Inst; dir Union Cold Storage Co, head Blue Star Line; *m* 1st 22 March 1882 Sarah (*d* 8 Aug 1923), dau of George Ellis, of Tranmere; *m* 2nd 9 Aug 1924 Evelyn (*d* 1941), dau of Hans Brodstone, of Superior, Neb., and *d* 10 Dec 1940, leaving by his 1st w:

1 SAMUEL, **2nd Baron**
2 George Ellis; *b* 9 Oct 1884; *m* 2 Sept 1909 Florence May (*d* 16 May 1964), dau of Thomas Webster, of Melling, Lancs, and *d* 14 Aug 1968, leaving:

  (1) Florence Mary; *b* 20 Nov 1913; WAAF WW II; *m* 10 July 1945 Maj Anthony Hugh Stevens, TD, RA (*d* 1979), s of Lt Col Hugh Clayton Stevens, and *d* 10 Aug 1994, leaving:

    1a *Hugh Charles [Hugh Stevens Esq, The Hall, Thorpe Arnold, Leics LE14 4RU]; *b* 26 Oct 1946; *educ* Winchester and U of Michigan (BA); *m* 1st 18 March 1972 (*divorce* 1993) Nicola Priscilla, dau of J C Bridgeman, of Staffs; *m* 2nd 22 May 1993 *Gabriele Maria Irmingard Nuesslein, of Munich, and by her has:

      1b *Robert Max William; *b* 16 June 1996
      1b *Delia Mary Susanne; *b* 12 Dec 1991
      2b *Sophie Clara Charlotte; *b* 19 June 1993

    1a *Angela Mary [Mrs Aubrey Adams, Vines Farm, Kidmore End, Oxon RG4 9AP]; *b* 9 Oct 1948; *m* 6 May 1972 *Aubrey John Adams, s of J W L Adams, of Henley, and has:

      1b *Katherine Mary Alicia; *b* 1975
      2b *Sara Angela Rose; *b* 1978
      3b *Felicity Nichole Elizabeth; *b* 1983

  (2) *Norah [Mrs William Dobbs, Sundial House, Greystones, Co Wicklow, Ireland]; *b* 16 March 1916; *m* 1st 7 March 1944 Maj William Bellingham Denis Dobbs, Roy Ulster Rifles (*d* 1982), s of William Bellingham Dobbs, of Dundrum, Co Dublin; *m* 2nd 17 Jan 1985 William Ronald Dobbs (*d* 9 Dec 1985) and by her 1st husb has:

    1a *George Denis Kildare; *b* 4 Sept 1947; *educ* Rugby; *m* 1975 *Prunella Osborne, dau of Osborne David Philips, of Dunganstown, Co Wicklow, and has:

      1b *Kildare Denis David; *b* 1979
      2b *Edward George; *b* 1982
      1b *Emily Norah; *b* 1977

    1a *Rosemary Florence [Mrs Michael Steen, Nevilles, Mattingley, Hants RG27 8JU]; *b* 21 Dec 1944; *m* 18 Dec 1971 *(David) Michael Cochrane Elsworth Steen and has issue (*see* COCHRANE, Bt)
    2a *Susan Norah [Mrs Nigel Atkinson, 43 Bramerton St, London SW3]; *b* 23 Feb 1951; *m* 1978 *Nigel Atkinson and has:

      1b *Anna Venetia; *b* 1980
      2b *Camilla Mary; *b* 1983

  (3) *Alice [Mrs Basil Beale, Appleton House, Appleton-le-Street, N Yorks YO17 0PG]; *b* 7 May 1918; *m* 1st 29 Sept 1939 William Ernest Legard (*see* LEGARD, Bt) and has issue; *m* 2nd 27 Nov 1943 Col Basil Perry Beale, OBE, MC, DL, RASC (*d* 30 Nov 1967), only surv s of Sydney Benjamin Beale, of Sutton Ho, Sutton, Surrey, and by him has:

    1a *Richard Basil William; *b* 1944; *m* 1981 *Siao-Li Liao and has:

      1b *Jennifer Mary Alice; *b* 1982
      2b *Alice Elizabeth May; *b* 1985

    2a *Stephen Dudley Norman; *b* 1950; *m* 1st 1972 (*divorce* 1978) Elizabeth Helen, dau of Peter Green, of The Rookery, Kirkby Malham, Yorks, and has:

      1b *Zoë Helen; *b* 1973

    2a (cont.) Stephen Beale *m* 2nd 1978 *Jo-Anna Mary Munt, dau of Arthur Harry Cook, of Church Farm, Wavendon, Bucks, and has:

      1b *Rollo Basil Arthur; *b* 1982

    1a *Elizabeth Alice; *b* 1947; *m* 1975 *Anthony David Stanbury, of Lewcombe Manor, E Chelborough, Dorset, and has:

      1b *Alexander George Basil; *b* 1978
      2b *Edward Samuel Joseph; *b* 1982
      1b *Caroline Alice; *b* 1976
      2b *Victoria Elizabeth Sophie; *b* 1984

3 Leonard; *b* 21 Dec 1888; Capt RFA; *m* 1st 21 Aug 1919 (*divorce* 1931) Hilda Dorothy (*d* 21 June 1943), dau of Thomas Thompson, of Grays, Essex; *m* 2nd 1931 Eleanor Margery (*m* 3rd 1955 Dr Richard Taylor; *m* 4th 19– Frank Fisher; *d* 1972), er dau of Edward Colman, of Three Ways, Chobham, Surrey, and widow of Capt F W H Simpson, RA, and *d* 1954, leaving:

(1) *Joyce [Mrs Thomas Strong, 19 Elamang Ave, Kirribilli, Sydney, NSW 2061, Australia]; *b* 2 Sept 1920; *m* 1st 16 Feb 1949 (*divorce* 1953) Henry Willis Maxwell Telling (*d* 1993), only s of Harry Maxwell Telling, and has:

1a *Michael Henry Maxwell; *b* 1950; *m* 1st 1978 (*divorce* 1981) Alison Ruth Webber and has:

1b *Matthew James Maxwell; *b* 1979

1a (cont.) Michael Telling *m* 2nd 1981 Monika Elizabeth (*d* 1983), dau of Louis Zumsteg, of Santa Rosa, Calif.

(1) (cont.) Mrs Joyce Telling *m* 2nd 1966 Dr Thomas Hugh Strong (*d* 1988)

(2) *Elizabeth Anne [Mrs Elizabeth Brougham, 26 Eldon Rd, London W8 5PT]; *b* 16 Dec 1923; *m* 30 March 1946 (*divorce* 1962) Lt-Cdr Patrick Brougham, RN, 3rd s of Capt John Hermann Brougham, DSC, RN, of Dulwich, and had:

1a *Christopher John, QC (1988) [Christopher Brougham Esq QC, 34 Launceston Place, London W8 5RN]; *b* 11 Jan 1947; *educ* Radley and Worcester Coll Oxford (BA 1968); barrister Inner Temple 1969; *m* 1974 *Mary Olwen, dau of Timothy Traherne Corker, of London NW1, and has:

1b *William Charles Rupert; *b* 1977

1b *Emily Clarissa; *b* 1979

2b *Miranda Jane Thérèse; *b* 1982

3b *Deborah Anne Rosemary; *b* 1988

2a Dominic James; *b* 28 March 1952; *d* 11 May 1953

3a *Nicholas Dominic Leonard [Nicholas Brougham Esq, Ampfield House, Blackheath, Surrey GU4 8RD]; *b* 13 April 1954; *educ* Radley; *m* 1982 *Susan Margaret Anne, dau of Thomas Frederick Vernon Mason, of Carbery Lodge, Farley Green, Surrey, and has:

1b *Thomas Edward Alexander; *b* 1988

1b *Caroline Fiona Jane; *b* 1984

2b *Claire Emma Louise; *b* 1986

1a *Margaret Elizabeth Jane [Mrs John Webber, 8 Elm Rd, Beckenham, Kent BR3 4JB]; *b* 17 July 1948; *m* 1st 1970 (*divorce* 1982) Hugh Robert John Simpson and has had:

1b *Antony John; *b* 1972; *d* 1986

1b *Tracey Jane; *b* 1975

1a (cont.) Mrs Margaret Simpson *m* 2nd 1982 *John Arthur William Webber

4 Frank; *b* 11 Jan 1893; *educ* Malvern and Clare Coll Cambridge; RASC; *m* 12 March 1918 Mary Vera (*d* 10 June 1972), 5th dau of Robert Archibald Brockle, of Carmarthen, and *dsp* 22 July 1950

The 1st BARON's er s,

SAMUEL VESTEY, **2nd Baron Vestey**; *b* 25 Dec 1882; *educ* Merton Coll Oxford (MA); High Sheriff Glos 1933; *m* 28 July 1908 Frances Sarah (*d* 16 Jan 1969), er dau of John Richard Howarth, of Freshfield, Lancs, and *d* 4 May 1954, having had:

1 William Howarth; *b* 24 April 1912; Capt Scots Gds WW II; *m* 27 Sept 1939 *(Helen) Pamela Fullerton (Melba) [The Rt Hon Pamela Lady Vestey, Coombe Cottage, Coldstream, Victoria, Australia] (granted March 1955 rank of baron's widow), dau of George Nesbitt Armstrong (*see* ARMSTRONG, Bt), and was *ka* Italy 25 June 1944, leaving:

(1) SAMUEL GEORGE ARMSTRONG VESTEY, **3rd and present Baron Vestey**

(2) +Mark William [The Hon Mark Vestey, Foxcote Manor, Andoversford, Glos GL54 4LP]; *b* 16 April 1943; *educ* Eton; late 2nd Lt Scots Grds, granted March 1955 rank of baron's yr s; *m* 6 Feb 1975 *Rose Amelia, yr dau of Lt-Col Peter Thomas Clifton, CVO, DSO, JP, DL (*see* BRUCE, Bt, of Downhill), and has had:

1a +Benjamin John; *b* 7 Aug 1979

2a A son; *b* and *d* 30 Jan 1983

1a *Tamara Pamela; *b* 3 March 1976

2a *Carina Patricia; *b* 15 Sept 1982

1 Kathleen Sarah; *b* 28 May 1909; *m* 1st 30 Oct 1928 (*divorce* 1936) Maj Philip Wilfred Cripps, KRRC (*d* 31 May 1965), 2nd s of Maj Sir Frederick William Beresford Cripps, DSO, of Ampney Park, Cirencester; *m* 2nd 18 Sept 1936 (*divorce* 1942) Capt Maurice John Kingscote (*d* in a car accident 5 June 1959), of Callingwood Hall, Burton-on-Trent, 2nd s of Thomas Arthur Fitzhardinge Kingscote, CVO, JP; *m* 3rd 3 May 1942 Maj Geoffrey Harbord, MC (*d* 3 Sept 1953), s of Rev Harry Harbord, of Colwood Park, Bolney, Sussex; *m* 4th 7 Feb 1955, as his 2nd w, Cdr William Canning Eykyn, RN (ret) (*d* 4 July 1972), s of William Eykyn, of Thames Ditton, Surrey, and *d* 198–, leaving issue

2 Joan Frances, MBE (1946); *b* 17 July 1914; *m* 1st 7 Nov 1934 (*divorce* 1944) Maj Hammon Paine, 60th Rifles (*d* 1987), of Little Coxwell, Faringdon, er s of Louis Paine, of Bourton, Shrivenham, Berks, and had:

(1) *Christopher Hammon; *b* 1935; *educ* Eton and Oxford (MA, DM, MSc, BCh); FRCP, FRCR; *m* 1959 *Susan, dau of D Martin, of Bridgwater, Somerset, and has:

1a *Edward Hammon; *b* 1960

2a *Simon John Hammon; *b* 1964

1a *Lucy Hammon; *b* 1962

2a *Alice Sarah; *b* 1968

2 (cont.) The Hon Mrs Joan Paine *m* 2nd 8 Sept 1954 John Lindesay Compton Shedden (*d* Jan 1994), er s of Lindesay Harry Compton Shedden, of Somerby, Leics, and *d* Oct 1991

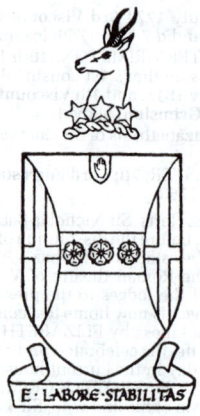

VESTEY, Bt

Arms: Argent on a fess between two flaunches gules, each charged with a cross throughout of the field, three roses also of the field.
Crest: In front of a springbok's head proper three mullets argent.
Motto: *E labore stabilitas* ('From work comes stability').
Creation: Bt. (UK) 27 June 1921.

SIR (JOHN) DEREK VESTEY, 2ND BT, of Shirley, Surrey [Sir Derek Vestey Bt, Park Penthouse, 355 King's Rd, London SW3 5ES]; *b* 4 Aug 1914; *s gf* 1953; *educ* Leys Sch Cambridge; F/Lt RAFVR WW II; *m* 21 June 1938 *Phyllis Irene, only dau of Harry Brewer, of Banstead, Surrey, and has:

1 +PAUL EDMUND [Paul Vestey Esq, 53 Cheval Place, London SW7]; *b* 15 Feb 1944; *educ* Radley; *m* 16 April 1971 *Victoria Anne Scudamore, 2nd dau of Sir John F E Salter, of Old Ford Ho, Tiverton, Devon, himself n of Baron Salter (LP, *see* 1970 edn), and has:

(1) *Joanna Clare; *b* 1972

(2) *Caroline Louise; *b* 2 Jan 1975

(3) *Georgina Jane; *b* 1977

1 *Rosamund Hope [Mrs Karl Arvidsson, Longdown Cottage, Longdown, Guildford, Surrey]; *b* 8 April 1940; *m* 1st 23 Sept 1961 (*divorce* 1980) Anthony Charles Brown, s of Frederick Charles Brown, of Bisley, Surrey, and has:

(1) *Mark Nigel Alastair; *b* 7 April 1964; *m* 1993 *Elizabeth Ann Julien and has:

1a *Vita Rosamund; *b* 1993

(1) *Julia Caroline; *b* 26 Aug 1962

1 (cont.) Mrs Rosamund Brown *m* 2nd 1982 *Karl Ove Arvidsson

Lineage: SAMUEL VESTEY, of Liverpool (*see* VESTEY, B); had a 3rd s:

Sir Edmund Hoyle Vestey, 1st Bt (UK), so *cr* 27 June 1921; *b* 3 Feb 1866; *educ* Liverpool Inst; chm Union International Co, head Blue Star Line; *m* 1st 15 Aug 1887 (*divorce* 1926) Sarah (*d* 2 July 1940), dau of Joseph Barker, of Formby, Lancs; *m* 2nd 10 March 1926 Ellen (*d* 11 Dec 1953), yst dau of Arthur Franklin Soward, of Sutton, Surrey, and *d* 18 Nov 1953, having had by his 1st w:

1 John Joseph; *b* 16 June 1888; *m* 8 May 1913 Dorothy Mary (*d* 11 Nov 1918), dau of John Henry Beaver, of Gawthorpe Hall, Bingley, Yorks, and *d* 20 Aug 1932, leaving:

(1) Sir (JOHN) DEREK VESTEY, **2nd and present Bt**

(2) Charles Gordon; *b* 30 Oct 1916; *educ* Leys Sch Cambridge; Lt RNVR WW II; *m* 27 May 1946 *Monica Hope [Mrs Charles Vestey, Little Haley, Oxenhope, Keighley, Yorks BD22 9PY], yr dau of Arthur John Parker Heaton, of Manorlands, Oxenhope, and *d* 1986, leaving:

1a *Diana Mary; *b* 6 May 1947; *m* 1st 4 May 1968 Kenneth Cameron Simm (*d* 1977), s of Douglas Simm, of Glasgow, and has:

1b *Gordon Christopher Cameron; *b* 8 March 1970

1b *Holly Ann Cameron; *b* 1971

1a (cont.) Mrs Kenneth Simm *m* 2nd 1987 *Thomas Mark Blackburn, of Prospect House, Bradley, N Yorks

2a *Rachel Margaret [Mrs Philip Hills, The Mill House, Gt Horkesley, Essex CO6 4AB]; *b* 23 May 1949; LRAM; *m* 2 May 1970 *Philip Anthony Hills, PhD, only s of F W Hills, of Gidea Park, Essex, and has had:

1b *Thomas Edmund; *b* 5 April 1977

2b *Matthew William; *b* 4 July 1979

2 Percy Charles; *b* 2 March 1893; *m* 9 May 1916 Dorothy Emmeline (*d* 1976), dau of Charles David Johnston, and *d* 8 April 1939, leaving:

(1) +Roger Edmund [Roger Vestey Esq, 11 Hyde Park Gdns, London W2 2LU]; *b* 4 April 1921; *educ* Harrow and Clare Coll Cambridge (BA 1946, MA 1951); Capt Berks Yeo WW II; *m* 5 April 1950 *Penelope Jane, only dau of Lt-Col Robert Arthur Little, DSO, ED, of Melbourne, Australia, and formerly w of G A Richardson, and has had:

1a *Charles Julian; *b* 13 April 1952; *educ* Harrow, Munich U and Sorbonne; *d* 1993

2a +James Patrick; *b* 13 April 1954; *educ* Harrow and Southampton U; BM, MRCP; *m* 1981 *Nicola Jane, dau of Harold Vernon Knight

(1) *Patricia [Mrs William Servaes, South Green House, Orford, Suffolk; Flat 10, 34 Bryanston Sq, London W1]; *b* 29 Nov 1922; *m* 16 Jan 1945 *Lt William Reginald Servaes, RN, only s of V-Adml Reginald Maxwell Servaes, CB, CBE, of Crocker Hill House, nr Chichester, Sussex, and has had:

1a Michael Maxwell; *b* 22 Jan 1947; *educ* Harrow; *d* 1986

2a *James William; *b* 14 April 1948; *educ* Harrow; *m* 1st 1972 (*divorce* 1975) Phoebe, dau of Keith Pither Cox, of Sydney; *m* 2nd 1978 *Harriet, yr dau of Maj Richard Neville Barclay, of Pond Ho, Boxted, Colchester, and by her has:

1b *Rebecca Mansel; *b* 1981

2b *Alice Harriet; *b* 1984

3a *Andrew Mark; *b* 30 April 1963

1a *Diana Patricia [Mrs James Hiddleston, 2 Chalfont Rd, Oxford OX2 6TH]; *b* 1951; *m* 1978 *James Norman Hiddleston and has:

1b *Thomas William; *b* 1981

1b *Sarah Alexandra; *b* 1979

2b *Emma Elizabeth; *b* 1986

2a *Elizabeth Mary [Mrs Timothy Fargher, The Old Rectory, Orford, Suffolk IP12 2NN]; *b* 1953; *m* 1978 *Timothy John Russell Fargher and has:

1b *Matthew Philip Michael; *b* 1981

2b *Edmund James Timothy; *b* 1986

1b *Zoe Clare; *b* 1979

2b *Anna Patricia; *b* 1984

(2) *Mary, JP (Bucks 1955) [Lady Verney JP, Ballams, Middle Claydon, Bucks MK18 2ET]; *b* 11 June 1925; LRAM; *m* 7 July 1948 *Sir Ralph Bruce Verney, 5th Bt, of Claydon House (*qv*) and has issue

3 Ronald Arthur, DL (Suffolk 1970); *b* 10 May 1898; *educ* Malvern; High Sheriff Suffolk 1961; *m* 18 Oct 1923 Florence Ellen McLean (*d* 16 Nov 1966), est dau of Col Theodore George Luis, VD, of Taychreggan, Broughty Ferry, and *d* 1987, leaving:

(1) +Edmund Hoyle, DL (Suffolk 1991, Essex 1978) [Edmund Vestey Esq DL, Little Thurlow Hall, Haverhill, Suffolk CB9 7LQ; Iolaire Lodge, Lochinver, Sutherland IV27 4LU; Sunnyside Farmhouse, Hawick, Roxburghshire TD9 9SS]; *b* 19 June 1932; *educ* Eton; 2nd Lt Queen's Bays 1951, late Lt City of London Yeo, High Sheriff Essex 1977, chm Associated Container Transportation (Australia) 1979–82 and 1985–88, Pres Gen Cncl Br Shipping (subsequently Chamber Shipping) 1981–82 and 1992–94, Jt MFH Thurlow, Chm MFH Assoc 1992–96, Pres Essex County Scout Cncl 1979–87, FRSA, FCIT 1982; *m* 21 April 1960 *Anne Moubray, yr dau of Gen Sir Geoffry Allen Percival Scoones, KCB, KBE, CSI, DSO, MC, of The Old Mill Ho, Wendover, Bucks, and has:

1a +Timothy Ronald Geoffry [Timothy Vestey Esq, Waltons, Ashdon, Essex]; *b* 23 April 1961; 2nd Lt Queen's Dragoon Gds, chm Metro Networks; *m* 31 March 1995 *Mrs Tessa Shepherd-Barron and has:

1b +Jack Arthur; *b* 8 Aug 1996

2a +James Edmund McLean; *b* 1 June 1962

3a +George Moubray William [George Vestey Esq, Gt Thurlow Hall, Haverhill, Suffolk]; *b* 17 Sept 1964; *m* 1989 *Rachel, yr dau of Patrick Osborne, of Currandooley, NSW, and has:

1b *Thomas (Tom) Hector Moubray; *b* 1993

2b *Edmund Arthur Valentine; *b* 16 Aug 1995

3b +Richard George Archibald; *b* 17 Dec 1997

1b *Ruby Constance; *b* 1991

4a +Robin John Henry; *b* 14 April 1968; *m* 1993 *Victoria Eileen Herbert, yst dau of Robin Waddell, of Edinburgh, and has:

1b +Harry Robin Edmund; *b* 15 Dec 1997

1b *Georgina; *b* April 1994

2b *Rose Elizabeth Jean; *b* 5 Feb 1996

(1) *Florence Elizabeth Lindsay [Mrs Robert Clifton-Brown, Little Bradley House, nr Haverhill, Suffolk]; *b* 10 Sept 1926; *m* 26 April 1952 *Robert Lawrence Clifton-Brown (*see* BROWN, Bt) and has issue

(2) *Jane McLean [Mrs John Baddeley, Great Butts, Cousley Wood, Wadhurst, Sussex]; *b* 8 April 1928; *m* 23 June 1956 *John Richard Baddeley, only s of Cyril Laud Baddeley, of The Coach Ho, Westcott, Surrey, and has had:

1a *Mark Christian Jon; *b* 18 June 1960; *m* 1987 *Brigette Susan Alfille and has:

1b *Matthew; *b* 1989

2b *Charles David James; *b* 1991

2a *Edward Christopher Francis later Gary Christopher (deed poll); *b* 3 April 1965; *m* 1989 *Cecilia Barker

1a Melissa Jane Elizabeth; *b* 28 Sept 1963; *d* 1980

(3) *Margaret [Mrs James Payne, Ardvar, Drumbeg, via Lairg, Sutherland]; *b* 12 Dec 1929; *m* 24 July 1954 *James Gladstone Payne, only s of Ralph Arthur Payne, of Putney, and has:

1a *Michael Edmund [Michael Payne Esq, Severals Farm, Arkesden, Essex]; *b* 12 April 1959; *m* 1986 *Sophie Corinne Banks, dau of Jeremy John Banks Skinner, of Stocking Farm, Stocking Pelham, Herts, and has:

1b *Fergus Edmund; *b* 1990

2b *Hector Cameron; *b* 1992

3b *Caspar James; *b* 1994

1a *Nichola Rosemary; *b* 23 June 1955; *m* 1981 *Alastair Ian McArthur and has had:

1b *Matthew James; *b* 1984

2b *Harry Simon; *b* 1987

3b *Samuel George; *b* 1988

1b Emily Clare; *b* and *d* 1983

2a *Phillippa Margaret; *b* 27 April 1963; *m* 1982 *Simon Hamilton Shirley-Beavan and has:

1b *Charles Michael; *b* 1984

2b *George Ronald Benjamin; *b* 1987

4 William; *b* 13 Dec 1902; *m* 20 Sept 1928 Ursula Frances Bowring (*d* 1993), dau of Edward Henry Bowring Skimming, of Taplow House, Taplow, and *d* 9 July 1971, leaving:

(1) +John [John Vestey Esq, 22 Hyde Pk Gdns, London W2 2LY]; *b* 5 Nov 1929; *educ* Eton; *m* 6 March 1958 (*divorce* 1977) Felicity Gay, 2nd dau of Kenneth Malcolm Crawford, of Mount Annan, Holbrook, NSW, and has had:

1a David William; *b* 26 Jan, *d* 6 Feb 1959

1a *Victoria Gay; *b* 19 May 1960; *m* 1986 *David Michael Russell-Hills and has:

1b *Mark William; *b* 1988

1b *Lucy Scarlett; *b* 1986

2a *Angela Caroline; *b* 31 March 1962; *m* 1987 *Paul Coleman and has:

1b *Luca John; *b* 1988

3a *Georgina Ann; *b* 11 Feb 1964

4a *Sara Frances; *b* 26 Oct 1966; *m* 1991 *Santiago Gaztambide

5a *Christina Mary; *b* 29 Dec 1969

1 Hannah; *b* 23 Jan 1897; *m* 31 March 1937 Lt-Col Eugene John O'Meara, OBE, FRCS, IMS (*d* 25 June 1962), s of Frederick Augustus O'Meara, of Brookfield, Colyton, Devon

2 Gladys Muriel; *b* 19 Sept 1900; *m* 1st 21 Oct 1926 Jack Llewellyn Barton, only s of Harry Barton, of Hollesley, Suffolk; *m* 2nd 15 June 1935 Charles Fleming (*d* 1 Sept 1959) and *d* 1973

VINCENT

Arms: Azure a chevron between two garbs in chief and in base a castle, all or. **Crest:** In front of two bird-bolts points downwards, saltirewise or, a Labrador retriever dog statant, sable. **Motto:** *Fortitudine et conatu* ('By fortitude and endeavour'). **Creation:** Bt. (UK) 18 Jan 1937.

SIR WILLIAM PERCY MAXWELL VINCENT, 3RD BT, of Watton, Co Norfolk [Sir William Vincent Bt, Whistlers, South Lane, Buriton, Hants GU31 5RU]; *b* 1 Feb 1945; *s* f 21 Oct 1963; *educ* Eton; 2nd Lt Irish Gds 1964, gen serv medal (Borneo) 1965; *m* 22 Sept 1976 *Christine Margaret , dau of Rev Edward Walton, and has:

1 +EDWARD MARK WILLIAM; *b* 6 March 1978

2 +Charles Michael Lacey; *b* 18 July 1979

3 +John James Robertson; *b* 1981

Lineage: LACEY ANDREWS VINCENT, of Watton, Norfolk; had:

Sir Percy Vincent, 1st Bt (UK), so *cr* 18 Jan 1937, JP City London; *b* 3 Sept 1868; City London: Alderman 1929–42, Sheriff 1926–27 and Ld Mayor 1935–36, ktd 1927; *m* 6 March 1901 Christine Emily (*d* 31 March 1949), dau of George Horatio Board, and *d* 22 Jan 1943, leaving:

1 **Sir Lacey Eric Vincent, 2nd Bt**; *b* 13 Jan 1902; *educ* Mill Hill; Lt RASC 1940 (invalided out 1941), chm L E Vincent & Ptnrs; *m* 18 Oct 1938 *Helen Millicent [Helen Lady Vincent, 179 Cranmer Court, Sloane Ave, London SW3], yr dau of FM Sir William Robert Robertson, 1st Bt (*see* ROBERTSON OF OAKRIDGE, B), and *d* 21 Oct 1963, leaving:

(1) Sir WILLIAM PERCY MAXWELL VINCENT, **3rd and present Bt**

(2) *Amanda Mildred [Mrs Gerald Ward, Park Farm, Chilton Foliat, Hungerford, Berks RG17 0SY]; *b* 22 Nov 1942; *m* 1st 5 Dec 1961 Capt John Barry Dinan, Irish Gds, s of Dermot A Dinan, of S Kensington; *m* 2nd, as his 2nd w, *Gerald John Ward (*see* DUDLEY, E) and by her 1st husb has:

1a *Mark Henry; *b* 9 March 1963

2a *Dominic John; *b* 27 June 1966

1 *Christina Ena Comfort [Mrs John Stevens, The Cottage, Flower Lane, Godstone, Surrey]; *m* 15 July 1931 *John S Stevens

VINCENT OF COLESHILL

Creation: B. (LP, UK) 15 June 1996.

THE BARON VINCENT OF COLESHILL, of Shrivenham, Co Oxon (FM Sir Richard Frederick Vincent, GBE (1990), KCB (1984), DSO (1972)) [FM The Rt Hon The Lord Vincent of Coleshill GBE KCB DSO, House of Lords, London SW1A 0PW]; *b* 23 Aug 1931; *educ* Aldenham (Govr 1987–) and RMC Sci Shrivenham (Mil Dir Studies 1974–75, Cmdt 1980–83); RA: Nat Serv 1951, Germany 1951–55, Gunnery Staff 1959, Radar Research Establishment Malvern 1960–61, BAOR 1962, Tech Staff Trg 1963–64, Staff Coll 1965 (Instr 1972–73), Cwlth Bde Malaysia 1966–68, MOD 1968–70, cmded 12th Light Air Def Regt 1970–72, Greenlands Staff Coll Henley 1974, cmded 19th Airportable Bde 1975–77, RCDS 1978, Dep Mil Sec 1979–80, Master-Gen Ordnance 1983–87, V-CDS 1987–91, CDS 1991–92, Chm Mil Ctee NATO 1993–96, Col Cmdt REME 1981–87 and RA 1983–, Govr Ditchley fndn 1992–, Visiting Fell Australian Coll Def and Strategic Studies 1995–, V-Pres Def Mfrs Assoc 1996–, Master Gunner St James's Pk 1996–, Chm: ICSTM 1996– (Govr 1995–), Hunting Def Ltd 1996–, MoDeM consortium 1997–; dir Hunting Engrg 1996–, Vickers Def Systems 1996–; Chllr Cranfield U 1998–; Freeman City London 1992 and Freeman Wheelwrights' Co 1997–, FRAeS 1990, FIMechE 1990, Hon DSc Cranfield 1985, Fell ICSTM 1996, Jordanian Order Merit (1st Cl) 1991, Cdr US Legn Merit 1993; *m* 1955 *Jean Paterson, dau of Kenneth Stewart, and has had two sons (one decd) and a dau

Lineage: FREDERICK VINCENT; *m* Frances Elizabeth Coleshill and had:

RICHARD FREDERICK, *cr* a **Baron**

VINSON

Arms: Per pale gules and azure a cross formy argent, on a chief per pale azure and gules two bull's heads cabossed argent, armed or and crowned with a crown rayonny, each straight ray ensigned by a mullet gold. **Crest:** Upon a helm with a wreath argent, azure and gules within a garland of vine leaves or, a demi-ounce azure. **Supporters:** Dexter, an ounce rampant sable semy of mullets or, gorged with a garland of vine leaves gold; sinister, a horse rampant argent, also gorged with a garland of vine leaves gold, the compartment comprising two grassy hillocks and in the valley between them water barry wavy of six azure and argent. **Motto:** No freedom without choice. **Creation:** B. (LP, UK) 1985.

THE BARON VINSON, of Roddam Dene, Co Northumberland (Nigel Vinson, LVO (1979), DL (Northumberland 1990)) [The Rt Hon The Lord Vinson LVO DL, Roddam Hall, by Alnwick, Northumberland NE66 4XY; 34 Kynance Mews, London SW7 4QR]; *b* 27 Jan 1931; *educ* Pangbourne Nautical Coll; Lt Queen's Roy Regt 1949–51; fndr Plastic Coatings Ltd 1952 (chm 1952–72), dir: Fleming High Income Tst 1972–, BAA 1973–80, CPS 1974–80, Electra Investment Tst 1975–98 (dep chm 1990–), Barclays Bank 1982–88; memb: Crafts Advsy Ctee 1971–77, Design Cncl 1973–80, Northumbrian Nat Parks Countryside Ctee 1977–89, Nat Tst Regnl Ctee 1977–84; Dep Chm CBI Smaller Firms Cncl 1979–84; Chm: Industrial Participation Assoc 1971–79 (Pres 1979–89), CoSIRA 1980–82, Rural Devpt Commn 1980–90 (Memb 1978–90) and RSA Industry Year Steering Ctee 1985–87; Hon Dir Queen's Silver Jubilee Appeal 1976–78; Tstee IEA 1972– (Chm Tstees 1989–96); Cncl memb St George's House Windsor Castle 1990–96; fndn donor Martin Mere Wildfowl Tst; FRSA, CIMgt; author: *Personal and Portable Pensions for All* (1984), *Owners All* (1985) and *Take upon Retiring* (1997); *m* 1972 *Yvonne Ann, dau of Dr Olaf Collin, of Forest Row, Sussex, and has:

1 *Bettina Claire; *b* 1974
2 *Rowena Ann; *b* 1977
3 *Antonia Charlotte; *b* 1979

Lineage: RONALD VINSON; *m* Bettina Southwell-Sander and had:

NIGEL, *cr* a **Baron**

VIVIAN

VIVE · REVICTURUS

Arms: Quarterly, 1st and 4th, or a chevron azure between three lion's heads erased proper as many annulets of the field; on a chief embattled gules a wreath of oak or between two medals, the dexter representing the gold medal and clasp given the first Baron following his conduct in the actions of Sahagun, Benevente and Orthes; the sinister, the silver Waterloo medal; 2nd and 3rd, barry of six ermine and gules (for HUSSEY). **Crest:** Issuant from a bridge of one arch embattled, and having at each end a tower, a demi-hussar in the uniform of the 18th Regt holding in his right hand a sabre, and in his left a pennon flying to the sinister gules, and inscribed with gold letters 'Croix d'Orade'. **Supporters:** Dexter, a grey horse caparisoned, thereon mounted a hussar of the 7th Regt of Light Dragoons habited, armed and accoutred, his sword drawn, proper; sinister, a bay horse guardant, caparisoned, thereon mounted a lancer of the 12th Regt, habited, armed and accoutred, supporting his lance, also proper. **Mottoes:** *Cor nobyle, cor immobyle* ('A heart both noble and unshakeable') and *Vive revicturus* ('Live as if about to be brought back to life'). **Creations:** Bt. (UK) 19 Jan 1828, B. (UK) 19 Aug 1841.

THE 6TH BARON VIVIAN OF GLYNN AND OF TRURO, Co Cornwall, and a **Baronet** (Sir Nicholas Crespigny Laurence Vivian, Bt) [Brig The Rt Hon The Lord Vivian, 5 Edith Terrace, London SW10 0TQ]; *b* 11 Dec 1935; *s f* 1991; *educ* Eton and Madrid U; Lt-Col 3rd Carabiniers, Roy Scots Dragoon Gds 1971, CO 16th/5th Queen's Roy Lancers 1976–79, Col MOD 1979–84, Dep Cdr Land Forces Cyprus and Ch of Staff 1984–87, Cdr Br Communicaton Zone NW Europe 1987–90, ret 1990 as Brig; *m* 1st 13 Dec 1960 (*divorce* 1972) Catherine Joyce, yst dau of James Kenneth Hope, CBE, DL, of W Park, Lanchester, Co Durham, and has:

1 +CHARLES CRESPIGNY HUSSEY; *b* 20 Dec 1966; *educ* Milton Abbey
1 *Henrietta Mary [The Hon Mrs Hoyland, 14 Starmead Dve, Wokingham, Berks; Box Green, Box, Nailsworth, Glos]; *b* 4 April 1963; *m* 21 July 1984 *Philip John Hoyland, s of Dr H J Hoyland, of Painswick, Glos, and has:
  (1) *Jack Nicholas Hope; *b* 1985
  (2) *George Hugh James; *b* 1991
  (1) *Francesca Mary Jane; *b* 1986

The 6th BARON *m* 2nd 6 Dec 1972 *Carol, er dau of (Frederick) Alan Martineau, MBE, JP, of Valley End Ho, Chobham, Surrey, and by her has:

2 *Natasha Sarah; *b* 17 Nov 1973
3 *Camilla Harriet; *b* 1 Oct 1976

Lineage: JOHN VIVIAN, of Trewan; *m* Mary Cavell and had a 2nd s:

THOMAS VIVIAN; *b* 1617; gf of:

THOMAS VIVIAN, of Comprigney; *m* Lucy Glynn and had:

Rev THOMAS VIVIAN, of Cornwood, Devon; *m* 1747 Mary (*d* 1807), dau of John Hussey, of Okehampton, barrister, and *d* 17 March 1793, leaving, with three yr sons (Thomas, *d* unm 1773; Rev Richard, JP, *b* 1754, Rector Bushey, Herts, *m* 1779 Mary Catherine (*d* 1843), dau of Edward John Willshire Emmett, of Dalton, Herts, and *d* 1825, leaving issue: Rev William Henry, *m* Frances Wingrove and *dsp* 13 Nov 1840):

JOHN VIVIAN, of Truro; V-Warden Stannaries; *m* 24 Aug 1774 Betsey (*d* 1816), only surv child of Rev Richard Cranch, and *d* 7 Dec 1826, leaving:

1 RICHARD HUSSEY, **1st Baron**
2 John Henry, of Singleton, Glam; had:
  (1) HENRY HUSSEY VIVIAN, 1st BARON SWANSEA OF SINGLETON (*qv*)
3 Thomas; *d* unm 1821

The est s,

Sir Richard Hussey Vivian, 1st Bt, and **1st Baron Vivian of Glynn and of Truro**, Co Cornwall (both UK), so *cr* 19 Jan 1828 and 19 Aug 1841 respectively, GCB (1837), KCB 1815), GCH (1831), KCH 1816), PC (I 1831, GB 1835); *b* 28 July 1775; *educ* Truro GS, Harrow and Exeter Coll Oxford; Ensign 20th Foot July

1793, Lt 54th Foot Oct 1793, Capt 28th Foot 1794, tfd 7th Light Dragoons 1798, Maj 1803, Lt-Col 25th Light Dragoons Sept 1804, tfd back to 7th Light Dragoons Dec 1804 (cmdg Corunna Campaign 1808–09), Col 1812, served Peninsular War again and France 1813–14, Maj-Gen 1814, cmded 6th Light Cavalry Bde Waterloo Campaign 1815 (despatches, thanks of Parl), Lt-Gen 1827, Col 12th Lancers 1827–37 and 1st Roy Dragoons 1837–42, Cdr Forces Ireland 1831–36, MP (Whig) Truro 1820–26 and 1832–34, Windsor 1826–31 and E Cornwall 1837–41, Master-Gen Ordnance 1835–41, DCL Oxon 1834; *m* 1st 14 Sept 1804 Eliza (*d* 15 July 1831), yst dau of Philip Champion de Crespigny, of Aldborough, Suffolk, and had:

1 CHARLES CRESPIGNY, **2nd Baron**

2 John Cranch Walker; *b* 18 April 1818; Capt 11th Hus, MP Truro, a Ld Treasury, U-Sec War; *m* 1st 31 March 1840 Louisa (*dsp* 5 May 1855), only dau of Henry Woodgate; *m* 2nd 18 June 1861 Florence Grosvenor (*m* 2nd 3 July 1872 5th Marquess of Waterford (*qv*) and *d* 4 April 1873), dau of Maj George Rowley (*see* ROWLEY, Bt); *m* 3rd 29 April 1876 Emma (*d* 10 May 1924), widow of Thomas Price, of Bayswater, and *d* 22 Jan 1879, having had by his 2nd w, with another dau (*d* unm):

(1) Sybll Agnes; *b* 2 April 1862; *m* 17 Aug 1889 Maj Heathfield Butler Dodgson, DSO, RA (*d* 31 Aug 1937), s of William Oliver Dodgson, of Sevenoaks, and *d* 28 Dec 1936, leaving issue

(2) Violet Jane Henrietta; *b* 8 Nov 1863; *m* 8 Nov 1887 William Somers Schuster (*d c* 1920), s of Samuel Lee Schuster, of The Grange, Leatherhead, Surrey, and *d c* 1917, leaving issue

1 Charlotte Eliza; *m* 14 Aug 1833 Gen Charles George James Arbuthnot (*d* 21 Oct 1870), est s of Rt Hon C Arbuthnot, and *d* 30 July 1877, leaving issue

2 Jane Frances Anne; *m* 12 Dec 1854 Henry John Wentworth Foley (*d* 23 April 1894), of Prestwood, Worcs, MP S Staffs, and *d* 2 Dec 1860, leaving issue

3 Georgina Agnes Augusta; *d* 1835

The **1st Baron** *m* 2nd 10 Oct 1833 Letitia (*d* 4 Jan 1885 aged 80), 3rd dau of Rev James Agnew Webster, of Ashford, Co Longford, and n of Sir Henry Brooke, 1st Bt, of Colebrooke (*see* BROOKEBOROUGH, V), and *d* 20 Aug 1842, leaving by her:

4 Lalage Letitia Caroline; *m* 26 March 1857 Henry Hyde Nugent Bankes (*d* 28 March 1895), s of George Bankes, PC, MP, of Kingston Hall, Dorset, and *d* 4 Oct 1875, leaving issue

The 1st BARON's est s,

CHARLES CRESPIGNY VIVIAN, **2nd Baron Vivian of Glynn and of Truro**; *b* 24 Dec 1808; *educ* Eton; Lt Rifle Bde 1825, Cornet 7th Hus 825, Lt 1826, Capt 1829, Brevet Maj 1834, MP Bodmin 1835–42, Dep Warden Stannaries 1852, Ld Lt Cornwall 1856–77; *m* 1st 2 July 1833 Arabella (*d* 26 Jan 1837), dau of Rev John Scott (*see* MEATH, E), and had:

1 HUSSEY CRESPIGNY, **3rd Baron**

2 John Brabazon; *b* 20 Oct 1836; *m* 6 May 1868 Alice Mary Disney Roebuck (*d* 5 May 1869) and *d* 12 Feb 1874

The **2nd Baron** *m* 2nd 21 Sept 1841 Mary Elizabeth (*d* 23 Jan 1907), est dau and heiress of Jones Panton, of Plas Gwyn, Pentraeth, Anglesey, and *d* 24 April 1886, having by her had:

3 Charles Hussey Panton; *b* 26 June 1847; *m* 6 Nov 1875 Irene Maud Shelah (*d* 18 June 1940, having *m* 2nd 8 April 1896 (*divorce* 1906, resumed former name) Walter Hayle Walshe), est dau of Capt John Farrer, of Gurthalougha, Co Tipperary, and *d* 12 March 1892, leaving:

(1) Gladys Irene Constance Camilla; *m* 1st 11 Dec 1900 (*divorce* 1907) Lewis Claud Leadbetter, s of Alfred Leadbetter; *m* 2nd 27 June 1919 Lt-Cdr Raymond George Francis Herault de Caen, DSC, RN (*d* 12 April 1922), only surv s of John Herault de Caen, of Jersey and Ceylon, and *d* 1 Oct 1954

4 Claud Hamilton, of Plas Gwyn, JP, DL Anglesey; *b* 18 March 1849; barrister, High Sheriff Anglesey 1899; *m* 29 April 1878 Constance Emily (*d* 20 Oct 1905), 2nd dau of Capt Jules Alexander Sartoris, of Hoppesford Hall, Warwicks, and *d* 8 May 1902, leaving:

(1) Anthony Hamilton, of Plas Gwyn; *b* 5 Dec 1880; Capt Rifle Bde; *d* 14 Feb 1937

(2) Claud Esme, MC, of Plas Gwyn, JP, DL Anglesey; *b* 18 June 1882; Lt-Col and Brevet Col 6th Bn Roy Welch Fus (TA), Capt RFA; *m* 26 Sept 1914 Emily, yst dau of Col Michael Rowand Gray-Buchanan, OBE, of Ettrickdale, Isle of Bute, and *d* 8 Jan 1928, leaving:

1a Claud Panton; *b* 5 June 1920; Capt RHA WW II; *m* 15 May 1943 Margaret Eleanor (*m* 2nd 10 Jan 1947 Charles Dundas Lawrie, of Plas Gwyn, yr s of Alfred Ainslie Lawrie, JP, of Edinburgh), only dau of Capt Alexander Edwin Baird, OBE, of Halles Brae, Colinton, Edinburgh, and *d* of wounds recd in action Normandy July 1944, leaving:

1b *Amanda Mary Panton; *b* 26 March 1944

1a *Elizabeth Frederica Amesbury [Mrs Claude Fanning-Evans, Plas Cadnant, Menai Bridge, Anglesey]; *b* 1916; *m* 17 July 1947 Maj Claude Fanning-Evans, DL, Durham LI, s of Maj Thomas Fanning-Evans, JP, DL

2a Esme Constance; *d* unm 29 June 1951

3a *Ann [Mrs Desmond Brennan, Cae Du, Dwyran, Anglesey]; *b* 1923; *m* 16 April 1953 Dr Desmond Brennan (*d* 1970), est s of Dr James Brennan, of Beech Hill, Patrickswell, Co Limerick, and has:

1b *Vincent Patrick Esme; *b* 21 Aug 1958

1b *Claire Patricia Ann; *b* 27 Oct 1956

2b *Hazel Mary; *b* 24 July 1961

(3) Cyril Panton VIVIAN later HAMPTON-VIVIAN (deed poll 1947), of Treffos, Llansadwru, Anglesey; *b* 12 Sept 1885; RN, RFC and RAF; *m* 2 Aug 1921 Sisli Myfanwy (*d* 2 Feb 1968 aged 84), widow of Capt Arthur Charles Davies and yst dau of Col Thomas Lewis Hampton-Lewis, JP, DL, and *dsp* 23 Nov 1960

(4) Eric Paul; *b* 8 Sept 1891; Capt RN, WWs I (despatches) and II; *m* 1 June 1922 Evelyn Audrey, est dau of Capt Thomas Pryse Arthur Holford, of Duntish Court, Buckland Newton, Dorset, and *d* 9 July 1961, leaving:

1a Desmond Walter Paul; *b* 14 May 1925; *educ* Harrow; Capt 12th Roy Lancers WW II (despatches twice); *m* 14 May 1949 Rose Gabrielle [Mrs Desmond Vivian, Langford Gate, Sydling St Nicholas, Dorset], yr dau of

---

Capt Charles John Houssemayne du Boulay, of Exton Ho, Exton, Hants, and *d* 2 July 1974, leaving:

1b +(Christopher) John Desmond; *b* 1 May 1956; *educ* Harrow; *m* 1984 *Alice Camilla, yst dau of John Brian Hollingsworth, of Cruea, Llanfrothen, Penrhyndeudraeth, Gwynedd, and has:

1c +Alastair Desmond; *b* 1991

1b *Vanda Rose; *b* 4 July 1950

1b *Clare Veronica; *b* 29 Oct 1952

2a +Patrick Cyril [Patrick Vivian Esq, Pumney, Sutton Courtenay, Oxon]; *b* 1 Nov 1929; *educ* Harrow and Cambridge (BA 1950, MA 1958, MB and BCh 1953); DRCOG 1958, late Capt RAMC; *m* 26 Aug 1961 *Pamela Mary, yst dau of Lt-Col Richard Rees Davies, JP, DL, of Ceris, Bangor, Caernarvs, and has:

1b +Simon Paul Richard [Simon Vivian Esq, 25 Rosebury Rd, London SW6 2NQ]; *b* 22 July 1962; *educ* Harrow and Nottingham U (LLB); slr 1987; *m* 1st 1988 (*divorce* 1991) Rose Rookmin, dau of Dr Balideo Bisseru, of Lusaka, Zambia, and Bromley, Kent; *m* 2nd 1997 *(Isobel) Suzy, dau of Edward Michael Thornton, of Ferndown, Dorset

1b *Susan Caroline; *b* 28 Aug 1964

3a +Charles Eveyln [Charles Vivian Esq, Hook Cottage, Hambledon, Hants]; *b* 23 Oct 1937; *educ* Haileybury

(5) Robert Crespigny Gwynedd; *b* 26 April 1898; *educ* Eton; Capt Life Gds; *m* 8 Dec 1925 Violet Clinton, 2nd dau of Clinton Holme, of Ruthin, Denbighs, and *d* 4 May 1984, leaving:

1a +Robin Audley Clinton [Robin Vivian Esq, B92 Res Amiral, Marina Baie des Anges, 06270 Villeneuve-Loubet, France]; *b* 24 Aug 1936; *educ* Eton; late Lt 12th Roy Lancers, jt md Marshall Cavendish 1976; *m* 13 May 1961 *Alice Penelope, only child of Lt Caesar Charles Hawkins, DSC, RN (*see* HAWKINS, Bt), and has:

1b +Rupert James; *b* 11 March 1970

1b *Claire Jennifer; *b* 2 June 1971

1a *(Edith) Eve(lyn) [Mrs Eve Clinton, Hawthorne Cottage, Pitmore Lane, Sway, Hants SO41 6BW]; *b* 10 Dec 1926; *m* 31 Dec 1954 (*divorce* 1975, took last forename as surname) Arnold Euston More Bloomer, of Eton, Bucks, er s of Leonard Bloomer, of Oak Cottage, Cunsey, Westmorland, and has:

1b *Anthony Leonard Clinton; *b* 24 April 1964; *m* 1993 *Harriet Ann, only dau of Timothy George Kirkbride (*see* BAKER-WILBRAHAM, Bt), and has:

1c *Alice Letitia Clinton; *b* 17 Sept 1996

1b *Angela Gwyneth More; *b* 7 Oct 1960; *m* 1988 *John Jardine Hearne Slater and has:

1c *Sophie Eve Hearne; *b* 15 Sept 1992

2c *Jessica Violet Hearne; *b* 19 Feb 1994

2a Pamela Blanche Gwynedd; *b* 7 Jan 1929; *m* 3 Dec 1955 (John) Charles Mark Fullerton, of Norwood Grange, Iver, Bucks, only s of Capt John Robert Rankin Fullerton, 19th Hus, of Boleskine Ho, Foyers, Inverness-shire, and had:

1b *John Robert Mark; *b* 16 April 1959

2b *David Adam Grey; *b* 3 March 1968

1b *Carolin Jane; *b* 1 Sept 1956

(1) Ursula Hermione Constance; *b* 31 Aug 1879; *d* unm 7 Sept 1945

5 Robert Champion; *b* 7 April 1854; Capt Cornwall Rangers Militia; *d* unm 29 Aug 1876

6 Walter Warrick, of Glyn, Bangor, and Cestyll, Cemaes Bay, Anglesey; *b* 18 May 1856; *d* unm 13 Sept 1943

1 Mary Charlotte Martha; *m* 13 Nov 1860 John Tremayne (*d* 7 April 1901), of Heligan, Cornwall, and Sydenham, Devon, and *d* 30 Oct 1917, leaving issue

2 Maude Frances; *m* 16 Feb 1876 Charles Garden Duff later Sir Charles Garden Assheton-Smith, 1st Bt (*d* 24 Sept 1914), and *d* 16 June 1893, leaving issue (*see* 1970 edn DUFF, Bt)

3 Edith; *m* 26 July 1873 Lt-Col Sir Audley Dallas Neeld, 3rd Bt (*d* 1 May 1941), and *d* 15 July 1926

The 2nd BARON's est s,

HUSSEY CRESPIGNY VIVIAN, **3rd Baron Vivian of Glynn and of Truro**, GCMG, GCMG (KCMG 1886), CB (1878), PC (1893); *b* 19 June 1834; *educ* Eton; FO 1851–93: Sr Clerk 1869–74, Consul-Gen Alexandria 1873, Moldavia and Wallachia 1874–76 and Egypt 1876–79, Min Berne 1879–81, Envoy Extrdy and Min Plen Denmark 1881–84 and Brussels 1884–92, Amb Rome 1892–93; *m* 8 June 1876 Louisa Alice (*d* 3 April 1926), only dau of Robert George Duff, of Wellington Lodge, Ryde, IoW, and sis of Sir Charles Garden Assheton-South, 1st Bt, of Vaynol (*see* 1970 edn DUFF, Bt), and *d* 21 Oct 1893, having had, with another s and dau (*d* in infancy):

1 GEORGE CRESPIGNY BRABAZON, **4th Baron**

1 Violet Mary, MBE (1945); Maid-of-Honour to HM QUEEN ALEXANDRA 1901–25; *d* unm 5 June 1962

2 Dorothy Maud (twin with Violet); LGStJ, Maid-of-Honour to TM QUEENs VICTORIA and ALEXANDRA 1899–1905; *m* 11 July 1905 1st Earl Haig (*qv*) and *d* 18 Oct 1939, having had issue

3 Alexandra Mary Freesia, CBE (1954, OBE 1945); *b* 27 Feb 1890 (HM QUEEN ALEXANDRA stood sponsor); Administrator No 12 Region WVS, Extra Woman Bedchamber to HM QUEEN ELIZABETH THE QUEEN MOTHER, Chm Victoria League 1948–53; *m* 31 Jan 1911 Lord Worsley (*ka* 30 Oct 1914), est s of 4th Earl of Yarborough (*qv*), and *dsp* 21 Sept 1963

The 3rd BARON's only s,

GEORGE CRESPIGNY BRABAZON VIVIAN, **4th Baron Vivian of Glynn and of Truro**, DSO (1918), TD (1920), JP, DL Cornwall; *b* 21 Jan 1878; *educ* Eton; ADC to HM GEORGE VI, Col cmdg 4th/5th Bn DCLI (TA), Maj 17th Lancers and Roy 1st Devon Yeo, Boer War 1900–01 (severely wounded), WW I (despatches twice), Legn Hon, Croix de Guerre France and Belgium, Order Leopold Belgium; *m* 1st 1 Aug 1903 (*divorce* 1907) Barbara, dau of William Atmar Fanning, and had:

1 ANTHONY CRESPIGNY CLAUDE VIVIAN, **5th Baron Vivian of Glynn and of Truro**; *b* 4 March 1906; *educ* Eton; Sgt RA WW II (invalided), Hants Special

Constabulary 1941 and 1943–44, war correspondent 1942, theatrical impresario; m 8 March 1930 Victoria Ruth Mary Rosamund (d 1985), est dau of Capt Henry Gerard Laurence Oliphant, DSO, MVO, RN, of Condie, and d 1991, leaving:

(1) NICHOLAS CRESPIGNY LAURENCE VIVIAN, **6th and present Baron Vivian of Glynn and of Truro**

(2) +Victor Anthony Ralph Brabazon [The Hon Victor Vivian, 26 Roehampton Close, Roehampton Lane, London SW15 5LU]; b 26 March 1940; educ Nautical Coll Pangbourne and Southampton U; theatre manager, late Merchant Navy; m 11 Feb 1966 *Inger Johanne, yr dau of Per Gulliksen, of Sandefjord, Norway, and has:

    1a +Thomas Crespigny Brabazon; b 17 Jan 1971; educ Marlborough and Grenoble U

    1a *Arabella Victoria; b 2 Feb 1973

(1) *Sally Anne Marie Gabrielle [The Hon Mrs Wilson, 150 Cranmer Ct, Whiteheads Grove, London SW3 5LU]; b 22 Sept 1930; m 1st 31 Aug 1954 (divorce 1962) (William) Robin Charles Edward Cecil Lowe, s of John Muir Lowe (the actor John Loder), of Chelsea; m 2nd 15 Nov 1963 Charles William Munro Wilson, s of Charles Skinner Wilson, of Hampstead, and by him has:

    1a *Alexander Vivian; b 16 Sept 1965; educ Shiplake Coll

1 Daphne Winifred Louise; b 11 July 1904; author: Before the Sunset Fades (1951), Mercury Presides (1954), The Adonis Garden (1961), The Duchess of Jermyn Street: the life and times of Rosa Lewis (1964), Emerald and Nancy (1968), The Nearest Way Home (1970), The Rainbow Picnic: a portrait of Iris Tree, The Face on the Sphinx: a portrait of Gladys Deacon, Duchess of Marlborough (1978): m 1st 27 Oct 1927 (divorce 1953) 6th Marquess of Bath (qv) and had issue; m 2nd 11 July 1953 (divorce 1978) Maj (Ale)Xan(der) Wallace Fielding, DSO (d 1991), s of Alexander Lumsden Wallace, of Kirkcaldy, and d 5 Dec 1997

The **4th Baron** m 2nd 5 Jan 1911 Nancy Lycett, OBE (1946, MBE 1918), CStJ, WVS Organiser Cornwall (d 6 May 1970), widow of Capt Adrian Rose, RHG (see ROSE, Bt, of Montreal and Hardwick Ho), and er dau of Sir Edward Lycett Green, 2nd Bt (qv), and d 28 Dec 1940, leaving by her:

2 Douglas David Edward, DSC; b 16 Jan 1915; Lt-Cdr RN WW II (despatches three times); m 3 April 1943 *Mary Alice [The Hon Mrs Douglas Vivian, Edington Cottage, Inmead, Edington, Wilts BA13 4QR], er dau of Francis John Gordon Borthwick (see BORTHWICK, L), and d 27 July 1973, leaving:

(1) *Deborah Mary, OBE, JP [Mrs Nicholas Hinton OBE JP, 22 Westmoreland Pl, London SW1V 4AE; Perhaver House, Cliff Rd, Gorran Haven, St Austell, Cornwall PL26 6JW]; b 15 Jan 1944; FRSA; m 18 Dec 1971 Nicholas John Hinton (d 1997), only s of Rev Canon John Hinton, of Bridport Rectory, Dorset, and has:

    1a *Josephine Mary Vivian; b 3 Aug 1984

(2) *Rose Emma Margaret [Mrs Benjamin Goodden, Ferryside, Riverside, Twickenham, Middx]; b 13 Sept 1945; m 1st 29 July 1965 (divorce 1973) James Collet Norman, yst s of Brig Hugh Ronald Norman, DSO, of St Clere, Kensing, Kent, and has:

    1a *Rupert Montagu; b 1966; m 1995 *Tasmin Fischer

    2a *Jason Douglas; b 1968

    1a *Melissa Rose; b 1970

(2) (cont.) Mrs Rose Norman; m 2nd 4 May 1973 *Benjamin Bernard Woulfe Goodden, only s of Cecil Phelips Goodden JP, of The Old Ho, N Cheriton, Templecombe, Somerset, and by him has:

    3a *Timothy Simon; b 1980

(3) *Eugenie Nancy Vivian [Mrs Eugenie Burne, Pear Tree Cottage, Bratton, Wilts]; b 20 Aug 1947; m 30 July 1966 (divorce 1988) Capt Simon Nicholas John Burne, 9th/12th Roy Lancers (Prince of Wales's), only s of Brig John Richard Burne, of Grove Cottage, Chiddingfold, Surrey, and has:

    1a *Thomas Edward Francis; b 1980

    1a *Lucy Caroline; b 7 Sept 1970; m 31 May 1997 *Timothy Fielding

(4) *Victoria Alice [Mrs Victoria Craig, The Lodge, Highfield, Co Durham DH8 9LQ]; b 20 Aug 1947; m 25 Nov 1972 (divorce Oct 1996) Nicholas Charlton Dudley Craig, s of (George) Dudley Craig, of Corbridge, Northumberland, and has:

    1a *Richard Nicholas Dudley; b 11 March 1976

    2a *Edward Douglas Charlton; b 1977

    3a *George David Vivian; b 1982

(5) *Charlotte Claire [Mrs Charles Dimpfl, 19 Gledhow Gdns, London SW5 0AZ]; b 5 Oct 1950; m 16 Oct 1971 *Charles Robert Dimpfl, er s of Robert Dimpfl, of Chelsea, and has:

    1a *Francesca Mary; b 3 April 1979

    2a *Daisy Charlotte; b 5 March 1985

    3a *Nancy Alice Rose; b 8 Aug 1990

2 (Ursula) Vanda Maud; b 16 July 1912; m 1st 1 Oct 1935 (divorce 1946) Maj Philip Alexander Clement Bridgewater, 5th Roy Inniskilling Dragoon Gds, only s of Capt Clement Bridgewater, Inniskilling Dragoons, and had:

(1) *Adrian Alexander Vivian [Adrian Bridgewater Esq, 5 Chaucer Rd, Cambridge]; b 1936; m 1st 1958 Charlotte, er dau of Rev Michael Ernest Christopher Pumphrey, Rector Hunsdon, Herts, and has:

    1a *Thomas George Michael; b 1964

    1a *Emma Mary; b 1960

    2a *Sophia Charlotte; b 1962

(1) (cont.) Adrian Bridgewater; m 2nd 1969 *Lucy Mary Le Breton, dau of Sir Basil Hardington Bartlett, 2nd Bt (qv), and has further issue

2 (cont.) The Hon Mrs Vanda Bridgewater m 2nd 22 Aug 1946 (divorce 1960), as his 1st w, Sir William Fane Wrixon-Becher, 5th Bt (qv), and had further issue; m 3rd 6 March 1962 9th Earl of Glasgow (qv) and d 1984

VYVYAN

Arms: Argent on a mound in base vert a lion rampant gules, armed sable. **Crest:** A horse passant, furnished proper. **Mottoes:** 1 Sapere aude ('Dare to be wise'), 2 Dum vivimus vivamus ('While we are alive let us live well'). **Creation:** Bt. (E) 12 Feb 1644/5.

SIR (RALPH) FERRERS ALEXANDER VYVYAN, 13TH BT, of Trelowarren, Cornwall [Sir Ferrers Vyvyan Bt, Trelowarren, Mawgan, Cornwall TR12 6AF]; b 21 Aug 1960; s f 1995; educ Charterhouse, RMC Sandhurst and Architectural Assoc; m 12 April 1986 *Victoria Arabella, yst dau of M B Ogle, of Skerraton, Buckfastleigh, Devon, and has:

1 +JOSHUA DRUMMOND; b 10 Oct 1986
2 +Frederick George; b 21 Dec 1987
3 +Rowan Arthur; b 23 Oct 1989
4 +Inigo Valentine; b 14 Feb 1994

Lineage: RALPH VYVYAN, of Trevidren, Cornwall, had:

JOHN VYVYAN; m Honor, dau and heir of Richard Ferrers, of Trelowarren, and had:

RICHARD VYVYAN, of Trelowarren; Sheriff Cornwall c 1493 and c 1505; m Florence, dau of Richard Arundel, of Trerice, and had an est s:

MICHAL VYVYAN; Sheriff Cornwall c 1507; m Thomasine, dau of John Glyn, of Murvayle, and had, with a dau (Florence, m c 1540 John Fortescue, of Spridlestone, Devon, and had issue):

JOHN VYVYAN; m Elizabeth, est dau of Thomas Trethurfe, and had:

JOHN VYVYAN; MP Helston c 1572; m Anne, dau of Baldwin Malet (probably one of the MALETs of St Audries; see MALET, Bt), and had:

HANNIBAL VYVYAN; Sheriff Cornwall, MP Helston, Truro and St Mawes temp ELIZABETH I and JAMES I; m Philippa, dau of Roger Tremaine, of Cullacomb, Devon, and had:

Sir FRANCIS VYVYAN; Sheriff Cornwall c 1618; m Loveday, dau of John Connock, of Treworgy, Cornwall, and d 11 June 1635, leaving:

Sir Richard Vyvyan, 1st Bt (E), so cr 12 Feb 1644/5, of Trelowarren; MP, royalist Master Mint at Exeter in Civil War; m 20 Oct 1636 Mary, dau of James Bulteel, of Barnstaple, Devon, and d 3 Oct 1655, having had:

1 Sir Vyell Vyvyan, 2nd Bt; MP Helston 1679–81, Sheriff Cornwall 1682; m 1st 30 June 1671 Thomasine, dau and coheir of James Robyns, of Glasney and Penryn; m 2nd 24 Feb 1683/4 June, dau of Thomas Melhuish, of Penryn, and dsp 24 Feb 1696/7

2 Charles, of Merthen, Cornwall; m 1674 Mary, est dau and coheir of Richard Erisye, of Trevanna, Cornwall, and was bur 12 Nov 1687, leaving:

    (1) RICHARD (Sir), **3rd Bt**

    (2) Charles; Army Capt; m Margaret Ash

    (3) John (Rev); Rector Tiverton, Devon

The 2nd Bt's n,

Sir Richard Vyvyan, 3rd Bt; MP Cornwall temp QUEEN ANNE; m 9 Nov 1697 Mary (bur 3 Dec 1736), dau and heiress of Francis Vivian, of Coswarth, and d 9 May 1724, having had, with another s and two other daus:

1 **Sir Francis Vyvyan, 4th Bt**; bapt 29 Sept 1698; High Sheriff Cornwall 1739; m 30 May 1730 Grace (d 3 Nov 1740), only dau and heiress of Rev Carew Hoblyn, and was bur 29 Dec 1745, leaving:

    (1) **Sir Richard Vyvyan, 5th Bt**; b 11 May 1732; m 6 Dec 1754 Jane, dau of Christopher Hawkins, of Trewinnard, Cornwall, and dsp 13 Oct 1781

    (2) **Rev Sir Carew Vyvyan, 6th Bt**; bapt 11 Jan 1736/7; MA Oxon; dsp 4 Oct 1814

2 Richard, of Tresmarrow; b 5 Feb 1701; Recorder Launceston; m 16 July 1728 Philippa (d 7 May 1771), er dau and coheir of Philip Piper, of Tresmarrow, Cornwall, and d 14 Jan 1771, leaving:

    (1) Philip Pursan, of Tresmarrow; b 1 May 1731; m 22 Sept 1766 Mary (d 13 Oct 1794), dau and heiress of Sheldon Walter, of Tremea, Cornwall, and d March 1791, leaving:

        1a VYELL (Sir), **7th Bt**

2a Francis; Capt Gren Gds; m Harriett (d 11 Dec 1851), dau of Tremenheere Johns, of Helston, and dsp 1804

1a Harriett; m Stephen Luke

(2) Richard (Rev); Vicar Lamerton; m Anne Downe and had:

1a Richard, JP, DL, of Trewan, Cornwall; Lt-Col; m 1st Jane Ballard and had a dau (Mary); m 2nd Margaret Anne, dau of Hugh Edwards, and by her had:

1b Richard Henry Stackhouse, of Trewan, JP, DL; b 3 Dec 1832; dsp 1882

2b William Courtenay; b 1834; Ensign 4th Regt; m 1859 Catherine Horlor (d 1891), dau of John Stafford, and d March 1870, leaving:

1c Kate Courtenay; b 13 March 1865; m 1890 Harold Oxley Chamberlain Smith (d 1919), of Southernhay, Exeter, and d 21 Feb 1957, having had issue

1a (cont.) Richard Vyvyan m 3rd 2 June 1859 Henrietta Charlotte, dau of T L Crickitt, and d 14 May 1860

2a Philip VYVYAN later VYVYAN-ROBINSON, DL, of Nansloe, Cornwall; b 14 Sept 1777; served 88th Regt; m 1818 Mary Elizabeth, dau of Henry Hance, and d 1870, leaving:

1b Philip (Rev), of Nansloe; b 21 Sept 1820; BA Cantab; m 1st 13 June 1851 Augusta Baker (d 29 Feb 1860), dau of Henry Norris, of Taunton, and had:

1c Philip Augustus, of Carn Towan, Sennen, Cornwall, and Cardiff; b 19 April 1852; m 1879 Susan (d 1897), dau of Arthur Pring, and d 2 July 1911, leaving:

1d Arthur Claude; b 8 Sept 1880; educ Repton; Lt S Lancs Regt WW I (wounded); m 27 June 1923 Patricia (d 1982), only child of Frederick Theodore MacDonnell, of Bradbourne, Rustington, and d 14 July 1960, leaving:

1e Arthur Frederick, RD, JP; b 27 Nov 1925; educ Nautical Coll Pangbourne and Pembroke Coll Cambridge (MA); Lt-Cdr RNR WW II; Headmaster: Woodbridge Sch Suffolk, Roy Masonic Sch Bushey; m 27 Dec 1951 Patricia Jill, er dau of Ivor William Gerwyn Freeman, of Ashwood Grange, Woking, and d 20 Jan 1999, leaving:

1f +Patrick John; b 14 June 1955; educ Radley; late Maj Roy Fus; m 30 Dec 1978 *Rosamund Mary, er dau of Maj Acton Henry Gordon Gibbon, GM, of Errington, Trillick, Co Tyrone, and has:

1g *Rachel Louise; b 1981

2g *Joanna Elizabeth; b 1983

3g *Tamsin Sarah; b 1987

4g *Henrietta Frances; b 1989

2f +James Courtenay, MBE (1988); b 21 Jan 1958; late Maj RGJ; m 1988 *Nicola, dau of N Poston, of Waltham St Lawrence, Berks, and has:

1g +Christopher Courtenay; b 1994

1g *Jessica Josselyn; b 1990

3f +David Augustus; b 13 Dec 1960; m 1988 *Charlotte, dau of Oscar Husum, of Cascais, Portugal

1f *Amanda; b 22 Jan 1953; m 1974 *Charles Philip Metcalfe Yeoman, ARICS, er s of P M Yeoman, FRCS, of Monkton Combe, Bath, and has:

1g *Charles William Metcalfe; b 1978

2g *Thomas Frederick Metcalfe; b 1980

3f *Harriet Vyvyan; b 1983

2e +Cecil Courtenay [Cecil Vyvyan-Robinson Esq, The Old House, Horsham, Worcs WR6 6PN]; b 5 Sept 1928; educ Charterhouse and Jesus Coll Cambridge (MA); late Capt RA (TA); m 11 June 1955 *Ann Leonora Dirom; er dau of Victor Berwyn Jones, MRCVS, of Frocester Lodge, Stonehouse, Glos, and has:

1f +Peter Dirom Courtenay, TD [Maj Peter Vyvyan-Robinson TD, 85 Finlay St, London SW6 6HF]; b 3 April 1958; Maj HAC; m 1994 *Elizabeth Anne Mary, dau of Derek Guy, of Backwell, Bristol

1f *Frances Jane [Mrs Michael Berrett, 49 Charlton Village Rd, Wantage, Oxon OX12 7HQ]; b 12 Jan 1957; AGSM; m 1981 *Michael Vincent Berrett, BA, slr, only s of I V Berrett, of Woodford Green, Essex, and has:

1g *Peter Michael Vyvyan; b 1990

2g *Joseph Benedict Vyvyan; b 1994

1g *Elizabeth Tamsin Mary; b 1985

2g *Anna Rosamunde Dirom; b 1987

2f *Katherine Armorel [Mrs Mark Stanford, 12b Arterberry Rd, London SW20 8AJ]; b 27 Sept 1959; m 1986 *Mark Peter Stanford, est s of P J Stanford, of Dartford, Kent, and has:

1g *Charlotte June; b 1987

2g *Sarah Vyvyan; b 1989

3f *Diane Elizabeth [Mrs Ian Cornock, The Tile House, Hadley, Worcs WR9 0AU]; b 24 July 1963; BA; m 1990 *Ian Charles Cornock, ARICS, er s of Maj-Gen Charles Gordon Cornock, CB, MBE, of Cranleigh, Surrey, and has:

1g *Harriet Lucy; b 1993

2g *Pippa Ann; b 1995

3g *Camilla Fran; b 1997

3e +Richard, MBE (1968); b 22 March 1937; educ Bradfield; Maj late LI, formerly SCLI; m 14 Sept 1968 *Virginia Ann, 2nd dau of Lt-Col William Maitland Brewster Dunn, KOSB, of Berwick-upon-Tweed, and has had:

1f Charles Arthur; b 1970; d 1989

2f +Mark William; b 1972; educ Blundell's and Sidney Sussex Coll Cambridge (BA)

1e *Susan Philippa [Mrs John Dugmore, 816 Ely Boulevard S, Petaluma, CA 94952, USA]; b 27 Oct 1924; WRNS WW II; m 17 April 1954 *John Dugmore, est s of William Dugmore, of Cardiff, and has:

1f *Neil Vyvyan; b 2 Nov 1957

2f *Geoffrey Roland; b 16 June 1959

3f *Christopher John; b 1 Sept 1965

2e *Jane Theodora [Mrs David Cox, Preston Farm, Drewsteignton, Devon]; b 1 Jan 1930; m 5 Nov 1955 *David Kenneth Wilton Cox, 2nd s of Richard Wilton Cox, of Harefield Grove, Harefield, and has:

1f *Timothy Michael Wilton; b 17 April 1959

2f *Richard Wilton; b 31 Dec 1961

1f *Sarah Lamorna; b 4 June 1957

2f *Victoria Tamsin; b 25 Feb 1964

3e *Claudia Frances [Mrs Henry Tom, Lower Trewiggett, St Teath, Cornwall]; b 29 Feb 1932; m 30 Sept 1957 *Henry Graham Tom, late Capt Coldstream Gds, only s of William Howard Graham Tom, of Penhill, St Kew, Cornwall, and has:

1f *Elizabeth Vyvyan; b 17 March 1959

2f *Juliet Vyvyan; b 15 Feb 1965

2d Cecil Albert VYVYAN-ROBINSON later VYVYAN (deed poll 7 Sept 1912); b 1883; Maj Roy Mon RE WW I and Staff GHQ France 1920–21; m 1 Oct 1923 Brigit (m 2nd 31 Dec 1929 (divorce 1945) William Vernon Squire Sinclair, barrister, and d 5 Oct 1959), 2nd dau of Lt-Col William Allen Stokes, RE, of Barnfield, Gillingham, Kent, and d 25 Aug 1928, leaving:

1e Jennifer Brigit; FRAM, operatic soprano; m 2 March 1962 *Leon Crown, er s of Maurice Crown, and d 5 April 1974, leaving:

1f *Jonathan Courtenay Langdon Maurice; b 16 Sept 1964

3d Hugh; b 1884; Capt Glam RGA (TF); d unm 25 Jan 1941

4d Courtenay; b 1886; Maj Glam RGA (TF); d France 22 Jan 1919

5d Francis, MC; b 4 June 1897; Lt Roy Mon RE, Lt-Col RE, WW I and WW II; m 4 Sept 1926 *Aileen [Mrs Francis Vyvyan-Robinson, 3 Pinewood Close, Dawlish, Devon], only dau of Dr Richard Henry Powers, of Southend-on-Sea, and d 1975, leaving:

1e +Henry Francis [Henry Vyvyan-Robinson Esq, Konia Village, 8300 Paphos, Cyprus]; b 9 March 1928; educ King's Coll Taunton; late F/O RAuxAF, civil pilot; m 12 Jan 1957 *Susan Rosamond, dau of P A H Pettman, of Bournemouth, and has:

1f +Hugh [Hugh Vyvyan-Robinson Esq, Riverhead House, Brixham Rd, Kingswear, Devon TQ6 0OD]; b 5 Sept 1958; m 1 June 1996 *Nora Joanna Watson

2f +Peter Francis [Peter Vyvyan-Robinson Esq, 5 Rue des Paquis, Geneva 1201, Switzerland]; b 6 Aug 1963; m 6 July 1996 *Catherine Elizabeth Boehler and has:

1g +Tristan Francis; b 13 May 1997

1f *Sally [Mrs Walter Albrecht, Ob der Mur 18, 8173 Riedt, Switzerland]; b 30 Dec 1960; m *Walter Albrecht and has:

1g *Yannik Vyvyan; b 1991

2g *Michael; b 1993

1g *Stefanie; b 1987

2g *Jennifer; b 1989

3g *Melanie; b 1993

1e *Loveday [Mrs Keith Fergusson, Cranmere, South Rd, Newton Abbot, Devon]; b 12 Jan 1930; m 8 Dec 1951 *Dr Keith Maxwell Fergusson, er s of Dr Alec Everett Fergusson, of Banbury, Oxon, and has:

1f *Neil Vyvyan; b 9 Nov 1952; educ Marlborough

2f *Graham Moore; b 18 April 1955; educ Marlborough

1f *Fiona Margaret; b 12 May 1959

2f *Elizabeth Loveday; b 6 July 1963

2e *Caroline [Mrs James Pryde, Arden Cottage, 19 Harefield Ave, Cheam, Surrey]; b 21 May 1934; m 7 Sept 1957 *James Caruth Moore Pryde, s of Capt Robert Moore Pryde, and has:

1f *Catherine Ann; b 14 July 1960

2f *Juliet Clare; b 31 Oct 1968

1d Vera; m 19 Jan 1922 Charles Lane Vicary (d July 1953), er s of Charles G Vicary, and d 23 Feb 1968, leaving issue

2d Evelyn; m 18 April 1931 Vernon Hallam (d 19–), only s of George Hallam, of Pendleton, Manchester, and d 10 Jan 1969, having had issue

2c Hugh Norris; b 21 Nov 1853; m 21 Sept 1889 Constance Ethel (d 17 Sept 1954), dau of James Haughton, UK Consul Newport, Va., and d 30 Aug 1931, leaving:

1d Hugh Wren, MC; b 19 Dec 1890; Capt Roy Canadian Ordnance Corps, Capt DCLI, QMS Scots Gds, WW I 1914–16 (wounded, despatches); m 1st 21 Oct 1917 Mary (d 30 Aug 1930), dau of Patrick Lowe, of Bridge of Allan; m 2nd 12 May 1945 *Nellie Ryan Sibson [Mrs Hugh Vyvyan, 1162 Fort Street, Victoria, BC, Canada] and d 19 Sept 1966, having had by his 1st w:

1e +Patrick Hugh [Patrick Vyvyan Esq, 71 Mary St, Barrie, Ont, Canada]; b 21 Oct 1918; Sgt Roy Signals WW II (wounded, despatches), Assist Supt Police Malaya Fedn; m 1959 (divorce 19–) Angela, dau of Viggo Christensen, of London, and has:

1f +Patrick Hugh Beresford; b 1959

2e Peter Gerald; b 12 Aug 1921; Capt RCEME; m 19– *Marjorie Thurman and d 23 Dec 1962, leaving:

1f +Peter Hugh; b 19–

1f *Rosemary Ann; b 19–

3e +Beresford Haughton; b 12 Oct 1929; m 19– *Enid Baker and has:

1f +Geoffrey; b 19–

1f *Maryann; b 19–

2f *Wendy; b 19–

3f *Laura; b 19–

1e Pamela Alice; b 21 Feb 1926; m Clyde Hunt and had issue

2e *Rosemary Constance; b 12 Oct 1929; m June 1959 *Richard David Messano and has issue

2d Beresford Haughton; b 7 March 1893; educ Jesus Coll Oxford; T/Capt RFA WW I 1915–17 (despatches, wounded); d 18 Aug 1917 of wounds recd in action

3d Malcolm, MC; b 21 Nov 1895; educ Queen's Coll Oxford; Capt RAF and Glam RGA (TA), WW I (despatches) and WW II 1939–41; m 23 June 1920 Fairy (d 1971), yst dau of Col John Birrell, of Allender House, Milngavie

1d Gertrude Nevillia; b 13 May 1906; m 24 Sept 1927 Capt Rupert Taylor, RA, slr, s of Lt-Col Herbert Taylor, TD, and had issue

3c Henry (Rev); b 3 March 1855; educ St John's Coll Cambridge; Rector Grade and Ruan Minor Cornwall; m 1880 Lucy Nugent (d 19 Jan 1929), 2nd dau of Jerry Colley Grattan, Consul in Canary Islands, and d 16 Jan 1937, leaving:

1d (Philip Henry) Nugent Norris, OBE (1919), MC; b 30 Aug 1881; Lt-Col RASC WW I (despatches, Croce di Guerra Italy); m 11 Nov 1917 Mary Caroline (d 16 June 1982), 2nd dau of Rev John Stephen Flynn, and d 16 July 1967, leaving:

1e *Lalage Nugent [Mrs John Boustead, Well Cottage, White Chimney Row, Westbourne, Hants]; b 25 Aug 1921; m 18 March 1943 Lt John Derek Atheling Boustead, Roy Ulster Rifles (ka Normandy 7 June 1944), er s of Cedric Boustead, of Kingston Hill and Ceylon, and has:

1f *Tamsin Lalage [Mrs Richard Lee, c/o Well Cottage, White Chimney Row, Westbourne, Hants]; b 26 Dec 1943; m 22 Aug 1964 *Capt Richard Hugh Lee, RE, s of Lt-Cdr Carol William Phipson Lee, of Revesby Park, Boston, Lincs, and has:

1g *James Nugent; b 9 Dec 1968

2g *Nicholas Harry Atheling; b 1984

1g *Angela Caroline; b 8 June 1967

2d Albert O'Donnel Colley; b 1884; Capt RASC WW I (despatches, Greek MC); m 1st 9 June 1909 Cecilia (d 27 July 1949), only dau of William Henry Armitage, JP, of Banney Royd, Huddersfield; m 2nd 1951 *Greta Sylvia, dau of Arthur John Dooel, of Brandeston, Suffolk, and d 13 March 1971, having had by his 1st w:

1e Henry O'Donnel, OBE (1957); b 28 March 1910; educ Pembroke Coll Cambridge (BA); Col REME WW II (POW 1941–45), ret 1957, AMIME; m 25 June 1936 *June [Mrs Henry Vyvyan, Try-le-Bois, Greencliff, St Martin, Jersey, CI JE3 6BP], only dau of John Humphries, of Napier, NZ, and d 2 March 1998, leaving:

1f *Wendy [Mrs Graham Bell, Try-le-Bois, Greencliff, St Martin, Jersey, CI]; b 3 Oct 1937; m 9 Nov 1957 *Capt Graham George Bell, RASC, only s of Henry George William Bell, of Worcester Park, Surrey, and has:

1g *Christopher Graham Vyvyan; b 26 March 1960

2g *Simon Bruce O'Donnel; b 4 Nov 1961

3g *Robin Benjamin; b 5 Nov 1963

4g *Bruce St John; b 1966

2f *Valerie Cecilia [Mrs Henry Thoresby, 12 Wexford Rd, London SW12 8NH]; b 3 Feb 1941; m 1st 3 Sept 1966 (divorce 19–) David Henry La Cagnina, est s of Henry La Cagnina, of Jupiter, Fla.; m 2nd 1979 *Henry Fielding Thoresby and has by her 1st husb:

1g *Adam Vyvyan; b 1970

2g *Dominic Vyvyan; b 1973

2e +George Nugent Grattan; b 26 May 1914; educ Pembroke Coll Cambridge (BA 1936); Maj (ret) RASC; m 1st 1944 Cecilia Violet Vincent (d 1956); m 2nd 2 April 1957 (divorce 1961) Mrs H C Anderson, née Hooper

1d Lucy Kathleen Grattan; b 1889; m 25 Aug 1917 Capt Stewart Edward Pixley, RFA (d 1972), er s of Maj Stewart Aikin Pixley, VD, and had issue

4c Charles Shimmin VYVYAN-ROBINSON later VYVYAN (deed poll 1879) (Rev); b 4 Dec 1856; Rector Landewednack and Ruan Major Cornwall; m 18 April 1881 Rose Mary (d 16 Feb 1950), dau of Rev John Sidney Boucher, Rector Gedding, Suffolk, and d 3 Oct 1930, having had:

1d Charles Sidney Philip; b 6 Jan 1882; d unm 18 July 1902

2d Norris; b 21 June 1900; m 4 June 1925 Florence Elizabeth (d 9 Oct 1967), er dau of Rev W J Tristram, and d 23 Sept 1963, leaving:

1e +Bertram Charles Boucher [Bertram Vyvyan Esq, 39 Ridgemere Rd, Pensby, Wirral, Cheshire]; b 3 Jan 1930; m 30 Oct 1965 *Jean Margaret, dau of Charles Duncan Taylor, of Pensby, Wirral, and has had:

1f Michael Ian; b 7 Oct 1969; d 19–

1f *Catherine Margaret; b 17 April 1967

1d Phyllis Norah; b 7 Feb 1887; m 22 Nov 1906 Arthur William Catling (d 1932), 4th s of Frederick James Catling, and had issue

2d Dorothy Kildare; b 6 Feb 1890; m 21 June 1920 Alfred Lucas Hughes (d 2 July 1942), s of Herbert Maddock Hughes, of Bundaberg, Qld, and had:

1e *Charles Lucas [Mr Charles Hughes, Jinks St, Miriamvale, Qld, Australia]; b 21 April 1921

2e *Philip Herbert [Philip Hughes Esq, Tarebarre, Rockhampton, Qld, Australia]; b 23 Oct 1928; m July 1955 *Palma, dau of Hector Gibson, of Southport, Qld, and has:

1f *Alastair Lucas; b 18 June 1955; m *Donna Byers, of Woodlea, Bluff, Qld, and has:

1g *Lincoln Lucas; b 1990

2g *Harrison John; b 1995

1g *Natalie Maree; b 1988

1f *Marelle; b 26 Feb 1957; m 19– *Robert Lee, of Howard Springs, N Territory, Australia, and has:

1g *Darian Philip; b 1986

2g *Haydn Bryce; b 1990

3g *Shane; b 1991

2f *Jocelyn; b 9 April 1959; m 19– *Scott McGregor, of Rockhampton, Qld, and has:

1g *Curtis; b 1991

1g *Jessie; b 1989

2g *Stephanie; b 1994

3g *Frances; b 1997

3e *Christopher Maddock; b 2 June 1933; m Aug 1968 *Alice Jane, dau of C O'Dell Hill, of Gadsden, Ala., and has:

1f *Vyvyan Lorraine; b 1970

1e *Rosemary Eleanor [Ms Rosemary Hughes, 12 Helena St, Biggera Waters, Qld, Australia]; b 13 Nov 1922

2e *Norah Vyvyan; b 6 Jan 1926; m Jan 1950 *Max Maurice Shannon, s of Maurice Roland Shannon, of Mackay, Qld, and has:

1f *Roland James; b 1 Feb 1951; m 19– *Debbie Hardy, of Lake Manmorah, NSW, Australia, and has:

1g *Dean Ryan; b 1989

2g *Eliott Leslie; b 1993

1f *Sue Dorothy; b 3 Nov 1953; m 19– *Aurillo Rocca, of Walkamin, Qld, and has:

1g *Michael; b 1975

1g *Lorraine; b 1971; m 19– *Alan Scott, of Charters Towers, Qld

3e *Katherine Ellen [Mrs James Davidson, Belivah Rd, Belivah, Qld 4207, Australia]; b 13 March 1928; m Jan 1953 *James Maclean Davidson and has:

1f *Peter Maclean; b 24 Aug 1959; m 19– *Suellen Klan and has:

1g *Katrina Louise; b 1990

2g *Rebecca Kay; b 1995

2f *James Mclean; b 10 May 1964

1f *Penelope Rothwell [Mrs Ross Abell, Cattermull Ave, Kalkie, Bundaberg, Qld, Australia]; b 31 Jan 1957; m 19– *Ross Anthony Abell and has:

1g *Gregory Ross; b 1984

2g *Lucas Anthony; b 1989

1g *Louise Penelope; b 1982

2g *Ellen Ruth; b 1991

3d Violet; b 23 Sept 1891; d 19–

4d Elsie; b 14 Nov 1892; m 4 Aug 1923 Eric William Thomson Cossar (d 10 March 1945), yst s of James William Cossar, and d 21 Jan 1959, leaving issue

5c Frederick Albert; b 3 March 1858; m 30 Oct 1888 Mary Agnes (d 12 May 1957 aged 95), yst dau of William Baynham, of New Orleans, and d 18 April 1939, having had:

1d Henry Norris; b 21 Nov 1890; d 5 Sept 1903

2d Philip; b 19 April 1892; Lt Roy W Surrey Regt WW I; m 14 Sept 1926 Mary Jacqueline (d 5 Sept 1970), dau of John Milberne Leacock, and d 1985, having had:

1e +John Philip (Rev) [The Rev John Vyvyan, The Vicarage, 13 Dog Close, Adderbury, Oxon OX17 3EF]; b 6 Jan 1928; educ Charterhouse and New Coll Oxford (MA); late Lt DCLI (Res) Malaya 1947, Overseas Civ Serv N Borneo 1952–57, Priest Anglican Church of Borneo 1961–64; m 9 Feb 1957 *Monica Yin Tsu, dau of Fu Yun Fatt, of Sandakan, N Borneo, and has had:

1f +Richard Mark Augustine; b 17 April 1960

2f +Henry Arthur Luke; b 17 Oct 1961

3f Francis Tristan Vyell; b 2 March 1967; d 19–

4f +Francis Michael Hannibal; b 26 Feb 1971

1f *Honor Mary Anastasia; b 9 May 1968

2e +Bernard Jeremy [Bernard Vyvyan Esq, 37 West Hill Avenue, Epsom, Surrey KT19 8JX]; b 7 July 1930; educ Charterhouse and London U (BSc Eng 1955); FICE, late REME; m 7 Feb 1964 *Constance Joan Steel, dau of Ronald Ismay Pattinson, of Stanwix, Carlisle, and has:

1f +David Jeremy; b 1972

1f *Mary Louise; b 11 Nov 1965; m 17 Aug 1996 *Iain Edward Gibb

2f *Juliet Penelope; b 3 Nov 1967

1d Eleanor Augusta; b 4 Aug 1889; d 7 May 1978

2d Mary Gertrude; b 24 May 1897; m 12 March 1926 S/Ldr Eric Charles Delamain, MC, RAF (d 10 Jan 1927), yr s of W G Delamain, and d 31 Dec 1936, leaving issue

1b (cont.) The Rev Philip Vyvyan-Robinson m 2nd 22 Oct 1862 Elizabeth Maria (d 1887), dau of Joseph Vivian, of Roseworthy, Cornwall, and d 20 Sept 1888, having by her had:

6c Edwin; b 2 April 1866; m 21 April 1894 Florence (d 1968), dau of William White, of Dublin, and d 20 Feb 1943, leaving:

1d Henry Edwin; b 1896; d 19–

1d Eileen; b 1895; m 17 Aug 1920 Alfred William Skerritt, MC (d 1968), Lt AIF, s of Alfred Pemberton Skerritt, of Sydney, NSW, and had issue

1c Mary Elizabeth; b 6 Oct 1864; m 1892 Ernest Edward Collins (d 1902)

2b Henry (Rev); b 12 Dec 1821; educ Cambridge (BA); Vicar Dawlish; m 11 Sept 1853 Elizabeth Jane, dau of Thomas Carnsew, and d 24 March 1907, leaving:

1c Millicent; *d* unm 1 Aug 1925

2c Alice; *d* unm 14 Oct 1944

3a Thomas; Capt 102nd Regt; *dsp*

(3) Charles (Rev); *b* 9 March 1704; Rector Withiel; *m* Mary, dau of Harry Bond, of Tresunger, Cornwall, and was *bur* 30 March 1768, leaving three sons and a dau

(4) Thomas; *b* 20 Aug 1706; *m* 1st Loveday (*d* 12 May 1768), dau and heiress of Nicholas Boguns, of Treleague, and had issue; *m* 2nd Margaret, dau of Charles Vyvyan, of Merthen, and by her had issue

(5) John; *m* Sarah Cousins

(1) Loveday Vyvyan; *m* 3 July 1753 Richard Porter, est s of William Porter, of St Stephens-by-Saltash, and *dsp*

(2) Bridget; *m* Richard Sawle, of Pelynt

The 6th Bt's cousin,

Sir Vyell Vyvyan, 7th Bt; *b* 12 July 1767; *m* 14 Aug 1799 Mary (*d* 5 Sept 1812), only dau of Thomas Hutton Rawlinson, of Lancaster, and *d* 27 Jan 1820, having had, with another dau (*d* unm):

1 **Sir Richard Rawlinson Vyvyan, 8th Bt**; *b* 6 June 1800; MP Cornwall, Okehampton, Bristol and Helston; *d* unm 15 Aug 1879

2 Vyell Francis (Rev); *b* 2 June 1801; Rector Withiel, Cornwall; *m* 21 July 1825 Anna (*d* 19 March 1888 aged 84), yst dau of John Vych Rhys Taylor, and *d* 30 Jan 1877, having had, with four other sons and another dau (all *d* unm):

(1) **Rev Sir Vyell Donnithorne Vyvyan, 9th Bt**; *b* 16 Aug 1826; Rector Withiel; *m* 16 April 1857 Louisa Mary Frederica (*d* 12 Jan 1907), 3rd dau of Richard Bourchier, of Brook Lodge, Dorset, and *d* 27 May 1917, having had:

1a **Sir Courtenay Bourchier Vyvyan, 10th Bt**; CB (1906), CMG (1915), JP, DL (Cornwall); *b* 5 June 1858; Lt-Col and Brevet Col Roy E Kent Regt, 1st Boer War 1879 (medal with clasp), Matabele War 1896 (despatches, Brevet Maj, medal), (2nd) Boer War 1899–1902 (despatches twice, two medals, three clasps, Brevet Lt-Col), WW I (despatches thrice), Order St Stanislas Russia 2nd Cl with swords; *m* 1st 17 Feb 1887 Eva Catharine Forestier (*d* 3 Jan 1928), dau of Maj-Gen George Edmond Lushington Walker, RE (*see* FORESTIER-WALKER, Bt); *m* 2nd 21 Nov 1929 Clara Coltman (*d* 1 March 1976 aged 90), authoress: *Arctic Adventure, Down the Rhone on Foot, The Old Place*, and *Letters from a Cornish Garden*, 2nd dau of Edward Powys Rogers, of Toorilla, Qld, and Cornwall, and *d* 15 Nov 1941, having had by his 1st w:

1b Vyell; *b* 25 and *d* 30 May 1898

2a Richard Walter Comyn, JP (Cornwall); *b* 16 Sept 1859; T/Lt-Col Res Service Bn Welch Regt WW I; *m* 16 Dec 1885 Mary, dau of Edward S Foster, of Dowbury, Lincs, and *d* 10 Sept 1931, having had:

1b Walter Drummond; *b* 20 March 1887; Lt Salop LI WW I (despatches); *ka* 2 March 1915

2b **Sir Richard Philip Vyvyan, 11th Bt**; *b* 21 Nov 1891; *d* unm 15 May 1978

1b Muriel Alice; *b* 1890; *d* 1891

3a Wilmot Lushington (Rt Rev); *b* 12 Aug 1861; MA, DD Cantab; Warden Community Resurrection Grahamstown; Bp Zululand 1903–29; *m* 21 Nov 1921 Edith Emily (*d* 15 April 1961), 2nd dau of Capt John Sumpter Mitchell, of Southampton, and *d* 26 Aug 1937

1a Mary Louisa; Sister Community Epiphany Truro; *d* 20 July 1950

(2) Thomas Henry, JP (Cornwall); *b* 17 Sept 1827; 52nd Regt; *m* 25 June 1850 Mary Ellen (*d* 1912), 2nd dau of Edward Dodson Salusbury, JP, of Middleton Tower, Lancs, and *d* 27 April 1908, having had, with other issue:

1a Robert Trefusis Salusbury; *b* 19 March 1865; *d* unm 27 Nov 1945

1a Mary Ellen Salusbury; *d* unm 5 Oct 1952 aged 95

2a Elizabeth Salusbury; *m* 19 Feb 1891 Henry Dudley Willimott and had issue

(3) Herbert Francis (Rev); *b* 17 May 1834; Rector Withiel; *m* 6 Dec 1860 Augusta Clara (*d* 9 Jan 1919), only dau of Baron de Schmiedern, KH, and *d* 13 Feb 1894, having had:

1a James Donnithorne; *b* 30 Sept 1861; Lt 1st Bn Roy Welch Fus; *d* 1890

2a Herbert Reginald, OBE (1928); *b* 8 Dec 1862; Capt Devonshire Regt, Ch Constable Devon 1907–31, APM Boer War 1900–02 (Queen's medal with clasp, King's medal with two clasps); *m* 1st 1889 Caroline Jane (*d* 27 Sept 1935), dau of Edward Hunt, of Belmore, Co Kilkenny; *m* 2nd 14 April 1938 Emmeline Mabel (*d* 1948), only dau of Richard Brighton, HM CS, and widow of Lt-Col A F Carlyon, RAMC, and *d* 19 Dec 1949, having had by his 1st w:

1b Ralph Ernest, CBE (1944), MC; *b* 28 Jan 1891; *educ* Stubbington, Exeter, and RMC Sandhurst; Col and Hon Maj-Gen, Worcs Regt and Roy Signals, WW I (despatches), WW II as Dir Signals India, and in Burma, Ceylon and Iraq; Registrar RUSI Museum 1948–58, ed RUSI Journal 1950–57; *m* 1st 3 April 1915 (*divorce* 1930) Vera Grace (*d* 1 Dec 1956), er dau of Robert Arthur Alexander, of Portglenone House, Co Antrim, and had:

1c **Sir John Stanley Vyvyan, 12th Bt**; *b* 20 Jan 1916; *educ* Charterhouse and SOAS London U; with BAT, Maj Roy Signals WW II India and Arakan; *m* 1st 1940 (*divorce* 1948) Joyce Lilia, dau of Frederick Marsh, of Kailan Mining Admin, Peking, and had:

1 Lorraine; *b* 1942; *d* 1983

1c (cont.) **Sir John** *m* 2nd 1948 (*divorce* 1958) Marie, only dau of Dr O'Shea, of Hamilton, Ontario; *m* 3rd 1958 *Jonet Noel [Jonet Lady Vyvyan, Trelowarren, Mawgan, Cornwall TR12 6AF], est dau of Lt-Col Alexander Hubert Barclay, DSO, MC (*see* MITCHELSON, Bt), and *d* 6 Oct 1995, leaving by her:

1d Sir (RALPH) FERRERS ALEXANDER VYVYAN, **13th and present Bt**

1d *Amanda Clare [Mrs David Judson, Chytodden, Kenwyn Rd, Truro, Cornwall]; *b* 22 Aug 1959; *m* 1984 (*divorce* 1988) Mark Ian Richard, Baron von Brockdorff, s of Lt-Col Baron Eduard von Brockdorff, of Malta, and has:

1e *Alexander Mark Edward John Vyvyan; *b* 1984

1d (cont.) Baroness Amanda von Brockdorff *m* 2nd 1991 *David John Judson and by him has:

2e *Josiah Barclay; *b* 1992

1e *Mariana; *b* 1995

2c Michael Stuart; *b* 10 May and *d* 6 July 1919

1b (cont.) Ralph Vyvyan *m* 2nd 12 Sept 1930 Kathleen Antonia (*d* 12 Jan 1995), only dau of Haskett Farquhar Haskett-Smith, of Starcross, S Devon, and *d* 31 Jan 1971, having by her had:

1c *(Mary) Virginia, JP [Mrs Douglas Redrup JP, Little Compton, Samarkand Close, Camberley, Surrey GU15 1DG]; *b* 2 Jan 1934; *m* 1st 9 June 1956 (*divorce* 1963) Harold Markham Mills (*d* 20 April 1995), only s of Harold Edward Mills, of Woodbridge, Suffolk; *m* 2nd 1975 (*divorce* 1978) William Archibald Wilson (*d* 14 Aug 1995); *m* 3rd *Douglas Frederick Redrup and has by her 1st husb:

1d *Julian Maximilian Vyvyan; *b* 20 June 1957

1d *Antonia Helen; *b* 16 July 1958

2d *Charlotte Elisabeth; *b* 5 Nov 1960

1b Avis; *b* 2 Nov 1893; *m* 20 July 1917 (*divorce* 1932) Capt Robert Rose, RFA (*d* 1943), 2nd s of Thomas Rose, of Kensington, and *d* 27 March 1983, having had:

1c Victor Hunter Vyvyan; *b* 7 June 1918; *m* 7 Dec 1940 *Janet [Mrs Victor Rose, Fairfield Hall, Fairfield Rd, Framlingham, Suffolk IP13 9LE], 2nd dau of James McGowan, of Dumfriesshire, and *d* 18 May 1976, having had:

1d *Winter James Robert Vyvyan [Winter Rose Esq, The Moat Farm, Framlingham, Suffolk]; *b* 2 March 1943; *educ* Eton

2d Bruce Alastair Vyvyan; *b* 1 Sept 1948; *d* 10 April 1960

1d *Jacqueline Avis Vyvyan; *b* 14 Sept 1946

2d *Suzanne Jane Vyvyan; *b* 2 May 1952

1c *Myfanwy Avis [Mrs Brian Bleach, 31 Birch Grove, Windsor, Berks SL4 5RT]; *b* 23 March 1920; *m* 22 Sept 1958 Brian George Underwood Bleach (*d* 12 Feb 1998), only s of George Bleach, of Dorking, and has:

1d *Cameron James Vyvyan; *b* 25 Jan 1966

3a Percy Edmund; *b* 19 Dec 1865; Lt 1st Bn DCLI; *d* 27 June 1892

4a Stanhope Trefusis; *b* 11 Feb 1867; *m* 18 Nov 1904 Ella Graham (*d* 28 Jan 1957), dau of Stirling Graves, and *d* 1 July 1961, having had:

1b Lester Trefusis; *b* 31 March 1905; Sr Supt Police Tanganyika Territory; *m* 10 April 1934 *Mary Clare Frances [Mrs Lester Vyvyan, 2 Trenoweth, Carwinion Rd, Mawnan Smith, Falmouth, Cornwall], dau of John Leeming, of Chalfont St Peter, Bucks, and *d* 27 Feb 1952, leaving:

1c +Anthony Beville [Anthony Vyvyan Esq, Merthen Manor, Constantine, Cornwall TR11 5RU]; *b* 20 Feb 1935; *educ* Downside; *m* 23 April 1960 *Mary Winifred, only dau of Arthur Joseph Quin-Harkin, OBE, of Richmond, Surrey, and has:

1d +Richard Trefusis; *b* 3 March 1961; *m* 1993 *Claire Susan, yr dau of David Willietts, of Fairfield Cottage, Middleton, Warwicks

2d +Jonathan Vyell; *b* 18 Aug 1962

3d +Simon Courtney; *b* 23 April 1964; *m* 1992 *Jane, er dau of Michael Lodge, of Lighthorne Rough, Lighthorne, Warwicks, and has:

1e +Edward Michael Trevidren; *b* 30 April 1995

1e *Alexandra; *b* 5 Dec 1993

2e *Georgia; *b* 16 Nov 1997

4d +Charles Bevil; *b* 1 Sept 1965; *m* 1990 *Amelia Jane, only dau of G A Boyd, of Threshfield, N Yorks, and has:

1e +George Anthony Bevil; *b* 21 April 1993

1e *Isabella Mary; *b* 17 April 1991

5d +Paul Grenville; *b* 27 June 1969

6d +James Hannibal; *b* 24 Aug 1972

7d +Hugh Donnithorne; *b* 8 Sept 1976

1d *Katharine Anne; *b* 3 Oct 1967; *m* 1996 *Robert Wall, only s of Brian Wall, of Perth, Australia, and has:

1e *Demelza Jane; *b* 12 Nov 1997

5a Charles Beauchamp; *b* 18 Feb 1872; Lt 4th Bn Devon Regt, DC Lagos; *d* unm 16 April 1904

6a William Geoffrey; *b* 21 Jan 1876; Capt Roy Welch Fus, China 1900 (medal with clasp) and WW I; *m* 12 Nov 1904 Frances Mary (*d* 11 Aug 1964), er dau of Edmund Salwey Ford, of Pengreep, Cornwall, and Bayswater, and was *ka* 24 Oct 1914, leaving:

1b +James Graham, DL (Denbighs 1965) [Lt-Col James Vyvyan DL, Weston House, Gresford, Wrexham, Clwyd LL12 8EN]; *b* 23 Oct 1905; *educ* Wellington and RMC Sandhurst; Maj, Hon Lt-Col Roy Welch Fus; *m* 6 Oct 1934 *Guenilda Mary, yr dau of Rev Arthur Thursby-Pelham, and has:

1c +Anthony Geoffrey [Anthony Vyvyan Esq, Villa Marguerite, 3 Ave Fabre, 06270 Villeneuve-Loubet, France]; *b* 27 April 1940; *educ* Wellington, RMA Sandhurst, Magdalen Coll Oxford (BA 1964, MA) and INSEAD (Diploma 1970); late Capt Roy Welch Fus; *m* 29 Aug 1970 *Miranda, yr dau of Rev Robnett Walters, BD, of N Tamerton, Cornwall, and has:

1d +Philip James; *b* 3 May 1975

2d +David Robnett; *b* 1977

3d +Nicholas George; *b* 1980

1c *Cicely Mary [Mrs Peter Rawll, The Gables, 39 Cotswold Green, Stonehouse, Glos GL10 2ET]; *b* 25 Jan 1936; *m* 9 Dec 1961 *Maj Peter Leslie Rawll, RM, er s of Reginald Henry Rawll, of Harborne, Birmingham, and has:

1d *Andrew Charles Vyvyan; *b* 28 March 1963

1d *Katherine Frances; *b* 26 Sept 1965

2c *Daphne Elizabeth; *b* 9 Dec 1937; *m* 3 April 1965 *Edward Christopher Mumford, only s of H E Mumford, of Sevenoaks, and has:

1d *Robert Vyvyan; *b* 1970

1d *Alison Clare Mary; b 30 Jan 1966; m 1991 *Timothy Robert Hazlitt Love, s of Col Stephen Love, of Brixham, S Devon, and has:

1e *James Robert; b 19–

2d *Jane Myfanwy Mary; b 27 April 1968; m 19– *Ian Thomson, of Hong Kong

2b Frederick Richard; b 15 May 1913; educ Wellington; Lt Roy Welch Fus WW II; m 21 July 1937 (divorce 1957) Barbara, dau of Montague Jones, of Hartpury, Glos, and d 1991, having had:

1c +Charles Richard; b 9 July 1938; educ Clifton and Trin Coll Cambridge (BA 1960, MA 1964); Assist at L'Ecole International, Geneva

1c *Priscilla Mary [Mrs John Cherry, Mill House, Iping, W Sussex]; b 16 Oct 1941; m 1972 *John Loraine Cherry and has:

1d *Tarquin Loraine; b 1974

1d *Amanda Clare; b 1978

2c *Clare Angelica [Mrs Richard Clarke-Hall, Greenway Manor, Luppitt, Devon]; b 7 June 1944; m 1st 12 Feb 1966 (divorce 1978) Martin Austrey Kendall, only s of Dr David Kendall, of Haslemere, Surrey, and has:

1d *Jonathan Austrey; b 27 Dec 1966

2d *Charles Vyvyan; b 1971

3d *Robert Bradley; b 1973

2c (cont.) Mrs Clare Kendall m 2nd 1984 *Richard Clarke-Hall and by him has:

1d *Henrietta; b 1986

1b *Opre [Lady MacLean, Deepdale Old Rectory, Brancaster Staithe, Norfolk PE31 8DD]; b 27 Sept 1910; m 1933 *V-Adml Sir Hector Charles Donald MacLean, KBE, CB, DSC, DL, s of Donald Charles Hugh MacLean (see LINLITHGOW, M), and has:

1c *Charles David Hector [Charles MacLean Esq, 8 Eardley Crescent, London SW5]; b 1 March 1936; educ Wellington and RMA Sandhurst; A/Major HAC, late Capt Roy Scots, with Imp Life Assur of Canada; m 20 Nov 1966 *Judith Patricia, er dau of Norman Donald Maclehose, of Clynder, Dunbartonshire, and has:

1d *Charles Hector; b 7 Aug 1968

2d *James Lachlan; b 1970

1c *Sara [Mrs Anthony Everett, Enford Grange, Pewsey, Wilts]; b 19 Sept 1934; m 7 May 1955 *Maj Anthony Michael Everett, Wilts Regt, s of C F C Everett, and has:

1d *Simon Anthony Cunningham; b 1956; educ Ampleforth

2d *Rupert Hector; b 1959; educ Ampleforth; actor

2c *Katherine Mary; b 10 May 1937

2b *Joan Mary [Lady Ford, 14 Wyndham Place, London W1H 1AQ]; b 27 Sept 1910; m 27 April 1937 *Sir (Richard) Brinsley Ford, CBE, FSA, er s of Capt Richard Ford, Rifle Bde, and has:

1c *Francis Vyvyan; b 1941; educ Eton and Ch Ch Oxford; m 1979 *Katherine Elizabeth, dau of John Owen, of Playden, Rye, Sussex, and has:

1d *Arthur Richard; b 1988

1d *Lily Rosamund Elizabeth; b 1980

2d *Gloria Frances Mary; b 1983

3d *Sylvia Agnes Helen; b 1985

2c *(Richard) Augustine; b 1943; educ Ampleforth; m 1978 *Elizabeth, dau of Edward Frost, and has:

1d *Thomas Augustine; b 1978

2d *Edward Brinsley; b 1980

3d *(Richard) Sebastian; b 1983

1d *Susanna Clare; b 1986

1c *Marianne Adele Hermione; b 1937; m 1966 (divorce 1973) Patrick Martin Laver and has:

1d *Harriet Joanna Veronica; b 1967

1a Clara Frances; m 20 April 1898 Frederick Arthur Cameron Smith (d 4 Jan 1937) and d 27 Feb 1953, leaving issue

(4) Richard Octavius; b 21 June 1840; Col Bengal Inf; m 1871 Marie (d 15 Jan 1922), dau of Richard Sleman, FRCS, and d 17 Nov 1919, leaving:

1a Richard Trefusis; b 30 Nov 1872; Maj 1st Bn Oxon and Bucks LI, formerly Rifle Bde and DCLI, Egypt, Salonika and Palestine WW I, Assist Cmdt POW Camp Heliopolis 1916; m 3 Feb 1925 Edith Madeline (d 14 June 1969 aged 94), yst dau of Daniel de la Cherois, DL, of Donaghadee, Co Down, and dsp 11 June 1957

2a (Arthur) Vyell (Sir), KCB (1923, CB 1918), DSO (1916); b 12 March 1875; Benin Expdn 1897 (medal with clasp), WW I (despatches twice), AVM, Cmdt Coastal Area 1919, Govt Dir Imperial Airways 1925–33, Legn Hon, Orders Rising Sun Japan 3rd Cl, St Anne Russia, St Saviour and Redeemer Greece, US DSM; m 17 Nov 1914 Frances Clare (d 27 Dec 1952), dau of Gen Sir Aeneas Perkins, KCB, RE, and d 30 Sept 1935

1a Edith Frances Grey; m 8 Jan 1902 V-Adml Arthur Kenneth Macrorie, CMG, MVO (d 25 Nov 1947), 2nd s of Rt Rev William Kenneth Macrorie, DD, DCL, Bp Maritzburg, and d 8 June 1955

(5) Beville Granville; b 13 May 1842; Col Bengal Inf Egyptian War 1882 (medal and star); m 15 March 1875 Maria Lydia (dsp 25 Jan 1889), dau of Archibald William Blane, and d 5 Jan 1920

(1) Anna Frances; m 17 Sept 1861 Rev Edward Lister Salisbury, Vicar St Agnes, and d 13 March 1865, leaving issue

(2) Sophia Marion; m 17 Sept 1861 Charles Hussey Williams (d 1896), of Truro, and d 8 April 1919, leaving issue

(3) Agatha Georgina Florence; m 3 Nov 1870 Henry Elliot James, 41st Regt (d 1886), and d 10 July 1919, leaving issue

3 Thomas Hutton (Rev); b 3 March 1803; m 1835 Mary Williams (d 14 Oct 1876), dau of George Grenfell, and d 4 Sept 1844, having had, with a dau (d unm):

(1) Thomas Grenfell (Rev); b 13 Jan 1837; MA Cantab, Fell Caius Coll; m 6 Aug 1874 Edith May (d 3 Oct 1940), dau of Lt-Gen Henry Man, and d 5 March 1924, leaving:

1a Richard Norman; b 2 Dec 1876; Engr-in-Ch Marconi Wireless Telegraph Co; m 16 Jan 1902 Mildred (d 14 Jan 1948), dau of Charles Henry Tawney, CIE, of Oatlands Grange, Weybridge, and d 14 Dec 1946, having had:

1b John Michal [sic] Kenneth; b 10 June 1907; educ Uppingham and Balliol Coll Oxford (BA 1928); Fell and Tutor Trin Coll Cambridge, 2nd Sec Dip Serv, WW II with Black Watch and Commandos; m 10 Nov 1941 (divorce 1971) Elizabeth Mary Lowder (sic) (d 1992), yr dau of Hugh Gordon Lowder, and d 28 Oct 1991, having had:

1c +Charles Gerard Courtenay, CB (1998), CBE (1990, MBE 1974); b 29 Sept 1944; educ Winchester and Balliol Coll Oxford (BA 1966); Maj-Gen, Ch Staff UK Land Forces 1994–97, Hd Br Def Staff Washington 1997–, Col Cmdt 1 RGJ; m 1989 *Mrs Elizabeth Frances Blair, LVO, dau of Sir John Starr Paget, 3rd Bt (see PAGET, Bt, of Cranmore Hall)

2c +(George) James Tawney, TD [James Vyvyan Esq TD, 63 Ramsden Rd, London SW12 8RA]; b 9 June 1951; educ Eton and RMA Sandhurst; barrister, late Capt RGJ, Maj TA; m 1st 1980 (divorce 1991) Diana Elizabeth Mary, dau of Richard Desmond Hill, OBE, of Kingston Bagpuize, Oxon; m 2nd 1993 *Venetia Ruth Caroline, er dau of John Philip Turner, of Chelsea, and by her has:

1d *Charlotte Elisabeth Constance; b 10 May 1996

1c *Caroline Mary Louise [Mrs Stephen Pryor, Bracken Garth, Keasden, Lancs]; b 5 Nov 1942; m 24 Aug 1963 *Stephen Charles Archibald Pryor, 3rd s of Rev Archibald Selwyn Pryor, and has:

1d *Henry Charles Lister; b 24 Jan 1965

2d *Charles James Archibald; b 1971

3d *William Tawney Charles; b 1973

4d *Richard Charles Stephen; b 1976

5d *James Charles Edward; b 1979

1d *Rachel Elizabeth; b 11 Oct 1966

2c Jane Elizabeth Charlotte; b 7 Nov 1949; d 3 May 1950

1b Constance Cristina; d unm 1 Feb 1935

2a Kenneth Man; b 30 April 1878; Border Mounted Rifles Natal; d Ladysmith 9 March 1900

3a Vyell Kingsley; b 6 Dec 1881; educ Charterhouse; d unm 3 Sept 1968

4a Maurice Courtenay; b 24 May 1891; educ Gonville and Caius Coll Cambridge (BA 1914, MA 1920); Lt MGC WW I (wounded); DSc Lond 1940; m 18 Sept 1916 Hilda May, dau of Harry Frederick William Bradbury, BCS

1a Beatrice Edith; d unm 25 Aug 1949

2a Dorothea Margaret; m 15 Oct 1935 Capt Arthur William Bernard Perceval (see EGMONT, E) and dsp 27 March 1961 aged 81

3a Irene Victoria; m 19 April 1956 Dr John Sextus Matthews (d 1972) and d 19–

(2) George Rawlinson (Sir), KCMG, JP (Kent); b 10 Sept 1838; Cdr RNR, Capt Merchant Serv, Er Bro Trin Ho 1883 and Dep Master 1898–1910; m 17 May 1873 Blanche Henrietta (d 9 Oct 1915), dau of Most Rev Robert Gray, DD, Bp Cape Town, and dsp 22 Oct 1914

4 Edward Walter; b 16 Oct 1808; m 20 Nov 1851 Agnes Margaret (d 13 April 1886), est dau of Joseph Reid, and d 30 Aug 1901, having had:

(1) Edward Reid; b 4 Sept 1854; m 11 June 1884 Susan Geraldine Eini (m 2nd 1890 Robert Hughes Humphreys), dau of John Harrison Watson, and d 1888, having had:

1a Edward Courtenay Ferrars; b 1887; educ Cambridge (BA); barrister Inner Temple, Capt KRRC WW II; m 11 Oct 1924 Beatrix Georgina, widow of H A Bush, of Maidenhead, and was ka 14 Nov 1940

1a Sibyl Geraldine Margaret; b 4 Sept and d 22 Oct 1885

1 Harriet Elizabeth; m 4 Sept 1832 Christopher Wallis Popham (d 1872), of Trevarno, Cornwall, and d Dec 1898, leaving issue

WADDINGTON

Arms: Ermine on a cross azure a lion's head gardant or, langued gules, between four roses gules, barbed and seeded proper. **Crest:** An arm embowed, vested azure, issuing from the sleeve of a silk's gown sable, the hand proper holding a wreath of four roses gules, barbed and seeded proper, enfiled by a sword, point upwards, argent, hilt, pommel and quillons gold. **Supporters:** Dexter, a lion in trian aspect; sinister, a griffin, both or, armed and langued gules, gorged with a bar dancetty ermine edged azure, each statant erect amid reeds growing from a grassy mount proper. **Motto:** *Deus noster refugium et virtus* ('God is our refuge and courage').
Creation: B. (LP, UK) 1990.

THE BARON WADDINGTON, of Read, Co Lancaster (Sir David Charles Waddington, GCVO (1994), PC (1987), DL (Lancs 1991)) [The Rt Hon The Lord Waddington GCVO PC DL, Stable House, Sabden, nr Clitheroe, Lancs; Flat 4, 39 Chester Way, London SE11 4UR]; *b* 2 Aug 1929; *educ* Sedbergh and Hertford Coll Oxford; 2nd Lt 12th Roy Lancers 1951–53; barrister Gray's Inn 1951, QC 1971, Recorder 1972, Bencher 1985; MP (C) Nelson and Colne 1968–74, Clitheroe 1979–83, Ribble Valley 1983–90; a Ld Commr Treasury 1979–81, Parly U-Sec Employment 1981–83, Min State Home Office 1983–87, Parly Sec Treasury 1987–89, Govt Ch Whip 1987–89, Home Sec 1989–90, Ld Privy Seal and Leader Lds 1990–92; dir: J J Broadley Ltd, J and J Roberts Ltd, Wolstenholme Rink Ltd; Govr and C-in-C Bermuda 1992–97; *m* 1958 *Gillian Rosemary, dau of Alan Green, CBE, of The Stables, Sabden, Lancs, and has:

1 *James Charles; *b* 1960
2 *Matthew David; *b* 1962
3 *Alistair Paul; *b* 1965
1 *Jennifer Rosemary; *b* 1965
2 *Victoria Jane; *b* 1971

Lineage: CHARLES WADDINGTON; *m* Mrs Minnie Hughan and had an only *s*:

DAVID CHARLES, *cr* a **Baron**

WADE OF CHORLTON

Creation: B. (LP, UK) 1990.

THE BARON WADE OF CHORLTON, of Chester, Co Cheshire (Sir (William) Oulton Wade, JP (Cheshire 1967)) [The Rt Hon The Lord Wade of Chorlton JP, Chorlton House, 1 Rectory Close, Farndon, Chester CH3 6PS]; *b* 24 Dec 1932; *educ* Birkenhead Sch and Queen's U Belfast; farmer and cheese-maker; memb Cheshire CC 1973–77, Jt Treas C Party 1982–90; dir: Murray Vernon Hldgs, John Wilman Ltd; Chm: NIMTECH, Marlow Wade and Partners, Campus Ventures Ltd, English Cheese Export Cncl 1982–84, Parly Rural Ec Gp; Pres: Combined Heat and Power Assoc; Freeman City London 1980, Liveryman Farmers' Co 1980–, ktd 1982; *m* 1959 *Gillian Margaret, dau of Desmond Leete, of Buxton, Derbys, and has:

1 *Christopher James; *b* 1961
1 *Alexandra Jane; *b* 1964

Lineage: SAMUEL NORMAN WADE; *m* Joan Ferris Wild and had:

(WILLIAM) OULTON, *cr* a **Baron**

WAKE

Arms: Or two bars gules, in chief three torteaux. **Crest:** The Wake knot. **Motto:** *Vigila et ora* ('Watch and pray').
Creation: Bt. (E) 5 Dec 1621.

SIR HEREWARD WAKE, 14TH BT, of Clevedon, Somerset, MC (1942) [Sir Hereward Wake Bt MC DL, The Old School House, Courteenhall, Northants NN7 2QD]; *b* 7 Oct 1916; *s* f 1963; *educ* Eton and RMC Sandhurst; Maj KRRC WW II (wounded); High Sheriff Northants 1955, V-Ld Lt Northants 1984–91 (DL 1969–84); *m* 6 Feb 1952 *Julia Rosemary, JP, DL, yr dau of Capt Geoffrey William Martin Lees, of Falcutt House, nr Brackley, Northants, and has:

1 +HEREWARD CHARLES; *b* 22 Nov 1952; *educ* Eton; *m* 1st 1977 (*divorce* July 1995) Lady Doune Mabell Ogilvy, est dau of 13th Earl of Airlie (*qv*); *m* 2nd May 1998 *Joan Elizabeth, dua of Kenneth McCall, of Caitloch, Dumfries-shire, and formerly w of John Raymond Barrow, of Farmington, Glos, and by his 1st w has:

  (1) +John Hereward; *b* 6 Oct 1978
  (2) +Henry; *b* 1980
  (3) Tom; *b* 1984; *d* 1985
  (1) *Laura Katherine; *b* 1986

1 *Diana Julia; *b* 20 March 1955; *m* 1979 *Roderick John Fleming and has issue (see WYFOLD, B)
2 *Caroline Jane; *b* 19 July 1957; *m* 1979 *Adam Richard Fleming and has issue (see WYFOLD, B)
3 *Sarah Jennifer; *b* 28 May 1960; *m* 1985 *Rodney C H Morgan-Giles, s of R-Adml Sir Morgan Charles Morgan-Giles, DSO, OBE, GM, of Upton Park, Alresford, Hants, and has:

  (1) *August George H; *b* 1988
  (2) *Julius; *b* 10 Sept 1995
  (3) *Max Arthur Xan; *b* 11 May 1998
  (4) *George Miles Atticus; *b* 11 May 1998
  (1) *Tilia Julia C; *b* 1990

Lineage: GEOFFREY WAC/WAKE; *b* by 1100; allegedly of Flemish extraction and possibly kin to the Vicomtes of the Bessin, Normandy; held lands nr Bayeux in the Bessin, also in the Channel Islands, where after Geoffrey of Anjou, husb of the EMPRESS MAUD, wrested Normandy from KING STEPHEN in 1142 the Guernsey fief of the forfeited Vicomte of the Bessin (Ranulf of Bayeux, Earl of Chester) was divided between the WAKEs and the Abbey of Mont St Michel (see SAINT LEVAN, B, section Seat); probably *m* twice and *d* by 1168, probably as early as 1142, leaving an est s:

HUGH WAC/WAKE; Seigneur de Négreville, nr Valognes, Cotentin Peninsula; as well as his Norman and Guernsey fiefs held over 16 knight's fees in England; living 1142, fndr 1168 Benedictine Abbey of Longues, Calvados; gave Wilsford, Lincs, to Le Bec Abbey; *m* Emma (becoming through her feudal Ld of Bourne, Lincs), er dau and coheir of Baldwin Fitz Gilbert/de Clare (bro of 1st Earl of Pembroke of the 1138 *cr* (see PEMBROKE and MONTGOMERY, E, preliminary remarks) and s of Gilbert, feudal Ld of Clare, Suffolk, and Cardigan, whose f Richard was s of the Count of Brionne, of an illegitimate line of the Dukes of Normandy), by Adeline (dau of Richard de Rollos, Chamberlain to HENRY I, apparently by Godiva, dau of Hugh d'Envermeu by Turfrida, dau and heiress of the Mercian Thegn Hereward, who led Anglo-Saxon resistence to WILLIAM I (THE CONQUEROR) 1071 and who apparently got back his pre-Conquest lands at Witham, Barholm and Rippingale about the time of the Domesday Survey 1086), and *d* probably between early autumn 1175 and early autumn 1176, leaving:

BALDWIN WAKE; feudal Ld of Bourne; benefactor of Bourne, Vandry, Longues, Mont St Michael and Prudhomme Abbeys; King's Constable in England; as well as Hereward's old lands at Witham and Barholm, held Deeping, also in the Fens; *m* Agnes (*m* 2nd Randulph de Vernay and *d* in or after spring 1224), dau of William du Hommet, hereditary Constable of Normandy; and *d* by early autumn 1198, leaving:

BALDWIN WAKE; feudal Ld of Bourne; apparently imprisoned by KING JOHN 1207; pardoned by 1210 and regranted his English lands, retaining also his Guernsey ones but losing his Norman ones (his efforts to retain which by currying favour with the French probably occasioning his quarrel with JOHN) following the overrunning of JOHN's territory in Normandy by the French 1206; *m* Isabel (*d* in or after 1224), eventual coheiress of estates that included the Manor of Blisworth, Northants, which remained with the WAKEs till HENRY VIII's reign, widow of Foubert de Douvres and dau of William Briwerre, Sheriff Bucks, Berks, Derbys, Devon, Nottingham and Oxon and Derby, and was allegedly *k* by a crossbow bolt before 20 July 1213 while besieging a castle in Gascony, leaving:

HUGH WAKE; feudal Ld of Bourne; Sheriff Yorks, Constable Scarborough Castle 1239; *m* by 29 May 1229 Joan (*m* 2nd by 5 Feb 1243/4 Hugh Bigod, Ch Justiciar England, and *d* 1276, being by him mother of Roger Bigod, 5th and last Earl of Norfolk (*see* NORFOLK, D, preliminary remarks) of the 1140–41 *cr*), est dau and coheir of Nicholas de Stuteville by Devorguille, dau of Roland, feudal Ld of Galloway and Constable of Scotland, and *d* by 18 Dec 1241 on Crusade in the Holy Land, leaving:

1 Baldwin; *b c* 1238; feudal Ld of Bourne and Liddell, Cumberland; also held Buttercrambe, Cottingham and Kirkby Moorside, Yorks, through his mother and Market Deeping and Skellingthorp, Lincs; opposed HENRY III in the Barons' War, hence taken prisoner when the latter's forces recovered Northampton 1264, following which he was held captive till released after the baronial victory over HENRY of Lewes; taken prisoner again by the future EDWARD I at Kenilworth just before the royalist victory of Evesham 1265; regained his freedom once more but again defeated by royalist forces at Chesterfield May 1266, following which he made his peace with HENRY; campaigned in Wales 1277; *m* 1st Ela (*d* by 10 June 1266/7), dau of William de Beauchamp, feudal Baron of Bedford, by his 2nd w Ida, dau of William Longespee, Earl of Salisbury (*see* SALISBURY, M, preliminary remarks), and had:

(1) Joan; *m* 1st Michael Picot, feudal Ld of Dodington, and had issue; *m* 2nd Ralph Paynel (*dsp* 1317)

(2) Ida; *m* John de Steynegreve and *d* 1295, leaving issue

(3) Elizabeth; *m* John de Horbury and *dsp* 1314

1 (cont.) Baldwin Wake *m* 2nd by 5 Feb 1267/8 Hawise (*d* by 27 March 1284/5), dau and coheir of Robert de Quincy (yst s of 1st Earl of Winchester of the *c* 1206–07 *cr*; *see* WINCHESTER, M, preliminary remarks), by Helen, dau of LLYWELYN AP IORWERTH, Prince of N Wales, and *d* just prior to 10 Feb 1281/2, leaving by her:

(1) JOHN WAKE, 1st LORD (Baron) WAKE (E), so *cr* (according to later doctrine) by writ of summons to Parl 24 June 1295; *b* probably towards the end of 1268; campaigned Gascony between 1288 and 1297 and against Scots 1297–1300, Jt Capt March of Scotland in Cumberland and Westmorland 1297, fought Battle of Falkirk 1298; *m* by 24 Sept 1291 Joan (*d* just prior to 26 Oct 1309), allegedly dau of Sir John FitzBernard, of Kingsdown, Kent, or William de Fenes, a Spanish Count, and possibly a relative of EDWARD I, and *d* just prior to 10 April 1300, leaving:

1a THOMAS WAKE, 2nd LORD (Baron) WAKE; *b c* 20 March 1297/8; campaigned against Scots 1318–23 and 1333, also in Gascony 1325; supported QUEEN ISABELLA and her lover Mortimer against EDWARD II but deserted them 1328 for his f-in-law HENRY, EARL OF LANCASTER (gs of HENRY III); Justice Forest South of Trent 1326–28, Keeper Tower London 1326–28, Constable Hertford Castle 1326, fndr 1326 Haltemprice Priory, nr his Castle of Cottingham, Yorks; Keeper Channel Islands Oct 1331–Feb 1332/3; *m* by 9 Oct 1316 Blanche of Lancaster (*dsp* just prior to 12 July 1380) and *dsp* 30/31 May 1349

2a John; living 1320; *dsp*

1a MARGARET Wake, BARONESS WAKE in her own right according to later doctrine; *m* 1st John Comyn of Badenoch (*dsp*, *ka* Battle of Bannockburn 24 June 1314), s of 'The Red' Comyn, a claimant to the Scottish throne; *m* 2nd *c* Christmas 1325 EDMUND OF WOODSTOCK, 1st EARL OF KENT of the 1321 *cr* (beheaded for treason 19 March 1329/30), 6th and yst s of EDWARD I, and by him had:

1b EDMUND, 2nd EARL OF KENT; *dsp* aged *c* five by 5 Oct 1331

2b JOHN, 3rd EARL OF KENT and according to later doctrine 4th LORD (Baron) WAKE; *b* 7 April 1330; *m c* 3 April 1348 Elizabeth, dau of Willem, Duke of Juliers, and *dsp* 26/27 Dec 1352

1b JOAN, called 'The Fair Maid of Kent', COUNTESS OF KENT and BARONESS WAKE, both in her own right; *m* 1st by 1339 Sir Thomas De HOLAND, KG, of Broughton, Bucks (*see* ZOUCHE, B), considered to be EARL OF KENT in right of his w, and had:

1c THOMAS De HOLAND, 2nd/5th EARL OF KENT and 6th LORD (Baron) WAKE, KG (1376); *b c* 1351; ktd 1367, Marshal of England March 1379/80–85; *m* a little while after 10 April 1364 Alice, dau of 10th/3rd Earl of Arundel (*see* NORFOLK, D), and *d* 25 April 1397, leaving:

1d THOMAS De HOLAND, 3rd/6th EARL OF KENT and 7th LORD (Baron) WAKE, KG (1397/99), also 1st and last DUKE OF SURREY (E), so *cr* 29 Sept 1397; *b c* 1371; Marshal of England Jan 1397/8, Lt Ireland 1398; m a little while after 20 Oct 1392 Joan, dau of 2nd Earl of Stafford (*see* STAFFORD, B), and was beheaded by a mob at Cirencester following a failed plot to lay hands on HENRY IV

2d EDMUND De HOLAND, 4th/6th and last EARL OF KENT and 8th LORD (Baron) WAKE, KG (*c* 1404), JP Hants, Kent, Surrey, Sussex (all 1406–07) and Dorset (1407); *b* seemingly 6 Jan 1382/3; Adml of the Fleet West and North 1407; *m* 24 Jan 1406/7 Lucy, 10th and yst dau of Barnabo Visconti, Ld of Milan, and *dspl* 15 Sept 1408, *ka* in an invasion of Brittany, when the Earldom expired and the Barony fell according to later doctrine into abeyance between his sisters or their issue, leaving illegitimately by Constance, dau of EDMUND OF LANGLEY, 1ST DUKE OF YORK of the 1385 *cr* (5th s of EDWARD III):

1e Alianore/Eleanor; *m* (papal dispensation 16 March 1429/30), as his 2nd w, 5th Lord (Baron) Audley (*b c* 1398; Ch Justice 1423 and Chamberlain S Wales 1438/9 and 1441, supported HENRY VI in Wars of Roses; *m* 1st (papal dispensation March 1415) Margaret, dau of 6th Lord (Baron) De Ros (*qv*) of Helmsley and had issue; *see* 1970 edn) and had:

1f William (Sir); *k* Battle of Tewkesbury 1471

2f Edmund, Bp Rochester 1480, Hereford 1493 and Salisbury 1502; *d* 23 Aug 1524

1f Margaret; *m* 1st Sir Roger Vaughan; *m* 2nd 1st Lord (Baron) Grey (of Powis) and had issue by one or other of her husbs (*see* VERNON, B)

1d Joan; *m* 1st as his 2nd w EDMUND OF LANGLEY (*d* 1 Aug 1402), 1st DUKE OF YORK of the 1385 *cr* and 5th s of EDWARD III; *m* 2nd after 1 Aug 1402 but before 9 Aug 1404, as his 2nd w, 5th Lord (Baron) Willoughby de Eresby (*qv*); *m* 3rd *c* 6 Sept 1410 3rd Lord (Baron) Scrope (of Masham) (*dsp*, beheaded 5 Aug 1415); *m* 4th between autumn 1415 and 27 April 1416, as his 1st w, 1st and last Lord (Baron) Vessy and *dsp* 12 April 1434

1b (cont.) JOAN, COUNTESS OF KENT, *m* 2nd 10 Oct 1361 EDWARD, (THE BLACK) PRINCE OF WALES (*dvp* 3 June 1376), est s of EDWARD III, and *d* 8 Aug 1385, leaving by him, with an er s (*d* aged seven):

1c RICHARD II; *m* twice, deposed 30 Sept 1399; *dsp*, murdered 14 Feb 1399/1400

(2) Hugh (Sir), of Winterbourne Stoke, Wilts; *m* Joan, dau of Baldwin de Bolany, and was ancestor of the WAKEs of Winterbourne Stoke, extinct in the male line in the 15th century

(1) A dau; *m* by 2 Nov 1299 1st and last Lord (Baron) Grelle (*dsp* by 11 Oct 1311)

2 Nicholas (Sir); Kt Banneret; taken captive by royalist forces, like his er bro, at their recovery of Northampton 1264

3 Hugh (Sir), of Blisworth, Northants, and Deeping, Lincs; MP Northants 1309, 1311 and 1313; pardoned for his part in death of Piers Gaveston 1313; *d* 31 May 1315, leaving:

(1) Thomas (Sir), of Blisworth and Deeping; Sheriff Northants 1329–30 and 1335–36; Ch Falconer to EDWARD III 1343–46, fought Battle of Crécy 1346; *m* Elizabeth, widow of John of Heigham and dau and heiress of Hugh Cransley, of Cransley, Northants, and *d* by 15 March 1346/7 while at Siege of Calais, leaving an er s:

1a Thomas (Sir), of Blisworth and Deeping; *m* Alice (d by 25 Sept 1398), dau and coheir of Sir John de Pateshull by Mabel, dau and ultimate coheir of 1st Lord (Baron) Grandison, and had, with an illegitimate s (John Wake, Vicar Bolton)

1b THOMAS (Sir)

1b Anne; *m* Sir Philip Courtenay and had issue (*see* DEVON, E)

The s,

Sir THOMAS WAKE, of Blisworth and Deeping; *m* Maud, dau of Sir John Pigot, of Cardington, Beds, and *d* 14 Aug 1383, leaving, with an er s (John, of Blisworth and Deeping, *dsp* by 1398):

THOMAS WAKE, of Blisworth and Deeping; Esq of the Body to HENRY VI 1400, Sheriff Northants 1413 and 1418; *m* Margaret, sis of Sir John Philpot, Ld Mayor London (opposed JOHN OF GAUNT in Peasants' Revolt), and *d* by 1425, leaving:

THOMAS WAKE, of Blisworth and Deeping; called 'Great Wake', *b c* 1402; Sheriff Northants 1434, 1446 and 1450; *m* Agnes (*d* 14 Oct 1471), dau and coheir of Thomas Lovel, of Clevedon, Somerset, and *d* 10 Dec 1458, leaving:

THOMAS WAKE, of Blisworth, Deeping and Clevedon; Sheriff Northants 1461 and 1463; *m* 1st —; *m* 2nd Elizabeth (*d* by 2 Oct 1480), 3rd dau and coheir of 13th Earl of Warwick (*see* WARWICK, BROOKE and, E) of the 1088 *cr* and widow of 1st Lord (Baron) Latymer (*qv*), and *d* 20 May 1476, having by his 1st w had an est s:

ROGER WAKE, of Blisworth, Deeping and Clevedon; *b c* 1452; Sheriff Northants 1483; fought for RICHARD III at Bosworth 1485, hence attainted and his lands forfeited, although some manors later restored him; *m* Elizabeth (*m* 2nd Lord John Grey, yr s of 1st Marquess of Dorset, KG), dau of Sir William Catesby, of Ashby St Legers, and *d* 16 March 1503/4, leaving, with other issue:

1 Thomas, of Deeping; imprisoned Tower of London till his mother bribed him free, he being pardoned 1512; sold to his mother 1507 the Clevedon estate, which she settled on her 2nd s Richard, also Blisworth 1523 and other manors, retaining only Deeping; *m* Isabel, dau of Thomas Sapcotes, of Burley, Rutland, and *d* by 1536, leaving:

(1) Thomas, of Deeping; *b c* 1515; *d* 17 Dec 1567, leaving:

1a Thomas; sold Deeping 1574 to 1st Baron Burghley (*see* EXETER, M); *m* Jane, dau of Francis Fitzwilliam, of Fenton, and had issue, which through poverty faded into obscurity

2 Richard, of Clevedon, also Salcey Forest and Hartwell, Northants; *m* 1st Dorothy, dau of Sir John Dyve, of Bromham, Sheriff Beds and Bucks; *m* 2nd Lady Margaret Grey (*dsp*), dau of 2nd Marquess of Dorset, and *d* 10 Aug 1558, having by his 1st w had, with 11 other sons (including Richard, *d* 9 March 1580/1, ancestor of the WAKEs of Hartwell, extinct in the male line 1628; Robert, London mercer, *d* 1593, leaving issue; Francis, living W R Yorks 1564) and six daus:

JOHN WAKE, of Clevedon, Salcey Forest and Piddington, Northants; *b c* 1519; *m* Elizabeth, dau of Sir Edward Gorges, and *d* 15 Sept 1572, having had, with four other sons (including Rev Arthur, Canon Ch Ch Oxford 1567, Rector Gt Billing 1565, deprived for nonconformity 1573, *m* Christian (*d* 16 June 1609), dau of Sir William Wigston, of Wolston, Warwicks, and *d* 12 July 1596, leaving, with other issue, Sir Isaac, *b c* 1581, *educ* Ch Ch Oxford, Fell Merton Coll Oxford 1598, Sec Embassy Venice *c* 1610, Envoy Turin 1615–30, ktd 1619, MP Oxford U 1624, Amb France 1631–32, *m* Dec 1623 Anna, dau of Edmund Bray, of Barrington, Glos, and *dsp* June 1632): and five daus:

JOHN WAKE, of Clevedon, Salcey Forest and Piddington; *b c* 1541; *m* Margaret, dau of Robert Goodwin, of Portbury, Somerset, and *d* 23 June 1621, leaving:

Sir Baldwin Wake, 1st Bt (E), so *cr* 5 Dec 1621 of Clevedon and Piddington; *bapt* 6 Oct 1574; *m* 1st 11 Nov 1600 Abigail (*d* by 6 Feb 1630/1), only dau of Sir George Digby (*see* DIGBY, B); m 2nd Elizabeth — and *d* 1627, having by his 1st w had, with three yr sons (including Sir Baldwin, *bapt* 13 Aug 1611, royalist naval Cap Civil War, cmdg frigate *Black Proud Eagle* that bore the future CHARLES II to safety in the Channel Islands 1646, Govr Castle Cornet, Guernsey, 1646–48, *d* by 15 Nov 1649) and two daus:

Sir John Wake, 2nd Bt; *bapt* 31 Jan 1601/2; royalist Col of horse Civil War; *m* 1st Bridget, dau of Henry Sandys, of Plumpton, Northants; *m* 2nd Anne, dau and coheir of Gregory Brokesby, of Frisby, Leics, and widow of Thomas Gifford, of Burstall, and *d c* 1663, having by his 1st w had, with a yr s and three daus:

Sir William Wake, 3rd Bt; *b c* 1632; sold Piddington; built a house at Westhall, Preston; *m* Diana (*d* 25 Jan 1674/5), dau and eventual heiress of Sir Dru Drury, 2nd Bt, of Riddlesworth by Susan, sis and coheir of Sir Samuel Jones, of Courteen Hall, Northants, and *d* Jan 1697/8, having had, with four other sons and four daus:

1 **Sir John Wake, 4th Bt**; *bapt* 19 July 1661; *educ* Merton Coll Oxford and Gray's Inn 1679; *m* Mary — and *dsp* 1714

2 William; *bapt* 13 July 1663; allegedly *k* by his yr bro

3 **Sir Baldwin Wake, 5th Bt**, of Fritwell, Oxon; *bapt* 19 June 1665; allegedly pardoned for killing his er bro William (but one of the Wake bts is said to have *k* in anger not a bro but a s, the blame being taken by a yr s who fled abroad until the f confessed on his deathbed, so it is possible that William was *k* accidentally by their f, the **3rd Bt**); *m* 1st *c* 10 July 1686 Anne Derham (*d* Feb 1695/6), dau of Elizabeth Derham/Read; *m* 2nd by licence 24 June 1697 Mary Hart, of Burford, Oxon, and *d* 1747, having had two illegitimate daus by a woman or women unknown and by her:

(1) Baldwin; *m* Mary, dau and coheir of Edward Lane, of Hanslope, Bucks, and *dvp* 14 March 1734/5, leaving:

1a Sir CHARLES later WAKE-JONES (under terms of will of his unc Charles WAKE-JONES), **6th Bt**, of Courteen Hall, Waltham Cross and Nazeing, Essex; Sheriff Northants 1752–53; *m* 16 June 1753 Mary, sis of Samuel Jackson, and *dsp* Jan 1775

(2) Charles WAKE later WAKE-JONES (under terms of will of his unc Sir Samuel Jones, who left him the Courteen Hall, Nazeing and Waltham Cross estates); *bapt* 19 Jan 1701/2; *m* Elizabeth, dau of Sir Samuel Sambrooke, Bt, and *dsp* 22 March 1739, leaving his estates to the **6th Bt**

(1) Diana; *m* Rev — Tinley

(2) Mary; *m* Henry Jones and *d* 17 March 1728/9

4 Robert (Rev); *bapt* 23 June 1666; *educ* BNC Oxford; Rector Buxted with Cuckfield, Sussex, Dean Bocking; *m* 23 July 1699 Elizabeth, dau of William Greenfield, of Marlborough, Wilts, and *d* 11 Oct 1725, leaving an only surv s:

(1) WILLIAM (Sir), **7th Bt**

5 Samuel WAKE later JONES (under terms of will of his great-uncle Sir Samuel Jones, of Courteen Hall, from whom he inherited large estates); *bapt* 7 Sept 1670; Sheriff Essex 1699; m Elizabeth Champion and *d* 1712

6 Drury; *bapt* 20 Oct 1673; Capt; allegedly hanged for killing an innkeeper at Reigate

The 6th Bt's 1st cousin once-removed,

Sir William Wake, 7th Bt, of Riddlesworth Hall; *m* 19 April 1738 Sarah Walker, of Weston, Yorks, and *d* 26 Sept 1765, having had:

1 WILLIAM (Sir), **8th Bt**

2 Charles

3 Drury; *m* Frances Pratt and *d* 4 July 1787, leaving:

(1) Baldwin; *b* 3 Aug 1774; MD; *m* Sarah (*d* 7 April 1856), dau of James Spedding, and *d* 3 March 1842, leaving:

1a James Hare (Rev); *b* 10 Feb 1805; Vicar Sutton-in-Forest, Yorks; *m* 1st 10 June 1839 Caroline Elizabeth (*d* 23 May 1863), dau of Rev Anthony Eyre, and had, with another dau (*d* unm):

1b Baldwin Eyre (Rev); *b* 20 March 1840; *educ* Trin Coll Oxford (MA); Vicar Ruswarp, Yorks; *m* 16 June 1868 Adelaide Bowles (*d* 7 July 1935), dau of Rev Henry Cleveland, and *d* 29 Oct 1911, leaving:

1c Hereward Eyre (Rev); *b* 8 June 1869; *educ* Worcester Coll Oxford (MA); Vicar Burnham, Somerset, Preb Wells, RD Shepton Mallet; *m* 18 April 1899 Mary Frances (*d* 29 Oct 1959), dau of James Sealy Lawrence, CE, of W Kensington, and *d* 8 Aug 1934, leaving:

1d Hereward Baldwin Lawrence; *b* 26 Aug 1900; *educ* Marlborough and Keble Coll Oxford (MA); Housemaster Cheltenham 1923–48, War Office WW II, Lt-Col Glos Regt (TA), Headmaster St John's Leatherhead 1948–59; *m* 5 Aug 1926 Sheila Winifred Lilian (*d* 1991), dau of Capt Henry William Fraser Harris, and *d* 1983, leaving:

1e +(Hereward) Michael Wilfred [Michael Wake Esq, High Ridge, Knoll Wood, Godalming, Surrey GU7 2EW]; *b* 2 Dec 1927; *educ* Cheltenham and Oriel Coll Oxford

2e +Robin Eyre [Robin Wake Esq, Polgreen Farm, St Mawgan-in-Pydar, Cornwall TR8 4AG]; *b* 8 May 1933; *educ* Down House Sch; ornithologist; *m* 29 Dec 1962 *Judith Ann (Judith Wake, NDD, artist), dau of Eric Hayden Barry, of W Chiltington Common, Sussex

1d Torfrida Marjory; *b* 11 May 1909; *m* 1st 30 June 1927 James Salmond Robinson, FRCS (*d* 1 April 1951), s of Andrew Robinson, CBE, MVO; *m* 2nd 19— Dr Noel Chilton, and *d* 1973

1c Torfrida Mary; *d* unm 29 April 1928

2c Margaret Gladys Hermione; *b* 1885; *m* 18 April 1921 Maj Clement William Robert Little, Tank Corps (*d* 18 Dec 1969 from wounds recd WW I), s of Robert Little, and *d* 1981, having had issue

2b Herewald Bentinck; *b* 17 July 1851; *m* 1877 Frances Elizabeth (*d* 23 March 1884), dau of Alexander Balmer, and *d* 9 March 1900, leaving:

1c Frank Eyre; *b* 23 Jan 1879; Lt Worcs Regt WW I; *m* 23 Feb 1909 Elizabeth Helen, dau of Joseph Nash, of Birmingham, and had:

1d Hereward Francis; *b* 1912; *d* 13 June 1943

3b Gervas Fountayne; *b* 14 April 1853 his cousin Amy Rosamond, dau of Capt Baldwin Arden Wake, RN (*see below*), and *d* 26 March 1942, having had:

1c Hereward Eyre; *b* 16 July 1888; *d* unm 23 Aug 1913

1c Rosamond Adelaide Alice; *b* 1882; *m* 14 Aug 1907 Frederick Paget Norbury, JP (*d* 19 Feb 1940), of Sherridge, Worcs, and *d* 26 March 1966, leaving issue

2c Gladys Maude Mary; *b* 1883; Nursing Sis Canadian AMC; *d* 21 May 1918 of wounds recd France

1b Emily Honor; *m* 15 Sept 1868 Arthur Charles Cleveland and *d* 25 Dec 1933, leaving issue

2b Lucy Joan

3b Edith Caroline; *m* 29 Nov 1864 Capt Martin Budd Lewin, 51st Regt, and *d* 18 Feb 1928, leaving issue

4b Gertrude Maude; *d* unm 1939

1a (cont.) The Rev James Wake *m* 2nd 21 June 1864 Elisabeth (*dsp* 2 Aug 1875), 2nd dau of Maj James Spedding, JP, DL, of Summergrove, Hensingham, and *d* 5 Dec 1874

2a Charles Hamilton; *b* 4 Sept 1808; Lt-Col; *d* unm 14 Feb 1872

3a Baldwin Arden; *b* 4 Jan 1813; Capt RN; *m* 16 June 1850 Ada Maria (*d* 20 Nov 1894), dau of Rev George Hough, and *d* 17 Jan 1880, having had:

1b Hereward Robert; *b* 7 Feb 1851; *d* 13 Nov 1871

2b Baldwin Hough; *b* 30 Jan 1852; *m* 7 Jan 1884 Amelia, dau of Frederick Morris, of Bridlington, Yorks, and *dsp* 19 May 1904

3b George Fenton; *b* 4 Jan 1859; *d* unm 6 May 1937

1b Ada Mary; *m* 24 Jan 1871 George Croker Fox (*d* 26 Feb 1902) and *d* 12 Nov 1892, leaving issue

2b Amy Rosamond; *m* 9 June 1881 her cousin Gervas Fountayne Wake (*see above*) and *d* 20 Dec 1938

3b Florence Myra; *m* 1 June 1886 Henry Colborne Maunoir Ridley and *d* 30 Sept 1949, leaving issue (*see* RIDLEY, V)

4a Carlisle William; *b* 18 Oct 1815; *d* Jan 1890

5a Fenton; *b* 15 March 1819; *m* 17 July 1856 Catherine Jolliffe (*d* 1889), dau of William Dobbinson, and *d* 5 Jan 1901, leaving a s and two daus (*d* unm)

1a Anne Lucy; *m* 8 Dec 1853 Maj George Seton (*d* 25 Dec 1905), yst s of Alexander Seton of Mounie, and *d* 6 June 1893, leaving issue

(2) Charles; MD; *m* Anne (*d* 1824), 3rd dau of James Spedding, of Summergrove, Hensingham, Cumberland, and *d* Jan 1852, leaving:

1a Elizabeth; *m* 1852 James Power

2a Cecilia; *m* 19 June 1845 Algernon O'Brien and had issue

(1) Frances; *m* John Walker and *d* 1812, leaving issue (*see* WALKER, Bt, of Oakley House)

1 Baldwin (Rev); Rector Riddlesworth, Norfolk; *m* 1st Elizabeth, dau of Gen Schuyler, US Army; *m* 2nd Anne —; *m* 3rd *c* Sept 1812 Elizabeth Bridge and *dsps* 14 June 1815

1b Mary; *m* 5 April 1796 William Clarke, of Brome, Suffolk

The 7th Bt's est s,

Sir William Wake, 8th Bt; *b* 1742; MP Bedford; *m* 6 June 1765 Mary (*d* 10 Dec 1823), only dau and heiress of Richard Fenton, of Bank Top, York, and *d* 29 Oct 1785, leaving:

1 WILLIAM (Sir), **9th Bt**

2 Richard William (Rev); *b* 16 July 1775; Rector Courteenhall; *m* 1st 17 Nov 1798 Jane (*d* 8 June 1823), dau of Sir William Dunkin, Judge Supreme Court Calcutta, and had, with another dau (*d* unm):

(1) William Fenton; *b* 31 March 1800; *d* 18–

(2) Richard William; *b* 5 July 1805; Lt-Col; *d* unm 5 April 1894

(3) Charles Dunkin; *b* 18 Feb 1807; *m* his cousin Jane Sophia, est dau of **Sir William Wake, 9th Bt** and *d* 24 Aug 1866

(1) Mary; *d* unm 22 Oct 1825

2 Jane Helena; *d* unm 30 Nov 1822

2 (cont.) The Rev Richard Wake *m* 2nd 6 April 1836 Harriet (*dsp* 2 Jan 1865), yst dau of Rt Hon Henry Grattan

1 Mary Anne; *b* 1773; *m* Col Roger Elliot Roberts

2 Charlotte; *d* unm 28 Feb 1853, aged 74

The 8th Bt's er s,

Sir William Wake, 9th Bt; *b* 5 April 1768; DCL; *m* 1st 1 July 1790 Mary (*d* 22 Nov 1791), only dau of Francis Sitwell (*see* SITWELL, Bt); *m* 2nd 22 April 1793 Jenny (*d* 7 May 1837), dau of V-Adml James Gambier, and *d* 27 Jan 1846, having by her had, with other issue (*d* young or unm) a s (Rev John William, *b* 19 April 1801, *d* unm 14 Feb 1829) and two daus (Jane Sophia, *m* Charles Dunkin Wake (*see above*) and *d* 2 July 1892 aged 90; Cecilia, *m* 30 July 1835 Henry Newcome, of Upper Wimpole St, London), and by his 1st w:

Sir Charles Wake, 10th Bt; *b* 21 Nov 1791; *m* 1st 23 Aug 1815 Mary Alice (*dsp* 3 Feb 1816), est dau of Sir Sitwell Sitwell, 1st Bt (*qv*); *m* 2nd 1 June 1822 Charlotte (*d* 31 March 1888), 2nd dau of Craufurd Tait of Harviestoun and Castle Campbell, Clackmannan, and sis of Archibald Tait, DD, Archbp Canterbury, and *d* 23 Feb 1864, having by her had, with other issue:

1 WILLIAM (Sir), **11th Bt**

2 Charles; *b* 23 Oct 1824; Adml; *m* 18 Feb 1860 Emma (*d* 15 March 1920), sis of 1st Baron Saint Levan (*qv*), and *d* 26 March 1890, leaving:

(1) Charles St Aubyn, CMG (1899); *b* 9 Feb 1861; Capt 18th Bn Roy Irish Rifles and 3rd Bn Devon Regt Uganda 1897–98 (despatches), Maj Suffolk Regt, Recruiting Offr Bristol, WW I, V-Consul at Mombasa; *d* unm 22 Nov 1938

(2) Edward St Aubyn, CMG (1919); *b* 20 July 1862; Lt-Col cmdg 21st Serv Bn Middx Regt and IA Burma War 1885–86 (medal with clasp), Samana Expdn 1897 (despatches, medal with two clasps), Tirah Expdn 1897–98 (despatches, medal with two clasps), WW I; 1st Cl Kaisar-i-Hind and clasp, Coronation Medal 1911; *m* 12 June 1913 Vera Cecilia (*d* 17 June 1968), yst dau of Francis Johnston, of Dunsdale, Westerham, and *d* 20 Oct 1944, leaving:

1a Hugh (Rev); *b* 23 March 1916; *educ* RNC Dartmouth; *m* 4 Sept 1944 *(Catherine) Marigold (3rd Offr WRNS) [Mrs Hugh Wake, 3 Queen's Court, Queen's Close, Sudbury, Suffolk CO10 6US], yr dau of Adml Sir (William) Frederic Wake-Walker, KCB, CBE (*see* WALKER, Bt, of Oakley House), and *d* 13 Oct 1993, leaving:

1b +Vincent Hugh [Vincent Wake Esq, 800 Crow Rd, Glasgow G13 1LY]; *b* 16 April 1947; *educ* Clayesmore; SRN, RSCN; *m* 17 Sept 1977 *Ruth, dau of William McAulay, of Glasgow, and has:

1c *Christine Grace; *b* 6 July 1978

2c *Rebekah Sarah; *b* 22 Feb 1980

2b +(Cedric) Philip [Philip Wake Esq, 22 Lytton Grove, London SW15]; *b* 2 May 1950; *educ* Roy Hosp Sch Holbrook; MSc, MNI, Master Mariner, Lt-Cdr RNR (ret); *m* 22 July 1978 *Claire Susan Woodburn, er dau of William Vinten, OBE, of Hartest, Suffolk, and has:

    1c *Charlotte Elizabeth Vinten; *b* 9 Aug 1982

    2c *Suzannah Catherine Vinten; *b* 1985

    3c *Henrietta Claire Vinten; *b* 1992

3b +Thomas Baldwin [Thomas Wake Esq, 30 Moss Gdns, Leeds, W Yorks LS17 7BH]; *b* 27 July 1960; BSc; *m* 20 Sept 1986 *Valerie, dau of Harry Green, of Aston, Sheffield, and has:

    1c +Alexander Harry; *b* 26 Jan 1996

    2c +Christopher Edward; *b* 18 May 1998

1b *Catherine Frances [Mrs Vernon Nott, 2 Springfield Terr, Sudbury, Suffolk CO10 6TS]; *b* 5 July 1945; *m* 1st 12 Nov 1966 Michael Edward Turpin (*d* 1972), s of John Edward Turpin, and has:

    1c *Edward; *b* 29 Sept 1969; *m* Nov 1994 *Maayan Aviram and has:

        1d *Sayana; *b* 22 July 1996

    1c *Sarah Jane; *b* 29 April 1967; *m* 5 Dec 1998 *Francois Esterhuyse

    2c *Rosanna Elspeth; *b* 28 Aug 1972; has:

        1d *George Thomas; *b* 23 Jan 1996

1b (cont.) Mrs Michael Turpin *m* 2nd 25 Oct 1973 (*divorce* July 1986) Vernon Charles Nott, BSc, MIAgrE, s of Kenneth Nott, and by him has:

    2c *Benjamin Porter; *b* 20 Sept 1976

(3) Drury St Aubyn (Sir), KCIE, CB; *b* 16 Sept 1863; Adml, served Egypt 1882 (medal with clasps, bronze star), WW I (despatches, CB, CIE, KCIE); 5th Cl Medjidie, Humane Soc medal, Cdr Order of St Maurice and St Lazarus, 4th Cl Russian Order of St Vladimir, and Tuscan medal; *m* 1896 Edith Rose Mary (*d* 15 Feb 1949), dau of Rev Thomas White Boyce, MA, and *d* 23 Sept 1935, having had issue:

1a Charles Baldwin Drury; *b* 1897; 2nd Lt KRRC; *ka* 25 Sept 1918

(4) Hugh St Aubyn, MVO; *b* 27 March 1870; Maj IA, Tirah Expdn 1897–98 (medal with clasp) and WW I; *m* 16 Nov 1899 Kathleen Mary (*d* 11 Oct 1938), 2nd dau of Lt-Col Edward Evans Grigg, of Ouselea, Bedford, Commr Kumaon, NW FP, India, and was *ka* 1 Nov 1914, leaving:

1a Hugh Edward William; *b* 1900; *m* 1928 June Brotherton and *d* 1967, leaving:

    1b Charles Hugh Edward; *b* 1930; *d* USA 1976

1a *Kathleen Josephine; *b* 7 April 1909; *m* 1 Feb 1934 *Lt-Col George Douglas James McMurtrie, Somerset LI, er s of George Edwin James McMurtrie, of Eastfield House, Westbury-on-Trym, nr Bristol, and has:

    1b *Hugh Wake [Hugh McMurtrie Esq, W Cottage, Oakley, Aylesbury, Bucks]; *b* 22 Aug 1936; *educ* Clifton, RAC Cirencester and Wolverhampton Tech Teachers' Coll; 1st Bn Roy Hants Regt 1954–56, anti-terrorist ops Malaya; ag lecturer

    2b Michael St Aubyn, OMM; *b* 22 Aug 1936; *educ* Clifton; Maj 3rd Bn Princess Patricia's Canadian LI; *m* 19 Dec 1958 *Bridget Constantia, dau of Capt L E Rubery, of W Malvern, Worcs, and has:

        1c *Nigel Andrew James; *b* 7 Sept 1959

        2c *Paul Marcel; *b* 1971

        1c *Marcia Kathleen; *b* 27 Sept 1961

    3b *Jonathan Philip James; *b* 14 April 1941; *educ* Clifton; *m* 1975 *Anne Kelly and has:

        1c *Andrew; *b* 1975

        1c *Jane; *b* 1977

(5) William St Aubyn, DSO; *b* 26 Oct 1871; Lt Middx Regt; *d* 4 Feb 1900 from fever contracted on serv Nigeria

(6) Arthur Leofric St Aubyn; *b* 31 Oct 1879; Lt N Somerset Yeo and Devon Regt; *m* 27 Sept 1911 Elma Claribel (*d* 26 Jan 1971 aged 80), only dau of William Edward Highett, of Melbourne, Victoria, and *d* 9 Nov 1957, leaving:

1a +Geoffrey St Aubyn [Geoffrey Wake Esq, 43 Kooyong Rd, Armadale SE3, Victoria, Australia]; *b* 24 Aug 1914; Capt (Res Offrs) Roy Corps Signals and 22nd Field Regt Artillery AIF WW II; *m* 1943 *Lois Ivan-Smith and has:

    1b *Carolyn Fearnley St Aubyn; *b* 1 Jan 1945

    2b *Cheryl Anne; *b* 1949

1a *Elma Thurfrida; *b* 1912

2a *Diana; *b* 1913; *m* 15 Jan 1940 Desmond George Grace, 2nd s of George Beresford Grace, of Hampton, and has:

    1b *Simon George; *b* 3 Sept 1948

    1b Diana Gillian [Mrs David Greig, 76 Centre Rd, E Brighton, S6, Victoria, Australia]; *b* 12 Sept 1941; *m* 9 Oct 1964 *David Hunter Greig, s of David William Greig, of Kew, Australia, and has:

        1c *Christopher David; *b* 1 Nov 1968

    2b *Susan Elizabeth [Mrs William Catmull, 24 Ryan's Rd, Eltham, 3095 Melbourne, Victoria, Australia]; *b* 18 Oct 1943; *m* 23 Dec 1964 *William Thomas Catmull, only s of Leonard Robert Catmull, of New Zealand, and has:

        1c *Matthew Brinnin; *b* 10 Jan 1968

        1c *Bridie Erin [Mrs Leonard Rutzou, 21 Hobson St, Newport, Victoria 3015, Australia]; *b* 5 Jan 1970; *m* 19– *Leonard Brian Rutzou

3a *Audrey; *b* 1916; *m* 4 Sept 1946 *Angus Manning Watson, yst s of Herbert Watson, of Glenelg, S Australia

(1) Emma Sybil; *m* 26 June 1894 Sir Hugh Molesworth-St Aubyn, 13th Bt (*qv*), and *d* 4 April 1929, leaving issue

(2) Isabel Violet; *m* 26 July 1894 Nevile Gwyn Gwynne, CBE (*d* 9 July 1951), of Piddinghoe, Sussex, and *d* 24 April 1955, leaving issue (*see* MORRISON-BELL, Bt)

(3) Emma Blanche; *m* 22 Feb 1898 Guy Shorrock, of Calcutta, and *d* 1909, leaving issue (*see* WELBY, Bt)

(4) Christabel Edith; *m* 29 April 1920 (John) Sheldon Withers, JP, MRCS (*d* 11 March 1934), and *d* 5 April 1974 aged 99

3 Drury, of Pitsford House, Northants; *b* 1827; barrister; *m* 20 Aug 1874 Louisa Julia Harriet (*d* 23 Sept 1913), yst dau of Henry Osmond Nethercote, of Moulton Grange, Northants, and *d* 22 April 1891, leaving:

(1) Drury; *b* 25 Dec 1875; *educ* Ch Ch Oxford (BA); Capt Rifle Bde; *m* 3 Aug 1904 Dorothy Caroline (*d* 15 Dec 1956), er dau of Sir Courtenay Knollys, KCMG, and *d* 3 June 1947, leaving:

    1a Drury; *b* 14 July 1906; *educ* Sherborne; Maj Sudan Def Force; *m* 1 Nov 1950 *Margaret [Mrs Drury Wake, Glebe Cottage, Upper Beeding, W Sussex], dau of Richard Henderson Owen Garbutt, LRCP, LRCS, of Newcastle, and *dsp* 14 April 1962

    1a Elizabeth; *b* 14 Sept 1907; VAD, ARRC WW II in; *d* 10 April 1978 aged 70

    2a Catherine; *b* 4 March 1914; Jr Cdr ATS WW II; *m* 21 April 1953 *Lt-Col Brian Walton Rowe, OBE, MC, s of George Frederick Rowe, JP, of Hampstead, and *d* 1972

(1) Emily Matilda; *b* 21 March 1876; civ serv 1916–1947; *d* unm 11 March 1959

(2) Susan Ellen; *m* 25 Oct 1909 Col John Carden, CMG (*ka* Gallipoli 10 Aug 1915), Cmdt N Rhodesia Police Force, s of Capt Charles W Carden, 36th Regt, of Brixworth, Northants, and *d* 26 April 1961, leaving issue

(3) Mary Alice; *d* unm 9 April 1962 aged 82

4 Herwald Craufurd, CB; *b* 10 March 1829; BCS; *m* 18 Aug 1860 Charlotte Lucy Hurt (*d* 17 Aug 1907), 4th dau of Sir George Sitwell, 2nd Bt (*qv*), and *d* 9 Dec 1901, leaving:

(1) Herwald; *b* 23 July 1862; *m* 18 July 1914 Katherine Frances Margaret (*d* 16 July 1961), er dau of William Hutton, of Beetham House, Milnthorpe, Westmorland, and *d* 12 Nov 1938, leaving:

    1a Herwald Molyneux Sitwell; *b* 10 April 1917, Lt Roy Signals WW II; *das* Egypt 31 Dec 1942

(2) Richard Frederick Robert; *b* 24 Sept 1865; *k* 7 Dec 1888 while war correspondent Egypt

5 Edward Baldwin; *b* 14 Dec 1833; Col 21st Hus; *m* 1st 26 Jan 1861 Mary (*d* 9 Dec 1868), 2nd dau of Ross Donnelly Mangles, of Woodbridge, Surrey, and had:

(1) Gerald Baldwin; *b* 29 Nov 1862; Boer War 1899–1902 (wounded, two medals, six clasps); *m* 17 March 1909 Violet Alice, yst dau of Henry Froom, of Isleworth, and *d* 1919

(1) Mildred Emily Baldwin; *m* 4 March 1890 Archibald Cameron Norman (*d* 2 Aug 1948), of Bromley Common, Kent, and *d* 14 Sept 1940, leaving issue

(2) Ethel Torfrida Baldwin; *m* 6 April 1895 Frank Marchant (*d* 13 April 1946), 4th s of Stephen Walter Marchant, of Matfield House, Kent, and *d* 17 Dec 1947, leaving issue

5 (cont.) Edward Wake *m* 2nd 19 Aug 1871 Ellen Mary (*d* 26 Sept 1912), est dau of Henry Osmonde Nethercote, of Moulton Grange, Northants, and *d* 7 Aug 1883, having by her had:

(3) Mary Charlotte Baldwin; *d* unm 12 April 1965 aged 92

(4) Henrietta Louisa Baldwin; *m* 12 Aug 1908 Sir Henry Hamond Dawson Beaumont, KCMG (*d* 15 Dec 1949), Min Plen Dip Serv, and *d* 8 June 1964, leaving issue

(5) Dorothy Blanche Baldwin; *m* 30 Jan 1901 Col John Henry Lang Sims, OBE, TD (*d* 30 Sept 1928), s of Samuel Sims, of Blackheath, and *d* 25 March 1950, leaving issue

6 Chattie Baldwin; *m* 8 June 1904 Maj Michel Hewitt Salaman, Roy N Devon Hus Yeo, s of Myer Salaman, and *d* 18 May 1971 aged 92, leaving issue

The 10th Bt's est s,

Sir William Wake, 11th Bt; *b* 1823; *m* 21 Sept 1844 Margaret Anne (*d* 12 Dec 1866), est dau of Henry Fricker, of Southampton, and *d* 13 April 1865, having had, with other issue (*d* young or unm):

1 HEREWALD Sir, **12th Bt**

2 Archibald James (Rev); *b* 4 July 1857; *educ* Trin Coll Oxford; Rector Courteenhall; *d* unm 1 Aug 1925

3 Charles Baldwin; *b* 1858; civ engr; *d* unm 9 May 1886

4 Thomas Herbert Drury; *b* July 1862; *d* 31 May 1938

1 Amy Margaret; *m* 27 Jan 1883 Allen Charles Ball (*d* 13 Sept 1891), of Ste Adresse, Havre, and *d* 27 Jan 1925

The 11th Bt's est s,

Sir Herewald Wake, 12th Bt, JP, DL (Northants); *b* 19 July 1852; High Sheriff Northants 1879, Ld Manors of Waltham Abbey and Nazeing; City of London acquired 1874 Epping Forest from him, making it a public Park; Capt 4th Bn Northants Regt; *m* 14 April 1874 Catharine (*d* 18 Jan 1944), sis of 1st Baron Saint Levan (*qv*), and *d* 5 Jan 1916, leaving:

1 HEREWARD (Sir), **13th Bt**

2 Godwin Rupert, of Vigila, S Rhodesia; *b* 7 June 1879; *educ* Eton; Maj KRRC Boer War 1899–1902 (medal with four clasps), WW I (despatches four times); *d* unm 8 Dec 1949

3 Baldwin St Aubyn (Sir), KBE (1944), CB (1935); *b* 1 Nov 1882; China War 1900 (medal), WW I, ADC to HM GEORGE V 1933, Dir Naval Equipment 1934–36, Adml Supt contract-built ships 1937–44, V-Adml; Russian Order of St Anne 3rd Cl with swords, Kt Cdr Order King George I of Greece; *d* unm 1 Oct 1951

1 Thurfrida; *b* 28 March 1875; *d* unm 24 Jan 1965

2 Joan, CBE (1960); *b* 29 Feb 1884; FSA, FRHistS, Hon MA Oxon 1953, Hon LLD Leicester 1959, Hon Sec and Gen Ed Northants Record Soc 1920–63; *d* unm 15 Jan 1974

3 Phyllis Katheren Wake; *b* 20 Feb 1887; nurse WW I France, MI5 and Min Info WW II; *m* 19 April 1919 Richard Montgomery Archdale, MBE, MC, 19th Hus (*d* 15 Nov 1965), est s of George Montgomery Archdale, and had:

(1) *Nicholas Montgomery [Nicholas Archdale Esq, Penbedwllchaf, Mold, Flints]; *b* 5 Feb 1924; 60th Rifles and Para Regt WW II; *m* 10 Nov 1953 *Patricia, dau of Herbert William Thomas, of Pentref, Nannerch, Flints, and has:

    1a *Edward Montgomery; *b* 6 July 1954

    2a *Christopher; *b* 13 April 1959

    1a *Catherine; *b* 22 Feb 1956

(1) *Felicity Clare [Mrs Robin von der Heyde, Vigila Farm, PO Box 80, Mvurwi, Zimbabwe]; *b* 25 July 1922; FANY WW II; *m* 1957 *Robin von der Heyde and has:

 1a *Nicholas Fearne; *b* 8 Oct 1961, *m* 19 Sept 1987 *Sarena Ann Versfeld, and has:

  1b *Johnathan; *b* 24 Dec 1991
  1b *Katherine Ann; *b* 18 Sept 1989

 1a *Amanda Claire; *b* 1 May 1960, *m* 9 Sept 1995 *Robert Frederick Milbank, and has:

  1b *Sabrina Joan; *b* 29 Aug 1997

The 12th Bt's est s,

Sir Hereward Wake, 13th Bt, CB (1933), CMG (1918), DSO (1900), JP, DL (Northants); *b* 11 Feb 1876; *educ* Eton and RMC Sandhurst; KRRC 1897–1924 (Lt-Col 4th Bn 1922), Boer War 1899–1902 (wounded, despatches three times, two medals, seven clasps), WW I (despatches four times, brevet), Cdr: 162nd Inf Bde (TA) 1928, 12th Inf Bde 1929–32 and 46th (N Midland) Div 1934–37; ADC to HM GEORGE V 1930–32, Maj-Gen 1932 (ret 1937), Col-Cmdt: 1st Bn KRRC 1938–46, Northants ACF 1942–44; King's Messenger and Cdr Northants HG (ret 1947) WW II, High Sheriff Northants 1944, Freeman Dover, Cdr Legn Hon and Order Crown Italy, Roy Humane Soc medal; *m* 30 Oct 1912 Margaret Winifred (Daisy) (*d* 21 June 1976), er dau of Robert Henry Benson, JP, of Buckhurst, Sussex, and *d* 4 Aug 1963, having had:

1 Sir HEREWARD WAKE, **14th and present Bt**

2 Roger; *b* 19 Sept 1918; *educ* Eton; Lt RN WW II (wounded, despatches); dir Kleinwort Benson, chm Carpets Interest; *m* 22 July 1944 (*divorce* 1970) Olwyn Mary, yr dau of Lt-Col John Charles Wynne Finch (*see* AYLESFORD, E); *m* 2nd 1984 *Belinda Joan [Mrs Roger Wake, Newton House, Lochmaddy, N Uist, Scotland], dau of Charles Patrick Crossley and formerly w of Timothy Michael Nicholl, and *d* 1988, leaving by his 1st w:

 (1) +John [John Wake Esq, L'Aumonerie, 49124 St Barthelemy d'Anjou, France]; *b* 8 Aug 1945; *educ* Eton; *m* 7 March 1969 *Isabelle, dau of Comte de Dreux-Brézé, of Paris, and has:

  1a +Christopher; *b* 18 Aug 1969
  2a +Jeremy Alistair; *b* 1974
  1a *Charlotte; *b* 1971
  2a *Annabelle; *b* 25 Sept 1986

 (2) +(Charles) Julian; *b* 16 Feb 1947; *educ* Eton and U of BC Canada; *m* 1977 *Josie Alata, of Canada, and has:

  1a *Callum; *b* 1983
  1a *Rowena; *b* 1978

 (3) +William [William Wake Esq, 57 Macfarlane Rd, London W12]; *b* 23 Jan 1949; *educ* Eton; *m* 1986 *Jehanne Deirdre Alexandra, biographer, only dau of James Hamilton Williams, of Anderidan House, Curtisden Green, Kent, and has:

  1a +David; *b* 1991
  1a *Catherine Mary; *b* 1986

 (1) *Jane [Mrs Hugh Potter, Cuckoo Bush Farmhouse, Reybridge, nr Lacock, Wilts]; *b* 30 Oct 1950; *m* 1977 *(Simon) Hugh Arnold Potter, 3rd s of Arnott Potter, of Wellington Coll, Berks, and has:

  1a *Simon; *b* 1982
  1a *Emma; *b* 1978

3 Peter; *b* 19 July 1921; *educ* Eton; Capt KRRC WW II (wounded), banker; *m* 8 March 1960 *Marion Margaret, DL [Mrs Peter Wake DL, Fairfield House, Hambledon, Hants PO7 4RY], yr dau of Col John Henry Bevan, CB, MC, TD (*see* LUCAN, E), and *d* 1993, leaving:

 (1) +Edward; *b* 21 June 1965; *m* 1991 *Katherine Yvonne, only dau of John Alfred Leavett-Shenley (*see* AMHERST OF HACKNEY, B)

 (2) +Philip Hereward; *b* 10 Feb 1967; *educ* Eton

 (1) *Susan; *b* 16 April 1963; *m* 1994 *John Mervyn Edward Pugh, s of John Mervyn Cullwick Pugh, of Fernhill Heath, Worcs

1 *Margaret [Lady Turner, 3 The Grove, London N6]; *b* 24 July 1913; *m* 15 April 1939, as his 2nd w, Sir (Ronald) Mark Cunliffe Turner (*d* 1970), only s of Christopher Rede Turner, Clerk Jrnls H of C, of Green Hedges, Sheringham, Norfolk, and has:

 (1) *Christopher; *b* 7 Sept 1942; *educ* Eton; *m* 18 July 1964 *Katrina, 3rd dau of Capt Harold Keith Salvesen, DL, of Inveralmond, Cramond, Edinburgh

 (2) *Richard Wake; *b* 12 July 1949; *educ* Eton; *m* 1985 *Celia Anne, dau of David Carr, of Little Bookham, Surrey, and has:

  1a *Imogen Sarah; *b* 1993

 (3) *Roger Cunliffe; *b* 12 July 1949; *educ* Eton; *m* 1974 *Rosemary Jane, est dau of Rt Rev Richard Fox Cartwright, DD, Bp Plymouth

 (1) *Catherine; *b* 22 June 1940
 (2) *Margaret; *b* 8 Oct 1947

2 Diana; Jr Cdr ATS WW II; *b* 14 Nov 1915; *k* in a riding accident at Bicester Hunt Races 11 March 1950

3 Patricia; *b* 23 Nov 1919; *m* 6 Sept 1939 Lt-Col Christopher Payan Dawnay (*see* DOWNE, V) and had issue

4 *Mary [Mrs James Weatherby, Cleeve House, E Knoyle, Wilts]; *b* 15 Sept 1927; *m* 18 Feb 1947 *Capt James Howard Weatherby, 10th Hus, er s of Lt-Col James Thorpe Weatherby, DSO, of Stanton Ho, Stanton St John, Oxon, and has:

 (1) *Jeremy James; *b* 3 May 1949; *educ* Eton
 (1) *Susan [The Rt Hon The Viscountess Ullswater, The Old Rectory, Docking, Norfolk PE31 8LJ]; *b* 21 Nov 1947; *m* 10 June 1967 *2nd Viscount Ullswater (*qv*) and has issue

WAKEFIELD

Arms: Argent two barrulets sable between three owls proper. **Crest:** A bat displayed proper, charged on each wing with a crescent argent. **Motto:** Be just and fear not. **Creation:** Bt. (UK) 10 March 1962.

SIR (EDWARD) HUMPHRY TYRRELL WAKEFIELD, 2ND BT, of Kendal, Co Westmorland [Sir Humphry Wakefield Bt, Chillingham Castle, Alnwick, Northumberland NE66 5NJ]; *b* 11 July 1936; *s* f 1969; *educ* Gordonstoun and Trin Coll Cambridge (BA 1960, MA Hons); exec v-pres Mallett America Ltd 1970–75, dir: Mallet & Son (Antiques) Ltd 1971–78, Spoleto Festival of Two Worlds USA and Italy 1973–80, Tree of Life Fndn 1976–, chm: Tyrell and Moore Ltd 1978–92, Sir Humphry Wakefield and Ptnrs, Nicolai Patricia Co Ltd 1978–; Fell Pierpont Morgan Library, fndr Stately Homes Collection of Antique Furniture and Objects of Art, joined NZ Everest team on first ascent of Mt Wakefield 1991, attempted Everest 1992, memb Norman Vaughan Antarctic Expdn 1993, pres: Northumberland Nat Park Search and Rescue Team, Avison Tst; memb Standing Cncl Btage; Lt 10th Hus (Res); *m* 1st 17 Sept 1960 (*divorce* 1964) Priscilla, est dau of (Oliver) Robin Bagot, JP (*see* BAGOT, B); *m* 2nd 1 July 1966 (*divorce* 1971) Hon Elizabeth Sophia, est dau of 1st Viscount De L'Isle (*qv*) and formerly w of (George Silver) Oliver Annesley Colthurst (*see* COLTHURST, Bt), and by her has:

 1 +MAXIMILIAN EDWARD VEREKER; *b* 22 Feb 1967; *educ* Milton Abbey and RMA Sandhurst; Lt Roy Hussars (PWO); *m* 19– *Lucinda Pipe and has:

  (1) +William; *b* 9 May 1998

Sir HUMPHRY *m* 3rd Dec 1974 *Hon Katharine Mary Alice, er dau of 1st Baron Howick of Glendale (*qv*), and by her has had:

 2 +John Humphry Baring; *b* 1977; *educ* Eton
 3 A son; *b* and *d* 19–
 1 *Mary Elizabeth Lalage; *b* 1975; *educ* Wycombe Abbey and Edinburgh U

Lineage: ROGER WAKEFIELD, of Challon Hall, Preston Patrick, Westmorland; *m* Isabel — and *d* in or after 1592, leaving:

NICHOLAS WAKEFIELD; had:

ROGER WAKEFIELD, of Challon Hall; *m* 21 March 1665 Hannah Preston (*d* 1732), of Farleton, and *d* 1724, leaving an est s:

ROGER WAKEFIELD, of Stricklandgate, Kendal, Westmorland; *b* 1677; *m* Mary Haig, of Brighouse, Yorks, and was *bur* 30 Nov 1731, having had, with two other sons and five daus:

1 ROGER

2 Edward; *b* 1715; *m* Isabella Gibbon, a relative of the historian, and *d* 1756, leaving, with a yr s:

 (1) Edward; *m* Pricilla [*sic*] Bell, author as Pricilla Wakefield of some 20 books on miscellaneous subjects and a fndr of various savings banks, and had:

  1a Edward; *b* 1744; *m* Susanna Crash and *d* 1854, leaving, with other issue:

   1b Edward Gibbon; *b* 1796; originator of concept of Adelaide, Australia, as a convict-free settlement; fndr Christchurch, Wellington, Nelson and New Plymouth in New Zealand; *m* Eliza Pattle and *d* 1826, having had, with a dau (*d* young):

    1c Edward Jerningham; adventure writer

   2b William; *b* 1797; Gen Spanish Army, colonial administrator NZ; *m* 1826 Emily, dau of Sir John Shelley Sidney, 1st Bt (*see* DE L'ISLE, V), and *d* 1849, leaving:

    1c Emily; *m* Sir John Stafford, 1st PM NZ

The er s,

 ROGER WAKEFIELD, of Stricklandgate; *b* 14 Aug 1706; *m* 1st 2 April 1730 Margaret (*d* 26 June 1736), dau of Thomas Willan, of Sedbergh, Yorks, and had two sons and two daus; *m* 2nd 4 Oct 1737 Mary (*m* 2nd William Dilworth), dau of John Wilson, of Kendal, and *d* 14 Aug 1756, having by her had, with two er sons and two daus:

JOHN WAKEFIELD, of Stricklandgate; *b* 18 Dec 1738; *m* 1760 Margaret Hodgson (*d* 8 Dec 1812) and *d* 26 May 1811, having had, with four yr sons:

JOHN WAKEFIELD, of Stricklandgate; *b* 13 March 1761; *m* 16 May 1787 Mary (*d* 10 Feb 1824), dau of John Beakbane, and *d* 30 Oct 1829, having had, with two er sons (John, *b* 18 May, *d* 7 July 1791; John, of Sedgwick House, Kendal, *b* 1 June 1794, High Sheriff Westmorland 1854, *m* 30 June 1823 Fanny, dau of Dr MacArthur, of Glasgow, and *d* 8 April 1866, leaving two sons and four daus) and a yst s (William Henry, *b* 25 Feb 1804, *d* 3 Aug 1827), a 3rd s:

EDWARD WILLIAM WAKEFIELD, of Birklands, Kendal; *b* 7 Oct 1799; *m* 1822 Susanna (*d* 1898), dau of William Birkbeck, of Settle, Yorks, and *d* 6 Feb 1858, having had:

1 John Edward; *b* 1823; *d* 1829

2 WILLIAM

3 Thomas Birkbeck, of The Hall, Moate, Co Westmeath; *b* 3 Sept 1828; *m* 13 May 1851 Sophia, dau of David Espinette, of Tenterden, Kent, and *d* 19 April 1898, leaving:

(1) Edward; *b* 2 June 1862; *m* 14 May 1891 Frances (*d* 11 Dec 1942), dau of Owen Thomas Conolly, of Dublin, and *d* 3 Sept 1920, having had:

1a Roger Birkbeck; *ka* 1914

1a Kathleen de Carte; *m* 1 March 1921 Cecil William Johnson, of Moate, and had:

1b *Edward Brabazon Wakefield, MC; *b* 11 Feb 1922; *educ* St Columba's; Capt Roy Irish Fus, formerly Roy Ulster Rifles, WW II; *m* 7 March 1951 *Ruth, dau of Hans Wagner, of Liestal, Switzerland, and has:

1c *Suzanne Elizabeth; *b* 27 Aug 1952

2c *Veronica Ruth; *b* 30 Aug 1953

3c *Marianne Patricia; *b* 13 Nov 1957

2a Noel Patricia; *m* 29 May 1920 Lt-Gen John Conyers D'Arcy, CB, CBE, MC (*d* 1 Feb 1966), only s of Most Rev Charles Frederick D'Arcy, Primate All Ireland, and *d* 11 July 1968, leaving two sons

(1) Editha Susan; *d* unm 1873

(2) Eva Margaret; *m* Feb 1877 John Crofton Rainey and had issue

(3) Ada Sophia; *m* Sept 1879 Herbert Knott, of Stalybridge, Cheshire, and had issue

(4) Kathleen Jemima; *m* April 1878 Edward ffrench, MD, of Glason, Athlone, and *dsp*

4 John Edward, of Birklands, Kendal; *b* 8 Aug 1839; *m* 13 Sept 1854 Rachel Crewdson (*d* 20 Sept 1887), er dau of Henry Fox, of Tonedale, Cornwall, and *d* 30 July 1858, leaving:

(1) John Edward William; *b* 31 March 1858; *m* 9 Aug 1882 Nora, dau of Richard Drake, and *d* 1934, leaving:

1a John Hylbert; *b* 9 Oct 1886; *m* and *dsp*

1a Nora Muriel

2a Cicely Corner

(1) Rachel Mary; *m* 25 April 1878 Christopher Elliott, MD, of Clifton, and had issue

5 Jacob Henry; *b* 1831; *d* 1833

6 George Henry, of Wavertree, Liverpool; *b* 29 April 1835; *m* 31 Aug 1858 Susan, dau of Stafford Stratton Baxter, of Mancetter Manor, Atherstone, and *d* 4 Feb 1903, having had:

(1) Mary Constance; *m* 19 Jan 1882 Maj George Morley Saunders, Durham LI (*d* 1918), yst s of William Allen Francis Saunders, of Wennington Hall, Lancs, and had, with a s:

1a Margaret Georgina; *b* 1915; *m* Maj Thomas Willes and had:

1b *Olda Ann; *b* 1939; *m* 1979 as his 2nd w, *Desmond John Villiers Fitz Gerald, 29th Knight of the Glin (*see also* DURHAM, E)

(2) Maude; *d* unm

(3) Ethel; *d* umn

(4) Beatrice; *d* unm

1 Rachel Mary; *b* 1826; *d* 1843

EDWARD WAKEFIELD's 2nd s,

WILLIAM WAKEFIELD, JP, DL (Westmorland), of Birklands; *b* 30 April 1825; *m* 16 Oct 1861 Marianne, dau of Edmund Minson Wavell, of Field House, Halifax, and *d* 19 April 1893, having had:

1 Edward William, JP (Kendal), DL, of Stricklandgate; *b* 8 Sept 1862; *educ* Trin Coll Cambridge (BA 1883); barrister Inner Temple 1893, High Sheriff Westmorland 1900–01, Capt 11th Bn Cheshire Regt 1914–15 and 4th Res Bn Border Regt 1916, 37th Labour Co France 1917–18, Chev Order Crown Italy, Mayor Kendal 1925–26, Freeman Kendal 1937, Ld Manor Seaton, Cumberland; *m* 8 Sept 1886 Mary, MA Edin (*d* 30 March 1921), dau of J R Wilkinson, of Burnside, Skipton, and *d* 3 Aug 1941, leaving:

(1) Marian Alice; *b* 6 July 1887; *m* 26 Sept 1912 Peter Christian Gordon (*d* 21 April 1956), yr s of James Edward Henry Gordon, and had a s and dau

2 George Henry; *b* 10 Aug 1864; *d* 29 April 1868

3 ROGER WILLIAM

4 William Birkbeck, MBE; *b* Aug 1867; FRGS; *m* 14 Oct 1919 Elizabeth, dau of Robert Davison, of S Shields, and *d* 3 Nov 1941, leaving:

(1) Robert Edward William; *b* 8 July 1920; *m* 30 Jan 1945 *Yannoulla, dau of Sir Panayotis Loizou Cacoyannis, LLB, of Limassol, and *d* following a car crash 14 March 1970

5 Arthur William; *b* 13 April 1876; *educ* Sedbergh, Trin Coll Cambridge (MA) and London Hosp (MD, BCh, MRCS, LRCP); Trooper 70th Co Imp Yeo Boer War; MO to Roy Nat Mission to Deep Sea Fishermen in Labrador 1908–14, Lt Newfoundland Regt and Capt RAMC WW I (despatches), memb Mt Everest Expdn 1922, pres Northern Counties branch BMA 1930, Lt-Col MO HG WW II; *m* 1 June 1910 Marjorie (*d* 13 Jan 1976), dau of James D Younger, of Montreal, and *d* 23 Feb 1949, leaving:

(1) Robert William; *b* 3 March 1914; *educ* Sedbergh and McGill; Lt RA WW II; *m* 7 June 1940 *Harriet Margaret Towers, dau of Alfred Towers Settle, of London, and had:

1a *Allan Gale; *b* 28 Dec 1941; *educ* Trin Coll Sch Port Hope, Yale (BA) and Harvard (MBA); assist to exec v-pres (Finance) Alcan Aluminium; *m* 17 June 1967 *Susan Elizabeth Weatherhead, of Ottawa

2a *Charles James; *b* 25 July 1945; *educ* Trin Coll Sch Port Hope and McGill

1a *Sally Anne; *b* 6 June 1947

(2) (James) Roger; *b* 19 May 1921; *educ* Sedbergh; *m* 1st 16 Jan 1943 (*divorce* 1958) Elizabeth Mary, dau of Wilfred Clarke, of Halstead, Essex, and had:

1a *Michael James Mark [Michael Wakefield Esq, 57c Canfield Gdns, London NW6]; *b* 29 April 1944; *educ* Downside; *m* 11 Oct 1968 *Veronica Marie Quah Wai Ling, est dau of Maj Francis Edmund C C Quah, Hong Kong Regt

2a *Simon Roger Sebastian; *b* 10 Nov 1947; *educ* The Oratory Sch

1a *Virginia Sarah Veronica; *b* 4 July 1950

(2) (cont.) Roger Wakefield *m* 2nd 13 April 1963 *Penelope Anne [Mrs Roger Wakefield, Fox House, 77 High St, Whitwell, Herts SG4 8AH], yr dau of Frank Arthur Jackman, OBE, BSc, FRIC, of Pinner, Middx, and *d* 27 Jan 1973, leaving by her:

2a *Rachel Frances; *b* 22 Sept 1964; *m* 25 April 1998 *Andrew James Luck, of Hitchin, and has:

1b *Phillipa Anne; *b* 14 Nov 1997

3a *Katherine Penelope; *b* 18 March 1968; *m* 3 Oct 1992 *Gregory James Rataj, of Hitchin, and has:

1b *Megan Grace; *b* 1 April 1996

4a *Susannah Ruth; *b* 31 Dec 1970

(1) *Elizabeth Marianne [Mrs William Hill, Applecote, Applethwaite, Keswick, Cumberland]; *b* 24 Aug 1917; consultant, sci dir Cumberland Worm Farms Ltd; *m* 12 Dec 1940 W/Cdr William Owen Hill, RAF, s of Albert Charles Hill, of Colwyn, Denbighs, and has:

1a *Anthony William Garnet Wakefield; *b* 31 March 1942; *educ* Sedbergh and Flint Hill Sch, USA

1a *Elizabeth Mari-Anne Gale [Mrs Patrick Osborne, Raysdale House, Castle Carrock, Cumberland]; *b* 21 Oct 1944; *m* 6 June 1964 *Patrick Tom Hamilton Osborne, s of F O B Osborne, of Burgh-by-Sands, Cumberland, and has:

1b *Christian Elizabeth; *b* 30 March 1966

2b *Joanna Kate; *b* 13 May 1968

2a *Jennifer Marjorie [Mrs Robert Taylor, The Garden Flat, 7 Redcliffe Square, London SW10]; *b* 9 July 1946; *m* 2 Sept 1967 Robert Mortimer James Taylor, BA, s of C R Taylor, of Shave House, Bantry, Co Cork

1 Marianne Isabel; *b* 31 Aug 1869; *d* unm 3 Sept 1953

2 Rachel Mary; *m* 4 Jan 1900 William Douglas Monro, yr s of James Monro, CB, Bengal CS, and *d* 28 June 1919, leaving two sons and a dau

3 Frances Marget; MB, ChB; MO EMS Hosp Omdurman 1917–18, Women's Civil Hosp Basrah 1919; *d* unm 1970

WILLIAM WAKEFIELD's 3rd s,

ROGER WILLIAM WAKEFIELD, JP (Lancs 1924), of Birklands; *b* 1 Nov 1865; *educ* Sedbergh and Trin Coll Cambridge (MA); MB; *m* 12 Jan 1897 Ethel Mary (*d* 19 Dec 1960 aged 86), dau of John Frederick Knott, of Stalybridge, and *d* 1958, having had:

1 (WILLIAM) WAVELL WAKEFIELD, 1st and last BARON WAKEFIELD OF KENDAL, of Kendal, Co Westmorland (UK), so *cr* 15 Nov 1963; *b* 10 March 1898; *educ* Sedbergh and Pembroke Coll Cambridge (BA 1923, MA 1927); RNAS 1916–18, RAF 1918 WW I, Res of Offrs 1923, MP (C) Swindon 1935–45, St Marylebone 1945–63, PPS to: Sec State Dominions 1936–38, Sec Dept Overseas Trade 1939–40, U-Sec for Air 1940–42; Dir ATC 1942–44, chm Parly and Scientific Ctee 1952–55; ktd 1944; *m* 19 Nov 1919 Rowena Doris, dau of Llewellyn Lewis, OBE, MD, of Neath, Glam, and *d* 1983, when the Barony expired, leaving:

(1) *Joan Rosemary, OBE (1981) [The Hon Mrs Raynsford OBE, Milton Malsor Manor, Northampton NN7 3AR]; *b* 18 Nov 1920; *m* 18 March 1944 Capt Anthony Edward Montague Raynsford, DL, RN (*d* 1993), er s of Lt Col Richard Montague Raynsford, DSO, JP, DL, of Milton Manor, and has:

1a *Richard Wakefield; *b* 1945; *m* 1979 *Rosemary, dau of Brig Thomas Hayward Evill, CBE, DSO, and has:

1b *Thomas Lindsay Wakefield; *b* 1980

1b *Clementina Daisy; *b* 1982

1a *Julia Daphne [Lady Boyd, Churchill Coll, Cambridge CB3 0DS]; *b* 1948; *m* 1977, as his 2nd w, *Sir John Dixon Iklé Boyd, KCMG, and has:

1b *Jessica; *b* 1978

2b *Alice Clara; *b* 1979

3b *Olivia Wakefield; *b* 1982

(2) *Mary Sheila, OBE (1992) [The Hon Mrs Hensman OBE, Lindum Holme, Stricklandgate, Cumbria LA9 4QG]; *b* 29 April 1922; *m* 6 July 1945 Brig Richard Frank Bradshaw Hensman, CBE (*d* 1988), er s of Capt Melvill Hensman, RN, and has:

1a *Peter Richard Wavell; *b* 1948; *m* 1973 *Claire Theresa, dau of Peter Wallace Henderson, MC, BM, BCh, and has:

1b *Roger Edward Wavell; *b* 1981

1b *Lucinda Carolyn Barrett; *b* 1978

2b *Joanna Mary Bradshaw; *b* 1980

1a *Suzannah Mary; *b* 1953; *m* 1977 *William Ian Simpson and has:

1b *Thomas James; *b* 1981

1b *Victoria Jane; *b* 1979

(3) *Ruth Isabel [The Hon Mrs Adorian, Buckstone House, Carnforth, Lancs]; *b* 12 Oct 1932; *m* 1st 1 June 1955 Maj Nigel James Clarkson Webb, Gren Gds (*d* 1987), yst s of William Thomas Clarkson Webb; *m* 2nd 1992 *Paul Anthony Adorian and has by her 1st husb:

1a *Edward James; *b* 1966

1a *Georgina Anne; *b* 1957; *m* 1981 *Christopher Campbell Townsend, er s of Eric L Townsend, of Sandford Orcas, Dorset, and has:

1b *Alexander Peard; *b* 1984

1b *Rosanna Campbell; *b* 1987

2a *Carolyn Mary; *b* 1958; *m* 1983 *Jeremy Simon Seel, yst s of Kenneth Seel, of Gt Rollright Manor, Chipping Norton, Oxon, and has:

1b *Annabel Lucy; *b* 1987

2b *Natasha Mary; *b* 1989

2 John Dickins; *b* 17 Dec 1899; *educ* Oundle; *m* 23 Sept 1925 *Celia (*m* 2nd 2 July 1940 Basil Radclyffe), dau of John Penny, of Lyndale, Que Que, Zimbabwe, and *d* 10 Feb 1938, leaving:

(1) *John Roger [John Wakefield Esq, 39 Newport Road, Parkwood, Johannesburg, S Africa); *b* 2 Oct 1926; *educ* Plumtree Sch Rhodesia and U of Cape Town (BA); RN WW II 1945–46, Colonial Admin Serv 1954–59, sub-ed *The Star* Johannesburg 1961–66, assist ed *The Post* Johannesburg 1967–69, PR dir and manager edtl servs Unimark Internat S Africa 1969–; *m* 1st 31 Jan 1951 (*divorce* 1961) Heath Katharine, dau of Frank Rosselli, of Bulawayo, Rhodesia, and has:

1a *Richard James Wavell; *b* 22 March 1953; *educ* Milton Sch Bulawayo

2a *Roger William; *b* 14 May 1955; *educ* Milton Sch

3a *Peter John; *b* 5 Jan 1958

(1) (cont.) John Wakefield *m* 2nd 17 June 1961 *Ruth Kirkham, yst dau of William Gluck, of Mafeking, and by her has issue

4a *Roger Nicholas; *b* 9 Oct 1963

1a *Nicola Margaret; *b* 21 March 1962

(1) *Basil Birkbeck [Basil Wakefield Esq, Piedmont, PB 915, Bindura, Zimbabwe]; *b* 20 Feb 1934; *educ* Plumtree Sch Rhodesia and U of California Ag Faculty; *m* 5 July 1958 *Deirdre Penelope Anne, est dau of Sidney Walton Hinde, of Warren Beach, Natal, by his 1st w Freda Violet Henrietta, only child of Sir William Willoughby Williams, 5th Bt, of Bodelwyddan (*qv*), and has:

1a *Dean Roger; *b* 28 Nov 1960

2a *Clive Basil; *b* 30 Nov 1964

3a *Richard Owen; *b* 18 Sept 1967

4a *Darryl William; *b* 18 Sept 1967

1a *Deborah Odile; *b* 13 April 1959

(1) *Mary Celia Margaret [Mrs Eric Owen, 15 Epping Rd, Mount Pleasant, Harare, Zimbabwe]; *b* 3 April 1932; *m* 4 Jan 1947 *Eric Cyril Coxon Owen, s of Cyril Coxen Owen, of Selukwe, S Rhodesia, and has four daus

3 EDWARD BIRKBECK (Sir), **1st Bt**

4 Roger Cuthbert, CMG (1953), OBE (1950); *b* 27 June 1906; *educ* Sedbergh and Trin Coll Cambridge (BA 1928); FRICS (1949), Dir Surveys Khartoum 1946–55; *m* 6 June 1936 *Elizabeth Rhoda, yr dau of Sidney Richard Davie, of W Byfleet, Surrey, and had:

(1) *Deirdre Eva Preston; *b* 9 Nov 1943; *m* 29 Oct 1966 Lt William Lawrance Tosco Peppé, RN, est s of Lt-Col William Tosco H Peppé, of Castle Cottage, Clun, Salop, and has:

1a *William Roger Tosco; *b* 24 Dec 1968

2a *Alasdair; *b* 26 Dec 1970

ROGER WAKEFIELD's 3rd s,

Sir Edward Birkbeck Wakefield, 1st Bt (UK), so *cr* 10 March 1962, CIE (1945); *b* 24 July 1903; *educ* Haileybury and Trin Coll Cambridge (BA 1925, MA 1941); joined ICS 1927, Ch Minister Kalat State 1933–36, Nabha State 1939–41 and Rewa State 1943–45, MP (C) Derbyshire W Feb 1950–March 1962, Assist Govt Whip 1954, a Ld Commr Treasury 1956–58, Comptroller Household 1958–59, V-Chamberlain 1959–60, Treasurer 1960–62, UK Commr Malta 1962–64, HC Malta 1964–65; Bronze Medal for saving life from drowning 1936; *m* 7 Dec 1929 *(Constance) Lalage [Dowager Lady Wakefield, 13 St Mary Abbot's Terrace, London W14], er dau of Sir John Perronet Thompson, KCSI, KCIE, chm Union of Britain and India, and *d* 14 Jan 1969, having had:

1 Sir (EDWARD) HUMPHRY TYRRELL WAKEFIELD, **2nd and present Bt**

2 +Gerald Hugo Cropper [Gerald Wakefield Esq, Bramdean House, Alresford, Hants SO24 0JU]; *b* 15 Sept 1938; *educ* Eton and Trin Coll Cambridge (BA 1961); late Lt 12th Lancers, chm: Guy Carpenter & Co Inc, New York, J & H Marsh & McLennan (Hldgs); *m* 4 Dec 1971 *Victoria Rose, er dau of Maj Cecil Henry Feilden, Coldstream Gds, and has:

(1) +Edward Cecil; *b* 7 March 1973; *educ* Eton and Durham U (BSc 1995)

1 Frances Imogen; *b* 4 Dec 1930; *k* earthquake Quetta 31 May 1935

2 Xanthe; *b* 6 Nov 1932; *educ* Somerville Coll Oxford; BBC TV producer; *d* unm 4 Dec 1962

WAKEHAM

Arms: Per fess embattled azure and argent a pale counter-changed, in the azure a lion's head guardant or, langued gules, in the argent a bugle horn azure, garnished and stringed gold. **Crest:** A greyhound statant or, crowned with a mural crown checky azure and argent and supporting by the dexter foreleg a cross raguly argent, nailed of three gold. **Supporters:** Dexter, a sea-lion azure, mane and head in trian aspect argent, langued gules, crowned with a crown tridenty gold; sinister, a sea-horse azure, head and neck argent and crowned also with a crown tridenty gold, the compartment comprising three bars wavy azure, argent and azure, in front thereof a grassy mount, growing therefrom three double roses argent upon gules, barbed and seeded, stalked and leaved proper. **Motto:** *Vigilo* ('I watch').
Creation: B. (LP, UK) 1992.

THE BARON WAKEHAM, of Maldon, Co Essex (John Wakeham, PC 1983, JP (Inner London 1972), DL (Hants 1997)) [The Rt Hon The Lord Wakeham PC JP DL, House of Lords, London SW1A 0PW]; *b* 22 June 1932; *educ* Charterhouse; CA; MP (C) Maldon 1974–83, Colchester S and Maldon 1983–92, Assist Govt Whip 1979–81, Govt Whip (Ld Commr Treasury) 1981, Parly U-Sec Industry 1981–82, Min State Treasury 1982–83, Parly Sec Treasury and Govt Ch Whip 1983–87, Ld Privy Seal 1987–88 and 1992–94, Leader H of C 1987–89, Ld Pres Cncl 1988–89, Sec State Energy 1989–92, Minister Govt Policies 1990–92, Leader Ho Lds 1992–94; memb Lloyd's and RNLI Mgmt Ctee 1995–, Chm: Br Horseracing Bd 1995–98, Press Complaints Commn 1995– and Alexandra Rose Day 1998–, Chllr Brunel U 1998–; Sec Small Businesses Ctee; FCA; *m* 1st 1965 Anne Roberta (*k* 1984), dau of Harold Edwin Bailey, and has:

1 *Jonathan Martin; *b* 1972; *educ* Charterhouse

2 *Benedict Ian; *b* 1975; *educ* Charterhouse

THE BARON WAKEHAM *m* 2nd 1985 *Alison Bridget, MBE, yr dau of Ven Edwin James Greenfield Ward, LVO (see BUXTON, Bt), and has:

3 *David Robert; *b* 1987

Lineage: WALTER JOHN WAKEHAM; Maj; *m* E R — and had:

JOHN, *cr* a **Baron**

WAKEHURST

Arms: Quarterly 1st and 4th, grand quarters: azure on a fess between in chief a portcullis chained and in base a martlet or three stag's heads cabossed proper (for LODER); 2nd grand quarter, the arms of CHARLES II, viz., quarterly 1st and 4th France and England quarterly, 2nd quarter Scotland, 3rd quarter Ireland, over all a baton sinister gules charged with three roses argent, barbed and seeded proper (for BEAUCLERK); 3rd grand quarter, quarterly gules and or, in the first quarter a mullet argent (for DE VERE). **Crest:** A stag's head cabossed, transfixed by an arrow bendwise point downwards, all proper, between two escallops or. **Supporters:** Dexter, a Russian brown bear proper; sinister, a greyhound argent, gorged with a collar chequy of the last and azure. **Motto:** *Murus aeneus conscientia sana* ('A sound conscience is a wall of brass'). **Creation:** B. (UK) 29 June 1934.

THE 3RD BARON WAKEHURST, of Ardingly, Co Susssex ((John) Christopher Loder) [The Rt Hon The Lord Wakehurst, Trillinghurst Oast, Ranters Lane, Goudhurst, Kent TN17 1HL]; *b* 23 Sept 1925; *s f* 1970; *educ* Eton, King's Sch NSW and Trin Coll Cambridge (BA 1948, LLB 1949, MA 1953); Sub-Lt RANVR and RNVR W Pacific WW II, barrister Inner Temple 1950, md Brown Harriman and Internat Bank, 1968–73, chm: Continental Illinois Ltd 1973–84, Anglo & Overseas Tst plc 1980–96, Overseas Investment Tst plc 1980–95, Morgan Grenfell Equity Income Tst plc 1991–95, Morgan Grenfell Latin American Tst plc 1994–96, Philadelphia National Ltd 1985–90, dep chm London and Manchester Gp 1981–95, CStJ; *m* 1st 27 Oct 1956 Ingeborg Krumbholz-Hess (*d* 14 Feb 1977), dau of Walter Otto Krumbholz, and has:

1 +TIMOTHY WALTER; *b* 28 March 1958; *educ* Millfield; *m* 1987 (*divorce* 1997) Susan Elaine Hurst

1 *Christina Anne [The Hon Mrs MacCarthy, Wiveton Hall, Holt, Norfolk NR25 7TE]; *b* 13 Dec 1959; *educ* Millfield and RCA (MD 1985); *m* 1993 *Desmond James MacCarthy and has issue (*see* BUXTON, Bt)

The 3rd BARON *m* 2nd 10 Sept 1983 *(Francine) Brigid, yr dau of William Noble, of Cirencester, Glos

Lineage: Sir ROBERT LODER, 1st Bt (*qv*), had a 5th s:

GERALD WALTER ERSKINE LODER, **1st Baron Wakehurst**, of Ardingly, Co Sussex (UK), so *cr* 29 June 1934, JP, DL (Sussex); *b* 25 Oct 1861; *educ* Trin Coll Cambridge (MA); LLB, barrister Inner Temple 1888, MP (C) Brighton 1889–1905, Assist Priv Sec to: Pres Local Govt Bd 1888–92 and Sec State India 1896–1901, Jr Ld Treasury 1905, v-chm Sussex TA, chm Southern Rlwy 1932–35 (jt dep chm 1922–32, chm London Brighton and S Coast Rlwy 1922 at its merger to become SR and dir LBSCR from 1896), pres RHS 1929–31, author: *Wakehurst Place, Sussex* (1907); *m* 25 Oct 1890 Lady Louise de Vere Beauclerk (*d* 15 Dec 1958), est dau of 10th Duke of Saint Albans (*qv*), and *d* 30 April 1936, leaving:

1 JOHN DE VERE WAKEHURST, **2nd Baron**

1 Dorothy Cicely Sybil; *b* 1896; *m* 13 May 1922 Capt Hon (William Jocelyn) Lewis Palmer, yst s of 2nd Earl of Selborne (*qv*), and *d* 1986, leaving issue

2 Victoria Helen; *b* 1899; *m* 17 Dec 1928 Maj Alan Rees Colman, ATA, Norfolk Yeo (*kas* ferrying aircraft 17 Jan 1943), of S Kensington, yst s of Russell James Colman, of Crown Point, and *d* 198–, having adopted:

*Anthony Hugh [Anthony Colman Esq, South Repps Hall, Norwich, Norfolk]; *m* 24 Aug 1957 *Eli Inger, dau of Einar Englesen, of Norway, and has:

1a *Olav Anthony; *b* 28 Dec 1961

1a *Clare Angela Eli; *b* 22 Sept 1958

2a *Nina Jane; *b* 13 June 1960

Ben(edict) James; *d* Oct 1995

2 Diana Evelyn (twin); *b* 1899; *m* 25 Oct 1922 3rd Baron Strathcona and Mount Royal (*qv*) and *d* 1985, leaving issue

3 Mary Irene; *b* 1 May 1902; NRD; *d* unm 7 Jan 1970

The 1st BARON's only s,

JOHN DE VERE LODER, **2nd Baron Wakehurst**, KG (1962), KCMG (1937); *b* 5 Feb 1895; *educ* Eton; Capt 4th Bn Roy Sussex Regt and Intell Corps WW I (Galli-

poli, Egypt (despatches) and Palestine), Capt TAR, Clerk FO 1919–21, MP (C) E Leicester 1924–29 and Lewes 1931–36, Govr: NSW 1937–46, NI 1952–64 and Roy Ballet 1957–70, chm ESU 1946–51, Prior OStJ 1948–69, Tstee ROH 1949–57, Hon LLD Queen's U Belfast, Hon Air Cdre No 22 (Sydney), author: *The Truth about Mesopotamia, Syria and Palestine* (1923), *Industry and the State* (1927), *Bolshevism in Perspective* (1931), *Colonsay and Oronsay* (1935), *Our Second Chance* (1944) and *Preparations for Peace* (1945); *m* 3 June 1920 Margaret, DBE (1965), GCStJ (1970) (*d* 19 Aug 1994), dau of Sir Charles Tennant, 1st Bt (*see* GLENCONNER, B), and *d* 30 Oct 1970, leaving:

1 (JOHN) CHRISTOPHER LODER, **3rd and present Baron Wakehurst**

2 +(James) David Gerald [The Hon David Loder, Flat C, 45 Chesterton Rd, London W10 6ES]; *b* 24 March 1928; *educ* Geelong GS and Trin Coll Cambridge (BA 1950); Lt Coldstream Gds, RARO, barrister Inner Temple 1952, OStJ

3 +Robert Beauclerk, CBE (1990) [The Hon Robert Loder CBE, 14 Ladbroke Grove, London W11 3BQ]; *b* 24 April 1934; *educ* Eton and Trin Coll Cambridge (BA 1955); 2nd Lt Coldstream Gds, farmer 1966–, chm Mental Health Fndn 1982– and Sheringham Hldgs 1982–, dir: Transcontinental Servs Gp NV 1970–86 and Precious Metals Tst 1981–; *m* 1973 *Josette, dau of Josef Bromovsky by Brigid, dau of Sir Philip Gordon Dunn, 2nd and last Bt (*see* 1970 edn DUNN, Bt), of Ottmanach, Pischeldorf, Carinthia, Austria, and has:

(1) +John ('Jan') James; *b* 1977

(2) +Nicolai; *b* 1986

(1) *Nell Marguerite; *b* 1983

1 Henrietta Marguerite Jean; *b* 5 Feb 1922; *educ* Sydney U (Dip Social Studies); *m* 21 April 1953 John Wilmot Reader-Harris (*d* 1975), s of Montgomery Reader-Harris, of Hong Kong, and *d* 16 Dec 1995, leaving:

(1) *Michael John [Michael Reader-Harris Esq, 27 Brownside Rd, Cambuslang, Glasgow G72 8NJ]; *b* 26 Oct 1957; *m* 6 July 1985 *Susan Mary, est dau of Lt-Col J L Wilson Smith, OBE, of Cumledge, Duns, Berwicks, and has:

1a *Peter John; *b* 28 Nov 1989

1a *Rachel Katharine Hope; *b* 25 Jan 1992

(1) *Sarah Margaret [Mrs Erik van Hove, Landsroemlaan 24, 1083 Brussels, Belgium]; *b* 22 Dec 1959; *m* 1982 *Erik van Hove and has:

1a *Hannah Jean; *b* 1987

2a *Rebecca Claire; *b* 1989

3a *Laura Iris; *b* 1991

WAKELEY

Arms: Argent, on a chevron sable between in chief two eagles displayed azure and in base a rod of Aesculapius proper three crescents of the field. **Crest:** A demi-horse argent supporting between the legs a rod of Aesculapius proper. **Motto:** *Nihil sine labore* ('Nothing comes without work'). **Creation:** Bt. UK) 1952.

SIR JOHN CECIL NICHOLSON WAKELEY, 2ND BT, of Liss, Co Southhampton [Sir John Wakeley Bt, Mickle Lodge, Mickle Trafford, Chester CH2 4EB]; *b* 27 Aug 1926; *s f* 1979; *educ* Canford and London U (MB, BS 1950); anatomy lecturer King's Coll London 1950–52, S/Ldr RAF 1953–54, Ch Inspr City London Special Constabulary 1955–61, Sr Registrar Surgery Roy Post Grad Hosp Hammersmith 1955, Urological Registrar then Sr Registrar King's Coll Hosp, Consultant Surgn W Cheshire Gp Hosps 1961–88, memb: cncl RCS 1971–83, Mersey RHA 1974–78, LRCP 1950, FRCS 1955 (MRCS 1950), FACS 1973, Liveryman Barbers' Co and Soc Apothecaries, Civilian Consultant Advsr Surgery RAF 1981–89, CStJ 1959; *m* 10 April 1954 *June, only dau of Donald Frank Leney, of Shottermill, Haslemere, Surrey, and has:

1 +NICHOLAS JEREMY; *b* 17 Oct 1957; *m* 1991 *Sarah Ann, dau of Air V-Marshal Brian Lewis Robinson, of Cheldon Ho, Cheldon, Devon, and has:

(1) +Joshua Jeremy; *b* 27 Sept 1993

(2) +Samuel Nicholas; *b* 24 Feb 1998

(1) *Joanna Constance; *b* 23 Sept 1995

2 +Charles John [Charles Wakeley Esq, Old Bittern Barn, West Harptree, Somerset BS40 6HQ]; *b* 3 May 1959; BSc 1980, MB, BS 1983, FRCS 1987, FRCSEd 1987, FRCR 1991; *m* 1984 *Rachel Morag Louise, yr dau of George Penrose, of Ormsby Lodge, N Ormsby, Lincs, and has:

(1) +Rupert William; *b* 1990

(2) +Arthur Charles; *b* 1993

1 *Amanda Jane[Mrs Neil Gillon, 13 Queen's Gate Mews, London SW7 5QS]; *b* 15 Sept 1962; fashion designer; *m* 1st 1985 (*divorce* 1987) Alan Louis Bresler, er s of Judge Max Bresler, of Memphis, Tenn.; *m* 2nd *Neil David Gillon, s of Norman Keith Gillon, of Perth, W Australia

Lineage: THOMAS WAKELEY, of Rainham, Kent; *b* 1798; *m* Mary Butcher (*b* 1803) and *d* 20 May 1849, leaving:

THOMAS STANLEY WAKELEY, of Rainham; *b* 1 Dec 1832; *m* 12 Dec 1855 Mary Anne Dodd (*d* 3 Jan 1900) and *d* 27 May 1899, leaving, with other issue:

PERCY WAKELEY, of W Dulwich; *b* 28 May 1880; *m* 3 April 1890 Mary Sophia Pembrey (*d* 22 Feb 1940) and *d* 13 Nov 1954, leaving an est s:

Sir Cecil Pembrey Grey Wakeley, 1st Bt (UK), so *cr* 30 June 1952, KBE (1946), CB (1941), of Liss, Hants; *b* 5 May 1892; *educ* Dulwich and King's Coll London; FRCS 1921, DSc London 1932, FRS Edinburgh, FRSA, FACS 1937, FRASC 1937, LRCP 1915, Surgn-Lt RN WW I, T/Surgn R-Adml RN WW II, KStJ, Cdr US Legn Merit 1950, Order Nile 2nd Cl 1951, Order Southern Cross Brazil 1952, Pres RCS 1949–54, Consulting Surgn: King's Coll Hosp, Masonic Hosp and Belgrave Hosp for Children, also RN, Treasurer GMC, Master: Soc Apothecaries and Barbers' Co, chm: Cncl Imp Cancer Research Fund, Medical Sickness Soc, v-pres Br Empire Cancer Campaign, Hunterian Prof, Erasmus Wilson Lecturer and Arnott Demonstrator RCS, Hon LLD: Glasgow 1952 and Leeds 1954, Hon DSc Delhi 1955; *m* 21 July 1925 Elizabeth Muriel, MRCS, LRCP, CStJ (*d* 1985), dau of James Nicholson-Smith, of Blackheath, and *d* 5 June 1979, leaving:

1 Sir JOHN CECIL NICHOLSON WAKELEY, **2nd and present Bt**

2 +Richard Michael [Richard Wakeley Esq, 1 Wordsworth Mansions, Queen's Club Gdns, London W14]; *b* 31 Jan 1933; *educ* Winchester and London U (MB, BS 1957)

3 +William Jeremy [William Wakeley Esq, Popes Hall, Hartlip, nr Sittingbourne, Kent]; *b* 23 Nov 1935; *educ* Radley; late JP Kent; *m* 4 April 1959 *Veronica Mary Dunning, 3rd dau of John Dunning Aysh, of Hardham Priory, Hardham, W Sussex, and has:

  (1) +James Richard William; *b* 25 Nov 1963; *m* 19– *Gaynor Rowena, dau of David Morgan, of The Hollow, Caister Lane,Tealby, Lincs, and has:

    1a *Alice Angharad; *b* 1991

    2a *Imogen Cross; *b* 1993

  (2) +Adam John Paul [Adam Wakeley Esq, Moor St Ho, Seymour Rd, Rainham, Kent ME8 8PY]; *b* 23 May 1965; *m* 1991 *Melanie Henrietta, dau of Michael David Brash Dingley, of Foxcote Hill, Ilmington, Warwicks, and has:

    1a *Lily Evelyn; *b* 1993

  (1) *Miranda Elizabeth; *b* 9 May 1967; *m* 1992 *John Edgar Segar, s of Martin Segar, of Stanhill, Godalming, Surrey

WAKEMAN

TOUT SANS FAILLIR ET SANS LUCRE

Arms: Paly wavy of six vert and argent, a saltire engrailed ermine.
  Crest: Between two palm branches proper a lion's head erased argent, vomiting flames, gorged with a collar engrailed and cotised vert and charged with three ermine spots or. **Mottoes:** 1 *Nec temere, nec timide* ('Neither rashly nor timidly'), 2 *Tout sans faillir et sans lucre* ('All without failing and without greed').
    Creation: Bt. (UK) 20 Feb 1828.

SIR EDWARD OFFLEY BERTRAM WAKEMAN, 6TH BT, of Perdiswell Hall, Worcs [Sir Edward Wakeman Bt, c/o Peverey House, Bomere Heath, Salop SY4 3AT]; *b* 31 July 1934; *s* half-brother 1991

Lineage: THOMAS WAKEMAN, of Worcester; *m* Mary, dau of Henry Parry, and had a 2nd s:

Sir Henry Wakeman, 1st Bt (UK), so *cr* 20 Feb 1828, of Perdiswell, Worcs; *b* 27 Feb 1753; HEICS; *m* 1st 25 Aug 1787 (*divorce* 18 Dec 1795) Theodosia, dau of John Freeman, of Gaines, Herefs, and had:

  1 Anne; *m* 1st Thomas Snepp; *m* 2nd 22 May 1835 George Jones, MD

Sir Henry *m* 2nd 29 June 1797 Sarah (*d* 15 Feb 1843), dau and heiress of Richard Ward Offley, of Hinton, and Rorrington, Salop, and by her had:

  1 OFFLEY PENBURY (Sir), **2nd Bt**

2 Edward Ward (Rev), of Coton Hall, Bridgnorth, Salop; *b* 13 May 1801; *educ* Wadham Coll Oxford (MA); Perpetual Curate Claines, Worcs; *m* 28 April 1935 Louisa (*d* 12 March 1881), dau of Allan Thompson, of Lansdown, and *d* 8 Sept 1855, leaving:

  (1) Offley Francis Drake; *b* 27 April 1836; *d* unm 20 July 1865

  (2) Henry Allan WAKEMAN later WAKEMAN-NEWPORT (1862 under terms of will of his cousin Thomas Henry Newport, of Hanley Court, Worcs, and Thorneloe House, Worcester), of Sandbourne, Bewdley, Worcs, JP (Salop, Staffs and Worcs); *b* 11 Nov 1841; Ld Manor of Hanley William, High Sheriff Worcs 1895; *m* 1887 Louise (*d* 8 July 1930), dau and heiress of W Essington-Essington, of Ribbesford House, Bewdley, and *dsp* 8 April 1923

  (3) Edward Maltby, of Coton Hall, JP (Salop); *b* 19 Nov 1846; *educ* Ch Ch Oxford (MA); Maj then Hon Lt-Col 3rd Bn KSLI; CA Salop; *m* 16 June 1874 Edith Mary (*d* 26 Jan 1914), dau of Phillips Buchanan, of Hales Hall, Staffs, and *d* 18 March 1926, having had:

    1a Edward Offley; *b* 1886; *d* 1887

    1a Gladys Louisa; *m* 9 Jan 1906 Capt Hugh Davenport COLVILLE later WAKEMAN-COLVILLE (added 1927), RN (*d* 19 July 1962), 2nd s of Hugh Ker Colville, of Ballaport, Salop, and *d* 15 Jan 1959, leaving issue

  (1) Mary Louisa; *b* 1838; *m* 12 Aug 1869 Col Henry Steuart Tomson, s of Rev M Tomson, of Alderminster, Warwicks, and *d* 6 May 1900, leaving issue

2 Emily Offley; *m* 1 May 1832 Capt William Lucius Cary, 96th Regt (*d* 10 March 1869), and *d* 20 Dec 1879, having had issue

Sir HENRY *d* 23 April 1831; his er s,

Sir Offley Penbury Wakeman, 2nd Bt; *b* 17 May 1799; *m* 19 Dec 1848 Mary (*d* 3 Oct 1852), only dau of Thomas Adlington, of Bradenham, Norfolk, and had:

  1 OFFLEY (Sir), **3rd Bt**

  2 Henry Offley; *b* 25 Sept 1852; MA Oxon, Fell All Souls; barrister; *m* 16 Aug 1898 Violet Mary (*d* 24 July 1942), dau of Francis John Johnston, of Dunsdale, Westerham, Kent, and *d* 27 April 1899, leaving:

    (1) Mary Catherine; *b* posthumously 14 Oct 1899; *m* 9 Oct 1918 Cdr Mark Peregrine Charles Kerr, RN, and had issue (*see* LOTHIAN, M)

Sir OFFLEY *d* 21 Sept 1858; his er s,

Sir Offley Wakeman, 3rd Bt, JP, DL; *b* 15 Nov 1850; *educ* Ch Ch Oxford (MA); barrister; Salop: CA, High Sheriff 1887, Chm QS 1889–1914; *m* 1st 29 Jan 1885 Catherine Mary (*d* 27 Dec 1925), dau of Sir Charles Henry Rouse-Boughton, 11th Bt, of Lawford Hall (*see* 1963 edn), and had:

  1 OFFLEY (Sir), **4th Bt**

  2 Edward Offley Rouse; *b* 15 Jan 1889; *educ* St John's Coll Oxford (BA); Lt Gren Gds (SR) WW I 1915; *ka* 16 May 1915

Sir Offley *m* 2nd 30 Jan 1929 Ruth Margaret (*d* 28 July 1930), dau of Ralph Dalyell, CB, of Tickneven, Co Kildare, and widow of Capt Gerard Lysley Derriman, Gren Gds, and *d* 9 Feb 1929

His er son,

Sir Offley Wakeman, 4th Bt, CBE (1957), JP (1927), DL (1941); *b* 19 Oct 1887; *educ* Eton and Ch Ch Oxford (BA 1908, MA 1913); Capt Gren Gds WW I (wounded), ADC to Govr NSW 1914 and Viceroy India 1918–19; Salop: CA, V-Lt 1950, High Sheriff 1934, V-Chm CC 1921, Chm 1943–63, Chm Fin Ctee 1940–45, Chm Educn Ctee 1938–40 and 1945–67; memb Church Assembly Hereford Diocese, Chm Govrs Shrewsbury Sch, Priv Sec to Sec for Mines; *m* 1st 25 Nov 1920 Winifred Anne (*d* 19 March 1924), 2nd dau of Col Charles Robert Prideaux-Brune, of Prideaux Place, Cornwall, and had:

  1 **Sir (Offley) David Wakeman, 5th Bt**; *b* 6 March 1922; *educ* Canford; *m* 16 Nov 1946 *Pamela Rose Arabella [Lady Wakeman, Peverey House, Bomere Heath, Salop SY4 3AT], only dau of Lt-Col Cecil Hunter Little, DSO, MBE, Somerset LI, of The Old Post House, How Caple, Herefs, and *dsp* Feb 1991

Sir Offley *m* 2nd 4 Sept 1929 Josceline Etheldreda (*d* 28 Jan 1996), est dau of Maj-Gen Bertram Revely Mitford, CB, CMG, DSO (*see* REDESDALE B), and widow of Cdr Walter Leeke, RN (*see* MANNERS, B), and *d* 17 Sept 1975, leaving by her:

  2 Sir EDWARD OFFLEY BERTRAM WAKEMAN, **6th and present Bt**

WALDEGRAVE

Arms: Per pale argent and gules. **Crest:** Out of a ducal coronet or a plume of five ostrich feathers, the first two argent, the third per pale argent and gules, the last two gules. **Supporters:** Two talbots sable, eared or, each gorged with a mural crown argent. **Motto:** *Passes avant* ('Press forward'). **Creations:** Bt. (E) 1 Aug 1643, B. (E) 20 Jan 1685/6, E. and V. (GB) 13 Sept 1729.

THE 13TH EARL WALDEGRAVE, Co Northampton, **Viscount Chewton**, **Baron Waldegrave of Chewton**, Co Somerset, and a **Baronet** (Sir James ('Jamie') Sherbrooke Waldegrave, Bt) [The Rt Hon The Earl Waldegrave, Chewton House, Chewton Mendip, Bath BA3 4LQ]; *b* 18 Dec 1940; *s f* 1995; *educ* Eton and Trin Coll Cambridge (Pres U Boat Club); runs cheese-making business; *m* 1986 (*divorce* June 1996) Mary Alison Anthea, former jnlst *Evening Standard* and philosophy lecturer, dau of Sir Robert Furness, KBE, of Little Shelford, Cambs, and has:

1 +EDWARD ROBERT, *Viscount Chewton*; *b* 10 Oct 1986

2 +Robert Arthur Riversdale; *b* 1989

Lineage: Sir RICHARD WAL(DE)GRAVE, of Smallbridge, Suffolk; MP Suffolk Feb 1375/6, 1377, 1378, 1381, 1382, 1383, 1386, 1388 and Jan 1389/90, Speaker H of C 1381; *m* Joan, dau and heiress of — Silvester, of Bures, Suffolk, and *d* 2 May 1402, leaving:

Sir RICHARD WAL(DE)GRAVE; heir to his mother, feudal Ld Bures and Silvesters; served Hundred Years War: appointed 1402 with 4th Lord (Baron) Clinton (*qv*), 5th(?) Lord (Baron) Fauconberge (*see* YARBOROUGH, E) and Sir John Howard (*see* NORFOLK, D) to keep the seas, landing 10,000 men in Brittany, captured Conquet and the Isle of Rhé; *m* Jane, dau and of Sir Thomas Montechensy (probably cognate with Munchensy), of Edwardstone, Suffolk, and *d* 1436, leaving:

Sir WILLIAM WAL(DE)GRAVE; *d* 1461, leaving:

Sir THOMAS WAL(DE)GRAVE; ktd for valour at Battle of Towton (major Yorkist victory) 20 March 1461 during Wars of the Roses; *m* Elizabeth, est dau and coheir of Sir John Fray, Ld Ch Baron Exchequer, and *d* 1500, having had, with an est s (William), a yst s (Richard) and three daus:

EDWARD WALDEGRAVE; settled at Bor(e)ley, Essex; *m* Elizabeth, dau and coheir of John Cheyney, of Devon, and *d* 1514, leaving an only s:

JOHN WALDEGRAVE; *m* Lora, dau of John Rochester and sis of Sir Robert Rochester (*b* 1494?; a leading advsr and Comptroller Household to QUEEN MARY, also Chllr Duchy Lancaster; *d* 1557), and *d* 6 Oct 1543, leaving a 2nd s:

Sir EDWARD, PC (1553); *b c* 1516/7; granted manor and rectory of West Haddon, Northants, 1547/8, memb PRINCESS (later QUEEN) MARY's household and imprisoned 1551–52 first in the Fleet then Tower London, together with his unc Sir Robert Rochester and Sir Francis Englefield, for refusing to carry out the Privy Cncl's ban on her having mass said in her house of Copt Hall, Epping, Essex; Master Gt Wardrobe on MARY's accession, granted manors of Navestock, Essex, and Chewton, Somerset; MP Wilts 1553, Somerset 1554, Essex Jan 1557/8, ktd Oct 1553, Jt Receiver-Gen Duchy Cornwall Nov 1553, granted manor of Hever Cobham, Kent, 1557, Lt Waltham/Epping Forest 1557, *s* his unc Sir Robert Rochester as Chllr Duchy Lancaster 28 Nov 1557, but after MARY's death was dismissed his posts and committed to the Tower for allowing mass to be celebrated in his house; *m* Frances (*d* 1599), dau of Sir Edward Nevill(e) (*see* ABERGAVENNY, M), and *d* 1 Sept 1561, having had, with a yr s (Nicholas, ancestor of the WALDEGRAVEs of Borley) and three daus (Mary, *m* 1st Baron Petre (*qv*); Magdalene, *m* Sir John Southcote, of Witham, Essex; Catherine, *m* Thomas Gawen, of Wilts):

CHARLES WALDEGRAVE, of Staininghall, Norfolk, and Chewton, Somerset; *m* Jeronyma, dau of Sir Henry Jerningham, PC, of Cossey Hall, V-Chllr and Master Horse *temp* MARY, and *d* 25 Jan 1580(?), leaving an only s:

Sir Edward Waldegrave, 1st Bt (E), so *cr* 1 Aug 1643 (the *cr* was declared invalid by Parl and only became effective after the Restoration), of Hever Castle, Kent; *b c* 1568; MP(?) Sudbury 1584/5, ktd 1607; though over 70 when the Civil War broke out, cmded a regt of royalist horse, chiefly in Cornwall, being present at the impounding in that county 1644 of the army of the 3rd Earl of Essex (of the 1572 *cr*; *see* HEREFORD, V), also with his regt keeping the pass at Saltash, on which

occasion, being charged by the Parliamentarian cavalry in an attempt to break through, he thrice rallied his men, and although twice unhorsed, eventually succeeded in taking 40 prisoners; by his fervent royalism in the Civil War he lost £50,000 (*c* £3,700,000 in late-1990s terms) in fines and sequestrations together with two sons; *m c* 19 July 1598 Eleanor (*d* 12 Dec 1604), dau of Sir Thomas Lovell and sis and heiress of Sir Francis Lovell, of Harling, Norfolk, and *d* after 1647, leaving an est s:

Sir Henry Waldegrave, 2nd Bt; *b* 1598; *m* 1st Anne, dau of Edward Paston, of Appleton, and had 11 children; *m* 2nd Catherine (*d* by 1695), dau of Richard Bacon, and *d* 10 Oct 1658, having had 12 further children; his est s:

Sir Charles Waldegrave, 3rd Bt; *m* Eleanor, dau of Sir Francis Englefield, 2nd Bt, of Englefield, Berks (*cr* 1612; extinct 1822), and *d* after 26 May 1684, leaving an est s:

Sir Henry Waldegrave, 4th Bt, and **1st Baron Waldegrave of Chewton**, Co Somerset (E), so *cr* 20 Jan 1685/6 as a consequence of his marriage with a royal bastard; *b* 1661; Comptroller JAMES II's Household 9 Feb 1686/7–Dec 1688 in England and thereafter till 1689/90 at the Jacobite court in exile at St Germain, France; Ld Lt Somerset July 1687–Nov 1688, Envoy Extrdy France Nov 1688; *m* 29 Nov 1683 Henrietta FitzJames (*b c* 1667; *m* 2nd by 26 March 1695 3rd Viscount of Galmoye (*see* MOUNTGARRET, V) and *d* 3 April 1730), illegitimate dau of JAMES II by Arabella Churchill, sis of 1st Duke of Marlborough (*qv*), and *d* St Germain 14/24 Jan 1689/90, leaving, with a yr s (Henry, *b* 15 Feb 1688, *bur* 4 March 1726/7) and a dau (Arabella, *b* 10 May 1687, nun, *d* 30 April 1740):

Sir James Waldegrave, 5th Bt, and **1st Earl Waldegrave**, so *cr* 13 Sept 1729, as also VISCOUNT CHEWTON, Co Somerset (both GB), KG (20 Feb 1737/8), PC (12 Feb 1734/5); *b* 1684; built Navestock Hall, Chipping Ongar, *c* 1720; brought up RC but conformed to C of E following death of his w (an RC), thus able to take his seat in Ho Lds 12 Feb 1721/2; Ld Bedchamber (Whig) 1723 and 1730–41, Amb: Paris 1725 and 1730–40, Vienna 1728–30; V-Adml Essex 1735; *m c* 20 May 1714 Mary (*d* in childbirth 22 Jan 1718/19), 2nd dau of Sir John Webb, 3rd Bt, of Hatherop, Glos, and *d* 11 April 1741, having had:

1 JAMES WALDEGRAVE, **2nd Earl Waldegrave**, KG (1757), PC (1752); *b* 4 March 1714/15; *educ* Eton; Ld Bedchamber 1743–52, Govr to PRINCE OF WALES (later GEORGE III) and PRINCE EDWARD (later DUKE OF YORK) 1752–56, Ld Warden Stannaries 1751–62,Teller Exchequer 1757–63, 1st Ld Treasury 8–12 June 1757 (thus becoming, if one accepts the fact that in the time available he could at least allocate posts, if not govern, the briefest-serving PM in history); author: *Historical Memoirs* 1754–58; FRS 1749, LLD Cambridge 1749; *m* 15 May 1759, as her 1st husb, Maria (said by one contemporary source to have been the handsomest woman in England), 2nd illegitimate dau of Hon Sir Edward Walpole, KB (*see* WALPOLE, B), by Dorothy/Maria Clement(s), used-clothes-seller, and *d* 13 April 1763, leaving:

  (1) Elizabeth Laura; *b* 25 March 1760; *m* 5 May 1782 her cousin **4th Earl Waldegrave** (*see* below) and *d* 29 Jan 1816

  (2) Charlotte Maria; *b* 11 Oct 1761; *m* 16 Nov 1784 4th Duke of Grafton (*qv*) and *d* 1 Feb 1808, leaving issue

  (3) Anna Horatia; *m* 2 April 1786 Lord Hugh Seymour and *d* 12 June 1801, leaving issue (*see* HERTFORD, M)

2 John; *b* and *d* 17 Jan 1715/6

3 JOHN, **3rd Earl**

1 Henrietta; *b* 2 Jan 1716/7; *m* 1st 7 July 1734 Lord Edward Herbert (*see* POWIS, E) and had issue; *m* 2nd 1738/9 John Beard, a prominent singer at Covent Gdn, and *d* 31 May 1753

The 2nd EARL 's yr bro,

JOHN WALDEGRAVE, **3rd Earl Waldegrave**; *b* 28 April 1718; Ensign 1st Regt Foot Gds 1735, Lt and Capt Jan 1738/9, Capt and Lt-Col 3rd Regt Foot Gds 1743 (saw action at Fontenoy (French victory in War of Austrian Succession) 1745, where wounded), 2nd Maj 1748, 1st Maj 1749 Col: 9th Regt Foot 1750–55, 8th Dragoons 1755–58, 5th Dragoon Gds 1758–59, Maj-Gen 1757, saw action at Battles of Minden (Anglo-Hanoverian victory over French in Seven Years War) 1759 and Warburg (Allied victory over French) 1760, Lt-Gen 1759, Gen 1772, Col 2nd Dragoon Gds 1759–73 and Coldstream Gds 1773–84; MP (Whig) Orford 1747–54 and Newcastle-under-Lyme 1754–63, Govr Plymouth 1760, Groom Bedchamber to GEORGE III 1760–63, Master Horse to QUEEN CHARLOTTE 1770–84, Ld Lt Essex 1781–84; *m* 7 May 1751 Lady Elizabeth Leveson-Gower (*d* 28 April 1784), 5th dau of 1st Earl Gower (*see* SUTHERLAND, D), and *d* 22 Oct 1784, having had, with another dau:

1 GEORGE, **4th Earl**

2 WILLIAM WALDEGRAVE, 1st BARON RADSTOCK OF CASTLETOWN, in Queen's Co (I), so *cr* 20 Dec 1800, GCB (1815); *b* 9 July 1753; *educ* Eton; joined RN 1766, Capt 1776, Col RM April–June 1794, R-Adml July 1794, V-Adml 1795 (3rd ic Battle of Cape St Vincent (British victory over Spain) 1797, hence offered btcy but declined it on the grounds that as s of an earl he was already of higher station), Adml the Blue 1802, the White 1805 and the Red 1810, Govr Newfoundland; *m* 28 Dec 1785 Cornelia (Woman Bedchamber to QUEEN CHARLOTTE 1799–1816; *d* 10 Nov 1839), 2nd dau of David Van Lennep, Ch Dutch factory Smyrna, Greece, and *d* 20 Aug 1825, leaving:

  (1) GRANVILLE GEORGE WALDEGRAVE, 2nd BARON RADSTOCK OF CASTLETOWN, CB (1815); *b* 24 Sept 1786; joined RN 1798, Capt 1807, R-Adml 1841, V-Adml: the White 1853, the Red 1855, Naval ADC to WILLIAM IV and HM QUEEN VICTORIA 1831–41; *m* 7 Aug 1823 Esther Caroline (*b* 23 May 1800; *d* 16 March 1874), yst dau of James Puget, of Totteridge, Herts, a Dir Bank England, and *d* 11 May 1857, leaving:

    1a GRANVILLE AUGUSTUS WILLIAM WALDEGRAVE, 3rd BARON RADSTOCK OF CASTLETOWN; *b* 10 April 1833; *educ* Harrow and Balliol Coll Oxford (BA 1854, MA 1857); raised and cmded as Lt-Col W Middx Rifles 1860–66, memb 1st Cncl Nat Rifle Assoc, lay evangelist (briefly one of Plymouth Brethren) and fndr Victoria Homes for Working Men in Whitechapel and Victoria Hostel for Women in S London; *m* 16 July 1858 Susan Charlotte (*b* 14 Sept 1833; *d* 8 Dec 1892), yst dau of John Hales Calcraft (*see* MANCHESTER, D), and *d* 8 Dec 1913, leaving:

    1b GRANVILLE GEORGE WALDEGRAVE, 4th BARON RADSTOCK OF CASTLETOWN, CBE (1918); *b* 1 Sept 1859; *educ* Repton and Trin Coll

Cambridge (BA 1884); Pres Br Sailors' Soc, Egypt Rep Nat Cncl YMCA 1915–21; *d* unm 2 April 1937

2b MONTAGU WALDEGRAVE, 5th and last BARON RADSTOCK OF CASTLETOWN; *b* 15 July 1867; *educ* Monkton Combe and Trin Coll Cambridge (BA 1889); *m* 15 July 1898 Constance Marian (*d* 5 Nov 1936), est dau of James Campbell John Brodie, of Lethen, Nairn, and *dspms* 17 Sept 1953, when the Barony expired, having had:

1c John Montagu Granville, DSC; *b* 29 Aug 1905; Cdr RN WW II 1939–44; *m* 29 June 1940 Lady Hersey Margaret Boyle (*m* 2nd 24 July 1947 John Goring (*see* GORING, Bt) and *d* 1993), 2nd dau of 8th Earl of Glasgow (*qv*), and was *ka* in HMS *Penelope* 18 Feb 1944, leaving:

   1d *Horatia Marion [Mrs Oliver Diggle, Waterfall House, Swanton Morley, Norfolk NR20 4QD]; *b* 1 Aug 1941; *m* 5 Dec 1970 *Oliver John Diggle, s of Lt-Col I W Diggle, of Orchard Grange, Old Warden, Beds, and has:

     1e *John Wyndham Hugh [John Diggle Esq, Waterfall House, Worthing Rd, Swanton Morley, Norfolk NR20 4QD]; *b* 1974; *educ* Eton

     1e *Rowena Mary; *b* 1972

     2e *Emma Georgiana; *b* 1977

   2d *Griselda Hyacinthe; *b* 6 June 1943; *m* 15 July 1967 *Charles David Stephen Drace-Francis, CMG, yr s of Alan David Francis, CBE, MVO, of Chelsea, and has:

     1e *James; *b* 14 Oct 1969

     2e *Alexander John; *b* 5 Feb 1971

     1e *Teresa; *b* 1979

1c Rachel Elizabeth; *b* 12 May 1899; *d* 6 Jan 1900

2c Esther Constance; *b* 11 Nov 1900; *m* 28 June 1938 Adolph Charles Kunz, Austrian Dip Serv, s of Adolph Kunz, of Vienna, and *dsp* 17 April 1957

3c *Elizabeth Alexandra Sophia [Baroness Fritz von Bültzingslöwen, Planken, Principality of Liechtenstein]; *b* 22 Sept 1902; *m* 15 Jan 1940 Baron Fritz von Bültzingslöwen, Maj 7th Cuirassiers (*d* 30 Nov 1943), s of Wulff von Bültzingslöwen, and has:

   1d *Friedrich Johannes Helmart; *b* 16 March 1941; *m* 1966 *Ursula von Willert and has issue

3b John; *b* 30 Dec 1868; LLB Cantab; barrister; *d* serving with Imp Yeo Boer War 4 April 1901

1b Katherine; *d* 4 Dec 1874

2b Edith Caroline; *b* 30 Dec 1868; *m* 10 April 1889 Alister Gilian Fraser, of Leigh, Surrey and London SE19, 2nd s of Arthur Fraser, and *d* 15 Nov 1925

3b Mabel; *d* 12 Dec 1929

4b Constance; *d* unm 19 June 1945

5b Mary; *m* 25 April 1896 Edwyn Robert Bevan, OBE, yst s of Robert Cooper Lee Bevan, JP, of Trent Park, Middx, and *d* 17 Nov 1935, leaving issue

1a Elizabeth Cornelia; *d* unm 16 April 1903

2a Caroline Esther; *m* 15 June 1852 Sir Thomas William Brograve Proctor-Beauchamp, 4th Bt (*qv*), and *d* 3 July 1898, leaving issue

(2) William, CB; *b* 7 June 1796; Capt RN; *m* 25 Sept 1820 Amelia (*d* 1846), dau of Humphrey Allport, and *d* 18 Dec 1838

(1) Emily Susanna Laura; *m* 25 Aug 1815 Nicholas Westby, of Thornhill, Co Dublin, and *d* 12 April 1870

(2) Isabella Elizabeth; *d* 21 Oct 1866

(3) Harriet Anne Frances; *d* unm 26 July 1880

(4) Caroline; *m* 16 Dec 1830 Ven Carew St John-Mildmay and *d* 7 Jan 1878, leaving issue (*see* ST JOHN-MILDMAY, Bt)

1 Elizabeth; *b* 26 May 1758; Ldy Bedchamber to QUEEN CHARLOTTE 1793–1809; *m* 18 April 1791, as his 2nd w, 5th Earl of Cardigan (*see* AILESBURY, M) and *dsp* 23 June 1823

The 3rd EARL's est s,

GEORGE WALDEGRAVE, **4th Earl Waldegrave**, PC (1782); *b* 23 Nov 1751; *educ* Eton; Ensign 3rd Regt Foot Gds 1768, Lt and Capt 1773, served American War Independence 1776–77, Lt-Col Coldstream Gds 1778, cmded 87th Foot 1779–83, MP (Pittite near-Tory) Newcastle-under-Lyme 1778–80, ADC to GEORGE III and Col 1782, V-Chamberlain Household 1782–4, Master Horse to QUEEN CHARLOTTE 1784–89, Col: 63rd Foot 1788–89, 14th Foot Aug-Oct 1789; *m* 5 May 1782 his cousin Lady Elizabeth Laura Waldegrave (*see* above) and *d* 22 Oct 1789, leaving:

1 GEORGE WALDEGRAVE, **5th Earl Waldegrave**; *b* 13 July 1784; *educ* Eton; drowned while bathing in the Thames nr Eton 29 June 1794

2 JOHN JAMES WALDEGRAVE, **6th Earl Waldegrave**; *b* 31 July 1785; *educ* Eton; Ensign 3rd Foot Gds 1802, Lt 39th Foot March 1804 and 7th Hus April 1804 (Capt 1805), Maj 72 Foot 1808 and 15th Hus 1809, served Peninsular War and Flanders, Lt-Col cmdg 54th Foot 1812–19 including Waterloo campaign; Ld Bedchamber (Tory) 1830–31; *m* 30 Oct 1815 Anne (*b* 1790; *m* 2nd 2 Feb 1839 Dr Algernon Hicks, of Henrietta St, London W, and *d* 22 Aug 1852), dau of John William King, of Hastings, and *d* 31 July 1835, having had, with a dau (*d* unm) and several children born before their marriage:

(1) GEORGE EDWARD WALDEGRAVE, **7th Earl Waldegrave**; *b* 8 Feb 1816; *educ* Ch Ch Oxford; served six-month prison sentence *c* 1840–41 for assault; *m* 28 Sept 1840, as her 2nd husb, his dead er (but illegitimate) bro's widow Frances Elizabeth Anne (*b* 4 Jan 1821; *m* 1st 25 May 1839 John James Waldegrave (*d* April 1840), s of **6th Earl Waldegrave** and Anne King before their marriage; lived with her 2nd husb in the Queen's Bench Prison during his sentence; *m* 3rd 30 Sept 1847 George Granville Harcourt, of Nuneham Courtenay (*see* VERNON, B), as whose w she became a (arguably the) leading Whig hostess, a feat she brought off also as a leading Lib hostess when *m* to her 4th husb; she also restored and reopened Strawberry Hill, the celebrated Gothick mansion at Twickenham which Horace Walpole had left her 2nd husb but which had become derelict; *m* 4th 20 Jan 1863 1st and last Baron Carlingford, KP, and *dsp* 5 July 1879), dau of John Braham, a famous tenor in his day (he was the original Max in Weber's *Der Freischütz*); *dsp* 28 Sept 1846

---

(1) Annette Laura Maria; *m* 27 Feb 1841 Lt-Gen Archibald Money, CB (*d* 1856), of Crown Point, Norfolk, and *d* 28 Feb 1856

(2) Horatia Elizabeth; *m* 1st 17 May 1847 Capt John Joseph Webbe Weston (*d* 24 Sept 1849); *m* 2nd 28 Nov 1854 John Wardlaw, of 44 Prince's Gdns, London, s of Lt-Gen and Hon Mrs Wardlaw, and *d* 24 June 1884 aged 60

3 Edward William; *b* 29 Aug 1787; Lt 7th Dragoons, served Peninsular War; missing presumed drowned off Falmouth 22 Jan 1809

4 WILLIAM, **8th Earl**

1 Maria Wilhelmina; *m* 26 Jan 1804 Nathaniel Micklethwait, of Taverham, Norfolk, and *d* 20 Feb 1805

The 7th EARL's unc,

WILLIAM WALDEGRAVE, **8th Earl Waldegrave**, CB (1840); *b* 27 Oct 1788; *educ* Eton; RN 1801–46: Midshipman 1802, Lt 1806, Cdr 1809, Capt HMS *Macedonian* 1811–12, HMS *Seringapatam* 1829–32, HMS *Revenge* 1839–42, ret as R-Adml 9 Nov 1842, V-Adml 1858, MP (Whig) Bedford 1815–18; *m* 1st 10 Aug 1812 Elizabeth (*b* 20 Dec 1791; *d* 1 March 1843), est dau of Samuel Whitbread (*see* GREY, E), and had issue; *m* 2nd 8 Dec 1846 Sarah (*dsp* 18 April 1873), dau of Rev William Whitear, Preb Chichester, and widow of Edward/William Milward, of Hastings, and *d* 24 Oct 1859, having had by his 1st w, with three other daus (*d* unm):

1 William Frederick, *Viscount Chewton*; *b* 29 June 1816; *educ* Cheam Sch and Trin Coll Cambridge 1835–37; RN: Midshipman aboard f's ship HMS *Seringapatam* 1829–31, emigrated to Canada to farm, served Militia in putting down French-Canadian insurgents 1837, Lt Huntingdon Frontier Cav, Ensign Roy Canadians 1841, Lt 3rd Foot 1843 and 53rd Foot 1845, fought Battle of Sobraon (Sikh War) 1846, Capt 6th Foot 1847, Lt and Capt Scots Fus Gds 1848, Crimean War 1854; *m* 2 July 1850 Frances, VA 4th Class (1892) (Woman Bedchamber to HM QUEEN VICTORIA 1855; *d* 11 April 1902), only dau of Capt John Bastard, RN, of Sharpham, Devon, and *dvp* 8 Oct 1854 of wounds recd Battle of the Alma 20 Sept preceding, having had, with a dau (*d* an infant):

   (1) WILLIAM FREDERICK WALDEGRAVE, **9th Earl Waldegrave**, VD, PC (1897), JP (Westminster and Middx), DL; *b* 2 March 1851; *educ* Eton and Trin Coll Cambridge (BA 1873, MA 1877); Maj 9th Vol Bn KRRC, ret as Lt-Col, Hon Col Somerset Vol Regt, Ld in Waiting (C) 1886–92 and 1895–96, C Ch Whip Ho Lds 1896–1911, Capt Yeomen Gd 1896–1905, CA Somerset, Lunacy Commr 1899; *m* 5 Aug 1874 Lady Mary Dorothea Palmer, DBE (1918) (*d* 8 Nov 1933), 2nd dau of 1st Earl of Selborne (*qv*), and *d* 12 Aug 1930, leaving:

     1a WILLIAM EDWARD SEYMOUR WALDEGRAVE, **10th Earl Waldegrave**; *b* 2 Oct 1882; *d* unm 30 Jan 1933

     1a Mary Wilfreda; *m* 15 May 1900 Rev Richard Aubrey Chichester Bevan (*d* 7 Jan 1925), Chaplain Br Legation The Hague, yst s of Richard Lee Bevan, JP, of Brixworth Hall, Northants, and *d* 25 Dec 1947, leaving issue

     2a (Laura) Margaret; *m* 1st 19 July 1899 Alfred Millington Knowles (*ka* 9 Aug 1900 Boer War), only surv s of Robert Millington Knowles, JP, DL, of Colston Bassett Hall, Notts; *m* 2nd 7 June 1904 Reginald Nicholson and *d* 8 Nov 1959, leaving issue (*see* NICHOLSON OF WINTERBOURNE, B)

   (2) HENRY NOEL, **11th Earl**

2 Samuel (Rt Rev); *b* 13 Sept 1817; *educ* Cheam Sch and Balliol Coll Oxford (BA 1839, Fell All Souls 1839, MA 1842, DD 1860); Deacon 1842, Curate St Ebbe's Oxford, Rector Barford St Martin Wilts 1844, Canon Sarum 1857, Bp Carlisle 1860, fndr Carlisle Diocesan Church Extension Soc 1862; *m* 23 Jan 1845 Jane Anne (*d* 6 June 1877), dau of Francis Pym (*see* PYM, B), and *d* 1 Oct 1869, leaving:

   (1) Samuel Edmund (Rev); *b* 21 May 1856; BA Cantab; Rector Oborne Dorset; *m* 14 Jan 1886 Alice, MBE (*d* 12 April 1941), dau of Charles D Millett, of Marazion, Cornwall, and *d* 6 Jan 1907, leaving:

     1a Samuel Charles (Rev), MC; *b* 14 May 1887; *educ* Repton and Emmanuel Coll Cambridge (BA 1910, MA 1914); Hon CF, Lt 6th Bn King's Liverpool Regt, T/CF 1914–18, Munitions Area Chaplain to Bp Coventry 1918–19, Vicar Fillongley, Coventry, 1919–23, Chaplain 7th Roy Warwicks Regt (TA) 1922, Warden Birmingham City Union of Boys' and Girls' Clubs 1924–26, Priest-in-Charge Out Districts Matabeland and Curate St John Bulawayo 1926–30, Missions to Seamen Chaplain Port London 1930–33, Curate Holy Trinity Wimbledon 1933–36 and Holy Trinity Winchester 1936, France with Church Army Mobile Canteens 1940, Assist Chaplain to Mersey Missions to Seamen 1941–44, Area Organiser Northern Counties King George's Fund for Sailors 1944–49; *m* 1st 10 Jan 1918 Muriel Vesteinn (*d* 7 June 1943), only dau of Rev Canon Edmund McClure; *m* 2nd 7 April 1945 Katharine Joyce Maddison, 2nd dau of Rev George Clement Maddison Hall, and *dsp* 7 Jan 1965

     2a George Turner (Rev), MBE (1934), *b* 18 March 1889; *educ* Repton and Emmanuel Coll Cambridge (BA 1911, MA 1916); Vicar Sholing Hants 1935–59, Hon Chaplain RN WW I and Officiating Minister RN WW II, Hon Canon Winchester 1952; *d* unm 15 Jan 1966

     3a Frederick Arthur; *b* 2 April 1892; Coastal Def WW I; *d* unm 9 June 1960

     4a Edmund John; *b* 10 May 1899; 2nd Lt RFA WW I; *ka* 10 Aug 1918

   (1) Elizabeth Janet; *b* 8 Nov 1858; *m* 23 Feb 1886 Rev Reginald Fawkes (*d* 28 Jan 1939), Rector Poole, Dorset, and *d* 14 June 1890, leaving issue

3 George WALDEGRAVE later WALDEGRAVE-LESLIE, JP, DL (Fife and Kinross); *b* 30 Sept 1825; barrister, MP Hastings 1864–68, FRS, LLD; *m* 22 Jan 1861 Henrietta, Countess of Rothes in her own right (*see* ROTHES, E) and *d* 8 July 1904

1 Laura Waldegrave; *m* 2 Feb 1848 1st Earl of Selborne (*qv*) and *d* 10 April 1885, leaving issue

2 Maria Waldegrave; *m* 2 Oct 1844 Rev William Brodie (*see* BRODIE, Bt) and *d* 31 Jan 1911, leaving issue

The 10th EARL's unc,

Rev HENRY NOEL WALDEGRAVE, **11th Earl Waldegrave**; *b* posthumously 14 Oct 1854; *educ* Eton and Trin Coll Cambridge (Pres Union, BA 1878, MA 1881); Rector Stoke d'Abernon, Surrey, 1890–98, Marston Bigot, Somerset, 1905–12 and Orchardleigh-with-Lullington, Somerset; *m* 27 Oct 1892 Anne Katherine (*d* 21 March 1962 aged 94), dau of Rev William Pollexfen Bastard, of

Buckland Court, Ashburton, Devon, and Kitley, Devon, and *d* 30 Dec 1936, leaving:

1 GEOFFREY NOEL, **12th Earl**

1 Dorothy Caroline Frances, JP (Surrey 1942–52); *b* 1 March 1894; *m* 26 June 1915 Capt Thomas Granville Randolph, MC, RE (*d* 14 July 1961), s of Granville Walter Randolph, and *d* 25 Feb 1973, leaving issue

2 Irene Grace; *b* 14 June 1895; *d* unm 18 July 1972

3 Elizabeth Katharine; *b* 7 May 1897; *m* 16 March 1918 her bro-in-law Rev George Algernon Randolph (*d* 11 Aug 1977), s of Granville Walter Randolph, and *d* 19–, leaving issue

4 (Gabrielle) Sophia Annette; *b* 7 June 1908; *m* 20 Dec 1935 Maj John Stephen Schilizzi, RASC (*d* 1985), only s of Stephen Schilizzi, of Loddington Hall, Kettering, Northants, and *d* 8 Jan 1998, leaving:

  (1) *Stephen Noel John [Stephen Schilizzi Esq, Chacombe House, Chacombe, Oxon OX17 2JL]; *b* 1937; *educ* Eton; *m* 1959 *Diana, only dau of Eustace Allfrey, of Chacombe Priory

  (1) *Gabrielle Anne Mary [Mrs Gordon Hedley, Turweston Glebe, Brackley, Northants]; *b* 1936; *m* 1957 *Capt Gordon Shafto Hedley, late 17th/21st Lancers, and has:

    1a *Nicholas Edward John; *b* 1962

    1a *Caroline Mary; *b* 1957; *m* 1984 *George Adam Traill

    2a *Anne Penelope; *b* 1959; *m* 1983 *Timothy Christopher Thompson-Royds and has issue (*see* THOMPSON, Bt, of Park Gate)

    3a *Helena Margaret; *b* 1939

The 11th EARL's only s,

GEOFFREY NOEL WALDEGRAVE, **12th Earl Waldegrave**, KG (1971), GCVO (1976), TD (1946), JP (1936), DL (Somerset 1951); *b* 21 Nov 1905; *educ* Winchester and Trin Coll Cambridge (BA 1928); Maj RA (TA) WW II, Offr US Legn Merit 1945; Somerset: CC 1937–58, CA 1949–58, V-Lt 1955–60, Chm Ag Exec Cncl 1948–51, Jt Parly Sec MAFF 1958–62, Chm Forestry Commn 1963–65, MAFF Liaison Offr Somerset, Wilts and Glos 1952–57; Ld Warden Stannaries 1965–76; memb: Prince's Cncl Duchy Cornwall 1951–58 and 1965–76, Bristol U Ct, Cncl Roy Bath and W Southern Counties Soc, Ch Sec Gen Advsy Cncl 1963–66; dir: Lloyds Bank 1964–76 (chm Bristol Regnl Bd 1966–76), Bristol Waterworks Co; chm: English Farms Ltd, Advsy Ctee on Meat Research 1969–73; Pres Somerset Tst Nature Conservation 1964–80; Govr: Nat Fruit and Cider Inst, Wells Cathedral Sch; Tstee Partis Coll Bath 1935–88; Hon LLD Bristol 1976; *m* 22 Oct 1930 Mary Hermione (*d* Nov 1995), est dau of Lt-Col Arthur Morton Grenfell (*see* GRENFELL, B), and *d* 1995, leaving:

1 JAMES SHERBROOKE WALDEGRAVE, **13th and present Earl Waldegrave**

2 +William Arthur, PC (1990), JP (1975) [Rt Hon William Waldegrave PC JP, 66 Palace Gdns Terr, London W8 4RR]; *b* 25 Aug 1946; *educ* Eton, Corpus Christi Coll Oxford (Pres Union 1968, BA, Fell All Souls 1971–86) and Harvard; CPRS, Cabinet Office 1971–73, Political Staff 10 Downing St 1973–74, Hd Leader Oppn's Office 1974–75, with GEC 1975–81, MP (C) Bristol W 1979–97, Parly U-Sec: DES 1981–83 and DOE 1983–85, Min State DOE: Environment and Countryside 1985–87, Planning 1986–88, Housing 1987–88, Min State FCO 1988–90, Sec State Health 1990–92, Chllr Duchy Lancaster 1992–94, Sec State AFF 1994–95, Ch Sec Treasury 1995–97; memb IBA Advsy Cncl 1980–81, dir Bristol and West Bldg Soc 1997– and corporate fin div Dresdner Kleinwort Benson 1998–; author: *The Binding of Leviathan* (1977); *m* 25 July 1977 *(Linda Margaret) Caroline, yr dau of Maj Richard Burrows, of Tunbridge Wells, Kent, and has:

  (1) +James Victor; *b* 1984

  (1) *Katharine (Katie) Mary; *b* 15 Sept 1980

  (2) *Elisabeth Laura; *b* 27 Oct 1983

  (3) *Harriet Horatia; *b* 1988

1 *Sarah Caroline, JP (Somerset 1974), DL (Somerset 1998) [The Lady Sarah Wright JP DL, Honibere Farmhouse, Burton, Stogursey, Somerset TA5 1PZ]; *b* 23 Oct 1931; *m* 19 Feb 1955 *Ernest George Wright, GM, CPM, est s of Thomas Bennet Wright, of Jesmond, Northumberland, and has:

  (1) *Thomas Geoffrey; *b* 15 Jan 1956; *educ* Wells Cathedral Sch and Durham U; served RGJ; *m* 1986 *Sophia Louise, yst dau of J F P Tate, of Boscombe, Wilts, and has:

    1a *Matthew Adam Christopher; *b* Nov 1988

    1a *Katherine Elizabeth; *b* April 1992

  (2) *David James; *b* 22 July 1957; *educ* Wells Cathedral Sch and Durham U

2 *Jane Mary [The Lady Jane Howard, 17 Durand Gdns, London SW9 0PS]; *b* 25 Jan; *m* 1st 20 Feb 1954 (*divorce* 1977) 4th Baron Strathcona and Mount Royal (*qv*) and has issue; *m* 2nd 22 Sept 1977 (*divorce* 1979, resumed 1st husb's name) Duncan McIntosh, OBE, AFC, s of Duncan McIntosh, of Edinburgh

3 *Elisabeth Jeronima [The Rt Hon The Lady Forteviot, Aberdalgie House, by Perth]; *b* 4 April 1936; *m* 17 Oct 1963 *4th Baron Forteviot (*qv*) and has issue

4 *Anne Hermione [The Lady Anne Boles, Rydon House, Talaton, Devon EX5 2RP]; *b* 24 Dec 1937; *m* 20 Feb 1971 *Sir John (Jack) Dennis Boles, MBE, only s of Cdr Geoffrey Boles, OBE, RN

5 *Susan Katharine, DCVO (1984, CVO 1971) [The Lady Susan Hussey DCVO, Flat 15, 47 Courtfield Rd, London SW7]; *b* 1 May 1939; Woman Bedchamber to HM THE QUEEN Nov 1960–; *m* 25 April 1959 *Baron Hussey of North Bradley (LP, *qv*) and has:

  (1) *James Arthur; *b* 15 Aug 1961 (HM THE QUEEN stood sponsor); *educ* Harrow; Page of Honour to HM THE QUEEN 1975–77; *m* 1st 1988 (*divorce* 1993) Jacqueline, dau of Dr (George) Hugh Barrington Baker; *m* 2nd 1993 *Emma, dau of John Shelley, of Wimbledon, and by her has:

    1a *Arthur; *b* 19–

    1a *Rose Rachel; *b* 29 Aug 1994

  (1) *Katharine Elizabeth; *b* 1 Feb 1964; *m* 1989 *Sir Francis George Windham Brooke, 4th Bt, of Summerton (*qv*), and has issue

WALEY-COHEN

Arms: Quarterly, 1st and 4th, arg. on a chevron gu. cotised az. between in chief two roses gu. barbed and seeded ppr. and in base a buck's head couped also ppr., three annulets or (for COHEN); 2nd and 3rd, arg. a chevron az. cotised sa. between in chief two eagles displayed sa. and in base on a mount vert a hind trippant ppr. **Crests:** 1 A buck's head couped arg. attired or, holding in the mouth a rose slipped gu., the neck encircled by a wreath of oak ppr. between four barrulets gu. (for COHEN), 2 Out of a bush of fern a hind's head ppr., in the mouth a rose arg., stalked and leaved also ppr. **Motto:** All for the best. **Creation:** Bt. (UK) 11 Dec 1961.

SIR STEPHEN HARRY WALEY-COHEN, 2ND BT, of Honeymead, Co Somerset [Sir Stephen Waley-Cohen Bt, 1 Wallingford Ave, London W10 6QA]; *b* 22 June 1946; *s f* 1991; *educ* Eton and Magdalene Coll Cambridge (BA 1968, MA); fin jnlst *Daily Mail* 1968–73, ed *Money Mail Handbook* 1973 and 1974, dir Euromoney Publications Ltd 1969–77, publisher Euromoney 1977–83, ch exec Maybox Gp plc 1984–89, md Victoria Palace Theatre 1989–; dir: St Martin's Theatre Ltd, Soc London Theatres, Exeter Preferred Capital Investment Tst, Portsmouth and Sunderland Newspapers Ltd 1994–; chm: Policy Portfolio plc, Willis Faber and Dumas (Agencies) Ltd, JCA Charitable Fndn, Portsmouth and Sunderland Newspapers and UK Exec Ctee Br American Project for Successor Generation 1986–92, Govr Wellesley Ho Sch 1974–97, Tstee Theatres Tst 1998–; *m* 1st 10 April 1972 (*divorce* 1986) Pamela Elizabeth, yr dau of J E Doniger, of Bracken Ho, Tabley Mews, Knutsford, Cheshire, and has:

1 +LIONEL ROBERT; *b* 7 Aug 1974; *educ* Eton and Bath U

2 +Jack David; *b* 1979; *educ* Eton

1 *Harriet Ann; *b* 20 June 1976; *educ* Wycombe Abbey, St Paul's Girls' Sch and UCL

Sir STEPHEN *m* 2nd 1986 *Josephine Burnett, yr dau of Duncan M Spencer, of Bedford, NY, and by her has:

2 *Tamsin Alice; *b* 1986; *educ* St Paul's Girls' Sch

3 *Freya Charlotte; *b* 1989

Lineage: BENJAMIN COHEN, living *c* 1660; had:

1 Ezechiel (Esegiel), of Amersfoort, Netherlands; *m* Marritje (Meerle) (*d* 1746), dau of Abraham Levi Victoria (Italiaander), and *d* by 1746, leaving, with several other sons and daus:

  (1) Jonas; *b* 1698; *m* 1st Sara, dau of Benjamin Italiaander; *m* 2nd Esther, dau of Simon Butenheim, and *d* 1780, leaving, with other issue:

    1a Caotje (Chailes); *m* 1743 Joseph Meyer Goldsmit and had issue

    2a Rebecca; *b* 1738; *m* 1763 George (Gershom) Goldsmit and *d* 1808, leaving issue. He *d* 1812

2 Isaac; had:

  (1) Selig; had:

    1a Barnet (Bernard), of Amsterdam and Amersfoort; *b c* 1710; had:

      1b Solomon; *d* by 1808, leaving five daus

      2b LEVI BARENT

      3b Hyman Cohen Wessels; had:

        1c Solomon Hyman Cohen Wessels; *m* 1797 Fanny, dau of Levi Barent Cohen (*see* below), and had issue

The 2nd s,

LEVI BARENT COHEN, of 11 Angel Court, Throgmorton Street, EC, and Richmond, Surrey; *b* 1747; Presiding Warden Gt Synagogue 1794; naturalised Br subject Nov 1800; *m* 1st Fanny, dau of Joseph Diamantschleifer, of Amsterdam, and had:

1 JOSEPH

2 Solomon; *b* 1776; *m* 1802 Hannah (*d* 1871), dau of Moses Samuel, and *d* 1864, leaving:

  (1) Barent; *b* 1806; *d* 1808

  (2) Abraham; *b* 1808; *d* unm 1879

  (3) Levi (Lewis Barent); *b* 1812; *d* 1826

(4) Joshua; *b* and *d* 1818

(1) Jeannette; *b* 1803; *m* 18 April 1825, as his 1st w, Sir David Solomons, 1st Bt, MP, Ld Mayor London 1855–56 (*see* 1925 edn GOLDSMID-STERN-SALOMONS, Bt), and *dsp* March 1867. He *d* 18 July 1873

(2) Harriet; *b* 1804; *m* 1836 John Wagg and *d* 1879, leaving issue. He *d* 1878

(3) Emily; *b* 1809; *m* 1835 Solomon Isaac Joseph, of New York, and *d* 1841, leaving issue. He *d* 1866

(4) Hannah; *b* 1816; *m* 1845 Benjamin Moses Merton and *d* 1898, leaving issue. He *d* 1881

1 Fanny; *m* 1797 Solomon Hyman Cohen Wessels (*see* above) and had issue

LEVI COHEN *m* 2nd Lydia (*d* 1818), dau of Joseph Diamantschleifer, and *d* between 14 April 1807 and 20 June 1808, having by her had:

3 Barent; *b* 1780; *d* unm 1807

4 Benjamin; *b* 1789; *m* 3 March 1819 Justina (*d* 1873), dau of Joseph Elias Montefiore, and *d* 1867, leaving:

(1) Lionel Benjamin; *b* 1826; *m* 1st 17 Jan 1849 Henrietta Rachel (*d* 27 April 1859), dau of Joseph Salomons (*see* 1925 edn GOLDSMID-STERN-SALOMONS, Bt); *m* 2nd 1860 Bertha (*d* 1917), dau of Philip J Salomons, and *d* 1890, having by his 1st w had:

1a Florence Justina; *b* 1857; *m* 1st 1876 Abraham de Mattos Mocatta (*d* 1891); *m* 2nd 1892 Sir David Brynmor Jones, PC, KC, MP, est s of Rev Thomas Jones, of Swansea, and *dsp* 1 Aug 1920. He *d* 6 Aug 1921

(2) Nathaniel; *b* 1827; *m* 1860 Rebecca (*d* 1890), dau of Philip Lucas, and *d* 1911, having had:

1a Philip Arthur; *b* 1866; *d* unm 1937

1a Justina Rachel; *b* 1864; *m* 1888, as his 1st w, John Felix Waley and *d* 1889

2a Ethel; *b* and *d* 1869

3a Marguerite Abigail; *b* 1871; *m* 30 July 1890 Sir Benjamin Arthur Cohen, KC, and had issue (*see below*)

4a Elsie Juliana; *b* 1872; *d* 1875

(3) Arthur, PC (1905), KC; *b* 18 Nov 1830; *educ* UCL and Magdalene Coll (Hon Fell) Cambridge (MA, Pres Union 1852); HMG's Counsel Alabama and Venezuela Arbitrations, Standing Counsel Cambridge U 1879, MP Southwark 1880–87, Counsel to Sec State India 1893, memb Roy Commns on Unseaworthy Ships and TUs, Chm Roy Commn on Shipping Rings, memb Br Acad, memb of Senate London U, Judge Cinque Ports to 1914; *m* 1860 Emmeline (*d* 1888), dau of Henry Nicholls, and *d* 3 Nov 1914, leaving:

1a Benjamin Arthur (Sir), KC (1914); *b* 24 Dec 1862; barrister Inner Temple 1887, Bencher 1923, ktd 1929; *m* 30 July 1890 Marguerite Abigail, dau of Nathaniel Cohen (*see below*), and *d* 22 Dec 1942, leaving:

1b Charles Benjamin; *b* 1894; *m* Winifred Dorothy, dau of W Ernest Lord, and *d* 9 Feb 1954, leaving:

1c *John; *b* 1924

1c *Anne

2b Nathaniel Arthur Jim, JP; Judge

3b Arthur Neville; *b* 1898; *m* 31 May 1927 Judith Alexandra Grace, dau of Capt Sandford William Luard, and had two sons

1b Margery Emmeline; *m* 1926 Charles Clifton Roberts and had issue. He *d* 1935

2a William Herbert; *b* 1866; *d* unm 1914

3a Harry Montefiore; *b* 1877; *m* 1912 Elsa, dau of Moritz Levisseur, of Bloemfontein, and *d* 1946, leaving:

1b *John Arthur Levisseur; *b* 1915

1b *Josephine Lucy Brunette; *m* 1937 Malcolm Baird

1a Lucy; *b* 1861; *d* unm 1951

2a Margaret; *b* 1864; *m* 21 Oct 1895 Sir Theodore Morison, KCSI, KCIE, CBE, s of James Cotter Morison, of Hampstead, and *d* 10 Sept 1931, leaving issue. He *d* 14 Feb 1936

3a Mary Freda; *b* 26 Dec 1871; *m* 28 July 1914, as his 2nd w, Sir Thomas Colyer Colyer-Fergusson, 3rd Bt (*qv*), and *d* 11 Nov 1964

4a Katherine; *b* 2 Sept 1875; *m* 3 Nov 1897 Col Jacob Waley Cohen, CMG, CBE, DSO, TD (*see below*), and *d* 26 May 1924, leaving issue

5a Winifred Emmeline; *b* 1881; *m* 24 July 1905 Col Bernard Arnold Barrington Butler, CMG, DSO (*d* of wounds recd in action 23 Oct 1918), 6th s of Spencer Percival Butler, and *d* 10 July 1965, leaving issue

(1) Lucy; *b* 1820; *d* 1838

(2) Justina Rachel; *b* 1822; *m* 1843 Sampson Lucas Behrens and *d* 1854, leaving issue. He *d* 1876

(3) Hannah; *b* 1823; *m* 1841 Ippolito Leonino and *d* 1891, leaving issue. He *d* 1877

5 Isaac; *b* 1791; *m* 1st 1818 Rebecca (*d* 1819), dau of Dr Joseph Hart Myers; *m* 2nd 1827 Sarah (*d* 1879), dau of Phineas Samuel, and *d* 1846, having by her had:

(1) John; *b* 1828; *d* 1836

(1) Juliana; *b* 1831; *m* 26 June 1850 Mayer Amschel Rothschild and had a dau (*see* ROTHSCHILD, B)

(2) Anna Louisa; *b* 1835; *d* unm 1902

(3) Lucy; *b* 1839; *d* unm 1906

6 Hyman; *b* and *d* 1793

2 Esther; *b* 1782; *m* 1803 Samuel Moses Samuel, bro of Baron de Samuel, and *d* 1859, leaving issue. He *d*

3 Hannah; *b* 1783; *m* 22 Oct 1806 Nathaniel Mayer Rothschild and *d* 1850, leaving issue (*see* ROTHSCHILD, B)

4 Judith; *b* 1784; *m* 10 June 1812 Sir Moses Montefiore, 1st and last Bt (*d* 28 July 1885), and *dsp* 24 Sept 1862

5 Jessie; *b* 1795; *m* 1816 Meyer Davidson and *d* 1869, leaving issue. He *d* 1846

6 Adeline; *b* 1799; *m* 1817 John Helbert and *d* 1877, leaving issue. He *d* 1861

The est son,

JOSEPH COHEN, of London; *b* 1774; *m* 1 May 1796 Marianne (*d* 1840), dau of Elias Joachim, and *d* 24 July 1838, leaving, with an est s (Barent, *b* 1798, *d* an

infant) and two yst sons (Francis (Sheina), *b* 1801, *m* 1820 Louis Lucas (*d* 1851), s of Sampson Lucas, of Jamaica, and *d* 1868, leaving issue; Anna (Gererdel), *b* 1802, *d* unm 1891) a 2nd s:

LOUIS COHEN, of 84 Gloucester Pl, London; *b* Sept 1799; *m* 28 April 1824 Rebecca Floretta (*d* 2 Jan 1859), dau of Assur Keyser, and *d* 15 March 1882, having had:

1 Albert Assur; *b* and *d* 1825

2 Henry Louis; *b* 1827; *m* 1861 Ellen (*d* 1924), dau of Hananel de Castro, and *dsp* 1893

3 George Louis; *b* and *d* 1829

4 Lionel Louis; *b* 1832; MP N Paddington 1885–87, a manager Stock Exchange; *m* 1856 Esther (*d* 1894), dau of Jacob Henry Moses, and *d* 1887, leaving:

(1) Edward Joseph

(2) Leonard Lionel (Sir), KCVO (1930); *b* 17 April 1858; *educ* privately and King's Coll Sch London; ptnr Louis Cohen and Sons, foreign bankers and of Stock Exchange till its dissolution 1901, memb Ctee Stock Exchange 1896–1904, dir Bengal and NW Rlwy and Rohilkund and Kumaon Rlwy, memb Jewish Bd Guardians 1888 (Pres 1900–1920), Jt Hon Sec King Edward's Hosp Fund for London; *m* 1885 Eliza Henrietta (*d* 1935), dau of Sigismund Schloss, of Bowdon, Cheshire, and *d* 10 April 1938, leaving:

1a LIONEL LEONARD (Sir), BARON COHEN (LP), of Walmer, Co Kent (UK), so *cr* 12 Nov 1951, PC (1946), KC (1929); *b* 1 March 1888; *educ* Eton (Fell 1950–63) and New Coll Oxford (BA 1909, MA 1913, Hon Fell); 13th Princess Louise's Kensington Regt 1913–23, barrister Inner Temple 1913, Bencher Lincoln's Inn 1934 (Treas 1954), High Court Judge (Chancery) 1943, ktd 1943, Ld Justice Appeal 1946, Ld of Appeal in Ordinary 1951–60, Staff Min Ec Warfare WW II 1939–43, Chm Company Law Amendment Ctee 1943–45, Roy Commn on Awards to Inventors 1946–73, presided Comet Enquiry 1954, Assoc KStJ, Hon Fell UCL, Hon LLD London, Chm Coll Ctee UCL 1953–63, Capt Roy and Ancient Golf Club St Andrews 1960–61; *m* 9 April 1918 Adelaide (*d* 29 Dec 1961), dau of Sir Isidore Spielmann, CMG, by Emily, dau of Sir Joseph Sebag-Montefiore, and *d* 1973, leaving:

1b *Leonard Harold Lionel, OBE (1995) [The Hon Leonard Cohen OBE, Dovecote House, Swallowfield Pk, nr Reading, Berks RG7 1TG]; *b* 1 Jan 1922; *educ* Eton and New Coll Oxford (BA 1945, MA 1946); Capt Rifle Bde WW II 1941–45 (wounded Middle East 1943), barrister Lincoln's Inn 1948, dir Hill Samuel & Co Ltd 1961–76, Master Skinners' Co 1971–72, High Sheriff Berks 1987–88; *m* 14 July 1949 *Eleanor Lucy, dau of Philip Quixano Henriques, and has:

1c *Jonathan Lionel; QC (1997); *b* 8 May 1951; *educ* Eton; *m* 1983 *Bryony Frances Carfrae, and has issue

2c *Andrew Philip Lionel; *b* 28 May 1957

1c *Catherine Gillian; *b* 28 April 1953

2b Hugh Lionel; *b* 14 Jan 1925; *educ* Eton and New Coll Oxford; RNVR 1943–46; *m* 7 Oct 1953 *Jane [The Hon Mrs Hugh Cohen, Overbrook House, Devil's Highway, Crowthorne, Berks RG45 6BJ], yr dau of Rt Hon Lord Justice Sir Seymour Edward Karminski, and *d* 1992, leaving:

1c *James Seymour Lionel; *b* 19 Jan 1958; *m* *Sarah Frampton and has issue

2c *Charles Benjamin Lionel; *b* 13 April 1959; *m* 17 May 1990 *Sarah van Laun and has issue

3c *William Arthur Lionel; *b* 15 April 1961; *m* 10 May 1996 *Louise Wheatley and has issue

1b Elizabeth Adelaide; *b* 31 Dec 1919; *m* 1st 20 June 1940 Brig-Gen Eric Pearce-Serocold, CMG (*ka* N Africa Dec 1942); *m* 2nd 20 March 1946 *Maj Hon Peter Montefiore Samuel, MC, TD, 2nd s of 2nd Viscount Bearsted (*qv*), and *d* 14 July 1983, leaving issue

1a Irene Catherine; *b* 1891; ARRC; *m* 11 Dec 1919 Col Thomas Henry Sebag-Montefiore, DSO, MC, 4th s of Arthur Sebag-Montefiore, and *d* 3 Dec 1933, leaving issue. He *d* 11 June 1954

(3) Frank Lionel; *b* 1865; *m* 1896 Bertha (*d* 1930), dau of Simon Waley Waley, and *d* 29 June 1955, leaving:

1a Harold Lionel; *b* 1901

2a Richard Henry Lionel; *b* 1907; *m* *M Deas and *d* 1998, leaving:

1b *James; *b* 1942

1a Constance Esther; *b* 1898; *d* unm 9 March 1969

2a Beatrice Hendelah; *b* 1899; *m* 1922 Albert Isaac Polack, housemaster Clifton 1923–49, and had issue

3a *Mary; *b* 1911; *m* D W Lucas, Fell King's Coll Cambridge, and has issue

(4) Walter Samuel; *b* 1870; *m* 1903 Lucy Margaret (*d* 1942), dau of Henry Cobb, and *d* 29 Aug 1960, having had:

1a Oliver Henry Lionel; *b* 1904; *d* 15 March 1966

2a Andrew Benjamin (Sir), KCMG (1952), KCVO (1954), OBE; *b* 7 Oct 1909; *educ* Malvern and Trin Coll Cambridge; Assist U-Sec Colonial Office 1947–51, Govr and C-in-C Uganda 1952–57, Perm UK Rep UN Tsteeship Cncl 1957–61, Dir-Gen Dept Tech Co-opn 1961–64, Perm Sec Min Overseas Devpt 1964–68; Hon LLD Belfast 1960, KStJ; *m* 24 April 1949 *Helen Phoebe, JP (Co of London 1962), CStJ (*m* 3rd 29 May 1969 Michael Hope), formerly w of Prof Robert Donington and dau of G G Stevenson, and *d* 17 June 1968, leaving:

1b *Richard Hugh Rodel; *b* 15 Sept 1950

3a John Walter; *b* 1909; *d* 1910

1a Ruth Louisa; *b* 10 Nov 1906; Pncpl Newnham Coll Cambridge 1954

2a Esther Elizabeth; *b* and *d* 1912

3a *Catherine Floretta, JP; *b* 5 March 1915; *m* 5 April 1938 Arthur James Hunt, 2nd Master Rugby, s of Dr S Hunt, of Spondon, Derbys, and has:

1b *James Andrew; *b* 26 March 1942

1b *Margaret Ruth; *b* 10 July 1943

2b *Jennifer Mary; *b* 15 Sept 1946

3b *Susan Elizabeth; *b* 22 Feb 1949

(5) Harold Albert; *b* 1871; *d* unm 1894

(1) Floretta Marianna; *b* 1861; *m* 1880 Henry Edward Beddington and had, with other issue, a dau (*see below*). He *d* 1926

5 Alfred Louis; *b* 1836; *m* 1869 Louise Marie Sophie (*d* 1902), dau of Joseph Javal, of Paris, and *d* 1903, having had:

(1) Henry Alfred; *b* 1870; *d unm* 1895

(2) George Alfred; *b* 1884; *m* 1905 Gertrude Hannah, dau of Grenville Myer, and *d* 1942, leaving:

1a *Gladys; *m* Robert Hunter Codrington and has issue

2a *Lucy; *m* 1939 Leonard Solomon Falk and has issue

3a *Elizabeth Marjorie; *m* 1930 Ellis James Castello, MC, and has issue

(1) Margaret Louise; *b* and *d* 1871

(2) Susan Louise (Lily); *b* 1873; *m* 1895 Maj Harry Barned Lewis-Barned and had:

(3) Caroline; *b* 1875; *m* 1897 James Henry Solomon and had issue

6 Joseph Louis; *b* and *d* 1839

7 Samuel Louis; *b* 1840; *d* 1841

8 David Louis; *b* 1842; *d* 1843

9 Sir BENJAMIN LOUIS COHEN, 1st Bt (UK), so *cr* 19 Dec 1905, of Highfield, Shoreham, Kent, JP London and Kent; *b* 18 Nov 1844; memb LCC 1888–1901, MP E Islington 1892–1906, Pres London Orphan Asylum, Govr St Bart's, Bridewell and Bethlem Hosps, Lt City London; *m* 27 April 1870 Louisa Emily (*d* 20 Nov 1931), dau of Benjamin Moses Merton, and *d* 8 Nov 1909, leaving:

(1) Sir HERBERT BENJAMIN COHEN, 2nd and last Bt, OBE (1919), TD; *b* 26 April 1874; *educ* Clifton and King's Coll Cambridge (BA 1895, MA 1899); barrister Inner Temple 1898, Maj 4th Bn Roy W Kent Regt, Assist Embkn SO 1916–19 and Embkn SO 1919, Govr St Bart's Hosp, Master Salters' Co 1936–37; *m* 26 March 1907 Hannah Mildred (Nina) (*d* 27 March 1963), 2nd dau of Henry Behrens, of Gloucester Sq, W, and *d* 23 April 1968, when the btcy expired, having had:

1a Nigel Benjamin; *b* 18 Jan 1908; *educ* King's Coll Cambridge (BA); *dvp unm* 18 Sept 1931

2a Stephen Behrens; *b* 27 Feb 1911; *educ* King's Coll Cambridge (MA); barrister Inner Temple 1934, Capt Upper Sind Force (IA) WW II; *das unm* India 10 Feb 1943

(2) Arthur Merton, TD; *b* 16 June 1876; *educ* Harrow and King's Coll Cambridge (BA 1898, MA 1905); Maj 4th Bn Roy W Kent Regt; *d unm* 3 Feb 1966

(3) Ernest Merton; *b* 26 July 1877; *educ* Trin Coll Cambridge (MA); *d unm* 23 April 1955

(1) Hannah Floretta, OBE (1920); *d unm* 21 Nov 1946

10 Isaac; *b* 1844; *d* 1860

11 NATHANIEL LOUIS

12 Edward Louis; *b* and *d* 1848

1 Louisa; *b* and *d* 1826

2 Adelaide; *b* 1830; *m* June 1851 Sir Joseph Sebag-Montefiore, of E Cliff Lodge, Ramsgate, and *d* Feb 1895, having had issue. He *d* 18 Jan 1903

3 Julia; *b* 1834; *m* 1858 Henry Jessel and *d* 1905, leaving issue. He *d* 1870

4 Frances; *b* and *d* 1835

5 Henrietta; *b* 1838; *m* 1855 Assur Henry Moses and *d* 1876, leaving issue. He *d* 1918

6 Ellen; *b* 1843; *m* 5 March 1862 1st Baron Swaythling (*qv*) and *d* 15 March 1919, leaving issue

The 11th s,

NATHANIEL LOUIS COHEN, of Bayswater and Courtlands, E Grinstead, Sussex; *b* 26 May 1846; memb LCC for City London, ptnr Louis Cohen and Sons, bankers; philanthropist; *m* 3 June 1873 Julia Matilda (*d* 17 Dec 1917 aged 64), dau of Prof Jacob Waley, and *d* 14 Jan 1913, having had:

1 Jacob Waley, CMG (1919), CBE (1926), DSO (1916), TD; *b* 30 Oct 1874; *educ* Clifton and Merton Coll Oxford; Queen's Westminster Rifle Vols 1893, Boer War 1900, City London Imp Vols (CIV) as Signal Offr then Bde Signalling Offr 21st Inf Bde (despatches, medal and four clasps), WW I with Queen's Westminster Rifles and Army Signals (despatches, Croix de Guerre), WW II Army Welfare Offr Eastern Cmd 1940–45, Col Roy Corps Signals (TA); *m* 1st 3 Nov 1897 Katherine (*d* 26 May 1924), 4th dau of Rt Hon Arthur Cohen, KC (*see* above), and had:

(1) James Arthur Waley; *b* 11 Nov 1898; Liveryman Drapers' Co; *d unm* 12 Dec 1962

(2) Ian Nathaniel Waley; *b* 15 Aug, *d* 17 Aug 1900

(1) Emmeline Nora; *b* 25 Nov 1902

1 (cont.) Col Jacob Cohen *m* 2nd 18 June 1934 Evelyn Susanna (*d* 27 Feb 1976), widow of Cdr Noel Grabowsky-Atherstone, AFC, RN, and dau of Lt-Col H M A Hales, of Manchester, and *d* 12 July 1948

2 ROBERT WALEY (Sir)

3 Charles Waley, CMG (1919); *b* 26 Sept 1879; *educ* Clifton and Balliol Coll Oxford; barrister Inner Temple 1903, memb Colonial Office Ctee of Emigrants Information Bd 1904–10, Sec Select Ctee on Post Office Servants 1906–07 and 1912–13, Actg Judge High Court Karachi 1910–11, Lt-Col WW I 1915–21 (despatches, Legn Hon); *m* 28 Oct 1910 Ethel Alice (*d* 16 Aug 1956), dau of Hermann M Kisch, CSI, and *d* 16 Jan 1963

1 Henrietta; *b* 29 Dec 1875; *d unm* 7 Jan 1914

2 Margaret; *b* 21 June, *d* 28 June 1881

3 Dorothea Waley; *b* 17 Dec 1882; scientific writer; *m* 20 July 1910 Prof Charles Singer, DLitt, MD, Hon DSc, FRCP, FSA, son of Rev Simeon Singer, and *d* 24 June 1964. He *d* 10 June 1960

4 Matilda Waley; *b* 23 Sept 1885; *m* 11 March 1908 Frank George Joseph (*d* 6 Dec 1944), of Bayswater, and *d* 15 Jan 1945, leaving two sons and three daus

The 2nd s,

Sir ROBERT WALEY COHEN, KBE (1920), of Caen Wood Towers, Highgate, and Honeymead, Simonsbath, Somerset; *b* 8 Sept 1877; *educ* Clifton and Emmanuel Coll Cambridge (BA 1898); md Shell Tport and Trading, chm: Anglo-Egyptian Oilfields, Utd Br Oilfields of Trinidad; dir Baldwins Ltd, English and Scottish Investors; Petroleum Adviser War Office 1914–18, Order St Sava Yugoslavia; *m* 9 June 1904 Alice Violet (*d* 24 Jan 1935), dau of Henry Edward

Beddington, of Bayswater and Heathside, Newmarket, by Floretta Marianne, only dau of Lionel Louis Cohen, MP (*see* above), and *d* 27 Nov 1952, leaving:

1 BERNARD NATHANIEL (Sir), **1st Bt**

2 *Matthew Henry, TD; *b* 14 Aug 1916; *educ* Clifton; Shell Petroleum 1936–54, TA 1937, Liveryman Clothworkers' Co 1937 (Sr Warden 1973), BEF and BLA RA and RE WW II (wounded, despatches), memb Hornsey Borough Cncl 1953–62, Somerset: CC 1959, High Sheriff 1975, Kt Order Orange-Nassau Netherlands; *m* 1st 1 June 1943 (*divorce* 1950) Barbara Mabel, er dau of George H Wenham, of Plymouth; *m* 2nd 9 Oct 1950 *Gwynedd Mary, er dau of Henry Gwyn Davis-Scourfield, of the Mote, Pembroke, and has:

(1) *Helen Alice; *b* 22 Feb 1952

2 (cont.) Mr and Mrs Matthew Waley-Cohen also adopted 24 Oct 1955: *Geoffrey Michael; *b* 12 Dec 1954

1 *Henrietta Floretta; *b* 30 May 1914; *educ* Roedean and Newnham Coll Cambridge (MA); *m* 17 Sept 1937 Col Oliver Robert Marne Sebag-Montefiore, TD, 2nd s of Charles Edward Montefiore Sebag-Montefiore, OBE, of Kensington, and has:

(1) *Nathaniel Charles; *b* 14 Dec 1938; *educ* Wellington and King's Coll Cambridge (BA 1962, MA 1965); 2nd Lt RA 1957–59, Lt Essex Yeo RHA (TA) 1959–66, Liveryman Spectacle Makers' Co 1960, Fell Roy Anthropological Inst, export manager Alginate Industs; *m* 25 Oct 1965 *Annabel Victoria, only dau of Robert Alexander Bennet Gosling, of Mutton Hall, Wetherden, Suffolk, and has issue

(1) *Alice Floretta; *b* 1 Jan 1941; *m* 16 Oct 1961 *David Gestetner, er s of Sigmund Gestetner, of Mayfair, and has issue

(2) *Charlotte Hannah; *b* 1 Oct 1944; *educ* Cranborne Chase and Newnham Coll Cambridge (BA 1966); *m* 28 March 1968 *Christopher Kenneth Green, s of Frederic Ray Hilton Green, of Epsom, Surrey

Sir ROBERT COHEN's est s,

Sir BERNARD NATHANIEL WALEY COHEN later WALEY-COHEN (deed poll 1950), **1st Bt** (UK), so *cr* 11 Dec 1961; *b* 29 May 1914; *educ* HMS *Britannia* (RNC Dartmouth), Clifton (memb Cncl and Fin Ctee 1952) and Magdalene Coll Cambridge (BA 1941, MA 1950); Liveryman 1936 (Memb Court Assistants 1966, Master 1975) Clothworker's Co, Gunner HAC 1937–38, underwriting memb Lloyd's 1939, Pncpl Min Fuel and Power 1940–47, memb Coll Ctee and Finance Ctee UCL 1953 (Treas 1962), chm Simo Properties Ltd 1955, memb London Regnl Bd Lloyds Bank, dir: Burston & Texas Commerce Bank, Bray Gibb (Agencies) Ltd, Kleeman Industl Hldgs, Tudor Accessories; chm Devon and Somerset Staghounds 1953, ktd 1957, Pres: Bath and West and Southern Counties Soc 1962–63, Devon Cattle Breeders' Soc, Senate 1962 and Court 1966 London U, City London: Lt, Alderman, Sheriff 1955–56, Ld Mayor 1960–61, chm Public Works Loan Commrs, Hon LLD London 1961, Hon Fell UCL 1963, Hon Liveryman Farmers' Co 1961, Assoc KStJ 1961; *m* 21 Dec 1943 *Hon Joyce Constance Ina, JP Middx 1949–59 and Somerset 1959–86 [The Hon Lady Waley-Cohen, Honeymead, Simonsbath, Somerset TA24 7JX], only dau of 1st Baron Nathan (*qv*), and *d* 1991, leaving:

1 Sir STEPHEN HARRY WALEY-COHEN, **2nd and present Bt**

2 +Robert Bernard [Robert Waley-Cohen Esq, 18 Gilston Rd, London SW10 9SR]; *b* 10 Nov 1948; *educ* Eton; exec Christie's 1969–81, chm Alliance Medical Ltd, Steward Jockey Club 1983; *m* 9 Dec 1975 *Hon Felicity Ann, only surv dau of 3rd Viscount Bearsted (*qv*), and has:

(1) +Marcus Richard; *b* 25 May 1977; *educ* Eton and Edinburgh U

(2) +Sam Bernard; *b* 15 April 1982

(3) +Thomas Andrew; *b* 22 June 1984

(1) *Jessica Suzanna; *b* 30 Jan 1979

1 *Rosalind Alice [Mrs Philip Burdon, 140 Straven Rd, Christchurch, New Zealand]; *b* 19 Jan 1945; *educ* Cranborne Chase Sch; *m* 8 Dec 1966 *Philip Ralph Burdon, Min Trade and Industry NZ 1991–97, 2nd s of Cotsford Burdon, of S Canterbury, NZ, and has:

(1) *Miranda Ruth; *b* 21 Aug 1970

(2) *Rebecca Joyce; *b* 15 July 1972

(3) *Josephine Virginia; *b* 12 April 1975

2 *(Eleanor) Joanna; *b* 10 June 1947; *educ* Cranborne Chase and Girton Coll Cambridge (MA); Prof New York U 1997–; *m* 30 May 1977 *Keith Brad Gallant, of Branford, Conn., s of Edward Gallant, of Stoney Creek, Branford, and has:

(1) *Christopher (Kit) Edward Bernard; *b* 1988

(1) *Isobel Claire; *b* 1993

WALKER of Oakley House

READY AND FAITHFUL

Arms: Gules on a chevron between three cross-crosslets argent an anchor sable, on a chief of the second three stag's heads cabossed proper, a canton azure, thereon a representation of the diamond decoration appropriate to the rank of Pasha of the Ottoman Empire conferred on Sir Baldwin Wake Walker by the Sultan for his services in Syria. **Crest:** Out of a naval crown azure a stag's head proper, gorged with an eastern crown or. **Motto:** Ready and faithful. **Creation:** Bt. (UK) 19 July 1856.

SIR (BALDWIN) PATRICK WALKER, 4TH BT, of Oakley House, Co Suffolk [Sir Patrick Walker Bt, 5 Voortrekker Rd, Blanco 6531, S Africa]; *b* 10 Sept 1924; *s gf* 1928 and as hereditary Pasha Ottoman Empire; *educ* Gordonstoun; RN 1943–48, rejoined as Lt (Flying Duties) 1951, ret 1958; *m* 1st 4 Sept 1948 (*divorce* 1954) Joy Yvonne, yr dau of Sir Arrol Moir, 2nd Bt (*qv*); *m* 2nd 25 March 1954 (*divorce* 1961) Sandra, dau of Henry Stewart; *m* 3rd 1966 Rosemary Ann, dau of Henry Hollingdrake; *m* 4th 1980 *Vanessa Hilton and has by his 3rd w:

1 +CHRISTOPHER ROBERT BALDWIN; *b* 25 Oct 1969

1 *Amanda Jane; *b* 1967; *m* 1993 *Michael Grant Fenner-Solomon, and has:

  (1) *Alexandra Helen; *b* 28 Aug 1995
  (2) *Christine Jane; *b* 23 July 1997

Lineage: JOHN WALKER; had:

Rev DAVID WALKER; Vicar Deeping St James, Lincs; *m* Sarah Garfit and had:

JOHN WALKER, of Whitehaven; *m* Frances (*d* 1812), dau of Drury Wake, 17th Dragoons, 2nd s of Sir William Wake, 7th Bt (*qv*), and *d* 1822, leaving an only surv s:

Sir BALDWIN WALKER later WAKE-WALKER, **1st Bt** (UK), so *cr* 19 July 1856, KCB; *b* 6 Jan 1802; Comptroller RN 1847–60, cmded Cape of Good Hope Station 1860–64, Adml Turkish Serv, Pasha Ottoman Empire, Kt St Anne Russia, Chev Legn Hon, Kt Red Eagle Prussia, Greek Order Redeemer and Austrian Order Iron Crown; *m* 9 Sept 1834 Mary Catherine Sinclair (*d* 14 Nov 1899), only dau of Capt John Worth, RN, of Oakley, Suffolk, by Catherine Sinclair of Durran (*see* CAITHNESS, E), and *d* 1876, leaving:

  1 **Sir Baldwin Wake-Walker, 2nd Bt**, CMG, CVO; *b* 24 Sept 1846; V-Adml; *m* 31 Oct 1877 Fanny Augusta, JP (*d* 13 Aug 1951), est dau of Capt Cowper Coles, CB, RN, and *d* 28 June 1905, leaving:

    (1) Irene Catherine; *b* 1889; *m* 1st 3 June 1909 Capt Philip Francklin, MVO, RN (lost aboard HMS *Good Hope* in action off Chile 1 Nov 1914), yr s of John Leill Francklin, of Gonalston, Notts, and had issue; *m* 2nd 7 June 1917 Sir Osmond de Beauvoir Brock, GCB, KCMG, KCVO (*d* 14 Oct 1947), s of Capt Osmond de Beauvoir Brock, RN, and *d* 12 Nov 1939, leaving further issue

  2 Charles Sinclair; *b* 31 May 1849; lost at sea 7 Sept 1870 aboard HMS *Captain*

  3 FRANCIS ELLIOT (Sir), **3rd Bt**

  4 Arthur Hotham; *b* 1 May 1853, *d* 18 Jan 1857

  5 Frederic George Arthur; *b* 2 Oct 1857, *m* 12 April 1883 Mary Eleanor (*d* 18 Oct 1928), dau of William Forster, barrister, and *d* 10 Oct 1931, having had:

    (1) Charles Sinclair Wake; *b* 1884; *d* unm 1 June 1902

    (2) William Frederic (Sir), KCB (1943, CB 1940), CBE (1941, OBE 1916); *b* 24 March 1888; Adml, served WW I, 3rd Sea Ld and Controller RN WW II also R-Adml i/c afloat Dunkirk Beaches 1940, in HMS *Norfolk* in *Bismarck* action; *m* 19 Jan 1916 Muriel Elsie (*d* 28 Nov 1963), only dau of Sir Collingwood Hughes, 10th Bt (*qv*) *d* 24 Sept 1945, leaving:

      1a Christopher Baldwin WAKE-WALKER later HUGHES-WAKE-WALKER later still WAKE-WALKER again, DL (Suffolk 1983); *b* 16 May 1920; *educ* RNC Dartmouth; served WW II, Cdr RNC Greenwich 1959–61, Naval Attaché Paris 1962–64, Capt Dartmouth Training Sqdn 1964–66, Dir Naval Signals 1966–68, Capt RN, ret 1968, High Sheriff Suffolk 1985; *m* 10 Feb 1944 *Lady Anne Spencer [Lady Anne Wake-Walker, E Bergholt Lodge, E Bergholt, Suffolk CO7 6QU], late 3rd Offr WRNS, only dau of 7th Earl Spencer (*qv*), and *d* 5 April 1998, leaving:

        1b +David Christopher; *b* 11 March 1947; *educ* St Andrews U (MA); Page of Honour to HM THE QUEEN 1960–62; dir Kleinwort Benson Gp; *m* 14 July 1979 *Jenni Rosemary, only dau of Capt Patrick Vaulkhard, of Stone Cottage, Snape, Suffolk, and has:

          1c +Frederic David; *b* 25 Oct 1981
          2c +Nicholas John; *b* 5 July 1985

        2b +Richard Anthony; *b* 25 June 1951; *educ* Winchester and St Andrews (MA); Sr Regnl Controller Centl Selling Organisation; *m* 1980 *Sharon Pamela, yr dau of Gordon Stuart Little, of Crowborough, Sussex, and has:

          1c +Robert Michael; *b* 6 July 1990
          1c *Kate Louise; *b* 14 Oct 1982
          2c *Olivia Rose; *b* 21 Oct 1984

        3b +Michael John [Michael Wake-Walker Esq, 22 Prairie St, London SW8 3PP]; *b* 11 April 1958; *educ* Winchester and RMA Sandhurst; Capt Coldstream Gds; *m* 23 Sept 1992 *Catherine Patricia, est dau of Basil Rodney Hazlitt, of Billingshurst, Sussex, and has:

          1c +George; *b* 9 March 1995

        1b *Elizabeth Sarah [Mrs Anthony Duckworth-Chad, Pynkney Hall, East Rudham, Norfolk PE31 6TF]; *b* 2 Dec 1944 (HM QUEEN ELIZABETH THE QUEEN MOTHER stood sponsor); *m* 6 May 1970 *Anthony Nicholas George Duckworth-Chad, DL, High Sheriff Norfolk 1992, and has:

          1c +James Anthony de L'Etang; *b* 9 July 1972
          2c +William George Christopher; *b* 14 March 1975
          1c *Davina Alice; *b* 18 May 1978

        2b *Diana Mary; *b* 11 April 1958; *m* 1980 *Maj Charles Keble Macfarlane, Coldstream Gds, and has:

          1c +Thomas Christopher Keble; *b* 2 March 1983
          1c *Georgina Cynthia; *b* 20 Jan 1986

      2a +Cedric Collingwood [Lt-Cdr Cedric Wake-Walker RN, Terwick Wood, Rogate, Hants GU31 5DD]; *b* 23 Aug 1923; RN WW II and Korea 1950–51 (despatches), ret 1963, Sec-Gen to Comité International Radio Maritime; *m* 20 April 1949 *Margaret Iona Letitia, MBE, JP, DL, est dau of Capt John Cassilis Maclean, RN, of The Close, Chichester, and has:

        1b +Edward Collingwood [Edward Wake-Walker Esq, 5 West St, Kingston, Wareham, Dorset BH20 5LH]; *b* 22 Oct 1952; *educ* Marlborough; Head PR RNLI; *m* 1982 *Fiona Margaret, dau of Cdr Michael J Hodgson, DSC, RN, of Hill Ho, Turleigh, Bradford-on-Avon, Wilts, and has:

          1c +Thomas Collingwood; *b* 1987
          1c *Eleanor May; *b* 1989

        1b *Susanna [Mrs Mark Dancy, 41 Berwyn Rd, Richmond, Surrey]; *b* 2 June 1950; *m* 1974 *Christopher Mark Dancy, MA, BM, BCh, FRCP, and has:

          1c *Luke Henry; *b* 1983
          1c *Arabella Clare; *b* 6 July 1977
          2c *Martha Caroline; *b* 1979

        2b *Corinna Elizabeth [Mrs Fred Carr, 49 Moore Park Rd, London SW6 2HP]; *b* 28 April 1957; *m* 1983 *Francis Christopher (Fred) Carr, s of A E J Carr, of San Francisco, and has:

          1c *Polly Catherine Alice; *b* 1985
          2c *Matilda Rose; *b* 1987

     1a *Penelope Hughes [Lady Eley, The Change House, Gt Yeldham, Essex]; *b* 12 Sept 1917; *m* 4 Sept 1937 Sir Geoffrey Cecil Ryves Eley, CBE (*d* 1990), 2nd s of Charles Cuthbert Eley, JP, FLS, of E Bergholt Place, and has:

        1b *Piers David Christopher [Piers Eley Esq, 35 Montague Rd, Richmond, Surrey]; *b* 20 May 1941; *educ* Eton, Trin Coll Cambridge (BA 1964, MA 1967) and London Grad Sch Business Studies (MSc 1969); *m* 1 April 1967 *Sarah Cloudesley, only dau of Lt-Col David Edward Long-Price, OBE, of Little Baddow, Essex, and has:

          1c *Damian Edward Piers; *b* 24 Jan 1970
          1c *Thalia Catherine; *b* 9 Sept 1971

        2b *Gavin Michael Geoffrey [Gavin Eley Esq, 40 Woolmead Ave, London NW5]; *b* 21 Oct 1945; *educ* Eton; *m* 1st 1974 (*divorce* 1984) Mary Belinda (Holly), er dau of Maj Bruce Edward Arthur Urquhart of Craigston, Craigston Castle, Aberdeenshire, and formerly w of Fabrizio Pratesi; *m* 2nd 1994 *Virginia Jo, dau of Peter Williams, of W Hampstead

        1b *(Susan) Ianthe; *b* 3 June 1938; *m* 1st 18 Dec 1963 (*divorce* 1985) Paul Edward Cornwall-Jones, 3rd s of Brig Arthur Thomas Cornwall-Jones, CMG, of Henley-on-Thames, Oxon; *m* 2nd 1985 *Peter R del Tufo, est s of Sir Vincent del Tufo, KBE, and has by her 1st husb:

          1c *Imogen Annabel; *b* 24 Dec 1967; *educ* Edinburgh U (MA)
          2c *Theresa Hermione Chloë; *b* 13 July 1971

        2b *Chloe Sarabella [Mrs Peter Blegvad, 22 Anley Rd, London W14]; *b* 27 Nov 1950; *m* 1st 1971 Richard Christian Wynne Fremantle (*see* COTTESLOE B); *m* 2nd 1986 *Peter Blegvad, s of Eric Blegvad, of Wardsboro, Vt., and has by him:

          1c *Kaye Eley; *b* 11 Sept 1987
          2c *Alec Viggo Eley; *b* 18 March 1990

     2a *(Catherine) Marigold; *b* 25 Aug 1921; 3rd Ofrr WRNS WW II; *m* 4 Sept 1944 Lt-Cdr Rev Hugh Wake, RN (*see* WAKE, Bt), and has issue

    1b Marjorie Ella; *d* unm 18 Feb 1963
    2b Freda Evelyn; *d* unm 14 Nov 1954
    3b Joan Mary; *m* 17 Oct 1914 Maj John Glendinning Bryden Shand (*d* 14 Aug 1960), IMS, s of James Shand, and *d* 8 Dec 1965, leaving:
    4b Ruth Barbara; *m* 22 Aug 1916 Maj William Henry Lowe Watson, DSO, DCM (*d* 16 Dec 1932), s of Rev Patrick Watson, and had issue

  1 Mary Anne; *m* 4 Nov 1854 Frederick Bacon Frank, DL (*dsp* 27 Aug 1911), of Earlham Hall, Norfolk, and Campsall Hall, Yorks, and *d* 12 July 1902

  2 Emily; *m* 26 July 1870, as his 2nd w, Rev Francis William Peel (*d* 1895), Rector Burghwallis, and *d* 1916, leaving issue

  3 Florence Charlotte; *m* 17 Nov 1875 Rev Canon Charles Robertson Manning (*d* 7 Feb 1899), Rector Diss, Norfolk, and *d* 30 Oct 1920, leaving issue

4 Evelyn Laura; *m* 1st 25 Aug 1864 Capt Hugh Talbot Burgoyne, VC, RN (*d* 7 Sept 1870, lost in HMS *Captain*), only s of FM Sir John Fox Burgoyne, 1st Bt, GCB (*see* 1871 edn); *m* 2nd 30 July 1874 Wilson Fox, MD, FRS (*d* 1887), of Mayfair, and *d* 1889

The 2nd Bt's bro,

Sir Francis Elliot Wake-Walker, 3rd Bt; *b* 9 March 1851; Lt RN; *m* 5 April 1883 Helen Constance (*d* 15 Oct 1901), dau of Rev Archibald Paris, and *d* 27 July 1928, having had:

1 Baldwin Charles; *b* 7 Jan 1884, Cdr RN WW I (despatches, Legn Hon); *m* 22 Nov 1923 Mary (*m* 3rd 14 Nov 1928 S/Ldr Aubrey William Graham Martin, RAF, only s of Brig-Gen Herbert Martin, CB, of Torquay; *m* 4th Capt C Black; *m* 5th her 3rd husb, who *d* 1973), formerly w of — Bold and dau of Frederick Piere Barnett, of Whalton, Northumberland, and *d* 9 April 1927, leaving:

(1) Sir (BALDWIN) PATRICK WALKER, **4th and present Bt**

(2) Francis Donald Baldwin; *b* posthumously 18 July 1927; Lt 60th Rifles KRRC 1945–48; *m* 1st 12 March 1955 Joanna Mary, only dau of Sir John Weir Russell, of Kensington, and had:

1a *Caroline Lucy Marjorie; *b* 21 Jan 1957

(2) (cont.) Francis Walker; *m* 2nd 1965 *Jennifer Mary, only dau of Lt-Cdr Eric Stokoe, RN, and *d* 24 Nov 1994, leaving by her:

1a +Anthony Eric Charles; *b* 1966

1 Helen Marjorie; *d* unm

WALKER of
Pembroke House

Arms: Ermine on a chevron engrailed plain cotised azure, between three hurts, each charged with a portcullis or, as many trefoils slipped of the last. **Crest:** On a Roman fasces or, banded azure, a dove of the last, holding in its bill a trefoil slipped of the first. **Motto:** *Premo ad honorem* ('I aim for honour'). **Creation:** Bt. (UK) 12 July 1906.

SIR HUGH RONALD WALKER, 4TH BT, of Pembroke House, Dublin [Maj Sir Hugh Walker Bt, Ballinamona, Hospital, Kilmallock, Co Limerick, Ireland]; *b* 13 Dec 1925; *s* f 1964; *educ* Wellington; Maj RA (ret), 2 i/c RA Range Benbecula, Outer Hebrides, 1964–66, cmdg No 1 Army Information Team Aden and Hong Kong 1966–68, Larkhill 1969–73; memb Assoc Supervisory and Exec Engrs; *m* 14 Aug 1971 *Norma, er dau of Lt-Cdr R D Baird, RNR, of Yardford Orchards, Kingston St Mary, Somerset, and has:

1 +ROBERT CECIL; *b* 26 Sept 1974

2 +Roy Edward; *b* 10 Aug 1977

Lineage: ALEXANDER WALKER, of Grove Port, Co Westmeath; Capt; had with another s (Gen Mark Walker, VC, late 30th Regt, decorated for saving Regtl Collours at Battle of Inkerman 1854):

Sir Samuel Walker, 1st Bt (UK), so *cr* 12 July 1906, PC (I 1885), QC (1872), JP (Co Westmeath), of Pembroke House, Dublin; *b* 19 June 1832; barrister King's Inns Dublin 1855; MP Londonderry 1883–85, Slr-Gen Ireland 1883–85, Attorney-Gen 1885–86, Ld Chllr 1892–95 and 1905–11, Ld Justice Appeal 1895–1905; *m* 1st 9 Oct 1855 Cecilia Charlotte (*d* 18 June 1880), dau of Arthur Greene, and had:

1 **Sir Alexander Arthur Walker, 2nd Bt;** *b* 21 Jan 1857; RNR, Sr Examiner Masters and Mates for Port of London, Sec and Supt Local Marine Bd Dublin; *m* 1st 24 Oct 1885 Emily Florence (*d* 8 May 1908), dau of William L Crother, MD; *m* 2nd 20 Jan 1914 Dorothy (*d* 6 Sept 1957), only dau of William Douglas Phillipps, JP, of The Lea, Eccleshall, Staffs, and *dsp* 22 Nov 1932

2 Herbert; *b* 20 Dec 1867; *d* 30 March 1923

1 Alice Elizabeth

2 Elizabeth; *m* 23 Oct 1884 Edward Fitzgerald Hickson, RM, of Limerick, and *d* 5 March 1927, leaving issue

3 Mabel Elvira; *m* 17 Nov 1901 Maj Herbert Charles Owen, OBE, MC, Middx Regt

4 Eileen Emily; *m* 21 Oct 1913 Lt-Col Herbert William Allan Collum, DSO, RASC, s of Rev Hugh Robert Collum, Vicar Leigh, Kent, and *d* June 1966

Sir Samuel *m* 2nd 17 Aug 1881 Eleanor (*d* 22 Feb 1947), dau of Rev Alexander MacLaughlin, and *d* 13 Aug 1911, leaving by her:

3 CECIL EDWARD (Sir), **3rd Bt**

5 Ina Eleanor; *b* 3 Dec 1883; *m* 18 Feb 1911 Lt Charles William Sheridan, 5th Dragoon Gds (*d* 8 March 1942), only s of Charles William Sheridan, and had issue

The 2nd Bt's half-brother,

Sir Cecil Edward Walker, 3rd Bt, DSO (1919), MC; *b* 6 Aug 1882; *educ* Rugby; Maj RA WW I (despatches, Legn Hon); *m* 22 Oct 1924 Violet (*d* 26 Aug 1961), yr dau of Hugh Dunbar McMaster, of Dunbarton House, Gilford, Co Down, and *d* 2 July 1964, leaving:

1 SIR HUGH RONALD WALKER, **4th and present Bt**

1 *Sheilagh Rosemary [Mrs Wilfred Andrews, Oxleaze Farm, W Knoyle, Wilts]; *b* 20 May 1928; *m* 11 Oct 1969 *Wilfred James Andrews, s of A F Andrews, of The Cott, Kilmington, Wilts

WALKER of
Sand Hutton

Arms: Argent on a chevron gules between three crescents azure as many annulets or. **Crest:** Out of a battlement argent a dexter arm embowed in armour azure, in the hand proper a lizard vert. **Motto:** *Honesta quam magna* ('How great is honesty'). **Creation:** Bt. (UK) 9 Dec 1868.

SIR JAMES HERON WALKER, 5TH BT, of Sand Hutton, Co York, and Beachampton, Co Buckingham [Sir James Walker Bt, Oakhill, Port Sodderick, IoM IM4 1AP]; *b* 7 April 1914; *s* f 1930; *educ* Eton and Magdalene Coll Cambridge; *m* 1st 22 April 1939 (*divorce* 1972) Angela Margaret (*d* 1993), only dau of Victor Alexandre Beaufort, OBE, MC, and Mrs C F Burnard, of Steephill, Jersey, CI, and has had:

1 +VICTOR STEWART HERON [Victor Walker Esq, 6 Hill St, St Helier, Jersey JE4 6DX]; *b* 8 Oct 1942; *educ* Eton; 2nd Lt Gren Gds 1962–65, Lt Roy Wilts Yeo 1965–73; *m* 1st 24 July 1969 (*divorce* 1982) Caroline Louisa (*m* 2nd 1983 Jonathan Blackburn), yst dau of Lt-Col Frederick Barton Wignall, of Poulton Fields, Cirencester, Glos, and Cambusmore, Sutherland; *m* 2nd 7 May 1982 *Svea, only dau of Captain Ernst Hugo Gothard Knutson Borg, and by his 1st w has:

(1) +James Frederick Heron; *b* 14 Feb 1970

(2) +Andrew Robert Heron; *b* 6 Jan 1973

(1) *Rosanna Celia Louisa; *b* 29 May 1979

1 Celia Elizabeth Synolda; *b* 27 April 1948; *k* car crash S Africa 10 Feb 1969

Sir JAMES *m* 2nd 28 Sept 1972 *Sharonne Babette, dau of David Philip Read, of Clanfield, Oxon, and by her has:

2 +Simon Peter; *b* 13 Jan 1974; *educ* Eton and Leeds U (BA)

Lineage: JAMES WALKER, of Manchester; *b* 11 Oct 1680; merchant; *m* 1st Anne — and had:

1 John, of Manchester; *b* 5 Nov 1707; merchant; *d* unm 19 March 1757

1 Elizabeth; *m* Thomas Gardner

JAMES WALKER; *m* 2nd 16 Jan 1716 Mary, widow of Dr Waterhouse and dau of John Carter by Sarah Morewood, of Hallows, Derbys, and *d* 12 Feb 1753, leaving by her:

2 James, of Springhead, nr Hull; *b* 15 April 1719; FRS; *m* 1st 6 Dec 1744 Alice, dau of Rev Richard Goodwin, DD, Rector Tankersley, Yorks, and Prestwich, Lancs, and had, with another dau:

(1) JAMES

(1) Mary; *m* 1st John Wadman, of Imber, Wilts; *m* 2nd William G Burslem

2 (cont.) James Walker *m* 2nd Elizabeth, dau of Sir William Wentworth, 4th Bt, of Bretton, Yorks, and *d* 22 Feb 1789

His only s,

JAMES WALKER, of Springhead and Beverley; *b* 26 Dec 1753; *m* 12 Dec 1789 Jane, only dau and heiress of John Porter, of Kingston-Upon-Hull, and *d* 24 Feb 1829, leaving, with two daus (Jane, *m* 1819 Richard Hill, of Thornton (*d* 1855);

Harriet, m 7 April 1818 Joseph Robinson Pease (d 27 May 1866), of Hesslewood, nr Hull)

Sir James Walker, 1st Bt (UK), so cr 9 Dec 1868, of Sand Hutton, Co York, and Beachampton, Co Buckingham, JP, DL Yorks; b 30 May 1803; High Sheriff Yorks 1846; m 1st 13 Jan 1829 Mary (d 29 Sept 1830), 4th dau of Robert Denison, of Killnwick Percy, Yorks and had:

1 JAMES ROBERT (Sir), **2nd Bt**

Sir JAMES m 2nd 16 April 1833 Maria (d 9 Jan 1878), 2nd dau of Rev Robert Stephen Thompson (see MEYSEY-THOMPSON, Bt), and d 8 Oct 1883, having by his 2nd w had:

2 Frederick James, MVO, JP, DL (N RYorks); b 1 Feb 1835; educ Exeter Coll Oxford (MA); m 9 July 1861 Grace Charlotte (d 11 Oct 1923), dau and coheir of George Champney, of Middlesthorpe Manor, Yorks, by Harriet, er dau of Rev R S Thompson, of Bilbrough (see above), and d 7 Nov 1913, having had, with a dau (d unm):

(1) Frederick William George; b 4 Oct 1862; d unm 11 Nov 1906

(2) Hugh Edward; b 22 Aug 1865; Capt Roy Welch Fus Burma (medal with clasp); m 24 June 1913 Hon Marjory Winifred Forbes (d 14 Sept 1945), only dau of 21st Lord Forbes (qv), and d 26 Sept 1935, leaving:

1a Peter Hugh Frederick, TD; b 3 Feb 1916; educ Ampleforth and London U (BSc (Eng) 1937; C Eng, MICE, Capt RE WW II; m 17 Dec 1947 Geraldine Elizabeth May (d 27 Aug 1992), only dau of Maj Carlos Barron Lumsden of Clova, and d 8 March 1990, having had:

1b Elizabeth Mary; b 17 Aug, d 21 Aug 1950

1a (cont.) Mr and Mrs Peter Walker also adopted:

*Rozanne Mary [Mrs Windsor Charlton, Wells Cottage, Moniaive, Dumfriesshire]; b 11 Sept 1949; m 25 Aug 1973 *Windsor Lyndon Charlton, and has (by Godfrey Mrgodo):

1c *Oliver Hugh; b 6 Aug 1986

1c *Alexandra; b 24 Dec 1989

*Caroline Georgina Mary [Mrs Alan Clyde, 114 Braid Rd, Edinburgh EH10 6AS]; b 14 Nov 1953; m 11 Sept 1976 *Alan Stewart Clyde and has:

1c *James Alexander; b 4 June 1982

1c *Sophie Louise; b 4 June 1980

1a *Rosemary Alice Champney [Mrs Hugh Le Messurier, Thornton Grange, Thornton Steward, N Yorks HG4 4BQ]; b 9 July 1917; m 7 Aug 1948 Lt-Col Hugh Shelley Le Messurier, Duke of Wellington's Regt, s of Hugh Arnott Le Messurier, of Newfoundland, and has:

1b *Jacquine Shelley [Mrs Jeremy Gaskell, The Rose House, Wykeham, Old Malton, N Yorks YO17 0RF]; b 16 June 1949; m 18 Oct 1969 *Lt Jeremy John Gaskell, King's Regt, s of Maj John Rodney Gaskell, of Stourton Ford, Ilkley, Yorks, and has:

1c *Victoria Jacquine; b 28 Aug 1971

2c *Joanna Louise; b 7 Jan 1973; m 23 Sept 1995 *Guy Standring Marsh

2b *Susan Rosemary [Mrs John Green-Armytage, The Cedars, Barnes Common, London SW13]; b 16 Sept 1950; m 1976 *John McDonald Green-Armytage, of Winnipeg, Canada, and has:

1c *Matthew Whitla; b 1978

1c *Anna Claire; b 1981

2c *Camilla Rose; b 1983

3c *Elizabeth Caroline; b 1985

2a *Marguerite Helena Mary [Mrs Giles Tweedie, Glencairn, Church Cres, Dunscore, Dumfries DG2 0TA]; b 20 Oct 1919; m 27 June 1942 *Capt Giles Grierson Tweedie, Argyll and Sutherland Highrs, yst s of Col William Tweedie, CMG, CBE, of Beechwood, Dunblane, Perths, and has:

1b *Marion Veronica; b 8 May 1943; m 1978 *Michael Frank Walter and has:

2c *Patrick Douglas; b May 1980

2b *Jacqueline Alice; b 26 Oct 1944

3b *Rosalind Mary [Mrs Derek Evans, 9 Linden Drive, Mold, Clwyd]; b 19 Aug 1947; m 1979 Derek Gwynn Evans (d 9 April 1994) and has:

1c *Mark Edward; b 13 March 1982

2c *Eifion Charles; b 24 Oct 1983

1c *Alison Margaret; b 29 April 1985

2c *Pamela Sian; b 3 July 1988

3a *Daphne Elizabeth [Sister Daphne Walker SHCJ, 3 Barford St, London N1 0QB]; b 8 July 1926; sister Holy Child Jesus

3 Charles Francis, JP (E R Yorks); b 9 Feb 1836; R-Adml; m 22 April 1873 Edith Frances (d 9 Oct 1906), dau of Adml Hon Arthur Duncombe (see FEVERSHAM, B), and d 8 Aug 1925, having had:

(1) Edgar Wilmer; b 3 Aug 1875; barrister Inner Temple; Capt 3rd Bn E Yorks Regt; m 17 April 1906 Charlotte Rankin (d 2 April 1954, having m 2nd 8 July 1919 7th Viscount Lifford, qv), yr dau of Sir Robert Maule, JP, of Edinburgh, and was ka nr Armentieres by 28 Oct 1914, leaving:

1a +Francis Robert; b 21 Feb 1910

(2) Philip Charles (Rev); b 1 Sept 1878; educ Trin Coll Oxford (MA); Rector Lockington Beverley 1917–33; m 20 June 1916 Dorothy Ann (d 4 Oct 1936), dau of Col Frederick Compton-Howard (see CARLISLE, E), and d 3 July 1933, leaving:

1a +Anthony Charles Howard [Anthony Walker Esq, 58 Balfour Rd, Blackbird Leys, Oxford]; b 21 Oct 1917; educ Wellington; m 1st 5 Sept 1939 (divorce 1946) Lorna, dau of Hedley Crabtree; m 2nd 1 Aug 1952 *Peggy Foster, dau of John Thomas Hewes, of Cambridge, and by her has:

1b +Timothy Heron; b 5 Sept 1954

1b *Elizabeth Cavendish; b 22 Feb 1956

2b *Ann Cavendish; b 22 Feb 1958

2a +Philip James [Philip Walker Esq, Halse Springs, Macheke, Zimbabwe]; b 13 Sept 1920; educ Uppingham; RAF WW II; m 2 Aug 1951 *Helen Gibson, dau of Dr Harley P Milligan, of Hessle, E Yorks

4 Edwyn; b 6 Sept 1837; Capt 15th Hus; m 11 Aug 1874 Elizabeth (d 25 Oct 1915), dau of William Froggatt Bethell, of Rise, Yorks, and d 22 Aug 1919, having had:

(1) Oswald Bethell; b 28 May 1875; Capt 15th Hus WW I; m 14 Dec 1910 Marcia Eugenia (d 30 Dec 1970, having m 2nd 17 Feb 1920 Francois de Juge Montespieu, who d 30 Dec 1940), er dau of Lt-Col John Delalynde Mansel (see MANSEL, Bt), and was ka 28 Sept 1914, having had:

1a *Lois Adeline Walker [Mrs George Nickerson, Burnt Fen, Horning, Norfolk]; b 6 Feb 1912; m 11 Jan 1932 George Nickerson (d 1976), Coldstream Gds, s of George Augustus Nickerson and Hon Lady Hood, and has:

1b *David George François [David Nickerson Esq, 4 Ladbroke Terrace, London W11]; b 24 March 1933; educ Eton; m 31 Aug 1957 *Sara Elizabeth, dau of Col John Howlett Jewson, MC, TD, DL, of Mergate Hall, Norwich, and has:

1c *William John George [William Nickerson Esq, 20 Stowe Rd, London W10]; b 23 Aug 1958; m 16 May 1989 *Jayne, est dau of Roland Pickering, and has:

1d *Joshua; b 4 Nov 1992

2c *James David Rivers [James Nickerson Esq, 131 Hemingford Rd, London N1]; b 3 Aug 1960; m 14 Aug 1993 *Ann Reynolds

1c *Camilla Marcia; b 29 Sept 1965; m 30 July 1994 *Neville Wakefield

2b *Mark Oswald Julian [Mark Nickerson Esq, Boxted Lodge, Colchester, Essex CO4 5QR]; b 16 April 1935; educ Eton; m 1974 *Elizabeth, dau of F P Burch, and has:

1c *Emma Katherine Françoise; b 13 Nov 1975

2c *Caroline Alice Juliet; b 25 Nov 1978

2a Corisande Elizabeth; b 6 Aug 1913; m 29 July 1937 Gerard Walter Anthony Denny (d 21 Jan 1976), Capt 17th/21st Lancers, est s of Maj Ernest Wriothesley Denny, DSO, of Garboldisham Manor, Norfolk, and d following a hunting accident 16 March 1958, leaving:

1b Timothy John Anthony; b 6 July 1938; m 2 June 1962 *Elizabeth Ann North Powell and d 1993, leaving:

1c *Anthony; b 7 Oct 1964

1c *Melissa; b 24 Oct 1969

2c *Katherine

1b *Lois Marcia; b 27 Dec 1939; m 18 Oct 1962 *Jeremy Carr and has:

1c *James

1c *Anna Lois; b 23 Dec 1968

(2) Wilfred Beckett; b 5 Aug 1876; MajYorks Regt Boer War 1899–1902 (despatches, Queen's medal with five clasps, King's medal with two clasps) and WW I; ka 29 Oct 1914

(3) Edwyn Geoffrey; b 17 Oct 1879; barrister Middle Temple; d unm 4 April 1910, k in a steeplechase at Hindhead

(4) Roger Beverley, MC; b 23 June 1886; Capt Yorkshire Hus WW I (despatches); d 13 Nov 1918 of wounds recd in action

(1) Dorothy Katherine; b 12 July 1883; m 7 Aug 1907 Lt-Col Francis Bertie Brewis (d 21 Oct 1949), KOYLI, 4th s of Samuel Richard Brewis, of Obstone Ho, Oxon, and had:

1a Henry John; b 8 April 1920; m 20 April 1949 *Faith Agnes Devorguilla, dau of Sir Edward Orde MacTaggart Stewart, 2nd and last Bt (see SAINT DAVIDS, V), and d 25 May 1989, leaving:

1b *Francis Roger MacTaggart [Francis Brewis Esq, Flat 3, 1 White Horse Close, 27 Canongate, Edinburgh EH8 8BU; Ardwell House, Ardwell, By Stranraer]; b 30 Jan 1950; m 12 Dec 1981 *Marion Theresa Anderson and has issue

2b *Ralph Michael Rodney [Ralph Brewis Esq, Flat 2, 35 Montpellier Villas, Cheltenham, Glos GL50 2XQ; 17 Woodthorpe Rd, London SW15 6UQ; Norton Grove, Scarborough Rd, Norton, N Yorks YO17 8EF]; b 17 May 1951; m 10 Feb 1979 *Valerie Anne Gerard and has:

1c *Katharine Anne; b 24 Aug 1981

2c *Mairi Fiona; b 26 Oct 1984

3b *Christopher Mark John [Christopher Brewis Esq, 10 Beresford Park, Sunderland SR2 7JU; Sth Ardwell Cottage, Ardwell By Stranraer, Wigtown DG9]; b 7 Dec 1956; m 3 July 1982 *Aileen Teresa Rowland and has:

1c *David John; b 16 March 1988

1c *Catherine Flora; b 19 April 1985

1b *Sylvia Katharine Moira [Mrs Murray Watson, Trebles, Holford Seven Ash, Combe Florey, Somerset]; b 13 Dec 1952; m 1st 8 July 1978 Timothy Harrison (d 11 Dec 1981) and had:

1c *Wesley John; b 27 Nov 1979

1c *Abigail Katharine; b 3 June 1981

1b (cont.) Mrs Timothy Harrison m 2nd 26 Sept 1986 *Murray Michael Thomas Lloyd Watson and by him has:

2c *Alexander Guy Timothy Michael; b 22 Aug 1989

2c *Alice Pamela Charlotte; b 15 Aug 1987

1a Frances Elizabeth Edwyna; b 24 Nov 1908; m 17 Sept 1929 Sir Kenelm Henry Ernest Cayley, 10th Bt (qv), and d 21 Jan 1974, leaving issue

2a *Philippa Dorothy Annora; b 28 Aug 1911; m 8 Nov 1947 Walter Staves (d 19 March 1979) and has:

1b *Andrew; b 3 Aug 1948; m Aug 1970 *Deborah Lesley Tuck and has:

1c *William Robert Anderson; b 29 Dec 1975

2b *Gregory [Gregory Staves Esq, 26 Glamorgan Rd, Hampton Wick, Surrey KT1 4HP]; b 14 June 1951; m 4 Aug 1973 *Jane Pilgrim and has:

1c *Corinne Elizabeth; b 8 June 1979

2c *Rosemary Jane; b 20 April 1981

3a *Olivia Hester Rachel [Mrs Henry Dodds, 6 Ryndle Walk, Northstead, N Yorks YO12 6JU]; b 12 Jan 1916; m 7 July 1971 *Henry Hopkins Dodds

5 Gerald, JP (Yorks); b 14 Sept 1841; Capt 15th Hus; m 28 Sept 1869 Harriet Louisa (d 23 May 1930), 3rd dau of Henry Darley, of Aldby Park, Yorks, and d 13 July 1927, leaving:

(1) Bertram James, CMG (1919), DSO (1918); b 25 June 1880; Lt-Col Roy Sussex Regt WW I; m 1st 21 April 1909 (divorce 1926) Josepha Margaret (d 1 Feb 1972), yst dau of Sir George Donaldson, of Hove; m 2nd 1940 Countess Lucie Marie Reventlow née von Haugwitz-Hardenburg (d 1984 aged 99), of Denmark, and d 8 March 1947, leaving by his 1st w:

1a +Anthony Gerald Bartholomew [Lt-Col Anthony Walker, Chattis Hill Ho, Stockbridge, Hants SO20 6JS]; b 24 Aug 1912; educ Harrow and RMC Sandhurst; Lt-Col Somerset LI; m 24 Aug 1939 Margaret Cumberland (d 18 Oct 1987), only dau of Col Charles Perry Templeton, CB, DSO, of Victoria, BC, and has had:

1b Bertram Gerald Templeton; b 15 April, d 15 June 1941

2b +Christopher James Anthony (Rev) [The Rev Christopher Walker, Horseshoe Meadow Farm, Cholderton, Wilts SP4 0ED]; b 25 Aug 1943; educ Harrow and RMA Sandhurst; Lt-Col 17th/21st Lancers (ret 1984); Roy Army Chaplains Dept 1987; m 8 May 1971 *Ronwen Melody, er dau of Lt-Col E C Barton, MC, and has:

1c +Rupert Anthony Edward; b 14 Aug 1972; m 13 July 1996 *Helen Christine, only dau of David Jones, of The Almshouses, Throwley, Kent

1c *Alice Melody Margaret; b 2 Jan 1974

2c *Lavinia Verity Rose; b 24 Jan 1977

3c *Cicely Primrose Amy; b 2 April 1979

3b +Robin Charles Andrew [Robin Walker Esq, The Gdn Flat, 30 Maida Ave, London W2 1ST]; b 3 Aug 1944; educ Harrow and McGill (BA); m 30 Aug 1975 *Selina Margaret, er dau of Maj Patrick Dudley Erskine Riall, of Ballyorney Ho, Enniskerry, Co Wicklow, and has:

1c *Lucinda Margaret Riall; b 4 Oct 1983

2c *Sophie Claire Riall; b 3 Aug 1985

4b +Peter Gerald Edward [Peter Walker Esq, Binghams Farmhouse, Bower Chalke, Wilts SP5 5BW]; b 24 April 1948; educ Harrow; m 19 July 1980 *Anne Susan Lyon, only dau of Capt N Fellowes, and has:

1c +Harry Bertram Templeton; b 25 Nov 1984

2c +Charles Peter Templeton; b 13 Aug 1987

1c *Emily Rose Cumberland; b 2 April 1983

2c *Amelia Anne Cumberland; b 14 April 1989

5b +John Perry Donaldson [John Walker Esq, 9 Tanjong Rhu Rd, #20–04 The Waterside, Singapore 1543]; b 16 May 1951; educ Harrow; Capt 17th/21st Lancers

1b *Morella Cumberland [Mrs Robert Cottam, 7 Stanford Rd, London SW8 5PP]; b 13 April 1942; educ Cranborne Chase; m 7 Oct 1967 *Robert Gwynne Cottam, s of Maj-Gen Rev Algernon Edward Cottam, CB, CBE, MC, of Bodiam, Sussex, and has:

1c *Charles Robert Edward; b 1 June 1969

2c *Henry Gerald Alexander; b 4 Oct 1973

1c *Rosemary Margaret Cumberland; b 22 July 1971

(2) Victor Arthur; b 20 Oct 1882; brevet-maj 1917; m 14 Nov 1918 Annette (d 30 July 1954), widow of Maj Montagu Abrahams and sis of 1st and last Baron Duveen (see 1939 edn), and dsp 21 Feb 1945

(1) Geraldine May; b 6 Dec 1871; m 6 July 1895 Gerald M Soames and d 16 Dec 1950

6 Francis Henry (Rev); b 6 June 1843; d 18 April 1870

7 Henry Stephen; b 31 May 1845; 13th Hus; m 12 Oct 1870 Emma Ada, est dau of Henry Mason, of Coburg, formerly of Kingston-Upon-Hull, and d 7 July 1923, leaving:

(1) Augustus Henry; b 4 March 1872

(1) Sybil Ada

8 Arthur; b 4 Feb 1855; m 4 July 1881 Louisa Janet Dundas (d 1954), dau of Ven James Palmes, DD, Archdeacon E R Yorks, and d 30 April 1911, having had:

(1) Edward Arthur; b 9 April 1883; m 4 Nov 1911 Frances Beatrice (d 5 March 1961), dau of James Davies, and d 1 Dec 1950, leaving:

1a Harold Edward Palmes, TD; b 13 Sept 1917; educ Birkenhead Sch; Maj IA WW II Burma; m 24 Feb 1951 *Phyllis Nora, dau of Charles Green, of Heswall, and d 27 Dec 1990, leaving:

1b +Michael Heron Palmes [Michael Walker Esq, Springwood, Tower Rd, N Heswall, Wirrall L60 6RT]; b 1951; educ St David's Coll Llandudno; m 1983 *Frances Helen Price, of Australia, and has:

1c +James Heron Palmes; b 1986

1c +Rose Frances; b 1988

1a Joan Olive Beatrix; b 28 Aug 1912; m 20 April 1940 Geoffrey Norman Booth [Geoffrey Booth Esq, 77 Palm Grove, Oxton, Birkenhead, Cheshire L43 1TG], slr, s of Parkin Stanley Booth, of The Wirral, and d 6 Jan 1994, leaving:

1b *David Parkin; b 15 Sept 1943; educ Shrewsbury and Newcastle U (BA, BArch); m 2 April 1971 *Jane Hilary Wood and has:

1c *Matthew Shaw; b 18 Oct 1977

2a *Stella Rowena Palmes [Mrs Harold Dugdale, 3 Halifax Cl, Wellesbourne, Warwicks]; b 15 May 1920; m 27 June 1944 Lt-Cdr Harold Jack Edmund Dugdale, RNR (d 1975), s of Lt-Col W Dugdale, RAMC, and has:

1b *Janet Beatrice; b 10 April 1947; educ Upton Hall Convent; m 1972 *Robert Lewes Sinkinson and has:

1c *Mark Luis; b 1985

2c *James Alexander; b 1991

2b *Diana Elizabeth; b 12 Aug 1952, educ Upton Hall Convent; m 1989 *Jan Ryszard Kacperek and has:

1c *Paul Anthony; b 19—

(2) Henry; b 20 Aug 1885; m 1913 Margaret (d 1974), dau of Robert Rowlands, and d 8 Nov 1965, leaving:

1a Henry Arthur, JP (Kenya 1936); b 15 Nov 1913; educ Stubbington Ho and Brighton Coll; Maj KAR and RARO WW II and Staff E African Cmd, dir Harmans Uxbridge Brewery; m 1st 8 Nov 1935 (divorce 1947) Rose Vivien (d 5 Sept 1993), er dau of Raymond Robert Ulyate, of Arusha, Tanzania, and had:

1b +Robert Christopher Arthur [Robert Walker Esq, PO Box 835, Robertson 6705, Western Cape, S Africa]; b 13 June 1938; educ King's Sch Bruton; with Anglo-American Corp of S Africa; m 29 Feb 1964 *Melody Gloriana Mignonette, yst dau of Gustavus Adolfus Carl de Friedland, of Cape Town, and has:

1c +Grant Robert James; b 22 Sept 1968; educ St Martin's Johannesburg

1c *Juanita Marguerite Vivien [Mrs Ferdinando Carlos, PO Box 824, Jwaneng, Botswana]; b 8 Jan 1965; m 1983 *Ferdinando Ganchinho Carlos, of Johannesburg, and has:

1d *Sheyne Robert Martins; b 21 Aug 1984

2d *Ivan Anibal Christopher; b 16 March 1986

3d *Ricardo Ferdinando; b 18 Nov 1987

2c *Karine Madelaine Mignonette Tanya [Karine Walker, PO Box 249, Sunninghill, Johannesburg 2157, S Africa]; b 30 Nov 1965; has:

1d *Devon Christopher WALKER; b 22 June 1994

1a (cont.) Henry Walker m 2nd 1 June 1948 Christine Mabel (d 20 March 1973), yst dau of Ollive Edward Hollingworth, of Step Cottage, Witchampton, Dorset, and by her had:

1b *Mary Woodroffe Margaret [Mrs John Lucas, Wychwood, 4 Field Way, Corfe Mullen, Wimbourne, Dorset BH21 3XH]; b 15 Jan 1957; m 6 Sept 1980 *John Stephen Lucas and has:

1c *Emma Annabel Mary; b 11 Sept 1983

2c *Sophie Elizabeth; b 11 March 1985

1a (cont.) Henry Walker m 3rd 6 Dec 1980 *Patricia Blanche Neville [Mrs Henry Walker, The Bridge Ho, Spetisbury, Dorset DT11 9EB]), dau of Ralph Neville Neville-Jones, of Broadstone, Dorset, and widow of Capt C H Hammer MBE, RN, and d 15 Feb 1994

1a *Monica Diana [Mrs Archibald McMillan, 5 Bon Accord, Victoria Ave, Swanage, Dorset]; b 24 Oct 1915; m 25 Feb 1939 Archibald Robert Octavius McMillan, OBE (d 1988), s of Robert James McMillan, of Nottingham

2a *Margaret Patricia Walker [Mrs Margaret Larner, 5 Richmond Lodge, Victoria Ave, Swanage, Dorset]; b 27 Feb 1919; m 15 March 1944 (divorce 1966) Eugene Larner (d 1989), s of Eugene Layard Larner, of Norfolk, and has:

1b *Felicity Gay [Mrs Felicity McKinney, 15 Gayford Rd, London W12 9BY]; b 3 July 1945; m 1980 (divorce 1985) William McKinney and has:

1c *Clinton William Eugene; b 1981

(3) Ernest, JP Kenya; b 11 June 1887; Capt KAR German E Africa WW I (1914 Medal, Allies and Victory Medals, African GS Medals), Maj WW II in Ethiopia and Madagascar; m 1st 14 April 1921 Mildred Katherine Grace (d 26 May 1952), 3rd dau of Lt-Col Sir Charles Henry Brabazon Heaton-Ellis, CBE, of Wyddiall Hall, nr Buntingford, Herts; m 2nd 6 Jan 1953 Dorothy Hyacinthe (d 1993), only child of Maj Cecil William Bunbury Eames, JP, DL, RE, and d 9 Nov 1970, having by his 1st w had:

1a +Peter Martin Brabazon, CBE [Dr Peter Walker CBE, Drumlaggan, The Ross, Comrie, Perthshire PH6 2JT]; b 1 May 1922; educ Haileybury and Trin Coll Cambridge; MA, PhD, DSc; Prof Natural History Edinburgh U; m 1 May 1943 *Violet Norah Wright, dau of Wright, of Hadleigh, Suffolk, and has:

1b +Robin John; b 2 Aug 1947

1b *Marian Elizabeth; b 11 Dec 1943

2b *Sonia Elidh; b 12 July 1954

3b *Caroline Jane Palmes; b 3 Sept 1960

2a Timothy Robin Charles; b 22 Jan 1925; educ Nautical Coll Pangbourne; Lt-Cdr RN WW II Mediterranean and Far East; m 18 Feb1958 Dilys, dau of Brig John Victor Dykes Radford, OBE, MC, and was k with her in an air accident 29 Feb 1964, leaving:

1b *Sabrina Louise Walker; b 12 March 1963; m 1983 (divorce 1986) Maj Roderick Alexander Ingleby-Mackenzie, Scots Gds

3a +Jonathan Mungo Palmes [Maj Jonathan Walker, Lythhanger, Empshott, Hants GU33 6HT]; b 17 Feb 1929; educ Prince of Wales Sch Kenya and RMA Sandhurst; Maj Black Watch; m 12 May 1955 *Diana Mary, er dau of Brig Otho William Nicholson, TD, DL (see NICHOLSON OF WINTERBOURNE, B), and has:

1b +Timothy William Mungo; b 20 June 1956; educ Millfield; m 21 Oct 1989 *Julia Suzanne, est dau of John Clifford Groves, of Lundie Castle, Edzell, Angus, and has:

1c +Max John Mungo; b 25 Nov 1990

2b +Jonathan Alexander James; b 27 Nov 1961; educ Millfield

1b +Juliette Elisabeth Charmian; b 11 July 1958; educ St Mary's Calne and Homerton Coll Cambridge; m 22 April 1989 *Hon William Edward Alexander Wilson, yr s of 2nd Baron Moran (qv)

1 Jane Maria; b 1834; m 13 March 1877, as his 2nd w, Adml Hon Arthur Duncombe (d 6 Feb 1889; see FEVERSHAM, B) and dsp 23 Aug 1917

2 Emily Mary; b 1848; m 28 April 1874 Rev Charles Maude Meysey-Thompson (d 12 Sept 1881), s of Sir Harry Stephen Meysey-Thompson, 1st Bt (qv), of Kirby Hall, and d 18 Dec 1937, leaving issue

3 Charlotte; b 1851; m 14 July 1879 Col Richard Frederick Meysey-Thompson (d 1 Sept 1926), 2nd s of Sir Harry Stephen Meysey-Thompson, 1st Bt (qv), and d 3 March 1935, leaving issue

The 1st Bt's est s,

Sir James Robert Walker, 2nd Bt, JP, DL; b 19 Oct 1829; MA, MP Beverley 1859–65; m 23 June 1863 Louisa Susan Marlborough Heron (d 13 Jan 1920), dau of Sir John Heron-Maxwell, 6th Bt (qv), and d 12 June 1899, leaving:

1 JAMES HERON (Sir), **3rd Bt**

2 Reginald Edmund (Rev), JP BC; b 27 June 1866; educ Ch Ch Oxford (MA); Rector Frant, Sussex; m 10 Sept 1895 Lady Emily Mary Seymour (d 7 Nov 1948), 2nd dau of 6th Marquess of Hertford (qv), and d 23 Aug 1945, having had:

(1) Francis Hugh Seymour; b 20 July 1897; d 27 April 1913

(2) Lionel Reginald; b 9 Nov 1898; Lt 88th Victoria Fus and Cadet RFC; accidentally k whilst flying 11 Aug 1917

(3) Eric Henry James; *b* 16 May 1904; *d* 7 June 1934

(4) Rupert Alexander Seymour; *b* 17 April 1910; *m* 23 May 1942 *Edith May, dau of Robert Fergerson Sutherland, and *d* 28 April 1973, leaving:

  1a +Jack Mervyn; *b* 29 Jan 1946; *m* 29 June 1968 *Marjorie Aline, 4th dau of Herbert Buske, of Pembroke, and has had:

    1b Jack Raymond; *b* and *d* 18 Jan 1972

    1b *Victoria Edith; *b* 1974

  2a +Raymond Earle; *b* 27 Jan 1950

(1) *Margaret Edith Mary; *b* 26 Oct 1901; *m* 1st 21 Feb 1920 Frank Caffrey; *m* 2nd 1941 William Derbyshire and by her 1st husb has had:

  1a Reginald Francis; *b* 17 Aug 1923; *d* 3 Jan 1944

  1a *Kathleen Ethel Mary; *b* 10 March 1934; *m* 1st 25 Nov 1949 Robert Coates; *m* 2nd 19–*John Jeffrey, of Burnaby I, BC, Canada, and by her 1st husb has:

    1b *Edward Francis [Edward Coates Esq, 1311 Tagish, Whitehorse, Yukon Territory, Canada]; *b* 5 Sept 1950; *m* 1970 *Jo-Ann Shepherd and has:

      1c *Jolene Mary; *b* 1974

    2b *Douglas Colin Paul [Douglas Coates Esq, 85 Takhina Trailer Court, Whitehorse, Yukon Territory, Canada]; *b* 2 Sept 1953

    3b *Robert James; *b* 14 Sept 1958

    1b *Kathleen Wendy Maki; *b* 27 July 1952; *m* 1972 *Matthew Mackie and has:

      1c *Matthew Maki; *b* 1974

    2b *Anita Marie; *b* 14 Jan 1955; *m* 1973 *George Polburn and has:

      1c *Shayne Gregory; *b* 1974

    3b *Sharon Leigh; *b* 3 Dec 1957

    4b *Phyllis Margaret; *b* 23 Sept 1959

    5b *Debra Joan; *b* 6 Oct 1960

3 Harold Maxwell, JP and DL Yorks; *b* 18 April 1869; Capt 1st Life Gds Imp Yeo Boer War 1902, Maj W R RHA WW I; *m* 4 Oct 1904 Marie Albreda Blanche (*d* 14 April 1963), est dau of Hon Henry Wentworth Fitzwilliam, of Wigganthorpe, Yorks (*see* 1970 edn FITZWILLIAM, E), and *d* 6 Aug 1938, having had:

  (1) *Marya Constance [Mrs Reginald Lund, Blythe, Douglas Rd, Melrose, Roxburghs]; *b* 25 Oct 1905; *m* 3 Dec 1935 Reginald Dekyn Lund (*d* 24 May 1975), 2nd s of Reginald William Lund, of Ashfield, Malton, and has:

    1a *Rosemary Diana [Mrs Thomas Dalziel, Crailing Bhan, Crailing, Jedburgh, Roxburghshire TD8 6TP]; *b* 18 Jan 1937; *m* 24 July 1961 *Thomas Kennedy Dalziel, yr s of Ralph Kennedy Dalziel, of Nether Hallrule, Bonchester Bridge, and gs of Sir Kennedy Dalziel, of Kinnedar, Fife, and has:

      1b *Ralph Kennedy; *b* 5 May 1964; *m* 23 April 1988 *Annette Margaret, yr dau of Trevor Taylor, of Marsden, Yorks, and has:

        1c *Richard Ralph; *b* 10 Sept 1991

        2c *Donald Kennedy; *b* 24 Sept 1993

      2b *Michael Kennedy [Michael Dalziel Esq, Top Floor Flat Right, 11 Eyre Cres, Edinburgh EH3 5ET]; *b* 7 May 1966; *m* 22 May 1995 *Helen Elizabeth Strachan

  (2) Ellenor Mildred Kathleen; *b* 1 Sept 1908; *d* 20 Feb 1991

  (3) Rachel Marie Gabrielle; *b* 13 May 1913; *d* unm 27 Nov 1997

  (4) Albreda Mary; *b* 8 Oct 1922; *d* unm 22 Dec 1976

4 Francis Henry; *b* 26 Oct 1870; *m* 7 July 1904 Frances Mary Theresa (*d* 19 June 1961), est dau of Francis Palmes, formerly of Mill Mount, York, and *d* 15 Aug 1944, leaving:

  (1) *Evelyn Lindsay [Mrs Gerard Horton, Eastbury House, nr Sherborne, Dorset]; *b* 13 April 1905; *m* 29 June 1926 Lt-Col Gerard Thomas Scofield Horton, MC, Queen's Bays (*d* 25 Feb 1982), s of Thomas Horton, of Bilton Ho, Rugby, and has:

    1a *Michael Scofield [Michael Horton Esq, Lansdowne Ho, Sheep St, Shipston-on-Stour, Warwicks]; *b* 21 June 1929; *educ* Eton; *m* 15 May 1965 *Elizabeth Anne, er dau of Sir (Frederick) Philip Alfred William Wombwell, 6th Bt (*qv*), and has had:

      1b Charles Edward Scofield; *b* and *d* 6 March 1966

      2b *James Frederick; *b* 1968

      3b *Peter Michael; *b* 20 Sept 1969

    1a *Patricia Lindsay [Mrs Thomas Woods, Poyntington Manor, Sherborne, Dorset DT9 4LF]; *b* 13 Aug 1927; *m* 15 Jan 1955 Maj Thomas Pickering Salisbury Woods, MBE, RA (*d* 19 Dec 1978), s of Dr Rex Salisbury Woods, of Manor Court, Cambridge, and has had:

      1b Simon Salisbury; *b* 2 Feb 1956; *educ* Eton; *m* 15 July 1983 *Fiona Bevan and *d* 26 Oct 1991, leaving:

        1c *Oliver James; *b* 19 April 1988

        1c *Georgina Charlotte; *b* 16 April 1986

        2c *Iona; *b* 15 Nov 1990

      2b *Robert Gerard Salisbury; *b* 20 Feb 1965

      1b *Caroline Lindsay; *b* 25 Jan 1958; *m* 10 Sept 1982 *Richard William Jackman and has:

        1c *Connie Patricia; *b* 24 July 1984

        2c *Rosanna; *b* 29 Dec 1987

        3c *Charlotte Margaret; *b* 23 Dec 1988

    2a *Linda Mary [Mrs Ronald Crowther, Bishops Caundle House, Sherborne, Dorset]; *b* 29 Feb 1936; *m* 7 April 1956 *Ronald Oakes Crowther, s of Stanley Crowther, of George, CP, and has:

      1b *James Robert; *b* 23 July 1964

      2b *Charles Gerard Oakes; *b* 8 June 1967

      1b *Nicola Jane; *b* 3 Aug 1957; *m* 19–*Jeremy Mainwaring Burton and has:

        1c *Alexandra; *b* 1 Sept 1983

      2b *Miranda; *b* 30 May 1959; *m* 1989 *David Howard Tripp and has:

        1c *Rupert Howard; *b* 1991

        1c *Abigail; *b* 1993

5 Ernest Robert; *b* 10 May 1872; *m* 10 Oct 1901 Beatrice Mary (*d* 11 April 1938), yst dau of Sir Herbert Eustace Maxwell, 7th Bt (*qv*), and *d* 17 May 1942, leaving:

(1) James Herbert; *b* 17 Feb 1905; *d* 9 Feb 1980

(1) Silvia Mary; *b* 12 April 1903; *m* 12 June 1924 Lt-Col Llewellyn William Dean Wathen (*d* 2 Nov 1970), 8th KRI Hus, s of John Hancocke Wathen, of Sea Walls, Bristol, and *d* 19–, leaving:

  1b *Guy Llewellyn; *b* 5 April 1925; *educ* Marlborough; Lt-Col 5th Roy Inniskilling Dragoon Gds; *m* 1st 7 Jan 1953 (*divorce* 1970) Jean Maureen, dau of William Lancelot Dawes, of Malmains Manor, Pluckley, Kent; *m* 2nd 22 Jan 1971 Hilary Margaret, adopted dau of Joyce Marjorie Wigram (*see* WIGRAM, Bt) and formerly w of Stephen James Stuart Oxlade; *m* 3rd 1985 *Sarah Elizabeth, dau of W D Hancock, of Sherborne Hall, King's Lynn, Norfolk, and formerly w of Charles Thomas Bunbury (*see* BUNBURY, Bt), and by his 1st w has:

    1c *Julian Peter Guy; *b* 7 May 1954; *educ* Gordonstoun; Lt-Col Roy Dragoon Gds

    2c *Nigel Charles James [Maj Nigel Wathen, 14 Summerfield Rd, Saffron Walden, Essex CB11 4AJ]; *b* 12 Oct 1955; *educ* Gordonstoun; Maj 9th/12th Roy Lancers

  2b *David Anthony [David Wathen Esq, Torr a' Mhullaich, Dervaig, Isle of Mull PA75 6QR; Skirkton Muir, Bunchrew, by Inverness IV3 6RH]; *b* 18 May 1928; *educ* Marlborough and RAC Cirencester; *m* 1st 3 Feb 1954 (*divorce* 1974) Barbara Jean, dau of Thomas Horsburgh Gibson, of Manor Hill, Selkirk; *m* 2nd 1974 (*divorce* 1981) Patricia Gilbert Ros Croasdale, dau of Charles Ros Munton, of Knutsford, Cheshire, and by his 1st w has had:

    1c *Richard Llewellyn [Richard Wathen Esq, 6 Whitebrean Yard, Canute Place, Knutsford, Cheshire WA16 6BL]; *b* 24 April 1959

    2c Alistair Michael David; *b* 26 Oct 1966; *d* 23 Aug 1970

    1c *Wendy Anne [Mrs Matthew Wilson, Claggan, Morvern, by Oban, Argyll PA34 5XS]; *b* 21 March 1956; *m* 3 May 1986 *Matthew Wilson

  3b Ronald James; *b* 16 Nov 1934; *educ* Marlborough and Trin Coll Dublin; 2nd Lt 8th KRI Hus; *m* 1st 1959 (*divorce* 1961) Eliza Chase Collins, of Providence, RI; *m* 2nd 1983 *Asta Kristinsdottir [Mrs Ronald Wathen, 53 Bousfield Rd, London SE14 5TP], of Reykjavik, and *d* 5 Sept 1993, leaving by her:

    1c *Seàn Ronaldsson; *b* 1967

    1c *Sunna Ronaldsdottir; *b* 1964

  (2) *Kathleen Elizabeth Jean [Miss Kathleen Walker, Cannons, Tibberton, Glos GL19 3AB]; *b* 9 June 1908

1 Mary Louisa; *b* 25 May 1864; *m* 14 April 1891 Brig-Gen Edgar Alan Lambart (*d* 30 June 1930) and *d* 31 Jan 1948, leaving issue (*see* CAVAN, E)

2 Mildred Caroline; *b* 8 Dec 1867; *m* 23 July 1889 Arthur Herbert Kerr (*d* 8 Jan 1930), and *d* 8 Oct 1926, leaving issue (*see* LOTHIAN, M)

3 Beatrix Jane Frances; *b* 23 Dec 1873; *m* 18 Feb 1901 Rev Preb William Geoffrey Pennyman (*d* 12 March 1943), Rector St Mary-le-Bow, EC, and Preb St Paul's, and *d* 17 July 1959, leaving:

  (10 Joan Mary; *b* 10 Feb 1904; *m* 29 Oct 1925 Francis Edgar Hugonin and *d* 5 March 1967, leaving:

    1a *William Francis Pennyman; *b* 3 Aug 1926; *m* 9 Dec 1949 *Daphne Marjorie Oldham and has:

      1b *James William; *b* 5 Oct 1950

      1b *Serena Jane; *b* 28 Sept 1953

      2b *Camilla Frances Mary; *b* 22 Aug 1959

    2a *David Christian; *b* 28 March 1928; *m* 10 June 1952 *Delia Loftus and has:

      1b *Peter James; *b* 12 Aug 1954

      2b *Richard Francis; *b* 12 Aug 1954

      3b *Anthony David; *b* 12 Aug 1954

      1b *Susan Mary; *b* 17 March 1953

    1a *Lavinia Mary; *b* 8 July 1936; *m* 3 July 1957 *Sir John Robert Mowbray, 6th Bt (*qv*), and has issue

  (2) Angela Beatrix; *b* 9 Jan 1906; *m* 1 Nov 1927 2nd Baron Brocket (*qv*) and *d* 1975, leaving issue

4 Olive Cecil; *b* 26 Aug 1875; *m* 21 April 1897 Lt-Col Seymour Campbell Johnston (*d* 8 April 1939), yst s of Capt Frederick Erskine Johnston, RN, and *d* 3 Sept 1961, leaving:

  (1) Conway Bruce Campbell; *b* 23 April 1898; *m* 1st 20 June 1931 Helen Winifred Karslake Bruton (*d* 13 July 1969); *m* 2nd 18 Nov 1969 *Olive Zoe Strachey and by his 1st w had:

    1a *George Frederick Bruce [George Campbell Johnston Esq, Winscott, Cholderton, Wilts SP4 0EG]; *b* 15 May 1937; *m* 1st 10 Sept 1965 Victoria Betsy Gordon Wilson and had:

      1b *James Andrew Campbell; *b* 18 March 1968

      2b *Edward William Campbell; *b* 18 Dec 1970

    1a (cont.) George Campbell Johnston *m* 2nd 4 Oct 1974 *Jane Evill and by her has:

      1b *Charles Frederick; *b* 15 Aug 1976

The 2nd Bt's est s,

Sir James Heron Walker, 3rd Bt, JP; *b* 23 May 1865; Capt and Hon Maj 3rd Bn Hants Regt; *m* 12 June 1889 Violet Maud Cecil (*m* 2nd 15 June 1907 Lt-Col George Davey Symonds, RA, and *d* 24 Oct 1926), dau of Maj-Gen Cecil Robert St John Ives, of Moyns Park, Essex, and *d* 25 Nov 1900, leaving:

1 ROBERT JAMES MILO (Sir), **4th Bt**

2 John Percy Ernest; *b* 8 Sept 1891; *educ* Eton and Trin Coll Cambridge (BA 1914); Lt RSG (SR) WW I (despatches, Croix de Guerre); *m* 15 Nov 1927 Bridget Fleetwood (*d* 28 April 1955), est dau of Sir John Michael Fleetwood Fuller, 1st Bt (*qv*), and *d* 13 Dec 1951, having had:

  (1) John Cecil Fleetwood; *b* 17 Jan 1929; Lt 8th KRI Hus; *kas* Korea 6 Oct 1951

3 Ronald Heron; *b* 20 Nov 1896; *educ* Eton and RMC Sandhurst; Capt Rifle Bde WW I; *m* 2 June 1921 Noel (*d* 1972), only dau of Maj Guy Edward Wentworth, of Woolley Park, Wakefield, and *d* 24 Sept 1964, leaving:

  (1) +Michael Anthony [Michael Walker Esq, 11 Dornton Rd, London SW12 9NB]; *b* 6 Oct 1924; *educ* Nautical Coll Pangbourne; *m* 1st 7 April 1948 Ann

(*d* June 1978), est dau of John Edward Ferguson, of Bushbridge Wood, Godalming, Surrey, and has:

1a *Caroline Margaret [Mrs Ian Doulton, The Homestead, W Green, Hartley Wintney, Hants RG27 8JG]; *b* 22 Aug 1950; *m* 2 Aug 1969 *Ian D Doulton, yr s of Maj Peter Duke Doulton, RA, by Elizabeth, est dau of Francis Stewart Cokayne (*see* CULLEN OF ASHBOURNE, B), and has:

1b *David Peter Michael; *b* 1974; *m* 19– *Laura Ruth, yst dau of Dr Lloyd Caldwell, and has:

1c *Jack Peter; *b* 23 May 1998

2b *Jonathan Duke; *b* 1980

1b *Lucy Catherine; *b* 1971; *m* 31 Dec 1995 *Gavin Alan Tyte

2a *Rosemary Ann; *b* 11 Nov 1954; *m* 1981 *Cdr Robert Lincoln Guy, MVO, RN, and adopted:

*Laura Jade; *b* 8 Jan 1992

*Anna Caroline Sandy

3a *Frances Mary; *b* 17 July 1965

(1) (cont.) Michael Walker *m* 2nd 1978 *Anne Lavinia, er dau of Capt John Henderson, and by her has:

1a +John Michael; *b* 10 Sept 1979

2a +Andrew James; *b* 10 Sept 1979

3a +James; *b* 1980

4a *Ruth; *b* 19 April 1982

(1) *Diana Mary [Mrs Simon Turner, The Garden Cottage, Achnashellach, by Strathcarron, Ross-shire IV54 8YU]; *b* 20 Jan 1923; *m* 21 July 1969 Simon Neville Turner (*d* 20 July 1990), s of David Neville Turner, JP, of Walton Lodge, Chesterfield, Derbys

4 Patrick Bruce, MBE (1944); *b* 11 Sept 1898; *educ* Eton; Maj RA (TA) Italy WW II (despatches); *m* 19 June 1928 Sybil (*d* 1986), only dau of Charles Byron Turner, MRCS, of Ashby-cum-Fenby, Lincs, and *d* 1988, leaving:

(1) *Susan Anne Maud [The Hon Lady Butler, Penny Pot, Halstead, Essex CO9 1RY]; *b* 3 Aug 1930; *m* 5 July 1952 *Hon Sir Richard Clive Butler, est s of Baron Butler of Saffron Walden, KG, CH, PC (LP, *see* 1970 edn), and has:

1a *Richard Michael; *b* 29 May 1956; *m* 20 Oct 1984 *Christina Anne Blackwell and has:

1b *Richard Benjamin; *b* 23 Jan 1986

2b *Charles Robert; *b* 28 Sept 1987

1b *Rose Olivia; *b* 3 Oct 1993

2a *Christopher Patrick; *b* 29 May 1956; *m* 10 Sept 1983 *Tania Gaye Clarabut and has:

1b *David Mark; *b* 18 March 1987

1b *Anna Louise; *b* 9 Nov 1985

2b *Kimberley Jane; *b* 2 Dec 1988

1a *Antonia Mary; *b* 11 July 1954; *m* 1st 29 July 1978 Nicholas Lees; *m* 2nd 9 Dec 1983 *Timothy P Finch and by him has:

1b *Sophie Louise; *b* 19 Jan 1985

2b *Lucy Charlotte; *b* 15 July 1986

1 Cecily Etha Mary; *m* 30 Jan 1917 2nd Baron Cornwallis (*qv*) and *d* 10 Oct 1943, leaving issue

The 3rd Bt's est s,

Sir Robert James Milo Walker, 4th Bt; *b* 18 March 1890; *educ* Trin Coll Cambridge (MA); Maj Coldstream Grds; *m* 1st 5 June 1913 (*divorce* 1922) Emily Synolda (*d* 27 June 1975), yr dau of James Augustine Harvey Thursby Pelham, JP, DL, of Chelsea and Upton Cressett, Salop; *m* 2nd 23 Jan 1923 Esme Ethel Alice (*m* 2nd 26 Feb 1948 2nd Baron Cornwallis (*qv*) and *d* 5 June 1969), dau of Capt Grenville Montmorency d'Beaumont, 5th (Roy I) Lancers, and *d* 11 Feb 1930, leaving by his 1st w:

1 Sir JAMES HERON WALKER, **5th and present Bt**

2 Peter Arthur; *b* 7 Oct 1918; *educ* Eton; *d* 6 May 1994

WALKER OF DONCASTER

Creation: B. (LP, UK) 2 Aug 1997.

THE BARON WALKER OF DONCASTER, of Audenshaw, Co Gtr Manchester (Sir Harold Walker, PC (1979), DL (S Yorks 1997)) [The Rt Hon The Lord Walker of Doncaster PC DL, House of Lords, London SW1A 0PW]; *b* 12 July 1927; *educ* Manchester Tech; RN 1946–48; MP (Lab) Doncaster 1964–83, Doncaster Centl 1983–97; Assist Govt Whip 1967–68, Jt Parly U-Sec Employment and Productivity 1968–70, Oppn Spokesman: Industl Rels 1970–74, Employment 1979–83, Parly U-Sec Employment 1974–76, Min State Employment 1976–79; Chm Ways and Means and Dep Speaker H of C 1983–92, ktd 1992; *m* 1st 19– — and has a dau; *m* 2nd 1984 *Mary Griffin

Lineage: HAROLD WALKER; *m* Phyllis — and had:

HAROLD, *cr* a **Baron**

WALKER OF WORCESTER

Arms: Per pale sable and or semy of portcullises and three-turreted towers all counterchanged. **Crest:** Growing from a grassy mound proper, over which curls a footpath, a cedar tree all proper, irradiated or. **Supporters:** Dexter, a dragon gules; sinister, a sea lion proper, the head and mane or, supporting a trident also proper, a compartment per bend dexter a grassy mound, growing therefrom red and yellow cowslips all proper, sinister water barry-wavy azure and argent, over all in bend a footpath proper. **Motto:** *Diligentia cum humanitate* ('Diligence with humanity'). **Creation:** B. (LP, UK) 1992.

THE BARON WALKER OF WORCESTER, of Abbots Morton, Co Hereford and Worcester (Peter Edward Walker, MBE (1960), PC (1970)) [The Rt Hon The Lord Walker of Worcester MBE PC, Abbots Morton Manor, Gooms Hill, Worcs WR7 4LT]; *b* 25 March 1932; *educ* Latymer Upper Sch; Memb Nat Exec C Party 1956–70, Nat Chm YCs 1958–60, MP (C) Worcester 1961–92, PPS to Leader H of C 1963–64, Oppn Spokesman: Fin and Ec matters 1964–66, Tport 1966–68, Local Govt, Housing and Land 1968–70, Trade, Industry and Consumer Affrs 1974, Defence 1974–75, Min Housing and Local Govt 1970, Sec State: Environment 1970–72, Trade and Industry 1972–74, MAFF 1979–83, Energy 1983–87, Wales 1987–90; a fndr Slater-Walker, chm: Walker Young & Co, Thornton Gp 1991–97, Cornhill Insur 1992–, Kleinwort Benson 1997– and Carlton Club; dir: MCC to 1991, Worcester Gp, Tate & Lyle 1990–, Smith New Court 1990–95, Dalgety 1990–96, Br Gas 1990–96, LIFFE 1995–; author: *The Ascent of Britain* (1977), *Trust The People* (1987), *Staying Power* (1991); *m* 1969 *Tessa, dau of Geoffrey Ivan Prout, and has:

1 *Jonathan Peter; *b* 1970; *educ* St Paul's and Balliol Coll Oxford

2 *Timothy Rupert; *b* 1975; *educ* St Paul's and Exeter U

3 *Robin Caspar; *b* 1978; *educ* St Paul's and Balliol Coll Oxford

1 *Shara Jane; *b* 1971; *educ* Francis Holland Sch and BNC Oxford

2 *Marianna Clare; *b* 1985; *educ* Francis Holland Sch

Lineage: SYDNEY WALKER; *m* Rose — and had:

PETER EDWARD, *cr* a **Baron**

WALKER-OKEOVER

Arms: Quarterly, 1st and 4th, erm. on a chief gu. three bezants (for OKEOVER); 2nd and 3rd, or three pallets gu. surmounted of a saltire arg. charged with a stag's head erased ppr., on a chief az. a garb between two stars of six points of the first (for WALKER).
Crests: 1 On a wreath or and gu. an oak tree eradicated ppr., fructed or, mantled gu., doubled arg., 2 Out of a ducal coronet or a demi-dragon erm., armed az., langued gu., mantled gu., doubled arg. (for OKEOVER), 3 A cornucopia ppr. (for WALKER).
Motto: *Esto vigilans* ('Be vigilant'). **Creation:** Bt. (UK) 12 Feb 1886.

SIR PETER RALPH LEOPOLD WALKER-OKEOVER, 4TH BT, of Gateacre, Co Lancaster, and Osmaston Manor, Co Derby, DL (Staffs 1992) [Sir Peter Walker-Okeover Bt DL, Okeover Hall, Ashbourne, Derbyshire DE6 2DE; House of Glenmuick, Ballater, Aberdeenshire]; *b* 22 July 1947 (HM LEOPOLD III OF THE BELGIANS stood sponsor); *s* f 1982; *educ* Eton and RMA Sandhurst; late Capt Blues and Royals; *m* 4 Feb 1972 (*divorce* 1991) Catherine Mary Maule, est dau of Col George Patrick Maule Ramsay (*see* DALHOUSIE, E); *m* 2nd 1993 *Patricia Margaret Sevier, er dau of Laurance Sanderson, and by his 1st w has:

1 +ANDREW PETER MONRO; *b* 22 May 1978
2 +(Patrick) Ralph; *b* 6 May 1982
1 *Georgina Elizabeth; *b* 30 March 1976

Lineage (of Walker): ANDREW WALKER, of Bonville House, Mary Hill, nr Glasgow; *m* Agnes Hart and had:

PETER WALKER, of Auchinflower, Ayrshire, and Warrington, Lancs, *b* 1795, *m* 1820 Mary (*d* 4 Nov 1846), est dau of Arthur Carlaw, of Ayr, and *d* 15 Nov 1879, leaving, with other issue:

Sir Andrew Barclay Walker, 1st Bt (UK), so *cr* 12 Feb 1886, JP Ayrshire, DL Lancs; *b* 15 Dec 1824; Mayor Liverpool 1873–74 and 1876–77, High Sheriff 1886, ktd 1877, *m* 1st 16 June 1853 Eliza (*d* 20 March 1882), est dau of John Reid, of Limekilns, Fife, and had:

1 PETER CARLAW (Sir), **2nd Bt**
2 John Reid, TD, JP Staffs; *b* 4 June 1855; High Sheriff Salop 1917–18, Hon Col 4th Bn S Lancs Regt; *m* 14 Oct 1885 Katharine Howard (*d* 21 May 1945), yst dau of John Cartland, of The Priory, King's Heath, Worcs, and *d* 6 March 1934, leaving:

(1) John Vincent Reid; *b* 18 Nov 1893; *educ* Harrow; *d* 1974
(2) Codrington Gwynne Reid; *b* 3 Jan 1895; *educ* Harrow; RFA WW I, RAF WW II, High Sheriff Salop 1949; *m* 3 Nov 1921 Gwendolen Phyllis (*d* 1974), yr dau of James Monro Walker (*see* below), and *d* 29 July 1963, having had:

1a Giles Reid, *b* 7 April 1925, *m* 1 June 1949 *Catherine Elaine [Mrs Patrick Hall, Cae Grugog, Trearddur Bay, Holyhead, Anglesey LL65 2UD], LRAM (*m* 2nd 14 June 1955 Patrick Campbell Hall, BA, MA (Oxon) (*d* 20 Dec 1997), *s* of John Hall, of Charnes Hall, Eccleshall, Staffs), yr dau of Maj Charles Edward Hickman (*see* HICKMAN, Bt), and was *k* in a car crash 31 Aug 1951, leaving:

1b *Gilean Phyllis, *b* posthumously 20 Sept 1951
1a *Jean Reid [Mrs Nicholas Knoop, Ville ès Normans South, Trinity, Jersey, CI JE3 5DE]; *b* 1922; WRNS 1942–45; *m* 3 June 1949 *Nicholas Knoop, BSc, FICE, late S/Ldr RAFVR, yr s of Baron John Knoop, of Langford, BC, Canada, late of Moscow, and has:

1b *Alexander Jonathan; *b* 20 June 1951; *educ* Harrow; *m* 1988 *Cheryl, dau of Achilles George, of New York
1b *Sandra [Mrs Jean-Paul Vonrospach, 11 rue des Etats, 54000 Nancy, France]; *b* 5 April 1950; *m* 1973 *Jean-Paul Vonrospach and has:

1c *Alexander Kerry; *b* 1982
2c *Melany Claire; *b* 1980

(1) Violet Eliza Reid; *b* 14 May 1887; *m* 28 Oct 1918 Brig-Gen Reginald Hoare, CMG, DSO, 4th Hus (*d* 14 Oct 1947), s of Thomas Rolls Hoare, and *d* 1 Oct 1966, leaving:

1a *Reginald Arthur Reid [Maj Reginald Hoare, 53 Geffries House, London Rd, Hook, Hants]; *b* 5 Jan 1920; *m* 1st 19– (*divorce*) Lucy Myrtel Corbett-Winder (*d* Sept 1990) and has:

1b *Patrick Reginald Andrew Reid (Rev) [The Rev Patrick Hoare, Leake Vicarage, Knayton, N Yorks YO7 4AZ]; *b* 22 Nov 1947; *m* 19– *Nicola, dau of Maj John Mangles, and has:

1c *Poppy; *b* 8 Oct 1969
2c *Brioni; *b* 11 Dec 1970
3c *Sorrel; *b* 11 Sept 1984

1b *Katherine Roberta [Mrs John Dyson, 26 The Terrace, London SW13]; *b* 1941; *m* 19– *John Dyson and has:

1c *John; *b* 19–
1c *Jemima; *b* 19–
2c *Jennifer; *b* 19–
3c *Kimia; *b* 19–

1a (cont.) Maj Reginald Hoare *m* 2nd 19– *Dorothy Mary Blin, dau of Herbert Blin Stoyle, of Kenya, and has:

2b *Anne Violet; *b* 21 July 1956
3b *Elizabeth Jean; *b* 24 Feb 1959

2a John Nigel; *b* 7 July 1923; *m* 19– *Edith Cunnigham and was *ka* Malaya Nov 1949, leaving:

1b *Nicholas; *b* 19–
1b *Caroline; *b* 19–; *m* 19– *— Bell
2b *Camilla; *b* 19–; *m* 19– *Capt K Lindsay

3a Robin Cecil; *b* 25 March 1927; *d* 1989
1a *Katherine Rosemary [Mrs Raymond Daniels, Landsker, Wood Village, Newgate, Pembs SA62 6AR]; *b* 30 April 1930; *m* 1st 19– (*divorce*) David Hodges; *m* 2nd 19– *Raymond Daniels and by her 1st husb has:

1b *John; *b* 21 May 1955
1b *Susan; *b* 1 July 1953; *m* 19– *Alberto Fioretti and has:

1c *Luca; *b* 29 Dec 1993
1c *Julia; *b* 13 Feb 1991

(2) Katharine Monica; *m* 15 April 1921 Lt-Col Dennis Coleridge Boles, RHG and 17th Lancers, MP Wells (*d* 25 April 1958), est s of Francis James Coleridge Boles, JP, of Redcliffe, Exmouth, Devon, and *d* Jan 1971, leaving:

1a Kenneth Coleridge; *b* 1922; Capt Gren Gds WW II; *m* 1948 (*divorce* 1958) Gian Laurian, dau of Capt Laurence Reynolds Palmer, DSO, RN, and *d* 1974, leaving:

1b *Nicholas Coleridge; *b* 20 May 1952; *educ* Eton
2b *Julian Coleridge; *b* 1954

2a Vernon Coleridge; *b* 4 April 1926; late RN; *m* 28 Jan 1956 *Elizabeth [Mrs Vernon Boles, Old Clune, Tomatin, Inverness IV13 7XZ], dau of William James Spence-Thomas, of Caepwcella, Shirenewton, Gwent, and *d* 17 Jan 1997, leaving:

1b *Timothy Coleridge; *b* 27 Nov 1958; *educ* Eton
1b *Olivia Catherine Ann; *b* 19 Dec 1959; *m* 1990 *Neville Hill Archer and has:

1c *James Coleridge Hill; *b* 5 July 1995

1a *Virginia Ann; *b* 1928; *m* 5 April 1965 Lt-Col Christopher D'Arcy Preston Consett, DSO, MC, KRRC (ret) (*d* March 1998), 2nd s of R-Adml Montagu William Warcop Peter Consett, CMG, JP, DL, of Brawith Hall, Thirsk, Yorks

3 WILLIAM HALL WALKER, 1st and last BARON WAVERTREE, of Delamere, Co Chester (UK), so *cr* 27 Oct 1919, TD, DL Lancs and Denbighs; *b* 25 Dec 1856; Hon Col W Lancs Div Engrs (TA) and RA Special Res, MP Widnes 1900–19, KGStJ; *m* 29 Sept 1896 Sophie Florence Lothrop, CBE (1918), DGStJ (*m* 2nd 1947 Francis Marion Bates Fisher (*d* 23 July 1960), of Makona, Ngongotaha, Rotorua, NZ, s of George Fisher, MP, FRSS, Italian Consul Wellington, and *d* 27 Nov 1952), yr dau of Algernon Thomas Brinsley Sheridan, JP, DL, of Frampton Court, Dorset, and *dsp* 2 Feb 1933, when the Barony expired

4 Arthur Carlaw, of Meadhill, Torquay; *b* 4 May 1859; *m* 1885 Mary Elizabeth (*d* 5 Oct 1900), dau of J W Ellison, CE, and *d* 13 Aug 1907, leaving:

(1) Peter Arthur Carlaw; *b* 1887; Lt Derbys Yeo; *d* unm 14 Sept 1914
(2) William Barclay Carlaw; *b* 1893; *d* 29 April 1954
(1) Ethel Carlaw; *m* 19 Oct 1910 John Balfour Caldwell, of Cariboo, BC, and had:

1a *Michael; *b c* 1915
1a *Margaret; *b c* 1917
2a *Molly; *b c* 1918; *m c* 1942
3a *Mary; *b c* 1920

5 Andrew Barclay; *b* 24 June 1865; *educ* Jesus Coll Cambridge (BA); Lt Lancs Hus, KGStJ; *m* 10 April 1895 Edith Marianne (judicial separation 1898 and *d* 2 Feb 1939), widow of John Robert Aitchison, and *d* March 1930

6 James Monro; *b* 26 Dec 1866; Lt Lancs Hus; *m* 1st 9 Aug 1893 (*divorce* 1900) Emily Eileen (*d* July 1943), only dau of Henry Hodgson Bardswell, of Southport, and had:

(1) Doris Eileen; *b* 1893; *m* 1st 21 May 1914 (*divorce* 1933) Lt-Col William Lewis Clark Kirby, DSO, OBE, 12th Roy Lancers (*d* 12 Feb 1962), s of William Kirby, FRGS; *m* 2nd 1 June 1933 Herbert Geoffry Burton (*d* 21 Feb 1968), s of Herbert Burton, of Fallgates, Linton-on-Ouse, Yorks, and *d* 1984
(2) Gwendolen Phyllis; *b* 9 Aug 1895; *m* 3 Nov 1921 Codrington Gwynne Reid Walker (*see* above) and *d* 1974, leaving issue

6 (cont.) James Walker *m* 2nd 14 Oct 1902 Gladys (*d* 21 June 1915), yst dau of Humphrey Brooke Firman, of Gateforth, Yorks; *m* 3rd 12 Feb 1917 Eleanor Hilda Jane (*d c* 1940), yst dau of Frederick Nicholas Cunningham, of Southsea, Hants, and *d* 24 June 1920

1 Mary Carlaw, JP; *b* 20 March 1858; *m* 17 Jan 1883 William Roylance Court, JP (*d* 18 May 1917), of Manor House, Middlewich, Cheshire, and *d* 17 Dec 1933, having had:

(1) William Hubert Roylance; *b* 1885; *ka* 1915

(1) Evelyn Roylance; *b c* 1884; *m* 1912 Brig-Gen Stuart Peter Rolt and *d* 1941, leaving:

  1a Anthony Peter Roylance; *b* 1918; POW June 1940; *m* 19– Lois Allan and had:

    1b *Stuart; *m* 19– *Debbie Butler

    2b *David; *m* 19– *Jade —

    1b *Angela; *m* 19– *Antony Thompson

    2b *Nikki; *m* 19– *Steven —

  1a Pamela; *b* 1913; *m* 1939 Richard Gaynor, RAF, and *d* 1985, leaving:

    1b *Robert; has, with other issue:

      1c *Oliver; *b* 19–

      2c *Harry; *b* 19–

    1b *Caroline Susan Verney; *b* 23 April 1941; *m* 19– *John Reid and has:

      1c *Peter; *b* 19–

      1c *Suzanne; *b* 19–

      2c *Katrina; *b* 19–

      3c *Amanda; *b* 19–

    2b *Alice; *m* 19– *Ross Mills and has:

      1c *William; *b* 19–

      1c *Lucy; *b* 19–

      2c *Sophia; *b* 19–

  2a *Suzanne Phyllis [Mrs Peter Vaux, The Flat, Brettanby Manor, Barton, N Yorks]; *b* 1915; *m* 1938 *Peter Vaux, RAF, and has:

    1b *Peter Roylance; *b* 25 Sept 1939

    2b Anthony; *b* 1 Feb 1941; *d* 1961

    1b *Jennifer; *b* 19–; *m*

    2b *Diana; *b* 19–; *m*

  3a *Sybil Mary; *b* 1917; *m* 1st 1939 Michael Mosley, RAF, and has:

    1b *Amanda Wendy; *b* 21 June 1941

    2b *Gail; *b* 1943

  3a (cont.) Mrs Mosley *m* 2nd 19– *Stanford Smith and by him has:

    3b *Tessa; *b* 1945

    4b *Kim; *b* 194–

(2) Dorothy Allen Roylance; *b* 188–; *m* 19– Lt-Col Douglas Hervey-Talbot, DSO, 17/21st Lancers (*d* 1927), and had:

  1a *Brian Harvey; *m* March 1940 Katherine Hughes (*d* 1978) and has:

    1b *Andrew; *b* 19–

    1b *Mary Louise; *b* 1941

    2b *Wendy; *b* 19–

2 Ethel Lisette; *b* 29 Sept 1872; *m* 3 Feb 1897 9th Earl of Kingston (*qv*) and *d* 18 April 1949, leaving issue

Sir Andrew *m* 2nd 11 Oct 1887 Hon Maude Okeover (*m* 2nd 30 July 1895 Lt-Col John Frederick Lort Phillips, JP, DL (*d* 15 May 1926), of Lawrenny Park, Pembs, and *d* 1 May 1943), Maid of Honour to HM QUEEN VICTORIA and 2nd dau of Haughton Charles Okeover (*see* below), and *d* 27 Feb 1893

His est s,

  Sir Peter Carlaw Walker, 2nd Bt, TD, JP, DL Derbys, DL Lancs; *b* 7 May 1854; High Sheriff Derbys 1896, Lt-Col and Hon Col Derbys Yeo; *m* 30 May 1899 Ethel Blanche (*d* 17 March 1935), dau of Haughton Charles Okeover (*see* below), and *d* 18 Oct 1915, leaving, with a dau (Enid, *b* 5 July 1900, *m* 1st 1928 Count Cosmo Diodono de Bosdari and had issue, *m* 2nd 7 Feb 1958 Bernard H Lofts-Constable, *d* 1988):

  Sir IAN PETER ANDREW MONRO WALKER later WALKER-OKEOVER (roy licence 20 Aug 1956 on inheriting property through his mother), **3rd Bt**, DSO and bar (1945), TD; *b* 30 Nov 1902; *educ* Eton and Ch Ch Oxford; Hon Attaché Brussels 1925–26, served WW II, Jt MFH Meynell 1937–49, Derbys: JP 1932, High Sheriff 1934, Ld Lt 1951–82 (DL 1948–51), Lt-Col (Hon Col 1951) cmdg Yeo; memb Roy Co Archers, OStJ 1974; *m* 28 June 1938 *Dorothy Elizabeth [Elizabeth Lady Walker-Okeover, Park Cottage, Osmaston, Derbys DE6 ILT], yr dau of Capt Josceline Reginald Heber-Percy (*see* NORTHUMBERLAND, D), and *d* 20 Feb 1982, leaving:

  1 Sir PETER RALPH LEOPOLD WALKER-OKEOVER, **4th and present Bt**

  1 *(Elizabeth) Anne; *b* 4 July 1940, *m* 20 Dec 1969 *Lt-Cdr Timothy William Clowes, RN (ret), est s of Cdr William Josceline Clowes, RN, of Cubley Cottage, Cubley, Derbys, and has:

    (1) *Catriona Helen; *b* 1971

    (2) *Sophie Fiona; *b* 1974

  2 *Jane Katharine; *b* 2 Nov 1942

Lineage (of Okeover): ORMUS HELSWEYN or HALESOEN *alias* ORME de ACOVERE (Okeover) (possibly s of Eddulph, the Domesday tenant of Okeover); living 1089–1138; enfeoffed of Okeover by Abbot Nigel of Burton-on-Trent by 1113; also tenant of Tutbury Priory; had:

RALPH fitz ORMUS, of Okeover and Stretton, Staffs, and Callow, Derbys (by grant of Robert, Earl Ferrers; *see* FERRERS, E, and DERBY, E, preliminary remarks); granted an hereditary feoffment of Okeover and Stretton by Robert, Abbot of Burton, *c* 1150, *m* 1st Lettice (who brought as her dowry the manor of Snelston, Derbys), sis of Walter de Montgomery, of Cubley, leaving, with a s (Richard, *m* Margaret, dau of Robert de Waterfall, and *dsp* by 1204) and dau (Alice); *m* 2nd a dau of Robert de Blore and by her had, with a yst s (Geoffrey, *m* Matilda — and had a s, Ralph):

Sir HUGH OKEOVER, of Okeover and Stretton, Staffs; bought 1189 the Manor of Shene, Staffs, from Bertram de Verdun; had, with another s (Hugh):

Sir ROBERT OKEOVER, of Okeover; *m* 1196 Sarra, dau of Sir John de Chandos by Margery, dau and coheir of Robert fitz Walkeline (from whom the OKEOVERs probably held the manor of Atlow) and in or after 1241, leaving, with two other sons (Hugh, *dsp* 1242; Robert, granted Wetton, Staffs, *m* Margery — and had two sons (William, of Stretton; Robert, of Mayfield, Staffs, living 1275) and two daus (Agatha, *m* Wiger de Dive; Joan, *m* William de Stratton)):

Sir HUGH OKEOVER, of Okeover and Stretton; High Sheriff Salop and Staffs 1256–57; had:

Sir ROBERT OKEOVER, of Okeover; living between 1269 and 1282; had:

JOHN OKEOVER, of Okeover; living between 1282 and 1293, *m* Margaret, dau of Sir Henry Fitzherbert, of Norbury (*see* STAFFORD, B), and had:

Sir ROGER OKEOVER, of Okeover; under age 1293; took part in rebellion of Earl of Lancaster 1322 and had to compound for his estates with Hugh le Despenser, Earl of Winchester (*see* FALMOUTH, V); one of the kts of Staffs summoned to attend the King on his expdn to Guienne 1324; Commr of Array Derbys for the Scottish campaign 1333, 1334 and 1335; *m* Christian, dau and heiress of Engelhard de Atlow, of Atlow, and *d* by April 1338, leaving:

Sir THOMAS OKEOVER, of Okeover, *d* by June 1372, leaving:

Sir PHILIP OKEOVER, JP (Derbys 1390), of Okeover; living between 1372 and 1399; served Gascony 1370 and in Spain with DUKE OF LANCASTER 1386–87, MP Derbys 1381 and 1391; *m* 1st Alice — and had issue; *m* 2nd Elizabeth, dau of 1st Lord (Baron) Grey (of Ruthin) (*see* GREY, B), and by his 1st w had:

THOMAS OKEOVER, of Okeover, MP Derbys 1407 and 1421, *m* 1st Margaret, dau of John Curzon (*see* SCARSDALE, V); *m* 2nd Thomasine, widow of George de Sallowe, and *d* 4 Jan 1460, having had:

THOMAS OKEOVER; *dvp* 1439, leaving:

PHILIP OKEOVER, of Okeover; High Sheriff Notts and Derbys 1464–65 and 1473; *m* 1439 Thomasine, dau of Sir Ralph Basset, and had, with two other sons and a dau (Elizabeth, *m* Ralph Burton, of Mayfield and Fauld, Staffs):

RALPH OKEOVER, of Okeover; High Sheriff Staffs 1490, *m* Agnes, dau of John Bradburne, of Bradburne, Derbys, and *d* 9 Oct 1495, leaving:

HUMPHREY OKEOVER, of Okeover; *m* Isabella, dau of John Aston, of Tixall, and *d* 5 April 1538, having had, with an er s (Ralph, *dvp*) a yst s (Nicholas, of Sturton, Derbys) and three daus (Jane, *m* John Pole, of Hartington, Derbys, and *d* 3 Feb 1524; Elizabeth, *m* Philip Leech, of Chatsworth, Derbys; Margaret, *m* John Parker, of Norton Lees, Derbys; *see* PARKER, Bt, of Shenstone Lodge):

PHILIP OKEOVER; *m* 1508 Elizabeth, dau of Thomas Babington, of Dethick, and *dvp* 1536, leaving:

  1 Ralph, of Okeover; *b* 1524; High Sheriff Derbys 1564; *m* 1st 1534 Matilda, dau of Sir William Basset, of Blore, Staffs, and had four daus; *m* 2nd Catherine, widow of Henry Leigh, of Rushall, Staffs, and dau of Sir John Dunham, of Kirtlington, Notts, and *d* 29 March 1571, having by her had another dau

  2 Philip, of Okeover; High Sheriff Derbys 1585; *m* Margaret, widow of Thomas Finden, of Finden, and dau of William Dethick, of Newhall, and *d* 1604, leaving:

    (1) Jane; *m* 1st Thomas Cokayne (probably one of the COKAYNEs of Derbys; *see* CULLEN OF ASHBOURNE, B, with whom, however, no precise kinship has been established); *m* 2nd Sir Anthony Ashley, 1st Bt (*see* SHAFTESBURY, E), and had issue

  3 ROWLAND

  1 Elizabeth, *m* John Dethick, of Newhall, Derbys

The 3rd s,

ROWLAND OKEOVER, of Okeover; *m* 1st Sibyl, dau of Henry White, of London and Bristol, and had four sons and three daus; *m* 2nd Anne (*m* 3rd Sir Oliver Cheyney), widow of — Needham, and *d* 7 May 1610, leaving by her:

HUMPHREY OKEOVER, of Okeover, High Sheriff Derbys 1631; *b* 1609; *m* Martha, dau of Sir Oliver Cheyney, and *d* 30 Dec 1639, having had, with three yr sons and four daus:

Sir ROWLAND OKEOVER, of Okeover; *b* 19 July 1624; MP Staffs 1683; *m* Mercy, dau of Edmund Goodyere, of Heythrop, Oxon, and *d* 1692, having had, with two daus:

  1 Humphrey; *b* 29 May 1648; *dvp*

  2 Rowland, of Okeover; *b* 21 Sept 1651; High Sheriff Derbys 1703; *m* Elizabeth (*d* Oct 1705), only surv child and heiress of Sir Thomas Pettus, 2nd Bt, of Rackheath, Norfolk, and *d* 1730, having had, with other issue:

    (1) Thomas; *b* 28 March 1679; High Sheriff Derbys 1703; *m* Catherine (*d* 1713), dau and heiress of William Leake, Baron of the Exchequer, and *dvp* 1710, leaving:

      1a Leake, of Okeover; *b* 1701; *m* Mary (*d* 1764), dau of John Nichol, and *dsp* 31 Jan 1765

      2a William; barrister; *dsp* Sept 1748

      1a Elizabeth; *b* 1703; *m* 1st Thomas Hollingshead; *m* 2nd — Higginbotham; *m* 3rd — Yeomans and *dsp* 1774

      2a Catherine; *m* Edward Wilson, of Cannock, Staffs, and had:

        1b Catherine; *m* Morton Walhouse, of Hatherton, Staffs, and had:

          1c Edward WALHOUSE later OKEOVER (assumed with arms on inheriting the estates), of Okeover; High Sheriff Derbys 1779; *m* Margaret, dau of William Bowyer, and *dsp* 30 June 1793

    3 Henry; *b* 28 Jan 1654

    4 Thomas, of Tilney St Laurence; *b* 10 Jan 1657; *m* Elizabeth, dau of John Farmer, of Oldbury, Warwicks, and *d* 1705, having had, with five daus:

      (1) Rowland, of Oldbury; *m* 1st Patience (*dsps* 25 July 1741), dau of Matthew Farmer, of Atherstone; *m* 2nd Alice, dau of John Gregory, and *d* 1761, having had:

        1a Rowland Farmer; *b* 1745; *m* 1st Bridget (*d* 1784), dau of James Haughton Langston, banker, of London, and had:

          1b Haughton Farmer, of Okeover; *b* 7 Sept 1776; High Sheriff 1800; *dsp* 18 July 1836

          2b Rowland; *d* at Eton 16 Nov 1792

        1a (cont.) Rowland Okeover *m* 2nd Judith, widow of John Holden, of Sheepy, Leics, and dau of William Robinson, of Hill Redware, Staffs, and *d* 3 Jan 1793, leaving by her:

          3b Charles Gregory (Rev); *b* 11 May 1792; *m* 17 Sept 1823 Mary Anne (*m* 2nd 14 Feb 1833 Robert Plumer Ward, of Gilston Park, Herts, and *d*

1875), est dau of Gen Sir George Anson, GCB, MP (*see* LICHFIELD, E), and *d* 2 Aug 1826, having had:

1c Haughton Charles, of Okeover (in which *s* his uncle Haughton Farmer Okeover), JP Staffs and Derbys, DL Warwicks; *b* 13 Nov 1825; High Sheriff Derbys 1862, *m* 12 July 1859 Hon Eliza Ann Cavendish (*d* 11 Dec 1921), er dau of 3rd Baron Waterpark (*qv*), and *d* 20 Oct 1912, having had issue:

1d Haughton Ealdred, MVO (1901), of Okeover, JP (Derbys 1900 and Staffs 1917); *b* 10 May 1875; *educ* Harrow; Capt 4th N Midland Ammunition Column 4th N Midland (Howitzer) Bde RAF (TF) 1908–09, 6th Bn Sherwood Foresters (Notts and Derby Regt) 1914, High Sheriff Derbys 1928, Chev Ordre du Mérite Agricole France; *m* 2 March 1922 Anne Wilberforce (*d* 9 Dec 1967), yst dau of Joseph Simpson, of Mayfield, Staffs, and *dsp* 22 Jan 1955, when the Okeover estate passed to his n **Sir Ian Walker, 3rd Bt** (*see* above)

1d Mabel Alice; *d unm* 21 July 1938

2d Maude; Maid of Honour to HM QUEEN VICTORIA; *m* 1st 11 Oct 1887, as his 2nd w, **Sir Andrew Barclay Walker, 1st Bt** (*see* above); *m* 2nd 30 July 1895 John Frederick Lort Phillips and *dsp* 1 May 1943

3d Ruth Isabel; *m* 3 Nov 1903 Major Sir Hervey Ronald Bruce, 5th Bt, of Downhill (*qv*), and *dsp* 27 Sept 1915

4d Edith Mary; *m* 11 Aug 1891 Capt Hon Herbert Tongue Allsopp, s of 1st Baron Hindlip (*qv*), and *d* 4 Sept 1935, leaving issue

5d Ethel Blanche; *m* 30 May 1899 **Sir Peter Carlaw Walker, 2nd Bt**, and *d* 17 March 1935, leaving issue (*see* above)

6d Mercy Lilian; *m* 20 July 1897 Hon Assheton Nathaniel Curzon and *d* 16 Oct 1936, having had issue (*see* SCARSDALE, V)

7d Mary Beatrice; *d* 13 Jan 1889

8d Victoria Alexandrina; *m* 19 Nov 1907 George Moreton Buckston, of Sutton-on-the-Hill and Bradbourne Hall, Ashbourne, Derbys, and *d* 2 Nov 1960, leaving issue. He *d* 24 Nov 1942

1c Mary Anne; *d unm* 6 Feb 1842

WALKER-SMITH

Arms: Quarterly, 1st and 4th, per fess or and arg. a portcullis sa. throughout, raised to the nombril point within a bordure per fess gu. and or, charged with ten acorns counter coloured (for SMITH); 2nd and 3rd, per pale az. and gu. a horse passant arg., hooved and crined or, between three caltrops gold (for WALKER). **Crests:** 1 Out of a mural crown gu., masoned or, a mount vert, thereon a lion statant arg., holding in the dexter forepaw an oak branch fructed gold (for SMITH), 2 Between two ostrich feathers gu., quilled or, a leg in armour az., garnished gold (for WALKER). **Motto:** *Lege et luce* ('By law and light'). **Creation:** Bt. (UK) 18 Aug 1960.

SIR (JOHN) JONAH WALKER-SMITH, 2ND BT, of Broxbourne, Co Hertford [The Hon Sir Jonah Walker-Smith Bt, 11 Doughty St, London WC1N 2PG]; *b* 6 Sept 1939; *s* f 1992; *educ* Westminster and Ch Ch Oxford; barrister Middle Temple 1963, Crown Court Recorder 1980–; *m* 26 Oct 1974 *Aileen Marie, only dau of Joseph Smith, of Glasgow, and has:

1 +DANIEL DEREK; *b* 26 March 1980

1 *Charmian Lucinda; *b* 1977

Lineage: JOHN JONAH SMITH, of Watford, Herts; *b* 18 June 1840; *m* Jane Elizabeth (*d* 20 Nov 1928), dau of William Watson, of Watford, and *d* 1915, leaving, with an est s (William Sydney, *d unm*) and three yst sons (Percy Watson, *d unm*; George Alfred, *d* 1958, leaving three sons and a dau; Frederick John, *dsp* 1941), a 2nd s:

JONAH SMITH WALKER SMITH later WALKER-SMITH (deed poll 12 Feb 1934) (Sir); *b* 1 Nov 1874; Controller Housing and Town Planning Local Govt Bd Scotland 1910–19, Dir Housing Min Health 1919–25, barrister Gray's Inn 1922, ktd 1925, MP Barrow-in-Furness 1931–45, MICE, MIMechE, FRICS, Hon ARIBA; *m* 27 April 1905 Maud Coulton (*d* 29 Dec 1966), dau of Coulton Walker Hunter, of Barrow-in-Furness and Barton Hall, Yorks, and *d* 23 Feb 1964, leaving:

1 *Coulton Walker; *b* 13 Sept 1908; *m* 5 Nov 1946 *Joan, dau of Eric Blyth, of Paddington, and has:

(1) *Michael Anthony; *b* 14 June 1947; *educ* Malvern and Pembroke Coll Cambridge

(1) *Carol Louise; *b* 5 April 1951

(2) *Emma Jane Nicole; *b* 12 March 1968

2 DEREK COLCLOUGH (Sir), **1st Bt**

1 Joan Coulton; *b* 28 Feb 1906; *m* 1st 25 April 1935 Maj John St Ledger Thornton (*ka* 18 Aug 1944), s of Rev Canon Claud Thornton, Archdeacon Richmond, Yorks, and had issue; *m* 2nd 10 July 1947 Maurice Campbell Hanna, s of Maurice Hanna, of CP, S Africa, and was *k* in a car crash 28 Feb 1961

The 2nd s,

Sir Derek Colclough Walker-Smith, 1st Bt, and BARON BROXBOURNE (both UK), so *cr* 18 Aug 1960 and 1983 respectively, PC (1957), TD; *b* 13 April 1910; *educ* Rossall and Ch Ch Oxford (BA 1931); barrister Middle Temple 1934, QC 1955, Lt-Col RA (TA) WW II, MP (C) Hertford 1945–55 and Herts E 1955–64, Chm 1922 Ctee 1951–55, C Advsy Ctee Local Govt 1954–55, Parly Sec BOT 1955–56, Ec Sec Treasury 1956–57, Min State BOT Jan–Sept 1957, Min Health 1957–60, memb C working party reform Ho Lds 1977, Legn Hon; *m* 26 May 1938 *Dorothy [The Rt Hon The Lady Broxbourne, 7 Kepplestone, King Edward's Pde, Eastbourne, E Sussex BN20 7JY], only dau of Capt Louis John Walpole Etherton, of Rowlands Castle, Hants, and *d* 1992, when the Barony expired, leaving:

1 Sir (JOHN) JONAH WALKER-SMITH, **2nd and present Bt**

1 *Deborah Susan [The Hon Mrs Sinclair-Stevenson, 3 South Terrace, London SW7 2TB]; *b* 15 June 1941; *m* 10 June 1965 *Christopher Terence Sinclair-Stevenson, publisher, s of George Sinclair-Stevenson, of Hong Kong

2 *Berenice Mary [The Hon Mrs Weston, 7 Royal Arcade, Albemarle St, London W1X 3HD]; *b* 25 June 1946; *m* 1 July 1967 *William Andrew Weston, s of William Guy Weston, CMG, of Wyfold Grange, nr Reading

WALLACE OF COSLANY

Arms: Or a turkey oak tree eradicated vert, in base a portcullis chained orlewise azure, on a chief of the last a representation of Norwich Castle argent, masoned proper, its portal or closed by a portcullis azure, all between in the flanks two roses gules, barbed, seeded, stalked and leaved proper. **Crest:** Statant within a chaplet of turkey oak vert a lion in trian aspect gules, head, mane and tail tufts or, supporting the shaft of a spear gules, headed or, pendant therefrom on a crossbar by a cord azure and or a gonfalon of the arms. **Supporters:** Dexter, a horse argent; sinister, a lion or, head and mane gules; each rampant on a hillock of two grassy mounts, the innermost higher than the other, both within a circular wall proper, masoned or, growing from the dexter hillock between two double roses argent upon gules an oak sprig proper, fructed or, and from the sinister hillock between two like oak sprigs another double rose, argent upon gules, all three roses barbed, seeded, stalked and leaved proper. **Motto:** *Usque ad finem* ('Right on to the end'). **Creation:** B. (LP, UK) 1974.

THE BARON WALLACE OF COSLANY, of Coslany in the City of Norwich (George Douglas Wallace, JP, DL) [The Rt Hon The Lord Wallace of Coslany JP DL, 44 Shuttle Close, Sidcup, Kent DA15 8EP]; *b* 18 April 1906; *educ* Cheltenham Centl Sch; Sgt RAF WWII; MP (Lab) Chislehurst 1945–50, Norwich N 1964–74, Jr Govt Whip 1947–50, memb Kent CC 1952–57, PPS to: Ld Pres Cncl 1964–66 and Cwlth Sec 1966–67, Min State Housing and Local Govt 1967–68, memb Speaker's Panel of Chairmen 1970–74, Del Cncl Europe and WEU 1975–77, Govt Whip Ho Lds 1977–79, Oppn Spokesman and Whip Ho Lds 1979–86; memb: Cwlth Parly Assoc, Cwlth War Graves Commn 1970–86; Pres: Radio Soc GB 1977, Friends of Queen Mary's Hosp Sidcup; *m* 1932 *Vera, dau of William Joseph Randall, of Guildford, Surrey, and has:

1 *Michael George [The Hon Michael Wallace, 17 Leamington Ave, Orpington, Kent]; *b* 1944; *m* 1974 *Susan, dau of Henry William Price, of Orpington, and has issue

1 *Elizabeth Anne [The Hon Elizabeth Wallace, 44 Shuttle Close, Sidcup, Kent DA15 8EP]; *b* 1933; Dep Headmistress St Mary's C of E Sch Swanley to 1993

Lineage: GEORGE WALLACE, of Cheltenham Spa, Glos; had an est s:

GEORGE DOUGLAS, *cr* a **Baron**

WALLACE OF SALTAIRE

Creation: B. (LP, UK) 18 Nov 1995.

THE BARON WALLACE OF SALTAIRE, of Shipley, Co W Yorks (William John Lawrence Wallace) [The Rt Hon The Lord Wallace of Saltaire, House of Lords, London SW1A 0PW]; *b* 12 March 1941; *educ* St Edward's Sch Oxford, King's Coll Cambridge, Nuffield Coll Oxford, Cornell; lecturer govt Manchester U 1967–77, Dep Dir Roy Inst Internat Affrs 1978–90, Sr Research Fell European Studies St Antony's Coll Oxford 1990–95, Prof Internat Studies Centl European U Budapest 1994–, Reader Internat Rels LSE 1995–; Lib Parly candidate Huddersfield W 1970, Manchester Moss Side Feb and Oct 1974 and Shipley 1983 and 1987, V-Chm Lib Party Policy Ctee 1977–87, ed *Journal of Common Market Studies* 1974–78, author: *Foreign Policy and the Political Process* (1972), *The Foreign Policy Process in Britain* (1977), *The Transformation of Western Europe* (1990), *Regional Integration: the West European experience* (1994), *Policy-Making in the European Union* (co-author 1996) and *Why Vote Liberal Democrat?* (1997); *m* 1968 *Helen Sarah Rushworth and has a s and dau

Lineage: WILLIAM E WALLACE; *m* Mary A Tricks and had:

WILLIAM JOHN LAWRENCE, *cr* a **Baron**

WALLER

HONOR · ET · VERITAS

Arms: Checky or and azure, on a canton gules a lion rampant double-queued of the first. **Crest:** Out of a ducal coronet a plume of five ostrich feathers, 2nd and 4th azure, 1st, 3rd and 5th argent, surmounted by an eagle's claw gules. **Motto:** *Honor et veritas* ('Honour and truth'). **Creation:** Bt. (I) 1 June 1780.

SIR ROBERT WILLIAM WALLER, 9TH BT, of Newport, Co Tipperary [Sir Robert Waller Bt, 5 Lookout Terrace, Lynnfield, MA 01940, USA]; *b* 16 June 1934; *s f* 1958; *educ* Newark Coll of Engrg and Fairleigh Dickinson U; business manager General Electric Co to 1991 (ret); *m* 1960 (*divorce* 1975) Carol Anne, dau of John E Hines, of Lynn, Mass., and has:

1 +JOHN MICHAEL [John Waller Esq, 22 Mountain Ave, Malden, MA 02148, USA]; *b* 14 May 1962; *m* 1986 *Maria Renee Gonzalez and has:
  (1) +John Michael; *b* 1990
  (2) +Patrick Joseph de Warren; *b* 1992
  (1) *Jocelyn Anne; *b* 1988
  (2) *Mary Katherine; *b* 1994
2 +David Peter; *b* 1963; *m* 1989 *Lynn Riddle
1 *Susan Carol; *b* 1968
2 *Kathleen Ann; *b* 1970

Lineage: RICHARD WALLER, of Cully, Co Tipperary; had:

WILLIAM WALLER, of Cully; *m* Blanche, dau of Mark Weeks, and had, with five other sons, including an est (Richard, of Castle Waller, *m* Elizabeth, dau of Adml Holland, and had issue) and a 3rd s (Edward, *m* a dau of Richard White, Ld Mayor Dublin, and had issue), also three daus (Jane, *m* Richard Maunsell; Blanche, *m* 1731 Arthur Vincent; Elizabeth, *m* George Greene, of Old Abbey, Co Limerick) a 4th s:

SAMUEL WALLER, of Newport, Co Tipperary; *b* 1705; barrister; *m* 20 June 1730 Anne (*d* June 1800), sis of 1st Viscount Jocelyn (*see* RODEN, E), and *d* 1 May 1762, leaving, with three other sons (George, of Prior Park, Co Tipperary, *m* 1st 16 Oct 1782 Jane, dau of Benjamin Gault, *m* 2nd 8 Oct 1801 Elizabeth, dau of George Studdert, of Kilkishen, Co Clare, and *d* 16 July 1833, leaving issue; the other two *dsp*) and three daus (Charlotte, *m c* 18 Jan 1765 John Bloomfield, of

Newport, and *d* 1 Feb 1828, leaving issue; Elizabeth, *m* Aug 1766 Cooke Otway and *d* 1807, leaving issue; Blanche, *m* 1772 James Poe (*d* 13 March 1784), of Solsborough, and was *bur* 26 Sept 1834, leaving issue; *see* 1959 edn POEDOMVILLE, Bt), an est s:

Sir Robert Waller, 1st Bt (I), so *cr* 1 June 1780, of Lisbrian; Commr Revenue, MP Dundalk 1761–80, LLD Dublin 1774; *m* 3 April 1766 Catherine (*m* 2nd 2 June 1783 Rev Jerome Alley), dau and coheir of Rev Charles Moore, and *d* Aug 1780, leaving, with four daus:

1 **Sir Robert Waller, 2nd Bt**; *b c* 1768; *educ* Trin Coll Dublin (BA); High Sheriff King's Co 1826; *m* 1st by licence 29 April 1796 Mary (*d* 16 July 1804), dau of Thomas Bernard, of Castle Bernard, King's Co; *m* 2nd by licence 9 Jan 1806 Elizabeth (*d* 1851), dau of Nicholas Biddulph, of Borrisolegh, Co Tipperary, and widow of Jonathan Willington, and *dsp* 5 June 1826
2 Samuel Hamilton; *d* unm Aug 1793
3 Rev Sir Charles Townshend Waller, 3rd Bt; *dsp* 1 June 1830
4 Jocelyn Macartney, of Montreal; *m* Elizabeth Willis, widow of — Cullen, MD, and *d* 1837, having had, with other issue:
  (1) **Sir Edmund Waller, 4th Bt**; *b* July 1797; *m* 1st 28 March 1828 Selina Maria (*d* 22 July 1840), 2nd dau of George Waller, of Prior Park, Co Tipperary, and had, with another dau (*d* unm):
    1a Adelaide Georgina; sis in St George's Mission Home
    2a Eliza Matilda; *m* 1859 Charles Walter Bastable (*d* 16 July 1878) and had issue
    3a Selina Maria; *m* 16 July 1862 William Henry Baldwin, Head Master St John's Coll Newport, and *d* 28 April 1879, leaving issue
  (1) (cont.) **Sir Edmund** *m* 2nd 13 June 1844 Rebecca (*d* 22 Nov 1870), sis of Sir Benjamin Lee Guinness, 1st Bt (*qv*), and *d* 9 March 1851, leaving by her:
    1a **Sir Edmund Arthur Waller, 5th Bt**; *b* 16 March 1846; Lt 84th Foot; *m* 1st 4 March 1869 Annie (*dsp* 27 Dec 1876), dau of George Parsons; *m* 2nd 2 Sept 1878 Jessie Marion (*m* 2nd 29 Nov 1890 John A Haig, who *d* 6 July 1933), dau of Henry James Purbrook, of Brighton, and *dsp* 22 Oct 1888
    4a Anna Blanche; *m* 20 July 1875 Rev William Joshua Fennell, Chaplain Bombay Presidency, and *dsp* 9 May 1914
  (2) Charles, of Brooklyn, NY; *b* 13 Jan 1802; *m* 8 June 1830 Maria, dau of Nicholas Burgher, of Staten Island, NY, and *d* 23 Jan 1885, leaving:
    1a **Sir Charles Waller, 6th Bt**; *b* 8 June 1835; *d* unm 25 May 1912
    2a William Edgar; *b* 11 Nov 1841; *m* 6 June 1861 Emma Daisy, dau of Thomas Eccleston, and *d* 21 Sept 1899, leaving, with a dau (*d* an infant):
      1b WILLIAM EDGAR (Sir), **7th Bt**
      2b Elwood Eccleston; *b* 26 April 1876; *m* 1895 Francina Claire Shaughnessy (*d* 1958) and *d* 1944, leaving:
        1c Elwood Eccleston; *b* 1896; *m* 1921 Jane Eden (*d* 1977) and *d* 1976, leaving:
          1d +Elwood Eccleston [Elwood Waller Esq, 3511 Hargill Dve, Orlando, FL 32806, USA]; *b* 1922; late Lt USAAF; *m* 1st 1946 Marie Maupin; *m* 2nd 1956 *Marie Benton and by his 1st w has:
            1e +Patrick; *b* 1949
            1e *Susan [Ms Susan Waller, 3019 Emerson St, Tampa, FL 33629, USA]; *b* 1947; has adopted:
              *David Duckworth WALLER; *b* 20 Aug 1995
              *Lauren Ansley Eden WALLER; *b* 10 May 1993
          1d *Janet; *b* 1924; *m* 1st 1943 Newman Sallings Harrison; *m* 2nd 1947 *Glenn Charles Wilson and has issue
        1c *Eunice Claire; *b* 11 Jan 1900; *m* 1922 Clifford Albert Nagle, of Bound Brook, NJ, and has issue
      1b Daisy Emma; *m* 21 Feb 1883 William R McCurdy (*d* 4 July 1942) and had issue
      2b Lilian Edith; *m* 12 June 1895 Wallace L Jones (*d* 23 Feb 1946) and had issue
      3b Florence Eunice; *m* 1902 William T Thurston and had issue
      4b Olive Euretta; *m* 1901 Lester L Thurston (*d* 1929)
    3a Edmund; *b* 10 Dec 1844; *m* 1861 and *d* 1891, leaving issue
      1a Catherine Elizabeth Burgher; *m* Joseph Russell Thomas and had issue
      2a Josephine Harrison; *m* 6 July 1854 John Stanton (*d* 2 Nov 1870) and had issue
      3a Maria Louise; *m* 12 Dec 1862 her cousin Samuel William Waller and *d* 26 March 1873, leaving issue (*see below*)
      4a Georgiana; *m* 16 Jan 1871 David Egbert Terry, of Brooklyn, NY, and had issue
  (3) Samuel, of Montreal, MD; *b* 12 Jan 1803; *m* 30 April 1833 Henrietta Eliza (*d* 1885), dau of Capt Guy Carleton Colclough, 103rd Regt, and *d* 1878, having had, with other issue:
    1a Jocelyn Waller; *b* 9 Dec 1841; *m* 11 June 1867 Mary, dau of E Smith, of Hamilton, Ontario, and had:
      1b Augustus Edmund; *b* 4 Sept 1871
      2b Philip Percy; *b* 6 July 1877
      1b Mary Beatrice
      2d Mary Ethel Maud
    2a Samuel William; *b* 10 Feb 1844
    3b Edmund Henry Colclough; *b* 27 Feb 1879; *m* 18 Dec 1906 Caroline Agnes, dau of John Mann, of Grand Valley, Ontario, and *d* 23 March 1970, leaving, with another s (*d* an infant):
      1c Herbert Montague; *b* 29 Sept 1907; *m* 1942 *Vera Germain and *d* 1971, leaving:
        1d +Edgar Herbert; *b* 1942; *educ* Lake Head U Ontario; *m* 1966 *Sandra Yvonne Egan and has:
          1e +Scott Edward; *b* 1967
        2d +Brian; *b* 1944; *m* 1965 *Joan Gloria Woodgate and has:
          1e *Faye Kathleen; *b* 1969
          2e *Karen Louise; *b* 1972

1d *Sharon [Mrs Robert Nicholl, RR 2, Devlin, Ontario, Canada]; *b* 1946; *m* 1965 *Robert Bruce Nicholl and has:

  1e *Laura Cecile; *b* 1966

  2e *Rhonda Jean; *b* 1968; has:

    1f *Robert Herbert; *b* 1989

2d *Jean Patricia; *b* 1952; *m* 1972 *John Charles Mayo, of Thunder Bay, Ontario, and has:

  *Jennifer Ann; *b* 1975

2c +Arthur Edmund [Arthur Waller Esq, 6711 Dover Rd, Nanaimo, BC, Canada V9T 2L9]; *b* 6 Jan 1909; *m* 1st 1941 (*divorce* 1967) Frances, dau of John Martin, of Vancouver; *m* 2nd 1968 *Mrs Alma Rickerby and by his 1st w has:

  1d *Lynne Dianne; *b* 24 July 1944

3c +William Hugh; *b* 11 June 1912; *m* 1944 *Alvina Koch

4c +Cedric Henry; *b* 14 April 1914; *m* 1939 *Flora Margaret, dau of John George Campbell, of Macdowall, Sask, and has:

  1d +Cedric Lorne [Cedric Waller Esq, 34030 Shannon Dve, Abbotsford, BC, Canada V2S 5C8]; *b* 18 Dec 1940; *educ* U of BC (BEd) and W Washington U, USA (MEd); sch adminr; *m* 1st 11 July 1964 (*divorce* 1977) Doris Lorraine, dau of E G Sweetman, of Trail, BC, and has:

    1e +Stephen Lorne; *b* 17 Dec 1966

    2e +Richard Lawrence; *b* 10 Nov 1968

    3e +Daniel Leonard; *b* 1970

  1d (cont.) Cedric Waller *m* 2nd 1977 *Julia Carolyn, dau of George Glanville, of W Vancouver, and by her has:

    1e *Jennifer Louise; *b* 1980

    2e *Allison Patricia; *b* 1982

  2d +Ronald Henry; *b* 22 Sept 1943; *educ* U of BC (BSP, MSc); *m* 21 Aug 1965 *Gwendolyn Anne, dau of William Wright, of Nelson, BC, and has:

    1e +Michael Ronald; *b* 13 Feb 1966

    2e +Donald William Henry; *b* 30 April 1969

    3e +Christopher Bradley; *b* 1970

    4e +Darren Lorne; *b* 1971

    1e *Heather Diane Habiza; *b* 1972

5c +Thomas Geoffrey [Thomas Waller Esq, 1107 Dahl St, Prince George, BC, Canada]; *b* 7 Nov 1916; Forestry Dept Supervisor BC Govt (ret); *m* 1947 (*divorce* 1975) Elizabeth Margaret Esther, dau of William J Brodie, of Nelson, BC, and *d* Sept 1997, leaving:

  1d *Donna Elaine; *b* 1949; *m* 1971*Edward Charles Anderson and has:

    1e *Nicole Dawn; *b* 1974

    2e *Tara Leigh; *b* 1979

  2d *Glowena Margaret; *b* 1950; *m* 1st 1969 Alan Lee Hutchinson; *m* 2nd 1986 *Leslie Alexander Cook and by her 1st husb has:

    1e *Celeste Marie; *b* 1969

    2e *Michelle Jeanette; *b* 1972

  3d *Judith Darlene; *b* 1953; *m* 1st 1973 (*divorce* 1977) Joseph Martin Walker and has:

    1e *Cassandra Lee; *b* 1981

  3d (cont.) Mrs Judith Walker *m* 2nd 1983 *Frederick Louis Tuttosi and has:

    1e *Michael Ryne; *b* 1984

5c (cont.) Thomas Geoffrey *m* 2nd 19– *Evie Coghill

6c +Arnold Blair [Arnold Waller Esq, 401–154 Promenade Dr, Nanaimo, BC, Canada V9R 6Y3]; *b* 28 June 1924; *educ* BC U (BSc); engrg consultant; *m* 24 March 1951 Janet Louise (*d* June 1994), dau of William Paton Montgomery, of Montreal, and has:

  1d *Laurie Jane [Mrs Christopher Benson, 63 Anne St, Cannington, Ont L0E 1E0, Canada]; *b* 27 April 1953; *m* 1984 *Christopher Benson and has:

    1e *Robin Patrick; *b* 1989

    1e *Mairen Rose Montgomery; *b* 1992

  2d *Elizabeth Sue; *b* 18 Sept 1958; *m* 1989 (*divorce* 1993) Christopher Thor Asp, of Neustadt, Ontario

6c (cont.) Mr and Mrs Arnold Waller also adopted:

  *Jonathan Blair; *b* 1962

1c Marjorie Gladys; *b* 27 July 1910; *m* 1st 24 Dec 1926 (*divorce* 1949) James Boyd Young; *m* 2nd 1952 *Ivor B Tucker and *d* 1996, leaving issue

2c *Evelyn Agnes; *b* 19 July 1918; *m* 1st 11 Jan 1937 (*divorce* 1954) James Donald Ross; *m* 2nd 1961 *William Wilson and by her 1st husb has:

  1d *Shirley Norma; *b* 1938; *m* 1st 1955 (*divorce* 1969) Allen William Wilson; *m* 2nd 1980 *Póvi Frederich Holm and by her 1st husb has:

    1e *Michael Allen; *b* 1963

    1e *Shelley Norma; *b* 1957; *m* 1983 *Michael Collins

3c *Beatrice Alice; *b* 14 Aug 1922; *m* 1st 1942 Robert Ragsdale, of Dallas, Tex.; *m* 2nd 1949 Ernest John Moretti (*d* 1971) and by him has:

  1d *Ernest James; *b* 1950

4b Hugh Jocelyn; *b* 11 June 1887; *m* 2 June 1909 Olive Maria (*d* June 1959), dau of John Mann, of Grand Valley, Ontario, and *d* 1978 leaving, with another dau (*d* an infant):

  1c +Hector Hugh; *b* 17 April 1910; Capt RCE; *m* 21 Sept 1946 *Mary Patricia, dau of Ivor John Everson, of Gravesend, Kent, and *d* May 1986, leaving:

    1d +Thomas Hector [Thomas Waller Esq, 622 Shannon Crescent, N Vancouver, BC, Canada V7N 2Y9]; *b* 1 Dec 1947; *m* 1969 *Margaret Quilliam and has:

      1e +Michael Hugh; *b* 1974

      2e +Ian Denny; *b* 1976

  2d +Sean Ivor; *b* 17 March 1957

1d Patricia Jocelyn; *b* 15 June 1946; *d* 9 March 1964

2d *Mary Kathleen; *b* 23 July 1950; *m* 1972 *Gerald St Laurent, of Tumbler Ridge, BC, and has:

  1e *Jocelyn Kathleen; *b* 1974

  2e *Tannis Patricia Marie; *b* 1977

3d *Valeria Jane; *b* 16 Oct 1952; *m* 1st 19– William Truttman; *m* 2nd 1988 *Pal Levitt

2c +Gordon Jocelyn; *b* 4 Nov 1912; *m* 6 March 1937 *Pearl Solie, of Wells, BC, and *d* 30 May 1992, leaving:

  1d +Dennis Raymond [Dennis Waller Esq, 6340 Douglas St, W Vancouver, BC, Canada]; *b* 1938; *m* 28 Nov 1965 (*divorce* 19–) Robin Muriel Joiner, of Orbost, Victoria, Australia

  2d +Gordon Edmund; *b* 1948; *m* 1985 *Dianne — and has:

    1e +Mark; *b* 1996

    1e +Erin; *b* 1991

3c +Robert Allen; *b* 26 April 1914; *d* 1980

4c +Hugh Macartney [Hugh Waller Esq, 119 Heritage Drive, Nanaimo, BC V9V 1H8, Canada]; *b* 15 Oct 1922; *m* 1st 1943 Betty Hallat; *m* 2nd 1950 *Florence M Lowe, of Austin, Manitoba, and by her has:

  1d +Kenneth Hugh; *b* 4 July 1953; *m* 1975 *Anne Beswetherwick, of New Haven, Sussex, and adopted:

    *Liam Kenan Hugh; *b* 1987

  2d +Gregory Allen; *b* 22 Sept 1955; *m* 1980 *Judith Anne Yule and has:

    1e +Sean Steven; *b* 1987

    2e +Tristan Hunter; *b* 1990

  3d +Douglas William; *b* 25 March 1959; *m* 1983 *Kathleen Freeman and has:

    1e +Nicholas Hugh; *b* 1986

    1e *Jessica Rachelle; *b* 1988

    2e *Dayna Florence Shirley; *b* 21 July 1995

1d *Denise Jean; *b* 6 June 1951; *m* 1973 *Arthur Stanley Webb and has:

  1e *Ryan Gregory; *b* 1980

  2e *Jaye Scott; *b* 1981

  1e *Lauren Ashley; *b* 1987

2d *Kathleen Marie; *b* 4 July 1953; *m* 1983 *Johannes Verhagen and has:

  1e *Gregory William; *b* 1986

  1e *Caitlin Johanna; *b* 1989

1c *Lillian Gladys [Mrs Clinton Geddes, 1685 Taylor Dve, Prince George, BC, Canada]; *b* 6 July 1911; *m* 15 Aug 1935 Clinton Geddes and has:

  1d *Gordon; *b* 1936; *m* 1958 *Judith Anne Hall and has:

    1e *Clinton Douglas; *b* 1965

    2e *Michael; *b* 1970

    1e *Cinda Marie; *b* 1959

    2e *Dyana; *b* 1960

2c *Olive Kathleen; *b* 20 Feb 1916; *m* 1941 Noel Hendry, of Vancouver, and has:

  1d *Kenneth Noel; *b* 1944; *m* 1st Charlotte —; *m* 2nd 1987 *Anne Marie — and has:

    1e *A son; *b* 1970

    2e *A son; *b* 1971

    1e *A dau; *b* 19–

  2d *Douglas; *b* 1948

3c *Muriel Eleanor [Mrs Charles Guignet, 2399 Dalhousie St, Victoria, BC, Canada]; *b* 8 June 1919; *m* 1941 Charles Guignet, Curator Birds and Mammals Provincial Museum Victoria, and has:

  1d *Mark Lawrence; *b* 1950; *m* 19– *Victoria — and has:

    1e *Colin; *b* 19–

    1e *Michelle; *b* 19–

  1d *Joan Muriel; *b* 1942

  2d *Patricia Lynda; *b* 1947; *m* 1969 *John — and has:

    1e *Matthew Guignet; *b* 1969

  2d *Suzanne Maria; *b* 1955; *m* 198– *Bryce — and has:

    1e *Tyson Bancroft; *b* 1987

4c *Jean Pearl; *b* 15 Nov 1923; *m* 1946 Lawrence G Cutler, of Houston, BC, Canada, and has:

  1d *Jerry; *b* 1947

  2d *Ross; *b* 1952

  3d *Gregory; *b* 1955; *m* 19– *Sherry and has:

    1e *Ryan; *b* 19–

  1d *Janet; *b* 1949; *m* 1968 *Len Thony and has:

    1e *Paul John; *b* 1970

    1e *Corry Lynne; *b* 1969

    2e *Dana Marie; *b* 1973

  2d *Debra; *b* 1957

1b Katharine; *b* 11 Sept 1889; *m* 10 June 1908 John Alexander Lawrie, of Wild Rose, Saskatchewan, and had issue

2b Alice Maude; *b* 9 March 1892; *m* 21 June 1912 Frederick Stuart (*d* 1935), of Rozilee, Saskatchewan

1a Amelia; *b* 23 May 1838; *m* James Royce Vansittart Forest, of Montreal, and *d* 1904

(4) Robert; *b* 4 Jan 1806; EICS; *m* 17 April 1834 Mary Anne (*d* 4 June 1846), sis of — Blowers, EICS, and *d* 9 Feb 1860, leaving:

1a Robert William, of Bombay; *b* 26 Oct 1835; *m* 3 April 1866 Emily (*d* 1895), dau of John Page, and *d* 1895, leaving:

1b Herbert Montagu; *b* 18 Aug 1868; *dsp c* 1935

2b Jocelyn Edmund; *b* 3 June 1870; *dsp* 1937

3b Frank Hastings; *b* 16 Oct 1871; Gen Manager Rlwys, Colonial CS Nigeria; *m* 23 April 1914 Elvie Grace (*d* as the result of enemy action 1940), 2nd dau of William Bedford, and *d* Aug 1953, having had:

  1c Jocelyn Grace; *b* 11 March 1915; *d* as the result of enemy action 1940

  2c *Marjorie; *b* 30 Jan 1919

4b Charles Robert [Charles Waller Esq, 7 Lilyvale Rd, Pinetown, Natal, S Africa]; *b* 10 May 1877; Natal CS; *m* 10 Oct 1905 Agnes Helen, dau of Francis Thorne, of Launceston, Cornwall, and Torvale, Victoria Co, Natal, and *d* 1933, leaving:

  1c Robert William; *b* 25 Nov 1910; driver S African Mech Tport Ethiopia WW II 1940–42 (invalided); *m* 10 Oct 1936 Daphne Mabel (*d* Oct 1992), est dau of Herbert Clifton Morton, of Pretoria, and *d* 20 Aug 1992, leaving:

    1d +Robert David [Robert Waller Esq, Morville Farm, Le Hurel, St Quen, Jersey CI]; *b* 27 June 1939; *m* 14 April 1961 *Rosalie Beryl, dau of Wilfred Easter, of Southampton, and has:

      1e +Hugh; *b* 5 Jan 1965

      1e *Vanessa; *b* 8 April 1963

      2e *Ursula; *b* 8 April 1963; *m* 19– *Douglas A Richardson, of Morville Farm

    2d +Leonard Harold [Leonard Waller Esq, 21 Langanhoven, King William's Town 5600, South Africa]; *b* 16 May 1953; *m* 1st 1976 Moira (*d* 1981), dau of Frank Ferreira, of Queenstown, and has:

      1e +Stephen; *b* 1976

      2e +Marc; *b* 1977

    2d (cont.) Leonard Waller *m* 2nd 1982 *Helen Louise, dau of Raymond George Hewson, of E London, and by her has:

      1e +Peter; *b* 1984

    1d *Delene Ruth [Mrs Edgar Esselen, 132 Golf Ave, Club View W, Pretoria, Transvaal 0157, S Africa]; *b* 5 Aug 1937; *m* 1961 Edgar E Esselen, s of L F E Esselen, of Pretoria, and has:

      1e *Deborah; *b* 7 Nov 1962; *m* 1980 *Gary Alan Gordon and has:

        1f *Justin; *b* 1984

        1f *Megan; *b* 1986

      2e *Ingrid; *b* 20 May 1965; *m* 1994 *Christof James van Fedyk

    2d *Thalia Lynette [Mrs Allan Griffin, 14 Hill Crescent, Amanzimtoti, Natal, S Africa]; *b* 14 Jan 1943; *m* 14 Jan 1965 *Allan Harry Griffin, s of L H Griffin, of Greytown, Natal, and has:

      1e *Helen Eileen; *b* 1969; *m* 4 April 1998 *Richard Neil Zulch

      2e *Louise Daphne; *b* 1971; *m* 22 April 1995 *John Dennison

    3d *Daphne Jess; *b* 12 March 1945; *m* *Peter Alan Anscombe, of Johannesburg

    4d *Heather Lynn; *b* 8 Nov 1949

  2c +Charles Jellicoe; *b* 1916; Gunner Light AA Regt S African Artillery WW II Ethiopia and Middle E

  3c +Edmund John [Edmund Waller Esq, 7 Broadway, Durban Natal, S Africa]; *b* 1919; W/O SAAF WW II Middle E, Malta, Sicily and Italy (despatches); *m* 1944 *Alma, yst dau of Edwin Treffry-Goatley, of Durban, and had:

    1d *Virginia Helen; *b* 1945

    2d *Hazel Louise; *b* 1948; *m* 1968 *John Robert Lockwood, of E Yorks, and has:

      1e *Edmund Sean; *b* 1973

      1e *Amanda Jane; *b* 1969

  1c *Catherine Jocelyn; *b* 23 Nov 1906; *m* 1935 Reginald Charles Oates and has:

    1d *Jillian Elizabeth; *b* 1937

    2d *Sandra Jocelyn; *b* 1941

  2c *Agatha Minnie; *b* 4 Feb 1908; *m* 1933 Willam U E Cook (*d* 1971) and has:

    1d *Richard Clive; *b* 1939

    1d *Valma Jean; *b* 1935

  3c *Ruth; *b* 22 July 1909; *m* 25 April 1935 Richard Dennis Goble, of Beaufort, Compensation, Natal, and has:

    1d *Denise Joy; *b* 1938

    2d *Sylvia Helen; *b* 1940

    3d *Carol Ruth; *b* 1943

1b Florence Minnie; *d* unm 1955

2d Emily Mary; *m* 1896 her cousin Robert Martin Jocelyn Waller and *d* 17 Sept 1951, leaving issue (*see below*)

3d Amy Beatrice; *d* unm 1960

2a Jocelyn; *b* 30 July 1838; Ind Postal Serv; *m* Dec 1861 Eliza (*d* 1903), dau of Martin Power, and *d* 1914, having had, with another dau (*d* unm):

1b Robert Martin Jocelyn; *b* 24 Aug 1862; Bombay Govt Sec; *m* 1896 his cousin Emily Mary Waller (*see above*) and *d* 17 March 1936, having had:

  1c Robert Hardress Jocelyn; *b* 24 Aug 1901; *d* 21 Aug 1921

  2c +Frank Martin Roden; *b* 18 Sept 1909; Sub-Inspr Bombay Dist Police 1933–48; *m* 3 April 1948 Nora Dale (*d* 29 May 1965), dau of Rev Cyril Edgington, of Bath, and has:

    1d +Robert Cyril Hardress Jocelyn; *b* 12 Dec 1949

  1c *Dorothy Minnie; *b* 18 Sept 1898; *m* 1919 Reginald Carp, of Highbridge, Somerset, and has:

    1d *Thomas Walter Waller; *b* 1924

    1d *Pamela Mary; *b* 1923

  2c Winifrid Roberta, *b* 17 May 1900; *m* John Banham, of Paignton, Devon, and *d* 11 March 1936, leaving issue

2b Edmund Edward; *b* 18 Oct 1865; *d* 1900

3b William Dillon; *b* 10 Aug 1868; *m* 1896 Annie, dau of Hans Nielson, of Denmark, and had, with another s (*d* young):

  1c Hans Jocelyn; *b* 9 Nov 1897; *m* 29 June 1922 Mildred Vivian Pennock, of Longmont, Colorado, and had:

    1d +Edmund Hugh [Edmund Waller Esq, 8656 W Progress Pl, Littleton, CO 80123, USA]; *b* 15 Dec 1929; *m* 1951 *Barbara Yetter and has:

      1e *Kenneth Scott; *b* 1959; *m* 1982 *Karen Staley and has:

        1f +Tyler Paul; *b* 1989

        1f *Danielle Renée; *b* 1986

      1e *Wendy Anne; *b* 1957; *m* 1st 1983 (*divorce* 1985) Randall J Brunko; *m* 2nd 1987 *Timothy Todd and by him has:

        1f *Joseph Lee; *b* 1988

    1d *Patricia Gene; *b* 27 Dec 1925; *m* 1948 *Vern L Klingman and has issue:

      1e *Stephen Wesley; *b* 1957

      1e *Nancy Rose; *b* 1955

      2e *Candice Martha; *b* 1961

4b Alfred Jocelyn (Rev); *b* 14 Feb 1870; *m* 1903 Katherine Tarrence and *d* 1950, leaving:

  1c +Richard; *b* 1915; *m* 1949 *Mildred Lucka and has:

    1d *Sharon Rose; *b* 1951; *m* 19– *Charles Counts

  1c *Alice; *b* 1908; *m* 1932 Joseph C Chiappetti, of Flagstaff, Ariz., and has:

    1d *Joanne; *b* 1935; *m* 1957 *Dr Robert Wilcox, of Medford, Oregon

    2d *Nancy Lou; *b* 1938; *m* 1958 *Fred Marsh, of Los Alamos, NM

5b Thomas Hutton; *b* 7 Aug 1878

6b Harry Bernard; *b* 1882; *m* 1920 Anna Kruger Jorgensen (*d* 1946), of Denmark, and *d* 1971, leaving:

  1c *Evelyn May [Mrs Selwyn B Hoah, 1350 Ridge Rd, Littleton, CO 80120, USA]; *b* 1923; *m* 1949 *Selwyn Barton Hoah and has:

    1d *Selwyn Barton; *b* 1950; *m* 1st 1972 Claudia Lukas; *m* 2nd 1978 *Lee Lacey and by her has:

      1e *Jason Henry; *b* 1979

    2d *Christopher Henry; *b* 1958

    3d *Anthony Wayne; *b* 1960

    1d *Eugenia Anne; *b* 1943; *m* 1st 1965 Laurence V Monniger; *m* 2nd 1981 *Dennis Homrighausen and by him has:

      1e *Darren Warren; *b* 1983

      1e *Amanda Anne; *b* 1981

    2d *Jocelyn Deane; *b* 1955; *m* 1981 *John Parker Mertens and has:

      1e *Charles Parker; *b* 1983

1b Eva Mary

2b May Maud

1a Jane Amelia; *m* 15 Jan 1859 Capt Henry Bryde (*d* 10 July 1907), 57th Regt, of Goytrey Ho, Mon, and *d* Sept 1892, leaving issue

2a Katherine

The 6th Bt's n,

Sir William Edgar Waller, 7th Bt; *b* 22 Nov 1863; *m* 23 July 1890 Mary Augusta (*d* 1 May 1950), dau of Charles Meyers, and *d* 16 April 1943, leaving:

1 ROLAND EDGAR (Sir), **8th Bt**

2 Donald William; *b* 18 Jan 1899; *d* 8 Oct 1958

1 Dorothy de Warrenne; *b* 29 March 1893; *m* 24 Sept 1919 James Alexander Smith (*d* 9 Feb 1961) and had two daus

2 Miriam Jocelyn; *b* 11 April 1896; *m* 1916 Heber Kelshaw Peniston, of Oregon, USA, and had two sons

The 7th Bt's er s,

Sir Roland Edgar Waller, 8th Bt; *b* 11 Jan 1892; *educ* Cornell; Ensign USNAF WW I, memb American Legion, Offr Catholic War Veterans of US, Excise Tax Offr Bureau Internal Revenue US Treasury Dept 1934; *m* 5 Feb 1919 Helen Madeline, of Seminole, Fla., dau of Joseph Radl, of Matawan, NJ, and *d* 20 May 1958, leaving:

1 Sir ROBERT WILLIAM WALLER, **9th and present Bt**

1 *Helen Mary [Mrs Warshauer, RFD 4, Box 154, Medford Farm, Goffstown, NH 03045, USA]; *b* 13 Feb 1924; *m* 11 Feb 1945 Arthur Paul Warshauer (*d* 1990) and has:

  (1) *Shaw Matthew; *b* 21 Oct 1962

  (1) *Sandra Anne; *b* 23 Nov 1946

  (2) *Mary Susan; *b* 27 Nov 1950

2 *Patricia Anne [Mrs Leonard Monroe, 3321 19th St, E Bradenton, FL 34208, USA]; *b* 29 May 1930; *m* 1st 1949 (*divorce* 1974) Howard George Schier; *m* 2nd 19– *Leonard Monroe and by her 1st husb has:

  (1) *Virginia Gail; *b* 24 Dec 1949

  (2) *Nancy Lee; *b* 22 Aug 1954

  (3) *Linda Jean; *b* 28 April 1957

WALPOLE

Arms: Or on a fess between two chevrons sa. three cross-crosslets of the field. **Crest:** A saracen's head in profile, couped at the shoulders ppr., ducally crowned or, and from the coronet flowing a red cap turned down in front, tasselled and charged with a catherine-wheel gold. **Supporters:** Dexter, an antelope arg.; sinister, a stag arg., each gorged with a collar checky or and az., and therefrom a chain reflexed over the back gold. **Motto:** *Sibi constat* ('Let him be true to himself'). **Creations:** B. (GB) 1 June 1723 (of Walpole) and 4 June 1756 (of Wolterton).

THE 10TH BARON WALPOLE OF WALPOLE and **Baron Walpole of Wolterton** (Robert Horatio Walpole, JP (Norfolk 1972)) [The Rt Hon The Lord Walpole JP, Mannington Hall, Norwich, Norfolk NR11 7BB]; *b* 8 Dec 1938; *s* f 1989; *educ* Eton and King's Coll Cambridge (BA 1961, MA 1966, Dip Ag 1962); CC Norfolk 1970–81 (chm various ctees), chm: Area Museums Serv for SE England 1976–79, Norwich Sch of Art 1977–87, Textile Conservation Centre 1981–88 (pres 1988), E Anglian Tourist Bd 1982–88; *m* 1st 30 June 1962 (*divorce* 1979) (Sybil) Judith (*d* 1993), yst dau of Theodore Thomas Schofield, FDS, MRCS, LRCP, of Harpenden, Herts, and has:

1 +JONATHAN ROBERT HUGH; *b* 16 Nov 1967; *educ* Eton and Manchester U
2 +Benedict Thomas Orford; *b* 1 June 1969; *educ* Eton
1 *Alice Louise; *b* 1 Sept 1963; *educ* Norwich High Sch and New Hall Cambridge; *m* 1990 *Dr Angel Cesar Carro, yr s of Herminio Carro Castrillo, of Geneva, and has:

   (1) *Inigo Robert; *b* 6 June 1996
   (1) *Hester; *b* 19–
   (2) *Beatrice; *b* 19–
   (3) *Isobel; *b* 19–

2 *Emma Judith; *b* 10 Oct 1964; *educ* Norwich High Sch and Durham U; *m* 29 Aug 1998 *Timothy Walsh, yr s of Brian Walsh, of Malvern, Adelaide, S Australia

The 10th BARON *m* 2nd 1980 *Laurel Celia, only dau of S T Ball, of Swindon, Wilts, and by her has:

3 +Roger Horatio Calibut; *b* 1980
4 +Henry William; *b* 18 Jan 1982
3 *Grace Mary; *b* 1986

Earldom of Orford (see below): An earlier creation of this title was in favour of Edward Russell, nephew of the 1st Duke of Bedford (*qv*).

Lineage: The Walpoles are said to descend from John de Walpole, who *fl c* 1250, and had their seat at Houghton, Norfolk, from the late 13th century.

THOMAS WALPOLE, of Houghton; *m* Jane, dau of William Cobbe, of Sandringham, Norfolk, and had, with a yr s (Henry) and dau (Agnes, *m* 1st Thomas Russell, *m* 2nd — Halliday):

EDWARD WALPOLE, of Houghton; *m* Lucy, dau of Sir Terry Robsart, of Sidestone, Norfolk, and had, with two yr sons (Richard; Terry) and a dau (Elizabeth, *m* Martin Cobb, of Snettisham, Norfolk):

JOHN WALPOLE, of Houghton; cousin and heir of Amy, Lady Dudley, dau and heir of Sir John Robsart; *m* Katherine, dau and coheir of William Callybutt, of Coxforthe, Norfolk, and had, with an er s (Edward, *dsp*) and three daus (Elizabeth, Bona, Katherine):

CALYBUT WALPOLE, of Houghton; *m* Elizabeth, dau of Edmond Bacon, of Hessert, Suffolk, and had, with three yr sons (John; Calybut; Bacon) and a dau (Elizabeth, *m* Thomas Clifton, of Toptrees, Norfolk):

ROBERT WALPOLE, of Houghton; *m* Susan, dau of Sir Edward Barkham, of Southacre, Norfolk, and had:

Sir EDWARD WALPOLE, KB (23 April 1661); MP in the Parl which restored CHARLES II; *m* 1649 Susan, 3rd dau of Sir Robert Crane, 1st and last Bt, of Chilton, Suffolk, and had, with a yr s (Horatio) and four daus (Ann; Dorothy; Susan; Mary):

ROBERT WALPOLE; *b c* 1650; MP Castle Rising, Norfolk, 1689–1700; *m* Mary, only dau and heiress of Sir Geoffrey Burwell, of Rougham, Suffolk, and was *bur* 18 Nov 1700, leaving, with two er sons (*d* young):

1 Sir ROBERT WALPOLE, 1st EARL OF ORFORD, Co Suffolk, so *cr* 6 Feb 1741/2, as also BARON OF HOUGHTON, Co Norfolk, and VISCOUNT WALPOLE, Co Suffolk (all GB), KG (1726), KB (1725), PC (1714); *b* 26 Aug 1676; *educ* Eton and King's Coll Cambridge (LLD 1728); MP Castle Rising 1701–02 and King's Lynn 1702–42, memb Cncl Ld High Adml 1705–08, Sec at War 1708–10, Treasurer Navy 1710–11, Paymaster Forces 1714–15 and 1720–21, Chllr Exchequer 1715–17 and 1721–Feb 1741/2 and 1st Ld Treasury (in effect PM, usually regarded as the first such), High Steward: Yarmouth 1733–45 and King's Lynn 1738–45; *m* 1st 30 July 1700 Catherine (*d* 20 Aug 1737), dau of John Shorter (s of Sir John Shorter, Ld Mayor London) by Elizabeth, dau of Sir Erasmus Philipps, 3rd Bt (*see* SAINT DAVIDS, V); *m* 2nd by 3 March 1737/8 his mistress Maria (*d* 4 June 1738), only child of Thomas Skerret, by whom he had apparently before their marriage a dau Maria (aged under 21 in Dec 1744), and *d* 18 March 1744/5, having by his 1st w had, with another dau (*d* unm):

(1) ROBERT WALPOLE, **1st Baron Walpole of Walpole**, Co Norfolk (GB), so *cr* 1 June 1723 *vp*, with remainder, in default of the issue male of himself, his bros and his f, to the male descendants of his gf, and 2nd EARL OF ORFORD, KB (1925); *b c* 1701; *educ* Eton; Clerk of the Pells 1721–39, Ld Lt Devon 1733–51, Auditor Exchequer 1739–51; *m* 1724 Margaret (who *s* eventually to the Barony of CLINTON (*qv*) and *m* 2nd Hon Sewallis Shirley (*see* FERRERS, E)), dau and sole heiress of Samuel Rolle, of Heanton, Devon, and *d* 31 March 1751, when he was *s* by his w's only *s* (it was said by more than one contemporary that the biological f was someone else, possibly Sir George Oxenden, 5th Bt):

  1a GEORGE WALPOLE, **2nd Baron Walpole of Walpole** and 3rd EARL OF ORFORD; *b* 2 April 1730; *educ* Eton and (?) King's Coll Cambridge; a Ld Bedchamber (Whig) 1755–82, Ranger St James's 1784–91 and Hyde Parks 1763–83; *d* unm (and insane from 1773) 5 Dec 1791

(2) Edward (Sir), KB; Ch Sec Ireland; *d* unm, leaving illegitimately:

  1a Laura or Louisa; *m* 13 Sept 1758 Rt Rev and Hon Frederick Keppel, s of 2nd Earl of Albemarle (*qv*), and *d* 27 July 1813, leaving issue

  2a Maria Walpole; *b* 3 July 1739; *m* 1st 17 May 1759 2nd Earl Waldegrave (*qv*) and had issue; *m* 2nd 6 Sept 1766 HRH WILLIAM HENRY DUKE OF GLOUCESTER, was mother of HRH WILLIAM FREDERICK DUKE OF GLOUCESTER and HRH PRINCESS SOPHIA MATILDA OF GLOUCESTER and *d* 22 Aug 1807

  3a Charlotte; *m* 2 Oct 1770 5th Earl of Dysart (*see* 1970 edn) and *dsp* 5 Sept 1789

(3) HORATIO (HORACE) WALPOLE, **3rd Baron Walpole of Walpole** and 4th and last EARL OF ORFORD; *b* 5 Oct 1717; *educ* Eton, King's Coll Cambridge and Lincoln's Inn; Ch Usher, Clerk of Estreats and Comptroller of the Pipe 1738–97, MP (Whig) Callington, Cornwall, 1741–54, Castle Rising 1754–57 and King's Lynn 1757–68, FRS Feb 1746/7, FSA 1753, belle-lettrist and novelist, accomplished the Grand Tour 1739–41 with the poet Thomas Gray (whose *Odes* he published from his private press 1757), bought a villa at Twickenham which he transformed into a Gothick mansion (the celebrated Strawberry Hill), author: *Catalogue of the Royal and Noble Authors of England* (1758), *The Castle of Otranto* (first of the Gothick novels 1764), *The Mysterious Mother* (blank verse tragedy 1768), *Description of the Villa of Horace Walpole* (1774), *Memoirs of the Last Ten Years of the Reign of George the Second* (1822), *Memoirs of the Reign of George the Third* (1845) and *Journal of the Reign of King George the Third from the Year 1771 to 1783* (1859), publisher/editor: *Aedes Walpolianae* (1747), *Catalogue of the Royal and Noble Authors of England* (1758), *Anecdotes of Painting in England* (1762–71), *Catalogue of Engravers who Have Been Born or Resided in England* (1763), *Historic Doubts of the Life and Reign of Richard III* (1768), *Essay on Modern Gardening* (1785) and an edn of Lucan's *Pharsalia* (1760, with notes by the classical scholar Richard Bentley); after his death he acquired an even wider reputation as a social historian, chiefly through his voluminous correspondence, most notably with Sir Horace Mann, then British Ambassador in Naples; *d* unm 2 March 1797, when all his honours expired bar the Barony of Walpole of Walpole

(1) Mary; *b c* 1705; *m* 14 Sept 1723 3rd Earl of Cholmondeley (*see* CHOLMONDELEY, M) and *d* 2 Jan 1731/2, leaving issue

2 HORATIO WALPOLE, **1st Baron Walpole of Wolterton**, Co Norfolk (GB), so *cr* 4 June 1756, PC (GB 1730, I 1720); *b* 8 Dec 1678; *educ* Eton, King's Coll Cambridge (BA, MA, Fell 1702–14) and Lincoln's Inn; MP (Whig) Lostwithiel 1710, Castle Rising 1710–15, Beeralston 1715–17, E Looe 1718–22, Gt Yarmouth 1722–34, Norwich 1734–56; diplomat (Min Plen The Hague Jan-April 1715, Oct 1715–Oct 1716 and May-July 1722, Envoy Extrdny Paris 1721 and Jan 1723/4, Amb Paris 1724–27 and 1727–30 and The Hague 1734–39), U-Sec North 1708–10 and 1714–15, Commr Revenue 1714–16, Sec Treasury 1715–17 and 1721, Surveyor and Auditor-Gen Revenue America (for life) 1717, Sec State Ireland 1720–21 and Cofferer Household 1730–41; *m* 21 July 1720 Mary Magdalen, dau and coheir of Peter Lombard, and *d* 5 Feb 1757, leaving, with other daus (*d* unm):

(1) HORATIO WALPOLE, **2nd Baron Walpole of Wolterton** and **4th Baron Walpole of Walpole**, as which *s* cousin 1797, *cr* also 10 April 1806 EARL OF ORFORD (UK); *b* 12 June 1723; MP (Whig) King's Lynn 1747–57; *m* 12 May 1748 Rachel (*d* 8 May 1805), 3rd dau of Duke of Devonshire (*qv*), and *d* 24 Feb 1809, having had, with other issue (*d* unm):

  1a HORATIO WALPOLE, **3rd Baron Walpole of Wolterton**, **5th Baron Walpole of Walpole** and 2nd EARL OF ORFORD; *b* 24 June 1752; *m* 1st 27 July 1781 Sophia (*d* 1797), dau of Charles Churchill, and had, with other issue:

    1b HORATIO WALPOLE, **4th Baron Walpole of Wolterton**, **6th Baron Walpole of Walpole** and 3rd EARL OF ORFORD; *b* 14 June 1783; High Steward Borough of Lynn, Col W Norfolk Militia; *m* 23 July 1812 Mary (*d* 4 Feb 1860), dau of William Augustus Fawkener, of Brocton Hall, Salop, and *d* 29 Dec 1858, having had:

      1c HORATIO WILLIAM WALPOLE, **5th Baron Walpole of Wolterton**, **7th Baron Walpole of Walpole** and 4th EARL OF ORFORD, DL; *b* 18 April 1813; *m* 11 Nov 1841 Harriet Bettina Frances (*d* 9 Nov 1886), only child of Hon Sir Fleetwood Broughton Reynolds Pellew (*see* EXMOUTH, V), and *d* 7 Dec 1894, leaving:

1d Dorothy Elizabeth Mary; m 25 Feb 1868 the Duke Del Balzo, of Naples, only s of the Marquis della Señora del Balzo, Grandee Spain 1st Cl, and d 1921

2d Maude Mary; m 11 Nov 1871 Count Salvatore Griefeo and Gravana, Prince Palagonia, Grandee Spain 1st Cl, and d 2 June 1874

2c Henry; b 1 May 1818; m 3 July 1845 Cecilia Elizabeth (d 20 May 1887), dau of John Macalister, of Strathaird, and dsp 6 Nov 1876

3c Frederick; b 18 Sept 1822; Cdr RN, MP N Norfolk; m 12 Feb 1852 his cousin Laura Sophia Frances (d 26 Jan 1901), only dau of Francis Walpole, and d 1 April 1876, leaving:

1d ROBERT HORACE WALPOLE, **6th Baron Walpole of Wolterton, 8th Baron Walpole of Walpole** and 5th and last EARL OF ORFORD, JP (Norfolk and Norwich), DL (Norfolk); b 10 July 1854; Lt RN and Capt 4th Bn Norfolk Regt, attd Special Embassy to King of Spain's wedding 1877 (Order Charles III Spain), Priv Sec to his cousin Sir Henry Wolff's E Roumelian Commn 1878 and his Special Mission to Egypt 1886; m 1st 17 May 1888 Louise Melissa (d 4 May 1909), dau of D C Corbin, of New York, and had:

1e Horatio Corbin; b 9 Jan 1891; d 20 May 1893

1e Dorothy Rachel Melissa; b 11 March 1889; FRGS, memb Portuguese Geographical Soc; m 22 June 1916 (divorce 1933) Capt Arthur Hobart Mills (d 18 Feb 1955), DCLI, est s of Rev Barton Reginald Vaughan Mills, and dsp 4 Dec 1959

1d (cont.) The **6th/8th Baron** and 5th EARL m 2nd 15 Sept 1917 Emily Gladys, yst dau of Rev Thomas Henry Royal Oakes, Rector Thurgarton, Norwich, and dspms 27 Sept 1931, when the Earldom expired, having by her had:

2e Gladys Grace Sophia; b 4 Sept 1918; d 9 June 1919

3e Anne Sophia, JP (1964) [The Lady Anne Berry JP, Hackfalls, PO Box 3, Tiniroto, via Gisborne, New Zealand]; b 11 Dec 1919; VMH 1986, Hon FRHS 1988, Hon DSc Exeter 1990, Chm Internat Dendrology Soc 1982–87, V-Pres Internat Dendrology Soc England 1988–; m 1st 25 Nov 1939 Col Joseph Eric Palmer, CBE, TD, JP, DL (d 1980), 2nd s of Joseph Palmer, of Lymm, Cheshire; m 2nd 1990 *Robert James Berry, of Tiniroto, NZ, and has by her 1st husb:

1f *John Robert [John Palmer Esq, Kirkmichael House, Blairgowrie, Perthshire PH10 7NS]; b 6 March 1943; educ Eton; Capt RHG 1962–68; m 1st 9 Oct 1971 Carolyn, only dau of William Henry Atkinson-Clarke, of Ashintully Castle, Kirkmichael, Blairgowrie; m 2nd *Mrs Alison Ann Allinson, dau of Dr Noel Ian Bartholomew, of The Old Vicarage, N Bavant, Wilts

2f *Anthony Eric Fletcher [Anthony Palmer Esq, Knowl Hill House, Kingsclere, Berks RG15 8NY]; b 4 Nov 1945; educ Eton; ACA; m 31 March 1970 *Nicola Mary, only dau of H Maude, of Gisborne, NZ

2d Clare Horatio; b 21 Nov 1858; m Ann Gardner, of Nelson, Va., and d 6 May 1906, leaving:

1e Amye; m Hugh Wheelwright Davis and d 19–, leaving:

1f *Walpole; b 8 April 1914; educ U of Virginia; m 30 Sept 1944 *Lucie Morton and has:

1g *Walpole; b 19 Sept 1948; educ Aiglon Coll Switzerland

1g *Anne Taylor; b 19 Sept 1949; educ Monte Rosa Coll Switzerland

2f *Horace Walpole; b 5 Aug 1921; educ U of Virginia; m 8 March 1956 *Caralee Burson, dau of Donald Leyland Young, of Pasadena, Ca.

1d Amye Rachel; m 16 April 1872 4th Viscount Canterbury and d 23 Jan 1935, leaving issue (see RUTLAND, D)

1c Rachel Katherine; m 24 Feb 1842 4th Earl of Mexborough (qv) and d 21 June 1854, leaving issue

2c Dorothy Fanny; m 2 Dec 1847 Reginald Henry Nevill and d 24 March 1913, leaving issue (see ABERGAVENNY, M)

1b Maria; m 9 Aug 1817 Martin John West, barrister, Commr Bankrupts Leeds Dist, Recorder Lynn, and d 6 Dec 1870

2b Harriet; m 17 April 1817 Sir William Hoste, 1st Bt, KBE, Post Capt RN (d 6 Dec 1828; see 1902 edn), and d 18 April 1875, leaving issue

3b Georgiana Mary; m 6 Feb 1827 Rev Joseph Wolff, DD, LLD (d 2 May 1862), Vicar Isle Brewers, Somerset, and d 16 Jan 1859, leaving:

1c Henry Drummond (Sir), GCB, GCMG; MP 1874–85; d 11 Oct 1908

1a (cont.) The **3rd/5th Baron** and 2nd EARL m 2nd 28 July 1806 Catherine Tunstall (d 1807), widow of Rev Edward Chamberlayne, and d 15 June 1822

2a George; b 20 June 1758; d May 1835

1a Mary; m 4 Aug 1777 Thomas Hussey, of Galtrim, Co Meath

(2) Thomas; b 6 Oct 1727; MP; m 14 Nov 1753 Elizabeth (d 9 June 1760), est dau of Sir Joshua Vanneck, Bt (see HUNTINGFIELD, B), and d March 1803, leaving, with two daus (d unm):

1a Thomas, of Stagbury Park, Surrey; b 23 May 1755; Envoy Extrdy and Min Plen Bavaria; m 1 Dec 1803 Margaret (d 12 Dec 1854), 5th dau of 2nd Earl of Egmont (qv), and d 3 Nov 1840, leaving:

1b Thomas (Rev); b 30 Sept 1805; MA Oxon; Rector Alverstoke, Hants, Hon Canon Winchester; m 15 Jan 1833 Margaret Harriet Isabella (d 29 June 1876), est dau of Col Henry Hugh Mitchell, and d 8 Feb 1881, having had, with another s (d young) and two daus (d unm):

1c Henry Spencer WALPOLE later VADE-WALPOLE (roy licence 27 Oct 1892), of Stagbury and Freethorpe, Norfolk; b 10 March 1837; barrister; m 19 July 1877 Frances Selina (d 17 Sept 1924), 2nd dau of Thomas Bourke and widow of Denzil Thomas Chamberlayne, and d 1 March 1913, leaving:

1d Thomas Henry Bourke; b 2 Sept 1879; Lt 10th Bn Gordon Highrs; d unm ka France 20 Sept 1915

2d Horatio Spencer WALPOLE later VADE-WALPOLE later still WALPOLE again (deed poll 1913); b 19 June 1881; educ New Coll Oxford (BA); Lt Coldstream Gds, slr; m 3 July 1906 Dorothea Frances

(d 10 Jan 1971), only dau of Frederick Molyneux Montgomerie, of S Kensington, and was ka 9 April 1918, leaving:

1e ROBERT HENRY MONTGOMERIE WALPOLE, **7th Baron Walpole of Wolterton** and **9th Baron Walpole of Walpole**, TD; b 25 April 1913; educ Eton, Wye Ag Coll and RAC Cirencester; Capt RA; m 14 July 1937 *Nancy Louisa, OBE (1977), JP (Norfolk 1941), past pres BRCS Norfolk, yst dau of Frank Harding Jones, of Kensington, and d 1989, having had:

1f ROBERT HORATIO WALPOLE, **8th and present Baron Walpole of Wolterton** and **10th Baron Walpole of Walpole**

2f Jonathan Henry; b 27 July 1951; d 26 Jan 1961

1f Mary; b 19 Nov, d 20 Nov 1948

2f *Phillida Ann [The Hon Mrs Hurn, Beck Farm, Calthorpe, Norwich NR11 7NG]; b 18 Jan 1950; m 1st 6 Jan 1973 (divorce 1981) Clive Grainger Morgan-Evans, only s of Clive Victor Evans, of Cheswardine, Salop, and has:

1g *Edward Grainger; b 25 June 1973; educ Framlingham Coll

2g *Daniel Rupert; b 2 May 1977; educ Framlingham Coll

2f (cont.) The Hon Mrs Phillida Morgan-Evans m 2nd 1983 *Anthony Hurn

1e Pamela Frances, OBE (1960, MBE 1949), JP (Norfolk 1949); b 22 Feb 1908; granted 22 July 1939 rank of baron's dau, memb: WLA 1939, RDC 1944–70 (chm Smallburgh RDC 1961–66); d 19–

2c Horatio John Thomas; b 26 July 1842; Lt-Col Rifle Bde; d 28 Feb 1924

3c Ralph Charles; b 5 June 1844; Librarian H of C; m 21 June 1924 Emily Fraser, widow of Latimer T Le Merchant, and d 20 Feb 1928

1c Henrietta Elizabeth; m 15 April 1856 Maj John James Charles Irby and d 17 Jan 1916, leaving issue (see BOSTON, B)

2b Spencer Horatio, PC; b 11 Sept 1806; MP Cambridge U 1856–82, QC, LLD, FRS, Home Sec 1852, 1858 and 1866; m 6 Oct 1835 Isabella (d 16 July 1886 aged 84), dau of Rt Hon Spencer Perceval (see EGMONT, E), and d 22 May 1898, leaving, with a dau (d unm):

1c Spencer (Sir), KCB; b 6 Feb 1839; Clerk War Office 1858, Inspr Fisheries 1867, Govr IOM 1893–99, Hon LLD Edinburgh, Hon LittD Oxon; m 12 Nov 1867 Marion Jane (d 9 May 1912), yr dau of Sir John Digby Murray, 10th Bt, of Blackbarony (qv), and d 7 July 1907, having had:

1d Spencer Digby; b 17 April 1869; d 22 Feb 1871

1d Maud Constance; b 6 May 1870; m 9 Nov 1897 Francis Caldwell Holland (see KNUTSFORD, V) and d 23 March 1949

2c Horatio George (Sir), KCB, JP; b 9 Sept 1843; Assist U-Sec India 1883–1907, Sec Roy Commn on Civil Establishments 1886–90; m 23 June 1870 Selina Maria (d 5 Nov 1925), dau of John Thomas Perceval (see EGMONT, E), and d 29 June 1923, leaving:

1d Reginald Horace; b 27 Oct 1875; educ New Coll Oxford (BA); barrister; m 16 Dec 1905 Agnes Edwardine Brewster (d 5 Feb 1952), er dau of Rev Preb F Hancock, of The Priory, Dunster, and dsp 24 March 1946

2d Robert Spencer Hobhouse; b 11 Jan 1881; educ Wellington; Maj Rifle Bde; m 5 June 1923 Edith Winifred (d 1978), yst dau of S H Keeling, of Parkfield, Kenilworth, and d 1975, leaving:

1e +Horace Jeremy Spencer [Lt-Cdr Horace Walpole RN, Old Forge, Ashton Keynes, Wilts SN6 6NX]; b 8 Sept 1924; educ RNC Dartmouth; Lt-Cdr RN; m 5 April 1950 *Mary Elizabeth Bruce, only dau of Harold Joseph Kidman, and has:

1f +Robert Charles Spencer [Robert Walpole Esq, Stocks Farmhouse, Meysey Hampton, Glos]; b 9 Aug 1955; educ Wellington; m 1st 14 Feb 1975 (divorce 1986) Diana Rosemary Bishop and has:

1g +Daniel Nicholas Spencer; b 15 Jan 1977

2g +Thomas James; b 7 May 1980

1g *Theresa; b 23 Oct 1975

1f (cont.) Robert C S Walpole m 2nd 5 Sept 1987 *Judith, dau of Carrick McLelland, of Wester Housebyes, Melrose, and by her has:

2g *Catherine Mary; b 4 March 1992

3g *Helen; b 11 July 1995

1f *Caroline Mary Bruce; b 20 Jan 1951

2f *Elizabeth Jane Bruce; b 11 Jan 1953; has by *Dr Peter Lawrence:

1g *Emma Victoria; b 4 March 1990

2g *Charlotte Alice; b 2 June 1991

3f *Lucy Margaret Bruce [Mrs Stephen 1 Down Ampney, Glos]; b 9 Aug 1955; m 12 Oct 1974 *Stephen Ashcroft and has:

1g *Simon James; b 16 Nov 1975

2g *Christopher Andrew Jeremy; b 23 April 1981

1g *Caroline Jennifer; b 14 June 1978

4f *Charlotte Victoria Bruce [Mrs James Trumper, The Bothy, The Whiteway, Cirencester, Glos]; b 16 March 1960; m 8 Aug 1987 *James Ronald Trumper, s of William Trumper, of Bloxham, Oxon, and has:

1g *Fiona Jane; b 25 Aug 1991

1e *Elizabeth Clare Selina; b 7 July 1932; m 1971 *John Whipp, of Bedfield, Suffolk

1d Margaret; b 28 July 1873; m 25 Oct 1907 Walter Yarowyck Wyndham (d 23 Dec 1942), yr s of William Trevelyan Wyndham, and d 8 Feb 1964

1c Isabella Margaretta Elizabeth; m 15 June 1869 George Parker Heathcote, 2nd s of Sir William Heathcote, 5th Bt, of Hursley (qv), and d 22 Oct 1938

1b Robert (Sir), KCB; b 1 Dec 1808; Col 65th Regt, Lt-Gen IA; m 29 Jan 1846 Gertrude (d 22 Nov 1903), yst dau of Gen William H Ford, and d 12 July 1876, having had, with two other daus (d unm):

1c Robert Edmund; *b* 11 Jan 1847; *d* 28 April 1867

2c George; *b* 16 Feb 1848; *d* 26 Nov 1872

3c Spencer Charles; *b* 10 Feb 1852; *m* 23 Dec 1885 Jessie Madeline (*d* 3 Oct 1926), dau of Rev Tressilian George Nicholas, Vicar W Molesey, Surrey, and *d* 2 Feb 1934, leaving:

 1d Geraldine Edith; *d* unm 21 Sept 1955

 2d Madeline Rachel; *b* 2 Feb 1889; *m* 26 Aug 1926 Rev Arthur Hugh Rawlins Robinson (*d* 25 Dec 1945), Vicar Ringmer, Sussex, s of Rev Canon Arthur James Robinson, and *d* 19–

 3d Lucy Gertrude; *d* 19–

4c William Henry; *b* 27 April 1862; *m* 20 Sept 1893 Minnie (*m* 2nd Feb 1905 Percy Henry Thomas Broad, er s of J M Broad, of Bristol), 2nd dau of Capt Frank T Thomason, RN, and *dsp* 31 Jan 1902

1c Geraldine Frances; *m* 10 Oct 1872 Sir Colman Battle Rashleigh, 3rd Bt (*qv*), and *d* 24 Dec 1876, leaving issue

2c Catherine Lucy; *b* 2 Aug 1865; *d* unm 4 March 1944

3c Gertrude Margaret; *b* 12 Feb 1867; *d* unm 16 June 1955

4b John VADE-WALPOLE; *b* 23 April 1810; Assist Sec Govt Emigration Bd; *m* 17 May 1841 Henrietta (*d* 8 Jan 1899), dau of Col Henry Browne Smith, and *d* 30 Jan 1892, having had:

 1c Thomas Arthur; *b* June 1845; *d* 19 May 1858

5b Charles VADE-WALPOLE, CB; *b* 16 Aug 1813; *m* 13 May 1846 Annette (*d* 3 April 1885), dau of R-Adml James Provost, and *d* 2 Nov 1891, leaving:

 1c Charles George VADE-WALPOLE later WALPOLE, JP; *b* 7 Sept 1848; *educ* Cambridge (MA); barrister Inner Temple 1873, Attorney-Gen Leeward Islands 1889–92, Ch Justice Gibraltar 1892–93 and Bahamas 1893–97; ktd 189–, CC Surrey, FRGS; *m* 1st 18 Aug 1877 Maria Elizabeth (*d* 24 Sept 1914), 2nd dau of Henry Ford, of Ford Green, Staffs; *m* 2nd 19 Jan 1922 Marie Bowles (*d* 5 Feb 1928), dau of Percy Hale Wallace and widow of Maj Henry James Seton (*see* SETON, Bt, of Abercorn), and *d* 24 May 1926, having by his 1st w had, with a dau (*d* unm):

  1d Charles Archibald, OBE (1919), *b* 25 March 1881; manager Anglo-Perslan Oil Co, Mohammerah, Persian Gulf, FRGS; *m* 16 Dec 1927 (divorce 1935) Dorothea Hume de Falloux, yr dau of Lt-Cdr B Critchley-Salmonson, RN, and *dsp* 2 Jan 1943

  2d John Robsart; *b* 26 Dec 1882; Capt 1/7th Serv Bn Queen's Roy W Surrey Regt; *ka* 1 July 1916

  1d Kathleen Cypria; *b* 2 Oct 1884; *m* 11 Feb 1920 Denis Arthur Turpin, of Lahore, Punjab, s of Capt W A Turpin, and *d* 20 Dec 1922

 1b Catherine Margaret; *m* 8 April 1861 Baron de Teissier and *d* 18 March 1876

2b Sophia Frances; *m* 21 Aug 1849 Rev Edward Riou Berens (*dsp* 31 July 1867) and *d* 8 Feb 1900

2a Lambert Theodore; *b* 28 Dec 1757; Lt-Col; *m* 11 Jan 1788 Margaret (*d* June 1814), dau of 1st Baron Clive of Plassey (*see* POWIS, E), and *d* 1798, leaving two daus (*d* unm)

(3) Richard; *b* 5 Dec 1728; MP Yarmouth; *m* 22 Nov 1757 Margaret (*d* 9 May 1818), sis of 1st Baron Huntingfield (*qv*), and *d* 18 Aug 1789, leaving:

1a Richard; *b* 16 June 1762; *m* 23 Jan 1792 Elizabeth, dau of Sir Benjamin Hammet, and *dsp* 15 Aug 1811

2a Robert; *b* 1768; *d* unm 18 May 1834

3a Edward; *b* 1776; *d* unm 1 Oct 1844

1a Mary Rachel; *m* 4 Jan 1798 Rev Aston Vade (*d* 26 May 1820), Chaplain to GEORGE IV when PRINCE OF WALES, and *d* 16 Sept 1827, leaving issue

2a Caroline; *m* 12 May 1787 Hon George Henry Nevill and *d* 21 Dec 1841, leaving issue (*see* ABERGAVENNY, M)

(4) Robert; *b* 3 May 1736; Clerk of PC, Envoy Extrdy and Min Plen Portugal; *m* 1st 8 May 1780 Diana (*d* 24 July 1784), dau of Walter Grosset, and had, with another s (*dsp*):

1a Robert (Robert); *b* 8 Aug 1781; Rector Ch Ch Marylebone; *m* 6 Feb 1811 Caroline Frances (*d* 11 Dec 1840), dau of John Hyde, and *d* 16 April 1856, having had, with two daus (*d* unm):

 1b Reginald Robert; *b* 8 Dec 1817; barrister; *m* 1st 1 May 1849 Anne Eliza (*d* 18 Nov 1854), 3rd dau of John Heaton, of Plas Heaton, Denbighs, and had:

  1c Emily Jessie Horatia; *m* 29 Oct 1879 John Lynch Fletcher and had issue

 1b (cont.) Reginald Walpole *m* 2nd 17 Jan 1856 Caroline (*d* 22 Feb 1899), dau of Rev Frederick Apthorp and widow of William Watts, of Hanslope Park, Bucks, and *d* 28 July 1880, leaving by her:

  2c Diana Caroline; *m* 18 April 1876 James Boughey Monk Lingard-Monk (*d* 19 Aug 1906), s of Richard Boughey Lingard-Monk, of Fulshaw Hall, Cheshire, and *dsp* 13 May 1891

  3c Regina Caroline; *m* 17 July 1883 Thomas Dewhurst Lingard (*d* 14 Jan 1925), of Fellside, Windemere, and had issue

  4c Caroline Emily; *m* 20 Jan 1881 William Martin Cunningham (*d* 7 Feb 1924) and had issue

 2b Robert Seymour (Rev); *b* 20 Sept 1820; Lt 77th Foot, Vicar Balderton, Notts, 1852–78; *m* 11 Aug 1848 Elizabeth, 4th dau of Rev Frederick Apthorp, Rector Gumley, and *d* 1910, having had, with a dau (*d* unm):

  1c Horatio Frederick William Seymour; *b* 4 Dec 1850; *m* 1877 Laura Anne, dau of Joseph Coombe, and *d* 17 Dec 1887, leaving:

   1d Robert Somerset George Reginald; *b* 25 Aug 1878; *d* 19–

   2d Horace Henry Vade; *b* 5 April 1883; *d* 19–

  2c Herbert Reginald Robert Seymour; *b* 6 Dec 1853; *m* 23 Aug 1882 Jane Sophia (*d* 1916), dau of W Palmer Kent, of Tasmania, and *d* 2 July 1928, leaving:

   1d Francis Seymour; *b* 1895; *d* 19–

   1d Beatrice Adelaide; *m* 16 March 1912 Maj Kenneth Stuart Cross, MD, MSc, Australian Army Medical Corps (Res), and *d* 18 Nov 1964, leaving issue

2d Florence Louise; *b* 1885; *d* 19–

3d Lucy Apthorp; *b* 1887; *m* 1912 Robert Balcombe Beggs (*d* 10 March 1954) and *d* 19–, having had issue

4d Gladys; *d* unm 12 Dec 1969

5d Agnes Jane; *b* 1893; *m* 3 Dec 1918 Theodore Beggs, JP (*d* 1940), MLC, and *d* 19–, having had issue

3c George Henry Somerset (Rt Rev); *b* 9 Nov 1854; *educ* Trin Coll Cambridge (MA), Hon DD (1891); Rector Lambeth 1903–10, Hon Canon Southwark 1906–10, Bp Edinburgh 1910–29; *m* 12 Sept 1882 Mildred Helen (*d* 23 June 1925), dau of Charles Foster Barham, and *d* 4 March 1929, leaving:

 1d Hugh (Seymour) (Sir), CBE (1918); *b* 13 March 1884; *educ* King's Sch, Canterbury, Bede Coll Durham and Emmanuel Coll Cambridge; Russian Red Cross WW I, ktd 1937, author: *The Wooden Horse* (1910), *Maradick at Forty* (1910), *Mr Perrin and Mr Traill* (1911), *Fortitude* (1913), *The Duchess of Wrexe* (1914), *Joseph Conrad* (1916), *The Dark Forest* (1916), *The Secret City* (1919, James Tait Black Memorial Prize), *Jeremy* (1919), *The Art of James Branch Cabell* (1920), *Jeremy and Hamlet* (1923), *The Crystal Box* (1924), *Jeremy at Crale* (1927), *Anthony Trollope* (1928), *Farthing Hall* (with J B Priestley, 1929), *Rogue Herries* (1930), *Judith Paris* (1931), *The Fortress* (1932), *The Apple Trees* (1932), *Vanessa* (1933) and *Roman Fountain* (1940) among more than 40 popular novels, biographies and autobiographical books; *d* unm 1 June 1941

 2d Robert Henry; *b* 18 Jan 1892; *educ* Westminster and Magdalene Coll Cambridge (BA 1914); Lt Rifle Bde WW I 1916–18; *d* unm 6 May 1963

 1d Dorothea Elizabeth; *b* 20 Feb 1887; MB, ChB (Edin) 1925; *d* unm 16 Nov 1959

4c Richard Herbert; *b* 13 Jan 1858; *m* 1885 Sophia Louise (*d* 19 May 1944), dau of Hatsell Mellersh Garrard, and *d* 19–

(4) (cont.) The Hon Robert Walpole *m* 2nd 10 May 1785 Sophia (*d* 12 June 1829), dau of Richard Stert, of Lisbon, and *d* 19 April 1810, having by her had, with other issue:

2a Henry; *b* 2 Oct 1787; Lt-Gen IA; *m* 21 Aug 1834 Elizabeth Carpenter (*d* 19 April 1879), dau of Maj-Gen C F Smith, HEICS and *d* 29 Jan 1854, leaving:

 1b Henry; *b* 23 Jan 1836; Lt Madras Service; *m* 1871 Sempe Georgina, dau of Matthew Templeton, of Calcutta, and *d* 1 May 1878, leaving:

  1c Henry; *b* 1873; *d* 19–

 1b Eliza; *d* unm 29 May 1917 aged 81

3a Edward; *b* 2 June 1791; *m* 24 Jan 1815 Ann Theresa (*d* 15 Jan 1878), dau of Daniel Gildermeester, and *d* 31 Oct 1857, having had, with two daus (*d* unm):

 1b Horatio Edward; *b* 27 Feb 1820; Maj-Gen Madras Army; *dsp* 22 Jan 1892

 2b Frederick Goulburn; *b* 30 May 1829; *m* 15 Jan 1864 Amalie Trafford Haughton (*d* 7 Oct 1895), dau of Dr Edward Binns, of Jamaica, by Charlotte, later w of Duke of Saldanha, Portuguese Min England, and *d* 3 Sept 1901, leaving:

  1c Horace Henry Maximilian; *b* 18 Sept 1867; Capt 9th Bn Rifle Bde; *d* unm 23 July 1910

  1c Gwendolen Anna; *b* 19 Oct 1864; nun; *d* 19 April 1934

  2c Maud Josephine Charlotte; *b* 11 Oct 1865; *d* unm 10 Dec 1944

  3c Adeline Mary; *m* 1898 William Edwin Williams (*d* 17 April 1914), of Ty Clyd Govilon, nr Abergavenny, s of John Jones Williams, of Coed Iorwg, Abertillery, Mon, and Llanhilleth, Mon, took by deed poll 18 June 1914 the name KEYNTON-WILLIAMS and *dsp* 7 July 1929

  4c Mary Pauline; *m* 1 Sept 1917 P Burd Jagger, of Marylebone, and *dsp* 31 March 1944

 1b Josephine Maria; *m* 1860 Henry Maximilian, Baron de Tuyll de Serooskerken (*d* 1888), and *d* 20 March 1907

4a Francis; *b* 1 Jan 1795; *m* 8 May 1828 Elizabeth (*d* 3 Aug 1860), dau of Thomas A Knight, of Downton Castle, and *d* 9 Jan 1861, having had:

 1b Horatio Andrew; *b* 21 Feb 1829; *d* 20 Jan 1855

 1b Laura Sophia Frances; *m* 12 Feb 1852 her cousin Hon Frederick Walpole (*see* above) and *d* 26 Jan 1901

5a John; *b* 14 July 1797; Maj-Gen RE; *d* 4 Jan 1864

6a Horatio; *b* 27 Aug 1799; Col; *m* 22 July 1835 Fanny Sophia (*d* 18 April 1873), est dau of Col Thomas Henry Somerset Conway, CB, and *d* April 1886, having had, with another s and a dau (*d* young):

 1b Horatio; *b* 1837; Army Capt; *d* 1873

 2b Henry; *b* 15 Nov 1846; Lt-Col Loyal N Lancs Regt; *d* –

(1) Mary; *b* 25 Feb 1725/6; *m* Capt Maurice Suckling, RN, the early patron of Adml Lord Nelson

3 Galfridus; *b* 16–; RN; *dsp* –

1 Mary; *m* Sir Charles Turner, of Warham, Norfolk (*see* NELSON, E)

2 Dorothy; *m* as his 2nd w, before 25 July 1713 2nd Viscount Townshend (*see* TOWNSHEND, M) and *d* 29 March 1726, having had issue

3 Susan; *m* Anthony Hamond (*d* 7 Feb 1743), of Wotton, Norfolk, and had issue

Seats: Mannington Hall, Mannington, Norwich; Wolterton Hall, Norfolk. A certain William Lumnor built Mannington in 1460, during the Wars of the Roses. But licence to crenellate is said to have been granted as far back as 1451 and if so some earlier building might conceivably have existed already, though on balance this is thought unlikely. The grey stone of the elevations, the moat, which may predate the present house, and a lightly battlemented top to the great southern central block above a cornice, culminating in a polygonal but not very substantial tower at the southwest corner which in turn is matched by a still smaller one the other side of a low-pitched gable further along towards the southeast corner, give Mannington great charm. But it is difficult to believe it could have been seriously defensible, especially given the generously proportioned mullion windows on three storeys. They have gently curved tops on the uppermost storey and straight horizontal ones surmounted by dripstones lower down but are of two to four bays wide and would not have kept a determined attacker out. They would appear to be 16th-century, however, so may have replaced narrower apertures after the newly arrived Tudor dynasty had restored peace to the Norfolk countryside.

Mannington passed down through families called Tirel and Dodge till the 17th-century Civil War, when it was owned by Sir John Potts, who was nevertheless related to the previous proprietors. It was bought by the **1st Baron Walpole of Wolterton** in 1720, but only for use as a dower house. (Mannington and Wolterton are on the same estate, which now extends to about 2,000 acres.) None of the Walpoles actually lived there till the mid–19th century, when the purchaser's descendant the **5th Baron Walpole of Walterton** and **7th Baron Walpole of Walpole** (who was also the 4th Earl of Orford of the 2nd creation) moved in. Like his namesake the 4th Earl of Orford of the first creation, better known as Horace Walpole, he was enthralled by the past, and refurbished and enlarged his new home. The northeast and northern wings date from his time. Their projection from the earlier part gives Mannington the shape of a question mark minus the dot, and with its trunk substantially thicker than its arched head. Subsequently the house was let and only reoccupied by the head of the family, the present Lord Walpole, in 1969. He has completely transformed the grounds, placing special emphasis on roses, which have an area all of their own. A variety of historical species are on display there, each in a setting landscaped to depict the English garden as it looked in the appropriate period.

Wolterton dates from the 1720s, being erected in Norfolk red brick with Portland stone facing by the **1st Baron Walpole of Wolterton**. He seems initially to have intended remodelling an earlier house on which his newly-bought estate centred. When that largely burned down he started afresh, enlisting the designs of Thomas Ripley, who had worked on Houghton (*see* CHOLMONDELEY, M) for his brother Sir Robert. The main elevation is a break-front one and consists of two storeys of five bays each over a basement enclosed in arches underneath a terrace with balustrades. The three central bays are surmounted by a pediment, to either side of which stretches a large balustraded parapet. During the 19th century G S Repton remodelled the house on its southern side and an extension culminating in a tower to the east was put up to designs by Philip Hardwick. After the **4th Baron Walpole of Wolterton** and **6th Baron Walpole of Walpole**, who was also 3rd Earl of Orford, died in 1858 and Mannington was adopted as the family seat, Wolterton was shut up for nearly half a century. The **6th Baron Walpole of Wolterton** and **8th Baron Walpole of Walpole** (who was also the 5th and last Earl of Orford of the second creation) moved back in after inheriting the titles. Having married a New York heiress, he could afford to refurbish. Wolterton's subsequent history is almost a catalogue of the 20th-century woes of the English country house: wartime requisitioning, a fire, dry rot and the sale of contents following the lingering illness of its last occupant the **7th/9th Baron**, who was thus prevented from caring for it. Happily the 1990s have seen a thorough restoration programme set in motion.

The core of the house contains the main staircase. As with so many mansions of the period, the grand apartments are on the first floor, or piano nobile. They include the Blue Drawing Room, the Boudoir, the Marble Hall, the Saloon, the State Bed Room with its adjacent Dressing Room, the State Dining Room and the Venetian Room.

WALSHAM

Arms: Quarterly, 1st and 4th, per pale azure and gules a griffin segreant, wings elevated or, supporting on a tilting spear a banner flowing to the dexter argent, charged with a cross couped sable (for GARBETT); 2nd and 3rd, sable on a cross voided or five crosslets patée-fitchée of the last (for WALSHAM). **Crest:** A demi-eagle with two heads displayed sable, pendant from the neck by a gold chain an escutcheon argent and thereon a Saracen's head erased at the neck proper, round the temples a wreath argent and azure.
Motto: *Sub libertate quietem* ('Rest under liberty').
Creation: Bt. (UK) 30 Sept. 1831.

SIR TIMOTHY JOHN WALSHAM, 5TH BT, of Knill Court, Herefordshire [Sir Timothy Walsham Bt, Beckford Close, Tisbury, Wilts SP3 6QT]; *b* 26 April 1939; *s f* 1992; *educ* Sherborne; with P&O 1960–67, Roy Fleet Aux Serv 1968–72

Lineage: JOHN WALSHAM, of Presteigne, Herefs; *m* Mary, gdau and coheir of Sir Jenkin Harvey, of Llanvair, Montgomeryshire, thus acquiring much property in Radnorshire, and *d* 1473, leaving:

RICHARD WALSHAM, of Presteigne; *m* Eleanor Powell and *d* 1496, leaving an only s:

JOHN WALSHAM, JP (Herefs), of Presteigne; *m* Jane, dau and coheir of Thomas Chapman, of Discoed, and *d* 1524, leaving:

JOHN WALSHAM, of Presteigne; *m* Anne, dau of Morgan Williams and sis of Sir Richard Williams *alias* Cromwell, ancestor of OLIVER CROMWELL, and *d* 1557, leaving an est s:

JOHN WALSHAM, of Presteigne; *m* Anne, dau of Peter Lloyd, of Boultbroke, Sheriff Radnorshire 1548 and 1557, and *d* 1599, leaving an est s:

JOHN WALSHAM, of Presteigne; *m* Barbara, dau and heir of Francis Knill, of Knill Court, Herefs, descended from Sir John de Knill, feudal Ld of Knill in the 12th century, and *d* 1639, leaving an est s:

JOHN WALSHAM, of Knill Court; of age 1643; *m* Margaret, dau of Roger Lyde, of Lyde's Court, Herefs, and *d* 1648, leaving an est s:

JOHN WALSHAM, of Knill Court; Sheriff Radnorshire 1653; *m* Joanna, dau of John Jones, of Llandetty Court, Breconshire, and sis of Col Jenkin Jones, a Puritan leader, and *d* 1667, leaving an only s:

JOHN WALSHAM, of Knill Court; Sheriff Radnorshire 1670; *m* 1st Elizabeth, dau of Sir William Lygon, of Madresfield Court (*see* 1970 edn BEAUCHAMP, E), but by her had no issue; *m* 2nd Elizabeth, dau of Sir William Childe, of Kinlet, Salop, and *d* 1695, leaving by her an only s:

JOHN WALSHAM, of Knill Court, DL (Radnorshire); *m* Hester, er dau and eventually coheir of Sir John Morgan, Bt, of Kinnersley Castle, Herefs, MP Herefs and Govr Chester, and *d* 1734, leaving an er s:

JOHN WALSHAM, DL, of Knill Court; *m* Elizabeth, dau and coheir of Alderman Ford, of Hereford, and *dspm* 1751, leaving an only child:

ELIZABETH Walsham; *m* 1767 Francis GARBETT, of Huntington Park, Herefs, Sheriff Radnorshire 1790, only s of Samuel Garbett, of Pool Hall, Warwicks, descendant and heir male of Robert Garbett, of Acton Burnel, Salop, Exon Yeomen Gd 1486, and *d* 1779, leaving, with three daus (Anne, *m* 3 Jan 1798 Sir Samuel Romilly, KC, MP, and *d* 29 Oct 1818; Mary, *m* John Whittaker, of Newcastle Court, Radnorshire; Sophia, *m* William Davies, of Cabalva, Radnorshire, and *dsp* 1838):

JOHN GARBETT later WALSHAM, of Knill Court, DL (Herefs and Radnorshire); *b* 26 June 1771; Col Radnorshire Militia; *m* 21 June 1804 Anna Maria (*d* 29 March 1863), dau and sole heiress of Hugh Hughes, of Bodwryn, Anglesey, and *d* 1819, leaving an only s:

Sir John James Walsham, 1st Bt (UK), so *cr* 30 Sept 1831 (in consideration of his being the est coheir and rep of Gen Sir Thomas Morgan, 1st Bt (title *cr* 1661; expired 1768), a prominent royalist), of Knill Court, DL (Herefs and Radnorshire); *b* 6 June 1805; High Sheriff Radnorshire 1870; Poor Law Inspr, Maj Herefs Militia; *m* 25 May 1826 Sarah Frances (*d* 19 Aug 1857), 2nd dau of Matthew Bell, of Woolsington Ho, Northumberland (nephew of Lords Auckland and Henley, *qqv*), and *d* 10 Aug 1874, leaving:

1 JOHN (Sir), **2nd Bt**

2 Francis (Rev); *b* 9 April 1832; MA Dunelm; Rector Knill; *m* 29 June 1865 Marianne (*d* 16 June 1928), est dau of Charles James Barnett, of Bays Lawn, Glos, MP Maidstone, and *d* 13 March 1914, having had:

  (1) John Charles; *b* 11 Sept 1866; *m* 22 May 1902 Alice Maude (*d* 30 Dec 1945), dau of John Headland and widow of Dr J A Pike, and *dsp* 22 March 1919

  (2) Arthur Brandling; *b* 10 March 1868; *d* 1895, having had:

    1a Percy; *d* young

  (1) Florence Augustus, OBE (1920); *m* 14 Sept 1892 Lt-Col John Cecil Thornhill, Roy I Rifles (*d* 27 Oct 1944), s of Rev William Thornhill, of Offord d'Arcy, Hunts, and *d* 26 Oct 1955, leaving issue

  (2) Mary Caroline; *m* 1897 Algernon Estcourt Keys-Wells, of Durham, and *d* 1945, having had issue

3 Arthur; *b* 16 June 1833; Lt RA; *ka* Battle of the Alma 20 Sept 1854

4 Charles; *b* 26 Aug 1837; Vicar Sculcoates, Hull; *m* 27 Aug 1867 Mary Caroline (*d* Dec 1872), yst dau of Henry Newmarch, MD, and *d* 18 Jan 1882

1 Anna; *m* 20 May 1855 Maj-Gen O'Brien Bellingham Woolsey (*d* 14 Jan 1910), of Milestown, RA, and *d* 18 Aug 1905, leaving issue

2 Fanny; *m* 30 Oct 1883, as his 2nd w, Thomas Edward Yorke JP, DL (*d* 24 March 1923), of Bewerley Hall, and Halton Pl, Yorks, and *d* 25 May 1926

The 1st Bt's est s,

Sir John Walsham, 2nd Bt, KCMG, JP, DL; *b* 29 Oct 1830; *educ* Cambridge (MA); Sec Legation: Peking 1873–75, Madrid 1875–78 and Berlin 1878–83, Envoy Extrdy and Min Plen China 1885–92 and Romania 1892–94; *m* 5 March 1867 Florence (*d* 21 Dec 1915), only dau of Hon Peter Campbell Scarlett, CB (*see* ABINGER, B), and *d* 10 Dec 1905, leaving, with a dau (*d* an infant):

1JOHN SCARLETT (Sir), **3rd Bt**

2 Percy Romilly; *b* 2 March 1871; Chinese Maritime Customs; *m* 21 Oct 1899 Charlotte Cunninghame (*d* 1945), dau of William Wykeham Myers, MB, CM, of Formosa, and *d* 22 April 1933, leaving:

  (1) +PERCY ROBERT STEWART [Percy Walsham Esq, 129 Ram Gorse, Harlow, Essex CH20 1QA]; *b* 6 April 1904; heir presumptive; *m* 1937 Tamara Ellis (*d* 1981) and has:

    1a +Gerald Percy Robert; *b* 1939; F/Lt RAF; *m* 1984 *Evelyn Niebes

    1a *Diana Charlotte; *b* 1938; *m* 1959 *SCM/Sgt Harley Ralph Linley, USAF, and has:

      1b *Paul Ralph; *b* 1961

      1b *Charlotte Diana; *b* 1960

  (1) Florence May; *b* 15 Aug 1900; *m* 21 Oct 1924 Capt Henry Neville Lake, DSO, DSC, RN, of Tinkers Hill Farm, Furneaux Pelham, Herts, yst s of E W Lake, of Bury St Edmunds, and had:

1a *Anthony Walsham Neville [Anthony Lake Esq, Highham Farm, Winbush, Saffron Waldon, Essex]; *b* 13 Feb 1926; *m* 30 March 1950 *Penelope Doune, er dau of Hon James Perrott Phillipps (*see* MILFORD, B), and has:

    1b *David Anthony; *b* 20 Jan 1953; *educ* Eton

    2b *Simon Neville; *b* 20 Feb 1956; *educ* Eton

    3b *Mark Philip; *b* 30 May 1958

2a *John Dewe Neville; *b* 24 July 1928; *m* 26 April 1952 *(Ann) Cherida, er dau of Sir Reginald Culcheth Holcroft, 2nd Bt (*qv*), and has:

    1b *Christopher John Neville; *b* 9 Jan 1954

    2b *Timothy Michael David; *b* 1955

(2) Gladys Newell; *b* 10 Feb 1908; *m* 1930 Lt-Col Henry Richard Hopking, MBE (*d* 1965), Suffolk Regt, and had:

    1a *Richard Scarlett; *b* 1936; *m* 1968 *Elizabeth Ann Fortin and has issue

    1a *Gillian Walsham; *b* 1933; *m* 1956 *James Scudamore Oakes and has issue

(3) Aline Joyce; *b* 25 Feb 1913; *m* 12 April 1939 Maj Cecil Ronald Patrick Barrow, RA, of Milestown, Castlebellingham, Co Louth, est s of Maj Ronald Edumnud Barrow, IA, of Milestown, and had:

    1a *Patrick Cecil Walsham [Patrick Barrow Esq, Listoke, Drogheda, Co Louth, Ireland]; *b* 19 March 1940; *educ* St Columba's; *m* 20 April 1968 *Patricia Mary, only dau of Capt Peter John Thornhill, OBE, RN, of Hazelwood House, Bath, Avon, and has:

        1b *Juliet Mary; *b* 8 May 1971

        2b *Marie Louise; *b* 21 June 1973

    2a *John Anthony; *b* 17 May 1943; *educ* St Columba's

    3a *Michael Scarlett; *b* 9 Feb 1948; *educ* St Columba's

The 2nd Bt's er s,

Sir John Scarlett Walsham, 3rd Bt; *b* 15 Oct 1869; Inspr Chinese Labour Transvaal, Capt Labour Corps; *m* 20 Nov 1906 Bessie Geraldine Gundreda (*d* 8 Dec 1941), est dau of V-Adml John Borlase Warren (*see* WARREN, Bt), and *d* 14 Feb 1940, leaving,

1 **Sir John Scarlett Warren Walsham, 4th Bt**, CB (1963), OBE (1944), of Knill Court; *b* 29 Nov 1910; *educ* Rugby; Supt Portsmouth Dockyard, served WW II, ret as R-Adml 1964; *m* 21 Nov 1936 *Sheila Christina [Lady Walsham, 19 Beckford Close, Tisbury, Wilts SP3 6QT], only child of Cdr Bertrand Bannerman, DSO, RN (*see* BANNERMAN, Bt), and *d* 1992, leaving:

    (1) Sir TIMOTHY JOHN WALSHAM, **5th and present Bt**

    (1) *Susan Elizabeth [Mrs Charles Robertson, Dromquinna Manor Hotel, Kenmare, Co Kerry, Ireland]; *b* 7 March 1941; *m* 1st 20 July 1963 Christopher James Harbour (*d* 3 March 1986), 2nd s of Harold Ernest Harbour, of St Albans, Herts; *m* 2nd 1988 *Charles Michael Robertson and by her 1st husb has:

        1a *Mark Christopher Bannerman; *b* 16 Feb 1964

        2a *Benedict David Walsham; *b* 22 March 1967; *m* 20 July 1996 *Georgina Ellen Mein-Smith and has:

            1b *Tiger Jackson; *b* 31 Jan 1997

        3a *Mathew Alexander Walsham; *b* 5 April 1969

        1a *Caroline Lucy Scarlett; *b* 16 June 1965; *m* 8 Oct 1997 *Dennis Brown, of NZ, and has:

            1b *Daisy; *b* 25 Feb 1998

    (2) *Jane Scarlett [Mrs David Nairne, The Bungalow, Ower Farm, Ower Lane, Upham, Hants SO32 1HN]; *b* 19 Sept 1942; *m* 17 Aug 1963 *Cdr David Colin Nairne, RN, s of Lt-Col Charles Sylvester Nairne, of Compton, nr Winchester, and has:

        1a *Charles David Scarlett; *b* 24 Oct 1965

        2a *Alexander John Dalmahoy; *b* 1970

        1a *Sarah Catriona; *b* 5 Aug 1964; *m* 1990 *John Alexander Santos and has:

            1b *Alexander James; *b* 8 March 1995

            1b *Anouska Beatriz; *b* 1992

1 Barbara Knill; *b* 23 April 19–; *d* 19 Dec 1908

2 *Gundreda Brydget Coytmore; *b* 12 May 1909; *m* 14 Feb 1931 Chichester Kennedy Crookshank, of Emsworth, Hants, est s of Maj Claude Kennedy Crookshank, of Grahamstown, S Africa, and has:

    (1) *John Kennedy; *b* 1932; *educ* Repton and RMA Sandhurst; Capt late 5th Roy Inniskilling Dragoon Gds; *m* 1963 *Phyllida Anne, yr dau of Capt Ernest Charles Mylne, of Godmanstone Manor, Dorchester, and has:

        1a *Charles James Chichester; *b* 1966

        1a *Antonia Scarlett; *b* 1969

    (2) *Peter Scarlett; *b* 1935; *educ* Sherborne; *m* 1958 *Susan, dau of Thomas George Watwood, of Stafford, and has:

        1a *Richard Chichester; *b* 1962

        2a *William Thomas; *b* 1965

WALSINGHAM

Arms: Barry of six argent and azure, in chief three annulets gules. **Crest:** A wyvern's head or. **Supporters:** Two wyverns regardant argent, collared azure, chained or, and charged on the breast with three annulets gules. **Motto:** *Excitari non hibescere* ('To be spirited, not inactive'). **Creation:** B. (GB) 17 Oct 1780.

THE 9TH BARON WALSINGHAM, of Walsingham, Norfolk [John de Grey, MC (1952) [The Rt Hon The Lord Walsingham MC, The Hassocks, Merton, Norfolk IP25 6QP]; *b* 21 Feb 1925; *s f* 1965; *educ* Wellington, Aberdeen U, Magdalen Coll Oxford (BA 1950, MA 1959) and RMC Sandhurst; Lt-Col RA, served WW II, Palestine 1947, Korea 1951–52, Hong Kong 1952–54, Malaya 1954–56, Cyprus and Suez 1956, Aden Protectorate 1957–58 and 1961–63 and Borneo 1963–65; *m* 30 July 1963 *Wendy Elizabeth, er dau of Edward Sidney Hoare, of Southwick, Sussex, and has:

    1 +ROBERT; *b* 21 June 1969; *educ* Exeter U (BSc 1992); *m* 15 July 1995 *Josephine Elizabeth, dau of Richard Haryott, of Brickendon, Herts, and has:

        (1) +Thomas; *b* 23 Jan 1997

    1 *Sarah Jane; *b* 24 Sept 1964; *educ* London U (BA 1986); *m* 1990 *Bryan Muggeridge, yr s of Percy Muggeridge, of Paarl, CP, S Africa

    2 *Elizabeth Anne; *b* 24 July 1966; *educ* Durham U (BA 1989); *m* 1993 *Stefan Jones, only s of Roger Jones, of Yarnton Ho, Peopleton, Worcs

Walsingham, previous creation: In 1722 the illegitimate dau of GEORGE I by the Duchess of Kendal (Ermengarde Melusina von der Schulenberg, supposedly his favourite mistress) was created Countess of Walsingham for life. Before her ennoblement Petronille Melusine, as she was christened, had borne her mother's maiden name. She married the 4th Earl of Chesterfield (*see* 1967 edn CHESTERFIELD and STANHOPE, E) and died in 1773, when the Walsingham title expired.

Lineage: HENRY de GREY (*see* GREY, B); *d* 1219, leaving a 3rd s:

WILLIAM de GREY, of Cavendish, Suffolk, Landford and Sandiacre, Derbys; *m* Amice — (*d* 1287) and had:

Sir JOHN de GREY; *m* Margaret Odyngseles and had:

Sir THOMAS de GREY; *m c* 1306 Alice, dau and heiress of Sir Richard de Cornerth, thus acquiring the estate of Cornerth, Suffolk, and *d* 1321, leaving an est s:

Sir THOMAS de GREY; *m* Isabel, dau and coheir of Fulk Baynard, of Merton, Norfolk, thus *c* 1377 acquiring that property, and had:

FULKE de GREY; *m* Margaret, dau of Sir Thomas Vernon, of Elme, and had:

FULKE de GREY; *m* Eleanor Barnardiston and had:

WILLIAM de GREY; *m* Christian, dau of John Manynge, of Gt Ellingham, and *d* 1474, leaving:

WILLIAM de GREY; *m* 1st Mary, dau of Thomas Bedingf(i)eld, of Oxburgh (*see* PASTON-BEDINGFELD, Bt); *m* 2nd Grace, dau of Thomas Teye, of Essex, and widow of Francis Heth, and *d* 1495, leaving by his 1st w:

THOMAS de GREY; *m* Elizabeth, dau of Sir Richard Fitz Lewes, of Thorndon, Essex, became a priest after her death in 1515 and *d* by 1 Sept 1556, having had:

EDMUND de GREY; *m* 1531 Elizabeth, dau of Sir John Spelman, of Narborough, and *dvp* 1548, leaving:

ROBERT de GREY; recusant; *m* Anne, dau of Sir Thomas Lovell, and *d* 1601, leaving:

Sir WILLIAM de GREY; *m* 1617 Anne, dau of Sir James Calthorpe, of Cockthorpe, and *d* 1632, leaving:

JAMES de GREY; *m* Elizabeth, dau of Sir Martin Stuteville, of Dalham, Suffolk, and *d* 1665, leaving:

WILLIAM de GREY; MP Thetford 1685; *m* Elizabeth, dau and coheir of Thomas Bedingfeld, of Darsham, Suffolk, and *d* 1687, leaving an est s:

THOMAS de GREY; MP Norfolk 5th and 6th GB Parls; *m* Elizabeth, dau of William Windham, of Felbrigge, Norfolk, and was *bur* 18 Dec 1765, leaving:

Sir WILLIAM de GREY, **1st Baron Walsingham**, of Walsingham, Norfolk (GB), so *cr* 17 Oct 1780, PC (1771), KC (1758); *b* 17 July 1719; *educ* Trin Hall Cambridge and Middle Temple; barrister 1742, Bencher 1768, MP (Tory) Newport, Cornwall, 1761–70 and Cambridge U 1770–71, Slr-Gen to QUEEN CHARLOTTE 1761–63, Slr-Gen 1763–66, Attorney-Gen 1766–71, Ld Ch Justice Common Pleas 1771–80, ktd 1771; *m* 12 Nov 1743 Mary (*d* 2 Sept 1800), dau of William Cowper, of Hertingfordbury Park, nr Hertford, and *d* 9 May 1781, leaving, with a dau (Charlotte, *m* 16 June 1769 Joseph Windham, of Earsham Ho, Norfolk, who *dsp* 21 Sept 1810), an only surv s:

THOMAS de GREY, **2nd Baron Walsingham**, PC (1783); *b* 14 July 1748; *educ* Eton and Trin Hall Cambridge; MP (Tory) Wareham Jan-Sept 1774, Tamworth 1774–80 and Lostwithiel 1780–81, a Ld Trade 1777–81, U-Sec Colonies 1778–80, Jt V-Treasurer Ireland 1784–87, memb Ctee Trade (forerunner of BOT) 1784–86, a Commr India Bd 1784–90, Jt PMG 1787–94, Chm Ctees Ho Lds 1794–1814; *m* 30 April 1772 Hon Augusta Georgiana Elizabeth Irby (*d* 28 May 1818), only dau of 1st Baron Boston (*qv*), and *d* 16 Jan 1818, leaving:

1 GEORGE de GREY, **3rd Baron Walsingham**; *b* 11 June 1776; Lt-Gen Peninsular War (wounded); *m* 16 May 1804 Matilda, est dau of Paul Cobb Methuen (*see* METHUEN, B), and *dsp* 26 April 1831 in a fire at his house in Upper Harley Street, London, while his w, who had jumped from an upstairs window to avoid the flames, *d* six hours later 27 April 1831 from injuries

2 THOMAS, **4th Baron**

1 Charlotte; *m* 18 Sept 1806, as his 2nd w, William Gosling (*d* 27 Jan 1835), of Roehampton, Surrey, and *d* 16 Oct 1839, having had issue

2 Augusta Mary; *d* unm 1830

The 3rd BARON's bro,

Rev THOMAS de GREY, **4th Baron Walsingham**; *b* 10 April 1778; *educ* Eton and St John's Coll Cambridge; Deacon 1801, Priest 1802, Archdeacon Surrey, Preb Winchester, Rector Fawley, Hants, and Merton, Norfolk; *m* 12 Aug 1802 Elizabeth (*d* 8 May 1845), yst dau of Rt Rev Hon Brownlow North (*see* GUILFORD, E), and *d* 1839, leaving, with another s (*d* young):

1 THOMAS, **5th Baron**

2 Brownlow North Osborn; *b* 3 July 1808; *m* 11 Feb 1858 Emma (*d* 6 April 1868), dau of George Kenyon, of Cefn, nr Wrexham, and *dsp* 8 April 1868

3 Frederick (Rev); *b* 2 Nov 1810; Rector Copdock; *d* 30 March 1881

4 George; *b* 15 Nov 1811; *d* 26 May 1871

5 Francis; *b* 12 Feb 1815; drowned 25 April 1836 trying to rescue people adrift in a boat on the Medway

1 Elizabeth Augusta; *m* 13 Aug 1832 Richard Heber Wrightson, of Warmsworth, Yorks, and *d* 22 Feb 1875

2 Henrietta Maria; *m* 3 Dec 1835 Lt Brownlow North Garnier, RN (*d* 28 June 1847), 3rd s of Rev William Garnier, of Rookesbury, Hants, and *d* 18 March 1833, leaving issue

3 Georgina; *m* 29 June 1833 3rd Lord Kenyon (*qv*), Baron of Gredington and *d* 22 April 1874, leaving issue

The 4th BARON's s,

THOMAS de GREY, **5th Baron Walsingham**; *b* 6 July 1804; *m* 1st 6 Aug 1842 Augusta Louisa (*d* 1844), est dau of Sir Robert FRANKLAND-RUSSELL formerly FRANKLAND, 7th Bt (*see* ZOUCHE, B), and *d* 31 Dec 1870, leaving:

1 THOMAS de GREY, **6th Baron Walsingham**, JP, DL; *b* 29 July 1843; *educ* Eton and Trin Coll Cambridge; MP (C) W Norfolk 1865–70, a Ld in Waiting 1874–75, Chm Norfolk QS, High Steward Cambridge U and King's Lynn, Tstee Br and Hunterian Museums, FRS, FLS, FZS, FES (Pres 1889–90); held record for slaughtering grouse of 535 brace in 858 minutes; *m* 1st 19 March 1877 Augusta Selina Elizabeth (Leila) (*d* 4 Nov 1906), dau of William Locke, widow of Ernest Fitzroy, Lord Burghersh (*see* WESTMORLAND, E), and formerly w of Don Luigi Caracciolo, Duke of San Teodoro; *m* 2nd 1908 Marion Gwytherne-Williams (*d* 31 Oct 1913), of Belvedere, St Lawrence, IOW, dau of Thomas Rhys Withers; *m* 3rd 12 Nov 1914 Agnes Baird (*d* 25 April 1926), dau of Frederick Shand Hemming, of Merrywood Hall, Somerset, and Lissahawley, Londonderry, and widow of Richard Dawson, of Lealands, Hellingly, Sussex, and *d* 3 Dec 1919

The **5th Baron** *m* 2nd 25 Oct 1847 Hon Emily Elizabeth Julia Thellusson (*d* 13 May 1879), est dau of 2nd Baron Rendlesham (*qv*), and by her had:

2 JOHN AUGUSTUS, **7th Baron**

3 Arnold (Rev); *b* 11 Sept 1856; Rector Copdock; *m* 17 April 1882 Margaret Maria (*d* 14 Dec 1935), dau of Hon Sir Spencer Cecil Brabazon Ponsonby-Fane (*see* BESSBOROUGH, E), and *d* 15 Nov 1889, leaving:

(1) Michael; *b* 17 June 1883; *d* 6 May 1897

(2) Nigel (Rev), CMG (1945), OBE (1918); *b* 27 March 1886; *educ* Eton; Lt-Cdr RNVR, Naval Intell Div Admlty, F/Sub-Lt RNAS, WW I (despatches, Order St Maurice and St Lazarus Italy), FO WW II; *m* 29 Dec 1910 Florence Emily Frances (*d* 28 May 1963), yr dau of Spencer William Gore (*see* ARRAN, E), and *d* 25 May 1951, leaving:

1a John; *b* 22 Dec 1911; *educ* Eton; *m* 4 July 1939 *Averil Mary, yst dau of Herman Walter de Zoete, of The Rookery, Sproughton, Ipswich, and *d* 24 Oct 1973, leaving:

1b +Michael John [Michael de Grey Esq, 42 Murray Rd, London W5 4XS]; *b* 6 Sept 1942; *educ* Eton; *m* 1st 16 April 1966 (*divorce* 1988) Carolyn Althea Jane, er dau of John Blackie, CB, of The Bell Ho, Alconbury, Hunts, and has:

1c *Rachel Emma; *b* 17 Jan 1969

2c *Helen Sarah; *b* 26 Sept 1970

1b (cont.) Michael de Grey *m* 2nd 19– Charlotte Ashe and by her has:

3c *Annabel; *b* 1994

2b +Anthony [Anthony de Grey Esq, 54 Abbotswood Rd, London SW16 1AW]; *b* 16 May 1948; *educ* Eton; landscape gardener; *m* 26 July 1975 (*divorce* 1985) Miranda Jane, est dau of Robert Murdoch, of Linton, Kent, and has had:

1c +Nigel John; *b* 28 Nov 1981; *educ* Eton

1c Georgina Sophia; *b* 13 Sept 1979 and *d* 6 Dec 1981

2c *Alexandra Mary Carena; *b* 14 March 1984

2a Roger (Sir), KCVO; *b* 18 April 1918; *educ* Eton; RA (1969), Capt RAC WW II (wounded, US Bronze Star), artist; Hon Dlitt Reading 1992; PRA 1984–93; *m* 2 May 1942 *Flavia Hatt, professional name Flavia Irwin, RA [Lady de Grey, 5-6 Camer St, Meopham, Kent DA13 0XR], yr dau of Lt-Col Clinton de la Cherois Irwin, MC, of Silver Bridge, Chideock, Dorset, and *d* 14 Feb 1995, leaving:

1b +Spencer Thomas, CBE; *b* 7 June 1944; *educ* Eton; *m* 3 Sept 1977 *Hon Amanda Lucy Annan, er dau of Baron Annan (*qv*), and has:

1c +Felix Nicholas; *b* 29 Aug 1992

1c *Georgia Catherine; *b* 22 Aug 1988

2b +Robert Fulke; *b* 22 Aug 1948; *educ* Eton; *m* 1974 *Muriel Janik, dau of Jean-Paul Schoendoerffer, of Paris, and has:

1c +Thomas George; *b* 28 April 1981

1c *Elisa Catherine; *b* 9 Sept 1976

2c *Alice Rose; *b* 8 April 1979

1b *Emilia Jane Mary; *b* 25 March 1952; *m* 1975 *Timothy Crawford, s of James Crawford, of Post Ho, Stroud, Hants, and has:

1c *George Oliver; *b* 4 Jan 1979

2c *Joseph Alexander; *b* 4 Sept 1988

1c *Harriet Frances; *b* 8 Aug 1982

1a Barbara; *b* 18 July 1915; *m* 5 Oct 1946 Patrick Alexander VANS of Barnbarroch formerly VANS AGNEW, of The Glebe Ho, Hawling, Glos, s of Patrick Alexander Vans Agnew, of Winter Park, Fla., and had:

1b *James Edward; *b* 23 April 1950; *educ* Shrewsbury

1b *Margaret Olivia; *b* 26 Jan 1948; *m* 6 April 1968 *John Francis Mills, of Cheltenham, Glos, s of Patrick Mills, of W Ewell, Surrey, and has issue

4 Robert Baynard; *b* 20 March 1858; *d* unm 7 Jan 1930

1 Emily Augusta Louisa; *m* 28 June 1882 Hon Alfred Chetwynd-Talbot, 4th s of 18th Earl of Shrewsbury and Waterford (*qv*), and *d* 26 Jan 1912, leaving issue

2 Beatrice; *m* 10 Feb 1887, as his 2nd w, Adml Hon Walter Cecil CARPENTER formerly CHETWYND-TALBOT, 2nd s of 18th Earl of Shrewsbury and Waterford (*qv*), and *d* 16 Oct 1927

3 Mabel; *d* unm 6 April 1942

4 Elizabeth Odeyne, OBE (1918); Sec and Cmdt Clopton War Hosp; *m* 3 June 1896 Rev Francis Henry Hodgson (*d* 24 March 1930), est s of Sir Arthur Hodgson, KCMG, and *d* 4 Dec 1947, leaving issue

The 6th BARON's half bro,

JOHN AUGUSTUS de GREY, **7th Baron Walsingham**; *b* 21 March 1849; BA Cantab; barrister, Chm E Suffolk QS, Recorder Sudbury 1896 and King's Lynn 1897, Met Police Magistrate 1905; *m* 1st 24 April 1883 Elizabeth Henrietta (*d* 12 April 1927), dau of Patrick Grant, HEICS, and gdau of James Murray Grant of Glenmoriston and Moy; *m* 2nd 1928 Marguerite (*d* 1931), dau of Walter Vernon, of Trematon Lodge, Anerley, London SE, and widow of Thomas Godley, of Scarborough, and *d* 21 March 1929, leaving:

1 GEORGE, **8th Baron**

2 Richard Patrick, TD (1951), JP (Norfolk 1959); *b* 17 March 1900; *educ* Eton and Trin Coll Cambridge (BA 1922, MA 1946); Capt Cambs Regt (TA) WW II; *m* 1st 3 July 1925 Cynthia Estelle (*d* 29 Dec 1967), dau of Thomas Hewitt Myring, of Mayfair; *m* 2nd 11 Jan 1969 Dorothy, est dau of Thomas Knight, of Sidcup

1 Elizabeth Helen; *b* 20 Dec 1885; *m* 6 Oct 1910 Maj Henry Wynter Blathwayt (*ka* 30 Nov 1917), RFA, s of Charles George Blathwayt, ICS, and had issue

2 Margaret Henrietta; *b* 15 Nov 1889; *m* 1st 20 July 1912 Bethel Godefroy Bouwens (*d* 24 Oct 1942), MA Cambridge, MIAE, MIMT, FSA, only s of Lt-Col Lambart Henry Bouwens, RHA; *m* 2nd 29 Sept 1948 Cyril Fabian Ratcliff Johnston (*d* 22 March 1958), 4th s of William Henry Johnston, of Bristol, and *d* 13 July 1978

3 Alice Mary; *b* 26 May 1893; *m* 2 June 1923 Philip Wade, MC (*d* 3 Dec 1950), s of Frank Wade, and *d* 17 May 1966, leaving issue

The 7th BARON's er s,

GEORGE de GREY, **8th Baron Walsingham**, DSO (1915), OBE, JP (Norfolk 1930), DL (1959); *b* 9 May 1884; *educ* Eton and RMC Sandhurst; Lt-Col Roy Norfolk Regt WW I (wounded three times, despatches four times), and WW II, OStJ; *m* 29 April 1919 Hyacinth Lambart (*d* 6 Feb 1968), only dau of Lt-Col Lambart Henry Bouwens, RHA, of Bosmoor Ho, Boxmoor, and *d* 29 Nov 1965, leaving:

1 JOHN de GREY, **9th and present Baron Walsingham**

1 *Lavender Hyacinth [The Hon Mrs Garnier, College Farm, Thompson, Thetford, Norfolk]; *b* 14 Oct 1923; First Aid Nursing Yeo WW II 1942–45 N Africa, Italy, India and Ceylon; *m* 9 April 1946 Col William d'Arcy Garnier, RA (*d* 1989), yst s of Brig Alan Parry Garnier, CB, MBE, MC, of Eyot Mead, Mayfield, Sussex, and has:

(1) *James Hugh; *b* 7 April 1948; *educ* Wellington; *m* 2 June 1984 *Katherine Hale, yr dau of J H Puckle, of Foxton Ho, Foxton, Cambs, and has:

1a *Louisa Hale; *b* 1986

2a *Sophia Elizabeth; *b* 1988

3a *Georgina Sarah; *b* 1989

4a *Olivia Caroline; *b* 1991

(2) *Richard Charles; *b* 13 June 1950; *educ* Wellington; *m* 1989 *Melissa (Minnie) Mary, est dau of Anthony Meyrick Denny, of Rose Cottage, Hattingley, Hants, and has:

1a *William; *b* 1989

2a *Robert Anthony; *b* 1993

(3) *Edward Henry, QC (1995) [Edward Garnier Esq QC MP, 1 Brick Court, Temple, London EC4Y 7BY]; *b* 26 Oct 1952; *educ* Wellington and Jesus Coll Oxford (MA); barrister Middle Temple 1976; MP (C) Harborough 1992–, Oppn Spokesman Legal Affrs 1997–; *m* 1982 *Anna Caroline, er dau of Michael James Mellows (*see* HEATHCOTE, Bt, of London), and has:

1a *George Edward; *b* 20 July 1986

2a *James William; *b* 21 Jan 1991

1a *Eleanor Katharine Rose; *b* 21 Sept 1983

(1) *Katharine Juliet; *b* 16 Oct 1958; *m* 1985 *Anthony Richard Ashmore Wolstenholme, er s of Michael Ashmore Wolstenholme, of W Kensington, and has:

1a *Florence Maud; b 1990

2a *Edwina Lavender; b 1991

2 *Margaret Isolda [The Hon Mrs North, Holmingham Farm, Bampton, Tiverton, Devon]; b 14 Aug 1926; WRNS WW II; m 9 March 1950 *Maj Geoffrey Ford North, MC, late 10th Hus, High Sheriff Devon 1990, only surv s of Stephen Thomas Ford North, of Woking, Surrey, and has:

(1) *David John Ford [David North Esq, Strattenborough Castle Farm, Coleshill, Oxon SN6 8TH]; b 16 Nov 1959; m 1986 *Sarah Jane, dau of Gerald Barrow, of Gustard Wood, Wheathampstead, Herts, and has:

1a *George Peter Ford; b 1988

1a *Rosanna Katharine; b 1990

2a *Perdita Alexandra; b 1991

(1) *Amanda Ford; b 7 March 1951; m 1st 1970 (divorce 1980) Anthony John Wigan, and has:

1a *Benjamin Mark; b 24 June 1972

2a *Samuel John; b 29 Aug 1974

(1) (cont.) Mrs Amanda Wigan m 2nd 1980 *Sir Anthony William Weldon, 9th Bt (qv), and has further issue

(2) *Joanna Katharine; b 17 Jan 1953; m 1975 *Hon Kim Maurice Fraser and has issue (see LOVAT, L)

(3) *Belinda Jane; b 2 March 1955; m 1994 *Simon Michael Weinstock and has:

1a *Abigail Louisa; b 31 March 1995

3 *Katharine Odeyne [The Rt Hon The Dowager Countess of Powis, Marrington Hall, Chirbury, Powys]; b 26 April 1928; m 26 July 1949 7th Earl of Powis (qv) and has issue

Seat: Merton Hall, Merton, Norfolk. The estate that came to the De GREYs by marriage with the Baynard heiress in the late 14th century had been held by the latter family since the Domesday Survey of 1086, so that in the present day it has had only two owners in over 900 years. Robert the Recusant and his son Sir William (see above) rebuilt the manor house about the end of ELIZABETH's reign and the beginning of JAMES I's, finishing the main stucture around 1613. The mansion was now laid out in the conventional Tudor E, with the stepped gables typical of East Anglia and with the principal facade pointing north. A few years later, towards the end of JAMES's reign, a charming triple-curvilinear-gabled gate house was placed slightly separate from the main front. It alone of the original Jacobethan work survived a disastrous fire in 1956. A 19th-century servants' wing by Edward Blore, who also restored Hampton Court and Windsor Castle and finished Nash's work on Buckingham Palace, survived too and the family took up residence in it after their modern house, elsewhere on the estate, burnt down 14 years later. The **3rd Baron** and his wife died in yet a third fire, that of their town house.

WALTON OF DETCHANT

Arms: Paly wavy argent and gules a castle triple-towered purpure, on a chief of the last three crosses formy quadrate gold. **Crest:** Issuant from clouds proper a seahorse argent, the piscine part proper, crined and finned or, holding between the forelegs a cross formy quadrate fitchy at the foot purpure. **Supporters:** Dexter, a boar gold, suspended from the neck by a riband purpure a clarion, pipes downward, gules; sinister, a greylag goose proper. **Motto:** Disce, doce, medere ('To learn, to teach, to heal'). **Creation:** B. (LP, UK) 1989.

THE BARON WALTON OF DETCHANT, of Detchant, Co Northumberland (Sir John Nicholas Walton, TD (1962)) [The Rt Hon The Lord Walton of Detchant TD, 13 Norham Gdns, Oxford OX2 6PS]; b 16 Sept 1922; educ Alderman Wraith GS and King's Coll Med Sch Durham (MB, BS 1945, MD 1952), Newcastle (DSc 1972), Oxon (MA 1983); Physician Roy Victoria Infirmary 1946–47 (Registrar 1949–51), RAMC 1947–49, research assist Durham U 1951–56, Nuffield Fndn Fell USA 1953–54, King's Coll Fell Neurological Research Unit Nat Hosp 1954–55, first assist Neurology Newcastle-upon-Tyne 1956–58, consultant neurologist Newcastle U Hosps 1958–83, CO 1 (N) Gen Hosp (TA) 1963–66, ed-in-ch Journal of Neurological Sciences 1966–67, Hon Col 201 (N) Gen Hosp (TAVR)

1968–73, Prof Neurology Newcastle U 1968–83 (Dean Medicine 1971–81), memb: MRC 1974–78, EEC Advsy Ctee Medical Educn 1975–83, Ho Lds Select Ctee Sci and Tech; Chm: Muscular Dystrophy Gp of GB 1970–95, Hamlyn Nat Commn Educn 1991–95, Ho Lds Select Ctee Medical Ethics 1993–94; ktd 1979; Pres: BMA 1980–82, Assoc for Study of Medical Educn 1982–94, GMC 1982–89 (memb 1971, Chm Educn Ctee 1975–82), Roy Soc Medicine 1984–86, Assoc Br Neurologists 1987–88, World Fedn Neurologists 1989–97 (1st V-Pres 1981–89); Warden Green Coll Oxford 1983–89; FRCP 1963 (MRCP 1950); Hon Fell: ACP 1980, RCPE 1981, RCP (Canada) 1984, Roy Soc Medicine 1988, RCPath 1993, RCPsych 1993, Inst Educn London U 1994; Hon DSc: Leeds 1979, Leicester 1980, Hull 1988, Oxford Brookes 1994; Hon MD: Sheffield 1987, Mahidol, Thailand, 1998; Hon DCL Newcastle 1988; Hon Laurea Genoa 1992; Freeman: City London 1978, Newcastle 1980; author: Subarachnoid Haemorrhage (with R D Adams, 1956), Polymyositis (1958), Essentials of Neurology (1961, 6th edn 1986), Brain's Diseases of the Nervous System (7th edn 1969, 10th edn 1993), Skeletal Muscle Pathology (with F L Mastaglia, 1982, 2nd edn 1991), The Oxford Companion to Medicine (jt ed, 1986), The Spice of Life (1993), The Oxford Medical Companion (jt ed, 1994); m 1946 *Mary Elizabeth, dau of Joseph Harrison, of Spennymoor, Co Durham, and has:

1 *Christopher John; b 21 Feb 1956

1 *Elisabeth Ann; b 28 Sept 1947

2 *Judith Mary; b 26 Oct 1950

Lineage: HERBERT WALTON; m Eleanor Watson Ward and had:

JOHN NICHOLAS, cr a **Baron**

WARD

Arms: Azure a cross moline argent between four keys, wards upwards, or. **Crest:** A demi-griffin azure in front of two keys in saltire, wards upwards, or. **Motto:** Animo et fide ('By courage and faith'). **Creation:** Bt. (UK) 20 June 1911.

SIR JOSEPH JAMES LAFFEY WARD, 4TH BT, of Wellington, New Zealand [Sir Joseph Ward Bt, 3 Regal Place, Milford, Auckland, New Zealand]; b 11 Nov 1946; s f 1970; m 27 April 1968 *Robyn Allison, dau of William Maitland Martin, of Rotorua, NZ, and has:

1 +JOSEPH JAMES MARTIN; b 20 Feb 1971

1 *Theresa Jane; b 1972

Lineage: WILLIAM THOMAS WARD; merchant; had:

Sir Joseph George Ward, 1st Bt (UK), so cr 20 June 1911, GCMG (1930, KCMG 1901), VD, PC (1907), JP (1887); b 26 April 1856; memb Ho Reps NZ 1887–1919 and Invercargill 1925, Colonial Sec, PMG, Min for Rlwys, Industries and Commerce, Min Public Health, PM 1906–12 and 1928–30; memb and chm Bluff Harbour Bd, raised and cmded Naval and Artillery Vols, Hon LLD Edinburgh and Dublin 1907, Cantab and Birmingham 1911, Hon DCL Oxon 1911; m 5 Dec 1883 Theresa Dorothea, CBE (d 7 Feb 1927), dau of Henry Joseph de Smidt, of NZ, and had:

1 CYRIL RUPERT JOSEPH (Sir), **2nd Bt**

2 Vincent Aubrey, CBE; b 4 Jan 1888; MP Invercargill 1930–31, MLC 1934, Silver Jubilee Medal 1935, Coronation Medal 1937; m 14 Dec 1926 Sybil Mary, dau of Robert George Petre (see PETRE, B), and dsp 9 Feb 1946

3 Gladstone William; b 14 May 1891; stock and sharebroker, Capt attd Tank Corps WW I; m 21 July 1913 Sophia, dau of Salem Polymedix, of Jerusalem, and d 10 Dec 1965, leaving:

(1) *Myrcine Josephine; b 15 June 1921; m 1942 *Dr Peter Mowbray Tripp, of Christchurch, NZ, and has:

1a *David Mowbray Ward; b 14 Feb 1949; m 1973 *Martha McQuilkin and has:

1b *Peter James; b 1977

1b *Sophie Catherine; b 1976

2a *John Peter; b 7 Sept 1950; m 1975 *Amanda Moore and has:

1b *Celia Jane; b 1980

2b *Jessica; b 1982

1a *Penelope Mary; b 29 Dec 1943; m 1974 *Phillip Klap and has:

1b *Nicola Sophie; b 1975

2b *Annabelle Marie-Therese; *b* 1976

2a Anthia Susan; *b* 25 May 1947; *m* 1969 *Richard Rollo Warburton and *d* 1993, leaving:

  1b *Richard John; *b* 1976

  1b *Tessa Myrcine; *b* 1970

  2b *Anna; *b* 1972

(2) *Eileen Dorothea [Mrs Patrick Hunter, Ardmore, 9 Vicarage Hill, Farnham, Surrey]; *b* 23 June 1922; *m* 27 Feb 1943 S/Ldr Patrick Sinclair Hunter (*d* 1981), s of Dr Peter Sinclair Hunter, of Singapore, and has:

  1a *Michael Sinclair Ward; *b* 17 April 1947; *educ* Radley; *m* 1970 *Carol Rosemary Shorter and has:

    1b *Piers Charles Sinclair; *b* 1974

    2b *Charles Patrick Sinclair; *b* 1977

    1b *Victoria Lucinda; *b* 1972

  1a *Patricia Ann [Lady Spicer, Cropthorne Manor, nr Pershore, Worcs WR10 3LT]; *b* 5 Dec 1943; *m* 8 April 1967 *Sir (William) Michael Hardy Spicer, MP, s of Leslie Hardy Spicer, of Compton Ho, Farnham, Surrey, and has:

    1b *Edward Sinclair Hardy; *b* 16 Jan 1969

    1b *Antonia Hardy; *b* 1971

    2b *Annabel Jane Hardy; *b* 1974

4 Awarua Patrick Joseph George; *b* 14 Jan 1901; *m* 1930 Marjorie, only dau of O M McCormack, of Detroit, and *d* Dec 1961, leaving:

  (1) *Patricia Eileen; *b* 16 May 1933; *m* 2 April 1955 Duncan Cameron Bryan (*d* 19–), of California, and has:

    1b *Sheryl Cameron; *b* 19 Jan 1956

    2b *Jennifer Ward; *b* 1 Feb 1958

    3b *Denise Eileen; *b* 29 July 1961

1 Eileen Josephine; *b* 12 Oct 1886; *m* 4 Dec 1913 Bernard Bedingfield-Wood, of Heretaunga, Wellington, NZ, and *d* 1952, leaving issue

The 1st Bt's est s,

Sir Cyril Rupert Joseph Ward, 2nd Bt; *b* 22 Sept 1884; with Kinsey and Co, shipping, general agents and stevedores, of Christchurch and Lyttelton, NZ; Hon Belgian Consul Christchurch; Jubilee Medal 1935; *m* 5 Dec 1908 Elinor Angela (*d* 11 Oct 1943), dau of James Henry Davidson, JP, of Brisbane, Qld, Australia, and *d* 10 Nov 1940, leaving:

1 **Sir Joseph George Davidson Ward, 3rd Bt**, of Wellington, NZ; *b* 17 Sept 1909; *educ* Christ's Coll Christchurch and Canterbury U Coll (LLB 1933, LLM 1934); memb Canterbury U Coll Cncl 1930–70 (chm 1948) and Christchurch Stock Exchange 1945–66, barrister and slr NZ 1934, notary public, Capt Transport Shipping Office WW II, Hon Belgian Consul 1940, Provincial Commr Boy Scouts 1942–61, Civil Medal 1st Cl Belgium 1966, Pres Roy Humane Soc NZ; *m* 10 June 1944 Joan Mary Haden WAAF (*d* 13 Jan 1993), dau of Maj Thomas Patrick Laffey, of Auckland, NZ, and *d* 4 Aug 1970, leaving:

  (1) Sir JOSEPH JAMES LAFFEY WARD, **4th and present Bt**

  (2) +Roderick Anthony [Roderick Ward Esq, 35 Coates Park Rd, Cobbitty, NSW 2570, Australia]; *b* 23 April 1948; *m* 1993 *Faye Mary Morrisson

  (3) +Michael John [Michael Ward Esq, RD1, Wallis Rd, Ruawai, New Zealand]; *b* 13 April 1954; *m* 1977 *Alamein Sharlene Connelly and has:

    1a +Christopher Davidson; *b* 1979

    1a *Felicity Te Puawai; *b* 1980

    2a *Joan Marie Ngaroma; *b* 1985

  (1) *Angela Mary Josephine, NZRN, Dip SPAT, interior designer [Miss Angela Ward, 31 Vauxhall Rd, Devonport, Auckland, New Zealand]; *b* 11 June 1945

  (2) *Felicity Elizabeth Elinor Joan [Mrs Graham Kidd, 243 Bleakhouse Rd, Howick, New Zealand]; *b* 29 Sept 1951; *m* 1979 *Dr Graeme Warren Kidd and has:

    1a *Guy George Joseph; *b* 1983

    1a *Cecille Mary; *b* 1981

  (3) *Catherine Josephine Mina; *b* 12 Aug 1963

2 Cyril James; *b* 9 Aug 1913; P/O RNZAF WW II; *m* 22 April 1939 *Janet Graham [Mrs Cyril Ward, 10 Queen's Ave, Fendalton, Christchurch 1, New Zealand], dau of Dr John Stevenson, of Fendalton, Christchurch, NZ, and *d* 1984, leaving:

  (1) *Joanna Theresa; *b* 20 Jan 1940; *m* 19 April 1968 *Sir Roger Joseph Clifford, 7th Bt (*qv*), and has issue

  (2) *Celia Mary Louise [Mrs Richard Craig, c/o 10 Queen's Ave, Fendalton, Christchurch 1, New Zealand]; *b* 11 March 1950; *m* 1968 *Richard John Craig and has:

    1a *Holly Louise; *b* 1984

    2a *Hannah Rose; *b* 1988

3 Bruce Murray William; *b* 16 July 1920; *d* 16 June 1945

4 David Brinsley; *b* 11 Aug 1924; RNZAF WW II 1941–44, Korea 1950; *d* unm 24 Feb 1967

5 +John Rannie [John Ward Esq, 47 Webb St, Christchurch, New Zealand]; *b* 11 Aug 1924; Lt RNZNVR; *m* 2 April 1948 *Adrienne Lascelles, dau of Herbert Hill, OBE, JP, of Christchurch, and has:

  (1) +Jeremy John [Jeremy Ward Esq, 6 Mortimer Terrace, Wellington, New Zealand]; *b* 20 Feb 1957; *m* 1985 *Anne Susan Lockhart and has:

    1a +Oscar Joseph; *b* 1989

    2a +Barnaby John Lockhart; *b* 1992

  (2) +Rubert Rannie; *b* 8 May 1964; *m* 1994 *Willimina Eilander

  (1) *Caroline Diana [Mrs Daniel von Dadelszen, Hinerangi, RD2, Waipukurau, New Zealand]; *b* 8 May 1950; *m* 1970 *Daniel Frederick von Dadelszen and has:

    1a *Samuel John; *b* 1973

    1a *Victoria Mary; *b* 1975

    2a *Lucinda Gretchen; *b* 1977

  (2) *Jennifer Ann [Mrs Julian Payton, 64 Cole St, Masterton, New Zealand]; *b* 4 Feb 1951; *m* 1973 *Julian Simon Cowper Payton and has:

1a *Joseph Simon; *b* 1979

2a *Toby James; *b* 1982

1a *Anna Caroline; *b* 1977

1 *Theresa Dorothea [Mrs John Corry, Lawn Bungalow, Bitchett Green, Sevenoaks, Kent]; *b* 2 Dec 1916; *m* 21 Oct 1941 *John Swaine Corry, est s of Herbert William Corry, of Yaldham Manor, Kemsing, Kent, and has:

  (1) *David Herbert Cyril; *b* 18 Sept 1949; *educ* Rugby

  (2) *Robert John; *b* 27 Jan 1953; *educ* Malvern

  (1) *Angela Susan, MCSP [Mrs Iain Ridge, 145 London Rd, Sevenoaks, Kent]; *b* 14 Nov 1942; *m* 24 April 1965 *Iain Anderson Ridge, s of Keith Anderson Ridge, of Sevenoaks, and has:

    1a *Angus James Anderson; *b* 30 Aug 1966

  (2) *Rosemary Ann; *b* 25 July 1946

WARDINGTON

Arms: Per fess azure and gules a fess nebuly ermine between two lambs passant in chief argent, in base upon a mount proper a dove rising argent, holding in the beak a pea stalk, the blossom and pods proper. **Crest:** Upon the capital of an Ionic column a dove rising, holding in the beak a pea stalk as in the arms. **Supporters:** On either side a fox or, charged on the shoulder with a bugle horn stringed sable. **Motto:** *Pax et spes* ('Peace and hope').
Creation: B. (UK) 17 July 1936.

THE 2ND BARON WARDINGTON, of Alnmouth, Co Northumberland (Christopher Henry Beaumont Pease) [The Rt Hon The Lord Wardington, Wardington Manor, Banbury, Oxon OX17 1SW]; *b* 22 Jan 1924; *s f* 1950; *educ* Eton; Capt Scots Gds WW II (wounded); memb London Stock Exchange 1949–, Stock Exchange Cncl 1963–81, Corp For Bond Holders 1967–81 and Public Works Loan Bd 1964–69 (commr 1969–73), ptnr Hoare, Govett 1950–86, Alderman City London 1960–63; chm: Athlone Tst and Friends BL, Tstee Roy Jubilee Tsts; *m* 9 Sept 1964 *Margaret Audrey, dau of John White, of Bradford, and formerly w of Jack Dunfee, and adopted:

  *Christopher William Beaumont; *b* 18 April 1970; *educ* Eton

  *Lucy Ann; *b* 23 Sept 1966; *m* 1991 *John Vallance Petrie, est s of Neil Petrie, of Sulphur Wells, NZ, and has:

    (1) *Christopher Beaumont; *b* 1993

    (2) *Angus Crawford; *b* 1994

    (1) *Abigail Lucy; *b* 1996

  *Helen Elizabeth; *b* 24 Dec 1967

Lineage: JOHN BEAUMONT PEASE, of N Lodge, Darlington; had a 2nd s:

JOHN WILLIAM PEASE, of Pendower, Newcastle, and Nether Grange, Alnmouth, Northumberland, JP, DL; *b* 13 Aug 1834; DCL; *m* 13 Sept 1860 Helen Maria (*d* 1 May 1928), 4th dau of Alfred Fox, of Falmouth, and *d* 25 March 1901, leaving:

  1 Howard; *b* 12 July 1863; *m* 27 Oct 1887 Margaret (*d* 31 Aug 1947), dau of Rev Canon Herbert Kynaston, and *d* 25 Jan 1928, leaving issue

  2 JOHN WILLIAM BEAUMONT, **1st Baron**

  1 Sarah Helen, OBE, JP, DStJ; *d* unm 6 Dec 1937

  2 Florence, JP (Herefs 1933); *m* 22 July 1896 Montague Francis Maclean (*d* 14 Jan 1951), JP, of The Chantry, How Caple, and *d* 24 March 1947, leaving issue

  3 Sophia Mabel, JP (Herefs); *m* 18 Nov 1891 Reginald Wilson Fox (*ka* 8 March 1916) and *d* Oct 1953

The yr s,

JOHN WILLIAM BEAUMONT PEASE, **1st Baron Wardington**, of Alnmouth, Co Northumberland (UK), so *cr* 17 July 1936; *b* 4 July 1869; *educ* Marlborough and New Coll Oxford (BA 1891); chm Lloyds Bank 1922–45 and Bank of London and S America 1922–47, alternate chm Lloyds and Nat Prov Foreign Bank Ltd, dir Alliance Assur; *m* 5 April 1923 Hon Dorothy Charlotte (*d* 15 May 1983 aged 92), est dau of 1st and last Baron Forster (*see* 1936 edn) and widow of Hon Harold Fox Pitt Lubbock (*see* AVEBURY, B), and *d* 7 Aug 1950, leaving:

  1 CHRISTOPHER HENRY BEAUMONT PEASE, **2nd and present Baron Wardington**

2 +WILLIAM SIMON PEASE [The Hon William Pease, 29 Upper Addison Gdns, London W14 8AJ; Lepe Ho, Exbury, Hants SO45 1AD]; *b* 15 Oct 1925; heir presumptive; *educ* Eton, New Coll Oxford (BA 1949, MA 1956) and St Thomas's Hosp Medical School (MB, BS (London) 1956); FRCS (Eng) 1960, Consultant Otolaryngologist Centl Middx Hosp, late Capt Gren Gds; *m* 26 Oct 1962 *Hon Elizabeth Jane Ormsby-Gore, yst dau of 4th Baron Harlech (*qv*)

WARDLAW

Arms: Quarterly, 1st and 4th, azure three mascles or (for WARDLAW); 2nd and 3rd, azure three water bouquets or (for VALANCE). **Crest:** An estoile or. **Motto:** *Familias firmat pietas* ('Domestic virtue strengthens families').
Creation: Bt. (NS) 5 March 1630/1.

SIR HENRY JOHN WARDLAW, 21ST BT, of Pitreavie, Fifeshire [Sir Henry Wardlaw Bt, Mandalay, 75–77 Two Bays Rd, Mount Eliza, Vict 3930, Australia]; *b* 30 Nov 1930; *s f* 1983; *educ* Melbourne U (MB, BS); *m* 1962 *Julie-Ann, dau of Edward Patrick Kirwan, and has:

1 +(HENRY) JUSTIN; *b* 10 Aug 1963
2 +Edward Patrick; *b* 1964
3 +Simon; *b* 1965
4 +Anthony James; *b* 1968
5 +Adrian Stewart; *b* 1971
1 *Janet Montgomerie; *b* 1969
2 *Marie Ellen; *b* 1977

Lineage: CUTHBERT WARDLAW, of Balmule, apparently a cadet of the WARDLAWs of Torrie; *m* by 1561 Catherine Dalgleish (*d* his widow 16 Feb 1621) and had, with an est s (Nicol, of W Luscar, *m* 1st —, dau and coheir of John Dewar of Foulford, *m* 2nd Margaret Hutton and *d* by 1 July 1645, leaving issue by both ws), three yr sons (Robert, *b* 23 March 1567/8, *m* 1st by 20 Dec 1600 Katherine (*d* between 19 Sept and 30 Nov 1601), dau of Robert Dalgleish of Tunnygask, *m* 2nd Marion Law, and *d* 4 Dec 1618, leaving issue; Thomas, of Logie, *b* 4 Sept 1569, Provost Dunfermline 1621, *m* 21 July 1601 —, dau of Thomas Alison, and had issue; John, living 1 Oct 1618) and a dau (Catherine), a 2nd s:

Sir Henry Wardlaw, 1st Bt (NS), so *cr* 5 March 1630/1, of Balmule and Pitreavie, which he bought 1596 and 1606 respectively; Chamberlain 1603 to ANN, consort of JAMES I; *m* Elizabeth Wilson, of Edinburgh, and *d* 5 April 1637, having had, with a dau:

1 **Sir Henry Wardlaw, 2nd Bt**; had a charter of Pitreavie 1617; *m* 1617 Margaret, dau of David Beaton of Balfour, and *d* 2 March 1653, leaving:

  (1) **Sir Henry Wardlaw, 3rd Bt**; *m* 9 June 1653 Margaret, dau of Sir John Henderson of Fordell, and *dsp* by 16 May 1654
  (1) Elizabeth; *m* 29 March 1646 her cousin **Sir Henry Wardlaw, 4th Bt**
2 William, of Balmule; *m* Christian, dau of James Foulis of Colinston, and *d* by 11 July 1650, leaving, with other issue:

  (1) HENRY Sir, **4th Bt**
  (2) John, ancestor of the WARDLAWs of Abden
  (1) Elizabeth; *bapt* 22 July 1624; *m* 1646 David Boswell of Balgonie

The 3rd Bt's cousin,
Sir Henry Wardlaw, 4th Bt; *m* 29 March 1646 his cousin Elizabeth (*see above*) and *d* 4 March 1680, having had, with three daus (including Margaret, *bapt* 26 March 1647, *m* 6 March 1663 James Kynninmond of that Ilk and of Craighall and had issue):

Sir Henry Wardlaw, 5th Bt; *bapt* 19 Oct 1648; *m* 24 April 1673 Elizabeth, dau of John Skene of Hallyards, and *d* on or after 16 May 1683, having had, with another s (Patrick):

1 **Sir Henry Wardlaw, 6th Bt**; *m* 13 June 1696 Elizabeth, author: *Hardyknute*, a poem, 2nd dau of Sir Charles Halkett, 1st Bt, of Pitfirran, and *d* by 5 Oct 1709, having had, with four daus and another s:

  (1) **Sir Henry Wardlaw, 7th Bt**; *dsp*
2 **Sir George Wardlaw, 8th Bt**; *m* — Oliphant and had an only s:

  (1) **Sir Henry Wardlaw, 9th Bt**; 2nd Foot Gds, *d* unm between 20 June and 15 July 1739

3 **Sir David Wardlaw, 10th Bt**; *b* 1679; *m* 1st Jean, only child and heiress of Rolland of Craighouse; *m* 2nd Jean Mercer, of Aldie, and had an only s:

  (1) **Sir David Wardlaw, 11th Bt**; *m* Janet Taylor and *d* Feb 1782, having had, with a yr s and five daus:

  1a **Sir David Wardlaw, 12th Bt**; *m* Margaret, dau of Andrew Symson, of Broomhead, and *d* 13 April 1793, having had, with four er sons (*d* young) and three daus:

  1b **Sir John Wardlaw, 13th Bt**; Lt-Col 64th Regt; *m* Jean (*d* 16 Feb 1880), 2nd dau of Charles Mitchell, of Pitcadie and Balbridge, and *d* 1 Jan 1823, leaving an only surv dau:

  1c Jane; *m* Andrew CLARKE later WELLWOOD-CLARKE, of Comrie Castle, Perthshire, and *dsp* 1855

4 William; *b* 1680; *m* Mary Bisset and had, with a dau (Margaret) and an est s:

  (1) Alexander; *m* Margaret Campbell, of Burnside, and had:

  1a **Sir William Wardlaw, 14th Bt**; *m* 12 July 1782 Elizabeth, dau of George Anderson, of Carlungie, Angus, and had, with two er sons (*d unm vp*):

  1b **Sir Alexander Wardlaw, 15th Bt**; *d unm* 1833
  2b **Sir William Wardlaw, 16th Bt**; *d unm* 23 Dec 1863
  3b **Sir Archibald Wardlaw, 17th Bt**; *b* 25 Jan 1796; *dsp* 29 Jan 1874
2a Henry; *b* 1746; Excise Offr; *m* Jean Gould (*d* 8 Jan 1847) and *d* 21 July 1820, leaving:

  1b James; *b* 1787; *m* 1st 1821 Margaret (*d* 1827), dau of John Monro, and had, with a dau (*d unm*):

  1c HENRY (Sir), **18th Bt**
  2c John, of Galt, Ontario; *b* 1824; *m* Mary (*d* 1907), dau of Thomas Davidson, and *d* 1903, leaving, with a dau (*d unm*):

  1d James Sime; *b* 27 Aug 1851; MD; *m* 1st 1891 Doreta (*d* 1893), dau of Dr Lundy; *m* 2nd 1904 Mary Helen (*d* 24 Oct 1932), dau of John Ritchie, of Beaverton, Ontario, and *d* 22 Feb 1935, leaving by her:

  1e Mary Davidson; *b* 1 Aug 1914; *m* 1st 8 June 1940 Lt-Col George Alexander MacKay Edwards, Highland LI (*d* 1960), s of Alexander MacKay Edwards, MP; *m* 2nd 1964 Harold S Dando, of Quebec, and by her 1st husb had:

  1f *James Clare [James Edwards Esq, 3563 University St, Montreal, Canada]; *b* 21 July 1941; *m* 1965 *Sharon A Ure
2d Thomas Davidson; *b* 24 Oct 1853; *m* 1881 Margaret (*d* 27 Nov 1929), dau of Thomas Miller, of Stratford, Ontario, and *d* 1943, leaving:

  1e John Walter; *b* 1882; *m* 1914 Iva, dau of W W Brigham, and *d* 1944, leaving:

  1f James Walter; *b* 1921; *m* 1951 *Carina Guenther and *d* 1983, leaving:

  1g *Jane Katherine; *b* 1958; *m* 1976 *Ralph Duek, of Olds, Alberta, and has:

  1h *Jason Brent; *b* 1981
  1h *Lori Anne; *b* 1977
  2h *Cheryl Lynn; *b* 1979
  2g *Judy Carina; *b* 1961; *m* 1982 *Kenneth Randall, of Edmonton, Alberta
1f *Mary Macallum; *b* 1914; *m* 1938 *Safford Emory Thorp, of New London, Conn., and has had:

  1g Walter Wakeman; *b* 1944; *m* 28 April 1967 *Cynthia Anne Szegda and *d* 1979, leaving:

  1h *Walter Allen; *b* 1970
  1h *Dawn Marie; *b* 28 Nov 1968
  2h *Kristy Louise; *b* 1976
1g *Mina Jane [Mrs Earl Ewers, Milner's Mobile Home Estate, Lot 20, Lynchburg, VA, USA]; *b* 1939; *m* 1st 12 March 1956 Cofer Lee Gray, of Ledyard, Conn.; *m* 2nd 1983 *Earl Ewers and has had by her 1st husb:

  1h *Safford Emory; *b* 3 April 1964
  1h Bonnie Inez; *b* 12 June 1957; *d* 11 Jan 1968
  2h *Ramona Lee [Mrs Donald Jeay, Rt 3, Box 95–A, Dillwyn, VA, USA]; *b* 28 April 1958; *m* 1983 *Donald Jeay and has issue

2g *Lorna Elizabeth; *b* 1947; *m* 14 Aug 1965 *Lee William Coleman and has:

  1h *Tina Marie; *b* 25 Nov 1966
  2h *Leah J; *b* 29 Oct 1969
2f *Margaret Brigham; *b* 1918; *m* 1949 *James Gethyn Jones, of Toronto, and has:

  1g *Richard Gethyn; *b* 1952; *m* 1981 *Maureen Grierson, of Vancouver
  1g *Elizabeth Davidson; *b* 1958
3f *Elizabeth Davidson [Miss Elizabeth Wardlaw, 56 Jedburgh Rd, Toronto, Ontario, Canada]; *b* 1926
2e James Macallum; *b* 1884; *m* 1923 Mary (*d* 1953), dau of Robert Law, and *d* 1967, leaving:

  1f +Thomas Davidson [Thomas Wardlaw Esq, 72 Main St N, Waterford, Ontario N0E 1Y0, Canada]; *b* 1924; *m* 1950 *Grace Smith and has:

  1g +David Macallum [David Wardlaw Esq, 316 Eunice Dve, Kingston, Ontario K7M 3N8, Canada]; *b* 1952; *m* 1st 1978 (*divorce* 1984) Jennifer Leigh, dau of Wilbur Garvie, of Oaville, Ontario; *m* 2nd 1985 *Margaret Ann, dau of Irvin Andrew Bartee, and by her has:

  1h +Andrew Thomas; *b* 1989
  1h *Alison Marie; *b* 1987
  1g (cont.) David Wardlaw adopted his stepdau:
  *Sarah Lynn; *b* 1980

2g +Robert Duncan [Robert Wardlaw Esq, 317 Roywood Cres, Newmarket, Ontario L3Y 1A6, Canada]; *b* 1954; *m* 1982 *Rita C, dau of William G More, of Ottawa, and has:

   1h +James More; *b* 1983

   2h +Daniel Robert More; *b* 1989

3g +Craig Davidson [Craig Wardlaw Esq, 2681 Jerseyville Rd, Jerseyville, Ontario, L0R 1R0, Canada]; *b* 1956; *m* 1979 *Flora Margaret, dau of Duncan Hector Allan Simpson, and has:

   1h +Duncan Ian Macleod; *b* 1992

   2h +Liethen Davidson; *b* 1996

4g +Jonathan Stewart; *b* 1959; *m* 1988 *Beth Yvonne, dau of Rev John William Houstoun, of Aurora, Ontario, and has:

   1h +Mackenzie Jonathan; *b* 1995

   1h *Rebecca Jillian; *b* 1992

2f +Robert Law [Robert Wardlaw Esq, 9 Oriole Dve, Glos, Ontario, Canada K1J 7E8]; *b* 13 April 1927; BASc U of Toronto 1949, Dip Electrical Engrg McGill 1963, MEng Carleton U Ottawa 1966; *m* 20 March 1954 *Felicia Jane, dau of Frank Hallett Milsum, of London N4, and has:

   1g +Stephen James; *b* 2 Feb 1957; *m* 30 Sept 1995 *Margaret Jane Wallace, dau of Norman Wallace

   2g +Michael John; *b* 24 Aug 1960

   1g *Anne Margaret; *b* 11 Nov 1958; *m* 20 Feb 1988 *Eric Steven Teutsch, of Nepean, Ontario, and has:

     1h *Jeffrey Stephen; *b* 17 July 1989

     2h *Alexander Robert; *b* 2 Nov 1992

     1h *Laura Jane; *b* 23 Sept 1994

   2g *Patricia Mary; *b* 18 Feb 1962; *m* 21 Sept 1985 *Peter Hermann Laurich, of Nepean, and has:

     1h *Jason Robert; *b* 27 March 1989

     2h *Andrew Anthony; *b* 30 Dec 1990

     3h *Bruce Patrick; *b* 3 April 1993

   3g *Laura Kathleen; *b* 9 April 1963; *m* 12 June 1993 *Allan Gregory Osborne, of Ottawa, and has:

     1h *Charles Isaac; *b* 5 Oct 1997

     1h *Shannon Rose; *b* 12 June 1996

1f *Janet Melville [Miss Janet Wardlaw, 20 Suffolk St W, Guelph, Ontario N1H 2H8, Canada]; *b* 1924

1e Mary; *b* 12 April 1892; *d* 29 May 1990

3d Henry John; *b* 1865; *m* Clara (*d* 7 Nov 1938), dau of W Wasson, of California, and *dsp* 26 Nov 1938

1b (cont.) James Wardlaw *m* 2nd 1833 Grace (*d* 1872), dau of Peter Dudgeon, of Dollar, and *d* 5 March 1867, having by her had:

   3c Peter; *b* 23 Nov 1833; *m* 1862 and *d* 28 May 1906, leaving:

     1d Robert; *b* 1875; *m* 1910 Jeanie Paterson

     1d Joanna Margaret

     2d Isabella Jane; *m* 19 July 1905 B Tait and had issue

   1c Jane; *m* 10 Nov 1856 David Drysdale (*d* 4 July 1893), of Lyndhurst, Tillicoultry, and *d* 1918, leaving issue

   2c Isabella; *m* 1870 William Ross, of Brookfield Villa, Stirling, and *d* 1912, leaving issue

The 17th Bt's cousin,

Sir Henry Wardlaw, 18th Bt; *b* 22 March 1822; *m* 24 July 1845 Christina (*d* 28 Nov 1902), 3rd dau of James Paton, and *d* 13 April 1897, having had:

1 James; *b* 30 Oct 1861; *dvp*

2 HENRY (Sir), **19th Bt**

1 Grace; *b* 21 Feb 1851; *m* 12 Nov 1873 James Pow, of Montreal, and *d* 1923, leaving issue

2 Christina; *b* 16 March 1853; *d* unm 17 Sept 1943

3 Margaret; *b* 12 April 1855; *d* unm 1933

4 Jane; *b* 6 May 1857; *d* unm 15 July 1943

5 Isabella; *b* 28 Sept 1859; *m* 24 July 1890 Alexander Wylie, of Craiginnan, Giffnock, Glasgow, and *d* 24 Nov 1935, leaving issue

6 Helen; *b* 5 July 1869; *m* 28 April 1896 Henry Albert Boedeker, MB, CM, MO Br E African Protectorate, and *d* 23 Sept 1935

The 18th Bt's only surv s,

Sir Henry Wardlaw, 19th Bt; *b* 8 Feb 1867; engr; *m* 22 June 1892 Janet Montgomerie (*d* 16 May 1962 aged 98), dau of James Wylie, and *d* 4 Feb 1954, leaving:

1 **Sir Henry Wardlaw, 20th Bt**, of Pitreavie; *b* 31 Aug 1894; *m* 1929 Ellen, dau of John Francis Brady, leaving:

(1) Sir HENRY JOHN WARDLAW, **21st and present Bt**

(2) +Robert Murdoch [Robert Wardlaw Esq, 4 Connemarra St, Bexley, NSW, Australia]; *b* 18 March 1940; *m* 1971 *Dale Edith, dau of Jospeh Fetherston, and has:

   1a +Dominic; *b* 1972

(3) +Andrew David Montgomerie [Andrew Wardlaw Esq, 24 Middlesex Rd, Surrey Hills, Victoria, Australia]; *b* 10 April 1941; *educ* Melbourne U (LLB); *m* 1965 *Elizabeth, dau of Dennis Leary, and has:

   1a +David; *b* 1965

   2a +Matthew; *b* 1966

   3a +Michael; *b* 1969

   4a +Timothy; *b* 1974

   1a *Louise; *b* 1971

(4) +Gregory Wylie [Gregory Wardlaw Esq, 15 Millicent Ave, Buleen, Victoria, Australia]; *b* 11 Oct 1943; *m* 19– *— and has:

   1a +Cameron; *b* 1970

   2a +Alistair; *b* 1973

(1) *Cynthia Mary; *b* 23 Dec 1931; BA, DipEd; *m* 19– *—, of St Andrew's, Victoria, and has:

   1a +Jeremy; *b* 19–

   1a *Melanie; *b* 19–

   2a *Abigail; *b* 19–

1 Christine Martha Madge; *b* 25 June 1893

2 Frances Ethel; *b* 1 Sept 1898

WARING

Arms: Argent on a bend engrailed azure, between two rods of Aesculapius proper three crescents. **Crest:** A demi-wolf resting the sinister paw on a rod of Aesculapius proper. **Motto:** Whatever you undertake, do well. **Creation:** Bt. (UK) 29 Jan 1935.

SIR (ALFRED) HOLBURT WARING, 3RD BT, of St Bartholomew's, City of London [Sir Holburt Waring Bt, Earl's Croft, 30 Russell Rd, Moor Park, Northwood, Middx HA6 2LR]; *b* 2 Aug 1933; *s f* 1981; *educ* Rossall and Leeds Coll of Commerce; dir SRM Plastics Ltd, Waring Investment Ltd, Rota Print Ltd; *m* 1 Sept 1958 *Anita, dau of Valentin Medinilla, of Madrid, and has:

1 +MICHAEL HOLBURT; *b* 3 Jan 1964

1 *Margaret Rose; *b* 2 June 1961

2 *Susan Caroline; *b* 23 March 1967

Lineage: ISAAC WARING, of Southport, Lancs; had:

Sir Holburt Jacob Waring, 1st Bt (UK), so *cr* 29 Jan 1935, CBE (1919); *b* 3 Oct 1866; *educ* Chorley GS Lancs and Owens Coll Manchester (BSc 1888, MB 1890, BS 1891); FRCS 1891 (Pres 1932–35), MS London 1893, Brevet-Col RAMC (T) WW I (despatches); ktd 1925, Offr Legn Hon; consultant surgn: St Bartholomew's Hosp, Min Pensions, Roy Dental Hosp and Met Hosp, Govr St Bartholomew's Hosp and Medical Coll (Chm 1923–31), memb Bd Management 1923–44 (Chm 1942–44, Treas 1923–44) London Sch of Hygiene and Tropical Medicine, Govs Imp Coll and Queen Mary's Coll, Hunterian Tstee Roy Coll Surgns, FRSM, Treas Imperial Cancer Research Fund, Hon MS U of Egypt, Hon LLD Bristol 1933, Hon DCL Durham 1934, Hon Fell Roy Australasian Coll Surgns; *m* 10 Dec 1900 Annie Cassandra (*d* 9 Oct 1948), dau of Charles Johnston Hill, of London W11, and *d* 10 Feb 1953, leaving:

1 **Sir Alfred Harold Waring, 2nd Bt**; *b* 14 Feb 1902; *educ* Winchester, Trin Coll Cambridge (BA 1924) and London U (BSc Engrg 1924); AMIMechE; *m* 2 Aug 1930 Winifred, dau of Albert Boston, of Stockton-on-Tees, and *d* 1981, leaving:

(1) Sir (ALFRED) HOLBURT WARING, **3rd and present Bt**

(1) *(Winifred) Anne [Mrs Michael Mark, The White Ho, Easingwold, Yorks YO6 3AA]; *b* 23 June 1931; *m* 3 Sept 1954 *Michael Scott Mark, s of Douglas Scott Mark, of Knaresborough, and has:

   1a *Jonathan Scott; *b* 7 Feb 1956; *educ* Repton

   2a *Christopher Edward; *b* 23 July 1959

(2) *(Joan Catherine) Cassandra; *b* 1 Jan 1937; *educ* Edinburgh U (MA); *m* 19 May 1962 (*divorce*) John Barry William Holderness, of Jersey, CI, s of Barry Layton Holderness, MBE, of Richmond, Surrey, and has:

   1a *Corinne Louisa Cassandra; *b* 28 March 1969

   2a *Marina Isabelle Cassandra; *b* 1974

WARMINGTON

Arms: Or a lion rampant sable, charged on the shoulder with two fleurs-de-lys palewise of the first, holding between the paws a full-bottomed wig proper. **Crest:** An owl or, holding in the beak a penna and ink horn sable. **Motto:** *Non mihi sed omnibus* ('Not for myself, but for all'). **Creation:** Bt. (UK) 28 July 1908.

SIR DAVID MARSHALL WARMINGTON, 5TH BT, of Pembridge Sq, Roy Borough of Kensington [Sir David Warmington Bt, 139 Norfolk House, Highlands Heath, London SW15 3TZ]; *b* 14 Feb 1944; *s* half-bro 1996; *educ* Charterhouse; *m* 1st 10 Dec 1966 Susan Mary, dau of Rev Canon Clifford Chapman, Dean of Exeter; *m* 2nd 1981 *Mrs Eileen Verdin (née Johnston) and by his 1st w has:

  1 +RUPERT MARSHALL; *b* 17 June 1969

  2 +Guy Denham; *b* 12 Feb 1972

Lineage: EDWARD WARMINGTON, of Colchester; *m* Mary Payne and had a 6th s:

Sir (Cornelius) Marshall Warmington, 1st Bt (UK), so *cr* 28 July 1908, QC (1881), JP (Sussex), of Pembridge Sq, Kensington; *b* 5 June 1842; *educ* London U; slr 1864, barrister Middle Temple 1869, Bencher 1885, Treas 1904; MP (Lib) W Mon 1885–95, memb Senate London U; *m* 4 Feb 1871 Ann (*d* 16 Jan 1925), yst dau of Edward Winch, of Chatham and Rochester, and *d* 12 Dec 1908, leaving, with another s (*d* young) and a dau (*d* unm):

  1 MARSHALL DENHAM (Sir), **2nd Bt**

  2 Herbert Andrew Cromartie; *b* 8 May 1874; Fell Surveyors' Inst; *m* 1st 23 July 1904 (*divorce* 1926) Elsie (*d* 28 Dec 1956), dau of John Stuart, of Ardingly, Sussex; *m* 2nd 1938 Helena, dau of Albert de Mersey, and by his 1st w had:

    (1) Anthony Marshall Stuart; *b* 4 May; *d* 5 May 1916

    (1) *Joan Pamela Stuart; *b* 8 Jan 1906; *m* 1st 6 May 1926 Cdr Nigel Bellairs Deare, RN; *m* 2nd 26 April 1934 (*divorce* 1953) Dr Vincenzo Bottari, of Taormina

  3 Edward Stephen, CE; *b* 15 Jan 1882; *educ* Trin Coll Cambridge (BA); *d* 23 Oct 1933

  1 Mary Agnes Marshall; *b* 2 Nov 1889; *m* 18 March 1911 Sir Harry Herbert Trusted, QC, Ch Justice Palestine 1937–41 and Federated Malay States 1941, only s of Rev Wilson Trusted, of Salisbury, and had issue

The 1st Bt's est s,

Sir Marshall Denham Warmington, 2nd Bt, JP Bucks; *b* 3 Nov 1871; *educ* Trin Coll Cambridge (MA); barrister Middle Temple 1895, Registrar Bankruptcy High Court 1926; *m* 1st 15 July 1908 Alice Daisy (*d* 29 Oct 1913), er dau of George Ing, of Edenbridge, Kent; *m* 2nd 14 Sept 1915 Ethel Graham (*d* 29 Aug 1957), yst dau of John Lawson Gillies, of Bradford, and *d* 2 Aug 1935, leaving by his 1st w:

  1 **Sir Marshall George Clitheroe Warmington, 3rd Bt**; *b* 26 May 1910; *educ* Charterhouse; Lt-Cdr RN WW II; *m* 1st 21 March 1933 (*divorce* 1941) Molly, est dau of Capt Malcolm Alfred Kennard, RN, of Wonham, Bampton, and had:

    (1) **Sir Marshall Denham Malcolm Warmington, 4th Bt**; *b* 5 Jan 1934; *educ* privately; *d* 29 Nov 1996

    (1) *Margaret Anne [Mrs Colin Bricknell, Camrose, 71A High St, Hurstpierpoint, W Sussex BN6 9RE]; *b* 2 Sept 1936; *educ* OU (BA), LIMA; late 3rd Offr WRNS; *m* 27 Oct 1962 *Lt-Cdr Colin Alan (Charles) Bricknell, RN, MBIM, only s of Christopher Alfred Bricknell, of Hawkern Ho, Otterton, Devon, and has:

      1a *Martin Charles Marshall; *b* 14 Dec 1963; *educ* Christ's Hosp; Capt RAMC

      2a *Julian John; *b* 1 June 1965; *educ* Christ's Hosp

      3a *Peter Marshall; *b* 20 Nov 1969; *educ* Hurstpierpoint

  1 (cont.) **Sir Marshall** *m* 2nd 18 July 1942 Eileen Mary (*d* 25 Oct 1969), late Ch Offr WRNS, dau of Percy John Howes and Mrs Christopher Heseltine, of Brambridge Park, Bishopstone, Hants, and by her had:

    (2) **Sir DAVID MARSHALL WARMINGTON, 5th and present Bt**

    (3) +Anthony Marshall; *b* 1 July 1946; *educ* Charterhouse; late Lt 1st The Queen's Dragoon Gds; stockbroker; *m* 1973 (*divorce* 1987) Carolyn Patricia (*d* 1993), er dau of J A H Simonds, of Rotherfield Greys, Oxon, and has:

      1a +Oliver Marshall Simonds; *b* 1974; *educ* Charterhouse

      1a *Katherine Louise; *b* 1977

  1 (cont.) **Sir Marshall** *m* 3rd 15 May 1972 (*divorce* 1977) Sheila (*d* 1988), 2nd dau of Stanley Brotherhood, JP, of Thornhaugh Hall, Peterborough, by Vera, 4th dau of Charles Durant Kemp-Welch, JP, DL, of Broadlands, Ascot, Berks, and widow of Adml Hon Sir Cyril Eustace Douglas-Pennant, KCB, CBE, DSO (*see* PENRHYN, B), and *d* 5 Feb 1995

  1 *Elisabeth Barbara Marshall [Mrs John Perfect, 18 Cryspen Court, Garland St, Bury St Edmunds, Suffolk IP33 1EP]; *b* 12 May 1909; *m* 1st 21 Dec 1933 Ian Somerled Macdonald (*d* 15 Nov 1958), only s of John Hutcheson Macdonald, of Gt Missenden; *m* 2nd 23 Sept 1961 *John Perfect, s of Capt Herbert Mosley Perfect, RN, of Warrenpoint, Co Down, and by her 1st husb has:

    (1) *John Marshall; *b* 1937

    (2) *Euan Ross; *b* 1940

    (1) *Elisabeth Margaret; *b* 1935

    (2) *Sheila Joy; *b* 1942

WARNER

Arms: Per bend argent and gules two bendlets between six roses, all counterchanged. **Crest:** A Saracen's head affrontée, couped at the shoulders proper, vested gules, on the head a cap checky argent and of the second, in front thereof three roses fesswise of the third. **Motto:** *Spero* ('I hope'). **Creation:** Bt. (UK) 9 July 1910.

SIR (EDWARD COURTENAY) HENRY WARNER, 3RD BT, of Brettenham Park, Suffolk [Sir Henry Warner Bt, The Grove, Gt Baddow, Essex CM2 7AB]; *b* 3 Aug 1922; *s* f 1955; *educ* Eton and Ch Ch Oxford; Lt Scots Gds WW II (wounded); *m* 8 Oct 1949 *Jocelyn Mary, 2nd dau of Cdr Sir Thomas Lubbock Beevor, 6th Bt, RN (*qv*), and has:

  1 +PHILIP COURTENAY THOMAS [Philip Warner Esq, Marden Grange, Devizes, Wilts]; *b* 3 April 1951; *educ* Eton; *m* 1982 *Penelope Anne, yr dau of John Lack Elmer, and has:

    (1) +Charles Thomas Courtenay; *b* 30 Sept 1989

    (1) *Alexandra Sarah Vivian; *b* 1985

    (2) *Katherine Jocelyn Rose; *b* 1987

    (3) *Eleanor Felicity Jane; *b* 1992

    (4) *Isabella Lucy Penelope; *b* 1995

  2 +Richard Edward Lubbock; *b* 17 May 1952; *educ* Eton; *m* 1976 (divorce 1992) Jennifer Claire Furlonger and has:

    (1) +Peter Edward Courtenay; *b* 1983

    (1) *Lucy Claire; *b* 1979

    (2) *Sarah Louise; *b* 1981

  3 +Robert Henry [Robert Warner Esq, Perrotts Hill Farm, nr Witney, Oxon]; *b* 3 April 1957; *educ* Eton; *m* 1983 *Sophie Anne Rosalie, dau of Timothy Davis, of Steeple Aston, Oxon, and has:

    (1) +Henry Francis; *b* 1986

    (2) +George William; *b* 1987

    (3) +John Robert; *b* 1994

    (1) *Rosalie Mary; *b* 1992

Lineage: EDWARD WARNER, of Leyton, Essex; *m* 1768 Sarah, dau of Rev T Brooke, of Cottingham, Yorks, and *d* 1815, leaving, with an er s (Thomas Courtenay, *dsp* 1823):

EDWARD WARNER, of The Clock Ho, Walthamstow, Essex; *b* 26 June 1779; *m* 1817 Ann Mary (*d* 5 Oct 1850), dau of George Pearson, of Jamaica, and had, with other issue:

EDWARD WARNER, of Highams, Walthamstow; *d* 17 Dec 1847, leaving an er s:

EDWARD WARNER, of Highams, JP, DL Essex, Middx and Westminster; *b* 8 April 1818; *educ* Wadham Coll Oxford (MA); MP Norwich 1852–57 and 1860–68, FRGS; *m* 27 April 1848 Maria (*d* 4 Nov 1884), widow of John Hibbitts and dau of Thomas Carr, of New Ross, Co Wexford, and *d* 7 March 1875, having had, with an er s (Edward, *d* an infant 9 Sept 1849):

Sir Thomas Courtenay Theydon Warner, 1st Bt (UK), so *cr* 9 July 1910, CB, JP (Somerset); *b* 19 July 1857; *educ* Eton and BNC Oxford; Ld Lt and custos rotulorum Suffolk, Pres Suffolk TAA, Alderman W Suffolk CC, High Sheriff Essex

1891, Dir Nat Serv (E Region) 1917–18, MP (Lib) N Somerset 1892–95 and Lichfield 1896–1923, Col Suffolk Vol Regt, Lt-Col and Hon Col cmdg 3rd Bn (SR) Oxon and Bucks LI, chm Warner Estate Ltd and Law Land Co; *m* 6 Dec 1883 Lady Leucha Diana Maude, LGStJ (*d* 23 Aug 1947), 6th dau of 1st Earl de Montalt (*see* HAWARDEN, V), and *d* 15 Dec 1934, leaving:

1 EDWARD COURTENAY THOMAS (Sir), **2nd Bt**

2 Cornwallis John; *b* 1 Feb 1889; barrister 1911, Lt 3rd Bn (attd 2nd Bn) Oxon and Bucks LI WW I; missing believed *k* 16 May 1915

3 Thomas Seymour Marius; *b* 5 Nov 1903; Capt Scots Gds; *m* 1st 19 Jan 1926 (*divorce* 1929) Mrs Dorothy Russell, only dau of William Durran, of Durran, Caithness, and formerly w of Sydney Russell; *m* 2nd 5 Dec 1929 (*divorce* 1938) Mrs Edith Dorothy Morrison, dau of Robert Bold, of Liverpool; *m* 3rd 26 March 1938 *Louise Cameron [Mrs Thomas Warner, Ely Cottage, Wharf Lane, Henley-on-Thames, Oxon], dau of Edward M Roberts, of New York, and *d* 26 Dec 1965, leaving by her:

(1) +Courtenay Forbes [Courtenay Warner Esq, 12/46 Lowndes Sq, London SW1]; *b* 24 Sept 1939; *educ* Eton; late Lt Scots Gds; *m* 1st 11 Dec 1969 (*divorce* 1974) Veronica Jane, dau of Lt-Col W M W Cooper, OBE, of Medlands Farm Ho, Hurstbourne Tarrant, Hants; *m* 2nd 1974 *Venetia Elizabeth, dau of Maj R Atkinson-Turner, of Worlington, Suffolk, and by her has:

1a +Harry Richard Courtenay; *b* 1975

1 Leucha Mary; *b* 25 Dec 1884; *d* unm 13 Dec 1960

2 Lilian Georgina; *b* 9 June 1892; *m* 1st 20 March 1915 Lt David Archibald James Chapman (*ka* 15 Sept 1916), Scots Gds, s of Col David Philips Chapman, MVO, JP, of Manor Ho, Ham, Surrey; *m* 2nd 4 Nov 1925 Charles Ronald Mansel Lewis (*d* 19 Sept 1960), 2nd s of Charles William Mansel Lewis, of Stradey, and had issue

The 1st Bt's est s,
Sir Edward Courtenay Thomas Warner, 2nd Bt, DSO (1917), MC (1915), JP, DL Suffolk; *b* 4 Jan 1886; *educ* Eton and Ch Ch Oxford; ADC to Ld Lt Ireland, served WW I (despatches seven times, Brevet Maj), Col Scots Gds, Lt-Col cmdg 1931–34, Brevet Col 1932, GSO(3) 1934–36, WW II: GSO France and Belgium 1940, Area Cdr Maidstone 1941, Sr Regl Offr London CD Region 1942–45; Suffolk Branch BRCS 1946–53, High Sheriff Suffolk 1947, Croix de Guerre, Orders Avis Portugal and Danilo Montenegro, chm Warner Estate Ltd; *m* 16 Feb 1920 Hon Nesta Douglas-Pennant (*d* 4 March 1970), dau of 2nd Baron Penrhyn (*qv*), and *d* 2 Oct 1955, leaving:

1 Sir (EDWARD COURTENAY) HENRY WARNER, **3rd and present Bt**

1 *Anne Philippa [The Hon Mrs Edward Boscawen, Garden Ho, High Beeches Lane, Handcross, Sussex]; *b* 27 Feb 1927; *m* 14 July 1951 *Hon (Henry) Edward Boscawen, 3rd s of 8th Viscount Falmouth (*qv*), and has issue

2 *Leucha Daphne Mary; *b* 24 Jan 1929; *m* 19 July 1962 *Mark Gerald Edward North Buxton (*see* BUXTON, Bt) and has issue

WARNOCK

Creation: B. (LP, UK) 1985.

THE BARONESS WARNOCK, of Weeke, Winchester (Dame (Helen) Mary Wilson, DBE (1984)) [The Rt Hon The Baroness Warnock DBE, 3 Church St, Gt Bedwyn, Wilts]; *b* 14 April 1924; *educ* St Swithun's Winchester and LMH Oxford (Hon Fell 1984); Fell and Tutor Philosophy St Hugh's Coll Oxford 1949–66 (Sr Research Fell 1976–84, Hon Fell 1985), Headmistress Oxford High Sch 1966–72; memb: IBA 1973–81, Ctee Inquiry Special Educn 1974–78, SSRC 1981–85, UK Nat Commn for Unesco 1981–84; memb Roy Commn Environmental Pollution 1979–84, Chm: Advsy Ctee Animal Experiments 1979–86, Ctee Inquiry into Human Fertilisation 1982–84; Mistress Girton Coll Cambridge 1985–91; author: *A Common Policy for Education* (1988*)*, *Universities: knowing our minds* (1989), *The Uses of Philosophy* (1992), *Imagination and Time* (1994), *Women Philosophers* (ed, 1995), *An Intelligent Person's Guide to Ethics* (1998); *m* 1949 Sir Geoffrey James Warnock (*d* 8 Oct 1995), Pncpl Hertford Coll Oxford 1971–88 and V-Chllr Oxford U 1981–85, and has:

1 *Felix Geoffrey [The Hon Felix Warnock, 5 Kingsbridge Rd, London W10 6PU]; *b* 1952; *educ* Winchester and RCM; *m* 1975 *Juliet, dau of Arthur Robert Lehwalder, of Seattle, WN, and has:

(1) *Daniel Arthur Richard; *b* 1985

(1) *Eleanor Denise; *b* 1982

(2) *Polly Patricia; *b* 1986

2 *James Marcus Alexander [The Hon James Warnock, 5 Cheltenham Ave, Liverpool L17 2AR]; *b* 1953; *educ* Winchester and UEA; *m* 1986 *Fiona Margaret, dau of Matthew Stewart Hair, and has a s and dau

1 *Kathleen; *b* 1950; *educ* Oxford High Sch and St Hugh's Coll Oxford

2 *Stephana (Fanny) [The Hon Mrs Branson, 19 Orchard Close, East Hendred, Oxon]; *b* 1956; *educ* Downe House, Oxford High Sch and Guildhall Sch of Music; *m* 1987 *David E (Bruno) Branson, s of W E Branson, of S Hill, Beds, and has:

(1) *Abigail Brigitte Edith; *b* 1989

3 *(Grizel) Maria [The Hon Mrs Jenkins, 22 Hayes Ct, Camberwell New Rd, London SE5 0TQ]; *b* 1961; *educ* Oxford High Sch and W Surrey Sch of Art and Design; *m* 1994 *Paul Jenkins, s of Keith Jenkins, of Kidlington, Oxford

Lineage: ARCHIBALD EDWARD WILSON; *m* Ethel Mary, est dau of Sir Felix Otto Schuster 1st Bt (*see* 1970 edn), and had:

(HELEN) MARY, *cr* a **Baroness**

WARREN

Arms: Arg. a fess checky or and az. between three talbots passant ppr. **Crest:** A lion rampant holding a crozier ppr. **Motto:** *Non mihi sed deo et regi* ('Not for me, but for God and the King').
Creation: Bt. (I) 7 July 1784.

SIR (BRIAN) CHARLES PENNEFATHER WARREN, **9TH BT**, of Warren's Court, Co Cork [Sir Charles Warren Bt, The Wilderness, Castle Oliver, Kilmallock, Co Limerick, Ireland]; *b* 4 June 1923; *s f* 1961; *educ* Wellington; Lt Irish Gds WW II 1942–45; *m* 4 June 1976 (*divorce* 1983) Nicola Louise, er dau of Capt Edward de Lérisson Cazenove (*see* KENNEDY, Bt)

Lineage: ROBERT WARREN, of Kennagh, E Carbery, Co Cork; Army Offr; *m* Margery — and *d* 1662, leaving, with other issue:

WALLIS WARREN, of Kilbarry (later Warren's Court), Co Cork; *m* 1684 Elizabeth, dau of Thomas Knolles, and had, with other issue:

ROBERT WARREN, of Kilbarry; *m* Anne, sis of William Crooke, and *d* 1743, having had, with other issue, including a yr s (William, of Cork, *m* Dorcas, sis of William Perry, and *d* 1761, leaving issue):

Sir Robert Warren, 1st Bt (I), so *cr* 7 July 1784, of Warren's Court and Crookstown House, Co Cork; *b* 20 Aug 1723; *m* 1st 1748 Mary, dau of Augustus Carre, and *d* 1811, having had, with other issue:

1 **Sir Augustus Louis Carré Warren, 2nd Bt**; *b* 1754; MP City of Cork 1783–90; *m* 1778 Mary (*d* 14 Nov 1825), sis of 1st Earl of Bandon (*see* 1970 edn), and *d* 30 Jan 1821, leaving:

(1) **Sir Augustus Warren, 3rd Bt**; *b* 17 May 1791; Col City of Cork Militia; *d* unm 28 April 1863

(2) **Sir John Borlase Warren, 4th Bt**; *b* 13 Sept 1800; *m* 23 Nov 1823 his cousin Mary, dau of Rev Robert Warren (*see* below), and *d* 4 Dec 1863, leaving:

1a **Sir Augustus Riversdale Warren, 5th Bt**, JP Cos Cork and Kerry, DL Co Cork; *b* 24 Aug 1833; Maj 20th Regt Crimea 1854–55 and Indian Mutiny 1857–78, Hon Col 4th Bn Roy Munster Fus, High Sheriff Co Cork 1867; *m* 1st 28 April 1864 Georgina (*d* 10 Nov 1893), est dau of Rev John Blennerhasset, Rector Ryme Intrinseca, Dorset, and n of Arthur Blennerhasset, of Ballyseedy, MP Co Kerry; *m* 2nd 5 Feb 1898 Ella Rosa (*d* 26 Oct 1946), dau of Gen John Octavius Chichester and formerly w of Col F W Clarkson, 39th Regt, and *d* 1 April 1914, leaving by his 1st w:

1b **Sir Augustus Riversdale John Blennerhasset Warren, 6th Bt**, JP Co Cork; *b* 11 March 1865; Lt 3rd Roy Munster Fus; *m* 12 Jan 1898 Agnes Georgina (*m* 2nd 21 May 1924 George I Hartt, s of Edward Hartt, of Whitehill, Riverstown, Co Sligo, and *d* Oct 1950), dau of George Maurice Ievers, of Inchera, Co Cork, and *d* 28 Aug 1914, leaving:

1c **Sir Augustus George Digby Warren, 7th Bt**, MBE (1945); *b* 23 Oct 1898; *educ* Harrow and RMC Sandhurst; Lt 7th Hus WW I, Maj 17th/21st Lancers WW II; *d* unm 20 Jan 1958

2a John Borlase; *b* 27 March 1838; V-Adml, Baltic and Chinese medals; *m* 12 Sept 1874 Mary Elizabeth St Leger (*d* 9 March 1935), 2nd dau of Maj St Leger Atkins, of Water Park, Co Cork, and *d* 29 Jan 1919, leaving:

1b Bessie Geraldine Gundreda; *m* 20 Nov 1906 Sir John Scarlett Walsham, 3rd Bt (*qv*), and *d* 8 Dec 1941, leaving issue

2b Mary Detta St Leger

3b Louisa Ursula St Leger; *d* unm 1 Oct 1949

3a Robert; *b* 11 Dec 1842; *m* 4 Sept 1872 Blanche Louise, dau of Capt Leonard Leader, JP, of Ashgrove, Co Cork, and *dsp*

1a Mary; *m* 10 May 1859 Rev Thomas Robert Hamilton (*d* 19 May 1906), Chaplain RN, 4th s of Rev Hugh Hamilton, Rector Innismacsaint, Co Fermanagh, and had issue

2a Margaret; *m* 14 Aug 1851 Charles Bosworth Martin and *d* 1881, leaving issue

3a Charlotte; *m* 1848 Robert Heard (*d* 12 Sept 1896), JP, Pallastown, Co Cork, and *d* 28 April 1886, leaving issue

4a Esther; *m* 1867 Ralph Fuller, of Kilkondy, Co Cork, and *d* 12 March 1877, leaving issue

5a Elizabeth; m 28 April 1868 William Massy Hutchinson Massy (d 1887), JP, of Mount Massy, and d 1899, leaving issue

6a Rose Catherine; m 10 April 1867 Capt George David Clayhills-Henderson, RN (d 13 July 1909), of Invergowrie, and dsp 7 Dec 1898

7a Frances Augusta; m 10 April 1867 Col Charles Henry Chauncy (d 15 Aug 1920), 22nd Regt, and d 1 Feb 1919, leaving issue

(1) Esther; m 30 July 1808 James Colthurst (d 1814), of Dripsey Castle, Co Cork, and d 22 July 1872, leaving issue

(2) Charlotte; m Rev Somers H Payne, of Upton, Co Cork

2 William, of Lisgoold, Co Cork; m 1st Margaret, dau of Robert Gordon, of Newgrove; m 2nd Mary Martin (dsp 1822), dau of Rev Thomas Bushe, DD; m 3rd Alice (dsp), dau of Walter Baldwin, and by his 1st w had:

(1) Anna Maria; m 30 May 1799 Hugh Lawton (d 1859)

3 Thomas, of Monkstown, Co Cork; MP Charleville 1776–83 and Castlebar 1783–90, barrister; m Anne (m 2nd Richard Townsend), dau of Edward Mansel Townsend, of White Hall, Co Cork, and had, with other issue:

(1) Edward Townsend, of Belleville, Co Cork; b 1790; Lt 90th Regt; m 9 Nov 1824 Penelope, dau of Rev Edward Mitchell Carleton, and d 16 July 1858, leaving:

1a Edward Carleton; b 27 Dec 1826; m 1892 Emily, 5th dau of Henry Baldwin Foott, of Carrigacunna Castle, Mallow, Co Cork, and d 24 July 1916

1a Elizabeth Louisa; m 15 June 1848 Harmer Devereux Spratt, JP Co Cork

(2) Thomas (Rev); b Jan 1793; Rector Baltimore; m May 1831 Jane Kellett (d 12 Jan 1878), dau of John Galwey, of Passage, Co Cork, and d 1 March 1838, leaving:

1a John Augustus, JP Cork; b 26 March 1834; Maj Duke of Cambridge's Own Regt; m 15 Sept 1869 Mary Spencer, dau of Thomas Thimbleby, and d 1914, leaving:

1b Harold Galwey, JP Cork and Sierra Leone; b 20 July 1874; Maj and Hon Lt-Col Res of Offrs Limerick City RFResA, DC 1st Cl Panjuma, Sierra Leone; d unm 6 Feb 1919

1b Milly Kathleen; m 1896 Maj Charles Henry Ashurst, Roy Sussex Regt (d Oct 1966)

2b Aileen; m 1st 1897 Capt Sydney John Brazier Creagh (d Aug 1904), of Coolcower Ho, Macroom, Co Cork, and had issue; m 2nd 1906 Col Dulas Bentley Parry, DSO, JP (d Sept 1947), and had further issue

2a Thomas Robert, JP; b 1839; Dep-Gen-Inspr Hosps RN; m 1884 Harriet Lavinia (m 2nd John Henry Gibson and d 22 Jan 1937), dau of Richard Pennefather, of Lakefield, Co Tipperary, and d 5 April 1906, leaving:

1b THOMAS RICHARD PENNEFATHER (Sir), **8th Bt**

2b William Robert Vaughton; b 23 Feb 1889, OBE (1919), MC; Lt-Col RASC, RGA, served WWs I (despatches) and II; m 1st 31 July 1914 (divorce 1926) Marjorie May, only child of Harold Briggs, of Chobham, Surrey; m 2nd 12 Oct 1926 Violet Elsie (d 1963), est dau of Lt-Col John Wallis Gill, JP, of St German's, Cornwall, and by his 1st w had:

1c Patrick Vaughton; b 11 Jan 1917; Maj RA; d 19–

2c +MICHAEL BLACKLEY [Michael Warren Esq, La Basse Ruol, Puget-Ville, Var, France]; b 12 Nov 1918; heir presumptive; m 16 June 1941 *Marie Noelle, est dau of Ernest Marcel Laffaille, OBE, Hon Capt French Navy, and has:

1d *Danielle Mary [Mrs Jean d'Adda, 63 Av Pasteur, La Valette, Var, France]; b 2 March 1943; m 5 Aug 1967 *Jean Pierre d'Adda, s of Antonio Constantino d'Adda, of Cornogicurine, Lodigiano, Italy, and has:

1e *Sebastian Marie; b 1973

1e *Catherine Marie; b 14 April 1970

1c *Bridget Macree [Mrs Ernest Beale, 32 Knapton Lane, Acomb, York]; b 4 May 1922; m 1st 16 June 1944 (divorce 19–) F/O Frank Walter Ladbrook, RAF, and has:

1d *Sara Virginia; b 1945; m 1974 *David Walter Hayward and has:

1e *Peter David; b 1978

2e *Robin William; b 1982

2d *Philippa Mary; b 1953; m 1972 *John David Mead and has:

1e *Christopher John; b 1974

2e *Thomas William; b 1980

1c (cont.) Mrs Bridget Macree Ladbrook m 2nd 19– Ernest William Beale (d 1994) and by him has:

1d *Andrew William; b 1958; m 1984 *April Michelle Mitchell and has:

1e *Martin Andrew; b 1987

2e *Richard; b 1991

3b Edward Galway, CBE (1940); b 3 May 1893; educ Eltham Coll and RMC Sandhurst; Brig Northants Regt 1912, WW I (wounded, despatches), N Kurdistan 1932, NWF India 1936–37 and WW II; m 8 Aug 1914 Gwendolen Agnes, dau of Brooke Richard Brasier, JP, of Ballygarrett, Mallow, Co Cork, and Rivers, Co Limerick, and d 19–

1a Emily Jane; d unm

(3) Charles Duncan; b 1797; Capt RN; m 5 April 1830 Harriet Webb (d 1848), dau of Jonathan Gilder and widow of Dr — Fallon, and d 17 July 1864, leaving:

1a Charles Duncan; m Ellen — (d 21 Aug 1917) and d 6 March 1930, having had:

1b Charles Duncan; d in America

2b George Herbert; m Catherine, dau of Christopher Michael Skelly by Elizabeth, dau of James Whelen, and d Sept 1948, having had:

1c *Doreen Catherine [Miss Doreen Warren, 4 Woodstock Ave, Golders Green, London NW11]

2c Patricia Helen; d in infancy

3b Augustus; b 1878; d unm July 1907

1b Sadie Henrietta; m 16 April 1898 Robert Leahy Atkins (d 8 April 1952), of Cork, s of Thomas R Atkins, and d 12 Jan 1944, leaving issue

2a George Hagar

1a Anne Townsend; d unm

2a Henrietta; d unm

3a Victoria; d unm

4a Jemima Charlotte Munro; d unm 17 Nov 1920

5a Eliza Mary; d unm

(4) Augustus; b 1798; m Sara (d 1866), dau of Townsend Gun, of Rattoo, Co Kerry, and d 1860, leaving:

1a Augustus; b 1828; m 11 Nov 1857 Elizabeth (d 1893), dau of Jonas Studdert, and d 1897, leaving:

1b Townsend Jonas; b 3 Sept 1858

2b Augustus Townsend; b 4 Jan 1866

1b Amelia Isabella

2b Evelyn; m 1885 Francis Richard Coffey, CE, and had issue

3b Gertrude; m 1887 William Cecil Ringwood and had issue:

2a Thomas Townsend; b 1834

3a Townsend; b 1836

4a William Albert; b 1846

1a Anne; m Richard Webb

2a Katherine; m Randal Borough and dsp

3a Gertrude; m 1871 Andrew Hamilton Bryan, LRCSI

4a Emma Mary; m Jonas Studdert and had issue

(5) William; b 30 April 1805; m 15 Dec 1835 Elizabeth, dau of Richard Townsend, and d 1885, leaving:

1a Thomas William

2a Richard Townsend

3a William Augustus; m 24 Oct 1875 Kathleen, dau of John Monteith, and d 1923, leaving:

1b Kate Ethel; d unm 1954

2b Elizabeth Monteith; m 1902 Frederick Strombom and d 1957, leaving issue

3b Minnow Felda Inez

4b Muriel Leila

5b Aileen Elvino; d unm 1956

6b Mildred Irene; m 1920 Charles H Baker and had:

1c *Derek Charles Kuke; b 1921

2c *William Thomas Neville; b 1923

7b *Ruby Augusta Grahaeme

1a Elizabeth Mellifont; m 1 Sept 1870 Marcus George Slade (d 1921) and had issue

(6) Brisbane; b 1807; m 14 Aug 1838 Mary (d 23 March 1853), dau of Philip Somerville, and d 19 Aug 1847, leaving, with other issue:

1a Thomas Brisbane (Very Rev); b 26 Oct 1843; Dean Cork; m 8 Aug 1882 Elizabeth Sarah Emily (d 1 June 1921), dau of Thomas Christopher Cole, of Woodview, Co Cork, and d 8 Jan 1894, leaving:

1b Brisbane Charles Somerville; b 1887; m 28 June 1922 Janey Neill (Joan) (d 1986), est dau of T F M Cartwright, of Brenchley, Kent, and d 1979, leaving:

1c *Elizabeth Joan Mary [Miss Elizabeth Warren, Flat 2, 31 Clifton Crescent, Folkestone, Kent CT20 2EN]; b 22 June 1929

1b Mary Townsend; d unm

2a Philip Somerville; b 6 Dec 1844; LRCP, LRCS, Surg RN; m 1886 Elizabeth Sherrard (d 8 March 1903), dau of Thomas Somerville, and d 1909, leaving:

1b Robert Desmond Eyre Somerville; b 31 Aug 1897; educ RMC Sandhurst; Lt Res Offrs S Wales Borderers

2b Dennis Patrick Somerville; b 2 Oct 1901; m 1946 Valerie Antonia Lloyd, dau of Frederick Lloyd Harper, and d 1974, leaving:

1c +Philip Digby WARREN later SOMERVILLE WARREN [Philip Somerville Warren Esq, Well Cottage, Cliffe Rd, Seaford, Sussex]; b 1948; educ Columba's Sch St Albans; m 1980 *Violette Khajenouri and has:

1d *Antonia Nooshin; b 1981

2d *Natasha Soussan; b 1982

1b Millicent Madeleine Somerville; m 6 Dec 1911 Capt Andrew Winstanley Newton, Roy Dublin Fus

2b Norah Creina Somerville; m 1919 (divorce 1944) Maj-Gen Sir Colin Gubbins, KCMG, DSO, MC (d 11 Feb 1976), and had issue

3b Harriette Millicent Townsend Somerville

1a Mary; m 27 Aug 1867 Rev Alexander Jackson Nicholson, Rector St Nicholas Cork, Canon St Patrick's Cathedral Dublin, and d 19 Jan 1913, leaving issue

4 John, of Codrum, Co Cork; m 1st Cherry, sis of Massey Hutchinson, of Mount Massey; m 2nd Helen (dsp 1840), dau of Daniel O'Donovan, The O'Donovan, and by his 1st w had:

(1) John; d 1866

(2) Robert Massey Hutchinson; m Bridget (d 19 Dec 1858), dau of Samuel Penrose, and had:

1a John Massey

2a Frederick Hutchinson, of Codrum, Co Cork

5 Robert (Rev), of Crookstown House; m Margaret (d 1833), dau of Kingsmill Pennefather, MP, and d 1830, leaving:

(1) Robert (Rev); b 7 March 1794; m 26 May 1824 Mary, dau of David Crawford, and d 7 May 1879, leaving, with other issue:

1a Robert; b 8 Oct 1826; m 6 Sept 1859 Helen Sophia Ponsonby (d 1924), dau of Henry Braddell, of Mallow, and d 6 May 1903, leaving:

1b Robert; b 22 May 1870; m 1 June 1904 Maria Frances Lumley (d 1969), dau of William Lumley Perrier, of Maryborough, Douglas, Co Cork, and d 1947, leaving:

1c Augustus John; b 8 Sept 1909; m 28 April 1949 *Irene Joyce [Mrs Augustus Warren, The Cottage, Dunmanway, Co Cork, Ireland], dau of

James Edwards Atkins, JP, of Brook Park, Dunmanway, and *d* 8 Jan 1969, leaving:

1d +Robert (Rev); *b* 12 Oct 1954; *educ* St Columba's Rathfarnham and Trin Coll Dublin; Priest 1979, Curate St Mary's Cathedral Limerick, Rector Adare, Co Limerick, 1981

1c *Gladys Irene [Miss Gladys Warren, Sprayfield, Kinsale, Co Cork, Ireland]; *b* 1908

1b Mary Frances; *d* unm 22 May 1941

2b Sophia Louise Clowser; *m* 1891 Lt Jasper Drury, RFA (*d* 1932), and *d* 28 June 1951, leaving issue

3b Alice Sarah; *m* 1893 Brig-Gen Arthur Phelps, CB, RASC (*d* 3 Sept 1940), s of Col Peyton Phelps, RE, and *d* 24 Sept 1944

4b Antoinette Maude; *m* 1931 Edward Charles Buckley (*d* 1935) and *d* 7 Aug 1951

2a Richard, of Westbourne, Queenstown, Co Cork; *b* 31 May 1828; Maj-Gen RE; *m* 1st 24 Feb 1852 Emily (*d* 7 Aug 1891), dau of William Lauder; *m* 2nd 27 Dec 1893 Martha Elizabeth (*d* 25 Jan 1922), widow of Robert Pitcairn, barrister, of Sydney, NSW, and *d* 8 Oct 1913, having by his 1st w had:

1b Robert Richard; *b* 25 April 1853; Midshipman RN; lost at sea 25 April 1870

2b Herbert Lauder; *b* 1 April 1855; Staff Paymaster RN; *m* 1885 Ella Christian Hoyer (*d* 12 March 1945), dau of Christian Hoyer Millar (*see* INCHYRA B), and *d* 9 Jan 1897, leaving:

1c Ella Christian Louise Lauder, MBE (1963)

2c Kathleen Pelham Lauder, MBE (1966); *b* 1892

3b Edward Albert; *b* 29 May 1856; *m* 1884 Emily, dau of Talbot Palmer, and *d* 27 Feb 1899, leaving:

1c Edward Richard Lauder; *b* 28 Oct 1888

2c Henry Charles Herbert; *b* 3 Nov 1898; *d* 7 Aug 1926

1c Emily Ruth; *b* 29 July 1885; *m* 12 Jan 1907 Patrick Hardy

2c Dorothy Talbot; *b* 16 April 1887; *m* 8 June 1907 Bernard Tweedale

3c Winifred Mary; *b* 6 April 1891; *m* 1st 1909 Rev Edmund Watts (*d* 1912); *m* 2nd 1912 Reginald Miller

4c Marjorie Anne; *b* 12 Sept 1897; *m* Benjamin Bousfield (*d* 1932), of Henschel, CP, and *d* 13 March 1936

4b Henry Herrick; *b* 22 Dec 1857; Matabeleland 1896 (medal), Boer War 1900 (medal, three clasps); *m* 18 July 1908 Elizabeth (*d* 18 March 1941), yst dau of John Leader, of Keale, Co Cork, and *d* 1923

5b Richard Augustus; *b* 31 March 1862; Natal CS; *m* 1st 1884 Rosetta Violet Courtel Collins; *m* 2nd 12 April 1898 Marie Charlotte Alice (*d* 19 Aug 1948), 3rd dau of Attwell Hayes Allen, of Seaview, Queenstown, and *d* 21 June 1931

6b Percy Bliss; *b* 23 April 1864; Lt-Col 3rd Brahmans IA; *m* 11 Jan 1892 Margaret Ellen (*d* 1951), dau of William Langdon Martin, and *d* 15 June 1911, leaving:

1c Richard Crawford, MC (1917) and bar; *b* 1898; Lt Oxon LI WW I (despatches); *d* from wounds recd in an ambush in Ireland 28 June 1921

2c Wallis Langdon; *b* 1900; *m* 15 Nov 1934 Barbara (*d* 1990), dau of Harold Henry Durell Christian, and *d* 1974, leaving:

1d +Robert Nicholas Christian [Robert Warren Esq, Willowcroft, Thicket Grove, Newlands Dve, Maidenhead, Berks SL6 4LW]; *b* 1945; *m* 1976 *Judith Catherine Harvey and has:

1e +David Nicholas Joseph; *b* 4 Feb 1985

1e *Victoria Catherine; *b* 7 March 1978

2e *Rebecca Louise; *b* 13 July 1981

3e *Christina Annette; *b* 7 June 1989

1d *Shirley Margaret Christian [Mrs Jacovas Koukoularides, 261 Brownhill Rd, London SE6]; *b* 5 April 1936; *m* 1958 *Jacovas Ioannou James Koukoularides, s of John Koukoularides, of Cyprus, and has:

1e *Panos John; *b* 24 March 1966; *m* 1996 *Clare —

1e *Janet Sophia; *b* 28 Oct 1958; *m* 19– *Steven Nelsey and has:

1f *Nicholas; *b* 19–

2f *Michael; *b* 19–

2e *Daphne Barbara; *b* 30 Jan 1963; *m* 19– *John Trainor and has:

1f *Alexander; *b* 19–

1f *Sophia; *b* 19–

2d *Jennifer Mary Christian [Mrs Keith Brown, 6 Bridgenorth Rd, PO Greendale, Harare, Zimbabwe]; *b* 24 March 1940; *m* Nov 1963 *Keith Dallas Brown and has:

1e *Mark Dallas; *b* 3 June 1966; *m* Aug 1993 *Alison Fiona, dau of Michael John Henry Beckett, of Choma, Zambia, and has:

1f *Sacha Keith Beckett; *b* Dec 1997

2e *Anton Dallas; *b* 1970

1e *Sherrill Anne; *b* 28 Aug 1968; *m* May 1998 *Hugh Grainger Taggart, s of Mick Taggart, of Zimbabwe

3d *Jocelyne Anne Christian [Mrs Michael Younghusband, 4 Falcon Crest, Quail St, Helderkruin Ext 20, 1724, S Africa]; *b* 1942; *m* 1969 *Michael Edward Younghusband and has:

1e *Sharon Leigh; *b* 1971; *m* 1996 *Mark Alan Holden

2e *Tracey Anne; *b* 1972

3c Geoffrey Martin; *b* 3 March 1908; Maj Roy Tank Regt India 1930–35; *m* 28 Sept 1938 *Margaret Rosemary (*m* 2nd 1948 George Arthur (*d* 23 Sept 1968), s of Col John Maurice Arthur, of Airdrie, Lanarks; *m* 3rd 1972 Robert George Alexander Hemming, of Pillarbank, Cardross, Dumbarton), only dau of Col Thomas Young Seddon, IA, and *d* of wounds recd in action Libya 21 Nov 1941, leaving:

1d Brian Richard; *b* 20 July 1939; *m* 8 May 1965 *Angela Jean, dau of Arthur Leslie Yarranton, of Eardiston, Worcs, and *d* 1987, leaving:

1e +Oliver Martin; *b* 23 March 1968

1e *Emily Claire; *b* 30 March 1966

2e *Lucy Maud; *b* 1970

1c Margaret Joan; *b* 1895; *d* 1991

7b William Waldegrave (Rev); *b* 5 Sept 1867; Sub-Lt RNR, Hon CF, Chaplain Seamen's Hosp *Dreadnought* 1918, Rector Wendens Ambo Essex 1928–32, Curate Frimley i/c Dist of St Paul's Camberley 1932–35, Vicar St Paul's Camberley 1935; *m* 1st 4 Sept 1901 Alice Matilda (*d* 1 April 1936), 2nd dau of Rev Joseph Barton, of E Leigh, Havant; *m* 2nd 12 Jan 1937 Alice Grace Cassan (*d* 13 Oct 1937), and *d* 1946, having by his 1st w had:

1c Arthur Lionel Waldegrave, DSC; *b* 1902; Lt RNR WW II; *m* 6 Feb 1926 Marguerite, dau of Henry Edward Faulkner, of Port Arthur, Canada, and was *ka* 5 Feb 1942

1b Emily Margaret; *m* 21 Jan 1891 Lt-Col Arthur Gambier Norris, RA, and *d* 3 Oct 1930

3a William Henry; *b* 22 Oct 1839; Maj 81st Regt; *m* 6 Nov 1867 Maud (*d* 22 Feb 1929), dau of James Lane and widow of M E Heathcote, and *dsp* 22 May 1882

4a Augustus Charles James; *b* 13 May 1846; *m* 10 Sept 1872 Isabella, dau of William Clarke, of Farren, Co Cork, and *dsp*

1a Sarah; *m* 15 July 1852 John Warren Payne-Sheares, of Monkstown, Co Cork, and *d* 14 Nov 1907, leaving issue

2a Margaretta; *m* 19 Jan 1858 Capt Edward Herrick (*d* 28 May 1879), 12th Foot, and *d* 8 Oct 1911, having had issue

3a Emma Elizabeth; *m* 31 March 1864 J Cochrane and *dsp* 1 April 1866

(2) Richard MD; *b* Feb 1795; *m* 1824 Margaret (*d* Dec 1873), dau of W Pennefather, and *d* Dec 1870, leaving:

1a Frances; *m* 1st Capt — Oldham, 2nd Foot; *m* 2nd 1859 William Connor

2a Augusta; *m* 22 Aug 1854 Richard Lane Warren and had:

1b Cherry Frances Pennefather; *m* Henry Foster Longfield

(3) Henry; *d* unm

(1) Mary; *m* 23 Nov 1833 **Sir John Borlase Warren, 4th Bt** (*see above*)

6 Edward Webber (Rev); Vicar Kilbonane; *m* 25 Sept 1814 Eliza, dau of James B Thornhill, and *d* 1833, leaving:

(1) Robert Edward (Rev); *b* 10 Nov 1826; *m* 9 Jan 1849 Elizabeth (*d* 28 March 1907), dau of Alexander Deane, of Cork, and *d* 29 Aug 1889, leaving, with other issue:

1a Edward Webber; *b* 6 April 1854; *d* unm 18 Dec 1948

1a Augusta Mary; *d* unm 8 Aug 1941

2a Edith Maude; *d* unm 3 Oct 1954

3a Alice Gertrude; *m* 17 April 1895 Cdr Thomas John Oswell, RN (*d* 15 March 1935), 4th s of Rev Henry Lloyd Oswell, Vicar Stoulton, Salop, and *d* 30 May 1940, leaving issue

Sir Robert *m* 2nd April 1780 Elizabeth, dau of John Lawton, of Cork, and by her had, with other issue:

7 Richard Benson, QC; *b* 22 March 1784; Serjeant-at-law; *m* 14 Sept 1812 Eliza (*d* 28 Feb 1867), dau of Philip Pendleton, of Moortown, Co Meath, and *d* 6 July 1848, having had, with other issue:

(1) Robert Augustus; *b* 26 Jan 1822; barrister, Capt Co Dublin Militia; *d* 1 Nov 1899

(2) Henry Edward; *b* 25 Nov 1824; Maj 60th Rifles; *m* 29 Aug 1868 Annie Margaret, dau of James Bessonet, QC, and *dsp*

(3) Augustus Edmund; *b* 15 Dec 1829; Maj-Gen Seaforth Highrs; *m* 20 Aug 1862 Emily Susannah (*d* 8 Sept 1885), dau of Col Robert Brudenell Smith, 15th Regt, and *d* 2 July 1916, having had:

1a Augustus Richard Charles; *b* 29 May 1864; drowned at sea 1896

2a Ernest Henry Edmund; *b* 21 June 1865; *m* 10 April 1895 Nora, dau of Leander Jackson Bryan, and *d* 22 Feb 1930, leaving:

1b Ernest Vivian Reese; *b* 26 Jan 1896; *m* 19 March 1930 Gordon Gerald

2b Bryan Riversdale; *b* 24 Nov 1897; *d* 21 Oct 1915

3a Robert Monsell; *b* 10 May 1868; *m* 26 April 1916 Millicent Mary Edith (*d* 28 Dec 1916), dau of Capt Horatio Nelson, RN

4a Charles Dryden Stuart; *b* 30 May 1870; *dsp* Dec 1896

5a Guy Cecil Webber; *b* 31 Dec 1871; *d* 22 March 1928

6a Oswald Hugh; *b* 7 Sept 1873; *d* 17 Jan 1922

7a Dudley Edward; *b* 18 Aug 1875; *m* 27 May 1913 Gundreda Agnes (*d* 16 July 1971), yst dau of Col Duncan Spiller, of Earley Lodge, Earley, Berks, and *d* 1949, leaving:

1b Dudley Gundred; *b* 1923

1b *Adèle Valerie; *b* 22 Jan 1928

8a Vivian Brudenell; *b* 6 Nov 1877; *m* 20 Dec 1906 Lillie Barrington (*d* 18 Nov 1937), dau of Capt C A G Heysham, RN, and *d* 1973, leaving:

1b Charles Vivian; *b* 28 Sept 1907; *m* 1st 1945 Maeve (*d* 1965), dau of John Davis, of Ballina, Ireland; *m* 2nd 1972 Jaqueta Maeve (*d* 1979), dau of Sir Arnold Henry Moore Lunn, and *d* 1975, leaving by his 1st w:

1c +Robert Augustus Michael Mary; *b* 1948; *m* 1977 *Jacqueline Olive Dawn Baynes and has:

1d +Dominic Charles Augustus Warren; *b* 1979

2d +Guy Andrew Francis Warren; *b* 1980

2c +Patrick Martin Vivian Mary [Patrick Warren Esq, 7 St Ann's Crescent, London SW18 2ND]; *b* 1951; *m* 1974 *Frances Ann, dau of Frederick Lloyd, and has:

1d +Luke Lloyd; *b* 1975

2d +Duncan Charles; *b* 1980

3d +Nathan Alexander; *b* 1982

1d *Camilla Elizabeth; *b* 1976

2d *Saskia Anne; *b* 1982

1b *Vivienne Ellen [Mrs George Shilling, 13 Upper Wimpole St, London W1]; *b* 18 Nov 1912; *m* 1943 *George Frederick Alston Shilling

1a Adele Augusta Elizabeth

(4) Latham Coddington (Ven); *b* 4 April 1831; *educ* Trin Coll Dublin (MA); Archdeacon Lismore, Rector St Mary's Clonmel, Canon St Patrick's

Cathedral, RD; *m* 1st 4 Jan 1855 Harriett (*d* 1883), dau of John Henry Davidson, MD, and had, with other issue:

1a Richard Benson; *b* 10 Oct 1855; *dsp* 31 July 1891

2a Henry Davidson; *b* 11 Oct 1858; *d* 19 March 1889

3a Donald Macleod; *b* 26 Oct 1860

4a Robert Augustus Monsell; *b* 24 April 1875

1a Florence Martha Caroline

(4) (cont.) The Ven Latham Warren *m* 2nd 1885 Mary Georgina (*d* 5 Nov 1912), dau of Hall Stirling, and *d* 5 Nov 1912, having by her had:

2a Beatrice Lilian Mary

3a Dorothy Edythe Mary

(5) Thomas Monsell; *b* 11 March 1837; Maj-Gen Black Watch; *m* 1 Oct 1885 Anne (*d* 7 April 1932), dau of Henry Courteny Selous, and *d* 20 Jan 1914

(1) Martha Elinor; *m* 27 Oct 1835 James R Stewart (*d* 10 Dec 1889), DL, of Gortleitragh, Co Dublin, and *d* 5 May 1865, leaving issue

8 Henry; *b* 25 March 1786; Capt 25th Reg; *m* 10 May 1816 Katherine, dau of Rev William Stewart, and *d* 18 Nov 1872, having had, with other issue:

(1) Robert Richard, PC, QC; *b* 3 June 1817; LLD, Judge Probate Court Ireland, MP Dublin U 1867–68; *m* 22 March 1846 Mary (*d* 17 June 1913), dau of Charles Perry, of Cork, and *d* 24 Sept 1897, having had:

1a Henry Charles Jackson; *b* 20 Jan 1852; barrister King's Inns Dublin 1874; *m* 29 Dec 1877 Florence (*d* 14 Dec 1944), dau of Col Hon Robert Handcock (*see* CASTLEMAINE, B), and *d* 5 Feb 1937, leaving:

1b Desmond Cecil Robert; *b* 21 April 1895; *m* 13 Aug 1929 Violet Arabella, dau of Dr. Frederick Oakley Lasbrey, of St George's Ho, Wethersfield, and had:

1c +Donal; *b* 25 Nov 1930; *educ* Clayesmore

1c *Jennifer Edyth Helen; *b* 11 July 1932

2c *Juliet Alice Louise; *b* 4 May 1938

1b Dorothy Mary Augusta; *m* 9 March 1912 (*divorce* 1957) Sir Christopher Henry Lynch-Robinson, 2nd Bt (*qv*), and *d* 24 June 1970, leaving issue

2b Winifred Annette; *m* 15 Oct 1917 Cdr Guy Edward Cooper, RN (*d* 21 Aug 1941), yr s of Maj Francis Edward Cooper, RFA, and *d* 1 Feb 1977, having had:

1a Edyth Gundred

2a Katherine Florence

3a Mary Gertrude Helen

(1) Jane Stewart; *m* 1840 Ven Henry Joseph Woodroffe (*d* 1889)

(2) Catherine; *m* 1874 Rev John Nunn Blacker Woodroffe, DD, and had issue

The 7th Bt's distant cousin,

Sir Thomas Richard Pennefather Warren, 8th Bt, CBE (1919), DL (1941 Bucks); *b* 12 Sept 1885; *educ* Burneys and RMC Sandhurst; Brevet-Col Res Offrs RASC WW I (despatches twice), RM N R Tipperary 1919–20, Ch Constable Bucks 1928–53, barrister 1937, OStJ; *m* 7 July 1906 Ada Bene Costello, yr dau of Col Charles Hely, Suffolk Regt, of Woodstock, Cappoquin, Co Waterford, and *d* 1961, leaving:

1 Sir (BRIAN) CHARLES PENNEFATHER WARREN, **9th and present Bt**

1 *Patricia Bene Pennefather [Mrs Frederick Dewhurst, Crapstone House, Buckland Monachorum, S Devon]; *b* 9 Sept 1908; *m* 1st 1 June 1934 F/Lt William Sharman Bull, RAFVR (*ka* 4 July 1940), and has:

(1) *Victoria [Mrs Robert Darwall, Rockmoor, Harrowbeer Lane, Yelverton, S Devon]; *b* 16 April 1939; *m* 7 Sept 1957 *Capt Robert Darwall, MC, RM, and has:

1a *William Robert Thomas; *b* 9 July 1961

1a *Antonia Mary; *b* 16 June 1958

1 (cont.) Mrs Patricia Bull *m* 2nd 8 Aug 1945 *Col Frederick Wynford Dewhurst, RM, and by him had:

(1) *Charles Frederick; *b* 29 Aug 1946; *educ* Milton Abbey

(2) *Sarah Elizabeth; *b* 22 March 1948

2 *Eileen Lavina Pennefather [Mrs George Spiers, Grange Farm, Puttenham, Tring, Herts]; *b* 4 Jan 1910; *m* 1st 2 June 1930 G/Capt Joseph Herbert Arthur Landon, DSO, OBE, RAF (*d* 8 Dec 1935), only s of Col Frank Landon, of Brentwood, Essex; *m* 2nd 22 March 1950 *George Joseph Spiers

WARWICK, BROOKE and

VIX · EA · NOSTRA · VOCO

Arms: Sable on a cross engrailed or five pellets, all within a bordure engrailed of the second. **Crests:** 1 Out of a ducal coronet gules a demi-swan, wings expanded and elevated argent, beaked of the first, 2 A bear sejant argent, muzzled gules, supporting a ragged staff of the first. **Supporters:** Two swans, wings inverted argent, legged, beaked and ducally gorged gules. **Motto:** *Vix ea nostra voco* ('I scarcely call these things ours'). **Creations:** B. (E) 29 Jan 1620/1, E. 13 Nov 1759 (Warwick) and 7 July 1746 (both GB).

THE 9TH EARL OF WARWICK, Earl Brooke of Warwick Castle and **Baron Brooke of Beauchamps Court**, Co Warwick (Guy David Greville) [The Rt Hon The Earl of Warwick, 3a Brown St, Claremont, WA 6010, Australia]; *b* 30 Jan 1957; *s* f 1996; *educ* Eton and Ecole des Roches; *m* 1st 25 July 1981 (*divorce* 19–) Susan (Susie) McKinley, dau of George William McKinley Wilson, of Melbourne, Australia, and formerly w of Nicholas Sydney Cobbold, and has:

1 +CHARLES FULKE CHESTER, *Lord Brooke*; *b* 27 July 1982; *educ* Eton

The 9th EARL *m* 2nd Oct 1996 *Louisa Heenan, of Perth, W Australia

Earldom of Warwick: Apart from the period 1618 to 1759 the various creations and descents of the Earldom of Warwick have been to and among grantees connected by blood, however tenuously. That is remarkable, given that the period stretches to nearly a thousand years.

Even in the period 1618–1759 there was a connection by marriage with the preceding Earls of Warwick. Robert Rich, grandson of that Richard Rich who perjured himself to bring about the judicial murder of St Thomas More, was created Earl of Warwick in 1618. According to contemporary gossip he more or less bought the title from JAMES I for £10,000 (some £415,000 in late-1990s terms). His choice of Warwick as designation was allegedly based on nothing more solid than its not being used by any other peer just then. (An earldom whose name was taken from a county remained more prestigious than one commemorating a town or even family, the distinction between Warwick and Warwickshire not being so clear then as today.)

On the other hand his aunt, the perjurer Richard Rich's daughter, had married a son of that Earl of Warwick who after being promoted to Duke of Northumberland tried to establish his daughter-in-law LADY JANE GREY on the throne at the death of EDWARD VI. Moreover Robert Rich's wife Penelope (the Stella of Sir Philip Sidney's *Astrophel and Stella*) was a great-great niece of ANNE BOLEYN, whose husband HENRY VIII was great-nephew of George Earl of Warwick, so created in 1472. So there were two family connections of a kind. Even the statement that the Earldom of Warwick was vacant needs partial qualification. The bastard descendants of John Dudley Duke of Northumberland's son Robert styled themselves Earls of Warwick (and Dukes of Northumberland) for over a century.

The earliest creation of the Earldom of Warwick was heritable according to the doctrines of the early Middle Ages by and through females as well as males. But when in the mid-14th century the then 11th Earl of Warwick entailed Warwick Castle and the lands that went with it to his heirs male and their heirs male he was probably trying to limit the descent of the Earldom in the same way as the real estate, this practice being by now the norm. Certainly his eldest son's daughters did not inherit the Earldom. Yet almost a century later it was held by contemporary doctrine to have been inherited by a female in the shape of Richard Nevill(e)'s wife, Richard Nevill(e) (*see* ABERGVENNY, M) being then confirmed in the title of Earl of Warwick.

Lineage (of de Beaumont, Mauduit, de Beauchamp, Dudley, Nevill(e) and Plantagenet): ROGER de BEAUMONT; Seigneur (feudal Ld) of Beaumont, Pontaudemer, Brionne and Vatteville, Normandy; *m* Adeline, sis of Hugh Count of Meulan and dau by his 1st w of Waleran Count of Meulan, and *d c* 1094, leaving:

1 ROBERT de BEAUMONT; allegedly 1st EARL OF LEICESTER (*qv*, preliminary remarks) of the *c* 1102 *cr*

2 HENRY de BEAUMONT, 1st EARL OF WARWICK (E), so *cr* between July and Dec 1088 and granted lands which up till two years previously had belonged to a Saxon Thane, Thurkill or Turchil of Arden (an ancestor of William Shakespeare); *b c* 1048; granted feudal Ldship of Gower, S Wales, by HENRY I some

time between 1106 and 1116; *m* Margaret (*d* in or after 1156), dau of Geoffrey, Count de Perche, and *d* most probably 20 June 1119, having had, with two daus:

(1) ROGER, 2nd EARL

(2) Robert de Neuborg; inherited his f's Norman lands, Ch Justiciar Normandy; *m* Godeheut, dau of Ralph de Toeni/Conches (*see* STAFFORD, B), and had, with other sons:

　1a Henry de Neuborg

(3) Rotrou; Bp Evreux, Archbp Rouen, Ch Justiciar and Steward Normandy

(4) Geoffrey

(5) Henry

The 1st EARL OF WARWICK's est s,

ROGER de BEAUMONT, 2nd EARL OF WARWICK; *b c* 1102; *m* Gundred, er dau of William de Warenne, 2nd Earl of Surrey, by Elizabeth/Isabel, widow of his (Roger's) unc, 1st Earl of Leicester, and *d* 1153, having had an est s:

1 WILLIAM de BEAUMONT, 3rd EARL OF WARWICK; *m* 1st Margery, dau of John d'Eivile; *m* 2nd by 28 Dec 1175 Maud, est dau and coheir of William de Percy (*see* NORTHUMBERLAND, D), and *dsp* in the Holy Land (15 Nov?) 1184

2 WALERAN de BEAUMONT, 4th EARL OF WARWICK; *m* 1st Margery, dau of Humphrey de Bohun by Margaret, est dau and ultimate coheir of 1st Earl of Hereford of the 1141 *cr* (*see* HEREFORD, V, preliminary remarks), and had:

(1) HENRY de BEAUMONT, 5th EARL OF WARWICK; *b c* 1195; *m* 1st after 1205 Margery, er dau of Henry de Oilly by Maud, dau of Humphrey de Bohun; *m* 2nd by 1 May 1220, as her 1st husb, Philippe, est dau and coheir of Thomas Basset, and *d* (10 Oct?) 1229, having by his 1st w had:

　1a THOMAS de BEAUMONT, 6th EARL OF WARWICK; *b* by 1208(?); ktd 22 May 1229; *m* as her 1st husb Ela, dau of William Longespee or Longsword, Earl of Salisbury, by Ela, Countess of Salisbury in her own right (*see* SALISBURY, M, preliminary remarks), and *dsp* 26 or 27 June 1242

　1a MARGERY de Beaumont, COUNTESS OF WARWICK in her own right; *m* 1st by 22 Aug 1242 John MARSHAL, Marshal of Ireland (*dsp* Oct 1242), who does not seem to have been known as Earl of Warwick (possibly because of doubt as to whether he was in possession of Warwick Castle) though it was common then for a husb of a countess in her own right to bear her title; *m* 2nd by 14 Sept 1243 John Du PLESSIS (who seems to have been officially acknowledged as (7th) EARL OF WARWICK (in right of his w) by late April 1245, although not so styled before Aug 1247; *d* 25 Feb 1262/3) and *dsp* 3 June 1253

(2) Waleran

(1) Alice

(2) Gundred

2 (cont.) The 4th EARL OF WARWICK *m* 2nd *c* 1196 Alice, apparently dau of Robert de Harcourt, of Stanton (subsequently Stanton Harcourt), Oxon (*see* VERNON, B), though if so either Alice and the 4th EARL's marriage date of *c* 1196 is far too early or her f's marriage date of *c* 1200 is far too late, and widow of John de Limesy, and *d* 24 Dec 1203(?), leaving by her:

(3) ALICE de Beaumont; *m* William MAUDUIT (*d* just before 14 Feb 1256/7), Hereditary Chamberlain of the Exchequer, of Hanslope, Bucks, and Hartley Mauduit, Hants, and *d* by 1263, leaving:

　1a WILLIAM MAUDUIT, 8th EARL OF WARWICK; *b c* 1220–21; Jt Hereditary Chamberlain of the Exchequer; *m* Alice, dau of Gilbert de Segrave and possibly sis of 1st Lord (Baron) Segrave (*see* MOWBRAY, SEGRAVE and STOURTON, B), and *dsp* 8 Jan 1267/8

　1a Isabel Mauduit; *m* William De BEAUCHAMP, of Elmley, Worcs, Hereditary Sheriff Worcs and Pantler (officer responsible for the bread) at the King's Coronation (*d* between 7 Jan and 21 April 1268), and *d* by 1268, having had:

　　1b WILLIAM de BEAUCHAMP, 9th EARL OF WARWICK; *b c* 1240; Hereditary Sheriff Worcs and Pantler at Coronations, Keeper Forest of Dean 1270, Capt Cheshire and Lancs 1276; led an English army which defeated the Welsh at Maes Moydog, Montgomeryshire, 5 March 1294/5; cdr in the English army which defeated the Scots at Dunbar 1296, Constable Rockingham Castle and Steward forest between Oxford and Stamford 1297–98; *m c* 1270 Maud (*d* April 1301), dau of Sir John fitz Geoffrey and widow of Sir Gerard de Furnivall(e) (*see* PETRE, B), and *d* 5 or 9 June 1298, having had, with five daus:

　　　1c GUY de BEAUCHAMP, 10th EARL OF WARWICK; *b c* 1270; Hereditary Sheriff Worcs and Pantler at Coronations, ktd 1296, fought in EDWARD I's Div at victory over the Scots of Falkirk 1298, at Sieges of Carlaverock 1300 and Stirling Castle 1304; for services such as these was granted Barnard Castle, Co Durham, Feb 1306/7; one of the chief opponents of EDWARD II's favourite Piers Gaveston; *m* 1st by 11 May 1297 (annulled, possibly due to non-completion or even non-consummation), as her 1st husb, Lady Isabel de Clare (*m* 2nd *c* 1316, as his 2nd w, 2nd Lord (Baron) Berkeley; *qv*), dau of 6th Earl of Gloucester and Hertford of the 1122 *cr*; *m* 2nd Jan or Feb 1309/10 Alice (*b c* 1283; *m* 3rd by 25 Feb 1316/7, as his 1st w, 1st Lord (Baron) Zouche (*qv*) (of Richard's Castle, Mortimer or Ashby) and *d* just before 8 Jan 1324/5), sis of 1st and last Lord (Baron) Tony (*see* STAFFORD, B) and widow of Thomas de Leyburn, and *d* 12 Aug 1315, having had:

　　　　1d THOMAS de BEAUCHAMP, 11th EARL OF WARWICK, KG (*c* 1348, fndr memb); *b* probably 14 Feb 1314/5; Hereditary Sheriff Worcs and Pantler at Coronations, ktd Jan 1328/9, Marshal of England Feb 1343/4–69, Sheriff Warwicks and Leics for life 1344, one of two Marshals of the English Army at Crécy 1346 (where jt cdr PRINCE OF WALES's Div) and Siege of Calais 1346–47, Adml of the Fleet from mouth of Thames towards West by March 1352/3, Constable English army in Gascony and cdr vanguard at victory over the French of Poitiers 1356; *m* after 22 Feb 1324/5 Lady Catherine de Mortimer, dau of 1st Earl of March by Joan, dau and heir of Piers de Geneville, and *d* of plague 13 Nov 1369, having had:

　　　　　1e Guy; ktd July 1355; *m* by 1353 Philippe de Ferrers, dau of 2nd Lord (Baron) Ferrers (of Groby) (*see* FERRERS, E, preliminary remarks), and *dspm* & *vp* 28 April 1360, leaving:

　　　　　1f Katherine; *b* 1353; nun at Shouldham Priory, Norfolk

　　　　　2f Elizabeth; *b c* July 1358; *d* by Dec 1369

　　　　2e THOMAS de BEAUCHAMP, 12th EARL OF WARWICK, KG (1373); *b* by 16 March 1338/9; Hereditary Sheriff Worcs and Pantler at Coronations, ktd 1355, Adml of the Fleet towards the North 1377, Guardian of RICHARD II *c* Feb 1379/80, one of the Lords Appellant who overthrew RICHARD II's advisers 1387–89, arrested on a charge of high treason against RICHARD II 1397, following which his estates and honours were forfeited, but restored on accession of HENRY IV; *m* by April 1381 Margaret, dau of 3rd Lord (Baron) Ferrers (of Groby), and *d* 8 April 1401, having had:

　　　　　1f RICHARD de BEAUCHAMP, 13th EARL OF WARWICK, KG (1403); *b* 25 or 28 Jan 1381/2; ktd 1399; fought against Owen Glendower in Wales 1403, Ld High Steward for HENRY V's Coronation 1413, Capt Calais Feb 1413/4, took charge of prisoners en route to Calais Sept–Oct 1415, hence (*pace* Shakespeare) absent at time of Agincourt; participated, however, in successful sea Battle of Harfleur 1416; also at Sieges of Caen 1417, Caudebec 1418 and Rouen Jan 1418/9, *cr* 19 May 1419 COUNT OF AUMALE (part of HENRY V's policy of creating English nobles with French titles and fiefs in English-occupied France); undertook further Sieges of Melun 1420 and Meaux 1421, also Gamaches 1422 and St Valéry-sur-Somme; Capt Rouen by end Jan 1422/3; took Pontorson, Brittany, 1427; beaten by French Battle of Montargis Sept 1427; victor over French at Beauvais 1431; apptd by HENRY VI Lt and Govr France and Normandy 1437; *m* 1st by 5 Oct 1397 Elizabeth (*dspm* 28 Dec 1422), Baroness Berkeley, Lisle and Teyes in her own right according to later doctrine, only dau of 5th Lord (Baron) Berkeley (*qv*), and had:

　　　　　　1g Margaret; *m* as his 2nd w 1st Earl of Shrewsbury and Waterford (*qv*) and *d* 14 June 1467, having had:

　　　　　　　1h Sir JOHN TALBOT, 1st VISCOUNT LISLE, also 1st LORD AND BARON OF LISLE, so *cr* 30 Oct 1451 and 26 July 1444 respectively; *b c* 1426; *m* Joan, dau and coheir of Thomas Chedder and widow of Richard Stafford, and was *ka* Battle of Castillon 17 July 1453, leaving, with a s and other dau:

　　　　　　　　1i ELIZABETH Talbot, BARONESS LISLE in her own right according to later doctrine on death of her bro and sis, especially as she held the manor of Kingston Lisle (*see* DE L'ISLE, V, preliminary remarks, also SHREWSBURY and WATERFORD, E, for this point); *m* Sir Edward GREY, 1st LORD AND BARON OF LISLE (so *cr* 14 March 1474/5) and 1st VISCOUNT LISLE (so *cr* 28 June 1483) (*d* 17 July 1492), 2nd s of Edward, Lord (Baron) Ferrers (of Groby), and *d* 8 Sept 1487, leaving, with other issue:

　　　　　　　　　1j ELIZABETH Grey, BARONESS LISLE in her own right according to later doctrine; *m* 1st *c* 1495 Edmund Dudley (beheaded 18 Aug 1510), the extortionate minister of HENRY VII; *m* 2nd 12 Nov 1511 Arthur PLANTAGENET (*cr* VICOUNT LISLE 25 Aug 1523), illegitimate s of EDWARD IV by a woman referred to in contemporary sources as 'Lady Elizabeth Lucy', alternatively Jane Shore or Elizabeth Waite, and *d c* 1530, leaving:

　　　　　　　　　　1k JOHN DUDLEY, 1st EARL OF WARWICK(E), so *cr* 16 Feb 1546/7, as also later 11 Oct 1551 Duke of Northumberland; *b* 1502; the chief power in England in the latter half of EDWARD VI's reign; *m* Jane, dau of Sir Edward Guilford by Eleanor, dau of 8th Lord (Baron) De La Warr (*see* DE LA WARR, E), and was attainted and his titles forfeited, then executed by beheading 22 Aug 1553, having had, with six other sons (including Robert Dudley, Earl of Leicester (*see* LEICESTER, E, preliminary remarks), who was the subject of a special remainder in the limitation of the Earldom of Warwick conferred on his bro Ambrose but who predeceased Ambrose and *dspsl*):

　　　　　　　　　　　1l JOHN DUDLEY, 2nd and last EARL OF WARWICK of the 16 Feb 1546/7 *cr*; *b* by 1528; ktd Feb 1546/7, Jt Ld Lt Warwicks 1552 and 1553; called up to Ho Lds *vp* 5 Jan 1552/3 in f's Earldom of Warwick; *m* 3 June 1550 Lady Anne Seymour, dau of 1st Duke of Somerset (*qv*), but was attainted and his titles forfeited 1553, though set free rather than executed; *dsp* 21 Oct 1554

　　　　　　　　　　　2l AMBROSE DUDLEY, 1st EARL OF WARWICK (E), so *cr* 26 Dec 1561, with remainder, failing issue of his body, to his bro Sir Robert Dudley, also assigned precedence of 'his ancestors, former Earls of Warwick', KG (1563); *b c* 1528; ktd 1549; sent to the Tower 1553 for attempting with his f to put LADY JANE GREY on the throne, condemned to death but pardoned Jan 1554/5 and restored in blood by Act of Parl 1557/8; Ld Lt Warwicks 1569–70 and 1587–Feb 1589/90; *m* 1st by 4 March 1545/6 Anne (*dsps* 1552), dau of William Whorwood, Attorney Gen to HENRY VIII; *m* 2nd by 10 Sept 1553 Elizabeth (*dsp* by 28 March 1563), Baroness Talboys in her own right and *de jure* Baroness Kyme in her own right; *m* 3rd 11 Nov 1565 Lady Anne Russell, est dau of 2nd Earl of Bedford (*see* BEDFORD, D), and *dsps* 21 Feb 1589/90, when the Earldom of Warwick and his other honours expired

　　　　　　　　　　　3l Henry (Sir); *m* 1st, as her 1st husb, Winifred (*m* 2nd 2nd Lord (Baron) North (*see* 1970 edn) and *d* shortly after Nov 1578), 6th dau of Richard Rich, 1st Baron Rich, and aunt of ROBERT RICH, 3rd Baron

Rich and 1st EARL OF WARWICK of the 1618 *cr*, and was *k* Siege of St Quentin Aug 1557

2g Eleanor; *m* 1st 8th Lord (Baron) Ros (*qv*) of Helmsley and had issue; *m* 2nd by 7 March 1437/8 1st Duke of Somerset of the 1448 *cr* (*see* BEAUFORT, D)

3g Elizabeth; *m* Feb 1436/7 George Nevill(e), 1st Lord (Baron) Latymer (*qv*), and *d* by 2 Oct 1480, having had, with other issue:

1h Henry (Sir); *m* Joanna, dau of 1st Lord (Baron) Berners (*qv*), and *dvp* 26 July 1469, leaving:

1i RICHARD NEVILL(E), 2ND LORD (Baron) LATYMER; had by his 1st w Anne Stafford, with other issue:

1j Margaret; *m* Edward (*dvp* Nov 1517), only s of 2nd Lord (Baron) Willoughby de Broke (*qv*) by his 1st w Elizabeth (dau of 2nd BARON BEAUCHAMP OF POWICK; *see* below), and had, with two yr daus (*dsp*):

1k Elizabeth, *de jure* Baroness Willoughby de Broke; *m* just prior to 11 April 1526 Fulke Greville (*see* **Lineage (of Greville)** below)

1f (cont.) The 13th EARL *m* 2nd 26 Nov 1423 Isabel, Baroness Burghersh in her own right according to later doctrine, widow of his cousin Richard de Beauchamp, Earl of Worcester, and sis and heir of Richard le Despenser (*see* FALMOUTH, V), *de jure* Lord (Baron) Burghersh, and *d* 30 April 1439 (his tomb at Warwick being justly famous for its beauty and splendour), leaving by her:

1g HENRY De BEAUCHAMP, 14th EARL OF WARWICK and 1st and last DUKE OF WARWICK (E), so *cr* 5 April 1445, having been granted 2 April 1444 precedence of Premier Earl of England, it is thought in recognition of his f's achievements; *b* 22 March 1424/5; *m* 1434 Cecily, 2nd dau of Richard Nevill(e), Earl of Salisbury (*see* ABERGAVENNY, M) and *dspm* 11 June 1464, when the Dukedom expired, leaving:

1h ANNE De BEAUCHAMP, apparently COUNTESS OF WARWICK in her own right (but *see* preliminary remarks above); *b* Feb 1443/4; *d* 3 Jan 1448/9

1g ANNE de Beauchamp, apparently also COUNTESS OF WARWICK in her own right (but *see* again above preliminary remarks); *b c* Sept 1426; *m* 1434 Richard NEVILL(E) ('The King-maker'; *see* ABERGAVENNY, M), 16th (if in right of his w) or 1st EARL OF WARWICK (by the instrument of 2 March 1449/50 creating him and his w EARL and COUNTESS OF WARWICK each for his or her life, with remainder after both parties' death to the heirs of ANNE's body, then to her half-sis Margaret Countess of Shrewsbury and the heirs male of her (Margaret's) body, then to the heirs general of her (Margaret's) body, then to a vaguely defined body of persons called the 'right heirs' of her (ANNE's) f Richard, late EARL OF WARWICK), and *dspm* just before 20 Sept 1492, having had:

1h ISABEL Nevill(e); *b* 5 Sept 1451; *m* 11 July 1469 George PLANTAGENET, 1st Duke of Clarence, yr bro of EDWARD IV, and 1st EARL OF WARWICK (and Earl of Salisbury), so *cr* 25 March 1472 (attainted 8 Feb 1477/8, when all his titles were forfeited), and *d* 22 Dec 1476, leaving, with other issue (*see* ABERGAVENNY, M):

1i EDWARD PLANTAGENET, 2nd EARL OF WARWICK under terms of the instrument of 2 March 1449/50 creating his grandmother ANNE and gf RICHARD ('The King-maker') COUNTESS and EARL OF WARWICK (*see* above) from *c* 20 Sept 1492; *b* 21 or 25 Feb 1474/5; inherited 22 Dec 1476 lands through his mother (these being unaffected by the attainder of his f) which included Warwick Castle and was accordingly (if perhaps unjustifiably) regarded as Earl of Warwick from that moment according to a notion that the title was by tenure; *ktd* 1483; kept in close confinement by HENRY VII due to his potential danger as a claimant to the throne; impersonated by Lambert Simnel 1487; executed by HENRY VII 28 Nov 1499 (when the Earldom expired) on a trumped up charge of traitorous plotting with Perkin Warbeck to overthrow the King and attainted post-humously Jan 1503/4 (attainder reversed 1514)

3e Reynbrun; had:

1f Alianore; *m* John Knight, of Hanslope, Bucks, and had:

1g Emma; *m* William Forster

4e John; *d* unm

5e Roger; *d* unm

1e Maud; *m* 5th Baron Clifford (*see* DE CLIFFORD, B)

2e Philippa; *m* by 1 March 1350/1 2nd Earl of Stafford (*see* STAFFORD, B)

3e Alice; *m* 1st by 1354/5 3rd Lord (Baron) Beauchamp (of Somerset) (*dsp* 1361); *m* 2nd 1371–74 Sir Matthew Gournay and *d* 26 Oct 1383

4e Joan; *m c* May 1338, as his 1st w, 3rd Lord (Baron) Basset (of Drayton) and *dsp*

5e Isabel; *m* 1st 2nd Lord (Baron) Strange/Lestrange of the 1360 *cr* and had issue (*see* SAINT DAVIDS, V); *m* 2nd by 12 June 1376, as his 2nd w, 2nd Earl of Suffolk (*dsps* 15 Feb 1381/2) of the March 1336/7 *cr* (*see* SUFFOLK and BERKSHIRE, E, preliminary remarks), became a nun 21 March 1381/2 and *d* 29 Sept 1416

6e Margaret; *m* Guy de Montford

7e Agnes; *m* 1st — Cokesay; *m* 2nd — Bardolf

8e Juliana; *d* unm

9e Catharine; nun at Wroxall, Warwicks

2d JOHN BEAUCHAMP, 1st and last LORD (Baron) BEAUCHAMP (of Warwick) (E), as which *cr* by writ of summons to Parl (according to later doctrine) 25 Nov 1350, KG (fndr memb 1344); present at

EDWARD III's victories over the French of Sluys 1340 and Crécy 1346 (where he bore the royal standard) and the successful Siege of Calais 1347, Kt Banneret March 1348/9, Adml Fleet off Calais 1349, Capt Calais Jan 1354/5, Adml Western Seas 1355 and N, S and W July-Dec 1360; *d* unm 2 Dec 1360 when the Barony expired

1d Maud; *m* 2nd Lord (Baron) Say (*see* SAYE AND SELE, B)

2d Emma; *m* Rowland Odingsels

3d Isabel; *m* John Clinton

4d Elizabeth; *m* Sir Thomas Astley (*see* 1970 edn ASTLEY, Bt)

5d Lucia; *m* Robert/Roger de Napton

2b Walter, of Alcester, Warwicks, and Powick, Worcs; *d* 1303, leaving, with two er sons (*dsp*):

1c Giles; *m* 1329 Catherine, dau and heiress of Sir John de Bures, Suffolk, and *d* Oct 1361, leaving:

1d John; *m* Elizabeth — (*d* 1411) and *d* between 1378 and 14091, leaving:

1e William (Sir); *m* by March 1414/5 Catherine, dau of Sir Gerard Ufflete, and *d* by 1431, leaving:

1f JOHN BEAUCHAMP, 1st BARON BEAUCHAMP OF POWICK, Co Worcester (E), so *cr* by patent 2 May 1447, KG (1445); Constable Gloucester Castle 1446, Justice S Wales 1447, Ld Treas of England 1450–52; *m* by 1434 Margaret, sis of Richard Ferrars, and *d* between 9 and 19 April 1475, leaving:

1g RICHARD BEAUCHAMP, 2nd BARON BEAUCHAMP OF POWICK; *b c* 1435; *m* 27 Jan 1446/7 Elizabeth, dau of Sir Humphrey Stafford, and *dspms* 19 Jan 1502/3, when the Barony expired, leaving:

1h Elizabeth; *m* 2nd Lord (Baron) Willoughby de Broke (*qv*) and had:

1i Edward, JP Devon and Cornwall 1512–15; *b* between *c* 1494 and 1500; *m c* 22 Nov 1505 Margaret, dau of 2nd Lord (Baron) Latymer (*qv*), and *dspm* & *vp* Nov 1517, leaving, with two other daus (*dsp*):

1j ELIZABETH, *de jure* Baroness Willoughby de Broke in her own right according to later doctrine; *m* just prior to 11 April 1526 Sir Fulke Greville (*see* **Lineage (of Greville)** below) and had issue

2h Anne; *b* between *c* 1462 and 1472; *m* Richard Lygon and *d* 1535, leaving issue (*see* 1970 edn BEAUCHAMP, E)

3h Margaret; *m* Richard Rede, of Glos, and had issue

2e Walter (Sir); *m* Elizabeth, dau and coheir of John Roches, and had:

1f WILLIAM BEAUCHAMP, 5th LORD (Baron) ST AMAND in right of his marriage by 1426, as her 1st husb, with ELIZABETH Braybroke (BARONESS ST AMAND in her own right according to later doctrine; *m* 2nd by July 1458 Sir Roger Tocketts/Tocotes and *d* 2 Dec 1491), 2nd but only surv dau of Gerard Braybroke, *de jure* 4th Lord (Baron) St Amand according to later doctrine, by his 1st w; King's Kt 1433, Carver to HENRY VI, Sheriff Wilts 1436, 1442 and 1447, Chamberlain N Wales 1437, Keeper Beaumaris Castle 1442, Steward and Constable Barnard Castle and Constable Painscastle, Radnorshire, 1446; *d* 19 March 1456/7, leaving:

1g RICHARD BEAUCHAMP, 6th and last LORD (Baron) ST AMAND; *b c* 1461; attainted by RICHARD III's only Parl *c* Jan 1483/4 but attainder soon reversed; *m* Anne — and *dspl* between 14 June and 15 July 1508, when the Barony expired, leaving illegitimately by Mary Wroughton:

1h Anthony ST AMAND; Jt Keeper Blackmoor Forest, Jt Steward Marlborough; living 1508

2f Richard; Bp Salisbury

Lineage (of Greville): JOHN GREVILL; *d* by 1350; had:

WILLIAM GREVILLE, of Campden, Glos; living 1398; had:

WILLIAM GREVILLE, of London; with his father lent RICHARD II £300 (over £72,000 in late–1990s terms), a debt acknowledged 10 Aug 1397; bought 1398 the manor of Milcote, Warwicks, from Sir Walter Beauchamp and *d* 10 Oct 1401, having had:

JOHN GREVILLE, of Campden; Sheriff Glam 1405; *m* 1st Sibil, dau and heiress of Sir Robert Corbet; *m* 2nd Joyce, dau of Sir Walter Cocksey, sis and heiress of Hugh Cocksey and widow of — Beauchamp; gf of:

Sir THOMAS GREVILLE later COCKSEY (adopted on inheriting land through his grandmother); *dsp* 1523, when Milcote and other Greville possessions passed to:

JOHN GREVILLE, of Drayton (ggs of Lewis Greville and his w Margaret, sole dau and heir of Sir Giles Ardene, of Drayton, Oxon); Justice for gaol-delivery Warwick 1503; *m* Jane, dau of Sir Humphrey Forster, of Harpsden, Oxon, and had an er s:

Sir EDWARD GREVILLE, of Milcote; fought Battle of Spurs 1513; obtained wardship of Elizabeth Willoughby, who was at the time reckoned the greatest heiress in England and whom his s Sir Fulke succeeded in marrying 1522; *m* Anne, dau of John Denton, of Amersden, Bucks, and had, with other issue:

1 John (Sir), of Milcote and Drayton; MP Warwicks; *m* Elizabeth, dau of John Spencer, of Hodnot, and had an only s:

(1) Edward (Sir), of Milcote and Drayton; *m* —, dau and coheir of William Willington, of Barcheston, Warwicks, and had an only s:

1a Lodovick; *m* Thomasine, dau of Sir William Petre, and had an only s:

1b Edward (Sir), of Milcote and Drayton; *m* Joan, dau of Sir Thomas Bromley, Ld Chllr and had several daus; sold his estate to Lionel Cranfield, Earl of Middlesex; with his death the sr branch of the GREVILLEs died out

2 Fulke (Sir), of Beauchamp's Court, Alcester, Warwicks, which came to him through his w; *educ* Shrewsbury and Jesus Coll Cambridge (MA); High Sheriff

Warwicks 1542–43 and Leics 1547–48, ktd by 1544, MP Warwicks 1545–52 and 1554–55; *m c* 1534 Elizabeth (*see* **Lineage (of de Beaumont, Mauduit, de Beauchamp, Dudley, Nevill(e) and Plantagenet)** above), *de jure* Baroness Willoughby de Broke in her own right, and *d* 10 Nov 1559, having had, with other issue:

(1) Fulke (Sir), of Beauchamp's Court; *b c* 1536; ktd 1565, Sheriff Warwicks 1572–73 and 1584–85; *m c* 1553 Anne, dau of 4th Earl of Westmorland of the 1397 *cr* (*see* ABERGAVENNY, M), and *d* 15 Nov 1606, leaving an only s:

1a Sir FULKE GREVILLE, **1st Baron Brooke of Beauchamps Court**, Co Warwick (E), so *cr* 29 Jan 1620/1 (with remainder to his 1st cousin's sons ROBERT and WILLIAM GREVILLE), KB (1603), PC (1614); *b c* 1554; *educ* Shrewsbury and Jesus Coll Cambridge; Gentleman Privy Chamber, Clerk Signet to Cncl of Wales 1581 (Sec 1603), Sec for Wales 1583, MP Hedon 1584–86 and Warwicks 1586–87, 1588–89, 1593, 1597–98, 1601 and 1620–21, Treas Navy 1598–1604, R-Adml the Fleet 1599, granted Warwick Castle 1604 and spent around £20,000 (nearly £1.3m in late-1990s terms) restoring it, Chllr Exchequer 1614–21, MP Warwicks 1620–21, Gentleman Bedchamber 1621, Recorder Warwick; a man of literary bent and a patron of among others the antiquary William Camden; *d unm* 30 Sept 1628

(2) Robert, of Thorpe Latimer, Lincs; *m* Blanche Whitney and had an only s:

1a Fulke; *m* 15 May 1602 Margaret, dau of Christopher Copley, of Wadworth, Yorks, and widow of Ralph Bosville, of Gunthwaite, York, and *d* 1632, leaving, with a yr s (William) and a dau (Dorothy, *m* as his 2nd w Sir Arthur Hesilrige, 2nd Bt; *see* HAZLERIGG, B):

1b ROBERT GREVILLE, **2nd Baron Brooke of Beauchamps Court**; *b* 1607; *educ* Cambridge; Col Parly Regt of Foot Edgehill Oct 1642, Maj-Gen 7 Jan 1642/43, Recorder Warwick 1641–43, Ld Lt Warwicks 1642; *m c* 1630 Lady Catherine Russell, dau of 4th Earl of Bedford (*see* BEDFORD, D), and was *k* by a musket ball in a successful assault upon Lichfield 1643, leaving:

1c FRANCIS GREVILLE, **3rd Baron Brooke of Beauchamps Court**; Recorder Warwick; *d unm* Nov 1658

2c ROBERT GREVILLE, **4th Baron Brooke of Beauchamps Court**; *b c* 1638; Recorder Warwick 1660–76, Ld Lt Staffs 1660–76; one of the six Commrs deputed by the Ho of Lds in conjunction with six MPs to invite CHARLES II back in 1660; *m* Ann (*m* 2nd Thomas Hoby and *d* Feb 1690/1), dau and eventually sole heiress of John Dodington, of Breamore, Hants, and *dspms* 17 Feb 1676, having had, with six sons (*d* young):

1d Anne; *m* 1st *c* 6 Jan 1684/5 4th Earl of Kingston (*qv*, preliminary remarks)-upon-Hull of the 1628 *cr* (*dsp* 17 Sept 1690); *m* 2nd, as his 1st w, William Pierrepont (*d* Sept 1706), of Nottingham, and *dsp, bur* 23 Sept 1702

2d Dodington; *m* 1st Duke of Manchester (*qv*)

3c FULKE GREVILLE, **5th Baron Brooke of Beauchamps Court**; *b* 1643; MP Warwick 1664–77, Recorder Warwick 1677–1710 and Coventry 1687–1706; *m* 12 Jan 1664/5 Sarah, dau of Francis Dashwood (*see* DASHWOOD, Bt, of West Wycombe), and *d* 22 Oct 1710, having had, with other issue:

1d Francis; *m* Lady Anne Wilmot, dau of 2nd Earl of Rochester and widow of Henry Baynton, and *dvp* 11 Oct 1710, leaving:

1e FULKE GREVILLE, **6th Baron Brooke of Beauchamps Court**; *b c* 1693; *educ* Univ Coll Oxford; *d unm* 24 Feb 1710/11

2e WILLIAM, **7th Baron**

2d Algernon; MP Warwick 1699–1705; *m* Mary, dau and coheir of Lord Arthur Somerset (*see* BEAUFORT, D), and had, with two daus (Mary, *m* Shuckburgh Boughton; Hester):

1e Fulke, of Wilbury, Wilts; author: *Maxims and Characters*, MP Monmouth 1747–52; *m* Frances (*d* 1789), author of *Ode to Indifference*, dau and coheir of James Macartney (cousin of Earl Macartney, KB), and had issue (in remainder to the Barony of Brooke of Beauchamps Court only), with a s (*d* young):

1f William Fulke; *b* 8 Nov 1751; Capt RN, MP Granard 1798; *m* Meliora, only child of Rev Hon Richard Southwell (*see* SOUTHWELL, V), and *d* 1837, leaving:

1g Richard; *b* 1787; *m* Sabine Matilda Paterson (*d* 22 March 1822) and *dsp* 15 May 1866

2g Algernon; *b* 1791; *m* Dec 1813 Caroline, er dau of Sir Bellingham Graham, 6th Bt, of Norton Conyers (*qv*), and *d* 23 Nov 1857, having had, with a dau (*d unm*):

1h Algernon William Bellingham, of Bayswater and Gerard, Co Longford; *b* 1815; Army Capt; *m* 1st 1 Oct 1844 Margaret (*d* 18 Aug 1845), yst dau of Alexander Petty, and had:

1i Annie Margaret Christina; *m* 13 July 1870 Ralph Dalyell, CB (*d* 12 April 1915), of Lingo, Fife, and *d* 25 Aug 1924, leaving issue

1h (cont.) Algernon Greville *m* 2nd 5 Oct 1847 Mary Fanny (*d* 15 Nov 1860), est dau of Christopher Idle, of Northfrith, and by her had, with another s (*d* young):

1i George (Sir), KCMG; *b* 12 May 1851; Dip Serv 1876–1905, Envoy Extrdy and Min Plen Mexico 1900–05; *m* 30 March 1897 Elisabeth Louise (*d* 7 June 1947), only dau of L Nicolays, of Frankfurt, and *d* 25 Oct 1937

2i Alice Gertrude; *m* 29 April 1873 Oscar Leslie Stephen (*d* 17 March 1911), of Belgravia, and *d* 5 Jan 1947, leaving issue

1h (cont.) Algernon Greville *m* 3rd 4 June 1863 Louisa Fanny (*d* 17 July 1904), dau of Maj-Gen Richard Parker, RA, and *d* 14 July 1887

2h FULKE SOUTHWELL GREVILLE later GREVILLE-NUGENT (roy licence 1866), 1st BARON GREVILLE OF CLONYN, Co Westmeath (UK), so *cr* 15 Dec 1869; *b* 17 Feb 1821; Ld Lt and custos rotulorum Co Westmeath, MP Co Longford 1852–69, Hon Col Westmeath Rifles; *m* 28 April 1840 Lady Rosa Emily Mary Anne Nugent (*d* 17 Jan 1883),

only child and heir of 1st and last Marquess of Westmeath (*see* WESTMEATH, E), and *d* 25 Jan 1883, having had:

1i ALGERNON WILLIAM FULKE GREVILLE-NUGENT later GREVILLE (roy licence 10 March 1883), 2nd BARON GREVILLE OF CLONYN, JP, DL (both Co Westmeath); *b* 11 Feb 1841; Capt 1st Life Gds, MP (Lib) Co Westmeath 1865–74, Groom-in-Waiting to HM QUEEN VICTORIA 1868–73, a Ld Treasury 1873–74; *m* 16 Dec 1863 Lady Beatrice Violet Graham (*d* 29 Feb 1932), dau of 4th Duke of Montrose (*qv*), and *d* 2 Dec 1909, having had:

1j Ronald Henry Fulke, MVO, JP, DL (Co Westmeath); *b* 14 Oct 1864; MP E Bradford 1896–1906, Capt 1st Life Gds then Yorks Dragoons, High Sheriff Co Westmeath 1899; *m* 25 April 1891 Margaret Helen Anderson, DBE (1922) (*d* 15 Sept 1942), dau of William McEwan, PC, and *dsp* 5 April 1908

2j CHARLES BERESFORD FULKE GREVILLE, 3rd BARON GREVILLE OF CLONYN, OBE (1919), JP, DL; *b* 3 March 1871; LCC 1912–16, Maj 7th Hus then Res Regt of Cav, Lovat's Scouts Yeo, ADC to Ld Lt Ireland 1892–93 and Govr Bombay 1900–04, Mil Sec to Govr-Gen Australia 1904–08, Chm St George's Hosp 1914–43; *m* 24 Nov 1909 Olive Grace (*d* 1 Oct 1959), dau of John W Grace, of Leybourne Grange, Kent, and widow of Henry Scanlon Kerr, of New York (*see* 1970 edn KERR, Bt), and *d* 14 May 1952, leaving:

1k RONALD CHARLES FULKE GREVILLE, 4th and last BARON GREVILLE OF CLONYN; *b* 11 April 1912; *educ* Eton and Magdalen Coll Oxford; *d* 1987, when the Barony expired

1j Camilla Dagmar Violet; *m* 1st 21 Jan 1890 (*divorce* 1908) Hon Alistair George Hay and had issue (*see* KINNOULL, E); *m* 2nd 4 July 1911 Count Hervé de Bernis, s of Marquis de Bernis, and *d* 7 July 1938

2j Veronique Lillian Violet; *m* 10 July 1907 Cdr Herbert Victor Creer, RAN, s of Capt Joseph Creer, of Sydney, NSW, and *d* 7 Feb 1956, leaving issue

2i George Frederick Nugent GREVILLE-NUGENT later GREVILLE (roy licence 6 June 1883), DL (Middx); *b* 11 Sept 1842; MP Co Longford 1870–74; *m* 17 Aug 1870 Cecil Aitcheson (*d* 9 June 1925), est dau of Lt-Gen Henry Aitcheson Hankey, and *dsp* 11 May 1897

3i Robert Southwell; *b* 26 March 1847; *d unm* 10 Feb 1912

4i Reginald James Macartney; *b* 27 Nov 1848; Capt Coldstream Gds; *m* Oct 1871 Louisa Maud (*m* 2nd 17 July 1879 James Charles Hope-Vere (*see* LINLITHGOW, M) and *dsp* 20 April 1882; sis of 2nd Baron Churston (*qv*), and *dsp* 28 Feb 1878

5i Patrick Emilius John, JP, DL, of Clonyn Castle, Delvin, Co Westmeath; *b* 6 Aug 1852; Lt Westmeath Militia, High Sheriff Co Westmeath 1884, CC 1899; *m* 5 June 1882 Ermengarde (*d* 9 July 1949), dau and heiress of Augustus Ogilvy of Cove, Dumfriesshire, and *d* 27 Feb 1925, having had:

1j Rosemary Ermengarda; *b* 17 March 1883; *d* 20 Nov 1922

1i Mildred Charlotte; *m* 26 Aug 1869 Alexis Huchet, Marquis de la Bedoyère, and *d* 1 Aug 1906, leaving issue

3h Southwell; *b* Feb 1822; Maj 1st Bengal Fus 1st Sikh War 1845 and Indian Mutiny 1857; *m* 23 March 1847 Jane (*d* 29 Aug 1861), dau of L Tronson, of Newry, and *d* 16 Feb 1910, having had:

1i Brooke Southwell; *b* 9 April 1855; Capt Zulu War 1878–79 (medal with clasp), Assist Embarkation Staff Offr 1914–19 (despatches), Chev Order Leopold Belgium, King's Messenger War Office 1919, Hon King's Messenger FO to 1931; *m* 1879 Charlotte Priscilla (*d* 6 March 1933), only dau and heiress of E B Clough, of Pietermaritzburg, Natal, and *d* 6 April 1945, leaving:

1j Brooke Southwell Edward Algernon Fulke; *b* 2 June 1882; Lt-Col IA, WW I Mesopotamia and Persia, 3rd Afghan War 1919 (medal and clasp), Waziristan 1919–24 (two clasps), Chev Order Leopold Belgium, Delhi Durbar medal 1911; *m* 7 July 1912 Olive Lois (*d* 20 June 1977), 4th dau of John Punshon Denton, of Darlington, Co Durham, and *dsp* 19 May 1956

2j Guy George Frederick Fulke, DSO (1919); *b* 19 Jan 1884; *educ* Sherborne; Lt-Col HLI, Actg Lt-Col cmdg 6th Bn Roy Inniskilling Fus 1918, WW I (wounded, despatches), WW II as GSO and offr cmdg troopship; *m* 1911 Esther Hope (*d* 1968), 2nd dau of Henry Erskine Gerard, and *d* 20 Aug 1966, leaving:

1k Guy Eric Fulke, MC, ERD; *b* 1912; Capt RTR (Res) WW II (POW, escaped); *m* 1st 1934 (*divorce* 1968) Mary Henrietta, dau of Sir Harry Waechter, 1st Bt, CMG (*see* 1970 edn), and *d* 1986, leaving:

1l +Jonathan Guy Fulke; *b* 20 Oct 1940; *educ* privately

2l +René Brooke Fulke [René Greville Esq, Fressingfield Hall, Fressingfield, Suffolk]; *b* 3 Jan 1947; *educ* privately; *m* 1976 *Marion Pearl Emma, only child of H E Ings, of Harrow Weald, Middx, and has:

1m +Beaufort Henry d'Arcy; *b* 1977

2m +Brooke Southwell Guy; *b* 1981

1l *Priscilla Mary Caroline [Mrs Richard Holmes, 20 Parkside, Cambridge]; *b* 1935; *m* 26 June 1957 *Dr Richard Michael Holmes, only s of Prof Eric Gordon Holmes, MD, of Mivanza, Tanganyika, and Dr Barbara Elizabeth Holmes, of Cambridge, and has:

1m *Guy Aladar; *b* 1960

2m *Michael Aristide; b 1966

1m *Jacquetta Noël Barbara; b 1959

2l *Charlotte Anne Esther [Mrs Bernard Morton-Stevens, 39 Greys Rd, Eastbourne, Sussex]; b 1937; m 30 Oct 1954 *Bernard Morton-Stevens, s of Bernard Morton-Stevens, of Highgate, and has:

1m *Robert Guy; b 1956

2m *Dominic Peter; b 1962

1m *Veronica Mary; b 1955

2m *Lesley Anne; b 1959

1k (cont.) Guy Greville m 2nd 19– *Rosalind Jessie Gwavas [Mrs Guy Greville, Treetops, Llandividdy Lane, Polperro, Cornwall PL13 2RT], dau of George Larritt Polsue and widow of John Mostyn-Walker, and d 1986, leaving by her:

3l *Peregrine Fulke; b 1966

4l +Hugh Tristan Maynard; b 1968

2k +Hugh Edward Arderne Fulke; b 1914

1j Charlotte Caroline Muriel; b 6 March 1880; m 24 April 1901 George McKechnie and d 19–

2j Irene Fanny Gwendolin Gertrude; b 16 Aug 1888; d 19–

3j Annie Gladys Clare; b 20 April 1894; d unm 10 March 1959

4j Cecil Violet Enid; b 2 June 1896; m 7 Dec 1927 W/Cdr Edward Irvine Russell, RAF, and d 19–

2i Charles Algernon Fergus; b 26 Jan 1857; Transvaal CS, Pretoria; m 23 Oct 1876 Amy (d 1 Feb 1938), dau of Francis Picard, and d 24 Nov 1929, leaving:

1j May Vivienne Gertrude Amy; b 13 Dec 1877; m 18 Feb 1903 Col Louis Raymond Acworth, CBE, RAOC (d 22 Feb 1934), s of George Brindley Acworth, of Rochester, and d 1932, leaving issue

1i Charlotte Caroline; m 19 Dec 1871 Sir Frederick Alexis Eaton (d 11 Sept 1913), s of Richard Eaton, of Teignmouth, Devon, and dsp 3 March 1893

2i Gertrude Ann; b 6 Sept 1859; m 29 Dec 1888 Harry Moncrieff Simpson, of Madras

1g Harriet Greville; m James Morier (d 1849) and d 1858

2g Caroline Greville; m 1814 1st Viscount Combermere (qv) of Bhurtpore and d 1837

2f James (Rev); b 27 June 1753; Rector Stockton-on-Tees

3f Henry Francis; b 10 Aug 1760; Lt-Col 4th Dragoons; m 1st 18 Aug 1791 Catherine (d 18 Jan 1803), dau of Sir Bellingham Graham, 5th Bt, of Norton Conyers (qv); m 2nd 14 Feb 1805 Sophia (d 21 March 1839), dau of Francis Xavier Whyte and widow of Sir Henry Lambert, 4th Bt (qv), and d 13 Jan 1816, leaving by his 1st w:

1g George Macartney; b 1793; Maj 38th Regt; m Elizabeth Mary (m 2nd 2 Dec 1847 James Loch, MP, and d 29 Dec 1848), dau of John Pearson, Judge Advocate Calcutta, and d 26 April 1834, leaving:

1h Stapleton John; b 28 June 1826; R-Adml; m 26 Oct 1852 Henriette (d 13 Nov 1897), dau of G Kolimunzer, Italian Consul Corfu, and d 26 March 1903, leaving, with two other daus (d unm):

1i Stapleton Fulke; b 13 Jan 1858; m 29 July 1895 Alice (d 23 May 1938), dau of John Blackman, and d 3 June 1936, leaving:

1j John Algernon Fulke; b 9 Feb 1896; educ Hurstpierpoint; Lt attd Notts and Derby Regt WW I, with Bank of England 1914–56; m 3 Sept 1929 Frances Alice (d 1989), only dau of Harry Bird Harper, and d 20 July 1968, leaving:

1k +John Brooke Fulke [John Greville Esq, 314 Robin Hood Lane, Hall Green, Birmingham 28]; b 3 Nov 1930; educ Strand Sch (King's Coll London); m 22 Nov 1958 *Maureen Constance, only dau of Leonard Arthur Parkhouse, of Walton-on-Thames, Surrey, and has:

1l +Robert John Fulke; b 6 Feb 1960

2i Guy Alwine John; b 31 Oct 1861; Lt RN, lost at sea in HMS Serpent 10 Nov 1890

3i Algernon Brooke Eden; Capt RN Egypt 1882 (medal, bronze star) and Vitu Expdn 1890 (medal and clasp); d 9 Sept 1934

4i Turketil George Pearson; b 13 March 1864; m 18 Sept 1899 Edith Lucy (d 27 July 1953), dau of Rev Edward Austin, and dsp 9 March 1958

5i Henry Brooke Macartney Crewe; b 1 Feb 1870; m 21 Aug 1906 Cecilia Ada (d 3 July 1959), est dau of Sir Frederick Thomas Arthur Hervey-Bathurst, 4th Bt (qv), and d 3 Jan 1944, having had:

1j Paul Guy Brooke; b 12 May 1907; d 21 June 1929

2j Ronald Cecil; b 1 June 1908; Capt RA (TA) WW II; presumed ka in Br E Indies probably in Feb 1942

1j Beatrice Sheila; b 22 May 1910; m 15 Feb 1936 Michael James Farrer (d 25 March 1960), yst s of Arthur Richmond Farrer, and d 26 June 1976, leaving issue

2j *Margaret Ishla [Miss Margaret Greville, Ridge Hill Cottage, Kingscote, East Grinstead, Sussex]; b 27 Aug 1914

6i Percy Drummond Whitmore; b 6 July 1872; d unm c 1955

1i Amy Marie; m 5 Oct 1880 Theodore Edward Bouwens, of Manor Cottage, Littleton, Shepperton, s of Rev Theodore Bouwens, and d 1 May 1928

2i Jessie Matilda; m 20 May 1885 Lt-Col Edmund Roger Allday Kerrison, CMG, OBE, JP, DL, RA (d 12 July 1944), and d 3 Feb 1944, leaving issue

2g Henry Francis, CB; b 1796; V-Adml; m 3 July 1816 Harriet Dorothea (d 28 Dec 1856), only child of Gen John Despard, and d 18 Oct 1864, having had, with two other daus (d unm):

1h Henry Lambert Fulke; b 18 Oct 1826; Maj-Gen RA, Equerry to HRH THE DUCHESS OF CAMBRIDGE; d unm 5 July 1898

1h Emma Maria; m 9 Aug 1845 Lord Augustus William Frederick Spencer Loftus and d 1 Jan 1902, leaving issue (see ELY, M)

2h Jessie Fanny, m 2 May 1844 Edward Howley Palmer (d 28 July 1901) and had issue

3h Fanny Cecilia; m 30 April 1866 Adml Sir Charles Eden, KCB (dsp 7 March 1878), and d 18 July 1912

3g Brooke; b 1798; m 23 Oct 1856 Emilie Anne (d 3 Nov 1875), dau of Charles Bouchez, and d 1884, having had, with another s (d young) and a dau (d unm):

1h Henry Algernon Fulke Charles Ferdinand Stephen; b 30 May 1864; Maj 18th Hus, Maj and Hon Lt-Col City London Yeo; m 28 Oct 1891 Eileen Mary (d 12 Oct 1940), dau of Col Francis McDonnell, CB, and d 16 Feb 1937, leaving:

1i Ronald Algernon Fulke, of Tichborne Park, Alresford, Hants; b 9 Feb 1904; educ Harrow; m 25 March 1928 *Doris Ethel, dau of William Chouffot, and d 19 June 1968, leaving:

1j June Denise; b 10 June 1929; d 19–

1h Denise Dorothy Marie Emilie; b 15 Nov 18–; m 25 June 1913 Sir Joseph Henry Bernard Doughty-Tichborne, 13th Bt, and d 24 Aug 1959, leaving issue (see 1967 edn)

4f Charles; b 2 Nov 1762; Army Capt; m 31 March 1793 Lady Charlotte Bentinck (d 28 July 1862), dau of 3rd Duke of Portland (see PORTLAND, E), and d 26 Aug 1832, leaving:

1g Charles Cavendish Fulke; b 1794; Clerk PC and Sec BOT; the celebrated diarist; d unm 18 Jan 1865

2g Algernon Frederick; b 29 Jan 1798; Bath King-of-Arms; m 7 April 1823 Charlotte Maria (d 3 April 1841), dau of R H Cox, and d 15 Dec 1864, having had, with a dau (d unm):

1h Arthur Charles, JP (Middx); b 18 May 1827; Lt-Col Scots Gds; dsp 27 May 1901

2h Cavendish Hubert; Coldstream Gds; ka Inkerman 5 Nov 1854

1h Frances Harriet; m 2 Nov 1843 6th Duke of Richmond and (1st Duke of) Gordon (qv) and d 8 March 1887, leaving issue

2h Augusta Mary; m 15 April 1858 George Montagu Warren Sandford, MP (d 19 June 1879), of Reever Hall, Essex, and d 28 Dec 1921, leaving issue

3g Henry William; b 28 Oct 1801; Gentleman Usher to HM QUEEN VICTORIA; d unm 12 Dec 1872

1g Harriet Catherine; m 18 June 1822 1st Earl of Ellesmere and d 17 April 1866, leaving issue (see SUTHERLAND, D)

1f Frances Anne; m 4 April 1766 1st Baron Crewe (see 1940 edn CREWE, M) and d 23 Dec 1818, leaving issue

The 6th BARON's yr bro,

WILLIAM GREVILLE, **7th Baron Brooke of Beauchamps Court**; b c 1694; educ Wadham Coll Oxford; m 8 Nov 1716 Mary (d 29 March 1720), dau and coheir of Hon Henry Thynne (see BATH, M), and d 28 July 1727, leaving an only surv s:

FRANCIS GREVILLE, **1st Earl of Warwick** (GB), so cr 13 Nov 1759 (two months after the Rich-held Earldom of Warwick had expired; in 1767 he petitioned the Ho Lds to be allowed to use this title solely but with precedence of the Earldom of Brooke; succeeding Earls have normally preferred to use the title Earl of Warwick alone) and **1st Earl Brooke of Warwick Castle** (GB), so cr 7 July 1746, KT (1753); b 1719; educ Winchester; Ld Lt Warwicks 1749–57, FSA 1768; m 15 May 1742 Elizabeth (m 2nd Gen Robert Clerk and d 24 Feb 1800), est dau of Lord Archibald Hamilton (see HAMILTON and BRANDON, D), and d 6 July 1773, having had, with a yr dau (d unm):

1 GEORGE, **2nd Earl**

2 Charles Francis; b 12 May 1749; d unm 1809

3 Robert Fulke; b 3 Feb 1751; m 19 Oct 1797, as her 2nd husb, Louisa (d 11 July 1843), Countess of Mansfield in her own right (qv), and d 27 April 1824, leaving:

(1) Robert Fulke; b 1 Dec 1800; Capt 35th Foot; m 25 April 1822 Georgina Cecilia (d 14 Sept 1867), dau of Charles Locke, and d 12 Sept 1867, having had:

1a William Hamilton; b 29 Oct 1826; 2nd Life Gds; dsp 30 April 1848

(1) Georgiana; m 12 May 1824 Lt-Gen Hon Sir George Cathcart, GCB, and d 12 Dec 1871, leaving issue (see CATHCART, E)

(2) Louisa; m 15 Dec 1825 Rev Hon Daniel Heneage Finch Hatton and d 11 April 1883, leaving issue (see WINCHILSEA and NOTTINGHAM, E)

1 Louisa Augusta; m 1770 William Churchill, of Henbury, Dorset

2 Frances Elizabeth; m 17 July 1762 Sir H Harpur, 6th Bt, MP (d 10 Feb 1789; see 1924 edn), and d 6 April 1825, leaving issue

3 Charlotte Mary; m 16 Aug 1762 7th Earl of Galloway (qv) and dsps 31 May 1763

The 1st EARL's est s,

GEORGE GREVILLE, **2nd Earl of Warwick** and **Earl Brooke of Warwick Castle**; b 16 Sept 1746; educ Ch Ch Oxford; MP (Tory) Warwick 1768–73, a Ld Trade 1770–74, Recorder Warwick 1773–1816, Ld Lt Warwicks 1795–1816, Col Warwicks Fencibles; FRS, FSA; m 1st 1 April 1771 Georgiana (d 1772), only dau of 1st Baron Selsey of Selsey (see 1838 edn), and had an only s:

1 George, Lord Brooke; b 25 March 1772; d unm 2 May 1786

The **2nd Earl** m 2nd 14 July 1776 Henrietta (d 22 April 1838), dau of Richard Vernon, of Hilton, Staffs, and d 2 May 1816, having by her had, with other issue:

2 HENRY RICHARD, **3rd Earl**

3 Charles John (Sir), KCB; Maj-Gen; d unm 1836

1 Henrietta; m 1805 2nd Earl of Clonmell (d 18 Jan 1838) and d 8 Nov 1858, leaving issue (see 1935 edn)

2 Augusta; m 5th Earl of Aylesford (qv) and d 2 March 1845, leaving issue

The 2nd EARL's 2nd s,

HENRY RICHARD GREVILLE, **3rd Earl of Warwick** and **Earl Brooke of Warwick Castle**, KT (1827); b 29 March 1779; educ Winchester; MP (Tory) Warwick 1802–16, Recorder Warwick 1816–35, Ld Lt Warwicks 1822–53, Ld Bedchamber

1828–30, Ld-in-Waiting 1841–46; DCL Oxon; *m* 21 Oct 1816 Lady Sarah (*d* 30 Jan 1851), dau of 2nd Earl of Mexborough (*qv*) and widow of 4th Baron Monson (*qv*), and *d* 10 Aug 1853, leaving:

GEORGE GUY GREVILLE, **4th Earl of Warwick** and **Earl Brooke of Warwick Castle**; *b* 28 March 1818; *educ* St John's Coll Oxford (MA); MP (C) S Warwicks 1845–53, Hon Col Warwicks Yeo Cav, Yeo ADC to HM QUEEN VICTORIA 1878–93; *m* 18 Feb 1852 Lady Anne Charteris (*d* 16 Aug 1903), dau of 9th Earl of Wemyss and (5th Earl of) March (*qv*), and *d* 2 Dec 1893, leaving:

1 FRANCIS RICHARD CHARLES GUY, **5th Earl**

2 Alwyn Henry Fulke, CVO (1918), JP (Essex); *b* 9 Feb 1854; Capt KRRC and Hon Lt-Col Warwicks ImpYeo, ADC to Ld Lt Ireland 1884–85, Equerry-in-Waiting to HRH THE DUKE OF CLARENCE 1884–88, Extra Equerry to HM EDWARD VII (when PRINCE OF WALES) 1885–1901 and 1901–10, Extra Equerry to HM GEORGE V; *m* 8 Aug 1888 Mabel Elizabeth Georgina, OBE (1918) (*d* 19 May 1940), only dau of Ernald Mosley Smith, of Selsdon Park, Croydon, and *d* 11 April 1929, leaving:

    (1) Charles Henry, DSO; *b* 28 May 1889; Gren Gds WW I (wounded, despatches); *m* 22 June 1918 Louise Gwendoline (*m* 2nd 28 Nov 1931 Adml of the Fleet Sir Rhoderick Robert McGrigor, GCB, DSO (*see* McGRIGOR, Bt), and *d* 11 Nov 1961), only surv child of Col Geoffrey Carr Glyn, CMG, DSO (*see* WOLVERTON, B), and *dsp* 1 March 1931

    (1) Phyllis Dorothy Lindsay; *m* 16 Oct 1916 Brig Guy Elland Carne Rasch (*see* RASCH, Bt) and *d* 25 March 1977, leaving issue

3 Louis George; *b* 1 Jan 1856; 2nd Sec Dip Serv 1882–87, High Sheriff Wilts 1920; *m* 12 July 1887 Lily (*d* 17 July 1898), dau of J H Gordon, and *d* 6 March 1941, having had:

    (1) George Gordon Francis; *b* 18 March 1890; Capt 4th Hus; *ka* 31 March 1918

4 Sidney Robert (Sir), KCVO (1912), CB (1899); *b* 16 Nov 1866; *educ* Marlborough; Assist Priv Sec to U-Sec State India 1887, Priv Sec to PM 1888–92 and 1896–98, Equerry to HM EDWARD VII when PRINCE OF WALES 1898–1901, Groom-in-Waiting to TM EDWARD VII 1901–10 and GEORGE V 1910, Priv Sec to HM QUEEN ALEXANDRA 1901–11, Paymaster Household 1911–15, Comptroller and Treas to HRH THE PRINCE OF WALES 1915–20, Groom-in-Waiting to HM GEORGE V 1920, Kt Order Charles III Spain, Cdr Order Dannebrog, Kt Cdr Franz-Josef Austria, Offr Legn Hon, Prussian Order Red Eagle 2nd Cl and Italian Order; *d* 12 June 1927

1 Eva Sarah Louisa; Extra Woman Bedchamber to HM QUEEN MARY; *m* 20 July 1895 Col Frank Dugdale, CVO, 2nd s of James Dugdale (*d* 26 Nov 1925), of Wroxall Abbey, Warwicks, and *d* 12 July 1940, having had issue

The 4th EARL's est s,

FRANCIS RICHARD CHARLES GUY GREVILLE, **5th Earl of Warwick** and **Earl Brooke of Warwick Castle**, JP (Essex and Somerset), DL; *b* 9 Feb 1853; *educ* Ch Ch Oxford; MP (C) E Somerset 1879–85 and Colchester 1888–92, Mayor Warwick 1894–96 and 1901, CA Essex and Warwicks, Tstee Rugby Sch, Ld Lt Essex 1901–19 and Pres Essex TFA, Hon Col 3rd Bn Essex Regt, Lt-Col Cmdg Warwicks Yeo, Dep Grand Master Freemasons England; *m* 30 April 1881 Frances Evelyn (Daisy) (*b* 10 Dec 1861; one of EDWARD VII's better-known mistresses; fought Warwick (Lab) 1923 gen election; *d* 26 July 1938), er dau and coheir of Col Hon Charles Henry Maynard, s of 3rd and last Viscount Maynard (*see* 1865 edn), and *d* 15 Jan 1924, having had:

1 LEOPOLD GUY FRANCIS MAYNARD, **6th Earl**

2 Charles Algernon Cromartie; *b* 22 Nov 1885; *d* 28 March 1887

3 Maynard; *b* 21 March 1898; Lt RAF WW I; *m* 19 Feb 1918 Dora (*d* 12 Dec 1957), only dau of Edward Pape, of Moor Hall, Battle, Sussex, and *d* 21 Feb 1960, leaving:

    (1) *Felice [Mrs Eric Spurrier, Perryfields, Easton Lodge, Dunmow, Essex]; *b* 18 Jan 1919; *m* 17 Aug 1940 Eric James Spurrier (*d* 1984), s of Dr Harrry Spurrier, of Maidenhead, and has:

        1a *Neil; *b* 24 May 1952; *educ* Stowe

        1a *Caroline Ann; *b* 18 July 1957

1 Marjorie Blanche Eva; *b* 25 Oct 1884; *m* 1st 19 Jan 1904 2nd Earl of Feversham (*see* FEVERSHAM, B) and had issue; *m* 2nd 1 Nov 1917 Hon Sir (William) Gervase Beckett, 1st Bt (*qv*), and *d* 25 July 1964, leaving further issue

2 Mercy; *b* 3 April 1904; *m* 1st 1 July 1925 (*divorce* 1933), as his 2nd w, Basil Herbert Dean, CBE, the film producer, of Little Easton Manor, Dunmow, Essex, s of Harding Hewer Dean, and had issue; *m* 2nd 14 Feb 1933 (*divorce* 1936) Patrick Henry Reginald Gamble, s of Very Rev Henry Reginald Gamble, DD, Dean Exeter; *m* 3rd 1936 Richard Maurice Marter (*d* 31 Oct 1964), only s of Capt W M Marter, Coldstream Gds, and *d* 21 Nov 1968

The 5th EARL's est s,

LEOPOLD GUY FRANCIS MAYNARD GREVILLE, **6th Earl of Warwick** and **Earl Brooke of Warwick Castle**, CMG (1915), MVO (1905), JP (Essex and Warwicks), DL (Warwicks); *b* 10 Sept 1882 (HRH THE DUKE OF ALBANY stood sponsor); *educ* Eton; Capt 1st Life Gds, Boer War 1899–1901, Russo-Japanese War (as Reuter's correspondent) 1904–05, WW I (despatches, Chev Legn Hon, wounded), ADC to Viscount Milner 1901–02 and Inspr-Gen Forces 1907–12, cmded 2nd Cav Bde Canada 1913, Priv Sec to CIGS 1912–14, ADC to GOC BEF 1914–15, Brig-Gen 1915, cmded 4th Canadian Inf Bde then 12th Canadian Inf Bde to 1918, Hon Lt-Col TAR, Hon Brig-Gen, Orders Rising Sun Japan 4th Cl, St Stanislas Russia 1st Cl with swords and Croix de Guerre Belgium and France; *m* 29 April 1909 Elfrida Marjorie, JP, DGStJ, Mayor Warwick 1929, 1930 and 1931 (*d* 10 Feb 1943), only dau of Sir William Eden, 7th Bt (*see* EDEN OF WINTON, B), and *d* 31 Jan 1928, leaving:

1 CHARLES GUY FULKE, **7th Earl**

2 Richard Francis Maynard, OBE (1955); *b* 4 July 1913; *educ* Radley, Chillon Coll and Ch Ch Oxford; Capt Rifle Bde, Govr Univ Coll Hosp 1952–68, dir: Schweppes Ltd, Schweppes Overseas Ltd and Kia-Ora Ltd; *d unm* 29 June 1968

3 John Ambrose Henry; *b* 2 Feb 1918; Lt KRRC and F/Lt RAFVR WW II; *ka* July 1942

The 6th EARL's est s,

CHARLES GUY FULKE GREVILLE, **7th Earl of Warwick** and **Earl Brooke of Warwick Castle**, JP (1952), DL (Warwicks 1952); *b* 4 March 1911; *educ* Eton and RMA Sandhurst; Lt Res Offrs Gren Gds, Merchant Navy, Admlty Small Vessels

Pool 1943–45; CC Warwicks 1934–36, Mayor Warwick 1951–52, Pres Warwick Co Cricket Club, Govr: Birmingham U, Warwick Kings' Schs, Roy Ag Soc, Roy Shakespeare Theatre and Univ Coll Hosp; CStJ; *m* 1st 11 July 1933 (*divorce* 1938) Rose (*d* 29 Dec 1972), only dau of David Cecil Bingham (*see* LUCAN, E); *m* 2nd 19 Feb 1942 (*divorce* 1949) Mary Kathleen, er dau of Percy Clifford Hopkinson, of Seabarn, Kingston Gorse, Sussex, and formerly w of Harold Edward Bell; *m* 3rd 25 Nov 1963 *Janine Josephine [The Rt Hon Janine Countess of Warwick, 201 via Appia Antica, Rome, Italy], dau of Georges Detry de Mares, and *d* 20 Jan 1984, leaving by his 1st w:

DAVID ROBIN FRANCIS GUY GREVILLE, **8th Earl of Warwick** and **Brooke of Warwick Castle**, JP (Warwicks 1970); *b* 15 May 1934; *educ* Eton; Warwicks Yeo (TA), 2nd Lt Life Gds, Govr Roy Shakespeare Theatre, V-Pres Midlands Assoc Bldg Socs; *m* 28 June 1956 (*divorce* 1967) Sarah Anne (*m* 2nd Harry Thomson (Tom) Jones, Newmarket racehorse trainer), dau of Alfred Chester Beatty, of Owley, Wittersham, Kent, and *d* 20 Jan 1996, leaving:

1 GUY DAVID GREVILLE, **9th and present Earl of Warwick** and **9th and present Earl Brooke of Warwick Castle**

1 *Charlotte Anne Greville [The Lady Charlotte Fraser, 1 Petyt Place, London SW3 5DJ]; *b* 6 June 1958; *m* 10 Sept 1979 Hon Andrew Roy Mathew Fraser (*k* on safari 15 March 1994), yst s of 17th Lord Lovat (*qv*)

WATERFORD

Arms: Quarterly, 1st and 4th, argent crusilly-fitchée three fleurs-de-lys within a bordure engrailed sable (for BERESFORD); 2nd and 3rd, argent a chief indented sable (for LA POER). **Crest:** A dragon's head erased azure, transfixed by a broken spear, the lower part through the neck, the upper part through the jaw, proper (for BERESFORD). **Supporters:** On either side an angel proper, vested argent, crined and winged or, holding in the exterior hand a sword erect, also proper. **Motto:** *Nil nisi cruce* ('Nothing unless by the Cross'). **Creations:** Bt. (I) 5 May 1665; B. (I) 9 Nov or 19 Dec 1767 ((La) Poer); B. (I) 4 Nov 1720 (Beresford), (GB) 21 Aug 1786 (Tyrone of Haverfordwest); V. (I) 4 Nov 1720; E. (I) 18 July 1746; M. (I) 21 Aug 1786.

THE 8TH MARQUESS OF WATERFORD, **Earl of Tyrone**, **Viscount Tyrone**, **Baron (La) Poer**, **Baron Beresford**, of Beresford, Co Cavan, **Baron Tyrone of Haverfordwest**, Co Pembroke, and a **Baronet** (Sir John Hubert de la Poer Beresford, Bt) [The Most Hon The Marquess of Waterford, Curraghmore, Portlaw, Co Waterford, Ireland]; *b* 14 July 1933; *s f* 1934; *educ* Eton; Lt RHG SR; *m* 23 July 1957 *Lady Caroline Olein Geraldine Wyndham-Quin, yr dau of 6th Earl of Dunraven and Mount-Earl (*qv*), and has:

1 +HENRY NICHOLAS De La POER, *Earl of Tyrone* [Earl of Tyrone, Luggershall Farm, Owlpen, Glos GL11 5BX]; *b* 23 March 1958; *educ* Harrow; *m* 1986 *Amanda, dau of Norman Thompson, of The Castle, Borris-in-Ossory, Co Laois, and has:

    (1) +Richard John, *Lord Le Poer*; *b* 19 Aug 1987

    (2) +Marcus Patrick; *b* 1990

    (1) *Camilla Juliet; *b* 25 July 1995

2 +Charles Richard de la Poer [The Lord Charles Beresford, Estancia el Pucara, 6409 Tres Lomas, Prov de Buenos Aires, Argentina]; *b* 18 Jan 1960; *m* 1984 *Maria Teresa, dau of Gabriel Donoso Phillips and Maria Isabelle Donosa Rosselot, of Santiago, Chile, and has:

    (1) +William; *b* 1990

    (2) +A son; *b* 2 June 1996

    (1) *Carolina; *b* 1989

2 +James Patrick de la Poer; *b* 10 Dec 1965; *educ* King's Sch Bruton; *m* 6 Sept 1989 *Avril, dau of Louis Murphy, of Baylough, Portlaw, Co Waterford

1 *Alice Rose de la Poer; *b* 31 July 1970

Tyrone, Earldom of, previous creations: *See* DECIES, B, preliminary remarks, and O'NEILL, B.

Lineage (of Le Poer): HENRY le POER (probably s of Philip le Poer, of St Lawrence, Pembs) was granted by KING JOHN a very large area centred on Dunhill in mid- and east Co Waterford; his descendants, known as (feudal) Barons of Dunhill, survived in a direct line to c 1360, but even by 1300 there were many important cadet branches, including that of:

MATTHEW (also called MAKIN, a diminutive of Matthew) le POER; had:

1 Eustace fitz Matthew; ancestor of the branch of the POWERs called MacEustace

2 Theobald fitz Matthew; Sheriff Waterford 1323–27; m Elena, widow of Walter de la Roche, and d 1327, leaving:

(1) Milo; m by 1322 Joan — and dsp 1329

(2) Matthew; dsp after 1330

3 Philip; dsp

4 Edward; dsp after 1312

5 John fitz Matthew, called in later genealogies Seoinín na Buile ('Mad Johnnie'); m Joan — and d c 1331, leaving, with a yr s (Geoffrey, d after 1356):

(1) Richard Mór ('The Great') fitz John fitz Matthew; Ch Serjeant Co Waterford 1350, Sheriff 1367–68; assumed chieftaincy of POWERs in their conflict with the citizens of Waterford after the death of the last Baron of Dunhill; d after 1376, having had:

1a John; hostage for his f 1345; dsp & vp

2a DAVID

3a Nicholas

The 2nd s,

DAVID ROTHE (i.e., Ruadh, or 'The Red'), to whom his f conveyed lands in and around Clonea in 1351 and 1354; apptd 8 Dec 1388 with his f-in-law to negotiate with those POWERs who were in open rebellion; m Ellen, dau and eventual heirof Nicholas le Poer, of Kilmeadon (whose estates passed by entail to her illegitimate bro but were unsuccessfully claimed by the 3rd Lord Power 1586), and had:

NICHOLAS POWER, called 'MacDavy Rothe'; Sherif Waterford 1425–45 but for a brief interval 1431 when Milo Power, last of the Barons of Dunhill (dspl) held that office, and converted it to a local lordship; known as the most hospitable of the Anglo-Normans of Munster; d 1445, leaving, with (a) yr son(s) (David; also probably Walter, preceptor of Crook):

RICHARD POWER; styled Chief of his name; s f as Sheriff of Waterford and held on to the post even though the I Parl tried in 1476 in response to his opponents the citizens of Waterford to oust him; m Elena, dau of Sir Edmond 'Mac Richard' Butler (see 1970 edn ORMONDE, M), and d 3 Oct 1483, having had, with two yr sons (Nicholas, of Curraghduff, d after 1537, ancestor of the POWERs of Curraghduff; John, cleric, Commendatory Abbot of Mothal 1520):

Sir PIERS POWER; Chief of his name; s f as Sheriff Co Waterford from 1482, apparently relinquishing his shrieval authority to his s Richard c 1500; m his cousin Katherine (d after 1525), dau of Sir Gerald FitzGerald, feudal Ld of the Decies (see DECIES, B, preliminary remarks), and d after 2 Aug 1521, having had:

1 RICHARD

2 Piers; dsp & vp in France

3 Thomas, of Ballycanavan; styled 'Tanist of the Powers'; d after 1549; ancestor of the the POWERs of Brenan

1 Katherine; m Sir Edmond Butler, of Cahir, and was mother of the 1st Baron Cahir

2 Joan; m Richard FitzGerald, called 'MacThomas', Chief of his sept

3 Elerna; m Walter Power, of Kilmeadon

4 Gilles/Julia/Sile; m John FitzGerald, of Strancally, gs of 7th Earl of Desmond (see DENBIGH and DESMOND, E, preliminary remarks)

5 A dau; m (Moriartogh?) Kavanagh, of Clanmullin

The est s,

RICHARD POWER, 1st BARON OF LE POER AND COROGHMORE, Co Waterford (I), so cr 13 Sept 1535; Chief of his name; acquired Curraghmore from another branch of the POWERs through m Katherine; m by 1526 Katherine (m 2nd 13th Earl of Desmond (see DENBIGH and DESMOND, E, preliminary remarks); d 17 March 1552/3), 2nd dau of 8th Earl of Ormonde and (1st Earl of) Ossory (see MOUNTGARRET, V), and was k by Connor O'Callaghan 10 Nov 1538 while intervening on the Crown's behalf in a struggle concerning the succession to the Earldom of Desmond, leaving, with two er illegitimate sons (Nicholas; Edmond, Commendatory Prior of St Katherine's, Waterford, and Abbot of Mothal):

1 PIERS POWER, 2nd BARON LE POWER AND COROGHMORE; b 1526; served Siege Boulogne (ktd 1544) and d there unm of wounds 16 Oct 1545

2 JOHN, 3rd BARON

3 Thomas, of Coolfin; m Joan (m 2nd Edmond FitzGibbon, the White Knight), dau of Thomas Tobin, called Lord of the Compshinnagh, and d 10 Oct 1564, leaving:

(1) Edmond, of Coolfin; b 1557; dsp after 31 Oct 1568

(2) William, of Coolfin; dsp by 1586

(3) James, of Coolfin; m 1st —, dau of Piers FitzHarris, of Macmine, Co Wexford, and had:

1a Thomas, of Coolfin; m Margaret, dau of Piers Butler, 2nd s of 1st Viscount Mountgarret (qv), and d 15 Dec 1637, leaving:

1b Piers, of Coolfin; m Katherine, dau of William Wall, of Coolnamucky, and was transplanted to Connaught 1654

2b Richard; m Gilles, dau of David Power, of Coolrae

3b John

4b James

1b Katherine

2b Gilles; m Geoffrey Fanning

3b Joan; dsp

4b Margaret; m Piers Power, of Ballincarnan

2a Edmond

(3) (cont.) James Power m 2nd Aine, dau of Turlough O'Brien, 2nd s of 2nd Earl of Thomond (see INCHIQUIN, B), and d 1625, leaving by her:

3a William, of Ballinkina; dsp by 1627

4a John, of Ballinkina; living 1641

(4) Nicholas; dsp

(1) Ellen; m Thomas Butler, 3rd s of 1st Viscount Mountgarret (qv)

(2) A dau; m Piers Og ('The Younger') Lacy, of Bruff, Co Limerick

(3) A dau; m as his 1st w Gerald FitzGerald, of Coolishill, Co Waterford

1 Katherine; m Sir Nicholas Devereux, of Balmagir, Co Wexford

2 Ellice; m Sir Thomas FitzGerald, of Conna, and had:

(1) James fitzThomas, self-styled 15th Earl of Desmond (despite the attainder of 1582 passed against the 14th Earl)

3 Margaret; m 1st William Bourke, of Ballyloggan, Co Tipperary, called Lord of Costure; m 2nd Walter Burke, of Cappagh, called Lord of Muskerryquirk

4 Ellen; m Teig MacBrien, of Ballytrasna, Co Limerick

The 2nd s,

JOHN POWER Mor, 3rd BARON LE POWER AND COROGHMORE; b c 1529–30; m 1st Eleanor, 3rd dau of 13th Earl of Desmond, and had:

1 RICHARD, 4th BARON

2 Piers, of Clondonil and Rathgormuck; m Margaret, dau of Piers Butler, of Grellagh (see DUNBOYNE, B), and d 26 May 1597; ancestor of the POWERs or De La POERs of Gurteen le Poer, Co Waterford

3 Thomas, of Cullinagh; m Margaret, dau of Richard FitzGerald, feudal Baron of Burnchurch, Co Kilkenny, and widow of Robert Power, of Dunhill, and d after 1630, leaving:

(1) John; living 1633

4 David, of Ballyloughmore; m Catherine Prendergast and d after 1624, leaving:

(1) Edmond, of Ballyloughmore; m by 1626 Mary, dau of Richard, Archdeacon of Corballymore, and was living 1642

(2) Maurice; living 1642

5 Maurice; m — FitzGerald and dsp after 1585

1 Gilles/Julia; m 1st Donal MacCarthy, Tanist of Muskerry; m 2nd Piers Butler, of Nodstown, gs of 9th Earl of Ormonde and (2nd Earl of) Ossory (see MOUNTGARRET, V)

2 Catherine; m Piers Butler, of Grantstown, 7th s of 9th Earl of Ormonde and (2nd Earl of) Ossory

3 Margaret; m 1st, as his 2nd w, Sir Donough MacCarthy Reogh; m 2nd 1585, as his 1st w, James FitzThomas FitzGerald, self-styled 15th Earl of Desmond, also called the Sugan or 'Straw' Earl

The 3rd BARON m 2nd Ellen, dau of Teig MacCormac Og ('The Younger') MacCartie, of Muskerry, and widow of 3rd Viscount Barry/Barrymore/Buttevant, and d 8 Nov 1592, leaving by her:

6 William; dsp after 1585

4 Ellen; m Gerald FitzGerald, of Dromane, Lord of the Decies, and dsp

5 Margaret; m (divorce) her 1st cousin James fitzThomas FitzGerald, self-styled 15th Earl of Desmond; m 2nd James Butler, of Derryluskan (see DUNBOYNE, B), uterine bro of 11th Earl of Ormonde and (4th Earl of) Ossory (see MOUNTGARRET, V)

The 3rd BARON's est s,

RICHARD POWER, 4th BARON LE POWER AND COROGHMORE; b c 1553; m Katherine, only dau and heiress of 3rd Viscount Buttevant, and d 8 Aug 1607, having had:

1 John Og; m Helen Barry, 2nd dau of 5th Viscount Buttevant, and dvp by 18 Dec 1600, leaving:

(1) JOHN, 5th BARON

(1) Ellen; m c 1625 8th Viscount Roche of Fermoy (see FERMOY, B, preliminary remarks) and was hanged by the Commonwealth regime 1652 on a trumped up charge of murder, leaving issue

2 Piers, of Monalargie (now Munsborough, Co Waterford); m Katherine, dau of 11th Earl of Ormonde and (4th Earl of) Ossory (see MOUNTGARRET, V), and had:

(1) Piers, of Monalargie, attainted for partcipating in 1641 uprising; had, with a dau (Ellen, m Edmond Power, of Curraghkelly and Gurteen):

1a John, styled Baron Le Power and Coroghmore after death of 3rd Earl of Tyrone, Col Dublin Regt of Foot, Mayor Limerick during Siege, attainted 1688 but returned to England and was afforded some help by QUEEN ANNE; m probably by 1692 Catherine Eustace and d Paris (allegedly murdered by a servant) 20 Aug 1725, leaving, with three er sons (3 d young) and two daus (Charlotte, Françoise-Clare, nuns):

1b Henry; bapt 17 April 1699; went to England; unsuccessfully petitioned to be recognised heir to the Earl of Tyrone's estates; Gentleman Privy Chamber 1726, insane by 1733; d unm 5 May 1742, when the representation of the Barony passed to distant cousins, no attempt to assume it being made till 1920, when Maj John William Rivallon de la Poer, of Gurteen, Co Waterford, petitioned the Crown for recognition as Baron Le Power and Coroghmore, the Ho of Lds Cttee for Privileges reporting 1922 that were it not for the attainder the said petitioner would indeed be the rightful holder of the title

3 Thomas; dsp after 1624

4 Edmond, of Graigueshoneen; dsp after 1627

1 Eleanor; m David Condon, of Ballymacpatrick, Co Cork, Chief of his family

2 Ellis; m 1st David Barry (dvp), by whom she was mother of 1st Earl of Barrymore; m 2nd Patrick Sherlock, s of Sir John Sherlock, of Ballynaclarahan, Co Tipperary

3 Catherine

4 Gille/Julia; m 1615, as his 2nd w, 17th Baron of Kerry and Lixnaw (see LANSDOWNE, M)

The 4th BARON's gs,

JOHN POWER, 5th BARON LE POWER AND COROGHMORE; b 1599; educ Inner Temple; disordered in his wits in later life; m Ruth, dau and heiress of Robert Pypho, of St. Mary's Abbey, Dublin, and had, with other issue:

1 RICHARD POWER, 6th BARON LE POWER AND COROGHMORE, also 1st EARL OF TYRONE and VISCOUNT DECIES (both I), so cr 9 Oct 1672, PC (I 1667–79 and 1686); b 1630; Capt Regt of Foot Feb 1660/1, Govr Waterford City and Co 1661, MP (I Parl) Co Waterford 1661–65/6, Col of Foot 1670; m 1654

Lady Dorothy Annesley, dau of 1st Earl of Anglesey (see ANGLESEY, M, preliminary remarks, also VALENTIA, V), and d a Jacobite prisoner in Tower of London 14 Oct 1690, having had, with another s and two daus:

(1) JOHN POWER, 2nd EARL OF TYRONE; d unm 14 Oct 1693

(2) JAMES POWER, 3rd and last EARL OF TYRONE of the 1672 cr; m 13 Dec 1692 Anne, est dau and coheir of Andrew Rickard, of Dangan Spidoge, Co Kilkenny, and dspm 19 Aug 1704, when the Viscounty and Earldom expired, while right to the Barony would but for the attainders against him have vested in John Power (see above), leaving:

1a Katherine; claimed 4 April 1763 a Barony of Le Poer or La Poer (the change from the former to the latter version occurring during proceedings in the I Ho Lds in apparent deference to the sex of the claimant, following medieval usage) that she alleged had been cr by writ to Nicholas fitz John le Poer 1375, claim allowed by resolution of I Ho of Lds 16 Nov 1767, confirmed by the Crown 19 Dec 1767, conceivably thereby creating a Barony of that name from either of the two dates in 1767 even though no such Barony ever existed before; m 16 July 1717 **1st Earl of Tyrone** (see below) and had issue

(1) Helen; m her cousin John Walsh, of Pilltown, Co Waterford

(2) Dorothy; d unm

2 David; dsp 17 Aug 1661

3 Piers, of Killowen; m Honora (m 2nd Charles MacCarthy Mór, of Pallis, Co Kerry), dau and heiress of 2nd Lord Bourke, Baron of Brittas, and d between 1 March and 10 May 1669, leaving:

(1) Piers, of Killowen

(1) Ruth; m (Richard?) Duckett (of Whitestown, Co Waterford?) and was living 1703

1 Eleanor; m Thomas Walsh, of Piltown, and had issue

2 Katherine; m 1658 John FitzGerald, of Dromana, feudal Ld of the Decies (d 1661/2; see DECIES, B, preliminary remarks), and d 22 Aug 1660

3 Mary; m Philip Magrath, of Sleady, Co Waterford

4 Margaret

Lineage (of Beresford): JOHN, of Beresford, Staffs, as mentioned by the Domesday Survey of 1086 (a charter to him of Beresford of 1087 was witnessed by one Christopher de Beresford, who is referred to as 'Senior', hence was perhaps his f); had a 2nd s:

HUGH de BERESFORD, of Beresford; living 1133; had:

ADEN de BERESFORD, of Beresford; living 1150; had:

JOHN de BERESFORD, of Beresford; living 1220; had, with a yr s (William, of Leek, Staffs, who himself had a s (Robert, of Leek) and dau, Juliana):

HUGH de BERESFORD, of Beresford; living 1260; had:

ADEN de BERESFORD, of Beresford; living 1296; had, with a yr s (William, of Himley, Staffs, and Langley, Warwicks, m Margaret — and had issue) and a dau (Ellen, Prioress Kingsmead, Derbys, 1304–34):

ADEN de BERESFORD, of Beresford; living 1341; m Beatrice de Malbank, of Nantwich, Cheshire, and had, with a yr s (Thomas):

JOHN de BERESFORD, of Beresford; living 1349; m Emma — and had:

ADEN BERESFORD, of Beresford; m Agnes — and had:

JOHN BERESFORD, of Beresford; m Cecilia — and had, with a yr s (Aden, dsp 1411):

JOHN BERESFORD, of Beresford, also of Enson, Staffs; m Elizabeth, dau of William Basset, of Blore, Staffs, and d 1475, having had, with an est s (Aden, dsp) and two yst sons (Henry; William):

1 John, of Beresford; living 1439; m Elizabeth, dau of Robert Davenport, of Bramhall, Cheshire, and was ancestor of:

(1) Edward, of Beresford; last male-line rep of his family; had a dau and heiress:

1a Olivia; b 1591; m 1608, as his 1st w, Sir John Stanhope, of Elvaston, Staffs (see HARRINGTON, E)

2 Thomas, of Newton Grange, Derbys; fought Agincourt; m Agnes (d 16 March 1467), dau and heiress of Robert Hassell, of Arcluyd, Cheshire, and d 21 March 1473, having had, with eight other sons and five daus:

(1) Aden, of Bentley; m Elizabeth, dau of Roger Eyre, of Keyton, Notts, and had issue, which failed in the male line in the 5th generation

(2) Thomas, of Newton; m 1st Margaret, dau and heiress of Roger Wolgattethorp; m 2nd Alice Basset, of Blore, and dsp by 1512

(3) Hugh, of Newton; m Agnes, dau of John Longsdore, of Little Longstone, Derbys, and d 1516, being ancestor of:

1a Richard, of Newton Grange, Fenny Bentley, and Ashbourne, Derbys; ggf of:

1b William Hugh, of Altonsfield, Esher, Surrey; MRCS, S African War medal and clasp, 3rd Cl Osmanieh and Medjidie

(4) HUMPHREY, for whom see further below

(5) Edward, of Barnborough, Yorks; Reader Gray's Inn c 1524; m Joan, only child of Pierce Claughton, and d 1531, leaving:

1a Dionysius, of Gray's Inn 1545

(6) Denys, of Cutthorpe, ancestor of the BERESFORDs of Rickmansworth

(7) Lawrence, of Lea Hall; m Anne, dau of Thomas Cockaine, of Lea, and dsp by c 1520

(8) James; Vicar Chesterfield 1484–1520, LLD, Canon Res and Preb Lichfield, founded 1512 Beresford's Chantry in Fenny Bentley Church and two fellowships and two scholarships at St John's Coll Cambridge (to be called Beresford Fellows for ever)

THOMAS BERESFORD's 4th s here noticed,

HUMPHREY BERESFORD, of Newton Grange; m Margery, dau of Edmond Bardesley, of Bardesley, and had a yr s:

GEORGE BERESFORD, of Newton Grange; Steward Nottingham; m Eleanor, dau of Thomas Greene, and had an est s:

MICHAEL BERESFORD, of Otford and the Squirres, Kent; living 1574; Offr Ct of Wards; m Rose, dau of John Knevitt, and had, with two er and four yr sons and four daus:

TRISTRAM BERESFORD; b 1574; manager Society of the New Plantation in Ulster temp JAMES I; settled Coleraine, Co Londonderry, and had an er s:

Sir Tristram Beresford, 1st Bt (I), so cr 5 May 1665, of Coleraine; MP (I Parl) Cos Derry, Donegal and Tyrone 1656–58 and Co Derry 1661–66; m 1st Anne, est dau of John Rowley, of Castleroe, Co Londonderry, and had, with two daus (d unm):

1 RANDAL (Sir), **2nd Bt**

Sir Tristram m 2nd Sarah Sackville and d 15 Jan 1673, having by her had, with other issue:

2 Michael; m 17– — and had:

(1) Sackville (Rev); MA

(1) Anne; m 17 Oct 1747 Thomas Taylor, Ld Mayor Dublin 1751

1 Sarah; m 1st Paul Brazier and had issue; m 2nd Edward Cary, of Dungiven, and d 13 April 1683

Sir TRISTRAM's est s,

Sir Randal Beresford, 2nd Bt; MP Coleraine; m 20 Feb 1662/3 Catharine (d 3 April 1701), yr dau of 1st Viscount Valentia (qv), and was bur 19 Oct 1681, having had:

1 TRISTRAM (Sir), **3rd Bt**

1 Jane; m Lt-Gen Frederick Hamilton (d 26 March 1732), of Walworth, Co Derry, and dsp 1716

2 Catherine; m 1697 Matthew Pennefather, MP Cashel, yr bro of Kingsmill Pennefather, of New Park, Co Tipperary

Sir RANDAL's s,

Sir Tristram Beresford, 3rd Bt; Cdr Foot Regt against JAMES II, attainted by 1689 Dublin Parl; m 1687 Nichola Sophia (m 2nd 1704, as his 1st w, Lt-Gen Richard Gorges, and d 23 Feb 1713 aged 46), yst dau and coheir of 1st Lord Hamilton, Baron of Glenawly, and d 16 June 1701, having had, with other issue:

1 MARCUS, **1st Earl**

1 Susanna Catherina; m 1703 Hyacinth Richard, self-styled 2nd Baron Nugent of Riverston (see WESTMEATH, E), and dsp 8 March 1733

2 Jane; m c 30 March 1711 Gorges Lowther, MP (d 11 June 1716), of Kilrue, Co Meath, and d 20 Oct 1764, leaving issue (see CROFTON, B)

Sir TRISTRAM's s,

Sir Marcus Beresford, 4th Bt, and **1st Earl of Tyrone**, so cr 18 July 1746, as also earlier 4 Nov 1720 BARON BERESFORD, of Beresford, Co Cavan, and VISCOUNT TYRONE (all I); b 16 July 1694; MP (I Parl) Coleraine 1715–20; m 16 July 1717 Katherine Poer, **Baroness La Poer** (d 27 July 1769), dau and heiress of 3rd Earl of Tyrone (see above), and d 4 April 1763, having had, with other issue:

1 GEORGE DE LA POER, **1st Marquess**

2 John, PC (GB and I); b 14 March 1737/8; barrister, Commr Revenue Ireland 1770, Pres Bd Revenue, Taster Wines Port of Dublin 1772; m 1st 12 Nov 1760 Anne Constantin (d 26 Oct 1770), dau of Gen Count de Ligondes, of house of Ligondes, Auvergne, France, leaving:

(1) Marcus; b 14 Feb 1764; m 25 Feb 1791 Lady Frances Arabella Leeson (d May 1840), dau of 1st Earl of Milltown (see 1970 edn), and d 16 Nov 1797, leaving, with a dau:

1a John Theophilus; b 1792; k in Spain 19 Jan 1812

2a William; b 17 April 1797; Maj, MP N Essex 1847–65, Sec for War 1852; m 19 Dec 1833 Catherine (d 16 June 1895 aged 88), yst dau of George Robert Heneage, of Hainton Hall, Lincs (see 1967 edn HENEAGE, B), and d 6 Oct 1883, leaving:

1b Mostyn de la Poer; b 6 Dec 1835; Lt-Gen, Col Seaforth Highrs; d unm 19 Aug 1911

2b Edward Marcus; b 11 Dec 1836; Maj-Gen; d unm 14 Jan 1896

1b Frances Arabella; m 27 Aug 1867 Hon Reginald Grimston Standish O'Grady (dsp Dec 1874; see 1953 edn GUILLAMORE, V) and d 7 May 1924

(2) George de la Poer (Rt Rev); b 19 July 1765; Bp Kilmore and Ardagh; m 1794 Frances (d May 1843), dau of Gervais Parker Bushe, of Kilfane, MP Kilkenny, and niece of Henry Grattan, and d 16 Oct 1841, having had:

1a John; b April 1796; Colonial Sec St Vincent; m 6 May 1822 Harriet Eliza (d 11 Oct 1857), est dau of Hon William Wylly, Ch Justice St Vincent, and d 10 Sept 1856, having had, with other issue:

1b George William de la Poer; b 5 June 1823; m 19 June 1848 Elizabeth Hannah Nicholson, dau of Capt Donald Maclean, and d 7 July 1903, having had:

1c Donald John de la Poer; b 6 Feb 1852; dsp 1896

2c Arthur George de la Poer; b 18 Nov 1853; m 7 April 1877 Ellen Stuart (d 3 Jan 1946), dau of George Mayo, FRCP, and d 1924, leaving:

1d Arthur Mordaunt de la Poer; b 16 Nov 1877; Canadian Forces WW I (twice wounded); m 1910 Mary Elizabeth (d 19–), dau of James Ryan, of Hazelgrove, NSW, and dsp 19–

2d George Stuart de la Poer; b 16 Nov 1877; mining engr; m 1st 9 Sept 1900 Margaret (d 24 Dec 1920), dau of Edward Hooper, of Melbourne, and had:

1e Arthur de la Poer; b 28 Sept 1903; m 1926 Helen (d 13 Feb 1973), dau of Thomas Cull, of Perth, W Australia, and d 6 March 1931, leaving:

1f +John de la Poer [John Beresford Esq, 3 Park Way, Murray Lakes, South Yunderup, W Australia 6208]; b 11 Aug 1927; sr tech offr Cwlth Sci and Industl Research Org (ret 1986); m 25 Aug 1951 *Pamela Mary, dau of Glen J Sloman, of Applecross, W Australia, and has:

1g +Marcus de la Poer [Marcus Beresford Esq, c/o 3 Park Way, Murray Lakes, South Yunderup, W Australia 6208]; b 10 Aug 1952; m 1991 *Rilla Commins and has:

1h *Celeste Pamela; b 6 Oct 1995

2h *Natasha Ray; b 6 Oct 1995

2g +Graham de la Poer [Graham Beresford Esq, 7 Characin Ct, Sorrento, W Australia 6020]; *b* 21 April 1954; *m* 1981 *Josephine Vasalo and has:

    1h *Laurin Louise; *b* 18 April 1987

3g +Simon Stuart de la Poer [Simon Beresford Esq, 28 Gill St, Nth Perth, W Australia 6006]; *b* 28 March 1961; *m* 1991 *Dr Elizabeth Parker and has:

    1h *Georgia Kate; *b* 4 May 1997

1g *Shelley Louise de la Poer [Mrs Graham Ekert, 10b Boya Cres, Boya, W Australia 6056]; *b* 13 Sept 1957; *m* 1980 *Graham Ekert and has:

    1h *Cassandra Clare; *b* 6 March 1985

    2h *Melissa Louise; *b* 5 May 1987

    3h *Alexandra Michelle; *b* 4 June 1990

1f *Margaret Pamela de la Poer [Mrs Eric McCormick, 12 Hawkesbury Cres, Farrer, ACT 2607, Australia]; *b* 21 May 1930; *m* 25 July 1953 *Lt-Col Eric McPherson McCormick, Roy Australian Regt (ret), and has:

    1g *Gordon Rory [Gordon McCormick Esq, 16 Beresford St, Deakin, ACT 2600, Australia]; *b* 14 June 1954; *m* 1982 *Alice Jeanette Robinson and has:

        1h *Fergus George; *b* 29 Nov 1984

        1h *Harriet Faith; *b* 23 Dec 1986

    2g *Peter James [Peter McCormick Esq, 11 McManus Pl, Calwell, ACT 2905, Australia]; *b* 4 March 1956; *m* 1983 *Jennifer Louise Spence and has:

        1h *Rory Michael; *b* 12 Feb 1984

        2h *Mitchell James; *b* 26 Jan 1986

        1h *Georgia Mae; *b* 7 Feb 1991

        2h *Isabella Grace; *b* 9 Jan 1995

    3g *Angus Rory [Angus McCormick Esq, 231 Namatjira Dve, Fisher, ACT 2611, Australia]; *b* 23 Sept 1957; *m* 1985 *Dianna Marie McKeough and has:

        1h *Thomas John; *b* 19 March 1990

        1h *Ashleigh Louise; *b* 10 Jan 1987

    4g *Hamish John [Hamish McCormick Esq, 9 Menkens Ct, Swinger Hill, ACT 2607, Australia]; *b* 15 Nov 1961; Dip Serv

2e Brian de la Poer, MC; *b* 28 Sept 1910; barrister, Maj Australian Forces WW II (despatches twice); *m* 10 April 1942 *Valmai (*m* 2nd G J Thomas (*d* 1987)), only dau of Merlyn B Jones, of Perth, W Australia, and was *ka* New Guinea 7 Dec 1942, leaving:

    1f +Brian George de la Poer [Brian Beresford Esq, 3 Circe Circle, Dalkeith, W Australia]; *b* posthumously 21 April 1943; barrister, slr; *m* 1964 *Deborah Frances, only dau of A F Gamble, of Koorda, W Australia, and has:

        1g +Brian James de la Poer; *b* 28 Sept 1967; *m* 30 Sept 1995 *Nina Jane Dempster

        1g *Victoria Jane de la Poer; *b* 12 Jan 1965; *m* 1993 *Ian Peter Rakich and has:

            1h *Georgia Grace; *b* 29 Dec 1994

            2h *Eliza Loveday; *b* 28 Feb 1998

1e Marjory Ellen de la Poer; *b* 10 Nov 1901; *d* 1988

2e *Rosemary de la Poer; *b* 28 Jan 1917; *m* 7 Feb 1948 *Reginald Harold Sutton, DFC and bar, Croix de Guerre, F/Lt RAAF (*d* 1991), and has:

    1f *David Beresford [David Sutton Esq, 79 Florence Rd, Nedlands, W Australia]; *b* 1953; consulting engr; *m* 1980 *Catherine Jane Brewster and has:

        1g *Hannah Catherine; *b* 1986

        2g *Brigitte Rose; *b* 1989

    1f *Georgia Jane [Mrs James Hutchison, Cottage Farm, Obi Obi Rd, Mapleton, Queensland, Australia]; *b* Dec 1948; *m* 1st 1979 (*divorce* 1987) Peter Jonathan Schofield; *m* 2nd 1991 *James Richard Hutchison and by her 1st husb has:

        1g *Jonathan Henry; *b* 1986

    1f Rosemary Ann; *b* 1950; *m* 1974 *William Richard Kilpatrick and *d* 19–, leaving:

        1g *Jane Regina; *b* 1977

        2g *Catharine Ann; *b* 1979

        3g *Annabel Clare; *b* 1984

2d (cont.) George Beresford *m* 2nd 10 April 1923 Kathleen (*d* 12 June 1950), dau of Thomas Cull, of Perth, W Australia; *m* 3rd 18 Nov 1950 Faith (*d* 1984), dau of Rev Frederick George O'Halloran, of Perth, W Australia, and widow of S/Ldr Preston Williams, MC, and *d* 1965

3d Marcus John de la Poer; *b* 6 June 1882; *m* 1st 4 Feb 1911 Alice Janet (*d* 17 Sept 1935), dau of John Smith, of Victoria, Australia; *m* 2nd 1936 *Edith, dau of Capt George Wilkins, of Young, NSW, and *d* 28 April 1952, having had by his 1st w:

    1e +Marcus de la Poer; *b* 13 Jan 1912; *m* 25 April 1937 *Marie, dau of Edward Helmers, of Jincumbilly, Ando, NSW, and has had:

        1f +Marcus Edward de la Poer; *b* 30 Jan 1938

        2f +Brian Ernest de la Poer; *b* 13 March 1942

        1f Margaret Emily de la Poer; *b* 14 June 1946; *d* 19–

    2e +John de la Poer; *b* 29 April 1913; AIF WW II 1944–45; *m* 1936 *Helen Wilson and has:

        1f +John de la Poer; *b* 1942

        1f *Helen de la Poer; *b* 1937

        2f *Barbara de la Poer; *b* 1940

4d Charles Clement de la Poer; *b* 10 Feb 1885; *d* 19–

5d Henry Mayo de la Poer; *b* 29 May 1889; AIF WW I (wounded); *m* 26 Jan 1921 Nathalie (*d* 6 April 1963), dau of Robert Muir, of Middle Brighton, Victoria, and *d* 3 Jan 1948, leaving:

    1e *Joan de la Poer [Mrs Ralph Bewick, Corner Cottage, Sandy Lane, Kingswood, Surrey KT20 6LZ]; *b* 10 Dec 1922; *m* 13 March 1965 Ralph Louis Bewick, MBE, TD, Roy Fus (*d* 1985)

    2e *Judith de la Poer [Mrs Judith Hone, Unit 1, 16 Alpha St, Kensington Pk, S Aust 5068, Australia]; *b* 24 April 1930; *m* 10 Feb 1954 (*divorce* 1983) Lt Col Robin William Hone, Roy Australian Regt (*d* 1992), s of Col Ronald Bertram Hone, ED, and has:

        1f *David Christopher [David Hone Esq, 57 Gainsford St, London SE1 2NB]; *b* 4 May 1958; *m* 13 Nov 1993 *Wendy Jane, dau of Barry Moss, and has:

            1g *Luke William; *b* 18 May 1995

        1f *Carolyn Louise [Mrs Andrew McLean, 1 Mitchell Rd, Mosman, NSW 2088, Australia]; *b* 29 Oct 1963; *m* 1984 *Andrew John McLean and has:

            1g *Christopher Andrew; *b* 27 Aug 1987

            1g *Alexandra Louise; *b* 7 Jan 1993

            2g *Anastasia Leah; *b* 30 May 1994

6d William Russell de la Poer, MC (1918); *b* 31 Oct 1893; Capt Australian Inf WW I (wounded, despatches); *m* 1923 Marie Isobel (*d* 19 Dec 1944), dau of Samuel Cowper Ward, of Adelaide, S Australia, and *d* 13 Sept 1938, leaving:

    1e *Diana Mary de la Poer [Mrs Arthur Watson, 139 Stanley St, N Adelaide, S Australia]; *b* 1924; *m* 6 July 1946 Arthur John Watson, AM (late Lt RANR), s of Arthur Harrison Edward Watson, MB, BS, of Yorketown, S Australia, and has:

        1f *Christopher John Beresford [Christopher Watson Esq, 69, Highlever Rd, London W10]; *b* 6 Nov 1948; *m* 1st 1970 (*divorce* 1976) Georgina Henry and has:

            1g *Michaela; *b* 1970

        1f (cont.) Christopher Watson *m* 2nd *Lalita Georgiana Williams, dau of W Peter Halliday, MBE, and by her has:

            2g *Adelaide Elizabeth Beresford; *b* 1982

            3g *Francesca Mary Beresford; *b* 1984

        1f *Johanna Mary Beresford [Mrs Geoffrey Scott, 11 Ferdinand St, Hunters Hill, NSW, Australia]; *b* 28 Sept 1950; *m* 1st 1973 (*divorce* 1979) Rolf Alexander Detmering; *m* 2nd 1992 *Geoffrey Robert Scott and by him has:

            1g *Georgia Anne Beresford; *b* 1992

        1f (cont.) Mrs Geoffrey Scott also has by Ian Darnton Hill:

            2g Phoebe Jane Beresford; *b* 1981

        2f *Robina Anne Beresford [Mrs Richard Daw, 40 Melville St, Hawthorn, Victoria, Australia]; *b* 19 Jan 1960; *m* 1986 *Richard Goldsmith Daw

    2e *Marie Suzanne de la Poer [Mrs David Heysen, Heysen Rd, Hahndorf, S Australia 5245]; *b* 1925; *m* 1946 Murray Frew Bonnin, LLB, BA, Capt AIF (*d* 1978); *m* 2nd 1979 *David Hans Heysen and has by her 1st husb:

        1f *John Frew; *b* 2 Jan 1951

        2f *David Frew; *b* 9 May 1952; *m* 1st Jennifer Crowe; *m* 2nd 1989 *Angela Jane Dunstan and has by her:

            1g *William Frew; *b* 1990

            2g *Annabel Beresford; *b* 1992

1d Isabel Marion de la Poer; *b* 8 Feb 1880; *m* Oct 1911 Herbert Woodham (*d* 1917), of Romsey, Hants, and *d* 19–, having had issue

3c Richard de la Poer; *b* 23 June 1856; barrister; *m* 15 June 1887 Sydney Julia (*d* 1920), dau of John Acraman, of Adelaide, and *d* 1917, leaving:

    1d Claude Richard de la Poer; *b* 9 March 1888; *m* 10 Nov 1915 Edith Marion (*d* 1977) dau of Christopher Beaven, of Adelaide, Australia, and *d* 1945, leaving:

        1e +Ben Richard de la Poer [Ben Beresford Esq, 36 Brunswick Street, N Walkerville, S Australia 5081]; *b* 1927; formerly RAN, ASA, memb Australian Stock Exchange; *m* 1955 *Janet Marcia, dau of John Essington Grime, of Erina, NSW, and has:

            1f +William Richard de la Poer [William Beresford Esq, 472 Argyle St, Moss Vale, NSW 2577, Australia]; *b* 29 May 1959; BVSc; *m* 1987 *Sally Isobel, dau of John Walsh, of Sutton Forest, NSW, and has:

                1g *Samantha Jane; *b* 1988

                2g *Georgia Kate; *b* 1993

            2f +John Ben de la Poer; *b* 25 Aug 1965; BAGSC

            3f +Charles Patrick de la Poer [Charles Beresford Esq, 67 First Ave, St Peters, S Australia 5069, Australia]; *b* 30 Oct 1966; LLB; *m* 1992 *Sarah Jane, dau of Colin Hagger, of N Adelaide, and has:

                1g *Kate Victoria; *b* 1995

                2g *Mary Alexandra; *b* 1997

            1f *Mary Lynne de la Poer [Mrs Stewart Teague, 354A Kensington Rd, Erindale, S Australia]; *b* 16 July 1956; *m* 1977 *Stewart Graham Teague and has:

            1g *Nicholas James; *b* 1982

            2g *Andrew Graham; *b* 1984

            3g *James Robert; *b* 1986

            4g *Benjamin Stewart; *b* 1988

            1g *Sarah Jane; *b* 1980

    2e +Donald Charles de la Poer [Donald Beresford Esq, 55/186 Sutherland St, Paddington, NSW 2021, Australia]; *b* 1933; *m* 1962 (*divorce* 1979) Ruth, dau of Charles Henry Tisdall, of Seaford, Sussex, and has:

        1f +Peter Mark de la Poer; *b* 1965

        1f *Susan Jane de la Poer; *b* 1964

1e *Sydney May de la Poer [Mrs Leonard Evans, 116 Walkerville Terrace, Walkerville, SA 5081, Australia]; *b* 1917; *m* 1937 Leonard Arthur Ranson Evans, CA (*d* 1989) and has:

  1f *Michael John de la Poer Beresford [Michael Evans Esq, 17 William St, Hawthorn, SA 5062, Australia]; *b* 15 Oct 1941; *m* 1971 *Rachel Anne, dau of Rev Robert Alexander Wyndham, of Richmond, S Australia, and has:

    1g *(David) Michael Wyndham; *b* 1974

    1g *(Kathryn) Mary; *b* 1973

  1f *Elizabeth Jane; *b* 23 July 1946; *m* 1971 (*divorce* 1993) Whalley de Quetteville Robin, s of Prof C R Robin, of U of Adelaide, and has:

    1g *Ben de Quetteville; *b* 1975

    1g *Anne Sutton; *b* 1973

    2g *Mary de Quetteville; *b* 1978

2e *Molly Clodagh de la Poer [Mrs Harold Amphlett, 50 Second Ave, St Peters, SA 5069, Australia]; *b* 1920; *m* 1940 Harold de Vall Amphlett (*d* 1988), AIF, and has:

  1f *John de Vall; *b* 1949; *m* 1976 Margaret, dau of Robert Stokes, and has:

    1g *Scott Francis; *b* 1980

    2g *Mark John de Vall; *b* 1982

    1g *Alice Louise; *b* 1988

  1f *Margaret de Vall; *b* 1947; *m* 1968 *Daniel Knight and has:

    1g *Andrew de Vall; *b* 1971

    1g *(Rebecca) Anne; *b* 1974

2d Guy Errol de la Poer; *b* 11 Oct 1889; AIF WW I (wounded); *m* 1921 Dorothy Margaret (*d* 1956), dau of W T McCoy, of Adelaide, and *d* 25 Jan 1944, leaving:

  1e +Richard de la Poer [Richard Beresford Esq, 5 George St, Norwood, SA 5067, Australia]; *b* 31 July 1922; RAAF WW II; *m* 20 Jan 1945 *Elizabeth Leitch and has:

    1f +Marcus Richard de la Poer [Marcus Beresford Esq, PO Box 113, Mitcham, SA 5062, Australia]; *b* 11 Nov 1950

    1f *Melanie de la Poer; *b* 24 Aug 1948

  1e *Margaret de la Poer; *b* 29 Dec 1925; *m* 6 Aug 1947 *Jan Edgar Marr, late AIF, and has:

    1f *Carolyn Ann; *b* 19–

    2f *Stephanie Jane; *b* 19–

    3f *Katrina Louise; *b* 19–

1d Eileen May de la Poer, MBE (1942); *b* 11 May 1894; Coronation medal; *m* 3 May 1916 Harold Rischbieth, FRCS (*d* 13 Nov 1943), s of Charles Rischbieth, of Glenelg, S Australia, and *d* 1978, having:

  1e *John Beresford Wills, VRD; *b* 17 Aug 1917; Lt RANR WW II; *m* 4 Aug 1944 *Joan, dau of Joseph Osborne Stephenson, of Claremont, W Australia, and has:

    1f *Ian Harold; *b* 10 Oct 1954

    1f *Peggy Jane; *b* 28 June 1956

  2e *Henry George, VRD; *b* 18 Jan 1920; FRACP, Surg Lt RANR WW II; *m* 25 Jan 1945 *Nancy Fearon [Mrs Henry Rischbieth, 306 Ward St, N Adelaide, S Australia], dau of Geoffrey Koeppen Henderson, MC, MM, of Adelaide, and *d* 4 Dec 1977, leaving:

    1f *Geoffrey John [Geoffrey Rischbieth Esq, 306 Ward St, N Adelaide, S Australia 5006]; *b* 17 Aug 1956; *m* 26 Nov 1983 *Catherine Louise, dau of John Price Cooper, of Belair, and has:

      1g *James Henry John; *b* 17 Aug 1990

      1g *Briony Anne; *b* 13 March 1994

    1f *Margot Henderson; *b* 13 April 1949; *m* 2 Dec 1972 *Bruce Alexander Rosser and has:

      1g *Andrew John Rischbieth; *b* 30 Dec 1982

      2g *Geoffrey Rischbieth; *b* 30 Sept 1986

      1g *Anne Rischbieth; *b* 7 Oct 1977

      2g *Jane Margaret Rischbieth; *b* 23 Jan 1981

    2f *Judith Anne; *b* 23 Jan 1951; *m* 21 Dec 1977 *Peter Haskett and has:

      1g *Matthew Henry Thomas; *b* 17 July 1980

      2g *Hugh Edwin Robert; *b* 6 Feb 1982

      3g *Mark Ashik; *b* 23 June 1987

      4g *Timothy Surresh; *b* 17 Aug 1983

      1g *Amy Louise; *b* 15 Sept 1978

      2g *Bridget Anne; *b* 16 March 1985

      3g *Natasha Carmel; *b* 20 Jan 1989

      4g *Lucy Claire; *b* 26 June 1992

    3f *Suzanne Joan; *b* 1 July 1955; *m* 27 Nov 1976 *James Harvey and has:

      1g *Henry Aberdein Richard; *b* 4 Nov 1980

      2g *Lachlan Mungo; *b* 22 Dec 1982

      3g *Declan Holroyd; *b* 20 March 1992

      1g *Georgina Llevelys; *b* 20 Nov 1985

3e *Richard Harold Charles [Dr Richard Rischbieth, 70A Church Terrace, Walkerville, S Australia]; *b* 4 Aug 1927; MB, BS, MRCP, FRACP; *m* 23 March 1957 *Judith Ann, dau of Robert K Wood, of Adelaide, and has:

  1f *Peter Robert [Dr Peter Rischbieth, St Margaret, Algate, S Australia]; *b* 25 Nov 1957; MBBS; *m* 27 Nov 1981 *Amanda Mary, dau of James Griggs, of Adelaide, and has:

    1g *Thomas James; *b* 12 March 1987

    2g *William Hugh; *b* 3 Dec 1989

2f *Henry Mark [Mr Henry Rischbieth, 7 Averel Gdns Rd, Medislie, S Australia]; *b* 7 Dec 1958; *m* 5 April 1986 *Elaine Gearing, dau of David Tomlin, and has:

  1g *Emma Iles; *b* 13 March 1987

3f *Thomas John Hugh, of Loveday, S Australia; *b* 9 March 1962; LLB; *m* 22 Dec 1990 *Careena Hoskins and has:

  1g *Jake Samuel David; *b* 7 Sept 1992

  1g *Brooke Storm; *b* 30 April 1995

1f *Anne Caroline [Mrs Philip Arnfield, 40 Church Terrace, Walkerville, S Australia]; *b* 6 May 1960; *m* 27 Sept 1981 *Philip Arnfield and has:

  1g *Patrick George; *b* 7 Sept 1989

  2g *Samuel Richard; *b* 15 March 1993

  1g *Sarah Rose; *b* 7 Sept 1989

4c George Clement de la Poer; *b* 8 March 1865; *d* 5 March 1877

1c May; *d* unm

2c Ethel Maude; *m* 1882 Alexander McCulloch (*d* 1932), and *dsp* 19–

3c Dora; *d* unm 12 April 1948

1b Marcus Wylly de la Poer; *b* 22 Feb 1825; Col 49th Foot; *m* 24 Jan 1852 Charlotte (*d* 31 Oct 1906), 3rd dau of Capt R Blakeney, and *d* 12 Feb 1902, leaving, with a dau (*d* unm):

  1c John Blakeney de la Poer; *b* 16 Sept 1856; Lt Madras SC, Capt and Hon Maj 3rd Roy Berks Regt, Lt-Col 1st Cadet Bn London Regt; *m* 18 March 1903 (*divorce* 1917) Mrs Amy Eva Burrows, dau of William Cameron Gourlay, and *d* 22 May 1930

  2c Marcus Henry de la Poer, CMG, ISO; *b* 1857; Sec N Nigeria Admin 1903–11; *m* 1st 8 June 1882 Margery Mary (*d* 18 Oct 1920), dau of Rev John Connell, and had:

    1d Marcus John de la Poer; *b* 1883; Colonial CS; *m* 29 Oct 1914 Agnes Emily, only dau of Robert Bulkeley Pitt, of Dormansland, Surrey, and *dsp* 9 July 1941

    2d Julian Walter de la Poer; *b* 1886; Capt Inland War Tport; *m* 1921 (*divorce* 1940) Henriette Josephine Amelie Geraldine, dau of Col Cmdt B Bochart, of Namur, Belgium

  2c (cont.) Marcus Beresford *m* 2nd 31 Dec 1921 Florence Mary (*d* 7 Oct 1922), dau of Edward Mitchell, and *d* 22 Feb 1934

  3c Charles George de la Poer; *b* 1861; *d* 11 July 1937

  1c Mary Maude; *m* 8 Nov 1883 Julian Russell Sturgis (*d* 13 April 1904) and *d* 30 April 1952, leaving issue

3b John Hill de la Poer; *b* 15 May 1832; Colonial Sec Tobago; *m* 26 March 1859 Emma, 4th dau of Alexander Macleod, and *d* 3 Aug 1863, leaving:

  1c Eva Matilda; *b* 18–; *d* 18–

1b Henry Clements, *b* 1835; Capt 69th Regt; *m* 23 June 1857 Matilda (*d* 1 Jan 1884), yst dau of Sir Francis Hincks, KCMG, Govr Windward Isles, and drowned 19 Sept 1865

1b Mary Bayley; *m* 29 April 1862 Col Shadwell Henry Clerke (*d* 1891), Gentleman-at-Arms to HM QUEEN VICTORIA, and *d* 4 June 1909, leaving issue

2a Marcus Gervais (Most Rev); *b* 14 Feb 1801; DD, Bp Kilmore, Elphin, and Ardagh 1854–62, Archbp Armagh, Ld Primate Ireland, Prelate Order St Patrick; *m* 1st 25 Oct 1824 Mary (*d* 31 Dec 1845), dau of Col Henry Peisley L'Estrange, of Moystown, King's Co, and widow of R E Digby, of Geashell, and had, with a dau (*d* unm):

  1b George de la Poer, JP, DL, of Aubawn, Co Cavan; *b* 22 April 1831; High Sheriff 1867, MP Armagh 1875–85; *m* 24 April 1860 Mary Annabella (*d* 11 July 1917), dau of Rev William Vernon Harcourt (*see* VERNON, B), and *d* 3 Aug 1906, having had, with a dau (*d* unm):

    1c Marcus William; *b* 8 May 1862; Capt Rifle Bde; *d* unm 7 Aug 1900

    2c Edward; *b* 11 Sept 1863; *m* 1st 1886 Emily Constance Frederica (*d* 30 Oct 1889), dau of Henry Beilby Milner (*see* MILNER, Bt), and had:

      1d Mary Emily; *m* 8 Aug 1907 Reginald Moreton and *d* 6 March 1935, leaving issue (*see* DUCIE, E)

      2d Aline Constance Caroline; *m* 1914 Allan Havelock-Allan (*d* 7 Nov 1949), 2nd s of Lt-Gen Sir Henry Marshman Havelock-Allan, 1st Bt (*qv*), and *d* 28 May 1967, leaving issue

    2c (cont.) Edward Beresford *m* 2nd 30 April 1903 Florence Lilian (*d* 16 Dec 1940), dau of Capt Hon Reynolds Moreton, DL, RN (*see* DUCIE, E), and *d* 18 June 1939, having by her had:

      1d George Henry William de la Poer; *b* 25 June 1904; *m* 17 Nov 1926 (*divorce* 1949) Mary Isobel (*d* 1969), dau of George Gibson Richardson, of E Molesey, and *d* 19 Oct 1961, leaving:

        1e +John George de la Poer [John Beresford Esq, Aubawn, Lamorna Cove, Penzance, Cornwall TR19 6XW]; *b* 9 Aug 1927; *m* 17 Sept 1960 *Jeanne Frances, dau of William T Steward, and has:

          1f +Stephen de la Poer; *b* 19 July 1961; *m* 1991 *Aline Rogers and has:

            1g +Jack George de la Poer; *b* 25 Aug 1993

            2g +Philip Alexander de la Poer; *b* 11 March 1996

          2f +Mark de la Poer; *b* 13 July 1962; *m* 1989 *Sophie Grissa and has:

            1g +Justin de la Poer; *b* 9 Sept 1989

            1g *Heloise; *b* 11 April 1992

          1f *Clare Jeanne; *b* 16 Sept 1964

        2e *Timothy Edward de la Poer; *b* 30 Nov 1931; *m* 20 Sept 1955 *Mary Thom Leburn (Maureen) [Mrs Matthew Forrester, Little Etchden, Bethersden, Kent TN26 3DS] (*m* 2nd 28 April 1965 Maj Matthew Alexander Forrester (*d* 5 May 1998)), only child of John Waugh, of Edinburgh, and *d* 7 Feb 1964, leaving:

          1f +Michael John de la Poer; *b* 29 Dec 1957

          1f *Karen Mary de la Poer; *b* 17 Nov 1959; *m* 1984 *Gordon James Findlay, er s of James Findlay

1c Kathleen Mathilda; *m* 3 Sept 1925 Henry Edward Harcourt Rice (*d* 10 April 1944), of Dane Court, Dover, and North Court, Eastry, and *d* 12 Nov 1948

1b Henry Marcus; *b* 2 March 1835; Maj 9th Foot; *m* 10 April 1861 Julia Ellen (*d* 13 Oct 1923), dau of Rev Francis Richard Maunsell, Rector Castle Island, Co Kerry, and *d* 5 Feb 1895, leaving:

1c Kennedy, of Charlton Lodge, Cheltenham; *b* 25 Jan 1862; Lt-Col Roy Irish Rifles; *m* 1st 7 March 1894 Grace (*d* 15 Sept 1931), 3rd dau of Maj J F Des Barres, and had:

1d +Gervais de la Poer, MBE (1942), MC, DSM; *b* 29 Nov 1895; Lt-Col RE WW I (despatches, 2nd Cl Order St Anne Russia with swords), WW II: Staff Offr RE W Cmd HQ 1939–44, Liaison Offr Belgian Forces in Belgium, Holland and Germany 1944–45, Br Resident Brunswick, Holzminden and Emden-Leek with CCG 1945–52; *m* 1st 1927 Nada Celina (*d* 2 March 1956), est dau of Harry L Wormald, and has:

1e +Michael Marcus Gervais de la Poer [Michael Beresford Esq, 26 Ladbroke Sq, London W11]; *b* 8 Aug 1928; *educ* Marlborough, Birmingham U (B Comm) and Harvard (MBA); Lt 8th Hus 1948–49; *m* 1975 *Ann Veronica Nieburg, of S Africa

1d (cont.) Gervais Beresford *m* 2nd 3 April 1957 *Rosemary Helen Arnaud, yr dau of Lt-Col G E Painter, RE, of Epsom, and formerly w of Derrick Newall Gange, and *d* 1979

1d Sybil; *m* 1st 24 May 1915 (*divorce* 1938) Capt Bernard de Lerisson Cazenove, MC, 3rd Bn Roy Scots (*d* 19 March 1947), and had issue; *m* 2nd 28 April 1938 Lt-Col Vincent Marcus Barron Scully, DSO, OBE, Border Regt, s of Vincent Scully, of Mantle Hill, Golden, Co Tipperary, and *d* 15 Nov 1970

1c (cont.) Kennedy Beresford *m* 2nd 29 Jan 1935 Rose Miriam (*d* 27 Nov 1951), 4th dau of Lt-Col Anthony Oliver Molesworth, RA (see MOLESWORTH, V), and *d* 25 April 1943

2c Marcus Francis; *b* 26 Dec 1862; *m* 10 April 1894 Fanny Catherine (*d* 3 Feb 1914), dau of Richard Robert Wingfield (see POWERSCOURT, V) and widow of 6th Earl of Wicklow (see 1970 edn), and *dsp* 12 Dec 1896

3c George Charles; *b* 10 July 1864; *d* 21 Feb 1938

4c Henry Lowry Lambert; *b* Nov 1869; MIME, Lt RE; *d* 25 Sept 1932

1c Eva Emily; *m* 27 April 1895 Anthony Fritz Maude (*d* 7 June 1935) and *d* 18 Feb 1960, leaving issue (see HAWARDEN, V)

1b Charlotte Henrietta; *m* 16 Aug 1853 Henry Beilby William Milner (*d* 7 June 1876), of W Retford, and *d* 15 Sept 1884, leaving issue (see MILNER, Bt)

2b Mary Emily; *m* 16 Aug 1853 Col Thomas Heywood, DL (*d* 2 April 1915), of Hatley St George, Worcs, and *d* 12 Aug 1858, leaving issue

2a (cont.) The Most Rev Marcus Beresford *m* 2nd 6 June 1850 Elizabeth (*d* 1 July 1870), only dau of James Trail Kennedy, of Annadale, Co Down, and widow of Robert George Bomford, of Rahenstown, Co Meath, and *d* 26 Dec 1885

3a George de la Poer; *d* unm 6 June 1826

1a Charlotte Mary; *m* 1st 2 May 1812 Frederick Lumley-Savile (*d* 27 Feb 1837), of Tickhill Castle, York, and had issue (see SCARBROUGH, E); *m* 2nd 20 July 1839 Robert Henry Southwell, MP (see SOUTHWELL, V), and *d* 1851

2a Frances; *m* 19 June 1824 Rev Hon Francis Howard (*d* 16 Feb 1857) and *d* 17 Nov 1833, leaving issue (see 1970 edn WICKLOW, E)

(3) John Claudius; *b* 23 Oct 1766; Alderman, Ld Mayor Dublin; *m* 3 March 1795 Elizabeth McKenzie, only child of Archibald Menzies, of Culdares, Peebles, and *d* 3 July 1846, leaving, with four daus:

1a John Claudius, of Craig Dhu Varren, Portrush; *b* 6 Dec 1799; *m* 7 April 1836 Catherine, dau of Lt William Cuddy, 69th Regt, and *dsp* 23 Nov 1866

(4) Charles Cobbe (Rev); *b* 2 Oct 1770; *m* 22 Nov 1795 Amelia (*d* 14 March 1839), dau of Sir William Montgomery, 1st Bt (see 1830 edn), and had, with other issue:

1a John Isaac (Rev); *b* 13 Oct 1796; *m* 13 June 1824 Sophia (*d* 27 Nov 1858), dau of Robert White, of Aghaboe, Queen's Co, and *d* 9 Feb 1847, leaving:

1b George Robert, of Macbie Hill, Peebles; *b* 18 Oct 1830; Capt 88th Foot, Chev Legn Hon; *d* unm 6 April 1871

1b Emily Sara, of Macbie Hill; *m* 6 May 1851 Very Rev John Maunsell MASSY later MASSY-BERESFORD (see MASSY, B) and *d* 28 July 1893

2b Harriette Selina; *m* 29 April 1856 William Allan Woddrop, of Dalmarnock, Glasgow, and Garvald House, Dolphington, W Lothian, and *d* his widow 13 Feb 1919

2a George John, of Woodhouse, Co Waterford; *b* 21 July 1807; Col RA; *m* 1st 12 Dec 1839 Jane Charlotte (*d* 6 April 1842), yst dau of Charles Riall, of Heywood, Co Tipperary, and had:

1b Jane Selina; *m* 18 Feb 1868 Rev William Power Cobbe (*d* 18 April 1889), Rector Clonegam, and *d* 10 Nov 1930, leaving issue

2a (cont.) George Beresford *m* 2nd 15 Nov 1844 Frances Constantia (*d* 29 Oct 1867), est dau of Robert Uniacke, of Woodhouse, Co Waterford, and *d* 11 Feb 1864, having by her had, with other issue:

1b Robert Henry, JP, DL (Waterford); *b* 8 Sept 1845; Lt 75th Foot; *m* 24 May 1880 Laura Ellen Flora (*d* 5 July 1920), yst dau of Sir John Henry Keane, 3rd Bt, of Cappoquin (*qv*), and widow of Capt B H Entwisle, 5th Dragoon Gds, and *dsp* 30 Jan 1903

2b John George, of Woodhouse, Stradbally, Co Waterford; *b* 10 June 1847; *m* 1st 21 Feb 1898 Emilie Eleanora (*d* 1916), dau of Adrian Iselin, of New York, and *m* 2nd 14 Feb 1922 Helen, dau of Alphonso Mason, of Philadelphia, and *d* 8 May 1925

3b Richard Uniacke (Rev); *b* 4 Sept 1858; Rector Inistioge, Co Kilkenny, Canon Leighlin, Canon and Precentor Ossory; *d* 30 Jan 1925

2b Mildred Anne; *b* 8 Sept 1845; *m* 18 Oct 1866 Rev William Carleton (*dsp* 1891), Rector Callan, Canon Ossory, and *d* 17 Nov 1922

3b Emily Frances Louisa; *m* 20 April 1911 Sir Robert Adair Hodson, 4th Bt (*qv*), and *d* 14 Feb 1933

3a Charles Claudius (Rev); *b* 14 Dec 1810; *m* 8 Aug 1838 Anna Maria, only dau of Rev Frederick Fitzpatrick, of Loch Scillan Glebe, Cavan, and *d* 29 Aug 1848, leaving, with two daus (*d* unm):

1b Charles Frederick Cobbe; *b* 3 May 1844; Col RE; *m* 18 Jan 1877 Edith Gertrude (*d* 3 March 1949), dau of Salisbury Baxendale, of Ware, Herts, and *d* 13 Dec 1925, having had:

1c Charles Claudius de la Poer; *b* 4 Oct 1879; Capt RE; *d* unm 30 May 1910

2c Salisbury de la Poer; *b* 6 Dec 1882; *educ* Balliol Coll Oxford (BA 1904); Lt RGA, Dist Control Offr E Prussian and Upper Silesian plebiscites 1920–22; *d* unm 4 Sept 1969

1c Edith Kathleen de la Poer; *m* 3 Sept 1918 Maj Norman Deakin, RAF (*d* 19 Oct 1930), of Leigh Grange, Netley Abbey, and *d* 6 Aug 1964 aged 86

2b Frederick John Isaac; *b* 1 Aug 1846; Capt 4th Bn Roy Irish Fus; *d* 15 Oct 1929

1a Harriet Louisa; *m* 15 Feb 1825 Rev John James Fox, gs of 1st Earl of Farnham (see FARNHAM, B) and *d* 24 Sept 1871, leaving issue

2a Selina Griselda; *m* 6 July 1837 3rd Earl of Erne (*qv*) and *d* 4 Sept 1884 aged 80, having had issue

3a Anne Constantia; *m* 2 March 1844 Lord John Thynne (see BATH, M) and *d* 22 April 1866

4a Charlotte Frances; *m* 4 Nov 1839 Rev Samuel Alexander, Rector Termon, and *d* his widow 27 Jan 1890, leaving issue

(1) Catharine; *m* 7 Aug 1778, as his 2nd w, Lt-Col Henry Theophilus Clements, PC (*d* 26 Oct 1795), and *d* 7 Jan 1836, leaving issue

(2) Annette Constantia; *m* 1st 1790 Robert Uniacke (*d* 1802), of Woodhouse, Co Waterford, and had issue; *m* 2nd 2 July 1805 Robert Doyne, JP, DL (*d* Dec 1850), of Wells, Co Wexford, and *d* 8 Aug 1836, having had further issue

(3) Jane; *m* 1788 Sir George Fitzgerald Hill, 2nd Bt (*qv*), and *dsp* 2 Nov 1836

2 John; *m* 2nd 4 June 1777 Barbara (*d* 2 Dec 1788), 2nd dau of Sir William Montgomery, 1st Bt (see 1830 edn), and *d* 5 Nov 1805, leaving, with other issue:

(5) James Hamilton; *b* 18 Feb 1782; Offr RN; drowned 7 Dec 1806 serving in HMS *Phoenix*

(6) Henry Barré, of Learmount Park, Co Derry; *b* 25 Sept 1784; *m* 29 Feb 1812 Eliza (*d* 22 Dec 1831), dau of John Baily, of Hambrook, Glos, and *d* 15 Dec 1837, leaving, with a dau (*d* unm):

1a John Barré, JP, DL, of Learmount Park; *b* 19 April 1815; MA Oxon; *m* 1st 23 April 1840 Sophia (*d* 21 March 1850), 3rd dau of Hugh Lyons-Montgomery, of Belhavel, Co Leitrim, and had:

1b Henry Barré Blacker; *b* 4 May 1848; Lt RN, Capt Mid-Ulster Art; *d* unm 14 Feb 1882

2b John Claudius Montgomery; *b* 3 Feb 1850; Maj RE, ADC to Ld Lt Ireland; *m* 16 Jan 1884 Rose Sophia Montgomery (*d* 15 Sept 1911), dau of Ralph Smith, of Greenhills, Co Louth, and *d* 19 Sept 1894, leaving:

1c Ralph Henry Barré de la Poer, DL, of Learmount Park; *b* 26 Nov 1886; Lt Roy Dublin Fus, High Sheriff 1942; *d* unm 18 Dec 1925

1a (cont.) John Beresford *m* 2nd 7 July 1853 Caroline (*d* 13 Jan 1901), only child of William and Lady Elizabeth Hamilton Ash, of Ashbrook, Londonderry, and *d* 30 Aug 1895, leaving:

3b William Randal Hamilton BERESFORD later BERESFORD-ASH (roy licence 1901), DL, of Ashbrook, Co Derry; *b* 19 July 1859; High Sheriff 1912, Lt-Col and Brevet Col 1st Bn Roy Welch Fus; *m* 23 Oct 1886 Lady Florence Marion Browne (*d* 22 Nov 1946), dau of 5th Marquess of Sligo (*qv*), and *d* 8 March 1938, leaving:

1c Douglas, DL (Co Londonderry); *b* 8 Sept 1887; *educ* Eton and RMC Sandhurst; Maj Roy Fus WW I (wounded, despatches), High Sheriff Co Lononderry 1950; *m* 17 Sept 1930 Lady Betty Helena Joanna Rous (*d* 4 Nov 1969), yst dau of 3rd Earl of Stradbroke (*qv*), and *d* 1976, leaving:

1d +John Randal [John Beresford-Ash Esq, Ashbrook, Co Londonderry]; *b* 21 Jan 1938; *educ* Eton; *m* 28 March 1968 *Agnes Marie Colette, yr dau of Comte Guy de Lamberterie, of Cannes, and has:

1e *Melanie Anne Helena Charlotte; *b* 1968

2e *Louisa-Jane Marie Caroline; *b* 7 July 1971

3e *Angélique Mary Elisa; *b* 1978

4b Marcus John Barré de la Poer, DSO, of Learmount Park; *b* 10 April 1868; *educ* Cheltenham; Lt-Col S Wales Bdrs, Mtd Inf Boer War 1900–02 (Relief Kimberley, ops in Transvaal, Paardeberg, etc; Queen's medal, four clasps, King's medal, two clasps), WW I 1914–16, cmdg 4th Bn S Wales Bdrs Gallipoli (despatches); *m* 19 Dec 1914 Alma (*d* 27 Oct 1968 aged 87), dau of David Methven, of Regent's Pk, London, and *d* as result of enemy action July 1944, leaving:

1c *Patricia Douglas Methven; *b* 5 March 1924; *m* 22 May 1974 *Maurice William Alfred Carter and has issue

1b Emma Clara; *m* 20 Dec 1881 Capt Francis Coffin Macky, JP, DL (*d* 6 Sept 1920), 3rd Dragoon Gds, and *d* 19 Nov 1927, leaving issue

2b Barbara Caroline; *d* unm 13 May 1937

3b Mary Elizabeth; *m* 6 Feb 1899 Henry Joseph Cooke (*d* 1 July 1923), of Boom Hall, Co Londonderry, and *d* 22 Jan 1936, leaving issue

4b Louisa Gertrude Douglas; *m* 22 Aug 1894 Maj John Edward Pine-Coffin, DSO, Loyal N Lancs Regt (*d* 22 Aug 1919), of Portledge, Devon, and *d* 12 March 1941, leaving issue

2a Henry Barré; *b* 23 July 1816; Cdr RN; *dsp* Jan 1871

3a William Montgomery (Rev); *b* 17 Oct 1817; Rector Lower Baldoney, Co Tyrone; *m* 18 Feb 1851 Rosa Ellen (*d* 31 May 1908), dau of John Turner, and *d* 4 April 1868, leaving, with a dau (*d* unm):

1b William James Montgomery; *b* 31 Aug 1859; Sec Turf Club Calcutta; *d* 24 April 1925

2b James Hugh Brownlow de la Poer; *b* 30 March 1862; Maj 3rd Sikhs, Punjab Frontier Force; *m* 5 Dec 1906 Grace Blanche (*d* 19–), dau of Capt Alfred Philip Beaumont, JP, of Testwood Park, Totton, Hants, and *d* 13 Nov 1924

1b Harriet Sarah; *b* 3 Sept 1852; *m* 3 Nov 1906, as his 3rd w, Herbert Winnington Domvile, DL (*d* 6 Feb 1910), of Loughlinstown House, Co Dublin, and *d* 6 Oct 1931

2b Florence Mary Anne; *m* 28 Sept 1876 Henry William Russell Domvile (*d* 17 Aug 1928), of Pentre Cottage, Abergavenny, and had issue

4a James David; *b* 2 April 1819; Maj 76th Foot; *m* 3 Oct 1868 Charlotte (*d* 17 Aug 1880), dau of W L Conyngham, of Spring Hill, and *dsp* 27 Oct 1878

5a George de la Poer; *b* 13 Feb 1826; Capt 16th Foot; *m* 15 Dec 1849 Anne (*d* 4 Oct 1854), dau of Lt-Gen Charles E Conyers, CB, and *d* 5 June 1865, having had, with another s (*d* young):

  1b Charles Edward de la Poer; *b* 23 Oct 1850; Lt-Col, Brevet Col, Mil Attaché St Petersburg, 2nd Cl Russian Order St Anne; *m* 17 Oct 1882 Solita Henrietta (*d* 29 Nov 1944), yst dau of Henry Cockburn Milne Ximenes, of Bear Place, Berks, and *d* 22 Aug 1921

  2b Tristram Henry Barré; *b* 5 Oct 1851; Lt RN; *m* 13 March 1878 Helen Frederica Conyers (*d* 21 Jan 1935), est dau of Lt-Col F H Lang, and *d* 10 Dec 1917, leaving:

    1c Annie Helen; *b* 20 May 1879; *d* unm 22 Feb 1940

    2c Mary Flora; *b* 16 Jan 1881; *d* 19–

    3c Maud Clara Emily; *b* 4 Dec 1882; *m* 1917 Capt T Lachasse, E African Regt (*ka* Jan 1918), and had issue

  1b Daphne Sarah; *b* 24 Sept 1854; *d* unm 27 April 1941

1a Mary Barbara; *m* 9 Feb 1836 Thomas William Fountaine, 2nd s of Andrew Fountaine, of Narford Hall, Norfolk, and *d* 8 July 1868, leaving issue

(4) Anna; *m* 1st Charles Gardiner; *m* 2nd 9 Oct 1822 Charles Edward Allen (calling himself Charles Edward Stuart, Count d'Albanie) (*d* 25 Dec 1880), and *d* 13 Nov 1862, leaving issue

3 WILLIAM BERESFORD, *cr* BARON DECIES (*qv*)

1 Anne; *m* 16 Aug 1738 1st Viscount Glerawly (*see* ANNESLEY, E)

2 Jane; *m* 10 Aug 1743 Edward Cary, of Dungiven, Co Derry, PC, MP, and *d* 1792

3 Catherine; *m* 1st 8 Dec 1748 Thomas Christmas (*d* 28 March 1749), of Whitefield, Co Waterford, MP Co Waterford; *m* 2nd 29 March 1754 Theophilus Jones, PC, of Headfort, and *d* 28 March 1763, leaving issue

4 Frances Maria; *m* 13 April 1762 Henry Flood, PC, MP, of Farmley, Co Kilkenny, and *dsp* 1815

5 Eliza; *m* 1751 Col Thomas Cobbe, of Newbridge, MP, and had issue

The 1st EARL's est s,

GEORGE De La Poer BERESFORD, **1st Marquess of Waterford** (I), so *cr* 19 Aug 1789, KP (1783), PC (I, 1763); *b* 8 Jan 1734/5; MP (I Parl) Co Waterford 1757–60, Coleraine 1761–63, Govr Co Waterford 1766 and custos rotulorum 1769–1800, *cr* also 21 Aug 1786 BARON TYRONE, of Haverfordwest, Pembs (GB); *m* 19 April 1769 Elizabeth, only dau and heiress of Henry Monck, of Charleville, Co Wicklow (*see* PORTLAND, E), and *d* 3 Dec 1800, having had, with an est s (*d* age 11 when thrown from his horse trying to jump a low fence at Curraghmore) and two daus (*d* unm):

1 HENRY De La POER, **2nd Marquess**

2 John George (Most Rev); *b* 22 Nov 1773; DD, Archbp Armagh, Primate of Ireland, Prelate Order St Patrick, Chllr U of Dublin; *dsp* 19 July 1862

3 George Thomas, GCH, PC, *b* 12 Feb 1781; Co Waterford: custos rotulorum, Col Militia; *m* 22 Nov 1808 Harriett (*d* 28 April 1860), dau of John Bacon Schutz, of Gillingham Hall, Beccles, Suffolk, and *d* 26 Oct 1839, leaving:

  (1) Elizabeth Harriet Georgiana; *m* 8 Feb 1849 Adml Henry Eden (*d* 30 Jan 1888 aged 90) and *d* 25 Jan 1889

  (2) Harriet Susan Isabella; *m* 13 April 1844 George Dunbar, DL, MP (*d* 12 Aug 1875), of Woburn, Co Down, and *d* 18 April 1859, leaving issue

  (3) Caroline Susan Catherine; *m* 19 Sept 1840 Hon Edward Kenyon and *d* 8 March 1866, leaving issue (*see* KENYON, B)

1 Isabella Anne; *m* 1 April 1812 Sir John William Head Brydges (*d* 6 Sept 1839) and *d* 7 May 1850

2 Elizabeth Louisa; *m* 1st 10 July 1816 Maj-Gen Sir Denis Pack, KCB (*d* 24 July 1823), and had issue; *m* 2nd 12 Feb 1831 Lt-Gen Sir Thomas Reynell, 6th Bt, KCB (*d* 10 Feb 1848; *see* 1850 edn), and *d* 6 Jan 1856

The 1st MARQUESS's 2nd but 1st surv s,

HENRY De La POER BERESFORD, **2nd Marquess of Waterford**, KP (1806), PC (I, 1801); *b* 23 May 1772; *educ* Eton and Ch Ch Oxford (MA); MP (I) Co Londonderry 1790–1800, Govr Co Waterford, custos rotulorum 1801, Col Waterford Militia; *m* 29 Aug 1805 Lady Susanna Carpenter (*d* 7 June 1827), only dau and heiress of 2nd Earl of Tyrconnel of the 1761 *cr* (*see* 1850 edn), and *d* 16 July 1826, having had, with other issue:

1 HENRY De La POER BERESFORD, **3rd Marquess of Waterford**, KP (1845); *b* 26 April 1811; *educ* Eton and Ch Ch Oxford; MFH Waterford; *m* 8 June 1842 Hon Louisa Stuart (*dsp* 12 May 1891), 2nd dau and coheir of 1st and last Baron Stuart de Rothesay (*see* BUTE, M), and was *k* 29 March 1859 by a fall from his horse at Corbally, nr Carrick-on-Suir, when out with the Waterford; under his will Ford Castle, Northumberland (inherited from his mother) passed for life to his widow, who also inherited High Cliffe, Hants, from her mother

2 JOHN DE LA POER, **4th Marquess**

1 Sarah Elizabeth; *m* 2 Nov 1828 18th Earl of Shrewsbury and Waterford (*qv*) and *d* 13 Oct 1884

The 3rd MARQUESS's bro,

Rev JOHN De La POER BERESFORD, **4th Marquess of Waterford**; *b* 27 April 1814; *educ* Eton and Trin Coll Cambridge (MA); incumbent Mullaghbrack, Co Armagh, RD, Preb Armagh; *m* 20 Feb 1843 Christiana (*d* 19 May 1905), 3rd dau of Col Charles Powell Leslie (*see* LESLIE, Bt), and *d* 6 Nov 1866, having had:

1 JOHN HENRY De La POER, **5th Marquess**

2 CHARLES WILLIAM De La POER BERESFORD, 1st and last BARON BERESFORD, of Metemmeh and Curraghmore, Co Waterford (UK), so *cr* 22 Jan 1916, GCB (1911), KCB 1903, CB 1885), GCVO (KCVO 1903, GCVO 1906); *b* 10 Feb 1846; joined RN 1859, Naval ADC to PRINCE OF WALES 1875–76, cmded HMS *Condor* at Alexandria 1882 (Govr after Bombardment; despatches, medal

with clasp, bronze star, Medjidie 3rd Cl), cmded Naval Bde Sudan with Nile Expdn 1884–85 and expdn relief Sir C Wilson 1885 (despatches three times for gallantry, medal with clasps), Jr Ld Admlty 1886–88, cmded Steam Reserve 1893–96, R-Adml 1897, Naval ADC to HM QUEEN VICTORIA 1897, 2ic Mediterranean Fleet 1900–02, V-Adml 1902, cmded Channel Sqdn 1903–05, Adml 1906, C-in-C: Mediterranean Fleet 1905–07, Channel Fleet 1907–09, retired 1911, Hon Col RM Bde 1914; MP (C) Co Waterford 1874–80, E Marylebone 1885–89, York 1897–1900, Woolwich 1902–03 and Portsmouth 1910–16; DCL Oxon, Hon LLD Liverpool, FRGS; three medals for saving life, Grand Cordon Medjidie, Legn Hon, Grand Cross Saviour Greece, St Olaf Norway; *m* 25 June 1878 Mina (*d* 26 May 1922), er dau of Richard Gardner, MP Leicester, and *dspm* 6 Sept 1919, when the Barony expired, leaving:

  (1) Kathleen Mary de la Poer; *m* 8 July 1913 Maj-Gen Edmund Raoul Blacque (*d* 4 Aug 1954), s of Edward Blacque, and *d* 30 Sept 1939, leaving issue

  (2) Eileen Theresa Lucy de la Poer; *d* unm 2 June 1939

3 William Leslie de la Poer, VC (1879), KCIE; *b* 20 July 1847; Col 9th Lancers, Battle of Ulundi, ADC and Mil Sec to Govr-Gen India 1881–94; *m* 30 April 1895 Lillian Warren (*d* 11 Jan 1909), dau of Cdre Cicero Price, USN, and widow of Louis Hammersley and 8th Duke of Marlborough (*qv*), and *d* 28 Dec 1900, leaving:

  (1) William Warren de la Poer; *b* 4 Feb 1897; *d* unm 28 Jan 1919

4 Marcus Talbot de la Poer, KCVO (1918); *b* 25 Dec 1848; Lt 7th Hus, Extra Equerry and manager thoroughbred stud and race horses to TM EDWARD VII 1890–1910 and GEORGE V 1910–22; *m* 28 Aug 1895 Louisa Katherine (*d* 1 Oct 1920), est dau of Maj-Gen Charles William Ridley, CB (*see* RIDLEY, V), and *dsp* 16 Dec 1922

5 Delaval James de la Poer; *b* 19 Jan 1862; Lt 3rd Bn Leics Regt; *d* unm 22 Dec 1906

The 4th MARQUESS's est s,

JOHN HENRY De La POER, **5th Marquess of Waterford**, KP (1868), PC (I 1879, GB 1885); *b* 21 May 1844; *educ* Eton; Capt 1st Life Gds, MP 1865–66, Ld Lt 1874–95 and custos rotulorum Co Waterford, Hon Col 6th Bde S Irish Div RA, Master Buckhounds 1885–86; *m* 1st 9 Aug 1872 Florence Grosvenor (*dsp* 4 April 1873), 2nd dau of Maj George Rowley (*see* ROWLEY, Bt) and formerly w of Hon John Cranch Walker Vivian (*see* VIVIAN, B); *m* 2nd 21 July 1874 Lady Blanche Elizabeth Adelaide Somerset (*d* 22 Feb 1897), only dau of 8th Duke of Beaufort (*qv*), and *d* 23 Oct 1895, having by her had:

1 HENRY De La POER, **6th Marquess**

1 Mary; *b* 30 April, *d* 31 May 1877

2 Susan de la Poer; *b* 30 April 1877; *m* 28 April 1902 Maj Hon Hugh Dawnay (*see* DOWNE, V) and *d* 30 Oct 1947, leaving issue

3 Clodagh de la Poer; *b* 6 Aug 1879; *m* 27 Feb 1901 Hon Claud Anson (*see* LICHFIELD, E) and *d* 17 April 1957, leaving issue

The 5th MARQUESS's s,

HENRY De La POER, **6th Marquess of Waterford**, KP (1902), DL (Northumberland and Waterford); *b* 28 April 1875; *educ* Eton; Lt RHG, Boer War 1902, Hon Col S Irish Horse, KGStJ; *m* 16 Oct 1897 Lady Beatrix Frances FitzMaurice, GBE (1919), DGSt J (*d* 5 Aug 1953, having *m* 2nd 19 Aug 1918 12th Duke of St Albans; *qv*), yr dau of 5th Marquess of Lansdowne (*qv*), and *d* 1 Dec 1911, having had:

1 JOHN CHARLES De La POER, **7th Marquess**

2 William Mostyn de la Poer; *b* 30 May 1905; *educ* Sherborne; Maj RA, ADC to Govr and C-in-C Malta 1931, served WW II; *m* 29 Nov 1945 *Rachel [The Lady William Beresford, Thatched Cottage, Church Lane, Stradbally, Co Waterford, Ireland], yr dau of George Kennett Page, JP, of Upton Lodge, Bursledon, Hants, and *d* 24 Nov 1973, leaving:

  (1) *Meriel Beresford [Mrs Joseph Power, Old Town House Stud, Shanballymore, Co Cork, Ireland]; *b* 12 Sept 1948; *m* 1970 *Joseph Power and has:

    1a *James Anthony; *b* 1972

    2a *Richard Joseph; *b* 1982

    1a *Rosemarie Ann; *b* 1970

    2a *Jennifer Alice; *b* 1986

  (2) *Nicola; *b* 7 Jan 1951; *m* 1976 (legally separated 1993) Andreas Minihan, of English Town, Stradbally, Co Waterford, est s of Andrew Minihan, and has:

    1a *Andrew Peter Mark de la Poer; *b* 1977

    2a *Ian Michael de la Poer; *b* 1980

    3a *William David de la Poer; *b* 1983

    1a *Anna Rachel; *b* 1984

3 Hugh Tristram de la Poer; *b* 1 Oct 1908; Lt-Cdr RN WW II; *ka* in HMS *Kelly* off Crete 23 May 1941

1 Blanche Maud de la Poer; *m* 26 Oct 1927 Richard Desire Girouard, only s of Col Sir Percy Girouard, KCMG, DSO, and *d* as result of a motor accident 29 Sept 1940

2 Katherine Nora de la Poer; *m* 14 Oct 1926 Maj-Gen Sir David Dawnay KCVO, CB, DSO (*d* 3 Oct 1971; *see* DOWNE, V), and *d* 1991, having had issue

3 (Beatrix) Patricia de la Poer; *m* 7 July 1926 Lynden Roberts Miller, barrister (*d* 1973), est s of Rt Rev Robert Miller, DD, Bp Cashel, and had:

  (1) *David; *b* 30 Sept 1929; Maj Blues and Royals; *educ* St Peter's Hall Oxford (BA, MA); *m* 2 April 1955 *Marigold Winifred, er dau of Maj Thomas John Arnott (*see* ARNOTT, Bt), and has:

    1a *David Mark; *b* 16 Nov 1958

    2a *Christopher Declan; *b* 19 July 1961

    1a *Victoria Jane; *b* 27 July 1968

  (1) *Jean [Mrs Hugh Bulley, Willow Cottage, Church Rd, Yapton, Sussex]; *b* 12 April 1932; *m* 1956 *Lt-Cdr Hugh Cyril Edmund Bulley, RN, s of Ivo Bulley, of Overmarsh House, Ness in Wirral, Cheshire, and has:

    1a *Sarah; *b* 7 Sept 1957

    2a *Henrietta; *b* 6 March 1959

    3a *Emma; *b* 24 Aug 1961

The 6th MARQUESS's est s,

JOHN CHARLES De La POER BERESFORD, **7th Marquess of Waterford**; *b* 6 Jan 1901; *educ* Winchester and Trin Coll Cambridge; Lt RHG Res; *m* 14 Oct 1930

Juliet Mary (m 2nd 17 Dec 1946 Lt-Col John Eric Durnford Silcock, s of Charles Silcock, of Cahir, Co Tipperary, and d 1987), 2nd dau of Maj David Balcarres Lindsay (see CRAWFORD and BALCARRES, E), and d 25 Sept 1934, having had:

1 JOHN HUBERT De La POER BERESFORD, **8th and present Marquess of Waterford**

2 +Patrick Tristram de la Poer [The Lord Patrick Beresford, Fairview Cottage, Wicks Green, Binfield, Berks RG42 5PF]; b 16 June 1934; educ Eton and RMA Sandhurst (Sword of Honour Feb 1953); Capt RHG and Gds Para Co; m 26 Nov 1964 (divorce 1971) Julia, dau of Col Thomas Cromwell Williamson, DSO, of Beaumont Hall, Thorpe-le-Soken, Essex, and formerly w of Capt Darel Carey, RHG, and has:

   (1) +Valentine Tristram de la Poer; b 10 Oct 1965; m 1993 *Evelyne, dau of John Hoskin, of Harlow, Essex

   (1) *Samantha Julia; b 18 Jan 1969

Seat: Curraghmore, Portlaw, Co Waterford, Ireland. The core of the building is a tower house of a kind that is very common in Ireland. This was extensively altered in the 18th and 19th centuries to form a classical centre block reminiscent of Blenheim, though on a much smaller scale. A house was built on to the base of the tower by the mid-17th century, again as often happens to old towers in Ireland, but this too was classicised in the 18th century. The enlarged version existing today consists of an enclosed court, of which the original tower forms one complete side. To the front of the house extend two flanking wings, designed as stable blocks by John Roberts (d c 1796), who also designed both the Catholic and Protestant cathedrals in Waterford city. Inside the main house are some splendid ceilings, some of which are thought to be by the celebrated stuccodore brother team of Paul and Philip Francini, who also worked on Carton and Castletown, both in Co Kildare. Among other artists of the front rank who are thought to have worked at Curraghmore are Antonio Zucchi and Angelica Kauffman. In the 1780s James Wyatt, the architect of Castlecoole (see BELMORE, E), carried out further alterations to Roberts's work.

WATERLOW of Harrow Weald

Arms: Argent a lion rampant within a bordure nebuly azure, on a chief sable two shin-bones saltirewise, the dexter surmounted by the sinister or. **Crest:** A demi-lion guardant azure, in the mouth a shin-bone in bend, and holding between the paws a human skull, both or. **Motto:** Per mortem vinco ('I conquer through death'). **Creation:** Bt. (UK) 28 Oct 1930.

SIR (JAMES) GERARD WATERLOW 4TH BT, of Harrow Weald, Co Middlesex [Sir Gerard Waterlow Bt, Rushall Lodge, Pewsey, Wilts SN9 6EN]; b 3 Sept 1939; s f 1982; educ Marlborough and Trin Coll Cambridge; management consultant; m 10 July 1965 *Diana Suzanne, yr dau of Sir (William) Thomas Charles Skyrme, KCVO, CB, CBE, TD, MA, JP, FRGS, of S Kensington and Villa Tomara, Porto Valtravaglia, Lake Maggiore, Italy, by Hon (Barbara) Suzanne née Lyle (see 1970 edn LYLE OF WESTBOURNE, B), and has:

1 +THOMAS JAMES; b 20 March 1970

1 *Amanda Jane; b 14 May 1968; m 1991 *Jason Patrick Howard (see SUFFOLK and BERKSHIRE, E)

Lineage: JAMES JAMESON WATERLOW, of 25 Park Crescent, London W (see WATERLOW, Bt, of London); had:

Sir William Alfred Waterlow, 1st Bt (UK), so cr 28 Oct 1930, KBE (1919), JP (Middx); b 23 April 1871; educ Marlborough; slr 1895; City London: Alderman Cornhill Ward, Sheriff 1928, Ld Mayor 1929–30, md Waterlow Bros and Layton, chm Waterlow and Sons, Pres Fedn Master Printers GB and Ireland 1914 and 1915 and London Master Printers' Assoc 1914, Kt Cdr Order Dannebrog, Cdr Orders Nile and Rising Sun Japan 2nd Cl; m 30 April 1904 Adelaide Hay (d 4 June 1957), yr dau of Thomas Gordon, of Edinburgh, and d 6 July 1931, leaving:

1 **Sir (William) James Waterlow, 2nd Bt**, CBE (1945), TD; b 20 March 1905; educ Marlborough and Trin Coll Cambridge (BA 1927, MA 1932); WW II (despatches), cmded Col City London Yeo Rifle Bde TA 1945–50 (Hon Col 1952–61), dir Evans Brothers Ltd, Upper Warden Stationers' Co, Chm Govrs Birkbeck Coll London U, Pres: Fedn Master Process Engravers 1951–53, Lon-

don Master Printers' Assoc 1953–54, Printers' Pension Corp 1958, Periodical Proprietors Assoc 1962–64; d unm 20 Nov 1969

2 **Sir Thomas Gordon Waterlow, 3rd Bt**, CBE (1946); b 2 Jan 1911; educ Marlborough and Trin Coll Cambridge (LLD); G/Capt RAuxAF WW II (despatches); dep chm Roy Bank Scotland, dir Williams and Glyns Bank 1974, chm Gen Time (Internat Ops) 1977, Pres Edinburgh Chamber Commerce 1963–65; m 21 April 1938 Helen Elizabeth (d 29 May 1970), yr dau of Gerard Arthur Howard Robinson, of N Ridge, Bix, Oxon, and d 8 Aug 1982, leaving:

   (1) Sir (JAMES) GERARD WATERLOW, **4th and present Bt**

   (2) +Simon Gordon [Simon Waterlow Esq, 208 Lewisburg Ave, Franklin, Nashville, TN, USA]; b 20 June 1941; educ Marlborough and Trin Coll Cambridge (MA); m 10 Sept 1971 *Jane Elizabeth, est dau of W/Cdr Cameron Underhill, RCAF, of Montreal, and has:

      1a *Caroline Elizabeth; b 1973

   (3) +John William [John Waterlow Esq, 81 Streathbourne Rd, London SW17]; b 14 Nov 1945; educ Marlborough; m 15 July 1972 *Camilla Dudley, dau of W/Cdr Dudley Farmer, DFC, of Frieth, Oxon, and has:

      1a +Rufus Dudley Robinson; b 2 April 1976

      2a +Alec Gordon Brownrigg; b 1980

WATERLOW of London

Arms: Azure a demi-eagle displayed, erased or, holding in the beak a cross-crosslet fitchée argent, on a chief of the last three wolf heads erased sable. **Crest:** Upon a mount vert an oak tree, in front thereof a plough, both proper. **Motto:** Labor omnia vincit ('Work overcomes everything'). **Creation:** Bt. (UK) 4 Aug 1873.

SIR CHRISTOPHER RUPERT WATERLOW, 5TH BT, of London [Sir Christopher Waterlow Bt, 26 Barfield Rd, Bickley, Kent BR1 2HS]; b 12 Aug 1959; s gf 1973; educ Stonyhurst; m 6 Sept 1986 *Sally-Ann, only dau of Maurice Bitten, of Abbey Wood, London SE2

Lineage: WALLERAN WATERLO, of Lille; settled in Canterbury by 1628; had:

WALRAN WATERLO; b Lille; m Canterbury 12 Sept 1633 Marguerite Wearre (d 8 Oct 1678) and d 12 May 1684, leaving, with six other children:

WALRAN WATERLO; bapt 31 Aug 1634; Freeman Weaver's Co London 1694; m 17 Aug 1656 Jeanne (bur 8 Nov 1715), dau of Matthieu de Lobarre, and was bur 12 Sept 1715, leaving:

SAMUEL WATERLO; b 25 Nov 1663; by a 1st w had:

SAMUEL WATERLO; bapt 14 Sept 1701; m c 1722 and had an only s:

JOSIAH WATERLO; m 2nd 1761 Sarah — and had an est s:

JOSIAH WATERLO; bapt 23 Nov 1762; m c 1786 Sarah Anne (b 1769; d c 1835), dau of John Robertson, and was bur 5 Sept 1817, leaving, with other issue:

JAMES WATERLOW, of Peckham; b 19 April 1790; m 17 Oct 1812 Mary (d 23 July 1872), dau of William Crakell, and d 11 July 1876, having had, with three daus:

1 Alfred James, JP, DL Surrey; b 19 June 1815; m 10 Feb 1838 Isabella (d 14 Dec 1903), dau of John Jameson, and d 30 Nov 1886, having had, with other issue:

   (1) Alfred Jameson; b 1842; Commr Ltcy for City London, Capt HAC; d 1925

   (2) James Jameson, of 25 Park Crescent, London W; b 31 May 1844; m 16 July 1868 Kate Frances (m 2nd Arthur William Wray and d 30 April 1931), 2nd dau of Rev Joseph Lawson Sisson, Rector Edingthorpe, Norfolk, and d 17 Jan 1871, having had, with other issue:

      1a James Francis, DSO, TD; b 25 April 1869; educ Charterhouse; Col 4th Border Regt (TA), formerly 5th Queen's Roy Regt, Hon Capt Boer War 1900 (despatches, Queen's medal with six clasps), WW I (despatches); m 1916 Rosalie Marie, dau of Alphonse Lorenz, of Monthey, Canton du Valais, Switzerland, and d 19 Nov 1942

      2a Sir WILLIAM ALFRED WATERLOW, 1st Bt, of Harrow Weald (qv)

2 Charles William; b 6 Feb 1817; m 10 Dec 1842 Louisa Mary (d 24 Sept 1900), dau of John Masters, of Esher, and d 11 June 1897

3 Walter Blandford, of High Trees, Surrey, JP, DL; b 17 April 1819; High Sheriff 1888; Commr Ltcy London; m 1st 27 Sept 1842 Rebecca (d 14 Feb 1869), dau of

J Stones; *m* 2nd 1876 Maria, dau of James Corss, of London, and widow of Albert C Waterlow, of Fairlawn, Redhill, and *d* 28 Aug 1891

4 SYDNEY HEDLEY (Sir), **1st Bt**

5 Albert Crakell; *b* 23 Dec 1824; *m* 23 July 1846 Maria (*m* 2nd 1876 Walter B Waterlow, *see* above), dau of James Corss, and *d* 25 Feb 1856, having had issue

JAMES WATERLOW's 4th s,

Sir Sydney Hedley Waterlow, 1st Bt (UK), so *cr* 4 Aug 1873, KCVO, JP, DL Kent, JP Londonderry and Middx; *b* 1 Nov 1822; Commr Ltcy London, MP Dumfries 1868–69, Maidstone 1874–80 and Gravesend 1880–85; gave Waterlow Park, Highgate, to LCC 1889; City London: Alderman 1863–83, Sheriff 1866–67, Ld Mayor 1872–77, Grand Cross Crown Italy, Legn Hon, Orders Medjidie Turkey and Lion and Sun Persia, ktd 1867; *m* 1st 7 May 1845 Anna Maria (*d* 21 Jan 1880), yst dau of William Hickson, of Fairseat, Kent; *m* 2nd 28 March 1882 Margaret (*d* 30 May 1931), dau of William Hamilton, of Napa, Calif., and *d* 3 Aug 1906, having had, with three other sons (*d* young):

1 Frank William; *b* 6 July 1846; *d* unm 4 Dec 1871

2 PHILIP HICKSON (Sir), **2nd Bt**

3 George Sydney, JP Middx; *b* 12 April 1852; Commr Ltcy London; *m* 1 Aug 1876 Charlotte Elizabeth (*d* 2 Feb 1944), dau of Henry Herron Beauchamp, of Bexley, Kent, and *d* 10 July 1925, having had, with a dau (*d* an infant):

(1) Sydney Philip Perigal (Sir), KCMG, CBE; *b* 22 Oct 1878; *educ* Eton and Trin Coll Cambridge (MA 1905); Cnsllr FO 1924–26, Envoy Extrdy and Min Plen Bangkok 1926–28, Addis Ababa 1928–29, Sofia 1929–33 and Athens 1933–39, Chev Legn Hon; *m* 1st 10 Nov 1902 (*annulled* 1912) Alice Isabella (*d* 28 June 1953), only dau of Sir Frederick Pollock, 3rd Bt (*qv*); *m* 2nd 27 Sept 1913 Helen Margery (*d* 5 June 1973 aged 90), est dau of Gustav Eckhard, of Disbury, Manchester, and *d* 4 Dec 1944, leaving by her:

1a +John Conrad, CMG (1970) [Prof John Waterlow CMG, Oare, Marlborough, Wilts SN8 4JA]; *b* 13 June 1916; *educ* Eton and Trin Coll Cambridge; BChir, MD, ScD, Prof Human Nutrition London Sch Hygiene and Tropical Med 1970–82, FRCP, FRS 1982; *m* 29 July 1939 *Angela Pauline Cecil, dau of George Wynter Gray, of Galhampton, Somerset, and has:

1b +Oliver Sydney; *b* 9 Sept 1943; *educ* Eton

2b +Richard John; *b* 25 Sept 1945; *educ* Eton

1b *Sarah Jean; *b* 3 Nov 1941

1a *Charlotte Mary, MBE (1950); *b* 31 May 1915; *educ* Newnham Coll Cambridge (MA); Admin Offr FO; GS teacher and author

2a Judith Matilda; *b* 7 Feb 1921; MB, BS London, Associate Memb Br Psycho-Analytical Soc, Child Psychiatrist NW and SE Met Regnl Hosp Boards; *d* unm 13 Feb 1966

(2) John Beauchamp, DSO; *b* 15 March 1880; Cdr RN WW I; *k* Battle of Jutland 31 May 1916

(3) Guy Walron; *b* 18 April 1884; Capt RASC, RTO; *d* 5 July 1925

(4) Cecil Beauchamp; *b* 4 Dec 1887; T/Capt RASC, Inspr Mechanical Tport; *d* 16 June 1936

(1) Margery; *b* 23 Oct 1881; *m* 12 June 1909 Lt-Col John Herbert Norton, 6th Dragoon Gds (*d* 23 April 1963), s of Edward Norton, JP, of Fareham, Hants, and had:

1a Peter John; *b* 9 Jan 1913; *educ* Winchester; Capt RN WW II (despatches), author and painter, teacher of art; *m* 29 April 1944 *Olive Mary, dau of Percy Courtney Deacon, and had:

1b *John William Beauchamp; *b* 1 Jan 1949; *educ* Hurstpierpoint

1b *Sarah Katherine; *b* 12 Jan 1946

2a *Richard Christopher [Richard Norton Esq, West Side, Chorleywood Rd, Rickmansworth, Herts]; *b* 19 April 1919; *educ* Winchester and Magdalene Coll Cambridge (MA, MB, BCh); Hon Capt RA; *m* 8 April 1945 *Margaret May, dau of William Thomas, and has:

1b *David Waterlow; *b* 13 Nov 1946

2b *Robert Thomas; *b* 16 Oct 1948

3b *Philip William; *b* 29 July 1953

1b *Anne Elizabeth; *b* 25 Jan 1951

1a Janet; *m* 22 Oct 1940 A/Cdre Henry Eeles, CB, CBE, RAF, of Sutton Veny, Wilts, s of Henry Eeles, of Newcastle, and *d* 30 Jan 1960, leaving issue

4 Charles Hickson, FZS, FRBS; *b* 9 Aug 1854; *m* 19 Nov 1881 Frances Anne (*d* 8 Oct 1921), gdau of Thomas Latimer, JP, of Exeter, and *d* 10 Nov 1920

5 David Sydney; *b* 18 Dec 1857; MP N Islington 1906–10, CC for London 1896–1900; *m* 2 June 1883 Edith Emma (*d* 1 Aug 1932), est dau of Frederick Maitland, of Primrose Hill, London, and *d* 25 Aug 1924, having had:

(1) Clive Maitland; *b* 9 Sept 1885; Capt and A/Lt-Col RE, W/Cdr RNAS; *m* 9 June 1917 *Winifred Joan (*m* 2nd 14 Sept 1922 Claude Waller, only s of Frederick Waller), yst dau of John Henry Clare, of Farlands Croft, Farnham, Surrey, and was *kas* in an airship accident 20 July 1917

(2) Mervyn Maitland; *b* 31 Jan 1887; Lt RN; *d* 30 Oct 1913

(1) Margaret Maitland; *b* 10 April 1889; *d* 30 May 1903

(2) Joan Maitland Waterlow; *b* 3 May 1897; *m* 13 April 1926 (*divorce* 1971) George Ernest Lambourn, s of Henry Lambourn, of London, and had:

1a *Simon [Simon Lambourn Esq, 13 Grey Cl, London NW11]; *b* 25 Sept 1927; *educ* Highgate and Trin Hall Cambridge (MA); CEng, dir Computer Offices Ltd; *m* 3 Nov 1951 *Hilary Margaret Buckley, dau of Herbert J Williams, and has:

1b *Caroline Helen; *b* 7 Sept 1959

2b *Sarah Margaret; *b* 6 Dec 1963

2a *Martin; *b* 27 July 1929; *m* 1st 1951 (*divorce* 1957) Diana Godfrey and has:

1b *Nikolas; *b* 1952

1b *Tamsin; *b* 1954

2b *Charlotte Nancy; *b* 1956

2a (cont.) Martin Lambourn; *m* 2nd 1958 *Jill Amanda, dau of Norman Broughton Stevenson, of Bristol, and by her has:

1b *Giles Timothy; *b* 1960

2b *Hugo Gavin; *b* 1963

1b *Emma Fanny; *b* 1962

1a *Jane Esther [Miss Jane Lambourn, Talbot Settlement, 48 Addington Sq, London SE5]; *b* 27 May 1931

(3) Sylvia Maitland; *b* 28 Oct 1898; *m* 29 July 1920 Cyril George Dennys, CB, MC, of Hampstead, only s of Lt-Col Alexander Harry Dennys, IA, and has had:

(4) *Rosalind Maitland; *b* 17 June 1911; *m* 12 Feb 1936 Sheriton Clements Swan, of Hexham, Northumberland, only s of Sir Charles Sheriton Swan, of Broomley Grange, Stocksfield, Northumberland, and has:

1a *David Sheriton; *b* 23 Jan 1940; *educ* Gresham's and Loughborough Coll

2a *Nicholas Clements [Nicholas Swan Esq, Brook Ho, Stocksfield, Northumberland]; *b* 22 Feb 1944; *educ* Christ's Coll Brecon; *m* 1970 *Susan, dau of F Wells, of Berwick-on-Tweed, and has:

1b *Catharine Victoria; *b* 1970

2b *Diana Rachel; *b* 1972

1a *Lesley Jean [Mrs Richard Hamments, Gypsy, Sandhills Meadow, Shepperton, Middx, TW17 9HY]; *b* 13 June 1942; *m* 27 June 1964 *Richard James Hamments, s of Henry John Hamments, of St John's Wood

6 Paul Langbourne; *b* 22 Feb 1863; Town Cncllr Tunbridge Wells, FRPS, FRHS; *m* 16 June 1892 Kathleen (*d* 2 July 1953), dau of T B Holmes, JP, of Elim Lodge, Hornsea, Yorks, and *d* 11 Feb 1928

1 Ruth; *b* 8 Aug 1850; *m* 7 May 1873 Francis Wilkes Homan (*d* 4 Jan 1880), s of Ebenezer Homan, JP, of Friern Watch, Barnet, and *d* 6 Nov 1938, leaving issue

2 Hilda Maria; *b* 10 April 1861; *m* 12 May 1886 Alfred Bernard Ford (*d* 1918) and had issue

3 Celia Agnes; *b* 24 Jan 1865; *d* unm 12 Sept 1944

The 1st Bt's est surv s,

Sir Philip Hickson Waterlow, 2nd Bt, JP Kent; *b* 30 Oct 1847; High Sheriff Surrey 1905, Lt City London; chm Waterlow and Sons; *m* 1st 10 June 1869 Amy Grace (*d* 29 Jan 1897), 2nd dau of Edgar Lutwyche, of Streatham; *m* 2nd 7 July 1898 Laura Marie (*d* 26 March 1929), dau of Frederick J Jones, of Dulwich, and *d* 20 Sept 1931, leaving by his 1st w:

1 EDGAR LUTWYCHE, **3rd Bt**

2 Kenneth Lutwyche; *b* 19 May 1883; served RNAS; *d* 18 Feb 1926

1 Emily Lutwyche; *b* 24 Oct 1878; *m* 18 April 1900 Alfred Clifton Clapin (*d* 21 Aug 1950), est s of Rev Alfred Charles Clapin, and had issue

2 Grace Evelyn Lutwyche; *b* 21 Feb 1880; *m* 28 June 1905 Archibald Edward Boyd (*d* 8 March 1937), s of James Boyd, and had issue

3 Irene Lutwyche; *b* 27 Jan 1881; *m* 8 Sept 1903 Lt-Col Arthur Mowbray Berkeley, CIE, VD, IA (Res Offrs), 2nd s of Maj-Gen Frederick George Berkeley (*d* 23 March 1937), of the Almners, Chertsey, and *d* 14 July 1948, leaving issue

4 Gladys Maud Lutwyche; *b* 8 July 1886; *m* 26 July 1910 Brig-Gen Frederick Fitzhugh Lance, IA, s of Gen Sir Frederick Lance, KCB, of Roehampton, Surrey, and *d* 31 Dec 1935, leaving issue

The 2nd Bt's only surv s,

Sir Edgar Lutwyche Waterlow, 3rd Bt; *b* 15 June 1870; *educ* Harrow and Trin Hall Cambridge (BA 1894, MA 1898); Pres Printers' Pension Corp Festival 1936, Govr Christ's Hosp, Dir French Hosp, Past Master Stationers' and Newspaper Mfrs Co; *m* 1st 6 June 1896 (*divorce* 1913) Martha (Pattie) (*d* 25 Jan 1963), dau of Robert Carter, and had:

1 PHILIP ALEXANDER (Sir), **4th Bt**

2 Derek Vaudrey; *b* 19 Feb 1902; *educ* Harrow

Sir Edgar *m* 2nd 8 May 1913 Harriet Victoria (*d* 4 Aug 1968 aged 81), dau of Joseph Gecks, Roy Welch Fus, and *d* 12 Jan 1954, leaving by her:

3 Anthony Edgar Russell; *b* 5 March 1914; *educ* Harrow; Lt KRRC WW II; *m* 31 Aug 1940 *Barbara Winifred, of Chelsea, est dau of Ronald Davy, of Limber Harborough, Lincs, and *d* 30 July 1946 following a car crash, leaving:

(1) +NICHOLAS ANTHONY RONALD [Nicholas Waterlow Esq, 58 Willoughby St, Kirribilli, Sydney 2061, NSW, Australia]; *b* 30 Aug 1941; heir presumptive; *educ* Harrow; *m* 8 May 1965 Rosemary (*d* 11 Jan 1998), only dau of W J O'Brien, of Vaucluse, Sydney, and has:

1a +Antony William Nicholas; *b* 14 Jan 1967

2a +Luke Frederick Ronald; *b* 17 Dec 1969

1a *Chloe Diana; *b* 25 Nov 1972

4 Ronald James Charlton; *b* 18 Aug 1916; *educ* Harrow; Maj RA WW II (despatches), Freeman City London; *m* 31 Jan 1953 *Ethel Florence, yst dau of Frederick George Chelsom, of Stevenage, Herts

1 Joyce Rosamond Amy Waterlow; *b* 18 Aug 1916; *m* 1st 27 July 1940 (*divorce* 1947) F/O Godfrey Ian Hutchinson, F/O RAF, yr s of Godfrey Charles Hutchinson, of Mayfair; *m* 2nd 29 Aug 1953 *David Ronald Mitchell, only s of Sir Frank Herbert Mitchell, KCVO, CBE, of Forest Ho, Crowborough, Sussex, and *d* 14 Sept 1997, having by her 1st husb had:

(1) *Diana Joy [Mrs Diana Perez-Gonzalez, 19 Priory Rd, Cambridge CB5 8HT]; *b* 20 March 1941; *m* 1962 (*divorce* 1984) José Perez-Gonzalez, of Torremolinos, Spain, and has:

1a *Antonio Salvador; *b* 20 Feb 1964; *m* 1986 *Nichole, est dau of Sydney Decaix, of Lewes, Sussex, and has:

1b *Marco Salvador; *b* 17 Nov 1990

2b *Sebastian Raphael; *b* 30 March 1992

1b *Isabella Miranda; *b* 5 July 1995

1a Samantha Rosa; *b* 18 Dec 1966; *m* 1989 *Peter Bartram and *d* 21 March 1992

2a *Zoë Amanda; *b* 4 Aug 1975

The 3rd Bt's est s,

Sir Philip Alexander Waterlow; 4th Bt; *b* 17 March 1897; *educ* Harrow and RMC Sandhurst; Lt 3rd King's Own Hus WW I, ADC to Mil Govr Cologne BAOR 1919–20, Capt HG WW II; chm and md Waterlow and Sons Ltd, Govr Christ's Hosp and Lloyd Memorial (Caxton) Home, Deal, Liveryman Stationers and Newspapers Mfrs Co, Freeman City London; *m* 1st 6 Jan 1923 (*divorce* 1937) Iris Gwendoline (*m* 2nd Campbell Shaw and *d* 1969), only dau of Charles Rupert Butler; *m* 2nd 19 May 1937 Annie Catherine (*judicial separation* 1951), er dau of John Hay and widow of Frederick Webber Tee; *m* 3rd 1972 Gwendoline Florence

Elizabeth (d 199–), yr dau of Leon Balanche and formerly w of Baden Robert Murch, and d 18 July 1973, having had by his 1st w:

(Peter) Rupert; b 1 Oct 1925; educ Harrow; dir Waterlow and Sons Ltd and Waterlow Automation Servs Ltd, Freeman City London, Sub-Lt RNVR WW II; m 1st 17 March 1956 Jill Elizabeth (d 4 Sept 1961), er dau of Eric Thornborough Gourlay, of S Kensington; m 2nd 1 Sept 1962 Ruth Margaret (m 3rd 9 Dec 1969 Sir Arthur Lionel Pugh Norrington, JP, dir Waterlow and Sons Ltd and Warden Winchester, s of Arthur James Norrington, of Kenley, Surrey), widow of Frank Davis, Perm Sec Enugu, Nigeria, and yst dau of Edmund Cude, of London N2, and dvp 18 Feb 1969, leaving by his 1st w:

Sir CHRISTOPHER RUPERT WATERLOW, **5th and present Bt**

WATERPARK

Arms: Quarterly, 1st and 4th, sable three stag's heads cabossed argent, attired or, within a bordure of the second (for CAVENDISH); 2nd and 3rd, argent two bendlets, the upper sable, the lower gules (for BRADSHAW). **Crest:** On a ducal coronet or a serpent nowed fesswise proper. **Supporters:** Dexter, a stag per fess indented gules and sable, attired and unguled or; sinister, a stag proper, attired and unguled or and gorged with a chaplet of roses argent and azure alternately. **Motto:** Cavendo tutus ('Secure by caution'). **Creations:** Bt. (GB) 7 May 1755, B. (I) 14 June 1792.

THE 7TH BARON WATERPARK, of Waterpark, Co Cork, Ireland, and a **Baronet** (Sir Frederick Caryll Philip Cavendish, Bt) [The Rt Hon The Lord Waterpark, 74 Elm Park Rd, London SW3 6AU]; b 6 Oct 1926; s unc 1948; educ Eton; late Lt 4th Bn Gren Gds, Foundation Pres Nairobi Gliding Club, Assist Dist Cmdt Kenya Police Reserve 1952–54, sales dir CSE Aviation Ltd 1962 (dep chm 1983–90, ch exec 1990), md CSE Internat Ltd 1985, dir Airborn Gp plc 1990–; m 17 April 1951 *Danièle Alice, dau of Roger Guirche, of Paris, and has:

1 +RODERICK (RORY) ALEXANDER; b 10 Oct 1959; educ Harrow and Vassar; m *Anne, dau of Hon Luke Asquith (see OXFORD AND ASQUITH, E), and has:

  (1) +Luke Frederick; b 17 Sept 1990
  (2) +Tom Matthew Arthur; b 26 Aug 1997

1 *Caroline Laurence Patricia; b 3 March 1952; m 13 Oct 1979 *George Michael Richard Goulding (see GOULDING, Bt) and has issue

2 *Juliet Enid Marie Gabrielle; b 17 Oct 1953; m 19– *Charles Dumaresq Nicholson, yr s of Arthur Wilfred Nicholson, of Hartham Park, Corsham, Wilts, and has:

  (1) *Isabel; b 1986
  (2) *Claire; b 1988

Lineage: HENRY CAVENDISH, of Tutbury Castle, Staffs; b 1549 (er bro of 1st Earl of Devonshire; see DEVONSHIRE, D); dspl 12 Oct 1616, leaving, with four yr sons (Thomas; Charles; William; Augustin; all took name CAVENDISH) and three daus (Anne, m Vincent Lowe, of Denby Old Hall, and had issue; Audrey; Elizabeth):

HENRY CAVENDISH; had settled on him the Doveridge estate, Derbys; m 14 Oct 1610 Bridget, dau of Sir Percival Willoughby, of Wollaton, Notts (see MIDDLETON, B), and had, with an er s (Charles, educ Magdalen Hall Oxford, dsp) and three daus (Grace, d unm; Mary, m 20 April 1648 John Broughton, of Whittington, Staffs, and had issue; Bridget, b 1613, m Samuel Mason, of Nottingham, and had issue):

FRANCIS CAVENDISH, of Doveridge; b 1618; m 1st 13 Nov 1642 Dorothy, dau of John Bullock, of Darley Abbey, and had a dau (Dorothy, m Gervase Nevill, of Beeston and Sheffield, Yorks); m 2nd Dorothy, dau of Thomas Broughton (see BROUGHTON, Bt), and d 17 June 1650, leaving by her, with a yr s (Charles, b 1649/50, dsp):

HENRY CAVENDISH, of Doveridge; b 1648; educ Ch Ch Oxford; m Mary, dau of Sir Timothy Tyrrell, of Shotover, Oxon, and d 23 May 1698, leaving, with three yr sons (all d unm) and 11 daus (including Dorothy, m William Calton; Elizabeth, m 1st Richard Horwell, m 2nd Samuel Odlfield and d 1731; Anne, m Brooke Boothby (see BOOTHBY, Bt) and d 2 July 1707, leaving issue; Margaret, m Rayner Bate, of Foston Hall, Derbys; Henrietta, m Richard Wilmot (see WILMOT, Bt); the rest d unm):

WILLIAM CAVENDISH, of Doveridge; b 20 Sept 1682; m 1st his cousin Mary, dau of Timothy Tyrrell, of Shotover; m 2nd 1709 Elizabeth, dau of John Holt, of Castleton, Lancs, and by his 1st w had:

1 **Sir Henry Cavendish, 1st Bt** (GB), so cr 7 May 1755, PC (I 1768); b 13 April 1707; educ Univ Coll Oxford; Sheriff Derbys 1741, apptd Teller Exchequer Ireland during his cousin 3rd Duke of Devonshire's term as Ld Lt Ireland 1737–45, Collector Cork 1743, Commr Revenue Ireland 1747, MP (I Parl) Tullagh 1756–60, Lismore 1761–68 and 1776; m 1st 9 June 1730 Anne, dau and coheir of Henry Pyne, of Waterpark, Co Cork, s of Sir Richard Pyne, Ch Justice King's Bench Ireland, and had:

  (1) HENRY (Sir), **2nd Bt**
  (1) Pyne; m 1766 Very Rev Hon Maurice Crosby, Dean Limerick
  (2) Caroline; m 1st George Quin (see DUNRAVEN and MOUNT-EARL, E); m 2nd 1792 Thomas Ahmuty and had issue
  (3) Frances; m 15 May 1769 Sir Frederick Flood, 1st and last Bt (dspms 1 Feb 1824)
  (4) Anne; m 9 Oct 1759 Sir Simon Bradstreet, 2nd Bt (see 1924 edn), and dspm
  (5) Catherine; m Thomas Burroughs, Master in Chancery

1 (cont.) **Sir Henry** m 2nd 4 Oct 1748 Catherine, dau of Henry Prittie (see DUNALLEY, B) and widow of Sir Richard Meade, 3rd Bt (see CLANWILLIAM, E), and d 31 Dec 1776, having by her had:

  (2) James; m Harriet Moore Coote, dau of Guy Moore, of Abbey, Co Tipperary, by Mary Coote, gdau of 1st Lord Coote, Baron of Coloony (see COOTE, Bt), and d 31 May 1776, having had two other sons and three daus

2 James; had:
  (1) James; Capt; had a 2nd dau:
    1a Theodosia; m Aug 1825 Allen Hurrell, 2nd s of William Hurrell, of Foxton Hall, Cambs

1 Frances; m Richard Green

The est s,

Sir Henry Cavendish, 2nd Bt, PC (I 1779); b 29 Sept 1732; educ Eton and Trin Coll Dublin; MP (I Parl) Lismore 1764–68, 1776, 1783–90 and 1798–1801 and Killybegs 1790–97, also (GB Parl, Whig) Lostwithiel 1768–74, Receiver-Gen Ireland 1779, sometime V-Treas Ireland; m 12 Aug 1757 SARAH (b 1 April 1740; cr 14 June 1792 **Baroness Waterpark**, of Waterpark, Co Cork (I), with remainder to her issue male by her husb; d 4 Aug 1807), only dau and heiress of Richard Bradshaw, of Cork, by Deborah, dau of William Thompson, of Cork, and d 3 Aug 1804, having had:

1 RICHARD, **2nd Baron**
2 George; b 26 Aug 1766; Sec to Lds Treasury Ireland; m 1st 26 Feb 1803 Letitia Catherine (dsp 3 Aug 1805), dau of James Caulfeild; m 2nd 15 Nov 1807 Catherine, dau of Ralph Smyth, of Gaybrook, and d 13 Feb 1849
3 Augustus CAVENDISH later BRADSHAW (1790); b 17 Feb 1768; FSA, Groom Bedchamber; m 15 Nov 1796 Mary Anne (d 14 Feb 1849), est dau of Maj James John Jefferyes, of Blarney Castle, Cork (see COLTHURST, Bt), and formerly w of 7th Earl of Westmeath (qv)
4 Frederick; b 1777; m 1st 1801 Eleanor (d 25 March 1812), dau of 2nd Earl of Arran (qv), and had:

  (1) Frederick (Rev); b 28 Aug 1803; m 1st 7 April 1834 Anne (d 23 Sept 1847), est dau of Brabazon Morris, of Mullaha; m 2nd 1848 Anne (d 12 Nov 1860), dau of Richard Armstrong
  (1) Sarah Anne; m 25 April 1834 Joseph Andrew Macdonnell, of Caher, Co Tipperary, and Abbeyville, Co Mayo, and d 1874, leaving issue
  (2) Catherine Elizabeth; m 1 March 1838 Roger Palmer (d 12 Oct 1884), of Carrowmore, Co Mayo, and d Aug 1889, leaving issue
  (3) Louisa Sophia; m 18 Aug 1832 Joseph William Morris, of Mullaha, and d 1 Oct 1834, leaving issue
  (4) Eleanor; m 1st Jan 1834 Walter James Burke, of Killala Castle; m 2nd 1849 Oliver Cuff Jackson and d 8 Feb 1866

4 (cont.) Frederick Cavendish m 2nd 5 Oct 1817 Agnes Catherine, est dau of Alexander Macdonnell, and d 10 March 1856, having by her had three sons

1 Catherine, m Baron de Ville and d 1800
2 Deborah; m 10 Nov 1782 Sir Richard Musgrave, 1st Bt, of Tourin (qv), and dsp
3 Sarah; m 20 Dec 1783 1st Earl of Mountnorris (d 4 July 1816; see VALENTIA, V) and d 2 Jan 1849, having had issue
4 Anne; m 25 July 1793 2nd Baron Kilmaine (qv) and d 6 July 1863

The 2nd Bt's est s and heir by BARONESS WATERPARK,

Sir Richard Cavendish, 3rd Bt, and **2nd Baron Waterpark**; b 13 July 1765; m 6 Aug 1789 Juliana (d 11 Oct 1847), est dau and coheir of Thomas Cooper, of Cooper's Hill and Mullaghmast Castle, Co Kildare, and d 1 June 1830, leaving, with a dau (d unm):

1 HENRY MANNERS CAVENDISH, **3rd Baron Waterpark**; b 8 Nov 1793; m 18 July 1837 Elizabeth Jane (d 15 Sept 1894), VA 3rd Cl, Extra Lady Bedchamber to HM QUEEN VICTORIA, sis of 1st Earl of Lichfield (qv), and d 31 March 1863, leaving, with a dau (d unm):

  (1) HENRY ANSON CAVENDISH, **4th Baron Waterpark**, JP, DL Derbys, JP Staffs; b 14 April 1839; Capt Staffs Yeo Cav; m 1873 Emily (d 27 Dec 1925), dau of John Stenning, and d 3 Aug 1912, having had:

    1a Henry; b 3 March 1875; 2nd Lt Rifle Bde; d unm vp 22 Oct 1897
    2a CHARLES FREDERICK CAVENDISH, **5th Baron Waterpark**; b 11 May 1883; Cdr RN WW I; d unm 27 Jan 1932
    1a Mary; m 14 May 1915 Lt-Col George Oldroyd Borwick (see BORWICK, B) and d 15 May 1967
    2a Winifred; m 8 March 1904 (divorce 1925) George Aston Strutt (d 25 March 1935), of Brailsford, Derbys, est s of George Strutt, of Bridgehill, and d 8 Dec 1971, leaving a dau
    3a Norah Lilian, d unm 12 Feb 1932

  (1) Eliza Anne; m 12 July 1859 Haughton Charles Okeover and d 11 Dec 1921, leaving issue (see WALKER-OKEOVER, Bt)

(2) Adelaide, Maid-of-Honour to HM QUEEN VICTORIA; *m* 3 Dec 1863 Samuel William Clowes (*d* 31 Dec 1808), JP, DL, of Broughton Old Hall, Lancs, and Norbury, Derbys, and *d* 20 April 1925, leaving issue

2 Richard, of Thornton Hall Bucks, and Crakemarsh Hall, Uttoxeter, Staffs, DL Bucks; *b* 1794; Envoy Nagpoor; *m* 22 July 1841 Elizabeth Maria Margaret (*d* 4 June 1858), only dau and heiress of Thomas Hart and n and heiress of Sir Thomas Cotton Sheppard, 2nd Bt, of Thornton Hall, Bucks, and *d* 18 March 1876, leaving, with another s and dau (*d* unm):

(1) William Thomas, of Thornton and Crakemarsh Halls, JP Bucks and Northants; *b* 29 July 1843; Lt 5th Dragoon Gds, Capt Bucks Yeo; *m* 1 May 1873 Cecilia Lafayette (*m* 2nd 18 Aug 1880 1st Baron Rathcreedan (*qv*) and *d* 11 Jan 1898), dau of James Kennedy, of The Limes, Co Down, and *d* 10 April 1878, leaving:

1a HENRY SHEPPARD HART CAVENDISH, 6th **Baron Waterpark**; *b* 18 May 1876; *educ* Eton; Lt 4th Bn Roy Warwicks Regt, Capt S African Light Horse, Boer War 1899–1902 and WW I, African traveller and explorer; FRGS, FRES; *m* 1st 16 April 1902 (*divorce* 1906) Isabel Emilie, actress, gold medallist RAM (*d* 26 Feb 1927), dau of John Wimburn Jay, and had:

1b *Cecilia Claribel [The Hon Mrs Anderson, Courtenay Beach, Kingsway, Hove, Sussex]; *b* 11 June 1903; *m* 29 July 1933 James Mitchell Anderson (*d* 11 June 1963), MD ChB (Edin), LRCP and S (Edin) LRCS (Glas), s of Philip Anderson, of Forres, Morayshire, and has:

1c *Isabel Juliet Cavendish; *b* 1937; *m* 1957 *Clifford Anthony Broom and has:

1d *Nicholas James; *b* 1959

2d *Christopher David; *b* 1961

2c *Annabel Fiona Macpherson Cavendish; *b* 1940; *m* 1st 1962 (*divorce* 1970) Manfred Seifert; *m* 2nd 1971 *Haven Lemar Dunn and has by her 1st husb:

1d *Jenny Elisabeth; *b* 1965

1a (cont.) The **6th Baron** *m* 2nd 12 Dec 1906 (*divorce* 1913) May (*d* July 1969 aged 83), dau of William Ernest Burbidge, of Bromley, Kent, and by her had:

2b *Margaret [The Hon Mrs Leaver, St Benet's, Beech Hill, Bridge, nr Canterbury, Kent]; *b* 24 Dec 1907; *m* 1 Sept 1934 Wallace Edward Thomas Leaver (*d* 1972), BSc Ag London, memb Convocation, s of Thomas Leaver, of Meadowcroft, Herne Bay, Kent, and has:

1c *Diana Cavendish; *b* 1938; *m* 1961 *Charles Peter Parnell Wiggins, of E Cross, Tenterden, Kent, and has:

1d *Rupert Alexander Cavendish; *b* 1963

1d *Philippa Cavendish; *b* 1962

2c *Elizabeth Cavendish; *b* 1942

3b *Winifred [The Hon Mrs Cavendish-Tribe, 27 Strickmere, Stratford St Mary, Essex CO7 6YG]; *b* 1 June 1909; *m* 13 Dec 1929 Capt Albert Frank TRIBE later CAVENDISH-TRIBE (deed poll 29 Sept 1944; quartered CAVENDISH and TRIBE arms by letters patent 23 Dec 1944), Trinity Ho Pilot (*d* 7 Dec 1962), 4th s of Lt-Cdr Arthur Ernest Tribe, RNR, Capt Merchant Navy, and has:

1c *Barrie [Barrie Cavendish-Tribe Esq, 27 Strickmere, Stratford St Mary, Colchester, Essex CO7 6YG]; *b* 22 Dec 1930; Capt Trinity Ho Pilot; *m* 2 Nov 1957 *Jane McGeorge, SRN, only dau of Surgn R-Adml David Duncan, CB, OBE, MD, ChB, DPH, of White Gates, Chailey, Sussex, and has:

1d *Alan [Eur Ing Alan Cavendish-Tribe Esq, 128 Hill Village, Four Oaks, Sutton Coldfield, W Midlands B75 5HN]; *b* 12 Dec 1960; BSc Eng, CEng, MIMechE, MWeldInst; *m* 25 May 1996 *Susan Mary, dau of Roy Willson, CEng, FIMin

1d *Sonia [Mrs David Ellis, Istana, Stockton Ave, Fleet, Hants GU13 8NP]; *b* 20 Oct 1963; BScChem; *m* 5 May 1990 *David Richard Ellis, BScChem, and has:

1e *Emily Jane; *b* 13 Jan 1996

2e *Karen Louise; *b* 13 Jan 1996

1a (cont.) The **6th Baron** *m* 3rd 30 Aug 1913 (*divorce* 1919) Elise, dau of Emmanuel Adolphe Herran, of Paris, late Sec French Embassy London; *m* 4th 2 June 1920 (*divorce* 1929) Georgette Zlateffmoloff, dau of Ivan Zlateffmoloff Chaudronnier, of Bulgaria; *m* 5th 7 Aug 1929 *Jeanne, dau of Pierre Lassallette, of Castillon-sur-Dordogne, Gironde, France, and *dspm* 26 Nov 1948

2a Frederick William Lawrence Sheppard Hart, CMG (1918), DSO (1916); *b* 11 Sept 1877; Boer War 1899–1902 (wounded, two medals, nine clasps) and WW I (despatches, brevet), Col 9th Lancers, Hon Brig-Gen 1928, Legn Hon, Croix de Guerre Belgium and France, Offr Order Leopold Belgium, Cdr Crown Belgium; *m* 18 June 1917 Enid Maude (*d* 5 Jan 1973, having *m* 3rd 3 Aug 1933 1st Viscount Furness (*see* 1970 edn) and 4th 26 Jan 1943 6th Earl of Kenmare; *see* 1949 edn), dau of Charles Lindeman, of Sydney, NSW, and widow of Roderick Cameron, of New York, and *d* 8 Dec 1931, leaving:

1b FREDERICK CARYLL PHILIP CAVENDISH, **7th and present Baron Waterpark**

1b *Patricia Enid [Mrs Frank O'Neill, Broadlands Stud, Somerset W, CP, S Africa]; *b* 30 June 1925; *m* 1st 30 Sept 1950 (*divorce* 1954) Frank Thomas O'Neill, a world swimming title-holder, of Nice; *m* 2nd 1 July 1957 Count Aymon de Roussy de Sales, s of Count Raoul de Roussy de Sales; *m* 3rd 1969 her 1st husb *Frank Thomas O'Neill

1a Elizabeth Mary Cecilia; *d* unm 25 March 1907

(2) Charles Tyrell, of Crakemarsh, JP and DL Staffs; *b* 17 Nov 1849; *m* 24 April 1873 Elizabeth Anne (*d* 28 Aug 1933), dau of Robert Dickinson, of Shotley Ho and Ebchester Hall, Co Durham, and *d* 18 Aug 1903, leaving:

1a Tyrell William; *b* 12 Oct 1875; *educ* Harrow; *m* 26 Dec 1906 Julia Florence (*d* 16 Jan 1963), only child of Henry Siegel, of New York, and *d* 15 April 1912 in the *Titanic* disaster, leaving:

1b Henry Siegel; *b* 29 Aug 1908; *educ* Eton and Trin Coll Cambridge; S/Ldr RAuxAF WW II; *m* 3 Feb 1940 *Diana Linda, est dau of Edward

Hewish Ryle, of Mortham Tower, Rokeby, Co Durham, and *d* 1 Oct 1995 leaving:

1c +William Henry Tyrell; *b* 6 Dec 1940; *educ* Eton

2b +Geoffrey Manners [Geoffrey Cavendish Esq, 7 Gema Cl, Allestree, Derby DE22 2UL]; *b* 3 Oct 1910; *educ* Stowe; CEng, MIEE, AMIBritRE; Dip Faraday Ho Engrg Coll, late Air Ministry Examiner in Scientific and Electrical Section of Aeronautical Inspn Directorates; *m* 1st 9 Oct 1937 Caecilia Frances Patricia (*d* 18 April 1968), yr dau of Godfrey Pharazyn, of Waewaepa, Dannevirke, Hawke's Bay, NZ; *m* 2nd 16 Oct 1967 *Pamela, dau of Capt George Ashby Chadwick Osborn, 7th Wilts Regt, and formerly w of Karl Klaus Neumann (Newman), and by his 1st w has:

1c *Caroline Anne; *b* 28 Aug 1938; *m* 24 July 1964 *Charles Grellan Aliaga-Kelly, BArch, ARIBA FRTPI, FRIAI, Dublin Planning Offr (ret), of Clare Villa, Coliemore Rd, Dalkey, Dublin, 2nd s of Ambrose Aliaga-Kelly, of Clonskeath, Dublin, and has:

1d *William John; *b* 18 Aug 1967; *educ* U Coll Dublin

2c *Caecilia Bridget [Mrs Henry Rokeby-Johnson, Kelsey Farm, PO Box 2001, Stellenbosch, CP 7601, S Africa; Arthingworth, PO Box 1513, Rancho Santa Fé, CA 92067, USA] *b* 16 Feb 1941; *m* 1979 *Henry Ralph Rokeby-Johnson and has:

1d *Henry Ralph Cavendish; *b* 14 Dec 1979

(1) Marianne; *m* 1st 6 Sept 1864 Capt Thomas Keane FitzGerald, of Shalstone Ho, Bucks; *m* 2nd 29 Jan 1872 John Hampson Jones and *d* 26 Sept 1888

(2) Catherine Elizabeth; *m* 20 July 1867 Thomas Cokayne Maunsell (*d* 26 Nov 1887), of Thorpe Malsor, and *d* 5 Aug 1931, leaving issue

(3) Emily Maria Georgiana; *m* 12 July 1864 Francis Noel Mundy (*dsp* 10 Jan 1903), of Markeaton Hall, Derbys, and *d* 6 Aug 1929

(4) Elizabeth Dorothy; *m* 12 Dec 1868 Sir William Smith-Marriott, 5th Bt (*qv*), and *d* 25 March 1904, leaving issue

(5) Cecilia Augusta; *m* 24 May 1883 Edward A Cousins (*d* 4 April 1931) and *d* 13 March 1909, leaving issue

3 George John; *b* 1796; V-Adml; *m* 14 Aug 1838 Caroline (*d* 13 July 1885), yst dau of Rev Charles Prideaux Brune, of Prideaux Place, Cornwall, and Plumber, Dorset, and *d* 23 Oct 1865, leaving, with two other daus:

(1) Frances Catherine Mary; *m* 17 Nov 1864 Rev Hugh Forbes Smith-Marriott (*see* SMITH-MARRIOTT, Bt), and *d* 4 Dec 1920

4 Augustus (Rev); *m* Dec 1830 Mary Anne, est dau of Thomas Legh, of Adlington, Cheshire, and *d* 9 May 1863, leaving:

(1) Thomas; *b* 31 Jan 1841

5 Frederick; Army Capt, *d* 24 May 1877 aged 77

6 Thomas (Rev); Vicar Doveridge; *m* 4 May 1835 Sophia (*d* 13 July 1891), 10th dau of Rev Sir John Robinson, 1st Bt, and *dsp* 26 March 1859

1 Sarah Georgiana; *m* 18 Nov 1819 Sir George Richard Philips, 2nd and last Bt (*d* 17 Sept 1874), and *d* 19 Sept 1874, having had issue

2 Juliana; *m* 28 Dec 1816 Frederick Farmer Taylor (*d* 24 June 1852), of Chyknell Ho, Salop, and *d* 19 Jan 1865, having had issue

3 Catherine; *m* 12 Dec 1839 Thomas Musgrave (*d* 1860), DD, Archbp York, and *d* 16 May 1863

WATSON

Arms: Azure on a fess dancetté between three crescents argent as many martlets sable. **Crest:** A gryphon's head erased azure, ducally crowned or, between two branches of palm proper.
Motto: Παθηματα μαθηματα ('Sufferings are lessons').
Creation: Bt. (UK) 27 June 1866.

SIR (JAMES) ANDREW WATSON, 5TH BT, of Henrietta St, Cavendish Sq, St Marylebone, Co Middx [Sir Andrew Watson Bt, Talton House, Newbold-on-Stour, Warwicks CV37 8UB]; *b* 30 Dec 1937; *s* f 1941; *educ* Eton; barrister Inner Temple 1966, Recorder 1989, late Lt Life Gds; *m* 12 Jan 1965 *Christabel Mary, est dau of Kenneth Ralph Malcolm Carlisle (*see* ABERCONWAY, B), and has:

1 +RONALD VICTOR; *b* 4 March 1966

2 +Alexander Bruce; *b* 25 Feb 1969

1 *Olivia Mary; *b* 11 Dec 1972

Lineage: JOSEPH WATSON, sometime of Thorpe-le-Soken, Essex; *m* 10 March 1791 Mary (*d* 24 May 1838), dau of Thomas Catton, of W Dereham, Norfolk, and *d* 14 Nov 1872, leaving, with two yr sons (Joseph, of Bocking Hall, Essex, *b* 27 Oct 1797, *m* 11 April 1822 Mary Ann (*d* 7 July 1872), dau of Abraham Cawston, of Shimpling Hall, Suffolk, and *d* 19 Sept 1878, leaving issue; Rev John, *b* 16 April 1800, Rector Hompton and Vicar Welwick, Yorks, *d* 23 June 1872) and a dau (*d* unm):

Sir Thomas Watson, 1st Bt (UK), so *cr* 27 June 1866, of Henrietta St, Cavendish Sq, London W; *b* 7 March 1792; MD; LLD, Pres Roy Coll Physicians, one of HM's Physicians in Ordinary; *m* 15 Sept 1825 Sarah (*d* 15 Sept 1830), dau of Edward Jones, of Brackley, Northants, and *d* 12 Dec 1882, leaving, with a dau (*d* unm):

Sir Arthur Townley Watson, 2nd Bt, KC; *b* 13 Sept 1830; MA Cantab; barrister, Bencher Lincoln's Inn; *m* 3 Oct 1861 Rosamond (*d* 24 June 1904), dau of Charles Powlett Rushworth, of Marylebone, and *d* 15 March 1907, leaving, with a yr s (Arthur Gordon WATSON later CATTON-WATSON, *b* 3 Aug 1870, Capt 4th Bn Roy Irish Rifles, *d* unm 7 March 1911) and two daus (Mabel Frederica, *m* 11 Aug 1887 Rev Reginald Fitz-Hugh Bigg-Wither (*d* 7 Nov 1929), Rector Wonston, Hants, and *d* leaving issue; Amy Catherine Rose):

Sir Charles Rushworth Watson, 3rd Bt; *b* 21 Sept 1865; *educ* Eton; *m* 19 Jan 1911 Evelyn Mary Elizabeth (*d* 23 March 1937), only dau of Aubrey Thomas Cartwright, JP, of Edgcote Park, Northants, and *d* 27 March 1922, leaving:

1 THOMAS AUBREY (Sir), **4th Bt**

2 John Rushworth; *b* 3 May 1913; *m* 6 Sept 1963 *Amy Diana, est dau of Maj Harold Petit Rushton, JP, of Phepson Manor, Worcs, TD, and formerly w of Maj Peter Wesley Dean, and *d* 1984, leaving:

  (1) *Camilla Mary; *b* 1967

1 Eleanor Mary; *b* 4 Aug 1914; *d* unm 19 April 1998

The 3rd Bt's er s,

  Sir Thomas Aubrey Watson, 4th Bt; *b* 7 Nov 1911; Lt Life Gds WW II; *m* 29 April 1935 Ella Marguerite (*d* 22 Aug 1996), yst dau of Sir George Farrar, 1st Bt (*see* 1915 edn), and was *kas* Middle East 10 Jan 1941, leaving:

Sir (JAMES) ANDREW WATSON, **5th and present Bt**

WATSON OF INVERGOWRIE

Creation: B. (LP, UK) 2 Aug 1997.

THE BARON WATSON OF INVERGOWRIE (Michael Goodall Watson) [The Rt Hon The Lord Watson of Invergowrie, House of Lords, London SW1A 0PW]; *b* 1 May 1949; *educ* Dundee High Sch and Heriot-Watt U Edinburgh; devpt offr WEA E Midlands 1974–77, official ASTMS then MSF 1977–89, MP (Lab) Glasgow Centl 1989–97, memb: H of C Public Accounts Ctee 1995–97 and Lab Pty Scottish Exec Ctee 1987–90, dir PS Communication Consultants Edinburgh, author: *Rags to Riches: the official history of Dundee United Football Club* (1985); *m* 1986 *Lorraine Therese, dau of William McManus

Lineage: CLARKE WATSON; *m* Senga Goodall and had:

MICHAEL, *cr* a **Baron**

WAVERLEY

Arms: Argent a saltire engrailed between a mullet in chief and a lotus flower in base, on each flank a crescent gules, on a chief sable three martlets of the field. **Crest:** A demi-lion rampant or, armed and langued azure, holding in his dexter forepaw a branch of olive proper. **Supporters:** Two horses argent, crined and unguled or.
Motto: *Beati pacifici* ('Blessed are the peacemakers').
Creation: V. (UK) 28 Jan 1952.

THE 3RD VISCOUNT WAVERLEY, of Westdean, Co Sussex (John Desmond Forbes Anderson) [The Rt Hon The Viscount Waverley, House of Lords, London SW1A 0PW]; *b* 31 Oct 1949; *s f* 1990; *educ* Malvern; *m* 1st 1969 Anne Suzette Davidson; *m* 2nd 1994 *Dr Ursula Helen Barrow, LLM, PhD, Belize HC to UK, dau of Raymond Hugh Barrow, SC, barrister, of Belize City

Lineage: JOHN ANDERSON, of The School House, Dunfermline; had:

DAVID ALEXANDER ANDERSON, of Westland House, Eskbank, Midlothian; *b* 17 June 1855; *educ* Dunfermline; publisher, dir Valentine & Sons Ltd, Dundee; *m* Sept 1881 Janet Kilgour (*d* 1929), dau of Charles Briglmen, of Edinburgh, and *d* 27 June 1948, leaving:

JOHN ANDERSON, **1st Viscount Waverley**, of Westdean, Co Sussex (UK), so *cr* 28 Jan 1952, GCB (1923, KCB 1919, CB 1918), OM (1957), GCSI (1937), GCIE (1932), PC (UK 1938, I 1920); *b* 8 July 1882; *educ* George Watson's Coll Edinburgh, Edinburgh U (BSc, MA 1903) and Leipzig U; Colonial Off 1905, Sec Nat Health Insurance Commn 1913, Sec Min Shipping 1917–19, Chm Bd Inland Revenue 1919–22, U-Sec to Ld Lt Ireland 1920–21 and Home Office 1922–32, Govr Bengal 1932–37, MP Scottish Us 1938, Ld Privy Seal 1938–39, Home Sec and Min Home Security 1939–40, Ld Pres Cncl 1940–43, Chllr Exchequer 1943–45, Chm PLA 1946; FRS 1945, Hon LLD: Aberdeen, Cantab, St Andrews, Edinburgh, Liverpool, Sheffield, Leeds and Kingston Ontario, Hon DSc McGill, KStJ, Grand Offr Legn Hon, Order Crown Italy, Kt Grand Cross Roy Order St Olaf Norway, Order Pole Star Sweden, Mil Order Christ Portugal, Order Dannebrog Denmark; *m* 1st 2 April 1907 Christina (*d* 9 May 1920), dau of Andrew Mackenzie, of Edinburgh, and had:

1 DAVID ALASTAIR PEARSON ANDERSON, **2nd Viscount**

1 *Mary Mackenzie (Dame), DBE (1970, MBE 1958) [The Hon Dame Mary Pihl DBE, 7 Kiln Gdns, Hartley Wintney, Hants RG27 8RG]; *b* 3 Feb 1916; *educ* Sutton High Sch and Brillamont, Lausanne; Brig WRAC, Dir WRAC 1967–70, Hon ADC to HM THE QUEEN 1967–70; *m* 8 July 1973 Frithjof Pihl (*d* 1988), of Norway

The **1st Viscount** *m* 2nd 30 Oct 1941 Ava (*d* 22 Dec 1974 aged 78), dau of John Edward Courtenay Bodley and widow of Ralph Follett Wigram, CMG (*see* WIGRAM, Bt), and *d* 4 Jan 1958

His only s,

DAVID ALASTAIR PEARSON ANDERSON, **2nd Viscount Waverley**; *b* 18 Feb 1911; *educ* Malvern, Pembroke Coll Cambridge (MA, MB, BChir 1938) and St Thomas's Hosp; FRCP 1957, MRCP 1946, MRCS Eng, LRCP 1936; consultant physician Reading Gp Hosps, FRSM, RAF Med Branch WW II, memb Reading Pathological Soc; *m* 13 Nov 1948 *Lorna Myrtle Ann [The Rt Hon The Dowager Viscountess Waverley, Chanders, Aldworth, Berks RG8 9RU], dau of Lt-Col Frederick Hill Ledgerwood, IA, by Mrs Alfred John Home Ross, and *d* 1990, having had:

1 JOHN DESMOND FORBES ANDERSON, **3rd and present Viscount Waverley**

1 Ida Christina Romaine; *b* 8 March 1952; *d* following a car crash 1972

2 *Patricia Mairead Janet [The Hon Mrs Clifton, Chanders, Aldworth, Berks RG8 9RU]; *b* 2 March 1955; *m* 1st 1 June 1979 (*divorce* 1983, resumed maiden name) Charles R Roberts, only s of Alan Roberts, of Eastwood Farm, Graffham, W Sussex; *m* 2nd 1989 *Leon Clifton, of Colorado, and by him has:

  (1) *William Scott; *b* 1990

  (1) *India Rose Veronica Romaine; *b* 1994

WEATHERILL

Arms: Azure a cross floretty or surmounting two lances in saltire proper, flying from each a forked pennon per fess gules and argent.
Crest: A horse rampant argent supporting a mace erect or.
Supporters: Dexter, a Captain in the 19th King George V's Own Lancers (Indian Army); sinister, a Knight of Justice of the Most Venerable Order of the Hospital of St John of Jerusalem, both proper. **Motto:** A stitch in time. **Creation:** B. (LP, UK) 1992.

THE BARON WEATHERILL, of NE Croydon, London Borough of Croydon ((Bruce) Bernard Weatherill, PC (1980), DL (Kent 1992)) [The Rt Hon The Lord Weatherill PC DL, Emmetts House, Ide Hill, Kent TN14 6BA]; *b* 25 Nov 1920;

educ Malvern; WWII: 2nd Lt 4th/7th Roy Dragoon Gds 1940, 19th King George V's Own Lancers 1941–45, Capt; joined Bernard Weatherill Ltd 1946–70 (md and chm 1957–70, pres 1992–); Chm: Guildford YCs 1946–49, Guildford C Assoc 1959–63, v-chm SE Area Prov Cncl 1962–64, memb Nat Union C Party 1963–64, MP (C) Croydon NE 1964–92, Ld Commr Treasury 1970–71, V-Chamberlain Household 1971–72 (Comptroller 1972–73, Treas [Dep Govt Ch Whip] 1973–74), Oppn Dep Ch Whip 1974–79, Chm Ways and Means and Dep Speaker 1979–83, Speaker H of C 1983–92; Chm: Cwlth Speakers and Presiding Offrs 1986–88, Parly Channel 1993, Industry and Parly Tst 1994–; Alternate Convenor Cross Bench Peers Ho Lds 1993 (Convenor 1995–); Pres Cwlth Parly Assoc 1986 and Lucifer Golfing Soc; High Bailiff Westminster Abbey 1989–; Hon LLD William and Mary Coll VA 1989; Hon DCL Kent U 1990, Denver 1992; Hon DL OU 1993; Hon Bencher Lincoln's Inn 1990; V-Chllr OStJ 1992–; Freeman: City London 1949, Borough Croydon 1983; *m* 1949 *Lyn, dau of Henry Thomas Eatwell, of Whitehall, Sandwich Bay, Kent, and has:

1 *Bernard Richard; *b* 1951; *educ* Malvern; *m* 1977 *Sally Maxwell Fisher and has:
   (1) *Thomas Bernard; *b* 1984
   (1) *Julia Rosemary; *b* 1982
2 *Henry Bruce; *b* 1953; *educ* Malvern; *m* 1978 *Susan Mary Dutton and has:
   (1) *James Edward Bruce; *b* 1983
   (2) *Benjamin Harry Charles; *b* 1986
   (1) *Sophie; *b* 1989
1 *Virginia; *b* 1955; *m* 1982 *Alan Charles Lovell and has:
   (1) *Emma Charlotte; *b* 1985
   (2) *Lucinda Mary; *b* 1986

Lineage: BERNARD WEATHERILL, of Spring Hill, Guildford; *m* Annie Gertrude Creak and had:

(BRUCE) BERNARD, *cr* a **Baron**

WEDDERBURN OF CHARLTON

Creation: B. (LP, UK) 1977.

THE BARON WEDDERBURN OF CHARLTON, of Highgate, Gtr London ((Kenneth) William Wedderburn) [The Rt Hon The Lord Wedderburn of Charlton, 29 Woodside Ave, London N6 4SP]; *b* 13 April 1927; *educ* Aske's Hatcham GS, Whitgift Sch and Queens' Coll Cambridge (LLB 1949, Chllr's medal English Law, MA 1951); RAF 1949–51 (F/Lt 1951); barrister Middle Temple 1953, QC 1990; Fell Clare Coll Cambridge 1952–64 (Tutor 1957–60, Hon Fell 1997–); assist law lecturer Cambridge U 1953–55 (lecturer 1955–64); Cassel Prof Commercial Law LSE 1964–92 (Emeritus Prof 1992–); Visiting Prof: UCLA Law Sch 1967, Harvard Law Sch 1969–70; gen ed *Modern Law Review* 1971–88; Hon Pres Industl Law Society 1997–; Ind Chm London and Provincial Theatre Cncls 1973–93; Chm Ind Review Ctee 1976–; memb: Ctee Industl Democracy 1976–77, Civil Service Arbitration Tbnl; Pres Inst Employment Rights 1989–95; FBA 1981; Hon DGiur Pavia 1990; Hon DEc Siena 1991, Hon LLD Stockholm 1996; author: *The Worker and the Law* (1965, 3rd edn 1986), *Torts, Clerk and Lindsell* (assist ed, 1969, 1975, 1982, 1989, 1995), *Industrial Conflict* (ed with B Aaron, 1972), *Democrazia Politca e Democrazia Industriale* (with S Sciarra et al, 1978), *Discrimination in Employment* (ed with Folke Schmidt, 1978), *Labour Law and Industrial Relations* (ed with W T Murphy, 1983), *Labour, Law and the Community* (1983), *Diritto del Lavoro in Europa* (with S Ghimpu and B Veneziani, 1987), *Social Charter, European Company and Employment Rights* (1990), *Employment Rights in Britain and Europe* (1991), *Labour Law and Freedom* (1995), *I Diretti del Lavoro* (1997); *m* 1st 1951 (*divorce* 1962) Nina, dau of Dr Myer Salaman, and has:

1 *David Roland; *b* 17 Sept 1956; BSc, ACA
1 *Sarah Louise [The Hon Mrs Faulkner, 3 Birley Rd, London N20 0HB]; *b* 9 June 1954; *m* 1st 1975 (*divorce* 1985) Michael Walsh; *m* 2nd 1992 *Hugh Edmund Brooke Faulkner
2 *Lucy Rachel; *b* 28 June 1960; MA

THE BARON WEDDERBURN OF CHARLTON *m* 2nd 1962 (*divorce* 1969) Dorothy Enid, dau of Frederick C Barnard and formerly w of William A Cole; *m* 3rd 1969 *Frances Ann, dau of Basil F Knight, and by her has:

2 *Jonathan Michael; *b* 29 Oct 1972; MA

Lineage: HERBERT J WEDDERBURN, of Deptford; *m* Mabel — and had:

(KENNETH) WILLIAM, *cr* a **Baron**

WEDGWOOD

Arms: Gules four mullets in cross, a canton argent. **Crest:** Upon a ducal coronet a lion passant argent. **Supporters:** On either side a lion double-queued argent, supporting a staff raguly gules. **Motto:** *Obstantia discindo* ('I split asunder obstacles'). **Creation:** B. (UK) 21 Jan 1942.

THE 4TH BARON WEDGWOOD, of Barlaston, Co Stafford (Piers Anthony Weymouth Wedgwood) [The Rt Hon The Lord Wedgwood, House of Lords, London SW1A 0PW]; *b* 20 Sept 1954; *s f* 1970; *educ* Marlborough and RMA Sandhurst; Offr Roy Scots 1973–80 (GSM (NI) 1976); *m* 1985 *Mary Regina Margaret Kavanagh, dau of Judge Edward Thomas Quinn, of Philadelphia, and has:
1 *Alexandra Mary Kavanagh; *b* 1987

Lineage: STEPHEN de WEGEWOOD, of Brerehurst, Manor of Tunstall, Staffs; living 1358–93; had:

RICHARD WEGEWOOD; living 1393; *m* 1st Margaret — and had:

STEPHEN WEGEWOOD, of Blackwood, Horton, Staffs; *m* Cicely — and *d* 1469, having had, with a yr s (Thomas, living 1470):

JOHN WEDGEWOOD, of Blackwood; *m* Margaret, dau and heiress of John Shaw, of Haracles, Horton, and *d* 1494, leaving:

RICHARD WEDGWOOD, of Blackwood and Haracles; had:

JOHN WEDGWOOD, of Blackwood and Haracles; *m* Anne, dau of William Bowyer, of Knypersley, Staffs, and *d* by 1556, having had:

1 John, of Blackwood and Haracles; Collector of Subsidy for Pirehill Hundred 1563; *m* Agnes — and *d* 1572, leaving:
   (1) John, of Haracles; arms confirmed and crest granted 1576; *m* Mary, dau of Thomas Egerton, MP, of Wall Grange, and *d* 6 April 1589, leaving:
   (2) Richard; Queen's Gd; *d* by 1588, leaving issue
   (1) Margery; *m* William Keelinge
2 Richard, of Mowle, Biddulph, Staffs; *m* Agnes — and *d* 1589, leaving:
   (1) Richard, of Mowle; *m* 14 Sept 1567 Margaret Boulton and *d* Dec 1626, leaving a yst s:
     1a Gilbert, of Burslem, Staffs; *b* 1588; master potter 1649; *m* 1612 Margaret (*d* 1655), dau and coheir of Thomas Burslem, of Burslem Overhouse, and *d* 1678, having had a 2nd s:
     1b Thomas, of Burslem Overhouse; master potter; *m* 9 April 1653 Margaret, dau and heiress of John Shaw, of The Churchyard Ho, Burslem, and *d* 1679, leaving a 2nd s:
     1c Thomas, of The Churchyard Ho; *b* 1660; master potter; *m* 28 June 1684 Mary (*d* 1718), dau of Thomas Leigh, of Burslem, and *d* 1716, leaving an est s:
     1d Thomas, of The Churchyard Ho; *b* 1686; master potter; *m* Mary (*d* 1766), dau of Josiah Stringer, Unitarian Min, and had, with other issue (including Catherine, *m* 1754 William Willet and was grandmother of Sir Henry Holland, 1st Bt; *see* KNUTSFORD, V), a 7th s:
     1e Josiah, of Etruria, Staffs; *bapt* 30 Aug 1730; FRS; master potter and creator of the eponymous pottery; *m* 25 Jan 1764 Sarah (*d* 15 July 1815), dau and heiress of Richard Wedgwood, of Spen Green, Astbury, Cheshire, and had, with other issue:
       1f John; *b* 28 March 1766; banker; *m* 12 Jan 1794 Louisa Jane, 5th dau of John Bartlett Allen, of Cresselly, Pembs, and *d* 1844, leaving issue
       2f JOSIAH
       3f Thomas; *b* 14 May 1771; chemist; *d* unm 10 July 1805
       1f Susannah; *b* 3 Jan 1765; *m* April 1796 Robert Waring Darwin, FRS, MD (*d* 13 Nov 1848), and *d* 15 July 1817, leaving issue

JOSIAH WEDGWOOD *d* 3 Jan 1795; his 2nd s,

JOSIAH WEDGWOOD, of Maer Hall, Staffs; *b* 3 Aug 1769; master potter of Etruria, first MP Stoke-on-Trent 1832–34; *m* 28 Dec 1792 Elizabeth (*d* 31 March 1846), est dau of John Bartlett Allen, of Cresselly, and had, with three daus (*d* unm):

1 Josiah, of Leith Hill Place, Surrey; *b* 12 Jan 1795; master potter of Etruria; *m* 1 Aug 1837 his cousin Caroline Sarah (*d* 5 Jan 1888), dau of Robert Waring Darwin, FRS, MD, and *d* 11 March 1880, leaving three daus (the 2nd of whom was mother of Ralph Vaughan Williams, the composer)

2 Henry Allen, of Hermitage, nr Woking; *b* 6 April 1799; barrister; *m* 26 Oct 1830 his cousin Jessie (*d* 1872), dau of John Wedgwood, and *d* 7 Oct 1885, leaving issue

3 FRANCIS

4 Hensleigh; *b* 22 Jan 1803; barrister, philologist and lexicographer; *m* 10 Jan 1832 his cousin Frances Emma (*d* 15 May 1889), dau of Sir James Mackintosh, Bt, PC, MP, and *d* 1 June 1891, leaving:

(1) James MacKintosh; *b* April 1834; mountaineer; *dsp* July 1874

(2) Ernest Hensleigh; *b* 17 June 1837; clerk Colonial Office; *m* 9 Aug 1887 Mary Louise Webster, dau of William Neward Bell, and *d* 4 Sept 1989, leaving issue

(3) Alfred Allen; *b* June 1842; *m* 10 Jan 1873 Margaret Rosena, dau of Richard Ingall, of Valparaiso, and *d* 9 Sept 1892, leaving issue

(1) Frances Julia; *b* Feb 1833; authoress; *d* 26 Nov 1913

(2) Katherine Euphemia; *b* Nov 1839; co-fndr with her cousin Margaret Vaughan Williams Leith Hill music festival; *m* 30 May 1873 1st Baron Farrer (*d* 11 Oct 1899; *see* 1963 edn) and *d* 2 Sept 1931

(3) Hope Elizabeth; *b* Feb 1844; *m* 14 Oct 1876 her cousin Godfrey Wedgwood (*see below*) and *d* 23 July 1935

1 Sarah Elizabeth; *b* 8 Dec 1793; *d* unm 7 Nov 1880

2 Mary Anne; *b* 14 June 1796; *d* Oct 1798

3 Charlotte; *b* 10 Nov 1797; *m* 22 March 1832 Rev Charles Langton (*d* 1886), s of George Langton, of Lincs, and *d* Jan 1862, leaving issue

4 Frances; *b* 24 April 1806; *d* unm 20 Aug 1832

5 Emma; *b* 2 May 1808; *m* 29 Jan 1839 her 1st cousin Charles Robert Darwin, JP, FRS (*d* 19 April 1882), the naturalist, of Downe, Farnborough, Kent, and *d* 2 Oct 1896, leaving issue

The 3rd s,

FRANCIS WEDGWOOD, of Barlaston and Etruria, JP (Staffs); *b* 24 Nov 1800; *educ* Rugby and Cambridge; master potter; *m* 26 April 1832 Frances (*d* 19 March 1874), dau of Rev John Peploe Mosley (*see* RAVENSDALE, B), and *d* 2 Oct 1888, leaving:

1 Godfrey, of Idlerocks, Stone, JP (Staffs); *b* 26 Jan 1833; master potter of Etruria, chm Josiah Wedgwood and Sons; *m* 1st June 1862 Mary Jane (*d* 7 April 1863), dau of Sir John Hawkshaw, of Hollycombe, Sussex, and had:

(1) Cecil, DSO (1902), of Woodhouse, Staffs; *b* 28 March 1863; *educ* Clifton; Maj 4th N Staffs Regt Boer War 1900–02, Maj 8th N Staffs Regt WW I; master potter of Etruria, first Mayor Stoke-on-Trent, chm Josiah Wedgwood and Sons; *m* 18 July 1888 Lucie (*d* 1939), dau of William Edward Gibson, of Cork, and was *ka* Somme 3 July 1916, leaving:

1a Phoebe Sylvia; *d* unm 12 May 1972 aged 78

2a Doris Audrey; *m* 31 July 1928 Lt-Col Thomas Geoffrey Rowland Makeig-Jones, MC, RE (*d* 26 March 1952), and *d* 27 Nov 1969, leaving issue

1 (cont.) Godfrey Wedgwood *m* 2nd 14 Oct 1876 his cousin Hope Elizabeth, dau of Hensleigh Wedgwood (*see above*), and *d* 9 Oct 1905, having by her had:

(1) Mary Euphrasia, MBE (1920); *educ* St Leonard's Sch St Andrews; VAD WW I (Italian Mil Cross); *m* 5 May 1937 William Mosley (*see* RAVENSDALE, B) and *d* 17 Feb 1952

2 CLEMENT FRANCIS

3 Laurence, of Barlaston; *b* 24 Oct 1844; *educ* Edinburgh U; master potter of Etruria; *m* April 1871 Emma (*d* 6 Jan 1929), dau of John Houseman, of London, and *d* 5 May 1913, having had:

(1) Kennard Laurence; *b* 11 Nov 1873; *educ* Uppingham; chm Josiah Wedgwood and Sons Ltd, pres Josiah Wedgwood and Sons of America; *m* 15 July 1908 Kathleen (*d* 4 Feb 1961), dau of Ormson David Wright, of Johannesburg, and *d* 19 Jan 1950, leaving:

1a *Esmé Alice; *b* 19 March 1910; *educ* Rosemont, Pa. (BA 1931) and Columbia U (MA 1935); dir Josiah Wedgwood and Sons Inc (of America) 1965–

(2) Gilbert Henry, DSO (1918); *b* 19 June 1876; *educ* Clifton; Lt-Col Yorks and Lancs Regt, Boer War 1900–02, WW I; *m* 21 July 1920 Dorothy (*d* 20 July 1971), dau of Walter Salmond, and *d* 21 Dec 1963

(3) Clement John; *b* 29 Dec 1877; *educ* Clifton; WW I 1916–19; *m* 23 April 1902 Violet Constance (*d* 20 Jan 1952), 2nd dau of Edwin Douglas, of Foxdown, Findon, Sussex, and *d* 7 Sept 1954, leaving:

1a Godfrey Josiah; *b* 14 Dec 1907; *educ* Sutton Valence and Edinburgh U; *m* 6 Nov 1937 *Gwendoline Mary, dau of Laurence Welch, of London, and *d* 10 Aug 1970, leaving:

1b *Judith Imogen; *b* 12 April 1942; *m* 6 Nov 1962 *Miguel de Serra Vacquer, of The Cafeteria, Bramber, Sussex, and has issue

1a Sybil Marguerite Alison; *b* 15 May 1911; hosp nurse; *m* 1st 29 June 1935 Francis Gordon Lyle (*d* 27 April 1971), s of Charles Alexander Lyle, of Chatswood, Tunbridge Wells, Kent; *m* 2nd 22 Aug 1968 Anthony Herbert Karasinski, of Dewponds, Vines Cross, Hatfield, Sussex, s of — Karasinski, of Bydgoszcz, Poland, and *d* 7 May 1985, having by her 1st husb had:

1b *Ian Alexander Douglas; *b* 20 July 1937; *m* and has issue

1b *Alison Camilla Wedgwood; *b* 1 May 1936; *m* and has issue

2a *Eileen Violet; *b* 2 Feb 1913; *m* 6 Aug 1934 Robert Henry Burgess, of Pembury, Kent, and has:

1b *Rollo Michael Trevor Clive; *b* 14 Nov 1939; *m* and has issue

1b *Felicity Ann; *b* 8 Jan 1935; *m* and has issue

2b *Jennifer Blanche Wedgwood; *b* 19 Oct 1936; *m* and has issue

3b *Julie Alison; *b* 1946; *m*

4b *Victoria Susan; *b* 4 July 1950; *m* and has issue

(4) Geoffrey Walter; *b* 2 Aug 1879; *d* 12 Oct 1897

(1) Mary Frances; *b* 17 Dec 1874; *m* 12 June 1902 Ernald George Justinian Hartley (*d* 23 Dec 1947), only s of George Thompson Hartley, of Wheaton Aston, Staffs, and *d* 19 July 1969, leaving issue

1 Amy; *d* unm 25 Jan 1910

2 Cicely Mary; *m* 12 Oct 1865 John Clarke Hawkshaw, of Hollycombe, Sussex, and *d* 6 Sept 1917, leaving issue

3 Constance Rose; *b* 4 Aug 1846; *m* 26 July 1880 Johann Herman Franke (*d* 1912), of Dresden, Germany, and *dsp* 5 May 1903

4 Mabel Frances; *b* 19 Jan 1852; *m* 7 July 1880 Arthur George Parson (*d* 1907), of Haslemere, Surrey, and *dsp* 10 March 1930

The 2nd s,

CLEMENT FRANCIS WEDGWOOD, of Barlaston Lea; *b* 25 Feb 1840; master potter of Etruria; Capt 4th N Staffs Militia; *m* 6 Nov 1866 Emily Catherine (*d* 6 April 1921), dau of James Meadows Rendel, FRS, civil engr, and sis of 1st and last Baron Rendel (*see* 1913 edn), and *d* 24 Jan 1889, having had:

1 Francis Hamilton, of Barlaston Lea, JP, DL (Staffs); *b* 9 Oct 1867; *educ* Clifton and Trin Coll Cambridge; Capt 4th N Staffs Regt Boer War 1900–02; chm Josiah Wedgwood and Sons 1916–30, dir LMSR, High Sheriff 1929; *m* 11 Sept 1902 Katharine Gwendoline (*d* 20 Aug 1958), dau of Rev Edmund Vincent Piggott, of Doddershall Park, and *d* 29 Oct 1930, leaving:

(1) Clement Thomas (Tom); *b* 10 Nov 1907; *educ* Charterhouse and Trin Coll Cambridge (BA 1930); dir Josiah Wedgwood and Sons, farmer S Rhodesia; *m* 2 Dec 1934 Katharine Sarah, dau of Arthur B Rendel, MD, of Postbridge, Devon, and *d* 24 April 1960, leaving:

1a *Francis Alan [Francis Wedgwood Esq, The Dairy Farm House, Wallingford Rd, Cholsey, Berks]; *b* 16 May 1937; *educ* Marlborough and Worcester Coll Oxford (BA; DPhil 1962); physicist, non exec dir Waterford Wedgwood PLC; *m* 4 June 1966 *Janet Joyce, only dau of Dudley Merer, of Bo'ness, and has:

1b *Thomas Dudley; *b* 24 Jan 1971; civil engr

1b *Joyce Katherine; *b* 21 July 1969; MB, ChB; *m* 17 July 1993 *Andrew Greer McConkey

2b *Ruth Frances; *b* 7 Nov 1972

2a Stephen; *b* 28 April 1945; civil engr; *m* 19– *Judy Alice Jackson and *d* 30 Sept 1986, leaving:

1b *Thomas Roland; *b* 23 March 1969; sales dept Waterford-Wedgwood; *m* 28 May 1994 *Cheris Kim Miner

2b *Matthew Charles; *b* 6 June 1977

1b *Veronica; *b* 31 March 1970; nurse; *m* 12 April 1996 *Harold Aloysius Carroll

2b *Sarah Marjorie; *b* 16 Sept 1975

3a *Nicholas Robert; *b* 1 Aug 1953; airline pilot; *m* 20 Dec 1984 *Janette Angela Fuller and has:

1b *Samuel Stephen; *b* 17 april 1987

1b *Sophie Camilla; *b* 30 May 1989

1a *Susan Frances; *b* 28 Sept 1935; *m* 2 Aug 1958 *Mogens Christian Christoph Vind, farmer, Zimbabwe, yst s of Kammertherre Ove Holger Christian Vind, of Denmark, and has:

1b *Christian Tom; *b* 7 Sept 1959; salesman; has issue

2b *Ivor Henrik; *b* 6 Dec 1961; farmer; *m* and has issue

1b *Kirsten Frances; *b* 7 July 1964; *m*

(1) Frances Dorothy (Joy); *b* 12 July 1903; *m* 29 Aug 1941 Jack L W Fynn (*d* 1954), s of Sir Percival Donald Leslie Fynn, of Salisbury, S Rhodesia, and *d* 5 July 1996, leaving issue

(2) Cecily Stella; *b* 29 Oct 1904; *m* 30 June 1937 Maj Frederic Maitland Wright, MBE (*d* 5 May 1993), and *d* 18 Feb 1995, leaving issue

2 Clement Henry; *b* 1 Oct 1870; *d* 29 May 1871

3 JOSIAH CLEMENT, **1st Baron**

4 Sir RALPH LEWIS WEDGWOOD, 1st Bt (*see* WEDGWOOD, Bt)

5 Arthur Felix; *b* 18 July 1877; *educ* Clifton and Trin Coll Cambridge; Capt 5th N Staffs Regt; *m* 20 April 1911 Katherine (*d* 5 Dec 1976), dau of Lt-Col Llewellyn Wood Longstaff, of Wimbledon, and was *ka* 14 March 1917, leaving:

(1) Cecil Felix Nivelle; *b* 12 Dec 1916; *educ* Eton; farm manager; *d* 9 Sept 1996

(1) *Katherine Frances; *b* 11 July 1912; *m* 18 June 1936 Rev John Colpoys Cunningham (*d* 15 Oct 1991), est s of Maj John Francis Cunningham, OBE, FRCS, of London W1 and Sector, Axminster, Devon, and has:

1a *Colin John Kirkaldy [Colin Cunningham Esq, Camascoille, Achnahaird, Achiltibuie, Ullapool, Wester Ross]; *b* 31 Jan 1942; *educ* Sherborne; architectural historian Open U; *m* 1 Nov 1969 *Alisoun Elizabeth, dau of Rev Canon William Ernest Purcell, of Worcester, and has:

1b *Alastair William Felix; *b* 18 June 1971

1b *Margaret Sophia; *b* 6 Oct 1973

1a *Henrietta Mary; *b* 14 July 1940; *m* 22 Aug 1964 *Colin Charles Morath, design engr, and has:

1b *Timothy Charles; *b* 18 Aug 1965; musician

1b *Katharine Mary; *b* 11 March 1967; TV sound recordist

2b *Diana Frances; *b* 19 Feb 1972

2a *Anna-Lisa Karen; *b* 27 March 1948; C of E priest; *m* 29 May 1978 *Gordon Elliott Keith Garvie, only s of James Garvie, and has:

1b *Peter Francis; *b* 18 Nov 1984

1b *Sarah Kate; *b* 2 Oct 1980

(2) *Felicity Emily; *b* 1 Nov 1913; *m* 16 Jan 1943 *Charles Everard Cradock Royds, of Tyruched, Glasbury-on-Wye, er s of Rev Charles Cradock Twemlow Royds, Rector Heysham, and has:

1a *John Felix Cradock; *b* 30 Jan 1947; *educ* Christ's Coll Brecon; *m* 19– *Carol Lancaster *née* Nuttall and has:

1b *Stephen Felix; *b* 13 July 1971; chef

2b *Julian; *b* 10 Nov 1973; electrician

1b *Stephanie; *b* 4 Oct 1979

2b *Vivien; *b* 4 Oct 1979

3b *Jacqueline; *b* 4 Oct 1979

2a *Richard Clement; *b* 31 Dec 1948; *educ* Christ's Coll Brecon; teacher; *m* 25 March 1970 *Dr Janice Anne Lund and has:

1b *Martin David; *b* 8 Dec 1973

2b *Christopher Wedgwood; *b* 16 Aug 1987

1b *Rachel Helen; *b* 10 Aug 1972

3a *Tom Longstaff; *b* 3 Feb 1952; *educ* Christ's Coll Brecon; electronic engr; *m* 12 April 1977 *Jane Ann Sibley and has:

1b *Peter Longstaff; *b* 6 Jan 1979

2b *Michael Ryan; *b* 7 Aug 1980

1b *Felicity Christina; *b* 29 Oct 1982

1a *Caroline Felicity [Mrs James Cobb, c/o Gatty Marine, Laberably, St Andrews, Fife]; *b* 7 April 1944; *educ* St Andrews (MA); *m* 21 Aug 1965 *James Leslie Stiles Cobb, BSc, PhD, zoologist, s of Sidney John Cobb, of Nant Digeddi, Llanigon, nr Hay-on-Wye, Herefs, and has:

1b *Emily Jane; *b* 11 March 1967; MD; *m* 6 July 1991 *Iain Alistair MacLean, MRCVS

2b *Caroline Joan; *b* 13 Sept 1969; MD

3b *Victoria Joanna Toke; *b* 30 Jan 1971

2a *Beatrice Daisy; *b* 6 Sept 1945; *m* 4 Nov 1967 *David William Andrew Morgan, farmer, and has:

1b *Katharine; *b* 10 July 1968; MD; *m* 4 April 1992 *Dr Krishna Kandasamy

2b *Camilla Rebecca; *b* 1 Oct 1972

3b *Alexandra Louise; *b* 15 April 1978

1 Cecily Frances; *m* 26 Dec 1903 Maj-Gen Sir Arthur Wigram Money, KCB, RA (*d* 25 Oct 1951), and *d* 22 Sept 1904

CLEMENT WEDGWOOD *d* 24 Jan 1889; his 3rd s,

JOSIAH CLEMENT WEDGWOOD, **1st Baron Wedgwood**, of Barlaston, Co Stafford (UK), so *cr* 21 Jan 1942, DSO (1915), PC (1924), JP, DL (Staffs); *b* 16 March 1872; *educ* Clifton and RNC Greenwich; Assist Constructor Portsmouth Dockyard 1895–96, Naval Architect Elswick Shipyard 1896–1900, Capt Elswick Bn Boer War 1900–01 (medal and three clasps), RM Ermleo Transvaal 1902–04, Col WW I 1914–16 (wounded, despatches twice), CC 1910–19, MP (Lib, Lab then Ind) Newcastle-under-Lyme 1906–42 (Mayor 1930–32), V-Chm Lab Party 1921–24 Chllr and Ch Civil Commr Duchy Lancaster 1924, Chm Ctee on H of C Records 1929–42, Hon Sec William Salt Archaeological Soc, Pres English League for Taxation of Land Values; *m* 1st 3 July 1894 (*divorce* 1919) his 1st cousin Hon Ethel Kate BOWEN later BOWEN-WEDGWOOD (deed poll 24 June 1919; *d* 26 Nov 1952), only dau of Baron Bowen, PC (*see* 1894 edn); *m* 2nd 25 June 1919 Florence Ethel (*d* 1 July 1969), dau of Edward Guy Willett, of London, and by his 1st w had:

1 FRANCIS CHARLES BOWEN, **2nd Baron**

2 Josiah; *b* 20 Oct 1899; *educ* Bedales and London U (BSC 1922); chm Josiah Wedgwood and Sons (md 1930–60), dir: Bank of England 1942–46, District Bank 1948; chm Cncl RCA 1948, 2nd Lt RFA; *m* 19 Jan 1919 Dorothy Mary, OBE (1969) (*d* 13 Dec 1974), dau of Percy James Winser, of Knutsford, Cheshire, and *d* 5 May 1968, leaving:

(1) +JOHN, CBE [Dr John Wedgwood CBE, 156 Ashley Gdns, Thirleby Rd, London SW1P 1HW]; *b* 28 Sept 1919; heir presumptive; *educ* Abbotsholme and Trin Coll Cambridge (BA 1948, MA 1954), MD, FRCP; Surgn-Lt RNVR 1944–47, consultant physician; *m* 1st 17 June 1943 (*divorce* 1971) Margaret, dau of Alfred Sidell Mason, of Thurston Lodge Flat, Bury St Edmunds; *m* 2nd 20 May 1972 *Jo Alice Tamlyn, dau of Harold Swan Ripsher, of Stanmore, Middx, and by his 1st w has:

1a +Antony John [Antony Wedgwood Esq, 10 Milner Pl, London N1]; *b* 31 Jan 1944; *educ* Marlborough and Trin Coll Cambridge (BA 1965, MA 1967); *m* 18 July 1970 *Angela Margaret Mary Page and has:

1b +Josiah Thomas Antony; *b* 20 April 1978

1b *Elizabeth Helen Katherine; *b* 15 July 1975

2b *Caroline Phoebe Margaret; *b* 7 July 1981

2a +Simon James Josiah [Simon Wedgwood Esq, 35 Grafton St, Cambridge]; *b* 3 Oct 1949; *educ* Culford Sch, Bury St Edmunds; interior designer

3a +Nicholas Ralph [Nicholas Wedgwood Esq, 24 Camden High St, London NW1]; *b* 30 June 1951; *educ* Culford Sch, Bury St Edmunds; engr

1a *Judith Margaret Susanna; *b* 24 Aug 1946; *m* 1st 23 July 1966 (*divorce* 1986) Christopher Anthony Wingfield Tracy, of Wimbledon, s of David Quinn Wingfield Tracy, of Bickley, Kent, and has:

1b *Emma Sarah Honor; *b* 27 Dec 1970

2b *Victoria Jane Camilla; *b* 13 Dec 1974

3b *Charlotte Rose Christabel; *b* 20 Sept 1976

1a (cont.) Mrs Judith Tracy *m* 2nd 1986 *(Kevin) Dominic Hall Brennan, slr, and by him has:

1b *Alexander John Clement; *b* 4 Oct 1987

2b *Roland Kevin Dominic; *b* 4 Oct 1987

2a *Katherine Sarah [Mrs Ian Stanbury, Harewood Cottage, Chicksgrove, Wilts]; *b* 24 Nov 1955; *m* 22 April 1988 *Ian Reed Stanbury, property developer, and has:

1b *Jack Benjamin; *b* 22 Oct 1988

2b *Matthew John; *b* 9 Nov 1990

(2) +Josiah Ralph Patrick [Dr J Wedgwood, 3717 41st Ave NE, Seattle, WA 98105, USA]; *b* 25 May 1924; *educ* Harvard (MD); Capt MC, USAR 1951–53, Prof Pediatrics, memb Nat Advsy Research Cncl Nat Inst Health, US Public Health Serv, chm Jt Cncl Nat Pediatric Serv USA, memb Exec Ctee Cncl of Academic Socs of American Assoc of Med Colls; *m* 25 Oct 1943 *Virginia Lloyd, dau of Edward Eyre Hunt, of Washington, DC, and has had:

1a +Josiah Francis [Dr Josiah Wedgwood, 240 St Ronan, New Haven, CT 06510, USA]; *b* 1 Feb 1950; PhD, MD; Asst Prof Mount Sinai, NY; *m* 30 May 1982 *Prof Ruth Anne Glushien, Prof Constitutional and Internat Law Yale, dau of Morris Glushien, of Great Neck, Long Island, and has:

1b +Josiah Ruskin; *b* 25 Aug 1998

2a James Cecil; *b* 29 Aug 1951; *d* 27 June 1973

3a +Jeffrey Galton [Dr Jeffrey Wedgwood, 1837 127th St SE, Bellevue, WA 98005, USA]; *b* 30 Jan 1953; *m* 1st 1974 (*divorce* 1984) Cynthia Baird; *m*

2nd 1 Jan 1985 *Susan Singer, dau of Pierce D Smith, of Darien, Conn., and by his 2nd w has:

1b +Josiah Smith; *b* 5 March 1986

1b *Grace Madeleine; *b* 24 March 1989

4a +John Ralph Christopher[John Wedgwood, 7922 208th Ave NE, Redmond, WA98053, USA]; *b* 4 Sept 1964; computer engr; *m* 30 May 1987 *Kathleen, dau of William Turner, of Kirkland, WA, and has:

1b +James Turner Berkeley; *b* 8 Dec 1997

(1) Jennifer Susan; *b* 2 Dec 1927; *educ* Radcliffe (BA 1948); musician; *m* 28 Oct 1945 *Emil Wendel Lehmann [Emil W Lehmann, 205 Bedens Brook Rd, Skillman, NJ, USA], MSc Harvard, s of Emil Wilhelm Lehmann, and *d* 6 Sept 1992, leaving:

1a *John Winser; *b* 20 April 1951; *m* 23 June 1973 *Kathleen, dau of Francis Sehn, of Bloomfield Hills, MI, and has:

1b *Nora Fances; *b* 12 Feb 1977

2b *Claire Wedgwood; *b* 3 May 1980

3b *Anne Celeste; *b* 7 July 1983

2a *Mark Wedgwood; *b* 12 July 1954; *m* 8 Nov 1980 *Elizabeth Hollenbeck (Holly), dau of James Graves of San Juan, Puerto Rico, and New York, and has:

1b *John Ashford; *b* 20 April 1988

2b *Nicholas Wedgwood; *b* 30 March 1991

1 Helen Bowen, JP (1925); *b* 4 July 1895; *educ* Newnham Coll Cambridge (MA 1953); CC (1937), CA (1964) Cambs; *m* 24 Feb 1920 Michael Stewart Pease, OBE (*d* 27 July 1966), est s of Edward Reynolds Pease, of Limpsfield, Surrey, and *d* 17 June 1981, having had issue

2 Rosamund; *b* 19 Nov 1896; *m* 28 Feb 1920 Janos Békássy, son of István Békássy de Bekás, of Kis-Sennye, Rum Vas, Hungary, and *d* 5 Oct 1960

3 Camilla Hildegarde; *b* 25 March 1901; *educ* Orme Girls' Sch Newcastle-under-Lyme, Newnham Coll Cambridge (BA 1924, MA 1927) and Bedford Coll London U; Pncpl Women's Coll Sydney U Australia 1935–44, Lt-Col Australian Women's Serv in Directorate of Research and Sch Civ Affrs 1944–46; *d* unm 17 May 1955

4 Elizabeth Julia; *b* 1 May 1907; *dsp* 14 April 1993

5 Gloria; *b* 24 Dec 1909; *m* 1st 1 March 1937 (*divorce* 1940) Paul August Oppenheim, est s of Louis Oppenheim, of Kassel, and had:

(1) *(Paul) Felix OPPENHEIM later WEDGWOOD-OPPENHEIM (deed poll 1945) [Felix Wedgwood-Oppenheim Esq, 156 All Saints Rd, King's Heath, Birmingham 14]; *b* 8 Oct 1938; *educ* Prince of Wales Sch Christopher Sch Letchworth, Keele U (BA 1964) and Birmingham U (MSc 1968); lecturer Operational Research Inst of Local Govt Studies, Birmingham U; *m* 24 June 1961 *Helen Frances Anne, er dau of Dr John Stuart Glashan Shotwell, of NY, and Ottawa, Canada, and has:

1a *Mark Felix; *b* 30 Jan 1964; computer specialist

2a *Bruce Andrew; *b* 24 Oct 1967; geneticist

5 (cont.) The Hon Mrs Gloria Oppenheim *m* 2nd 15 April 1940 (*divorce* 1958, took name WEDGWOOD-MICHAEL by deed poll Nov 1968) Heinz Peter Michael, BSc, er s of Dr Otto Michael, of Leipzig, and *d* 7 July 1974, having by him had:

(2) *Otto Clement Wedgwood; *b* 5 June 1947; *educ* Imp Coll London (BSc 1969); civil engr with Essex River Authority; *m* 4 July 1970 (*divorce* 1995) Jane Elizabeth, er dau of Dr Rushmer, of Outwell, Cambs, and has:

1a *Helen Catherine; *b* 5 Jan 1978

2a *Susannah Rachel; *b* 3 June 1980

(1) *Elizabeth Ann Wedgwood; *b* 18 Sept 1944; *m* 27 July 1963 *Peter Newman Hard, of Bygrave, Herts, er s of John F Hard, and has:

1a *Newman Paul Wedgwood; *b* 12 March 1968; *m* 3 Sept 1994 *Belinda Vivien Webb

2a *Tarek John Wedgwood; *b* 25 May 1970

The 1st BARON *d* 26 July 1943; his s,

FRANCIS CHARLES BOWEN WEDGWOOD, **2nd Baron Wedgwood**; *b* 20 Jan 1898; *educ* Bedales and Slade; WW I as Sub-Lt RNVR and Lt RFC (wounded); artist; *m* 28 May 1920 Edith May (*d* 5 Feb 1977), dau of William Telfer, of Glasgow, and *d* 22 April 1959, leaving:

HUGH EVERARD WEDGWOOD, **3rd Baron Wedgwood**; *b* 20 April 1921; *educ* Bedales and Trin Coll Cambridge; Kenya Regt 1939; *m* 1st 20 March 1945 (*annulled* 1947) Jean Annette Heather, only child of Ralph S Leake, of Bournemouth; *m* 2nd 5 Oct 1949 *Jane Weymouth [The Rt Hon The Dowager Lady Wedgwood, Harewood Cottage, Chicksgrove, Wilts], 2nd dau of William James Poulton, of Kenjockety, Molo, Kenya, and *d* 25 April 1970, leaving by her:

1 PIERS ANTHONY WEYMOUTH WEDGWOOD, **4th and present Baron Wedgwood**

1 *Susan Margaret; *b* 22 Sept 1950; *m* 6 June 1994 *Hubert Ribeiro de Santana, artist and travel writer

2 *Sarah Jane Edith; *b* 11 July 1958; *m* 4 May 1983 *Paul J Bitove, of Toronto, s of James Bitove, of Toronto, and has:

(1) *Olivia Charlotte; *b* 7 Feb 1988

WEDGWOOD, Bt

Arms: Gules, four mullets in cross, a canton argent. **Crest:** Upon a ducal coronet, a lion passant argent. **Motto:** *Obstantia discindo* ('I split asunder obstacles'). **Creation:** Bt. (UK) 20 Jan 1942.

SIR (HUGO) MARTIN WEDGWOOD, 3RD BT [Sir Martin Wedgwood Bt, Pixham Mill, Pixham Lane, Dorking, Surrey]; *b* 27 Dec 1933; *s f* 1989; *educ* Eton and Trin Coll Oxford (BA); memb Stock Exchange 1973–91, ptnr Laurence, Prust and Co 1973–84, dir Smith New Court Int Ltd 1986–91; *m* 20 July 1963 *Alexandra Mary Gordon, FSA, authoress and architectural archivist Palace of Westminster, er dau of Judge Alfred Alexander Gordon Clark (*see* LAWRENCE, Bt, of Ealing Park), and has:

1 +RALPH NICHOLAS; *b* 10 Dec 1964; *educ* Westminster, Magdalen Coll Oxford (BA), King's Coll London (MPhil) and Cornell; PhD, Assist Prof Philosophy MIT 1995–

1 *Julia Mary; *b* 10 Nov 1966; *educ* St Theresa's Effingham and SS. Hild and Bede Coll Durham (BA); *m* 2 Sept 1995 *Nicholas Dominic Bernard Johnson, advertising exec, only s of Bernard Johnson, of Colchester, and has:

  (1) *Daniel Lawrence; *b* 10 Nov 1997

2 *Frances Veronica Mary; *b* 28 Oct 1969; *educ* Sutton High Sch, Christ's Coll Cambridge (BA) and UCL; MBBA, MRCP; *m* 4 Jan 1997 *Gareth Melindwr Edwards, TV producer, only s of John Edwards, of Bristol, and has:

  (1) *Joseph Josiah Emrys; *b* 23 June 1998

Lineage: **Sir Ralph Lewis Wedgwood, 1st Bt** (UK), so *cr* 20 Jan 1942, CB (1918), CMG (1917), TD; *b* 2 March 1874 (3rd s of Clement Francis Wedgwood; *see* WEDGWOOD, B); *educ* Clifton and Trin Coll Cambridge (BA 1895, MA 1939); WW I: Col cmdg Engr and Rlwy Staff Corps, Dir Docks with rank of Brig-Gen (despatches, Orders SS. Maurice and Lazarus Italy Crown Belgium, Legn Hon, Croix de Guerre), Dep Gen Manager NER 1919–21, Gen Manager 1922–23, Ch Gen Manager LNER 1923–39, ktd 1924, memb: Centl Electricity Bd 1930–45, Chinese Govt Purchasing Commn 1930 and Cncl Roy Soc Arts 1939, memb Delegacy King's Coll London 1942–45 (Chm 1945), Pres Nat Confedn Employers' Organisations 1929–30, memb Weir Ctee on Main Line Electrification 1930–31, Chm: Indian Rlwy Inquiry Ctee 1936–37, Air Raid Def League Ctee 1938–39 and Rlwy Exec Ctee 1939–41, Chm Assoc Br Picture Corp 1941–42, OStJ, Cdr Order Dannebrog Denmark, Kt Cdr Order St Olav Norway, Cdr Orders Orange Nassau Holland and Leopold II Belgium, Order Brilliant Jade China; *m* 24 Oct 1906 Iris Veronica (*d* 17 Feb 1982 aged 95), novelist and travel writer, dau of Albert Henry Pawson, of Farnley, Leeds, and had:

1 JOHN HAMILTON (Sir), **2nd Bt**

1 (Cicely) Veronica, DBE (1968, CBE 1956), OM (1969); *b* 20 July 1910; *educ* Norland Sch London and LMH Oxford (BA 1931, Hon Fell 1962); Pres English PEN 1951–57, Soc Authors and English Assoc 1955–56, memb Cncl V&A 1958–68, Ctee Soc Arts, Arts Cncl and Roy Comm Historical MSS., Tstee Nat Gallery, ed with Jonathan Cape, dep ed *Time and Tide*, author: *Thomas Wentworth, Earl of Strafford* (1934, revised edn 1961), *The Thirty Years War* (1939), *Oliver Cromwell* (1940), *William The Silent, Prince of Orange* (1944, James Tait Black Memorial Prize), Velvet Studies (essays, 1946), trans Elias Canetti's *Auto da Fé* (1946), *Richelieu and the French Monarchy* (1948), *Seventeenth Century Literature* (1950), *The Last of the Radicals* (biography of her uncle 1st Baron Wedgwood (*qv*), 1951), *A Life of Montrose* (1952), *The King's Peace* (1955), *The King's War* (1959), *Poetry and Politics Under the Stuarts* (1960), *The Trial of Charles I* (1964, revised edn 1980), *Milton and His World* (1969), *The Spoils of Time: a short history of the world vol I* (1984) and other historical works, Hon LLD Glasgow 1955, Hon DLitt Sheffield 1960, Smith 1962, Harvard 1964, Oxford 1965 and Keele 1966, Hon Fell UCL, FBA 1975, memb American Acad Arts and Letters and Acad Arts and Science, Offr Order Orange Nassau 1946, Goethe Medal Fedl Republic Germany 1958; *d unm* 9 March 1997

The 1st Bt *d* 5 Sept 1956; his only s,

Sir John Hamilton Wedgwood, 2nd Bt, TD (1948), JP (Stone 1951–59); *b* 16 Nov 1907; *educ* Winchester and Trin Coll Cambridge (BA 1929); Maj N Staffs Regt and on Gen Staff WW II; dep chm Josiah Wedgwood and Sons to 1966, dir Wedgwood Housing Assoc Ltd and Wedgwood Estate Co to 1966, memb Br Nat Export Cncl 1964–66, Chm Anglo-American Community Rels Lakenheath Base 1972–76, memb advsy body Harlaxton Coll Lincs 1975–89, Pres: Utd Commer-

cial Travellers Assoc 1959, Samuel Johnson Soc (Lichfield) 1959, FRSA 1968, FRGS 1973, Liveryman Painter-Stainers' Co 1971, Hon LLD Birmingham 1966, Hon DLitt William Jewell Coll Kansas; *m* 1st 6 April 1933 his 2nd cousin Diana Mildred (*d* 3 Oct 1976), dau of Lt-Col Oliver Hawkshaw, of Chisenbury Priory, Marlborough, Wilts; *m* 2nd 30 April 1982 *Pamela, PhD, FSA [Pamela Lady Wedgwood, 9 St Anne's Cres, Lewes, E Sussex BN7 1SB], dau of Herbert Wynn Reeves and widow of (Algernon) James Riccarton Tudor-Craig, FSA, and *d* 8 Dec 1989, having by his 1st w had:

1 Sir (HUGO) MARTIN WEDGWOOD, **3rd and present Bt**

2 +(John) Julian [Julian Wedgwood Esq, 528 Wandsworth Rd, London SW8]; *b* 17 June 1936; *educ* Stowe and McGill U; *m* 28 Dec 1961 *Sheila Mary Green, est dau of George Robert Meade, and had:

  (1) +(John) Adam; *b* 4 Aug 1962; artist

  (2) +Rupert Julian; *b* 11 April 1964; Park Warden

  (3) +Felix Hawkshaw; *b* 15 March 1966; photographer

3 +Oliver Ralph [Oliver Wedgwood Esq, 908 Independence Ave SE, Washington DC 20003, USA]; *b* 27 April 1940; *educ* Eton; textile trader

4 Adrian Charles Hamilton; *b* 10 June 1948; *educ* Eton and Trin Coll Oxford; lost at sea sailing off Sydney, NSW, 9 June 1974

1 *(Germaine) Olivia; *b* 5 May 1944; *m* 17 July 1965 David Louis Posner (*d* 1985), poet and author, only s of Louis S Posner, of New York, and has:

  (1) *Piers Oliver; *b* 3 May 1966; by Lora Olsen has issue

  (2) *Dominic Tobias, of Sydney, Australia; *b* 9 Sept 1968; *m* 13 Feb 1994 *Cvetanka Dimoska

WEIDENFELD

Arms: Per fess or and vert a fess embattled argent masoned proper, over all a weeping willow eradicated. **Crest:** A demi-wolf regardant sable, holding in its mouth a scroll argent. **Supporters:** Dexter, an old man proper, bearded argent, habited in a gown and cap sable supporting in his exterior hand a tablet proper; sinister, a youth proper habited in a blouse argent and breeches or, boots and peaked cap sable, holding in the sinister hand a rapier, point downwards, the scabbard sable. **Motto:** *Cedant arma togae* ('Let arms yield to the gown'). **Creation:** B. (LP, UK) 1976.

THE BARON WEIDENFELD, of Chelsea, Gtr London (Sir (Arthur) George Weidenfeld) [The Rt Hon The Lord Weidenfeld, 9 Chelsea Embankment, London SW3 4LE]; *b* 13 Sept 1919; *educ* Piaristen Gymnasium Vienna, Vienna U and Konsular Akademie; BBC: Monitoring Serv 1939–42, BBC news commentator 1942–46; fndr Contact Magazine and Books 1945, chm Weidenfeld & Nicolson 1948–; political advsr and Ch of Cabinet to Pres Weizman of Israel; chm Bd Govrs Ben Gurion U of the Negev 1996– (v-chm 1976–96); jt v-pres Oxford U Devpt Prog; Govr: Weizman Inst Sci 1964–, Tel Aviv U 1980–, Bezalel Acad Arts Jerusalem 1985–; memb: South Bank Bd 1986–, ENO Bd 1988–; Tstee Nat Portrait Gallery 1988–, ktd 1969; Jt V-Pres Campaign for Oxford 1992–95; Hon Fell: St Peter's Coll Oxford 1992, St Anne's Coll Oxford 1994; Hon PhD Ben Gurion U of the Negev 1984; Hon MA Oxon; Hon Senator Bonn U 1996; Golden Knight's Cross with Star Order of Merit Austria 1989, Chev Leg Hon 1990, Kt Cdr Order Merit Germany 1991; author: *The Goebbels Experiment* (1943), *Remembering My Good Friends* (1994); *m* 1st 1952 Jane, dau of J Edward Sieff, and has:

1 *Laura Miriam Elizabeth; *b* 1953; *m* 1976 *Christopher Andrew Barnett, s of Peter Alan Barnett and Joan Cullis, and has:

  (1) *Benjamin; *b* 1979

  (2) *Rowan; *b* 1981

  (3) *Nathaniel Peter Edward; *b* 1984

  (1) *Clara Aurjana; *b* 1986

THE BARON WEIDENFELD *m* 2nd 1956 (*divorce* 1961) Barbara (*d* 1996), dau of Maj George Skelton and formerly w of Cytril Connolly (*see* CRAIGAVON, V); *m* 3rd 1966 (*divorce* 1976) Sandra, dau of Charles Shipman Payson; *m* 4th 1992 *Annabelle, dau of Cdr Nicholas Whitestone.

Lineage: MAX WEIDENFELD; *m* Rosa —, and had an only s:

(ARTHUR) GEORGE WEIDENFELD, *cr* a **Baron**

WEINSTOCK

WEIR

Arms: Dancetty argent and gules on each of three piles, two issuant in chief and one in base azure, a sun in splendour, its straight rays each tipped with flame gold. **Crest:** Upon a wreath argent, or and azure on a mount vert two musical pipes saltirewise or between two stakes entwined by vines fructed proper and ensigned by a crown rayonny gules. **Supporters:** Dexter, a male griffin azure, beaked, rayed and gorged with a crown tridenty and forelegs or; sinister, a horse or, gorged with a wreath of trefoils, the stalks entwined vert. **Creation:** B. (LP, UK) 1980.

THE BARON WEINSTOCK, of Bowden, Co Wilts (Sir Arnold Weinstock) [The Rt Hon The Lord Weinstock, 7 Grosvenor Sq, London W1X 9LA]; *b* 29 July 1924; *educ* London U (BSc Econ); admin offr Admlty 1944–47; with Radio and Allied Industries 1954–63, md GEC 1963–96 (dir 1961–), ktd 1970; dir Rolls-Royce (1971) Ltd 1971–73, Friends of Ravenna Festival 1993; Tstee: Br Museum 1985–96, Roy Philharmonic Soc Fndn Fund 1984–92; FSS, Hon FRCR, Hon DSc: Salford 1975, Aston 1976, Bath 1978, Reading 1978; Hon LLD: Leeds 1978, Wales 1985, Keele 1997; Hon DTech Loughborough 1981; Hon Fell: Peterhouse Cambridge and LSE; DUniv Anglia Poly U 1994; Hon D Econ Sci London 1997; Hon Master Bench Gray's Inn; Cdr Order Merit Italy 1991, Offr Legn Hon 1992; *m* 1949 *Netta, dau of Sir Michael Sobell, and has had:

1 *Simon Andrew; *b* 24 Feb 1952; *educ* Winchester and Magdalen Coll Oxford (MA); GEC: commercial manager 1983–87, commercial dir 1987–96; *m* 1979 *Laura Helen, only dau of Maj Hon Sir Francis Michael Legh, KCVO, and *d* 8 May 1996, leaving issue (*see* NEWTON B)

1 *Susan Gina; *b* 1955; *educ* Cranborne Chase, St Hilda's Coll Oxford and LSE (PhD); *m* 1980 *Laurent Lacroix and has:

  (1) *Jerome Humphrey Andrew; *b* 1992

  (1) *Clare Marguerite Pamela; *b* 1985

  (2) *Karis Anne; *b* 1989

Lineage: SIMON WEINSTOCK; *m* Golda — and had:

ARNOLD, *cr* a **Baron**

Arms: Azure a cog wheel or, winged argent, in chief the sun in his splendour of the second. **Crest:** A wing argent charged with a thistle slipped proper. **Supporters:** A pair of winged horses argent, armed and crined or. **Motto:** (over the crest) Forwards towards the light. **Creations:** B. (UK) 26 June 1918, V. (UK) 25 June 1938.

THE 3RD VISCOUNT WEIR, of Eastwood, Co Renfrew, and **Baron Weir**, of Eastwood, Co Renfrew (William Kenneth James Weir) [The Rt Hon The Viscount Weir, Rodinghead, Mauchline, Ayrshire KA2 5TR]; *b* 9 Nov 1933; *s f* 1975; *educ* Eton and Trin Coll Cambridge (BA 1955); chm Weir Group plc 1983– (v-chm 1981–83, chm and ch exec 1972–81); dir St James's Place Capital plc, chm Gt Northern Investment Tst 1975–82 (dir from 1970); dir: BSC 1972–76, Hambro Life 1984–86, Canadian Pacific Ltd 1989–; memb: Court Bank England 1972–84, London Advsy Ctee Hong Kong and Shanghai Banking Corp 1980–92, Engrg Industries Cncl 1975–81 and Roy Co Archers; chm BICC plc 1996–, Br Bank of Middle East 1977–79; FRSA, Hon DEng Glasgow 1993, Hon FEng 1993; *m* 1st 25 April 1964 (*divorce* 1974) Diana Lucy, only dau of Peter Lewis MacDougall, of Rockcliffe, Ontario, and has:

1 +JAMES WILLIAM HARTLAND; *b* 6 June 1965

1 *Lorna Elizabeth; *b* 17 May 1967

The 3rd VISCOUNT *m* 2nd 6 Nov 1976 (*divorce* 19–) Jacqueline Mary, er dau of Baron Louis de Chollet, of Le Guintzet, Fribourg, Switzerland, by Mrs Frances Tate, of Easton, Md., and formerly w of Donald Alexander Cameron Marr; *m* 3rd 1989 *Marina, dau of Marc Sevastopoulo, of New York, and by her has:

2 +Andrew Alexander Marc, *b* 1989

Lineage: JAMES WEIR, of Over Courance, Dumfriesshire; *m* Mary (*d* May 1931), dau of William Douglas, of Kilmarnock, and *d* 10 July 1920, leaving:

WILLIAM DOUGLAS, **1st Viscount Weir**, of Eastwood, Co Renfrew, so *cr* 25 June 1938, as also earlier 26 June 1918 BARON WEIR, of Eastwood, Co Renfrew (both UK), GCB (1934), PC (1918), JP, DL Glasgow and Renfrew; *b* 12 May 1877; hon pres G and J Weir Hldgs Ltd of Glasgow (engineers), dir Internat Nickel Co of Canada; Dir Munitions Scotland 1915–16, ktd 1917, Controller Aero Supplies and memb Air Board 1917–18, Dir-Gen Aircraft Production Min Munitions 1917–18, Sec State Air Force and Pres Air Cncl 1918–19, Chm Advsy Ctee Civil Aviation 1919, industl advsr to Br Delegn Imp Conf Ottawa 1932, advsr to Govt on Nat Def measures 1936–37, Dir-Gen Explosives Min Supply 1939–41, Chm Tank Bd 1942; LLD Glasgow, Hon Col RE (TA), Cdr Legn Hon, Grand Offr Order Crown Italy, US DSM; *m* 2 June 1904 Alice Blanche (*d* 9 Nov 1959), dau of John MacConnachie, of Glasgow, and *d* 2 July 1959, leaving:

1 (JAMES) KENNETH WEIR, **2nd Viscount Weir**, CBE (1944); *b* 10 Sept 1905; *educ* Oundle and Trin Coll Cambridge (BA 1926); Chm 25–Pdr Field Gun Production Ctee Min Supply 1940–43, 6–Pdr Ordnance Ctee 1941–44, memb Industl Advsy Panel Min Production 1942–45; chm Weir Gp 1955–72 (dir 1937, md 1944), dir: Dunlop, Internat Nickel Co of Canada, Roy Bank Scotland, Caledonian Insur, Scottish TV, Guardian Assur Gp; Hon LLD Strathclyde 1967, Hon FRCOG 1968; *m* 1st 2 March 1929 (Dorothy Isabel) Lucy (*d* 12 Feb 1972), only dau of James Fuidge Crowdy, MVO, of Ottawa; *m* 2nd 3 March 1973 *Dorothy [The Rt Hon Dorothy Viscountess Weir, Little Pennbrook, Lake Rd, Far Hills, NJ 07931, USA], dau of William Yerrington Dear and widow of Edward F Hutton, of New York, and *d* 16 Aug 1975, having had by his 1st w:

  (1) WILLIAM KENNETH JAMES WEIR, **3rd and present Viscount Weir**

  (2) +Douglas Nigel; *b* 6 Oct 1935; *educ* Eton and Trin Coll Cambridge; *m* 29 Feb 1964 *Penelope Anne, dau of Gp/Capt John Whitehead, of Waltham St Lawrence, Berks, and has:

    1a *Juliet Anne; *b* 20 Dec 1964

    2a *Lucy; *b* 8 July 1966

    3a *Nicola Jean; *b* 17 Nov 1969

    4a *Joanna; *b* 1978

  (3) +George Anthony [The Hon George Weir, Kilmany, Cupar, Fife]; *b* 27 April 1940; *educ* Winchester, Trin Coll Cambridge (BA 1960) and MIT (SM, PhD); dir CF Taylor (Hldgs) (Weir Corp) 1973–; *m* 28 July 1962 (*divorce* 1992) Hon Jane Caroline Anstruther-Gray (*see* ANSTRUTHER, Bt) and has:

    1a +William John; *b* 5 Feb 1971

2a +Edward Kenneth; *b* 1972

1a *Belinda Jane; *b* 6 May 1974

(4) +James Richard Canning [The Hon James Weir, 17 Pimlico Rd, London SW1]; *b* 1 May 1949; *educ* Winchester; *m* 1977 *Haude Chantal Gabrielle, yst dau of Marc Charpentier, of Château de Bagateue, Mortaux, France, and has:

1a *Victoria Dorothy Sabine; *b* 1978

2a *Kate; *b* 1980

(1) Lucy Elspeth Anne; *b* 26 Dec 1929; *d* 10 Dec 1937

(2) *Janet Sibella [The Hon Mrs Valentine, The Gate House, Astrop, nr Banbury, Oxon]; *b* 13 April 1947; *m* 11 Nov 1978 *Francis Anthony Brinsley (James) Valentine (*see* LANESBOROUGH, E) and has:

1a *Robert Harris; *b* 1983

1a *Sibella Margaret; *b* 1981

2 John William; *b* 3 April 1907; *educ* Oundle and Univ Coll Oxford; Capt 4th Bn Cameron Highrs (TA); *m* 19 April 1950 Irene Marguerite Robertson (*d* 1987), 3rd dau of James Mckecknie, JP, of Glasgow, and *dsp* 18 Jan 1953

1 Elspeth Marjory Jessie; *b* 18 March 1912; *m* 1st 31 Jan 1933 Richard Fairfax William Cartwright, JP (*d* 31 March 1954), of Aynhoe Park, Banbury, Oxon, only s of Sir Fairfax Leighton Cartwright, GCMG, GCVO, PC, and had:

(1) Edward Fairfax; *b* 23 April 1936; *educ* Eton; *d* 31 March 1954

(1) *Elizabeth Armine Julia [Mrs Jeremy Cartwright-Hignett, Iford Manor, Bradford-on-Avon, Wilts BA15 2BA]; *b* 21 Feb 1939; *educ* Inst Archaeology London U, Goldsmith's Coll London U and Tavistock Clinic London; *m* 21 April 1979 (combining his name with hers) *(John) Jeremy Worthington Hignett, er s of Gerald Hignett, of Southstoke Manor, Bath, and has:

1a *William Fairfax; *b* 13 Sept 1982

1 (cont.) The Hon Mrs Cartwright *m* 2nd 29 Nov 1957 Eustace Benyon Hoare (*d* 9 July 1961), er s of Alfred Ernest Hoare, OBE, JP, DL, of Chelsworth Hall, Suffolk (*see* 1959 edn TEMPLEWOOD,V), and *d* 1989

WELBY

Arms: Sable a fess between three fleurs-de-lys argent. **Crest:** A cubit arm in armour issuing in bend sinister from clouds, holding a sword, pommel and hilt or, over flames of fire issuant from a wreath proper. **Motto:** *Per ignem per gladium* ('By fire, by sword').
Creation: Bt. (E) 27 June 1801.

SIR (RICHARD) BRUNO GREGORY WELBY, 7TH BT, of Denton Manor, Co Lincoln [Sir Bruno Welby Bt, 20 St Mary Abbot's Terrace, London W14]; *b* 11 March 1928; *s* f 1977; *educ* Eton and Ch Ch Oxford (BA 1950); *m* 8 Feb 1952 *Jane Biddulph, yst dau of Ralph Wilfred Hodder-Williams, MC, and has:

1 +CHARLES WILLIAM HODDER [Charles Welby Esq, Stroxton House, Grantham, Lincs NG33 5DD]; *b* 6 May 1953; *educ* Eton and RAC Cirencester; Lt TAVR 1977; FRICS; *m* 30 Sept 1978 *Suzanna Fiona, only dau of Maj Ian Stuart-Routledge, of Harston Hall, Grantham, and has:

(1) *Venetia Victoria; *b* 1981

(2) *Zinnia Louisa; *b* 1985

(3) *Isadora Barbara Pia; *b* 1993

2 +Dominic John Earle; *b* 4 July 1960; *m* 10 July 1982 *Camilla Janet, yr dau of Christopher Gerald Pole-Carew (*see* POLE, Bt, of Shute House), and has:

(1) +Hector George; *b* 1993

(1) *Maria Elizabeth; *b* 1987

(2) *Octavia Lind; *b* 1990

3 +Richard Henry Gregory; *b* 28 Dec 1970

1 *Miranda Lind; *b* 21 June 1955; *m* 1st 1977 (*divorce* 1989) Gavin Laird-Craig, er s of W/Cdr A J Laird-Craig, DSO, MBE, DFC, AFC; *m* 2nd 1991, as his 2nd w, her cousin *Col Hugh Earle Welby-Everard, MBE (*see* below), and has by her 1st husb:

(1) *Oliver John Gregory; *b* 1985

(1) *Emma le Flay; *b* 1981

Lineage: RANNULF; tenant of Guy de Credun, in Wellebi, nr Grantham, as recorded in Domesday Survey 1086; possibly kin to:

JOHN fitz ROGER (*i.e.*, s of Roger); gave lands and woods in Wellebi to Valle Dei Abbey at its foundation 1147; in 1166 a JOHN de WELLEBI (possibly the same person) held one and a half kts' fees in Wellebi parish under Maurice de Crun, they having been the subject of enfeoffment (possibly to him) by 1135; his yr s or bro settled in the Parts of Holland and was ancestor of the WELBYs of Fossdyke, Gedney, Kirton, London, Multon, Pinchbeck, Rutland, Stixwold and Sutton Woodhead; of the Multon line were Roger Welby (Sheriff Lincs 1397), Richard Welby (MP Lincs 1422), Richard Welby (MP Lincs 1450–52), Richard Welby (Sheriff Lincs 1471 and MP 1472–77), Richard Welby (Sheriff Lincs 1487) and Thomas Welby (Sheriff Lincs 1491); of the Gedney line were Richard Welby (living 1216), Adlard Welby (Sheriff Lincs 1562) and Sir William Welby, KB (1603), Sheriff Lincs 1606; the sr line continued at Harlaxton, Harrowby, Ropsley and Welby.

JOHN WELBY; Collector Subsidy Denton, Lincs, 1523; *m* —, sis and heiress of Robert Symond, who had a house and land in Denton 1492, and had, with two yr sons (Symon; Richard):

JOHN WELBY; bought another house and some lands in Denton 1539; *bur* 1547, leaving an only s:

WILLIAM WELBY; *m* Alice, dau of R Worsley, and *d* 1613, leaving:

WILLIAM WELBY; *m* Judith, dau of William Newton, of Gonerby, Lincs, and cousin of Sir Isaac Newton, and *d* 1627, leaving:

WILLIAM WELBY; bought 1648 the Manor of Denton from Sir William Thorold (*see* THOROLD, Bt) and moved into the manor house; elected MP Lincs 1654 but forbidden by CROMWELL to take his seat; *m* Ellinor, dau of William Williams, of Denton, and *d* 1657, leaving, with an er s (William, one of 11 Lincs gentlemen candidate membs Order of Royal Oak (a chivalric sodality mooted by CHARLES II but never established), *d* unm 1704), a yst s:

RICHARD WELBY; *b* 1658; Sheriff Lincs 1705; Ld Manors of Denton, Saperton, Stragglethorpe, Swinstead and Welby; *m* his cousin Mary, dau and heiress of John Towers, of Haddenham, Isle of Ely, and *d* 1713, leaving an er s:

WILLIAM WELBY, of Denton; Sheriff Lincs 1746, Col S Lincs Militia; *m* Catharine, dau of James Cholmeley, of Easton, Lincs, and *d* 29 June 1792, leaving an only s:

Sir William Earle Welby, 1st Bt (UK), so *cr* 27 June 1801, of Denton; MP Grantham; *m* 1st Penelope (*d* Feb 1771), 3rd dau of Sir John Glynne, of Hawarden Castle, Flints, and *d* 6 Nov 1815, having had:

1 WILLIAM EARLE (Sir), **2nd Bt**

1 Penelope; *m* Thomas Northmore (*d* 20 May 1851), of Cleve, Devon, and *d* 7 Nov 1792, leaving issue

Sir William *m* 2nd, March 1773 Elizabeth (*d* 18 Feb 1825), dau of Robert Cope, of Spondon, Derbys, and widow of Thomas Williamson, of Allington Hall, Lincs, and by her had, with other issue:

2 John Earle (Rev); *b* 11 Sept 1786; Rector Harston, Leics; *m* 20 May 1819 Felicia Elizabeth (*d* 9 Nov 1888), only dau of Rev George Hole, of Chulmleigh, Devon, and *d* 9 July 1867, having had:

(1) John Earle, JP (Lincs and Leics), of Allington Hall, Grantham; *b* 2 March 1820; MA Oxon; *m* 2 June 1873 Catherine Mary (*d* 7 April 1918), dau of Rev George Hutton, Rector Gate Burton and Knaith, and *dsp* 8 May 1905

(2) George Earle (Rev), JP (Lincs); *b* March 1821; *educ* Trin Coll Cambridge (BA); Rector Barrowby, Grantham, Canon Lincoln; *m* 9 July 1847 Augusta (*d* 26 Jan 1904), dau of Rev William Woodall, of Branston, and *d* 16 May 1916, leaving:

1a George Earle (Sir), CMG, JP; *b* 9 Jan 1851; *educ* Cambridge (BA); Dip Serv 1874–1906: Sec Legation Buenos Aires 1892, Stockholm 1894, Brussels 1897, Resident Min and Consul Gen Bogota 1898–1906, Mayor Westminster 1915–19 and Grantham 1919–20; *d* 25 Aug 1936

1a Felicia Mary; *m* 17 Sept 1884 Sir George E Dallas, 3rd and last Bt (*dsp* 27 Nov 1918), and *d* 5 Nov 1940

2a Emily; *m* 22 April 1891 Maj-Gen Hon Sir Savage Lloyd-Mostyn, KCB, s of 2nd Baron Mostyn (*qv*), and *d* 28 May 1956, leaving issue

(3) William Earle, JP, of Bainton House, Stamford; *b* 13 Oct 1823; *m* 24 Nov 1864 Adeline (*d* 19 June 1897), dau of William Fane (*see* WESTMORLAND, E), and *d* 5 May 1915, leaving:

1a Louisa Felicia; *m* 28 April 1927, as his 3rd w, Robert Mowbray Howard (*see* NORFOLK, D) and *dsp* 13 Oct 1956

(4) Montague Earle (Rev); *b* 17 Dec 1827; *educ* Oxford (MA), Fell Magdalen Coll 1854; Rector Uffington 1893–98; *m* 12 Aug 1857 Mary (*d* 29 Nov 1906), yr dau of Lewis Weston Dillwyn, MP, of Sketty Hall, Glam, and *dsp* 31 Dec 1910

(5) REGINALD EARLE WELBY, 1st and last BARON WELBY OF ALLINGTON, Co Lincoln (UK), so *cr* 16 April 1894, GCB (1892, KCB 1882, CB 1874), PC (1913); *b* 3 Aug 1832; *educ* Eton and Trin Coll Cambridge (BA 1855); Treasury: joined 1856, Priv Sec to Fin Sec 1859–71, Pncpl Clerk Fin Dept 1871–80, Auditor Civil List and Assist Fin Sec 1880–85, Perm Sec 1885–94; Chm LCC 1899–1900 (Alderman 1894–1907, V-Chm 1898–99), Pres Roy Statistical Soc 1914, a Commr 1851 Exhibition, memb Met Water Bd, dir: Grand Trunk Canada and Grand Trunk Pacific Rlwy and Standard Bank S Africa; *d* unm 30 Oct 1915, when the Barony expired

(1) Sarah Maria; *m* 11 July 1850 Joseph Livesay (*d* Jan 1854), of Stourton Hall, Lincs, and *d* 16 Jan 1854, leaving three sons

(2) Felicia Elizabeth; *m* 30 May 1854 11th Earl of Lindsey (*see* LINDSEY and ABINGDON, E) and *d* 16 March 1927, having had issue

The 1st Bt's s,

Sir William Earle Welby, 2nd Bt; *b* 14 Nov 1768; MP Grantham; *m* 30 Aug 1792 Wilhelmina (*d* 4 Feb 1847), only dau and heiress of William Spry, Govr Barbados, and *d* 3 Nov 1852, having had, with three other daus (*d* unm):

1 GLYNNE EARLE (Sir), **3rd Bt**

2 Thomas Earle (Rt Rev); *b* 11 July 1810; Offr 13th Light Dragoons; DD, Bp St Helena,; *m* 1837 Mary (*d* 1896), dau of A Browne, and was accidentally *k* 6 Jan 1899, having had:

(1) Henry; *b* 1838; *m* 1866 Cecilia (*d* 22 Jan 1923), dau of T Bland, of Cape of Good Hope, and *d* 16 June 1869, leaving:

  1a Hugh Earle; *b* 1867; *m* 17 Oct 1908 Evelyn Borradaile, MBE (*d* 1972), dau of Adam Bell, Rhodesian CS, and *d* 23 March 1952, having had:

    1b Edward Hugh Earle; *b* 2 Aug 1915; Sgt/Pilot RAF WW II; *kas* 13 June 1942

    1b *Gwynyth Mary; *b* 27 Jan 1910; *m* 18 Sept 1937 Arthur Wyatt Aust (*d* 1975), Inspr Br S African Police S Rhodesia, and has:

      1c *John Charles Wyatt; *b* 28 April 1942; Capt Rhodesian Army; *m* 12 April 1969 *Pamela Drusilla, dau of George Maberley Phillips, of Essexvale, Rhodesia, and has:

        1d *Patrick Welby; *b* 1975

        1d *Caroline Joyce; *b* 1970

        2d *Cherith Mary; *b* 1972

      1c *Elizabeth Mary; *b* 5 April 1940; *m* 22 Sept 1966 *Brian Tozer, of Harare, Zimbabwe, and has:

        1d *Ian Richard; *b* 26 Sept 1968

        2d *Nigel Stewart; *b* 1970

        3d *Timothy Charles; *b* 1975

  2a Edward Earle; *b* 1869; *k* Matabele War 1897

(2) William Glynne Earle; *dsp*

(3) Charles Earle; *b* 26 Dec 1850; Inspr schs, Fell Allahabad U NWP India, Capt Agra Vols; *m* 21 June 1880 Annie Williams (*d* 1912), widow of Walter Conroy, CE, PWD India, and *d* 1913, leaving:

  1a Thomas Earle; *b* 18 July 1881; *m* 1st 17 Oct 1909 Theodora Louise Knight (*d* 24 July 1925), er dau of Rev J F T Hallowes; *m* 2nd 23 April 1928 Dorothea (*d* 21 April 1972), dau of Arthur Wilbraham George, and *d* 21 Feb 1933

(4) Arthur Thomas Earle; *b* 1855; v-pres Denver L and NW Rlwy USA; *m* 1st 1874 Phoebe (*d* 1895), dau of Capt de Cew, and *d* 1908, having had:

  1a Wilhelmina Cecilia; *d* 19–

  2a Helena Beatrice; *d* 19–

(4) (cont.) Arthur Welby *m* 2nd 1898 Maria, dau of J F Mitchell, and *d* 8 Aug 1909, leaving by her:

  1a Alfred Earle; *b* 1899; *d* 1912

  2a Charles Earle; *b* 1901; *m* 1926 Lydia Elizabeth (*d* 1984), dau of Harry L Hunt, of Casper, Wyo., and *d* 1975, leaving:

    1b +Arthur Earle [Arthur Earle, 58 Oak Ridge Lane, Barrington, IL 60010, USA]; *b* 1927; *m* 1947 *Giuliana, dau of Alfredo Bruni, of Pisa, and has:

      1c +Allan Earle; *b* 1958; *m* 1984 *Sandra Capriotti, of Kanakee, Ill., and has:

        1d +Adam Earle; *b* 1988

        1d *Adriana Eda; *b* 1990

      2c +Steven Earle; *b* 1961

      1c *Janet Rose; *b* 1955; *m* 1979 *Dennis Joseph Sullivan and has:

        1d *Dennis Arthur; *b* 1985

        2d *Charles Orlando; *b* 1990

    2b +Charles Earle [Mr Charles Welby Esq, 1357 Oxford Way, Upland, CA 91786, USA]; *b* 1935; *m* 1955 *Doris Annen, of Madison, Wisc., and has:

      1c +Charles Earle; *b* 1959; *m* 1984 *Laura Helen Wood, of Claremont, Calif., and has:

        1d *Megan Neville; *b* 1988

      2c +Peter Thomas Earle; *b* 1962

      1c *Susan Kaye; *b* 1958; *m* 1982 *William Scott Jones, of Zephyr Cove, Nev., and has:

        1d *William Scott; *b* 1986

        1d *Margaret Ashley; *b* 1983

      2c *Joanne Marie; *b* 1960; *m* 1988 *Ricardo Aguilar, of Ontario, Calif.

    1b *Mary Elizabeth [Mrs Bruce Ringey, 1204 Airfield Lane, Midland, MI 48640, USA]; *b* 1931; *m* 1954 *Bruce W Ringey and has:

      1c *David Bruce; *b* 1967

      1c *Lynn Marie; *b* 1954; *m* 1977 *Philip J Baker III and has:

        1d *Andrew; *b* 1979

        2d *Patrick; *b* 1981

        1d *Laura; *b* 1985

        2d *Erin; *b* 1988

      2c *Catherine Ann; *b* 19–; *m* 1977 *Mark Willbur and has:

        1d *Matthew Paul; *b* 1980

        1d *Kimberly; *b* 1982

        2d *Travis; *b* 1988

      3c *Karen Elizabeth; *b* 1960; *m* 1985 *Roger Brandi

      4c *Diane Lea; *b* 1963

  3a *Muriel; *m* 26 May 1921 Maj Harold Godfrey St George Morgan, RMA (*d* 12 Sept 1929), and has issue

(5) Frederick Earle; *b* 1858; FRCSE, Colonial Surgn St Helena; *m* 1883 Janet Ann (*d* 11 April 1935), dau of F Henderson, of Wick, and *d* 21 Oct 1900, leaving:

  1a Francis Thomas Glynne Earle; *b* 1888; *d* 19 March 1919

  1a Mary Caroline; *d* unm 8 Sept 1913

  2a *Edith Jessie; *m* 1st 1920 William Adams (*d* 19–); *m* 2nd 19– — and *d* 19–, leaving issue

  3a Gladys; *m* 1st 1911 Edward Fanslow, of Minnesota; *m* 2nd 1930 Norman Harold Verge (*d* 1931) and *d* 19–, leaving issue

(1) Penelope; *b* 1863; *m* Maj-Gen John Haughton, RA (*d* 1889), and had issue

(2) Wilhelmina; *m* 14 Jan 1864 Maj-Gen Robert Barton, RE (*d* 11 Aug 1904), and *d* 19 Dec 1912

(3) Elizabeth; *d* 1934

(4) Caroline; *m* 1st 17 Sept 1867 Charles Fowler, MD (*d* 1877), and had issue; *m* 2nd 25 June 1884 Rev Francis William Carre (*d* 1901), Vicar St Katherine's Marlborough, and had further issue

(5) Katherine; *m* 1873 Saul Solomon (*d* 1896), of St Helena, and *d* 23 March 1937, leaving issue

(6) Edith Frances; *m* 19 Feb 1884 Surgn-Lt-Col Robert Mark Bradford (*d* 1915) and *d* 7 Jan 1929

3 Arthur Earle (Rev); *b* 22 Aug 1815; Rector Newton, Lincs, and Holy Trinity Hulme, Manchester; *m* 13 May 1843 Julia Catherine (*d* 18 Oct 1892), dau of Capt George Macdonald, and *d* 1884, leaving:

(1) Arthur Earle; *b* 15 Feb 1844; *m* 25 Feb 1894 Edith Adela Emily Louisa, yst dau of Rev James Cooper Farmborough, Rector Moreton Baggot, Warwicks, and *d* 1899

(2) William Macdonald Earle; *b* 22 Nov 1845; *m* 1st 1874 Mary (*d* 1875), dau of G W Pilkington, and had a s (*d* young); *m* 2nd 1878 Jessie, dau of Frederick Lucas, of Grahamstown, Cape Colony, and *d* 4 Oct 1885, leaving by her:

  1a Spencer Earle; *b* March 1879; *d* 19–

  2a Glynne Earle; *b* 1881; *d* 19–

  1a Isabel Florence; *d* 19–

  2a May; *d* 19–

(3) George Henry Francis Earle; *b* 31 Dec 1846

(4) Charles Earle; *b* 12 May 1848

(5) Frederick Earle; *b* 1851; *d* 27 March 1868

(6) Richard Earle; *b* 3 Jan 1854; Capt 5th Bn Rifle Bde and 3rd Bn Suffolk Regt 1st Boer War 1877–79 (medal and clasp), Basutoland 1880–88 (medal and clasp), WW I (star, medal); *m* 1st 1886 Mary Isabella (*d* 1892), dau of Thomas Paget, of Forton, Lancs, and had a dau (*d* an infant); *m* 2nd 1899 Alice Frances, 3rd dau of Lt-Col Cyril Blackburne Tew, 15th Regt, and widow of V-Adml Frederick Charles Bryan Robinson; *m* 3rd 3 Dec 1918 Helen Mary, only dau of Capt Creagh Scott, and *d* 8 Dec 1932, leaving by her:

  1a +Glynne Richard Earle [S/Ldr Glynne Welby RAF, c/o Lloyds Bank plc, 3 Sidney St, Cambridge]; *b* 14 Aug 1921; *educ* Cambridge (BA 1948, MA 1957); Capt E Yorks Regt, WW II Rifle Bde and E Yorks Regt; late S/Ldr RAF, ACIS 1962, with Directorate Educnl Servs Air Ministry 1960, Head Internat Studies RAF Coll Cranwell 1966–68, Sr Lecturer Mary Ward Coll Educn Notts; *m* 1st 12 March 1945 Hilarie Elizabeth (*d* 13 Aug 1957), er dau of H Cecil Rowse, of St Austell, Cornwall, and has:

    1b *Elizabeth Anne; *b* 4 June 1947

    2b *Rosalyne Mary; *b* 4 Dec 1950

    3b *Penelope Jane; *b* 28 June 1954

  1a (cont.) Glynne Welby *m* 2nd 2 Aug 1958 *Margaret Mary, yr dau of Pius C Broderick, of Bolton, Lancs, and by her has:

    1b +Richard Edmund Charles; *b* 16 Sept 1961

    4b *Elizabeth Mary; *b* 18 Nov 1959

(1) Julia Gertrude; *m* 21 June 1894 Richard John Linton (*d* 1920), of Folkestone, and *d* 1931

(2) Caroline Charlotte; *m* 12 Aug 1874 Richard Evans and had issue

(3) Sarah Wilhelmina Mary; *d* 1925

1 Wilhelmina; *m* 17 May 1825 Rev F Browning (*d* 3 Dec 1858), Preb Salisbury, and *d* 1874

2 Penelope; *m* 2 May 1825 Clinton James FYNES-CLINTON later FIENNES-CLINTON (*see* LINCOLN, E) and *d* 5 June 1834

3 Katherine; *m* 13 May 1822 her cousin Rev Thomas Welby Northmore (*d* 16 July 1829) and *d* 11 May 1869, leaving issue

4 Elizabeth; *m* 17 Feb 1829 Thomas James Ireland (*d* 1863), of Ousden Hall, and *d* 18 Nov 1888 aged 84, leaving issue

The 2nd Bt's s,

Sir GLYNNE EARLE WELBY later WELBY-GREGORY (roy licence 1861 under terms of will of Gregory Gregory, of Harlaxton), **3rd Bt**; *b* 26 June 1806; MP Grantham; *m* 6 March 1828 Frances (*d* 9 Oct 1881), yst dau of Sir Montague Cholmeley, 1st Bt (*qv*), and *d* 23 Aug 1875, having had:

1 WILLIAM EARLE (Sir), **4th Bt**

2 Henry Glynne Earle; *b* 15 Oct 1830; Capt 48th Regt; *d* 2 July 1876

3 Walter Hugh Earle (Rev), JP (Leics); *b* 19 Aug 1833; *educ* Corpus Christi Coll Oxford (MA); Rector Harston, Grantham; *m* 1st 1 Oct 1861 Frances (*d* 3 Jan 1875), yst dau of Rt Rev Alfred Ollivant, Bp Llandaff, and had a surv dau:

  (1) Frances Alice; *d* unm 24 Feb 1947

3 (cont.) The Rev Walter Welby *m* 2nd 8 Oct 1878 Florence Laura (*dsp* 17 Sept 1913), est dau of Rev George Sloane Stanley, Rector Branstone, Lincs, and *d* 8 Feb 1912

4 Edward Montague Earle, JP (Lincs); *b* 12 Nov 1836; *educ* Corpus Christi Coll Oxford (MA); barrister, Stipendiary Magistrate Sheffield 1874–1915; *m* 3 Feb 1870 Sarah Elizabeth (*d* 25 Feb 1909), only child of Robert Everard, of Fulney House, Lincs, and *d* 25 Jan 1926, having had:

  (1) Edward Everard Earle WELBY later WELBY-EVERARD (roy licence 6 April 1894), JP, DL, of Gosberton House, nr Spalding, Lincs; *b* 22 Dec 1870; *educ* Eton and Corpus Christi Coll Oxford (BA 1893, MA 1929); barrister Inner Temple 1896, High Sheriff Lincs 1935, Dep Chm (Chm 1939–42) Holland (Lincs) QS, memb Holland War Ag Exec Ctee, Chm Spalding RD Food Control Ctee, Pres Holland with Boston C and U Assoc, memb Ho Laity Ch Assembly; *m* 27 June 1899 Gwladys Muriel Petra (*d* 2 June 1946), yst dau of Rev George W Herbert, and *d* 20 July 1951, leaving:

    1a Philip Herbert Earle, OBE, DSC, JP (Leics 1956), DL (Lincs 1957); *b* 7 May 1902; Capt RN WW II, High Sheriff Lincs 1972, CStJ, Cdr St John Amb Lincs, V-Chm Assoc Drainage Authorities; *m* 24 July 1928 *Lilla Anna Maree Castell, JP [Mrs Philip Welby-Everard JP, 29 High St, Caythorpe, Lincs], est dau of Magnus Spence, of S Rhodesia, and *d* 1985, having had:

      1b Glynne Earle; *b* 10 July 1935; *educ* Eton; *m* 26 Oct 1963 Jan Plaisette (*d* 18 Nov 1973), dau of Milton Lee Stroud, of Texarkana, Tex., and *d* 1990, leaving:

        1c +Ariel Edward Earle; *b* 11 Jan 1970

        1c *Amanda Gray; *b* 9 June 1971

2c *Ariadne Melissa; *b* 28 Sept 1972

2b +Roger Earle [Roger Welby-Everard Esq, Owl's House, Frieston, Lincs]; *b* 11 Jun 1942; *educ* Eton; Lt RN (ret); *m* 2 April 1966 *Isabel Anne, yr dau of Maj Henry Lloyd Fielding Bucknall, of Branscombe, Devon, and has:

1c +Julian Richard Earle; *b* 1 July 1967

2c +Patrick Jonathan Earle; *b* 16 Dec 1969

1c *Anna Christabel; *b* 1974

1b (Elizabeth) Janet; *b* 16 July 1929; *m* 10 April 1948 Capt James Agnew, RM, yr s of Sir Andrew Agnew, CBE, of Glenlee Park, New Galloway, and *d* 19–, leaving:

1c *Richard; *b* 6 April 1950; *educ* Winchester and Pembroke Coll Oxford

2c *Malcolm; *b* 26 Aug 1952

1c *Nicolette; *b* 14 April 1958

2b *Susan [Mrs George Durrant, Tintern, Long St, Sherborne, Dorset]; *b* 14 April 1931; *m* 12 Aug 1959 George William Charles Algernon Durrant, er s of George Durrant, of Marsh End, Walberswick, Suffolk, and has:

1c *Henry William Welby; *b* 24 Aug 1960

1c *Lucinda Sarah; *b* 16 Aug 1963; *m* 1987 *Peter Stockley and has:

1d *Timothy Charles George; *b* 1993

1d *Laura Amber Maree; *b* 1990

2c *Georgina Jane; *b* 1 Oct 1965; *m* 1992 *Miles Bodimeade

1a Christopher Earle (Sir), KBE (1965, OBE (1945)), CB (1961), DL (Lincs 1966); *b* 9 Aug 1909; *educ* Charterhouse and Corpus Christi Coll Oxford (BA 1932); Maj-Gen Roy Lincs Regt, WW II (wounded), cmded 264th Scottish Beach Bde (TA) 1954–57, BGS HQ BAOR and N Army Gp 1957–59, Ch Staff to C-in-C Allied Forces N Europe 1959–61, GOC Nigerian Army 1962–65, High Sheriff Lincs 1971; *m* 1 June 1938 Sybil ('Peggy') Juliet Wake (*d* 1994), dau of Guy Shorrock (*see* WAKE, Bt), and *d* 10 May 1996, leaving:

1b +Peter Rodney Earle [Peter Welby-Everard Esq, 27 Milcote Rd, Solihull, W Midlands]; *b* 28 Dec 1942; *educ* Charterhouse and RMA Sandhurst; Lt Roy Anglian Regt (ret 1969); *m* 7 Oct 1972 *Jennifer Frances, dau of Lt-Col S T C Parsons-Smith, of Wildhem, Hants, and has:

1c +Christopher Nicholas Earle; *b* 1976

2c +Peter George Earle; *b* 21 Nov 1982

1c *Patricia Christabel; *b* 22 Sept 1974

2b +Hugh Earle, MBE [Col Hugh Welby-Everard MBE, Church Farm Cottage, Hurstbourne Tarrant, Andover, Hants SP11 0AX]; *b* 23 July 1944; *educ* Charterhouse and RMA Sandhurst; Col late RA; *m* 1st 25 April 1970 Virginia Gresley (*d* 1989 as result of motor accident), er dau of Maj-Gen John Edward Longworth Morris, CB, CBE, DSO, of Marshgate, Tolleshunt D'Arcy, Essex; *m* 2nd 20 July 1991, as her 2nd husb, his cousin *Miranda Lind, only dau of **Sir (Richard) Bruno Gregory Welby, 7th Bt** (*see* above), and has by his 1st w:

1c +Guy John Earle; *b* 9 Jan 1979

1c *Louisa Gresley Wake; *b* 17 April 1975

1a Clemence Penelope Olga, JP (Mon 1954); *b* 26 Jan 1905; *m* 11 May 1929 R-Adml St John Aldrich Micklethwait, CB, DSO, DL (*d* 31 July 1977), est s of St John Gore Micklethwait, KC, and has:

1b *John Douglas Pelham [John Micklethwait Esq, Latches, Ibthorpe, Hants SP11 0BJ]; *b* 27 Feb 1933; *educ* Eton; *m* 7 Feb 1959 *Clarinda Margaret, dau of Lt-Col Michael Trethowan, OBE, of Haven Hill, St Mary Bourne, Hants, and has:

1c *John Julian Pollard; *b* 1 Nov 1961; *m* 9 Aug 1996 *Laurence Isobel Raillard

2c *Michael St John; *b* 7 March 1964

2b *Richard; *b* 11 Oct 1938; *educ* Radley and RAC Cirencester

1b *Diana [Lady Tritton, River House, Heytesbury, Warminster, Wilts BA12 0EE]; *b* 18 April 1931; *m* 12 Oct 1957 *Maj Sir Anthony John Ernest Tritton, 4th Bt (*qv*), and has issue

(2) Glynne Everard Earle; *b* 24 Nov 1872; Maj S Wales Borderers; *ka* 26 Sept 1914

(3) Hugh Robert Everard Earle, CMG (1936), JP (Parts of Kesteven, Lincs 1937); *b* 27 July 1885; *educ* Eton and Corpus Christi Coll Oxford (BA 1907); Kenya Admin 1911–36 (Prov Commr 1933, MLC 1934), Capt E African Forces WW I 1916–18, Div Coal Offr Mines Dept 1939–41, Maj HG 1941–46; *m* 19 Oct 1915 Dorothea Margaret (*d* 2 March 1965 aged 87), only surv dau of Charles Martin Green, of Spalding, Lincs, and *dsp* 18 April 1970

(1) Cicely Elizabeth; *m* 15 June 1910 William Ernest Tweedie, est s of David Tweedie, of Morningside, Edinburgh, and *d* 4 June 1928, leaving issue

(2) Margaret Sarah; *d* unm 21 April 1948

5 Philip James Earle (Rev); *b* 28 July 1842; Rector Stroxton, Lincs; *d* 25 Aug 1873

6 Hugh Richard Earle; *b* 1845; RN; *d* 28 May 1862 aboard HMS *James Watt*

7 Alfred Cholmeley Earle (Sir), KBE (1918) JP (Lincs); *b* 22 Aug 1849; Lt Col 2nd Dragoons, Scots Greys, MP Taunton 1895–1906, memb LCC for E Finsbury 1907–10, 2nd Cl Order St Anne Russia; *m* 15 Feb 1898 Alice Desirée (*d* 27 Feb 1969 aged 91), 2nd dau of Arthur Edward Copland-Griffiths, and *d* 18 May 1937, having had:

(1) Rannulf Alfred Earle, TD; *b* 23 Nov 1902; *educ* Eton; Hon Maj RA (TA) WW II; *m* 22 April 1938 *Elizabeth Marjorie Buchanan, er dau of James Smith, of Crosbie Tower, Troon, and *d* 19–

(1) Helen Cicely Desirée; *b* 14 Dec 1898; *d* 25 June 1902

(2) Amyse Mary; *b* 5 Oct 1900; *m* 23 April 1929 Capt Geoffrey Whitaker, Coldstream Gds, yst s of Arthur Whitaker, JP, and had:

1a *Camilla Jean Amyse; *b* 2 Feb 1934; *m* 6 Feb 1960 *Renaud Louis Thomas, s of Roger Alexandre Thomas, of La Gara, Jussy, Switzerland, and has:

1b *Benjamin Louis; *b* 30 Sept 1961

2b *Guy Alexander; *b* 1 July 1964

1b *Letitia Juliette; *b* 24 July 1966

(3) *Desirée Ann Eda; *b* 17 May 1904; *m* 23 April 1932 Capt Gerald Richard de Capell-Brooke Guinness (*see* GUINNESS, Bt) and has issue

1 Frances Wilhelmina; *m* 18 Aug 1857 Lt-Col John Reeve (*d* 2 Jan 1897, leaving issue), of Leadenham Ho, Lincs, and *dsps* 20 Oct 1858

2 Mary Elizabeth; *m* 1st 22 March 1860 John Richards Homfray (*d* 8 Aug 1882), of Penllyn Castle, Glam, and had issue; *m* 2nd 13 Nov 1893 Col George Shirley Maxwell (*d* 13 Aug 1911) and *d* 29 Nov 1919

3 Alice; *m* 19 Sept 1860 George Troyte BULLOCK later CHAFYN-GROVE (roy licence 1892) (*d* 27 Sept 1913), of North Coker Ho, Somerset, and *d* 27 Dec 1915, leaving issue

4 Cicely; *d* unm 14 Aug 1869

The 3rd Bt's est s,

Sir WILLIAM EARLE WELBY later WELBY-GREGORY (roy licence 27 Dec 1875), **4th Bt**, JP, DL (Lincs); *b* 4 Jan 1829; MP S Lincs 1868–84, Chm Lincs (Kesteven) CC, High Sheriff 1890; *m* 4 July 1863 Hon Victoria Alexandrina Maria Louisa Stuart (*d* 29 March 1912), Maid of Honour to HM QUEEN VICTORIA, only dau of Hon Charles James Stuart-Wortley (*see* WHARNCLIFFE, E), and *d* 26 Nov 1898, having had, with an er s (Victor Albert William, *b* 24 July 1864 (HM QUEEN VICTORIA stood sponsor), *d* 5 Feb 1876) and a dau (Emmeline Mary Elizabeth, *b* 5 Aug 1867, *m* 11 Oct 1893 Henry John Cockayne Cust (*see* BROWNLOW, B) and *dsp* 29 Sept 1955):

Sir Charles Glynne Earle Welby, 5th Bt, CB (1897), JP, DL; *b* 11 Aug 1865; *educ* Ch Ch Oxford (MA); MP Newark 1900–06, Assist U-Sec War Office 1900–02, CA Lincs, Chm Kesteven CC 1921–34; *m* 11 July 1920 Lady Maria Louisa Hervey (*d* 11 July 1920), sis of 4th Marquess of Bristol (*qv*), and *d* 19 March 1938, having had, with an er s (Richard William Gregory, *b* 16 Oct 1888, Lt Gren Gds WW I, *ka* 16 Sept 1914) and four daus (Dorothy Geraldine, *b* 1890, *m* 8 June 1920 19th Lord Saltoun (*qv*) of Abernethy and *d* 1985, having had issue; Katherine Winifred, *d* young 10 April 1895; Katherine Amothe, *b* 7 April 1895, *d* unm 11 Feb 1950; Joan Margaret Welby, *b* 10 April 1898, *m* 22 July 1919 1st Viscount Portal of Hungerford (*see* PORTAL, Bt) and *d* 19 June 1996, leaving issue):

Sir Oliver Charles Earle Welby, 6th Bt, TD, JP (Parts of Kesteven 1931); *b* 26 Jan 1902; *educ* Eton and Ch Ch Oxford (MA); CC Kesteven 1931–45, Hon Capt RA (TA) WW II, High Sheriff Lincs 1953; *m* 18 April 1927 Barbara Angela Mary Lind (*d* 19–), dau of John Duncan Gregory, CB, CMG, and *d* 6 Oct 1977, having had:

1 Sir (RICHARD) BRUNO GREGORY WELBY, **7th and present Bt**

2 Julian Philip Earle; *b* 4 Sept 1931; *educ* Eton; *d* unm 31 March 1974

WELCH

Arms: Or on a fess gules between six martlets azure two lions passant respectant or. **Crest:** A heraldic antelope's head erased or, armed gules, gorged with a collar composed of six pierced mullets azure, chained also gules. **Motto:** *Ne cede arduis* ('Do not give in to hardship'). **Badge:** A sword erect gules, enfiled by a circlet of six pierced mullets or, chained azure. **Creation:** Bt. (UK), 16 Dec 1957.

SIR JOHN READER WELCH, 2ND BT, of Chard, Co Somerset [Sir John Welch Bt, 28 Rivermead Court, Ranelagh Gdns, London SW6 3RU]; *b* 26 July 1933; *s* f 1980; *educ* Marlborough and Hertford Coll Oxford (BA 1957, MA 1961); late Roy Corps of Signals; slr 1960, ptnr Bell, Broderick and Gray 1961–71, Wedlake Bell 1972–96, Ward Clerk Walbrook Ward City London 1961–74, Registrar Archdeaconry London 1967–, Liveryman Haberdashers' Co 1955 (Court of Assistants 1973, Master 1990), Freeman Parish Clerks' Co 1954 (Master 1967), Chm Management Ctee London Homes for Elderly 1981–90, Memb Ct Common Cncl City London 1975–86 and Chm Planning and Communications Ctee 1981 and 1982, chm John Fairfax (UK) Ltd 1977–90, Pres Grand Charity of Freemasons 1985–95, CStJ, FRSA; *m* 25 Sept 1962 *Margaret Kerry, only dau of Kenneth Victor Douglass, of Killara, Sydney, NSW, and has:

1 +JAMES DOUGLASS CULLUM; *b* 10 Nov 1973

1 *Margaret Trudy Cullum [Mrs Anthony Jervoise, Rowden Manor Farm, Sampford Courtenay, Devon EX20 2SJ]; *b* 17 Jan 1965; *m* 1992 *Anthony Richard Loveys Jervoise, yr s of John Loveys Jervoise, of Herriard Park, Hants, and has:

(1) *Elizabeth Antonia; *b* 4 Jan 1995

(2) *Cecily Jane; *b* 11 Nov 1996

2 *Jane Olive Comrie Cullum [Mrs David Waller, Vine Farm, Headcorn, Kent TN27 9JJ]; *b* 17 Jan 1965; *m* 1992 *David Ross Waller, er son of John Waller, of Clarencefield, Dumfries, and has:

    (1) *Maximilian Douglass; *b* 5 March 1998

    (1) Phoebe; *b* and *d* 5 March 1998 (stillborn)

Lineage: GEORGE WELCH; *m* Catherine Gerard Sheppard and had:

JAMES READER WELCH; *b* 7 Dec 1868; slr; *m* 11 Sept 1894 Harriet (*d* 28 April 1953), dau of Benjamin Cullum, and *d* 26 Dec 1944, leaving:

Sir (George James) Cullum Welch, 1st Bt (UK), so *cr* 16 Dec 1957, OBE (1944), MC (1918), of Chard, Co Somerset; *b* 20 Oct 1895; *educ* Alleyn's Sch Dulwich; Capt Roy Berks Regt WW I, Lt-Col WW II, memb City London TA&AFA 1941–65, ktd 1952, Hon Col City London Bn Roy Fus (TA) 1953–65 and City of London Army Cadet Force 1956–65; slr 1920, memb Cncl Law Soc 1951–63, Registrar Archdeaconry London 1953–67; memb Court Common Cncl City London 1931–47, Ch Commoner 1946, a Lt City London 1947–70, Alderman 1947–70, Sheriff 1950, Ld Mayor 1956–57, Liveryman and memb Court Assists Haberdashers' Co (Past Master), Liveryman Spectacle-makers' Co, Past Master: Slrs', Parish Clerks' and Paviors' Cos, Pres City Livery Club 1943–44, Chm Florence Nightingale Hosp 1954–63, V-Chm Govrs Bethlem Roy Hosp and Maudsley Hosp 1953–66, Dep Chm Exec Ctee King George VI Fndn, Chm Ld Mayor of London's Nat Hungarian and Centl Relief Fund 1956–60; Hon Freeman Borough Chard, Bangor, Co Down, and London, Ontario; Chm London Homes for the Elderly, Hon Treas UNICEF 1964–68, Tstee Wakefield (Tower Hill, Trinity Sq) Tst, Chm Tstees Morden Coll, Govr Hon Irish Soc 1967–70, KStJ, Order Mercy, Cdr Order Dannebrog Denmark, Offr Order Orange Nassau Netherlands, Cdr 1st Cl Order Lion Finland, Grand Ufficiale Al Merito Italy; *m* 1st 23 April 1921 Gertrude Evelyn Sladin (*d* 12 Dec 1966), dau of John William Harrison, of Stubbins, Lancs, and Eastbourne, Sussex; *m* 2nd 25 Feb 1969 Irene Avril (*d* 2 March 1996), dau of John Foster, OBE, and *d* 28 July 1980, leaving by his 1st w:

1 Sir JOHN READER WELCH, **2nd and present Bt**

    1 *Rosemary Avril [Mrs Leighton Jones, 6 Dunleary Court, Westcote Rd, Reading, Berks RG30 2DJ]; *b* 22 April 1927; *m* 1st 5 June 1952 (*divorce* 1963) John Osmond; *m* 2nd 2 Sept 1963 Leighton Griffith Jones (*d* 1983)

WELDON

Arms: Arg. a cinquefoil pierced gu., on a chief of the second a demi-lion issuant of the first. **Crests:** 1 A demi-lion rampant arg., guttée de sang, 2 The bust of QUEEN ELIZABETH I (granted Sir Anthony Weldon, Clerk of the Spicery). **Motto:** *Bene factum* ('Well done'). **Creation:** Bt. (I) 11 July 1723.

SIR ANTHONY WILLIAM WELDON, 9TH BT, of Dunmore, Co Carlow [Sir Anthony Weldon Bt, c/o White's Club, 37 St James's St, London SW1]; *b* 11 May 1947; *s f* 1979; *educ* Sherborne; 2nd Lt Irish Gds 1966–69 (GSM S Arabia), ret as Lt 1974; *m* 1980 *Amanda, dau of Maj Geoffrey Edward Ford North, MC (see WALSINGHAM, B), and formerly w of Anthony John Wigan, of Rackenford, Tiverton, Devon, and has:

    1 *Alice Louise Iona; *b* 13 Nov 1981

    2 *Oonagh Leonie Isobel; *b* 6 Oct 1983

Lineage (of Weldon): HUGH WELTDEN; Sewer to HENRY VII; had, with two er sons (Hugh, ancestor of the WELTDENs of Shottesbrooke, Berks; Edward WELDON, Master of the Household to HENRY VIII and f of Sir Anthony Weldon, Clerk of the Spicery and Bd of Green Cloth, to whom ELIZABETH I granted the Manor of Swanscombe and who was ancestor of the WELDONs of Swanscombe) and a yst s (William, ancestor of the WELDONs of Thornby, Northants), a 3rd s:

THOMAS WELDON (presumably the person of that name who Cofferer to EDWARD VI and ELIZABETH I and ancestor of the WELDONs of Cookham, Berks); had, with other issue:

WALTER WELDON, of St John's Bower, Co Kildare; MP Athy 1613; *m* Jane, dau of John Ryder, Bp Killaloe, and *d* 9 Dec 1634, leaving, with other issue:

1 Thomas, of St John's Bower; *m* Mary (*d* 26 April 1668), dau of Jacob Newman, and *d* intestate 20 May 1647, leaving:

    (1) John, of Rosscomroe and Gurteen; *b* 1629/30; *m* by licence 3 June 1667 (*divorce* 4 Nov 1675) Rebecca, only dau of Roger Lloyd, of Kilmacdogh, Co Galway, and *dsp* intestate by 13 Feb 1707

    (1) Rose; *m* Henry Ponsonby (*d* 1681), of Stacktown and Crotto, Kerry, and had issue

2 William, of Rahinderry; MP Athy 1668; *m* 1st Elizabeth Robinson (*d* 18 April 1669) and had:

    (1) Walter, of Rosscomroe and Gurteen; *m c* 2 May 1683 Celia (*m* 2nd James Eustace; *m* 3rd Adam Kidder), dau of Thomas Loftus, of Killyan, Co Meath, and *dsp* 1686

    (1) Elizabeth; *m c* 28 April 1663 Thomas Pigot, of Dysart, and had issue

    (2) Jane; *m* 1675, as his 2nd w, Rev John Moore, Archdeacon Cloyne

2 (cont.) William Weldon *m* 2nd (licence 31 March 1673) Elizabeth Watson (*m* 2nd 1682 Garret Wall, of Athy) and by her had:

    (2) Robert; *b* May 1675; *m* 1702/3 Celia (*d* 21 Oct 1733 aged 46), 6th dau of Alexander Cosby, of Stradbally, and had, with other issue:

        1a William; High Sheriff, King's Co 1761; *m* 15 Oct 1730 Elizabeth, dau of Henry Westenra (*see* ROSSMORE, B), and had, with other issue:

            1b Robert; *m* Mary (*m* 2nd 1772 Claudius Cathcart), dau of William Parsons (*see* ROSSE, E), and had:

                1c Mary; *m* 1786 Erasmus Grace, of Prospect, King's Co

            1b Elinor; *m* as his 2nd w her bro's f-in-law William Parsons and had issue

3 ARTHUR, of whom presently

1 Sarah; *m* Sir Erasmus Borrowes, 1st Bt, of Gilltown (*see* 1939 edn), and had issue

2 Frances; *m* 1st William Savage, of Rheban; *m* 2nd Sir William Flower (*see* ASHBROOK, V) and *d* 26 Dec 1673, leaving issue by both husbs

The 5th s,

ARTHUR WELDON, of Park, Co Carlow; *m* Mary (*d* between 18 May 1683 and 9 March 1685), sis of Sir Thomas Harman, of Athy, and widow of Sir John Dunbar, of Dunbar, Co Fermanagh, and had:

WALTER WELDON, of Rahinderry; MP Carlow 1692–1715; *m* Anne, sis and in her issue ultimate heir of **Sir Thomas Burdett, 1st Bt** (*see* **Lineage (of Burdett)** below), and had:

1 ARTHUR

2 Thomas; *m* 1st 5 March 1732 Charlotte (*d* 1741), dau of William Paston, 2nd Earl of Yarmouth by Charlotte Jemima Henrietta Maria, illegitimate dau of CHARLES II by Elizabeth, Countess of Shannon, and widow of Thomas Herne, of Heverland, Norfolk; *m* 2nd (by licence 14 Sept 1747) Elizabeth Portland, of Norwich; *m* 3rd (by licence 23 Feb 1747/8) Mrs Mary Wingfield, widow, who surv him

3 John; *b* 24 Dec 1694; *m* 18 Nov 1729 Mary, dau of Sir Stephen Glynne, 3rd Bt, and *d* 8 Oct 1759, having had issue:

    (1) Anna Maria; *m* 1st Rev John Burgh, of Donore, Co Kildare; *m* 2nd Rev John Peile, of Norwich

4 George; *m* 26 Nov 1729 Anne, dau of Maj Achilles La Columbine, of Carlow, and *dsp* (*bur* at St John's, Athy) 8 Sept 1732

WALTER WELDON *d* 16 May 1728/9; his est s,

ARTHUR WELDON, of Rahinderry; *m* 1st Hon Bridget Ponsonby (*dsp*), dau of 1st Viscount Duncannon (*see* BESSBOROUGH, E); *m* 2nd 20 Dec 1721 Mary, dau of Anthony Dopping, DD, Bp of Meath, and by her had with other issue:

1 Walter, of Rahinderry, MP Athy 1745; *b* 1 July 1724; *m* 1st Mary, dau of Col John Steuart, of Leighlinsbridge, and had:

    (1) Stewart, of Kilmorony; MP Ennis; *m* 11 Dec 1777 Helen, sis of 1st Marquess Conyngham (*qv*), and *d* 2 Jan 1829, having had:

        1a Walter Francis; *b* 1 Dec 1781; *d* 12 March 1782

1 (cont.) Walter Weldon *m* 2nd Anne (*d* 4 Dec 1809 aged 83), dau of Sir Samuel Cooke, Bt, MP Dublin (*ext*), and *d* 23 Aug 1773, leaving by her:

    (2) Samuel Cooke; *dsp* 19 April 1798

    (1) Mary; *m* 1786 Very Rev Thomas Trench, Dean Kildare

    (2) Jane; *b* Oct 1766; *m* 1797 Lt-Col Hon John Crichton and had issue (*see* ERNE, E)

2 Thomas; *b* 3 Jan 1726; Army Capt; *m* 21 Aug 1776 Mrs Elinor Agnew, widow, and *d* 9 Nov 1788, leaving:

    (1)Thomas; *dsp* 13 Sept 1793

3 ANTHONY, of whom presently

1 Jane; *b* 4 Sept 1725; *m* Richard Despard, of Cranna, Queen's Co, and *d* Sept 1793

2 Mary; *m* 8 Aug 1751 James Molony, of Kiltanon, Co Clare, and had issue

The 3rd s,

Rev ANTHONY WELDON; *b* 30 Dec 1728; Rector Athy; *m* 1st (licence 21 April 1759) Mrs Katherine Lewis, widow (*bur* 23 Jan 1766); *m* 2nd Anne, dau of John Coghlan, and *d* 1803, having by her had, with other issue, including two er sons (Rev Arthur Jocelyn, Rector Killaban, *m* Isabella, dau of John Barrington and widow of John Cuffe, and *dsp* 1826; Walter, *dsp* 1810):

Sir Anthony Weldon, 4th Bt, as which *s* cousin **Sir William Bagenal Burdett, 3rd Bt**, of Rahen or Rahinderry and Kilmorony, Co Kildare; *b* 16 June 1781; Sheriff Queen's Co 1839, Col Madras Artillery 1855; *m* 4 Jan 1824 Harriet, yst dau of Col Thomas Hockley, of Bury St Edmunds, Suffolk, and had, with other issue:

1 Arthur; *d* unm July 1853

2 ANTHONY CROSDILL (Sir), **5th Bt**

3 Walter; *b* 11 May 1828; Maj-Gen Madras Army; *m* 1st 4 July 1861 Louisa Acheson (*d* 16 Aug 1873), 2nd dau of Sir James Macaulay Higginson, KCB, of Brookhill, Co Antrim, and had, with other issue:

    (1) Helen Mary; *d* unm

    (2) Alice Frances; *m* 1 Nov 1911 Lt-Col Oswald Mosley Croshaw, DSO, 19th Hus (*d* 26 Sept 1917 of wounds recd in action), and *d* 14 June 1950

    (3) Louisa Elinor; *m* 14 Feb 1900 Maj-Gen George Walker, CB, CBE, DSO, RE (*d* 5 Dec 1936), s of Maj G R Walker, RE, and *d* 21 Sept 1938

(4) Evaleen Maud Mary; *m* 2 April 1910 Capt Ralph Blackett, Roy Inniskilling Fus (*d* 20 June 1964), 3rd s of Sir Edward William Blackett, 7th Bt (*qv*), and *d* 21 Nov 1952

3 (cont.) Walter Weldon *m* 2nd 3 June 1876 Annie Homan (*d* 1913), dau of Daniel Molloy, of Clonbela, King's Co, and *d* 7 July 1907, leaving by her:

(1) Arthur Steuart; *b* 1 March 1877; Maj N Staffs Regt Boer War 1900–02 (two medals and five clasps) and WW I; *ka* 25 March 1917

(5) Harriet Hockley; *m* 8 June 1910 Thomas Loftus Uniacke Townshend (*d* 1953) and *d* 26 Aug 1941, leaving issue

(6) Gertrude Wilmer; *m* Aug 1916 Capt Conway Higginson, RA, and *d* 15 Feb 1927

4 Edmund Courtney; *b* 1830; *d* unm

5 Thomas, CIE; *b* 9 Sept 1834; Col IA; *m* 16 Feb 1865 Helen Rachel Louisa (*d* 16 Oct 1931), only child of Gen George William Young Simpson, RA and *d* 9 Nov 1905, having had:

(1) George Anthony; *b* 1 Feb 1866; Capt Roy Dublin Fus; *ka* Boer War 20 Oct 1899

(2) Francis Harry, DSO; *b* 24 April 1869; Maj Sherwood Foresters, Derbyshire Regt, Boer War 1899–1902 (despatches, two medals with five clasps); *m* 16 Sept 1902 Eveleen (*d* 25 April 1955), dau of Thomas Fielden Campbell, of Devonshire Place, London, and *d* 8 April 1920, leaving:

1a George Anthony Thomas; *b* 5 June 1908; *d* unm Aug 1963

1a Sybil May; *b* 20 Nov 1906

(3) Walter Ivan; *b* 2 16 July 1871; *educ* Emmanuel Coll Cambridge; Lt 4th Bn Manchester Regt; *m* 5 July 1899 Edith Lucy (*d* 10 June 1956), dau of Clifton Whiting, of Ashstead Grange, Surrey, and *d* 6 March 1934, leaving:

1a Violet Iva; *b* 30 June 1900

(1) Mary Helen Meikle; *m* 1889 Charles Sewell and *d* 7 Nov 1889

(2) Louie Harriet Grace; *m* 16 July 1895 Maxmilian McKenzie Litkie and *d* his widow 14 Jan 1932, leaving issue

6 Francis; *b* 30 July 1836; Col IA; *m* 1 Aug 1871 Henrietta Frances Alicia (*d* 31 Oct 1922), only dau of Langford Kennedy, and *d* 24 June 1926, having had, with other issue:

(1) Walter Langford; *b* 30 July 1872; *educ* Selwyn Coll Cambridge (BA, LLM); barrister Bombay; *m* 1st 1 Dec 1904 Emma (*dsp* 25 May 1905), dau of John Henry Tod; *m* 2nd 5 Jan 1910 Muriel Stewart (*m* 2nd 3 March 1924 Lt-Col William Weldon Herring-Cooper, CBE, DSO (*d* 11 Jan 1953), s of Harman Herring-Cooper, of Shrule Castle, Co Carlow, and *d* 26 Feb 1966), dau of William Richardson, of Tunbridge Wells, and *d* 15 June 1922, leaving:

1a Francis William Charles, MVO (1952), MBE (1946), MC; *b* 2 Aug 1913; *educ* Wellington; Lt-Col RA WW II 1939–40 (despatches, POW), ret 1958; *m* 9 March 1946 *Diana Geraldine [Mrs Francis Weldon, Stable Cottage, Wickwar, Glos], dau of Stephen Anderson, of Starloch by Blairgowrie, Perthshire, and had:

1b +George Francis Daryl [George Weldon Esq, 102 Kew Green, Surrey TW9 3AP]; *b* 9 Dec 1946; *educ* Wellington Coll, Keble Coll Oxford and Carnegie-Mellon U USA; *m* 1981 *Jane Margaret, er dau of Maurice William George Knapman, of Stoke Gabriel, Devon, and has:

1c *Claire Elizabeth; *b* 1984

2c *Sarah Jane; *b* 1987

2b +David Walter; *b* 10 May 1949; *educ* Wellington; *m* 1975 *Tessa Herron and has:

1c *Emilio; *b* 1982

1c *Sophie; *b* 1976

2a +Patrick Langford Daryl, MC (1952) [Maj Patrick Weldon MC, 18 Westbourne Park Rd, London W2 5PH]; *b* 26 Sept 1917; *educ* Wellington and Trin Coll Cambridge (BA); Maj RA WW II, Wilts Regt Korea 1950–51 (despatches); *m* 20 Aug 1955 *Pamela Jane, yst dau of Col Leonard Bishopp Grant, CIE, TD, ED, of Burnt House, Benenden, Kent, and has:

1b +Thomas Daryl; *b* 1963

2b +Guy Patrick; *b* 27 April 1967

1b *Anna Grant [Mrs Andrew Reed, 58 Strathville Rd, London SW18]; *b* 17 May 1958; *m* 1987 *Andrew William Gadsden Reed, s of Gp/Capt William Reed, of Eydon, Northants, and has:

1c *Louisa Charlotte Weldon; *b* 1991

2b *Sarah Kate [Mrs Andrew Wilkinson, 48 Woodstock Rd, London W4 1UB]; *b* 14 May 1960; *m* 1984 *Andrew James Durham Wilkinson and has:

1c *Lucy Natasha; *b* 1988

2c *Amelia Grace; *b* 1990

3c *Matilda Rose; *b* 1994

1a Evelyn Stewart; *b* 30 Sept 1910; Kaisar-i-Hind medal; *m* 5 Sept 1931 Brig Arthur Francis Gordon Forbes (*d* 20 March 1970), MC, Indian Cav, only s of Brig Gen Sir Arthur William Forbes, KBE, CB, and had issue

2a Joan Valerie; *b* 25 Nov 1921; *m* 31 July 1965 Maj Derrick Peter Henry Dyson, RA, yr s of Henry Dyson, of Carshalton Beeches, Surrey

(2) Ernest Steuart, CBE (1923), DSO, (1919); *b* 6 Jan 1877; Lt-Col Dorsetshire Regt, Boer War 1899–1902 (two medals with six clasps), WW I (despatches), Malabar 1923; *m* 16 March 1916 Helen Cecilia (*d* 12 Sept 1966), dau of Alfred Greaves, of Haversham, Bucks, and *d* 12 Jan 1946, leaving:

1a Arthur Reginald; *b* 4 Dec 1918; *educ* Wellington; Maj RA WW II, ret 1958; *m* 4 Oct 1945 *Dorothy Ann [Mrs Arthur Weldon, Beanlands Park, Irthington, Carlisle], only child of William Monkhouse Pratchitt, of Eden Grove, Crosby-on-Eden, Carlisle, and *d* 9 Oct 1982, leaving:

1b +Steuart William Pratchitt [Steuart Weldon Esq, 96 Taybridge Rd, London SW11 5PS]; *b* 24 April 1947; *educ* Wellington; *m* 1984 *Carola Helen Victoria, er dau of John Hugh Loch, of The Market House, Aldbourne, Wilts, and has:

1c *Helen Ann Freda; *b* 1986

2b +Robert Arthur de Weltden; *b* 13 May 1950; *educ* Wellington; *m* 1993 *Clare Frances, yr dau of Richard Killingworth Hedges, of Charlton House, Shaftesbury, Dorset

2a Hugh de Weltden; *b* 15 June 1925; *educ* Wellington and Christ's Coll Cambridge (BA 1949, MA 1954); Housemaster Marlborough, proprietor *The Bryant Index to Country Houses*; *d* unm 25 May 1983

(1) Ethel Olive; *d* unm 13 Jan 1951

(2) Winifred Edith; *m* 29 Jan 1916 Capt Montagu Herbert Hartcup, RASC (*d* 22 June 1957), er surv s of Herbert James Hartcup, of Upland Hall, Bungay, Suffolk, and had:

1a *Guy Rider Monyns; *b* 30 May 1919; *educ* Lancing and St Catharine's Coll Cambridge (BA 1947, MA 1949); Roy Berks Regt and RIASC WW II; *m* 30 May 1953 *Henrietta, dau of Baron Johann Ludwig Alfons Pereira-Arnstein, of Vienna, and widow of Leonard Greaves

7 Lewen Burton (Rev Canon); *b* 17 Aug 1840; DD; Canon Salisbury and Christchurch Cathedral Dublin, Vicar Holy Trinity Weymouth 1894–1914, RD 1903–14, Rector and RD Bridport; *m* 13 June 1871 Olivia Maria (*d* 15 April 1921), 2nd dau of Sir Croker Barrington, 4th Bt (*qv*), and *d* 5 Jan 1914, leaving:

(1) Lewen Francis Barrington, MC; *b* 15 Oct 1875; *educ* St Edward's Sch Oxford and Trin Coll Dublin; Capt Intell Corps WW I (despatches twice), Surveyor-Gen Egypt 1919–23, Order Nile; *m* 29 Oct 1904 Mary Macaulay (*d* 29 June 1946), est dau of Lawrence Bomford Molloy, DL, of Clonbeale, King's Co, and *d* 13 June 1958, leaving:

1a Olivia Mary; *b* 1 Dec 1905; Jr Cdr ATS WW II; *d* 19 Sept 1978

(2) Kenneth Charles, DSO (1917); *b* 25 April 1877; *educ* St Edward's Sch Oxford and Trin Coll Dublin (BA 1899); Lt-Col Sherwood Foresters, Maj and Brevet Lt-Col Roy Dublin Fus, Boer War 1899–1902 (two medals and five clasps), WW I (despatches), Offr Legn Hon; *m* 14 Nov 1906 Elizabeth Constance Jane (*d* 17 Sept 1960), only dau of Maj William Croker, Roy Inniskilling Fus and Roy Irish Fus, of Byblox, Doneraile, Co Cork, and *d* 11 April 1958, leaving:

1a Anthony Croker; *b* 26 Sept 1907; Lt Sherwood Foresters, Capt Roy Irish Fus, T/F/Lt RAF; *d* unm 20 June 1939

1a Aphra Elizabeth; *b* 23 May 1911; WAAF WW II

2a *Elinor Constance; *b* 8 May 1913

3a *Clemence Jane [Miss Clemence Weldon, 28 Leamington Rd, Charminster, Hants]; *b* 21 Feb 1915

(1) Mary Caroline; *m* 28 Sept 1912 Brian James Gwynn, Dept Industry and Commerce Ireland, s of Rev John Gwynn, DD, Regius Prof Divinity Dublin, and *d* 22 Dec 1944, having had issue

(2) Hilda Frances; Cmdt VAD Dorset 1914–18; *m* 24 June 1918 Rev Cyril Summerfield Pugh (*d* 9 May 1953), Rector Winfrith, Dorchester, s of Samuel S Pugh, of Heathcote House, Devizes, Wilts, and *d* 8 Oct 1962 aged 89

(3) Anna Felicia; *m* 19 June 1908 Lt-Col William Harley Macalpine-Leny (*d* 4 March 1951), DSO, DL, RGA, of Duror, Argyll, yst s of William Macalpine-Leny, DL, of Dalswinton, and *d* 6 Oct 1926, leaving issue

1 Harriet; *m* 15 Aug 1849 Weldon S Molony (*d* 1890), of Upper Mount St, Dublin, and *d* 1870, leaving issue

2 Anna Maria; *m* 1895 John Chapman (*d* 1885), of Lonford Terrace, Monkstown, and *d* 1895, leaving issue

3 Selina; *m* 27 April 1865 Harman Herring-Cooper (*d* 1887), of Shrule, and *d* 1899, leaving issue

4 Ellinor Emma; *m* 1 June 1869 Abraham Hobson (*d* 1887), MD, FRCSI, and *d* 23 March 1913, leaving issue

The 4th Bt *d* 21 Dec 1858; his 2nd s,

Sir Anthony Crosdill Weldon, 5th Bt, of Rahinderry and Kilmorony, JP, DL; *b* 16 March 1827; *m* 12 June 1862 Elizabeth Caroline Thomasina (*d* 16 April 1914), est surv dau of Lt-Col Arthur Kennedy, 18th Hus, and had, with other issue:

1 ANTHONY ARTHUR (Sir), **6th Bt**

2 Thomas Hamilton; *b* 7 July 1864; Capt 3rd Bn Leinster Regt, Boer War 1899–1900 (medal and clasp), Lt Sub Miners RE; *d* unm 1 Nov 1903

3 Bertram de Weltden, MC; *b* 16 Nov 1872; Capt 3rd Bn Leics Regt attd Egyptian Army, ADC to GOC The Curragh 1900–01, Maj 10th Serv Bn Lancs Fus Boer War 1899 (wounded, despatches, medal with clasp); *d* 7 Oct 1922

4 Ralph Lewen; *b* 17 June 1875; Imp Yeo Boer War 1900 (medal and clasps); *d* unm 25 July 1912

5 Henry Walter, DSO (1919); *b* 2 Nov 1878; Lt-Col Beds and Herts Regt and Prince of Wales's Leinster Regt, Boer War 1901–02 and WW I (despatches, Croix de Guerre); *m* 19 Aug 1909 Helen Louise Victoria (*d* 12 April 1965), yst dau of Sir Edward Porter Cowan, of Craig-a-vad, Co Down, and *d* 2 June 1925, leaving:

(1) Hamilton Edward Crosdill, CBE (1961, OBE 1950), DL (Gtr London 1967); *b* 14 Sept 1910; *educ* Charterhouse and RMA Woolwich; Brig RA WW II (despatches twice), Cdr 33 AA Bde 1958–60, Cdr Sch Artillery Manorbier 1960–62, BRAN Cmd but ret to become Sec Co of London T&AFA Nov 1962 (Sec Gtr Lond TA&VRA 1968), Hon Col 265 Lt AD Regt RA (TA), ADC to HM THE QUEEN 1961–85, Croix de Guerre; *m* 1st 31 Oct 1935 (*divorce* 1946) Margaret Helen Katherine, dau of Maj Frederic Passy, of Blachford Cornwood, Devon, and had:

1a *Wendy Juliet; *b* 14 July 1937; *m* 19 Nov 1960 *Capt Ian Fothergill Grant, RN, and has:

1b *Jonathan James Fothergill; *b* 23 Feb 1962; *m* 3 Sept 1995 *Kathryn Jean, yr dau of C P Wood-Mallock, of Altrincham, Cheshire, and has:

1c *Jemima Beatrice; *b* 18 Sept 1997

2b *Andrew William Edward Fothergill; *b* 5 Oct 1963; *m* 1989 *Katrina Louise, dau of Henry Evill, of London, and has issue

1b *Amanda Katherine Linley; *b* 2 March 1968

(1) (cont.) Brig Hamilton Weldon *m* 2nd 3 Jan 1948 *Elwyne Priscilla [Mrs Hamilton Weldon, 3 Burnt Hill Rd, Wrecclesham, Surrey], 2nd dau of Harold Richards Chaldecott, OBE, of Chantry, Leyburn, Yorks, and *d* 17 May 1985, leaving by her:

1a +KEVIN NICHOLAS; *b* 19 April 1951; heir presumptive; *educ* Haileybury; *m* 1973 *Catherine Main, of Fontenay le Comte, France, and has:

1b +Alexander Nicholas *b* 6 Jan 1977

2a +Mark Henry de Weltden; *b* 31 July 1953; *educ* Haileybury; Maj RHA (1974); *m* 1980 *Catherine M, yr dau of Lt-Col D J P Weld, of Manor Farm, Apethorpe, Northants, and has:

  1b +John; *b* 4 Nov 1981

  1b *Lucinda Katie; *b* 14 June 1983

2a *(Andrea) Sari Victoria [Mrs Michael Smith, 53 Green Lane, Farnham, Surrey GU9 8QE]; *b* 30 Nov 1948; *m* 1st 1974 (*divorce* 1983) Richard Amyas Evetts; *m* 2nd 28 Nov 1998 *Michael John Smith, and by her 1st husb has:

  1b *Benjamin George; *b* 27 Feb 1976

  2b *Thomas Edward; *b* 21 April 1979

(1) *Aurea Elizabeth [Mrs Humphrey Stuart, Southwood, Baltonsborough, Somerset]; *b* 1 Sept 1915; *m* 7 Nov 1942 Capt Humphrey John James Stuart, RA (*d* 22 May 1969), only s of Maj William Stuart, IA, of Merecombe, Kemerton, nr Tewkesbury, by Hon Dorothy Evelyn, 5th dau of 2nd Baron Norton (*qv*), and has:

  1a *Julian de Weltden; *b* 1947

1 Mabelle Harriet Lucy; *m* 23 June 1921 Maj Francis Philip Kirkpatrick (*d* 13 Dec 1929), MC, and *dsp* 2 March 1954

2 Murielle Nina Eva; *d* unm 30 Aug 1952

The 5th Bt *d* 14 Jan 1900; his est s,

Sir Anthony Arthur Weldon, 6th Bt, CVO, DSO, JP, DL Queen's Co; *b* 1 March 1863; *educ* Trin Coll Cambridge (BA); HM's Lt Co Kildare, High Sheriff 1906, Lt-Col and Brevet Col 4th Bn Prince of Wales's Leinster Regt Roy Canadians, ADC to C-in-C 1895–1900, Boer War 1899–1900 (despatches twice, Queen's medal with two clasps), WW I (despatches, Brevet of Col), V-Chamberlain to Ld Lt Ireland 1905–08, State Steward and Chamberlain 1908–17; *m* 11 Feb 1902 Winifred Bruce Blakeney, OBE (1920) (*m* 2nd 17 Dec 1938 Wilfred Fitzgerald (*d* 26 July 1943), of Dublin, and *d* 19 Feb 1951), dau of Col — Varty-Rogers, of Broxmore Park, Romsey, Hants, and *d* 29 June 1917, leaving:

1 **Sir Anthony Edward Wolseley Weldon, 7th Bt**, of Rahinderry and Kilmorony; *b* 1 Dec 1902; *educ* Charterhouse; S/Ldr AAF and RAF Regt WW II, Staff Offr to Govr Trinidad, OStJ; *d* unm 9 Jan 1971

2 THOMAS BRIAN, (Sir), **8th Bt**

3 Terence Gordon Mackworth de Weltden, AE; *b* 16 May 1909; *educ* Sherborne; RAuxAF 1938–46, PA to C-in-C Technical Trg Cmd (AM Sir John Tremayne) 1941–42, RAF Intell 1942–44, N Africa 1943, Italy 1943 and France 1944, Air Tport Cmd Paris 1945, attached Br Embassy; *m* 1st 10 July 1941 (*divorce* 1946) Suzanne Marie, yr dau of Percy Clifford Hopkinson, of Sea Barn, Kingston Gorse, Sussex; *m* 2nd 26 Sept 1946 (*divorce* 1969) Simonne Mireille, dau of Armand Philippon, of Aix-en-Provence, France, and *d* 24 July 1970, leaving:

(1) *Oonagh Serena Elizabeth [Ms Oonagh Weldon, Parc Voltina, Mas des Nigelles Bat B, Route du Tholonet, 13100 Aix-en-Provence, France]; *b* 28 Nov 1947; has:

  *Sarah Ilitch WELDON; *b* 1984

The 7th Bt's bro,

Sir Thomas Brian Weldon, 8th Bt; *b* 19 May 1905; *educ* Sherborne and Magdalene Coll Cambridge; Capt 2nd Bn Princess Louise Kensington Regt WW II; *m* 21 July 1942 *Marie Isobel (WRNS) (*m* 2nd 1984, as his 2nd w, 6th Earl Cathcart; *qv*) [The Rt Hon The Countess Cathcart, Moor Hatches, W Amesbury, Salisbury, Wilts], est dau of Capt Hon William Joseph French (see DE FREYNE, B), and *d* 5 Aug 1979, leaving:

1 Sir ANTHONY WILLIAM WELDON, **9th and present Bt**

1 *Tara Louise Winifred [Mrs Alan Elliot, The Old Rectory, Chilton Foliat, Hungerford, Berks RG17 0TF]; *b* 27 Sept 1943; *m* 20 Jan 1967 *Alan Christopher Elliot and has:

  1a *Dominic Ian Christopher; *b* 10 April 1975

  1a *Sacha Louise; *b* 25 Dec 1968

  2a *Larissa Mary; *b* 1 Oct 1970

  3a *Natalya Isobel; *b* 11 Feb 1978

Lineage (of Burdett): ROBERT BURDETT, London Alderman and merchant (alleged by some sources to be the Robert Burdett who was 2nd s of Sir Francis Burdett, 1st Bt, of Foremark, Derbys (see 1949 edn), though proof is lacking); granted 1630 *c* 20 townlands in Co Carlow; *m* Mary, dau of — Wright, London Alderman, and had an est s:

THOMAS BURDETT, of the Old Castle, Garrahill, Co Carlow; Sheriff Co Carlow 1662; *m* 2 July 1653 Catherine, dau of Sir Robert Kennedy, 1st Bt, of Mount Kennedy, Co Wicklow, and *d* between 2 Jan 1685 and 16 Aug 1701, leaving, with an er s (*d* young):

1 **Sir Thomas Burdett, 1st Bt** (I), so *cr* 11 July 1723, with remainder to the heirs male of his sis Anne, of Dunmore, Co Carlow; *b* 14 Sept 1668; *educ* Trin Coll Dublin; Sheriff Co Carlow 1701, MP (I Parl) Co Carlow 1704–13 and 1715–27 and Carlow town 1713–14, Govr Co Carlow 1725–27; *m* 1st, as her 3rd husb, probably *c* 1700 Honora, widow of (a) 3rd Earl of Ardglass (see CROMWELL, B, preliminary remarks) and (b) Francis Cuffe, MP (I Parl) Co Mayo and sis of 1st Viscount Blesington of the 1673 *cr* (see CORK and ORRERY, E), but by her had no issue; *m* 2nd by 1715 Martha, 4th dau of Bartholomew Vigors, Bp Ferns and Leighlin, and *d* 14 April 1727, leaving by her an only s:

(1) **Sir William Vigors Burdett, 2nd Bt**, of Dunmore; *b* 8 June 1715; *m* 1st by Aug 1739 —, n of Robert Jones, of Mount Kennedy, Co Wicklow, and had a s (Thomas, *d* young 1 March 1755); *m* 2nd 5 Oct 1769 Henrietta, dau of Hon James O'Brien (see INCHIQUIN, B), and widow of Terence O'Loghlin, and *d* 17 Dec 1798, leaving by her a 2nd but est surv s:

  1a **Sir William Bagenal Burdett, 3rd Bt**; *bapt* 16 July 1770; *educ* Magdalen Coll Oxford; *m* 1st 7 March 1800 Maria, dau of Rev Henry James Reynett, DD, and had at least three sons (living 1811); *m* 2nd 18 July 1820 Esther, est dau of Thomas Smith, of Castleton Hall, Lancs, and *dspms* 14 Dec 1840, when the btcy passed to his distant cousin (see **Lineage (of Weldon)** above)

1 Anne; *m* WALTER WELDON and had issue (see **Lineage (of Weldon)** above)

WELLINGTON

Arms: Quarterly: 1st and 4th, gules a cross argent between five plates in saltire in each quarter (for WELLESLEY); 2nd and 3rd, or, a lion rampant, gules (for COLLEY); as honourable augmentation in chief an escutcheon charged with the crosses of St George, St Andrew and St Patrick conjoined (union badge of United Kingdom of Great Britain and Ireland). **Crest:** Out of a ducal coronet or a demi-lion rampant gules, holding a forked pennon of the last flowing to the sinister, one-third per pale from the staff argent charged with the cross of St George. **Supporters:** Two lions gules, each gorged with an eastern crown and chained or. **Motto:** *Virtutis fortuna comes* ('Fortune is the companion of valour').

Creations: B. (I) 9 July 1746 (Mornington), V. (Wellesley of Dangan Castle) and E. (Mornington) (I) 2 Oct 1760, (UK) 4 Sept 1809 (Douro of Wellesley) V. (UK) 4 Sept 1809 (Wellington of Talavera and of Wellington), E. (I) 2 Oct 1760 (Mornington), E. (UK) 28 Feb 1812 (Wellington), M. (Wellington) (UK) 3 Oct 1812, D. and M. (Douro) (UK) 11 May 1814, also Count (Portugal) 18 Oct 1811, Marquis (Portugal) Aug 1812, D. (Portugal) 18 Dec 1812 (Vittoria), D. (Spain) Jan 1812 (Ciudad Rodrigo), P. (Netherlands) 18 July 1815 (Waterloo).

THE 8TH DUKE OF WELLINGTON, Marquess of Wellington, Marquess Douro, Earl of Wellington, Co Somerset, **Earl of Mornington**, Co Meath, **Viscount Wellington of Talavera and of Wellington**, Co Somerset, **Viscount Wellesley of Dangan Castle**, Co Meath, and **Baron Douro of Wellesley**, Co Somerset, also **Prince of Waterloo, Count of Vimeiro, Marquis of Torres Vedras** and **Duke of Vittoria, Duke of Ciudad Rodrigo** and a Grandee of the 1st Class (1968) (Sir Arthur Valerian Wellesley, KG (1990), LVO (1952), OBE (1958), MC (1941), DL (Hants 1975)) [His Grace The Duke of Wellington KG LVO OBE MC DL, Apsley House, 149 Piccadilly, London W1V 9FA; Stratfield Saye House, Basingstoke, Hants RG27 0AS]; *b* 2 July 1915; *s f* 1972; *educ* Eton and New Coll Oxford; RHG WW II Middle East, Italy and NW Europe, Lt-Col cmdg RHG 1954–58, Lt-Col cmdg Household Cav and Silver Stick-in-Waiting 1959–60, cmded 22nd Armd Bde (TA) 1960–61, RAC 1st (Br) Corps BAOR 1963–64, Def Attaché Madrid 1964–68, ret as Brig 1968, Col-in-Ch Duke of Wellington's Regt 1974–, Hon Col 2nd Bn Wessex Regt 1974–80; CC Hants 1967–73; dir: Massey Ferguson Hldgs 1967–89, Massey Ferguson Ltd 1973–84 and Motor Iberica SA (Spain) 1967–, Pres: Game Conservancy 1976–81 (Dep Pres 1981–87), S E Branch Roy Br Legn 1978–, BSJA 1980–82, Rare Breeds Survival Tst 1984–87, Cncl for Environmental Conservation 1983–87, Atlantic Salmon Tst 1983–, V-Pres Zoological Soc London 1983–89, memb cncl RASE 1976– (Dep Pres 1993) and Ctee of Honour Passports for Pets, HM's Rep Appointee Bd of Tstees Armouries 1983–95, Tstee WWF (UK) 1985–90, Govr Wellington Coll 1965–, Chm Pitt Club; OStJ, Offr Legn Hon, Kt Grand Cross Order St Michael of the Wing Portugal, Order Isabel La Catolica Spain; sold 1972 the estates in Wellington, Somerset, and the Ldship of the Manor bought by the **1st Duke** 1812; *m* 28 Jan 1944 *Diana Ruth, only dau of Maj-Gen Douglas Fitzgerald McConnel, CB, CBE, DSO, of Knockdolian, Colmonell, Ayrshire, and has:

1 +ARTHUR CHARLES VALERIAN, *Marquess of Douro* [Marquess of Douro, The Old Rectory, Stratfield Saye, Berks RG7 2DA]; *b* 19 Aug 1945; *educ* Eton and Ch Ch Oxford; C parly candidate Islington N Feb 1974, memb Basingstoke Borough Cncl 1978–79, MEP (C) Surrey 1979–84 and Surrey W 1984–89, chm: Deltec Securities (UK) Ltd 1985–89, Dunhill Hldgs 1991–93, Framlington Gp 1994–, Sun Life & Provincial Hldgs plc 1996; dep chm: Thames Valley Bdcasting 1975–84, Deltec Panamerica SA 1985–89, Guinness Mahon Hldgs 1988–91, Vendôme Luxury Gp plc 1993–; dir: Antofagasta and Bolivia Railway Co 1977–80, Eucalyptus Pulp Mills 1979–88, dir Transatlantic Hldgs plc 1983–96, Global Asset Management Worldwide Inc 1984–, Continental and Industrial Tst plc 1987–90, Sun Life Corp 1988–96, Rothmans Internat 1990–93; memb cncl RCA 1992–; *m* 3 Feb 1977 *HRH Princess Antonia Elizabeth Brigid Luise of Prussia, yr dau of HRH Prince Friedrich Georg Wilhelm Christoph of Prussia (see 1967 edn ROYAL FAMILY) and has:

  (1) +Arthur Gerald, *Earl of Mornington*; *b* 31 Jan 1978; *educ* Eton

  (2) +Frederick Charles; *b* 1992

  (1) *Honor Victoria; *b* 25 Oct 1979

(2) *Mary Luise; *b* 1986

(3) *Charlotte Anne; *b* 1990

2 +Richard Gerald [The Lord Richard Wellesley, Knockdolian, Colmonell, Girvan, Ayrshire]; *b* 20 June 1949; *educ* Eton; *m* 14 July 1973 *Joanna Marion, est dau of John Sumner, of Marston St Lawrence, Banbury, Oxon, and has:

  (1) *Natasha Doone; *b* 5 Oct 1975

  (2) *Davinia Chloe; *b* 10 Oct 1977

3 +John Henry [The Lord John Wellesley, 15 Ensor Mews, London SW7 3BT]; *b* 20 April 1954; *educ* Eton; *m* 7 May 1977 *Corinne, dau of HE Baron Vaes, KCMG, late Belgian Amb UK, and has:

  (1) +Gerald Valerian; *b* 6 June 1981

  (1) *Alexandrina Sofia; *b* 23 July 1983

4 +(James) Christopher Douglas; *b* 16 Dec 1964; *educ* Eton; *m* 1994 *Laura Elizabeth, only dau of T E Wedge, and has:

  (1) *Eleanor Rose; *b* 9 Dec 1995

1 *(Caroline) Jane [The Lady Jane Wellesley, 42 Clarendon Rd, London W11]; *b* 6 July 1951; racing driver, antique business, researcher *Radio Times*, independent TV producer

Lineage: The WELLESLEYs take their name from Wellesley, Somerset, which they held under the Bps of Bath and Wells down to 1352. The first of the family in Ireland seems to have been:

Sir WALERAN de WELLESLEY; Justice Itinerant in Ireland 1261–68; acquired various lands in Cos Kildare and Wexford as well as other places; *m* Maud — and *d* by 1 Aug 1264, leaving:

MICHAEL de WELLESLEY; *b* 1245; *d* by 1290, leaving:

Sir WALERAN de WELLESLEY; in service of Bp of Bath and Wells 1291; *k* in Ireland 22 Oct 1303, leaving, with a yr s (Sir William, Constable Kildare Castle 1309–16, Keeper of the Peace Kildare 1346, *d* at Carlow between 17 Feb and 25 March 1348):

Sir JOHN de WELLESLEY, of Pollardstown, Conall and Kineagh, Co Kildare; Sheriff Kildare 1313; Keeper Peace Co Kildare 1346; *m* 1st —; *m* 2nd Rose Calf (who released her right to dower in Wellesley and the other Somerset lands July 1351; it was possibly by descent from her rather than through a later marriage that a junior branch of the WELLESLEYs inherited the feudal barony of Narragh, Co Kildare, after the death of Elizabeth Calf in 1442) and *d c* 1349, leaving:

Sir JOHN de WELLESLEY, of Pollardstown, Conall and Kineagh; released his lands in Wellesley, Dulcote and Eston to the Bp of Bath and Wells 1352; *m* Elizabeth — (who released her right to dower in the English lands 1353) and *d* 1353, leaving:

JOHN de WELLESLEY, of Pollardstown, Conall and Kineagh; *b* 1336; *d* by 1369, leaving:

Sir WILLIAM de WELLESLEY, of Pollardstown etc; summoned to the I Parl 1375, 1378 and 1393; intermittently Sheriff and Keeper of the Peace Co Kildare *c* 1388–1402; summoned to I Parl 1375; *d* after 1404, leaving:

Sir RICHARD de WELLESLEY; one of the reps sent to England by the I Parl Oct 1429; Sheriff Co Kildare; *m* by 27 Jan 1412/3 Joan, dau and heiress of Sir Nicholas de Castle Martin, of Dunsany, and heir to her kinsman Christopher Southern, of Dangan and Mornington (originally called Mariners' Town), Co Meath, whereby these last two estates came to the WELLESLEYs, and widow of Richard FitzGerald (*see* LEINSTER, D), by whom she had a dau (*m* 1st Baron Dunsany, *qv*), and *d* 1437, having shortly beforemade his Co Kildare lands over to his est s, leaving:

1 William; *m* Katherine Cusack and *dsp* by 22 Sept 1440

2 CHRISTOPHER

3 Gerald; *dsp* 1443

4 Waleran; had a crown grant of Blackcastle and Donaghmore, Co Meath, 1465; *dsp* after 1468

5 James, of Newcastle Macormigon, Co Meath; guardian to his n William 1465; *m* and had:

  (1) Edward; *dsp*

  (2) John; had:

    1a John; *dsp*

The 2nd s,

CHRISTOPHER WELLESLEY, of Dangan; had livery 22 Sept 1449 as heir to his bro; sold Kineagh to Sir Rowland Eustace, Lord Portlester, 1461; *d c* 1464, leaving, with a yr s (Edmond, possibly ancestor of the WELLESLEYs of Barrettstown and Blackhall, Co Kildare):

Sir WILLIAM WELLESLEY, of Dangan; minor at his f's death; sold Pollardstown to the Earl of Kildare (*see* LEINSTER, D) 1497; *m* 1st Ismay, dau of Sir Thomas Plunkett, of Rathmore (*see* DUNSANY, B); *m* 2nd by 3 May 1497, as her 2nd w, Meadhbh (Maeve or Maud) O'Toole (*m* 3rd Patrick Hussey), widow of Gerald *Bacach* ('The Lame') FitzGerald (*d* 1493), and *d* by 29 April 1502, having by his 1st w had:

1 Piers; *dsp & vp*

2 Garret/Gerald, of Dangan; *m* 1st Margaret, dau of Sir Thomas FitzGerald, of Lackagh, Co Kildare (*see* LEINSTER, D); *m* 2nd Amy/Anne Bermingham, widow of 3rd Baron Dunsany (*qv*), and *d* 1538, having had by his 1st w:

  (1) William, of Dangan; *m* (contract 30 July 1526) Elizabeth, dau of James Cusack, of Portrane, Co Dublin, and *d* 6 July 1550, leaving, with three yr sons (Walter, of Hurdlestown; Edward; James; all *dsp*) and three daus (Margaret; Ismay; Margery/Marcella):

    1a Garret/Gerald, of Dangan; *b* 1538; *m* 1st his cousin Genet, dau of Sir Thomas Cusack, and had:

      1b William; *m* Ellice Wakeley, dau of his stepmother Anne by her 1st husb, and *d* by 15 Nov 1595, leaving, with other issue:

        1c Valerian (a Latinisation of Waleran), of Dangan; *b* Dec 1592; contracted by his gf 1602 to *m* Mary, dau of Sir Patrick Barnewall, of Tunvey, a marriage he disavowed (as was his right in law) on reaching the age of 14; *m* 1st — and had:

          1d William; *m* (settlement 30 June 1637) Mary, dau of Sir Gerald Kempe, of Slindon, Sussex, and *d* 1638, leaving:

1e Garret/Gerald , of Dangan; *b* posthumously 1638; *educ* Trin Coll Dublin; Sheriff Co Kildare 1671; *m* Elizabeth (*d* 8 Sept 1678), dau of Dudley Colley (*see* below), and *d* 1682, having had, with four yr sons (Dudley; Valerian; Colley; Christopher; all *d* young):

  1f William, of Dangan; *m* —, dau of Maurice Keating, of Narraghmore, Co Kildare, and *dsp*

  2f Garret, of Dangan; MP Trim and Co Meath; *m* his er bro's sis-in-law Katherine (*d* 14 April 1745), dau of Maurice Keating, and *dsp* 23 Sept 1728, leaving his estates to his cousin RICHARD COLLEY later WESLEY, **1st Baron of Mornington** (*see* below)

  1f Margaret; *m* Oct 1679 Wentworth Harman, of Moyle, Co Longford, and *d* 15 June 1683

1c (cont.) Valerian Wellesley *m* 2nd Anne, dau of Edward Cusack, of Lismullen, and widow of (a) Sir Ambrose Forth and (b) Christopher Nugent (*d* 3 July 1626), bro of 1st Earl of Westmeath (*qv*), and *d* May 1655

1a (cont.) Garret/Gerald Wellesley *m* 2nd Anne, dau of 1st Baron Louth (*qv*) and widow of John Wakeley, of Ballyburley, and *d* 14 May 1603, leaving by her:

  2b Christopher; possibly a priest

  3b Edward, of Kill and Painstown, Co Kildare; *m* (contract 12 June 1602) Mary, dau of Richard Fagan, Dublin Alderman, and had:

    1c Joseph, of Kill; living 1641

  4b Patrick, of Newtown, Co Kildare

  1b Ismay; *m* Richard Cusack, of Lismullen

(2) Robert; *dsp & vp*

(3) Piers, of Blackhall, Co Meath; *m* Ismay, dau of John Cusack, of Cushinstown, by his 2nd w, and *dsp* between 6 Nov 1582 and 30 June 1583

(4) Maurice, of Danestown, Co Kildare, and Growtown, Co Meath; *m* Mary, dau of Walter Cusack, of Kilcarn, and was living April 1597; had, with other issue:

  1a Garret; *dsp & vp*

  2a Oliver, of Growtown; *m* Margaret — and *d* 18 April 1609, leaving:

    1b Maurice, of Growtown; *b* 1595

  (1) Genet; *m* Philip FitzGerald, of Allen, Co Kildare

  (2) Maud; *m* Walter Tuit, of Moneylea, Co Westmeath

1 Margaret; *m* Robert Kent, of Danestown, Co Meath

2 Alison; *m* John Cusack, of Cushinstown, Co Meath, and had:

  (1) Thomas (Sir), of Lismullen; Ld Chllr Ireland; *m* 1st —; *m* 2nd Maud, dau of George Darcy, of Platten, and widow of (a) James Marward, feudal Baron of Skreen, and (b) of Richard FitzGerald, 6th s of 8th Earl of Kildare (*see* LEINSTER, D), and *d* 1 April 1471, having had, with other issue:

    1a Katherine; *m* 1st Sir Henry Colley/Cowley, PC (I), DL (King's Co 1574), of Castle Carbery, Co Kildare, and Edenderry, King's Co, Steward King's Co, ktd 1576, Seneschal King's Co and Constable Fort of Philipstown, Capt in English forces Ireland *temp* ELIZABETH I (*d* by 2 Oct 1584, having *m* 1st 1560 — D'Arcy and had a s); *m* 2nd William Eustace, of Castlemartin, Co Kildare, and *d* 19 Jan 1597/8, leaving by her 1st husb::

      1b Henry (Sir), of Castle Carbery; *m* Anne (*m* 2nd Capt George Blount, of Kidderminster, and had issue; *m* 3rd by 13 June 1605 1st Lord Blayney, Baron of Monaghan; *see* 1874 edn), 5th dau of Adam Loftus, Archbp Dublin, and *d* by 17 Oct 1601, leaving, with a yr s (Edmond, of Ardee, Co Louth) and two daus:

        1c Henry (Sir), of Castle Carbery; MP Monaghan 1613, ktd 1615; *m* Anne, dau and heiress of Christopher Peyton, Auditor-Gen Ireland, and widow of Sir Richard Cooke, Pncpl Sec and Chllr Exchequer Ireland, and *d* 1637, leaving, with four yr sons and three daus:

          1d Dudley, of Castle Carbery; *b c* 1621; MP Phillipstown *c* 1660; *m* 1st Anne, dau of Henry Warren, of Grangebegg, Co Kildare; *m* 2nd Elizabeth, dau of George Sankey, of Ballenrath, King's Co, and widow of Henry Bollard, of Dublin, and *d* July 1674, having by her had three daus (including Grace, *m* 1st Anthony Brabazon, of Kellystown, Co Louth, *m* 2nd Caleb Gay, Collector Drogheda), and had by his 1st w, with seven yr sons and six other daus (including Ellen, *m* 1669 Thomas Moore, of Croghan, and had issue (*see* 1875 edn CHARLEVILLE, E); Mary, *m* 1st William Ashe, of Ashefield, Co Meath, *m* 2nd James Brabazon, *see* MEATH, E):

            1e Henry, of Castle Carbery; *m* 1st Mary, only dau of Sir William Usher, of Dublin; *m* 2nd Aug 1694 Sarah (*dsp* 1719), dau of John Boswell, of Kilcorey, Co Wicklow, and *d* 1700, leaving by his 1st w, with other issue:

              1f Henry; MP Strabane; *m* 1719 Mary, 3rd dau of 6th Earl of Abercorn (*see* ABERCORN, D), and *d* 1723, leaving a s (*d* an infant) and two daus (the yr of whom, Mary, *m* 20 Oct 1747 1st Viscount Harberton, *qv*)

              2f RICHARD COLLEY/COWLEY later WESLEY (roy licence 15 Nov 1728 on inheriting estates from his cousin Garret Wesley; *see* below), **1st Baron of Mornington** (I), so *cr* 9 July 1746; *b c* 1690; *educ* Trin Coll Dublin; Auditor and Registrar Roy Hosp nr Dublin, 2nd Chamberlain Court Exchequer Ireland 1713, MP Trim 1729–46, High Sheriff Co Meath 1734; *m* 23 Dec 1719 Elizabeth (*d* 17 June 1738), est dau of John Sale, LLD, MP Carysfort, and *d* 31 Jan 1758, having had, with other issue (*d* young):

                1g GARRET, **1st Earl**

                1g Elizabeth; *m* 1743 Chichester Fortescue, of Dromisken, Co Louth, and had issue

                2g Frances; *m* 1750 William Francis Crosbie (*d* 11 Sept 1768) and had issue

              1f Anne; *m* — Pole and had:

                1g William, of Ballyfin, Queen's Co; *d* Dec 1801, leaving his estate to his cousin **3rd Earl of Mornington** (*see* below)

             1e Elizabeth; *m* Garret/Gerald Wellesley and had issue (*see* above)

2b Gerald; had an only dau (m William Moore, of Barmeath, Co Louth)
1b Mary; m 1st 1st Viscount Moore of Drogheda (see DROGHEDA, E); m 2nd 1st Viscount Wilmot of Athlone
2b Eleanor; m Robert Talbot, of Templeoge, Co Dublin

The 1st BARON's only s,
GARRET WESLEY, **1st Earl of Mornington**, Co Meath, so cr 2 Oct 1760, as also VISCOUNT WELLESLEY OF DANGAN CASTLE (both I), PC (I 1776); b 19 July 1735; educ Trin Coll Dublin (BA 1754, MA 1757, MusDr 1764, Prof Music 1764–74, his proficiency in music winnng him GEORGE III's admiration and allegedly the promotion to an Earldom); MP Trim 1757–58, custos rotulorum Co Meath 1759; m 6 Feb 1759 Anne (d 10 Sept 1831), est dau of 1st Viscount Dungannon (see TREVOR, B), and d 22 May 1781, leaving:
1 RICHARD WESLEY later WELLESLEY (1789), **2nd Earl of Mornington**, also 1st and last MARQUESS WELLESLEY OF NORRAGH (I), so cr 2 Dec 1799, as also earlier 20 Oct 1797 BARON WELLESLEY OF WELLESLEY, Co Somerset (GB), KG (1812), KP (1783–1812), PC (I 1784, GB 1793); b 20 June 1760; educ Harrow, Eton and Ch Ch Oxford; MP (I Parl) Trim 1780–81, Beeralston (GB Parl) 1784–86, Saltash 1786–87, Windsor 1787–96 and Old Sarum 1796–97, custos rotulorum Co Meath 1781‑1842, a Ld Treasury 1786–97, a Commr Indian Affrs 1793–97, Govr Madras 1797 and Govr-Gen Bengal 1797–1805 and C-in-C India 1800–05, as which took Seringapatam and overthrew the Mysore Empire under Tippoo Sultan; Ch Remembrancer Court Exchequer Ireland 1798, Amb Spain 1809, For Sec 1809–12, Ld Lt Ireland 1821–28 and 1833–34, Ld Steward Household 1830–33, Ld Chamberlain April–May 1835; LLD Glasgow 1804, Kt Crescent Ottoman Empire 1805, Kt Lion and Sun Persia 1812; m 1st 29 Nov 1794 his mistress Hyacinthe Gabrielle (d 7 Nov 1816), only dau of Pierre Roland, of Paris; m 2nd 29 Oct 1825 Marianne (d 17 Dec 1853), Ldy Bedchamber to QUEEN ADELAIDE, dau of Richard Caton, Baltimore merchant, and widow of Robert Patterson (whose sis Elizabeth was 1st w of JEROME BONAPARTE, KING OF WESTPHALIA; see Introduction (p.23), American Presidential Families, 1994, Morris Genealogical Books SA), and dspl 26 Sept 1842, when the Marquessate and 1797 Barony expired, leaving five children by his 1st w b before their marriage, including:
(1) Richard WELLESLEY; educ Eton; MP; d in or after 1864
(2) Gerald WELLESLEY; educ Eton; Bengal CS; d by 1864
(1) Hyacinthe Mary; m 21 Dec 1812, as his 1st w, 1st Baron Hatherton (qv) and d 4 June 1849 leaving issue
2 WILLIAM WESLEY later WELLESLEY (in or after 1784) later still WELLESLEY-POLE (on inheriting from his cousin William Pole 1801; see above), **3rd Earl of Mornington**, also 1st BARON MARYBOROUGH OF MARYBOROUGH, Queen's County (UK), so cr 17 July 1821, GCH (1830), PC (I 24 Oct 1809, GB 18 Dec 1809); b 20 May 1763; educ Eton; MP (I Parl, Tory) Trim 1783–90 and (UK Parl) E Looe 1790–95 and Queen's Co 1801–21, Clerk Ordnance 1802–06 and March–July 1807, Ch Sec Ireland 1809–12, a Ld Treasury 1809–11 and Nov–Dec 1834, Chllr Exchequer Ireland 1811–12, Master Mint 1814–23, Constable Maryborough Castle and Custos Rotulorum Queen's Co 1823–45, Master Buckhounds 1823–30, PMG 1834–35, Capt Deal Castle 1838–43; m 17 May 1784 Katherine Elizabeth (d 23 Oct 1851 aged 91), est dau and coheir of Adml Hon John Forbes (see GRANARD, E), and d 22 Feb 1845, leaving:
(1) WILLIAM WELLESLEY-POLE later POLE-TYLNEY-LONG-WELLESLEY (roy licence 14 Jan 1812), **4th Earl of Mornington**; b 22 May 1788; Sec Embassy and Min Constantinople and Copenhagen, MP (Tory to 1830, Whig 1830–32) St Ives 1812–18 and 1830–31, Wilts 1818–20 and Essex 1831–32, Gentleman Usher and Daily Waiter to GEORGE IV 1822–24; m 1st 14 March 1812 Catherine (d 12 Sept 1825), est dau and eventual heiress (to the tune of £25,000 [over £575,000 in late-1990s terms] p.a. and £300,000 [nearly £7m in late-1990s terms] ready cash) of Sir James Tylney-Long, 7th Bt, of Draycot, Wilts (by his 2nd w Catherine Sidney, dau of 4th Earl of Plymouth; qv); m 2nd 10 Nov 1828 Helena (d 7 April 1869), 3rd dau of Col Thomas Paterson and widow of Capt Thomas Bligh, Coldstream Gds, and d a pauper through his extravagance 1 July 1857, having by his 1st w had, with a dau (d unm):
1a WILLIAM RICHARD ARTHUR POLE-TYLNEY-LONG-WELLESLEY, **5th Earl of Mornington**; b 7 Oct 1813; educ Eton; d unm Paris 25 July 1863, when the Barony of Maryborough expired
2a James FitzRoy Henry William; b 11 Aug 1815; 12th Lancers; d unm 30 Oct 1851
(1) Mary Charlotte Anne; m 22 July 1806 Rt Hon Sir Charles Bagot, GCB (see BAGOT, B), and d 2 Feb 1845, leaving issue
(2) Emily Harriet; m 13 March 1814 1st Baron Raglan (qv) and d 6 March 1881, leaving issue
(3) Priscilla Anne; m 26 June 1811 11th Earl of Westmorland (qv) and d 18 Feb 1879, leaving issue
3 ARTHUR, **1st Duke**
4 Gerald Valerian (Rev); b 7 Dec 1770; DD, Rector Chelsea, Preb Durham, Chaplain Roy Household; m 2 June 1802 Emily Mary (d 22 Dec 1839), est dau of 1st Earl Cadogan (qv), and d 24 Oct 1848, having had:
(1) Arthur Richard; b 1804; Capt Rifle Bde; dvp 21 Aug 1830
(2) William Henry Charles; b 14 Feb 1813; Col 10th Foot; m 1 Nov 1849 Jane Malet (d 3 May 1901), dau of Thomas Hayden, and d 14 Nov 1888, having had:
1a Arthur George Henry; b 8 Oct 1850; m 14 Aug 1879 Alice Sarah (d 1921), only child of Lt-Col Thomas Richardson Humphrey, and d 12 Aug 1893, leaving:
1b Garret Gerald Henry; b 28 Feb 1880; d 7 Aug 1915
1b Valerie Olivia; m 9 May 1906 Maj Reginald Dashwood-Tandy, Lancs Fus, s of Cdr Dashwood-Tandy, RN, and d 7 Aug 1958, leaving issue
2a Gerald Valerian; b 2 Sept 1852; Lt-Col, Staff Paymaster APD; m 6 Feb 1878 Kathleen (d 5 Aug 1910), dau of Edward Christopher Carleton, and d 20 June 1914, leaving:
1b Cyril Gerald Valerian; b 24 June 1879; Capt Lincs Regt; m 4 Feb 1909 Lilias Mason (m 2nd 6 Feb 1919 Col Reginald Bastard, DSO, DL (d 20 May 1960), of Kitley, Yealmpton, Devon, and d 30 Nov 1974), only dau of James Woolley Summers, MP, of Cam-yr-Alyn, Rossett (see 1970 edn SUMMERS, Bt), and was ka 14 March 1915

2b Frederick Henry Burton; b 23 Aug 1880; educ RMC Sandhurst; Lt-Col Duke of Wellington's W R Regt WW I (wounded); m 2 Oct 1907 Helen Evelyn (d 4 Nov 1960), dau of William Henry Cobb, of South Wood's Hall, Thirsk, Yorks, and d 7 Sept 1955, having had:
1c Frederic Henry Valerian; b 10 Aug 1908; educ Winchester and RMC Sandhurst; Maj Duke of Wellington's Regt; m 12 Feb 1938 *Nancy Evelyn, yr dau of Percy Saunders, of Halifax, and d 21 Sept 1978, leaving:
1d *Evelyn Angela Juliana [Mrs John Searle, Southlands, Market Bosworth, Leics CV13 0LS]; b 4 Dec 1938; m 2 April 1961 *John Albert Searle, only s of A J Searle, of Grays, Essex
2d *Helen Christabel Kate [Mrs Daniel Levasseur, Church Hill, Crayke, York]; b 14 July 1947; m 1975 *Daniel Levasseur
3d *Rosalind Jane [Mrs Alfred Walshaw, The Cottage, 1 High Mickley, Stocksfield, Northumberland]; b 4 March 1954; m 1978 *Alfred Peter Walshaw
1c Kathleen Helen Valerie; b 29 Dec 1910; d unm 17 July 1934
2c Evelyn Geraldine Ruth; b 5 Oct 1917; m 16 June 1951 *John Frederick Akroyd, only s of Fred Akroyd, of Enfield, Middx, and d 19–, leaving:
1d *Ailsa Evelyn Margaret; b 5 May 1954
2d *Cecilia Ruth Lorraine; b 17 Oct l960
1b Kathleen Geraldine Helen; b 14 March 1882; m 31 March 1910 Capt Walton Mellor, Roy Irish Regt (ka Mons 23 Aug 1914), s of Col John Edward Mellor, of Tan-y-Bryn, Abergele, and d 9 Dec 1982, leaving issue
3a Edmond Ernest Charles; b 25 April 1858; Capt Hants Yeo Cav; m 29 Nov 1882 Florence Sarah Louisa (m 2nd 28 Jan 1890 Rev Arthur J Burr and d 4 Feb 1937), 5th dau of John Platt, MP, of Werneth Park, Lancs, and d 11 Aug 1886, leaving:
1b Gerald Valentine; b 25 May 1885; 2nd Lt Suffolk Regt WW I; m 12 June 1918 *Christina Adelina (m 2nd 16 Jan 1937 Capt Ronald Douglas Boyd, Roy Munster Fus and RA (TA), dau of F G Jelley, of Wandsworth Common, London, and d 29 Jan 1933, leaving:
1c Edmund Gerald Valerian; b 23 Sept 1919; d unm 8 June 1944
2c Philip Vernon Charles; b 10 April 1921; Immigration Offr Mombasa; m 3 Sept 1952 *Marguerite Victoria [Mrs Philip Wellesley, 50A Ellerslie Rd, Barnstaple, N Devon], dau of Alfred Cameron Clark, of London, and d 1992, leaving:
1d *Barbara Victoria [Mrs Roger Sandwell, 25 Lynhurst Ave, Barnstaple, N Devon EX31 2ER]; b 27 Feb 1958; m 1985 *Roger John Sandwell
1c *Eileen Valerie Christine; b 7 June 1922
2c *Florence Geraldine Joan; b March 1924; m 21 Sept 1946 *Capt John Gabriel Combe, s of Robert Combe, of Hutton-le-Hole, Yorks, and has:
1d *Michael Valerian Wellesley; b 24 Feb 1948
2d *Jeremy Vernon Wellesley; b 21 Dec 1952
1d *Patricia Daphne Eastburn; b 24 Feb 1950
2d *Diana Muriel Davenport; b 31 May 1960
2b Edmond Ernest Charles; b 9 July 1886; Capt 9th Bn Norfolk Regt; m 6 April 1916 Gwendolyn, dau of Maj John Samuels, VC, RGA (TFR), of Edenfield, Llanfairfechan, N Wales, and was ka 30 April 1916
1b Muriel Alice; m 17 April 1906 Percival William Clifford Goodchild (d 5 Feb 1968) and d 19–, leaving issue
4a Herbert Arthur; b 15 Aug 1867; m 29 Feb 1892 Charlotte Elizabeth, dau of Archdale Villiers Palmer, of Nazeing Park, and was lost at sea with his w in the wreck of the Hilda off St Malo 18 Nov 1905, leaving:
1b Ronald Arthur; b 17 Nov 1894; Cadet RN; d unm 19 Sept 1914
2b Eric George; b 1 May 1896; ka WW I 1915
1b Violet Evelyn, MBE (1946); b 15 Aug 1897; Maj WRAC (TA), WWs I and II; d unm Sept 1971
5a Cecil George, OBE (1919); b 30 Sept 1869; Lt-Col 3rd Bn E Yorks Regt, Boer War 1902 (medal with three clasps), WW I (despatches); m 1 Nov 1906 Winifred Mary (m 2nd 24 Oct 1933 Lt-Col Clifford Charles Horace Twiss, DSO (d 13 Feb 1947), of Barn Hill, Strumpshaw, Norfolk, and d 26 Feb 1959), yst dau of Hon Reginald Parker (see MACCLESFIELD, E), and d 14 July 1932, leaving:
1b Lettice Jane Katharine; b 1908; m 23 April 1930 Peter Jocelyn Lambert, MC (d 1970), s of Frank F Lambert, and d 1995, leaving:
1c *(Peter) Miles [Maj Miles Lambert, Half Moon House, Rectory Lane, Halesworth, Suffolk 1P19 8AF]; b 1931; late Maj Gren Gds; m 1959 *Armorel Madeleine Frances Tress, dau of Maj Sir Rupert Barry, 4th Bt (qv), and has:
1d *Peter Tobin; b 24 Nov 1966
1d *Annabel Madeline Jane [Mrs Jonathan Manuel, 64 Ridgway Place, London SW19 4SW]; b 29 July 1960; m 1992 *Jonathan Reinier Manuel and has:
1e *Olivia Victoria Greta; b 1993
2e *Venetia Elizabeth Emily; b April 1995
2d *Miranda Caroline Tress; b 23 Dec 1961
1c *April Daphne Claire [Mrs Michael Falcon, Keswick Old Hall, Norwich, Norfolk NR4 6TZ]; b 1934; m 1954 *Michael Gascoigne Falcon, CBE, DL, and has:
1d *Michael [Michael Falcon Esq, Stalham Hall, Norwich NR12 9PP]; b 1956; m 1983 *Katharine Miranda, dau of Peter Thomas Thistlethwayte, of E Donyland Hall, Colchester, Essex, and has:
1e *Emily; b 1987
2e *Isabella; b 1989
3e *Amy Lucinda; b 1993
2d *Andrew [Andrew Falcon Esq, Bridge Farm, Reymerston, Norwich NR9 4QD]; b 1958; m 1991 *Victoria, only dau of Maj Peter Noel de Bunsen (see CARRINGTON, B), and has:
1e *Billy; b 1994

2e *Frank; b 1998

1e *Ruby; b 1993

1d *Claire Isabella [Mrs Simon Garrett, Ffynnon Felen, Cwm Bach, Whitland, Dyfed]; b 1960; m 1990 *Simon N Garrett, s of J Garrett and Mrs R Quint, of Ventura, Calif., and has:

  1e *George Francis; b 1993

  1e *Isabel; b 1991

  2e *Laura; b 1996

2b *Pamela [Mrs Edward Estcourt, Stone Cottage, Woolage Green, Kent CT4 6SD]; m 16 April 1938 Maj-Gen Edward Noel Keith Estcourt, DSO, OBE, RA (d 1982), s of Ernest Alfred Estcourt, ICS, of Folkestone, and has:

  1c *Edward James; b 1939; Lt-Col RA; m 1963 *Jennifer Clare, dau of Lt-Col C A McLaren, of Cornwood, S Devon, and has:

    1d *Edward Rory Charles; b 1965

    2d *Angus James; b 1968

  2c *Adrian Charles; b 1942; late Lt Para Regt; m 1967 (divorce 1991) Judith Mary, dau of Col G W Preston, of Menethorpe, N Yorks, and has:

    1d *Suzannah Jane; b 1970

    2d *Charlotte Pamela; b 1972

  1c *Hermione Jessica Jane [Mrs Christopher Cousins, Stone Cottage, Woolage Green, Kent CT4 6SD]; b 1947; m 1970 *Christopher Hugh James Cousins and has:

    1d *Elizabeth Pamela Julia; b 1977

    2d *Victoria Edwina Jane; b 1982

1a Florence Jane Helen, OBE (1918); m 5 Oct 1871 1st Baron Nunburnholme (qv) and d 8 Dec 1932, leaving issue

2a Alice Jane; m 3 Sept 1873 Charles Edward Sanderson (dsp 1893) and d 2 May 1936

3a Evelyn Jane; m 10 Jan 1878 Bernard Edward Cammell (d 19 Nov 1932), of The Gate Ho, Merrow, Guildford, and d 17 May 1931, leaving issue

4a Cecilia Louisa Jane; m Sept 1880 Lt-Col Walter Harry Sykes, RE (d 12 Nov 1932), of Firfield, Merrow, Guildford, and d 2 Nov 1944, leaving issue

5a Dora Penelope Jane

6a Ethel Caroline Jane; m 1st 31 May 1883 Maj Bernard Hamilton Gunston (see GUNSTON, Bt) and had issue; m 2nd 28 July 1909 Sir George Francis Fleetwood Cradock-Hartopp, 8th Bt (qv), and d 8 May 1953

7a Winifred Charlotte Jane; m 3 Feb 1903 Lt-Col Harold Platt Sykes (d 13 Feb 1942), Queen's Bays, of Beckbury Hall, Shifnal, Salop, s of Thomas Hardcastle Sykes, DL, of Cringle, Cheshire, and d 21 April 1955, leaving issue

(3) George Greville (Sir), GCB; b 2 Aug 1814; joined RN 1834, Supt Portsmouth Dockyard 1865–69, C-in C N American Station 1869, cmded Channel Sqdn 1870, Adml 1875, 1st Sea Ld 1877–79; m 25 Oct 1853 Elizabeth Doughty (d 9 Jan 1906), yst dau of Robert Lukin, and d 6 April 1901, leaving:

  1a Olivia Georgiana; b 29 Sept 1857; DGStJ, Medaille de la Reine Elisabeth of Belgium; m 15 Oct 1890 Lt-Col Sir Henry Trotter, KCMG, CB, RE (d 25 Sept 1919), and d 28 Feb 1956, leaving issue

(1) Emily Ann Charlotte; m 26 Jan 1836 Rev Hon Robert Liddell, 5th s of 1st Baron Ravensworth (qv), and d 22 Oct 1876, leaving issue

(2) Georgiana Henrietta Louisa; m 21 April 1827 Rev George Darby St Quintin (d 22 Dec 1872), of St Leonards, Sussex, and d 1 March 1879

(3) Mary Sarah; m 12 July 1836 4th Earl Cadogan (qv) and d 11 Feb 1873, leaving issue

(4) Cecil Elizabeth; m 11 May 1842 Hon George Augustus Liddell, 6th s of 1st Baron Ravensworth (qv), and d 12 July 1883, leaving issue

5 HENRY WELLESLEY, cr BARON COWLEY OF WELLESLEY (see COWLEY, E)

1 Anne; m 1st 7 Jan 1790 Hon Henry FitzRoy, 4th s of 1st Baron Southampton (qv), and had issue; m 2nd 2 Aug 1799 Culling Charles Smith, of Hampton, and d 16 Dec 1844

The 1st EARL OF MORNINGTON's 3rd s,

ARTHUR WESLEY later WELLESLEY (from May 1798), **1st Duke of Wellington**, so cr 11 May 1814, as also MARQUESS OF DOURO (with £400,000 [over £10.75m in late-1990s terms] to augment his earlier sum for the acquisition of an estate; see below), and earlier 4 Sept 1809 BARON DOURO OF WELLESLEY, Co Somerset, and VISCOUNT WELLINGTON OF TALAVERA AND WELLINGTON, Co Somerset (plus Feb 1810 annuity of £2,000 [just over £42,000 in late-1990s terms] to himself and next two holders of those peerages), 28 Feb 1812 EARL OF WELLINGTON, Co Somerset (with additional annuity identical to that of 1810 [by now, with inflation due Napoleonic War, worth just over £46,000 p.a. in late-1990s terms]), and 3 Oct 1812 MARQUESS OF WELLINGTON (with £100,000 [some £2.3m in late-1990s terms] to buy an estate with] (all UK); cr 18 Oct 1811 COUNT OF VIMEIRO (Portugal), Jan 1812 DUKE OF CIUDAD RODRIGO and a Grandee 1st Cl (Spain), Aug 1812 MARQUIS OF TORRES VEDRAS and 18 Dec 1812 DUKE OF VITTORIA (both Portugal) and 18 July 1815 PRINCE OF WATERLOO (Netherlands), KG (1813), GCB (1815, KB 1804), GCH (1816), PC (GB 8 April 1807, I 28 April 1807); b 1 May 1769; educ Eton at Brussels and Acad at Angers (later the École de Cavalerie Saumur); Ensign 73rd Foot 1787, ADC to Ld Lt Ireland 1787–93, Lt 76th Foot Dec 1787 (exchanged into 41st Foot 1788 and 12th Light Dragoons 1789), MP (I Parl) Trim 1790–97, Capt 58th Foot 1791 (exchanged into 18th Light Dragoons 1792), Maj April 1793 and Lt-Col 1793–1806 33rd Foot (Holland Campaign 1794–95), Col 1796, campaigned India 1797–1805 (Govr Seringapatam and Mysore 1799–1805), Maj-Gen 1802, won Battles of Assaye 23 Sept and Argaum 29 Nov 1803 Mahratta War (also took fortress of Gawilghur 15 Dec, thus subjugating Sind and defeating the Rajah of Berah), Bde Cdr Hanover 1805–06, Col 33rd Foot (later Duke of Wellington's W R Regt) 1806–12, RHG 1813–27 and Gren Gds 1827–52, Div Cdr Zealand Expdn 1807 which resulted in Copenhagen's capitulation and that of the entire Danish Navy, Lt-Gen and Ch Cdr Iberian Peninsula 1808 (won Battles of Roliça and Vimeiro 17 and 21 Aug respectively), C-in-C Br Forces Portugal and Marshal-Gen Portuguese Army 1809 (won Battle of Talavera

27–28 July 1809), Capt-Gen Spanish Army Aug 1809, a Regent Portugal 1810, won Battles of Busaco 27 Sept 1810, Fuentes de Oñoro 5 May 1811, Salamanca 22 July 1812, Vittoria 21 June 1813, Nivelle 10 Nov 1813, Orthez 27 Feb 1814 and Toulouse 10 April 1814, Gen 31 July 1811, took Ciudad Rodrigo 19 Jan 1812, Badajoz 6 April 1812, Madrid 12 Aug 1812, San Sebastian 31 Aug and Pampeluna 31 Oct 1813, Generalissimo Spanish Armies Sept 1812, FM 1813, FM Hanover 1815, C-in-C Allied Forces Continent of Europe 28 March 1815, winning Battle of Waterloo 18 June 1815 (following which granted by Parl £200,000 [more than £5.75m in late-1990s terms] over and above his previous sums (see above), FM Netherlands Army July 1815, C-in-C Allied Forces of Occupation France 1815–18, FM Austria, Russia and Prussia 1818, Master-Gen Ordnance with Cabinet Seat 1818–27, Col-in-Ch Rifle Bde 1820–52, C-in-C Forces Jan–March 1827, Aug 1827–28 and 1842–52; MP (Tory) Rye April-Oct 1806, St Michael Jan–April 1807 aand Newport IoW 1807–09, Ch Sec to Ld Lt Ireland 1807–09, Amb Extrdy and Plen Paris Aug 1814–Jan 1815, First Plen Congress of Vienna Jan–March 1815, Jt Plen Conf Aix-la-Chapelle Aug-Nov 1818, Govr Plymouth 1819–26, Ld Lt Hants 1820–52, Ld High Constable 1821, 1831 and 1838 Coronations, Plen to Conf Verona 1822, Constable Tower London and Ld Lt Tower Hamlets 1826–52, PM 1828–30 and (caretaker pending return of Peel from Rome, also Home, For and Colonial Sec, remaining For Sec after Peel's return till April 1835) Nov-Dec 1834, Constable Dover Castle and Ld Warden Cinque Ports 1829–52, Er Bro 1829 and Master 1837–52 Trin Ho, Chllr Oxford U 1834–52, DCL Oxon 1814, LLD Cantab 1835, Cabinet Min without portfolio 1841–46, FRS 1847, Ranger St James's and Hyde Pks 1850–52; m 10 April 1806 Hon Catherine Pakenham (d 25 April 1831), 2nd dau of 2nd Baron Longford (see LONGFORD, E), and d 14 Sept 1852, giving his name to the eponymous apple, Barracks, boot, capital of NZ, sch for offrs' sons and species of sequoia tree, leaving:

1 ARTHUR RICHARD WELLESLEY, **2nd Duke of Wellington**, also **6th Earl of Mornington** etc, as which s cousin 1863, KG (1858), PC (1853); b 3 Feb 1807; educ Eton, Ch Ch Oxford and Trin Coll Cambridge; Ensign 81st Foot 1823 and 71st (Highland) Foot May 1825, Cornet RHG June 1825, Lt 1827, Capt May 1828, Capt 60th (KRRC) Foot July 1828, MP (Tory) Aldeburgh 1829–32 and Norwich 1837–52, Maj 1830 (exchanging into Rifle Bde 1831), Lt-Col 1834, ADC to C-in-C (his f) 1842–52, Brevet Col 1846, Master Horse 1853–58, Lt-Col Victoria (Middx) Rifle Vol Corps 1853–70, Maj-Gen 1854, Lt-Gen 1862, ret 1863, Ld Lt Middx 1868–84, Hon LLD Cantab, ed his f's correspondence: Despatches (23 vols); m 18 April 1839 Elizabeth, VA 3rd Cl, Ldy Bedchamber to HM QUEEN VICTORIA 1843–58 and Mistress Robes 1861–68 and 1874–80 (dsp 13 Aug 1904), dau of 8th Marquess of Tweeddale (qv), and dsp 13 Aug 1884

2 Charles; b 16 Jan 1808; Maj-Gen, Ch Equerry and Clerk Marshal to HM QUEEN VICTORIA, MP S Hants 1847 and Windsor 1852; m 9 July 1844 Augusta Sophia Anne (d 13 July 1893), only child of Rt Hon Henry Manvers Pierrepont, of Conholt Pk, Wilts, 3rd s of 1st Earl Manvers (see 1953 edn), and d 9 Oct 1858, having had:

  (1) Arthur; b 5 May 1845; d 7 July 1846

  (2) HENRY WELLESLEY, **3rd Duke of Wellington**, DL (Hants); b 5 April 1846; educ Eton; Ensign and Lt Gren Gds 1865, Lt and Capt 1868, MP (C) Andover 1874–80, Capt and Lt-Col 1876, Maj 2nd Bn 1881–82, when ret, Hon Col 2nd Bde S Div RA Militia 1884 and 3rd and 4th Bns Duke of Wellington's W R Regt 1886–1900, Chm Mendicity Soc; m 7 March 1882 Evelyn Katrine Gwenfra (m 2nd 1904 Col Hon Frederick Arthur Wellesley (see COWLEY, E) and d 11 March 1939), yst dau of Col Thomas Peers Williams, MP, of Temple Ho, Berks, and dsp 8 June 1900

  (3) ARTHUR CHARLES, **4th Duke**

  (1) Victoria Alexandrina (HM QUEEN VICTORIA stood sponsor); granted with siblings 1884 rank of duke's dau/yr s; m 6 Sept 1877 1st Baron Holmpatrick (qv) and d 31 July 1933, leaving issue

  (2) Mary Angela; m 7 Sept 1875 George Arthur Jervoise Scott (see SCOTT, Bt, of Rotherfield Park) and d 26 April 1936

  (3) Georgina; m 22 July 1874 William Rolle Malcolm (d 3 Feb 1923), 3rd s of John Malcolm of Poltalloch, and d 3 Feb 1880, leaving issue

The 3rd DUKE's yr bro,

ARTHUR CHARLES WELLESLEY, **4th Duke of Wellington**, KG (1902), GCVO (1902), DL (Hants); b 15 March 1849; educ Eton; Ensign and Lt Gren Gds 1868, Capt 1871, Lt-Col 1879, Maj and Col 1887, cmdg 1st Bn 1891–95, ret as Col 1900; Chm Hants QS, Grand Cross Charles III Spain and Tower and Sword Portugal; m 24 Oct 1872 Kathleen Emily (d 24 June 1927), n of Sir Richard Bulkeley Williams-Bulkeley, 11th Bt (qv), and d 18 June 1934, having had:

1 ARTHUR CHARLES WELLESLEY, **5th Duke of Wellington**, JP (Hants); b 9 June 1876; educ Eton; Lt Gren Gds, Boer War 1900, WW I; m 23 March 1909 Hon Lilian Maud Glen Coats (d 3 May 1946), yr dau of 1st Baron Glentanar (see 1970 edn), and d 11 Dec 1941, leaving:

  (1) HENRY VALERIAN GEORGE WELLESLEY, **6th Duke of Wellington**; b 14 July 1912 (HM THE QUEEN OF SPAIN stood sponsor); educ Stowe; 2nd Lt Duke of Wellington's W R Regt 1935, WW II: attd KAR 1939–42 Abyssinia and No 2 Commando Centl Mediterranean Forces; ka Salerno 16 Sept 1943

  (1) *Anne Maud; b 2 Feb 1910; s bro (as did her husb) 1943 in Spanish honours; renounced them in favour of her unc **7th Duke** 1949; m 23 March 1933 (divorce 1963) Hon David Reginald Rhys (d 1991), 3rd s of 7th Baron Dynevor (qv), and has issue

2 Richard; b 30 Sept 1879; Capt Gren Gds, S Africa 1900 and WW I; m 30 April 1908 Louise Nesta Pamela (m 2nd her bro-in-law George (see below) and d 21 Feb 1946), only dau of Sir Maurice FitzGerald, 2nd Bt, of Valentia (qv), 20th Kt of Kerry, and was ka 29 Oct 1914, leaving:

  (1) Pamela; b 14 May 1912; m 1st 12 June 1933 (divorce 1943) Lt Charles Robert Archibald Grant, RN, only s of Gen Sir Charles John Cecil Grant, KCB, KCVO, DSO, and had:

    1a *Anthony Richard Charles; b 22 May 1934

    1a Louise Margaret; b 11 July 1936; d 9 Oct 1942

  (2) (cont.) Mrs Pamela Grant m 2nd 24 July 1947 Maj Hon Denis Gomer Berry (see KEMSLEY, V), and d 31 March 1987, having had further issue

  (2) *Mary [Miss Mary Wellesley, 12 Clarence Terrace, London NW1 4RD]; b posthumously 8 Jan 1915

3 GERALD, **7th Duke**
4 George, MC (1916); *b* 29 July 1889; *educ* Wellington; Lt-Col RFC and RAF WW I (despatches), S/Ldr RAFVR WW II, md Coxeter and Son, Roy Humane Soc Medal; *m* 1st 12 March 1917 his er bro's widow Louise; *m* 2nd 25 Nov 1955 Jean (*d* 25 June 1989), dau of John McGillivray, of The Braes of Glenlivet, Banffshire, and *d* 31 July 1967, leaving by his 1st w:

  (1) Richard, MC (1941), DL (Berks 1954); *b* 22 June 1920; *educ* Wye Coll; High Sheriff 1955, Maj RA (TA) WW II; *m* 1st 30 April 1948 (*divorce* 1970) Ruth, 3rd dau of Peter Haig-Thomas (*see* NORMANTON, E); *m* 2nd 1970 *Jill [Mrs Richard Wellesley, Buckland Mead, Buckland, Oxon SN7 8QR], dau of Gp Capt E Burton, and *d* 1984, leaving by his 1st w:

    1a +Charles [Charles Wellesley Esq, The Dower Ho, Buckland, Oxon SN7 8QR]; *b* 21 Oct 1955; *educ* Milton Abbey; *m* 1981 *Louise Charlotte, dau of Cdr Allan Miles Brittain Buxton, of Shalbourne House, Shalbourne, Wilts, and has:

      1b *Rosanna; *b* 12 Oct 1989

      2b *Charlotte; *b* 15 Oct 1992

    2a +John; *b* 25 Jan 1962; *educ* Eton; *m* 1994 *Sarah Catriona Grantham, dau of Dr David Duncan

    1a *Nesta [Mrs Richard Hawes, St Mary's, Latton, Wilts SN6 6DS]; *b* 27 Feb 1951; *m* 5 Sept 1985 *Richard Sidney Hawes, only s of Sidney Hawes, of Cirencester, Glos, and has:

      1b *David Richard; *b* 1 Aug 1992

      2b *John Sidney; *b* 1 Aug 1992 (twin)

    2a *Lucy; *b* 15 May 1953; *m* 26 Jan 1991 *Charles Robert Collin, only s of Robert Frederick Dura Collin, of Wheatsheaf House, Hook Norton, Oxon

  1 Evelyn Kathleen; *b* 30 July 1973; *m* 18 June 1900 Hon Robert James, 3rd s of 2nd Baron Northbourne (*qv*), and *d* 19 Jan 1922, leaving issue

  2 Eileen; *b* 13 Feb 1887; *m* 11 Sept 1916 Cuthbert Julian Orde (*d* 19 Dec 1968), Capt RFC, 2nd s of Sir Julian Walter Orde, of Aveley Ho, Bromley, and *d* 31 Oct 1952, leaving issue

The 6th DUKE's unc,

GERALD WELLESLEY, **7th Duke of Wellington** (*s* niece in Spanish honours on her renunciation 1949 but ceded them to his s 1966), KG (1951); *b* 21 Aug 1885; *educ* Eton; Dip Serv: joined 1908, 3rd Sec 1910–17, 2nd Sec 1917–19: Petrograd, Constantinople and Rome; Surveyor King's Works of Art 1936–43; Lt-Col Gren Gds WW II, Ld Lt Co London 1944–49 and Hants 1949–60, Pres London Playing Fields Assoc 1945, Tstee Nat Gallery 1950–59, Chllr Southampton U 1951–62, Govr IOW 1956–65, V-Pres GB/USSR Assoc 1959–72, Chm Govrs Wellington Coll, KStJ, FRIBA 1921, FSA 1935, Hon LLD Southampton 1953; gave to the nation 1947 Apsley House, Hyde Park Corner, London W1 (formerly known as 'No 1, London', originally built by 2nd Earl Bathurst (*qv*) 1771–78 to designs by the brothers Adam, sold 1810 to the 1st and last Marquess Wellesley (*see above*) and by him to his bro the **1st Duke**; after its presentation to the public it housed the Wellington Museum), reserving an apartment in it for the donor's use and that of subsequent dukes; author: *The Iconography of the First Duke of Wellington* (with J Steegmann 1935), *The Diary of a Desert Journey* (1938), *The Journal of Mrs Arbuthnot* (ed with F Bamford 1950) and *A Selection from the Private Correspondence of the First Duke of Wellington* (ed, 1952); *m* 30 April 1914 Dorothy Violet (*d* 11 July 1956), dau of Robert Ashton (*see* ASHTON OF HYDE, B), and *d* 4 Jan 1972, leaving:

1 ARTHUR VALERIAN WELLESLEY, **8th and present Duke of Wellington**
1 *Elizabeth [The Lady Elizabeth Clyde, Oliver's Farm, Bramley, Basingstoke, Hants]; *b* 26 Dec 1918; *m* 18 Nov 1939 (*divorce* 1960) Maj Thomas Clyde, RHG (*m* 2nd 1961 May Peach, actress, of S Africa), s of William Pancoast Clyde, of New York, and has had:

  (1) *(Michael) Jeremy Thomas; *b* 22 March 1941; *educ* Eton and Central Sch of Speech and Drama; '60s pop singer (as Jeremy, of Chad (Stuart) and Jeremy), actor (roles include Dick in ITV's comedy *Is It Legal?*), memb Nat Theatre Co 1973; *m* 1970 (*divorce* 1990) Vanessa, dau of Harold Field, and has:

    1a *A son; *b* 19–; *educ* Bryanston

    1a *Lucy; *b* 5 Dec 1971; *educ* Bryanston

  (2) Robin; *b* 19 April 1943; drowned 13 Feb 1950

  (3) *William Jonathan; *b* 27 May 1949; *educ* Eton

Seat: Stratfield Saye, Stratfield Mortimer, Hants. The central block, including the inner wings at either end, dates from early in CHARLES I's reign, being erected by Sir William Pitt, ancestor of the two great 18th-century prime ministers the Earl of Chatham and Pitt the Younger (*see* JERSEY, E). The outer wings, with their Dutch-looking pedimented gables, were attached later, as were perhaps similar pediments to the gables of the inner wings. This was probably in the second half of the 17th century, either under CHARLES II or his successors, an era culminating in the occupancy of the throne by a Dutch King, WILLIAM III, which would have lent them an aura of fashion. But Stratfield Saye is a comfortable rather than glamorous house, squirearchical rather than ducal, in pleasing but not outstandingly beautiful countryside (the environs have been likened to a Low Countries battlefield), in keeping with its most famous owner's simple tastes.

Before being bought by the **1st Duke** it had already had its old mullion windows replaced by sash ones and its brickwork covered over in rendering. Apart from a conservatory and real tennis court, the front porch alone dates from Stratfield Saye's ownership by the WELLESLEYs, being put up in 1838 by Benjamin Wyatt, who had wanted to pull the whole thing down and replace it with something more like Blenheim but had to be content with this small commission.

Internally the staircase alone remains from Strafield Saye's earliest days, but the Hall contains one feature very much older still: Ancient Roman mosaic paving from Silchester, a few miles to the west and one of the chief centres of Britain when it was a mere imperial province (and as it might have become again had the **1st Duke** lost the day at Waterloo). Most of the rest of the rooms are either mid- or late-18th century. It is conventional to remark that their contents commemorate the **1st Duke**'s career, and so they do. But they also commemorate NAPOLEON's, for not only do his battle colours and his bust as First Consul by Jean Antoine Houdon adorn the Hall, but much of the furniture, paintings and other pretty things are French and were assembled by the Emperor's uncle, Cardinal Fesch,

or in the case of the Sèvres dinner service given the **1st Duke** by LOUIS XVIII after starting life as a gift offering by NAPOLEON to Josephine to commemorate his Egyptian escapade. The style of much of the contents is Empire, but not all. The Ancien Régime gets a look in with boulle marquetry by Etienne Levasseur. In the Drawing Room even the wall paper is French. And many of the paintings, though by Low Countries artists and belonging at one time to the Kings of Spain (who had formerly held the Low Countries), came to the **1st Duke** as booty when JOSEPH BONAPARTE decamped from Madrid, the restored Bourbon KING FERDINAND subsequently waiving his rights out of gratitude to the man who had put him back on his throne. Stratfield Saye should be seen as a monument, not to the Grandeur of War, as Blenheim is, but to its Perquisites.

WELLS

Arms: Gules between two pallets a garb or, bound with a ribbon azure, buckled of the second, pendant therefrom a hunting horn sable, stringed of the third, between two fountains. **Crest:** A demi-bear sable, muzzled gules, the sinister paw resting on a portcullis chained or. **Motto:** *Qui patitur vincit* ('He who endures patiently conquers'). **Creation:** Bt. (UK) 21 Jan 1944.

SIR CHARLES MALTBY WELLS, 2ND BT, of Felmersham, Co Bedford, TD (1960) [Sir Charles Wells Bt TD, 41 Sherwood Ave, Toronto, Ontario M4P 2A6, Canada]; *b* 24 July 1908; *s f* 1956; *educ* Bedford Sch and Pembroke Coll Cambridge; Lt-Col RE (TA) WW II; *m* 2 Sept 1935 *Katherine Boulton, only dau of Frank Matthew Boteler Kenrick, of Toronto, and has:

1 +CHRISTOPHER CHARLES [Dr Christopher Wells, 6 Silverbirch Ave, Toronto, Ontario M4E 3K9, Canada]; *b* 12 Aug 1936; *educ* McGill (BSc) and Toronto U (MD); *m* 1st 16 July 1960 (*divorce* 1983) Elizabeth Florence Vaughan, dau of Isaac Foulkes Griffiths, of Outremont, Quebec, and has:

  (1) +Michael Christopher Gruffydd; *b* 24 Oct 1966

  (2) +Geoffrey Charles Vaughan; *b* 1970

  (1) *Felicity Elizabeth Boulton; *b* 28 Sept 1964

  (2) *Megan Sarah Kenrick; *b* 9 Feb 1969

1 (cont.) CHRISTOPHER WELLS *m* 2nd 1985 *Lynda Anne, dau of R Cormack, of Toronto, and by her has:

  (3) +Andrew Christopher Brennan; *b* 1983

2 +Anthony Richard; *b* 2 July 1947; *m* 1st 21 Aug 1969 (*divorce* 1974) Frances Jane, dau of Brig Gerard Boycott, of Berwick, Victoria, Australia, and has:

  (1) +Matthew Kenrick; *b* 1970

2 (cont.) Anthony Wells *m* 2nd 19– *Judith, dau of Rev Arthur Hamilton, and by her has:

  (2) +Charles Hamilton; *b* 1978

Lineage: THOMAS WELLS; *b* 1775; had nine children; the 2nd:

GEORGE WELLS; *b* 1800; *m* 1837 Sarah Hayward Waldron and had six children; the 3rd:

CHARLES WELLS, of Bedford; *b* 1842; *m* 1872 Josephine, dau of Dr Grimbly, and *d* 1914, leaving, with seven other children, including (Guy Franey, *b* 1882, Ika June 1915; Mabel Mary, *b* June 1873, *d* unm 16 April 1960; Edith Josephine, *b* Dec 1880, *m* Thomas Britton), an est s:

Sir (Sydney) Richard Wells, 1st Bt (UK), so *cr* 21 Jan 1944, DL (Beds 1940); *b* 3 Aug 1879; *educ* Bedford Sch; MP (C) Bedford 1922–1945, V-Chm Primrose League 1928–46 (Chllr 1946–48), Chm Brewers' Soc 1940–42, ktd 1938; *m* 17 Sept 1907 Mary Dorothy (*d* 13 May 1956), est dau of Christopher James Maltby, of Travancore and Bedford, and *d* 26 Nov 1956, leaving:

1 CHARLES MALTBY (Sir), **2nd and present Bt**

2 Christopher Hayward; *b* 26 Sept 1909; Lt-Cdr RN WW II; *m* 18 Sept 1937 *Christina Hilary (*m* 2nd 23 Feb 1949 Sir James Holmes Henry, 2nd Bt; *qv*), est dau of Sir Hugh Oliver Holmes, KBE, CMG, MC, QC, of Alexandria, and was *ka* 8 June 1940, leaving:

  (1) +John Hayward [John Wells Esq, The Old Rectory, Shelton, Hunts]; *b* 16 Nov 1938; *educ* Harrow and Pembroke Coll Cambridge; *m* 7 Jan 1965 *Heather Donriel, er dau of John Gordon Christie Kelly, MC, of Riebeck West, CP, S Africa, and has:

    1a +Christopher Hayward; *b* 6 Feb 1966

2a +Richard Michael; *b* 26 June 1967

3a +Peter John; *b* 1970

3 James Michael; *b* 28 Feb 1911; *educ* Bedford Sch and Pembroke Coll Cambridge; S/Ldr RAF WW II; *ka* over Holland 10 May 1940

4 +David Franey, MC [Maj David Wells MC, 43 Day's Lane, Biddenham, Bedford MU40 4AE]; *b* 6 Jan 1913; *educ* Bedford Sch and RMA Woolwich; Maj RA WW II; *m* 21 Oct 1948 *Patricia Mary, dau of Rev Reginald Henry Goode, Rector Marston Morteyne, Beds, and has had:

(1) +Thomas Franey; *b* 9 Oct 1951; *educ* Shiplake Coll Henley-on-Thames and Mander Coll Bedford

(1) Priscilla Jane; *b* 28 July 1949; *d* car crash 21 May 1969

5 +George Crichton [Dr George Wells, Abbots Lodge, Sibton, Saxmundham, Suffolk IP17 2NB]; *b* 13 July 1914; *educ* Bedford Sch and Pembroke Coll Cambridge (MB and BCh 1939), MRCP London 1946, FRCP London 1959; Maj RAMC WW II; *m* 10 Oct 1951 *Margaret Caroline, dau of Dr Lewis Campbell Bruce, of Perth

6 Thomas Capper; *b* 15 April 1916; *educ* RNC Dartmouth; Maj Beds and Herts Regt WW II; *ka* Singapore 13 Feb 1942

7 +Oliver John, OBE, DL (Beds 1964) [W/Cdr Oliver Wells OBE DL, Ickwell Grange, Biggleswade, Beds]; *b* 10 March 1922; *educ* Uppingham; W/Cdr RAF WW II; High Sheriff Beds 1970; *m* 6 Aug 1949 *Felicity Anne, yr dau of Brig Maurice Edward Mascall, DSO, OBE, RA, of Lewes, Sussex, and has:

(1) +Michael Mascall; *b* 14 April 1951; *educ* Uppingham and Oriel Coll Oxford

(2) +Paul Richard; *b* 22 Aug 1958

(1) *Joanna Felicity; *b* 6 March 1953

1 *Sydney Mary [Mrs George Milburn, Sibton, Saxmundham, Suffolk]; *b* 4 Oct 1917; *m* 28 July 1938 *Cdr George Edward Pollington Milburn, RN, s of Dr. George Leslie Milburn, of St Kitts, and has:

(1) *Edward Barnaby Pollington; *b* 1944

(1) *Philippa; *b* 1939

(2) *Georgina; *b* 1940

2 *Sarah Jospehine [Mrs Michael Gibson, The Garden House, Piddlehinton, Dorset DT2 7TE]; *b* 10 March 1922; WRNS WW II; *m* 24 June 1947 *Michael Oliver John Gibson, MD, FRCP, only s of Lt-Col Alan Keith Gibson, OBE, MC, of Wykeham, Lymington, Hants, and has:

(1) *James Michael; *b* 12 June 1950; *educ* Winchester

(2) *Timothy Wells; *b* 21 Nov 1952; *educ* Winchester

WEMYSS and MARCH

Arms: Quarterly, 1st and 4th, argent a fess azure within a double tressure flory counter-flory gules (for CHARTERIS of Amisfield); 2nd and 3rd, or a lion rampant gules, armed and langued azure (for WEMYSS). **Crest:** A dexter hand holding up a dagger paleways, proper. **Supporters:** Two swans wings elevated proper, gorged with Earl's coronets about their necks. **Motto:** (in an escroll above) This is our charter. **Creations:** L. (S) 1 April 1628 (Wemyss of Elcho), E. (Wemyss) and L. (Elcho and Methil) (S) 25 June 1633, E., V. and L. (Douglas of Neidpath, Lyne and Munard) 20 April 1697, B. (UK) 17 July 1821.

THE 10TH EARL OF WEMYSS and 8TH EARL OF MARCH, also **Viscount of Peebles, Lord Douglas of Neidpath, Lyne and Munard, Lord Wemyss of Elcho, Lord Elcho and Methil** and **Baron Wemyss,** of Wemyss, Co Fife (UK) (Sir (Francis) David Charteris, KT (1966), JP (E Lothian 1957)) [The Rt Hon The Earl of Wemyss and March KT JP, Gosford House, Longniddry, East Lothian EH32 0PX]; *b* 19 Jan 1912; *s gf* 1937; *educ* Eton and Balliol Coll Oxford (BA 1933); Colonial Admin Serv Basutoland 1937–44, WW II: Lt Lovat Scouts, Union Def Force, Maj with Basuto Troops Middle East; Ld Lt E Lothian 1967–87 (DL 1959–67), Ld HC to Gen Assembly Ch Scotland 1959, 1960 and 1977, memb: Roy Co Archers, Roy Commn Historical MSS. 1975–; Chm: Cncl Nat Tst Scotland 1947–69 (Pres 1967–), Roy Commn Ancient and Historical Monuments & Constructions Scotland 1949–, Ctee for Scotland Marie Curie Meml Fndn 1952–, Scottish Churches' Cncl 1964–, Pres: Roy Scottish Geographical Soc 1958–62, Nat Bible Soc of Scot-

land 1960–; Ld Clerk Register Scotland 1974–; Hon LLD St Andrews 1953, D Univ Edinburgh 1983, late dir: Standard Life Assur, Scottish TV; *m* 1st 24 Feb 1940 Mavis ('Babs') Lynette Gordon (*d* 1988), er dau of Edwin Edward Murray, of Hermanus, CP, S Africa; *m* 2nd 29 April 1995 *Shelagh Kennedy, property manager Nat Tst Scotland's Georgian House Edinburgh, and by his 1st w has had:

1 Iain David, *Lord Elcho*; *b* 20 June 1945; *d* in an accident 3 April 1954

2 +JAMES DONALD, *Lord Neidpath* [Lord Neidpath, Stanway House, Cheltenham, Glos GL54 5PQ]; *b* 22 June 1948; *educ* Eton, Univ Coll (BA 1969) and St Antony's Coll Oxford (DPhil 1975) and RAC Cirencester (Dip 1978); Page of Honour to HM QUEEN ELIZABETH THE QUEEN MOTHER 1962–64; author: *The Singapore Naval Base and the Defence of Britain's Eastern Empire 1919–41* (1981); *m* 1st 16 July 1983 (*divorce* 1988) Hon Catherine Ingrid Guinness, dau of 3rd Baron Moyne (*qv*); *m* 2nd 29 Dec 1995 *Amanda Claire, yst dau of Basil Feilding (*see* DENBIGH and DESMOND, E), and by his 1st w has:

(1) +(Francis) Richard (Dick); *b* 15 Sept 1984

(1) *Mary Olivia; *b* 1987

1 *Elizabeth Mary [The Lady Elizabeth Benson, 11 Brunswick Gdns, London W8; Cucumber Farm, Singleton, Chichester, Sussex]; *b* 2 July 1941; *m* 17 Oct 1964 *David Holford Benson, yr s of Lt-Col Sir Reginald Lindsay (Rex) Benson, DSO, MVO, MC, of 30 Cadogan Place, London SW1, and Cucumber Farm, Singleton, nr Chichester, Sussex, and has:

(1) *Matthew James; *b* 26 June 1966

(1) *Henrietta Katherine; *b* 29 March 1969

(2) *Katherine Emma; *b* 7 May 1972

2 Caroline Letty; *b* 5 Nov, *d* 22 Nov 1946

Lineage: MICHAEL, of Wemyss and Methil; *b c* 1165; *d c* 1214, having had, with another s (Duncan):

Sir JOHN WEMYSS of Wemyss and Methil; *b* by 1202; ktd between 1231 and 1240; *d c* 1263, leaving, with a yr s (John, of Upper and Nether Cameron, Fifeshire, *m c* 1289 Amabilla, dau of Sir John of Anesley, and had issue):

Sir MICHAEL WEMYSS of Wemyss; *b* by 1231; supported John Balliol's candidacy for the crown 1291; did homage to EDWARD I 1296; allegedly *m* the heiress of Sir David Lochore of Lochore and *d c* 1320, leaving:

Sir DAVID WEMYSS of Wemyss; of age by 1290; *m* 1st Annabella Sinclair, widow of Sir Robert Bisset; *m* 2nd by 1304 Marjory, dau of Walter Ramsay, and *d* by 1332, leaving, presumably by her:

1 Michael (Sir), of Wemyss; ktd *c* 1316, captured by the English at their victory over the Scots of Halidon Hill 1333 but set free on swearing fealty to EDWARD III; *d* 1342, leaving, with two other daus (from whose descendants Robert Livingston and John Boswell the Sir JOHN WEMYSS who *d c* 11428 bought back their share of the former WEMYSS lands):

(1) Margaret; *m* Sir John Inchmartin of that Ilk and had:

1a Isabel; *m* Sir Alan Erskine of Inchmartin and had:

1b Isabel; *m* her cousin Sir JOHN WEMYSS (*see below*)

2 John (Sir); had charters from ROBERT I (THE BRUCE) of a 3rd of the (territorial) Barony of Leuchars and from Sir Alexander Abernethy of the lands of Kincaldrum; *d c* 1392, leaving a gs:

(1) John (Sir), of Leuchars, Kincaldrum, Reres and Methil, the last two of which he acquired from his kinsman Sir David Wemyss of Cameron; Constable Castle and town of St Andrews; *m* 1st — and had:

1a Duncan, of Reres and Leuchars; ancestor of the WEMYSSes of Reres, WEMYSSes of Pittencrieff and WEMYSSes of Logie

2a Alexander, of Kilmanym; ancestor of the WEMYSSes of Lathocker, Fifeshire

3a Michael, of Pittmeddil, Perths; *dsp*

(1) (cont.) Sir John *m* 2nd *c* 1386 his cousin Isabel, dau of Sir Alan Erskine of Inchmartin, and by her had:

4a DAVID, for whom *see* below

5a Andrew; had:

1b (John

1a Elizabeth; *m* (contract 31 Aug 1418) 1st Lord Gray (*qv*) and had issue

2a Isabel; *m* by Dec 1432, as his 2nd w, Hugh Fraser, 6th of Lovat (*see* LOVAT, L)

(1) (cont.) Sir John *m* 3rd Christian, dau of Sir Patrick Ogilvy of Auchterhouse (*see* AIRLIE, E), and *d c* 1428

His est s by his 2nd w:

DAVID WEMYSS of Methil and Wemyss; *m c* 4 Feb 1423/4 Christian Douglas (*m* 2nd Sir James Auchinleck of that Ilk) and *d c* Sept 1430, having had, with two daus:

JOHN WEMYSS of Wemyss; *b c* 1425; tried to buy back more of the family lands; *m c* 1448 (*divorce* 1489) Margaret (*d* 1494), dau of Sir Robert Livingstone of Drumry; *m* 2nd Helen Dunbar (*m* 3rd Andrew Moncur of that Ilk), widow of Alexander Melvill of Kirkcaldy, and *d* 22 Feb 1502/03, leaving by her no issue but by his 1st w, with a yr s (David, of Aucherleven, Aberdeenshire) and a dau (Grisel, *m* 1466 David Boswell of Glassmonth and had issue):

Sir JOHN WEMYSS of Wemyss, Strathardle, Inchmartin, Elcho and Dron, etc; *m* 1468 Christian, dau of 2nd Lord Saltoun (*qv*) of Abernethy, and *d c* May 1508, having had, with three yr sons and two daus:

Sir DAVID WEMYSS of Wemyss; his lands of Wester Wemyss etc, Fifeshire, also Elcho, Balhepburn and Strathardle, Perths, and Balhall, Forfarshire, erected into the (territorial) Barony of Wemyss 1511; *m* 1st *c* 11 May 1493 Euphemia, dau of John Lundy of that Ilk; *m* 2nd *c* 1512 Janet (*m* 3rd William Keith and had issue (*see* KINTORE, E); *m* 4th James Campbell of Lawers), dau of 2nd Lord Gray (*qv*) and widow of John Charteris of Cuthill, and was *ka* Flodden 9 Sept 1513, leaving by his 1st w, with two yr sons (James, of Newton and Cameronmill, living 1535; Robert, of Easter Lathrisk, *m* Janet, sis and coheir of Henry Symsoun, of Lathrisk, and *d c* 24 Oct 1542, leaving issue) and a dau:

DAVID WEMYSS of Wemyss; *m* 1st (contract 27 Jan 1511/2) Katherine, dau of 3rd Lord Sinclair (*qv*), and had:

1 JOHN (Sir)

2 James, of Caskieberran; *m* Janet Durie (*d* July 1578), widow of David Martin of Carden, Fifeshire, and had:

(1) James, of Caskieberran; *d c* 1608, leaving:

1a James (Sir); Master Gunner England, Gen Artillery Scotland; *d* 1666, leaving:

1b JAMES WEMYSS, LORD BURNTISLAND (S), so *cr* 15 April 1672, having had previously a charter of the Castle of Burntisland; *m* 28 March 1672 his cousin Lady Margaret Wemyss, dau of **2nd Earl of Wemyss** and following his death **Countess of Wemyss** in her own right, and *d* Dec 1682, leaving issue (*see* below)

1 Margaret; *m* her cousin James Wemyss of Pittencrieff

2 Grisel; *m* 1st Andrew Kinninmonth; *m* 2nd David Ramsay of Brackmonth

DAVID WEMYSS of Wemyss *m* 2nd (contract 7 March 1526) Mariota (*m* 2nd Bernard Hamilton of Bogwood), dau of John Towers of Inverleith, and *d c* 27 May 1544, leaving by her:

3 David, of Dron and Strathardle; Army Capt; *m* 1st 1553 Margaret Cunningham; *m* 2nd 1577 Janet (*d* 22 Jan 1578/9), dau of John Beaton of Auchmithie and widow of James Lundy of Conland; *m* 3rd Eupheme Kinninmonth and *d* Feb 1593/4, leaving issue by his 1st w

3 Jonet; *m* 1st (contract 28 April 1540) Thomas Clephane, Yr. of Carslogie; *m* 2nd Robert Boswell

4 Mariota; *m* (contract 26 Nov 1549) Robert Fairlie of Braid and had issue

The est s,

Sir JOHN WEMYSS of Wemyss; present defeat by English of Pinkie 10 Sept 1547 and Battle of Langside for MARY QUEEN OF SCOTS 13 May 1568; *m* 1st *c* 20 Oct 1534 (*divorce* 1556) Margaret, dau of Sir Adam Otterburn of Redhall; *m* 2nd *c* 21 Feb 1557/8 Janet, dau of Alexander Trail of Blebo and widow of John Ramsay of Ardbekie, and *d c* 25 Jan 1571/2, leaving by her two sons (Gavin, of Powguild in Auchterderran, *m* Catherine, dau and heiress of David Wemyss of Unthank in Cameron, thus acquiring that estate, and was ancestor of the WEMYSSes of Wemysshall; Patrick, Burgess of Dysart, *d* in or after 1596) and by his 1st w, with a yr s (John, living 1572) and four daus (Margaret, *m* (contract 27 Nov 1555) David Barclay of Collaimie, Fifeshire, and *d* Sept 1608, leaving issue; Agnes, *m* 1567 John Aytoun of Dynmure; Elizabeth, *m* 1st David Balfour of Balbuthy, *m* 2nd Robert Carnegie; Eupheme, *m* (contract 4 Oct 1568) David Carnegie of Colluthie, s of Sir Robert Carnegie, and *d* 16 Nov 1593, leaving issue):

DAVID WEMYSS of Wemyss; served heir 14 May 1572; *m* (contact 7 May 1556) Cecilia (*d* 8 July 1589), dau of 2nd Lord Ruthven (*see* CARLISLE, E), and *d* 22 Feb 1596/7, having had, with five yr sons (Sir James, of Bogie, Fifeshire, ancestor of the WEMYSS, Bts of Bogie, who following the **2nd Earl of Wemyss**'s death 1679 are thought to be heirs to the btcy *cr* 1625; Andrew, of Newton, Fifeshire, *dsp*; Patrick, of Rumgay, ancestor of the WEMYSSes of Crighsall, Fifeshire; David, ancestor of the WEMYSSes of Fingask, Dairsie, Fifeshire; Henry, of Wester Dron, ancestor of the WEMYSSes of Foodle, Fifeshire) and five daus (Margaret, *m* (contract 5 April 1578) James Beaton of Creich and *d* 1636, leaving issue; Jean, *m* (contract 18 April 1578) James Makgill of Rankeillour (*d* 6 Nov 1602), and had issue (*see* OXFUIRD, V); Cecilia; *m* 1st 1585 Andrew Kinninmonth of that Ilk, *m* 2nd William Learmonth of Clatto; Elizabeth, *m* (contract 1 Aug 1597) Alexander Wood of Lamlethan; Isobel, *m* 1st (contract 10 Dec 1590) John Auchmoutle (*d* 11 Oct 1608) and had issue, *m* 2nd Stephen Orme):

Sir JOHN WEMYSS of Wemyss; *m* 1st (contract 17 April 1574) Margaret (*dsp*), est dau of 6th Earl of Morton (*qv*); *m* 2nd *c* Aug 1581 Mary, dau of 1st Lord Doune (*see* MORAY, E), and *d c* June 1622, leaving by her, with an er s (David, *m* 1608 Elizabeth (*m* 2nd *c* 13 Feb 1610, as his 1st w, 1st Earl of Findlater; *see* SEAFIELD, E), dau of 5th Earl of Rothes (*qv*), and *dsp* Aug 1608) and four daus (Cecilia, *m* 1599 2nd and last Earl of Tullibardine of the 1606 *cr* (*see* ATHOLL, D) and *dsp*; Janet, *m* 1st Lord Colville of Ochiltree and *dsp* 1655; Isabel, *m* 1614 7th Lord (Fraser of) Lovat (*qv*) and *d* 1636, leaving issue; Catherine, *m* 1624 Sir John Haldane of Gleneagles and had issue):

Sir JOHN WEMYSS, 1st Bt (NS), and **1st Earl of Wemyss**, so *cr* 29 May 1625) and 25 June 1633 respectively, as also on the latter date LORD ELCHO AND METHIL, as well as previously 1 April 1628 LORD WEMYSS OF ELCHO (all S, with remainder to heirs male bearing the name and arms of Wemyss), PC (S 1641); *b* 1586; ktd between 1615 and 1618; was a supporter of the Covenanters by 1638; *m* (contract 8 and 15 Sept 1609) Jean, dau of 6th Lord Gray (*qv*), and *d* 22 Nov 1649, having had, with five other children, an only surv s:

DAVID WEMYSS, **2nd Earl of Wemyss**, PC (S March 1649/50); *b* 6 Sept 1610; Covenanter, Col Fifeshire Foot in Scots Army at Newcastle 1640–41 and 1643, defeated by royalist forces under Montrose (*qv*) at encounters of Tippermuir 1 Sept 1644, Alford 2 July 1645 and Kilsyth 15 Aug 1645; Sheriff Fifeshire 1656–57; after his last surv s's death 1671 got 23 Aug 1672 a regrant of his peerage honours and lands in favour of his yst dau and the heirs male of her body; *m* 1st 4 Feb 1626/7 Anna (*d* 10 Nov 1649), dau of 2nd Lord Balfour of Burleigh (*qv*), and had, with 10 other children (*d* young or unm):

1 Jean; *m* 1st 1649 Archibald, Earl of Angus, s of 1st Marquess of Douglas (*see* HAMILTON and BRANDON, D); *m* 2nd 11 Aug 1659 15th Earl of Sutherland (*qv*) and *d* 5 Jan 1715, leaving issue

The **2nd Earl** *m* 2nd (contract 4 April 1650) Lady Eleanor Fleming (*dsp* 20 April 1642), dau of 2nd Earl of Wigtoun; *m* 3rd 13 Jan 1652/3 Margaret (*d* Feb 1688), dau of 6th Earl of Rothes (*qv*) and widow (a) of Alexander, Lord Balgonie (*see* LEVEN and MELVILLE, E), and (b) 2nd Earl of Buccleuch (*see* BUCCLEUCH and QUEENSBERRY, D), and *dspms* after 6 July 1679, when the btcy became dormant, having by her had, with two other sons (*d* young) an only surv dau:

2 LADY MARGARET Wemyss, **Countess of Wemyss** in her own right; *b* 1 Jan 1658/9; *m* 1st (contract 25 Dec 1671) her distant cousin LORD BURNTISLAND; *m* 2nd 29 April 1700 1st Earl of Cromartie (*qv*) and *d* 11 March 1705, having by him had a dau (*d* unm) and by her 1st husb, with other issue (*d* young):

(1) DAVID, **4th Earl**

(1) Anne; *b* 18 Oct 1675; *m* (contract 3 Sept 1691) 5th Earl of Leven and (2nd Earl of) Melville (*qv*) and *d* 9 Jan 1702, leaving issue

(2) Margaret; *m* 29 Jan 1697 4th Earl of Northesk (*qv*)

The COUNTESS's s,

DAVID WEMYSS, **4th Earl of Wemyss**; *bapt* 29 April 1678; Ensign Roy Co Archers 1703 (Lt-Gen 1713, Capt-Gen 1715), Fell Coll Physicians Edin 1705, Commr Union S and E Parls 1706–07, last Ld High Adml Scotland March 1705/6–07, V-Adml Scotland 1707 and 1708–14, rep S peer 1707–10; *m* 1st (contract 13 Aug 1697) Anne (*d* 23 Feb 1700), dau of 1st Duke of Queensberry (*see* QUEENSBERRY, M) and sis of William, 1st Earl of March, and had:

1 David, *Lord Elcho*; *b* 3 Oct 1698; memb Roy Co Archers; *dvp* unm 16 Dec 1715

2 JAMES, **5th Earl**

The **4th Earl** *m* 2nd 5 Jan 1708/9 Mary (*dsp c* 8 Sept 1712), er dau of Sir John Robinson, 2nd Bt, of Farming Woods, Northants; *m* 3rd (contract 5 July 1716) Elizabeth (*d* 1721), dau of 1st/10th Lord Sinclair (*qv*), and *d* 15 March 1720, leaving by her:

1 Elizabeth; *m* 17 April 1734 17th Earl of Sutherland (*qv*) and *d* 20 Feb 1747, leaving issue

2 Margaret; *m* 24 April 1740 8th Earl of Moray (*qv*) and *d* 31 Aug 1779, leaving issue

The 4th EARL's only surv s,

JAMES WEMYSS, **5th Earl of Wemyss**; *b* 30 Aug 1699; memb Roy Co Archers 1714 (Brig 1724, Lt-Gen 1726, Capt-Gen 1743); Burgess Perth 1726; his est s having been attainted 1746 for participation in the 1745 Uprising, he made over Wemyss Castle and its associated estates to his 3rd s 31 July 1750 and sold the Elcho estate to his 2nd s the same year for £8,500 (nearly £500,000 in late-1990s terms); *m* 17 Sept 1720 (separated shortly after 1732) Janet (*d* 1 March 1778), only dau and heiress of Col Francis Charteris of Amisfield (formerly Newmills), Haddingtonshire, and *d* 21 March 1756, when his titles became forfeited by virtue of his s's attainder, having had, with three other daus (*dsp*):

1 David, *Lord Elcho*, also self-styled 6th Earl of Wemyss; *b* 21 Aug 1721; *educ* Winchester and Acad Angers; made Col of Dragoons by titular James III Feb 1743/4, memb Roy Co Archers 1742, ADC to Bonnie Prince Charlie throughout 1745 Uprising, being present at Preston Pans 21 Sept 1745 (made Col 1st Troop Horse Gds there), Siege of Stirling and Battles of Falkirk 17 Jan 1745/6 and Culloden 16 April 1746, following which he fled to France and was attainted 1746, Capt Regt of FitzJames 1752, Col Roy Scots 1756–63 in French Serv, Order Mil Merit France 1770; *m* 9 Sept 1776 — (*d* 26 Nov 1777), dau of Baron d'Uxhull, of Neuchâtel, Switzerland, and *dspms* 29 April 1787

2 Francis WEMYSS later CHARTERIS (on death 24 Feb 1731/2 of his maternal gf 1729; by Act of Parl 1771 he was allowed to keep the surname and arms of CHARTERIS and the entailed estates of his maternal gf in the event of his succeeding to the Earldom of Wemyss or any other dignity despite the provision to the contrary in the entail); known in error as Earl of Wemyss on the death of his er bro under the widespread belief that he was not affected by the attainder as he did not descend from his bro; *b* 21 Oct 1723; memb Roy Co Archers 1747; *m* 13 Sept 1745 Catherine (*d* 21 Jan 1786), dau of 2nd Duke of Gordon (*see* HUNTLY, M), and *d* 24 Aug 1808, having had, with four other daus (*d* unm):

(1) Francis, mistakenly styled *Lord Elcho* after 1787; *b* 31 Jan 1748/9; MP Haddington Burghs 1780–87, memb Roy Co Archers 1786; *m* 18 July 1771 Susan (*d* 25 Feb 1835), dau of Anthony TRACY-KECK formerly TRACY (*see* HAMILTON and BRANDON, D), and *dvp* 20 Jan 1808, leaving:

1a FRANCIS, **6th Earl**

1a Henrietta Charlotte Elizabeth; *b* 3 Feb 1773; *m* 23 Dec 1797 6th Earl of Stamford (*d* 26 April 1845; *see* 1970 edn) and *d* 30 Jan 1838, leaving issue

2a Susan; *m* 23 Nov 1799 Lt-Gen Sir Henry Clinton, GCB (*see* LINCOLN, E), and *d* 17 Aug 1816

3a Katharine; *m* 19 Nov 1805 Hon Edward Richard Stewart (*see* GALLOWAY, E) and *d* 8 Oct 1863, leaving issue

4a Augusta; *m* 3 June 1819 2nd Baron Rossmore (*qv*) and *dsp* 28 July 1840

(1) Frances; *m* 29 April 1799 Rev William Traill, DD (*d* 1831), Chllr Down and Connor, and *d* 1848

3 James; *b* 23 Feb 1726; MP Sutherland; *m* 29 Aug 1757 his cousin Elizabeth (*d* 24 Jan 1803), dau of 17th Earl of Sutherland (*qv*), and *d* 10 May 1786, having had, with other issue (*d* unm):

(1) William, of Wemyss; *b* 9 April 1760; Lt-Gen; *m* 16 Sept 1788 Frances (*d* 1 Feb 1798), dau of Sir William Erskine, Bt, of Torrie (*see* 1839 edn), and *d* 4 Feb 1822, leaving:

1a James, of Wemyss; *b* 9 July 1789; MP 1820–47, R-Adml, Ld Lt and Sheriff-Pncpl Fife; *m* 8 Aug 1826 Emma (*d* 17 July 1841), dau of 17th Earl of Erroll (*qv*), and *d* 3 April 1854, having had, with another s (*d* young):

1b James Hay WEMYSS later ERSKINE-WEMYSS, of Wemyss Castle; *b* 29 Aug 1829; Ld-Lt and MP Fife; *m* 17 May 1855 Millicent Ann Mary (*d* 11 Feb 1895), dau of Hon John Kennedy Erskine of Dun (*see* AILSA, M), and *d* 29 March 1864, leaving:

1c Randolph Gordon, DL; *b* 11 July 1858; *m* 1st 18 July 1884 (*divorce* 1898) Lilian Mary (*d* 11 Nov 1952), only dau of 14th Marquess of Winchester (*qv*), and had:

1d Michael John, of Wemyss Castle, JP, DL (Fife 1936); *b* 8 March 1888; confirmed Chief of the name of Wemyss by Lyon Court 1910; Capt RHG WW I (wounded); *m* 25 Nov 1918 Victoria Alexandrina Violet, CVO (*d* 1994 aged 104), only dau of 6th Duke of Portland (*see* PORTLAND, E), and *d* 1982, leaving:

1e +David [David Wemyss of that Ilk, Invermay, Forteviot, Perthshire PH2 9DA]; *b* 11 Feb 1920; *educ* Eton and Magdalene Coll Cambridge; Capt Roy Signals WW II; *m* 21 July 1945 *Lady Jean Christian Bruce, 2nd dau of 10th Earl of Elgin and (14th Earl of) Kincardine (*qv*) and has:

1f +Michael James, DL [Michael Wemyss Yr of that Ilk DL, Wemyss Castle, East Wemyss, Fife KY1 4TE]; *b* 10 Nov 1947; *educ* Gordonstoun and RAC Cirencester; FRICS 1985; *m* 7 June 1975 *Charlotte Mary, dau of Lt-Col Royle Bristowe, of Brookhampton Hall, Ickleton, Cambs, and has:

1g *Hermione Mary; *b* 23 April 1982

1g *Leonora Anne; *b* 25 Sept 1986

2f +Charles John; *b* 26 July 1952; *educ* Eton; *m* 21 Oct 78 *Fiona Elizabeth, dau of Lt-Col Sir Eric Penn, GCVO, OBE, MC, of Sternfield House, Saxmundham, Suffolk, and has:

1g +James Michael; *b* 1987

1g *Mary Victoria; *b* 1981

2g *Elizabeth Katherine; *b* 1985

2e +Andrew Michael John [Andrew Wemyss Esq, Torrie House, Newmills, Dunfermline, Fife KY12 8HH]; *b* 3 Oct 1925; *educ* Eton; *m* 8 Feb 1967 *Janet Alethea, only dau of Maj John Swire Scott, of Eredine House, Dalmally, Argyll, and has:

1f +William John; *b* 8 Oct 1970

1f *Isabella Alethea; *b* 22 Feb 1968

1d Mary Millicent; *b* 15 May 1885; *m* 30 April 1917 Ernest Caswell Long, Lt Gren Gds

1c (cont.) Randolph Erskine-Wemyss of Wemyss *m* 2nd 23 Nov 1898 Lady Eva Cecilia Margaret Wellesley (*d* 4 March 1948), dau of 2nd Earl Cowley (*qv*), and *d* 17 July 1908

2c Hugo; *b* 31 May 1861; Hon Attaché Dip Serv; *d* unm 12 March 1933

3c ROSSLYN ERSKINE WEMYSS, 1st and last BARON WESTER WEMYSS, of Wemyss, Co Fife (UK), so *cr* 18 Nov 1919, GCB (1918, KCB 1916), CMG (1911), MVO (1901); *b* 12 April 1864; Extra Equerry to HM GEORGE V, R-Adml 2nd Battle Sqdn 1912 and 3rd Fleet 1914, cmded Base at Mudros Feb–Dec 1915, led attack and landing at Gallipoli 25 April 1916, C-in-C Egypt and E Indies 1916–17, 2nd Sea Ld 1917, 1st Sea Ld and Ch Naval Staff 1917–19, Grand Cross Legn Hon, Adml of the Fleet, Hon LLD Cambridge, Hon DCL Oxon, Hon LLD and Freeman St Andrews 1922; *m* 21 Dec 1903 Victoria (*d* 22 April 1945), only dau of Rt Hon Sir Robert Morier, GCB, GCMG, and *dspm* 24 May 1933, when the Barony expired, leaving:

1d Alice Elizabeth Millicent; *b* 1906; Dr ès Lettres Toulouse; *m* 11 Feb 1953 Maj Francis Henry Cunnack, RA (*d* 5 Jan 1974), yr s of Francis Henry Cunnack, JP, of Helston, Cornwall, and *d* 31 Dec 1994

1c Dora Mina; *m* 21 April 1887 Lord Henry George Grosvenor (*see* WESTMINSTER, D) and *d* 24 Dec 1894, leaving issue

2c Mary Frances; *m* 28 Feb 1882 Cecil Stratford Paget and had issue (*see* ANGLESEY, M)

1b Frances Harriet; *m* 16 May 1850 Capt Charles James Balfour, RN (*d* 3 Feb 1878), s of Gen Robert Balfour, 6th of Balbirnie, and *d* 14 Dec 1877, leaving issue

2a William; *b* 5 Sept 1790; Lt-Gen, Equerry to HM QUEEN VICTORIA; *m* 14 April 1820 Isabella (*d* 28 July 1868), dau of 17th Earl of Erroll (*qv*), and *d* 30 Nov 1852, leaving issue:

1b James Henry; Army Capt; *d* unm June 1857

2b Charles Thomas; Army Capt; *d* unm 19 March 1883

1b Isabella Harriet Jane; *m* 11 May 1859 Karl, 2nd Count Reventlow-Criminil (*d* 10 Jan 1908), and *d* 7 Dec 1894, leaving issue

1a Frances; *m* 10 Oct 1826 3rd Earl of Rosslyn (*qv*) and *d* 30 Sept 1858, leaving issue

(2) James, BCS; *b* 4 May 1778; *m* 6 Sept 1805 Caroline Charlotte (*d* 30 Jan 1863), 5th dau of Rev Henry Binfield, Vicar Albrighton, Salop, and *d* 22 Aug 1849, having had, with other issue (*d* young or unm):

1a James; *b* 11 Jan 1807; Maj; *m* Helen (*d* 1898), dau of James Reilly, and *d* 27 June 1865, leaving:

1b Binfield; *b* 10 March 1844; Maj-Gen ISC; *m* 25 Nov 1876 Mildred (*d* 13 April 1921), dau of Henry Unwin, Judge in India, and *d* 27 Feb 1904, leaving:

1c Hubert Gordon; *b* 12 Aug 1878

2c Alan Binfield; *b* 1886; Capt and Admin Offr Roy Signals (TA), Capt 4th Bn Dorset Regt; *m* 30 March 1921 Caroline Ethel, only dau of Cdr E A Constable, RN, and had:

1d +John Michael; *b* 28 Sept 1924

1b Mary; *m* 27 Jan 1870 Col Thomas James Quin, IA

2b Elizabeth Helen; *m* 3 Dec 1867 Col Grey Townsend Skipwith and *d* 27 Dec 1878, leaving issue (*see* SKIPWITH, Bt)

2a William Binfield; *b* 15 Feb 1810; Gen 9th Bengal Light Cav; *m* 24 March 1832 Martha Rose Diana (*d* 23 Oct 1876), est dau of Lt-Gen Samuel Smith, Bengal Cav, and *d* 24 May 1890, having had, with other issue (*d* young or unm):

1b James; *b* 26 May 1833; Lt 93rd Highrs; *d* 13 June 1855

1b Mary Harriett; *b* 7 March 1845

2b Caroline Binfield; *b* 24 July 1848; *d* unm 6 May 1942

3b Katherine Jane; *b* 23 June 1851; *m* 9 Oct 1873 Lt-Col William Barrington Browne, DCLI, and *d* his widow 3 June 1937

3a Francis; *b* 18 Nov 1814; Lt-Col Bengal Engrs; *m* 1848 Selina (*d* 6 Oct 1910), dau of George Pye, and *d* 1887, leaving:

1b Selina Elizabeth Pye; *m* 25 Oct 1879 Henry Whatley Estridge (*d* 15 Jan 1902)

1a Caroline Charlotte; *m* Maj-Gen Charles Campbell of Kinloch and *d* 23 Aug 1841, leaving issue

2a Mary; *m* 1 May 1833 Maj-Gen Charles F Havelock (*see* HAVELOCK-ALLAN, Bt)

3a Elizabeth Huntly; *m* 1840 Sir William Muir, KCSI (*d* 11 July 1905), and *d* 17 Oct 1897, leaving issue

4a Katherine Harriett; *m* 20 Feb 1845 Maj Octavius Henry St George Anson and *d* 18 May 1849, leaving issue

(1) Elizabeth Margaret; *m* 16 Aug 1793 Alexander Brodie of Arnhall, Kincardineshire, and *d* 19 July 1800, leaving issue

1 Frances; *m* 14 Oct 1743 Sir James Steuart-Denham, Bt, of Coltness, and *d* 29 June 1789, leaving issue

2 Helen; *m* 2 May 1754 Capt Hugh Dalrymple, RN (*see* STAIR, E)

The 5th EARL's ggs,

FRANCIS CHARTERIS later CHARTERIS-WEMYSS-DOUGLAS (on inheriting the Peeblesshire estates of his cousin 4th Duke of Queensberry (*see* QUEENS-

BERRY, M), which included the Castle and (territorial) Barony of Neidpath), **6th Earl of Wemyss**, as which recognised on reversal of attainder 26 May 1826 though he had styled himself *Lord Elcho* 20 Jan–24 Aug 1808 and Earl of Wemyss thereafter till 1810, when he styled himself Earl of Wemyss and (4th Earl of) March on the grounds that the Earldom of March and its associated titles *cr* 1697 (*see* QUEENSBERRY, M) had been with extended limitation ensuring that they would pass with the lands, an argument which has been pronounced probable but which has not been proven in a court of law so that he was not immediately recognised as possessing such titles, though the Roll of Scottish peers allowed to vote for representatives of themselves in the House of Lords has included the Earldoms both of Wemyss and March as late as 1960, shortly before Scottish peers were all admitted to that body, and this official document has been taken as tantamount to recognition of the right of the Earls of Wemyss to the Earldom of March as well; *b* 15 April 1772; *educ* Eton; ADC to his great-uncle Lord Adam Gordon when latter Cdr Forces Scotland; Ld Lt Peeblesshire 1821–53; *cr* 17 July 1821 BARON WEMYSS OF WEMYSS, Co Fife (UK); *m* 31 May 1794 Margaret (*d* 25 Jan 1850), dau of Walter Campbell of Shawfield, and *d* 28 June 1853, having had, with other issue:

1 FRANCIS, **7th Earl**

2 Walter; *b* 26 May 1797; *d* 8 Aug 1818

1 Eleanor; *b* 7 July 1796; *m* 14 Jan 1820 her cousin Walter Frederick Campbell of Shawfield, MP Argyll, s of Col John Campbell and gs maternally of 5th Duke of Argyll (*qv*), and *d* 16 Sept 1832, leaving issue

2 Margaret; *b* 8 Feb 1800; *m* Dec 1824 Col John Wildman and *d* 22 Oct 1825

3 Katharine; *b* 20 Aug 1801; *m* 20 Dec 1824 George Harry, Lord Grey (*dvp* 24 Oct 1835), s of 6th Earl of Stamford (*see* 1970 edn), and *d* 4 Jan 1844, leaving issue

4 Charlotte; *b* 20 Aug 1806; *m* 7 Sept 1825 Andrew Fletcher of Saltoun (*d* 9 April 1879) and *d* 3 March 1886, leaving issue

5 Louisa Antonietta; *m* 14 Aug 1832 William Forbes of Callendar (*d* 10 Feb 1855) and *d* 2 July 1854, leaving issue

6 Harriett; *m* 3 Sept 1829 Sir George Grant-Suttie, 5th Bt (*qv*), and *d* 30 May 1858, leaving issue

The 6th EARL's only surv son,

FRANCIS CHARTERIS later WEMYSS-CHARTERIS-DOUGLAS, **7th Earl of Wemyss**; *b* 14 Aug 1795; *educ* Ch Ch Oxford; memb Roy Co Archers (Lt-Gen 1842–83), Ld Lt Peeblesshire 1850–80; *m* 22 Aug 1817 Louisa (*d* 16 April 1882), dau of 2nd Earl of Lucan (*qv*), and *d* 1 Jan 1883, having had, with another s and dau (*d* infants):

1 FRANCIS RICHARD, **8th Earl**

2 Richard Charteris, DL (Co Tipperary); *b* 25 July 1822; Lt-Col Scots Gds; *m* 2 Aug 1858 Lady Margaret Butler (*d* 21 Feb 1915), only surv dau and heiress of 2nd and last Earl of Glengall (*see* 1858 edn), and *d* 10 March 1874, leaving:

(1) Richard Butler, TD, JP, DL Co Tipperary, of Cahir Castle; *b* 12 Oct 1866; High Sheriff 1919, Lt-Col Warwicks Yeo, Imp Yeo Boer War, ADC to Inspr-Gen Cav 1907–08; *m* 8 Aug 1890 Pamela (*d* June 1932), dau of Robert Dyer, of Layham, Suffolk, and *dsp* 15 Aug 1961

(2) Edmund Butler; *b* 28 Sept 1870; Capt RHG (Blues), Priv Sec to Sec of War Office, Legn Hon; *m* 1st 1918 (*divorce* 1921) Lilian Clare (*d* 19 Dec 1962), dau of Andrews Knox Rickards, JP, of Monmouth; *m* 2nd 20 March 1939 Dorothy Alice, dau of James Dean and formerly w of Joseph Steedon Sheldon, and *d* 2 July 1939

(1) Elinor Margaret; *m* 12 July 1888 Maj-Gen Inigo Richmund Jones CVO, CB, Scots Gds (*d* 20 July 1914), of Kelston Pk, Somerset, and *d* 31 Oct 1940, leaving issue

(2) Maud Emily; *m* 29 Oct 1889 Lt-Col Charles Arthur Wynne Finch and *d* 2 Aug 1945, leaving issue (*see* AYLESFORD, E)

3 Walter; Capt 92nd Highrs; *ka* Balaclava 25 Oct 1854

4 Frederick William; *b* 28 Feb 1833; Capt RN; *m* 30 Nov 1864 Louisa (*d* 12 March 1930), dau of 6th Earl of Albemarle (*qv*), and *d* 10 Oct 1887, leaving:

(1) Nigel Keppel, CMG (1919), DSO (1917), OBE (1943); *b* 10 March 1878; *educ* Winchester and Ch Ch Oxford; Col cmdg 1st Bn Roy Scots Boer War (despatches), WW I (despatches three times, Brevet Lt-Col), WW II cmdg 24th Bn Hants HG 1942–43, Ch Instr Small Arms Sch Hythe 1921–25; *m* 6 Jan 1904 Katharine Margaret (*d* 12 Feb 1961), est dau of Sir John Walter Buchanan Riddell, 11th Bt (*qv*), and *d* 28 Feb 1967, leaving:

1a +John Douglas [Maj John Charteris, Glen Lorne House, Muirfield Drive, PO Chisipite, Harare, Zimbabwe]; *b* 6 May 1914; *educ* Radley; Maj Roy Scots WW II; *m* 1st 8 May 1943 Mrs Catherine Pitcairn Colley (*d* 1 Feb 1957), dau of Capt W P Nunneley, Black Watch, and has:

1b *Sarah Keppel; *b* 8 Feb 1945; *m* 1970 *Peter Guthrie Brown and has issue

1a (cont.) Maj John Charteris *m* 2nd 18 Feb 1958 (*divorce* 1971) Jean Haigh and by her has:

1b +Martin Ian [Martin Charteris Esq, Wingtip Farm, Box 534, Marondera, Zimbabwe]; *b* 31 May 1960; *m* 7 Oct 1989 *Dr Helen Elizabeth Heath and has:

1c +Michael John Samuel; *b* 27 July 1990

2c +Andrew Philip; *b* 7 July 1992

2b *Bridget Alison [Mrs Ian Donovan, 20 Clairwood Rd, Alexandra Park, Harare, Zimbabwe]; *b* 8 Dec 1958; *m* 1983 *Ian Donovan and has issue

1a (cont.) Maj John Charteris *m* 3rd 1982 *Mrs Rosemary Gillian Druscilla Perry (*née* Edmonds), of Zimbabwe

2a +David Nigel [David Charteris Esq, Longstone Cotts, South St, Little Avebury, Wilts SN8 1QX]; *b* 13 Sept 1920; *educ* Lancing; Lt RNVR WW II; *m* 1st 5 July 1952 Euphemia Mary (*d* 24 June 1969), dau of Maj-Gen Sir Drummond Inglis, KBE, CB, MC, of The Old Manor, Chelsworth, Suffolk, and has:

1b +Nigel Drummond Keppel [Nigel Charteris Esq, c/o PO Box CH 172, Chisipite, Harare, Zimbabwe]; *b* 24 Oct 1958; *m* 1988 *Phillipa Margaret, dau of Maj Robert Edward Paton, of Harare, and has:

1c +James David; *b* 1992

1c *Alice Fiona; *b* 1990

1b *Angela Katharine Keppel [Mrs Nigel Butler, Mufaro, 56 Kent Rd, Chisipite, Harare, Zimbabwe]; b 16 Oct 1953; m 1980 *Nigel Butler and has:

　　1c *Katharine Emma; b 5 May 1981

　　2c *Sabrina Charlotte; b 19 Feb 1983

　　3c *Belinda Alexandra; b 11 Feb 1986

　　4c *Joanna Mary Tessa; b 27 March 1988

2b *Helen Mary Keppel; b 10 Jan 1956; m 1984 *Richard William Lewis Groves, s of Capt P W Groves, of Cardiff, and has issue

2a (cont.) David Charteris m 2nd 1982 *Astrid Henrietta Vivian Alys (neé Cooper), widow of Dr A Henderson-Begg

1a *Margaret Olive [Mrs Eric Copner, 16 Clare Pk, Crondall, Surrey GU10 5DT]; b 1 Feb 1905; m 1st 11 Jan 1930 Cdr Michael Richard Hallam Murray, RN (d 15 Aug 1938), yr s of Alexander Henry Hallam Murray, of Hythe, Kent, and has:

　　1b *Christopher Philip Hallam [Christopher Murray Esq, Manor Farm, Little Barugh, N Yorks YO17 0UY]; b 3 May 1937; educ Marlborough and Pembroke Coll Cambridge (BA 1961); m 22 July 1967 *Judith Mary, dau of Lt-Col Ian David MacInnes, and has:

　　　　1c *James Michael Hallam; b 9 Aug 1968

　　　　2c *Justin Richard; b 1973

　　　　1c *Harriet Alexandra; b 1970

　　1b *Susan Barbara; b 30 Oct 1930; m 1974 Leslie Max Pritchard (d 1990)

　　2b *Katharine Bridget [Mrs Nigel Davison, 3 South Dene, Stoke Bishop, Bristol BS9 2BW]; b 5 Oct 1934; m 1st 26 Oct 1956 Lt John Charles Brian Taite, RN (d 1975), of Windsor, Berks, s of Cdr John Charles Taite, RN, and has:

　　　　1c *Roderick Michael James; b 29 Sept 1966

　　　　1c *Clare Bridget; b 27 April 1959

　　　　2c *Caroline Rachel; b 22 Aug 1960

　　2b (cont.) Mrs John Taite m 2nd 18 Oct 1997 *Dr Nigel St John Davison

1a (cont.) Margaret Olive m 2nd 28 Jan 1954 Maj Eric Cecil Lewis Copner (d 12 Aug 1968), late Devonshire Regt, yr s of Dr Arthur Lewis Copner, of Ilfracombe, Devon

2a *Anne Louisa; b 17 May 1909; m 30 Dec 1939 Maj John Arkwright Bonham-Carter, CVO, DSO, OBE, ERD, of Redbridge House, Crossways, Dorset, Roy Tank Regt, s of Capt Guy Bonham-Carter, and has:

　　1b *Richard Francis [Richard Bonham-Carter Esq, Maybank, Monkwood, Alresford, Hants SO24 0HB]; b 4 Oct 1940; educ Winchester; MICE (1970); m 27 Jan 1968 Josephine Ann (d 22 May 1998), er dau of Alfred Smithson Gallimore and Mrs J Rankine, of Burton Hall, Carlow, and has:

　　　　1c *Nicola Jane; b 5 Aug 1969; m 14 Oct 1994 *Alex Roads

　　　　2c *Claire Helen; b 2 March 1972

　　2b *Nigel John [Nigel Bonham-Carter Esq, Dowlands, Thorndon, Eye, Sussex]; b 12 April 1945; educ Winchester and King's Coll Cambridge (BA 1966, MA 1970)

(2) Ronald Louis; b 24 Sept 1879; Lt Norfolk Imp Yeo Boer War, Capt RAF WW I; m 1st 27 June 1907 (divorce 1918) Edith Augusta Muriel (d 22 June 1960), only child of Capt Henry Tryon (see TRYON, B); m 2nd 3 July 1919 Louise Eileen (d 21 April 1971), dau of Maj-Gen George Williams Knox, CB, and widow of Lt-Col James Valentine, DSO, RAF, and dsp 26 Nov 1950

(1) Clare Susan; b 21 March 1884; m 18 Nov 1909 V-Adml Sidney Robert Drury-Lowe, CMG (d 24 Jan 1945), s of Lt-Gen Robert Henry Drury-Lowe, Gren Gds, and d 3 Dec 1945, leaving issue

1 Anne; b 29 July 1829; m 18 Feb 1852 4th Earl of (Brooke and of) Warwick (qv) and d 16 Aug 1903, leaving issue

2 Louisa; b 28 Sept 1830; m 7 Dec 1854 Capt William Wells (d 1 May 1889), JP, DL, MP, 1st Life Gds, of Holmewood, Hunts, and dsp 16 March 1920

The 9th EARL's est s,

FRANCIS RICHARD CHARTERIS-WEMYSS-DOUGLAS later CHARTERIS, **8th Earl of Wemyss**, GCVO (1909), DL (Haddington and Selkirk); b 4 Aug 1818; educ Eton and Ch Ch Oxford (BA); memb Roy Co Archers 1838 (Ensign-Gen), MP (C) E Glos 1841–46 and Haddington 1847–83, a Ld Treasury 1853–55, Tstee Nat Portrait Gallery 1856–66, Lt-Col London Scottish Rifles Vols 1859–79 (Hon Col 1879–1900), First Chm Cncl Nat Rifle Assoc 1860–67 and 1869–70, Vol ADC to TM QUEEN VICTORIA 1881–1901 and EDWARD VII 1901–10, Hon LLD Edin, Legn Hon; m 1st 29 Aug 1843 Anne Frederica (d 22 July 1896), 2nd dau of 1st Earl of Lichfield (qv), and had:

1 Francis; b 11 Nov 1844; d unm 22 July 1870

2 Arthur; b 30 Aug 1846; d 1847

3 Alfred Walter; b 2 June 1847; Lt 71st Foot; d at sea 24 Nov 1873 of illness caught while on Staff during Ashanti War

4 HUGO RICHARD, **9th Earl**

5 Alan Dudley; b 19 March 1860; Lt Coldstream Gds; d unm 9 Jan 1901

6 Evan Edward (Sir), KC (1919); b 29 Jan 1864; Lt Coldstream Gds, Staff Capt RTC 1916; barrister Inner Temple 1891, Bencher Inner Temple 1924, Tstee Nat Portrait Gallery (Chm 1928), Nat Gallery, Tate Gallery (Chm 1934) and Wallace Collection, Chm Standing Commn Museums and Galleries 1937, author: *Affairs of Scotland 1744–46, William Augustus, Duke of Cumberland* and other works; m 9 Aug 1930 Dorothy Margaret (d 8 March 1961), dau of 5th Earl of Kenmare (see 1949 edn) and widow of Lord Edward Arthur Grosvenor (see WESTMINSTER, D), and d 16 Nov 1940

1 Evelyn; b 17 Oct 1851; m 4 June 1872 4th Viscount de Vesci (qv) and d 18 June 1939, having had issue

2 Lilian Harriet; m 1st 27 Nov 1872 Sir Henry Carstairs Pelly, 3rd Bt (d 4 June 1877; qv), and had issue; m 2nd 31 July 1882 Sir Henry Francis Redhead Yorke, KCB (d 12 Jan 1914), of Iver Heath, Bucks, and d 11 April 1914, leaving further issue

3 Hilda; b 13 Oct 1854; m 4 Dec 1880 1st Earl of Midleton (see MIDLETON, V) and d 1 Aug 1901, leaving issue

The **8th Earl** m 2nd Dec 1900 Grace (d 13 Feb 1946), 3rd dau of Maj John Blackburn and niece of Baron Blackburn of Killearn (see 1896 edn), and d 30 June 1914

His est surv s,

HUGO RICHARD CHARTERIS, **9th Earl of Wemyss**, DL (Peeblesshire); b 25 Aug 1857; educ Harrow and Balliol Coll Oxford; MP (C) Haddingtonshire 1883–85 and Ipswich 1886–95, memb LCC 1904–10, Ld Lt Haddingtonshire 1918–37, Hon Col 7th Vol Bn Roy Scots; m 9 Aug 1883 Mary Constance (d 29 April 1937), dau of Hon Percy Scawen Wyndham, MP (see EGREMONT, LECONFIELD and, B), and d 12 July 1937, having had:

1 Hugo Francis, Lord Elcho; b 28 Dec 1884; Capt Glos Yeo Egypt WW I; m 1 Feb 1911 Lady Violet Catharine (Letty) Manners (m 2nd 9 July 1921 Guy Holford Benson, of Winchcombe, Glos (d 30 April 1975), and d 23 Dec 1971), dau of 8th Duke of Rutland (qv), and was ka 23 April 1916, leaving:

　　(1) (FRANCIS) DAVID CHARTERIS, **10th and present Earl of Wemyss**

　　(2) +MARTIN MICHAEL CHARLES CHARTERIS, cr BARON CHARTERIS OF AMISFIELD (qv)

2 Guy Lawrence; b 23 May 1886; educ Eton and Trin Coll Cambridge (BA 1911); Capt Scots Gds (SR), 4th Cl Order St Sava Serbia; m 1st 23 July 1912 Frances Lucy (d 5 Nov 1925), est dau of Francis John Tennant (see GLENCONNER, B), and had:

　　(1) Hugo Francis Guy, MC; b 11 Dec 1922; educ Eton and Oxford; Capt Scots Gds WW II; writer, TV playwright; m 24 April 1948 *Virginia Mary [Mrs Hugo Charteris, The Elms Bubwith, Selby, Yorks], dau of Colin Forbes Adam (see FORBES ADAM, Bt), and d 1970, leaving:

　　　　1c Richard Hugo; b 3 Feb 1949; d 31 Oct 1951

　　　　2c +James Hugo Desmond; b 13 Sept 1958; m 1990 *Kathryn Helen, dau of G B Shaw of Fourstones, Hexham, Northumberland, and has:

　　　　　　1b +Felix Guy; b 1992

　　　　　　1b +Esmé Iris; b 12 March 1995

　　　　　　2b *Ruby Rose; b 1 Jan 1997

　　　　1c *Frances Irene Ann [Mrs Val Chong, 705 Driggs Ave, Brooklyn, New York, NY, USA]; b 16 Oct 1950; m 1983 *Val Chong and has issue

　　　　2c *Virginia Jane; b 19 April 1953; m 1984 *Peter Charles Clark, er s of F C Clark of Streatham

　　　　3c *Perdita Rosemary; b 11 Sept 1955; m 29 July 1978 *Jeremy Rupert Beckett and has issue (see BECKETT, Bt)

　　(1) Ann Geraldine Mary; b 19 June 1913; m 1st 6 Oct 1932 3rd Baron O'Neill (ka 24 Oct 1944; qv) and had issue; m 2nd 28 June 1945 2nd Viscount Rothermere (qv); m 3rd 24 March 1952 Ian Lancaster Fleming (d 12 Aug 1964), Cdr (Sp) RNVR, writer, 2nd s of Maj Valentine Fleming, DSO, MP, of Arnisdale House, Loch Hourn, Inverness-shire, and d 1981, having had issue by him

　　(2) *(Frances) Laura; b 10 Aug 1915; m 1st 14 Nov 1933 (divorce 1942) 2nd Viscount Long (ka 23 Sept 1944; qv) and has issue; m 2nd 25 Feb 1943 (divorce 1954) 3rd Earl of Dudley (qv); m 3rd 13 June 1960 Michael Temple Canfield (d 20 Dec 1969), yr s of Cass Canfield, of Mount Kisco, New York; m 4th 26 Jan 1972, as his 2nd w, *10th Duke of Marlborough (qv)

　　(3) Mary Rose; b 10 Feb 1919; m 1st 21 Sept 1940 (divorce 1946) Capt Roderic Miles Doughty Thesiger (see CHELMSFORD, V); m 2nd 15 Dec 1949 Nigel Francis Egerton Grey (see GREY, E) and d 21 Dec 1962, leaving issue

2 (cont.) The Hon Guy Charteris m 2nd 5 Oct 1945 *Violet, dau of Alfred Charles Masterton Porter, of Dundee, and d 21 Sept 1967

3 Colin Charteris; b 1 June 1889; d 27 Dec 1892

4 Ivo Alan; b 6 Oct 1896; 2nd Lt 1st Bn Gren Gds; ka 17 Oct 1915

1 Cynthia Mary Evelyn; b 27 Sept 1887; m 28 July 1910 Hon Herbert Asquith (d 5 Aug 1947), 2nd son of 1st Earl of Oxford and Asquith (qv), and d 31 March 1960, leaving issue

2 Mary Pamela Madeline Sibell; b 24 Oct 1895; m 1st 4 Dec 1915 Algernon Walter Strickland (see STRICKLAND-CONSTABLE, Bt) and had issue; m 2nd 4 April 1943 Maj John George Lyon (see STRATHMORE AND KINGHORNE, E)

3 Irene Corona; b 31 May 1902; Sr Cmdt ATS, GCStJ; m 14 July 1921 2nd Earl of Plymouth (qv) and had issue

March, previous creations: An English peerage of this name was conferred in October 1328 on Roger de Mortimer, one of the party opposed to EDWARD II's favourites the Despensers (see FALMOUTH, V) and the lover of his Queen, ISOBEL. March is the first Earldom in the history of the peerage of England given a name other than that of a county or county town (for the interchangeability of which in the Middle Ages, see WINCHESTER, M, preliminary remarks). The March in question referred to the border lands of England and Wales where Mortimer held large estates.

EDWARD III, who had long resented his mother's lover's high-handedness, had March arrested in mid-October 1330, following which he was attainted and his titles forfeited, then executed in the fashion reserved for common criminals, being drawn to Tyburn gallows and hanged there.

Roger's grandson, another Roger de Mortimer, had the Earldom restored to him in 1354, when the attainder on his grandfather was reversed, after a military career in the Hundred Years War of considerable distinction, particularly during the Crécy Campaign of 1346. His later feats were less spectacular, though he did manage to capture the towns of Saint-Florent and Tonnerre in the 1359 campaign in France which had as its chief aim the reduction of Rheims. On his death the following February his son Edmund inherited the Earldom. The latter married Philippa, daughter of LIONEL DUKE OF CLARENCE, second son of EDWARD III (see also ROYAL FAMILY, section GLOUCESTER, subsection **Ulster, previous creations**), and had a son Roger, the 4th Earl, who was killed on active service in 1398 while campaigning in Ireland against the natives of that country.

Due to the royal marriage connection two generations back his son and successor, Edmund, the 5th Earl, was looked on by RICHARD II's followers after the latter's deposition as rightful heir to the throne. He was leniently treated by HENRY IV, nevertheless, being kept under house arrest first at Windsor Castle then at Berkhamsted Castle. HENRY V freed him completely, made him a Knight of the Bath and took him to France at the start of the Agincourt Campaign in 1415. A year later he helped defeat a French fleet besieging the port of Harfleur, occupied by the English since the previous autumn, and continued campaigning in France till HENRY V's death in 1422, two years after which he died himself.

He had no children and the title passed to his sister Anne's son by her husband Richard Earl of Cambridge. The latter, created Duke of York in 1426, became head of the Yorkist party during the Wars of the Roses and was father of EDWARD IV, with whose accession the Earldom of March merged in the Crown.

The title was revived as one of the subsidiary honours of EDWARD V before his accession. For the extant creation under this title in the peerage of England, see RICHMOND and GORDON, D. For further creations involving the name March in the peerage of Scotland see DUNBAR, Bt, of Mochrum, MORAY, E, against both the Earldom of Lennox of the 1578 creation and the Dukedom of Richmond of the 1641 creation, and LAUDERDALE, E, against the Dukedom of Lauderdale created in 1672.

Seat: Gosford House, Longniddry, East Lothian. Robert Adam designed the earliest part of the house, working on the project between 1790 and his death two years later, although it was not finished till 1800. His plans provided for a domed central block with a pavilion, also domed, either end. The proximity to the Firth of Forth, a somewhat bleak setting which nevertheless justified the curving skyline in mimicry of the waves, must have made it look like a sea serpent from far inland. In the 1840s, during the **6th Earl**'s time, these outer curves were removed. Nearly half a century elapsed before William Young's extension in the Italianate style. The Marble Hall, his most noticeable feature, announces the precise year of its construction, 1890, in roman numerals on the arch over the fireplace. The marble is very light in colour, so that what with its glass dome above and high windows facing south over a courtyard the Hall is well lit even on a Scottish midwinter afternoon. Light is always a preoccupation so far north, and in Gosford's case the original Adam windows were found to be too small to allow proper viewing of the art collection. They were accordingly replaced by larger apertures.

In the 20th century Gosford has been a hotel and army quarters. In 1940, during the latter phase, fire destroyed the Saloon, one of Adam's original three huge central chambers. A few years later it became evident that dry rot had set in. The house was reroofed in the 1980s and restoration of the entire property was reported in late 1997 to be continuing.

WESTBURY

Arms: Argent on a chevron engrailed azure between three boar's heads couped sable an estoile or, all within a bordure of the third.
Crest: Out of a crown vallery or an eagle's head sable between two wings azure, charged on the breast with an estoile as in the arms.
Supporters: On either side, an eagle, wings addorsed, azure, ducally crowned, collared and charged on the breast with an estoile or.
Motto: '*Ap Ithel*' (i.e., the old Welsh family name).
Creation: B. (UK) 27 June 1861.

THE 5TH BARON WESTBURY, of Westbury, Co Wilts (David Alan Bethell, CBE (1994), MC (1943), DL (N Yorks 1973)) [The Rt Hon The Lord Westbury CBE MC DL, Barton Cottage, Malton, N Yorks YO17 0AT; 8 Ropers Orchard, Danvers St, London SW3]; *b* 16 July 1922; *s* bro 1961; *educ* Harrow and RMC Sandhurst; Capt Scots Gds WW II (wounded, despatches three times), Equerry to HRH THE 1st DUKE OF GLOUCESTER 1947–49; KStJ 1977, Bailiff Egle OStJ 1988–92, Bailiff Grand Cross 1988; *m* 21 Oct 1947 *Ursula Mary-Rose, JP (N Yorks 1962), er dau of Hon Robert James (see NORTHBOURNE, B), and has:

1 +RICHARD NICHOLAS, MBE (1979) [Maj The Hon Richard Bethell MBE, Clarendon House, Manor House Stables, Middleham, Leyburn, N Yorks DL8 4QL]; *b* 29 May 1950 (HRH THE DUCHESS OF GLOUCESTER stood sponsor); *educ* Harrow and RMA Sandhurst; Maj Scots Gds (ret), NI and S Atlantic Campaign 1982 (despatches twice, wounded); Offr Bro OStJ; *m* 1st 11 Dec 1975 (*divorce* 1991) Caroline Mary, only dau of Richard John Palmer (see PALMER, B), and has:

  (1) +ALEXANDER; *b* 21 Dec 1986
  (1) *Alice Mary; *b* 11 Aug 1979
  (2) *Rose; *b* 9 Jan 1984

1 (cont.) Maj The Hon Richard Bethell *m* 2nd 1993 *Charlotte Sarah-Jane, dau of Jack Gore

2 +James David William; *b* 22 Feb 1952; *educ* Harrow; *m* 1st 3 April 1974 Emma Hermione, yr dau of Malise Allen Nicolson, MC, of Frog Hall, Tilston, Cheshire, and has:

  (1) *Clare Angelina Serena; *b* 23 Oct 1977
  (2) *Lucinda Emma; *b* 1 April 1979

2 (cont.) The Hon James Bethell *m* 2nd 1987 *Mrs Sally Le Gallais, dau of John Roberts (see ROBERTS, Bt, of Milner Field), and by her has:

  (1) +Edward David John; *b* 1994
  (3) *Jessica Mary; *b* 1988

1 *Celia Mary [The Hon Mrs Holliday, Mount St John, Felixkirk, N Yorks]; *b* 5 March 1955; *m* 28 June 1980 *(Lionel) Brook Holliday, yr s of Maj Lionel Brook Holliday OBE, TD, JP, of Copgrove Hall, Yorks, and has:

  (1) *Lucy; *b* 1983
  (2) *Serena; *b* 1990

Lineage: RICHARD BETHELL, MD, of Bristol (s of Samuel Bethell, of Bradford, Wilts, and gs of Thomas Bethell, of Bradford, who *d* 1755); *m* Jane Baverstock and had, with a yr s (John, *m* 1833 Louisa, 2nd dau of Robert Abraham and sis of Lady Westbury (*see* below) and had surv issue):

RICHARD BETHELL, **1st Baron Westbury**, of Westbury, Co Wilts (UK), so *cr* 27 June 1861, PC (1861); *b* 30 June 1800; *educ* Wadham Coll Oxford (BA 1818, MA 1822, Fell 1822, DCL 1860); barrister Middle Temple 1823, Bencher and QC 1840, Ldr Chancery Bar 1841, V-Chllr Co Palatine Lancaster 1851–52, MP (Lib) Aylesbury 1851–59 and Wolverhampton 1859–61, Slr-Gen 1852–56, ktd 1853, Attorney-Gen 1856–58 and 1859–61, Ld Chllr 1861–65; *m* 1st 19 Nov 1825 Ellinor Mary (*d* 17 March 1863), est dau of Robert Abraham, architect, of Bloomsbury, and had:

1 RICHARD AUGUSTUS, **2nd Baron**
2 Slingsby, CB, JP, DL (Middx); *b* 4 Oct 1831; barrister 1857, Registrar Bankruptcy, Clerk Ctees Ho Lds 1861–96; *m* 1st 9 May 1855 Caroline (*d* 28 July 1886), 5th dau of William Chaplin, MP, of Ewhurst Park, Hants, and had:

  (1) Slingsby Westbury, JP; *b* 5 Nov 1861; *m* 12 Feb 1890 Sophia Isabella (*d* 2 Sept 1940), est dau of Capt John Hobhouse Inglis Alexander, CB, RN (*see* HAGART-ALEXANDER, Bt), and *d* 30 April 1936, leaving:

    1a Christopher Alick; *b* 3 April 1893; Capt Roy Scots Fus, Brevet-Maj Roy Tank Corps, WW I (wounded), WW II; *m* 1 Jan 1921 Esmée Clare (*d* 6 June 1967), dau of Campbell Dillon, and was *ka* 2 July 1940
    2a Jocelyn Slingsby, CBE (1943); *b* 8 March 1897; Capt RN, WW I (despatches) and WW II (despatches), US Legn Merit; *m* 6 April 1929 *Violet Monica, 2nd dau of William George Peareth-Kincaid-Lennox, of Campsie Glen, Stirlingshire

  (2) Guy Vivian; *b* 5 Nov 1861; *m* 12 Aug 1892 Ethel (*d* 1 Sept 1932), 3rd dau of John Coutts Fowlie, and *dsp* 8 Sept 1932

  (3) Lionel Beresford; *b* 29 Jan 1864; *m* 5 Aug 1896 Jemima Amy (*d* 20 Sept 1961), yst dau of Col Richard Bomford George Bolton, RHG (The Blues), of Brook Lodge, Co Meath, and *d* 7 Dec 1928, having had:

    1a Vivian Lionel Slingsby; *b* 4 June 1897; *educ* Wellington and RMA Woolwich; Hon Maj RA, WW I 1916–18 and WW II 1939–42; *m* 19 Jan 1928 *Joan Ker, only child of John Manwell, and *d* 28 Aug 1967, leaving:

      1b +Richard Ker Slingsby, OBE (1973), DL (Somerset 1991) [Capt Richard Bethell OBE DL RN, Court Farm House, Nunney, Frome, Somerset]; *b* 4 Aug 1928; Capt RN; *m* 29 July 1953 *Anne, dau of Harry Frost, of Amwell, Herts, and has:

        1c *Helena Susan Mary [Mrs Nicholas Harland, Quinces, Piddle Hinton, Dorset]; *b* 7 Jan 1955; *m* 1978 *Cdr Nicholas J G Harland, RN, and has:

          1d *Rupert Slingsby; *b* 1981
          1d *Francesca; *b* 1984

        2c *Theresa Jane [Mrs Michael Stephenson, Napier Lodge, Napier Ave, London SW6]; *b* 2 July 1956; *m* 1979 *Michael J Stephenson and has:

          1d *Edward; *b* 1982
          1d *Emily; *b* 1984

        3c *Jane Ker [Mrs David Fletcher, 18 Rusholme Rd, London SW15 3JZ]; *b* 28 March 1959; *m* 1981 *David F Fletcher and has:

          1d *Charles; *b* 1991
          1d *Rosanna; *b* 1987

      1b *Deirdre Anne; *b* 1929; *m* 6 Dec 1952 (*divorce* 1964) Sir Hugo Giles Edmund Sebright, 14th Bt (*qv*), and has issue; *m* 2nd 1965 Anthony Melbourne-Hart (*d* 1988)

    2a Rupert Patrick Slingsby; *b* 9 Sept 1902; *d* 11 Nov 1925

  (1) Violet Isabel Slingsby; *b* 28 Feb 1859; *m* 5 Jan 1888 Maj Archibald William Hicks Beach and *d* 19 Sept 1891, leaving issue (*see* SAINT ALDWYN, E)

2 (cont.) The Hon Slingsby Bethell *m* 2nd 6 Sept 1888 Laura Beatrice (*d* 16 July 1925), est dau of Rev Frederick Webster Maunsell, Rector Symondsbury, Dorset, and *d* 3 April 1896, leaving by her:

  (4) Llewelyn Slingsby; *b* 22 July 1889; *educ* Winchester and Univ Coll Oxford (BA 1912); Nigeria and Gold Coast Regts WW I 1917–19; *m* 6 July 1914 Margery Gladys (*d* 1985 aged 99), only child of George Stanley Farnell, Pncpl Victoria Coll Jersey, and *d* 5 Jan 1971, leaving:

    1a *Margaret Eve Slingsby; *b* 9 Aug 1915; *m* 10 June 1939 *Cdr Warwick Seymour Bracegirdle, DSC, RAN, er s of R-Adml Sir Leighton Seymour Bracegirdle, KCVO, CMG, DSO, RAN, of NSW, and has:

      1b *Simon Warwick Slingsby; *b* 1941
      2b *Nicholas; *b* 1944
      1b *Phillida Ann; *b* 1946

  (5) Richard Alfred Slingsby; *b* 7 July 1892; Cdr RN WW II; *m* 15 Feb 1930 *Frances Elizabeth (Betty), only child of Lt-Col Charles Maxwell Shurlock Henning, and *d* 9 Nov 1975, leaving:

    1a +Maxwell Slingsby [Dr Maxwell Bethell, Overhill Cottage, Sutton, Cheshire SK11 0NA]; *b* 28 Jan 1931; *educ* Wellington and Peterhouse Coll Cambridge (BA 1952, MB, ChB 1955, FRCPsy 1961); *m* 25 June 1953 *Pamela Mary, dau of Hubert Fletcher, and has:

      1b +Charles Maxwell Slingsby; *b* 7 May 1957

1b *Nicola Slingsby; *b* 1953; *m* 19– *Nicholas Winer and has:

1c *A son; *b* 1982

2b *Juliet Slingsby; *b* 25 April 1955

3b *Zoe Melisande Slingsby; *b* 4 Nov 1958

2a +David Slingsby; *b* 8 June 1934; *educ* Wellington and Peterhouse Coll Cambridge (BA 1958, MA 1962); late Lt The Cameronians; *m* 5 Sept 1964 *Sadie Patricia Melfort, est dau of Lt-Col Guy Melfort Baldwin, of Ottery St Mary, Devon, and has:

1b +Richard Slingsby; *b* 12 June 1965

2b +Christopher Maunsell Slingsby; *b* 18 Nov 1966

1b *Zillah Slingsby; *b* 15 Aug 1968

(2) Eleanor Love Slingsby; *b* 1 Dec 1890; *m* 27 Dec 1915 Maj Humphrey Le Fleming Fairfax Harvey, MC, RFA, only s of H Fairfax Harvey, of Warden House, Weymouth, and *d* 15 June 1943, leaving issue

3 Arthur Howard; *b* 31 Jan 1833; *d* April 1834

4 Walter John; *b* 11 Dec 1842; BA Oxon; barrister; *m* 11 Dec 1900 Ada Mary (*d* 31 July 1929), dau of Rev Charles Welfitt Blathwayt and widow of Thomas Hole, of Moorlands, Crewkerne, and *dsp* 26 Dec 1907

1 Ellen; *m* 9 May 1845 Rev Thomas Edward Abraham, Rector Risby, and *d* 25 March 1880, leaving issue

2 Eliza Jane; *m* 22 June 1850 Capt Christopher Baldock Cardew, 74th Highrs (*d* 1893), of Broomfield, Hants, and *d* 22 May 1916, having had issue

3 Emma Louisa; *m* 14 Sept 1854 Mansfield Parkyns (*d* 12 Jan 1894), of Woodborough Hall, Notts, and *d* 2 Sept 1877

4 Augusta; *m* 1st 23 Jan 1874 Henry Charles Adamson Kenyon-Parker (*d* 1881); *m* 2nd 13 Aug 1890 Thomas Arthur Nash, barrister (*d* 20 Aug 1921), and *d* 20 Dec 1931

The **1st Baron** *m* 2nd 25 Jan 1873 Eleanor Margaret (*d* 19 Dec 1894), 3rd dau of Henry Tennant, of Cadoxton, Glam, and *d* 20 July 1873

His est s,

RICHARD AUGUSTUS BETHELL, **2nd Baron Westbury**; *b* 11 March 1830; *m* 5 July 1851 Mary Florence (*d* 14 Aug 1901), yr dau of Rev Alexander Fownes Luttrell, JP, BCL, of E Quantoxhead, Somerset, and had, with two daus (*d* unm):

1 RICHARD LUTTRELL PILKINGTON, **3rd Baron**

2 Alexander Edward (Sir), GCMG, KCB; *b* 28 Aug 1855; Somaliland 1903–04, ADC to HM EDWARD VII 1907–08, Dir Naval Intell 1909–12, C-in-C E Indies 1912, cmded RN War Coll 1913–14, V-Adml Cmdg battleships 3rd Fleet 1914, Pres RNC Greenwich 1914–15, V-Adml cmdg Channel Fleet 1915, Adml cmdg Coastguard and Reserves 1915–16, C-in-C Plymouth 1916–18 with rank of Adml, Order of Aviz Portugal 1st Cl; *m* 11 March 1890 Hilda Mary (*d* 1 Dec 1928), yst dau of Benjamin Huntsman, DL, of W Retford Hall, Notts, and *d* 13 June 1932, having had:

(1) Edward Walter; *b* 17 Dec 1891; Capt Roy W Surrey Regt WW I (wounded, star); *ka* 21 Sept 1918

(2) Maurice John; *b* 9 March 1894; Lt RN WW I (despatches); *ka* Battle of Jutland 31 May 1916

(1) Agatha Hilda; Assist Pncpl WRNS WW I 1918–19, Ch Cdr ATS WW II; *m* 25 Jan 1922 Cdr John Bertram Aubrey Marsden-Smedley, RN (*d* 23 Aug 1959), s of John Bertram Marsden-Smedley, of Lea Green, Derbys, and had issue

3 Arthur John; *b* 17 June 1860; *d* 1921

4 Albert Victor; *b* 8 Jan 1864; *m* 17 Oct 1918 Eleanor Violet (*d* 2 March 1933), dau of Stephan Egan and widow of Charles Brett, Coldstream Gds, and *d* 20 July 1927

The 2nd BARON *d* 28 March 1875; his est s,

RICHARD LUTTRELL PILKINGTON BETHELL, **3rd Baron Westbury**; *b* 25 April 1852; Lt Scots Fus Gds; *m* 24 July 1882 Lady Agatha Manners Tollemache (*d* 8 Jan 1941), sis of 9th Earl of Dysart (*qv*), and *d* 21 Feb 1930, having had:

1 Richard; *b* 26 April 1883; Capt Scots Gds, WW I 1914–16 (wounded); *m* 10 Oct 1911 Evelyn Lucia Millicent (*d* 23 June 1956), dau of Col George Morland Hutton, CB, of Gate Burton Hall, Lincs, and *d* 15 Nov 1929, leaving:

(1) RICHARD MORLAND TOLLEMACHE BETHELL, **4th Baron Westbury**; *b* 9 Oct 1914; *educ* Stowe and Trin Coll Cambridge; Maj RE WW II; *d* unm 26 June 1961

(2) DAVID ALLAN BETHELL, **5th and present Baron Westbury**

(1) *Veronica Wenefryde Nefertari [The Hon Mrs Innes, 25 Beaufort Close, London SW15 3TL]; *b* 15 July 1917; granted 1930 with her er bro rank of baron's dau/yr s; *m* 14 Jan 1941 *Lt-Col James Innes, Coldstream Gds, est s of Lt-Col James Archibald Innes, DSO, of Horringer Manor, Bury St Edmunds, and Inchgary, N Berwick, and has:

1a *James Richard [Lt-Col James Innes, Romanys, Lawbrook Lane, Peaslake, Guildford, Surrey]; *b* 13 Sept 1943; *educ* Eton and RMA Sandhurst; Lt-Col Coldstream Gds

2a *Peter David [Peter Innes Esq, Boon House, Lauder, Berwicks]; *b* 25 Aug 1952; *educ* Eton; Capt Coldstream Gds; *m* 1980 *Carolyn Ann Darley, dau of Julian Blackwell, of Osse Field, Appleton, Oxon, and has:

1b *James David; *b* 1982

1b *Sarah Clementine; *b* 1984

2b *Laura Mary; *b* 1987

1a *Elizabeth Mary [Mrs Edward Nicholl, Trewhitt Hall, Thropton, Northumberland NE65 7ET]; *b* 8 May 1947; *m* 1st 30 March 1967 (*divorce* 1972) James Keith Alan Rugge-Price and has issue (*see* RUGGE-PRICE, Bt); *m* 2nd 1973 *Edward Rice Nicholl, of Trewhitt Hall, and by him has:

2b *Katherine Sarah; *b* 1974

3b *Emily Mary; *b* 1977

WESTMEATH

Arms: Ermine two bars gules. **Crest:** A cockatrice, wings elevated and displayed vert, tail nowed, combed and wattled gules. **Supporters:** Two cockatrices, wings elevated vert. **Motto:** *Decrevi* ('I have resolved'). **Creation:** B. (I) 1451, E. (I) 4 Sept 1621.

THE 13TH EARL OF WESTMEATH and **Baron Delvin** (William Anthony Nugent) [The Rt Hon The Earl of Westmeath, Farthings, Rotton Row Hill, Bradfield, Berks RG7 6LL]; *b* 21 Nov 1928; *s* f 1971; *educ* Marlborough and RMC Sandhurst; Capt RA (ret 1961); staff St Andrew's Sch Pangbourne 1961–88 (Sr Master 1980–88); *m* 31 July 1963 *Susanna Margaret, only dau of His Hon Judge (James Charles Beresford Whyte) Leonard, of Sutton Courtenay, Berks, and has:

1 +SEAN CHARLES WESTON (does not use courtesy title); *b* 16 Feb 1965; *educ* Ampleforth

2 +Patrick Mark Leonard; *b* 6 April 1966; *educ* Douai

Lineage: FULKE de BELLESME; feudal Ld of Nogent le Rotrou, Normandy; had:

GILBERT de NUGENT; feudal Ld of Nogent; had a 2nd s:

FULKE de NUGENT; had:

HUGH de NUGENT; went to Ireland with Hugh de Lacy and Gilbert and Richard de Nugent, his cousins, 1st and 2nd feudal Barons of Delvin, and was granted lands at Bracklyn, Co Westmeath; *m* Theffania — and *d* 1213, leaving:

GILBERT de NUGENT, of Bracklyn; a minor 1215; had:

HUGH de NUGENT, of Bracklyn and Platyn; had:

NICHOLAS de NUGENT, of Bracklyn; living 1325; had:

RICHARD de NUGENT, of Bracklyn; *m* Juliana, dau and eventual heiress of Nicholas Drake, of Albrytestown, Co Meath, and had:

NICHOLAS NUGENT, of Bracklyn; living 1391; had:

1 Thomas, of Bracklyn; living 1454; had:

(1) Lavalin, of Bracklyn; living 1517; *m* Elizabeth Plunket (*d* 3 Jan 1528/9) and had:

1a Christopher; *dvp*, leaving:

1b Thomas, of Bracklyn; *m* Alicia, dau of George Barnewall, of Arrodstown, and *d* 20 Dec 1553, leaving:

1c Edward, of Bracklyn; *m* Ismay Barnewall and *d* 1599, leaving:

1d Thomas: had:

1e Edward, of Bracklyn; *m* Frances Nugent and had:

1f Gilbert, of Bracklyn; *m* Rose, dau of James Walsh, of Shenganagh, and had:

1g Edward, of Bracklyn; *m* Mary Green and had:

1h Edward; ancestor of the Princes and Counts Nugent of Austria

2 William (Sir); Sheriff Co Meath 1401; ktd by late Nov 1401, Justice of Assize Feb 1411/2; *m* Katharine (*d c* 1406), dau of John FitzJohn, feudal Baron of Delvin, thereby acquiring the Manor of Delvin by 27 Sept 1385, and *d* by 1415, leaving:

(1) RICHARD, **1st Baron**

(2) William; *m* Joane, dau and heiress of Richard Talbot, thus acquiring Moyrath; ancestor of the NUGENTs of Moyrath (*cr* Bts 1621), NUGENTs of Dardistown, the NUGENTs of Culvin and the NUGENTs of Gillstown, Co Roscommon

The er s,

Sir RICHARD NUGENT, **1st Baron Delvin** (I), so *cr* 1451; feudal Baron of Delvin; Sheriff Co Meath 1428, Dep to Lt of Ireland 1448/9; *m* Julian/Katherine, dau and of Thomas Drake, of Carlanstown, Co Westmeath, and *d* 1475, having had, with two yr sons:

1 James; *m* Elizabeth (*m* 2nd Sir Thomas Dowdall; *m* 3rd Peter Travers, of Courtlough), dau and coheir of Sir Robert Holywode, of Artane and Holywood, Co Dublin, and *dvp* 1458, leaving:

(1) CHRISTOPHER, **2nd Baron**

(2) Robert, of Drumcree, Co Westmeath; *m* Anna Cusack and was ancestor of the NUGENTs of Drumcree and New Haggard, Co Meath

(3) Lavallin, of Dysert, Co Westmeath; *d* 10 March 1532/3; ancestor of the NUGENTs of Dysert, Farthingstown, Ballynacorr, Portaferry, etc

(4) Andrew, of Donore, Co Westmeath; *m* Mary, dau of James Tuite, and had:

1a Walter, of Donore; ancestor of the NUGENTs, Bts, of Donore (*qv*)

2a Andrew Og ('The Younger'), of Clonlost, Co Westmeath; *m* Anne, dau of George Darcy; his 2nd s:

1b Christopher, of Clonlost; *m* the dau of William fitz Laurence Nugent Multifarnha, and *d* 1 March 1613/4, leaving, with a yr s (Oliver):

1c James, of Clonlost; *m* Marion, dau of Redmond Petit, of Ballinderry, Co Westmeath, and *d* between 22 Oct 1625 and 10 Dec 1626; his er s:

1d Thomas, of Clonlost; had confirmation of his estate 1684/5; *m* Ismay, dau of Theobald Nugent, of New Haggard, and widow of Walter Pollard; his er s:

1e James, of Clonlost; living 1710; *m* Anne, dau of John Cook, of Moygallen, Co Westmeath, and had:

1f Thomas; *m* (settlement 20 Sept 1693) Mary, dau of Thomas Smyth, of Drumcree, Co Westmeath, and *dvp* between 5 May 1710 and 20 Feb 1712, leaving an er surv s:

1g James, of Clonlost; *m* (settlement 2 July 1719) Jane (*d* between 20 Jan 1756 and 9 Feb 1757), dau of John Cook, of Cooksborough, Co Westmeath, and *d* between 15 Aug 1746 and 11 Feb 1748, leaving, with another s (*d* young) and four yr daus (Anne; Jane; Cassandra; Martha, m 21 Oct 1762 Thomas Burrows):

1h John, of Clonlost; *m* (settlement 1 Oct 1753) Elizabeth Power, dau of Richard Trench (*see* CLANCARTY, E), and *d* between 1 Nov 1769 and 9 March 1770, leaving four sons and seven daus

2h James; Capt in the army; *dsp*

3h Nicholas; army offr, *ka sp*, seige of Havana

4h Walter, of Ballyburr, Co Kilkenny; *m* 29 Oct 1762 Mary, dau of John Smith, of Griffinstown, and *d* 1789, leaving a yr s:

1i John, of Merrion Sq, Dublin; *m* 27 Jan 1798 Mary (*d* 28 Dec 1831), dau of John Gregg, of Belfast, and *d* 17 Aug 1827, having had, with a yr s (Henry, *d* unm):

1j Walter Nugent, 1st Baron Nugent, so *cr* with descent to legitimate issue of either sex by Imperial Austrian letters patent 25 Aug 1859; *m* 1st 4 Dec 1830 Louisa Maria (*d* 19 June 1832), 2nd dau of Rev John Digby and sis and coheir of John William Digby, of Landenstown, Co Kildare, and had:

1k Louisa Maria Digby; *b* 7 June 1832; *d* 30 Oct 1922

1j (cont.) The 1st Baron *m* 2nd 24 Oct 1833 Georgina Elizabeth, dau and coheir of Sir Charles Jenkinson, 10th Bt (*qv*), and *d* 24 Oct 1864, having had, with other issue (*d* young or unm):

1k Reginald Boothby; *b* 3 Feb, *d* 24 Aug 1835

2k Walter Ruthven Nugent, 2nd Baron Nugent; *b* 31 May 1836; Offr in Austrian Serv, ADC to FM Prince Nugent; *d* 25 July 1907

4k ALBERT LLEWELLYN NUGENT, 3rd BARON NUGENT, which title was granted by roy licence 22 July 1908 right to bear for himself and the heirs male of his body in HM EDWARD VII's realms; *b* 8 Jan 1841; *educ* Charterhouse; served RN; *m* 7 April 1862 Elizabeth (*d* 11 March 1899), est dau of Theodore Baltazzi, of Constantinople, and *d* 2 Feb 1909, having had:

1l ALGERNON JOHN FITZROY NUGENT, 4th BARON NUGENT; *b* 5 Oct 1865; *educ* Winchester and Trin Coll Cambridge; ceased use of title 1915, being so authorised by roy warrant 1920; *m* 13 Aug 1895 Clara (*d* 20 April 1937), dau of Sir George Elliott Meyrick Tapps-Gervis-Meyrick, 3rd Bt (*qv*), and *d* 15 March 1922

2l George Frederick Edward; *b* 5 Feb 1867; Cdr RN; *d* unm 26 April 1901

3l Albert Beauchamp; *b* 12 Feb 1874; *educ* Winchester and Heidelberg U; Lt Intell Corps WW I; *m* 29 April 1914 Frances Every Douglas (*d* 1950), dau of Douglas Campbell, of Blythswood (*see* 1939 edn BLYTHSWOOD, B), and *d* 26 Feb 1938, leaving:

1m Guy Patrick Douglas John; *b* 1 July 1915; *educ* Stowe; *ka* Italy WW II 1944

2m David James Douglas; *b* 24 Nov 1917; *educ* Lancing; 2nd Lt Green Howards; *m* 1st 17 May 1958 (*divorce* 1960) C A Rosemary, only dau of William F Edwards; *m* 2nd 26 March 1968 Mary Louise (Maidie), JP (*d* 1975), dau of William Henry Wroth, of Devon, and widow of Howard Seys-Phillips; *m* 3rd 16 Jan 1979 Evelyn Diana (*d* 1996), widow of Sir Hector Lethbridge, 6th Bt (*qv*), and dau of Lt-Col Francis Arthur Gerard Noel (*see* GAINSBOROUGH, E), and *d* 1988

4l Frank Henry NUGENT later BURNELL-NUGENT (deed poll 1916), CB (1933), DSO (1916), OBE (1919); *b* 5 Sept 1880; *educ* Winchester and RMC Sandhurst; Brig-Gen Rifle Bde, served Boer War (wounded, medal), WW I (wounded, despatches), Iraq Rebellion 1920, Brig cmdg Tientsin area N China 1930–33; Hon MA Manchester 1914; *m* 25 Sept 1905 Ellen Mary (*d* 20 Aug 1941), only dau of Thomas Coke Burnell, of St

Cross Grange, Winchester, and *d* 12 March 1942, leaving:

1m Anthony Frank, DSC (1939); *b* 9 July 1906; Cdr RN WW II (despatches); *m* 11 June 1941 *Gian Mary, dau of R-Adml Charles Otway Alexander, of Wilford Rise, Woodbridge, and *d* 21 Aug 1976, leaving:

1n +Charles Anthony [Baron Nugent, 10 Radley Lodge, 25 Inner Park Rd, London SW19 6DG]; *b* 26 June 1942; *educ* Brickwall

2n +James Michael; *b* 20 Nov 1949; *educ* Stowe and Corpus Christi Coll Cambridge; Lt RN; *m* 18 Aug 1973 *Henrietta Mary, yst dau of Rt Rev Robert Wilmer Woods, KCMG, KCVO, and has:

1o +Anthony James; *b* 1980

2o +Rupert Michael; *b* 30 April 1982

3o +Thomas Alexander; *b* 1986

1o *Henrietta Marie; *b* 10 March 1978

1n *Mary [Mrs John Lloyd, Argent Manor, Stutton, Ipswich, Suffolk IP9 2SY]; *b* 25 March 1947; *m* 28 Oct 1967 *John Richard Conway Lloyd, only s of William Rhys Lloyd, and has:

1o *John Conway; *b* 16 May 1970

1o *Lucy Ellen; *b* 1972; *m* 22 Nov 1997 *Maj Crispin Alexander Lockhart, Blues and Royals, s of Lt-Col Brian Lockhart

2n *Sheila Jane; *b* 9 March 1951; *m* 1980 *Marino Gianella, of Florence, and has:

1o *Francesco; *b* 1981

1l Mary Helen Elizabeth; DGStJ; Kaiser-i-Hind Gold Medal; *m* 1 July 1886 Lord Carmichael, of Skirling (*d* 16 Jan 1926; *see* 1925 edn), and *dsp* 22 March 1947

2l Zoë Virginie; *m* 1st 14 June 1892 Claude Hume Campbell Guinness (*see* GUINNESS, Bt) and had issue; *m* 2nd 5 Sept 1922 3rd Baron Manners (*qv*) and *d* 28 Nov 1953

3l Florence Agnes Louisa; *m* 8 April 1896 Sir Michael Culme-Seymour, 4th Bt (*qv*), and *d* 17 Jan 1956, leaving issue

2k Ismania Catherine, VA; *b* 23 Sept 1838; Ldy Bedchamber to HM QUEEN VICTORIA; *m* 25 Feb 1862 3rd Baron Southampton (*qv*) and *d* 18 Aug 1918, leaving issue

3k Helen Georgina; *b* 10 July 1842; *m* 30 July 1873 Dacre Mervyn Archdall Hamilton (*d* 24 Dec 1899), of Corncassa, Co Monaghan, and had issue

1h Eliza Catherine; *m* Rev Arthur Reynell, Rector Churchtown, est s of Richard Reynell, of Killough, and had issue

3a Theobald; ancestor of the NUGENTs of Ballingelott

2 John, of Killagh, Co Westmeath; ancestor of the NUGENTs of Killagh

3 Edward; executed Dublin 1473; ancestor of the NUGENTs of Balreagh, Co Westmeath

RICHARD NUGENT's gs,

CHRISTOPHER NUGENT, **2nd Baron Delvin**; had Parly livery of his lands 1475; was presumably recognised as a peer of Parl in succession to his gf; *m* Anne, dau of 1st Viscount Gormanston (*qv*), and *d* 1478 of plague, leaving:

RICHARD NUGENT, **3rd Baron Delvin** (I); called to Parl 1486 and among 11 Irish peers summoned to Greenwich 1489; V-Dep Ireland 1527–28; *m* 1st Elizabeth/Isabel, dau of 8th Earl of Kildare (*see* LEINSTER, D); *m* 2nd Elizabeth St Lawrence, probably dau of 3rd Baron Howth (*see* 1909 edn HOWTH, E), and *d* 28 Feb 1537/8, having had:

1 Christopher (Sir); *m* Marion (*m* 2nd Sir Gerald FitzGerald, Kt Marshal of Ireland), dau of 3rd Baron Howth, and *dvp* 1531, leaving:

(1) RICHARD, **4th Baron**

(2) James; *d* 10 June 1603; ancestor of the NUGENTs of Coolambey, Co Longford

(3) Oliver, of Ballina; *m* Katherine, dau of 5th Baron Dunsany (*qv*), and was ancestor of the NUGENTs of Ballina and NUGENTs of Farrenconnell, Co Cavan, of whom the last male rep, Oliver St George Percy Nugent, of Farrenconnell, *d* 11 Feb 1929

(4) Gerald, of Tristernagh; *k* 1565

(5) Nicholas, of Kilmore, Co Dublin; Ch Justice Common Pleas Ireland; executed on very dubious charges of high treason 1582; ancestor of the NUGENTs of Robinstown, Co Westmeath

(1) Ismay; *m* Sir John Bellew, of Castletown, Co Louth, and Bellewstown, Co Meath

(2) Katherine; *m* 1st Robert Cusack, of Cushinstown, 2nd Baron of the Exchequer Ireland (s of Sir Thomas Cusack, Ld Chllr Ireland); *m* 2nd 6th Baron Trimlestown (*qv*)

(3) Elizabeth; *m* James Nugent, of Donore

(4) Margery/Marcella; *m* 1st (? If so, subsequently divorced) Philip O'Reilly, Commendatory Prior of Drumlane, Co Cavan, s of Mulmore O'Reilly, Ch of his name; *m* 2nd(?) Connla Mageoghagan, Ch of his name, and *d* after 1582

2 Thomas (Sir), of Carlanstown, Co Westmeath; *m* Katherine, dau of Sir George Fleming, of Stephenstown, 2nd s of 7th (Baron) Slane, and *d* after 1569, being ancestor of ROBERT NUGENT, 1st EARL NUGENT, so *cr* 21 July 1776 (*see* TEMPLE OF STOWE, E), and leaving, with other issue:

(1) Eleanor; *m* 1st John Plunket, s of 4th Baron Dunsany; *m* 2nd her (illegitimate) cousin Sir Gerald Fleming, of Ballylagan

3 William; Rector Trim and Ardnurgher, Commendatory Prior of Fore, till resigning it to HENRY VIII 1540; *d* just prior to June 1547, leaving an illegitimate dau

The 3rd BARON's gs,

RICHARD NUGENT, **4th Baron Delvin**; *b c* 1523; *m* Elizabeth, est dau of 3rd Viscount Gormanston (*qv*), and *d* 10 Dec 1559, leaving:

1 CHRISTOPHER, **5th Baron**

2 William, of Ross, Co Meath; rebelled against ELIZABETH I 1581, hence attainted but eventually pardoned and restored 1606; a poet in Irish and English who improbably has been suggested as the true author of the writings usually attributed to William Shakespeare; *m* Janet (*d* 1 Aug 1629), dau and heir of Walter Marward, last feudal Baron of Skreen, and *d* 30 June 1626, leaving issue

1 Mary; *m* 1st Sir Thomas Nugent, of Moyrath; *m* 2nd William Eustace, of Castlemartin, Co Kildare, and *d* 25 May 1588

The est s,

CHRISTOPHER NUGENT, **5th Baron Delvin**; of age by 22 Nov 1565; *educ* Clare Hall Cambridge; ktd 1565; imprisoned Tower London 1580–*c* 1585 for suspected disaffection; *m* 6 May 1575 Mary (*d* 1 Oct 1610), dau of 11th Earl of Kildare (*see* LEINSTER, D), and *d* a prisoner in Dublin Castle 26 Aug 1602, leaving, with other issue:

1 RICHARD, **1st Earl**

2 Christopher, of Corbetstown; *m* Anne, widow of Sir Ambrose Forth (*m* 3rd Valerian Wellesley; *see* WELLINGTON, D), and *dsp* 3 July 1626

3 William, of Killasonna, Co Longford; *m* Margaret Leigh and was ancestor of Count Nugent, of Killasonna

The 5th BARON's est s,

RICHARD NUGENT, **1st Earl of Westmeath** (I), so *cr* 4 Sept 1621; *b* 1583; ktd 1603; briefly imprisoned Dublin Castle late 1607 on suspicion of complicity in the rebellious activities of the Earl of Tyrconnell, but escaped over the walls on a rope said to have been 35 yards long; pardoned 1608 and granted large tracts of land 1611; led RC oppn in 1613 I Parl and after but refused to join 1641 Uprising, an event that probably exacerbated his already terminal illness; *m* by 1604 Jane (*d* on or after 24 Jan 1626/7), sis of 1st Earl of Fingall (see 1970 edn), and *d* shortly after May 1642 after being dragged from his coach nr Trim, Co Meath, and manhandled by insurgents during the 1641 Uprising, having had:

1 Christopher, *Lord Delvin*; *b* 1604; *m* Anne (*m* 2nd by 18 Jan 1626/7 14th Lord (Baron) Slane), est dau of 1st Earl of Antrim (*qv*) of the 1620 *cr*, and *dvp* 10 July 1625, leaving:

(1) RICHARD, **2nd Earl**

2 Francis; *dsp*

3 John, of Dromeng; ancestor of the Princes and Counts Nugent of Austria

4 Lawrence

5 Ignatius; Col in French Serv; *m* Jane, dau of 5th Baron Louth (*qv*), and *d* Feb 1671, leaving:

(1) Jane; *m* Daniel Dunne, of Brittas

(2) Mary; *m* Andrew Palles, of Mount Palles, Co Cavan, and had issue

The 1st EARL's gs,

RICHARD NUGENT, **2nd Earl of Westmeath**; *b* 1621–23; arrested late Dec 1641 while on his way back to Ireland from London on suspicion of complicity in 1641 Uprising and remanded in custody till midsummer 1642; cavalry cdr Ireland Civil War, as which captured by opposing forces at Battle of Dungan Hill 8 Aug 1647; joined Confederate Irish by midsummer 1646, Gen all forces in Leinster 1650–52; *m* by 1641 Mary (*d* 19 May 1672), dau of Sir Thomas Nugent, 1st Bt, of Moyrath, and widow of Christopher Plunkett, est s of 9th (Baron) Dunsany (*qv*), recovered little of his estates after the Restoration, and *d* just prior to 25 Feb 1683/4, having had, with other issue:

1 Christopher, *Lord Delvin*; *m c* 1665 Mary (*d* 28 March 1737), 2nd dau of Richard Butler, of Kilcash (*see* MOUNTGARRET, V), and *dvp* well before 1680, leaving, with three daus:

(1) RICHARD NUGENT, *de jure* 3rd EARL OF WESTMEATH, but apparently never assumed the title; Capuchin friar in France; *d* April 1714

(2) THOMAS NUGENT, **4th Earl of Westmeath**, assumed title in er bro's lifetime on grounds that as a professed religious the latter was civilly dead; *b* 1669; Col of Foot in JAMES II's Army in Ireland, hence outlawed 11 May 1691; cmded a cavalry regt during Siege of Limerick and benefited from articles of its capitulation, hence his outlawry reversed by late 1697; *m* 1684 Margaret (*d* 1700), only dau of 1st Baron Bellew (*qv*) of Duleek, and *dspms* 30 June 1752, having had:

1a Christopher, *Lord Delvin*; *d* unm at Bath 12 April 1752

2a John; *d* unm 21 July 1725:

1a Mary; *m* 22 Sept 1716, as his 1st w, 14th Lord (Baron) Athenry and had issue

2a Catherine; *m* Andrew Nugent, of Dysert, and had issue

(3) JOHN NUGENT, **5th Earl of Westmeath**; *b* 1671; allegedly served in JAMES II's forces at Battle of Boyne and Siege Limerick, certainly later in French Serv as Lt King's/Sheldon's Horse, campaigning Flanders, Supernumerary Capt Sheldon's New Regt of Horse Feb 1697/8, later known as Nugent's Horse or FitzJames's Horse, as which campaigned Italy 1701–02 and in Flanders again at Battles of Ramillies 1706, Oudenarde 1708, Malplaquet 1709 and Denain 1712, also Sieges of Douai and Quesnoy 1712, then in Germany at Sieges of Landau and Freiburg, Brevet Maj Jan 1719/20 and Mestre-de-Camp de Cavalerie Feb 1720/1, campaigning again in Germany 1733–35, Lt-Col 1736, Brevet Brig Jan 1739/40, campaigned Germany again and Bohemian borders War Austrian Succession early 1740s, Maréchal-de-Camp 1744, ret 1748; Equerry of Stables to titular James III 1707; *m* 7 Jan 1710/1 Marguerite Jeanne (*d* 11 Feb 1776), dau of Count Charles Molza, of Modena, Gentlman Usher to MARY OF MODENA (w of JAMES II), and *d* 3 July 1754, leaving, with four other sons (James; John Christopher; Richard; Edward, all *d* young) and two daus (Marie Charlotte, *d* young; Françoise Christine):

1a THOMAS NUGENT, **6th Earl of Westmeath**, KP (1783), PC (I 1758–71 and 1774 on); *bapt* 18 April 1714; in French Serv when young but returned to Ireland and conformed to the C of I, custos rotulorum Co Westmeath

1765–88; *m* 1st *c* 1741 Mary, only dau and heiress of Walter Durand Stapleton, of Hispaniola, and had:

1b Richard, *Lord Delvin*; *b* 1742; Cornet 1st Horse 1758, MP (I Parl) Fore 1759–60; *dvp* unm 6 Aug 1761 of wounds sustained in a duel on Marlborough Green

1a (cont.) The **6th Earl** *m* 2nd 7 Aug 1756 Catherine (*d* 7 Aug 1772), dau and coheir of Henry White, of Pitchfordstown Co Kildare, and *d* 7 Sept 1792, leaving by her, with an er s (*d* young):

2b GEORGE FREDERICK NUGENT, **7th Earl of Westmeath**, PC (I 1793); *b* 18 Nov 1760; MP (I Parl) Fore 1780–92, Sec Order St Patrick 1783–92, Auditor For Accounts and Imprests Ireland 1784–98, custos rotulorum Co Westmeath 1788–1814, rep I peer 1801–14, Clerk of Crown and Hanaper 1807–14; *m* 1st 27 April 1784 (*divorce* by Act of Parl Oct 1796) Mary Anne, est dau of Maj James St John Jefferyes, of Blarney Castle, Co Cork (*see* COLTHURST, Bt), and had:

1c GEORGE THOMAS JOHN NUGENT, **8th Earl of Westmeath** and 1st and last MARQUESS OF WESTMEATH (I), so *cr* 12 Jan 1822; *b* 17 July 1785; *educ* Eton and Rugby; Ensign Coldstream Gds 1800 (served Egyptian campaign 1801), Capt 3rd E Kent Regt of Foot 1803, Lt and Capt Coldstream Gds 1803–04, then exchanging into 88th Foot, Commr Barracks Ireland 1813–15, Ld Lt Co Westmeath 1831–71, rep I peer 1831–71, Col Co Westmeath Militia; *m* 1st 29 May 1812 (*divorce* 1827) Emily Anne Bennet Elizabeth (*d* 21 Jan 1858), 2nd dau of 1st Marquess of Salisbury (*qv*); *m* 2nd 18 Feb 1858 (*divorced* 1862) Maria Jarvis; *m* 3rd 12 July 1864 Elizabeth Charlotte (*dsp* 18 Sept 1882), 2nd dau of David Verner (and n of Col Sir William Verner, 1st Bt, KCH, MP; *see* 1970 edn), and *dspms* 5 May 1871, when the Marquessate expired, leaving an only surv child by his 1st w:

1d Rosa Emily Mary Anne; *b* May 1814; *m* 28 April 1840 1st Baron Greville of Clonyn (*see* WARWICK, BROOKE and, E) and *d* 17 Jan 1883, leaving issue

2b (cont.) The **7th Earl** *m* 2nd 2 Feb 1797 Elizabeth Emily (*d* 18 March 1841), dau of 1st Marquess of Drogheda (*see* DROGHEDA, E), and *d* 30 Dec 1814, leaving by her:

2c Robert Seymour; *b* 2 June 1805; *dsp*

3c Thomas Hugh; *b* 3 Sept 1807; *m* 26 Sept 1843 Mary Anne Bush and *dsp* 3 Feb 1849

1c Elizabeth Emily; *m* 15 Sept 1820 Hon Lionel Charles Dawson, 4th s of 1st Earl of Portarlington (*qv*), and *d* 6 Sept 1863, leaving issue

2c Catherine Anne; *b* 10 May 1801; *m* 1823 Francis Bruen, JP, DL, MP (*d* 15 Dec 1867), 2nd s of Col Henry Bruen, of Oak Park, Co Carlow, and *d* 16 Oct 1864

3c Mary Frances; *m* 4 May 1837 Hon James Hope-Wallace and *d* 23 May 1904, leaving issue (*see* LINLITHGOW, M)

1b Catherine; *m* 4 July 1784 Capt Hon John Rodney, 3rd s of 1st Baron Rodney (*qv*), and *d* 26 Feb 1794, leaving issue

2 THOMAS NUGENT, 1st BARON NUGENT OF RIVERSTON, Co Westmeath (I), so *cr* 3 April 1689 by JAMES II after he had been declared by the English Parl to have vacated the throne of that Kingdom (*i.e.*, after 11 Dec 1688) but before his defeat at the Battle of the Boyne in Ireland and during a period when he both reigned and ruled in the latter Kingdom; moreover the title was acknowledged by 1st Earl of Athlone of the March 1691/2 *cr* (*see* 1844 edn), C-in-C WILLIAM III's Forces Ireland, in a document of 5 Oct 1691 and as late as an order of 5 July 1701 by the Commrs of Irish forfeitures, of Pallas, Co Galway, PC (1686–90), KC (1685); 3rd Puisne Judge King's Bench Ireland 1686, Ld Ch Justice Ireland 1687, Commr Treasury Ireland 1689; initially outlawed as Jacobite but benefited from terms of capitulation of Limerick and got back his landed property; *m c* Sept 1680 Marianna (*d* 16 Sept 1735), dau of 2nd Viscount Barnewall of Kingsland, and *d* 2 April 1715, leaving:

(1) Hyacinth Richard, self-styled 2nd Baron Nugent of Riverston despite his having been outlawed for high treason 1694, when less than 10 years old; conformed to C of I 1703, Cornet Lord Peterborough's Dragoons serving Spain; recovered his estate Feb 1736/7 by Act of Parl 1728; *m* 1703 Susanna Catharina (*d* 30 March 1763), sis of 1st Earl of Tyrone (*see* WATERFORD, M), and *dsp* 6 March 1737/8

(2) William, self-styled 3rd Baron Nugent of Riverston, of Pallas; conformed to C of I by late Jan 1738/9; *m* March 1719 Bridget (*d* 14 April 1768), dau of Charles Daly, of Cloghan, King's Co, and widow of Patrick Kirwan, and *d* 11 May 1756, leaving a 3rd but only surv s:

1a Anthony, self-styled 4th Baron Nugent of Riverston, of Pallas; *b* 28 Aug 1730; *m* 25 June 1772 Olivia, dau of Arthur French, of Tyrone Ho, Co Galway, and *d* Sept 1814, having had issue:

1b William Thomas, self-styled 5th Baron Nugent of Riverston (claimed title 1839 but the Ho Lds Privileges Ctee adjourned 30 July 1839 *sine die* and no further steps were taken), of Pallas; *b* 29 Sept 1773; *m* 1799 Mary Catherine (*d* 1855), only dau of Michael Bellew (*see* GRATTAN-BELLEW, Bt), and *d* 6 Sept 1851, having had:

1c ANTHONY FRANCIS, **9th Earl**

2c Michael William Bellew, of Earl's Park, Co Galway; *b* 28 Aug 1808; *m* 29 Dec 1838 Emily (*d* 5 June 1856), only dau of Charles Morrall, of Plâs Yolyn, Salop

1c Jane Olivia; *m* 24 Jan 1814 Lt-Col James FitzGerald Kenney, JP (*d* 29 Feb 1852), of Kilclogher, Co Galway, and *d* 27 Dec 1842, leaving issue

2b Arthur Anthony, of Cranna, Co Galway; *b* 29 Aug 1774; *m* 1801 Maria (*d* 5 Aug 1844), dau of Richard Gore, of Cloghatanna, and *d* 14 April 1858, having had, with four daus:

1c Arthur, of Cranna, JP; *b* 27 Nov 1805; *m* 16 Feb 1847 Ella, only dau of Thomas Lalor Cooke, of Parsonstown, and *d* 5 June 1885, having had:

1d Arthur St George; *b* 20 April 1848; *d* 20 Oct 1854

2d William Arthur Antisel; *b* 8 May 1859; *d* 10 Nov 1884

3d Richard Charles Antisel; *b* 3 May 1861; *d* 13 July 1874

1d Ella Rosa; *b* 10 April 1851

2d Olivia Lucinda; *b* 17 Dec 1853; *m* 13 Jan 1885 Sir Charles Haughton Rafter, KBE (*d* 23 Aug 1935), Ch Constable Birmingham, and *d* 10 Feb 1914, leaving issue

2c Anthony; *b* 9 April 1809; *d* 7 March 1876

3c Charles; *b* 7 Sept 1813; *m* 1838 Frances, est dau of John Burke, of Clareville, Co Galway, and *d* 29 Aug 1839, leaving a dau (*d* young)

1b Olivia Emilia; *m* 27 Oct 1794 Christopher Dillon Bellew and *d* Sept 1856, leaving issue (*see* GRATTAN-BELLEW, Bt)

The self-style 5th BARON NUGENT OF RIVERSTON's est s,

ANTHONY FRANCIS NUGENT, **9th Earl of Westmeath**; *b* 1 Nov 1805; *educ* Trin Coll Dublin; *m* 3 Oct 1829 Anne Catherine (*d* 27 Sept 1871), er dau and coheir of Malachy Daly, of Raford, Co Galway (*see* BURKE, Bt), and *d* 12 May 1879, having had:

1 WILLIAM ST GEORGE, **10th Earl**

2 Malachy Daly; Capt 67th Regt; *das* unm China 20 Oct 1862 in Taiping War

3 Charles Anthony, of Flower Hill, Tynagh, Co Galway, JP; *b* 10 March 1836; *m* 15 June 1875 Gertrude (*d* 28 June 1921), est dau of Denis O'Conor, of Mount Druid, Co Roscommon, and *dsp* 8 Nov 1906

4 Richard Anthony, JP Co Galway; *b* 12 Nov 1842; *m* 20 Dec 1877 Theresa Henrietta (*d* 28 April 1935), er dau of Richard Gradwell, JP, of Dowth Hall, Co Meath, and *d* 19 Jan 1912, having had, with a dau (*d* unm):

(1) Anthony Charles St George; *b* 15 Dec 1882; *d* 20 Oct 1891

(2) Richard Francis Robert; *b* 3 Oct 1884; Lt Scots Gds (SR); *ka* 18 Dec 1914

(3) Hugh Fulke George Riverston; *b* 21 Oct 1897; *d* March 1901

(1) Mary Theresa; *b* 27 Sept 1880; *m* 30 April 1925 Capt Michel Popoff (*d* 14 Feb 1984), 8th Russian Hus, s of Serge Popoff, Cncllr of State, Odessa, and *d* 26 March 1973

(2) Anne Christian; *m* 14 Feb 1906 Capt Charles Edmund Arden Law Rumbold and *d* 3 April 1928, leaving issue (*see* RUMBOLD, Bt)

1 Julia Catherine Anne; *b* 3 June 1830; *m* 20 July 1858 3rd Marquess of Sligo (*qv*) and *d* 25 June 1859, leaving issue

2 Mary Frances; *b* 3 Oct 1831; *m* 21 Feb 1857 Sir Thomas John Burke, 3rd Bt (*qv*), and *d* 1 Sept 1892, leaving issue

3 Olivia Jane; *b* 20 March 1838; *m* 1 March 1859 Patrick Joseph Mahon Power, DL (*d* 18 Feb 1913), of Faithlegg, Co Waterford, and *d* 21 Jan 1903, leaving issue

4 Anne Elizabeth Charlotte; *b* 5 Oct 1839; *m* 30 April 1864 Col John Archer Daly, JP, DL (*d* 13 June 1917), of Raford and Furbough, Co Galway, and *d* 1 Dec 1906, having had issue

The 9TH EARL's est s,

WILLIAM ST GEORGE NUGENT, **10th Earl of Westmeath**; *b* 28 Nov 1832; *educ* Oscott; Capt 9th Foot Crimean War (Br, Turkish and Sardinian medals); High Sheriff Co Galway 1875; *m* 24 July 1866 his cousin Emily Margaret (*d* 7 July 1906), dau of Andrew William Blake, JP, DL of Furbough, Co Galway, and *d* 31 May 1883, having had, with three other daus (*d* in infancy or unm):

1 ANTHONY FRANCIS NUGENT, **11th Earl of Westmeath**, PC (I 1902), JP, DL Co Galway; *b* 11 Jan 1870; *educ* Oratory Sch and Ch Ch Oxford; Hon Attaché Washington 1895–97, A/Sec to Roy Commn to inquire into French Treaty Rights in Newfoundland 1898, Assist Priv Sec to Sec State Colonies 1898–1901, rep I peer 1901–33, Hon LLD and memb Senate of Roy U of Ireland and *dsp* 12 Dec 1933

2 William Andrew; *b* 11 March 1876; Capt 15th Hus WW I (despatches); *m* 25 June 1913 Kathleen (*m* 2nd 14 Feb 1917 Capt Gerald McKay, MC, and *d* 13 Nov 1955), er dau of John Jacob STEIN later STONER, and *das* 29 May 1915, having had a dau (*d* an infant)

3 GILBERT CHARLES, **12th Earl**

1 Emily Theresa; *m* 4 Oct 1906 Brig-Gen Gardiner Humphreys, CB, CMG, DSO, RA (*d* 6 Feb 1942), and *d* 23 Sept 1935, leaving issue

The 11th EARL's bro,

GILBERT CHARLES NUGENT, **12th Earl of Westmeath**; *b* 9 May 1880; Maj RA WW I (wounded twice, despatches), CD WW II; *m* 20 Nov 1915 Doris (*d* 9 April 1968), 2nd dau of Charles Imlach, of Liverpool, and *d* 20 Nov 1971, leaving:

1 WILLIAM ANTHONY NUGENT, **13th and present Earl of Westmeath**

1 *Pamela Joan [The Lady Pamela Barbary, Briar Rose Cottage, 17 Landeryon Gdns, Penzance, Cornwall]; *b* 31 Jan 1921; Section Offr WAAF WW II; *m* 23 Sept 1950 Lt-Col Peter John Barbary, OBE, GM, TD, DL, FRIBA (*d* 20 June 1969), est s of Brig John Ewart Trounce Barbary, CBE, TD, DL, ADC, of Gwennap, Cornwall, and has:

(1) *Michael John Nugent; *b* 24 June 1951; *educ* King's Coll Taunton

(1) *Joanna Clare Nugent; *b* 16 March 1955

WESTMINSTER

Arms: Quarterly, 1st and 4th, azure a portcullis with chains pendant or; on a chief of the last, between the united roses of York and Lancaster proper, a pallet of the first charged with a cross flory between five martlets also or, being the arms of the City of Westminster, granted as a coat of augmentation; 2nd and 3rd, azure a garb or (for GROSVENOR). **Crest:** A talbot statant or. **Supporters:** On each side a talbot regardant or, gorged with a plain collar azure. **Motto:** *Virtus non stemma* ('Virtue not pedigree'). The Sir Robert Grosvenor who served in France under the Black Prince and in Scotland later in the 14th century bore arms of azure a bend or. In 1385 his right to bear these was challenged by Sir Richard Scrope, 1st Lord (Baron) Scrope (of Bolton); the matter was referred to the Court of Chivalry presided over by the Constable of England, the Duke of Gloucester, who in 1389 decided in Lord Scrope's favour but allowed Sir Robert Grosvenor to bear the arms differenced with a bordure argent. Sir Robert appealed to RICHARD II, who in 1390 not only confirmed Lord Scrope's right to the arms but also disallowed the Constable's grant to Grosvenor of a differenced version of the arms of Scrope. Sir Robert thereupon assumed the arms azure a garb or, which his descendants have ever since borne. The sobriquet 'Bendor' of the **2nd Duke** was therefore something of a misnomer. **Creations:** Bt. (E) 23 Feb 1621/2, B. (GB) 8 April 1761, V. and E. (GB) 5 July 1784, M. (UK) 13 Sept 1831, D. (UK) 27 Feb 1874.

THE 6TH DUKE OF WESTMINSTER, **Marquess of Westminster, Earl Grosvenor, Viscount Belgrave, Baron Grosvenor of Eaton**, Co Chester, and a **Baronet** (Sir Gerald Cavendish Grosvenor, Bt, OBE (1995), TD (1994) DL (Cheshire 1982) [His Grace The Duke of Westminster OBE TD DL, Eaton Hall, Eaton, Cheshire CH4 9EJ]; *b* 22 Dec 1951; *s f* 1979; *educ* Harrow and Sunningdale Sch; Lt-Col and OC Queen's Own Yeo (TAVR) 1992; dir: Int Students' Tst 1976–93, Claridge's 1981–93, Grosvenor Estate Hldgs 1989–, Marcher Sound Ltd 1982–, Westminster Christmas Appeal Trust Ltd 1989–, Sutton Ridge Pty Ltd, N W Business Leadership Team Ltd 1990–, BITC 1991–, Manchester Olympic Games Co-ord Ctee Ltd 1991–; Sun Alliance 1996–, Govr: Roy Ag Soc England, Chester Teacher Training Coll 1979–; Pro-Chllr U of Keele 1986–93, Chllr Manchester Metropolitan U 1993–; Pres: London Tourist Bd 1983–, N W Industrialists' Cncl 1979–93, Chester City C Assoc 1977–93, RNIB 1986–, The Spastics Soc 1985–, Arthritis Care 1987–, Game Conservancy, London Fedn of Boys' Clubs, Abbeyfield Soc 1989–, Nat Kidney Research Fund, BLESMA, Youth Clubs UK, BASC, and Drug and Alcohol Fndn; V-Pres: Cheshire Ag Soc, Kings Sch Chester, incorporated Liverpool Sch of Tropical Medicine 1980–; Tstee: Civic Tst 1983–, TSB Fndn for England and Wales, Grosvenor Estate, Prince's Youth Business Tst, Westminster Abbey Tst, Westminster Fndn, Westminster Housing Tst; ctee memb: Business in the Community, Nat Army Museum, Rural Target Team; Freeman: Cities Chester 1971 and London 1981; KStJ 1991; *m* 7 Oct 1978 *Natalia Ayesha, yst dau of Lt Col Harold Pedro Joseph Phillips, FRGS (*see* 1970 edn WERNHER, Bt), of Checkendon Court, Oxon, and has:

1 +HUGH RICHARD LOUIS, *Earl Grosvenor*; *b* 29 Jan 1991

1 *Tamara Katherine; *b* 1979

2 *Edwina Louise; *b* 1981

3 *Viola Georgina; *b* 1992

Other creations: A titular Earldom of Westminster was conferred on 12 Aug 1759 on Alexander Murray (*see* ELIBANK, L), a notorious Jacobite, by the Old Pretender, James III. James was apparently a little hesitant about creating a title which had so many associations with the location of the court and initially issued a blank warrant in case the august nomenclature of the proposed designation should overwhelm the grantee.

Lineage: ROBERT le GROSVENOR, of Budworth, Cheshire, which he was granted, probably some time in the 1170s, by Hugh of Kevelioc, 3rd Earl of Chester of the 1120 *cr*; *m* Alice (*m* 2nd William de Stretton) and had, with another s (Robert):

RANDLE le GROSVENOR, of Budworth, *d* by 1232, leaving:

RICHARD le GROSVENOR, of Hulme, Cheshire; living 1234–69; had:

ROBERT le GROSVENOR, of Hulme; High Sheriff Cheshire 1284–87; *m* Margery — and was *bur* 1293, leaving:

ROBERT le GROSVENOR; of age by 1305, when he did homage for his Manor of Lostoke (later Allostock) to the Abbot of Vale Royal; High Sheriff Cheshire 1307–12, served Scottish Wars *temp* EDWARD II; *m* Margery — and *d* 1328, leaving:

ROBERT le GROSVENOR, of Rudheath, Cheshire, later of Hulme; did homage for his lands 1328; *m* by 1323 Emma (living 1366), dau and coheir of William de Modburlegh, and *d* by 1342, leaving, with a yr s (Robert):

RALPH le GROSVENOR, of Hulme; *m* Joan — and *d* by 1356, leaving:

Sir ROBERT le GROSVENOR, of Hulme; did homage for his lands 1373, High Sheriff Cheshire 1389 and 1394; served France under the Black Prince and in Scotland 1385; *m* 1st Margaret (*dsp* June 1370), dau of Sir John Danyell or Danyers; *m* 2nd Joan, dau and heiress of Robert de Pulford and widow of Thomas Belgrave, and *d* 22 April 1396, leaving by her:

Sir THOMAS GROSVENOR, of Hulme; living 1423; *m* Katherine (*m* 2nd Sir Thomas Roch), dau and heiress of Sir William Fesant, and had, with an er s (Robert; *dspm*):

RAUFE le GROSVENOR; living 1447; *m* Joan, only dau and heir of John Eton, of Eton (later Eaton), Cheshire, and had, with two other sons:

ROBERT GROSVENOR, of Eaton; *m* Johan, dau of Thomas Fitton, of Gawsworth, Cheshire, and *dvp*, leaving:

ROBERT GROSVENOR; *m* Catherine, dau of Sir William Norris, of Speke, Lancs, and had, with other issue, including an er s (Thomas, *m* Elizabeth, dau of Sir Hugh Calverley, of Calverley, and *dsp*):

RICHARD GROSVENOR, of Eaton; *m* 1509 Catherine, 3rd dau and coheir of Richard Cotton, of Ridware, Hampstall, Staffs, and *d* 1542, having had, with three yr sons (Richard, *m* Elizabeth, Lady Puleston, dau of Piers Puleston, of Hatton, and had issue; John, *dsp*; Anthony, *m* Uriel, dau of Sir Roger Puleston, and had a dau (Amy, *m* Edward Bellott, of Moreton)) and 10 daus:

Sir THOMAS GROSVENOR, of Eaton; *m* 1529 Maud (*m* 2nd Robert Fletcher, of Ince), dau of Sir William Poole, of Poole, Cheshire, and *d* 1549, having had, with a yr s (Richard, *d* unm) and three daus (Elizabeth, *m* Richard Masterson, of Nantwich; Catherine, *m* 1st Richard Hunt, *m* 2nd Richard Shawcross; Grace, *m* John Massie, of Codington):

THOMAS GROSVENOR, of Eaton; *m* Anne, dau of Roger Bradshaigh, of Haigh, Lancs, and *d* 1579, leaving, with three daus:

RICHARD GROSVENOR, of Eaton; High Sheriff Cheshire 1602; *m* Christian, dau of Sir Richard Brooke, of Norton, Cheshire, and *d* 18 Sept 1619, leaving, with six daus (Anne, *m* John Massie Jnr, of Godington; Christian, *m* Peter Danyel, of Tabley; Frances, *m* Samuel Bisphan, MD; Catharine, *m* 1st Thomas Ravenscroft and had issue (*see* GREY EGERTON, Bt), *m* 2nd Thomas Glynne; Eleanor, *m* Arthur Chambre, of Petton; Margaret, *m* 1st Henry Brereton, *m* 2nd Hugh Wilbraham):

Sir Richard Grosvenor, 1st Bt (E), so *cr* 23 Feb 1621/2; *b* 9 Jan 1584/5; BA Oxon, ktd, Cheshire: MP 1621–29, High Sheriff 1623, also Denbighs 1624; *m* 1st Lettice (*bur* 20 Jan 1611), 2nd dau of Sir Hugh Cholmondeley (*see* CHOLMONDELEY, M); *m* 2nd 1614 Elizabeth (*bur* 26 June 1621), dau of Sir Thomas Wilbraham, of Woodhey; *m* 3rd Elizabeth (*d* 12 March 1627/8), dau of Sir Peter Warburton and widow of Sir Thomas Stanley, of Alderley (*see* STANLEY OF ALDERLEY, SHEFFIELD and, B), and *d* 14 Sept 1645, having by his 1st w had, with three daus (Christian, *m* Sir Francis Gamul; the other two *d* unm):

Sir Richard Grosvenor, 2nd Bt; High Sheriff Cheshire 1644, royalist Civil War, estates sequestrated; *m* 1628 Sydney, dau of Sir Roger Mostyn (*see* MOSTYN, B), and *d* 31 Jan 1664, having had, with four daus (*d* unm bar the yst, Sydney, who *m* 1st Thomas Hesketh (*see* HESKETH, B), *m* 2nd Col Spencer) and four yr sons (*d* unm):

ROGER GROSVENOR; royalist; one of 13 Cheshire gentlemen nominated to be Kts of the Royal Oak 1660; *m* 1654 Christian, dau of Sir Thomas Myddelton, of Chirk Castle, and *dvp* 22 Aug 1661, leaving, with three yr sons (Robert, *d* young; John, High Sheriff Merioneths, *m* twice, *dsp* 1691; Roger, *d* young) and a dau (Sydney):

Sir Thomas Grosvenor, 3rd Bt; MP Chester 1679–1700, Mayor Chester 1685; *m* 8 Oct 1677 Mary (*d* 12 Jan 1730), only dau and heiress of Alexander Davis, of Ebury, Middx, thus acquiring the lucrative London property centred on what is now Mayfair and Belgravia, and was *bur* 2 July 1700, having had, with two other sons and two other daus:

1 **Sir Richard Grosvenor, 4th Bt**; MP Chester 1715–32, Mayor Chester 1715; as holder of the Manor of Wymondeley, Herts, was Grand Cup-Bearer Coronation of GEORGE II; *m* 1st 1708 Jane (*bur* 6 Feb 1719), dau of Sir Edward Wyndham, 1st Bt, of Orchard Wyndham, Somerset; *m* 2nd 1724 Diana (*d* 18 Feb 1729/30), only dau of Sir George Warburton, 3rd Bt, of Arley, Cheshire, and *dsps* 13 July 1732

2 **Sir Thomas Grosvenor, 5th Bt**; *b* 7 Dec 1693; MP Chester 1727–33; *d* unm 31 Jan 1733

3 ROBERT (Sir), **6th Bt**

1 Anne; *m* 26 May 1730 Hon William Leveson Gower and had issue (*see* SUTHERLAND, D)

The 5th Bt's yr bro,

Sir Robert Grosvenor, 6th Bt; *b* 7 May 1695; MP Chester 1733–55; *m* 21 July 1730 Jane (*bur* 25 May 1791), only surv child and heiress of Thomas Warre, of Shepton Beauchamp and Swell Court, Somerset, and *d* 1 Aug 1755, having had, with two other daus:

1 RICHARD, **1st Earl**

2 Thomas, of Swell Court; *m* 21 Sept 1758 Deborah, dau and coheiress of Stephen Skynner, of Hoe Street, Walthamstow, and had, with two daus (*d* unm):

(1) Richard GROSVENOR later ERLE-DRAX-GROSVENOR (added with arms on marriage); *m* 11 March 1788 Sarah Frances (*d* 15 June 1822), dau and heir of Edward Drax, of Charborough Park, Dorset, and *d* 8 Feb 1819, leaving:

1a Richard Edward, of Charborough; *d* unm 13 Aug 1828

1a Jane Frances; *m* 1 May 1827 John Samuel Wanley SAWBRIDGE later SAWBRIDGE-ERLE-DRAX (roy licence 13 Aug 1828), of Olantigh, Wye, Kent, who subsequently inherited Charborough

(2) Thomas; *b* 1764; FM, Col 65th Regt; *m* 1st 1797 Elizabeth, dau of Sir Gilbert Heathcote, 3rd Bt, of London (*qv*); *m* 2nd 1831 Anne, dau of George Wilbraham, of Delamere, Cheshire, and *dsp* 20 Jan 1851

(3) Robert; *b* 7 June 1767; MA, Fell All Souls Oxford; *d* 17 Dec 1842

1 Dorothy; *m* 6 Feb 1766 1st Viscount Curzon of Penn and *d* 25 Feb 1774, leaving issue (*see* HOWE, E)

The 6th Bt's er s,

Sir Richard Grosvenor, 7th Bt, and **1st Earl Grosvenor**, so *cr* 5 July 1784, as also VISCOUNT BELGRAVE and earlier 8 April 1761 BARON GROSVENOR OF EATON, Co Chester (all GB); *b* 18 June 1731; MP (Whig) Chester 1754–61; *m* 19 July 1764 Henrietta (*m* 2nd 15 Sept 1802 George PORTER later HOCHEPIED, Baron de Hochepied in the Kingdom of Hungary, and *d* 2 Jan 1828), dau of Henry Vernon, of Hilton Park, Staffs, and *d* 5 Aug 1802, leaving:

ROBERT GROSVENOR, **1st Marquess of Westminster**, so *cr* 13 Sept 1831 (GB), KG (1841), PC (1793); *b* 22 March 1767; *educ* Westminster, Harrow and Trin Coll Cambridge (MA); MP (Tory) E Looe 1788–90, Chester 1790–1802, a Ld Admlty 1789–91, Commr Indian Affrs 1793–1801, Ld Lt Flints 1798–1845; Col Flints Militia 1798, FRS; *m* 28 April 1794 Eleanor (*d* 29 Nov 1846), only dau of 1st Earl of Wilton (*qv*), and *d* 17 Feb 1845, having had:

1 RICHARD, **2nd Marquess**

2 THOMAS GROSVENOR later EGERTON, *s* maternal gf as 2nd EARL OF WILTON (*qv*)

3 ROBERT GROSVENOR, *cr* BARON EBURY (*qv*)

The est s,

Sir RICHARD GROSVENOR, **2nd Marquess of Westminster**, KG (1857), PC (1850); *b* 27 Jan 1795; *educ* Westminster and Ch Ch Oxford (MA); MP (Lib) Chester 1818–30, Cheshire 1830–34, S Cheshire 1832–35, Maj Cmdg Flints Yeo 1831, Ld Lt and custos rotulorum Cheshire 1845–67, Ld Steward Household 1850–52; *m* 16 Sept 1819 Elizabeth Mary (*d* 11 Nov 1891), 2nd dau of 1st Duke of Sutherland (*qv*), and *d* 31 Oct 1869, having had, with another s (*d* an infant) and dau (*d* unm):

1 HUGH LUPUS, **1st Duke**

2 Gilbert Norman; *b* 6 Jan 1833; RN; *d* 20 March 1854

3 RICHARD De AQUILA GROSVENOR, 1st BARON STALBRIDGE, of Stalbridge, Co Dorset (UK), so *cr* 22 March 1886, PC, JP (Dorset and Flints); *b* 28 Jan 1837; MA Cantab; MP Flintshire 1861–86, V-Chamberlain Household 1872–74, Patronage Sec Treasury 1880–85, Hon Col Queen's Own Dorset Yeo Cav, chm LNWR 1891–1911, FRGS; *m* 1st 5 Nov 1874 Hon Beatrice Charlotte Elizabeth Vesey (*d* 15 Jan 1876), yst dau of 3rd Viscount de Vesci (*qv*), and had:

(1) Elizabeth Emma Beatrice; *b* 7 Dec 1875; *m* 1 June 1899 Adm Sir Aubrey Clare Hugh Smith, KCVO, KBE, CB, DL (*d* 6 Oct 1957), s of Hugh Colin Smith, of Mount Clare, Roehampton, Surrey, and *d* 31 Jan 1931, leaving issue

3 (cont.) The 1st BARON STALBRIDGE *m* 2nd 3 April 1879 Eleanor Francis Beatrice Hamilton (*d* 21 March 1911), dau of Robert Hamilton Stubber, JP, DL, of Moyne, Queen's Co, and *d* 18 May 1912, leaving by her:

(1) HUGH GROSVENOR, 2nd and last BARON STALBRIDGE, MC, JP; *b* 5 May 1880; *educ* Eton; Lt 14th Hus and Northants Yeo Boer War 1899–1902 (despatches twice), Personal Staff with Northants Yeo WW I (despatches twice); *m* 10 Nov 1903 Gladys Elizabeth (*d* 21 March 1960), yst dau of Brinsley de Courcy Nixon, and *dsp* 24 Dec 1949, when the title expired

(2) Gilbert; *b* 22 Aug 1881; Lt Rifle Bde Boer War 1900–02, Capt 2nd Regt King Edward's Horse, T/Maj Nottingham Yeo WW I; *m* 4 July 1913 Effie E (*d* 6 Feb 1938), dau of Rev D C Cree, and *dsp* 15 June 1939

(3) Richard Eustace, MC; *b* 27 Jan 1883; Capt RHA WW I (despatches); *ka* 13 Oct 1915

(1) Blanche; *b* 5 May 1880; *m* 2 July 1901 Lt-Col James Henry Edward Holford, CMG, DSO (*d* 17 June 1936), s of Thomas Holford, of Duntish Court, Dorset, and *d* 4 April 1964, leaving issue

(2) Eleanor Lilian; *b* 18 Jan 1885; *m* 26 July 1906 Maj Josceline Charles Henry Grant, 3rd Roy Scots (*d* 8 April 1947), est s of Sir Charles Grant, KCSI, and *d* Aug 1977, leaving issue

1 Eleanor; *m* 25 Aug 1842 4th Duke of Northumberland (*qv*) and *d* 4 May 1911

2 Mary Frances; Extra Ldy Bedchamber to HM QUEEN ALEXANDRA; *m* 25 Aug 1842 6th Earl of Macclesfield (*qv*) and *d* 2 Jan 1912, leaving issue

3 Elizabeth; *m* 28 Nov 1846 2nd Baron Wenlock (*d* 6 Nov 1880) and *d* 16 Dec 1899, leaving issue (*see* 1932 edn)

4 Caroline Amelia; *m* 22 Aug 1848 2nd Baron Leigh (*qv*) and *d* 24 March 1906, leaving issue

5 Octavia; *m* 28 Dec 1852 Sir Michael Robert Shaw-Stewart, 7th Bt (*qv*), and *d* 29 May 1921, leaving issue

6 Agnes; *m* 1st 1 July 1858 Sir Archibald Ilay Campbell, 3rd Bt, of Succoth (*qv*); *m* 2nd 5 Dec 1871 Philip Frank, MD, FRCP, of 3 Elvaston Place, London SW, and *dsp* 22 Jan 1909

7 Jane Louisa Octavia; *m* 1st 2 Aug 1855 4th Baron Muncaster (*dsps* 18 June 1862); *m* 2nd 3 Oct 1863 Hugh Barlow Lindsay (*see* CRAWFORD and BALCARRES, E) and *d* 13 July 1921, leaving issue

8 Theodora; *m* 8 March 1877 Thomas Merthyr Guest (*see* WIMBORNE, V) and *d* 24 March 1924, leaving issue

The 2nd MARQUESS's est surv s,

HUGH LUPUS GROSVENOR, **1st Duke of Westminster**, so *cr* 27 Feb 1874 (UK), KG (1870), PC (1880); *b* 13 Oct 1825; *educ* Eton and Balliol Coll Oxford; MP (Lib) Chester 1847–69, Master Horse 1880–85, Yeo ADC to HM QUEEN VICTORIA 1881–99, Ld Lt Cheshire 1883–99 and London 1889–99, High Steward Westminster 1884–99; *m* 1st 28 April 1852 Constance Gertrude (*d* 19 Dec 1880), yst dau of 2nd Duke of Sutherland (*qv*), and had, with two other sons and a dau (all *d* in infancy):

1 Victor Alexander, *Earl Grosvenor*; *b* 28 April 1853 (HM QUEEN VICTORIA stood sponsor in person); *educ* Eton; Lt Cheshire Yeo Cav; *m* 3 Nov 1874 Lady Sibell Mary Lumley, DJStJ, Pres League Mercy (*m* 2nd 7 Feb 1887 George Wyndham (*see* EGREMONT, LECONFIELD and, B) and *d* 4 Feb 1929), dau of 9th Earl of Scarbrough (*qv*), and *dvp* 22 Jan 1884, leaving:

(1) HUGH RICHARD ARTHUR GROSVENOR, **2nd Duke of Westminster**, GCVO (1907), DSO (1916); *b* 19 March 1879; *educ* Eton; Lt RHG, ADC to Govr Cape Good Hope 1899 and C-in-C S Africa 1900–01 Boer War (despatches, Queen's medal with five clasps), WW I: T/Cdr RNVR with armoured cars France 1915 (despatches) and N Africa 1916, personal assist to Controller Mechanical Warfare Dept Min Munitions 1917; Lt-Col and Hon Col Cheshire Yeo, Hon Col 16th Bn Co of London Regt, Ld Lt Cheshire 1907–20; Order Isabella Spain 1st Cl and Cdr Legn Hon 1934; *m* 1st 16 Feb 1901 (*divorce* 1919) Constance Edwina, CBE (1918) (*d* 21 Jan 1970), yr dau of Col William Cornwallis-West (*see* DE LA WARR, E), and had:

1a Edward George Hugh, *Earl Grosvenor*; *b* 16 Nov 1904 (HM EDWARD VII stood sponsor); *d* 13 Feb 1909

1a Ursula Mary Olivia; *b* 21 Feb 1902; *m* 1st 23 July 1924 (*divorce* 1940) William Patrick Filmer-Sankey, 1st Life Gds, s of Cdr Filmer-Sankey, RN, and had issue; *m* 2nd 5 Oct 1940 Maj Stephen Vernon, s of Bernard Morris Vernon, and *d* 5 June 1978, leaving further issue

2a *Mary Constance [The Lady Mary Grosvenor, Saighton Lodge, Saighton, Chester, Cheshire]; *b* 27 June 1910

(1) (cont.) The **2nd Duke** *m* 2nd 26 Nov 1920 (*divorce* 1926) Violet Mary, yst dau of Sir William Nelson, 1st Bt (*qv*), and formerly w of George Richard Francis Rowley, Coldstream Gds; *m* 3rd 20 Feb 1930 (*divorce* 1947) Hon Loelia Mary Ponsonby, author of *Grace and Form*, only dau of 1st Baron Sysonby (*qv*); *m* 4th 7 Feb 1947 *Anne Winifred [Her Grace Anne Duchess of Westminster, Eaton Lodge, Eaton Park, Eccleston, Chester CH4 9JF], only dau of Brig-Gen Edward Langford Sullivan, CB, CMG, of Jersey, and *d* 19 July 1953

(1) Constance Sibell; granted with her sisters rank of duke's daus 20 Aug 1900; *b* 22 Aug 1875; Extra Ldy Bedchamber to HM QUEEN MARY; DJStJ; m 15 July 1899 9th Earl of Shaftesbury (*qv*) and *d* 8 July 1957, leaving issue

(2) Lettice Mary Elizabeth; *b* 25 Dec 1876; *m* 26 July 1902 7th Earl Beauchamp, KG (*d* 15 Nov 1938; *see* 1970 edn), and *d* 28 July 1936, leaving issue

2 Arthur Hugh, TD, JP, DL Cheshire; *b* 31 May 1860; *educ* Eton and Ch Ch Oxford; Lt-Col 3rd Bn Cheshire Vol Regt, Hon Capt Army, Lt-Col and Hon Col cmdg Cheshire Yeo Boer War 1900–01; *m* 12 April 1893 Helen, RRC, JP (Cheshire) (*d* 12 July 1950), 2nd dau of Sir Robert Sheffield, 5th Bt (*qv*), and *d* 29 April 1929, leaving:

(1) Robert Arthur, MC (1918) and bar; *b* 25 May 1895; *educ* Wellington; Capt Res Offrs Queen's Bays, Hon F/Lt RAF, WW I (despatches), WW II 1939–40 (invalided); *m* 9 Dec 1925 Doris May (*d* 13 Nov 1975), only dau of Frederick William Wignall, JP, DL, of The Rookery, Tattenhall, Cheshire, and Cambusmore, Sutherland, and *d* 12 June 1953, having had:

1a Hugh Frederick; *b* 19 Oct 1927; 2nd Lt Life Gds; accidentally *k* 9 April 1947

1a *Robina Jill [Mrs Ronald Mills, Court Farm, Kenchester, Herefs]; *b* 28 Aug 1930; *m* 1st 19 Sept 1951 (*divorce* 1961) Michael Philip Forsyth-Forrest, er twin s of Maj Philip Forsyth-Forrest, of Kineton, Warwicks, and has:

1b *Anita; *b* 20 Oct 1952

2b *Teresa; *b* 25 Feb 1955; *m* 1984 *Hon Harry St Clair Fane, yr s of 15th Earl of Westmoreland (*qv*)

1a (cont.) Mrs Robina Forsyth-Forrest *m* 2nd 1961 *Ronald Mills and by him has:

1b *Robin; *b* 1962

3b *Serena Laura; *b* 1965

(1) Constance Isolde; *b* 12 Jan 1900; *m* 2 June 1930 Maj William Reginald James Alston-Roberts-West, Gren Gds (*ka* May 1940), of Alscot Park, Stratford-on-Avon, and had:

1a *James William; *b* 12 Nov 1935; late Gren Gds; *m* 22 Oct 1958 *Camilla Audrey, yst dau of Anthony Seymour Bellville, of The White House, Bembridge, IoW, by Hon Mrs Peter Pleydell-Bouverie (*see* RADNOR, E), and has issue

2a *George Arthur; *b* 23 Nov 1937; Maj Gren Gds; *educ* Eton; *m* 20 May 1970 *Hazel Elizabeth Margaret, yst dau of Lt-Col Sir Thomas Russell Albert Mason Cook, JP, of Sennowe Park, Guist, Norfolk

(2) Barbara; *b* 17 Aug 1901; *m* 15 Jan 1929 4th Earl of Stradbroke (*qv*) and *d* 30 Aug 1977, leaving issue

3 Henry George; *b* 23 June 1861; *m* 1st 21 April 1887 Dora Mina (*d* 24 Dec 1894), est dau of James Erskine Wemyss of Wemyss (*see* WEMYSS, E), and had:

(1) WILLIAM GROSVENOR, **3rd Duke of Westminster**; *b* 23 Dec 1894; invalid; *d* unm 22 Feb 1963

(1) Millicent Constance; *b* 14 Jan 1889; *m* 1st 15 Nov 1909 (*divorce* 1919) William Molyneux Clarke, s of Stephenson Clarke, of Brook House, Ardingly, Sussex, and had issue; *m* 2nd Aug 1919 Capt Frank Billinge, DFC (*d* 28 Sept 1928), Manchester Regt and RAF, and had issue; *m* 3rd 6 Aug 1932 Maj John Finlay Dew, DSO, MC, of Iringa, Tanganyika Territory, s of Rev Edward Parker Dew, of Breamore, Hants, and *d* 24 Aug 1944

(2) Dorothy Alice Margaret Augusta; *b* 22 Aug 1890; granted rank of duke's dau 20 April 1954; *m* 1st 15 April 1909 (*divorce* 1919) 6th Earl of Rosebery (*qv*) and had issue; *m* 2nd 16 March 1920 (*divorce* 1927) Capt Robert Bingham Brassey, s of Albert Brassey, MP (*d* 14 Nov 1946), of Heythrop; *m* 3rd 23 May 1929 (*divorce* 1938) Chetwode Charles Hamilton Hilton-Green (*d* 31 Dec 1963), s of Francis Hilton-Green, JP, of Alderley, Wotton-under-Edge, Glos; *m* 4th 7 Feb 1938 Cdr Richard Herbert Mack, RN (*d* 16 Sept 1967), 3rd s of Philip Paston Mack, of Paston Hall, Norfolk, and *d* 11 Jan 1966

3 (cont.) Lord Henry Grosvenor *m* 2nd 19 Oct 1911 Rosamund Angharad, CBE (1918) (*d* 16 April 1941), only child of Edward Lloyd, of Tyn-y-Rhyl, Flints, and widow of Edward Seymour Greaves, of Glenetive, Argyll, and *d* 27 Dec 1914

4 Robert Edward; *b* 19 March 1869; *d* Constantinople 16 June 1888

5 Gerald Richard; *b* 14 July 1874; Capt Scots Gds, Boer War 1900 (despatches) and WW I (wounded); *d* unm 10 Oct 1940

1 Elizabeth Harriet; *m* 2 Feb 1876 3rd Marquess of Ormonde (*see* MOUNTGARRET, V) and *d* 25 March 1928, leaving issue

2 Beatrice Constance; *m* 1st 13 Nov 1877 3rd Baron Chesham (*qv*) and had issue; *m* 2nd 4 Oct 1910 Maj John Alexander Moncreiffe (*see* ERROLL, E) and *d* 12 Jan 1911

3 Margaret Evelyn; *b* 1 April 1873; *m* 12 Dec 1894 1st Marquess of Cambridge, GCB, GCVO, CMG (*see* 1970 edn), and *d* 27 March 1929, leaving issue

The **1st Duke** *m* 2nd 29 June 1882 Hon Katherine Caroline Cavendish, CBE (*d* 19 Dec 1941), dau of 2nd Baron Chesham (*qv*), and *d* 22 Dec 1899, leaving by her:

6 Hugh William; *b* 6 April 1884; Capt 1st Life Gds; *m* 21 April 1906 Lady Mabel Florence Mary Crichton, MBE (*d* 15 Aug 1944, having *m* 2nd 29 Sept 1920 Maj Robert Hamilton Stubber, DSO (*d* 27 Jan 1963), s of Robert Hamilton Hamilton Stubber, of Moyne, Durrow, Queen's Co, and *d* 15 Aug 1944, leaving further issue), yr dau of 4th Earl of Erne (*qv*), and was *ka* 30 Oct 1914, leaving:

(1) GERALD HUGH GROSVENOR, **4th Duke of Westminster**, DSO, PC, DL (Cheshire 1967); *b* 13 Feb 1907; *educ* Eton and RMC Sandhurst; Lt-Col 9th Lancers, Col TA 1950, Hon Col Cheshire Yeo 1955, High Sheriff Cheshire 1959, Col 9th/12th Lancers 1961, memb Yeomen Gd 1964, Ld Steward Household 1964–67; *m* 11 April 1945 Sally (*d* 1990), twin dau of George Perry, and *dsp* 25 Feb 1967

(2) ROBERT GEORGE, **5th Duke**

7 Edward Arthur, MC; *b* 27 Oct 1892; S/Ldr RAF, Lt RHG, Offr Order St Maurice and St Lazarus Italy; *m* 5 Aug 1914 Lady Dorothy Margaret Browne (*d* 8 March 1961, having *m* 2nd 9 Aug 1930 Hon Sir Evan Charteris (*see* WEMYSS, E)), er dau of 5th Earl of Kenmare (*see* 1949 edn), and *d* 26 Aug 1929, leaving:

(1) Beatrice Elizabeth Katharine, CBE (1952); *b* 6 Nov 1915; Assist Supt-in-Chief St John Ambulance Bde WW II (despatches), DStJ, Dep Supt-in-Chief St John's Ambulance Bde 1954–58; *m* 3 June 1944 (*divorce* 1945) Maj Richard Desiré Girouard, Welsh Gds, only s of Maj-Gen Sir Percy Girouard, KCMG, DSO, and *d* 19–

(2) Rosemary Helen; *b* 4 March 1918; *m* 23 July 1945 Maj Hon George William Folkes Dawnay, MC, JP, yr s of 9th Viscount Downe (*qv*), and *d* 19 Sept 1969, leaving issue

4 Mary Cavendish; *b* 12 May 1883; *m* 1st 10 June 1903 Henry William, Viscount Crichton, MVO, DSO (*ka* 31 Oct 1914), and had issue (*see* ERNE, E); *m* 2nd 18 April 1918 Col Hon Algernon Francis Stanley, DSO (*d* 10 Feb 1962), and *d* 14 Jan 1959, leaving further issue (*see* DERBY, E)

5 Helen Frances; *b* 5 Feb 1888; *m* 10 Nov 1915 Brig-Gen Lord Henry Charles Seymour, DSO, 2nd s of 6th Marquess of Hertford (*qv*), and *d* 21 Oct 1970, leaving issue

The 4th DUKE's bro,

ROBERT GEORGE GROSVENOR, **5th Duke of Westminster**, DSO (1942), TD, JP (Co Fermanagh 1953), DL (Cheshire 1950); *b* 24 April 1910; *educ* Eton; Lt-Col RA 1943 WW II (wounded), Lt-Col cmdg NI Horse 1953–56, Hon Col (RAC) TAVR 1973; High Sheriff Co Fermanagh 1952, ADC to Govr NI 1953–55, MP (U) Fermanagh and S Tyrone 1955–64, PPS to For Sec 1957–59, Senator NI 1964–67, Freeman: Chester, City London; CStJ (1951); *m* 3 Dec 1946 Hon Viola Maud Lyttelton (*k* car crash 1987), est dau of 9th Viscount Cobham (*qv*), and *d* 1979, leaving:

1 GERALD CAVENDISH GROSVENOR, **6th and present Duke of Westminster**

1 *Leonora Mary, LVO (1997) [Leonora Countess of Lichfield, Cranborne Lodge, Cranborne, Dorset]; *b* 1 Feb 1949; Extra Ldy in Waiting to HRH THE PRINCESS ROYAL; *m* 8 March 1975 (*divorce* 1986) 5th Earl of Lichfield (*qv*) and has issue

2 *Jane Meriel [The Lady Jane Dawnay, Hillington Hall, Hillington, Norfolk PE31 6BW]; *b* 8 Feb 1953; *m* 1st 1977 (*divorce* 1990) 10th Duke of Roxburghe (*qv*) and has issue; *m* 2nd 11 June 1996 her cousin *Edward (Ned) Dawnay (*see* DOWNE, V)

Seat: Eaton Hall, Cheshire. The Eaton estate has been held by the GROSVENORs since the 15th century and in the last decade of CHARLES II's reign the **3rd Baronet** commissioned a well-born amateur, William Samwell, to put up a brick-built mansion. Traces of this were still extant as late as the early 1960s but long before that the place had been completely transformed by the **1st Marquess of Westminster**, for whom during the Napoleonic Wars William Porden confected a Gothick extravaganza. In the mid-1820s Benjamin Gummow added a couple of wings but the **2nd Marquess** truncated them, employing William Burn in mid-century to restore an atmosphere of true gravity, in keeping with High Victorian ideals. All this was swept away by Alfred Waterhouse in the early 1870s, when he erected a tour de force of late neo-Gothic for an outlay of £600,000 (just under £2m in late-1990s terms). Waterhouse's stable yard, clock tower and domestic chapel survive.

The present Eaton is one of the 100 or so country seats built in Britain since World War II. It replaced a graceless building put up in 1973 after the old gigantic and sprawling Eaton Hall was pulled down in the years 1961 to 1965. The latter had been occupied by the Army as a training establishment for officer cadets. Under the terms of the lease negotiated by the Grosvenor Estate the Army was obliged to pay a large sum for dilapidations. These were judged so heavy that the building was demolished. The replacement, finished some hundred years after Waterhouse's effort, won little favour. The current building is essentially a thorough embellishment of the 1973 structure. It uses cladding of locally quarried rose-coloured sandstone to conceal the concrete of 1973 and a pitched roof (whereas the original 1973 building had had a flat one). Curvilinear window copings replaced the older straight ones. The overall effect is curiously Germanic, as if a Schloss had been designed by Rennie Mackintosh. The interior has been remodelled with the assistance of Sir Hugh Casson.

WESTMORLAND

Arms: Az. three dexter gauntlets, back affrontée or. **Crest:** Out of a ducal coronet or a bull's head argent, pied sable, armed of the first, charged on the neck with a rose gules, barbed and seeded proper. **Supporters:** Dexter, a griffin per fess argent and or, gorged with a plain collar and lined sable; sinister, a bull argent, pied sable, collared and lined or, at the end of the line a ring and three staples of the last. **Motto:** *Ne vile fano* ('Let there not be vileness in church'). **Creations:** E. and B. (E) 29 Dec 1624.

THE 16TH EARL OF WESTMORLAND and **Baron Burghersh**, Co Sussex (Anthony David Francis Henry Fane) [The Rt Hon The Earl of Westmorland, 31 Langton St, London SW10 0JL]; *b* 1 Aug 1951; *s* 1993; *educ* Eton; memb Orbitex N Pole expdn 1990, Life Pres St Moritz Sporting Club, Govr Guild of Veteran Pilots and Racing Drivers, dir Phillips Internat Auctioneers, FRGS; *m* 1985 *Caroline Eldred, dau of Keon Hughes and formerly w of Charles Fairey, and has:

1 *Daisy Caroline; *b* 1989

Earldom of Westmorland: For the previous creation under this title *see* ABERGAVENNY, M.

Lineage: The Heralds' Visitation of Kent of 1574 traces the FANEs from Howell ap Vane, of Monmouthshire, but the earliest certain ancestor is:

HENRY A-VANE, of Tonbridge, Kent; living 1426; *m* Isabel Persall or Peshall; made his will 26 Jan 1455 or 1456/7 and had, with other issue:

JOHN VANE or FANE, of Tonbridge; *m* Isabel, dau of Sir John Darell, of Calehill, Kent, made his will 16 April 1488 and had, with three yr sons (Henry, *dsp c* 1536; Thomas; John, *see* BARNARD, B) and three daus:

RICHARD FANE, of Badsell in Tudeley, Kent; inherited from his f the Manor of Snergate and other extensive property; *m* Agnes, dau and heiress of Thomas Stidolph, of Badsell, and *d* 1540, leaving an only s:

GEORGE FANE, of Badsell; Sheriff Kent 1557–58; *m* 1557 Joan, dau of William Waller, of Groombridge, Kent, and *d* 1571, leaving an er s:

Sir THOMAS FANE; ktd 1573; *m* 1st Elizabeth (*dsp*), dau of Thomas Colepepper, of Bedgbury; *m* 2nd 12 Dec 1574 Mary Nevill(e), Baroness le Despenser in her own right, only dau and heiress of 4th Lord (Baron) Bergavenny, himself eggs of Edward Nevill(e), yst s of the 1st Earl of Westmorland of the 1397 *cr* (*see* ABERGAVENNY, M), and *d* 13 March 1589, having had, with three other sons and two daus:

FRANCIS FANE, **1st Earl of Westmorland**, so *cr* 29 Dec 1624, as also BARON BURGHERSH, Co Sussex (both E), in addition 4th LORD (Baron) LE DESPENSER (as which *s* mother 1626), KB (1603); *b* Feb 1579/80; *educ* Queens' Coll Cambridge; MP Kent 1601, Maidstone 1604–11, 1614 and 1620–22 and Peterborough 1624; *m* just after 15 Feb 1598/9 Mary (*d* 9 April 1640), only surv dau and heiress of Sir Anthony Mildmay (*see* ST JOHN-MILDMAY, Bt), and *d* 23 March 1628, having had, with other issue:

1 MILDMAY FANE, **2nd Earl of Westmorland** and 5th LORD (Baron) LE DESPENSER, KB (1 Feb 1625/6); *b* 24 Jan 1601/2; *educ* Emmanuel Coll Cambridge (MA 1619); MP Peterborough 1620–22, 1626 and 1628–29, royalist Civil War, Capt Prince of Wales's Regt of Horse, arrested by Parl and imprisoned Tower of London Oct 1642–April 1643; at Restoration raised a Tp of Vol Horse for CHARLES II, Jt Ld Lt Northants 1660–65; *m* 1st 6 July 1626 Grace (*d* 29 June 1636), dau of Sir William Thornhurst, of Herne, Kent (and maternal gdau of 1st Viscount Howard of Bindon), and had, with five daus:

(1) CHARLES FANE, **3rd Earl of Westmorland** and 6th LORD (Baron) LE DESPENSER; *b* 6 Jan 1634/5 (CHARLES I stood sponsor); cmded a troop of vol horse under his f 1660 and 1662, MP Peterborough 1660 and 1661–62; *m* 1st 15 June 1665 Elizabeth, dau and coheir of Charles Nodes, of Shephall Bury, Herts; *m* 2nd Dorothy (*m* 2nd 3rd Viscount of Dunbar and *d* 26 Jan 1739/40), dau of 2nd Earl of Cardigan (*see* AILESBURY, M), and *dsp* 18 Sept 1691

1 (cont.) The **2nd Earl** *m* 2nd 21 June 1638 Mary, dau and coheir of 1st Baron Vere of Tilbury (*see* SAINT ALBANS, D) and widow of Sir Roger Townshend, 1st Bt (*see* TOWNSHEND, M), and *d* 12 Feb 1665/6, having by her had, with four daus:

(2) VERE FANE, **4th Earl of Westmorland** and 7th LORD (Baron) LE DESPENSER, KB (23 April 1661); MP (Whig) Peterborough 1671–79, Kent 1679–81 and 89–91, Lt Govr Dover Castle, Jt Ld Lt Kent 1692–93; *m* 13 July 1671 Rachel (*d* 17 Feb 1710/11), only dau and heiress of John Bence, Alderman City London, and *d* 29 Dec 1693, having had, with six daus (*see* DASHWOOD, Bt, of West Wycombe):

1a John; *bapt* 16 April 1676; *dvp* young and *bur* 22 Jan 1677/8

2a VERE FANE, **5th Earl of Westmorland** and 8th LORD (Baron) LE DESPENSER; *b* 25 May 1678; Guidon and est Cornet 1st Life Gds; *d* unm 19 May 1698

3a THOMAS FANE, **6th Earl of Westmorland** and 9th LORD (Baron) LE DESPENSER, PC (16 April 1717); *b* 3 Oct 1683; Gentleman Bedchamber (Whig) to QUEEN ANNE's husb PRINCE GEORGE OF DENMARK 25 April 1704, becoming with him Dep Govr Dover Castle and Dep Warden Cinque Ports 1705–08, Ld Bedchamber to GEORGE I 1715, First Ld Trade and For Plantations 1719–35, Ld Lt Northants 1735; *m* June 1707 Catherine (*d* 4 Feb 1729/30), dau and heiress of Thomas Stringer, of Sharleston, Yorks, and widow of Richard Beaumont, of Whitley, and *dsp* 4 July 1736

4a JOHN FANE, **7th Earl of Westmorland** and 10th LORD (Baron) LE DESPENSER; *bapt* 24 March 1685/6; *cr* 4 Oct 1733 BARON CATHERLOUGH (I); MP (Whig) Hythe 1708–11, Kent 1715–22 and Buckingham 1727–34; 5th Dragoon Gds 1708–14 Battle of Malplaquet and ensuing campaigns, Col various Gds regts 1715–37, Maj-Gen and Lt-Gen 1742, Gen Horse 1761, DCL 1749, High Steward 1754–59, Chllr Oxford U 1759–62; *m* Mary (*d* 29 July 1778), dau and heiress of Lord Henry Cavendish (*see* DEVONSHIRE, D); *dsp* 26 Aug 1762, when the Irish peerage expired, the Earldom of Westmorland passed to his cousin and the Barony of le Despenser fell into abeyance between the descendants of his sisters until terminated 19 April 1763 in favour of Sir Francis Dashwood, 2nd Bt, of West Wycombe (*qv; see* also FALMOUTH, V)

2 Francis (Sir), KB, of Fulbeck, Lincs, and Aston, Yorks; Govr Doncaster and Lincoln Castles, dramatist and poet; *m* Elizabeth (*d* 1669), est dau of William West, of Firbeck, Yorks, coheir to her bro John West and widow of 3rd and last Baron Darcy (of Aston) of the 1548 *cr* restoration, and *d* by Sept 1681, leaving:

(1) Francis (Sir), KB, of Henbury, Glos; *m* 16 Feb 1663/4 Hannah, dau of John Rushworth, and *d* by Sept 1691, leaving:

1a Henry, of Brympton, Somerset; *b* 1669; *m* Anne (*d* 1720), dau of Thomas Scrope, of Bristol, and sis and coheir of John Scrope, MP, of Wormsley, Oxon, Sec Treasury, and *d* 19 Dec 1726, leaving:

1b Francis; barrister, MP 1727–57; *d* unm 28 May 1757 aged 59

2b THOMAS, **8th Earl**

3b Henry, of Wormsley, Watlington, Oxon; *b* 1703; MP Lyme Regis 1757–77; *m* 1st 17 July 1735 Charlotte (*d* 29 Sept 1739), only dau of Nicholas Rowe, poet, and had:

1c Charlotte; *m* Sir William St Quintin

3b (cont.) Henry Fane *m* 2nd 20 May 1742 Anne, dau of John Wynn, DD, Bp Bath and Wells, and by her had:

2c Mary; *m* 27 Nov 1765 Sir Thomas Stapleton, 5th Bt (*see* 1970 edn, also FALMOUTH, V), of Greys Court, and had issue

3b (cont.) Henry Fane *m* 3rd Sept 1748 Charlotte (*d* April 1758), sis and coheir (with Rebecca, w of John Taylor, of the Circus, Bath), of John Luther, of Myles's, Essex, and *d* 31 May 1777, having by her had, with a yr s (Francis, of Myles's, MP Dorchester):

1c John, of Wormsley; *b* 6 Jan 1751; DCL 1797, MP 1796–1824; *m* 16 Nov 1773 Lady Elizabeth Parker (*d* 10 June 1829), dau of 3rd Earl of Macclesfield (*qv*), and *d* 8 Feb 1824, leaving, with a dau (*d* unm):

1d John, of Wormsley; *b* 9 July 1775; High Sheriff Oxon 1836, DCL 1824, MP 1824–31; *m* 6 June 1802 Elizabeth (*d* 20 Nov 1865), dau of William Lowndes Stone, of Brightwell Park, and *d* 4 Oct 1850, leaving:

1e John William, of Wormsley, JP, DL (Oxon); *b* 1 Sept 1804; MP Oxford, High Sheriff Oxon 1861, Lt-Col Oxon Militia, DCL 1854; *m* 1st 30 Nov 1826 Catherine (*d* 6 Nov 1828), dau of Sir Benjamin Hobhouse, 1st Bt (*qv*), and had:

1f Sophia; *m* 29 July 1851 Arthur Henry Clerke Brown (*d* 16 March 1889), of Kingston Blount, Oxon, and *d* 26 Aug 1886, leaving issue

1e (cont.) John Fane *m* 2nd 3 Nov 1829 his cousin Lady Ellen Catherine Parker (*d* Sept 1844), 3rd dau of 5th Earl of Macclesfield (*qv*), and by her had:

1f John Augustus, of Wormsley, JP (Oxon); *b* 23 Sept 1830; Maj and Adj 2nd Bn Oxon Rifle Vols, Capt 46th Regt; *m* 21 June 1860 Eleanor (*d* 31 March 1902), dau of Thomas Thornhill, of Woodleys, Oxon, and *d* 19 Aug 1908, having had:

1g John Henry Scrope, of Wormsley; *b* 24 June 1861; Lt 3rd Bn Oxon LI; *d* 30 May 1928

2g Francis Luther, of Wormsley; *b* 31 March 1865; *m* 1st 6 Feb 1906 Mary (*d* 18 June 1927), yst dau of John Henry Harris, of Ballarat, Australia; *m* 2nd 12 Feb 1929 Beatrice Jane (*d* 31 March 1961), est dau of Harry Coppleston, of Lostwithiel, Cornwall, and *d* 9 Dec 1954, leaving:

1h +John Coppleston Luther [John Fane Esq, The White House, North End, Henley-on-Thames, Oxon]; *b* 27 Aug 1933; *educ* Harrow and Emmanuel Coll Cambridge; late Lt Welsh Gds, High Sheriff Oxon 1977

1h *Anne Isabel [Mrs Anne Richmond-Watson, Castle Minor, Tintagel, Cornwall PL34 0DG]; *b* 11 April 1931; *m* 5 June 1954 (*divorce* 1976) Colin Irving Richmond-Watson, yst s of Richmond Watson, of Chalfont Grove, Bucks, and has had:

1i *Harry Fane; *b* 24 May 1956; *educ* Gresham's; *m* 1976 *Sylvia Alexander and has:

1j *Paul Alexander; *b* 25 July 1979

2i Angus Colin John; *b* 1 March 1958; *educ* Gresham's; *d* 1984

1i *Elizabeth Frances Aves; b 1960; m 1978 (*divorce* 1982, resumed maiden name) Stuart Hogan and has:

     1j *Gareth Michael Colin; b 1978

2i *Sarah Eleanor; b 7 Oct 1962; m 1987 (*divorce* 1992) Kerry C Baxley, of New York

3g Augustus Walter; b 1866; d 20 Dec 1873

4g Sydney Algernon; b 27 Oct 1867; m 12 July 1894 Selina Violet (d 23 Sept 1939), only child of Loftus Fitzwygram (*see* WIGRAM, Bt), and d 16 May 1929, leaving:

1h Aubrey Francis Sydney, TD; b 9 May 1895; Capt Northumberland Fus, Lt-Col cmdg 43rd Wessex Div Sigs WW I, Roy Sigs (TA), King's Messenger; m 3 June 1926 Geraldine Marion, dau of Adml Gerald Charles Langley, and was k in a plane crash Dallas, Tex., 29 Nov 1949

2h Gerard William Reginald, DSC; b 7 Aug 1898; Capt RAF, F/Sub-Lt RNAS, WW I (despatches); m 1st 1 Oct 1919 Constance Rhoda Elizabeth (d 26 March 1969), dau of Sir Nicholas Henry Bacon, 13th Bt (qv); m 2nd 22 July 1970 *Phyllis Jane [Mrs Gerard Fane, Feering Place, Feering, Essex CO5 9QX], dau of Hugh Jackson, of Chevington, Suffolk, and d 1979, having had by his 1st w:

1i Peter Gerard Scrope; b 1 April 1921; educ Eton; Lt RNVR; m 1st 20 Dec 1948 (*divorce* 1955) Cecilie Kirsten, only dau of Einar Walter Nansen, of Oslo; m 2nd 1 June 1961 (*divorce* 1962) Juliet, dau of Brig George Maitland Edwards, DSO, and widow of W/Cdr Trevor Freeman, DSO, DFC; m 3rd 27 Nov 1963 *Anne Barclay, dau of Lt-Col Henry Gamble, OBE, of Instow, N Devon, and formerly w of Lt-Cdr Anthony Stuart Melville-Ross, DSC, RN, and d 3 Sept 1977

2i +Julian Raymond [Julian Fane Esq, Feering Place, Feering, Essex CO5 9QX]; b 18 April 1925

3h Kenneth Cecil; b 16 Sept 1902; educ Wellington; m 5 Oct 1927 Jessie (d 31 March 1970), 3rd dau of Edwin Owen Davies, of Bulawayo, Rhodesia, and dsp 14 Jan 1970

4h Nigel Loftus Henry, RD; b 25 July 1904; educ RNCs Osborne and Dartmouth; Cdr RNR WW II in HMS Fervent (1939–41) and staff of AOC-in-C, Coastal Cmd RAF (1941–45); underwriting memb Lloyd's, memb Hon Co Master Mariners; m 1st 12 Jan 1935 (*divorce* 1959) Catherine Henrietta (d 22 July 1968), dau of Henry Percy Hussey, of Bricklehurst Manor, Stonegate, Sussex; m 2nd 11 May 1960 (*divorce* 1971) Dorothy Mai, dau of John Farrington and widow of Borras Noel Hamilton Whiteside (*see* BELHAVEN AND STENTON, L), and d 4 June 1973, having had by his 1st w:

1i William Nigel Sydney; b 26 Oct 1938; d 18 Jan 1939

1i Patricia Margaret; b 17 March 1936; m 21 June 1958 *Charles Henry David Denning [Charles Denning Esq, The Old Vicarage, Stonegate, Wadhurst, Sussex], yr s of Lt-Gen Sir Reginald Francis Stewart Denning, KBE, CB, of Delmonden Grange, Hawkhurst, Kent, and d 1996 leaving:

     1j *James Henry; b 1 June 1959

     2j *Guy William; b 16 April 1962

     1j *Sophia Jane; b 23 March 1964

     2j *Venetia Mary; b 25 Feb 1966

1g Catharine Elizabeth Agnes; b 30 Oct 1862; m 27 Aug 1887 Albert Butter, yst s of Archibald Butter (d 17 Jan 1920), of Faskally, Perthshire, and d 16 Sept 1948, leaving issue

2g Isabel; b 7 April 1864; m 14 April 1885 Maj-Gen Francis Hugh Plowden, CB (d 24 Aug 1911), and d 27 Feb 1914, leaving issue

3g Amy Eleanor; b 13 Nov 1868; d unm 20 Feb 1932

2f Ellen; m 24 Nov 1853 George Stratton (d July 1895) and d 18 Nov 1900, leaving issue

1e (cont.) John Fane m 3rd 18 Nov 1845 Charlotte (d 19 May 1855), dau of Theodore Henry Broadhead, and by her had:

2f Henry George; b 10 Sept 1846; Capt 52nd Regt; m 5 July 1876 Blanche Louisa (d 24 Feb 1919), only dau of Col Hon Robert Charles Henry Spencer (*see* CHURCHILL, V), and d 29 May 1924, having had:

1g Adrian Henry; b 31 Oct 1877; d 5 Feb 1882

2g Hubert William, JP; b 9 Nov 1878; educ Uppingham; associate Roy Sch of Mines, Mayor Kensington 1934–37; m 19 June 1911 Mathilde Emilie Aloise (d 12 Sept 1953), dau of Victor August Josef von Adametz, and d 7 Nov 1949, leaving:

1h Robert William Augustus, MBE (1944); b 26 April 1913; educ Oundle and Emmanuel Coll Cambridge (BA 1934, MA 1950); MICE, AMIMechE, Maj RA WW II; m 15 Oct 1949 *Elinor Valerie [Mrs Robert Fane, Hoo Lodge, Hoo, Woodbridge, Suffolk], er dau of Hon William Borthwick (*see* BORTHWICK, Bt), and d 1989, leaving:

1i +Andrew William Mildmay [Andrew Fane Esq, Hoo House, Hoo, Woodbridge, Suffolk]; b 9 Aug 1949; educ Radley and Emmanuel Coll Cambridge (MA); FCA; m 1989 *Clare Lucy, MB, BS, FRCS, yr dau of Francis Marx, of Coventry

2i +Peter Robert Spencer; b 31 May 1956; educ Radley and RAC Cirencester (MSc); ARICS; m 1997 *Dorothy, only dau of Thomas Harris, of Brighton, and has:

     1j *Thomas Robert; b 8 Dec 1997

1i *Priscilla Margaret; b 1943; m 1975 *R Christopher Brewer, yr s of Kenneth Brewer, of Reigate, and has:

     1j *Simon Robert; b 1976; educ Eastbourne Coll and Emmanuel Coll Cambridge

     2j *Charles Thomas; b 1979; educ Charterhouse

2i *Lavinia Anne; b 1947; m 1974 *Stephen Wright, PhD, and has:

     1j *Matthew David Robert; b 1975; educ Roy Grammar Sch, Guildford, UCL and Merton Coll, Oxford (BA)

     1j *Catherine Frances; b 1977

3i *Angela Elizabeth; b 24 April 1954; barrister

1h *Dorothy Louisa [Mrs John Freeland, 25 Amesbury Crescent, Hove, E Sussex BN3 5RD]; b 8 Feb 1917; m 1st 28 Sept 1938 Capt Frederick James Colville (ka Dunkirk June 1940; *see* COLVILLE OF CULROSS, V); m 2nd 27 Dec 1941 (*divorce* 1962) Lt-Cdr Clifford John Maddocks, MIMechE, RNVR, only s of John Maddocks, of Rhymney House, Monmouth, and has:

1i *Cynthia Diana [Mrs John Orchard, Honington Glebe, Honington, Shipston-on-Stour, Warwicks]; b 20 April 1944; m 12 Aug 1967 *John Charles Johns Orchard, MA, LLB, yr s of Ronald Stark Orchard, of St John's Wood, and has:

     1j *Alister Mildmay Heywood; b 1971

     1j *Alexandra Rosemary Fane; b 27 Sept 1969

2i *Anne Susan; b 12 July 1948; m 1st 5 Oct 1968 (*divorce* 1988) Richard Fullerton Evetts, er s of Desmond Frederick Evetts, of Liss, Hants, and has had:

     1j *Toby James Fullerton; b 11 Feb 1970

     2j David Jason Clifford; b and d 1974

1h (cont.) Mrs Dorothy Maddocks m 3rd 8 Sept 1962 (*divorce* 1974) Lt-Col John Anthony Russell Freeland, Queen's Roy Regt (d 1989), only s of Col John Cavendish Freeland, CB, CBE, IA

3g Almeric Cecil; b 7 Jan 1880; d unm 30 March 1907

4g Arthur George Cecil, MC (1918); b 29 Dec 1880; educ Marlborough and Cooper's Hill; PWD India 1902–30, Maj IA Res WW I (despatches); m 3 Nov 1909 Daisy Geraldine (d 29 Sept 1947), est dau of Harry Victor Samps Baker, MInstCE, and dsp 3 April 1974

5g Robert Gerald; b 8 April 1882; Cdr RN, Italian Medal for Valour; ka May 1917

6g Horatio Alfred, MC; b 25 Feb 1884; Lt (T/Capt) Oxon Yeo; d 11 Aug 1918 of wounds recd in action

7g Francis John, JP; b 13 April 1885; educ Marlborough; m 15 Oct 1915 Violet (d 31 Dec 1970 aged 80), dau of George Clifford Bower, of Bromley, Kent, and d 18 Feb 1963, leaving:

1h +Peter Francis George [Peter Fane Esq, Wildermere, Haughurst Hill, Hants RG26 5TR]; b 15 Dec 1917; educ Marlborough and Emmanuel Coll Cambridge (MA); Capt RA WW II (POW); m 31 Oct 1939 *Diana, only dau of Col George Holden Hodgkinson, of Bembridge, IoW, and has had:

1i +Francis Michael George [Francis Fane Esq, Murreyfields, Reading Rd, Burghfield Common, Berks RG7 3BU]; b 5 Feb 1941; educ Peterhouse, Rhodesia, and Emmanuel Coll Cambridge (MA); m 1st 28 Oct 1967 (*divorce* 1989) Anne Bridget, dau of Maj John Alfred Gordon Gribble, of Fleet, Hants; m 2nd 1989 *Irene, dau of Maurice Frederick Osborne Johnston, and has by his 1st w:

     1j +Thomas Francis; b 23 Nov 1968

     1j *Suzanne; b 1972

2i David; b and d 24 March 1953

1i *Victoria [Mrs Martin Cardale, Castle View Hotel, Chepstow, Gwent]; b 14 April 1947; m 1 Oct 1966 *Martin Richard Cardale, yr s of Alfred George Cardale, of Ashfold Hill, Newbury, and has:

     1j *George Martin; b 1970; m 1998 *Annica, dau of Bo Henning, of Stockholm

     1j *Miranda Lucy [Mrs Stuart Nicholson, 6 Malcolm Rd, Borrodale, Harare, Zimbabwe]; b 8 June 1968; educ Exeter U (BA 1989); m 1994 *Stuart James Nicholson

     2j *Zara Diana; b 1980

2i *Sarah Lucy; b 1962; educ Exeter U; m 1998 *Frederic Fournier, of Provence

2h Henry John, MC; b 27 Dec 1919; educ Marlborough; Maj RA WW II; m 1st 7 June 1945 (*divorce* 1970) Donna Agatina, dau of Count Francesco Saverio D'Ayala and Countess Dora D'Ayala Vergara di Craco, of Rome; m 2nd Mrs Anne Barclay Fane, widow of Peter Gerard Scrope Fane (*see* above) and d 1993 leaving:

1i +Richard John George; b 3 Nov 1946; educ The Oratory; m 1989 *Anne, yst dau of Peter Knox

2i +Patrick Henry; b 1 May 1949; educ The Oratory; m 1976 *Stephanie Anne, er dau of A R Matanle, and has:

     1j +Edward Henry; b 1978

     2j +George Arthur; b 1981

     1j *Heloise Anne; b 1982

1h *Elizabeth Daphne [Mrs John Dickson, 1 Mytchett Heath, Mytchett, Camberley, Surrey GU16 6DP]; b 10 Oct 1916; m 29 June 1940 Lt-Col John David Logan Dickson, MC, RHA (d 14 Oct 1958), yr s of Lt-Col John Macausland Dickson, of N Warnborough, Hants, and has:

1i *Jeremy David Fane [Jeremy Dickson Esq, 8 Alan Rd, London SW19 7PT]; b 23 June 1941; educ Marlborough and Emmanuel Coll Cambridge (MA); m 9 Oct 1965 *Patricia, dau of Laurence Cleveland Martin, MD, FRCP, of Cambridge, and has:

1j *James David Laurence; *b* 30 Jan 1970; *educ* Marlborough and Pembroke Coll Cambridge (BA); *m* 7 Oct 1995 *Fern, dau of Rhidian Graesser, of N Wales

1j *Lucy Camilla; *b* 1971

1i *Sally Ann; *b* 16 July 1942; *m* 1975 *Lt-Col John Alan Cubitt Blakiston, 13th/18th Roy Hus, and has issue (*see* BLAKISTON, Bt)

8g Octavius Edward, DSO, MC; *b* 15 Oct 1886; Maj RGA WW I (despatches twice); *das* 18 Sept 1918

3f Charlotte Elizabeth; *m* 2 March 1871 George Henry Phillpotts (*d* 1914), of Earls Court, and *d* 20 Nov 1928, leaving issue

1e (cont.) John Fane *m* 4th March 1856 Victoria (*m* 2nd 29 June 1880 Lt-Col Sir John Terence O'Brien, KCMG (*d* 25 Feb 1903), and *d* 28 Feb 1912), yst dau of William Temple, and *d* 19 Nov 1875, having by her had:

3f Frederick William; *b* 26 July 1857; *m* 30 Oct 1880 Annie Henrietta (*d* 13 April 1936), sis of 8th and last Earl of Clonmell (*see* 1935 edn), and *d* 12 March 1933

4f Cecil; *b* 27 June 1859; *educ* Eton; *m* 1st 25 April 1892 Alice Mary (*d* 1 Feb 1899), only dau of Rev Thomas Ward Goddard, Vicar Nazeing, Essex, and had:

1g Valentine Cecil; *b* 30 Jan 1893; *d* unm 11 Jan 1977

4f (cont.) Cecil Fane *m* 2nd 30 Sept 1913 Florence Marjorie (*d* 15 July 1967), dau of William Ferrand, DL, of St Ives, Yorks, and *d* 6 Sept 1948, having by her had:

2g Adrian Cecil; *b* 25 April 1916; *educ* Eton; Lt Glos Regt (SR); *m* 22 Oct 1952 *Elizabeth Muriel [Mrs Adrian Fane, Carrickmanor Haven, Carrickbrennan Rd, Monkstown, Co Dublin, Ireland], dau of Henry Wheeler, of Garbally, Bruff, Co Limerick, and *d* 1987, having had:

1h +Henry Cecil; *b* 19 April 1954; *educ* Kilkenny Coll; *m* 1st 1979 (*divorce* 1991) Roisin Elizabeth, dau of Donald Mooney, of Delgany, Co Wicklow, and has:

1i +Edwyn Charles; *b* 1979

2i +Gareth John; *b* 1981

1h (cont.) Henry Fane *m* 2nd 1991 *Celia Margaret Wreford, dau of Brian Councell, of Clevedon, Avon, and formerly w of Anthony Wreford

1h *Gwendoline Anne [Mrs Michael Harrison, 36 Pearson St, Narara, NSW 2250, Australia]; *b* 9 March 1953; *m* 1988 *Michael John Harrison

3g John William; *b* 14 Sept 1919; *m* 1st 12 Feb 1944 (*divorce* 19–) Doreen, dau of Albert Lawrence, of Waltham Abbey, Essex; *m* 2nd 1963 *Gwendoline-Ann [Mrs John Fane, 84 Addison Rd, Enfield, Middx], widow of Gerald Francis Kelly, and *d* 1982, leaving by his 1st w:

1h +Anthony John; *b* 20 Feb 1948

1h *Sheila Rosamund [Mrs John Johnson, 3 Manton Rd, Lincoln LN2 2JL]; *b* 1 May 1951; *m* 19– *John Johnson

1g *Kathleen Marjorie; *b* 17 July 1914; *m* 28 Feb 1944 *Maj Michael Charles Selfe Langdon, Roy Sussex Regt, s of Rev Charles Godfrey Langdon, and has:

1h *Christopher Michael Fane [Christopher Langdon Esq, 211 Harley Shute Rd, St Leonards, Sussex]; *b* 10 April 1945; *educ* St Edward's Sch Oxford and Queens' Coll Cambridge (BA); slr 1970, Lt 5th (Vol) Bn Queen's Regt (TA); *m* 8 July 1967 *Penelope Diana, er dau of Merton Wall, of Guestling, Sussex, and has:

1i *Rupert Christopher Fane; *b* 1971

2i *Tobias John; *b* 1975

2h *Patrick John [Patrick Langdon Esq, 36 Gillsmans Park, St Leonards, Sussex]; *b* 25 March 1947; *educ* St Edward's Sch, Oxford; *m* 1973 *Hilary Peers Carter and has:

1i *James Michael Peers; *b* 1976

2i *Richard Patrick Thomas; *b* 1978

3g *Winifred Anne [Mrs Philip Stuart, 35 Front St South, Apt 1806, (Port Credit) Mississauga, Ontario, Canada]; *b* 19 Dec 1917; F/O WAAF WW II; *m* 26 March 1949 *Philip William Dacre Stuart, er s of Capt Robert Spurrel Dacre Stuart, of Stroud, Glos, and has:

1h *Peter Robin [Peter Stuart Esq, 17 Wellington St, Goderich, Ontario N7A 2W6, Canada]; *b* 27 June 1953; *m* 1979 *Susan Blaker Clinkard and has:

1i *Tyler John; *b* 1985

1i *Amanda Michelle; *b* 1981

1h *Penelope Anne [Mrs Eric Honsberger, 90 Quantrell Trail, Scarborough, Ont M1B 1L8, Canada]; *b* 18 April 1951; *m* 1970 *Eric Douglas Honsberger and has:

1i *Philip John Walter; *b* 1974

2i *Stuart Douglas; *b* 1979

1i *Margaret Anne; *b* 1972

2i *Alison Michelle; *b* 1976

2e Frederick Adrian Scrope (Rev), of Priors, Essex; *b* 8 Dec 1810; Vicar Norton Mandeville, Essex; *m* 10 June 1834 Joanna (*d* 8 April 1878), yst dau of Sir Benjamin Hobhouse, 1st Bt (*qv*), and *d* 5 Oct 1894, leaving, with a dau (*d* unm):

1f Edward; *b* Aug 1836; *d* unm 22 June 1868

2f Frederick John; *b* 30 Jan 1840; Col Glos Regt, and 102nd Regtl Dist; *m* 13 Nov 1873 Annie Louisa (*d* 9 Feb 1939), est dau of Thomas Abbott, of Halifax, NS, and *d* 4 June 1923, leaving

1g Frederick Luther, MC; *b* 27 April 1875; *educ* Charterhouse and Magdalen Coll Oxford (BA 1898, Cricket Blue 1897–98); Capt W Yorks Regt WW I (despatches); *m* 19 Sept 1938 Edna

Mary (*d* 1982), dau of Henry James Meads, of Eastbourne, and *d* 27 Nov 1960, leaving:

1h *Elizabeth Anne; *b* 2 Aug 1946

2h *Rosemary Enid [Miss Rosemary Fane, Hoo House, Hoo, Woodbridge, Suffolk]; *b* 24 April 1952

1f Isabella Elizabeth; *m* 10 June 1857 Rev Almeric John Churchill Spencer (*see* MARLBOROUGH, D) and *d* 8 Dec 1924

2f Joanna Amelia; *m* 14 March 1874 Arthur Henry Capel Waters (*d* 10 Dec 1931), of Epping, and *d* 19–, having had issue

3e George Augustus Scrope; *b* 29 March 1817; *m* 3 June 1843 Frances Sophia Pole (*d* April 1909), dau of John Phillips, of Culham, Oxon, and *d* 14 Aug 1960, leaving surv issue, with a dau (*d* unm):

1f Charles Augustus; *b* 1846; *m* 18– — and *d* 7 March 1923, having had:

1g Charles Eugene; *b* 1872; *m* 1909 Florence Beatrice Yeates and *d* 1955, leaving:

1h +Alexander Eugene; *b* 1913; *m* 1942 *Nancy Lorna, dau of Ray Carron, of Brighton, Victoria, and has:

1i +Russell [Russell Fane Esq, 21 Knox Dr, Barwon Heads, Victoria, Australia]; *b* 1952

1i *Sylvia [Mrs Donald Shaw, 37 Kent St, Gladstone, Queensland, Australia]; *b* 1943; *m* 1966 *Donald B Shaw

2i *Gwendoline; *b* 1948; *m* 1966 (*divorce* 1981) Ray Leggett

2h +George Augustus [George Fane Esq, 159 George Rd, Geraldton 6530, W Australia]; *b* 1916; *m* 1st 19– (*divorce* 19–) Eileen Byers and has:

1i *Brenda; *b* 19–

2i *Joy; *b* 19–

2h (cont.) George Fane *m* 2nd 19– *Lena Campbell and has:

1i +Peter Eugene [Peter Fane Esq, 230 Barker Rd, Subiaco, W Australia]; *b* 1959; *educ* U of W Australia and Australian Nat U; *m* 1983 *Debra Barnes and has:

1j *Kristy Caroline; *b* 1983

2i +Donald Lorne [Donald Fane Esq, 4 Lazarus St, Geraldton 6530, W Australia]; *b* 1960; *m* 1982 *Gae Pepperell and has a s and two daus

3i *Shirlee Margaret [Mrs Allan Rose, 8 Duclas Pl, Geraldton 6530, W Australia]; *m* 1983 *Allan Rose and has:

1j *Maggie Lee; *b* 17 Oct 1985

2j *Katherine Anne; *b* 4 April 1987

1h *Iolanthe Florence [Mrs Ronald Dunlop, 130 Abbett St, Scarborough, W Australia]; *b* 1918; *m* 1945 *Ronald Le-Grange Dunlop and has:

1i *Diana Iolanthe [Mrs John Pauley, 10 Rainbow View, Ocean Reef 6027, W Australia]; *b* 1946; *m* 1970 *John Joseph Pauley and has:

1j *David John; *b* 1974

1j *Helen Diana; *b* 1973

2i *Margaret Chase [Mrs John Lanyon, Yarrabee, One Tree Hill Rd, Ferny Creek, Victoria 3786, Australia]; *b* 1950; *m* 1979 *John Robin Lanyon and has:

1j *James John; *b* 1982

2j *Thomas Charles; *b* 1985

2h *Beatrice Mary [Mrs Laban Johnson-Head, 1046 McConnell Dr, Decatur, GA 30033, USA]; *b* 1922; *m* 1944 *Laban Johnson-Head and has:

1i *Stephen Johnson; *b* 1945; *m* 1970 (*divorce* 1985) Betsy Holter and has:

1j *Charles Johnson; *b* 1974

1i *Susan Gail [Mrs Brian Kreider, 5134 Timber Trail, Atlanta, GA 30342, USA]; *b* 1947; *m* 1st 1976 (*divorce* 1983) Elgin M Wells, Jr, and has:

1j *Laurel Brooke; *b* 1978

1i (cont.) Mrs Susan Johnson-Head *m* 2nd 1988 *Brian Wealand Kreider

2i *Julia Kathleen [Mrs Charles Adams, 2839 Tahoe Dr, Merced, CA 95340, USA]; *b* 1952; *m* 1980 *Capt Charles David Adams, USAF, and has:

1j *Royce Henry; *b* 1988

2i (cont.) Mr and Mrs Charles Adams also adopted:

*Quinton Lee; *b* 1984

*Royal Dawn; *b* 1980

*Jennifer Renée; *b* 1982

3h *Gloria Sybil [Mrs Noel Gleed, 12 Grosvenor Rd, Meltham 6053, W Australia]; *b* 1924; *m* 1958 *Noel Gleed

4h *Deborah Kathleen [Mrs Murray Henderson, MS 115, Harchs Rd, Gympe 4570, Qld, Australia]; *b* 1927; has:

1i Margaret Enid [Mrs Margaret Fane, 15B 55 Herdsman Pde, Wembley, WA 6014, Australia]; *b* 1950; SFO (Third Order of St Francis); *m* 1973 (*divorce* 1981, took name FANE 1982) Steven James Kirkman and has:

1j *James Murray; *b* 1977

1j *Genevieve Margaret; *b* 1974

2j Priscilla Norma [Miss Priscilla Kirkman, 39 Mistral St, Falcon, WA 6210, Australia]; *b* 1976

3j Kathleen Deborah; *b* 1979

4h (cont.) *Deborah Fane; *m* 1951 *Murray Henderson and has:

1i *Murray; *b* 1953

2i *John; *b* 1955

1i *Fiona; *b* 1957

5h *Mary Patricia [Mrs Donald McLaren, 104 Nollamara Ave, Nollamara, WA 6061, Australia]; b 1929; m 1955 Donald Whiteford McLaren (d 1976)

2f Augustus; b 1847; Capt RN; d 12 Jan 1924

1f Ellen; b 1855; m 1879 William Matthews (dsp 1887) and d 20 Sept 1903

1e Elizabeth; m 8 March 1842 Rev John Ballard

2e Anne; m 23 Sept 1824 John Billingsley Parry, QC (d 28 March 1876), and d 21 Nov 1829

3e Charlotte; m 16 Nov 1852 Rev Frederick Fyler (d 1864), s of J C Fyler, of Heffleton

2d Francis William; b 14 Oct 1778; R-Adml; m 20 July 1824 Anne (m 2nd 5 Jan 1847 3rd and last Marquess of Thomond (see INCHIQUIN, B) and d 22 Oct 1874), only dau of William Flint, of Old Sauchie, Clackmannanshire, and sis of Sir Charles Flint, Sec to 1st Duke of Wellington, and dsp 28 March 1844

1d Elizabeth Sarah; m 21 Dec 1813 Lt-Col Thomas Drake (d 1851), DQMG Mediterranean, s of Rev Dr Drake, of Amersham, Bucks

2d Charlotte; m 28 Dec 1813 Col John Potter Hamilton and had issue

3d Georgiana; m 1816 Rt Hon Joseph Warner Henley, JP, DL (d 9 Dec 1884), of Waterperry, Oxon, and d 15 June 1864, having had issue

4d Augusta; m 25 April 1815 Benjamin Keene and dsp

3 Anthony; b 1613; m Amabel/Annabella (m 2nd 1 Aug 1644 10th Earl of Kent (see GREY, B, and LUCAS OF CRUDWELL, B) and d 17 Aug 1698 or 1699), dau and heiress of Sir Anthony Benn, of Kingston-on-Thames, Recorder London, and d 1643, having had Anthony and Jane (both bur Kingston-on-Thames)

1 Grace; m 2nd Earl of Home (qv) and dsp

2 Mary; m 3rd Baron Gerard (qv) and had issue

3 Elizabeth; m 1st Sir John Cope, 3rd Bt, of Hanwell; m 2nd William Cope, of Icombe, Glos, and had issue

4 Rachael; m 1st 13 Dec 1638 5th Earl of Bath (see BATH, M, preliminary remarks); m 2nd May 1655 3rd Earl of Middlesex and dsp 11 Nov 1680

The 7th EARL's 2nd cousin once-removed,

THOMAS FANE, 8th Earl of Westmorland; bapt 8 March 1700/1; Bristol merchant, Clerk to Soc of Merchant Venturers; attorney and later barrister Middle Temple 1759, MP (Whig) Lyme Regis 1753–62; m 8 Aug 1727 Elizabeth (b Aug 1708; d 17 Nov 1782), dau of William Swymmer, Bristol merchant, by Mary Anne, dau of Sir John Lane, of Bristol, and widow of Samuel Kentish, Clerk in Chancery, of St Dunstan's, London, and d 12 Nov 1771, having had, with two daus:

1 JOHN, 9th Earl

2 Henry; b 4 May 1739; educ Westminster; MP; m 12 Jan 1778 Anne (d 19 Jan 1838), dau of Edward Buckley Batson, banker, of Avon Tyrell, Hants, by Mary, est dau of John Michel, of Kingston Russel Manor, Dorset, and d 4 June 1802, having had:

(1) Henry (Sir), GCB; b 26 Nov 1779; Gen, Col 1st Dragoon Gds and C-in-C E Indies, ADC to WILLIAM IV; dsp 24 March 1840

(2) Charles; Col 59th Regt; ka Vittoria 1813

(3) Edward (Rev); b 7 Dec 1783; Rector Fulbeck, Lincs, Preb Lincoln and Salisbury; m 7 Oct 1816 Maria (d 11 Nov 1850), dau of Walter Parry Hodges, of Dorchester, and d 28 Dec 1862, having had, with two daus (d unm):

1a Henry Edward FANE later HAMLYN-FANE, of Clovelly Court, Devon, and Avon Tyrrell, Hants; b 5 Sept 1817; MP, Lt-Col 4th Light Dragoons; m 9 April 1850 Susan Hester (d 19 May 1869), est dau and coheir of Sir James Hamlyn-Williams, 3rd Bt, MP, of Clovelly, Devon (see 1850 edn), and Edwinsford, Carmarths, and d 27 Dec 1868, having had, with a s (d young) and dau (d unm):

1b Nevile Hamlyn Batson, of Clovelly Court and Avon Tyrrell; b 21 Nov 1858; Lt 3rd Bn Northants Regt; d 10 March 1884

1b Marion Elizabeth; m 5 Feb 1879 Sir William Lewis Stucley, 2nd Bt (qv), and d 3 Aug 1934

2b Christine Louisa, of Clovelly Court; b 29 Nov 1855; m 11 June 1889 Frederick GOSLING later HAMLYN, DL (dsp 22 July 1904), and d 12 Nov 1936

4b Constance Edwina Adeline; b 28 Sept 1861; m 12 Aug 1885 3rd Baron Manners (qv) and d 4 March 1920, leaving issue

2a Edward George Robert; b Sept 1819; Madras CS; d unm 10 March 1891

3a Charles Thorold, JP (Middx), of Fulbeck Manor, Grantham, and Kelton Manor Rd, Bournemouth; b 14 Aug 1822; m 1st 24 Sept 1866 Emma (dsp 12 March 1897), widow of Capt Walter Davis; m 2nd 2 June 1898 Caroline Anne (d 27 March 1931), est dau of Maj-Gen Charles Edward Michel, JP, DL, and dsp 23 Nov 1901

4a Francis Augustus, of Fulbeck Hall, Lincs; b 22 March 1824; Col; m 10 Feb 1863 Augusta (d 14 June 1895), dau of William Fane (see below) and d 1 Feb 1893, leaving issue:

1b Mildmay; b 29 Dec 1863; Lt Rifle Bde; d unm 14 March 1886

2b Ralph Nevile; b 6 Jan 1870; Capt 4th Bn N Staffs Regt; d unm Africa 27 May 1900

1b Hester; b 12 May 1865; m 22 Aug 1907 Algernon Henry Mackworth Praed, of Owsden Hall, Suffolk, and d 30 May 1923

2b Rachel Louisa; b 30 Jan 1869; m 21 May 1889 Sir Edmund Royds, OBE, DL, MP (d 31 March 1946), of Stubton Hall, Newark, and d 18 Dec 1943, leaving issue

5a Frederick (Rev), of Moyles Court, Hants; b 11 July 1825; m 1st 19 Aug 1851 Elizabeth (d 11 May 1861), dau of James Peel Cockburn, est s of Sir William Cockburn, 9th Bt, of Langton, and had:

1b Cicely Grace Augusta; m 2 Dec 1875 William Robert Phelips (d 23 Nov 1919), of Montacute, Somerset, and d 4 March 1877, leaving issue

2b Florence Mary Anna; m 10 Sept 1873 Wynne Albert Bankes (d 16 April 1913), of Wolfeton, Dorset, and d 25 Feb 1947, leaving issue

3b Lilla Gertrude; m 12 Jan 1886 Capt Hon Arthur Grenville Fortescue and d 30 Oct 1913, leaving issue (see FORTESCUE, E)

5a (cont.) The Rev Frederick Fane m 2nd 28 Oct 1864 Fanny Eliza (d 5 May 1903), dau of Hollingworth Magniac, and d 22 Feb 1902, having by her had:

4b Helen Violet; b 29 July 1865; m 24 Aug 1909 John Wentworth Garneys Bond, CB, JP, DL (d 8 Oct 1948), of Creech Grange, Wareham, Dorset, and d 17 Aug 1952

6a Walter, CB; b 6 Jan 1828; Maj-Gen; m 4 Aug 1879 Agnes (d 17 Nov 1912), dau of Sir Henry Bold Hoghton, 8th Bt, and dsp 17 June 1885

1a Mary Eliza Caroline; m 24 June 1845 Anthony Willson, MP (d 5 June 1866), of Rauceby Hall, Lincs, and d 26 Jan 1888 aged 68

(4) Vere; b 5 April 1785; MP Lyme Regis; m 2 June 1815 Elizabeth (d 6 Jan 1865), est dau of Charles Chaplin, MP, of Blankney (see 1970 edn CHAPLIN, V), and d 18 Jan 1863, having had:

1a Nevile; b 17 May 1820; d unm 8 March 1852

1a Emily; m 5 Sept 1849 Col Edward Birch Reynardson, CB (d 10 May 1896) and d 5 March 1893, leaving issue

2a Emma; m 14 Aug 1845 Westley Richards, of Ashwell, Rutland, and d 14 Dec 1847, leaving issue

3a Georgiana Ellen; m 20 Feb 1856 Sir Henry Bromley, 4th Bt (qv), and d 17 June 1906

(5) William; b 5 April 1789; HEICS; m 12 Jan 1811 Louisa Hay (d 14 Nov 1855), dau of Thomas Dashwood (see DASHWOOD, Bt, of Kirtlington Park), and d 7 March 1839, leaving:

1a William Dashwood, JP (Derbys and Notts), of Fulbeck Hall; b 21 Oct 1816; educ Cambridge (MA); barrister; m 7 Aug 1861 Susan Millicent (d 12 Dec 1877), er dau of Gen John and Lady Susan Reeve, and d 29 Nov 1902, having had:

1b William Vere Reeve FANE later KING-FANE (roy licence Sept 1920), of Fulbeck Hall, JP, DL; b 29 Oct 1868; educ Cambridge (MA); High Sheriff 1908; barrister, Brevet-Col 3rd Bn Lincs Regt; m 16 May 1895 Helen Beatrice (d 8 March 1962 aged 94), 2nd dau of Rev Thomas Houldsworth Newman (see NEWMAN, Bt, of Mamhead), and d 5 Nov 1943, leaving:

1c Henry William Newman FANE, OBE, JP (1937), DL (Lincs 1951); b 6 Feb 1897; educ Charterhouse and RMA Woolwich; Capt RA WW I (1915–19) and WW II; CC (1937), CA (1952) Parts of Kesteven, Lincs, High Sheriff Lincs 1952, V-Chm CC Parts of Kesteven, Lincs, 1957–62, Chm 1962–67, Chm Lincs Police Authority 1968; m 14 Dec 1946 Dorothy ('Dotty') Mary (d 1986), only dau of Alexander Ogilvy Findlay, of Llantarnam, Mon, and d 23 May 1976, leaving:

1d *Mary Helen Fane [Mrs Michael Fry, Fulbeck Hall, Grantham, Lincs]; b 3 Oct 1947; m 1982 *Michael Robin Fry, graphic designer and inventor, and has:

1e *Marcus Fane; b 1985

2e *Samuel Henry Fane; b 1987

2c Francis Christopher FANE; b 9 June 1900; Lt RN (ret); m 11 Aug 1931 *Joyce Patricia [Mrs Vincent Tofts, Scots Hill, Fulbeck, Grantham, Lincs] (m 2nd 16 March 1957 Maj Vincent Glenton Tofts, TD, late IA (d 1983), s of Charles Tofts), 2nd dau of Rev William Hugh Munely Hancock, Vicar Leadenham, Lincs, and was lost at sea 17 June 1947, leaving:

1d +Julian Francis, DL (Lincs 1997) [Julian Fane Esq DL, Fulbeck Manor, Grantham, Lincs]; b 2 Oct 1938; educ Marlborough and Emmanuel Coll Cambridge (MA 1966); High Sheriff Lincs 1981; m 5 June 1965 *(Mary) Julia, yr dau of Michael William Allday, of The Shrubbery, Hartlebury, Worcs, and has:

1e +Andrew Julian; b 5 Dec 1967; educ Marlborough

1e *Alexandra Julia; b 23 Sept 1969

1d *Susan Cicely [Mrs John Dymoke, Scrivelsby Court, Horncastle, Lincs LN9 6JA]; b 9 Nov 1932; m 4 Sept 1953 *Lt-Col John Lindley Marmion Dymoke, MBE, V-Ld Lincs, late Roy Anglian Regt, 33rd of Scrivelsby and 7th of Tetford, Hereditary Sovereign's Champion by virtue of possession of Scrivelsby, est s of Lionel Marmion Dymoke, of Heydour Priory, Grantham, and has:

1e *Francis John Fane Marmion [Francis Dymoke Esq, Scrivelsby Grange, Horncastle, Lincs]; b 19 Jan 1955; educ Marlborough; m 1982 *Rosalie Mary, only dau of Maj Anthony Goldingham, of Marsh Farm, Uley, Glos, and has:

1f *Henry Francis Marmion; b 1984

2f *Thomas Anthony Marmion; b 1989

1f *Emily Rachel Marmion; b 1984

2e *Philip Henry Marmion; b 10 Sept 1957; Maj Welsh Gds; m 1982 *Arabella, yr dau of Sir Ralph Jordan Dodds, 2nd Bt (qv), and has:

1f *Edward Philip Marmion; b 1985

2f *William Thomas Marmion; b 1988

3e *Charles Edward Marmion; b 19 Aug 1961; m 1990 *Kathryn Jane, yst dau of Rex Topham, of Otford, Kent, and has:

1f *Jasper Rex Fane; b 1993

2f *Angus John Topham; b 1994

3f *Archie Charles Lindley; b 1997

2d *Rosemary Lilias, JP; b 10 April 1934; BA (1987); m 27 Feb 1954 *Derek Cecil Stevenson, MB, BS, FRCS, LRCP, MRCS, 2nd s of Capt Cecil Y Stevenson, of Jersey, and has:

1e *Christopher Peter; b 5 Feb 1956; B Juris, LLB, LLM (Lond); m 1985 *Evelyn Bowen, MB, BS, DObst (RCOG), and has:

1f *Richard Vere; b 1990

2f *Harry Bowen; b 1994

1f *Georgina Bowen; b 1988

1e *Melody Jane; b 7 Jan 1958; m 1980 *Christopher John Chipper and has:

1f *Simon Derek; b 1984

1f *Jasmin Melody; b 1982

2e *Catherine Fane [Ms Kate Stevenson, 63 Alderbury St, Floreat Pk, W Australia 6014]; b 17 Aug 1960; m 1985 *Peter Charles Kiel, MB, BS, and has:

1f *Michael William Fane; *b* 1989

2f *David Peter Stevenson; *b* 1991

1f *Sarah Jane Mary; *b* 1987

3e *Mary-Louise [Ms Mary-Louise Stevenson Hardwick, 35 Liddelow Rd, Banjup 6164, W Australia]; *b* 28 Oct 1969; BSc, Grad DipEd; *m* 1993 *Russell Paul Hardwick and has:

1f *Hayley Louise; *b* 1997

3d *Belinda Joyce [Mrs Belinda Phillips, 26a Cumberland Way, Bassendean, W Australia]; *b* 2 Oct 1938; *educ* Sydney U (Th A 1976, Th Dip 1988); *m* 1971 (*divorce* 1981) Gary Douglas Phillips

3c Charles William; *b* 2 Feb 1904; *educ* Charterhouse; underwriting memb Lloyd's, RNVR WW II; *m* 1st 15 Sept 1931 (*divorce* 1966) Pauline Margaret (*d* 10 Nov 1994), er dau of Rt Rev Ernest Morell Blackie, Dean Rochester, and had:

1d +Peter William [Peter Fane Esq, 22 Cheyne Row, London SW3 5HL]; *b* 17 April 1939; *educ* Eton; underwriting memb Lloyd's, High Sheriff Lincs 1983–84; *m* 28 June 1969 *Ruth, dau of John Paske Yeomans, of Hill Croome, Upton-on-Severn, Worcs, and adopted:

*Maximilian William; *b* 1978

1d *Angela Pauline [Mrs Patrick Bruce-Gardyne, The Old Rectory, Meonstoke, Hants]; *b* 9 June 1936; *m* 11 April 1964 *Lt-Cdr Kenneth Patrick Bruce-Gardyne, RN, yst s of Capt Evan Bruce-Gardyne, DSO, RN, of Middleton by Arbroath, Angus, and has:

1e *James Patrick; *b* 7 Sept 1965

2e *Vere Alexander; *b* 1973

1e *Victoria Sophia; *b* 8 Aug 1969

3c (cont.) Charles Fane *m* 2nd 29 July 1966 Pamela Mary (*d* Sept 1997), er dau of Capt Robert Millington Synge (*see* SYNGE, Bt), and *d* 15 March 1976, having by her had:

2d *Eleanor Mary; *b* 1965

3d *Georgina Rachel; *b* 1966; *m* 17 June 1995 *Jocelyn Andrew Denison-Pender (*see* PENDER, B) and has issue

4d *Rose Christabel; *b* 31 March 1968

1c Elizabeth Christine; *b* 6 April 1906; *m* 13 Oct 1931 Col Jeffrey Maurice Lambert, OBE, late RE (*d* 19 June 1967), yst s of Col Joseph Alexander Lambert, Queen's Bays, of Brookhill, Co Mayo, and *d* 30 May 1997, leaving:

1d *John Alexander [John Lambert Esq, 40 The Avenue, Greenacres, Aylesford, Kent ME20 7LE]; *b* 24 Nov 1932; *educ* St Lawrence Coll Ramsgate; *m* 30 Sept 1961 *Iris Elaine, only dau of James Balfour Craig, of Belfast, and has:

1e *Alastair James; *b* 2 Jan 1966

1e *Rachel Elizabeth; *b* 9 Dec 1962; and has issue

1d *Janetta Grace; *b* 2 Sept 1936

1b Grace Susan; *b* 27 Sept 1862; *m* 10 Feb 1887 Col Joseph Alexander Lambert, DL, 2nd Dragoon Gds (*d* 25 Sept 1907), of Brookhill, Co Mayo, and *d* 2 Nov 1947, leaving issue

2b Millicent Emma Rachel; *b* 4 Feb 1864; *m* 17 Aug 1898 Thomas Dalton Lawrance (*d* 1930) and *d* 19 Nov 1939, leaving issue

2a Henry Prinsep; *b* 27 Aug 1822; BCS; *d unm* 8 Jan 1894

1a Louisa Anne Fleming; *b* 7 Oct 1814; *m* 26 Dec 1840 Henry Porter Sherbrooke, JP, DL (*d* 11 June 1887), of Oxton, Notts, bro of 1st and last Viscount Sherbrooke, GCB, PC (*see* 1892 edn), and *d* 5 Dec 1893, leaving issue

2a Caroline; *b* 7 July 1818; *m* 22 Jan 1838 Gen Marcus Beresford and *d* 8 Jan 1895, leaving issue (*see* DECIES, B)

3a Emily Maria; *b* 10 Dec 1820; *m* 26 April 1859 Bulkeley John Mackworth Praed (*d* 12 March 1876), of Owsden Hall, Suffolk, and *d* 11 May 1905, leaving issue

4a Julia Charlotte; *m* 23 July 1844 Robert Alexander (*d* 23 Oct 1863) and *d* 1903, leaving issue

5a Adeline; *b* 6 Sept 1830; *m* 24 Nov 1864 William Earle Welby and *d* 29 June 1897, leaving issue (*see* WELBY, Bt)

6a Augusta; *b* 3 Nov 1831; *m* 10 Feb 1863 her cousin Col Francis Augustus Fane and *d* 14 June 1895, leaving issue (*see* above)

(6) Mildmay; *b* Sept 1794; Gen, Col 54th Foot; *k* 12 March 1868 by a fall from his horse while hunting

(7) Robert George Cecil; *b* 8 May 1796; Commr Court Bankruptcy; *m* 1st 24 June 1835 Isabella Mary (*dsp* 15 Dec 1838), yst dau of Adml Sir Eliab Harvey, GCB, of Rolls Park, Essex; *m* 2nd 7 Sept 1841 Harriette Anne, only dau of Adml Hon Sir Henry Blackwood, 1st Bt, and *d* 4 Oct 1864, having by her had, with two daus (*d unm*):

1a Lionel Arthur Cecil; *b* 10 March 1851; *d unm* 1 April 1872

2a Cecil Francis William; *b* 7 Oct 1856; Lt Gren Gds; *m* 1st 8 May 1880 (*divorce* 1904) Lady Augusta Fanny Rous (*d* 10 Feb 1950), est dau of 2nd Earl of Stradbroke (*qv*), and had:

1b Charles George Cecil; *b* 8 April 1881; *m* 21 April 1942 Rebecca (*d* 9 Oct 1961), dau of Henry Jephson and widow of Maj Hugh Ward, of Lereko, Naivasha, Kenya, and *d* 26 Sept 1950

2b Richard Lionel Richards; *b* 2 Jan 1884; *m* 30 July 1928 Barbara Kathleen (*m* 3rd 20 Sept 1947 Maj Bryan Northam Gibbs, MBE (*d* 23 Jan 1965), s of Arthur Gibbs, of Tunbridge Wells; reverted to her former married name FANE by deed poll 1965; *m* 4th 16 June 1969 John Sidney Mason (*d* 1974) and *d* 1980), est dau of Falconer Lewis Wallace, OBE, of Candacraig, Strathden, Aberdeenshire, and formerly w of Capt Oliver Henry Douglas Vickers, and *d* 25 Oct 1945, leaving:

1c Vere John Alexander; *b* 21 April 1935; *educ* Eton and Trin Coll Cambridge; Lt Coldstream Gds; *m* 30 May 1964 *Tessa Helen Murray [Mrs Vere Fane, 18 Empire Ho, Thurloe Sq, London SW7 2RU], only dau of John Murray Prain, DSO, OBE, DL, of Longrigg, St Andrews, Fife, and *d* 23 July 1997, leaving:

1d +Rupert John Alexander; *b* 27 April 1967; *m* 7 Nov 1998 *Nicola, dau of Jens Dowling, of Sydney, NSW

1d *Miranda Helen; *b* 2 Sept 1968; *m* 10 May 1997 *Jamie Landale, 3rd s of Sir David Landale, KCVO, of Dalswinton, Dumfries-shire

1c *Venetia Sophia Diana, MBE [Miss Venetia Fane MBE, Drumwhill, Mossdale, by Castle Douglas, Kirkcudbrightshire DG7 2NL]; *b* 24 Feb 1930

2a (cont.) Cecil Fane *m* 2nd 19 Nov 1904 Muriel Ellen (*d* 3 June 1938), est dau of John Selwyn Harvey, MD, and formerly w of Onslow Powell Traherne, and *d* 30 Jan 1914

(1) Anne; *b* 19 Jan 1780; *m* 29 Sept 1803 Lt-Gen John Michel (*d* 1844), of Dewlish and Kingston Russell, Dorset, and *d* March 1831, leaving issue

(2) Caroline; *b* 28 Dec 1791; *m* 17 Sept 1812 Charles Chaplin, MP, of Blankney, Lincs (*dsp* 31 May 1859; *see* 1970 edn CHAPLIN, V)

(3) Harriett; *b* 10 Sept 1793; *m* 31 Jan 1814 Rt Hon Charles Arbuthnot, KC, MP (*d* 1850), and *d* 1834

The 8th EARL's est s,

JOHN FANE, 9th Earl of Westmorland; *b* 5 May 1728; *educ* Westminster; Commr Taxes 1760–62, MP (Tory) Lyme Regis 1762–71, LLD Cantab 1769; *m* 1st 26 March 1758 Augusta (*d* 4 Feb 1766), dau of Lord Montague Bertie, s of 1st Duke of Ancaster and Kesteven (*see* LINDSEY and ABINGDON, E), and had:

1 JOHN, **10th Earl**

2 Thomas; *b* 6 July 1760; Field Offr Army; *m* 27 July 1789 Anne Lowe and *d* 15 April 1807, leaving:

(1) John Thomas; *b* 27 April 1790; Lt-Col, MP Lyme Regis; *m* 10 Aug 1816 Marianne Shrimpton (*d* 15 April 1836), est dau of John Mills Jackson, of Southampton, and *d* 1833, leaving an only s (*dsp*)

(2) William; *b* 2 July 1793; Capt 84th Foot; *das* Peninsular War 27 Feb 1815

1 Augusta; *b* 18 Sept 1761; *m* 12 July 1781 1st Earl of Lonsdale (*qv*) and *d* 6 March 1838, leaving issue

The **9th Earl** *m* 2nd 28 May 1767 Susan (*m* 2nd 28 Dec 1778 Lt-Col John Woodford and *d* 11 Dec 1814), dau of 3rd Duke of Gordon (*see* RICHMOND and GORDON, D), and *d* 26 April 1774, having had by her:

2 Susan; *b* 3 Oct 1768; *m* 20 July 1788 John Drummond of Megginch and *d* 8 March 1793, leaving issue (*see* STRANGE, B)

3 Elizabeth; *b* 7 Jan 1770; *m* 4 Sept 1790 Sir John Lowther, 1st Bt (*qv*), and *d* 19 May 1844, leaving issue

4 Mary; *b* 19 Sept 1772; *m* 16 Jan 1792 George Fludyer (*d* 18 April 1837), 2nd s of Sir Samuel Fludyer, 1st Bt, Ld Mayor London (*see* 1917 edn), and *d* 27 June 1885

The 9th EARL's er s,

JOHN FANE, 10th Earl of Westmorland, KG (1793), PC (1789); *b* 1 June 1759; Jt PMG 1789, Ld Lt Ireland 1789–95, Master Horse 1795–98, Ld Privy Seal 1798–1806 and 1807–27, Ld Lt Northants 1828–41; *m* 1st (at Gretna Green against wishes of his f-in-law) 20 May 1782 Sarah Anne (*d* 9 Nov 1793), only dau and heiress of Robert Child, banker, of Osterley Park, Middx, and had:

1 JOHN, **11th Earl**

1 Sarah Sophia (who inherited the immense fortune of her maternal gf); *b* 4 March 1785; *m* 23 May 1804 5th Earl of Jersey (*qv*) and *d* 26 Jan 1867

2 Augusta; *b* 17 March 1786; *m* 1st 20 June 1804 (*divorce* 1809) 1st Earl of Morley (*qv*); *m* 2nd 16 Feb 1809 Rt Hon Sir Arthur Paget, GCB (*see* ANGLESEY, M)

3 Maria; *b* 11 May 1787; *m* 16 Nov 1805 4th Earl of Bessborough (*qv*) and *d* 19 March 1834, leaving issue

The **10th Earl** *m* 2nd 24 March 1800 Jane (*d* 26 March 1857), dau and coheir of Richard Huck Saunders, MD, and *d* 15 Dec 1841, having by her had, with two daus:

2 Charles Saunders John; *b* 8 May 1802; *d* 23 Oct 1810

3 Henry Sutton; *b* 18 Sept 1805; Lt-Col

4 Montague Villiers; *b* 18 Sept 1805

The 10th EARL's est s,

JOHN FANE, 11th Earl of Westmorland, GCB (1846, KCB 1838, CB 1815), GCH (1817); *b* 3 Feb 1784; MP Lyme Regis 1806–16, Extra ADC Peninsular War to Duke of Wellington, present Battles of Talavera and Busaco, Gen 1854; Envoy Extrdy and Min Plen Florence 1814–30, Prussia 1841 and Vienna 1851, special Plen Vienna Conference 1855; Grand Cross Order Leopold; fndr and pres RAM 1823; *m* 26 June 1811 Priscilla Anne (*d* 18 Feb 1879), dau of 4th Earl of Mornington (*see* WELLINGTON, D), and *d* 16 Oct 1859, having had, with another dau (*d unm*):

1 John Arthur; *b* 12 Feb 1816; *dvp* 29 Aug 1816

2 George Augustus Frederick John, *Lord Burghersh*; *b* 18 June 1819; *d* 29 April 1848

3 Ernest Fitzroy Neville, *Lord Burghersh*; *b* 7 Jan 1824; Capt Scots Fus Gds; *m* 17 Oct 1849 Augusta Selina Elizabeth (Leila) (*m* 2nd 31 Aug 1854 (*divorce* Nov 1876) Luigi Caracciolo, Duke di Santo Teodoro, and had a dau Teresa (*m* Prince Colonna and had a dau Vittoria Colonna, Duchess of Sermoneta, author); *m* 3rd 19 March 1877 6th Baron Walsingham (*qv*) and *d* 4 Nov 1906), only child of Capt William Locke (subject of *Boy and Dog* by Sir Thomas Lawrence, RA), by Selina, 6th dau of Adml Tollemache (*see* TOLLEMACHE, B), and *dsp* 22 Jan 1851

4 FRANCIS WILLIAM HENRY, **12th Earl**

5 Julian Henry Charles; *b* 10 Oct 1827; Sec Embassy Vienna and Paris; *m* 29 Sept 1866 Adine Eliza Anne, 3rd dau of 6th Earl Cowper (*see* LUCAS OF CRUDWELL, B), and *d* 19 April 1870, leaving:

(1) John Francis Henry; *b* 18 July 1868; *d* 9 March 1876

(1) Ethel Anne Priscilla; *b* 27 June 1867; Extra Ldy Bedchamber to HM QUEEN MARY; *m* 17 Feb 1887 1st and last Baron Desborough and *d* 28 May 1952, leaving issue (*see* GRENFELL, B)

1 Rose Sophia Mary; *m* 15 Aug 1866 Henry Weigall, DL, of Southwood, St Lawrence, Isle of Thanet, and *d* 14 Feb 1921, leaving issue (*see* 1949 edn WEIGALL, Bt)

The 11th EARL's est surv s,

FRANCIS WILLIAM HENRY FANE, 12th Earl of Westmorland, CB (10 July 1855), DL (Northants); *b* 19 Nov 1825; *educ* Westminster and RMC Sandhurst;

Col Coldstream Gds, ADC to his unc Lord Raglan in Turkey and Crimea 1854–55, brought home despatches after Battle of Alma 20 Sept 1854, ADC to HRH THE DUKE OF CAMBRIDGE 1856–60; *m* 16 July 1857 Lady Adelaide Ida Curzon (*d* 22 March 1903), dau of 1st Earl Howe (*qv*), and *d* 3 Aug 1891, having had:

1 George Neville John, *Lord Burghersh*; *b* 3 Sept 1858: *d* 31 July 1860

2 ANTHONY MILDMAY JULIAN, **13th Earl**

1 Grace Adelaide; *m* 11 Aug 1887 2nd Earl of Londesborough (*see* LONDESBOROUGH, B) and *d* 13 June 1933, leaving issue

2 Margaret Mary; *m* 2 Oct 1888 Capt John Edmund Philip Spicer, 1st Life Gds (*d* 31 March 1928), of Spye Park, Chippenham, Wilts, and *d* 22 Nov 1949, leaving issue

The 12th EARL's yr s,

ANTHONY MILDMAY JULIAN FANE, **13th Earl of Westmorland**, CBE (1919), JP (Northants); *b* 16 Aug 1859; *educ* Eton; Maj 3rd Bn Northants Regt Boer War 1902, Lt Col cmdg 3rd Bn Northants Regt 1907–14, ADC to HM GEORGE V 1911, Lt-Col 3rd Bn Lancs Fus WW I; *m* 1st 28 May 1892 Lady Sybil Mary St Clair-Erskine (*d* 21 July 1910), dau of 4th Earl of Rosslyn (*qv*), and had:

1 VERE ANTHONY FRANCIS ST CLAIR, **14th Earl**

2 Mountjoy John Charles Wedderburn, TD (1944), DL (Lincs 1952); *b* 8 Oct 1900; *educ* RNCs Osborne and Dartmouth; Maj RASC (TA); *m* 29 April 1926 Agatha Isabel Acland-Hood, JP (*d* 1993), dau of Lt-Col Arthur Acland-Hood-Reynardson, OBE, JP,DL, (*see* 1970 edn FULLER-ACLAND-HOOD, Bt); *d* 9 Oct 1963, leaving:

(1) +Antony Charles Reynardson [Lt-Cdr Antony Fane RN, Ridgemead House, Shrubbs Hill Lane, Sunningdale, Berks SL5 0LD]; *b* 11 Oct 1927; *educ* RNC Dartmouth; *m* 17 Jan 1956 *Caroline Mary Rokeby, dau of Hugh Delano Holland, of Englefield Green, and has:

1a +Edward Hugh Reynardson [Edward Fane Esq, 15 Kyrle Rd, London SW11 6BD]; *b* 11 June 1957; *m* 10 July 1982 *Suki Serena, only dau of Sir David Mitchell, MP, of Odiham, Hants, and has:

1b +Arthur Charles Reynardson; *b* 1992

1b *Elizabeth Helen Clementine; *b* 1986

2b *Helena Evelyn Cecily; *b* 1988

1a *Olivia Mary Rokeby; *b* 9 May 1960; *m* 1st 11 Sept 1982 (*divorce* 1992) Adam Nicolson (*see* CARNOCK, B)

2a *Charlotte Evelyn Langham; *b* 9 Sept 1967

(1) *Daphne Sybil [Miss Daphne Fane, Little Paddocks, Careby, Stamford, Lincs]; *b* 25 March 1929

1 Enid Victoria Rachel; *b* 24 May 1894; *m* 1st 25 Aug 1914 Hon Henry Cecil Vane (*dsp* & *vp* 9 Oct 1917 in France), est s of 9th Baron Barnard (*qv*); *m* 2nd 1 Sept 1922 Maj Herbert Broke Turnor, MC, DL, 17th Lancers, est s of Algernon Turnor, CB (*see* GALLOWAY, E), and *d* 9 Sept 1969, leaving issue

2 (Violet) Gloria Sybil; *b* 11 April 1902; *d* 19–

The 13th Earl *m* 2nd 22 April 1916 Catherine Louise (*d* 21 Aug 1973), er dau of Rev John Samuel Geale, and *d* 9 June 1922

His er s,

VERE ANTHONY FRANCIS ST CLAIR FANE, **14th Earl of Westmorland**; *b* 15 March 1893; Lt-Cdr RN WW I in HMS *Lion* at Jutland, ret 1919; gentleman rider and trainer; *m* 7 June 1923 Hon Diana (*d* 3 Dec 1983), dau of 4th and last Baron Ribblesdale (*see* 1925 edn) and widow of (a) Percy Lyulph Wyndham (*see* EGREMONT, LECONFIELD and, B) and (b) Capt Arthur Edward Capel, CBE, and *d* 12 May 1948, having had:

1 DAVID ANTHONY THOMAS, **15th Earl**

2 +Julian Charles [The Hon Julian Fane, Rotten Row House, Lewes, E Sussex BN7 1TN]; *b* 25 May 1927; *educ* Harrow; author, FRSL; *m* 7 Jan 1976 *Gillian, yr dau of John Kidston Swire, DL, of Hubbards Hall, Harlow, Essex

1 Rose; *b* 4 Jan 1931; *m* 3 Nov 1950 (*divorce* 1969) Capt John Macdonald-Buchanan, MC, Scots Gds, er s of Maj Sir Reginald Narcissus Macdonald-Buchanan, MBE, MC, Scots Gds, of Cottesbrooke Hall, Northants, and Egerton House, Newmarket; *m* 2nd 9 May 1972 *John V Bardsley, s of R V Bardsley, CMG, OBE, and *d* 1984, leaving by her 1st husb:

(1) *Alastair Reginald; *b* 25 Nov 1960

(1) *Fiona Mary; *b* 12 Jan 1954

(2) *Serena; *b* 17 April 1956

The 14th EARL's est s,

DAVID ANTHONY THOMAS FANE, **15th Earl of Westmorland**, GCVO (1991), KCVO (1970), DL (Glos 1991); *b* 31 March 1924; *educ* Eton; Lt RHG WW II 1944 (wounded), a Ld-in-Waiting 1955–78, Master Horse 1978–91, Ld-in-Waiting 1991–93, dir: Sotheby Parke Bernet Gp 1965–, (dep chm 1979, chm 1980–82), Sotheby Hldgs Inc 1983–, Sotheby Advsy Bd 1987–, Pres: S of England Ag Soc 1973–93 and Anglo American Sporting Club; *m* 20 June 1950 *Jane Barbara, DL [The Rt Hon The Dowager Countess of Westmorland, DL, The Old Vicarage, Badminton, Glos GL9 1DG], only child of Col Sir Roland Lewis Findlay, 3rd Bt (*see* 1970 edn), and *d* 1993, leaving:

1 ANTHONY DAVID FRANCIS HENRY FANE, **16th and present Earl of Westmorland**

2 +HARRY ST CLAIR [The Hon Harry Fane, 14 Trevor St, London SW7]; *b* 19 March 1953; heir presumptive; *educ* Harrow; Page of Honour to HM THE QUEEN 1966–68; *m* 6 Jan 1984 *Tessa, 2nd dau of Capt Michael Philip Forsyth-Forrest (*see* WESTMINSTER, D) and formerly w of Christopher Baldwin, and has:

(1) +Sam Michael David; *b* 1989

(1) *Sophie Jane; *b* 1987

1 *Camilla Diana [The Lady Camilla Hipwood, Fosse Tillery Farm, Brokenborough, Wilts SN16 0HY]; *b* 26 Dec 1957; *m* 24 Sept 1985 *Howard J Hipwood and has:

(1) *Sebastian John; *b* 15 Aug 1988

(1) *Rosanna Charlotte; *b* 22 Aug 1986

WESTWOOD

Arms: Argent a lion rampant gules between three lymphads sable, flags flying to the dexter of the second. **Crest:** A mullet argent, charged with a thistle slipped and leaved proper. **Supporters:** On either side a sea-lion argent, charged on the shoulder with two anchors in saltire sable. **Motto:** Deeds not words. **Creation:** B. (UK) 29 Jan 1944.

THE 3RD BARON WESTWOOD, of Gosforth, Co Northumberland (William Gavin Westwood) [The Rt Hon The Lord Westwood, Ferndale, Clayton Rd, Newcastle-upon-Tyne NE2 1TL]; *b* 30 Jan 1944; *s f* 1991; *educ* Fettes; ACA; *m* 21 June 1969 *Penelope, FCA, est dau of Dr Charles Edgar Shafto, VRD, MD, of Newcastle 7, and has:

1 +WILLIAM FERGUS; *b* 24 Nov 1972; *educ* Roy GS Newcastle

2 +Alastair Cameron; *b* 28 June 1974; *educ* Roy GS Newcastle

Lineage: WILLIAM WESTWOOD, of Broughty Ferry, nr Dundee; *m* Elizabeth Shaw (*d* 4 April 1932) and *d* 29 July 1923, leaving:

WILLIAM WESTWOOD, **1st Baron Westwood**, of Gosforth, Co Northumberland (UK), so *cr* 29 Jan 1944, OBE (1920), JP (Northumberland and City of Dundee); *b* 28 Aug 1880; *educ* elementary schs Dundee; started work in jute mills aged 10, shipbldg apprentice Dundee, Sec Dundee Labour Rep Ctee and political agent, Chm Scottish Lab Advsy Cncl 1918–19, Supervisor Ship Constructors' and Shipwrights' Assoc 1913–29 (Gen Sec 1929–45), CC 1937–46, Pncpl Labour Advsr Bd of Admlty 1942, Dir Contract Labour Admlty 1941–42, Ch Industl Advsr Bd of Admlty 1942–45, a Ld-in-Waiting 1945–47, Chm Mineral Devpt Ctee Min Fuel and Power 1946 and Newcastle Exec Cncl under NHS Act 1946, dir Olympia Ltd, Covent Garden Properties Ltd, Investment Registry Ltd and Kaye and Stewart Ltd, chm and dir Century Insur (Newcastle Bd) and Newcastle Utd FC, Pres: Engrg and Shipbuilding Trades Fedn 1933–36, Confedn Shipbldg and Engrg Unions 1936–39 and Inst of Engrg Draughtsmen and Designers, V-Pres Bldg Socs Assoc, Liveryman and Freeman Shipwrights' Co, Freeman City London, FRSA, FRES; *m* 1st June 1905 Margaret Taylor (*d* Oct 1916), dau of William Young, of Dundee, and had:

1 WILLIAM, **2nd Baron**

2 Douglas Wilkie; *b* 13 Sept 1910; *educ* Allan Glen's Sch Glasgow, FRSA; 2nd Mate Merchant Navy 1930–32; *m* 18 Aug 1939 Mary Katherine (*d* 1987), dau of John Carter, of Durham, and *d* 1 May 1968, leaving an adopted dau:

*Carol Margaret [Baroness Staël von Holstein, 4 Penzance Place, London W11]; *b* 17 Jan 1945; *m* 1st 4 Oct 1966 (*divorce* 1978) Maj John Stephen Ralli and has issue (*see* RALLI, Bt); *m* 2nd Robert Alexander Karl Constantin, Baron Staël von Holstein

3 James Young Shaw; *b* 19 Sept 1915; *educ* Queen's Park Acad Glasgow; Capt Merchant Navy; *m* 22 March 1941 (*divorce* 1969) Joan, only child of Raymond Potts, of Newcastle, and *d* 1989, leaving:

(1) +Roger Douglas [Roger Westwood Esq, Swallowtail Cottage, Hobbs Lane, Beckley, E Sussex TN31 6TT]; *b* 16 Sept 1943; *educ* Westminister and New Coll Oxford (MA, DipEd); P/O RAFVR

1 Davina Young; *b* 3 Dec 1911; *m* 1st 31 Oct 1931 (*divorce* 1946) John William Lamb, s of John William Lamb, of Jesmond, and had issue; *m* 2nd 27 March 1947 Edward Ronald Norman, formerly RNVR, of Manningtree, Essex, s of Alfred Ernest Norman, of Manningtree, and *d* 26 Dec 1961

2 *Margaret Taylor Young, MBE [The Hon Mrs Campbell MBE, 2 Ethorpe Crescent, Gerrards Cross, Bucks SL9 8PW]; *b* 15 Dec 1913; WRNS; *m* 1st 18 Jan 1934 (*divorce* 1943) William Blackbird Lynn, s of John Lynn, of S Shields; *m* 2nd 14 Feb 1945 (*divorce* 1974) John Bruce Campbell, RCA, s of George Howard Campbell, of Port Hope, Ontario, and has:

(1) *Robert Bruce; *b* 15 June 1948; *educ* privately

(1) *Helen Jean Laura; *b* 19 April 1946; *educ* Southampton U (BA)

The **1st Baron** *m* 2nd 26 April 1918 Agnes Helen Flockhart (*d* 28 Jan 1952), dau of James Downie, of Dundee, and *d* 13 Sept 1953

His est s,

WILLIAM WESTWOOD, **2nd Baron Westwood**, JP (Newcastle upon Tyne 1949); *b* 25 Dec 1907; *educ* Queen's Park Acad Glasgow, FCIS, FRSA; Chm Newcastle Utd FC, Pres Football League and a V-Pres FA 1974–91; *m* 9 June 1937 *Marjorie [The Rt Hon The Dowager Lady Westwood, 55 Moor Court, Westfield, Newcastle-upon-Tyne NE3 4YD], only child of Arthur Bonwick, of Heaton, Newcastle, and *d* 1991, leaving:

1 WILLIAM GAVIN WESTWOOD, **3rd and present Baron Westwood**

2 +Nigel Alistair [The Hon Nigel Westwood, 7 Fernville Rd, Gosforth, Newcastle-upon-Tyne NE3 4HT]; *b* 30 April 1950; *educ* Fettes; Kt 1st Cl Order Merit Norway; FRICS, FRSA; Hon Roy Norwegian Consul; *m* 11 June 1977 *Joan Elizabeth, dau of Reginald Ibison, CBE, of Gosforth, Northumberland, and has:

   (1) +David Alistair; *b* 1983

   (2) +Peter Robert; *b* 1986

WHADDON

Arms: Quarterly vert and or on a fess engrailed ermine, between in dexter chief a mullet and in sinister base a harp or, and in sinister chief and dexter base a rose gules, barbed and seeded proper, three garbs gold. **Crest:** Upon a wreath or, vert and gules a crown vallary or, issuing therefrom, within a chaplet vert set with roses gules barbed and seeded proper, a triple trefoil slipped vert. **Supporters:** Dexter, a lion guardant proper winged or; sinister, a mermaid proper crined and with a tail fin or, a round shield with its boss gold on her forearm and holding in the hand proper a sword point upward argent hilt, pommel and quillons gold. **Motto:** *Caveat qui certuses* ('Take care that you are right'). **Creation:** B. (LP, UK) 1978.

THE BARON WHADDON, of Whaddon, Co Cambridge ((John) Derek Page) [The Rt Hon The Lord Whaddon, The Old Vicarage, Whaddon, Royston, Herts]; *b* 14 Aug 1927; *educ* St Bedes Coll Manchester and London (BSc); MP (Lab) King's Lynn 1964–70; chm: Cambridge Chemical Co 1991– (dir 1962–), Rindalbourne Ltd 1983–90, Daltrade Ltd 1983–, Skorimpex-Rind Ltd 1985–; memb: Cncl Management CoSIRA 1975–82, E Anglia Ec Planning Cncl 1975–80; Golden Insignia Order Merit Poland 1989; *m* 1st 1948 Catherine Audrey (*d* 1979), dau of John William Halls, and has:

   1 *John Keir; *b* 1955; *m* 1976 *Gale Masterman

   1 *Eve-Ann; *b* 1952; *m* 1972 *Patrick Prentice

The BARON WHADDON *m* 2nd 1981 *Angela Rixson, dau of Luigi della Bella, of Treviso, Italy

Lineage: JOHN PAGE; *m* Clare Maher and had:

(JOHN) DEREK, *cr* a **Baron**

WHARNCLIFFE

Arms: Quarterly, 1st and 4th, arg. on a bend, between six martlets gu., three bezants, a canton or charged with the arms of STUART, being those of the 2nd quarter (for WHORTLEY); 3rd, arg. three lozenges conjoined in fess gu. within a bordure sa. (for MONTAGU). **Crests:** 1 A demi-lion rampant gu. and in an escrol over the motto *Nobilis ira* ('Noble in anger', for STUART), 2 An eagle's leg erased or, issuant therefrom three ostrich feathers ppr., charged on the thigh with a fess chequy az. and arg. (for WHORTLEY), 3 A griffin's head couped or, wings addorsed and beak sa. (for MONTAGU). **Supporters:** Dexter, a horse argent, bridled gu.; sinister, a stag proper, attired or, each gorged with a collar flory counter-flory of the second. **Motto:** *Avito viret honore* ('He flourishes with the honour of his ancestors'). **Creations:** B. (UK) 12 July 1826, E. and V. (UK) 15 Jan 1876.

THE 5TH EARL OF WHARNCLIFFE, West Riding of Co York, **Viscount Carlton**, of Carlton, West Riding of Co York, and **Baron Wharncliffe of Wortley**, Co York (Richard Alan Montagu Stuart Wortley) [The Rt Hon The Earl of Wharncliffe, 270 Main St, Cumberland, ME 04021, USA]; *b* 26 May 1953; *s* kinsman 1987; *educ* Wesleyan U, Conn; builder; *m* 1979 *Mary Elizabeth, dau of Rev William Wellington Reed, of Keene, NH, and has:

   1 +REED, *Viscount Carlton*; *b* 5 Feb 1980

   2 +Christopher James; *b* 1983

   3 +A son; *b* 19–

Lineage: The 1st EARL OF SANDWICH (*qv*) had a 2nd s:

SIDNEY MONTAGU later WORTLEY-MONTAGU; *m* Anne Newcomen alias Wortley, illegitimate dau and heir of Sir Francis Wortley, 2nd and last Bt (*dspl* 14 March 1665/6), of Wortley Hall, Yorks, and *d* 11 Nov 1727, having had, with other issue, including an er s (Francis, MP Huntingdon, *dvp*):

EDWARD WORTLEY-MONTAGU; Ld Commr Treasury, Amb Constantinople; *m* by licence 12 Aug 1715 Lady Mary Pierrepont (*d* 1762), celebrated for introducing small-pox inoculation into England 1719, having previously had her own children treated thus in Constantinople, est dau of 1st Duke of Kingston-upon-Hull, KG (*see* KINGSTON, E, preliminary remarks), and *d* 1761, having had, with a s (Edward, MP Bossiney, Cornwall, *dsp* & *vp*):

MARY Wortley-Montagu, BARONESS MOUNT STUART OF WORTLEY, Co York (GB), so *cr* 3 April 1761, with remainder to the heirs male of her body by her then husb; *b* Feb 1718; *m* 13/24 Aug 1736 John STUART, 3rd Earl of Bute (*see* BUTE, M), and *d* 6 Nov 1794, when the Barony passed to her est s, leaving a 2nd s:

JAMES ARCHIBALD STUART later STUART-WORTLEY (roy licence 17 Jan 1795, on inheriting mother's estates in Cornwall and Yorks) later still STUART-WORTLEY-MACKENZIE (1803 on inheriting the Scottish estates of his uncle Rt Hon James Stuart Mackenzie; added also the arms of MACKENZIE of Rosehaugh); *b* 19 Sept 1747; Lt-Col, MP Bute 1774, 1784 and 1806; *m* 8 June 1767 Margaret, dau of Sir David Cunynghame, 3rd Bt (*qv*), and had:

   1 John; MP Bossiney; *d* unm 14 Jan 1797

   2 JAMES ARCHIBALD, **1st Baron**

   3 George; *b* 1783; *d* 1813

   1 Mary; *m* 1 June 1813 Rt Hon William Dundas (*d* 1845), MP Edinburgh, and *d* 9 March 1855

   2 Louisa Harcourt; *m* 23 June 1801 5th Duke of Northumberland (*qv*) and *d* 30 June 1848

JAMES STUART-WORTLEY-MACKENZIE *d* 1 March 1818; his s,

JAMES ARCHIBALD STUART later STUART-WORTLEY (roy licence 17 Jan 1795) later still STUART-WORTLEY-MACKENZIE (1826), **1st Baron Wharncliffe of Wortley**, Co York (UK), so *cr* 12 July 1826, PC (1834); *b* 6 Oct 1776; *educ* Charterhouse; Capt and Lt-Col 1st Foot Gds 1797, MP (Tory) Bossiney 1802–18 and Yorks 1818–26, Ld Privy Seal 1834–35, Ld Pres Cncl 1841–45, Ld Lt W R Yorks 1841–45; *m* 30 March 1799 Lady Elizabeth Caroline Mary Crichton (*d* 23 April 1856), dau of 1st Earl of Erne (*qv*), and had:

   1 JOHN, **2nd Baron**

2 Charles James; *b* 3 June 1802; *m* 17 Feb 1831 Emmeline Charlotte Elizabeth (*d* 30 Oct 1855), 2nd dau of 5th Duke of Rutland (*qv*), and *d* 22 May 1844, leaving:

(1) Archibald Henry Plantagenet; *b* 26 July 1832; Col, Chev Legn Hon, Medjidie and St Maurice and St Lazarus; *m* 15 June 1879 Lavinia Rebecca (*d* 21 Nov 1937), dau of Samuel Gibbins, and *d* 30 April 1890

(1) Victoria Alexandrina; Maid of Honour to HM QUEEN VICTORIA; *m* 4 July 1863 Sir William Earle Welby-Gregory, 4th Bt, and *d* 29 March 1912, leaving issue (*see* WELBY, Bt)

3 James Archibald STUART-WORTLEY, PC; *b* 3 July 1805; QC, MP, Recorder City London, Slr-Gen 1856–57; *m* 6 May 1846 Hon Jane Lawley (*d* 4 Feb 1900), only dau of 1st Baron Wenlock (*see* 1932 edn), and *d* 22 Aug 1881, leaving, with two other sons (*d* young):

(1) Archibald John; *b* 27 May 1849; *m* 1883 Eleanor Edith Bromley (*d* 27 Oct 1939) and *dsp* 11 Oct 1905

(2) CHARLES BEILBY STUART-WORTLEY, 1st and last BARON STUART OF WORTLEY, of the City of Sheffield (UK), so *cr* 1 Jan 1917, PC (1896), QC (1892); *b* 15 Sept 1851; *educ* Rugby and Balliol Coll Oxford (BA 1875, MA 1878); barrister Inner Temple 1876, MP (C) Sheffield 1880–85 and Sheffield Hallam 1885–1916, Parly U-Sec Home Dept 1885–86 and 1886–92, T/Chm Ctees H of C 1895–1916; *m* 1st 16 Aug 1880 Beatrice (*d* 26 July 1881), only child of Thomas Adolphus Trollope (*see* TROLLOPE, Bt), and had:

1a Beatrice Susan Theodosia; *b* 15 July 1881; *m* 1 Dec 1906 Arthur William James Cecil and *d* 30 Dec 1973, leaving issue (*see* SALISBURY, M)

(2) (cont.) The 1st and last BARON STUART OF WORTLEY *m* 2nd 6 Jan 1886 Alice Sophia Caroline (*d* 1 Jan 1936), dau of Sir John Everett Millais, 1st Bt (*qv*), and *dspm* 24 April 1926, when the title expired, leaving by her:

2a Clare Euphemia; *b* 16 Oct 1889; *d* unm 15 Jan 1945

(1) Mary Caroline; *m* 30 Dec 1880 2nd Earl of Lovelace (*qv*) and *d* 18 April 1941

(2) Margaret Jane; *m* 8 May 1877 Maj-Gen Hon Sir Reginald Arthur James Talbot, KCB (*see* SHREWSBURY and WATERFORD, E), and *d* 6 Oct 1937

(3) Blanche Georgina; *m* 26 Feb 1895 Col Frederick Firebrace, RE (*d* 21 Sept 1917), and *d* 7 July 1931

(4) Caroline Susan Theodora, CBE (1920); Chm Women's Farm and Garden Assoc, author: *The Bands of Orion* and *The First Lady Wharncliffe and her Family 1799–1856*; *m* 25 June 1881 Norman de l'Aigle Grosvenor, 3rd s of 1st Baron Ebury (*qv*), and *d* 7 Aug 1940, leaving issue

(5) Katharine Sarah; *m* 1 Oct 1883 Gen Rt Hon Sir Neville Gerald Lyttelton, GCB, GCVO, and *d* 27 March 1943, leaving issue (*see* COBHAM, V)

1 Caroline Jane; *m* 30 Aug 1830 Hon John Chetwynd Talbot and *d* 12 June 1876, leaving issue (*see* SHREWSBURY and WATERFORD, E)

The 1st BARON *d* 19 Dec 1845; his est s,

JOHN STUART-WORTLEY-MACKENZIE, **2nd Baron Wharncliffe**; *b* 23 April 1801; *educ* Harrow and Ch Ch Oxford (BA 1822); Lt-Col SW Yorks Yeo; MP Bossiney 1823–30 and 1831–32, Perth Burghs 1830 and W R Yorks 1841–45; *m* 12 Dec 1825 Georgiana Elizabeth (*d* 22 Aug 1884 aged 80), 3rd dau of 1st Earl of Harrowby (*qv*), and *d* 22 Oct 1855, leaving:

1 EDWARD MONTAGU STUART GRANVILLE STUART-WORTLEY later STUART-WORTLEY-MACKENZIE (1855) later still MONTAGU-STUART-WORTLEY-MACKENZIE (roy licence 18 Oct 1880), **1st Earl of Wharncliffe**, West Riding of Co York, so *cr* 15 Jan 1876, as also VISCOUNT CARLTON, of Carlton, West Riding of Co York (both UK, with remainder in both cases to his bro Francis and the latter's heirs male of the body), JP, DL; *b* 15 Dec 1827; *educ* Eton; Lt Gren Gds, Hon Col 1st Vol York and Lancaster Regt; *m* 4 July 1855 Lady Susan Charlotte Lascelles (*d* 18 May 1927), dau of 3rd Earl of Harewood (*qv*), and *dsps* 13 May 1899, having had:

(1) John Henry Montagu; *b* 8 April 1856; *d* 19 Jan 1857

2 Francis Dudley MONTAGU-STUART-WORTLEY, DL (Yorks); *b* 23 July 1829; *m* 28 Aug 1855 Maria Elizabeth (*d* 26 Sept 1891), est dau of William Bennet Martin, of Worsborough Hall, Yorks, and *d* 21 Oct 1893, having had, with another s and dau (*d* in infancy):

(1) FRANCIS JOHN MONTAGU-STUART-WORTLEY-MACKENZIE, **2nd Earl of Wharncliffe**, JP, DL (W R Yorks); *b* 9 June 1856; *educ* Eton; Cdr RN; *m* 17 Aug 1886 Ellen (*d* 12 March 1922), dau of Lt-Gen Sir Thomas Lionel John Gallwey, KCMG, Govr Bermuda, and *d* 8 May 1926, having had:

1a George Francis Dudley; *b* 25 May 1889 (HRH THE DUKE OF CORNWALL AND YORK stood sponsor); *d* 6 Oct 1894

2a ARCHIBALD RALPH MONTAGU STUART WORTLEY MACKENZIE, **3rd Earl of Wharncliffe**, JP, DL (W R Yorks); *b* 17 April 1892; *educ* Eton and RMC Sandhurst; Capt Res Offrs Life Gds and Gds MG Regt WW I, ADC to Govr-Gen S Africa 1915–16; *m* 24 March 1918 Lady (Maud Lillian) Elfreda Mary Wentworth Fitzwilliam (*d* 1979), ran her own munitions works WW II, Master Ecclesfield Beagles 1930–79, est dau of 7th Earl Fitzwilliam, KCVO, DSO (*see* 1970 edn), and *d* 16 May 1953, leaving:

1b ALAN JAMES MONTAGU STUART WORTLEY MACKENZIE, **4th Earl of Wharncliffe**; *b* 23 March 1935; *educ* Eton; RN 1953–55, later RNVR; Master Ecclesfield Beagles, able seaman, drummer in rock band, motor mechanic, publican, salesman; *m* 25 July 1957 *Aline Margaret [The Rt Hon Aline Countess of Wharncliffe, Wharncliffe House, Wortley, Sheffield], only dau of Robert Fernie Dunlop Bruce, of Dyson Holmes House, Wharncliffe Side, nr Sheffield, and *d* June 1987, having had:

1c Joanna Margaret; *b* 15 July 1959; *k* car crash 1981

2c *Rowena [The Lady Rowena Stuart Wortley Hunt, Minety House, Minety, Wilts]; *b* 14 June 1961; *m* 1986 *John Hunt, s of Dr G H Hunt, of Greenwich, and has:

1d *Somerset Carlton Gerald; *b* 1987

1b *Ann Lavinia Maud [The Lady Ann Bowlby, Sutton Stables, Felixkirk Rd, Sutton-under-Whitestonecliffe, N Yorks YO7 2PU]; *b* 25 Jan 1919; MTC WW II; *m* 26 Sept 1939 Cdr Vivian Russell Salvin Bowlby, RN (*d* 23 July 1972), s of Col Robert Russell Bowlby, of Tunbridge Wells, and has:

1c *Michael Robin Salvin; *b* 1947; *educ* Malvern

2b (Mary) Diana; *b* 2 June 1920; MTC WW II, MFH Wylye Valley 1955 on, jockey; *m* 30 Nov 1946 (*divorce* 1959), as his 2nd w, 9th Duke of Newcastle, OBE (*see* LINCOLN, E), and *d* 19 Sept 1997, leaving issue

3b *Barbara Maureen [The Lady Barbara Ricardo, Rose Cottage, Wortley, Sheffield S35 7DB]; *b* 26 Aug 1921; WLA and Remount Depot Melton Mowbray WW II; *m* 23 June 1943 *David Cecil Ricardo, late Lt 8th King's Roy Irish Hus, only s of Maj Louis Ferdinand Ricardo, 8th Hus, of New Rawdon, Iringa, Tanganyika, and has:

1c *Dorrien Harry Ralph; *b* 22 Sept 1952; *educ* Scarborough Coll

2c *Richard Michael David; *b* 28 Sept 1955; *educ* Ackworth Sch; *m* 1986 *(Charlotte) Miranda, dau of Michael Evelyn Brown, of E Bergholt, Suffolk, and has:

1d *Frederick Michael David; *b* 1989

1d *Corisande Barbara Emily; *b* 1991

4b *Mary Rosemary Marie-Gabrielle, OBE (1983), JP (1974) [The Lady Mary Mansel Lewis OBE JP, Stradey Castle, Llanelli, Dyfed SA15 4PL]; *b* 11 June 1930; *m* 15 April 1952 *Sir David Courtenay Mansel Lewis, KCVO (1994), JP, KStJ, Ld Lt Dyfed, only s of Charles Ronald Mansel Lewis, of Stradey Castle, by Lillian Georgina, yr dau of Sir Courtenay Warner, 1st Bt (*qv*), and has:

1c *Patrick Charles Archibald [Patrick Mansel Lewis Esq, Capel Isaf, Manordeilo, Llandeilo, Dyfed]; *b* 25 Nov 1953; *educ* Eton; *m* 1985 *Claire Mary, only dau of (Alexander) William Houston (*see* SWANSEA, B), and has:

1d *Edward Vivian; *b* 21 Jan 1987

2d *Robert William; *b* 6 Nov 1989

3d *John David; *b* 20 Aug 1992

1c *Catherine Maud Leucha [Ms Catherine Mansel Lewis, Laurel Cottage, Welsh Newton Common, Monmouth, Herefs]; *b* 9 Nov 1955; *m* 1985 (*divorce*, resumed maiden name) Christopher N Hamilton, s of P N Hamilton, of Florence, and has:

1d *Archie Balthazar; *b* 12 Dec 1985

2c *Annabel Lillian Elfrida; *b* 10 July 1962; *m* 1st 19– (*divorce* 19–) Anthony Scott; *m* 2nd 1990 *Guy W C Herbert, er s of H R Herbert, of Alderbury, Wilts, and has:

1d *Benson; *b* 20 March 1991

3a Edward Thomas; *b* 25 April 1900; *m* 1921 Lucy Perrin (*m* 2nd 1925 Frank Leslie Russell) and *d* 21 March 1923

1a Elizabeth Jane; *b* 19 Aug 1887; *d* 23 March 1897

2a Mary Violet; *b* 2 Feb 1891; *d* unm 16 March 1937

3a (Ellen) Rachel; *b* 26 Feb 1894; *m* 9 July 1914 Sir Mark Beresford Russell STURGIS later GRANT-STURGIS (deed poll 1935), KCB (*d* 29 April 1949), er s of Julian Sturgis, and *d* 12 May 1968, leaving issue

4a Joan Margaret; *b* 22 Nov 1895; *m* 27 Feb 1917 Thomas Gordon Audley Miles (*d* 7 Feb 1960), er s of Audley Charles Miles, of Bayswater, and *d* 27 June 1960, leaving issue

(2) Edward James, CB, CMG, DSO, MVO, DL (Hants), of Highcliffe Castle, Christchurch, Hants; *b* 31 July 1857; granted 25 April 1900 with surv sis rank of earl's dau/yr s; Maj-Gen KRRC cmdg 10th Inf Bde 1908–12 and 46th and 65th Divs 1914–18, Mil Attaché Paris 1901–04, Orders Medjidie, Legn Hon and 2nd Cl Red Eagle Germany with star, served Afghan War 1879–81 (despatches), Egypt 1882 (medal with clasp, bronze star), Sudan 1884–85 (despatches twice, two clasps, brevet), Nile 1897–98 (despatches, medal), Boer War 1899–1900 (despatches, medal with six clasps, brevet), WW I (despatches); *m* 5 Feb 1891 Violet Hunter, CBE (1918), JP (*d* 11 Feb 1953), dau of James Alexander Guthrie, of Craigie, Dundee, and *d* 19 March 1934, having had:

1a Nicholas Rothesay, MC; *b* 9 Jan 1892; Capt Hants Yeo and Maj RAF; *m* 12 Nov 1919 Marie Louise Lucienne Juliette (*d* 13 Nov 1948), dau of François Xavier Martin, of Vancouver, and widow of Capt Hon Cecil Edwardes (*see* KENSINGTON, B), and *d* 28 Dec 1926

1a Louise Violet Beatrice; *b* 18 July 1893; DGStJ; *m* 23 Oct 1924 Sir Percy Lytham Loraine, 12th and last Bt, GCMG, PC (*d* 23 May 1961), and *dsp* 8 June 1970

2a Elizabeth Valetta (Bettine); *b* 1 Aug 1896; Chev Legn Hon; *m* 1st 14 Aug 1917 (*divorce* 1922) Capt Allastair Edward George Grant, 9th Lancers (*d* 27 Sept 1947), s of Sir Charles Grant, KCSI; *m* 2nd 11 Aug 1928 13th Earl of Lindsey and (8th Earl of) Abingdon (*qv*)

(3) Ralph Granville; *b* 4 July 1864; *m* 22 Jan 1891 Virginia Maria (*d* 10 Dec 1941), dau of Adml Winfield Scott Schley, USN, and *d* 1 March 1927, leaving:

1a Ralph; *b* 12 March 1897; *m* 24 May 1924 Isabella, dau of George Edward Wood, of Bedford Village, NY, and *d* 8 Feb 1961, leaving:

1b Alan Ralph; *b* 22 July 1927; *m* 23 Feb 1952 Virginia Anne(*d* 1993), dau of (William) Martin Claybaugh, of Brownsville, Pa., and *d* 1986, leaving:

1c RICHARD ALAN MONTAGU STUART WORTLEY, **5th and present Earl of Wharncliffe**

2c +William Ralph [William Montagu Stuart Wortley Mackenzie Esq, 18 Nola Ave, Rochester, NH, USA]; *b* 18 April 1959; *m* 1985 *Dorothea Jane, dau of Ronald Riley, of Rochester, and has:

1d +Brian Alan; *b* 1988

1d *Dorothea Jayne; *b* 1987

1c *Anne Steele; *b* 30 Jan 1955; *m* 1987 *Robert Losty, s of Bruce Losty, of Cheshire, Conn., and has:

1d *Michelle Anne; *b* 1988

1b Elizabeth Anne; *b* 8 May 1925; BS, MS; *m* 27 Nov 1948 (*divorce* 1963) Chester Lyman Kingsbury Jr, s of Chester Lyman Kingsbury, of Middletown, Ohio, and *d* 19 June 1993, leaving:

1c *Chester Lyman [Chester Kingsbury Esq, 9430 N Bald Eagle Ave, Tucson, AZ 85742, USA]; *b* 14 Feb 1950

1c *Meredith Ellen [Mrs James Lambert, 269 Williamsburg Circle, Idaho Falls, Idaho 83404, USA]; *b* 1 May 1952; *m* 19– *James Lambert and has:

1d *Jessica

2c *Michelle Elizabeth [Michelle Kingsbury, 2404 Amigo Ct, Virginia Beach, VA 23456, USA]; *b* 8 Oct 1957; *m* 19– *John Walker and has:

1d *Zeb; *b* 11 Dec 1996

2b *Joan Isabella [Mrs Harry Bishop,18 Webber Ave, Bath, ME 04530, USA]; *b* 20 July 1928; *m* 1 Dec 1951 *Harry Atwood Bishop Jr, s of Harry Atwood Bishop, of Gorham, NH, and has:

    1c *Harry Atwood III [Harry Bishop III, 9 Colony Dve, Turner, ME 04282, USA]; *b* 1 Feb 1957; *educ* U of NH, Plymouth; *m* 1982 *Julie Sayre, dau of Leonard Mulligan, and has:

        1d *Alex MacKenzie; *b* 28 July 1986

        1d *Erin Sayre; *b* 5 April 1984

    2c *Alan Stuart Wortley [Alan Bishop Esq, 25 Kerry Hill, Fairport, NY 14450, USA]; *b* 3 June 1959; *educ* Syracuse U (BA); *m* 19– *Lisa, dau of Anthony Marconi and has:

        1d *Andrew Anthony; *b* 27 Dec 1992

        1d *Colleen Joan; *b* 4 Oct 1994

    1c *Wendy Ann Isabella [Mrs Dennis Gillespie, 19 Woodhaven Dve, Andover, MA 01810, USA]; *b* 16 June 1952; *educ* U of NH, Durham (BA); *m* 1975 *Dennis Charles Gillespie and has:

        1d *Kelly Isabella; *b* 2 Nov 1977

        2d *Meghan Therese; *b* 27 April 1980

    2c *Linda Walters [Mrs Nicolo Bimbo, 15B Orchard Ave, Haverhill, MA 01830, USA]; *b* 16 Oct 1953; *educ* Springfield Coll Mass. (BS, MSM); *m* 1981 *Nicolo Bimbo and has:

        1d *Katherine Anne; *b* 11 Feb 1985

1a Anne; *b* 23 Dec 1907; *m* 1st 26 April 1930 (*divorce* 1941) Davenport Plumer Jr, only s of Davenport Plumer, of N Hill Manor, N Hill, Pa., and had issue; *m* 2nd 30 May 1941 Edmund R Sawtelle (*d* 1964), s of Capt Edmund M Sawtelle, and had further issue

(4) (Alan) Richard (Sir), KCB, KCMG, DSO, of Home Close, Highclere, Newbury; *b* 20 Jan 1868; *educ* Wellington; Lt-Gen KRRC, Hon Col Engrs and Rlwy Staff Corps 1924–48, GSO(3) 1904–07, GSO(2) 1907–08, Assist Dir Movements 1914–15, Dir Movements War Off 1915–17 (T/Brig-Gen), cmded 19th and 32nd Divs 1917, DQMG Mesopotamia 1917–19, Maj-Gen i/c Admin 1919–23, QMG India 1924–27, Col Cmdt 1st Bn KRRC 1925–38, Lt-Gen 1924, served Chitral 1895 (medal and clasp), Boer War 1899–1900 (severely wounded, despatches, medal with three clasps), WW I (despatches three times), Cdr Crown Italy and Belgium and Legn Hon; *m* 31 May 1900 Hon Maud Julia Mary Winn (*d* 17 June 1938), yst dau of 1st Baron Saint Oswald (*qv*), and *d* 23 Sept 1949, leaving:

    1a Henry James; *b* 10 May 1906; *educ* Winchester; with Cunard Steam Ship Co 1924–35, Imperial Airways and BOAC 1936–49 and E African Airways 1949–54; *d* unm 16 June 1982

    1a Marjorie Susan; *b* 4 March 1901; *m* 6 Feb 1929 Maj Roger Orlando Bridgeman and had issue (*see* BRADFORD, E)

(1) Mary Susan; *m* 17 Sept 1884 Sir George Everard Arthur Cayley, 9th Bt (*qv*), and *d* 11 Dec 1941, leaving issue

3 James Frederick; *b* 16 Jan 1833; *d* unm 27 Nov 1870

1 Mary Caroline; *m* 25 Aug 1847 3rd Marquess of Drogheda (*see* DROGHEDA, E) and *dsp* 2 April 1896

2 Cecily Susan; *m* 1 Aug 1865 1st Baron Montagu of Beaulieu (*qv*) and *d* 2 May 1915, leaving issue

WHARTON

Arms: Quarterly, 1st and 4th grand quarters, quarterly, 1st and 4th gules, a lion couchant between six cross crosslets argent (for TYNTE); 2nd and 3rd, vert on a chevron argent three pheons sable (for KEMEYS), 2nd and 3rd grand quarters, sable a maunch argent, on a bordure or eight pairs of lion's gambs erased in saltire gules (for WHARTON). **Supporters:** Dexter, a bull argent, armed and unguled gules, crined sable, gorged with a ducal coronet per pale gules and gold; sinister, a lion gules, fretty or. **Motto:** *Plaisir en faits d'armes* ('Pleasure in feats of arms'). **Creation:** B. (E) 30 Jan 1544/5.

THE BARONESS WHARTON (11th holder of the title) (Myrtle Olive Felix (Ziki) Robertson) [The Rt Hon The Baroness Wharton, 9 Gipsy Lane, London SW15 5RG]; *b* 20 Feb 1934; *s* mother 1990 on termination of abeyance; Co-V-chm Ho Lds All Party Media Gp 1994–; V-Pres RSPCA 1997–; *m* 17 Nov 1958 Henry Macleod Robertson (*d* 17 Jan 1996), composer and film producer, s of Henry Robertson, of Elgin, Morayshire, and has:

    1 +MYLES CHRISTOPHER DAVID; *b* 1 Oct 1964; *educ* King's Coll Wimbledon

    2 +Christopher James; *b* 24 Dec 1969; *educ* Claysmore

    3 +Nicholas Charles; *b* 24 Dec 1969; *educ* Claysmore

    1 +Patricia Lesley; *b* 26 May 1966

Lineage: HENRY WHARTON; living *temp* HENRY V; feudal Ld of Wharton and Nateby, in Kirkby Stephen, Westmorland; *m* Elizabeth, dau of 1st Lord (Baron) Musgrave (*see* MUSGRAVE, Bt, of Hartley Castle) by his 2nd w, and had, with a yr s (Gilbert, ancestor of the WHARTONs of Skelton Castle):

THOMAS WHARTON, of Wharton and Croglin, Cumberland; MP Appleby 1436–37; *m* —, dau of Lowther of Lowther, and had:

HENRY WHARTON, of Wharton; *m* Alice, dau of Sir John Conyers, of Hornby, Yorks, and had:

THOMAS WHARTON, of Wharton; *m* Agnes, dau of Reginald Warcop, of Smardale, Westmorland, and apparently *d c* 1520, having had an er s:

THOMAS WHARTON, **1st Baron Wharton**, of Wharton, Co Westmorland (E), so *cr* by 5 March 1543/4; *b c* 1495; ktd *c* 1528, MP Appleby 1529–36 and Cumberland 1542–44, Sheriff Cumberland 1529–30, 1535–36 and 1539–40, Dep Warden W Marches 1537, Govr Carlisle 1541 and Berwick 1557; gave a good account of himself at the Battle of Solway Moss 24 Nov 1542, which is thought to have played a large part in winning him a peerage and certainly is what earned him the honourable augmentation to his arms from EDWARD VI 23 April 1553; Warden W March spring 1543/4–49, memb Cncl of North *c* Jan 1544/5, Dep Warden E, W and Middle Marches 1552 and 1553, Warden Middle March and Capt Berwick, Constable Alnwick Castle and Ch Steward Hexham, all 1555, Keeper Berwick Castle 1556–57; *m* 1st by 4 July 1518 Eleanor, dau of Sir Bryan Stapilton, of Wighill, Yorks; *m* 2nd 18 Nov 1561 Anne (*dsp* 1584), dau of 5th Earl of Shrewsbury and Waterford (*qv*) and widow of 2nd Lord (Baron) Braye (*qv*) and by his 1st w had:

    1 THOMAS, **2nd Baron**

    2 Henry (Sir); *m* Jane, dau and heiress of Sir Thomas Mauleverer

    1 Joane; *m* William Pennington, of Muncaster, Cumberland

    2 Anne; *m* Sir Richard Musgrave (*see* MUSGRAVE, Bt, of Hartley Castle)

    3 Florence; *m* Thomas Forster, of Etherston, Northumberland, and had issue

The 1st BARON *d* 23/24 Aug 1568; his er s,

THOMAS WHARTON, **2nd Baron Wharton**, PC (1553); *b* 1520; ktd 1545, MP Cumberland 1545–52 and 1553, Hedon 1554 and Northumberland 1555, 1558 and 1559, Sheriff Cumberland 1547–48, Master Queen's Henchmen 1553–58, memb Cncl North 1558; imprisoned Tower of London for illegal religious activities, presumably Catholicism, June–July 1561 but was too prudent to take part on either side in the 1569 Rebellion of the Northern Earls (*see* NORTHUMBERLAND, D, and ABERGAVENNY, M); *m* May 1547 Lady Anne Radcliffe (*d* 7 June 1561), dau of 1st Earl of Sussex (*see* FITZWALTER, B), and *d* 14 June 1572, having had, with three daus:

PHILIP WHARTON, **3rd Baron Wharton**; *b* 23 June 1555; *educ* Jesus Coll Cambridge and Gray's Inn (also by a tutor, with whom he was in Paris at the time of the Massacre of St Bartholomew 1572, and who was among those killed); Commr Anglo-Scottish Border 1618 and 1619; *m* 1st 24 June 1577 Lady Frances Clifford (*d* 1592), dau of 2nd Earl of Cumberland (*see* DE CLIFFORD, B); *m* 2nd 1597 Dorothy (*d* 4 April 1621), dau and heiress of Thomas Colby, of Sherfield-on-Loddon, Hants, and widow of (a) John Tamworth, of Leake, Lincs, and (b) Sir Francis Willoughby, of Wollaton, Notts, and by his 1st w had:

1 George (Sir), KB (1603); *b* 1583; both *k* and was *k* by the Master of Blantyre (*see* 1899 edn BLANTYRE, L) in a duel over cards 1609; *d unm*

2 Thomas (Sir), of Aske, Yorks; *b* 1587/8; ktd 1611, MP Westmorland 1614 and 1621–22; *m* 11 April 1611 Lady Philadelphia Carey, dau of 1st Earl of Monmouth, and *dvp* 17 April 1622, having had:

(1) PHILIP, **4th Baron**

(2) Thomas (Sir), of Edlington, Yorks; *b* 1615; *m* Lady Mary Carey, dau of 1st Earl of Dover, and *d* 1684, having had issue

1 Margaret; *b* July 1581; *m* Sept 1603, as his 2nd w, 1st Baron Wotton of Marley, and *dsps* 10 March 1658/9

2 Eleanor; *m* William Thwaytes, of Long Marston

3 Frances; *m* Sir Richard Musgrave, 1st Bt, of Hartley (*qv*), and had issue

The 3rd BARON *d* 26 March 1625; his gs,

PHILIP WHARTON, **4th Baron Wharton**, PC (Feb 1688/9); *b* 8 April 1613; *educ* Eton, Exeter Coll Oxford and Lincoln's Inn; Parly appointee as Ld Lt Lancs and Bucks 1642 and Westmorland 1644, Speaker Ho Lds May–Aug 1642 and Feb-June 1645, Parliamentarian Civil War (present Edgehill 1642), called to CROMWELL's 'Other House' 1657 and RICHARD CROMWELL's Parl Jan 1658/9 but did not obey the summons; *m* 1st 23 Sept 1632 Elizabeth, dau of Sir Rowland Wandesford, of Pickhill, Yorks, and had:

1 ELIZABETH; *m* 3rd Earl of Lindsey (*see* LINDSEY and ABINGDON, E)

The **4th Baron** *m* 2nd 7 Sept 1637 Jane (*d* 21 April 1658), dau and heiress of Arthur Goodwin, MP, of Upper Winchendon, Bucks (*see* GREY, B), and by her had, with other issue:

1 THOMAS WHARTON, **5th Baron Wharton** and 1st MARQUESS OF WHARTON, Co Westmorland, and 1st MARQUESS OF MALMESBURY, Co Wilts (both GB), so *cr* 15 Feb 1714/5, as also earlier 23 Dec 1706 VISCOUNT WINCHENDON, Co Buckingham, and EARL OF WHARTON, Co Westmorland (both E), and 12 April 1715 MARQUESS OF CATHERLOUGH, also BARON OF TRIM, Co Meath, and EARL OF RATHFARNHAM, Co Dublin (all I), PC (Feb 1688/9); *b* Aug 1648; MP Wendover 1673–79 and Bucks 1679–81, 1685–87 and 1689–96; wrote the lyrics to the celebrated Protestant propagandist song *Lilliburlero*; one of the first to join WILLIAM III on his landing 1688, Comptroller Feb 1688/9–1702, Ld Lt Oxon 1697–1702 and Bucks Jan–June 1702, memb of the Whig Junto in QUEEN ANNE's reign, a Commr for the Union of E and S Parls 1706, Ld Lt Ireland 1708–10 (his Ch Sec being Joseph Addison, the essayist), Ld Privy Seal 1714–15; *m* 1st 16 Sept 1673 Anne (like her husb a versifier; *dsp* 29 Oct 1685), yr dau and coheir of Sir Henry Lee, 5th Bt, of Ditchley, Oxon; *m* 2nd July 1692 Lucy (*d* 5 Feb 1715/16), dau and heiress of Adam Loftus, Viscount Lisburne (*see* ELY, M), and *d* 12 April 1716, leaving by her:

(1) PHILIP WHARTON, **6th Baron Wharton** and 1st and last DUKE OF WHARTON, Co Westmorland, so *cr* 28 Jan 1717/8 in an attempt by the authorities to wean him from his Jacobitism and make him a good Whig like his father, he having while touring Europe written a flattering letter to the titular James III which procured him on 22 Dec 1716 the Jacobite titles of Duke of Northumberland, Marquess of Wooburn, Co Buckingham, Earl of Malmesbury, Co Wilts, and Viscount Winchendon, Co Buckingham, all in the notional E peerage; PC (I 1717–26); *bapt* 5 Jan 1698/9; his GB Dukedom did at least make him for a while speak and vote with the Tories in the Ho Lds, for instance in debates on the South Sea Bubble; but in June 1725 he left the country and was made the titular James III's Envoy to Vienna in Aug and to Madrid March 1725/6, also made a titular KG by James III; cmded a Spanish detachment Siege of Gibraltar (now held by the English) 1727, hence outlawed (though without due regard for procedure) and his titles and such estates as he still held in Britain forfeited 3 April 1729; *m* 1st 2 March 1714/5 Martha (*d* 14 April 1726), dau of Maj-Gen Richard Holmes, and had:

1a Thomas, *Marquess of Malmesbury*; *bapt* 29 March 1718/9; *d* 1 March 1719/20

(1) The **6th Baron** *m* 2nd 22 or 26 July 1726 (becoming an RC at the same time) Maria Theresa O'Neill (*dsp* 13 Feb 1777), a Maid of Honour to the Queen of Spain, dau of Col Henry O'Beirne, and *dspms* 31 May 1731, when all his titles, which were in any case forfeited, albeit in irregular fashion, expired bar the Barony of Wharton, which was deemed by the Ho Lds 1915 to have been *cr* by writ hence descendible to heirs general, which could include females

(1) JANE; *m* 1st John Holt (*d* by 20 Feb 1728/9), of Redgrave Hall, Suffolk; *m* 2nd 13 June 1733 Robert Coke, of Hillingdon, Middx, bro of 1st Earl of Leicester of the 1744 *cr* (*see* LEICESTER, E), and *dsp* between 22 Dec 1757 and 19 Jan 1761, when her right to the Barony (as declared *ex post facto* 1915) fell into abeyance among the reps of the daus of the **4th Baron Wharton**

(2) Lucy; *m* Sir William Morice, and *dsp* 2 Feb 1738/9

2 Margaret; *m* 1st Maj Dunch (*d* 27 Sept 1679), of Pusey, Berks; *m* 2nd Sir Thomas Seyliard/Sulyarde, 2nd Bt (*bur* 4 May 1692); *m* 3rd by Sept 1695, as his 2nd w, 12th Lord Ross (*d* 15 March 1738) and by her 1st husb had a s and two daus (all *dsp*)

3 MARY Wharton; *b* 1649; *m* 1st (settlement 14 Feb 1672/3) William Thomas (*see* THOMAS, Bt, of Wenvoe) and had:

(1) Edmund (Sir), of Wenvoe and Ruperra; *bapt* 20 Aug 1674; ktd 1686; *d* unm, *bur* 24 Jan 1692/3

(1) Anne; *b* 10 Aug 1675; *d* unm 1694

3 (cont.) Mrs (MARY) Thomas *m* 2nd 1678 Sir Charles KEMEYS, 3rd Bt, of Cefn Mably, MP Monmouth (*m* 2nd 1701 Mary, dau and coheir of William Lewis, and widow of (a) William Jephson and (b) Sir John Aubrey, 2nd Bt (*see* AUBREY-FLETCHER, Bt), and was *bur* 22 Dec 1702), and *d* between 27 March 1698/9 and 16 May 1699, having had by him, with other issue (*dsp*):

(2) Sir CHARLES KEMEYS, 4th and last Bt, of Cefn Mably; *b* 23 Nov 1688; High Sheriff Glam 1712–13, MP Mon 1713–15 and 1716–34; *d* unm 29 Jan 1734/5, when the btcy expired

(2) JANE Kemeys, of Cefn Mably; *m* 25 Dec 1704 Sir John TYNTE, 2nd Bt, of Halswell, Somerset (*d* 5 March 1709/10), and was *bur* 16 Oct 1747, having had:

1a Sir HALSWELL TYNTE, 3rd Bt; *b* 15 Nov 1705; MA Oxford; MP Bridgewater 1727–30; *m* 28 Sept 1727 Mary (*m* 2nd 1 Oct 1736 Sir Paulet St John, 1st Bt (*see* ST JOHN MILDMAY, Bt), and *d* 17 Dec 1758), dau and heiress of John Waters, of Brecon, and *dsps* 12 Nov 1730

2a Rev Sir JOHN TYNTE, 4th Bt; *b* 27 March 1707; Rector Goathurst; *d* unm 15 Aug 1740

3a Sir CHARLES KEMEYS TYNTE, 5th and last Bt; *b* 19 May 1710; DCL Oxford; MP Monmouth 1745–47 and Somerset 1747–74; *m* March 1737/8 Anne (*bur* 24 March 1798), dau and coheir of Rev Thomas Busby, LLD, Rector Addington, Bucks, and *dsp* 25 Aug 1785, when the btcy expired

1a Jane; *m* 23 April 1737 Maj Ruisshe Hassell, RHG (The Blues) (*m* 2nd Charlotte, dau of 3rd Baron Stawell of Somerton), and *d* 1741, having had an only dau and heiress:

1b JANE HASSELL later KEMEYS-TYNTE; *m* 1765 Col John Johnson, 1st Foot Gds (*d* 1807), Groom Bedchamber and Comptroller to PRINCE OF WALES (later GEORGE IV), s of Lt-Gen Johnson, of Burhill, Surrey, and Glaston, Rutland, and *d* 1825, having had, with two daus (Jane; Anne Georgina; both *d* unm):

1c CHARLES KEMEYS-TYNTE, of Halswell, Somerset, and Cefn Mably, Glam; *b* 29 May 1778; Col W Somerset Yeo; MP Bridgewater 1820–37; declared by Ho Lds Privileges Ctee 1845 to be coheir of the whole blood to the Barony of Wharton, the outlawry of which was annulled 3 May 1845 by Writ of Error in the Court of Queen's Bench; no further action was taken in the matter at that time, however; *m* 25 April 1798 Anne (*d* 1835), dau of Rev Thomas Leyson, Vicar Bassaleg, Mon, and widow of Thomas Lewis, of St Pierre, Mon, and *d* 22 Nov 1860, having had:

1d CHARLES JOHN, for whom *see* below

1d Anne; *m* 10 April 1827 Sir William Henry Cooper of Cogar, 5th Bt (*dsp* 14 Jan 1836), and *d* 17 Sept 1880

2d Jane; *d* unm

3d Louisa; *m* 1834 Simon Fraser Campbell (*d* March 1872) and *d* 31 Aug 1872

4d Henrietta Anne; *m* 14 Sept 1833 Capt Thomas Arthur Kemmis, Gren Gds (*d* 25 Dec 1858), MP E Looe, and *d* 24 March 1880, leaving issue

4 Philadelphia; *m* 1st (settlement 2 Sept 1679) Sir George Lockhart of Carnwath; *m* 2nd Capt John Ramsay and *d* by 19 Nov 1703, leaving issue by both marriages

The **4th Baron** *m* 3rd 24 or 26 Aug 1661 Anne (*d* 13 Aug 1692), dau of William Kerr (yr bro of 1st Earl of Ancram; *see* LOTHIAN, M) and widow of Col Edward Popham, and *d* 4/5 Feb 1695/6, having by her had:

2 William; *d* unm, *k* in a duel 14 Dec 1687

Col CHARLES KEMEYS-TYNTE's only s,

CHARLES JOHN KEMEYS-TYNTE, of Halswell, Somerset, Cefn Mably, Glam, and Burleigh Hall, Leics; *b* 1800; Col Roy Glamorgan LI, MP W Somerset 1832–37 and Bridgewater 1847–65; *m* 1st 18 July 1820 Elizabeth (*d* 10 May 1838), dau and coheir of Thomas Swinnerton, of Butterton Hall, Staffs, and had, with two daus (*d* unm):

1 CHARLES KEMEYS

2 Milborne; *b* 1823; Lt 4th Roy Irish Dragoon Gds; *k* by a fall from his horse 10 March 1845

Col CHARLES JOHN KEMEYS-TYNTE *m* 2nd 15 April 1841 Vincentia (*d* 14 Oct 1894), dau of Wallop Brabazon (*see* MEATH, E), and by her had:

3 John Brabazon; *b* 24 June 1842; RN and 5th Fus, served Baltic 1854 (medal); *d* 16 Dec 1916

4 Clifford Wharton Charles; *b* 2 Aug 1843; Lt 11th Foot; *d* India 8 April 1866

5 St David Morgan; *b* 1 March 1846; Lt W Somerset Yeo; *m* 21 April 1897 Alice (*d* 16 June 1942), yr dau of Rev Thomas Lee, Vicar Ch Ch Luton, and widow of Anthony Hammond, JP, of Bath, and *d* Sept 1927

6 Arthur Marcus Philipps; *b* 22 March 1850; Capt Roy Glam Militia Zulu War 1879 and Canada 1885 (three medals); *m* Dec 1889 Ruby (*d c* 1930), dau of R Clark, of Ottawa, and *d* 4 Nov 1943

7 Fortescue Tracy Freke; *b* 31 Jan 1856; *m* 1st 17 Aug 1899 Gertrude (*d* 1 Dec 1911), dau of J D Waterbury, of Ozralan, Wis.; *m* 2nd 25 April 1917 Antoinette King (*d c* 1936), dau of James Lawrence Montgomery, of Culpepper, Va., and widow of Rev Benjamin Staunton, and *d* 17 Jan 1919

8 Edward Plantagenet; *b* 13 Sept 1858; Capt Roy Glam Militia Zulu War 1879 (medal and clasp); *m* 21 Feb 1889 Beatrice Mary (*d* 7 Oct 1933), dau of Lansdowne Daubeney, of Norton Malreward, and *d* 4 April 1929, leaving:

(1) Mary Vincentia Blanche Edwardrina; *m* 12 June 1915 William Arnold Riley, MM (*d* 24 Aug 1967), only surv s of Rev William Riley, of Barrow-in-Furness, and *d* 13 Dec 1976, leaving:

1a +Priscilla Ann; *m* 3 Dec 1942 *Rev Desmond Agar-Ellis Ker, of Torquay, 2nd s of Reginald Arthur Ker, of Edinburgh, and has:

1b +Stephen Charles; *b* 7 Dec 1958

2a +Brigid Alison; *m* 10 Oct 1959 *John Derrick Benjamin Griffin, of Salisbury, Wilts, s of Dudley Alipore Griffin, of Trusham, S Devon, and has:

1b +Andrew John; *b* 8 Nov 1962

2b +Edward James; *b* 19 April 1965

3a +Eleanor Rose Aldersey

(2) Beatrice Margaret Gladys Clare; *m* 27 April 1910 Eric Blake Herbert Johnson, JP, only s of George Herbert Johnson, MD, FRCS, of Teignmouth, and had:

1a Rosemary Ann; *b* 19 Feb 1932; *m* 5 Nov 1955 *James Oliver Young, 2nd s of William Allen Young, of Worthy Ho, Winchester, and *d* 18 Oct 1964, leaving:

1b +Jane Elizabeth; *b* 21 Oct 1956

2b +Caroline Anne; *b* 18 Jan 1960

1 Maude Maria; *m* 23 July 1885 Amherst Henry Gage Morris (*d* 13 Feb 1919) and *d* 18 July 1936

2 Blanche Elizabeth Plantagenet; *m* 22 Sept 1909 Edgar Dewdney, PC (*d* 8 Aug 1916), Lt-Govr BC, and *d* 27 March 1936

Col CHARLES JOHN KEMEYS-TYNTE *d* 16 Sept 1882; his est s,

CHARLES KEMEYS KEMEYS-TYNTE, of Halswell, Cefn Mably and Burleigh Hall, JP, DL (Mon and Somerset); *b* 16 March 1822; Col 1st Somerset Militia, Capt 11th Hus and Gren Gds; *m* 1st 2 Nov 1848 Mary (*d* 1864), dau of Rev George Frome, of Pucknoll, Dorset, and had:

1 HALSWELL MILBORNE, for whom *see below*

2 Charles Harley Morton; *b* May 1864; *d* unm 1893

1 Rachel Elizabeth Henrietta

Col CHARLES KEMEYS KEMEYS-TYNTE *m* 2nd 18 Dec 1873 Hannah (*d* 17 Feb 1875), widow of T Lewis; *m* 3rd 18 Sept 1879 Elizabeth (*d* 18 March 1933), dau of Richard Fothergill, MP, of Tenby and Lowbridge Ho, Westmorland, and *d* 10 Jan 1891, leaving by his 2nd w:

2 Grace

His er s,

HALSWELL MILBORNE KEMEYS-TYNTE, of Halswell, Cefn Mably and Burleigh Hall, JP, DL (Mon); *b* 1852; Capt Somerset Militia; *m* 25 Sept 1875 Rosabelle Clare (*m* 2nd 2 June 1900 Col Rawlins, 2nd Bn Scottish Rifles (*d* 11 Jan 1909), and *d* 18 Aug 1931), dau of Theobald Walsh, of Tyrrelston, Co Kildare, and had:

1 CHARLES THEODORE HALSWELL, **8th Baron**

2 Eustace; *b* 10 April 1878; *m* 13 Aug 1902 Ann, dau of John Emerson, and *d* 1949, leaving:

   (1) +Nicholas Halswell; *b* 4 Aug 1903

   (1) +Eleanor Vanessa Rosabelle; *b* 27 Dec 1904

1 Mary Arabella Swinnerton; *b* 6 April 1884; *m* 21 April 1909 Maj Sir Guy Colin Campbell, 4th Bt (*qv*), and *d* 1 July 1948, leaving issue

Mr HALSWELL MILBORNE KEMEYS-TYNTE *d* 18 Feb 1899; his er s,

CHARLES THEODORE HALSWELL KEMEYS-TYNTE, **8th Baron Wharton**, on termination of abeyance in Barony in his favour and writ of summons to Parl issued 15 Feb 1916, JP (Mon and Somerset); *b* 18 Sept 1876; Hon Lt Army 1915–18, Lt Roy Mon RE; *m* 10 Aug 1899 Dorothy (*d* 3 Aug 1944), yst dau of Maj-Gen Sir Arthur Edward Augustus Ellis, GCVO (*see* HOWARD DE WALDEN, B), and *d* 4 March 1934, leaving:

1 (CHARLES) JOHN HALSWELL KEMEYS-TYNTE, **9th Baron Wharton**; *b* 12 Jan 1908; *educ* Ch Ch Oxford; F/Lt RAFVR WW II; *m* 1 Sept 1967 *Joanna [Mrs Bruce Yorke, Casa la Concha, Rocio de Naguèles, Marbella (Malaga), Spain] (*m* 4th 1971 Bruce Yorke), only dau of Walter Henry Law-Smith, of Adelaide, S Australia, widow of 6th and last Baron Tredegar (*see* 1959 edn) and formerly w of Cdr Archibald Boyd Russell, DSO, RN, and *dsp* 11 July 1969

1 ELIZABETH DOROTHY, **Baroness Wharton** in her own right; *b* 1907; *m* 1st 17 May 1933 (*divorce* 1946) David George Arbuthnot (*see* ARBUTHNOT, Bt, of Edinburgh); *m* 2nd 1946 (*divorce* 1958) St John Vintcent and *d* 4 May 1974, when the Barony fell into abeyance between her daus until determined in favour of the er one 1990, leaving:

   (1) MYRTLE OLIVE FELIX (ZIKI) ARBUTHNOT later ROBERTSON, **present Baroness Wharton**

   (2) +Caroline Elizabeth [The Hon Mrs Appleyard-List, The Birches, Stanford Common, Pirbright, Surrey GU24 0DG]; *b* 28 Aug 1935; *m* 1970 *Capt Jonathan Cecil Appleyard-List, CBE, RN, s of Cecil Rhodes List, of Wimbledon, and has:

   1a +Zoë; *b* 13 Oct 1973

dolen Alice, dau of Alfred Ernest Oram, of Walberton, Kirby Muxloe, Leics, and has:

1 +JOHN FREDERICK [John Wheeler Esq, Round Hill, Aldeburgh, Suffolk]; *b* 3 May 1933; *educ* Bedales and London Sch of Printing; late Life Gds; *m* 11 May 1963 *Barbara Mary, dau of Raymond Flint, of Stoneygate, Leicester, and has:

   (1) +John Radford; *b* 27 Dec 1965

   (2) +Andrew Charles; *b* 12 April 1969

   (1) *Jane Louise; *b* 21 May 1964

2 +Benjamin [Benjamin Wheeler Esq, Benscliffe Hay Cottage, Newtown Lindford, Leics]; *b* 2 Oct 1935; *educ* Bedales and Leicester Coll of Art and Tech; *m* 26 May 1962 *Brenda Mary, dau of Arthur Goodman, of Syston, Leics, and has:

   (1) +Miles John; *b* 12 Dec 1962

   (2) +Edward James; *b* 11 March 1964

   (3) +Matthew Benjamin; *b* 26 March 1966

   (1) *Rebecca Mary; *b* 1972

Lineage: CHARLES WHEELER, of Fairford and Kempsford, Glos; *m* Frances — (*d* Jan 1714) and *d* Nov 1712, having had a yst s:

JOHN WHEELER, of Fairford; *b* Jan 1691; *m* 12 July 1713 Elizabeth Hicks (*d* 1747) and *d* Aug 1765, having had a 2nd s:

JOHN WHEELER, of Fairford; *b* March 1721; *m* 4 May 1747 Mary Herbente and had, with other issue:

JOHN WHEELER, of Fairford and later Little Compton; *b* Feb 1749; *m* 9 Aug 1767 Elizabeth Speckford (*d* April 1822) and had a yst s:

Rev FRANCIS WHEELER, of Moulton, Northants; *b* 11 Jan 1788; *m* Elizabeth Rogers and *d* 22 Sept 1853, leaving:

BENJAMIN WHEELER, of Northampton; *b* 1 July 1824; *m* 18 Jan 1848 Mary (*d* 26 June 1890), dau of John Hieron Radford, of Nottingham, and *d* 2 Dec 1889, leaving, with an er s (Benjamin Francis, *b* 10 Dec 1856, *m* and had issue) and seven daus (Sarah Elizabeth, *d* unm 22 Jan 1924; Annie Hieron, *d* unm; Mary Ellen, *m* 30 Oct 1890 Arthur Kingham, JP, of Rounton, Nascot Wood, Watford, Herts, and had issue; Alice, *m* 4 Aug 1897 Arthur Winton Thorpe, OBE, and *d* 2 June 1934, leaving issue; Catherine Grace, *m* 12 Sept 1895 Arthur Gavin Stevenson, LLB (*d* 11 May 1927), estate agent LNER and CA, and *d* 15 March 1951, leaving issue; Bertha Radford, *m* Jan 1891 Rev Frederick Olinthus Sutton (*d* 1949) and *d* 21 Jan 1947, leaving issue; Emily Martin, *d* unm 26 Nov 1954):

Sir Arthur Wheeler, 1st Bt (UK), so *cr* 7 Feb 1920, JP, DL (Leics); *b* 18 Sept 1860; High Sheriff Leics 1922; *m* 19 March 1896 Mary (*d* 21 April 1938), est dau of Frederick Pullman, JP, Sheriff Nottingham 1889, Mayor 1894, and *d* 20 May 1943, leaving:

1 **Sir Arthur Frederick Pullman Wheeler, 2nd Bt**; *b* 10 Dec 1900; *educ* Charterhouse; *m* 7 Jan 1938 *Alice Webster [Alice Lady Wheeler, E12 Marine Gate, Marine Drive, Brighton, Sussex BN2 5TQ], yst dau of George Heath Stones, of Rutherglen, Lanarks, and *dsp* 16 Dec 1964

2 Sir JOHN HIERON WHEELER, **3rd and present Bt**

1 Catherine Mary Victoria; *m* 25 Aug 1921 John Reginald Leeson, s of John Leeson, of Leicester, and *d* 28 June 1959, leaving issue

2 Nancie Radford; *d* unm 6 Dec 1997

WHEELER

Arms: Sable a chevron between in chief two talbot's heads erased, and in base an eagle displayed, all or. **Crest:** A talbot's head sable, eared and charged on the neck with a catherine-wheel or.
Motto: *Promisso sto* ('I stand by my promises').
Creation: Bt. (UK) 7 Feb 1920.

SIR JOHN HIERON WHEELER, 3RD BT, of Woodhouse Eaves, Co Leicester [Sir John Wheeler Bt, 39 Morland Ave, Stoneygate, Leics LE2 2PF]; *b* 22 July 1905; *s* bro 1964; *educ* Charterhouse; Volunteer Trooper 49 RTR WW II; chm and md Raithby Lawrence and Co (De Montfort Press) (ret 1973); *m* 24 July 1929 *Gwen-

WHELER

Arms: Or a chevron between three leopard's faces sable. **Crest:** Out of a ducal coronet or an eagle displayed gules. **Motto:** *Facie tenus* ('Up to the mark'). **Creation:** Bt. (E) 11 Aug 1660.

SIR EDWARD WOODFORD WHELER, 14TH BT, of City of Westminster, Co London [Sir Edward Wheler Bt, 34 St Carantoc Way, Crantock, Newquay, Cornwall TR8 5SB]; *b* 13 June 1920; *s* f 1986; *educ* Radley; Capt Roy Sussex Regt (attd 10th/15th Punjab Regt IA 1941–45) WW II; Overseas Audit Serv Uganda and Ghana 1948–58, AA E Africa 1958–70, Benson & Hedges 1971–81 (dir 1979–81), Co Sec Robert Lewis (St James's) Ltd 1981–90, Liveryman Pipe-makers and Tobacco Blenders' Co 1980, Freeman City London 1980; *m* 2 July 1945 *Molly Ashworth, dau of Thomas Lever, Gold Coast CS, and has had:

1 +TREVOR WOODFORD [Trevor Wheler Esq, 83 Middle Park, Inverurie, Aberdeenshire]; *b* 11 April 1946; *educ* St Edmund's Canterbury and St Mary's

Nairobi; RAF; *m* 1st 25 Oct 1969 Christine Ann, dau of Leonard Durkin; *m* 2nd 1974 *Rosalie Margaret, dau of Ronald Thomas Stunt, and by her has:

(1) +Edward William; *b* 14 June 1976

(2) +Andrew Robert; *b* 1978

1 *Dinah Margaret [Mrs Bernard Tomlinson, 32 St Carantoc Way, Crantock, Cornwall TR8 5SB]; *b* 25 May 1947 (twin with a dau who *d* at birth); *m* 1st 17 Feb 1968 (*divorce* 1983) Clive Richard Knight, s of Walter George Knight, of Lechlade, Glos; *m* 2nd 1987 *Bernard Teasdale Tomlinson and by her 1st husb has:

(1) *Anthony Clive; *b* 5 Nov 1969

(2) *Simon Mark; *b* 1972

Lineage: HENRY WHELER, of St Mary Magdalen, Milk St, London; citizen and grocer; *m* Agnes (*m* 2nd Nov 1565 Thomas Elliott, of London, citizen and draper, and was *bur* 28 Oct 1613) and was *bur* 20 Feb 1564/5, leaving:

1 John, of London and Holland; *bapt* 17 March 1559/60; London citizen, grocer and goldsmith; *m* 1st Anne, dau of Henry Hervey, of Chessington, Surrey (s of Sir Nicholas Hervey, of Ickworth; *see* BRISTOL, M), and sis of 1st and last Baron Hervy [*sic*] of Rosse, and widow of — Ingelar, and had issue; *m* 2nd Sarah (*m* 2nd Lawrence Goffe and was *bur* 8 March 1642/3), and *d* on or after 14 Nov 1617; his only s by his first w:

(1) **Sir William Wheler, 1st Bt** (E), so *cr* 11 Aug 1660, with special remainder to his cousin, Charles Wheler, of Martin Husingtree, and the heirs male of the latter's body, of Westminster; MP Westbury 1640–48 and 1659 and Queenborough 1660; *m* Elizabeth (*bur* 20 Sept 1670), dau of Michael Cole, of Kensington, and *dsp* 6 Aug 1666

2 William, of Martin Husingtree, Worcs, and Nantwich, Cheshire; *m* Eleanor (*d* 1 June 1678), dau of Edward Puleston, of Allington, Denbighs, by Winifred, sis of Sir Thomas Trevor, Baron Exchequer 1625–49, and had:

(1) **Sir Charles Wheler, 2nd Bt,** of Birdingbury, Warwicks; *b* 1620; MA Cantab; Gentleman Privy Chamber, Col 7th Regt, MP Cambridge U 1667–79, Govr Leeward Islands; *m* by licence 7 Aug 1648 Dorothy (*d* 16 Aug 1684), dau of Sir Francis Bindlosse, of Borwick Hall, Lancs, and sis of Sir Robert Bindlosse, 1st and last Bt, and had:

1a Trevor, Maj 7th Foot; *dvp* unm 12 Oct 1678

2a WILLIAM (Sir), **3rd Bt**

3a Francis (Sir); Adml, Govr Deal Castle; *m* 12 Nov 1685 Arabella Clifton and was drowned 1693, leaving issue (his gs, Francis Wheler, of Warwicks, left an only dau and heiress Jane, *m* 10 Sept 1772 2nd Viscount Hood (*qv*) and *d* 6 Dec 1847, having had issue)

1a Dorothy Elizabeth; Mid of Honour to QUEEN CATHERINE of Braganza; *m* Count of Nassau

Sir CHARLES *d* 26 Aug 1683; his est surv s,

Sir William Wheler, 3rd Bt; *m* 15 Jan 1695/6 Teresa (*bur* 7 May 1718), dau of Hon Edward Widdrington, s of 1st Baron Widdrington of Blankney, and *d* 23 Feb 1708/9, having had, with two other sons and five daus:

1 **Sir Trevor Wheler, 4th Bt**; *bapt* 25 Nov 1697; *d* unm and was *bur* 17 Oct 1718

2 **Sir William Wheler, 5th Bt**; *m* 1726 Penelope (*bur* 23 Jan 1739/40), dau of Sir Stephen Glynne, Bt, of Hawarden Castle, and was *bur* 4 June 1763, having had:

(1) **Sir William Wheler, 6th Bt**; *b* 16 July 1726; *m* 1754 Lucy (*bur* 27 March 1791), only dau and heiress of Giles Knightley, of Woodford, and was *bur* 16 April 1790, having had, with other issue:

1a Lucy; *m* 1777 E S Wilmot Sitwell, of Stainsby, Derbys

(2) Francis; Army Offr; *dsp*

(3) CHARLES (Sir), **7th Bt**

(4) Edward; memb Supreme Cncl Calcutta; *m* 1st Harriet Chicheley Plowden (*dsp*); *m* 2nd Charlotte, dau of George Durnford, of Winchester, and *d* Calcutta 10 Oct 1783, leaving:

1a Charlotte; *d* 1861

2a Penelope; *m* 1817 Charles John Craven (*see* CRAVEN, E) and *d* 1857

(5) John; Preb Westminster; *d* unm

The 6th Bt's bro,

Rev Sir Charles Wheler, 7th Bt; *b* 22 Dec 1730; MA Cantab; Preb York, Vicar Leamington Hastings; *m* 20 Jan 1762 Lucy (*d* 22 Dec 1800), dau and eventually coheiress of Sir John Strange, Master of the Rolls, and had:

1 TREVOR (Sir), **8th Bt**

2 Charles John; *b* 14 April 1766; *m* 13 Nov 1797 Isabel (*d* 30 Sept 1841), dau of John Close, of Easby, Yorks, and *d* 26 Sept 1856, having had, with two other sons (*d* young) and two daus (*d* unm):

(1) Edward, JP; *b* 27 Sept 1798; *m* 31 Dec 1845 Elizabeth Anne (*d* 7 Jan 1906), dau of Samuel Tertius Galton, of Duddeston Ho, Warwicks, and *d* 16 Nov 1879, leaving:

1a Edward Galton WHELER later WHELER-GALTON (roy licence 11 Jan 1913), of Claverdon Leys, Warwicks, JP (Northumberland and Warwicks); *b* 12 June 1850; *m* 13 Nov 1890 Mary Louisa, MBE (1918), dau of James Dugdale, JP, DL, of Wroxall Abbey, Warwicks, and *d* 28 July 1935

1a Lucy Elizabeth; *m* 26 Sept 1889 Col Thomas James Charles Aylmer Studdy, RA (*d* 1 Oct 1920), and *d* 5 Feb 1928

(3) Henry Trevor (Rev); *b* 9 Aug 1804; Rector Berkeley, Somerset; *m* 11 Dec 1834 Charlotte (*d* 30 Aug 1885), 4th dau of Rev Charles Euseby Isham, Rector Polebrook, Northants, and *d* 28 April 1860, having had, with other issue:

1a Henry Isham; *b* 1 April 1840; Col Bengal SC, Bhutan Campaign 1864–65 (medal with clasp); *m* 1st 15 Sept 1869 Frances Catherine (*d* 18 May 1904), 4th dau of Col James Charles Innes, Bengal Inf; *m* 2nd 17 April 1906 Alice, yr dau of Edmund Malpas, of Worcester, and *d* 28 July 1918, having by his 1st w had:

1b Laura Evelyn; *b* Nov 1878; *d* unm Feb 1948

2a Charles Trevor; *b* 16 Dec 1841; *m* 18 Dec 1861 Elizabeth Anne (*d* 23 April 1872), dau of John Fleming Martin Reid, Bengal CS, and *d* 7 Feb 1874, having had, with two other daus (*d* unm):

1b Edith Trevor; *m* 15 Sept 1891 Rev Aston Legh Whitlock, BCL (*d* 1927), Rector Sidlow Bridge, Reigate, and *dsp* 1941

3a William Alfred; *b* 28 Oct 1843; Indian Navy, Cdre P&O Fleet, served Egypt 1882 (medal and Khedive's Star); *m* 3 July 1879 Mary Margaret (*d* 10 Feb 1918), dau of William John Cumming, MRCS, and *d* 23 March 1933, having had:

1b Frederick Trevor; *b* 27 April 1880; *educ* Rugby; *m* 20 Sept 1905 Romana Gertrude (*d* 2 Jan 1969), only dau of William Bemrose, FSA, of Elmhurst, Derby, and *dsp* 12 Oct 1952

1b Winifrede Margaret; *m* 21 April 1915 Rev Edward Powell, s of Rev George B Powell, and *d* 1955, leaving issue

2b Mary Glynne; *b* 7 June 1887; *m* 27 April 1914 Rev John Augustus Kirby (*d* 2 June 1962), Vicar Marystowe and Rector Coryton, Devon, Hon CF, only s of John Kirby, of Stamford Bridge, Yorks, and had:

1c *Mary Aline Glynne; *b* 1915; *m* 1935 (*divorce* 1949) Lt-Cdr George Robert May Robertson, RN, and has:

1d *Ian Antony; *b* 1937

2d *Robert Edward; *b* 1939

1d *Elizabeth Janine; *b* 1946

4a John Mordaunt; *b* 18 July 1845; MRCS, LSA; *m* 1st 16 Oct 1872 (*divorce* 1881) Caroline Martha Anne, only dau of Josiah Cash, MD, of Matlock; *m* 2nd 1882 Ellen Victoria (*d* 1891), dau of John Coates, of Seedley, nr Manchester, and widow of Sydney Smith, and *d* 18 Jan 1910, having by his 1st w had:

1b Annie Rose; *m* 1892 Harvey Kinnersley Bradbury, MRCS, LRCP (*d* 21 March 1938)

2b Gertrude Caroline; *m* 1895 Joseph Ebenezer Wright, and had issue

1a Caroline Emma; *m* 10 Aug 1869 Rev William Handcock (*d* 18 April 1897) and *d* 1919, leaving issue

2a Rosa Penelope; *m* 25 June 1874 Rev Arthur Beauclerc Tarbutt (*d* 1888) and *d* 20 Nov 1933, leaving issue

(4) Frederick (Rev); *b* 25 May 1812; Vicar Dunchurch, Rugby; *m* 27 Oct 1863 Catherine Emma (*d* 26 Aug 1900), dau of William Plowden, of Ewhurst Park, Hants, and *dsp* 31 Dec 1898

(1) Isabella Penelope; *m* 30 Dec 1833 Rev Percy Powlett (*d* 23 Sept 1894) and had issue

(2) Sophia Wheler; *m* 1823 Rev Henry Wilmot-Sitwell (*d* 1874), of Stainsby Ho, Derbys, and *dsp* 23 Nov 1869

3 William (Rev); *b* 3 Nov 1770; *m* 1807 Charlotte, dau of William Harding, of Baraset, Warwicks, and *d* 30 May 1834, leaving:

(1) William; *dsp*

(2) John; *b* 1812; Bengal CS; *m* Jane Elizabeth, dau of Christopher Rowland Richardson, of Kumtoul, Tirhoot, and *d* 1850, leaving a dau (*d* unm)

(1) Teresa; *m* 3 Nov 1836 Rev George Rudston-Read (*d* 31 Dec 1864), Rector Sutton-on-Derwent, 2nd s of Rev Thomas Cutler Rudston-Read, of Hayton, Yorks

(2) Charlotte; *d* 13 Aug 1896

1 Penelope; *m* William Wilberforce Bird, of the Spring, Kenilworth, Warwicks, and *d* 11 March 1839

2 Jane; *m* George Dandridge, of The Commandery, Worcester

3 Sarah; *m* Abraham Hume, of Bilton Grange, Warwicks, and *d* 5 April 1839

4 Lucy; *m* Rev John Wise, 2nd s of Matthew Wise, of Leamington Priors, Warwicks

5 Sophia; *m* Rev John Biddulph (*d* 18 Feb 1863) and *d* 19 Aug 1837

The 7th Bt *d* 12 July 1821; his s,

Sir Trevor Wheler, 8th Bt; *bapt* 23 June 1763; *m* 20 March 1792 Harriet (*d* 29 Aug 1806), dau of Richard Beresford, of Ashbourne, Derbys, and *d* 4 Feb 1830, having had, with four daus (*d* unm):

1 **Sir Trevor Wheler, 9th Bt**; *b* 20 Dec 1792; Lt-Col cmdg N Devon Mounted Rifle Yeo; *m* 1st 15 Oct 1817 Lucy (*d* 25 April 1859), only dau of George Dandridge, of The Commandery, Worcs; *m* 2nd 14 Dec 1865 Frances (*d* 6 Oct 1872), dau of Rev W Carus-Wilson and widow of Rev Jocelyn Willey, of Camblesforth Hall, Yorks, and *d* 6 Sept 1869, having by his 1st w had:

(1) Trevor; *b* and *d* 1818

(1) Lucy Penelope; *m* 11 Jan 1854 Pierce Wynne Yorke, DL (*d* 10 Dec 1891), of Dyffryn Aled, Denbighs, and *dsp* 2 Sept 1906

(2) Jane; *m* 26 June 1856 Edward William Brydges Willyams, MP, of Carnanton, Cornwall, and *d* 2 March 1877

2 FRANCIS (Sir); **10th Bt**

1 Lucy; *m* 15 April 1828 James Molony (*d* 7 July 1874), of Kiltanon, Co Clare, and *d* 14 May 1855, having had issue

The 9th Bt's bro,

Sir Francis Wheler, 10th Bt, CB; *b* 9 Nov 1801; Gen Bengal Cav; *m* 1st Feb 1827 Caroline (*d* Jan 1833), dau of Rev C Palmer, and had:

1 TREVOR (Sir); **11th Bt**

1 Harriet Anne; *m* 1829 Dr J G Kemp, HEICS (*d* 1858), and had issue

Sir Francis *m* 2nd 18 Nov 1841 Elizabeth (*d* 1 March 1900), dau of William Bishop, and by her had:

2 Francis Henry; *b* 3 July 1848; Lt-Col 2nd Bn Loyal N Lancs Regt; *m* 22 April 1885 Jane (*d* 9 March 1932), dau of John Highett, JP, DL, of Weymouth, Dorset, and Highton, Victoria, and *d* 16 March 1932, leaving:

(1) Trevor; *b* 16 Sept 1888; *educ* Cheltenham; Capt The Buffs WW I (star, two medals); *m* 28 May 1935 Enid F (*d* 1983), dau of H R Stokes, and *d* 6 June 1967, leaving:

1a +Glynne Henry Trevor; *b* 20 Feb 1941

1a *Jane Frances Trevor [Mrs Kenneth Thompson, Nesscroft, Box 381, PO Griffith, NSW, Australia]; *b* 6 Oct 1938; *m* 1962 *Kenneth Ross Thompson and has:

1b *John Kenneth Glynne; *b* 1967

1b *Susan Jane; *b* 1963

2b *Jennifer Anne Frances; *b* 1965

(2) Francis Glynne; *b* 8 Aug 1891; *educ* Wellington; *m* Winifred Ethel, dau of N B White

(1) Doris Laura; *d* unm 15 Aug 1966

3 Charles Stuart; *b* 25 Aug 1851; Col 6th Bengal Cav, IA, Egyptian Expdn 1882 (medal and star), Tirah 1897–98 (clasp); *m* 25 April 1876 Alice Lilian (*d* 20 June 1927), dau of Lt-Col James Spence Ogilvie, Bengal SC, and *d* 10 Dec 1923, leaving:

(1) Aubrey Stuart; *b* 15 April 1877; RE WW I (Croix de Guerre avec palme); *m* 3 Nov 1904 Blanche Christina (*d* 1 Jan 1946), only dau of Samuel Watson Jameson and n of Rt Hon Sir Starr Jameson, 1st and last Bt, CB, PC (see 1917 edn), and *d* 26 Aug 1934, having had:

1a Stephen Jameson; *b* 21 Sept 1907; *educ* Radley; WW II as Maj Reconnaissance Corps RAC; *m* 22 July 1950 Annette (*d* 1968), yr dau of Frank Eden Smith, and *d* 2 March 1967, leaving:

1b *Amanda [Mrs Robert Kenhard, The Summer House, Lodge Lane, Keymer, W Sussex BN6 8NA]; *b* 7 Feb 1952; *m* 28 Dec 1996 *Robert Brindley Kenhard

2b *Jacqueline [Mrs Christopher French, 714 N W 2nd Ave, Del Ray Beach, FL 33444, USA]; *b* 24 Feb 1956; *m* 1987 *Christopher French, of Florida, and has:

1c *William; *b* 6 Oct 1995

2a Glynne Jameson; *b* 21 Sept 1907; *d* 11 Feb 1908

1a Elinor Jameson; *b* 26 Feb 1906; *m* 1st 10 July 1926 (*annulled* 1932) Capt Edward Fraser Walter, AFC (*d* 19 Nov 1965), IA and RAF, 2nd s of Edmund Walter, of Croft, Leicester; *m* 2nd 19 Sept 1936 Charles Peter Graham Engelbach, MA, AFRAeS, yr s of Cdr Charles Richard Fox Engelbach, OBE, RNVR, of Quarry Farm, Northfield, Warwicks, and by him had:

1b *(Flora Caroline) Starr [Mrs Douglas Wallis, 3 rue de Chateau, Chissay en Touraine, 41400 Montrichard, France]; *b* 27 Sept 1942; *m* 25 Sept 1965 Douglas Alan Spencer Wallis, s of George Spencer Wallis

2b *Sally Elinor [Mrs Kelly Calladine, 8338 Chalet Dve, Whistler, BC, Canada]; *b* 6 Aug 1944; *educ* Bath Acad of Art (Dipl Art and Design); *m* 1988 *Kelly Calladine and has:

1c *Charles; *b* 1988

2a Rosemary Blanche Jameson; *b* 19 June 1919; *m* 20 July 1948 *Douglas Victor Gordon Feltham, MA, MB, BCh, s of Douglas Feltham, of Highgate, and *d* 14 Sept 1995 leaving:

1b *John Leander [John Feltham Esq, 77 Honeywell Rd, London SW11]; *b* 9 Aug 1955; *educ* Crookham Court Sch, BA; *m* 1982 *Michele Carla Fabian-Jones

1b *Hoonie Rosemary Anne [Mrs Hoonie Feltham, Knapp House, Shenington, Banbury, Oxon OX15 6NE]; *b* 25 Oct 1950 and has:

1c *Leander Charles FELTHAM; *b* 1979

1b (cont.) She married 1986 *Hugh Cecil Palmer (but retains maiden name) and has further issue:

2c *Gerald Hugh Feltham PALMER; *b* 1987

1 Dorothy; *m* 21 May 1913 Gerald B Deakin (*d* 1944), of S Hill Pk, Bracknell, Berks, and had issue

Sir FRANCIS *d* 4 April 1878; his est s,

Sir Trevor Wheler, 11th Bt; *b* 12 March 1828; Col Bengal SC (medals and clasps for Aliwal, Sobraon, Burma, Indian Mutiny); *m* 21 June 1852 Cordelia Mary (*d* 15 May 1893), dau of Maj John A Scott, Bengal Cav, and had:

1 Trevor Francis; *d* young

2 EDWARD (Sir), **12th Bt**

1 Dorothy Kathleen; *b* 7 Jan 1879; *d* 20 March 1883

Sir TREVOR *d* 10 Jan 1900; his only surv s,

Sir Edward Wheler, 12th Bt; *b* 5 Dec 1857; Lt-Col 1st Bn Roy Sussex Regt; *m* 4 July 1883 Mary Leontine (*d* 30 March 1917), dau of Sir Richard Wood, GCMG, CB, and had:

1 TREVOR WOOD (Sir), **13th Bt**

1 Feridah Audrey Mary; *m* 1915 Julian Nathan (*d* 1948), Roy Sussex Regt and The Buffs, and had:

(1) Trevor Anthony; *b* 15 Nov 1919; RA WW II; *ka* 1944

(1) *Christine Mary; *b* 13 Aug 1916; *m* 21 Sept 1957 John Robert Carden Teale and has:

1a *Mary Christina Beatrice; *b* 1959

2 Cordelia Edmé Mary; *m* 29 July 1907 Capt Oliver Plunkett (*d* 2 May 1971), Colonial Serv 1923–45, Supreme Court Judge, Judge Mixed Courts Egypt, s of Patrick Joseph Plunkett, of Dublin, and *d* 19–, having had issue

Sir EDWARD *d* 11 Aug 1903; his only s,

Sir Trevor Wood Wheler, 13th Bt; *b* 20 Sept 1889; *educ* Radley; Capt 6th Bn Roy Sussex Regt WW I, attd IA 1918–20, Lt HG 1940, Capt Movement Control RE, WW II; CCG 1947–50, E Africa 1952, Kenya Police Res throughout Mau Mau Emergency; *m* 4 Dec 1915 Margaret Idris (*d* 1982), yst dau of Sir Ernest Woodford Birch, KCMG, and *d* 1986, having had:

1 Sir EDWARD WOODFORD WHELER, **14th and present Bt**

1 *Audrey Idris [Mrs John Wightwick, 34A Coombe Rd, Croydon, Surrey]; *b* 6 Sept 1916; *m* 16 March 1940 Maj John Humphrey Wightwick (*d* 1970), Suffolk Regt, only s of Lt-Col Herbert Milner Wightwick, Indian Political Service, and has:

(1) *Christopher Kennneth Wheler [Christopher Wightwick Esq, c/o Coutts & Co, 1 Old Park Lane, London W1]; *b* 31 Dec 1940; *educ* abroad; *m* 1st (*divorce* 19–) 1 Oct 1966 Sarah Gordon, only dau of Gordon MacDonald, of Hampstead; *m* 2nd 1978 *Sheila Gay Morton-George and by his 1st w has:

1a *Katherine Jennifer; *b* 15 June 1969

(2) *Simon John Patrick Wheler; *b* 3 Sept 1949; *educ* Stoneham Sch, Reading; *m* 1973 *Annee Alfsen, of Oslo

(3) *Nigel Martin Humphrey Wheler; *b* 17 Feb 1951; *educ* Stoneham Sch, Reading

(1) *Vanessa Ann Margaret Wheler; *b* 25 Oct 1947; *m* 25 April 1970 *John Bray Needham, only s of John William Needham, of Upper Whiston, Yorks, and has:

1a *Gavin Timothy; *b* 1971

2 *Diana Edmée; *b* 4 Sept 1918; *m* 29 March 1941 Leslie Francis Gordon Pritchard, MBE, TD (*d* 1977), late Colonial Serv, only s of Lt-Col Hugh Robert Norman Pritchard, CIE, OBE, IA, and has:

(1) *Caroline Jane; *b* 17 April 1943; *m* 12 Nov 1966 *Dean Edward Fischer

(2) *Susan Letitia; *b* 15 Jan 1947; *m* 1972 *Roderic Hill

(3) *Anne Charlotte; *b* 20 Aug 1948; *m* 1973 *Todd Civardi

(4) *Rachel Sarah; *b* 12 April 1955; *m* 1978 *Henry Mark Wyndham (*see* EGREMONT, LECONFIELD and, B) and has issue

WHITAKER

Arms: Per pale argent and azure a chevron embattled between three mascles counterchanged. **Crest:** A horse passant argent, gorged with a collar gemel and resting the dexter foreleg on a mascle azure.
Motto: *Spes et fides* ('Hope and faith').
Creation: Bt. (UK) 15 July 1936.

SIR JAMES HERBERT INGHAM WHITAKER, 3RD BT, of Babworth, Co Nottingham, OBE (1996) [Sir James Whitaker Bt OBE, Garden House, Babworth, Retford, Notts DN22 8EW; Auchnafree, Dunkeld, Perthshire]; *b* 27 July 1925; *s* f 1957; *educ* Eton; Lt Coldstream Gds 1944–47, NW Europe, Egypt, Palestine, Maj Sherwood Rangers Yeo (TA); late dir Halifax Bldg Soc (v-chm 1973–94), Economic Forestry Gp, Barrow Barnsley (Hldgs) and Barnsley and Dist Coking Co; *m* 26 July 1948 *Mary Elisabeth Lander, dau of Ernest Johnston, of Cockshut, Reigate, Surrey, and widow of Capt David Urling Clark, MC, and has:

1 +JOHN (JACK) JAMES INGHAM [John Whitaker Esq, Babworth Hall, Retford, Notts DN22 8EP]; *b* 23 Oct 1952; *educ* Eton and Bristol U (BSc); FCA, AMIEE; *m* 1981 *Elizabeth Jane Ravenscroft, dau of L J R Starke, of New Zealand, and has:

(1) +Harry James Ingham; *b* 1984

(1) *Lucy Harriet Ravenscroft; *b* 1982

(2) *Alix Catherine Hepburn; *b* 1987

(3) *Eleanor Mary Harvie; *b* 1989

1 *Shervie Ann Lander; *b* 28 March 1950; *m* 27 Feb 1971 *David William James Price, of Harrington Hall, Spilsby, Lincs, only s of R J E Price, of Quinta da Romeria, Bucelas, Portugal, and has:

(1) *William James Emlyn; *b* 1973

(1) *Hesther Jane Lander; *b* 1971

Lineage: JOSEPH WHITAKER, of Hesley, Notts, had a 9th s:

Sir Albert Edward Whitaker, 1st Bt (UK), so *cr* 15 July 1936 CBE (1919), TD, JP, DL (Notts); *b* 9 May 1860; Capt Northumberland Fus, Afghan War 1870–90, WW I (despatches), Lt-Col cmdg Notts (Sherwood Rangers) Yeo, Hon Col 1931; High Sheriff 1921, Chm QS, Ld High Steward E Retford, ktd 1928; *m* 29 April 1896 Eileen Gertrude Celeste, MBE (*d* 5 May 1947), dau of Col John Croker, Scots Fus, of Co Limerick, and of Bithia M Croker (authoress), and *d* 11 June 1945, leaving:

Sir John Albert Charles, 2nd Bt, CB (1945), CBE (1942), JP, DL (Notts); *b* 5 March 1897; *educ* Eton; Maj-Gen Coldstream Gds WW I, cmded Coldstream Gds 1937–39, WW II as a Bde Cdr (despatches twice), Dir Mily Trg 1942–45; High Sheriff 1950, Ld High Steward E Retford 1951; *m* 18 Dec 1923 Pamela Lucy Mary (*d* 13 Sept 1945), er dau of Herbert Guy Snowden, and *d* 5 Oct 1957, leaving:

1 Sir JAMES HERBERT INGHAM WHITAKER, **3rd and present Bt**

2 +David Arthur Edward (Rev) [The Rev David Whitaker, The Cottage, Hereford Rd, Weobley, Herefs HR4 8SW]; *b* 8 Nov 1927; *educ* Eton and New Coll Oxford (BA); Lt Coldstream Gds 1947–49; *m* 7 April 1956 *Susan Mary, er dau of Ven Richard Hamilton Babington, Archdeacon Exeter, and has:

(1) +Robert John; *b* 7 April 1957

(2) +Michael Benjamin (Rev); *b* 6 Oct 1960; *m* 19– *—

(3) Richard Dominic; *b* 18 Oct 1966; *d* 19–

(4) +Jonathan; *b* 7 Dec 1972

(1) *Caroline Lucy; *b* 22 May 1959

(1) *Iona Ruth; *b* 6 Aug 1963

2 +Ben(jamin) Charles George [Ben Whitaker Esq, 16 Adamson Rd, London NW3 3HR]; *b* 15 Sept 1934; *educ* Eton and New Coll Oxford (BA); 2nd Lt Coldstream Gds; barrister Inner Temple 1959; MP (Lab) Hampstead 1966–70, PPS to: Min Overseas Devpt 1966, Min Housing and Local Govt 1966–67, Parly Sec

Overseas Devpt 1969–70; exec dir Minority Rights Gp 1971–88, Dir Gulbenkian Fndn (UK) 1988–; author: *The Police* (1964), *A Radical Future* (1967), *Crime and Society* (1967), *Participation and Poverty* (1968), *Parks for People* (1971), *The Foundations* (1974), *The Police in Society* (1979), *UN Report on Slavery* (1982), *A Bridge of People* (1983) and *The Global Connection* (1987); *m* 18 Dec 1964 *Janet Alison, dau of Alan Henry Stewart, of The Small House, Station Rd, Beeston, Notts, and has:

   (1) +Daniel Peter Alan; *b* 8 April 1966
   (2) +Rasaq Andrew Ian; *b* 2 June 1972
   (1) *Quincy Rachel Suzy; *b* 5 April 1968

WHITE, Baroness

Creation: B. (LP, UK) 1970.

THE BARONESS WHITE, of Rhymney, Co Monmouth (Eirene Lloyd Jones) [The Rt Hon The Baroness White, 64 Vandon Court, Petty France, London SW1H 9HF; 22 Bailey Court, Hereford Rd, Abergavenny, Gwent NP7 5PQ]; *b* 7 Nov 1909; *educ* St Paul's Girls' Sch and Somerville Coll Oxford (Hon Fellow 1966); offr Min of Labour 1933–37 and 1941–45; Political Corr *Manchester Evening News* 1945–49; MP (Lab) E Flint 1950–70; Nat Exec Ctee Labour Party 1947–53 and 1958–72 (Chm 1968–69); Parly Sec Colonial Office 1964–66; Min of State: For Affrs 1966–67 and Welsh Office 1967–70; Dep Chm, Metrication Bd 1972–76; Dep Speaker House of Lords 1979–80; Memb Roy Commission on Environmental Pollution 1974–81, Br Waterways Bd 1974–80; Govr Nat Library of Wales 1950–70; BFI and NFT 1959–64; Pres Cncl for Protection of Rural Wales 1974–89; Memb Cncl U of Wales Coll of Cardiff 1981–93 (Chm 1983–88, Pres 1987–88, V-Pres 1988–93); author: *The Ladies of Gregynog* (1985); *m* 1948 John Cameron White (*d* 1968)

Lineage: Dr THOMAS JONES, CH, LLD; had issue:

EIRENE LLOYD, *cr* a **Baroness**

WHITE, Bt, of Boulge Hall

Arms: Gules a chevron nebuly between three boar's heads couped, two flaunches argent, each charged with a cross patée of the field.
   Crest: In front of a demi-tower gules, issuant therefrom a boar's head argent, tusked and maned or, charged on the neck with a cross patée also gules, three crosses patée also argent. **Motto:** *Non sibi sed aliis* ('Not for self but for others'). **Creation:** Bt. (UK) 14 June 1937.

SIR CHRISTOPHER ROBERT MEADOWS WHITE, 3RD BT, of Boulge Hall, Co Suffolk [Sir Christopher White Bt, c/o Mrs Edwin Steinschaden-Silver, Pinkney Ct, nr Malmesbury, Wilts SN16 0PD]; *b* 26 Aug 1940; *s f* 1972; *educ* Bradfield and Imp Russian Ballet Sch Cannes; Lt (TA) Norfolk 1969, sch master 1961–72, taught EFL Shenker Inst Rome and Scuola Specialista Aeronautica Macerata 1962–63, Housemaster St Michael's Sch Ingoldisthorpe Norfolk 1963–69, Hon Pres Warnborough House Oxford 1973–; *m* 1st 14 April 1962 (*divorce* 1967) Anne Marie Ghislaine, yr dau of Maj Tom Brown, OBE, MC, by Mrs RW Taggart-Browne, of Hove, Sussex; *m* 2nd 1968 (*divorce* 1972) Dinah Mary Sutton; *m* 3rd 1976 *Ingrid Carolyn, er dau of Eric Jowett, of Gt Baddow, Essex

Lineage: ROBERT WHITE, of Ludham, Norfolk; *b* 1644; *m* Margaret (*d* 5 Feb 1685/6), dau of William Burton, clerk, and *d* May 1727, leaving:

ROBERT WHITE, of Burgh in Flegg, Norfolk; *b* 28 Oct 1683; clerk; *m* Anne Gostlin (*d* 1758) and *d* 26 Sept 1765, leaving:

ROBERT WHITE, of Burgh; *b* 23 Sept 1711; surgn; *m* Clementina Barchard (*m* 2nd Joseph Hindermarsh and *d* 1807) and *d* 1764, leaving:

ROBERT WHITE, of Gt Yarmouth and Bury St Edmunds; *b* 23 Feb 1738/9; surgn, physician; *m* 17 Sept 1761 Sarah (*d* 1814), dau of John Nuthall, of Caister, Norfolk, and *d* July 1814, having had:

ROBERT GOSTLIN WHITE, of Halesworth, Suffolk; *b* 6 Jan 1763; slr; *m* 1st Mary Yarrington (*d* 1795) and had issue; *m* 2nd 6 March 1797 Elizabeth (*d* 1831), dau

of Martin Meadows, of Wenhaston Grange, Halesworth, and *d* 18 Oct 1828, having by her had, with other issue, including an er s (Rev Robert Meadows, *b* 8 Jan 1798, DD, Rector Slimbridge, Glos, *d* unm 31 Jan 1865):

JOHN MEADOWS WHITE, of Halesworth, Suffolk, and Bayswater; *b* 20 Jan 1799; slr; *m* Anne, dau of Robert Crabtree, of Halesworth, and *d* 19 March 1863, leaving:

ROBERT HOLMES WHITE, of Boulge Hall, Suffolk; *b* 24 Jan 1834; *m* 10 July 1862 Elizabeth Sarah (*d* 29 Dec 1905), dau of John Griffith Frith, of Minchinhampton, Glos, and *d* 23 Nov 1901, having had:

  1 ROBERT EATON (Sir), **1st Bt**
  2 Herbert Meadows Frith; *b* 9 Dec 1867; *educ* Eton and New Coll Oxford; slr 1892; WW I; *m* 26 July 1893 Annie Laura (*d* 7 Aug 1953), est dau of Maj-Gen Herbert Charles Borrett, CB, and *d* 12 March 1954, leaving:

    (1) Herbert John Frith; *b* 15 April 1895; *educ* Eton and Seafield Pk Eng Coll Fareham; Lt-Col Roy Signals, Internat Refugee Org, previously with UNRRA, WW I (wounded) and WW II (despatches) Liaison Offr to Ch Signal Offr Forces Europe 1944–1946, Offr US Legn Merit; *m* 16 June 1917 Marie Kathleen (*d* 4 Jan 1970), dau of Dr Anthony Blanc, and *d* 24 Jan 1963, leaving:

      1a *Anthony John Frith [Anthony White Esq, Flat 12, 4 Cranley Place, London SW7]; *b* 21 March 1925; RNVR WW II, exec dir British-American Educnl Fndn 1966–

    (2) Robert Percy Frith, MC; *b* 31 May 1896; *educ* Eton and RMC Sandhurst; Lt-Col King's Own Roy Regt WW I (wounded), also WW II; *m* 1st 3 April 1919 Eleanor Clare Hargrave (*d* 31 July 1952), est dau of Ven Ernest Newton Sharpe, Archdeacon London, and had:

      1a *Eleanor Anne Love [Mrs Michael de Halpert, Barns House, Lower Durford Wood, Petersfield, Hants GU31 5AS]; *b* 22 March 1923; *m* 23 Nov 1944 *Lt-Cdr Michael Francis de Halpert, DSC, RN, only s of Cdr Roger Vincent de Halpert, RN, of France Lynch, Glos, and has:

        1b *Simon David; *b* 27 Dec 1945; *educ* Canford and RNC Dartmouth; Cdr RN; *m* 19 Dec 1970 *Katherine, yr dau of James Daly, of Nairobi, and has:

          1c *Michael James Robert; *b* 1 May 1974
          2c *Christopher Vincent; *b* 2 Oct 1975
          1c *Natasha Frances; *b* 3 Oct 1972

        2b *Jeremy Michael; *b* 9 July 1947; Cdre RN; *m* 8 July 1972 *Jane, dau of Joseph Fattorini, of Ilkley, and has:

          1c *Peter Alexander; *b* 11 Feb 1974
          2c *Benjamin Jeremy; *b* 21 Oct 1978
          1c *Anna Mary; *b* 12 March 1976

        1b *Susan Anne Clare; *b* 5 Nov 1953; *m* 1st 29 July 1978 (*divorce* 1986) Samuel Higgins, er s of J R C Higgins; *m* 2nd 8 July 1988 *John Rachkind, yr s of Harold Rachkind

    (2) (cont.) Lt-Col Robert Percy Frith White *m* 2nd 14 Oct 1954 *Joyce Margaret, only child of Stanley Unwin Embery, of London, and *d* 16 Jan 1981

    (3) Cecil Meadows Frith, CB (1945), CBE (1943), DSO (1941); *b* 29 Aug 1897; *educ* Eton and RMA Woolwich; Maj-Gen Roy Signals, WW I in RA (despatches), WW II (despatches six times) cmded 4th Ind Div Signals 1939–41, Ch Sigs Offr E African Forces 1941, Ch Sigs Offr 8th Army 1941–44, Sigs Offr in Ch 21st Army Gp 1944, Cdr US Legn Merit; *m* 26 March 1925 *Elizabeth Rennie, 2nd dau of Dr Herbert Rennie Robertson, of Tientsin, and had:

      1a *Elizabeth Nancy Rennie [Mrs Peter Chalk, Haresdown, Holcombe, Burnell, nr Exeter, Devon]; *b* 11 April 1927; *m* 17 Aug 1956 *Peter John Chalk, s of Lawrence Chalk, DPhil, of W Hanney House, Wantage, Berks, and has:

        1b*Christopher Martin, *b* 5 Aug 1958
        2b *Stephen Peter, *b* 24 Dec 1965
        1b *Alison Phoebe, *b* 7 July 1960
        2b *Gillian Clare, *b* 18 Dec 1963

  3 Ralph Layard (Very Rev); *b* 16 Feb 1872; *educ* New Coll Oxford (MA); Dean Maritzburg and Vicar Cathedral Ch St Saviour Pietermaritzburg 1929–34 Rector Peakirk Peterborough and RD 1934–39; *m* 1 Nov 1910 Ruth Boswell (*d* 20 Dec 1961 aged 90), dau of Rev E D Stone, and *d* 25 Dec 1954, leaving:

    (1) *Mary Layard [Miss Mary White, St Katharine's House, Wantage, Oxon OX12 8EA]; *b* 22 May 1912; ARCM 1936, LRAM 1937, Sec Gloucester Diocesan Bd Women's Work 1947–60

  4 Cecil Arbuthnot; *b* 17 Aug 1874; Lt Suffolk Regt; *ka* Boer War 6 Jan 1900
  1 Margaret; *d* unm 11 Jan 1949
  2 Caroline Henrietta; *d* unm 29 March 1934
  3 Agnes Mary; *d* unm 5 March 1945

The est s,

Sir Robert Eaton White, 1st Bt (UK), so *cr* 14 June 1937, VD, JP, DL; *b* 6 Nov 1864; Lt-Col 14th Suffolk Regt (TF), Chm E Suffolk QS and E Suffolk CC; *m* 6 June 1903 Rose Dorothy (*d* 15 May 1967), dau of Charles Pearce-Serocold, of Taplow Hill, Bucks, and *d* 5 Aug 1940, having had:

  1 Robert Charles Meadows; *b* 30 Dec 1904; Lt-Cdr RN; *das* 13 Dec 1939
  2 (ERIC) RICHARD MEADOWS (Sir), **2nd Bt**
  1 Elizabeth Margaret; *b* 1906; *m* 15 Sept 1941 S/Ldr William Elwyn Francis Evans, RAFVR (*d* 1983), only s of William Edward Evans, of Milford Haven, and *d* 19 Oct 1995, leaving:

    (1) +Charles William [Dr Charles Evans, Wayton House, Landulph, Cornwall PL12 6QQ], *b* 18 Aug 1942, *educ* Radley and St Bartholomew's Hosp; MB, BS, MFOM, MRCS, LRCP, Surg-Cdre RN, *m* 30 Aug 1975 *Christina M Cameron, er dau of Maj A J Cameron, of Allangrange, Ross-shire and has:

      1a *Marion Elizabeth Victoria; *b* 8 Sept 1976
      2a *Rachel Fiona Clare; *b* 4 Oct 1978
      3a *Veronica Lucy Margaret; *b* 19 March 1982

    (1) *Sarah Margaret [Mrs Edwin Steinschaden-Silver, Pinkney Court, nr Malmesbury, Wilts SN16 0PD]; *b* 2 June 1946; *m* 1st 1976 (*divorce* 1993) Maj Peter Hibbert; *m* 2nd 1993 *Edwin Steinschaden-Silver and has by her 1st husb:

      1a *Venetia Sarah; *b* 1977

2 *Esther Dorothy; *b* 1914; 3rd Offr WRNS WW I; *m* 15 May 1943 Lt-Cdr (John) Michael Chappell, RN, only s of Percy Chappell, of Stourbridge, and has:

(1) *Rodney Guy Eaton [Rodney Chappell Esq, Clathy House, Crieff, Perthshire]; *b* 18 Feb 1944; *educ* Nautical Coll Pangbourne and RNC Dartmouth; Lt RN; *m* 27 Feb 1971 *Sarah Mary Bromhead, est dau of Maj John Bromhead, of Timberley Farm, Bury, W Sussex, and has:

1a *Katherine Mary; *b* 1972

2a *Isobel Dorothy Denise; *b* 1975

3a *Emily Jane; *b* 1980

(2) *David Nigel; *b* 2 Nov 1946; *educ* Radley and RMA Sandhurst; Lt 9th/12th Roy Lancers (PWO)

The 1st Bt's gs,

Sir (Eric) Richard Meadows, 2nd Bt; *b* 29 June 1910; *educ* Eton and RAC Cirencester; Lt Roy Suffolk Hus 1938–41 and Lt RNVR 1943–46 WW II; FZS; *m* 1st 20 Oct 1939 (*divorce* 1947) Elizabeth Mary Gladys (*d* 31 Dec 1950), only dau of 6th Marquess Townshend (*qv*); *m* 2nd 11 Sept 1947 *Ann Heron, er dau of Alexander Gerald Eccles, of Caldy, W Kirby, Cheshire, and *d* 26 April 1972, leaving by his 1st w:

Sir CHRISTOPHER ROBERT MEADOWS WHITE, **3rd and present Bt**

WHITE, Bt, of Cotham House

Arms: Barry wavy of six argent and azure, over all a lymphad sable, on a chief of the second two roses of the first. **Crest:** Upon a mount vert a beacon fired proper, pendant therefrom a sail azure charged with a rose as in the arms. **Motto:** Ever watchful. **Creation:** Bt. (UK) 26 Aug 1904.

SIR GEORGE STANLEY JAMES WHITE, 4TH BT, of Cotham House, Bristol, JP [Sir George White Bt, The Clock Room, Guildhall Library, Aldermanbury, London EC2]; *b* 4 Nov 1948; *s f* 1983; *educ* Harrow; FSA, High Sheriff Avon 1989, JP Bristol 1991–95, Pres Gloucestershire Soc 1993–, Chm Advsy Gp Bldg Conservn Bristol U 1996–, Jt Warden Clockmakers' Co 1997–98 (Keeper of its Collection 1988–); *m* 1st 1974 (*divorce* 1979) Susan Elizabeth, dau of J L Ford, of Mawnan Smith, Cornwall, and has:

1 *Caroline Morwenna; *b* 1978

Sir GEORGE *m* 2nd 1979 *Elizabeth Jane, dau of Sir (William) Reginald Verdon-Smith and formerly w of Robert George Clinton, and by her has:

1 +GEORGE PHILIP JAMES; *b* 19 Dec 1987

2 *Kate Elizabeth; *b* 1983

Lineage: HENRY WHITE, of Honiton, Devon; *b* 7 Oct 1787; *m* 4 June 1811 Elizabeth Tucker (*d* 26 April 1863) and *d* 8 March 1862, leaving an est s:

HENRY WHITE, of Bristol; *b* 10 Jan 1815; *m* 10 Aug 1843 Eliza, dau of John Tippetts, of Bristol, and *d* 25 Oct 1872, leaving a 2nd s:

Sir George White, 1st Bt (UK), so *cr* 26 Aug 1904, of Cotham House, Bristol, JP; *b* 28 March 1854; head George White and Co, Bristol, aeroplane mfrs; introduced Bristol biplanes and monoplanes 1910, also pioneer electric street traction, introducing it into London, Dublin, Bristol and Middlesbrough; Pres: Bristol Stock Exchange and Cncl Assocd Stock Exchanges UK, Bristol Roy Infirmary (and Treas), Queen Victoria Memorial Hosp Nice, Dolphin Soc and Bristol and W of England Aero Club; Charity Tstee and Govr Bristol GS and other schs; Hon LLD U of Bristol; *m* 14 June 1876 Caroline Rosena (*d* 9 Nov 1915), dau of William Thomas, of Bristol, and had:

1 GEORGE STANLEY (Sir), **2nd Bt**

1 Daisy May; *m* 1st 3 Dec 1902 Maj Ernest John Hudson, OBE, Queen's Own Roy W Kent Regt (*d* 10 Sept 1943), of Hungerford; *m* 2nd 27 Sept 1945 Brig-Gen Edward Hall Stevenson, CMG, DSO (*d* 3 Jan 1964), s of Col Edward Macdonald Stevenson, IA, and *dsp* 20 Oct 1969

The 1st Bt *d* 22 Nov 1916; his only s,

Sir (George) Stanley White, 2nd Bt; *b* 31 July 1882; *educ* Clifton; with George White and Co, dep chm Bristol Aeroplane Co; *m* 3 June 1908 Kate Muriel (*d* 26

Oct 1971 aged 91), yst dau of Thomas Baker, of Bristol, and *d* 18 Jan 1964, leaving:

Sir George Stanley Midelton White, 3rd Bt; *b* 11 April 1913; *educ* Harrow and Magdalene Coll Cambridge; chm and md Bristol Cars Ltd, with George White, Evans and Co, of Bristol; *m* 22 July 1939 *Diane Eleanor [Diane Lady White, Acton House, Park St, Iron Acton, nr Bristol], only dau of Bernard Abdy Collins, CIE, ICS, formerly of Deccan House, Aldeburgh, Suffolk, and *d* 1983, leaving:

1 Sir GEORGE STANLEY JAMES WHITE, **4th and present Bt**

1 *Daphne Eleanor; *b* 19 April 1945; *m* 19 April 1969 *Jonathan Wheeler, Lt RNR, est s of Surgn-Cdr Stanley John Wheeler, RN, of Wareham, Dorset

WHITE, Bt, of Salle Park

Arms: Quarterly, 1st and 4th, argent a fess chequy gules and or, over all on a bend engrailed azure an arrow point downwards of the field (for WHITE); 2nd and 3rd, azure a lion rampant between four estoiles or (for DYMOCK). **Crest:** A boar's head erased proper, pierced through the mouth with an arrow or. **Motto:** *Progredere ne regredere* ('Progress not retreat'). **Creation:** Bt. (UK) 29 June 1922.

SIR JOHN WOOLMER WHITE, 4TH BT, of Salle Park, Norfolk [Sir John White Bt, Salle Park, Norwich, Norfolk NR10 4SG]; *b* 4 Feb 1947; *s f* 1971; *educ* Cheltenham and RAC Cirencester; *m* 1987 *Joan, dau of T D Borland, of Flemington, W Linton, Peeblesshire, and by her has:

1 +KYLE DYMOKE WILFRID; *b* 16 March 1988

Lineage: JOHN WHITE, of Harrow Weald, had, with other issue:

THOMAS WHITE, of St Luke's, Middx; *m* 1st —; *m* 2nd Jane, widow of — Smith and dau of James Honeyman, and *d* July 1912 aged 79, leaving, with other issue:

JOSEPH WHITE, of Northwood Hall, Middx; *b* 3 Oct 1778; *m* 1806 Mary Adams, of Pegwell, Kent, and *d* 16 Oct 1829, having had, with other issue, including two er sons (Thomas, of Halliford-on-Thames, *b* 28 May 1812, *m* 1849 Marian, est dau of Joseph Rownson, of City of London, and *d* 1890, leaving issue; Benjamin, of Upper Thames St, London, *b* 19 May 1820, *m* 1849 Jane, yst dau of Thomas Moore, of Coleshill, Berks, and *d* 1875, leaving issue):

TIMOTHY WHITE, of Salle Park, Norfolk; *b* 11 April 1824; Maj 2nd Hants Artillery Vols; *m* 1846 Emily Celestina, yst dau and coheir of Francis Dymock, of City of London and Stroud, Glos, and *d* 8 May 1908, leaving, with other issue:

Sir Woolmer Rudolph Donati White, 1st Bt (UK), so *cr* 29 June 1922, JP (Hants); *b* 21 Aug 1858; High Sheriff Norfolk 1914, CC 1912–22, Capt Hants TF; *m* 3 July 1883 Edith Wittcomb (*d* 4 Sept 1934), yr dau of George Dawes Monck, of Hilsea, Hants, and had:

1 Lynton Woolmer; *b* 5 May 1886; BA Cantab; Lt King's Dragoon Gds; *m* 29 June 1911 Dorothea (*d* 19 Aug 1926), only dau of W R Haughton, VD, MInstCE, Engr-in-Ch E Bengal State Rlwy, and *d* 4 Sept 1914 of wounds recd in action

2 (RUDOLPH) DYMOKE (Sir), **2nd Bt**

1 Marguerite; *m* 14 June 1915 Lt-Col Christopher Victor Bulstrode, DSO, TD, MA, MD Cantab, RAMC (TA), attd Warwicks Yeo (*d* 18 March 1949), and *d* 24 Nov 1952, leaving issue

2 Pauline

Sir WOOLMER *d* 6 Dec 1931; his 2nd s,

Sir (Rudolph) Dymoke White, 2nd Bt, JP, DL (Hants); *b* 11 June 1888; *educ* Cheltenham and Trin Coll Cambridge (BA 1910, MA 1944); Hants: CA, High Sheriff 1935, Maj Carabiniers WW I (Hon Col 1954); MP Fareham 1939–50; Hon Col 457 (Wessex) Heavy AA Reg RA (TA) HCY 1963; *m* 26 June 1912 Isabelle Stuart, yr dau of James George MacGowan, of Paris, and had:

1 HEADLEY DYMOKE (Sir), **3rd Bt**

2 +Lynton Stuart (Sir), MBE (1943), TD, DL (Hants) [Lt-Col Sir Lynton White MBE TD DL, Oxenbourne House, E Meon, Hants]; *b* 11 Aug 1916; *educ* Harrow and Trin Coll Cambridge (MA); Maj RA WW II (despatches), Hon Lt-Col RA (TA) 1946; memb Hants CC 1970 (V-Chm 1976, Chm 1977–85), ktd 1985; *m* 17 Jan 1945 *Phyllis Marie Rochfort, er dau of Sir Newham Arthur Worley, KBE, and has:

(1) +Anthony Douglas; *b* 13 Oct 1946; *educ* Harrow

(2) +Richard Lynton; *b* 28 June 1953; *educ* Winchester

(3) +Robert Newnham Stuart; *b* 10 Sept 1956; *educ* Winchester; *m* 1989 *Jennifer Elizabeth Anne, dau of Rev Barry Hughes-Gibbs, of Pretoria, S Africa

(4) +Philip Dymoke [Philip White Esq, Chidden Farmhouse, Hambledon, Hants PO7 4TD]; *b* 19 April 1958; *educ* Winchester and RAC Cirencester; *m* 1984 *Fiona Elizabeth, dau of James Lunn, of W Meon, and has:

    1a +Alexander Stuart Dymoke; *b* 1988

    1a *Emelia Louise; *b* 1990

    2a *Annabel Madeleine; *b* 1994

(1) *Katharine Anne Rochfort; *b* 16 Feb 1949; *m* 1976 *Christopher John Wernham, of Sydney, NSW

1 *Marguérite Isabelle [Lady Martell, 2 Marcuse Fields, Bosham, W Sussex PO18 8NA]; *b* 12 July 1920; *m* 11 Jan 1941 (*divorce* 1983) V-Adml Sir Hugh Colenso Martell, KBE, CB, yr s of Engr-Capt Albert Arthur Green Martell, DSO, RN, of Emsworth, Hants, and has:

(1) *Richard James [Richard Martell Esq, Little Court Farm, Hambrook, W Sussex]; *b* 9 Jan 1942; *educ* Shrewsbury and RAC Cirencester; *m* 24 Sept 1966 (*divorce* 1991) Theresa Hannah, 2nd dau of John Frederick Wickins, of Eastergate, W Sussex, and has:

    1a *Jonathan James; *b* 22 March 1969

    2a *Jeremy Paul; *b* 1971

    1a *Emma Jane; *b* 1979

(2) *Stuart [Stuart Martell Esq, Flat 26, Neville's Court, Dollis Hill Lane, London NW2]; *b* 25 May 1943; *m* 1st 22 June 1968 (*divorce* 1976) Penelope Gay, only dau of Christopher Hunt, of North Farm, Washington, Sussex; *m* 2nd 1978 *Carol, only dau of Lt-Col R H N Simonds, of Aldwick Bay, W Sussex, and has by his 1st w:

    1a *Benjamin Stuart; *b* 1969

    2a *Christopher Hugh Stuart; *b* 1973

(3) *Charles; *b* 7 April 1946; *m* 1968 *Monica, dau of Martin Gillman, of Gloucester, and has:

    1a *Charles Edward; *b* 1971

    1a *Elizabeth; *b* 1969

(4) *Timothy Hugh; *b* 30 Sept 1952; *m* 1973 *Elizabeth Grazyna, dau of Frank Szostak, and has:

    1a *Marcus Timothy; *b* 1977

    2a *John Robert; *b* 1981

(5) *Michael Gordon; *b* 30 Sept 1952; *m* 1981 *Fiona Jane, dau of W C Dack, of Worthing, and has:

    1a *William Michael; *b* 1986

    1a *Natalie Fiona; *b* 1981

(1) *Sarah Jessica; *b* 21 Sept 1957

2 *Hélène Pauline [Mrs Neville Cairns, The Mews House, Beechwood Park, Nenagh, Co Tipperary, Ireland]; *b* 24 July 1924, MA; *m* 24 July 1954 Lt-Col (William) Neville Cairns, 1st King's Dragoon Gds (*d* 1973), 2nd s of Maj Thomas Russell Cairns, TD, FCS, of Hackwood, Hexham, Northumberland, and has:

(1) *Jeremy Dymoke Russell; *b* 25 July 1955; *m* 1984 *Teresa Jane, dau of Gene L Lewis, of Rocky Mount, NC, USA, and has:

    1a *Neville Gene Patrick; *b* 1989

    2a *Jeremy Rudland Lee; *b* 1994

(2) *Patrick Neville; *b* 15 May 1957; *m* 1990 *Monica Frances, dau of James Kelly, of Aylwardstown House, Glenmore, Co Kilkenny, and has:

    1a *Isabelle Nicola; *b* 1993

    2a *Sophie Hélène; *b* 1997

Sir DYMOKE *d* 25 May 1968; his er s,

Sir Headley Dymoke White, 3rd Bt; *b* 15 April 1914; *educ* Winchester and Trin Coll Cambridge; Maj Intell Corps WW II; *m* 9 Jan 1943 Elizabeth Victoria Mary (*d* 29 June 1996), er dau of Wilfred Ingram Wrightson (*see* WRIGHTSON, Bt), and *d* 25 Feb 1971, leaving:

1 Sir JOHN WOOLMER WHITE, **4th and present Bt**

1 *Morna; *b* 20 Feb 1944

2 *Isabelle Sarah; *b* 9 June 1948

Seat: Salle Park, Salle, Norfolk. This house dates from 1761, being constructed by Edward Hase, brother of Sir John Lombe, 1st Bt, and father-in-law of Richard Jodrell, a classical scholar, dramatist, philologist, poet and Old Etonian who died insane. Lombe's baronetcy was created with remainder to the heirs male of his niece Vertue (Edward Hase's daughter) so that on his death it passed to his great-nephew, another Richard Jodrell, son of the Renaissance man already mentioned. Salle was inherited on the 3rd (Jodrell) Baronet's death without issue in 1882 by his sister Amelia, from whom it passed eight years later to Timothy White (*see* above), the possessor of the reversion. **Sir Woolmer White, the 1st Baronet** and Timothy's son, added two low wings designed according to the then fashionable Queen Anne revival school of architecture. Despite this extension the central block remains somewhat stark, especially given its position in the flat Norfolk terrain.

WHITE, Bt, of Wallingwells

Arms: Gules a chevron vair between three lions rampant or.
Crest: Out of a ducal coronet argent a demi-eagle with wings expanded sable. **Motto:** Loyal unto death.
Creation: Bt. (UK) 20 Dec 1802.

SIR NICHOLAS PETER ARCHIBALD WHITE, 6TH BT, of Wallingwells, Co Nottingham [Sir Nicholas White Bt, The Stables, Canon Lane, Wateringbury, Kent ME18 5PQ]; *b* 2 March 1939; *s* unc 1996; *educ* Harrow; 2nd Lt 2nd/10th POW Gurkha Rifles 1957–59, with Courage Ltd 1959–84, wine merchant 1984–94, with Gulf Eternit Industs Dubai 1994–; *m* 1970 *Susan Irene, dau of G W B Pollock, of Blackrock, Dublin, and has:

1 +CHRISTOPHER DAVID NICHOLAS; *b* 20 July 1972

2 +Simon Richard William; *b* 1974

1 *Annabelle Victoria Jocelyn; *b* 1976

Lineage: JOHANNES WHITE, of N Colyngham, Notts; in a list of Notts gentry drawn up by order of HENRY VI 1428; had:

JOHN WHITE; bought lands at Tuxford, Notts; had:

THOMAS WHITE; bought the Manor of Tuxford 1545 but lived chiefly at Woodhead, Rutland; presumably the person of the same name granted three manors in Somerset by QUEEN MARY and her husb PHILIP OF SPAIN in gratitude for help against their opponents; *m* Anne, est sis of 1st Baron Burghley (*see* EXETER, M), and had:

Sir JOHN WHITE, of Tuxford; Sheriff Notts *c* 1623; *m* Dorothea, dau of Sir John Harpur, Bt, of Swarkeston, Derbys, and *d* 1625, leaving:

THOMAS WHITE, of Tuxford; *m* Anne, dau of Sir Edward Hartopp, 1st Bt, of the 1619 *cr* (*see* CRADOCK-HARTOPP, Bt), and *d* 1638, leaving:

JOHN WHITE, of Tuxford; MP Notts 1678–98; *m* Jane, dau of Sir Thomas Williamson, 1st Bt, of East Markham, Notts (*qv*), and had, with two daus (Anne, *m* Thomas Westby, of Ravensfield; Rebecca, *m* 7 Nov 1728 Sir Griffith Boynton, 3rd Bt; *see* 1963 edn):

THOMAS WHITE, of Tuxford; MP E Retford; *m* 28 July 1698 Bridget, only dau and heiress of Richard Taylor, of Wallingwells (s of Samuel Taylor, Govr Tangier, of the TAYLORs of Bolsover, Derbys), and *d* 24 Feb 1730, leaving, with an er s (John, of Tuxford and Walling Wells, MP E Retford, *d* unm 1769) and three daus (Bridget, *m* 5 Aug 1720 Sir John Heathcote, 2nd Bt, of London (*qv*); Anne, *m* 5 April 1742, Sir Griffith Boynton, 5th Bt (*see* 1963 edn); Mary, *d* unm):

TAYLOR WHITE; *b* 21 Dec 1701; barrister Lincoln's Inn, Judge Chester, Recorder Stamford, Dep-Recorder Nottingham, Steward E Retford, first Treas Foundling Hosp; *m* 1st May 1729 Anne, dau of Thomas Errington, of Errington and Beaufront, Northumberland; *m* 2nd 18 Sept 1739 Frances (*d* 17 March 1763), dau and coheir of Maj-Gen John Armstrong, of Ballyard, King's Co, and by her had, with two yr sons (Thomas, barrister, Steward E Retford, *d* unm 19 Feb 1786; Rev Stephen, LLD, of Castor, Northants, *b* 14 Jan 1750, Rector Conington, Hunts, *m* 5 April 1774 Elizabeth Hannah (*d* 29 March 1814), dau of Rev William Sellon (*d* 27 March 1772) and *d* 30 Sept 1824, leaving issue) and two daus (*d* unm):

TAYLOR WHITE, of Tuxford; *b* 5 Nov 1743; *m* April 1765, Sarah (*d* 29 Oct 1802), est dau and eventual coheir of Sir Isaac Wo(o)llaston, Bt, of Loseby, Leics, and St Ives, Hunts, and *d* July 1795, having had, with other issue, including a yr s (Taylor, *b* 21 Aug 1771, Lt-Col, *m* 9 Feb 1803 Sophia Jewell and *d* 11 Sept 1847, leaving five sons (Isaac Woollaston, *b* 21 Aug 1805, *d* Feb 1846, leaving issue; Charles Lawrence, *b* March 1813; Thomas, *b* 1816; William Cecil, *b* 1822; Rowland Humberstone, *b* 1824) and at least two daus (Lydia, *m* 1789 Col James Worsley and *d* 19 April 1832, leaving issue; Elizabeth, *m* 14 March 1801 her sis's bro-in-law Adml Richard Worsley (*dsp* 25 Jan 1838) and *d* 18 Nov 1841)):

Sir Thomas Woollaston White, 1st Bt (UK), so *cr* 20 Dec 1802, with remainder to his f's male issue, of Wallingwells; *b* 20 Jan 1767; *m* 31 Jan 1801 Elizabeth, dau of Thomas Blagg, of Tuxford, and had:

1 THOMAS WOOLLASTON (Sir), **2nd Bt**

2 Taylor (Rev); *b* 9 June 1805; Vicar Norton Cuckney, Notts; *m* 1st Aug 1828 Dorothy Letitia (*d* 2 Sept 1840), dau of Col John Kirke, of Markham Hall, Notts, and had, with two daus (*d* unm):

(1) Thomas Woollaston; *b* 25 May 1829; *m* 9 March 1858 Charlotte Letitia (*d* 11 April 1935), est dau of Rev Francis Arthur Jackson, Vicar Riccall, Yorks, and *dsp* 8 April 1887

(2) Taylor, of Angora Park, Wimbledon, Hawke's Bay, NZ; *b* 20 Dec 1837; *d* unm 24 July 1914

(3) John, of Glenesk, Turriff, Aberdeenshire; *b* 25 June 1839; *m* 30 Nov 1876 his cousin Louisa Caroline (*d* 15 June 1915), dau of George Towry White, barrister, and *d* 12 Dec 1911, having had, with other issue:

1a Taylor Woollaston, of Glenesk; *b* 20 April 1879; *m* 11 April 1906 Mary (*d* 25 Aug 1921), dau of George Broadbent, and *d* 25 Aug 1921

2a George Towry; *b* 22 Jan 1889; NZ Mounted Rifles WW I; *m* 31 March 1922 Evangeline, dau of John Arthur, of Feilding, NZ, and had:

1b +John Woollaston [John White Esq, 74 Broadway, Waitara 4656, New Zealand]; *b* 16 Feb 1923

2b +George Towry; *b* 18 April 1925

3b +Louis Arthur Taylor [Louis White Esq, RD 4, Te Kuiti, New Zealand]; *b* 12 Jan 1928; *m* 1957 *Gladys Daphne, only dau of John Stokes, of Kinohaku, NZ, and has:

1c +Stanley George; *b* 17 July 1958

2c +Norman John; *b* 14 Dec 1959

3c +Jeffrey Taylor; *b* 22 April 1964

1c *Jocelyn Amy Anne *b* 28 Feb 1961

2c *Miriam Una; *b* 26 Sept 1962

3c *Patricia Gladys; *b* 22 April 1964

4c *Eva Marie; *b* 16 Nov 1966

1b *Marion Penelope; *b* 7 Sept 1926

2b *Harriet Cicely; *b* 14 July 1929; *m* 28 May 1960 *Robert Wallace Geange and has issue

3a John Mervyn; *b* 19 Sept 1892; Capt 4th Bn Hants Regt WW I, Pioneer Corps WW II; *d* unm 7 May 1966

1a Louisa Mary Maxwell; *d* unm 29 April 1957

2a Frances Armstrong; *d* unm 13 Dec 1965

3a Amy Anne Cecil; *b* 1884

4a Penelope Errington; *b* 1885

5a Isabella Georgina Sarah; *b* 1889

6a Joanna Caroline Decima; *b* 1891

7a Cicely Bridget Heathcote; *b* 1894

8a Joyce Alice Finderne; *b* 1897

(1) Letitia; *m* 1875 Henry Kirke Hodge, of Te Owhanga, Feilding, NZ, and *d* 23 Sept 1913

2 (cont.) The Rev Taylor White *m* 2nd 5 Nov 1850 Charlotte Bates (*m* 2nd 10 Feb 1857 Henry Sweet Hodding, of Harners Grove, Notts, and *d* 25 Jan 1887), only child of Robert Crofts, of Dumpton Park, Isle of Thanet, and *d* 8 June 1853, having by her had:

(2) Charlotte Crofts; *m* 8 April 1880 William James Chalk, of Crawley, Sussex, and *d* 6 Aug 1945, leaving issue. He *d* 18 Dec 1933

(3) Bridget; *m* 20 April 1876 Rev Preb William John HUMBLE later HUMBLE CROFTS (on his w's inheriting the Dumpton Park estate from her maternal gf), Rector Waldron, Sussex, Canon Chichester, and *d* 11 Feb 1932, leaving issue. He *d* 1 July 1924

1 Anne; *m* 10 Dec 1827 William Kirke, JP, of Markham Hall, Notts, and *d* 11 Oct 1874, leaving issue. He *d* 15 March 1843

2 Sarah; *m* 5 April 1836 Rev Buchan Warren Wright, Vicar Norton Cuckney, Notts, and *dsp* 4 Jan 1879

3 Lydia; *d* unm 1827

The 1st Bt *d* 28 Oct 1817; his er s,

Sir Thomas Woollaston White, 2nd Bt, JP, DL; *b* 3 Oct 1801; High Sheriff Notts 1839, Lt-Col Sherwood Rangers Yeo; *m* 1st 4 March 1824 Georgina (*d* 2 Dec 1825), dau of George Ramsay, of Barnton, Edinburgh, by Jean Hamilton, sis of 7th Lord Belhaven and Stenton (*qv*), and had:

1 Georgina; *m* 16 Oct 1856 Lt-Col Hon Horace Monckton (*see* GALWAY, V) and *d* 7 July 1879, leaving issue

Sir Thomas *m* 2nd 31 March 1827 Mary Euphemia (*d* 3 June 1861), dau of William Ramsay, of Gogar, Edinburgh, by Bethia, another sis of 7th Lord Belhaven and Stenton (*qv*), and *d* 7 Aug 1882, leaving by her:

1 **Sir Thomas Woollaston White, 3rd Bt**, JP Notts; *b* 7 Feb 1828; Lt-Col 16th Lancers; *d* unm 20 May 1907

2 William Knight Hamilton Ramsay, of Leahurst, Tickhill, Yorks; *b* 23 Jan 1834; *m* 5 July 1876 Edith Laura (*d* 15 March 1926), est dau of Rev Archibald Paris, Rector Ludgvan, Cornwall, and *d* 11 June 1900, leaving:

(1) ARCHIBALD WOOLLASTON (Sir), **4th Bt**

(2) William Taylor, MC; *b* 9 Feb 1880; Capt Yorks Regt; *d* 3 April 1937

(3) Charles Ramsay, DSO (1918); *b* 11 May 1881; Lt-Col 3rd Bn Yorks Regt; *d* 31 March 1921

(4) John Broughton, MC; *b* 8 March 1889; Capt Notts and Derby Regt WW I

(1) Bridget, MBE, JP (E R Yorks); *m* 18 Jan 1906 Lt-Col Alfred George William Wright, TD, JP, DL (*d* 2 Sept 1923), of Bessingby Hall, Bridlington, Yorks, s of Alfred Wright, of Bessingby Hall, and *d* 11 May 1960, leaving issue

2 Mary Elizabeth; *d* unm 15 Sept 1894 aged 65

3 Fanny Lucy Fowke; *m* 12 May 1869 Sir James Ramsay-Gibson-Maitland, 4th Bt (*see* MAITLAND, Bt), and *d* 17 March 1896, leaving issue

The 3rd Bt's n,

Sir Archibald Woollaston White, 4th Bt, TD; *b* 14 Oct 1877; Capt Yorks RGA (M), Lt-Col RHA; *m* 12 Aug 1903 Gladys Becher Love (*d* 5 Oct 1954), yr dau of Rev Edward Augustus Bracken Pitman, FSA, Rector Stonegrave, Yorks, and *d* 16 Dec 1945, leaving:

1 **Sir Thomas Astley Woollaston White, 5th Bt**, JP (Wigtownshire 1952); *b* 13 May 1904; *educ* Wellington; FLAS; *m* 8 July 1935 *Daphne Margaret [Daphne Lady White, Ha Hill, Wigtown, Wigtownshire DG8 9DJ], er dau of Col Francis

Remi Imbert Athill, CMG, OBE, DL, of Brinkburn High House, Longframlington, Northumberland, and *d* 1996, leaving:

(1) *Bridget Juliet [Mrs Charles Orr Ewing, Torhousemuir, Wigtown, Newton Stewart DG8 9DJ]; *b* 4 Aug 1962 *Lt-Cdr Charles David Orr Ewing, RN and has issue (*see* ORR EWING, Bt)

2 Richard Taylor, DSO (1940) and two bars (1941, 1942); *b* 29 Jan 1908; *educ* RNC Dartmouth; Capt RN WW II (despatches); *m* 2 Sept 1936 *Gabrielle Ursula [Mrs Richard White, Lavenders, Lavenders Rd, W Malling, Kent ME19 6HP], yr dau of Robert Henry Style (*see* STYLE, Bt), and *d* 3 March 1995, leaving:

(1) Sir NICHOLAS PETER ARCHIBALD WHITE, **6th and present Bt**

(2) +Robert Leslie; *b* 19 Aug 1945; *educ* Eton; *m* 1989 *Hong Chen

(3) +Richard Mark [Richard White Esq, 60 Bessborough Place, London SW1]; *b* 19 Aug 1945; *educ* Eton; *m* 1988 *Catherine Anne Isobel, only dau of Judge Karl Roy Barrington Brandon, of Fairwater, Chew Stoke, Somerset

(1) *Victoria Rosamond; *b* 5 July 1937; *m* 1st 1 May 1965 (*divorce* 1983) David Ashton BOSTOCK later ASHTON-BOSTOCK (roy licence), yr s of Cdr John Bostock, DSO, RN, of Wormshill House, nr Sittingbourne, Kent; *m* 2nd 1984 Sir Hugo Giles Edmund Sebright, 14th Bt (*d* 1985), and has had by her 1st husb:

1a *(Henrietta) Sophia; *b* 1967; *m* 1990 *Dominic Bertram Charles Taylor, s of Michael Taylor, of the Old Parsonage, Aust, nr Bristol

1a Ralph Nicholas Swinford; *b* 27 April, *d* 29 April 1966

(2) *Jocelyn Henrietta [Mrs Michael Mallock, Manor Lodge, Bringhurst, Market Harborough, Leics LE16 8RJ]; *b* 12 Jan 1943; *m* 8 Jan 1966 *Michael Christopher Mallock, only s of Brig Christopher Courtenay Mallock, OBE, of Stanton St Bernard, Wilts, and has had:

1a Katharine Grace; *b* 4 June, *d* 7 July 1969

1a *James Rawlyn; *b* 26 Jan 1972

2a *Sarah Penelope; *b* 27 Oct 1970; *m* 1 Aug 1992 *Lt James Edward Buck, RN, est s of W A Buck, of Stamsall, Staffs, and has:

1b *Nicholas James; *b* 5 Oct 1997

3 Archibald John Ramsay, CBE (1963), DSC (1943); *b* 17 Sept 1910; Capt RN WW II (despatches); *m* 7 July 1949 *Marguerite Elise [Mrs Archibald White, Stonewalls, Evenlode, Moreton-in-Marsh, Glos], only dau of Sir Ernest Nathaniel Bennett, JP, MP, of Cwmllecoediog, Montgomery, and *d* 1991, leaving:

(1) +Thomas Charles Ramsay; *b* 1 June 1952; *educ* Winchester; Capt 9th/12th R Lancers (ret); *m* 1981 *Mary, yr dau of Edward Ross-Hime, of E Malling, Kent, and has:

1a +Charles Thomas Ramsay; *b* 1988

1a *Elizabeth Susannah; *b* 1983

2a *Clare Marguerite; *b* 1986

(2) +John Woollaston; *b* 22 Sept 1958

(1) *Caroline Marguerite; *b* 4 Sept 1950

(2) *Sarah Elizabeth; *b* 19 March 1960

WHITEHEAD

Arms: Per pale azure and sable on a fess invected plain cotised or between three fleurs-de-ly of the last a fasces erect between two eagle's heads erased proper. **Crest:** An eagle, wings expanded proper, each wing charged with a fasces erect or, supporting with the dexter claw an escutcheon of the arms. **Motto:** *Virtute et labore* ('By valour and exertion'). **Creation:** Bt. (UK) 26 Nov 1889.

SIR ROWLAND JOHN RATHBONE WHITEHEAD, 5TH BT, of Highfield House, Kent [Sir Roland Whitehead Bt, Walnut Tree Cottage, Fyfield, Glos GL7 3LT; Sutton House, Chiswick Mall, London W4 2PR]; *b* 24 June 1930; *s f* 1953; *educ* Radley and Trin Hall Cambridge (BA 1953); late 2nd Lt RA; Chm: Standing Cncl Btage 1984–87 (memb Ctee 1981–), Rowland Hill Benevolent Fund 1982– (and Tstee), The Baronets' Tst 1984– (and Fndr); Govr Appleby GS, Freeman City London, Liveryman Fruiterers' Co (Master 1995–96, memb Court 1993–), Pres: Inst of Translation and Interpreting 1996–, Rising Stars Fndn Romania; *m* 3 April 1954 *Marie-Louise, dau of Arnold Christian Gausel, of Stavanger, Norway, and has:

1 +PHILIP HENRY RATHBONE [Philip Whitehead Esq, 8 Herbert Crescent, London SW1X 0EZ]; *b* 13 Oct 1957; *educ* Eton and Bristol U; late Welsh Gds; *m* 1987 *Emma Charlotte, dau of Capt Alexander Michael Darley Milne Home, RN (*see* MINTO, E), of Sydney, NSW, and has:

  (1) +Orlando James Rathbone; *b* 8 Oct 1994

  (2) +Caspar Henry Rathbone; *b* 1 Oct 1996

1 *Philippa Martha Gausel [The Hon Mrs Frederick Hamilton, c/o Coutts and Co Ltd, 15 Lombard St, London EC3]; *b* 15 Feb 1955; *m* 1st 14 Sept 1976 (*divorce* 1988) Capt Brian James Douglas Abdy Collins (*see* MORTON, E) and has:

  (1) *Henry James Abdy; *b* 1980

  (1) *Rosie Alice Louise; *b* 1978

1 (cont.) Mrs Philippa Collins *m* 2nd 1991, as his 2nd w, *The Master of Belhaven (*see* BELHAVEN AND STENTON, L) and has further issue

Lineage: JOHN WHITEHEAD, of Raisbeck, Orton, Westmorland; *m* 1620 Agnes Thompson, of Orton, and *d* 1636, leaving:

JOHN WHITEHEAD, of Raisbeck; *b* 1629; *d* 1715, leaving:

JAMES WHITEHEAD, of Raisbeck; *b* 1665; *m* 1704 Isabell Atkinson, of Bretherdaile, and *d* 1728, leaving:

JOHN WHITEHEAD, of Raisbeck; *b* 1707; *m* 1732 Agnes Taylor and *d* 1743, leaving:

JAMES WHITEHEAD, of Raisbeck; *b* 1733; *m* 1764 Dorothy, dau of John Farrer, of Bousfield, and *d* 1784, leaving:

JOHN WHITEHEAD, of Raisbeck; *b* 1765; *m* 1792 Eleanor, dau of Robert Wilson of Midfield, and *d* 1851, leaving:

JAMES WHITEHEAD, of Raisbeck and Appleby; *b* 1793; *m* 1822 Agnes, dau of Robert Atkinson, of Hutton Le Hay, and *d* 1861, leaving, with an er s (John, *b* 1824, Mayor Appleby):

Sir James Whitehead, 1st Bt (UK), so *cr* 26 Nov 1889, of Catford, Kent, JP, DL (Westmorland), JP (Cos London and Kent); *b* 2 March 1834; High Sheriff Kent 1890, Lt City London, Alderman Cheape 1882–96, Sheriff London and Middx 1884–85, Ld Mayor 1888–89, MP (Lib) Leicester 1892–94, Cdr Legn Hon, Grand Cordon Order St Sava and Kt Cdr Takovo Serbia, Lion and Sun Persia 2nd Cl, Kt Offr Order Leopold Belgium, Tablet of Honour China; *m* 30 May 1860 Mercy Matilda (*d* 8 May 1911), 4th dau of Thomas Hinds, of St Neots, and *d* 20 Oct 1917, having had:

  1 **Sir George Hugh Whitehead, 2nd Bt**, JP (Kent); *b* 30 Oct 1861; *educ* Clifton and Trin Coll Oxford (MA); a Lt City London, Govr Appleby GS; *m* 5 Sept 1889 Gertrude Grace (*d* 4 April 1949), dau of Sir William Ashcroft, JP, of Overleigh House, Preston, Lancs, and The Wyke, Grasmere, Westmorland, and *dspms* 21 May 1931, having had:

    (1) James Hugh Edendale; *b* 8 July 1890; *educ* Clifton and Trin Coll Oxford; Lt Roy W Kent Regt; *d* 13 March 1919 from disease contracted WW I

    (2) George William Edendale; *b* 27 Aug 1895; *educ* Clifton and RMA Woolwich; Lt RFA attd RAF; *ka* 17 Oct 1918 flying over German lines

    (1) Christobel; *m* 10 Feb 1917 Pierre de Putron, OBE (*d* Oct 1950), Jurat Roy Court Guernsey, only s of Rev Godfrey Pierre de Putron, of Guernsey, and *d* 12 Jan 1982 having had:

      1a Peter; *b* 14 Jan 1920; 2nd Lt 60th Rifles; *ka* Tobruk 10 April 1941

      2a *John Whitehead [John de Putron Esq, Lower Bertozerie, Guernsey, CI]; *b* 3 Feb 1929; *educ* Eton and Trin Coll Oxford (MA); FCA, MIMC; *m* 26 Sept 1959 *Evelyn Hastings, est dau of Arthur Sidney Fitzgerald Pruen, of Cheltenham, and has:

        1b *Peter Nicholas; *b* 15 Oct 1963

        2b *Timothy Richard; *b* 29 Sept 1964

        1b *Frances Alison; *b* 31 May 1961

      1a *Mary, OBE [Mrs Clive Russell Vick OBE, Ameroak, Seal, Sevenoaks, Kent]; *b* 16 July 1922; *educ* Somerville Coll Oxford (MA 1948); *m* 2 Dec 1944 Clive Compston Russell Vick (*d* 11 Sept 1990), slr, er s of His Honour Sir Godfrey Russell Vick, QC, of Wildernesse Chase, Seal, Kent, and has:

        1b *Rosemary Russell [Mrs John Scott, Sunnybank, Little Budworth, Cheshire]; *b* 21 Sept 1945; *m* 14 Sept 1968 *John Gabriel Valentine Scott, MSc, PhD, s of Walter Lambert Scott, BSc, ARCS, of West End, Ingworth, Norwich, and has:

          1c *Sarnia Isabel; *b* 2 Nov 1974; *educ* Glasgow U (BA Hons 1996)

          2c *Catriona Caroline; *b* 29 Dec 1978; *educ* St Hilda's Coll Oxford

        2b *Susan Russell [Mrs Anthony Clear, 62 St Bernard's Rd, Oxford]; *b* 28 Feb 1950; *educ* St Hugh's Coll Oxford (MA, MSc); *m* 5 May 1973 *Anthony Earland Clear, ARICS, s of Frederick Earland Clear, MA, AMICE, and has:

          1c *Philip Earland; *b* 9 May 1976; *educ* Uppingham and Magdalen Coll Oxford (BA 1997)

          2c *Michael Russell; *b* 12 Jan 1979; *educ* Uppingham and Edinburgh U

          3b *Christabel Russell; *b* 1 Sept 1956

    (2) Joan Gertrude; *b* 20 March 1894; *d* 15 Oct 1971

    (3) Sylvia Mercy Ascroft; *m* 17 July 1933 Rev James Walter Herbert Nankivell, BLitt, author (*d* 4 Nov 1953), s of Ernest James Patch Nankivell, and *d* 16 Feb 1989 having had:

      1a Hensley Robert George; *b* 5 May 1934; *educ* Cheltenham and Trin Coll Oxford; *d* 31 Jan 1987

  2 ROWLAND EDWARD (Sir), **3rd Bt**

  3 Gilbert Hinds; *b* 26 May 1866; *m* 10 April 1901 Helena Emmeline (*d* 1949), only dau of Henry A Langford, of Plymouth, and *d* 18 Dec 1908, leaving:

    (1) *Margaret Joy; *m* 1st 5 May 1928 Lt-Cdr John Brett, DSC, RN (*ka* in HMS *Gloucester* off Crete 22 May 1941), er s of Michael Brett, of Bishop's Stortford, and had issue; *m* 2nd 24 July 1965 Lt-Col Robert Clement Giles, RM (*d* 1970), only s of Rev Clement Douglas Giles

  4 Wilfred James, DSO (1917); *b* 6 Jan 1873; *educ* Rugby and Trin Coll Oxford (MA); Lt-Col 6th City London Regt WW I (wounded, despatches); *m* 16 April 1907 Dona Margaret (*d* 4 July 1944), dau of T A N Chase, ICS, and *d* 22 Dec 1934, leaving:

(1) John Chase, MBE (1945); *b* 23 May 1913; *educ* Rugby and RMC Sandhurst; barrister Inner Temple 1938; Maj Roy W Kent Regt WW II; *m* 15 Nov 1941 *Lorna Davey [Mrs John Whitehead, Abbotsleigh, Dalton Rd, Eastbourne, Sussex], dau of Walter Rupert Belk, of Newbury, and *d* 22 June 1956, leaving:

  1a *Carolyn; *b* 30 Sept 1946; *m* 1967 *Patrick Geoghegan Smyth and has:

    1b *Dominic; *b* 1970

    1b *Siobhan; *b* 1972

    2b *Bridget; *b* 1974

  2a *Saffron Ann [Mrs John Davies, 265 Burntwood Lane, London SW17 0AW]; *b* 13 Feb 1948; BSc, PhD; *m* 1st 1974 (*divorce* 1977) Christopher Butler, BSc, PhD; *m* 2nd 1978 *John Kenneth Davies, BSc, and has by him:

    1b *Thomas John; *b* 1978

    2b *Daniel Lloyd; *b* 1980

    3b *Lewis Robert; *b* 1983

  3a *Nicola Jane [Ms Nicola Whitehead, 265 The Parkway, Iver Heath, Bucks SL0 0RJ]; *b* 15 March 1956; BSc, PhD, ARCS, DIC, CBiol, MIBiol; has by *Ian Stuart Thomas Fisher:

    1b *Benjamin Alexander; *b* 1991

    1b *Rebecca Emily; *b* 1990

(1) Elizabeth Dona; *b* 22 June 1910; *m* 5 July 1939 Maj Lionel William Skipwith Tayler, Roy Sussex Regt, er s of Lt-Col Francis Lionel Tayler, DSO, IA, and *d* 22 Aug 1953, leaving a s and dau

1 Leila Isabel Mercy, JP (Kent); *d unm* 11 March 1956

2 Florence Marion; *d unm* 2 Dec 1958

The 2nd Bt's bro,

Sir Rowland Edward Whitehead, 3rd Bt, KC, JP (Berks); *b* 1 Sept 1863; *educ* Clifton and Univ Coll Oxford (MA); Lt 2nd Vol Bn City London Regt, Master Fruiterers' Co 1904, MP (Lib) SE Essex 1906–10, PPS to Parly U-Sec Home Dept 1906–09 and Attorney-Gen 1909–10, Lt City London, Bencher Lincoln's Inn, CC Berks, Chm Clifton Cncl Tstee Rowland Hill Benevolent Fund GPO, Govr Appleby Grm Sch, memb Ctee Work Nat Importance 1916–19; *m* 18 May 1893 Ethel Mary Leonie (*d* 26 Feb 1945), dau of Philip Henry Rathbone, JP, of Greenbank Cottage, Wavertree, Liverpool, and had:

1 PHILIP HENRY RATHBONE (Sir), **4th Bt**

2 Gilbert Rathbone, TD (1950); *b* 15 Oct 1910; *educ* Clifton and Univ Coll Oxford (BA 1933, MA 1938); Lt-Col RA (TARO) WW II; Govr Clifton Coll and Appleby GS, Liveryman Fruiterers' Co, Tstee Rowland Hill Benevolent GPO; *m* 15 Sept 1934 Adeline Joy, only child of Sydney Frederick Rumball, of The Slyce, St Leonards-on-Sea, and *d* 18 May 1968, leaving:

  (1) *Gilla Fleur [Mrs Gilla Slocock, 11 Fyfield Rd, Oxford]; *b* 29 March 1936; *educ* St Anne's Coll Oxford (MA Oxon) (BSc London); *m* 20 Aug 1960 (*divorce* 19–) Martin Oliver Slocock, only s of Oliver Charles Ashley Slocock, of Woking, Surrey, and has:

    1a *Oliver Rowland Benjamin; *b* 8 July 1964

    2a *Thomas Gilbert; *b* 13 Aug 1969

    1a *Eleanor Sophia; *b* 8 July 1964

  (2) *Celia Lynette [Mrs Edward Rowe, 23 Portsmouth Ave, Thames Ditton, Surrey KT7 0RU]; *b* 5 Aug 1939; *m* 2 July 1970 *Edward Raphael Rowe, 3rd s of Stephen Joseph Rowe, of Dublin, and has:

    1a *Russell Stephen; *b* 1978

    1a *Anthea Rosalind; *b* 1976

  (3) *Anthea Margaret Joy [Mrs John Hutchinson, 2 The Green North, Warborough, Oxford]; *b* 16 Sept 1943; *educ* Edinburgh U (MA); memb Dip Serv; *m* 1972 *John Valentine Hutchinson

1 Hermione Elfrida Mary; *m* 24 April 1930 Maj Edmund Kell Blyth, Oxon and Bucks LI, s of Charles Frederick Tolme Blyth, CMG, of Felden, Boxmoor, Herts, and had:

  (1) *Philip Henry, MC [Philip Blyth Esq MC, Starbank House, High St, Thame, Oxon]; *b* 6 May 1931; *educ* Shrewsbury and Queen's Coll Oxford (MA); late Lt Oxon and Bucks LI Korean war (wounded); *m* 3 July 1959 *Mary Elizabeth, est dau of Maurice Bennett, of Wootton Rivers, Wilts, and has:

    1a *William James; *b* 23 June 1968

    1a *Sarah Jane; *b* 8 May 1960

    2a *Carey Ann; *b* 26 Feb 1962

    3a *Eleanor Mary; *b* 25 March 1964

    4a *Lucy Rosalind; *b* 28 Oct 1965

  (2) *Thomas Whitehead [Thomas Blyth Esq, 20 Brooksby St, London N1]; *b* 4 May 1938; *m* 5 Sept 1964 *Caroline Ruth, dau of Charles Victor Bowden, of Shepton Mallet, Somerset, and has:

    1a *Charles Kell Howard; *b* 8 May 1967

    2a *Paul Barnabas; *b* 12 April 1969

  (1) *Elizabeth Lawrence [Mrs Jack Griffin, 60 Alexandra Dve, Surbiton, Surrey]; *b* 25 Sept 1932; *educ* Roedean; SRN, NNEB; *m* 17 Dec 1955 *Jack Nicolas Griffin and has:

    1a *Nicola Jane; *b* 26 Dec 1958

    2a *Celia Rachel; *b* 13 Sept 1960

    3a *Clare Patricia; *b* 16 Dec 1963

  (2) *Jane Rathbone [Mrs Maqbul Caleb, Mehboob Villa, Dalhousie, HP, India 176304]; *b* 29 April 1936; *m* 1962 *Rev Maqbul Caleb, Bp Delhi 1982–90, and has:

    1a *Michael Sunil; *b* 20 Nov 1963

    1a *Leila; *b* 11 Feb 1966

2 Eileen Isabel; *m* 7 June 1921 Thomas Stephen Leach, CMG, MC, yst s of Henry Robert Leach, of Rickmansworth, and had:

  (1) *John Hugh Whitehead [John Leach Esq, 40 Bedford Rd, Letchworth, Herts]; *b* 10 Sept 1926; *educ* Gresham's; *m* 6 Dec 1957 *Heather, only dau of John Houston, of Kildonan, Conan Bridge, Ross-shire, and has:

    1a *Fiona Jane; *b* 22 Jan 1963

    2a *Anne Marie; *b* 11 Aug 1966

(2) *Martin Hilary; *b* 10 Aug 1931; *educ* Gresham's; *m* 15 July 1967 *Ruth, only dau of John Frederick Pidcock, of Bakewell, and has issue
(1) *Anne Joscelyn [Mrs Eric Williams, Drive Lodge, Keele University, nr Newcastle, Staffs]; *b* 21 Dec 1923; *m* 12 April 1952 *Eric Williams, s of William Victor Williams, of Standon, Staffs, and has:
1a *Michael Philip; *b* 21 May 1954; *educ* Wolstanton GS
2a *Christopher Stephen; *b* 3 May 1956; *educ* Wolstanton GS
3a *Timothy John; *b* 12 Oct 1960

The 3rd Bt *d* 9 Oct 1942; his er s,
Sir Philip Henry Rathbone Whitehead, 4th Bt; *b* 24 July 1897; *educ* Clifton and RMC Sandhurst; Maj Res Offrs Oxon and Bucks LI WW I (wounded) and Intell Corps WW II; Tstee Rowland Hill Benevolent Fund GPO; *m* 1st 17 Sept 1929 (*divorce* 1938) Gertrude, dau of John C Palmer, of Wheeling, WVa., and had:
1 Sir ROWLAND JOHN RATHBONE WHITEHEAD, **5th and present Bt**
2 Peter James Palmer; *b* 24 June 1930; *educ* Radley and Trin Hall Coll Cambridge (BA 1953), PhD; late 2nd Lt RA; Pncpl Sci Offr Br Museum (Natural History), author: *Drawings of fishes from Captain Cook's Voyages* (1969) and *A Dutch 17th-Century Portrait of Brazil* (1989); *m* 1st 1953 (*divorce* 1960) Monica (*d* 1969), only dau of James O'Dwyer, of Tipperary; had by Mrs Mavis Argwings-Kodhek (*d* 1968), of Armagh and Kenya:
(1) *Paul James [Paul Whitehead Esq, 51 Lydalls Rd, Didcot, Oxon]; *b* 19 Dec 1961; *m* 1993 *Anne-Marie Mulcahy and has:
1a *Thomas Harrison; *b* 1991
(1) *Amanda Oonagh [Mrs Paul Griffiths, 22 Tavistock Ave, Didcot, Berks]; *b* 9 Nov 1960; *m* 1987 *Paul Lloyd Griffihs and has:
1a *William Kai; *b* 1987
2a *Luke Aidan; *b* 1989
2 (cont.) Dr Peter Whitehead *m* 2nd 12 Oct 1967 *Greta Maureen Caecelia [Mrs Peter Whitehead, Sud-de-Village, 65670 Monleon Magnoac, Hautes Pyrenées, France], dau of Capt Frederick J Ransom, of Greenwich, and *d* 1992, leaving by her:
(2) Peter Rathbone Palmer; *b* 21 Aug 1970; *d* 19 May 1998
(2) *Victoria-Augusta Gordon Rathbone Williams Palmer; *b* 21 April 1968; composer for TV and films

Sir Philip *m* 2nd 3 Oct 1946 *Margery (*m* 4th 30 July 1959 Capt Sydney Alick Harrison-Smith, CBE, RN, s of Paymaster R-Adml Sir Francis Harrison-Smith, KCB), dau of Edward Weston Hickes, of Brasted Hall, Kent, and formerly wife of (a) Francis R Ronald Dresser and (b) Christopher Langlands, and *d* 31 Dec 1953

WHITELAW

Arms: Sa. a chevron engrailed or between three boar's heads couped arg., armed and langued or. **Crest:** A bee erect ppr. **Supporters:** On either side a Charolais bull in trian aspect ppr., each with a garland about the shoulder of roses gu., barbed and seeded, slipped and leaved, and thistles, stalked and leaved ppr., and interlaced in front with two pairs of golf clubs fretted saltirewise gold, the compartment comprising three mounts, seeded, stalked and leaved ppr., growing from each of these to the fore two roses and as many thistles, the roses gu., barbed and seeded, stalked and leaved ppr., the thistles stalked and leaved also ppr. **Motto:** *Solertia ditat* ('Prudence enriches'). **Creation:** V (UK) 1983.

THE 1ST VISCOUNT WHITELAW, of Penrith, Co Cumbria (Sir William Stephen Ian Whitelaw, KT (1990), CH (1974), MC (1944), PC (1967), DL (Dunbartonshire 1952–66, Cumberland 1967–74, Cumbria 1974–) [The Rt Hon The Viscount Whitelaw KT CH MC PC, Ennim, Penrith, Cumbria]; *b* 28 June 1918; *educ* Winchester and Trin Coll Cambridge; Maj Scots Gds WW II, MP (C) Penrith and the Border 1955–83, PPS to Pres BOT 1956 and Chllr Exchequer 1957–58, Assist Govt Whip 1959–61, Ld Commr Treasury 1961–62, Parly Sec Min Labour 1962–64, Oppn Ch Whip 1964–70, Ld Pres Cncl and Leader H of C 1970–72, Sec State NI 1972–73 and Employment 1973–74, Dep Leader Oppn 1975–79, Home Sec 1979–83, Ld Pres Cncl and Leader Lds 1983–88; Chm Govrs St Bees Cumbria 1984– and Carlton Club 1986–; Visiting Fell Nuffield Coll Oxford 1970–, Pres GB-USSR Assoc 1988–, author: *The Whitelaw Memoirs* (1989); *m* 1943 *Cecilia

Doriel, yr dau of Maj Mark Sprot, RSG, of Riddell, Melrose, Roxburghs, by Meliora, dau of Sir John Adam Hay, 9th Bt, of Smithfield and Haystoun (*see* 1963 edn), and has:
1 *(Elizabeth) Susan; *b* 1944; *m* 1966 (*divorce* 19–) Hon Nicholas John Cunliffe-Lister and has issue (*see* SWINTON, E)
2 *Carolyn Meliora [The Hon Mrs Graves-Johnston, 54 Stockwell Park Rd, London SW9]; *b* 1946; *m* 1st 1973 (*divorce* 1979) Robert Donald Macleod Thomas and has:
(1) *Miranda Cecilia; *b* 1974
(2) *Rhoda Mary Macleod; *b* 1977
2 (cont.) The Hon Mrs Carolyn Thomas *m* 2nd 1983 *Michael Francis Graves-Johnston and has by him:
(3) *Cleopatra Frances; *b* 1985
(4) *Helen Mercedes; *b* 1987
3 *Mary Cecilia; *b* 1947; *m* 1972 *David Alexander Coltman (*see* HOTHFIELD, B) and has issue
4 *Pamela Winifred; *b* 1951; *m* 27 April 1974 *Malise Charles Richard Graham (*see* GRAHAM, Bt, of Netherby)

Lineage: W A WHITELAW; had:

WILLIAM STEPHEN IAN WHITELAW, **1st and present Viscount Whitelaw**

WHITMORE

Arms: Quarterly, 1st and 4th, vert fretty or; 2nd and 3rd, vert fretty and a canton or charged with a cinquefoil azure, pierced of the second. **Crests:** Dexter, a falcon sitting on the stump of a tree with a branch springing from the dexter side, all proper; sinister, an arm couped at the elbow erect and habited or, doubled azure, holding in the hand proper a cinquefoil of the second, slipped vert, all within two wings expanded gold. **Motto:** *Incorrupta fides* ('Unbreakable faith'). **Creation:** Bt. (UK) 28 June 1954.

SIR JOHN HENRY DOUGLAS WHITMORE, 2ND BT, of Orsett, Essex [Sir John Whitmore Bt, Southfield, Leigh, nr Tonbridge, Kent TN11 8PJ]; *b* 16 Oct 1937; *s* f 1962; *educ* Eton, RMA Sandhurst and RAC Cirencester; chm Orsett Estate Co, racing driver (ret), sports psychologist; Dep Dir Centre for Internat Peacebuilding; author: *The Winning Mind* (1987), *Superdriver* (1988), *Coaching for Performance* (1992) and *Need, Greed or Freedom* (1997); *m* 1st 2 Nov 1962 (*divorce* 1969) Ella Gunilla, est dau of Sven A Hansson, OV, KLH, of Sweden, and has:
1 *Tina; *b* 31 March 1966

Sir JOHN *m* 2nd 1977 *Diana Elaine, er dau of Fred A Becchetti, of California, and by her has:
1 +JASON; *b* 26 Jan 1983

Lineage: JOHN de WHYTENMERE (northwest part of the parish of Bobbington in the manor of Claverley, Salop); living *temp* HENRY III and EDWARD I; had:

PHILIP de WHYTMERE; *d* 1300, leaving:

JOHN de WHYTEMERE; living 1361; had:

RICHARD de WHYTEMERE, of Claverley and Whytmere; *m* Margery, dau and heir of William Attetrall, of Claverley, and *d c* 1385, leaving:

RICHARD de WHYTEMERE; had:

RICHARD de WHYTEMERE; *m* Joan — and *d* 1441, leaving:

THOMAS WYTEMERE, of Claverley; *d* 1482, leaving:

RICHARD WHYTEMERE; *m* Agnes — (*d* 1522) and *d* 1504, leaving:

RICHARD WHITMORE, of Claverley; *b* 1495; *m* Frances Barker and *d* 1549, having had, with a yr s (Thomas, ancestor of the WHITMOREs of Ludstone in Claverley):

WILLIAM WHITMORE; London merchant; *m* Anne (*d* 9 Oct 1615), dau of William Bond, Alderman London, and *d* 8 Aug 1593, having had:
1 WILLIAM (Sir)
2 George (Sir), of Balmes, Hackney, Middx; Ld Mayor London 1631–32; royalist Civil War

3 Thomas, *dsp*

1 Elizabeth; *m* Sir William Craven and had issue (*see* CRAVEN, E)

2 Anne; *m* Francis Baber, of Chute, Wilts

3 Margaret; *m* Sir Richard Grubham

4 Mary; *m* Sir Charles Montagu, bro of 1st Earl of Manchester (*see* MANCHESTER, D)

5 Frances; *m* Sir John Weld (*d* 1622), of Arnolds Court, Middx, and *d* 1656, having had issue

6 Jane; *m* N Still

The est s,

Sir WILLIAM WHITMORE, of London; *b* 1572; bought the estate of Apley, Salop; High Sheriff Salop 1620, MP Bridgnorth 1621, 1624 and 1625; *m* 1st Margaret (*d* 31 Jan 1608), dau of Rowland Mosley, of Houghend, Lancs (*see* RAVENSDALE, B), and had:

1 George; *dsp*

1 Anne; *m* Sir Edmund Sawyer (*d* 1670), of Heywood, Berks, MP Berwick-on-Tweed, and *d* 1666, having had issue

Sir WILLIAM *m* 2nd Dorothy (*d* 1626), dau of John Weld, of London, and *d* Dec 1648, having by her had:

2 Sir THOMAS WHITMORE, 1st Bt (E), so *cr* 28 June 1641, of Apley; *b* 28 Nov 1612; *educ* Trin Coll Oxford (BA 1631); barrister Middle Temple 1639, MP Bridgnorth April-May 1640 and 1640–44; *m* 16 April 1635 Elizabeth (*d* 1666), dau and heir of Sir William Acton, Alderman and Ld Mayor London, and *d* 1653, leaving:

(1) Sir WILLIAM WHITMORE, 2nd and last Bt, of Apley; *b* 8 April 1637; MP Salop 1660 and Bridgnorth 1661–99; *m c* 1658 Mary (*d* 30 Jan 1710/11), dau of Elias Harvey, of London, and *dsp* 1699, when the btcy expired

(2) Thomas (Sir), of Bridgnorth

(1) Anne; *m* 1650 Sir Francis Lawley, 2nd Bt (*d* Oct 1696), of Spoonhill, Salop, MP Wenlock, and had issue (*see* 1932 edn WENLOCK, B)

(2) Elizabeth; *m* John Bennett

(3) Dorothy; *m* Sir Elias Harvey

3 Richard, of Lower Slaughter, Glos; *b* 21 June 1614; High Sheriff Glos 1667; *m* Catherine (*d* 30 Nov 1673), dau and coheir of Robert Deards, of London, and *d* 20 Aug 1667, leaving:

(1) Richard, of Lower Slaughter; *m* Anne, dau of Sir John Weld, of Willey, Salop, and *d* by 1694, leaving:

1a WILLIAM, for whom *see* further below

1a Anne; *m* Walter Jones, of Chastleton, Oxon, and *d* 1738, leaving issue

The 2nd Bt's cousin,

WILLIAM WHITMORE, of Lower Slaughter, and Apley, which he inherited 1699; MP Bridgnorth 1705–10 and 1713–25; *m* Elizabeth (*d c* 1736), dau of Roger Pope, of Wolstanton, Salop, and *d* 24 May 1725, having had:

1 William; *d* an infant 1710

2 Thomas (Sir), KB, of Apley; *m* Anne (*d* 1775), dau of Sir Jonathan Cope, 1st Bt, of Brewern, and *d* 15 April 1773, leaving:

(1) Mary; *m* her cousin Thomas Whitmore (*see below*)

(2) Anna Sophia; *m* Anthony Deane

(3) Elizabeth; *m*, as his 2nd w, Rev Charles Edward Holden, of Aston, Derbys, and *dsp* 7 Aug 1795

3 William, of Lower Slaughter; *b* 1714; Lt-Gen, first Col 53rd Regt; MP Bridgnorth; *d* 1771, leaving:

(1) George, of Lower Slaughter; *m* 8 March 1774 Mary, dau of John Wall, MD, by Catherine Sandys, and *d* 19 Nov 1794 at Amiens, a prisoner and victim of the French Revolution, having had:

1a George (Sir), KCH, of Lower Slaughter; *b* 12 May 1775; Gen, Col Cmdt RE; *m* 16 Jan 1798 Cordelia (*d* 19 Dec 1857), dau of George Ainslie, and *d* 2 April 1862, having had:

1b George St Vincent; *b* 28 Nov 1798; Maj RE; *m* 22 Feb 1827 Isabella Maxwell (*d* 18 April 1885), dau of Sir John Stoddart, LLD, Ch Justice Malta, by Isabella, er dau of Rev Sir Henry Wellwood Moncreiff, 8th Bt DD (*see* MONCREIFF, B), and *dvp* 12 Nov 1851, having had:

1c George Stoddart (Sir), KCMG (1882, CMG 1869); *b* 30 May 1829; *educ* Edinburgh Acad; Hon Col NZ Militia 1868, Maj 62nd Regt; MLC NZ 1863–1903, Colonial Sec and Def Min NZ 1877–79, joined Cape Mounted Rifles 1847, served Kaffir Wars 1847 and 1851–53, Boer War 1848, Crimean War 1855–56, last Maori War 1866–69, cmdg Hawke's Bay Militia, Cmdt Colonial Forces 1868–88, Maj-Gen 1874; *m* 11 March 1865 Isabella, dau of William Smith, of Roxeth, Rugby, Warwicks, and *dsp* 16 March 1914

2c Montagu Stopford; *b* 11 Jan 1831; Capt RE; *dsp* 17 Oct 1880

3c Henry Ainslie; *b* 20 June 1837; Lt 47th Regt; *d* unm 14 Sept 1857

4c Charles William; *b* 13 Aug 1838; *d* 21 April 1839

5c John; *b* 8 Sept 1845; *educ* Merton Coll Oxford; Judge ICS, barrister Inner Temple; *m* 22 May 1901 Clara (*d* 29 Nov 1948), dau of Michael Roach, and *d* 17 May 1904, leaving:

1d George Montagu John Llewelyn; *b* 31 July 1903; *educ* Cheltenham and Balliol Coll Oxford (BA 1925); barrister Inner Temple 1927; F/Lt RAFVR WW II 1940–45; inherited the Lower Slaughter estate 1944 from Eva, widow of his cousin Edmund Henry Whitmore (*see below*); Glos: CC 1949, High Sheriff 1956; *m* 5 Jan 1954 Pamela Mary, dau of Walter London, and *d* 22 Sept 1964, leaving:

1e *George John Walter; *b* 3 Jan 1955

1e *Clara Pamela; *b* 9 Sept 1957

1c Cordelia Nugent; *b* 16 Jan 1828; *d* unm

2c Mary Moncreiff; *b* 8 May 1833; *m* Rev Thomas Llewelyn Griffith, of Penynant, Ruabon, Denbighs, Rector Deal, Kent, and had issue

3c Annette Dashwood; *b* 22 July 1834; *d* 14 Sept 1835

4c Emily Atkinson; *b* 27 Sept 1840; *d* unm 8 July 1924

2b Ainslie Henry; *b* 28 Sept 1800; *d* 1 April 1843

3b Charles Shapland, of Lower Slaughter, QC, JP (Glos); *b* 25 July 1805; MA; Recorder Gloucester, Bencher Inner Temple, Judge County Court Circuit No 46; *m* 2 Dec 1845 Elizabeth Katharine (*d* 11 Feb 1883), dau of Lt-Col Robert James Brownrigg and sis of Sir Robert Brownrigg, 2nd Bt (*qv*), and *d* 17 May 1877, leaving:

1c Charles Algernon, of Lower Slaughter, JP (Glos); *b* 24 Feb 1851; *educ* Eton and Balliol Coll Oxford; Fell All Souls 1874, barrister Inner Temple 1876, MP Chelsea 1886–1906, Alderman LCC; *d* unm 10 Sept 1908

2c William Walter, of Lower Slaughter; *b* 19 May 1853; *educ* Eton and BNC Oxford; *d* unm 21 Oct 1925, having willed the Lower Slaughter estate to his sis-in-law

3c Edmund Henry; *b* 16 Aug 1858; *educ* Eton; *m* 26 April 1898 Eva (*d* 19 April 1944), of Lower Slaughter, only dau of Cdr Sidmouth Stowell Skipwith, RN (*see* SKIPWITH, Bt), and *dsp* 23 Feb 1905

4b William Lechmere; *b* 4 July 1807; *m* 17 Oct 1837 Sara Patience Mee (*d* 27 Sept 1890) and *d* 6 May 1866, having had:

1c George Ainslie Lechmere Aston; *b* 26 Dec 1841; *m* Georgina Long and *d* 18 Oct 1878, leaving:

1d Frances

2d Constance

2c Mortimer Durant; *b* 28 May 1848; Maj RE; *m* 4 April 1888 Elizabeth Georgina Mary (*d* 11 April 1954), dau of Rev Thomas Llewelyn Griffith, Rector Deal, and *d* 29 Aug 1892, leaving:

1d Zarina Mary; *b* 1 Jan 1889; *d* unm 11 March 1977

1c Marian Serena; *b* 22 March 1844; *m* Arthur Long and had issue

2c Grace Emily; *b* 17 Jan 1854; *m* 21 Nov 1881 Arthur Payne, est s of Dr A J Payne, and had issue

5b Mortimer Robert Sandys; *b* 22 Feb 1809; Maj-Gen; *m* 22 Nov 1836 Cecilia Hall (*d* 17 April 1900), dau of Adml Hon Henry Byng (*see* TORRINGTON, V), and *d* 30 Dec 1884, having had:

1c Ada Byng; *b* 9 Jan 1838

6b Francis Locker; *b* 31 July 1814; Lt-Gen; commnd 1st Foot (Roy Scots) 1835, served Canada and Crimea, First Cmdt Roy Mil Sch Music Kneller Hall 1857–80; *m* 18 Jan 1848 Eliza, dau of John Ledsam, 7th Fus, and *d* 23 Dec 1894, having had:

1c Winifred Mary; *b* 1 June 1851; *d* unm 27 Oct 1934

2c Maud Mildred; *b* 12 May 1862; *d* unm 21 Sept 1944

7b Edmund Augustus (Sir), KCB; *b* 8 July 1819; Gen, served Crimea, Mil Sec; *d* unm 14 Dec 1890

1b Mary Wall; *b* 31 Aug 1802; *m* 3 Feb 1827 Nicolas Orlando Walter Tyrell Leroux Nugent

2b Cordelia Winifreda; *b* 27 Feb 1804; *m* 22 Aug 1827 Adml Hon Sir Montagu Stopford, KCB, s of 3rd Earl of Courtown (*qv*), and *d* 4 Sept 1851, leaving issue

3b Emily Harriet Octavia; *b* 24 Nov 1812; *d* unm 5 Nov 1870

1a Mary Hanway; *b* 25 Aug 1777; *m* Rev Joseph Shapland and *d* 2 May 1837

4 George, of Apley; *dsp* 1775

5 Charles, of Southampton; *m* Mary Kelly (*d* 1799) and *d* 1770, having had, with other issue:

(1) Thomas, of Apley, which he acquired through his 1st w; MP Bridgnorth 1771–95; *m* 1st his cousin Mary (*d* 1776), est dau of Sir Thomas Whitmore, KB (*see above*), and had:

1a Mary Anne; *m* Thomas Wylde Browne, of Caughley, Salop, and *d* 1844, leaving issue

2a Anna Sophia; *d* unm

3a Georgiana; *d* unm

(1) Thomas Whitmore *m* 2nd Mary (*d* 1817), dau of Capt Thomas Foley, RN (*see* FOLEY, B), and *d* 1795, having by her had:

1a Thomas, of Apley, JP, DL (Salop); *b* 16 Nov 1782; MP Bridgnorth 1806–31; High Sheriff Salop 1825; *m* 19 July 1804 Catherine (*d* 20 Aug 1887), only dau and heiress of Thomas Thomason, of York, by Catherine, dau of James Grierson, and *d* 6 Feb 1846, leaving:

1b Thomas Charlton, of Apley; *b* 5 Jan 1807; MP Bridgnorth 1832–52; *m* 11 April 1833 Lady Louisa Anne Douglas (*d* 31 Aug 1871), est dau of 5th Marquess of Queensberry (*qv*), and *d* 13 March 1865, having had:

1c Thomas Charles Douglas, of Gumley, Leics (which he bought 1867 but later sold), and Orsett Hall, Essex (which he inherited 1884 from Capt Digby Hanmer Richard Wingfield-Baker), formerly of Apley, Salop (which he sold 1867), JP, DL (Leics), JP (Essex); *b* 26 May 1839; *educ* Eton; Capt RHG (The Blues), High Sheriff Leics 1875; *m* 11 May 1867 Louisa Margaret Emily (*d* 29 Nov 1892), 5th dau of Sir William Edmund Cradock-Hartopp, 3rd Bt (*qv*), and *d* 16 Feb 1907, leaving:

1d FRANCIS HENRY DOUGLAS CHARLTON (Sir), **1st Bt**

1d Mildred Louisa Lucy; *b* 30 Aug 1868; *m* 12 June 1899 Hugh Bertie Craven (*d* 26 March 1944), of Wheathills House, Kirklangley, Derbys, son of John Albert Craven, of Whilton Lodge, Northants, and *d* 17 Feb 1931, leaving issue

2d Ethel Mary Alberta; *b* 3 Sept 1870; *m* 20 July 1899 Col Sir William Thomas Reginald Houldsworth, 3rd Bt (*qv*), and *d* 7 May 1937, leaving issue

2c Walter Henry; *b* 21 Aug 1842; *d* 19 Aug 1880

1c Caroline Louisa; *m* 24 May 1866 John William Scott, of Delgany, Co Wicklow, 3rd s of John Scott, QC, and *d* his widow 29 June 1909, leaving:

2c Mary Catherine; *d* unm 30 Nov 1898

3c Emily Harriet; *m* 24 Oct 1877 Maj-Gen William Tweedie, CSI, IA (*d* 20 Sept 1914), of Lettrick, Dumfriesshire, est son of Rev W K Tweedie, DD, of Edinburgh, and *dsp* 16 Oct 1912

4c Louisa Dorothea; *d* 11 Oct 1839

5c Lucy Albinia; *d* unm 8 June 1911

6c Edith Georgina; *d* unm 23 Aug 1898

7c Cecil Elizabeth; *m* 14 June 1887 Lt-Col Duncan Stewart, 92nd Gordon Highrs (*d* 19 Dec 1909), and *d* 17 Oct 1925

8c Evelyn Octavia; *d* 14 Nov 1929

2b George (Rev), JP; *b* 13 Aug 1812; Rector Stockon Shifnal, Salop; *m* 6 Jan 1848 Sarah, 3rd dau of John Deacon, of Mabledon Park, Kent, and *d* 20 Sept 1900, having had:

1c Algernon George Bernard; *b* 18 Oct 1849; *d* 22 July 1877

2c Henry Eardley; *b* 26 April 1855; *m* 16 April 1907 Katharine Maud (*d* 9 Aug 1930), est dau of John Tayleur, JP, DL, of Buntingsdale Hall, Salop, and *d* 22 Feb 1909

1c Katherine Mildred; *d* 25 Oct 1925

2c Dora Louisa Mary

3c Geraldine Ellen Georgina; *m* 23 April 1895 Percy Robert Kenyon-Slaney and *d* 7 Sept 1947, leaving issue (*see* KENYON, B)

3c Henry, of Sunnyside, Coalbrookdale, Salop; *b* 13 Oct 1813; MP Bridgnorth 1852–70, a Ld Treasury; *m* 15 April 1852 Adelaide Anna, dau and coheir of Francis Darby, of Coalbrookdale, and *d* 1876

1b Catherine Mary; *m* 16 Aug 1832 3rd Earl of Bandon, DCL (*d* 17 Feb 1877; *see* 1970 edn), and *d* 15 Dec 1873, leaving issue

2b Emily Elizabeth; *m* 13 Feb 1855 Lt-Gen Eardley Nicholas Wilmot (*see* WILMOT, Bt) and *dsp* 26 April 1900

3b Lucy Georgiana; *m* 27 Dec 1849 Col John Forbes, Coldstream Gds, 2nd son of William Forbes of Callendar, Stirlingshire, and *d* 28 Oct 1872, having had issue

2a Charles Blaney Cavendish (Rev); *b* 9 March 1787; Rrector Stockton, Salop; *m* 1829 Anne Barbara (*d* 23 Nov 1834), 4th dau of Thomas Giffard, of Chillington, Staffs, and *d* 30 Oct 1856, leaving three daus

4a Elizabeth; *m* Jan 1818 Rev John Storer, Rector Hawksworth, Notts

(2) William, of Dudmaston, Salop

(3) George, DD, Fell St John's Coll Cambridge; *d* 25 Nov 1805

(1) Elizabeth; *m* Launcelot Shadwell and had, with other issue:

1a Launcelot Shadwell (Sir), KC, LLD; MP, last V-Chllr of England

6 John, of London; *m* 1st Sarah Stevens (*d* 1748) and had two daus; *m* 2nd Elizabeth Henkell (*d* 1788) and *d* 1791, having by her had:

(1) John, of London; *b c* 1750; MP Bridgnorth 1795–1806; *m* Caroline Williams (*d* 1833) and *d* 1826, having had, with other issue (*dvp*):

1a John, of London; *m* Mary Stainforth and *d* 1842

2a Edward, of London; *m* 1st Frances Kensington (*d* 1833) and had issue; *m* 2nd Elizabeth Davison and by her had issue

3a Robert, of Lincoln's Inn; *m* Elizabeth Kaye and had issue

4a Frederick, of London

(2) William; ptnr Whitmore, Wells & Co (Maidstone), bankers; *m* Elizabeth, dau of Montagu Booth, of Upton, and had, with other issue:

1a William, of Beckenham, Kent, JP; *m* 1st 18 May 1830 Charlotte (*d* 15 Feb 1855), est dau of George Norman, of Bromley Common, Kent; *m* 2nd 11 July 1866 Frances Maria (*d* 18 May 1900), dau of Francis Holles Brandram, DL, of Underriver Ho, Kent, and widow of Rev Aretas Akers (*see* CHILSTON, V)

THOMAS CHARLES DOUGLAS WHITMORE's only s,

Sir Francis Henry Douglas Charlton Whitmore, 1st Bt (UK), so *cr* 28 June 1954, KCB (1941), CMG (1918), DSO (1917), TD (1918), JP (Essex 1899), DL (Essex 1907); *b* 20 April 1872; *educ* Eton; Ld Manors of Orsett, Stifford, Corringham, N Benfleet and Little Thurrock; Lt 1st Essex Vols RA 1892–95, Maj Essex Imp Yeo 1901, memb Essex TAA 1908–62 (chm 1929–36, pres 1936–62), WW I (despatches four times) as Lt-Col cmdg Essex Yeo 1915–18 and 10th (PWO) Roy Hus 1918–19, memb TA Advsy Ctee War Off 1935–37, Hon Col Essex Gp AA Searchlight Cos RE 1926–33, 104th (Essex Yeo) Regt RHA 1936–47, 147th (Essex Yeo) Field Regt RA 1940–47, 17th Light AA Regt RA 1941, 517th Light AA Regt RA 1947, 304th (Essex Yeo) Field Regt RA 1947–50, WW II as Hon Cdr Essex Zone HG 1940, Hon Cdr J and K Zones HG London Dist 1940, with RA Field and Light AA Regts, memb Allotments Advsy Ctee Min Ag 1924–48; CC Essex 1918–26, High Sheriff Essex 1922, Ld Lt Essex and Custos Rotulorum 1936–58, KGStJ 1936, KJStJ 1937; *m* 1st 28 June 1900 Violet Frances Elisabeth, OBE (*d* 13 June 1927), yst dau of Sir William Henry Houldsworth, 1st Bt (*qv*); *m* 2nd 1 Oct 1931 *Ellis Christensen, DStJ [Ellis Lady Whitmore, 7 Parc de Bude, Geneva, Switzerland], dau of Herr Direktor Knud Christian Johnsen, of Bergen, Norway, and *d* 12 June 1962, leaving by her:

1 Sir JOHN HENRY DOUGLAS WHITMORE, **2nd and present Bt**

1 *Anne Catherine; *b* 5 Sept 1933; MAOT, SROT; *m* 9 Aug 1966 *Daniel Jose Emilio O'Connell, er s of Jose Maria O'Connell, of Buenos Aires, and has:

(1) *Lucy Elizabeth; *b* 25 May 1967

(2) *Patricia Elena; *b* 1969

(3) *Anna Elisa; *b* 1970

WHITTY

Creation: B. (LP, UK) 21 Aug 1996.

THE BARON WHITTY, of Camberwell, London Borough of Southwark ((John Lawrence (Larry) Whitty) [The Rt Hon The Lord Whitty, House of Lords, London SW1A 0PW]; *b* 15 June 1943; *educ* Latymer Upper and St John's Coll Cambridge; with Hawker Siddeley Aviation 1960–62, Min Aviation Tech 1965–70, TUC 1970–73, GMBATU 1973–85; Lab Pty: Gen Sec 1985–94, European Co-ordinator 1994–97, Govt Whip Ho Lds May 1997–98, Parly U-Sec Environment and Tport 1998–; *m* 1st 1969 (*divorce* 1986) Tanya Margaret — and has two sons; *m* 2nd 1993 *Angela Forrester

Lineage: FREDERICK JAMES WHITTY; *m* Kathleen May - and had:

(JOHN) LAWRENCE (LARRY), *cr* a **Baron**

WIGAN

Arms: Vair on a pile or a mount in base vert, thereon a mountain ash proper. **Crest:** On a mount vert a mountain ash surmounted by a rainbow, all proper. **Motto:** *Carpe diem* ('Make use of your opportunity'). **Creation:** Bt. (UK) 9 March 1898.

SIR MICHAEL IAIN WIGAN, 6TH BT, of Clare Lawn, Mortlake, Surrey, and Purland Chase, Ross, Co Hereford [Sir Michael Wigan Bt, Borrobol, Kinbrace, Sutherland KW11 6UB]; *b* 3 Oct 1951; *s f* 1996; *educ* Eton and Exeter Coll Oxford; *m* 1st 1984 (*divorce* 1985) Frances, dau of F/Lt Angus Barr Faucett and Mrs Antony Reid, of Balnakilly, Kirkmichael, Perths; *m* 2nd 1989 *Julia Teresa, est dau of John de Courcy Ling, CBE, MEP, and by her has:

1 +FERGUS ADAM; *b* 30 April 1990

2 +Thomas Iain; *b* 4 May 1993

3 +Finnbarr Frederick; *b* 17 Sept 1997

1 *Lilias Margaret; *b* 9 March 1992

Lineage: EDWARD WIGAN, of Highbury Terrace, Islington Middx; Lt-Col 1st Middx Militia; *m* 11 April 1782 Jane Bond (*d* 1826) and *d* 22 March 1814, leaving, with other issue:

JOHN ALFRED WIGAN, of Clare House, E Malling, Kent, JP; *b* 11 Sept 1787; *m* 21 Sept 1815 Elizabeth Pratt (*d* 25 July 1864), dau and heiress of William Lewis, of Lion House, Stamford Hill, Middx, and *d* 16 Nov 1869, having had, with 14 other children:

Sir Frederick Wigan, 1st Bt (UK), so *cr* 9 March 1898, of Clare Lawn, E Sheen, Surrey, and Purland Chase, Ross, Herefs, JP, DL (Surrey); *b* 4 Dec 1827; dir N London Rlwy, High Sheriff Cos London and Surrey 1894, ktd 1894; *m* 26 April 1857 Mary Harriett (*d* 10 April 1915), dau of Joseph Blunt, of W Park, Kew, Surrey, and had:

1 FREDERICK WILLIAM (Sir), **2nd Bt**

2 Henry Charles; *b* 14 Jan 1864; *d* 10 Oct 1866

3 Arthur Lawford; *b* 27 April 1868; *educ* Eton and Balliol Coll Oxford (MA); *m* 29 July 1896 Beatrice (*d* 4 Sept 1959), dau of Col Charles Hervey Bagot, CB, RE, and *d* 26 Aug 1944, leaving:

(1) Joyce Madeline; *b* 22 Jan 1898; *m* 14 April 1917 Capt Paul Randle Feilden Mason, King's Regt (*d* 24 May 1944), only s of Col Henry Paul Mason, DL, of Eden Place, Kirkby Stephen, Westmorland, and had:

1a Maurice Randle; *b* 4 Dec 1919; *d* 2 Dec 1920

2a Anthony Feilden MASON later MASON-HORNBY (roy licence 1966); *b* 9 March 1921; *educ* Eton; *m* 11 June 1960 *Cecily Barbara [Mrs Anthony Mason-Hornby, Dalton Hall, Burton-in-Kendal, Cumbria LA6 1NJ], dau of Lt-Col Henry Gordon Carter, MC, DL, of Bodlondeb, Beaumaris, Anglesey, and *d* 5 Oct 1994, leaving:

1b *Francis Anthony; *b* 14 Aug 1961; *m* 24 July 1998 *Charlotte M L, dau of Michael Tinné

2b *Christopher Randle; *b* 12 March 1963

1b *Catherine Cecily [Mrs David Bertie, Seven Acres, Church Hill, Binfield, Berks RG42 5PY]; *b* 7 May 1964; *m* 1994 *David Montagu Albemarle Bertie and has issue (*see* LINDSEY and ABINGDON, E)

1a *Pamela Marcia [Miss Pamela Mason, Grove House, Latton, Wilts SN6 6DP]; *b* 10 July 1923

2a *Virginia Cicely [Miss Virginia Mason, Grove House, Latton, Wilts SN6 6DP]; *b* 2 Feb 1926

4 Edgar Clare; *b* 28 Nov 1876; *educ* Eton and Lincoln Coll Oxford; Capt 7th Bn Rifle Bde; *m* 2 Feb 1909 his er bro's sis-in-law Cicely Margaret (*d* 14 Oct 1960), 2nd dau of Col Charles Hervey Bagot, CB, RE

1 Amy Mary; *d* 28 May 1919

2 Katherine; *d* unm 20 July 1942

3 Ellen Mary; *m* 19 May 1900 Rev William Alexander Birkbeck (*d* 31 Dec 1952), s of John A Birkbeck, and *d* 15 May 1923, leaving issue

4 Ethel Harriet; *m* 23 April 1891 Egerton Spencer Grey, CB, and *d* 20 July 1949, leaving issue (*see* GREY, E)

5 Madeleine; *b* 29 June 1870; *d* 23 Oct 1893

6 Constance Helen; *m* 4 Dec 1913 Rev Francis Nathaniel Hill (*d* 4 March 1947), Canon Bombay, and *d* 4 Sept 1951

Sir FREDERICK *d* 2 March 1907; his est s,

Sir Frederick William Wigan, 2nd Bt; *b* 18 March 1859; *m* 10 Nov 1885 Elizabeth Adair (*d* 12 Nov 1902), est dau of Lt-Col Francis Douglas Grey (*see* GREY, E), and had:

1 RODERICK GREY (Sir), **3rd Bt**

2 Adair Grey; *b* 9 April 1889; *d* 9 May 1896

3 Denis Grey, JP (E Suffolk); *b* 21 June 1893; *educ* Eton and Magdalen Coll Oxford; Capt KRRC WW I; *m* 21 Oct 1915 Madeline Mabel Ambrose (*d* 5 March 1969), 3rd dau of Charles Robert Whorwood Adeane, CB, of Babraham Hall, Cambs, and *d* 31 Dec 1958, having had:

(1) Adair Michael Charles; *b* 30 Sept 1916; *educ* Eton; Maj (RARO) Coldstream Gds WW II; *m* 13 Sept 1939 *Dawn Patrine [Mrs Adair Wigan, West Blagdon, Cranborne, Dorset BH21 5RY], 3rd dau of Charles Wilfred Gordon, of Boveridge Park, Cranborne, and *d* 1993, having had:

1a Charles Grey; *b* 25 Dec 1948; *d* 6 Feb 1949

2a +James Adair [James Wigan Esq, Biddlesgate Farm, Cranborne, Dorset BH21 5RS]; *b* 18 Jan 1950; *educ* Eton; *m* 1977 (*divorce* 1991) Rose Cecilia, er dau of John Johnston Kirkpatrick (*see* LODER, Bt), and has:

1b +Harry Edward; *b* 1986

2b +Thomas Adair; *b* 1986

1b *Emma Charlotte; *b* 1983

3a +Dominic Richard Ludlow [Dominic Wigan Esq, Hyde Farm, Damerham, Fordingbridge, Hants]; *b* 18 Aug 1951; *educ* Milton Abbey; *m* 1989 *Julia, only dau of Richard Russell, of Newnham Manor, Daventry, Northants, and has:

1b *Anna Jessie; *b* 1991

2b *Nesta; *b* 199–

1a *Lola Dawn; *b* 28 Aug 1940; *m* 18 June 1987 *John Hobbs

2a *Camilla Rose; *b* 28 Feb 1944; *m* 1977 *Michael Charles Thomas and has:

1b *Archie Charles; *b* 13 Feb 1978

2b *Reuben; *b* 3 Nov 1982

(2) Michael Grey; *b* 5 Nov 1919; *d* 13 April 1920

(1) *Elizabeth Sibell Isabel [Mrs Humphrey Gascoigne, Ashe Abbey, Campsea Ashe, Suffolk]; *b* 21 Dec 1918; *m* 17 July 1937 Humphrey Edward Crisp Gascoigne (*d* 1992), yst s of Brig-Gen Sir (Ernest) Frederick Orby Gascoigne, KCVO, CMG, DSO, of Ashtead Lodge, Ashtead, Surrey, and has:

1a *David Clive; *b* 1939; *educ* Eton; Maj RGJ Res Offrs; *m* 1964 *Deirdre Cecil Hermione, dau of Lt-Col Alec C S Moore, of Whites Meadow, Bicknoller, Somerset, and has:

1b *Dominic William Wigan; *b* 1965

2b *Tobias Charles Humphrey; *b* 1971

1b *Nichola Elizabeth Blanche; *b* 1968

2a *Martin Wyndham; *b* 1944; *educ* Eton

3a *Anthony Grey; *b* 1947; *educ* Gordonstoun; *m* 1970 (*divorce* 1985) Hon Olivia Clare Teresa Brett, dau of 4th Viscount Esher (*qv*), and has issue

1 Eira Grey; *b* 3 Oct 1897; *m* 27 May 1931 Lewis Gretton Graham-Wigan, 13th/18th Hus (*d* 6 Oct 1961), 2nd s of John Graham Wigan, of Oakwood Park, Maidstone, and *d* 30 Sept 1940, leaving issue

Sir FREDERICK *d* 6 April 1907; his est s,

Sir Roderick Grey Wigan, 3rd Bt, JP (Northumberland); *b* 11 Nov 1886; *educ* Eton and Magdalen Coll Oxford; T/2nd Lt RASC WW I, Croix de Guerre; *m* 27 Jan 1909 Hermina Mary Graham (Ina) (*d* 22 Jan 1977), only child of Lewis Davis Wigan, JP, of Brandon Park, Suffolk, and *d* 16 Jan 1954, leaving:

1 **Sir Frederick Adair Wigan, 4th Bt**; *b* 13 April 1911; *educ* privately; *d* unm Jan 1979

2 **Sir Alan Lewis Wigan, 5th Bt**; *b* 19 Nov 1913; *educ* Eton and Magdalen Coll Oxford; Capt KRRC Res Offrs WW II (wounded, POW), dir Charrington & Co 1939–70, Master Brewers' Co 1958–59; *m* 1950 *Robina [Robina Lady Wigan, Field House, Badingham, Suffolk IP13 8JP], dau of Lt-Col Sir Iain Colquhoun of Luss, 7th Bt (*qv*), and *d* 3 May 1996, leaving:

(1) Sir MICHAEL IAIN WIGAN, **6th and present Bt**

(1) *Rebecca [Mrs Nicholas Camu, Badingham House, Woodbridge, Suffolk IP13 8JP]; *b* 1953; *m* 1st 1976 (*divorce* 1978) John Dominic Spearman (*see* SPEARMAN, Bt); *m* 2nd 1980 (*divorce* 1986) James Alwyne Compton (*see* NORTHAMPTON, M); *m* 3rd 1991 *Nicholas Pascal Camu (*see* CROSSLEY, Bt)

1 Joan Yvonne; *b* 6 Dec 1914; *m* 10 July 1957 Hubert Frederick Pascoe Rutter (*d* 1983), s of Sir Frederick Pascoe Rutter, and *d* 1980

WIGGIN

To thine ownself be true

Arms: Gules three mullets of six points argent, on a chief invected or two spurs sable. **Crest:** Over a fleur-de-lys sable a spur or between two wings erect proper, each charged with a fleur-de-lys sable. **Motto:** To thine own self be true.
Creation: Bt. (UK) 17 June 1892.

SIR CHARLES RUPERT JOHN WIGGIN, 5TH BT, of Metchley Grange, Harborne, Staffordshire [Maj Sir Charles Wiggin Bt, c/o Child and Co, 1 Fleet St, London EC4Y 1BD]; *b* 2 July 1949; *s* f 1992; *educ* Eton; Maj Gren Gds, T/Equerry to HRH THE DUKE OF EDINBURGH 1977–79; *m* 1979 *Mrs Mary Burnett-Hitchcock, only dau of Brig Samuel Craven Chambers, CBE, and has:

1 +RICHARD EDWARD JOHN; *b* 1 July 1980

1 *Cecilia Charlotte; *b* 1984

Lineage: RICHARD WIGAN, of Chebsey, Staffs; *d* 1744, leaving:

RICHARD WIGGIN; *m* 1 May 1739 Rachel Addison (*d* 1785) and *d* 10 Jan 1786; his 2nd s:

SAMUEL WIGGIN; *b* 1755; *m* Elizabeth Bratt, of Stafford Castle, and had an only s:

WILLIAM WIGGIN, of Cheadle, Staffs; *b* 1783; *m* 18 April 1815 Elizabeth (*d* 19 Dec 1832), dau of William Milner, of Tean, and *d* 14 Jan 1862, having had, with an er s (William Milner, *b* 28 April 1822, *d* 4 May 1856) and four daus:

Sir Henry Samuel Wiggin, 1st Bt (UK), so *cr* 17 June 1892, of Metchley Grange, Staffs, and Garth Gwynion, Montgomeryshire, JP, DL (Staffs), JP (Worcs and Birmingham); *b* 14 Feb 1824; MP (Lib) E Staffs 1880–85 and Handsworth 1885–92; *m* 11 June 1851 Mary Elizabeth (*d* 24 Feb 1911), 2nd dau of David Malins, JP, of Edgbaston, and had:

1 HENRY ARTHUR (Sir), **2nd Bt**

2 William Malins; *b* 5 Aug 1854; *d* 8 July 1856

3 Walter William, JP (Worcs and Staffs); *b* 29 Sept 1856; Capt 3rd Bn N Staffs Regt, Lt-Col Worcs Yeo; *m* 13 Oct 1886 Edith (*d* 3 Jan 1950), 4th dau of George Charles Adkins, JP, and *d* 4 Nov 1936, having had:

(1) George Robert; *b* 22 Feb 1889; *educ* Eton and Trin Coll Cambridge; Capt Worcs Yeo; *ka* Egypt 23 April 1916

(2) Christopher; *b* 1891; *d* 1895

4 Alfred Harold, of Bordesley Hall, Alvechurch, JP (Worcs); *b* 20 Jan 1864; *educ* Trin Coll Cambridge (BA); High Sheriff 1923; *m* 5 May 1887 Margaret (*d* 25 May 1932), 4th dau of Edward John Nettlefold, of Highgate, and *d* 29 Jan 1933, leaving:

(1) William Henry (Sir), KCB (1948), DSO (1916) and bar (1918), TD, JP, DL Worcs; *b* 26 Feb 1888; *educ* Eton and Trin Coll Cambridge (BA 1909); Lt-Col and Brevet Col RA (TA) WW I (despatches), Chm Worcs TA&AFA; dir Barclays Bank; *m* 28 Oct 1935 Elizabeth Ethelston (*d* 28 April 1959), only dau of Capt John Danvers Power, MVO, of Thurloxton, Somerset, and *d* 11 Sept 1951, leaving:

1a +Alfred William (Jerry) (Sir), TD (1970) [Sir Jerry Wiggin TD, The Court, Axbridge, Somerset BS26 2BN]; *b* 24 Feb 1937; *educ* Eton and Trin Coll Cambridge; 2nd Lt QO Warwicks and Worcs Yeo (TA) 1959, Maj Roy Yeo 1975–78, Hon Col Warwicks and Worcs Yeo (A) Sqdn, Roy Mercian and Lancastrian Yeo 1992–; MP (C) Weston-super-Mare 1969–97, Jt Hon Sec C Def Ctee 1974–75, Parly Sec MAFF 1979–81, Parly U-Sec MOD 1981–83, Chm Select Ctee Ag 1987–97 and Ec Ctee N Atlantic Assembly 1990–94, ktd 1993, memb Ct Assists Goldsmiths' Co 1995–; *m* 1st 28 July 1964 (*divorce* 1982) Rosemary Janet, only dau of David Lewis Davidson Orr, of Wormley, Surrey; *m* 2nd 1991 *Morella C M, *née* Kearton, formerly w of James Esmond Bulmer, and by his 1st w has:

1b +William David; *b* 4 June 1966

2b +Thomas Henry; *b* 27 Feb 1969

1b *Audrey Mary; *b* 22 March 1974

2a +Henry Walter [Henry Wiggin Esq, Brockweir Farm, nr Chepstow, Gwent NP6 7NG]; *b* 12 Aug 1939; *educ* Eton and Trin Coll Cambridge (MA); late Capt Warwicks and Worcs Yeo; slr 1965; *m* 1st 3 April 1962 (*divorce*

1978) Hon Julia Redmond Vaughan-Morgan, er dau of Baron Reigate (LP; *see* 1970 edn VAUGHAN-MORGAN, Bt), and has:

    1b *Lucy Redmond; *b* 25 Aug 1965; *m* 1990 *Joel Patrick Ford, s of Roy B Ford, San Antonio, Tex.

    2b *Caroline Julia; *b* 25 Nov 1970

  2a (cont.) Henry Wiggin *m* 2nd 1978 (*divorce* 1985) Robin Margaret, dau of A Campbell B Linwood, of Wanganui, NZ, and formerly w of David Erskine Tolhurst, and by her has:

    1b +Jonathan Henry; *b* 1978

  2a (cont.) Henry Wiggin *m* 3rd 1986 *Diana, dau of Adml Sir Robin Leonard Francis Durnford-Slater, KCB, and formerly w of Simon Anstey, of Toronto

(2) Richard Arthur, TD, JP (Worcs 1946), DL (Worcs 1958); *b* 4 July 1903; *educ* Eton and Trin Coll Cambridge (BA 1924); Lt-Col cmdg Worcs Yeo WW II (despatches), Hon Col Birmingham U OTC, High Sheriff 1958, dir Harry H Payne Ltd, Guardian Standard of Wrought Plate Birmingham, Birmingham U: Dep Pro-Chllr, Hon LLD; *m* 24 Jan 1952 Joan Mary (*d* 1979), only dau of Smith Whitehead, of The Croft, Nelson, and *d* 14 April 1977, leaving:

    1a *Margaret Joan; *b* Jan 1954; *m* 14 June 1979 *Christopher J Heath, s of Lt-Gen Sir Lewis Macclesfield Heath, and has:

      1b *William Henry Christopher; *b* 1983

(1) Hilda Margaret; *b* 1 Aug 1889; *m* 26 March 1918 Maj Noel Stanley Wilson, JP, yr s of William Wilson, of S Kensington, and *d* 13 Oct 1955, leaving issue

(2) Nancy; *b* 21 Jan 1892; *m* 18 Jan 1928 Maj Douglas Warner Turner (*d* 20 April 1956), er s of Thomas Warner Turner, of Cuckney Ho, Mansfield, Notts, and *d* 15 Feb 1945, having had issue

5 Edgar Askin, DSO (1917), JP, DL (Warwicks); *b* 26 Nov 1867; Maj and Brevet Lt-Col 13th Hus Boer War 1899–1902 cmdg Mtd Inf Regt (despatches, two brevets), WW I cmdg 5th Mtd Bde 1914–17 (despatches, Offr Legn Hon), Hon Brig-Gen, High Sheriff 1930; *m* 27 March 1906 Emilie Margaret (*d* 27 Jan 1951), yst dau of Arthur Keen, of Edgbaston, and *d* 11 Nov 1939, leaving:

(1) +Peter Milner, JP (Hants 1955) [Lt-Col Peter Wiggin JP, Chapel Cottage, Plaistow Green, Berks]; *b* 9 April 1907; *educ* Eton and RMC Sandhurst; Lt-Col 11th Hus (PAO) WW II; *m* 17 Oct 1933 *Margaret Frances, er dau of Capt Noel Christian Livingstone-Learmonth, JP, of St James's, and has:

    1a George David Henry; *b* 1 Dec 1934; *educ* Eton; Lt 11th Hus (PAO); *m* 24 June 1958 *Jennifer (*m* 2nd 1993 Charles Arthur Smith-Bingham), er dau of Capt Ian Stanley Akers-Douglas (*see* CHILSTON, V), and *d* 1990, leaving:

      1b +David Peter; *b* 5 Jan 1960; *educ* Harrow; Lt Roy Hus; *m* 1991 *(Susan) Emma, yst dau of Maj Robert Philip Burrowes, of Dorrington Priory, Lincs, and has:

        1c +George Robert; *b* 1994

        2c +Nicholas Peter; *b* 20 Aug 1996

      2b +James George; *b* 5 June 1968; *educ* Eton; 2nd Lt Roy Hus

      1b *Davina Jane; *b* 8 Jan 1962; *m* 1986 *Michael Gatehouse, yr s of Capt Richard Gatehouse, DSC, RN, of Easton Farm Ho, Newbury, Berks, and has:

        1c *James Richard; *b* 1987

        1c *Sophie Charlotte; *b* 1989

        2c *Emily Alice; *b* 16 Aug 1994

    2a +Michael Peter [Michael Wiggin Esq, Downton Hall, Ludlow, Salop]; *b* 22 Nov 1937; *educ* Eton; late 2nd Lt 11th Hus (PAO); *m* 26 April 1962 *Victoria Zara, dau of Malcolm Septimus Vaughan, of Old Westfield Farm, Moreton Morrell, Warwicks, and has:

      1b +Mark David; *b* 1 Aug 1963; *educ* Eton; *m* 1991 *Philippa A, dau of David Burrows, of Tetbury, Glos, and has:

        1c +Max David Boughton; *b* 6 July 1998

        1c *Tara Daisy; *b* 1994

        2c *Camilla Victoria; *b* 20 Oct 1995

      2b +Rupert Michael; *b* 1969; *educ* Wellington

      1b *Miranda Zara; *b* 1965; *m* 1990 *Graham J Walsh, s of Walter Walsh, of Barrow-in-Furness, Cumbria, and has:

        1c *Luke Walter; *b* 1992

        1c *Zara Patricia (twin); *b* 1992

      2b *Kate Victoria; *b* 3 Feb 1972

    1a *Sara Margaret [The Rt Hon The Viscountess Allenby, Newnham Lodge, Newnham, Hants]; *b* 28 Dec 1942; *m* 29 July 1965 *3rd Viscount Allenby (*qv*) and has issue

1 Mary Elizabeth; *m* 5 Dec 1884 Brig-Gen Richard Charles Bernard Lawrence, CB, CMG, 1st Dragoon Gds (*d* 22 May 1923), and *d* 23 April 1945, leaving issue

2 Ethel Malins; *m* 20 Jan 1897 Brig-Gen St John Fancourt Michell Fancourt, CB, JP, Bengal Lancers (*d* 11 June 1917), of Danecroft, Stowmarket, Suffolk, and *d* 10 April 1939, having had issue

The 1st Bt *d* 12 Nov 1905; his est s,

Sir Henry Arthur Wiggin, 2nd Bt, JP, DL (Staffs); *b* 3 May 1852; High Sheriff 1896; *m* 12 Sept 1878 Annie Sarah (*d* 9 June 1937), dau of Charles Rogers Cope, of Kinnerton Court, Radnorshire, and Metchley Ho, Edgbaston, and had:

1 CHARLES RICHARD HENRY (Sir), **3rd Bt**

1 Margaret Annie *b* 12 July 1879; *d* unm 7 April 1948

2 Elinor Mary; *b* 27 March 1882; *m* 17 Jan 1905 Lt-Col Sir Thomas Anderdon Salt, 2nd Bt, of Weeping Cross (*qv*), and *d* 11 Jan 1974, leaving issue

Sir HENRY *d* 2 May 1917; his only s,

Sir Charles Richard Henry Wiggin, 3rd Bt, TD, JP, DL (Warwicks 1931) (both); *b* 21 March 1885; *educ* Eton and Trin Coll Cambridge (BA 1907); WW I (despatches), Lt-Col and Brevet Col cmdg Staffs Yeo 1921–25 (Hon Col Staffs Yeo 1951–54), MFH Brocklesby 1921–25, Warwicks: CC High Sheriff 1942; *m* 24 July 1916 Mabel Violet Mary (*d* 25 Dec 1961), only dau of Sir William Jaffray, 2nd Bt (*qv*), and *d* 16 Sept 1972, leaving:

Sir John Henry Wiggin, 4th Bt, MC (1946), JP (Berks 1966); *b* 3 March 1921; *educ* Eton and Trin Coll Cambridge; Maj Gren Gds WW II (POW); *m* 1st 30 Sept 1947

(*divorce* 1961) Lady Cecilia Evelyn Anson (*d* 16 Jan 1963), yr dau of 4th Earl of Lichfield (*qv*), and had:

1 Sir CHARLES RUPERT JOHN WIGGIN, **5th and present Bt**

2 +Benjamin Henry Edward; *b* 23 Aug 1951; *educ* Eton and McGill

Sir John *m* 2nd 8 Feb 1963 *Sarah [Sarah Lady Wiggin, Honington Hall, Shipston-on-Stour, Warwicks CV36 5AA], er dau of Brig Stewart Arthur Forster, of Winkfield, Berks, and *d* 1992, leaving by her:

3 +Daniel Mark; *b* 21 Jan 1964; *educ* Eton; *m* 3 Aug 1996 *Simone, yr dau of Malcolm Hooper, of Cornwall

4 +Jeremy James; *b* 16 July 1966; *educ* Milton Abbey

WIGODER

Arms: Gules a chevron engrailed ermine between three wigs or, a chief or. **Crest:** On a wreath or and gules upon a mount vert a gosling or, supporting by the dexter foot a daffodil proper, mantled gules, doubled argent. **Supporters:** Dexter, a seahorse; sinister, a sea-griffin; both or, their piscine parts scaled azure, finned and tailed or, each gorged with a collar sable, pendant therefrom a chain ending in a broken ring sable. **Motto:** *Medio tutissimus ibis* ('You will go most safely the middle way'). **Creation:** B. (LP, UK) 1974.

THE BARON WIGODER, of Cheetham, City of Manchester (Basil Thomas Wigoder) [The Rt Hon The Lord Wigoder, House of Lords, London SW1A 0PW]; *b* 12 Feb 1921; *educ* Manchester GS and Oriel Coll Oxford (MA); Lt RA WW II 1942–45; barrister Gray's Inn 1946, QC 1966, Master Bench 1972, Recorder Crown Court 1972–84, Treasurer 1989 (V-Treasurer 1988); BOT Inspr Pinnock Finance 1967; Memb: Cncl Justice 1960–, Gen Cncl Bar 1970–74, Crown Court Rules Ctee 1971–77, Cncl on Tbnls 1980–86, Home Office Advsy Ctee on Service Candidates 1984–; Chm: Lib Party Exec 1963–65, Lib Party Organising Ctee 1965–66, Chief Lib Whip Ho Lds 1977–84 (Dep Whip 1976–77); V-Pres: Lib Party 1966, BUPA 1992 (Chm 1981–92, V-Pres 1992–), Nuffield Hosps 1981–92, Statute Law Soc 1984–90; Chm: Health Servs Bd 1977–80, Securities Assoc Tbnl 1988–92; dir BUPA Hosps 1981–92; memb Ct Nene Coll 1982–90; Tstee Oxford Union Soc 1982–92; *m* 1948 *Yoland, dau of Ben Levinson, and has:

1 *Justin; *b* 1951; *m* 1981 *Heather J—, dau of J H Bugler, and has:

  (1) *Annabel Miriam Jane; *b* 1986

  (2) *Charlotte Abigail Lucy; *b* 1991

2 *Charles Francis; *b* 1960; ch exec Peoples Phone 1988–96; *m* 1988 *Elizabeth Sophia, only dau of Elmar Duke-Cohan, of Totteridge, and has:

  (1) *Benjamin Marcus James; *b* 1990

  (1) *Natasha Sarah; *b* 1992

  (2) *Clarissa Emma; *b* 1995

3 *Giles; *b* 1963; *m* 1993 (*divorce* 1996) Louisa, est dau of Prof Gerald Westbury

1 *Carolyn (twin); *b* 1963

Lineage: P I WIGODER; LRCPI, LRCSI; *m* Rebecca Rachel Jacobs, JP Manchester, and had:

BASIL THOMAS, *cr* a **Baron**

WIGRAM, Baron

1 Anne; *b* 27 Sept 1913; *m* 25 Jan 1939 Lt-Col John Leslie Harvey, MBE, Scots Gds (Res Offrs), er s of Col John Harvey, DSO, of Ringstead Bury, Norfolk, and *d* 12 July 1958, leaving issue

WIGRAM, Bt

Arms: Argent on a pale gules three escallops or, over all a chevron engrailed counterchanged, on a chief waves of the sea, thereon a ship representing an English vessel of war of the 16th century, with four masts, sails furled proper, colours flying gules. **Crest:** On a mount vert a hand in armour in fess couped at the wrist proper, charged with an escallop and holding a fleur-de-lys erect or. **Supporters:** On either side a Bengal lancer holding in the exterior hand a lance proper. **Motto:** *Dulcis amor patriæ* ('Sweet is the love of one's country'). **Creation:** B. (UK) 25 June 1935.

THE 2ND BARON WIGRAM, of Clewer, Co Berks ((George) Neville Clive Wigram, MC (1945), JP (Glos 1959), DL (Glos 1969)) [The Rt Hon The Lord Wigram MC JP DL, Poulton Fields, Cirencester, Glos GL7 5SS]; *b* 2 Aug 1915; *s* f 1960; *educ* Winchester and Magdalen Coll Oxford (MA); Page of Honour to HM GEORGE V 1925–32, Lt-Col Gren Gds WW II, Mil Sec and Comptroller to Govr-Gen New Zealand 1946–49, cmded 1st Bn Gren Gds 1955–56, ret 1957, Govr Westminster Hosp 1967–74; *m* 19 July 1941 Margaret Helen (*d* 1986), yr dau of Gen Sir Augustus Francis Andrew Nicol Thorne, KCB, CMG, DSO and two bars, DL (*see* PENRHYN, B), and has:

1 +ANDREW FRANCIS CLIVE, MVO [Maj The Hon Andrew Wigram MVO, Poulton Fields Farms, Poulton, Glos GL7 5SS]; *b* 18 March 1949; *educ* Winchester, RMA Sandhurst and RAC Cirencester; late Maj Gren Gds, Extra Equerry to HRH THE DUKE OF EDINBURGH 1982–86; *m* 26 Feb 1974 *Gabrielle Diana, yst dau of R D Moore, of Wellington, NZ, and Knightsbridge, and has:

   (1) +Harry Richard Clive; *b* 20 May 1977
   (2) +Robert Christopher Clive; *b* 29 Feb 1980
   (3) +William Michael Clive; *b* 3 Jan 1984
   (1) *Alice Poppy Louise; *b* 31 Oct 1989

1 *(Margaret) Cherry; *b* 24 April 1942; *m* 22 Jan 1972 (*divorce* 1993) Capt Greville John Wyndham Malet and has issue (*see* MALET, Bt)
2 *(Anne) Celia [The Hon Mrs Webb-Carter, Horcott House, Fairford, Glos]; *b* 23 April 1945; *m* 20 Jan 1973 *Maj-Gen Evelyn John Webb-Carter, OBE, late Gren Gds (*see* HOOD, V) and has:

   (1) *Alexander Clive; *b* 5 April 1975
   (1) *Helen Celia; *b* 8 April 1978
   (2) *Rose Evelyn; *b* 25 Aug 1983

Lineage: Sir ROBERT WIGRAM, 1st Bt (*qv*); had by his 2nd w a 9th s:

Rev WILLIAM PITT WIGRAM; had:

HERBERT WIGRAM; had:

CLIVE WIGRAM, **1st Baron Wigram**, of Clewer, Co Berks (UK), so *cr* 25 June 1935, GCB (1933, KCB 1931, CB 1918), GCVO (1932, KCVO 1928, CVO 1915, MVO 1903), CSI (1911), PC; *b* 5 July 1873; *educ* Winchester (Fell 1938) and RMA Woolwich; joined RA 1893 and 18th Lancers IA 1897, ADC to Viceroy India 1894–95 and 1899–1904, Tirah Expdn NW Frontier 1897–98 and Boer War 1900 (despatches), Brevet Maj 1906, Mil Sec to GOC-in-C Aldershot 1908–10, Brevet Lt-Col 1915, Brevet Col 1919, Col 19th KGO Lancers 1932–46, Equerry to HM GEORGE V when PRINCE OF WALES 1906–10, Assist Priv Sec and Equerry 1910–31, Priv Sec and Extra Equerry 1931–35, Priv Sec and Keeper Privy Purse 1935–36), Extra Equerry to HM EDWARD VIII 1936 and Priv Sec to July 1936, Extra Equerry to HM GEORGE VI 1937–45, Dep Constable and Lt Govr Windsor Castle 1936–45, Keeper HM's Archives 1936–45, Perm Ld-in-Waiting to HM GEORGE VI 1936–52, Permanent Ld-in-Waiting and Extra Equerry to HM THE QUEEN 1952–60, Roy Victorian Chain 1937, dir: Midland Bank and LMSR, FRGS, FRHS, FZS, V-Patron Westminster Hosp, memb: Cncl King George's Jubilee Trust, Gen Cncl King Edward's Hosp Fund, Imp War Graves Commn 1945–60, V-Pres Wellington Coll 1940–45, Govr ISC Jr Sch; *m* 5 Dec 1912 Nora Mary (*d* 5 Jan 1956), only child of Col Sir Neville Francis Fitzgerald Chamberlain, KCB, KCVO (*see* 1970 edn CHAMBERLAIN, Bt), and *d* 3 Sept 1960, having had:

1 (GEORGE) NEVILLE CLIVE WIGRAM, **2nd and present Baron Wigram**
2 Francis; *b* 19 March 1920; Capt Gren Gds WW II; *ka* Sept 1943

Arms: Argent on a pale gules three escallops or, over all a chevron engrailed counterchanged; on a chief waves of the sea, thereon a ship representing an English vessel of war of the 16th century, with four masts, sails furled proper, colours flying gules. **Crest:** On a mount vert a hand in armour in fess, couped at the wrist proper, charged with an escallop and holding a fleur-de-lys erect or. **Supporters:** On either side an eagle, wings elevated argent, collared gules, charged on the breast with a shamrock vert. **Motto:** *Dulcis amor patriae* ('Sweet is the love of one's country'). **Creation:** Bt. (UK) 30 Oct 1805.

REV SIR CLIFFORD WOOLMORE WIGRAM, 7TH BT, of Walthamstow, Essex [The Rev Canon Sir Clifford Wigram Bt, Flat 8, Emden House, Barton Lane, Headington, Oxford OX3 9JU]; *b* 24 Jan 1911; *s* unc 1935; *educ* Winchester, Trin Coll Cambridge (BA 1932, MA 1936) and Ely Theological Coll; Assist Priest St Ann's Brondesbury 1934–37, Chaplain Ely Theological Coll 1937–40, Vicar Marston St Lawrence 1945 on, non-res Canon Peterborough 1973–83, Canon Emeritus 1983–; *m* 24 Aug 1948 Christabel Joan (*d* 1983), widow of Eric Llewellyn Marriott, CIE, Indian Police, of Fullands Ho, Taunton, Somerset, and yst dau of William Winter Goode, of Curry Rivel, Somerset.

Lineage: JOHN WIGRAM, of Bristol; *m* Mary, dau of Robert Clifford, of Co Wexford, by Mary, dau of Highgate Boyd, of Rosslare (*see* ELY, M), and had:

Sir Robert Wigram, 1st Bt (UK), so *cr* 30 Oct 1805, of Wexford; *b* 30 Jan 1743; London druggist, took shares in HEIC ships, shipbuilder, ptnr Blackwall Yard, Deptford; MP Fowey 1802–06 and Wexford 1806–07; *m* 1st 19 Dec 1772 Catherine (*d* 22 Jan 1786), yst dau of Francis Brodhurst, of Mansfield, Notts, and had, with other issue:

1 Sir ROBERT WIGRAM later FitzWYGRAM (roy licence 1832), **2nd Bt**; *b* 25 Sept 1773; *m* 3 Aug 1812 Selina (*d* 22 Aug 1866), dau of Sir John Hayes, 1st Bt (*see* 1902 edn), and *d* 1843, having had, with another s and dau (*d* unm):

   (1) **Sir Robert Fiztwygram, 3rd Bt**; *b* 7 Aug 1813; *d* unm 3 Sept 1873
   (2) **Sir Frederick Wellington John Fitzwygram, 4th Bt**, JP, DL Hants; *b* 29 Aug 1823; Col 15th Hus (Crimean and Turkish medals), Hon Col 2nd Vol Bn Hants Regt, Inspr-Gen Cavalry, Lt-Gen, CA Hants, MP S Hants 1884–1900; *m* 17 Oct 1882 Angela Frances Mary (*d* 5 Aug 1935), dau of Thomas Nugent Vaughan (*see* GRANARD, E), and *d* 9 Dec 1904, leaving:

      1a **Sir Frederick Loftus Francis Fitzwygram, 5th Bt**, MC; *b* 11 Aug 1884; *educ* Magdalen Coll Oxford (MA); Maj Scots Gds WW I (wounded twice, despatches); *d* unm 5 May 1920
      1a Angela Catherine Alice; *b* 11 Sept 1885

   (3) John Fitzroy (Rev); *b* 16 April 1827; Vicar New Hampton, Middx; *m* 29 Nov 1866 Alice (*d* 9 March 1912), yst dau of Sir Henry George Ward, GCMG, and *dsp* 13 Aug 1881
   (4) Loftus; *b* 7 April 1832; barrister; *m* 3 July 1866 Lady Frances Georgina Butler, sis of 6th Earl of Lanesborough (*qv*), and *d* 3 July 1904, leaving:

      1a Selina Violet; *b* 6 Feb 1870; *m* 12 July 1894 Sydney Algernon Fane (*see* WESTMORLAND, E) and *d* 23 Sept 1939, leaving issue
      (1) Augusta Catherine; *m* 16 Nov 1858 Sir George Baker, 3rd Bt (*see* BAKER-WILBRAHAM, Bt), and *dsp* 19 Nov 1893

1 Catherine, *m* 21 Oct 1803 Charles Tottenham (*d* 6 July 1843), of Ballycurry, MP New Ross, and *d* 22 Sept 1865 aged 90, leaving issue

Sir Robert *m* 2nd 23 June 1787 Eleanor (*d* 23 Jan 1841), yst dau of John Watts, and *d* 6 Nov 1830, having by her had, with other issue (amounting to 23 children by his two ws):

   2 Money; *b* 14 March 1790; *m* 19 April 1822 Mary (*d* 1886), dau of Charles Hampden Turner, of Rook's Nest, Surrey, and *d* 24 March 1873, leaving, with two daus (*d* unm):

      (1) Money, of Esher Place, Surrey; *b* 25 Jan 1823; *m* 30 July 1851 Anne Whitaker (*d* 25 Feb 1890), dau of William Whitaker Maitland, of Loughton Hall, Essex, and *d* 25 Feb 1881, leaving, with with other issue:

1a Alfred Money, JP (Essex); *b* 21 July 1856; MP S Essex 1894–97; *m* 11 June 1882 his cousin Venetia Mary (*d* 18 Feb 1911), est dau of Rev John Whitaker Maitland, of Loughton Hall, and *d* 13 Oct 1899, having had, with another dau (*d* an infant):

  1b Venetia Gladys, *m* 2 Dec 1908 Christian Augustine Everard Greene, s of David Greene, of Loughton, and had issue

  2b Vera Maitland; *m* 15 Oct 1917 Max Gardner Valentine Browne, AFA, 3rd s of Valentine Edward Browne, MD, of Melbourne, and *d* 7 Sept 1938, leaving issue

  3b Ruth Constance; *d* unm 28 Nov 1964

  1a Mary; *d* unm 30 Dec 1945

  2a Constance Maitland; *m* 14 July 1881 J Topham Richard Lodge, s of Hilton Lodge, and *d* 1901, leaving issue

  3a Florence Emily; *d* unm 3 Jan 1950

(2) Heathcote; *b* 1824; drowned 1836 when pupil at Shrewsbury

(3) Charles Hampden (Sir), JP, DL; *b* 12 April 1826; *m* 14 July 1857 Beatrice (*d* 25 March 1909), dau of Rev Philip Hall Palmer, and *d* 30 Oct 1903, leaving:

  1a Henry Hampden; *b* 3 Oct 1858; *educ* Trin Coll Cambridge (BA); Maj Scots Gds; *m* 5 Nov 1891 Dorothy Isabel (*d* 21 Dec 1960), dau of George William Liddell, of Keldy Castle, Yorks, and *d* 1 May 1919, leaving:

    1b Violet; *b* 1893; ARRC; *m* 1 Feb 1928 Rev Allan Augustin de Vere (*d* 15 Jan 1949), Vicar Ch Ch Ealing 1939–49, s of George Lewis de Vere, of Salt Rd, Bath, and had issue

    2b Myrtle; *b* 1894; ARRC

    3b Lettice Rosalind; *b* 1897; *d* unm 24 July 1928

(4) Clifford, DL (London); *b* 9 April 1828; a Dir Bank of England, Col 9th Vol Bn Rifle Bde; *d* 1898

(5) Woolmore (Rev); *b* Oct 1831; MA Cantab; Rector St Andrew's Hertford, Hon Canon St Albans; *m* 23 July 1863 Harriet Mary (*d* 11 Oct 1927), dau of Rev Thomas Ainger, and *d* 19 Jan 1907, leaving, with two other daus (*d* young or unm):

  1a **Sir Edgar Thomas Ainger Wigram, 6th Bt**; *b* 23 Nov 1864; *educ* Trin Hall Cambridge (MA); Mayor St Albans 1926; *d* unm 15 March 1935

  2a Robert Ainger; *b* 10 Aug 1866; BA Cantab; *m* 19 April 1910 Evelyn Dorothy (*d* 21 June 1960), dau of Cecil William Edward Henslowe, PWD India, and *d* 18 March 1915, leaving:

    1b Rev Sir CLIFFORD WOOLMORE WIGRAM, **7th and present Bt**

    2b +EDWARD ROBERT WOOLMORE [Maj Edward Wigram, 1 Skipster Hagg, Sinnington, York YO6 6SP]; *b* 19 July 1913; heir presumptive; *educ* Winchester and Trin Coll Cambridge (BA 1934); late master Westminster Sch (Maj CCF), Maj Special List, late 19th King George V's Own Lancers IA; *m* 12 Aug 1944 Viva Ann (*d* 15 June 1997), yr dau of Douglas Bailey, of Laughton Lodge, Sussex, and has:

      1c *Ann Catherine; *b* 22 April 1945; *m* 1973 *Fredrik Procopé and has:

        1d *Robert Hjalmar; *b* 1974

        2d *Christopher Creswell; *b* 1976

        2d *Harry Michael; *b* 1977

  3a William Ainger (Rev); *b* 16 May 1872; *educ* Trin Hall Cambridge (BA 1894, MA 1907, BD 1914); DD Lambeth 1910, Hon Chaplain to Archbp Canterbury, Chaplain Br Legation Athens; *d* unm 16 Jan 1953

  4a Arthur Woolmore, JP Straits Setts; *b* 23 Dec 1875; MIEE, MIME; *m* 3 Oct 1911 Avis Marion (*d* 2 Feb 1972 aged 89), dau of Hartley Hartley-Smith, of Upwey, Dorset, and *d* 24 April 1946, leaving:

    1b Peter Woolmore; *b* 1 Jan 1913; *educ* Gresham's, Dean Close Cheltenham and Trin Hall Cambridge (BA 1934); *m* 1st 24 July 1936 (*divorce* 1953) Ellen Brenda, dau of William Hill, of Rockferry, Cheshire; *m* 2nd 16 Sept 1953 *Sylvia Mary [Mrs Peter Wigram, Red Lodge, 22 Chiltern Hills Rd, Beaconsfield, Bucks HP9 1PL], dau of Rev John Smithson Barstow, of Woolsthorpe by Belvoir, and *d* 11 Feb 1998, leaving by her:

      1c +John Woolmore [John Wigram Esq, 11 Doneraile St, London SW6 6EL]; *b* 25 May 1957; *m* 18 May 1996 *Sally Jane, dau of Tom Winnington, of Abingdon, Oxon and has:

        1d +James Woolmore; *b* 10 Feb 1997

      1c *Caroline Judith [Mrs Roderick Evans, 12 Broadway Rd, Bishopton, Bristol BS7 8ES]; *b* 11 May 1955; *m* 1984 *Roderick Evans and has:

        1d *Matthew James; *b* 25 Feb 1993

        1d *Nicola Charlotte; *b* 24 Dec 1990

      2c *Sylvia Clare [Mrs Lee Chapman, 112 Sherbrooke Rd, London SW6]; *b* 16 Jan 1963; *m* 1998 *Lee Chapman

    1b Avis Betty Woolmore; *b* 19 July 1914; *d* unm 14 Oct 1958

    2b *Daphne Marion Woolmore; *b* 23 Sept 1919

  1a Adelaide Mary; *d* 23 Feb 1958

(6) Robert; *b* 23 Aug 1833; *m* 29 June 1867 Mary Edith (*d* 16 May 1919), 2nd dau of Samuel Solly, FRS, and *d* 5 Nov 1918, leaving:

  1a Robert; *b* 24 June 1874; *educ* Charterhouse and Merton Coll Oxford; 2nd Lt 9th Lancers and KRRC WW I; *m* 1st 21 Oct 1920 Adela Mary (*d* 19 Aug 1923), dau of Richard Reid, of Bramcote, Weybridge, and had:

    1b Robert Money; *b* 17 Aug 1923; *educ* Eton and New Coll Oxford; Hon Capt KRRC; *d* unm 14 Oct 1953

  1a (cont.) Robert Wigram *m* 2nd 11 April 1925 Winifred (*d* 1987), est dau of Capt Phipps, 24th Foot, and *d* 3 May 1932, leaving by her:

    2b +Francis John [Francis Wigram Esq, Cotters Barn, Penn, Bucks]; *b* 11 April 1926; *educ* Eton

  2a Percy Solly (Rev), MC; *b* 10 Jan 1878; *educ* Trin Coll Cambridge (BA 1899, MA 1904); Vicar St Anne's Nanango Qld, Hon CF 1918, SSJE Bombay 1923–28, Superior St Edward's Ho SW1; *d* unm 2 Sept 1953

  3a Francis; *b* 20 June 1879; *d* unm 28 May 1918

  1a Eleanor Dorothea; *d* unm 24 May 1915

  2a Eirene; *d* unm 16 April 1928

  3a Enid; *d* unm 14 May 1907

  4a Beatrice; *d* unm 18 July 1945

5a Hilda; *m* 25 Aug 1914 Alfred Ollivant (*d* 19 Jan 1927), 2nd s of Col Edward Ollivant, RA, and *d* 4 Feb 1959, leaving issue

6a Maud Fanny; *m* 19 June 1901 Reginald John Salt (*see* SALT, Bt, of Weeping Cross) and *d* 13 June 1962, leaving issue

(7) Percy, BCS; *b* 2 Jan 1836; *d* 13 Sept 1910

(8) Reginald, JP W R Yorks; *b* 16 Jan 1843; *educ* Marlborough; dir Gt Northern Rlwy; *m* 17 Oct 1872 Isabella (*d* 8 Jan 1913), dau of John Spencer, of Newcastle, and *d* 18 April 1915, leaving:

  1a Reginald Spencer; *b* 17 Sept 1874; *educ* Shrewsbury; FSI; *m* 25 June 1904 Olive Eleanor (*d* 9 March 1955), yst dau of Rev Edward Charles Lister, and *d* 12 Jan 1943, leaving:

    1b Reginald Edward Money; *b* 22 Feb 1908 *educ* Shrewsbury; *m* 10 Feb 1945 Joan Norah (*m* 3rd 22 March 1955 John David Paton, s of William Roger Paton, of Grandhome), widow of Capt Alan Macleod, Queen's Own Cameron Highrs, and dau of Capt Jersey de Knoop, and *d* 8 Feb 1950

    2b Francis Loftus; *b* 7 Jan 1911; *educ* Shrewsbury; *d* unm 16 March 1971

    1b Isabelle Georgiana; *b* 19 July 1906; *m* 10 Dec 1949 Charles James Askham (*d* 18 Jan 1964), s of Stanley James Askham

  2a Walter Gott; *b* 30 April 1877; *educ* Shrewsbury; AMIMechE, dir John Fowler and Co, Leeds; *d* 8 May 1937

3 James (Sir), PC; *b* 5 Nov 1793; *m* 24 Dec 1818 Anne (*d* 3 Feb 1844), dau of Richard Arkwright, of Willersley Castle, Derbys, and *d* 29 July 1866, leaving:

(1) James Richard; *b* 9 Oct 1819; Capt Coldstream Gds; *m* 31 July 1845 Margaret Helen (*d* 5 Nov 1883), dau of Peter Arkwright, and *d* 12 Aug 1892, leaving, with two other sons and another dau (*d* unm):

  1a Henry James; *b* 25 Dec 1847; Lt Coldstream Gds, Capt 2nd Somerset Rifle Vols; *m* 19 Jan 1870 Penelope Helen (*d* 17 Sept 1934), dau of George Eyre, JP, of Warrens, Wilts, and *d* 17 Aug 1902, leaving:

    1b George Montagu; *b* 9 May 1871; Capt 3rd Bn HLI, Maj 8th (Serv) Bn KRRC; *m* 11 Feb 1902 Esther (*d c* 1957), dau of J Heydenrych, JP, of Jansenville, Cape Colony, and *d* 16 Jan 1921

    2b Ronald Scott Jervoise, DSO (1917); *b* 23 Sept 1874; Capt RN WW I (Croix de Guerre); *m* 28 Feb 1911 Ethel Rosa (*d* 13 Oct 1940), est dau of Rev Frederick Charles Kinglake, and *d* 19 Oct 1944, leaving:

      1c Henry Frederick James; *b* 1 Feb 1916; *educ* Wellington; Maj DCLI; *m* 15 Sept 1938 (Helen) Enid (*d* Oct 1984), er dau of Frank Clyde-Smith, of Netherclay Ho, Bishop's Hull, Somerset, and *d* Dec 1984, leaving:

        1d +Roger Charles Kinglake [Capt Roger Wigram, 15 Redwood Dve, Bradley, Huddersfield, W Yorks HD2 1PW]; *b* 23 June 1940; *educ* Wellington; late Capt Somerset and Cornwall LI; *m* 1st May 1965 (*divorce* 1982) Wendy Joan (*d* 1985), er dau of Brig Philip Herbert Richardson DSO, MBE, of Manor House, Merriott, Somerset; *m* 2nd 1983 *Christine, dau of James Kenneth Pratt, and by his 1st w has:

          1e *Giselle Rose; *b* 3 April 1966

          2e *Susanna Nicola; *b* 29 Dec 1968

        2d +Peter Henry; *b* 9 Dec 1944

        3d +James Somerset [James Wigram Esq, Hilary House, Ashburton Rd, Bovey Tracey, Devon]; *b* 9 Feb 1950; *educ* Nautical Coll Pangbourne; 2nd Lt RM; *m* 1974 *Susan Jane, only dau of Bryan Braithwaite-Exley, of Pant Head, Austwick, Yorks, and has:

          1e +Thomas Peter James; *b* 1978

          2e +William Henry James; *b* 1981

          1e *Tessa Vera Joyce; *b* 1988

        1d *Sally Kinglake [Mrs Robin Atton, 581 Doyle Rd, RR#3, Victoria, BC V8X 3X1, Canada]; *b* 20 July 1939; *m* 1st 1972 (*divorce* 1982) William Arthur Rose (*d* 1987); *m* 2nd Nov 1989 *Robin Atton and by her 1st husb has:

          1e *Alan Kindred; *b* 1972

          2d *(Janet) Gail [Mrs Timothy Kyle, Zirlden, 51 Broomleaf Rd, Farnham, Surrey GU9 8DQ]; *b* 12 Feb 1953; *m* 2 Aug 1975 *Timothy Wallace Kyle, Lt RN (ret), yst s of ACM Sir Wallace Kyle, GCB, KCVO, CBE, DSO, DFC, and has:

          1e *Robert Henry Remington; *b* 1986

          1e *Laura Rachel; *b* 1977

          2e *Thea Helen; *b* 1981

    3b Cyril Charles; *b* 18 March 1882; *educ* Winchester; Lt Somerset LI Boer War 1901–02, S/Cdr RFC WW I, S/Ldr RAFVR WW II 1939–42 (POW); *m* 1st 2 March 1912 (*divorce* 1918) Mabel Mary Adams; *m* 2nd Sept 1918 (*divorce* 1928) Olivia Marie (*d* 29 July 1970), dau of Maj-Gen William Robinson Truman, and had:

      1c *Isolde Marianne [Miss Isolde Wigram, Greathed Manor, Lingfield, Surrey RH7 6PA]; *b* 18 Dec 1919

    3b (cont.) S/Ldr Cyril Wigram *m* 3rd Dec 1932 Mrs Dorothy Scott (*d* Dec 1937); *m* 4th 5 Dec 1946 Elizabeth (*d* 1970), widow of J W New, OBE, of East Ho, Wentworth, Surrey, and yst dau of Dr Frederic Sondern, of New York, and *d* 16 May 1952

    1b Florence Margaret Penelope; *b* 29 Nov 1872; *m* 2 June 1898 Capt Edmund Moore Cooper Cooper-Key, CB, MVO, RN (*d* 25 July 1933), s of Adml Rt Hon Sir Astley Cooper-Key, GCB, and had issue

    2b Kathleen Alice; *b* 22 June 1876; *m* 17 Aug 1899 Brig-Gen Tyrell Other William Champion de Crespigny, 15th Hus (*d* 25 Feb 1946), s of Sir Claude William Champion de Crespigny, 3rd Bt (*see* 1949 Edn), and *d* 4 Oct 1965, leaving issue

    3b Rachel Winifred; *b* 22 July 1878; *m* 12 Aug 1908 Lt-Col Edward Harry Arkwright, RA (*d* 6 Jan 1956), 2nd s of Canon William Harry Arkwright, and had issue

  1a Janet Mary; *d* unm 21 Jan 1953

(2) Robert James; *b* 23 April 1832; *m* 4 Sept 1854 Leonora Jane (*d* 1897), dau of Henry Alexander, HEICS, and *d* 6 Oct 1886, having had:

  1a Herewald Robert; *b* 14 Jan 1858; Maj KOSB; *d* 11 Sept 1935

  2a Alexander Robert; *d* 30 May 1883 aged 24

  3a Cecil Robert; *b* 3 Feb 1861; *d* 1892

  4a Lionel Robert; *b* 20 Feb 1867

1a Ada Leonora; *d* 17 July 1935

2a Ethel Margaret; *d* unm 30 Aug 1943

3a Amabel Mary; *m* 7 Jan 1903 Rev Roland Edward Chesshyre Walker (*d* 25 April 1936), Rector Graveley Herts 1899–1933, and had issue

(3) Arthur James; *b* 11 Jan 1834; *d* unm 5 Nov 1874

(4) Godfrey James, CB; *b* 3 June 1836; Col cmdg Coldstream Gds, Maj-Gen; *d* unm 16 Sept 1908

(1) Mary; *m* 3 Aug 1847 Alfred Smith (*d* 1886), s of George Smith, of Selsdon, Surrey, and n of 1st Baron Carrington (*qv*), and *d* 23 Nov 1869

(2) Anne Emma; *m* 27 May 1851 Edward Daniell (*d* 6 July 1875), of Little Berkhamsted, Herts, and *d* 1910, leaving issue

(3) Frances Maria; *m* 21 Dec 1848 Unwin Unwin Heathcote (*d* 1893), of Shephalbury, Herts, and *d* 1900, leaving issue

(4) Elizabeth Anne; Superior All Saints' Sisterhood Eastbourne; *d* 12 Dec 1918 aged 89

(5) Alice Jane; *m* 15 Oct 1868 R-Adml Samuel Long (*d* 25 April 1893) and *d* 8 Nov 1928, leaving issue

4 Octavius; *b* 18 Dec 1794; *m* 24 March 1824 Isabella Charlotte (*d* 1 Oct 1863), dau of Rt Rev Hon William Knox (*see* RANFURLY, E), and *d* 20 May 1878, having had, with three daus (*d* unm):

(1) William Knox, JP; *b* 13 Sept 1825; barrister; *m* 2 March 1856 Mary Ann (*d* 19 April 1883), dau of 5th Viscount Harberton (*qv*), and *d* 3 Aug 1885, having had:

1a Henry Francis (Sir); *b* 18 Jan 1857; MLC NZ 1903–20; *m* 31 March 1885 Agnes Vernon, OBE (1918) (*d* 23 Sept 1957), dau of Henry Eden Sullivan (*see* SULLIVAN, Bt), and *d* 6 May 1934

2a William Arthur; *b* 7 Oct 1860; *m* 6 Sept 1888 Edith Constance (*d* 11 Nov 1941), dau of Col Hon Sir Wellington Patrick Manvers Chetwynd-Talbot, KCB (*see* SHREWSBURY and WATERFORD, E), and *d* 12 Dec 1943, leaving:

1b Charles Knox; *b* 6 Aug 1889; *educ* Wellington and Trin Coll Cambridge (BA 1911); T/Lt RASC WW I, T/Maj RASC WW II; *m* 1st 12 June 1914 (*divorce* 1931) Gladys Mary (*d* 25 Jan 1954), dau of Rev Robert Edward Baynes, of Edgehill, Teignmouth, Devon, and had:

1c James Robert Knox; *b* 25 May 1915; *educ* Harrow; 2nd Lt 53rd (City London) AA Bde, RA (TA), Hon Maj RASC, WW II (despatches); *m* 31 Oct 1942 Beatrice Elizabeth (*d* 1984), yr dau of Rev William Arthur Sandford, of Dunstable, Beds, and *d* 1984, leaving:

1d +Brian Arthur Knox [Brian Wigram Esq, 1 Chevin Bank, Hazlewood Rd, Duffield, Derby DE6 4AA]; *b* 11 Nov 1947; *educ* Wellington; *m* 1982 *Glynnis Anne, dau of Maurice Owens, of Kilburn, Derbys

1d *Michele Anne; *b* 30 July 1946; *educ* Reading U (BA)

2c +Valentine Knox [Valentine Wigram Esq, c/o Barclays Bank, Horsham, Sussex]; *b* 11 Aug 1920; *educ* Haileybury; Cpl RAF WW II, ARICS

1b (cont.) Charles Wigram *m* 2nd 24 June 1931 Margaret Esther (*d* 2 Dec 1974), dau of Capt Henry Valentine Simpson, CMG, RN, and *d* 28 Feb 1966, leaving by her:

3c Patrick Knox; *b* 17 May 1937; *educ* Wellington and RNC Dartmouth; late Lt RN, ACII 1967; *m* 18 April 1964 *Susan Mary Fyers, dau of Col Alexander Robert Fyers Martin, of Camberley, Surrey, and *d* 10 Aug 1992, leaving:

1d +Charles Robert Knox; *b* 17 Aug 1968

1d *Sandra Fyers; *b* 30 Aug 1965

2d *Julia Margaret Fyers; *b* 8 April 1967

1c *Susan Alice Ann [Mrs Colin Scorer, 11 Stuart Grove, Teddington, Middx TW11 8RR]; *b* 18 March 1932; *educ* London U (BA 1953); *m* 1 May 1965 Colin Scorer, s of Percy Scorer, of Biddenham, Bedford, and adopted:

*Andrew Michael; *b* 23 Feb 1968

*Jane Sarah; *b* 1971

2c *Jennifer Jane [Mrs Allen Griswold, 3022 Linda Vista, Alameda, CA 94502, USA]; *b* 30 April 1935; *educ* Godolphin Sch Salisbury; *m* 4 Aug 1967 Allen Griswold (*d* 7 May 1998), yst s of E S Griswold, of Mansfield, Mass.

1b Ivy Margaret; *b* 1890; *m* 27 Sept 1923 Lt-Col Herbert Bowater Vernon, MC, IA, s of Mark H H Vernon, of Horsham, and *d* 28 Feb 1956, leaving issue

1a Eleanor Mary; *m* 6 April 1880 Francis Hughes Gibb (*d* 1917), of Manor Ho, Tarrant Gunville, Blandford, est s of Col Charles John Gibb, RE, and had issue

2a Helen Isabella; *d* unm 24 July 1877

3a Margaret Esther; *m* 22 Oct 1889 Arthur Edgell Eastwood, JP, of Leigh Court, Taunton, and *d* 13 Dec 1912

4a Madeline Clara; *b* 10 Aug 1871; *d* unm 15 Dec 1936

(2) Francis Spencer, BCS; *b* 25 March 1829; *d* unm 26 June 1918

(3) Spencer Robert (Rev); *b* 22 Aug 1835; MA Oxon; Vicar Prittlewell Essex 1864–80, Rector W Ilsley Berks 1896–99; *m* 30 April 1867 Elizabeth Pearson (*d* 30 July 1915), dau of Rev William Dalby, Preb Sarum, and *d* 13 Jan 1909, leaving, with another dau (*d* an infant):

1a Alice Margaret Spencer, Sis of Charity, Wantage; *d* 31 March 1927

2a Evelyn Frances Spencer; *d* unm 8 June 1925

3a Rosamond Edith Spencer; *d* unm 5 May 1958

4a Lilian Agnes Spencer; *m* 13 April 1910 Brevet Maj Francis Herbert Howe, Welsh Regt (*d* 29 May 1931), yst s of Edward Russell James Howe, of Chart Place, Kent, and *d* 26 May 1960, leaving issue

5 Joseph Cotton (Rt Rev); *b* 26 Dec 1798; DD, Bp Rochester 1860 on; *m* 1 March 1837 Susan Maria (*d* 27 June 1864), dau of Peter Arkwright, and *d* 6 April 1867, having had, with another s (*d* an infant) and dau (*d* unm):

(1) Alfred Joseph; *b* 8 May 1839; *d* 14 April 1904

(2) Arthur Henry; *b* 1840; *d* 1842

(3) Gerrard Andrewes; *b* 24 Jan 1842; *educ* Trin Coll Cambridge; *m* 10 June 1873 Selina Maria, dau of Edmund Wilmot (*see* WILMOT, Bt), and *d* 9 Nov 1917, leaving:

1a Gerrard Edmund (Rev); *b* 6 Oct 1877; *educ* Jesus Coll Cambridge; Vicar Leamington, Hastings, Warwicks 1928 on; *m* 11 Oct 1902 Maria Isména (*d* 4 Sept 1944), 2nd dau of William Townson Mayne, and *d* 31 Oct 1947, leaving:

1b +Francis Gerrard Mayne [Francis Wigram Esq, 132 Bridgewater Manor, Somerset West 7130, CP, S Africa]; *b* 13 May 1905, AMInstF; *m* 17 Oct 1934 Helen Frances (*d* 1990), yr dau of Dr Sidney Worthington, of Warwick, and has:

1c +Gerrard Charles [Gerrard Wigram Esq, Lenana, 25 Duckitt Ave, Constantia 7800, S Africa]; *b* 10 Jan 1936; FCA 1970, CA (SA); *m* 8 May 1965 Joan Patricia, yst dau of James Lang, of Nairobi, and has:

1d +Keith Gerrard [Keith Wigram Esq, 3/141 Celtic Cresc, Ellerslie, Auckland 1005, New Zealand]; *b* 4 Jan 1969; *m* 13 Jan 1996 *Lynn Marie, dau of Hamilton Bennet

1d *Zena Patricia Jean; *b* 14 July 1966; *m* 7 June 1997 *Roger Hugh Knight, only s of Hugh Knight

1d *Eileen Frances; *b* 1972; *m* 7 Dec 1996 *David Kenneth Murdoch Putterill, only s of Kenneth Putterill

2c +Nigel Francis [Nigel Wigram Esq, 8 Heseldon Ave, Rondebosch, Cape Town, S Africa]; *b* 26 Sept 1939; CCS, BCom, MBA, PhD; *m* 1974 *Lynette Monique, dau of Dr Leon Stern, of Kenilworth, Cape Town, and has:

1d +Andrew David; *b* 1976

1c *Deborah Helen [Mrs Richard Farnfield, Rydings, Park Rd, Forest Row, E Sussex RH18 5BX]; *b* 7 June 1938; *m* 15 April 1961 *Capt Richard Hugh Farnfield, RN, only s of Capt Gilbert Lescombe Farnfield, DSO, DSC, RN, of Bridge of Weir, Renfrewshire, and has:

1d *Anthony Gilbert; *b* 6 Jan 1963

2d *Andrew Richard *b* 26 March 1970

3d *Timothy Francis; *b* 30 July 1971; *m* 28 Aug 1993 *Belinda Alice Irene, dau of Oliver Preston Benn (*see* BENN, Bt)

1d *Helen Rosemary; *b* 1 Feb 1965; *m* 22 May 1993 *Mark Jeremy Moore-Gillon, PhD, s of J A Moore-Gillon, of Surbiton, and has:

1e *Charles William; *b* 24 Jan 1996

1e *Katherine Lucy; *b* 2 April 1997

1b Margaret Isména Wilmot; *b* 12 Oct 1903; *m* 15 June 1939 Arthur Carrington, s of Lindow Carrington, of Nantwich, Cheshire, and had:

1c *Michael Anthony; *b* 30 Aug 1940; *educ* Brentwood and Imp Coll Sci and Tech London; *m* 16 Oct 1965 *Cynthia Denise, dau of Eric Clifford, and has:

1d *Richard Anthony; *b* 5 May 1969

1d *Elizabeth Louise; *b* 20 June 1966

1c Margaret Ann; *b* 1 March 1942; *d* 30 Jan 1947

2b *Marion Rochford [Mrs William Richardson, Quarndon Hill, 78 The Common, Quarndon, Derbys DE6 4JY]; *b* 31 Aug 1909; *m* 3 Sept 1930 William Hadden Richardson (*d* 22 May 1968), est s of William Henry Richardson, of Leylands, Derby, and has:

1c *James Hadden [James Richardson Esq, Fern Hill, Quarndon, Derbys DE22 5JY]; *b* 15 Aug 1937; *educ* Uppingham; *m* 27 May 1961 *Susan Mary, dau of James Harry Keith Thomson, of Derwent Ho, Duffield, Derbys, and has:

1d *Nicholas Hadden [Nicholas Richardson Esq, Quarndon Hill, 76 The Common, Quarndon, Derby DE22 5JY]; *educ* Uppingham; BSc, ARICS; *b* 20 July 1963; *m* 1991 *Lynn Clements and has:

1e *William Hadden Henry; *b* 16 Sept 1996

1e *Katherine Jane; *b* 16 June 1992

2e *Susannah Mary; *b* 2 May 1994

2d *Timothy James Keith; *b* 1970

1d *Wendy Diana; *b* 16 Oct 1965

1c *Judith Mary [Mrs Judith Yeomans, Flat 4B, Flower Lillies, Windley, Belper, Derbys DE56 2LQ]; *b* 14 April 1934; *m* 11 May 1963 (*divorce* 19–) John Swain Yeomans, s of Harry Mountford Yeomans, of Allestree, Derby, and has:

1d *Philip Hadden [Philip Yeomans Esq, The Woodlands, Belper Rd, Sturston, Derbys DE6 1LL]; *b* 6 May 1964; *m* 1990 *Louise Dale and has:

1e *Daniel Hadden; *b* 1995

1e *Bethany Angela; *b* 1991

2e *Charlotte Rowena; *b* 1993

3b *Janet; *b* 8 Jan 1916 *m* 26 May 1956 *Hon Valentine Henry Okes Herbert, 2nd s of 1st Baron Hemingford (*qv*)

(4) John; *b* 23 July 1846; FSI; *m* 30 April 1872 Gertrude Eliza (*d* 18 June 1929), dau of Rt Rev Henry Mackenzie (*see* MACKENZIE, Bt, of Coul), and *d* 4 Dec 1943, leaving:

1a Henry Joseph; *b* 28 March 1873; *m* 1st 19 April 1898 (*divorce* 1909) Alice Laura, dau of Thomas Jarvis, of Mount Jarvis, Antigua, and had:

1b John Jarvis; *b* 25 April 1900; *m* 28 Oct 1929 Ivy Harley, dau of George Hayes, of Cressy, Tasmania

2b Richard Henry; *b* 25 Feb 1903; *m* 1st Dec 1928 Aimée Fairlam (*d* 1946), dau of William Hall, of Beauty Point, Tasmania; *m* 2nd 1947 Sheelah Mary Veronica, dau of William J Gowans, of Glengarry, Tasmania

1b Daphne; *b* 13 Jan 1899; *m* 24 July 1924 Douglas Cecil FitzHerbert (*see* FITZHERBERT, Bt) and had issue

2b *Lorna; *b* 12 Dec 1904; *m* 21 June 1932 Cdr William Luard Bond, RN, s of Rev Charles Harold Bond, of Eakring Rectory, Newark, and has issue

1a (cont.) Henry Wigram *m* 2nd 16 July 1910 Beatrice Mary (*d* 1945), dau of B J Baylis Garrard, of Haydon Manor, Somerset, and *d* 3 March 1926

1a Edith Margaret, JP; *m* 29 May 1900 William Nathaniel Brooks (*d* 11 April 1946), s of William Brooks, of Odiham, Hants, and *d* 28 March 1958, leaving issue

2a Mary Helen; *d* unm 24 July 1907

3a Agnes Gertrude; *m* 11 Jan 1905 Thomas Zachary Lloyd (*d* 24 Sept 1939), 3rd s of Sampson Zachary Lloyd, of Areley Hall, nr Stourport, and *d* 22 March 1958, leaving issue

4a Bertha Caroline; *m* 23 April 1904 Francis Austin Langton Hodgkinson (*d* 29 Dec 1955), s of Rev Canon George Langton Hodgkinson, and had:

1b Edward Thomas Langton; *b* 18 Jan 1905; *d* 22 March 1908

2b David Anthony; *b* 14 April 1909; *m* 22 Dec 1939 Jacqueline, dau of M Dutoit, of Vevey, Switzerland, and *d* 29 Dec 1958, leaving:

1c *Edward; *b* 23 Aug 1942

2c *Mark; *b* 3 March 1946

3b *John Francis Nicholas; *b* 17 Dec 1918; *m* 1st 1945 (*divorce* 1946) Genevieve Borland; *m* 2nd 15 Sept 1947 Dorothy Mary Gertrude, dau of W F D Leonard, and by her has:

1c *Simon Nicholas; *b* 14 Aug 1948

2c *Patrick Francis; *b* 12 Jan 1950

3c *David John Tresilian; *b* 15 July 1951

1b *Catherine Sidgwick; *b* 29 Nov 1906; *m* Dec 1938 Marvin McCord Lowes (*d* 23 June 1960), and has:

1c *Marvin Langton; *b* 12 Feb 1944

1c *Susan; *b* 22 Jan 1941

2c *Gillian; *b* 23 Feb 1946; *m* 24 Dec 1969 *Daniel Hamilton, PhD, of USA

5a Katherine Muriel; *d* 9 April 1975 aged 94

6a Rachel FitzHerbert; *m* 25 Jan 1910 Rev Bernard Rambold Keir Moilliet, MA (*d* 14 Sept 1956), s of James Keir Moilliet, of Abbotsleigh, Malvern, Worcs, and has:

1b *Rachel Mary Keir; *b* 16 Oct 1911

2b *Madeline Gertrude Keir; *b* 12 Oct 1913; *m* 6 Oct 1942 Ven Denis James (*d* 28 July 1965), Archdeacon Emeritus Exeter, s of Francis James, of Cirencester, Glos, and has:

1c *Francis Bernard Wigram; *b* 6 Jan 1944; *educ* Sherborne and Exeter Coll Oxford

2c *David Alistair; *b* 2 March 1946; *educ* Grenville Coll Bideford

3b *Faith Keir; *b* 22 Jan 1916

4b *Jacqueline Keir; *b* 2 Oct 1920; *educ* King's Coll of Household and Social Sci (BSc)

(5) William Loftus; *b* 24 Oct 1852; *m* 6 Aug 1879 Clara Anne, dau of John Bell, of Rushpool Hall, Yorks, and *dsp* 20 May 1897

(6) Walter Augustus; *b* 11 Dec 1856; *educ* Trin Coll Cambridge (BA); barrister; *m* 21 July 1883 Ethel Rosa (*d* 2 June 1960, aged 98), dau of William Henry Brace, MD, of S Kensington, and *d* 5 Feb 1921, having had:

1a Dennis; *d* an infant

1a Audrey Eleanor; *b* 18 Aug 1885; *m* 1st 1 Aug 1907 (*divorce* Scotland 1936) John Fletcher Campbell (*d* 31 Dec 1942), s of Hugh Fletcher Campbell, and had issue; *m* 2nd 31 Aug 1943 James Stuart Bull (*d* 15 March 1949), yr s of Rev Benjamin Bull, and *d* 19 Nov 1973

(7) Eustace Rochester; *b* 26 Jan 1860; Lt Coldstream Gds; *m* 2 July 1889 Mary Grace (*d* 14 March 1951), dau of Col Ralph Bradford-Atkinson, of Angerton, Morpeth, and *d* 11 Feb 1940, having had, with a dau (*d* young):

1a Ralph Follett, CMG (1933); *b* 23 Oct 1890; T/Capt Special List WW I, Counsellor FO 1933; *m* 28 Feb 1925 Ava (*m* 2nd 30 Oct 1941 1st Viscount Waverley (*qv*) and *d* 1974), dau of John Edward Courtenay Bodley, and *d* 31 Dec 1936, leaving:

1b Charles Edward Thomas Bodley; *b* 27 Nov 1929; *d* 14 Aug 1951

(1) Susan Caroline; *m* 20 June 1861 Maj George Gooch Clowes, 8th Hus (*d* 7 Nov 1891), and *dsp* 17 Jan 1923

(2) Edith Katharine; *m* 9 Sept 1873 Atkinson Holden (*d* 9 June 1876), of Nuttall Temple, Notts, and *dsps* 17 Nov 1878

6 Edward; *b* 30 Sept 1802; *m* 10 Aug 1830 Catherine (*d* 31 Aug 1876), 4th dau of George Smith, of Selsdon (*see* CARRINGTON, B), and *d* 3 Dec 1870, leaving, with another dau (*d* unm):

(1) Frederic Edward (Rev), of Hampstead; *b* 1 June 1834; Hon Gen Sec CMS; *m* 31 May 1859 Frances (*d* 16 Feb 1914), 4th dau of Francis Wright, of Osmaston Manor, Derbys, and *d* 10 March 1897, leaving:

1a Edmund Francis Edward (Rev); *b* 13 Dec 1864; MA Cantab; Hon India Sec CMS 1915–32; *m* 3 Aug 1904 Violet, est dau of Sir Thomas Charles Dewey, 1st Bt (*qv*), and *d* 15 Sept 1933, leaving:

1b Oswald Thomas Edward (Rev); *b* 9 Aug 1905; *educ* Marlborough; CMS; *m* 9 March 1935 Margaret [Mrs Oswald Wigram, Scotleigh Lodge, 76 Old Exeter St, Chudleigh, Devon TQ13 0JX], dau of Robert Nicolls Barnes, of Sutton Coldfield, and *d* 1990, leaving:

1c +Robert Edmund [Robert Wigram Esq, 93 Investigator St, Red Hill, Canberra, ACT 2603, Australia]; *b* 13 Feb 1936; *educ* Prince of Wales Sch Nairobi; *m* 8 June 1963 *Patricia, dau of L C Collisson, of Liverpool, NSW, and has:

1d +Simon Andrew; *b* 4 Sept 1967; *m* 1987 *Caroline Threlfall

2d +Christopher Anthony; *b* 1977

1d *Frances Elizabeth; *b* 19 Nov 1964

2d *Louise Annette; *b* 27 Jan 1966; *m* 1987 *Anthony Fryer and has:

1e *Amy Louise; *b* 1994

2e *Ashley Jane; *b* 1997

2c +Paul Frederic [Paul Wigram Esq, PO Box 10, Limuru, Kenya]; *b* 29 July 1937; *educ* Marlborough and Pembroke Coll Cambridge (MA); *m* 27 July 1963 *Christian Virginia, twin dau of Maj H A R Bucknall, MC, and has:

1d +Thomas Paul Henry; *b* 13 July 1964

1d *Lucy Helen Gabrielle; *b* 23 Feb 1966

2d *Bronwen Serena Christian; *b* 1971

3c +Andrew Oswald (Rev) [The Rev Andrew Wigram, The Vicarage, 2 Dobbin Close, Cropwell Bishop, Notts NG12 3GR]; *b* 31 July 1939; *educ* Marlborough and London U (BD 1964); *m* 18 July 1964 *Catherine Mary Howden, yr dau of Rev Canon Geoffrey John Rogers, of Combe Down, Bath, and has:

1d +John Michael; *b* 30 May 1967; *m* 1989 *Rachel, dau of Rev Guy Chapman, and has:

1e +David James; *b* 1991

2e +Peter Jonathan; *b* 1996

1e *Hannah Catharine; *b* 1992

1d *Susanna Dora; *b* 25 Jan 1966; *m* Sept 1998 *Stener Vogt, of Oslo

2d *Margaret Jane Majala; *b* 10 Feb 1970

4c +Francis Aidan [Francis Wigram Esq, Riggles Farm, Upottery, Honiton, Devon EX14 0SP]; *b* 24 July 1949; *educ* Marlborough and Seale Hayne Ag Coll; *m* 1973 (*divorce* 1995) Christine Susan, dau of T E Abbey, of Tilney, Sellicks Green, Taunton, and has:

1d +Timothy Francis; *b* 1974

2d +Richard James; *b* 1976

3d +Nicholas Mark; *b* 1977

1c *Ruth Margaret (Rev) [Rev Ruth Wigram, The Vicarage, St Paul's Dve, Brompton-on-Swale, N Yorks DL10 7HQ]; *b* 18 Nov 1941; *educ* St Michael's Limpsfield and Salisbury Training Coll

2b Aidan Frederic; *b* 27 May 1907; BA Cantab; Lt (A) RNVR WW II; *m* 9 April 1938 Marjorie Joyce (*d* 16 April 1963), yr dau of Lt-Col Ernest Richard Inglis Chitty, IA, and was *k* on air ops 11/12 Nov 1941, leaving:

1c (Aidan) David [David Wigram Esq, High Timbers, Hartley Rd, Cranbrook, Kent TN17 3QX]; *b* 13 Dec 1938; *educ* Marlborough and U Coll N Wales (BSc); *m* 26 July 1968 *Jennifer Ann, only dau of Ernest Noel Firmager, of Godstone, Surrey, and has:

1d *Lesley Rosalind; *b* 20 June 1969

2c (Aidan) Patrick; *b* 29 Oct 1940; *educ* Thomas Delarue Sch Tonbridge; *d* 25 Jan 1983

3b Edmund Hugh Lewis; *b* 4 July 1911; MB, BCh Cantab; MRCS, LRCP, memb 1935 and 1936 Everest Expdns, Lt-Col RAMC WW II; *m* 39 Sept 1938 Kathleen Maud (*m* 2nd 6 Nov 1948 (*divorce* 1968) Christopher Henry Kaye, BA, MRCS, LRCP, 4th s of Henry Wynyard Kaye (*see* below)), yr dau of L C S Hallam, of Port Arthur, Canada, and *d* following a climbing accident 2 Dec 1945, leaving:

1c +Peter Hallam [Peter Wigram Esq, PO Box 1557, Banff, Alberta, Canada]; *b* 27 June 1939; *m* 1st 1966 (*divorce* 1976) Michelle —; *m* 2nd 1987 *Catherine Hardie

2c +(Edmund) William [William Wigram Esq, Boghouse Farmhouse, Blagdon, Seaton Burn, Newcastle NE13 6DB]; *b* 5 May 1942; *educ* Winchester and Trin Coll Cambridge (BA 1963); *m* 3 July 1965 *Diana Frances, only dau of Anthony Douglas Bell, MB, BS, of Sunday Is, via Kirkwall, Orkney, and has:

1d +Anthony Christopher; *b* 23 Aug 1966

1d *Clare Frances; *b* 18 Nov 1969

1b Joy Frances; *b* 11 July 1909; *educ* Sherborne Sch for Girls and Newnham Coll Cambridge (BA 1931); CMS; *m* 20 April 1937 Fortescue Eric Vesey Ross (*d* 24 Dec 1996), yr s of Rev Edmund Francis Vesey Ross, and *d* 12 March 1992, leaving:

1c *Brian Patrick Edmund; *b* 20 Jan 1942; *educ* Bryanston and Queen's U Belfast (BA); *m* 9 July 1966 (*divorce* 19–) Theodolinda Maria Theresa, dau of Ernest Appleton, of Stockport, Cheshire

2c *Ian Ronald Francis; *b* 28 Sept 1945; *educ* Marlborough and Edinburgh U; *m* 9 Sept 1967 Laura, dau of Hugh Stevenson, of Penicuik, Midlothian

3c *Michael John; *b* 16 Nov 1947; *educ* Felsted and Manchester U

1c *Wendy Joy [Miss Wendy Ross, 14 Gilwell Close, Putnoe, Bedford MK41 8BS]; *b* 22 Jan 1939; *educ* Sherborne Sch for Girls

2a Beresford Edward (Rev); *b* 17 May 1870; MA Cantab; *m* 12 March 1901 Jessie Violet (*d* 20 Jan 1939), 4th dau of Walter Scott, of Bramley Hill, Croydon, and *d* 19 Oct 1917, leaving:

1b Arthur Frederic; *b* 24 March 1903; *educ* RNCs Osborne and Dartmouth; signal engr BR, Maj Inns of Ct (TA) Regt; *m* 21 Oct 1939 Nadina Grace, dau of Engr Cdr Frank Lloyd Newhouse, RN, of Thorpe St Andrew, Norfolk, and *d* 15 Sept 1973, having had:

1c Anthony Beresford; *b* 12 Dec 1941; *d* 15 Feb 1942

2c Andrew Beresford; *b* 21 March 1947; *d* 20 Sept 1951

1c *Judy

2b Winstone Beresford; *b* 3 June 1908; *educ* St Lawrence Coll Ramsgate and Queens' Coll Cambridge (BA 1930, MA 1947); Colonial CS Kenya; *m* 17 March 1942 Adelaide Joyce (Dair), BA Oxon (*d* 1966), er dau of Rev William Aldworth Ferguson, DD, of Victoria, BC, and *d* 1988, leaving:

1c *Erica Joyce [Mrs Ian Sharpe, Slough House, Bishops Nympton, S Molton, N Devon]; *b* 9 Dec 1943; *educ* Bristol U (BA); *m* 4 April 1970 *Ian Ferguson Sharpe, RAOC, and has:

1d *Jasper Henry Ferguson; *b* 1971

2d *Daniel William; *b* 1973

3b Marcus Walter; *b* 23 Feb 1917; *educ* Haileybury and Gonville and Caius Coll Cambridge (BA 1938); Lt Queen's Roy Regt, Dir Music Ottershaw Sch; *m* 8 Feb 1941 *Christina [Mrs Marcus Wigram, 5 Riverway, S Cerney, Cirencester, Glos GL7 6HZ], dau of Bertram William Cantrell, and *d* 1989, leaving:

1c *Ann Margaret Joyce [Mrs Derek Blandford, 176 Watleys End Rd, Winterbourne, Bristol]; *b* 2 Jan 1942; *m* 1964 *Derek William F Blandford, er s of W F Blandford, of Shroton, Dorset, and has:

1d +Andrew Paul; *b* 12 Oct 1966

2d +Ian Keith; *b* 8 March 1969

3d +Kieron John; *b* 1971

2c *Carol Frances Violet [Miss Carol Wigram, 8 Saxon Rd, Faversham, Kent]; *b* 20 Nov 1946; *m* 1976 (*divorce* 1994. resumed maiden name) Peter Guilderoy Croskin and has:

    1d *Jonathan Guilderoy; *b* 1978

3c *Sarah Christina Agnes [Mrs Humphrey Lane, Huckstones, Cottons Lane, Ashton-under-Hill, Worcs]; *b* 1 July 1949; *m* 1970 *Humphrey David Lane and has:

    1d *Bridget Anna; *b* 1972

    2d *Corrinne Victoria; *b* 1972

    3d *Kathryn Alice; *b* 1978

4c *Jane Eleanor Bridget; *b* 23 March 1954; *m* 1st 1971 (*divorce* 1986) Mark Christian Eckersley; *m* 2nd 1988 *Kenneth William Augustus Robeson and by her 1st husb has:

    1d *Naomi Jane; *b* 1974

    2d *Samantha Claire; *b* 1979

1b Eleanor Violet; *b* 10 Jan 1902; *d* unm 15 May 1927

2b Joyce Marjorie; *b* 21 Feb 1905; *educ* London U (MB, BS 1930); adopted:

*John Martin; *b* 19 June 1943; *educ* Leighton Park; *m* *Mary Rose, only dau of Mrs K Williams, of Sevenoaks, and has:

    1d *Patrick; *b* 1969

    2d *David; *b* 1970

    1d *Eleanor; *b* 1962

    2d *Rachel; *b* 1964

    3d *Rebecca; *b* 1967

*Hilary Margaret; *b* 2 March 1941; *educ* St George's Sch Harpenden and Dartington Hall; *m* 12 Sept 1964 *Stephen James Stuart Oxlade, only s of Norman Stuart Oxlade, of Ewhurst, Sussex, and has:

    1d *Samantha Gay; *b* 8 April 1969

3a Harold Frederic Edward (Rev); *b* 9 Sept 1873; *educ* Trin Coll Cambridge (MA); Vicar Goodnestone Kent; *m* 18 July 1913 Gladys Christine (*d* 14 June 1985), dau of Sir Howard Warburton Elphinstone, 3rd Bt, of Sowerby (*qv*), and *d* 19 March 1946, leaving:

1b Howard Beresford; *b* 31 Oct 1917; *d* 30 Sept 1991

2b +Andrew Harold [Maj Andrew Wigram 17 Albury Rd, Newcastle-upon-Tyne NE2 3PE]; *b* 30 Nov 1919; *educ* Wellington and Trin Hall Cambridge (BA 1940); Maj RHA, 1st Airborne Div; *m* 18 April 1953 Alice Jefferson (*d* 1989), est dau of Charles Guttidge Trewhitt, of Roker, Sunderland

3b +Alexander (Sandy) Robert [Sandy Wigram Esq, Le Bons Bay, Rural Delivery, Akaroa Banks Peninsula, New Zealand]; *b* 24 Dec 1925; *educ* Wellington and BNC Oxford (BA 1949, MA 1953); late Lt Roy Signals and P/O Hong Kong AuxAF; *m* 14 Feb 1958 *Virginia Claire, dau of Gp/Capt Philip Patrick Strachan Rickard, OBE, and has:

1c +Kester Jonathan; *b* 28 Feb 1959; *educ* U of Canterbury NZ (BE Chem); CEng, IChemE; *m* 1983 (*divorce* 1989) Lynn, dau of James Davidson, and has:

    1d +Elliot Simon; *b* 1984

2c +Simon Nicholas; *b* 16 Dec 1960

3c +Luke; *b* 15 Nov 1977

1c *Sarah Christine; *b* 28 March 1963

2c *Aroha Kirsty; *b* 12 May 1975

1b *Gladys Veronica [Mrs Reginald Fennell, The Old Vicarage, Moulsford, Oxon OX10 9JB]; *b* 17 Jan 1916; *m* 1st 17 Sept 1938 Lt William George Player Brigstocke, RNVR (*d* of wounds recd in action July 1940), er s of George Robert Brigstocke, of Ferryside, Carmarthen; *m* 2nd 9 June 1943 Maj Reginald Charles Grisdale Fennell, TD, KOYLI, s of Charles William Fennell, of Cliff Hill Ho, Wakefield, and has:

1c *Robert John [Robert Fennell Esq, Kilve House, 315 Andover Rd, Newbury, Berks RG150WY]; *b* 22 March 1944; *educ* Oundle; *m* 1975 *Phoebe Joscelyn, dau of Gordon Wilfred Langley-Smith, of Gloucester, and has:

    1d *Thomas Edward; *b* 1979

    1d *Anthea Sarah; *b* 1977

    2d *Megan; *b* 1986

2c *William Richard Kenneth [William Fennell Esq, 22 Place Farm Way, Monks Risborough, Bucks HP17 9JH]; *b* 11 Jan 1952; *educ* Oundle and Birmingham U (BSc); FRICS; *m* 1979 *Sylvia Mary, BA, dau of Wilfred Fletcher, and has:

    1d *Margaret Anne; *b* 1983

2b *Rose Eleanor [Mrs Richard Barry, 37 Bennells Ave, Tankerton, Whitstable, Kent CT5 2HL]; *b* 16 June 1923; *m* 16 Oct 1954 *Richard Edward Barry, s of Edward Charles Barry, and has:

1c *John Andrew [John Barry Esq, 125 The Knole, Faversham, Kent ME13 7QJ]; *b* 16 Nov 1958; *m* 1982 *Marion, dau of Julian Warwick, and has:

    1d *Alistair James; *b* 1988

    1d *Elaine Christine; *b* 1990

1c Sylvia May; *b* 22 May 1956, BA; *m* 1976 *Kim Marsh [Kim Marsh Esq, 127 Dene Rd, Wylam, Northumberland NE41 8EZ] and *d* 24 June 1996 leaving:

    1d *Philip Robert; *b* 1977

4a Marcus Edward (Rev); *b* 18 June 1875; *educ* Harrow and Trin Coll Cambridge (BA 1897, MA 1901); Curate St Matthew's Fulham 1899–1901, CMS Missionary NW India 1901–37, Sec CMS Lahore and Hon Canon Lahore 1932–37, Silver Jubilee 1935 and Coronation Medals 1937; *m* 29 Dec 1910 Mary, MB (*d* 26 Feb 1952), dau of James Townsend, of Exeter, and *d* 29 March 1953

5a Loftus Edward; *b* 31 May 1877; *educ* Harrow and Trin Coll Cambridge (BA 1899, MA, MB, and BCh 1903); CMS Peshawar 1904–09, taught Livingstone Coll to 1946; *m* 23 July 1912 Constance Emma Letitia (*d* 5 Nov

1970 aged 89), dau of Rev Canon William Gilbert Edwards, of Ch Ch Oxford, and *d* 3 July 1963, leaving:

1b +Gerald Frederic [Gerald Wigram Esq, Calverleigh Cottage, Tiverton, Devon EX16 8BB]; *b* 30 Dec 1916; *educ* Marlborough; late Capt KAR; *m* 11 Dec 1948 Anne Christal (*d* 1981), er dau of Brig-Gen Hon Lesley James Probyn Butler (*see* DUNBOYNE, B), and has:

1c *Carolyn Lesley; *b* 22 Aug 1950; *m* 1986 *John Eastman Perry and has:

    1d *Mark Andrew; *b* 1987

    2d *Ben Jack; *b* 1988

2c *Marylee Anne; *b* 16 March 1952; *m* 15 Nov 1997 *Maj Mark Ravnkilde, Roy Scots Dragoon Gds, s of Knud Ravnkilde, of Greenham, Wellington

3c *Bridget Margaret; *b* 5 Feb 1954; *m* 1982 *Jonathan Patrick Simmons and has:

    1d *Michael Anthony; *b* 1987

    1d *Anne Julia; *b* 1985

2b Michael; *b* 30 Aug 1919; *educ* Marlborough and St Peter's Coll Oxford (BA 1941); MRCS, LRCP 1945, Fndn MRCGP; *m* 25 April 1945 Margaret Edith Ann [Mrs Michael Wigram, Crickerton, Buckfastleigh, S Devon TQ11 0BL], dau of Wilfred Ernest Watson-Baker, of Toddington, Beds, and was *k* in a car crash 23 Nov 1973, leaving:

1c *Laurette [Mrs Brian Guest, Wateroak, Ludgores Lane, Danbury, Essex]; *b* 11 June 1946; *m* 1971 Brian Guest (*d* May 1998) and has:

    1d *William Andrew; *b* 1974

    1d *Josephine Briony; *b* 1972; *m* July 1996 *Paul Murrell

2c *Sarah Margaret, of Ashburton, S Devon; *b* 27 June 1949; *m* 1973 (*divorce* 1994) Timothy Veise, of Rectortown, Va., and has:

    1d *Katherine Anne Bovington; *b* 1975

    2d *Emily Sarah; *b* 1978

3c *Jennifer Rose; *b* 28 April 1953; *m* 1994 *Robert Lawson-Peebles, PhD

3b Robert, MC; *b* 1 Nov 1922; Lt RAC (Inns of Ct) WW II; *ka* Normandy 7 June 1944

1b *Lettice Margaret [Mrs Edward Hadow, 2 Highlands Park, Chudleigh, Devon TQ13 0JZ]; *b* 27 Nov 1920; *educ* LMH Oxford (BA 1942); Section Offr WAAF WW II; *m* 18 Aug 1951 Maj Edward Arthur Hadow late RE, only surv son of Lt-Col Arthur Lovell Hadow, CMG (*see* ANGLESEY, M), and has:

1c *John Wigram; *b* 6 Aug 1959; *m* 1988 *Susan Frances, yr dau of F W Naylor, of Totnes, Devon, and has:

    1d *George Louis; *b* 1992

    2d *Patrick William; *b* 11 Oct 1994

    3d *Angus John; *b* 3 May 1997

2c *Robert Edward; *b* 19 Jan 1968

1c *Rosemary Maude; *b* 12 April 1953; *m* 1st 1974 (*divorce* 1988) David Ericson and has:

    1d *Daniel; *b* 1985

1c (cont.) Mrs Rosemary Ericson *m* 2nd 1989 *Graham John White and by him has:

    1d *Rebecca Hadow; *b* 1991

2c *Juliet Letitia; *b* 3 March 1955; *m* 1979 *Graham Paul Herbert and has:

    1d *Mark Graham; *b* 1985

    1d *Emma Letitia; *b* 1983

    2d *Rosanna Bethan; *b* 1987

3c *Celia Catherine; *b* 6 June 1957; *m* 1984 *Ian Cranston Shields and has:

    1d *Joe; *b* 1988

    1d *Kerry Mohira; *b* 1985

1a Eleanor Selina; *m* 29 Dec 1896 Rev Edmund Stileman Carr (*d* 10 June 1954), 2nd s of Rev Edmund Carr, of Holbrooke Hall, Derbys, and Boscobel, Salop, and *dsp* 16 June 1901

2a Agnes Margaret; *d* unm 4 Jan 1952

(1) Catherine Frances; *m* 5 May 1859 Rev John Barton and *d* 15 May 1860

7 Loftus Tottenham, QC; *b* 6 Nov 1803; MP Cambridge 1850–59; *m* 23 Jan 1849 Ldy Katherine Jane Douglas, yst dau of 5th Earl of Selkirk (*qv*), and *dsp* 19 Sept 1889

8 George Vicessimus; *b* 28 March 1805; *m* 1st 23 March 1830 Fanny (*d* 11 March 1834), dau of Thomas Cherbury Bligh, and had a dau (*d* unm); *m* 2nd 18 Aug 1835 Catherine, only dau of William Parnell (*see* CONGLETON, B) and *d* 1 Feb 1879

9 William Pitt (Rev); *b* 2 Dec 1806; *m* 13 Nov 1837 Sophia Sarah (*d* 1883), 5th dau of George Smith, of Selsdon (*see* CARRINGTON, B), and *d* 18 Sept 1870, leaving:

(1) Ernest (Rev); *b* 3 May 1840; Rector Whitby; *d* 1876

(2) Herbert; *b* 16 Jan 1842; MA Oxon; Madras CS 1863–84; *m* 27 July 1872 Amy Augusta (*d* 10 Jan 1935) dau of Lt-Gen John Wood Rideout, IA, and *d* 1 Oct 1914, leaving:

1a CLIVE WIGRAM, *cr* BARON WIGRAM (*qv*)

2a Kenneth (Sir), GCB, CSI, CBE, DSO; *b* 5 Dec 1875; *educ* Winchester; IA: Tirah Expdn 1897–98 (medal two clasps), Waziristan Expdn 1901–02 (clasp), Tibet 1904 (medal with clasp), WW I (despatches seven times, two brevets, Legn Hon, Orders Crown Belgium, Crown Siam 3rd Cl, Croix de Guerre Belgium): GSSO(1) 1916–17, Brig-Gen Gen Staff 1917–18, A/Brig-Gen Air Staff 1918–19, T/Brig-Gen and Col Staff AHQ 1919–21, cmdg Delhi Bde Area 1922–24, Maj-Gen 1923, DA&QMG N Cmd India 1924–26 and cmdg Waziristan Dist 1926–29, Lt-Gen 1929, Col 2nd KEO Gurkha Rifles 1930–45, Gen 1932, CGS India 1931–34, ADC Gen to HM GEORGE V 1933–36, GOC-in-C N Cmd India 1934–36, Chm Roy Cancer Hosp; *d* unm 11 July 1949

3a Ernest, CMG, (1918), DSO (1916); *b* 16 April 1877; RN: WW I (despatches, Order Crown Belgium, Croix de Guerre), V-Adml, Naval ADC to HM GEORGE V 1926; *d* unm 29 Oct 1944

1a Hilda; *b* 20 Oct 1874; *d* unm 12 April 1929

2a Amy; *b* 15 Nov 1878; *m* 7 May 1906 Henry Wynyard Kaye, MD (*d* 21 April 1922), yr s of Joseph Kaye, Master Supreme Ct, and had issue

(3) Lewis; *b* 14 May 1844; MA Oxon; *m* 10 Sept 1872 Mary (*d* 15 April 1924), dau of Rev Lewis Deedes, Rector Bramfield, Herts, and *d* 31 May 1915, having had:

1a Roland Lewis; *b* 26 Aug 1874; *educ* Winchester and New Coll Oxford (BA); *m* June 1907 Mildred Gladys (*m* 2nd 4 Feb 1930 Lennox Chaplin Prendergast and *d* 1973), er dau of Rev Robert Peel Willock, Rector Warmington, and *d* 10 Aug 1918, leaving:

  1b Derek Roland; *b* 18 March 1908; *educ* Marlborough and Peterhouse Cambridge (BA 1929, MA 1933); housemaster and careers master Bryanston 1936–46, BSc Econ London 1943, Headmaster Monkton Combe Sch 1946–68, Chm Headmasters' Conf 1963 and 1964; *m* 11 Jan 1944 *Catharine Mary [Mrs Derek Wigram, The Old Schoolhouse, The Common, Swardeston, Norfolk NR14 8EB], dau of Very Rev William Ralph Inge, KCVO, DD, of Brightwell Manor, Berks, and *d* 6 Feb 1996, leaving:

    1c +Richard Inge [Richard Wigram Esq, Woodlynch, Branksomewood Rd, Fleet, Hants]; *b* 28 Oct 1944; *educ* Marlborough and Roy Coll of Art (MDes); industrial designer Mather & Platt, Manchester, sr ptnr Wigram Tivendale Assocs; *m* 1971 *Angela Patricia, dau of Capt M D Rahilly, RN, of Upper Westwood, Wilts, and has:

      1d +David Roland; *b* 1976

      1d *Helen Marguerite; *b* 14 July 1974

    1c *Janet Catharine Inge [Mrs Nicholas Miller, The Old Schoolhouse, The Common, Swardeston, Norfolk NR14 8EB]; *b* 3 July 1948; *m* 1975 *Nicholas Charles Miller, MA, MSc, and has:

      1d *Lydia Catharine; *b* 1980

      2d *Emily Joy; *b* 1984

  2b Mervyn Roland; *b* 31 Jan 1916; *educ* Marlborough and Peterhouse Cambridge (BA 1938, MA 1946); RAMC and Capt Intell Corps WW II, Schs Inspr 1959–78, Staff Inspr 1974–78, dir modern languages and housemaster Mill Hill Sch; *m* 3 April 1947 *Beryl Margaret [Mrs Mervyn Wigram, 27 Glasshouse Lane, Kenilworth, Warwicks CV8 2AH], yr dau of Howard Morriss, of Letchworth, and *d* 1994, leaving:

    1c +Christopher Edward Mervyn; *b* 2 March 1954; *educ* Monkton Combe; *m* 1982 *Susanne Ruth, dau of Paul Johannes Schnabel, of Grossbottwar, Germany, and has:

      1d +Michael Lake; *b* 1986

      1d *Jessica Jade; *b* 1983

      2d *Stephanie Rachel; *b* 1989

    1c *Rowena Margaret; *b* 17 Feb 1949; *m* 1978 *Francisco Muñoz Ramirez, of Ciudad Real, Spain

    2c *Diana Catharine; *b* 7 Jan 1956; *m* 1991 *Paul Francis McGuire

  1b *Nora Phyllis; *b* 22 April 1909; *m* 10 Aug 1939 Rev Kenneth Philpott Stewart, only s of Alan J Stewart, of Wimbledon

2a Oswald Lewis; *b* 27 July 1878; *educ* Marlborough; *m* 14 Jan 1914 Lucy Claire Elaine (*d* 16 July 1962), er dau of Rev Thomas Wilkinson Stephenson, and *d* 6 Oct 1960, leaving:

  1b Michael Lewis; *b* 29 April 1918; *educ* St Bee's Sch; Maj RA (TA); *m* 7 Sept 1950 Dorothea Mary (*d* 10 Oct 1964), er dau of Yorke Wood, of Georgeham, N Devon, and *d* 1983, leaving:

    1c +Anthony Lewis [Anthony Wigram Esq, 18 Spencer Gate, St Albans, Herts]; *b* 13 Aug 1953; *educ* St Lawrence Coll Ramsgate; *m* 1976 *Jennifer Hilary, dau of Albert Thorn, and has:

      1d +Robert Alexander Lewis; *b* 1981

      2d +Michael Anthony Yorke; *b* 1983

      3d +David Arthur Kennedy; *b* 1986

    1c *Mary Elaine [Mrs Anthony Tucker, 50 Woodcote Rd, Caversham, Reading RG4 7BB]; *b* 5 Dec 1951; *m* 1977 *Anthony Laurence Tucker and has:

      1d *John Michael; *b* 1982

      2d *Mark Andrew Laurence; *b* 1987

      1d *Sarah Frances; *b* 1979

  1b *Margaret Elaine

1a Grace; *d* unm 1900

2a Maud; *d* unm 27 June 1951

3a Ruth; *d* unm 9 July 1952

4a Joan; *d* unm 6 Feb 1932

1 Maria Catherine; *m* 7 Aug 1866 Rev Alfred Snell (*d* 6 April 1899), Rector Wickham Bishops, Essex, and *d* 19 Jan 1900, leaving issue

2 Anne; *b* 22 Feb 1796; *m* 29 Oct 1818 Rev Joseph Arkwright (*d* 23 Feb 1864), of Markhall, Essex, and Normanton Turville, Leics, and *d* 21 May 1863, leaving issue

3 Anna Maria; *b* 20 Jan 1812; *m* 11 April 1839 Ven Charles Maitland Long (*d* 6 Oct 1875), yr s of Samuel Long, of Carshalton, and n of 1st and last Baron Farnborough (*see* 1886 edn), and *d* 11 March 1856, leaving issue

WILBERFORCE

Creation: B. (LP, UK) 1964.

THE BARON WILBERFORCE, of City and Co of Kingston-upon-Hull (Sir Richard Orme Wilberforce, OBE (1944), CMG (1956), PC (1964)) [The Rt Hon The Lord Wilberforce OBE CMG PC, House of Lords, London SW1A 0PW]; *b* 11 March 1907; *educ* Winchester and New Coll Oxford (Fell All Souls 1932–, Hon

Fell New 1965 and Wolfson Colls 1991, Hon DCL 1967, High Steward 1967–90, Visitor Wolfson 1974–90 and Linacre Colls 1983–90); WW II: RA, Hon Brig; U-Sec Control Office Germany and Austria 1946–47; barrister Middle Temple 1932, QC 1954, Bencher 1961, High Court Judge Chancery 1961–64, ktd 1961, Ld Appeal in Ordinary 1964–82; Chm: Exec Cncl Internat Law Assoc 1966–88, Court Inquiry Power Workers' Dispute 1970; memb Permanent Ct Arbitration; Pres: Fédération Internationale du Droit Européen 1978, Appeal Tbnl Lloyd's 1983–87; Chllr Hull U 1978–94; Jt-Pres Anti Slavery Soc, Jt V-Pres RCM and David Davies Meml Inst; Hon LLD: London 1972, Bristol 1983; Hon FRCM; Hon Companion Roy Aeronautical Soc; Hon Memb Scottish Faculty Advocates 1978; author: *The Law of Restrictive Trade Practices* (1956); *m* 1947 *Yvette Marie, dau of Roger Lenoan, Judge Cour Cassation, of Paris, and has:

1 *Samuel Herbert; *b* 1951; *educ* Eton; *m* 1978 *Mrs Sarah L Scorer, dau of Arthur Allen, of Northampton

1 *Anne Catherine; *b* 1948; *m* 1975 *Lindsay Stuart Burn

Lineage: S WILBERFORCE; had:

RICHARD ORME, *cr* a **Baron**

WILCOX

Creation: B. (LP, UK) 18 Nov 1995.

THE BARONESS WILCOX, of Plymouth, Co Devon (Judith Ann Freeman) [The Baroness Wilcox, House of Lords, London SW1A 0PW]; *b* 19–; *educ* St Dunstan's Abbey Devon, St Mary's Convent Wantage, Plymouth Poly; fin dir Capstan Foods 1979–84, Chm: Channel Foods 1984–89, Morinie et Cie France 1991–94 (Pres Dir Gen Pecheries de la Morinie 1989-91), Nat Consumer Cncl 1990–96, Citizen's Charter Complaints Task Force 1993–95 and Ho Lds All-Party Gp Consumer Affrs and Trading Standards; memb: Advsy Panel Citizen's Charter 1992–97, Bd AA 1991–, Bd Inland Revenue 1992–95, Ld Chllr's Review of Ct Appeal 1996–, Tax Law Review Ctee and PLA 1993–; dir: Carpetright plc 1997–, Cadbury Schweppes plc 1997–; *m* 1st 1961 Keith Davenport and has a s; *m* 2nd 1986 Sir Malcolm George Wilcox, CBE (*d* 1986)

Lineage: JOHN FREEMAN; *m* Elsie — and had:

JUDITH ANN, *cr* a **Baroness**

WILKINSON

Arms: Quarterly, argent and vair sable and or, a cross gules, in the 1st and 4th quarters a lion rampant of the fourth, on a chief also of the fourth three mullets of the third. **Crest:** Issuant from a chaplet of roses argent, barbed and seeded proper, a demi-unicorn or.
Motto: *Honorem custode* ('Guard thy honour').
Creation: Bt. (UK) 8 Dec 1941.

SIR (DAVID) GRAHAM BROOK WILKINSON, 3RD BT, of Brook, Witley, Co Surrey [Sir Graham Wilkinson Bt]; *b* 18 May 1947; *s* f 1972; *educ* Millfield and Ch Ch Oxford; *m* 1st 26 July 1977 (*divorce* 1996) Sandra Caroline, dau of Dr Richard Rossdale, of Kensington; *m* 2nd 17 April 1998 *Mrs Hilary Griggs and by his 1st w has:

1 *Louise Caroline Sylvia; *b* 1979

2 *Tara Katherine Juliet; *b* 1982

Lineage: Sir George Henry Wilkinson, 1st Bt (UK), so *cr* 8 Dec 1941, KCVO (1956); *b* 20 July 1885 (s of George Henry Wilkinson, of Dulwich); City London: memb Court Common Cncl (Queenhithe Ward) 1923–33, Chm County Purposes Ctee 1928, Licensing Planning Ctee and City of London and Westminster Disablement Advsy Ctee, Alderman (Aldersgate Ward) 1933, Sheriff 1931–32, memb Employment Ctee 1928–32 (Chm 1942–47) and LCC 1937–43, Lt, Ld Mayor 1940–41; Govr Freemason's, St Bartholomew's, St Thomas's and King's Coll Hosps 1929–45, memb: Archbp Canterbury's Ctee on Ecclesiastical Commrs as Ground Landlords 1938, Bp of London's Commn on City Churches 1941–46 and YMCA War Emergency Ctee 1940–45, Chm: Min Home Security Deep Shelter Ctee 1941–44, King George VI National Memorial Fund, Govrs Nat Corp Care of Old People, London and Home Counties Conciliation Bd Cinematograph

Industry 1941–46 and Nat Arbitration Bd Cinematograph and Theatrical Employees; Govr Christ's Hosp Sch, Roy Holloway Coll 1941–47; Tstee Morden Coll 1943–47, Tstee and Treas Ld Mayor's Air Raid Distress Fund, Dep Chm and Tstee King George VI Fndn and WVS Residential Clubs and Stationers' and Paper Mfrs' Provident Soc, Dep Chm Ld Mayor's UN Appeal for Children, V-Pres Roy Bridewell and Bethlem Hosps and Roy Gen Dispensary Cncl St Bartholomew's Medical Coll, LLD London 1957, KStJ, Grand Cross Order Phoenix Greece, ktd 1932; m 11 Sept 1912 Freda Dorothy, CStJ, dau of Robert Volland, of Dulwich, and had:

1 (LEONARD) DAVID (Sir), **2nd Bt**

2 *Eileen [Mrs John Sidey, 28 Hathaway Common, New Canaan, CT 06840, USA]; b 17 March 1916; m 1 March 1941 *John MacNaughton Sidey, DSO, er s of John Sidey, of Collingwood House, Exeter, and has had:

(1) *Ian MacNaughton; b 19 July 1947; educ Marlborough; BSc (Eng), MBA; m 17 Jan 1970 *Christina Willing Ashdown and has:

1a *Jamie MacNaughton; b 19 Sept 1975

2a *Guy Xavier; b 4 Sept 1979

(1) Jennifer Anne; b 4 Jan 1944; d 8 Feb 1954

Sir GEORGE d 27 June 1967; his only s,

Sir (Leonard) David Wilkinson, 2nd Bt, DSC (1943); b 18 Jan 1920; educ Eton and Ch Ch Oxford; joined RNVR 1939, WW II: cmded 801 Sqdn 1944 and 803 1st Roy Canadian Naval Air Sqdn, Lt-Cdr 1944; Hon Treas Ex-Servs Welfare Soc 1947–56, memb Cncl for Music in Hosps 1948–54, Hon Dir Thermega 1947–58, Govr Bridewell Roy Hosp 1958–72, Assist Dir-Gen St John Ambulance Assoc 1964–68, KStJ (memb Chapter Gen); m 20 July 1946 (divorce 1967) Sylvia Ruby Eva Anne, only dau of Prof Bosley Alan Rex Gater, of Greatham Mill, Liss, Hants, and d 1 Nov 1972, leaving:

1 Sir (DAVID) GRAHAM BROOK WILKINSON, **3rd and present Bt**

1 *(Sylvia) Davinia Gay [Marchesa Grimaldi, Tyne Hall, Bembridge, IoW PO35 5NH]; b 23 June 1948; m 1978 *Peter Martin Gort Beaufort Grimaldi, FRCS, 16th Marchese Grimaldi, of, only s of Philip R B Grimaldi, 15th Marchese (d 1983), and has:

(1) *Alicia Anne Davinia; b 19 Dec 1979

(2) *Carina Rose Anne; b 8 Sept 1981

(3) *Sophia Anne Camilla; b 7 June 1987

WILLIAMS of Bodelwyddan

Arms: Argent two foxes counter-salient in saltire gules, a crescent for difference. **Crest:** An eagle displayed or. **Motto:** *Y Cadarn ar cyfrwys* ('Strong and crafty'). **Creation:** Bt. (GB) 24 July 1798.

SIR LAWRENCE HUGH WILLIAMS, 9TH BT, of Bodelwyddan, Denbighs [Sir Lawrence Williams Bt, Old Parciau, Marianglas, Anglesey LL73 8PH]; b 25 Aug 1929; s half-bro 1995; educ RNC Dartmouth; Capt RM Korea 1951, Cyprus 1955, Nr East 1956 (ret 1964); farmer, High Sheriff Anglesey 1970, Lt-Cdr RNXS 1965–87, chm Parciau Caravans Ltd 1964–, underwriting memb Lloyd's 1977–97; m 13 Sept 1952 *Sara Margaret Helen, 3rd dau of Prof Sir Harry Platt, 1st Bt, of Rusholme (see 1970 edn), and has:

1 *Emma Louise; b 5 June 1961; BA, ACII; m 1988 (divorce 1998) Radcliffe Percy Royds and has:

(1) *Harry Lawrence Percy; b 26 Jan 1991

(2) *Jack Michael William; b 25 July 1992

(1) *Mollie Isabella Rose; b 22 May 1995

2 *Antonia Margaret; b 4 March 1963; m 12 Sept 1998 *Antonin Leif Peter Markutza Svensson, s of Gothleij Svensson, of Sweden

Lineage: Sir WILLIAM WILLIAMS, 1st Bt (see WILLIAMS-WYNN, Bt); had a 2nd s:

JOHN WILLIAMS, of Chester; barrister; m Catherine, dau of Sir Hugh Owen, 1st Bt (qv), and had an est surv s:

JOHN WILLIAMS, of Bodelwyddan; Ch Justice Brecon, Glam and Radnor 1741; m Elizabeth, dau and heiress of Henry Bennett, and d 1788, having had:

BENNETT WILLIAMS; b 1735; m 1758 Sarah (d 18 Aug 1824), dau of Roger Hesketh, of Rossall, Lancs, and dvp 1786, leaving:

1 JOHN (Sir), **1st Bt**

2 William WILLIAMS later WILLIAMS-EDWARDS (Rev); Rector St George, Denbighs; m Jennett, dau of Edward Edwards, of Cerrigllewydion, Llanyns, Denbighs, and dsp

3 Roger Hesketh Fleetwood; m Elizabeth Statham and had issue

1 Emma; m Rev Hugh Davies-Griffith (d 20 July 1802), of Caer-Rhûn Hall, Conway, Caernarvs, and d 4 March 1858, leaving issue

2 Margaret

BENNETT WILLIAMS' est s,

Sir John Williams, 1st Bt (GB), so cr 24 July 1798; High Sheriff Flints 1794; m 21 Oct 1791 Margaret (d 6 March 1835), dau and heiress of Hugh Williams, of Tyfry, Anglesey, and d 9 Oct 1830, having had, with two other daus (d unm):

1 Sir JOHN HAY WILLIAMS later WILLIAMS-HAY (roy licence 1842), **2nd Bt**; b 9 Jan 1794; m 8 Sept 1842 Sarah Elizabeth (d 8 Aug 1876), only dau of 1st Earl Amherst (see 1970 edn also AMHERST OF HACKNEY, B), and d 10 Sept 1859, leaving:

(1) Margaret Maria; m 14 Jan 1868 Sir Edmund Hope Verney, 3rd Bt, of Claydon House (qv), and d 7 Oct 1930, leaving issue

(2) Maude Sarah; m 8 June 1870 Frederic William Verney (see VERNEY, Bt, of Claydon House) and d 28 Aug 1937, leaving issue

2 **Sir Hugh Williams, 3rd Bt**; b 8 Jan 1802; m 16 April 1843 his cousin Henrietta Charlotte (d 28 May 1878), only dau of Sir Watkin Williams-Wynn, 5th Bt (qv), and d 10 May 1876, having had, with two other daus (d unm):

(1) **Sir William Grenville Williams, 4th Bt**, JP (Denbighs), JP, DL (Flints); b 30 May 1844; Capt 1st Life Gds, Col Montgomeryshire Yeo, High Sheriff Flints 1883; m 16 Sept 1884 Elinor Harriet Hurt (d 30 April 1894), only dau of William Willoughby Hurt Sitwell (see SITWELL, Bt), and d 28 Aug 1904, having had:

1a **Sir William Willoughby Williams, 5th Bt**; b 11 Feb 1888; m 1st 29 April 1912 (divorce 1922) Violet Henrietta, yst dau of Thomas Hector Powell, of Singapore; m 2nd 8 March 1925 Mildred Georgina (m 2nd 1 Sept 1939 Col Philip William French Brown, s of William Brown, of Salisbury, Wilts, and d 20 July 1962), dau of Henry Collins, of Dulwich, and d 18 Jan 1932, leaving by his 1st w:

1b *Freda Violet [Mrs William Hodgson, Box 1914, Gaberone, Botswana]; b 26 Sept 1913; m 1st 6 Feb 1937 (divorce 1950) Sydney Walton Hinde (d 1967), BSA Police; m 2nd 16 July 1959 *William Vere Hodgson and by her 1st husb has:

1c *Richard Courtney Buckley [Richard Hinde Esq, Madilla Farm, Centenary, Zimbabwe]; b 14 Dec 1939; m 1st 1961 (divorce 1977) Sally Makins and has:

1d *Stephen Ross; b 1962; m 1994 *Noirin Fitzpatrick

2d *Craig Sydney; b 1964; m 1989 *Amanda Dalkin and has:

1e *Darren; b 1991

1e *Tamsan; b 1993

1d *Felicity Anne; b 1957; m 1992 *Glen Mirams and has:

1e *Shelby; b 1993

1c (cont.) Richard Hinde m 2nd 1978 *Jeanette Kramburger and by her has:

3d *Glen Richard; b 1979

4d *Douglas Patrick; b 1981

4d *Patrick Christopher; b 1985

1c Deirdre Penelope Anne [Mrs Basil Wakefield, Piedmont, P/Bag 915, Bindura, Zimbabwe]; b 20 Jan 1938; m 5 July 1958 Basil Birkbeck Wakefield (see WAKEFIELD, Bt) and was k by terrorists 1979, leaving issue

2c *Patricia Rosamund [Mrs Patrick Hyde-Smith, 25 Belfast Rd, Emerald Hill, Harare, Zimbabwe]; b 14 May 1941; m 9 April 1961 *Patrick David Spaid Hyde-Smith, s of Samuel Newburgh Hyde-Smith, of London, and has:

1d *Vaughan Christopher; b 16 May 1962; m 1989 *Sandra Egeland and has:

1e *Ryan Patrick; b 1992

2e *Craig; b 20 June 1996

2d *Brent Richard; b 5 Feb 1964; m June 1995 *Joanna Banks

1d *Natasha Jane; b 1967

2d *Samantha; b 1971

3c *Caroline Bryer; b 6 Sept 1946; m 1st 1970 Emmanuel Riez (d 1971); m 2nd 1981 (divorce 1992) William Rooke and by him has:

1d *Amber Zuleika; b 1987

2a **Sir Hugh Grenville Williams, 6th Bt**, MC and bar; b 26 March 1889; educ Malvern; KRRC and Montgomeryshire Yeo WW I (despatches); MLA Gwanda S Rhodesian 1933–61; m 1st 1914 (divorce 1921) Charlotte Kebbell; m 2nd 1922 Maud Beatrice Fraser Marie (d 26 Sept 1966), dau of Comte de Marillac St Julien, and d 9 Dec 1961, having by her had:

1b Hugh Richard Grenville; b 5 March 1927; m 30 Oct 1948 Jaqueline Ferney, dau of John Davidson, of Livingstone, Zambia, and d 11 March 1952, leaving:

1c *Jennifer Mary; b 28 May 1949; m 1st 19– E Stead; m 2nd 19– *John Manning

2c *Melanie Jane; b 14 Sept 1950; m 19– *J Krienke

3c *Richardyne Megan; b 10 Oct 1952; m 19– *D Van Emmenis

3a Francis Idris; b 17 Aug 1891; d unm 10 Sept 1910

4a Owen Arthur; b 19 April 1894; d 21 March 1895

1a Elinor Henrietta; b 7 June 1886; m 12 Oct 1909 Col Lawrence Williams, OBE, and had issue (see below)

2a Megan Louise; b 30 March 1890; drowned Rhuddlan, nr Rhyl, 20 Feb 1902

3a Olwen Harriet; b 6 March 1893; drowned Rhuddlan 20 Feb 1902

(2) Watkin Herbert (Rt Rev); *b* 22 Aug 1845; *educ* Westminster and Ch Ch Oxford (BA 1870, MA 1872); DD, Vicar Bodelwyddan 1872–92, Canon and Archdeacon St Asaph 1889–92, Dean St Asaph 1892–99, Bp Bangor 1899–1924; *m* 30 April 1879 Alice (*d* 15 Jan 1937), dau of Gen Henry Monckton (*see* GALWAY, V), and *dsp* 19 Nov 1944

(2) Robert ap Hugh, of Plâs Llwyn On, Anglesey, JP, DL; *b* 25 Oct 1849; Hon Lt-Col Roy Anglesey Militia, High Sheriff 1884; *d* 1898

(3) Owen John, JP (Denbighs); *b* 16 Nov 1850; Capt Denbighs Yeo Cav; *d* unm 4 Oct 1908

(4) Charles Henry Bennett, of Eyrl, St Asaph, JP (Salop and Flints); *b* 8 March 1854; Capt and Hon Maj 4th Bn Oxon LI Zulu War 1879 (medal with clasp); *m* 18 April 1882 Hon Mabel Emma Boscawen, dau of 6th Viscount Falmouth (*qv*), and *d* 17 Sept 1944, having had, with another dau (*d* young):

1a Evelyn Hugh Watkin, DSO (1918), DL (Flints); *b* 21 March 1884; Maj 10th Hus, Hon Col 5th Bn Roy Welch Fus WW I (despatches); *m* 19 July 1910 Florence Jane, only dau of G A Brett, of Ryde, IOW, and *d* 9 Aug 1934, leaving:

1b *Gwenllian Elizabeth Anne; *b* 26 June 1911; *m* 1st 9 Dec 1935 Cdr Christopher Ryle WOOD later WILLIAMS (deed poll 28 Feb 1936), RN; *m* 2nd 1948 Campbell Sherston SMITH later WILLIAMS (name by deed poll and WILLIAMS arms by roy licence 27 May 1949), s of Herbert Smith, and has by her 1st husb:

1c *Jane; *b* 1936

2c *Prudence; *b* 1938; *m* 1960 *David Turnbull and has:

1d *Christopher Neil; *b* 1962

1d *Catherine Fiona; *b* 1965

1a Mary Nesta Harriet; *b* 31 Jan 1883; *m* 20 June 1916 Lt-Col Charles Ralph Borlase Wingfield, 3rd Bn KSLI (*d* 1 Feb 1923), of Onslow, Salop, and *d* 15 June 1947, leaving issue

(1) Henrietta Margaret; *m* 1 Feb 1866 Edmund Peel (*d* 27 March 1903), of Bryn-y-Pys, and *d* 29 July 1885, leaving issue

(2) Edith Sarah; *m* 30 May 1869 Salusbury Kynaston Mainwaring (*d* 22 Aug 1895), of Oteley, Salop, and *d* 6 Sept 1920, leaving issue

3 William; *b* 20 Sept 1805; *m* 1st 30 June 1855 Arabella (*dsp* 1867), yst dau of Rev George Thomas Pretyman, LLB, Chllr Lincoln; *m* 2nd 3 Aug 1871 Marian (*d* 18 April 1920), est dau of Gen William Henry Scott, and *d* 18 Aug 1892, leaving by her:

(1) Lawrence, OBE (1938), of Parciau, Marianglas, Anglesey, JP, DL (Anglesey); *b* 25 April 1876; *educ* Harrow and Trin Coll Cambridge; Col DCLI Boer War 1901, WWs I (despatches, Col) and II; Alderman Anglesey CC (Chm 1935–37); *m* 1st 1897 Catherine Elizabeth Anne (*d* 1 Feb 1905), dau of Col George Phibbs, and had:

1a **Sir Reginald Lawrence William Williams, 7th Bt**, MBE (1945), ED; *b* 3 May 1900; *educ* Malvern; mining engr; W African Engrs RWAFF WW II; Cmdt Army Leave Station Nigeria 1946–48 with rank of Maj, High Sheriff Caernarvs 1968; *m* 15 Aug 1936 Elinor Meriol Enriqueta, only dau of Frederic Pelham Trevor, DCLI, of Anglesey, and *d* 30 Jan 1971, leaving:

1b *Laurelie Meriol Winifrida; *b* 20 July 1939; *m* 14 Sept 1968 *Robert Bayley Emilius Laurie (*see* LAURIE, Bt)

2b Juliet Elizabeth Rosamund; *b* 28 Jan 1942; *m* 18 June 1966 *Brian Derek Price [Brian Price Esq, 52 Hazlewell Rd, Putney, London SW15 6LR], er s of Gp/Capt Derek Price, and *d* 22 July 1997, leaving:

1c *Edmund Hugh Owain; *b* 16 Jan 1969

2c *Henry William Frederick; *b* 11 Dec 1973

2a **Sir Francis John Watkin Williams, 8th Bt**, QC 1951, JP (Denbighs 1951); *b* 24 Jan 1905; *educ* Malvern and Trin Hall Cambridge (MA); W/Cdr RAFVR; barrister Middle Temple 1928, High Sheriff Denbighs 1957 and Anglesey 1963, Dep Chm: Anglesey 1949–60 (Chm 1960–95), Cheshire 1952–95 and Flints QS 1953–61 (Chm 1961–95); Recorder: Birkenhead 1950–95, Chester 1958–95, Chllr Diocese of St Asaph 1966; *m* 23 July 1932 Brenda Beryl, JP, yr dau of Sir John Jarvis, 1st Bt (*see* 1963 edn), and *d* 3 Jan 1995, leaving:

1b *Jennifer Frances Ann; *b* 27 May 1933; *m* 1st 20 Nov 1954 (*divorce* 1975) Lt-Col Ivan Wise Lynch, RGJ, of Woking, Surrey, only s of Percy Wise Lynch; *m* 2nd 1979 *Maj Basil Hugh Philips Heaton, MBE, of Rhûal, Mold, Clwyd, and by her 1st husb has:

1c *Francis William Adrian [Francis Lynch Esq, Lower Grove Cottage, Little Horwood, Bucks]; *b* 3 April 1957; *m* 1982 *Julia Mary Battram and has:

1d *James Lawrence Francis; *b* 1983

2d *Nicholas John Richard; *b* 1985

2c *William John Ivan [William Lynch Esq, 13 Atheldene Rd, London SW18 3BN]; *b* 31 May 1965; *m* 1990 *Charlotte, dau of John Michael Howard, of Cramond Ho, Pirbright, Surrey

1b (cont.) Lt-Col and Mrs Lynch also adopted:

*Amanda-Jayne Charlotte; *b* 10 Feb 1961

2b *Tessa Gillian Rosamond, MBE [Mrs Tessa Preece MBE, Plas Llanddyfnan, Talwrn, Llangefni, Anglesey LL77 7TH]; *b* 27 Oct 1935; High Sheriff Gwynedd 1990; *m* 20 Sept 1958 (*divorce* 1996) Michael John Stewart Preece, est s of Lt-Col James Preece, OBE, TD, of Jersey, and has:

1c *James Francis Stewart [James Preece Esq, The Gate House, Chelford, Cheshire SK11 9AH]; *b* 28 Sept 1964; *m* 1990 *Annabelle Katherine, est dau of John Hartley Beckett, of Belton, Whitchurch, Salop, and has:

1d *Barnaby James Francis; *b* 1997

1d *Daisy Angela Tessa; *b* 1993

2d *Katie Angharad; *b* 1995

2c *Hugh Michael Stewart; *b* 25 Oct 1969

2b (cont.) Mr and Mrs Preece also adopted:

*Emily Margaret [Mrs Christopher Foden, 108 Ramsden Rd, London SW12 8RB]; *b* 28 Nov 1961; *m* 1993 *Christopher Starkie Foden and has:

1d *Harrison Francis Starkey; *b* 1996

1d *Madeline Tessa; *b* 1993

*Rosamond Alice [Mrs Robert Woolf, Rose Cottage, Gt Shelford, Cambs CI32 5EH]; *b* 12 Aug 1963; *m* 1990 *Robert James Woolf and has:

1d *Sophie Antonia; *b* 1995

3b *Antonia ('Anna') Kathleen Brenda; *b* 31 May 1939; *m* 1st 9 July 1960 (*divorce* 1974) Timothy Roy Henry Kimber (*see* KIMBER, Bt) and has issue; *m* 2nd June 1974 *Timothy G Emanuel and by him has:

1c *Harry Sebastian; *b* 1975

4b *Victoria Elizabeth Alice [Mrs Andrew Paterson, Kirk Stile, Town End, Radnage, Bucks HP14 4DY]; *b* 22 Feb 1944; *m* 19 June 1965 *Andrew Walter Loraine Paterson, yr s of Harry Douglas Loraine Paterson, of Woodcote Ho, Windlesham, Surrey, and has:

1c *Harry Adrian Loraine; *b* 13 Sept 1968

2c *Douglas Watkin Loraine; *b* 1972

1c *Lucinda Mona Alice; *b* 15 Oct 1966; *m* 1990 *James Frederick Foster and has:

1d *Sophie Jessie; *b* 5 Dec 1997

2c *Jessie Brenda Antonia; *b* 26 Sept 1970; *m* 1997 *Duncan James Sillence

1a Mona Rosamond Alice; *m* 30 Sept 1920 (*divorce* 1933) Maj Gerald Hartley Lees, MC, RWF, only s of Hartley Lees, of Hendregyda, Abergele, Flints, and *d* 18 Oct 1956, leaving issue

2a *Violet Kathleen Mary [Mrs Thomas Pearson, Meadow Croft, Cae Mawr, Beaumaris, Anglesey]; *b* 1902; *m* 21 April 1926 Lt-Cdr Thomas Arthur Pearson, RNVR (*d* 3 May 1974 aged 86), only s of Arthur Pearson, of Soldiers Point, Holyhead, and has:

1b *David Arthur [David Pearson Esq, Banastre Cottage, Parkgate South, Wirral, Cheshire]; *b* 10 Sept 1931; *educ* Harrow; *m* 1st 29 Oct 1960 (*divorce* 1977) Carolyn Frances, est dau of Frank Hilary Minoprio, of Hessle Well Ho, Heswall, Merseyside; *m* 2nd 1981 *Gillian Mary, dau of G Buckley, of Wirral, and by his 1st w has:

1c *Charles David; *b* 2 Aug 1961; *m* 1989 *Zöe Louise Hancox

1c *Joanna Mary; *b* 17 Sept 1963

2c *Lucy Alexandra; *b* 25 Feb 1968

2b *(Thomas) Martin [Martin Pearson Esq, 40 Rutland Gate, London SW7]; *b* 18 Aug 1933; *educ* Harrow

(1) (cont.) Col Lawrence Williams *m* 2nd 2 Oct 1909 his cousin Elinor Henrietta (*d* 1980), only surv dau of **Sir William Grenville Williams, 4th Bt** (*see* above), and *d* 6 June 1958, leaving by her:

3a Sir LAWRENCE HUGH WILLIAMS, **9th and present Bt**

3a Penelope Lawrence; *b* 24 June 1925; *m* 31 Aug 1950 Maj Thomas William Edward Corrigan, MBE, Queen's Bays (*d* 25 Aug 1961), s of Thomas William Edward Corrigan, of The Beacon, Tiverton, Devon, and *d* 8 April 1992, leaving:

1b *Henrietta Louise; *b* 10 Sept 1954

(1) Margaret; *b* 4 July 1874; *m* 24 Oct 1894 William Edward Southwell Sotheby (*d* 20 March 1950), of Menaifron, Dwyran, Anglesey, est s of Adml Sir Edward Sotheby, KCB, and *d* 21 April 1922, leaving issue

(2) Rosamond; *b* 9 April 1877; *d* unm 28 Feb 1957

1 Margaret; *m* 10 March 1829 16th Baron Willoughby de Broke (*qv*) and *dsp* 3 Aug 1880

2 Mary Elizabeth; *m* 2 Dec 1823 George Lucy (*see* RAMSAY-FAIRFAX-LUCY, Bt) and *d* 15 March 1890

3 Ellen; *m* 14 Feb 1832 Hon William Owen Stanley (*see* STANLEY OF ALDERLEY, SHEFFIELD and B) and *d* 24 Nov 1876

WILLIAMS of Bridehead

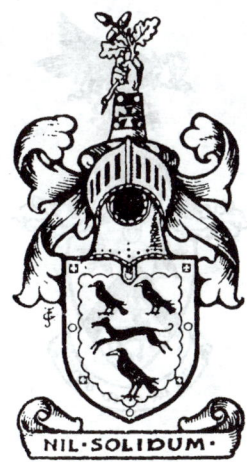

Arms: Argent a greyhound between three Cornish choughs sable, beaked and membered purpure; on a bordure engrailed gules, four crosses formée or between as many bezants. **Crest:** A dexter arm couped, the sleeve barry of four sable and argent, charged with a cross formée per fesse counterchanged between four bezants, the hand proper grasping a branch of oak vert, fructed or.
Motto: *Nil solidum* ('There is nothing permanent').
Creation: Bt. (UK) 9 Feb 1915.

SIR (ROBERT) PHILIP NATHANIEL WILLIAMS, 4TH BT, of Bridehead, Dorset, JP (W Dorset 1992), DL (Dorset 1995) [Sir Philip Williams Bt JP DL, Bridehead, Littlebredy, Dorset DT2 9JA]; *b* 3 May 1950; *s f* 1970; *educ* Marlborough and St Andrews (MA); *m* 1979 *Catherine Margaret Godwin, dau of Canon C G R Pouncey, of Church Walk, Littlebredy, and has:

1 +DAVID ROBERT MARK; *b* 31 Oct 1980
1 *Sarah Catherine Anne; *b* 23 July 1982
2 *Margaret Jane Louise; *b* 1 March 1984
3 *Clare Elizabeth Philippa; *b* 20 Aug 1987

Lineage: JOHN WILLIAMS, of Dorchester; High Sheriff Dorset *c* 1508; had:

JOHN WILLIAMS, of Herringston, Dorset, which he bought 1513 from Sir William Filiol; *b* 1473; *m* 1st Margery, dau and coheir of Thomas Baker, of Lyme, Dorset; *m* 2nd Alice, dau of Alexander Cheney, of Isle of Sheppey, Kent, and widow of Sir Thomas de la Lynde, of Winterbourne Clenston, Dorset, and *d* 1549; his er s by his 1st w:

ROBERT WILLIAMS, of Herringston; *b* 1509; High Sheriff Dorset 1567; *m* 1st Anne, dau of Henry Trenchard, of Lychet, and had an only child (Jane, *m* Robert Bingham; *see* LUCAN, E)); *m* 2nd Anne, dau of Sir Thomas de la Lynde abovementioned, and *d* 1569, having had by her (with three daus):

Sir JOHN WILLIAMS, of Herringston; *b* 1545; High Sheriff Dorset *c* 1582 and *c* 1592, MP Dorset 1603; *m* Eleanor, dau of Henry Uvedale, of More Critchel, Dorset, and had, with an est s and two yst sons:

ROBERT WILLIAMS; *m* Mary (*d* 1630), dau and heiress of John Argenton, of Shitterton, Bere Regis, Dorset, and *d* 1631; his est s:

LEWIS WILLIAMS, of Shitterton; *b* 1604; *m* Honor, dau of Robert Grove, of Ferne, Wilts, and *d* 1656; his est s:

ROBERT WILLIAMS, of Herringston, which he inherited on the extinction of the er branch of the family descended from his ggf Sir JOHN's est s; *m* 1638 Margery (*d* 1661), only dau of John Browne, of Frampton, and *d* 1697; his only s:

JOHN WILLIAMS, of Herringston; *b* 1660; Maj; *m* 1678 Margaret, dau and heiress of Thomas Fulford (s and heir of Thomas Fulford, of Thorn St Margaret, Somerset, 3rd s of Sir Thomas Fulford, of Gt Fulford, Devon), and *d* 1722, having had, with an er s (John, *b* 1680, *m* Jane, dau of Humphrey Sydenham, of Combe, Somerset, and *dvp* (*k* Spain 1703), being ancestor of the WILLIAMSes of Herringston, heirs male of the family) and five daus:

ROBERT WILLIAMS, of Charminster, Dorset; *b* 1694; *m* 1st Frances (*dsp*), dau of Rev Henry Hooton, Vicar Puddletown; *m* 2nd Anne Shaw, of Manchester, and by her had, with three daus:

1 John, of Avery Hatch; *m* Anne, dau of William Guy, of Wellclose Sq, London, and *d* 1774, leaving issue
2 Thomas, of Warfield Lodge, Berks; *m* Elizabeth Topsell, of Bracknell, Berks, and *d* 1793; ancestor of WILLIAMSes of Rucham Hall, Northants
3 George, of Bath; *m* Mary Beer, of Lyme, Dorset, and had issue
4 ROBERT
5 Stephen, of London; Dir HEIC; *m* Charlotte (*d* 1813), dau of Rev Sir Hadley D'Oyly, 5th Bt (*qv*), and *d* 1805, leaving issue

The 4th s,

ROBERT WILLIAMS, of Bridehead, Dorset, and Moor Park, Herts; *b* 1739; MP Dorchester, High Sheriff Dorset, banker in London; *m* 27 Oct 1764 Jane (*d* 8 Oct 1841 aged 101), dau of Francis Chassereau, and had, with two other daus:

1 ROBERT
2 William, of Belmont, Surrey; *b* 28 March 1774; MP Weymouth and Melcombe Regis; *m* 30 Nov 1797 Anne (*d* 19 April 1855), er dau of John Rashleigh (*see* RASHLEIGH, Bt), and *d* Feb 1839; ancestor of the WILLIAMSes of Woolland, Dorset

1 Harriet; *m* 24 May 1808 Sir John Colman Rashleigh, 1st Bt (*qv*), and *d* 7 July 1831, having had issue

ROBERT WILLIAMS *d* 17 Jan 1814; his er s,

ROBERT WILLIAMS, of Bridehead, JP, DL Dorset; *b* 11 Feb 1767; MP Dorchester, banker in London and Dorchester, London Alderman, Sheriff 1796–97; *m* 28 Aug 1794 Frances (*d* 25 Sept 1841), yst dau of John Turner, of Putney, and *d* 10 March 1847, leaving, with a dau (Frances, *m* 15 Sept 1835 Arthur Henry Dyke ACLAND later TROYTE (*see* ACLAND, Bt, of Columb John), and *d* 4 Aug 1856, leaving issue):

ROBERT WILLIAMS, of Bridehead, JP, DL Dorset; *b* 23 Jan 1811; banker, High Sheriff 1855, MP Dorchester; *m* 1st 7 Sept 1847 Mary Anne (*d* 1 Sept 1855), dau of Rev John William Cunningham, Vicar Harrow; *m* 2nd 18 Nov 1858 Emily Maria (*dsp* 10 March 1896), est dau of 9th Earl of Leven and (6th Earl of) Melville (*qv*), and *d* 7 June 1890, leaving by his 1st w, with a yr s (John Arthur, *b* 29 Aug 1849, *d* 8 Dec 1892) and three daus (*d* young or unm):

Sir Robert Williams, 1st Bt (UK), so *cr* 9 Feb 1915; *b* 15 June 1848; Col 4th Bn Dorset Regt, CA, MP (C) W Dorset 1895–1922, Chm Public Accounts Ctee 1907–19, Lt City London, dir Williams Deacon's Bank; *m* 7 Sept 1869 Rosa Walker (*d* 26 Dec 1916), dau of Nathaniel Simes, of Strood Park, Horsham, and had:

1 Robert; *b* 10 Sept 1874; *d* 22 May 1881
2 John Nathaniel; *b* 24 Jan 1878; MA Oxon; Capt 4th Bn Dorset Regt, in ranks of NZ contingent WW I; *ka* Gallipoli 25 April 1915
3 PHILIP FRANCIS CUNNINGHAM (Sir), **2nd Bt**
1 Mary Anne Frances; *m* 2 Jan 1896 Rt Rev John Wordsworth, DD, LLD (*d* 16 Aug 1911), Bp Salisbury, s of Rt Rev Christopher Wordsworth, Bp Lincoln, and *d* 2 Sept 1938, leaving issue
2 Margaret Emily Jane; *m* 23 Oct 1894 Rt Rev Frederic Wallis, DD (*d* 24 June 1928), Bp Wellington, NZ, 1895–1911, Archdeacon Wilts 1911–12 and Sherborne 1916–19, s of Rev Joseph Wallis, and *d* 28 Feb 1967
3 Rosa Ruth; *d* an infant
4 Rachel Sophia; *m* 6 Aug 1914 Col Henry John Madocks, RWF (*ka* 25 Sept 1915), of Old Basing Ho, Basingstoke, s of Henry Robarts Madocks, of Llay Hall, Denbighs, and *d* 11 Sept 1963
5 Dorothy Rhoda; *m* 4 March 1924 Maj Robert Leatham Barclay, CBE (*d* 22 May 1939), of Gaston Ho, Bishops Stortford, Herts, and Higham, Suffolk, and had issue

Sir ROBERT *d* 15 April 1943; his only surv s,

Sir Philip Francis Cunningham Williams, 2nd Bt; *b* 6 July 1884; *educ* Eton and Trin Coll Oxford; High Sheriff Dorset 1949; *m* 1 Oct 1908 Margaret (*d* 5 Sept 1948), dau of Sir Cuthbert Edgar Peek, 2nd Bt (*qv*), and had:

1 DAVID PHILIP (Sir), **3rd Bt**
2 (Robert) Mark Edgar; *b* 25 April 1913; *educ* Radley; *m* 10 Oct 1942 *Juliet Susan Harriet [Mrs Mark Williams, 5 Winters Lane, Portesham, Dorset], only dau of Cdr Kenneth Berkeley Mackenzie Churchill, RN, of Muston Manor, Dorchester, and *d* 22 Feb 1969, leaving:
  (1) +Robert Norrie]; *b* 21 Aug 1943; *educ* Radley; *m* 3 July 1971 *Nesta Rosemary, yr dau of T Stewart Bell, of Stretton, Broadway, Llandrindod Wells, and has:
    1a +Andrew John Mark; *b* 1975
    1a *Ann Margaret; *b* 1973
  (2) +John Philip Mackenzie; *b* 25 March 1947; *educ* Radley; *m* 1978 *Louise Beverly, dau of David Douglas, of Vancouver, and has:
    1a +Jonathan Mark; *b* 1988
    1a *Hayley Michelle; *b* 1992
  (1) *Marcia Jane [Mrs Robert Machin, Grey Cottage, Askerswell, Dorset]; *b* 27 Aug 1945; *m* 1st 1977 (*divorce* 1979) Christopher Maples; *m* 2nd 1983 *Robert Machin and by him has:
    1a *Luke Robert; *b* 1983
    2a *Mark George; *b* 1984
    1a *Sarah Ann; *b* 1984
3 Nathaniel Roger Cunningham; *b* 30 June 1917; *educ* Blundell's; late S Rhodesia Regt; *d* 24 Jan 1979
1 Ann Margaret Augusta; *b* 22 Oct 1910; *m* 3 Nov 1932 (*divorce* 1966) Edward Fox Gundry, s of Edward Pearkes Gundry, and *d* 10 April 1982, leaving issue
2 Mary Felicity Rosa; *b* 13 Dec 1911; *m* 29 April 1939 V-Adml Sir William Godfrey Crawford, KCB, DSC [V-Adml Sir William Crawford KBE DSC, Broadlands, Whitchurch Canonicorum, Bridport, Dorset], 2nd s of Henry Edward Venner Crawford, JP, of Wyld Cour, Hawkchurch, Devon, and *d* 11 April 1995, leaving:
  (1) *Edward Philip; *b* 29 April 1940; *educ* Gordonstoun; BSA Police Zimbabwe; *m* 21 Aug 1965 *Rosamond Helen, dau of W Frank Wynne, of Greensykes, Ruwa, Zimbabwe, and has:
    1a *Alastair; *b* 1974
    1a *Heather; *b* 1968
    2a *Felicity; *b* 1970
  (2) *(David) Alexander; *b* 1 Feb 1942; *educ* Allhallows; *m* 29 June 1968 *Penelope Ann, yst dau of Cdr Claude Everard John Streatfield, OBE, DL, of Denhay, Broadoak, Bridport, Dorset, and has:
    1a *David William; *b* 1970; *m* 11 July 1998 *Sophie Umney
    2a *Mark Jonathan; *b* 1972
    3a *Richard Henry; *b* 1977

(3) *(Michael) James; *b* 28 May 1951; *educ* Radley and London U; m 1974 *Margaret Cotton and has:
   1a *Robert; *b* 1982
   1a *Louise; *b* 1979
(1) *Prunella Marion Pharazyn; *b* 1 Feb 1942; *m* 16 Oct 1965 *Neboysha Ranko Brashich, er s of Dr Ranko Brashich, of Flushing, NY, and has:
   1a *Alexander; *b* 1970
   2a *Nicholas; *b* 1972
3 Jane Elizabeth Rhoda; *b* 25 March 1915; *m* 4 Jan 1941 Lt-Col Richard Leslie David Weber, RA (*d* 1967), yr s of Col William Hermann Frank Weber, CMG, DSO, of Birkin, nr Dorchester, and *d* 1994, having had:
   (1) David; *b* 8 May 1942; *educ* Radley and Trin Coll Oxford; *d* 16 Dec 1974
   (2) *Jeremy; *b* 16 Sept 1944; *educ* Radley and Trin Coll Dublin
   (3) *George [George Weber Esq, Scotsgrove House, nr Thame, Oxon]; *b* 26 April 1946; *educ* Radley; *m* 3 May 1969 *Elizabeth, adopted dau of Lt-Col Hon Alexander Money-Coutts (*see* LATYMER, B), and has:
      1a *Thomas Richard; *b* 19 Jan 1976
      1a *Charlotte Mary; *b* 8 Feb 1980
   (1) *(Philippa) Emily Margaret; *b* 8 March 1950
4 Rachel Prunella Peace; *b* 15 May 1919; *d* 3 April 1936
5 Frances Honor Ruth; *b* 16 Jan 1922; *d* 25 July 1989
6 (Eleanor Sarah) Joy; *b* 9 April 1927; *m* 1st 27 Nov 1948 (*divorce* 1963) John Henry Fownes Luttrell (*d* 1991), er s of Claude Mohum Fownes Luttrell, JP; *m* 2nd Peter MacGregor Coleman (*d* 1979) and *d* 6 March 1996, leaving by her 1st husb:
   (1) *Charlotte Rose [Mrs Jonathan Yorke-Long, Shrob Lodge, Old Stratford, Northants MK19 6BA]; *b* 1954; *m* 1977 *Jonathan C Yorke-Long and has:
      1a *Marcus John Alexander; *b* 19 Oct 1983
      1a *Lucy Eleanor; *b* 23 June 1986
7 *Juliet Dorothea Chassereau; *b* 26 Feb 1933; *m* 14 June 1956 *John Douglas Young Hickman, est s of John Douglas Hickman, of Rothesay, NB, Canada, and has:
   (1) *(Philip) Douglas; *b* 25 Nov 1956; *m* 1981 *Pamela Mary Hunter and has:
      1a *Angela Lindsay; *b* 1986
      2a *Connie Marie; *b* 1988
      3a *Jennifer Lee; *b* 1990
   (2) *Stephen James; *b* 29 Aug 1958; *m* 1988 *Catherine Jean King and adopted:
      *Alexander James; *b* 1991
      *Sarah Ann; *b* 1998
   (3) *Charles Nicholas; *b* 17 July 1960; *m* 1987 *Gay Giselle Augustin Drescher and has:
      1a *Nicholas; *b* 1993
      1a *Katherine Ashley; *b* 1990

Sir PHILIP *d* 6 May 1958; his est s,

Sir David Philip Williams, 3rd Bt, DL (Dorset 1968); *b* 5 Oct 1909; *educ* RNC Dartmouth and Trin Coll Oxford; Lt RNVR WW II; *m* 1st 6 Sept 1937 Kathleen (*d* 31 Aug 1945), only dau of Maj Reginald Walker, RE, and had:
   1 A son; *b* and *d* 19 Feb 1943
   1 *(Mary) Venetia Honor [Mrs John Peake, Corscombe Court, Corscombe, Dorset]; *b* 28 July 1939; *m* 18 July 1964 *John Copson Peake, yr s of Geoffrey Copson Peake, of Northfield, Priestlands, Dorset

Sir David *m* 2nd 3 April 1948 *Elizabeth Mary Garneys, JP (Dorset 1959), DL (Dorset), High Sheriff Dorset 1979 [Elizabeth Lady Williams JP DL, Stable House, Moigne Combe, Owermoigne, Dorset], only dau of William Ralph Garneys Bond, of Moigne Combe, and *d* 31 Oct 1970, leaving by her:
   (2) Sir (ROBERT) PHILIP NATHANIEL WILLIAMS, **4th and present Bt**
   (3) +(David) Michael Ralph; *b* 1 Feb 1955; *educ* Marlborough and Durham U; *m* 17 Oct 1992 *Charlotte Prudence Elizabeth, only dau of Capt Malcolm Syms (*see* PASLEY, Bt), and has:
      1a +James Mark Edward; *b* 3 Nov 1995
      1a *Emily Honor; *b* 3 July 1997
   (2) *(Elizabeth Margaret) Ruth [Mrs Michael Widén, Batsford House, St Mary Bourne, Hants]; *b* 28 June 1951; *educ* Downe House; *m* 1975 *Michael Widén and has:
      1a *William David Alexander; *b* 1978

WILLIAMS of Castell Deudraeth

Arms: Argent a chevron between two pierced mullets in chief and in base a stag trippant sable. **Crest:** A gryphon segreant sable, holding between the fore claws a stag's head cabossed or. **Motto:** *Nid da onid Duw* ('No good but God'). **Creation:** Bt. (UK) 28 July 1909.

SIR (MICHAEL) OSMOND WILLIAMS, 2ND BT, of Castell Deudraeth and Borthwen, Co Merioneth, MC (1944), JP (1960) [Sir Osmond Williams Bt MC JP, Borthwen, Minffordd, Penrhyndeudraeth, Gwynedd LL48 6EN]; *b* 22 April 1914; *s* gf 1927; *educ* Eton and Freiburg U; Maj RSG WW II (Chev Order Leopold II Belgium, Belgian Croix de Guerre); *m* 12 July 1947 *Benita Mary, yr dau of George Henry Booker, of Mayfair, and has:
   1 *Sarah Theresa Ceridwen [Mrs Leo Kay, 179 Ière Rue Mont Suisse, St Sauveur des Monts, Quebec J0R 1R2, Canada]; *b* 29 Aug 1948; *m* 1981 *Leo Kruidbos *alias* Kay
   2 *Julia Mary Myfanwy [Mrs Richard O'Conor, 31 Clarendon Rd, London W11]; *b* 13 April 1952; *m* 1982 *Richard Shaun O'Conor

Lineage: WILLIAM JONES, of Hirdre, Llangoed, Breconshire; *m* Gwen Hughes and had an er s:

JOHN WILLIAMS *alias* JONES, of Saethon, Caernarvs; *b* 1713; *m* 7 Aug 1742 Ann, dau of Robert Davids, of Lonfydr, and *d* 1796, having had, with two er sons and four daus:

DAVID WILLIAMS, of Lonfydr and Saethon; *b* 4 Sept 1754; *m* 19 June 1792 Jane, dau of Edward Jones, of Carnarvon, and *d* 28 March 1823, having had, with four daus:
   1 Edward; *b* 4 Aug 1794; surgn at Bala; *d* unm
   2 John, of Llanfyllin, Montgomeryshire; *b* 17 June 1797; *m* 27 June 1818 Ann, dau of John Smith, and *d* 22 Nov 1846, leaving issue
   3 DAVID
   4 Robert, of Penrhynisso; *b* 1 March 1804; *d* 1869
   5 Abraham Jones; *b* 2 June 1812; Sheriff Caernarvs 1867–68; *m* 1853 Sarah Elizabeth Margaret, yst dau of Lt-Gen Sir Loveday Parry Jones-Parry, KH, of Madryn, Penarth and Wernfawr Rhydolion

The 3rd s,

DAVID WILLIAMS, of Deudraeth Castle, Merionethshire, JP, DL; *b* 30 June 1799; High Sheriff 1861, MP Merioneths; *m* 25 Sept 1841 Annie Louisa Loveday (*d* 16 June 1904), only dau of William Williams, barrister, of Pennarthuchaf, Merioneths, and *d* 15 Dec 1869, having had:
   1 William Edward Wynne; *b* 6 July 1842; *dvp*
   2 (ARTHUR) OSMOND (Sir), **1st Bt**
   3 Edward Herbert Vychan; *m* Rosa Dymock and *d* 11 Oct 1930
   4 Edmund Trevor Lloyd, JP (Merioneths and Bucks); *b* 1859; *m* 30 April 1895 Alice Le Poer (*d* Dec 1948), yst dau of David Fullerton, JP, and Mrs. David Fullerton, of Pennington House, and *d* 8 Dec 1946, leaving issue
   5 Llewellyn Leonard Bulkeley, MD; *b* 2 Oct 1861; *m* Antonia Beavan and *d* 20 Aug 1939, leaving issue
   1 Angharad Wynn; *m* Augustus Henry Reid and *d* 13 Jan 1927
   2 Dora Louisa; *m* 24 July 1879 Romer Williams, DL, of Dolmelynllyn, Merioneths, and *d* 1 Dec 1933, leaving issue
   3 Fanny Caroline; *m* John Bell
   4 Harriet Gertrude; *m* 6 Feb 1879 Robert Clover Beazley (*d* 9 Aug 1925), 2nd s of James Beazley, of Fern Hill, Oxton, Cheshire, and *d* 7 March 1945, leaving issue
   5 Florence Gay Octavia; *m* 1882 Sir Ernest de la Rue, KCVO (*d* 18 Aug 1929; *see* DE LA RUE, Bt), and *d* Aug 1942, leaving issue
   6 Blanche Winefred Wynn; *m* Perceval Currey
   7 Alice Helena Alexander, CBE; *d* unm 15 Aug 1957

The est surv s,

Sir Arthur Osmond Williams, 1st Bt (UK), so *cr* 28 July 1909, JP, DL (Caernarvs); *b* 17 March 1849; *educ* Eton; Constable Harlech Castle, Merioneths: Col

Vol Regt, MP (Lib) 1900–10, Ld Lt 1909–27, Chm QS; *m* 3 Aug 1880 Frances Evelyn (*d* 10 Aug 1926), 4th dau of John Whitehead Greaves, DL, of Bericote, Warwicks, and *d* 28 Jan 1927, having had:

1 David Osmond Deudraeth; *b* 6 Feb, *d* 18 March 1882

2 Osmond Trahairn Deudraeth, DSO; *b* 26 Feb 1883; Lt 19th Hus Boer War 1901–02 (Queen's medal with four clasps), Capt Welsh Gds WW I (despatches three times); *m* 5 Feb 1912 Gladys Margaret (*d* 30 May 1964), only dau of 13th Earl of Winchilsea and (8th Earl of) Nottingham (*qv*), and *d* 30 Sept 1915 of wounds recd in action at Loos 27 Sept 1915, leaving:

  (1) Sir (MICHAEL) OSMOND WILLIAMS, **2nd and present Bt**

  (1) *Elizabeth Anne [Miss Elizabeth Williams, Seafield Lodge, 124 Dorset Rd, Bexhill-on-Sea, E Sussex TN40 2HT]; *b* 28 Aug 1915

3 Lawrence Trevor Greaves; *b* 26 Aug 1885; Capt ASC WW I; *d* unm 26 July 1930

1 Evelyn Olwen; *b* 24 May 1884; *m* 23 July 1918 Maj-Gen Sir Neville Maskelyne Smyth, VC, KCB (*d* 21 July 1941), 2nd s of Sir Warington Smyth, FRS, of Marazion, Cornwall, and *d* 29 Sept 1960, leaving issue

2 Ellen Dolgar Dormie; *b* 14 Nov 1891; *m* 3 June 1915 Capt Robert Gordon Beazely, King's Liverpool Regt (*d* 9 Aug 1953), 2nd s of Robert Clover Beazley, of Birkenhead, and had issue

WILLIAMS of
Cilgeraint

Creation: Bt. (UK) 3 July 1953.

SIR ROBIN PHILIP WILLIAMS, 2ND BT, of Cilgeraint, Co Caernarvon [Sir Robin Williams Bt, 1 Broadlands Close, London N6 4AF]; *b* 27 May 1928; *s f* 1954; *educ* Eton and St John's Coll Cambridge (BA 1950, MA 1955); 2nd Lt RA 1948; barrister Middle Temple 1954, insur broker 1952, memb Lloyd's; V-Chm Fedn of U C and Unionist Assocs 1951–52 (acting Chm 1952), Chm Bow Group 1954 and Anti-Common Market League 1969–84, Borough Cncllr Haringey 1968–74, Hon Sec Campaign for an Independent Britain 1989–; *m* 19 Feb 1955 *Wendy Adele Marguerite, only dau of Felix Joseph Alexander, of Hong Kong and London, and has:

1 +ANTHONY GERAINT [Anthony Williams Esq, 6 Willow Bridge Rd, London N1 2LB]; *b* 22 Dec 1958; *m* 1990 *Rachel J, er dau of Norman Jennings, of Fenny Drayton, Warwicks, and has:

  (1) +A son; *b* 19–

  (2) +A son; *b* 19–

  (1) +A dau; *b* 19–

2 +Stephen Robin Alexander; *b* 1 May 1962

Lineage: THOMAS WILLIAMS; *b* 1847; *educ* Cambridge (MA, LLD); Headmaster Hooton GS Cheshire; *m* Mary Anne — (*d* 1931) and *d* 1896, leaving:

1 Charles Thomas; barrister Inner Temple; *d* 1935

2 John David Ellis; PhD; schoolmaster, *d* 1954

3 **Sir Herbert Geraint Williams, 1st Bt** (UK), so *cr* 3 July 1953; *b* 2 Dec 1884; *educ* Hooton GS and Liverpool U (Rathbone Scholar, BEng 1906, BSc 1907, MSc 1908, MEng 1911); marine and electrical engr; Alderman LCC 1940–44; MP (C) Reading 1924–29, S Croydon 1932–45 and E Croydon 1950–54, Parly Sec BOT 1928–29, Memb Select Ctee H of C on Nat Expenditure 1939–44, Jt Sec Engrg and Shipbuilding Hours of Labour Investigation Ctee 1920–22, Sec and Manager Machine Tools Trades Assoc 1911–28, Dir Empire Industries Assoc 1926–28 and 1931–41, Chm Exec London C Union 1939–48, Chm Nat Union C and U Assocs 1948; *m* 29 Jan 1916 Dorothy Frances (*d* 14 June 1957), dau of Barton Jones, and *d* 25 July 1954, leaving:

  (1) Sir ROBIN PHILIP WILLIAMS, **2nd and present Bt**

  (1) Rosemary; *b* 12 April 1927; *m* 1st 18 June 1946 (*divorce* 1969) Sir Ian Auld Mactaggart, 3rd Bt (*qv*); *m* 2nd 20 June 1973 (*divorce* 1986), as his 2nd w, 13th Lord Belhaven and Stenton (*qv*) and *d* 1992

WILLIAMS of
Tregullow

Arms: Vair three crescents or. **Crest:** A demi-eagle azure, wings elevated sable, each wing charged with four bezants. **Motto:** *Nil desperandum* ('Never despair'). **Creation:** Bt. (UK) 4 Aug 1866.

SIR DONALD MARK WILLIAMS, 10TH BT, of Tregullow, Cornwall [Sir Donald Williams Bt, Upcott House, Barnstaple, N Devon EX31 4DR]; *b* 7 Nov 1954; *s f* 1976; *educ* W Buckland Sch Devon; *m* 15 May 1982 *Denise, only dau of Royston H Cory, of Kashmir, Raleigh Hill, Bideford, Devon, and has had:

1 Matthew; *b* and *d* 1985

1 *Hannah Louise; *b* 6 Aug 1987

2 *Michelle Ruth; *b* 13 Nov 1994

3 *Natasha Elizabeth; *b* 24 July 1997

Lineage: JOHN WILLIAMS (allegedly the er of two bros who moved from Wales to Cornwall for the mining opportunities there); *b c* 1684; settled Burncoose, Gwennap, 1715; *m* 1st Thomasine Paynter; *m* 2nd — and *d* 1761, leaving by her, with other issue:

MICHAEL WILLIAMS; *b* Aug 1730; *m* 30 Nov 1752 Susanna (*d* Feb 1814), dau of Henry Harris, of Cusgarne, Gwennap, and *d* Feb 1775, leaving an est s:

JOHN WILLIAMS, of Burncoose and Scorrier Ho; *b* 23 Sept 1753; bought 1806 Manor of Calstock, Devon; *m* 23 Jan 1776 Catherine (*d* Sept 1826), dau of Martin Harvey, of Kenwyn, Cornwall, and *d* April 1841, having had, with other issue:

1 Michael, of Scorrier Ho and Caerhays Castle, Cornwall, and Gnaton Hall, Devon, DL Cornwall; *b* 3 June 1784; High Sheriff Glam 1840, MP W Cornwall 1853–58, Dep-Warden Stannaries; *m* 5 March 1813 Elizabeth (*d* 30 July 1852), er dau of Richard Eales, of Eastdon, Devon, and *d* 15 June 1858, leaving issue

2 Edward; *b* 20 Aug 1786; *m* 15 July 1814 Elizabeth (*d* 25 Dec 1851), dau of John Pearson Foote, of Harwood, nr Tavistock, and *d* 1822, leaving issue

3 **Sir William Williams, 1st Bt** (UK), so *cr* 4 Aug 1866, DL Cornwall; *b* 3 Aug 1791; High Sheriff 1851, Dep-Warden Stannaries; *m* 26 Sept 1826 his er bro's sis-in-law Caroline (*d* 17 Feb 1886), yr dau of Richard Eales, and had, with three other daus (*d* young or unm):

  (1) William John; *b* 3 Nov 1827; *d* 25 Sept 1847

  (2) FREDERICK MARTIN (Sir), **2nd Bt**

  (3) Richard Michael; *b* 18 Dec 1830; Lt-Col 3rd Hus; *m* 19 Jan 1858 Georgiana Sophia (*d* 13 Jan 1923), dau of Rev Thomas Phillpotts, of Porthgwidden, Cornwall, Hon Canon Truro and n of Henry Phillpotts, Bp Exeter, and *d* 25 Dec 1867, leaving:

    1a William Phillpotts; *b* 9 Aug 1860; Capt 2nd Bde W Div RA; *m* 8 Aug 1901 Edith Bonella, 2nd dau of Rev James Harvey Simpson, Preb Chichester, and *d* 29 Aug 1916, leaving:

      1b Elizabeth Georgiana Phillpotts; *b* 6 Sept 1904

    2a Lionel Arthur; *b* 29 Dec 1861; Lt 3rd Bn Yorks LI, Capt Res Offrs; *d* unm 17 Feb 1911

    1a Georgiana Caroline Mary; *m* 17 Aug 1882 5th Baron Henley (*qv*) and *dsp* 26 Aug 1888

  (4) Arthur Edward; *b* 28 Aug 1832; *d* unm 9 July 1893

  (5) Charles Henry WILLIAMS later BASSET (roy licence 1880), JP, DL, of Pilton Ho, Umberleigh, and Watermouth Castle, Devon; *b* 16 Nov 1834; Maj Roy N Devon Hus, Lt RN 1848–60; MP Barnstaple 1868–74; *m* 7 Jan 1858 Harriet Mary (*d* 12 May 1920), dau of Arthur Davie Basset, of Watermouth Castle, and *d* 1 Feb 1908, having had:

    1a Walter Basset; *b* 20 Sept 1863; Lt RN; *m* 18 Nov 1890 Ellen Caroline Charlotte (*d* 5 March 1945), dau of Adml Sir William Montagu Dowell, GCB, and *dsp* 27 May 1907

    1a Edith Basset, CBE (1918); *m* 18 Oct 1882 Maj Ernest Charles Penn Curzon and *d* 30 April 1943, leaving issue (*see* HOWE, E)

  (6) Michael, JP (Cornwall); *b* 10 Jan 1839; *educ* Oriel Coll Oxford (MA); *d* unm 24 April 1905

(1) Catherine Anne; *m* 9 June 1859 Lt-Col James Hornby Buller (*d* 7 Aug 1895), of Down Hall, Epsom, est s of Rev Richard Buller, of Lanreath, Cornwall, and *d* 9 Dec 1874, leaving issue

Sir WILLIAM *d* 24 March 1870; his est surv s,

Sir Frederick Martin Williams, 2nd Bt, DL (Cornwall); *b* 25 Jan 1830; Dep-Warden Stannaries, MP (C) Truro 1865–78; *m* 10 June 1858 Mary Christian (*d* 22 May 1892), dau of Rev Robert Vanbrugh Law, Rector Christian Malford, Wilts, Treas and Preb Wells, Canon Chester (s of George Henry Law; *see* ELLENBOROUGH, B), and *d* 3 Sept 1878, leaving, with other issue:

1 **Sir William Robert Williams, 3rd Bt**, of Tregullow, Cornwall, DL Devon; *b* 32 Feb 1860; CC Devon, Capt 3rd Bde W Div RA; *m* 13 July 1881 Matilda Frances, Order Elisabeth Belgium (*d* 25 May 1946), dau of Edmund Beauchamp Beauchamp, DL, of Trevince, and *d* 16 May 1903, leaving:

(1) **Sir William Frederick Williams, 4th Bt**; *b* 17 May 1886; *d* unm 20 Sept 1905

(2) **Sir Frederick William Williams, 5th Bt**; *b* 15 Jan 1888; *d* unm 1 Oct 1913

(3) **Sir Burton Robert Williams, 6th Bt**; *b* 7 July 1889; Lt 3rd Bn Devon Regt WW I (despatches twice); *ka* 3 Oct 1917

(1) Frances Maria; *m* 29 June 1909 (*divorce* 1926) Capt John Franklin Richardson, Lincs Regt, only s of Maj-Gen J B Richardson, RA, of Hulton Ho, Spilsby, Lincs, and *dsp* 27 March 1949

2 **Sir Frederick Law Williams, 7th Bt**; *b* 10 May 1863; Capt Dorset Regt; *m* 1899 Emily (*d* 26 Nov 1959), dau of William Reid, of Downpatrick, and *d* 20 Dec 1921, leaving:

(1) **Sir William Law Williams, 8th Bt**; *b* 1 May 1907; *educ* Sherborne and St John's Coll Cambridge (BA 1930); Capt RWF WW II; *m* 22 April 1950 Betty Kathleen, dau of John Taylor, of Hitchin, Herts, by Mrs J Nowell Philip, of The Haven, Torquay, and *dsp* 1 July 1960

(1) Eva Kathleen Victoria Daisy; *b* 1900; *m* 21 Dec 1935 Lt-Cdr Christopher Ernest Inman Gibbs, RNR (*d* 1947), and had issue

(2) Winifred; *b* 1901

3 Edward Harvey, JP Cornwall; *b* 2 Feb 1865; Sarawak CS 1882–97; *m* 19 Oct 1897 Annie Caroline (*d* 10 Feb 1943), yr dau of Rev Sir St Aubyn Hender Molesworth-St Aubyn, 12th Bt (*qv*), and *d* 4 Nov 1938

4 Leonard Alfred (Rev); *b* 9 April 1867; *educ* Pembroke Coll Cambridge (BA 1889); Vicar Hessenford Cornwall 1924–32; *m* 16 Oct 1894 Margaret Hay (*d* 28 June 1950), yst dau of Lt-Col Eugene Hay Cameron, RA, and *d* 10 Oct 1956, leaving:

(1) David Cameron; *b* 10 Dec 1898; Lt-Cdr RN; *m* 7 Aug 1929 Violet Mary (*m* 2nd 17 June 1946 Humphrey Douglas Tyringham, 2nd s of Roger William Giffard Tyringham, of Trevethoe Ho, Lelant, Cornwall, formerly of Tyringham, Bucks, and *d* 7 Jan 1998), er dau of Rev Canon Arthur Townshend Boscawen (*see* FALMOUTH, V), and *d* 26 Sept 1931, leaving:

1a *Susan Mary [Mrs Michael Halford, 31 Knowle Rd, Knowle, Budleigh Salterton, Devon EX9 6AR]; *b* 20 Aug 1931; *m* 18 Dec 1954 *Maj (John) Michael Halford, RM, s of S/Ldr W Halford, DFC, of Datchet, Bucks, and has:

1b *John Wallis Williams; *b* 7 Dec 1955

2b *Peter David [Peter Halford Esq, The Cottage, Philpotts Lane, Hildenborough, Kent TN11 8PB]; *b* 31 Jan 1957; *educ* Wellington; *m* 1985 *Caroline Smith and has:

1c *Edward David; *b* 1988

1c *Lucy Alexandra; *b* 1991

1b *Julia Karenza; *b* 4 March 1961; *m* 1988 *Michael Peter Mansergh and has:

1c *Annabel Karenza; *b* 1990

2c *Philippa Louise; *b* 1991

(2) Michael Leonard (Rev); *b* 25 Feb 1907; *educ* Pembroke Coll Cambridge (BA 1928, MA 1934); Curate St John the Baptist Bognor Regis 1941–46 and Horsham 1946–54, Vicar Woodingdean Sussex 1954–56; *d* unm 5 April 1956

(1) Margaret; *b* 15 June 1900; *m* 15 Feb 1930 Brig George William Marshall Findlay, CBE, MD, DSc, FRCP (*d* 14 March 1952), only s of George Findlay, of Brailes, nr Banbury, and has:

1a *Isabella Anne Marshall [Mrs Angus Hewat, Templemead, Pulborough, Sussex]; *b* 26 Feb 1931; *m* 1st 2 April 1955 (*divorce* 1966) John Patrick Henry Goodison, er s of E H Goodison, of Radlett, Herts, and has:

1b *Simon James Findlay; *b* 10 July 1956; *educ* Marlborough

1b *Sarah Louise Katharine; *b* 3 Feb 1958

1a (cont.) Mrs Isabella Goodison *m* 2nd 23 Feb 1967 *Angus Davidson Hewat, 5th s of Aubrey Middleton Hewat, MD, of Bexhill-on-Sea, Sussex, and by him has:

2b *Harry William Davidson; *b* 4 Feb 1968

2b *Sophie Anne; *b* 18 Jan 1969

2a *Julia Margaret Marshall; *b* 19 March 1933; *educ* St Andrews (MA); *m* 1 March 1958 *Lt-Col Brian Hugh Clare Emsden, Roy Anglian Regt, 2nd s of Col Leslie George Emsden, OBE, JP, of Clare, Suffolk, and has:

1b *Clare Emma Margaret; *b* 12 Jan 1960

2b *Annabel Julia Clare; *b* 14 June 1962

5 Ernest Martyn; *b* 17 Dec 1871; *m* 22 Jan 1898 Leila, dau, of Lewis Coultis, and *d* 3 June 1926, leaving:

(1) Ernest Claude, CS; *b* 5 Nov 1898; *m* 5 June 1922 Theresa Gertrude, dau of R Graefer, and *d* 26 June 1933, leaving:

1a ROBERT ERNEST (Sir), **9th Bt**

1a *Leila June; *b* 8 Aug 1926; *m* 1st 1952 (*divorce* 1972) Norman E Hambley, police constable, and has:

1b *Kenneth Charles Claude; *b* 18 June 1953

2b *Keith Thomas; *b* 17 Jan 1957

1b *Kim Lee Ann; *b* 21 March 1959

1a (cont.) Mrs Leila Hambley *m* 2nd 1972 *Adam Casson

(2) Percival Martyn; *b* 12 Aug 1900; *m* 11 Sept 1950 Margaret Elsie Davidson

(3) Edward Law (Rev); *b* 7 July 1903; Rector St John's Episcopal Ch, Midland, Mich.; *d* unm 1 Feb 1960

---

(1) Beatrice Lavinia; *b* 8 Feb 1902

(2) Matilda Maud; *b* 12 Dec 1909; *m* 1942 Robert McFadyen and had:

1a *Diane Beatrice; *b* 29 Nov 1942

6 Victor George; *b* 28 Jan 1874; MD; *m* 1895 Marion Elizabeth (*d* 15 June 1949), dau of Godfrey Phipps Baker, of Woodrooff, Ottawa, and *d* 31 May 1944, having had:

(1) Frederick Martyn Charles; *b* 15 July 1898; *m* 21 Feb 1935 Maud Ann, dau of Dennis Bawif, of Winnipeg, Canada, and *d* 1961, leaving:

1a +Martyn Dennis Victor [Martin Williams Esq, 8-9 Ipswich Cres, Willodale, Toronto, Canada]; *b* 5 Jan 1936; *educ* Toronto U (BSc Mech Eng 1961); *m* 26 Jan 1968 *Beth Diane, dau of E John Koch, of Kitchener, Ontario, and has:

1b *Robin Lynn; *b* 1972

2b *Michael David; *b* 1978

1b *Sandra Diana; *b* 1975

2b *Karen Patricia (twin); *b* 1978

(2) Victor George Bertram; *b* 2 Aug 1900; *m* (*divorce*) Helen Donald Moir, of Winnipeg, and *dsp* 1968

(1) Marion Christian Victoria; *b* 22 March 1897

(2) Dorothy Ellenborough; *b* 21 Oct 1902; *m* Brig George Edward Robert Smith, RASC, and *d* 16 May 1939, leaving issue

7 Bertram Leopold; *b* 27 May 1878; *m* 1st 3 Jan 1906 (*divorce*) Vera Mary, only dau of Arthur Venables, JP, of Wooburn Ranche, BC, and had:

(1) William Bertram; *b* 3 Nov 1906; *m* 1932 Agnes (*d* 1968), dau of John Allen, of Vancouver, and *d* 1960, leaving:

1a *Judith Patricia [Mrs William McLean, 4537 Portland St, Burnaby, BC V5J 2P1, Canada]; *b* 13 July 1934; *m* 1954 *William Demuth McLean and has:

1b *Douglas William; *b* 1958; has by *Patricia Kensington:

1c *Alicia Lareina; *b* 1991

1b *Kay Elizabeth; *b* 1956; *m* 1983 *Gordon Gray and has:

1c *Kristin Patricia; *b* 1985

1c *Andrea Barbara; *b* 1987

2b *Lynn Marion; *b* 1960; *m* 1990 *Paul Kirkpatrick and has:

1c *Michael William; *b* 1992

2a *Barbara Anne; *b* 1939; *m* 1959 *Douglas Norman Tartaglio and has:

1b *Norman William; *b* 1962; has:

1c *Ryan Wayne; *b* 1982

2b *Neil Joseph; *b* 1964; *m* 1987 *Mary Kathleen, dau of Walter MacNeill

1b *Joanne Denise; *b* 1967; *m* 1993 *Peter Bukacell

(2) Claude Martin; *b* 21 Jan 1911; Engr 1st Cl; *m* 1 May 1944 Hannah Louisa Mary, dau of Capt William Massey, of Courtown Harbour, Gorey, Co Wexford, and *d* 1977, leaving:

1a +Bertram Douglas [Bertram Williams Esq, 20571 49 A Ave, Lengley, BC V3A 574, Canada]; *b* 30 March 1945; *m* 19– *Wanda Charlotte, only dau of Capt Trim, of Nanimo, BC, and has:

1b *Brianne Kathleen; *b* 1979

2b *Colleen Kate; *b* 1981

3b *Leaerin Elizabeth; *b* 1982

2a +William Claude [William Williams Esq, 2640 Moss Ave, Prince George, BC V2L 5J3, Canada]; *b* 28 Feb 1947; *m* 19– *Leslie Gaye, dau of Norman Steward, of Delta, BC, and has:

1b *Matthew Stewart; *b* 1980

2b *Andrew James; *b* 1982

(3) +Peter Robert [Peter Williams Esq, RR1 Big Maple, Sechelt, BC V05 380, Canada]; *b* 21 July 1913

7 (cont.) Bertram Williams *m* 2nd 23 Oct 1926 Amy Muriel Douglas, yr dau of Douglas Fourdrinier, of Teddington, Middx, and *d* 21 April 1962

1 Caroline Sydney, DBE, JP Co Dublin; DGStJ; *m* 27 Sept 1881 Sir John Alexander Arnott, 2nd Bt (*qv*), and *d* 28 Dec 1933, having had issue

2 Mary Christian, CBE; *m* 15 Oct 1884 John Charles Williams (*d* 29 March 1939), of Caerhays Castle, St Austell, Burncoose, Gwennap, and Werrington Pk, Cornwall, and *d* 1 Oct 1922, leaving issue

3 Beatrice Julia, OBE (1918); *m* 12 Jan 1892 Sir Charles Henry Cave, 2nd Bt (*qv*), and *d* 7 Nov 1951, leaving issue

The 8th Bt's cousin,

Sir Robert Ernest Williams, 9th Bt; *b* 6 June 1923; *educ* McKenzie High Sch, Dauphin, Manitoba; with Canadian Nat Rlwys 1944–60; *m* 3 July 1948 *Ruth Margaret [Ruth Lady Williams, Upcott House, Barnstaple, N Devon], dau of Charles Edwin Butcher, of Hudson Bay, Saskatchewan, and *d* 1976, having had:

1 Robert Tracy; *b* 31 March 1950; *k* car crash Canada 3 Aug 1969

2 Sir DONALD MARK WILLIAMS, **10th and present Bt**

3 +BARTON MATTHEW; *b* 20 Nov 1956; heir presumptive; *m* 1st 1980 (*divorce* 19–) Karen Robinson and has:

(1) +Ashley; *b* 19–

(1) *Fay Marie; *b* 19–

3 (cont.) BARTON WILLIAMS *m* 2nd 1985 (*divorce* 19–) Sarah — and by her has:

(2) *Elizabeth; *b* 19–

1 *Phyllis June; *b* 4 March 1949

WILLIAMS OF CROSBY

WILLIAMS OF MOSTYN

Arms: Per chevron azure and or three lions passant guardant in pale counter-changed, a bordure engrailed ermine. **Motto:** *Quamdiu* ('Until'). **Creation:** B. (LP, UK) 1993.

THE BARONESS WILLIAMS OF CROSBY, of Stevenage, Co Herts (Shirley Vivien Teresa Brittain, PC 1974) [The Rt Hon The Baroness Williams of Crosby PC, House of Lords, London SW1A 0PW]; *b* 27 July 1930; *educ* Summit Sch Minnesota, St Paul's Girls' Sch, Somerville Coll Oxford (Hon Fell 1970) and Columbia U New York; MP (Lab) Hitchin 1964–74 and Hertford and Stevenage 1974–79, PPS to Min Health 1964–66, Parly Sec Min Labour 1966–67, Min State: DES 1967–69 and Home Office 1969–70; Sec State: Prices and Consumer Protection 1974–76, Educn and Sci 1976–79 (also Paymaster-General), Chm Fabian Soc 1980–81 (Gen Sec 1960–64), Memb Lab NEC 1970–81, Co-Founder SDP 1981, Pres 1982–88 and MP (SDP) Crosby 1981–83, Fellow Inst Politics Harvard 1979–80, Memb Sr Advsy Ctee 1988–; Research Fellow PSI 1979–85, Prof Elective Politics Kennedy Sch Government Harvard 1988–, Dir Project Liberty 1990–, Memb Cncl Advsrs to Praesidium Ukraine 1991–97, dir Rand Europe 1993–, FBA, author: *Politics Is For People* (1981), *Jobs for the 1980s*, *Youth Without Work* (1981), *Unemployment and Growth in the Western Economies* (co-author, 1984), *A Job to Live* (1985), *Snakes and Ladders: a political diary* (1996); *m* 1st 1955 (*divorce* 1974) Prof Bernard Arthur Owen Williams; *m* 2nd 1987 *Prof Richard E Neustadt and has by her 1st husb:

  1 *Rebecca Clare; *b* 1961; barrister; *m* 20 June1992 *Christopher Simon Honey

Lineage: Prof Sir GEORGE EDWARD GORDON CATLIN; *m* Vera Brittain and had:

SHIRLEY VIVIEN TERESA, *cr* a **Baroness**

WILLIAMS OF ELVEL

Creation: B. (LP, UK) 1985.

THE BARON WILLIAMS OF ELVEL, of Llansantffraed in Elvel, Co Powys (Charles Cuthbert Powell Williams, CBE 1980) [The Rt Hon The Lord Williams of Elvel CBE, 48 Thurloe Sq, London SW7 2SX; Pant-y-Rhiw, Llansantffraed in Elvel, Powys LD1 5RH]; *b* 9 Feb 1933; *educ* Westminster, Ch Ch Oxford and LSE; with BP 1958–64, Bank of London and Montreal 1964–66, Eurofinance SA Paris 1966–70, Baring Bros & Co 1970–77 (md 1971–77); Chm: Price Commn 1977–79; md Henry Ansbacher & Co 1980–82 (chm 1982–85), ch exec Henry Ansbacher Hldgs 1982–85; dir: Pergamon Hldgs 1985–91, Mirror Gp Newspapers 1985–92; fndr memb Lab Ec Fin and Taxation Assoc (V-Chm 1975–77, 1979–83); Pres: Campaign Protection Rural Wales 1989–95 (v-pres 1995–), Fedn Ec Devpt Authorities 1990–95 (v-pres 1995–); Ho Lds Oppn Spokesman: Trade and Industry 1986–92, Energy 1988–90, Def 1990–97, Environment 1992–97; Dep Leader Oppn Ho Lds 1989–92; author: *The Last Great Frenchman: a life of General de Gaulle* (1993), *Bradman: an Australian hero* (1996); *m* 1975 *Jane Gillian, DL, dau of Lt-Col Gervase Edward Portal and formerly w of Gavin Bramhall Bernard Welby and has a step-s

Lineage: Dr NORMAN POWELL WILLIAMS, DD; *m* Mrs Muriel de Lérisson Williams (*née* Cazenove) and had:

CHARLES CUTHBERT POWELL, *cr* a **Baron**

Arms: Ermine on a pile flory at the point sable a lion rampant or, armed and langued gules. **Crest:** A portcullis or in front of an arm embowed vested and the cuff braided sable, frilled at the wrist, the hand proper holding by its blade upwards argent a sword palewise to the front of the portcullis, its hilt, pommel and quillons gold. **Supporters:** Dexter, upon a grassy mount, growing therefrom two sweet pea flowers proper, a griffin statant erect gold; sinister, upon a like mount a dragon statant erect, also gold, both armed and langued gules. **Motto:** *Y gwir yn erbyn y byd* ('The truth against the world'). **Creation:** B. (LP, UK) 1992.

THE BARON WILLIAMS OF MOSTYN, of Great Tew, Co Oxon (Gareth Wyn Williams) [The Rt Hon The Lord Williams of Mostyn, House of Lords, London SW1A 0PW]; *b* 5 Feb 1941; *educ* Rhyl GS and Queens' Coll Cambridge (MA 1965, LLB 1964); barrister Gray's Inn 1965, Recorder Crown Court 1978–, QC 1978, Leader Wales and Chester Circuit 1987–90, Bencher Gray's Inn 1991; Memb: Bar Cncl 1986 (Chm 1992–), Cncl Justice 1993–; Oppn Spokesman Ho Lds NI, Home and Legal Affairs 1992–97, Parly U-Sec Home Office 1997–98, Min State 1998–; Pres: Prisoners Advice Serv 1992–, Cwlth and Ethnic Bar Assoc 1993–; Tstee NSPCC 1993–; Patron Redress Tst 1993–; Pro-Chllr U of Wales 1994–, Fell Wales U Aberystwyth 1993–; *m* 1st 1962 (*divorce* 19–) Pauline, dau of Ernest Clarke, and has:

  1 *Daniel; *b* 1969
  1 *Martha; *b* 1963
  2 *Emma; *b* 1966

The BARON WILLIAMS OF MOSTYN *m* 2nd 1994 *V M Russell and by her has:
  3 *Imogen; *b* 199–

Lineage: ALBERT THOMAS WILLIAMS; *m* Selina Evans and had:

GARETH WYN, *cr* a **Baron**

WILLIAMS-BULKELEY

Arms: Quarterly, 1st and 4th, sable a chevron between three bull's heads cabossed argent, a canton ermine (for BULKELEY); 2nd and 3rd, gules a chevron ermine between three Saracen's heads couped at the shoulders proper (for WILLIAMS). **Crests:** 1 Out of a ducal coronet or a bull's head argent, horned or, charged with a chevron sable (for BULKELEY), 2 A stag's head cabossed argent (for WILLIAMS). **Motto:** *Nec temere nec timide* ('Neither rashly nor fearfully'). **Creation:** Bt. (E) 28 May 1658 (Interregnum) and again (after Restoration) 17th June 1661.

SIR RICHARD THOMAS WILLIAMS-BULKELEY, 14TH BT, of Penrhyn, Caernarvonshire [Sir Richard Williams-Bulkeley Bt, Red Hill, Beaumaris, Anglesey LL58 8YT]; *b* 25 May 1939; *s f* 1992; *educ* Eton; Capt Welsh Gds 1963, FRICS, High Sheriff Gwynedd 1993; *m* 14 May 1964 *Sarah Susan, er dau of Rt Hon Ld Justice Phillimore (*see* PHILLIMORE, B), and has:

1 +RICHARD HUGH; *b* 8 July 1968; *educ* Eton and Reading U (BSc); Capt Welsh Gds; *m* 24 June 1995 *Jacqueline, er dau of David Edwards, of Kenn, Devon, and has had:

  (1) +Richard David Harry; *b* 26 April 1996

  (2) +Oliver Hugh; *b* 8 Feb 1998

2 +Harry David; *b* 8 July 1968; *educ* Eton and Manchester U (BA)

2 *Victoria Mary; *b* 1973; *educ* St Mary's Wantage

Lineage (of Williams): COEL HEN or COEL CODEBOG; KING OF RHEGED; *fl c* 330; had (according to a largely oral tradition):

CENEU Ap COEL HEN; had:

MOR Ap CENEU; had:

ARTHWYR ARTHWYS Ap MOR, KING OF RHEGED; had:

CYNFELYN Ap ARTHWYR ARTHYS; had:

CYNWYD CYNWDION Ap CYNFELYN; had:

CADROD CALCHFYNYDD Ap CYNWYD CYNWYDION; had:

YSBWYS Ap CADROD CALCHFYNYDD; had:

YSBWYS MWYNTYRCH Ap YSBWYS; had:

MYNAN Ab YSBWYS; had:

MORAP MYNAN; had:

ELFYN Ap MOR; had:

CYNAN Ab ELFYN; had:

MARCHUDD Ap CYNAN; *fl c* 840–70; Ld (apparently on a heriditary basis) of Brynffanigland later Abergele, in what was to become Denbighs; had, with other issue:

CARWED Ap MARCHUDD; *fl c* 903?; Ld of Brynffanigl, as were his successors till the late 13th century; had:

JAPETH Ap CARWED; *fl c* 949?; had:

NEITHON Ap JAPETH; *fl c* 997?; had:

ERUD Ap NEITHON; *fl c* 1039?; had:

IDNERTH Ab EDRUD; *fl c* 1080; had, with three other sons (Bradwen; Iddon; Madog Miniaw):

GWRGAN Ab IDNERTH; *fl c* 1128; had:

IORWERTH Ap GWGON; *fl c* 1178; *m* Gwenllian, dau of Rhirid ap Pasgen; had with a dau (Gwenllian; *m* Iorwerth ap Hwfa ap Cynddelw):

CYNFRIG Ab IORWERTH; *fl* 1200; minister to LLYWELYN II Ab IORWERTH, PRINCE OF GWYNEDD; *m* Angharad, dau of Hwfa ap Cynfrig, Ld of Cristionydol, Powys, and had:

  1 Heilyn *Sais* ('The Englishman'); drowned Hiraethog

2 EDNYFED FYCHAN

3 Goronwy *Foel* ('The Bald')

4 Einion *Ddu* ('The Black')

1 Gwenllian

2 Gwenllian (possibly so called because her er sis predeceasd her)

The est(?) s,

EDNYFED FYCHAN Ap CYNFRIG; *b c* 1173?; Ld of Brynffanigl, Cellan, Cwmllanerch, Dinorwig, Erddreiniog, Gwredog, Llanrhystud, Llansadwrn, Penmynydd, Penrhyn Creuddyn and Trecastell; steward to LLYWELYN THE GREAT, DAFYDD Ap LLYWELYN and LLYWELYN Ap GRUFFUDD III, PRINCES OF GWYNEDD, *c* 1216–46; Seneschall of Gwynedd *c* 1215–46; *m* 1st Efa (sometimes called Tangwystyl), dau of Llywarch ap Brân, Ld of Menai, Anglesey, and had:

  1 TUDUR (Sir)

  2 Llywelyn; Ld of Creuddyn, Penthyn

  3 Cynfrig; *fl* 1275; Ld of Creuddyn, Iâl

  4 Hywel; Bp St Asaph 1240–47; *d* 1247

  5 Iorwerth, called 'The Leprous', Ld of Abermarlais, Glandowy

  6 Madog

  1 Angharad; *m* Einio Fychan ab Einon, of Plas-y-nant, Anglesey

  2 Gwenllian; *m* Llywelyn Fawr, Ld of Meirlonydd, s of GRUFFUDD III Ap CYNAN, PRINCE OF GWYNEDD UWCH CONWY 1194–1200

EDNYFED FYCHAN *m* 2nd Gwenllian (*d* 1236), dau of RHYS Ap GRUFFUDD, PRINCE OF DEHEUBARTH (more or less coextensive with S Wales), and *d* 1246, having had by her:

  7 Goronwy; Seneschall of Gwynedd 1246–68; Ld of Erddreiniog, Gwredog, Penmynydd and Trecastell; Minister to LLYWELYN III Ap GRUFFUDD, PRINCE OF WALES; *m* Morfudd, dau of Meurig ab Ithel, Ld of Gwent, and *d* 17 Oct 1268

  8 Gruffudd; *fl* 1222–47; Ld of Dinorwig, Henglawdd, Llanrhystudd, Llansadwrn and Tregarnedd; *m* 1st —; *m* 2nd Gwenllian, dau of Hywel ap Ifan ap Trehaearn ap Gwgan, Ld of Brycheinig

  9 Rhys; Ld of Garth Garmon; *d* 1269

  3 Angharad; *m* 1st Tegwared Bais Wen, illegitimate s of LLYWELYN II Ap IORWERTH, PRINCE OF GWYNEDD; *m* 2nd Einion (*fl* 1170–1220) Ap Gwalchmai, of Trefeilir, Ld of Malltraeth y Gwladus; *m* Tegwared ap Cynfrig ap Rhotpert Fawr

EDNYFED FYCHAN's est(?) s,

  Sir TUDUR Ap EDNYFED, Ld of Llangynhafal, Nant, Maenam and Trysglwyn; Steward to LLEWELYN Ap GRUFFUDD, PRINCE OF N WALES, and Seneschall of Gwynedd 1268–78; *m* Ales, dau of Rhisiart ap Cadwaladr ap Gruffudd II ap CYNAN, KING OF GWYNEDD (by Alice, dau of Richard fitz Gilbert de Clare, Ld of Clare and Cardigan), and *d* 1278, leaving:

HEILYN Ap TUDUR; *fl* 1242–82; Ld of Dinallaen, Llangynhafal, Nant and Trysglwyn; hostage of HENRY III 1246–63; granted lands by GRUFFUDD 1281; *m* Annes, dau of Bleddyn, Ld of Abertanat and Dinmael, Denbighs, Baron of Rûg, and *d c* 1298, leaving, with two daus:

  1 GRUFFUDD

  2 Lyweln

  3 Goronwy

The est s,

  GRUFFUDD Ap HEILYN; Ld of Llangynhafel and Nant; Minister to LLYWELYN III Ap GRUFFUDD, PRINCE OF N WALES; *m c* 1305 Gwenhwyfa, dau of Ievan ap Gruffudd ap Madog Fychan, of Maengwynydd, Merioneths, and *d c* 1340, leaving:

GWILYM Ap GRUFFUDD; *b c* 1306; Ld of Llangynhafel and Nant; *m c* 1340 Efa (*d* 1352), dau and heiress of Gruffudd ap Tudur, of Penwnllys, Llengoed, Anglesey, and *d c* 1375, leaving, with an er s (Bleddyn):

GRUFFUDD Ap GWILYM; *b c* 1342; Ld of Nant; inherited lands from his unc Gwilym ap Tudur; *m c* 1360 Generys Fychan, dau and heiress of Madog ap Goronwy, of Erddreiniog and Gwredog, Anglesey, and *d* 1405 in Owen Glendower's rebellion against English rule, leaving (order of birth conjectural):

  1 Gwilym; *d* 1431; ancestor of the OWENs of Penmynydd and GRIFFITHs of Penrhyn

  2 ROBIN

  3 Rhys; had his f's lands in Flints

The 2nd(?) s,

  ROBIN Ap GRUFFUDD Ap GWILYM, of Cochwillan, Llanllechid, Caernarvs; *b c* 1362; settled in Bodfaeo, Llanllechid, Caernarvs; *m* 1st Angharad, dau of Rhys ap Gruffudd, of Penmaenmawr, Caernarvs, and had:

  1 GRUFFUDD

  2 Hywel

ROBIN Ap GRUFFUDD Ap GWILYM *m* 2nd Lowri (English 'Laura'), dau of Goronwy ab Ieuan, of Eifionydd, Merioneths, and *d c* 1445, leaving by her:

  3 Thomas; beheaded Conwy 1468 as Lancastrian in Wars of Roses

The est s,

  GRUFFUDD Ap ROBIN, of Cochwillan; *m* Mallt (English 'Matilda'), dau of Gruffudd Derwas ap Meurig, of Cemmaes, Merioneths, and *d c* 1475, leaving, with three daus:

GWILYM Ap GRUFFUDD Ap ROBIN; *b c* 1429; Sheriff of Caernarvs for life 1485; *m* Angharad, dau of Dafydd ab Ieuan, of Pengwern, Merioneths, and *d c* 1500, leaving, with several daus and an illegitimate s (Morgan) and dau (Alice, *m* as his 1st w Maredudd ab Ieuan; *see* WILLIAMS-WYNN, Bt):

  1 WILLIAM

  2 Thomas Gethin; DCL; *d* by Dec 1556, leaving an illegitimate dau (Gwenllian, *m* Rhys Wynn, of Clegyr, Llanbeulan, Anglesey, and had issue)

  3 Robert

  4 Dafydd

The est s,

WILLIAM WILLIAMS, of Cochwillan; Sheriff Caernarvs 1542, 1547 and 1553, MP Caernarvs 1558; *m* Lowri, dau of Henry Fychan Salesbury, of Llanrhaeadryng-Nghinmeirch, Denbighs, and *d* between 22 June 1558 and 3 June 1559, having had, with nine daus:

1 WILLIAM

2 Thomas, of Faenol, Carmarths; *m* Jane, dau of William Stanley, of Hooton, Cheshire, and *d* 1592, leaving:

(1) Sir WILLIAM WILLIAMS, 1st Bt (E), so *cr* 15 June 1622, of Faenol; *m* 1st his cousin Ellen, dau of WILLIAM WYN Ap WILLIAM (*see below*); *m* 2nd Dorothy, dau of Edward Dymock, of Willington, Flints, and *d c* 1630, leaving by one or other of his ws:

1a Sir THOMAS WILLIAMS, 2nd Bt, of Faenol; *m* Katharine, dau of Robert Wynne, and *d c* 1650, leaving:

1b Sir WILLIAM WILLIAMS, 3rd Bt, of Faenol; *m* 1st Margaret, dau of John Wynne, of Mell; *m* 2nd Margaret, dau and heiress of Richard Jones, of Castle March, and *d c* 1659, leaving by one or other w:

1c Sir GRIFFITH WILLIAMS, 4th Bt, of Faenol; allegedly *m* Penelope Bulkeley, dau of 1st VISCOUNT BULKELEY OF CASHEL (*see* **Lineage (of Bulkeley)** below), and *d c* 1663, leaving:

1d Sir THOMAS WILLIAMS, 5th Bt, of Faenol; *d c* 1670 a minor unm

2d Sir WILLIAM WILLIAMS, 6th and last Bt, of Faenol; MP Caernarvs 1689–*c* 1696; *m* Ellen Bulkeley, dau of 2nd VISCOUNT BULKELEY OF CASHEL, and *dsp c* 1696, when the btcy expired

3 John WILLIAMS/WYNNE; *m* Elen, dau of Hywel ap Rhobert, of Bodsilin in Malltreath (Llanfeirian) Anglesey; ancestor of the WILLIAMSes, of Bodlew

4 Edward, of Maesycastell; High Sheriff Caernarvs 1569; *d* unm *c* 1601

5 Harry, of Llangoed; living 1569

6 Robert; *d* by 1550

The est s,

WILLIAM WILLIAMS/WYNN, of Cochwillan; *m* Dorothy, 4th dau of Sir William Griffith, of Penrhyn, Caernarvs, by Jane, dau of Thomas Stradling, of St Donat's, Glam, and *dvp* by 14 May 1557, leaving, with three daus:

1 William WILLIAMS, of Cochwillan; JP; High Sheriff Caernarvs 1571 and 1592 and Montgomeryshire 1569 and 1596; *m* 1st Agnes, dau of John Wynn ap Meredith, of Gwydyr, and had:

(1) Owen Williams; disinherited; *m* Mary, dau of John Leigh, of The Ridge, Cheshire, and *dvp c* 1590 leaving a dau

(1) Ellen; *m* as his 1st w her cousin Sir WILLIAM WILLIAMS, 1st Bt (*see above*)

1 (cont.) William WILLIAMS *m c* 1569 2nd Barbara, sis of 1st and last Baron Lumley of the 1547 *cr* (*see* SCARBROUGH, E) and widow of Humphrey Lloyd/Llwyd (by whom she was grandmother of 1st VISCOUNT BULKELEY OF CASHEL's w; *see* **Lineage (of Bulkeley)** below), and *d* Feb 1612; had:

(2) Henry; of Cochwillan, which he sold to the (1st or 2nd?) Earl of Pembroke (*see* PEMBROKE and MONTGOMERY, E), who sold it on for £10,000 (a little over £800,00 in late-1990s terms) to Henry's cousin John (*see* below); Henry; James, dau and heiress of Thomas Salusbury, of Denbigh, 3rd s of Sir John Salusbury, of Llewenni, Denbighs, MP Denbighs *temp* HENRY VIII and MARY, and had:

1a Lumley; *m* Dorothy, dau and heir of Rhys Thomas, of Ystym Colwyn, Montgomeryshire, and *d* 1638, leaving issue

2 John, of Llanllechid

3 Rhys

4 Rowland

5 EDMUND

6 Thomas

7 Arthur (Rev), of Meillionydd, Caernarvs; Precentor Bangor Cathedral; *m* Anne, dau of John Lewis, of Chwaen Wen, Llantrisant, Anglesey, and widow of Owen Wynn, of Ystumcegid, LLanfihangel-y-Pennant, Caernarvs, and *d* 3 July 1621; ancestor of the WILLIAMSes of Meillionydd and Ystym Colwyn, whose heiress Anne *m* Sir Robert Howel Vaughan, Bt, of Nannau (*see* 1859 edn), and *d* 4 March 1791

8 Richard

The 4th s,

EDMUND WILLIAMS; Alderman Conwy; *m* Mary (*d* 10 Oct 1585), dau of Owen Wynn, of Disserth, Caernarvs, and *d* 13 Jan 1601, leaving:

1 ROBERT

2 John; *b* 22 March 1582; DD, Dean Sarum and Westminster, Ld Keeper Gt Seal 1620, Bp Lincoln 1621–41, Archbp York 1641–50; bought back Cochwillan (*see above*) and Penrhyn from his cousin Pierce Griffith; *d* unm 25 March 1650, leaving those estates to his n the **1st Bt**

1 Dorothy; *m* 1st Capt Hugh Williams, of Wegg; *m* 2nd Sir William Powel, Surveyor Rolleston Park

2 Ellen; *m* 1st Evan Griffith, of Pengwern, Flints; *m* 2nd Sir Peter Mytton, of Llanerch Park, Denbighs, Ch Justice N Wales and MP Carmarthen, and by him had, with another dau:

(1) Anne, of Llanerch Park; *m* Robert Davies, of Gwysaney, Flints, and was ancestor of the DAVIESes of Gwynsaney and Llanerch Park

The er s,

ROBERT WILLIAMS, of Pen-yr-allt in Dwygyfylchi, Caernarvs; *m c* 1601(?) Elizabeth (*d* 26 April 1608), dau of Gruffudd ap John Gruffudd, of Cefnamwlch, Tudweiliog, Caernarvs, and *d* 1613, leaving, with three daus:

Sir Griffith Williams, 1st Bt (E), so *cr* 28 May 1658 during the Interregnum and again 17 June 1661, of Penrhyn; High Sheriff Caernarvs 1651, 1662; *m* by 1627 Gwen (*bur* 12 Nov 1674), dau of Hugh Gwyn Bodwrda, of Bodwrdda [*sic*], Aberdaron, Caernarvs, and *d* between 3 Sept and 3 Dec 1663, leaving, with at least four other daus:

1 **Sir Robert Williams, 2nd Bt**; *b c* 1627; MP Caenarvs 1656–58 and Carnarvon 1659, High Sheriff Caernarvs 1669–70; *m* 1st 1652 Frances, sis of Sir William Glynne, 1st Bt (*see* 1874 edn); *m* 2nd 12 June 1671 Frances (*dsp*), dau of Sir

Edward Barkham, 1st Bt, and perhaps widow of Col Whyte, of the Friars, Anglesey, and *d* probably 10 Dec 1680, leaving by his 1st w:

(1) **Sir John Williams, 3rd Bt**; *d* unm 4 Jan 1682 aged 19

(2) **Sir Griffith Williams, 4th Bt**; *d* unm a minor 29 Dec 1684

(1) Frances; *m* 1st Robert Lloyd, of Esclusham (*d* 4 Nov 1675) and had issue; *m* 2nd Lord Edward Russell, s of 1st Duke of Bedford (*qv*)

(2) Anne; *m* Thomas Warburton, of Winnington (*bur* 26 Feb 1727), and had:

1a Hugh, of Winnington and Penrhyn; Lt-Gen; *m* Susanna, dau of Edward Norris, MD, of Speke, Lancs, and had:

1b Anne Susanna; *m* 16 Nov 1765 1st and last Baron Penrhyn (*qv*) of the 1783 *cr* and *d* 1 Jan 1816

(3) Gwen; *m* (licence 15 June 1691), as his 2nd w, Sir Walter Yonge, 3rd Bt, of Culliton, Devon (*d* 18 July 1731), and had issue

2 **Sir Hugh Williams, 5th Bt**, of Marle, nr Conwy; *b* 1628; *m* Anne, dau and coheir of Henry Vaughan, of Pant Glas, Ysbyty Ifan, Caernarvs, and *d* 22 March 1686, leaving:

(1) **Sir Griffith Williams, 6th Bt**, of Marl and Pant Glas in Ysbyty Ifan; High Sheriff Caernarvs 1707–08; *m* 7 April 1697 Catherine (*d* 1726), est dau and coheir of Owen Anwyl, s of Robert Anwyl, of Parc, Llanfrothen and Penrhyndeudreath, Merioneths, and *d* July 1734, leaving:

1a **Sir Robert Williams, 7th Bt**, of Llwyn, Marle, Pant Glas and Parc; *dspl* unm Nov 1745 leaving illegitimately by Margaret Roberts:

1b William ROBERTS, of Fleet, Hants; *b* 1742; Lt RN; *m* 1st 3 Nov 1767 —, his f's sis's maid, and had seven children; *m* 2nd 26 Oct 1784 Anne Payton and *d* 7 July 1791, leaving four children by her

1a Anne; *m* 1st 11 Jan 1739 Sir Thomas Prendergast, 2nd and last Bt (*see* GORT, V); *m* 2nd 1761 (separated 1762) Capt Terence PRENDERGAST later PRENDERGAST later WILLIAMS (indenture 27 Jan 1761) (*dsp* 30 Oct 1776) and *dsp* 15 Dec 1770

3 Edmund of Eirianws; *m* Mary, dau of William Wood, of Tal-y-llyn, Dothan, Anglesey, and was *bur* 1 Aug 1714, leaving:

(1) Griffith, of Eirianws; Col; *m* Mary, dau of Robert Williams, of Roe, and *d* by 1725, leaving:

1a HUGH WILLIAMS (Sir), **8th Bt**

4 Roger

5 John

1 Dorothy; *m* John Jeffreys (*see* JEFFREYS, B)

The 7th Bt's 2nd cousin,

Sir Hugh Williams, 8th Bt, of Plas-y-nant, Bettws Garmon, Caernarvs, and Fryars, Llanfores, Anglesey; Lt-Col 53rd Foot 1761; MP Beaumaris 1768–80 and 1785–94; *m* 28 June 1760 Emma Bridget (*d* 13 Aug 1770), only dau and heiress of Thomas Rowlands, of Plas-y-nant, Bettws Garmon, Caernarvs, and widow of 6th VISCOUNT BULKELEY OF CASHEL (*see* **Lineage (of Bulkeley)** below), and *d* 19 Aug 1794, having had, with other issue:

Sir Robert Williams, 9th Bt, JP; *b* 20 July 1764; MP Caernarvs 1790–1826 and Beaumaris 1826–30; *m* 11 June 1799 Anne (*d* 11 Sept 1837), dau of Rev Edward Hughes, of Kinmel Park, Denbighs, and descended via the LEWISes of Llysdulas from the BULKELEYs of Brynddu, and had, with other issue:

1 RICHARD BULKELEY (Sir), **10th Bt**

2 Robert Griffith; *b* 26 July 1809; Army Capt, Comptroller Household of Ld Lt Ireland; *m* 1833 Mary Anne (*d* 1894), dau of Piers Geale, of Dublin, and *d* 13 April 1865, having had, with another dau (Frances Elizabeth, *d* unm):

(1) Laura Anne; *m* 28 Feb 1854 Sir Thomas Gresley, 10th Bt (*see* 1970 edn), and *d* 8 May 1910, leaving issue

(2) Charlotte Maria; *m* 20 July 1861 Capt William Robert Gamul Farmer, Coldstream Gds, JP, DL (*d* 19 May 1910), of Nonsuch Park, Surrey, and *d* 18 Dec 1906, leaving issue

(3) Louisa Gwyn; *m* 15 Aug 1878 Hon Marcus Piers Francis Caulfeild and *d* 14 Nov 1916, leaving issue (*see* CHARLEMONT, V)

(4) Kathleen Emily Bulkeley; *m* 24 Oct 1872 4th Duke of Wellington (*qv*) and *d* 24 June 1927, leaving issue

3 Arthur Wellesley; *b* 6 Oct 1817; Maj 10th Hus; *m* 11 Dec 1854 Rose Charlotte (*d* 18 June 1918), dau of Rev William Stoddart, Vicar Arksey, Yorks, and widow of Richard Breeks, and *d* 17 Nov 1891, leaving:

(1) Arthur Richard Llewellyn; *b* 15 Sept 1859; *d* unm 9 Feb 1952

(2) Rupert Owain Glendwr, JP (Dorset); *b* 22 Oct 1866; *m* 25 Oct 1899 Marion Winkworth (*d* 23 July 1937), only dau of Henry Hammond, of Duncton, Sussex, and *d* 9 Jan 1939, leaving:

1a Elizabeth Marion; *b* 8 July 1903; *m* 4 Jan 1928 Baron Fernand André de Watteville (*d* 6 Aug 1990), s of Baron Oscar de Watteville, of Berne, Switzerland, and *d* 21 March 1974, leaving:

1b *Jean-Jacques Oscar [Baron de Watteville, Chemin du Château 11, CH–1023 Crissier, Vaud, Switzerland]; *b* 25 April 1931; Col Swiss Army (ret); *m* 5 Nov 1970 *Laure, dau of Léon de Sépibus, of Mörel, Valais, Switzerland, and has:

1c *Christian; *b* 22 Sept 1970

1c *Patricia Laurence; *b* 5 June 1973

1b *Elizabeth-Anne [Mme Jean-Pierre Marendaz, 1 Ave Victor Ruffy 1, CH–1012 Lausanne, Vaud, Switzerland]; *b* 14 Aug 1929; *m* 23 July 1953 *Jean-Pierre Arnold Edmund Marendaz, s of Georges Marendaz, of Mathod, Vaud, Switzerland and has:

1c *Thierry Pierre [Thierry Marendaz, Ave Florimont 6A, CH–1006 Lausanne, Vaud, Switzerland]; *b* 1 June 1954; *m* 20 Oct 1979 *Anne Elisabeth, dau of Georges Müller, of Monthey, Valais, Switzerland, and has:

1d *Arnaud Julien; *b* 2 March 1985

1d *Aude Christelle; *b* 4 Oct 1981

1c *Chantal Elisabeth [Mme Jean-Marie Lack, Rue de l'Hotel de Ville 47, CH–2300 La Chaux-de-Fonds, Neuchâtel, Switzerland]; *b* 28 Feb 1956; *m* 31 Aug 1985 *Jean-Marie Lack, s of Maurice Lack, of Neuchâtel, Switzerland, and has:

1d *Nathanäel; *b* 16 Oct 1985

2d *Timothée; b 30 Oct 1991

1d *Noémie; b 3 June 1989

2b *Hélène Antoinette [Mrs Colin Huggett, 5313 Palos Verdos Boulevard, Torrance, CA 90505, USA]; b 20 July 1939; m 29 April 1965 *Colin Edward Huggett, s of Thomas Huggett, of Epsom, Surrey, and has:

1c *Keith Andrew [Keith Huggett, Vacaville, California, USA]; b 1 Aug 1968; m 22 April 1994 *Allyson, dau of Edward Banfield, of Torrance Calif.

1c *Marie-Hélène [Mrs Marie-Hélène Leseux, Boulder, CO, USA 7]; b 2 July 1966; m 19– (divorce 19–) Pascal Leseux, s of Pierre Leseux, of Tours, France, and has:

1d *Austin Pierre; b 9 June 1991

2a Sylvia Mary; b 23 Aug 1905; d unm 17 June 1976

(1) Mabel Rose; b 11 Oct 1856; m 25 Oct 1884 Rev Richard Ernest Ricketts and d 2 Nov 1956, leaving issue (see RICKETTS, Bt)

(2) Annie Frances; b 1858; m 8 Jan 1885 Edward Miles (d Jan 1890), of Birstall, Leics, slr, s of Rev Lomas Miles, Vicar Willow-by-Waterless, Leics, and d 13 Dec 1945, leaving issue

(3) Edith Nina; b Nov 1860; d unm 12 June 1953

(4) Selina Rachel; b 6 June 1868; m 15 April 1903 Henry Francis Field (d 27 June 1941), s of Rev James Field, Rector Braybrooke, Northants, and dsp 9 June 1966 aged 98

(5) Marguerite Fanny; b 21 Sept 1872; m 4 Oct 1905 Capt Frederick William Stoddart, 1st Bn Wilts Regt (ka 27 Oct 1914), er s of Col William Stoddart, Madras SC, and d 15 March 1973, leaving issue

1 Emma; m 17 Aug 1828 V-Adml Sir Charles Eden, KCB (see EDEN OF WINTON, B), and d 8 Jan 1865

2 Charlotte Jemima; m 27 Feb 1834 Stewart Paget (see ANGLESEY, M) and d 3 March 1895

3 Eliza Martha; m 27 April 1839 Sir John Eardley Eardley-Wilmot, 2nd Bt (qv), and d 23 Oct 1887

4 Amelia Jane; m 13 June 1846 Gen Mark Wood, Coldstream Gds (d 18 March 1883), and d 17 Oct 1898, leaving issue

Sir ROBERT d 1 Dec 1830; his est s,

Sir RICHARD BULKELEY WILLIAMS later WILLIAMS-BULKELEY (roy licence 26 June 1827 after inheriting 1822 7th and last VISCOUNT BULKELEY OF CASHEL's estates; see **Lineage (of Bulkeley)** below), **10th Bt**, of Baron Hill, Beaumaris, JP; b 23 Sept 1801; MP Beaumaris 1831–33, Anglesey 1832–37 and 1847–68 and Flints Boroughs 1841–47, Ld Lt Caernarvs 1851–66, High Sheriff 1870; m 1st 7 May 1828 Charlotte Mary (dsp 11 May 1829), dau of 1st Baron Dinorben of Kinmel Park (see 1852 edn); m 2nd 30 Aug 1832 Maria Frances (d 4 March 1889), only dau of Sir Thomas Stanley-Massey-Stanleley, 9th Bt, of Hooton (see 1893 edn ERRINGTON, Bt), and by her had:

1 RICHARD LEWIS MOSTYN (Sir), **11th Bt**

2 Robert Stanley; b 17 April 1836; Capt 9th Lancers; d 1 Feb 1861

3 Thomas James; b 13 March 1840; Col 10th Hus; d 12 Sept 1881

4 Charles William; b 29 Aug 1841; m 22 May 1871 Mary Henrietta (d 1878), dau of Gen Henry S Stephens, KH, and d 1 Feb 1892

The 10th Bt d 28 Aug 1875; his est s,

Sir Richard Lewis Mostyn Williams-Bulkeley, 11th Bt; b 20 May 1833; Capt RHG (Blues); m 1st 11 May 1857 (divorce 1864) Mary Emily, est dau of Henry Bingham Baring (see NORTHBROOK, B); m 2nd 12 Aug 1866 Margaret Elizabeth (d 10 Aug 1909), est dau of Col Thomas Peers Williams, MP, of Temple Ho, Berks, and d 28 Jan 1884, leaving by her a dau (Bridget Henrietta Frances, m 8 Dec 1902 Benjamin Seymour Guinnes (see GUINNESS, Bt) and d 5 Jan 1931, leaving issue) and by his 1st w:

Sir Richard Henry Williams-Bulkeley, 12th Bt, KCB (1922, CB 1916), VD, JP (Carnarvon); b 4 Dec 1862; Anglesey: High Sheriff 1887, Chm QS 1889–1929, Ld Lt 1896; Mayor Beaumaris 1885–88 and 1893; Lt cmdg Liverpool Bde RNAV, Pres TAA 1908, Chm Admlty Vol Ctee 1914, Hon Col Roy Anglesey RE (SR), Cdre RNR Depot 1914, Cdr Mersey Div RNVR, Cdre Roy Yacht Sqdn 1927, Yr Bro Trin Ho, CStJ; m 10 Dec 1885 Lady Magdalen Yorke (d 27 Jan 1940), dau of 5th Earl of Hardwicke (qv), and had:

1 Richard Gerard Wellesley, MC; b 21 July 1887; Lt Gren Gds, Maj Welsh Gds; m 27 Aug 1909 Victoria Alexandrina Stella (m 2nd 28 Sept 1921 (divorce 1944, resumed 1st husb's name by deed poll 1946) Capt Roland Frank Holdway Norman, Leics Regt and RAF (d 2 June 1958), and d 22 April 1965), only dau of Col Hon Sir Henry Charles Legge, GCVO (see DARTMOUTH, E), and d 28 March 1918 of wounds recd in action, leaving:

(1) RICHARD HARRY DAVID (Sir), **13th Bt**

(2) David; b 19 Aug 1915; d unm 27 Feb 1937

(1) Victoria Sylvia Jane; b 8 March 1910; m 3 June 1938 Hubert Alfred Cleary (d 1965), only s of James Cleary, of Brighton, and d 1988

1 Generis Alma Windham; b 17 May 1889; m 12 June 1913 Sir Harry Stapleton Mainwaring, 5th and last Bt (see 1934 edn), and d 14 June 1946, leaving issue

2 Eira Helen; b 2 Jan 1891; m 24 Sept 1921 John Chadwick (d 10 July 1962), 2nd s of T S Chadwick, of Anglesey, and d 3 Aug 1964, leaving a dau

3 Siriol Penelope Diana Katherine; b 23 June 1902; m 11 June 1924 (divorce 1947) Capt Vivian Bulkeley-Johnson, Rifle Bde (d 14 Feb 1968), only s of Francis Head Bulkeley-Johnson

The 12th Bt d 7 July 1942; his gs,

Sir Richard Harry David Williams-Bulkeley, 13th Bt, of Penryhn, TD, JP (Anglesey 1934); b 5 Oct 1911; educ Eton; Maj RWF (TA) WW II, Lt-Col cmdg Caernarvon and Anglesey Army Cadet Force 1946–47, Anglesey: CA 1936, Ld Lt and custos rotulorum 1947–73 (Ld Lt Gwynedd 1974–92),V-Pres T&AFA 1947–92, memb CC 1946 (Chm 1955–57); Mayor Beaumaris 1949–52, CStJ; m 8 June 1938 Renée Arundell (d 1994), yr dau of Sir Thomas Lewis Hughes Neave, 5th Bt (qv), and d 1992, leaving:

1 Sir RICHARD THOMAS WILLIAMS-BULKELEY, **14th and present Bt**

2 +Michael [Michael Williams-Bulkeley Esq, Rhiwlas, Pentraeth, Anglesey LL75 8YG]; b 2 April 1943; educ Eton; late Lt Welsh Gds; m 4 May 1968 *Ellen-Marie, er dau of L Falkum-Hansen, of Oslo, and has:

(1) +James; b 12 Dec 1970; educ Rugby and Reading U (BSc)

(2) +David Haakon; b 20 Oct 1973; educ Eton

Lineage (of Bulkeley): Sir RICHARD BULKELEY, of Baron Hill, Beaumaris; Constable Beaumaris Castle, MP Anglesey 1571, 1603–11 and 1614, Sheriff Anglesey 1570–71, Mayor Beaumaris; m 1st Margaret/Mary, dau of 2nd Lord (Baron) Burgh (qv); m 2nd Catherine, dau of Sir William Davenport, of Broom Hall, Cheshire and d 28 June 1621, leaving by his 1st w, with a dau (Jane, m Morus Wynn; see WILLIAMS-WYNN, Bt):

THOMAS BULKELEY, 1st VISCOUNT BULKELEY OF CASHEL, Co Tipperary (I), so cr 6 Jan 1643/4; b 10 Aug 1585; Sheriff Anglesey 1641–42; m Blanche, dau of Robert Coetmor, of Coetmor, Llanllechid, Caernarvs, by Lumley, dau of Humphrey Lloyd/Llwyd (by Barbara, sis of 1st and last Baron Lumley of the 1547 cr; see SCARBROUGH, E), and d by 1659, leaving, with two other children:

1 Richard; royalist Col Civil War, as which held Beaumaris Castle till 1646; dsp & vp 19 Feb 1649/50, murdered by Richard/Thomas Cheadle, Dep Constable Beaumaris Castle, who was accordingly hanged

2 ROBERT BULKELEY, 2nd VISCOUNT BULKELEY OF CASHEL; High Sheriff Anglesey 1660, MP Anglesey 1660 and 1685–87 and Caernarvs 1675–79, V-Adml N Wales 1679–88; m by 1655 Sarah, dau of Daniel Harvey, of Coombe, Croydon, London Turkey merchant, and d 18 Oct 1688, leaving:

(1) RICHARD BULKELEY, 3rd VISCOUNT BULKELEY OF CASHEL; b 1658; MP (Tory) Beaumaris 1679 and Anglesey 1679–81 and 1690–1704, V-Adml N Wales 1701; m 1st by 1682 Mary, dau of Sir Philip Egerton, of Oulton, Cheshire (see GREY EGERTON, Bt); m 2nd 1 March 1687/8 Elizabeth, widow of Thomas Lort, of Stackpoole, Pembs (m 3rd Thomas Ferrers, of Bangeston, Pembs, MP Pembroke; m 4th, as his 2nd w, John Hooke, of Bangeston, and d July 1757), dau of Humphrey White, of Henllan, Pembs, and d 9 Aug 1704, leaving by his 1st w an only s:

1a RICHARD BULKELEY, 4th VISCOUNT BULKELEY OF CASHEL; b 19 Sept 1682; MP (Tory) Anglesey 1704–15 and 1722–24, Constable Beaumaris Castle and Chamberlain N Wales, V-Adml N Wales 1708–10 and 1711–15, Constable Carnarvon Castle 1713–14; m (licence 12 Feb 1702/3) Bridget, dau of 1st Earl of Abingdon (see LINDSEY and ABINGDON, E), and d 4 June 1724, leaving:

1b RICHARD BULKELEY, 5th VISCOUNT BULKELEY OF CASHEL; b 18 April 1707; MP (Tory) Beaumaris 1730–March 1738/9, Constable Beaumaris Castle and Chamberlain N Wales; m 8 Jan 1739 Edward Williams; see WILLIAMS-WYNN, Bt), dau of Lewis Owen, of Peniarth, Merioneths (see WILLIAMS-WYNN, Bt), and dsp 15 March 1738/9

2b JAMES BULKELEY, 6th VISCOUNT BULKELEY OF CASHEL; b 17 Feb 1716/7; MP (Tory) Beaumaris 1739–52, Constable Beaumaris Castle and Chamberlain N Wales; m 5 Aug 1749 Emma Bridget (m 2nd **Sir Hugh Williams, 8th Bt**; see **Lineage (of Williams)** above), dau and heiress of Thomas Rowlands, of Plas-y-nant, Bettws Garmon, Caerau, Llanfairynghornwy, and Castellior, Llansadwrm, Anglesey, and d 23 April 1752, leaving:

1c THOMAS JAMES BULKELEY later WARREN-BULKELEY (roy licence 20 Sept 1802), 7th and last VISCOUNT BULKELEY OF CASHEL; b 12 Dec 1752; MP (Whig to 1783, Pittite thereafter, hence his peerage) Anglesey 1774–84, cr 14 May 1784 LORD BULKELEY, BARON OF BEAUMARIS, Co Anglesey (GB); Ld Lt Caernarvs 1785–1802; m 26 April 1777 Elizabeth Harriet (d 23 Feb 1826), dau of Sir George Warren, KB, of Poynton, Cheshire, and dsp 3 June 1822, when both peerages expired

(1) Ellen; m Sir WILLIAM WILLIAMS, 6th and last Bt, of Faenol (see **Lineage (of Williams)** above)

1 Penelope; allegedly m Sir GRIFFITH WILLIAMS, 4th Bt, of Faenol (see **Lineage (of Williams)** above)

2 Katherine; b c 1637; m Richard Wynn (see WILLIAMS-WYNN, Bt) and was bur 5 Sept 1706, having had two sons and a dau (d in infancy)

WILLIAMS-WYNN

Arms: Quarterly, 1st and 4th, vert three eagles displayed in fess or (for OWEN GWYNEDD, PRINCE OF N WALES), armed and langued gules; 2nd and 3rd, argent two foxes counter-salient in saltire gules, the dexter surmounted of the sinister (attributed to CADROD HARDD, a 9th-century figure from whom since the 17th century the WILLIAMSes latterly WILLIAMS-WYNNs have claimed descent), a crescent azure in chief for difference. **Crest:** An eagle displayed or, armed and langued gules. **Motto:** *Eryr eryrod eryri* ('The eagle of the eagles of Snowdonia'). **Creation:** Bt. (E) 6 July 1688.

SIR (DAVID) WATKIN WILLIAMS-WYNN, 11TH BT, of Wynnstay, Co Denbigh, DL (Clwyd 1966) [Sir Watkin Williams-Wynn Bt DL, Plâs-yn-Cefn, St Asaph, Clwyd LL17 0EY]; *b* 18 Feb 1940; *s f* 1988; *educ* Eton; Roy Dragoons 1958–63, OC Cheshire Yeo Sqdn QOY 1971–77; MFH: Sir W W Wynn's 1971–77 and 1991– and Flint and Denbigh 1978–90, High Sheriff Clwyd 1990; *m* 1st 26 Oct 1968 (*divorce* 1981) (Harriet) Veryan Elspeth, dau of Gen Sir Norman Hastings Taylour, KCB, DSO, of Ale Farm, Sutton-by-Dover, Kent, and has:

1 +CHARLES EDWARD WATKIN; *b* 16 Sept 1970
2 +Robert Euan Watkin; *b* 10 Sept 1977
1 *Alexandra June *b* 18 Dec 1972
2 *Lucinda Jean *b* 18 Dec 1972

Sir WATKIN *m* 2nd 1983 *Victoria Jane, dau of Lt-Col Ian Dudley De Ath, DSO, MBE, and formerly w of Lt-Col R E Dillon, RM, and by her has:

3 +Nicholas Watkin; *b* 1988
4 +Harry Watkin (twin); *b* 1988

Lineage (of Williams): Notwithstanding the claim to descent from CADROD HARDD (*see* **Arms** above), the most reliable pedigree starts with:

ADDA FAWR, of Genau'r-glyn, Cards; had:

EINION FELYN, of Llanbadarn, Cards; had:

ADDA FOEL; held lands at Rhoscolyn, Menai, Anglesey, 1352; had:

IORWERTH; had:

IEUAN; had:

IOLYN; *m* Myfanwy, dau of Ieuan ap Gruffudd Llwyd, of Llanfair-yng-Nghornwy, Anglesey, and had:

WILLIAM; *m* Anharad, dau of Ieuan ap Hywel, and had:

IEUAN, of Bryngwellan, Rhodogeidio, Anglesey; *m* Margred, dau of Iorwerth ab Ieuan Llwyd, and had:

WILLIAM; *m* Catrin, dau of Richard ap Huw, of Nantanog, Llantrisaint, Anglesey, and had:

IEUAN; *m* Jonet, dau of John ap Gwilym ap Llewelyn, of Ffrasallt, Anglesey, and had:

WILLIAM; *m* Margaret, dau of John ap Rhydderch, of Tregaean, and had:

WILLIAM WILLIAMS; *m* 1st Margaret, dau of John Wynn Owen, of Plas Ucha, Llanfaethlu, Anglesey; *m* 2nd Jane, dau of John Wynn, of Bodewryd, Anglesey, and by her had, with an er s (John, of Chwaen Isaf, Llantrisaint, Anglesey, *d* 1661):

Rev HUGH WILLIAMS, of Nantanog; *b* 1596; DD, Rector Llantrisaint, Preb Bangor and St Asaph; *m* Emma, dau and heiress of John Dolben, of Caeau Gwynion, Denbighs, and *d* 28 Sept 1676, leaving, with two yr sons (John, dsp; David, of Glanalaw, m Anne, dau and heiress of William Maurice, of Cefn-y-braich) and two daus (Margaret, m John Owen, of Pen-rhos, and had a s (Richard) and dau, Margaret):

Sir William Williams, 1st Bt (E), so cr 6 July 1688, KC (1689); *b c* 1634; *educ* Jesus Coll Oxford and Gray's Inn (Treasurer 1681); barrister 1658, Recorder Chester 1667–84 and 1687–1700, MP (Whig) Chester 1675–81, Montgomery 1685 (election declared void) and Beaumaris 1689–90 and 1695–98, Speaker H of C 1680–March 1680/1; ktd 1687, Slr-Gen 1687, as which unsuccessfully led for the

Crown June 1688 in the Trial of the Seven Bishops (for seditious libel, the seditious libel in question consisting of their petitioning JAMES II to be let off having to order their diocesan clerics to promulgate the 2nd Declaration of Indulgence (which in effect permitted RC worship) and claiming as illegal JAMES's arrogation to himself of the power to suspend legislation he disliked), his efforts nevertheless earning him his btcy; despite his promotion under JAMES he supported the Glorious Revolution, though he never again held office, apart from that of Ld Lt Merioneths Oct 1689–March 1690; *m* 14 April 1664 Margaret, est dau and coheir of Watkin Cyffin, of Glascoed, Denbighs, and had:

1 WILLIAM (Sir), **2nd Bt**

2 John, of Chester; barrister; *m* on or after 27 May 1693 Catherine, est dau of Sir Hugh Owen, 2nd Bt (*qv*), and had:

  (1) Hugh; MP Anglesey; *m* 1st Ursula, dau of Sir John Bridgeman, 3rd Bt (*see* BRADFORD, E); *m* 2nd —, dau of Edward Norris, MD, MP Liverpool, and *dsp*

  (2) Cyffin; *m* Mary Bunbury, and *dsp*

  (3) John; Judge; ancestor of the WILLIAMS Bts of Bodelwyddan (*qv*)

  (4) Arthur; Archdeacon St David's; *d* unm

  (5) Edward; *m* 1739 Jane, dau of Lewis Owen and widow of 5th Viscount Bulkeley of Cashel (*see* WILLIAMS-BULKELEY, Bt), and had, with two other daus:

    1a Jane; *m* William Wynne, of Wern, and had:

      1b William, of Peniarth

  (1) Elizabeth; *m* Sir William Owen, 4th Bt (*qv*), and had issue

  (1) Emma; *m* Sir Arthur Owen, 3rd Bt (*qv*)

Sir WILLIAM *d* 11 July 1700; his er s,

  Sir William Williams, 2nd Bt; *b c* 1665; MP Denbigh 1708–10; *m* 1st 1689 Jane, dau and heiress of Edward Thelwall, of Plâs-y-Ward, Denbighs (*see* below **Lineage (of Wynn)**); *m* 2nd Catharine (*dsp*), dau of Mytton Davies, of Gwysanau, Flints, and by his 1st w had:

1 WATKIN (Sir), **3rd Bt**

2 Robert, of Erbistock, Denbighs; MP Montgomeryshire; *m* Meriel, dau of Arthur Williams, of Ystymcolwyn, and *dsp* 1763

3 Richard, of Penbedw, Denbighs; MP Flint; *m* 1st —; *m* 2nd Charlotte, dau and coheir of Richard Mostyn (*see* MOSTYN, B), and had a s (*d* young); *m* 3rd Annabella, dau and heiress of Charles Lloyd, of Drenewydd, Salop, and had four sons (all *dsp*; *see* LANGFORD, B) and, with two other daus:

  (1) Annabella; *m* Rev Philip Puleston, DD, of Pickhill, Denbighs, and had issue

  (2) Jane; *m* Robert Lloyd, of Swan Hill, and had issue

1 Margaret; *m* Lewis Owen and had issue (*see* WILLIAMS-BULKELEY, Bt)

2 Sydney; *m* 7 April 1713 John Wynne, of The Abbey, Denbighs, MP Denbighs

Sir WILLIAM *d* Oct 1740; his est s,

Sir WATKIN WILLIAMS later WILLIAMS-WYNN (on inheriting 7 Jan 1718/9 the Wynnstay and other estates from his mother's cousin Sir John Wynn, 5th and last Bt; *see* **Lineage (of Wynn)** below), **3rd Bt**; *b* 1692; *educ* Jesus Coll Oxford; MP Denbigh 1716–49 (supported both Walpole and the Jacobites), Mayor Oswestry 1728 and Chester 1732; *m* 1st Anne (*dsp*), dau and coheir of Edward Vaughan, of Llwydiarth, Montgomeryshire, and Llangedwin, Denbighs, thus acquiring those estates; *m* 2nd 19 July 1748 Frances (*d* 19 April 1803), dau of George Shakerley (*see* SHAKERLEY, Bt), and *d* 26 Sept 1749, having by her had, with a yr s:

Sir Watkin Williams-Wynn, **4th Bt**; *b* 1749; *educ* Oriel Coll Oxford; MP Salop 1772–74 and Denbighs 1774–89; *m* 1st 11 April 1767 Henrietta, 5th dau of 4th Duke of Beaufort (*qv*); *m* 2nd 21 Dec 1771 Charlotte (*d* 29 Sept 1832), dau of Rt Hon George Grenville (*see* KINLOSS, L), and by her had, with another dau (*d* unm):

1 WATKIN (Sir), **5th Bt**

2 Charles Watkin, PC, of Llangedwin, Denbighs; *b* 9 Oct 1775; MP Montgomeryshire, DCL, FSA, Chllr Duchy Lancaster, Pres Bd Control, Sec at War; *m* 9 April 1806 Mary (*d* 14 June 1838), est dau of Sir Foster Cunliffe, 3rd Bt (*qv*), and *d* 2 Sept 1850, having had, with another s (*d* young) and two daus (*d* young or unm):

  (1) Charles Watkin, of Coed-y-Maen, Welshpool, Montgomeryshire; *b* 4 Oct 1822; MP Montgomeryshire 1862–80, Recorder Oswestry; *m* 18 Aug 1853 Lady Annora Charlotte Pierrepont (*d* 22 March 1888), yr dau of 2nd Earl Manvers (*see* 1953 edn), and *d* 1896, having had:

    1a Arthur Watkin, of Coed-y-Maen, DL Montgomeryshire; *b* 2 June 1856; *educ* Ch Ch Oxford (MA); barrister, Montgomeryshire: High Sheriff 1901, Hon Lt-Col Imp Yeo; *m* 23 July 1892 Alice Mary (*d* 3 March 1956), dau of Hon George Wentworth Fitzwilliam (*see* 1970 edn FITZWILLIAM, E), and *d* 27 Jan 1946, having had:

      1b Charles Watkin; *b* 19 May 1896; Lt SR Coldstream Gds WW I; *ka* 29 Oct 1914

      1b Maud Annora; *b* 10 Aug 1893; *m* 8 April 1920 1st Baron Harvey of Tasburgh (*qv*) and *d* 21 Feb 1970, leaving issue

      2b Alice Nesta Margaret; *b* 10 Nov 1894

    2a Charles Hugh Watkin; *d* an infant 18 July 1858

    3a Henry Cunliffe; *b* 26 July 1863; Maj RFA, Dep Assist Dir Remounts 1911–14; *d* 6 April 1914

    4a Frederick Rowland, CB (1927); *b* 19 Feb 1865; *educ* Univ Coll Oxford (BA); Capt Montgomery Imp Yeo Boer War 1900, Maj Roy W Surrey Regt (TF) WW I, Pncpl Clerk Ctee Office H of C 1921–30; *m* 31 July 1907 Beatrice Kathleen (*d* 6 Oct 1913), est dau of Maj Francis Cooper, RFA, of Markree Castle, Co Sligo, and *d* 18 July 1940, leaving:

      1b John Francis WILLIAMS-WYNN later WILLIAMS-WYNNE (deed poll 1940), CBE (1972), DSO (1944), JP (1951); *b* 9 June 1908; *educ* Oundle and Magdalene Coll Cambridge (BA 1929, MA 1946); commnd RA 1929, served Waziristan 1936 and WW II, Col 1954, Ld Lt Merioneths 1957–74 and Gwynedd 1974–84 (V-Ld Lt 1984–), Constable Harlech Castle 1964–, FRAgS 1970, Pres Timber Growers Assoc 1974; *m* 29 Sept 1938 Margaret Gwendolen Hayward (*d* 1991), dau of Rev George Eliot Roper, and *d* 20 Jan 1998, leaving:

1c +William Robert Charles, JP (1972) [William Williams-Wynne Esq JP, Peniarth, Tywyn, Gwynedd]; *b* 7 Feb 1947; *educ* Eton; FRICS 1972; *m* 18 Oct 1975 *Hon Veronica Frances, 3rd dau of Baron Buxton of Alsa (*qv*), and has:

  1d *Chloë Frances; *b* 1978

  2d *Leonora Mary; *b* 1980

  3d *Rose Margaret; *b* 1981

1c *Virginia (renounced forenames Merion Beatrice by deed poll 1968); *b* 17 Nov 1941; *m* 1st 18 Nov 1964 Maj (Thomas) Peter Anthony DAVIES later ABBOT-DAVIES (deed poll 1969 at mother's request; *d* 1979), only s of Col Thomas Emanuel Herbert Davies, and has:

  1d *Orion Jonathan; *b* 11 Oct 1965

  2d *Hardwin Thomas; *b* 17 Feb 1968

1c (cont.) Mrs Abbot-Davies *m* 2nd 1980 *HH Sayyid Fayer bin Taimur al Said, Dep Omani PM Security and Defence, and by him has:

  1d *Latifah; *b* 1981

2c *Jane Margaret [The Rt Hon The Countess of Home, 99 Dovehouse St, London SW3 6JZ]; *b* 20 Feb 1949; *m* 10 Oct 1972 *15th Earl of Home and has issue (*qv*)

1b Kathleen Charlotte; *b* 26 Jan 1910; *m* 30 April 1931 Maj Christopher William Stewart Blackett, DL, Coldstream Gds, only s of Capt William Stewart Burdett Blackett, Gren Gds, and had:

  1c Archibald Frederick Stewart; *b* 12 Sept 1933; *educ* Eton; Actg Capt Coldstream Gds (Res Offrs); *m* 6 June 1959 *Camilla Joy Victoria, yr dau of Capt Harold George Bissell Thomas, of Jersey, and *d* 20 Feb 1970, leaving:

    1d *Cynthia; *b* 11 June 1960

  2c *John Beauchamp; *b* 6 May 1939; *educ* Eton; late Capt Coldstream Gds; *m* 15 Jan 1964 *Sarah Jennifer, dau of James Trevor Gridley Withycombe, of Bury Farm, Studham, Beds, and has:

    1d *James William Beauchamp; *b* 17 Oct 1964

    2d *Edward John Christopher; *b* 3 Feb 1969

    1d *Annabel Hope; *b* 3 Oct 1966

  1c *Beatrice Olivia [Lady Bland, Totties, Mill Hill, Edenbridge, Kent TN8 5DB]; *b* 7 March 1932; *m* 2 March 1954 Lt-Col Sir Simon Claude Michael Bland, KCVO, Scots Gds, only surv child of Sir Nevile Bland, KCMG, KCVO, and has:

    1d *David Nevile William; *b* 7 Dec 1959

    1d *Catherine Mary; *b* 15 May 1955

    2d *Rachel Corinna; *b* 25 Feb 1957

    3d *Henrietta Portia; *b* 17 April 1967

  2c *Cicely Catherine Victoria; *b* 18 Feb 1946

2b *Annora Beatrice [Mrs Charles Wainman, The Tower House, Hinton St George, Somerset TA17 8SS]; *b* 21 Aug 1911; *m* 1st 7 June 1934 (*divorce* 1945) Lt-Col David Sacheverell Curtis and has issue (*see* CURTIS, Bt); *m* 2nd 4 May 1945 Charles George Gordon Wainman (*d* 1988), s of Capt Philip Stafford Gordon Wainman, of Otterington Hall, Northallerton, Yorks, and by him has:

  1c *(Annora) Mary; *b* 14 April 1946; *m* 21 Feb 1970 *Evangelos N Koemtzopoulos, er s of Gen Koemtzopoulos, of Athens, and has had:

    1d *Nicholas; *b* 1974

    2d *Mark; *b* 1979

    1d Laura; *b* 1971; *d* 1978

    2d *Marina; *b* 1981

1a Mary; *m* 1 June 1886 Henry Goulbourn Chetwynd-Stapylton and *d* 9 Jan 1951, leaving issue (*see* CHETWYND, V)

2a Agnes Sophia; *d* unm 12 July 1954 in her 96th year

3a Annora Margaret; *m* 17 Jan 1901 William Douglas Watson Smyth (*d* 5 Feb 1918), of Wadhurst Castle, Sussex, and Edwin's Hall, Essex, and *d* 21 Dec 1954, leaving issue

4a Constance Hariott; *d* unm 24 June 1950

(1) Mary; *m* 16 May 1832 James Milnes Gaskell, JP, DL, MP (*d* 5 Feb 1873), of Thornes Ho, Yorks, and *d* 21 April 1869, leaving issue

(2) Hariot Hester; *m* 31 May 1836 John Lindsay, of Loughry, Co Tyrone, and *d* his widow 18 March 1878

(3) Sidney; *m* 12 Dec 1844 Sir Francis Hastings Doyle, 2nd Bt (*d* 8 June 1888; *see* 1970 edn), and *d* 23 Nov 1867, leaving issue

3 Henry Watkin (Rt Hon Sir), KCB, GCH; *b* 16 March 1783; Envoy Denmark; *m* 30 Sept 1813 Hester Frances, 6th dau of 1st Baron Carrington (*qv*), and *d* 28 March 1856, having had, with another dau (*d* an infant):

(1) Grenville Watkin; *b* 1816; *d* 7 Jan 1865

(2) Arthur Watkin; *b* 1819; Maj 23rd RWF; *k* cmdg Regt at Battle of Alma 20 Sept 1854

(3) Henry Bertie Watkin, of Howbery Park, Oxon, and Nant-y-Melched, Montgomeryshire, JP, DL; *b* 23 Sept 1820; High Sheriff 1871; *m* 20 Sept 1848 Marion (*d* 25 July 1907), dau of Maj-Gen Sir James Limond, CB, and *d* 4 Oct 1895, having had, with a s and other dau (*d* young):

  1a Jessie Marie; *m* 27 Aug 1873 Stanley Leighton and *d* 18 Dec 1939, leaving issue (*see* LEIGHTON, Bt)

  2a Frances Caroline; *m* 6 Nov 1872 Samuel Richard Brewis, JP (*d* 4 March 1897), of Ibstone Ho, Oxon, and *d* 3 May 1918, leaving issue

  3a Bertha Marion; *m* 4 March 1886 Joseph Godman (*d* 18 Sept 1896), of Park Hatch, Surrey, and *d* 27 Dec 1936, leaving issue

  4a Henrietta Catherine Letitia; *m* 14 Sept 1882 Hon Robert William Henry Rodney, s of 6th Baron Rodney (*qv*), and *d* 18 Nov 1948, leaving issue

(1) Charlotte Henrietta; *m* 14 June 1847 Count Frederick Bismarck (*d* 16 April 1893) and *d* 17 Sept 1873, leaving issue

(2) Katharine; *m* 11 Sept 1840 Gen John Studholme Brownrigg, CB (*d* 1 April 1889; *see* 1881 edn BROWNRIGG, Bt)

(3) Marie Emily; *m* 28 April 1852 her cousin **Sir Watkin Williams-Wynn, 6th Bt** (*see* below), and *d* 21 Sept 1905, leaving issue

1 Charlotte; *m* 1806 Lt-Col William Shipley (*see* LANGFORD, B) and had issue

2 Henrietta Elizabeth; *m* 17 Dec 1810 1st Baron Delamere (*qv*) and *d* 18 Aug 1852, leaving issue

The 4th Bt *d* 29 July 1789; his only s,

  Sir Watkin Williams-Wynn, 5th Bt; *b* 25 Oct 1772; *educ* Ch Ch Oxford; MP Beaumaris 1794–96 and Denbighs 1796–1840, Ld Lt Denbighs and Merioneths, ADC to WILLIAM IV; *m* 4 Feb 1817 Henrietta Antonia, est dau of 1st Earl of Powis (*qv*), and *d* 6 Jan 1840, leaving:

1 **Sir Watkin Williams-Wynn, 6th Bt**; *b* 22 May 1820; *educ* Westminster and Ch Ch Oxford; 1st Life Gds 1839–43, ret as Lt; MP Denbighs 1841–85, Hon Col Montgomery Yeo Cav, Lt-Col 1st Denbigh Rifle Vol Corps, ADC to HM QUEEN VICTORIA; *m* 18 April 1852 his cousin Mary Emily (*see* above) and *d* 9 May 1885, having had, with another dau (*d* unm):

  (1) Louise Alexandra; *m* 26 Aug 1884 (*divorce* 1898) her cousin **Sir Watkin Williams-Wynn, 7th Bt**, and *d* 18 Aug 1911, leaving issue (*see* below)

2 Herbert Watkin; *b* 29 April 1822; Col, MP Montgomeryshire; *m* 26 July 1855 Anna (*d* 23 Jan 1926), dau and heiress of Edward Lloyd, of Cefn, Denbighs, and *d* 22 June 1862, leaving:

  (1) Edward Watkin; *b* 3 June 1857; Lt Scots Gds; *d* 8 Sept 1880

  (2) **Sir (Herbert Lloyd) Watkin Williams-Wynn, 7th Bt**, CB, TD, JP Salop and Merioneths, JP, DL Denbighs; *b* 6 June 1860; *educ* Trin Coll Cambridge (BA); High Sheriff Denbighs 1890, Ld Lt Montgomeryshire, Pres TAA, MP Denbighs May–Nov 1885, Lt-Col cmdg 7th RWF (TA), KGStJ; *m* 26 Aug 1884 (*divorce* 1898) Louise Alexandra, dau of **Sir Watkin Williams-Wynn, 6th Bt**, and *d* 24 May 1944, leaving:

    1a **Sir Watkin Williams-Wynn, 8th Bt**, JP, DL Denbighs; *b* 25 Jan 1891; *educ* Eton and Trin Coll Cambridge (BA 1913); Lt 1st Roy Dragoons and Personal Staff WW I (wounded); Denbighs: High Sheriff 1948, V-Lt 1949; *m* 14 Sept 1920 Daisy, OBE (1957) (*d* 24 Nov 1977), yr dau of John Johnson Houghton, of Westwood, Neston, Cheshire, and *d* 9 May 1949, having had:

      1b Watkin; *b* 6 April 1925; *educ* Eton; Lt 1st Roy Dragoons WW II; *d* following an accident 18 Jan 1946

      1b (Margaret) Helen; *m* 1st 23 July 1941 (*divorce* 1950) Capt (Hubert Charles) Paul(et) Hamilton, Roy Irish Fus, only s of Judge Hubert Charles Hamilton, KC, of Moyne, Durrow, Queen's Co, and Carolside, Berwicks, and had:

        1c *Andrew Paulet; *b* 24 Oct 1943; *educ* Millfield

      1b (cont.) Mrs Helen Hamilton *m* 2nd 16 Oct 1950 Lt-Col Sir Richard Bertram Verdin, OBE, TD, JP, DL (*d* 16 Aug 1978), of Stoke Hall, Nantwich, Cheshire, Garnstone, Weobley, Herefs, and Darnhall, Winsford, Cheshire, est s of Lt-Col Richard Norman Harrison Verdin, TD, JP, DL, of Garnstone, and by him had:

        2c *Allister Richard Norman; *b* 29 Aug 1963

      2b Bronwen Mary; *m* 24 Sept 1946 (*divorce* 1951) Capt Michael Rowland Godfrey Llewellyn, Gren Gds, only s of Col Sir Robert Godfrey Llewellyn, 1st Bt, CB, CBE, MC, TD, JP, DL (*see* 1970 edn LLEWELLYN, Bt, of Baglan), of Tredilion, Park, Abergavenny, Mon, and *d* 29 Aug 1965

      3b Joan; *m* 9 June 1951 Maj Geoffrey Richard Michael Sewell, Gren Gds, of Tysoe Manor, Tysoe, Warwicks, only surv s of Brig-Gen Horace Somerville Sewell, CMG, DSO, of Arcadia, Duncans, Jamaica, and had:

        1c *David Nigel Wynn; *b* 4 April 1953; *educ* Harrow

        2c *Mark Geoffrey; *b* 27 May 1955; *educ* Harrow

        3c *Charles Percy; *b* 22 Dec 1958

    1a Gwladys Elin; *b* 4 Sept 1885; *m* 11 June 1912 Maj Walter Roger Owen Kynaston, TD, JP, DL (*d* 24 Sept 1935), of Hardwick, Salop, and *d* 8 May 1956, leaving issue

    2a Constance Mary; *b* 20 Sept 1895; *m* 28 April 1925 Maj Guy Charles Mostyn-Owen, 12th Lancers (Res), 2nd s of Charles Roger Mostyn-Owen, of Erway, Ellesmere, Salop

  (3) ROBERT WILLIAM HERBERT WATKIN (Sir), **9th Bt**

  (1) Helen Florentia; *b* 5 Nov 1858; *d* unm 16 Nov 1956 aged 98

1 Henrietta Charlotte; *m* 16 April 1843 Sir Hugh Williams, 3rd Bt, of Bodelwyddan (*qv*), and *d* 28 May 1878, leaving issue

The 8th Bt's uncle,

  Sir Robert William Herbert Watkin Williams-Wynn, 9th Bt, KCB (1938), DSO (1902), TD (1909), JP Denbighs and Flints; *b* 3 June 1862; *educ* Wellington and Ch Ch Oxford (BA 1891); MFH Flint and Denbigh 1888–1945, Denbighs: Ld Lt, Pres TAA, Hon Capt, Lt-Col and Brevet Col Montgomery Yeo, Hon Col 61st Carnarvon and Denbigh Yeo (TA), Boer War 1900–01 (despatches twice) and WW I (despatches three times), KStJ; *m* 28 Jan 1904 Elizabeth Ida, MBE (1918), JP (Flints 1932) (*d* 28 Nov 1970 aged 95), 2nd dau of George William Lowther (*see* LOWTHER, Bt), and had:

1 OWEN WATKIN (Sir), **10th Bt**

2 Edward Watkin, OBE (1945); *b* 26 Nov 1908; *educ* Eton and RMC Sandhurst; Maj TARO Welsh Gds WW II, ADC to Maj-Gen cmdg 9th and 11th Armoured Divs 1941–44, Mil Sec: Br Mil Mission USSR 1944 and C-in-C W African Forces 1945, FRAGS; *m* 10 Feb 1949 Roma Sunderland, dau of Kenneth Murray Matheson, of Western District, Victoria, Australia, and *dsp* 8 Sept 1977

1 *Joyce; *b* 2 Oct 1906; *m* 6 Feb 1929 Duncan Robertson (*d* 1987), of Llanlysilio Hall, Llangollen, Denbighs, 2nd s of Sir Henry Beyer Robertson, JP, DL, of Palé Llandderfel, Merioneths, and has had:

  (1) Sheila Ann; *b* 1929; *m* 1st 1953 (*divorce* 1975) Henry Saxon Tate and had issue (*see* TATE, Bt); *m* 2nd 1976 Humphrey Sandford, of The Isle, Shrewsbury, Salop, and *d* 1987

  (2) *Jean Margaret [Mrs Peter Greenwell, Tregeiriog, nr Llangollen, Clywd LL20 7HU]; *b* 1932; *m* 1956 *Capt Peter Miles de Wend Greenwell and has had:

    1a *Rupert Peter; *b* 1959; *educ* Milton Abbey

    2a James Robertson; *b* 1963; *educ* Eton; murdered in Zimbabwe 1982

    3a *Duncan Charles de Wend; *b* 1966; *educ* King's Sch Bruton

  (3) *Bridget Jennifer [The Rt Hon The Lady de Clifford, Riggledown, Pennymoor, Devon EX16 8LR]; *b* 1935; *m* 1959 27th Baron de Clifford (*qv*)

2 *Margaret; *b* 21 March 1911; *m* 4 Oct 1934 Maj Hon Peter Hotham (*see* HOTHAM, B) and has issue

The 9th Bt *d* 23 Nov 1951; his er s,

Sir (Owen) Watkin Williams-Wynn, 10th Bt, CBE (1969), of Wynnstay, Denbighs, JP (Denbighs 1937); *b* 30 Nov 1904; *educ* Eton and RMA Woolwich; WW II (despatches twice, POW), Maj RHA (Res), Lt-Col cmdg 361 Med Regt RA (TA) 1947, Hon Col 361 Med Regt RA 1952, MFH: Flint and Denbigh 1946–61, Sir W W Wynn's 1957, Liaison Offr Min Ag N Wales 1961, Ld Lt Clwyd 1974–88 (Ld Lt Denbighs 1966–74, V-Lt 1957–66, DL 1947–57, High Sheriff 1954), FRAGS; *m* 1st 21 Feb 1939 Margaret Jean, OStJ (*d* 4 Sept 1961), dau of Col William Alleyne Macbean, RA; *m* 2nd 18 March 1968 *Gabrielle Haden [Dowager Lady Williams-Wynn, Eryl, Llangedwyn, Oswestry, Salop], formerly w of W/Cdr Matheson, RAF, and dau of Herbert Alexander Caffin, and *d* 1988, having had by his 1st w:

1 Sir (DAVID) WATKIN WILLIAMS-WYNN, **11th and present Bt**

2 Robert Watkin; *b* 11 April 1948; *educ* Eton; 2nd Lt 14th/20th King's Hus; *kas* Belfast 13 July 1972

Lineage (of Wynn): GRUFFUDD Ap CYNAN; *b c* 1055; PRINCE OF GWYNEDD; *m c* 1095 Angharad (*d* 1162), dau of Owain ab Edwin, of Tegeingl (modern Englefield, Flints), and *d* 1137, leaving:

OWEN GWYNEDD; *b c* 1100; PRINCE OF GWYNEDD; *m* 1st (*annulled* due consanguinity) his 1st cousin Cristin, dau of Gronwy ab Owain, of Tegeingl, and had:

1 RHODRI

2 Dafydd; *m* Emma, illegitimate dau of Geoffrey, Count of Anjou and fndr of the PLANTAGENET dynasty, and *d* 1203

1 Angharad

OWEN GWYNEDD, PRINCE OF GWYNEDD, *m* 2nd Gwladus, dau of Llywarch ap Trahaearn, of Arwystli, Powys, and by her had:

3 Iorwerth *Drwyndwn* ('Crooked Nose') ap Owen Gwynedd; *m* Margaret, dau of Madoc, Prince of Powys, and had an only s:

(1) LLEWELYN Ap IORWERTH, called 'The Great'; recovered 1194 the crown of N Wales from his uncle DAVID; *d* 1240; gf of:

1a LLEWELYN Ap GRIFFITH, called 'Llewelyn The Last', being the last native Sovereign Prince of Wales; *k* Builth 11 Dec 1282

2 Gwenllian; *m* OWAIN CYFEILIOG, PRINCE OF POWYS

OWEN GWYNEDD, PRINCE OF GWYNEDD, had allegedly by more wives several other children and without doubt illegitimately by Angharad, dau of Peredur:

4 Cynan; *d* 1173

His est s,

RHODRI ap OWEN GWYNEDD; *m* 1st Gwenllian, dau of RHYS Ap GRUFFUDD, PRINCE OF DEHEUBARTH (roughly coterminous with S Wales); *m* 2nd —, dau of REGINALD, KING OF THE ISLE OF MAN, and *d* 1195, having had probably by his 1st w, with an est s (Gruffud, granted land by KING JOHN OF ENGLAND 1214, living 1240) and a yst s (Einion):

THOMAS Ap RHODRI; *m* Margred, dau of Einion ap Seisyll, of Merioneth, and had:

CARADOG Ap THOMAS; perhaps the person of that name who was envoy from LLYWELYN THE GREAT to HENRY III 1221 and 1237; *m* Efa, dau of Gwyn ap Gruffudd, of Cegidfa, Montgomeryshire (modern Guisfield, Powys), and had:

GRUFFUDD Ap CARADOG; granted land on privileged terms by LLYWELYN Ap GRUFFUDD, PRINCE OF WALES; *m* Lleucu, dau of Llywarch Fychan ap Llywarch Goch, and had:

DAFYDD Ap GRUFFUDD Ap CARADOG, of Nanconwy; held 1350 lands in Bryncelyn, Lleyn, Caernarvs, which had been granted with privileged tenure by LLYWELYN Ap GRUFFUDD, PRINCE OF WALES; *m* Efa, dau of Gruffudd Fychan ap Gruffudd ap Moriddig, of Penyfed, Dolbenmaen, Caernarvs, and had:

HYWEL Ap DAFYDD; *m* 1st Efa, dau of Ieuan ap Hywel, of Henllys, Cefn-y-fan (*i.e.*, Ystumcegid), Dolbenmaen; *m* 2nd —, dau of Hywel ap Cynwrig Fychan, and by her had a s (Tudur); also had by one or other wife several other children and by his 1st w:

MAREDUDD Ap HYWEL, of Cefn-y-fan; living 1353; *m* Morfudd, dau of Ieuan Goch ap Dafydd Goch, of Penllech, Leyn, and had, with an er s (Ieuan, of Ystumcegid, *d* 1403) and three daus:

ROBERT Ap MAREDUDD; living 1403; *m* aged 80 Angharad, dau of Dafydd ap Llywelyn, of Cefnmelgoed, Llanychaiarn, Cards, and had:

IEUAN Ap ROBERT; *fl* 1437–68; *m* Catrin, dau of Rhys ap Hywel Fychan, of Bron-y-foel, Ystumllyn, Cricieth, Caernarvs, and had:

MAREDUDD Ab IEUAN Ap ROBERT; bought Gwydir, nr Llanrwst, Caernarvs, from Dafydd ap Hywel, of Coytmore; *m* 1st Alice, illegitimate dau of Gwilym ap Gruffudd ap Robin, of Cochwillan, Caenarvs (*see* WILLIAMS-BULKELEY, Bt); *m* 2nd Gwenhwyfar, dau of Gruffudd ap Hywel *y Farf* ('of the beard') and by her had a dau (Elsbeth); *m* 3rd Margaret, dau of Morus ap John, of Clenennau, Dolbenmaen, and *d* 1525, having by her had two sons (Humphry Wyn; Cadwaladr) and seven daus, several other children by a variety of mistresses and by his 1st w, with three yr sons (Rhys Wyn; William Wyn; Rhydderch) and six daus:

JOHN WYN Ap MAREDUDD, of Gwydir; High Sheriff Caernarvs 1544; *m* Elen, dau of Morus ap John, of Clenennau, and *d* 9 July 1559, leaving:

MORUS WYN, of Gwydir; MP Caernarvs 1553, 1554, 1559, 1563–677, High Sheriff Caernarvs 1555, 1570 and 1578; *m* Jane, dau of Sir Richard Bulkeley (*see* WILLIAMS-BULKELEY, Bt), and *d* 10 Aug 1580, leaving, with three yr sons (Elis; Edward, of Ystrad, ancestor of the WYNNs of Llwyn; Robert) and several daus:

Sir JOHN WYN, 1st Bt (E), so cr 29 June 1611, of Gwydir; *b* 1553; ktd 1606, author: *The History of the Gwydir Family* (not published till 1770); *m c* 1575 Sidney, dau of Sir William Gerard, Ld Chllr Ireland, and *d* 1 March 1626, having had, with eight other sons and two daus:

1 Sir RICHARD WYN, 2nd Bt, of Gwydir; *b c* 1588; Gentleman Privy Chamber to CHARLES I when Prince of Wales, MP Caernarvs 1619, Ilchester 1621–22, 1624–25 and 1625, Andover April-May 1640 and Liverpool 1640–49; *m* 16

June 1616 Anne, dau and coheir of Sir Francis Darcy, of Isleworth, Middx, and *dsp* 19 July 1649

2 Sir OWEN WYNN, 3rd Bt, of Gwydir; *m* Grace, dau of Hugh Williams, of Werg, Caernarvs, and *d c* 1660, leaving:

(1) Sir RICHARD WYNN, 4th Bt, of Gwydir; MP Caernarvs 1647–48 and 1661–74, Sheriff Caernarvs 1657–58; *m* Sarah, dau of Sir Thomas Middleton, 1st Bt, of Chirk Castle, Denbighs, and *dspm* by 18 Nov 1674, leaving:

1a Mary; *m* 30 July 1678, as his 1st w, 4th Earl of Lindsey (*see* LINDSEY and ABINGDON) and had issue

2 William (6th s); Prothonotary Wales, bought Branas, Ederirnion, Merioneths, from Humphrey Branas; *m* between 26 Oct 1622 and 20 March 1628 Jane, dau and heiress of Thomas Lloyd, of Milton, Kent, and had:

(1) Richard, of Branas and Garthgynan; High Sheriff Merioneths 1667; *m* Katherine (*bur* 5 Sept 1706 aged 69), dau of Thomas, Viscount Bulkeley, and had two sons and a dau (*d* in infancy)

(1) Sidney; *m* Edward Thelwall, of Plâs-y-Ward, Denbighs, and had:

1a Jane; *b* 25 Dec 1665; *m* 1689 **Sir William Williams, 2nd Bt** (*see* **Lineage (of Williams)** above) and had issue

2a Sidney; *m* Cadwallader Wynn, of Foelas

3a Mary; *m* Edward Vaughan

3 Henry (10th and yst s); had:

(1) Sir JOHN WYNN, 5th and last Bt, of Watstay, which he renamed Wynnstay, Denbighs; *b c* 1628; Sheriff Caernarvs 1674–75, MP Merioneths 1678–79, 1679–81, 1685–87, 1689–90 and 1690–95; *m* Jane, dau and heiress of Eyton Evans, of Watstay, and *dsp* 7 Jan 1718/9, when the btcy expired

WILLIAMSON

Arms: Or a chevron gules between three trefoils slipped sable.
Crest: Out of a mural crown gules a wyvern's head, wings addorsed or. **Creation:** Bt. (E) 3 June 1642.

SIR NICHOLAS FREDERICK HEDWORTH WILLIAMSON, 11TH BT, of East Markham, Co Nottingham [Sir Nicholas Williamson Bt, Abbey Croft, Mortimer, Berks RG7 3PE]; *b* 26 Oct 1937; *s* unc 1946; *educ* Eton; late 4th/7th Roy Dragoon Gds

Lineage: ROBERT WILLIAMSON, of E Markham, Notts; *m* Faith, 5th dau of Sir Edward Ayscough, of S Kelsey, Lincs, and had an est s:

Sir Thomas Williamson, 1st Bt (E), so cr 3 June 1642, of E Markham; *bapt* 14 May 1609; *m* 1st 27 Aug 1633 Jane (*bur* 22 Aug 1642/43), est dau of Sir Edward Hussey, 1st Bt, of Honington, Lincs; *m* 2nd 5 May 1647 Dionysia (*dsp* 1684), dau of William Hale, of King's Walden, Essex, and *d* 14 Oct 1657, leaving by his 1st w, with other issue:

1 **Sir Thomas Williamson, 2nd Bt**; *bapt* 10 May 1636; *m* Dorothy (*d* 4 Nov 1699), yst dau and coheir of George Fenwick, of Brinkburne, Northumberland, thus acquiring the Monkwearmouth estate, and *dsp* 23 April 1703

2 **Sir Robert Williamson, 3rd** Bt; *m* Rebecca, dau of John Burrows, of London, and was *bur* 25 May 1707, leaving:

(1) **Sir William Williamson, 4th** Bt; *bapt* 9 Oct 1681; High Sheriff Co Durham 1723–47; *m* 1st 1703 Elizabeth (*d* 1736), yst dau and coheir of John Hedworth, of Harraton, Co Durham; *m* 2nd Mary (*dsp* 17 April 1752), dau and heiress of William Featherstonhaugh, of Brancepeth, Co Durham, and by his 1st w had, with other issue:

1a HEDWORTH (Sir), **5th Bt**

2a William (Rev); DD, Fell Merton Coll Oxford, Rector Whickham, Co Durham; *m* 9 Oct 1748 Frances Barras (*bur* 8 June 1761) and *d* 23 Aug 1763, leaving:

1b William; *d* unm

1b Anne; *m* 26 Oct 1782 Robert HOPPER later WILLIAMSON (*d* 13 Jan 1835), Recorder Newcastle, and *d* 28 Sept 1829, leaving issue

Sir WILLIAM *d* April 1747; his est surv s,

Sir Hedworth Williamson, 5th Bt; High Sheriff Co Durham 1747–88; *m* 1747 Elizabeth (*d* 10 Oct 1793), dau and heiress of William Hudleston, of Millom Castle, Cumberland, and had:

1 William Hudleston; *dvp* 12 April 1782

2 HEDWORTH (Sir), **6th Bt**

3 Thomas (Rev); Rector Stoke Damerel, Devon; *d* 16 Feb 1828, leaving:

(1) Ferdinand Thomas; Capt 73rd Regt; *m* 16 July 1827 Frances Caroline (*m* 2nd 31 Aug 1835 Hamilton Gyll, of Shenley Lodge and Salisbury Hall, Herts), dau and coheir of Sir John Murray, 8th Bt, of Stanhope (*see* 1878 edn), and *dsp* 16 Dec 1834

(2) Henry William; *m* 1829 Margaret, 2nd dau of Philip Augustus Browne, of Devonshire Place, London, and *d* 1844, leaving, with two daus:

1a Augustus Henry; *b* 1831; Capt 30th Foot; *d* 1900

2a Ferdinand Hedworth, DL (Sussex); *b* 1835; Lt 4th Foot; *d* 1 Jan 1893

(3) Hedworth; Lt 73rd Regt; *d* 12 Nov 1828

(1) Mary; *m* 21 Aug 1824 Frederick Solly Flood, of Ballynaslaney Ho, Co Wexford, and *d* 1864

The 5th Bt *d* 9 Jan 1788; his er s,

Sir Hedworth Williamson, 6th Bt; MA Oxon; High Sheriff Co Durham 1788–1810; *m* 23 Oct 1794 Maria (*d* 10 Jan 1848), dau of Sir James Hamilton, of Co Monaghan, and had, with another dau (*d* unm):

1 HEDWORTH (Sir), **7th Bt**

2 William Hamilton; *b* 3 Aug 1800; *m* 25 April 1854 Mary, est dau of Robert William Brandling, of Low Gosforth, and *d* 2 April 1884

3 Robert Hudleston; *b* 5 April 1810; EICS; *m* July 1843 Margaret Grace, 2nd dau of William Gordon, of Millrig, Ayrshire, and *d* 14 Aug 1869, leaving:

(1) Cecil Hedworth; *b* 18 Oct 1845; Capt 6th Dragoon Gds; *m* 24 Feb 1886 Charlotte Campbell, DGStJ (*d* Jan 1941), only dau of Alexander Campbell-Johnston, of Pimlico, and *d* 27 June 1909, leaving:

1a Hudleston Noel Hedworth, DSO (1920), MC (1917); *b* 27 Dec 1886; *educ* Eton and RMA Woolwich; Col (Hon Brig) RA, WWs I (despatches three times, wounded, Croix de Guerre Belgium, Orders St Vladimir and St Stanislas Russia) and II (despatches), Assist Controller BOT 1946; CC 1961 and CA 1970 W Sussex; *m* 1st 20 Feb 1923 (*divorce* 1926) Helen Marjorie (*d* 14 Oct 1969), only dau of Arthur Edward Lord, of The Mount, Hallow, Worcester; *m* 2nd 20 Jan 1926 Leila Isabel (*d* 1983), only dau of Lt-Col Robert William Peter Lodwick, of Camberley, and *d* 19 April 1971, leaving by her:

1b *Mary [Lady Nicholas Gordon-Lennox, South Nore, W Wittering, W Sussex PO20 8AT]; *b* 20 March 1934; Extra Ldy-in-Waiting to HRH PRINCESS ALEXANDRA 1990–; *m* 14 Jan 1958 *Lord Nicholas Charles Gordon Lennox, KCMG, KCVO (see RICHMOND and GORDON, D), and has issue

1 Maria Dorothea; *m* 20 Oct 1818 David Barclay (*d* 1 July 1861) of Eastwick Pk, Surrey, and *d* 1846, leaving issue

2 Sophia Jane; *m* 6 Sept 1823 2nd Earl of Zetland (*see* ZETLAND, M) and *dsp* 21 May 1865

The 6th Bt *d* 14 March 1810; his est s,

Sir Hedworth Williamson, 7th Bt; *b* 1 Nov 1797; MA Cantab; MP Durham 1831–37 and Sunderland 1847–52; *m* 18 April 1826 Hon Anne Elizabeth Liddell, 3rd dau of 1st Baron Ravensworth (*qv*), and had:

1 HEDWORTH (Sir), **8th Bt**

2 William Henry; *b* 14 Oct 1828; BA Oxon; *d* unm 6 July 1904

3 Charles; *b* 1 Sept 1833; Lt-Col 60th Rifles; *m* 20 April 1871 Isabella Henrietta (*d* 1874), yst dau of Edmund H Shipperdson, of Hermitage, Co Durham, and *dsp* 4 March 1877

4 Victor Alexander, CMG, DL (Co Durham 1865); *b* 28 June 1838; MA Oxon; barrister Inner Temple, MLC and MEC Fiji; *d* 16 Sept 1924

The 7th Bt *d* 24 April 1861; his est s,

Sir Hedworth Williamson, 8th Bt; JP, DL (Co Durham); *b* 25 March 1827; Attaché St Petersburg and Paris (resigned June 1854), MP N Durham 1864–74, High Sheriff Co Durham 1877, Capt Durham Vol Artillery; *m* 3 Feb 1863 Elizabeth Jane (*d* 1 Jan 1920), 4th dau of 1st Earl of Ravensworth (*see* RAVENSWORTH, B), and *d* 26 Aug 1900, leaving:

1 **Sir Hedworth Williamson, 9th Bt**; JP, DL (Co Durham); *b* 23 May 1867; High Sheriff 1904; *d* unm 27 Oct 1942

2 Adolphus Hudleston, CMG (1917), MVO (1909); *b* 5 July 1869; Capt RN, Naval Attaché Rome 1908–10, served WW I (despatches); *d* 14 July 1918

3 Frederick Charles; *b* 22 Sept 1872; *m* 28 June 1900 Phyllis (*d* Sept 1948), dau of Lt-Col Charles Edward Hunter, JP, DL, and *d* 22 March 1907, leaving:

(1) **Sir Charles Hedworth Williamson, 10th Bt**; *b* 6 Sept 1903; Lt Northumberland Hus Yeo; *d* unm 8 April 1946

(2) William Hedworth; *b* 9 Sept 1906; *educ* Ch Ch Oxford (BA); Maj Northumberland Hus Yeo WW II; *m* 10 Dec 1936 Diana Mary (*m* 2nd 7 June 1945 1st Baron Hailes, PC, GBE; *see* BUCHAN-HEPBURN, Bt), only dau of Brig-Gen Hon Charles Lambton, DSO (*see* DURHAM, E), and was *ka* Middle East 31 Oct 1942, leaving:

1a **Sir NICHOLAS FREDERICK HEDWORTH WILLIAMSON, 11th and present Bt**

(1) Elizabeth Mary; *b* 15 April 1901

1 Beatrice Ann; *m* 12 June 1887 Col Edward William Herbert, CB, and *d* 8 June 1928, leaving issue (*see* POWIS, E)

2 Horatia Dorothy; *m* 1 June 1896 Arthur Herbert Meysey-Thompson (*see* MEYSEY-THOMPSON, Bt) and *d* 4 April 1949, leaving issue

WILLINK

Arms: Az. three acorns on one stem slipped or. **Crest:** Issuant from a wreath of oak leaves or a dexter cubit arm bendwise grasping in the hand a chaplet of laurel ppr. **Motto:** *Fides et amor* ('Faith and love'). **Creation:** Bt. (UK) 20 July 1957.

SIR CHARLES WILLIAM WILLINK, 2ND BT, of Dingle Bank, City of Liverpool [Sir Charles Willink Bt, 22 North Grove, London N6 4SL]; *b* 10 Sept 1929; *s f* 1973; *educ* Eton and Trin Coll Cambridge (MA, PhD); master Eton 1954–77 (housemaster 1964–77); *m* 7 Aug 1954 *Elizabeth, er dau of Humfrey Andrewes, of Highgate, and has:

1 +EDWARD DANIEL; *b* 18 Feb 1957; *educ* Eton

1 *Penelope Jane; *b* 23 April 1959; *m* 1987 *Simon John Lawrence Linnett, only s of Prof John Linnett, of Brookside, Cambridge, and has:

(1) *John Lawrence Humfrey; *b* 1991

(2) *Henry Simon Albert; *b* 1993

Lineage: DANIEL WILLINK; *b* 29 July 1779; Dutch Consul Liverpool, Kt Order Lion Netherlands; *m* 16 March 1808 Anne Latham (*d* 8 Nov 1870) and *d* 6 Jan 1859, having had, with other issue:

1 William Willimson, of Bayswater; *b* 9 Dec 1808; *m* 4 June 1844 Catharine Harriet (*d* 15 July 1851), dau of Sir George Nicholls, KCB, and *d* 11 Dec 1883, leaving:

(1) William Nicholls; *b* 10 July 1847; *m* 22 Nov 1878 Cecilia Jane Frances de Chantal Wingfield and *d* 9 April 1894, leaving issue

(2) Henry George, of Hillfields, Burghfield, Berks, JP; *b* 10 July 1851; *educ* Eton and BNC Oxford (MA 1877); CA, barrister Lincoln's Inn 1877; *m* 9 Sept 1880 Mary Grace (*d* 10 Feb 1918), dau of Rev Peter Thomas Ouvry, Vicar Wing, Bucks, and *d* 28 April 1938, having had:

1a John Ouvry; *b* 9 July 1884; *d* 13 June 1885

2a George Ouvry, MC; *b* 1 Feb 1888; *educ* Eton and Corpus Christi Coll Oxford; barrister Inner Temple, Capt 2nd/4th Roy Berks WW I; *ka* France 28 March 1918

3a Francis Arthur, OBE (1942); *b* 14 Feb 1891; *educ* Eton and BNC Oxford (MA); Capt Roy Berks Regt WW I, Lt-Col HG 55th Lancs Bn WW II, dep chm Manchester Collieries Ltd 1944–48; *m* 7 May 1930 (Alma) Marion, JP (Manchester 1949), dau of Rev Hendrick Chignell, and *d* 20 July 1973

1a Catharine Dorothy; *b* 15 Oct 1885; *m* 28 Jan 1914 Edward Fielden Pilkington, OBE, JP, est s of Charles Pilkington, of The Headlands, Prestwich, Lancs, and had two sons and two daus

(1) Harriet Anne; *b* 11 Oct 1845; *d* 18 Aug 1846

2 Jacob, of Hindeton, Cheshire; *b* 1819; *m* Christina E Bushby (*d* 1874) and *d* 1901, leaving, with two yr daus:

(1) Daniel; *b* 1851; *m* Alma Foster (*d* 1921), dau of Col John Scriven, of Chelsea, and *d* 1917, leaving, with five other daus:

1a Derick; *b* 8 May 1882; *m* Oct 1911 Marjorie (*d* 12 Aug 1956), dau of Rev Francis Burton Shepherd, of Essex, and *d* Oct 1947, leaving:

1b *Mary Alma CHAMBERLAIN (deed poll); *m* 2 Aug 1934 Henry Selby-Wright, of Hartlepool

2b *Hester E; *m* 8 June 1963 *Patrick Walter Rowlandson Butler, s of Harry Butler, of N Lancing

3b *Helen Frances Ramsey; *m* April 1945 *Peter Magnus

1a Dorothy; *m* 1912 Robert St John (*see* SAINT JOHN OF BLETSO, B) and *b* 31 March 1958, leaving issue

(2) Wilhem; *b* 1853; *d* 1918

(1) Cecilia; *m* 1876 Conrad Adolphus Wallroth, of Mickleover House, Derby, est s of Charles William Herman Wallroth, of Lee, Kent, and had issue

3 Arthur (Rev); *b* 27 March 1824; *educ* St John's Coll Cambridge; Vicar St Paul's Tranmere; *m* 6 Sept 1849 Sarah Wakefield (*d* 21 June 1890), 2nd dau of John Cropper, of Dingle Bank, Liverpool, and *d* 21 Nov 1862, leaving:

(1) Arthur; *b* 1 July 1850; *educ* Emmanuel Coll Cambridge; *m* 2 July 1878 Margaret (*d* 19 April 1935), dau of Rev Thomas Briggs Dickson, of Eastchurch, and *d* 3 Jan 1913, leaving:

1a Arthur Charles Eric; *b* 28 Jan 1881; *educ* Uppingham and Emmanuel Coll Cambridge; *m* 3 June 1924 Ellen Maud Vigers (*d* 10 Jan 1948) and *d* 1957

2a Herman James Lindale; *b* 14 Sept 1884; *educ* Tonbridge and Caius Coll Cambridge; Capt W R Regt WW I; *m* 14 Aug 1912 Mary Elizabeth, JP (Westmorland 1931), er dau of Sir John Weston, 1st and last Bt, of Kendal (*see* 1926 edn), and *d* of wounds recd in action 5 Nov 1918, leaving:

  1b Christopher Alfred, JP; *b* 10 July 1913; *educ* Stowe and Trin Coll Cambridge; *m* 20 July 1945 Rachel Anne (*d* 3 Sept 1997), dau of Henry Christopher Pinckney, of The Mount, Papcastle, Cumberland, and had:

    1c *James Christopher; *b* 14 June 1954; *educ* Sedbergh

    1c *Judith Kate; *b* 19 Oct 1946

    2c *Elizabeth Anne; *b* 24 Sept 1948

    3c *Patricia Mary; *b* 10 Oct 1950

  2b Peter John; *b* 2 May 1916; *educ* Stowe; 2nd Lt Border Regt WW II; *ka* June 1940

1a Margaret Dorothea Rose; STh, theologian; *d* unm 23 July 1970 aged 91

2a Hilda Mary; CSMMG; *d* unm 10 Jan 1960 aged 76

(2) James Cropper; *b* 7 June 1853; *educ* Uppingham; *d* 13 June 1876

(3) Charles Daniel; *b* 3 Nov 1854; *d* 19 July 1860

(4) WILLIAM EDWARD

(5) John Wakefield (Very Rev); *b* 24 Oct 1858; *educ* Clifton and Pembroke Coll Cambridge; DD, Dean Norwich 1919–27; *m* 27 July 1887 Ruth Agnes (*d* 15 Sept 1937), dau of James Duncan Sim, CSI and *d* 22 Sept 1937, leaving:

  1a Arthur James Wakefield; *b* 17 May 1890; *educ* Repton and King's Coll Cambridge; Headmaster Preparatory Sch Christ's Hosp; *m* 7 April 1927 Rachel Marian, dau of Rev Maurice Tanner, of Cheltenham, and *d* 1 Jan 1964, having had:

    1b Ian Wakefield; *b* 1928; *d* an inf

    2b *Simon Wakefield (Rev) [The Rev Simon Willink, 6 Ridgeway Close, Sidbury, Devon EX10 0SN]; *b* 29 Oct 1929; *educ* Leighton Park and Magdalene Coll Cambridge; *m* 1st 31 March 1959 Kathleen Ann Hyatt; *m* 2nd 16 Feb 1985 *Blanche Elsie Alice, dau of Thomas Moore, and by his 1st w has had:

      1c *Timothy Wakefield; *b* 4 Feb 1960; *m* 27 Feb 1982 *Jeanine Rebecca, dau of Ian Flemming, of Napier, NZ, and has issue

      2c *Robin Daniel; *b* 29 May 1961

      1c Clare Theresa Ann; *b* 12 Jan 1963; *d* Jan 1970

    1b *Janet Wakefield; *b* 27 Dec 1936; *m* 30 June 1956 *David Gaston Martineau, s of Bernard Gaston Martineau, of Westington Pound, Chipping Campden, Glos, and has:

      1c *Philip Maurice; *b* 5 June 1959

      2c *Stephen James; *b* 29 Sept 1966

      1c *Judith Jane; *b* 21 Dec 1957

      2c *Jennifer Gay; *b* 9 July 1962

  2a John Humphrey Wakefield, CBE (1952); *b* 20 April 1898; *educ* Rugby; Col Coldstream Gds, WW I 1916–18 and WW II, Sec Roy Met Soc, Fell Inst Br Photographers; *m* 29 Oct 1937 *Mrs Agnes Marjorie Rowden, only dau of Richard Philip Myers, consulting engr, of Hornsey, and *dsp* 19 Nov 1972

  1a (Mary) Cecilia Wakefield, OBE (1948), JP (Darlington 1941); *b* 2 July 1893; CStJ; *m* 17 Oct 1929, as his 2nd w, Sir Charles Walter Starmer (*d* 27 June 1933), of Danby Lodge, Darlington, s of Charles William Starmer, of Loftus-in-Cleveland, Yorks, and *d* 1979

  2a Helen Dorothy Wakefield, JP; *b* 22 Jan 1895; *m* 31 July 1919 Capt (Cyril) Ivan Horton, RN (*d* 8 May 1968), s of Percy Henry Horton, of Mawnan, Cornwall, and *d* 1989, leaving:

    1b *Rosemary Wakefield [Mrs Rodney Cundall, Flat 18, Providence Place, Chapel St, Chichester, W Sussex PO19 1BS]; *b* 12 May 1920; *m* 15 Dec 1942 Cdr Rodney Cundall, RN (*d* 1981), s of R-Adml John Rowley Cundall, CBE, of Emsworth, Hants, and has:

      1c *David Richard; *b* 13 May 1951; *educ* Lancing; *m* 1982 *Ann Jung

      1c *(Patricia) Jane; *b* 12 Sept 1943; *m* 2 April 1966 *Capt Maxwell John Barrett, RM, of Emsworth, Hants, s of Edward Barrett, of Plymouth, and has:

        1d *Jonathan Ivan; *b* 13 March 1968

        1d *Susan Katherine Patrica; *b* 12 July 1969

        2d *Sarah Elisabeth Jane; *b* 1981

      2c *Janet Rosemary; *b* 24 April 1946; *m* 25 April 1970 (*divorce* 199–) Richard Thornton Booth Dykes, of Earls Court, s of Alan Dykes, of Ascog, Isle of Bute and has:

        1d *Nicholas Thornton; *b* 1972

      3c *Cherry Anne Elizabeth; *b* 23 Oct 1948; *m* 19– *Christopher John Conway-Hughes, s of Dr Conway-Hughes and has:

        1d *Benjamin Andrew; *b* 1977

        2d *Toby Michael; *b* 1980

    2b *Helen Doreen Wakefield; *b* 29 Aug 1927; *m* 5 Aug 1949 *Cdr Colin Mayne Robinson, CEng, MIMechE, RN, s of Cdr Charles Vernon Robinson, OBE, CEng, FIEE, RN, and has:

      1c *Christopher Paul; *b* 11 Nov 1950; *educ* Hurstpierpoint; Midshipman RN

      2c *Rupert Mark; *b* 7 May 1953; *educ* Hurstpierpoint

(6) Alfred Henry, of Whitefoot, Burneside, Kendal, Westmorland, JP (1898); *b* 24 May 1860; *educ* Pembroke Coll Cambridge; CA and CC, High Sheriff Westmorland 1931, Capt TF; *m* 19 April 1885 Beatrice Amy (*d* 1924), dau of Maj Robert Luard-Selby, RA, of The Mote, Ightham, Kent, and *dsp* 18 Sept 1947

  (1) Clara Cecilia; *m* 28 July 1881 Rev Norman Frederick McNeile, yst s of Very Rev Dr Hugh Boyd McNeile, Dean Ripon 1868–75, and *dsp*. He *d* 9 May 1929

  (2) Amy; *d* an infant

The 4th s,

WILLIAM EDWARD WILLINK, of Liverpool; *b* 17 March 1856; *educ* King's Coll Cambridge; FRIBA; *m* 16 Feb 1893 Florence Macan (*d* 6 Dec 1933), yst dau of Col Henry Brabazon Urmston, IA, and *d* 11 March 1924, leaving:

---

1 HENRY URMSTON (Sir), **1st Bt**

2 Derek Edward, JP (Westmorland 1937); *b* 23 Oct 1902; *educ* Eton and King's Coll Cambridge; CA and CC Westmorland; *m* 24 July 1928 Joan Leslie, dau of Dr Matthew Edmund Smallwood, of Wheathampstead, Herts, and had:

  (1) *William Alfred [William Willink Esq, Dalton House, Burton, Kendal]; *b* 11 July 1931; *educ* Marlborough and St John's Coll Oxford; *m* 7 April 1956 *Hester Anne Dymond, only dau of W E Mounsey, of Brigsteer, Westmorland, and adopted:

    *Daniel Patrick; *b* 17 May 1961

    *(Helen) Jessica; *b* 14 Oct 1963; *m* 1994 *James Walker and has:

      1b *Harry James; *b* 13 Aug 1997

      2b *Nicholas John; *b* 23 Dec 1998

    *Priscilla Marian; *b* 18 Sept 1965; *m* 1993 *Nurettin Yilmaz

  (2) *Nicholas Warren [Nicholas Willink Esq, Greenhills, Crook, nr Kendal, Westmorland]; *b* 25 April 1935; *educ* Marlborough and Magdalene Coll Cambridge; *m* 30 April 1960 *Jennifer Wendy, er dau of Allan James Marr (*see* MARR, Bt), and has:

    1a *Patrick John; *b* 18 Dec 1964; *m* 7 Sept 1996 *Katie Middleton and has:

      1b *Oliver Hal; *b* 27 June 1997

    1a *Amanda Frances; *b* 1 May 1961; *m* 1984 *Peter Trickett, of Wike, nr Leeds, and has:

      1b *James; *b* 13 Dec 1985

      2b *Robin; *b* 13 Dec 1985

      3b *Alastair; *b* 7 Jan 1987

    2a *Susan Joan; *b* 3 Aug 1963; *m* 5 Sept 1992 *Ian Harrison and has:

      1b *Gemma Elizabeth; *b* 3 Nov 1994

      2b *Rosemary Clare; *b* 8 March 1996

  (3) *John Dingle; *b* 13 April 1938; *educ* Marlborough and Magdalene Coll Cambridge, ACA; *m* 21 Sept 1963 *Judith Mary, er dau of Michael Barkway, of Westmount, Montreal, and has:

    1a *Michael Derek; *b* 23 June 1964

    2a *David Christopher; *b* 21 Sept 1969

    1a *Patricia Janet; *b* 31 Aug 1966

  (1) *Anne Julia; *b* 6 Sept 1932; *m* 28 April 1962 *Michael Sykes, er s of Harry Sykes, of Chantry, Chute, Hants, and has:

    1a *Jonathan; *b* 10 April 1965

    1a *Caroline; *b* 18 April 1963

  (2) *Sarah Louise; *b* 9 Aug 1940; *m* 29 June 1963 *Michael John Stone, of Waltry, Milton of Campsie, Stirlingshire, er s of Robert George Stone, of Priorscleve, Yetminster, and has:

    1a *Richard John Benedict; *b* 29 April 1968

    1a *Emma Christina; *b* 18 May 1965

1 Beatrice Cropper; *m* 15 July 1919 Rt Rev Christopher Maude Chavasse, OBE, MC, TD, DD, Bp Rochester 1939–60, est s of Rt Rev Francis James Chavasse, Bp Liverpool, and *d* 1 Aug 1977, leaving three sons and two daus. He *d* 10 March 1962

2 Mary Christina; *m* 26 May 1926, as his 2nd w, Herbert Morley Fletcher, MD, FRCP, 2nd s of Alfred Evans Flecher, of Combe Lea, Dorking, Surrey, and had two daus. He *d* 11 Sept 1950

3 Anna Wakefield; *b* 24 Oct 1906; *d* 16 Dec 1926

The er s,

Sir Henry Urmston Willink, 1st Bt (UK), so *cr* 20 July 1957, MC, PC (1943), KC (1935); *b* 7 March 1894; *educ* Eton (Fell 1946–56) and Trin Coll Cambridge (BA 1919, MA 1933); WW I: Capt RA 1916, Maj W Lancs Regt TA (Res Offrs) 1923–38, barrister Inner Temple 1920, Bencher 1942, DCL Lambeth 1955, MP (C) N Croydon 1940–48, Min Health 1943–45, Master Magdalene Coll Cambridge 1948–66, V-Chllr Cambridge U 1953–55, Chllr Dioceses of Norwich, St Edmundsbury and Ipswich 1948–55, Dean Arches 1955–70, Hon Liveryman Goldsmiths' Co 1943, chm: Roy Commn on Betting, Lotteries and Gaming 1949–51, Commn on Minorities Nigeria 1957–58 and Roy Commn on Police 1960–62; Hon LLD Liverpool and Melbourne; *m* 1st 11 Dec 1923 his cousin Cynthia Frances (*d* 2 Dec 1959), 4th dau of Herbert Morley Fletcher (*see* above); *m* 2nd 8 Aug 1964 *Mrs Doris Campbell Preston, dau of William Campbell Sharman, of Leicester, and *d* 1 Jan 1973, leaving by his 1st w:

1 Sir CHARLES WILLIAM WILLINK, **2nd and present Bt**

2 +Stephen Henry [Stephen Willink Esq, 7 Clifton St, Plymouth, PL4 8JA]; *b* 16 Sept 1932; *educ* Eton and Trin Coll Oxford; *m* 18 July 1970 *Mary Louise, dau of Ernest R Royston, and has:

  (1) +Henry Augustine; *b* 12 May 1971

  (1) *Annabella Mary Victoria; *b* 13 Jan 1975

1 Rachel Frances [Mrs Michael Kinchin Smith, The Old Bakery, Epwell, Banbury, Oxon OX15 6LA]; *b* 27 June 1925; *educ* St Mary's Calne and LMH Oxford; *m* 20 Sept 1947 *Michael Kinchin Smith, OBE, s of Francis John Kinchin Smith, of S Kensington, and has:

  (1) *Christopher Henry [Christopher Kinchin Smith Esq, 5 Naisby Dve, Gt Brickhill, Bucks MK17 9BL]; *b* 24 Jan 1950; *educ* Westminster and Nottingham U; *m* 1974 *Susan Valerie, yr dau of William G Adams, of W Wickham, Kent, and has:

    1a *Holly Rebecca; *b* 1983

    2a *Katherine Alice; *b* 1988

  (2) *John Michael (Rev) [Rev John Kinchin Smith, The Rectory, Mursley, Bucks MK17 0RT]; *b* 27 Jan 1952; *educ* Bradfield and Cambridge; *m* 1981 *Caroline Anne, yr dau of G Francis Harris, of Copdock, Suffolk, and has:

    1a *Joseph Francis; *b* 1983

    2a *Samuel John; *b* 1988

    3a *David Luke; *b* 1990

    1a *Eleanor Mary; *b* 1985

  (3) *David Francis; *b* 5 March 1954; *educ* Westminster and Sussex U; *m* 1976 *Rosalind Jane, yr dau of Dr Frank Holden, of Bessacarr, Yorks

  (4) *Robert Mark; *b* 6 Oct 1960; *educ* UCS and Birmingham U (MSc)

(1) *Lavinia Mary; *b* 28 June 1948; *educ* Putney High Sch and LMH Oxford; *m* 1975 *John Cunningham, s of William Henry Cunningham, of Minchin-hampton, Glos, and has:
   1a *Anna Clare; *b* 1980
   2a *Ruth Elizabeth; *b* 1983
   3a *Helen Mary; *b* 1984
(2) *Juliet Clare [Mrs Malcolm Hancock, King Charles Vicarage, 5D Frant Rd, Tunbridge Wells, TN2 5SB]; *b* 11 May 1957; *educ* Twickenham Co GS and Sussex U; *m* 1985 *Rev Malcolm James Hancock, s of Isaac Hancock, of Newark, and has:
   1a *James Timothy Michael; *b* 1989
   2a *Benjamin Andrew; *b* 1991
2 *Elisabeth Mary [Mrs Frank Bell, Stables Barn, Trimnells, Colerne, Wilts SN14 8EP]; *b* 6 April 1927; *educ* St Mary's Calne and LMH Oxford; *m* 31 March 1951 *Frank Erskine Bell, OBE, of Cambridge, s of Sir Ernest Albert Seymour Bell, CIE, and has:
(1) *Nicholas John; *b* 13 Dec 1953; *educ* Perse Sch Cambridge
(1) *Catharine Elisabeth; *b* 30 Jan 1955; *m* 1986 *Timothy Cutting, s of George Cutting, of Cambo, Northumberland, and has:
   1a *Daniel Christopher Frank; *b* 1993
   1a *Amber Charlotte; *b* 1997

WILLOUGHBY DE BROKE

Arms: Quarterly: 1st and 4th, gules three crosses recercellée or, a chief vairé, ermine and ermines (for VERNEY); 2nd and 3rd quarterly, argent and gules, a bear sejant sable, muzzled and collared or (for BARNARD). **Crests:** 1 A Saracen's head couped at the shoulders and affrontée proper, ducally crowned or (for VERNEY), 2 A demi-bear couped sable, muzzled and collared, holding between the paws a mascle or (for BARNARD). **Supporters:** Two antelopes argent, semée of torteaux, armed and unguled or. **Motto:** *Vertue vaunceth* ('Virtue prevails'). **Creation:** B. (E) 12 Aug 1491.

THE 21ST BARON WILLOUGHBY DE BROKE and *de jure* 28th/29th LORD (Baron) LATIMER (of Corby) ((Leopold) David Verney) [The Rt Hon The Lord Willoughby de Broke, Ditchford Farm, Moreton-in-Marsh, Glos GL56 9RD]; *b* 14 Sept 1938 (HM KING LEOPOLD III OF THE BELGIANS stood sponsor); *s f* 1986; heir general to the Barony of Latimer, *cr* by writ of summons 20 Dec 1299; *educ* Le Rosey and New Coll Oxford; memb Ho Lds Select Ctee EC; *m* 1 May 1965 *(divorce* 1989) Petra Daphne, 2nd dau of Col Sir John Renton Aird, 3rd Bt (*qv*), and has had:

1 +RUPERT GREVILLE; *b* 4 March 1966
2 +John Mark; *b* 9 Oct 1967
3 +Edmund Peyto; *b* 1973
1 A dau; *b* and *d* 6 Dec 1971

Lineage: ROBERT WILLOUGBY, **1st Lord** (Baron) **Willoughby de Broke** (E), so *cr* (according to later doctrine) by writ of summons to Parl 12 Aug 1491, also *de jure* 8th/9th LORD (Baron) LATIMER (*qv*) (of Corby) (*c* 1489); *b* 1452; ktd by mid-Feb 1471/2, Sheriff Cornwall 1478–79 and Devon 1480–81 and 1487–88; attainted 1483/4 and stripped of his lands for having supported the Duke of Buckingham's rising of autumn 1483 (*see* STAFFORD, B), but returned with the future HENRY VII and fought at Bosworth 22 Aug 1485, Receiver Duchy Cornwall and Steward Roy mines of precious metals Devon and Cornwall Sept 1485 and soon had his lands restored, Kt of the Body by Christmas 1485, Ld Steward Household 1488–1502, Jt Cdr an expdn to Brittany against the French 1488–89, Jt Amb Brittany 1490, Adml Fleet against France July 1490 and again 1492 (also Marshal of the Army); *m* by 1472 Blanche, dau and heiress of Sir John Champernowne, and *d* 22 Aug 1502, leaving, with a dau (Elizabeth, *m* as his 2nd w 7th Lord (Baron) Dinham):

ROBERT WILLOUGHBY, **2nd Lord** (Baron) **Willoughby de Broke** and *de jure* 9th/10th LORD (Baron) LATIMER (of Corby), KB (1509); *b* 1472; Steward Duchy Cornwall and Warden Stannaries in Devon and Cornwall 1502–09, ktd by sum-

mer 1504; *m* 1st by 28 Feb 1494/5 Elizabeth, est dau and coheir of 2nd and last Baron Beauchamp of Powick (*see* WARWICK, BROOK and, E), and had:

1 Edward, JP (Devon and Cornwall 1512–15); *m c* 22 Nov 1505 Margaret Nevill(e), dau of 2nd Lord (Baron) Latymer (*qv*), and *dspm* & *vp* Nov 1517, leaving:
(1) ELIZABETH Willoughby, according to later doctrine *de jure* BARONESS WILLOUGHBY DE BROKE (3rd holder of the title) and *de jure* BARONESS LATIMER (of Corby) (10th/11th holder of the title), both in her own right, following death of her surv sis and coheir; *m* just prior to 11 April 1526 Sir Fulke GREVILLE (*see* WARWICK, BROOK and E) and *d* seemingly Nov 1562, leaving:
  1a Sir FULKE GREVILLE, *de jure* 4th LORD (Baron) WILLOUGHBY DE BROKE and 11th/12th LORD (Baron) LATIMER (of Corby); *b c* 1536; *m c* 1553 Anne, dau of 4th Earl of Westmorland of the 1397 *cr* (*see* ABERGAVENNY, M), and *d* 15 Nov 1606, leaving:
   1b Sir FULKE GREVILLE, *de jure* 5th LORD (Baron) WILLOUGHBY DE BROKE and *de jure* 12th/13th LORD (Baron) LATIMER (of Corby); *cr* 29 Jan 1620/1 BARON BROOKE OF BEAUCHAMPS COURT, Co Warwick (E); *b c* 1554; *d unm* 30 Sept 1628
   1b MARGARET Greville, *de jure* BARONESS WILLOUGHBY DE BROKE (6th holder of the title) and *de jure* BARONESS LATIMER (13th/14th holder of the title), both in her own right, according to doctrine developing about now; *b c* 1561; *m* 29 Oct 1582 Sir Richard VERNEY (*d* 7 Aug 1630), of Compton Murdak/Verney, Warwicks, bro of Sir Edmund Verney (*see* BRAYE, B), and *d* 26 March 1631, leaving:
    1c Sir GREVILLE VERNEY, *de jure* 7th LORD (Baron) WILLOUGHBY DE BROKE and 14th/15th LORD (Baron) LATIMER (of Corby); *b c* 1586; *educ* possibly at Cambridge and certainly at Gray's Inn; MP Warwick 1614 and 1620–22, ktd 1617, Sheriff Warwicks 1635–36; *m* 13 May 1618 Katherine, dau of Sir Robert Southwell (*see* SOUTHWELL, V), and *d* 12 May 1642, leaving, with another s:
     1d GREVILLE VERNEY, *de jure* 8th LORD (Baron) WILLOUGHBY DE BROKE and *de jure* 15th/16th LORD (Baron) LATIMER (of Corby); *b* 1619; *educ* Jesus Coll Cambridge and Middle Temple; Sheriff Warwicks 1647–48; *m* Elizabeth, dau and coheir of 2nd Viscount Wenman of Tuam, and *d* 9 Dec 1648, leaving:
      1e Sir GREVILLE VERNEY, *de jure* 9th LORD (Baron) WILLOUGHBY DE BROKE and *de jure* 16th/17th LORD (Baron) LATIMER (of Corby), KB (1661); *b* posthumously 26 Jan 1648/9; *m* 29 Aug 1667 Diana (*m* 2nd 15 July 1675 3rd Baron Alington of Killard and *d* 13 Dec 1701), dau of 1st Duke of Bedford (*qv*), and *d* 23 July 1668, leaving an only child:
       1f WILLIAM VERNEY, *de jure* 10th LORD (Baron) WILLOUGHBY DE BROKE and *de jure* 17th/18th LORD (Baron) LATIMER (of Corby); *b* 12 June 1668; *d unm* 13 Aug 1683
    2d John; *b* and *d* 11 Aug 1620
    3d RICHARD VERNEY, **11th Lord** (Baron) **Willoughby de Broke**, as which recognised 13 Feb 1695/6, and *de jure* 18th/19th LORD (Baron) LATIMER (of Corby), of Allexton, Leics, which Manor he bought *c* 1652, and Belton, Rutland, which Manor he bought a little while after 1672; *b* 28 Jan 1621/2; *educ* Jesus Coll Cambridge; Sheriff Rutland 1681–82 and Warwicks 1683–84, ktd 1685, MP Warwicks 1685–87 and 1689–90; *m* 1st *c* 21–29 Nov 1651 Mary, dau of Sir John Pretyman, 1st Bt, of Lodington and Horninghold, Leics (*see* 1840 edn); *m* 2nd Frances, dau of Thomas Dove, of Upton, Northants, and *d* 18 July 1711, having by her had a s (Richard, *d unm* 23 June 1698 aged *c* 21) and a dau (Diana, *m* Sir Charles Shuckburgh, 2nd Bt; *qv*) and by his 1st w, with three other sons (*d* young by 1681) and two daus:
     1e John, of Allexton; *b c* 1652; *educ* Jesus Coll Cambridge and Middle Temple; barrister 1677, MP Leics 1695–1701 and 1702–07; *m c* 13 July 1683 Christian, dau of John Breton, of Norton, Northants, and *dsps* & *vp* 31 Oct 1707, having had:
      1f John; *b c* 1685; *dvp unm* 15 May 1700
      2f Greville; *dvp unm*
     2e GEORGE, **12th Lord**
     3e Thomas; *b c* 1663; London merchant; *d unm* at Lisbon
    1d Elizabeth; *m* William Peyto, of Chesterton, Warwicks
    2c John
(2) Anne; *d unm* by 12 Nov 1528
(3) Blanche; *m* by 25 Jan 1534/5 Sir Francis Dawtrey, of Hunston, Sussex, and Portswood, S Stoneham, Hants, and *dsp* by 1545, perhaps as early as 1536

The **2nd Lord** *m* 2nd Dorothy, dau of Thomas Grey, 1st Marquess of Dorset, by his 2nd w Cicely, Baroness Harington and Bonville in her own right according to later doctrine, and *d* 10 Nov 1521 of the pestilence, when the Barony of Willoughby de Broke and right to that of Latimer (of Corby) fell according to later doctrine into abeyance among his three gdaus and coheirs by his s, having by her had, with other issue:
1 Elizabeth; *m* 2nd Marquess of Winchester (*qv*)
2 Anne; *m* 5th Lord (Baron) Mountjoy (for whose early ancestry *see* BLOUNT, Bt)

The 11th LORD's only surv s,
Rev GEORGE VERNEY, **12th Lord** (Baron) **Willoughby de Broke** and *de jure* 19th/20th LORD (Baron) LATIMER (of Corby); *b* 10 March 1660/1; *educ* Winchester and New Coll Oxford; Rector Hallaton, Leics, 1683, Kimcote, Leics, 1696, Southam, Warwicks, 1700, BD and DD 1699, Canon Windsor 1701, Dean Windsor and Register Order Garter 1714–28; *m* 2 Dec 1688 Margaret, dau and heiress of Sir John Heath, of Brasted, Kent, Attorney-Gen Duchy Lancaster, and *d* 26 Dec 1728, leaving:

1 George; *b* 13 Oct 1689; *dvp* 16 March 1696/7
2 Philip; *b* 1690; *educ* Rugby; *dvp* young
3 Thomas; *b* 1691; *educ* Rugby and New Coll Oxford; *m* Eleanor, yst dau of 2nd Baron Leigh (*qv*) of Stoneleigh of the 1643 *cr*, and *dvp* 1710, leaving:
(1) Eleanor; *b* 1710; *m* 1 Oct 1724, as his 1st w, George Bowes, of Streatlam Castle and Gibside, Co Durham (*dspm* 17 Sept 1760, leaving by his 2nd w a

dau and heiress Mary Eleanor, who *m* 7th Earl of Strathmore and Kinghorne, (*qv*)

4 RICHARD VERNEY, **13th Lord** (Baron) **Willoughby de Broke** and *de jure* 20th/21st LORD (Baron) LATIMER (of Corby); *b* 1693; *educ* Rugby and New Coll Oxford; *m* 1st Penelope (*dsp* 31 Aug 1718), est dau of Clifton Packe, of Prestwold, Leics; *m* 2nd by 1735 Elizabeth/Margaret, dau of Nehemiah Walker/Williams, of Newport, Mon, and *dsps* 11 Aug 1752, having had:

(1) George; *dvp* an infant by 1735

5 John, PC (1738); *b c* 1700; Attorney-Gen to GEORGE II's w QUEEN CARO-LINE, Ch Justice Co Palatine of Chester, Master Rolls 1738–41; *m* Abigail, sis of 3rd Earl of Oxford and Earl Mortimer (see OXFORD AND ASQUITH, E, preliminary remarks), and *d* 5 Aug 1741, leaving:

(1) JOHN, **14th Lord**

1 Margaret; *m* 1 Jan 1715/6, as his 1st w, 1st and last Lord Feversham, Baron of Downton, and *d* 9 Oct 1755, having had issue (*see* FEVERSHAM, B)

The 13th LORD's n,

JOHN VERNEY later PEYTO-VERNEY (under terms of will of his cousin Margaret Peyto, of Chesterton, Warwicks), **14th Lord (Baron) Willoughby de Broke** and *de jure* 21st/22nd LORD (Baron) LATIMER (of Corby); *b* 4 Aug 1738; *educ* Ch Ch Oxford; a Ld Bedchamber; *m* 8 Oct 1761 Louisa (*d* 1798), dau of 1st Earl of Guilford (*qv*), and *d* 15 Feb 1816, having had, with two yst sons (William; Francis; *d* young) and four other daus (*dsp*):

1 JOHN PEYTO-VERNEY, **15th Lord** (Baron) **Willoughby de Broke** and *de jure* 22nd/23rd LORD (Baron) LATIMER (of Corby); *b* 28 June 1762; *educ* Ch Ch Oxford; *d unm* 1 Sept 1820

2 George; *b* 25 June 1763; *d* 11 June 1773

3 Francis; *b* 13 May, *d* July 1772

4 HENRY PEYTO-VERNEY, **16th Lord** (Baron) **Willoughby de Broke** and *de jure* 23rd/24th LORD (Baron) LATIMER (of Corby); *b* 5 April 1773; *educ* Oriel Coll; Capt Warwicks Yeo Cav 1803, Maj 1807, Lt-Col 1814, Groom Bedchamber 1804–15; High Sheriff Warwicks 1817–18; *m* 10 March 1829 Margaret (*d* 3 Aug 1880), 3rd dau of Sir John Williams, 1st Bt, of Bodelwyddan (*qv*), and *dsp* 16 Dec 1852

1 Louisa; *b* 20 June 1769; *m* 31 Oct 1793 Rev Robert Barnard, Preb Winchester (*d* 25 Feb 1834), 2nd s of Rev Thomas Barnard, Rector Withersfield, Suffolk, and *d* 3 Feb 1835, leaving:

(1) Robert; *b* 31 Aug, *d* Sept 1806

(2) ROBERT JOHN, **17th Lord**

(1) Louisa; *m* 9 June 1835 Joseph Townsend (*d* 29 April 1870), bro of Henry Townsend, of Honington Hall, Warwicks, and *d* 22 April 1863, leaving issue

The 16th LORD's n,

ROBERT JOHN BARNARD later VERNEY (roy licence 17 May 1853), **17th Lord** (Baron) **Willoughby de Broke** and *de jure* 24th/25th LORD (Baron) LATIMER (of Corby); *b* 17 Oct 1809; *educ* Eton and Ch Ch Oxford; MFH Warwickshire 1839–65 and Jt MFH 1861–62; Capt Warwicks Yeo Cav 1848; *m* 25 Oct 1842 Georgiana Jane (*d* 7 March 1889), 3rd dau of Maj-Gen Thomas William Taylor, CB, of Ogwell, Devon, and *d* 5 June 1862, leaving:

1 HENRY, **18th Lord**

2 Walter Robert (Rev); *b* 18 March 1846; MA Oxon; Rector Lighthorne, Vicar Chesterton, Warwicks, Hon Chaplain Warwicks Imp Yeo; *m* 5 June 1879 Elizabeth Georgina (*d* 29 Oct 1941), only dau of Maj Robert Wilberforce Bird, of Barton House, Warwicks, and *d* 20 Oct 1912, leaving:

(1) Robert Barnard; *b* 5 Nov 1881; *d unm* 14 Aug 1956

(2) Reynell Henry, CBE (1937, OBE 1919), DL (Warwicks 1952); *b* 12 Jan 1886; *educ* Seafield Coll and ISC; A/Cdre RAF WW I (despatches), Dir Tech Devpt Air Min 1934–38, Dep Dir-Gen Dept of Supply (Aircraft) Govt of India 1943–46; *m* 28 Nov 1942 Hon Dorothy Cecily (*d* 16 Dec 1994), est dau of 3rd Baron Tollemache (*qv*), and *dsp* 27 Oct 1974

(1) Clare; *b* 1 June 1887; *d unm* 12 March 1976

3 Robert Reynell; *b* 8 Aug 1850; Lt 52nd Foot; *d unm* 6 Oct 1872

1 Margaret Louisa; *m* 30 Sept 1874 Jervoise Smith, MP (*d* 21 July 1884), est s of John Abel Smith, and *d* 8 April 1920, leaving:

(1) Dorothy Anne; *b* 29 March 1883; *d unm* 9 Feb 1963

2 Alice Jane; *m* 30 Sept 1874 Edward William Tritton (*see* TRITTON, Bt) and *d* 8 Jan 1882, leaving issue

3 Susan Emma; *m* 11 June 1885 Edmund Temple Godman, JP, DL (*d* 22 March 1894), 6th s of Joseph Godman, JP, of Park Hatch, Surrey, and Merston, Sussex, and *d* 21 March 1941, leaving:

(1) John, CBE (1957), JP, DL; *b* 9 May 1886; *educ* Eton; Lt-Col 15th Hus WW I, Glos: Chm CC 1946–56, High Sheriff 1942, Chm Severn River Board 1952 on; *d* 19–

4 Mabel; *b* 6 Oct 1855; *d unm* 7 May 1937

The 17th LORD's est s,

HENRY VERNEY, **18th Lord** (Baron) **Willoughby de Broke** and *de jure* 25th/26th LORD (Baron) LATIMER (of Corby), JP, DL (Warwicks); *b* 14 May 1844; *educ* Eton and Ch Ch Oxford; Warwicks Yeo Cav: Capt 1863, Maj 1880, Lt-Col cmdt 1891–1900, MFH Warwickshire 1876–90; *m* 17 Oct 1867 Geraldine (*d* 21 Dec 1894), est dau of James Hugh Smith Barry, of Marbury Hall, Cheshire, and Fota Island, Co Cork, and *d* at sea 19 Dec 1902, having had, with two other daus (*d* young or unm):

1 RICHARD GREVILLE, **19th Lord**

2 Henry Peyto; *b* 19 June 1870; Lt 7th Hus; *d unm* 25 June 1893

1 Blanche; *m* 13 April 1898 Capt Michael Granville Lloyd Lloyd-Baker, JP, Glos Yeo (*ka* 23 April 1916), est s of Granville Edwin Lloyd-Baker, JP, DL, of Hardwicke Court, Glos, and *d* 5 Oct 1947, leaving:

(1) Olive Katherine Lloyd, CBE (1958), JP (1943), of Hardwicke Court; *b* 15 Aug 1902; Glos: CC 1940–48, High Sheriff 1970, Co Chm NFU 1942–43, Co Chm CLA 1954–56; *d* 19–

(2) +Audrey Pamela Lloyd; *b* 8 May 1908

2 Patience, JP (Warwicks); *m* 4 June 1896 her bro's bro-in-law Lt-Col Basil Hanbury, TD (*d* 20 Dec 1933), 3rd s of Charles Addington Hanbury, JP, DL, of Bel-

---

mont, E Barnet, and Strathgarve, Ross-shire, and *d* 27 April 1965 aged 91, leaving:

(1) Harold Greville; *b* 19 June 1896; *educ* Charterhouse and BNC Oxford (BCL 1923, MA 1924, DCL 1936); Lt Warwicks Yeo WW I, Staff Capt S Midland Dist WW II, Vinerian Prof English Law and Fell All Souls 1949–64, QC 1960, Hon Fell Lincoln Coll, Hon Master Bench Inner Temple, author; *m* 21 July 1927 Anna Margaret Geelmuyden, dau of Hannibal Dreyer, of Copenhagen, and *d* 19–

The 18th LORD's only surv s,

RICHARD GREVILLE VERNEY, **19th Lord** (Baron) **Willoughby de Broke** and *de jure* 26th/27th LORD (Baron) LATIMER (of Corby), TD, JP, DL (Warwicks); *b* 29 March 1869; *educ* Eton and New Coll Oxford (BA); Warwicks Yeo Cav: Lt 1891, Capt 1903, Maj 1908, ret 1910; MP (U) Rugby 1895–1900; MFH Warwickshire 1900–23; Maj 1914–16 and Lt-Col 1916–18 Warwicks Yeo 2nd Line Regt WW I; author: *Hunting the Fox* (1920), *The Sport of Our Ancestors* (anthology, 1921), *The Passing Years* (autobiography, 1924); *m* 2 July 1895 Marie Frances Lisette, OBE (*d* 14 Oct 1941), yst dau of Charles Addington Hanbury (*see* also above), and *d* 16 Dec 1923, leaving:

JOHN HENRY PEYTO VERNEY, **20th Lord** (Baron) *Willoughby de Broke* and *de jure* 27th/28th LORD (Baron) LATIMER (of Corby), MC (1918), AFC (1940), AE, JP (Warwicks 1922), DL (Warwicks 1931); *b* 21 May 1896; *educ* Eton and RMC Sandhurst; Lt 17th/21st Lancers WW I (wounded) (ret as Capt 1929), ADC to Govr Bombay 1920–22, Adj Warwicks Yeo 1925–29 (Hon Col 1942–63), S/Ldr cmdg 605 Sqdn AAF 1936–39, WW II: W/Cdr II (F) Gp 1940 (despatches), Gp Capt 1941, Dir PR Air Min 1945–46 (Dep Dir 1941–44), ret as A/Cdre RAF 1946; Warwicks: Ld Lt 1939–67 (V-Lt 1938–39), Co Pres Assoc Boys' Clubs, Pres Boy Scouts Assoc and Cncl of St John 1946–67, Steward Jockey Club 1944–47 and 1954–56, Steward Nat Hunt Ctee 1942–45, 1950–52 and 1964–67, Chm Tattersalls Ctee 1948–54, Pres Hunters Improvement Soc 1957–58, Chm: Wolverhampton Racecourse Co, The Steeplechase Co (Cheltenham) and Racecourse Tech Servs; KStJ; *m* 4 Oct 1933 Rachel (*d* 1991), Chev Order Crown Belgium, only child of Sir (Robert) Bourchier Sherard Wrey, 11th Bt (*qv*), and *d* 1986, leaving:

1 (LEOPOLD) DAVID VERNEY, **21st and present Lord** (Baron) **Willoughby de Broke**

1 +Susan Geraldine [The Hon Mrs Lascelles, Giffords Hele, Meeth, Devon EX20 3QN]; *b* 2 Dec 1942; *m* 1st 25 April 1964 (*divorce* 1969) Jeremy James Wagg, 2nd s of Kenneth Arthur Wagg, of Mayfair, by his 1st w (Rachel) Katherine (*see* HORLICK, Bt); *m* 2nd 10 March 1972, as his 2nd w, Robie David Corbett Uniacke, only surv child of Lt-Col Robie Dennis Woodgate Uniacke, RTR; *m* 3rd 1990, as his 2nd w, *Rupert John Orlando Lascelles (*see* HAREWOOD, E) and has had by her 2nd husb:

(1) +Casper John; *b* 14 March 1973

(1) Kate Rachel; *b* 1975; *d* 10 July 1979

WILLOUGHBY DE ERESBY

Arms: Quarterly, 1st and 4th, or fretty azure (for WILLOUGHBY); 2nd, or three bars wavy gules (for DRUMMOND); 3rd, ermine three pomals, each charged with a cross or (for HEATHCOTE).
Motto: *Loyauté me oblige* ('Loyalty binds me').
Creation: B. (E) 26 July 1313.

THE BARONESS WILLOUGHBY DE ERESBY ((Nancy) Jane Marie Heathcote-Drummond-Willoughby, DL (Lincs 1993)) [The Rt Hon The Baroness Willoughby De Eresby DL, Grimsthorpe, Bourne, Lincs PE10 0LZ; Drummond Castle, Crieff, Perthshire]; *b* 1 Dec 1934; *s* f 1983 as 28th holder of title; Jt Hereditary Ld Gt Chamberlain of England; Train Bearer to HM THE QUEEN Coronation 1953

Lineage (of Willoughby): WILLIAM de WILLOUGHBY; held land at Sloothby, Willoughby-in-the-Marsh, Lincs, *temp* RICHARD I and a kt's fee at Willoughby-in-the-Marsh 1212; *m* Maud, dau of William de Fulletby, and *d* by 1227, having had:

1 Hugh; *m* Frethesancia, dau and coheir of William de Scoteney, and *dvp*, leaving:

(1) William; not yet of age in 1227; ancestor of the WILLOUGHBYs, feudal Lds of Cumberworth, Lincs

2 Robert; allegedly *m* — Orreby, dau of one of the feudal Lds of Orby and Ingoldmells, Lincs, and *d* between 3 Feb 1256/7 and 21 Feb 1257/8, leaving:

(1) William (Sir), JP Lincs 1279–80; *m c* 1250–60 Alice, est dau and coheir of 1st and last Lord (Baron) Beke, of Eresby, Lincs (*see* **Lineage (of Bec/Beke)** below), and *d* by 29 March 1300, leaving:

1a ROBERT de WILLOUGHBY, **1st Lord** (Baron) **Willoughby de Eresby** (E), so *cr* 26 July 1313 (according to later doctrine) by writ of summons to Parl made out to 'Roberto de Wylghby' (*i.e.*, Willoughby) alone, with the addition of 'de Eresby' not occurring till the 1350–Jan 1370/1 Parl of EDWARD III, and then only in the period 1350–60, presumably because a similarly named personage, Richard de Willoughby, was also called to that Parl, the next version of the title to included the suffix 'de Eresby' occurring in 1580 (when the 2nd BARON WILLOUGHBY OF PARHAM (*see* below) was sitting in Parl), the Barony from then on being held with superior peerages till 1870 but referred to in the declaratory patent of 18 March 1780 as 'Willoughby of Eresby' and only as 'Willoughby de Eresby' from the 1871 termination of the abeyance onwards, though for convenience's sake this form has been adhered to throughout this article; *b c* 1250–60; campaigned against Scots, being present Siege of Carlavrock 1300; *m* by 1303 Margaret, dau of 1st Lord (Baron) Deincourt, and *d* just prior to 25 March 1316/7, leaving:

1b JOHN de WILLOUGHBY, **2nd Lord** (Baron) **Willoughby de Eresby**; *b* 6 Jan 1303/4; kt banneret Jan 1326/7; campaigned in Gascony, Scotland Brittany and France, where present Battle of Crécy 1346 and possibly also the ensuing Siege of Calais; *m* by 2 July 1323 Joan, dau of Peter Roscelyn, of Edgefield, Norfolk, and *d* 13 June 1349, leaving, with at least one yr s (Robert):

1c JOHN de WILLOUGHBY, **3rd Lord** (Baron) **Willoughby de Eresby**; *bapt* 6 Jan 1328/9; ktd by May 1347; thought to have assisted at Siege of Calais 1347; fought Battle of Poitiers 19 Sept 1356, campaigning again in France 1359–60 and Gascony 1371; *m* by 1349 Cecily, 2nd dau of Robert de Ufford, 1st Earl of Suffolk (*see* SUFFOLK and BERKSHIRE, E, preliminary remarks), and *d* 29 March 1372, leaving, with at least one other yr s (William):

1d ROBERT de WILLOUGHBY, **4th Lord** (Baron) **Willoughby de Eresby**; *b c* 1349; campaigned France 1373–74, Scotland 1385 and Spain 1386–87; *m* 1st by 1370 Alice, allegedly er dau of Sir William Skipwith (*see* SKIPWITH, Bt), and had:

1e WILLIAM, **5th Baron**

1d (cont.) The **4th Lord** *m* 2nd by 29 March 1372 Margery, dau of 2nd Lord (Baron) Zouche (*qv*) (of Haryngworth), and had, it is thought by her:

2e Robert

3e Thomas (Sir); *m* his stepsister Elizabeth, dau of Elizabeth, *de jure* Baroness Latimer (*qv*) (of Corby) in her own right, by her 1st husb 3rd Lord (Baron) Neville (of Raby) (*see* ABERGAVENNY, M), and with her was ancestor of the Lords (Barons) Willoughby de Broke (*qv*)

4e John; had issue (*see* 1850 edn WILLOUGHBY Bt, of Baldon House, Oxon)

5e Bryan; *b c* 1384

1d (cont.) The **4th Lord** *m* 3rd Elizabeth, *de jure* Baroness Latimer (*qv*) (of Corby) in her own right according to later doctrine, and *d* 9 Aug 1396, leaving:

1e Margaret; thought to have *dsp* or unm by 1430

2b William; *b c* 1306; *d* between 28 May 1345 and 13 July 1346

1b Joan; *m* as his 1st w Gilbert de Umreville, 3rd/10th Earl of Angus (*see* HAMILTON and BRANDON, D, preliminary remarks) of the line first recognised as such *c* 1114–15, and *d* 16 July 1350, leaving or having had issue

The 4th LORD's est s,

WILLIAM de WILLOUGHBY, **5th Lord** (Baron) **Willoughby de Eresby**, KG (*c* 1401); *b c* 1370; assisted usurpation of Duke of Lancaster (later HENRY IV) 1399 and attended the abdication of RICHARD II in the Tower of London 29 Sept 1399; *m* 1st by 23 April 1383 Lucy, dau of 5th Lord (Baron) Strange (of Knokyn) (*see* SAINT DAVIDS, V); *m* 2nd after 1 Aug 1402 but before 9 Aug 1404, as the 2nd of her four husbs, Joan, sis and coheir of 4th/6th and last Earl of Kent of the 1321 *cr* (*see* WAKE, Bt), having by his 1st w had, with four daus (including Margery, *m* 14 Nov 1406 5th Lord (Baron) FitzHugh and had issue; *see* DACRE, B):

1 ROBERT (de) WILLOUGHBY, **6th Lord** (Baron) **Willoughby de Eresby**, KG (*c* 1417); *b c* 1385; joined expdn to Normandy and Bordeaux 1412–13, also Agincourt Campaign 1415 and France generally from 1417: successful Sieges of Caen, Rouen, Meaux, Ivry, Le Mans, Bonneval and St Valéry and relief of Cravant; fought Battle of Verneuil 17 Aug 1424, hence granted Comtés of Vendôme 20 Sept 1424 and Beaumont-sur-Oise 4 Oct 1430, with remainder in each case to the heirs male of his body, also Dreux Feb 1427/8; lost Battle of Vivoin to French while King's Lt Normandy; Capt of Bayeux 1433–37 and Pont de l'Arche *c* 1434; held Paris 1435–36 till forced to capitulate (having holed up in the Bastille) 17 April 1436; *m* 1st by 21 Feb 1420/1 Elizabeth de Montagu, yst dau of 3rd Earl of Salisbury of the 1337 *cr* (*see* SALISBURY, M, preliminary remarks), *m* 2nd by 9 Jan 1448/9 Maud, dau of Sir Richard Stanhope, of Rampton, Notts (*see* CROMWELL, B, also 1967 edn CHESTERFIELD and STANHOPE, E), and *dspm* 25 July 1452, when his French honours expired, leaving by his 1st w:

(1) JOAN Willoughby, *de jure* BARONESS WILLOUGHBY DE ERESBY in her own right according to later doctrine; *b c* 1425; *m* probably by 1446 and certainly by 9 Jan 1448/9, as his 1st w, Sir Richard de WELLES, recognised as **7th Lord** (Baron) **Willoughby de Eresby** by summons to Parl from 26 May 1455, s of 6th Lord (Baron) Welles (attainted 31 Dec 1461 following his death at Battle of Towton 29 March 1460/1) by his 1st w and on the reversal of his f's attainder 1467 7th Lord (Baron) Welles) also (beheaded 12 March 1469/70 following his s's rebellion and posthumously attainted Jan–March 1474/5

backdated to 12 March 1469/70, though this attainder too was reversed 1485–86), and *d* just prior to 13 Feb 1461/2, leaving:

1a ROBERT de WELLES, **8th Lord** (Baron) **Willoughby de Eresby** and 8th LORD (Baron) **WELLES**; cmded a Lincs contingent of Lancastrians at defeat by Yorkists under EDWARD IV of Empingham ('Losecoat Field') 12 March 1469/70 and was beheaded 19 March following; *m* Elizabeth, dau of 1st Lord (Baron) Berners (*qv*), and *dsp*

1a JOAN de Welles, *de jure* BARONESS WILLOUGHBY DE ERESBY in her own right according to later doctrine; *m* as his 1st w Sir Richard Hastings (*dsp* 1503; *see* HUNTINGDON, E), *cr* Lord (Baron) Hastings (of Welles)/Lord (Baron) Welles by virtue of a writ of summons of 15 Nov 1482 but on the reversal of the attainder of the 7th and 8th Lords (Barons) Welles 1485–86 was no longer recognised as holding the Welles Barony and instead styled 'Lord Willoughby' without formal creation, to the detriment of the rights of the *de jure* 10th LORD (Baron) WILLOUGHBY DE ERESBY (*see* below), who nevertheless styled himself such late in his life, and *dsp* probably just prior to the Act of Attainder of Jan–March 1474/5 that stripped her f of his peerages

2 Thomas (Sir), KB; *m* Joan, dau and coheir of Sir Richard Arundell, and *d* by 1 July 1439, leaving an er s:

(1) Robert (Sir); *m* Cicely (d 1380), 2nd dau of 6th Lord (Baron) Welles, and *d* 30 May 1465, leaving:

1a Robert; *d* unm 24 March 1466/7

2a CHRISTOPHER WILLOUGHBY, *de jure* 10th LORD (Baron) WILLOUGHBY DE ERESBY, KB (1483), of Parham, Suffolk; *b* 1453; *m* by 28 March 1482 Margaret, dau of Sir William Jenney, of Knoddishall, Suffolk, and *d* between 1 Nov 1498 and 13 July 1499, leaving, with apparently two other sons (John; Richard, *m* and *d* between 20 Sept 1499 and 25 Sept 1500):

1b WILLIAM WILLOUGHBY, **11th Lord**

2b Christopher; *m c* May 1512 Elizabeth, yst dau of Sir George Tailboys, *de jure* 9th Lord (Baron) Kyme, and *d* between July 1538 and Oct 1540, leaving:

1c WILLIAM WILLOUGHBY, 1st BARON WILLOUGHBY OF PARHAM, Co Suffolk (E), so *cr* 20 Feb 1546/7; *b c* 1515; ktd 1542, Esq for the Body by 1545, Ld Lt Lincs by 10 Aug 1557–late Oct 1558 (Jt Ld Lt 1559 on), Dep of Calais 1550–52, Ch Steward Duchy Lancaster Feb 1552/3–70; *m* 1st *c* 1535 Elizabeth, dau of Sir Thomas Heneage, of Hainton and Knaith, Lincs; *m* 2nd on or after 20 Aug 1559 Margaret, dau of Robert Garneys, of Kenton, Suffolk, and widow of 1st Viscount Hereford (*qv*), and *d* 30 July 1570, leaving by his 1st w:

1d CHARLES WILLOUGHBY, 2nd BARON WILLOUGHBY OF PARHAM; *b* 1536–37; *educ* St John's Coll Cambridge; *m* Margaret, 3rd dau of 1st Earl of Lincoln (*qv*), and *d* between Oct 1610 and 26 Oct 1612, having had:

1e William, of Little Coates, Lincs, and Parham; *b* on or after 11 Jan 1551/2; perhaps *educ* Eton; *m* by 1582 Elizabeth, dau of Sir Christopher Hildyard, of Winestead in Holderness, Yorks, and *dvp* 1 June 1601, leaving:

1f WILLIAM WILLOUGHBY, 3rd BARON WILLOUGHBY OF PARHAM; *b* 1584; ktd 1603; *m c* 4 Feb 1602/3 Frances, dau of 4th Earl of Rutland (*see* RUTLAND, D), and *d* 28 Aug 1617, leaving:

1g HENRY WILLOUGHBY, 4th BARON WILLOUGHBY OF PARHAM; *b c* Nov 1612; *d* in infancy

2g FRANCIS WILLOUGHBY, 5th BARON WILLOUGHBY OF PARHAM; *b* 1613–14; *educ* Eton; Parly Ld Lt Lindsey (in Lincs) and all Lincs 5 and 26 March 1642 respectively, Col Parly regt of horse1642–Jan 1643/4, defeating a royalist contingent nr Ancaster Jan 1642/3 but being forced to capitulate when having held Gainsborough against a siege 30 July 1643; took Bolingbroke Castle Nov 1643; voted earldom by H of C Dec 1645; Speaker Ho Lds 1647; impeached by H of C for alleged high treason 1647 and escaped to Holland, where threw in lot with CHARLES II, who made him Govr Barbados, which he held against attacking Parly forces late April 1650–11 Jan 1651/2, when obliged to surrender, the terms negotiated allowing his return to England and involving the restoration to him of his estates, previously confiscated; frequently conspired throughout rest of Interregnum to restore the monarchy, hence imprisoned Tower London 1655–57; the Restoration saw the renewal of his governorship of Barbados, which he accordingly ruled more or less as despot 1663–66; *m c* 1628–29 Elizabeth, dau of 1st and last Viscount Wimbledon (*see* EXETER, M) by his 1st w, and *dspms c* 23–24 July 1666 in a hurricane that destroyed his ship the *Hope* and all in her, having had two sons (*d* young)

3g WILLIAM WILLOUGHBY, 6th BARON WILLOUGHBY OF PARHAM; *b c* 1616; *educ* Eton and Middle Temple; apparently pro-Parl in Civil War; Capt-Gen and Govr Caribbee Islands (*i.e.*, English-controlled West Indies) Jan 1666/7–73; *m* by 1638 Anne, 3rd dau of Sir Philip Cary (*see* FALKLAND, V), and *d* 10 April 1673, leaving:

1h GEORGE WILLOUGHBY, 7th BARON WILLOUGHBY OF PARHAM; *b* 18 March 1638/9; *m* 9 Oct 1666 Elizabeth, dau of Henry Clinton/Fiennes, s of Sir Henry Clinton/Fiennes, of Kirkstead, Lincs (*see* CLINTON, B), and *d* 1674, leaving:

1i JOHN WILLOUGHBY, 8th BARON WILLOUGHBY OF PARHAM; *b* 16 July 1669; *d* early 1667/8

1i Elizabeth; heiress to family estates 1679; *m* James Bertie, s of 2nd Earl of Abingdon (*see* LINDSEY and ABINGDON, E), and had issue

2h Edward; *b* 9 Feb 1639/40; *dvp*

3h Henry; *b* 16 Dec 1640; Lt-Gen, Govr Antigua; *dvp* unm and was bur 1 Dec 1669

4h William; *b* 24 Nov 1641; Lt-Govr Barbados; *dvp* unm and was *bur* 22 May 1669

5h JOHN WILLOUGHBY, 9th BARON WILLOUGHBY OF PARHAM; *b* 29 Dec 1643; Col of Foot Barbados; *m* Anne Bolterton, of Bermuda, and *dsp* Sept 1678

6h James; *b* 3 Aug 1647; *dvp* unm by 23 March 1669/70

7h Car(e)y; *b* 5 April 1649; *d* unm Dec 1676

8h CHARLES WILLOUGHBY, 10th BARON WILLOUGHBY OF PARHAM; *b* 6 Oct 1650; *m* Mary, 2nd dau of Sir Beaumont Dixie, 2nd Bt (*see*), and *dsp* 9 Dec 1679, when the Barony technically became dormant

2e Ambrose (Sir), of Matson, Glos; *b* on or after 11 Jan 1551/2; ktd 1603; *m* Susanna, dau of Richard Brooke, of Matson, and *d* by 24 Nov 1608, leaving:

1f Edward, of Soulbury, Bucks; *m c* 5 May 1625 Rebecca, dau of Henry Draper, and *d* by 30 Sept 1650, leaving:

1g HENRY WILLOUGHBY, *de jure* 11th BARON WILLOUGHBY OF PARHAM, of Minsterworth, Glos, and Rappahannock, Va.; *bapt* 14 Nov 1626; emigrated to America 1675–76; *m* 25 June 1661 Mary —, of Nailsworth, Glos, and *d* 26 or 28 Nov 1685 in Va, by which time Sir Ambrose's male line was thought extinct, otherwise he would have inherited the Barony of 20 Feb 1546/7; instead it, or rather an almost identically worded but fresh creation, was 'allowed' to (unjustifiably, so in effect *cr* in favour of) the jr branch (*see* below), leaving:

1h HENRY WILLOUGHBY, *de jure* 12th BARON WILLOUGHBY OF PARHAM; *bapt* 13 April 1665; *educ* Free Sch Gloucester; cutler's apprentice Tower Hill, London; full cutler by autumn 1695; *m* 28 July 1695 Elizabeth, dau of William Pi(d)geon, of Stepney, and *d* 22 Oct 1722, leaving:

1i HENRY WILLOUGHBY, 13th BARON WILLOUGHBY OF PARHAM, as which recognised 20 March 1767, though he had claimed it as far back as 1733; *b* 14 May 1696; cutler and brewer; Col 2nd Regt Trained bands Tower Hamlets; *m* 6 Jan 1725/6 Susanna, dau of Robert Greswell, of E Smithfield, and *dspms* 29 June 1775, having had a s (*dvp* an infant)

2i William; *m* 1723 Elizabeth — and *d* 27 Dec 1729, leaving:

1j William; *m* Mary, widow of Richard Bray, and *dsp* by 3 Aug 1754

3i Edward; *dsp* by 3 Aug 1754

4i Joseph; *m* Anne de Graves, of St Katherine-by-the-Tower, and *dsp* between 3 Aug 1754 and 3 Nov 1766

5i Fortune; *m* 7 Feb 1746 Hannah, dau of Thomas Barrow, of Deptford, and formerly w of Cook Tollet, of Swanscombe, Kent, and was *bur* 20 June 1750, leaving:

1j GEORGE WILLOUGHBY, 14th and last BARON WILLOUGHBY OF PARHAM; *b* 24 April 1748; *educ* Warrington Acad and Queens' Coll Cambridge; *d* unm 29 Oct 1779, when the Barony expired

3e Edward; *b* on or after 11 Jan 1551/2

4e Thomas (Sir), of Newton-on-Trent; *m* Mary, dau of John Thornhagh, of Fenton, Notts, and had:

1f THOMAS WILLOUGHBY, 1st LORD (Baron) WILLOUGHBY OF PARHAM (E), so *cr* according to later doctrine 21 Oct 1680, of Shaw Place, Horwich, Lancs; *b c* 1602; *m c* 22 Feb 1639/40 Eleanor/Ellen, dau of Hugh Whittle, of Horwich, and *d* 29 Feb 1691/2, leaving:

1g HUGH WILLOUGHBY, 2nd LORD (Baron) WILLOUGHBY OF PARHAM; *b* 1640; Unitarian; *m* 1st 29 Dec 1663 Anne, dau of Laurence Halliwell, of Tockholes, Lancs; *m* 2nd *c* 5 Oct 1692 Honora, sis of 2nd Baron Leigh (*qv*) of Stoneleigh of the 1643 *cr* and widow of Sir William Egerton, KB (*see* GREY EGERTON, Bt), and *dsps* 1 Aug 1712, having by his 1st w had an only s (*dvp* unm)

2g Thomas; *bapt* 19 Dec 1641

3g Francis; *m* Eleanor, dau of Thomas Rothwell, of Haigh, Lancs, and *d* 1704, leaving:

1h EDWARD WILLOUGHBY, 3rd LORD (Baron) WILLOUGHBY OF PARHAM; *b* 12 April 1676; *d* unm 13 April 1713

2h CHARLES WILLOUGHBY, 4th LORD (Baron) WILLOUGHBY OF PARHAM; *b* 25 Dec 1681; *m* Hester, yst dau of Henry Davenport, of Darcy Lever, Lancs, and *d* 12 June 1715, leaving:

1i HUGH WILLOUGHBY, 5th LORD (Baron) WILLOUGHBY OF PARHAM; *b c* 1714; *educ* Rivington GS; FRS (V-Pres 1752) Feb 1744/5, FSA (Pres 1754–65) 1748, Chm Ctees Ho Lds; *d* unm 21 Jan 1765, when the Barony of 1680, being by writ of summons, fell into abeyance between his sisters

1i Helena; *m* Baxter Roscoe, of Anglezark in Bolton, Lancs

2i Elizabeth; *m* John Shaw, of Shaw Place, Heath Charnock, Lancs

1e Katherine; *b* on or after 11 Jan 1551/2

2e Margaret; *b* on or after 11 Jan 1551/2

3e Anne; *m* Sir William Pelham (*see* YARBOROUGH, E)

3b George; had issue, now extinct

4b Thomas (Sir); had issue (*see* MIDDLETON, B)

The *de jure* 10th LORD's s,

WILLIAM WILLOUGHBY, **11th Lord** (Baron) **Willoughby de Eresby**, KB (1501), JP (Lincs 1497); Master Hart Hounds 1508; *m* 1st Mary (*dsp*), dau of Sir

William Hussey, of Sleaford, Lincs; *m* 2nd 5 June 1516 Maria de Salinas, Maid of Honour to CATHERINE OF ARAGON, and *dspms* 19 Oct 1526, having had by her, with a s (*d* young):

KATHERINE Willoughby, *de jure* BARONESS WILLOUGHBY DE ERESBY in her own right according to later doctrine; *b* 22 March 1518/9 or 1519/20; *m* 1st possibly 7 Sept 1533 or 1534, as his 4th w, Charles BRANDON, 1st Duke of Suffolk of the 1514 *cr* (*d* 21 Aug 1545; *see* SUFFOLK and BERKSHIRE, E, preliminary remarks), and had two sons (Henry, 2nd Duke of Suffolk; Charles, 3rd and last Duke of Suffolk; both *d* young); *m* 2nd 1553 Richard Bertie (*d* 9 April 1582) and *d* 19 Sept 1580, leaving by him:

PEREGRINE BERTIE, **13th Lord** (Baron) **Willoughby de Eresby**; *b* 12 Oct 1555; *educ* Gray's and Staple Inns; served with English forces in Low Countries, Govr Bergen-op-Zoom 1586–87, Capt-Gen there 1587–89, Lt-Gen English forces France sent to aid the Protestant leader HENRY OF NAVARRE (later HENRY IV OF FRANCE) 1598–Jan 1598/90, Govr Berwick-on-Tweed and Warden E Marches March 1597/8, memb Cncl of North 1599; *m* between Christmas 1577 and 12 March 1577/8 Mary, sis and heiress of Edward, 17th Earl of Oxford, Ld High Chamberlain of England (*see* SAINT ALBANS, D), whereby right to the hereditary post of Ld Gt Chamberlain ultimately came to the WILLOUGHBYs and their descendants and *d* 25 June 1601, having had, with four yr sons and a dau (Catherine, *m* 1609, as his 1st w, 1st Baron Rockingham, of Rockingham Castle, Northants, and *dspms* 15 Feb 1610/1):

ROBERT BERTIE, **14th Lord** (Baron) **Willoughby de Eresby** and 1st EARL OF LINDSEY, Co Lincoln (E), so *cr* 22 Nov 1626 (*see* LINDSEY and ABINGDON, E); had:

MONTAGU BERTIE, **15th Lord** (Baron) **Willoughby de Eresby** and 2nd EARL OF LINDSEY; had:

ROBERT BERTIE, **16th Lord** (Baron) **Willoughby de Eresby** and 3rd EARL OF LINDSEY; had:

ROBERT BERTIE, **17th Lord** (Baron) **Willoughby de Eresby** and 1st DUKE OF ANCASTER AND KESTEVEN (GB), so *cr* 26 July 1715; had:

PEREGRINE BERTIE, **18th Lord** (Baron) **Willoughby de Eresby** and 2nd DUKE OF ANCASTER AND KESTEVEN; had:

PEREGRINE BERTIE, **19th Lord** (Baron) **Willoughby de Eresby** and 3rd DUKE OF ANCASTER AND KESTEVEN; had:

1 ROBERT BERTIE, **20th Lord** (Baron) **Willoughby de Eresby** and 4th DUKE OF ANCASTER; *d* unm 8 July 1779, when the Dukedom and its associated titles passed to his unc (*see* LINDSEY and ABINGDON, E) and the Barony of Willoughby de Eresby fell into abeyance between his surv sisters

1 Mary Catharine; *b* 14 April 1754; *d* 12 April 1767

2 PRISCILLA BARBARA ELIZABETH Bertie, **Baroness Willoughby de Eresby** in her own right, becoming so on termination of abeyance 18 March 1780; *b* 16 Feb 1761; Joint Hereditary Ld Gt Chamberlain of England with her sis by a judgement of 25 May 1781; *m* 23 Feb 1779 Sir Peter BURRELL, 2nd Bt (*qv*), of the 1766 *cr* (ktd 1781, made Dep Ld Gt Chamberlain 14 Aug 1781), also 1st BARON GWYDIR, of Gwydir, Co Carnarvon (GB), so *cr* 16 June 1796, reflectinghis w's inheritance of the Gwydir estate from her bro, and *d* 29 Dec 1828, leaving:

(1) PETER ROBERT BURELL later DRUMMOND-BURRELL (roy licence 5 Nov 1807), **22nd Lord** (Baron) **Willoughby De Eresby**, as which s mother, and 2nd BARON GWYDIR, as which s f 29 June 1820, PC (1821); *b* 19 March 1782; *educ* St John's Coll Cambridge; MP (Whig) Boston 1812–20, Dep Ld Gt Chamberlain GEORGE IV's and QUEEN VICTORIA's coronations; *m* 19 Oct 1807 Clementina Sarah (*d* 26 Jan 1865), dau and sole heiress of 1st and last Lord Perth, Baron Drummond (*see* PERTH, E), and *d* 22 Feb 1865, having had:

1a ALBERIC DRUMMOND-BURRELL later DRUMMOND-WILLOUGHBY (roy licence 26 June 1829), **23rd Lord** (Baron) **Willoughby de Eresby** and 3rd BARON GWYDIR; *b* 25 Dec 1821; *d* unm 26 Aug 1870, when the Barony of Willoughby de Eresby fell into abeyance between his sisters

1a CLEMENTINA ELIZABETH Drummond-Burrell later (by marriage) HEATHCOTE later still HEATHCOTE-DRUMMOND-WILLOUGHBY (roy licence 4 May 1872), **Baroness Willoughby de Eresby** in her own right, becoming so on termination of abeyance 13 Nov 1871; *b* 2 Sept 1809; *m* 8 Oct 1827 1st Baron Aveland of Aveland (*see* HEATHCOTE, Bt, of London), and *d* 13 Nov 1888, leaving:

1b GILBERT HENRY HEATHCOTE later HEATHCOTE-DRUMMOND-WILLOUGHBY (roy licence 4 May 1872), **25th Lord** (Baron) **Willoughby de Eresby**, as which s mother, 2nd BARON AVELAND OF AVELAND, as which s f 6 Sept 1867, and 1st EARL OF ANCASTER (UK), so *cr* 22 Aug 1892, PC (1880), JP, DL (Lincs, Rutland); *b* 1 Oct 1830; *educ* Harrow and Trin Coll Cambridge; MP Boston 1852–56 and Rutland 1856–57; Dep Ld Gt Chamberlain for his mother and aunt (Lady Carrington) 24 Jan 1871–22 Jan 1901 (*i.e.*, within life of reigning sovereign, QUEEN VICTORIA); CA Rutland, Chm QS Parts of Kesteven, Lincs; *m* 14 July 1863 Evelyn Elizabeth (*d* 16 March 1921), 2nd dau of 10th Marquess of Huntly (*qv*), and *d* 24 Dec 1910, leaving:

1c GILBERT, **26th Lord**

2c Charles Strathavon, CB (1918), CMG (1916); *b* 18 May 1870; Maj Scots Gds Boer War 1899–1902, Lt-Col cmdg 6th London Inf Bde 1912–15 WW I, Hon Brig-Gen; *m* 7 Jan 1903 Muriel Agnes, est dau of 14th Earl of Buchan (*qv*), and *d* 15 Dec 1949, leaving:

1d Charles Peregrine; *b* 13 Sept 1905; *m* 19 April 1939 Anne Evelyn (*d* 1983), yr dau of James Fitzsimons, of Cootehill, Co Cavan, and *d* 1 Oct 1965, leaving:

1e +(Anne) Leueen [Mrs Willoughby, 509 Broadview Ave, Toronto, Canada M4K 2N5]; *b* 9 June 1949; *m* 1985 (but retains maiden name) *David Reid Brown and has:

1f +Peregrine WILLOUGHBY-BROWN; *b* 1985

1f +Breanne WILLOUGHBY-BROWN; *b* 1988

1d Rosalie; *b* 10 July 1908; *m* 25 April 1935 1st and last Baron Nugent (*see* NUGENT, Bt, of Waddesdon) and *dsp* July 1994

3c Claud; *b* 15 Oct 1872; Boer War, MP Stamford 1910–18 and Rutland and Stamford 1918–22, Lt-Col Coldstream Gds, T/Lt-Col cmdg Bn MGC TF WW I; *m* 17 June 1905 Florence (*d* 28 Jan 1946), yst dau of 3rd Marquess Conyngham (*qv*) and widow of Bertram Frankland-Russell-Astley (*see* HASTINGS, B), and *dsp* 24 Feb 1950

4c Peter Robert; *b* 2 Nov 1885; Lt-Cdr RN; *m* 4 June 1913 Pamela May (*m* 2nd 31 July 1917 Capt William Duncan Phipps, CVO, RN (*d* 2 June 1967), 2nd s of William Wilton Phipps, er dau of Brig-Gen Sir Walter Charteris Ross, KBE, CB, CMG, of Cromarty, Ross-shire, and *das* 1 Nov 1914 aboard HMS *Monmouth* off Chile, leaving:

  1d Peter Gilbert; *b* 8 June 1914; *d* 2 Nov 1916

1c Evelyn Clementina; *b* 26 Aug 1864; *m* 3 Nov 1888 Maj-Gen Sir Henry Peter Ewart, 1st and last Bt, GCVO, KCB (*d* 16 April 1928), and *d* 15 Jan 1924, having had issue

2c Margaret Mary; *b* 23 March 1866; *m* 5 June 1902 Gideon Macpherson Rutherford (*d* 31 July 1907), barrister, and *d* 15 Nov 1956, leaving:

  1d Margaret Evelyn; *b* 3 Aug 1903; *m* 16 April 1930 (*divorce* 1944) Lt-Cdr Reginald Arthur Forbes, RN (*see* STUART-FORBES, Bt), and *d* 1984, leaving issue

  2d Christine Jane [Mrs William Poole, Ascot, 7 Thamesfield Court, Wargrave Rd, Henley-on-Thames, Oxon RG9 2ND]; *b* 5 Jan 1906; *m* 19 Dec 1934 Gp/Capt William Henry Poole, AFC, MM, RAF (*d* 1971), s of John Edward Poole, of Seven Kings, Essex, and has:

    1e +David Rutherford [David Poole Esq, Wainbridge House, Malt Hill, Warfield, Berks RG12 6PL]; *b* 25 April 1939; *educ* Charterhouse; *m* 1962 *Julie Anne, dau of Gp/Capt Hoskins, of Forecourt, Hewley, and has:

      1f +Jennifer Alice; *b* 3 March 1968

  3d Nina; *b* 11 May 1869; *d* unm 5 Dec 1940

4d Cecile; *b* 24 June 1874; *m* 15 April 1896 Thomas Clarence Edward Goff, DL (*d* 13 March 1949), s of Thomas William Goff, DL, of Oakport, Co Roscommon, and *d* 27 July 1960, leaving:

  1e Thomas Robert Charles, OBE (1959); *b* 16 July 1898; *educ* Eton and Ch Ch Oxford (BA); Lt Scots Gds WW I, ADC to Govr-Gen Canada, barrister Middle Temple 1922

  1e Elizabeth Moyra; *b* 30 May 1897

5d Alice; *b* 27 June 1876; memb Oakham RDC; *d* unm 13 Oct 1951

6d Mary Adelaide; *b* 25 April 1878; *m* 14 July 1903 14th Earl of Dalhousie (*qv*) and *d* 23 May 1960, leaving issue

1b Clementina Charlotte; *m* 5 April 1869 V-Adml Sir George Tryon, KCB, and *d* 8 Nov 1922, leaving issue (*see* TRYON, B)

2b Elizabeth Sophia

2a Elizabeth Susan; *b* 21 Sept 1810; *d* unm 10 Oct 1853

3a Charlotte Augusta Annabella; *b* 3 Nov 1815; *m* 10 Aug 1840 2nd Baron Carrington (*qv*) and *d* 26 July 1879, leaving issue

(2) Merrick Lindsey; *b* 20 June 1786; *m* 13 July 1807 Frances, yst dau of James Daniell, Madras CS, and *d* 1 Jan 1848, leaving:

  1a Sir PETER ROBERT BURRELL, 5th Bt, and 4th BARON GWYDIR; *b* 27 April 1810; *educ* St John's Coll Cambridge; Sec to hereditary Ld Gt Chamberlain 1837–70, High Sheriff Suffolk 1858, High Steward Ipswich 1884–1909; *m* 1st 10 Sept 1840 Sophia (*d* 14 March 1843), only child of Frederick William Campbell, of Barbreck, Argyllshire; *m* 2nd 8 May 1856 Georgina, 2nd dau of George Peter Holford, of Westonbirt, Glos, and *d* 3 April 1909, leaving by his 1st w:

    1b WILLOUGHBY MERRICK CAMPBELL BURRELL, 5th and last BARON GWYDIR; *b* 26 Oct 1841; *educ* Eton; Capt Rifle Bde; *m* 1st 4 Sept 1873 Mary (*d* 26 June 1898), only child of Sir Thomas Bankes, KCB, MD, of Merrion Sq, Dublin; *m* 2nd 4 June 1901 Anne, dau of John Ord, of Overwhitton, Roxbughshire, and *dspms* 15 Feb 1915, when his titles expired, having had:

      1c Randulphus Clement Robert; *b* 2 Nov 1876; *d* 13 Nov 1882

      2c John Percy; *b* 11 Feb 1878; Dip Serv; *d* unm 17 Aug 1902

(3) William Peregrine Peter; *b* 1 Oct 1788; *d* 27 July 1852

(1) Elizabeth Julia Georgiana; *m* 14 April 1826 2nd Earl of Clare (*dsp* 18 Aug 1851) and *d* 30 April 1879

2 Georgiana Charlotte; *m* 25 April 1791 1st Marquess of Cholmondeley (*qv*) and *d* 23 June 1838, leaving issue

The 25th LORD's est s,

GILBERT HEATHCOTE-DRUMMOND-WILLOUGHBY, **26th Lord** (Baron) **Willoughby de Eresby** and 2nd EARL OF ANCASTER, GCVO (1937), TD, JP Lincs, DL Perths; *b* 20 July 1867; *educ* Eton and Trin Coll Cambridge (MA); MP Horncastle 1894–1910, Parly Sec Min Ag and Dep Min Fisheries 1921–24, Ld Gt Chamberlain 1937–50 (when post assumed by his s due his own ill health), *i.e.*, for reign of HM GEORGE VI; Lt-Col Lincs Yeo, Rutland: Ld Lt and custos rotulorum, Chm CC, Chm QS Parts of Kesteven 1912–33, memb Roy Commn Historical MSS. 1935; *m* 6 Dec 1905 Eloise Laurence, OBE (1920), JP (Kesteven) (*d* 12 Dec 1953), er dau of William Lawrence Breese, of New York, and *d* 19 Sept 1951, leaving:

1 (GILBERT) JAMES HEATHCOTE-DRUMMOND-WILLOUGHBY, **27th Lord (Baron) Willoughby de Eresby**, as which called up to Ho Lds *vp* 16 Jan 1951, and 3rd EARL OF ANCASTER, JP (Lincs 1937)); *b* 8 Dec 1907; *educ* Eton and Magdalene Coll Cambridge (BA 1929, MA 1934); MP Rutland and Stamford 1933–50; Maj Leics Yeo (TA) WW II (wounded, despatches); apptd Ld Gt Chamberlain for rest of HM GEORGE VI's reign 1950; Lincs: Ld Lt and custos rotulorum 1950–75 (DL 1947–50), CC 1950, CA Kesteven 1954; *m* 27 July 1933 Hon Nancy Phyllis Louise Astor (*d* 2 March 1975), only dau of 2nd Viscount Astor (*qv*), and *d* 29 March 1983, when the Barony of Aveland and Earldom expired, having had:

  (1) Timothy Gilbert, *Lord Willoughby de Eresby*; *b* 19 March 1936; *educ* Eton; lost in Mediterranean 19 Aug 1963

  (1) (NANCY) JANE MARIE, **present Baroness Willoughby de Eresby**

2 John, of Brooklyn House, Kingsclere, Hants; *b* 14 March 1914; *educ* Stowe and Magdalene Coll Cambridge; *d* unm 1 March 1970

---

1 Catherine Mary Clementina; *b* 25 Sept 1906; *m* 1st 20 Feb 1935 (*divorce* 1947) John St Maur Ramsden (*see* RAMSDEN, Bt) and had issue; *m* 2nd 8 April 1948 Charles Wedderburn Hume (*d* 1974), 2nd s of Thomas Levi Hume, of Washington, DC, and *d* 19 Feb 1996 leaving by him:

  (1) +Carola Eloise [Mrs Robert Philippi, The Mains of Drummond, Crieff, Perthshire]; *b* 26 Oct 1938; coheiress presumptive; *m* 1st 5 April 1961 George Filmore Miller III, s of George Filmore Miller, Jr, of Princeton, Mass., and has:

    1a +Sebastian St Maur; *b* 7 Feb 1965; Capt Blues and Royals; *m* 1991 *Emma Caroline, dau of John Harries, of Esher, Surrey

  (1) (cont.) Mrs Miller *m* 2nd 4 July 1974 *Robert Ernest James Philippi, s of Col George Philippi, of Madrid, and by him has:

    2a +James Jeremy George; *b* 10 June 1975

2 +PRISCILLA [The Lady Priscilla Aird, Wingrove House, Chipping Campden, Glos]; *b* 29 Oct 1909; coheiress presumptive; *m* 26 April 1939 Col Sir John Renton Aird, 3rd Bt (*qv*), and has issue

Lineage (of Bec/Beke): WALTER de BEC; *m* Agnes, dau and heir of Hugh fitz Pincheon (living 1167), s of Pinco, feudal Ld of Tatshull, Lincs, thus acquiring the feudal Ldship of Eresby, Lincs, and had:

HENRY de BEC or BEKE, of Eresby; *m* Alice/Hawise, sis of Thomas de Muleton, and had:

WALTER BEKE, of Eresby; *m* 1222 Eve, n of Walter de Grey, Archbp York, and had, with two yr sons (Anthony, Bp Durham 1283, Patriarch Jerusalem 1305, fndr collegiate church Chester, *d* 2 March 1310/1; Thomas, Bp St Davids 1280, *d* 20 April 1293) and two daus:

JOHN BEKE, 1st and last LORD (Baron) BEKE (E), so *cr* 24 June 1295 (according to later doctrine) by writ of summons to Parl, of Eresby; *b* by 1230; *dspms* 1303–04, when any barony *cr* by the writ of summons must be deemed by later doctrine to have fallen into abeyance between his daus, leaving:

1 Walter; *dsp* & *vp* shortly after 1 Aug 1301

1 Alice; *m* Sir William de Willoughby (*see* **Lineage (of Willoughby)** above)

2 Margaret/Milisent; *m* Richard de Harcourt (*see* VERNON, B, section **Lineage (of Harcourt)**)

3 Mary; *d* unm

Seat: Grimsthorpe Castle, Bourne, Lincs. The **11th Lord**'s second marriage in 1516, with the Spaniard Maria de Salinas, was the occasion of his being granted in reversion the Manor of Grimsthorpe among other Lincolnshire estates. A Cistercian monastery seems to have existed there previously, for among the features of the present-day park is a stewpond, said to date from the 12th century. (Others were subsequently joined up to form the nucleus of the lake facing the west front.) The south front, with tall chimneys interspersed among a row of high-pitched gables, appears to be 16th-century. It is flanked by two square, crenellated towers, one 13th-century in origin (part of the old lookout tower, now refaced), the other 16th-century. The windows of the entire front, both on the ground and first floors are later.

The north front is the chief glory of Grimsthorpe. It dates from the 1st Duke of Ancaster and Kesteven's time and was commissioned by him from Sir John Vanbrugh to celebrate his step up in the peerage in 1715, though the project was not completed till 1723. Vanbrugh's love of plinth-like towers, almost keeps in bulk though high baroque as to finish, is much in evidence, as also is his use of finials to break up that bulk. Here he has placed two relatively low towers well forward of the main part of the building, joining them to their larger brothers by a low wall. They are of two storeys but the way they are surmounted by balustrades and urn-shaped finials at the corners, as with those on the main building, has the effect of raising them almost half a storey again. The two larger versions are of three storeys, the single top window to the north having a triangular pediment, the single middle storey drawing the eye with a tripartite window, the centre bay of which rises above its fellows to an arched top. The sides of these larger towers are of three bays, also with triangular pediments.

The central block on this north facade is a tour de force. Though capable of sustaining three storeys it actually has only two, a double row of seven arched windows divided from a single further window on each storey to either side by gigantic twin columns. These rise higher than the top of the second storey windows anyway but are then finished off with huge plinths on which sit armorial figures. They thus soar well above the skyline even of the high-pitched roof. The central seven bays are prevented from seeming too low for the height of the block by a decorative cornice below the balustrade, the balustrade itself and lastly the finials above it climaxing in a huge coat of arms at the centre.

Internal features include the magnificent hall, with its arches and gallery. The state rooms contain items from the House of Lords before the fire of 1834 that destroyed both houses of Parliament. They were acquired through the parliamentary connection that stemmed from the post of Lord Great Chamberlain's being hereditary in the family.

WILLS of Blagdon

Arms: Gules a sun in splendour between two gryphons passant in pale or. **Crest:** Issuant from an annulet or a demi-gryphon gules, holding in the dexter claw a battleaxe gold. **Motto:** *Pro aris et focis* ('For our altars and our hearths'). **Creation:** Bt. (UK) 19 July 1923.

SIR JOHN VERNON WILLS, 4TH BT, of Blagdon, Co Somerset, KCVO (1988), TD, JP (Somerset 1962) [Sir John Wills Bt KCVO TD JP, Langford Court, Langford, nr Bristol, Somerset BS40 5DA]; *b* 3 July 1928; *s* bro 1945; *educ* Eton; Lt Coldstream Gds Malaya 1948–49, Lt-Col cmdg Somerset and Bristol Yeo 1965–67, Brevet Col 1967; Hon Capt RNR 1988; Lt-Col cmdg Somerset and Bristol Yeo 1965–67, Brevet Col 1967; Hon Capt RNR 1988; dir Bristol Water Hldgs plc (dir 1963–98), dep chm Bristol Evening Post and Bristol Utd Press (dir 1973–), memb Nat Water Cncl and chm Wessex Water Authority 1973–82; dir Bristol and W Bldg Soc 1969–93 (Pres 1993–98); High Sheriff Somerset 1968, Ld Lt and Keeper Rolls Avon 1974–96, Ld Lt Somerset 1994– (DL 1968–94), Pro-Chllr Bath U 1979–, Hon LLD Bristol U 1986, Hon LittD Bath U 1993; KStJ 1978; *m* 24 Oct 1953 *Diana Veronica Cecil (Jane), only dau of Douglas Ryan Midelton Baker, of The Close, Winsford, Minehead, Somerset, and has

1 +DAVID JAMES VERNON [David Wills Esq, Vale Cottage, Blagdon, Somerset BS40 7TQ]; *b* 2 Jan 1955; *educ* Stanbridge Earls Sch

2 +Anthony John Vernon [Anthony Wills Esq, Kinlochruel House, Colintraive, Argyll PA22 3AH]; *b* 10 Dec 1956; *educ* Millfield; *m* 9 Oct 1983 *Katherine A, 3rd dau of Thomas Wilks, of Laggan, Bowmore, Isle of Islay, and has:

(1) +George Edward Vernon; *b* 26 May 1985

(2) +James Douglas Vernon; *b* 26 April 1987

(3) +Peter John Vernon; *b* 15 July 1989

3 +Rupert Charles Vernon [Rupert Wills Esq, 22 Perryn Rd, London W3 7NA]; *b* 11 April 1959; *educ* Eton; *m* 20 May 1989 *Kathryn A, 2nd dau of Gordon Board Matthews and Mrs W Clarke Graham, of Binoxica, Menorca and has:

(1) +Harry James Vernon; *b* 16 Aug 1990

(2) +Thomas Edward Vernon; *b* 4 Sept 1992

4 +Julian Robert Vernon [Julian Wills Esq, Lodge Farmhouse, Langford, Somerset BS40 5BW]; *b* 5 March 1963; *educ* Blundell's; *m* 8 July 1989 *Fiona E R, est dau of T R Thom, of The Forge, Lower Langford, nr Bristol, and has:

(1) *Alice Elizabeth Vernon; *b* 16 Sept 1991

(2) *Fiona Diana Vernon; *b* 8 Aug 1994

Lineage: PETER WILLS, of Salisbury; had (with other issue by his 1st w Anne):

THOMAS WILLS; *b* 14 June 1705; *m* 1730 — and had:

EDMUND WILLS; *b* 1731; *m* 10 Aug 1756 Rebecca, dau of Henry Overton, of Andover, Hants, and had:

HENRY OVERTON WILLS, of Bristol; *b* 2 March 1761; *m* 24 June 1790 Anne, est dau of William Day, of Bristol, and *d* 1 Dec 1826, having had, with other issue:

1 William Day, of Portland Sq, Bristol; *b* 6 June 1797; co-fndr W D & H O Wills, tobacco mfrs; *m* 1820 Mary (*d* 20 Nov 1872), 3rd dau of Robert Steven, of Glasgow and Camberwell, Surrey, by Jane, dau of Thomas Dawson, of Cirencester, Glos, and *d* 13 May 1865, having had, with a dau (*d* an infant):

(1) Robert Steven; *b* 1821; *d* 1833

(2) Sir WILLIAM HENRY WILLS, 1st and last Bt, also 1st and last BARON WINTERSTOKE, of Blagdon, Co Somerset, so *cr* 12 Aug 1893 and 1 Feb 1906 respectively (both UK), JP Kent and Bristol, JP, DL Somerset; *b* 1 Sept 1830; *educ* Mill Hill and London U; joined W D & H O Wills 1858, 1st Chm Imp Tobacco Co 1901, Sheriff Bristol 1877–78, MP (Lib) Coventry 1880–85 and E Bristol 1895–1900; dir GWR, Pres Bristol Fine Arts Acad, Chm Bristol Chamber of Commerce, Pro-Chllr Bristol U, High Sheriff Somerset 1905–06; *m* 11 Jan 1853 Elisabeth (*d* 10 Feb 1896), yst dau of John Stancomb, of Trowbridge, Wilts, and *dsp* 29 Jan 1911, when his titles expired

2 Henry Overton, of Bristol; *b* 13 July 1800; co-fndr W D & H O Wills; *m* 7 Jan 1828 Isabella (*d* 23 June 1843), dau of William Board, of Bristol, and *d* 23 Nov 1871, leaving, with other issue:

(1) HENRY OVERTON

(2) Sir EDWARD PAYSON WILLS, 1st Bt, of Hazelwood (*qv*)

(3) Sir FREDERICK WILLS, 1st Bt, so *cr* 1897 (*see* DULVERTON, B)

The est s,

HENRY OVERTON WILLS, of Kelston Knoll, nr Bath, JP; *b* 22 Dec 1828; Chllr Bristol U; *m* 1853 Alice Hopkinson (*d* 1881), and *d* 4 Sept 1911, leaving with other issue:

1 GEORGE ALFRED (Sir), **1st Bt**

2 Henry Herbert, of Barley Wood, Wrington, Somerset (which he sold to his n Douglas 1921), JP (Somerset); *b* 1856; *educ* Clifton; Somerset: CA, High Sheriff 1910, Pro-Chllr Bristol U 1919, Freeman Bristol 1921, dir Imp Tobacco Co 1901–22; *m* 29 April 1886 Mary Monica Cunliffe, DBE (1925), DGStJ (*d* 2 April 1931), 2nd dau of Sir Francis Philip Cunliffe-Owen, KCB, KCMG, CIE (*see* CUNLIFFE-OWEN, Bt), and *dsp* 1922

3 Walter Melville, of Bracken Hill, Leigh Woods, Somerset, and Killilan, Ross and Cromarty; *b* 28 June 1861; *educ* Clifton and Emmanuel Coll Cambridge; *m* 15 March 1887 Louisa Gertrude (*d* 10 April 1936), dau of Robert Wilson, and *d* 26 Jan 1941, having had:

(1) (Walter) Douglas Melville, CBE (1948), JP (Somerset 1927), of Barley Wood; *b* 16 Dec 1887; *educ* Charterhouse and Trin Coll Cambridge (BA 1909); Capt N Somerset Yeo WW I; Somerset: CC 1925, CA 1940–48, High Sheriff 1946, Chm War Ag Exec Ctee 1940–48, Jt MFH Mendip 1929–32, Master Clifton Foot Harriers 1938; *m* 1st 14 April 1921 (*divorce* 1930) Penelope Wilhelmina, only dau of Charles Onslow Master, of Flax Bourton, Somerset, and had:

1a Charles Overton Melville; *b* 7 June 1922; *educ* Eton and RMC Sandhurst; Lt Gren Gds, WW II; *ka* Tunisia 3 Feb 1943

1a *Elizabeth Penelope Melville; *b* 7 Sept 1924; *m* 18 Sept 1948 Maj George Thomas Ponsonby and has issue (*see* BESSBOROUGH, E)

(1) (cont.) Douglas Wills *m* 2nd 5 April 1931 Pamela Violet (*d* 3 Aug 1944), yr dau of Capt Charles Clement Tudway, N Somerset Yeo Cav, JP, DL, of Stoberry Park, The Cedars and Milton Lodge, Wells, Somerset, and by her had:

2a *Simon Melville; *b* 19 June 1933; *educ* Eton; High Sheriff Avon 1976; *m* 30 April 1955 *Philippa Dorothy Mary, only dau of Robert Hamlyn Mervyn Drake, of Musbury Farm, Axminster, Devon, and has:

1b *Caryl Peter Melville; *b* 10 March 1957; *educ* Millfield; *m* 1st 6 Sept 1980 (*divorce* 1990) Caroline Buckland, est dau of Michael Hall, of Truro, Cornwall; *m* 2nd 14 July 1990 *Rebecca Gabrielle, dau of Roger Edward Marshall Foulds, of Hewish, Somerset, and has:

1c *Joshua Simon Melville; *b* 27 Dec 1990

1c *Nina Isabella Melville; *b* 28 Sept 1992

1b *Lisa Susan Melville; *b* 18 Jan 1959; *educ* Millfield; *m* 1st Oct 1980 (*divorce* 1990) John Rushing Grant, only s of William Ray Grant, of Denver, Colo.; *m* 2nd July 1994 *Peter James Lawford, s of Reginald James Lawford, of Wimbledon and by her 1st husb has issue

2a *Jennifer Susan Melville; *b* 25 May 1937; *m* 21 Jan 1961 *David William Fattorini, s of E W Fattorini, of Arundel Lodge, Ilkley, Yorks, and has issue

(1) (cont.) Douglas Wills *m* 3rd 18 Nov 1949 Cynthia Melanie Agnes, dau of Harry Grimshaw Barlow, of Clifton, Bristol, and widow of Edward Wilson Thomas, JP, of Bourne, Burrington, Somerset

(2) Robert Bruce Melville; *b* 26 May 1890; *educ* Charterhouse and Trin Coll Cambridge; Capt 2nd Wessex Field Co RE WW I 1914–15; *m* 16 June 1914 Beryl Emmeline, est dau of John Robert Sutton, of Clifton, Bristol, and was *ka* 15 Feb 1915, leaving:

1a Ione Bruce Melville; *b* 16 July 1915; *m* 1st 20 June 1942 (*divorce* 1946) W/Cdr Hamish Mackenzie Kerr, RAF, est s of James Kerr, of Irvine, Ayrshire, and had a dau; *m* 2nd 16 May 1960, as his 2nd w, Ralph Luttrell, yr s of Alexander Fownes Luttrell, JP, DL, of Dunster Castle and Court House, East Quantoxhead, Somerset

(3) (Maitland) Cecil Melville, MC (1915), JP (Hants 1937), late of Sherfield Court, Basingstoke, Hants; *b* 30 Nov 1891; *educ* Charterhouse and Manchester U; Capt RE TF WW I, Maj Gen Staff War Off WW II; author detective novels and other works; *m* 5 May 1915 Gladys Amy Fothergill (*d* 12 June 1964), dau of Reginald Hughes, of Weston-super-Mare, Somerset, and *d* 12 March 1966, leaving:

1a *Robin Michael Melville; *b* 8 Aug 1928; *educ* Stowe; *m* 17 Sept 1949 *Françoise, 2nd dau of Raoul Lubcké, of Juan-les-Pins, France, and has:

1b *Richard Melville Lubcké; *b* 18 Oct 1950; *educ* The Oratory Sch

1b *Penelope Anne Gladys; *b* 1 June 1953

1a *(Aimée) Hyacinth Melville; *b* 22 Jan 1916; *m* 14 Feb 1936 (*divorce* 1961) Brig Hugh Marlborough Hale Ley, OBE, 3rd Carabiniers, s of Col Arthur Edwin Hale Ley, of St Erme, Cornwall, and has issue

2a *Gladys Rosemary Melville; *b* 29 May 1918; *m* 1st 5 Sept 1939 Charles Cubitt, Lt 3rd Carabiniers attd King's Dragoon Gds (*ka* 5 Feb 1941), 2nd s of James Edward Cubitt, of Camberley, Surrey, and has issue; *m* 2nd 18 March 1944 Col Richard Totman, US Army, s of Curtis Revel Totman, of Lancaster, Wisc., and has further issue

3a *Pamela Doreen Melville; *b* 3 Nov 1919; *m* 1st 3 Sept 1939 (*divorce* 1946) Charles Larking, s of Capt Dennis Larking, RN, of Sunningdale, Berks, and has issue; *m* 2nd 5 March 1947 Samuel Morrell, s of Samuel Barant Morell, of Gloversville, NY

4a *Elaine April Melville; *b* 2 April 1921; *m* 1st 5 Jan 1939 (*divorce* 1944) Maurice Rétout, marquis du Trevou, of Paris, and has issue; *m* 2nd 11 Sept 1945 Maj Colin Kerr-Peterson, BSc, CEng, MIMechE, AMIEE, REME, 2nd s of Ivan Emile Kerr-Peterson, CEng, MIEE, of Torquay, Devon, and has further issue

5a *Ailsa Viola Melville; *b* 23 May 1923; *m* 30 May 1942 *Adolphe D'Hondt, s of Gustave D'Hondt, of High Down, Hindhead, Surrey, and has issue

6a *Hermione Anne Melville; *b* 8 March 1926; *m* 1st 23 July 1951 Merfyn Evans (drowned Cannes 20 June 1953), 2nd s of David Owen Evans, of Moneifion, Morfa Nevin, Pwlheli, Caernarvs, and had issue; *m* 2nd 26 March 1955 *Maj Henry Stoner Ball, 3rd Carabiniers (Prince of Wales's Dragoon Gds), only s of Percy Ball, of Colombo, Ceylon, and had further issue

(4) Harold Edgar Melville; *b* 23 Oct 1896; *educ* Charterhouse and Ch Ch Oxford; *k* by an avalanche 11 Feb 1925

(1) Elsie Gertrude Melville; *b* 17 Sept 1902; *m* 10 June 1930 James Broom Douglas, MB, ChB, DMR (*d* 1 Jan 1940), s of William Douglas, of St Andrews, and had issue

4 (Arthur) Stanley; *b* 13 Dec 1862; *educ* Clifton and Trin Coll Cambridge; barrister; dir Imp Tobacco; *m* 30 July 1890 Hilda (*d* 1956), dau of John Bonny Dewhurst, of Airville, Yorks, and *d* 6 Feb 1935, leaving:

(1) Ronald Dewhurst, of Hill House, Corston, Wilts; *b* 23 June 1891; *educ* Marlborough and Trin Coll Cambridge; Capt Somerset LI WW I, also RFC, RAF 1919; late parly candidate (C) Frome; *d* unm 22 Sept 1937, having adopted:

Gerald (Sir), MBE (1945), JP (Wilts 1946), formerly of Hatch House, Tisbury, Wilts; *b* 3 Oct 1905; *educ* privately and Trin Coll Cambridge (MA); barrister Middle Temple 1932; underwriting memb Lloyd's 1935, Maj RA WW II, also on Staff (DAAG S Cmd); MP (C) Bridgewater 1950–1969, Assist Whip 1952–54, Ld Commr Treasury 1954–57, Comptroller Household 1957–58, ktd 1958; *m* 19 July 1927 Amy Mary Louise (Toddie) (*d* 1993), est dau of Ivo Peters, of Corston, Wilts, and *d* 31 Oct 1969, leaving:

1b (Ronald) Henry Nicholas; *b* 22 Dec 1936; *educ* Eton; Lt Gren Gds; insur broker, underwriting memb Lloyd's; *m* 5 April 1961 *Susan Eleanor Mary [Mrs Jeremy Armitage, Pigeon House Farm, Hatherden, Hants SP11 0HJ] (*m* 2nd 25 Jan 1985 *(Robert) Jeremy Armitage), yr dau of Lt-Col Hugh Humphreys, RA, of Croft House, Manorbier, Pembs, and *d* 19 Sept 1982, leaving:

1c *Nicholas Henry Charles; *b* 21 May 1963; *educ* Eton and RMA Sandhurst; Maj Queen's Roy Lancers (2nd Lt 1983), UK, Germany, NI, Cyprus, Gulf War, RMC Sci Shrivenham and Staff Coll Camberley (MA Def Studies, U of Cranfield, psc) 1994–95, MOD (Op requirements) 1996–; *m* 19 May 1990 *Emma Victoria, dau of Lt-Col Michael Balfour Scott, Scots Gds, and has:

1d *Harry Nicholas Balfour; *b* 20 July 1991

2d *Thomas Henry Charles; *b* 18 Sept 1992

1d *Molly Isabella Primrose; *b* 19 April 1995

1b (cont.) Mr and Mrs Henry Wills also adopted:

*Arabella Mary Louise; *b* 19 Feb 1969; *educ* Croft House, Dorset; *m* 15 April 1995 *Andrew Stone, s of Frederick Stone, of Portland, Dorset

1b Caroline Louise; *b* 21 Jan 1931; *educ* Hatherop Castle; *m* 1 Nov 1952 *Maj (Francis) James Johnston, Coldstream Gds (ret) (*m* 2nd 15 May 1976 *Joan, dau of Capt John Hamilton and widow of Edmund Sharpe), est s of Francis Benjamin Johnston, of Shamley Wood, Shamley Green, Surrey, and *d* 21 Oct 1974, leaving:

1c *(Francis) Rupert Gerald [Maj Rupert Johnston, 9 Avenue Rd, Caterham, Surrey CR3 5TR]; *b* 31 Aug 1953; *educ* Eton and RMA Sandhurst; Maj (RARO) Coldstream Gds (2nd Lt 1973), UK, NI, Germany, Cyprus and Kenya, ret 1990; ptnrship manager and sec Tweedie and Prideaux (slrs); *m* 30 March 1978 *Jane Morley, yst dau of Charles William Morley Saunders (*d* 1996), of Wennington, Lancs, and has:

1d *(Francis) Gerald Charles; *b* 24 Nov 1980; *educ* Caterham and St Bede's

1d *Signe Louise; *b* 10 Oct 1983; *educ* St Bede's

2c *Andrew James Benjamin, MBE (1991) [Maj Andrew Johnston MBE, High Brow House, Motcombe, Dorset SP7 9HU]; *b* 15 Sept 1960; *educ* Eton and RMA Sandhurst; Maj Coldstream Gds (2nd Lt 1977), UK, Germany, NI, Canada, Cyprus, T/Equerry to HM THE QUEEN 1987–89, RMC Sci Shrivenham and Staff Coll (psc) 1989–90, MOD (Directorate Army Plans and Programme) 1990–1992, Bosnia-Herzegovina (active serv) 1993–94 (Queen's Commendation for Valuable Serv 1994), invalided 1995; *m* 21 Aug 1982 *Catherine Millicent Frances, yr dau of Maj-Gen Lionel Harrod, OBE (*d* 1995), Gren Gds and Roy Regt of Wales, of The Grange, Marnhull, Dorset, and has:

1d *Alexander James Edward; *b* 6 May 1985

1d *Katherine Mary Frances; *b* 13 March 1987

3c *George Henry Murray [George Johnston Esq, 75E Duke's Ave, London W4 2AQ]; *b* 23 Jan 1963; *educ* Eton; insur underwriter (Lloyd's 1983–93, Liberty Mutual Insurance 1993–)

1c *Henrietta Mary Louise [Mrs Peter Reeve, Leadenham House, Lincs LN5 0PU]; *b* 27 April 1956; *educ* Heathfield; *m* 8 Sept 1978 *Peter Richard Reeve, yst s of Lt-Col William Reeve, OBE, JP, DL, Gren Gds (*d* 11 Jan 1993), of Leadenham House, and has:

1d *William Francis; *b* 22 May 1980; *educ* Eton

2d *James Henry; *b* 6 Oct 1981; *educ* Eton

1d *Caroline Mary Louise; *b* 18 Nov 1983; *educ* Heathfield

2d *Eleanor Susan Katharine; *b* 4 June 1985; *educ* Heathfield

(2) Wilfrid Dewhurst; *b* 15 Oct 1898; *educ* Cheltenham and RMC Sandhurst; Lt 5th Dragoon Gds WW I 1916–19, Lt-Cdr RNVR WW II; MP Batley and Morley 1931–35; *d* unm 20 April 1954

The est s,

Sir George Alfred Wills, 1st Bt (UK), so *cr* 19 July 1923, JP (Somerset); *b* 3 June 1854; Pres Imp Tobacco, Chm Cncl and Pro-Chllr Bristol U, dir GWR, Sheriff Bristol 1899–1900, Hon DCL Oxford 1926, Hon LLD Bristol; *m* 12 Sept 1878 Susan Britton (*d* 20 June 1904), er surv dau of Robert Proctor, of Clifton, Bristol, and *d* 11 July 1928, leaving:

1 (GEORGE) VERNON PROCTOR (Sir), **2nd Bt**

1 Hilda Proctor; *d* unm 13 May 1946

2 Alice Lilian Proctor; *m* 16 Sept 1919 Rt Rev St John Basil Wynne Willson, DD (*d* 15 Oct 1946), Bp Bath and Wells 1921–37, s of Rev William Wynne Willson, and *dsp* 4 Nov 1950

3 Mary Vera Proctor; *d* unm 3 Feb 1940

4 Margaret Aline Proctor; *m* 6 Feb 1929 Ellison Fuller Eberle (*d* 2 May 1968), 2nd s of Alderman James Fuller Eberle, OBE, of Clifton, Bristol, and *d* 30 March 1950

Sir GEORGE's only s,

Sir (George) Vernon Proctor Wills, 2nd Bt; *b* 21 March 1887; dir Imp, Hon Capt TAR; *m* 15 Nov 1919 Nellie Jeannie, ARRC, JP (Somerset) (*d* 28 Jan 1961), yst dau of John Thomas Rutherford, of Abergavenny, and *d* 1 Feb 1931, leaving:

1 **Sir (George) Peter Vernon Wills, 3rd Bt**; *b* 8 Jan 1922; *educ* Eton and Trin Coll Cambridge; Lt Coldstream Gds WW II; *ka* N Italy 19 April 1945

2 Sir JOHN VERNON WILLS, **4th and present Bt**

1 *Jean Mary Vernon [Mrs Richard Hill, Harptree Court, East Harptree, nr Bristol]; *b* 1925; *m* 17 April 1948 *Richard Hill, yr s of Charles Loraine Hill, JP, of Grove House, Alveston, Glos, and has:

(1) *Charles Peter Loraine; *b* 30 March 1954; *educ* Millfield; *m* 1980 *Linda Elizabeth Anne, dau of Alan Beresford Gordon, of Little Tumnerscourt, Godalming, and has:

1a *Matthew; *b* 1989

1a *Katie; *b* 1983

2a *Emily; *b* 1986

(1) *Angela Lorraine; *b* 2 Feb 1949; *m* 1971 *James Anderson Darling, yr son of Gordon Darling, of S Yarra, Victoria, Australia

(2) *Caryll Lorraine; *b* 4 April 1951

(3) *Sarah Lorraine; *b* 13 April 1956

WILLS of Hazelwood

Arms: Gules three suns in splendour fesswise between two gryphons passant, all or. **Crest:** Issuant from an annulet or a demi-gryphon gules charged with a sun in splendour and holding in the dexter claw a battleaxe, also or. **Motto:** *Quo Deus vult* ('As God wills'). **Creation:** Bt. (UK) 19 Aug 1904.

SIR (DAVID) SETON WILLS, 5TH BT, of Hazelwood, Stoke-Bishop, Bristol [Sir Seton Wills Bt, Eastridge House, Ramsbury, Wilts SN8 2HJ; Inchrory Lodge, Glenavon Estate, Tomintoul, Banffshire]; *b* 29 Dec 1939; *s unc* 1983; *educ* Eton; FRICS, QALAS; *m* 2 March 1968 *Gillian, twin dau of Albert Percival Eastoe, of Windmill Cottage, Aldbourne, Wilts, and has:

1 +JAMES SETON; *b* 24 Nov 1970

1 *Sarah Elizabeth; *b* 4 Nov 1969; *m* 1994 *Dominic E Pearson, son of Edward J Pearson, of Barbican, London EC2, and has:

(1) *Thomas Edward; *b* 4 April 1995

2 *Victoria Lucy; *b* 1975

3 *Alice Louise; *b* 1980

Lineage: HENRY OVERTON WILLS (*see* WILLS, Bt, of Blagdon) had a 2nd s:

Sir Edward Payson Wills, 1st Bt (UK), so *cr* 19 Aug 1904, of Hazelwood, Stoke-Bishop, Bristol, Westbury-on-Trym, Glos, and Clapton in Gordano, Somerset, KCB, JP (Glos); *b* 12 June 1834; dir Imp Tobacco, Govr Bristol Gen Hosp; *m* 2 Sept 1858 Mary Ann (*d* 25 Jan 1891), est dau of Joseph Chaning Pearce, MLCS, FGS, of Montague House, Bath, and *d* 13 March 1910, having had, with another s and dau (*d* in infancy):

1 **Sir (Edward) Chaning Wills, 2nd Bt**; *b* 25 April 1861; *educ* Emmanuel Coll Cambridge (MA); High Sheriff Devon 1915, first Pres Devonshire Regt VTC 1915, FCS; *m* 7 April 1891 Isabella Sommerville, est dau of Peter Fabyan Sparke Evans, JP, of Trinmore, Clifton Down, Bristol, and *dsp* 14 Oct 1921

2 ERNEST SALTER (Sir), **3rd Bt**

3 Arnold Stancomb, DL Ross and Cromarty; *b* 24 Nov 1877; Capt 18th Hus WW I; High Sheriff Northants 1935; *m* 11 Oct 1905 Hilda Caroline (*d* 19 Aug 1965), dau of Edward Lyon, of London and New York, and *d* 19 Jan 1961, leaving:

(1) Arnold Cass Lycett; *b* 17 July 1906; *educ* Harrow; WW II: 2nd Lt 9th Queen's Roy Lancers, Capt and Adj 24th Lancers 1940, Instr RMC Sandhurst 1943–45; *d* unm 28 Feb 1978

(2) +John Lycett [Maj John Wills, Allanbay Park, Binfield, Berks; 12 Montpellier Sq, London SW7]; *b* 29 May 1910; late Maj Life Gds; High Sheriff Berks 1958; *m* 25 July 1936 *Hon Jean Constance Buller-Fullerton-Elphinstone, 2nd dau of 16th Lord Elphinstone (*qv*), and has had:

1a Andrew Arnold Lyon; *b* 15 Aug 1937 (HM QUEEN ELIZABETH THE QUEEN MOTHER stood sponsor); *educ* Harrow; Capt Life Gds; *m* 19 Jan 1961 *Hon Elizabeth Anne Cecil [The Hon Mrs Wills, Gavelacre, Longparish, Hants SP11 7AL], only dau of 2nd Baron Rockley (*qv*), and *d* 5 Jan 1998, leaving:

 1b +Richard Arnold [Richard Wills Esq, Middleton House, Longparish, Hants SP11 6NX]; *b* 5 March 1962; *m* 1988 *Netta, er dau of Lt-Col Trevor Morris, of Butlers, Donhead St Mary, Dorset, and has:

  1c +Edward Henry Arnold; *b* 15 June 1994

  1c *Anna Rose Constance; *b* 23 May 1990

  2c *Charlotte Caroline; *b* 23 Sept 1991

 2b +Alexander John; *b* 23 May 1967; *m* 1992 *Wendy A, er dau of Robin H Leach, of Ugley Park, Essex

 1b *Tessa Elizabeth; *b* 1 Oct 1963; *m* 1993 *Richard E M Affleck, s of Michael Affleck, of Park Farm, N Moreton, Oxon

 1a *Susan Griselda Anne Lyon; *b* 8 April 1940; *m* 20 April 1960 *(Charles) Peregrine Albemarle Bertie and has issue (*see* LINDSEY and ABINGDON, E)

 2a Marilyn Emma Margaret; *b* 30 Nov 1947 (HRH PRINCESS MARGARET, COUNTESS OF SNOWDON stood sponsor); *m* 10 Feb 1970 *Trelawny Reginald Courtenay Gayer, s of Lt-Col Lionel Courtenay Gayer, of White Meads, Cranleigh, Surrey, and *dsp* 25 June 1970

 3a Georgina Rose; *b* 18 April, *d* 26 April 1951

1 Ella Marian; *m* 25 Nov 1905 Francis T T Rowcroft, s of Lt-Col F F Rowcroft, Bengal Army, and *d* 26 Jan 1941

2 Amelia Isabella; *d* unm

3 Violet Edith, DBE (1937), OStJ; *d* unm 26 Oct 1964

4 Ethelwyn Annie; *d* unm 1960

The 2nd Bt's brother,

Sir Ernest Salter Wills, 3rd Bt, JP (Somerset and Wilts); *b* 30 Nov 1869; dir Imp Tobacco, Ld Lt Wilts 1930–42, Pres TAA, Silver Jubilee 1935 and Coronation Medals 1937, CStJ; *m* 6 June 1894 Caroline Fanny Maud, OStJ (*d* 11 Feb 1953), dau of William Augustine de Winton, of Westbury Lodge, Durdham Down, Bristol, and *d* 14 Jan 1958, leaving:

1 **Sir (Ernest) Edward de Winton Wills, 4th Bt**; *b* 8 Dec 1903; *educ* Eton; WW II: Lt Scots Gds, Lt-Col Middx Regt (Res) and cmdg 5th Bn Manchester Regt TA 1943–45; *m* 1st 26 Jan 1926 Sylvia Margaret (*d* 26 Jan 1946), dau of William Barker Ogden, and had:

 (1) *Venetia Dawn [Mrs Alan Hopkins, Chalet Topaze, Anzere, Valais, Switzerland]; *b* 5 Dec 1927; *m* 1st 15 April 1948 (*divorce* 1962) Charles Robert Cecil Weld-Forester and has issue (*see* FORESTER, B); *m* 2nd 14 Sept 1962 *Alan Cripps Nind Hopkins, s of Sir Richard Valentine Nind Hopkins, GCB, PC, of Chelsea, and by him has:

  1a *Mark Edward Wills; *b* 1 Aug 1963

  2a *Peter Alan Wills; *b* 1 Aug 1963

 (2) *Edwina Sylvia [Mrs Christopher Bonn, La Maison du Coin, St Ouen, Jersey, CI]; *b* 13 March 1933; *m* 1st 17 March 1952 (*divorce* 1961) 8th Marquess of Ailesbury (*qv*) and has issue; *m* 2nd 23 Feb 1963 *Maj Christopher Leslie Leo Bonn, Welsh Gds (ret), yr s of Maj Walter Bonn, DSO, MC, of Jersey, and by him has had:

  1a *Philip Edward Leo; *b* 9 Feb 1964

  1a *Camilla Georgina Alexandra; *b* 22 April 1965

  2a Melanie Marina Roselle; *b* 4 Dec 1968; *d* 14 Nov 1971

  3a *Melanie; *b* 3 Nov 1974

1 (cont.) **Sir Edward** *m* 2nd 29 June 1949 Juliet Eve (*d* 11 Nov 1996), yr dau of Capt John Eagles Henry Graham-Clarke, JP, of Frocester Manor, Gloucester, and *d* 19 Aug 1983

2 George Seton, TD; *b* 18 May 1911; Maj Roy Wilts Yeo WW II (despatches); *m* 1st 30 Oct 1935 (*divorce* 1946) Lilah Mary (*m* 2nd, as his 2nd w, Col Nigel Victor Stopford Sackville; *see* COURTOWN, E), yst dau of Capt Percy Richard Hare (*see* LISTOWEL, E), and had:

 (1) **Sir (DAVID) SETON WILLS, 5th and present Bt**

2 (cont.) Maj George Wills *m* 2nd 23 June 1961 *Mrs Victoria Katherine Allbut [Mrs George Wills, Eastridge, Ramsbury, Wilts], 3rd dau of Capt Percy Richard Hare (*see* LISTOWEL, E), and *d* 1979

1 Doris Maud de Winton; *b* 9 Aug 1896; *m* 1st 12 Jan 1916 Rev William Alexander White (*d* 9 July 1916), Vicar Ramsbury, and had issue; *m* 2nd 14 June 1920 Norman Carl Haag (*d* 8 Dec 1950), formerly Consul-Gen Basle, and *d* Oct 1968, leaving further issue

2 Margaret Joyce de Winton; *b* 21 June 1898; *m* 19 June 1918 Capt John Trevor Kyffin, RAF (*d* 18 July 1969), s of Dr John Kyffin, of Penrhyn, Alverstoke, Hants, and had issue

3 Barbara Joan de Winton; *b* 23 Feb 1902; *m* 1st 28 Oct 1925 (*divorce* 1943) Capt Thomas Ansell Fairhurst, Life Gds (*d* 18 Aug 1955), s of Col James Ashton Fairhurst, TD, JP, DL, of Arlington Manor, Newbury, and had issue; *m* 2nd 11 Feb 1943 Jack Morton, 7th QO Hus, s of George Arthur Morton, of Harpley, Norfolk

WILMOT

Arms: Sable on a fess or between three eagle's heads couped argent as many escallops gules; a canton vaire ermine and of the fourth.
Crest: An eagle's head couped argent, gorged with a mural coronet sable, in the beak an escallop gules. **Creation:** Bt. (GB) 15 Feb 1759.

SIR HENRY ROBERT WILMOT, 9TH BT, of Chaddesden, Co Derby [Sir Henry Wilmot Bt, Beck House, Gt Broughton, Stokesley, N Yorks]; *b* 10 April 1967; *s f* 1974; *educ* Eton; *m* 1995 *Susan Clare, er dau of John Malvern

Lineage: ROBERT WILMOT, of Derby; *m* 1539 — and had, with two yr sons (Henry, of Derby, living 1562; Richard):

ROBERT WILMOT; Derby merchant; *m* Elizabeth, dau of Edward Linley, of London, and had, with a yr s (Edward, of Chaddesden, Derbys, had a s Samuel, of London, *b* 1605, living 1632):

ROBERT WILMOT, of Derby; *m* Elizabeth, dau of Edward Smith, of Derby, and had:

ROBERT WYLMOT, of Chaddesden; *m* Dorothea, dau of Lawrence Shrigley, of Cheshire, and *d* 8 Feb 1638, leaving, with an est s (Robert, *m* Mary, dau of William Newton, and *dsp*), two yst sons (John, of Osmastonby, Derbys, *d* unm 1646; Sir Nicholas, *see* EARDLEY-WILMOT, Bt) and two daus, a 2nd s:

EDWARD WILMOT (Rev), of Chaddesden; *b* 1606; *educ* Magdalen Hall Oxford (DD); Vicar All Saints Derby; *m* Dorothy, dau of Sir George Gresley, Bt (*see* 1970 edn), and had, with an er s (Robert, of Chaddesden, High Sheriff Derbys 1671, *d* unm) and two daus (Elizabeth, *bapt* 18 July 1636; Dorothy, *m* Thomas Robey, of Denby Old Hall and Castle Donington, and had issue):

EDWARD WILMOT, of Spondon and Chaddesden; *b* 1638; barrister; *m* 30 May 1667 Susanna, 2nd dau of Richard Coke, of Trusley, and had, with two yr sons (Edward, of Spondon and Derby, barrister, *m* 27 Dec 1718 his cousin Catherine Cassandra Isabella, est dau and coheir of William Coke, of Trusley, and was ancestor of the WILMOTs of Trusley; Richard, of Derby, *b* 1675, MD, *m* 8 Sept 1709 Henrietta, dau of Henry Cavendish (*see* WATERPARK, B), and had four sons (*dsp*) and seven daus):

ROBERT WILMOT; *b* 16 July 1668; rebuilt the mansion of Chaddesden; *m* 13 Sept 1691 Joyce, dau and ultimate coheir of William Sacheverell, of Staunton and Morley, and had, with an er s (Robert, of Chaddesden, *d* unm 1755), a yr s (Rev Richard, *b* 1682, DD, Canon Lichfield, Rector Morley and Mickleover, Derbys, *m* 17 Oct 1746 Dorothy, only dau of Simon Degge, of Abbot's Hill, Derby, and *d* 2 Dec 1771, being ancestor of the WILMOT-SITWELLs of Stainsby House) and two daus (Elizabeth, *bapt* 30 Oct 1701, *m* Rev Samuel Davison, Rector Dalbury, and had issue; Susannah, *m* — Lichford, of Lincoln, and had issue):

Sir Edward Wilmot, 1st Bt (GB), so *cr* 15 Feb 1759 for attending as physician on GEORGE II's family; *b* 15 Oct 1693; Physician-Gen Army, Physician-in-Ordinary to GEORGE III; *m* Sarah Marsh (*d* 10 Sept 1785), dau of Richard Meade, MD, Physician-in-Ordinary to GEORGE II, and *d* 21 Nov 1786, having had, with two daus:

Sir Robert Meade Wilmot, 2nd Bt; *b* 19 Sept 1731; *m* 13 May 1759 Mary (*d* 18 March 1811, dau and heiress of William Woollett, and had, with three other daus (*dsp*):

1 ROBERT (Sir), **3rd Bt**

2 Edward Sacheverel (Rev); *b* 16 Sept 1766; *m* April 1797 Anne (*d* 1818), only child of Dr Chambers, of Stretton, and *d* March 1809, leaving:

 (1) Francis Sacheverel, of London; *b* 2 May 1804; *m* 26 April 1843 Anne, dau of Benjamin Broomhead

 (1) Anna Maria; *m* 22 Feb 1819 Edward Sacheverell Chandos-Pole, of Radbourne Hall, Derby, and *d* 19 Jan 1863, leaving issue

 (2) Mary Frances; *m* 1st Rev John Biddulph (*see* BIDDULPH, Bt); *m* 2nd 15 Nov 1838 Gen George Dixon (*d* 15 May 1874) and *d* 23 Nov 1839

 (3) Emma Matilda; *m* 1st 24 Dec 1822 Henry Dixon (*d* 3 Aug 1838), of Gledhow, Yorks; *m* 2nd 30 April 1850 Rev Henry John Towe (*d* 2 Feb 1904) and *dsp* 25 June 1874

1 Louisa; *m* 4 Jan 1793 Sir William Cave-Browne-Cave, 9th Bt (*qv*), and *d* 23 April 1824

2 Augusta; *m* 1 July 1816 2nd Earl of Kenmare (*d* 31 Oct 1853; *see* 1949 edn) and *dsp* 26 Aug 1873

Sir ROBERT *d* Sept 1793; his er s,

Sir Robert Wilmot, 3rd Bt; *b* 5 July 1765; *m* 1st 29 March 1796 Lucy (*d* May 1812), est dau of Robert Grimston, of Neswick, Yorks, and had, with another s and three daus:

1 Roberts Robert; *b* 2 July 1799; Lt 2nd Dragoon Gds; *d* unm *vp* 24 Feb 1822

2 HENRY SACHEVEREL (Sir), **4th Bt**

3 Richard Coke (Rev); *b* 18 May 1802; *m* 3 July 1828 Ellenor (*d* 18 June 1895), 2nd dau of Rev Kyrle Ernle Money, Vicar Much Marcle, Herefs, and n of Maj-Gen Sir James Kyrle-Money, Bt, of Much Marcle (*see* 1843 edn MONEY-KYRLE, Bt), and *dsp* 16 Nov 1856

4 John WILMOT later GRIMSTON (roy licence 21 July 1860), of Neswick, Yorks; *b* 10 May 1807; *m* 23 Sept 1835 Jane (*d* 18 Dec 1889), dau of Thomas Bewes, MP, of Beaumont, Plymouth, and *d* 3 May 1879, leaving:

(1) John Robert; *b* 30 June 1836; Capt 29th Foot; *m* 10 Feb 1863 Lucy Anne (*d* 13 Nov 1894), est dau of Robert Bazley, and *dsp* 1895

(2) Henry Archer; *b* 4 July 1837; Lt RN; *d* unm July 1889

(1) Fanny; *m* 9 July 1868 Walter Francis Wrangham (*d* 12 Dec 1893), of Hotham Ho, Brough, Yorks, and *d* 15 July 1929, leaving issue

5 Edward Woollett, of Buxton; *b* 3 Aug 1808; *m* 1st 3 Feb 1831 Augusta Matilda, only dau of Charles Champion, of Beaumont Chase, and had two sons and a dau (*dsp*); *m* 2nd 13 Jan 1841 Emma Elizabeth (*d* 22 Dec 1898), 2nd dau of Sir Francis Sacheverel Darwin, JP, DL, of Breadsall Priory, Derbys, and *d* 25 June 1864, leaving by her, with another dau (*d* unm):

(1) Darwin (Rev), VD; *b* 14 Oct 1845; MA Oxon; Chaplain 5th Vol Bn Cheshire Regt, Headmaster Macclesfield Sch 1876–1910; *m* 3 Oct 1876 Louisa Lilla (*d* 19 Jan 1919), dau of Rev Charles Bickmore, DD, and *d* 5 Sept 1935, having had:

  1a Edward Darwin; *b* 19 March 1882; MB Edinburgh 1907; *d* unm 11 Nov 1908

  2a Sacheverel Darwin; *b* 22 Feb 1885; *educ* Rugby and RMA Woolwich; Capt RGA WW I, Order White Eagle Serbia 5th Cl with swords; *m* 18 Nov 1912 Annie Dudley (*d* 3 April 1960), dau of Maj-Gen Henry Strover, RA, and *das* 14 Oct 1918, leaving:

    1b +MARTYN SACHEVEREL [Maj Martyn Wilmot, Foxlair, Fifehead St Quintin, Sturminster Newton, Dorset]; *b* 2 Sept 1914; heir presumptive; *educ* Rugby and RMA Woolwich; Maj RA WW II 1939–41 (POW, escaped 1945); *m* 24 April 1948 Mona ('Jackie') Elizabeth (*d* 6 Sept 1996), yr dau of Stanley David Milnes Horner, of Farnham, Surrey, and has:

      1c +Brian Sacheverel; *b* 25 March 1949; *educ* Rugby; *m* 1979 *Beatrice, dau of Dr Ormonde George Pickard, CBE, of Dunwich, Suffolk, and has:

        1d +Thomas Sacheverel; *b* 1980

        1d *Lucy Eleanor; *b* 19–

      2c +Robin Woollett; *b* 26 Oct 1950; *educ* Rugby

      1c *Annabel Sarah; *b* 23 Sept 1960

    2b +Gordon Darwin [Maj Gordon Wilmot, Bruern End, Milton-under-Wychwood, Oxon OX7 6LL]; *b* 30 March 1918; *educ* Rugby and RMC Sandhurst; Maj late Roy Scots Fus; *m* 25 Jan 1941 *Margot Virginia, dau of Robert Murray Thorburn, of Peebles, and has:

      1c +Patrick Gordon; *b* 14 Jan 1954; *educ* Rugby

      1c *Virginia Ann [Mrs Jeremy Hill, Peyton Hall, Bures, Suffolk]; *b* 29 Dec 1942; *m* 24 April 1965 *Jeremy Adrian Hill, yr s of Lt-Col Cecil Vivian Hill, DSO, RA, of Greystones, Methven, Perthshire, and has:

        1d *Edward Justin; *b* 4 May 1969

        2d *Tristram Darwin; *b* 1970

        3d *Marcus Jeremy; *b* 1977

      2c *Felicity Joyce [Mrs Anthony Ziegler, Titcombe, Burford, Oxon]; *b* 29 Nov 1944; *m* 8 Aug 1964 *Anthony Peter Ziegler, s of Harold Colin Ziegler, of New Place, Haslemere, Surrey, and has:

        1d *Thomas Pippin; *b* 4 May 1965

        2d *Nicholas Martyn; *b* 4 May 1967

  1a Dorothy; *d* unm 24 Jan 1945

  2a Cicely, JP; *d* unm 26 Feb 1958

(2) Woollett; *b* 1847; Lt RM; *d* 31 July 1879

(3) Reginald Mead; *b* May 1852; *m* 14 March 1893 Melinda (*d* 1943), dau of George Daniel, of Burford, Ontario, and *d* 17 Dec 1920, leaving:

  1a Garton Woollett; *b* 2 Dec 1900; *m* 1831 Ivason White, of Toronto

  2a +Ronald Keith; *b* 11 March 1907; *m* 10 April 1937 *Stella Irene Shellington, of Woodstock, Ontario

  1a Frances Ellen; *b* 23 June 1895; *m* 1st 23 June 1915 Charles William Radloff (*d* 8 Aug 1939), s of John Radloff, of Princeton, Ontario; *m* 2nd 1958 Walter H Evans and by her 1st husb had:

    1b *Irma Doreen; *b* 23 March 1919; *m* 26 March 1943 *Herbert Watts, s of Alfred John Watts, and has:

      1c *William Terence; *b* 7 Jan 1944

      2c *Donna Frances; *b* 10 March 1946

(1) Emma Maria; *m* 11 Oct 1866 Godfrey Franceys Meynell (*d* 18 Feb 1921), of Meynell Langley, Derbys, and *d* 26 June 1927, leaving issue

6 Edmund, JP, DL; *b* 15 Oct 1809; *m* 1 June 1848 Ann (*d* 1 Nov 1893), yst dau of Francis Edward Hurt, of Alderwasley, Derbys, and *d* 29 June 1869, leaving, with a dau (*d* unm):

(1) Francis Edmund William (Rev); *b* 21 May 1849; *educ* Trin Coll Oxford (MA); Rector Monnington-on-Wye, Herefs; *m* 25 July 1878 Katharine (*d* 1 Dec 1939), dau of Col Thomas Coningsby Norbury, CB, and *d* 12 Jan 1911, having had:

  1a Robert Coningsby; *b* 14 July 1886; T/Capt Sherwood Foresters WW I; *ka* 29 Oct 1917

  2a Henry Cecil; *b* 13 June 1891; Private Worcs Regt WW I; *das* 1917

3a Edward; *b* 24 April 1893; Capt Herefs Regt TF WW I, Capt RWF WW II; *m* 7 Sept 1921 Marjorie (*d* 21 June 1961), only dau of Gwilym Saunders Edmunds, of Nigeria and Llandow, Glam, and *dsp* 29 Jan 1965

4a Thomas Norbury, MC; *b* 18 March 1896; 2nd Lt Worcs Regt WW I; *d* 25 Aug 1916 of wounds recd in action

5a Laurence Mead; *b* 10 Aug 1898; Lt Herefs Regt TF WW I; *d* unm 18 April 1971

1a Winifred Anne; *b* 6 Oct 1879; *d* unm 13 Aug 1909

2a Mary Sacheverel; *b* 24 May 1881; *m* 30 July 1904 George Robins Joyce, of Bath Coll, and *d* 24 Jan 1911, leaving issue

3a Gertrude; *b* 7 Oct 1882; *m* 21 May 1912 Rev Francis Edward Sutcliffe (*d* 18 July 1933), Rector Byford, Herefs, Chaplain RN, and *d* 26 Sept 1960, leaving issue

4a Audrey; *b* 17 July 1884; *m* 28 Oct 1913 Rev Charles Henry Jones Wilton (*d* 3 Nov 1940), Vicar Foy, Ross, Herefs, s of Rev Charles Turner Wilton, and *d* 7 April 1966, leaving a dau

5a Katharine Joyce; *b* 10 May 1888; *m* 27 Dec 1930 Hency Sutcliffe Crook (*d* 8 Feb 1945), s of Rev James Sutcliffe Crook, of Weobley, Herefs, and had:

  1b *Faith Marygold; *b* 17 Oct 1931

6a Meriel; *b* 4 Nov 1900; *m* 8 June 1931 Ariston St John Diamant (*d* 1951)

(2) Edmund Mead; *b* 17 Oct 1860; Capt 4th Bn Derbys Regt Boer War 1900–01 (medal and three clasps); *m* 1885 Agatha Georgiana (*d* 21 Aug 1931), dau of Francis J Jessopp, and *d* 20 March 1935, having had:

  1a Edmund Sacheverel; *b* 9 Feb 1892; 2nd Lt S Staffs Regt WW I; *ka* 13 Nov 1916

  2a Francis Hurt; *b* 8 Aug 1894; *m* 28 Aug 1935 Dorothy Fownes, er dau of Harry W Keith, MD, of Enderby, BC, Canada, and had:

    1b *Penelope; *b* 19–

(3) Richard Hurt (Rev); *b* 1 March 1864; *educ* Merton Coll Oxford (MA); Rector Bishopstone Herefs 1907–16; *m* 19 April 1893 Hon Charlotte Frances Sugden (*d* 16 Aug 1938), dau of Hon Henry Sugden (*see* 1970 edn ST LEONARDS, B), and *d* 3 Nov 1941

(1) Rose; *m* 19 Feb 1873 John Henry Fox (*d* 19 June 1892), s of Rev Samuel Fox, of Morley Rectory, Derbys, and *d* 15 Sept 1934, leaving issue

(2) Selina Maria; *m* 10 June 1872 Gerrard Andrewes Wigram and *d* 21 Nov 1934, leaving issue (*see* WIGRAM, Bt)

(3) Dora May *m* 1880 Arthur Popham Hyde Parker and *d* 3 Nov 1921, leaving issue (*see* PARKER, Bt, of Melford Hall)

Sir Robert *m* 2nd 26 May 1817 Bridget (*d* 30 Dec 1844), widow of Daniel Craufurd and dau of Henry Holland, and *d* 13 July 1842, leaving by her:

1 Ellen Frances; *m* 10 May 1837 William John Sawrey Morritt (*d* 13 April 1874), of Rokeby Pk, Yorks

His est son,

Sir Henry Sacheverel Wilmot, 4th Bt; *b* 11 Feb 1801; Cdr RN; *m* 13 Dec 1826 Maria (*d* 24 Dec 1865), est dau of Edward Miller Mundy, of Shipley Hall, Derbys, and *d* 11 April 1872, having had, with three other daus (*d* unm):

1 Robert Edward Eardley; *b* 29 Jan 1830; *d* unm *vp* 22 Oct 1861

2 **Sir Henry Wilmot, 5th Bt**, VC, KCB, JP; *b* 3 Feb 1831; Maj Rifle Bde (medal and clasp for Lucknow, medal and two clasps for China), MP S Derbys 1869–85, Hon Col 1st Vol Bn Sherwood Foresters, Derbys Regt, Chm Derbys CC 1895, CA; *m* 15 July 1862 Charlotte Cecilia (*d* 5 May 1891), dau of Rev Frederick H Pare, and *dsp* 7 April 1901

3 Edward; *b* 12 March 1833; Cdr RN; *ka* aboard HMS *Euryalus* off Japan 15 Aug 1863

4 Arthur Alfred (Rev); *b* 14 Feb 1845; Rector Morley with Smalley, Derbys; *m* 16 Jan 1872 Harriet Cecilia, 3rd dau of Rev Alleyne FitzHerbert (*see* FitzHERBERT, Bt), and *d* 11 May 1876, leaving:

(1) RALPH HENRY SACHEVEREL (Sir), **6th Bt**

1 Maria; *m* 15 June 1854 James William Mitchell and *d* 1 Nov 1897

The 5th Bt's n,

Sir Ralph Henry Sacheverel Wilmot, 6th Bt; *b* 8 June 1875; Capt Coldstream Gds, Boer War 1899–1902 (two medals, eight clasps), WW I; *m* 12 Dec 1905 Ada Marian (*m* 2nd 21 June 1921 Arnold), dau of 13th Earl of Lauderdale (*qv*), and had:

1 ARTHUR RALPH (Sir), **7th Bt**

2 Henry Frederick; *b* 13 Dec 1910; *educ* Wellington; RCASC WW II; *m* 23 March 1946 Patricia Bridget, dau of Thomas Wall, of Nelson, BC, and had:

(1) *Sheila Marion; *b* 4 June 1947

1 Ada Snowdrop; *b* 1 Feb 1907; *m* 27 Oct 1934 Rev Walter William Pulford, yr s of Stephen Wilkinson Pulford, and *d* 31 Dec 1963, leaving two sons and a dau

Sir RALPH *d* 14 Jan 1918 of wounds recd on active service; his er s,

Sir Arthur Ralph Wilmot, 7th Bt; *b* 2 Feb 1909; *educ* Wellington; Maj 1st Bn Black Watch (Adj 1941) WW II 1939–42; *m* 1 Oct 1936 Pamela Vera (*m* 2nd 15 Feb 1955 Lt-Col Charles Frederick Cathcart; *see* CATHCART, E)), twin dau of Mary Harry Sebastian Garrard, of Welton Pl, Daventry, and had:

ROBERT ARTHUR (Sir), **8th Bt**

1 *Pamela Ann [The Rt Hon The Lady Norrie, Chapel-on-the-Water, Ramsbury, Wilts SN8 2QE]; *b* 26 Nov 1937; *m* 1st 1 April 1959 (*divorce* 1967) Capt William James Stockton, RSG, only s of Lt-Col John Stockton, of Hagley Hall, Stourbridge, Worcs, and has:

(1) *Adela Louise; *b* 28 May 1961

(2) *Henrietta Maria Caroline; *b* 5 Jan 1963

1 (cont.) Mrs Pamela Stockton *m* 2nd 26 Sept 1967 (*divorce* 1982) Anthony Paul McCaffry, yst s of Loftus Joseph McCaffry, of Amherst Ho, E Grinstead, Sussex, and by him has:

(3) *Sophie Claire; *b* 13 June 1968

1 (cont.) Mrs Pamela McCaffry *m* 3rd 29 May 1997 *2nd Baron Norrie (*qv*)

Sir ARTHUR *d* following an accident in N Africa 3 Oct 1942; his only s,

Sir Robert Arthur Wilmot, 8th Bt; *b* 8 Oct 1939; *educ* Eton; Capt Scots Gds (ret 1966), Equerry to HRH the late DUKE OF GLOUCESTER 1963–65; *m* 25 May

1965 (*divorce* 1974) Juliet Elivira [Mrs Juliet Wilmot, The Garden Lodge, Chittoe, Wilts SN15 2EW] (*m* 2nd 1976 (*divorce* 1980 took 1st husb's name by deed poll 1980) Richard James Stanes), er dau of Capt Michael Neville Tufnell, DSC, RN, of Curdridge Grange, Botley, Hants, and *d* following a hit and run accident 14 Nov 1974, leaving:

1 Sir HENRY ROBERT WILMOT, **9th and present Bt**
2 Charles Sacheverel; *b* 13 Feb 1969; *d* 1993
1 *Zoë Meriel; *b* 21 April 1971

WILSON, Baron

Arms: Sable a wolf salient or, on a chief of the last a pale of the first charged with a fleur-de-lys argent between two pellets. **Crest:** A demi-wolf or, the sinister paw resting on a pellet charged with a fleur-de-lys gold. **Supporters:** Dexter, a rifleman; sinister, a bugler; both of the Rifle Brigade, in full dress proper. **Motto:** Wil sone wil. ('Get one's way'). **Creation:** B. (UK) 12 March 1946.

THE 2ND BARON WILSON (Patrick Maitland Wilson), of Libya and of Stow-langtoft, Co Suffolk [The Rt Hon The Lord Wilson, c/o Barclays Bank, Cambridge CB2 3PZ]; *b* 14 Sept 1915; *s* f 1964; *educ* Eton and King's Coll Cambridge; Lt-Col Rifle Bde WW II (despatches); *m* 12 Jan 1945 Storeen Violet (*d* 1990), est dau of Maj James Hamilton Douglas Campbell, OBE, by Hon Anna Leonora Beatrice Massey, 4th dau of 5th Baron Clarina (*see* 1949 edn)

Lineage: THOMAS WILSON, of Highbury Place; *m* Mary Remington (*d* 26 July 1816) and had, with an er s and a dau:

JOSEPH WILSON, of Highbury Hill, Middx, Little Massingham, Norfolk, and Stowlangtoft, Suffolk; *b* 7 Aug 1766; *m* 1st 10 July 1792 Mary Anne (*d* 26 May 1798), est dau of Robert Maitland, of Blue Stile, Greenwich, W Indian merchant; *m* 2nd 19 Feb 1800 Emma (*dsp* 11 March 1851), est dau of John Welford, of Black-heath, and by his 1st w had, with two daus:

HENRY WILSON, of Stowlangtoft Hall, JP, DL Suffolk; *b* 27 Aug 1797; High Sheriff 1845, MP W Suffolk 1835–37; *m* 1st 29 July 1824 Mary Fuller, er dau of Ebenezer Fuller Maitland, of Park Place, Henley-on-Thames, and had:

1 FULLER MAITLAND
2 Henry Maitland; *b* 1 March 1827; *m* 2 Aug 1854 Mary Elizabeth (*d* 12 July 1856), est dau of Charles Wriothesley Digby, of Meriden, Warwicks
3 Joseph Edward Maitland, DL; *b* 22 Feb 1833; V-Adml; *m* 15 Feb 1860 Mary (*d* 12 Aug 1906), dau of Arthur Kelly, of Kelly, Devon, and *d* 17 April 1920, having had, with other issue:
   (1) Edith; *d* 24 Dec 1920
1 Mary Maitland; *m* 21 Aug 1851 her cousin Henry Grace Wilson Sperling (*d* 24 May 1879), of Grovehurst, Tunbridge Wells, and had issue
2 Adela Maitland; *d* unm 8 April 1910
3 Ellen Maitland; *m* 10 Sept 1861 William Arthur Smith (*d* 28 Dec 1921), of Colebrook, and had issue (*see* below)
4 Fanny Maitland; *m* 22 April 1852 her bro's bro-in-law Edward Leigh Kindersley (*d* 16 Oct 1907), est s of Sir Richard Torin Kindersley, PC, and *d* 9 Dec 1913, leaving issue
5 Janet Maitland; *m* 22 June 1858 Reginald Kelly (*d* 14 Aug 1899), of Kelly, Devon, and *dsp* 5 Feb 1911

HENRY WILSON *m* 2nd 18 May 1839 Caroline, only dau of Rev Lord Henry FitzRoy (*see* GRAFTON, D), and *d* 1866, leaving by her:

4 FitzRoy; *b* 28 Jan 1840; Rifle Bde; *m* 18 Sept 1861 Annie, dau of Col Laughton, Bengal Engrs
5 Cyril FitzRoy (Rev); *b* 21 May 1841; Rector Stowlangtoft; *m* 7 Aug 1866 Fanny Isabella Smith (*see* SMITH-MARRIOTT, Bt) and had:
   (1) Amy Mary; Deaconess St Hilda's Lahore; *d* 10 Sept 1932
6 Caroline FitzRoy
7 Amy FitzRoy

His est s,
  FULLER MAITLAND WILSON, of Stowlangtoft Hall, JP (Suffolk); *b* 27 Aug 1825; Lt-Col W Suffolk Militia, MP W Suffolk 1875, High Sheriff 1873; *m* 20

April 1852 Agnes Caroline, 2nd dau of Sir Richard Torin Kindersley, PC, and had:

1 ARTHUR MAITLAND
2 Henry Fuller Maitland (Sir), KCB (1915), KCMG (1918); *b* 18 Feb 1859; *educ* Eton and RMC; Afghan 1878–79 and Boer Wars 1899–1902, WW I, Col Cmdt 2nd Bn Rifle Bde 1921–29, ret as Lt-Gen, Chev Legn Hon, Order White Eagle Serbia, Order Redeemer Greece 2nd Cl, Greek Mil Cross, Italian Croce di Guerra; *m* 29 April 1884 Charlotte Elise (*d* 17 Aug 1942), dau of Gen Sir Hugh Gough, VC, GCB, and *d* 16 Nov 1941, having had:
   (1) Arthur Henry Maitland; *b* 22 Jan 1885; accidentally *k* 29 Jan 1918
   (2) Hugh Maitland; *b* 6 April 1886; Maj; *d* 17 Oct 1955
   (1) Muriel Maitland; *d* unm 25 June 1950
3 Joseph Maitland, CBE (1918), JP, DL Suffolk; *b* 22 Dec 1868; *educ* Eton and Ch Ch Oxford; Capt and Hon Maj PWO Norfolk Artillery, Hon Lt-Col Med Vol Corps, Boer War 1899–1901, Hon Freeman Bury St Edmunds, KGStJ; *m* 15 June 1937 Constance, dau of Percy Eagle, of Risby, and *dsp* 14 Sept 1940
1 Agnes Katherine Maitland; *m* 25 Sept 1894 Rev Canon J W D Brown, Rector Stowlangtoft
2 Ethel Maitland; *d* unm 1 Jan 1950
3 Ellen Maitland; *d* unm 5 July 1955
4 Constance Maitland; *m* her cousin H W Smith, only s of William Arthur Smith (*see* above)
5 Ida Maitland; *m* Maj John Alan le Norreys Daniell, JP, 11th Hus (*d* 7 July 1932), of Eyston Hall, Sudbury, Suffolk, and *dsp c* 1943
6 Amy Maitland; *d* unm 20 Oct 1959 aged 93
7 Alice Maitland; *d* unm 25 March 1954

Lt-Col FULLER WILSON *d* 1875; his est s,
  ARTHUR MAITLAND WILSON, OBE, of Stowlangtoft Hall, JP, DL Suffolk; *b* 16 June 1857; *educ* Eton and Ch Ch Oxford; Ld Manors and Patron Livings Stow-langtoft and Langham, High Sheriff 1913, Capt 3rd Bn Suffolk Regt; *m* 21 July 1880 Harriet Maude Isabella (*d* 14 March 1906), est dau of Col Sir Nigel Robert FitzHardinge Kingscote, GCVO, KCB, of Kingscote, Glos, and *d* 4 Nov 1934, leaving:

1 HENRY MAITLAND, **1st Baron**
2 Nigel Maitland, CB (1938), DSO (1916), OBE (1924); *b* 6 April 1884; *educ* Eton and RMC Sandhurst; IA: WW I 1914–16 (despatches), Waziristan 1922–23 (despatches), cmdg Sind Bde Area 1935, Dir Personal Servs AHQ India 1936–38, DAAG AHQ India 1938–41, ret as Maj-Gen 1941, Col RWF 1942–47; *m* 3 Feb 1909 Lady Violet Freddie (*d* 30 June 1974 aged 86), sis of 10th Duke of Grafton (*qv*), and *d* 24 Feb 1950, leaving:
   (1) Barbara; *b* 4 Sept 1910; *m* 19 Oct 1929 Lt-Col John Henry Beckwith Evatt, RA (*ka* El Alamein Oct 1942), only s of Charles Beckwith Evatt, of Bathwick Hill, Bath, and had:
     1a *Judith Rosemary; *b* 4 Feb 1933; *m* 12 April 1960 William Granville Wingate, QC, County Ct Judge, yst s of Col George Wingate, CIE, IA (*see* 1970 edn WINGATE, Bt), and has issue
     2a *Jancis Primrose; *b* 7 Aug 1935; *m* 23 Oct 1965 *Maj Anthony Lyle Hayes-Newington, 22nd (Cheshire) Regt, only s of Lt-Col Bertram Yorke Hayes-Newington, OBE, DL, of Beech Cottage, Marfold, nr Wrexham, and has:
       1b +Mark Evatt; *b* 8 Aug 1966
       2b +Adam Lyle; *b* 10 June 1968
     3a *Jennifer Beckwith [Mrs Richard Brett, White Gates Farm, Mundon, Essex]; *b* 5 Feb 1943; *m* 31 July 1965 *Richard Patrick Brett, only s of Patrick Brett, of Scarr Cottage, Stow Maries, Essex, and has:
       1b *Robin Charles Beckwith; *b* 6 July 1967
       1b *Nicola Hope; *b* 21 Sept 1968
3 Reginald Maitland; *b* 17 Jan 1889; *m* 15 Oct 1923 Monica Towers, dau of William Towers Mynors, of Berry Hill, Tixell, Staffs, and *dsp* 22 Sept 1945

ARTHUR WILSON's est s,
  HENRY MAITLAND WILSON, **1st Baron Wilson**, of Libya, and of Stow-langtoft, Co Suffolk (UK), so *cr* 12 March 1946, GCB (1944), KCB 1940, CB 1937), GBE (1941), DSO (1917); *b* 5 Sept 1881; *educ* Eton and RMC Sandhurst; 2nd Lt Rifle Bde 1900 (cmded 1st Bn 1927–30, Col Cmdt 2nd Bn 1939–51), Boer War 1900–02, WW I (despatches three times, Brevet Lt-Col), cmded 6th Inf Bde 1934–35 and 2nd Div 1937–39, Maj-Gen 1935, Lt-Gen 1939, GOC-in-C Br Troops Egypt 1939–41, Mil Govr and GOC-in-C Cyrenaica 1941, GOC-in-C Br Troops Greece 1941, Gen 1941, GOC Br Troops Palestine and Transjordan 1941, GOC-in-C Allied Forces Syria 1941, GOC 9th Army 1941, C-in-C Persia-Iraq Cmd 1942–43 (despatches), C-in-C Middle East 1943, SAC Mediterranean 1944, FM 1944, Head Br Jt Staff Mission Washington 1945–47, ADC Gen to HM GEORGE VI 1941–52, Constable Tower London 1955–60, Pres Army Cadet Force Assoc 1947–, Freeman Bury St Edmunds, Ch Cdr US Legn Merit, US DSM, Orders Crown Belgium and Belgian Croix de Guerre, Mil Valour Poland 5th Cl, Mil Cross Greece 1st Cl, Gd Offr Mil Merit Brazil, Kt Gd Cross Orange Nassau; *m* 15 Dec 1914 Hester Mary (*d* 1979), yst dau of Capt Philip James Digby Wykeham, JP, DL, of Tythrop Ho, Oxon, and *d* 31 Dec 1964, leaving:

1 PATRICK MAITLAND WILSON, **2nd and present Baron Wilson**
1 Maud ('Timmy') Maitland; *b* 19 Nov 1917; *d* unm 10 June 1996

WILSON, Bt, of Airdrie

Arms: Argent a lion rampant between three mullets sable, on a chief vert a crescent of the first between two mullets pierced or. **Crest:** A demi-lion sable, charged on the body with a crescent argent between two mullets pierced or, all in pale. **Motto:** *Semper vigilans* ('Ever watchful'). **Creation:** Bt. (UK) 27 July 1906.

SIR JAMES WILLIAM DOUGLAS WILSON, 5TH BT, of Airdrie, New Monkland, Lanark [Sir James Wilson Bt, Lillingstone Lovell Manor, Buckingham MK18 5BQ]; *b* 8 Oct 1960; *s f* 1984; *educ* Marlborough and London U (BA); *m* 1 June 1985 *Julia Margaret Louise, dau of Joseph Charles Francis Mutty, of Mulberry Hall, Melbourn, Herts, and has:

1 +THOMAS EDWARD DOUGLAS; *b* 15 April 1990
2 +Harry William Patrick; *b* 17 March 1995
1 *Jessica Sarah; *b* 11 May 1988
2 *Katrina Elizabeth; *b* 6 March 1992

Lineage: JOHN WILSON, of Eastforth, Lanarks; living 1599; had:

JAMES WILSON; bought 1655 the lands of Hinschelwood and Cleugh, Carnwath, from William Inglis of Eastsheil; *m* 1655 Janet Somerville (*d* 1674) and had, with a yr s (Thomas, of E Hinschelwood):

WILLIAM WILSON, of Cleugh and W Hinschelwood; *m* 1666 Agnes Cunninghame (*bur* Dec 1696) and was *bur* Jan 1697, having had, with two yr sons (James, in Eastforth, had a s, William, an Edinburgh writer (legal practitioner); John, Baillie and merchant of Edinburgh, bought Cleugh 1744 from his bro William, had three sons, of whom John and William started 1779 one of Scotland's earliest coal and iron works called Wilsontown, Parish of Carnwath):

WILLIAM WILSON; sold W Hinschelwood to William Weir of Waysateshaw; *m* 1702 Margaret, dau of John Somerville of Spittal, and had:

WILLIAM WILSON; *b* Feb 1704; *m* 31 Nov 1730 Euphan Inglis and had, with a yr s and a dau:

THOMAS WILSON; *b* 28 Jan 1733; *m* 1770 Janet Tod and had:

JAMES WILSON; *b* 10 Aug 1777; *m* 1806 Helen Menzies and had:

JAMES WILSON of Airdrie, New Monkland, Lanarks; *b* 30 May 1809; *m* 1st Dec 1840 Agnes (*d* 18 July 1847), dau of William Motherwell of Airdrie, thus acquiring that property; *m* 2nd 17 April 1855 Agnes Paul (*d* 12 June 1867), dau of Robert Millar, of Airdrie, and *d* 27 Sept 1887, leaving issue by her and a 2nd s by his 1st w:

Sir John Wilson, 1st Bt (UK), so *cr* 27 July 1906, of Airdrie, JP, DL Lanarks, JP Fife and Glasgow; *b* 26 June 1843; MP (Lib U and Lib) Falkirk Burghs 1895–1906; *m* 1st 26 Sept 1878 Margaret Bell (*d* 27 March 1885), dau of James Robertson, of Glasgow, and had:

1 **Sir James Robertson Wilson, 2nd Bt**, JP, DL Perths; *b* 5 May 1883; *educ* Uppingham and Balliol Coll Oxford (BA 1906); memb Inner Temple; Capt Lanarks Yeo WW I 1915–17 Gallipoli and Egypt, AA Battery RA WW II 1939–40, memb Roy Co Archers; *m* 15 Jan 1908 Helen Rae Fife (*d* 24 May 1971), er dau of Archibald Bulloch Graham, JP, of Auldhouse, Crieff, Perthshire, and *d* 30 Sept 1964, having had:

  (1) John; *b* 13 April 1911; *educ* Eton; Maj Lanarks Yeo (RA) WW II; *m* 20 June 1936 *Zoe Jane (*m* 2nd 10 May 1943 Guy Cecil Turner, AFC, of Orange Grove, Littleton, Surrey), 2nd dau of George Simpson Orr, of Kilduff House, Drem, E Lothian, and was *ka* Malaya Jan 1942, leaving:

    1a *Sarah Jane [Mrs Michael Ogilvie-Thomson, Hengist Hearth, 38 North Hinksey Lane, Oxford]; *b* 2 May 1937; *m* 5 Sept 1959 her cousin Michael Claude Ogilvie-Thomson, WS (*d* 21 June 1967), yr and only surv s of V-Adml Evelyn Claude Ogilvie Thomson, CB, DSO (*see below*), and has:

      1b *David John; *b* 22 Nov 1961
      1b *Sheelagh Jane; *b* 23 May 1960

2 **Sir John Menzies Wilson, 3rd Bt**; *b* 12 Feb 1885; *educ* Uppingham; Hon Attaché St Petersburg 1911–12, Washington 1912–14 and Constantinople 1914; Lt Scots Greys, Capt 2nd Life Gds, WW I; *m* 5 Jan 1921 (*divorce* 1948) Silvia Helena, 3rd dau of William Dodge James, CVO, JP, DL, of West Dean Park, Chichester, and *d* 22 Oct 1968, leaving:

  (1) *Daphne Margaret; *b* 8 Feb 1922; *m* 1 Sept 1945 Thomas Morton Macdonald, of Coanwood, Jordans, Bucks, s of Mark Macdonald, of Middlesbrough, Yorks, and has had:

    1a *Ian James; *b* 8 Jan 1946; *educ* Stowe
    2a *Neil Stuart; *b* 1 Oct 1947; *educ* Oakham; *m* 16 Nov 1968 *Alice Adair, dau of Leslie Montgomerie
    3a Alastair; *b* 5 May and *d* 8 May 1950
1 Margaret Bell Millar; *b* 6 April 1881; *d* 17 June 1896

Sir John *m* 2nd 25 June 1889 Emma Alexandrina (*d* 6 July 1948), dau of David Binnie, of Glasgow, and *d* 28 July 1918, having by her had:

3 Thomas Douglas; *b* 25 Sept 1890; *educ* Fettes; 2nd Lt 7th Bn Argyll and Sutherland Highrs; *m* 4 June 1914 Kathleen Elsie, 3rd dau of Henry Edward Gray, JP, of Peterstone Court, Brecon, and was *ka* 23 April 1917, leaving:

  (1) THOMAS DOUGLAS (Sir), **4th Bt**
  (1) *Aileen [Mrs Roger Constant, 16 Bramble Close, Oaklands Park, Redhill, Surrey]; *b* 23 June 1915; *m* 20 April 1939 Roger Benjamin Constant, of Merstham, Surrey, est s of Benjamin Constant, of Cape Town, and has had:

    1a *Roger Clive; *b* 24 Aug 1945; *educ* Sherborne
    1a *Stella; *b* 28 April 1943
    2a Elizabeth; *b* 31 July 1949; *d* 14 July 1953

2 Jane Robertson; *m* 1st 23 April 1914 Lt-Col John Cassels Monteith, Beds Regt (*ka* 30 Sept 1915), s of Rev John Monteith, Minister Glencairn, and had issue; *m* 2nd 9 July 1932 Gen Sir Reginald Seaburne May, KCB, KBE, CMG, DSO, and *d* 20 May 1970

3 Agnes (Motherwell, dropped 1942); *m* 10 April 1918 V-Adml Evelyn Claude Ogilvie Thomson, CB, DSO (*d* 21 Dec 1941), s of Andrew Thomson, of Edinburgh, added OGILVIE to her married surname 1942 and *d* 24 July 1957, leaving issue (*see above*)

The 3rd Bt's n,

Sir Thomas Douglas Wilson, 4th Bt; *b* posthumously 10 June 1917; *educ* Marlborough and RMC Sandhurst; Capt 15th/19th Hus WW II; *m* 16 June 1947 *Pamela Aileen [Lady Wilson, Lillingstone Lovell Manor, Bucks MK18 5BQ], 2nd dau of Sir Edward Hanmer, 7th Bt (*qv*), and *d* 1984, leaving:

1 Sir JAMES WILLIAM DOUGLAS WILSON, **5th and present Bt**
1 *Sarah Ann [Mrs Michael Fleming, Ye Olde Malting House, Bengal Lane, Greens Norton, Northants NN12 8BE]; *b* 29 Aug 1950; *m* 20 March 1976 *Michael James Fleming and has:

  (1) *Simon James; *b* 6 May 1982

2 *Susan Mary [Mrs Robert Nield, 5 Belle Vue Rd, Exmouth, Devon]; *b* 13 Jan 1954; *m* 1978 *Robert James Nield and has:

  (1) *Timothy James; *b* 1979
  (2) *Michael Jonathan; *b* 1980
  (1) *Emilia Mary; *b* 1984

3 *Margaret Rose [Mrs Jonathan Gurney, Mount Mill, Stratford Rd, Wicken, Bucks MK19 6DG]; *b* 11 Jan 1957; *m* 1983 *Jonathan Kendal James Gurney, er s of Brian Gurney, of Handley Park, Towcester, and has:

  (1) *Joseph Brian Thomas; *b* 1985
  (1) *Olivia Kate; *b* 1987

WILSON, Bt, of Carbeth

Arms: Argent a chevron gules between two mullets in chief and in base a trefoil slipped vert. **Crest:** A demi-lion rampant gules, armed and langued azure. **Motto:** *Semper vigilans* ('Ever watchful'). **Creation:** Bt. (UK) 11 Feb 1920.

SIR DAVID WILSON, 3RD BT, of Carbeth, Killearn, Stirling [Sir David Wilson Bt, Tandem House, Queen's Drive, Oxshott, Surrey KT22 0PH]; *b* 30 Oct 1928; *s f* 1975; *educ* Deerfield Acad Mass., Harrow and Oriel Coll Oxford; barrister Lincoln's Inn 1954–61, slr 1962; *m* 25 Feb 1955 *Eva Margareta, est dau of Tore Lindell, of Sweden, and has:

1 +THOMAS DAVID [Thomas Wilson Esq, 120 Balham Park Rd, London SW12 8EA]; *b* 6 Jan 1959; *educ* Harrow; *m* 21 July 1984 *Valerie, er dau of Vivian David Davies Stogdale, of Monks Farm, Shotover, Oxon, and has:

  (1) +Fergus; *b* 24 April 1987

(2) +Oscar; *b* 10 June 1989

2 +Andrew [Andrew Wilson Esq, Mulberry Cottage, 4 Fairway, Merrow, Surrey GU1 2XG]; *b* 16 Dec 1959; *m* 1984 *Penelope May, 2nd dau of Brig William Turner, of The Holt, Woolton Hill, Newbury, Berks, and has:

  (1) +Charles; *b* 1989
  (2) +George; *b* 1994
  (1) *Jemima; *b* 1988

1 *Annika [Mrs David Ratcliffe, 63 Winchester Rd, Walton-on-Thames, Surrey KT12 2RH]; *b* 14 Oct 1961; *m* 1984 *Dr David Malcolm Ratcliffe, s of M Ratcliffe, of Worcester, and has:

  (1) *Camilla; *b* 1992
  (2) *Tegaela; *b* 1995

Lineage: DAVID WILSON, of Edington, Berwicks; *m* Helen Murray and had:

GEORGE WILSON, of Foulden-Greenlaw; *b* 1678; *m* 12 Aug 1697 Jean Richardson (*d* 14 March 1753) and *d* 6 Feb 1729, leaving:

JAMES WILSON, of Foulden-Newton; *b* 1721; *m* July 1753 Helen (*d* 17 Jan 1796), dau of James Murray, of Flemington, Berwicks, and *d* 18 Nov 1796, leaving:

DAVID WILSON, of Linthaughlee, Roxburghshire; *b* 5 Jan 1760; *m* 1796 Margaret (*d* 13 July 1831), dau of Lt-Col Thomas Currie, RM (*d* Sept 1806), and *d* 23 March 1839, leaving:

DAVID WILSON, of Carbeth; *b* 25 May 1805; *m* 10 Aug 1852 Jane (*d* 4 Dec 1903), dau of William Harvey, of Yoker, Renfrewshire, and *d* 16 June 1898, leaving an only s:

Sir David Wilson, 1st Bt (UK), so *cr* 11 Feb 1920, JP, DL Stirling; *b* 4 April 1855; MA, DSc; Convener Stirlingshire CC, memb Advsy Ctee Scottish Bd Ag; *m* 5 June 1896 Susan Main (*d* 14 March 1944), dau of Rev John Mitchell Harvey, DD, and had:

  1 David; *b* 16 Sept 1897; Lt 2nd Bn Argyll and Sutherland Highrs; *d* of wounds recd in action 28 Dec 1916

  2 JOHN MITCHELL HARVEY (Sir), **2nd Bt**

  3 (Thomas) George (Sir), KBE (1959), JP (Stirling); *b* 24 Nov 1900; *educ* Harrow and Trin Coll Cambridge (MA 1922); CC Stirling, Chm Govrs W of Scotland Ag Coll, memb: Herring Industry Bd 1944–63 and Cncl Hannah Dairy Research Inst, dir Br Linen Bank, Hon LLD Glasgow 1950, ktd 1944

  4 Archibald; *b* 1 May 1903; *educ* Harrow; *d* unm 31 May 1965

  1 Mary Baird; *b* 20 April 1907; *m* 1 Nov 1938 Sir Arthur Stretton Gaye, CB, OBE (*d* 22 Sept 1960), s of Arthur Gaye

Sir DAVID *d* 8 March 1930; his est surv s,

  Sir John Mitchell Harvey, 2nd Bt, KCVO (1957, CVO 1950); *b* 10 Oct 1898; *educ* Harrow and New Coll Oxford; 2nd Lt Coldstream Gds WW I; barrister; Keeper Roy Philatelic Collection 1938–69, Pres Roy Philatelic Soc 1934–40, author: *The Royal Philatelic Collection* (1952), Hon LLD U of Western Ontario; *m* 17 Dec 1927 Mary Elizabeth, er dau of William Richards, CBE, of Chelsea, and *d* 6 Feb 1975, leaving:

  (1) Sir DAVID WILSON, **3rd and present Bt**

  (2) +John Richards [John Wilson Esq, Heron's Court, Killearn, Stirlingshire]; *b* 6 April 1930; *educ* Harrow and New Coll Oxford; *m* 6 Feb 1969 *(Helen) Jane, dau of Maj Gilbert Bernard Rahr, of Huntbourne Farm, Tenterden, Kent

  (3) +Andrew George [Andrew Wilson Esq, Little Carbeth, Killearn, by Glasgow]; *b* 12 Jan 1933; *educ* Harrow and Trin Coll Oxford; *m* 1967 his bro's w's sister *Anne-Marie Tekla, 3rd dau of Tore Lindell

WILSON, Bt, of Eshton Hall

Arms: Sable a wolf rampant or, gorged with a collar gemel of the field between four mullets of six points, three in chief, and one in base of the second. **Crest:** A demi-wolf or, gorged with a collar genel sable, resting the sinister paw on an escutcheon of the last, charged with a mullet as in the arms. **Mottoes:** 1 *Res non verba* ('Facts not words'), 2 *Loyal en tout* ('Loyal in everything').
Creation: B. (UK) 16 March 1874.

SIR MATHEW JOHN ANTHONY WILSON, 6TH BT, of Eshton Hall, Co York, OBE (1979, MBE 1971), MC (1972) [Brig Sir Mathew Wilson Bt OBE MC, c/o Military Secretary, MOD, Whitehall, London SW1]; *b* 2 Oct 1935; *s* unc 1991; *educ* Trin Coll Sch Port Hope Ontario; Brig King's Own Yorks LI (ret 1983); Exec Dir Wilderness Leadership Fndn (UK) 1983–85, late V-Pres Internat Wilderness Leadership Fndn, Pres Dolphin Voyaging Inc 1995–, author: *Taking Terrapin Home: a love affair with a small catamaran* (1994); *m* 1 Dec 1962 *Janet Mary, er dau of Edward Worsfold Mowll, JP, of Walmer, Kent, and has:

  1 +(MATHEW) EDWARD AMCOTTS; *b* 13 Oct 1966; *educ* King's Canterbury and King's Coll London; late Capt LI (despatches 1993); mktg mngr Earthwatch Europe; *m* 11 March 1995 *Imogen, dau of Tom Wilson, of Bagnols, France, and Mrs Judith Wilson, of Uggeshall, Suffolk

  1 *Victoria Mary; *b* 1968; *educ* King's Canterbury and New Hall Cambridge; slr

Lineage: ROBERT WILSON, of Brigsteare, Haversham, Westmorland; *m* Alice — and had:

MATHEW WILSON; London merchant; bought 1646 the Eshton Hall estate from Sir Robert Bindlosse, 1st and last Bt; *d* Nov 1656, leaving:

JOHN WILSON, of Eshton Hall; *m* Dorothy — (*bur* 9 Oct 1684) and *d* 7 May 1706, leaving, with two yr sons and two daus:

MATHEW WILSON, of Eshton Hall; *m* 28 June 1699 Anne (*d* 1722–23), dau of Timothy Blackburne, of Blackburne Hall, Swaledale, and *d* 1717, leaving, with four other sons and four daus:

MATHEW WILSON, of Eshton Hall; *bapt* 14 Oct 1706; *m* Margaret, dau of Harry Wiglesworth, of Slaidburn, and had:

  1 MATHEW

  2 Henry (Rev); *bapt* 23 Jan 1723; Rector Slaidburn, Vicar Otley; *m* Anne, dau and heiress of Thomas Fourness, of Otley, and *d* 13 Dec 1781, leaving:

    (1) Thomas Fourness (Rev), JP, of Burley Hall, nr Otley; *b* 22 July 1769; Perpetual Curate Silsden and White Chapel; *m* 1 March 1813 Eleanor (*d* 22 Nov 1864), dau of Sir John Eden, 4th Bt (*see* EDEN OF WINTON, B), and *d* 17 Oct 1837, leaving:

    (2) Mathew, JP, DL W R Yorks and Lancs; *b* 10 Aug 1772; *m* 24 Nov 1800 his 1st cousin Margaret Clive (*d* 29 May 1848), widow of Rev Henry Richardson and only dau and heiress of Mathew Wilson, and *d* 15 Oct 1854, leaving issue (*see* below)

    (1) Rebecca; *m* 27 Aug 1811 John Tennant Stansfield Tennant, of Chapel Ho, Yorks, and had issue (*see* below)

  1 Margaret; *m* 15 Aug 1763 Rev Thomas Butler, Rector Bentham and Whittington, Archdeacon Chester

MATHEW WILSON *d* 27 March 1769; his s,

  MATHEW WILSON, of Eshton Hall; *b* 12 Feb 1730; barrister; *m* 7 July 1759 Frances (*d* 3 Oct 1798), 4th dau of Richard Clive, of Styche, Salop (*see* POWIS, E), and *d* 16 April 1802, leaving an only dau and heiress:

  1 Margaret Clive, of Eshton Hall; *b* 23 April 1764; *m* 1st 3 Feb 1783 Rev Henry RICHARDSON later CURRER (on inheriting estates of Sarah Currer), Rector Thornton (10 Nov 1784), and had:

    (1) Frances Mary; rep of the RICHARDSONs of Brierley and CURRERs of Kildwick; *d* unm 28 April 1861

1 (cont.) Mrs Henry Richardson *m* 2nd 24 Nov 1800 her 1st cousin Mathew Wilson (*see* above) and *d* 29 May 1848, leaving by him, with a dau (*d* unm):

    (1) MATHEW (Sir), **1st Bt**

    (2) Henry Currer (Rev); *b* 8 Oct 1803; Rector Marton-in-Craven, Vicar Tunstale-in-Lunedale; *d* unm 1 Dec 1866

      2a Frances Mary; *m* 28 May 1839 her 1st cousin John Robert Tennant

      3a Henrietta Fourness; *m* 10 Nov 1829 Charles Hampden Turner (*d* 23 Sept 1842), of Leigh Place, Godstone, only s of Charles Hampden Turner, of Rook's Nest, Godstone, Surrey, and had an only surv s

The er s,

  Sir Mathew Wilson, 1st Bt (UK), so *cr* 16 March 1874; *b* 29 Aug 1802; MP Clitheroe 1841–42 and 1847–53, N Yorks 1874–85 and Skipton 1885–86; *m* 1st 15 June 1826 Sophia Louisa Emerson Amcotts (*d* 29 Sept 1833), only dau and coheir of Sir Wharton Emerson Amcotts, Bt, of Kettlethorpe Park, Lincs (*see* INGILBY, Bt, also 1854 edn INGILBY, Bt); *m* 2nd 20 Aug 1878 Frances (*d* 5 Aug 1909), widow of Col Pedler, of Brunswick Sq, Brighton, and *d* 18 Jan 1891, leaving by his 1st w a surv s:

  Sir Mathew Wharton Wilson, 2nd Bt, JP Glos and W R Yorks; *b* 20 March 1827; Lt 11th Hus; *m* 13 Nov 1850 Gratiana Mary (*d* 25 March 1922), only dau of Adml Richard Thomas, of Stonehouse, and had:

    1 MATHEW AMCOTTS (Sir), **3rd Bt**

    2 Richard Henry Francis Wharton, DSO; *b* 18 Aug 1855; served RN then Army: Maj 10th Hus, Ashanti War, Afghanistan, Sudan, Suakin and Boer War, Hon Lt-Col; *m* 17 Jan 1889 Annabella Margaret (*d* 28 Aug 1936), dau of John Forbes Walker Drummond, of Ednam House, Kelso (*see* 1970 edn WILLIAMS-DRUMMOND, Bt), and *d* 14 Dec 1936, leaving a dau (*d* unm)

    1 Gratiana Sophia Margaret; *m* 9 Sept 1884 Rev Henry Madan Pratt, JP (*d* 28 Aug 1934), and *d* 11 April 1928, leaving issue

The 2nd Bt *d* 1 March 1909; his er s,

  Sir Mathew Amcotts Wilson, 3rd Bt, JP N and E R, JP, DL W R Yorks, DL City and Co York; *b* 2 Jan 1853; Maj 3rd KOYLI; *m* 8 Oct 1874 Georgina Mary (*d* 4 April 1929), est dau of Richard Thomas Lee, of Grove Hall, Yorks, and had:

    1 MATHEW RICHARD HENRY (Sir), **4th Bt**

    2 Robert Amcotts, DSO (1915); *b* 25 June 1882; Capt RN, F/Cdr RNAS, WW I, cmdg HMS *Mersey* in ops against the *Königsberg* off E Africa 1915 (despatches), cmded Anti-Submarine Vessels WW II 1939–41, Naval Attaché Brazil and Venezuela 1941–45; *m* 1st 30 April 1912 Gladys (*d* 1 Dec 1918), yst dau of William Gillian, of Kensington, and had:

      (1) David Amcotts; *b* 17 Feb 1913; Gren Gds WW II; *ka* N Africa 22 April 1942

    2 (cont.) Capt Robert Wilson *m* 2nd 19 July 1928 Marjorie, widow of E Clarence Jones, of New York, and *d* 26 June 1960

3 Alec Thomas Lee, JP, DL Breconshire; *b* 21 Oct 1883; Cdr RN (Emerg List), KJStJ; *m* 7 Aug 1913 Margaret; DStJ (*d* 16 June 1966), dau of Leopold Hirsch, of Kensington, and *d* 19 Dec 1956, leaving:

(1) James Thomas Amcotts, JP Dorset; *b* 1 Jan 1916; *educ* Sherborne and McGill; Lt-Col KOYLI WW II (despatches); *m* 20 Sept 1947 *Judy [Mrs James Wilson, Manor Farm, Wraxall, Dorset]; er dau of Maj Pierre Elliot Inchbald, MC, of Wraxall Manor, and *d* 1992, having had:

1a Alec Amcotts; *b* 20 Sept 1960; *d* 10 Jan 1962

1a *Carol Anne [Mrs David Parry, Broomhill, Rampisham, Dorset]; *b* 26 Dec 1948; *m* 1972 *David John Hugh Parry, s of Alan Wheeler Parry, of Liverpool, and has:

1b *James Alan David; *b* 1976

2b *Benjamin Alec; *b* 1979

2a *Pamela Gay [Mrs Edward Lewis, 77 Lexham Gdns, London W8 6JN]; *b* 18 May 1951; *m* 1974 *Edward Trevor Gwyn Lewis, barrister, s of Rev Gwyn Lewis, and has:

1b *Frances Leone; *b* 28 Feb 1975

2b *Kim Olivia; *b* 23 Jan 1979

3b *Tamsin Gwynne (twin); *b* 1979

3a *Vianna Jane [Mrs John Dene, Manor Farm, Higher Wraxall, Dorset DT2 0HR]; *b* 9 Jan 1959; *m* 1988 *John Michael Dene, s of Lt-Col John Anthony Dene, of Kilteelagh Stud, Dromineer, Co Tipperary, and has:

1b *Polly Alexandra; *b* 1990

(2) +Francis Amcotts [Francis Wilson Esq, Garth House, Llangammarch Wells, Powys]; *b* 3 April 1922; *educ* Shrewsbury; Sub-Lt RNVR WW II; *m* 1 March 1968 *Katherine Mary, formerly w of Capt John James Scott, Argyll and Sutherland Highrs, and only dau of Robert Charles Bruce, MC (*see* ELGIN and KINCARDINE, E), and adopted:

*Robert Mathew; *b* 6 April 1978

*Jane Mary; *b* 1972

(1) *Iris; *b* 28 May 1914; *m* 1st 19 Dec 1936 (*divorce* 1948) Col David Llewellin Rhys, OBE, MC, DL, 24th S Wales Borderers, er s of Col Owen Rhys, of Cardiff, and has issue; *m* 2nd 1 July 1948 *John Lewtas Longworth, of Andwell Mill, Basingstoke, Hants, s of Harold Longworth, of Chalkfield, Friston, Sussex

(2) *Peggy Amcotts; *b* 11 Nov 1917; *m* 15 Nov 1947 *David Altham Bayford, yr s of Robert Frederic Bayford, OBE, KC, of Ashbridge, Compton, Hants, and has:

1a +Robin Alec; *b* 22 Sept 1949; *educ* Aiglon Coll Switzerland and Trin Hall Cambridge

1a *Georgina Catharine Margaret; *b* 16 Oct 1952

1 Gwendolin Georgiana Frances Mary; *m* 1 June 1897 Rev John Arthur Victor Magee (*d* 8 Feb 1923), Vicar St Mark's Maida Vale, s of Most Rev William Connor Magee, Archbp York, and *d* 5 Jan 1965, leaving issue

2 Beatrice Maud; *m* 29 Nov 1898 Col Richard Foulis Roundell, Northumberland Fus (*d* 5 Jan 1940), s of William Roundell, of Gledstone, Yorks, and *d* 31 Jan 1960, leaving issue

3 Freda Ethel Louisa; *b* 1 April 1889; *m* 23 Nov 1915 Capt Rollo Samuel Barrett, JP, BA, RE (TA), FRICS, MIME (*d* 30 June 1963), er s of Charles Rollo Barrett, of Whitehill Hall, Co Durham, and *d* 6 March 1971, leaving issue

The 3rd Bt *d* 18 Jan 1914; his est s,

Sir Mathew Richard Henry Wilson, 4th Bt, CSI (1911), DSO (1918), JP W R Yorks; *b* 25 Aug 1875; *educ* Harrow; Maj 10th Hus Boer War 1899–1902, MP (C) SW Bethnal Green 1914–22, Lt-Col cmdg 1st Co London Yeo (Middx Hus) WW I (despatches); *m* 7 Sept 1905 Hon Barbara Lister (*d* 22 Dec 1943), est dau of 4th and last Baron Ribblesdale (*see* 1925 edn), and *d* 1958, leaving:

1 **Sir Matthew Martin Wilson, 5th Bt**; *b* 2 July 1906; *educ* Eton; *d* 1991

2 Anthony Thomas; *b* 15 Nov 1908; *educ* Eton; *m* 29 Dec 1934 (*divorce* 1939) Margaret (*d* 1980), formerly w of Vernon Motion and dau of Alfred Holden, and *d* 1979, leaving:

(1) Sir MATHEW JOHN ANTHONY WILSON, **6th and present Bt**

3 Peter Cecil, CBE (1970); *b* 8 March 1913; *educ* Eton and New Coll Oxford; dir Sotheby's 1938 (chm 1958–80); *m* 10 Jan 1935 (*divorce* 1951) Grace Helen, dau of Arthur Ranken, and *d* 1984, leaving:

(1) +Richard Thomas [Richard Wilson Esq, Le Cepède, Lotissement de Clavary, 06810 Auribeau-sur-Siagne, France]; *b* 5 Aug 1937; *educ* Gordonstoun, Millfield and Trin Hall Cambridge (MA); MICE; *m* 12 Sept 1964 (*divorce* 1974) Judith Anne, only dau of Ford Jenkins, of N Landing, Oulton Broad, Suffolk, and has:

1a *Alice Thomasina; *b* 27 Jan 1966

2a *Imogen Nancy; *b* 12 March 1967

(2) +(Edward) Philip [Philip Wilson Esq, 24 Highbury Place, London N5]; *b* 2 Nov 1940; *educ* Bryanston and Conservatoire de Musique Paris; ed: *The International and British Antiques Yearbooks*, *Art at Auction* and *The Gardener's Yearbook*; *m* 21 May 1970 *Alexandra Patricia Gwendoline, er dau of 2nd Earl Jellicoe (*qv*), and has:

1a +(Anthony) Benedict; *b* 1980

2a +(Peter) Patrick; *b* 1984

WILSON OF TILLYORN

Arms: Sable on a chevron argent, between a dragon passant guardant or in chief and a demi-wolf argent holding in its forepaws a pearl proper in base, a Celtic cross azure. **Crest:** A talbot's head erased sable, langued gules, gorged of a collar argent charged with two mullets gules. **Motto:** *Semper vigilans* ('Always watchful').
Creation: B. (LP, UK) 1992.

THE BARON WILSON OF TILLYORN, of Finzean, in the District of Kincardine and Deeside, and of Fanling in Hong Kong (Sir David Clive Wilson, GCMG (1991, KCMG 1987, CMG 1985)) [The Rt Hon The Lord Wilson of Tillyorn GCMG, House of Lords, London SW1A 0PW]; *b* 14 Feb 1935; *educ* Trin Coll Glenalmond, Keble Coll Oxford (MA), Hong Kong U, Columbia U (visiting scholar) and London U (PhD 1973); Nat Service: Black Watch 1953–55; Dip Serv: joined 1958, 3rd Sec Vientiane 1959–60, language studies Hong Kong 1960–62, 2nd Sec Peking 1963 (1st Sec 1965), FCO 1965–68, ed *The China Quarterly* 1968–74, rejoined Dip Serv 1974, Cabinet Office 1974–77, Political Advsr to Govr Hong Kong 1977–81, Head S European Dept 1981–84, Assist U-Sec for Asia and Pacific FCO 1984–87, Govr and C-in-C Hong Kong 1987–92; chm Scottish Hydro-Electric 1993–, dir Martin Currie Pacific Tst 1993–; memb: Bd Br Cncl 1993– (Chm Scottish Ctee 1993–), govrng bdy SOAS 1992–97, Cncl Glenalmond Coll 1994–; Pres: Bhutan Soc UK 1993–, Hong Kong Assoc 1994–, Chllr Aberdeen U 1997– (Chllr's Assessor 1993–97) (Hon LLD 1990), V-Pres RSGS 1996–, Hon DLitt Sydney U 1991, Abertay Dundee 1994; KStJ 1987; *m* 1967 *Natasha Helen Mary, dau of Bernard Gustav Alexander, and has:

1 *Peter Michael Alexander; *b* 1968

2 *Andrew Marcus William; *b* 1969

Lineage: Rev WILLIAM SKINNER WILSON; *m* Enid Sanders and had:

1 DAVID CLIVE, *cr* a **Baron**

1 *Ruth Georgina; *b* 1929; *m* 1951 *Rev Hugh McIntosh

2 *Monica Joan; *b* 1931; *m* 1955 *Rev Donald Eric Nelson Cameron

WILTON

Arms: Argent a lion rampant gules between three pheons, points downwards sable. **Crest:** Three arrows, points downwards, one in pale and two in saltire or, barbed and fledged sable, band gules and tasseled or. **Supporters:** Dexter, a wyvern, wings inverted or; sinister, a lion argent, ducally crowned or. **Motto:** *Virtuti non armis, fido* ('I trust in virtue, not arms').
Creations: E. and V. (UK) 26 June 1801.

THE 7TH EARL OF WILTON OF WILTON CASTLE, Co Hereford, and **Viscount Grey de Wilton** (Seymour William Arthur John Egerton) [The Rt Hon The Earl of Wilton, House of Lords, London SW1A 0PW]; *b* 29 May 1921; *s f* 1927; *educ* Eton; *m* 24 March 1962 *Diana Elizabeth Lea, only dau of Roy Galway, of St Ronans, Winkfield Row, Berks, and formerly w of (Alick) David Yorke Naylor-Leyland, LVO (*see* NAYLOR-LEYLAND, Bt)

Lineage: Sir ROLAND EGERTON, 1st Bt (*see* GREY EGERTON, Bt); *m* Bridget, only sis of 15th and last Lord (Baron) Grey (of Wilton) (*see* GREY, B), and was ancestor in the 5th generation of:

Sir THOMAS EGERTON, 7th Bt, of Egerton and Oulton, Cheshire, **1st Earl of Wilton of Wilton Castle**, Co Hereford, so *cr* 26 June 1801, as also VISCOUNT GREY DE WILTON (both UK, with, as regards these two peerages only, remainder, failing heirs male of his body (something which had already happened, since his sons both *dvp*), to the 2nd and all yr sons successively of his dau by her then husband, Ld Belgrave (afterwards Marquess of Westminster), or to her male issue by any future husband) and earlier 15 May 1784 BARON GREY DE WILTON, Co Hereford (GB); *b* 14 May 1749; *educ* Westminster and Ch Ch Oxford; MP (Tory) Lancs 1772–84; *m* 12 Sept 1769 Eleanor, yst dau and coheir of Sir Ralph Assheton, 3rd Bt (*see* CLITHEROE, B), and *dspms* 23 Sept 1814, when the btcy passed to a cousin and the Barony of Grey de Wilton expired, leaving, with other issue:

ELEANOR Egerton; *m* 28 April 1794 Robert GROSVENOR, 1st MARQUESS OF WESTMINSTER (*see* WESTMINSTER, D) and *d* 29 Nov 1846, leaving, with other issue (*see* also EBURY, B):

THOMAS GROSVENOR later EGERTON (roy licence 27 Nov 1821), **2nd Earl of Wilton of Wilton Castle**, GCH (1835), PC (1835); *b* 30 Dec 1799; *educ* Westminster and Ch Ch Oxford (DCL 1834); Ld Steward Household Jan–April 1835, Col London Militia LI 1840, Kt Crown Rue Saxony; *m* 1st 29 Nov 1821 Mary Margaret (*d* 16 Dec 1858), dau of 12th Earl of Derby (*qv*); *m* 2nd 12 Sept 1863 Isabella (*d* 23 Jan 1916), only child and heiress of Maj Elton Smith, Madras Army, of Ilminster, Somerset, and *d* 7 March 1882, leaving by his 1st w, with two er sons (*d* infants):

1 ARTHUR EDWARD HOLLAND GREY EGERTON, **3rd Earl of Wilton of Wilton Castle** and 1st BARON GREY DE RADCLIFFE, in the Co Palatine of Lancaster (UK), so *cr* 14 June 1875; *b* 25 Nov 1833; *educ* Eton and Ch Ch Oxford; Lt 1st Life Gds 1854–59, MP (C) Weymouth 1859–65 and Bath 1873–74, Lt-Col 1882 (later Hon Col) 5th Bn Prince Consort's Rifle Bde and Duke of Lancaster's Own Yeo Cav; *m* 11 Aug 1858 Elizabeth Charlotte Louisa (*m* 2nd 14 Sept 1886 Arthur Vickris Pryor (*d* 18 June 1927), of Hylands, nr Chelmsford, Essex, s of Arthur D Pryor, DL, of Hylands, and *d* 8 March 1919), est dau of 2nd Earl of Craven (*qv*), and *dsp* 18 Jan 1885, when the Barony of Grey de Radcliffe expired

2 SEYMOUR JOHN GREY, **4th Earl**

1 Elizabeth Grey; *m* 12 Oct 1853 23rd Lord (Baron) de Ros (*qv*) of Helmsley and *d* 14 March 1892, leaving issue

2 Katherine Grey; Woman Bedchamber to HM QUEEN MARY; *m* 22 July 1861 Hon Henry John Coke (*see* LEICESTER, E) and *d* 28 Jan 1920, leaving issue

3 Alice Magdalene Grey; *m* 13 Aug 1863 Sir Henry Dalrymple des Voeux, 5th Bt (*see* 1940 edn), and *d* 21 Dec 1925, leaving issue

The 3rd EARL OF WILTON's yr bro,

SEYMOUR JOHN GREY EGERTON, **4th Earl of Wilton of Wilton Castle**, DL; *b* 20 Jan 1839; *educ* Eton; 1st Life Gds 1855–68, ret as Capt; *m* 9 Aug 1862 Laura Caroline (*m* 2nd 7 June 1899 Sir Frederick John William Johnstone, 8th Bt (*qv*), and *d* 15 June 1916), dau of William Russell (*see* BEDFORD, D), and *d* 3 Jan 1898, leaving, with a dau (Elizabeth Emma Geraldine, *m* 17 Nov 1887 George William Taylor (*d* 14 July 1929), Coldstream Gds, of Orchards, Godalming, Surrey, and *d* 2 Oct 1953, leaving issue):

ARTHUR GEORGE EGERTON, **5th Earl of Wilton of Wilton Castle**, TD; *b* 17 May 1863; Hon Col 4th Bn Manchester Regt; *m* 28 Aug 1895 Hon Mariota Thellusson (*d* 19 March 1924), yst dau of 5th Baron Rendlesham (*qv*), and *d* 26 April 1915, leaving:

1 SEYMOUR EDWARD FREDERIC, **6th Earl**

2 George Arthur; *b* 25 Jan 1898; Sub-Lt RN; *m* 1st 14 April 1928 (*divorce* 1947) Claire Frederique, dau of Jean Richard Stickelbaut, of Oudenarde, Flanders, and formerly w of Jack William Crawshay, MC; *m* 2nd 19 Aug 1947 Pamela Yolanda (*m* 2nd 29 July 1950 Maj George Rowland Hill Cholmley, MC, of Grange Garth, Wintringham, Malton, Yorks), yr dau of Maj Henry Algernon Cholmley Darley, and *dsp* 17 Nov 1947

1 Mary Cecilia; *b* 10 May 1901; *m* 11 Jan 1923 Roderick Bulteel Boyd (*d* 9 July 1968), yst s of Maj Walter Boyd, of W Par, Ermington, Ivybridge, Devon, and had issue

The 5th EARL's er s,

SEYMOUR EDWARD FREDERIC EGERTON, **6th Earl of Wilton of Wilton Castle**; *b* 1 Aug 1896; Lt RN WW I; *m* 31 Aug 1917 Brenda (*d* 12 Jan 1930), dau of Sir William Petersen, KBE, of Portland Pl, London, and Eigg, Inverness, and *d* 12 Oct 1927, having had:

1 SEYMOUR WILLIAM ARTHUR JOHN EGERTON, **7th and present Earl of Wilton of Wilton Castle**

1 A dau; *b* and *d* 11 June 1918

2 Alexandra Mariota Flora; *b* 9 Nov 1919; *m* 1 Aug 1939 (*divorce* 1962) Patrick Thomas Beasley, s of Henry Herbert Beasley, of Eyrefield Ho, Curragh, Co Kildare, and *d* 28 July 1991, leaving:

  (1) *Lavinia Mary [Mrs Richard Aykroyd, Molino del Cancon, Casares, Malaga, Spain]; *b* 17 Feb 1945; *m* 1st 13 Oct 1966 (*divorce* 1971) Confrey Adolphus Phillips, musician, er s of John Phillips, of Calcutta, and has:

    1a *Emma Bernadette; *b* 28 Jan 1968; *m* 7 Jan 1989 *André Radwan and has:

      1b *Maximilian Blake; *b* 7 May 1998

      1b *Imogen Kate; *b* 25 July 1996

  (1) (cont.) Mrs Lavinia Phillips *m* 2nd 28 Nov 1974, as his 2nd w, (John) Richard Aykroyd (*d* 1 Feb 1997; *see* AYKROYD, Bt, of Lightcliffe), and has further issue

WIMBORNE

Arms: Azure on a chevron or, between three swan's heads erased proper, as many crosses-moline sable. **Crest:** A swan's head erased proper, gorged with a collar or and underneath charged with a cross-moline as in the arms, between two ostrich feathers gold. **Supporters:** On each side a figure habited as Vulcan, resting his exterior hand on an anvil and holding in front thereof a sledge-hammer, all proper. **Motto:** *Ferro non gladio* ('By iron, not by the sword'). **Creations:** Bt. (UK) 14 Aug 1838, B. (UK) 30 April 1880 (Wimborne), B. (UK) 15 March 1910 (Ashby St Ledgers), V. (UK) 15 June 1918.

THE 4TH VISCOUNT WIMBORNE, **Baron Wimborne**, of Canford Magna, Co Dorset, **Baron Ashby St Ledgers**, of Ashby St Ledgers, Co Northampton, and a **Baronet** (Sir Ivor Mervyn Vigors Guest, Bt) [The Rt Hon The Viscount Wimborne, House of Lords, London SW1A 0PW]; *b* 19 Sept 1968, *s f* 1993; *educ* Eton; composer

Lineage: JOHN GUEST; left Broseley, Salop, *c* 1758, and set up iron works at Dowlais, Glam, the largest in Wales till they closed 1930; *d* 25 Nov 1785, leaving:

THOMAS GUEST, of Dowlais; *m* Jemima, dau of Thomas Phillips, of Shifnal, and *d* 1809, leaving an er s:

Sir Josiah John Guest, 1st Bt (UK), so *cr* 14 Aug 1838, of Dowlais; *b* 2 Feb 1785; MP Honiton 1825–31 and Merthyr Tydfil 1832–52; *m* 1st 14 March 1817 Maria Elizabeth (*dsp* Jan 1818), dau of William Ranken; *m* 2nd 29 July 1833, as her 1st husb, Charlotte Elizabeth, only dau of 9th Earl of Lindsey (*see* LINDSEY and ABINGDON, E), and by her had:

1 IVOR BERTIE, **1st Baron**

2 Thomas Merthyr, of Inward Ho, Somerset, JP, DL; *b* 18 Jan 1838; *educ* Trin Coll Cambridge (BA); Maj Dorset Yeo Cav; *m* 8 March 1877 Lady Theodora Grosvenor (*see* WESTMINSTER, D) and *d* 5 Nov 1904, leaving:

(1) Elizabeth Augusta Grosvenor, of Inward Ho (which she left to the Comte de Pelet), JP; *b* 18 Sept 1879; *d* unm 16 June 1960

3 Montague John, JP Middx, JP, DL Dorset; *b* 29 March 1839; Lt Rifle Bde, Hon Maj Dorset Yeo Cav, MP Youghal 1869–74 and Wareham 1880–85; *d* unm 9 Nov 1909

4 Augustus Frederick; *b* 12 Aug 1840; *d* 23 May 1862

5 Arthur Edward, JP, DL Glam; *b* 7 Nov 1841; MP Poole 1868–74; *m* 23 April 1867 Adeline Mary (*m* 2nd 30 Dec 1899 Cecil Maurice Chapman and *d* 20 Jan 1931), yst dau of David Barclay Chapman, of Downshire Ho, Roehampton, and *d* 17 July 1898, leaving:

(1) (Arthur) Rhuvon; *b* 16 Dec 1869; Lt RN; *m* 22 April 1901 Hilda Eugenia (*d* 15 April 1959), yst dau of Adml Hon Keith Stewart, CB (*see* GALLOWAY, E), and *d* 24 Feb 1946, leaving:

1a Evan Rhuvon; *b* 24 Jan 1902; *educ* Eton and Roy Coll Sci London (BSc 1924); *m* 1st 10 Sept 1935 (*divorce* 1952) Mrs Columba Mary Dolores Heathcote, MB, BCh, MRCS, LRCP (*d* 1 Dec 1955), dau of Joseph Francis O'Carroll, MD, FRCPI, LRCSI, of Dundrum, Co Dublin; *m* 2nd 30 July 1952 Christabel, formerly w of Benjamin George Wingate Wiggett and dau of John Thomas Kelly

2a Alan Keith; *b* 4 April 1908; *educ* Eton; 2nd Lt KOYLI; *d* unm 12 Oct 1944

1a *Mary Adeline [Mrs Henry Bousfield, 39 Argyll Rd, London W8]; *b* 31 Aug 1904; *m* 26 Nov 1929 Capt Henry Thomas Wishart Bousfield, IA (*d* 1 Jan 1967), only s of Rev Stephen Bousfield

2a *Pamela Margaret [Miss Pamela Guest, Windrush Cottage, Inkpen, nr Newbury, Berks]; *b* 28 Oct 1905; Probation Offr London Juvenile Ct to 1965

(1) Mildred Ella; *b* 6 July 1868; *m* 24 April 1888 Lt-Col John Delalynde Mansel and *d* 11 March 1942, leaving issue (*see* MANSEL, Bt)

1 Charlotte Maria; *b* 3 July 1834; *m* 9 Aug 1859 Richard Du Cane (*d* 29 Jan 1904), est s of Richard Major Du Cane, 20th Light Dragoons, and *d* 5 June 1902, leaving issue

2 Katharine Gwladys; *m* 9 Feb 1861 Rev (Frederick) Cecil Alderson (*d* 3 Dec 1907), Hon Chaplain to HM EDWARD VII, Rector Lutterworth, Residentiary Canon Peterborough, yst s of Hon Sir Edward Hall Alderson, Baron of the Exchequer, and *d* 5 Dec 1926, leaving issue

3 Mary Enid Evelyn; *m* 9 March 1869 Sir Austen Henry Layard, GCB, PC, DCL (*dsp* 5 July 1894), and *d* 1 Nov 1912

4 Constance Rhiannon; *m* 26 Oct 1865 Col Hon Charles George Cornwallis Eliot (*see* SAINT GERMANS, E) and *d* 22 March 1916, leaving issue

5 Blanche Vere, CBE; *m* 22 April 1875 8th Earl of Bessborough (*qv*) and *d* 10 Oct 1919, having had issue

Sir JOHN *d* 26 Nov 1852; his est s,

Sir Ivor Bertie Guest, 2nd Bt, and **1st Baron Wimborne**, of Canford Magna, Co Dorset (UK), so *cr* 30 April 1880, JP, DL Dorset, JP Glam, DL Ross-shire; *b* 29 Aug 1835; *educ* Trin Coll Cambridge (MA); Dorset: CA, High Sheriff 1862, Mayor Poole 1896; *m* 25 May 1868 Cornelia Henrietta Maria, OBE (*d* 22 Jan 1927), est dau of 7th Duke of Marlborough (*qv*), and had:

1 IVOR CHURCHILL, **1st Viscount**.

2 (Christian) Henry Charles; *b* 15 Feb 1874; *educ* Eton; Boer War 1900–02, MP E Dorset June–Dec 1910, Pembroke and Haverfordwest Dec 1910–Nov 1918, N Bristol Nov 1922–Nov 1923 and Plymouth Drake June 1937–June 1945, PPS to Fin Sec Treasury and Chllr Duchy Lancaster 1911–15; WW I: Lt-Col 1st Dragoons, GSO(3) War Office 1914, GSO(1) 1916; *m* 12 July 1911 Frances Henrietta, 2nd dau of 8th Viscount Cobham (*qv*), and *d* 9 Oct 1957, leaving:

(1) John Spencer Churchill; *b* 14 May 1913; *educ* Eton and Trin Coll Cambridge (MA 1937); WW II (despatches); *m* 23 Oct 1948 Margaret Hetherington (*d* 21 May 1997), yr dau of Henry Craft Houck, of Schenectady, NY, and *d* 14 May 1997, leaving:

1a +Richard Lyttelton [Richard Guest Esq, 7 James St, Norwalk, CT 06850, USA]; *b* 30 July 1954; *m* 1983 *Cynthia Rogers, dau of William Shelton Vaiden, of Los Osos, Calif., and has:

1b *Sarah Frances Vaiden; *b* 1984

1a *Cornelia Schermerhorn [Mrs Robert Mitchell, 148 June Rd, North Salem, NY 10560, USA]; *b* 12 Sept 1952; *m* 1986 *Robert Allan Mitchell and has:

1b *Andrew Moses Leonard; *b* 1993

2b *John Henry Guest; *b* 1993

3b *Aune Elizabeth Houck (triplet); *b* 1993

3 Frederick Edward, CBE (1919), DSO (1917), PC (1920); *b* 14 June 1875, Capt 1st Life Gds, Nile Expdn 1899 (despatches), Boer War 1901–02, WW I; MP E Dorset 1910–22, Stroud 1923–24, Bristol N 1924–29 and Plymouth Drake 1931, Jr Ld Treasury 1911–12, Treas Household 1912–15, Patronage-Sec Treasury 1917–21, Sec State Air 1921–22, Hon A/Cdre AAF 1931–37, Chev Legn Hon; *m* 28 June 1905 Amy (*d* 7 Oct 1959), dau of Henry Phipps, of Pittsburgh, and *d* 28 April 1937, leaving:

(1) Winston Frederick Churchill; *b* 20 May 1906; Capt US Marines; *m* 1st 2 June 1934 (*divorce* 1944) Helena Woolworth, dau of Charles Edward Francis McCann, of NY, and had:

1a +Winston [Winston Guest Esq, 152 Wells Rd, Palm Beach, FL 33480, USA]; *b* 4 Jan 1936; *m* 4 Nov 1967 *Helen Mane Elizabeth, dau of Joseph Vincent Shields, of NY, and has:

1b +Winston Frederick Churchill; *b* 6 Oct 1968

2b +Spencer Randolph Harrison; *b* 1984

1b *Helena Woolworth; *b* 27 May 1970

2a +Frederick Edward (II) [Frederick E Guest II, c/o Bessemer Trust Co, 630 5th Ave, New York, NY 10111, USA]; *b* 13 Feb 1938; *m* 1st 21 Aug 1963 Stephanie, dau of Walter F Wanger, of New York, by Joan Bennett, the actress; *m* 2nd 1988 *Carole, dau of Frank Baldoff, of Pitsburgh, and by his 1st w has:

1b +Frederick Edward (III); *b* 1975

2b +Andrew Churchill; *b* 1976

1b *Victoria Woolworth; *b* 23 Oct 1966

2b *Vanessa Wanger; *b* 1973

(1) (cont.) Winston Guest *m* 2nd 8 March 1947 *Lucy Douglas, dau of Alexander Lynde Cochrane, of Boston, Mass., and *d* 1982, leaving by her:

3a +Alexander Michael Dudley Churchill; *b* 10 Sept 1954; *m* 1986 *Elizabeth, dau of Cyril Geacintov, and has:

1b +Gregory Winston Churchill; *b* 1990

1a *Cornelia Cochrane; *b* 28 Nov 1963

(2) Raymond Richard; *b* 25 Nov 1907; Senator Va, US Amb Ireland, racehorse owner; *m* 1st 25 June 1935 Elizabeth Sturgis (*d* 1990), dau of Frank Lyon Polk, and *d* 1991, leaving:

1a +Raymond Richard (Jr) [Raymond R Guest Jr, Rock Hill Farm, Front Royal, VA, USA]; *b* 29 Sept 1939; *m* 1st 1962 Patricia, dau of David R Donovan; *m* 2nd 1979 *Mary Scott, dau of Butler Carbon Derrick, and by his 1st w has:

1b +Raymond Richard (III); *b* 1965

1b *Mary Elizabeth; *b* 21 Sept 1964

1a *Elizabeth Polk [Mrs George Stevens, 3050 Avon Lane NW, Washington, DC 20007, USA]; *b* 4 Oct 1937; *m* 1st Edward B Condon and has:

1b *Caroline; *b* 19 March 1959

1a (cont.) Mrs Condon; *m* 2nd 5 July 1965 *George C Stevens Jr and by him has:

1b +Michael Murrow; *b* 21 Nov 1966

2b +David Averill; *b* 22 May 1968

2a *Virginia [Mrs E Massie Valentine, 102 Tonbridge Rd, Richmond, VA 23221, USA]; *b* 24 June 1946; *m* 1st 1975 (*divorce* 1978) William L Van Alen, Jr, of Newtown Sq, Pa.; *m* 2nd 1991 *E Massie Valentine

(2) (cont.) Raymond R Guest *m* 2nd 30 April 1953 Ellen Tuck, formerly w of John Jacob Astor and dau of Francis Ormond French; *m* 3rd 1960 HH Princess Caroline Cécile Alexandrine, yr dau of HH Prince Alexandre Michel Eugène Joachim Napoléon Murat, and *d* 1991, leaving by his 3rd w:

2a +Achille Murat; *b* 23 March 1961

3a *Laetitia Amelia [Mrs Laurie Oppenheim, 4 Tregunter Rd, London SW10]; *b* 1965; *m* 19– *Laurie Oppenheim

(1) Diana; *b* 1 Nov 1909; *m* 1st 21 Nov 1934 (*divorce* 1937, resumed maiden name by deed poll 30 June 1938) Marc Sevastopoulo, s of Charles Sevastopoulo, of Odessa, and had:

1a Diane Lorraine; *b* 17 Oct 1935; *m* 1st 29 Sept 1955 Pierre Firmin-Didot, of Paris; *m* 2nd 1967 *Arthur Peter Perkins and *d* 19–, leaving by her 1st husb:

1b *Isabelle Marie; *b* 20 Jan 1962

2b *Christine Aimée; *b* 22 Oct 1963; *m* 1987 *Antonio Bulridge

(1) (cont.) Mrs Diana Guest *m* 2nd 20 Feb 1943 Count Jean de la Valdène, of Château St Georges, Eure, France, s of Count Henri de Gaillard de la Valdène, of Château de Bellevue, Vaucluse; *m* 3rd 1970 *Allen Manning and *d* 1996, leaving by her 2nd husb:

1a *Guy Winston de Gaillard; *b* 8 May 1944; *m* 1965 *Thérèse Anderson and has:

1b *Jean Pierre; *b* 1967

1b *Valery Elaine; *b* 1966

2a *(Lorraine) Aimée de Gaillard; *b* Feb 1946; *m* 1978 *Christian Odasso and has:

1b *Fréderic Christian; *b* 1978

1b *Diana Melody Christina; *b* 1979

4 Lionel George William, OBE (1919); *b* 16 Nov 1880; Capt (A/Maj) RAF WW I, memb LCC 1928–31; *m* 6 July 1905 Flora (*d* 16 June 1964), formerly w of Charles Stuart Dodge, of New York, and dau of Hon John Bigelow, of New York, US Amb France, and *d* 27 Sept 1935

5 (Oscar) Montague; *b* 24 Aug 1888; *educ* Harrow and Trin Coll Cambridge (BA 1910); Maj Lothians and Border Horse Yeo and RAF WW I (wounded), MP Loughborough 1918–22 and Camberwell NW 1935–45, PPS to PMG 1921–22; *m* 19 Jan 1924 Kathleen Susan (*d* 1982), only child of Graham Paterson (*see* HUNTINGDON, E), and *d* 8 May 1958, leaving:

(1) +Bertie Warner [Bertie Guest Esq, Cabalva House, Whitney-on-Wye, Herefs]; *b* 4 June 1925; *educ* Stowe; Lt Welsh Gds 1944–47, Dir Public Relations Cncl 1974–; *m* 5 Nov 1949 (*divorce* 1970) Margaret Rose, only dau of Charles Lamond Henderson, JP, QC, of Tilsworth Ho, Leighton Buzzard, Beds, and has:

1a +Jonathan Bertie; *b* 24 June 1952; *educ* Canford

1a *Veronica Susan; *b* 20 April 1953; *m* 25 Aug 1978 (*divorce* 1989, resumed maiden name) J Crowder, s of Frank Crowder

2a *Harriet Clare; *b* 5 Dec 1955

3a *Diana Charlotte; *b* 23 Aug 1959; *m* 1988 *Charles Hicks

(2) +Patrick Henry [Patrick Guest Esq, Upper Bettwys Farm, Clyro, Herefs HR3 6JY]; *b* 17 March 1927; *educ* Stowe; *m* 8 Dec 1951 *Juliet Marian, dau of Harold Morton James, and has:

1a +Peter Hugh [Peter Guest Esq, 170 Goldhurst Terrace, London NW6]; *b* 2 Nov 1952; *educ* Stowe; *m* 1988 *Donna Jean, dau of Donald Lee Macfarlane, of Piedmont, Calif.

2a +Matthew James; *b* 5 April 1954; *educ* Stowe

3a +David Christian; *b* 15 July 1960; *m* 1986 *Henrietta Mary, dau of John Giles Selby Coode-Adams (*see* BUXTON, Bt), and has:

1b *Imogen Victoria; *b* 1993

(1) *Cornelia Rowena (Cara) [Mrs Peter Denman, Duke's House, 23 Lawrence St, London SW3]; *b* 7 May 1928; *m* 1st 9 June 1948 (*divorce* 1955) Hugh Dearman Janson (*see* SUTHERLAND, E) and has issue; *m* 2nd 6 Sept 1957 *Peter Frederick Arthur Denman (*see* DENMAN, B) and has further issue

(2) *Revel Sarah [Mrs Robert Albert, Cabalva, Whitney-on-Wye, Herefs]; *b* 14 Sept 1931; coauthor *Lady Charlotte: a Biography of the Nineteenth Century* (1989); *m* 22 Aug 1963 *Robert Alan Albert, only s of James Albert, of Boston, Mass., and has:

1a +Justin Thomas [Justin Albert Esq, Cabalva Farmhouse, Whitney-on-Wye, Herefs HR3 6EX]; *b* 19 Feb 1965; *m* 1991 *Hester Amanda Jessica, est dau of Michael Selby Gray, of Argyll, and has:

1b +Oscar Timothy; *b* 9 March 1996

1b *Charlotte Revel; *b* 27 March 1992

1a *Corisande Charlotte; *b* 10 March 1967

1 Frances Charlotte, CI (1916), GBE (1918); *m* 27 Jan 1894 1st Viscount Chelmsford (*qv*) and *d* 24 Sept 1957, leaving issue

2 Corisande Evelyn Vere, CBE; *m* 24 Jan 1891 (*divorce* 1902) 7th Baron Rodney (*qv*) and *d* 1 Sept 1943, leaving issue

3 Elaine Augusta; *m* 1st 30 April 1884 Ernest Amherst Villiers (*see* CLARENDON, E) and had issue; *m* 2nd 28 July 1933, as his 3rd w, Robert Lewin Hunter, (*d* 16 May 1942), slr, 2nd s of Richard Hunter, of Wimbledon

4 Rosamond Cornelia Gwladys, DBE (1918); *m* 8 Feb 1899 2nd Viscount Ridley (*qv*) and *d* 2 Dec 1947, leaving issue

The 1st BARON *d* 22 Feb 1914; his est s,

IVOR CHURCHILL GUEST, **1st Viscount Wimborne**, of Canford Magna, Co Dorset, so *cr* 15 June 1918, as also earlier 15 March 1910 BARON ASHBY ST LEDGERS, of Ashby St Ledgers, Co Northampton (both UK), PC (1910), JP Glam and Dorset; *b* 16 Jan 1873; High Sheriff Glam 1900, Capt and Hon Maj Dorset and 7th Bn Imp Yeo Boer War 1900, MP Plymouth 1900–06 and Cardiff 1906–10, Paymaster-Gen 1910–12, Ld-in-Waiting to HM GEORGE V 1913–15 and Ld Lt Ireland 1915–18; *m* 10 Feb 1902 Hon Alice Katherine Sibell Grosvenor, yr dau of 2nd Baron Ebury (*qv*), and had:

1 IVOR GROSVENOR, **2nd Viscount Wimborne**.

1 Rosemary Sibell; *b* 7 March 1906; *m* 1st 12 July 1926 (*divorce* 1955, resumed maiden surname) 6th Baron Kilmarnock (*qv*) and had issue; *m* 2nd 4 May 1955 John Peter Berger and *d* 21 March 1971

2 *Cynthia Edith; *b* 24 Oct 1908; *m* 14 Dec 1933 Thomas Talbot (*see* SHREWSBURY and WATERFORD, E) and has issue

The 1st VISCOUNT *d* 14 June 1939; his only s,

IVOR GROSVENOR GUEST, **2nd Viscount Wimborne**, OBE (1953), JP (Co London 1946), DL (1948); *b* 21 Feb 1903; *educ* Eton and Trin Coll Cambridge; Maj RAC WW II 1939–43, MP Brecon and Radnor Nov 1935–June 1939, PPS to U-Sec State for Air 1943–45, Lib Whip Ho Lds 1944–48, Chm Govrs Stowe 1952–60; *m* 22 Nov 1938 (Mabel) Edith, yr dau of 6th Earl of Ilchester (*qv*), and *d* 7 Jan 1967, leaving:

1 IVOR FOX-STRANGWAYS GUEST, **3rd Viscount Wimborne**; *b* 2 Dec 1939; *educ* Eton; md Harris & Dixon Gp 1967–71 (chm 1972–76), Jt MFH Pytchley 1968–76; *m* 1st 20 Dec 1966 (*divorce* 1981) Victoria Ann (*m* 2nd 1982 Vincent Poklewski-Koziell), only dau of Col Mervyn Doyne Vigors, DSO, MC, IA, and had:

(1) IVOR MERVYN VIGORS GUEST, **4th and present Viscount Wimborne**

1 (cont.) The **3rd Viscount** *m* 2nd 1983 *Venetia Margaret [The Rt Hon Venetia Viscountess Wimborne, Château Fontaine l'Abbé, 27470 Serquigny, France], formerly w of Capt Frederick Grant Barker, 11th Hus, and dau of Richard Bridges St John Quarry, of Orchard Ho, Odiham, Hants, and *d* 1993, leaving by her:

(1) *Ilona Charlotte; *b* 24 Feb 1985

2 +JULIAN JOHN [The Hon Julian Guest, c/o White's Club, 37 St James's St, London SW1]; *b* 12 Oct 1945; heir presumptive; *educ* Stowe; *m* 1st 28 Jan 1970 (*divorce* 1978) Emma Jane Arlette, er dau of Cdr Archibald Gray, DSO, RN, of Tilbridge, Gt Staughton, Hunts; *m* 2nd 16 Nov 1983 *Jillian, dau of Ninian Stuart Gray Bannatine

3 *Charles James [The Hon Charles Guest, Truckwell Manor Farm, Lydeard St Lawrence, Somerset TA4 3PT]]; *b* 10 July 1950; *educ* Harrow and RMA Sandhurst; Lt 9th/12th Roy Lancers 1974, Capt Roy Wessex Yeo, memb Securities Inst, with Rathbone Neilson Cobbold Ltd; *m* 28 Feb 1976 *Simone Katherine, dau of Patrick Whinney, of Grand Havre, Guernsey, and has:

(1) +Henry Charles; *b* 1978; *educ* Harrow

(2) +William Patrick; *b* 1981; *educ* Harrow

(1) *Catherine Elizabeth; *b* 1987

1 *Frances Ann [Mrs Rao Gaddipati, Apt 6R, 5440 Little Neck Parkway, Little Neck, NY 11362, USA]; *b* 18 Nov 1942; *m* 1st 1 May 1971 (*divorce* 1987) Ernest Martin Johnson, s of Ernest Martin Johnson, of Gardner, Mass.; *m* 2nd 1991 *Rao Gaddipati

WINCHESTER

AYMEZ · LOYAULTE

Arms: Sable, three swords in pile, points downwards, proper, pommels and hilts or. **Crest:** A falcon, wings displayed or, belled of the same, and ducally collared gules. **Supporters:** Two hinds purpure, semée of estoiles and ducally gorged or. **Motto:** *Aymez loyaulte* ('Love loyalty'). **Creations:** B. (E) 9 March 1538/9, E. (E) 19 Jan 1549/50, M. (E) 12 Oct 1551.

THE 18TH MARQUESS OF WINCHESTER, **Earl of Wiltshire** and **Baron St John** (Nigel George Paulet) [The Most Hon The Marquess of Winchester, 6A Main Rd, Irene 1675, Transvaal, S Africa]; *b* 23 Dec 1941; *s* cousin 1968; premier Marquess of England; dir: Rhodesia Mineral Ventures (Pvt) Ltd, Sani-Dan Services (Pvt) Ltd, and Rhodesia Prospectors (1969) (Pvt) Ltd; *m* 25 Nov 1967 *Rosemary Anne, dau of Maj Aubrey John Hilton, of Salisbury, Rhodesia, and has:

1 +CHRISTOPHER JOHN HILTON, *Earl of Wiltshire*; *b* 30 July 1969; runs a chemical company; guitarist with pop group Wizard

2 +Richard George; *b* 16 Aug 1971

1 *Susan; *b* 1976

Winchester, previous creations under title of: Before the 16th century no distinction was made between the earldom of such historic cities within a county as Winchester and that of the county itself. Accordingly, just as the Earl of Salisbury in the 12th century might also be known as the Earl of Wiltshire (*see* SALISBURY, M, preliminary remarks), so too the Earl of Winchester might also be called Earl of Southampton (Hampshire being then called Co Southampton). That is why the de Quincy Earls of Winchester, who held the title from 1207 to 1264, the Despenser Earls of Winchester, who held the title from 1322 to 1326 and the Bruges Earls of Winchester, who held the title from 1472 to 1500, are sometimes found referred to as Earls of Southampton.

Saher de Quency or Quincy, created Earl of Winchester in or about Feb 1207/8 or possibly recognised officially then as Earl following an earlier creation, had been a close associate of KINGS RICHARD I and JOHN, particularly in France and Normandy. He later turned against JOHN and was one of the magnates who forced him to observe Magna Carta in 1215. After HENRY III's accession he submitted to the Crown. On his son Roger's death the Earldom reverted to the Crown. In the next century Hugh le Despenser, one of EDWARD II's favourites, was briefly Earl of Winchester but was soon liquidated by Queen Isabel, EDWARD's forceful wife.

In 1472 EDWARD IV conferred the Earldom of Winchester on Louis Le Bruges, a Flemish Prince who had been his host when in exile two years earlier. Louis' son surrendered the title to HENRY VII in 1500.

Earldom of Wiltshire: Hervey de Leon, also known as Hervey Le (The) Breton (*i.e*, a native of Brittany), was a supporter of STEPHEN in the Time of Troubles after HENRY I's death. STEPHEN created him Earl of Wiltshire in 1140. He was later forced to flee from England and since he lost possession of the lands which were then considered a necessary concomitant to an earldom, his title was deemed to have reverted to the Crown. For the next two centuries the Earldom of Wiltshire was indistinguishable from that of Salisbury (*see* above remarks and SALISBURY, M, preliminary remarks).

In 1397 William le Scrope was created Earl of Wiltshire. The wording of the document creating him Earl left out the words 'of his body' when limiting inheritance to heirs male, so that in 1859 a collateral descendant claimed the Earldom. The House of Lords Privileges Committee rejected the claim, doing so rightly but on the wrong grounds. Thirty years earlier it had been even less precise (*see* DEVON, E).) Scrope was a loyal supporter of RICHARD II right up till the latter's deposition in 1399 and was accordingly executed by HENRY IV.

In 1449 James Butler, eldest son of the 4th Earl of Ormond (*see* 1970 edn ORMONDE, M), was created Earl of Wiltshire. He was a Lancastrian in the Wars of the Roses and after the Yorkist victory at Towton 1461 was executed and posthumously attainted. The Earldom of Wiltshire would have expired anyway because he died without issue. In January 1469/70 an adherent of EDWARD IV, John Stafford, a younger son of the 1st Stafford Duke of Buckingham (*see* STAFFORD, B), was created Earl of Wiltshire. His son died without issue, whereupon this creation too became extinct. The title was conferred upon another member of the Stafford family in January 1509/10 but this grantee also died without issue.

Yet another first holder of the earldom of that county died without male issue with the demise of ANNE BOLEYN's father Thomas, who was a Butler of the Earl of Ormond's family through his mother and who had been promoted Earl of Wiltshire in 1529.

Lineage: The family who currently hold the Earldom of Wiltshire and Marquessate of Winchester are a branch of the Paulets, Poulets or Powletts who were in addition created Earls Poulett in 1706 (*see* 1970 edn). The 1st Marquess used to be portrayed as the archetypal Vicar of Bray figure of the mid-16th century, bending every way necessary to ensure his own survival (and material enrichment). A maturer view, initiated by the late 19th–early 20th-century historian A F Pollard and continued by the late Sir Geoffrey Elton, sees him as the prototypical Permanent Under Secretary, an able civil servant (particularly in finance) who carried on competent administration no matter what the outlook of his sovereign, be it Protestant, Catholic, Erastian, Ultramontane, pro-French, pro-Spanish, inflationary or in favour of sound money. (Paulet's great-grandson was less methodical, nearly bankrupting himself; the **16th Marquess** actually did so in 1930).

Sir JOHN PAULET, of Paulet and Got(e)hurst, Somerset; *m* Elizabeth, dau of Sir Thomas Reyney, of Rowd and Shyrston, Somerset, and *d* 1356, leaving:

Sir JOHN PAULET; ktd 1381; *m* Elizabeth, dau and heiress of Sir John Creedy, of Creedy, Devon, and had:

1 Thomas (Sir); *m* Margaret, dau of Henry Boulton, and had an est s:

(1) William (Sir); ktd by HENRY VI; *m* Elizabeth, dau of John Deneland, of Hinton St George, Somerset, through whom he acquired the manor of Hinton St George, and had, with four daus (*see* DONEGALL, M):

1a Amyas (Sir), JP; Sheriff Dorset and Somerset 1485, ktd 1487 following HENRY VII's defeat of Lambert Simnel Battle of Stoke, Treasurer Middle Temple 1521; *m* 1st Margaret, dau of Sir John Paulet, of Nunney Castle, Somerset, but by her had no issue; *m* 2nd Laura, dau of William Kellaway, of Roeborne, Hants, and *d* 1538, leaving, with a yr s John (*b* 1509(?); *educ* Oxford; last pre-Reformation Dean Jersey; *d* 1565):

1b Hugh (Sir), JP (Somerset 1532); *b* after 1500; Sheriff Dorset and Somerset 1536, 1542 and 1547, ktd 1537, Treas English Army Siege Boulogne 1544, Govr Jersey 1550–72, V-Pres Cncl Welsh Marches 1559, MP Somerset 1572; *m* 1st *c* 1528 Philippa, dau of Sir Lewis Pollard, of King's Nympton, Devon, and had three sons and two daus; *m* 2nd by Dec 1560 Elizabeth, dauof Walter Blount, of Blount's Hall, Staffs, and widow of Sir Thomas Pope (fndr Trin Coll Oxford), and *d* probably Dec 1572, leaving by his 1st w an est s:

1c Amyas (Sir), PC (1585); *b c* 1536; Lt-Govr Jersey under his f 1559–71, full Govr thereafter, ktd 1576, Amb France 1576, Custodian MARY QUEEN OF SCOTS on ELIZABETH I's behalf 1585, Chllr Order Garter 1587–88; *m* Margaret, dau of Anthony Hervey, of Columb-John, Devon, and *d* 26 Sept 1588, leaving, with an est and yst s and three daus:

1d Anthony (Sir); Govr Jersey, Capt ELIZABETH I's Gd; *m* 1583 Catherine, only dau of 1st Lord (Baron) Norris (*see* LINDSEY and ABINGDON, E), and *d* 22 July 1600, having had, with two yr sons and two other daus:

1e JOHN POULETT, 1st BARON POULETT OF HINTON ST GEORGE (*see* 1970 edn POULETT, E)

1d Sarah; *m* Sir Francis Vincent, 1st Bt, and had:

1e Elizabeth; *m* Sir John Acland, (?)1st Bt(?), of the 1644 *cr* (*see* ACLAND, Bt, of Columb-John)

2 William, of Melcomb Paulet, Somerset, Serjeant-at-law *c* 1416; *m* Eleanor, dau of Philip de la Mere, of Nunney Castle, Somerset, and sis and heiress of Sir Elias de la Mere, of Nunney, and *d* 8 Aug 1435, leaving:

(1) John (Sir), of Nunney; *m* Constance (*dvp* by 10 Feb 1427/8), dau and coheir of Sir Hugh de Poynings (*d* on or after 27 Nov 1427), est s and heir of Thomas de Poynings, 5th Lord (Baron) St John (of Basing), and *d* 11 Jan 1436/7, leaving:

1a John (Sir), of Nunney; *m* Eleanor, dau and coheir of Robert Roos, of Gedney and Irby, Lincs, and *d* 5 Oct 1492, leaving, with a dau (Margaret, *m* her cousin Sir Amyas Paulet; *see* above):

1b John (Sir), KB (1501), of Basing, Hants, and Nunney, Somerset; cdr HENRY VII's troops Battle of Blackheath 1497; *m* by June 1468 his cousin Alice, dau of Sir William Paulet, of Hinton St George, s and heir of Thomas Paulet, 2nd s of Sir John Paulet, of Pawlett, Somerset, and er bro of the William Paulet mentioned above, and had:

1c WILLIAM, **1st Marquess**

2c Thomas, *dsp*

3c George (Sir), of Crondall, Hants; *m* three times and *d* 1558, leaving four sons and five daus

4c Richard, of Herriard, Hants, whose male line died out with his gs, Richard, who left two daus and coheirs

1c Eleanor; *m* Sir William Gifford, of Itchell

2c Katherine; *m* Sir William Fermor, of Summertown, Oxford (*see* HESKETH, B)

Sir JOHN's est s,

WILLIAM PAULET or POWLETT, **1st Marquess of Winchester**, so *cr* 11 Oct 1551, as also earlier 9 March 1538/9 BARON S(EYN)T JOHN and 19 Jan 1549/50 EARL OF WILTSHIRE (all E), KG (1543), PC (1542); *b c* 1483, Sheriff Hants 1511–12, 1518–19 and 1522–23, ktd 1523–25, MP Hants 1529–36, Comptroller Household 1532–37, Treasurer Household Oct 1537–March 1538/9, Master Court of Wards 1540–42 and Court of Wards and Liveries 1542–54, Ld Chamberlain 1543–*c* 1545, Ld Steward Household and Ld Pres Cncl *c* Nov 1545–Feb 1549/50, Ld Treasurer Feb 1549/50–March 1571/2, Ld Keeper Gt Seal March-Oct 1547, Ld Lt Hants 1552, 1559 and Hants and Middx 1569, Jt Ld Lt London 1569, Speaker Ho Lds March 1558/9 and Oct 1566; *m c* 1509 Elizabeth, dau of Alderman Sir William Capel, Ld Mayor London, and *d* 10 March 1571/2 at his seat of Basing, nr Basingstoke, Hants, having had, with three yr sons (Thomas, of Cossington, Somerset, had issue; Chidiock, of Wade, Hants, had issue; Giles, of Cokels, Wilts, had issue (and four daus (Alice, *m* Richard Stawell, of Cotherston, Somerset; Margaret, *m* Sir William Berkeley; Margery, *m* Sir Richard Waller, of Oldstoke, Hants; Eleanor, *m* Sir Richard Pecksail, of Beaurepaire, Hants):

JOHN PAULET, **2nd Marquess of Winchester**; *b c* 1510; Sheriff Hants 1533–34 and Somerset and Dorset 1543–44, ktd 1544, called up to Ho Lds *vp* in f's barony 3 Oct 1544, Ld Lt Dorset 1557, Govr IoW Jan–Oct 1558; *m* 1st by 20 Oct 1528 Elizabeth, est dau of 2nd Lord (Baron) Willoughby de Broke (*qv*) by his 2nd w; *m* 2nd March/April 1554 Elizabeth, widow of (a) Sir Anthony Ughtred and (b) 1st Baron Cromwell of the 1536 *cr* (*see* CROMWELL, B, preliminary remarks) and dau of Sir John Seymour (also sis of HENRY VIII's w JANE; *see* SOMERSET, D); *m* 3rd by 30 Sept 1568 Winifred, widow of Sir Richard Sackville (*see* SACKVILLE, B) and dau of Sir John Brug(g)es/Brydges, Ld Mayor London, and *d* 4 Nov 1576, leaving solely by his 1st w, with three yr sons (Sir George, Govr Londonderry, murdered there May 1608; Richard; Thomas, *dspm*) and a dau (Mary, *m* by 1560 2nd Baron Cromwell of the 1536 *cr* (*d* 20 Nov 1592) and *d* 10 Oct 1592, leaving issue):

WILLIAM PAULET, **3rd Marquess of Winchester**, KB (1553); *b* 1532/3; Sheriff Hants 1560–61, Jt Ld Lt (sole Feb 1585/6 on) Dorset 1569 and Hants 1585, MP Dorset 1571, called up to Ho Lds *vp* in f's barony 5 May 1572; a man of letters and poet; *m* between 20 June 1544 and 10 Feb 1547/8 Agnes, dau of 1st Baron Howard of Effingham (*see* EFFINGHAM, E), and *d* 24 Nov 1598, leaving, with three daus (Anne, *m* Sir Thomas Dennis, of Holcome, Devon; Katherine, *m* Sir Giles Wroughton; Elizabeth, *m* Sir Edward Hoby) and at least one illegitimate child (Sir William Paulet, whose dau Elizabeth was 2nd w of 4th Viscount Hereford, *qv*):

WILLIAM PAULET, **4th Marquess of Winchester**; entertained ELIZABETH I at Basing nearly two weeks 1601, an episode so expensive his finances never wholly recovered; *m* 28 Feb 1686/7 Lucy, dau of 1st Earl of Exeter (*see* EXETER, M), and *d* 4 Feb 1628/9, having had, with two other sons:

1 William, *Earl of Wiltshire*; *b* early 1587/8; *m* just prior to 17 Feb 1613/4 Mary Browne (m 2nd by 22 Oct 1627 William Arundell, 2nd s of 1st Baron Arundell of Wardour; *see* 1940 edn), dau of 2nd Viscount Montagu (*see* SACKVILLE, B), and *dsp* & *vp* Aug 1621

2 JOHN PAULET, **5th Marquess of Winchester**; *b c* 1598; allegedly *educ* Exeter Coll Oxford; MP St Ives 1620–22; called up to Ho Lds *vp* in f's barony 10 Feb 1623/4; held Basing for CHARLES I in Civil War (said to be the last royalist stronghold to survive), but the house was at length burnt by the Parliamentarians and the Marquess's plate, jewels, etc, destroyed to the amount of £200,000 (over £8m in late-1990s terms); *m* 1st (licence 18 Dec 1622) Jane Savage, dau of 1st Viscount Savage, and had an only s:

(1) CHARLES PAULET/POWLETT, **6th Marquess of Winchester** and 1st DUKE OF BOLTON (E), so *cr* 9 April 1689, PC (1679); *b c* 1630; MP Winchester 1660 and Hants 1661–75; *m* 1st 28 Feb 1651/2 Christian (*d* 22 May 1653), est dau and coheir of 1st and last Baron Frescheville of Staveley, by whom he had no surv issue; *m* 2nd 12 Feb 1654 Mary (*d* 1 Nov 1680), widow of Henry Carey, Lord Leppington (s of 2nd and last Earl of Monmouth; *see* FALKLAND, V), and est illegitimate dau of Emanuel Scrope, 1st and last Earl of Sunderland of the 1627 *cr*, and *d* 27 Feb 1698/9, having by her had, with two daus (one of whom *m* as his 2nd w 3 Earl of Bridgwater, *see* GREY EGERTON, Bt):

1a CHARLES PAULET, **7th Marquess of Winchester** and 2nd DUKE OF BOLTON, KG (1714), PC (1690); *b* 1661; MP (Whig) Hants 1681, 1685–87 and 1689–98, Ld Chamberlain 1715–17, Ld Lt Ireland 1717–19; *m* 1st 10 July 1679 Margaret (*dsp*), dau of 3rd Baron Coventry (*see* COVENTRY, E); *m* 2nd 8 Feb 1682/3 Frances (*d* 1696), sis of Sir John Ramsden, 1st Bt (*qv*), and by her had:

1b CHARLES POWLETT, **8th Marquess of Winchester** and 3rd DUKE OF BOLTON, KG (1722), PC (1725); *b* 3 Sept 1685; MP (Whig) Lymington 1705–08, Hants 1708–10 and Carmarths 1715–17, Constable Tower London 1725–26, Ld Lt: Carmarths and Glam 1715, Hants and Dorset 1722–33 and Hants 1742–54, Govr IoW 1726–33 and 1742–46, Lt-Gen 1745, having raised a foot regt to suppress the Jacobites; it was intended to call him up to the Ho of Lds *vp* in his f's barony of St John but the writ was worded wrongly so that a fresh creation of PAWLET OF BASING (GB) was conferred 12 April 1717; *m* 1st 21 July 1713 Lady Anne Vaughan (*dsp* 20 Sept 1751), dau and sole heiress of 3rd Earl of Carbery (*see* CARBERY, B, preliminary remarks); *m* 2nd 20 Oct 1751 his longtime mistress Lavinia, dau of Lt — Beswick, RN, better known as the actress Lavinia Fenton (noted for her performances as Polly Peachum in *The Beggar's Opera*; *d* 17 Jan 1760), and *dspl* 26 Aug 1754, when the Barony of Pawlet of Basing expired, having by her had before their marriage (all of whom took the name POWLETT):

1c Charles (Rev); Rector Itchen, Hants, and St Martin's, nr Looe, Cornwall; *b* 28 Dec 1728; *d* 39 Jan 1809

2c Percy, RN; had:

1d Charles (Rev); Rector Roding, Essex

3c Horatio Armand; Lt Col; *m* Jane — and had:

1d Charles; *b* 24 Feb 1763; *d* 26 Jan 1776

2b HARRY POWLETT, **9th Marquess of Winchester** and 4th DUKE OF BOLTON, PC (1755); *b* 24 July 1691; MP (Whig) St Ives 1715–22 and Hants 1722–54, a Ld Admlty 1733–42, Lt Tower London 1742–54, Ld Lt Glam 1754–55 and Hants 1754–58; *m* Catharine (*d* 25 April 1744), dau of Charles Parry, of Oakfield, Berks, and *d* 9 Oct 1759, having had:

1c CHARLES POWLETT, **10th Marquess of Winchester** and 5th DUKE OF BOLTON, KB (1753), PC (1758); *b c* 1718; *educ* Winchester; MP (Whig) Lymington 1754–59, Lt Tower London 1754–60, Ld Lt Hants 1758–63, Col Northern Bn Hants Militia, *d* by his own hand (shooting himself) unm 5 July 1765, leaving an illegitimate dau (*see* BOLTON, B)

2c HARRY POWLETT, **11th Marquess of Winchester** and 6th and last DUKE OF BOLTON, PC (1766); *b* 6 Nov 1720; *educ* Winchester; MP (Whig) Christchurch 1751–54, Lymington 1755–61 and Winchester 1761–65, Adml the White 1775; *m* 1st 7 May 1752 Mary Munn, of Eltham, Kent (*d* 31 May 1764), and had:

1d Mary Henrietta; *m* 25 April 1772 5th Earl of Sandwich (*qv*) and *d* 30 March 1779, leaving issue

2c (cont.) The **11th Marquess** *m* 2nd 8 April 1765 Katharine (*d* 21 March 1809), sis of 1st Earl of Lonsdale (*qv*), and *d* 24 Dec 1794, when the Dukedom expired, leaving by her:

2d Katherine Margaret; *m* 17 Sept 1787 5th Baron Barnard (*qv*) of Barnard's Castle and *d* 17 June 1807, leaving issue

   3d Amelia; *d unm*

1c Henrietta; *m* 12 July 1741 Robert Colebrooke (*d* 10 May 1784), of Chilham Castle, Kent, and *dsp* 22 Dec 1753

2c Catherine; *m* 1st William Ashe (*dsp*); *m* 2nd 1734 Adam Dummond of Megginch (see also STRANGE, B) and *d* 1775

1b Mary; *m* 1st Charles O'Neill (*see* O'NEILL, B); *m* 2nd Capel Moore, 6th s of 3rd Earl of Drogheda (*qv*)

2b Frances; *m* 1708 John, Lord Mordaunt, s and heir of 3rd Earl of Peterborough, and *d* 30 July 1715, leaving issue (see MORDAUNT, Bt)

1a (cont.) The **7th Marquess** *m* 3rd 1697 Henrietta Crofts, est illegitimate dau of 1st and last Duke of Monmouth (*see* BUCCLEUCH and QUEENSBERRY, D) by Eleanor, yst dau of Sir Robert Needham, and *d* 21 Jan 1721/2, having by her had:

3b Nassau; *m* Isabella, dau of 6th Earl of Thanet (*see* DE CLIFFORD, B), and *d* 1741, leaving:

   1c Isabella; *m* 4 June 1765 3rd Earl of Egmont (*qv*) and *d* 8 Sept 1821, leaving issue

2a William; MP Winchester; *m* 1st Louisa, dau of the Marquis Monpouillon, yr s of the Duke de la Force, and had:

1b William, of Easton, Hants; MP Lymington and Winchester; *m* 10 Feb 1721 Annabella (*d* 21 Nov 1769), dau of 1st Earl of Tankerville (*qv*), and *d* Feb 1757, having had, with a s (*d unm vp*):

   1c William; *m* Rev Richard Smyth, of Itchen and Crux Easton, Hants, Rector Myddle, Salop (*m* 2nd 12 July 1786 Susannah Baskett, of Leatherhead), and *d* April 1761, leaving:

      1d William Powlett SMYTH later POWLETT; *b* 16 March 1758; *m* 15 Aug 1779 Mary, of Hurstbourne, Hants (*d* 15 May 1817), yst dau of Richard Dalton, of Leatherhead and Knaith, Lincs, and *dsp* 8 March 1821

      1d Mary; *d* 1762

      2d Camilla; *m* Rev Barton Wallop (*see* PORTSMOUTH, E)

      3d Annabella; *m* 1st Baron Bayning of Foxley (*see* TOWNSHEND, M)

2c Charles Armand (Sir); Maj-Gen, MP Christchurch; *m* June 1738 Elizabeth (*d* Sept 1756), widow of Richard Dashwood (*see* DASH-WOOD, Bt, of Kirtlington Park) and dau of Thomas Lewes, of Stanford, Notts, and *dsp* Nov 1751

   1c Mary; *m* 25 June 1714 1st Earl of Rosse (*qv*) of the 1718 *cr* and *d* 15 Oct 1718

   2c Jane

2a (cont.) Lord William *m* 2nd Oct 1699 Anne (*d* 1737), dau and coheir of Randolph Egerton, of Betley, Staffs, and *d* 25 Sept 1729, leaving by her:

3b Henrietta; *m* 29 May 1725 Hon William Townshend (*see* TOWNSHEND, M) and *d* 1755, leaving issue

1a Jane; *m* 2 April 1673 3rd Earl of Bridgwater and *d* 23 May 1716, leaving issue (*see* GREY EGERTON, Bt)

2 (cont.) The **5th Marquess** *m* 2nd by 4 Oct 1633 Honora (*d* 10 March 1661), widow of Garratt McCoghlan and dau of 4th Earl of Clanricarde (*see* SLIGO, M), and by her had four sons and three daus; *m* 3rd 1669 Isabel (*bur sp* 5 Sept 1691), dau of 1st and last Viscount Stafford (*see* STAFFORD, B), and *d* 5 March 1674/5

3 Henry, of Amport, Hants; *m* Lucy, dau of Sir George Philpot, of Thruxton, Hants, and *d* 1672, leaving:

(1) Francis, of Amport; *b c* 1645; *m* 20 May 1674 Elizabeth, dau and heiress of Sir Richard Norton, 2nd Bt, of Rotherfield, Hants, and *d* 25 Feb 1695/6, leaving an only s:

1a Norton, of Amport; *b c* 1679; *m* Jane, dau of Sir Charles Morley, of Droxford (*see* POWIS, E), and *d* 6 June 1741, having had:

1b Norton; *b c* 1705; *educ* Exeter Coll Oxford; MP Winchester 1730–34; *m* Anne — and *dspl* 14 March 1759, leaving:

   1c Thomas Norton PAULET

2b Henry; Capt 3rd Foot Gds; *d unm* and was *bur* 13 April 1743

3b John: Army Offr; *d unm c* 1750

4b Charles; Capt RN; *d unm* 4 April 1762

5b William; Lt RN; *d unm* 15 Nov 1772

6b Herbert; Army Capt; *d unm* and was *bur* 29 March 1746

7b Francis; *b c* 1721; *educ* Peterhouse Cambridge; *d unm* and was *bur* 10 Dec 1742

8b GEORGE, **12th Marquess**

4 Charles; had, possibly illegitimately:

(1) Jane; allegedly *m* Sir John Huband, 1st Bt, of Ipsley, Warwicks

The 11th MARQUESS's 3rd cousin once-removed,

  GEORGE PAULET, **12th Marquess of Winchester**; *b* 7 June 1722; Gentleman Usher to PRINCE OF WALES 1750, MP (Tory) Winchester 1765–74, Groom Porter to GEORGE II 1757, 1st Commr Ltcy Hants 1793–98, V-Adml Hants 1797; *m* 7 Jan 1762 Martha (*d* 14 March 1796), dau of Thomas Ingoldsby, of Waldridge, Bucks, and had:

1 CHARLES INGOLDSBY, **13th Marquess**

2 Henry (Sir), KCB; *b* 31 March 1767; V-Adml the White, a Ld of Admlty; *m* 26 Oct 1813 Anne Maria (*d* 15 April 1876), dau of George Ravenscroft, and *d* 28 Jan 1832, leaving:

(1) Sir HENRY CHARLES PAULET, 1st and last Bt (UK), so *cr* 18 March 1836, of W Hill Lodge, Hants; *b* 1 Aug 1814; Capt Dragoon Gds; *d unm* 11 Dec 1886, when the btcy expired

(2) Edward; *b* 28 Feb 1825; *d* 6 Nov 1838

(1) Anna Maria; *m* 3 June 1845 Rev Wellesly Pole Pigott, Rector Bemerton, Wilts, and *d* 19 Dec 1851

(2) Urania Elizabeth; *m* 1 Feb 1844 Hon Sir Edward Butler (*see* DUNBOYNE, B) and *d* 2 Dec 1858, leaving issue

1 Urania Anne; *b c* 1767; *m* 1st 17 March 1785 1st Marquess of Clanricarde (*see* SLIGO, M); *m* 2nd 28 Oct 1799 Col Peter Kington (*ka* 6 July 1807 in attacking Buenos Aires); *m* 3rd 22 May 1813, as his 2nd w, V-Adml Sir Joseph Sidney Yorke, KCB (*see* HARDWICKE, E), and *d* 27 Dec 1843

The 12th MARQUESS *d* 22 April 1800; his e *r* s,

  CHARLES INGOLDSBY PAULET later BURROUGHS-PAULET (roy licence 8 Aug 1839 under terms of will of Dame Sarah Salusbury, of Offley Place, Herts), **13th Marquess of Winchester**, PC (1812); *b* 27 Jan 1764; *educ* Eton and Clare Hall Cambridge; Ensign 1st Foot Gds 1784–86, MP Truro 1792–96, Lt-Col N Hants Militia 1796, Ld Lt Hants 1798–1800, last holder of post of Groom of the Stole, as such serving GEORGEs III and IV and WILLIAM IV; *m* 31 July 1800 Anne (*d* 21 March 1841), 2nd dau of John Andrews, of Shotley Hall, Northumberland, and *d* 29 Nov 1843, leaving:

1 JOHN PAULET, **14th Marquess of Winchester**; *b* 3 June 1801; *educ* Eton; Cornet 10th Hus 1817, Lt 1820, Capt 35th Foot 1823 June and 8th Hus Dec 1823, Maj June 1826, Lt-Col Infantry Dec 1826, Col Hants Militia 1843 and Hon Col 1873, Ld Lt Hants 1852–87; *m* 29 Nov 1855 Hon Mary Montagu (*d* 6 Sept 1868), dau of 6th Baron Rokeby of Armagh, and *d* 4 July 1887, leaving:

(1) AUGUSTUS JOHN HENRY BEAUMONT PAULET, **15th Marquess of Winchester**, DL (Hants); *b* 6 Feb 1858; *educ* Eton; 2nd Lt Coldstream Gds 1879, Lt 1881, Suakin campaign 1885, Capt 1890, Maj 1897, Boer War 1899; *ka* Battle of Magersfontein 11 Dec 1899

(2) HENRY WILLIAM MONTAGU PAULET, **16th Marquess of Winchester**; *b* 30 Oct 1862; Lt 3rd Bn Hants Regt, Hants: Capt Imp Yeo 1902–05, Ld Lt 1904–17, Chm CC 1905–09, Pres TAA 1907–17; Maj 13th Bn Rifle Bde WW I; *m* 1st 23 Feb 1892 Charlotte Josephine, GBE (1918) (*d* 28 Dec 1924), widow of Samuel Garnett, of Arch Hall, Co Meath, and dau of Col John Stanley Howard, of Ballina Park, Co Wicklow; *m* 2nd 19 Jan 1925 Caroline (*d* 10 Feb 1949), widow of Maj Claud Marks, DSO, Highland LI (TF), and dau of Abraham Hoffnung, of Rawdon Hall, Holyport, Berks; *m* 3rd 2 July 1952 Bapsy (*b* 1902; *d* 6 Sept 1995), MA Columbia, New York Litterature, Order Merit Iran (1955), memb Cncl World Alliance for Internat Peace through Religion and various international organisations for promoting friendly relations between nations, author: *Heroines of Ancient Iran* (1930), dau of Most Rev Khurshedji Erachji Pavry, Parsi High Priest of Bombay, and *d* 28 June 1962

(1) Lilian Mary; *b* 26 July 1859; *m* 28 July 1884 (*divorce* 1898) Randolph Gordon Erskine Wemyss of Wemyss and *d* 11 Nov 1952, leaving issue (*see* WEMYSS and MARCH, E)

2 Charles (Rev); *b* 13 Aug 1802; Preb Salisbury, Vicar Wellesbourne, Warwicks; *m* 1st 18 Aug 1831 Caroline Margaret (*d* 6 Oct 1817), 3rd dau of Sir John Ramsden, 4th Bt (*qv*), and had:

(1) Charles William, of Wellesbourne; *b* 27 Sept 1832; Capt 7th Hus, Hon Col Warwicks Yeo Cav; *m* 1st 3 Dec 1863 Susan Amelia Georgina (*d* 18 Oct 1885), 4th dau of William Standish Standish, of Duxbury, Lancs, and had:

1a Charles Standish, MVO (1917); *b* Oct 1873; *educ* Eton; Capt Warwicks Yeo, Imp Yeo Boer War 1900–01 (despatches), Maj and Dep Dir-Gen Supply Dept Min Munitions 1915–19, Orders Crown Italy and Rising Sun Japan; *m* 24 Oct 1901 Lillian Jane Charlotte (*d* March 1972), dau of Maj William Thomas Exham Fosbery, 77th Regt, and *d* 18 Feb 1953, leaving:

   1b RICHARD CHARLES PAULET, **17th Marquess of Winchester**; *b* 8 July 1905; *educ* Eton; Lt Roy Fus; *d unm* 5 March 1968

   1b Pamela; *b* 1909; *m* 197– Hans Nieter O'Leary (*d* 1978) and *d* 1991

2b *Eileen Cecil Theo [The Lady Eileen Fitton, 470 Sonora Crescent, Campbell River, BC V9W 6V3, Canada]; *m* 1st Harry Evan Martin (*d* 1947) and has had:

   1c *Gillian Jane [Mrs Lipot Winter, 1193 S Alder St, Campbell River, BC V9W 1Z8]; *b* 1942; *m* 1964 *Lipot Gyula Winter and has:

      1d *Edward Steven; *b* 1966

      2d *Robert Ferenc; *b* 1974

      3d *Peter James; *b* 1978

      1d *Elizabeth Jane; *b* 1964

   2c *Elizabeth Susan [Mrs Luis Correia, 21 Kenton Gdns, Kenton, Middx HA3 8DE]; *b* 1945; *m* 24 Sept 1971 *Luis Correia and has:

      1d *Chrisol Luis; *b* 1 April 1973

      2d *Michael Felipe; *b* 13 July 1974

      1d *Alice Anne Theofile; *b* 7 Feb 1978

2b (cont.) Lady Eileen Martin *m* 2nd 1949 *Joseph Fitton and by him has had:

   1c *Francis Peter [Francis Fitton Esq, Box 454, Quathiaski Cove, Quadra Is, BC V0P 1N0, Canada]; *m* 1985 *Victoria Lynn, dau of Donald Ralph Gregory, BEM, and has:

      1d *Kala Louise; *b* 1985

      2d *Deanna Eileen; *b* 1987

   2c *Jonathan Paul [Jonathan Fitton Esq, 359 Simms Rd, Campbell River, BC V9W 1P2, Canada]; *b* 1952; *m* 1991 *Lona Dianne, dau of Reuben Emil Croissant, and has:

      1d *Jeffrey Duggan; *b* 1983

      2d *William Elliot; *b* 1984

   1c *Theresa Mary [Mrs Neil Marson, 500 Quadra St, Campbell River, BC V9W 6V1, Canada]; *m* 1992 *Neil Andrew Marson

   2c *Margaret Anne [Mrs Kenneth Clippingdale, Box 203, Heriot Bay, BC V0P 1H0, Canada]; *m* 1982 *Kenneth Dodd Clippingdale and has:

      1d *Robert Nathan; *b* 1974

      2d *Andrew Dodd; *b* 1983

      3c *Catherine Louise; *b* 1958

   4c Judith Ellen; *b* 1961; *d* 1985

2a Cecil Henry; *b* March 1875; 2nd Lt Dorset Yeo; *m* 6 Sept 1898 Ethel Frances (*d* 3 Sept 1961), dau of Capt Walter Frederick James Cowan, of Alveston Lodge, Warwicks (*see* 1956 edn COWAN, Bt), and was *ka* 26 Feb 1916, leaving:

   1b George Cecil; *b* 25 Feb 1905; *m* 23 Aug 1937 Hazel Margaret (*m* 2nd 1962 George Meyer and *d* 19–), only dau of Maj Danvers Wheeler, RA, of Salisbury, S Rhodesia, and *d* 9 Aug 1961, leaving:

1c NIGEL GEORGE PAULET, **18th and present Marquess of Winchester**

2c +Timothy Guy; *b* 26 Jan 1944; *m* 1973 *Gillian Margaret, dau of Capt Thomas Preacher, 8th Bn DLI, and has:

   1d +Timothy Guy; *b* 1975

   2d +Michael Raoul; *b* 1976

1c *(Angela) Jane; *b* 15 Nov 1939; *m* 1972 *Christopher John Fisher

2b John Valentine; *b* 14 Feb 1909; *m* 5 March 1945 *Mira Elisabeth, only dau of Edmund Francis Smith, of Mossel Bay, CP, S Africa, and *d* 1970, having had:

   1c Michael John; *b* 19 Nov 1945; Br S Africa Police S Rhodesia; *m* 19 Aug 1967 *Gail Lisbeth, yr dau of John Blackwood Ward, of Bulawayo, and *d* 19–

   1c *Pamela Elizabeth; *b* 26 Sept 1947

1b *Violet Susan Mary [Miss Violet Paulet, Lydford Hall, Lydford-on-the-Fosse, Somerton, Somerset]; *b* 12 Jan 1903

(1) (cont.) Col Charles Paulet *m* 2nd 25 Sept 1890 Mary (*dsp* 19 Feb 1901), 2nd dau of Capt Mildmay Clerk, of Spratton, Northants, and *d* 8 April 1897

(2) Frederick John; *b* 7 Aug 1830; *d* 26 Sept 1846

(3) Cecil Henry; *b* 14 Oct 1841; 60th Rifles; *d* 1864

2 (cont.) The Rev Lord Charles Paulet *m* 2nd 10 Aug 1850 Joan Frederica Mathewana (*d* 10 Dec 1918), est dau of Bernard Granville, of Wellesbourne Hall, Warwicks, and *d* 23 July 1870, having by her had:

(4) Ernest Ingoldsby; *b* 22 Aug 1851; *d* 5 Feb 1853

(1) Adela; *b* 22 Feb 1854; *m* 5 June 1886 Frederick La Coque Thorne, MD, of The Manor Ho, Adderbury East, Banbury, and *d* 15 July 1893

(2) Eleanor Mary; *m* 1 June 1889 Lt-Gen Sir Edward Thomas Henry Hutton, KCB, KCMG, s of Edward Thomas Hutton, of Beverley, and *d* 27 March 1950. He *d* 4 Aug 1923

3 George, CB; *b* 12 Aug 1803; Adml, ADC to HM QUEEN VICTORIA, Offr Legn Hon, Kt Medjidie; *m* 11 July 1835 Georgina (*d* 17 Jan 1889), dau of Maj-Gen Sir George Wood, KCB, of Ottershaw Park, Surrey, and niece of Sir Mark Wood, 1st Bt, of Gatton (*see* 1837 edn), and *d* 22 Nov 1879, leaving:

(1) George; *b* 16 June 1836; 2nd Life Gds; *d unm* 12 Nov 1891

(2) St John Claude; *b* 30 April 1839; 5th Dragoon Gds; *d unm* 9 July 1908

4 William (Sir), GCB; *b* 7 July 1804; Col 1st Bn Durham LI Crimean War, FM, Offr Legn Hon, Kt Medjidie; *d unm* 9 May 1893

5 Frederick, CB; *b* 12 May 1810, Lt-Gen Coldstream Gds and 32nd Foot, Offr Legn Hon, Kt Medjidie, Comptroller Household and Equerry to HRH THE DUCHESS OF CAMBRIDGE; *d* 1 Jan 1871

1 Annabella; *m* 6 Aug 1827 R-Adml William Ramsden (*see* RAMSDEN, Bt) and *d* 26 May 1855

2 Cecilia; *m* Dec 1842 Sir Charles des Voeux, 2nd Bt (*see* 1940 edn), and *d* 23 Aug 1890, leaving issue. He *d* 28 Sept 1858

WINCHILSEA and NOTTINGHAM

NIL CONSCIRE SIBI

Arms: Quarterly, 1st and 4th, az. a chevron between three garbs or; 2nd and 3rd, arg. a chevron between three griffins passant, wings addorsed sa. **Crests:** 1 A griffin passant sergreant sa., 2 A pegasus courant arg., winged, maned and hoofed or, ducally gorged of the last. **Supporters:** Dexter, a pegasus arg., wings, mane and hoofs or, ducally gorged of the last; sinister, a griffin, wings addorsed sa., ducally gorged or. **Mottoes:** 1 *Nil conscire sibi* ('Conscious of no guilt'), 2 *Virtus tutissima cassis* ('Virtue is the safest protection').
Creations: Bt. (E) 29 June 1611 and 7 June 1660, V. (E) 8 July 1623, E. (E) 11 July 1628 and 12 May 1681, B. (E) 10 Jan 1673/4.

THE 16TH EARL OF WINCHILSEA and 11TH EARL OF NOTTINGHAM, Viscount of Maidstone, Co Kent, **Baron Finch of Daventry**, Co Northampton, and a **Baronet** (Sir Christopher Denys Stormont Finch Hatton, Bt) [The Rt Hon The Earl of Winchilsea and Nottingham, South Cadbury House, nr Yeovil, Somerset

BA22 7HA]; *b* 17 Nov 1936; *s f* 1950, also as hereditary Ld Roy Manor of Wye; *educ* Eton and Gordonstoun; *m* 23 June 1962 *Shirley, est dau of Bernard Hatfield, of Sutton Coldfield, Warwicks, and has:

   1 +DANIEL JAMES HATFIELD, *Viscount Maidstone*; *b* 7 Oct 1967

   1 *Alice Nan Christiane; *b* 2 May 1970

Nottingham, previous creations: Some early medieval references to Earls of Nottingham are on the whole to be considered as pertaining to such Earls of Derby (*qv*, preliminary remarks) as resided or were of origins in Nottingham. (A single shrievalty covered both Derbyshire and Nottinghamshire.) In the later Middle Ages the distinction was clearer and in 1377 and January 1385/6 specific Earldoms of Nottingham were conferred respectively on the 5th and 6th Lords (Barons) Mowbray (*see* MOWBRAY, SEGRAVE and STOURTON, B), the former having predeceased without issue the latter, his younger brother, so that the title had to be revived rather than passed on by inheritance.

On the death without male issue of the second grantee's great-grandson in January 1475/6 the Earldom once more expired. It was revived yet again, this time for Richard Duke of York, the younger of EDWARD IV's sons and one of the two Princes in the Tower, in the early summer of 1476 in anticipation of his marriage with Anne, the infant daughter of the last Earl of the January 1385/6 creation. His death, presumably by murder on the orders of RICHARD III, has been assigned to the first half of 1483, not least because in late June of that year Lord Berkeley (*qv*) was created Earl of Nottingham. If the Prince had still been alive the title would not have been vacant. The new Earl was promoted to a Marquessate some six years later but both titles expired on his death without surviving issue in 1492.

HENRY VIII in 1525 conferred an Earldom of Nottingham on his illegitimate son Henry FitzRoy as a subsidiary title to the Dukedom of Richmond and Somerset, the title by which the boy is better known, though he died childless aged only 17 in any case, so had little chance to play any very great role in English history. For the last pre-Finch-held Earldom of Nottingham, which had been extinct only just over two weeks before being revived in favour of HENEAGE FINCH, *see* EFFINGHAM, E.

Lineage: VINCENT HERBERD; *fl* 1292–1306; Burgess of Winchelsea and wine merchant; connected with (possibly as f-in-law, the change of name, whether due to marriage or otherwise, occurring by 1341):

HENRY FINCH; Mayor Winchelsea 1341; bought *c* 1345–50 the Manors of Netherfield and Icklesham, Sussex; had, with other issue, including a yr s (Sir Richard, of Orleston, Kent, *dsp*) and a dau (Joane; *m* Sir William Scott, of Scot's Hall, Kent, Sword Bearer to HENRY V):

WILLIAM FINCH, of Netherfield, Sussex; Sheriff Sussex and Surrey *c* 1430; *m* Agnes, dau of Walter Roo, of Dartford, and had, with an er s (John Herbert *alias* Finch, of Icklesham, *dsp* on or after 2 Dec 1457):

HENRY FINCH, of Netherfield; *m* Alice, only dau and heiress of Philip Belknap, of The Moat, nr Canterbury, and had:

Sir WILLIAM FINCH; granted lands formerly held by the Austinian monastery nr Canterbury; *m* 1st Elizabeth, widow of Sir Richard Lovelace, of Bethersden, Kent, and dau of Sir James Crowmer, of Tunstal; *m* 2nd Catherine, dau of Sir John Gaynsford, of Crowhurst, Surrey, and by her had issue, as also by his 1st w, with two other sons (including Lawrence, *m* Mary, dau and helress of Christopher Kemp, and *dsp*):

Sir THOMAS FINCH; ktd 1553, Kt Marshal Newhaven, then besieged by the French; *m* 1547 Catherine (*d* 9 Feb 1586/7), er dau and coiheir of Sir Thomas Moyle, of Eastwell, Kent, Chllr Ct Augmentations, and *d* in the wreck of the *Greyhound* 19 March 1562/3 off Rye while crossing to France, leaving, with other issue:

1 MOYLE (Sir), **1st Bt**

2 Henry (Sir), Serjeant-at-law; *m* Ursula, dau of John Thwaites, and *d* 11 Oct 1625, leaving:

   (1) JOHN FINCH, 1st BARON FINCH OF FORDWICH, Co Kent (E), so *cr 7 April 1640*; *b* 17 Sept 1584; *educ* Gray's Inn (Bencher 1617, Autumn Reader 1618); barrister 1611, Recorder Canterbury 1617–20, MP Canterbury 1620–22 and 1625–26 and Winchelsea 1624–25, ktd 1625, KC and Attorney Gen to QUEEN HENRIETTA MARIA 1626, Speaker H of C 1628–29, Ch Justice Common Pleas 1634–40, High Steward Cambridge 1640, Ld Keeper Gt Seal 1640–41; *m* 1st his cousin Eleanor, dau of Sir George Wyatt (*see* below); *m* 2nd by 14 March 1644/5 Mabel, dau of Very Rev Charles Fotherby, Dean Canterbury, and *dspm* 20 Nov 1660, when the Barony expired, leaving:

      1a A dau; *m* Sir George Radcliffe, of Ireland

   1 Jane; *m* Sir George Wyatt, of Boxley, Kent, and had at least one dau:

      (1) Eleanor; *m* as his 1st w her cousin 1st and last BARON FINCH OF FORDWICH

Sir THOMAS *d* Feb 1563; his est s,

Sir Moyle Finch, 1st Bt (E), so *cr* 29 June 1611, of Eastwell; *b c* 1550/1; *educ* Gray's Inn; MP Weymouth 1575–83, Kent 1593 and Winchelsea 1601, ktd 1584, Dep or Under Treas at Wars and Col of a foot regt 1588–89 during the period of threat of invasion by the Armada, Sheriff Kent 1596–97 and 1606–07; *m* by 1573 Elizabeth, **Countess of Winchilsea** (E) in her own right (*b* 9 July 1556; *d* 23 March 1633/4), so *cr* 11 July 1628, as also earlier 8 July 1623 VISCOUNTESS OF MAIDSTONE, with remainder in both cases to the heirs male of her body, dau and heiress of Sir Thomas Heneage, PC, of Copt Hall, Essex, V-Chamberlain to ELIZABETH I and Chllr Duchy Lancaster, by his 1st w Anne, 3rd dau of Sir Michael/Nicholas Poyntz, of Iron Acton, Glos, and *d* 18 Dec 1614, leaving, with other issue:

   1 **Sir Theophilus Finch, 2nd Bt**; *b* 2 Oct 1573; *educ* Magdalen Coll Oxford (BA); served Ireland, where ktd 1599, MP Gt Yarmouth 1614; *m* 16 July 1596 Agnes (*bur* 16 Feb 1620/1), dau of Sir Christopher Heydon, of Baconsthorpe, Norfolk, and *dsp vm c* 1619

   2 Heneage; *b* 25 Sept 1576; *d* young

   3 **Sir Thomas Finch, 3rd Bt**, and **2nd Earl of Winchilsea**, as which s mother; *b* 13 June 1578; *educ* Trin Coll Cambridge; ktd Jan 1608/9, MP Winchelsea 1621–22 and Kent 1628–29; *m* 1609 Cicely (*d* 1642), sis of Sir John Wentworth, 1st Bt (*see* LYTTON, E, section **Lineage (of Wentworth)**), and *d* 4 Nov 1639, having had, with an er s (*d* young):

(1) **Sir Heneage Finch, 4th Bt**, and **3rd Earl of Winchilsea**; b 1627–28; educ Queens' Coll Cambridge, Govr Dover 1660, ktd May 1660, cr 26 June 1660 BARON FITZHERBERT OF EASTWELL, Co Kent (E), Ld Lt Kent 1660–62, Jan 1672/3–87 and 1689 (also Somerset 1675–83) and Jt Ld Lt 1668–72, Levant Co rep Constantinople 1660–69 (effectively E Amb), V-Adml Kent Jan 1672/3–87; m 1st 21 May 1645 Diana (dsps), dau of 5th Baron Willoughby of Parham (see WILLOUGHBY DE ERESBY, B); m 2nd by 1649 Mary, dau of 2nd Duke of Somerset (qv), and by her had, with 10 other children:

1a William, *Viscount Maidstone*; bapt 20 Jan 1651/2; educ Westminster and St John's Coll Cambridge; m by 26 Dec 1666, perhaps as early as 1665, Elizabeth, dau of Thomas Windham, of Felbrigg Hall, Norfolk, and dvp in the sea Battle of Sole Bay 28 May 1672 during the Third Dutch War, leaving:

1b **Sir Charles Finch, 5th Bt**, and **4th Earl of Winchilsea**, PC (1711); b 26 Sept 1672; Lt-Govr Dover Castle, Dep Warden Cinque Ports and V-Adml Kent 1702–05, Envoy Extrdy Hanover Sept 1702–March 1702/3, Ld Lt Kent 1704–05, Fist Ld Trade 1711–12; m 26/28 Sept 1692 Sarah, dau of Henry Nourse, of Woodlands, Wilts, and dsps 14 Aug 1712, having had:

1c Charles, *Viscount Maidstone*; b Aug 1703; dvp an infant 1705

2a **Sir Heneage Finch, 6th Bt**, and **5th Earl of Winchilsea**; b 3 Jan 1656/7; Capt Coldstream Gds 1682, Lt-Col 1687, Groom Bedchamber to JAMES II 1683–88, DCL Oxon 1683, MP Hythe 1685–87; resigned commission 1689 and attempted to leave the country for France but was apprehended, only to be set free on bail, FSA Jan 1723/4; nonjuror, hence never took seat in Ho Lds; m c 14 May 1684 Anne (d 5 Aug 1720), minor poetess (Pope's 'Ardelia', her best-known work being 'The Spleen', dau of Sir William Kingsmill, of Sydmonton, Hants, and dsp 30 Sept 1726

(1) (cont.) The **3rd Earl** m 3rd 10 April 1673 Catherine (dspm late summer 1678), formerly w of (a) Christopher Lister, of Thornton, Yorks, and (b) Sir John Wentworth, of Elmshall, Yorks, and dau of Sir Thomas Norcliff, of Langton, Yorks; m 4th c 29 Oct 1681 Elizabeth (d 10 April 1745), only dau and heiress of John Ayres, of London, and d 28 Aug 1689, leaving by her:

3a **Sir John Heneage, 7th Bt**, and **6th Earl of Winchilsea**; b 24 Feb 1682/3; educ Ch Ch Oxford; d unm 9 Sept 1729, when the Barony of FitzHerbert of Eastwell expired

3 Heneage (Sir); Serjeant-at-law, Recorder City London, Speaker H of C; m 1st Frances, dau of Sir Edmund Bell, of Beaupre Hall, Norfolk, and had issue; m 2nd Elizabeth, widow of Richard Bennet (see TANKERVILLE, E) and dau of William Cradock, of Staffs, and d 5 Dec 1631, leaving issue by her and by his 1st w:

(1) **Sir Heneage Finch, 1st Bt** (E), so cr 7 June 1660, and **1st Earl of Nottingham**, so cr 12 May 1681, as also earlier 10 Jan 1673/4 BARON FINCH OF DAVENTRY, Co Northampton (all E), of Raunston (i.e., Ravenstone), Bucks, PC (1673, S 1674 and 1676); b 23 Dec 1621; educ Westminster and Ch Ch Oxford; barrister Inner Temple Jan 1644/5 (Treas 1661–72), Slr-Gen 1660, ktd June 1660, MP (Tory) Canterbury 1660 and Oxford U 1661–73, Attorney-Gen 1670–73, Ld Keeper Gt Seal 1673–75, Ld Chllr 1675–82, Speaker Ho Lds Jan 1673/4; m 30 July 1646 Elizabeth, dau of Daniel Harvey, a Folkestone grocer and Turkey merchant based in London, and d 18 Dec 1682, having had, with other issue:

1a **Sir Daniel Finch, 2nd Bt**, and **2nd Earl of Nottingham**, as both of which s f, and **8th Bt** and **7th Earl of Winchilsea**, as both of which s 2nd cousin 1729, PC (Feb 1679/80–March 1695/6), 1702–07 and 1714–Jan 1729/30); b 2 July 1647; educ Westminster, Inner Temple and Ch Ch Oxford; MP Gt Bedwyn 1673–79 and Lichfield 1679–81, a Ld Admlty 1679–84 and 1st Ld 1680–84, Sec State for South March 1688/9–93 and 1702–04, Ld res Cncl 1714–Feb 1715/6; m 1st 16 June 1674 Lady Essex Rich, 3rd dau and coheir of 3rd Earl of Warwick of the 1618 cr (see WARWICK, BROOKE and, E, preliminary remarks), and had, with seven other children:

1 Mary; m 1st 2nd Marquess of Halifax; m 2nd 1 Jan 1707/8 1st Duke of Roxburghe (qv)

1a (cont.) The **2nd/7th Earl** m 2nd 29 Dec 1685 Anne Hatton (d 26 Sept 1743), only dau (and in her issue sole heiress) of 1st Viscount Hatton of Gretton (Isee DE CLIFFORD, B), and d 1 Jan 1729/30, having by her had with, seven other children:

1b DANIEL FINCH, **8th Earl of Winchilsea** and **3rd Earl of Nottingham**, KG (1752), PC (1725); b 24 May 1689; educ Westminster and Ch Ch Oxford; MP (Whig) Rutland 1710–30, a Ld Bedchamber to PRINCE OF WALES later GEORGE II 1714–16, a Ld Treasury 1715–16, Comptroller Household 1725–30, 1st Ld Admlty March 1741/2–44 and Apriil-June 1757, Er Bro Trin Ho 1743, Ld Pres Cncl 1765–66; m 1st 1720 Frances (bur 3 Oct 1734), dau of 4th Earl of Denbigh and (3rd Earl of) Desmond (qv), and had:

1c Charlotte; d unm

1b (cont.) The **8th/3rd Earl** m 2nd 18 Jan 1737/8 Mary (d 8 Aug 1757), dau and coheir of Sir Thomas Palmer, 4th Bt, of Wingham, Kent (see 1838 edn), and dspm 2 Aug 1769, having by her had, with other issue:

2c Heneage; m 22 Aug 1788 Sir George Osborn, 4th Bt (qv), and dsp 4 May 1918

2b William, PC; MP, Envoy Extrdy Sweden 1724, V-Chamberlain Household 1742–65; m 1st 23 Jan 1733 Anne (dsp), dau of 4th Marquess of Queensberry (qv); m 2nd 9 Aug 1746 Charlotte (d 11 July 1813), 2nd dau of 1st Earl of Pomfret (see HESKETH, B), and d 25 Dec 1766, having had, with other issue:

1c GEORGE FINCH, **9th Earl of Winchilsea** and **4th Earl of Nottingham**, KG (1805), PC (1804); b 4 Nov 1752; educ Eton and Ch Ch Oxford; Maj 87th Foot 1779, Lt-Col 1780, served War American Independence, a Ld Bedchamber 1777–1812, Ld Lt Rutland 1779–1826, Pres Roy Inst 1799–1813; noted cricketer: fndr MCC, sponsored the acquisition by one Thomas Lord of a cricket ground in Marylebone, hence the name 'Lord's'; dspl unm 2 Aug 1826, leaving by a Mrs Thomson:

1d George FINCH; b 2 Sept 1794; inherited his f's Burley-on-the-Hill estate; had issue, with whom it remained into the second half of the 20th century

3b John; d 1763, leaving:

1c Elizabeth; m John Mason, of Greenwich

4b Henry; d unm

5b Edward FINCH later FINCH-HATTON (on inheriting 5 Oct 1764 the Hatton estate of Kirby Hall, Northants, and other property), also of Eastwell Park, which he inherited 1769; MP Cambridge U, diplomat, Groom Bedchamber, Master Robes; m 6 Sept 1746 his er bro's sis-in-law Elizabeth, 3rd dau and coheir of Sir Thomas Palmer, 4th Bt, of Wingham, Kent, and d 16 May 1771, leaving, with other issue:

1c George, of Eastwell Park and Kirby Hall; b 1747; m 10 Dec 1785 Elizabeth Mary (d 1 June 1825), est dau of 2nd Earl of Mansfield (qv), and d 17 Feb 1823, leaving, with other issue:

1d GEORGE WILLIAM, **10th/5th Earl**

2d Daniel Heneage (Rev); b 1795; Rector Gt Weldon Northants, Chaplain to HM QUEEN VICTORIA; m 15 Dec 1825 Louisa (d 11 April 1883), 2nd dau of Louisa, Countess of Mansfield (qv) in her own right by her 2nd husb Hon Robert Fulke Greville (see WARWICK, BROOKE and, E), and d Jan 1866, leaving, with two other daus (d unm):

1e Edward Hatton; b 21 Oct 1826; d 6 April 1887

2e William Robert (Rev); b 12 Dec 1827; Rector Gt Weldon; m 4 Aug 1852 Agnes Graham (d 18 April 1916), 2nd dau of Rev Montagu Oxenden and sis of Sir Percy Dixwell-Oxenden, 10th Bt (see 1924 edn), and d 24 Jan 1909, having had, with two other daus (d unm):

1f Greville Oxenden; b 14 May 1853; dsp 15 Feb 1896

2f George Daniel; b 8 April 1856; d 23 Oct 1921

3f William David FINCH later FINCH-BESLEY (roy licence 1893) later still FINCH again; b 27 Nov 1857; m 1st 18 July 1893 Frances Caroline (dsp 26 May 1901), widow of E H Wood and dau of W H Besley, of Dunmore, Devon; m 2nd 21 July 1902 Violet Louisa (d 23 Dec 1944), dau of Maj-Gen A H Utterson, CB, of Sidbrook, Somerset, and d 13 Dec 1914

4f Nigel Montagu; b 15 June 1859; d 22 June 1937

5f Daniel Heneage Edward; b 3 May 1866; d 26 Feb 1807

6f Edward Heneage, CMG, DSO; b 4 Jan 1868; Boer War 1899–1902 (despatches), Hon Brig-Gen 1st Bn The Buffs (E Kent Regt), T/Brig-Gen and Bde Cdr 1916 WW I (wounded, despatches), Mil Kt Windsor 1931; m 25 Jan 1912 Dagmar Gladys (d 1975), est dau of Col Francis George Archibald Wiehe, 68th Durham LI, and d 22 May 1940, leaving:

1g *Ann Zephine [Mary Maurice Newnham, Briar Cottage, Duck Lane, Liss, Hants]; b 12 Dec 1912; m 17 Dec 1943 *G/Capt Maurice Ashdown Newnham, OBE, DFC, RAFVR, and has:

1h *Nicola Ann; b 17 April 1946

2g *Essex Dagmar; b 4 Dec 1916

1f Ethel Beatrice; m 17 Oct 1888 Brig-Gen Sir Charles Vere Gunning, 7th Bt (qv), and d 24 Feb 1958, leaving issue

2f Elizabeth Anne; m 17 April 1901 Lt-Col Davidson Bruce Stewart, DSO, RFA, and d 16 June 1905

1e Isabella; m 26 Nov 1868 Sir Percy Dixwell Nowell Dixwell-Oxenden, 10th and last Bt (d 12 July 1924), and d 25 June 1927, leaving issue

1d Louisa Anne; m 30 April 1807 Gen Hon Charles Hope and d 1 March 1875, leaving issue (see LINLITHGOW, M)

2c John Emilius Daniel Edward; b 19 May 1755; barrister, Bencher Inner Temple; d 10 Jan 1841

1c Harriet Frances Charlotte; m 1781 Sir Jenison William Gordon, Bt, KCB, and d 1821

2b Essex; m 20 July 1703 Sir Roger Mostyn, 3rd Bt (qv), and d 23 May 1721, leaving issue

3b Charlotte; m 4 Feb 1725/6 6th Duke of Somerset (qv) and d 21 Jan 1773, leaving issue

4b Mary; m 22 Sept 1716 1st Marquess of Rockingham and d 30 May 1761, leaving issue

5b Henrietta; m 22 Jan 1731/2 3rd and last Duke of Cleveland of the 1670 cr (see JERSEY, E) and dsp 14 April 1742

6b Elizabeth; m 20 Sept 1738 1st Earl of Mansfield (qv) and d 10 April 1784

2a HENEAGE FINCH, cr EARL OF AYLESFORD (qv)

1a Elizabeth; m as his 1st w Sir Samuel Grimston, 3rd and last Bt (see VERULAM, E)

4 Francis, barrister

The 9th EARL's cousin,

GEORGE WILLIAM FINCH-HATTON, **10th Earl of Winchilsea** and **5th Earl of Nottingham**; b 19 May 1791; educ Westminster and Christ's Coll Cambridge; m 1st 26 July 1814 Georgiana Charlotte (d 13 Feb 1835), est dau of 3rd Duke of Montrose (qv), and had:

1 GEORGE JAMES FINCH-HATTON, **11th Earl of Winchilsea** and **6th Earl of Nottingham**; b 31 May 1815; educ Eton and Ch Ch Oxford; MP (C) N Northants 1837–41, published several books of poetry; m 1st 6 Aug 1846 Constance Henrietta (d 5 March 1878), dau of 2nd Marquess of Anglesey (qv); m 2nd 16 Feb 1882 Elizabeth Georgiana (d 2 Feb 1904), widow of George Leopold Bryan, of Jenkinstown, Co Kilkenny, and dau of 2nd Marquess Conyngham (qv), and dspms 9 June 1887, leaving by his 1st w:

(1) George William Heneage, *Viscount Maidstone*; b 26 Dec 1852; RA; m 28 Dec 1876 Louisa Augusta (m 2nd 22 Dec 1917 Lt-Col Francis James Ashburner (d 10 Jan 1934), 2nd Dragoon Gds, and d 21 Dec 1932), yst dau of Sir George Jenkinson, 11th Bt (qv), and dsp & vp 3 Feb 1879

(1) Constance Eleanora Caroline; m 3 June 1871 Hon Frederick Charles Howard (see EFFINGHAM, E) and d 15 April 1910, leaving issue

(2) Mabel Emily; m 6 July 1872 4th Baron Auckland (qv) and dsp 6 Nov 1872

(3) Hilda Jane Sophia; m 23 April 1877 Henry Vincent Higgins, CVO, 1st Life Gds, s of Matthew James Higgins by Emily Blanche, yst dau of Sir Henry

Tichborne, 8th Bt (*see* 1967 edn DOUGHTY-TICHBORNE, Bt), and *d* 8 Feb 1893, leaving issue

1 Caroline; *m* 2 Feb 1837 Christopher Turnor, JP, DL (*d* 7 March 1886), of Stoke Rochford and Panton Ho, Lincs, and *d* 13 March 1888 aged 71, leaving issue

The **10th/5th Earl** *m* 2nd 15 Feb 1837 Emily Georgiana (*dsp* 10 July 1848), 2nd dau of Rt Hon Sir Charles Bagot, GCB (*see* BAGOT, B); *m* 3rd 17 Oct 1849 Fanny Margaretta (*d* 26 April 1909), est dau of Edward Royds Rice, MP, of Dane Ct, Kent, and *d* 8 Jan 1858, leaving by her:

2 MURRAY EDWARD GORDON FINCH-HATTON, **12th Earl of Winchilsea** and **7th Earl of Nottingham**, DL Lincs; *b* 28 March 1851; *educ* Eton and Balliol Coll Oxford (Fell Hertford Coll); Sheriff Lincs 1879, MP (C) S Lincs 1884–85 and Spalding 1885–87, KJStJ; *m* 27 Oct 1875 Edith (*d* 6 Jan 1944), only dau of Edward William Harcourt (*see* VERNON, B), and *d* 7 Sept 1898, having had:

(1) George Edward Henry Murray, *Viscount Maidstone*; *b* 3 Sept 1882; *dvp* 6 March 1892

(1) Muriel Evelyn Vernon, CBE; *b* 19 Aug 1876; DGStJ, Cdr Latvian Order Three Stars, Order Lithuanian Grand Duke Gediminas and Estonian, Russian Red Cross and Czechoslovak Order White Lion 5th Cl; *m* 31 May 1897 Sir Richard Arthur Surtees Paget, 2nd Bt, of Cranmore (*qv*), and *d* 16 June 1938, leaving issue

3 HENRY STORMONT, **13th/8th Earl**

4 Harold Heneage; *b* 23 Aug 1856; MP Newark 1895–98, High Sheriff Merioneths 1903; *d* unm 16 May 1904

2 Evelyn Georgiana; *m* 28 Feb 1883 4th Viscount Templetown (*see* 1970 edn) and *d* 15 Jan 1932, leaving issue

The 12th/7th EARL's bro,

HENRY STORMONT FINCH-HATTON, **13th Earl of Winchilsea** and **8th Earl of Nottingham**; *b* 3 Nov 1852; *educ* Eton and Balliol Coll Oxford; Qld cattle-farmer and gold prospector; *m* 12 Jan 1882 Annie Jane (*d* 20 June 1924), dau of Adml of the Fleet Sir Henry John Codrington, KCB (*see* CODRINGTON, Bt, of Dodington (1876)), and had:

1 GUY MONTAGUE GEORGE, **14th/9th Earl**

2 Denys George, MC; *b* 24 April 1887; BA Oxon; T/Capt E African Protectorate Forces and ADC WW I (despatches); *k* flying in E Africa 14 May 1931

1 Gladys Margaret; *b* 8 Dec 1882; *m* 5 Feb 1912 Capt Osmond Trahairn Deudraeth Williams, DSO, Welsh Gds (*see* WILLIAMS, Bt, of Castell Deudraeth), and *d* 30 May 1964, leaving issue

The 13th/8th EARL *d* 14 Aug 1927; his er s,

GUY MONTAGU GEORGE FINCH-HATTON, **14th Earl of Winchilsea** and **9th Earl of Nottingham**, OBE (1919), DSC; *b* 28 May 1885; *educ* Eton and Magdalen Coll Oxford; Lt Roy E Kent Yeo 1908, Lt-Cdr RNVR and Lt-Col RAF WW I (despatches), memb London stock exchange; *m* 8 June 1910 Margaretta Armstrong (*d* 22 Dec 1952), only surv dau of Anthony Joseph Drexel, of Philadelphia, and had:

1 CHRISTOPHER GUY HENEAGE, **15th/10th Earl**

1 *Daphne Margarita; *b* 1913; *m* 17 July 1935 A/Cdre Whitney Willard Straight, CBE, MC, DFC, RAuxAF (*d* 1979), and has:

(1) *Camilla Caroline; *b* 1937; *m* 22 June 1960 *Maj Michael Ian Vansittart Bowater and has issue (*see* BOWATER, Bt, of Friston)

(2) *Amanda Betsy; *b* 1952

2 (Henrietta) Diana Juanita; *m* 26 April 1938 Peter Frank Tiarks, MC (*d* 17 April 1975), s of Frank Tiarks, of Loxton Lodge, Axbridge, Somerset, and *d* 7 March 1977, leaving issue

The 14th/9th EARL *d* 10 Feb 1939; his est s,

CHRISTOPHER GUY HENEAGE FINCH-HATTON, **15th Earl of Winchilsea** and **10th Earl of Nottingham**; *b* 2 Aug 1911; *educ* Eton; Lt RNVR WW II; *m* 1st 11 June 1935 (*divorce* 1946) Countess Gladys Szechenyi, 3rd dau of Count Laszlo Szechenyi, Hungarian Min UK; *m* 2nd 17 June 1946 Agnes Mary (*d* 22 June 1964), dau of Patrick Joseph Conroy, JP, of Malvern Ho, Wigan, Lancs, and *d* 7 March 1950, leaving by his 1st w:

1 CHRISTOPHER DENYS STORMONT FINCH-HATTON, **16th and present Earl of Winchilsea and 11th and present Earl of Nottingham**

2 +Robin Heneage [The Hon Robin Finch-Hatton, Town House Farm House, Clemsfold, W Sussex RH12 3PP]; *b* 1 Nov 1939; *educ* Gordonstoun; *m* 7 Sept 1962 *Molly Iona, yr dau of Col Palgrave Dawson Turner Powell, MBE, TD, of Damson Hill Cottage, Swanmore, Hants, and has had:

(1) +Christopher Benjamyn; *b* 17 July 1966

(2) +Rupert Stormont; *b* 14 May 1968

(1) Nicola Jane; *b* 21 June 1964; *d* 24 July 1967

(2) *Louisa Henrietta Mari (Mariska); *b* 14 Feb 1971

WINDLESHAM

Arms: Gu. a boar passant ppr., on a chief or a trefoil slipped vert between two roses of the field, barbed and seeded, also ppr.
Crest: In front of a dexter arm embowed in armour, the hand grasping a battle-axe, a trefoil slipped and a red rose, stalked and saltirewise, all ppr. **Supporters:** On either side an officer of the Irish Brigade in the service of the King of France in the 18th century ppr., the dexter supporting with the exterior hand a gold mounted and tasselled staff ppr. **Motto:** *Vi vivo et armis* ('I live by force and arms').
Creations: Bt. (UK) 24 Jan 1927, B. (UK) 22 Feb 1937.

THE **3RD BARON WINDLESHAM**, of Windlesham, Co Surrey, and a **Baronet** (Sir David James George Hennessy, Bt, PC (1973), CVO (1981)) [The Rt Hon The Lord Windlesham PC CVO, House of Lords, London SW1A 0PW]; *b* 28 Jan 1932; *s* f 1962; *educ* Ampleforth and Trin Coll (Hon Fell 1982) Oxford (MA 1958, DLitt 1995, Visiting Fell All Souls 1986, Pncpl BNC 1989–); memb Westminster City Cncl 1958–62, V-Pres: Fedn U C and U Assocs 1959–60 and 1962–63 and Br Cancer Cncl, Chm Bow Gp 1959–60 and 1962–63, md Grampian TV 1967–70, Min State Home Office 1970–72 and NI 1972–73, Ld Privy Seal and Leader Ho Lds 1973–74, ATV: jt md 1974–75, md 1975–81, chm 1981–, dir: *The Observer* 1981–89 and W H Smith Gp 1986–95, chm Parole Bd 1982–88, Pres Victim Support 1992–, Tstee: Charities Aid Fndn 1977–81, Br Museum 1981–96 (Chm 1986–96), The Roy Collection 1993–; Govr and memb Cncl Management Ditchley Fndn 1983– (V-Chm 1987–); author: *Communication and Political Power* (1966), *Politics in Practice* (1975), *Broadcasting in a Free Society* (1980), *Responses to Crime*, vols I–III (1987, 1993, 1996); *m* 22 May 1965 Prudence Loveday (*d* 1986), fashion ed *The Times* (1966–81), yr dau of Lt-Col Rupert Trevor Wallace Glynn, MC, of Harlesford Ho, Tetsworth, Oxon, and has:

1 +JAMES RUPERT; *b* 9 Nov 1968; *educ* Eton and Bristol U

1 *Victoria Jane; *b* 17 July 1966; *educ* London U (BA)

Lineage: JAMES HENNESSY, of Ballymacmoy, Co Cork; *m* Helen Nagle and had, with a dau (Barbara, *m* 1739 Edmund Roche; *see* FERMOY, B):

GEORGE HENNESSY, of Ballymacmoy; *m* Mary O'Phelan, of Co Tipperary, and had:

1 JAMES

2 Charles, of Brussels, and Ostend; *m* Margaret O'Murphy and had:

(1) James; *m* Ellen Barrett (*m* 2nd 1763 Richard Hennessy, of Cognac (*see* below), and *dsp*

(2) Patrick Michael; *m* — Danout, of Brussels, and had:

1a Patrick, of Brussels

1 A dau; *m* Henry Goold (*see* GOOLD, Bt)

The er s,

JAMES HENNESSY, of Ballymacmoy; *m* 1758 Catherine Barrett (*d* 1770), descended from Sir William Barrett, of Castlemore Barrett, Co Cork, and had:

1 George, of Ballymacmoy; *m* his cousin Anastasia, dau of John Comerford, of Cork, and had:

(1) John, of Ballymacmoy; *b* 1761; *m* Margaret, dau of Philip Barry, of Burton, and had issue

(2) Christopher; *m* Mary, only dau of — Seton, of Santa Cruz, and *dsp* W Indies

(3) James; *d* at sea 1782

(1) Bridget; *b* 1760; *m* 1780 Patrick Lawson, of Banff, Capt of the *Lord Holland*, E Indiaman, aboard which her bro *d*, and had issue

(2) Catherine; *b* 1764; *m* Samuel Flanrey, of London, and had issue

2 RICHARD

3 James, of Cork; *m* Ellen, dau of Athanasius Nagle, of Ballyegan, Co Cork, and had:

(1) George, of Cork; *m* 1794 — Stackpole and had:

1a James; *d* young

1a Mary; nun

2a Georgina; *m* John Coxon, of Flesk Priory, Co Kerry

(2) Athanasius; *b* 1761; Col HEICS, Town Maj Fort William, ADC to Govr-Gen India; *d* unm 1830

(1) Eleanor; *d* unm 1831

1 Mary; *m* 1746 John Shea, Cork merchant

2 Bridget; *m* MacWalter Burke, of Curraghnabouly, Co Tipperary

3 Anne; *d* unm

4 Elizabeth; *m* John Comerford, of Cork

JAMES HENNESSY's 2nd s,

RICHARD HENNESSY; *b* Ballymacoy 1720; Offr Dillon's Regt in French Serv (fought Battle of Fontenoy 1745), fndr at Cognac, France, 1765 Hennessy brandy firm *m* 1763 his cousin Ellen, widow of James Hennessy, of Brussels (*see below*), and dau of James Barrett by Margaret, sis of Garret Nagle, of Monanymy and Ballyduff, Co Cork, and aunt of the political philosopher Edmund Burke, and *d* 1800, leaving, with a dau (Bridget, *b* 1767, *d* France):

JAMES/JACQUES HENNESSY, of Cognac; *b* Ostend 11 Oct 1765; memb Charente Chamber Deps till his death; *cr* a Peer of France though an Irishman and never naturalised; *m* Martha, dau of Frédéric Gabriel Martell, of Cognac, Dep for Libourne, and *d* 22 April 1843, having had:

1 James, of La Billarderie, Cognac; *b* 1795; *m* Sophia, dau of Joseph Alexandre Jacques Durant, Comte de Mareuil, French Amb Naples, and *d* 1845, leaving:

(1) Maurice; *b* 1834; *m* Jeanne Foussat (*d* 1896) and *d* 1905, having had:

1a James Richard, of La Billarderie; *b* 1867; Dep Cognac 1906, Senator Charente 1920–45; *m* 1893 his cousin Alice (*d* 1901), dau of Richard Hennessy (*see below*), and *d* 1945, having had:

1b Raymond; *b* 1895; Lt French Navy; *das* 1916

2b Maurice; *b* 1896; *m* 1923 Viviane, dau of Comte du Pontavice, and had:

1c James; *b* 1923, *m* 1949 *Lucie, dau of Olivier Flornoy, and *d* 1990, leaving:

1d *Maurice; *b* 1950

2d *Frédéric; *b* 1953

1d *Anne; *b* 1952; *m* *Etienne de Soyres and has:

1e *Axelle

2d *Isabelle; *b* 1958

2c Raymond; *b* 1926; *m* *Jeanne-Marie, dau of André Terrasson, Baron de Senevas, and *d* 26 Sept 1965, leaving:

1d *Jacques; *b* 11 May 1957

2d *Philippe, *b* 1 Dec 1958

3d *François, *b* 11 July 1961

1c *Irène [Comtesse Armand, 3 rue Louis Bailly, 75 Paris 16eme, France]; *m* 1954 *Comte Charles Antoine Armand and has:

1d *Patrick

2d *Nicolas

1d *Caroline

2c *Marie-Alice

3c *Evelyne

1b Irène; *b* 1894; *m* Baron Armand d'Etchegoyen

2b Madeleine (twin); *b* 1894; *m* Comte Guy de Pracomtal and had issue

3b Isabelle; *b* 1898; *m* 1919 Jean, Marquis de Geoffre de Chabrignac, and had issue

2a Jean Patrick, of Château de St Brice; *b* 1873; Amb of France, Dep for Barbezieux, Charente, 1910; *m* 1901 Marguerite, dau of Comte de Mun, memb Academie Française and a Dep, and *d* 1944, leaving:

1b Patrick; *b* 1902; *m* Geneviève Bouchayer and had:

1c Eric; *b* 1945

1c Catherine; *b* 1943

2b *Kilian; *b* 1907; *m* 1st Gunnel Skogstedt and has:

1c *Moira; *b* 1937; *m* 1957 Charles René, Duc de Mortemart

2b (cont.) Kilian Hennessy *m* 2nd 1948 (*divorce*) Peggy, formerly w of John de Laszlo and dau of Sir Richard Robert Cruise, GCVO, FRCS, LRCP; *m* 3rd *Sylvia de Castilleja and by his 2nd w has:

1c *Gilles; *b* 1949

2c *Gerald; *b* 1951

1b Jacqueline; *b* 1904; *m* 1923 Prince Jean de Caraman Chimay (*d* 29 April 1968)

1a Marguerite; *b* 1868; *m* 1889 Comte Bruno de Boisgelin (*d* 1933) and *d* 1892, leaving issue

2a Jacqueline; *b* 1870; *d* unm 1886

(1) Sophia; *m* Baron Jard Panvillier and had issue

(2) Alice; *m* 1855 Charles Edmond, Vicomte Ruinart de Brimont, and had issue

2 AUGUSTE RICHARD

3 Frederick, of Cognac; *b* 1807; *m* 1842 Julia, dau of Frederick Perkins, of Chipstead Park, Kent, and *d* 1878, leaving:

(1) Armand; *b* 1845; *dsp* 1899

(2) Robert; *b* 1846; *dsp* Jan 1908

(3) Gerard; *b* 1859; *dsp* 1880

(1) Martha Lucy; *b* 1854; *m* 1st 1872 her cousin Richard Hennessy, of Bagnolet (*see below*), and had issue; *m* 2nd 4 Sept 1888 Lord James Edward Sholto Douglas (*see* QUEENSBERRY, M) and *d* 31 Jan 1941

4 George; twin with Ernest; *d* young

5 Ernest; twin; *d* young

6 Patrick; *d* young

1 Lucy; *b* 1808; *m* Jean Gabriel Martell, of Cognac, Dep Charente, and *dsp* 1843

JAMES HENNESSY's 2nd s,

AUGUSTE RICHARD HENNESSY, of Cognac; *b* 1800; Col Nat Gd, Pres Chamber Commerce, Dep Charente 1845–65, Senator 1876–79, Chev Legn Hon; *m* 1832 Irène, dau of Jean-Baptiste César, Baron d'Anthes, of Burgundy, and *d* 1879, having had, with two yr sons (Jacques François, *b* 1841, *dsp* 1929; Raymond, *b*

1842, *dsp* 1884) and two daus (Marguerite, *b* 1834, *m* 1854 Auguste-Charles Denys, Comte de Danremont, French Amb Russia, and *d* 1887, leaving issue; Henriette, *b* 1844, *d* unm 1864):

RICHARD HENNESSY, of Bagnolet, Cognace; *b* 1835; Vol Regt Horse Gds Franco-Prussian War and Siege of Paris 1870; *m* 1872 his cousin Martha Lucy (*d* 31 Jan 1941), dau of Frederick Hennessy (*see above*), and *d* 24 March 1886, leaving:

1 Richard; *b* 1876; *educ* Wellington; Gordon Highrs, joined 3rd Bn Gordon Highrs 1897, Capt 2nd Bn Boer War 1899–1902 (wounded, two medals, six clasps), Capt 8th Bn 1914, BEF 1915–19, WW I (despatches, Croix de Guerre avec palme Belgium); *m* 29 July 1902 Ethel Frederica (*d* 27 Oct 1930), dau of Charles Selmes, of Playden, Sussex, and *d* 28 Aug 1953, leaving:

(1) Francis Richard Blennerhasset; *b* 26 July 1907; *educ* Eton

(2) Robert Angus Martin, MVO (1963), DSC; *b* 26 Sept 1914; *educ* RNC Dartmouth; Cdr RN WW II (despatches); *m* 19 July 1941 *Valerie Marion, er dau of Capt Vaughan Adrian Philip Stokes, 10th Hus, of St Botolphs, Pembs, and *d* 19–, leaving:

1a *Caroline Bridget; *b* 4 April 1942; *m* 16 Dec 1969 *Carlos Perez de Jauregui, of Madrid, only s of Carlos Perez de Jauregui, of Asturias, and has:

1b *A son; *b* 23 June 1971

(1) Aileen Frederika; *b* 15 April 1903

(2) Sheilah Irene Alice; *b* 19 June 1905; *d* unm 23 June 1984

2 GEORGE RICHARD, **1st Baron**

1 Henriette-Lucie Frédérique; *b* 1873; *m* 1st 1892 Comte Gabriel-Louis Venantille Bailly de la Falaise (*d* 1910), s of the Marquis de la Falaise de la Coudraye, and had issue; *m* 2nd 1912 Comte Antoine Hocquart de Turtot (*d* 1954) and *d* 1965, leaving further issue

2 Alice; *b* 1874; *m* 1893 her cousin James Richard Hennessy and *d* 1901, leaving issue

3 Lucy; *b* 1880; *m* 1901 René Formey de St Louvent and *d* 1908, leaving issue

RICHARD HENNESSY's 2nd s,

Sir George Richard James Hennessy, 1st Bt, and **1st Baron Windlesham**, of Windlesham, Co Surrey (both UK), so *cr* 24 Jan 1927 and 22 Feb 1937 respectively, OBE (1919), JP Hants; *b* 23 March 1877; *educ* Eton; Maj 3rd Bn Cheshire Regt Boer War (medal and three clasps), MP (U) Winchester 1910–31, High Sheriff Hants 1910–11, T/Maj 9th (Serv) Bn KRRC 1914–17 and Gen List, ADC to GOC 8th Div 1917–19 WW I (despatches twice), PPS to Min Labour 1921–22, Jr Ld Treasury 1922–Jan 1924 and Nov 1924–25, V-Chamberlain Household 1925–27, Treas Household 1928–29 and Sept–Nov 1931, Civil Commr Liverpool and NW England Gen Strike May 1926, V-Chm C Party Organisation 1931–41, raised and cmded Farnham Co HG WW II, Army Welfare Offr N Aldershot Dist 1940–45; *m* 14 Dec 1898 Ethel Mary (*d* 10 July 1951), dau of Charles Reginald Wynter, and had:

1 JAMES BRYAN GEORGE, **2nd Baron**

2 Frederick Francis George, MBE (1945); *b* 10 Oct 1906; *educ* Eton and Magdalene Coll Cambridge; Maj Gren Gds WW II; *m* 23 July 1932 Merritt Jean (*d* 21 May 1976), yst dau of Alfred Allen Longsdon, and *d* 16 May 1969, leaving:

(1) +Peter Grant Auguste [Peter Hennessy Esq, Cradle House Farm, Wigginton, Oxon]; *b* 10 Aug 1944; *educ* Eton; *m* 25 July 1968 *Sally Ann Royden, yr dau of Dr Clarence Laverne Johnson (*see* ROYDEN, Bt), and has:

1a +James George; *b* 27 Nov 1970

2a +Benedict John; *b* 18 Feb 1978

1a *Katherine Ann; *b* 5 Nov 1973

2a *Sophie Elizabeth; *b* 1981

(1) *Maunagh Jean [Mrs Timothy Koch de Gooreynd, Blacksmiths Cottage, Idbury, Oxon OX7 6RU]; *b* 10 Aug 1933; *m* 17 Sept 1953 Timothy William Jacques Leopold Koch de Gooreynd (*d* 1987; *see* QUEENSBERRY, M) and has:

1a *Peter Frederick Leopold; *b* 31 Aug 1958; *m* 1990 *Carolynn Antonia N, yr dau of Ambrose Parker, and has:

1b *Timothy Luke Ladislas; *b* 14 March 1995

2b *Anthony; *b* 1 Jan 1998

1b *Tamara Manuela; *b* 1992

2a *Alexander Francis William; *b* 21 Oct 1969

1a *Stella Antoinette Jeanne; *b* 20 Aug 1954; *m* 1976 *Kenneth Mannering and has:

1b *William; *b* 1977

2b *Maximilian Timothy George; *b* 1 March 1997

1b *Olivia; *b* 1981

2b *Alexia; *b* 1983

3b *Miranda; *b* 1986

2a *Manuela Enriqueta Maria; *b* 18 Aug 1957

3a *Annabel Maria Therese; *b* 10 Nov 1963; *m* 1990 *Christopher Alexander and has:

1b *Joseph Timothy Lloyd; *b* 24 July 1994

(2) *Susan Jane [Mrs Charles Morley-Fletcher, 16 Paradise Walk, London SW3 4JL]; *b* 14 May 1938; *m* 25 July 1963 Charles Edward Morley-Fletcher (*d* 19–), only s of Edward Morley-Fletcher, TD, of Richmond, Surrey, and has:

1a *Michael Francis; *b* 1964; *m* 1991 *Elisabeth Anne, er dau of David Quintin Gurney (*see* BOUGHEY, Bt), and has:

1b *Oliver Charles; *b* 1994

2a *Patrick Edward; *b* 1966

3a *Frederick Maurice; *b* 1969

1a *Caroline Angela Elisabeth; *b* 1971

1 Dorothy Lucy; *m* 14 Oct 1924 (*divorce* 1949) Cdr William Frederick George North, RN (*see* 1970 edn NORTH, B), and *d* 15 Jan 1961, leaving issue

2 Violet Ethel Mary; *m* 29 April 1935 Capt Charles Elphinstone Fordyce, Seaforth Highrs, of Bracken Lodge, Church, Surrey, only s of Boston Elphinstone Fordyce, of Ashogee, and had:

(1) *John Stewart Elphinstone; *b* 13 Sept 1936; *educ* Ampleforth; *m* 13 Sept 1961 *Patricia Rose, er dau of A G Noyce, of Billericay, Essex, and has:

1a *Andrew John Elphinstone; *b* 20 Jan 1963

2a *Nicholas Charles; *b* 1 May 1965

3a *Dominic James; *b* 1 May 1967

(1) *Sheila Mary Rose; *b* 2 May 1939; *m* 1st 24 Nov 1960 (*divorce* 1971) Jeremy Charles Peel (*see* PEEL, E) and has issue; *m* 2nd Nov 1976 *Michael J Foster

3 *Noreen Madeleine Mary; *b* 1910; *m* 27 July 1931 (*divorce* 1948) Michael Bull (*d* 9 Oct 1962), 3rd s of William Perkins Bull, KC, of Toronto, and has:

(1) *(Michael) Matthew, MBE; *b* 25 Aug 1932; *educ* Ampleforth; late Maj Coldstream Gds; *m* 3 March 1962 *Jane, only dau of Harry Inglis, of Slough, and has:

1a *Richard Matthew Charles; *b* 1963

2a *Philip Henry; *b* 1969

1a *Emma Jane; *b* 1964

(2) *George Jeffrey (Sir) [Sir George Bull, The Old Vicarage, Arkesden, Essex CB11 4HB]; *b* 16 July 1936; *educ* Ampleforth; ktd 1998, chm: Grand Met 1996–98 (ch exec 1993–96), J Sainsbury plc 1998–; *m* 7 Jan 1960 *Fleur-Thérèse (Tessa), only dau of Patrick Freeland, of Zimbabwe, and has:

1a *George Sebastian Matthew; *b* 8 Oct 1960

2a *Rupert Frederick Alain; *b* 12 May 1963

3a *Justin Bartholomew Peter; *b* 4 Sept 1964

4a *Cassian Michael Thomas; *b* 7 March 1967

1a *Tasmin Emily Mary; *b* 1972

4 *Kathleen Irene Mary [The Hon Mrs Barnett, The Stables, The Grange, Benenden, Kent TN17 4DN]; *b* 1914; *m* 22 Nov 1947 Wilfred Ernest Barnett (*d* 1992) and has:

(1) *Robin George [Robin Barnett Esq, Ponds House, Hurst Green, E Sussex]; *b* 31 May 1951; *educ* Worth Abbey Sch; *m* 1973 *Carolyn Seward, est dau of Ronald E Plummer, of Wadhurst, Sussex, and has:

1e *Max Robin Nicholas; *b* 1983

1a *Annabel Penelope; *b* 1978

2a *Julia Seward; *b* 1980

3a *Stephanie Lucinda; *b* 1987

(2) *Nicholas James [Nicholas Barnett Esq, 27 Mysore Rd, London SW11 5RY]; *b* 11 Jan 1955; *educ* Worth Abbey Sch; *m* 1998 *Margaret Katherine, dau of Colin Morrison, of Benenden

The 1st BARON *d* 8 Oct 1953; his er s,

JAMES BRYAN GEORGE HENNESSY, **2nd Baron Windlesham**; *b* 4 Aug 1903; *educ* Eton and RMC Sandhurst; Brig Gren Gds WW II (Croix de Guerre, Cdr Order George I Greece, Order Leopold II Belgium); *m* 1st 6 June 1929 Angela Mary (*d* 13 March 1956), 2nd dau of Julian Duggan, of Buenos Aires and S Kensington; *m* 2nd 25 March 1957 Pamela Joan (*m* 3rd 9 Dec 1966 William Marsden Elverston-Trickett), formerly w of Dermot A Dinan and yr dau of Francis Kennedy, and *d* 16 Nov 1962, leaving by his 1st w:

1 DAVID JAMES GEORGE HENNESSY, **3rd and present Baron Windlesham**

1 *Marie Louise [The Hon Lady de Zulueta, Flat 5, 7 Princes Gate, London SW7 1QL]; *b* 9 March 1930; *m* 14 Sept 1955 Sir Philip Francis de Zulueta (*d* 1989), only s of Prof Francis de Zulueta, of Chelsea, and has:

(1) *Francis Philip Harold [Francis de Zulueta Esq, 39 Lyford Rd, London SW18 3LU]; *b* 10 Feb 1959; *m* 1st 1981 Miranda Jane, dau of Philip Alexander Howden, of Worminghall, Bucks; *m* 2nd 1987 *Pandora, formerly w of Hon Edward Abdy Wodehouse (*see* KIMBERLEY, E) and est dau of Mrs W J Germing, of Mortlake, and by her has:

1a *Sebastian Philip William; *b* 1990

1a *Gala Marie-Louise Philomena; *b* 1988

(1) *Louise Angela Mary; *b* 27 Oct 1956; *m* 1982 *Mark Donald Seligman and has:

1a *Jocelyn David; *b* 1983

1a *Lucinda Marie Joanne; *b* 1985

2a *Iona Louise; *b* 1990

2 *Rosalie Ann [The Hon Mrs Elwes, 75 Murray Rd, London SW19 4PF]; *b* 18 Feb 1934; *m* 7 May 1960 *Peter John Gervase Elwes, est s of Simon Edmund Vincent Paul Elwes, RA, Lt-Col 10th Hus, of The Old Place, Amberley, Sussex, and has:

(1) *Luke Andrew Cary; *b* 26 July 1961; *m* 1987 *Anneke Lucille, only dau of Hans du Moulin, of Farnham, Surrey, and has:

1a *Jake Peter; *b* 1993

2a *Toby Robert; *b* 1996

(2) *Benedict James; *b* 4 May 1963; *m* 1991 *Georgina Claire, only dau of Michael Rapinet, of Northend, Henley-on-Thames, Oxon, and has:

1a *Jasper Simon; *b* 1996

2a *Samuel Joseph; *b* 1997

(3) *Marcus David; *b* 27 Nov 1964; *m* 1995 *Sandra, dau of John Gray, and has:

1a *Thomas William; *b* 1998

(1) *Harriet Clare, *b* 3 Dec 1968

3 *Annabel Jane [The Hon Mrs Chisholm, The Manor Ho, Stratton-on-the-Fosse, Bath BA3 4QU]; *b* 20 Dec 1937; *m* 4 May 1963 *Dr Ian Duncan Chisholm, MRCP, DPM, and has:

(1) *Rory Bryan Duncan; *b* 18 March 1964

(2) *Daniel Hugh; *b* 1 Aug 1966; *m* 1995 Juliette Elizabeth Chalmers Dow (*see* STAMP, B)

(3) *Alexander James; *b* 2 Jan 1968; *m* 1993 *Eliza, yr dau of Thomas Frank Dermot Pakenham (*see* LONGFORD, E), and has:

1a *Aidan Carus; *b* 29 July 1996

(4) *John Malcolm; *b* 7 July 1970

WINNINGTON

Arms: Quarterly, 1st and 4th, arg. an orle between eight martlets sa. (for WINNINGTON); 2nd and 3rd, sa. a saltire engrailed or (for SALWEY). **Crest:** A Saracen's head full-faced, couped at the shoulders ppr., wreathed about the temples arg. and sa. **Motto:** *Grata sume manu* ('Take with a grateful hand'). **Creation:** Bt. (GB) 15 Feb 1755.

SIR FRANCIS SALWEY WILLIAM WINNINGTON, 6TH BT, of Stanford Court, Co Worcester [Sir Francis Winnington Bt, Brockhill Court, Shelsey Beauchamp, Worcs WR6 6RH]; *b* 24 June 1907; *s* gf 1931; *educ* Eton; Lt Res Offrs Welsh Gds WW II 1939–40 (despatches, POW); *m* 22 April 1944 *Anne Beryl Jane, only dau of Capt Lawrence Robert Charles Drury-Lowe, Scots Gds, and has:

1 *Charmian Anne; *b* 4 March 1945

Lineage: FRANCIS WINNINGTON; royalist Col Civil War; had:

Sir FRANCIS WINNINGTON; *b* 1635; MP Worcester and Tewkesbury, Slr-Gen; *m* 1st Elizabeth Herbert and had:

1 Elizabeth; *m* 1676 Richard Dowdeswell, MP Busshley, Worcs

Sir FRANCIS *m* 2nd Elizabeth, sis and coheir of Edward Salwey, of Stanford, Worcs, and *d* 1 May 1700, leaving by her:

1 Salwey; *m* 1690 Anne, sis of 1st Baron Foley (*qv*) of Kidderminster of the Jan 1711/2 *cr* and *d* 6 Nov 1736, having had, with other issue:

(1) Francis; *d* Vienna 1718

(2) Thomas, PC; *b* 1696; MP Worcester, Paymaster-Gen; *m* 6 Aug 1719 Love, 4th dau and heiress of Sir James Reade, 2nd Bt (*qv*), of the March 1641/2 *cr*, and *dsps* 23 April 1746

2 Francis, of Broadway, Worcs; MP Droitwich 1747; *m* Anne, dau of Thomas Jackson, of London, and had, with other issue:

(1) Edward, of Broadway; *m* Sophia Boote (*d* 24 Feb 1770), of Wantage, and had:

1a EDWARD (Sir), **1st Bt**

3 John; *d* unm

4 Edward; MP Droitwich, barrister, Judge; *m* Anne Blome, neice and heiress of Henry Jeffereys, of Ham Castle, and *dsp*

2 Honora; *m* — Bruen, of Bruen Stapleford, Cheshire

3 Mary; *m* (licence 28 July 1689) Felix Calvert (*see* VERNEY, Bt, of Claydon House)

Sir FRANCIS's ggs,

Sir Edward Winnington, 1st Bt (GB), so *cr* 15 Feb 1755, of Standford Court, Worcs; *b c* 1728; MP Bewdley 1761–74; *m* 1749 Mary, dau of John Ingram, of Ticknell, and *d* 9 Dec 1791, leaving:

Sir Edward Winnington, 2nd Bt; *b* 14 Nov 1749; MP Droitwich 1777–1805; *m* 12 Sept 1776 Anne (*d* 9 Dec 1794), dau of 1st Baron Foley (*qv*) of Kidderminster, and had, with other issue:

1 THOMAS EDWARD (Sir), **3rd Bt**

2 Edward WINNINGTON later WINNINGTON-INGRAM (under terms of will of his relative on his paternal grandmother's side Mr Ingram, of Ribbesford, Worcs) (Rev); Canon Worcester, Rector Ribbesford; *m* 7 Aug 1810 Jane (*d* 10 Dec 1850), dau of Very Rev Arthur Onslow (*see* ONSLOW, E), and *d* 7 May 1851, leaving, with other issue:

(1) Francis Edward; Capt 6th Dragoons; *d* unm 31 July 1843

(2) Edward (Rev), of Ribbesford; *b* 17 Oct 1814; Rector Stanford-on-Teme; *m* 16 Dec 1847 Maria Louisa (*d* 11 Jan 1924 aged 96), dau of Rt Rev Henry Pepys (*see* COTTENHAM, E), and *d* 30 April 1891, leaving, with other issue:

1a Edward Henry (Ven); *b* 13 March 1849; *educ* Trin Coll Cambridge (MA); Rector Ribbesford 1876–93 and Ross-on-Wye Herefs 1893–1910, Vicar Bewdley 1891–93 and Bristow Herefs 1910–17, Preb 1898, Archdeacon Hereford 1910–23 and Canon Residentiary Hereford 1917–25; *m* 1st 24 July 1879 Elizabeth Ruscombe (*d* 9 Jan 1892), dau of John-Anstice, of Madeley Wood, Salop; *m* 2nd 2 June 1898 Harriet Anne (*dsp* 8 Feb 1912), dau of Rev Thomas Dehaney Bernard, Canon and Chllr Wells, of High Hall, Wimborne, Dorset, and *d* 27 April 1930, leaving by his 1st w:

1b Edward Francis (Rev); *b* 1 July 1883; *educ* Repton and Keble Coll Oxford (BA 1905, MA 1909); Assist Chaplain S Africa Rlwy Mission 1914–19, Vicar Ch Ch Notting Hill 1920–22, Tenbury 1922–24 and Cherbury 1924–33, Rector Holy Trinity Wistanstow Salop 1933–63, RD Stokesay, Preb Hereford 1947, CF 1941–63, Preb Emeritus 1959; *m* 5 Nov 1924 Gladys, dau of John Armstrong, of Tenbury Wells, and *d* 13 April 1963, leaving:

1c +(Edward) John [John Winnington-Ingram Esq, Old Manor Farm, Cottisford, Northants NN13 5SW]; *b* 20 April 1926; *educ* Shrewsbury and Keble Coll Oxford (BA 1949); Sub-Lt RNVR 1945–47; *m* 1st 12 Sept 1953 Shirley Yvonne, est dau of Gerald Lamotte, of Denham, Bucks; *m* 2nd 21 June 1973 *Mrs Elizabeth Linda Few Brown, dau of Geoffrey Milling, of Brading, IoW, and formerly w of Peter Few Brown, and by his 1st w has:

1d +Edward Nicholas; *b* 22 Feb 1957

2d +Gerald Francis; *b* 29 Jan 1960; *m* 1987 *Rebecca Susan, dau of Terence Cocks, of Geneva, Switzerland, and has:

1e *Lucy Margaret; *b* 1990

1c *Gladys Ann [Mrs Francis Bartlett, Eaton Cottage, Eaton Hill, Baslow, Derbys]; *b* 8 Aug 1929; *m* 19 Aug 1952 *Lt Cdr (E) Francis Nigel Oldfeld Bartlett, RN, er s of S/Ldr Charles Philip Oldfield Bartlett, DSC, of Cheltenham, and has:

1d *Charles Nicholas Oldfield; *b* 27 March 1954; *educ* Dauntseys

1d *Sarah Frances; *b* 4 July 1955

2d *Rachel Victoria; *b* 1 April 1957

3d *Joanne Elizabeth; *b* 16 Feb 1959

2b Arthur John (Ven); *b* 14 June 1888; *educ* Hereford Catherdral Sch and St John's Coll Oxford (BA 1911, MA 1914); Vicar Corsham Wilts 1916–21, Pncpl St Aidan's Theol Coll Ballarat Victoria 1921–28, Vicar Kimbolton Herefs 1929–36, Rector Ledbury Herefs 1936–45, RD Leominster 1934–36 and Ledbury 1937–42, Archdeacon Hereford 1942–59, Archdeacon Emeritus 1959, Canon Res Hereford 1945–61; *m* Aug 1938 Joan Mary, only dau of Rev Richard Arundell Lyne, of Pye's Nest, Ledbury, and *dsp* 1 June 1965

1b Constance Maud; V-Pres Cheltenham Ladies Coll; *d* unm 18 Feb 1972 aged 92

2b Ethel Mary; *educ* London U (BA); Pncpl Norwich Trg Coll to 1958

3b Laura Evelyn; *m* 21 Sept 1918 Maj Thomas Horatio Westmacott, OBE, VD (*d* 1951), Calcutta Light Horse, 2nd s of Edward Vesey Westmacott, ICS, and *d* 1968, leaving issue

2a Francis Herbert; *b* 8 June 1854; *m* 1880 Emily Jane (*d* 4 Feb 1926), dau of William Hankinson, of Grovesend, Ontario, and *d* July 1928, leaving:

1b Charles William Edward; *b* 1881; *m* 1902 Maud Esther, dau of Richard R Jones, of Copenhagen, Ontario, and *d* 1958, leaving:

1c +(Francis) Herbert; *b* 24 Oct 1906; *m* 16 Aug 1930 *Ruth Agnes, dau of Newton Newell, of Aylmer, Ontario, and has:

1d +Gerald Newell [Gerald Winnington-Ingram Esq, PO Box 464, 58 McMurray St, Bracebridge, ON, Canada]; *b* 10 June 1935; *m* 6 July 1957 *Lillian Tremblay and has:

1e +James Brian; *b* 1 Sept 1959

2e +Douglas Michael; *b* Aug 1964

1e *Phyllis Anne; *b* 28 Sept 1958

2e *Angela Marie; *b* 30 April 1969

2d +Charles Edward; *b* 11 June 1938; *m* 19– *Dorothy — and has:

1e +A son; *b* 19–

3d +Philip Herbert; *b* 29 June 1943; *m* 19– *Bea —

2c +Arthur Foley [Arthur Winnington-Ingram Esq, RR6, Aylmer, ON, Canada]; *b* 1 June 1908; *m* 6 July 1927 *Ruby Louisa, dau of Edward Herries, of Luton, Ontario, and has:

1d +Donald Foley [David Winnington-Ingram Esq, RR6, Aylmer, ON, Canada]; *b* 23 Aug 1935; *m* 1957 *Dawn Marlyn, dau of Rev Garnet Husser, of Aylmer, Ontario, and has:

1e *Cheryl Lyn; *b* 26 March 1962

1d (cont.) Mr and Mrs Donald Winnington-Ingram also adopted: *Allan Foley; *b* 19 Dec 1968

3c +(Charles) Alexander; *b* 16 Nov 1912; *m* 20 Sept 1939 Doris Marjorie Buck (*k* 30 Nov 1969) and has:

1d +Alexander Grant; *b* 8 Oct 1940; *m* 7 May 1966 *Carolyn Fuschia Johnston and has, with other issue:

1e *Sherri Lynn; *b* 30 Dec 1966

2d +David Gary; *b* 10 May 1943; *m* 16 Oct 1965 *Mary Ilene McClure and has:

1e +David; *b* 19–

1e *Deborah; *b* 19–

4c +Cecil Harold; *b* 30 Dec 1918; *m* 2 Aug 1947 *Patricia Howse Green and has:

1d +William Edward; *b* 1 Oct 1948

2d +Brian Charles *b* 10 March 1959

3d +Frank Barton; *b* 10 March 1959

1d *Beth Arlene; *b* 24 March 1952

2d *Beverley Irene; *b* 5 July 1953

5c +Gerald; *b* 9 May 1926; *m* 20 Sept 1947 *Edna Arletta Johnson and has:

1d *Judith Susanne; *b* 19 Feb 1949; *m* 19– *— Jones and has:

1e *Jennifer; *b* 19–

2d *Janet Marie; *b* 16 Sept 1951

1c *Vera Louise; *b* 31 Oct 1903; *m* Kenneth McGregor Hatch (*d* 19–) and has:

1d *Kenneth Herbert; *b* 3 May 1931; *m* 1953 *Pamela Diane House and has:

1e *Steven Kenneth; *b* 5 Aug 1955; *m* 19– *Kati Mary McClung and has:

1f *Kenneth Robert; *b* 1982

2f *Gregory; *b* 1984

2e *Peter Donald; *b* 18 May 1957; *m* 19– *Wendy Elizabeth Vaughan and has:

1f *Keven Donald; *b* 1989

3e *Thomas Alan; *b* 1966

1e *Nancy Laura; *b* 18 May 1957; *m* 19– *Stuart William Jackson and has:

1f *Jason Blair; *b* 1988

2e *Wendy Vivian; *b* 22 March 1962; *m* 1987 *Edward Evans Etchelles

1d *Donna Lucille; *b* 19 Sept 1928; *m* 1949 *Clayton Vickers McKechnie, of Hanover, Ontario, and has:

1e *Stewart Douglas; *b* 12 March 1952; *m* 1972 *Kathleen Haskey and has:

1f *Christopher Stewart; *b* 1974

2f *Erin; *b* 1979

2e *Dean Charles; *b* 5 March 1958

1e *Janice Louise; *b* 16 Sept 1953; *m* 1971 *Edward Adrian Vanherk and has:

1f *Pamela Jenifer; *b* 1971

2c Constance Maude; *b* 19 Jan 1905; *m* 15 July 1933 *Fergus Arnold Hatch and had:

1d *Robert Fergus; *b* 20 Jan 1945

1d *Carolyn Jane; *b* 22 Oct 1936; *m* 29 Sept 1956 *Roy Travis Billson and has:

1e *Douglas Frederick; *b* 8 Oct 1957

1e *Barbara Jane; *b* 22 July 1959

3c *Helen Patricia; *b* 1914; *m* 2 Sept 1938 James Arthur Ferris (*d* 1989) and has:

1d *Charles David; *b* 31 March 1942

2d *James Edward; *b* 13 May 1945; *m* 1968 *Maureen O'Keefe and has:

1e *Jennifer Rebecca; *b* 1970; *m* 19– *Richard Hartney, of Vancouver, and has:

1f *Kirk Russell; *b* 19–

2f *Kody James Ferris; *b* 19–

2e *Danielle Jacqueline; *b* 1973

1d *Heather Anne; *b* 13 Jan 1956; *m* 1980 *Rolf Larsen, of Sudbury, Ontario

4c *Marjorie; *b* 21 Feb 1920; *m* 7 Dec 1946 John M Hale and has:

1d *John Maitland; *b* 6 Oct 1947; *m* 19– *Johanna — and has:

1e *Jonathon; *b* 19–

1e *Jennifer; *b* 19–

1d *Barbara Lyn; *b* 1 Jan 1951; *m* 19– *Wayne Stafford and has:

1e *Adam; *b* 19–

2e *Jorden; *b* 19–

5c *Audrey Lucille [Mrs William Ozarko, 632 Lime Ridge Rd, RR3, Hamilton, ON, Canada]; *b* 12 June 1921; *m* 12 June 1948 *William Ozarko and has:

1d John Douglas; *b* 20 Sept 1950; *d* 19–

2d *William Edward; *b* 22 Dec 1955

1d *Catherine Lucille; *b* 10 Sept 1954

6c *Pauline; *b* 22 July 1928; *m* 28 Oct 1948 *Edward Golibashi and has:

1d *Paul Edward; *b* 20 May 1949

1d *Linda Marline; *b* 17 Dec 1950

2b Herbert Arthur; *b* 1882; *m* June 1912 Anna (*d* 24 Feb 1924), dau of Capt — Grant, of Edmonton, Alberta, and *d* 1941, leaving:

1c Herbert Grant; *b* 21 July 1914; *m* *Florence Beatrice Lea and *d* 16 Nov 1995, leaving:

1d +Donald Grant [Donald Winnington-Ingram Esq, 6092 Oakland Rd, Halifax, Nova Scotia B3H 1N8, Canada]; *b* 30 May 1947; *m* 1977 *Ethel Langille, of Pugwash, Nova Scotia, and has:

1e +Daniel Grant; *b* 1979

1e *Megan Elizabeth; *b* 1981

2e *Emily Hope (twin); *b* 1981

2d +Robert Craig; *b* 1 June 1952; *m* 1987 *Hélène Dobrowolsky, of Whitehorse, Yukon, and has:

1e *Joelle Xenia Aunalea; *b* 1988

1d *Lea Gordon; *b* 30 March 1946; *m* 1978 *Lovie Mohammed, of Toronto

2c Charles Gordon; *b* 12 Aug 1918; *m* 1st 1944 Marion Winkler (*d* 19–); *m* 2nd 19– *Joan Youngand [Mrs Charles Winnington-Ingram, 66 Glenhaven Cres, St Albert, AB T8N 1A5, Canada] and *d* 4 Dec 1990, leaving by his 1st w:

1d +Robert Gordon; *b* 16 Dec 1943; *m* 1st 19– (*divorce* 19–) Jane Bennett and has:

1e +Robert Paul; *b* 16 April 1966

1e *Jill; *b* 13 Jan 1969

1d (cont.) Robert Winnington-Ingram *m* 2nd 19– *Sharon Mills and by her has:

2e +Graham Gordon; *b* 1978

3e *Mathew James; *b* 1981

2e *Laura Sharon; *b* 1982

2d +James Hugh; *b* 14 June 1948; *m* 1968 (*divorce* 19–) Joan Smith

1d *Donna Marion [Mrs Gerrard Lemieux, 10217–132 St, Edmonton, Alberta T5N 1Y8, Canada]; *b* 14 July 1946; *m* 19– *Gerrard Lemieux and has:

1e *André Gerard; *b* 1971

1e *Alène Margaret; *b* 1973

2e *Collette Marie; *b* 1977

1c *Marion Elizabeth [Mrs William Duff, 14515 84th Ave, Edmonton, AB T5R 3X1, Canada]; *b* 12 Sept 1920; *m* 1945 *William Niven Duff and has:

  1d *William Neil; *b* 1948; *m* 1st 1969 (*divorce* 1971) Christine Judy Melmoth and has:

    1e *Shae Nancy Marion; *b* 1967; *m* 23 March 1991 *Robert Paul Watkins, of Greenwood, NS, and has:

      1f *Robert Michael Scott; *b* 1993

      2f *Daniel Thomas; *b* 1996

      1f *Chelsea Megan Elizabeth; *b* 1994

  1d (cont.) William Duff *m* 2nd 1973 Joanne Margaret Fedorow; *m* 3rd 19– *Marlene Anane Hyilker and by his 2nd w has:

    1e *William Michael Scott; *b* 1977

    2e *Brindy Veronica; *b* 1981

  2d *David Duff; *b* 1954; *m* 1976 *Elizabeth Maria, dau of John Van Lier, of Edmonton, and has:

    1e *Erin Nicole; *b* 1985

    2e *Rebecca Anne; *b* 1990

  1d *Nancy Marion; *b* 1947; *m* 1969 (*divorce* 1997) Derek David Nash and has:

    1e *Katharine Elizabeth; *b* 1976

    2e *Margaret Lindsey; *b* 1979

2c *Nancy Anna; *b* 14 Feb 1922; *m* 1947 *Raymond Benjamin Hager and has:

  1d *Richard Raymond; *b* 1949; *m* 1982 *Lesley Jane Etty, of Edmonton

  2d *Douglas Gordon; *b* 1951; *m* 19– Melanie Lissa Jahrig, of Ontario, and has:

    1e *Natalie Bree; *b* 1985

  3d *Donald Benjamin; *b* 1957; *m* 19– *Dolores Freda Patterson, of Alberta Beach, and has:

    1e *Jarret Benjamin; *b* 1986

    2e *Jamie Donald; *b* 1988

  1d *Laura Lillian; *b* 1954; *m* 1977 *Darryl Bruce Smith, of Edmonton, and has:

    1e *Joel Jeffrey; *b* 1982

    1e *Jess Cole; *b* 1981

3b Francis Harold; *b* 1885; *ka* 1915

4b John Gordon Gerald; *b* 1889; *m* 4 March 1922 Florence Byron (*d* 1985) and *d* 1945, leaving:

  1c *(Florence) Maxime; *b* 12 March 1923; *m* 5 May 1945 *Alexander Harold Clark and has:

    1d *David Gerald; *b* 7 Sept 1946; *m* 4 July 1970 *Linda Jeffery, of Devon, and has:

      1e *Scott Jeffery; *b* 7 June 1973

      1e *Cindi Jennifer; *b* 1975

    2d *Randall Gregory; *b* 17 April 1957; *m* 1988 *Debora Ann Degryse, of Winnipeg, and has:

      1e *Carly Anne; *b* 1992

    1d *Kathleen Laura; *b* 1 March 1948; *m* 13 June 1969 *Robert Kenneth Chalmers, of Winnipeg, and has:

      1e *Laura Susan; *b* 1970; *m* 1993 *Cornelius Vandertop and has:

        1f *Devonny Katherine; *b* 1994

      2e *Barbara Ruth; *b* 31 March 1973

  2c *Kathleen Hazel; *b* June 1931; *m* 1956 *Rev Gordon Samuel Jardine and has:

    1d *Edwin Jones; *b* 1961

    2d *Arthur John; *b* 1964

    1d *Bonnie Jean; *b* 1959; *m* 1984 *Hugh McLellan and has:

      1e *Stephen Patrick; *b* 1985

      1e *Kathleen Joan; *b* 1987

    2d *Donna Jean; *b* 1965

    3d *Naomi Kathleen; *b* 1972

5b Alfred Ernest (Rev); *b* 1891; Rector Midland, Ontario,1929–45, 2nd Lt RGA (SR); *m* 28 Aug 1926 Elizabeth Frances, dau of Edward William Roberts Hill, of Brantford, Ontario, and *dsp* 5 Aug 1945

1b Constance Evelyn; *b* 1884; *m* 1914 Edward Peyton Breay (*d* Oct 1918), s of Rev Christopher Breay, of Madras, and *d* 5 Sept 1952, leaving issue

2b Dora Blanche; *b* 1886; *m* 25 Dec 1912 Howard Dodds McClennan (*d* June 1955), s of Kenneth McClennan, of Grovesend, Ontario, and *d* April 1959, leaving issue

3b Ethel Grace; *b* 1888; *m* Aug 1926 Capt Harold Rigg Carradus and has issue

4b Frances Hazel; *b* 1893; *m* 1919 F Widmer Ball, of Toronto, and *d* 11 March 1930, leaving issue

3a Charles William; *b* 7 June 1856; R-Adml; *m* 6 Feb 1894 Ida Vere Maude (*d* 30 Jan 1945), yr dau of Charles Harcourt Chambers, and *d* 18 Jan 1923, leaving:

1b Charles Harcourt; *b* 23 July 1895; *d* 24 Jan 1913

2b Reginald Pepys; *b* 22 Jan 1904; *educ* Clifton and Trin Coll Cambridge (BA 1925, Fell 1928, MA 1929); Fell King's Coll London, Prof Classics Westfield Coll London U 1948–53, Prof Greek Language and Literature King's Coll London U 1953; FBA 1958, Hon DLitt Glasgow 1969; *m* 26 July 1938 Edith Mary, dau of Thomas Cousins

1b Ida Modwyn; *m* 19 July 1923 Rev Ambrose Douglas Adams, s of Samuel Allen Adams, JP, DL, of Northlands, Carrickmacross, and *d* 18 Sept 1926

2b Joyce Constance; *educ* St Hugh's Coll Oxford (MA 1950); *m* 30 Dec 1961 *Ven Ronald Percy Frank Plaistowe, Archdeacon Christchurch, NZ

4a Arthur Foley (Rt Rev), KCVO (1915), PC (1901); *b* 26 Jan 1858; *educ* Marlborough and Keble Coll Oxford (BA 1881, MA 1885, DD 1898); ordained 1884, Curate St Mary's Shrewsbury 1884–85, Chaplain to Bp Lichfield 1885–88, Head Oxford Ho Bethnal Green 1888–97, Chaplain to Archbp York 1891–97 and Bp St Albans 1890–97, RD Spitalfields and Rrector St Matthews Bethnal Green 1896–97, Canon St Paul's 1897–1901, Treas 1898–1901, Bp Stepney 1897 and London 1901–39, Chaplain TF 1909–22 (Hon Chaplain 1922) and RNVR 1904, Prelate Order Br Empire 1917–39, Chm C of E Temperance Soc, Dean Chapels Roy, Bp London, Hon LLD Toronto 1907 and Cantab 1908, Hon DD Durham 1913 and NWU USA 1926, Hon STD Columbia U 1928, Grand Cross Redeemer Greece 1918, Order St Sava Serbia 1st Cl 1919, author: *Work in Great Cities*, *Old Testament Difficulties*, *The Men Who Crucify Christ*, *The Potter and The Clay*, *Re-Building the Walls*, *The Sword of Goliath*; *d* unm 26 May 1946

5a George Frederick; *b* 29 Oct 1859; *m* 1901 Mary Beatrice (*d* 1957), dau of John Burridge, of Charminster, Bournemouth, and *d* March 1929, leaving:

1b Robin; *b* 19 June 1903; *m* 27 June 1942 *Hilda Edith, dau of John Diamond Jones, of Denmead, Hants, and *d* 4 Dec 1964

2b +John Felix; *b* 7 May 1909

1b Phyllis Mary; *b* 2 Dec 1906

6a Alfred (Rev); *b* 15 Sept 1861; *educ* Keble Coll Oxford (MA); Rector Enville, Staffs; *m* 11 July 1906 Julia Margaret (*d* 14 Oct 1958), est dau of William Augeraud, of Eastbourne, and *d* 20 Oct 1920, having had:

1b Arthur Francis; *b* 24 Sept 1907; WW II; *d* unm 7 June 1961

2b Charles Alfred; *b* 3 Feb 1909; Hon Lt E Africa Cmd WW II

3b Henry Edward (Rev); *b* 14 Sept 1911; *educ* Trin Coll Cambridge (BA 1934, MA 1937); Lt Worcs Regt, Vicar Awbridge, Rector Mottisfont Hants; *m* 15 Feb 1950 Florence Emily, dau of John Judd, of The Elms, Market Harborough

4b Cecil, MBE (1950); *b* 14 Dec 1914; *educ* Keble Coll Oxford (BA 1936); Colonial Admin Serv Tanganyika 1937–54, Nyasaland 1955–63, Administrator RSPB 1964–69, Dep Dir 1970; *m* 21 Dec 1954 *Maude Ethel May [Mrs Cecil Winnington-Ingram, 14 Main Rd, Biddenham, Beds MK40 4BB], yr dau of James Bartlett Lee, of Portsmouth, and *d* 1990, leaving:

  1c +Charles Pepys; *b* 6 Oct 1955

  2c +(Francis) Christopher; *b* 1 June 1957

5b +John Harold; *b* 14 Oct 1916

6b +Richard Sullivan [Maj Richard Winnington-Ingram, Supuko, 36 Barnton Ave, Edinburgh EH4 6JL]; *b* 16 Aug 1919; *educ* RMA Woolwich; Maj RE WW II (despatches), Assist Bursar Fettes; *m* 6 Sept 1952 *Isobel Margaret, only dau of Robin McCrae, of Nairobi, and has:

  1c +David Robert [The Rev David Winnington-Ingram, The Rectory, Offwell, Devon EX14 9SB]; *b* 24 April 1959; *m* 1990 *Carol Jarvis and has:

    1d +Jonathan Richard; *b* 1992

    2d +Christopher Edward; *b* 1995

  2c +Peter Richard [Peter Winnington-Ingram Esq, 4 Home Farm Cottages, Malshanger, Hants RG23 7ET]; *b* 16 Nov 1960; *m* 1989 *Mrs Sarah L J Addie, yst dau of Archie Weir, of Edinburgh, and has:

    1d +Archie; *b* 1993

    1d *Kitty Rose; *b* 1992

  1c *Julia Caroline [Mrs Peter Gregson, 15 Harling Bank, Kirkby Lonsdale, Lancs LA6 2DJ]; *b* 18 Nov 1954; *m* 1982 *Peter Derek Gregson, 2nd s of W D H Gregson, of Edinburgh, and has:

    1d *Heather Mary; *b* 1986

    2d *Sheila Rosalind; *b* 1988

  2c *Mary Cynthia [Mrs Edward Hundert, 8 Fuller Rd, Wellesley, MA 02181, USA]; *b* 6 April 1956; *m* 1985 *Dr Edward Mark Hundert, s of Irwin Hundert, of E Brunswick, NJ, and has:

    1d *Carol Grace; *b* 1991

1b Joan Constance; *b* 18 March; *d* 11 Aug 1910

7a Gerald Constantine; *b* 26 June 1869; *educ* New Coll Oxford (MA); ICS; *m* 1896 Ethel Hawthorne (*d* 13 April 1919), dau of Frederick Pollen, BCS, and *d* 11 May 1918, leaving:

1b Eric Alfred; *b* 4 Aug 1902; *educ* Keble Coll Oxford (BA. 1924); *m* 9 Aug 1930 Jean Emma Caroline (*d* 19 April 1998), yr dau of Frederick Gardnor Hopkins, of Christchurch, Hants, and *d* 1986, leaving:

  1c *Marianne Jean [Mrs Roderick MacBeath, The Pines, Deanland Rd, Balcombe, W Sussex]; *b* 6 Jan 1933; *m* 1968 *Roderick MacBeath

  2c *Iris Hawthorne [Mrs John Field, Yewtrees Farm, Balcombe, W Sussex]; *b* 25 May 1935; *m* 20 April 1964 *John Awberry Field, s of Charles Awberry Field, of Newick, Sussex, and has:

    1d *Fiona Clare; *b* 4 June 1967

    2d *Alison Joyce; *b* 18 April 1969

1b Enid Kathleen; *b* 6 Aug 1897; *educ* Cheltenham Ladies' Coll; *m* 26 April 1920 Christopher Francis Wood, ICS (*d* 7 July 1955), and *d* 12 May 1984, leaving:

  1c *Christopher Winnington; *b* 29 March 1926; *m* 15 Dec 1951; *educ* Gresham's and Christ's Coll Cambridge (MA) *Rhodope Margaret, dau of Rudolph Milner-White, ICS, and has:

    1d *John Chilion Gurney; *b* 21 Nov 1952

    2d *Peter Gerald Winnington; *b* 6 Aug 1954

    1d *Mary Halcyon Meredith; *b* 31 July 1965

  1c *Rosemary Anne Meredith; *b* 26 March 1921

2b *Madge Meredith; *b* 25 Oct 1909

1a Constance Jane; *m* 2 June 1877 George Walter Thomas Coventry and *d* 3 May 1907, having had issue (*see* COVENTRY, E)

2a Alice Mary; *d* unm 17 May 1949

(3) Thomas Onslow; *b* 16 March 1816; Lt-Col 97th Foot, Chev Legn Hon; *m* 8 April 1847 Jessie Maria (*d* 1891), dau of Lt-Col John Whitehill Parsons, CMG, and *d* 14 March 1858, leaving:

1a Edward John; *b* 30 Aug 1849; Maj Roy Warwicks Regt; *m* 3 June 1884 Jessie (*d* 10 June 1937), dau of Sir William Edmonstone, 4th Bt (*qv*), and *dsps* 5 Aug 1892

2a Thomas Frederick; *b* 13 July 1856; Cdr RN; *d* unm 8 May 1894

1a Jessie; *m* 3 Dec 1895 John Lennox Peareth (*d* 30 Dec 1932), of Lennox Castle, Campsie Glen, and *d* 8 Sept 1926, leaving issue

(4) Arthur Henry (Rev); JP; *b* 5 Oct 1818; Hon Canon Worcester, Rector Harvington, Worcs; *m* 25 Jan.1849 Sophia Mary (*d* Dec 1900), only dau of Lt-Col George Arnold, Bengal Cav, and *d* 6 March 1887, leaving, with other issue:

1a Arthur Rogers (Rev); *b* 2 Jan 1850; Rector Lassington, Glos; *m* 1st 24 Nov 1884 Rose Clare (*dsp* 1906), widow of J R S Knott, barrister; *m* 2nd 20 Jan 1910 Elizabeth (*d* 21 Oct 1960), dau of Henry Wheeler, of Bleak Ho, Churcham, Glos, and *d* 2 July 1928, leaving:

1b Sophia Elizabeth; *b* 30 May 1916; *m* 28 Oct 1944 *Charles Herbert Hammond and *d* 12 Feb 1969, leaving issue

(5) Herbert Frederick; *b* 12 Dec 1820; R-Adml; *m* 6 Sept 1856 Catherine (*d* 6 April 1910), dau of Charles Twining, of Halifax, Nova Scotia, and *d* 13 Sept 1889, leaving:

1a Herbert Edward; *b* 14 Nov 1869; *m* 7 Feb 1899 Agnes Maud (*d* 6 Sept 1956), 2nd dau of George Bevington Foster, and *d* 1958, leaving:

1b Winifred Florence; *b* 4 Dec 1899; *m* April 1923 Robert Charles Kennedy and *d* 24 Aug 1955

2b Marjorie Agnes; *b* 21 Feb 1901

1a Pauline Frances; *m* 10 June 1879 Charles Alexander Gallop (*d* 1890) and *d* 14 Nov 1923, leaving issue

2a Florence Herbert; *m* 3 April 1883 Thomas Hill (*d* 20 Dec 1920) and *d* 22 March 1946, leaving issue

3a Katherine Mary; *m* 1886 Henry Leslie Bates, LRCP, of St Albans, Herts, and *d* 18 July 1932, leaving issue

4a Annie Georgina; *m* 1897 Arthur George Loraine Gamlen (*d* 1954), slr, and *d* 23 Oct 1955, leaving issue

(1) Frances; *m* 27 Sept 1838 Henry Barry Domvile (*d* 4 Aug 1843), n of Sir Compton Domvile, 1st Bt, and had issue (*see* 1956 edn POË-DOMVILLE, Bt)

(2) Marianne Elizabeth; *m* May 1843 Rev John Ryle Wood, Canon Worcester, and *d* 1844, leaving issue

3 Francis (Rev); Rector Sapey, Herefs

4 Charles Fox (Rev); Rector Stanford; *m* 16 April 1819 Elizabeth (*d* Feb 1842), est dau of Robert Thornton Heysham, of Stagenhoe Park, Herts, and *dsp* June 1841

5 Henry Jeffries, JP; Capt 39th Foot, MP W Worcs 1833–41; *d* 25 Aug 1873

Sir EDWARD *d* 9 Jan 1805; his est s,

Sir Thomas Edward Winnington, 3rd Bt; *b* 1780; *m* 11 Nov 1810 Joanna (*d* 23 Dec 1853), dau of John Taylor, of Moseley Hall, Worcs, and had, with other issue:

1 THOMAS EDWARD (Sir), **4th Bt**

2 John Taylor; *b* 17 Jan 1814; Capt 3rd York Militia; *m* 27 Oct 1842 Emma (*m* 2nd Capt Henry Barre Phipps and *d* 6 Feb 1901), dau of Thomas Prothero, of Malpas Ct, and *d* 12 May 1844, leaving:

(1) John Taylor; *b* Aug 1843; Capt 1st Dragoons; *m* 29 April 1875 Rose (*m* 2nd 23 Sept 1880, as his 2nd w, Maj Herbert Winnington Domvile (*d* 6 Feb 1910) and *d* 14 Oct 1905), 2nd dau of Adml of the Fleet Sir George Rose Sartorius, GCB, and *d* 1877, leaving:

1a John Francis Sartorius, DSO; *b* 17 Sept 1876, Maj Boer War 1899–1900 (Queen's medal with four clasps), Brevet Lt-Col Worcs Regt, Assist Inspr Recruiting 1917, WW I (despatches); *m* 20 July 1910 Joyce Mary (*d* 25 Jan 1970), yst dau of David Marriage, of Wood Hall, Norton, Worcs, and *d* 22 Sept 1918 of wounds recd in action, leaving:

1b *Susanne [Mrs John Duerdin, Affcot Manor, Church Stretton, Salop SY15 6RL]; *b* 14 Dec 1913; *m* 1st April 1937 (*divorce* 19–) Russell Cowell (*d* 10 July 1964); *m* 2nd March 1950 *John Duerdin, s of John Duerdin, JP, of Little Haven, Cleator St Mary, Salop, and by him has:

1c *John Patrick; *b* 2 Aug 1952; *educ* Grenville Coll; *m* 1986 *Judy Mary Trow, of Little Stretton, and has:

1d *Emma Mary; *b* 1988

2d *Sophy Elizabeth

1c *Joanna Elizabeth; *b* 15 March 1950; educ Acton Reynald; *m* 1st 1978 (divorce 1992) R Wise; *m* 2nd 1996 *Andrew Crofts, OBE, chartered engr, and by her 1st husb has:

1d *George John; *b* 1988

1d *Suzanna Frances; *b* 1986

2c *Frances June; *b* 1 June 1951; educ Acton Reynald; *m* 1973 *Graham Bowcher and has:

1d *Sian Monique; *b* 1977

2d *Ceri Anne; *b* 1979

2b *Patricia Rose [Mrs Robin Unwin, Longdon Hall, Tewkesbury, Glos GL20 6AS]; *b* 16 Jan 1917; *m* 17 Sept 1949 Robin Darell Unwin, OBE (*d* 1991), s of Frederic Herbert Unwin, of Longdon Hall, and has:

1c *Carol John; *b* 30 Jan 1951; *educ* Grenville Coll

2c *Guy Darell; *b* 4 Nov 1952; *educ* Harrow; *m* 1984 *Patricia Ann, dau of Alan Derek Boydell, of Winchcombe, Glos, and has:

1d *William Francis; *b* 1988

1d *Sally Victoria; *b* 1986

2d *Elizabeth Laura Dorothea; *b* 1990

3c *Barry James; *b* 13 Jan 1956; *educ* Harrow; *m* 1984 *Susan Louise, dau of George Dennis Gilbert, of Redmarley, Glos, and has:

1d *Louise Rose; *b* 1987

2d *Rosanna Helen; *b* 1989

3d *Phoebe Grace; *b* 1994

Sir THOMAS *d* 24 Sept 1839; his est s,

Sir Thomas Edward Winnington, 4th Bt; *b* 11 Nov 1811; *educ* Ch Ch Oxford (BA); MP Bewdley 1837–47 and 1852–68, High Sheriff Worcs 1851; *m* 21 June 1842 Anna Helena, *d* 28 March 1883 aged 66), est dau of Sir Compton Domvile, 1st Bt (*see above*), and *d* 18 June 1872, having had, with other issue, including an er s (Thomas Edward, b Jan 1848, *dvp* unm April 1869) and a dau (Helena Caroline, *m* 8 Sept 1870 Hon Frederick Stephen Archibald Hanbury-Tracy and *d* 13 Sept 1916, leaving issue, *see* SUDELEY, B):

Sir Francis Salwey Winnington, 5th Bt, JP, DL Worcs; *b* 24 Sept 1849; High Sheriff 1894, 66th Foot; *m* 5 Feb 1879 Jane (*d* 20 June 1940), est dau of Lord Alfred Spencer-Churchill, 2nd s of 6th Duke of Marlborough (*qv*), and *d* 4 March 1931, having had:

1 Francis Salwey; *b* 4 May 1881; Lt Coldstream Gds; *m* 19 Oct 1904 Blanche Emma (*m* 2nd 18 May 1915 Douglas Giles Rooke, Coldstream Gds (*d* 2 Nov 1918), s of Col Harry William Rooke, of Haynford Hall, Norwich, and *d* 24 Jan 1968), dau of Cdr William John Casberd-Boteler, RN, of Eastry, Kent, and *d* 4 Feb 1913, leaving:

(1) Sir FRANCIS SALWEY WILLIAM WINNINGTON, **6th and present Bt**

(2) +THOMAS FOLEY CHURCHILL, MBE (1948) [Col Thomas Winnington MBE, 182 Rivermead Ct, Ranelagh Gdns, London SW6 3SG]; *b* 16 Aug 1910; heir presumptive; *educ* Eton and Balliol Coll Oxford; Col Gren Gds WW II; *m* 20 May 1944 *Lady Betty Marjorie Anson, er dau of 4th Earl of Lichfield (*qv*), and has:

1a +Anthony Edward [Anthony Winnington Esq, 20 Baskerville Rd, London SW18 3RW]; *b* 13 May 1948; *educ* Eton; *m* 5 Dec 1978 *Karyn, dau of Francis Hubbs Kettles and Mrs Alan Dayton, of Palm Beach, Fla., and has:

1b +Edward Alan; *b* 15 Nov 1987

1b *Victoria Elizabeth; *b* 1981

2b *Sophia Rose; *b* 1985

2a +Henry Thomas; *b* 19 Feb 1961

1a A dau; *b* and *d* 19 Jan 1947

2a *Sarah Rose, LVO (1996) [Viscountess Campden LVO, Exton Park, Oakham, Rutland LE15 8AN]; *b* 29 April 1951; *m* 23 May 1972 *Anthony Baptist, Viscount Campden, est s of 5th Earl of Gainsborough (*qv*), and has issue

3a *Emma Elizabeth; *b* 26 Feb 1956; *m* 1981 *Christopher J Milne and has:

1b *Rupert John; *b* 1986

1b *Isabella Katherine; *b* 1984

2b *Lucinda Alice; *b* 1991

2 Charles Alfred Edward; *b* 28 June 1882; *educ* Cheltenham; *m* 1st 1915 Mary Margaret (*d* 1928), dau of William O'Connor; *m* 2nd 5 Jan 1929 Charlotte Ida Frederica, MBE (1919) (*d* 28 June 1961), er dau of Adml of the Fleet Sir Gerard Henry Uctred Noel, GCB, KCMG (*see* GAINSBOROUGH, E), and *dsp* 19 Jan 1968

3 John Winston Foley; *b* 22 Aug 1883; *educ* Cheltenham; Lt Worcs Regt WW I; *m* 5 July 1910 Gladys Cooke and *d* 29 Aug 1961, leaving:

(1) Jessie Babette; *b* 16 March 1912; *m* 8 July 1933 Michael Thomond Wilson, MBE, est s of Sir Roy Wilson, of Pyrford, Surrey, and had:

1a *Michael John Francis Thomond; *b* 9 Sept 1934; *educ* Rugby and Oriel Coll Oxford (BA); slr 1961; *m* 4 May 1968 *Katharine Mary Rose, only child of Lt-Col Robert Macaulay Fanshawe, of the Vine Stanton, Broadway, Worcs, and has:

1b *James Robert Thomond; *b* 2 March 1970

2a *(Patrick) Simon; *b* 29 March 1937; *educ* Rugby

1a *Patricia Jane; *b* 29 March 1937; *m* 10 Dec 1966 Maj Charles Dalzell Craigie Halkett, RHF, s of Brig-Gen Hugh Marjoribanks Craigie Halkett, CMG, DSO, and has:

1b *Hugh Dalzell; *b* 28 Oct 1968

1 Frances Jane; *b* 13 Jan 1880; OStJ; *m* 2 Aug 1902 Capt Andrew Mansel Talbot Fletcher, DL (*d* 21 Feb 1950), 2nd Life Gds, of Saltoun, and *d* 25 June 1953, leaving issue

2 Iris Harriet Helena; *b* 8 Feb 1887; *m* 1st 27 April 1909 (*divorce* 1922) Lt Robert Reginald Fairfax Wade-Palmer, 3rd Reserve Regt Cav, est s of Fairfax Blomfield Wade-Palmer, JP, of Holme Pk, Berks; *m* 2nd 28 March 1925 Gerald Owen Weaver Joynson, 2nd s of Harold Mead Joynson, of Springfields, Banbury, Oxon, and *d* 12 May 1965

WINSTON

Creation: B. (LP, UK) 18 Nov 1995.

THE BARON WINSTON, of Hammersmith, London Borough of Hammersmith and Fulham (Robert Maurice Lipson Winston) [The Rt Hon The Lord Winston, 11 Denman Drive, London NW11 6RE]; *b* 15 July 1940; *educ* St Paul's and London Hosp Med Coll London U (MB, BS 1964); Registrar and Sr Registrar Hammersmith Hosp 1970–74 (Sr Lecturer 1978–81, Consultant Obstetrician and Gynaecologist 1978– also Roy Masonic Hosp 1988–), Reader 1982–86 and Prof 1987– Fertility Studies Roy Postgrad Medical Sch Inst of Obstetrics and Gynaecology London U, Visiting Prof U of Leuven Belgium 1976–77, Prof Gynaecological Studies U Texas San Antonio 1980–81, Clyman Visiting Prof Mt Sinai Hosp New York 1985, Pres Internat Fallopius Soc 1987–, V-Pres Progress 1992–, memb: (fndr) Br Fertility Soc 1975–, also Cncl RPMS 1992–, MRCS, LRCP 1964, FRCOG 1983 (MRCOG 1971), author: *Reversibility of Sterilization* (1978), *Tubal Infertility* (co-author, 1981), *Infertility, a Sympathetic Approach* (1987); *m* 1973 *Lira Helen Feigenbaum and has two sons and a dau

Lineage: LAURENCE WINSTON; *m* 1938, as her 1st husb, *Ruth, MBE (1996), JP (Middx 1954) [Mrs Ruth Winston-Fox MBE JP, 4 Morton Crescent, London N14 7AH], dau of Maj Rev Solomon Lipson, and *d* 1949, leaving, with another s and a dau:

ROBERT MAURICE LIPSPON, *cr* a **Baron**

WINTERTON

Arms: Ermines on a cross quarterly, pierced argent, four fers de moline sable. **Crest:** A lion passant guardant argent, holding in the dexter forepaw a fer de moline sable. **Supporters:** Two lions argent, semée of fers de moline sable. **Motto:** *Esse quam videri* ('To be, rather than seem'). **Creations:** B. (I) 10 April 1761, E. and V. (I) 12 Feb 1766.

THE 8TH EARL WINTERTON, Viscount Turnour and **Baron Winterton**, of Gort, Co Galway ((Donald) David Turnour) [The Rt Hon The Earl Winterton, 6672 Mockingbird Lanes, Mississauga, Ontario, Canada L5N 5K1]; *b* 13 Oct 1943, *s* uncle 1991; *educ* Waterloo Lutheran U Ontario (BA); *m* 1968 *Jill Pauline, dau of John George Esplen, of Bala, Ontario, and has:

1 *Michele Susan; *b* 25 April 1973
2 *Amy Elizabeth; *b* 28 March 1976

Lineage: EDWARD TURNOUR; *m* Anne, dau of James Morice, of Ongar, Essex, and had:

ARTHUR TURNOUR; *b c* 1588; Serjeant-at-law; *m* Anne, dau of John Jermy, of Gunton, Norfolk, and *d* 1 July 1651, leaving:

Sir EDWARD TURNOUR; Attorney-Gen to JAMES II when DUKE OF YORK, Speaker H of C, Slr-Gen, Prime Serjeant-at-Law, Ld Ch Baron Exchequer 1661–76; *m* 1st Sarah, dau of Alderman — Gore, of London; *m* 2nd Mary, dau and heiress of Henry Ewer, of S Mimms, Middx, and widow of William Ashton, of Tingrey, Beds, and *d* 1675, leaving by her no issue but by his 1st w, with a dau:

1 Eedward (Sir); MP; *m* Isabella, dau of 7th Earl Marischal (*see* KINTORE, E), and *d* 3 Dec 1721, having had surv issue:

(1) Charles, of Shillinglee Park, Sussex, and Little Parndon, Essex; *m* Dorothy, dau of William Fenwick, of Bywell, Northumberland, and *d* 1 Aug 1726, leaving two daus (*dsp*)

(1) SARAH Turnour; *m* Francis GEE and had an only surv dau:

1a SARAH Gee; *m* Joseph GARTH, of Shillinglee, which he acquired through his w, and *d* 22 Sept 1744, leaving:

1b EDWARD TURNOUR GARTH later GARTH-TURNOUR, **1st Earl Winterton**, so *cr* 12 Feb 1766, as also VISCOUNT TURNOUR OF GORT, Co Galway, and earlier 10 April 1761 BARON WINTERTON OF GORT, Co Galway (all I); *b* 1734; *educ* Trin Coll Oxford; MP Bramber 1761–69, FRS 1767; *m* 1st 13 March 1756 Hon Anne Archer (*d* 20 June 1775), dau of 1st Baron Archer of Umberslade, and had, with six other daus:

1c EDWARD, **2nd Earl**
2c Gerard; RN; *d* unm 21 June 1824
3c George; *b* 4 Feb 1768; *m* Emilie de Beaussett (*d* Aug 1846), n of Cardinal Duc de Beaussett, and *d* 1813, leaving two sons and three daus
4c Henry; *b* 1769; RN; *d* unm Sept 1805
5c Charles; *b* 1775; Lt 60th Regt; *d* 23 Feb 1816
1c Anne; *m* 1st George Gordon Brown; *m* 2nd F Remington, MD, and *d* 1824
2c Catherine; *m* 1778 William Bacon Foster and *d* 1778
1b (cont.) The **1st Earl** *m* 2nd 28 Feb 1778 Elizabeth (*m* 2nd 30 March 1791 William Richardson and *d* 1 Dec 1841), dau of John Armstrong, of Godalming, Surrey, and *d* 20 Aug 1788, leaving by her:

6c Edward John (Rev); *b* 8 Nov 1778; *m* 1st 16 Nov 1799 Elizabeth, dau of his step-f William Richardson, Accountant-Gen HEICS, and had surv issue (with two daus *d* unm):

1d Edward; *b* 4 May 1802; *m* April 1831 Elizabeth Maunsell, dau of William Crease, and *dsp* 7 July 1837
2d Arthur Edward George; *b* 26 Sept 1804; *dsp*
3d Francis Edward (Rev); *b* 26 Jan 1808; *d* unm 13 July 1869
4d Edmund Edward; *b* 3 Feb 1813; Cdr RN; *m* 18 June 1845 Helen (*d* 4 March 1886), yst dau of William Davies, of Little Strawberry Hill, London, and *d* 22 Dec 1874, leaving, with three other daus:

1e Elizabeth Frances Annette; *m* 5 Aug 1880 Capt Henry Henzell F Pidcock Henzell, 10th Regt (*d* 7 Aug 1931), est s of Henry Pidcock, of Oakfield, Worcs, and *d* 1892

6c (cont.) The Rev Edward Garth-Turnour *m* 2nd 21 May 1825 Rebecca (*d* 11 Aug 1887 aged 92), est dau and coheir of Rev David Jones, of Longhope, Glos, and *d* 10 May 1844, having by her had, with a dau (*d* unm):

5d Henry Edward; *b* 19 April 1826; MD; *m* 15 April 1857 Mary, est dau of Rev James Reece, and *dsp* 1 May 1885
6d Nicholas Edward Brooke; *b* 21 May 1827; Capt RN; *d* unm 10 July 1870
7d George Arthur Edward; *b* 18 March 1832; *d* unm 2 Feb 1871
1d Frances Helen; *m* 1 June 1861 her cousin Arthur Edward Turnour, MD (*d* 7 Aug 1894), and *d* 20 Dec 1867, leaving issue (*see* below)
3c Elizabeth; *m* 1798 Francis, s of William Richardson, and *d* 1818

2 Arthur; *d* 4 April 1724, leaving:

(1) Edward; inherited Shillinglee but *dsp* 1736 having willed it to his cousin Sarah, Mrs Joseph Garth (*see* above)

The 1st EARL's s,
EDWARD GARTH-TURNOUR later TURNOUR, **2nd Earl Winterton**; *b* 11 May 1758; *educ* Harrow and Trin Coll Oxford; *m* 1st 6 Nov 1781 Jane (*d* 1792), dau of Richard Chapman, of London; *m* 2nd 1795 Harriet, est dau of William Board, of Paxhill Park, Sussex, and widow of Rev John Bodicote, and *d* 23 April 1831, having by his 1st w had, with two other daus (*d* unm):

1 EDWARD TURNOUR, **3rd Earl Winterton**; *b* 13 June 1784; *m* 28 May 1809 Lucy Louisa (*d* 26 Oct 1846), dau of John Heys, of Upper Sunbury, and *d* 6 Jan 1833, leaving:

(1) EDWARD TURNOUR, **4th Earl Winterton**; *b* 18 May 1810; *m* 19 Jan 1832 Maria (*d* 25 June 1904), 3rd dau of Sir Peter Pole, 2nd Bt (*qv*), and *d* 1 March 1879, leaving, with five other daus (*d* unm):

1a EDWARD TURNOUR, **5th Earl Winterton**, TD, PC, JP, DL (Sussex); *b* 15 Aug 1837; *educ* Eton; Capt 6th Sussex Roy Vols; *m* 16 March 1882 Georgiana Susan (*d* 23 March 1913), 5th dau of 1st Duke of Abercorn (*qv*), and *d* 5 Sept 1907, leaving:

1b EDWARD TURNOUR, **6th Earl Winterton**, TD, PC (1924), JP, DL (Sussex); *b* 1 April 1883; *educ* Eton and New Coll Oxford; MP (C) Horsham 1904–18 and 1945–51 and Horsham and Worthing 1918–45, PPS to Fin Sec Admlty 1905, Parly U-Sec India 1922–24 and 1924–29, Chllr Duchy Lancaster 1937–39 with Cabinet seat 1938–39, additional memb Air Cncl March–May 1938, Assist to Home Sec 1938–39, Paymaster Gen Jan–Nov 1939, Maj TFR Sussex Yeo WW I Gallipoli and Imp Camel Corps Egyptian Expdny Force 1916–18, Hedjaz Ops 1918 (Orders Nile 4th Cl and El Nahda), memb Sussex TAA, Chm and Br Govt Rep Inter-Govtl Ctee for Refugees 1938–45, Br Delegate Burma Round Table Conf 1931 and Third India Round Table Conf 1932, *cr* 15 Feb 1952 BARON TURNOUR, of Shillinglee, Co Sussex (UK); *m* 28 Feb 1924 Hon (Cecilia) Monica Wilson (*d* 9 Nov 1974), only dau of 2nd Baron Nunburnholme (*qv*), and *dsp* 26 Aug 1962, when his UK barony expired

2a Keith TURNOUR later TURNOUR-FETHERSTONHAUGH (roy licence 1896), JP (Sussex); *b* 23 Feb 1848; Lt-Col KRRC, Red River Expdn 1870 (medal), Zulu Campaign 1879 (medal with clasp), Miranzai Expdn 1891 (despatches, medal with clasp), Hazara Expdn 1891 (clasp); *m* 23 Dec 1879 Caroline Chester (*d* 4 March 1920), 2nd dau of Strachan Bethune, KC, of Montreal, and *d* 16 Dec 1930, having had:

1b Henry Keith; *b* 23 June 1885; *d* 11 Feb 1892
1b Beatrice Winterton; *b* 31 Oct 1881; *d* unm 2 Nov 1965
3a Archer; *b* 11 Nov 1852; *m* 10 April 1877 Florence Emma (*d* 24 May 1925), dau of John Bryant, of S Kensington, and *d* 27 April 1905, leaving:

1b Gerard Archer; *b* 30 Jan 1878; Maj TA; *m* 8 June 1905 Amy (*d* 16 Feb 1953), dau of Col S P Woodfull, RA, and *dsp* 18 Sept 1957
1b Muriel Audrey; *b* 1 Sept 1886
1a Georgiana; *m* 2 Oct 1862 George Hanbury Field (*d* 24 July 1901), of Ashurst Park, Kent, and *d* 19 Aug 1891, leaving issue
(2) Heys; *b* 31 Dec 1931; *m* 15 June 1837 Anne (*d* 31 Jan 1857), dau of Augustus Barker, and *d* 27 Aug 1882, leaving issue:

1a Edward Heys; *b* 4 Feb 1839; *d* 24 Feb 1885
2a Charles Bulkeley; *b* 31 May 1843; *d* unm 23 Dec 1889
1a Louisa Anne; *m* 4 April 1888 Rev Frederick Augustus Bright (*d* 2 April 1907), Rector Caterham, and *d* Dec 1926
2a Frances Jane; *d* unm 8 Sept 1911
3a Emily Isabella; *m* 21 Sept 1870 Capt William George England, RN (*d* 1905), only child of William England, of Hindringham, Norfolk, and *d* 16 July 1922, leaving issue
(1) Charlotte Emily Harriet Anne; *m* 4 July 1840 Rev James Beckford Nevill Heard, Rector Caterham, and *d* his widow 24 April 1892
(2) Lucy Louisa Maria; *m* 12 Sept 1835 Cdr George William Rabett, RN, and *d* 26 Nov 1879, having had issue
2 Arthur Richard; *b* 14 Jan 1787; Cdr RN; *m* 1 Sept 1829 Charlotte FitzHerbert (*d* 12 Feb 1871), dau of Peter Daysh, of Petworth, and *d* 20 Aug 1853, leaving:

(1) Garth Edward George; *b* 9 March 1831; *m* 20 July 1852 Emily Jane Baker, of Brighton (*d* 6 Nov 1903), and *dsp* 7 March 1903
(1) Georgiana Charlotte Daysh; *m* 27 July 1854 William Powell Murray (*d* 20 Aug 1885) and *d* 29 Feb 1884 aged 49
3 Adolphus Augustus (Rev); *b* 3 Aug 1789; Vicar Beesthorpe, Rector Tatterset, Norfolk; *m* 9 Nov 1812 Jessie (*d* 25 Aug 1877), dau of John Dewar, and *d* 5 March 1857, leaving:

(1) Charles Chad; *b* 21 Nov 1815; *m* 4 Jan 1848 Frances Louisa (*d* 9 March 1865), yst dau of Lt-Col Harcourt Master, of Catton, Norfolk, and *d* 21 March 1878, leaving:

1a Charles Chad; *b* 2 June 1853; *m* 11 Nov 1879 Elizabeth Ethel, dau of William Downer, of Petworth, and *d* 30 June 1885, leaving:

1b Cecil; *b* 1880; *m* 1913 Effie Annie (*d* 1956), dau of Robert McMillan, of London, Ontario, and *d* 1953, leaving:

1c ROBERT CHAD TURNOUR, **7th Earl Winterton**; *b* 13 Sept 1915; *educ* Nutana Coll; Flt/Sgt RCAF WW II, with Canadian NATO Force Sqdn Sardinia 1957–58; *m* 1941 Kathleen Ella (*d* 30 April 1969), dau of

D B Whyte, of Saskatoon; *m* 2nd 16 Oct 1971 *Marion Eleanor [The Rt Hon Marion Countess Winterton, 1326 55th St, Delta, BC, Canada], dau of Arthur Phillips, of Belleville, Ontario, and *d* 1991

2c Cecil Noel, DFM, CD; *b* 11 Dec 1919; *educ* Nutana Collegiate and Saskatchewan U; late F/Lt RCAF; *m* 16 July 1941 *Evelyn Isobel [Mrs Cecil Turnour, 47 Kenmore Ave, Cambridge, Ontario N1S 3H4, Canada], dau of Dr CA Oulton, of Saskatoon, and *d* 1987, leaving:

    1d (DONALD) DAVID TURNOUR, **8th and present Earl Winterton**

    2d +ROBERT CHARLES [Robert Turnour Esq, 553 Duke St, Cambridge, Ontario N3H 3T2, Canada]; *b* 30 Jan 1950; heir presumptive; *educ* Conestoga Coll, Kitchener, Ontario; *m* 1st 1974 (*divorce* 1976) Sheila, dau of Garth H Stocking, of Brampton, Ontario; *m* 2nd 1983 *Patricia Ann, dau of William Avery, of Cambridge, Ontario, and by her has:

        1e *Sarah Elizabeth; *b* 1983

        2e *Megan Ann; *b* 1985

    3d +Murray John [Dr Murray Turnour, 4 Lansdowne South, Cambridge, Ontario N1S 2T3, Canada]; *b* 6 Feb 1951; *educ* U of Waterloo, Onrario (OD 1975, MSc 1979); Dr of Optometry; *m* 1980 *Brenda Jill, dau of Dr James Alexander Tremayne Behan, of Orillia, Ontario, and has:

        1e +Jonathan Winterton Behan; *b* 18 April 1985

    1c *Margaret Ethel [Mrs Donald McGeary, 58 St Andrews Ct, Aurora, Ontario L4G 3B1, Canada]; *b* 1917; *m* 1939 *Donald S McGeary and has issue

  1b Noel Charles; *b* 1882; *m* 1904 Sarah Maria (*d* 13 May 1955), dau of W Hawthorne, of Deloraine, Manitoba, and *d* 27 March 1920, leaving:

    1c Doris Ethel Anne; *m* 29 June 1933 Kenneth William Frederick Cooper, of Saskatoon, and *d* 15 Dec 1953, leaving issue

  1a Jessie Sophia; *d* 1879

  2a Frances Anne; *m* 25 April 1871 Rev Henry Nelson (*d* 1881), Vicar Legsby, Lincs, and *d* 16 April 1934, leaving issue

(2) Arthur Edward, of Denbigh; *b* 31 Jan 1819; MD; *m* 1 June 1861 his cousin Frances Helen (*d* 20 Dec 1867), dau of Rev Hon Edward John Turnour (*see* above), and *d* 7 Aug 1894, leaving:

  1a Arthur Henry (Rev); *b* 5 Oct 1862; Vicar St Augustine Stockport; *m* 4 July 1893 Alice Mary (*d* 12 April 1927), dau of Rev Josiah Turner Lea, Vicar Far Forest, Worcs, and *d* 1896, leaving:

    1b Arthur William Winterton; *b* 31 March 1894; Lt Rifle Bde; *ka* 25 Sept 1915

    2b Edward Keith Henry; *b* 2 March 1896; RNAS WW I (despatches); *m* 21 Feb 1924 Jeanie, est dau of John F Burton, of Gwaynynog, Denbighs, and *dsp* 8 April 1968

  2a Edward Adolphus; *b* 13 May 1864; Lt 1st Vol Bn Roy Welch Fus; Mayor Denbigh 1898; *d* unm 8 June 1899

  1a Anne Mary; *m* 2 July 1903 John Pryse Lewis, er s of Rev L Lewis, Rector Denbigh, and *d* 1 Feb 1904

(3) Edward Winterton, CB; *b* 18 Sept 1821; Adml; *m* 4 Jan 1866 Emma Elizabeth (*d* 18 Feb 1891), yst dau of R W Hodgson, of N Dene, Gateshead, and *dsp* 8 Oct 1901

(4) Adolphus Augustus (Rev); *b* 22 April 1823; Vicar Ellenhall, Staffs; *m* 26 Sept 1850 Mary Anne Elizabeth Grace (*d* 1 Dec 1909), only child of Alexander Pearson, of Park House, Stainmore, Westmorland, and *d* 7 July 1888, leaving, with two daus (*d* unm):

  1a Mary Jessie; *b* 5 June 1851; *m* 4 Sept 1873 Harcourt Master and *d* 28 April 1906, leaving issue

  2a Caroline; *b* 20 Nov 1852; *m* 19 April 1887 Rev Alfred Corrie Almack, (*d* 6 July 1930), Rector Blandford St Mary Dorset 1907–23, and *d* 27 Jan 1933, having had issue

(5) John Horatio; *b* 17 Oct 1830; *m* 1st 28 July 1853 Marianne, est dau of Robert R Wilson and step-dau of F W Keppel (*see* ALBEMARLE), and had:

  1a Keppel Arthur; *b* 31 Oct 1856; barrister; *m* 2 April 1878 Margaret (*d* 15 March 1901), only dau of C C Wallace, of Greenbank, Isle of Bute, and *d* 1930, having had:

    1b Arthur Wallace; *b* 6 May 1879; *d* of wounds recd in action 1917

    2b Donald Winterton; *b* 27 June 1882

    3b James Owen; *b* 1884

    4b Keppel Ernest; *b* 1885

    5b John Edward Garth; *b* 1893; *d* of wounds recd in action 1917

    1b Alice; *b* 16 March 1881; *m* 10 Dec 1910 Cecil Henry Henty, and has issue

    2b Marion Margaret Keith; *b* 1886; *d* June 1907

    3b Sybil Ruth; *b* 1890

  2a Edward Edmund Hewitt; *b* 5 Oct 1864; *m* 29 June 1900 Mary Ann, dau of Duncan C Milne, of Adelaide, S Australia, and *d* 1915, leaving:

    1b *Marjorie Balman Winterton; *b* 30 Nov 1906

  3a Frederick John; *b* 13 April 1866; *dec*

  1a Florence Winterton; *d* unm

  2a Harriet Dashwood Balmain; *m* 18 Oct 1879 James Blackwood (*d* Aug 1916), of Homecroft, Foot's Cray, Kent, son of John Blackwood, and *d* 13 Nov 1952, leaving issue

  3a Mildred Augusta Maria; *d* 1875

(6) John Horatio Turnour *m* 2nd 1896 Sarah Margaret (*d* 20 Dec 1919), dau of John Brown, MD, HEICS, of Langholm, Dumfriesshire, and *d* 11 Dec 1904

(1) Anne Chad; *m* 31 Oct 1844 Rev William Dack Daniel and *d* 17 Sept 1853

1 Anne; *m* Sir Charles Chad, 2nd Bt (*see* 1855 edn), and *d* 1832

WISE

Creation: B. (UK) 24 Dec 1951.

THE 2ND BARON WISE, of King's Lynn, Co Norfolk (John Clayton Wise) [The Rt Hon The Lord Wise, Lynn Cottage, Castle Hill, Hemyock, Devon EX15 3RU]; *b* 11 June 1923; *s* f 1968; *educ* Bury Sch Suffolk; farmer; *m* 1st 21 Sept 1946 (*divorce* 1986) Margaret Annie, dau of Frederick Victor Snead, of Banbury, Oxon; *m* 2nd 1993 *Janice Harman Thompson, and by his 1st w has:

  1 +CHRISTOPHER JOHN CLAYTON [Dr The Hon Christopher Wise, Demeter, Woodmancote, Cirencester, Glos]; *b* 19 March 1949; *educ* Norwich Sch and U of Southampton (BSc 1971); PhD 1978

  2 +Martin Highfield [The Hon Martin Wise, 3 Rosedale Close, Titchfield, Hants]; *b* 18 April 1950; *educ* Norwich Sch and U of Bristol (MB, ChB 1973); MD, FRCS

Lineage: EDWARD WISE, of Bury St Edmunds, Suffolk; *b* 11 May 1861; *m* 11 May 1884 Ellen Clayton, JP, memb W Suffolk CC and Bury St Edmunds RC (*d* May 1952 aged 90), dau of John Joel, and *d* 16 May 1952, leaving:

1 Edward Frank, CB (1919), of Hazeldene, Wendover, Bucks; *b* 3 July 1885; *educ* Guildhall Feoffment Sch, King Edward VI Sch Bury St Edmunds and Sidney Sussex Coll Cambridge (BA 1906); barrister Middle Temple 1911; Jr Clerk H of C 1907, Acting Pncpl Clerk Nat Health Insur Commn 1912, Sec War Off Ctee Anglo-Russian Supplies 1914–15, Assist Dir Army Contracts Clothing and Raw Materials 1916, Pncpl Assist Sec Min Food 1917, Chm Inter-Allied Oilseeds Exec and memb Food Cncl 1918, Delegate Supreme Ec Cncl and Chm Sub-Ctee Germany, Paris 1919, Ec Advsr All-Russian Centl Union Consumers' Co-op Socs 1923–33, MP (Lab) E Leicester 1929–31; *m* Dorothy Lilian Owen, MA (London) (*m* 2nd 1950 Ernest Cox, of Merries Bungalow, Steep, Petersfield, Hants), and *d* 5 Nov 1933, leaving:

  (1) Thomas Frank; Ch Economist Dept Indian Affrs and Northern Devpt Govt of Canada, Dean Ec and Social Studies U of Khartoum, Sudan; *m* and had two daus

  (1) Margaret Dorothy; *m* Rev William Jack Jenner, AKC, and had:

    1a *William John Francis; *b* 5 Oct 1940

    2a *Peter Julian; *b* 3 March 1943

  (2) *Mary Frances; *m* *Eric Murray, Trinidad and Tobago High Commr, Kingston, Jamaica, and has:

    1a *Jelka Brigid; *b* 1 Oct 1952

    2a *Anna Katherine; *b* 11 Nov 1953

    3a *Frances Margaret; *b* 3 Nov 1956

  (3) *Helen Irene; *m* *William Keith Struthers and has:

    1a *William Anthony Keith; *b* 2 July 1943

    2a *Stephen John Richard; *b* 16 Oct 1949

    3a *Robert Andrew Frank; *b* 7 Jan 1951

    4a *Philip Alexander James; *b* 27 Jan 1956

2 FREDERICK JOHN WISE, **1st Baron Wise**, of King's Lynn, Co Norfolk (UK), so *cr* 24 Dec 1951, DL (Norfolk 1954); *b* 10 April 1887; *educ* King Edward VI Sch Bury St Edmunds; FRICS; RFC, Suffolk Regt and RAF WW I, RAF WW II; MP (Lab) King's Lynn 1945–51; Comptroller Fndn Govrs King Edward VI Sch, chartered surveyor, land agent and farmer, memb Oxfordshire CC and Bombay Borough and RDCs; *m* 25 Nov 1911 Kate Elizabeth, dau of John Michael Sturgeon, of Horringer, Bury St Edmunds, and *d* 20 Nov 1968, leaving:

  1 JOHN CLAYTON WISE, **2nd and present Baron Wise**

  1 *Joan Mary [The Hon Mrs Wood, Small Acre, Hewish, Weston-super-Mare, Somerset]; *b* 27 Sept 1912; *m* 2 April 1938 *John Reginald Wood, s of Reginald George Wood, of Staunton Harold, Leics, and has:

    1a *Michael George; *b* 12 Jan 1939

    2a *David Clayton; *b* 26 Jan 1946

    3a *Roger John; *b* 7 April 1947

    1a *Mary Janet; *b* 17 April 1941

  (2) *Jean Phyllis [The Hon Mrs Turrill, 12 Woburn Close, Caversham, Berks]; *b* 11 July 1914; *m* 1939 *Lt-Col John Patrick Turrill, OBE, TD, RA, s of H Turrill, of Stadhampton, Oxon, and has:

    1a *John Ewen; *b* 2 Dec 1948

    1a *Judith Elizabeth; *b* 16 Aug 1946

    1a *Ruth Eleanor; *b* 29 Nov 1947

  (3) *Eileen Ellen [The Hon Mrs Hastings, Bridge Cottage, Rousden, Lyme Regis, Dorset]; *b* 28 Sept 1916; *m* 7 Sept 1940 *S/Ldr Gerald Edmund Hastings, RAF, s of Alfred Philip Hastings, of Leamington Spa, Warwicks, and has:

    1a *Tanera [Mrs Tree, 3 Meganna Way, Braishfield, nr Romsey, Hants]; *b* 10 Aug 1943; *m* — Tree

    2a *Eileen Mary; *b* 17 Feb 1948

    3a *Bridget Talmine; *b* 24 March 1950

WISEMAN

Arms: Sa. a chevron erm. between three cronels arg. **Crest:** A castle triple-towered or, port open arg., out of the top a demi-Moor issuant, armed ppr., in his right hand a dart arg., barbed and flighted or, in his left a Roman target of the last. **Motto:** *Sapit qui Deo sapit* ('He is wise who is wise through God'). **Creation:** Bt. (E) 29 Aug 1628.

SIR JOHN WILLIAM WISEMAN, 11TH BT, of Canfield Hall, Essex [Sir John Wiseman Bt, 395 North Rd, Sudbury, MA 01776, USA]; *b* 16 March 1957; *educ* Millfield and Hartford U, USA; *s f* 1962; *m* 1980 *Nancy, dau of Casimer Zyla, of New Britain, Conn., and has:

1 *Elizabeth; *b* 1983
2 *Patricia Alison; *b* 1986

Lineage: Sir JOHN WISEMAN, of Much Canfield Pk, Essex; Auditor Exchequer *temp* HENRY VIII, ktd *c* 1513; *m* Agnes, dau of Ralph Joscelyn, of Gt Canfield, and *d* 17 Aug 1558, leaving:

JOHN WISEMAN; *m* Margery, dau of Sir William Waldegrave, of Smallbridge, Suffolk, U-Treasurer Calais, and *d* 17 Oct 1602, having had, with other issue:

THOMAS WISEMAN; *m* Alice, dau and heiress of Robert Myles, of Sutton, Suffolk, and *d* 1624, having had, with another s (Robert, *dsp*):

Sir William Wiseman, 1st Bt (E), *so cr* 29 Aug 1628; *m* 6 Nov 1628 Elizabeth (*d* 6 April 1660), dau of Sir Henry Capel (*see* ESSEX, E), and *d* 1 July 1643, leaving:

1 **Sir William Wiseman, 2nd Bt**; *b* 1630; Sheriff Essex 1659–60; *m* 1st 26 Oct 1659 Anne (*dsp* 11 May 1662), dau and coheir of Sir John Prescot; *m* 2nd 16 May 1664 Arabella (*d* 1705), sis and coheir of 1st and last Viscount Hewytt of Goran (*see* LYTTON, E), and *d* 14 Jan 1684/5, leaving, with other issue:

1 **Sir Thomas Wiseman, 3rd Bt**; *d* unm 1 May 1733
2 **Sir Charles Wiseman, 4th Bt**; *bapt* 27 Aug 1676; *d* unm 3 June 1751
3 John, of the Middle Temple; *bapt* 14 Dec 1679; *m* Penelope — and had:

(1) **Sir William Wiseman, 5th Bt**; *dsp* 25 May 1774

2 Edmund (Sir); *b* 1633; *m* (licence 18 April 1670) Elizabeth (*d* 8 Dec 1694), dau of Daniel Waldo, citizen of London, and *d* 8 May 1704, leaving, with other issue:

(1) Edmund, of Tewkesbury; *b* 1671; *m* (licence 3 Nov 1697) Maria, dau of Edmund Harnage, of Bellyard, Salop, and *d* Oct 1741, leaving, with other issue:

1a Edward; *b* 21 Dec 1700; *d* 1767, leaving by his 1st w Mary Jones:

1b THOMAS (Sir), **6th Bt**

3 Capel (Very Rev); Dean Raphoe, Bp Dromore; *d* Sept 1683
1 Theodosia; *m* 7 April 1662 Sir William Craven, Bt
2 Elizabeth; *m* Robert Tyderleigh

The 5th Bt's 1st cousin once-removed,

Sir Thomas Wiseman, 6th Bt; *m* 1st 1 Dec 1757 Mary (*d* 11 June 1776), dau of Michael Godden, Master Attendant Chatham Dockyard, and had:

1 Edmund; *m* 1783 Jemima (*m* 2nd 5 Jan 1792 Peter Reynolds), dau of Michael Arne, and *d* 7 May 1787, leaving:

(1) WILLIAM SALTONSTALL (Sir), **7th Bt**

(1) Mary Anne; *m* 23 Oct 1806 Thomas Frid (*d* 10 Oct 1850) and *d* 21 Nov 1828, leaving issue

2 Thomas, of Northfleet, Kent; *b* 24 April 1760; *m* 13 Jan 1778 Susannah, dau of Alexander Bookham, and *d* 1830, leaving:

(1) Thomas; *b* 1778; had:

1a Edward Thomas; had:

1b Thomas Edward; *b* 1851; *m* 1877 Ellen Justinia, dau of George Ware, and *d* 1918, leaving:

1c Thomas Edward; *b* 1878; *m* 1916 Annie (*d* 1970), dau of George William Allen, and *d* 1959, leaving:

1d +THOMAS ALAN [Thomas Wiseman Esq, 14 Havisham Rd, Chalk, Gravesend, Kent DA12 4UN]; *b* 8 July 1921; heir presumptive; *educ* Gravesend Co Sch; late Admin Offr Forest Products Ltd, late

Staff Sgt RAOC; *m* 11 Dec 1946 Hildemarie (*d* 1991), dau of Gustav Domnik, of Allenstein, E Prussia, and has had:

1e Thomas Eldred; *b* 22, *d* 26 Dec 1947
1e Susan; *b* 5 March; *d* 17 April 1949

2c Wallis Julian; *b* 1879, Pte QO Roy W Kent Regt WW I; *ka* 1916
3c Frank Eldred; *b* 1880; *m* 1923 Lily Amy (*d* 1957), dau of Harry Lewis Littlewood, of Gravesend, Kent, and *d* 1938, leaving:

1d Wallis Littlewood; *b* 1924; *m* 1st 1951 Brenda Doris (*d* 1990), dau of Arthur Allanson; *m* 2nd 1991 *Margaret-Ann [Mrs Wallis Wiseman, Box 5689, Walmer 6070, Port Elizabeth, S Africa], dau of Malcolm Edward Rittenhouse, of Osgood, Indiana, and *d* 1993, leaving by his 1st w:

1e +Jonathan Charles [Jonathan Wiseman Esq, 11 Huilboom St, Randpark, Johannesburg, S Africa]; *b* 28 Feb 1953; *m* 1980 *Rita Hilda, dau of L A Williams, of Port Elizabeth, and has:

1f *Lauren Ann; *b* 1983
2f *Nicola Jane; *b* 1986

2e +Richard Christopher; *b* 20 July 1954; *m* 1986 *Dawn Lorraine, dau of Patrick Hart, of Springs, S Africa, and has:

1f +Christopher Philip; *b* 1987

3e +Barry James [Barry Wiseman Esq, 19 Pamela Crescent, Walmer Downs, Port Elizabeth, S Africa]; *b* 10 June 1956; *m* 1979 *Brigitte, dau of Hans Bülbring, of Port Elizabeth, and has:

1f +Jarrod; *b* 1984
2f *Paul Mark; *b* 1986

1e *Margaret Alexandra [Mrs Peter Newton, 19 Barrydale Rd, Miramar, Port Elizabeth, S Africa]; *b* 23 Aug 1960; *m* 1985 *Peter Wilson Newton, son of Michael Newton, of Nairobi, and has:

1f *Matthew Michael; *b* 1987
2f *Bailey Louise; *b* 1985

4c Louis Gerald; *b* 1881; *m* Agnes — and had:

1d +Edward Thomas; *b* 19–
2d +Louis George; *b* 19–
1d *Teresa; *b* 19–
2d *Audrey; *b* 19–

5c Frederick William; *b* 1885; *m* 1914 Charlotte Ward (*d* 1966) and *d* 1954, leaving:

1d +John Henry Ware [John Wiseman Esq, 258 Murray St, Rockhampton 4700, Queensland, Australia]; *b* 1924; WW I Roy Aust Artillery Pacific (wounded); *m* 1962 *Delma Margaret, dau of Douglas James Lung, of Bundaberg, Qld

1d *Marie Eleanor [Mrs Stanley Shaw, 14 Ryrie St, N Ryde, Sydney, NSW, Australia]; *b* 1919; *m* 1941 Capt Stanley Thornton Shaw, RAA (*d* 1956), and has:

1e *John Alexander; *b* 1943
2e *Philip Thornton; *b* 1945
3e *Laurence Edward; *b* 1946

1c Henrietta Clara; *b* 1888; *m* 1918 Herbert William Russell, of Gravesend, Kent, and had issue

2a Charles Pierce; had:

1b William Henry; *b* 1831; *m* 1857 Mary Johnson (*d* 1892) and *d* 1912, leaving:

1c Edwin Wycliffe; *b* 1864; *m* 1st 1893 Rosa (*d* 1926), dau of Leonard Leonard, and had:

1d Edwin Leonard; *b* 1897; *m* 1921 *Winifred May [Mrs Edwin Wiseman, 27 Davis Ave, Northfleet, Kent], dau of Edward William Bassant, and *d* 1964, leaving:

1e *Mary; *b* 1933

1d Ethel Emma; *b* 1895; *m* 1st 1928 William Luttrell (*d* 1930); *m* 2nd 8 July 1950 Henry Smart (*d* 7 Jan 1959)

1c (cont.) Edwin Wiseman *m* 2nd 1928 Alice Maud Mary (*d* 1966), dau of Horace Plant, and *d* 29 Jan 1954, leaving by her:

2d *Alice Rosa [Miss Alice Wiseman, 47 Pelham Rd S, Gravesend, Kent]; *b* 1930

2b Pierce; *b* 1844; *m* 1871 Elizabeth Catherine (*d* May 1928), dau of Thomas Wells, and *d* April 1928, leaving:

1c Thomas Charles; *b* 1873; *m* 1896 Eliza, dau of Charles Carpenter, and *d* 1940, leaving:

1d William Henry; *b* 1910; Capt RA, bank official; *m* 1937 Winifred (*d* 1988), dau of William Charles Ambrose Knight, and *d* 1979, leaving:

1e *Susan Marjorie [Mrs Ian Crowe, 12A West End Grove, Farnham, Surrey GU9 7EG]; *b* 1940; *m* 1977 *Ian Crowe

2d +Albert Victor; *b* 1915; police offr, late F/O RAF; *m* 1941 *Nicola, dau of Leonard Foreman, and has:

1e +Jonathan Thomas Charles; *b* 1946
2e +Simon Pierce; *b* 1949
1e *Elizabeth Victoria; *b* 1942

1d Amy Gertrude; *b* 1898; *m* 1932 Frederick Gulliford and had issue
2d May Constance; *b* 1899; *m* 1938 George Durling, of Chatham, Kent
3d *Gertrude Minnie; *b* 1903; *m* 1936 Thomas Jarvis (*d* 1976) and has:

1e *Michael [Michael Jarvis Esq, Glenview House, Leith Park Rd, Gravesend, Kent]; *b* 1942; *m* 1972 *Brenda Shaffoe and has:

1f *Alton James; *b* 1976
1f *Julia Simone; *b* 1975

2e *Trevor; *b* 1946; *m* 19– *Patricia English and has:

1f *Charles Alexander; *b* 1977

2c Albert Edward; *b* 1882; *m* 1908 Charlotte, dau of Charles Morgan, and *d* 6 March 1966, leaving:

1d Violet Doris; *b* 1909; *m* 1930 Frederick Beach, of Handsworth Wood, Birmingham, and had issue

1c Alice; *b* 1877; *m* 1898 James John Heaver (*d* 1930), and *d* Aug 1952, leaving issue

2c Edith Eleanor; *b* 1880; *m* 1902 Thomas William Whyte Shaw (*d* Oct 1948) and had issue

3c Sarah Ann; *b* 1887; *d* unm 27 July 1962

4c Ethel Maud; *b* 1893

(2) Edmund; had:

1a Thomas Palmer; had:

1b Charles John; *b* 1862; *m* 1890 Lillie Jane, dau of William Oakley, and *d* 1936, leaving:

1c William Thomas; *b* 1891; 8th London Bde WW I

2c Thomas Charles; *b* 1897; *m* 1919 — and *d* 1928, leaving:

1d Ronald Henry; *b* 1924; WW II; *m* 1943 — and *d* 14 Dec 1974, leaving:

1e *Dawn

1d Constance Queenie; *b* 1921; *m* 1940 —

2d Betty Thomasina; *b* 1928; *m* 1946 —

3c Charles John; *b* 1904; *m* 1937 *Jessie [Mrs Charles Wiseman, 17 Holburne Gdns, Kidbrooke, London SE3], dau of James Arthur Laming, and *d* 1990, leaving:

1d +David John; *b* 1939; Lt Parachute Regt TRAVR; *m* 1st 1964 (*divorce* 1968) Susan Anne, dau of Charles William Tait; *m* 2nd 1977 *Ann, dau of Dr Henry James Walls

4c Alfred; *b* 1906; *m* 1st 1931 (*divorce* 1946) Rose Knight; *m* 2nd 1946 *Enid May Hurford and *d* 1979, leaving by her:

1d Linda; *b* 1949; *m* 1970 *Michael Ramsay

5c +John Robert, ISM; *b* 1908; *m* 1931 *Ethel, dau of Joseph Thomas Beecham

1c Lily Mary; *b* 1893; *m* 1913 Alfred Taylor, of Woolwich, and had:

2c Maud Elizabeth; *b* 1893; *m* 1916 — Parr and had issue

3c Annie Elizabeth; *b* 1896; *m* 1918 Zacharia William Coles, of The Queen's Arms, Mortlake, Surrey, and had:

1d *Nancy Joan [Mrs Edward Willard, The Cock, Church St, Staines, Middx]; *b* 1921; *m* 1944 *Edward Henry Willard and has:

1e *Paul William; *b* 1946

4c Grace Mary; *b* 1900; *m* 1923 Walter Jefferies and had issue

5c May Lily; *b* 1901; *m* 1925 Alfred Preston, of Woolwich, and had:

1d *Ronald Walter; *b* 1925

2d *Dennis Gordon; *b* 1927; *m* 19– *— and has:

1e *Beverley; *b* 1952

6c Violet Mary; *b* 1903; *m* 1930 Frank Tranter and has:

1d *Jean Alma; *b* 1931

3 William, of Brompton, Kent; *b* 23 April 1762; *m* Elizabeth, dau of John Robertson, of London, and had:

(1) George Augustus; *b* 20 Oct 1808

Sir Thomas *m* 2nd 2 Dec 1769 Sarah (*d* 4 Dec 1777), dau of Thomas King, of Gravesend, and *d* 1810, leaving:

1 Anne; *m* Joseph Lawford

His gs,

Sir William Saltonstall Wiseman, 7th Bt; *b* 5 March 1784; Capt RN; *m* 1st 8 Jan 1812 Catherine (*d* 27 Oct 1862), dau of Sir James Mackintosh; *m* 2nd 5 April 1827 Eliza, est dau of Rev George Davies, BD, Rector Cranfield, nr Newport Pagnell, and *d* 1 July 1845, leaving by his 1st w, with other issue:

Sir William Saltonstall Wiseman, 8th Bt, KCB; *b* 4 Aug 1814; R-Adml; *m* 25 Oct 1838 Charlotte Jane (*d* 23 May 1891), only dau of Adml — Paterson, of E Cosham Ho, Hants, and *d* 14 July 1874, leaving, with a dau (Eliza Frances Charlotte, *m* 22 Oct 1865 R-Adml Henry McClintock Alexander, of Dunduan, Coleraine, and *d* 1 April 1875, leaving issue):

Sir William Wiseman, 9th Bt; *b* 23 Aug 1845; Capt RN; *m* 20 Sept 1878 Sarah Elizabeth (*d* 13 Sept 1925), 3rd dau of Lewis Langworthy, of Putney, and had:

1 WILLIAM GEORGE EDEN (Sir), **10th Bt**

1 Winifred May; *b* 1880; *m* 24 Sept 1919 Maj John Muspratt-Mood, OBE, MC (*d* 4 Dec 1927), Roy Dublin Fus and MGC, er s of W R Mood, of Chapel Ho, nr Kirkcaldy, and *d* 17 Oct 1969, leaving issue

2 Dorothy Lilian; *b* 17 Oct 1881; *m* 14 Dec 1910 Charles Stephen Ascherson, yr s of Edward Ascherson, of Pett Pl, Charing, Kent, and had:

(1) *Janet Elizabeth; *b* 22 May 1914; WAAF WW II; *m* 30 April 1947 *Raoul William Raphael Martin, of Toulon, s of Henri Martin

(2) *Dorothy Renée; *b* 19 May 1915; actress; *m* 1953, as his 2nd w, (Frederick) Robert Donat (*d* 9 June 1958), actor, s of Ernst Emil Donat

3 Margery Elizabeth; *b* 4 Nov 1883; *m* 1 July 1919 Capt Arnold John Dick (*d* 1955), RAF, and *d* 10 March 1967

4 Joan Hilda Marion; *b* 13 Dec 1890; *m* 30 Sept 1911 Capt Arthur Robert Montgomery Roe, Dorset Regt (*d* of wounds 16 Sept 1914), s of Sir Charles Roe, and *d* 9 May 1955, leaving issue

Sir WILLIAM *d* 11 Jan 1893; his only s,

Sir William George Eden Wiseman, 10th Bt, CB (1918), CMG (1917); *b* 1 Feb 1885; *educ* Winchester and Jesus Coll Cambridge; Capt 6th (Serv) Bn DCLI, Lt Cardigan Artillery RGA, Lt-Col Staff MI Peace Conf, Ch Adviser American Affrs to Br Delegn Paris 1918–19, memb Dollar Exports Bd 1950; *m* 1st 16 Sept 1908 (*divorce* 1925) Marjorie Florence Hulton (*d* 4 May 1961), 3rd dau of Rev George Frederick Sams, Rector Emberton, Bucks, and had:

1 Honour Marjorie; *b* 18 Jan 1910; *d* unm 4 Aug 1954

2 Margaret; *b* 21 Feb 1913; *m* 19 Sept 1936 *Ramsay William Rainsford Hannay [Ramsay Rainsford Hannay Esq, Cardoness, Gatehouse-of-Fleet, Kirkcudbrightshire DG7 2EP], s of Col Frederick Rainsford Hannay, CMG, DSO, RA, of Kirkdale, Kirkcudbrightshire, and *d* 14 Nov 1994, leaving:

(1) *David Wiseman Ramsay Rainsford HANNAY (dde poll); *b* 3 Jan 1939; *educ* Winchester and Trin Coll Cambridge; MA, MB, BChir, DCH; *m* 25 Sept

---

1963 *Janet Mary, er dau of Canon Patrick Nevile Gilliat, of Winchester, and has:

1a *Mark Gilliat Rainsford; *b* 4 April 1966; *m* 9 Nov 1991 *Fiona MacPherson, dau of James Parker, of Millrig, Skelmorlie, Ayrshire, and has:

1b *James David Rainsford; *b* 29 May 1998

1b *Jessica Margaret Rainsford; *b* 29 May 1998

2a *Neil Maxwell Rainsford; *b* 13 Aug 1969; *m* 27 July 1996 *Kirsten Joanne, dau of John Doughty, of Edinburgh

3a *Stephen Ramsay Rainsford; *b* 1972

(1) *Jessica Margaret; *b* 2 Sept 1937; *m* 1978 *Colin Russell

3 *Rosemary [Mrs Frederick Hulton, Firles, Chyngton Rd, Seaford, Sussex BN25 4HH]; *b* 13 Jan 1916; *m* 5 March 1936 *Lt-Col Frederick Richard Hulton, RA, s of Col Frederick Courtenay Longuet Hulton, CB, King's Dragoon Gds, and has:

(1) *Frederick William; *b* 3 Aug 1938; *m* 1973 *Ruth Parsons and has:

1a *Mark; *b* 3 July 1975

2a *Dominic; *b* 3 July 1975

(2) *Peter Richard; *b* 12 Aug 1941; *m* 26 July 1969 *Dorinda Stewart and has:

1a *Anna Sky; *b* 9 Oct 1979

(3) *Thomas Michael; *b* 29 Sept 1943; Capt 1st Queen's Dragoon Gds; *m* 14 Dec 1968 *Susan Oldman and has:

1a *Claire; *b* 1 Jan 1973

2a *Kathleen; *b* 22 Jan 1975

(1) *Rosemary Jane; *b* 27 Dec 1949; *m* 2 May 1970 *Christopher Eliot and has:

1a *James; *b* 20 Sept 1975

2a *David; *b* 10 March 1978

3a *Peter; *b* 22 May 1984

Sir William *m* 2nd 5 Dec 1925 (*divorce* 1933) Patrice (*d* 1951), dau of Elliott B Clark, and by her had:

4 *Sheila; *b* 4 July 1928; jnlst

Sir William *m* 3rd 10 Feb 1944 *Joan Mary [Joan Lady Wiseman, 32 Victoria Rd, London W8], formerly w of Lawrence E Lesureur and dau of Arthur Phelps, of Woodridge, Harrow, and *d* 16 June 1962, leaving by her:

1 Sir JOHN WILLIAM WISEMAN, **11th and present Bt**

WOLFSON

Arms: Per pale dovetailed vert and or on a chevron counter-changed between in chief two roses, also or and gu. respectively, and in base an ancient hand bell ppr., two pears sa. and gold. **Crest:** In front of two rods of Æsculapius in saltire ppr. a torch inflamed, also ppr. **Motto:** *Omnibus rebus cura et provide*. ('Care and provide for all things'). **Creations:** Bt. (UK) 19 Feb 1962; B. (LP, UK) 1985.

THE BARON WOLFSON, of St Marylebone, City of Westminster, and a **Baronet** (Sir Leonard Gordon Wolfson, Bt) [The Rt Hon The Lord Wolfson, 18–22 Haymarket, London SW1Y 4DQ]; *b* 11 Nov 1927; *s* f as 2nd Bt 1991; *educ* King's Sch Worcester; chm GUS 1981–96 (dir 1952–, md 1963–81, hon pres 1996–) and Burberrys Ltd 1968, Chm and Fndr Tstee Wolfson Fndn, Hon Fell St Catherine's Coll Oxford, Wolfson Coll Cambridge, Wolfson Coll Oxford, Worcester Coll Oxford, UCL, Patron Roy Coll Surgns 1976, Hon FRCP, Hon PhD Tel Aviv 1971, Hebrew U 1978, Hon DCL Oxon 1972, Hon LLD Strathclyde 1972, Dundee 1979, Canterbury 1982, London 1982, Hon DSc Hull 1977, Hon DHL Bar Ilan U 1983, ktd 1977; *m* 1st 14 Nov 1949 (*divorce* 1991) Ruth, dau of Ernest A Sterling; *m* 2nd 1991 *Estelle (*née* Feldman), widow of Michael Jackson, FCA, and by his 1st w has:

1 *Janet [The Hon Mrs de Botton, c/o GAM, 12 St James's Pl, London SW1A 1NX]; *b* 31 March 1952; *m* 1st 1972 (*divorce* 1989) Michael Philip Green (*m* 2nd 1990 Tessa Buckmaster), chm Carlton Communications; *m* 2nd 1990 *Gilbert de Botton, investment banker, and by 1st husb has:

(1) *Rebecca Sarah Wolfson; *b* 1974

(2) *Catherine Victoria Wolfson; *b* 1976

2 *Laura [The Hon Mrs Townsley, c/o Townsley & Co, 44 Worship St, London EC2A 2JT]; *b* 7 June 1954; *m* 1975 *Barry Stephen Townsley and has:

(1) *Charles Ralph Wolfson; *b* 1984

(1) *Alexandra Jane Wolfson; *b* 1977

(2) *Georgina Kate Wolfson; *b* 1979

(3) *Isabella Edith Wolfson; *b* 1994

3 *Deborah; *b* 5 Jan 1959; *m* 19– *G— Davis

4 *Elizabeth; *b* 9 Aug 1966; *m* 1991 *Daniel Peltz, s of Dr Sam Peltz, of London W1, and has:

(1) *Max; *b* 19–

(1) *Francesca Edith; *b* 1992

Lineage: SOLOMON WOLFSON, JP, of 16 Campbell Ave, Glasgow; *b* 1868; *m* 1894 Naelia (*d* Dec 1943), dau of — Williamovsky, and *d* Dec 1941, leaving:

1 Samuel; *b* Oct 1896

2 ISAAC (Sir), **1st Bt**

3 Charles; *b* 9 Feb 1899; *m* Hylda — and *d* 3 April 1970, leaving:

(1) DAVID WOLFSON, *cr* BARON WOLFSON OF SUNNINDALE (*qv*)

1 Jeannie; *m* 5 July 1924 Max Williams and had issue

2 Edith; *m* Ralph Hyman, of New York, and had a s and dau

3 Rose; *m* 4 March 1930 *Samuel Martyn and had issue

4 Bette; *m* 1942 Harold Schapiro, of Larchmont, NY, s of Nathan Schapiro, and had issue

5 Dolly; *m* 1st 5 Dec 1937 Dr Jason Jacobson (*d* 14 Feb 1953), sn of Harry Jacobson, of New York; *m* 2nd 24 Feb 1957 *Robert K Raisler, of New York, s of Sam Raisler, and had:

(1) *Gordon Anthony; *b* 13 March 1941

(2) *Steven Ronald; *b* 3 April 1944; *m* 16 June 1968 *Lynn, dau of Harold Kaplan, of Larchmont, NY

6 Hannah Anne; *m* 8 Feb 1938 *Jack Steinberg, of London W1, and had:

(1) *Raymonde; *m* 19– *Ian Jay and has issue

(2) *Kathrine; *m* 19– *Jean-Louis de Gunzburg

SOLOMON WOLFSON's 2nd s,

Sir Isaac Wolfson, 1st Bt (UK), so *cr* 19 Feb 1962; *b* 17 Sept 1897; *educ* Queen's Park Sch Glasgow; chm GUS 1946 (md 1934); FRS 1963, Hon DCL Oxon 1963, Hon LLD London 1959, Glasgow 1963, Cantab 1966, Manchester 1967, Strathclyde 1969, Brandeis 1969, Nottingham 1971, Hon PhD Jerusalem 1970, Hon FRCP 1959, Hon FRCS 1969, Hon Fell St Edmund's Coll Oxford 1961, Weizmann Inst Sci, Jews Coll, LMH Oxford, Fndr Fell Wolfson Coll Oxford, Pres Utd Synagogue, memb Pattenmakers' Co, Fndr Tstee Wolfson Fndn 1955–, memb Grand Cncl Br Empire Cancer Campaign, Tstee Religious Centre Jerusalem, Hon Treas Victoria League Cwlth Friendship, Einstein Award USA 1967, Herbert Lehmann Award USA 1968, Freeman City Glasgow 1971; *m* 17 Feb 1926 Edith (*d* 1981), dau of Ralph Specterman, and *d* 1991, leaving:

Sir LEONARD GORDON WOLFSON, **2nd and present Bt**, *cr* a **Baron**

WOLFSON OF SUNNINGDALE

Creation: B. (LP, UK) 1991.

THE BARON WOLFSON OF SUNNINGDALE, of Trevose, Co Cornwall (Sir David Wolfson) [The Rt Hon The Lord Wolfson of Sunningdale, House of Lords, London SW1A 0PW]; *b* 9 Nov 1935; *educ* Clifton, Trin Coll Cambridge (MA) and Stanford U CA (MBA); with GUS 1960–78, 1993– (dir 1973–78, 1993–); Sec to Shadow Cabinet 1978–79, Ch Staff Political Office 10 Downing St 1979–85, ktd 1984; chm: Alexon Gp 1982–86; Next plc 1990–; non-exec dir: Stewart Wrightson Hldgs 1985–87, Next 1989–90; Hon Fell Hugh's Hall Cambridge 1989, Hon FRCR 1978, Hon FRCOG 1989; *m* 1st 1962 (*divorce* 1967) Patricia Elizabeth, dau of Louis Rawlings; *m* 2nd 1967 *Susan E, dau of Hugh Davis, and has by her:

1 *Simon Adam; *b* 1967

2 *Andrew Daniel; *b* 1969

1 *Deborah Sarah; *b* 1973

Lineage: *See* WOLFSON, B

WOLSELEY of Mount Wolseley

Arms: Arg. a talbot passant gu., a crescent for difference. **Crest:** Out of a ducal coronet or a wolf's head ppr. **Motto:** *Homo homini lupus* ('Man is as a wolf towards his fellow man'). **Creation:** Bt. (I) 19 Jan 1744/5.

SIR JAMES DOUGLAS WOLSELEY, 13TH BT, of Mount Wolseley, Co Carlow [Sir James Wolseley Bt, 4317 Clay St, Fort Worth, TX, USA]; *b* 17 Sept 1937; *s* kinsman 1991; *educ* Texas Christian U (BBA); *m* 1st 29 May 1965 (*divorce* 1971) Patricia Lynn, dau of William R Hunter, of Mount Shasta, Calif.; *m* 2nd 1984 *Mary Anne, dau of Thomas G Brown, of Hilo, USA

Lineage: Sir CHARLES WOLSELEY, 2nd Bt, of Wolseley (*qv*); had a yst s:

RICHARD WOLSELEY, to whom his f left his Irish estates; had a 3rd s:

Sir Richard Wolseley, 1st Bt (I), so *cr* 19 Jan 1744/5, of Mount Wolseley, Co Carlow; *b* Feb 1696; MP Carlow 1727–68; *m* 1st (licence 25 Feb 1722/3) Mrs Anne Smith, widow (*dsp*); *m* 2nd (licence 5 May 1727) Alice (*d* 17 Aug 1778), dau of Sir Thomas Molyneux, 1st Bt, of Castle Dillon, Co Armagh (*see* 1940 edn), and widow of William Rogerson, yr s of Sir John Rogerson, and *d* 8 April 1769, leaving by her:

1 **Sir Richard Wolseley, 2nd Bt**; *b* 10 Jan 1729; *m* 31 Jan 1765 Letitia (*d* Aug 1788), only dau of Anthony Marlay, of Celbridge, Co Kildare, and *d* 28 July 1781, having had, with other issue:

(1) **Sir William Wolseley, 3rd Bt**, BA Oxford; *b* 26 Jan 1775; *d* unm 30 Aug 1819

(1) Matilda; *m* 1790 her cousin Clement Wolseley (*see* below) and *d* 1820, leaving issue

2 Clement, of Wolseley Bridge, Co Carlow; High Sheriff 1770, Col; *m* Catherine, dau of Very Rev Arthur St George, Dean Ross, and *d* 1811, leaving:

(1) **Rev Sir Richard Wolseley, 4th Bt**; *b* 15 June 1760; MA Dublin; Precentor Down 1796–1823; *m* 1st Aug 1786 Mary Anne, dau of Rev Jeremiah Symes, of Ballybeg, Co Wicklow; *m* 2nd Mary, dau of William Richard Middlemore, of Grantham, Lincs; *m* 3rd Elizabeth (*d* 15 July 1880), dau of William Smith, of Golden Bridge Ho, Co Dublin, and *dsp* 3 May 1852

(2) John Rogerson; Maj Carlow Militia; *m* Mary, dau of Arthur Baillie, of Kilbride, Co Carlow, and had with other issue:

1a **Sir Clement Wolseley, 5th Bt**; *b* 27 Oct 1794; 80th Regt India, Maj Carlow Militia, High Sheriff Co Carlow 1852; *m* 30 April 1833 Alice Elizabeth (*d* 25 April 1889), est dau of Peter Van Homrigh, MP Drogheda, and *d* 30 Oct 1857, having had, with other issue:

1b **Sir John Richard Wolseley, 6th Bt**, JP, DL; *b* 24 June 1834; 18th Roy Irish Regt Crimea 1854–55; *m* 6 Dec 1859 Frances Annabella (*d* 30 May 1907), yst dau of Arthur Blennerhasset, of Ballyseedy, Co Kerry, MP, and *d* 20 June 1874, having had, with another dau (*d* unm):

1c Ada Frances Alice; *m* 18 June 1885 Lt-Col Charles Bradford Harries JENKINS later WOLSELEY-JENKINS (roy licence 15 Nov 1894), 19th Hus (*d* 14 Dec 1922), yst s of Gen Charles Vanbrugh Jenkins, of Cruckton Hall, Salop, and *d* 11 March 1940, leaving issue

2c Amelia Cecilia Louisa

2b **Sir Clement James Wolseley, 7th Bt**, JP, DL; *b* 25 July 1837; barrister; Col 3rd Bn Prince of Wales's Leinster Regt; *m* 12 Sept 1872 Constance Louisa (*d* 18 Aug 1899), est dau of Lt-Gen Robert Parker Radcliffe, RA, and gdau and coheir of Sir John Head Brydges, MP, of Wootton Ct, Kent, and *dsp* 16 Oct 1889

1a Wilhelmina; *m* 22 Sept 1821 Thomas Belmore St George (*d* 14 Jan 1863), of Esker, Co Kilkenny, and *d* 8 April 1883

2a Mary Joan; *m* Rev James Alexander Emerton, DD, of Hanwell Ho, Middx, and had issue

(3) Arthur; *m* 1800 Jane (*d* 1 Dec 1843), dau of Arthur Griffiths, of Tregaron, Cards, and *d* 28 May 1842, leaving:

1a Very Rev Sir John Wolseley, 8th Bt; *b* 9 June 1803; MA Dublin; Dean Kildare 1859–90, Rector St Michael's Portarlington; *m* 13 Oct 1832 Anne (*d* 14 Dec 1860), dau of John Maunsell, of Portarlington, and *dsp* 26 Jan 1890

2a David; *b* 17 April 1804; *m* 1st Jane, dau of Abraham Peters, of Towyn, Mon; *m* 2nd Bridget Dorothy, dau of William Hughes, of Llanfihangel, Cards; *m* 3rd 16 April 1873 Ann Eliza, dau of Edward Edwards, of Chirk, Denbighs, and *dsp* June 1876

1a Mary Anne; *m* 23 Nov 1831 Rev Thomas Lewis (*d* 12 Jan 1872), Rector Manavon, Montgomeryshire, and *d* 18 Jan 1875, leaving issue

(4) Clement, of Weston, Co Meath; *m* 1790 his cousin Matilda (*see above*) and *d* 1809, leaving:

1a Clement (Rev), of Sandbrook, Co Carlow; *m* Maria (*d* 1864), dau of Francis Fetherston, of Whiterock, Co Longford, and had, with other issue:

1b Mary Magdalene; *m* John William Lambert

2b Emily Catherine; *m* Ambrose Cox, DL (*d* 1863), of Clara, King's Co, and had issue

3b Clementina; *m* 1867 Lt-Col George Hamilton Evans, Devonshire Regt (*d* 1900), and *d* 1935, leaving issue

3 William (Rev); Capt 8th Hus Germany Seven Years War, Rector Tullycorbet; *m* Jane, dau of Samuel Hulbert, of Corsham, Wilts, and *d* 1800, leaving, with other issue:

(1) William (Rev); Rector Glenarm; *m* Winifred (*d* 3 Oct 1851), dau of Cadwallader Edwards, of Ballyshire, and had:

1a Cadwallader (Ven); *b* 12 Feb 1806; Archdeacon Glendalough; *m* Oct 1833 Anna Maria (*d* 28 Nov 1870), dau of Isaac D'Olier, and *d* 4 Nov 1872, leaving, with other issue:

1b William Charles; *b* Dec 1834; Maj 6th Foot; *m* 10 July 1869 his cousin Annie (*d* 29 May 1938), dau of Rev Capel Wolseley (*see below*), and *d* 28 Nov 1878, leaving, with other issue:

1c Sir Capel Charles Wolseley, 9th Bt; *b* 24 Aug 1870; Br V-Consul Archangel Russia 1900–09, Capt 3rd Bn E Surrey Regt Gallipoli, Egypt and Palestine WW I and Army of Occupation, Albania and N Russia Expdn 1919; *m* 9 May 1907 Beatrice Sophia (*d* 23 June 1947), er dau of Col William Wallingford Knollys (*see* KNOLLYS, V), and *dsp* 27 Aug 1923

1c Alice Mary; *d* unm 4 April 1932

2c Winifred Annie

2b Cadwallader Brooke; *b* 9 April 1845; MB Dublin; *m* 12 Jan 1871 Katie Maria (*d* 2 Nov 1929), dau of Thomas Edward Beatty, MD, and *d* 22 July 1884, leaving:

1c Sir Reginald Beatty Wolseley, 10th Bt; *b* 31 Jan 1872; *m* 25 May 1930 Marian Elizabeth (*d* 20 June 1934), est dau of William Alfred Baker, JP, of Avishays, Newport, Monmouth, and *dsp* July 1933

1c Winifred Katie; *m* 23 Aug 1904 Frederic Montagu Russell, and *d* 1 Feb 1946, leaving issue

2c Ethel Henrietta; *d* unm 21 Oct 1959

3c Honoria Violet Bessie; *m* 24 Feb 1915 Col William Davenport Crawley Kelly, DSO, MB, RAMC (*d* 18 Dec 1951), s of William Pierce Kelly, of Co Clare, and *d* 13 Dec 1955, leaving issue

2a William; *b* 12 Feb 1806; *m* Marcia Daly and *dsp*

3a Charles, of Demerara; *b* 12 Nov 1809; *m* 19 April 1859 Margaret (*d* Feb 1905), dau of Thomas FitzGerald, of Kilberry Lodge, Athy, Co Kildare, and *d* June 1889, leaving:

1b Rev Sir William Augustus Wolseley, 11th Bt; *b* 19 April 1865; *educ* Rathmines and Trin Coll Dublin (BA 1887, Wall Hebrew Scholar 1888, 1st Theological Exhibitioner 1889); Rector Ravensthorpe W Australia 1906–10, Denmark W Australia 1910–20, Sr Curate Ch Ch Felling 1921–23, Vicar Alnham Northumberland 1932–42; *m* 16 June 1932 Sarah Helen (*d* 29 March 1959), dau of William Cotton Grummitt, of Grantham, Lincs, and *dsp* 19 Feb 1950

1b Anna Augusta; *d* 1866

2b Jane Josephine; *d* unm 5 Jan 1945

3b Meta Theodosia; *d* unm 1913

4b Anne Augusta; *m* 1890 her cousin Thomas Beard, MD, and *d* 1907, leaving issue

4a Capel (Rev); *b* 10 Oct 1814; Rector Sacred Trinity Salford; *m* 16 Dec 1847 Anne Jane (*d* July 1900), dau of N Proctor, and *d* 10 Feb 1885, leaving, with other issue:

1b William Owen; *b* 4 April 1854; Col RAMC; *m* 7 Dec 1899 Mary Seton, dau of Wensley Tyrrell Jacob, and *dsp* 3 June 1905

1b Annie; *m* 10 July 1869 her cousin Maj William Charles Wolseley and *d* 29 May 1938, leaving issue (*see above*)

(2) George Rogerson; *b* 1777; MD Dublin; *m* 12 Jan 1804 Catherine, dau of Robert Brown, of Clough, Co Down, and *d* 11 May 1857, leaving:

1a Robert Brown; *b* 1809; civ engr; *m* 1st 1838 Elizabeth Ann (*d* 21 Sept 1851), widow of Hugh Jones and dau of John Hughes, MD, of Liverpool, and had:

1b John St George; *b* 19 Dec 1839; Lt-Col Cheshire Regt; *d* unm 23 May 1913

2b Robert Hughes; *b* June 1841; *m* 1861 Fanny (*d* 21 April 1901), dau of Charles James Clarke, and *d* 13 April 1912, leaving:

1c Arthur Hugh; *b* 6 Dec 1862; *m* 1897 Mary Bryan Grace Smith and *dsp* 28 June 1942

2c Frank St George; *b* 13 July 1868; *d* unm 21 Sept 1901

1c Marian Josephine; *b* 1870; *m* 12 June 1902 Arthur Greene Brinton, FRCS, LRCP (*d* July 1945), and had issue

2c Gertrude Isabel; *b* 1877; *m* 10 June 1909 Frederick Oliver Timmins, of Oakley, Beds, s of Frederick Henry Timmins, of The Old Bell Ho, Northfield, Worcs, and *d* 24 April 1948, having had issue

1b Isabel; *m* 1869 William King, of Dublin, and had issue

2b Kathleen Maria Charlotte; *b* 1845; *m* 25 May 1868 John Charles, of Donnycarney, Co Dublin, and *d* 1924, leaving issue

1a (cont.) Robert Brown *m* 2nd 1852 Lalla Marcella (*m* 2nd 29 Oct 1862 Edward McDowell and *d c* 1880), dau of Capt George Oliver Bingham, 26th Regt, and *d* 6 July 1858, having by her had:

3b Richard Bingham; *b* 13 Dec 1853; *m* 1st 28 Sept 1878 Jane Wilkinson (*d* 7 Feb 1907), dau of William Dickson, of Liscard, Cheshire, and had:

1c Richard Bingham; *b* 29 Sept 1879; *m* 1907 Edith, dau of James Haigh, of Birkenhead, Cheshire, and *d* 14 Feb 1948, having had:

1d Arthur St George; *b* 31 Oct 1909; *d* unm 9 April 1936

2c Reginald Gordon; *b* 13 May 1883; *m* 12 Oct 1918 Lilian Wallace, dau of Charles Rankin Fyffe, of Natal, S Africa, and *d* 3 Sept 1925, leaving issue

1d Ronald Wilkinson; *b* 26 May 1920; Roy Durban LI S African Mil Force WW II; *d* unm a POW 19 April 1945

3b (cont.) Richard Bingham *m* 2nd 8 June 1908 Mary Alexandra, dau of John Edward Read, and *d* 20 Dec 1938, leaving by her:

3c Sir Garnet Wolseley 12th Bt; *b* 27 May 1915; *educ* Wallasey Centl Sch; Northants Regt WW II Madagascar, Sicily, Italy and Germany; emigrated to Canada 1951; *m* 5 Aug 1950 *Lilian Mary [Dowager Lady Wolseley, 73 Dorothy St, Brantford, ON N3S 1H1, Canada], dau of William Bertram Ellison, of Wallasey, Cheshire, and *dsp* Oct 1991

1c Rubina Bingham; *b* 18 April 1909; *m* 1st 25 May 1946 Walter Leonard Openshaw (*d* 1951); *m* 2nd 1952 Frank Whitby (*d* 1960)

2c Lalla; *b* 7 Feb 1914

2a Richard John; *b* 1821; civ engr; *m* Elizabeth Ann Hughes (*d* 13 May 1887), dau of Hugh Jones by his w Elizabeth Ann Hughes (*m* 2nd Robert Brown Wolseley (*see above*), and *d* 11 July 1865, leaving:

1b Richard Francis; *d* unm 25 May 1869

2b William Robert; *b* 1849; *educ* Trin Coll Dublin; *m* 9 Dec 1885 Lillie Eustace (*d* 1911), dau of Rev John W Dockray, and *d* 9 Feb 1906, leaving:

1c Noel Cecil; *b* 14 Dec 1887; naturalized US citizen 1920; *m* 21 June 1913 Mae Evelyn (*d* 1965), dau of John J O'Connell, and *d* 28 Dec 1969, leaving:

1d *Eileen Rita; *b* 1916; Dir Nursing Serv Concord Hosp, Concord, NH, USA

3b Francis Ernest; *b* 1854; *m* 1 July 1874 Fanny Elizabeth, dau of Henry Byrne, CE, of Dublin, and *d* 17 Dec 1914, leaving:

1c Francis Richard; *b* 30 March 1877; chartered accountant; *m* 1906 Elizabeth Ellen (*d* 1966), dau of John Abbot Shippey, and *d* 26 Jan 1934, leaving:

1d *Frances Hilda; *b* 18 July 1908; *m* 1938 *Hugh Wynn Jones and has:

1e *Kathleen Margaret; *b* 1939

2d *Eulalie Jacqueline Patricia; *b* 17 March 1911; *m* 1932 *John Lewis Jones and has:

1e *Jane Eulalie; *b* 1942

2e *Anne Jessie Alexandra; *b* 1947

2c Albert George; *b* 2 Nov 1878; *m* Alethia Gardner and *dsp* 18 Aug 1941

3c Walter Henry; *b* 24 June 1880; *d* unm 11 July 1931

4b Edwyn Hulbert; *b* 1855; *m* 1888 Anna Sophia (*d* 1917), dau of Judge Kristian Filip Mortimer Lang, of Vastergotland, Sweden, and *d* 22 Nov 1942, leaving:

1c Eileen Anna; *b* 1890; *d* unm 30 Oct 1948

2c Sigrid Dagmar; *b* 1892; *m* 1914 (*divorce* 1946) Capt Eric Erskine Campbell Tufnell, RN, and *d* 5 Jan 1952, leaving issue

5b Athelstan George, of Dublin; *b* 1858; Irish Land Commr; *d* unm 8 Oct 1933

1a Maria Jane; *m* 1st 1838 George Cook; *m* 2nd H Taylor and had issue

2a Catherine Emily; *m* 31 Dec 1830 Francis Fetherstonhaugh, of Whiterock, Co Longford, and *d* 8 Jan 1845, leaving issue

(3) Garnet Joseph; *b* 1778; Maj 25th Bdrs Guadaloupe and W Indies; *m* 1825 (Frances) Anne (*d* 7 Oct 1883), dau of William Smith, of Golden Bridge Ho, Co Dublin, and *d* 1840, having had, with other issue:

1a GARNET JOSEPH WOLSELEY, 1st VISCOUNT WOLSELEY, of Wolseley, Co Stafford, so *cr* 28 Sept 1885, with remainder in default of male issue, to his dau and her male issue, as also earlier 25 Nov 1882 (plus thanks of Parl and grant of £30,000 [over £1.4m in late-1990s terms]) BARON WOLSELEY OF CAIRO AND OF WOLSELEY, Co Stafford (both UK), with remainder to heirs male of his body, KP (1885), GCB (KCB 1874, CB 1871), OM, GCMG (1874, KCMG 1870), VD, PC (I 1850); *b* 4 June 1833; Ensign 12th (E Suffolk) Foot March 1852, tfd to 80th (Staffs Regt) Foot April 1852, Burmese War 1852–53 (severely wounded, despatches), Lt 1853, tfd to 84th (York and Lancaster) Foot Jan 1854 and 90th (Perths Vol LI) Foot Feb 1854, Crimean War 1854–56 (despatches twice, wounded four times, Legn Hon 5th Cl, Medjidie), Capt 1855, DAQMG Light Div 1855, Indian Mutiny 1857–59, DAQMG Oudh Div 1858–60, Brevet Maj 1858, Brevet Lt-Col 1859 (despatches five times), DAQMG Chinese War 1860–61, AQMG 1862–67, DQMG 1867–70 Canada, cmded Red River Expdn Canada 1870, AAG War Office 1871–73, local rank of Maj-Gen Gold Coast Ashanti Expdn 1873–74 (thanks of Parl, grant of £25,000 [over £900,000 in late-1990s terms], Freedom City London), Maj-Gen 1874, Inspr-Gen Aux Forces 1874–76, Commr Natal 1875, memb Indian Cncl 1876–78, Lt-Gen 1878, HC and C-in-C Cyprus 1878–79, Govr Natal and Transvaal and HC and C-in-C 1879–80, QMG 1880–82, Gen 1882, Adj-Gen 1882–84 and 1885–90, C-in-C Forces Egypt 1882, GOC Egypt 1884–85, Nile Expdn 1885, C-in-C Forces Ireland 1890–95, C-in-C all HM's Forces 1895–1900, FM, Col Roy Irish Regt and Prince of Wales's Leinster Regt (Roy Canadians) and 2nd Vol Bn Roy Fus, Hon Col Queen's Rifle Vol Bde, Roy Scots, Col RHG (The Blues) and Gold Stick to TM QUEEN VICTORIA 1895–1901 and EDWARD VII 1901–07, Hon DCL Oxon, Hon LLD Cantab, Dublin and Edinburgh; author: *Soldier's Pocket-Book for field service* (1869), *The Life of John Churchill, Duke of Marlborough* (1894), *The Decline and Fall of Napoleon* (1895) and *Story of a Soldier's Life* (1903); *m* 4 June 1867 Louisa (*d* 10 April 1920), probably illegitimate dau of Alexander Erskine Holmes, and *d* 25 March 1913, when the Barony expired, leaving:

1b FRANCES GARNET WOLSELEY, VISCOUNTESS WOLSELEY; *b* 15 Sept 1872; Fndr Glynde Coll Gdning, author: *Gardening for Women* and other works, Freedom City London 1913; *d unm* 24 Dec 1936, when the Viscounty expired

2a Richard; *b* 3 June 1834; Surgn-Gen PMO Meerut; *m* 1852 Mary (*d* 13 Nov 1887), dau of John Ingram, and *d* Jan 1887

3a Frederick York, JP NSW; *b* 16 March 1837; *m* — and *d* Jan 1899

4a George Benjamin (Sir), GCB; *b* 11 July 1839; Indian Mutiny 1858–59, Afghan War 1878–79, Egyptian Expdn 1882, Col York and Lancaster Regt Sudan 1884–85, ADC to HM QUEEN VICTORIA 1882–92, Burmese Expdn. 1887–91, Brig-Gen Madras 1889–94, Maj-Gen India 1895–98, Lt-Gen cmdg Madras forces 1898–1903, 3rd Cl Medjidie; *m* 11 Nov 1867 Esther Louise (*d* 11 March 1902), dau of William Andrews, and *d* 10 May 1921, having had:

    1b Garnet John; *b* 1873; Lt Sherwood Foresters; *d* 24 June 1896

    1a Matilda Emily Victoria; *m* 23 Feb 1854 John Bagwell Creagh (*d* 9 Oct 1906), of Ballyandrew, Doneraile, Co Cork, and *d* 5 Oct 1914, leaving issue

    2a Frances Jane; *m* 1857 Gavin Ralston Caldwell (*d* 1868), of Grennon Castle, Ayrshire, and *d* 19 April 1912, having had issue

(4) Robert Benjamin; *b* 1790; Maj 25th Bdrs; *m* 1820 Alice (*d* 1870), dau of Sir Robert Warren, 1st Bt (*qv*), and *d* 1870, leaving:

    1a William Hulbert (Ven); *b* 16 June 1821; Rector Kilrush, Archdeacon Kilfenora; *m* 1st 15 Jan 1847 Elizabeth, dau of John Dawson, of Annamartin, Co Fermanagh; *m* 2nd March 1899 Nina, dau of William Sadleir, of Scallahen and *d* 9 May 1899, having had by his 1st w, with other issue:

        1b Robert Benjamin (Rev), of NY; *b* 20 Nov 1847; *m* 1872 Ellen Pierce and *d* 1895, leaving:

            1c Robert Benjamin; *b* 1873

            2c William Warlock; *b* 1874

            1c Annie Louise; *m* 1905 Henry Clark Baker

        2b Richard Warren; *b* 26 Sept 1849; Dist Registrar in Probate Ct Cork; *m* 4 July 1883 Ruth, dau of Rev Lawrence Painting, and *d* 18 May 1923

        3b William Burdett Morony; *b* 6 Jan 1860; *d* 23 Aug 1887

        4b John Francis; *b* 29 March 1862; Egypt 1897 (despatches, medal and two clasps) and 1898–1900 (despatches, promoted, medal with three clasps and Br medal), Boer War 1900–02 (despatches, two medals, five clasps), Maj (T/Lt-Col) The King's Own Regt, APM 1916, T/Lt-Col cmdg 5th Garrison Bn Roy Welch Fus; *m* 12 April 1904 Beatrice (*d* 30 Jan 1945), widow of William Fox, of St Bees, Cumberland, and yst dau of Col C C Grantham, 89th Regt, and *dsp* 28 April 1947

        1b Grace; *m* 11 June 1868 Maj-Gen Thomas Staples and had issue (*see* STAPLES, Bt)

        2b Alice Warren; *m* 1883 William Milward Newport and had issue

        3b Elizabeth Dawson; *m* 22 Aug 1877 Frederick John Leech, of Enniscorthy, Co Wexford, and had issue

    2a Robert Warren (Rev); *b* 27 Dec 1823; *educ* Trin Coll Dublin (BA); Vicar Dunton Bassett; *m* 1st 10 March 1847 Georgina (*d* 3 Feb 1881), dau of James Nixon, of Prospect, Co Fermanagh, and had:

        1b Robert Warren St John; *b* 25 Jan 1848; *m* Marianne Dezendorf, of Newburgh, NY (*d* 1937), and *d* 1910, leaving:

            1c Douglas St John; *b* 1875; *m* 1900 Annie Elizabeth (*d* 1959), dau of Jared Edward Stallings, and *d* 1943, leaving:

                1d James Douglas; *b* 1903; *m* 1935 *Olive, dau of Carroll Walter Wofford, and *d* 23 Oct 1960, leaving:

                    1e Sir JAMES DOUGLAS WOLSELEY, **13th and present Bt**

                1d Margaret; *b* 1906; *m* 18 June 1941 Oscar Hughes King, of Fort Worth

                2d Ann; *b* 1910; *m* 1936 (*divorce* 1954) William Anson Hines and *d* 29 Sept 1961

            1c Georgina Christina; *b* 1870; *m* Robert Preston Conner and *d* 1948, leaving issue

        2b Henry William Falloon; *b* 3 Nov 1849; *m* — and *d* Sept 1924, leaving:

            1c Alice

            2c Nellie; *m* — Vories, of Chicago

        3b Edward St George, slr; *b* 31 Dec 1852; *m* 13 Aug 1877 Hannah Mary (*d* 26 Jan 1916), dau of Colin Douglas Robertson, and *d* 5 Aug 1907, leaving:

            1c Kathleen Mary; LRAM

        4b Herbert Falkner; *b* 30 Dec 1854; Lt 44th Regt

        1b Alice Elizabeth Jane; *d unm*

    2a (cont.) Rev Robert Wolseley; *m* 2nd 8 Aug 1882 Jean Ruskin (*d* 22 May 1926), dau of William Richardson, MD, of Gloucester Gdns, W, and *d* 15 Nov 1909, having by her had:

        5b Garnet Ruskin; *b* 24 May 1884; *m* 14 April 1937 Joan Alys (*d* 10 April 1943), dau of Sir Walter John Trevelyan, 8th Bt, of Nettlecombe (*qv*), and *d* 16 Nov 1967, leaving:

            1c +JOHN WALTER [John Wolseley Esq, Nettlecombe, Williton, Somerset TA4 4HS]; *b* 21 April 1938; heir presumptive; *educ* Westminster; *m* 1964 (*divorce* 1978) Patricia Ann Newland and has:

                1d +William [William Wolseley Esq, c/o Anglesey Post Office, Victoria, Australia]; *b* 24 Jan 1967

                2d +Thomas; *b* 2 Oct 1969

            1c Jane Alys; *b* 30 July 1939; *m* 6 April 1963 (*divorce* 1976, took surname TREVELYAN) Nicolas Alexander, architect, and *d* 1993, leaving:

                1d *Julius Diccon; *b* 1968

                1d *Tamsyn Trevelyan; *b* 1966

            2c Jennifer Ann Ruskin; *b* 18 Aug 1941; *m* 1979 *Baron Roman Heinrich Gamotha, of Venice, and *d* 1983, leaving:

                1d *Tatiana Romana; *b* 1982

        6b Horace Carter; *b* 1886; *d* 20 June 1912

        2b Eirene Eva; *b* 27 April 1888; LCC London Ambulance Serv WW II

1 Catherine; *m* 1st June 1752 Thomas Burgh, MP (*d* 23 June 1759), of Oldtown, and had issue; *m* 2nd Ven Caulfeild Byrne Caulfeild, Archdeacon Clogher

WOLSELEY of Wolseley

Arms: Argent a talbot passant gules. **Crest:** Out of a ducal coronet or a wolf's head erased proper. **Motto:** *Homo homini lupus* ('Man is as a wolf towards his fellow man'). **Creation:** Bt (E) 24 Nov 1628.

SIR CHARLES GARNET RICHARD MARK WOLSELEY, 11TH BT, of Wolseley, Co Stafford [Sir Charles Wolseley Bt, Wolseley Park, Rugeley, Staffs WS15 2TU]; *b* 16 June 1944; *s gf* 1954; *educ* Ampleforth and RAC Cirencester; FRICS; consultant Smiths Gore (chartered surveyors) 1987– (assoc ptnr 1974, ptnr 1979–87); *m* 1st 15 June 1968 (*divorce* 1984) Anita Maria, er dau of Hugo J Fried, of Epsom, Surrey, and has:

  1 +STEPHEN GARNET HUGO CHARLES; *b* 2 May 1980; *educ* Worth Abbey

  1 *Annabelle Clare Maria; *b* 26 April 1969; *educ* Roy Naval Sch

  2 *Emily Lavinia; *b* 7 March 1972; *educ* Roy Naval Sch

  3 *Louise Margaret; *b* 7 March 1977; *educ* Mayfield

Sir CHARLES *m* 2nd 5 June 1984 *Mrs Imogene (Jeannie) E Brown

Lineage: EDRIC/EADRICHT de WULSELLEGH; living *temp* WILLIAM II (RUFUS); had, with two er sons (Reinner, held Wolseley, Staffs, under Nigel de Stafford, and granted land at Gailey, nr Penkridge, to the nuns of Blithbury 1158–65; Hervey) and a dau (Beatrice, *m* Sir Ralph de Hintes, of Hintes):

SIWALD/SIWARD de WULSISLEE; *d* by 1165, leaving:

WILLIAM Fitz SIWARD de WULSISLEE; feudal Ld of Wolseley; *m* Matilda (a widow in 1199), dau of Stephen de Davenport, and *d* on a pilgrimage to St James of Compostela, Spain, leaving:

  1 Robert; living 1203/4; *dvp unm*

  2 Richard; feudal Ld of Wolseley; had:

    (1) Richard; *d unm* by *c* 1255

    (1) Agnes; *m* Hugh de Langnad

    (2) Felicia; *m* Richard — and had:

      1a Nicholas

      2a William

      3a Stephen

  3 Stephen; had:

    (1) Robert fitz Stephen de WOLSELEY; feudal Ld of Wolseley; jt heir with Agnes de Langnad and Richard de Hintes, living 1248; *m* Matilda de Bishton, of Staffs, an heiress, and had:

      1a Robert; *d* by 1266, leaving:

        1b Robert; feudal Ld of Wolseley; juror 1255, Verderer Cannock Forest 1286; *m* Hawise — and had:

          1c RICHARD

          2c William, of Bradley, Staffs; *d c* 1344

          3c Geoffrey; *b* 1270

The est s,

RICHARD de WOLSELEY; feudal Ld of Wolseley; *m* 1297 Sybilla (*m* 2nd Richard de Wenlock), dau of Roger de Aston, feudal Ld of Heywood, Staffs, through whom he acquired Bishton, Staffs, and *d* 1320, leaving:

  1 Geoffrey; priest, fndr Trinity Chantry at Wolseley; *d c* 1341

  2 JOHN

  3 William, of Bishton; had illegitimately by Alice Norice:

    (1) Anna; *d unm* 1338

  4 Richard, of Rugeley, Staffs; had:

    (1) William

    (2) John

  5 Robert; had:

    (1) John; Esq to THE BLACK PRINCE

The 2nd s,

JOHN de WOLSELEY; feudal Ld of Wolseley; *m* Joan — and *d* 1350, leaving:

JOHN de WOLSELEY, feudal Ld of Wolseley; *m* Eleanor de Allaton, of Pillaton Hall, Staffs, and *d* by 1381, leaving, with two other sons:

RALPH de WOLSELEY; living 1397; *m* Maud — and had:

THOMAS de WOLSELEY; MP Staffs 1465; *m* 1419 Margery, dau of William Brocton, of Longdon, Staffs, and *d c* 1469, leaving:

RALPH WOLSELEY; had licence to crenellate Wolseley Hall 1469; fourth Baron of the Exchequer and Lt of Calais *temp* EDWARD IV; *m* 1st Agnes (*dsp*), dau of Thomas Blount, of Edlaston, Derbys, and sister of 1st Lord (Baron) Mountjoy; *m* 2nd 1468 Margaret, dau of Sir Robert Aston, of Heywood, Staffs, and widow of John Kynardesley, of Loxley, Staffs, and by her had:

JOHN de WOLSELEY; *b* 1475; *m* Elizabeth, dau of George Stanley, of Bromwich, Staffs, and *d* 1553, leaving, with an est s (Anthony, *m* Margaret, dau of William Blythe, of Norton, Derbys, and was ancestors of the WOLSELEYs of Wolseley, whose male line died out with Sir Thomas Wolseley, a recusant so impoverished by fines for his religious conservatism that he had had to sell his estate over the years 1624 to 1627, doing so, however, to his distant cousin **Sir Robert Wolseley, 1st Bt**, a yst s (Rev John, LLB, Rector Ecton Montgomery, Northants) and six daus, a 2nd s:

RALPH WOLSELEY, of Shugborough, Staffs; *m* Joyce, dau and heiress of John Salwey, of Stanford, and widow of William Ashby, and had, with a yr s (*dsp*):

JOHN WOLSELEY, of Morton, Staffs; living 1614; *m* Isabella, dau of John Porter, of Chillington, Staffs, and had a 2nd s:

Sir Robert Wolseley, 1st Bt (E), so *cr* 24 Nov 1628, of Morton and Wolseley, which he acquired from his cousin (*see above*); *b* 1587; *m* 1630 Mary, 2nd dau of Sir George Wroughton, of Wilcot, Wilts, and *d* 21 Sept 1646, having had, with other issue, including a yr s (William, PC (I), Col of Horse, accompanied WILLIAM III to Ireland 1690, cmded the Inniskillen men at the Battles of Newtown Butler and the Boyne, Brig-Gen 1690, Master Ordnance 1692, Ld Justice 1696, *d* unm 1697):

Sir Charles Wolseley, 2nd Bt, of Wolseley, Staffs; MP Oxford 1653, Stafford 1654–58 and 1660, memb CROMWELL's 'Other House'; *m* 1649 Anne, yst dau of 1st Viscount Saye and Sele (*qv*), and *d* 9 Oct 1714, having had, with eight other daus:

  1 Robert; *b* 1650; Envoy to Brussels *temp* WILLIAM III; *d* unm 1697

  2 Charles; *dsp*

  3 **Sir William Wolseley, 3rd Bt**; *d* unm, accidentally drowned 8 July 1728

  4 **Sir Henry Wolseley, 4th Bt**; *d* unm, *bur* 5 Sept 1730

  5 Richard; Capt Williamite forces Ireland, bought part of the estate of Charles Butler, Earl of Arran, and established himself at Mount Arran (later Mount Wolseley), Co Carlow; MP Co Carlow 1703–13 and 1715–24; *m* by licence 16 Jan 1688/9 Frances, dau and heiress of John Burneston, and *d* 1724, having had, with other issue:

    (1) WILLIAM (Sir), **5th Bt**

    (2) Robert; *m* Annek, dau of Ebenezer Warren, of Lodge, Co Kilkenny, and *d* 30 Jan 1733, having had:

      1a William Neville; Sheriff Kilkenny 1767–69; *m* Anne Cosby and had:

        1b William, of Rostrevor; Adml the Red; *m* 1795 Jane, dau of John Moore, of Clough, Co Down, and *d* 1842, having had:

          1c John Hood; RN; *d* 14 June 1827

          2c William Cosby; *d* 11 March 1868

          1c Mary Jervis; *m* 15 May 1829 Arthur Innes and *d* 24 Jan 1886, leaving issue (*see* ROXBURGHE, D)

          2c Sydney Anne; *m* 8 Oct 1835 John Madden, of Hilton Park, Co Monaghan (*d* 8 July 1844), and *d* 24 Sept 1870, leaving issue

    (3) **Sir RICHARD WOLSELEY, 1st Bt**, of Mount Wolseley, Co Carlow (*qv*)

  1 Elizabeth; *m* Robert Somerville, of Edstone, Warwicks, and had:

    (1) William; author *The Chase*

  2 Mary; *m* Richard Edwards, of Old Court, Co Wicklow, MP

The 4th Bt's n,

Sir William Wolseley, 5th Bt; *b c* 1692; *m* 1st 1738 Ann (*d* 1752), dau of John Fieldhouse; *m* 2nd 23 Sept 1752 Anna (allegedly *m* 3rd John Robins, of Stafford; *m* 4th — Hargreaves), only dau of William Northey, of Compton Bassett, Wilts, and widow of John Whitby, of Cresswell Hall, Staffs, and *d* 12 May 1779, leaving by her no issue but by his 1st w, with two yr sons (Charles, *b* 25 Oct 1741, Adml the Red, *d* unm 10 April 1808; James, *bapt* 12 Oct 1751, Lt 17th Foot, *d* unm in Ireland 18 May 1773) and a dau (Sophia, *bapt* 31 March 1749, *m* 1768 William Pigott, of Doddershall, Bucks (*d* 26 Feb 1802), and *d* 1801, leaving issue:

Sir William Wolseley, 6th Bt; *b* 24 Aug 1740; *m* 2 July 1765 Charlotte Barbara, only child of Zachary Chambers, of Wimbledon, Surrey, and niece of Ephraim Chambers, and had, with other issue:

  1 CHARLES (Sir), **7th Bt**

  2 Robert (Rev); *b* 3 Aug 1770; *m* Mary Ann, dau of Archdeacon Hand, and *dsp* 1 Sept 1815

  3 Henry; *b* 16 Aug 1771; Capt Army; *m* 2 Dec 1793 Charlotte Elizabeth (*d* 1826), only dau of Maj John Delap Halliday (*see* DYSART, E), and *d* 1836, having had, with a dau (*d* unm):

    (1) Henry John; *b* 1795; RN; *d* 1823

    (2) William Bertie; *b* 17 Aug 1797; served RN and Civ Serv Br Guiana; *m* 1st 11 July 1818 Eliza Earle (*d* 21 March 1851), dau of William Nicholas Daniell, of Monstserrat, barrister, and had:

      1a William Augustus; *b* 2 June 1819; MD; Staff Surgn Turkish Contingent Crimea 1854–55; *m* 1 Jan 1843 Mary Maria, dau of William Flockhart, and *d* 13 Feb 1859, leaving, with other issue:

        1b Henry John; *b* 9 March 1846; MB, MCH; Prof Medicine Codrington Coll Barbados; *m* 14 Nov 1872 Fanny Carlyon (*d* 6 Feb 1936), dau of John Gittens, and *d* 17 Jan 1931, leaving:

          1c Ellen Graham; *b* 26 Sept 1876; *d* unm 15 Jan 1957

          2c Emily Bertie; *b* 11 Dec 1879

          3c Alice Hamilton; *b* 30 Dec 1883

          4c Minnie Bathurst; *b* 19 May 1885; *m* 6 Sept 1924 Edward Archer Wood (*d* 15 Dec 1957), MRCS, LRCP, s of Louis Henry Wood, of Marlborough

          5c Janet Porter; *b* 30 May 1889

        2b William Augustus (Daniel); *b* 3 Oct 1847; MEC Guiana 1893–1901; *m* 1st 20 Aug 1891 Harriet (*dsp* 15 Jan 1894), dau of D Fraser Luckie; *m* 2nd 2 Feb 1895 Lilian Laura (*d* 2 June 1941), dau of Horatio Bethune Leggatt, of Worth, Sussex, and *d* 18 April 1929, leaving:

        1c William Bertie; *b* 7 July 1896; Lt RFA WW I; *d* of wounds recd in action 5 July 1916

        1c Cecilia Lucy Cavendish; *b* 14 Oct 1903; barrister Gray's Inn 1930; memb IOJ; *d* unm 14 Jan 1972

        2c *(Lilian) Patricia Dysart [Mrs Patricia Archdale, Flat 6, Chester Mansions, 151 Oakhill Rd, London SW15 2QW]; *b* 8 Jan 1908; *m* 25 March 1933 (*divorce* 1948) Alexander Mervyn Archdale, s of Lt-Col Theodore Montgomery Archdale, DSO, RA, and has:

          1d *Dominic Edward Wolseley; *b* 8 Jan 1937; *educ* St Paul's and Downing Coll Cambridge (BA 1961, MA, 1965); late RAF; manager product planning, Process Computer Dept, GEC, USA; *m* 1st 1959 (*divorce* 1974) Ruth Selby, dau of Charles Johnstone, of Bloomery, WVa.; *m* 2nd 1976 *Donna, dau of Albert Leroy Baird, of Sun City, Ariz.

          2d *Anthony Quintin Wolseley [Anthony Archdale Esq, Flat 6, 151 Oakhill Rd, London SW15 2QW]; *b* 23 March 1940; *educ* Saltus GS Bermuda

      1b Eliza Porter; *m* 1867 Lynch Thomas, MD, and *d* Nov 1921, leaving issue

      2b Mary Jane Bourne; *m* 1873 John Shine Wilson (*d* 1900), and *d* 21 Feb 1937, leaving issue

      2a John Henry; *b* 1 Nov 1820; *d* 11 Nov 1840

      1a Charlotte Elizabeth; *m* 7 Oct 1840 Thomas Porter, est s of Thomas Porter, of Rockbeare House, Devon, and *dsp* 9 April 1906

      2a Frances Anne; *m* 1st 23 Jan 1845 George Noble Bredin (*d* 1852), s of Maj-Gen Bredin, RA; *m* 2nd 1854 J Frederick Hills and had issue

      3a Cecilia Lewis Pauline; *m* 1st 23 Jan 1845 Edmund Hayter Bingham (*dsp* 9 Oct 1856), s of Col Charles Cox Bingham, RA; *m* 2nd 22 Aug 1860 Dr Henry Hutson and had issue

      4a Eliza Jane; *m* 23 Jan 1845 Rev John Frederick Bourne, s of John Henry Bourne, of Dalby Hall, Spilsby, Lincs, and *d* 15 Dec 1848, leaving issue

      5a Catharine Norval Magdalene Dysart; *m* 18 May 1854 Harry Grosvenor Butts, MD, s of R G Butts, of Demerara, and had issue

      6a Louisa Tollemache; *m* 3 Nov 1853 John Rose Daniell (*dsp* 6 May 1866), s of Hon Meade Home Daniell, Pres Cncl Antigua, and *d* 7 Dec 1879

      7a Henrietta Augusta Meade; *m* 3 Feb 1857 Edward Poulton Wells, s of A Wells, of Bermuda, and had issue

    (2) (cont.) William Wolseley *m* 2nd 14 Sept 1852 Charlotte (*d* 12 Nov 1887), dau of Rev Charles Prowett, Rector Stapleford, Herts, and *d* 7 Jan 1881

    (1) Charlotte; *m* Gen Sir Thomas Browne, KCB, and *d* his widow 10 Feb 1861 aged 88

    (2) Caroline; *m* Robert Haig, of Roebuck, Co Dublin, and of Kilan, Co Cavan, and *d* 1833, leaving issue

    (3) Cecilia; *m* 1812 Rev Charles Prowett, Rector Stapleford, and *d* 27 Nov 1857, having had issue

Sir WILLIAM *d* 5 Aug 1817; his est s,

Sir Charles Wolseley, 7th Bt; *b* 20 July 1769; *m* 1st 13 Dec 1792 Mary (*d* 16 July 1811), dau of Hon Thomas Clifford (*see* CLIFFORD OF CHUDLEIGH, B), and had two sons and a dau (*dvp*); *m* 2nd 2 July 1812 Anne (*d* 24 Oct 1838), yst dau of Anthony Wright, of Wealdside, Essex, and by her had:

  1 CHARLES (Sir), **8th Bt**

  2 Henry; *b* 21 Oct 1819; *dvp* 18 Aug 1843

  3 Edward; *b* 30 April 1821; *dvp* Brussels 6 March 1827

  1 Marianne; *m* 25 Nov 1834 Francis, Marques de Lousada de San Miniato (*d* 17 March 1870), Br Consul Boston, and *d* 1 Nov 1881, leaving issue

  2 Caroline; *m* 22 Aug 1845 Marmaduke Salvin, DL (*d* 27 Dec 1885), of Burnhall, Co Duham, and *d* 23 Sept 1880, leaving issue

Sir CHARLES *d* 3 Oct 1846; his only surv s,

Sir Charles Wolseley, 8th Bt; *b* 6 May 1813; *m* 23 Sept 1839 Mary Anne (*d* 18 Jan 1873), est dau of Nicholas Selby, of Acton House, Middx, and had:

  1 William Henry; *d* 16 Jan 1852

  2 CHARLES MICHAEL (Sir), **9th Bt**

  3 Edward Talbot, of Maryland, Ascot; *b* 13 Oct 1848; Capt 3rd Stafford Militia; *m* 23 Jan 1872 Florence Mary (*d* 20 Aug 1939), 3rd dau of Edward Joseph Weld, of Lulworth Castle, Dorset, and *d* 2 Feb 1935, having had, with a dau (*d* an infant):

    (1) Mervyn Joseph Witham; *b* 23 Nov 1873; *m* 19 Sept 1907 Dorothy Mary (*d* 12 March 1956), est dau of Philip Witham, of Whitmoor House, Sutton Place, Surrey, and *d* 30 Nov 1956, leaving:

      1a Ursula Mary; *b* 13 Sept 1908; *m* 9 Jan 1937 John Henry Spencer (*d* 8 Oct 1963), only s of Cdr Henry Spencer, RN, and had issue

      2a Evelyn Mary; *b* 1 May 1913; *m* 18 March 1939 Bela Garzulay, late of Hungarian Min of For Affrs

    (2) Hubert Joseph; *b* 17 Nov 1874; *ka* Elandslaagte 27 Oct 1899 while with Imp Light Horse Boer War

    (3) Charles Joseph; *b* 15 Feb 1877; *m* Jan 1902 Isobel (*d* 27 April 1961), dau of A Drummond, of Newcastle, and *d* 25 May 1933, leaving:

      1a Charles Edward (Peter); *b* 9 Oct 1913; *educ* Ampleforth; *m* 7 Aug 1954 *Marie, dau of Arthur John Locke, of Newcastle

      1a Gundred Etheldreda; *b* 31 May 1903; *m* Sept 1944 Stanley Horrocks (*d* 1956)

    (4) Edward Joseph; *b* 17 April 1880; Capt 1st Bn E Lancs Regt Boer War 1900–02 (despatches, severely wounded, Queen's medal with three clasps, King's medal with two clasps), N Nigeria 1906–07 (despatches, medal and clasp); *m* 29 April 1919 Viola, only dau of Lorenzo Mancine, of Durban, and *d* 4 June 1920

    (5) William Spencer Joseph; *b* 30 March 1886; Lt 2nd Bn E Lancs Regt; *ka* 14 March 1915

(6) Robert Francis Joseph; *b* 23 July 1890; Maj and T/Lt-Col 3rd Bn E Lancs Regt, WW I (wounded) and WW II; *m* 9 Jan 1917 Helen Congreve (*d* 16 June 1963), dau of Maj R P Congreve Schneider, IA, and *das* 18 Dec 1940

(1) Florence Mary Josephine; *m* 24 Oct 1906 Oswald Francis Gerard Stonor and *d* 3 June 1956, leaving issue (*see* CAMOYS, B)

4 Robert Joseph (Rev); *b* 21 June 1850; RC priest; *d* 24 March 1920

5 Henry Olivier; *b* 1851; *d* 1855

Sir CHARLES *d* 15 May 1854; his est surv s,

Sir Charles Michael Wolseley, 9th Bt, JP, DL Staffs; *b* 4 July 1846; Lt Staffs Militia and Yeo Cav; *m* 18 July 1883 Anna Theresa (*d* 11 Oct 1937), dau of Daniel T Murphy, of San Francisco, and had:

1 EDRIC CHARLES JOSEPH (Sir), **10th Bt**

2 William Ralph Joseph, TD, JP (Salop 1939); *b* 1 July 1887; Capt Staffs Yeo WW I (despatches), Roy Pioneer Corps WW II 1942 on; *m* 10 Nov 1923 Ruth Gertrude (*d* 7 Dec 1962), yst dau of Lt-Col Robert Halstead Hargreaves, JP, DL, of Knightley Grange, Staffs, and Barnside, Lancs, and *d* 1977, leaving:

(1) Robert William Hargreaves; *b* 13 Dec 1924; *educ* Canford; Gren Gds and Roy Fus WW II 1942 on; *m* 24 July 1965 *Beryl Marjorie [Mrs Robert Wolseley, Dodhill Firs, Nailsbourne, Somerset TA2 8AT], dau of Frederick George Harvey, of Woodside, Pitsminster, Taunton, and *d* 17 Jan 1998, leaving:

  1a +Alistair Robert Hargreaves; *b* 25 May 1969

  1a *Heather Frances; *b* 25 Aug 1967

(1) *Veronica Ruth Theresa Rose; *b* 22 Oct 1928

Sir CHARLES *d* 30 Jan 1931; his er s,

Sir Edric Charles Joseph Wolseley, 10th Bt, JP; *b* 7 April 1886; ARSM; Lt Staffs Yeo WW I; *m* 19 Aug 1916 Clare Mary Annette (*d* 27 June 1978 aged 82), er dau of Charles Edmond de Trafford (*see* DE TRAFFORD, Bt), and *d* 17 Sept 1954, having had:

1 Stephen Garnet Hubert Francis; *b* 17 May 1918; Capt RA WW II 1939–44; *m* 12 Jan 1942 *Pamela Violette Barry Power [Pamela Lady Wolseley, The Cottage, Wolseley Bridge, Stafford, Staffs ST17 0XR], granted rank of bt's widow 1955, yr dau of Capt F Barry, of Co Cork, and Mrs W N Power, of Wolseley Park, Rugeley, Staffs, and was *ka* France 31 Aug 1944, leaving:

(1) Sir CHARLES GARNET RICHARD MARK WOLSELEY, **11th and present Bt**

(1) *Mary Patricia Anne [Mrs Steuart Moore, Park Side, 4 Cliff Rd, Stamford, Lincs PE9 1AH]; *b* 23 Nov 1942; *m* 24 Feb 1973 *Steuart Martin Moore, TD, FRICS, s of J B Moore, of Little Court Hellidon, Northants, and has issue:

  1a *Theresa Mary Geraldine; *b* 1974

  2a *Sonya Mary Elizabeth; *b* 1976

  3a *Caroline Stephanie Elaine; *b* 1978

2 +Basil Charles Daniel Rudolph [Basil Wolseley Esq, Moor Oak, Dymock, Glos]; *b* 16 Nov 1921; *educ* Ampleforth; F/Lt RAF WW II; *m* 6 Oct 1950 *Ruth Key, est dau of Col William Tom Carter, OBE, of The Old Forge, W Malling, Kent, and has:

(1) *Ann Therese Margaret; *b* 7 July 1951; *m* 1980 *Robert Hext-Fremlin, of Southborough, Kent, and has:

  1a *Shelley Naomi; *b* 1980

(2) *Susanna Elizabeth Mary; *b* 10 Sept 1952

(3) *Sarah Angela Clare; *b* 24 Oct 1954

(4) *Joanna Ruth; *b* 16 Aug 1958

3 +George John Carlos [George Wolseley Esq, Rosethorpe, Finmere, Bucks MK18 4AT]; *b* 28 Jan 1925; *educ* Ampleforth, Santa Barbara Sch Calif., U of New Brunswick and U of BC, Canada; RAF (India Cmd) WW II 1943 on

4 Richard Edric Vincent; *b* 6 Oct 1928; *educ* Ampleforth and U of New Brunswick; land surveyor; Rifle Bde and RCN; *m* 25 Nov 1950 (*divorce* 1969, remarried 1971) Alice Baltazzi (*d* 1987), only dau of Amos Tuck French, of Walker St, Falmouth, Mass., and Mrs Hunter Dominguez, of Catherine St, Newport, RI, and *d* 1991, leaving:

(1) +Stephen Richard Dulany; *b* 28 Feb 1954; *m* 1993 *Kathleen Frances O'Ahern

(2) +Christopher Michael Garnet; *b* 23 April 1956; *m* 1989 *Cheryl M McCormick

(1) *Carlotta Andrea Tuck [Mrs Carlotta Wolseley-Lahchiouach, 313 Old Main Rd, PO Box 74, N Falmouth, MA 02556, USA]; *b* 7 June 1951; *m* 1972 (*divorce* 1982) Abdelhadi Lachiouach, of Essaioura, Morocco

(2) *Heather Maria Warner; *b* 26 June 1957; *m* 1975 (*divorce* 1981, resumed maiden name 1983) James de Mello, of N Falmouth, Mass., and has:

  1a *Tara Maria French; *b* 13 Jan 1976; has by *Manuel Lindo:

  1b *Brianna Maria; *b* 12 May 1993

1 *Frances Mary Mona Clare [Mrs Bernhard Wolseley-Wilmsen, Casas Cortijo 139, 11310 Sotogrande (Cadiz), Spain]; *b* 19 May 1920; late WRNS; *m* 12 Sept 1953 Bernhard WILMSEN later WOLSELEY-WILMSEN (deed poll, *d* 1983), only s of Bernhard Wilmsen Jr, of Philadelphia, and Mrs K McConnell, of Shamokin, Pa., and has:

(1) *Anthony Edric Charles [Anthony Wolseley-Wilmsen Esq, Villa Gosen, 11310 Sotogrande (Cadiz), Spain]; *b* 10 March 1955; *educ* St Christopher's Sch, Letchworth, U of Wales and U of Granada, Spain

2 *Agnes Mary Anne Hilda [Miss Agnes Wolseley, Rosethorpe, Finmere, Bucks MK18 4AT]; *b* 27 March 1923

WOLVERTON

Arms: Arg. an eagle displayed with two heads sa., guttée d'or. **Crest:** An eagle's head erased sa., guttée d'or, holding in the beak an escallop arg. **Supporters:** Two eagles, wings elevated sa., guttée d'or, each gorged with a collar gemel gold, and holding in the beak an escallop arg. **Motto:** *Fidei tenax* ('Firm to my trust'). **Creation:** B. (UK) 14 Dec 1869.

THE 7TH BARON WOLVERTON, of Wolverton, Co Buckingham (Christopher Richard Glyn) [The Rt Hon The Lord Wolverton, 97 Hurlingham Rd, London SW6 3NL]; *b* 5 Oct 1938; *s* f 1988; *educ* Eton; late Lt Gren Gds; FRICS, memb Jockey Club; *m* 1st 7 Dec 1961 (*divorce* 1967) Carolyn Jane, 2nd dau of Anthony Noel Hunter, of Kensington, and has:

1 *Sara-Jane; *b* 23 May 1963; *m* 1993 *John Francis O'Callaghan, yr son of James O'Callaghan, of Co Clare

2 *Amanda Camilla; *b* 15 March 1966

The 7th BARON *m* 2nd 1975 (*divorce* 1989) Mrs Frances Sarah Elizabeth Stuart Black, est dau of Robert Worboys Skene, of Kensington; *m* 3rd 1990 (*divorce* 199–) Gillian Konig (*m* 2nd 16 July 1997 Colin Edwards)

Lineage: Sir RICHARD CARR GLYN, 1st Bt, of Gaunts, Dorset (*qv*); had a 4th s:

GEORGE CARR GLYN, **1st Baron Wolverton**, of Wolverton, Co Buckingham (UK), so *cr* 14 Dec 1869; *b* 27 March 1797; *educ* Westminster; ptnr Glyn, Mills, Currie & Co, bankers, chm London and NW Rlwy 1837–52, MP (Lib) Kendal 1847–68, Govr Harrow Sch; *m* 17 March 1823 Marianne (*d* 30 March 1892), dau of Pascoe Grenfell, MP, of Taplow Ho (*see* GRENFELL, B), and *d* 24 July 1873, having had, with another s (*d* an infant) and a dau (*d* unm):

1 GEORGE GRENFELL GLYN, **2nd Baron Wolverton**, PC (1873); *b* 10 Feb 1824; *educ* Rugby and Univ Coll Oxford; ptnr Glyn, Mills & Currie, chm Rlwy Clearing House, MP (Lib) Shaftesbury 1857–73, Jt Sec Treasury (Whip) 1868–73, Paymaster-Gen 1880–85, PMG Feb-Aug 1886; *m* 22 June 1848 Georgiana Maria (*d* 10 Jan 1894), est dau of Rev George Tufnell, of Uffington, Berks, and *dsp* 6 Nov 1887

2 St Leger Richard; *b* 3 Oct 1825; *m* 5 June 1855 Florence Elizabeth (*d* 14 Sept 1887), dau of James Wilmot Williams, of Herringston, Dorset, and *d* 16 April 1873, having had, with a dau (*d* young):

(1) Constance Gertrude; *m* 5 June 1889 George Henry Eyre Matcham, of Newhouse, Wilts, and *d* 12 April 1933, leaving issue (*see* NELSON, E)

(2) Florence Elizabeth Mary, CBE (1920), DGStJ; *m* 23 June 1880 Sir William Wyndham Portal, 2nd Bt (*qv*), and *d* 30 Dec 1931, leaving issue

(3) Edith Theodosia; *m* 25 July 1896 Henry Thomas Timson, of Stydd Ho, Lyndhurst, Hants, s of Capt Henry Timson, JP, of Tatchbury Mount, and *d* 28 March 1913

(4) Mabel; *m* 2 June 1890 Capt Robert Henry Fowler, Shropshire LI (*d* 11 May 1957 aged 99 yrs 11 months), of Rahinston, Co Meath, and *d* 3 Feb 1919, leaving issue

(5) Beatrice Ellerie; *m* 11 Oct 1888 Maj Frederick Howard Wingfield Fetherstonhaugh, The Cameronians (*d* 29 July 1931), Extra Equerry to HM GEORGE V, manager HM's thoroughbred stud, s of Howard Fetherstonhaugh, and *d* 15 April 1951

3 Henry Carr, CB, CSI; *b* 17 April 1829; V-Adml, ADC to HM QUEEN VICTORIA, Kt Medjidie 3rd Cl, gold medal for distinguished services on the Danube under Omah Pasha in 1854, present 1854 and 1855 with naval bde before Sebastopol and at its bombardment; *m* 23 Sept 1858 Rose (*d* 21 July 1870), widow of John Pennefather and dau of Rev Denis Mahony, JP, of Dromore Castle, Co Kerry, and *d* 16 Feb 1884, leaving, with a dau (*d* unm):

(1) HENRY RICHARD GLYN, **3rd Baron Wolverton**; *b* 18 July 1861; *d* unm 2 July 1888

(2) FREDERIC GLYN, **4th Baron Wolverton**, JP, DL Dorset; *b* 24 Sept 1864; *educ* Eton and Oxford; sr ptnr Gllyn, Mills & Currie; Ld in Waiting 1892–93, Memb LCC Fulham 1898–1901, Lt N Som Imp Yeo Boer War 1900, V-Chamberlain Household 1902–05, Steward Jockey Club 1913, Maj TFR, Hon Col 10th Bn Middx Regt WW I 1914–16; *m* 5 Jan 1895 Edith Amelia, CBE (*d* 6 June 1956), only dau of 1st Earl of Dudley (*qv*), and *d* 3 Oct 1932, having had:

1a George Edward Dudley Carr; *b* 18 Aug 1896; Lt 10th Hus Gen Res Offrs WW I (wounded); *d* unm 30 July 1930

2a NIGEL REGINALD VICTOR GLYN, **5th Baron Wolverton**; *b* 23 June 1904; *educ* Eton; Capt RA (TA); *d* unm 1986

1a Marion Feodorovna Louise, DCVO (1961, CVO 1945); *b* 23 Aug 1900; Woman Bedchamber to HM QUEEN ELIZABETH THE QUEEN MOTHER 1937–61, Extra Woman Bedchamber 1961–70; *m* 18 April 1932 Lord Hyde, er s of 6th Earl of Clarendon (*qv*), and *d* 13 Dec 1970, leaving issue

2 Esmé Consuelo Helen, OBE (1946); *b* 20 Sept 1908; *m* 1 Aug 1950 (Evelyn) Nigel Chetwode Birch (*d* 1981), PC, OBE, MP (*cr* Baron Rhyl of Holywell, Co Southampton (LP) 1970), s of Gen Sir Noel Birch, GBE, KCB, KCMG, RHA (*see* CHETWODE, B)

(1) Rose Riversdale; granted rank of baron's dau 1889; *m* 25 July 1885 Montagu Charles Francis, Lord Norreys, and *d* 21 Dec 1933, leaving issue (*see* LINDSEY and ABINGDON, E)

4 Richard Riversdale; Maj Rifle Bde, Kt of the Medjidie; *d* 11 Dec 1859

5 Pascoe Charles; *b* 12 April 1833; Commr Ltcy London, MP E Dorset 1885–86; *m* 1st 5 Oct 1858 Horatia Louisa (*d* 15 Nov 1858), dau of Ven Carew St John Mildmay (*see* ST JOHN-MILDMAY, Bt); *m* 2nd 19 Feb 1861 Carolina Henrietta (*d* 22 Aug 1912), dau of Capt William Amherst Hale, 52nd Regt, and *d* 3 Nov 1904, having by her had, with another s (*d* young):

(1) Geoffrey Carr, CMG, DSO, MVO, TD; *b* 19 April 1864; Hon Col N Som Yeo, Boer War 1900–02 (medal with four Clasps) and WW I 1914–16 (wounded, despatches), Priv Sec to Govr Transvaal 1903–06, Mil Sec to Govr Madras 1906–08; *m* 20 July 1889 Hon Winifred Harbord (*d* 6 Jan 1949), 6th dau of 5th Baron Suffield (*qv*), and *d* 12 Jan 1933, having had:

1a Louise Gwendoline; *b* 21 Sept 1891; *m* 1st 22 June 1918 Maj Charles Henry Greville (Isee WARWICK, BROOKE and, E); *m* 2nd 28 Nov 1931 Adml of the Fleet Sir Rhoderick Robert McGrigor, GCB, DSO (*see* McGRIGOR, Bt), and *d* 11 Nov 1961

2a Winifred Alice; *b* 7 June, *d* 19 July 1893

(2) Maurice George Carr; *b* 12 March 1872; High Sheriff Herts 1912, Alderman, London CC, Lt Dorset Yeo Cav; *m* 6 Oct 1897 Hon Maud Grosvenor, JP Herts (*d* 2 June 1948), est dau of 2nd Baron Ebury (*qv*), and *d* 20 Aug 1920, leaving:

1a Christopher Pascoe Robert; *b* 8 Oct 1899; 2nd Lt Gen Res Offrs Gren Gds; *d* 25 April 1921

2a Francis Maurice Grosvenor (Sir), KCMG (1954), JP (Herts); *b* 9 Aug 1901; *educ* Eton; dir Glyn Mills and Co, memb London Midland Area Bd Br Tport Commn, dir Bank of London and S America Ltd, dep chm Advsy Cncl Export Credits Guarantee Dept BOT; *m* 1st 15 Feb 1926 (*divorce* 1937) Jane (*d* 2 July 1964), dau of William D Perkins, of Seattle, USA, and had:

1b Jeremy Christopher; *b* 1 Oct 1930; *educ* Eton and Worcester Coll Oxford (MA 1960); *m* 8 Dec 1956 *Robina Elspeth [Mrs Jeremy Glyn, Upton Farm, Upton, Andover, Hants SP11 0JS], only dau of Sir George Arthur Harford, 2nd Bt (*qv*), and *d* 1984, leaving:

1c *Lucinda Mary; *b* 3 June 1958

1b Pamela Jane; *b* 9 Aug 1928; *m* 29 June 1950 (*divorce* 1972) Geoffrey William Pooley, 2nd s of Dr J S Pooley, and *d* 1983, leaving:

1c *Alexander Pascoe; *b* 17 May 1951; *m* 19 Aug 1978 *Jennifer Cathcart and has:

1d *John; *b* 1989

1d *Clare; *b* 1980

2d *Amanda; *b* 1984

2c +Hilary John; *b* 21 May 1953; *m* 1983 (*divorce* 1993) Jane Copsey

2a (cont.) Sir Francis Glyn *m* 2nd 30 July 1941 Mary Elspeth (*d* 13 Aug 1966), formerly w of Kenneth James Miln and dau of Tom Garnett, of Waddow Hall, Clitheroe, and *d* 15 Dec 1969

3a Martin St Leger; *b* 6 Dec 1902; *d* 15 June 1924

4a Pascoe Anthony George; *b* 11 June 1911; Lt Gren Gds; *m* 18 April 1934 Katharine Florita (*m* 2nd 23 Sept 1936 Lt-Col Patrick Lort-Phillips, DSO, DL, FRGS, Gren Gds (*d* 1979), s of Maj-Gen Thomas Herbert Shoubridge, CB, CMG, DSO), 3rd dau of Lt-Col Arthur Morton Grenfell, DSO, TD (*see* GRENFELL, B), and *d* 15 June 1935, leaving:

1b Mary Georgina; *b* 21 May 1935; *m* 1st 3 April 1954 (*divorce* 1963) Lt-Cdr John William Talbot Lewes, RN (*see* SHREWSBURY and WATERFORD, E), and had issue; *m* 2nd 19– Capt R D S Drew-Smythe, and *d* 1992

5a JOHN PATRICK RIVERSDALE, **6th Baron**

6a +Hilary Beaujolais; *b* 12 Jan 1916; *educ* Eton; Capt RASC (Res Offrs), md Gallaher Ltd (ret 1976); *m* 16 Feb 1938 *Caroline, yst dau of William Perkins Bull, QC, of Lorne Hall, Rosedale, Toronto, and has:

1b +James Hilary [James Glyn Esq, PO Box 139, Jawan, Sabah, Malaysia]; *b* 23 Aug 1939; *educ* Eton; md N Borneo Timbers; *m* 12 Dec 1964 (*divorce* 1983) Lucinda March, only dau of W/Cdr Gordon Stanley Keith Haywood, RAF (*see* DARNLEY, E), and has:

1c +Caspar Hilary Gordon; *b* 1969; *m* 25 Jan 1997 *Christine Agnew

1c *Marina Jane [Mrs Robert Furniss-Roe, 14 rue des Renaudes, Paris 75017, France]; *b* 23 Sept 1966; *m* 1991 *Robert P Furniss-Roe, s of Henry Furniss-Roe, of Bishopsteignton, Devon, and has:

1d *Olivia Sophie; *b* 18 Aug 1993

2d *Emma Caroline; *b* 27 June 1995

3d *Charlotte Anne; *b* 27 June 1995

1b *(Caroline) Ann [Mrs Gowri Shankar, Castle Hill Cottage, Boothby Graffoe, Lincs]; *b* 1 Aug 1941; *m* 1st 8 July 1968 (*divorce* 1979) Padmanabh Vijai Pillai, of Ann Arbor, Mich., yr s of Dr P P Pillai, of New Delhi; *m* 2nd 1980 *Gowri Shankar

2b *Sarah [Mrs Robert Henson, Ermine House, Boothby Graffoe, Lincs LN5 0LD]; *b* 5 May 1948, *m* 1st 8 July 1967 (*divorce* 1971) Richard Patrick King, only s of Richard Francis King, of Assam, India; *m* 2nd 1979 (*divorce* 1982) Nicholas John Turner, s of John Turner, and by him has:

1c *James William Hilary; *b* 12 Jan 1980

2b (cont.) Mrs Sarah Turner *m* 3rd 1984 *Robert Gino Henson, s of John Gordon (Gino) Henson, of Ermin Ho, Boothby Graffoe, and by him has:

1c *Jessica Ann Frances; *b* 12 Feb 1985

2c *Cecilia Sarah; *b* 29 June 1990

(1) Maud Louisa; *m* 12 Oct 1887 Henry Percy St John and *d* 28 Oct 1938, leaving issue (*see* BOLINGBROKE and SAINT JOHN, V)

(2) Agnes Mary; *m* 23 Feb 1884 Col Francis Onslow Barrington Foote, RA (*d* 26 Feb 1911), of Manor Ho, Barnes, Surrey, s of Gen William Francis Foote, and *d* 21 Sept 1954, leaving issue

6 Sidney Carr; *b* 11 Oct 1835; Capt Rifle Bde Crimea (medal), MP Shaftesbury 1880–85; *m* 31 Dec 1868 Fanny (*d* 9 March 1907), yst dau of Adolphe Marescaux, of St Omer, France, and *d* 26 Feb 1916, having had:

(1) Arthur St Leger; *b* 11 Nov 1870; Maj Gren Gds Res Offrs, Lt-Col cmdg 10th Bn Middx Regt Boer War 1899–1900 (medal with four clasps) and WW I (despatches, brevet, Offr Legn Hon); *m* 7 July 1908 Amy Frances, JP Suffolk, CA W Suffolk (*m* 2nd 5 Dec 1929 Maj-Gen Frank William Ramsay, CB,CMG, DSO; *see* RAMSAY, Bt); *m* 3rd 5 Feb 1955 Noel John Dawson (*d* 14 May 1966), s of Horace Spurling Dawson, and *d* 8 April 1958), dau of Frederick Scott Hohler, of 30 Lowndes Sq, London SW, and *d* 30 Nov 1922, leaving:

1a Rosemary Frances; *b* 28 Feb 1913; *m* 1st 18 Nov 1935 (*divorce* 1947) Olof Erik Haakon Carlsson Wijk, 4th Queen's Own Hus, yr s of Carl Olof Wijk, of Gothenburg, Sweden; *m* 2nd 11 Feb 1948 Lt-Col David Rew Elkington, OBE, TD, er s of Lt-Col John Ford Elkington, DSO, of Adbury Holt, Newbury, and *d* 31 Dec 1971, leaving:

1b *Robert John; *b* 7 Oct 1949; *educ* Eton and Exeter U

2a Lavender Amy; *b* 5 Feb 1922; *m* 1st 19 April 1941 P/O Hon William Richard Christopher Boyle Parker, RAFVR (*kas* Dec 1941), 2nd s of 7th Earl of Macclesfield (*qv*); *m* 2nd 12 Sept 1947 Michael Fulwar Horne, of Park Cottage, Moulton, nr Newmarket, Suffolk, 2nd s of Rev Francis Herbert Horne, and *d* 3 Nov 1964, having had issue

(2) George Carr; *b* 13 Aug 1872; *m* 13 July 1894 Kate Alice, only dau of George Ashmead, and *dsp* 12 March 1905

7 Ashley Carr; *b* 20 Nov 1839; barrister; *m* 21 Feb 1871 Mary Louisa (*d* 20 Nov 1917) (*m* 2nd 22 June 1886 Rt Rev Isaac Hellmuth, DD, DCL, Bp Huron, who *d* 28 May 1901), dau of Adml Hon Arthur Duncombe (*see* FEVERSHAM, B), and *d* Sept 1875, leaving:

(1) Delia Mary; *m* 7 Jan 1897 Paul Winsloe Phillipps (*d* 6 Aug 1952) and *d* 5 Jan 1958

(2) Mildred; *m* 4 Oct 1899 Rev Raymond Alured Bond (*d* 26 Jan 1941), of Holme Priory, Wareham, Vicar Iwerne Minster, Blandford, Dorset, and *d* 4 March 1963 aged 88, leaving issue

8 Edward Carr (Rt Rev); *b* 21 Nov 1843; DD Oxon,Vicar and RD Kensington 1878–96, Chaplain in Ordinary to HM QUEEN VICTORIA 1884–96, Bp Peterborough 1897–1916, Chaplain to OStJ 1915; *m* 4 July 1882 Lady Mary Campbell (*d* 22 March 1947), dau of 8th Duke of Argyll (*qv*), and *d* 14 Nov 1928, leaving:

(1) Sir RALPH GEORGE CAMPBELL GLYN, 1st and last Bt, and 1st and last BARON GLYN, of Farnborough, Co Berks (UK), so *cr* 21 Jan 1934 and 29 June 1953 respectively, MC, DL; *b* 3 March 1884; *educ* Harrow and RMC Sandhurst; Maj Rifle Bde, MP Clackmannan 1918–22 and Abingdon 1924–53, High Steward Wallingford, dir LMSR to 1 Jan 1948, PPS to: PM Aug 1931–June 1935, Ld Pres Cncl June 1935–May 1937, served WW II (despatches, Legn Hon, US DSM, Russian Order of St Anne, Serbian Order White Eagle); *m* 25 April 1921 Hon Sibell, OBE (*d* 23 March 1958), widow of Brig-Gen Walter Long, CMG, DSO (*see* LONG, V), and dau of 2nd Baron Derwent (*qv*), and *dsp* 1 May 1960, when his title expired

(1) Margaret Isabel Frances; *b* 22 Feb 1888; *m* 6 July 1911 Adml Hon Sir Herbert Meade-Fetherstonhaugh, GCVO, CB, DSO, 3rd son of 4th Earl of Clanwilliam (*qv*), and *d* 15 June 1977, leaving issue

(2) Alice Mary Sybil, MBE (1950), JP (Denbighs 1940); *b* 1 May 1889; *m* 17 Feb 1914 Col John Charles Wynne-Finch and *d* 31 March 1970, leaving issue (*see* AYLESFORD, E)

1 Alice Carr; *m* 4 Aug 1870 5th Earl of Chichester (*qv*) and *d* 1 Feb 1934, leaving issue

The 5th BARON's cousin,

JOHN PATRICK RIVERSDALE GLYN, **6th Baron Wolverton**; *b* 17 April 1913; *educ* Eton and New Coll Oxford (BA); Maj Gren Gds Res Offrs WW II (wounded), md Glyn, Mills & Co; *m* 3 April 1937 *Audrey Margaret (does not use title) [Mrs Audrey Glyn, 1 Lower Upton Farm Cottage, Burford, Oxon OX18 4LN], dau of Richard Stubbs, of Haseley Manor, Oxford, and *d* 1988, leaving:

1 CHRISTOPHER RICHARD GLYN, **7th and present Baron Wolverton**

2 +ANDREW JOHN [Andrew Glyn Esq, 167 Divinity Rd, Oxford], Fell Corpus Christi Coll Oxford; *b* 30 June 1943; heir presumptive; *educ* Eton and New Coll Oxford; *m* 1st 1965 (*divorce* 1986) Celia Laws, and has:

(1) +Miles John; *b* 1966

(1) *Lucy Abigail; *b* 1968

2 (cont.) The Hon ANDREW GLYN *m* 2nd 1986 *Wendy Carlin and by her has:

(2) +Jonathan; *b* 1990

(2) *Tessa; *b* 1987

1 *Susan [Mrs Nicholas Mills, Lower Upton Farm, Burford, Oxford]; *b* 10 Aug 1940; *m* 16 June 1962 *Nicholas Greenaway Mills, yr s of Lt-Col Robert Breynton Yarnton Mills, OBE, MC, of Barrington Grove, Burford, and has:

(1) *Charlotte Sophia; *b* 13 April 1964; *m* 1991 *Capt James D T Bainbridge, 16th/5th Roy Lancers, yr s of David Bainbridge, of Hurworth Hall, W Darlington, and has:

1a *Charlotte Isabelle Greenaway; *b* 1993

(2) *Maria Louise Greenaway; *b* 8 Sept 1967

2 *Joanna Caroline [Miss Joanna Glyn, Fourways, Station Rd, Chinnor, Oxon OX9 4QB]; *b* 22 June 1955

WOMBWELL

IN·WELL·BEWARE

Arms: Gu. a bend between six unicorn's heads couped arg.
Crest: A unicorn's head couped arg. **Motto:** In well beware.
Creation: Bt. (GB) 26 Aug 1778.

SIR GEORGE PHILIP FREDERICK WOMBWELL, 7TH BT, of Wombell, Yorks, MBE (1977) [Sir George Wombwell Bt, Newburgh Priory, Coxwold, York YO6 4AS]; *b* 21 May 1949; *s f* 1977; *educ* Repton; *m* 31 Aug 1974 *(Hermione) Jane, er dau of T S Wrightson, of Ulshaw Grange, Middleham, Yorks, and has:

  1 +STEPHEN PHILIP HENRY; *b* 12 May 1977

  1 *Sarah Georgina; *b* 1980

Lineage: GEORGE WOMBWELL, of Wombwell, Yorks; *m* Hannah, dau of William Waugh, and had:

  1 William; *m* 1696 Elizabeth, est dau of Sir Michael Wentworth, of Wolley, Yorks, and *d* 1682, leaving:

    (1) William; *b* 1700; *m* Margaret, dau of Sir Thomas Standish, 2nd Bt, and had:

      1a Margaret; *m* 1761 Anthony St Leger, who thus acquired Wombell, and *dsp* 1776

      2a Elizabeth; *m* Sir Charles Turner, 1st Bt, of Kirkleatham, York

    (2) George; Vicar Norton; *d* unm 1756

    (3) Michael, of Wakefield; *d* 1742

  2 John; *b* 1672; *m* Elizabeth, dau of Richard Nottingham, and had, with other issue:

    1 George; *b* 1701; Br Consul Alicante; *m* Anne, dau and heiress of John Nottingham, and had:

      1a John; *b* 1748

      1a Anne; *m* 14 Nov 1770 Ven John Strachey, LLD, FSA, Archdeacon Suffolk (*see* 1970 edn STRACHIE, B), and had issue

    2 ROGER

  3 Thomas; *d* 1740

JOHN WOMBWELL's 2nd s,

  ROGER WOMBWELL, of Barnsley, Yorks; *b* 31 May 1708; *m* Mary, dau of Francis Chadwick, and *d* at sea 1740 en route to Gibraltar, leaving, with a yr s (John, of Alicante, merchant, *m* 1st 24 Oct 1783 Elizabeth, est dau of Joshua Grigsby, MP Suffolk, *m* 2nd Frances, dau of Richard Baker, and by her had issue):

Sir George Wombwell, 1st Bt (GB), so *cr* 26 Aug 1778; *bapt* 11 June 1734; bought back the Wombwell estate; MP Huntingdon 1774–80; Chm HEIC; *m* 4 June 1765 Susannah (*d* 27 Sept 1816), only dau of Sir Thomas Rawlinson, Alderman City London and Ld Mayor 1746, and *d* 2 Nov 1780, leaving, with other issue:

Sir George Wombwell, 2nd Bt; *b* 14 March 1769; *educ* Trin Coll Cambridge (MA); Sheriff Yorks 1809–10; *m* 1st 19 July 1791 Lady Anne Belasyse (*d* 7 July 1808), dau and coheir of 2nd and last Earl Fauconberg of Newborough, and had, with other issue:

  1 GEORGE (Sir), **3rd Bt**

  2 Henry Walter; *b* 24 May 1795; *d* 17 Feb 1835

Sir George *m* 2nd 1813 Eliza (*d* 21 March 1856), yst dau of T E Little, of Hampstead, and by her had, with other issue:

  3 Charles Orby; *b* 3 April 1813; Offr 10th Hus; *m* 1st 21 May 1836 Charlotte, dau of Orby Hunter, of Crowland Abbey, Lincs, and had:

    (1) Frances Charlotte; *m* 20 Sept 1864 Lt-Col Clifton Gascoigne, Gren Gds (*d* 27 Sept 1903), and *d* 6 March 1920, leaving issue

  3 (cont.) Charles Wombwell *m* 2nd 7 Sept 1865 Frances Jane (*d* 11 Aug 1876), est dau of David Baillie, and *d* 14 Sept 1898, leaving by her:

    (1) Arthur Charles; *b* 4 July 1866; Lt Gren Gds; *m* 23 Nov 1898 Violet Bridget Heron (*d* 5 Sept 1929), only dau of Capt John Heron Maxwell-Heron (*see* HERON-MAXWELL, Bt), and *d* 18 Feb 1921, leaving:

      1a Claude Ronald; *b* 27 Feb 1900; *educ* Harrow and RMC Sandhurst; Maj Seaforth Highrs; *m* 9 July 1936 Eva Mabel (*d* 1988), only dau of Lt-Col Gerald Hugh Charles Madden, Irish Gds (*see* 1970 edn MACPHERSON-GRANT, Bt), and *d* 5 July 1959, leaving:

1b +Gerald Arthur [Gerald Wombwell Esq, 40 Quarrendon St, London SW6 3SU]; *b* 24 Dec 1937; *educ* Wellington; *m* 6 March 1968 *Elizabeth Ann, SRN, RSCN, er dau of John Victor Gent, of Thika, Kenya, and has:

    1c +Richard Brian; *b* 3 Aug 1973

    1c *Camilla Susan; *b* 4 Oct 1970

  2a Michael Henry; *b* 2 June 1907; *educ* Harrow and Trin Coll Cambridge (BA 1929); *m* 1st 19 July 1932 Joy Evelyn Georgina (*d* 23 April 1954), dau of Algernon Seymour Bernard Oakley, of Chadlington, Oxon; *m* 2nd 6 Oct 1962 Grace Margaret (*d* 30 Dec 1976) dau of David Willis, of Headley, Surrey, and *d* 1 March 1977

1 Louisa; *m* Aug 1840 as his 2nd w Henry William Beauclerk (*see* SAINT ALBANS, D) and *d* 28 Dec 1882

Sir GEORGE *d* 28 Oct 1846; his est s,

  Sir George Wombwell, 3rd Bt; *b* 13 April 1792; *m* 23 June 1824 Georgiana (*d* 10 May 1875), 2nd dau of Thomas Orby Hunter, of Crowland Abbey, Lincs, and *d* 14 Jan 1855, leaving:

    1 **Sir George Orby Wombwell, 4th Bt**, JP, DL N R Yorks; *b* 23 Nov 1832; Lt 17th Lancers Crimean War, High Sheriff Yorks 1861; *m* 3 Sept 1861 Julia Sarah Alice (*d* 24 Oct 1921), er dau of 6th Earl of Jersey (*qv*), and *d* 16 Oct 1913, having had:

      (1) George; *b* 1 Nov 1865; Lt KRRC; *dvp* unm 16 Jan 1889

      (2) Stephen Frederick; *b* 19 Feb 1867; *educ* Trin Hall, Cambridge (BA); Lt Yorks Hus Yeo Cav, Capt Imp Yeo Boer; *das & vp* of enteric fever Vryburg, S Africa, 1 Feb 1901

      (1) Julia Georgiana Sarah; *m* 1st 29 Aug 1882 2nd Earl of Dartrey (*see* 1933 edn) and had issue; *m* 2nd 29 April 1933 2nd Baron Saint Levan (*qv*) and *d* 7 Feb 1938

      (2) Mabel Caroline; *m* 31 July 1897 Henry Robert Hohler (*d* 7 June 1906), est s of Henry Booth Hohler, of Fawkham Manor, Kent, and *dsp* 19 Dec 1948

      (3) Cecilia Clementina; *m* 28 July 1890 William Dudgeon Graham Menzies (*d* 24 Oct 1944), of Hallyburton, Coupar, Angus, Perthshire, and *d* 20 Jan 1948, leaving issue

    2 Adolphus Ulick; *b* 17 May 1834; Lt-Col 12th Lancers; *m* 28 Sept 1862 Mary Caroline (*d* 20 Sept 1890), 2nd dau of Col Myddelton Biddulph, MP, of Chirk Castle, and *d* 21 June 1886, leaving:

      (1) Mary Alexina Florence; *b* 23 Oct 1870; *m* 19 Nov 1890 Louis St Julien Prioleau and *d* 1897

    3 **Sir Henry Herbert Wombwell, 5th Bt**; *b* 24 Sept 1840; 7th Hus and Capt RHG; *m* 8 Feb 1902 Hon Myrtle Mabel Muriel Mostyn (*d* 26 March 1956), sis of 7th Baron Vaux of Harrowden (*qv*), and *dsp* 1 Feb 1926

    4 Frederick Charles; *b* 12 July 1845; *m* 12 Jan 1868 Marie (*d* 30 Sept 1913), dau of M Boyer, and *d* 7 July 1869, leaving:

      (1) Frederick Adolphus; *b* 8 April 1869; Capt 16th Lancers; *m* 6 July 1909 Gertrude May (*m* 2nd 28 Jan 1920 Thomas Stamford Booth (*d* 11 July 1928), of Leam, Avon Castle, Ringwood, s of Thomas Booth, of Leam Hall, Derbys, and *d* 1 March 1948), est dau of Alfred Harrison Smith, of Carlton Hall, Worksop, and *d* 17 Feb 1912, leaving:

        1a FREDERICK PHILIP ALFRED WILLIAM (Sir), **6th Bt**

      (1) Almina Victoria Marie Alexander; *m* 1st 26 June 1895 5th Earl of Carnarvon (*qv*) and had issue; *m* 2nd 19 Dec 1923 Lt-Col Ian Onslow Dennistoun, MVO, Gren Gds (*d* 22 May 1938), and *d* 8 May 1969 aged 92

Sir HENRY's gn,

  Sir (Frederick) Philip Alfred William, 6th Bt, MBE (1944); *b* 6 July 1910; *educ* Repton; Maj RE WW II Movement Control; *m* 1 Feb 1936 Ida Elizabeth, er dau of Frederick John Leitch, of Branksome Pk, Bournemouth, and Belfast, and *d* 4 April 1977, leaving:

    1 Sir GEORGE PHILIP FREDERICK WOMBWELL, **7th and present Bt**

    1 *(Elizabeth) Anne [Mrs Michael Horton, Kings Lea, Kemerton, Tewkesbury, Glos]; *b* 25 Nov 1938; *m* 15 May 1965 *Michael Scofield Horton, only s of Lt-Col Gerard Thomas Scofield Horton, MC, of Bishops Caundle Ho, nr Sherborne, Dorset, and has had:

      (1) Charles Edward Scofield; *b* and *d* 6 March 1966

      (2) *Peter Michael; *b* 20 Sept 1969

    1 (cont.) Mr and Mrs Michael Horton also adopted:

      *James Frederick; *b* 22 March 1968

    2 *Hazel Maureen; *b* 26 Sept 1947; took name WILLIAMSON by deed poll 1977

WOMERSLEY

Creation: Bt. (UK) 3 Sept 1945.

SIR PETER JOHN WALTER WOMERSLEY, 2ND BT, of Grimsby, Co Lincoln, JP (Worthing and Dist) [Sir Peter Womersley Bt JP, Broomfields, 23 Goring Rd, Steyning, W Sussex BN44 3GF]; *b* 10 Nov 1941; *s gf* 1961; *educ* Charterhouse and RMA Sandhurst; Lt (ret 1968) King's Own Roy Border Regt; personnel manager Beecham Gp 1972–89, Human Resources Manager SmithKline Beecham 1989–96, Job Evaluation Project Manager 1996–97, Human Resources Consultant 1997–; author (with Neil Grant): *Collecting Stamps* (1980); *m* 7 Sept 1968 *Janet Margaret, dau of Alastair Forbes Grant, of Fir Tree House, Drayton, Norwich, and has:

1 +JOHN GAVIN GRANT; *b* 7 Dec 1971
2 +Matthew Alastair Peter; *b* 1973
1 *Margaret Frances; *b* 1969
2 *Helen Kathryn; *b* 1974

Lineage: WILLIAM WOMERSLEY, of Bradford; *m* Mary Ann (*d* Jan 1919), dau of William Green, of Northampton, and *d* 1908, leaving:

Sir Walter James Womersley, 1st Bt (UK), so *cr* 3 Sept 1945, PC (1941), JP (Grimsby); *b* 5 Feb 1878; *educ* Usher St Bd Sch Bradford; sr ptnr Womersley and Stamp (house furnishers), Grimsby, Cncllr Grimsby 1911, Mayor Grimsby 1922–23, High Steward Grimsby 1950, MP (C) Grimsby 1924–1945, PPS to Sir Kingsley Wood Aug–Oct 1931, a Jr Ld Treasury and Govt Whip 1931–35, Assist PMG 1935–39, Min Pensions 1939–45, Pres Nat Chamber Trade 1946, Pres Grimsby Chamber Trade, V-Pres Municipal Corps Assoc, Kt Cdr Order Dannebrog Denmark 1950, ktd 1934; *m* 23 Jan 1905 Annie (*d* 12 March 1952), dau of John Stamp, of Bradford, and *d* 15 March 1961, having had:

1 John; *b* 19 May 1906; *d* 23 Feb 1910
2 John Walter; *b* 22 May 1919; Capt Lincs Regt WW II; *m* 12 Feb 1941 *Betty [Mrs Peter Garrini, 23 River Park, Boxmoor, Hemel Hempstead, Herts] (*m* 2nd 1948 Gordon Shuttlewood (*d* 1980); *m* 3rd 1981 Peter Garrini (*d* 1996), dau of Cyril Williams, of Elstead, Surrey, and was *ka* Forli, Italy, 14 Nov 1944, leaving:

(1) Sir PETER JOHN WALTER WOMERSLEY, **2nd and present Bt**
1 *Dorothy [Mrs Cyril Moseley, 23 Burnmill Rd, Market Harborough, Leics LE16 7JF]; *b* 16 Jan 1911; *educ* Grimsby High Sch and London U; memb Market Harborough UDC 1950–59 (Chm 1956–57), CC Leics 1952–61; *m* 4 April 1934 Cyril Howard Moseley (*d* 15 June 1979), s of Howard Francis Moseley, of Westbrooke House, Market Harborough, and has:

(1) *Walter Howard; *b* 22 June 1941; *educ* Radley and Magdalene Coll Cambridge; assist master Eton
(1) *Lavinia Anne; *b* 26 Sept 1938; *m* 9 Feb 1971 *George Anthony Mitcheson, s of Thomas Broughton Mitcheson, of Hadley Wood, and has:
  1a *Thomas George Moseley; *b* 6 June 1972
(2) *Philippa Clare [Mrs Derrick Woodcock, Stone House Farm, Saturna Island, BC, Canada]; *b* 17 April 1944; *m* 11 Sept 1965 *Derrick William Woodcock, s of George William Woodcock, of The Walnuts, East Norton, Leics, and has:
  1a *Philip Howard; *b* 13 March 1972
  1a *Frances Louise; *b* 18 Aug 1967
  2a *Sonja Clare; *b* 29 Nov 1969

WOOLF

Creation: B. (LP, UK) 1992.

THE BARON WOOLF, of Barnes, London Borough of Richmond (Sir Harry Kenneth Woolf, PC (1986)) [The Rt Hon The Lord Woolf PC, Royal Courts of Justice, Strand, London WC2A 2LL]; *b* 2 May 1933; *educ* Fettes and UCL (LLB); 2nd Lt 15th/19th Roy Hus 1954, Capt Army Legal Serv 1955; barrister Inner Temple 1954, Bencher 1976, Recorder Crown Court 1972–79, Jr Counsel Inland Revenue 1973–74, First Treasury Jr Counsel 1974–79, High Court Judge Queen's Bench 1979–86, ktd 1979, Presiding Judge SE Circuit 1981–84, Ld Justice Appeal 1986–92, Ld Appeal in Ordinary 1992–96, Master Rolls 1996–, Memb Senate Bar and Bench 1981–85; Chm: Ld Chllr's Advsy Ctee Legal Educn 1986–91, Middx Advsy Ctee on JPs 1986–90, Bd Management Inst Advanced Legal Studies 1986–94 (memb 1986–94), Tstees Butler Tst 1992– (tstee 1991–), St Mary's Hosp Special Tstees 1993–97; Pres: Assoc Law Teachers 1985–90, Centl Cncl Jewish Soc Servs 1987–, SW London Magistrates' Assoc 1987–92, Assoc Membs Bd Visitors 1994–; Govr Emeritus Oxford Centre Hebrew Studies 1988–; Pro-Chllr London U 1994–; Fell UCL 1981; Hon LLD Buckingham 1992, Bristol 1992, London U 1993, Anglia Poly 1994, Manchester Metropolitan 1994; Hon Fell Leeds U; Hon memb SPTL 1988; author: *Protecting the Public: the new challenge* (1990), *Declaratory Judgement* (with J Woolf, 2nd edn, 1993), *Prison Report* (1993), *De Smith Judicial Review of Administrative Action* (jt ed, 5th edn, 1995), *Access to Justice* (1996); *m* 1961 *Marguerite, dau of George Sassoon, and has:

1 *Jeremy Richard George; *b* 1962; *educ* Clifton, Sussex U and Trin Hall Cambridge; *m* 19– *Wendy — and has:
  (1) *Benjamin; *b* 1996
2 *Andrew James David; *b* 1965; *educ* Clifton, St Paul's, Southampton U and Woolfson Coll Cambridge
3 *Eliot Charles Anthony; *b* 1967; *educ* Eton and Robinson Coll Cambridge

Lineage: ALEXANDER WOOLF; *m* Leah Cussins and had:

HARRY KENNETH, *cr* a **Baron**

WOOLTON

Arms: Sable on a bend engrailed between two garbs or a rose gules barbed and seeded proper between two lions rampant of the field.
Crest: Suspended from and between the antlers of a stag proper a stirrup and leather. **Supporters:** On either side a lion or, gorged with a riband azure, pendant therefrom by a chain also or an escutcheon azure charged with a liver bird argent. **Motto:** *Fortitudine virtute dabitur* ('By fortitude and courage it shall be given').
Creations: B. (UK) 7 July 1939, V. (UK) 2 July 1953 (Woolton), E. and V. (Walberton) (UK) 9 Jan 1956.

THE 3RD EARL OF WOOLTON, Viscount Woolton, of Liverpool, Co Lancaster, **Viscount Walberton**, of Walberton, Co Sussex, and **Baron Woolton**, of Liverpool, Co Lancaster (Simon Frederick Marquis) [The Rt Hon The Earl of Woolton, Auchnacree House, Glenogil, by Forfar, Angus DD8 3SX]; *b* 24 May 1958; *s f* 1969; *educ* Eton and St Andrews (MA 1981); *m* 1987 (*divorce* 13 May 1997) Hon Sophie Frederika, only child of 3rd Baron Birdwood (*qv*), and has:

1 *Olivia Alice; *b* 1990
2 *Constance Elizabeth; *b* 1991
3 *Claudia Louise; *b* 3 March 1995

Lineage: THOMAS ROBERT MARQUIS, of Kirkham, Lancs; *b* 21 Nov 1857; *m* Margaret Ormerod, of Manchester, and *d* 3 Dec 1944, leaving an only child:

FREDERICK JAMES MARQUIS, **1st Earl of Woolton**, so *cr* 9 Jan 1956, as also VISCOUNT WALBERTON, of Walberton, Co Sussex, and earlier 7 July 1939 BARON WOOLTON, of Liverpool, Co Lancaster, then 2 July 1953 VISCOUNT WOOLTON, of Liverpool, Co Lancaster (all UK), CH (1942), PC (1940), JP, DL Liverpool; *b* 24 Aug 1883; *educ* Manchester GS and Manchester U (BSc 1906, MA 1912); Research Fell Ec Manchester U 1910; WW I in War Office on Allied Commn (Raw Materials Section) and Sec to Leather Control Bd, Controller Civilian Boots; Sec Boot and Shoe Fedn 1918–20; md and chm Lewis's Investment Tst 1926–39 and 1945–51 (Hon Pres 1951–64); Pres Incorporated Assoc of Retail Distributors 1930–33, memb Advsy Cncl Overseas Devpt Ctee 1928–31 and BOT 1930–34, memb Advsy Cncl GPO 1933–47, Hon Col Armoured Div RE (TA) 1939, Hon Advsr to Sec State War April–Sept 1939, Dir-Gen Equipment and Stores Min of Supply Sept 1939–April 1940, Min Food 1940–43, Min Reconstruction and memb War Cabinet 1943–45, Ld Pres Cncl May–July 1945 and 1951–52, Chllr Duchy Lancaster 1952–55, Min Materials 1953–54, Chm C Party 1945–55, Chllr Manchester U 1944–64 (Chm Convocation 1939); Chm: Exec Ctee BRCS 1943 and Govrs Manchester GS, memb Court Liverpool U 1928–64 (Treas 1937–40), Tstee Nat Centl Library, Warden U Settlement Liverpool, memb: Hambledon Ctee on teaching of industrial art, Home Office Ctee to enquire into organization of Fire Bde Service, Cadman Ctee on Civil Aviation, V-Pres Nat Inst for the Blind 1944, Hon Freeman and memb Court Salters' Co, Hon Freeman Liverpool, past Pres and Fell Roy Statistical Soc, Hon LLD Manchester 1943, Hon LLD Liverpool 1944, Hon LLD Cambridge 1952, Hon LLD McGill, Hon LLD Hamilton Coll USA, Cdr Legion of Honour, KStJ, ktd 1935; *m* 1st 19 Oct 1912 Maud (*d* 13 Sept 1961), yr dau of Thomas Smith, of Manchester, by Augusta Mathews, and had:

1 ROGER DAVID, **2nd Earl**
1 Margaret Judith, TD; *b* 21 Aug 1917; Jr Cdr ATS WW II; *m* 7 April 1945 Maj John Hele Sandeman-Allen, RA (*d* 19 Oct 1958), only s of Col John Sandeman-Allen, OBE, MC, TD, of The Priory, Hethersett, Norfolk, MP Birkenhead, and had:

(1) John Marquis; *b* 8 Dec 1952; *educ* Harrow; *d* 28 Aug 1967
(2) *Charles James; *b* 16 March 1954; *educ* Harrow
(1) *Judith; *b* 6 Dec 1947; *m* 2 Dec 1967 (*divorce* 1973) Sir (George) Hugh Pigot, 8th Bt (*qv*), and has issue
(2) *Hilary; *b* 23 June 1949; SRN; *m* 21 July 1973 *Donald William Robertson Boyd, er s of D J Boyd

The **1st Earl** *m* 2nd 19 Oct 1962 Margaret Eluned, MB, ChB (*d* 1983), only dau of Richard Thomas, of N Wales, and *d* 14 Dec 1964

His only s,

ROGER DAVID MARQUIS, **2nd Earl of Woolton**; *b* 16 July 1922; *educ* Rugby and Trin Coll Cambridge (BA 1943); F/Lt RAFVR WW II; *m* 1st 9 Nov 1946 (*divorce* 1953) Hon Lucia Edith Lawson, only dau of 4th Baron Burnham (*qv*); *m* 2nd 25 June 1957 *Cecily Josephine (*m* 2nd 22 Sept 1969 (*divorce* 1974) 3rd Baron Forres (*qv*); *m* 3rd 1982 3rd Earl Lloyd George of Dwyfor; *qv*), er dau of Maj Sir Alexander Penrose Gordon-Cumming, 5th Bt (*qv*), and *d* 7 Jan 1969, leaving by her:

1 SIMON FREDERICK MARQUIS, **3rd and present Earl of Woolton**
1 *Alexandra Susan [The Lady Alexandra Elletson, The Old Rectory, Huish, Wilts SN8 4JN]; *b* 12 Jan 1961; *m* 1984 *Philip Roger Chandos Elletson, s of Roger Elletson, of The Grey House, Forton, Lancs, and has:
   (1) *Edward Roger Chandos; *b* 23 Aug 1990
   (1) *Laura Katherine Elizabeth; *b* 17 March 1985
   (2) *Sophie Josephine Rose; *b* 5 June 1986

WORSLEY

Arms: Arg. a chief gu. **Crest:** A wyvern vert. **Motto:** *Quam plurimis prodesse* ('Do good to as many people as possible').
Creation: Bt. (UK) 10 Aug 1838.

SIR (WILLIAM) MARCUS JOHN WORSLEY, 5TH BT, of Hovingham Hall, Co York, JP (1957), DL (N R Yorks 1978) Ld Lt N Yorks 1987–) [Sir Marcus Worsley Bt, Hovingham Hall, York YO6 4LU]; *b* 6 April 1925; *s f* 1973; *educ* Eton and New Coll Oxford (BA 1949, MA 1955); Lt Green Howards WW II; Programme Assist BBC European Serv 1949–53, MP (C) Keighley 1959–1964 and Chelsea 1966–74, PPS to: Min Health 1960–61, Min without Portfolio 1962–64 and Ld Pres Cncl 1970–72; 2nd Ch Estates Commr 1970–74; Delegate to Cncl Europe 1964 and 1968–70; Pres Roy Forestry Soc of England, Wales and NI 1980–82; Dep Chm Nat Trust 1986–92 (Chm Properties Ctee 1980–90), High Sheriff N Yorks 1982; *m* 10 Dec 1955 *Hon Bridget Assheton, only surv dau of 1st Baron Clitheroe (*qv*), and has:

1 +WILLIAM RALPH [William Worsley Esq, Wool Knoll, Hovingham, York YO6 4NA]; *b* 12 Sept 1956; *educ* Harrow and RAC Cirencester; late Lt QOY (TAVR); FRICS; *m* 1987 *Marie-Noëlle, yr dau of Bernard H Dreesmann, of Miramar, AM, France, and has:
   (1) +Marcus William Bernard; *b* 2 Nov 1995
   (1) *Isabella Claire; *b* 24 Oct 1988
   (1) *Francesca Sylvia; *b* 5 March 1992
2 +Giles Arthington [Dr Giles Worsley, 86 Cambridge Gdns, London W10 6HS]; *b* 22 March 1961; *ed Perspectives on Architecture* 1995–98, architectural writer; *m* 21 Sept 1996 *Joanna, dau of Peter Pitman, and has:
   (1) *Alice Beaufort; *b* 19 June 1998
3 +Peter Marcus; *b* 15 Sept 1963 (HRH THE DUCHESS OF KENT stood sponsor)
1 *Sarah Marianne [Mrs Martin Elwes, Holywell House, Shellingford, Oxon SN7 7PN]; *b* 25 June 1958; *m* 1984 *Martin Stephen Robert Elwes, er s of Capt Robert Valentine Gervase Elwes and Mrs J H Taylor, of The White Ho, Sowerby, N Yorks, and has:
   (1) *James Robert; *b* 1986
   (2) *Hugo Marcus; *b* 1991
   (1) *Sophie Bridget; *b* 1988

Lineage: ELIAS de WORSLEY, whose name derives from the town of Worsley, Lancs, near Manchester, had:

RICHARD de WORSLEY; living 1203–19; was granted Manors of Worsley and Hulton; had:

GEOFFREY de WORSLEY; living 1254; *m* Agnes — and *d* by 1268, leaving:

RICHARD de WORSLEY; living 1268–92; *m* probably as his 2nd w Maud, dau of Alice, dau of William the Clerk, of Eccles, and had:
1 Richard
2 HENRY
3 Jordan; granted Wardley; living 1292–1305; had:

(1) Margaret; ward of Richard de Worsley; carried off by a number of neighbours and *m* soon after 1331 to Thurstan, s of Richard de Tyldesley, the Wardley estates thus passing to his family

The 2nd s,
HENRY de WORSLEY; living 1292–1303; *m* 1st Joan (*d* by 1293) and had:
1 Richard de Worsley; living 1295–1332; Commr of Array 1327; *m* by 1295 Margaret — and *d* by 1334, having had, with a dau (Ellen, *m* Robert de Radcliffe):
   (1) Henry; living 1296–1305; *m* Alice (living 1354) and *d* by 1350, having had:
     1a Geoffrey; living 1341; *m* Anabel (*m* 2nd by 1359 John le Comyn), dau of Gilbert de Haydock, and *dvp* by 1350, leaving, with a dau (Alice, *m c* 1372 Sir John Massey, of Tatton):
     1b Geoffrey (Sir); of age by 1356; fought in 100 Years War, ktd in Spain; *m c* 1376 (*divorce* 1381) Mary, dau of Thomas de Felton; *m* 2nd Isabel (*m* 2nd Sir John Stanley (*see* DERBY, E), whose family thus acquired Lathom and Knowsley), dau and heiress of Sir Thomas de Lathom, and *d* 1385, leaving by her:
       1c Elizabeth; *b c* 1384; declared illegitimate after her f's death, the Manors of Worsley and Hulton passing to her aunt Alice, Lady Massey; *m* her cousin Arthur Worsley (*see* below)

HENRY de WORSLEY *m* 2nd Margaret de Shoresworth (living 1318, *m* 2nd Robert de Radcliffe) and *d* by 1304, leaving by her:
2 Robert; living 1299–1346; was granted the Ldship of Booths 1323; had:
   (1) William; living 1350–66; *m* Ellen, dau of John de Hulton, of Farnworth, and had:
     1a Robert; MP Lancs 1386 and 1391, imprisoned Tower of London 1388–89 as supporter of Lords Appellant, Commr of Array 1400; *m* by 1376 Isabel, dau of Henry de Trafford and widow of John Worthington, of Blackrod, and *d* 1402, leaving:
       1b Arthur; *m* his cousin Elizabeth, dau and heiress of Sir Geoffrey de Worsley (*see* above) and *d* Dec 1415, leaving:
         1c Geoffrey; *b c* 1409
         2c ROBERT
         3c William; *d* by 1460

The 2nd s,
ROBERT de WORSLEY; of age by 1432; was accused 1460 with his s Robert of complicity in the death of Robert Derbyshire; *m* Margaret, dau of Thomas Booth, of Barton, and had:

ROBERT de WORSLEY; *m* 1st Hellen/Elenor, dau of Robert Hulton, of Park, and had:
1 ROBERT
2 Adam
3 Gilbert
4 Giles
1 Clemence; *m* John Redish (living 1533)

ROBERT de WORSLEY *m* 2nd Mabell, dau of Richard Duckett, of Grayling, Westmorland, and *d* 1497, leaving by her:
5 Thomas

The est s,
ROBERT de WORSLEY; *b c* 1467; *m* Alice, dau and coheir of Hamlet Massey, of Rixton, and *d* 1533, leaving:

Sir ROBERT de WORSLEY; *b* by 1512; ktd 1544, MP Lancs 1553 and 1559; *m* by 1553 Alice, dau of Thurstan Tyldesley, of Wardley; *m* 2nd (and probably bigamously) by 1547 Margaret Beetham and *d* 1585, having had three illegitimate sons (Richard; Robert; Thomas) and by his 1st w:

ROBERT WORSLEY; Keeper Fleet Prison, Salford, *c* 1579; MP Callington 1589; bought Manor of Hovingham, Yorks, 1563 but was forced through debt to sell many of his ancestral estates in Lancs; *m* Elizabeth, dau of Sir Thomas Gerard, of Bryn, and *d* 1605, leaving:
1 THOMAS
2 Robert
3 Gilbert, of Upholland
1 Margaret; *m* Robert Henley, of Henley
2 Elizabeth; *m* William Leicester, of Toft, Cheshire
3 Mary; *m* John Assheton, of Ashton-under-Lyne
4 Katherine; *m* George Hilton, of Farnsworth
5 Dorothy; *m* John Cardinal
6 Anne
7 Jane
8 Frances

The est s,
THOMAS WORSLEY; described as of Booths 1609; recovered the Manor of Hovingham from Charles Cavendish 1610, described as of Hovingham 1623; *m* 1580 Katherine, dau and coheir of Henry Kighley, and *d* 1659, having had:
1 Thomas, of Beeston; *m* 1623 Elizabeth, dau of John Wood, of Beeston, and *d* 1626, leaving:
   (2) THOMAS
2 John, of Cripplegate, Lancs; *m* Elizabeth, dau of Robert Heywood, of Heywood, Lancs
3 Edmund; *d* unm
1 Elizabeth; *d* unm
2 Jane; *m* William Lascelles

The gs,
THOMAS WORSLEY; *b c* 1624; *m* 1st Alice, dau of John Holcroft, and had:
1 THOMAS
2 John; *b* 1651; *d* 1680
3 Charles; *b* and *d* 1654

THOMAS WORSLEY *m* 2nd Penelope, dau of Peter Egerton, and *d* 3 Nov 1664, leaving:

4 Charles; *b* 30 March 1665

The est s,

THOMAS WORSLEY; *b* 1649; MP Malton 1685 and 1698, Lt-Col Militia 1689; *m* Mary, dau and coheiress of Henry Arthington, of Arthington Hall, Yorks, and *d* 3 May 1715, leaving, with a dau (Mary; *m* Francis Foljambe, of Aldwarke, ancestor of Francis John Savile Foljambe, of Osberton and Aldwarke):

THOMAS WORSLEY, of Hovingham; *b* 16 Nov 1686; MP Thirsk 1711; *m* 1718 Mary (*bur* 4 Sept 1722), est dau of Sir Thomas Frankland, 2nd Bt (*see* ZOUCHE, B), by (Elizabeth) Frances, dau of Sir John Russell, 4th Bt, by Frances, 4th dau of OLIVER CROMWELL, and had:

1 THOMAS

2 James (Rev); *bapt* 28 Aug 1722; Rector Stonegrave, Yorks; *m* 17 Dec 1761 Dorothy (*d* 14 Nov 1811), dau of Sir James Pennyman, 5th Bt, of Ormesby Hall (*see* 1852 edn), and *d* 19 Aug 1777, leaving issue: his gs Capt James While WORSLEY *s* to Ormesby Hall and took the name and arms of PENNYMAN

1 Mary; *m* Marmaduke Constable (*d* 1762), of Wassand, and had issue

2 Frances; *m* 13 July 1737 1st Baron Grantham (*d* 30 Sept 1770) and had issue (*see* LUCAS OF CRUDWELL, B)

THOMAS WORSLEY *m* 2nd Anne (*d* 15 Jan 1768), sis of 1st Baron Grantham, and was *bur* 2 March 1750/1, leaving by her:

3 Anne; *m* William Bastard (*d* 1782), of Kitley, Devon, and had issue

The er s,

THOMAS WORSLEY, of Hovingham; *b* 22 Nov 1710; Equerry to GEORGE II, Surveyor-Gen Bd Works 1760–1778, MP Orford 1761–68 and Callington 1768–74; *m* 5 July 1757 Elizabeth (*d* 19 Nov 1809), dau of Rev J Lister, and *d* 13 Dec 1778, having had surv issue, with an er s (Edward, of Hovingham, *d* unm 21 March 1830):

Rev GEORGE WORSLEY; *b* 15 Nov 1761; *educ* Trin Coll Cambridge (MA); Rector Stonegrave and Scawton, N R Yorks; *m* Anne (*d* 31 Aug 1854), 4th dau of Sir Thomas Cayley, 5th Bt (*qv*), and *d* 4 Feb 1815, having had, with other issue:

1 WILLIAM (Sir), **1st Bt**

2 Marcus, of Terrington, Yorks; *b* 1794; Capt RN; *m* Harriet (*d* 19 Nov 1858), widow of Andrew Barlow and dau of Joshua Hamer, and *d* 6 Feb 1878, leaving:

(1) Harriet Philadelphia; *m* 4 July 1854 her cousin **Sir William Cayley Worsley, 2nd Bt** (*see* below), and *dsp* 11 Aug 1893

3 Thomas (Rev); *b* 15 July 1797;, MA, DD Cantab; Master Downing Coll, V-Chllr Cambridge U, Rector Scawton Yorks; *m* 20 June 1842 Katherine, dau of Stansfeld Rawson, of Wastdale Hall, Cumberland, and *dsp* 16 Feb 1885

4 Frederick Cayley; *b* 1803; *m* 29 Jan 1840 Juliana (*d* 15 Jan 1889), dau of John Wright, and *d* 22 July 1884, having had issue

5 Henry Francis; *b* 1806; *m* 1st Catherine, dau of B Blackden; *m* 2nd Mrs Caroline Hankinson, *née* Cust, widow, and *d* 24 July 1876, having had issue

6 Charles Valentine; *b* 1808; barrister; *m* 4 May 1848 Mrs Sophia Kent, widow, dau of John Kemble, and *d* 1878, leaving issue

7 Arthur; *b* 10 May 1810; Lt 51st NI; *m* 11 Nov 1858 Winifred Sherring, only dau of Rev J W Evans, Vicar Bassingthorpe, Lincs, and had issue

The Rev GEORGE WORSLEY's est surv s,

Sir William Worsley, 1st Bt (UK), so *cr* 10 Aug 1838, of Hovingham; *bapt* 26 Aug 1792; *m* 18 Jan 1827 Sarah Philadelphia (*d* 23 April 1885 aged 82), dau of Sir George Cayley, 6th Bt (*qv*), and *d* 5 March 1879, having had, with other issue:

1 Thomas Robinson; *b* 28 Oct 1827; *d* 17 Oct 1855

2 **Sir William Cayley Worsley, 2nd Bt**, JP, DL N R Yorks; *b* 6 Dec 1828; barrister; *m* 1st 4 July 1854 his cousin Harriet (*see* above); *m* 2nd 11 March 1896 Susan Elizabeth (*d* 14 May 1933), 2nd dau of Henry Wyndham Phillips, of Greenroyd, Ripon, and *dsp* 10 Sept 1897

3 Arthington; *b* 21 Dec 1830; *m* 13 March 1860 Marianne Christina Isabella (*d* 11 Aug 1893), dau of Hon Henry Hely-Hutchinson (*see* DONOUGHMORE, E), and *d* 3 June 1861, leaving:

(1) WILLIAM HENRY ARTHINGTON (Sir), **3rd Bt**

(2) Arthington, JP; *b* posthumously 9 Dec 1861; CC Middx; *m* 5 Jan 1900 Helen (*d* 7 Feb 1949), widow of Frank Thomas Bartlett Griffiths, of Stourbridge, and *d* 13 Jan 1943, leaving:

1a Marcus Rurik; *b* 28 May 1901

1 Catherine Louisa; *m* 5 July 1859 Sir George Allanson Cayley, 8th Bt (*qv*), and *d* 19 Jan 1907, leaving issue

2 Emma Frances; *m* 20 Aug 1861 Col Rt Hon Edward Robert King Harman (*d* 10 June 1888), MP Isle of Thanet, and *d* 15 May 1893, leaving issue

Sir WILLIAM's n,

Sir William Henry Arthington Worsley, 3rd Bt, JP, DL N R Yorks; *b* 12 Jan 1861; *educ* New Coll Oxford (BA); CA N R Yorks, Hon LLD Leeds U 1923, Maj 2nd Vol Bn Yorks Regt; *m* 13 Oct 1887 Augusta Mary Chivers (*d* 25 July 1913), est dau of Edward Chivers Bower, DL, of Broxholme, Scarborough, and had:

1 WILLIAM ARTHINGTON (Sir), **4th Bt**

2 Edward Marcus; *b* 13 June 1891; *educ* Eton and Univ Coll Oxford; T/Capt KRRC, WWs I (wounded twice) and II; *m* 7 June 1941 *Joyce Marian [Mrs Edward Worsley, Cawton Hall, Cawton, York YO62 4LW], only child of Stanley Graham Beer, of Northernhay, Bickley, Kent, and *d* 2 Sept 1971, leaving:

(1) +Thomas Edward [Thomas Worsley, 35D Gibson Sq, London N1 0RB]; *b* 26 March 1947; *educ* Eton; *m* 1989 *Sheila Christie and has:

1a +Nicholas Richard; *b* 1990

2a +Charles Robert; *b* 1993

(1) *Susan Marian [Mrs Christopher Oliver, 46 Woodville Rd, Richmond, Surrey TW10 7QN]; *b* 7 Dec 1942; *m* 29 April 1989 *Christopher Edwin Oliver, only s of Edwin John Charles Oliver, of Bournemouth

(2) *Angela Joyce [Mrs Ian Strickland-Skailes, Harston Hall, Grantham, Lincs NG32 1PS]; *b* 8 Dec 1950; *m* 22 Sept 1973 *Ian Michael Downing Strickland-Skailes, twin s of Frank Strickland-Skailes, of Lea Hall, Hatfield

Heath, Herts, and Mrs E J Strickland-Skailes, of Almington Hall, Market Drayton, Salop, and has:

1a *Robin Edward; *b* 1977

1a *Lucinda Isabel; *b* 1979

(3) *Diana Rosalind; *b* 16 Aug 1953

1 Winifred Mary; *b* 9 Dec 1888; *m* 1st 30 April 1912 Capt Francis Percy Campbell Pemberton, 2nd Life Gds (*ka* 19 Oct 1914), only s of Rev Canon Thomas Percy Hudson Pemberton, of Trumpington Hall, Cambridge; *m* 2nd 22 Nov 1917 Sir Arthur Colegate (*d* 10 Sept 1956) and *d* 3 April 1955, leaving issue

2 Ethel Isabel; *b* 19 Oct 1892; *m* 7 Sept 1933 Charles Frederick Ratcliffe Brotherton, of Kirkham Abbey, Yorks, and Greycount, Roundhay, Leeds, and *d* 4 Sept 1935

3 Victoria; *b* 23 Feb 1900; *m* 12 Nov 1932 Arthur Roland King-Farlow (*d* 1 Aug 1974), FCA, only s of Arthur Richard King-Farlow, FCA, of Sandgate, Kent

Sir WILLIAM *d* 27 Nov 1936; his er s,

Sir William Arthington Worsley, 4th Bt, JP (1922), DL (N R Yorks 1942); *b* 5 April 1890; *educ* Eton and New Coll Oxford; Col Green Howards, WWs I (wounded, POW) and II 1939–41, Capt Yorks Co Cricket Club 1928–29 (Pres 1960–73), Col cmdg NR Army Cadets 1942–49, Zone Cdr HG 1942–44, CA NR Yorks, Ld Lt 1951–65, Hon LLD Leeds 1968, Pres Yorks Ag Soc 1959, Pres MCC 1961–62, KStJ; *m* 20 May 1924 Joyce Morgan (*d* 3 Jan 1979), dau of Sir John Fowler Brunner, 2nd Bt (*qv*), and *d* 4 Dec 1973, leaving:

1 Sir (WILLIAM) MARCUS JOHN WORSLEY, **5th and present Bt**

2 +(George) Oliver, TD [Maj Oliver Worsley TD, Midgley House, Heslington, Yorks YO10 5DX]; *b* 22 Feb 1927; *educ* Eton and Trin Coll Oxford (BA 1949, MA 1955); Maj Queen's Own Yorks Yeo, late KRRC; *m* 29 Oct 1966 *Penelope Suzanne Fleetwood, est dau of Lt-Col Christopher Herbert Fleetwood Fuller (*see* FULLER, Bt), and has had:

(1) +David Christopher; *b* 27 April 1969

(2) Richard Oliver Arthington; *b* 11 Oct 1972; *educ* Uppingham and RMC Sandhurst; Lt Light Dragoons; *k* car crash 25 Nov 1996

(1) *Georgina Joyce; *b* 9 Nov 1967 (HRH THE DUCHESS OF KENT stood sponsor); *m* 10 Sept 1990 (*divorce* 1994) Tjden Lane and has:

1a *Marcus Oliver; *b* 10 Sept 1993

1a *Molly; *b* 14 Dec 1991

(2) *Anne Penelope; *b* 27 Sept 1974

3 +John Arthington [John Worsley Esq, RR2, Uxbridge, ON, Canada]; *b* 15 July 1928; *educ* Eton and Trin Coll Oxford (MA 1955); pres Morgan Tst Co Canada; *m* 16 Jan 1954 *Hon Carolyn Mary Wynyard Hardinge, er dau of 4th Viscount Hardinge (*qv*), and has:

(1) +Henry John; *b* 2 May 1958

(2) +Jonathan Hugh; *b* 3 Oct 1960

(3) +Dickon Carol; *b* 16 Dec 1966

(1) *Willa Victoria; *b* 24 May 1955

(2) *Katharine Margot; *b* 24 May 1968

1 *KATHARINE LUCY MARY, GCVO (1977) (HRH THE DUCHESS OF KENT) [HRH The Duchess of Kent, York House, St James' Palace, London SW1]; *b* 22 Feb 1933; Chllr Leeds U 1965, Controller Comdt WRAC 1967, Col-in-Ch 4th/7th Roy Dragoon Gds, Prince of Wales' Own Regt of Yorks, Army Catering Corps and Hon Col Yorks Vol; Patron: Kent Co Playing Fields Assoc, Spastics Soc, Cancer Relief Macmillan Fund and Samaritans; *m* York Minster 8 June 1961 *2nd DUKE OF KENT (*see* ROYAL FAMILY) and has issue

WRAXALL, Baron

Arms: Argent three battleaxes erect sable within a bordure nebuly of the last. **Crest:** A dexter arm embowed in armour, the hand in a gauntlet proper bearing a battleaxe bendwise sinister sable. **Supporters:** On either side a St Kilda sheep proper, each charged on the shoulder with a portcullis chained or. **Motto:** *Tenax propositi* ('Firm of purpose'). **Creation:** B. (UK) 11 Jan 1928.

THE 2ND BARON WRAXALL, of Clyst St George, Co Devon ((George) Richard Lawley Gibbs, DL (Avon 1974)) [The Rt Hon The Lord Wraxall DL, Tyntesfield, Wraxall, Bristol BS48 1NU]; *b* 16 May 1928 (HM QUEEN MARY stood sponsor); *s*

f 1931; *educ* Eton and RMA Sandhurst; late Capt Coldstream Gds (RARO) and Maj N Somerset and Bristol Yeo, Chm North Somerset C Assoc 1970–74

Lineage: ANTONY GIBBS, of Tyntesfield (*see* ALDENHAM and HUNSDON OF HUNSDON, B); had an est s:

GEORGE ABRAHAM GIBBS, **1st Baron Wraxall**, of Clyst St George, Co Devon (UK), so *cr* 11 Jan 1928, TD, PC (1923), JP, DL Somerset; *b* 6 July 1873; *educ* Ch Ch Oxford (MA), Ld Manor of Wraxall, Somerset, Col TAR, cmded N Somerset Yeo Boer War 1900 (medals, four clasps); MP (C) Bristol W 1906–28, PPS to Sec State Colonies 1917, Treasurer Household 1921–24 and 1924–28; *m* 1st 26 Nov 1901 Victoria Florence de Burgh, CBE (*d* 29 March 1920), est dau of 1st Viscount Long (*qv*), and had:

  1 George Antony; *b* and *d* 5 Sept 1911

  2 Antony Eustace Long; *b* 24 Sept *d* 29 Nov 1916

  1 *Doreen Albinia de Burgh [The Hon Mrs Norman, Villa Villetri, Vallée des Vaux, St Helier, Jersey, CI]; *b* 17 Sept 1913; *m* 12 Nov 1937 Charles Bathurst Norman, barrister, yr s of Rev Harry Bathurst Norman, of Iwood Manor, Somerset, and has:

    (1) *George Alfred Bathurst [His Honour Judge Norman, 3 Hare Ct, Temple, London EC4]; *b* 15 Jan 1939; *educ* Harrow and Magdalen Coll Oxford (BA); barrister Inner Temple 1961; Met Stipendiary Magistrate 1981–86, Circuit Judge 1986–; *m* 1st 29 July 1967 (*divorce* 1967) Prudence Veronica, dau of F H Keenlyside, of Salisbury, Rhodesia; *m* 2nd 14 Sept 1973 *Susan Elizabeth, dau of Thomas Ball, of Bromley, Kent, and by her has:

      1a *Charles Canning Bathurst; *b* 1979

      1a *Harriet Anstice Bathurst; *b* 1977

    (1) *Victoria Mary Bathurst [Mrs Patrick Eyre, 8 Cheyne Gdns, London SW3]; *b* 29 Sept 1940; *m* 1st 30 Sept 1961 (*divorce* 1967) Capt Raymond Edward Barthop, Northants Regt, yr s of Maj John Amyas Fielding Barthop, Northants Regt, of The Quinta, Bentley, Hants, and has:

      1a *Nicola Vivien; *b* 11 May 1964

    (1) (cont.) *Mrs Victoria Barthop *m* 2nd 1977 *Patrick Eyre (*see* ACTON, B) and has further issue

The **1st Baron** *m* 2nd 21 July 1927 Hon Ursula Mary Lawley, OBE (1945), RRC, SSStJ, Maid of Honour to HM QUEEN MARY 1912–27 (*d* 1979), er dau of 6th and last Baron Wenlock (*see* 1932 edn), and *d* 28 Oct 1931, leaving by her:

  3 (GEORGE) RICHARD LAWLEY GIBBS, **2nd and present Baron Wraxall**

  4 +EUSTACE HUBERT BEILBY (Sir), KCVO (1986), CMG (1982) [The Hon Sir Eustace Gibbs KCVO CMG, Coddenham House, Coddenham, Suffolk IP6 9TY]; *b* 3 July 1929; heir presumptive; *educ* Eton and Ch Ch Oxford (MA 1965); Dip Serv 1954: Bangkok, Rio de Janeiro, Berlin, Vienna, Caracas, Paris, RCDS 1974, V-Marshal Dip Corps 1982–86, ret 1986; *m* 23 Oct 1957 *Evelyn Veronica, only dau of Sydney Keith Scott, of Reydon Grove Farm, Southwold, Suffolk, and has:

    (1) *Antony Hubert [Antony Gibbs Esq, The Coachhouse, 1 Grace Mews, London SE5]; *b* 19 Aug 1958; *educ* Eton and New Coll Oxford; *m* 1st 1988 (*divorce* 1994) Caroline Jane, dau of Arthur Gould, and has:

      1a *India Florence Aurelia; *b* 28 March 1989

      2a *Cosima Eleanore; *b* 3 March 1992

    (1) (cont.) Antony Gibbs *m* 2nd 15 March 1995 *Virginia, dau of Colin Gilchrist, of Knightsbridge and Viscountess Dilhorne (*qv*), and by her has:

      1a +Orlando Hubert; *b* 19 May 1995

    (2) +Andrew Christopher; *b* 17 May 1965; *educ* Eton and Peterhouse Cambridge; *m* 1 July 1995 *Diahann Lesley Alison, dau of J E Brown, of Brighton, and has:

      1a *Eleanore Frances; *b* 25 March 1998

    (3) +Jonathan Charles William; *b* 27 April 1969; *educ* Eton and Bristol U

    (1) *Miranda Caroline; *b* 26 Jan 1961; *educ* Benenden; *m* 1993 *Andrew David Fox Jolliffe, only s of B R Jolliffe, of Bedford

    (2) *Alexander Mary Henrietta; *b* 28 May 1971; *educ* Wycombe Abbey and Edinburgh U

WRAXALL, Bt

Arms: Lozengy erminois and azure, on a chevron gules three estoiles of eight points or. **Crest:** A buck's head cabossed and erased gules, charged on the breast with two lozenges in fess and between the attires an estoile or. **Creation:** Bt. (UK) 21 Dec 1813.

SIR CHARLES FREDERICK LASCELLES WRAXALL, **9TH BT**, of Wraxall, Somerset; *b* 17 Sept 1961; *s* 1978; *educ* Archbishop Tenison's GS Croydon; civ serv; *m* 1983 *Lesley Linda, dau of William Albert Allan, and has:

  1 +WILLIAM NATHANIEL LASCELLES; *b* 3 April 1987

  1 *Lucy Rosemary Lascelles; *b* 1992

Lineage: NATHANIEL WRAXALL, of Mayse Hill, nr Bristol; *b* 1687; merchant, High Sheriff; *m* 1708 Anne (*d* 1764), dau of John Goddard, of Cork, and *d* 24 March 1731, leaving, with four daus:

NATHANIEL WRAXHALL, of Mayse Hill; *b* 1725; Bristol merchant; *m* 1749 Anne (*d* 1800), dau of William Thornhill, of Bristol, and great-niece of the architect Sir James Thornhill, and *d* 1781, leaving, with two daus:

Sir **Nathaniel William Wraxall, 1st Bt** (UK), so *cr* 21 Dec 1813, of Wraxall, Somerset; HEICS 1769–72, Judge Advocate and Paymaster Forces Gujerat 1771, MP Hindon 1780, Ludgershall 1784 and Wallingford 1790–94, author: *Historical Memoirs* and other works; *m* 30 March 1789 Jane (*d* 9 Aug 1839), dau of Peter Lascelles, of Knights House, Herts, and *d* 7 Nov 1831, leaving:

  1 Sir **William Wraxall, 2nd Bt**; *b* 5 Sept 1791; *d* unm 2 May 1863

  2 Charles Edward; *b* 9 Aug 1792; Lt RA; *m* 1827 Ellen Cecilia (*d* Nov 1840), dau of John Madden, of Richmond, Surrey, and *d* 1849, leaving:

    (1) Sir **Frederick Charles Lascelles, 3rd Bt**; *b* 2 Jan 1828; Assist Commissary Turkish Contingent, author; *m* May 1852 Mary Anne (*d* 27 Nov 1882), dau of J Herring, and *dsp* 11 June 1865

    (2) Sir **Horatio Henry, 4th Bt**; *b* 17 Dec 1832; *m* 28 Feb 1855 Laura, 2nd dau of Edward Hammond, of Richmond, Surrey, and *dsp* April 1882

    (3) MORVILLE WILLIAM NATHANIEL (Sir), **5th Bt**

    (1) Emilie Fanny; *b* 20 Nov 1830; nun convent Isleworth, Middx; *d* 1851

The 4th Bt's bro,

Sir **Morville William Nathaniel, 5th Bt**; *b* 5 Oct 1834; *m* 1860 Susannah Hariet Claringbold, of Walmer, Kent (*d* 1884), and *d* 20 Oct 1898, leaving, with two yr sons (Charles Edward Lascelles, *b* 27 May 1868; Horatio Henry Edwin, *b* 1869) and a dau (Emilie Elizabeth, *b* 1861, RRC, Army nursing sister WW I, *d* unm 1 Sept 1955):

Sir **Morville William Wraxall, 6th Bt**; *b* 23 Jan 1862; Commissariat and Tport Corps Nile Expdn 1884–85 (medal with two clasps, bronze star); Lt Egyptian Coastguard Serv 1891; *m* 6 Aug 1892 Honorine Herminia (*d* 24 Jan 1920), dau of John Lanzon, of Alexandria, and had:

  1 CHARLES FREDERICK LASCELLES (Sir), **7th Bt**

  1 Aida Mary Elizabeth; *b* 21 May 1893; *m* 11 Jan 1919 Anthony Joseph Bertuchi, FRGS (*d* 25 Nov 1957), s of Anthony Bertuchi, of Gibraltar, and *d* 29 Oct 1967, leaving a s and five daus

  2 Alice Elvira Herminia; *b* 21 Jan 1895; *m* 1st 21 Jan 1916 John Johnstone, of Ayr (*d* 1927); *m* 2nd Dec 1929 W/Offr Walter Huckvale, RAF, and *d* 1993 having had:

    (1) *Ronald Dennis; *b* 2 June 1932; Lt-Col RCAF; *m* June 1953 *Lucinda Russell, of Somerset, and has:

      1a *Robert; *b* 1961

  3 Emily Irene Honorine; *b* 21 Jan 1895; *m* 23 Feb 1916 Aubrey Slade Roberts (*d* 11 May 1968), s of Capt Thomas John Roberts, Sub-Commr Pilotage, of Polruan-by-Fowey, Cornwall, and *d* 10 May 1963, leaving a dau

  4 *Lesley Mary Virginia; *b* 20 Jan 1902; *m* 1st 31 March 1928 (*divorce* 1955) Herbert Cecil Thorpe, F/Lt RAF, s of Cecil Thorpe, of Southsea, and has:

    (1) *Leslie William [Leslie Thorpe Esq, 39 Morland Rd, Addiscombe, Surrey]; *b* 9 Dec 1928; *m* 18 July 1952 *Pamela Deirdre, dau of Christopher Connolly, of Kingston, Surrey, and has:

      1a *Karen Leslie Wraxall; *b* 5 Nov 1954

4 (cont.) Mrs Lesley Thorpe *m* 2nd July 1971 — Hollingsworth, of Worcester Pk, Surrey

5 Vera Jane; *b* 20 Jan, *d* 1 Aug 1902

Sir MORVILLE *d* 12 Oct 1902; his only s,

Sir Charles Frederick Lascelles Wraxall, 7th Bt; *b* 28 Sept 1896; *m* 20 Jan 1921 Marceline (*d* 28 Oct 1959), dau of O Cauro, of Cauro, Corsica, and had:

1 MORVILLE WILLIAM LASCELLES (Sir), **8th Bt**

  1 *Gwendolyn Aileen [Mrs John Hunter, 110 Devonshire Way, Shirley, Croydon, Surrey]; *b* 16 Nov 1927; *m* 14 Oct 1945 John Hunter, F/Lt RAFVR, CEng, FIMechE, AFRAeS, FInstPet (*d* 1987), and has:

    (1) *Kenneth Charles John Wraxall [Kenneth Hunter Esq, Flat 10, Beech Ct, 46 Copers Cope Rd, Beckenham, Kent BR3 1LD]; *b* 28 Nov 1951; BSc Hons (Warwick); MInstPet; *m* 1976 (*divorce* 1998) Gillian Margaret Sutton, of Billericay, Essex, and has:

      1a *Martin Robert; *b* 1981

      2a *Simon Richard; *b* 1985

      1a *Alicia Jennifer; *b* 1988

    (2) *Keith Philip Wraxall [Keith Hunter Esq, 1 Tower Gdns, Bearsted, Kent ME14 4JQ]; *b* 12 July 1957; BSc Hons (London U); *m* 24 June 1983 *Louise Bernadette Maria Baede, of Amsterdam, and has:

      1a *Nicholas John; *b* 2 April 1988

      2a *Christopher Marinus; *b* 18 Jan 1990

      3a *Alexander Keith; *b* 24 May 1993

      4a *Sebastian Nicholas; *b* 4 March 1996

Sir CHARLES *d* 7 July 1951; his only s,

Sir Morville William Lascelles Wraxall, 8th Bt; *b* 11 June 1922; *educ* St Mark's Coll Alexandria; RASC 1940–46; *m* 6 Oct 1956 *Irmgard Wilhelmina Maria, dau of Alois Larry Schnidrig, of Prattein, Switzerland, and *d* 19 July 1978, leaving:

1 Sir CHARLES FREDERICK LASCELLES WRAXALL, **9th and present Bt**

2 +Peter Edward Lascelles [Peter Wraxall Esq, 8 Glendower Rd, Table View, 7441 Cape Town, South Africa]; *b* 30 March 1967

  1 *Sylvia Laura [Mrs Andrew Lack, 112 Park Ave North, Abington, Northants NN3 2BX]; *b* 6 Aug 1957; *m* 1st 19– Peter Buckby; *m* 2nd 19– *Andrew Lack, and by her 1st husb has:

    (1) *Matthew Peter; *b* 1982

    (1) *Natalie Sarah; *b* 1983

WRENBURY

· TO · MY · UTMOST ·

Arms: Azure a chevron cotised between two stag's heads cabossed in chief and a garb in base all or, on a chief engrailed ermine a buckle between two crosses patée fitchée gules. **Crest:** On a mount vert a demi-stag at gaze gules, attired and gorged with a collar, thereto attached a chain reflexed over the back or, supporting a garb of the last. **Supporters:** On either side a buck at gaze gules, collared, attired and chained or. **Motto:** To my utmost. **Creation:** B. (UK) 12 April 1915.

THE 3RD BARON WRENBURY, of Oldcastle, Co Sussex (Rev John Burton Buckley) [The Rev and Rt Hon The Lord Wrenbury, Oldcastle, Dallington, E Sussex TN21 9JP]; *b* 18 June 1927; *s f* 1940; *educ* Eton and King's Coll Cambridge (BA 1948, MA 1953); slr 1952; dep legal advsr Nat Tst 1955–56; ptnr: Freshfields, slrs, 1956–74; Thomson Snell and Passmore 1974–90; Deacon C of E 1990, Priest 1991, non-stipendiary incumbent Brightling, Dallington, Mountfield and Netherfield 1990–; *m* 1st 10 March 1956 (*divorce* 1961) Carolyn Joan Maule, only child of Lt-Col Ian Burn-Murdoch, OBE, of Gartincaber, Doune, Perths; *m* 2nd 6 Oct 1961 *Penelope Sara Frances, only dau of Edward Dimond Fort, of The White Ho, Sixpenny Handley, Dorset, and by her has:

1 +WILLIAM EDWARD; *b* 19 June 1966; *m* 6 July 1996 *Emma L, dau of Peter Clementson, of W Wittering, Sussex, and Mrs Antony Robinson, of S Clifton, Notts

  1 *Elizabeth Margaret; *b* 21 May 1964; *m* 1st 1988 (*divorce* 1991) Capt Andrew Murray Macnaughton, Argyll and Sutherland Highrs, er s of R M Macnaugh-

ton, of Edinburgh; *m* 2nd 1993 *Dr Timothy Grey Morgan, s of Prof Colyn Grey Morgan, of Meyols, Swansea

  2 *Katherine Lucy; *b* 13 Nov 1968

Lineage: TIMOTHY BUCKLEY; *m* 4 July 1603 Mary Gray and had:

WILLIAM BUCKLEY, of New Hall, Wrenbury, Cheshire; had, with a dau (Elizabeth, *bapt* 1710):

WILLIAM BUCKLEY; *bapt* 19 March 1697; *m* 1st Mary — and had a s (William, *bapt* 7 June 1724); *m* 2nd Anne — and by her had, with a yr s (Thomas, *m* 7 June 1756 Elizabeth Unwin):

JOHN BUCKLEY, of New Hall; *bapt* 16 May 1731; *m* 25 Nov 1754 Ann Penny (*bur* 24 July 1797) and was *bur* 12 Oct 1801, having had, with two yr sons and a dau (Mrs Whittingham):

THOMAS BUCKLEY, of Grosvenor St, London, and Waterloo House, Kilburn; *b* 20 April 1757; *m* 1st — Vaudrey (*d* 3 Feb 1801); *m* 2nd 25 Aug 1803 Arabella Wall Callcott (*d* 29 June 1831) and by her had, with another dau (*d* unm):

  1 JOHN WALL

  2 Thomas Wall; *b* 17 Feb 1811; *d* 22 Feb 1902

  3 William Augustus; *b* 26 July 1813; *m* 20 April 1843 Emily Bush (*d* 12 Aug 1857) and *d* 10 March 1893, leaving three sons and two daus

  1 Ann Wall; *b* 25 April 1806; *m* 25 April 1838 Capt Robert Duncan Stuart (*d* 13 Oct 1842) and *d* 15 March 1859

THOMAS BUCKLEY was *bur* 8 Sept 1819; his est s,

Rev JOHN WALL BUCKLEY; *b* 31 July 1809; MA Cantab; Vicar St Mary's, Paddington Gn, 40 years; *m* 25 Sept 1832 Elizabeth (*d* 2 Feb 1889), dau of Thomas Burton, and *d* 22 Aug 1883, having had, with another s (*b* and *d* the same day):

  1 William Burton (Rev); *b* 22 March 1835; *d* 28 April 1888

  2 Charles Burton, of Singapore, Straits Settlements; *b* 30 Jan 1844; *d* 22 May 1912

  3 HENRY BURTON, **1st Baron**

  4 Robert Burton, CSI; *b* 23 Aug 1847; MICE; U-Sec India PWD 1887–89, Suptg Engr 1892, Ch Engr and Sec to Govt Bengal 1898–1902; *m* 29 July 1880 Ada Marion Sarah (*d* 23 Feb 1929), dau of Maj B K Finnimore, RA, and *d* 19 Dec 1927, leaving surv issue:

    (1) Donald Finnimore; *b* 4 June 1887; BA Cantab; slr; *m* 22 Feb 1915 Edith May, only dau of Sidney A Boulton, of Bayswater

    (1) Elsie Finnimore; *b* 1 Aug 1882; *m* 20 March 1920 Anthony Ludovici and *d* 6 June 1959

    (2) Winifred Finnimore; *b* 18 Oct 1883; MRCS, LRCP; *d* unm 10 April 1959

    (3) Margery Finnimore; *b* 26 April 1893; *m* 10 July 1913 George Edward Hughes

  5 Arthur Burton; *b* 11 June 1849; *m* 10 Oct 1872 Ada Maria Bacci and *d* 7 Aug 1937, leaving:

    (1) Arthur Burton, OBE, of Dorchester Ho, Park Hill, Carshalton; *b* 15 Aug 1877; *m* 7 Aug 1907 Stuarta Frances, dau of Franz Weyermann, of The Hagerhof, Honnef, and *d* 23 Oct 1964, leaving issue

    (2) Hugh Gianpaolo; *b* 30 April 1881

    (3) John Wall; *b* 30 Oct 1883

    (4) Peter Frederick Joseph; *b* 29 March 1891; *m* 27 Aug 1915 Mary Marjorie, 2nd dau of Richard Tuson Heneker, KC, of Montreal

    (1) Cecilia Elizabeth; *d* unm 6 Oct 1940

    (2) Jane Julia; *m* George le Messurier and *d* 29 Dec 1918

    (3) Ada Maria Agnes

  1 Elizabeth Burton; *b* 7 July 1833; *m* 28 April 1859 Rev Henry Lettsom Elliot, Vicar Gosfield, Essex, and had issue

  2 Julia Burton; *b* 25 Jan 1839; *m* 21 March 1863 Charles Adhemar Roselli Clauson (*d* 6 March 1895) and *d* 1 May 1924, leaving issue

  3 Arabella Burton; *b* 24 Oct 1840; *m* 6 March 1884 Thomas Fisher, MD (*d* 28 Jan 1895), of Christchurch, NZ, and *d* 9 Feb 1929

The Rev JOHN WALL BUCKLEY's 4th s,

HENRY BURTON BUCKLEY, **1st Baron Wrenbury**, of Old Castle, Co Sussex (UK), so *cr* 12 April 1915, PC (1906); *b* 15 Sept 1845; barrister 1869, QC 1886, Bencher 1891, High Court Judge Chancery Div 1900–06, Ld Justice Appeal 1906–15, ktd 1900, alleged by Sir Osbert Lancaster to have been the last man in London to wear Dundreary whiskers; *m* 12 April 1887 Bertha Margaretta (*d* 23 Nov 1960 aged 94), 3rd dau of Charles Edward Jones, of S Kensington, and had:

  1 BRYAN BURTON, **2nd Baron**

  2 Guy Burton; *b* 21 June, *d* 9 July 1892

  3 Colin Burton; *b* 16 Oct 1899; *educ* Eton and King's Coll Cambridge (BA 1922, MA 1927, MB and BCh 1927); *m* 15 Sept 1925 Evelyn Joyce (*d* 1987), est dau of Sir Hugh Calthrop Webster, of Newlands, Hadley Wood, and *d* 1981, having had:

    (1) +Martin Christopher Burton [Martin Buckley Esq, Crouchers, Rudgwick, Sussex RH12 3DD]; *b* 5 Oct 1936; barrister Lincoln's Inn 1961, Registrar Bancruptcy Companies Court 1988–; *m* 2 May 1964 *Victoria Gay, dau of Dr Stanhope Edward Furber, of 14 Wimpole St, London W1, and Oak Cottage, Bracknell, Berks, and has:

      1a +Arthur Burton; *b* 2 May 1967; *m* 1992 *Amanda Jane Ridley

      2a +Samuel Burton; *b* 1973

      1a *Hannah Kate; *b* 22 Sept 1965

      2a *Amanda Victoria; *b* 12 Dec 1968; *m* 1991 *Anthony Clarke

      3a *Jessica Beth; *b* 1971

    (1) Susan Mary; *b* 2 Nov 1926; *d* 19 March 1939

    (2) *Bridget Elizabeth [Miss Bridget Buckley, 22 Gunter Grove, London SW10]; *b* 21 Aug 1929

    (3) *Jessica Margaret [Mrs Michael Knott, Seaton Mill, Ickham, Canterbury, Kent]; *b* 24 June 1932; *m* 3 Oct 1957 *Michael John Knott, s of Claude Carrington Knott, of Wychbold, Worcs, and has issue

    (4) *Alison Rachel [Mrs Benjamin Fisher, 133 Victoria Rd, Fulwood, Preston, Lancs]; *b* 6 Sept 1933; *m* 6 June 1959 *Benjamin Fisher, s of B T Fisher, of Preston, and has issue

(5) *Hazel Charlotte [Sister Ancille Buckley, Ladywell Convent, Ashtead Lane, Godalming, Surrey GU7 1ST]; *b* 28 Dec 1934; nun from 1958

4 +Denys Burton (Sir), PC (1970), MBE (1945); *b* 6 Feb 1906; *educ* Eton and Trin Coll Oxford (BA 1929, MA 1932, Hon Fell 1969); Maj RAOC and GSO(2) Directorate Signals War Office WW II (US Medal Freedom); barrister Lincoln's Inn 1928, bencher 1949 (Treasurer 1969), High Court Judge Chancery Div 1960–70, ktd 1960, Judge Restrictive Practices Court 1962–70 (Pres 1968–70), memb Law Reform Ctee 1963–73, Pres Senate Four Inns of Court 1970–72, Ld Justice Appeal 1970–81, Master Merchant Taylors' Co 1972, CStJ; *m* 23 July 1932 Gwendolen Jane (*d* 1985), yr dau of Sir Robert Armstrong-Jones, CBE, JP, DL (*see* SNOWDON, E), and has:

(1) *Jane Gwenllian Armstrong [Lady Slade, 16 Elthiron Rd, London SW6 4BN]; *b* 22 May 1936; *m* 30 May 1958 *Sir Christopher John Slade, PC, est s of George Penkivil Slade, KC, of Painswick, Glos, and has:

1a *Richard Penkivil; *b* 12 July 1963; *m* 1994 *Lucy Jane, dau of George Cacanas, of Upper Swainswick, Bath

1a *Lucinda Jane; *b* 15 Nov 1959; *m* 1985 *Christopher Charles Tite, s of Leslie J Tite, of Wandsworth, and has:

1b *William Christopher James; *b* 1990

2b *Oliver Henry Charles; *b* 1992

1b *Serena Catherine Lucinda; *b* 1994

2a *Victoria Albinia; *b* 15 Jan 1962; *m* 1988 *Hugh J Henderson-Cleland, s of J G W Henderson-Cleland, of Clapham, and has:

1b *Archibald Hugh; *b* 1994

1b *Georgia; *b* 1989

2b *Charlotte May; *b* 1991

3b *Octavia Jane; *b* 1997

3a *Amelia Caroline; *b* 4 Oct 1966; *m* 1992 *Capt Matthew Jackson, RE, s of Cdr M E Jackson, RN, of Old Portsmouth, Hants

(2) *Catherine Elizabeth Armstrong [Mrs Charles Nunneley, 19 Rosaville Rd, London SW6 7BN]; *m* Fyfield House, Pewsey, Wilts]; *b* 28 Dec 1961 *Charles Kenneth Roylance Nunneley, only s of Robin Michael Charles Nunneley, of Chelsea, and has:

1a *Luke James Charles; *b* 25 April 1963; *m* 1990 *Katherine Ruth, 2nd dau of B F Panter, of Walton-on-Thames, Surrey, and has:

1b *Rebecca; *b* 1992

1a *Alice Georgina; *b* 22 June 1964; *m* 1989 *Nicholas Bruce Chapple and has:

1b *Ben; *b* 1994

2a *Clare Sabina; *b* 27 May 1967

3a *Frances Mary; *b* 12 June 1969

(3) *(Marion) Miranda Armstrong; *b* 7 March 1945

1 Joyce Burton; *b* 10 Feb 1889

2 Muriel Burton; *b* 30 March 1894; MRCS, LRCP; *m* 20 May 1920 Bernard Warren Williams, MB, ChB, FRCS, 3rd s of James Rowland Williams, MLC, Dir Educn Jamaica, and had issue

3 Olive Burton; *b* 25 Jan 1896; *educ* Somerville Coll Oxford (BA 1922, BM 1925, DM 1932); LRCP, MRCS 1925, MRCP 1928; *m* 15 Sept 1949 Ven Archdeacon Stephen Romney Maurice Gill (*d* 26 March 1954), s of Arthur Tidman Gill

4 Ruth Burton, DBE (1959), JP (1935); *b* 12 July 1898; barrister Lincoln's Inn 1926; E Sussex: CA, V-Chm CC 1949, Chm 1952

The 1st BARON *d* 27 Oct 1935; his est s,

BRYAN BURTON BUCKLEY, **2nd Baron Wrenbury**; *b* 24 May 1890; *educ* Eton and King's Coll Cambridge (BA 1912, MA 1926); Lt London Regt; barrister Lincoln's Inn 1913; *m* 7 April 1925 Helen Malise (*d* 1981), 2nd dau of His Honour John Cameron Graham, of Ballewan, Blanefield, Stirlingshire, and *d* 30 May 1940, leaving:

1 JOHN BURTON BUCKLEY, **3rd and present Baron Wrenbury**

1 *Mary Graham [The Hon Mrs Homan, 30 High St, Ticehurst, Sussex TN5 7AS]; *b* 30 May 1929; *m* 8 April 1961 *John Richard Seymour Homan, CBE (1985), yr s of Capt Charles Edward Homan, Er Bro Trin House, of Honey Lane Cottage, Burley, Hants, and has:

(1) *Robert Seymour; *b* 21 July 1964

(1) *Frances Mary; *b* 1967

(2) *Rosalind Claire; *b* 1969

WREY

Arms: Sable a fess between three pole-axes argent, helved gules.
Motto: *Le bon temps viendra* ('The good times will come').
Creation: Bt. (E) 20 June 1628.

SIR (GEORGE RICHARD) BOURCHIER WREY, 15TH BT, of Trebitch, Cornwall [Sir Bourchier Wrey Bt, 60 The Chase, London SW4 0NH; Hollamoor Farm, Tawstock, Barnstaple, N Devon]; *b* 2 Oct 1948; *s f* 1991; *educ* Eton; *m* 1981 *Lady Caroline Janet, only dau of 15th Earl of Lindsay (*qv*), and has:

1 +HARRY DAVID; *b* 3 Oct 1984

2 +Humphrey George; *b* 1991

1 *Rachel Pearl; *b* 1987

Lineage: JOHN WREY, of North Russell, Devon; *m* Blanche (*d* 14 Dec 1596), dau and heiress of Henry Killigrew, of Wolston, Cornwall, thus acquiring the Manor of Trebitch, Cornwall, and *d* April 1577, leaving a 4th s:

Sir William Wrey, 1st Bt (E), so *cr* 20 June 1628, of Trebitch; High Sheriff Cornwall 1612–13; *m* 1600 Elizabeth, dau of Sir William Courtenay, *de jure* 3rd Earl of Devon (*qv*), and *d* June 1636, leaving:

Sir William Wrey, 2nd Bt; ktd 1634; *m* (licence 6 Oct 1624) Elizabeth, yst dau of 1st Viscount Chichester (*see* DONEGALL, M), and *d* Aug 1645, having had, with three daus:

Sir Chichester Wrey, 3rd Bt; *b* 1628; MP Lostwithiel 1661–68, Govr Sheerness and Col Duke of York's Regt; *m* by 1653 Anne (*bur* 9 Sept 1662), 3rd dau and coheir of Edward Bourchier, 4th Earl of Bath (*see* BATH, M, preliminary remarks), and widow of James Cranfield, 2nd Earl of Middlesex, and had:

1 BOURCHIER (Sir), **4th Bt**

2 Chichester; Col; *k* in the defence of Fort Monjuich, Spain, 1706

3 Edward

4 John; *k* before Tangier

1 Anne; *m* 26 July 1688 Sir Francis Northcote, 3rd Bt (*see* IDDESLEIGH, E), and *dsp*

Sir CHICHESTER was *bur* 17 May 1668; his est s,

Sir Bourchier Wrey, 4th Bt, KB; Col of Horse; MP Liskeard 1677–78 and 1689–96 and Devon 1685–87; *m* 3 May 1681 Florence, dau of Sir John Rolle, KB, of Stevenstone, and had:

1 BOURCHIER (Sir), **5th Bt**

2 Chichester (Rev); MA Oxon; Rector Tawstock 1710; *m* and had issue

1 Florence; *m* 10 July 1707 John Cole (*see* ENNISKILLEN, E) and had issue

The 4th Bt *d* 28 July 1696; his er s,

Sir Bourchier Wrey, 5th Bt; MP Camelford 1712–3; *m* 28 Feb 1707/8 Diana, dau of John Rolle, of Stevenstone, and widow of John Sparke, and was *bur* 12 Nov 1726, having had, with four yr sons and four daus:

Sir Bourchier Wrey, 6th Bt; Col N Devon Militia, MP Barnstaple 1749–54; *m* 1st 10 July 1749 Mary (*bur* 3 Sept 1751), dau of John Edwards, of Highgate; *m* 2nd 1 May 1755 Ellen (*d* Nov 1813), dau of John Thresher, of Bradford, Wilts, by Ellen, dau of Henry Long, of Melksham, and by her had:

1 BOURCHIER (Sir), **7th Bt**

2 Bourchier William (Rev); *b* 6 May 1761; MA Oxon, Fell All Souls, Rector Tawstock and Combe-in-Teignhead, Devon; *s* to the Melksham estate of his Long ancestors; *m* Nov 1789 Sophia, dau and coheir of George Bethell, of Bradford, Wilts, and *d* 27 Aug 1839, having had, with three daus:

(1) William Long; *b* 1792; Lt 19th Dragoons

(2) Edward Bourchier; *b* 7 Jan 1794; barrister, Judge in India; *m* 9 Feb 1818 Juliana (*d* 11 March 1829), dau of Rev George Wilson, Vicar Corbridge, and *d* 30 May 1840, leaving, with a dau:

1a George Bourchier; *b* 4 Jan 1820; *m* 8 July 1848 Sarah (*d* 29 July 1869), dau of Col John Cuninghame, of Caddel, Ayrshire, and *d* 9 March 1854, leaving:

1b George Edward Bourchier, of Thornton; *b* 9 March 1851; *educ* Trin Coll Cambridge (BA); *m* 24 Feb 1886 his cousin Anne Maud, dau of Rev Arthur Bourchier Wrey (*see* below), and *d* 9 Aug 1926, leaving:

1c Edward Charles, OBE (1919); *b* 30 March 1889; Cdr RN, WWs I (despatches) and II; *m* 11 Dec 1914 Grace Elsie (*d* 14 Dec 1940), yr dau of James Cook Rimer, of Kelvin Grove, Newlands, Cape Colony, and *d* 1972, leaving:

1d *Elizabeth Anne [Mrs William Flexner, 9 Paultons St, London SW3 5DP]; *b* 31 Aug 1917; *educ* Oxford (MA); *m* 11 Oct 1946 *William Welch Flexner, BS (Harvard), PhD (Princeton), s of Dr Simon Flexner, of New York

2d *Marie Jean; *b* 9 Sept 1919; *m* 1st 16 May 1940 Capt David Cecil Patrick Hastings (*das* Burma 29 March 1943), yr s of Sir Patrick Hastings, QC, of Thurston Hall, Framfield, Sussex, and has:

1e *Judith Maryanne [Mrs Colin Dickinson, The Old Vicarage, Coaley, Dursley, Glos GL11 5EB]; *b* 15 Sept 1941; *m* 10 Aug 1963 *Colin Etienne Boileau Shearme Dickinson, er s of Lt -Col Richard Ridley Boileau Dickinson, of Woodbridge, Suffolk, and has:

1f *Anthony David Richard; *b* 27 Sept 1965; *m* 10 June 1996 *Sarah Flanakin

1f *Charlotte Lucy; *b* 27 Sept 1965; *m* 3 Aug 1996 *Ian Wilson and has:

1g *Ella Marie; *b* 17 May 1998

2f *Sophie Louise; *b* 8 Sept 1971

2d (cont.) Mrs David Hastings *m* 2nd 5 March 1949 (Frank Herbert) Michael Dowden (*d* 1972), s of Frederick Charles Patrick Dowden, and by him has:

1e *Edward David Michael [Edward Dowden Esq, 11 Bath Rd, Bradford-on-Avon, Wilts BA15 1SN; *b* 27 July 1950; *educ* Uppingham and Newcastle U; *m* 3 Jan 1970 *Sarah Anne, dau of Kenneth Arthur Sherwin, of Ipswich, Suffolk, and has:

1f *Benjamin Thomas Edward; *b* 6 Jan 1978

1f *Emma Mary; *b* 15 March 1973

2f *Matilda Jane; *b* 24 May 1975

(3) John (Rev); *b* Sept 1797; *m* 1st 1826 Anne Burnett (*d* 15 Sept 1860), only dau and heiress of Rev Thomas Yeomans, Vicar Bishop's Tawton and Braunton; *m* 2nd 6 Nov 1866 Elizabeth Dorothea (*d* 1885), widow of Thomas Potts, of St Mary Church, Devon, and *d* 30 Oct 1872, leaving by his 1st w, with other issue:

1a Charles Joseph, of Stoodley Knowle, Torquay; *b* 20 Dec 1828; Capt RN; *m* lst 9 May 1867 Caroline Rashleigh (*d* 16 Dec 1870), dau and heiress of Rev Charles Harward Archer, of Lewannick, and had:

1b Douglas Edward Archer; *b* 25 March 1869; *m* 1888 Mary Thomasine (*d* 18 Aug 1905), dau of Henry Archdale Owen, and *dsp* 6 Jan 1931

1a (cont.) Capt Charles Wrey *m* 2nd 21 Oct 1875 Henrietta Jane (*dsp* 13 Aug 1909), dau of Adml Charles Aldridge, and *d* 23 Aug 1891

2a Arthur Bourchier (Rev); *b* 17 April 1831; *educ* Trin Coll Cambridge (MA); Vicar St Mary Church 1876–1905; *m* lst 18 Jan 1859 Helen (*d* 10 May 1878), dau of Rev Thomas Phillpotts, Hon Canon Truro, and had, with a s (*d* an infant):

lb Emily Florence; *d* unm 8 Sept 1947

2b Cicely Helen; *m* 20 April 1893 Rev Henry Charles Wilder (*d* 26 Oct 1948), Rector Sulham, Berks, RD Bradfield, and *d* 15 Nov 1947, leaving issue

3b Anne Maud; *m* 24 Feb 1886 her cousin George Edward Bourchier Wrey and *d* 30 May 1950, leaving issue (*see* above)

2a (cont.) The Rev Arthur Wrey *m* 2nd 24 Aug 1881 Claudine Maud (*d* 6 Jan 1904), dau of Charles Twining, KC, and *d* 8 Sept 1918, leaving by her:

lb Wilfrid Arthur Bourchier; *b* 20 March 1885; Capt RE; *d* 1 March 1922

2b Hugh Bourchier; *b* 19 July 1888; Cdr RN; *m* 25 April 1925 Ruth (*d* 23 Sept 1951), dau of William Jackson, of Elmwood, Harrogate, and widow of Arthur Lord, MC, and *d* 13 Jan 1940

3b Mary Claudine; *m* 1st 11 June 1913 Capt Humphrey Richard Locke Lawrence, 34th Sikh Pioneers (missing presumed *kas* 30 Dec 1915), s of Maj-Gen William Alexander Lawrence, of Kensington, and had issue; *m* 2nd 13 Aug 1928 Heathcote Dicken Statham, MusD, FRCO (*d* 1973), s of Henry Heathcote Statham, of Wimbledon, and by him had:

1c *Michael Heathcote Wrey; *b* 1929

1 Ellen; *m* Rev Edward Henry Whinfield

2 Dyonisia; *m* Robert Harding, of Upcott

3 Florentina; *m* Richard Godolphin Long (*d* 1835), of Rood Ashton, Wilts, and *d* 1835, having had issue

4 Anne Maria; *m* 1791 Nicholas Roundell Toke (*d* 19 Feb 1837), of Godinton, Kent

The 6th Bt *d* 13 April 1784; his er s,

Sir Bourchier Wrey, 7th Bt; *b* 22 Feb 1757; *m* 1st 14 March 1786 Anne (*d* Sept 1791), est dau of Sir Robert Palk, 1st Bt (*see* 1940 edn), of Haldon, Devon, and had:

1 **Sir Bourchier Palk Wrey, 8th Bt**, JP, DL; *b* 10 Dec 1788; barrister; *m* 1st 14 March 1818 and (there being some uncertainty as to the legality of the earlier ceremony) a 2nd time 10 July 1832 Ellen Caroline (*née* O'Brien; *d* 23 July 1842), his sister Mrs Edward Hartopp's child's nanny and supposedly widow by 1818 of — Johnson, who at that time had disappeared for seven years but who subsequently turned up again, revealing himself to be Riddle rather than Johnson and a groom to Lord Adare (*see* DUNRAVEN AND MOUNT-EARL, E); he *d* 1826; **Sir Bourchier** *m* 2nd 11 Sept 1843 Eliza Coles (*dsp* 11 May 1875), allegedly lady's maid to her predecessor and dau of the lodge-keeper on the Tawstock estate, and *dspm* 11 Sept 1879, leaving by his 1st w:

(1) Ellen Caroline; *b* 1819; *m* 9 Aug 1838 Edward Joseph Weld (*d* 8 Dec 1877), of Lulworth Castle, Dorset, and *d* 13 Oct 1866, leaving issue

2 Robert Bourchier; *b* 1790; *m* 1821 Mary Anne (*d* 22 Dec 1886, aged 92), dau of Capt James, RN, and *dsp* 29 March 1872

1 Anna Eleanor; *m* 1st 19 July 1806 Edward Hartopp, of Little Dalby, Leics; *m* 2nd 9 Dec 1815 Sir Laurence Vaughan Palk, 3rd Bt (*see* 1940 edn HALTON, B), and *d* 25 Jan 1846, leaving issue

Sir Bourchier *m* 2nd 1793 Anne (*d* 26 Jan 1813), dau of John Osborne, and *d* 20 Nov 1826, leaving by her:

3 HENRY BOURCHIER (Sir), **9th Bt**

2 Eleanora Elizabeth; *m* 1st 2 March 1815 Albany Savile (*d* Feb 1831), of Oaklands, Devon, and had issue; *m* 2nd Rev Richard Fayle (*d* 26 March 1872), of Torquay, and *d* 12 Jan 1882

The 8th Bt's half-bro,

Rev Sir Henry Bourchier Wrey, 9th Bt, JP; *b* 5 June 1797; *educ* Balliol Coll Oxford (MA); Rector Tawstock; *m* 1st 27 Sept 1827 Ellen Maria (*d* 1 March 1864), only dau of Nicholas Roundell Toke, of Godington, Kent; *m* 2nd 5 Jan 1865 Jane (*d* 26 July 1889), dau of Humble Lamb, of Ryton House, Co Durham, and widow of John Stevenson, of Newcastle, and by his 1st w had:

1 HENRY BOURCHIER TOKE (Sir), **10th Bt**

2 Bourchier William Toke (Rev); *b* 7 Aug 1830; BCL Cantab; Rector Combe-in-Teignhead, Devon, 1864–1906; *m* 8 Sept 1859 Anne Caroline (*d* 1896), dau of Thomas Crosthwait, of Dublin, and *d* 13 June 1918, having had, with two other sons (*d* infants) and four daus (*d* unm):

(1) Henry Bourchier (Rev); *b* 13 Jan 1863; Rector Ideford, S Devon; *m* 11 Sept 1895 Helen Esmé (*d* 29 Jan 1961), dau of Frederick Charles Ernest Griffin, of Gorsty Hayes Manor Ho, Tettenhall, Wolverhampton, and *d* 2 May 1936, leaving:

1a Mary Caroline Bourchier; *m* 1st 16 Oct 1923 Robert Harry Cresswell Edwards (*d* 24 Sept 1925), late of Ceylon, 3rd s of Rev Robert Stafford Edwards, of Solihull, and had issue; *m* 2nd 19 April 1932 Rev Cyril Lucian O'Ferrall, Rector Shillingford St George, Exeter, s of James Eaton O'Ferrall, of Hartley Lodge, Market Harborough, Leics, and had issue

2a Helen Edith Bourchier; *d* unm 1 Nov 1962

3a Dorothy Esmé Bourchier; CStJ

(1) Evelyn Maria; *d* unm 31 March 1956 aged 90

(2) Henrietta Sophie; *b* 1 Aug 1875; *d* unm 9 Aug 1970

1 Anna Maria Toke; *m* 3 Sept 1857 Very Rev Isaac Morgan Reeves, Dean Ross, est s of Thomas Somerville Reeves, of Trammore Ho, and *d* 7 March 1867, leaving issue

The 9th Bt *d* 23 Dec 1882; his est s,

Sir Henry Bourchier Toke Wrey, 10th Bt, JP, DL; *b* 27 June 1829; *educ* Trin Coll Oxford (BA); Maj 4th Bn Devonshire Regt; High Sheriff Devon 1891; *m* 6 July 1854 Marianne Sarah (*d* 16 Feb 1896), only child of 9th Baron Sherard (*see* 1931 edn), and *d* 10 March 1900, leaving:

1 **Sir Robert Bourchier Sherard Wrey, 11th Bt**, JP, DL; *b* 23 May 1855; Capt RN and Roy Def Force, Maj and Hon Lt-Col Roy N Devon Yeo, Zulu, Egyptian, Burmese and Chinese Campaigns; *m* 26 Oct 1905 Jessie Maud (*m* 2nd 2 Nov 1918 Maj Godfrey Heseltine, 6th Dragoon Gds (*d* 5 Aug 1932) and *d* 20 Dec 1955), dau of William Thomson Fraser and gdau of John Fraser, of Mongewell Park, Oxon, and *d* 26 Jan 1917, leaving:

(1) Rachel; SSStJ, Chev Order Crown Belgium; *m* 4 Oct 1933 20th Baron Willoughby de Broke (*qv*) and *d* 1991, leaving issue

2 **Sir Philip Bourchier Sherard Wrey, 12th Bt**, CBE; *b* 28 June 1858; *m* 14 Aug 1889 Alice Mary (*d* 12 July 1950), dau of Capt Borton, RA, and *d* 8 May 1936, leaving:

(1) Florence Muriel Phyllis; *m* 14 Aug 1914 Lt John Lamb, RE (*ka* 17 Oct 1917), s of Rev John Lamb, Rector Blofield, Norfolk, and had issue

(2) *Barbara Marion Celia; *m* 1st 12 Aug 1925 F/O Robert Darley Whelan, RAF (*d* 3 Dec 1927), est s of Rev Percy Scott Whelan, Vicar Brenchley, Kent; *m* 2nd 22 May 1929 Sir Andrew Henry Strachan, CBE, FCA (*d* 1976), s of Andrew Douglas Strachan, of Dublin, and by him has:

1a *Richard Neville; *b* 25 Feb 1930

1a *Judith Meriel; *b* 21 Jan 1936; *m* 2 Dec 1961 *Alexander Colin Campbell, s of Cdr William Alexander John Campbell, OBE, RN, of Withygate, Brayford, N Devon

3 **Rev Sir Albany Bourchier Sherard Wrey, 13th Bt**, JP (Devon); *b* 4 Jan 1861; *educ* Hertford Coll Oxford (BA 1886, MA 1889); Rector Tawstock-with-Harracott 1893–1948, RD Barnstaple 1912–18, Chaplain to Roy N Devon Hus, CC Devon, memb Devon Co Educn Ctee, Chm Barnstaple RDC 1916–48, Silver Jubilee Medal 1935, Coronation Medal 1937; *m* 5 Aug 1896 Isabel Frances Sophia (*d* 29 April 1921), dau of Thomas Horn Fleet, JP, DL, of Darenth Grange, nr Dartford, and *dsp* 10 April 1948

4 William Bourchier Sherard, CMG (1917), CBE (1919); *b* 2 April 1865; Capt RN, Egypt 1882 (medal, two clasps, bronze star), China 1900 (medal, clasp, promotion), WW I as Pncpl NTO Southampton with rank of Cdre (despatches), Offr Order Leopold Belgium, Japanese Order Sacred Treasure, US DSM, Br War and Victory Medals; *m* 3 June 1897 Flora Bathurst (*d* 1 April 1954), yr dau of V-Adml William Samuel Greive, of Ord Ho, Berwick-on-Tweed, and *d* 8 Jan 1926

5 Gerald Bourchier Sherard; *b* 12 Dec 1870; *m* 12 July 1899 Jane Ellen (*d* 1 May 1945), dau of William Handford, ICS, and *dsp* 9 Sept 1902

6 Arthur Henry; *b* 18 June 1872; *m* 11 Dec 1897 Florence (*d* 29 April 1959), yst dau of Thomas Radmall, and *dsp* 26 Dec 1940

7 Edward Castell; *b* 9 Feb 1875; *m* 11 April 1901 Katherine Joan (*d* 30 Dec 1966 aged 84), 2nd dau of Rev John Dene (*see* MOLESWORTH-ST AUBYN, Bt), and *d* 28 Jan 1933, leaving:

(1) CASTEL RICHARD BOURCHIER (Sir), **14th Bt**

(2) Christopher Bourchier, TD (1946); *b* 27 Jan 1906; *educ* Blundell's; Maj 3rd Co of London Yeo (The Sharpshooters) WW II; *m* 8 June 1932 (*divorce* 1947) Ruth, only dau of Sir Harold Bowden, 2nd Bt (*qv*), and *d* 1976, leaving:

1a *Timothy Christopher Bourchier [Timothy Wrey Esq, c/o Lloyds Bank, Berkeley Sq, London W1X 6BJ]; *b* 2 Jan 1937; *educ* Blundell's and Clare Coll Cambridge; *m* 18 Sept 1964 *Susan Mary Bonita, only dau of Reginald Lancaster, of Kensington, and has:

1b +Marcus Valerian Bourchier; *b* 27 May 1969

1b *Camilla Melusine; *b* 20 Aug 1966

2a +Benjamin Harold Bourchier [Benjamin Wrey Esq, 8 Somerset Sq, Addison Rd, London W14 8EE]; *b* 6 May 1940; *educ* Blundell's and Clare Coll Cambridge (BA 1963, MA 1966); *m* 19 Feb 1970 *Mrs Anne Christine

Aubrey Cherry, only dau of Col Christopher Bushnell Stephenson, of Hurstbourne Tarrant, Hants, and has:

1b *Tanya Serena; *b* 1971

(1) *Katharine Augusta; *m* 30 June 1926 Harry Robert Wells, s of Henry Wells, of Fleet, Hants, and has:

1a *Christopher Richard Henry; *b* 24 Feb 1929; *educ* Blundell's; Capt RASC; *m* 9 March 1957 *Elizabeth Anne, only dau of Lt-Col Edward R Daglish, of Thurston, Suffolk, and has:

1b *Christopher Edward James; *b* 3 Dec 1958

1b *Philippa Frances Katharine; *b* 1961

1a *Cordelia Joan; *b* 28 Aug 1930; *m* 2 June 1956 *Alan John Douglas Wheeldon, MA, FIEE, er s of Douglas Parker Wheeldon, and has:

1b *Robert Alan Douglas; *b* 3 May 1957

1b *Virginia Margaret; *b* 1 Jan 1961

(2) *Diana Joan [The Hon Mrs William Rollo, Barleythorpe, Oakham, Rutland LE15 7EQ]; *m* 1st 27 Jan 1932 (*divorce* 1946) Jocelyn Abel Smith (*d* 1966), er s of Col Bertram Abel Smith, DSO, MC (*d* 1 May 1966), of 45 Montagu Sq, London W1, and Cossington, Leics, and has:

1a *John William; *b* 1933; *m* 1st 1957 Ruth, dau of Sir John Huggins, GCMG, MC; *m* 2nd 1965 (*divorce* 1974) Christine, only dau of Keith Taylor, of Adelaide; *m* 3rd 1975 *Mary Chichester Mills

2a *(Bertram) Robin; *b* 1938; *m* 1st 1961 (*divorce* 1976) Anne, yst dau of Walter Kidman, of Adelaide, S Australia, and has:

1b *William Walter; *b* 1964

1b *Rachel Muriel; *b* 1969

2a (cont.) Robin Abel Smith; *m* 2nd 1978 (*divorce* 1991) Kathleen Eugenie, dau of George Cecil Houghton Cowell, of Elms Farm, Ashley, Newmarket, and widow of Robert Bibby Collie; *m* 3rd 1993 *Diana Marjorie Fielder, dau of Patrick Forsell, and by her has:

2b *Thomas Patrick; *b* 1993

(2) (cont.) Mrs Diana Abel Smith *m* 2nd 21 Nov 1946 Hon William Hereward Charles Rollo, MC (*k* in a hunting accident 3 Oct 1962), bro of 12th Lord Rollo (*qv*)

8 Reginald Charles; *b* 17 June 1876; Maj 1st Bn Devon Regt, Boer War 1900–02 and WW I; *m* 17 April 1912 Evelyn (*d* 27 April 1931), est dau of Rev Charles William Herbert Kenrick, Vicar Holy Trinity, Barnstaple, and *d* 19 March 1931, leaving:

(1) Denys Charles Bourchier, TD (1954); *b* 14 March 1913; *educ* Eton; Capt Derbys Yeo WW II; *m* 31 March 1942 *Katherine Frances Theodora (Peggy), yr dau of Rev William Francis Eliot (*see* DEVITT, Bt), and *d* 1991, leaving:

1a +Charles Bourchier [Charles Wrey Esq, Breach House, Compton Basset, Calne, Wilts]; *b* 11 Jan 1949; *educ* Eton; *m* 1982 *Catriona Anne, er dau of Ian Wilson, and has:

1b +Thomas Alexander; *b* 1983

2b +Edward Charles; *b* 1986

3b +Maximilian George Bourchier; *b* 1989

2a +Mark Eliot Bourchier [Mark Wrey Esq, The Quag, Midhurst, W Sussex GU29 0JH]; *b* 13 April 1955; *educ* Harrow; *m* 1985 *Loveday Elizabeth, yr dau of Maj Simon Bolitho, of Trengwainton, Penzance, Cornwall, and has:

1b +Alexander Mark Bourchier; *b* 1986

2b +Simon Sherard Bourchier; *b* 1992

1b *Charlotte Loveday; *b* 1989

1 Annie Marian; *d* unm 4 Aug 1926

2 Emma Henrietta; *d* unm 14 Nov 1932

3 Augusta Eleanora; *d* unm 10 Aug 1951

4 Florence Amelia; *d* unm 18 Dec 1932

5 Beatrice Alexandra; *d* unm 4 Jan 1961

6 Isabel Maria; *d* unm 1958

The 13th Bt's nephew,

Sir (Castel Richard) Bourchier Wrey, 14th Bt; *b* 27 March 1903; *educ* Oundle; 2nd Lt RASC 1939–40 (invalided), Ordinary Seaman RN 1940, Lt RNVR 1942 WW II; *m* 15 March 1947 *Sybil Mabel Alice [Sybil Lady Wrey, 511 Currie Rd, Durban, S Africa; Les Bellevue de Mougins, Val de Mougins, S France], er dau of Dr George Lubke, of Durban, and *d* 1991, leaving:

1 Sir (GEORGE RICHARD) BOURCHIER WREY, **15th and present Bt**

2 +(Edward) Sherard Bourchier; *b* 27 Feb 1961; *educ* Durham Coll; *m* 1992 *Hon Catherine Margaret Baring, yst dau of 5th Baron Northbrook (*qv*), and has:

(1) *Tallulah Kitty; *b* 6 Jan 1996

WRIGHT OF RICHMOND

Arms: Per fess gules and or, on a pale counterchanged between in chief two oak leaves or, each charged with a quaver azure, and in base as many oak leaves gules, each charged with a quaver gold, a doric column proper, and overall a chevron per pale azure and gules. **Crest:** Beneath a palm tree a pelican in its piety with its young all proper. **Supporters:** Dexter, a bichon frisé rampant and in trim aspect proper; sinister, a stag guardant gold. **Motto:** *Constantia et fidelitate* ('By constancy and fidelity'). **Creation:** B. (LP, UK) 1994.

THE BARON WRIGHT OF RICHMOND, of Richmond-upon-Thames, London (Sir Patrick Richmond Henry Wright, GCMG (1989, KCMG 1974, CMG 1978)) [The Rt Hon The Lord Wright of Richmond GCMG, House of Lords, London SW1A 0PW]; *b* 28 June 1931; *educ* Marlborough and Merton Coll Oxford; Lt RA 1950–51; FO: joined 1955, Middle East Centre for Arabic Studies 1956–57, 3rd Sec Beirut 1958–60, Private Sec to: Amb Washington 1960–65, PUS FO 1965–67, 1st Sec Cairo 1967–70, Dep Political Resident Bahrain 1971–72, Head Middle East Dept FCO 1972–74, Priv Sec Overseas Affrs to PM 1974–77; Amb: Luxembourg 1977–79, Syria 1979–81, Dep U-Sec FCO 1982–84, Amb Saudi Arabia 1984–86, PUS FCO and Head Dip Serv 1986–91; dir: Barclays Bank 1991–, Unilever 1991–, BP 1991–, De La Rue 1991–, BAA 1991–; Memb: Cncl RCM 1991–, ICRC Consultative Gp 1992–93, Security Commn 1993–, Atlantic Coll 1993–; V-Pres Home Start 1991–; Govr: Ditchley Fndn 1986–, Wellington Coll 1991–; Chm RIIA 1995– (Memb Cncl 1992–); KStJ 1990 (Registrar OStJ 1991–95, Dir Overseas Rels 1995–); Hon Fell Merton Coll Oxford 1987; FRCM 1994; *m* 1958 *Virginia Anne, step-dau of Col Samuel John Hannaford, of Hove, and has:

1 *Marcus; *b* 1959

2 *Angus; *b* 1964

1 *Olivia; *b* 1963

Lineage: HERBERT H S WRIGHT of Haslemere, Surrey; *m* Rachel Green and had:

PATRICK RICHMOND HENRY, *cr* a **Baron**

WRIGHTSON

Arms: Or a fess invected chequy azure and argent between two eagle's heads erased in chief sable and a saltire couped in base gules.**Crest:** In front of a saltire gules a unicorn salient or.
Motto: *Veritas omnia vincit* ('Truth conquers all things').
Creation: Bt. (UK) 13 July 1900.

SIR (CHARLES) MARK GARMONDSWAY WRIGHTSON, 4TH BT, of Neasham Hall, Co Durham, and Eryholme, Co York [Sir Mark Wrightson Bt, Neasham Hall, Darlington, Co Durham; 39 Westbourne Park Rd, London W2 5QD]; *b* 18 Feb 1951; *s* f 1983; *educ* Eton and Queens' Coll Cambridge (BA 1972); barrister Middle Temple 1974, with Hill Samuel 1977–96 (dir 1984–96); *m* 1975 *Stella Virginia, dau of George Dean, MPS, of Garden Cottage, Middleton Tyas, N Yorks, and has:

  1 +BARNABY THOMAS GARMONDSWAY; *b* 5 Aug 1979
  2 James George; *b* 1982
  3 +William John; *b* 1985

Lineage: JOHN WRIGHTSON, of Eryholme, Wapentake of Gilling East, N R Yorks; had:

RICHARD WRIGHTSON, of Eryholme; *bur* 22 July 1578, leaving an er s:

JOHN WRIGHTSON, of Eryholme and N Cowton, N R Yorks; involved in the Rebellion of the Northern Earls 1569 (*see* ABERGAVENNY, M, and NORTHUMBERLAND, D); *m* Agnes — (*bur* 5 Jan 1537/8) and was *bur* 19 Feb 1585/6, leaving:

EDMUND WRIGHTSON, of Eryholme and N Cowton; *m* 29 Nov 1573 Isabel Winspear (*bur* 22 July 1642) and was *bur* 10 April 1630, having had, with a yr s and four daus:

JOHN WRIGHTSON, of Eryholme; *bapt* 7 March 1575/6; *m* lst Elizabeth — (*bur* 20 April 1618) and had issue (including an er s John, *bapt* 15 Dec 1611); *m* 2nd Margaret (*dsp, bur* 3 Aug 1623); *m* 3rd Barbara (*bur* 7 March 1631/2) and was *bur* 17 Sept 1757, having by her had two other sons; his yr s by his 1st w:

THOMAS WRIGHTSON, of Eryholme and Richmond, Yorks; *bapt* 30 July 1615; *m* 29 Nov 1649 Anne Robinson and had, with three yr sons and two daus:

JOHN WRIGHTSON, of Spring House, Long Newton, Co Durham; *bapt* 23 May 1652; *m* 1st and had issue, including an er s (John, of Middleton-one-Row, Co Durham, and Spring Ho, Co Durham, *m* 1 May 1711 Margaret — (*bur* 10 June 1766), dau and coheir of Thomas Robinson, of Middleton-one-Row, and was *bur* 23 May 1727, having had issue, now extinct); *m* 2nd 22 Jan 1697/8 Ann Simpson and was *bur* 16 Sept 1723; his yr s by his 1st w:

THOMAS WRIGHTSON, of Over Dinsdale, Sockburn, Yorks, and White Ho and Sedgefield, both Co Durham; *bapt* 15 March 1691; *m* 18 June 1717 Elizabeth (*d* 10 April 1774), dau and coheir of Thomas Robinson, of Middleton-one-Row, and *d* 5 Nov 1768, leaving:

  1 John, of Over Dinsdale, Little Smeaton and Easingwold, Yorks; *bapt* 23 March 1717/8; *m* 19 April 1748 Ann (*bur* 15 Aug 1762), dau of John Cornforth, of Coxhoe, Co Durham, and was *bur* 15 Nov 1803, leaving, with other issue:
    (1) John, of Thirsk; *d* 1817, leaving issue (all *dsp*)
    (1) Ann; *m* Liscombe Price, of Lincoln's Inn, barrister, and had issue
  2 THOMAS
  3 William, of Sedgefield; *bapt* 25 June 1723; *m* Mary — (*bur* 28 Oct 1790) and was *bur* 7 April 1810

The 2nd s,
  THOMAS WRIGHTSON, of White Ho, Co Durham; *bapt* 23 Feb 1719/20; *m* 19 Nov 1754 Margaret (*d* 21 Jan 1797), dau of William Garmonsway, of Great Burdon, Houghton, Co Durham, and *d* 4 Nov 1803, leaving, with a dau:

WILLIAM WRIGHTSON, of Neasham Hall, Hurworth-on-Tees, and Morton Palmes, Co Durham; *bapt* 4 Oct 1755; *m* 23 July 1795 Mary (*d* 20 Jan 1818), est dau of Robert White, of Norton, Co Durham, and *d* 8 July 1826, having had, with three yr sons (John, *b* 25 June 1804, *d* unm 26 Aug 1881; William, *b* 10 March 1806, *d* unm 30 Sept 1878; Robert White, *b* 2 Dec 1807, Bengal Med Serv, *m* 2 May 1844 Anna Maria (*d* 12 May 1886), dau of Frederick Lumley, of Stockton-on-Tees, Co Durham, and *d* 13 Feb 1853, leaving issue) and five daus:

THOMAS WRIGHTSON, of Neasham Hall and Spring Ho, Co Durham; *b* 16 July 1799; *m* 16 June 1834 Rebecca Gilchrist (*d* 24 Sept 1884), 4th dau of William Potter, of Walbottle Ho, Northumberland, and *d* 12 April 1872, leaving, with a dau (*d* unm):

  1 William Garmondsway (Rev), of The Old Hall, Hurworth, and Spring Ho; *b* 24 June 1836; MA Cantab; Vicar St Paul's Beckenham Kent; *m* 4 Dec 1866 Priscilla Anne (*d* 3 Nov 1914), est dau and coheir of Alfred Head, of Bayswater, and *d* 8 March 1900, leaving issue
  2 THOMAS (Sir), **1st Bt**
  3 John; *b* 9 Sept 1840; Pres Downton Coll of Ag Wilts; *m* 23 July 1872 Maria Isabel (*d* 11 Oct 1923), only dau of Charles Norleigh Hulton, of Little Broughton, Stokesley, Yorks (*see* 1970 edn HULTON, Bt), and had issue
  1 Rebecca Ingram; *m* 26 Sept 1860 Jeremiah Head, MICE (*d* 10 March 1899), of Coatham, Redcar, and *d* 1 Sept 1899, leaving issue

The 2nd s,
  Sir Thomas Wrightson, 1st Bt (UK), so *cr* 13 July 1900, JP, DL Co Durham; *b* 31 March 1839; MP (C) Stockton 1892–95 and E St Pancras 1899–1906; *m* 23 June 1869 Elizabeth (*d* 30 April 1931), est dau of Samuel Wise, of Ripon, Yorks, and had:

  1 THOMAS GARMONDSWAY (GUY) (Sir), **2nd Bt**
  2 Charles Archibald Wise, CBE (1919); *b* 17 July 1874; Capt RN WW I; *d* unm 7 Feb 1953
  3 Wilfrid Ingram, JP (Co Durham 1925); *b* 20 Feb 1876; *educ* Charterhouse and Trin Coll Cambridge (BA 1898, MA 1902); Lt Durham LI WW I; *m* 23 April 1913 Victoria (*d* 8 Feb 1966 aged 85), dau of Frederick Charles Winby, of 47 Portland Pl, London W1, and *d* 30 July 1949, leaving:
    (1) Elizabeth Victoria Mary; *b* 22 Jan 1914; *m* 9 Jan 1943 Maj Sir Headley Dymoke White, 3rd Bt, of Salle Park, Norfolk (*qv*), and *d* 29 June 1996, leaving issue
    (2) *Ann Winby [Mrs Robin White, Cross Gates, High Lorton, Cockermouth, Cumbria CA13 9UL]; *b* 27 Feb 1917; *m* 26 Jan 1952 Robert (Robin) le Rougetel White, BArch (Liverpool), ARIBA, AMTPI, LRAM (*d* 1979), er s of Robert Prosser White, MD, of Wigan, and Ainsdale, Lancs
  1 Mary Isabella Edith; *m* 18 Oct 1893 George Frederick Lloyd Mortimer, KC (*d* 5 Sept 1928), Recorder Rotherham, s of Rev M L Mortimer, and *d* 24 Oct 1960 aged 90, leaving issue
  2 Lucy Elizabeth; *b* 26 Jan 1873; *m* 16 June 1904 Sir Fredric Wise, MP (*d* 26 Jan 1928), est s of Alexander Josiah Patrick Wise, DL, of Belleville Park, Cappoquin, Co Waterford, and *d* 23 Oct 1963, leaving issue
  3 Margaret Justina; Fell Roy Soc Br Sculptors
  4 Grace Evelyn Spencer; *m* 18 July 1906 Frederic Kelly Gascoyne, 20th Hus and W African FF (*d* 8 Sept 1944), son of William Gascoyne, of Bapchild Court, Kent, and had issue
  5 Rebecca Hope Gilchrist, OBE (1956); *m* 21 Feb 1923 her er sis's bro-in-law Maj Alexander Wise, Connaught Rangers, s of Alexander Josiah Patrick Wise
  6 Jocelyn Bruce

The 1st Bt *d* 18 June 1921; his er s,
  Sir Thomas Garmondsway (Guy) Wrightson, 2nd Bt, TD, JP, DL Co Durham, JP N R Yorks; *b* 21 Aug 1871; *educ* Marlborough and Trin Coll Cambridge (BA 1892, MA 1897); Maj 5th Bn Durham LI, Hon Col 1926; High Sheriff 1926; *m* 6 Oct 1909 Gwendolin Cotterill (*d* 17 April 1964), 3rd dau of George Harding Neame, of Belgravia, and had:

  1 JOHN GARMONDSWAY (Sir), **3rd Bt**
  2 Peter, OBE (1945); *b* 20 Feb 1914; *educ* Eton; Lt-Col Durham LI WW II; *m* 31 Aug 1946 *Pamela, JP [Mrs Peter Wrightson JP, Manfield Grange, Manfield, nr Darlington, N Yorks DL2 2RE], yst dau of Sir Murrough John Wilson, KBE, of Cliffe Hall, Piercebridge, and *d* 27 Aug 1995, leaving:
    (1) +Simon Murrough [Simon Wrightson Esq, Manfield Grange, Manfield, N Yorks DL2 2RE]; *b* 7 Sept 1954; *educ* Eton; *m* 1975 *Elisabeth Yvonne, dau of Hubert Marcel Michelin, of France, and has:
      1a +Richard Charles Peter; *b* 22 May 1985
      1a *Emma Mary Rose; *b* 10 Aug 1982
    (1) *Joanna Mary; *b* 11 Sept 1947; *m* 9 Aug 1969 (*divorce* 1990) Peter Jonathan Howard, er s of Robin Cecil Howard, of Norwoods Farm, Ticehurst, Sussex, and had:
      1a *Benjamin Simon; *b* 28 May 1975
      2a *James Edward Peter; *b* 19 April 1979
      1a *Penelope Sarah; *b* 6 July 1971
      2a *Alison Rebecca; *b* 8 Sept 1972
    (1) (cont.) Mrs Joanna Howard *m* 2nd 12 April 1995 Arthur Goodwin (*d* 25 Sept 1995)
    (2) *Susan Jennifer [Mrs Montague Style, 27 rue des Romains, 68480 Bettlach, Alsace, France]; *b* 27 May 1948; *m* 18 July 1970 *Montague William Style and has issue (*see* STYLE, Bt)
  3 Rodney; *b* 16 April 1916; Cdr RN WW II (despatches); *m* 1st 7 May 1940 Florence Jean (*d* 13 Feb 1944), er dau of James Dunn Dunn, of Ferniecraig, Skelmorlie, Ayrshire, and *d* 1992, leaving:
    (1) +Jeremy Rodney [Jeremy Wrightson Esq, 29 Lynn Close, Leigh Sinton, Malvern, Worcs WR13 5DU]; *b* 22 Dec 1941; *educ* Eton; *m* 27 June 1970 *Lindsay Margaret Glen, dau of Dr John Milroy Glen Parker, of Malton, Yorks, and has:
      1a +Rufus Guy; *b* 1975
      2a +Christopher John; *b* 1985
      1a *Amy Jean; *b* 1974
  3 (cont.) Cdr Rodney Wrightson *m* 2nd 20 Feb 1947 *Janet Elizabeth [Mrs Rodney Wrightson, 22 West St, Wilton, Wilts SP2 0DE], est dau of Brig Raymond Henry Arnold Davison Love, RA, of Overcroft, Mayford, Surrey, and formerly w of Brig William Branfoot Wilson, OBE, and *d* 1992, leaving by her:
    (1) *Lucinda [Mrs John Abbott, White Abbott, Mas De Juston, Serviers 30700, Uzés, France]; *b* 8 May 1948; *m* 1st 17 April 1969 Jonathan Philip Hudson, est s of Philip Hudson, of Newbridge Mill, Coleman's Hatch, Sus-

sex; *m* 2nd 1985 *John Riddell White Abbott, only s of John Nesbitt White Abbott, MBE, TD, and by her 1st husb has:

    1a *Henry Andrew; *b* 1972

    1a *Emily Alice; *b* 1974

4 Oliver; *b* 28 May 1920; *educ* Eton and Balliol Coll Oxford; barrister Lincoln's Inn 1950; late Capt Coldstream Gds; *d* 1988

Sir GUY *d* 7 Jan 1950; his est s,

Sir John Garmondsway Wrightson, 3rd Bt, TD (1953), DL (Co Durham 1961); *b* 18 June 1911; *educ* Eton; Maj Durham LI (TA) WW II in France 1940 with 23rd Div, Belgium and Germany with 6th Airborne Div (despatches); High Sheriff Co Durham 1959; *m* 30 Nov 1939 Hon Rosemary Monica Dawson (*d* 13 June 1998), yst dau of 1st and last Viscount Dawson of Penn, GCVO, KCB, KCMG, PC (*see* 1940 edn), and *d* 1983, leaving:

1 Sir CHARLES MARK GARMONDSWAY, **4th and present Bt**

1 *Penelope Linda; *b* 21 Dec 1940

2 *Juliet Diana; *b* 24 Sept 1943

3 *Elizabeth Anne [Mme Laurent Tisné, La Roche Abilen, St Georges du Bois, Maine et Loire, France]; *b* 25 Dec 1946; *m* 1978 *Laurent Tisné and has:

    (1) *Martin; *b* 1979

    (2) *Louis; *b* 1981

WRIXON-BECHER

BIS · VIVIT · QUI · BENE

Arms: Vair, arg. and gu., on a canton or a stag's head, couped sa. **Crest:** Out of a ducal coronet or a demi-lion erm., gorged with a plain collar vair. **Motto:** *Bis vivit qui bene* ('He lives twice who lives well'). **Creation:** Bt. (UK) 30 Sept 1831.

SIR WILLIAM FANE WRIXON-BECHER, 5TH BT, of Ballygiblin, Co Cork, MC (1943) [Sir William Wrixon-Becher Bt MC, 13 Montpelier Cres, Brighton, E Sussex BN1 3JF]; *b* 7 Sept 1915; *s* f 1934; *educ* Harrow and Magdalene Coll Cambridge (BA); Lt and T/Maj Rifle Bde SR Offrs WW II (wounded twice); *m* 1st 22 Aug 1946 (*divorce* 1960) Hon (Ursula) Vanda Maud (*d* 1984), 2nd dau of 4th Baron Vivian (*qv*) and formerly w of Maj Philip Alexander Clement Bridgewater, and has:

1 +JOHN WILLIAM MICHAEL [John Wrixon-Becher Esq, 28 Atherton St, London SW11]; *b* 29 Sept 1950; *educ* Harrow and U of Neuchâtel; with Lloyd's 1971–87, dir Wise Speke Fin Servs 1987–93, HSBC Gibbs Consulting Ltd 1993–

1 *Susannah Elizabeth [Mrs Timothy Jackson, Forth Lodge, Hill Rd, Gullane, E Lothian, Scotland EH31 2BE]; *b* 27 Jan 1948; *m* 1st 3 Oct 1970 Gordon M A P Whitson (*d* 1974), er s of H Whitson, of Edmonston, Biggar, Lanarks, and has:

    (1) *James Alexander; *b* 1973

1 (cont.) Mrs Gordon Whitson *m* 2nd 7 June 1975, as his 2nd w, *Timothy Jackson, OBE, s of Col W H Jackson, CBE, DL, and by him has had:

    (2) *William Harry; *b* 1978

    (1) Lucy Alexandra Esther; *b* 1983; *d* 1984

Sir WILLIAM *m* 2nd 6 July 1960 *Yvonne Margaret, yst dau of Arthur Stuart Johnson, JP, of Henshall Hall, Congleton, Cheshire, and formerly w of 5th Baron Mostyn (*qv*)

Lineage: HENRY WRIXON, of Ballygiblin, Co Cork; *m* Catherine — and *d* between 13 April and 9 Oct 1714, leaving a 4th s:

NICHOLAS WRIXON, of Ballygiblin; *m* —, dau of Charles Bastable, of Castle Magner, and *d* 1740, leaving:

HENRY WRIXON, of Assolas, Co Cork; *m* 1747 Anna, dau of William Mansfield, and *d* 1794, leaving:

WILLIAM WRIXON, of Cecilstown, Co Cork; *m* 1778 Mary, dau of John Townsend Becher, of Annisgrove, Co Cork, and had an est s:

Sir WILLIAM WRIXON later WRIXON-BECHER, **1st Bt** (UK), so *cr* 30 Sep 1831, of Ballygiblin; *b* 31 July 1780; MP Mallow, Co Cork; *m* 18 Dec 1819 Elizabeth, actress (*d* 29 Oct 1872), dau of John O'Neill, and *d* Oct 1850, having had, with other issue:

1 Sir Henry Wrixon-Becher, 2nd Bt, DL; *b* 1826; *m* 20 Feb 1878 Florence Elizabeth Hannah (*m* 2nd 8 March 1894 Arthur Denis Henry Heber Reynell-Pack, of Netherton, Newton Abbot (*d* 27 Oct 1937), and *d* 26 Sep 1912), est dau of Frederick John Walker, and *dsp* 25 Nov 1893

2 JOHN (Sir), **3rd Bt**

3 William Nicholas, DL Co Cork; *b* 1831; MA Cantab; Lt 62nd Regt; *m* 1888 Georgina Henrietta, dau of Capt William Henry Herrick, RN, of Shippool, Innishannon, Co Cork, and *dsp* 12 Dec 1912

The 2nd Bt's bro,

Sir John Wrixon-Becher, 3rd Bt, JP, DL Co Cork; *b* 16 Aug 1828; MA Cantab; High Sheriff Co Cork 1867; *m* 6 May 1857 Emily Catherine (*d* 31 Dec 1916), 2nd dau of 2nd Earl of Listowel (*qv*), and *d* 24 April 1914, having had:

1 EUSTACE WILLIAM WINDHAM (Sir), **4th Bt**

2 Edgar; *b* 12 Oct 1862; *d c* 1920

3 Henry, DSO (1917); *b* 27 July 1866; Maj Duke of Wellington's W R Regt Boer War 1899–1902 (despatches, brevet), Lt-Col 12th Bn Yorks Regt WW I (despatches, wounded), Croix de Guerre Belgium; *d* unm 9 Jun 1951

4 Arthur Nicholas; *b* 3 Aug 1868; presumed to have *d* in USA

5 Charles Edward; *b* 27 Nov 1871; *d* 5 May 1882

1 Victoria Emily; *d* unm 6 Aug 1930

2 Mary; *d* unm 27 June 1939

3 Cecil Eleanor; *m* 28 March 1894, as his 1st w, Percy Hope Murray, MB (*d* 28 April 1957), of Oakhurst, Hambledon, Hants, and *d* 18 March 1927, leaving issue

4 Barbara Elizabeth; *d* unm 8 March 1943

5 Adelaide Maud; *m* 1 June 1899 William Norton Barry, JP (*d* 5 Dec 1935), of Castle Cor, Co Cork, s of William Norton Barry, JP, of Castle Cor, and *dsp* 3 July 1959

6 Alice Elizabeth; *m* 28 June 1899 Hon Horace George Lysaght, JP (*d* 30 Sept 1918), only s of 6th Baron Lisle (*qv*), and *d* 8 Sep 1941, leaving issue

7 Georgiana Victoria; *m* 23 Aug 1898 Brig-Gen Edward Wilfrid Spedding, CMG, OBE, RA (*d* 4 Jan 1939), s of John James Spedding, JP, DL of Windebrowe, Keswick, Cumberland, and *d* 5 Jan 1966 aged 89, leaving issue

8 Hilda Mary; *m* 27 Sept 1927 her dead sister's widower Percy Hope Murray (*see* above) and *d* 1 Dec 1958

The est s,

Sir Eustace William Windham Wrixon-Becher, 4th Bt, DL Co Cork; *b* 27 Dec 1859; High Sheriff 1916; *m* 8 Oct 1907 Hon Constance Gough-Calthorpe (*d* Oct 1957), 2nd dau and coheir of 6th Baron Calthorpe (*see* 1970 edn), and *d* 14 Oct 1934, having had:

1 Sir WILLIAM FANE WRIXON-BECHER, **5th and present Bt**

1 Muriel Mary; *b* 21 Feb 1909; *m* 29 July 1932 James Reginald Dorrington Salusbury-Trelawny (*see* SALUSBURY-TRELAWNY, Bt) and *d* 25 April 1970, leaving issue

2 Aileen; *b* 2 July 1910

3 *Sheila [Miss Sheila Wrixon-Becher, Rowdell, Washington, W Sussex]; *b* 5 Feb 1913

4 *Rosemary [Mrs Rosemary Watson, Ashways, Stogumber, Somerset]; *b* 12 Aug 1914; *m* 16 Feb 1938 (*divorce* 1948) Cyril Jeremy Taylor Watson (*d* 1974), yr s of Cyril F Watson of Greysouthern, Cockermouth, Cumberland, and has:

    (1) *Ann Maree; *b* 23 Feb 1939

    (2) *Joy Rosemary; *b* 14 May 1941

    (3) Susan Brenda; *b* 16 Aug 1942; *m* 27 July 1963 Simon George Barff, MICE, s of Lt-Col George Frederick Alistair Barff, MC, RA, of Old Priors, Partridge Green, Sussex, and had:

        1a *Patrick George; *b* 22 June 1966

        1a *Katherine Jane; *b* 23 Feb 1968

WROTTESLEY

Arms: Or three piles sable, a canton ermine. **Crest:** Out of a ducal coronet or a boar's head ermine (sometimes borne azure), armed and crined gold. **Supporters:** Two unicorns proper, ducally gorged and chained or, pendant from the coronet of each a shield of the arms. **Motto:** *Vis unita fortior* ('Strength is increased by union'). **Creations:** Bt. (E) 30 Aug 1642, B. (UK) 11 July 1838.

THE 6TH BARON WROTTESLEY, of Wrottesley, Co Stafford, and a **Baronet** (Sir Clifton Hugh Lancelot de Verdon Wrottesley, Bt) [The Rt Hon The Lord Wrottesley, House of Lords, London SW1A 0PW]; *b* 10 Aug 1968; *s* gf 1977; *educ* Eton, Edinburgh U and RMA Sandhurst; Capt Gren Gds, ret 1995; investment broker

Lineage: RALPH, bro of Walter, the first Norman Abbot of Evesham after the Conquest; had:

WILLIAM de COCTUNE/COCTON/COUGHTON, of Warwicks; had, with an er s (Ralph):

SIMON de COUGHTON; enfeoffed by the Abbot of Evesham *c* 1164 with the Manors of Wrottesley and Livington/Loynton, Staffs; *d* by 1199, leaving:

WILLIAM de VERDON later de WROTTESLEY; *m* Ingrith, dau and coheir of Robert FitzAdam, of Waterfall and Butterton-on-the-Moors, and *d c* 1242, leaving:

Sir HUGH de WROTTESLEY; lived 1242–75; sided with Simon de Montfort (*see* LEICESTER, E), hence his estates confiscated after the Battle of Evesham 1265, though these restored under the Dictum of Kenilworth; *m* Idonia, dau of Ralph de Perton, and had:

Sir WILLIAM de WROTTESLEY; living 1276–1313; *m* 1st Petronilla, dau of Sir John Audley, of Blore; *m* 2nd Katherine, dau of 1st Lord (Baron) Strange (of Knokyn) (*see* SAINT DAVIDS, V) and widow of Sir Alan de Glaseley, and by his 1st w had:

Sir WILLIAM de WROTTESLEY; ktd 1306, served EDWARD I's Scottish campaign 1306; *m* Joan, dau of Sir Roger Basset, and *d* 1320, leaving, with a yr s:

Sir HUGH de WROTTESLEY, KG (original memb); served BLACK PRINCE's Div Battle of Crécy 1346; *m* 1st Elizabeth, dau of Sir John de Hampton, of Elderstoke; *m* 2nd Mabel, dau and coheir of Sir Philip ap Rees, of Talgarth; *m* 3rd Isabella, dau of Sir John Arderne, of Aldford, and *d* 1381, having by her had, with an er s (Hugh, *d* young):

JOHN de WROTTESLEY; *b c* 1379; *m* Elizabeth, dau of Sir Robert de Standish, and *d* 1402, leaving:

HUGH WROTTESLEY; *m* Thomasine, dau of Sir John Gresley, of Drakelowe, and *d* 1464, leaving:

Sir WALTER WROTTESLEY; Chamberlain Exchequer *temp* EDWARD IV, follower of Richard Nevill(e), Earl of Warwick ('The Kingmker') (*see* ABERGAVENNY, M); proclaimed a traitor 1470; on brief restoration of HENRY VI 1471 held Calais as Warwick's Lt but after Warwick's death at Battle of Barnet gave up Calais to EDWARD IV on condition he and the garrison were pardoned; *m* Jane, dau and heiress of William Baron, of Reading, and *d* 1473, having had, with other issue, including a yr s (William, Esq of the Body to HENRY VII) and three daus (Thomasine, allegedly *m* as his 2nd w 5th Lord (Baron) Stourton (*see* MOWBRAY, SEGRAVE and STOURTON, B); Anne, *m* Sir Anthony St Amand; Margaret, *m* Sir John Scrope, of Castle Combe):

RICHARD WROTTESLEY, of Wrottesley; High Sheriff Staffs 1492, 1502 and 1516; *m* Dorothy, dau of Sir Edmund Sutton (*see* DUDLEY, B), and *d* 1521, leaving an est s:

WALTER WROTTESLEY; High Sheriff Staffs 1531 and 1546; *m* Isabel, dau of John Harcourt, of Ranton, and *d* 1563, leaving, with other issue, including a dau (Elizabeth, *m* Sir John Talbot, of Albrighton, *see* SHREWSBURY and WATERFORD, E):

JOHN WROTTESLEY; High Sheriff Staffs 1564; *m* Elizabeth, dau of Thomas Astley, of Patshull, and *d* 1578, leaving:

WALTER WROTTESLEY; High Sheriff Staffs 1597; *m* 1st Mary, dau and heiress of Hugh Lee, of Woodford, Staffs; *m* 2nd Joyce, dau of Sir Edward Leighton, of

Wattlesborough, and widow of Francis Bromley, of Hallon, Salop, and *d* 1630, leaving by his 1st w:

Sir HUGH WROTTESLEY; *m* 1st Mary, sis of 5th Viscount Hereford (*qv*); *m* 2nd Clara, dau of Sir Anthony Colclough, of Tintern Abbey, Co Wexford, and widow of William Sneyd, of Keele, and *d* 1633, leaving by his 1st w:

Sir Walter Wrottesley, 1st Bt (E), so *cr* 30 Aug 1642; *bapt* 6 May 1606; royalist Civil War; *m* Mary, dau of Ambrose Grey, of Enville, Staffs, and *d* Nov 1659, leaving, with two yr sons (Edward, *m* Martha, dau of Sir Thomas Hewit, of Shire Oaks, Notts; John, merchant in Portugal) and two daus (Elizabeth, *m* Sir Francis Wolrich, 2nd Bt, of Dudmaston; Mary, *m* Sir Edward Littleton, 2nd Bt, *see* HATHERTON, B):

Sir Walter Wrottesley, 2nd Bt; *b c* 1632; *m* Margaret, dau of Sir Thomas Wolrich, 1st Bt, and *d* 1686, leaving an est s:

Sir Walter Wrottesley, 3rd Bt; *b* 1659; *m* 1st 27 June 1678 Eleanora, dau of Sir John Archer, of Coopersall, Essex, Judge Court Common Pleas; *m* 2nd Anne, dau of Mr Justice Burton, of Longnor, Salop, and *d* 1712, leaving by her a s (Walter) and two daus (Margaret; Anne, *m* — Hutchinson, of Woodhall, Herefs) and by his 1st w, with a yr s (Hugh, had issue, *see* below) and two daus (Elizabeth, *m* Anthony Collins, of Baddow, Essex; Eleanora,; *m* William Eyre and s to Coopersall):

Sir John Wrottesley, 4th Bt; *b* 1683; MP Staffs 1708–10; *m* 1703 Frances (*d* 1769), gdau of 1st Earl of Stamford (*see* 1970 edn), and *d* Oct 1726, having had, with two other sons and two other daus:

1 **Sir Hugh Wrottesley, 5th Bt**; *d* a minor 1729

2 **Sir Walter Wrottesley, 6th Bt**; *d* a minor Feb 1732

3 RICHARD (Sir), **7th Bt**

1 Frances; *m* Heigham Bendish, of East Ham, Essex

2 Elizabeth; *m* her cousin Thomas Wrottesley, s of Walter Wrottesley (3rd s of **3rd Bt**)

3 Henrietta; *m* Theodore William Inge, of Thorpe

The 6th Bt's bro,

Very Rev Sir Richard Wrottesley, 7th Bt; *b* 1721; *educ* Winchester and St John's Coll Oxford; MP Tavistock 1747–54, Pncpl Clerk Bd Green Cloth 1749; Chaplain to GEORGE III 1763, Dean Worcester 1765–69; *m c* 1744 Mary (*d* 30 April 1778), dau of 1st Earl Gower (*see* SUTHERLAND, D), and *d* 20 July 1769, leaving, with five daus (Mary, Maid-of-Honour to QUEEN CHARLOTTE, *d* unm 1769; Frances, *m* Adml Pigot, bro of 1st Baron Pigot of Patshull (*see* PIGOT, Bt), and *d* 13 April 1811; Elizabeth, *m* 1769 3rd Duke of Grafton (*qv*); Dorothy, *m* 1780 Christian, Baron von Kutzleben, Min to Hesse-Cassel; Harriet, Maid-of-Honour to QUEEN CHARLOTTE, *m* 1779 Gen William Gardiner, bro of Luke, 1st Viscount Mountjoy of Mountjoy, and *d* 8 Dec 1824):

Sir John Wrottesley, 8th Bt; *b* 1744; Lt-Col 1st Foot Gds, Col 45th Foot, Page of Honour to GEORGE III, Master Horse to HRH THE DUKE OF YORK, Maj-Gen, MP Newcastle-under-Lyme 1768 and Staffs 1768–87, DCL Oxon 1773; *m* 7 June 1770 Hon Frances Courtenay (*d* 24 Feb 1828), 2nd dau of 1st Viscount Courtenay (*see* DEVON, E), and had, with five daus:

1 JOHN, **1st Baron**

2 Henry; *b* 1772; barrister, MP Brackley 1810–25; *d* unm 1825

3 Hugh; *b* 1782; Lt-Col Bengal establishment; *d* 18 Oct 1830, leaving a s (Hugh, *dsp*) and dau

4 Charles (Rev); *b* 1783; Rector E Knoyle, Wilts; *d* unm 17 Feb 1848

5 Edward; *b* 19 Oct 1785; Cdr RN; *m* 1812 Anne (*d* 15 May 1853), dau of Rev Thomas Tringham, and *d* 29 July 1814, leaving:

(1) Edward John (Rev); *b* 9 Nov 1814; MA Oxon; Preb Lichfield, Vicar Brewood, Staffs; *m* 8 April 1847 Maria Eugenia (*d* 11 Jan 1892), dau of John Jeffreys, of Fynone, Swansea, and *d* 19 Jan 1901, leaving:

1a Francis John (Rev); *b* 19 May 1848; MA Oxon; Vicar Denstone, Uttoxeter; *m* 3 Oct 1876 Agnes Mabel Stilwell (*d* 18 Jan 1917), dau of Frederic John Freeland, and *d* 27 Dec 1922, leaving:

1b Francis Robert, DSO (1919); *b* 8 June 1877; Capt RN WW I (despatches), Order St Anne Russia; *m* 17 Aug 1911 Leila (*d* 28 Nov 1961), 2nd dau of Gen Sir Charles William Dunbar Staveley, GCB, and *dsp* 13 Nov 1954

2b Edward Algernon; *b* 30 April 1879; *m* 12 Dec 1906 Mabel Letitia (*d* 25 Oct 1955), yr dau of Francis Clowes, JP, of Sutton Hall, Stalham, Norfolk, and *d* 1 Nov 1957, leaving:

1c (Arthur) John Francis; *b* 18 June 1908; *educ* Wellington and Univ Coll Oxford (BA 1929, MA 1933); barrister Inner Temple 1932, Capt Roy Norfolk Regt WW II (JAG's Dept 1942); Br Tport Commn Legal Serv 1953 (Br Rlwys Bd 1962); *m* 22 Aug 1936 Marjorie Mary, MBE (1973), only dau of Frank Wilde, of Edgbaston, and *d* 14 July 1996, leaving:

1d +David John [David Wrottesley Esq, 29 Twentywell Rd, Bradway, Sheffield, Yorks]; *b* 9 May 1940; *educ* Mill Hill; *m* 7 June 1969 *Christine Ann, only dau of Henry Smith, of Sheffield, and has:

1e *Angela Jane; *b* 1977

2d +Michael Francis [Michael Wrottesley Esq, 17 Ordnance Hill, London NW8 6PR]; *b* 23 Oct 1945; *educ* Mill Hill; *m* 1973 *Francesca Jacqueline, only dau of Jack Miller, and has:

1e +Alexander Francis; *b* 1976

2e +Maxim George; *b* 1980

1d *Elizabeth Mavis [Mrs MacLeod, Anvil House, Hook Norton, Oxon OX15 5NH]; *b* 1 May 1938; *educ* St Mary's Coll Durham U (BA 1960); *m* 1st 16 June 1962 Capt John Michael Parr, RAEC, only s of James Ronald Parr, of Arch Ho, Newsham, Yorks, and has:

1e *Richard John; *b* 1 Jan 1964; *m* 1988 *Alison Jane, yr dau of Graham Massey, of Comberbach, Cheshire, and has:

1f *James Richard; *b* 7 Jan 1991

1f *Sophie Rebecca; *b* 19 July 1993

2f *Grace Florence; *b* 3 July 1997

1e *Sarah Anne Elizabeth [Mrs Stephen Ross, Brookdale, 28 Hawthorn Lane, Wilmslow, Cheshire SK9 5DD]; *b* 12 Nov 1965; *m* 1992 *Stephen John Ross, and has:

1f *Magnus Alexander; *b* 15 March 1998

1f *Amy Freya; *b* 27 July 1994

2e *Rosalind Mary; *b* 1975

1d (cont.) Mrs Parr *m* 2nd 1982 *I Breac C MacLeod

2d *Letitia Marjorie [Mrs Graeme Lythe, 38 Vicarage Rd, London SW14 8RU]; *b* 23 Oct 1945; *m* 23 March 1968 *Graeme Allan Lythe, only s of Allan Edgar Lythe, of Auckland, NZ, and has:

1e *Edward Graeme; *b* 18 March 1970; Lt Queen's Own Hus

2e *James Edgar; *b* 1972

3e *Henry Frederick; *b* 1975

3b Frederic John (Sir), PC (1947), KC 1926, JP Staffs; *b* 20 March 1880; *educ* Tonbridge and Lincoln Coll Oxford (MA, Hon Fell 1937); Maj 3rd N Midland Bde RFA WW I (despatches); barrister Inner Temple 1907, Recorder Wolverhampton 1930–37, Bencher Inner Temple 1934, High Court Judge 1937–47, Ld Justice Appeal 1947–48, chm Staffs QS 1939–48, Rlwy and Canal Commr 1938, ktd 1937; *m* 26 Nov 1915 Marion Cecil (*d* 26 Dec 1955), dau of Lt-Col W Patterson, DCLI, and *dsp* 14 Nov 1948

1a Anna Caroline; *m* 31 July 1873 Rev Edward Salt (*d* 29 April 1907), Rector Standon, Staffs, and *d* 16 Feb 1941, leaving issue

The 8th Bt *d* 23 April 1787; his est s,

Sir John Wrottesley, 9th Bt, and **1st Baron Wrottesley**, of Wrottesley, Co Stafford (UK), so *cr* 11 July 1838; *b* 25 Oct 1771; *educ* Westminster and Mil Acad Angers; Capt 13th Lancers Holland and France, Lt-Col W Staffs Militia, MP (Whig) Lichfield 1799–1806, Staffs 1823–32 and S Staffs 1832–37, FSA; *m* 1st 23 June 1795 Caroline (*d* 7 March 1818), dau of 4th Earl of Tankerville (*qv*); *m* 2nd 19 May 1819 Julia (*d* 29 Sept 1869), dau of John Conyers, of Copt Hall, Essex, and widow of his former bro-in-law Capt Hon John Astley Bennet, RN, and by his 1st w had, with two daus (*d* unm):

1 JOHN, **2nd Baron**

2 Charles Alexander; *b* 20 Oct 1799; Lt-Col 29th Foot; *d* unm 24 Feb 1861

3 Robert (Rev); *b* 2 June 1801; *m* 1828 Georgiana, dau of Sir George Pigot, 3rd Bt, of Patshull (*qv*), and *dsp* 20 Jan 1838

4 Walter; *b* 8 April 1810; Fell All Souls; *m* 22 June 1843 Marianne Lucy (*d* 29 March 1848), only dau of Col Archer, 16th Lancers, and *d* 2 May 1872, leaving:

(1) Walter Francis (Rev); *b* 27 Nov 1845; *d* unm 16 Feb 1873

(1) Lucy Edith; *m* 9 Sept 1869 Charles Gilbert Heathcote (*see* WILLOUGHY DE ERESBY, B) and *d* 11 Feb 1918, leaving issue

5 Edward Bennet, DL; *b* 26 July 1811; *m* 8 Jan 1846 Ellen Charlotte (*d* 29 Oct 1878), dau of George Rush, of Elsenham Hall, Essex, and *d* 20 Jan 1892, leaving, with a dau (*d* unm):

(1) Alfred Edward; *b* 29 Dec 1855; Maj RE; *m* 20 April 1881 Ellen Mary Isabel (*d* 29 Sept 1934), er dau of Maj-Gen Alfred Wilkes Drayson, RA, and *d* 26 Oct 1899, leaving, with a dau (*d* an infant):

1a Hugh Edward; *b* 12 Feb 1882; Lt Rifle Bde; *d* unm 9 Aug 1942

1a Maud Ellen; *b* 20 Sept 1884; *m* 14 Dec 1911 Brig Francis Harry Stapleton, CMG, Oxon LI (*d* 13 Aug 1956), and *d* 19 Feb 1960, leaving issue (*see* 1970 edn STAPLETON, Bt)

(1) Ellen Maria; *m* 10 July 1884 Rev Canon Charles Rowland Haydock Hill (*d* 15 July 1911), Rector Holy Trinity, Dorchester, and had issue

1 Henrietta; *m* 10 Jan 1832 Henry van Straubenzee (*d* 31 May 1892), of Spennithorne, Yorks, and *d* 13 May 1893 aged 88, leaving issue

The 1st BARON *d* 16 March 1841; his est s,

JOHN WROTTESLEY, **2nd Baron Wrottesley**; *b* 5 Aug 1798; *educ* Westminster and Ch Ch Oxford (BA 1819, MA 1823, DCL 1860); fndr Roy Astronomical Soc 1820 (Sec 1831–41, Gold Medallist 1839, Pres 1841–43), Pres Roy Soc 1854–58; *m* 28 July 1821 Sophia Elizabeth (*d* 13 Jan 1880), 3rd dau of Thomas Giffard, of Chillington, Staffs, and had:

1 ARTHUR, **3rd Baron**

2 Charles; *b* 23 Feb 1826; MA Oxon, Fell All Souls; Maj 1st King's Own Staffs Militia; *d* unm 19 June 1907

3 George; *b* 15 June 1827; Maj-Gen RE; *m* 1st 7 Jan 1854 Margaret Anne (*dsp* 3 May 1883), dau of FM Sir John Fox Burgoyne, 1st Bt, GCB; *m* 2nd 21 Feb 1889 Nina Margaret (*d* 30 Jan 1941), dau of John William Philips, of Heybridge, Staffs, and *dsp* 4 March 1909

4 Henry; *b* 4 March 1829; Lt 43rd Regt; *ka* Kaffir War 11 March 1852

5 Cameron; *b* 19 Dec 1834; Lt RE; *ka* siege of Bomarsund 15 Aug 1854

1 Caroline; *b* 24 Feb 1832; *m* 28 Dec 1859 Edward Wallace Goodlake, of the Inner Temple, and *d* 1 Sept 1860

The 2nd BARON *d* 27 Oct 1867; his est s,

ARTHUR WROTTESLEY, **3rd Baron Wrottesley**, JP, DL; *b* 17 June 1824; *educ* Rugby and Ch Ch Oxford (BA 1846); Ld Lt Staffs 1871–87, Ld-in-Waiting (Lib) 1869–74 and 1880–85, MFH Albrighton; *m* 18 July 1861 Augusta Elizabeth (*d* 20 Jan 1887), 4th dau of 1st Baron Londesborough (*qv*), and *d* 28 Dec 1910, having had:

1 William; *b* 17 May 1863; Capt 4th Dragoon Gds; *dvp* unm 7 Oct 1899

2 Bertram Francis; *b* 20 July 1864; *dvp* 26 Oct 1875

3 VICTOR ALEXANDER WROTTESLEY, **4th Baron Wrottesley**; *b* 18 Sept 1873; *educ* Eton and Ch Ch Oxford; *d* unm 1 Sept 1962

4 Walter Bennet; *b* 28 Sept 1877; *educ* Eton; Lt S Staffs Regt WW I (wounded); *m* 19 May 1917 (*divorce* 1926) Kate May, only dau of Douglas Howard Harris, of Craddock, Cape Colony, S Africa, and *d* 25 May 1962, leaving:

(1) RICHARD JOHN, **5th Baron**

1 Evelyn Henrietta; *b* 10 Oct 1866; *m* 8 June 1910 2nd and last Viscount Wolverhampton (*dsp* 9 March 1943; *see* 1940 edn) and *d* 30 Oct 1947

The 4th BARON's n,

RICHARD JOHN WROTTESLEY, **5th Baron Wrottesley**, MC; *b* 7 July 1918; *educ* Harrow and RMC Sandhurst; Maj (RARO) RHG (Blues) WW II, OStJ; *m* 1st

25 Jan 1941 (*divorce* 1949) Roshnara Barbara [Mrs Wingfield-Stratford-Orr, Lakeview House, Station Lane, Kirby Bellars, Melton Mowbray, Leics LE14 2ED] (*m* 2nd 1950 Lt-Col Norman David Melville Johnstone, MBE, Gren Gds (*d* 9 Oct 1995); *m* 3rd 9 May 1998 *Ronald Henry Davidson Orr, and took by deed poll the name Wingfield-Stratford-Orr), only dau of Capt Esmé Cecil Wingfield-Stratford (*see* POWERSCOURT, V), and had:

1 A son; *b* and *d* 29 Aug 1941

2 Richard Francis Gerard; *b* 16 Aug 1942; *educ* Stowe and King's Coll Cambridge; Lt Parachute Regt; Jt MFH Bermingham and N Galway 1970; *m* 6 Nov 1967 *Georgina Anne [Mrs Jonathan Seddon-Brown, The Coach House, Dauntsey, Wilts, SN15 4HP] (*m* 2nd 1982 Lt-Col Jonathan Lovett Seddon-Brown, Scots Gds), er dau of Lt-Col Peter Thomas Clifton, DSO, JP, DL (*see* BRUCE, Bt, of Downhill), and *dvp* 9 Nov 1970, leaving:

(1) CLIFTON HUGH LAUNCELOT De VERDON WROTTESLEY, **6th and present Baron Wrottesley**

1 A dau (twin); *b* and *d* 29 Aug 1941

The **5th Baron** *m* 2nd 9 Dec 1949 (*divorce* 1953) (Joyce) Marion, dau of Dare Frederick Alexander Wallace, and formerly w of Maj Sean Rainey, and by her had:

3 Mark; *b* 21 June 1951; *educ* St Andrew's Grahamstown, S Africa; *m* 1st 1974 (*divorce* 1978) Marie Louise de Plooy and had:

(1) *Caroline May; *b* 19–

(2) *Veronica; *b* 19–

3 (cont.) The Hon Mark Wrottesley *m* 2nd 1981 *Judy Matthews and *d* 1986

The **5th Baron** *m* 3rd 5 March 1955 *Mary Ada van Echten [The Rt Hon The Lady Wrottesley, 18 Sonnehoogte, Thomas Rd, Kenilworth, CP 7708, S Africa], only dau of Edgar Dryden Tudhope, of Kenilworth, and *d* 1977, leaving by her:

4 +STEPHEN JOHN [The Hon Stephen Wrottesley, 1 Lodge Rd, Orangezicht, Cape Town 8001, S Africa]; *b* 21 Dec 1955; heir presumptive; *educ* Harrow; jnlst; *m* 1982 *Mrs Rosamund Clare Fletcher (*née* Taylor) and has:

(1) *Alexandra Wynne Marie; *b* 1985

(2) *Stephanie Victoria; *b* 1988

5 +Nicholas Charles [The Hon Nicholas Wrottesley, 88 Stredwick Dve, Torbay, Auckland, New Zealand]; *b* 24 Sept 1963; *educ* Harrow and Cape Town U (BA 1985, LLB 1987, LLM 1992); *m* 1991 *Denny Marian Welman, and has:

(1) *Mary Jane; *b* 28 Nov 1994

WYFOLD

Arms: Sable a lion couchant erminois holding between the paws a bale of cotton proper. **Crest:** An eagle, wings addorsed and inverted or, supporting with the dexter claw an increscent argent, and looking at the rays of the sun issuant from clouds proper. **Supporters:** On either side a trooper of the Oxfordshire Yeomanry (Queen's Own Oxfordshire Hussars). **Motto:** *Praemium virtutis gloria* ('Glory is the reward of valour'). **Creations:** Bt. (UK) 5 Aug 1902, B. (UK) 17 May 1919.

THE 3RD BARON WYFOLD, of Accrington, Co Lancaster, and a **Baronet** (Sir Hermon Robert Fleming Hermon-Hodge, Bt) [The Rt Hon The Lord Wyfold, Sarsden House, Churchill, Oxon; Les Trois Couronnes, Vevey, Switzerland]; *b* 26 June 1915; *s* f 1942; *educ* Eton and Le Rosey, Switzerland; Capt Gren Gds (Res) WW II; dir Robert Fleming Holdings 1949–85

Lineage: ROWLAND HODGE, of Newcastle; *b* 1752; *m* 29 July 1780 Jane Cram (*d* 30 Jan 1827), and *d* 16 Nov 1802, leaving:

ROWLAND HODGE, of Newcastle; *b* 18 July 1781; *m* 21 July 1808 Jane (*d* 2 Nov 1858), dau of Jonathan Cram, of Newcastle, and *d* 3 June 1855, leaving, with a 2nd s (*see* HODGE, Bt):

GEORGE WILLIAM HODGE, of Newcastle; *b* 17 Dec 1817; *m* 13 June 1850 Sarah Eliza, dau of David Green, of Ainderby, Yorks, and *d* 11 April 1880, leaving:

1 ROBERT TROTTER, **1st Baron**

2 George William Baldwin, of Richmond, Surrey; *b* 23 Feb 1855; *m* 25 April 1888 Constance Lucie, dau of John Hardie, and had:

(1) Marjorie Frances Baldwin; *b* 28 March 1890; *d* 10 March 1958

1 Blanche; m 1874 Rev Cameron Churchill (d 20 Jan 1901), Vicar Crockham Hill, Kent, and d 1 Aug 1933, leaving issue

The er s,

Sir ROBERT TROTTER HODGE later HERMON-HODGE (roy licence 3 Jan 1903), **1st Bt**, and **1st Baron Wyfold**, of Accrington, Co Palatine of Lancaster (both UK), cr 6 Aug 1902 and 17 May 1919 respectively, TD, JP, DL Oxon; b 23 Sept 1851; educ Clifton and Worcester Coll Oxford (BA 1873, MA, SCL 1881); Lt-Col and Hon Col cmdg Oxon Yeo, memb Oxon TAA; MP (C) NE Lancs 1886–92, S Oxon 1895–1906 and S 1917–18 and Croydon 1909–10, Alderman CC; m 16 May 1877 Frances Caroline (d 5 Feb 1929), only dau of Edward Hermon, of Wyfold Court, Oxon, MP Preston, and had:

1 ROLAND HERMON, **2nd Baron**

2 Robert Edward Udny, DSO (1919); b 11 April 1882; Lt Oxon LI, Maj Oxon Yeo, WW I; m 27 July 1934 Sybil Rika, dau of Capt Percy Richard Hare (see LISTOWEL, E), and dsp 2 May 1937

3 George Guy; b 22 Aug 1883; Capt RHA; d unm 7 July 1916 of wounds recd in action

4 Harry Baldwin; b 4 Oct 1885; educ Magdalen Coll Oxford (BA); Resident N Nigeria, WW I with Nigerian FF; d unm 9 Jan 1947

5 Claude Preston, DSC; b 20 Jan 1888; WW I (despatches twice), Assist Sec to CID 1924–28, Dep Dir Naval Intell Admlty 1936–38, R-Adml; m 20 Nov 1918 Gwendoline Rose (d 14 Sept 1949), dau of James Goulding Davis, PWD, of Bahawalpur, and d 25 March 1952, having had:

(1) Anthony Claude; b 1 Aug 1920; Sub-Lt RNVR WW II; ka aboard HMS Grove 12 June 1942

(1) *Pauline Frances Gwendoline; b 6 Aug 1921; m 27 Dec 1947 *Maj Meyrick James Magrath, DFC, Croix de Guerre, RA, of The Old Rectory, Croom, Co Limerick, only s of Maj Meyrick Myles Magrath, and has:

1a *Carol Rose; b 27 April 1949

(2) *Stella Riette; b 17 July 1925; m 4 Feb 1949 David Charles Courtenay (d 1983), of Woodcutters, Ambersham Common, Midhurst, W Sussex, only s of Ashley Reginald Courtenay, of Little Powderham, Aldwick Bay, Sussex, and has had:

1a A son; b 23, d 24 June 1951

2a A son; b and d 27 April 1955

3a *David Anthony Orin; b 19 Feb 1958

1a Gwendoline; b 14, d 15 July 1950

2a *Geraldine; b 5 Jan 1953; m 1977 *Rev Douglas John Dales and has:

1b *Christopher St John Douglas; b 1981

2b *Basil Michael Dunstan; b 1987

1b *Gwendoline Clare Courtenay; b 1984

6 John Percival; b 18 July 1890; 2nd Lt 1st/4th Oxford and Bucks LI; ka 28 May 1916

7 Leonard St Leger, MC (1919); b 8 Sept 1892; Capt Gren Gds (SR) WW I; d following an accident 31 Jan 1940

1 Marguerite; b 6, d 9 June 1879

2 Nona Carol; b 20 Nov 1897; m 8 April 1924 Harold Montagu Hermon-Worsley, MC (d 24 April 1956), s of Canon Edward Worsley, of Evenly, Brackley, Northants

The 1st BARON d 3 June 1937; his est s,

ROLAND HERMON HERMON-HODGE, **2nd Baron Wyfold**, DSO, MVO, JP, DL Oxon; b 10 July 1880; Capt Gren Gds, Maj and Brevet Lt-Col Res Offrs, Boer War 1900–02, WW I on Staff; m 26 June 1906 Dorothy (d 7 Aug 1976), er dau of Robert Fleming, of Joyce Grove, Oxon, and d 14 Oct 1942, leaving:

1 HERMON ROBERT FLEMING HERMON-HODGE, **3rd and present Baron Wyfold**

1 Pamela Kate; b 27 Nov 1908; m 1st 26 April 1938 Viscount Fincastle (ka vp France June 1940), only s of 8th Earl of Dunmore (qv), and has issue; m 2nd 27 June 1944 Capt Follett Watson Bell, RA (d 2 Oct 1982), s of Frederick Norman Bell, and d 1978, having by him had:

(1) *Ewan Follett [Ewan Bell Esq, Easter Coul, Auchterarder, Perth PH3 1DS]; b 11 March 1945; educ Harrow; late 2nd Lt Roy Scots Greys; m 9 June 1979 *Angela Frances, er dau of Maj Francis Blackett (see BLACKETT, Bt) and has:

1a *Archibald John; b 2 March 1981

2a *Caspar; b 24 Aug 1989

1a *Georgia Elizabeth; b 16 Jan 1983

(2) *Donald [Donald Bell Esq, 1008–1330 Harwood St, Vancouver, V6E I5C BC, Canada]; b 26 Sept 1948; educ Harrow; m 1st 3 July 1971 Elizabeth, dau of Frederick Browne, of Montreal; m 2nd 19 Aug 1987 *Sabine, dau of Peter Ullrich, of Glücksburg, Germany, and has:

1a *Andrew Simon; b 12 March 1981

2a *Alexander Peter; b 11 May 1987

1a *Natalie; b 30 May 1989

(1) *(Lorna) Marilyn [Miss Marilyn Bell, Dalness Cottage, Glen Etive, Ballachulish, Argyll PA39 4JA]; b 19 April 1951

2 *Lorna Frances; b 25 Feb 1911; m 14 April 1941 Maj John Schuster, TD, DL, Oxon Yeo (d 20 June 1984), of The Manor Farm, Nether Worton, Oxon, est s of Sir George Ernest Schuster, KCSI, KCMG, CBE, MC, of Nether Worton House, Middle Barton, Oxon, and adopted:

*Peter Jonathan [Peter Schuster Esq, The Homestead, Kingham, Chipping Norton, Oxon]; b 4 March 1952; educ Gordonstoun; m 30 June 1984 *Emma, er dau of Christopher Codrington, of Manor Farm House, Petersham, Surrey, and has:

1a *George Barkley; b 1989

1a *Hannah Frances; b 1986

*Richard Douglas [Richard Schuster Esq, The Grange, Over Worton, Oxon OX7 7ES]; b 4 June 1953; educ Eton; m 1986 *Jennifer C, dau of David G W Barham, of Hole Park, Rolvenden, and formerly w of Simon Francis Mann (see MANN, Bt)

*Joanna Valentine [Mrs Joanna Clarke, Nether Worton House, Chipping Norton, Oxon OX7 7AT; 63 Bourne St, London SW1W 8JD]; b 15 June 1950; m 31

July 1971 (divorce 1989) Orme Roosevelt Clarke (d 21 Oct 1992) and has issue (see CLARKE, Bt, of Dunham Lodge)

3 *(Dorothy) Charmian; b 4 Jan 1913; m 12 May 1938 Maj Richard Evelyn Fleming, MC, TD, Lovat Scouts (d 14 Aug 1977), of Leygore Manor, Northleach, Glos, and 12 Hyde Park Sq, London W2, 3rd s of Maj Valentine Fleming, DSO, MP (see ROSE, of Rayners), and had:

(1) *James Roland; b 26 Feb 1944; educ Eton and Magdalen Coll Oxford; m 1975 *Kathryn Alice, dau of D A Rooksby, and has:

1a *Christian Peter; b 1977

2a *Thomas Roland; b 1980

(2) *Adam Richard; b 15 May 1948; educ Eton; m 1979 *Caroline Jane, dau of Sir Hereward Wake, 14th Bt (qv), and has:

1a *Hector Adam; b 1982

2a *Angus Richard; b 1988

1a *Eleanor Kate; b 1985

(3) *George Andrew [George Fleming Esq, York Cottage, Churchill, Oxon OX7 6UL]; b 16 Dec 1950; educ Gordonstoun; m 1979 (divorce 1987) Elaine, dau of Peter Owen, of The Old Rectory, Mixbury, Oxon, and has:

1a *Frederick Richard; b 1981

(4) *Roderick John [Roderick Fleming Esq, The Dower House, Sarsgrove, Churchill, Oxon]; b 12 Nov 1953; educ Eton; m 1979 *Diana Julia, est dau of Sir Hereward Wake, 14th Bt (qv), and has:

1a *Chloe Dorothy; b 1989

2a *Hermione Kisty; (twin) b 1989

(5) *Fergus Hermon Robert; b 13 Oct 1959

(1) *Kathleen Alexandra [Mrs Kathleen Loder, Sydenham Farm, Broadwell, Moreton-in-Marsh, Glos GL56 0YE]; b 10 Jan 1941; m 23 June 1962 (divorce 1979) Capt Simon John Loder and has issue (see LODER, Bt)

(2) *Mary Fern; b 3 Oct 1942; m 1971 *Jeremy Donnithorne Taylor, of Coldharbour Farm, N Aston, Oxon, only son of Lt-Col Anthony Donnithorne Taylor, DSO, MC, of N Aston Manor, Oxford, and has:

1a *James Fionn; b 1971

1a *Katherine Clare Romayne; b 1973

(3) *Dorothy Frances; b 21 June 1955

4 Valentine Kathleen; b 2 Feb 1918

WYNFORD

Arms: Sa. a cinquefoil within an orle of cross-crosslets or, on a canton of the last a portcullis of the first. **Crest:** Out of a ducal coronet or a demi-ostrich rising arg., in its beak a cross-crosslet fitchée gold, gorged with a plain collar and pendant therefrom a portcullis sa. **Supporters:** Two eagles regardant, wings elevated, each standing on a Roman fasces, all ppr. **Motto:** Libertas in legibus ('Liberty in the laws'). **Creation:** B. (UK) 5 June 1829.

THE **8TH BARON WYNFORD**, of Wynford Eagle, Dorset (Robert Samuel Best, MBE (1952), DL (Dorset 1970) [Lt-Col The Rt Hon The Lord Wynford MBE DL, Wynford House, Wynford Eagle, Dorchester, Dorset]; b 5 Jan 1917; s f 1943; educ Eton and RMC Sandhurst; Lt-Col RWF 1937, WW II (wounded, Croix de Guerre 1943), Instr Staff Coll 1945–46, War Off 1947–49, OC Roy Welch Fus Depot 1955–57, Instr JSSC 1957–60, RARO 1960; m 6 May 1941 *Anne Daphne Mametz, only dau of Maj-Gen John Randle Minshull-Ford, CB, DSO, MC, of The White Cottage, Windlesham, Surrey (see 1970 edn HARMOOD-BANNER, Bt), and has:

1 +JOHN PHILIP ROBERT [The Hon John Best, The Manor, Wynford Eagle, Dorchester, Dorset DT2 0ER]; b 23 Nov 1950; educ Radley and Keele U; ARICS (1979); m 10 Oct 1981 *Fenella Christian Mary, only dau of Arthur Reginald Danks (see GIFFORD, B), and has:

(1) +Harry Robert Francis; b 9 May 1987

(1) *Sophie Hannah Elizabeth; b 18 Nov 1985

1 *Caroline Anne Sabina [The Hon Mrs Gundry, 15 Genoa Ave, London SW15]; b 28 March 1942; m 24 Oct 1964 *Edward Patrick Gundry, er s of Edward Fox Gundry (see WILLIAMS, Bt, of Bridehead), and has:

(1) *David Edward Patrick; b 14 April 1976

(1) *Rachel Anne; b 13 Nov 1965

(2) *Alexandra Clare Victoria; b 13 Sept 1967

2 *Jacqueline Dorothy Mametz [The Hon Mrs Pope, Field Cottage, Compton Abbas W, Maiden Newton, Dorset]; b 9 Nov 1946; m 7 June 1969 *Jeremy James Richard Pope, OBE, FRSA, and has:

(1) *Rory Christian Robert; b 9 Dec 1970

(2) *Rupert Philip; b 22 Dec 1973

(3) *Toby Francis; b 29 Sept 1977

Lineage: THOMAS BEST, of Haslebury Plucknett, Somerset; had a 3rd s:

WILLIAM DRAPER BEST, **1st Baron Wynford**, of Wynford Eagle, Co Dorset (UK), so cr 5 June 1829, PC (1824); b 13 Dec 1767; educ Crewkerne Sch and Wadham Coll Oxford; barrister Middle Temple 1789, Serjeant-at-law 1800, MP (Whig) Petersfield 1802–06 and (Tory) Bridport 1812–17 and Guildford 1818–19, King's Serjeant 1806, Recorder Guildford 1809, Slr-Gen and Attorney-Gen to PRINCE OF WALES 1813–16 and 1816–19 respectively, 2nd Justice and Ch Justice Chester 1817–18 and Jan-Nov 1818 respectively, Judge King's Bench 1818–24, ktd 1819, Ch Justice Common Pleas 1824–29, Dep Speaker Ho Lds 1829, DCL Oxon 1834; m 6 May 1794 Mary Anne (d 5 March 1840), 2nd dau of Jerome Knapp, Clerk Haberdashers' Co, and d 3 March 1845, leaving:

1 WILLIAM SAMUEL BEST, **2nd Baron Wynford**; b 19 Feb 1798; educ Eton and BNC Oxford; barrister Inner Temple 1814, MP St Michael's 1831–32; m 21 July 1821 Jane (d 23 Feb 1895 aged 92), dau of William Thoyts, of Sulhampstead, Berks, and d 28 Feb 1869, leaving, with other issue:

(1) WILLIAM DRAPER MORTIMER BEST, **3rd Baron Wynford**, JP, DL; b 2 Aug 1826; Ensign 70th Foot May and Rifle Bde July 1844, Lt 1847, Capt 1854, ret 1856; m 17 Dec 1857 Caroline Eliza Montague (d 16 Jan 1913), dau of Evan Baillie of Dochfour (see BURTON, B), and d 27 Aug 1899, having had:

1a Algernon; b 26 Dec 1858; d 18 Jan 1859

(2) Frederick Barnewall; b 18 Aug 1827; Capt 2nd Bengal Fus, memb Gentlemen-at-Arms; m 1st 9 June 1864 Charlotte Elizabeth (d 28 May 1865), est dau of Francis Haft Dyke, and had:

1a A son; b and d 13 March 1865

(2) (cont.) The Hon Frederick Best m 2nd 24 Nov 1870 Frances Hinton (m 3rd 19 Sept 1882 Sir Thomas Fraser Grove, 1st Bt (qv), and d 9 Aug 1912), widow of Capt Herbert Edward George Crosse, 59th Regt, and only child of Henry Northcote, of Okefield, Crediton, and d 5 Jan 1876

(3) HENRY MOLYNEUX BEST, **4th Baron Wynford**; b 9 Nov 1829; d unm 28 Oct 1903

(4) Robert Rainy; b 21 Aug 1834; Capt Gren Gds; m 1st 8 March 1856 Maria Addison (dsp 12 Jan 1881), dau of T A Swaysland, of Crawley, Sussex; m 2nd 18 April 1882 Meynella Katherine Hilda (d 7 Feb 1899), dau of Capt Frederick A P Wood, RM, and d 2 Feb 1903, leaving by her, with other issue:

1a Muriel Henrietta Louisa; b 8 Oct 1884; m 2 July 1907 Maj John William Rivallon de Poher de la Poer, JP, 2nd Count de la Poer (Papal cr 19 Aug 1864) (d 27 March 1939), and d 19 Jan 1936, leaving issue (see 1935 edn EMLY, B)

(1) Anne Louisa; m April 1858 Maj-Gen Patrick Yule, RE (d 1873), and d 22 April 1899

2 Thomas; b 12 Aug 1799; V-Adml; m 25 Aug 1835 Marianne (d 18 Sept 1866), 2nd dau of 2nd Baron Kenyon (qv), and d 4 Sept 1864

3 Samuel (Rev); b 2 Dec 1802; Rector Abbots Anne, Hants; m 1st 11 April 1826 Charlotte Willis (d 23 Sept 1833), dau of Sir James Burrough, Judge Ct Common Pleas; m 2nd 21 Feb 1835 Emma (d 7 Sept 1891), dau of Lt-Col Charles Duke, and d 20 Jan 1873, having by her had:

(1) GEORGE, **5th Baron**

(2) John Charles, JP Denbighs and Merioneths; b 13 May 1842; granted 6 May 1904 with siblings rank of baron's dau/yr s; Capt RN, High Sheriff Denbighs 1888; m 2 April 1873 Mary (d 28 Jan 1927), dau of William Wagstaff, of Plas yn Vivod, Llangollen, and d 25 May 1907, leaving:

1a William, JP, DL Denbighs; b 24 June 1874; educ Eton and RMC Sandhurst; Capt Roy Welch Fus; High Sheriff 1928; m 9 July 1903 Constance Adela (d 26 March 1963), dau of Col Charles Wingfield, of Onslow, Salop, and d 18 April 1950, leaving:

1b Harry George, TD, JP (Denbighs 1946); b 14 Nov 1904; educ privately and Clare Coll Cambridge; MIEE; late Capt RA, WW II (despatches); High Sheriff 1956; d 4 June 1975

2b Frank Charles, OBE (1964); b 19 Jan 1906; educ privately and Christ's Coll Cambridge; Forestry Commn Conservator N Wales 1947–66; d 19 Dec 1987

3b +John William, MBE (1946) [John Best Esq MBE, Lawton Hall, Leominster, Herefs HR6 9AX]; b 6 Aug 1912; educ Stowe; F/Lt RAFVR (POW) WW II 1939–41; m 1st 6 Aug 1938 (divorce 1959) Mary Constance, dau of Robert Charles Otter, JP, DL, of Royston Manor, Notts; m 2nd 19 May 1959 *Mary Elisabeth, dau of Dr Edward Lancelot Bunting, of Hardwicke Manor, Worcs, and formerly w of John Ogilvie Corbin, and by his 1st w has:

1c +Robert John [Robert Best Esq, Plas Yn Vivod, Llangollen, Denbighs LL20 7LS]; b 25 July 1946; educ Marlborough; m 1976 *Juliet, dau of Peter John Owen, of Mixbury, Northants, and has:

1d +William; b 1981

1d *Lucinda Emma; b 1977

2d *Candida Mary; b 1979

1c *Antonia Mary [Mrs Christopher Wilson-Clarke, Greenbanks, Coptiviney, Salop SY12 0NB]; b 29 Feb 1948; m 28 Feb 1970 *Christopher Duncan Steuart Wilson-Clarke, s of Maj Cyril John Wilson-Clarke, of Achareidh, Nairn, and has:

1d *Alpha Georgia; b 1978

2d *Laura Alice; b 1979

1b Hilda Mary; b 14 July 1909; m 15 June 1935 Ranald Macdonald Brodie Macalister (d 1980), yr s of Maj Matthew Charles Brodie Macalister, JP, of Glenbarr and Cour, Argyll, and d 18 March 1995, leaving:

1c *Angus Charles [Angus Macalister Esq, Glenbarr Abbey, Glenbarr by Tarbert, Argyll, Scotland]; b 27 March 1937; educ Gordonstoun; m

---

1st 20 April 1963 (divorce 1981) Gustava, dau of Ulrich Liebing, of Eckernforde, Germany; m 2nd 1986 *Jeanne Cummings, dau of Clinton Barclay-Allardice, of Providence, RI, and by his 1st w has:

1d *Duncan Joachim; b 30 Jan 1964

2d *Kai-Donald; b 1970

1d *Elke Maree; b 30 May 1966

1c *Fiona Anne; b 24 June 1947; m 1973 (divorce 1981, resumed maiden name) William Lorimer, s of Robert Lorimer, of Edinburgh, and has:

1d *Siobhan Macalister; b 1976

1d *Ciaran Sorcha; b 1978

(3) Thomas William; b 23 Jan 1844; Maj W R Regt, Ch Constable Merioneths 1883–1907; m 16 Sept 1879 Harriet Royds (d 8 July 1935), 3rd surv dau of Henry Anthony Grey, JP, of Brent Ho, Meole Brace, Salop, and d 3 Jan 1909, leaving:

1a John Samuel, JP (Glos 1930); b 28 July 1883; educ Shrewsbury and Ch Ch Oxford; tea planter Assam; m 7 Sept 1912 Anne Stewart (d 30 Oct 1969), dau of James Topp Jamieson, JP, of Assam and Aberdeen, and dsp 21 April 1940

2a Humphrey Willie, CBE (1944), DSO (1919); b 2 July 1884; Capt RN WW I, recalled as Cdre 1939; m 28 July 1914 Helen Grace (d 1975), dau of Lewis James Meakin, of Ashby-de-la-Zouch, and d 29 April 1959, leaving:

1b +Walter John [Walter Best Esq, 10 Cronk Drean, 2nd Ave, Douglas, IOM]; b 30 Sept 1917; educ HMS Worcester; Marine Pilot Trinidad and Tobago, Roy Fleet Aux Serv WW II Far East (despatches); m 15 April 1941 *Jessie Mackintosh, yst dau of Kenneth Mackintosh Simpson, of Port of Spain, Trinidad, and has:

1c *Anne Mackintosh [Mrs Robert Massey, 8 Gilwell Rd, Valsayan Park, Curepe, Trinidad, West Indies]; b 3 April 1944; m 23 April 1966 *Robert Brian Massey and has:

1d *Stewart John; b 8 Nov 1967

2d *Ian James; b 1972

1d *Catherine Anne; b 1975

2c *Fiona Elizabeth [Mrs Anthony Cotter, Trewalla Farm, Commonmoor, Liskeard, Cornwall, PL14 6ED]; b 22 Nov 1949; m 1972 *Anthony John Cotter and has:

1d *Andrew John; b 1976

1d *Heather Jane; b 1979

2b +Peter Anthony [Peter Best Esq, White House, Trevilson, St Newlyn East, Cornwall TR8 5JF]; b 1 Oct 1922; educ Allhallows; F/Lt RAF WW II (POW); m 1st 1 March 1948 Sheelah Gillian Vernon St John (d 1979), dau of Lt-Col Darrel St John Baxter, of Hambrook, W Sussex; m 2nd 1979 *B Smyth and by his 1st w has:

1c +Peter Kimble; b 28 Jan 1952; educ Allhallows; F/O RAF; m 1974 *Georgina Alison Gibson and has:

1d +Oliver Giles; b 1977

2d +Timothy Tristan; b 1978

1d *Gemma Lucy Gillian; b 1982

2c +Jeremy Dean [Jeremy Best Esq, Brambles, Mitchell Fruit Garden, Mitchell, Cornwall]; b 10 March 1954; educ Allhallows; horticulturalist; m 1978 *Claudia Anhalies Roost and has:

1d +Timothy Peter; b 1985

1d *Christine Sara; b 1984

2d *Miriam Anna; b 1987

1c *Hilary Jane; b 1 April 1949; m 17 June 1971 *Robert Dale Johnson and has:

1d *Dale Anthony; b 1974

2d *Jeremy Ross; b 1976

1b *Pamela Grey [Mrs Philip Hawkins, Veryan, 6 Shuteleigh, Wellington, Somerset TA21 8PG]; b 1 Feb 1920; m 5 April 1947 *Philip Henry Hawkins, s of Col Horatio Hawkins, of Disley, Cheshire, and has:

1c *Jonathan Edward Spencer [Jonathan Hawkins Esq, Whitmore Cottage, Shawford, Winchester SO21 2BL]; b 18 June 1953; educ Aldenham; m 1998 *Sarah Sants Smith and has:

1d *Catherine Sarah; b 1980

2d *Emily Elizabeth; b 1982

1c *Caroline Tessa [Mrs James Bradnock, Russets, 8 Shuteleigh, Wellington, Somerset TA21 8PG]; b 15 June 1948; m 30 July 1971 *James Harvey Bradnock and has:

1d *Thomas Philip; b 23 June 1975; educ Exeter Coll Oxford; barrister Gray's Inn 1997

2d *Edward James Peter; b 7 March 1978

(1) Mary Margaret; m 5 May 1859 Rev Sir James Erasmus Philipps, 12th Bt, and d 5 Sept 1913, leaving issue (see SAINT DAVIDS, V)

(2) Grace Emma; m 27 Feb 1862 Rev Florence Thomas Wethered and d 10 Oct 1864

(3) Fanny Gertrude Sophia; d unm 26 Nov 1904

4 John Charles; b 9 Dec 1810; Capt 50th Regt; drowned 13 Feb 1840

1 Grace Anne; m 1814 Philip Lake Godsal (d 1858) and d 1868, leaving issue

2 Ann; m 1826 Adml Sir William Fanshawe Martin, 4th Bt, KCB, of Lockynge, Berks (see 1910 edn), and d 1836, leaving issue

The 4th BARON's cousin,

GEORGE BEST, **5th Baron Wynford**, JP Wilts and Dorset; b 14 Dec 1838; educ Rugby and RMA Woolwich; RA: joined 1858, Capt RHA 1871, Maj 1879, ret as Lt-Col 1883, Chm Wilts Ag Ctee; m 7 Sept 1870 Edith Anne (d 31 May 1924), dau of Matthew Henry Marsh, of Ramridge, Andover, Hants, MP Salisbury, and d 27 Oct 1904, leaving:

1 PHILIP GEORGE BEST, **6th Baron Wynford**, DSO, JP, DL Dorset; b 27 Aug 1871; Capt RHA, Lt-Col RA and Dorset Yeo TA, WW I (wounded, despatches); m 16 Oct 1906 Hon (Eva) Lilian Cecilia Napier (d 23 March 1974), only child of 2nd Baron Napier of Magdala (qv), and d 15 Dec 1940, leaving:

(1) *Grace Janet Mary [The Hon Mrs Hilleary, Lordington Park, Chichester, W Sussex PO18 9DX]; b 27 Aug 1907; m 12 Nov 1930 *Edward Kenneth Macleod Hilleary, MVO, 2nd s of Maj Edward Langdale Hilleary, OBE, TD, DL, of The Lodge, Edinbane, Skye, and has:

   1a *Shena Sarah [Mrs Harry Cornell, The Walled House, Droxford, Hants SO32 3PT]; b 16 Aug 1931; m 11 Dec 1954 *Lt-Cdr Harry R Cornell, RN, and has:

      1b *Nicola Anne; b 23 Jan 1956; m 198– *Richard Staveley, s of Adml of Fleet Sir William Staveley, GCB, and has issue

   2a *Wendy Jemima [Mrs Ian Hedderwick, Lot 35, Robinson Rd, Albany, WA 6330, Australia]; b 27 March 1933; m 1954 *Ian Hedderwick

   3a *Gillian Marianne [Mrs J Bengough, White Lodge, Church St, Sidbury, Devon EX10 0SB]; b 9 June 1936; m 1975 *Maj J D Bengough, Black Watch

(2) *Eva Constance Edith [The Hon Mrs Mackinnon, Barton Lodge Retirement Home, Cerne Abbas, Dorset]; b 11 Feb 1909; m 23 April 1932 (divorce 1961) Philip Valentine Mackinnon, only s of Rt Hon Sir Frank Douglas Mackinnon, Ld Justice Appeal, and has had issue

(3) *Mary Jemima [The Hon Mrs Hendy, 1 Portherras Cross, Pendeen, Cornwall TR19 7DY]; b 23 Aug 1912; m 2 Sept 1944 *Jack Hendy and has:

   1a *John Giles; b 1948

   2a *Peter Gerard; b 1953

2 SAMUEL JOHN, 7th Baron

3 Matthew Robert (Hon Sir), KCB, DSO and bar, MVO; b 18 June 1878; RN WW I, ADC to HM GEORGE V 1927–28, R-Adml cmdg 2nd Cruiser Sqdn 1929–31, R-Adml-in-Charge Malta, Adml Supt Malta Dockyard 1931–34, C-in-C America and WI Station 1934–37, memb Cncl Malta 1931, V-Adml 1932, Adml 1936, Russian Order St Stanislas 2nd Cl with swords, Japanese Order Rising Sun 3rd Cl; m 2 Jan 1908 Annis Elizabeth (d 12 May 1971), 2nd dau of Charles Frederic Wood, of Twyford Ho, Winchester, and d 13 Oct 1940, leaving:

(1) George Frederic Matthew, OBE (1985); b 14 Dec 1908; Capt RN WW II (despatches), Dep Dir Naval Intell 1956–58, Cdre Arabian Seas and Persian Gulf 1958–60, ADC to HM 1960, CC Dorset 1962–70; m 26 July 1940 *Rosemary Elizabeth [Mrs George Best, Wallhayes, Nettlecombe, Bridport, Dorset DT6 3SX], er dau of Maj John Chadwick Brooks, OBE (1919), of Chiswick, and d 7 March 1994, leaving:

   1a +John Vincent Matthew [John Best Esq, 29 Folkstone Rd, London E17]; b 20 Dec 1948; educ Sherborne and Sussex U (BSc, MBA); m 18 Dec 1970 *Penelope Ann, dau of John H Williams, of Washington, DC, and Isle of Arran, and has:

      1b +Tobias Graham; b 3 Sept 1974

      2b +Crispin Alex Sebastian; b 15 July 1983

      1b *Philippa Hannah; b 1 Sept 1972

   1a *Annis Rosemary Georgina; b 28 Nov 1944; m 12 June 1971 *Col Richard M Connaughton, MPhil Cantab, and has:

      1b *Michael Thomas George; b 27 June 1972

      1b *Emma Caroline Jane; b 5 March 1974

(1) *Margaret Annis [Mrs Godfrey French, Mollyl Bawn, Stoke Abbott, Dorset DT8 3JT]; b 16 Jan 1913; m 1st 18 May 1937 Cdr Alexander Pollock Gibson, RN (ka 23 Aug 1940), s of Dr Henry Wilkes Gibson, of The Gables, Emsworth, Hants; m 2nd 17 Oct 1941 Capt Godfrey Alexander French, CBE, RN (d 1988), s of Alexander Weatherhead French, of Torcross, Kingsbridge, S Devon, and has:

   1a *Matthew [Lt-Cdr Matthew French RN, Beechfield Farm, Curry Rivel, Somerset TA10 0NP]; b 11 Aug 1945; educ Sherborne and RNC Dartmouth; Lt-Cdr RN, FRGS, MInstN; m 1983 *Nicola Mary, dau of Eustace Arthur McNaught, and has:

      1b *Annis Evelyn; b 1984

      2b *Eleanor Winifred; b 1986

      3b *Charlotte Imogen; b 1990

   2a *David [David French Esq, 21 Prospect Rd, St Albans, Herts AL1 2AT]; b 20 June 1947; educ Sherborne and Durham U (BA 1969); dir Relate 1987–95, Dir-Gen Cwlth Inst 1997–; m 1974 *Sarah Anne, dau of the Rt Rev Henry David Halsey, Bp Carlisle, and has:

      1b *Thomas Weatherhead; b 1978

      2b *Alexander Matthew; b 1980

      3b *William Sholto; b 1983

      4b *Henry Kenneth Robert; b 1993

   1a *Jenny Margaret [Mrs Peter Crossley, The Old Vicarage, Henton, Wells, Somerset BA5 1PD]; b 29 June 1950; educ St Mary's Calne and Homerton Teachers Training Coll Cambridge; m 1982 *Peter Bigham Crossley, s of T Crossley, OBE, ICS, and has:

      1b *Giles Bigham; b 1983

      2b *James Bigham; b 1988

      1b *Hannah Margaret; b 1986

4 James William, OBE (1919), VD, JP Dorset; b 3 May 1882; educ Wellington and Cooper's Hill; India Forest Serv, Capt Auxiliary Force India, Verderer New Forest; m 11 Aug 1914 Florence Mary Bernarda (d 3 Dec 1961), dau of Sir Elliott Lees, 1st Bt, of Lytchet Manor (qv), and d 16 July 1960, leaving:

(1) Thomas William, CB (1966); b 1 Sept 1915; RN: WW II (despatches) and in Far E 1951–52 (despatches), ADC to HM THE QUEEN 1964, Flag Offr Gibraltar 1964–66, ret as R-Adml 1967; m 28 April 1942 *Brenda Joan [Mrs Thomas Best, Hincknowle, Melplash, Dorset DT6 3UG], only dau of Frederick Alan Hellaby, of Auckland, NZ, and d 10 July 1984, leaving:

   1a +Rupert Thomas Nicholas [Cdr Rupert Best RN, 39 Beach Rd, Emsworth, Hants PO10 7HR]; b 15 May 1943; educ Winchester, RNC Dartmouth and London Business Sch; RN active serv incl Brunei 1962, Borneo 1963–65 and Falklands/S Atlantic 1982, ret 1989 as Cdr; Yr Bro Trin Ho, FIMgt; Pingat Perjuangan Brunei 1962; m 1971 *Margaret, dau of Maj Alan L Murray, and has:

      1b +Thomas Matthew; b 8 Nov 1973

      2b +William Rupert; b 20 May 1982

      1b *Sarah Margaret; b 27 Nov 1976

2a +James Frederick; b 1 Sept 1948; educ Malvern, BA Oxon; m 1980 *Sara Victoria, dau of Brian Cole, of Kilburn, and has:

   1b +Harry James; b 1983

   2b +Tom; b 1987

   1b *Mary-Rose Victoria; b 1981

1a *Joanna Mavis; b 10 Dec 1945; educ Downe Ho and St Mary's Coll Durham (BA); m 18 July 1970 *Maj Thomas James Knott, RE, 2nd s of Lt-Gen Sir Harold Knott, KCB, OBE, MD, of Jersey, and has:

   1b *Felicity Anne; b 1971

   2b *Alison Joanna; b 1973

   3b *Amelia Mary; b 1982

(2) Giles Bernard; b 19 Oct 1925; educ Wellington and Jesus Coll Oxford; barrister Inner Temple 1951, Dep Chm Dorset QS 1967–71, Recorder Crown Ct 1972–75, Circuit Judge 1975–97; d unm 27 Aug 1997

(3) Samuel James; b 9 June 1927; educ Wellington; m 25 Sept 1954 *Jennifer Elspeth Mary [Mrs Samuel Best, Kings House, Powerstock, Dorset], er dau of Max Herbert Heilbut, of Baker's Barn, Touchen End, Berks, and d 1974, leaving:

   1a +Crispin John; b 7 May 1955; educ Sherborne

   1a *Jane Mary; b 25 March 1957

   2a *Susannah Catherine; b 29 June 1962

   3a *Deborah Gabriel; b 1966

(4) +Henry Nicholas [Henry Best Esq, Whitelackington House, Ilminster, Somerset TA19 9EF]; b 3 May 1930; educ Wellington; late md Anglo Blackwells Ltd and SKW Metals UK; m 30 July 1963 *Elisabeth Rose Ursula, er dau of Hans Joachim Druckenbrodt, of Marburg, Germany, and has:

   1a +Frederick Henry Achim; b 21 June 1964

   2a +Thomas Bernard Nicholas; b 10 Dec 1968

   1a *Isabel Florence Christina; b 1972

(1) *Alice Mary [Mrs Christopher Dilke, Valehouse Farm, Whitchurch Canonicorum, Dorset DT6 6RP]; b 19 Aug 1919; m 15 Aug 1939 Christopher Wentworth Dilke (d 2 Nov 1987) (see DILKE, Bt) and has issue

(2) *Helen Margaret; b 14 Nov 1923

1 Margaret Mary, CBE (1938); b 6 Oct 1872; Hon Sec Sch Empire Tour Ctee, Fell Roy Empire Soc; d unm 30 Nov 1941

2 Gertrude Emma, MBE (1941); b 10 Nov 1876; ARRC, SRN, Assist Matron St Thomas's Hosp 1913–24, Matron EMS Hosp Salisbury 1940–45; d unm 19 Oct 1953

3 Grace Edith; b 1 Sept 1879; d 20 May 1899

4 Helen; b 5 Nov 1880; m 12 July 1910 Gerald Wilson (d 7 Sept 1918), s of Rev Charles Wilson, of Bickley, Kent, and d 7 Jan 1959, leaving issue

5 Bertha Beatrice; b 26 June 1884; m 7 Jan 1920 Lt-Col Guy Montague Atkinson, DSO, JP, DL, 60th Rifles (d 1 May 1956), of Penleigh Ho, Westbury, Wilts, er s of Lt-Col Guy Newcomen Atkinson, of Cangort, King's Co, and dsp 10 June 1961

6 Marion Frances; b 27 July 1887; d unm 6 Sept 1969

The 6th BARON's bro,

SAMUEL JOHN BEST, 7th Baron Wynford; b 24 June 1874; Lt RNVR; m 1st 26 Aug 1914 Evelyn Mary Aylmer (d 28 March 1929), 2nd dau of Maj-Gen Sir Edward Sinclair May, KCB, CMG, RA; m 2nd 5 June 1930 Marguerite Jane (d 28 March 1966), widow of William Kenneth Allies and dau of Charles Pratt, and d 29 Aug 1943, leaving by his 1st w:

1 ROBERT SAMUEL BEST, 8th and present Baron Wynford

2 John Philip; b 14 March 1919; Sub-Lt RN WW II; presumed ka 16 Aug 1940

3 +Patrick George Matthew [The Hon Patrick Best, Monk's House, Durford Wood, Petersfield, Hants]; b 5 Oct 1923; educ Wellington; Lt RNVR WW II; chm/md Wiggins Teape Gp; dir BAT Industries, RHM; Past Master Ironmongers' Co; FRSA; Offr Order Crown Belgium 1980; m 29 March 1947 *Heather Elizabeth, yr dau of Hamilton Gardner, of S Kensington, and has had:

   (1) +Christopher John Patrick [Christopher Best Esq, 27 Warwick Rd, London N11 2SB]; b 20 Dec 1948; educ privately; m 1st 1973 (divorce 1977) Anna Marion Richmond Rowe, only dau of David Rowe Mitchell; m 2nd 1977 *Margherita Antonietta, dau of Alberto Pietro Toninato, and by her has:

      1a *Francesca Victoria; b 1984

   (2) Michael Hamilton; b 23 May 1951; d 28 June 1952

   (3) +David Robert; b 5 May 1953; educ Lancing

   (4) +Philip Edward Fraser; b 15 Jan 1960; m 10 June 1995 *Catherine, yst dau of Claude Legoux, of Lyon

   (1) *Clare Phyllis; b 15 July 1955; m 1992 *Philip A Willatt, yst s of Ian Duncan Willatt, MD, of Lavant, W Sussex

1 Edith Joy Marion; b 14 Aug 1915; m 3 April 1937 Cdr Walpole John Eyre, RN, s of Rev George Frederick Eyre, of West Hill, Lyme Regis, and had:

   (1) *Charles George Samuel; b 6 June 1948; educ Bradfield; m 1971 *Carol Anne Spink and has issue

   (1) Evelyn Joy Ruth; b 4 Sept 1938

1 (cont.) Cdr and the Hon Mrs Eyre also adopted:

   *Elizabeth Mary; b 17 April 1940; m 19– *H Goodwill, of Auckland, NZ

YARBOROUGH

VINCIT · AMOR · PATRIÆ

Arms: Quarterly, 1st and 4th, azure three pelicans argent vulning themselves proper; 2nd and 3rd, gules two belts erect argent decorated with buckles and studs or. **Crest:** A peacock in his pride argent. **Supporters:** Dexter, a bay horse regardant, charged on the body with three antique buckles or; sinister, a water spaniel dog regardant or, charged on the body with three crosses-flory sable. **Motto:** *Vincit amor patriæ* ('Patriotism prevails'). **Creations:** B. (GB) 13 Aug 1794 (of Yarborough) and (UK) 30 Jan 1837 (of Worsley), E. (UK) 30 Jan 1837.

THE 8TH EARL OF YARBOROUGH, **Baron Yarborough**, of Yarborough, Co Lincoln, and **Baron Worsley**, of Appuldurcombe, IoW (Charles John Pelham) [The Rt Hon The Earl of Yarborough, Brocklesby Park, Habrough, S Humberside DN37 8PL]; *b* 5 Nov 1963; *s f* 1991; *educ* Eton and Bristol U; *m* 26 Jan 1990 *Anna-Karin, dau of George Zecevic, of Chelsea, and has:

1 +GEORGE JOHN SACKVILLE, *Lord Worsley*; *b* 9 Aug 1990

2 +William Charles John Walter; *b* 28 Dec 1991

3 +James Marcus; *b* 8 March 1994

1 *Margaret Ann Emily; *b* 30 Jan 1997

Lineage: Sir WILLIAM PELHAM, of Laughton, E Sussex (*see* CHICHESTER, E); had by his 2nd w Mary Sandys:

Sir WILLIAM PELHAM; *b c* 1530; Capt Pioneers Siege of Leith 1560 in the English army sent to assist the Scots against the French; cmded Pioneers Havre Nov 1562; sent to help French Huguenots under Adml Coligny Feb 1562/3; at taking of Caen, Normandy, late winter 1562/3; Lt-Gen Ordnance; Envoy Netherlands 1578; on mil service Ireland 1579–80, being particularly involved in reduction of Munster; ktd 1579; Ld Justice Ireland *ad interim* Oct 1579–Sept 1580 with authority of Ld Deputy; Marshal of army in Netherlands *c* 1586; *m* 1st Eleanor (*d* 1574), dau of 5th Earl of Westmorland (*see* ABERGAVENNY, M); *m* 2nd Dorothy, dau of Anthony Catesby, of Whiston, Northants, and widow of Sir William Dormer (*see* DORMER, B), and *d* 24 Nov 1587, leaving by her a s (Peregrine) and dau (Ann) and by his 1st w:

Sir WILLIAM PELHAM, of Brocklesby, Lincs; *m* Anne, est dau of 2nd Baron Willoughby of Parham (*see* WILLOUGHBY DE ERESBY, B), and had an est s:

Sir WILLIAM PELHAM, of Brocklesby; *m* Frances, dau of 1st Viscount Conway of Conway Castle (*see* HERTFORD, M, preliminary remarks), and had, with at least two daus (Anne, *m* 1654, as his 3rd w, Sir George Wynne, 1st Bt of the Dec 1660 cr; Elizabeth, *m* as his 1st w her er sister's stepson Sir Edmund Winn, 2nd Bt; *see* SAINT OSWALD, B), an est surv s:

CHARLES PELHAM, of Brocklesby; *m* 1st Anne, dau of Sir Edward Hussey, 1st Bt, of Honington, Hunts, by whom he had no surv issue; *m* 2nd his distant cousin Elizabeth (*dsp*), dau of Sir Thomas Pelham, 2nd Bt (*see* CHICHESTER, E); *m* 3rd Elizabeth, dau of Michael Wharton, of Beverley, Yorks, and sis and coheir of Sir Michael Wharton, and by her had, with two yr sons and four daus:

1 Charles, of Brocklesby; *b c* 1679; *m* twice and *dsps* 6 Feb 1763, leaving his estates to his gn Charles

1 MARY Pelham; *m* Francis ANDERSON, of Manby, Lincs, gggs of Sir Edmund Anderson, Ld Ch Justice Court Common Pleas 23 years *temp* ELIZABETH I, and had an est s:

(1) Francis, of Manby; *b c* 1711; *m* Eleanor (*m* 2nd 5 May 1768 Robert Vyner, MP, of Gautby), dau of Thomas/William Carter and sis of Rev Robert Carter-Thelwall, of Kinmel and Bathavern, Denbighs, and *d* 23 Oct 1758, having had:

   1a CHARLES, **1st Baron**

   2a Francis Evelyn; Lt-Col; *m* Caroline (*d* 18 June 1823), dau of Gen James Johnston

   1a Frances Maria; *d* 1761

   2a Harriott; *m* Paul Moss

FRANCIS ANDERSON's er s,

  CHARLES ANDERSON later PELHAM (1763 under terms of will of great-uncle Charles Pelham on inheriting latter's estates), **1st Baron Yarbor-**

ough, of Yarborough, Lincs (GB), so *cr* 13 Aug 1794; *b* 3 Feb 1748/9; *educ* Eton; MFH Brocklesby 1763–1816, MP (Whig) Beverley 1768–74 and (Whig then Pittite) Lincs 1774–94, Sheriff Lincs 1771, Recorder Grimsby 1786, FRS 1777, DCL Oxon 1793, FSA 1796; *m* 21 July 1770 Sophia (*d* 25 Jan 1786 aged 33), only dau and heiress of George Aufrère, MP, of Chelsea, and *d* 22 Sept 1823, having had:

1 CHARLES, **1st Earl**

2 George; *b* 15 Sept 1785; *d unm* 1835

1 Sophia; *m* 1802 Dudley Long North (*see* GUILFORD, E), of Glemham Hall, Suffolk

2 Caroline; *m* 12 Oct 1797 Robert Cary Elwes (*d* 1852), of Roxby and Brigg, Lincs, Great Billing, Northants, and Egton, Yorks, and *d* July 1812, leaving issue

3 Maria Charlotte; *m* 1804 William Tennant, of Aston Hall, and *d* 1840, leaving issue

4 Arabella; *m* 1802 Thomas Fieschi Heneage, 2nd s of George Fieschi Heneage, of Hainton, Lincs (*see* 1967 edn HENEAGE, B), and *d* 16 May 1871

5 Georgiana Anne; *m* 14 Aug 1811 Francis John Bateman Dashwood, of Well, Lincs, and *dsp* his widow 15 Sept 1861

The 1st BARON's est s,

  CHARLES ANDERSON-PELHAM, **1st Earl of Yarborough** so *cr* 30 Jan 1837, as also BARON WORSLEY, of Appuldurcombe, in the Isle of Wight (both UK); *b* 8 Aug 1781; *educ* Eton and Trin Coll Cambridge (MA 1801); MP (Whig) Gt Grimsby 1803–07 and Lincs 1807–23, MFH Brocklesby 1816–46, Recorder: Gt Grimsby 1823–32 and Newport IoW 1825–32, Provincial Grand Master IoW Freemasons 1826–46, Lt-Col N Lincs Yeo Regt 1831, V-Adml IoW and Hants 1831, Cdre RYS; *m* 11 Aug 1806 Henrietta Anna Maria Charlotte (*b* 24 April 1788; *d* 30 June 1813), 2nd dau of Hon John Bridgeman Simpson (*see* BRADFORD, E) and heiress to her maternal unc Sir Richard Worsley, Bt, and *d* 5 Sept 1846, leaving:

1 CHARLES ANDERSON WORSLEY, **2nd Earl**

2 Dudley Worsley; *b* 20 April 1812; Capt RN; *m* 15 Oct 1839 Madalina, 2nd dau of Adml Sir John Gordon Sinclair, 8th Bt (*see* SINCLAIR-LOCKHART, Bt), and *d* 13 April 1851, leaving:

  (1) Edith Charlotte; *m* 10 Aug 1875 Capt Gilbert Joshua Smith and *d* 26 March 1936, leaving issue (*see* SPENCER-SMITH, Bt)

1 Charlotte, VA; *m* 19 Nov 1831 Sir Joseph William Copley, 4th and last Bt (*d* 3 Jan 1883; *see* 1883 edn), and *d* 10 Aug 1875

The 1st EARL's er s,

  CHARLES ANDERSON WORSLEY ANDERSON-PELHAM, **2nd Earl of Yarborough**; *b* 12 April 1809; *educ* Eton; MP (Whig) Newtown IOW 1830–31, Lincs 1831–32 and N Lincs 1832–46, Capt N Lincs Yeo 1831, MFH Brocklesby 1846–62, Provincial Grand Master Lincs Freemasons 1949–62, V-Adml Lincs 1854–62, Ld Lt 1857–62, High Steward Gt Grimsby; it is after him that the term 'Yarborough' is named, a Yarborough in bridge being a hand with no honours (*i.e.*, knave, queen, king or ace); in the 2nd Earl's day bridge had not been invented but whist, bridge's ancestor, was popular and the odds of being dealt a 'Yarborough' are in any case identical, at 1,827–1, whichever game is played; the 2nd Earl, however, frequently found gamblers foolish enough to take his offered odds of 1,000–1 against an honourless hand turning up; *m* 19 Dec 1831 Maria Adelaide (*m* 2nd 7 Aug 1869 1st Viscount Oxenbridge of Burton (*see* 1898 edn); *d* 24 Dec 1897), dau of 3rd Viscount Hawarden (*qv*), and *d* 7 Jan 1862, leaving:

1 CHARLES, **3rd Earl**

2 Evelyn Cornwallis, JP (Hants and Lincs), DL (Hants); *b* 16 Sept 1851; *m* 24 Oct 1872 Harriett Frances (*d* 13 July 1813), yst dau of Rev George Hutton, Rector Gate Burton, Lincs, and *d* 6 March 1908, leaving, with two other daus:

  (1) Cecil Henry, OBE (1919); *b* 25 Jan 1874; Capt and Hon Maj Lincs and Northants Yeo, formerly 12th Lancers, Boer War 1899–1901, WW I, Dep Assist Dir Remounts Eastern Cmnd 1931–38, Hon Sec MFH Assoc 1926; *m* 12 Nov 1902 Georgina, OBE (1920) (*d* 20 Dec 1960), 2nd dau of 1st Baron Holmpatrick (*qv*), and *dsp* 14 Nov 1945

  (2) Charles Cornwallis ANDERSON-PELHAM later ANDERSON-PELHAM-WELBY (roy licence 16 April 1937), CVO (1945); *b* 30 Sept 1876; Lt Leics Yeo, Lt 11th Hus (SR) and T/Capt RFA WW I, Order Star Romania; *d unm* 5 Oct 1959

  (3) Reginald Evelyn ANDERSON-PELHAM later WELBY-PELHAM (dropped ANDERSON by deed poll, added WELBY by roy licence Sept 1960), JP (Beds); *b* 29 Nov 1883; *educ* Haileybury; served E Africa WW I, Colonial Service 1916–31; *m* 1st 21 Nov 1921 Diana Marian (*d* 21 June 1951), dau of William Frederick Lee, of Grove Hall, Knottingley, Yorks; *m* 2nd 22 Nov 1951 Sylvia Augusta, 6th dau of Sir John Ralph Starkey, 1st Bt (*qv*), and widow of Capt Eustace Ruffel Drake Long, CBE, RN, and *dsp* 19 March 1965

  (4) Alfred Ronald, OBE (1918); *b* 7 June 1880; Capt RFA WW I; *d* 27 Jan 1928

  (1) Adelaide Muriel; *b* 25 April 1878; *m* 12 Dec 1906 William Francis Henry Lyon, JP (*d* 30 Dec 1925), of Goring Hall, Worthing, and *d* 25 Aug 1945

  (2) Eleanor Blanche; *b* 10 Jan 1885; *m* 12 Feb 1907 Capt Nugent St Clair Allfrey, Queen's Bays (*d* 5 Aug 1939), yr s of Goodrich Holmsdale Allfrey, JP, of Wokefield Park, Berks, and *dsp* 6 May 1941

1 Sophia Adelaide Theodosia; *m* 6 Dec 1862 14th Earl of Eglinton and (2nd Earl of) Winton (*qv*) and *d* 21 Sept 1886, leaving issue

The 2nd EARL's er s,

  CHARLES ANDERSON-PELHAM, **3rd Earl of Yarborough**; *b* 14 Jan 1835; *educ* Eton; Capt Roy N Lincs Militia 1853–58 and Denbighs Yeo 1859, MP (Lib) Gt Grimsby 1857–62, Lt-Col 1st Bn Lincs Rifle Vols 1860, MFH Brocklesby 1862–75; *m* 3 Aug 1858 Victoria Alexandrina, MFH Brocklesby 1875–80 (*m* 2nd 16 July 1881 John Maunsell Richardson, DL, MP, of Edmondthorpe Hall, Oakham, Rutland, winner Grand National 1873 and 1874 (*d* 22 Jan 1912), and *d* 7 March 1927, leaving further issue), 4th dau of 2nd Earl of Listowel (*qv*), and *d* 6 Feb 1875, having had, with another dau (*d* an infant):

1 CHARLES ALFRED WORSLEY, **4th Earl**

2 Victor Ralph ANDERSON-PELHAM later PELHAM (roy licence 26 Oct 1905); *b* 30 Jan 1866; Lt 9th Lancers and Capt Middx Yeo Cav; *m* 1893 Gertrude Emma (*dsp* 22 March 1911), dau of Charles Gordon Adams, and *d* 5 July 1927

3 Henry Cornwallis ANDERSON-PELHAM later PELHAM (roy licence 26 Oct 1905); *b* 31 Aug 1868; *m* 16 July 1892 Edith Katharine (*d* 12 June 1966 aged 94),

only dau of Col William Arthur Roberts, RHA, Ch Constable Met Police, and *d* 5 Dec 1924, leaving:

(1) Harry Francis; *b* 27 May 1905; *educ* Eton; F/Lt RAFVR WW II; *d* 19–

(1) Esmé Marcia Rose; *b* 9 June 1893; *m* 12 Aug 1914 William Laidlaw (*d* 7 Feb 1959), s of John Laidlaw, of Kippilaw, St Boswells, Roxburghs, and *d* 19–, leaving issue

(2) Marjorie Edith; *b* 23 May 1897; *m* 28 April 1919 Henry George Dacres Dixon (*d* 23 Jan 1947), s of George Gough Dixon, of Greenfield, Watlington, Oxon, and had:

1a *Michael George Dacres; *b* 1922; Capt KRRC WW II (wounded and invalided out); *m* 1st 1946 (*divorce* 1960) Evelyn Nancy, dau of Maj (William) Bertram Bell, 12th Lancers, and has:

1b *Henry George; *b* 1948

1b *Annabel Jane; *b* 1954

1a (cont.) Michael Dixon *m* 2nd 1960 Azneve, dau of Martin Takajian, of Long Island, NY; *m* 3rd 1983 *Trudy, dau of Irving Stern, of Cleveland, Ohio

2a *Robin Charles Dacres; *b* 1926; late Lt KRRC; *m* 1956 *Sarah Manners Baron and has:

1b *Charles Richard; *b* 1960; *m* 1985 *Angela Dickinson

1b *Anna Mary; *b* 1957; *m* 1980 *Mark Lilly

2b *Sophie (twin); *b* 1957; *m* 1988 *Richard T Maylam, s of Thomas Maylam, of Tonbridge, Kent

4 Dudley Roger Hugh ANDERSON-PELHAM later PELHAM (roy licence 26 Oct 1905), DSO, JP, DL Lincs; *b* 5 July 1872; Maj 10th Hus, Boer War 1899–02 (despatches) and WW I (despatches, Brig Maj 1916), High Sheriff Lincs 1938; *m* 9 Feb 1907 Evelyn Elizabeth (*d* 18 April 1973), yst dau of Montagu Richard Waldo-Sibthorp, JP, DL, and *dsp* 13 Sept 1953

1 Gertrude Augusta; *b* 11 May 1861; *m* 5 June 1882 Sir Francis Edmund George Astley-Corbett, 4th Bt (*d* 5 Feb 1939; *see* 1949 edn), of Elsham Hall, Lincs, and *d* 6 July 1920, leaving issue

The 3rd EARL's est s,

CHARLES ALFRED WORSLEY ANDERSON-PELHAM later PELHAM (roy licence 26 Oct 1905), **4th Earl of Yarborough**, KG (1935), PC (22 Nov 1890); *b* 11 June 1859; *educ* Eton and Trin Coll Cambridge (BA 1881, MA 1884); sat as Lib initially but became Conservative over Irish Home Rule, MFH Brocklesby 1880–1936, FSA 1888, V-Adml Lincs 1883, Capt Gentlemen-at-Arms 1890–92, Provincial Grand Master Lincs Freemasons 1895–1936, Lt-Col cmdg Lincs Yeo 1901–07, Ld Lt 1921–36 and Co Alderman Lindsey Div, High Steward Gt Grimsby, Hon Col 3rd Bn Lincs Regt 1922–36, KJStJ, Pres Roy Ag Soc; *m* 5 Aug 1886 Marcia Amelia Mary, OBE (1920) (*b* 18 Oct 1863; LJStJ, *s* her *f* 8 June 1892 as BARONESS CONYERS (*see* below, also DARCY DE KNAYTH, B) in her own right on the termination of the abeyance in that title between her and her only surv sis, became also BARONESS FAUCONBERG (*see* below) in her own right 29 Sept 1903 on termination in her favour of that title's abeyance; she brought to her husb's family 153 armorial quarterings and all her descendants, whether male or female, are in remainder to the two Baronies of Conyers and Fauconberg, so that the + sign against females and their issue from now on in this article does not signify their being in remainder to the Earldom of Yarborough or the Baronies of Yarborough and Worsley; *d* 17 Nov 1926), and *d* 12 July 1936, having had:

1 Charles Sackville, *Lord Worsley*; *b* 14 Aug 1887; *educ* Eton and RMC Sandhurst; 2nd Lt RHG 1908, Extra ADC to Gen Sir Douglas Haig (*see* HAIG, E) Aldershot 1912–13, Lt RHG WW I; *m* 31 Jan 1911 Hon Alexandra Mary Freesia Vivian, CBE (1954, OBE 1945) (*d* 21 Sept 1963), yst dau of 3rd Baron Vivian (*qv*), and was *ka* Zandvoorde, Belgium, 30 Oct 1914

2 SACKVILLE GEORGE ANDERSON-PELHAM later PELHAM, **5th Earl of Yarborough**, also 14th LORD (Baron) CONYERS and 7th LORD (Baron) FAUCONBERG, as both of which latter *s* mother 17 Nov 1926 (though chose to be styled Lord Conyers rather than Lord Worsley or Lord Fauconberg from then till he *s* to the Earldom 1936), MC, DL (Lincs); *b* 17 Dec 1888; *educ* Eton and Trin Coll Cambridge; 2nd Lt 11th Hus 1910, Lt 1914, Capt 1916, WW I (wounded, despatches), ret 1919, Maj Notts Yeo 1926, Lt-Col cmdg Notts Yeo (TA) 1936–40, served WW II, MFH Brocklesby 1936–48; *m* 23 Sept 1919 Nancye (*d* 27 Oct 1977), yst dau of Alfred Brocklehurst, of The Spinney, Melton Mowbray, and n of 1st and last Baron Ranksborough (*see* 1921 edn), and *dspm* 7 Feb 1948, when the Baronies of Fauconberg and Conyers fell into abeyance between his two daus:

(1) +Diana Mary [The Lady Diana Miller, c/o Zimbank, Box 2270, Harare, Zimbabwe]; *b* 5 July 1920; SRN 1945; *m* 15 Nov 1952 Robert Miller (*d* 1990 in a car crash in Zimbabwe), s of Capt Gordon Molineux Miller, of Rio, Cavendish, Suffolk, and has:

1a +Marcia Anne (adopted by Maj Michael and Lady Wendy Lycett (*see* below) and renamed Anthea Theresa LYCETT; she retains her right of *s* to the baronies); *b* 21 June 1954

2a +Beatrix Diana Miller [Mrs Simon Armstrong, Box 49, Gilgil, Kenya]; *b* 23 Aug 1955; *m* 1991 *Simon William Jones Armstrong, only s of Christopher Wyborne Armstrong, OBE, of Kwetu Farm, Gilgil, Kenya

(2) +(June) Wendy Pelham [The Lady Wendy Lycett, West Grange, Scots Gap, Morpeth, Northumberland NE61 4EQ]; *b* 6 June 1924; 3rd Offr WRNS WW II, Jt MFH Tynedale 1974–77; *m* 12 Oct 1959 *Maj Michael Hildesley Lycett Lycett, CBE, late Roy Scots Greys, s of Rev Norman Lycett, of E Dean, Sussex, by Ruth Edith, yst dau of Jonas Lindow Burns-Lindow, JP, DL, of Irton Hall, Holmbrook, Cumberland, and has adopted her niece (*see* above)

3 D'Arcy Francis; *b* 15, *d* 19 Feb 1892

4 MARCUS HERBERT ANDERSON-PELHAM later PELHAM, **6th Earl of Yarborough**, JP, DL (both Lincs 1950); *b* 30 June 1893; *educ* Eton and Trin Coll Cambridge (BA 1914); Capt Res of Offrs, Lt 1st Life Gds WWs I and II; *m* 3 Sept 1919 Hon Pamela Douglas-Pennant (*d* 31 Jan 1968), 2nd dau of 3rd Baron Penrhyn (*qv*), and *d* 2 Dec 1966, leaving:

(1) JOHN EDWARD, **7th Earl**

(1) Janet Marcia Rose; *b* 17 Oct 1923; *m* 20 March 1948 *John Charles HARPER later DOUGLAS PENNANT (roy licence 1950 with arms), LLB [John Douglas Pennant Esq, Penrhyn, Bangor, Gwynedd LL57 4HN], only s of Sir Charles Henry Harper, KBE, CMG, and *d* 28 Nov 1997 leaving:

1a +Richard Charles; *b* 19 Feb 1955; *educ* Stanbridge Earls Sch; *m* 1978 *Georgia, yst dau of Theodorus Giorgiou, of Limassol, Cyprus, and has issue

2a +Edmond Hugh; *b* 2 May 1960; *educ* U of Wales, Bangor (BA, MPhil)

The 6th EARL's only s,

JOHN EDWARD PELHAM, **7th Earl of Yarborough**, JP (Lincs 1965), DL (Lincs 1956); *b* 2 June 1920; *educ* Eton and Trin Coll Cambridge (BA 1940); Maj Gren Gds WW II, V-Lt Lincs 1964–91, High Sheriff 1964, Hon Col 440 Light AD Regt RAC (TA) 1965–69, Hon Col Humber Regt RA T&AVR 1969–71, Dep Hon Col 2nd Bn Yorks Vols 1971–72, Pres: Midland Area Br Legion 1959–60, E Midland Area Br Legion 1960–62; Nat Exec Cncl Br Legion 1962–73, Patron E Midlands Area 1974–91; *m* 12 Dec 1957 *(Florence) Ann Petronel [The Rt Hon Ann Countess of Yarborough, Flat 6, St Albans Mansions, Kensington Court Place, London W8 5QH], 3rd dau of John Herbert Upton, JP, of Ingmire Hall, Yorks, and Lew House, Oxon, and formerly w of Lt Charles John Riddell Duffin, Scots Gds, and *d* 1991, leaving:

1 CHARLES JOHN PELHAM, **8th and present Earl of Yarborough**

1 +Sophia [The Lady Sophia Kinmont, Manor Farmhouse, Rodmarton, Glos GL7 6PE]; *b* 15 Oct 1958; *m* 24 Sept 1983 *(Patrick William) John Kinmont, s of Dr Patrick Kinmont, of Carlton Ashes House, Hough-on-the-Hill, Lincs

2 +Arabella [The Lady Arabella Casey, Park Wood Farm, Leighterton, Glos GL8 8UQ]; *b* 20 Jan 1960; *m* 2 June 1984 *Christopher Casey, only s of Ronald Casey, of Pecklands Farm, Stansted, Kent, and has:

(1) Thomas Edward Ronald; *b* 7 Sept 1993; *d* 11 Nov 1995

(1) +Laura Alexandra; *b* 1986

(2) +Emma Olivia; *b* 1988

3 +Vanessa Petronel [The Lady Vanessa Brown, Flat 7, 56 Redcliffe Sq, London SW10 9HQ]; *b* 21 Sept 1961; *m* 1987 (*divorce* 1994) Timothy Colin Brown, only s of Peter Brindley Brown

Lineage (of Faucomberge/Fauconberg(e)): A person known in the Latin of the time as *Franco homo Drogonis* ('Drogo's freeman') seems to have been related to a family who were feudal Lds of Fauquembergue in Normandy; this person held Rise and Catfoss, Yorks (now Humberside), from Drogo or Dreue de Bevrere the Fleming at the time of the Domesday Survey (1085–86); he was an ancestor of the later Faucomberges and his successor was:

ROBERT de FAUCOMBERGE, of Rise and Catfoss; *m* Agnes, Ldy of Appleton, fndr Nunkeeling Priory, dau of Osbern d'Arches, and had:

PIERS de FAUCOMBERGE; *m* Beatrice — and had:

WALTER de FAUCOMBERGE, of Rise, Withernwick and Catwick; *m* Agnes, Ldy of Whitton and Risby, Lincs, dau and coheir of Simon Fitz Simon, and had:

Sir PIERS de FAUCOMBERGE, of Rise and Withernwick; living April 1230; *m* 1st, as her 2nd husb, Margaret (*m* 1st Hugh de Bolebek), dau of Richard de M(o)untfichet, of Stansted, Essex, and had a s; *m* 2nd Ellen and had by her a s (Piers de Faucumberge [*sic*]); his s by his 1st w:

Sir WALTER de FAUCOMBERGE, 1st LORD (Baron) FAUCOMBERGE (E), so *cr* by writ of summons to Parl (according to later doctrine) 24 June 1295, of Rise and Withernwick; accompanied Simon de Montfort, notional 6th Earl of Leicester of the equally notional 1107(?) *cr* (*see* LEICESTER, E, preliminary remarks) when latter HENRY III's Vicegerent in Gascony 1254, later rebelled with Simon and thereby forfeited his estates, though they were restored to him 1268; *m* by Nov 1242(?) Agnes (*d* by 25 May 1280?), sis and coheir of Sir Piers de Brus, of Skelton and Danby, Cleveland, and *d* 1–2 Nov 1304, leaving, with an er s:

WALTER de FAUCOMBERGE, 2nd LORD (Baron) FAUCOMBERGE; *b c* 1254; *m* 1st Isabel, sis of 1st Lord (Baron) De Ros (*qv*) of Helmsley; *m* 2nd Alice (*m* 2nd, probably as his 2nd w, by 11 Feb 1318/9 Sir Ralph de Bulmer, notional 1st and last Lord (Baron) Bulmer; *d* 22 June 1356), dau of Sir John de Killingholm, of Boythorpe, Yorks, and *d* 31 Dec 1318, leaving by his 1st w:

1 Walter (Sir); ktd 1306; *m* Anastase (*d* in or after 1315), dau of 1st Lord (Baron) Nevill(e) (of Raby) (*see* ABERGAVENNY, M), and *dsp* & *vp*, *k* at the Scots victory over the English of Bannockburn 24 June 1314

2 JOHN de FAUCOMBERGE, 3rd LORD (Baron) FAUCOMBERGE; *b* by 24 June 1290; Escheator and Sheriff Yorks 1341–42, Keeper Berwick-on-Tweed 1342; *m* his step sister Ivod or Eve, dau of Sir Ralph de Bulmer, notional 1st and last Lord (Baron) Bulmer, by his 1st w, and *d* 17/18 Sept 1349, leaving a s and heir:

(1) WALTER (de) FAUCOMBERG(E), 4th LORD (Baron) FAUCOMBERGE; *b c* 1319; *m* 1st *c* Dec 1330 Maud (*d* by 28 Sept 1359), sis and coheir of William de Pateshulle, of Bletsoe and Keysoe, Beds, Rothersthorpe, Heyford and Pattishall, Northants, N Crawley, Bucks, and Firsby, Lincs; *m* 2nd by 15 Jan 1359/60 Isabel (*dsp* 19 May 1401), dau of Sir Roger Bigod, of Settrington, Yorks, and widow of Sir Roger de Burton, and *d* 29 Sept 1362, leaving by his 1st w a s and heir:

1a Sir THOMAS FAUCOMBERGE, 5th LORD (Baron) FAUCOMBERGE, of Skelton, Yorks; *b* 20 July 1345; joined French in Hundred Years War *c* 1376 and was imprisoned in Gloucester Castle 1378–91, thereafter became allegedly an imbecile though when examined by the King and Cncl *c* 1406 appeared of sound mind; *m* 1st by 17 Nov 1366 Constance (*d* May or June 1402), dau and heir of John de Felton, of Edlingham, Northumberland, and had:

1b John (Sir); participated in the uprising of 1405 (*see* NORTHUMBERLAND, D); *m* as her 2nd husb Joan (*m* 3rd by 28 July 1408 her 2nd husb's stepmother's bro Sir Thomas (II) Brounflete, s of Sir Thomas (I) Brounflete (*see* below); *d* 6/7 Nov 1438), dau of Sir Robert Conyers, of Ormesby, Yorks, and widow of Robert del Bowes (*d* by 22 Dec 1399), and *dsp* & *vp* 20 July 1405, being beheaded for treason

1a (cont.) The 5th LORD (Baron) FAUCOMBERGE *m* 2nd Joan (*d* 4 March 1408/9), dau of Sir Thomas (I) Brounflete, of Londesborough and Weighton, Yorks, and *dspms* 9 Sept 1407, leaving by her:

2b JOAN/ALICE Faucomberge, according to later doctrine BARONESS FAUCOMBERGE in her own right; *b* 18 Oct 1406; an imbecile; *m* 1st by 28 April 1422 Sir William NEVILL(E) (considered according to later legal doctrine 6th LORD (Baron) FAUCOMBERGE or FAUCONBERGE in right of his w, in addition 1st and last EARL OF KENT of the 1461 *cr*; *dspml* 9

Jan 1462/63, when the Earldom expired), 8th s of 1st Earl of Westmorland of the 1397 *cr* (*see* ABERGAVENNY, M), and had:

1c Joan; *b c* 1433; *m* by 1463 Sir Edward Bethom/Bethum (*dsp* before his w 22 Feb 1472), of Beetham and Hazleslack, Westmorland, and *dsp* & *vm*

2c Elizabeth; *b c* 1435; *m* by 1463, as his 1st w, Sir Richard Strangways (*d* 13 April 1488), of W Harlsey, Yorks, Hadstone, Northumberland, and Eckington, Derbys, and had:

1d James (Sir); *b c* 1460; a coheir to his grandmother; living 17 May 1491

3c Alice; *b c* 1437; *m* by 1463 John CONYERS (*dvp* 26 July 1469, *k* Battle of Edgcot, nr Banbury, Oxon (victory of pro-Earl of Warwick ('the Kingmaker') faction (*see* ABERGAVENNY, M) over pro-Woodville faction among Yorkists in Wars of Roses), of Hornby, Yorks, s of Sir John Conyers, KG (*see* below), and had:

1d WILLIAM CONYERS, 1st BARON CONYERS, a coheir to his grandmother, for whom *see* further below

2b (cont.) JOAN Countess of Kent *m* 2nd by 14 March 1462/3 John Berwyke and *d* 11 Dec 1490, when according to later doctrine the Barony of Faucomberge fell into abeyance between her gs Sir James Strangways and the 1st BARON CONYERS and the representation of the latter devolved with the Barony of Conyers (*see* below).

Lineage (of Conyers): (*Note*: This section should be studied in conjunction with the article DARCY DE KNAYTH, B, which it complements.) Sir HUMPHREY CONYERS; gave lands to Rievaulx Abbey, Yorks; had:

Sir JOHN CONYERS; *d* 1299, leaving a 2nd s:

Sir ROGER CONYERS, of Sockburne; *d* 1323, leaving:

Sir JOHN CONYERS, of Sockburne; *m* by March 1388/9, as her 2nd husb, Elizabeth (*m* 1st Sir William Place and by him had issue), 3rd and yst dau and coheir of 1st Lord (Baron) Aton (*cr* according to later doctrine 1359; the Barony became abeyant between representatives of his three daus and coheirs, also according to a later doctrine, on his death *c* March 1388/9), and *d* by 6 March 1395/6, leaving:

ROBERT CONYERS; feudal Ld of Sockburne; living 1437; *m* Isabel, dau and coheir of William Pert, and had, with three er sons:

Sir JOHN CONYERS, of Hornby, Yorks, in right of his w Margaret, dau and heiress of Anthony St Quinton, of Hornby; had:

CHRISTOPHER CONYERS, of Hornby; *m* Ellene, dau and coheir of — Rylestone (*d* 1443), and had, with a yr s (Sir William, of Marske, Yorks, identified by some historians (others prefer his er bro Sir John) with 'Robin of Redesdale', leader 1469 of an insurrection fomented by the 1st and last Earl of Warwick ('Warwick the Kingmaker') of the March 1449/50 *cr* (*see* ABERGAVENNY, M) against EDWARD IV, in particular his favourites and in-laws the Woodvilles, *d* 1495):

Sir JOHN CONYERS, KG (1483), of Hornby; either he or his bro as 'Robin of Redesdale' collected an army of Nevill(e) retainers and supporters in the North of England and in the summer of 1469 marched south, both to support the Earl of Warwick ('the Kingmaker') and to cut off EDWARD IV from London; at Edgecot (*see* above) he and his forces captured the 1st Earl of Pembroke of the 1468 *cr* (*see* POWIS, E) and his brother Sir Richard Herbert, both of whom were presently beheaded; Sir John was also one of the Lancastrian cdrs at Barnet (Yorkist victory) 14 April 1471, where he fought under the defeated Earl of Warwick; *m* by 20 Nov 1431 Margery (*b* posthumously 1 Sept 1418; *d* 20 March 1468/9–20 April 1469), yr dau and coheir of 6th Lord Darcy (*see* DARCY DE KNAYTH, B), and *d* 14 March 1489/90, leaving:

JOHN CONYERS; *m* Alice, dau and coheir of 1st and last Earl of Kent (*see* above) by Joan, dau of 5th Baron Faucomberge, and had, with an er s (John, *d* after 4 July 1472) and a dau (Anne, *m* 3rd Lord (Baron) Lumley and had issue; *see* SCARBROUGH, E):

WILLIAM CONYERS, 1st LORD (Baron) CONYERS (E), so *cr* by writ of summons to Parl (according to later doctrine) 17 Oct 1509, though styled Lord Conyers 1506–07; *b* 21 Dec 1468; ktd 1497; Constable Richmond Castle 1509, fought at English victory over Scots of Flodden 1513; *m* 1st Mary, dau of 5th Lord (Baron) Scrope (of Bolton) by his 1st w Joan Fitzhugh; *m* 2nd, as her 1st husb, Anne (*m* 2nd as his 1st w Anthony Saltmarsh, of Hornby), dau of 3rd Earl of Westmorland of the 1397 *cr* (*see* ABERGAVENNY, M), and *d* by 14 April 1524, leaving (whether by 1st or 2nd w is unclear):

CHRISTOPHER CONYERS, 2nd LORD (Baron) CONYERS; ktd 1523; *m* 28 Sept 1515 Anne (*d* 16 Dec 1547–21 April 1548), dau of 8th Lord (Baron) Dacre (of Gilsland) (*qv*), and *d* 14 June 1538, leaving:

JOHN CONYERS, 3rd LORD (Baron) CONYERS; *b c* 1524; served Siege of Leith in war against Scots 1544, ktd there, Warden W Marches and Govr Carlisle *temp* EDWARD VI and Warden E Marches and Govr Berwick *temp* MARY; *m* by 28 Oct 1539 Maud, dau of 1st Earl of Cumberland (*see* DE CLIFFORD, B), and *dspms* 30 June 1557, having had, with two sons (*dsp* & *vp*, so that the Barony of Conyers fell into abeyance between the surv daus and subsequently their representatives):

1 Anne; *m* Anthony Kempe, of Slindon, Sussex, and had an only s:

(1) Henry; *dsp*

2 Elizabeth; *m* Thomas Darcy (*d* 6 Nov 1605), Lt Tower of London, 2nd s of Sir Arthur Darcy (*see* DARCY DE KNAYTH, B), and *d* 6 June 1572, leaving:

(1) CONYERS (Sir), 4th LORD (Baron) CONYERS, for whom *see* further below

3 Katherine; *m* John Atherton, of Atherton, Lancs; their issue became extinct on the death *sp* 13 July 1644 of their gdau Anne, w of Sir William Pennyman, 1st and last Bt

4 Margaret; *d* unm, presumably *vp*

The 3rd BARON CONYERS's gs,

Sir CONYERS DARCY, 4th LORD (Baron) CONYERS and 7th LORD (Baron) DARCY DE KNAYTH; *b* 27 Aug 1570; *educ* Caius Coll Cambridge; ktd 1603, confirmed by letters patent 10 Aug 1641 in the Barony of Darcy de Knayth and 11 Aug 1641 in the Barony of Conyers, which a later judgement (1903) decided amounted to a determination of abeyance in both Baronies; in both cases the 1641 letters patent stipulated that the remainder should be to his *heirs male*, rather than remainder to heirs general (*i.e.*, so as to include females in certain circumstances). That is because the later legal doctrine ascribing remainder to heirs general to baronies *cr* by writ of summons (which both Conyers and Darcy originally had been) had not fully evolved in 1641. As it happened, by the death of Lady Prettyman three years later he became sole heir to the Conyers Barony anyway, since all other coheirs or their representatives had died out. The effect of the 1903 decision, however, was to resuscitate the ability of the two titles to descend to heirs general (*i.e.*, including females) and the fact that the Barony of Conyers had been allowed in the late 18th century to a descendant in the female line of its holder in 1641 anticipated that decision; *m c* 1594 Dorothy (*bur* 11 May 1653), dau of Sir Henry Bellasis, 1st Bt, of Newborough, Yorks, and *d* 3 March 1653/4, leaving, with other issue:

1 CONYERS DARCY, 5th LORD (Baron) CONYERS, 8th LORD (Baron) DARCY DE KNAYTH and 1st EARL OF HOLDERNESSE within the parts of the East Riding, Co York (E), so *cr* 5 Dec 1682 (the day before the burial of the last Earl of Holderness [*sic*], otherwise known as Prince Rupert, whose title was of a completely different *cr*, that of 1644); *bapt* 24 June 1598/9; Constable Middleham Castle 1660–71; *m* 14 Oct 1616 Grace (*bur* 4 Jan 1658), only dau and heir of Thomas Rokeby, of Skiers, Yorks, and *d* 14 June 1689, having had, with two er sons, three yr sons and four daus (all *dvp*):

(1) CONYERS DARCY, 6th LORD (Baron) CONYERS, 9TH LORD (Baron) DARCY DE KNAYTH and 2nd EARL OF HOLDERNESSE; *bapt* 3 March 1621/2; *educ* Univ Coll Oxford and Gray's Inn; MP Boroughbridge 1660 and Yorks 1661–79, Capt Prince Rupert's Horse 1667, Constable Middleham Castle 1671; called up to Ho of Lds 1 Nov 1680 in his f's junior Barony of Conyers before latter's promotion to an Earldom, a unique instance of a summons *vp* of an heir apparent of a baron holding no higher peerage title; *m* 1st 14 May 1645 Lady Catherine Fane (*dsp* and *bur* 30 Aug 1649), dau of 1st Earl of Westmorland (*qv*) of the current *cr*; *m* 2nd 8 Feb 1649/50 Frances (*b c* 1627; *d* 9 April 1670), dau of 1st Earl of Berkshire (*see* SUFFOLK and BERKSHIRE, E); *m* 3rd *c* 1676 Frances (*dsp* and *bur* 5 Jan 1680/1), dau of 2nd Duke of Somerset (*qv*) and widow of (a) 2nd Viscount Molyneux of Maryborough and (b) 4th and last Earl of Southampton (*see* SOUTHAMPTON, B, preliminary remarks); *m* 4th 8 Jan 1684/5 Elizabeth (*b* 1 Jan 1634/5; *dsp* 22 Feb 1689/90), 2nd dau and coheir of 1st and last Baron Frescheville of Staveley and widow of Philip Warwick, and *d* 13 Dec 1692, having had:

1a John; *bapt* 5 Nov 1659; MP Richmond; *m* Bridget Sutton, only dau of 1st Baron Lexington, and *dvp* 6 Jan 1688/9, leaving, with an er s:

1b ROBERT DARCY, 7th LORD (Baron) CONYERS, 10th LORD (Baron) DARCY DE KNAYTH and 3rd EARL OF HOLDERNESSE, PC (Feb 1717/8); *b* 24 Nov 1681; Constable Middleham Castle 1702, Ld Lt N R Yorks 1714–22, 1st Ld Trade (Whig) 1718–19, Ld of Bedchamber 1719–22; *m* 26 May 1715, as her 1st husb, Frederica, Countess of Mertola (Portugal, *cr* 1668) in her own right (*m* 2nd 18 June 1724 19th Lord (Baron) FitzWalter, *qv*), dau and coheir of 3rd Duke of Schomberg by Caroline Elizabeth, an illegitimate dau of Karl Ludwig, the Elector Palatine (himself n of CHARLES I), and *d* 20 Jan 1721/2, leaving, with an er s and one or more yr sons (*dvp*):

1c ROBERT DARCY, 8th LORD (Baron) CONYERS, 11th LORD (Baron) DARCY DE KNAYTH and 4th EARL OF HOLDERNESSE, PC (1751); *b* 17 May 1718; *educ* Westminster and Trin Coll Cambridge; Constable Middleham Castle 1739, Ld Lt N R Yorks 1740–77, a Ld Bedchamber 1741–51, Amb Venice 1744–46, Min The Hague 1749–51, Sec of State for South 1751–54 and North 1754–61, Whig till *c* 1770, in effect Tory thereafter, Ld Warden Cinque Ports 1765–78, Govr to THE PRINCE OF WALES 1771–76; *m* 29 Oct 1743 Mary (*d* 13 Oct 1801), dau of Francis Doublet, of Groenevelt, Memb of States of Holland, and *dspms* 16 May 1778, when the Earldom expired, having had, with two sons (George, *Lord Darcy and Conyers*, *b* Sept 1745, *d* 27 Sept 1747; Thomas, *d* young) and a yr dau (Margaret, *m* Sir Thomas Harrison and had issue; *see* MUSGRAVE of Hartley):

1d AMELIA Darcy, *de jure* BARONESS CONYERS and *de jure* BARONESS DARCY DE KNAYTH according to later legal doctrine, though Amelia herself was unaware she had any right to the latter title; in addition *de jure* Countess of Mertola; *b* 12 Oct 1754; *m* 29 Nov 1773 (eloped with her 2nd husb 13 Dec 1778, *divorce* from her 1st husb May 1779) Francis Godolphin OSBORNE, then styled Marquess of Carmarthen, later 5th Duke of Leeds (*b* 29 Jan 1750/1; For Sec 1783–89; *d* 31 Jan 1799; *see* 1963 edn); *m* 2nd 9 June 1779, as his 1st w, Capt John Byron (f of the poet; *see* BYRON, B) and *d* 27 Jan 1784, leaving by him a dau (Augusta, *b* 1782, Woman of the Bedchamber to QUEEN CHARLOTTE, *m* 17 Aug 1807 her cousin Lt-Col George Leigh, 10th Dragoons, and *d* 18 Oct 1851, having had (with other issue), quite possibly by her half-bro 6th Baron Byron a dau, (Elizabeth) Medora, *b* 15 April 1814, *d* 1849) and by her 1st husb:

1e GEORGE WILLIAM FREDERICK OSBORNE, 10th LORD (Baron) CONYERS, as which recognised 27 April 1798 (having *s* mother 27 Jan 1784 as *de jure* holder of the title), *de jure* 12th LORD (Baron) DARCY DE KNAYTH (though he was not aware of any right to the title) and 6th DUKE OF LEEDS, KG (1827), PC (1827); *b* 21 July 1775 (GEORGE III stood sponsor); Govr Scilly Isles 1801–38, Ld Lt N R Yorks 1802–38, Master Horse 1827–30; *m* 17 Aug 1797 Lady Charlotte Townshend (*b* 16 March 1776; *d* 30 July 1856), dau of 1st Marquess Townshend (*qv*), and *d* 10 July 1838, having had:

1f FRANCIS GODOLPHIN D'ARCY OSBORNE later D'ARCY-OSBORNE (roy licence 6 Aug 1849), 11th LORD (Baron) CONYERS, *de jure* 13th LORD (Baron) DARCY DE KNAYTH and 7th DUKE OF LEEDS; *b* 21 May 1798; *educ* Ch Ch Oxford; Capt 2nd Life Gds 1828, MP (Tory) Helston 1826–30, as a peer voted with Whigs or Libs; *m* 24 April 1828 Louisa Catherine (*d* 8 April 1874), 3rd dau of Richard Caton, merchant at Baltimore, Md., USA (by Mary, dau of Charles Carroll, of Carrollstown, Md.), sis of Marchioness Wellesley (*see* WELLINGTON, D) and Baroness Stafford (*qv*) and widow of Sir Felton Hervey-Bathurst, 1st Bt (*qv*), and *dsp* 4 May 1850, when the Dukedom passed to his cousin (*see* 1963 edn LEEDS, D), but the Conyers Barony and right to the

Barony of Darcy de Knayth and Countship of Mertola devolved upon his sis Charlotte's s (*see below*)

2f Conyers George Thomas William Godolphin; *b c* 1812; *educ* Oxford; *dsp* & *vp* 16 Feb 1831

1f CHARLOTTE MARY ANNE GEORGIANA Osborne; *b* 16 July 1801; *m* 22 June 1826 Walter Sackville LANE-FOX, Gren Gds Offr and MP (*b* 24 March 1797; *d* 18 Aug 1874), 3rd s of James Fox-Lane or Lane-Fox, MP Horsham, of Bramham Park, Yorks, and *d* 17 Jan 1836, leaving, with two daus:

1g SACKVILLE GEORGE LANE-FOX, 12TH LORD (Baron) CONYERS and *de jure* 15th LORD (Baron) DARCY DE KNAYTH (*qv*); *b* 14 Sept 1827; joined army 1854, Lt 87th Foot 1855, fought Sebastopol (medal, clasp), sat as C Ho Lds; *m* 14 Aug 1860 Mary (Ho Lds Privileges Ctee having affirmed 27 July 1903 her late husb's right to the Barony of Darcy de Knayth, she took the style Lady Darcy de Knayth and Conyers; *d* 12 Nov 1921), est dau of Capt Reginald Curteis, 1st Dragoons, of Windmill Hill, Sussex, and *dspms* 24 Aug 1888, when the Baronies of Conyers and Darcy de Knayth fell into abeyance, having had:

1h Sackville Fitzroy Henry; *b* 9 May 1861; *dvp* unm 27 Aug 1879

1h MARCIA AMELIA MARY, BARONESS CONYERS (on termination of abeyance 8 June 1892) and BARONESS FAUCONBERGE; *b* 18 Oct 1863; the Ho of Lds Committee for Privileges declared 23 July 1903 her coheir with her sis, the Countess of Powis, to the Baronies of Fauconberg and Darcy de Knayth, the abeyance of the former being terminated in her favour (and the latter in favour of her yr sis) 29 Sept 1903; *m* 5 Aug 1886 **4th Earl of Yarborough** (*see above*) and had issue

1h VIOLET IDA EVELINE, BARONESS DARCY DE KNAYTH (*qv*)

2g Charles Pierrepoint D'Arcy; *b* 25 Aug 1830; granted 9 July 1859 with his sisters rank of baron's dau/yr s; *m* 22 June 1859 Louisa Emma (*d* 30 Jan 1870), 2nd dau of Thomas Fairfax, of Newton Kyme, Yorks, and *d* 13 Sept 1874, leaving, with another dau:

1h Charlotte Catherine Marcia; *m* 14 May 1884 Charles Joseph Weld-Blundell, JP (*d* 5 Aug 1927), of Ince Blundell, Lancs, and *d* 4 March 1926, leaving:

1i Richard Shirburne; *b* 1887; 2nd Lt 7th Bn Liverpool Regt; *m* 11 Feb 1915 Mary Angela (*m* 2nd 27 Sept 1927 the poet Alfred Noyes), dau of Capt Jasper Graham Mayne, CBE, Ch Constable E Suffolk, and *d* 1 Jan 1916, leaving:

1j +Agnes Mary [Lady Grey, Holmwood House, Elstead, Surrey GU8 6DB]; *b* 2 Dec 1915; *m* 27 Oct 1936 Sir Paul Francis Grey, KCMG, and has issue (*see* GREY, E)

2i Louis Joseph; *b* 1889; Queen's Westminster Rifles; *d* 8 Feb 1919

1i Mary Teresa; *s* jointly with her sister Alice Mary to the Ince Blundell estates on death of her f; *m* 15 Oct 1912 Capt George Frederick MONTAGU later WELD-BLUNDELL (roy licence Nov 1923), RN (*d* 21 Feb 1958), 2nd s of Robert Acheson Cronie Montagu (*see* MANCHESTER, D), and *d* 6 June 1957, leaving:

1j +Frederica Mary Montagu later Weld-Blundell [Mrs Jocelyn Pereira, 20 St Leonards Terrace, London SW3]; *b* 16 Dec 1918; *m* 26 Aug 1966 *Jocelyn Philip Pereira, yst s of Maj-Gen Sir Cecil Edward Pereira, KCB, CMG

2i Alice Mary; *m* 10 Jan 1923 John Joseph Humphrey WELD later WELD-BLUNDELL (roy licence 1923) (*d* 13 June 1960), 4th s of Walter Weld, of Birkdale, Lancs, and *d* 9 Jan 1947, leaving:

1j +Charles Joseph Ignatius [Charles Weld-Blundell Esq, Pinehurst, Tongland, Kirkcudbright DG6 4NA]; *b* 18 Feb 1928; *educ* Stonyhurst; High Sheriff Lancs 1989; *m* 21 Feb 1951 *Veronica Mary, dau of the poet Alfred Noyes (*see above*), and has:

1k +John Joseph Thomas; *b* 20 June 1955; *educ* Stonyhurst

2k +Peter Alfred; *b* Nov 1956; *educ* Stonyhurst

3k +George Edric [George Weld-Blundell Esq, Loud Mythom, Little Bowland Rd, Chipping, Lancs PR3 2TS]; *b* 15 Nov 1967; *educ* Ampleforth and Liverpool U (BSc); *m* 1985 *Buddug, dau of G Selwyn-Lloyd, and has:

1l +Joseph Charles; *b* 1993

1l +Laura Sian; *b* 1987

2l +Philippa Kate; *b* 1989

1k +Mary Alice; *b* 27 Aug 1952

2k +Lucy Ann; *b* 1 Dec 1953

3k +Diana Celia; *b* July 1958; *m* 1990 *Charles E Hothersall, s of H E Hothersall

4k +Fiona Ann [Mrs Robert Armstrong, 20 Balmoral Court, 43–45 Clarence Parade, Southsea, Hants]; *b* 21 July 1962; *m* 1991 *Robert Armstrong, s of Warwick Armstrong, of Southsea

5k +Elizabeth; *b* 14 March 1969

1j +Theresa Mary Katherine [Miss Theresa Weld-Blundell, 10 Archery Steps, St George's Fields, London W2 2YF]; *b* 12 June 1926; Dame of Honour and Devotion SMO Malta

2j +Mary Geraldine [Mrs Anthony Davies, Primrose Cottage, 31 Fife Rd, London SW14]; *b* 29 March 1930; *m* 19

Dec 1957 *Antony St John Davies, slr, s of Very Rev Dr Arthur Davies, of Berkhamsted, Herts, and has:

1k +Benedict Antony John Whitcliffe; *b* 20 May 1960

2k +Simon; *b* 27 March 1963

1k +Hermione Anne; *b* 18 Nov 1958

2k +Catherine; *b* 6 May 1971

3j +Anne Mary [Mrs Thomas de Pentheny-O'Kelly, 34 Thornhill Rd, Mannamead, Plymouth, Devon]; *b* 3 Aug 1933; *m* 20 Feb 1960 *Thomas Frederick de Pentheny-O'Kelly, yr s of Col Edgar John de Pentheny-O'Kelly, DSO, of Hambledon House, Childe Okeford, Dorset, and has:

1k +Edmund Thomas; *b* 29 Dec 1962

1k +Maureen Louise; *b* 20 March 1961

2k +Carmel Anne; *b* 3 Aug 1964

3k +Mary Clare; *b* 8 July 1967

2h Edith Isabella Georgina; *m* 2 Feb 1893 Hon William Reginald Wentworth Fitzwilliam (*d* 7 July 1906; *see* 1970 edn FITZWILLIAM, E) and *dsp* 19 June 1904

3h Louisa Emma; *d* unm 20 Jan 1943

1g Elizabeth Catherine; *m* 7 July 1864 Rev Robert Wentworth Cracroft (*d* 22 March 1905), Rector Harrington, Lincs, and *dsp* 26 Oct 1879

2g Lora Mary; *d* unm 12 Feb 1908

YARROW

Arms: Azure in base on the sea proper an ancient three-masted ship sailing to the sinister argent, in chief two swallows volant of the last, each holding in the beak a harebell slipped also proper. **Crest:** Above clouds proper a swallow volant argent, holding in the beak a yarrow flower slipped also proper. **Badge:** A kingfisher volant proper. **Mottoes:** 1 Be just and fear not, 2 *Sans Dieu rien* ('Without God nothing'). **Creation:** Bt. (UK) 29 Jan 1916.

SIR ERIC GRANT YARROW, 3RD BT, of Homestead, Co Surrey, MBE (1946), DL (Renfrewshire 1970) [Sir Eric Yarrow Bt MBE DL, Cloak, Kilmacolm, Renfrewshire PA13 4SD]; *b* 23 April 1920; *s* f 1962; *educ* Marlborough and Glasgow U; Maj RE WW II 1942–45 Burma, chm: Clydesdale Bank 1985–91 (dep chm 1975–85, dir 1962–91), Yarrow & Co 1962–85 (assist manager 1946, dir 1948, md 1958–67), pres Yarrow plc 1985–87, dir: (sometime) Upper Clyde Shipbuilders, Standard Life Assur 1958–91 and Nat Australia Bank 1987–91, memb Gen Ctee Lloyd's Register Shipping 1960–87, Pres Scottish Convalescent Home for Children 1957–70, Deacon Inc of Hammermen Glasgow 1961–62, Prime Warden Worshipful Co of Shipwrights 1970, Hon V-Pres RINA 1972– (memb Cncl 1957–, V-Pres 1965), V-Chm Water Tube Boilermakers' Assoc, memb cncl IOD 1983–90, Hon Pres Princess Louise's Scottish Hosp at Erskine 1986 (Chm 1980–86), Prime Warden Shipwrights' Co, Pres Burma Star Assoc Scottish Area 1990–, OStJ, FRSE; *m* 1st 28 April 1951 Rosemary Ann (*d* 10 Jan 1957), yr dau of Henry Thomas Young, of Roehampton, and has had:

1 Richard Grant; *b* 21 March 1953; *educ* Marlborough; *m* 1982 *Sheila Elizabeth [Mrs Richard Yarrow, Edgebrook House, 13 E Fettes Ave, Edinburgh EH4 1DN], er dau of Ronald William Paul Allison, CVO, and *dvp* 1987, leaving:

(1) +ROSS WILLIAM GRANT; *b* 14 Jan 1985

(2) +Thomas Christopher; *b* 1987

Sir ERIC *m* 2nd 23 May 1959 (*divorce* 1975) Annette Elizabeth Françoise, only dau of Alasdair James Elwes Steven, of Grianach, Ardgay, Ross-shire, formerly of Munnar, S India, and by her has:

2 +Norman Murray; *b* 5 Feb 1960; *m* 1988 *Carol Jane, er dau of Nicholas Hawkins, and has:

(1) +Richard Eric; *b* 1994

(1) *Katie Diana; *b* 1990

(2) *Lucy Carol; *b* 1992

3 +Peter Harold; *b* 5 Feb 1960; *m* 1998 *Sara, yr dau of Peter Parry

4 +David Eric; *b* 8 Feb 1966

Sir ERIC m 3rd 1982 *Caroline Rosa Joan, dau of R F Masters, of Piddinghoe, Sussex, and formerly w of Philip Botting, of Allington Farm, Offham, Sussex

Lineage: EDGAR WILLIAMS YARROW, of Barnsbury, London N; had:

Sir Alfred Fernandez Yarrow, 1st Bt (UK), so, cr 29 Jan 1916; b 13 Jan 1842; engr, chm Yarrow & Co (shipbuilders) to 1922, FRS 1922, Hon LLD Glasgow 1924; m 1st 24 March 1875 Minnie Florence Franklin (d 20 Aug 1922) and had:

1 HAROLD EDGAR (Sir), **2nd Bt**

2 Norman Alfred; b 10 July 1891; engr and shipbuilder, dir BC Electrical Co Ltd, advsy bd memb Roy Tst Co, Victoria, BC; m 9 Nov 1915 Ada Hope (m 2nd 9 July 1959 Sir Eric Stuart Taylor, 2nd Bt (see STUART TAYLOR, Bt), and d 1990), dau of Forrest Bertram Leeder, MRCS, LRCP, of Victoria, BC, and d 25 June 1955, having had:

(1) John Alfred Forrest; b 30 July 1916; d car crash 11 Feb 1938

(1) *Cynthia Hope [Mrs Cynthia Pinckard, 638 Transit Rd, Victoria, BC, Canada V85 4Z5]; b 1921; m 1st 27 May 1944 (divorce 1954) Lt Clifton Thomas Williams Hyslop, RCNVR, s of David Allan Hyslop, of Hamilton, Ontario, and has:

    1a *John David Allan; b 8 June 1946

    2a *Andrew Peter; b 9 June 1951

    1a *Gillian Cynthia; b 19 Aug 1948

(1) (cont.) Mrs Cynthia Hyslop m 2nd 12 Oct 1955 (divorce 19–) William Ferdinand Pinckard, step-s of Capt Jocelyn Arthur Hobday, of Victoria, BC, and by him has:

    3a *Christopher William Norman; b 17 March 1958

    4a *Jonathan Mark; b 3 April 1960

(2) *Daphne Veryan [Mrs Howard Clark, 2440 Chiltern Place, Victoria, BC V8R 3S8 Canada]; b 1924; m 13 Sept 1952 *Lt-Cdr Howard Victor Clark, RCN (ret), er s of Maj Cecil Allan Clark, of Stratford, Ontario, and has:

    1a *Susan Veryan; b 2 Oct 1954

    2a *Stephanie Jane; b 26 March 1958

3 Eric Fernandez; b 5 Jan 1895; 7th Argyll and Sutherland Highrs WW I; ka 8 May 1915

1 Florence; m 5 Nov 1898 Adml Sir Percy Molyneux Rawson Royds, CB, CMG (d 25 March 1955), s of Ernest Molyneux Royds, of Rochdale, and d 8 March 1948, leaving issue

2 Evelyn; m 18 April 1903 Alfred Ernest Yarrow (d 2 April 1943), er s of Frederick John Yarrow and gs of John Guthrie, MD, of Brechin, and d 13 Jan 1963, leaving issue

3 (Minnie) Ethel, OBE (1918), DGStJ; m 18 Dec 1900 1st and last Viscount Dawson of Penn (d 7 March 1945; see 1940 edn) and had issue

Sir Alfred m 2nd 2 Dec 1922 Eleanor Cecilia (d 15 March 1953), dau of W Goodwin Barnes, of Foxley, Bishops Stortford, Herts, and d 24 Jan 1932

His est s,

Sir Harold Edgar Yarrow, 2nd Bt, GBE (1958, CBE 1918); b 11 Aug 1884; educ Bedford Sch and Tech Coll; engr and shipbuilder, chm Yarrow and Co and Clydesdale and N of Scotland Bank, dir Midland Bank, chm: Instn of Eng and Shipbuilders Scotland, V-Pres Instn Naval Architects, Hon LLD Glasgow 1953; m 1st 27 Feb 1906 Eleanor Etheldreda (d 1 June 1934), dau of Rev Canon William Hay Macdowall Hunter Aitken, and had:

1 Sir ERIC GRANT YARROW, **3rd and present Bt**

1 *Eleanor Audrey [Mrs Harry Boyd, Balauchen Lodge, Milngavie, Glasgow G62 8EJ]; b 10 Feb 1907; m 16 Aug 1934 Maj Harry Duncanson Boyd, MBE, TD, RA (d 24 Dec 1964), only s of Harry Watson Boyd, and has:

(1) *Eleanor Margaret [Mrs Peter Hutt, Strathisla, Box 33, PO Hillcrest 3650, Natal, S Africa]; b 27 March 1937; m 26 Sept 1959 *Peter Murray Bruce Hutt, er s of Sir (Alexander McDonald) Bruce Hutt, KBE, CMG, of Natal, and has:

    1a *Colin Murray Bruce; b 17 July 1960

    2a *Nigel Duncan; b 3 May 1964; m 6 April 1994 *Fiona Anne Cameron

    1a *Nichola Margaret; b 20 Aug 1966; m 25 April 1992 *James William John Baker and has:

      1b *Luke Frank; b 26 June 1994

      1b *Tamzyn Skye; b 1 June 1996

(2) *Eda Daphne [Mrs Christopher Enslin, 5 Bothwell Close, Tokai 7945, nr Cape Town, S Africa]; b 11 Jan 1940; m 24 May 1963 *Christopher Roche Enslin, s of Roche Enslin, of Constantia, and has:

    1a *Michael Roche; b 27 Aug 1967

    2a *Ian Boyd; b 27 March 1970

    1a *Camilla Fiona; b 15 Sept 1964

(3) *Sylvia Audrey [Mrs David Norris, Graghvar, Milngavie, Glasgow G62 8EJ]; b 2 April 1944; m 1st 15 June 1967 (divorce 1983) Alexander Baird Fergus Morton, s of Alexander Fergus Morton, of Bearsden, and has:

    1a *Peter Fergus; b 7 March 1970

    1a *Anita Audrey; b 1973

(3) (cont.) Mrs Sylvia Morton m 2nd 1983 *David Charles Alan Norris

2 *Beryl Winifred Ethne [Mrs Graeme Hardie, Netherblane, Blanefield, Glasgow G62 8EJ; b 12 May 1910; m 1st 30 April 1932 Charles Wood Scott (d 17 Aug 1960), s of Charles Scott, of Dunarbuck, Bowling, Dunbartonshire, and has:

(1) Grahame Charles Wood; b 18 May 1933; educ Leys Sch Cambridge and St Andrews (BSc 1955); m 14 Sept 1962 *Jean Isabel Mary, CA (1961) [Mrs Grahame Scott, 10 Mosspark Av, Milngavie, Glasgow G62 8NL], dau of Robert L Manners, of Cruach, Bearsden, Dunbartonshire, and d 1981, leaving:

    1a *Alan Charles Wood; b 5 Nov 1966

    1a *Fiona Anne Wood; b 2 June 1963

    2a *Lorna Jean Ethne Wood; b 2 July 1965

(1) *Avril Eleanor Yarrow [Mrs James Meighan, Fernbrae, Strathblane, Stirlingshire G63 9EY]; b 15 April 1936; m 5 Sept 1959 *James Alistair Spence Meighan, s of Dr S Spence Meighan, BSc, MC, ChB, FRSPSG, of Kenly, Blanefield, Stirlingshire, and has:

    1a *Andrew Alistair Spence; b 1 March 1963

    1a *Marjorie Eleanor Spence; b 14 April 1961; m 1984 *Ranald Morton White and has:

      1b *Sarah Jane; b 1987

      2b *Alice Jennifer; b 1990

    2a *Avril Gillian Spence; b 1 April 1966

2 (cont.) Mrs Charles Scott m 2nd 25 Sept 1969 Graeme Hardie, BEM (d 1973), s of Henry David Hardie, of Glasgow

3 Sheila Marion; b 14 Sept 1914; m 3 April 1937 Maj John Henry Atkinson, of Craiglea Ho, Gerrards Cross, Bucks, yr s of William James Garnier Atkinson, of The Downs, Woldingham, Surrey, and had:

(1) *Christopher John Garnier; b 1 July 1940; educ Stowe and St Edmund Hall Oxford (BA 1964); m 1 May 1965 *Philippa Daphne Mountsteven, dau of Lt-Col Patrick George Wright, TD, RA, of Drive House, Datchet, Berks, and has:

    1a *Adam Edward Garnier; b 19 July 1967

    2a *William John Patrick; b 20 Oct 1969

    3a *Marcus Christopher George; b 23 April 1971

(2) *Anthony Harold Garnier [Anthony Atkinson Esq, Craiglea Ho, Gerrards Cross, Bucks]; b 15 Dec 1941; educ Stowe; ACA

Sir Harold m 2nd 6 Feb 1935 Rosalynde, twin dau of Sir Oliver Lodge, LLD, DSc, MA, FRS, and d 19 April 1962, leaving by her:

4 *Angela Mary Rosalynde [Mrs Clive Griffiths, Wyfold Grange, Wyfold, Reading, Berks]; b 23 June 1937; m 5 May 1961 *(David) Clive Griffiths, s of Ivor Karn Griffiths, of Park End, Cardiff, and has:

(1) *David William Yarrow; b 13 June 1969

(1) *Rosemary Kate; b 18 Aug 1962

(2) *Amanda Mary; b 14 Sept 1964

YOUNG

Creation: B. (LP, UK) 1971.

THE BARONESS YOUNG, of Farnworth, Co Palatine of Lancaster (Janet Mary Baker, PC 1981, DL Oxon 1989) [The Rt Hon The Baroness Young PC DL, House of Lords, London SW1A 0PW]; b 23 Oct 1926; educ Headington Sch Oxford, Prospect Hill Sch New Haven, Conn., Mt Holyoke Coll USA and St Anne's Coll Oxford (MA, Hon Fell); memb Oxford City Cncl 1957–72 (Alderman 1967–72, Leader C Gp Oxford City Cncl 1967–72); Baroness-in-Waiting 1972–73; Parly U-Sec Environment 1973–74; V-Chm C Party Organisation 1975–83 (Dep Chm 1977–79, Co-Chm Women's Nat Ctee 1979–83); Min State DES 1979–81, Chllr Duchy Lancaster 1981–82 and Leader Ho Lds 1981–83, Ld Privy Seal 1982–83, Min State FCO 1983–87; dir Nat Westminster Bank plc 1987–96, Marks & Spencer plc 1987–97; Tstee Lucy Cavendish Coll Cambridge, Chm Ind Schs Jt Cncl; V-Pres W India Ctee 1988–; Chllr Greenwich U 1993–, Memb Court Cranfield U 1991–; m 1950 *Dr Geoffrey Tyndale Young and has:

1 *Alexandra Janet [The Hon Mrs Slater, 34 Southmoor Rd, Oxford OX2 6RD]; b 1951; m 1974 *John Douglas Slater and has a s and a dau

2 *Rosalind Ann [The Hon Mrs McIntyre, 48 Taleworth Rd, Ashtead, Surrey]; b 1954; m 1977 *Stephen McIntyre and has:

(1) *Peter James; b 1981

(2) *David Edward; b 1984

3 *Juliet Marguerite; b 1962; m 1986 *Stephen Paul Brown, er s of Dr Stanley Brown, of Harborne, Birmingham, and has:

(1) *Simon Richard; b 1989

Lineage: JOHN NORMAN LEONARD BAKER; m Phyllis Marguerite Hancock and had:

JANET MARY, cr a **Baroness**

YOUNG, Bt, of Bailieborough

Arms: Argent three piles sable, each charged with a trefoil slipped or, on a chief of the second three annulets of the third. **Crest:** A demi-lion rampant gules, charged on the shoulder with a trefoil slipped or and holding in the dexter paw a sprig of three maple leaves, all proper. **Motto:** *Prudentia* ('Prudence').
Creation: Bt. (UK) 28 Aug 1821.

SIR JOHN KENYON ROE YOUNG, **6TH BT**, of Bailieborough, Co Cavan [Sir John Young Bt, 159 Chatham Rd, Maidstone, Kent ME14 2ND]; *b* 23 April 1947; *s* f 1981; *educ* Hurn Court Sch, Christchurch, Hants, and Napier Coll; RN 1963–79 (Hydrographic Branch 1970–79), purchasing manager, FIPM, memb Hydrographic Soc; *m* 1977 *Frances Elise, only dau of W R Thompson, and has:

  1 +RICHARD CHRISTOPHER ROE; *b* 14 July 1983

  1 *Tamara Elizabeth Eve; *b* 1986

Lineage: The Rev JOHN YOUNG; Rector Urney, Co Tyrone; *m* Elspa Douglas and had an est s:

JAMES YOUNG, of Co Donegal; defended Derry 1688–89 in siege by Jacobites, attainted by JAMES II's I Parl May 1689; had, with several daus and eight yr sons:

JOHN YOUNG, of Coolkeiragh, Co Londonderry; *m* Catherine Knox, sis of Thomas Knox, of Lough Esk, Co Donegal, and gdau of Rt Rev Andrew Knox, 2nd post-Reformation Bp Raphoe, and *d* 1730, having had, with a dau and er s (William, of Coolkeiragh; ancestor of the YOUNGs of Coolkeiragh):

THOMAS YOUNG, of Lough Esk, an estate he inherited *c* 1721 from his unc Thomas Knox; *m* 1740/1 Rebecca, dau of Oliver Singleton, of Fort Singleton, Co Monaghan, by a dau of Oliver Anketel, of Anketel Grove, Co Monaghan, and had, with an est s (Thomas, *m* 1768 Elizabeth, dau of Rev Arthur Forde, Rector Segor, Co Armagh, and had issue), a yst s (William, *m* Rebecca, dau of Laurence O'Hara, of Brookfield, Co Donegal) and four daus:

Rev JOHN YOUNG, of Eden, Co Armagh; *m* April 1766 Anne, dau of John McClintock (*see* RATHDONNELL, B), and had, with other issue, including an er s (Thomas, Offr HEICS Madras Presidency, memb Duke of Wellington's staff Battle of Assaye (British victory in India over Mahrattas) 1803, lost at sea 1808 in a storm off Mauritius) and a yr s (Rev John, Rector Killishil, Co Tyrone, *m* his cousin Margaret (*d* Jan 1845), dau of Thomas Young, of Lough Esk, and widow of J Lendrum, of Magheracross, Co Fermanagh, and *d* 21 Aug 1844):

Sir William Young, 1st Bt (UK), so *cr* 28 Aug 1821, of Bailieborough Castle, Co Cavan; Dir HEIC; *m* 20 Sept 1806 Lucy (*d* 8 Aug 1856), yst dau of Lt-Col Charles Frederick, est s of Sir Charles Frederick, KB, himself yr bro of Sir John Frederick, 4th Bt (*qv*), and *d* 10 March 1848, having had, with a dau (d unm):

  1 **Sir John Young, 2nd Bt**, and 1st and last BARON LISGAR OF LISGAR AND BAILIEBOROUGH, Co Cavan (UK), so *cr* 26 Oct 1870, GCB (1868, KCB 1859), GCMG (1855), PC (I and GB 1852); *b* 31 Aug 1807; *educ* Eton and Corpus Christi Coll Oxford (BA 1829); barrister Lincoln's Inn 1834, MP (Tory then C) Co Cavan 1831–55, a Ld of Treasury 1841–44, Jt Sec Treasury 1844–46, Ch Sec to Ld Lt Ireland 1852–55, Ld High Commr Ionian Isles 1855–59, Govr: NSW 1860–67 and Canada 1868–72, Ld Lt Co Cavan 1871–76; *m* 8 April 1835 Adelaide Annabella (*m* 2nd 3 Aug 1878 Sir Francis Charles Fortescue Turville, KCMG, of Bosworth Hall, Leics (*d* 20 Dec 1889), and *d* 19 July 1895), dau of Edward Tuite Dalton by Olivia (*m* 2nd 2nd Marquess of Headfort (*qv*)) and *dsp* 6 Oct 1867, when the barony expired

  2 Thomas; *b* Jan 1810; with Bengal CS; *m* 24 June 1844 Mary J Duncan, dau of William Pitt Muston, and *d* 1846, leaving:

    (1) WILLIAM MUSTON NEED (Sir), **3rd Bt**

    (1) Lucy Frances; *d* unm Feb 1929

  3 Charles; *b* 3 June 1811; *d* Calcutta 18 March 1838

  4 William; *b* June 1817; Bengal Cav Offr; *d* unm Sept 1850

  5 Helenus Edward; *b* June 1822; Bengal Cav Offr; *m* 4 Dec 1844 Frances (*m* 2nd 1 July 1853 Col Charles Nedham), est dau of Capt Frederick Nepean Skinner, and *dsp* Jan 1851

---

  1 Anna; *m* 14 June 1860 Adolphe Christophe Edouard Baron von Barnekow (*d* 21 May 1862) and *d* 7 June 1882

  2 Augusta Maria; *m* 3 April 1841 George Rolleston (*d* 22 Oct 1870) and *d* 29 Nov 1899, leaving issue

The 2nd Bt's n,

  Sir William Muston Need Young, 3rd Bt, JP; *b* posthumously 20 Jan 1847; with Telegraph Dept ICS 1870 (ret 1897), served Afghan Campaign 1878–79 (medal and clasp), Burma Expdn 1885–87 and 1887–89 (medal and two clasps), cmded F Co Rangoon Vol Bn 1882–84; *m* 1st 24 Nov 1870 Isabella (*d* 1925), dau of John Leach, of Torrington; *m* 2nd 27 Sept 1932 Sarah, dau of James Hallinan, and *d* 31 March 1934, having had by his 1st w:

  1 John Edgar Harington; *b* 4 Sept 1871; Capt RGA; *m* 11 June 1896 Mildred Annie Ferrers (*m* 2nd 3 Aug 1911 Col Patrick Alexander Vansittart Stewart, CBE, DSO, DL, late KOSB (*d* 13 July 1960), s of Lt-Gen John Mackie Stewart, IA, and *d* 31 July 1928), only dau of Tom Ferrers Guy, of Kensington, and *dvp* 14 Feb 1902, leaving:

    (1) John Ferrers Harington; *b* 22 March 1897; Lt 1st Bn King's Own Roy Lancaster Regt; *ka* 1916

  2 CYRIL ROE MUSTON (Sir), **4th Bt**

  1 Jessy May Annette; *d* 5 March 1874

  2 Ella Louise; *m* 8 June 1905 Henry Reynolds, PhD, s of John Henry Reynolds, of Cheadle Hulme, Manchester, and *d* 1957, leaving issue

The 3rd Bt's 2nd s,

  Sir Cyril Roe Muston Young, 4th Bt; *b* 21 Aug 1881; MInstCE, with Butterfield and Swire, Shanghai merchants; *m* 17 Dec 1912 Gertrude Annie (*d* 9 March 1994), dau of John Elliott, of Braunton, N Devon, and *d* 15 June 1955, leaving:

  1 JOHN WILLIAM ROE (Sir), **5th Bt**

  2 +Patrick Elliott [Patrick Young Esq, 1151 North Shore Rd, Lake Oswego, Oregon 97034, USA]; *b* 6 March 1917; *m* 14 May 1946 *Sadie Reid, only dau of Laurence Beattie, of Prestwick, Ayrshire, and has:

    (1) +Christopher Brian Harrington; *b* 13 March 1965

    (1) *Patricia Louise Elliott; *b* 29 June 1947

    (2) *Veronica Anne Reid; *b* 22 April 1949

    (3) *Nancy Gay Lisgar; *b* 7 Sept 1952

  3 +Michael Cyril Harrington [Michael Young Esq, 35 Woodland Rd, Terrigal 2260, NSW, Australia]; *b* 7 Aug 1928; *educ* St Paul's; AICS, assist branch manager Australian Nat Line; *m* 1st 12 Feb 1955 Anita Patricia (*d* 1994), only dau of C H Duff, of Hong Kong; *m* 2nd 4 Feb 1995 *Elaine Ada, dau of Frank Norman Langley, of Balgowlah, NSW, and by his 1st w has:

    (1) +Peter Charles Harrington; *b* 2 June 1956

    (2) +Anthony Michael; *b* 24 Aug 1961

    (1) *Gail Louraine; *b* 4 June 1960

  1 Margaret Isobel; *b* 22 May 1920; *m* 26 July 1947 (*divorce* 1971) Lt-Cdr Stanley Stopford Claremont, RCN, only s of Capt E M S Claremont, RN, and Mrs Claremont, MBE, and had two sons (one deceased) and a dau

The 4th Bt's est s,

  Sir John William Roe Young, 5th Bt, of Bailieborough Castle; *b* 28 June 1913; *educ* Elizabeth Coll Guernsey; Sub-Lt RNVR Hong Kong (POW 1941–45); *m* 1st Aug 1946 Joan Minnie Agnes (*d* 20 Dec 1958), dau of M M Aldous, of Camelot, Parranport; *m* 2nd 1960 Joy Maureen, dau of A G Clarke, of Southsea, Hants, and *d* 1981, leaving by his 1st w:

  1 Sir JOHN KENYON ROE YOUNG, **6th and present Bt**

  1 *Eve Maureen Aldous; *b* 19 April 1949; *m* 1976 (*divorce* 1989) — Robertson

YOUNG, Bt, of Dominica

Creation: Bt. (GB) 2 May 1769.

SIR WILLIAM NEIL YOUNG, **10TH BT**, of Dominica, West Indies [Sir William Young Bt, Penchrise Peel, Hawick, Roxburghshire TD9 9UA]; *b* 22 Jan 1941; *s* gf 2 March 1944; *educ* Wellington and RMA Sandhurst; late Capt 16th/5th Queen's Roy Lancers; *m* 4 Sept 1965 *Christine Veronica, only dau of Robert Boland Morley, of Maida Vale and Buenos Aires, and has:

  1 +WILLIAM LAWRENCE ELLIOT; *b* 26 May 1970; *educ* Eton and Edinburgh U (MA)

  1 *Catherine Clare; *b* 2 Dec 1967; *educ* Somerville Coll Oxford (BA); *m* 1993 *Hugh E Powell, s of Sir Charles Powell, KCMG

Lineage: WILLIAM YOUNG, MD, of the WI, whither he had allegedly migrated from Scotland after the Jacobite rising of 1715; *m* 1720 Margaret Nanton, of Antigua, and had:

Sir William Young, 1st Bt (GB), so *cr* 2 May 1769; *b* 1725; Lt Govr Dominica, bought 1767 Delaford Manor, Iver, Bucks; *m* 1st Sarah (*dsp*), sis of Sir William Fagge, 5th Bt (*qv*); *m* 2nd 1747 Elizabeth (*b* 1729; *d* 12 July 1801), only child of Brook Taylor, DCL, FRS (and Sec), of Bifrons, Kent, and *d* 8 April 1788, having by her had, with five daus:

Sir William Young, 2nd Bt, of Delaford; *b c* 1750; *educ* Univ Coll Oxford; sold Delaford and rented 1790–c 1807 from Sir George Lee, 6th Bt (*see* 1826 edn) Hartwell Ho, nr Aylesbury, Bucks (subsequently residence of LOUIS XVIII of France), MP St Mawes 1784–1806 and Buckingham 1806–07, Govr Tobago 1807–15, FRS, FSA; *m* 12 Aug 1777 Sarah (*d* 6 Jan 1791), dau and coheir of Charles Lawrence (gs of Dr Thomas Lawrence, 1st Physician to QUEEN ANNE, and ggn of Henry Lawrence, Ld Pres of CROMWELL's Cncl 1653); *m* 2nd 22 April 1793 Barbara (*dsp* 1 Feb 1830), est dau of Baroness Talbot of Malahide (*qv*), and *d* 10 Jan 1815, having by his 1st w had:

  1 WILLIAM LAWRENCE (Sir), **3rd Bt**

  2 Brook Harry; Lt-Col; *d* 1813

  3 Charles; Lt RN; *d* 1815

4 George; Maj; *m* 4 Aug 1821 Mary, dau of John Harrison, of Derby, and had issue

1 Sarah Elizabeth; *m* Sir Richard Ottley, Ch Justice Ceylon, and *d* 16 Oct 1849

2 Caroline; *m* Thomas Robson, of Holtby Ho, Yorks

Sir WILLIAM's est s,

Sir WILLIAM Lawrence Young, 3rd Bt; *b c* 1778; *educ* BNC Oxford; Lt-Col Bucks Militia; *m* 21 Dec 1805 Anna Louisa (*d* 4 March 1844), sis of John Jolliffe Tufnell, of Langley, Essex, and *d* 3 Nov 1824, having had:

1 WILLIAM LAWRENCE (Sir), **4th Bt**

2 Henry Tufnell (Rev), of Mallard's Court, Stokenchurch, Oxon; *b* 9 Oct 1810; Vicar Mundon, Essex; *m* 1st 16 July 1841 Josephine Isabella (*d* 19 Aug 1852), dau of Joseph Savill, of Waltham Lodge, Essex; *m* 2nd 11 May 1854 Sarah Anne (*dsp* 25 March 1859), only dau of Rev Thomas Leigh; *m* 3rd 3 June 1862 Emma (*dsp* Oct 1884), dau of Philip Hills, of Colne Park, Essex, and *d* 24 Feb 1888, having had by his 1st w, with a dau (*d* unm):

(1) Henry Savill (Rev), of Mallard's Court; *b* 20 Sept 1843; *educ* BNC Oxford (MA); Rector Englefield, Berks; *m* 23 July 1868 Rebecca Isabella (*d* 28 Jan 1912), dau of Samuel Brewis, of Prestwich, and *d* 29 April 1906, having had, with a s and dau (*d* young):

1a Henry Brook (Rev); *b* 9 Nov 1869; *educ* Selwyn Coll Cambridge (MA); Rector St Andrew's Romford and St Mary's Newmarket 1904–20; *m* 14 March 1920 Emmie (*d* 1 Jan 1934), dau of Henry Everitt, of Exning, Suffolk, and *d* 28 Jan 1937, leaving:

1b +William Brook Charles [William Young Esq, 2 Chugg's Orchard, Cloutman's Lane, Croyde, Braunton, Devon EX33 1NG]; *b* 25 June 1922; *educ* St John's Leatherhead; S/Ldr RAF Bomber Cmd WW II India and Burma, Queen's Commendation for Valuable Serv in Air; *m* 3 Dec 1949 *Alma Evelyn, dau of Francis Charles Harvey, of Reading, and has:

1c +Paul Anthony Brook; *b* 17 Dec 1950; *m* 1st 1975 Barbara Inkley; *m* 2nd 1993 *Lyn White

2c +Christopher Charles Brook; *b* 9 April 1953; *m* 1975 *Mary Patricia Walls

1c *Amanda Jane Brook; *b* 14 March 1956; *m* 1st 1975 Delwyn Dowse; *m* 2nd 1982 *Randall Dobbs

2a Lawrence Charles Hills; *b* 25 Nov 1876; *educ* Oxford (BA); *d* unm 8 Sept 1907

3a Basil Arthur; *b* 30 April 1880; *d* unm 24 May 1939

4a Hugh Greville, DSO (1915); *b* 4 Nov 1882; *educ* Marlborough and RMA Woolwich; Lt-Col RHA WW I (despatches four times); *m* 15 Jan 1919 Constance, dau of Brig Gen Neil Douglas Findlay, CB, RA, and *d* 5 Nov 1950, leaving:

1b Hugh Findlay; *b* 13 Nov 1919; *educ* Wellington and RMA Woolwich; Maj RHA WW II (despatches); *m* 19– *Angela Elaine [Mrs Hugh Young, 15 Gloucester Rd, Coleford, Glos GL16 8BH], dau of R G M Whigham and Mrs Howard Davies, of St Briavels, Glos, and *d* 1987, leaving:

1c +James Greville [James Young Esq, Hampshire Ho, Hampshire Gdns, Coleford, Glos]; *b* 11 June 1957; *m* 1990 *Samantha, dau of Lawrence Edward Sillet, of Hill Park, Stag Hill, Yorkley, Glos, and has:

1d *Cecilia Angela; *b* 1990

2d *Matilda Judith Alice; *b* 199

3d *Christabel Mary Rose; *b* 24 June 1998

2c +Giles Hugh Findlay [Giles Young Esq, 172 Ruspidge Rd, Cinderford, Glos GL14 3AR]; *b* 20 Feb 1964; *m* 1996 *Sarah Jane, dau of Alan Leach of Blakeney Hill, Glos

3c +Piers Jonathan [Piers Young Esq, 170 Abertillery Rd, Blaina, Gwent NP3 3DY]; *b* 19 May 1965; *m* 1993 *Julia Marie, dau of Sidney Charles Barnfield, of Tewkesbury, Glos

1c *Mary Rose Frederica [Mrs Philip Butcher, Oak Ho, The Folly, Parkend, Lydney, Glos GL15 4JQ]; *b* 14 June 1958; *m* 1995 *Philip Gerald Butcher

2b Basil Neil; *b* 28 Sept 1921; *educ* Wellington; Capt 7th (Queen's Own) Hus WW II; *d* 1990

3b Jonathan George; *b* 5 Nov 1924; *educ* Wellington; Capt RA WW II; *m* 16 Feb 1965 *Margaret Helen, dau of Archibald Abbott, of Colinton, Edinburgh, and widow of Ian Miller Roberts, and *d* 1989

5a George Edward Savill; *b* 20 Jan 1884; *educ* Corpus Christi Coll Oxford (BA); Maj Irish Gds; *m* 10 Dec 1914 Alison Jane (*d* 12 Sept 1957), only dau of Rev Frederick John Poole, and *d* 31 March 1917 of wounds recd in action, leaving:

1b +Henry Lawrence Savill, DSO (1944) [Brig Henry Young DSO, The End House, Pilton, Somerset]; *b* 19 Oct 1915; *educ* Harrow and RMC Sandhurst; Brig Irish Gds WW II (despatches); *m* 19 Sept 1939 *Noreen de Vere, only dau of Thomas Brabazon Ponsonby (*see* BESSBOROUGH, E), and has:

1c +(George Trevor) Savill [Savill Young Esq, 37 Lessar Av, London SW4 9HW]; *b* 24 Oct 1941; *educ* Harrow and Trin Coll Dublin; late Lt Irish Gds; *m* 1983 *Marion Sonia, dau of Jean Paul Koch, of Rome, and has:

1d *Sophie Georgiana; *b* 1984

1c *Verona [Mrs Colin Fraser-Mackenzie, Cedar House, Pilton, Somerset BA4 4DB]; *b* 6 July 1943; *m* 1976 *Colin Lionel Angus Fraser-Mackenzie and has:

1d *Richard Savill Thomas; *b* 13 April 1981

2d *Peter Alexander Francis; *b* 8 May 1983

1b Josephine Isabella; *m* 8 Aug 1901 Marcus Warre Slade (*d* 28 Nov 1941) and had issue (*see* SLADE, Bt)

2b Evelyn Lucy; Headmistress Queen Ethelburga's Sch Harrogate 1911–36; *d* unm 10 May 1960

3b Frances Irene; *m* 15 Dec 1910 Sir Archibald Young Gipps Campbell, KCIE, CSI, CBE, VD (*see* CAMPBELL, Bt, of Auchinbreck), and *d* 30 Dec 1967, leaving issue

4b Olive Portia; *m* 19 May 1920 Bruce Waring Smith (*d* 1976), s of Hamilton Alan Smith, of Church Farm, Eversley, Hants, and had a dau

3 Brook; *b* 16 Aug 1813; served RN; *d* 23 Feb 1879

4 George Augustus; *b* 28 April 1822; *m* 20 June 1848 Isabella Marianne (*d* 1890), dau of Rev George Moore, Canon Canterbury, and *d* 25 Jan 1898, having had:

(1) William Henry; *b* 6 May 1849; Col cmdg 16 Regtl Dist Beds Regt; *d* unm 25 April 1906

(2) George Brooke; *b* 27 Nov 1857; Maj Beds Regt Zulu War 1879 (medal with clasp); *m* 28 Jan 1893 Anna Georgina (*d* 15 Dec 1925), dau of Townley Filgate, of Arthurstown, Co Louth, and *d* 19 May 1934, leaving a dau (*d* unm)

(3) Arthur; *b* 4 Feb 1859; *d* 1889

(4) Harold Lawrence; *b* 29 May 1866; *m* 1894 Beatrix Kinsey (*m* 2nd 1911 George Gully), est dau of William Kinsey Hayward, of Caernarvon, and *d* 27 Jan 1909, leaving:

1a Dorothy; *b* 13 March 1903; *m* 1928 Walter Adam, MB

(5) Wilfred Edward; *b* 12 July 1868; Lt-Col IA; *m* 1st 18 Nov 1903 his sis-in-law Edith Steuart (*d* 29 Aug 1917), dau of Robert Gladstone, of Woolton Vale, Liverpool; *m* 2nd 30 Sept 1932 Dorothy, dau of Col G F A Norton, RA, and widow of Col Arthur Edward Cave Burney, DSO, MC, RA, and *dsp* 23 Oct 1942

(1) Louisa Harriet; *m* 11 Oct 1876 Rev John FitzAlan Cornwall, Rector Witcombe (*d* 18 May 1929), and *d* 13 March 1928, leaving issue

(2) Emily Mary; *m* 18 Aug 1880 Edmund Waller, of Kirkby Fleetham, Yorks (*d* 1898), and *d* 12 May 1923

(3) Blanche Caroline; *d* unm 17 Feb 1939

(4) Isabella Georgina; Sister Community of Holy Trinity, Ascot; *d* 3 March 1929

(5) Agnes Augusta; *d* unm 25 March 1910

(6) Bertha Margaret; *d* unm 9 Aug 1947 aged 90

(7) Mildred Alice; *d* unm 3 March 1924

(8) Mabel Josephine; *d* unm 27 Jan 1941

(9) Maude Eugenie; *m* 1899 Arthur Steuart Gladstone, of S Kensington and Hungerford, Berks, est s of Robert Gladstone, of Woolton Vale, and *d* 30 March 1929, leaving issue

1 Sophia Louisa; *m* 14 June 1831 Rev Sir Thomas Bridges, 7th Bt (*d* 28 Feb 1895; *see* 1899 edn), and *d* 11 Jan 1850

2 Mary Ann; *m* 30 Dec 1835 Henry Plumptre Gipps, of Lincoln's Inn, and *d* 9 Nov 1874

3 Emma Catherine; *m* 24 July 1847 Rev John Laurence Prior, Rector Linby (*d* 30 Oct 1879), only s of Andrew Redmond Prior, and *d* 20 Oct 1905, leaving issue

The 3rd Bt's est s,

Sir William Lawrence Young, 4th Bt, of Hughenden; *b* 29 Sept 1806; Lt 8th Hus, MP Bucks 1835–42; *m* 27 March 1832 Caroline (*d* 16 Feb 1871), dau and coheir of John Norris, of Hughenden Ho, Bucks (following whose death 1845 it was bought by Benjamin Disraeli, subsequently 1st and last Earl of Beaconsfield), and *d* 27 June 1842, leaving:

1 **Sir William Norris Young, 5th Bt**; *b* 15 Jan 1833; *educ* Charterhouse; 1st Lt 23rd Foot (Roy Welch Fus) 1852; *m* 10 March 1854 Florence (*m* 2nd 10 April 1860 John Soltau and *d* 13 Aug 1894), 2nd dau of Erving Clarke, of Efford Manor, Plymouth, and was *ka* the Alma 20 Sept 1854

2 **Sir George John Young, 6th Bt**; *b* 1 March 1835; Lt RA; *d* unm of cholera 22 Oct 1854

3 CHARLES LAWRENCE (Sir), **7th Bt**

1 Elizabeth Sophia; *m* 29 April 1858 James George Ferguson Russell, JP, of Aden, Aberdeenshire (*dsp* 1887), and *d* 1 Aug 1915

2 Caroline Louisa; *m* 30 Oct 1860 Bertram Wodehouse Currie (*d* 1896) and *d* 16 April 1902, leaving issue

Sir GEORGE's yr bro,

Sir Charles Lawrence Young, 7th Bt; *b* 31 Oct 1839; *educ* Cheltenham and New Coll Oxford (BA 1862); barrister Inner Temple 1865, Commr Copyholds 1876–77, v-chm Grand Trunk Rlwy Canada 1879–87, playwright: *Jim the Penman* (first performed 1886); *m* 1st 11 Aug 1863 Mary Florence (*d* 21 July 1870), yr dau of Henry Hayman Toulmin, of Childwickbury, Herts; *m* 2nd 3 Aug 1871 Margaret Alice Mary (*d* 21 Jan 1923), est dau of Rev William Serocold Wade, and *d* 12 Sept 1887, leaving by his 1st w:

1 **Sir William Lawrence Young, 8th Bt**; *b* 3 Aug 1864; *educ* Charterhouse; memb LCC 1895; *m* 12 April 1887 Helen Mary (*d* 4 March 1939), dau of Hon Henry William Petre (*see* PETRE, B), and *dsp* 11 June 1921

2 (CHARLES) ALBAN (Sir), **9th Bt**

1 Mary Agnes; *b* 18 Sept 1868; *m* 1st 19 Aug 1880 William Henry Makins (*dvp* 1 Dec 1889), est s of Sir William Thomas Makins, 1st Bt (*qv*), and had issue; *m* 2nd 18 March 1891 Warine Martindale, of Haistwell Ho, Sunningdale, Surrey, s of Col Martindale, CB, RE, of Bickley, Kent, and *d* 18 July 1915, leaving further issue

Sir WILLIAM's yr bro,

Sir (Charles) Alban Young, 9th Bt, KCMG (1918), MVO (1906); *b* 18 Nov 1865; Dip Serv 1890–1925: Cncllr Teheran 1910–13, Envoy Extrdy and Min Plen and Consul-Gen Guatemala, Honduras, Nicaragua and Salvador 1913–19 and Belgrade 1919–25; *m* 18 July 1908 (Frances) Clara (*d* 28 Nov 1967), dau of Sir Frances Edmund Hugh Elliot, GCMG, GCVO (*see* MINTO, E), and *d* 2 March 1944, leaving:

1 William Elliot; *b* 6 Sept 1910; Capt RAMC WW II; *m* 1 Sept 1939 *Mary [Mrs George Nash, 2 Douro Rd, Cheltenham, Glos] (*m* 2nd 15 Aug 1945 Lt-Col George Herbert Nash, OBE, IA, s of Albert Edward Nash), dau of Rev John Macdonald, of Tongue, Sutherland, and was *ka* Libya 27 May 1942, leaving:

(1) Sir WILLIAM NEIL YOUNG, **10th and present Bt**

1 Helen; *b* 29 April 1909; *m* 24 June 1938 Capt Thomas Newman (*see* NEWMAN, Bt, of Mamhead) and had issue

2 *Joan Persica; *b* 17 Oct 1912; *m* 25 July 1936 *George Rupert Raw, s of Capt Rupert George Raw, DSO, Northumberland Fus, and has:

(1) *(Charles) Rupert [Rupert Raw Esq, 38 Ripplevale Grove, London N1]; *b* 4 Aug 1940; *educ* Eton and BNC Oxford; *m* 20 Feb 1965 *Nicola Henrietta St John, er dau of Dr Hans Henry Winterstein Gillespie

(1) *Victoria; *b* 3 May 1939

(2) *Susan Augusta; *b* 18 Aug 1949

YOUNG, Bt, of Formosa Place

Arms: Per fess sa. and arg. in chief two lions rampant-guardant and in base an anchor with cable, all counterchanged. **Crest:** A demi-unicorn couped erm., maned, armed and hoofed or, gorged with a naval crown az., supporting an anchor sa. **Motto:** Be right and persist. **Creation:** Bt. (UK) 24 Nov 1813.

SIR GEORGE SAMUEL KNATCHBULL YOUNG, 6TH BT, of Formosa Place, Berks, PC (1993) [The Rt Hon Sir George Young Bt PC MP, House of Commons, London SW1A 0AA]; *b* 16 July 1941; *s* f 1960; *educ* Eton and Ch Ch Oxford (BA 1963, MA 1967), MPhil Surrey (1969); economist NEDC 1966–67, Kobler Research Fell U of Surrey 1967–69, Ec Advr Post Office Corp 1969–74, Cncllr Lambeth 1968–71, memb GLC for Ealing 1970–73, MP (C) Ealing Acton 1974–97, Hants NW 1997–, Oppn Whip 1976–79, Parly U-Sec: DHSS 1979–81, DoE 1981–86, Comptroller HM Household 1990, Min State DoE 1990–94, Fin Sec Treasury 1994–95, Tport Sec 1995–97, Shadow Def Sec 1997–98, Shadow Ldr H of C 1998–; chm Acton Housing Assoc 1986–90, dir Lovell Partnerships Ltd 1987–90, tstee Guiness Tst 1986–90; author: *Accommodation Services in the UK 1970–80* (1970), *Tourism, Blessing or Blight?* (1973); *m* 11 July 1964 *Aurelia, er dau of Oscar Nemon, the sculptor, and Mrs Nemon-Stuart, of Boars Hill, Oxford, and has:

  1 +GEORGE ('GERRY') HORATIO [George Young Esq, Flat 4, 27 Elsham Rd, London W14 8HB]; *b* 11 Oct 1966; *educ* Windsor CFE and Ch Ch Oxford

  2 +Hugo Patrick; *b* 23 Sept 1970

  1 *Sophia Angelica; *b* 23 May 1965; *m* 27 July 1996 *David Butler, yr s of Ian Butler, of Kingston-upon-Thames

  2 *Camilla Mary; *b* 1975

Lineage: Sir GEORGE YOUNG, of Formosa Place, Cookham, Berks; *b* 17 June 1732; Adml the White, served taking of Louisburg 1758 (gold medal), Quebec 1759, Havana 1762 and Pondicherry 1778 (sword of honour); *m* 1st Elizabeth (*d* 19 Feb 1779), dau of Samuel Bradshaw, of Great Marlow, Bucks, and had two sons and two daus; *m* 2nd Anne (*dsp* 16 Oct 1830), dau of William Battie, MD, and *d* 28 June 1810; his er s by his 1st w:

Sir **Samuel Young, 1st Bt** (UK), so *cr* 24 Nov 1813; *b* 23 Feb 1776; EIC Madras CS; *m* 28 April 1796 Emily (*d* 13 Dec 1847), dau of Charles Baring, of Exmouth, and *d* 14 Dec 1826, having had, with a s (*d* young) and a dau (*d* unm):

  1 GEORGE (Sir), **2nd Bt**

  2 Charles Baring; *b* 7 Nov 1801; *m* 25 Jan 1843 Elizabeth (*d* 1897), 2nd dau of Stephen Winthrop, MD, and *d* 1882, leaving, with a dau (*d* unm):

    (1) Charles Edward Baring, of Daylesford House, Chipping Norton, and Oak Hill, E Barnet; *b* 1850; *educ* Trin Coll Cambridge (MA); barrister, MP Christchurch 1885–92; *d* 22 Sept 1928

    (2) Arthur William; *b* 1852; *educ* Trin Coll Cambridge (MA); barrister; *d* 7 June 1936

    (1) Caroline Susan; *m* 16 Feb 1887 William Frederic Lawrence, MP (*d* 15 Jan 1935), of Cowesfield House, Salisbury, and *d* 21 Nov 1925

  3 Henry; *b* 9 Oct 1803; HEIC's Bombay CS; *m* 17 April 1838 Catherine Anne (*d* 1875), est dau of John H Eccles, and *d* 14 Oct 1881, leaving issue, with a dau (*d* unm):

    (1) Henry Cathcart Arthur; *b* 2 Sept 1850; *m* 17 April 1902 Florence (*d* 23 July 1968), yst dau of Alfred Eccles, FRCS, of Holyrood Terrace, The Hoe, Plymouth, Devon, and *d* 23 Dec 1940, having had:

      1a Malcolm Henry Cathcart; *b* 30 June 1903; Lt-Cdr RN, served WW II; *m* 17 July 1930 Gwenda (*m* 2nd 22 Jan 1946 Rev Arthur Alan Western Gray, s of Rev Selby Arthur Gray, LLD, Vicar E Finchley, and *d* 23 April 1953), only dau of William Bromley Taylor, and was *ka* 18 Aug 1940, leaving:

        1b +Christopher Malcolm [Christopher Young Esq, South Sea Farm, Kington Langley, Chippenham, Wilts]; *b* 4 May, 1936; *educ* Geelong GS, Victoria, Australia, and Magdalene Coll Cambridge (BA 1959, MA 1963); *m* 30 April 1960 *Mary, dau of Ralph Lindsay, of Herstmonceux, Sussex, and has:

          1c +Richard Malcolm; *b* 7 April 1966

          1c *Caroline Mary; *b* 29 Jan 1962

          2c *Victoria Jane; *b* 16 March 1964

        2a Arthur Colin Everard; *b* 26 March 1914; *d* 3 June 1923

        1a *Katharine Elizabeth [Miss Katharine Young, 8 Campden House, 29 Sheffield Terrace, London W8 7NE]; *b* 9 July 1908; VAD Emergency and RAF Hosps WW II

  (2) Horace Edward Broughton; *b* 13 July 1853; *m* 1882 Ellen Elizabeth (*d* 27 April 1938), dau of George Thorne, and *d* 3 Oct 1924, having had:

    1a Percy Horace Broughton; *b* 13 Oct 1883; *d* 16 April 1919

    2a George Arnold; *b* 1886; Lt RFA (SR) and on Personal Staff 1916; *ka* 4 Oct 1917

    3a +Henry Herbert; *b* 13 Jan 1895; Lt RGA (SR) WW I (wounded); *m* Feb 1920 *Margaret Caroline Britannia, dau of Capt James Somerville Murray, of Wentworth Falls, NSW, and had:

      1b +Andrew Broughton [Andrew Young Esq, Comrie, Garra, NSW, Australia]; *b* 17 Dec 1920; 2nd/5th Field Artillery AIF WW II Middle East, New Guinea and Borneo; *m* 14 March 1956 *Julia Gray, dau of Geoffrey Gray Cambridge, of Clifton Gardens, Sydney, NSW, and has:

        1c +Nicholas Garth Broughton; *b* 23 Aug 1957

        2c +Graeme Arnold; *b* 12 Oct 1964

        1c *Vanessa Frances Caroline; *b* 26 Dec 1960

      2b +Arnold Somerville [Arnold Young Esq, PO Box 74, Molong, NSW 2866, Australia]; *b* 20 July 1923; 2nd/12th Field Artillery AIF New Guinea and Borneo WW II; *m* Feb 1956 *Erica Joy, dau of Joseph Little, of Wembley, Perth, W Australia, and has:

        1c +Michael Robert; *b* 17 Feb 1957

        2c +Graeme Arnold; *b* 13 Oct 1964

        1c *Gillian Brita; *b* 27 Aug 1958

        2c *Susan Margaret; *b* 5 March 1960

      3b +Horace Anthony [Horace Young Esq, The Rocky, Mendooran, NSW 2842, Australia]; *b* 6 Feb 1925; RAN WW II; *m* June 1946 *Margaret Jean, dau of M Bryce, of Cooparoo, Brisbane, and has:

        1c +Malcolm Herbert; *b* 27 Dec 1948; *m* 1st 14 Jan 1970 (*divorce* 1980) Dorothy Madeleine Stephenson, and had:

          1d *Sarah-Jean Dorothy; *b* 1 Feb 1970

        1c (cont.) Malcolm Young *m* 2nd Sept 1982 *Marcelle Kathleen Robinson, and by her has:

          1d +Henry Malcom Macarthur; *b* 5 June 1986

          2d *Phoebe Alice Macarthur; *b* 12 Jan 1991

        2c +James Forbes; *b* 18 July 1952

        3c +Angus Anthony; *b* 23 Aug 1957; *m* 9 Sept 1978 *Hilary Ruth Venton, and has:

          1d +Timothy Robert; *b* 3 July 1980

          2d +Andrew Lloyd; *b* 8 July 1982

          1d *Helen Brita; *b* 23 Jan 1985

        1c *Lisa Margaret; *b* 15 April 1954; *m* 23 Aug 1980 *Darryl Maxwell-Yeo, and has five sons and a dau

      4b +Robert Alexander; *b* 7 Feb 1927; *m* Oct 1956 Rosemary, dau of Thomas Mostyn Jasper, of Hamilton, Victoria, and has:

        1c +Justin Mark; *b* 2 Nov 1960

        2c +Martyn Andrew; *b* 2 Nov 1960

        1c *Lesley Philippa; *b* 6 Feb 1958

      1b *Janet Elizabeth; *b* 29 Oct 1931; *m* 1952 *Dr John Saxton, late RAN, s of Dr William Saxton, of Wickham Terrace, Brisbane, and has:

        1c *Jeremy John; *b* 9 March 1956

        2c *William Bevan; *b* 1 June 1963

        1c *Julie Belinda; *b* 13 Oct 1953

        2c *Fiona Jane; *b* 26 June 1958

        3c *Georgina Margaret; *b* 10 Dec 1961

    1a Evelyn Florence Broughton; *m* April 1926 Arthur Liddon Webb, MB, BS, FRCS, 3rd s of Rev Frederick Webb, of Adelaide, S Australia, and *d* 19–, having had three daus

    2a Doris Emily Broughton; *m* 28 July 1911 Rev Canon David James Knox (*d* 1960), Canon St Andrew's Cathedral Sydney, and had three sons and two daus

    3a Constance Elizabeth Broughton; *d* unm 24 Oct 1924

    4a *Winifred Elinor Broughton [Mrs David Nicholson, c/o 99 Copeland Rd, Beecroft, NSW, Australia]; *m* 1920 David Theodore Field Nicholson (*d* 1955) and has:

      1b *Peter Theodore [Peter Nicholson Esq, 99 Copeland Rd, Beecroft, NSW, Australia]; *b* 1926; *educ* Sydney U (BSc, BE); FIE Aust, MIEE; *m* 1949 *Patricia May Ohlsson, BSc, and has issue:

        1c *Peter Timothy James; *b* 1952; *educ* Sydney U (BSc)

        2c *Philip Theodore; *b* 1954; *educ* Sydney U (BSc, BE), U of NSW (ME)

        1c *Catherine Jane; *b* 1955; *educ* Macquarie U (BA); *m* 1979 *Bruce Kevin Coffee and has:

          1d *Matthew Bruce; *b* 1983

        2c *Anne Elizabeth; *b* 1957

        3c *Alison Patricia; *b* 1961; *educ* Sydney U (MB, BS)

      2b *Donald Ian; *b* 1928; *educ* Sydney U and Aust Forestry Sch (BSc Forestry 1949); *m* 1956 *Grace Mary, dau of Rev Harold Dennis Powley, and has:

        1c *Graham John; *b* 1957

        2c *Robert Christopher; *b* 1965

        1c *Stephanie Jane; *b* 1959

        2c *Joanne Christine; *b* 1962

      3b *John David; *b* 1934; *m* 1974 *Alice Louise, dau of Robert Kurwen Campbell, and has:

        1c *David Theodore Campbell; *b* 1975

        1c *Frances Bryony; *b* 1978

1b *Sheila Constance; b 1921; m 1949 *John Wallace Knox, FRCS, MRCOG

2b *Elinor Catherine; b 1924; educ Sydney U (MB, BS); ChB NZ, DObstRCOG Sydney, FRCOG; m 1950 *Reginald Henry James Hamlin, OBE, MB, ChB, FRCOG, and has:

   1c *Richard Havelock James; b 1953

3b *Alisa Mary; b 1931; m 1959 *Bruce Graham Pottie, of Turrawonga, Lairas Lee, NSW, and has:

   1c *Dougal John; b 1960

   2c *James Theodore Graham; b 1961

   3c *Angus Bruce; b 1965

(3) Charles Ernest; b 14 Jan 1855; m 19 Feb 1891 Margaret Elsé (d 12 Dec 1952), dau of John Shedden Adam, of Ellerslie, Turramurra, NSW, and d 26 April 1927, leaving:

1a Henry Shedden Baring, MC; b 15 April 1894; Capt RA WW I 1915–18; m 1st 2 Oct 1929 Eva Theodora (d 28 July 1940), dau of T C Maltby, of Tauranga, New Zealand, and had:

  1b +James Ernest Baring [James Young Esq, 11 Upper Rosemount Rd, Nambour, Qld 4560, Australia]; b 18 Nov 1933; educ Sydney GS and Canterbury Ag Coll NZ; m 1st 9 April 1959 (divorce 1975) Florence Annette, only dau of Kenneth R Lane, of St Ives, NSW; m 2nd 1976 *Cheryl Beverley Price and has by his 1st w:

   1c +Timothy James Baring; b 30 June 1960

   2c +Michael Henry Baring; b 24 Feb 1962

   3c +David Kenneth; b 28 Aug 1969

   4c +Anthony Baring; b 1971

   1c Jennifer Anne; b 29 May, d 13 Dec 1966

  1b *Dorothy Joan Baring [Mrs John Wheeler, 34 Irvines Rd, Bonville, NSW 2441, Australia]; b 31 Oct 1930; educ Sydney U (BSc Ag 1953) and London U (MSc Ag 1957); m 1957 *John Lionel Wheeler, PhD, BSc Ag, BCouns and has:

   1c *Philip John Henry (Rev); b 1961; m 1985 *Dr Jillian Margaret Collins, and has issue

   2c *Ian Charles Andrew; b 1963; m 1986 *Dianne Topham, and has issue

   1c *Rosemary Helen; b 1959; m 1982 *Rev Andrew John Sempell, Chap Australian Army, and has issue

1a (cont.) Henry Young m 2nd 25 Feb 1953 *Janet Mary [Mrs Henry Young, 20 Lamington St, Deakin, ACT 2600, Australia], only dau of Rev J Milton Thompson, of Tonbridge, Kent, and d 1976, having by her had:

  2b +Stephen Henry Baring; b 24 Nov 1954; m 1st 1976 (divorce 1989) Grace Marianne, dau of Stewart Dinnen; m 2nd 1992 *Nicola Helen, dau of William Main, of Turramurra, NSW, and has by his 1st w:

   1c *Rachel Grace Marie; b 1981

   2c *Clare Ruth Mary; b 1983

  2b *Angela Mary Katherine [Mrs Mark Diesendorf, PO Box 48, O'Connor, ACT, Australia]; b 22 May 1957; m 1988 *Dr Mark Oliver Diesendorf and has:

   1c *Joseph James; b 1993

2a Charles Arthur Noel, AM; b 23 Dec 1899; educ Tonbridge and Sydney GS; chm and md Fairymead Sugar Co, Bundaberg, executive memb and v-pres Australian Sugar Producers Assoc; m 24 Jan 1923 *Margery Bisdee Maynard, dau of Dr Maynard Pain, of Sydney, and d 1992, having had:

  1b +Charles Edward Christopher [Charles Young Esq, M/S 827 Moore Pk Rd, Bundaberg, Qld 4670, Australia]; b 20 Feb 1926; m 1st April 1949 Margaret Florence (d 1976), dau of W Guilford, of Killara, Sydney; m 2nd 1986 *Beverley Gaze, dau of Arthur W Edwards, of Leamington Spa, by Margaret Allison (see MACARA, Bt), and has:

   1c +Christopher Roderick [Christopher Young Esq, 4 Edzell Pl, Carindale, Brisbane, Qld, Australia]; b 8 March 1950; educ Brisbane Anglican GS and U of Queensland (BCom); Company Sec Bundaberg Sugar Co; m 1973 Jennifer Ann, dau of J Mackrill of Bunderberg, Qld, and has:

    1d +Benjamin Roderick; b 1982

    1d *Bianca Margaret; b 1979

   2c +Timothy Charles; b 31 Jan 1952; educ Brisbane Anglican GS and U of Qld (BBus); AASA; m 1979 *Leonie, dau of R McDowell, of Bundaberg, Qld, and has:

    1d *Erin Nancy; b 1983

    2d *Vanessa Megan; b 1985

   3c +Gregory Mark (Rev); b 27 April 1955; educ Brisbane Anglican GS; m 1983 *Michelle Suzanne, dau of A Baster, of Perth WA, and has:

    1d +Adam Christopher; b 1991

    1d *Hayley Clare; b 1985

    2d *Alyce Nicole; b 1988

   4c +Nicholas William; b 4 March 1961; educ N Bund HS; m 1991 *Wendy Lee, dau of R W Basmin, of Penshurst, Sydney

  1b *Margery Marian [Mrs Margery Berry, Box 181 PO, Moss Vale, NSW 2577, Australia]; b 22 Sept 1924; educ Abbotsleigh Sch; SRN; m Sept 1949 (divorce 1976) Norman Bruce Berry and has:

   1c *Andrew Bruce [Dr Andrew Berry, PO Box 301, Westmead, NSW 2145, Australia]; b 13 July 1950; educ Sydney U and Adelaide U; MB, BS, FRACP, State Dir NSW Newborn and Paediatric Emergency Transp serv; Med Dir 'Child Flight' helicopter rescue serv

   2c *Simon Mark [Simon Berry Esq, RMB 2352, George Bass Dve, Broulee, via Moruya, NSW 2537, Australia]; b 11 March 1956; educ ANU (BEc); m 1982 *Sue Imrie

   3c *Hugh Jonathan [Hugh Berry Esq, Montage, 62 Albany St, Crowsnest, NSW, Australia]; b 3 March 1962; m 1992 *Jennifer Green

   1c *Susan Marian; b 22 July 1952; educ Macquarie U (BA); m 1984 *William Alexander Ryan and has:

    1d *Alexander Cheyne; b 1985

    1d *Phoebe Imogen; b 1987

   2d *Clare Margery Frances; b 1989

  2c *Philippa Jane [Mrs David Palmer, 8 Downes Pl, Hughes, Canberra, ACT, Australia]; b 19 July 1954; educ Scegg Sch; SRN; m 1979 *David William Learmonth Palmer and has:

   1d *Angus Norman Learmonth; b 1980

   2d *Simon David; b 1982

   1d *Olivia Jane; b 1984

  2b *Elizabeth Wendy [Mrs Neil Yorkston, 59 Blackwell, Darlington, Co Durham DL3 8QT]; b 6 June 1927; m Feb 1957 *Neil James Yorkston, MB, BS, FRACP, FRCPsych, and has:

   1c *Ian Charles [Ian Yorkston Esq, 1 Deerness Hts, Brandon, Co Durham DH7 8TQ]; b 23 Dec 1961; m 1985 *Valerie Dunford, of Edmonton, Alberta

   1c *Catherine Judith [Mrs John Allinson, 31 Kingsmead Rd, London SW2 3HV]; b 30 Jan 1958; educ Blackheath HS and U of Br Columbia (BA); m 1985 *John Christopher Allinson, s of James Allinson, of Bradford, and has:

    1d *Simon James; b 1992

    1d *Emma Charlotte; b 1988

   2c *Ruth Elizabeth; b 21 Sept 1959; educ Blackheath HS and London U (BSc)

   3c *Ann Margery; b 2 June 1965; educ Blackheath HS and U of Br Columbia

  3b *Lois Margaret [Mrs Arthur Pennington, 119 Kissing Point Rd, Dundas, NSW 2117, Australia]; b 29 Jan 1929; educ Macquarie U; SRN; m Nov 1957 *Arthur Pennington, MB, BS, and has:

   1c *Jeremy Arthur; b 15 Aug 1958; m 198– *Denise, dau of John Pountney, of Sydney, and has:

    1d *Jennifer Grace; b 1989

    2d *Melanie Denis; b 1991

   2c *Martin Frederick; b 14 Dec 1961; m 1984 *Heath, dau of Brian Richards, of Adelaide, and has:

    1d *Huon Frederick; b 1994

    1d *Elise Patricia; b 1988

    2d *Myanna Ellen; b 1991

   1c *Judith Charis; b 20 April 1960; m 1989 *Malcolm Rundle, of Boronia Pk, Melbourne, and has:

    1d *Julia Helen; b 1993

   2c *Mary Priscilla; b 3 April 1964; m 1986 *Rev Richard Lane and has:

    1d *Sebastian Arthur; b 1992

    1d *Emily Cassandra; b 1991

   3c *Fiona Margaret; b 1974

  4b *Catherine Anne; b 29 May 1930; ThL (Aust); SRN, V-Pncpl Redcliffe Missionary Training Coll

  5b *Alison Jennifer; b 30 July 1932; m 8 Oct 1960 W J Douglas Cribb and d 19–, having had:

   1c *Charles Wilfrid; b 3 March 1964

   1c *Margery Jennifer; b 3 July 1962

   2c *Felicity Judith; b 15 May 1966

   3c *Prudence Elizabeth; b 30 Dec 1969

  6b Judith Guinevere Constance; b 24 Dec 1933; accidentally k 19 Dec 1954

  7b *Philippa Lucia Charis [Mrs Donald Thorn, 28 Rubens Grove, Canterbury, Vic, Australia]; b 13 June 1937; m 19 April 1963 *Donald Campbell Thorn, FRAIA, and has:

   1c *Christopher Ian; b 6 April 1964; educ Melbourne U (BCom); m 1990 *Rosalind Heather Mills and has:

    1d *Benjamin Lawrence; b 1993

   2c *Samuel Douglas; b 1967; educ Melbourne U (BEng); m 1990 *Jane, dau of Brian Willis, of Hawthorn, and has:

    1d *Maxwell David; b 1992

    2d *Harrison Campbell; b 1993

   1c *Bronwen Margery; b 18 Nov 1965; educ Melbourne U (MB, BS); FRACGP; m 1993 *Robert Graham Wilson, of S Perth, Australia

   2c *Sarah Penelope Joan; b 1972; educ Monash U

  8b *Helen Rosalind [Mrs Helen Deck, 618 Windermere Ave, Toronto, Ont M6S 3L8, Canada]; b 4 June 1939; educ U of Toronto (BA, MA); m 28 Nov 1959 (divorce 19–) John Henry Northcote Deck, MD, FRCP (C), gs of John Field Deck (see below), and has:

   1c *Wilbert John Northcote; b 5 Dec 1960; educ Upper Canada Coll and McGill U (BSc, MB); m 1986 *Carmen Leger and has:

    1d *Max Antonio; b 1991

    1d *Zoë Lise; b 1987

    2d *Anouk; b 1989

    3d *Emma; b 1993

   2c *Philip Charles; b 23 March 1962; educ U of Toronto (BA)

   3c *Roger Norman; b 5 Dec 1964; educ Upper Canada Coll and U of Toronto (BCom)

   1c *Kathleen Margery; b 8 April 1963; educ U of Toronto (BA) and U of Ottawa (BSocSc)

   2c *Rachel Frances; b 1971

   3c *Jennifer Luci Maynard; b 1973

  9b *Adrienne Penelope [Mrs Wilfrid Galbraith, Medway, Oldbury Road, Moss Vale, NSW 2577, Australia]; b 17 April 1943; m 1976 *Wilfrid Galbraith and has:

   1c *Thomas Charles; b 1977

   2c *James Wilfrid; b 1978

   3c *Barnaby Donald; b 1984

   1c *Annabel Christiana; b 1980

   2c *Clarissa Bisdee; b 1982

10b *Carolyn Bronwen [Mrs Carolyn Wolfson, 7 Pickford Ave, East-wood, Sydney, NSW, Australia]; b 7 Jan 1945; m 1971 (divorce 19–) Keith Wolfson and has:

1c *Robin Lawrence; b 1978

2c *Asher David; b 1981

1c *Chlöe Samantha; b 1977

3a +Ernest Stafford [Ernest Young Esq, 13 Karranga Ave, Killara, Sydney, NSW 2071, Australia]; b 25 July 1903; educ Sydney U (BE); formerly missionary in Borneo, served WW II as F/Lt RAAF; m 2 April 1946 *Lilian Olive, JP, dau of C E Mumford, of Cremorne, Sydney, NSW, and has:

1b +David Hilton [David Young Esq, 23 Greenhill Cresc, St Ives, NSW 2075, Austrialia]; b 11 Jan 1947; educ Sydney U (BEc); m 1st 1972 (divorce) Katherine Beatrice, dau of Dr E L A Rod, of Gordon, Sydney, m 2nd 19 Sept 1998 *Sharon Watts, and by his 1st w has:

1c +Jeremy Andrew; b 1973

1c *Virginia Bronwyn; b 1976

2c *Amanda Penelope; b 1977

1b *Lesley Anne [Mrs Rodney Allen, 55 Kensington Rd, Bolwarra, NSW 2320, Australia]; b 12 April 1949; educ Sydney U (BA, DipEd) and Newcastle U (MEd Studies); m 1972 *Rodney Elkington Allen, MB, BS, DipObs, FRACGP, and has:

1c *Matthew James Elkington; b 1974; m 1998 *Maggie Mulliardy

2c *Benjamin Mark Elkington; b 1976

3c *Andrew Stephen Elkington; b 1979

2b *Rosemary Frances; b 10 March 1953

3a Geoffrey Lawrence; b 4 Jan 1910; educ Emmanuel Coll Cambridge; Dr London 1938, RAAF WW II; m 19 Jan 1935 *Irene, OAM, BSc, 3rd dau of P W Petter, of Swallowcliffe, Yeovil, and d 1993, having had:

1b +Peter Lawrence [Peter Young Esq, 4 Narelle Ave, Pymble, NSW 2073, Australia]; b 4 Dec 1935; FCILA, FCPA; m 29 April 1961 *Jennifer Mary, dau of J M Clift, and has:

1c +Michael Lawrence; b 8 Oct 1968; educ Sydney U (BE, BSc)

1c *Judith Anne; b 1971

2b +Geoffrey Branscombe; b 31 July 1942

1b *Susan Irene; b 16 June 1938; educ Abbotsleigh and Sydney U (BA, Dip Ed); m 19 Dec 1966 (divorce 1977) William Werden Wilson, s of Capt William Werden Wilson, and has:

1c *John William Werden; b 20 April 1968

1c *Anthea; b 4 July 1969

2b *Kathleen Patricia [Mrs Stuart Braga, 52 Seaview St, Ashfield, NSW 2131, Australia]; b 3 May 1940; educ Abbotsleigh, Sydney U (BSc) and U of New England (Dip Ed); m 11 Jan 1969 *Stuart Braga, MA, M Ed Admin, FACE, only s of Hugh Braga, of Castlecrag, NSW, and has:

1c *David Hugh; b 5 May 1970

2c *Christopher Stuart; b 1972

3c *Andrew Geoffrey; b 1975

3b *Jocelyn Olivia; b 19 Sept 1946; m 1 March 1969 *Wayne Mackenzie, est s of R Mackenzie, and has:

1c *Malcolm Geoffrey; b 1972

1c *Barbara Lorraine; b 1970

1a Marjorie Lucia; b 19–; d 19–

2a Charis Elsé; b 19–; d 19–

(1) Emily Baring; m 24 Aug 1865 John Feild Deck, MD, of Sydney, NSW, and d 23 Dec 1914, leaving issue

(2) Florence Selina Harriett; b 18–; d –

4 Horatio Beauman; b 24 April 1806; Adml; m June 1860 Elizabeth (d 10 March 1924), only dau of Samuel Pretor, of Wyke House, Dorset, and d 17 Dec 1879, leaving:

(1) Alfred Horace; b 5 Nov 1861; d unm 10 Oct 1911

(2) Alan Rowley; b 23 Feb 1863; Glam Imp Yeo Boer War 1899–1902 (medal with four clasps) and WW I; m 25 July 1903 Isabel Louisa (d 2 Feb 1917), dau of Col James George, Gordon Highrs and 21st Lancers, and dsp 11 Dec 1942

(1) Eleanor Theresa; m 1895 Rev William Gilbert Walshe and d 26 Sept 1943, leaving issue

(2) Eva Gertrude; d unm 26 Aug 1944

(3) Agnes; b 18–; d unm 19–

5 William Jackson; b 10 July 1809; m 22 May 1845 Annie (m 2nd 1850 Stephen Digby Murray and d 1905), dau of Thomas Eaton, and d 3 June 1848, leaving:

(1) William Eaton, JP (Somerset); b 7 Feb 1848; educ Queen's Coll Oxford (BCL, BA); barrister; m 1st 29 July 1874 Mary Cecil Augusta (d 20 Dec 1920), only dau of Rev Sir Cecil Bisshopp, 9th Bt (see ZOUCHE, B), and had, with a yst s (d an infant):

1a Cecil Digby Hillyar; b 18 Nov 1875; d April 1932

2a Heugh Gerard Montagu; b 15 Jan 1878; d 13 March 1926

(1) (cont.) William Young m 2nd 12 Sept 1927 Ethel (d 19–), est dau of W F Randall of The Triangle, Bath, and d 13 Jan 1934

1 Lucia; m 24 July 1839 Rev Charles Washington Lawrence (d 30 Nov 1861), s of Charles Lawrence, of Mossley Hill, Liverpool, and d 1890

2 Louisa Caroline; m 20 Aug 1846 Rev Joseph Webster Harden (d 1873), Vicar Condover, Salop

Sir SAMUEL's est s,

Sir George Young, 2nd Bt; b 19 Aug 1797; Capt RN; m 23 June 1835 Susan (d 20 May 1895 aged 90), only surv dau of William Mackworth-Praed, Serjeant-at-law, and d 8 Feb 1848, having had:

1 GEORGE (Sir), **3rd Bt**

2 Edward Mallet (Rev); b 24 Jan 1839; MA Cantab; Rector and RD Rothbury, Northumberland, Hon Canon Newcastle, Fell Trin Coll Cambridge, Headmaster Sherborne, Canon Sarum; m 15 Aug 1882 Augusta Melita (d 29 Aug 1920),

dau of Gen Hon Sir Augustus Almeric Spencer, GCB (see CHURCHILL, V), and widow of Lt-Col Sussex Vane Stephenson, Scots Gds, and dsp 19 Dec 1900

3 William Mackworth (Sir), KCSI, JP (Sussex); b 15 Aug 1840; MA; Fell King's Coll Cambridge; Bengal CS 1863–1902, memb Viceroy's Legislative Cncl 1893, Resident Mysore, Ch Commr Coorg 1895–97, Lt-Govr Punjab 1897–1902; m 1st 17 Aug 1869 Isabel Maria (d 28 May 1870), 3rd dau of Rev Charles Boileau Elliott, FRS, and had:

(1) Isabel Mary; m 21 April 1897 Archibald Vere Monro (d 19 Feb 1944), s of Rev Horace George Monro, of Binfield, Berks, and d 14 Dec 1929, leaving issue

3 (cont.) Sir William m 2nd 21 April 1881 Frances Mary (d 8 March 1932), dau of Sir Robert Eyles Egerton, KCSI, CIE (see GREY EGERTON, Bt), and d 10 May 1924, having by her had:

(1) Gerard Mackworth YOUNG later MACKWORTH-YOUNG (deed poll 1947), CIE (1929); b 7 April 1884; educ Eton and King's Coll Cambridge (BA 1906, MA 1912); ICS (ret 1934), U-Sec to Govt of India Home Dept 1916–19, Dep Commr Delhi 1921–24, Sec Govt of India Army Dept 1926–32, Dir British Sch Archaeology Athens 1936–46, in Govt of India War Dept 1941–44, Archaeological Survey of India 1944–45, FSA; m 9 May 1916 Natalie Leila Margaret (d 1981), dau of Sir Walter Francis Hely-Hutchinson, GCMG (see DONOUGHMORE, E), and d 28 Nov 1965, leaving:

1a +Robert ('Robin') Christopher Mackworth (Sir), GCVO (1985, KCVO 1975, CVO 1968, MVO 1961) [Sir Robin Mackworth-Young GCVO, c/o Baring Bros & Co Ltd, 8 Bishopsgate, London EC2]; b 12 Feb 1920; educ Eton and King's Coll Cambridge (BA 1948, Pres Union 1948, MA 1952); S/Ldr RAFVR WW II, For Serv 1948–55, Dep Librarian Windsor Castle 1955–58, Librarian Windsor Castle and Assist Keeper Roy Archives 1958–85, Librarian Emeritus to HM THE QUEEN 1985–, Bd memb Br Library 1984–90; m 17 Dec 1953 *Helen Editha Rosemarie, yr dau of Werner Charles Rudolf Aue, of Menton, France, and has:

1b *Charles Gerard [Dr Charles Mackworth-Young, 18 The Chase, London SW4]; b 6 July 1954; educ Eton and Magdalene Coll Cambridge (MA); MRCP, MD; m 28 June 1983 *Lady Iona Sina Lindsay, yr dau of 29th Earl of Crawford and (12th Earl of) Balcarres (qv), and has:

1c *Rose Bettina Natalie; b 1987

2c *Constance Ruth Sina; b 1990

2a Gerard William; b 10 Oct 1926; educ Eton; Lt RARO Welsh Gds, memb London Stock Exchange, ptnr Rowe & Pitman 1953–73, v-chm Morgan Grenfell Holdings 1973–84, chm Morgan Grenfell 1980–84 (dir 1974–84, dep chm and ch exec 1975–79), dir: Union Discount Co 1974–84, Willis Faber Ltd, London Bd Halifax Bldg Soc, Lloyds Bank Ltd; chm Industrial Devpt Advisory Bd 1980–84; m 14 July 1949 *Lady Evelyn Leslie [The Lady Evelyn Mackworth-Young, Fisherton Mill, Fisherton de la Mere, Warminster, Wilts BA12 0PZ], yr dau of 20th Earl of Rothes (qv), and d 1984, leaving:

1b *Angela Clare; b 11 Feb 1951

2b *Susan Charlotte [Mrs Susan Tribolini, 5625 Beach Drive SW, Seattle, WA 98136, USA]; b 14 April 1953; barrister Inner Temple 1975; m 1987 (divorce 1996) Andrew Tribolini, s of A L Tribolini, of Milwaukee, Wisconsin

3b *Lucinda Jane [Mrs Oliver Sells, 5 Paper Bldgs, Temple, London EC4 7HB]; b 4 Jan 1957; m 1st 1981 (divorce 1984) Charles J Lumsden; m 2nd 30 Aug 1986 *Oliver Matthew Sells, QC, s of Sir David Perronet Sells, and by him has:

1c *Hugo William; b 17 June 1988

1c *Rosanna Mary; b 30 June 1991

4b *Tessa Natalie [Mrs Michael Hardingham, 9 Finlay St, London SW6 6HE]; b 6 Oct 1959; m 8 Nov 1986 *Michael G Hardingham, yst s of Maj M L Hardingham, of E Harting, W Sussex, and has:

1c *Robin Matthew; b 29 April 1990

2c *Luke Charles; b 14 Dec 1993

1c *Clara Louise; b 4 March 1992

1a *Honor Margaret; b 22 Oct 1917; m 6 Sept 1938 Maj Archibald Douglas George Braithwaite, RA (see FORESTIER-WALKER, Bt), er s of William Douglas Braithwaite, of Brockenhurst, Hants, and has:

1b *Richard William [Richard Braithwaite Esq, Tayvallich, Argyll]; b 29 Sept 1944; educ Shrewbury and Queen's Coll Dundee; m 26 March 1970 (divorce 1975) Claire Patricia, dau of A H Sangster, of Kilmarnock, Ayshire; m 2nd *Belinda Anne, dau of D F Sheerman, of Truro, and has by her:

1c *Iain Dudley; b 1986

1c *Shuna Anne; b 1986

2b *Gerard Nicholas; b 2 Jan 1954; educ Stanbridge Earls

1b *Janis Mary; b 13 June 1942; m 1973 *James Mattinson, of Keswick, and has:

1c *Hamish Edward; b 1973

1c *Sarah Jane; b 1976

2b *Sarah Helen; b 23 March 1948

2a *Lucia May; b 15 Dec 1931; m 30 March 1966 *Paul Mayersberg, only s of Denis Mayersberg, of Brent, and has:

1b *Zoltan Alexander; b 7 March 1969

1b *Natasha Catherine; b 9 Oct 1966

(2) Hubert Winthrop (Sir), KCMG (1934), DSO (1919); b 6 July 1885; educ Eton and RMA Woolwich; Maj IA WW I Mesopotamia as Assist Pol Offr and Dep Dir Local Resources (despatches), special duty with Hedjaz ops (despatches, Order of El Nahda), Eastern Dept FO 1919–20, Assist Sec Middle East Dept Colonial Office 1921–26, Colonial Sec Glbraltar 1927–29, Counsellor to HC Iraq 1929–32, Envoy Extrdy and Min Plen Iraq 1932, Govr and C-in-C: Nyasaland 1932–34, Northern Rhodesia 1934–38 and Trinidad and Tobago 1938–42, in Relief Dept 1943 and in UNRRA 1944–45, Cdr Order Orange Nassau 1949, Chm Roy Free Hosp and W Wilts Hosp Management Ctee and Consultative Cncl S Electricity Area; ktd 1932; m 7 Feb 1924 Margaret Rose Mary (d 1981), dau of Col Frank Romilly Reynolds, RE, and d 20 April 1960, leaving:

1a Nicholas; *b* 22 Dec 1924; *educ* Eton and Trin Coll Cambridge; Capt RA, attd RIA WW II (despatches); with Shell Internat Petroleum Co; *m* 25 Sept 1969 *Antonia Rosetta [Mrs Nicholas Young, 7 Hamilton Terr, London NW8 9RE], er dau of Brig Nigel Dugdale, CBE, 17th/21st Lancers, and *d* 1992, leaving:

    1b +Thomas Daniel Noah; *b* 1972

    1b *Zoe Alexandra; *b* 1970

2a +Martin Francis [Martin Young Esq, Finca La Magdalena Baja, Apartado 13, 29400 Ronda, Malaga, Spain]; *b* 27 Feb 1927; *educ* Eton and King's Coll Cambridge (BA 1948, MA 1957); For Serv 1948–63; *m* 1988 *Catherine Carlotta, only dau of John Marshall, of Jacksonville, Fla.

3a Simon Bainbridge; *b* 6 July 1928; *educ* Eton and King's Coll Cambridge (BA 1952, MA 1957); dir John Murray (publishers) Ltd; *m* 1 May 1954 *Diana Tyndale [Mrs Simon Young, Martins, Whitehill, Bradford-upon-Avon, Wilts BA15 1SQ], only dau of Oswald Lewis, of Beechwood, Highgate, N6, and *d* 1984, leaving:

    1b +James Hubert; *b* 6 Sept 1955; *educ* Marlborough

    2b Mark; *b* 17 April 1957; *d* 26 June 1987

    3b +Stephen; *b* 24 March 1959; *m* 1991 *Margaret, dau of Peter McBride, of Donegal, and has:

        1c *Caoimhe; *b* 1993

        2c *Fionnuala; *b* 1994

    1b *Emma; *b* 15 April 1961; *m* 1991 *Stephen Lewis-Dale, yr s of Douglas Lewis-Dale, of Cheshire

(3) Mark Aitchison (Sir), GCMG (1946); *b* 30 June 1886; *educ* Eton and King's Coll Cambridge (BA 1908); Ceylon CS 1909–28, T/Capt Rifle Bde WW I, Colonial Sec Sierra Leone 1928–30, Ch Sec Palestine 1930–33, Govr and C-in-C Barbados 1933–38 (Admin Govt of Trinidad 1937), Govr and C-in-C: Tanganyika Territory 1938–41 and Hong Kong 1941 and 1946–47 (Japanese POW 1942–45), KStJ; *m* 26 Nov 1919 Josephine Mary, CStJ (*d* 10 April 1977), er dau of Walter Cromwell Price, and *d* 12 May 1974, leaving:

    1a Brian Walter Mark (Sir) [Sir Brian Young, Hill End, Woodhill Ave, Gerrards Cross, Bucks SL9 8DJ]; *b* 23 Aug 1922; *educ* Eton and King's Coll Cambridge (MA); Lt RNVR WW II, assist master Eton 1947–52, Headmaster Charterhouse 1952–64, dir Nuffield Fndn 1964–70, Dir-Gen IBA 1970–82, chm Christian Aid 1983–90, memb Arts Cncl 1983–88, ktd 1976; *m* 10 July 1947 Fiona Marjorie (*d* 14 Feb 1997), only dau of Allan Winslow Stewart, 16th Chief of Appin, and has:

    1b +Timothy Mark Stewart; *b* 6 Oct 1951; *educ* Eton and Magdalene Coll Cambridge (MA); Headmaster Roy GS Guildford; *m* 1990 *Alison M, yr dau of Geoffrey Keightley, of Wellingborough, Northants, and has:

        1c +Dugald Robert; *b* 1992

        2c +Rowland Mark Keightley; *b* 1993

    1b *Joanna Margaret; *b* 4 July 1949; *educ* Durham U (BA); Headmistress St George's Sch, Ascot; *m* 20 April 1974 *Brig A Peter Grant-Peterkin, OBE (1990), s of Brig James Alexander Grant-Peterkin, DSO and bar, DL, of Grangehall, Forres, Morayshire, and has:

        1c *James Mark; *b* 1977

        1c *Alexandra; *b* 1975

    2b *Deborah Jane [Mrs Geoffrey Hudson, 26 Bolton Ave, Windsor, Berks SL4 3JF]; *b* 7 April 1953; *m* 1979 *Geoffrey Robert François Hudson, 2nd s of Richard Thomas Erskine Hudson, of Wimbledon, and has:

        1c *Thomas Geoffrey Mark; *b* 1980

        1c *Charlotte Jane; *b* 1983

        2c *Sophie Emma; *b* 1988

2a +Denis Egerton; *b* 22 June 1926; *educ* Winchester and King's Coll Cambridge (BA 1949, MA 1953); RNVR WW II 1944–45, housemaster and head history Strathallan Sch 1952–79, antique dealer 1979– ; *m* 21 Dec 1957 *Judith Mary, est dau of Dr Edward Russell Matthews, of Nettleton, Wilts, and has:

    1b +Matthew Egerton; *b* 13 Nov 1959

    2b +Walter Samuel Egerton; *b* 27 Jan 1965

    1b *Emma Faith; *b* 23 Nov 1960

    2b *Cecilia Frances; *b* 15 May 1962; *m* 1982 *Paul John Thompson, of London, and has:

        1c *Matthew Harry William; *b* 1983

1a Eleanor Mary; *b* 26 April 1921; WRNS WW II; *d* 18 June 1985

2a *Janet Cecilia Josephine [Mrs R J Owens, 22 Norman Rd, Hout Bay 7806, S Africa]; *b* 17 Aug 1930; MB, BS London 1955, LRCP and MRCS 1955; *m* 1973 Dr R J ('Jerry') Owens MA, PhD (*d* 21 Aug 1995)

(4) Norman Egerton, CB (1953), CMG (1946), MC (1919); *b* 27 Feb 1892; *educ* Eton and Corpus Christi Coll Oxford (BA 1919, MA 1951); T/Capt Roy Sussex Regt WW I (despatches), Treasury 1919, Assist Fin Sec Sudan 1929–31, Fin Advsr Br Embassy Paris 1939–40, Br Govt Dir Suez Canal Co 1939–45, Comptroller Gen Nat Debt Office 1951–54; presumed *drowned* off coast of Mozambique 30 June 1965

(1) Lucia Katharine; *educ* London U (BA 1917, BD 1958), B Litt Oxford 1966, ARCM; *m* 26 July 1924 Arthur John Beamish, MA (*d* 13 Sept 1957), 2nd s of Lt-Col Alten Augustus William Beamish, and *d* 1 Sept 1969, leaving issue

4 Albert Stewart Winthrop (Rev), VD; *b* 16 March 1842; *educ* King's Coll Cambridge (MA and Fell); Vicar Kingston-on-Thames 1877–1918, RD 1887–1909, Chaplain 6th Bn E Surrey Regt; *d* unm Feb 1918

5 Bulkley Samuel; *b* 2 Dec 1843; *d* 23 Aug 1866

1 Elizabeth Susan; *m* 27 July 1865 Col William Paston Purnell, CB (*d* 14 May 1869), and *d* 11 Oct 1925, leaving issue

The 2nd Bt's est s,

Sir George Young, 3rd Bt, JP (Berks 1860); *b* 15 Sept 1837; *educ* Trin Coll Cambridge (MA, Fell), LLD (Hon) St Andrews; barrister 1864, Commr: British Guiana Immigration 1870, Friendly Socs 1875, Factory Acts 1875, Irish Land Acts 1881, Charity Commr 1882, Ch Commr for England and Wales 1903–06, Govr Reading U 1926; *m* 10 Oct 1871 Alice Eacy (*d* 22 Aug 1922), dau of Evory Kennedy, MD, of Belgard, Co Dublin, and widow of Sir Alexander Hutchinson Lawrence, 1st Bt (*see* LAWRENCE, Bt, of Lucknow), and *d* 4 July 1930, having had:

1 GEORGE (Sir), **4th Bt**

2 Geoffrey Winthrop; *b* 25 Oct 1876; *educ* Marlborough and Trin Coll Cambridge (BA 1898, MA 1902); Offr ic Br Aux Units Flanders 1914–15 and Italy 1915–18 (despatches, severely wounded), Chev Legn Hon, Orders Leopold Belgium and Crown Italy, Croix de Guerre Belgium and Italy, Italian Silver Medal for Valour (twice), assist master Eton, lecturer comparative educn London U 1932–58; pres: Alpine Club, Gordonstoun Govt, Outward Bound Mountain Sch, Br Mountaineering Cncl 1944–47, author *Mountain Craft, On High Hills*, etc; Hon D Litt Durham, FRSL; *m* 25 April 1918 Eleanor, yst dau of William Cecil Slingsby, of Heversham, Westmorland, and *d* 6 Sept 1958, leaving:

(1) +Jocelin Slingsby Winthrop, OBE (1960) [Jocelin Young Esq OBE, Gräfin Hildegard Str 9, 78354 Sipplingen, Germany]; *b* 25 Oct 1919; *educ* Gordonstoun and U of Geneva; Lt RNVR WW II, tutor to Crown Prince of Greece 1948–58, Headmaster and fndr Anavryta Sch Athens 1949–59, FO 1959–63, Headmaster Salem 1964– , memb Cncl Gordonstoun, Cdr Order St George and St Constantine of Greece; *m* 1st 11 March 1951 (*divorce* 1974) Countess Ghislaine (*d* 1987), dau of Count Gustaf De la Gardie, of Malmö, Sweden, and has:

    1a +Mark Gustav [Mark De La Gardie-Winthrop-Young Esq, Holbein Str 16, 88212 Ravensburg, Germany]; *b* 25 April 1952 (HM KING PAUL OF THE HELLENES stood sponsor); *educ* Gordonstoun

    2a *Geoffrey Hubert [Dr Geoffrey Young, University of Waterloo, Ontario, Canada]; *b* 26 Dec 1960 (HRH PRINCE KARL OF HESSE stood sponsor)

    1a *Sophie [Mrs Roger Weidlich, Gräfin Hildegart Str 9, 78354 Sipplingen, Germany]; *b* 30 July 1954 (HRH PRINCESS SOPHIE OF GREECE stood sponsor); *m* 1985 *Roger Weidlich and has:

        1b *Amelie Ebba Ghislaine; *b* 1989

(1) (cont.) Jocelin Young *m* 2nd 1975 Countess Sibylle, D Phil, dau of Count von der Schulenburg, of Duisburg

(1) *Marcia Eacy Winthrop [Mrs Peter Newbolt, Green Banks, Cley-next-the-Sea, Norfolk NR25 7RX]; *b* 11 March 1925; *m* 3 July 1948 *Peter Newbolt, late T/Capt The Rifle Bde, s of Francis Newbolt, CMG, of Ockham, Surrey, and has:

    1a *Thomas Winthrop; *b* 24 Aug 1951; *educ* Winchester

    2a Harry Triffitt; *b* 9 Aug 1953; *educ* Bradfield; *d* 2 Aug 1978

    3a *Barnaby Charles Slingsby; *b* 4 Jan 1955; *educ* Winchester

    1a *Catherine Eacy; *b* 23 Nov 1956

3 EDWARD HILTON YOUNG, *cr* BARON KENNET (*qv*)

1 Eacy; *b* 23 Dec 1873; *d* 25 Dec 1888

Sir GEORGE's est s,

Sir George Young, 4th Bt, MVO (1906); *b* 25 Oct 1872; *educ* Eton and Us in Russia and Germany; Dip Serv 1896–1915, Admiralty Intelligence 1915–18, Driver RFA and Lt RMA 1918, Prof Portuguese and examiner in Ottoman Law London U 1919–23, visiting Prof in Int Law and Political Science various American Us 1928–30; *m* 1st 24 Nov 1904 Jessie Helen (*d* 6 Dec 1946), dau of Sir Courtenay Ilbert, GCB, KCSI, CIE; *m* 2nd 23 June 1948 Dorothy Joan, only surv dau of Rev Frank Bullock-Webster, and *d* 26 Sept 1952, having had by his 1st w:

1 GEORGE PEREGRINE (Sir), **5th Bt**

2 Courtenay Trevelyan; *b* 2 Aug 1914; *educ* Trin Coll Cambridge; Lt-Col Intelligence Corps WW II, Assist Sec to UK HC Canberra 1949–51, attd Office of Commr Gen for SE Asia in Singapore 1952–55, attd IDC 1960; *m* 23 April 1942 *June [Mrs Courtenay Young, Browne's Lodge, West Street, Reigate, Surrey], dau of Gordon Brinley Richards, and *d* 1974, having had:

(1) +Frederick Courtenay; *b* 11 June 1948; *educ* Charterhouse; *m* 1971 *Heather Brunskell and has:

    1a +Daniel Justin; *b* 1972

    2a +Jude Aaron; *b* 1976

    1a *Gudrun Rachel; *b* 1974

(1) Caroline June; *b* 7 June 1945; *d* 14 Nov 1948

(2) *Jessica Catherine [Mrs Paul Staddon, 7 Chepstow Rd, London W2 5BP]; *b* 13 June 1950; *m* 1976 *Paul Staddon, and has:

    1a *Anthony David; *b* 1988

1 *Joan Alison [Mrs Robert Mathew, 8 Wyndham Way, Oxford OX2 8DF]; *b* 5 March 1910; *m* 8 July 1933 Robert Mathew (*d* 24 March 1954), 4th s of Theobald Mathew, and *d* 25 June 1996, leaving:

(1) Theo(bald) David; *b* 7 April 1942; *educ* Downside and Balliol Coll Oxford (BA 1964); sometime Windsor Herald, Green Staff Offr at Investiture of HRH THE PRINCE OF WALES 1969, OStJ; *d* unm 24 Dec 1998

(1) *Perdita Mary [Mrs Michael Dawson, Leasgill, Amberley, Glos GL5 5AA]; *b* 23 Sept 1944; *educ* Hengrave Hall and Sussex U *m* 16 Feb 1965 *Michael Ivar Royal Dawson and has:

    1a *Daniel Cyrus; *b* 6 Sept 1965

    2a *Robert Caspar; *b* 3 Nov 1966

    1a *Cressida Ruth; *b* 8 Sept 1968

    2a *Jessie Charlia; *b* 1975

2 *Virginia Jacomyn; *b* 6 April 1911; *m* 28 May 1936 Sir Noel Kilpatrick Hutton, GCB, QC (*d* 1984), yr s of William Hutton, of Crutherland, E Kilbride, Lanarks, and has:

(1) *William Noel; *b* 8 March 1937; *educ* Rugby and Clare Coll Cambridge (MA, MB, BChir); FRCP (London); inventor; *m* 23 Jan 1960 *Doris Mary, dau of Stephen Hilton Nesfield, of Sevenoaks, Kent, and has:

    1a *Timothy Noel; *b* 9 Jan 1963

    2a *Duncan Neil; *b* 9 July 1964

    3a *Rupert MacIntyre; *b* 1971

    1a *Virginia Rozanne; *b* 17 Feb 1961

    2a *Julia Mary; *b* 18 May 1967

(2) *Charles Edward Ilbert [Charles Hutton Esq, The Cottage, Church Lane, Hornton, Oxon]; *b* 4 March 1943; *educ* Rugby and Keble Coll Oxford; *m* 18 Feb 1967 *Alison Victoria Fetherstone, yr dau of John Alan Harvey, and has:

    1a *Samuel Barnaby; *b* 1968

    2a *William Gabriel; *b* 1970

    1a *Pegotty Alice; *b* 1974

(1) *Melissa Grace [Mrs James Perot, 316 Maple Ave, Doylestown, PA 18901, USA]; *b* 12 Feb 1939; *m* 2 Feb 1963 *James Perot, 3rd s of Thomas Morris Perot III, and has:

    1a *James Blair; *b* 23 May 1965
    1a *Noelle Melissa; *b* 25 Oct 1963
    2a *Sczerina Alice; *b* 1968

(2) *Dorothea Eacy; *b* 10 Oct 1948

Sir GEORGE's e s,

Sir George Peregrine Young, 5th Bt, CMG (1951); *b* 8 Sept 1908; *educ* Westminister and Ch Ch Oxford (BA 1929), Laming Fell Queen's Coll Oxford 1929; head Western Dept FO 1950–51, Min Rome 1951–53, Assist Sec Cabinet Office 1953–55, Head News Dept FO 1955–56, Min Paris 1956–60, Cdr Legn Hon; *m* 14 Feb 1939 Elisabeth (*d* 15 Aug 1957), er dau of Sir Hughe Montgomery Knatchbull-Hugessen, KCMG (see BRABOURNE, B), and *d* 17 March 1960, leaving:

1 Sir GEORGE SAMUEL KNATCHBULL YOUNG, **6th and present Bt**

2 +Charles Evory [Charles Young Esq, 62 Old Rd, Oxford OX3 7LL]; *b* 15 Nov 1943; *educ* Eton and Ch Ch Oxford; *m* 1973 *Wiltrud, dau of H J Frömbling, and has:

    (1) *Emily Lucinde; *b* 1974
    (2) *Juliet; *b* 1975

1 *Helen Mary [Mrs Tom Winnifrith, 50 Sheep St, Shipston-on-Stour, Warwicks CV36 4AE]; *b* 23 Nov 1947; *educ* St Anne's Coll Oxford (BA 1968); *m* 26 July 1969 (*divorce* 1986) Digby Robert William Norton, s of Rev Alan James Norton, of Addington Vicarage, Surrey; *m* 2nd 1988 *Dr Tom Winnifrith, 2nd s of Sir John Winnifrith, KCB, and has by her 1st husb:

    (1) *Thomas Alan Hughe; *b* 1975
    (1) *Joanna Elisabeth; *b* 1972
    (2) *Felicity Margaret; *b* 1979

YOUNG, Bt, of Partick

Arms: Argent, on three piles issuant from a chief sable, charged with three lymphads or under full sail argent flagged gules, as many annulets of the third. **Crest:** A lymphad or under full sail, its sail charged of the arms, having a pennon gules with the badge of Scotland, *viz.*, azure a saltire argent, in the hoist. **Motto:** ('Serve wisely with faith'). **Creation:** Bt. (UK) 7 Sept 1945.

SIR STEPHEN STEWART TEMPLETON YOUNG, 3RD BT, of Partick, Co of the City of Glasgow [Sheriff Sir Stephen Young Bt, Glen Rowan, Shore Rd, Cove, Dunbartonshire G84 0NU]; *b* 24 May 1947; *s f* 1963; *educ* Rugby, Trin Coll Oxford and Edinburgh U; advocate Scotland, Sheriff Glasgow and Strathkelvin March-June 1984, Sheriff N Strathclyde at Greenock 1984–; *m* 1974 *Viola Margaret, dau of Prof P H Nowell-Smith by his 1st w Perilla (*m* as her 2nd husb and as his 2nd w Baron Roberthall (LP, see 1970 edn)), and has:

1 +CHARLES ALASTAIR STEPHEN; *b* 21 July 1979
2 +Alexander David; *b* 1982

Lineage: DANIEL HENDERSON LUSK YOUNG, of Glasgow; *m* E Alice Templeton and had:

Sir Arthur Stewart Leslie Young, 1st Bt (UK), so *cr* 7 Sept 1945, JP (Glasgow); *b* 10 Oct 1889; *educ* Fettes; Maj Scottish Rifles WW I, MP (U) Partick Nov 1935–50, PPS to U-Sec State Scotland 1937–39 and Sec of State Scotland 1939–42, Scottish Unionist Whip 1941, a Ld Commr Treasury 1942–44, V-Chamberlain Household 1944–45; *m* 21 Nov 1913 Dorothy (*d* 16 June 1966), dau of Sir Walter Baldwin Spencer, KCMG, and *d* 14 Aug 1950, leaving:

1 ALASTAIR SPENCER TEMPLETON (Sir), **2nd Bt**

2 Patrick Templeton; *b* 5 July 1925; *educ* Rugby; ARIBA; *m* 3 Aug 1950 *Jenny Loxton [Mrs Patrick Young, 3F Lansdowne Rd, London, W11 3AL], only dau of Sir Walter Eric Bassett, KBE, MC, of Melbourne, Australia, and *d* 1992, leaving:

    (1) +Roger Spencer Masson; *b* 28 April 1954; *educ* Radley; *m* 1979 *Margaret Alice Wilhelmina —

    (1) *Jane Templeton; *b* 21 July 1952; has:

        1a *Gemma Lucy; *b* 1983

---

1 *Barbara Mary [Mrs William Grayburn, 12 Lee Rd, Aldeburgh, Suffolk]; *b* 25 March 1916; *m* 20 May 1939 William Echlin Hollington Grayburn (*d* 1988), est s of Lionel Markham Grayburn, of Roughwood Farmhouse, Chalfont St Giles, Bucks, and has had:

    (1) Jon Alastair; *b* 11 Feb 1943; *educ* Sherborne and Trin Coll Oxford; *m* 1970 *Valerie Irlam and *d* 1978, leaving:

        1a *William Alastair George; *b* 1973

    (1) *Lesley Mary; *b* 11 April 1949

2 Anne Stewart; *b* 29 Oct 1919; *m* 8 July 1946 James Gray Workman, late 14th Sikhs, est s of William Orr Workman, and *d* 1990, leaving:

    (1) *Robert Stewart Gray [Robert Workman Esq, 32 West Kensington Mansions, Beaumont Cres, London W14 9PF]; *b* 28 June 1947; *educ* Fettes

    (2) *Hugh Stewart Gray; *b* 18 Sept 1951; *educ* Fettes

    (3) *Douglas Templeton; *b* 23 June 1956; *educ* Fettes

    (1) *Katrina Margaret; *b* 11 Aug 1948

Sir ARTHUR's er s,

Sir Alastair Spencer Templeton Young, 2nd Bt, DL (Dunbartonshire); *b* 28 June 1918; *educ* Rugby and Trin Coll Oxford; Lt Highland LI WW II, chm James Templeton & Co Glasgow; *m* 10 Nov 1945 (Dorothy Constance) Marcelle (*d* 17 Jan 1964), dau of Lt-Col Charles Ernest Chambers and widow of Lt John Hollington Grayburn, VC, 43rd LI (att Parachute Regt), and *d* 15 Oct 1963, leaving:

1 Sir STEPHEN STEWART TEMPLETON YOUNG, **3rd and present Bt**

1 *Clare Elizabeth [Mrs Stephen Beaty, 35 Chestnut Rd, London SE27 9EZ]; *b* 4 March 1953; *m* 1975 *Stephen John Beaty and has issue:

    (1) *Thomas Alastair Stephen; *b* 1977
    (1) *Corinne Elizabeth; *b* 1979
    (2) *Josepha Isobel; *b* 1981

YOUNG OF DARTINGTON

Creation: B. (LP, UK) 1978.

THE BARON YOUNG OF DARTINGTON, of Dartington, Co Devon (Michael Young) [The Rt Hon The Lord Young of Dartington, 18 Victoria Park Sq, London E2 9PF]; *b* 9 Aug 1915; *educ* Dartington Hall (Tstee 1942–92, Dep Chm 1980–) and London U (MA, PhD); barrister Gray's Inn 1939; Dir: Political and Ec Planning Lab Party 1941–45 (Sec Research Dept 1945–51), Inst Community Studies 1953–, Mauritius Coll of the Air 1972; Fell Churchill Coll Cambridge 1961–66; Chm: SSRC 1965–68, Dartington Amenity Research Tst 1967–, Internat Extension Coll 1970–, Nat Consumer Cncl 1975–77, Mutual Aid Centre 1977–, Tawney Soc 1982–84, Coll of Health 1983–90, Argo Venture 1984–, Health Info Tst 1987–, Open Coll Arts 1987–90, Open Sch 1989–, Language Line 1989–Educn Extra 1990–; Pres: Consumers Assoc 1965– (Chm 1956–65), Nat Extension Coll 1971– (Chm 1962–71), ACE 1976– (Chm 1959–76), Birkbeck Coll London U 1989–92; memb: Centl Advsy Cncl Educn 1963–66, NEDC 1975–78, SDP Policy Ctee 1981–83; Visiting Prof Ahmadu Bello U Nigeria 1974; Regent's Lecturer UCLA 1985; Hon DLitt Sheffield 1965, Keele 1991; Hon D OU 1973; Hon DLitt Adelaide 1974; Hon Fell LSE 1978, Plymouth Poly 1980, QMC 1983; Hon LLD Exeter 1982; Hon FBA 1995; author: *Family and Kinship in East London* (with Peter Willmott, 1957), *The Rise of the Meritocracy* (1958), *Family and Class in a London Suburb* (with Peter Willmott, 1960), *Innovation and Research in Education* (1965), *Learning Begins at Home* (with Patrick McGeeney, 1968), *Forecasting and the Social Sciences* (ed, 1968), *The Symmetrical Family* (with Peter Willmott, 1973), *The Poverty Report* (ed, 1974 and 1975), *Mutual Aid in a Selfish Society* (with Marianne Rigge, 1979), *Distance Teaching for the Third World* (co-author, 1980), *The Elmhirsts of Dartington: the creation of an Utopian Community* (1982), *Revolution from Within: co-operatives and co-operation in British Industry* (with Marianne Rigge, 1983), *Social Scientist as Innovator* (1984), *The Metronomic Society* (1988), *The Rhythms of Society* (with Tom Schuller, 1988), *Life After Work* (with Tom Schuller, 1991), *Your Head in Mine* (1994); *m* 1st 1945 (*divorce* 1959 or 1960) Joan Lawson and has:

1 *Christopher Ivan; *b* 1946
2 *David Justin [The Hon David Young, 18 Camden Rd, London NW1]; *b* 1949
1 *Emma Dorothy; *b* 1956

The BARON YOUNG OF DARTINGTON *m* 2nd 1960 Sasha (*d* 1993), broadcaster and novelist, dau of Raisley Stewart Moorsom and sis of Christopher Moorsom (see also LINDSEY and ABINGDON, E), and has by her:

3 *Toby Daniel Moorsom [The Hon Toby Young, 67 Gibson Sq, London N1]; *b* 1963; jnlst
2 *Sophie Ann; *b* 1961

The BARON YOUNG OF DARTINGTON *m* 3rd Nov 1995 *Dorit Uhlemann, milliner, and by her has a dau

Lineage: GIBSON YOUNG; musician; had:

MICHAEL, *cr* a **Baron**

YOUNG OF GRAFFHAM

Creation: B. (LP, UK) 1984.

THE BARON YOUNG OF GRAFFHAM, of Graffham, W Sussex (David Ivor Young, PC (1984)) [The Rt Hon The Lord Young of Graffam PC, Young Assocs Ltd, Harcourt House, 19 Cavendish Sq, London W1M 9AB]; *b* 27 Feb 1932; *educ* Christ's Coll Finchley and UCL (LLB); slr 1956; exec GUS 1956–61; chm: Eldonwall 1961–75, Manufacturers Hanover Property Servs 1974–84, Br Organisation for Rehabilitation by Training 1975–80 (Pres 1980–82), Cambridge Display Technology; dir: Town & City Properties Ltd 1972–75, Salomon Inc 1990–94, CPS 1979–82 (memb Management Bd 1977); industl advsr DTI 1979–80 (special advsr 1980–82), Min without Portfolio 1984–85, Sec State: Employment 1985–87, Trade and Industry 1987–89, Dep Chm C Party 1989–90; Memb English Industl Estates Corp 1980–82, NEDC 1982–89; Chm: Internat Cncl Jewish Social and Welfare Servs 1981–84, Manpower Servs Commn 1982–84, Bd Govrs Oxford Centre Postgrad Hebrew Studies 1989–93, Central Cncl for Jewish Community Servs 1993–, UCL Devpt Bd 1994– (Chm Cncl 1995–), London Philharmonic Tst 1995–; Pres: World Organisation for Rehabilitation by Training Union 1990–93 (Chm Admin Ctee 1980–84), IOD 1992–, Jewish Care 1990–; exec chm Cable & Wireless plc 1990–95; chm Young Assocs Ltd 1996–; Dir ROH Tst 1990–95; Hon FRPS 1981; Fell UCL 1988; author: *The Enterprise Years* (1990); *m* 1956 *Lita Marianne, dau of Jonas Shaw, and has:

  1 *Karen Debra; *b* 1957; *m* 1983 *Sir Bernard Anthony Rix (Hon Mr Justice Rix), s of Otto Rix, of London, and has:

    (1) *Jacob; *b* 19–
    (2) *Gideon; *b* 19–
    (3) *Jonathan; *b* 19–
    (1) *Hannah; *b* 19–
    (2) *Rachel Elsie; *b* 1994

  2 *Judith A—; *b* 1960; *m* 1st 1989 Jeremy A Amias, yr s of Alan Amias, of London; *m* 2nd 1 May 1997 *Guy Robert Beacroft, s of Ronald Beacroft

Lineage: JOSEPH YOUNG; *m* Rebecca — and had:

DAVID IVOR, *cr* a **Baron**

YOUNG OF OLD SCONE

Creation: B. (LP, UK) 2 Aug 1997.

THE BARONESS YOUNG OF OLD SCONE (Barbara Scott Young) [The Rt Hon The Baroness Young of Old Scone, House of Lords, London SW1A 0PW]; *b* 8 April 1948; *educ* Perth Acad, Edinburgh U and Strathclyde U; Sector Administrator Gtr Glasgow Health Bd 1973–78, Dir Planning and Devpt St Thomas's Health Dist 1978–79, Gen Administrator NW District Kensington and Chelsea and Westminster AHA 1979–82, Dist Administrator Haringey HA 1982–85, Dist Gen Manager: Paddington and N Kensington HA 1985–88, Parkside HA 1988–91; memb: BBC Gen Advsy Cncl 1985–88, Ctee King's Fund Inst 1986–90, Delegacy St Mary's Hosp Med Sch 1991–; Pres Inst Health Servs Management 1987–88; Internat Fell King Edward VII Hosp Fund Coll 1985–87 and 1990; Tstee Wytham Hall 1990–92; Ch Exec RSPB 1991–, Chm English Nature 1998–; memb Bd Tstees NCVO 1993–; Patron Inst Ecology and Environment Management 1993; DUniv Stirling 1995; FRSA

Lineage: GEORGE YOUNG; *m* Mary Scott and has:

BARBARA SCOTT, *cr* a **Baroness**

YOUNGER

Arms: Or on a bend azure between two martlets sable three roses argent, barbed and seeded vert, on a chief gules a crescent between two mullets of the first. **Crest:** A dexter hand holding a lance in bend sinister proper. **Motto:** *Tout prest* ('Quite ready').
Creation: Bt. (UK) 14 Feb 1911.

SIR JOHN WILLIAM YOUNGER, 3RD BT, of Auchen Castle, Co Dumfries, CBE (1969, MBE 1945) [Maj-Gen Sir John Younger Bt CBE, 23 Cadogan Sq, London SW1X 0HU]; *b* 18 Nov 1920; *s f* 1973; *educ* Canford and RMC Sandhurst; Coldstream Gds: 2nd Lt 1939, Middle East WW II 1939–42 (POW), Staff Coll Camberley 1949, Lt-Col 1959, cmded 1st Bn, AQMG HQ London Dist 1961–63, Col 1963, AAG War Office 1963–65, Brig 1967, Dep Dir Army Staff Duties MOD 1967–70, Dir Quartering MOD 1970–73, Maj-Gen 1971, Dir Management and Support Intelligence 1973–76, Commr-in-Ch St John Ambulance Bde 1980–85 (Dep Commr London 1978), KStJ 1980; *m* 1st 23 Jan 1948 *Stella Janet, only dau of Rev Canon John George Lister and formerly w of Chris Dodd, and has:

  1 +JULIAN WILLIAM RICHARD [Julian Younger Esq, 6 Country Club Lane, Pelham Manor, NY 10803, USA]; *b* 10 Feb 1950; *educ* Eton and Grinnell U USA; *m* 1981 *Deborah Ann Wood and has:

    (1) *Andrew William; *b* 14 Jan 1986

  1 *Joanna Jane [Mrs Timothy Binnington, Thakeham Place, Thakeham, W Sussex]; *b* 12 Aug 1951; *m* 1972 *Timothy John Binnington and has:

    (1) *Nicholas William David; *b* 1977

    (1) *Kate Louise Frances; *b* 1975

Sir JOHN *m* 2nd 30 Sept 1953 Marcella Granito (*d* 1989), dau of Professor Avvocato (*i.e.*, 'Advocate') Roberto Scheggi and formerly w of Prince Pignatell di Belmonte; *m* 3rd 1991, as her 2nd husb, *Anne Henrietta Maria St Paul, only dau of Horace George St Paul Butler and formerly w of Timothy Seely (see SEELY, Bt)

Lineage: JAMES YOUNGER; Baillie (elective local magistrate) of Linton, Peeblesshire, 1678, Linton being then a burgh of regality (chief town of a territorial jurisdiction granted direct by the sovereign) with a council; *m* 25 Feb 1658 Isobel Purdie and had, with three yr sons and a dau:

WILLIAM YOUNGER, of Linton; *bapt* 20 Feb 1659; *d* by 22 July 1710, leaving:

JOHN YOUNGER, of Oxgale, Peeblesshire; *b* 1672; writer (legal practitioner) in Edinburgh; *m* 2 Nov 1700 Helen, dau of James Douglas, of Linton, and had, with two yr sons:

WILLIAM YOUNGER; *b* 1702; Baillie of Linton 1731; *m* Margaret Mitchell and *d* 1755, having had, with three yr sons and four daus:

WILLIAM YOUNGER; *b* 1733; *m c* 1756 Grizel Cochran-Syme (*m* 2nd — Anderson and *d* 1821 aged 90) and *d* 1770, having had, with two er sons (Archibald, of Ardyne, Argyllshire, *b* 4 March 1757, *d* unm 1819; Richard, *b* 1762, *m* Mary Ross and *d* 1806, leaving issue, extinct 1880) and two daus (Jane, *m* — Ryrie and *d* 1817; Grize; *m* John Somervail (*d* 1826), of W Morham, Haddingtonshire, and *dsp* 1849):

WILLIAM YOUNGER, of Craigielands, Dumfriesshire, and Ardyne; *b* 31 Aug 1767; *m* 1800 Janet (*d* 14 June 1843), 5th dau of John Hunter by Jacobina Yorston, and *d* 28 Nov 1842, having had, with a yr s (John, *b* 1809, *d* unm 1829) and a dau (Jamima, *b* 1804, *m* 1823 Alexander Allen (*d* 1884) and had issue):

WILLIAM YOUNGER, of Craigielands; *b* 21 June 1801; *m* 1827 Isabella, 3rd dau of Henry Johnston, MD, of Corstorphine House, Edinburgh, and *d* 5 June 1854, having had:

  1 WILLIAM

  2 Henry Johnston, JP, DL, of Benmore, Kilmun, Argyllshire; *b* 5 Oct 1832; Commr of Supply; *m* 1st Emma (*d* 9 March 1874), dau of Richard Lowman, and had issue; *m* 2nd 1876 Jane Edith (*d* 1 July 1929), dau of T Richardson, of Wentworth House, Mill Hill, and *d* 6 March 1913, having by her had:

    (1) Eda Georgina May; *m* 7 Nov 1906 Sir William Jardine, 9th Bt, of Applegirth (*qv*), and *dsp* 30 Dec 1960

  3 John, JP (Dumfries), of Langshaw Bush, Moffat; *b* 7 June 1840; Col RA and Hon Col West of Scotland RFA; *m* 1st 3 Jan 1878 Caroline Isabella, dau of Maj-Gen George Bucknal Shakespear, RA, and had issue; *m* 2nd 30 April 1906 Lou-

isa Grace Campbell, dau of Archibald Brown, DL, of Johnstownburn, E Lothian, and *d* 1 Sept 1925

4 David; *b* 1 Sept 1844; *m* 1870 Memé Isidora (*d* 6 May 1931), dau of Kenneth Macleay, and *d* 1883, leaving issue

1 Isabella; *m* 1854 Lt-Col George Allan, 5th Fus

2 Janet; *d* unm 12 April 1909

3 Henrietta; *m* 28 Dec 1861 Sir Alexander Jardine, 8th Bt, of Applegirth (*qv*), and *d* 13 June 1925, leaving issue

4 Jamima; *m* 1870 Rev Frederick Stainton Tireman, Rector Kirk Sandall, Yorks, and had issue

5 Grace Margaret

The est s,

WILLIAM YOUNGER, JP, of Auchen Castle, Moffat, Dumfriesshire; *b* 8 March 1831; Commr of Supply; *m* Oct 1861 Margaret (*d* 29 July 1900), er dau of John Wyld Brown, of Sydney, NSW, and *d* 4 Aug 1886, leaving:

Sir William Younger, 1st Bt (UK), so *cr* 14 Feb 1911, JP (Dumfriesshire), DL (Dumfriesshire and Leics); *b* 28 June 1862; Lt 16th Lancers, Capt Lanarks Yeo, Maj Sherwood Rangers (Notts ImperialYeo), MP (C) Stamford 1895–1906 and (Lib) Peebles and Selkirkshire Jan–Dec 1910, memb Roy Commn Housing in Scotland 1913–17, Hon LLD Edinburgh 1932; *m* 24 Jan 1888 Helen (Nellie) Caroline Benyon (*d* 17 Dec 1925), est dau of Col Sir Robert Gunter, 1st Bt (*see* 1970 edn), and *d* 28 July 1937, having had:

1 **Sir William Robert Younger, 2nd Bt**, of Auchen Castle; *b* 27 Oct 1888; *educ* Harrow and Ch Ch Oxford; Dip Serv: Hon Attaché St Petersburg, The Hague and Rome 1912–18; *m* 1st 7 April 1915 (*divorce* 1923) Joan Gwendoline, yr dau of Hon Louis Vanden-Bempdé-Johnstone (*see* DERWENT, B), and had:

(1) William Anthony; *b* 16 May 1917; *educ* Canford and Ch Ch Oxford; *m* 25 July 1945 Nancy Elizabeth, 3rd dau of Lt-Col Harold Ernest Brassey (*see* BRASSEY OF APETHORPE, B) and widow of S/Ldr Reginald Frederick Stuart Leslie, DSC, DFC, AFC, and *dsp* 13 Feb 1961

(2) Sir JOHN WILLIAM YOUNGER, **3rd and present Bt**

(1) *Margaret Elizabeth [Mrs John Moller, 4 Cherriman's Orchard, Haslemere, Surrey GU27 1NP]; *b* 11 Jan 1916; *m* 3 Sept 1937 John Howard Moller, Queen's Own Cameron Highrs (*d* 1983), s of Pierre Howard Moller, and has:

1a *Christopher Pierre William Howard; *b* 27 Aug 1943; *educ* Charterhouse; *m* 1973 *Susan Maria Scougal Burdette, dau of Alban Miller Ross-Smith, of Heyshott, Sussex, and has:

1b *Cassandra Maria; *b* 1975

2b *Tara Elizabeth; *b* 1976

1a *Caroline Victoria Margaret; *b* 19 May 1939

2a *Maxine Faith Alexandra; *b* 31 May 1940; *m* 18 June 1966 (*divorce* 1978) Rory Bryan Mario Nicholas, s of A/Cdre Bryan David Nicholas, CBE, of Villa Romani, Maidenhead Court, Berks

(2) *Diana Joan; *b* 29 July 1919; *m* 1st 6 June 1940 (*divorce* 1947), as his 1st w, 8th Earl of Clancarty (*qv*); *m* 2nd 21 April 1947 *H(anford) Wentworth Eldredge, AB, PhD, Prof Sociology Dartford Coll, NH, and has:

1a *James Wentworth; *b* 15 Aug 1950

2a *Alan Wentworth; *b* 7 March 1953

1 (cont.) **Sir William** *m* 2nd 4 July 1930 Nellie Elizabeth (*d* 4 April 1960), dau of John Archbold, of Portsmouth, and *d* 25 May 1973

2 John Malcolm; *b* 15 Aug 1889; Capt Coldstream Gds; accidentally drowned 31 Aug 1918

YOUNGER OF LECKIE

Arms: Per saltire or and gu. a rose counterchanged, in base a martlet sa., on a chief az. three covered cups or. **Crest:** An armed leg couped at the thigh ppr., garnished and spurred or. **Supporters:** Dexter, a lion rampant sa.; sinister, a wolf arg., both armed and langued gules. **Mottoes:** 1 *Celer et audax* ('Swift and bold'), 2 *Labentibus junior annis* ('Younger as the years go by'). **Creations:** Bt. (UK) 12 July 1911, V. (UK) 20 Feb 1923, B. (LP, UK) 1992.

THE 4TH VISCOUNT YOUNGER OF LECKIE, of Alloa, Co Clackmannan, **Baron Younger of Prestwick**, of Ayr, District of Kyle and Carrick, and a **Baronet** (Sir George Kenneth Hotson Younger, KT (1996), KCVO (1993), TD (1964), PC (1979), DL (Stirlingshire 1968) [The Rt Hon The Viscount Younger of Leckie KT KCVO TD PC DL, Leckie House, Gargunnock, Stirlingshire]; *b* 22 Sept 1931; *s* f in Viscountcy and btcy 1997; *educ* Winchester (Fell 1992–, Warden 1997–) and New Coll Oxford (MA); Maj Argyll and Sutherland Highrs 1950, BAOR and Korea 1951, 7th Bn TA (T&AVR) 1951–65, Hon Col 154th Regt RCT (V) 1977–85, Brig Roy Co Archers; dir: Geo Younger & Son 1958–68, J G Thomson & Co 1962–66, Maclachlans Ltd 1968–70, Tennant Caledonian Breweries 1977–79; Govr Roy Scottish Acad Music 1962–70; MP (C) Ayr 1964–92, Scottish C Whip 1965–67, Dep-Chm Scottish C & U Assoc 1967–70, Parly U-Sec Scottish Office 1970–74, Min State Def 1974, Chm C Party Scotland 1974–76 (Dep Chm 1967–70), Sec State Scotland 1979–1986, Def 1986–89, Pres Nat Union C and U Assocs 1987–88; dir: Roy Bank Scotland 1989– (chm 1990–), Scottish Equitable Life Assur 1990–98, Roy Bank Scotland Gp 1991–, SPEED Ltd 1992–98; chm: Roy Anniversary Tst 1990–, Romanian Orphanage Tst 1990, Edinburgh Festival Theatre Tst 1991–, Siemens Plessey (UK) Ltd 1991–98, Murray Johnston Investment Tsts 1993– (dir 1989–), PIK Ltd 1991–98, Royal Armouries 1994–; Chllr Napier U 1993–; FRSE; Hon LLD Glasgow 1992, Hon DLitt Napier U 1992, Hon DU Edinburgh 1992; *m* 1954 *Diana Rhona, est dau of Capt Gerald Seymour Tuck, DSO, RN, of Little London, W Sussex, and has:

1 +JAMES EDWARD GEORGE [The Hon James Younger, The Old Vicarage, Dorton, Bucks HP18 9NH]; *b* 11 Nov 1955; *educ* Winchester and St Andrews (MA); MBA, MCIM; personnel manager Coats Patons plc 1984–86; consultant Angela Mortimer Ltd 1984–86; assist dir Stephens Consultancies 1986–92; dir MacInnes Younger 1993–94, dir Union Bank of Switzerland 1994–; memb Roy Co Archers 1997; *m* 1988 *Jennie Veronica, dau of William Edward James Wootton, of Chanters Ho, Pilton, Somerset, and has:

(1) +Alexander William George; *b* 13 Nov 1993

(1) *Emily Evelyn; *b* 1990

(2) *Alice Elizabeth; *b* 1992

2 +Charles Gerald Alexander; *b* 1959; *educ* Winchester; *m* 1986 *Sally Elizabeth, er dau of Kenneth Mackenzie Neil Fergusson, of Blinkbonny Ho, Haddington, E Lothian, and has had:

(1) Freddie; still born 23 April 1995

(2) +Geordie Charles Kenneth; *b* 19 Dec 1997

(1) *Arabella Emily; *b* 1987

(2) *Katrina Louise; *b* 1990

(3) Georgina Harriet; *b* and *d* 1993

(4) *Francesca Claire; *b* 26 June 1996

3 +Andrew Seymour Robert [The Hon Andrew Younger, Fernhill House, Cradley, Worcs WR13 5LN]; *b* 1962; *educ* Winchester; *m* 1989 *Hilary Margaret, yst dau of Philip Alexander Forbes Chalk, of The Barn House, Hurstbourne Priors, Hants, and has:

(1) *Rosanna Lucy; *b* 1994

(2) *Isobel Alexandra; *b* 26 May 1996

1 *Joanna Rosalind [The Hon Mrs Davidson, Easter Leckie, Gargunnock, Stirling FK8 3BN]; *b* 1958; *m* 1st 1986 (*divorce* 1989) Gregory William Rossiter Cooper, s of Brian Cooper, of Ealing; *m* 2nd 25 March 1995 *John S M Davidson and has:

(1) *Molly Diana Audrey; *b* 6 May 1996

(2) *Lucy Harriet Alice; *b* 18 Aug 1997

Lineage: THOMAS YOUNGER, of Craigton, Clackmannan (probably s of Thomas Younger, of Leit Green, Kincardine); *m* 21 June 1598 Marjorie, dau of Andrew Schaw, of Knockhill, and had a 2nd s:

THOMAS YOUNGER, of Culross; *bapt* 18 Jan 1609; *m* by 1641 Elizabeth Miller, of Clackmannan, and *d* by 1666, leaving, with two yr sons (James, *bapt* 30 Nov 1644, *m* 28 Feb 1672 Agnes, dau of George Tilloch, and had issue; John, of Powside, Clackmannan, *bapt* 3 Jan 1658, *m* Margaret Hutcheson and had issue) and two daus:

THOMAS YOUNGER, of Culross; *bapt* 22 Jan 1642; *m* 21 Aug 1680 his yr bro's sis-in-law Jane, dau of George Tilloch, and had, with three daus:

GEORGE YOUNGER; *bapt* 14 Feb 1694; *m* 27 Feb 1721 Jean, dau of Thomas Thomson, in Grange, and had, with a yr s (Thomas, tenant of The Grange 1771, had issue):

GEORGE YOUNGER, of Alloa, Clackmannanshire; *bapt* 17 Feb 1722; fndr George Younger and Son, brewers; *m* 14 April 1755 Catherine Allan (*d* 14 April 1785) and *d* 28 Sept 1788, leaving a 4th s:

JAMES YOUNGER, of Alloa; *b* 1 July 1763; *m* 4 Dec 1789 Mary Bleloch (*d* 15 Nov 1837), of Clackmannan, and *d* 19 Feb 1809, leaving an est s:

GEORGE YOUNGER; *b* 19 Aug 1790; *m* 16 Dec 1816 Jane, dau of James Hunter, and *d* 25 Sept 1853, leaving an est s:

JAMES YOUNGER, of Alloa; *b* Feb 1818; *m* Nov 1850 Janet (*d* 2 April 1912), er dau of John McEwan, of Alloa, and *d* 5 Aug 1868, leaving:

1 GEORGE, **1st Viscount**

2 John McEwan; *b* 1852; *d* 1867

3 James, of Mount Melville, St Andrews, and Arnsbrae, Cambus, DL Fife; *b* 20 Jan 1856; Freeman St Andrews; *m* 18 Feb 1886 Annie (*d* 21 Aug 1942), dau of John Thomson Paton, of Alloa, and *d* 27 Nov 1946, leaving:

(1) James Paton (Sir), CBE (1945), JP (Clackmannanshire 1933), of Mount Melville and Arnsbrae; *b* 19 June 1891; *educ* Eton and Balliol Coll Oxford; Capt 3rd Bn Argyll and Sutherland Highrs WWI, chm: Patons Scottish Knitwear Hldgs, George Younger and Sons, United Caledonian Breweries and Western Regnl Hosp Bd Scotland 1955–63, dir Charrington United Breweries, Ld Lt Clackmannanshire 1955–66, ktd 1961, memb Roy Co Archers; *m* 30 April 1921 Rachel Howard, er dau of Paul Waterhouse, PRIBA, of Yattendon Court, Berks, and *d* 17 Sept 1976, leaving:

1a James Andrew; *b* 26 Oct 1924; *educ* Eton and Balliol Coll Oxford; *m* 1st 8 June 1950 (*divorce* 1955) Portia Mary, only dau of Bruce Ottely; *m* 2nd 28 Nov 1963 *Moira Robertson Peterson, *née* Bell, and *d* 5 Aug 1868, leaving:

1b *Elizabeth Rachel; *b* 28 Sept 1951

2b *Mary Clare; b 9 March 1953

1a Mr and Mrs James Younger also adopted 9 Dec 1964:
*Peter Brian; b 29 April 1961

2a *Robert Paul [Robert Younger Esq, 6 Seymour Walk, London SW10]; b 20 Aug 1928; educ Eton; m 17 July 1952 *Gillian Mary, dau of Maj A Savory, and has:

1b *Katherine Mary; b 7 Oct 1956
2b *Lorna Louise; b 10 April 1959

3a *Stephen John; b 27 Dec 1931; educ Eton and Balliol Coll Oxford; m 27 Sept 1958 *Jean Maxwell, er dau of Brig Eric Brickham, DSO, of Denork, St Andrews, and has:

1b *Michael James; b 8 Aug 1960
2b *Alastar Stephen Eric; b 10 Feb 1962

1a *Mary Elizabeth [Mrs Denis Mackay, Millfield Ho, Hexham, Northumberland]; b 27 March 1922; m 13 July 1946 Cdr Denis Handcock Mackay, DSC, RN, est s of Lionel Mackay, of Nelson, NZ, and has:

1b *Lionel James; b 28 Jan 1949; educ Eton and Churchill Coll Cambridge
1b *Mariele Grace; b 7 Oct 1952
2b *Rachel Jane; b 20 Aug 1954

(1) Mary Graeme; b 26 June 1881; m 14 Nov 1911 Eric FitzGeorge Boothby (d 17 March 1919), s of Capt George FitzRobert Boothby (see 1970 edn BOOTHBY, B) and d 7 Dec 1916, leaving issue

(2) Dorothy Janet; b 14 Nov 1892; m 27 May 1919 Maj Edward Owen Rutter (d 1 Aug 1944), Wilts Regt, est s of Engr-Cdr E W Rutter, RD, RNR and d 25 July 1961, leaving issue

4 William; b 1857; m 4 June 1902 Katherine Theodora (d 1 June 1961), dau of Cdr Adam Alexander Duncan Dundas of Dundas, RN and d 22 Aug 1925, leaving:

(1) Ralph, CB (1957) CBE (1954) DSO, MC, JP (1961), DL (Roxburghs 1962); b 12 July 1904; educ Charterhouse and Trin Coll Cambridge (BA 1926); WW II, Col 7th QO Hus 1952–58, Maj-Gen 1955, Col QO Hus 1958–62, memb Roy Co Archers; m 1st 6 Jan 1932 (divorce 1932) Mary Cynthia, only dau of Charles Remington Mills; m 2nd 21 July 1938 *Greta Mary [Mrs Ralph Younger, Ravenswood, Melrose, Roxburghshire], dau of Alfred Turnbull, of Clifton Maubank, Yeovil, Somerset, and had by her:

1a *David John; b 23 Oct 1939; educ Eton; Lt-Col QOH; m 6 Dec 1966 *Jennifer Ann, only dau of Thomas Lewis Dewey (see DEWEY, Bt), and has:

1b *William Grahame Ralph; b 22 Jan 1970
2b *James David; b 1972
1b *Catherine Belinda; b 27 Dec 1967

1a *Rosemary Anne; b 18 Aug 1948

(2) Sir WILLIAM McEWAN YOUNGER, 1st Bt (qv)

(1) *Charlotte Mary; m 14 April 1936 13th Lord Reay (d 10 March 1963) and has issue

5 ROBERT YOUNGER, BARON BLANSBURGH, of Alloa, Co Clackmannan (LP, UK), so cr 12 Oct 1923, GBE (1917), PC (1919); b 12 Sept 1861; educ Edinburgh Acad and Balliol Coll (BA 1883, MA 1909, Hon Fell 1916, Visitor 1934, Hon DCL); barrister Inner Temple 1884, QC 1900, Bencher Lincoln's Inn 1907, Treas 1932, High Court Judge Chancery 1915–19, Ld Justice Appeal 1919–23, Ld Appeal in Ordinary 1923–37, Pncpl Br Del Reparation Commn 1925–30, LLD Edin and St Andrews, Fell King's Coll London and Chm Delegacy, V-Pres and FRCM, Hon Memb RWCS, Prime Warden Goldsmiths' Co 1931–32; d unm 17 Aug 1946, when the Barony expired

1 Anne; m 1878 Rev D McLean and d 1924 leaving issue

The est s,

Sir George Younger, 1st Bt, and **1st Viscount Younger of Leckie**, of Alloa, Co Clackmannan (both UK), so cr 12 July 1911 and 20 Feb 1923 respectively, JP Clackmannanshire; b 13 Oct 1851; educ Edinburgh Acad; chm George Younger and Son 1897, Ld Lt Stirling, V-Lt Clackmannanshire (Convener 1895–1906), Pres CCs Assoc Scotland 1902–04 and Nat Union of C Assocs Scotland 1904, MP (U) Ayr Burghs 1906–22 (previously fought 1904, also Clackmannan and Kinross 1895, 1899 and 1900), Chm U Party Organisation 1916–23, Treas U Party 1923, dir: Nat Bank Scotland, Lloyds Bank, N Br and Mercantile Insur and Southern Rlwy Co; m 10 June 1879 Lucy (d 26 May 1921), dau of Edward Smith, MD, FRS, of Harley St, London, and Heanor Fall, Derbys, and d 29 April 1929, having had, with two yr sons (Edward John, b 1 July 1882, 2nd Lt 16th Lancers, ka Boer War 23 Dec 1901; Charles Frearson, b 9 Sept 1885, educ New Coll Oxford (BA), Lt Lothians and Border Horse, m 23 June 1913 Marjory Caroline (d 29 April 1971), dau of Thomas Middleton Murray, of Geanies, Ross-shire, and was ka 21 March 1917):

JAMES YOUNGER, 2nd Viscount Younger of Leckie, DSO (1919), TD (1919), JP, DL Stirling; b 19 May 1880; educ Winchester and New Coll Oxford; with George Younger and Son, Fife and Forfar Yeo: joined 1902, Maj 1909, Lt-Col 1918, WWI (wounded despatches), V-Lt Clackmannanshire, Brig Roy Co Archers; m 7 Feb 1906 Maud (d 28 Dec 1957), er dau of Sir John Gilmour, 1st Bt, of Lundin and Montrave (qv), and d 1946, leaving:

1 EDWARD GEORGE YOUNGER, 3rd Viscount Younger of Leckie, OBE (1940), TD (1941); b 21 Nov 1906; educ Winchester and New Coll Oxford (BA 1928); Lt 7th Bn Argyll and Sutherland Highrs, Col Gen Staff WW II, Ld Lt Stirlingshire 1964–79 (DL 1947–64), also CD Organiser, TA 1926–46, dir George Younger and Son to 1963, Tstee Nuffield Fndn, Chm Scottish Multiple Sclerosis Soc; m 7 June 1930 Evelyn Margaret, MBE (1963) (d 23 July 1983), est dau of Alexander Logan McClure, KC, LLB, of Edinburgh, and d 25 June 1997, leaving:

(1) GEORGE KENNETH HOTSON YOUNGER, **4th and present Viscount Younger of Leckie**

(2) Alexander James [The Hon Alexander Younger, Wester Leckie, Kippen, Stirlingshire FK8 3JL]; b 5 May 1933; educ Winchester and Worcester Coll Oxford (BA 1956); Capt Argyll and Sutherland Highrs, attd Black Watch, Korea 1952–53 (wounded), Capt 7th Argylls TA, dir Sir Joseph Causton and Sons 1963–68 and Key Europe Ltd 1977–80, md Robert MacLehose and Co Ltd, University Press of Glasgow 1968–1977, mktg dir The Simpson Label Co Ltd, Dalkeith 1980–96, pres FINAT (European Assoc of Label Printers)

1994–96; m 20 June 1959 *Annabelle Christine, only dau of Gerald Furnivall, LLB of Middle Brook, Bishop's Waltham, Hants and has:

1a +Nicholas Gerald Gilmour; b 6 Feb 1963; educ privately

2a +Rupert Edward Alexander; b 12 May 1966; educ Winchester and King's Coll Aberdeen; m 1 July 1995 *Catherine E P, dau of David de Borman, of London, and has:

1b +Alec Gilmour; b Oct 1998

1a *Amanda Charlotte Frances; b 4 Feb 1961; m 1st 1981 (divorce 1986) Simon John Miller Richard; m 2nd 1989 *William Alexander Clark, er s of Dr Alister Clark, of Hammersmith, and has:

1b *Ruari Alexander; b 1990
2b *Harry Edward; b 1992

2a *Araminta Lucy; b 27 Dec 1967

(3) +Robert Edward Gilmour [The Hon Robert Younger, Old Leckie Ho, Gargunnock, Stirling]; b 25 Sept 1940; educ Winchester and New Coll Oxford (BA), Edinburgh U and Glasgow U; advocate 1968, Sheriff Glasgow and Strathkelvin 1979–82 and Tayside, Centl and Fife 1982–; m 16 Dec 1972 *Helen Jane, dau of Capt Eric Gerald Hayes, DFC (see MUIR, Bt), and has:

1a +Fergus Robert; b 5 Feb 1975
1a *Meriel Charlotte; b 30 Nov 1973

(1) *Rosalind Evelyn [The Hon Mrs Cropper, Greenhills, Willow Tree, NSW 2339, Australia]; b 12 Oct 1937; educ Priorsfield; m 14 May 1960 *Thomas Ross Charles Cropper, JP, s of Cecil Howe Cropper, DSO, MC, of Sydney, NSW, and has:

1a *Charles Thomas Howe; b 23 July 1962; educ King's Sch Sydney and U of Sydney; m 1994 *Sophia, dau of Antony de Mestre
2a *Robert Douglas; b 27 June 1969

1a *Jill Marion; b 15 May 1961; educ Ascham Sch Sydney and U of Sydney; m *Michael John Hawker and has:

1b *William Thomas George; b 1990
1b *Annabel Kate; b 1988
2b *Emma Louise; b 1993

2a *Annabel Rosalind; b 20 July 1966; educ Ascham Sch; m 1998 *Craig Kennedy Williamson, s of Lorne Williamson

2 Kenneth Gilmour (Sir), KBE (1972), PC (1951); b 15 Dec 1908; educ Winchester and New Coll Oxford (BA 1930, MA 1961); barrister Inner Temple 1932, Maj Intell Corps WW II, MP (Lab) Grimsby 1945–59, PPS to Min State 1945–46 and Sec State Air 1946–47, Parly U-Sec Home Office 1947–50, Min State FO 1950–51, Memb Ctee Security Procedures, Chm: European Ctee UNRRA 1946–48, Govrs St George's Hosp 1966, Advsy Cncl Penal Treatment 1966–69, Ctee on Privacy 1970, Dir-Gen RIIA 1959, author: The Public Service in New States (1960) and Changing Perspectives in British Foreign Policy (1964); m 23 Aug 1934 *Elizabeth Kirsteen [The Hon Lady Younger, 3 New Buildings, Shore Rd, Old Bosham, W Sussex PO18 8JD], only dau of William Duncan Stewart, JP, of Achara, Duror, Argyll, and d 19 May 1976, leaving:

(1) +(James) Samuel [Samuel Younger Esq, 28 Rylett Crescent, London W12 9RL]; b 5 Oct 1951; educ Westminster and New Coll Oxford; m 1984 *Katharine Anne, dau of C K Spencer, of Abergavenny, Gwent, and has:

1a +Edward Kenneth Spencer; b 1986

(1) *Susannah Mary; b 5 June 1936; educ Somerville Coll Oxford (BA 1958, MA 1961)

(2) *Christina Lucy; b 18 Feb 1950; educ St Hilda's Coll Oxford

1 Elizabeth Maud; b 22 May 1913; m 31 March 1937 Lt-Col Kenneth Bulstrode Lloyd Davidson, Argyll and Sutherland Highrs, Lt-Col UDR, only s of Col Charles Lloyd Davidson, DSO, of The Manor House, Eglinton, Co Londonderry, and had:

(1) *Charles Kenneth Lloyd [Charles Davidson Esq, 2205 Barbara Ave, Kamloops, BC, Canada]; b 19 Oct 1938; educ Haileybury and ISC; m 16 June 1961 *Diana Margaret, only child of Harold Christopher Watts, of Lansdown, Bath, and has:

1a *Ilona Margaret; b 24 Nov 1969
2a *Rosemary Nicole; b 1971

(2) *Andrew James Lloyd [Andrew Davidson Esq, The Manor House, Eglinton, Co Londonderry]; b 30 Nov 1944; educ St Columba's Coll and Trin Coll Dublin

(3) *Claude John Lloyd; b 3 Dec 1947; educ St Columba's Coll and RMA Sandhurst; Lt Roy I Rangers 1971; m 1971 *Bridget Jane Phyllis, yr dau of Raymond Salmon, of Kenya and has a s and dau

(4) *Alastair Michael Lloyd; b 16 July 1954

(1) A dau; b and d 22 May 1951

(2) A dau; b and d 22 May 1951

(3) *Anne Elizabeth [Miss Anne Davidson, Garden Flat, 1 Redcliff St, London SW10]; b 20 Nov 1952

2 Anne Margaret; b 10 March 1920; m 13 March 1943 Capt James Timothy Noel Price (see O'BRIEN, Bt) and had:

(1) *Timothy James; b 15 Sept 1945; educ Ampleforth and Magdalene Coll Cambridge

(2) Simon Anthony Carew; b 15 Jan 1951; educ Ampleforth; late Capt Scots Gds; m 16 Aug 1975 *Primrose E, dau of J G B Thompson, of Church Farm, Brattan Seymour, Somerset

(1) *Jenifer Mary [Mrs Walter Gilbey, Ballacallin Mooar, Crosby, Marown, Isle of Man]; b 6 Jan 1944; m 2 April 1964 *Walter Anthony Gilbey (see GILBEY, Bt) and has issue

(2) *Jacqueline Anne; b 15 Jan 1948; m 23 Sept 1972 *Andrew Ducker

(3) *Mary Elizabeth; b 26 April 1953

ZETLAND

Arms: Argent a lion rampant within a double tressure flory counter-flory gules, all within a bordure azure. **Crest:** A lion's head affrontée, struggling through an oak bush, all proper, fructed or, crowned with an antique crown of the last. **Supporters:** Two lions proper crowned with antique crowns or and gorged with a chaplet of oak leaves vert, fructed gold an escutcheon pendant from each; the dexter argent, a saltire and chief gules, on a canton of the field a lion rampant azure (for BRUCE); the sinister lozengy or and gules (for FITZWILLIAM). **Motto:** *Essayez* ('Strive'). **Creations:** M. (UK) 22 Aug 1892, E. (Zetland) 2 July 1838 and (Ronaldshay) 22 Aug 1892 (both UK), B. (GB) 13 Aug 1794, Bt. (GB) 16 Nov 1762.

THE 4TH MARQUESS OF ZETLAND, Earl of Zetland, Earl of Ronaldshay, Co Orkney, **Baron Dundas of Aske**, Co York, and a **Baronet** (Sir Lawrence Mark Dundas, Bt, of Kerse, Co Stirling, DL (N Yorks 1994)) [The Most Hon The Marquess of Zetland DL, Aske, Richmond, N Yorks DL10 5HJ; 9 Crescent Place, London SW3]; *b* 28 Dec 1937; *s* f 1989; *educ* Harrow and Christ's Coll Cambridge; 2nd Lt Gren Gds, Steward Jockey Club 1992–95, dir Br Horseracing Bd 1993–97; *m* 4 April 1964 *Susan Rose, Pres Cancer Relief Macmillan Fund, 2nd dau of Guy Richard Chamberlin, of Shefford House, Shefford, Newbury, Berks, and has:

1 +ROBIN LAWRENCE, *Earl of Ronaldshay*; *b* 5 March 1965; *educ* Harrow and RAC Cirencester; dir: Catterick Racecourse Co 1988–, Redcar Race Co 1989–; md Musks Ltd (sausage mfrs) 1993–; *m* 12 April 1997 *Heather, er dau of Robert Hoffman and Mrs Richard Cazenove, and has:

  (1) *Eliza Constance; *b* 31 March 1998

2 +James Edward [The Lord James Dundas, The Fishing Cottage, Stitchcombe, Marlborough, Wilts SN8 2EU]; *b* 2 May 1967; *educ* Harrow and RAC Cirencester; *m* 13 July 1991 *Melanie Clare, est dau of Robert Henry Whitefield, of The Old Rectory, Stocking Pelham, Herts, and has:

  (1) +Milo James; *b* 21 May 1998
  (1) *Poppy Alice; *b* 19 June 1993
  (2) *Emily Rose; *b* 21 Nov 1994

1 *Henrietta Kate [The Lady Henrietta Stroyan, 77 Bramfield Rd, London SW11 6PZ]; *b* 9 Feb 1970; *m* 10 Dec 1994 *James Mark Ptarmigan Douglas Stroyan, s of Judge Ronald Stroyan, QC, of Boreland, Killin, Perthshire, and has:

  (1) *Clementine; *b* 10 Feb 1997

2 *Victoria Clare; *b* 2 Jan 1973; *educ* Oxford Sch of Drama; voly social worker with Family Friends, co-fndr Stripey Demon theatre co

Lineage: Sir JOHN DUNDAS of Fingask, Perthshire (modern Tayside), some five miles SE of Perth; had a gs and heir:

THOMAS DUNDAS of Fingask; *m* Bethia, dau of John Baillie, of Castlecary, Stirling, and *d* 1762, leaving:

1 Thomas, of Fingask and Carron Hall, Larbert, Stirlingshire; MP Orkney and Shetland 1768–71, Police Commr Scotland 1771; *m* 1st 1737 Ann (*dsp*), dau of Hon James Graham; *m* 2nd 11 Nov 1744 Janet (*d* 29 Dec 1805), dau of 6th Earl of Lauderdale (*qv*), and *d* 16 April 1786, leaving:

  (1) Thomas, of Fingask and Carron Hall; *b* 30 June 1750; MP Orkney and Shetland 1771–84, Maj-Gen 80th Regt (served N America as Lt-Col 1779–81, commr to arrange Br surrender Yorktown 1781), cmded troops in capture from French of Guadeloupe, Martinique and St Lucia, WI, 1794; *m* 9 Jan 1784 Elizabeth Eleanor (*d* 10 April 1837), dau of 9th Earl of Home (*qv*), and *d* Guadeloupe 3 June 1794, leaving:

    1a Thomas, of Carron Hall; Lt-Col 15th Hus; *m* 18 Feb 1815 Charlotte Anna (*d* 9 Jan 1862), dau of Joseph Boultbee, and *d* 24 May 1860, leaving:

    1b Joseph, JP, DL, of Carron Hall; *b* 28 Nov 1822; Maj Stirling Militia; *m* 28 Nov 1850 Margaret Isabella (*d* 25 Oct 1905), dau and coheir of Charles G Moir, and *d* 7 July 1872, leaving, with another s (*d* young) and two daus (*d* unm):

      1c Thomas George, of Carron Hall; *b* 14 May 1853; 52nd Regt; *m* 3 Dec 1879 Mary (*d* 28 Oct 1923), dau of Lt-Col Duncan Henry Caithness Reay Davidson of Tulloch, and *d* 12 June 1929, leaving:

      1d Thomas Archibald; *b* 22 Dec 1880; *m* 14 Dec 1903 (*divorce* 19–) Sybil Katherine, yst dau of F R Hampshire, and had:

        1e +Thomas Archibald David
        1e *Christobel; *b* 16 Oct 1904

      2d Ronald George; *b* 14 June 1886; *m* 21 Aug 1912 Olive Mary, dau of Robert Scott-Day, of Victoria, BC, and had:

        1e *Eleanor Mary; *b* 24 June 1914; *m* a US Naval Offr

     2c Laurence Armine; *b* 4 Oct 1854; Capt Merchant Navy; *m* 26 June 1882 Isabel (*d* 15 July 1915), dau of Don St Iago Noguez, and *d* 4 June 1901, leaving:

      1d Laurence George Dionicio; *b* 9 Oct 1892; *m* 1st 16 Feb 1925 (*divorce* 1932) Margaret Fay, er dau of Dr B F Sandow, of Berkeley, Calif.; *m* 2nd 19 Sept 1959 Kathleen Agnes (*d* 2 May 1969), dau of Oswald White, CMG, of S Kensington, and *dsp* 8 Feb 1971

      1d Leonore; *b* 25 March 1885; *d* unm 1916

      2d Margarita Maria Teresa; *b* 17 June 1894; *d* unm

     3c Arthur Bruce; *b* 3 March 1860; *m* 1st 10 Feb 1891 Margaret Seton Steuart (*d* 28 Jan 1912), dau of William Montgomery (*see* MONTGOMERY, Bt); *m* 2nd 11 Oct 1913 Janetta Elizabeth Frances, est dau of John James Smyth, JP, of Rathcoursey Ho, Ballinacurra, Co Cork, and *dsp* 14 June 1937

     4c Charles; *b* 17 April 1861; *d* unm 1937

     5c George Joseph; *b* 26 Nov 1866; *d* unm 6 Nov 1943

     1c Isabella; *m* 13 Dec 1888 George Royce Allen (*d* 17 June 1945), s of Sir George Wigram Allen, KCMG, of Toxteth Park, Sydney, NSW, and *d* 13 June 1947, leaving issue

    1b Charlotte Anna; *m* 1st 12 Feb 1845 Col Armine Mountain, CB (*d* 8 Feb 1854); *m* 2nd 12 May 1860 Gen Sir John Henry Lefroy, KCMG, CB (*d* 1890), and *d* 4 June 1903

    2b Clementina; *m* 1856 Vincenzo Bartolucci and *d* 1867, leaving issue

(2) CHARLES DUNDAS, 1st and last BARON AMESBURY, of Kintbury-Amesbury and Barton Court, Berks, and Aston Hall, Co Flint (UK), so *cr* 16 May 1832; *b* 5 Aug 1751; *educ* Trin Coll Cambridge (BA 1773, MA 1776); barrister, MP (Whig) Richmond (N Yorks) 1775–80 and 1784–86, Orkney and Shetland 1781–84 and Berks 1794–1832, nominated as Speaker H of C 1802 but withdrew, Cncllr of State Scotland to PRINCE OF WALES (later GEORGE IV), Col White Horse Vol Cavalry; *m* 1st Anne (*dspm* 29 Nov 1812 aged 59), dau and heiress of Ralph Whitley, of Aston Hall, Flints, acquiring considerable property in Kintbury-Amesbury thereby; *m* 2nd 25 Jan 1822 his cousin Margaret (*d* 21 April 1841), dau of Hon Charles BARCLAY formerly MAITLAND (*see* LAUDERDALE, E) and widow of (a) Charles Ogilvy and (b) Maj Archibald Erskine, and *d* 30 June 1832, leaving by his 1st w:

  1a Janet; *m* 28 April 1808, as his 1st w, her cousin James DEANS later Adml Sir James WHITLEY-DEANS-DUNDAS, GCB, Adml the White 1861, MP (Whig) Greenwich 1832–34 and 1841–52 and Devizes 1836–38, ch naval cdr Mediterranean on outbreak of Crimean War, being criticised for insufficent energy in bombardment of Sebastopol 1854 (*m* 2nd Lady Emily Morton, dau of 1st Earl of Ducie (*qv*) and *d* 3 Oct 1862 aged 76), and *d* 30 April 1846, having had issue

(1) Margaret; *m* A Gibson
(2) Berthea; *m* George Haldane of Gleneagles
(3) Mary; *m* James Bruce of Kinnaird
(4) Janet; *m* James Deans, MD, of Calcutta, and had

  1a Adml Sir James DEANS later WHITLEY-DEANS-DUNDAS (*see* above)

2 Sir Lawrence Dundas, 1st Bt (GB), so *cr* 16 or 23 Nov 1762, with remainder in default of male issue to his er bro, PC (1771), of Kerse, Upleatham and Aske, both Yorks; *b c* 1710; MP Linlithgow Burghs 1747–48, Newcastle-under-Lyme 1762–68 and Edinburgh 1768–80 and Feb–Sept 1781, Commissary Gen and contractor to Army 1748–59 with such adroitness that he left personal property worth £900,000 (nearly £38,290,000 in late-1990s terms) and an estate worth £16,000 a year (just over £680,000 in late-1990s terms), V-Adml Shetland and Orkney; *m* 9 April 1738 Margaret (*d* 11 Oct 1802 aged 67), only dau of Brig-Gen Alexander Bruce, of Kennet, by Mary, dau of 4th Lord Balfour of Burleigh (*qv*), and *d* 21 Sept 1781, leaving:

(1) THOMAS DUNDAS, **1st Baron Dundas of Aske**, Co York (GB), so *cr* 13 Aug 1794; *b* 16 Feb 1741; MP (Whig) Richmond 1763–68 and Stirlingshire 1768–94, FRS 1768, FSA 1784, Cncllr of State to PRINCE OF GEORGE IV), Ld Lt and V-Adml Orkney and Shetland 1794–1820; *m* 14 May 1764 Charlotte (*d* 11 Feb 1833), 2nd dau of 3rd Earl Fitzwilliam (*see* 1970 edn), and *d* 14 June 1820, having had:

  1a LAWRENCE, **1st Earl**
  2a Thomas Lawrence; *b* 13 Dec 1768; *d* an infant
  3a William Lawrence; *b* 18 May 1770; Lt-Col; *d* Santo Domingo 1796
  4a Charles Lawrence; *b* 18 July 1771; *m* 16 Feb 1797 Caroline (*d* 23 Nov 1838), dau of 5th Duke of St Albans (*qv*), and *d* 25 Jan 1810, leaving, with a dau (*d* unm):

    1b Frederick; *b* 14 June 1802; MP and Lt Orkney and Shetland; *m* 2 June 1847 Grace (*d* 15 Jan 1868), est dau of Sir Ralph St George Gore, 7th Bt (*qv*), and *dsp* 26 Oct 1872

    1b Catherine Elizabeth; *m* 21 Aug 1832 Lt-Gen Freeman Murray (*d* 14 April 1885) and *d* 12 Feb 1876

    2b Charlotte Amelia; *m* 14 May 1846 Ralph Thomas Fawcett and *d* 27 Jan 1881

  5a Thomas Lawrence (Rev); *b* 12 Oct 1775; Rector Harpole, Northants; *m* 25 July 1816 Mary Jane (*d* 15 Dec 1827), est dau of Rev James Bousquet, and *d* 17 March 1848, leaving:

    1b Thomas James; *b* Nov 1818; *d* unm 28 Dec 1838

    2b Robert Bruce (Rev); *b* 1821; *educ* Cambridge (MA); Rector Harpole; *d* 6 Feb 1912

    1b Charlotte Mary; *m* 6 July 1852 Capt Frederick Thompson, 6th Dragoons (*d* 1886), and had issue

    2b Louisa; *m* 14 Dec 1847 George Gilpin Brown (*d* 28 Nov 1889), of Sedbury Park, Yorks, and had issue

3b Anne; *m* 24 Aug 1854 Hon C W W Fitzwilliam, MP (*dsp* 20 Dec 1894; *see* 1970 edn FITZWILLIAM, E) and *d* 20 Dec 1925

6a George Heneage Lawrence, CB; *b* 8 Sept 1778; R-Adml; *d* unm 7 Oct 1834

7a Robert Lawrence (Sir), KCB; *b* 27 July 1780; Lt-Gen; *d* unm 23 Nov 1844

1a Anne; *b* 3 April 1767; *d* an infant

2a Margaret; *m* 24 Jan 1794 Archibald Spiers (*d* 2 Nov 1832), of Elderslie, Renfrews, and *d* 8 May 1852, leaving issue

3a Charlotte; *m* 19 April 1808 Rev William Wharton (*d* 26 May 1842), Vicar Gilling, Richmond, Yorks, and *d* 5 Jan 1855, leaving issue

4a Frances Laura; *m* 24 Jan 1805 Robert Chaloner, MP (*d* 7 Oct 1842), and *d* 27 Nov 1844, leaving issue (*see* GISBOROUGH, B)

5a Dorothy; *b* 13 Aug 1785; *d* 24 Dec 1790

6a Mary; *m* 8 July 1806 4th Earl Fitzwilliam, KG (*d* 4 Oct 1857; *qv*), and *d* 1 Nov 1830, leaving issue

7a Isabella; *m* 4 May 1814 John Charles Ramsden, MP, est s of Sir John Ramsden, 4th Bt (*qv*), and *d* 6 Dec 1887 aged 97, leaving issue

The 1st BARON's est s,

LAWRENCE DUNDAS, **1st Earl of Zetland** (UK), so *cr* 2 July 1838; *b* 10 April 1766; *educ* Harrow and Trin Coll Cambridge (MA 1786, Hon LLD 1811); MP (Whig): Richmond (N Yorks) 1790–1802 and 1808–11 and York 1802–07 and 1811–20, Lt-Col N R Militia and Col Army 1791, Alderman York 1808 (Ld Mayor 1811–12), FSA 1812, Dep Grand Master and Pro Grand Master Freemasons 1821–22 and 1834–39, Ld Lt and V-Adml Orkney and Shetland 1831–39; *m* 21 April 1794 Harriot (*b* 16 June 1769; *d* 18 April 1834), 3rd dau of Gen John Hale (*see* GISBOROUGH, B), and *d* 19 Feb 1839, having had, with two other sons (*d* young unm):

1 THOMAS DUNDAS, **2nd Earl of Zetland**, KG (1872, KT 1861–72); *b* 5 Feb 1795; *educ* Harrow and Trin Coll Cambridge (MA 1815); MP (Whig): Richmond 1818–30 and 1835–39 and York 1830–32 and 1833–34, Ld Lt N R Yorks 1839–73, Freemasons: Dep Grand Master 1839–40, Pro Grand Master 1840–43, Grand Master 1844–70; *m* 6 Sept 1823 Sophia Jane (*b* 21 Nov 1803; *d* 7 May 1865), yst dau of Sir Hedworth Williamson, 6th Bt (*qv*), and *dsp* 6 May 1873

2 John Charles, of Woodhall, Wetherby, Yorks; *b* 21 Aug 1808; MP Richmond, Ld Lt Orkney and Shetland; *m* 27 March 1843 Margaret Matilda (*d* 8 Dec 1907), dau of James Talbot, of Maryville, Co Wexford, yst s of Matthew Talbot, of Castle Talbot, and *d* 14 Feb 1866, having had issue, with two other sons (*d* young) and two daus (*d* unm):

(1) LAWRENCE, **1st Marquess**

(2) John Charles; *b* 21 Sept 1845; MP Richmond 1873–85, Ld Lt Orkney and Shetland; granted 1873 with siblings rank of earl's daus/yr sons; *m* 2 Aug 1870 Alice Louisa (*d* 3 June 1934), 2nd dau of 1st Viscount Halifax (*see* HALIFAX, E), and *d* 13 Sept 1892, leaving:

1a Charles Lawrence; *b* 18 Aug 1871; ICS; *m* 11 Oct 1896 Georgina (*d* 30 Sept 1950), dau of George Butt and widow of Capt Charles Mordaunt Stevens, and *d* 26 April 1922, leaving:

1b Margaret; *b* 1899; *m* 22 July 1920 (*divorce* 1940) Brig Sir John George Smyth, 1st Bt (*qv*), and had issue

2a Frederick James; *b* 9 Jan 1877; *m* 27 March 1913 Sylvia Mary (*d* 30 Dec 1976), est dau of Hugh March Phillipps, of Chapel Court, Kenn, nr Exeter, and *d* 16 June 1950, leaving:

1b John Charles, DFC and bar; *b* 19 Aug 1915; *educ* Stowe and Ch Ch Oxford (BA); A/F/Lt 609 Fighter Sqdn AAF WW II; *ka* 28 Nov 1940

2b Hugh Spencer Lisle (Sir), CBE (1977), DSO (1944) and bar (1945), DFC (1941), DL (Surrey 1968); *b* 22 July 1920; *educ* Stowe; G/Capt RAuxAF WW II (despatches), cmded 601 (Co of London) Flying Sqdn RAuxAF 1948–49, md: Rediffusion Ltd 1969–74, Br Fleet Traction Co, chm Redifon, High Sheriff Surrey 1989; *m* 28 Jan 1950 *Enid Rosamond Lawrence [The Hon Lady Dundas, 55 Iverna Court, London W8 6TS], 2nd dau of 3rd Baron Trevethin and (1st Baron) Oaksey (*see* OAKSEY, TREVETHIN and, B), and *d* 10 July 1995, leaving:

1c +James Frederick Trevor [James Dundas Esq, 16 Norland Sq, London W11 4PX]; *b* 4 Nov 1950; *educ* Eton; *m* 28 June 1979 *Jennifer A, dau of Lt-Col John Daukes, and has:

1d +David Lawrence Charles; *b* 2 May 1989

1d *Clare Jessica; *b* 27 April 1984

2d *Lucy Rose; *b* 7 Jan 1986

1c *Sarah Jane [Ms Sarah Dundas, 190 Crawford St, Toronto, Ont M6J 2V6, Canada]; *b* 15 Jan 1953; *m* Oct 1977 (*divorce* 1994, has resumed maiden name) Terence McGlade, s of Eugene McGlade, of Toronto, and has:

1d *Victoria Rose Clare; *b* 1983

2d *Charlotte Amanda; *b* 1984

2c *Amanda Rose [Mrs Thomas Service, 30 Baskerville Rd, London SW18 3RS]; *b* 28 March 1956; *m* 1986 *Thomas Nicholas McKinlay Service, s of Ian McKinlay Service, and has:

1d *George; *b* 1992

1d *Katherine (Katie) Mary Rose; *b* 1987

2d *Louisa Amy; *b* 1989

1b *Elizabeth Mary [Dowager Lady Muir, Bankhead, Blair Drummond, Perthshire]; *b* 1 Jan 1914; *m* 24 Oct 1936 Sir John Harling Muir, 3rd Bt (*qv*), and has issue

2b Alice; *b* 4 June 1918; *m* 1st 27 July 1939 (*divorce* 1950) Patrick John Macdonald, 3rd s of Dr Peter Macdonald, of York, and had issue; *m* 2nd 7 Feb 1952 Surg-Cdr Dennis Charles Drake, RN (ret) (*d* 1976), and *d* 19–

3b *Charmian [Mrs Maurice Snowden, Manor Cottage, Milton, Banbury, Oxon OX15 4HH]; *b* 20 May 1931; *m* 28 April 1955 *Maurice Ronald Snowden, yst s of Cyril Ralph Snowden, of Tiverton, and has:

1c *John Frederick Hugh [John Snowden Esq, 7 Paradise Terrace, Chipping Norton, Oxon OX7 5HN]; *b* 22 Oct 1955; *educ* Eton

2c *Mark Lawrence; *b* 15 July 1957

1c Katherine Mary; *b* 17 Feb, *d* 21 Feb 1959

1a Evelyn Mary; *b* 15 Jan 1873; *m* 26 June 1895 Maj Herbert Peake and *d* 26 July 1945, having had issue (*see* INGLEBY, V)

2a Margaret; *b* 5 Jan 1875; *m* 26 Sept 1889 Col Edward Bunbury North, CMG, DSO, JP, Roy Fus (*d* 23 July 1944), of Summerdale Ho, Holme, Carnforth, Lancs, and *d* 7 July 1954, leaving issue

3a Alice Katharine; *b* 21 Dec 1883; *m* 21 Dec 1907 (*divorce* 1924) Maj Kenneth George Bittleston, DSO, RFA, est s of Col G H Bittleston, BA, and *d* 1 Jan 1933, leaving issue

(3) William Fitzwilliam James, DL (Yorks); *b* 8 May 1860; *educ* Trin Hall Cambridge; sub-agent in Cleveland, Yorks, to **1st Marquess of Zetland** 1892–96 and resident agent on Goodwood estates to 6th and 7th Dukes of Richmond and (1st and 2nd Dukes of) Gordon (*qv*), Clerk of Course Goodwood race meeting 1896–1908; *m* 20 June 1892 Mary Maud (*d* 2 Sept 1945), yst dau of Lt-Col Henry Auriol Prinsep, and *d* 23 Nov 1906, having had issue:

1a Geoffrey William Seymour; *b* 12 Jan 1896; Capt Rifle Bde WW I (wounded); *d* 2 Jan 1937

2a Robert Bruce; *b* 11 Aug 1900; *educ* Uppingham; *m* 18 April 1934 Enid Mary (*d* 19–), est dau of Cdr Francis William Roberts, RN, and *d* 1980, leaving:

1b +David Lawrence; *b* 15 May 1936; *educ* Shrewsbury and Balliol Coll Oxford (MA 1966); geologist with Hunting Surveys & Consultants Ltd; *m* 14 Dec 1968 *Fay or Faith Dorine, dau of Harold Scott, of Friendship, Jamaica

1b *Jennifer Elizabeth Mary; *b* 23 April 1942; *m* 10 Aug 1963 *John Warren Williams, er s of John O Williams, of Friday St, Eastbourne, and has had:

1c Peter Robert; *b* 3 April 1969; *d* 19–

1c *Patricia Helen; *b* 8 July 1965

1a (Margaret) Beryl; *b* 27 April 1893; *m* 12 April 1920 Capt James Chaigneau Colvill, RN (*d* 29 Nov 1976), s of Robert Frederick Stewart Colvill, of Coolock Ho, Coolock, Co Dublin, and had issue

2a Mary Gwendolen; *b* 22 Nov 1894

3a *Janet Elizabeth [Miss Dundas, 6 Dunwich Road, Southwold, Suffolk]; *b* 29 July 1911

(4) Cospatric Thomas, JP (N R Yorks), DL (Orkney and Shetland); *b* 5 Nov 1862; Lt Yorks Hus; *m* 18 July 1892 Maud (*m* 2nd 2 Oct 1912 Maj Sir Harry Edward Spiller Cordeaux, KCMG, CB, and *d* 15 July 1949), yr dau of Hon George Wentworth Fitzwilliam (*see* 1970 edn FITZWILLIAM, E), and *d* 23 Nov 1906, having had, with a dau (*d* unm):

1a John George Lawrence, CB (1945), CBE (1942); *b* 3 Nov 1893; V-Adml WWs I and II, Ch Staff Mediterranean 1942–44, Assist Ch Naval Staff 1944–45, Offr Legn Hon, Croix de Guerre with palms, US Legn Merit, Grand Cross Phoenix Greece; *m* 22 Sept 1928 *Ruth Northrop, dau of Archibald Coleman, of Minneapolis, and *d* 26 March 1952, leaving:

1b +John Archibald Lawrence [Dr John Dundas, 151 Concord St, Apt 13, Newton Lower Falls, MA 02162, USA]; *b* 30 June 1942; *educ* Groton and Harvard; MD; *m* 1967 (*divorce* 1985) Dorothy Polk, dau of H Bradford Washburn, of Boston, and has:

1c +Michael Henry Lawrence; *b* 29 July 1969

2c +Patrick George Bradford; *b* 1973

3c +Matthew Colgate; *b* 1976

1c *Jennifer Deirdre; *b* 1971

1b *Elgiva Ruth [Dr Elgiva Watson, 4408 Pamlico Dve, Raleigh, NC, USA]; *b* 22 June 1929; *m* 7 June 1951 *Penn Thomas Watson, only s of Penn Watson, of Wilson, NC, and has:

1c *Rom Purefoy [Rom Watson, 378 Central St, Newton, MA 02166, USA]; *b* 1955; *m* 1981 *Susan Bazett

1c *Ruth Coleman [Mrs Jeffrey Scheuer, 56 West 10th St, New York, NY 10011, USA]; *b* 1952; *m* 1st 1974 (*divorce* 1978) Jack Barry Tanenbaum; *m* 2nd 1982 *Jeffrey Scheuer

2c *Clare Thomas [Mrs Louis Gallo, 544 Riverside Dr, Ormond Beach, FL 32176, USA]; *b* 1958; *m* 1st 1982 (*divorce* 1992) James Acker, MD; *m* 2nd 1993 *Louis Gallo

2b *Rosemary Maud [Mrs Robert Patton, 85 Parker Ave, San Francisco, CA 94118, USA]; *b* 16 Dec 1933; MA; *m* 2 Oct 1954 *Dr Robert Gray Patton, only s of Dr Lewis Patton, of Durham, NC, and has:

1c *Mary Gray; *b* 1956; *m* 1986 *Roger T Phelps

2c *Sarah Dundas; *b* 1959; *m* 1991 *Peter Feichtmeir

3c *Susannah MacRae; *b* 1964

3b *Deirdre Clare [Mrs Walter Newton Jr, 406A Cocos Pl, Honolulu, Hawaii 96818, USA]; *b* 13 Feb 1935; MA; *m* 1st 26 July 1958 (*divorce* 1960) Clifford Enright, only s of Joseph Clifford Enright, of Falls Church, Va., and has:

1c *Iva Margaret; *b* 1959

3b (cont.) Mrs Deirdre Enright *m* 2nd 16 July 1961 *Dr Walter Monroe Newton, Jr, only s of Walter Monroe Newton, of Bennettsville, SC, and has:

1c *Walter Monroe; *b* 1962

2c *Elisabeth Dundas; *b* 1970

4b *Alexandra Mary; *b* 18 April 1946; PhD; *m* 1st 4 June 1965 (*divorce* 1973) John Andrew Todd, yr s of Dr Richard Todd, of Washington, DC, and has:

1c *John Andrew; *b* 1970

4b (cont.) Dr Alexandra Todd *m* 2nd 1988 Stephen Russell Fox, PhD

1a Elgiva Margaret; *b* 9 Nov 1897; *m* 11 Oct 1920 5th Baron de Mauley (*qv*) and *d* 1987, leaving issue

2a Ida Victoria Alice; *b* 24 May 1905

(1) Harriot Emily; *m* 7 April 1875 Col Charles Thomas Bunbury, Rifle Bde (*d* 4 Oct 1917), 4th s of Hugh Mill Bunbury, of West Hill, Wandsworth, and *d* 11 Dec 1939, having had issue

(2) Mary; *m* 12 Oct 1874 William Francis Plowden (*see* PLOWDEN, B) and *d* 19 Sept 1911, leaving issue

(3) Laura Octavia; *m* 8 Feb 1877 4th Baron de Freyne (*qv*) and *d* 19 Jan. 1881, leaving issue

(4) Alice; *d* unm 3 April 1950

1 Margaret Bruce; *m* 5 Feb 1816 her cousin Henry Walker Yeoman (*d* 14 Sept 1875), of Woodlands, and *d* 13 Sept 1860, having had issue

2 Harriott Frances; *m* 8 Dec 1825 Col Henry Lane and *d* his widow 13 Oct 1878 aged 77

3 Charlotte Jane; Ldy of Bedchamber to HRH THE DUCHESS OF KENT; *d* unm 29 Nov 1866

The 2nd EARL's n,

LAWRENCE DUNDAS, **1st Marquess of Zetland**, so *cr* 22 Aug 1892, as also EARL OF RONALDSHAY, Co Orkney (both UK), KT (1900), PC (1889), JP, DL (Stirling); *b* 16 Aug 1844; *educ* Harrow and Trin Coll Cambridge; RHG: Cornet 1866, Lt 1869, ret 1872, MP (Lib) Richmond 1872–73, Provincial Grand Master N and E Rs Yorks Freemasons 1874–1923, Capt Yorks Hus Yeo Cav 1874, MFH Zetland 1876–1911, a Ld-in-Waiting May–Sept 1880, Col cmdg 1st N R Yorks Vol Artillery 1881–94, Steward Jockey Club 1881–84, Ld Lt Ireland 1889–92, CA N R Yorks 1894, Mayor Richmond 1895–97, Hon Col 3rd Bn Yorks Regt; *m* 3 Aug 1871 Lilian, DGStJ (*d* 24 Dec 1943), 3rd dau of 9th Earl of Scarbrough (*qv*), and *d* 11 March 1929, having had:

1 Thomas, styled *Lord Dundas*; *b* 19 Jan, *d* 11 Feb 1874

2 LAWRENCE JOHN LUMLEY, **2nd Marquess**

3 George Heneage Lawrence; *b* 1 July 1882; *educ* Harrow; Capt Argyll and Sutherland Highrs Boer War 1900–02, RFC and F/Lt RAFVR, Instr CFS 1916, T/Maj and Sqdn Cdr 1918, WWs I (despatches) and II; *m* 23 Dec 1905 Ivy Winifred (*d* 20 March 1969 aged 86), dau of Col Malachy McDee Hanley, and *dsp* 30 Sept 1968

1 Hilda Mary; *b* 24 Nov 1872; *m* 9 July 1892 4th Baron Southampton (*qv*) and *d* 19 May 1951, leaving issue

2 Maud Frederica Elizabeth, OBE (1920); *b* 9 July 1877; CStJ, Nat Pres Br Legion, Scout Commr S Yorks 1921–40; *m* 24 June 1896 7th Earl Fitzwilliam, KCVO, CBE, DSO (*see* 1970 edn), and *d* 15 March 1967, leaving issue

The 1st MARQUESS's er surv s,

LAWRENCE JOHN LUMLEY, **2nd Marquess of Zetland**, KG (1942), GCSI (1922), GCIE (1917), PC (21 April 1922), JP, DL N R Yorks; *b* 11 June 1876; *educ* Harrow and Trin Coll Cambridge (Hon LLD 1926); ADC to Viceroy India 1900, Capt 1st N R Yorks (W Div) RA, MP (C) Hornsey 1907–16, memb Roy Commn Public Servs India 1912–14, Maj 4th Bn Yorks Regt 1915–23, Col 62nd (Northumbrian) AA Bde RA (TA), Govr Bengal 1916–22, Provincial Grand Master Freemasons N and E Yorks 1923–56, Sec State: India 1935–37, India and Burma 1937–40, Ld Lt N R Yorks 1945–51, Pres: RGS 1922–25 (Tstee 1925–47), Roy Asiatic Soc 1928–31, Roy India Soc, Dep Govr then Govr Nat Bank Scotland 1923–35 and 1940–51, Chm Exec Ctee Nat Tst 1931–45, KGStJ, Hon DLitt Leeds U 1923, Hon LLD Glasgow U 1924, FBA, author: *Sport and Politics under an Eastern Sky* (1902), *On the Outskirts of Empire in Asia* (1904), *A Wandering Student in the Far East* (1908), *An Eastern Miscellany* (1911), *Lands of the Thunderbolt* (1923), *India: A bird's-eye view* (1924), *The Heart of Aryâvarta* (1925), *The Life of Lord Curzon* (1928), *The Letters of Disraeli to Lady Bradford and Lord Chesterfield* (1929), *Lord Cromer* (1932) and *Steps Towards Indian Home Rule* (1935); *m* 3 Dec 1907 Cicely (*d* 11 Jan 1973), 2nd dau of Col Mervyn Henry Archdale, 12th Lancers, and *d* 6 Feb 1961, having had:

1 LAWRENCE ALDRED MERVYN, **3rd Marquess**

2 Bruce Thomas; *b* 18 Oct 1920; *educ* Harrow; F/Sgt RAFVR WW II; *kas* Feb 1942

1 Viola Mary; *b* 4 Jan 1910; *d* unm 21 March 1995

2 Lavinia Margaret; *b* 31 Dec 1914; *m* 1st 19 Oct 1939 Capt John Creagh Rogerson, 15th/19th Hus (*d* 24 Oct 1945), s of John Edwin Rogerson, of Mount Oswald, Co Durham; *m* 2nd 20 Feb 1947 Jack Green (*d* 9 Feb 1961), est s of Louis Green, of W Hampstead; *m* 3rd 19 April 1962 Brig Francis ('Tim') Wyld Sandars, DSO and bar, DLI (*d* 1986), s of Canon George Russell Sandars, of Cedar Court, Farnham, Surrey, and *d* 4 Jan 1974

3 Jean Agatha; *b* 4 May 1916; *m* 2 Sept 1939 Capt Hector Lorenzo Christie, MBE (*d* 18 Oct 1969), only s of William Lorenzo Christie, JP, of Jervaulx Abbey, and *d* 13 May 1995, leaving:

(1) *William Lawrence [William Christie Esq, 21 Chiddingstone St, London SW6 3TQ]; *b* 1948; *educ* Eton; *m* 1st 1976 (*divorce* 1979) (Pamela Rosalind) Grace, dau of William R D Coddington and formerly w of Michael Chow; *m* 2nd 1991 *Amanda Kate Victoria Howard, only dau of Derek Nimmo, actor, and former w of Hon Nicholas Paul Geoffrey Howard (*see* CARLISLE, E), and has:

1a *Charles Hector Lorenzo; *b* 24 June 1994

1a *Florence Ella Kate; *b* 15 Dec 1991

(1) *Carolyne Anne; *b* 27 Dec 1946; *m* 1st 1966 (*divorce* 1970) John Julian Reynolds (*see* REYNOLDS, Bt); *m* 2nd 1974 (*separated* 1975, *divorce* 1981) Robert Scully, of San Francisco; *m* 3rd 1986 (*divorce* 1992) (George) Roger Waters, and by him has:

1a *Harry William; *b* 16 Nov 1976

1a *India Rose; *b* 25 April 1978

The 2nd MARQUESS's er s,

LAWRENCE ALDRED MERVYN DUNDAS, **3rd Marquess of Zetland**, ED (1945), DL (N R Yorks 1965); *b* 12 Nov 1908; *educ* Harrow (Govr to 1972) and Trin Coll Cambridge (BA 1930); ADC to Viceroy India 1930–31, Maj Yorks Hus Yeo WW II (despatches), Jr Grand Warden Utd Grand Lodge Freemasons, Provincial Grand Master Freemasons N and E Yorks 1956–89, dep chm R K Dundas Gp 1974–89; *m* 2 Dec 1936 *(Katherine Mary) Penelope, 2nd dau of Col Ebenezer John Lecky Pike, CBE, MC (*d* 1965), of Little Glebe, Fontwell, Sussex, and *d* 5 Oct 1989, leaving:

1 (LAWRENCE) MARK DUNDAS, **4th and present Marquess of Zetland**

2 +David Paul Nicholas [The Lord David Dundas, 17 Mandeville Courtyard, 142 Battersea Park Rd, London SW11 4NB]; *b* 2 June 1945; *educ* Harrow and Central Sch of Speech and Drama; song writer (works include 'Jeans On', no. 1 hit 1976); *m* 1st 17 Dec 1971 Corinna Maeve Wolfe, dau of Denys Martin Scott; *m* 2nd 21 Nov 1997 * Taina, dau of Kurt Eberhard Philip Breuckmann and has:

(1) +(Thomas) Harry Django; *b* 15 Jan 1981

(1) *Daisy Star; *b* 6 Nov 1975; *educ* North Foreland Lodge and Frances Holland Sch; singer

3 +(Richard) Bruce [The Lord Bruce Dundas, 28 Overstrand Mansions, Prince of Wales Dve, London SW11 4EZ]; *b* 6 Jan 1951; *educ* Harrow; *m* 1st 15 June 1974 (*divorce* 1981) Jane Melanie, yst dau of Ernest Frederick Wright, and has:

(1) +Max Charles; *b* 13 April 1978

(1) *Emily Louisa; *b* 2 Oct 1980

3 (cont.) Lord Bruce Dundas *m* 2nd 9 April 1983 (*divorce* 1992) Sophie Caroline, only dau of Henry Giles Francis Lascelles (*see* HAREWOOD, E), and by her has:

(1) *Flora India Esmé; *b* 29 May 1986

(3) *Tallulah Lily; *b* 27 Oct 1988

3 (cont.) Lord Bruce Dundas *m* 3rd 30 June 1995 *Ruth Anne, yr dau of Sir Francis Kennedy, KCMG, CBE

1 *Serena Jane Dundas [The Lady Serena Kettlewell, The Old Rectory, Newton Toney, Wilts SP4 0HA]; *b* 10 Sept 1940; *m* 15 Aug 1964 *Capt Nigel Ion Charles Kettlewell, JP, RN, only s of Cdr Charles Kettlewell, RNR, and has:

(1) *Robert James; *b* 27 May 1965; *educ* Sherborne

(1) *Melissa Jane; *b* 29 June 1968; *m* 25 April 1992 *John S Nicholson, yr s of C J Nicholson, of E Lambrook, Somerset

(2) *Charlotte Rose; *b* 25 Sept 1970

ZOUCHE

Arms: Azure, a dolphin naiant embowed or, on a chief of the second two saltires gules. **Crest:** A dolphin hauriant argent and entwined round an anchor erect proper. **Motto:** *Franke lande Franke mynde* ('A free country makes for a free spirit'). **Creations:** B. (E) 16 Aug 1308, Bt. (E) 24 Dec 1660.

THE 18TH LORD (BARON) **ZOUCHE** (of Haryngworth) and a **Baronet** (Sir James Assheton Frankland, Bt) [The Rt Hon The Lord Zouche,The Abbey, Charlton Adam, Somerton, Somerset TA11 7BE]; *b* 23 Feb 1943; *s f* 1944 as 12th Bt and paternal grandmother 1965 as 18th holder of the Barony; *educ* Lycée Jaccard, Lausanne; Capt 15th/19th KRH 1963–68, ADC to Govr Tasmania 1965–68 (Hon ADC 1975–), Pres Multiple Sclerosis Soc Victoria 1981–84; *m* 15 Dec 1978 *Sally Olivia, yr dau of Roderic M Barton, of Brook House, Pulham St Mary, Norfolk, and has:

1 +WILLIAM THOMAS ASSHETON; *b* 23 July 1984

1 +Lucy Victoria; *b* 23 Nov 1982

Lineage (of Zouche): GEOFFREY, VISCOMTE de PORHOËT in Brittany; *m* Hawise, dau of Alan Fergant, Duke of Brittany, and *d* 1141, leaving:

1 EON/EUDON, VISCOUNT de PORHOËT; acknowledged as DUKE OF BRITTANY in right of his w 1148–56; granted a charter to the Abbey of Marmoutier 1153

2 Alan CEOCHE/LA COCHE/LA ZOUCHE; mentioned in connection with his er bro's grant (*see* above); also witnessed the latter's grant of a charter founding Lantenac Abbey; had established himself in England by 1172, where he seems to have held land in Devon and Northants, if not elsewhere, being referred to in the Devon instance as Alan la Zouche; *m* Alice, dau and eventual heir of Philip de Belmeis, of Tong, Salop, and Ashby, Leics, among other places, and *d* 1190, leaving:

(1) William de BELMEIS; undertook mily service in Normandy *c* 1194, held land in Sussex; confirmed a charter to Lilleshall Abbey, Salop; *m* Bonenée (*d* after her husb) and *dsp* 1199

(2) Roger LA ZOUCHE, of Ashby-de-la-Zouche, Leics; served in Poitou, possibly under Geoffrey (*d* 1205), an illegitimate s of KING JOHN who held the honour of Perche and led an expedition of mercenaries to France in 1205, and again 1214, though under some other leader; served in Ireland 1210; took an oath to uphold the baronial enforcement of Magna Carta 1215 but witnessed a charter issued by JOHN in 1216, hence had presumably switched support to the King by then; benefited from substantial land grants in Cambs, Devon, Hants and Norfolk at JOHN's and HENRY III's hands; Sheriff Devon 1228–31; a witness to HENRY III's confirmation of Magna Carta Jan 1236/7;

m Margaret (*d* in or after 1220 or even as late as 1232 or after) and *d* by 14 May 1238, leaving:

1a Alan; undertook mil service Gascony 1242–43; Justice Chester and the four cantrefs (administrative subdivisions, precursors of counties) of N Wales 1250 and as Deputy under PRINCE EDWARD (later EDWARD II) Feb 1253/4–55, Justiciar Ireland 1256–58, Justice Forest S of Trent and Constable Rockingham Castle 1261–64, Constable Northampton Castle 1261–63 and Feb-June 1267, Sheriff Northants 1261–64, Warden of the City and Constable Tower London 1267–68; *m* by 1242 Ellen/Helen (*d* by 20 Aug 1296), 3rd dau of 2nd Earl of Winchester (*see* WINCHESTER, M, preliminary remarks) of the Feb 1206/7 *cr*, and *d* 10 Aug 1270 of injuries inflicted by the 7th Earl of Surrey of the 1088 *cr* (*see* NORFOLK, D, preliminary remarks), the said Earl being one of the parties to a lawsuit in which Alan was involved, leaving, with four yr sons:

1b Roger; *b c* 1240–42; *m* by 1267 Ela (*d* by 19 July 1276), dau of Stephen Longespee, himself s of William Longespee Earl of Salisbury (illegitimate s of HENRY II; *see* SALISBURY, M, preliminary remarks), and *d* just prior to 15 Oct 1285, leaving:

1c ALAN LA ZOUCHE, 1st LORD (Baron) (LA) ZOUCHE (E), so *cr* (according to later doctrine) by writ of summons to Parl 6 Feb 1298/9; *b* 9 Oct 1267; undertook mil service in Flanders, Gascony and Scotland; fought in vanguard at Battle of Falkirk (EDWARD I's victory over William Wallace) 1298; Constable Rockingham Castle and Keeper forests between Oxford and Stamford bridges Feb 1311/2–Feb 1313/4; *m* (?)Eleanor, dau of 1st Lord (Baron) Segrave (*see* MOWBRAY, SEGRAVE AND STOURTON, B), and *dspm* just prior to 25 March 1314, when according to later doctrine such hereditary honour as was *cr* by the writ of Feb 1298/9 fell into abeyance between his daus and coheirs:

1d Ellen; *b c* 1288; *m* 1st by 1314, as his 2nd w, NICHOLAS De SAINT MAUR (*d* 8 Nov 1316), summoned to Parl 1314 as LORD (Baron) ST MAUR (E) (it is thought because of his w's position as coheir to her f, since among other reasons Nicholas's s by his 1st w was not summoned to Parl after his death); *m* 2nd by Nov 1318 Sir Alan de Cherleton (*d* Dec 1360), of Apley, Salop, and *d* in or after Oct 1334, having had by her 1st husb:

1e Alan; *dvp*

2e NICHOLAS de SAINT MAUR or SEYMOUR, 2nd LORD (Baron) SAINT MAUR, JP (Somerset 1351); fought in Hundred Years War at Crécy 1346 and ensuing Siege of Calais 1346–47; *m* MURIEL (*d* by 1361), dau of James Lovel, gdau of 1st Lord (Baron) Lovel (of Castle Cary) and according to later doctrine BARONESS LOVEL in her own right, and *d* 8 Aug 1361, leaving:

1f NICHOLAS SEYMOUR, 3rd LORD (Baron) SAINT MAUR and 3rd LORD (Baron) LOVEL (of Castle Cary); *b c* 1351/2; *d c* Jan 1361/2

2f RICHARD SEYMOUR, 4th LORD (Baron) SAINT MAUR and 4th LORD (Baron) LOVEL (of Castle Cary); involved in a mil expedition to Brittany 1379–80, ktd by 1382; *m* Ella (*d* 28 Nov 1409–13 Feb 1409/10), er dau and coheir of Sir John de Saint Lo and widow of Thomas de Bradeston, and *d* 15 May 1401, leaving, with two yr sons:

1g RICHARD SEYMOUR, 5th LORD (Baron) SAINT MAUR and 5th LORD (Baron) LOVEL (of Castle Cary), JP (Somerset 1405); served Ireland 1398 and Aquitaine 1401; *m* Mary, dau of Thomas Peyvre, of Toddington, Beds, and widow of John Broughton, and *d* Jan 1408/9, leaving posthumous issue:

1h ALICE Seymour, according to later doctrine BARONESS SAINT MAUR and BARONESS LOVEL (of Castle Cary), both in her own right; *b* 24 July 1409; *m* by 8 March 1423/4, as his 1st w, her distant cousin 5th LORD (Baron) ZOUCHE (of Haryngworth) (*see* below) and *d* in or after 1430/1, leaving issue

2d Maud; *b c* 1290; *m* by 1314 Sir Robert de Holand, 1st LORD (Baron) Holand (E), so *cr* (according to later doctrine) by writ of summons 29 July 1314 (*b c* 1270; in retinue of Thomas, 2nd Earl of Lancaster (gs of HENRY III), who substantially advanced his career and with whom he sided (though not apparently without tergiversation) in the latter's disputes with EDWARD II, notably at the final battle between Lancaster and the royal forces at Boroughbridge March 1321/2; after Boroughbridge his lands were confiscated but were restored him on EDWARD III's coming to the throne; ktd 1307; Justice Chester intermittently 1307–20, Govr Beeston Castle, Cheshire, 1312; served Scottish campaigns 1314 and 1316; Commr Array Lancs 1316; among his many grants of land was the Manor of Thorpe Waterville, Northants, which he acquired 1319; he also held land in Pendleton, Lancs, from the Priory of St Thomas Stafford; decapitated 7 Oct 1328 by followers of his old leader Lancaster, who not unnaturally resented his less than whole-hearted support, after being taken in Boreham Wood, Herts, s of Sir Robert de Holand, of Upholland, Lancs (s of Thurstan, s of Robert de Holand), by Elizabeth, dau and coheir of William de Samlesbury, and *d* 31 May 1349, leaving:

1e ROBERT de HOLAND, 2nd LORD (Baron) HOLAND (E); *b c* 1312; ktd by 1336, served Hundred Years War (thought to have been at Crécy); *m* Elizabeth — and *d* 16 March 1372/3, leaving:

1f Robert; served in the Crécy and Siege of Calais campaign 1346–47; *m* by 1355 Alice/Joan — and *dspm* & *vp* by 1373, leaving:

1g MAUD de Holand, BARONESS HOLAND in her own right according to later doctrine; *b c* 1356; *m c* 1372 5th LORD (Baron) LOVEL (of Titchmarsh) (*d* 10 Sept 1408) and *d* 7 May 1423, having had, with at least one other s:

1h JOHN LOVEL, 6th LORD (Baron) LOVEL (of Titchmarsh); *b c* 1378; *m* Eleanor (?)Zouche, dau(?) of 3rd Lord (Baron) Zouche (of Haryngworth) (*see* below) and *dvm* 19 Oct 1414, leaving:

1i WILLIAM LOVEL, 7th LORD (Baron) LOVEL (of Titchmarsh) and on his grandmother's death 4th LORD (Baron) HOLAND, JP (1441); *b* 1397; Constable Wallingford Castle 1450; *m* by 31 Aug 1422, as her 1st husb, Alice (*b* 25 Feb 1403/4; *m* 2nd 1463 1st and last Baron Sudeley (*qv*) of the 1441 *cr*; *d* 10 Feb 1473/4), dau of 5th Lord (Baron) Deincourt and sis and ultimate heir of 6th Lord (Baron) Deincourt, thus according to later doctrine Baroness Deincourt in her own right, also according to the same doctrine Baroness Grey (of Rotherfield) through her mother, and *d* 13 June 1455, leaving, with three yr sons and a dau:

1j JOHN LOVEL, 8th LORD (Baron) LOVEL (of Titchmarsh) and 5th LORD (Baron) HOLAND; *b c* 1433; Lancastrian Wars of Roses; *m* Joan, dau of 1st Viscount Beaumont (*see* BEAUMONT, Bt), and *d* 9 Jan 1464/5, leaving issue

2f Thomas; *dsp* & *vp*

3f Gilbert; monk

4f John

2e Alan; *dsp c* 1339

3e THOMAS de HOLAND, 1st LORD (Baron) HOLAND (E), so *cr* March 1353/4–57 (according to later doctrine) by writ of summons to Parl, KG (1348?, fndr memb); served Hundred Years War: Battle of Sluys (English naval victory) and Siege of Tournai 1340, Crécy 1346, Lt and Capt Brittany and neighbouring parts of Poitou for duration of war March 1353/4, Keeper: Channel Islands 1356, Crocy (Normandy) 1357 and Castle of Saint Sauveur le Vicomte Feb 1358/9, Jt Lt and Capt Duchy of Normandy 1359, Capt and Lt France and Normandy 1360; *m* by 1339, as her 2nd of three husbs, Joan ('The Fair Maid of Kent'), Countess of Kent in her own right and gdau of EDWARD I, and in consequence was summoned to Parl 20 Nov 1360 as EARL OF KENT, although the Parl in question did not meet till 24 Jan 1360/1, by which time he had *d* 26 or 28 Dec 1360, leaving issue (*see* WAKE, Bt)

4e Otes (Sir), KG (fndr memb); *dsp*

5e John (Sir), 'of' Thorpe Waterville, which, however, he appears to have occupied as a kind of grace and favour tenant rather than outright owner since the records show that Manor as having passed to the descendants of his er bro THOMAS, EARL OF KENT; had, with a yr s (Thomas, ancestor of the HOLLANDs of Weare, Devon):

1f John (Sir), 'of' Thorpe Waterville; *d c* 1421, leaving, with a dau (Margaret, *m* John Beauchamp):

1g John (Sir), 'of' Thorpe Waterville; *d c* 1451; possibly f of:

1h John, of Nassington, Northants (a manor then held by his putative cousin John de Holand, Duke of Exeter), by 1449; *d* between 1499 and *c* 1520, leaving, with a possible er s (John):

1i Robert, of Gorthall Houses and Newhall, Pendleton, Lancs; living 1534; had:

1j Otho, of Newhall; by 1553 held also Nassington, Northants; had:

1k George, of Nassington and Newhall, also of Salford, Lancs; *m* Isabel, dau of Adam Byrom, and *d* 1585, leaving, with other issue:

1l Otho, of Nassington, Newhall and Salford; *m* 1597 Katherine, dau of George Linne or Lynne, of Southwick, Northants, and *d* 26 Jan 1619/20, leaving:

1m George, of Newhall; *b* 22 June 1599; *m* Alice, dau of Sir Henry Bunbury, of Stanney, Cheshire (*see* BUNBURY, Bt), and had issue

2m James, of Newhall, which he acquired, possibly on the extinction of his er bro George's male-line issue; *bapt* 25 Jan 1600; *m* Mary, dau of John Blomfield, of Redenhall, Norfolk, and *d* 1667, leaving:

1n Otho, of Pendleton; *m* 15 Aug 1678 Alice, dau of Ferdinando Stanley, of Broughton, Lancs, and *d* Nov 1712, leaving a s (*d* young) and five daus

2l John; *m* 1st 1608 Elizabeth Peake (*d* 1613); *m* 2nd 1621 Isabel Seddon and had by her:

1m Thomas, of Whit Lane, Pendleton; *bapt* 13 April 1623; *m* 29 June 1641 Sisley, dau of John Travis, of Crumpsall, Lancs, and *d* 1676, leaving, with four yr sons and four daus:

1n John, of Newhall and Whit Lane; *bapt* 2 Jan 1641/2; *d* 1692, leaving, with a yr s (Thomas, *m* and had issue) and two daus:

1o Joseph, of Whit Lane; *bapt* 19 Sept 1675; *m* 18 June 1699 Maragret Chadwick (*d* 1723) and *d* 1731, leaving, with two er sons and six daus:

1p Samuel, of Salford; *bapt* 2 Feb 1717/8; check (*i.e.*, cloth)mfr; *m* 1 Aug 1741 Mary Birch (*d* 1785) and *d* 1791, leaving, with an er s and four daus:

1q Thomas, of Salford; *bapt* 14 March 1756; wine merchant; *m* 21 Oct 1777 Mary (*d* 18 Sept 1826), dau of Robert Jones, of Chester, and *d* 10 Feb 1811, leaving, with other issue (including an est s, Samuel, of Manchester, *bapt* 21 July 1780, wine merchant, *m* 24 Sept 1812 Mary Whittaker and *d* 23 Jan 1867, leaving issue) a 3rd s:

1r Robert, of Grahamstown, CP, S Africa; *bapt* 27 June 1792; cotton merchant; *m* 5 May 1825 Sarah Frances Tonge, of Runcorn, Cheshire, and *d* 27 May 1872, leaving, with another dau (*d* in infancy):

1s Thomas; *b* 5 April 1826; *d* 1893

2s Frederick; *b* 10 Nov 1827; *d* 5 Oct 1881

3s John Alfred; *b* 7 June 1829; *d* 24 June 1900

4s Robert Francis; *b* 22 Sept 1836; *d* 8 Jan 1892

5s Ben(jamin) Herbert, of Worsley, Kenilworth, Cape Town; *b* 19 July 1842; Registrar Deeds Cape Colony; *m* 22 Nov 1872 Agnes Hope, 3rd dau of Charles Hugh Huntly, CMG, of Grahamstown, Albany, S Africa, and had:

1t Arthur Herbert; *b* 11 Oct 1873; Personal Sec to Cecil Rhodes; Admin Sec S Rhodesia; *m* 22 Jan 1901 Madeleine Elise Emily (*d* 24 Aug 1922), 3rd dau of Joseph Millered Orpen, of Avoca, Barkly East, CP, and *d* 1956, leaving:

1u Douglas Orpen Huntly; *b* 7 Dec 1901; *educ* New Coll Oxford (Rhodes Scholar); GS Intell (despatches) WW II; *m* 11 Dec 1928 Eva Frances, 4th dau of Walter Gascoigne Shaw, of Camberley, Surrey, and *d* May 1964, leaving:

1v *André Sothern; *b* 30 Jan 1931; Rhodesian Nuffield Scholar 1960, memb: Rhodesian Nuffield Selection Ctee 1965, Cncl of Rhodesia NFU 1962–65, Ag Mktg Cncl 1964, Cncl of Nat Tst 1965, PM's Ec Cncl (Ag Section) 1965, Fell IPES (London) 1965; *m* 14 Dec 1956 *Susan Jessica, er dau of Jack Leslie Browning, of Fontainbleau, nr Salisbury, Rhodesia, and has:

1w *Michael Sothern; *b* 20 Dec 1963; *m* 19– *Lisa — and has:

1x *Fawn Skyla Madeleine; *b* 24 Sept 1996

1w *Anne Leonie; *b* 6 Sept 1958

2w *Jane Frances; *b* 28 April 1960

2v *Guy Huntly; *b* 30 Nov 1934

2t Sir (ALFRED REGINALD) SOTHERN HOLLAND, 1st Bt (UK), so *cr* 17 Feb 1917, JP (CP); *b* 15 March 1876; Cape Civ Serv 1894–1908, Admin Branch Colonial Office 1896, Native Affrs Dept 1899, Priv Sec to PM 1902–08, Perm Head PM's Dept 1905–08, Trade Commr S Africa 1908–14, organised High Explosives Dept War Office 1914, Dep Dir-Gen Explosives Supply Min Munitions 1915, Dir-Gen Inspections Munitions Dept 1916, Bd Inventions and Research Admlty 1917, memb Advsy Cncl Min Reconstruction 1917, Controller Cultivation Div Food Production Dept 1918, memb Commn for Disposal of War Stores, chm Centl Mining and Investment Corp 1925–31 and 1943–45, Rhodes Tstee 1932, Coronation Medal 1902, Chev Order Leopold Belgium, High Sheriff Oxon 1943; ktd 1912; *m* 30 April 1910 Stretta Aimee (*d* 15 Jan 1949), 2nd dau of Edward George Price, of Broadwater, Godalming, Surrey, and *d* 14 Sept 1948, leaving:

1u Sir JIM SOTHERN HOLLAND, 2nd Bt; *b* 31 March 1911; *educ* Marlborough and Trin Coll Oxford (BA 1932, MA 1934); Maj RA (TARO) City of London Yeo WW II, ADC to Govr and C-in-C Malta 1942–44, joined Centl Mining and Investment Corp 1932, Alternate Dir and Manager Charter Consolidated Ltd, dir: Price and Pierce (Finance) Ltd and Price and Pierce Ltd 1959–67; *m* 4 Sept 1937 *Elizabeth Hilda Margaret, only child of Thomas Francis Vaughan Prichard, CVO, JP, CA, of Dderw, Rhayader, Radnorshire, and *d* 1981, leaving:

1v *Jennifer Lisabeth Gwynllyn; *b* 22 Oct 1940

2v *Claerwen Belinda; *b* 4 March 1942

2u Sir GUY HOPE HOLLAND, 3rd and last Bt; *b* 19 July 1918; *educ* Ch

Ch Oxford; T/Capt RSG; *m* 12 May 1945 *Joan Marian [Lady Holland, Sheepbridge Barn, nr Eastleach, Glos GL7 3PS], only dau of Capt Herbert Edmund Street, 20th Hus, and *d* 2 Sept 1997, when the btcy expired, leaving:

1v *Davina Huntly; *b* 24 June 1946; *m* 1981 *Guy Timothy Geoffrey Conant (*see* CONANT, Bt) and has issue

2v *Georgiana [Mrs Nicholas Robertson, The Old Rectory, Thorpe Malsor, Northants NN14 1JS]; *b* 17 July 1951; *m* 1979 *Nicholas Antony Norman Stuart Robertson, s of Antony Stuart Robertson, CBE, and has:

1w *Ralph Edmund Sothern Stuart; *b* 1982

2w *Guy George Sothern Antony; *b* 1985

1s Frances Mary; *b* 15 March 1832

1e Alianore; *m* by 8 July 1332, as his 1st w, 2nd Lord (Baron) Darcy de Knayth (*qv*) and *dspm* by 21 Nov 1341

3d Elizabeth; *b c* 1294; nun at Brewood, Staffs, by 1314

2a William; *d* just prior to 3 Feb 1271/2, leaving:

1b Joyce; *m* Robert de Mortimer (*d* 7 April 1287), of Richard's Castle, Herefs, and was *bur* 13 March 1289/90, leaving:

1c HUGH De MORTIMER, 1st LORD (Baron) MORTIMER (E), so *cr* 6 Feb 1298/9 (according to later doctrine) by writ of summons to Parl; present Siege of Carlaverock 1300; *m* seemingly by 1290 Maud, thought to have been a niece of William le Marshal and a relative of QUEEN ELEANOR OF CASTILE, and *dspm* 20 July 1304 after his w had poisoned him (possibly inadvertently, but although she was pardoned for her part in her late husb's death the next year she was that same year tried for conspiracy to murder someone else, which suggests that on the whole she was homicidal rather than just careless), when the Barony fell according to later doctrine into abeyance between his daus, leaving:

1d Joan; *bapt* 24 Nov 1291; *m* 1st by 12 Aug 1305 Thomas de Bykenore (*dsp c* 1316); *m* 2nd Richard Talbot, (see SHREWSBURY and WATERFORD, E), who thus acquired Richard's Castle, and *d* by 12 Jan 1341/2, aparently leaving issue by him which died out by 1388

2d Margaret; *b* 14 Sept 1295; *m* 1st by 1309 Geoffrey de Cornwall (*d* by June 1355) and had issue (*see* GREY, B); *m* 2nd William de Evereys (*d* just prior to 6 March 1337/8) and *d* Dec 1345, apparently leaving further issue

2c WILLIAM De MORTIMER later LA ZOUCHE, 1st LORD (Baron) ZOUCHE (of Richard's Castle, Mortimer or Ashby, writs being addressed to him at various times under each of these three territorial qualifications) (E), so *cr* 26 Dec 1323 (according to later doctrine) by writ of summons to Parl; fought at Falkirk (*see above*) 1298; in autumn 1304 secured reversion of manor of Ashby-de-la-Zouche, Leics, and other lands in Cambs and Sussex from his cousin 1st LORD (Baron) (La) ZOUCHE of the Feb 1298/9 *cr*, coming into full possession of them 1314 on the latter's death *spm*; involved in the murder of EDWARD II's favourite Piers Gaveston but pardoned 1313; fought on EDWARD II's side at the Battle of Boroughbridge 16 March 1321/2, where the King temporarily defeated his opponents; Jt Keeper Caerphilly Castle Feb 1326/7, Keeper Glamorgan and Morganno and Chamberlain Cardiff Feb–June 1327, Keeper Tower London 1328–29, Justice Forest S of Trent 1328–29; *m* 1st by 25 Feb 1316/7, as her 3rd husb, Alice, sis of 1st and last Lord (Baron) Tony (*see* STAFFORD, B); *m* 2nd *c* Jan 1328/9 Lady Eleanor de Clare (*b* Oct 1292; *d* 30 June 1337), dau of 6th Earl of Gloucester and Hertford of the 1122 *cr* (*see* HERTFORD, M, preliminary remarks) by his 2nd w Joan (dau of EDWARD I) and widow of 1st Lord (Baron) Le Despenser of the 1314 *cr* (*see* FALMOUTH, V), and *d* 28 Feb 1336/7, leaving by his 1st w:

1d ALAN LA ZOUCHE, *de jure* 2nd LORD (Baron) ZOUCHE (of Richard's Castle, Mortimer or Ashby) but never summoned to Parl; *b* 1317; fought at Crécy; *m* by 1338, as her 1st husb, Eleanor — and *d* 12 Nov 1346, leaving:

1e HUGH LA ZOUCHE, *de jure* 3rd LORD (Baron) ZOUCHE (of Richard's Castle, Mortimer or Ashby) but never summoned to Parl; *b* 29 Sept 1338; *m* 1st Philippe — (*d* on or after 2 Jan 1374/5); *m* 2nd *c* 14 Sept 1391 Joan, dau of John Bramshott, of Gatcombe, IOW, and Bramshott, Hants, and *dsp* 11 July 1399

(?)2d Philip; allegedly f of:

1e John; allegedly f of:

1f John; allegedly f of:

1g Robert ZOUCHE or RAMMESFOLD, of Sussex; living 15 Feb 1411/2, but not mentioned as succeeding to the Barony of Zouche (of Richard's Castle, Mortimer or Ashby)

1d Joyce; *m* 2nd Lord (Baron) Botetourt (*d* 4 April 1386) and *d* on or after 4 May 1372, having had:

1e John; *m* Maud de Grey, dau of 2nd Lord (Baron) Grey (of Rotherfield) and *dvp* & *vm* 21 Sept 1369, leaving:

1f JOYCE DE BOTETOURT, *de jure* BARONESS BOTETOURT according to later doctrine, also *de jure* BARONESS ZOUCHE (of Richard's Castle, Mortimer or Ashby) according to the same later doctrine unless Robert ZOUCHE/RAMMESFOLD's pedigree is to be preferred (*see* above), in which case he would have had a better claim to the Barony of Zouche (of Richard's Castle etc) from 11 July 1399; *b c* 1364; *m* by 21 April 1386, as his 2nd w, 2nd Lord

(Baron) Burnell (*m* 3rd and *dspms* 27 Nov 1420) and *dsp* 1 Jan 1406/7, when such Barony of Zouche (of Richard's Castle, Mortimer or Ashby) as may have been *cr* by the 1323 writ of summons became abeyant between her f's five sisters (*see* BEAUFORT, D)

3a Eon (not necessarily a *younger* bro of William, though probably so of Alan); *m* by 13 Dec 1273 Millicent (*d* by 7 Jan 1298/9), dau of William de Cauntelo (*see* ABERGAVENNY, M) and widow of John de Mohaut, and *d* 28 April-25 June 1279, leaving:

1b WILLIAM LA ZOUCHE, **1st Lord** (Baron) (LA) **Zouche** (of Haryngworth), for whom *see* further below

1a Lora; *m* Gilbert de Stanford

2a Alice; *m* as his 1st w Sir William de Harcourt (*see* VERNON, B)

EON LA ZOUCHE's s,

WILLIAM LA ZOUCHE, **1st Lord** (Baron) (LA) **Zouche** (of Haryngworth) (E), so *cr* by writ of summons to Parl 16 Aug 1308–14 Feb 1347/8 first as LORD (Baron) LA ZOUCHE, later as LORD (Baron) LA ZOUCHE OF HARYNGWORTH; *b* 18 or 21 Dec 1276; ktd 1306, did mil service against Scots 1301–33 and in Ireland 1317 and 1332, also in Gascony 1324–25; *m* by 15 Feb 1295/6 Maud (*b c* 1280; *d* by 1346), dau of 1st Lord (Baron) Lovel (of Tichmarsh), and *d* 11/12 March 1351/2, having had:

1 Eon; *b* 1297–98; fought for EDWARD II at Battle of Boroughbridge (*see* also above); indicted for the killing 19 Jan 1325/6 in Leics (where outlawed following his own death) of one Roger Beler, of Kirby Bellars, and took flight to France; *m* by June 1322, as her 1st w, Joan (*b c* 1300; *m* 2nd, as his 1st w of two, by 6 Nov 1327 William Moton and *d* by Jan 1359/60), dau and eventually coheir of William Inge, Ch Justice King's Bench 1316–17, and *dvp* Paris 24 April 1326, leaving:

(1) WILLIAM, **2nd Lord**

2 William

3 John

4 Roger

5 Thomas

6 John

7 Edmund

1 Mil(l)icent; *m* by 26 March 1326 2nd Lord (Baron) Deincourt (*b c* 1301; *d* 2 June 1364) and *d* 22 June 1379, leaving issue (*see* above against Lovel, also NORFOLK, D)

2 Isabel

3 Thomasine

The 1st LORD (Baron) (LA) ZOUCHE (of Haryngworth)'s gs,

WILLIAM LA ZOUCHE, **2nd Lord** (Baron) (LA) **Zouche** (of Haryngworth); *b* (?)Christmas 1321; served in Gascony and Picardy Hunded Years War (present Siege of Calais 1347), called to Parl 20 Nov 1348–15 Nov 1351 in his gf's lifetime by writs of summons to 'William la Zouche of Haryngworth the younger' and 20 July 1352–24 March 1380/1 (after his gf's death) by the same designation without the words 'the younger'; this would under later doctrine be construed as constituting a fresh *cr*; *m* by 16 July 1334 Elizabeth (*d* between 16 May 1380 and 23 April 1382), dau of 2nd Lord (Baron) de Ros (*qv*) of Helmsley, and *d* 23 April 1382, leaving:

1 WILLIAM, **3rd Lord**

2 Thomas

3 Eon; Canon Linoln, thrice Chllr Cambridge U

1 Elizabeth; *m* — Basing

2 Margery; *m* by 29 March 1372, as his 2nd w, 4th Lord (Baron) Willoughby de Eresby (*qv*) and *d* 18 Oct 1391

The 2nd LORD (Baron) (LA) ZOUCHE (of Haryngworth)'s est s,

WILLIAM LA ZOUCHE, **3rd Lord** (Baron) (LA) **Zouche** (of Haryngworth); *b c* 1342; *m* 1st by 27 Oct 1351 Agnes (*d* on or after 2 Dec 1391), (?)dau of Sir Henry Green, Ch Justice King's Bench 1361–65, and had issue, including three yr sons (John; Edmund; Thomas); *m* 2nd after 28 April 1393 Elizabeth (*d* 10 or 11 April 1408), dau of 1st Lord (Baron) Le Despenser and widow of 2nd Lord (Baron) Arundel *de jure* (though he was never summoned to Parl), and *d* 13 May 1396, leaving another s Hugh and a dau (Eleanor, *m* 6th Lord (Baron) Lovel); his est s by his 1st w:

WILLIAM LA ZOUCHE, **4th Lord** (Baron) (LA) **Zouche** (of Haryngworth), KG (*c* 1415); *b c* 1373; attended HENRY IV's dau Blanche to Heidelberg June-July 1402 on her marriage to the Duke of Bavaria, also JOAN OF NAVARRE, DUCHESS OF BRITTANY, to England Nov 1402–Jan 1402/3 for her marriage to HENRY IV; Lt Calais 1413–14; commr to negotiate with envoys of KING OF ARAGON and DUKE OF BURGUNDY 1413; *m* by 1402, as her 1st husb, Elizabeth (*d* by 20 Nov 1425), (?)dau of Sir William Crosse, and *d* 3 Nov 1415, leaving:

1 WILLIAM LA ZOUCHE, **5th Lord**

2 John (Sir), of Bulwick, Northants; *m* Elizabeth, dau of 1st/4th Lord (Baron) Grey (*qv*) (of Codnor) and ultimately coheir of her n 4th/7th Lord (Baron) Grey (of Codnor) on the latter's death 1496, following which the Barony of Grey (of Codnor) (*qv*) fell into abeyance till abeyance terminated 1989; Sir John bought from his w's n the reversion of the Castle and Manor of Codnor, Derbys, and was ancestor of the ZOUCHEs of Codnor, among whom was Sir John Zouche (*d c* 1639); *see* also SHEFFIELD Bt

The 4th LORD (Baron) (LA) ZOUCHE (of Haryngworth)'s er s,

WILLIAM LA ZOUCHE, **5th Lord** (Baron) (LA) **Zouche** (of Haryngworth); *b c* 1402; *m* 1st by 8 March 1423/4 Alice, dau of 5th Lord (Baron) Saint Maur (*see* above) and by a later doctrine Baroness Lovel (of Castle Cary) and Baroness Saint Maur in her own right (*see* above); *m* 2nd by 2 April 1450 Elizabeth, dau of Sir Oliver St John, of Bletsoe, Beds (*see* SAINT JOHN OF BLETSO, B), and *d* 25 Dec 1462, leaving by his 1st w:

WILLIAM LA ZOUCHE, **6th Lord** (Baron) (LA) **Zouche** (of Haryngworth) and by a later doctrine *de jure* 7th LORD (Baron) LOVEL (of Castle Cary) and 7th LORD (Baron) SAINT MAUR; *b c* 1432; MP Northants 1455–56; *m* 1st(?) Katherine, dau of Sir Rowland Lenthall, of Hampton Court, Herefs, by his 2nd w Lucy, aunt and ultimately coheir of 4th/7th Lord (Baron) Grey (of Codnor) (*qv*); *m* 2nd(?), as her 1st husb, Katherine (*m* 2nd Sir Gilbert Debenham and *d* Oct 1470), dau of Sir William Plumpton, of Plumpton, Yorks, and *d* 15 Jan 1467/8, leaving by his 1st w, with a yr s (William) and two daus (Elizabeth; Margaret):

JOHN LA ZOUCHE, **7th Lord** (Baron) **Zouche** (of Haryngworth) and by a later doctrine *de jure* 8th LORD (Baron) LOVEL (of Castle Cary) and 8th LORD (Baron) SAINT MAUR; *b* 1459; captured by HENRY VII while fighting for RICHARD III at Battle of Bosworth (1485), attainted by Parl which met 7 Nov 1485, but attainder reversed 1489 and he restored to his previous dignities Oct–Dec 1495; participated in campaign against French 1492; *m* by 26 Feb 1486/7 Joan (*b c* 1458; *d* in or after 1507), sis and coheir of 1st/7th Lord (Baron) Dinham, and *d c* March 1525/6, leaving:

JOHN LA ZOUCHE, **8th Lord** (Baron) **Zouche** (of Haryngworth) and by a later doctrine *de jure* 9th LORD (Baron) LOVEL (of Castle Cary) and 9th LORD (Baron) SAINT MAUR; *b c* 1486; served in campaign against French 1513, ktd 1513, Lt Selwood Forest Somerset; *m* 1st Dorothy, dau of Sir William Capell (*see* ESSEX, E); *m* 2nd by 8 Oct 1527 Susan (*d* on or after 19 June 1569), dau and coheir of William Welby, of Hallstead, Lincs, and widow of Nicholas Davenport, of Bulwick, Northants, and *d* 10 Aug 1550, having had by his 1st w, with a yr s (Sir John) and a dau (Mary):

RICHARD LA ZOUCHE, **9th Lord** (Baron) **Zouche** (of Haryngworth) and by a later doctrine *de jure* 10th LORD (Baron) LOVEL (of Castle Cary) and 10th LORD (Baron) SAINT MAUR; *b c* 1510; *m* 1st *c* 1525 Joan, dau of Sir John Rogers, of Bryanston, Dorset, by his 1st w Elizabeth, dau of Sir William Courtenay (*see* DEVON, E); *m* 2nd after 1532 Margaret, est dau of John Cheney, of West Woodhay, Berks, by his w Jane, dau of Sir William Norris, of Yattendon, Berks, and *d* 22 July 1552, leaving an illegitimate dau (Dorothy, *m* 14th Lord (Baron) Grey (of Wilton), *see* GREY, B) and by his 1st w:

1 GEORGE LA ZOUCHE, **10th Lord** (Baron) **Zouche** (of Haryngworth) and by a later doctrine *de jure* 11th LORD (Baron) LOVEL (of Castle Cary) and 11th LORD (Baron) SAINT MAUR; *b c* 1526; *m* 1553/4 Margaret (*d* on or after 13 Sept 1569), dau and coheir of William Welby, of Multon, Lincs (*see* WELBY, Bt), and *d* 19 June 1569, leaving:

(1) EDWARD LA ZOUCHE, **11th Lord** (Baron) **Zouche** (of Haryngworth) and by a later doctrine *de jure* 12th LORD (Baron) LOVEL (of Castle Cary) and 12th LORD (Baron) SAINT MAUR, PC (11 May 1603, S 1617); *b* 6 June 1556; *educ* Trin Coll Cambridge (MA 1571) and Gray's Inn; Amb to Scotland Jan-April 1594 and Denmark June–July 1598, Dep Govr Guernsey 1600–01, Ld Pres Cncl of Wales 1602–07, Cncllr Virginia Co 1609 and New England 1620, Commr to negotiate with France 1610, Commr Treasury 1612–14, Constable Dover Castle and Ld Warden Cinque Ports 1615–24; *m* 1st *c* 1578 his cousin Eleanor (*bur* 3 April 1611), dau of Sir John Zouche, of Codnor, and had:

1a ELIZABETH

2a Mary; *bapt* 4 Nov 1582; *m* 1st 4 March 1602/3 Thomas Leighton and had five sons and two daus; *m* 2nd William Connard (*dsp*) and was *bur* 6 Oct 1652

(1) (cont.) The **11th Lord** *m* 2nd *c* Oct 1611, as her 3rd husb, Sarah (*m* 4th 1626 Sir Thomas Edmonds, Treasurer Household to CHARLES I), sis of 1st Baron Harington of Exton (*see* HARINGTON, Bt) and widow of (a) Francis Lord Hastings (s of 4th Earl of Huntingdon; *qv*) and (b) Sir George Kingsmill, Justice Common Pleas, and *dspm* 18 Aug 1625, leaving at least one other dau, when the Barony of Zouche (of Haryngworth) and right to the Baronies of Lovel (of Castle Cary) and St Maur fell into abeyance between his daus and coheirs Elizabeth and Mary and their representatives

The er dau,

ELIZABETH La Zouche; *bapt* 14 Feb 1578/9; *m* 27 Dec 1597 Sir William TATE, MP (*bur* 14 Oct 1617), of Delapré Abbey, Northants, and *dvp* and was *bur* 24 April 1617, leaving:

ZOUCHE TATE, of Delapré Abbey; *b* 1606; MP Northampton 1640; *m* Katherine (*d* 1700), dau of Sir Giles Alington, of Horseheath, Cambs, and was *bur* 8 Jan 1650/1, leaving, with other issue:

WILLIAM TATE, of Delapré Abbey; *m* Mary (*d* 1699), dau and coheir of James Stedman, of Lincoln's Inn, MP Chippenham, and was *bur* 20 June 1695, leaving, with other issue:

BARTHOLOMEW TATE, of Delapré Abbey; *b c* 1666; *m* Mary (*d* 1721), dau and coheir of Edward Noel, of the Inner Temple, Commr Excise, and *d* 6 July 1704, having had, with other issue, including a s (Bartholomew, sold Delapré Abbey, *m* 1st Arundel, dau and heiress of Henry Stratford, of Overston, Northants, *m* 2nd Mary, dau of Col Moyser, and *dsps* and was *bur* 5 Sept 1776) and a yr dau (Mary, *bapt* 14 Dec 1701, *m* 19 Sept 1723 Samuel Long, Capt Dragoons (*d* 1757), and *d* 16 June 1765, being ancestor of the LONGs of Hampton Lodge, Surrey):

CATHARINE Tate; *bapt* 7 May 1698; *m* 1720 Charles HEDGES, of Finchley, Middx, yst s of Sir William Hedges, Govr Bengal 1681–84 and Sheriff London 1693–94, and had:

SUSAN Hedges; *m* 8 Jan 1750 Sir Cecil BISSHOPP, 7th Bt (*cr* 24 July 1620), of Parham, Sussex (*bur* 12 Sept 1779), and *d* 1 Dec 1791, leaving, with other issue:

Sir CECIL BISSHOPP, 8th Bt, and **12th Lord** (Baron) **Zouche** (of Haryngworth), in favour of whom abeyance terminated and writ of summons issued 11 Aug 1815 following his claim 7 Feb 1804; took seat 1 Feb 1816; *b* 29 Dec 1752; MP (Tory) Shoreham 1780–90 and 1796–1806, FRS 1791, DCL (Oxon) 1810; *m* 27 July 1782 Harriett Anne (*b c* 1760; *d* 10 Dec 1839), only dau and heiress of William Southwell, of Frampton, Glos, unc of 20th Lord (Baron) De Clifford (*qv*) and descended from John Southwell, of Felix Hall, ancestor of Viscount Southwell (*qv*), and *dspms* 11 Nov 1828, when the btcy passed to his cousin Sir George Bisshopp, 9th Bt (*see* 1870 edn), while the Barony fell into abeyance between his two daus, having had:

1 Cecil; *b* 25 June 1783; MP Newport, IOW, 1811–12, Lt-Col 1st Foot Gds; *m* 6 April 1805 Charlotte Barbara (*d* 3 Oct 1807), est dau of 2nd Marquess Townshend (*qv*), and *dsp* & *vp* 11 July 1813 of wounds recd in action Black Rock, Upper Canada

2 Charles Cecil; *b* 1785; Lt RN; *d* unm Jamaica 10 May 1808

1 HARRIETT ANNE, for whom *see* further below

2 Katherine Annabella; *b* 1 Dec 1791; *m* 1 Aug 1826 V-Adml Sir George Richard Brooke-Pechell, 4th Bt (*d* 29 June 1860), and *dspms* 29 July 1871, leaving issue (*see* 1970 edn PECHELL, Bt)

The 12th LORD's er dau,

HARRIETT ANNE Bisshopp, **Baroness Zouche** (of Haryngworth) in her own right on termination of abeyance 9 Feb 1829; *b* Geneva 7 Sept 1787; *m* 14 Oct 1808 Hon Robert CURZON, MP, 3rd s of 1st Viscount Curzon (*see* HOWE, E), and *d* 15 May 1870, having had:

(1) ROBERT CURZON, **14th Lord** (Baron) **Zouche** (of Haryngworth); *b* 16 March 1810; *educ* Charterhouse and Ch Ch Oxford; MP (Tory) Clitheroe 1831–32, Attaché and Priv Sec to Br Amb Constantinople 1841, Commr to arrange Turco-Persian boundaries Erzerum 1843–44, Turkish Order of Nishan, Persian Orders of Lion and Sun, author: *Lay of the Purple Falcon* (1847), *Catalogue of Materials for Writing...*(1849), *Visits to Monasteries in the Levant* (1849), *Armenia* (1854) and *A Short Account of Some of the Most Celebrated Libraries of Italy* (1854); *m* 27 Aug 1850 Emily Julia (*b c* 1822; *d* 11 March 1866), dau of Sir Robert Wilmot-Horton, 3rd Bt, PC (*see* 1931 edn), and *d* 2 Aug 1873, leaving:

1a ROBERT NATHANIEL CECIL GEORGE CURZON, **15th Lord** (Baron) **Zouche** (of Haryngworth), JP (Staffs and Sussex), DL (Sussex); *b* 12 July 1851; *educ* Eton and Ch Ch Oxford (BA 1872); Lt 20th Bn Imp Yeo Boer War 1900–01, Capt and Hon Maj 4th Bn Roy Sussex Regt; *m* 15 July 1875 (*divorce* 8 Dec 1876 following her desertion of her husb three months after the marriage and an action for criminal conversation with the 7th Earl of Mayo; *qv*) Hon Annie Mary Eleanor Fraser (*b* 8 Feb 1857; *m* 2nd, as his 1st w, 2nd Baron Trevor (*qv*) of Brynkinalt and *d* 10 May 1895), 3rd dau of 18th Lord Saltoun (*qv*) of Abernethy, and *dsp* 31 July 1914

1a DAREA CURZON, **Baroness Zouche** (of Haryngworth); *b* 13 Nov 1860; *d* unm 7 April 1917

(2) Edward Cecil; *b* 8 Nov 1812; barrister; *m* 5 May 1834 Amelia Sophia Charlotte (*d* 29 March 1892), 6th dau of James Daniell, of Beddington House, Surrey, and *d* 12 Feb 1885, leaving:

1a George Augustus, JP (Hants); *b* 12 July 1836; *educ* Merton Coll Oxford; Col 2nd Life Gds, formerly Rifle Bde, served suppression Indian Mutiny Cawnpore and Lucknow; *m* 1st 7 May 1867 Mary Florence (*dsp* 21 July 1868), dau of Morgan Treherne, MP; *m* 2nd 19 March 1873 Mary Louisa Anne Frances Josephine Martha (*d* 2 Nov 1889), est dau of William Ince Anderton, of Euxton Hall, Lancs, and by her had:

1b MARY CECIL Curzon, **Baroness Zouche** (of Haryngworth) in her own right; *b* 15 May 1875; *m* 12 Nov 1901, as his 2nd w, **Sir Frederick William Francis George Frankland**, **10th Bt**, of Thirkleby (*d* 19 Dec 1937) (*see* **Lineage (of Frankland)** below), and *d* 25 Sept 1965, having had:

1c **Sir Thomas William Assheton Frankland**, **11th Bt**, of Thirkleby; *b* 18 Aug 1902; *educ* RNCs Osborne and Dartmouth; served Coldstream Gds 1921–26, ADC to: High Commr Egypt 1925–26 and GOC Southern Cmd 1930–33, Maj 15th/19th Hus WW II; *m* 1st 9 July 1931 (*divorce* 1941) Edna Maud, dau of Frederick Hynde Fox, JP, DL, of Inglewood, Ledsham, Cheshire; *m* 2nd 25 June 1942 Pamela Catherine Mabell (*m* 3rd 29 June 1946 (*divorce* 1968) Michael Barclay, s of Rev Humphrey Barclay, CVO, of Southrepps Rectory, Norwich; *m* 4th 1970 Robert Hugh Pardoe; *d* 1972), only dau of Hon Edward James Kay-Shuttleworth (*see* SHUTTLEWORTH, B) and formerly w of Hon William Keith Rous (*see* STRADBROKE, E), and *das* 5 Aug 1944 following a car crash, leaving:

1d Sir JAMES ASSHETON FRANKLAND, **12th and present Bt** and **18th and present Lord** (Baron) **Zouche**

2c Roger Nathaniel; *b* 11 April 1909; *educ* Charterhouse and Pembroke Coll Cambridge (BA 1930); W/Cdr RAuxAF (Res); *m* 1st 11 May 1931 (*divorce* 1947) Elizabeth Cecil (*d* 10 Feb 1968), dau of Arthur Cecil Sanday, of S Kensington, and *d* 1989, leaving:

1d +Timothy Cecil [Timothy Frankland Esq, c/o Hill Samuel, 100 Wood St, London EC2]; *b* 4 Oct 1931; *educ* Charterhouse; late Lt 15th/19th Hus, dir Hill Samuel 1967–; *m* 4 Sept 1957 (*divorce* 1968) Lynette, yr dau of Lt-Cdr Ian Hope Dundas, RNVR, and has:

1e +Nicholas Charles [Nicholas Frankland Esq, East Park House, Handcross, W Sussex RH17 6BD]; *b* 13 June 1958; *m* 1991 *Suzanne, only dau of Michael Race, of Tole House, Keymer, Sussex, and has:

1f +Tallulah Cecily; *b* 19 Sept 1992

2f +Tatjana Camellia; *b* 22 March 1994

2e +Mathew Curzon; *b* 25 April 1962

3e +Adam Christian; *b* 22 Feb 1965

2d +Frederick Mark; *b* 19 April 1934; *educ* Charterhouse and Pembroke Coll Cambridge (BA 1956)

2c (cont.) The Hon Roger Frankland *m* 2nd 16 April 1947 Olivia (*d* 1987), er dau of Rev Hon Nigel Campbell (*see* CAWDOR, E) and widow of Maj Samuel John Rennie Bucknill, Irish Gds

1c +Barbara Mary [The Hon Mrs Barbara Frankland, Ridge House, Stockland, Honiton, Devon]; *b* 1906; *m* 1st 6 July 1926 (*divorce* 1937) Brig (later Sir) Otho Leslie Prior-Palmer, DSO (*d* 1968), er s of Prior Spunner Prior-Palmer, of 32 Merrion Sq, Dublin, and has had:

1d Anthony Errol; *b* 23 May, *d* 20 Oct 1927

1d +Diana Mary Leslie; *b* 1 April 1929; *m* 1974 *Bruno de Marco

1c (cont.) The Hon Mrs Barbara Prior-Palmer *m* 2nd 5 July 1937 (*divorce* 1943) 5th Earl of Normanton (*qv*); *m* 3rd 4 Feb 1943 (*divorce* 1960; resumed maiden name by deed poll 1958) Peter Lucas, artist, er s of Herbert Lucas, tea planter, and gs of Sir Oswald Brierley, marine artist to HM QUEEN VICTORIA

1a (cont.) Col George Curzon *m* 3rd 2 Aug 1905 Mabel Isabel (*m* 2nd 29 Aug 1917 Lt-Col Francis John Paul Butler (*d* 17 May 1936), 3rd dau of Col Cornwallis Henry Chichester, 5th Lancers, of Oaklands, Ascot, and *dspm* 27 Nov 1912

2a William Southwell, JP (London); *b* 23 May 1838; Col RHA cmdg Woolwich dist 1889–94; *m* 9 Sept 1873 Walberga Mary (*d* 22 April 1920), yst dau of Joseph Samuel Lescher, of Boyles Court, Essex, and *d* 29 April 1919

1a Cecil; *d* unm 10 Dec 1913

2a Harriet Anne; *m* 18 May 1864 Maj James Johnes Bourchier, 52nd Regt (*d* 1886), and *d* 13 Sept 1924, leaving issue

3a Emily Anne; *m* 19 Sept 1861 Augustus Wentworth Gore, of Linwood, Hants, 7th Hus (*d* 1919), and *d* 5 Nov 1917 aged 75, leaving:

1b Charles Cecil Howard; *b* 1862; *m* 1897 Fanny (*d* 4 Sept 1957), only dau of Maj Philip Henry Knight, Roy Welch Fus, and *d* 1929, leaving:

1c Cecil Beryl Katharine; *b* 1898; *d* unm 1968

2b Frederick Wentworth; *b* 15 Sept 1865; *m* 1895 Edith (*d* 1962), dau of Harry Emans Pollard, and *d* Feb 1952, leaving:

1c Eileen Esmé; *b* 1900; *m* 1930 Denis Gordon Williams

3b Francis Southwell Cecil Charles; *b* 1879; Lt Middx Regt WW I; *m* 1904 Frances Rose Mary (*d* 1974), only dau of C Maybrook, and was *kas* 1917, leaving:

1c Frederick Edward Cecil; *b* 1905; *d* 19–

2c +Francis Norton Wentworth, CBE (1960, OBE 1947) [Brig Francis Gore CBE, Vine Cottage, Point Hill, Rye, E Sussex TN31 7NP]; *b* 8 June 1906; Brig RA; *m* 5 Sept 1939 *Else Gurli Astrid, dau of Evald Christensen, of Copenhagen, and has:

1d +Peter Wentworth [Peter Gore Esq, Saddlers, Mark Cross, Crowborough, Kent]; *b* 22 May 1946; *educ* Charterhouse, RMA Sandhurst and St John's Coll Cambridge; Capt QOH (ret 1976); *m* 1975 *Joanna Penelope, dau of John Guy Bedford, and has:

1e +Robert Edward Wentworth; *b* 1979

1e +Emily-Jane Wentworth; *b* 1977

1d +Frances Jane Wentworth [Mrs Colijn Thomson-Moore, 14 Clareville Court, Clareville Grove, London SW7 5AT]; *b* 2 Sept 1947; *m* 1970 *Major Colijn N R Thomson-Moore, Irish Gds, est s of Cdr R C V Thomson-Moore, of Barne, Clonmel, Co Tipperary, and has:

1e +Richard Charles Randal; *b* 1978

1e +Alexandra Louise; *b* 1977

4a Blanche Katharine; *m* 6 Dec 1892 Rev Charles Marriott (*d* 1912), Rector Charington, Glos, and *d c* 1930

Lineage (of Frankland): — FRANKLAND; had:

1 William; London clothworker, of Rye House, Herts, Roche Abbey, Thirkleby, Blubberhouses, Yorks, and Fewston, Yorks; *m* 1st Margery —; *m* 2nd Joyce (*d* without issue by him 23 Feb 1586), dau of Robert Trappes, of London, and widow of Henry Saxie, and *d* 21 Aug 1576, having had by his 1st w three sons (Henry; William; Joyce)

2 Richard, of Blubberhouses, had:

(1) Hugh, of Thirkleby and Rye House, heir also to his unc William; *m* 1st probably a dau of John Foxall; *m* 2nd Joan Trappes (*d* 1628, *bur* with her husband at Thirkleby), probably dau of John Trappes, gs of Robert Trappes, of London, by his 1st w, and *dsp* 1607

(2) Ralph; *s* his er bro; had:

1a William, of Thirkleby; MP Thirsk 1627–40; *m* Lucy, dau of Sir Henry Boteler, of Hatfield Woodhall, Herts, and *d* 1639, having had, with other issue, including a yr s (William, had issue, *d* Ireland) and a dau (Frances, *m* 1625 Sir Hugh Bethell, of Ellerton):

1b Henry (Sir), of Thirkleby; *b* 1609; ktd 1636; *m* Anne, dau of Sir Arthur Harris, of Cricksey, Essex, and had:

1c **Sir William Frankland, 1st Bt** (E), so *cr* 24 Dec 1660 *vp*, of Thirkleby; MP Thirsk 1671–81; *m* 1662 Arabella (*d* 26 Feb 1687), dau of Hon Henry Belasyse, est s of 1st Viscount Fauconberg of Henknowle of the Jan 1642/3 *cr*, and *d* 2 Aug 1697, having had:

1d THOMAS (Sir), **2nd Bt**

2d Henry, of Sowerby; Clerk Peace N R Yorks; *d* unm 1736

3d John (Rev);V-Chllr Cambridge U and Dean Ely; *m* Mary Turton and had:

1e John (Rev); Fell St John's Coll Cambridge, Vicar Eastbourne, Sussex, Rector Sundridge, Kent; *m* 1st Margaret, dau of Dr Green, Dean Ely; *m* 2nd Mrs Mary Pierson and *dsp*

1d Anne; *m* Leonard Smelt, of Kirkby-Fletham, and had issue

Sir WILLIAM's est s,

Sir Thomas Frankland, 2nd Bt; had a considerable estate at Chiswick made over to him by his unc Thomas, Earl Fauconberg; MP Thirsk 1685–95 and 1698–1711 and Hedon 1695–98, PMG 1690–1713; *m* (licence 14 Feb 1682/3) Elizabeth (*d* 20 July 1733), dau of Sir John Russell, 3rd Bt, of Chippenham, Cambs, by his w Frances, yst dau of OLIVER CROMWELL, and *d* 30 Oct 1726, having had, with other issue:

1 **Sir Thomas Frankland, 3rd Bt**; MP Harwich 1708–13 and Thirsk 1715–47; *m* 1st Dinah (*d* 2 Feb 1740/1), heir of Francis Topham, of Agelthorpe, Yorks, and by her acquired a large fortune; *m* 2nd 1743 Sarah (*d* 1783), dau of — Moseley, of Worcester, and *d* 17 April 1747, having had by his 1st w:

(1) Elizabeth; *m* John Morley Trevor, MP, of Glynde, Sussex

(2) Dinah; *b c* 1719; *m* 16 Jan 1744/5 3rd Earl of Lichfield (*qv*, preliminary remarks) of the 1674 and *d* 8 Jan 1779

2 William; FRS, Treasurer Stamp Office, Consul Biscay; *dsps* 28 Nov 1714

3 Henry; Govr Bengal; *m* Mary (*d* 14 Oct 1783), dau of Alexander Cross, and *d* 23 Aug 1728, having had, with other issue:

(1) **Sir Charles Henry Frankland, 4th Bt**; *b c* 1717; Collector Boston, Mass., 1741–57, Consul-Gen Lisbon 1757–67; *m* 1755 or 1756 Agnes (*m* 2nd Nov 1781 John Drew, banker, of Chichester, and *d* 23 April 1783), dau of Edward Surriage, of Marblehead, Mass., and *dsp* 11 Jan 1768

(2) THOMAS (Sir), **5th Bt**

(3) William, of Muntham, Sussex; MP Thirsk; *dsp* 28 Dec 1805

(4) Frederick Meinhar(d)t; MP, Govr Bank of England, barrister, a Commr Revenues Ireland and later of Excise in England; *m* 1st Elizabeth (*d* 17 Jan 1736/7), widow of Adam Cardonnel, sec to 1st Duke of Marlborough (*qv*); *m* 2nd Feb 1738/9 Ann (*dsp* 28 Feb 1739/40), dau of 1st Earl of Scarbrough (*qv*), and *d* 8 March 1768, having had by his 1st w:

1a Anne; *m* 15 June 1754 1st Earl of Chichester (*qv*) and *d* 5 March 1813, having had issue

Sir CHARLES's bro,

Sir Thomas Frankland, 5th Bt; MP Thirsk 1747–80 and 1784, Adml the White; *m* May 1743 Sarah Rhett (*d* 20 Sept 1808), gdau of Ch Justice S Carolina, and *d* 21 Nov 1784, having had, with other issue:

1 **Sir Thomas Frankland, 6th Bt**; *b* 1750; *educ* Merton Coll Oxford (MA); MP Thirsk 1774–80 and 1796–1801, High Sheriff Yorks 1792, FRS, scientist and botanist, built mansion at Thirkleby 1788; *m* 1773 Dorothy (*d* 19 May 1820), dau of William Smelt, and *d* 4 Jan 1831, leaving an only s:

(1) Sir ROBERT FRANKLAND later FRANKLAND-RUSSELL (roy licence 1837), **7th Bt**; *b* 16 July 1784; MP Thirsk 1815–34, High Sheriff Yorks 1838, inherited from the Russell family Chequers Court, Bucks (now the official coutry seat of the PM); *m* 30 Nov 1815 Louisa Anne (*d* 21 Feb 1871), 3rd dau of Rt Rev Lord George Murray (*see* ATHOLL, D), and *d* 11 March 1849, having had:

1a Augusta Louisa; *m* 6 Aug 1842 5th Baron Walsingham (*qv*) and *d* 28 April 1844

2a Caroline Agnes; *d* 18 May 1846

3a Emily Anne, of Thirkleby Park, Thirsk; *m* 10 Nov 1847 Sir William PAYNE-GALLWEY later PAYNE-FRANKLAND (roy licence 2 Oct 1882), 2nd Bt, and *d* 13 Sept 1913, leaving issue (*see* FRANKLAND-PAYNE-GALLWEY, Bt)

4a Julia Roberta; *m* 18 Sept 1845 Robert Neville Grenville, MP (*d* 20 Aug 1886), and *d* 17 Oct 1892, leaving issue

5a Rosalind Alicia, of Chequers Court; *m* 7 Sept 1854 Lt-Col Frances L'Estrange Astley (*see* HASTINGS, B; he *d* 9 April 1866), added 1872 the names FRANKLAND-RUSSELL to ASTLEY and *d* 27 Aug 1900, leaving issue

2 William; Fell All Souls; MP Thirsk 1801–06 and 1807–15 and Queenborough 1806–07, a Ld Admlty 1806; *d* unm 10 June 1816

3 Roger (Rev); Canon Wells, Rector Yarlington, Somerset; *m* 19 June 1793 Catherine (*d* 19 Sept 1843), dau of 7th Baron Colville (*see* COLVILLE OF CULROSS, V), and *d* 25 March 1826, having had, with other issue:

(1) FREDERICK WILLIAM (Sir), **8th Bt**

(2) George; *b* Jan 1800; Lt 65th Regt; *m* 18 July 1822 Anne, 3rd dau of Thomas Mason, and *d* 30 Dec 1838, leaving:

1a Augustus Charles; *b* 21 Sept 1826; 2nd Regt Bombay European LI; *m* 22 Sept 1851 Clara (*dsp* 17 Dec 1851), dau of H Williams, and was *ka* Battle of Kooshab 8 Feb 1857

1a Sophia Catharine; *b* 22 June 1823; *m* 1st 28 Sept 1846 Gore Boland Mumbee, Capt Bombay Engrs; *m* 2nd 2 July 1862 Col Charles Payne Barras, s of William Barras, of The Leam, Co Durham

2a Georgina Anne; *b* 22 June 1824; *m* 12 Sept 1847 Maj-Gen John T Francis, HEICS (*d* 1896), and *d* 1887

1 Mary; *m* Sir Boyle Roche, Bt, MP (*dsp* 5 June 1807)

2 Anne; *m* 1st John Lewis, of Harpton Court; *m* 2nd Rev Robert Hare, of Hurstmonceux, Sussex, and *d* 1842

3 Dinah; *m* William Bowles and had issue

4 Charlotte; *m* Robert Nicholas, MP, of Ashton Keynes, Wilts

The Bt's 1st cousin,

Sir Frederick William Frankland, 8th Bt, JP, DL (both Sussex); *b* 11 May 1793; *educ* Mil Coll Marlow and Woolwich; served Peninsula War Dec 1812 on and France and Low Countries thereafter, at blockade of Pamplona, Battles of Pyrenees, Nivelle, Nive and Bidassoa, skirmishes before Bayonne, Battles of Toulouse and Waterloo and the storming of Cambrai; afterwards served E and W Indies, returned to England 1825; inherited from his unc William Frankland the Muntham Court estate, Sussex, which he sold 1839; *m* 21 Aug 1821 Katherine Margaret (*d* 1 Nov 1871), only dau of Isaac Scarth, of Stokesby, Yorks, and *d* 11 March 1878, having had:

1 Frederick Roger; *b* 2 May 1824; Midshipman HMS *Winchester*; *d* of fever Sierra Leone 23 Jan 1845

2 Thomas; *b* 16 March 1828; Lt 48th Madras Inf, twice wounded at taking of Delhi; *k* 17 Nov 1857 while leading a co of 2nd Punjab Inf to assault of a tower in the Secunder Bagh at Lucknow

3 Harry Albert; *b* 11 April 1830; Midshipman HMS *Alarm*; *d* of fever off Vera Cruz 9 May 1847

4 WILLIAM ADOLPHUS (Sir), **9th Bt**

5 Colville; *b* 6 Nov 1839; Col 2nd Bn Roy Dublin Fus Indian Mutiny; *m* 22 Sept 1870 Mary Jay (*d* 25 Jan 1914), only dau of William Dawson, of New York, and *d* 22 Dec 1913, having had:

(1) William Jay Colville; *b* 14 April 1876; *d* unm Nov 1896

(2) Robert Cecil Colville; *b* 7 July 1877; Capt 3rd Bn N Staffs Regt Boer War 1899–1901 and WW I; *ka* 7 Aug 1915

(3) Thomas Hugh Colville; *b* 17 Oct 1879; Capt and Brevet Maj Roy Dublin Fus and F/O RFC (Res), Boer War 1899–1902 (Queen's medal with three clasps, King's medal with two clasps) and WW I (despatches); *ka* 25 April 1915

(1) Katherine Marian Colville; *d* unm 17 Sept 1950

(2) Margaret Lee Colville; *d* 26 Nov 1874

(3) Eleanor Colville; *m* 1st 6 April 1905 Thomas Maberley Cobbe (*d* 7 June 1914), of Newbridge House, Donabate, Co Dublin, s of Leuric Charles Cobbe, and had issue; *m* 2nd 28 Aug 1915 Cyril Corbally (*d* 10 March 1946), of Rathbeale, Co Dublin, and *d* 11 Sept 1964

(4) Beatrice Colville; *m* 14 Jan 1915 George Crosbie Dawson (*d* 1 Feb 1940), only s of G J Crosbie Dawson, CE, and *d* 11 Oct 1959

(5) Mary Olive Elsie Colville; *d* unm 26 March 1960

1 Catherine Frederica; *d* an infant at Poona

2 Eliza Henrietta Augusta; *m* 12 Jan 1861 Maj-Gen Frederick Smith Vacher (*d* 17 March 1893), 33rd (Duke of Wellington's) Regt, and *d* 25 April 1911, leaving issue

3 Maria Margaret Isabella; *d* unm 25 Aug 1860

Sir FREDERICK 's est surv s,

Sir William Adolphus Frankland, 9th Bt; *b* 12 Aug 1837; Lt-Col RE; *m* 25 Feb 1864 Lucy Ducarel (*d* 21 Feb 1928), est dau of Francis Adams, of Clifton and Cotswold Grange, Glos, and *d* 29 Nov 1883, having had, with other issue:

1 FREDERICK WILLIAM FRANCIS GEORGE (Sir), **10th Bt**

2 Arthur Pelham, DSO; *b* Dec 1874; Maj Lancs Fus, Boer War 1899–1901 (despatches, Queen's medal with four clasps), WW I; *m* 1st 12 Oct 1898 (*divorce* 1934) Margaret Annie Phoebe (*d* 2 Feb 1953), only dau of Charles Compton Seton (*see* SETON, Bt, of Abercorn); *m* 2nd 1 Aug 1934 Ethel Theresa Gerard (*d* 1962), dau of Humphrey Jeffreys Walmesley, JP, of Inglewood House, Hungerford, and *d* 26 Jan 1948, having had by his 1st w:

(1) Marion Annie Margaret; *m* 18 Dec 1930 Eric Stewart Grant, s of Charles Grant, of Putney, and had issue

(2) Rosalind Lucy Seton; *m* 29 Nov 1928 Lt-Col Augustus Cameron Hancocks, MC, RA (*d* 1970), only s of Maj A T Hancocks, JP, DL, of Wolverley Court, Worcs, and *d* 198–, leaving issue

1 Ethel Maud; *m* 1st 26 April 1906 Peter Macara-Meredith (*d* 21 Dec 1919), of Pentre, Bychan Hall, nr Wrexham; *m* 2nd 1925 Frank Large (*d* Feb 1933), of Court House, Pewsey, Wilts, took 1926 name of MEREDITH and *d* 21 Dec 1941

2 Frances Cromwell; *m* 12 June 1897 Claud Neville (*d* 15 Jan 1944) and *d* 9 April 1959 aged 93, leaving issue (*see* BRAYBROOKE, B)

Sir WILLIAM's er s,

Sir Frederick William Francis George Frankland, 10th Bt; *b* 2 Sept 1868; served Matabele War 1896 (medal), Boer War 1899–1900 (Queen's medal with four clasps), Maj 3rd Bn Beds Regt, Assist Provost Marshal 1914–17 and RTO 1917–18; *m* 1st 10 Dec 1890 Charlotte (*dsp* 24 March 1892), only dau of John Augustus di Zerega, of New York; *m* 2nd 12 Nov 1901 Mary Cecil Curzon **Baroness Zouche** (of Haryngworth), for whom *see* above

Index

This index purports to identify every living person mentioned in this edition of *Burke's Peerage & Baronetage* bar (a) peers and baronets, who are listed in the Contents pages, (b) divorced spouses of living persons who are members of *Burke's Peerage & Baronetage* families, and (c) subsequent spouses of former spouses of members of *Burke's Peerage and Baronetage* families. Persons included are listed by their surnames, even where they hold a title under some other designation, and are in strict alphabetical order of the said surname, such that 'Mac–' is a category listed ahead of 'Mc–'. The one exception is the form 'St –', as in St John or St Leger, which is treated as if spelled 'Saint'. Multiple-barrelled surnames appear after the listing of the first of the names, such that all the Sackville-Wests appear at the end of the Sackvilles. In certain cases two versions of a person's forenames may occur. This reflects the practice (*see* Reader's Guide) whereby an individual may be known by different forenames among various members of his or her circle of family and friends.

A

Aanonson, A John 1616
Aanonson, Margaret Caroline 1616
Aarvold, Angus David Merriman 1410
Aarvold, Camilla Louise 1409
Aarvold, Christopher Olaf 1409
Aarvold, Daniel Alexander 1409
Aarvold, Dominic Ralph Ole 1409
Aarvold, Douglas Henry Eric 1410
Aarvold, Eleanor Pippin 1409
Aarvold, Elizabeth 1410
Aarvold, James Hillary 1409
Aarvold, Jillian Stanley 1409
Aarvold, John Merriman 1410
Aarvold, Noeline Etienne 1409
Aarvold, Robert John Douglas 1410
Aarvold, Sandi 1409
Aarvold, Thomas William 1409
Aarvold, Tobias Carl 1409
Abberfield, Derk Beresford 392
Abberfield, Kenneth Beresford 392
Abberfield, Melissa Judith 392
Abbot, Jessica 658
Abbot, Kenneth Kyle 1719
Abbot, Lucy 658
Abbot, Mary Muriel 1719
Abbot, Michael William 1719
Abbot, Thomas Lindsay 1719
Abbot-Davies, Hardwin Thomas 3026
Abbot-Davies, Orion Jonathan 3026
Abbott, Benjamin Tobias 2844
Abbott, Clare 1691
Abbott, Frances Dorothea 1691
Abbott, Harold 1691
Abbott, John 1691
Abbott, John Riddell White 3076
Abbott, Judith Caroline 2844
Abbott, Justin 1450
Abbott, Kathleen 2844
Abbott, Lucinda 3075
Abbott, Mary Elizabeth Jane 2334
Abbott, Nicholas John Milford 2844
Abbott, Simon Milford 2844
Abbott, Stacie Joy 1450
Abbott, Tina Winifred 1450
Abdy, Robert Etienne Eric 1
Abdy Collins, Alice Susanna 2004
Abdy Collins, Anna Mary 2004
Abdy Collins, (Brian) James Douglas 2004
Abdy Collins, Christabel Lily 2004
Abdy Collins, Cicely Violet 2004
Abdy Collins, Eleanor Katherine 2004
Abdy Collins, Elspeth Peggy 2004
Abdy Collins, Emma Charlotte 2004
Abdy Collins, Esmond Gerald Beau 2004
Abdy Collins, Henry James Abdy 2004
Abdy Collins, Phoebe Helen 2004
Abdy Collins, Rose Alice Louise 2004
Abdy Collins, Thomas 2004
Abel Smith, Belinda Patricia 155
Abel Smith, (Bertram) Robin 3074
Abel Smith, Catherine 466
Abel Smith, Catherine Clare 1650
Abel Smith, Christopher 466
Abel Smith, Diana Marjorie 3074
Abel Smith, Elizabeth ('Libba') Sophia 797
Abel Smith, Henriette Alice 466, 2191
Abel Smith, John Lawrence 1650
Abel Smith, John William 3074
Abel Smith, Julia 82
Abel Smith, June Isabel 1650
Abel Smith, Karen Moireach Aileen 1061
Abel Smith, Lucy 82
Abel Smith, Lyam Paul Alexander 466
Abel Smith, Mary Chichester 3074
Abel Smith, Michael James 1061
Abel Smith, Rachel Muriel 3074
Abel Smith, (Robert) Sam(uel) Clive 797
Abel Smith, Susanna Mary 82, 155
Abel Smith, Thomas Patrick 3074
Abel Smith, Timothy Bertram 82, 155
Abel Smith, William Walter 3074
Abell, Alexandra 394
Abell, Alexandra Louise 427
Abell, Antony 427
Abell, Antony Philip Norman 394
Abell, Ellen Ruth 2900
Abell, Gregory Ross 2900
Abell, John Norman 394
Abell, Louise Penelope 2900
Abell, Lucas Anthony 2900
Abell, Martin George 394
Abell, Mora Delia 394
Abell, Nazare 394
Abell, Penelope 2900
Abell, Ross Anthony 2900
Abercromby, Andrew Frank 438
Abercromby, Carol Marguerite 438
Abercromby, Diana Marjorie 7
Abercromby, Jane 438
Abercromby, John Glen 438
Abercromby, Marguerite Lavinia 438
Abney-Hastings, Amanda Louise 1764
Abney-Hastings, Frederick James 1764
Abney-Hastings, Lisa Maree 1764
Abney-Hastings, Marcus William 1764
Abney-Hastings, Michael Edward 1764
Abney-Hastings, Noelene Margaret 1764
Abney-Hastings, Peter 1764
Abney-Hastings, Rebecca 1764
Abney-Hastings, Simon Michael 1764
Aboud, Angus Alfred McIntyre 392
Aboud, Annabelle Louise 392
Aboud, Jacqueline Lucinda 392
Aboud, Lucinda Marie 392
Abraham, Brian Lionel John 1705
Abraham, David Thomas 1705
Abraham, Diana Margaret 1705
Abraham, Helen Mary 1705
Abraham, James Bidwell 2029
Abraham, John Richard 2029
Abraham, Nicola Jane 1705
Abraham, Susan Winifred 1705
Abraham, Thomas Nelson 1705
Abrahams, Annika Kathryn Anne 2612
Abrahams, Elizabeth Ann Amanda 2475
Abrahams, Harriett Laila 2612
Abrahams, Kathryn Helen Anne 2612
Abrahams, Michael 2475
Abrahams, Sydney Anthony George 2612
Abrahams, Thomas Anthony Talbot 2612
Abram, Jillian Ruth 167
Abram, Kerry Ann Lois 167
Abram, Lois 167
Abram, Peter Geoffrey 167
Abram, Victor Geoffrey 167
Abram, William Geoffrey 167
Abrams, Anna 2063
Abrams, Mara Elizabeth 2063
Abrams, Peter Charles 2063
Abrams, Sarah Katherine Louise 2063
Abriawan, Fiona Juliet 810
Abriawan, Nyoman 810
Acchiappati, Chiara 2022
Acchiappati, Gaea Francesca 2022
Acchiappati, Gianantonio 2022
Acchiappati, Nicoletta 2022
Acchiappati, Pierluigi 2022
Acchiappati, Pierrille 2022
Acchiappati, Ugo 2022
Achache, Francis Maximilian Frederick 1520
Achache, George Jean 1520
Achache, Philippe Alphonse 1520
Achache, Victoria Marina Cecilie 1520
Acheson, Christopher 1187
Acheson, Cynthia Margaret 1187
Acheson, Emma Mary Camilla 1187
Acheson, Eric James Patrick 1187
Acheson, John Alexander Simon 1187
Acheson, Karen Erica 1187
Acheson, Katharine Genevieve 1187
Acheson, Kelly Lauren 1187
Acheson, Kendall Bate 1187
Acheson, Lisa Kimberley 1187
Acheson, Lynnette Redmond 1186
Acheson, Nicholas Hope Carter 1187
Acheson, Patricia 1187
Acheson, Patrick Bernard Victor Montagu 1187
Acheson, Sheryl 1187
Ackers, Annette Ruth 925
Ackers, Geoffrey Ross 925
Ackers, Margaret Lynne 925
Ackers, Stanley Ross 925
Ackner, Janet 22
Ackner, Joan 22
Ackner, Martin Stewart 22
Ackroyd, Andrew John Armitage 22
Ackroyd, Beatrice Alice Violet 1781
Ackroyd, Brant 22
Ackroyd, Caroline Rachael Josephine 22
Ackroyd, Christopher Lowell 22
Ackroyd, David Mark 1781
Ackroyd, Frederick William 1781
Ackroyd, (Lucinda) Kate 1781
Ackroyd, Marcus Lowell 22
Ackroyd, Nancy Caroline 1781
Ackroyd, Roy 22
Acland, Alastair Michael 25
Acland, Alexander John Dyke 26
Acland, Alexandra Evelyn 25
Acland, Alice Beatrice 22
Acland, Alison 24
Acland, Alison Jane 27
Acland, Amanda Joy 28
Acland, Ann Sarah 24
Acland, Anna Katherine Hornby 25
Acland, Annabel Emily 25
Acland, Anne Maureen 27
Acland, Anthony Robert 23
Acland, Antony Arthur 27
Acland, Arabella Catherine 27
Acland, Beatrice Maud 26
Acland, Benjamin Napier 25
Acland, Benjamin Thomas 26
Acland, Bridget 27
Acland, Carina 24
Acland, Charles Robert 27
Acland, Charlotte Emma Victoria 27
Acland, Christine Mary 26
Acland, Christopher John Dyke 25
Acland, Cindy 27
Acland, Daniel James 26
Acland, David Alfred 27, 1616
Acland, David James Dyke 28
Acland, David Quaife 25
Acland, Diana 27
Acland, Diana Marcia 27
Acland, Dominic Dyke 22
Acland, Dorothy Rosemary 25
Acland, Edward Francis Dyke 25
Acland, Elizabeth 25
Acland, Elizabeth Caroline 27
Acland, Elizabeth Vibert 25
Acland, Eloise 27
Acland, Emily Grace 26
Acland, Emily Mary 25
Acland, Emily Mary Dyke 25
Acland, Emily Rosanna 27
Acland, Finlay 22
Acland, Florence 22
Acland, Francis Oliver Dyke 25
Acland, Fredericka Scott 25
Acland, George Christopher 25
Acland, Georgina 24
Acland, Georgina Katharine 25
Acland, Hamish Ormond 25
Acland, Harriet 22
Acland, Harry Alexander 27
Acland, Henry Dyke 25, 26
Acland, Holly Dyke 22
Acland, Hugh 27
Acland, Hugh Anthony Waring Dyke 26
Acland, Hugh Thomas Dyke 25
Acland, Inez Amelia 23
Acland, Ion Andrew Dyke 28
Acland, Jennifer 27
Acland, Jessica Emily 25
Acland, Joanna 25
Acland, John Barton 25
Acland, John Barton Ormond 25
Acland, John Hugh Bevil 27
Acland, John William Brian Dyke 24
Acland, Joseph Peter Reynolds 24
Acland, Josephine 27
Acland, Judith Sarah 26
Acland, Judith Veronica 25
Acland, Julian Dyke 24
Acland, Katharine Elisabeth 27
Acland, Katherine 25
Acland, Kathleen 24
Acland, Kim Lin 25
Acland, Lorna May 24
Acland, Lucinda M 22
Acland, Lucy Elizabeth 25
Acland, Luke Simon Burgoyne 25
Acland, Margaret Ellen 25
Acland, Margaret Joan 28
Acland, Margot 25
Acland, Mark Arundell 25
Acland, Martin Edward 27
Acland, Martin Hilary Dyke 25
Acland, Mary 26
Acland, Michael Bernard Pavey 25
Acland, Michael Christopher Dyke 27
Acland, Michael Dyke 25
Acland, Miranda Jane Elisabeth 27
Acland, Molly 24
Acland, Monica 25
Acland, Myrtle Christian 27
Acland, Nicholas Antony Bevil 27, 606, 2769
Acland, Nina Catherine 25
Acland, Oliver Geoffrey Dyke 25
Acland, Olivia 27
Acland, Patrick 22
Acland, Paul Hobson 25
Acland, Peter 24
Acland, Peter Edward Dyke 27
Acland, Peter Geoffrey Dyke 25
Acland, Peter John 27
Acland, Peter McArthur 25
Acland, Peter Theodore 23
Acland, Peter Vivian 23
Acland, Philippa Mabel 25
Acland, Piers Dyke 22
Acland, Polly Jane 24
Acland, Richard Arthur Dyke 27
Acland, Richard Hugh 25
Acland, Robert Dyke 25
Acland, Robin Julian Dyke 25
Acland, Rory 27
Acland, Rosemary Anjelica 24
Acland, Sarah Anne 22
Acland, Sarah Burgoyne 25
Acland, Serena Elizabeth 27, 1616
Acland, Simon Henry Harper 25
Acland, Simon Hugh Verdon 27
Acland, Simon Nicholas Dyke 24
Acland, Sophia Caroline Annabel 27, 606, 2769
Acland, Susan Jean 28
Acland, Susanna Rose Juliet 27
Acland, Susannah 25
Acland, Sybil Marjorie 25
Acland, Tara Katherine Elisabeth 27
Acland, Thomas 27
Acland, Thomas Alexander 27
Acland, Thomas Alison Dyke 28
Acland, Thomas Dyke 25
Acland, Thomas Edward Dyke 25
Acland, Thomas Jeremy Dyke 24
Acland, Thomas St Hill 25
Acland, Timothy John Dyke 28
Acland, Virginia 22
Acloque, Alexander John Sebastian 1458
Acloque, Camilla Anne Bronwen 1458
Acloque, Guy 1458
Acloque, Henrietta Mary Rose 1458
Acloque, Laura Isabella Helen 1458
Acosta, Jaime 2696
Acosta, Nicolas 2696
Acosta, Sarah Margaret 2696
Acosta, Simon 2696
A'Court-Wills, Alice Victoria Anne 2698
A'Court-Wills, Jonathan 2698
A'Court-Wills, Patrick David Anthony 2698
A'Court-Wills, Sophie Caroline 2698
Acton, Anne 30
Acton, Christopher Michael 29
Acton, Christopher Richard Henri 30
Acton, Dennis Richard 29
Acton, Edward David Joseph 30
Acton, Emily 30
Acton, Frances 29
Acton, Helen Marie 30
Acton, Joan Cinnetta 688

Acton, John Charles 30
Acton, Julia Ann 29
Acton, Michele 30
Acton, Natalie Elizabeth 30
Acton, Patrick John Pascal 30
Acton, Paul Reginald 29
Acton, Peter Hedley 30
Acton, Robert Peter 30
Acton, Simon Richard 30
Acton, Stella Marie 30
Acton, Suzanne 29
Acton, William Benjamin 30
Acworth, Adam Buzzard 460
Acworth, Anna Claire 460
Acworth, Florence Mary 2883
Acworth, James Michael 460
Acworth, Jane Marion 460
Acworth, Julia Beale 460
Acworth, Juliet Rose 2883
Acworth, Robin 2883
Acworth, Simon Hugh Arden 2883
Acworth, Susan Esmé 460
Acworth, Susan Henrietta 460, 1218
Acworth, William Bernard 460
Acworth, William Farquhar 460, 1218
Adair, Andrew Patrick 96
Adair, Arbuthnot James 96
Adair, Catherine Elizabeth 96
Adair, Gillian Marjorie 96
Adair, Gloria Rosalind 96
Adair, (Henrietta) Julia 96
Adair, James William 96
Adair, Patrick Charles Hugh 96
Adair, William Henry 96
Adam, Angus Ronald 1889
Adam, Ann Caroline 559
Adam, Anna Joanna Elizabeth 1266
Adam, Charlotte 1266
Adam, David Ronald 1889
Adam, James Robert 1266
Adam, Mathew James 734
Adam, Michael C L 1266
Adam, Michele Jane 734
Adam, Patricia Anne 1086
Adam, Penelope 1086
Adam, Penelope Margaret 1889
Adam, Ronald Arthur 734
Adam, Ronald Eric Croll 559
Adam, Yasmin 1889
Adams, Abigail 597
Adams, Alison Rose 354
Adams, Amanda Jane 464
Adams, Angela Clare 1678
Adams, Angela Mary 2893
Adams, Annabella Jane 2192
Adams, Anne 2878
Adams, Anne Louise 2138
Adams, Anne Primrose Louise 2622
Adams, Anthony Neville 876
Adams, Aubrey John 2893
Adams, Barbara Joan 2747
Adams, Bradford Michael 354
Adams, Brian Roderic 2501
Adams, Carol 1858
Adams, Celia Ann 1096
Adams, Charles David 2620, 2988
Adams, Charles Michael Richard 1096
Adams, Cheralee 2747
Adams, Christine 597
Adams, Christopher Stephen 771
Adams, Clare Laura Catherine 597
Adams, Daniel Francis 107
Adams, David Alexander Ian 1173
Adams, David Bernard Butler 464
Adams, David Eric Stewart 2878
Adams, Donald Bruce 2636
Adams, Edith Jessie 2966
Adams, (Edward) Seymour 1860
Adams, Eileen Esther 519
Adams, Eleanor Mary 2125
Adams, Elizabeth 26
Adams, Elizabeth Mary 441
Adams, Ellen Catherine Jean 1860
Adams, Eric W 716
Adams, Euan George 143
Adams, Felicity Nichole Elizabeth 2893
Adams, Fiona Mary 464
Adams, Frances 597
Adams, Frederick Joseph 771
Adams, Gary Thomas 1858
Adams, Geoffrey Doyne 2138
Adams, George Miles Bramston 597
Adams, Georgina Penelope Anne 1096
Adams, Gillian Alison Joan 876
Adams, Gillian Merle 2878
Adams, Gregory Walter 2501
Adams, Guy Luke 107
Adams, Harriet Mary 2138
Adams, Hugh H C 2192
Adams, Hugh Robert 2620
Adams, Jacqueline Anne 2878
Adams, James Alexander Seton 530
Adams, James Arnold 1291
Adams, James Rolf 2125
Adams, James Ronald Creighton 354
Adams, Jean Ursula 1645
Adams, Jennifer Renée 2988
Adams, Jeremy J 1678
Adams, John Evelyn Creighton 354
Adams, John Rainier 2620
Adams, Julia Helena 771
Adams, Julia Kathleen 2988
Adams, Justin Alexander 2138
Adams, Kate Dawson 876
Adams, Katherine Charlotte 2125
Adams, Katherine Mary Alicia 2893
Adams, Kris 441
Adams, Leila 597
Adams, Lorraine Gladys 2636
Adams, Lucy Sylvia 530
Adams, Lucy Victoria 2138
Adams, Marguerite Gladys 2620
Adams, Marjorie Heather 771
Adams, Mark Henry Leo 363, 597
Adams, (Mary) Elizabeth 2138
Adams, Mary (Molly) Viola 1860
Adams, Matthew 441
Adams, Max Philip Erskine 1860
Adams, Michael Adam James 143
Adams, Michael James David 2747
Adams, Nancy Perena 716
Adams, Naomi 441
Adams, Niall Michael 519
Adams, Nicholas George Knox 1173
Adams, Nicholas Henry Harvey 597
Adams, Nicola 107
Adams, Patrick Joseph John 519
Adams, Philip Dawson 876
Adams, Philip George Doyne 2138
Adams, Philomena 790
Adams, Quinton Lee 2988
Adams, Richard George 26
Adams, Robert George Seton 530
Adams, Rosalie Annette 464
Adams, Rosalind Elizabeth 1860
Adams, Rose Evelyn 363
Adams, Rose June 2747
Adams, Rosemary Ella 1173
Adams, Ross Henley 143
Adams, Royal Dawn 2988
Adams, Royce Henry 2988
Adams, Ruth Susannah 2125
Adams, Sandra Claire 2878
Adams, Sara Angela Rose 2893
Adams, Sarah Ursula 143
Adams, Sebastian Thomas Maitland 1645
Adams, Siobhan Mary 519
Adams, Sophie Anne 464
Adams, Steven Edward 2501
Adams, Steven Mark 441
Adams, Terence Frank 519
Adams, Theresa Ann 530
Adams, William David 464
Adams-Beck, Mary Elizabeth Helen 268
Adamski, Anthony John 2878
Adamski, Damian Joseph 2878
Adamski, Frances Mary 2878
Adamski, Haiden James 2878
Adamski, Jordon Jessie 2878
Adamski, Kyle Jozef 2878
Adamski, Maria Ann 2878
Adamski, Marian Josef 2877
Adamski, Peter Bernard 2878
Adamski, Priscilla 2877
Adamson, Alison Mary 975
Adamson, Catherine Elizabeth 802
Adamson, Catherine Grace 975
Adamson, Gary Wesley 802
Adamson, Hugh A Campbell 975
Adamson, James William 975
Adamson, John McKenzie 802
Adamson, Rosemary Jane 975
Adamson, Vera Marie 802
Adar, Bey Yaltin 1728
Adar, (Mary) Catherine Elizabeth 1728
Adderley, Anthony John 2128
Adderley, Betty Margaret 2128
Adderley, Charles Henry 2128
Adderley, David Michael 2128
Adderley, Edward James Arden 2127
Adderley, Elizabeth Jane 2128
Adderley, Fleur Charlotte Alice 2128
Adderley, Frances Elizabeth 2127
Adderley, Nigel John 2128
Adderley, Olivia Fleur Elizabeth 2127
Adderley, Teresa 2128
Addington, Alexander William Russell 2617
Addington, Anna Frances 2616
Addington, Anne 2617
Addington, Antonia Veronica 2617
Addington, Benjamin Richard Francis 2617
Addington, Carol Jacqueline 2617
Addington, Charles Haviland 2617
Addington, Constance Victoria Nell 2617
Addington, Daniel Anthony Travers 2617
Addington, David Anthony Brian 2617
Addington, Deryn Victoria 2617
Addington, Donald Emile 2617
Addington, Edmund John 2617
Addington, Elizabeth Clare 2618
Addington, Emma Teresa 2617
Addington, Frances Clare 2617
Addington, Francis Henry 2617
Addington, Gurth Louis Francis 2617
Addington, Hiley William Dever 2617
Addington, Honor 2617
Addington, Jack Alexander 2617
Addington, Jason Robin Mark 2617
Addington, Jean Margaret 2617
Addington, Jeremy Francis 2616
Addington, Jessica Louise Susan 2617
Addington, John 2616
Addington, Laura Grete 2616
Addington, Lauren Elizabeth 2617
Addington, Leo Nicholas 2617
Addington, Leslie Richard Bagnall 2617
Addington, Lucy Anne 2617
Addington, Lynne Elizabeth 2617
Addington, (Marie) Thérèse 2616
Addington, Mark Nicholas Guy 2617
Addington, Martin Gerald Francis 2617
Addington, Mary-Anne 2617
Addington, Michael Peter 2617
Addington, Oliver Thomas 2617
Addington, Patience Gillian 2617
Addington, Paul Anthony 2617
Addington, Peter John Gerald 2617
Addington, Philippa Clare 2616
Addington, Raleigh 2617
Addington, Raleigh Thomas 2617
Addington, Raymond Thomas Casamajor 2617
Addington, Richard Charles Raymond 2617
Addington, Rita 2617
Addington, Robert Hiley 2617
Addington, Rosemary Anita 2617
Addington, Sally Jane 2617
Addington, Sarah Anne Clare 2617
Addington, Sasha Elizabeth Anna 2617
Addington, Steffan 2616
Addington, Una 2616
Addington, William Leslie Hume 2617
Addington, Zoe Veronica 2617
Addinsell, Shaunagh Gundrede 2139
Addis, Bronwen Margaret 2557
Addis, Harriet Jane 2557
Addis, Helen Mary 2557
Addis, Madeleine Rosemary 1601
Addis, Oliver 2557
Addis, Sarah Diana 1601
Addis, Sarah Elizabeth Ruth 2557
Addis, Thomas Oliver 2557
Addis, William Dickon 1601
Addison, Caroline Amy 32
Addison, Christine Julia 2398
Addison, Donald Andrew Plowden 2258
Addison, Dorothea 2258
Addison, John Fox 2398
Addison, Kathleen 32
Addison, Lesley Ann 32
Addison, Paul Wand 32
Addison, Philippa Jane 2258
Addison, Sarah Louise 32
Addyman, Oliver Dimitri 1151
Addyman, Oscar Titus 1151
Addyman, Tania Arabella 1151
Addyman, Thomas 1151
Adeane, Antony Charles 763
Adeane, Camilla Viola 763
Adeane, (George) Edward 556
Adeane, Henry R T 763
Adeane, Madeline Bridget 763
Adie, Kim 2124
Adie, Peter 2124
Adkins, Jennifer Claire 112
Adkins, Pamela Elizabeth 112
Adkins, Paul Everett 112
Adler, Abraham 1527
Adler, Ann 1527
Adler, Aviva 1527
Adler, Gila 1527
Adler, Joseph Samuel 1527
Adler, Michael William 1531
Adler, Nathan 1527
Adler, Pierre 1527
Adler, Tobi 1527
Adler, Tzippora 1527
Adorian, Paul Anthony 2908
Adorian, Ruth Isabel 2908
Advani, Diana 558
Advani, Madhu 558
Advani, Suresh 558
Advani, Yolanda 558
Affleck, Richard E M 3037
Affleck, Tessa Elizabeth 3037
Afia, Meriel Rose 453
Afia, Peter Maurice 453
Afsari, Ali Resa 2567
Afsari, Anna Rose 2567
Afsari, Eleanor Katharine Mary 2567
Agar, Antony Edward 55
Agar, Arabella Clare 2106
Agar, Charles Christopher Edward 2106
Agar, Daphne Marion 55
Agar, Francillia 56
Agar, James Shaun Christian Welbore Ellis 2105
Agar, Madeleine Carmel 55
Agar, Madeleine Daphne 56
Agar, Marisa Charlotte 2105
Agar, Mark Sidney Andrew 2106
Agar, Maurice Ashton 56
Agar, Max John Andrew 2106
Agar, Portia Caroline 2105
Agar, Stephen Kirwan 56
Agar, Victoria Susan 2105
Agassiz, Christine Mary 294
Agassiz, David John Lawrence 294
Agassiz, Fiona Margaret 294
Agassiz, Michael Lewis 294
Agerbak, Andrew Thomas 2213
Agerbak, Elinor 2213
Agerbak, Isobelle 2213
Agerbak, Rhoda Jane 2213
Agius, Katherine Juliette 2460
Agius, Lara Sophie Elizabeth 2460
Agius, Marcus Ambrose Paul 2460
Agius, Marie-Louise Eleanor 2460
Agnew, Alexander Christian Pepys 668
Agnew, Alexandra Isobel 35
Agnew, Amanda 34
Agnew, Amanda Barbara 33
Agnew, Amelia Elizabeth 33
Agnew, Andrew David Quentin 36
Agnew, Andrew Robert 35
Agnew, Anna Margaret 668
Agnew, Annabel J 33
Agnew, Anne Merete Louise 34
Agnew, Anne Meryl 36
Agnew, Antonia Jane 33
Agnew, Benjamin Geoffrey David Callander 33
Agnew, Bolton 34
Agnew, Carol Ann 33
Agnew, Caspar Jonathan William 33
Agnew, Catherine Penelope 34
Agnew, Charlotte Anne 33, 1453
Agnew, Charlotte Diana Pamela Geraldine 1160
Agnew, Charlotte Elizabeth 35
Agnew, Christina Jeanette 35
Agnew, Christina Margaret 35
Agnew, Christine 33
Agnew, Clare Elizabeth 34
Agnew, Clare Margaret 34, 457
Agnew, Clare Rosalind 1160
Agnew, Clarissa Virginia 33
Agnew, Crispin Hamlyn 2726
Agnew, Daisy Matilda 33
Agnew, David James 36
Agnew, David Richard Charles 1453
Agnew, Diana Margaret Zoë 34
Agnew, Diane Clyde 36
Agnew, Dickon James 33
Agnew, Dominic Geoffrey Paul 33
Agnew, Doreen Rosemary 33
Agnew, Edgar Christopher 34
Agnew, Eleanor Josephine 668
Agnew, Elizabeth Mary 35
Agnew, Ellen Frances Anna-Maria Josephine 1057
Agnew, Elspeth 34
Agnew, Emma Rachel Elizabeth 35
Agnew, Emma Victoria 35
Agnew, Fulke Quentin Ernesto 36
Agnew, Garth Stephen 34
Agnew, George Anthony 34
Agnew, George Archibald Quentin 36
Agnew, Georgina Catherine 35
Agnew, Gordon Alexander Mackay 36
Agnew, Hazel Patricia 36
Agnew, Hector Jonathan Timothy 33
Agnew, Ian Hervey 33
Agnew, Isabel Sevilla Wilhelmina 35
Agnew, James Brooks Close 34
Agnew, James Douglas 35
Agnew, James Ion Daniel 1160
Agnew, James Nicolai 37
Agnew, James Philip 33
Agnew, Jenny R 34
Agnew, Jeremy Andrew Derrick 33
Agnew, Jethro Luke 34
Agnew, Joanna 33
Agnew, John Benedict 36
Agnew, John Nevin 35
Agnew, John Stuart 34
Agnew, Jonathan Geoffrey William 33
Agnew, Jonathan Graeme 33
Agnew, Jonathan Herbert 36
Agnew, Jonathan Michael 35
Agnew, Judith Dianne 34
Agnew, Julian 33
Agnew, Katherine Agneta 33
Agnew, Katherine Mary 36
Agnew, Kathleen Diana 36
Agnew, Lara Joanna 33
Agnew, Leigh Diane 36
Agnew, Lesley Stair 35
Agnew, Louise Frances Elizabeth 34
Agnew, Luisa Beatriz 36
Agnew, Madeleine Elizabeth Demetria 34
Agnew, Malcolm 2967
Agnew, Margaret 35
Agnew, Marie-Clare 33
Agnew, Mark Douglas Noel 35
Agnew, Mark Walter 34
Agnew, Mark Wyndham 33
Agnew, Martin 33
Agnew, Mary Diana 33
Agnew, Mary Lorna 33
Agnew, Mary Sylvia 33
Agnew, Michael Stannus 36
Agnew, (Morland Herbert) Julian 730
Agnew, Nancy Veronica 1141, 2867
Agnew, Nicolette 2967
Agnew, Patricia 35
Agnew, Patrick William 36
Agnew, Peter Graeme 33
Agnew, Peter Jonathan 36
Agnew, Poppy Eily 36
Agnew, Richard 2967
Agnew, Richard Charles 33
Agnew, Robert Peter 668
Agnew, Robin Andrew 36
Agnew, Robin Andrew Patrick Mackay 36
Agnew, Ronan Samuel 36
Agnew, Roseanna Celia Nancy 35
Agnew, Rosemary Brooks 34
Agnew, Roy Duncan 35
Agnew, St John Kenneth 34
Agnew, Sarah K 1160
Agnew, Scott Andrew 36
Agnew, Shelley 37
Agnew, Shirley 36
Agnew, Stacy Ann 36
Agnew, Stephen Hardcastle 34
Agnew, Stephen William 34, 36
Agnew, Susan 35
Agnew, Susan Georgina 36

Arbuthnot, James Robert Yu-Ming 94
Arbuthnot, Jennifer Anne 97
Arbuthnot, Jennifer Mei-Chen 94
Arbuthnot, Jennifer Rosemary 96
Arbuthnot, Johanna Rachel 96
Arbuthnot, John Keith 95
Arbuthnot, (John Sten) Robin 94
Arbuthnot, Julia Grace 97
Arbuthnot, Katherine 98
Arbuthnot, Katherine Rose Joste 98
Arbuthnot, Kathleen Phyllis (Peggy) 97
Arbuthnot, Kezia Louise 96
Arbuthnot, Kitty Anne 95
Arbuthnot, (Margaret) Jean 98
Arbuthnot, Matthew Kennaway 96
Arbuthnot, Mia 96
Arbuthnot, (Nicole) Patricia 94
Arbuthnot, Patrick Hugh Alexander 95
Arbuthnot, Patrick Stephen FitzGerald 97
Arbuthnot, Patrick William Martin 93
Arbuthnot, Peter Geoffrey 94
Arbuthnot, Peter Kennaway 95
Arbuthnot, Phoebe Elizabeth 97
Arbuthnot, Richard Keith 95
Arbuthnot, Robert Hugh 95
Arbuthnot, Robert Hugh Peter 93
Arbuthnot, Robin Douglas 95
Arbuthnot, Rosanna Mary 97
Arbuthnot, Roseanna Louise 95
Arbuthnot, Rupert 95
Arbuthnot, Samaita 95
Arbuthnot, Sheelah Margaret 94
Arbuthnot, Simon Charles FitzGerald 97
Arbuthnot, Susan Elizabeth 95
Arbuthnot, Susan Philippa 95
Arbuthnot, Swee Lien Ong 94
Arbuthnot, Viola Jane 95
Arbuthnot-Leslie, Candida Mary Sibyl 1771
Arbuthnot-Leslie, John Alexander 1771
Arbuthnot-Leslie, Portia Elizabeth 1771
Arbuthnot-Leslie, Rose Eleanor 1771
Arbuthnot-Leslie, Sebastian Anthony 1771
Arbuthnot-Leslie, Sophia Louisa 1771
Arbuthnot-Leslie, William Anthony 1771
Arbuthnott, Albert Michael 101
Arbuthnott, Alison Mary 100
Arbuthnott, Ann 100
Arbuthnott, Anne Rosamund 101
Arbuthnott, Anthony St John Gordon 101
Arbuthnott, Arabella Elizabeth 101
Arbuthnott, Barbara Joan 100
Arbuthnott, Bernard David Ogilvy 100
Arbuthnott, Catherine 101
Arbuthnott, Charles Philip 101
Arbuthnott, Charles Robert 101
Arbuthnott, Christine Elizabeth 100
Arbuthnott, Christopher John 100
Arbuthnott, Christopher Keith 99
Arbuthnott, Clare Anne 99
Arbuthnott, David 100
Arbuthnott, David Barrington 101
Arbuthnott, Dawn Grace 100
Arbuthnott, Dominic Hugh 101
Arbuthnott, Dorothy 100
Arbuthnott, Edmund 101
Arbuthnott, Edmund Stephen 101
Arbuthnott, Edward Alexander Hugh 101
Arbuthnott, Elizabeth Christian 101
Arbuthnott, Elizabeth Jane 101
Arbuthnott, Elizabeth Nina 101
Arbuthnott, Florence (Flora) Lily 101
Arbuthnott, Florence Mary 101
Arbuthnott, George Arthur Harben 101
Arbuthnott, Georgina Margaret 101
Arbuthnott, Giles Sebastian 101
Arbuthnott, Hannah 100
Arbuthnott, Hugh Andrew 101
Arbuthnott, Hugh Frederick Archibald 101
Arbuthnott, (Hugh) James Hamilton 101
Arbuthnott, Hugh James 101
Arbuthnott, Hugh John 100
Arbuthnott, Hugh Sinclair 101
Arbuthnott, Ian 100
Arbuthnott, James Brooke 101
Arbuthnott, James Francis 101, 2515
Arbuthnott, Jane 100
Arbuthnott, Jennifer Ann 100
Arbuthnott, Jess Agnes 100
Arbuthnott, Jill Mary 99
Arbuthnott, John 100
Arbuthnott, John Patrick 101
Arbuthnott, Katharine Anne 101
Arbuthnott, Katherine Anne 101
Arbuthnott, Lindsay C 101
Arbuthnott, Louisa Nina 101, 2515
Arbuthnott, Lucy Margaret 101
Arbuthnott, Magnus Malcolm James 101
Arbuthnott, Margaret Georgina 100
Arbuthnott, Mary Elizabeth Darley 99
Arbuthnott, Molly Victoria 101
Arbuthnott, Nicholas Charles 101
Arbuthnott, Nicholas Octavius 101
Arbuthnott, Patricia Diane 101
Arbuthnott, Rachel Sarah 99
Arbuthnott, Robert 100
Arbuthnott, Robert Keith 100
Arbuthnott, Robert Marshall 101
Arbuthnott, Rose Elizabeth Marshall 101
Arbuthnott, Sally 101
Arbuthnott, Simon David 101
Arbuthnott, Sonja Mary 101
Arbuthnott, (Sophie) Robina 100
Arbuthnott, Susan 101
Arbuthnott, Suzanne Ruth 101
Arbuthnott, Thomas 101
Arbuthnott, Vanessa Julie 101
Arbuthnott, Vanessa Rose 101
Arbuthnott, Walter Francis 101
Arbuthnott, (William) David 101
Arcedeckne-Butler, Christopher Michael 902
Arcedeckne-Butler, Emily Julia Garnier 902
Arcedeckne-Butler, Jacqueline 902
Arcedeckne-Butler, (Jacqueline) Jean 902
Arcedeckne-Butler, John Patrick 902
Arcedeckne-Butler, Mark Piers 902
Arcedeckne-Butler, Nathalie Catherine 902
Arcedeckne-Butler, St John Terence 902
Arcedeckne-Butler, (St John) Patrick 902
Arcedeckne-Butler, Timothy Garnier 902
Archdale, Anne Alicia 102
Archdale, Anthony Quintin Wolseley 3063
Archdale, Audley Mervyn 2255
Archdale, Aureole Helen 102
Archdale, Caroline Anne 102
Archdale, Catherine 2906
Archdale, Christopher 2906
Archdale, Denis Theodore 2255
Archdale, Dominic Edward Wolseley 3063
Archdale, Donna 3063
Archdale, Edward Montgomery 2906
Archdale, Geraldine Angel 102
Archdale, Gilbert Humphrys 102
Archdale, Jonathan Talbot 102
Archdale, Judith Penelope 102
Archdale, Kathryn Emma 102
Archdale, (Lilian) Patricia Dysart 3063
Archdale, Mary 2255
Archdale, Mervyn Talbot 102
Archdale, Nicholas Edward 102
Archdale, Nicholas Henry 2255
Archdale, Nicholas Montgomery 2906
Archdale, Patricia 2906
Archdale, Peter Charles Alexander 102
Archdale, Peter Mervyn 102
Archdale, Rachael Mary 2255
Archdale, Susan Anne 102
Archdale, Thomas Robert Humphrys 102
Archer, Alexandra 417
Archer, Catherine Harriet 417
Archer, Catherine Mary 2203
Archer, David Birdwood 278
Archer, Edward John Harold 2203
Archer, Elizabeth Georgiana 417
Archer, Elizabeth Rosemary 417
Archer, Emily Elizabeth 417
Archer, Geoffrey Thynne Valentine 278
Archer, Gwenyth Daphne 278
Archer, Harry Thomas David 417
Archer, Henry David 416
Archer, Isabel Gwenyth 278
Archer, James Coleridge Hill 2923
Archer, James Geoffrey Birdwood 278
Archer, James Howard 103
Archer, James Norman 2203
Archer, Jasper Rodney 1676
Archer, John David 417
Archer, John Kingsley 103
Archer, Margaret Irene 103
Archer, Mary Doreen 103
Archer, Mary Ruth Elizabeth 2203
Archer, Matthew George 417
Archer, Michael Marcus 2203
Archer, Neville Hill 2923
Archer, Nicholas Jasper 1676
Archer, Olivia Catherine Ann 2923
Archer, Pauline Muriel 2648
Archer, Richard George 417
Archer, Richard Tudor 2648
Archer, Ronald Walter 2203
Archer, Ruth 417
Archer, Sally 417
Archer, Sonia Gina 278
Archer, Sophie Louise 1676
Archer, Thomas Benjamin Highley 278
Archer, Victoria Anne 1676
Archer, William 417
Archer, Will(iam) Harold 103
Archer-Shee, Mary Pauline Daphne Therese 2025
Archibald, Brian Mortimer 2000
Archibald, Elizabeth Frances 2000
Arculus, Caroline Sarah 67
Arculus, Henry William 67
Arculus, James Edward Gilman 67
Arculus, Robin Gilman 67
Ardeshir, Frainy Navai 2233
Ardeshir, Jer Navai 2233
Ardeshir, Navai J 2233
Ardeshir, Shireen Navai 2233
Ardeshir, Silla Sorab 2233
Ardeshir, Sohrab Navai 2233
Arends, Islah Valerie Touche 2835
Arends, Sebastian Valdimar Touche 2835
Arends, Siri Ouida Elizabeth Touche 2835
Arends, Susan Ruth 2835
Arends, Trevor B 2835
Argent, Jenna Charlotte 1890
Argent, Sally Dorothy 1890
Argles, Anne Henrietta 2360
Argles, Arthur Peter Kingston 2360
Argles, Christopher Jonathan Sneyd 2360
Argles, Edward Hugh Rashleigh 2360
Argles, Isobel Lydia Anne 2360
Argles, Peter B R 2360
Argue, Bruce Dugan 399
Argue, John Douglas 399
Argue, Nona Frances Evelyn 399
Argue, Sally 399
Aris, Dennis James 2806
Aris, Stella Marian 2806
Arkle, Alexander Edward Buxton 457
Arkle, Alwyn Gerald Buxton 457
Arkle, Bridget Ayliffe Buxton 457
Arkle, Morna Annabel 457
Arkwright, Annabel Georgia 2565
Arkwright, Anne-Louise Marie-Noële Miranda Josephine 2097
Arkwright, Arabella 2097
Arkwright, Cecilia Caroline Georgina 2565
Arkwright, Charles Richard Francis 2097
Arkwright, Charlotte Mirabel 2097
Arkwright, Dominic Geoffrey Philip 2565
Arkwright, Francis Jocelyn Philip 2565
Arkwright, Harriet Marguerita 2097
Arkwright, Rebecca 2097
Arlaud, Anthony Stephen 590
Arlaud, Barbara 590
Arlaud, Christopher John 590
Arlaud, David Paul 590
Arlaud, Hilary Dawn 590
Arlaud, Kimberly Rose 590
Arlington, Alan Frederick 1031
Arlington, Diana Margaret 1031
Armanasco, Daniel Charles 969
Armanasco, Elizabeth 969
Armanasco, Kimberley Jane 969
Armanasco, Lindsay Clare 969
Armand, Charles Antoine 3051
Armand, Evelyne 3051
Armand, Irène 3051
Armand, Marie-Alice 3051
Armer, Adrian 2699
Armer, Catherine 2699
Armer, Graham 2699
Armer, Maree 2699
Armes, Elizabeth Felicia 2851
Armes, Philip Arthur Harcourt 2851
Armit, Jerome Nathan 472
Armit, Serena Helen Christian 472
Armit, Vashti Imogen 472
Armitage, Alexander James 2864
Armitage, Alexandra Margery Eileen 535
Armitage, Carolyn Margery 2864
Armitage, Charles Edward Marshall 2864
Armitage, Daisy Elizabeth Collette 2864
Armitage, Emma Victoria 3036
Armitage, Harry Nicholas Balfour 3036
Armitage, James Robert Perceval 2883
Armitage, Judith 2864
Armitage, Luke 1351
Armitage, Luke Robert 2883
Armitage, Mark Cecil Christopher 535
Armitage, Mary Esther 1351
Armitage, Molly Isabella Primrose 3036
Armitage, Nicholas Henry Charles 3036
Armitage, Oliver James 2883
Armitage, Richard Hugh Lyon 1351
Armitage, (Robert) Jeremy 3036
Armitage, Rosanna Catharine 2883
Armitage, Sophie Clare 2864
Armitage, Stephen Lyon 1351
Armitage, Susan Eleanor Mary 3036
Armitage, Susan Kathleen 1351
Armitage, Thomas Henry Charles 3036
Armitage, William John 2883
Armour, Emily Frances 1096
Armour, Georgina Elizabeth 1096
Armour, Nicholas Hilary Stuart 1096
Armour, Sophie Elizabeth 1096
Armson, Frederick Simon Arden 346
Armson, Katherine Geraldine 346
Armson, Marion Albinia 346
Armson, Meriel Albinia 346
Armson, Patrick David Arden 346
Armstrong, Alexander Edmund Roberto 107
Armstrong, Amanda 1229
Armstrong, Anne-Victoire Emily 107
Armstrong, Antonia Kathleen 2058
Armstrong, Barbara Dorothy 262
Armstrong, Beatrix Diana 3083
Armstrong, Bruce William 2058
Armstrong, Catherine Jill 1229
Armstrong, Catherine Julia Cecily 2722
Armstrong, Chantal 2058
Armstrong, Charles Andrew 106
Armstrong, Charles Ivan 818
Armstrong, (Christine) Caroline Catherine 2722
Armstrong, Christopher John Edmund Stuart 106
Armstrong, David Warwick 262
Armstrong, Deborah 1400
Armstrong, (Edmund Charles) Mark 106
Armstrong, Edward James Maxwell 2058
Armstrong, Elizabeth 988
Armstrong, Elsie 988
Armstrong, Eric Napier 2058
Armstrong, Fiona Ann 3085
Armstrong, Flora 1400
Armstrong, Geoffrey James 818
Armstrong, Geoffrey Read 988
Armstrong, Georgina Elizabeth 106
Armstrong, Graham Whitney 988
Armstrong, Hazel Claire 818
Armstrong, Henry Francis Arthur Rous 2722
Armstrong, Henry Napier 2058
Armstrong, Iain 1229
Armstrong, James Douglas 1400
Armstrong, James Hugo 106
Armstrong, Jane 2422
Armstrong, Jane Elizabeth Alice 2058
Armstrong, Jane Orlanda 107
Armstrong, Jane Winchester 2844
Armstrong, Jill J 2058
Armstrong, John Fortescue 2058
Armstrong, John George William Rous 2722
Armstrong, John Henry 1705
Armstrong, Johnny 988
Armstrong, Judith Anne 1705
Armstrong, Kate Amanda 1705
Armstrong, Kathleen Mary 2058
Armstrong, Madeleine Margaret 2058
Armstrong, Mark Harold Napier 2058
Armstrong, Mark Simon Warneford 107
Armstrong, (Mary) Patricia 107
Armstrong, Melvin Cooper 262
Armstrong, Niall John 818
Armstrong, Nicola Anne 1705
Armstrong, Nigel 1229
Armstrong, Patrick Austin 107
Armstrong, Philip Raymond 2058
Armstrong, Rachel Susan 2844
Armstrong, Richard John 818
Armstrong, Richard Michael Boris 2844
Armstrong, Richard Thomas 262
Armstrong, Robert 3085
Armstrong, Robert Walter 2422
Armstrong, Robert William Fortescue 2058
Armstrong, Roselyne Jeanne Thérèse 107
Armstrong, Rosemarie 2058
Armstrong, Sam Edward 106
Armstrong, Sarah Elizabeth 455
Armstrong, Sarah Jane 2844
Armstrong, Sarah Margaret 2648
Armstrong, Sean Andrew 107
Armstrong, Simon William Jones 3083
Armstrong, Teresa Brigid 107
Armstrong, Timothy 1229
Armstrong, Victoria Jane 106
Armstrong, William Edward O'Dowd 2058
Armstrong-Jones, Caroline Therese 2656
Armstrong-Jones, David Albert Charles 1320
Armstrong-Jones, Frances 2656
Armstrong-Jones, India Sophie 2656
Armstrong-Jones, Jenifer 2656
Armstrong-Jones, Lucy Mary 2656
Armstrong-Jones, Peregrine Thomas Owen Llewellyn 2656
Armstrong-Jones, Serena 1320
Armytage, Alexander Hugh Edward 109
Armytage, Antonia Cosima 109
Armytage, Brioni Katherine 109
Armytage, Charles David 109
Armytage, David George 109
Armytage, Diana Marion 108
Armytage, Edwina Frederica 108
Armytage, Gaye (Gee) 109
Armytage, Georgina Caroline 108
Armytage, Harry Charles George 109
Armytage, Hugh Anthony 109
Armytage, Jane Annette 109
Armytage, Julia 108
Armytage, Julian Ralph Fitzroy 108
Armytage, Katharine (Katie) Alexandra 109
Armytage, Marcus David 109
Armytage, (Maria) Margarete 109
Armytage, Maurice John Reginald 109
Armytage, Roderick (Roddy) Charles 109
Arnander, Christopher James Folke 49, 706
Arnander, Conrad David Folke 49
Arnander, Katharine Louise 49
Arnander, Magnus 49
Arnander, Michael Theodore Per 49
Arnander, Pamela Primrose 49, 706
Arnfield, Anne Caroline 2952
Arnfield, Patrick George 2952
Arnfield, Philip 2952
Arnfield, Samuel Richard 2952
Arnfield, Sarah Rose 2952
Arnold, Amanda Jane 1237
Arnold, Brooke Egerton Halley 1237
Arnold, Catherine Angela 607
Arnold, David James 607
Arnold, Elizabeth Jane Mary 2023
Arnold, Emily Minna Mary 2023
Arnold, Frances Helen 641
Arnold, Helen Maud 1237
Arnold, Hugh James 641
Arnold, John Christopher 641
Arnold, John Halley 1237
Arnold, Joseph William 1637
Arnold, Mary Elizabeth 1637
Arnold, Michelle Tracey 1237
Arnold, Penelope Clare 641
Arnold, Richard John Halley 1237
Arnold, William Henry 641
Arnott, Andrew John Eric 110
Arnott, Ann (Annie) 110
Arnott, Caroline 110
Arnott, Eric John 110
Arnott, Guy 110
Arnott, Isabella Anastasia 110
Arnott, Jean Barbara 109
Arnott, Jennifer Mary 109
Arnott, John Andrew 109
Arnott, John David 109
Arnott, Katherine Jane 110
Arnott, Lara Georgina Emma 110
Arnott, Myles Anthony 109
Arnott, Oliver Timothy John 110
Arnott, Peter John 110
Arnott, Robert Lauriston John 110
Arnott, Stephen John 110
Arnott, Veronica Mary 110
Aron, Diana Bridget Lilian 2544

B

Baird, Maria Florine 169
Baird, Mervyn Edward Hozier 170
Baird, Mirella Frances Hozier 170
Baird, Nichola Bridget Halsall 170
Baird, Nicola Laura 168
Baird, Petra Helen Stuart 169
Baird, Roderick 34
Baird, Roderick Frank Gardiner 170
Baird, Rosemary Alice 34
Baird, Senta Louise Stuart 169
Baird, Tara Francesca Stuart 169
Baird, Thomas Roderick 34
Baird, (William) Julian Gardiner 170
Bairstow, George Robert 1101
Bairstow, Katharine Selina 1101
Bairstow, Maria Elizabeth Jane 1101
Bairstow, Vivian 1101
Baker, Agnes Charlotte Gertrude 2143
Baker, Aidan Lee 1418
Baker, Alan 268
Baker, Albert Victor 2037
Baker, Alexander Duncan 1819
Baker, Andrew 2966
Baker, Andrew William St John 2519
Baker, Annabel Dorothy Primrose 2760
Baker, Anne Dorothy 2260
Baker, Archie John Midelton 2645
Baker, Barbara 254
Baker, Basil Lionel 1418
Baker, Boadicea Louisa Ann 2143
Baker, Bruce Stephen 92
Baker, Camilla Lucy 2519
Baker, Carl Gary 1855
Baker, Carol Lynn 92
Baker, Caroline 2844
Baker, Caroline Anne Christine 231
Baker, Catherine Ann 268
Baker, Charles Frederick Benno 265
Baker, Christine Mary 2037
Baker, Christopher J V R 609
Baker, Colin Freeman 1022
Baker, Colin Harris 2427
Baker, Constance Daffodil Bohemia 2143
Baker, Conyers Collingwood Massy 231
Baker, Cynthia Margaret 373
Baker, Daniel Sancroft 2260
Baker, Darcy Eryn 464
Baker, David 464
Baker, Derek Charles Kuke 2941
Baker, Eileen Ann 268
Baker, Eliza Rose 2143
Baker, Elizabeth 2602
Baker, (Elizabeth) Anne 609
Baker, Elizabeth Denise 913
Baker, Elizabeth Diana 2143
Baker, Erin 2966
Baker, Felicity Ruth 2519
Baker, Fiona 2427
Baker, Gavin Jeremy Wyndham 1819
Baker, Graham 906
Baker, Hannibal Eustace Pilate 2143
Baker, Harry Brian 989
Baker, Herbert Douglas Midleton 2645
Baker, Holly Sarah 1855
Baker, Hugh Honner Sancroft 2260
Baker, (Hugh) Lysander Luke 2143
Baker, James Carl 1855
Baker, James Paul 268
Baker, James William John 3086
Baker, Jamie 913
Baker, Janet Cynthia 373
Baker, Janet Finetta Campbell 89
Baker, Joanna Gwendoline 1819
Baker, John Andrew 92
Baker, John Paul Philip 373
Baker, Jonathan Piers Massy 231
Baker, Jonathon Mark Midelton 2645
Baker, Joshua Ralph 2143
Baker, Katherine 2037
Baker, Laura 2966
Baker, Lisa Renée 1819
Baker, Lucy Florence 609
Baker, Luke Frank 3086
Baker, Lynn Marie 2966
Baker, Margaret Jean 92
Baker, Marie 464
Baker, Marion Avery 1022
Baker, Mark Alexander Wyndham 1819
Baker, Martin 2427
Baker, Mary Elizabeth 170
Baker, Matthew Ronald Nicholas 2760
Baker, Melinda Elizabeth Eirène 2645
Baker, Meriel 1819
Baker, Michael Herbert 2844
Baker, Miranda Alice 2519
Baker, Miranda 1819
Baker, Miriam Arabella Elizabeth 2037
Baker, Myrtle Jesse 1418
Baker, Natalie 2092
Baker, Nichola Margaret 3086
Baker, Nicholas Sancroft 2260
Baker, Norah Mary 2260
Baker, Patrick 2966
Baker, Paul Bertram 373
Baker, (Penelope) Carol 2760
Baker, Penelope Elizabeth 2427
Baker, Peter Sherston 2602
Baker, Philip J 2966
Baker, Philip Massy 231
Baker, Priscilla Ann 2143
Baker, Rebecca Beatrice 1819
Baker, Richard St John 2519
Baker, Robert Alan 268
Baker, Robert Edward Nicolas 2587
Baker, Ruth 2427
Baker, (Samuel) Justin Francis 2143
Baker, Sandra Ann 906
Baker, Sara Mary 2587
Baker, Sarah 2427
Baker, Sarah Georgina 265
Baker, Sophia Victoria 265
Baker, Tamzyn Skye 3086
Baker, Terence Sancroft 2260
Baker, Victor George 2037
Baker, Virginia Dale 2519
Baker, Wendy Lynn 1855
Baker, (William) Gregory Francis Meath 2143
Baker, William Hugh 265
Baker, William Hugh Massy 231
Baker, (William John) Clovis 2143
Baker, William Thomas Neville 2941
Baker, William Thompson 2092
Baker Wilbraham, Alice Maria Elizabeth 171
Baker Wilbraham, Amanda Jane 171
Baker Wilbraham, Anne Christine 171
Baker Wilbraham, Charlotte Cecilia Anne 171
Baker Wilbraham, Joyce Katharine 171
Baker Wilbraham, Randle 171
Bakewell, Charlotte Alice 339
Bakewell, Constance Louise 339
Bakewell, Elisabeth Aylva 339
Bakker, Angela Kathleen 273
Bakker, Jeremy 273
Bakker, Norman Adrianus 273
Bakker, Sarah Antonia 273
Bakker, Vanessa 273
Balan, Gonzolo Daniel 574
Balan, Jorge Daniel 574
Balan, Rita Adela 574
Balding, Andrew Matthews 1476
Balding, Clare Victoria 1476
Balding, Emma Alice Mary 1476
Balding, Ian Anthony 1476
Baldock, Catherine Jane 200
Baldock, Jeremy John 200
Baldock, John Kingsley 200
Baldock, Judith Mary 200
Baldock, Mary Diane 200
Baldry, June Penson 1768
Baldry, Stanley Thomas 1768
Baldwin, Alison Mary 2832
Baldwin, Angus Oldham 2346
Baldwin, Anita Jane 2878
Baldwin, Anthony Ian Maxwell 1669
Baldwin, Benedict Alexander Stanley 172
Baldwin, Bruce Phillip 2878
Baldwin, Christina Helen 1669
Baldwin, Christopher William Kennard 59
Baldwin, Constance Agnes 2346
Baldwin, David Maurice 2832
Baldwin, Emma Margaret 59
Baldwin, George William Robert 1669
Baldwin, Ian Hugh Trevor 1669
Baldwin, Isabelle Rose 59
Baldwin, James Conrad 172
Baldwin, Jean Helen 1669
Baldwin, John Lindsay Alexander 59
Baldwin, Malcolm Ramsay 2346
Baldwin, Mark Thomas Maitland 172
Baldwin, Martin Trevor Maxwell 1669
Baldwin, Penelope Debra 2878
Baldwin, Petra Josephine 2832
Baldwin, Raymond William 190
Baldwin, Richard Arthur 2346
Baldwin, Rosalind Penelope 190
Baldwin, Ross Ramsay 2346
Baldwin, Sarah 172
Baldwin, Susan Joan 2346
Baldwin, Thomas Raymond 190
Balfour, Alan Ian 1608
Balfour, Alastair Albert David 1870
Balfour, Alexander John 2232
Balfour, Ann Shuyler 1534
Balfour, Anna Louise 2416
Balfour, Anthony John Chetwynd 1608
Balfour, Arthur Michael 2416
Balfour, Candida Rose 173
Balfour, Carolyn Margaret 2687
Balfour, Charles George Yule 173
Balfour, Christopher John Jellicoe 1534
Balfour, Consuelo Lily 1870
Balfour, Daphne Cecelia 2416
Balfour, David 914
Balfour, David Rowland 2416
Balfour, Derek Andrew 1608
Balfour, Edward Francis 2416
Balfour, Edward James Melville 2687
Balfour, Eleanor Cecily Isabelle 173
Balfour, Emily Kate Mary 2232
Balfour, Eustace Arthur Goschen 173
Balfour, Evelyn Mary 174
Balfour, Frances Christian 2416
Balfour, Francis Henry 2416
Balfour, George Eustace Charles 173
Balfour, Graeme Charles 914
Balfour, Harry Luke Chetwynd 1609
Balfour, Hilary Joan Gwendolen 1609
Balfour, James Charles Murray 914
Balfour, James Henry 2416
Balfour, James Melville John 2687
Balfour, Jeremy Ralph 2416
Balfour, Josephine Maria Jane 175
Balfour, Judith Ann Margaret 1609
Balfour, Kate Frances 2416
Balfour, Katharine Augusta 174
Balfour, Kinvara Clare Rachel 173
Balfour, Laura Elizabeth 2687
Balfour, Lila Camila 174
Balfour, Margaret Carolyn 2687
Balfour, Maria Alice Jubilee 173
Balfour, Mary Ainslie 176
Balfour, Mary Emma 914
Balfour, Maureen Ethné 19
Balfour, Maxwell James 1534
Balfour, Michael Patrick Keir 174
Balfour, Nancy Ann 2416
Balfour, Neil Roxburgh 1870
Balfour, Paula Susan 173
Balfour, Peter John Torquil 1609
Balfour, Peter Murray 914
Balfour, Rebecca Anne 2416
Balfour, Rita Ann 2416
Balfour, Robert Arthur 1406
Balfour, Robert Henry 2416
Balfour, Robert William Keir 174
Balfour, Roderick Francis Arthur 173, 2090
Balfour, Russell Miller 914
Balfour, Ruth Beverly 1609
Balfour, Ruth 2416
Balfour, Serena Mary 1870
Balfour, Susan Jane 1608
Balfour, Svea Maria Cecily Lucrezia 173
Balfour, Tessa Mary Isabel 173, 2090
Balfour, Wendy May 2416
Balfour-Paul, Alison Muriel 2143
Balfour-Paul, Ann 2143
Balfour-Paul, Catherine Angela 2143
Balfour-Paul, (Hugh) Glencairn 2143
Balfour-Paul, James Ogilvy 2143
Balkwill, Francis Martin 1229
Balkwill, Jennifer Anne Christine 1229
Balkwill, Michael Peter 1229
Balkwill, Sarah Louise 1229
Ball, Adrianne Elaine Patricia 1290
Ball, Alberto Carlos 2279
Ball, Alison Daphne 1662
Ball, Amelia Kate 177
Ball, Anna Frances 176
Ball, Anthony St Vincent 1290
Ball, Arabella Clare Lucy 2744
Ball, Aurelia Cary Rennie 2851
Ball, Aurelia Cary Roslyn 2851
Ball, Barry 2744
Ball, Benjamin Peter 810
Ball, Beth Sigrid 39
Ball, Beverly Ann 176
Ball, Christine 177
Ball, Christine Trilby 176
Ball, Christopher James 177
Ball, Christopher Nigel Morton 177
Ball, Claire Diana 810
Ball, David Jonathan 1290
Ball, Diana Margaret 176
Ball, Dorothy Lucia Annie 177
Ball, Elsie Nelly 2279
Ball, Emma Frances 177
Ball, Henry Stoner 3035
Ball, Hermione Anne 3035
Ball, James Irwin Hampson 177
Ball, Joanna Rachel 177
Ball, John Clement 1662
Ball, John Trollope Macintosh 2851
Ball, Jonathan Gresley 177
Ball, Jorge Eduard 2279
Ball, Josephine Grace 176
Ball, Katherine Elizabeth 177
Ball, Lesley Anne 39
Ball, Mary 176
Ball, Melanie 177
Ball, Molly 177
Ball, Peter Halley 176
Ball, Peter John 810
Ball, Peter Jonathan 177
Ball, Richard Bentley 176
Ball, Robert Grant 176
Ball, Robert J 39
Ball, Roberto 2279
Ball, Rosamond Eleanor 1662
Ball, Rupert Valentine 177
Ball, Stephen Jarvis 1290
Ball, Susana Beatriz 2279
Ball, Vincent George Jarvis 1290
Ballantyne, Priscilla Moira Angèle 1376
Ballard, Andrew James 100
Ballard, Ethel Ruth 923
Ballard, Frances S 2080
Ballard, Hugh William 100
Ballard, Marianne Jean Elspeth 100
Ballard, William Richard Woods 100
Ballarin, Antonia Barbara 2552
Ballarin, Caterina Teresa 2552
Ballingall, Alexandra Marjorie 2313
Ballingall, Andrew H C 2313
Ballot, Antonia Katherine 962
Ballot, Marcel 962
Bally, Alexander St John 403
Bally, David Anthony 403
Bally, Ian Stephen Edward 403
Bally, Jodie Marie 403
Bally, Kay Louise 403
Bally, Kay Therese 403
Bally, Louise Frances Joan 403
Bally, Madelaine Marie 403
Bally, Mark William 403
Bally, Sarah Ann Frances 403
Bally, Tabitha Louise 403
Bamber, Joanna 2196
Bamber, Mark 2196
Bamford, Alan Peter 2652
Bamford, Constance Amelia 2283
Bamford, Elizabeth Maria 2283
Bamford, Henrietta Mary 2283
Bamford, Lucy Mary 2283
Bamford, Richard John 2283
Bampfylde, Camilla 2273
Bampfylde, Charlotte Mary 2273
Bampfylde, David Cecil Warwick 2273
Bampfylde, Edward David Warwick 2273
Bampfylde, Henry Anthony Warwick 2272
Bampfylde, Jean Margaret 2273
Bampfylde, John Spencer Warwick 1897, 2273
Bampfylde, Lara Fiona Brita 2272
Bampfylde, Laura Margaret 2273
Bampfylde, Michael Hugh Warwick 798, 2273
Bampfylde, Nicola 1897
Bampfylde, Nicola 2273
Bampfylde, Oliver Hugh Coplestone 2272
Bampfylde, Richard Ian David 2273
Bampfylde, Sally Anne 2272
Bampfylde, Sarah Fenella 798, 2273
Banbury, Amanda Carol 272
Banbury, Charles Thomas 272
Banbury, Charlotte Rosa 177
Banbury, Inger Marianne Norton 177
Banbury, Poppy Isobel 177
Bancroft, Adam Fisher 2207
Bancroft, Angus 155
Bancroft, Anna Charlotte 155
Bancroft, Caroline Georgiana 2207
Bancroft, Imogen Georgiana Patricia 2207
Bancroft, Jonathan Guy 2207
Bancroft, Mary 155
Bancroft, Oliver Robert 2207
Bancroft, Paul Fisher 2207
Bancroft, William Harry 155
Band, Charlotte Louise 1166
Band, George Christopher 1166
Band, Nigel Edward 1166
Band, Rupert Alexander 1166
Band, Susan Maeve 1166
Banerji, Ranjit 2011
Banerji, Sara Ann 2011
Bangham, Alison Mary 1316
Bangham, Charles Richard Mark 1316
Bangham, Charles Stafford 1316
Bangham, Derek Raymond 1316
Bangham, Elizabeth Mary 1316
Bangham, Florence Clara Jocelyne 1316
Bangham, George Richard Derek 1316
Bangham, Guy Nicholas 1316
Bangham, Humphrey Bernard 1316
Bangham, Jocelyne Marie 1316
Bangham, Madeleine Edith Marie 1316
Bangham, Olivia Charlotte 1316
Banham, Frances Barbara 2608
Banham, John Michael Middlecott 2608
Banham, Mark Richard Middlecott 2608
Banham, Morwenna Bridget 2608
Banham, Serena Frances Tamsin 2608
Bankes, Althea 2678
Bankes, Ariane 74, 2678
Bankes, Fiona Gillian 1092
Bankes, Henry Francis John 2746
Bankes, John Jervis Murray 2746
Bankes, John Wynne 2678
Bankes, Juliet Anne 1092
Bankes, Louisa Juliet 1092
Bankes, Margaret Christine 2746
Bankes, Nigel John Eldon 1092, 2678
Bankes, William Nigel Wynne 1092
Banks, Ann 1600
Banks, Chloë Berenice Josephine 735
Banks, Edward Joseph 735
Banks, Elizabeth Christina 735
Banks, George Kenneth 1600
Banks, Georgina Emma 347
Banks, Janet Bridget 254
Banks, Justin Christopher 1600
Banks, Melanie Catherine 330
Banks, Michael 330
Banks, Nicola Claire 330
Banks, Richard George Fothergill 347
Banks, Richard Michael 735
Banks, Rosalind 330
Banks, Rowena Phyllis 361
Banks, Simon J 361
Banks, Thomas 254
Banks, William Ferdinand 735
Banks, (William) Lawrence 735
Banner, Elizabeth Gwendolen Teresa 700, 2326
Banner, Kenneth Harmood 2326
Bannerman, Andrew Henry 1412
Bannerman, Arabella Rose 182
Bannerman, Barbara Charlotte 183
Bannerman, Brendon Peter 1412
Bannerman, Cheryl 1412
Bannerman, Clodagh Isobel Rose 182
Bannerman, Dwayne Marcus 1412
Bannerman, Edna Gladys 183
Bannerman, Henrietta Jane 183
Bannerman, Jane Alison 183
Bannerman, Jenny Marie 1412
Bannerman, Joan Mary 183
Bannerman, Kevin Bruce 1412
Bannerman, Margot Charlotte 182
Bannerman, Myra Edith 1412
Bannerman, Natalie Ann 1412
Bannerman, Neville William 1412
Bannerman, Prudence Mary 182
Bannerman, Shane Bruce 1412
Bannero, Lorenzo Cavan 524
Bannero, Natasha Pepa 524
Banning, Joshua Charles 1563
Banning, Rachel Susan 1563

Barlow, Natasha Helen 190
Barlow, Nicholas Dalmahoy 190
Barlow, Nicholas Hugh 189
Barlow, Nicholas Philip 188
Barlow, Oscar Hugh 191
Barlow, Patricia Jennifer 189
Barlow, Pauline 188
Barlow, Pepita Elisabeth 191
Barlow, Peter Stephen 189
Barlow, Philip Thomas 190
Barlow, Rebecca Nora 190
Barlow, Richard Owen 189
Barlow, Rosemary Alexandra 188
Barlow, Rosemary Joan 188
Barlow, Rosemary Sylvia Mary 189
Barlow, Sacha Jane Anna 188
Barlow, Sarah Hilary 187
Barlow, Stephen Hugh 188
Barlow, Susan 1446
Barlow, Susan Jane 190
Barlow, Susan Marian Deborah 190
Barlow, Thomas Daniel 190
Barlow, Thomas David Bradwall 187
Barlow, (Thomas) Jeremy Erasmus 190
Barlow, Veronica 187
Barlow, Yvonne Rosalind 190
Barnard, Benjamin Philip 1520
Barnard, Christopher John 2583
Barnard, David Charles 2583
Barnard, Diana Eileen 2583
Barnard, Emma Lavinia 1520
Barnard, Emma Louise 668
Barnard, Gillian Valerie 1849
Barnard, James 1520
Barnard, Joanna Suzanne 2583
Barnard, Jonathan James 668
Barnard, Joy 668
Barnard, Louisa Jane 1520
Barnard, Simon William Leslie 667
Barne, Alasdair Michael Fitzroy 1815
Barne, Charles Miles 954
Barne, Christopher Miles 954
Barne, Elizabeth Beatrice 954
Barne, Hamish Nicholas Charles 1815
Barne, Janet Elizabeth 1815
Barne, Nicholas Michael Lancelot 1815
Barnes, Anna Clare 2859
Barnes, Christina Hermione 454
Barnes, Daphne 1198
Barnes, Elizabeth Gail 1176
Barnes, George Christopher 2859
Barnes, George Stanley Coote 657
Barnes, Gillian 1176
Barnes, Helen Rosalind 2655
Barnes, Ivy Joy 2671
Barnes, Jessie 1478
Barnes, Joan Marion 1175
Barnes, John 2167
Barnes, John David Millard 454
Barnes, John Picton Gorell 1176
Barnes, Jonathan David Batrick 2655
Barnes, Julie Ann 711
Barnes, Mark Richard 2859
Barnes, Mary Veronica 798
Barnes, Nicola Jane 711
Barnes, Peter Denis Ponsonby 798
Barnes, Priscilla Ann 657
Barnes, Rachel Mary 2859
Barnes, Robert Ogle Ball 176
Barnes, (Ronald Alexander) Henry Gorell 1176
Barnes, Samuel 1478
Barnes, Stella Elizabeth 176
Barnes, Thomas David 2859
Barnes, Thomas William Ponsonby 798
Barnes, Timothy James 711
Barnes, William Peter Ward 798
Barnett, Annabel Penelope 3052
Barnett, Barbara Joan 1793
Barnett, Benjamin 2963
Barnett, Bruce Sydney 237
Barnett, Carolyn Seward 3052
Barnett, Christopher Andrew 2963
Barnett, Clara Aurjana 2963
Barnett, Craig John 1793
Barnett, Erica Hazel 193
Barnett, Fiona Anne 237
Barnett, Gregory Mark 1793
Barnett, Hilton A 753
Barnett, John Sydney 1793
Barnett, Julia Seward 3052
Barnett, Kathleen Irene Mary 3052
Barnett, Laura Miriam Elizabeth 2963
Barnett, Leila Katharine 753
Barnett, Lilian Stella 193
Barnett, Margaret Katherine 3052
Barnett, Marie-Jane 2892
Barnett, Max Robin Nicholas 3052
Barnett, Natalie Aline 2892
Barnett, Nathaniel Peter Edward 2963
Barnett, Nicholas James 3052
Barnett, Oliver Louis 2892
Barnett, Robin George 3052
Barnett, Rory Nicholas 2892
Barnett, Rowan 2963
Barnett, Stephanie Lucinda 3052
Barnett, Sylvia Irina 2892
Barnett, Thomas 753
Barnett, Tracy Megan 1793
Barnett, Ulric David 2892
Barnewall, Alexandra Rose 195
Barnewall, Alison Louise 194
Barnewall, Allison Mae 195
Barnewall, Amy Louise 195
Barnewall, Ann Louise 195
Barnewall, Anthony Brian 195
Barnewall, Barbara Ruth Mary 195
Barnewall, Benjamin Scott 195
Barnewall, Brian Francis 194
Barnewall, Brooke 195
Barnewall, Christopher Patrick 193
Barnewall, Clare Therese 195
Barnewall, Daisy Mabel 195
Barnewall, Daniel Leigh 195
Barnewall, David Matthew 195
Barnewall, Dianne Margaret 194
Barnewall, Dianne Robyn 195
Barnewall, Frances Erica 194
Barnewall, Francis Richard 194
Barnewall, Glenda Michelle 195
Barnewall, Graeme David 195
Barnewall, Holly Renae 194
Barnewall, Jack 195
Barnewall, Jennifer 195
Barnewall, Jessica Kate 195
Barnewall, Jessica Rose 193
Barnewall, Joan Catherine 195
Barnewall, John Jeffrey 194
Barnewall, John Robert 194, 195
Barnewall, Judith Diane 194
Barnewall, Kathryn Jane 193
Barnewall, Kerry Teresa 194
Barnewall, Kevin Bruce 195
Barnewall, Kieran Gerard 195
Barnewall, Laura Mary 195
Barnewall, Lesley Christine 195
Barnewall, Linda Mary 194
Barnewall, Lindy Jean 195
Barnewall, Lisa 195
Barnewall, Madeleine Grace 195
Barnewall, Margaret Ann 193
Barnewall, Margaret Mary 194
Barnewall, Marie Patricia 194
Barnewall, Marietza Anne 194
Barnewall, Marietza Elizabeth 194
Barnewall, Marjorie Joyce 195
Barnewall, Mark Raymond 195
Barnewall, Mary 2847
Barnewall, Maureen Ellen 193
Barnewall, Mavis Leone 195
Barnewall, Michael James 195
Barnewall, Murray Charles 195
Barnewall, Naomi Patricia 194
Barnewall, Patrick Joseph 194
Barnewall, Peter Joseph 193
Barnewall, Rebecca Jayne 195
Barnewall, Rhianna Kate 194
Barnewall, Richard Joseph 193
Barnewall, Ronald William 195
Barnewall, Samantha Kate 195
Barnewall, Sarah Jane 195
Barnewall, Susan Jennifer 195
Barnewall, Tammie Elizabeth 194
Barnewall, Teena Merrie 194
Barnewall, Daphne Mavis 194
Barnsley, Louisa Frances 86
Barnsley, Rose Alice 86
Baron, Una Pamela 2015
Barone, Christina Marie 1598
Barone, David Spencer 1598
Barone, Gail Heather 1598
Barone, Lisa Ann 1598
Barr, Angus Haddon Dunstan 2877
Barr, George Arthur 2798
Barr, Gillian Mary 2798
Barr, Greig 338
Barr, Helen Marion 2660
Barr, James Haddon 2877
Barr, Jock Henry Hugh 2877
Barr, Sarah Mary Constance 2877
Barr, Valerie Winifred 338
Barr-Sim, Andrew John 440
Barr-Sim, Evelyn Susan 440
Barraclough, Amabel 1896
Barraclough, Hector 1896
Barran, Adrian Stuart Lechmere 197
Barran, Alastair Haworth 196
Barran, Alice Matilda 196
Barran, Amy Louise 197
Barran, Anthea Janet 196
Barran, Antony Nicholas 197
Barran, Camilla Violet 196
Barran, Charles Patrick Edward 197
Barran, Christabel Lucy 196
Barran, Cosmo Ralph 197
Barran, Daisy Charlotte 196
Barran, Daniel Nicholas 197
Barran, David Haven 197
Barran, Diana 197
Barran, Diana Buttercup 196, 870
Barran, Donald Austyn Nicholson 196
Barran, Elizabeth Margery 196
Barran, Emily Dolores 197
Barran, Emma Louise Moya 196, 2607
Barran, Estelle Elspeth 197
Barran, Feliksa 197
Barran, Ferdinand Roc 197
Barran, George Arthur Mansfield 196
Barran, George Wharton 196
Barran, Giuseppe Maria 197
Barran, Hebe Elisabeth 197
Barran, Hugh 197
Barran, Hugh Paull 196
Barran, Hugh Rowland Murray 196, 870
Barran, Hugo Jeremy 196
Barran, Jane 197
Barran, Jane Margaret 195
Barran, Jean 197
Barran, John Napoleon Ruthven 505
Barran, John Ruthven 195
Barran, Jonathan Haworth 196
Barran, Julian Mark Lechmere 197
Barran, Laurence Edward 197
Barran, Leo David 197
Barran, Lindsay 196
Barran, Lorna Marina 197
Barran, Marius Peregrine Lechmere 197
Barran, Milo 197
Barran, Miranda Clare Frances 197, 678
Barran, Miranda Jane 196, 2443
Barran, Nicholas Dudley Edward 197
Barran, Nicholas Eric Hugh 196, 2607
Barran, Nicholas George 196
Barran, Patricia Helen 197
Barran, Patrick Robin 196, 2443
Barran, Perdita Elizabeth 197
Barran, Petra Sely 197
Barran, Phoebe Alice 197
Barran, Rachel Louise 196
Barran, Richard Martin 196
Barran, Rosa 196
Barran, Rowland Paull 196
Barran, Sally Elizabeth 196
Barran, Stephen William Edward 197
Barran, Susannah Margaret 195
Barran, Tabitha Jane 197
Barran, Toby Nicholas Hugh 197
Barran, Veronica Tessa 197
Barrantes, Susan Mary 2304
Barratt, Caroline 504
Barratt, Charles William 504
Barratt, David John 504
Barratt, Elyned Barbara 504
Barratt, Fergus Ralph Legh 504
Barratt, Frederick David Nicholas 504
Barratt, John Legh 504
Barratt, Penelope Constance Isabel 504
Barratt, Samuel Charles Legh 504
Barratt, William James 504
Barrell, Louisa Roxane 2298
Barrell, Susanna Louise Roxane 2298
Barren, Jane Margaret 351
Barren, John Napoleon Ruthven 351
Barrett, Aileen Margaretta 1849
Barrett, Andrew 2418
Barrett, Anthony Charles 606
Barrett, April Joy 606
Barrett, Barbara Leone 2006
Barrett, Bryan Nicholas 478
Barrett, Claire Fiona 478
Barrett, Curtiss 448
Barrett, David McNaghten 2006
Barrett, Denis Hugh Bryan 478
Barrett, Edward Ronald 606
Barrett, Elizabeth Jane 2418
Barrett, Evelyn Mary 478
Barrett, George Robin 606
Barrett, Georgina Mary 478
Barrett, Hazel Jean 2671
Barrett, Hilary Mary 1391
Barrett, Hugh Yelverton Scott 236
Barrett, James McNaghten 2006
Barrett, Jonathan 61
Barrett, Jonathan Ivan 3029
Barrett, Joy 2336
Barrett, Karen Diana 236
Barrett, Leigh 2336
Barrett, Lorilee Faye 448
Barrett, Margaret Lloyd 1742
Barrett, Mark Hugh 2336
Barrett, Mary Elizabeth 1824
Barrett, Maxwell John 3029
Barrett, Michael Patrick Denis 478
Barrett, Neville Ramsay 2336
Barrett, Patricia Anne 2671
Barrett, (Patricia) Jane 3029
Barrett, Robert James Michael 606
Barrett, Robert John 1849
Barrett, Roger Hugh 2336
Barrett, Sally 2336
Barrett, Sarah Elisabeth Jane 3029
Barrett, Sarah Margaret 606
Barrett, Simon 61
Barrett, Susan Katherine Patrica 3029
Barrett, Taran John 448
Barrett, Tyler Richard Joseph 448
Barrett-Lennard, Alexander Dacre 199
Barrett-Lennard, Alison 198
Barrett-Lennard, Alix Louise 199
Barrett-Lennard, Amy 200
Barrett-Lennard, Ann Mary 199
Barrett-Lennard, Anthony Leslie 198
Barrett-Lennard, Antony John William 198
Barrett-Lennard, Audrey 199
Barrett-Lennard, Beatrice Elizabeth 201
Barrett-Lennard, Benjamin James 198
Barrett-Lennard, Berwine Ruth 199
Barrett-Lennard, Bethwyn Ruth 200
Barrett-Lennard, Brent 199
Barrett-Lennard, Brian 200
Barrett-Lennard, Cameron 199
Barrett-Lennard, Carmen Lesley 198
Barrett-Lennard, Catherine Jane 198
Barrett-Lennard, Christopher James Blake 198
Barrett-Lennard, Cicely Anne 198
Barrett-Lennard, Claire 198
Barrett-Lennard, Clare Lois 200
Barrett-Lennard, Clay 199
Barrett-Lennard, Constance Rosalie 200
Barrett-Lennard, Dacre 200
Barrett-Lennard, Dale Cameron 199
Barrett-Lennard, Daniel Thomas John 200
Barrett-Lennard, David Anthony 200
Barrett-Lennard, David John 199
Barrett-Lennard, David Thomas 199
Barrett-Lennard, Deanna Jane 199
Barrett-Lennard, Deborah Dacre 201
Barrett-Lennard, Derwent Thomas Keith 198
Barrett-Lennard, Dina 199
Barrett-Lennard, Donald 200
Barrett-Lennard, Dorothea Ann 199
Barrett-Lennard, Dorothy 200
Barrett-Lennard, Dorothy Marianne 198
Barrett-Lennard, Douglas Graham 199
Barrett-Lennard, Douglas John 198
Barrett-Lennard, Dymity Ann 200
Barrett-Lennard, Edmund George 199
Barrett-Lennard, Edmund Timothy Dacre 198
Barrett-Lennard, Edward Graham 199
Barrett-Lennard, Edward Guy 200
Barrett-Lennard, Edward William 200
Barrett-Lennard, Elizabeth Jane 201
Barrett-Lennard, Elizabeth May 200
Barrett-Lennard, Ethel Barbara Adams 198
Barrett-Lennard, Ferguson 200
Barrett-Lennard, Florence Ray 199
Barrett-Lennard, Frank St Aubyn 200
Barrett-Lennard, Fynes 199
Barrett-Lennard, Godfrey Trevor 199
Barrett-Lennard, Graham Francis 199
Barrett-Lennard, Gregory Dacre 199
Barrett-Lennard, Guy St Aubyn 200
Barrett-Lennard, Helen 199
Barrett-Lennard, Helen Mary 198
Barrett-Lennard, Holly Elizabeth 199
Barrett-Lennard, Hugh Anthony 199
Barrett-Lennard, Irwin Prescott 199
Barrett-Lennard, Jackson Dacre 199
Barrett-Lennard, James Dacre 198
Barrett-Lennard, James Irwin 199
Barrett-Lennard, James Thomas 201
Barrett-Lennard, Jane 200
Barrett-Lennard, Jennifer Jill 200
Barrett-Lennard, Jeremy 198
Barrett-Lennard, Jeremy Robert 199
Barrett-Lennard, Jillian Elizabeth 199
Barrett-Lennard, Jodie Louise 198
Barrett-Lennard, John 198
Barrett-Lennard, John Dacre 200
Barrett-Lennard, John Fiennes 202
Barrett-Lennard, John Graham 199
Barrett-Lennard, Josephine Albertina Elizabeth 202
Barrett-Lennard, Judith Anne 200
Barrett-Lennard, Judith Helen 199
Barrett-Lennard, Julie Louise 199
Barrett-Lennard, Julieanne 200
Barrett-Lennard, June Rosemary 202
Barrett-Lennard, Katherine Gail 199
Barrett-Lennard, Kathryn Faye 199
Barrett-Lennard, Kaye Julie 199
Barrett-Lennard, Kingsley Ian Michael 199
Barrett-Lennard, Krystelle Amy 199
Barrett-Lennard, Lance Godfrey 199
Barrett-Lennard, Lancelot 199
Barrett-Lennard, Leita Catherine 198
Barrett-Lennard, Lesley Vernon 199
Barrett-Lennard, Lorna Jean 198
Barrett-Lennard, Lorna Margaret 198
Barrett-Lennard, Lorraine 200
Barrett-Lennard, Lynette Marie 200
Barrett-Lennard, Maisie 200
Barrett-Lennard, Margaret 198, 200
Barrett-Lennard, Margaret Louise 199
Barrett-Lennard, Marie 198
Barrett-Lennard, Marika Joan 199
Barrett-Lennard, Mark Robert 200
Barrett-Lennard, Melissa 200
Barrett-Lennard, Michael Henry 202
Barrett-Lennard, Michael James 198
Barrett-Lennard, Michael John 200
Barrett-Lennard, Michael Scott 199
Barrett-Lennard, Monica Anne 202
Barrett-Lennard, Naomi Barbara 201
Barrett-Lennard, Nigel Dacre 200
Barrett-Lennard, Olive 199
Barrett-Lennard, Patricia Ida 199
Barrett-Lennard, Penelope Anne 198
Barrett-Lennard, Peter Dacre 199
Barrett-Lennard, Peter John 198, 200
Barrett-Lennard, Philip Francis Dacre 202
Barrett-Lennard, Philip St Aubyn 200
Barrett-Lennard, Rebecca Ann 199
Barrett-Lennard, Richard 198
Barrett-Lennard, Richard Dacre 202
Barrett-Lennard, Richard Fynes 198
Barrett-Lennard, Richard John Stirling 199
Barrett-Lennard, Richard St Aubyn 200
Barrett-Lennard, Robert Allan 200
Barrett-Lennard, Robert Villiers 202
Barrett-Lennard, Sandra 200
Barrett-Lennard, Simon Hugh 199
Barrett-Lennard, Simon James 198
Barrett-Lennard, Siri Anne 199
Barrett-Lennard, Sonja 198
Barrett-Lennard, Thomas Edmund 199
Barrett-Lennard, Thomas William Timothy 198
Barrett-Lennard, Timothy Stewart 200
Barrett-Lennard, Trevor Henry 199
Barrett-Lennard, Una 198
Barrett-Lennard, Vicki 199
Barrett-Lennard, Viva Dacre 198
Barrett-Lennard, Walter James 201
Barrett-Lennard, William Ashley Dacre 199
Barrett-Leonard, Alison Louise 199
Barrett-Leonard, Andrew Graham 199

Bateson, Janet 2806
Bateson, Simon Vivian Ranulf 2806
Bath, Beatrice Elizabeth 1153
Bath, Richard 1153
Bathhurst, Charlotte Anne 215
Bathhurst, James Seymour 216
Batho, Alexander Francis Ghislain 214
Batho, Bethany Frances Ghislaine 214
Batho, Charles William Ghislain 214
Batho, Cynthia Marion Blanche 1753
Batho, Georgina Catherine Ann Gwynne 214
Batho, Hugh Charles Ghislain 214
Batho, Jennifer 1753
Batho, Jo-Anne Louise 214
Batho, Julia Elizabeth 1754
Batho, Lucille Mary 214
Batho, Richard Ghislain 214
Batho, Rupert Sebastian Ghislain 214
Batho, Sarah Catherine Ghislaine 214
Batho, William Guy Pakenham 1754
Batho, William Nicholas Pakenham 1753
Batho, Zoe Elizabeth 214
Bathurst, Alexander Edward Seymour 215
Bathurst, Alice Patricia 215
Bathurst, Allen Christopher Bertram 215
Bathurst, Amanda Phyllis Vesey 2305
Bathurst, Anna Christian 215
Bathurst, Arabella Rose 292
Bathurst, Benjamin George Henry 215
Bathurst, Benjamin John 215
Bathurst, Charles Colin Addington 291, 2305
Bathurst, Charlotte Mary 291
Bathurst, Christopher Metcalfe Addington 291
Bathurst, (David) Benjamin 215, 2234
Bathurst, (Elizabeth) Ann 215, 2799
Bathurst, Emma Gae 215
Bathurst, Flora Elizabeth 292
Bathurst, George Bertram 216
Bathurst, Gloria 215
Bathurst, Harry John Seymour 215
Bathurst, Helen Winifred 1363
Bathurst, Henrietta Mary Lilias 215
Bathurst, Ianthe Elizabeth Sophie 2305
Bathurst, Ivy 291
Bathurst, Jane Elizabeth 291
Bathurst, Joan 292
Bathurst, Jonathan Chandos Seymour 215
Bathurst, Joseph John 291
Bathurst, Katherine 215
Bathurst, Katherine Joan 291
Bathurst, Lara Elizabeth 215
Bathurst, Lucilla Ruby 215
Bathurst, Lucy Celeste 292
Bathurst, Mark 291
Bathurst, (Mary) Cornelia (Nelly) 292
Bathurst, Matilda Blanche 291
Bathurst, Nicholas Charles George 291
Bathurst, Otto Benjamin Charles 291
Bathurst, Pamela Rosemary Alice 291
Bathurst, Philip Charles Metcalfe 291
Bathurst, Robert Guy 291
Bathurst, Rosie Meriel Lilias 215
Bathurst, Rupert Edward Ludlow 291
Bathurst, Sara 215
Bathurst, Sarah Christian Pandora 215, 2234
Bathurst, Sharon Elizabeth 215
Bathurst, Sophia Eleanor Frances 291
Bathurst, Sophie Mary Elizabeth 291
Bathurst, Susan 216
Bathurst, Theophilus Christopher Vesey 2305
Bathurst, Timothy Seymour 215
Bathurst, William Malcolm 216
Bathurst, William Nevile 291
Bathurst, William Ralph Seymour 1363
Batt, Camilla Louise 1561
Batt, Robert 751
Batt, Rosabelle Patricia 751
Batt, Rose Margaret Ruth 1561
Battell, Gwendoline Filumena 2100
Batten, Amanda Rose 2281
Batten, Annabell Jane Beardmore 1823
Batten, Anne 2469
Batten, Charles James 2281
Batten, David Henry Cary 625
Batten, Hope 1823
Batten, James Macdonald 2281
Batten, Joanna 625
Batten, Katherine Nicola Beardmore 1824
Batten, Michael John 625
Batten, Patrick John Beardmore 1823
Batten, Rachel Nancy 2469
Batten, Sally Elizabeth Beardmore 1824
Batten, Sarah 625
Batten, Stephen Duval 2469
Batten, Susan Helen Frances 625
Batten, Susan Mary Geraldine 2281
Batten, William Henry 625
Batterbury, Adrian William George 2440
Batterbury, Edward Anthony George 2440
Batterbury, Mark Richard George 2440
Batterbury, Susan 2440
Batterham, Alisoun Mary 1466
Batterham, Joanna 393
Batterham, Luke 1466
Battye, Alexander Robert 2480
Battye, (Elizabeth) Rose 695
Battye, Emma Alice 2480
Battye, Ian Richmond 695
Battye, Mary Jill 2480
Battye, Nell Aurore 695
Battye, Robert William Gerald 2480
Battye, Thomas Gathorne 695
Baudouin, Alexandre John 1460
Baudouin, Henrietta Margaret Mary 1460
Baudouin, Jacques 1460
Baudouin, Luke Jacques 1460
Baudouin, Maxime Roger 1460
Baudouin, Timothy Joseph 1460
Baudoux, Carol Anne Hingley 1144
Baudoux, Daphne Mary 1144
Baudoux, Everett Large 1144
Baudoux, Katherine Anne 1144
Baudoux, Michael Alfred 1144
Bauer, Arnold J 1473
Bauer, Claire Katy 362
Bauer, George William Frederick 362
Bauer, John William Neale 362
Bauer, Julia 1473
Bauer, Katy Louisa 362
Bauer, Rebecca 1473
Baughart, Richard Paul 1533
Bauhan, Patrick Lathrop 1078
Bauhan, Sarah Forbes 1078
Bauhan, William Lathrop 1078
Bauld, Jean Charlotte 491
Bavin, Anthony Julian 2562
Bavin, Jacqueline Anne 2562
Baxendale, David Hugh 1096
Baxendale, Elizabeth Joan 1096
Baxendale, Guy Jonathan 1096
Baxendale, Jacqueline Loveday 1096
Baxendale, (Patricia) Elizabeth 444
Baxendale, Peter Anthony 1096
Baxendale, Thomas Lloyd 1096
Baxley, Claudia Patricia 217
Baxley, Sarah Eleanor 2987
Baxter, Alexandra Adele (Zandra) 2792
Baxter, Ann Harriet 2275
Baxter, Belinda Mary Victoria 339
Baxter, Camilla Jane 455
Baxter, Charles Peter 1346
Baxter, Colin Andrew 2275
Baxter, Devorguilla 2507
Baxter, Donald 2507
Baxter, Edward 2507
Baxter, Edward Thomas 455, 2853
Baxter, Elizabeth Anne 2853
Baxter, (Elizabeth) June 2853
Baxter, Helen Margaretta 1346
Baxter, (Isobel) Laura 622
Baxter, Izaac Jeremy 622
Baxter, Jack Godfrey 2621
Baxter, Jacqueline 2621
Baxter, Jacqueline Tessa 1628
Baxter, James 2507
Baxter, James David 2792
Baxter, Jennifer Carly 1997
Baxter, Joshua James 622
Baxter, Luke 339
Baxter, Mark 339
Baxter, Mary Emma 2853
Baxter, Nicola Caroline 1346
Baxter, Nicola Jane 2792
Baxter, Patrick Ian 2275
Baxter, Robert 1628
Baxter, Robert Bryan 2621
Baxter, Sarah Evelyn 2853
Baxter, Susanna 2507
Baxter, Thomas 339
Baxter, Timothy Reginald 2621
Baxter, Tobias Andrew 622
Bay, Anthony David 2045
Bay, David Michael 2045
Bay, Eric A 342
Bay, Jane Lilly 2045
Bay, Nicholas Michael 2045
Bay, Patricia Kathleen 2045
Bay, Sandra Molly 342
Bayante, Alberto 201
Bayante, Annabel Joan 201
Bayante, Maxwell Arthur 201
Bayed, Clare 1826
Bayed, Penelope Mary 1826
Bayford, David Altham 3042
Bayford, Georgina Catharine Margaret 3042
Bayford, Hilda Elizabeth Mary 712
Bayford, Mary Elizabeth 712
Bayford, Peggy 3042
Bayford, Robert Michael Croft 712
Bayford, Robin Alec 3042
Bayler, Amelia Jane 112
Bayler, Helena Mary 112
Bayler, Michael J 112
Bayley, Andrew John 1648
Bayley, Benjamin George Robson 1648
Bayley, Catherine Anne 1648
Bayley, Catriona Louise Alicia Lucinda 72
Bayley, Edward Alexander Christian Lambart 72
Bayley, Edward Archibald Richard 72
Bayley, Ellen Elizabeth 1648
Bayley, Elspeth Henrietta 2106
Bayley, Emma Susan 1648
Bayley, Helena Mary 363
Bayley, James Francis Leslie 363
Bayley, John Richard 2106
Bayley, Jonathan 1648
Bayley, Mary Boyd 1648
Bayley, Michael John 1648
Bayley, Peter Charles 1648
Bayley, Rachel Helena 363
Bayley, Richard 2106
Bayley, Robin Kennett 1648
Bayley, Rosemarie Evelyn Gisela 72
Bayley, Ruth Fleur Annette 1648
Bayley, Sara 2106
Bayley, Sarah 1648
Bayley, Sarah Mary Helen 1648
Bayley, Thomas Francis 363
Bayley-Vandeleur, Joan 72
Baylis, Araminta Rose 1582
Baylis, Camilla Annabelle 1582
Baylis, Clive 699
Baylis, Emily Charlotte 1582
Baylis, Harriet Alicia 1582
Baylis, Henrietta Aeddan 1582
Baylis, Jennifer Lynette 699
Baylis, Russell 1582
Bayliss, Anna M 363
Bayliss, Caispar Jeremy Lyle 363
Bayliss, Charles Robert Bowes 363
Bayliss, Jeremy David Bagot 362
Bayliss, Jonathan Andrew Bagot 363
Bayliss, Mary Selina 362
Bayliss, Patrick Thomas Clive 363
Bayliss, Rebecca 363
Bayliss, Richard Charles 363
Bayliss, Sarah E 363
Bayliss, Walter Richard Bridgeman 363
Bayman, Alexander Christian Gray 2220
Bayman, Caroline Louise 2220
Bayman, John Edward 2220
Bayman, Linda Louise 2220
Baynard-Smith, Christopher Ruthven 505
Baynard-Smith, James 504
Baynard-Smith, Julia Woodley 505
Baynard-Smith, Peter James 505
Baynard-Smith, Rebekah Clare 505
Baynard-Smith, Sarah Constance Anne 504
Baynes, Adam John Stuart 216
Baynes, Alasdair William Merriman 216
Baynes, Anthony Edward George 217
Baynes, Christopher Rory 216
Baynes, Estelle Anne Gabrielle 216
Baynes, Fergus Joseph Malcolm 216
Baynes, Margaret Anne Mary 216
Baynes, Rory Nicholas Aimery 216
Baynes, Sandra 216
Baynes, Shirley 216
Baynes, Simon Robert Maurice 216
Baynes, Timothy Peter 216
Baynes, William John Walter 216
Bayntun-Coward, Charlotte Anne Wentworth 1136
Bayntun-Coward, Edward William George 1136
Bayntun-Coward, Emma Louise Wentworth 1136
Bayntun-Coward, Hylton Henry 1136
Bayntun-Coward, Jonathan Henry Alexander 1136
Bayntun-Coward, Laura Catherine 1136
Bayntun-Coward, Polly Jane Constance 1136
Bazely, Angela Clare 200
Bazley, Anthony Martin Christopher 217
Bazley, Carmen 217
Bazley, Catherine Elisabet Annemarie 217
Bazley, John Francis Alexander 217
Bazley, Virginia Isabella Marged 217
Bazley, Zoë Tulia 217
Beach, Atalanta Maria 2500
Beach, Aurora Ursula 2500
Beach, Charles Thomas FitzRoy 2340
Beach, Christine Diane 2382
Beach, Eugenia (Jenny) Anne 2500
Beach, Georgiana Emily Estelle 2340
Beach, Gilda Maria 2500
Beach, John Roberts 2340
Beach, Louise Charlotte 2340
Beachus, Geoffrena 276
Beachus, James William 276
Beachus, Justin Nicholas 276
Beachus, Lucinda 276
Beachus, Simon Jeremy James 276
Beachus, Tanya 276
Beachus, Timothy James 276
Beacroft, Guy Robert 3094
Beacroft, Judith A 3094
Bealby, Annabel Kate 1895
Bealby, Ashley J 1895
Beale, Alice 1670, 2893
Beale, Alice Elizabeth May 2893
Beale, Andrew Charles Robert 268
Beale, Andrew Macartney 1794
Beale, Andrew William 2941
Beale, April Michelle 2941
Beale, Bridget Macree 2941
Beale, Christopher William 1794
Beale, Francesca May 1794
Beale, Freddie James Robert 268
Beale, Jennifer Mary Alice 2893
Beale, Jo-Anna Mary 2893
Beale, Julian Macartney 1794
Beale, Louisa Margaret 268
Beale, Martin Andrew 2941
Beale, Polly Theodora 268
Beale, Richard 2941
Beale, Richard Basil William 2893
Beale, Rollo Basil Arthur 2893
Beale, Roseanna Mary Elizabeth 268
Beale, Siao-Li Liao 2893
Beale, Stephen Dudley Norman 2893
Beale, Zoë Helen 2893
Beament, Annabella Moira 1500
Beament, Anne Moira Olivia 1500
Beament, Edward Hugh Landale 1500
Beament, Emily Catherine Olivia 1500
Beament, John Michael Landale 1500
Beament, Karen 1500
Beament, Rachel Helen Olivia 1500
Beament, Roger 1500
Beament, Sarah 1500
Beament, Thomas Edward 1500
Beams, Alexander Thomas 2327
Beams, Catherine Alice 2327
Beams, Catriona 2327
Beams, Geoffrey Charles 2327
Beams, Michael Robert Charles 2327
Bear, Alexander George Philip Villiers 585
Bear, Christopher 1436
Bear, Edward James 1436
Bear, Mary Caroline 1436
Beard, Jeremy Nigel Thomas 1310
Beard, Laraine Susan 1310
Beardall, Fiona Carolyn 253
Beardall, Michael John Dodson 253
Beare, (Anthony) Julian Lyell 1121
Beare, Charlotte Julia Mary 1121
Beare, James Oliver Lyell 1121
Beare, Rosanna Sarah Cecil 1121
Bearman, Anthony Richard 2562
Bearman, Christopher Charles 2562
Beasley, Alexander Hendrik Vincent 2256
Beasley, Charlotte 2722
Beasley, George 2722
Beasley, Helena Sibyl 2722
Beasley, Katherine 2256
Beasley, Michael Clive Rashleigh 2722
Beasley, Thomas 2722
Beaton, Camilla Jane Moira 1766
Beaton, Donald Peter 1236
Beaton, Emily Rose Margaret 1766
Beaton, Gregory 1236
Beaton, Jane Belinda 1766
Beaton, John David 1766
Beaton, Joseph Finlay 1236
Beaton, Maxine 1236
Beatson-Hird, Digby George 2694
Beatson-Hird, Hubert John 2694
Beatson-Hird, Jonathan 2694
Beatson-Hird, Suzannah Clare 2694
Beattie, Amanda Jane 650
Beattie, Anne Marjorie 272
Beattie, Carol Woodman 428
Beattie, Elizabeth Angela Darwin 650
Beattie, James Brian David 650
Beattie, John Humphrey 428
Beattie, Martin John 650
Beattie, Nicola Jane 428
Beattie, Rosemary Ann 650
Beatty, Angela Miriam 219
Beatty, Anoma Corinne 219
Beatty, Benjamin George 1258
Beatty, Caroline Diana Charlotte 2557
Beatty, Catherine Louise 1258
Beatty, Diana 220
Beatty, Frances Elizabeth 2557
Beatty, Geraldine Alice 2557
Beatty, Jill Lucinda 219
Beatty, Joanna Elisabeth 219
Beatty, Katherine Margaret Barrett 2557
Beatty, Kathleen Eva Margaret Le Hunte 219
Beatty, Laura Mary Catherine 1465
Beatty, Mark George 1258
Beatty, Michael P K 2557
Beatty, Nicholas Duncan 1465
Beatty, Peter Wystan 219
Beatty, Rosanna Mary Gisborne 2557
Beatty, Samuel George 1258
Beatty, Sean David 219
Beaty, Clare Elizabeth 3093
Beaty, Corinne Elizabeth 3093
Beaty, Josepha Isobel 3093
Beaty, Stephen John 3093
Beaty, Thomas Alastair Stephen 3093
Beauchaine, Brenda Jeanne 1450
Beauchaine, Wade 1450
Beauchamp, Anna Maria Magdalena 2319
Beauchamp, Anthony Tremayne 2320
Beauchamp, Barbara Allison 2320
Beauchamp, Beryl Irene 2320
Beauchamp, Bruce Proctor 2320
Beauchamp, Catriona Clare 2319
Beauchamp, Christine 2320
Beauchamp, Christopher David 2320
Beauchamp, Christopher Tremayne 2320
Beauchamp, Daphne Helen 2319
Beauchamp, David Dohrmann 2320
Beauchamp, David FitzGerald 2319
Beauchamp, Elisabeth Margaret 2319
Beauchamp, Ellen Paris 2320
Beauchamp, Felicity Daphne Dorina 2319
Beauchamp, Geoffrey Frank 2320
Beauchamp, Gillian Alexandra 2319
Beauchamp, Hugh Alan Vernon 2319
Beauchamp, Jan 2320
Beauchamp, Jean Anita 2320
Beauchamp, John Christopher Michael 2319
Beauchamp, John Louis 431
Beauchamp, John Proctor 2320
Beauchamp, Julian Lawrence Stuart 2319
Beauchamp, Laura Ann 2320
Beauchamp, Lucien Willoughby 2319
Beauchamp, Mark Andrew 2320
Beauchamp, Mark David 2320
Beauchamp, Michael Douglas 2320
Beauchamp, Nancy Anne 2320
Beauchamp, Nancy Knight 2319
Beauchamp, Pamela Nerida 2320
Beauchamp, Peter Clare 2318
Beauchamp, Peter Willoughby 2319
Beauchamp, Robin Anthony Nicol 2320

Bigsby, Kirsty Jane 2438
Bigsby, Megan Carolyn 2438
Bigsby, Paul 2438
Bigwood, A G 2063
Bigwood, Anita Margaret 2063
Bihr, Jane Sarah 1877
Bihr, Rudolf 1877
Bihr, Sophia Violanta 1877
Billingsley, James Michael 1767
Billingsley, Nicola Jane 1767
Billingsley, Olivia Jane 1767
Billington, Caspar Leo 1751
Billington, Catherine Rose 1751
Billington, Chloe Margaret 1751
Billington, Craig Neville 1412
Billington, Janice Audrey 1412
Billington, Kevin 1751
Billington, Nathaniel Kevin 1751
Billington, Neville 1412
Billington, Philip John 1412
Billington, Rachel Mary 1751
Billson, Barbara Jane 3053
Billson, Carolyn Jane 3053
Billson, Douglas Frederick 3053
Billson, Roy Travis 3053
Billups, Molli Elizabeth 1171
Billups, Patti Jon 1171
Billups, Phyllis 1171
Bimbo, Katherine Anne 2994
Bimbo, Linda 2994
Bimbo, Nicolo 2994
Bindner, Daniel 902
Bing, Adam Laurence 101
Bing, Alan Charles 101
Bing, Alison Ursula 101
Bing, Andrew John Collingwood 101
Bing, Christian Frances 295
Bing, Christian Keith Arbuthnott 101
Bing, Eleanor Mary 101
Bing, Emma Florence 101
Bing, Henry Jarvis 101
Bing, Inigo Geoffrey 295
Bing, Isobel Donald (Zoë) 101
Bing, Julia Margaret 101
Bing, Katherine Isobel 101
Bing, Peter John 101
Bing, Richard Daniel 295
Bing, Robert Adrian 101
Bing, Sarah Frances 101
Bing, Sarah Lucy 101
Bing, Wendy Margaret 101
Bingham, Alexandra Louise Clare 579
Bingham, Alexandra Romina 1777
Bingham, Camilla 1776
Bingham, Catherine Elizabeth 869
Bingham, Catherine Violet 1777
Bingham, Charles Nigel 1777
Bingham, Charlotte Poppy 258
Bingham, Christopher Toby 869
Bingham, David Julian 1777
Bingham, Dorothea 1777
Bingham, Dorothy Blanche 709
Bingham, Eileen Gertrude 709
Bingham, Elizabeth 276
Bingham, Elizabeth Hilda 709
Bingham, Elizabeth Patricia 869
Bingham, Elizabeth Rosamund 1777
Bingham, Frances 1776
Bingham, George Charles 1776
Bingham, George Frederick 258
Bingham, George J C 258
Bingham, Georgina Mary Margaret 579
Bingham, Gizella Maria 578
Bingham, Hugh 1777
Bingham, (Jane) Victoria (Clare) 579
Bingham, Jean 579
Bingham, (John) Nigel 1777
Bingham, Lucy Katherine Gizella 578
Bingham, Madeleine Susannah 1777
Bingham, Nicholas Charles 1777
Bingham, Norah Frances 709
Bingham, Penelope Ann 1777
Bingham, Peter John 1777
Bingham, Philip Charles 1777
Bingham, Richard Patrick 1777
Bingham, (Robert) Derek de Burgh 579
Bingham, Rosamunde Jessica Elizabeth 579
Bingham, Sarah Charlotte 258
Bingham, Thomas Henry 869
Bingham, Veronica 1776
Bingham, Victoria Mary 579
Binnie, Alan 145
Binnie, Alastair 145
Binnie, Alison 1013
Binnie, Archie 145
Binnie, Ian 1013
Binning, Carina Lorraine 83
Binning, Gareth John 83
Binning, Gavin Douglas 83
Binning, John Bathurst Shaw 83
Binning, Madeleine Rachel 83
Binning, Nora Kathleen 83
Binnington, Joanna Jane 3094
Binnington, Kate Louise Frances 3094
Binnington, Nicholas William David 3094
Binnington, Timothy John 3094
Binny, Diana Heather 2030
Binny, John Anthony Francis 2030
Birch, Barbara Mary Elizabeth 556
Birch, George Anthony 556
Birch, James Lovel 687
Birch, John Montagu 556
Birch, Julian Wyndham 687
Birch, Magnus Courtenay 2849
Birch, Michael Edward Stafford 2023
Birch, Timothy Malcolm Stafford 2023
Birch, William 556
Birchall, Peter Birchall 1218
Birchall, Ruth Veronica 1218
Bird, Ann Geraldine 426
Bird, Anthony Donald 277
Bird, Anthony Nigel Godfrey 2876
Bird, Beverley Aldington 2872
Bird, Caroline Anne-Marie 1623
Bird, Caroline Fiona 2317
Bird, Catherine Veronica 276
Bird, Cecilia Mary 276
Bird, Christopher John Godfrey 2876
Bird, Christopher K St J 2317
Bird, Christopher Kenelm Anthony 1202
Bird, Christopher Robert 277
Bird, Clive Robert 2872
Bird, Denise Helen 276
Bird, Eileen Diana 2405
Bird, Elizabeth Mary 2876
Bird, Emma Louise 1623
Bird, Frances Bernadette 276
Bird, Garth Raymond Godfrey 2876
Bird, Georgina Jane 304
Bird, Helen Patricia 276
Bird, (Isobel) Theresa 2405
Bird, Jane Claire 2872
Bird, Joan Ethel 1623
Bird, John Andrew 276
Bird, John Anthony 2405
Bird, John Miles 254
Bird, John Ronald 1623
Bird, Julie Anne 925
Bird, Justyn 2015
Bird, Kathleen Elaine Vere 2872
Bird, Kaye Lorraine 925
Bird, Malcolm Harvey 925
Bird, Mark Richard 276
Bird, Murray Scott 925
Bird, Myles Fleetwood 2015
Bird, Patrick Jack 2405
Bird, Paul 304
Bird, Peter Donald Chapman 277
Bird, Rachel 1202
Bird, Roland Ernest 426
Bird, Rowena Clare 276
Bird, Sarah Jane 304
Bird, Simon Callum 304
Bird, Susan Katherine 254, 2015
Bird, Tiffany 254, 2015
Bird, Vera Mary 277
Birdwood, Alice Caroline 278
Birdwood, Anthony 277
Birdwood, Arabella Katherine 278, 2541
Birdwood, Beatty Hamilton 278
Birdwood, Charlotte 277
Birdwood, Cherry 278
Birdwood, Christopher Halhed Lovett 278
Birdwood, Christopher R Brodrick 277
Birdwood, Diana V 278
Birdwood, (Dorothy) Gaynor 277
Birdwood, Elizabeth Jane 278
Birdwood, George Fortune Brodrick 277
Birdwood, Gordon Thomas Riddell 278, 2541
Birdwood, Helen 278
Birdwood, Helen Sylvia 277
Birdwood, James Gresford Brodrick 277
Birdwood, Jennifer Alice 278
Birdwood, Joan 278
Birdwood, John Richard Gresford 277
Birdwood, Judith Helen 277
Birdwood, June 277
Birdwood, Katie 278, 2541
Birdwood, Nigel Fortune 277
Birdwood, Roger Halhed Bilbe 278
Birdwood, Sheila Kathleen 277
Birdwood, Travers John Durand 278
Birdwood, Victoria Rose 278
Birdwood, William Halhed 278
Birkbeck, Anthony William Savile 2657
Birkbeck, Davina Mary 2657
Birkbeck, Edward Harold 2036
Birkbeck, Elizabeth (Beth) 2657
Birkbeck, Elizabeth Mary 2036
Birkbeck, George Charles Edward 2036
Birkbeck, Hermione Ann 2036
Birkbeck, Hermione Anne 2813
Birkbeck, John Oliver 2813
Birkbeck, John Oliver Charles 2036
Birkbeck, Katherine (Kate) 2657
Birkbeck, Lucy Claire 2036
Birkbeck, Mary 2657
Birkbeck, Mary Joan 2036
Birkbeck, Nicola Susan 2036
Birkbeck, Sarah Ann 2036
Birkbeck, William 2657
Birkett, Alice Emily Rose 2785
Birkett, (Charles) John Ross 2785
Birkett, Charles Ross 2785
Birkett, Francesca Elisabeth 2785
Birkett, Gloria 279
Birkett, (Norah) Melanie 2785
Birkett, Rupert Francis William 2785
Birkett, Thomas 279
Birkin, Abigail Victoria Ann 280
Birkin, Alexander Kingdom 280
Birkin, Amanda Jane 280
Birkin, Andrew Timothy 280
Birkin, Benjamin Charles 279
Birkin, David Tristan 280
Birkin, Edmund Xavier 280
Birkin, Emma Louise 279
Birkin, James Francis Richard 280
Birkin, Jane Mallory 280
Birkin, Louie 279
Birkin, Susan 280
Birkmyre, Alexander 280
Birkmyre, David 280
Birkmyre, Doreen 280
Birkmyre, Gillian Mary 280
Birkmyre, James 280
Birkmyre, Lesley Amanda 280
Birkmyre, Margot 280
Birkmyre, Rebecca 280
Birley, Anthony Richard 2031
Birley, Jane Mary 2474
Birley, Mary Eileen 2474
Birley, Paul Hamish Aurelius 2031
Birley, Robin Marcus 1747
Birley, Susanna Jane 2474
Birley, Suzanna Mary 2031
Birley, Ursula Ann 2031
Birnie, (Marguerite) Kathleen 836
Birrell, Mary Louise 2516
Birtwell, Emily Jane 237
Birtwistle, Anthony Gerard Astley 2847
Birtwistle, Diana 2847
Birtwistle, Moya 2641
Bischoff, Charles Francis 1659
Bischoff, Christopher William 1659
Bischoff, Rosemary Elizabeth 1659
Bischoff, Win(fried) Franz Wilhelm 1659
Bishop, Alan Stuart Wortley 2994
Bishop, Alex MacKenzie 2994
Bishop, Andrew Anthony 2994
Bishop, Beverley Louise 296
Bishop, Caroline Mary Beverley Anne 851
Bishop, Charles Andrew Meynell 1269
Bishop, Charles Richard Maurice 2214, 2824
Bishop, Colleen Joan 2994
Bishop, Dennis 851
Bishop, Dennis John 851
Bishop, Erin Sayre 2994
Bishop, Harry Atwood 2994
Bishop, Joan Isabella 2994
Bishop, Julie Sayre 2994
Bishop, Kristi-Lee 296
Bishop, Lisa 2994
Bishop, Louise 1117
Bishop, Mary Janet 1269
Bishop, Mary Louie 851
Bishop, Mary Mitchell 912
Bishop, Mary Rhoda 1700
Bishop, Richard Charles 296
Bishop, Rosalind Jane 2214, 2824
Bishop, Rosanna Emily Margaret 2214, 2824
Bishop, Rosemary Janet 1269
Bishop, Russell Allan 296
Bishop, Sarah Rose 1269
Bishop, Thomas Richard Chilton 2214, 2824
Bishop, Victoria Oenone Jane 2214, 2824
Bishop, William Ernest John 2140
Bissell, John Philip 54
Bissell, Patricia Helen 54
Bissill, Charmaine Elizabeth Violet Cecilia 2134
Bissill, Eileen Grey 1627
Bitove, Olivia Charlotte 2962
Bitove, Paul J 2962
Bitove, Sarah Jane Edith 2962
Bizzarri, Carla 1307
Bizzarri, Giovanna 1307
Bizzarri, Joan Felicity 1307
Bizzarri, Mario 1307
Bizzarri, Paola Maria Augusta Audreina Giovanna 1307
Bjornsten, Janet 500
Blaauw, Carolyn Phyllis 1563
Blaauw, Jan Gerard Willemszoon 1563
Blaauw, Keir Alexander Kennedy 1563
Blaauw, Patrick Jan Kennedy 1563
Blaber, Marcus 1331
Black, Adam Sebastian 1775
Black, Alexander William Francis 464
Black, Brinsley Graham 1476
Black, Caroline 464
Black, Caroline Ann 2892
Black, Charles Archibald Adam 1775
Black, Charles Joshua Rokeby 464
Black, Crispin Nicholas 2892
Black, (Dorothy) Maureen 281
Black, Elizabeth Ann 2592
Black, Ernestine Emily 258
Black, Francis Rokeby 464
Black, Harrison John 2592
Black, Holly Patricia Louisa 1775
Black, James Pat Rokeby 464
Black, Jane Margaret 715
Black, John 2592
Black, Katherine 2592
Black, Kathleen Mary 281
Black, Melanie Fiona Louisa 1775
Black, Moorea 1476
Black, Natasha Caroline 464
Black, Octavius Orlando Irvine Casati 1476
Black, Peter Michael 715
Black, (Reginald) Baron (Barry) 2466
Black, Richard Mason 2592
Black, Rosemary Diana 1309
Black, Stuart Alexander 258
Black, Susan Elizabeth 464
Black, Susan Mary 715
Black, Thomas Charteris 715
Blackall, Jean Mary 89
Blackburn, Bridget Mary 628
Blackburn, David Peter 628
Blackburn, Emma Margrethe 2128
Blackburn, (Erica) Judith 406
Blackburn, Esther Joy 2203
Blackburn, James David 628
Blackburn, Jane Margrethe 2128
Blackburn, Kari Ruth 2203
Blackburn, Kenneth 2128
Blackburn, Lucy Patricia 2203
Blackburn, Paul Hamer 406
Blackburn, Richard Martin 406
Blackburn, Robert 2203
Blackburn, Robert Paul 406
Blackburn, Sara Elisabeth 2128
Blackburn, Thomas Mark 2894
Blacker, Barnaby Stewart Hugh 2360
Blacker, Caroline Susan 454, 2664
Blacker, Cecil Hugh 454
Blacker, Colleen 2360
Blacker, David Stewart Wellesley 2208, 2360
Blacker, Felicity Mary 454
Blacker, Julia Adelaide 2360
Blacker, Mary Rose 2208, 2360
Blacker, Philip 454
Blacker, Rohan David Peel 2360
Blacker, Susan 454
Blacker, Terence 454, 2664
Blacker, William O'Neill 2360
Blackett, Amelia 281
Blackett, Anna 281
Blackett, Annabel 282
Blackett, Annabel Hope 3026
Blackett, (Camilla Harriet) Eve 282
Blackett, Camilla Joy Victoria 3026
Blackett, Charlotte Elizabeth 282
Blackett, Cicely Catherine Victoria 3026
Blackett, Cynthia 3026
Blackett, Edward John Christopher 3026
Blackett, Flora 281
Blackett, Geva Charlotte Caroline 282, 2527
Blackett, (Helena) Charlotte Rose 282
Blackett, Hendrika Theresa 282
Blackett, Henry Douglas 281
Blackett, Isabella 281
Blackett, James Henry 282
Blackett, James William Beauchamp 3026
Blackett, Joan 282
Blackett, John Beauchamp 3026
Blackett, (John) Simon 2527
Blackett, Kate Elizabeth 282
Blackett, Letitia 282
Blackett, Lucia Georgia 282
Blackett, Marcus Henry 282
Blackett, Piers Rupert 282
Blackett, Rebecca Anne 282
Blackett, Rupert Beaumont 282
Blackett, Sarah Jennifer 3026
Blackett, Veronica Heath 282
Blackett, William Luke 282
Blackett Ogram, Theophania Eve 282
Blackler, Cristelle Irene 1413
Blackler, Holly Margaret 1413
Blackler, Julie Margaret Irene 1413
Blackler, Nigel John 1413
Blackler, Paige Marie 1413
Blacklock, Diana Frances 2546
Blackman, Anthony George 2701
Blackman, George Lewis 2701
Blackman, Hamish Flint 2701
Blackman, Henry David Stewart 2701
Blackman, Ian Arthur Floyd 2702
Blackman, Marion Evelyn Stewart 2701
Blackton, Charles Stuart 790
Blackwell, Arabella Clare 1142
Blackwell, Brenda 283
Blackwell, Catriona Charmiane 1203
Blackwell, Christopher 1203
Blackwell, Sarah Jean 1203
Blackwell, Susan Mary 1826
Blackwell, Thomas Charles 1142
Blackwood, Alexander Francis Winkle 888
Blackwood, Alice Kathleen Winkle 888
Blackwood, Anne Edith 888
Blackwood, Annette Kay 885
Blackwood, Arthur Frederick 96
Blackwood, Charles Temple 2892
Blackwood, Clare Mary 888
Blackwood, Diana 888
Blackwood, Doreen 1035
Blackwood, Ellen 888
Blackwood, Fiona Marjorie 96
Blackwood, Francis Senden 885
Blackwood, Frederick George 96
Blackwood, Freya Jodie 885
Blackwood, George 888
Blackwood, Henry 888
Blackwood, James Maurice Henry 888
Blackwood, James Temple 2892
Blackwood, Jennifer Anne 888
Blackwood, Jonathan Charles 2892
Blackwood, Kathryn 888
Blackwood, Kay Lynette 888
Blackwood, Lilian Margaret 888
Blackwood, Margaret 888
Blackwood, Maurice Henry 888
Blackwood, Michael Francis 888
Blackwood, Peter Maurice 888
Blackwood, Robert George Temple 888
Blackwood, Robin Henry 888
Blackwood, Susan 2892
Blades, Flavia Mary 580
Blair, Alexandra Charlotte 1092
Blair, Andrew 62
Blair, Audrey 62
Blair, Charles 1087

Butler, Nigel 2978
Butler, Norah Helen 1301
Butler, Norman David Thomas 221
Butler, Patricia Bolduc 448
Butler, Patricia Colleen 900
Butler, Patricia Honor 221
Butler, Patricia Julia 1628
Butler, Patricia Penelope 899
Butler, Patrick Barry Webb 900
Butler, Patrick Beauchamp Rupert 447
Butler, Patrick Colman 450
Butler, Patrick James Richard 448
Butler, Patrick Walter Rowlandson 3028
Butler, Penelope Cynthia 1097
Butler, Peter James Sydney 450
Butler, Peter Woods 450
Butler, Philippa Janice Victoria 510
Butler, Pierce Anders 2019
Butler, Pierce Richard 2019
Butler, Pierce Torsten 2019
Butler, Piers Edmund Theobald Lismalyn 510
Butler, Piers James Richard 2018
Butler, Piers Somerset Patrick 511
Butler, (Reginald) Paul 450
Butler, (Reginald) Richard Michael 450
Butler, Richard Benjamin 2922
Butler, Richard Clive 2922
Butler, Richard Michael 2922
Butler, Richard Percy 448
Butler, Richard Pierce Theobald 898
Butler, Robert Bruce Holgate 136
Butler, Robert David 221
Butler, Robert Patrick 903
Butler, Robert Pierce 449
Butler, Robin Carol Boaden 449
Butler, Rose Olivia 2922
Butler, Rosemary Elizabeth 1045
Butler, Rosena Marie 902
Butler, Rupert Dudley 446
Butler, Rupert Lionel Somerset 511
Butler, Ryan 449
Butler, Sabrina Charlotte 2978
Butler, Samuel Thomas Blake 899
Butler, Sarah Elizabeth 321
Butler, Scarlett Frances 510
Butler, Sean 1097
Butler, Sebastian Somerset Lionel 511
Butler, Shanda 449
Butler, Sheila Chevallier 1616
Butler, Simon Blake FitzWalter 899
Butler, Simon Laforey Butler 1541
Butler, Sophia Angelica 3089
Butler, Sophie Rosalind 869
Butler, Stephen Patrick 446
Butler, Susan 448
Butler, Susan Anne Maud 2922
Butler, Susan Elizabeth 136
Butler, Susan Margaret 901
Butler, Susannah May Frances 447
Butler, Tami 449
Butler, Tania Gaye 2922
Butler, Tanis Dawn 449
Butler, Tara Siobhan 511
Butler, Theobald FitzWalter 899
Butler, Theresa 450
Butler, Thomas David 449, 450
Butler, Thomas George 901
Butler, Thomas Pierce 446
Butler, Thomas Woods 450
Butler, Timothy 449
Butler, Toby George Ormonde 448
Butler, Tracey Penelope 1097
Butler, Tymandra Grace 446
Butler, Tyssen Desmond 448
Butler, Ulla 2019
Butler, Vera Elizabeth 903
Butler, Vicki Lynn 449
Butler, Victoria Marsland 511
Butler, Vivienne Claire 448
Butler, Walter 448
Butler, Walter Richard Courtenay 447
Butler, Walter Richard Pierce 448
Butler, William Grant 449
Butler, William Hans 449
Butler, William Neal 449
Butler-Cole, Christopher Thomas 2058
Butler-Cole, Jane Elizabeth 2058
Butler-Cole, Thomas Falcon 2058
Butler-Creagh, Michelle Edith 899
Butler-Creagh, Richard 899
Butler-Creagh, Simone Antoinette 899
Butler-Creagh, Therese Agnes 899
Butler-Creagh, Vincent 899
Butler-Creagh, Walter 899
Butler-Danvers, Alice Isabella 1629
Butler-FitzGerald, Frederick FitzGerald 448
Butler-FitzGerald, Geraldine 448
Butler-Henderson, Adina 1035
Butler-Henderson, Alan 1035
Butler-Henderson, Anne Elizabeth Mary 1033
Butler-Henderson, Benjamin 1035
Butler-Henderson, Chad Stuart 1035
Butler-Henderson, Clare 1035
Butler-Henderson, David James 1035
Butler-Henderson, Edward 1035
Butler-Henderson, Elizabeth Cassy 1035
Butler-Henderson, Eric Alexander 1035
Butler-Henderson, Gemma 1035
Butler-Henderson, Guy 1035
Butler-Henderson, Horatia 1033
Butler-Henderson, Jacqueline 1035
Butler-Henderson, Jason 1035
Butler-Henderson, Julian 1035
Butler-Henderson, Kenneth 1035
Butler-Henderson, Kerryn 1035
Butler-Henderson, Louise 1033
Butler-Henderson, Oliver Stephen 1035
Butler-Henderson, Pamela 1035
Butler-Henderson, Pauline Anne Lowe 1035
Butler-Henderson, Phyllis Daphne 1035
Butler-Henderson, Richard Ian 1033
Butler-Henderson, Timothy 1035
Butler-Henderson, Valerie 1035
Butler-Henderson, Virginia Anne 1033
Butler-Kearney, Catherine Mary 900
Butler-Kearney, James Davies Theobald 900
Butler-Kearney, Jean 900
Butler-Kearney, Juliet Mary 900
Butler-Kearney, Norma 900
Butler-Lloyd, Ann 900
Butler-Lloyd, Audrey Veronica 900
Butler-Lloyd, Carmel 900
Butler-Lloyd, Caroline 900
Butler-Lloyd, Charles 900
Butler-Lloyd, Florence 900
Butler-Lloyd, Geraldine 900
Butler-Lloyd, Henry John 900
Butler-Lloyd, Jacqueline Caroline 900
Butler-Lloyd, James 900
Butler-Lloyd, Jason James 900
Butler-Lloyd, Katherine Geraldine 900
Butler-Lloyd, Kathleen Leacky 900
Butler-Lloyd, Maggie-Jo 900
Butler-Lloyd, Mary 900
Butler-Lloyd, Mary Margaret 900
Butler-Lloyd, Thomas Henry John 900
Butler-Lloyd, Veronica 900
Butler-Lloyd, William Francis 900
Butler-Sloss, Robert Joseph Neville Galmoye 2493
Butler-Sloss, Sarah Jane 2493
Butler-Wheelhouse, Andrew 2653
Butler-Wheelhouse, Duncan 2653
Butler-Wheelhouse, Keith Oliver 2653
Butler-Wheelhouse, Pamela Anne 2653
Butroid, Mary 2349
Butt, Annabel Laura Mary 588
Butt, Ben Michael 2129
Butt, Imogen Hannah Joanell 2751
Butt, Jason Martin 2129
Butt, Johanna 2129
Butt, Kathryn Joanell 2751
Butt, Marie Josephine 450
Butt, Simon William Daniel 2751
Butt, Susannah Jane 588
Butt, Tobias Simon Benjamin 2751
Butter, Andrew Edward 1762
Butter, Archibald Simon 1762
Butter, Bridget 1762
Butter, David Charles 1762
Butter, Ian Peter 1762
Butter, John Henry 1762
Butter, Joyce 1762
Butter, Margaret Janet 1762
Butter, Rachel Mary Cecilia 1762
Butterfield, Isabel-Ann 451
Butterfield, Jeremy John Nicholas 451
Butterfield, Jonathan West Sanders 451
Butterfield, Lawrence 75
Butterfield, Mary Patricia 75
Butterfield, Toby Michael John 451
Butterini, Andrew Anthony 325
Butterini, Janelle May 325
Butterini, John 325
Butterini, Matthew John 325
Butterini, Nicholas James 325
Butterworth, Antonia Ruth 1557
Butterworth, (Charles) Richard 2581
Butterworth, Doris Crawford 451
Butterworth, Hazel 1557
Butterworth, Janet Helen 1763
Butterworth, Jessica 1557
Butterworth, John William Blackstock 451
Butterworth, Julian Richard Nigel 299, 876
Butterworth, Margaret Brora 2581
Butterworth, Mark F 1557
Butterworth, Nigel Hartley Dryden 876
Butterworth, Olivia 1557
Butterworth, Rachel 1557
Butterworth, Thomas William 1763
Buttery, Alexander Kevin 737
Buttery, Christopher (Kim) 737
Buttery, (Elizabeth) Rosemary 737
Buttery, Nigel Christopher 737
Button, Andrew 1984
Button, Brenda Maud 1984
Button, Carmel Elizabeth 2124
Button, Caroline Wendy 1984
Button, Catherine Gail 1984
Button, Christopher 1984
Button, Darren Scott 1168
Button, Dianne Joy 1168
Button, Ethne Patricia 1984
Button, Gary N 1168
Button, Gillian Sheila 1867
Button, James 1984
Button, James Edward 1984
Button, Jillian Leonie 1984
Button, Kelly Lou 1168
Button, Mary Ann Hofmeyr 1984
Button, Matthew James 1984
Button, Penelope 1168
Button, Peter David 2124
Button, Richard James Kenneth 1867
Button, Sarah Nicola 1867
Button, Stephanie Brianna 2124
Button, Sylvia Jean 1984
Button, Teresa Jane 1867
Button, Victoria Jane 1984
Buurman, Dirk Jacobus Gerhard 317
Buurman, Henriette 317
Buurman, Jacob Lucas 317
Buurman, Johan Willem Godard 317
Buxton, Adrian David 453
Buxton, Agnes Josephine 453
Buxton, Alexandra Mary 453
Buxton, Alison D 2088
Buxton, Amanda 459
Buxton, Amanda Evelyn 1042
Buxton, Amy 455
Buxton, Andrew Edward 456, 2781
Buxton, Andrew Ralph 999
Buxton, Andrew Robert Fowell 453, 932
Buxton, Andrew Wakefield 453
Buxton, Angharad Grace Jones 454
Buxton, Ann 453
Buxton, Ann Frances 452
Buxton, Annabel 2365
Buxton, Annabella 155, 456
Buxton, Anne 456
Buxton, Anne Caroline 457
Buxton, Anthony John 452
Buxton, Antony Leonard 453
Buxton, Asha Theresa 453
Buxton, Ashley 453
Buxton, (Aubrey) James Francis 459
Buxton, Aubrey Leland Oakes 458
Buxton, Barbara Anne 456, 2781
Buxton, Belinda Margaret 454, 1154
Buxton, Belinda Ruth 457
Buxton, Bennington Haille 456
Buxton, Betty 458
Buxton, Blake Mark Chee-Meng 453
Buxton, Bridget 457
Buxton, Bruce John 453
Buxton, Caragh Susan 453
Buxton, Carmela Mary Beatrice 456
Buxton, Caroline Mavis 458
Buxton, Carolyn Viola 454
Buxton, Cecile Moss 455
Buxton, Charles Benedict 458
Buxton, Charles Hubert Jex 455
Buxton, Charles Joseph 453
Buxton, Charles Robert James 452
Buxton, Christopher Godfrey Reader 455
Buxton, Christopher John Noel 2088
Buxton, Christopher Robert 453
Buxton, Colin 458
Buxton, Crispin Charles Gerard 458
Buxton, Daniel Elliot 453
Buxton, Daniel Richard 453
Buxton, Daphne Rosemary 457
Buxton, Darren Richard Blake 453
Buxton, David Adrian Leonard 453
Buxton, David Colleton 456
Buxton, David Edson 453
Buxton, David Grant 999
Buxton, David Mark Reford 452
Buxton, David Roden 455, 458
Buxton, Diana Mildred 999
Buxton, Douglas Edward 453
Buxton, Edmund Digby 453
Buxton, Edward 452
Buxton, Edward Guy Fowell 452
Buxton, Edward Leland 459
Buxton, Edward North 457
Buxton, Edward Robert 453
Buxton, Eleanor Charlotte 455
Buxton, Elinor Grace Alyson 452
Buxton, Elizabeth Caroline Tilden Whitelocke 457
Buxton, Elizabeth Edith Millicent 453
Buxton, Elizabeth 453
Buxton, Elmira Mary 453
Buxton, Emma Lucie Maria 459
Buxton, Fiona Anne 456
Buxton, Fiona Helen 457
Buxton, Francesca 458
Buxton, Francis 453
Buxton, Georgina Elizabeth 453
Buxton, Gerard St John Roden 458
Buxton, Gervase Michael 453
Buxton, Giles Aubrey 454
Buxton, Greig Daniel 453
Buxton, Guy Lawrence 457
Buxton, Harriet Faith Alyson 452
Buxton, Harry Desmond Gascoigne 456
Buxton, Heather Clive 453
Buxton, Heather Morwenna Marie 453
Buxton, Helen Celia 454
Buxton, Henrietta Louise 452
Buxton, Henry Adrian 453
Buxton, Henry Alexander Fowell 218, 452
Buxton, Henry Gurney 456
Buxton, Henry James Aubrey 459
Buxton, Hero Elizabeth 455
Buxton, Hilda 458
Buxton, Horatia Mary 454
Buxton, Hugh David 454
Buxton, Hugh Lawrence 457
Buxton, Ian Lyon 456
Buxton, Jaeden Laurence Chee-Kan 453
Buxton, James Andrew Denis 458
Buxton, James Anthony Fowell 70, 452
Buxton, James Desmond 155, 456
Buxton, James Geoffrey Pease 454
Buxton, James Patrick 454
Buxton, Jane Elizabeth 2088
Buxton, Jane Margery 453, 932
Buxton, Jane Mary 453
Buxton, Janet Susan Paine 456
Buxton, Jasper Francis 456
Buxton, Jean Carlile 455
Buxton, Jean Mary 456
Buxton, Jeremy Clifton Gurney 456
Buxton, Joanna Margaret Reader 455
Buxton, Jocelyn David 453
Buxton, Joe Grace 455
Buxton, John Arthur 453
Buxton, John Joseph 457
Buxton, Jonathan 458
Buxton, Jonathan Charles Fowell 453
Buxton, Jonathan Hugh 456
Buxton, Jonathan James 161, 453
Buxton, Joseph William Henry 453
Buxton, Josephine 453
Buxton, Judith Averil 458, 626
Buxton, Judith Mary 457
Buxton, Julia Grace 452
Buxton, Julia Victoria 454, 2203
Buxton, Julian Wilberforce 458
Buxton, Juliet Horatia 454
Buxton, Juliette Gaye 453
Buxton, Katharine Mary 452
Buxton, Katharine 453
Buxton, Katherine Helen 2088
Buxton, Katherine Louise 452
Buxton, Kathleen Hannah 453
Buxton, Kathleen 459
Buxton, Katriona Topaz Mary 453
Buxton, Keith Mervyn Lyon 456
Buxton, Kenneth Leonard 453
Buxton, Laura Elizabeth Verena 453
Buxton, Laura Joan 458
Buxton, Laura Juliet 455
Buxton, Laura Rose 453
Buxton, Leonie Carinna Rose 453
Buxton, Lettice Katharine 452
Buxton, Leucha Daphne Mary 457, 2940
Buxton, Liane Frances 454
Buxton, Linda Jane 458
Buxton, Lucinda (Cindy) Catherine 459
Buxton, Lucy Jane 453
Buxton, Lynley Anne 453
Buxton, Margaret Elizabeth 70, 452, 2088
Buxton, Margaret Evelyn 364, 455
Buxton, Mark Gerald Edward North 457, 2940
Buxton, Martin Patrick Mingulay 458
Buxton, Mary 454
Buxton, Mary Katharine 455
Buxton, Mary Violet 455, 458
Buxton, Matthew Thomas Gervase 453
Buxton, Maurice 458
Buxton, Mavis Jean 458
Buxton, Melinda 459
Buxton, Meriel Jessica 454
Buxton, Meriel Lavinia Margaret 452
Buxton, Nicholas Andrew 453
Buxton, Nicholas Edward North 457
Buxton, Nicholas Fowell 452
Buxton, Nicola Rachel Anne 456
Buxton, Nicola Wendy 2306
Buxton, Nigel Arthur 453
Buxton, Oliver 455
Buxton, Oliver Desmond 456
Buxton, Oliver Silas 458
Buxton, Olivia Louise 459
Buxton, Paul Kenneth 453
Buxton, Paul Stephen 458
Buxton, Paul William Jex 364, 455
Buxton, Penelope Ann Cecil 456
Buxton, Peter Hildred 455
Buxton, Phyllida Dorothy Roden 455, 458
Buxton, Priscilla Peronne 454
Buxton, Rachel Jane 455
Buxton, Rachel Susan 2088
Buxton, Regina Yuet Mei 453
Buxton, Richard Antony 453
Buxton, Richard Christopher 2365
Buxton, Richard Moberly 452
Buxton, Richard Ronan 458
Buxton, Robert 453
Buxton, Robert Hugh 456
Buxton, Robert Thomas 2306
Buxton, Robert Victor 455
Buxton, Robin Anthony 457
Buxton, Roden Arnold 458
Buxton, Ronald Carlile 455, 458
Buxton, Rosaleen Pleasance 161, 453
Buxton, Rosaleen Poppy 453
Buxton, Rose Emma 454
Buxton, Rose Vivian 454
Buxton, Sam 455
Buxton, Samuel Roden 458
Buxton, Sara 453
Buxton, Sarah Jane 458
Buxton, Shane Laurence Blake 453
Buxton, Simon Campden 2088
Buxton, Simon Cosmo Robert 452
Buxton, Simon Lyon 456
Buxton, Sophia Frances 455
Buxton, Sophie 455
Buxton, Susan 453
Buxton, Susan Margaret 453
Buxton, Susan Whiteway 458
Buxton, Terence Mark 457
Buxton, Teresa Constance 452
Buxton, Terri 453
Buxton, Tessa Rosa 453
Buxton, Thaddeus Alexander Wolf 453
Buxton, Thomas Archie 452
Buxton, Thomas Lyon 456
Buxton, Thomas Mark 453
Buxton, Thomas Michael 453
Buxton, Timothy James 453
Buxton, Timothy Leland 459, 1042
Buxton, Timothy Richard Blake 453

Buxton, Tobias Richard Valentine 455
Buxton, Toby Finbarr 458
Buxton, Vanessa Ann 455
Buxton, Veronica Juliet Mary 453
Buxton, Veronica Mary 453
Buxton, Victoria 218, 452, 453
Buxton, Victoria Jane 459
Buxton, Victoria Rose 453
Buxton, William Paul 453
Buxton, Xavier 455
Buxton, Yvo 455
Buzzard, Angela Caroline 459, 1566
Buzzard, Ann Sophia Madeline 459
Buzzard, Barbara Jean 459
Buzzard, Claire Judith 459
Buzzard, Heather Elizabeth 459
Buzzard, Jacqueline Frances 459, 1566
Buzzard, Jennifer Ann 459
Buzzard, Jennifer Anne 1566
Buzzard, Jennifer Mary 460
Buzzard, Jonathan Mark 460
Buzzard, Nicholas John 459, 1566
Buzzard, Rachel Mary 460
Buzzard, Sarah Jane 459
Buzzard, Sylvia 459
Buzzard, Timothy Macdonnell 460
Byatt, Alexandra Mary 1921
Byatt, Andrew Lorne Campbell 611
Byatt, Douglas Edward Campbell 2191
Byatt, Duncan 1921
Byatt, Duncan Ian Arthur Campbell 611
Byatt, Emma Alyson Campbell 2191
Byatt, Fiona Mary Mackenzie 611
Byatt, Hugh Campbell 611
Byatt, Leonard Joseph 2679
Byatt, Lucinda Margaret 611
Byatt, Sarah James 2679
Byers, James Paul Edward Murray 2042
Byers, Katharine Lucy Victoria 2042
Byford, Elizabeth-Anne 2878
Byford, Justin D 2878
Bygott-Webb, Mark William 1241
Bygott-Webb, Samuel John 1242
Byk, Camilla Christian 1090
Byk, Jennifer Merrill 2736
Byk, Robert 1090
Byk, Stephen 2736
Byng, Ann Maitland 2834
Byng, Anna 2724
Byng, Colin Hugh 2833
Byng, Eve Finola 2724
Byng, Francesca 1992
Byng, Francis Gustaf 2724
Byng, Francis John Stuart 1992
Byng, (George Michael) Alexander 2724
Byng, Georgina Isabel 2833
Byng, Henrietta Rose 2833
Byng, James Edmund 2723
Byng, Joan 2834
Byng, Joanne Rachel 2834
Byng, John Lancelot 2833
Byng, John Nicholas 2833
Byng, Julia Mary (Judy) 2723
Byng, Julian Francis 2724
Byng, Julian Michael Edmund 2724
Byng, Karen Elizabeth 2723
Byng, Leo Walter 2723
Byng, Leslea Anne 2833
Byng, Lisa Anne 2833
Byng, Malaika Anne 2833
Byng, Margaret Ellen 2833
Byng, Marley McVeigh 2723
Byng, Mary Margaret 2833
Byng, Maximillian Rupert Stuart 1992
Byng, Patrick James John Wentworth 2724
Byng, Peter Joseph 2833
Byng, Prudence Mary Kent 2724
Byng, Robert Michael Julian Wentworth 2724
Byng, Rupert Wingfield 1992
Byng, Sarah Jaine 2833
Byng, Saskia Ruth Jessica 2723
Byng, Sheila Margaret 2833
Byng, Susan Honour 2833
Byng, Thomas Francis Edmund Wentworth 2724
Byng, Toby James Findhorn 1992
Byng, Whitney Osborn 2723
Byng, William Robert 2723
Byrams, Bronwyn 1250
Byrams, Peter De Wyckoff 1250
Byrne, Andrea Carina 1650
Byrne, Anna Louise 285
Byrne, Anthony Gerard 1794
Byrne, Catherine Penelope 1650
Byrne, Christian Rory 1651
Byrne, Clare Joan 1084
Byrne, Damien Charles 1794
Byrne, Danny 1071
Byrne, Dominic Lawrence 1650
Byrne, Edward Alexander 1651
Byrne, Elliot James 1650
Byrne, Emily May 1071
Byrne, Fergus 625
Byrne, Fiona Georgina Mary 1650
Byrne, Frederick Michael 1794
Byrne, George Henry St Clare 1650
Byrne, Henry Charles Mogeridge 1650
Byrne, Jacqueline 2312
Byrne, James Vincent 1650
Byrne, Jessica Katherine 1651
Byrne, John 1650
Byrne, Juliet Elizabeth Anson 1650
Byrne, Katharine Letitia 1650
Byrne, Kevin 285
Byrne, Kirstie Mary Kate 1650
Byrne, (Margaret) Louise 1794
Byrne, Martin Gerard 1084
Byrne, Mary Gabriel 1650, 1894
Byrne, Nona Georgette 1650
Byrne, Paul Leonard Dominic 1794
Byrne, Philippa Elizabeth 285
Byrne, Robert Paul 2013
Byrne, Rory Shaun 1650
Byrne, Rosalie Julianne 285
Byrne, Rosanna Amber 2312
Byrne, Rosanna Clare 1650
Byrne, Rowena Catherine Anson 1650
Byrne, Simon Thomas 1084
Byrne, Susan Amanda 1650
Byrne, Susanna 1071
Byrne, Tamsin 1071
Byrne, Tara Mary Fiona 1650
Byrne, Teresa Frances Ida 1084
Byrne, Thomas Edward 1071
Byrne, Thomas Vincent Lawrence 1650
Byrne, Veronica 2013
Byrne, Victoria Mary 625
Byrne, (Vincent) Patrick 1650, 1894
Byrne-Hill, Cosmo George Nicholas 2356
Byrne-Hill, Damien John 2356
Byrne-Hill, Martha Louise 2356
Byrne-Hill, William Francis Stapleton 2356
Byron, Caroline Anne Victoria 460
Byron, Charles Richard Gordon 460
Byron, Emily Clare 460
Byron, Robyn Margaret 460
Byron, Sophie Georgina 460

C

Caba, Ali Kemâl 1192
Caba, Christina Margaret 1192
Caba, Elif Ina 1192
Caba, Ozan Sinan 1192
Cabbell-Manners, Diana (Dido) Dorothy Elizabeth 1845
Cabbell-Manners, Hugh 1845
Cabbell-Manners, Jessica 1845
Cabbell-Manners, Rupert 1845
Cabbell-Manners, (Thomas) Benjamin 1845
Cable, Andrew Duncan 1634
Cable, Gordon Ian Langrishe 1634
Cable, William H 1366
Cable-Alexander, Fergus William Antony 462
Cable-Alexander, Jane Mary 462
Cable-Alexander, Margaret Mabel 463
Cable-Alexander, Melanie Jane 462
Cabot, Ann Sophia Madeline 1566
Cabrol, Alice 2040
Cabrol, Danielle 2040
Cabrol, Elizabeth Anne 2040
Cabrol, Hélène 2040
Cabrol, Jacques 2040
Cabrol, Jean Louis 2040
Cabrol, Louis H 2040
Cabrol, Marie Thérèse 2040
Cadman, Angela Muir 464
Cadman, (Arthur) Denys 464
Cadman, Cary 464
Cadman, Cary Anne 464
Cadman, Constance St Clair 464
Cadman, Cynthia 464
Cadman, Elizabeth Jane 464
Cadman, Evelyn Lloyd 463
Cadman, Giles Oliver Richard 463
Cadman, James Patrick David 464
Cadman, James Rupert 464
Cadman, Janet Patricia 464
Cadman, Janet Valerie 463
Cadman, John Denys 464
Cadman, Julia Mary 463
Cadman, Kenneth John 464
Cadman, Lais Moreira de Castro 464
Cadman, Marie 464
Cadman, Marion Lloyd 463
Cadman, Marjorie Elizabeth 464
Cadman, Martin Henry 463
Cadman, Nicholas Anthony Janes 463
Cadman, Richard Edward Charles 464
Cadman, Richard James Allen 463
Cadman, Robert Andrew 464
Cadman, Susan Lesley 464
Cadman, Sybil Mary 463, 464
Cadman, Victoria Marion 1346
Cadman, William Martin 463
Cadman, William Stephen 1346
Cadogan, Alexander John 524
Cadogan, Ambrose Alec Patrick George 466
Cadogan, Camilla Mary 524
Cadogan, Caroline 466
Cadogan, Catharine Anne 466
Cadogan, Cecilia Margaret 466
Cadogan, Charles Gerald John 465, 2295
Cadogan, Charles John 466
Cadogan, Daphne Jane Richards 524
Cadogan, Dorothy (Dot) 465
Cadogan, Edward Charles 465
Cadogan, George Edward Charles Diether 465
Cadogan, Gerald 466
Cadogan, Henry Michael Edward 524
Cadogan, Jonathan Joseph 2701
Cadogan, Katharina Johanna Ingeborg 465
Cadogan, Leo 466
Cadogan, Lucy Dodd 466
Cadogan, Nancy 466
Cadogan, Oliver Roger 524
Cadogan, Pamela Mary 466
Cadogan, Patrick Michael 2701
Cadogan, Philippa Katharina 465
Cadogan, William John 465
Cadzow, Joan Margaret 1102
Cadzow, Nora Denise 1102
Cadzow, Sally Jean 1102
Caffell, Anna Margaret Juliet 2215
Caffell, Gillian Esmé 2215
Caffell, Timothy C 2215
Cafferkey, Clare Mary 1384
Cafferkey, Patrick Charles 1384
Cahill, Alice 2094
Cahill, Angela Violet 2094
Cahill, Anne Violet 2094
Cahill, Bryan Anthony Ernest 1428
Cahill, Colin Algar 2094
Cahill, Elizabeth Mary 2094
Cahill, Jeremy James 1428
Cahill, Joanne Amanda 1428
Cahill, John 2094
Cahill, John Anthony 2094
Cahill, Pamela Pixie Anne 1428
Cahill, Peter Francis 2094
Cahill, Rachel Louise 1428
Cahill, Rosemary 2094
Cahill, Timothy Joseph 1428
Cahn, Benjamin Albert 467
Cahn, Edward John 467
Cahn, Jessie Laura 467
Cahn, Julien Michael 467
Cahn, Malka 467
Cahn, Marietta 467
Cahn, Marilynne Janelle 467
Cahn, Richard Ian 467
Cain, Ann 374
Cain, Debra Rae 2009
Cain, John Corey Johnson 2009
Cain, Linder Harrison 2009
Cain, Michael 2009
Cain, Michell Mostyn Johnson 2009
Cain, Zachary Peter Johnson 2009
Caine, Michael Harris 2081
Caird, Adam Benjamin 2880
Caird, Edmund George 2880
Caird, George Caird 2880
Caird, Helen Fay 115
Caird, Iona Katherine Mary 2880
Caird, Oliver Ralph 2880
Caird, Peter William 116
Caird, Sarah Dorothy 2880
Cairns, Alison Margery Anna 337
Cairns, Alistair 21
Cairns, Alistair Benedict 467
Cairns, Amanda Mary 467, 1363
Cairns, Ann Camilla 468
Cairns, Barbara Jeanne 468
Cairns, Bertram Wilfrid Arthur 468
Cairns, Bridget 558
Cairns, Caroline Byng 1112
Cairns, Catriona Helen 468
Cairns, Conrad Thomas 337
Cairns, Daniel 558
Cairns, (David) Patrick 467
Cairns, Edmund Frederick 337
Cairns, Elizabeth 468
Cairns, Felix Timothy 467
Cairns, Francesca ('Fresci') L 467
Cairns, Francis John Hugh 468
Cairns, Hélène Pauline 3001
Cairns, Harriet 467
Cairns, Heather Mary 337
Cairns, (Hugh) Andrew David 468
Cairns, Hugh Sebastian Frederick 467
Cairns, Isabelle Nicola 3001
Cairns, Isobel 558
Cairns, Jeremy Dymoke Russell 3001
Cairns, Jeremy Rudland Lee 3001
Cairns, Julia Andrea 2147
Cairns, Juliet 467
Cairns, Juliet Frances Jean 2188
Cairns, Katherine Frances 468
Cairns, Monica Frances 3001
Cairns, Neville Gene Patrick 3001
Cairns, Oliver 558
Cairns, Oliver David Andrew 467
Cairns, Oscar 467
Cairns, Patrick Neville 3001
Cairns, Peter Granville 468
Cairns, Ruth 1729
Cairns, Simon Dallas 1363
Cairns, Sophie Hélène 3001
Cairns, Tara Davina Amanda 467
Cairns, Teresa Jane 3001
Cairns, Trevor 337
Cairns, Ulla Agneta 468
Cairns, William 1112
Calame, Antonia Anne 1272
Calame, Philippe Robert 1272
Caldecott, Dominic 2405
Caldecott, Frederick Arthur Nicholas 2405
Caldecott, Rufus George 2405
Caldecott, Sarah Caroline 2405
Caldecott, Thomas Andrew 2405
Calder, Andrew John Scott 2414
Calder, Casey Beresford 1067
Calder, Chloë Abigail 2414
Calder, Christine Doreen Orange 1067
Calder, Guy Leon 2414
Calder, John Beresford 1067
Calder, Jude Anthony 1067
Calder, Madeleine Clare 2414
Calder, Ngaire Beresford 1067
Calder, Peter McRobert 1067
Calder, Philippa Chrystal 1067
Calder, Poppy Marie 2414
Calder, Sandra Joy Welsh 1067
Calderbank, James 1180
Calderbank, Judith Cecilia Anne 1180
Calderbank, Rachel Claire Joanna 1180
Calderbank, William Michael 1180
Caldwell, Amy 155
Caldwell, Angela Mary 1413
Caldwell, Deborah Grace 1598
Caldwell, Duane Thomas 1598
Caldwell, E V 2213
Caldwell, Elizabeth Avarina Joan 1598
Caldwell, Hayden James 1413
Caldwell, Hazel Katharine 373
Caldwell, James Martin Stewart 373
Caldwell, Jane Louise Lake 155
Caldwell, Johanna Grace 1598
Caldwell, Kathleen Avarina Suzanne 1598
Caldwell, Kathleen Georgina 2213
Caldwell, Kieran John 1413
Caldwell, Marcus Stewart 373
Caldwell, Margaret 2923
Caldwell, Mary 2923
Caldwell, Mary Beatrice 155
Caldwell, Mary Rebecca Christine 1598
Caldwell, Megan Avarina-Mae 1598
Caldwell, Michael 2923
Caldwell, Molly 2923
Caldwell, Nadia Lauren 1413
Caldwell, Olivia Leah 1413
Caldwell, Rosemary Katharine 373
Caldwell, Russell 1413
Caldwell, Ryan Gerrard 1413
Caldwell, Stevan 155
Caldwell, Stewart Duane Sandes 1598
Caleb, Caroline Mary 1603
Caleb, Jane 3003
Caleb, Leila 3003
Caleb, Magdul 3003
Caleb, Michael Sunil 3003
Caleb, Penelope Frances 1603
Calladine, Charles 2998
Calladine, Kelly 2998
Calladine, Sally Elinor 2998
Callaghan, Audrey Elizabeth 474
Callaghan, Jennifer Mary Morris 474
Callaghan, Joseph Edwin James 474
Callaghan, Kate Elizabeth 474
Callaghan, Michael James 474
Callaghan, Sarah Jane 474
Callander, Amy Louise 2183
Callander, Emma Louise 2001
Callander, James Edward 2001
Callander, Louise Anne 2183
Callander, Mary Pamela 2001
Callander, Richard 2001
Callander, Sarah Mary 2001
Callander, Wayne Robert 2183
Callender, David Gordon 2746
Callender, Ella Jean Skuse 2746
Callender, Fiona Margaret 253
Callender, Hugh Royston 2746
Callender, Ian Stuart 253
Callender, Linda Margaret 2746
Callender, Mary Lorna Elliot 2746
Callender, Patricia Margaret 253
Callender, Richard Stuart 253
Callender, Robert Andrew 2746
Callender, Vivien Elliot 2747
Callender, Warwick Elliot 2747
Callender, William Stuart 2746
Callinicos, Alexander Theodore 30
Callinicos, Alice 30
Callinicos, Anastasius John 30
Callinicos, Helena Marie Immaculée 30
Callinicos, Joanna 30
Callinicos, John Alexander 30
Callinicos, Michael John 30
Calver, Ann Clementine 2381

Calver, Peter 2381
Calvert, Deborah Deirdre Anne 2357
Calvert, Edmund Archibald 394
Calvert, George Arbuckle 1457
Calvert, Henrietta Amelia 394
Calvert, Henry (Harry) Clifton 394, 988
Calvert, Ian Arbuckle 1457
Calvert, Jack Richard 2391
Calvert, Pamela Nanine 1457
Calvert, Paul 2357
Calvert, Piers Henry 394
Calvert, Robert Henry 456
Calvert, Ruth Margaret 394, 988
Calvert, Susan Arbuckle 1457
Calvert, Susannah Honor 2391
Calvert, Teresa Mary Claire 2391
Calvert, Thomas 2391
Calvin, Barbara Patricia Lee 464
Calvin, Graham Denys 464
Calvin, John Collamer 464
Calvin, Mary Betty 464
Calvin, Robert Alexander 464
Calvin, Robert Denys 464
Calvin, Sarah Emily 464
Calvo-Platero, Ariadne Grace 230
Calvo-Platero, Clio 230
Calvo-Platero, Mario 230
Calvo-Platero, Milo Alaric 230
Calvo-Platero, Oliver Guido 230
Calvocoressi, Andrew Matthew Ion 41
Calvocoressi, Barbara Dorothy 1373
Calvocoressi, Cristopher John 41
Calvocoressi, David Sebastian 1373
Calvocoressi, Francesca 41
Calvocoressi, Hermione Beatrice 41
Calvocoressi, James Melville Ion 41
Calvocoressi, Katherine 41
Calvocoressi, Matthew James 41
Calvocoressi, Natalia Katherine 41
Calvocoressi, Nujoji Peter 1373
Calvocoressi, Nuku Vanonyi 1373
Calvocoressi, Nuname Ankaret 1373
Calvocoressi, Paul Peter 1373
Calvocoressi, Peter John Ambrose 1373
Calvocoressi, Richard Edward Ion 41
Calvocoressi, Richenda Victoria Hanson 41
Calvocoressi, Rupert Benedict 41
Calvocoressi, Thomas David 41
Cambell, Judy Mary 280
Camden, Anthony Baptist 3055
Camden, Sarah Rose 3055
Cameron, Alan 771
Cameron, (Allan) Alexander 2013
Cameron, Alison Lesley 771
Cameron, Alistair Ewen David 2341
Cameron, Andreena Louise 241
Cameron, Andrew Lee 852
Cameron, Andrew Wyndham Armar 77
Cameron, Angus Duncan John 2670
Cameron, Angus Ewen 436
Cameron, (Angus) Iain 436
Cameron, Anna Rosalind 154
Cameron, Anthony Cameron 1320
Cameron, Archibald Charles 852
Cameron, Camilla Louise 476
Cameron, Candida 436
Cameron, Caroline 2033
Cameron, Catherine Alison 771
Cameron, Catherine Mary 694, 1759
Cameron, Catriona Louise 2670
Cameron, Cecil Nennella Therese 694, 1759
Cameron, Clare Elizabeth 2863
Cameron, Clare Louise 2013
Cameron, Clive Bremner 76
Cameron, Craig 2033
Cameron, Daniel 241
Cameron, David 852
Cameron, David W D 2597
Cameron, David William 771
Cameron, David William Donald 2013
Cameron, Diane Carol 241
Cameron, Donald 1376
Cameron, Donald Andrew John 694, 1759
Cameron, Donald Angus 694, 1759
Cameron, Donald Eric Nelson 3042
Cameron, Donald Marsh 2033
Cameron, Edward Richard Pyers 2670
Cameron, Eleanor Jessica Jane 1376
Cameron, Elizabeth Clare 2670
Cameron, Emily Frances 694, 1759
Cameron, Ewen Duncan 2473, 2863
Cameron, Ewen James Fassiefern 2341
Cameron, Fiona 436
Cameron, Gavin Ian 771
Cameron, Gemma Blair 2009
Cameron, Gillian Jane 2670
Cameron, Hamish 694
Cameron, Henrietta Jane 1320
Cameron, Hester Caroline 436
Cameron, Iain Donald Robert 2670
Cameron, Ian 2033
Cameron, Ian Donald 2013
Cameron, Imogen Clare 2013
Cameron, Jacqueline 2009
Cameron, James 2670
Cameron, James Allan Godfrey 2341
Cameron, James Paget 76
Cameron, James William 1320
Cameron, Jane 1376
Cameron, Jean Pamela 476
Cameron, Jennifer Dines 1418
Cameron, Jo-Ann Mirrielle 852
Cameron, Joan Mary Frances 1418
Cameron, Joanna Lee 852
Cameron, Joanna Margaret 2473, 2863
Cameron, Joel Aley Barry 717
Cameron, John 2670
Cameron, John Alastair Nigel 694
Cameron, John Bruce 1418
Cameron, Judith Evelyn Maud 436
Cameron, Julia R 694
Cameron, Katherine Elizabeth Phoebe 1376
Cameron, Keith 2033
Cameron, Kirsty Anne 694
Cameron, Kylie Jane 1668
Cameron, Lois Mary Maitland 2473
Cameron, Lorien 436
Cameron, Louisa Mary 2863
Cameron, Louise 2341
Cameron, Lucy Margot Therese 694, 1759
Cameron, Margaret Victoria 2670
Cameron, Mary Alexandra 943
Cameron, Mary Fleur 2013
Cameron, Maureen 771
Cameron, Michael Aylmer 154
Cameron, Michelle 2033
Cameron, Monica Joan 3042
Cameron, Murray Owen 1668
Cameron, Neil Robert David 943
Cameron, Robert Andrew 694
Cameron, Robert S 943
Cameron, Rosalind Alice 154
Cameron, Rosaline Louise 76
Cameron, Rose Phoebe Anne 1376
Cameron, Samantha Gwendoline 2597
Cameron, Sarah Louise 77, 2013
Cameron, Susan 1376
Cameron, Susan Fiona 2670
Cameron, Tania Rachel 2013
Cameron, Timothy Charles 852
Cameron, Zhan 2033
Cameron-Beaumont, Andrew Jon 2520
Cameron-Beaumont, Charlotte Lucinda 2520
Cameron-Beaumont, Lucinda Jill 2520
Cameron-Beaumont, Richard Peregrine 2520
Cameron of Lochiel, Donald Hamish 694
Cameron of Lochiel, Margaret Doris 694
Cameron-Ramsay-Fairfax-Lucy, Anna Margaret Barclay 2348
Cameron-Ramsay-Fairfax-Lucy, Duncan 2347
Cameron-Ramsay-Fairfax-Lucy, Janet Barclay 2347
Cameron-Ramsay-Fairfax-Lucy, Robin Spencer 2348
Cameron-Ramsay-Fairfax-Lucy, Spencer Angus James 2348
Cameron-Rose, Georgina Louise Stella 161
Cameron-Rose, Hugh Charles 161
Cameron-Rose, Jane Fiona 946
Camp, Claudia 1641
Campbell, Adelaide Elizabeth 36
Campbell, Ailsa Catherine 1795
Campbell, Alan 530
Campbell, Alan Leslie John Macartney 1795
Campbell, Alastair Colin Leckie 408, 626
Campbell, Alastair James Calthrop 488, 1755
Campbell, Alexander 530, 2082
Campbell, Alexander Colin 3073
Campbell, Alexander Edward Lindsay 482
Campbell, Alexander James Le Grand 482
Campbell, Alexander Leo 2214
Campbell, Alexander Nickson 2082
Campbell, Alice 2082
Campbell, Alice Violet 531
Campbell, Alida Virginie (Lilian) 481
Campbell, Alison Barbara Rose 527, 530
Campbell, Alistair Neil 2755
Campbell, Alister Neil 530
Campbell, Andrew 530
Campbell, Andrew P W 1860
Campbell, Angela Francesca 1408
Campbell, Angela Louise Vereker 627
Campbell, Angela Rosemary 1018
Campbell, Angus Charles Dundas 485
Campbell, Angus Mervyn 531
Campbell, Angus Neil Morgan 2755
Campbell, Anita Karen 530
Campbell, Anna Iona 485
Campbell, Anna Margaret 482
Campbell, Annabel Rose 408, 626
Campbell, Anne-Marie 222
Campbell, Annette Elizabeth 1240
Campbell, Arabella Louise Evelyn 530
Campbell, Araminta 2082
Campbell, Archibald Edward FitzGerald 479
Campbell, Archibald James 483
Campbell, Archibald Malcolm Scott 484
Campbell, Arthur Frederick 627
Campbell, Atholl 439
Campbell, Barbara Alison 482
Campbell, Barbara Mary 482
Campbell, Barnabas William Erskine 1860
Campbell, Benedict Robert Gordon 235
Campbell, Benjamin 1408
Campbell, Betty Yolande 2733
Campbell, Brian Barbrec 2863
Campbell, Bridget Nancy 1343
Campbell, Brigite 235
Campbell, Bruce Ronald 222
Campbell, Camilla Mary 2755
Campbell, Camilla Rose 2733
Campbell, Candace M 2128
Campbell, Cara Jenny 531
Campbell, Carol Patricia 286
Campbell, Carola Jane 481, 807
Campbell, Caroline Jean 1343
Campbell, Casper 1318
Campbell, Catherine 1343
Campbell, Catherine Janet Denman 481
Campbell, Catherine Rosemary 531
Campbell, Ceril Diana 530
Campbell, Charles 1318
Campbell, Charles Colin 480
Campbell, Charlotte Diana Pamela Geraldine 480
Campbell, Charlotte Fiona 286
Campbell, Charlotte Virginia 483
Campbell, Charmian Rachel 412, 481
Campbell, Chloe Elizabeth 531
Campbell, Christian Jean Mary 484
Campbell, Christine 480
Campbell, Christopher 480
Campbell, Christopher John 482
Campbell, Christopher Patrick 1343
Campbell, Christopher William John 2861
Campbell, Clarence Elwood 2816
Campbell, Claudia Jane 1173
Campbell, Colin 1240
Campbell, Colin Alan George 484
Campbell, Colin Guy Napier 412, 481
Campbell, Colin Ian Calthrop 488
Campbell, Colin Ivar 106
Campbell, Colin John Bruce 1018
Campbell, Colin MacLeod 500
Campbell, Colin Robert Vaughan 1320
Campbell, Colin Walter Joseph 1893
Campbell, Cosmo Thomas Aretas 235
Campbell, Daphne Jane 1584
Campbell, David Anthony 2732
Campbell, David Archibald 531
Campbell, David Michael Hay 2861
Campbell, David Richard Collingwood 1240
Campbell, Dermot John Hugh 1893
Campbell, Diana Mary 2863
Campbell, Diana Ruby 1795
Campbell, Dinah Mary 36
Campbell, Dominic Diarmid 1343
Campbell, Donald 222
Campbell, (Donald) Bruce le Strange 1822
Campbell, Donald James 482
Campbell, Donald le Strange 1822
Campbell, Duncan Alastair 125
Campbell, Edie Blanche 627
Campbell, Edward 488
Campbell, Edward Alastair Ian 531
Campbell, Eily Jane 36
Campbell, Elisabeth 530
Campbell, Elisabeth Joan 2128
Campbell, Elizabeth 481
Campbell, Elizabeth Gay Adair 486
Campbell, Elizabeth Janet 1804
Campbell, Elizabeth Mary 482, 483
Campbell, (Elizabeth) Poppy 1860
Campbell, Elizabeth St George 1173
Campbell, Elizabeth Topham 531
Campbell, Emma Mary 286
Campbell, Euan Henderson 2214
Campbell, Ewan Alexander 485
Campbell, Ewan Anton Hugh 484
Campbell, Ferdinand James Marc 488
Campbell, Fiona 1860, 2732
Campbell, Fiona Annelisa 1893
Campbell, Fiona Jane Alison 1018
Campbell, Fiona Madeline 485
Campbell, Fiona Mary St Clair 483
Campbell, Flann 1343
Campbell, Frances 186
Campbell, Fred(erick) William 531
Campbell, Frederick Hugh 531
Campbell, Gay Lindsey Helen 632
Campbell, George Richard Angus 2755
Campbell, Georgina Dorothy 481
Campbell, Georgina Louise Gore 1173
Campbell, Gerald Angus 2755
Campbell, Gerard Francis 1318
Campbell, Gillachrist 1343
Campbell, Gillian Susan 2128
Campbell, Glynis Kathleen 94
Campbell, Godfrey Garrett 1893
Campbell, Graham Duncan 125
Campbell, Guy 626
Campbell, Guy James Farquhar 530
Campbell, Hamish Adair 2880
Campbell, Hamish Iain 439
Campbell, Harriet Jane Sarah 479
Campbell, Harry David 531
Campbell, Helen Christina 531
Campbell, Helen Jean Laura 2991
Campbell, Helen Mary 1240
Campbell, Henry Mark 500
Campbell, Henry Neil Edward 2755
Campbell, Hugh 286
Campbell, Hugh Robin Farquhar 530
Campbell, Ian 629
Campbell, Ian Adair 2880
Campbell, Ian Angus Ralph 531
Campbell, Ian Neil 125
Campbell, Ian Robert 530
Campbell, Ilay Mark 1274
Campbell, Ion Edward FitzGerald 480
Campbell, Iona 2082
Campbell, Iona Lenor 484
Campbell, Iona Mary 103, 629
Campbell, Isabella Rachel 529, 1320
Campbell, Ishbel Elizabeth Rose 530
Campbell, Isla Rowena 2733
Campbell, Isla Sophia Rose 530
Campbell, Jacqueline 531
Campbell, James 530, 1804
Campbell, James Alexander 531
Campbell, James Alexander Moffat Bain 807
Campbell, James Charles Anthony 480
Campbell, James Farquhar Robin 530, 2142
Campbell, James Ian Somerset 2733
Campbell, James Ion Daniel 480
Campbell, James Malcolm 531
Campbell, James Robert 186
Campbell, James William Patrick 484
Campbell, Jamie John 94
Campbell, Jarvis Hunniford 36
Campbell, Jean Caroline 485
Campbell, Jenna Cherie 2732
Campbell, Jennifer Margaret 2732
Campbell, Jeremy George 2755
Campbell, Joan Esther Sybella 626, 1754
Campbell, Joan Margaret 632
Campbell, Joanna Frances 484
Campbell, Joanna Margaret 482
Campbell, John (Jack) Alexander 531
Campbell, John Agnew 36
Campbell, John Alexander 485
Campbell, John Alistair Chichester 482
Campbell, John Edward FitzGerald 480
Campbell, John Graham Colin 482
Campbell, John Howard 2266
Campbell, John Malcolm 632
Campbell, John Robertson 2861
Campbell, Joyce Margaret 2732
Campbell, Judith Meriel 3073
Campbell, Julia Margaret Rachel 480
Campbell, Julian 1826
Campbell, Julian James Noel 235
Campbell, Julian Simon 1343
Campbell, Juliet 125
Campbell, June 485
Campbell, K Dominique 627
Campbell, Kate Emily 485
Campbell, Katherine (Katie) J M 531
Campbell, Katherine June 485
Campbell, Katherine Laura 482
Campbell, Kathleen Adair 486
Campbell, Kathleen Mary 36
Campbell, Kiloran Diana Claire 627
Campbell, Kim Campbell 1408
Campbell, Kristine 1822
Campbell, Laura 480
Campbell, Laura Jane 531
Campbell, Lavinia Mary 579, 1343
Campbell, Leonora Mary Felicia 488
Campbell, Leslie James FitzGerald 480
Campbell, Leslie John 1795
Campbell, Liliana 531
Campbell, Linda Christine 2816
Campbell, Lorne Mary 486
Campbell, Louis Auchinbreck 483
Campbell, Louise Ann 530
Campbell, Louise Iona 103
Campbell, Louise Mary Walton 482
Campbell, Lucia Murdock 480
Campbell, Lucinda Louise 483
Campbell, Lucy 2082
Campbell, Lucy Catherine Isabel 480
Campbell, Lucy Catriona Margarette 485
Campbell, Lucy Georgia Elizabeth 531
Campbell, Luke Bingham 1343
Campbell, Lynn Nora Mary 2861
Campbell, Lynnette 235
Campbell, Malcolm Niall Kelso 484
Campbell, Marcus George Akers 235
Campbell, Margaret Alison 482
Campbell, Margaret Elizabeth 186, 1893
Campbell, Margaret Emily Robina 530
Campbell, Margaret Jean 500
Campbell, Margaret Minette Rohais 487, 1274
Campbell, Margaret 480
Campbell, Margaret Taylor Young 2991
Campbell, Margot 222
Campbell, Maria 1343, 2005
Campbell, Marina Caroline 530, 2142
Campbell, Marion Isobel 922
Campbell, Mark C 2214
Campbell, Martin Emmott 627
Campbell, Mary 531, 1343
Campbell, Mary Alison 483
Campbell, Mary Anne Chichester 482, 2157
Campbell, Mary Dorothy 2755
Campbell, Mary Lesley Griffin 482
Campbell, Maud Susan Rosemary 36
Campbell, May Alexandra 481
Campbell, Melfort 2082
Campbell, Michael James Douglas 6
Campbell, Moyra Jean 2732
Campbell, Moyra Kathleen 6
Campbell, Muriel Anne 627
Campbell, Muriel Elisabeth 480
Campbell, Neil Arthur 2755
Campbell, Neil Colin 485
Campbell, Neil Donald 627
Campbell, Neil Vanisittart 626
Campbell, Nicholas 530
Campbell, Nicholas C W 2779
Campbell, Nicholas Edward Angus 1343
Campbell, Nicholas John Muir 482
Campbell, Nicholas Robin 626
Campbell, Nicola Elizabeth Gina 488
Campbell, Nicola Frances 2880
Campbell, Nicole Mary 2779
Campbell, Noël Christabel 2732
Campbell, Nora Margaret 2861
Campbell, Norma Joyce 485
Campbell, Oliver Alistair 2880
Campbell, Orlando 1318

Christie, Ian 2083
Christie, Imogen Rose Lycett 1213
Christie, Isabel Nightingale 2083
Christie, Isabella Frances Mary 1771
Christie, James 2455
Christie, James Patrick Phillimore 2245
Christie, Jasmine Elisabeth Céline 2330
Christie, John Edward Phillimore 2245
Christie, Joseph Adrian Fortescue 2245
Christie, Laura Nightingale 2083
Christie, Lucinda Mary Rose 1771
Christie, (Marie) Jeanne 2330
Christie, Michael Ian Jerôme 2330
Christie, Michael Phillimore 2245
Christie, Patricia Ruth 2083
Christie, Paul James 1168
Christie, Robert Sylvester 1771
Christie, Thomas Alastair 1771
Christie, Wesley Alan 2330
Christie, William Lawrence 3099
Christie-Miller, Charlotte 855
Chubb, Alfred 1355
Chubb, Alice Christine 1355
Chubb, Andrew Harry 1355
Chubb, (Ann) Nicola 1355
Chubb, Charles Henry Thomas 1355
Chubb, David J 2827
Chubb, Edward James 189
Chubb, Elizabeth Anne 1355, 2475
Chubb, (George) William Michael 1355
Chubb, Georgia 1355
Chubb, Henrietta Joscelyne 2827
Chubb, Jack Charles 1355
Chubb, Jeremy David Knyvett 1355
Chubb, John Andrew 1355
Chubb, Josephine Anne 1355
Chubb, Lucinda Mary 189
Chubb, (Mark) Henry 1355
Chubb, Patrick David 1355
Chubb, Richard John 189
Chubb, Sandy 1355
Chubb, Thomas Frederik Flackl 1355
Chubb, Valerie Ann 1355
Chubb, Veronica 1355
Chubb, Waltaud 1355
Chubb, William Maurice 189
Chubb, Charles Henry Thomas 1355
Chumbley, Justin 2392
Chumbley, Lucy 2392
Chumbley, Margaret 2392
Chumbley, Roger 2392
Church, Jessica Jane 1349
Church, Susette Henrietta Mary 1349
Church, Theobald Frederick Stephen 1349
Church, William Henry Frederick 2430
Churcher, Catherine Elizabeth 2203
Churcher, Elizabeth Theresa 2203
Churchill, Alexandra 914
Churchill, Bryony 286
Churchill, Catherine Z 1869
Churchill, Charles ffleetwood 1859
Churchill, Daniel 914
Churchill, Deborah 286
Churchill, Diane Louise 253
Churchill, Glen 253
Churchill, Gratia Mary Anne ffleetwood 1859
Churchill, John (Jack) Gerard Averell 1869
Churchill, John Edward ffleetwood 1859
Churchill, John Malcolm Thorpe Fleming 812
Churchill, John ffleetwood 1859
Churchill, Jonathan 286
Churchill, Juliet Kathleen ffleetwood 1859
Churchill, Luce 1869
Churchill, Malcolm John Leslie 812
Churchill, Marina Spencer 1869
Churchill, Nicola 286
Churchill, Randolph Leonard Spencer 1869
Churchill, Rodney Alistair Gladstone 812
Churchill, Rosamund Margaret 812
Churchill, Serena Barbara Spencer 1869
Churchill, Stephen 286
Churchill, Violet Isabella Harriet 705
Churchill, Winston 1869
Churchill-Emery, Penelope Maud Valentine 1010
Churton, David Nigel Vardon Churton 1570
Churton, David Richard Harding 1043
Churton, Gelda Susan Marjorie 1042
Churton, Katherine 1570
Churton, Oscar Vardon 1570
Churton, Robert Harding 1042
Churton, Rollo Crispin 1570
Churton, Thomas Edward Harding 1042
Churton, Zara Fleur 1570
Chute, Nigel Anthony 1516
Chute, Rosalind Alexandra 1516
Chute, Valerie Evelyn 1516
Ciaralli-Parenzi, Andrew 146
Cincotta, John Gerard 491
Cincotta, Rosemary Ferelith 491
Cisneros, Carlos Alberto 307
Cisneros, José Alberto 307
Cisneros, José Maria 307
Cisneros, Josepha Margarita 307
Cisneros, Luis Eduardo 307
Cisneros, Marcela Inez 307
Cisneros, Maria Laura 307
Citkowitz, Ivana 887
Citrine, Mary 575
Citrine, Norman Arthur 575
Citrine, Patricia Deirdre 575
Citrine, Ronald Eric 575
Civardi, Anne Charlotte 2998
Civardi, Todd 2998
Cividiño, Clare Antoinette 1646
Cividiño, Oscar 1646
Civval, Bridget Elvira 2367
Clabburn, Elizabeth Mary Eilidh 435
Clabburn, Philip 436
Clacy, Mary Cyrilla 2650
Clancey, Christine Rose 2149
Clancey, Christopher 2149
Clapham, Adam John 2374
Clapham, Charles Marcus 2374
Clapham, Christopher Derek Charles 982
Clapham, Elsie Maree 325
Clapham, Melanie Alice 325
Clapham, Michael John Sinclair 2374
Clapham, Nicholas Walter Geoffey 982
Clapham, Nicolas 2374
Clapham, Stephen Geoffrey 982
Clapham, Susan Nesta Rosemary 982
Clapham, Thomas Anthony 325
Clapp, Barbara Ann 2703
Clapp, Enid Gwendolen 2703
Clapp, John William Maurice 2703
Clapp, Zoe Alice Katherine 2703
Clapton, Peter Thomas Archibald 908
Clapton, Thomas Robert 908
Clare, Brendan Marshall Foster 1542
Clare, Fay Margaret 1542
Clare, Jennifer Rose 2616
Clare, John Joseph 2616
Clare, Michael Charles Allen 1542
Clare, Paul Christopher 2616
Clare, Pauline Rosemary 2616
Clare, Tomas Aeron 2616
Clarfelt, Alice Nicola Irene 488
Clarfelt, Christina Marjorie 488
Clarfelt, Harriet 488
Clarfelt, Kate 488
Clarfelt, Mark Michael 488
Clarfelt, Max 488
Clarfelt, Tessa 488
Clargo, Frances Jane 2810
Clargo, Jeffrey Alex 2810
Claridge, Anna Louise 2488
Claridge, Evelyn Joanna Christian 2488
Claridge, Fabienne José 493
Claridge, Fergus 2488
Claridge, Hester Lucy 2488
Claridge, Jessica 2488
Claridge, Martin 2488
Claridge, Philip 493
Claridge, Rebecca 2488
Claridge, Simon Julian 2488
Claridge, Tobias James 2488
Claridge, Victoria 2488
Clark, Abel David 1419
Clark, Aidan Natis Miles King 2099
Clark, Alan Kenneth McKenzie 2569
Clark, Alexander Edward 2012
Clark, Alexander Harold 3054
Clark, Alexander Simon 2493
Clark, Alice 1946
Clark, Alison Tamsen 1355
Clark, Amanda Charlotte Frances 3096
Clark, Andrew David 1355
Clark, Andrew McKenzie 2569
Clark, Angela Madeline Gwynne 201
Clark, Ann Mary 527
Clark, Anna Camilla 1783
Clark, Anna Louise 657
Clark, Anne 589
Clark, Anne 2099
Clark, Anthea Mary 2537
Clark, Anthony Joseph 657
Clark, Anthony Miles Stapleton 2099
Clark, Anthony Phillip 201
Clark, Asa Alan III 1586
Clark, Asa Alan IV 1586
Clark, Ashton Thomas 657
Clark, Benedict John Innes 589
Clark, Benjamin Joseph 657
Clark, Bronwyn 2099
Clark, Bruce Shannon 1586
Clark, Bryan Stapleton 2099
Clark, Camilla Georgina Grace 589
Clark, Carly Anne 3054
Clark, (Caroline) Jane 2569
Clark, Catherine Mary 1419
Clark, Catherine Roseanne 201
Clark, Charles Adrian 1625
Clark, Charles Gavin 2469
Clark, Charles James Travers 1768
Clark, Christine 2179
Clark, Christopher 1586, 1946
Clark, Cindi Jennifer 3054
Clark, Cushla Kerr 657
Clark, Daphne Veryan 3086
Clark, David Crispin Stapleton 2099
Clark, David Gerald 3054
Clark, David Humphrey 1355
Clark, David James 1419
Clark, David Noah 1419
Clark, David William Francis 589
Clark, Debora Ann 3054
Clark, Deborah Mary Ann 588
Clark, Deborah 1586
Clark, Dominic 2012
Clark, Duncan A 472
Clark, Edward Drake 588
Clark, Elizabeth 1062
Clark, Elizabeth 657
Clark, Elizabeth Jane Delves 391, 1918
Clark, Emma Louise 1625
Clark, Emma Victoria 2179
Clark, Ezra David 1419
Clark, Fiona Elizabeth 587
Clark, Fiona Janet 2041
Clark, (Florence) Maxime 3054
Clark, Frances Clare 2785
Clark, Francis Malcolm 2041
Clark, Frederic William 1062
Clark, Garry Martin 588
Clark, Geoffrey Robert 657
Clark, Geoffrey Scott 2412
Clark, Georgina Jane 2041
Clark, Gerald Reginald 527
Clark, Geraldine Anne 2099
Clark, Geraldine Lesley 201
Clark, Gillian 588
Clark, Gordon Eric 369
Clark, Graham Leslie 2099
Clark, Hamish Douglas 589
Clark, Harry Edward 3096
Clark, Harry James Lothian 588
Clark, Hazel Yvonne Elizabeth 587
Clark, Hester Catherine 1419
Clark, Howard Victor 3086
Clark, Hugh Lothian 588
Clark, Hugh Roberts 1062
Clark, Hugo Ian Moberly 588
Clark, Ian Nicholas Harper 589
Clark, Irene Dorothy 589
Clark, James Alasdair Kenneth 2569
Clark, James Alexander 1521
Clark, James Auckland 1946
Clark, James Jackson 2493
Clark, Jamie Duncan 1783
Clark, Jamie Stewart 588
Clark, Jane Clare 2314
Clark, Jane 1062
Clark, Jean 587
Clark, Jean Margaret 1768
Clark, Jeffrey Wodehouse 1586
Clark, Jennifer Mary 2537
Clark, Jeremy John 657
Clark, Jeremy Scott 2412
Clark, Jessica 1783
Clark, John Charles Travers 1768
Clark, John Francis 2041
Clark, John Hatch 2179
Clark, John Jasper 2179
Clark, John Jeremy 201
Clark, John Joseph William 2537
Clark, John Maurice 588
Clark, Jonathan 507
Clark, Jonathan Thomas 2412
Clark, Joseph Trevor 657
Clark, Judith 201
Clark, Julia Jane 2012
Clark, Julie 2569
Clark, Justin 2012
Clark, Katherine Mary 1355
Clark, Katherine May 587
Clark, Katie Jane 588
Clark, Keith Charles Cave 527
Clark, Kenna Mary Rose 527
Clark, Kyle Hendrik Gorell 1175
Clark, Linda Helen 587
Clark, Linda 3054
Clark, Louise Elizabeth 1521
Clark, Lucy Caroline 589
Clark, Luke Edward Campbell 589
Clark, Margaret 588
Clark, Margaret Ellanor 369
Clark, Margie 1586
Clark, Marguerite Laura 1783
Clark, Marian Ruth 200
Clark, Mark James Macdonald 589
Clark, Mary 588
Clark, Mary-Jane 1625
Clark, Maura Teresa 1768
Clark, Michael 369
Clark, Michael Adam 1901
Clark, Michael James 2041
Clark, Michael John 2314
Clark, Michael Peter George 587
Clark, Mildred Pauahi 1586
Clark, Nancy Catherine 587
Clark, Nicholas James 200
Clark, Nicola Jane 472
Clark, Nicoletta Luisa Caroline 589
Clark, Nicolien 2099
Clark, Oliver Hamish William 589
Clark, Olivia Jessie 657
Clark, Paul Michael Frazer 588
Clark, Paul Robert 200
Clark, Peter Andrew 657
Clark, Peter Aubrey 587
Clark, Peter Charles 2978
Clark, Polly Caroline 587
Clark, Polly Catherine Isabel 589
Clark, Randall Gregory 3054
Clark, Richard Anthony 589
Clark, Richard Henry Frazer 587
Clark, Robert Alan 1521
Clark, Robin H A 1175
Clark, Roger 2493
Clark, Roger Ashton 200
Clark, Rosanne Felicity 369
Clark, Rosemary Cecilia 657
Clark, Rosemary Frazer 587
Clark, Ruari Alexander 3096
Clark, Ruth Christine 2099
Clark, Sandra Robyn 1901
Clark, Sarah G 2569
Clark, Sarah Tamsen 1355
Clark, Scarlett Alexandra 1946
Clark, Scott Jeffery 3054
Clark, Serena Elizabeth 589
Clark, Sheena Campbell 588
Clark, Sheila Campbell 588
Clark, Sheila Mary 2412
Clark, Shelley Marie 1901
Clark, Simon William 1355
Clark, Stephanie Jane 3086
Clark, Sue 589
Clark, Susan Elizabeth 1175
Clark, Susan Veryan 3086
Clark, Tessa Louise 587
Clark, Thomas Averell 1946
Clark, Thomas Edward 1783
Clark, Thomas George Nigel 588
Clark, Thomas George Ramsay Davidson 588
Clark, Thomas William 2537
Clark, Timothy Anthony 1625
Clark, Timothy Ian Hugh 588
Clark, Timothy John 1783
Clark, Vera Katharine 2469
Clark, Victoria Mary 507
Clark, Virginia Jane 2978
Clark, Wendy Ann 589
Clark, Wentworth Douglas 588
Clark, William Alexander 3096
Clark, Winnie 588
Clark-Maxwell, Alice Louise 382
Clark-Maxwell, James Michael Gilchrist 382
Clark-Maxwell, John William 382
Clark-Maxwell, Juliet Nina 382
Clarke, Alan Gerard 1084
Clarke, Alexander 590
Clarke, Alexandra Kathleen 591
Clarke, Alison Faith 2213
Clarke, Alison Stephenson 457
Clarke, Amanda Victoria 3071
Clarke, Andrea Rosalind 591
Clarke, Andrea 591
Clarke, Andrew John Patrick Stephenson 457
Clarke, Angela Mary 590
Clarke, Ann 1236
Clarke, Anthony 3071
Clarke, Anthony Clive 591
Clarke, Antony Graham 591
Clarke, Augusta Elfrida 589
Clarke, Barbary 591
Clarke, Barry Ian Charles 811
Clarke, Barry Michael 998
Clarke, Benjamin James 1236
Clarke, Betty Jocelyne 1889
Clarke, Bridget 1565
Clarke, Caroline Anne 590, 2013
Clarke, Caroline Stephenson 457
Clarke, Catherine Anne 543
Clarke, Charles Frederick Orme 590
Clarke, Charles Richard Spencer 1565
Clarke, (Charles Somerset) Lawrence 589
Clarke, Christine V 590
Clarke, Christopher Simon Courtenay Stephenson 2013
Clarke, Christopher Stephenson 457
Clarke, Clare Frances Elizabeth 108
Clarke, Cleone Rachen Vivien 1735
Clarke, Damian Anthony John 2237
Clarke, Desmond Walter Robert 2237
Clarke, Diana Susan Coningsby 811
Clarke, Dominic Michael Bernard 2237
Clarke, Dominic Wyndham 1735
Clarke, Dorothea 832
Clarke, Duncan Robert Petre 2237
Clarke, Edward 2013, 2237
Clarke, Edward Peter 590
Clarke, Eleanor Geraldine 1595
Clarke, Eleanor Margaret 998
Clarke, Elizabeth 590
Clarke, Elizabeth Anne 2501
Clarke, Elizabeth Charlotte 1889
Clarke, Elizabeth Lennox 591
Clarke, (Ernestine) Lucilla 591
Clarke, Fiona 2213
Clarke, Fiona Jane 1565
Clarke, Fiona Mary 590, 2237
Clarke, Francine 1180
Clarke, Francis Brookes 591
Clarke, Frederick William Michael 590
Clarke, Geoffrey Lindsay 204
Clarke, George 2237
Clarke, Geraldine Anne Danielle 1180
Clarke, Geraldine Coningsby 811
Clarke, Helen Rosalind 591
Clarke, Helena Margaret 590
Clarke, Henrietta 2013
Clarke, Henry 2237
Clarke, Imogen 2237
Clarke, Isabel Helen 590
Clarke, Ismay Elizabeth 1180
Clarke, James Alured 1565
Clarke, James William 1236
Clarke, Jane Caroline 1565
Clarke, Jason William 591
Clarke, Jennifer Frances 543
Clarke, Jennifer Jane 832
Clarke, Jessie Deakin 591
Clarke, Jill Maureen 457
Clarke, Joanna 591
Clarke, Joanna Grace 1084
Clarke, Joanna Valentine 3079
Clarke, John Elton 590
Clarke, Katherine Sybil 590
Clarke, Kathleen 590
Clarke, Lena Helen 2699
Clarke, Lilah Victoria Mary 590
Clarke, Linda Dawn 2699
Clarke, Louisa 2013

Coombes, Connemara Alice Mary 803
Coombes, Rowland William Sebastian 803
Coombes, Victoria Roque-Rebecca 803
Coombs, Arabella Sarah 869
Coombs, Augusta Elinor Lettice 2537
Coombs, Carolyn 2350
Coombs, Charles T Hardy 869
Coombs, Christopher Paternayan 2350
Coombs, David Paul 2350
Coombs, Dominic Nathaniel Thomas 2537
Coombs, Dorothy 2350
Coombs, Florence Margaret 1410
Coombs, Joan Vivian 2350
Coombs, Jolyon 869
Coombs, Linda Margaret 1410
Coombs, Malcolm D 2537
Coombs, Michele 2350
Coombs, Octavia Alexandra Elizabeth 2537
Coombs, Patricia Doreen 2162
Coombs, Paul Charles 2350
Coombs, Sarah 869
Coombs, Tessa Annette 1410
Coombs, Tracey Elizabeth 1410
Coombs, Victoria Margaret Daisy 869
Coombs, Vivien Gale 2350
Coombs, Walter Ramsden 2350
Cooper, Alexander Paton Astley 652
Cooper, Alexander Thomas 1932
Cooper, Alice Clare Antonia (Artemis) Opportune 2129
Cooper, Alice Teresa Mostyn 2010
Cooper, Angela Marjorie 653
Cooper, Anne Nicholson 2319
Cooper, Audrey Anne Jervoise 652
Cooper, Barbara Ann 1529
Cooper, Belinda Gay 654
Cooper, Belinda Jane 606
Cooper, Bobby Ryan 1006
Cooper, Burjor Sohrabji 1533
Cooper, Caroline Elisa Margaret 30
Cooper, Catherine Black 758
Cooper, Charles James Beauchamp Douglas 2319
Cooper, Charles Philip 1696
Cooper, Charmian Mary 2010
Cooper, Cheryl Ann 1450
Cooper, Christine Elisabeth 654
Cooper, Christopher Allan 597
Cooper, Christopher Colin 577
Cooper, Christopher Patrick Ashley 606
Cooper, Claudia 577
Cooper, Daisy 1786
Cooper, Daniel Alexander Westrow 655
Cooper, David Polwhele 622
Cooper, Derick Hetherington 2458
Cooper, Desmond Beauchamp 653
Cooper, Diana Geraldine 1098
Cooper, Donald Kenneth 1450
Cooper, Donald Stewart 758
Cooper, Doreen 2458
Cooper, Dorita Mae 1006
Cooper, Dorothy Frances Hendricka 654
Cooper, (Dorothy) Sarah 2252
Cooper, Dylan Michael 1450
Cooper, Edward James Ashley 606
Cooper, Edward Joshua 1098
Cooper, Elisabeth 2319
Cooper, Elizabeth Anne 2252
Cooper, Elizabeth Katherine 597
Cooper, Elizabeth Marie 758
Cooper, Elizabeth Mary 758
Cooper, Emma Lavinia 1932
Cooper, Felicity Anne 606
Cooper, George John 655
Cooper, Gerald 1448
Cooper, Gerald Nigel Astley 653
Cooper, Grace Irene 1521
Cooper, Harry Edward 1042
Cooper, Heather-Mary 758
Cooper, Helen Margaret 655
Cooper, Hester 1786
Cooper, Hugh Edward Keith 2877
Cooper, Ian Alexander Douglas 2329
Cooper, Isobel Rosalie 456
Cooper, James Alexander 2177
Cooper, James Paten 2319
Cooper, James Patrick Ashley 606
Cooper, Jane Alice 653
Cooper, Janet 1786
Cooper, Jason Alexander 597
Cooper, Jason Charles Duff Bede 2129
Cooper, Jean 655
Cooper, Joan 653
Cooper, Joanna Clare 1932
Cooper, John Craigmyle 2329
Cooper, Jonathan Francis Christie 225
Cooper, Jonquil Kate 2010
Cooper, Joseph 653, 1448
Cooper, Joyce Louise 1450
Cooper, Julia 577, 654
Cooper, Julie Rosalind Coghill 622
Cooper, Juliet Elizabeth 225
Cooper, Katherine Lois 597
Cooper, Katherine Teri Helen 655
Cooper, Kathleen 654
Cooper, Kenneth Lawrence 1450
Cooper, Kimball 653
Cooper, Laura Jean 882
Cooper, Louisa Clare 1932
Cooper, Lucinda Jane Coghill 622
Cooper, Lucy Elizabeth 653
Cooper, Margaret Elizabeth 2329
Cooper, Margaret Jane 2329
Cooper, Mary 2601
Cooper, (Mary) Elisabeth 655
Cooper, Mary Irene 1696
Cooper, Mary (Mollie) 2130
Cooper, Matilda 1786
Cooper, Matilda Alice 2877
Cooper, Maureen Isabel 577
Cooper, Michael Hetherington 2458
Cooper, Michael Joseph 1450
Cooper, Michael Keith 1006
Cooper, Minnie Margaret 652
Cooper, Neville John 1529
Cooper, Nicholas Keith 2877
Cooper, Nicola Elspeth 2177
Cooper, Nigel 456
Cooper, Patrick John Ashley 606
Cooper, Paul Andrew 1042
Cooper, Peter Charles 597, 758
Cooper, Peter Craigmyle 2329
Cooper, Peter S 2252
Cooper, Pirojbai 1533
Cooper, Pollyanna Fenella 225
Cooper, Randa 653
Cooper, Rebekah Jane 1448
Cooper, Richard Adrian 653
Cooper, Richard D B 1786
Cooper, Richard Gregory Christopher 655
Cooper, Robert 1006
Cooper, Robert James 2252
Cooper, Roy Charles 758
Cooper, Sally Muara Coghill 622
Cooper, Samuel Robert Paul 655
Cooper, Shaun David Coghill 622
Cooper, Sheila Mary 622
Cooper, Simon Christie 225
Cooper, Simon Richard Colin 577
Cooper, Sophie Maria 2010
Cooper, Stephen Frederick Louis 1521
Cooper, Stephen Jackson 1521
Cooper, Steven Alfonse 1450
Cooper, Susan Elizabeth Margaret 882
Cooper, Sydney Michael 655
Cooper, Tarquin Rupert Christopher Mostyn 2010
Cooper, Teresa Margaret 655
Cooper, Teri 655
Cooper, Thomas Hornby Graham 1932
Cooper, Thomas James Ashley 606
Cooper, Thomas William 1450
Cooper, Westrow Gerald Alan 655
Cooper, William Jeremy Daniel 655
Cooper, Zoe Catherine 758
Cooper-Key, Cara 2455
Cooper-Key, Cosmo 2455
Cooper-Key, Lorna Peggy Vyvyan 2455
Cooper-Key, Pandora Lorna Mary 2455
Coore, Anna-Claire 1782
Coore, Christopher George 1782
Coore, George Thomas 1782
Coote, Amber Danielle 659
Coote, Angela Mary 657
Coote, Anna 657
Coote, Anna May 657
Coote, Anne Georgiana 655
Coote, Barbara Jean 659
Coote, Belinda Jane 657
Coote, Bernadette Sophia 658
Coote, Catherine Alice 657
Coote, Cheryl 658
Coote, Chidley 657
Coote, Christopher Chenevix 658
Coote, Christopher Neil 658
Coote, David Brian 658
Coote, David Eyre 657
Coote, Deborah Michelle 657
Coote, Dermot Chenevix 658
Coote, Diana 2400
Coote, Dorothy 658
Coote, Eleanor Marianne 655
Coote, Elizabeth Helen 658
Coote, Elizabeth Joy 658
Coote, Ellen Jean 659
Coote, Emma Louise 658
Coote, Erica Lynette 658
Coote, Evan Blechynden 657
Coote, Gabrielle Alice 657
Coote, Glennis Susan 657
Coote, Inger Dahl 658
Coote, Jack Buchanan 657
Coote, Jack Eric 657
Coote, James Chenevix 658
Coote, Janet Patricia 657
Coote, Jennifer W 659
Coote, Joan May 658
Coote, Joanna Frances 658
Coote, Jody Susan 658
Coote, John Anthony Royds 657
Coote, John Edward 2400
Coote, John McDonald 657
Coote, John Robin 657
Coote, Jonathan Eyre 659
Coote, Jonathan Robert 657
Coote, Judith 657
Coote, Judith Sylvia 657
Coote, Justin Russell Royds 657
Coote, Kris Vollebrght 657
Coote, Linda Elizabeth 658
Coote, Logan Eyre 657
Coote, Lynne 658
Coote, Mary Patricia 657
Coote, Mavis Ellen 657
Coote, Michael Henry 657
Coote, Michael Philip John 659
Coote, Mona Rebecca 655
Coote, Nancy Bower-Playter 657
Coote, Nicholas Anthony 659
Coote, Nicholas Patrick 655
Coote, Noel Margaret Jephson 656
Coote, Patrick Shrubbs 658
Coote, Peter Mervyn Dahl 658
Coote, Peter Richard 659
Coote, Philip Arthur Cecil 657
Coote, Rhondda Beverly 657
Coote, Richard Anthony 658
Coote, Richard Eyre 657
Coote, Richard Philip 657
Coote, Robert Malcolm 657
Coote, Robin Maxwell 657
Coote, Roderic Norman 658
Coote, Rory Alasdair 655
Coote, Samuel Jack 659
Coote, Sarah Jane 659
Coote, Sarah Patricia 657
Coote, Sharon Ann 659
Coote, Sheila Mary 659
Coote, Stephanie 657
Coote, Stephen Arthur 658
Coote, Stephen Richard 657
Coote, Susan Barbara 658
Coote, Sylvia 657
Coote, Terence Eyre 659
Coote, Thomas Michael 659
Coote, Thomas Stanley Eyre 657
Coote, Timothy Charles 658
Coote, Timothy Philip 657
Coote, Tyler Lesley 657
Coote, Vanessa Jean 655
Coote, Wilbur 657
Coote, William Richard 658
Copage, Christopher 147
Copage, Lucinda Anne 147
Cope, Annabel Margaret 977
Cope, Djemila Lovell 659
Cope, G V (Charles) 977
Copeland, Elizabeth Margaret 2400
Copeman, Charlotte Anne 1587
Copeman, James Robert 1587
Copeman, Michael George Auchel 594
Copeman, Rachel Mary 1587
Copeman, Robert Charles 1587
Copleston, Elizabeth 2621
Copleston, Richard Guillemard 2621
Coplestone-Boughey, Clare Louise 330
Coplestone-Boughey, Gillian Beatrice 330
Coplestone-Boughey, John Fenton 330
Coplestone-Boughey, Katharine Elizabeth 330
Coplestone-Boughey, Mary 330
Coplestone-Boughey, Robert Fenton 330
Coplestone-Boughey, William Fenton 330
Copley, Alice Florence 1766
Copley, Anthony 1766
Copley, Bridget Griselda 1766
Copley, Diana Mary 1766, 2302
Copley, Jack Anthony Talbot 1766
Copley, Robert Anthony 1766, 2302
Copner, Margaret Olive 2978
Coppez, Henri Jean-Patric 1584
Coppez, Jean-Marc Guy 1584
Coppez, Jeannet Elizabeth 1584
Coppock, Andrew Joseph 2022
Coppock, David Michael 2022
Coppock, Michael Thomas 2022
Coppock, Sarah Louise 2022
Coppock, Susan Ann 2022
Copsey, Derek 1362
Copsey, Jenifer Clare 1362
Copsey, Kate 1363
Copsey, Thomas 1362
Copus, Kathleen Ann 491
Coradi, Andrew 1195
Coradi, Charlotte Elizabeth 1195
Coradi, Cregg 1195
Coradi, Daniel 1195
Coradi, Kenneth 1195
Coradi, Robert 1195
Corbally, Bernard Humphreys Clement 284
Corbally, Colin George Eric 284
Corbally, Erica Mary Josephine 284
Corbally, Linda Clare Cecilia 284
Corbally, Ruth Ida Mary 284
Corbally, Simon Herbert Arthur 284
Corbally Stourton, Beatrice Cicely 2025
Corbally Stourton, Edward Richard Plantagenet 2025
Corbally Stourton, Lavinia 2025
Corbally Stourton, Nicholas Simon 2025
Corbally Stourton, Nigel Edward 2025
Corbally Stourton, Patrick Henry 2025
Corbally Stourton, Vanessa Mary 2025
Corbett, Alexander James 706
Corbett, Benjamin Edward Thomas 2166
Corbett, Camilla Louise 466
Corbett, Catherine 30, 2461
Corbett, Claire 2461
Corbett, Clare Barbara 706
Corbett, Daisy Angelica 2029
Corbett, Doran Elizabeth Ann 2461
Corbett, Edmund Uvedale 826
Corbett, Edward John Patrick 2029
Corbett, George Alan Cameron 2462
Corbett, George Miles 1906
Corbett, Hannah 2166
Corbett, Janet Glencora 1906
Corbett, Jason William Polson Cameron 2461
Corbett, Jennifer Anne 1762
Corbett, Joanne Gwyn Alice Cameron 2461
Corbett, (Jonathan Arthur) Cameron 2461
Corbett, Joseph Mervyn 2461
Corbett, Laura 826
Corbett, Lucy Miranda 466
Corbett, Madeline Janet 1906
Corbett, Melanie June 2029
Corbett, (Patricia) Clare 826
Corbett, Patricia Elisabeth 466
Corbett, Patrick Michael 1762
Corbett, (Patrick) William Uvedale 826
Corbett, Peter-John Stewart 2029
Corbett, Poppy Ann 2029
Corbett, Robert Anthony 2166
Corbett, Robert Cameron 2462
Corbett, Sarah 2166
Corbett, Sarah Angela Josephine 2166
Corbett, Sebastian Antony 2461
Corbett, Simon Mark 466
Corbett, Soay Mairi Cameron 2461
Corbett, Stephen 1906
Corbett, Tom 2166
Corbishley, Benjamin James 34
Corbishley, Jonathan Piers 34
Corbishley, Linda Rosemary Anne 34
Corbishley, Rupert Charles 34
Corby, Christina 2300
Corby, Diana 2300
Corby, Roshnara 2300
Corby, Victoria Rose Charlotte 2300
Corby, William John 2300
Corby-Tuech, Catherine 2005
Corby-Tuech, Jacques Max Gillachrist 2005
Corby-Tuech, Michel Jean Jer(me 2005
Corby-Tuech, Poppy Colette 2005
Corcoran, Alexander Martin Desmond 49
Corcoran, Dale 2009
Corcoran, Judith Cynthia Aline 49
Corcoran, Mardi Anne 2009
Corcoran, Sandra 2009
Corcoran, Stephanie Jeanette 2009
Corcuera, Andres 1187
Corcuera, Camilla 1187
Corcuera, Carmen 1187
Corcuera, Felipe 1187
Corcuera, Fernando 1187
Corcuera, Jaime Marcos Pedro 1187
Corcuera, Juan Fernando Pedro 1187
Corcuera, Karl Sebastian 1187
Corcuera, Myriam Adelhaid Hugoline Omnes Sancti Marcus d'Aviano Melchiora 1187
Corcuera, Paloma 1187
Corcuera, Pedro Johannes 1187
Cordeaux, Charles Nicholas 196
Cordeaux, Elfrida Cicely 196
Cordeaux, Heather Claire 196
Cordeaux, Margaret Elizabeth 196
Cordeaux, Mark Edward 196
Cordeaux, Martin Bennett 196
Cordeaux, Michael Robert 196
Cordingley, Emma Geraldine Anne 2295
Cordingley, Gerald Thomas 2295
Cordingley, Jennifer Rose 2295
Cordingley, Katie Madeleine 2295
Cordingley, Venetia Ruth 2295
Cordle, Alexander Anthony 269
Cordle, Anthony John 1872
Cordle, Camilla Ann 269
Cordle, Hugo Andrew 269
Cordle, Jessica Grace Rosanne 1872
Cordle, Lucia Georgina Diana 1872
Cordle, Miranda Mary 1872
Cordle, Rachel Venetia 2302
Cordle, Rupert Alister Peter John 269, 2302
Cordle, Sophie Jane 2302
Cordy-Simpson, Angus John 653
Cordy-Simpson, Roderick Alexander 653
Cordy-Simpson, Virginia Rosemary 653
Cordy-Simpson, Zoë 653
Cork, Christopher Michael 1205
Cork, Deborah Katherine Louise 1205
Cork, Elizabeth Lily 1205
Cork, Ronald Stephen 1205
Corke, Anthea Lynda 2113
Corke, Cicely Catherine 364
Corke, Clive Edward Theo 2113
Corke, Daisy Elizabeth 993
Corke, Elizabeth Anne 993
Corke, Ella Clementine 993
Corke, Emma Lucy 364
Corke, Georgiana Phoebe 364
Corke, Hilary 364
Corke, Imogen Sally 993
Corke, Jaimie Coltart 993
Corke, Lynda Anne 2113
Corke, Madeleine Olga 364
Corke, Milo Jaimie 993
Corke, Philip Clive 2113
Corke, Shauna 2113
Corke, Shirley Frances 364
Corke, Sophie 364
Corke, William Edward Orlando 364
Corkey, Elizabeth Phyllis Mary 1012
Corkey, Jonathan Whitla Glover 1012
Corkey, Patrick William Isaac 1012
Corkran, Alexandra Frances Louise 76
Corkran, Claire Melanie 76
Corkran, Jane Melanie 76
Corkran, Richard Seymour 76
Cormack, Gwendoline Rita Jean 778
Cormack, Irvine 1787
Cormack, Valerie Jean 1787
Cornelius, Deborah Caswell Oliphant 2049
Cornelius, Katherine Caswell Oliphant 2049
Cornelius, Philippa Mary 1918
Cornelius, Richard Alan 1918
Cornelius, Stuart William Guy 1918
Cornell, Harry R 3081
Cornell, Lucy Elizabeth 2405
Cornell, Mark 2405

D

E

Emo, Caterina 2074
Emo, Gabriele Filippo 2074
Emo, Giorgio 2074
Emo, Giovanni 2074
Emo, Madeleine Maria 2074
Emo, Olimpia 2074
Emo, Pietro Antonio 2074
Emo, Rufina 2074
Empson, Alice 2353
Empson, Elizabeth Marianne 2353
Empson, Lucy 2353
Empson, Simon 2353
Empson, Victoria 2353
Emsden, Annabel Julia Clare 3020
Emsden, Brian Hugh Clare 3020
Emsden, Clare Emma Margaret 3020
Emsden, Julia Margaret 3020
Emslie, Derek Robert Alexander 986
Emslie, Elizabeth Jane 986
Emslie, (George) Nigel Hannington 986
Emslie, Heather Ann 986
Emslie, Lilias Ann 986
Emslie, Richard Hannington 986
Endall, Melissa Frances 491
Endall, Rodney Peter 491
Endresen, Anthony Finn 2197
Endresen, Isobel 2197
Endresen, Klaus 2197
Endresen, Kristian Gyamfi 2197
Endresen, Per Kojo 2197
Enfield Booth, Charles 312
Engel, Patricia Nesta 1960
Engel, Sarah Rosamund 161
Engeler, Helen Marina 1123
Engeler, Peter 1123
Engeler, Rebekah Freda 1123
Engeler, Sarah Thérèse 1123
England, Alexandra Sarah Camilla 1187
England, Caroline Margaret Fountayne 200
England, David 1187
England, Jane Anne Fountayne 200
England, John Dacre Fountayne 200
English, Georgina Frances 2058
English, Joseph Edward 1564
English, Lilian Mary 1564
English, Lucy Caroline 1450
English, Mopsa Mary 1564
English, Patricia Mary 2058
English, Philip Ernest Ricardo 2058
English, Philippa Katharine 2058
English, Richard Douglas 1564
English, Thomas Eliot 1564
English, Willard Wakeman 1450
Ennor, Charlotte Annabella 2367
Ennor, Daniel Lewis 2367
Ennor, Julian George 2367
Enright, Iva Margaret 3098
Enslin, Camilla Fiona 3086
Enslin, Christopher Roche 3086
Enslin, Eda Daphne 3086
Enslin, Ian Boyd 3086
Enslin, Michael Roche 3086
Enthoven, Alexandra Louise 685
Enthoven, Andrew James 685
Enthoven, Belinda Margaret 891
Enthoven, Dorothea Olivia 685
Enthoven, Fiona Valerie 685
Enthoven, James John 891
Enthoven, John Christopher 685
Enthoven, John Henry William 685
Enthoven, Penelope Margaret 891
Enthoven, Sally 685
Enthoven, Stephen Andrew 685
Enthoven, Thomas Samuel Donald 685
Entwistle, Melissa Ann 345
Entwistle, Scott Alan 345
Enzensberger, Ann 2368
Enzensberger, Anne Jennifer 2368
Enzensberger, Janet 2368
Enzensberger, Joseph 2368
Epps, Pamela Anne 1963
Epsom, Bryan L B 1970
Epsom, Guy Bryan 1970
Epsom, Henry Edmund 1135
Epsom, Hugh David 1970
Epsom, Juliette Nancy 1135
Epsom, Mary 1970
Epsom, Paul Robert 1970
Epstein, Edwina Maureen 2692
Epstein, (Joshua) Philip 2692
Erasmus, Anthony Charles 2066
Erasmus, Martina Kathleen 2066
Ericson, Daniel 3013
Erith, Charles R 456
Erith, Jemima Barbara 456
Erith, Laura Catherine 456
Ernest, Charlotte Maria 992
Ernest, Fenella Jane 992
Ernest, John 992
Erridge, Alison Ann 251
Erridge, Juliet Clare 251
Erridge, Simon 251
Errington, Andrew Davenport 993
Errington, Anne 993
Errington, (Anne) Jacqueline 993
Errington, Catherine Ann 993
Errington, Charles Stuart 993
Errington, David Grant 993
Errington, Diana Kathleen Forbes 993
Errington, Frederick Charles 993
Errington, Isabel Jane Davenport 993
Errington, John Davenport 993
Errington, Molly Wilhelmina 993
Errington, Nicholas David 993
Errington, Nicole 993
Errington, Prue 993
Errington, Robin Davenport 993
Errington, Stuart Grant 993
Errington, Timothy Grant 993
Erroll, Elizabeth 997
Erskine, Abigail Mia Thérèse 1860
Erskine, Aleda Grace Elizabeth 998
Erskine, Alexander 413
Erskine, Alexander Capel 1860
Erskine, Alexander David 414, 441, 1860
Erskine, Alexander Fitzgerald 416
Erskine, Alexander William Ian Marshall 415
Erskine, Alice 2451
Erskine, Alice Fiona 792
Erskine, Alice Maria 415
Erskine, Alison Gillian 414
Erskine, Alistair John 1860
Erskine, Alistair Robert 1860
Erskine, Andrew John Hodsoll 1860
Erskine, Andrew Stuart 416
Erskine, Angela Jane 416
Erskine, Angus Bruce 414
Erskine, Ann 998
Erskine, Anne Nicola 415
Erskine, Anthony John 417
Erskine, Archibald Walter Forbes 1860
Erskine, Audrey Rosemary 998
Erskine, Ava 417
Erskine, Belinda Ann 1860
Erskine, Belinda Anne 2045
Erskine, Belinda Mary Rosalind 1860
Erskine, Benjamin David 1860
Erskine, Beth Rosemary 1858
Erskine, Bronwyn Rebecca 417
Erskine, Bryan Andrew 1858
Erskine, Byron Thomas 416
Erskine, Carina 415
Erskine, Carl 415
Erskine, Caroline Mary 1313, 1860
Erskine, Carolyn 417
Erskine, Caspar James Pears 1860
Erskine, Catherine Ann 416
Erskine, Catherine 414
Erskine, Catherine Evelyn 1858
Erskine, Catherine Jean 998
Erskine, Chad Esmé 416
Erskine, Charles Malcolm 998
Erskine, Charles Nelson 416
Erskine, Charles Seymour 1858
Erskine, Charlotte 1860
Erskine, Charlotte Catherine Lucinda 413
Erskine, Charlotte Irene 998
Erskine, Charlotte Louise Annabelle 416
Erskine, Christine Maria 1858
Erskine, Claude Anthony 2753
Erskine, Claude Mark 2753
Erskine, Clive Patrick Monteith 998
Erskine, David Alexander John 1860
Erskine, David Boyd 416
Erskine, David Hervey 1313, 1860
Erskine, David Monteith 998
Erskine, David Stuart 417
Erskine, Debbie 1860
Erskine, Deborah Jane 415
Erskine, Diana Margery 2753
Erskine, Dominic James 998
Erskine, Donna 417
Erskine, Duncan FitzGerald 415
Erskine, Edmund Alexander 1860
Erskine, Elaine Joy 1858
Erskine, Eleanor Kathryn 1860
Erskine, Elizabeth (Elizavete Fyodorovna) 417
Erskine, Elizabeth Mary 998
Erskine, Emily Clare 1860
Erskine, Euan Stewart 1860
Erskine, Felix Benjamin 1860
Erskine, Fiona Sue 1860
Erskine, Florence Elizabeth 417
Erskine, Francis David Monteith 998
Erskine, Frederick Alastair 413
Erskine, Geordie James Donald 414
Erskine, George Lindley 416
Erskine, (George) Edward 415
Erskine, George St Vincent 416
Erskine, Gerald Conrad 417
Erskine, Gillian Christian 998
Erskine, Gillian Margaret 1860
Erskine, Gladys Evelyn 415
Erskine, Gratney Evelyn 1858
Erskine, Gratney Pierrepont 1858
Erskine, Gregory Bryce 1858
Erskine, Guy Francis 998
Erskine, Gyneth Alice 416
Erskine, Hamish Robert Coll Charles 415
Erskine, Harriet Alice 1860
Erskine, Harry Charles David 414
Erskine, Helen M 2450
Erskine, Henry Thomas Alexander 413
Erskine, Hilary Diana Cecil 413, 2298
Erskine, Hugh Walter Bushby 1858
Erskine, Ian Ross 417
Erskine, Imogen Felicia Anne 1860
Erskine, Isabel Katherine 1860
Erskine, James Alexander 1860
Erskine, James Dunbar 998
Erskine, James Francis 998
Erskine, James Malcolm Kenneth 414
Erskine, Jamie William 2450
Erskine, Janet Madeline 417
Erskine, Janine Gaye 1858
Erskine, Jean Meriel 416
Erskine, Jennifer 414
Erskine, Jennifer Lynn 416
Erskine, Jill 1860
Erskine, Joan Mary 1860
Erskine, (Joan Mary) Thérèse Frances 1860
Erskine, Joanna Christian 414
Erskine, Joanne Margaret 1858
Erskine, John Andrew 417
Erskine, John David 417
Erskine, John Steuart 417
Erskine, Jonathan 415
Erskine, Jonathon Montague 2753
Erskine, Joseph Christian 417
Erskine, Julia Rosemary 414
Erskine, Julian Benedict 417
Erskine, Juliet 998
Erskine, Karen Lynn 417
Erskine, Katherine Shawford 441, 1860
Erskine, Kathleen 998
Erskine, Kathrina Jane 998
Erskine, Keith Malcolm 414
Erskine, Kellie Knox 1858
Erskine, Keryn Maree 1858
Erskine, Laura Anne 1860
Erskine, LeAnn 417
Erskine, Leslie 417
Erskine, Lona Diane 416
Erskine, Lucia 2451
Erskine, Lucy Emmeline 1860
Erskine, Malcolm David Vernon 998
Erskine, Malcolm Harry 2298
Erskine, Malcolm John 415
Erskine, Margaret Ann 416
Erskine, Marilyn-Gene 416
Erskine, Mary 1857
Erskine, Mary Caroline 998
Erskine, Mary Douglas 1858
Erskine, Melanie 416
Erskine, Michael John 1860
Erskine, Mireille 998
Erskine, Montagu John 413
Erskine, Neil Steuart 417
Erskine, Oliver Stewart 1860
Erskine, Pamela Ann 1858
Erskine, Patrizia Pandora 998
Erskine, Paul Anthony 2753
Erskine, Paula Swanzie 416
Erskine, Peter Alexander 1860
Erskine, Philip Neil 415, 792, 998
Erskine, Rachel 413
Erskine, Rachel Diana Mary 417
Erskine, Rachel Joanna 417
Erskine, Robert John 1860
Erskine, Robert Keith 415, 946
Erskine, Robert William Hervey 1860
Erskine, Robin David 1860
Erskine, Robyn Ann 1858
Erskine, Rose Agnes Jessie 415
Erskine, Roy Alistair 415
Erskine, Sarah Laurel 417
Erskine, Sarah Margaret 416
Erskine, Sharyl LeAnn 417
Erskine, Sheelah Katherine 1858
Erskine, Simon David 998
Erskine, Stuart Graeme 416
Erskine, Susan 416
Erskine, Susan Eileen 998
Erskine, Susan Morag 415, 946
Erskine, Tessa Victoria 998
Erskine, Thomas Edward 417
Erskine, Thomas Georges 998
Erskine, Thomas Gerald 1860
Erskine, (Thomas) Peter Neil 998
Erskine, (Thomas) Struan 998
Erskine, Timothy Harold 2753
Erskine, Victoria Margaret 999
Erskine, William 998
Erskine, Yvonne Constance 1858
Erskine-Hill, Alice 1000
Erskine-Hill, Christine Alison 1000, 1548
Erskine-Hill, David 1000
Erskine-Hill, David John 1000
Erskine-Hill, Gwen Carolyne 1000
Erskine-Hill, Henry James 1000
Erskine-Hill, Kirsty Rose 999
Erskine-Hill, Lucy Diana Elspeth 1000
Erskine-Hill, Mark Colville 1000
Erskine-Hill, Myra Elizabeth 1000
Erskine-Hill, Robert Benjamin 999
Erskine-Murray, (Arthur) Sydney Elibank 968
Erskine-Murray, Antonia 966
Erskine-Murray, Clare Ruth 968
Erskine-Murray, Florence Duncan 968
Erskine-Murray, Isabella Valerie Elibank 966
Erskine-Murray, Jenny Mary Margaret 968
Erskine-Murray, Patrick Elibank 968
Erskine-Murray, Robert Francis 966
Erskine-Murray, Tim(othy) Alexander Elibank 966
Erskine-Tulloch, Charlotte Lucy 7
Erskine-Tulloch, Elspeth Jane 7
Erskine-Tulloch, Margaret Helen 7
Ervin, Craig Douglas 2103
Ervin, Henry Nichols 1125
Ervin, Kathleen Elizabeth 1125
Ervin, Kelly Patricia 2103
Escardo, Florencio Enrique 1542
Escardo, Florencio Julian 1542
Escardo, Irene 1542
Escardo, Monica Lena 1542
Escardo, Pilar 1542
Eschauzier, Hilda Susan 2380
Eschauzier, Johanna Elisabeth 2380
Eschauzier, Pierre George 2380
Escombe, Alan Rowland Lingard 2351
Escombe, Myra Patricia 2351
Esmonde, Aileen Mary 1003
Esmonde, Aisling Margaret Pamela Grattan 1002
Esmonde, Alice Mary Grattan 1003
Esmonde, Alngelda Barbara Mary Grattan 1003
Esmonde, Anne Caroline Grattan 1003
Esmonde, Anthony James Grattan 1003
Esmonde, Bartholomew Thomas Grattan 1003
Esmonde, Donal 1003
Esmonde, Eira Margaret Antonia 1003, 1805
Esmonde, Eithne Marion Grattan 1003
Esmonde, Eugene James 1003
Esmonde, Eugene Patrick Mackenzie 1003
Esmonde, Godfrey Christian 1003
Esmonde, Grania Adelaide 1003
Esmonde, Harold William Grattan 1003
Esmonde, Jennifer Ann 1003
Esmonde, Karen Maria Grattan 1003
Esmonde, Kevin Harold 1003
Esmonde, Lisa Marion Grattan 1003
Esmonde, Niamh Pauline Grattan 1002
Esmonde, Norah Marcia 1003
Esmonde, Pamela Mary 1003
Esmonde, Patrick 1003
Esmonde, Pauline Loretto 1002
Esmonde, Peter Witham 1003
Esmonde, Richard Anthony Grattan 1003
Esmonde, Sean Vincent Grattan 1002
Esplen, Fiona Mary 1004
Esplen, Mary Caroline 1004
Esplen, Wendy Anne 1004
Esplen, William John Harry 1004
Essayan, Geraldine ('Dina') 1254
Essayan, Joanna Consuelo 1255
Essayan, Martin Sarkis 1255
Essayan, Michael 1254
Esse, Barnaby Samuel Hare 1310
Esse, Elizabeth Florence 1310
Esse, William Nicholas 1310
Esselen, Delene Ruth 2928
Essex, Dinah Ross 2664
Essington-Boulton, Crystal 2482
Essington-Boulton, James Clive 2482
Essington-Boulton, Nicolette 2482
Estcourt, Adrian Charles 2973
Estcourt, Angus James 2973
Estcourt, Charlotte Pamela 2973
Estcourt, Edward James 2973
Estcourt, Edward Rory Charles 2973
Estcourt, Jennifer Clare 2973
Estcourt, Judith Mary 2503
Estcourt, Pamela 2973
Estcourt, Suzannah Jane 2973
Estep, Crystal Lila 744
Estep, Justin Chase 744
Estep, Lila Jane 744
Esterhuyse, Francois 2906
Esterhuyse, Sarah Jane 2906
Estevan, Annabel Marguerite Pamela 2216
Estevan, Orland 2216
Estlick, Daphne Alice 1121
Estlick, Nigel John Lincoln 1121
Estlick, Robin Monckton 1121
Estridge, Christopher Ivan 523
Estridge, Christopher Robert Ivan 523
Estridge, Lydia Margaret 523
Estridge, Patricia 523
Estripeau, Natalie Isabelle 2062
Estripeau, Tamsin Jame 2062
Etchelles, Edward Evans 3053
Etchelles, Wendy Vivian 3053
Etheridge, Albert George 1035
Etheridge, Charles Robert Guthrie 1583
Etheridge, Jane 1035
Etheridge, Jane Guthrie 1583
Etheridge, Lucy Kate 1583
Etheridge, Mark Charles 1583
Etheridge, Susan 1035
Etive, Ann Honoria Mary 1919
Etive, Wayne 1919
Eubank, Arthur 1446
Eubank, Henrietta Nora 1446
Eugster, Alexandra Marcia Gabrielle 1173
Eugster, Julia Clare Elizabeth 1173
Eugster, Maximilian Brian Michael 1173
Eugster, Maxine Marjorie 1173
Eugster, Timothy Basil Edward 1173
Eustace, Alicia Mary 2126
Eustace, Alys 2145
Eustace, Cassandra Mary 2145
Eustace, Catherine Helena 2145
Eustace, David James 2126
Eustace, Dorothy Anne 2126
Eustace, Emily Anne 2145
Eustace, Gay Rosemary 2126
Eustace, Henry Alan 2126
Eustace, James Maurice Percy 2126
Eustace, Margaret Alison 2145
Eustace, Thomas Robert Hales 2126
Evans, Adelaide Grace 101
Evans, Alexander Kenelm Singleton Cayley 535
Evans, Alexander Peter Sommerville 1534
Evans, Alexander Richard Andvord 2018
Evans, Alice Valerie Katherine 2292
Evans, Alison Daphne 456
Evans, Alison Margaret 2919
Evans, Allan Ashley 491
Evans, Amber 283
Evans, (Andrew) Michael 1401
Evans, Annabel Celia Dorothy 329
Evans, Annette Matilda 2505

F

Frederick, Janie Mary 1104
Frederick, Joan Olive 1104
Frederick, Joanne 1104
Frederick, John 1104
Frederick, John Peter Wynyard 1104
Frederick, Jonathan Denley 1104
Frederick, Laura Anne 1104
Frederick, Lia 1104
Frederick, Lourdes Mercedes 1104
Frederick, Luciana 1104
Frederick, Margaret Lilian 1104
Frederick, Maria Claudia 1104
Frederick, Maria de los Milagros 1104
Frederick, Marina 1104
Frederick, Marta Rose 1104
Frederick, Melba 1104
Frederick, Oscar Geoffrey 1104
Frederick, Rae Jervis 1104
Frederick, Rafael Daniel 1104
Frederick, Ricardo 1104
Frederick, Richard Frank 1104
Frederick, Roger Mansfield 1104
Frederick, Rosa 1104
Frederick, Rosemary 1103
Frederick, Sarah Ann 1104
Frederick, Sonia 1104
Frederick, Thomas Russell 1104
Frederick, Valerie Anne 1104
Fredrick, Camilla Elizabeth 1142
Fredrick, Christopher St John 1142
Free, Douglas Michael 781
Free, Harriet Susan Anne 781
Freeland, Caroline Mary 1914
Freeland, Denby Elizabeth Hay 1586
Freeland, Dorothy Louisa 2987
Freeland, (Florence) Elizabeth Hay 1586
Freeland, George Warren 1586
Freeland, Kimberley 1586
Freeland, Nohea Edward 1586
Freeman, Alison Hilary 1935
Freeman, Amanda Jane 2249
Freeman, Anthony Tresiddar 2249
Freeman, Bernard Keith 2519
Freeman, Charles Philip Broke 2096
Freeman, Chloe Anne 2249
Freeman, Christopher Scott Max 1105
Freeman, Cindy 2519
Freeman, Cordelia Mary Antonia 2096
Freeman, Dennis John 2009
Freeman, Eileen 1105
Freeman, Gabriella Eve 1279
Freeman, Heather 2249
Freeman, Hilary Jane 2096
Freeman, Isabella 2096
Freeman, Jack 2519
Freeman, Jennifer Margaret 1105
Freeman, John Glover 1935
Freeman, John Lynn 2519
Freeman, Kim Donna 2519
Freeman, Marjorie 2519
Freeman, Michael Edmund Piers 2249
Freeman, Mildred 2519
Freeman, Oliver Franklin 2519
Freeman, Patricia 1105
Freeman, Piers Anthony 2249
Freeman, Richard 2519
Freeman, Richard Andrew 1279
Freeman, Ronald Keith 2519
Freeman, Susanna Eve 1279
Freeman, Thomas 2096
Freeman, Thomas Michael Percy 1935
Freeman, William Griffin Henry 1935
Freeman, Winefride Alice 2096
Freeman-Attwood, Emily (Emmy) Magda 2458
Freeman-Attwood, Julian 2458
Freeman-Attwood, Marigold Diana Sneyd 2144
Freeman-Grenville, Bevil David Stewart Chandos 1602
Freeman-Grenville, Teresa Mary 1602
Freeman-Mitford, Sarah Georgina 2382
Freemec, Cyril 2408
Freemec, Diane Loraine 2408
Freemec, Morah Elizabeth 2408
Freke, Kate Emily 2067
Fremantle, Adam 676
Fremantle, Alice Marian 675, 2768
Fremantle, Alison 676
Fremantle, Anna Elizabeth 675
Fremantle, Anne Marie Huth 676, 1525
Fremantle, Caroline Mary 676
Fremantle, Charles Alan 676
Fremantle, Charles Ereld Patrick 675
Fremantle, Christopher Nicholas 676
Fremantle, Christopher Richard 675
Fremantle, Edmund Richard 676
Fremantle, Edna Maud 676
Fremantle, Edward Vigant Eardley 675
Fremantle, Edward Walgrave 677
Fremantle, Elizabeth Ann 674
Fremantle, Emily Teresa Alice 675
Fremantle, Francesca Mary 676
Fremantle, Gillian 676
Fremantle, Gillian Daphine 675
Fremantle, Gloria Jean Irene 677
Fremantle, Henry John 677
Fremantle, Holly 676
Fremantle, (Honor) Diana 565, 675
Fremantle, Hugh Dominic Christopher 677
Fremantle, James Justin 676
Fremantle, Jane Pamela 676
Fremantle, John Godfrey 675
Fremantle, Katharine Dorothy Honor 677
Fremantle, Katherine Fiona 675
Fremantle, Louisa Clare 677
Fremantle, Mark Thomas 675
Fremantle, Mary Grace 676
Fremantle, Patience Ann 735
Fremantle, Patricia Mary 676
Fremantle, Paul Zachary 676
Fremantle, Peter Thomas 676
Fremantle, Richard Christian Wynne 676
Fremantle, Richard William 676
Fremantle, Robin Patrick 565, 675
Fremantle, Samuel Patrick 676
Fremantle, Sara E 677
Fremantle, Sarah Maud 675
Fremantle, Serena Katherine 675
Fremantle, Stephen Antony 676
Fremantle, Susan 677
Fremantle, Susan Delia Aiton 676
Fremantle, Sydney Walter 676
Fremantle, Thomas David 675, 2768
Fremantle, Thomas Francis Henry 674
Fremantle, Timothy Charles 676
Fremantle, (Valerie Rosamond) Christina 676
French, Abigail Digna Joanna 788
French, Alexander James Charles 786
French, Alexander Matthew 3081
French, Alice Cecilia 788
French, Amelia Mary Katherine 1646
French, Anna-Louise Rosemary 1494
French, Anne Rosemary 1103
French, Anne Rosemary Maurice 1646
French, Annis Evelyn 3081
French, Arthur Edmund 788, 1722
French, Charles Peter 788
French, Charlotte Imogen 3081
French, Charlotte Mary 788, 1722
French, Christine 787
French, Christopher 2998
French, Christopher John 788
French, Claudia Rosemary 788
French, Coleen 787
French, David 3081
French, Denise Shirley 787
French, Dominic Arthur 788
French, Dominick George Maitland 1646
French, Edmund Peter 788
French, Eleanor Winifred 3081
French, Emily Mary Lucia 788
French, Francis Martin 1494
French, (Fulke) Charles Arthur John 786
French, Gerald Hugh 788
French, Henry Kenneth Robert 3081
French, Hilda Felicity 788
French, Jacqueline 2998
French, James Philip 788
French, Joan Patricia 1323
French, John 787
French, Joseph Miles French 1646
French, Julia Mary 786
French, Julia Winfred 788
French, Kerynne Diane 787
French, Kirsty Elizabeth 1494
French, Lance de Freyne 787
French, Lavinia Mary 788
French, Margaret Annis 3081
French, Mary Frances 788
French, Matthew 3081
French, Maurice Aloysius 788
French, Miles Arthur Maitland 1103, 1646
French, Miranda 788
French, Nanette 787
French, Naomi Hilda 1103, 1646
French, Nicola Mary 3081
French, Patrick Dominick Fitzstephen Jude 786
French, Patrick Rollo 788
French, Philip John 788
French, Raphael Maitland 1103, 1646
French, Richard Charles 788
French, Richard Maurice 788
French, Rosemary 1494
French, Sacha 788
French, Sarah Anne 3081
French, Sheelin Deirdre 786
French, Suszanna Frances 788
French, Thomas Tenzin 788
French, Thomas Weatherhead 3081
French, William 2998
French, (William) Rory Francis 786
French, William Sholt 3081
Frere, Anabel 2653
Frere, Jeremy Alexander Keble White 2653
Frere, Martin Adrian 2653
Frere, Patricia Gwyn 96
Frere, Toni Elaine 2653
Frere-Cook, Christine Margaret 394
Frere-Cook, David Bartle Cracroft 394
Frere-Cook, Guy Weston 394
Frere-Cook, Hugh Leonard 394
Frere-Cook, Jennifer Jane 394
Frere-Cook, Joanna Christine 394
Frere-Cook, Piers Gervis 394
Frere-Cook, Rosemary Grace 394
Frere-Cook, Sarah Jane 394
Frere-Cook, Simon Aubrey Cracroft 394
Freret, Julian Payne 1439
Freshman, Roger David Barry 206
Freshwater, Andrew 179
Freshwater, Clive 179
Freshwater, Duncan 179
Freshwater, Jane Elizabeth Mary 1404
Freshwater, Jonathan 179
Freshwater, Martin Walter James 1404
Freshwater, Michael David Latimer 1404
Freshwater, Sally 179
Frewen, Anita Louise 2577
Frewen, Antonia 2577
Frewen, Charles Grey Justin 2577
Frewen, Jennie Selina 2577
Frewen, Jerome Fergus d'Estoutville 2577
Frewen, Jonathan Briscoe Moreton 2577
Frewen, Mark K 2869
Frewen, Matthew 2869
Frewen, Robert Edward Jerome 1092, 2577
Frewen, Rolline Charlotte 1092, 2577
Frewen, Samantha Joy 2869
Frewen, Sarah Joy 2869
Frewer, Amanda Mary 1414
Frewer, Matthew 1414
Freyberg, Annabel Pauline 1106
Freyberg, Christina Marie-Gabriel 1106
Freyberg, Ivry Perronelle Katharine 1106
Frick, Adrian Bruno 2404
Frick, Geneviève Ann 2404
Frick, Max 2600
Frick, Rainer 2404
Frick, Sarah Jane 2600
Fried, Ben 1352
Fried, Elizabeth Grace 1352
Fried, Mark 1352
Fried, Sochi Bess 1352
Friedberger, Joanna Mary 2883
Friedberger, John Peter William 2883
Friedberger, Lucinda Jane 2883
Friedberger, Richard Mark 2883
Friedman, Eli 201
Friend, Alexander James 1328
Friend, Georgina Mary Flavia 1328
Friend, James Irvine Hinchliffe 1328
Friend, Josephine Lilian 1516
Friend, Nicholas Andrew Irvine 1328
Friend, Sanda Susan 1328
Friesen, Alexander Christian Edward 531
Friesen, Hero Arabella Mairi Elizabeth 531
Friman, Dorothy Mary 2518
Friman, Magnus Carl Olof 2518
Frisch, Tom 2507
Frisch, Wendy 2507
Frith, Lisa Marie 2699
Frith, Paul Laut 2699
Froggatt, Alison Clare 1726
Froggatt, Eric Charles 1726
Froggatt, Hayley Louise 1726
Froggatt, Ian Wilson 1726
Froggatt, Janet 1726
Froggatt, Michele 1726
Froggatt, Nigel Thomas 1726
Froggatt, Peter Webley 1726
Froggatt, Richard Wilson 1726
Frost, Alexander Fortescue 2209
Frost, Angela Judith 441
Frost, Carina Mary Gabrielle 2090
Frost, Carolyn Ann 2209
Frost, Charlotte Birgitta 2047, 2778
Frost, David Paradine 2090
Frost, Edward 2209
Frost, George Paradine 2090
Frost, Melanie Alaire 441
Frost, Miles Paradine 2090
Frost, Roger Harry Gosta 2048
Frost, Samuel Allan 441
Frost, Samuel Timothy Einar 2047
Frost, Thomas Alexander Fortescue 2209
Frost, Timothy Oliver 2047, 2778
Frost, Wilfred Paradine 2090
Frost, William 2209
Frost, Zachary Oliver Gustav 2047
Frost Pennington, Ewan Patrick 2351
Frost Pennington, Fraser Robert 2351
Frost Pennington, Iona Arabel 2351
Frost Pennington, Isla Rose 2351
Frost Pennington, Peter Edward 2351
Fry, Adam 848
Fry, Alan George 1010
Fry, Daniel 848
Fry, Edward James 603
Fry, Emily Catherine 2519
Fry, Emma Katherine 603
Fry, Georgina Sarah 603
Fry, Jillian Margaret 2519
Fry, Marcus Fane 2989
Fry, Mary Helen Fane 2989
Fry, Michael Robin 2989
Fry, Phoebe Rivers 2519
Fry, Polly Louise 2519
Fry, Rosemary Jane 603
Fry, Sam 2074
Fry, Samuel Henry Fane 2989
Fry, Susannah 848
Fry, Thomas Rivers 2519
Fry, Virginia Dawn 1010
Frye, John Maurice 144
Fryer, Amy Louise 3012
Fryer, Anthony 3012
Fryer, Ashley Jane 3012
Fryer, Christine Mary 2183
Fryer, Frederick Charles Horace 1235
Fryer, John 2183
Fryer, Kirsten 2183
Fryer, Louise Annette 3012
Fryer, Nicholas 2183
Fryer, Priscilla 1235, 2078, 2576
Fuchs, Albert Alois 1057
Fuchs, Julia Katherina Sonia Mariele 1057
Fuchs, Rose Sofia Iris Mary 1057
Fulford, Elizabeth 1559
Fullard, Glenys 1800
Fullard, Robert 1800
Fuller, (Katherine) Mary 1106
Fuller, Andrew William Fleetwood 1106
Fuller, Anthony Gerard Fleetwood 1106
Fuller, Caspar Furneau 2488
Fuller, Charles Christopher Fleetwood 1106
Fuller, Charlotte 2134
Fuller, Charlotte Beatrice 2328
Fuller, Edward Hamilton Fleetwood 1106
Fuller, Edward Richard Fleetwood 1106
Fuller, Elizabeth Mary 2828
Fuller, Geraldine Anne 2667
Fuller, Jessie Alison 556
Fuller, Joanna Elizabeth 556
Fuller, Jonathan 735
Fuller, Joshua FitzRoy 2667
Fuller, Julia Fleetwood 1106
Fuller, Julia Mary 1106
Fuller, Katharine Georgina 2488
Fuller, Katherine Ruth 2828
Fuller, Lorna Marian 1106
Fuller, Matilda Grace 2488
Fuller, Maurice John Arthur 2828
Fuller, Michael Arthur 2828
Fuller, Miranda 735
Fuller, Oliver 2667
Fuller, Pamela Jane Fleetwood 1106
Fuller, Pauline Elizabeth Lydia 1106
Fuller, Richard 2488
Fuller, Richard Gordon 2667
Fuller, Richard Hamilton Fleetwood 1106, 2134
Fuller, Victoria 2667
Fuller, William Gerard Fleetwood 1106
Fuller-Sessions, John Francis 1271
Fuller-Sessions, Marion 1271
Fuller-Sessions, Nicholas Francis Blair 1271
Fuller-Sessions, Ruth 1271
Fuller-Sessions, Sara 1271
Fullerton, Carolin Jane 2897
Fullerton, Daphne Elizabeth 1306
Fullerton, David Adam Grey 2897
Fullerton, John Robert Mark 2897
Fullerton-Carnegie, David Howard 1059
Fullerton-Carnegie, Frances May 1059
Fullerton-Carnegie, George Christopher Howard 1059
Fullerton-Carnegie, George Travers 1059
Fulton, Guy Charles Jeffreys 2602
Fulton, Robyn Frances Jeffreys 2602
Fulton, Veronica 2602
Furber, Eleanor Primrose 683
Furber, George Frederick Edward 683
Furber, Robin E 683
Furber, Victoria Cecilia 683
Furness, Christopher 1107
Furness, Colin Gerard 1107
Furness, Francis Christopher 1107
Furness, Georgeana Anne 1107
Furness, Grania Patricia Jane 1107, 1249
Furness, John Wilson 1107
Furness, Margaret Grace 1107
Furness, Mary 1107
Furness, Mary Jeffray 2700
Furness, Michael Fitzroy Roberts 1107
Furness, Simon John 1107
Furness, Virginia 1107
Furniss-Roe, Charlotte Anne 3065
Furniss-Roe, Emma Caroline 3065
Furniss-Roe, Marina Jane 3065
Furniss-Roe, Olivia Sophie 3065
Furniss-Roe, Robert P 3065
Furse, Alice Jane 2145
Furse, Corinna Margaret Dolignon 2145
Furse, Elizabeth Jane 2145
Furse, Heather 2145
Furse, Mark Nicolas Ralph Dolignon 2145
Furse, Nicolas Ralph Dolignon 2145
Furse, Samuel Robert 2145
Furse, Thomas Henry 2145
Fyfe, James Gordon 2037
Fyfe, Katherine Jean Wolfe 2037
Fyffe, Alice Catherine 88
Fyffe, Emma Cicely 88
Fyffe, Virginia Mary 88
Fynes-Clinton, Alan 1715
Fynes-Clinton, Alexander Geoffrey 1715
Fynes-Clinton, Amelia Jane 1715
Fynes-Clinton, Arthur Nevill 1715
Fynes-Clinton, Ben Thomas 1715
Fynes-Clinton, Charles John 1714
Fynes-Clinton, Christine Elisabeth 1714
Fynes-Clinton, Eleanor 1714
Fynes-Clinton, Elizabeth Jean 1715
Fynes-Clinton, Emma Mary 1715
Fynes-Clinton, Francis Bernard Peter 1714
Fynes-Clinton, Jacqueline 1715
Fynes-Clinton, Jamie 1715
Fynes-Clinton, Jane 1715
Fynes-Clinton, Janeece 1715
Fynes-Clinton, Joyce Kathleen 1714
Fynes-Clinton, Kate Margaret 1715
Fynes-Clinton, Laura Emily 1715
Fynes-Clinton, Margaret Julia 1714
Fynes-Clinton, Marissa Jane 1715
Fynes-Clinton, Matthew James 1715
Fynes-Clinton, Michael Peter 1714
Fynes-Clinton, Neil 1715
Fynes-Clinton, Oliver John 1714
Fynes-Clinton, Pauline Ruth 1714
Fynes-Clinton, Pelham 1714
Fynes-Clinton, Quenilda Margaret 1714
Fynes-Clinton, Rozanne Jean 1714

Garner-Clarke, Peter 161
Garnett, Adrian Charles Hugh 1155
Garnett, Anne Jeannetta Essex 791
Garnett, Anthony Eardley Douglas 294
Garnett, Charles Henry Esmond 120
Garnett, Conrad Peter Almeric 791
Garnett, Dariel 2370
Garnett, Elizabeth Ann 1155
Garnett, Elizabeth Jane 1155
Garnett, Harry John Gerard 2370
Garnett, Jeremy Paul 791
Garnett, John Robert Stewart 1155
Garnett, Natasha 2370
Garnett, Patricia 120
Garnett-Orme, Katharine 394
Garnham, Araminta 1204
Garnham, Belinda 1204
Garnham, Caroline 1204
Garnham, Emily Victoria 1204
Garnham, Jasper Meredydd 1631
Garnham, Meriel Ann 1631
Garnham, Piers Alexander 1204
Garnham, Robert 1204
Garnier, Anna Caroline 2934
Garnier, Edward Henry 2934
Garnier, Eleanor Katharine Rose 2934
Garnier, George Edward 2934
Garnier, Georgina Sarah 2934
Garnier, James Hugh 2934
Garnier, James William 2934
Garnier, Katherine Hale 2934
Garnier, Lavender Hyacinth 2934
Garnier, Louisa Hale 2934
Garnier, Melissa (Minnie) 2934
Garnier, Olivia Caroline 2934
Garnier, Richard Charles 2934
Garnier, Robert Anthony 2934
Garnier, Sophia Elizabeth 2934
Garnier, William 2934
Garnons-Williams, Elizabeth Mary Ellinor 2408
Garra, Gerard 988
Garra, Susan Joan 988
Garrett, Anthony Terence 961
Garrett, Caroline Edith Mary 961
Garrett, Claire Isabella 2973
Garrett, Craig Douglas 1806
Garrett, Edward James Sutcliffe 1738
Garrett, Gaynor 1738
Garrett, Geoffrey Keith 1806
Garrett, George Francis 2973
Garrett, Isabel 2973
Garrett, Jenifer Mary 1806
Garrett, Jeremy David 1806
Garrett, Laura 2973
Garrett, Lucinda Felicity 1738
Garrett, Melissa 1738
Garrett, Nicholas Edward Sutcliffe 1738
Garrett, Nikki Jane 1806
Garrett, Simon N 2973
Garrick, Emily Mary 1543
Garrini, Betty 3067
Garrod, Dylan Roy 258
Garrod, Jacob Thomas 258
Garrod, Sarah Jane 258
Garside, Alan Nigel 123
Garside, Douglas Paul 123
Garside, Gillian Elizabeth 2411
Garside, Ian Richard 123
Garside, Peter Dignus 2411
Garside, Philip Marshall 123
Garson, Elizabeth Lucy 622
Garson, Faith Patricia Elizabeth 622
Garson, James Leslie 622
Garson, Jeremy James 622
Garthwaite, Alice Sophie Elizabeth 1722
Garthwaite, Amanda Gabrielle Mary 1722
Garthwaite, Andrew William David 1127
Garthwaite, Caroline C 1127
Garthwaite, Caroline Sally 1127
Garthwaite, Felix Sebastian 1127
Garthwaite, George William Angus 1127
Garthwaite, James William John 1127
Garthwaite, Jemima Victoria 1127
Garthwaite, Joanna Rachel 1127
Garthwaite, John William Philip 1127
Garthwaite, Mark Edmond 1722
Garthwaite, Michael William Gladwyn 1127
Garthwaite, Nicholas Anthony William Mancroft 1127
Garthwaite, Oliver Julian 1127
Garthwaite, Patricia Merriel 1127
Garthwaite, Piers Marcus 1127
Garthwaite, Rebecca Elizabeth 1127
Garthwaite, Rosie Francesca 1127
Garthwaite, Sarah Elizabeth 1127
Garthwaite, Simon William James 1127
Garthwaite, Victoria Lisette 1127
Garthwaite, William Tuzo 1127
Garton, (Anthony Gavin) Charles Luis 2446
Garton, Anthony Richard Leslie 2133
Garton, Camilla Mary Eva 2446
Garton, Dorothy Margaret 651
Garton, Elizabeth Hera 651
Garton, Ines Monica 2133
Garton, James Anthony Leo 2446
Garton, Lucy Catherine Mary 2446
Garton, Patrick William 651
Garton, Tristan John Leslie 2133
Garvie, Anna-Lisa Karen 2961
Garvie, Gordon Elliott Keith 2961
Garvie, Peter Francis 2961
Garvie, Sarah Kate 2961
Garvin, Eliza Rose Clare 1797
Garvin, Emma Mary 1797
Garvin, James M 1797
Gary-Muir, Elizabeth Margaret 1974
Gaschet, Annik Marie Nicole 2024
Gaschet, Astrid 2024
Gaschet, Bruno 2024
Gaschet, Guillaume 2024
Gascoigne, Anna Jennifer 2033
Gascoigne, Anthony Grey 3007
Gascoigne, (Arthur) Bamber 2157
Gascoigne, Brian Alvary 2157
Gascoigne, Cecily 2033
Gascoigne, Christina Mary 2157
Gascoigne, Crispin 2885
Gascoigne, David Clive 3007
Gascoigne, Deirdre Cecil Hermione 3007
Gascoigne, Dominic William Wigan 3007
Gascoigne, (Elizabeth) Ann 2885
Gascoigne, Elizabeth Sibell Isabel 3007
Gascoigne, Fenn 1001
Gascoigne, Frederick William 2885
Gascoigne, Gemma Eva Pamela 2033
Gascoigne, James Neil Crispin 2033
Gascoigne, Julian Aubrey Harcourt 2885
Gascoigne, Margaret 2033
Gascoigne, Martin Wyndham 3007
Gascoigne, May 1001
Gascoigne, Michael Neil Clifton 2033
Gascoigne, Nichola Elizabeth Blanche 3007
Gascoigne, Oliva Clare Teresa 1000
Gascoigne, Patrick Edward Cecil 2033
Gascoigne, Penny 2033
Gascoigne, Peter John Hector 2033
Gascoigne, Ralph Edward 2885
Gascoigne, Robert Hugh 2033
Gascoigne, Susan Alexandra 2885
Gascoigne, Tobias Charles Humphrey 3007
Gascoigne, William Harcourt Crisp 2885
Gascoyne-Cecil, Alison Julia 2534
Gascoyne-Cecil, Andrew Peter 2534
Gascoyne-Cecil, Caroline Alison 2534
Gascoyne-Cecil, Christopher Anthony 2534
Gascoyne-Cecil, Elizabeth Carol 2534
Gascoyne-Cecil, Helen Elizabeth 2534
Gascoyne-Cecil, James Anthony 2534
Gascoyne-Cecil, Jonathan Michael 2534
Gascoyne-Cecil, Judith 2534
Gascoyne-Cecil, Marjorie (Mollie) Olein 917, 2531
Gascoyne-Cecil, Michael Anthony 253 4
Gascoyne-Cecil, Richard David 2534
Gascoyne-Cecil, Robert Edward Peter 917
Gascoyne-Cecil, Robert Michael James Cecil 2531
Gascoyne-Cecil, Victoria Ruth 2534
Gaselee, James Digby Charles 977
Gaselee, Sophie Elizabeth 977
Gash, Norah Susan 130
Gash, Walter Stuart 130
Gaskell, Andrew 1736
Gaskell, Anna Elizabeth 1736
Gaskell, Celia Elizabeth 1736
Gaskell, Charles Paul 1736
Gaskell, Charles Peter 2810
Gaskell, Jacquine Shelley 2919
Gaskell, James 1736
Gaskell, Jeremy John 2919
Gaskell, Joseph Gerald 2810
Gaskell, Joseph William 2810
Gaskell, Maureen Elizabeth Jane 2810
Gaskell, Thomas 1736
Gaskell, Victoria Jacquine 2919
Gasser, Beat 2660
Gasser, Elizabeth Kaye 2660
Gatacre, (Alice) Amelia 2186
Gatacre, Amelia Lettice 2186
Gatacre, Catherine Lucy Emily 2186, 2573
Gatacre, Cecily 2186
Gatacre, Dorothy (Dolly) Perpetua 2186
Gatacre, Elsebeth 2186
Gatacre, Jack Victor 2186
Gatacre, Maria Teresa 2186
Gatacre, Thomas Jerome 2186
Gatacre, William 2186, 2573
Gatcombe, Louise Christian 1655
Gatcombe, Michael 1655
Gatehouse, Davina Jane 3008
Gatehouse, Elizabeth Ann Cecilia 1408
Gatehouse, Emily Alice 3008
Gatehouse, James Peter Wright 1408
Gatehouse, James Richard 3008
Gatehouse, Juliet Ann Cecilia 1408
Gatehouse, Michael 3008
Gatehouse, Peter Oswald 1408
Gatehouse, Rosemary Hazel 2475
Gatehouse, Sophie Charlotte 3008
Gates, (Anna) Lee 1965
Gates, Catherine 1965
Gates, Christopher William 1705
Gates, Mary-Anne 1705
Gates, Rebecca Mary 1705
Gates, Stephanie Louise 1705
Gather, Charlotte Mairi 582
Gather, Felix Edinmore 582
Gather, Rupert Edinmore 582
Gathorne-Hardy, Alfred 695
Gathorne-Hardy, Alice 695
Gathorne-Hardy, Angus Edward 694
Gathorne-Hardy, Benjamin 695
Gathorne-Hardy, Caroline 580, 694
Gathorne-Hardy, Caroline Elizabeth 695, 2415
Gathorne-Hardy, Daisy 695
Gathorne-Hardy, Fidelity 695
Gathorne-Hardy, Flora 694
Gathorne-Hardy, Frederick Jasper 695
Gathorne-Hardy, Gathorne 580
Gathorne-Hardy, Grace 695
Gathorne-Hardy, Hugh 695, 2415
Gathorne-Hardy, John Jason 694
Gathorne-Hardy, Jonathan Gathorne 695
Gathorne-Hardy, Lydia 695
Gathorne-Hardy, Mary Catherine 695
Gathorne-Hardy, Nell 695
Gathorne-Hardy, Nicolette 695
Gathorne-Hardy, Penelope Rose 695
Gathorne-Hardy, Philippa 695
Gathorne-Hardy, Robert Dee 695
Gathorne-Hardy, Samuel Gathorne 695
Gatliff, John William 1720
Gatliff, Rosie Frances 1720
Gatliff, Sarah Frances 1720
Gatliff, Simon John 1720
Gatling, Anthony 336
Gatling, Mary Hamilton Victoria Ignatia 336
Gattai, Antonello 2074
Gattai, Cristina 2074
Gattai, Enrico Budini 2074
Gattai, Federico 2074
Gattai, Ferdinando 2074
Gattai, Francesca 2074
Gattai, Francesco 2074
Gattai, Giulia 2074
Gattai, Leopoldo 2074
Gattai, Maria Vittoria 2074
Gattai, Nicoletta 2074
Gattai, Roberto 2074
Gattai, Rodolfo 2074
Gattai, Ruggero 2074
Gatten, Arabella Ann 39
Gatten, Michael J 39
Gatten, Morgan 39
Gattertop, Virginia Charlotte Angela 626
Gatty, Cheryll 2371
Gatty, Jessica Margaret 2371
Gatty, Pamela 2371
Gatty, Richard George 2371
Gauguier, Fabrice 911
Gauguier, Jane 911
Gauld, Andrew James Mitchell 740
Gauld, Cynthia Rowena 740
Gauld, Fiona Rowena 740
Gault, Barbara Irene 952
Gault, Julie Heather 952
Gault, Karen Marie 952
Gault, Lindsay 952
Gault, Shane David 952
Gaussen, (Diana) Bridget 1380
Gaussen, Mariana Diana 1380
Gaussen, Robert Casamajor 1380
Gaussen, Samuel Charles Casamajor 1380
Gawlik, Clive Matthew 1899
Gawlik, Emma Frances Mary 1899
Gawlik, Millicent Victoria 1899
Gawne, Amanda Louise 2773
Gawne, Hilary Ann 2773
Gawne, John Francis 2773
Gawne, Kae 2773
Gawne, Kelly Robert 2773
Gawne, Kevin Donald 2773
Gawne, Nicola Caroline 2773
Gawne, Olinda Margaret 2773
Gawne, Robert Atholl 2773
Gayer, Trelawny Reginald Courtenay 3037
Gaymer, Adam Timothy 1071
Gaymer, Kathryn Helen Adams 1071
Gaymer, Kirsten Anne 1071
Gaymer, Nigel Anthony 1071
Gayner, Catharine Harriet Cecilia 1173
Gayner, John Robert Haydon 1173
Gayner, Richard Edward Geoffrey 1173
Gayner, William Richard Francis 1173
Gaynor, Harry 2924
Gaynor, Oliver 2924
Gaynor, Robert 2924
Gaztambide, Santiago 2895
Gaztambide, Sara Frances 2895
Geake, Elisabeth Marjorie 2321
Geake, Helen Mary 2321
Geake, Rosemary Jean 2321
Geake, Thomas Henry 2321
Geake, William Beauchamp 2321
Geange, Harriet Cicely 3002
Geange, Robert Wallace 3002
Gear, Michael Leishman 460
Gear, Nicola 460
Gear, Sarah 460
Gear, Susan Anne 460
Gearing, Alyson Maree 113
Gearing, Jack Ernest 113
Gearing, Sybil Dorothy 1122
Gebreyohanes, Axumawi 400
Gebreyohanes, Flora Rhalou 400
Gebreyohanes, Mike 400
Geddes, Acland Eric Anthony 1129
Geddes, Ailie Ford 1129
Geddes, Alexander James Campbell 1130
Geddes, Andrew Campbell 1130
Geddes, Angus John 1129
Geddes, Anne Mary 1129
Geddes, Barbara Gertrude 1129
Geddes, Beverley 1129
Geddes, Bridget Charlotte Helen 1130
Geddes, Camilla Joanna Isabella 1130
Geddes, Christopher Edward Frederick 1130
Geddes, Cinda Marie 2927
Geddes, Clinton Douglas 2927
Geddes, David Ford 1129
Geddes, Diana Elizabeth 1130
Geddes, Diana Elizabeth Campbell 1130
Geddes, Dominic Oliver Campbell 1130
Geddes, Donatella 1129
Geddes, Duncan Mackay 1129
Geddes, Dyana 2927
Geddes, Emily Claire Kateryna 1130
Geddes, Enid Mary 1130
Geddes, Erica 1129
Geddes, Ford Irvine 1129
Geddes, Gaia Irene Olga 1129
Geddes, Gavin Reay MacKay 1129
Geddes, Gerda 1130
Geddes, Gordon 2927
Geddes, Harriet Diana Christabel 3, 1130
Geddes, Hugh John Reay 3, 1130
Geddes, Ian David 1129
Geddes, James George Neil 1129
Geddes, Joan Catherine 1129
Geddes, Judith Anne 2927
Geddes, Julia 1525
Geddes, Katharine Arabella Campbell 1130
Geddes, Laura 1525
Geddes, Leo Patrick 1130
Geddes, Lillian Gladys 2927
Geddes, Luke John McLaren 1130
Geddes, Marcus 1129
Geddes, Margaret Clair 1129
Geddes, Mark Leys 1525
Geddes, Merryn Campbell 1129
Geddes, Michael 2927
Geddes, Nicholas Campbell 1130
Geddes, Piers Mackay 1129
Geddes, Roger Brian 1129
Geddes, Rorie Irvine 1129
Geddes, Sam Duncan McLaren 1130
Geddes, Stephen George 1130
Geddes, Susan Margaret 1129
Geddes, Vivien M 1130
Geddes, William Leys 1525
Geddes-Ablitt, Emma Irene Anne 1620
Geddes-Ablitt, Helen Angela Emma 1620
Geddes-Ablitt, Michael Henry 1620
Geddes-Ablitt, Sophie Hannah Rachel 1620
Geddes-Ablitt, Tessa Catherine Ruth 1620
Geddes-Ablitt, Zoë Christiana 1620
Gedye, Christopher John 2838
Gedye, Diana Vere 2838
Gedye, Michael Jonathan 2838
Gedye, Nichole Jade 2838
Gedye, Noel Trevor 2838
Gedye, Ranee Joy 2838
Gedye, Roseann 2838
Gedye, Shari Justin 2838
Gedye, Stephen Warren 2838
Gedye, Victoria Ruth Ohms 2838
Gee, Adrian 1417
Gee, Benedict Thomas Lewes 2607
Gee, Caroline Dorothy 142
Gee, Joan Mary 1417
Gee, Lisa Ann 2838
Gee, Loveday Elisabeth 2607
Gee, Mathew George Cooper 2607
Gee, Miranda 2607
Gee, Patrick Robert Cooper 2607
Gee, Peter Anthony 142
Gee, Robert George 2607
Gee, William Benedict Robert Cooper 2607
Gehman, Blair Lee 2206
Gehman, Christie Robin 2206
Gehman, Dane Robert 2206
Gehman, Iris Patricia 2206
Gehman, Lane Peel 2206
Gehman, Lorne Albert 2206
Gehman, Regan Corey 2206
Gehman, Shannon Dee 2206
Geidt, Christopher 781
Geidt, Emma Charlotte Angela 781
Geiringer, Alfred 1658
Geissler, Beatrice Alison 975
Geissler, Erik 975
Geissler, Judith Margery 975
Geissler, Leonie Elizabeth Pauline 975
Geissler, Stephen Francis 975
Gelber, Ann 1953
Gelber, David Aba 1866
Gelber, Henrietta Mary 1866
Gelber, Herman 1953
Gelber, Maximilian Henry 1866
Gelber, Sean Roderick 1953
Gelernter, Jake Oliver 1998
Gelernter, Linda Jane 1998
Gelernter, Paul M 1998
Gelernter, Theo Saul 1998
Gellatly, Betty Theodosia 186
Gellatly, Marilyn Fay 186
Gellatly, Paul 1638
Gellatly, Peter Russell 186
Gellatly, Russell 186
Geller, Stanley John 2501
Geller, Tomazin 2501
Gellhorn, Barbara Dorothea 1658
Gellhorn, Catherine 1658
Gellhorn, Martin Oliver 1658
Gellhorn, Mary Ann 1658
Gellhorn, Olive Shirley 1658
Gellhorn, Peter 1658
Gellhorn, Philip Nicholas 1658
Gelly, Anne Cordelia 901
Gelly, Bennett Butler Vaughan 901
Gelly, Clement Guthrie Estes 901
Gelly, James Vaughan 901
Gelly, Piers George Crampton 901
Gemell, Bruce 1412
Gemell, Claude 1412

Gibson, Cosmo David 1137
Gibson, Cynthia 2730
Gibson, David Hope 1137
Gibson, David Travers Worsley 1476
Gibson, Diana Madeleine 1137
Gibson, Dominic John Mulholland 931
Gibson, (Edward) Charles D'Olier 116
Gibson, Effie Dione 688
Gibson, (Elizabeth) Dione 688, 1136
Gibson, Emma Clare 2683
Gibson, Eric Nicholas Galbraith 2730
Gibson, Eric Osborne 2730
Gibson, Frances Phoebe 2245
Gibson, Frances Towneley 688, 2148
Gibson, Frederick 2530
Gibson, Frederick John Philip 2158
Gibson, Geoffrey Andrew 117
Gibson, Georgina Odette 1137
Gibson, Harriet Anne 2530
Gibson, Harry Maximilian 688
Gibson, Helen 1476
Gibson, Herbert 1137
Gibson, Herbert Mark 1137
Gibson, Hugh Marcus Thornley 688, 2148
Gibson, James Bruce 1137
Gibson, James Frederick 2530
Gibson, James Michael 2975
Gibson, Jasper Tallentyre 688
Gibson, Jennifer 1137
Gibson, John 2168
Gibson, John Carmichael 1138
Gibson, John Frederic 117
Gibson, John Hastings 2408
Gibson, Joseph Emerson 491
Gibson, Joseph Peter 2245
Gibson, Josephine Jean 1137
Gibson, Joy Beatrice 117
Gibson, Kate Louise 2356
Gibson, Lilian Lake 1137
Gibson, Lori Frances 688
Gibson, Lorna Mary 117
Gibson, Lucy Lavinia 688
Gibson, Lucy Victoria Cornelia 1926
Gibson, Madeleine 1137
Gibson, Margaret Jean 1137
Gibson, Maria Pia 1137
Gibson, Mark 777
Gibson, Martha Camilla 688
Gibson, Mary Ann Frances 2158
Gibson, Mary-Jane 2356
Gibson, Matthew Charles 688
Gibson, Melanie Jane Stella 688
Gibson, Michael 1137
Gibson, Michael Oliver John 2975
Gibson, Michel 1137
Gibson, Miles Cosmo Archdale 1136
Gibson, Monica Hastings 1476
Gibson, Neil Henry 117
Gibson, Noel Gerald 1137
Gibson, Olivia Emily Victoria 1926
Gibson, Pamela Cherry 117
Gibson, Patrick Clive 688
Gibson, Patrick Mayne 116
Gibson, Peter John Bradford 1926
Gibson, Peter Worsley 1476
Gibson, Philipa Constance 116
Gibson, Phyllida 1578
Gibson, Piers Nathaniel 688
Gibson, Ralph Alan 2408
Gibson, Rhoda Caroline 491
Gibson, (Richard) Patrick Tallentyre 688
Gibson, Robert Herbert 1136
Gibson, Rosie Alice 2530
Gibson, Roy Herbert 1137
Gibson, Sabina 116
Gibson, Sarah Claire 688
Gibson, Sarah Jospehine 2975
Gibson, Sebastian Thomas Maxmilian 1137
Gibson, Shari-Anne Joy 117
Gibson, Sharon 2730
Gibson, Simon John 117
Gibson, Stuart Barrie 1578
Gibson, Tessa 931
Gibson, Theodore Charles 688
Gibson, Thomas Herbert 1136
Gibson, Timothy C 2356
Gibson, Timothy Wells 2975
Gibson, Valerie 1137
Gibson, Victor Russell 117
Gibson, Victoria Lucy 2730
Gibson, Walter Alexander 2730
Gibson, William Barnaby Thomas 1136
Gibson, William H M 931
Gibson, William Knatchbull 688
Gibson, (William) Rodney Colles 116
Gibson, Yvonne Georgina 116
Gibson-Craig-Carmichael, Alasdair John 1139
Gibson-Craig-Carmichael, Andrew Charles 1139
Gibson-Craig-Carmichael, Emily Edith 1139
Gibson-Craig-Carmichael, Irene 1139
Gibson-Craig-Carmichael, Margaret Anne 1137
Gibson-Craig-Carmichael, Patricia 1137
Gibson-Craig-Carmichael, Peter William 1137
Gibson-Craig-Carmichael, Rosemary Anita 1139
Gibson-Watt, Andrew James 1278
Gibson-Watt, Anthony David 1139
Gibson-Watt, David Julian 1139
Gibson-Watt, Diana 1139, 1278
Gibson-Watt, Edward Ricardo 1139
Gibson-Watt, Guy Charles 1139
Gibson-Watt, James David 1278
Gibson-Watt, Marcia Susan 513, 1139
Gibson-Watt, Marie-Therese 1139
Gibson-Watt, Pamela 1278
Gibson-Watt, Phoebe Charlotte 1139
Gibson-Watt, Robin 513, 1139
Gidney, Alison Jane 1544
Gidney, David Guy 1543
Gidney, Mark Henry 1543
Gieve, Daniel Vereker 1183
Gieve, Edward John Watson 1183
Gieve, Katherine Elizabeth 1183
Gieve, Matthew Vereker 1183
Giffard, Adam Edward 1272
Giffard, Ellen 1272
Giffard, Emma Cole 1272
Giffard, Joanna Elizabeth 1272
Giffard, Phyllis 1273
Giffard, Sarah Cole 1272
Giffard-Lindsay, Mark Oliver 1718
Giffard-Taylor, Angela Maureen 2654
Giffard-Taylor, Barrie 2654
Giffard-Taylor, Emily Victoria 2654
Giffard-Taylor, James William 2654
Giffard-Taylor, Jemima Alice 2654
Gifford, Andrew Graham 1785
Gifford, Antony Patrick Carlyle 1785
Gifford, Carolyn Mortimore 1785
Gifford, Elean Roslyn 1140
Gifford, Griselda Mary Honoria 1919
Gifford, James Alexander Moncreiff 1963
Gifford, John Vernon 1785
Gifford, Lucinda Felicity Moncreiff 1963
Gifford, Margaret Letitia 1921
Gifford, Mark Richard Alexander 1919
Gifford, Mary 1785
Gifford, Nicola Jane 1919
Gifford, Patricia Anne 1963
Gifford, Patrick Antony Francis 1785
Gifford, Paul Julian David 1919
Gifford, Polly Anna 1140
Gifford, Robert James Moncreiff 1963
Gifford, Samantha Louise Moncreiff 1963
Gifford, Sheba Chanel 1140
Gifford, Thomas Adam 1140
Gifford, William Lyell 1785
Gilbart, Pamela 1678
Gilbart, William Stephen 1678
Gilbert, Anthony Guy Pakenham 338
Gilbert, Brenda Constance Mary 338
Gilbert, Christopher Guy 338
Gilbert, Christopher Peter 1357
Gilbert, Daphne Mary 565
Gilbert, Derek Gilbert 565
Gilbert, Edith Rosemary Patricia 2346
Gilbert, Erica Claire 565
Gilbert, Fiona Patricia 565
Gilbert, Flora Margaret 2214
Gilbert, Graham 2214
Gilbert, James Carl 2346
Gilbert, Jean Olive 1140, 2203
Gilbert, Joanna Catherine 565
Gilbert, John 2203
Gilbert, John David 1357
Gilbert, Kris Graham 2214
Gilbert, Leonard 842
Gilbert, Margaret Evelyn 2176
Gilbert, Margaret Julia 1357
Gilbert, Mary Agatha 2782
Gilbert, Patricia Jean 338
Gilbert, Patrick Charles 565
Gilbert, Peter Denby 2176
Gilbert, Richard John Michael 338
Gilbert, Rory Neil 2214
Gilbert, Susan Ruth 1357
Gilberto, Marcelo Esteban 574
Gilberto, Susana Hortensia 574
Gilbey, Amanda M 1141
Gilbey, Angela 1141
Gilbey, Angela Ruth 1142
Gilbey, Anne 1141
Gilbey, Anthony James 1141, 2722
Gilbey, Anthony William 2873
Gilbey, Barbara 1141
Gilbey, Beth 2873
Gilbey, Beverley Anne 2873
Gilbey, Beverley M A 1141
Gilbey, Caroline 2873
Gilbey, Caroline Anne 1142
Gilbey, Celia 1141
Gilbey, Charlotte 2873
Gilbey, Charlotte Katharine 2873
Gilbey, Christopher Sebastian Bruce 1142
Gilbey, Diana Mary 1142
Gilbey, Elizabeth Mary 1142
Gilbey, Elizabeth Muriel Emma 2873
Gilbey, Emma Lenora 1141
Gilbey, Francis Newman 1141
Gilbey, Giles Newman 1141
Gilbey, Guy Hugh 1141
Gilbey, Guy Newman 1141
Gilbey, Helen 1141
Gilbey, Henry John 2873
Gilbey, James Dennis 1141
Gilbey, James Newman 1141
Gilbey, James William 2873
Gilbey, Jasper Sebastian Christopher 1142
Gilbey, Jenifer Mary 1142, 3096
Gilbey, Jill Felicity 1141
Gilbey, Joan Carmen Simone 1141
Gilbey, Joan Irene 1141
Gilbey, Julian Sebastian 2873
Gilbey, Linda 1142, 2873
Gilbey, Lisa 1142
Gilbey, Lisa Maria 1142
Gilbey, Mary Agnes Margaret 2875
Gilbey, Maureen Pamela 2873
Gilbey, Medina 1142
Gilbey, Michael Christopher 1142, 2873
Gilbey, Pamela Maureen 1141
Gilbey, Paul Alfred 1141
Gilbey, Paul Hugh 1141
Gilbey, Penelope 1141
Gilbey, Penelope Anne 2722
Gilbey, Philip Alexander Charles 2873
Gilbey, Phyllis Anne 1141
Gilbey, Ralph Newman 1141
Gilbey, Richard Hubert Gordon 2873
Gilbey, Robert James Newman 1141
Gilbey, (Ronald) Nicholas Dashwood 1141
Gilbey, Rupert John 1142
Gilbey, Sara Jane 1142
Gilbey, Sarah Elizabeth 1142
Gilbey, Shirley A 1141
Gilbey, Simon Byas 1141
Gilbey, Simon Newman 1141
Gilbey, Simon Rupert 1142
Gilbey, Sophie 1142
Gilbey, Thomas Edward 2873
Gilbey, Thomas Newman 1141
Gilbey, Victoria Caroline 2873
Gilbey, Walter Anthony 1142, 3096
Gilbey, William Henry Newman 1141
Gilbey, William John 2873
Gilbey, William Michael Arthur 2874
Gilborson, Julia Ruth 2212
Gilborson, Mark Julian 2212
Gilborson, Sarah Lewise 2212
Gilborson, Terry 2212
Gilchrist, Catherine 636
Gilchrist, Catherine Anne 636
Gilchrist, Charles Warren 636
Gilchrist, David Warren 636
Gilchrist, John Drysdale 2419
Gilchrist, Julia Mary 636
Gilchrist, Rosemary Jane 2419
Gilchrist, Warren Llewellyn Russell Euan 636
Gile, Amos Webster 740
Gile, John Lockhart 740
Gile, Lorna Margaret 740
Gile, Pamela Jean 740
Giles, Alleyne Bruce 201
Giles, Anna Louise 1236
Giles, Arrabella Kathleen 1576
Giles, Ash Fomorrii Eaodraca 1576
Giles, Barbara 201
Giles, Benjamin-Peter Wesley 1236
Giles, Bronwen Davies 1576
Giles, Christine 201
Giles, Daniel Peter 201
Giles, Elizabeth Louise 1236
Giles, Frank Thomas Robertson 794
Giles, (Henry Frank) Sebastian 794
Giles, Ian Wesley 1236
Giles, John Nicholas 201
Giles, Katharine (Kitty) Pamela 794
Giles, Kelly Vanessa 201
Giles, Kirsten Jasmine 201
Giles, Lucas Charles O 794
Giles, Margaret Joy 3003
Giles, Maxwell Joseph W 794
Giles, Michael William 1576
Giles, Natalie Simone 201
Giles, Peter William 1576
Giles, Richard Courthope 201
Giles, Sally Elizabeth 1236
Giles, Sarah 794
Gilfillan, Claire Mary 92
Gilfillan, Edward Crawfurd 92
Gilfillan, Edward Hugh 92
Gilfillan, Edward Mounsey 92
Gilfillan, Mary 92
Gilfillan, Philip Mounsey 92
Gilfillan, Ross Mounsey 92
Gilfillan, Ruth-Mary 92
Gilfillan, Sydney James 1365
Gill, Angela Patricia 1420
Gill, Anthony Henry 791
Gill, David 716
Gill, Douglas George 1175
Gill, Fionn Paul 1175
Gill, Henrietta Patricia Mary 1176
Gill, Herbert 1472
Gill, Jeremy David Hallen 1420
Gill, John Laurence 791, 1184
Gill, Julia 1472
Gill, Juliet Flora 791, 1184
Gill, Katherine Elizabeth Louise 1176
Gill, Kim Elizabeth 716
Gill, Mabel Dorothy 616
Gill, Margaret Katherine Dorothy 1420
Gill, Marlene Elsie 1420
Gill, Michael David 716
Gill, Nicholas Anton Stephens 1420
Gill, Nicholas Charles Ronald 1176
Gill, Nichole May 716
Gill, Peter Douglas 1176
Gill, Peter Geoffrey Fiennes 616
Gill, Peter William 1420
Gill, Ralph John David 1420
Gill, Ryan David 1420
Gill, Samantha Jane 716
Gill, Shirley Anne 716
Gill, Trevor William Hugh 1420
Gillard, John Patrick 734
Gillard, Ruth Mary 734
Gillbanks, Prudence Caroline 2000
Gillespie, Alice Catherine Mary 2356
Gillespie, David Buchanan 2863
Gillespie, Dennis Charles 2994
Gillespie, Elisabeth Helena Anne 2356
Gillespie, Elizabeth Mary 2863
Gillespie, Giles Peter Seton 2583
Gillespie, Hamish Peregrine Curzon 2863
Gillespie, Hugh Rollo 2356
Gillespie, James Hugh 2356
Gillespie, Joanna Mary 2583
Gillespie, Kelly Anne Isabella 2994
Gillespie, Meghan Therese 2994
Gillespie, Peter 2583
Gillespie, Richenda Antoinette 458
Gillespie, Simon Rollo 2356
Gillespie, Wendy Ann Isabella 2994
Gillett, Adam Holmes 1143
Gillett, Alan Henry Puckridge 1143
Gillett, Andrew Jonathan 1143
Gillett, Andrew William Tollemache 2830
Gillett, Chris(topher) John 1143
Gillett, Clara Elizabeth 2830
Gillett, David 2830
Gillett, Edward 2830
Gillett, Ella Clare 2830
Gillett, Esther 2830
Gillett, Haylie 1143
Gillett, John Chetwynd 2830
Gillett, Lucy 1143
Gillett, Nicholas Danvers Penrose 1143
Gillett, Oliver James 1143
Gillett, Patricia 1143
Gillett, Priscilla Joan 2830
Gillett, Robert John Chetwynd 2830
Gillett, Rosemary 2830
Gillett, Sarah Lucy 1143
Gillett, Sophie Louise 2830
Gillett, Susannah Rachel 1143
Gillett, Tessa 1143
Gillett, Timothy Richard Puckridge 1143
Gillford, Patrick James 1211
Gillford, Serena Emily 1211
Gillies, Clare 2514
Gillies, Helen 2514
Gillies, Jane Caroline 88
Gillies, John 2514
Gillies, Sarah 2514
Gilligan, Arran Thomas 1391
Gilligan, Dominic Francis 1391
Gilligan, Liam Patrick 1391
Gilligan, Michael 1391
Gilligan, Susan Margaret 1391
Gillissie, Michael Gerald 1938
Gillissie, Phyllida Fiona 1938
Gillmore, Lucile Morin 1143
Gillon, Amanda Jane 2911
Gillon, Neil David 2911
Gilmour, Aivin 1144
Gilmour, Alexander Clement 1145
Gilmour, Alexander Ian Michael 1144
Gilmour, Alexandra Ruth 1145
Gilmour, Andrew Frank 254, 1144
Gilmour, Andrew James 1145
Gilmour, Andrew Robert Campbell 1144
Gilmour, Archie John Ludo 1145
Gilmour, Barbara Marie-Louise Constance 1557
Gilmour, Caroline Margaret 412, 1144
Gilmour, Christian Alexander 1145
Gilmour, Christopher Simon 1145
Gilmour, Corinna Valerie 1144
Gilmour, David Edward 1144
Gilmour, David Robert 1144, 1345
Gilmour, Elizabeth 536
Gilmour, Emma 1145
Gilmour, John 1144
Gilmour, (John) Nicholas 1144
Gilmour, Katherine Victoria Mary 1144
Gilmour, Laura Elizabeth Rose 1144
Gilmour, Leonora Rose Bonnie 1145
Gilmour, Mardi 1145
Gilmour, Mary 254, 1144
Gilmour, Natalia Clare 1145
Gilmour, Nigel Christopher 536
Gilmour, Oliver John 1145
Gilmour, Patrick George William 1144
Gilmour, Rachel Anne Caroline 1144
Gilmour, Rory Calvyn 1145
Gilmour, Sarah Anne 1144, 1345
Gilmour, Susan Janet 1145
Gilmour, Ursula 1144
Gilmour, Valerie 1144
Gilmour, (Victoria) Juliet 1144
Gilmour, Xan 1145
Gilpin, Beatrice May Edith 63
Gilpin, Henrietta 252
Gilpin, Joanna Clare 252
Gilpin, Patricia Margaret Aline 63
Gilpin, Susan 252
Gilpin, Timothy Ernle 252
Gilroy, Angus Hugh 706
Gilroy, Caspar Alexander 1330
Gilroy, Elizabeth 706
Gilroy, Fergus Hugh 706
Gilroy, Margaret Cecilia 706
Gimena, Anne-Marie Ines 881
Gimena, Laureano Perez-Andujar 881
Gimlette, Edward Timothy 2031
Gimlette, Henrietta Miranda 2031
Giorgi, Charles 1348
Giorgi, Penelope Jane 1348
Girdlestone, Katie Serena Margaret 1071
Girdlestone, Michael Owen 1071
Girdlestone, Philip David Alexander 1071
Girdlestone, Robert Brook Pennant 1071
Girdlestone, Sarah Fariana Mary Agnes 1071

Guinness, Matthew Richard 2028
Guinness, Maureen 1253
Guinness, Michael Damon 1250
Guinness, Molly Louise 2028
Guinness, Murtogh David 2028
Guinness, Niall Owen Shane 1253
Guinness, Patrick Desmond Karl Alexander 2028
Guinness, Paul Dennis 1253
Guinness, Paul Rohio 1252
Guinness, Pauline 1843
Guinness, Pauline Vivien 1251
Guinness, Peggy Stephaich 2027
Guinness, Penelope ('Penny') 2028
Guinness, Peter Brian 1252
Guinness, Richard Mackay 1252
Guinness, Richard de Zoete 1249
Guinness, Robert Chapman 1249
Guinness, Robin Arthur 1252
Guinness, Rory Michael Benjamin 1520
Guinness, Rupert 1253
Guinness, Rupert Edward Roger 1251
Guinness, Sabrina Jane 1251
Guinness, Samuel Hugo 2028
Guinness, Samuel Walter 1249
Guinness, Sarah Jane 1249
Guinness, Sean St Lawrence Lee 1249
Guinness, Sebastian Walter Denis 2027
Guinness, Selina Karen Elizabeth 1253
Guinness, Shaunagh Mary 1250
Guinness, Sheridan William 1250
Guinness, Stella 1252
Guinness, Susan Elizabeth Jennifer 1253
Guinness, Susan Petronella 1252
Guinness, Susan ('Shoe') Mary 2027
Guinness, Suzanne 2027
Guinness, Tania Caroline 1252
Guinness, Tara Victoria 2027
Guinness, (Thomas) Seymour 1250
Guinness, Thomasin Margaret 2028
Guinness, Timothy Roberts 1252
Guinness, Timothy Whitmore 1254
Guinness, Tom 2028
Guinness, Valentine Guy Bryan 2027, 2419
Guinness, Valerie Susan 1247, 1251
Guinness, Vivienne 2028
Guinness, William Loel Seymour 1250
Guinney, Ann 1117
Guinney, Carl Stewart 1117
Guinney, Mark Stewart 1117
Guinney, Michael Victor 1117
Guiot-Pascau, Daniel François 2641
Guiot-Pascau, Grant Ivan 2641
Guiot-Pascau, Heal Gregory 2641
Guiot-Pascau, Jane Ann Louise 2641
Guiot-Pascau, Marie Denise 2641
Guise, Amanda Frances 1256
Guise, Anselm Mark 1257
Guise, Anselm Neison 1256
Guise, Anthony John 1255
Guise, Caitlin Ruth 1256
Guise, Carole 1257
Guise, Christopher Francis 1256
Guise, (Christopher) James 1257
Guise, Christopher John 1256
Guise, Christopher Patrick 1256
Guise, Christopher Rivett 1256
Guise, Daphne Jean 1256
Guise, David Johnathan 1256
Guise, David Nigel 1256
Guise, Dianne Elizabeth 1256
Guise, Edward William 1256
Guise, Eileen Mary 1256
Guise, Gertrude Joyce 1256
Guise, Gladys Constance 1256
Guise, Gwynneth 1256
Guise, Hannah 1257
Guise, Holly Rebecca 1256
Guise, James Nicholas 1256
Guise, John Francis 1256
Guise, Judith Anne 1255
Guise, Larry Steven 1256
Guise, Marion Florence 1256
Guise, Megan Isabella 1256
Guise, Morfydd Meredydd 1256
Guise, Neil Reginald 1256
Guise, Nicola 1256
Guise, Nikki 1255
Guise, Patricia Frederica 1256
Guise, Peter Rivett John 1256
Guise, Rhian 1256
Guise, Ruth Victoria Margaret 1257
Guise, Sally 1255
Guise, Samuel Benjamin 1256
Guise, Simone Renée 1256
Guise, Susan 1256
Guise, Wendy Nola 1256
Guiver, Catherine Mary 210
Guiver, Ian 210
Gull, Angus William John 1257
Gull, Gillian Lee 1257
Gull, Jacqueline Mary 1257
Gull, Katie Alexandra 1257
Gull, Margaret 1257
Gull, Margaretha Catherine Johanna 1258
Gull, Mark Capel James 1257
Gull, Olivia 1257
Gull, Victoria Yvonne 1257
Gulliver, Christopher Ronald 1784
Gulliver, Patricia Jean 1784
Gulliver, Penelope Daphne 1784
Gulliver, Ronald 1784
Gully, Andrew Donald Mackenzie 2577
Gully, Catherine Mary Albinia 2577
Gully, Christopher Rolf Thomas 2576
Gully, Fiona Margaret 2577
Gully, (James) Edward Hugh Grey 2577
Gully, James Ian Mackenzie 2577
Gully, Mary Theresa 2577
Gummer, John Selwyn 537
Gummer, Penelope Jane 537
Gummer, Peter Selwyn 537
Gummow, Bruce 900
Gummow, Ian Andrew 900
Gummow, Rosalind Jane 900
Gundry, Alexandra Clare Victoria 3080
Gundry, Caroline Anne Sabina 3079
Gundry, David Edward Patrick 3080
Gundry, Edward Patrick 3079
Gundry, John Charles 2546
Gundry, Mark Alexander 2546
Gundry, Rachel Anne 3080
Gundry, Vyvien Frances 2546
Gundry-White, Charmian Eunice 2230
Gundry-White, George Geoffrey 2230
Gundry-White, Henry Simon 2230
Gundry-White, Jasper 2230
Gundry-White, Katherine Jane Louise 2230
Gundry-White, Laura 2230
Gundry-White, Madelaine Anne 2230
Gundry-White, Patrick 2230
Gundry-White, Timothy 2230
Gunn, Ann Veronica 964
Gunn, David James Paul 964
Gunn, Jennifer Mary 489
Gunn, Marcus Charles 2102
Gunn, Miranda Rosalind 2102
Gunn, Munro James 2102
Gunn, Nicola 964
Gunn, Paul Munro 2102
Gunn, Pauline Miranda 2102
Gunn, Petronella Clare 2102
Gunn, Reuben Harry 489
Gunn, Sarah Louise 489
Gunning, Alina 1259
Gunning, Angela Marion 1259
Gunning, Anthony Andrew Simon 1259
Gunning, Bernard Christopher 1259
Gunning, Brodie Adam 1259
Gunning, Caroline Anne 1258
Gunning, Christopher John Ross 1259
Gunning, Claudette 1259
Gunning, David Laurence 1259
Gunning, Derek John Robert 1259
Gunning, Diana Elizabeth 1259
Gunning, Eleanor 1259
Gunning, Elizabeth 1259
Gunning, Evelyn Briliana 1259
Gunning, George Bryce 1259
Gunning, George Peter 1259
Gunning, Heather Jean 1259
Gunning, Helen Nancy 1259
Gunning, Henry Michael 1259
Gunning, Hilda 1259
Gunning, Holly Michelle 1259
Gunning, Jennifer Christina 1259
Gunning, John Robert 1259
Gunning, Joseph Jeremy 1259
Gunning, June 1259
Gunning, Kevin Philip 1259
Gunning, Kristina Jaclyn 1259
Gunning, Leslie Anita 1259
Gunning, Lilian Jessie Isabella 1259
Gunning, Linda 1258
Gunning, Lori-Ann 1259
Gunning, Melanie Dawn 1259
Gunning, Michelle Wendy 1259
Gunning, Patricia Mary 1259
Gunning, Pauline Maud 1259
Gunning, Richard Ross 1259
Gunning, Rita 1259
Gunning, Susan Mary 1259
Gunning, Theressa Kathleen 1259
Gunning, Timothy Robin 1259
Gunston, Doris Gwendoline 1259
Gunston, Richard St George 1259
Gunston, Rosalind 1259
Gunston, Veronica Elizabeth 1259
Gupta, Anil Kumar 2629
Gurdon, (Brampton) Charles 695
Gurdon, Frances Henrietta 412, 695
Gurdon, Louisa-Jane 695
Gurdon, Philip Bertram 412
Gurdon, (Sacha William) Robin 695
Gurney, Alexandra Victoria 1389
Gurney, Ann 2143
Gurney, Anne Marie 995
Gurney, Carol James Hay 610
Gurney, Christopher Hay 610
Gurney, David Quintin 330
Gurney, Elizabeth Anne 330, 995
Gurney, Elizabeth Sara Ann 610
Gurney, Henry Robert Timothy 1389
Gurney, Isabel Margaret 1389
Gurney, Jacqueline 330
Gurney, Jonathan Kendal James 3040
Gurney, Joseph Brian Thomas 3040
Gurney, Margaret Elizabeth Diana 34, 1389
Gurney, Margaret Rose 3040
Gurney, Mariota Susan 1060
Gurney, Michael Jeremy 995
Gurney, Mungo 2821
Gurney, Nicola Ruth 330
Gurney, Oliver Samuel 1389
Gurney, Olivia Kate 3040
Gurney, Richard Eustace Thomas 34, 1389
Gurney, Richenda Victoria Amelia 1389
Gurney, Rowan 2821
Gurney, Sarah Carolyn 330
Gurney, William Ivan 995
Gurowich, Aaron Finbar Simon 2541
Gurowich, Celia Mary 2541
Gurowich, Paul Maxwell 2541
Gurowich, Timothy Peter 2541
Gurowski, Anya 1064
Gurowski, Richard Melchior Beaumont 1064
Gurowski, Rosanna 1064
Gush, Andrew 92
Gush, Camilla Mary 92
Gush, Giles Joseph Guerney 92
Gush, Henry Guerney 92
Guthe, Alexander 2503
Guthe, Annabel Mathilda 2503
Guthe, Sarah Jane 2503
Guthrie, Alexander Valentine Connop 1260
Guthrie, Anna 24
Guthrie, Barnaby Fairbairn 23
Guthrie, Barnaby Giles 1260
Guthrie, Diana Mary 1260
Guthrie, Elizabeth Dorothy Margaret 1260
Guthrie, Giles Malcolm Welcome 1260
Guthrie, Ian Benjamin 24
Guthrie, Ione Vivienne 23
Guthrie, Islay Mary 1260
Guthrie, Jennifer Sarah 24
Guthrie, Nicholas Bruce 24
Guthrie, Rhona Leslie 1260
Guthrie, Ross Cameron 24
Guthrie, Russell Sean 24
Guthrie, Ryan David 24
Guthrie, Victoria 1260
Guthrie-James, Christopher Leslie Donan 848
Guthrie-James, Diana Mary 848
Guthrie-James, Jaquetta Mary Theresa 848
Guthrie-James, Kenelm Henry Thomas 848
Guthrie-James, Marina 848
Guthrie-James, Michael David Ashworth 848
Guthrie-James, Namrata 848
Guthrie-James, Peter Edward 848
Guthrie-James, Sarah 848
Gutierrez, Alberto Juan 2747
Gutierrez, Andrew Ryan 2747
Gutierrez, Bryoni Kate 2747
Gutierrez, Cecily Louise 745
Gutierrez, Julio Jesus 745
Gutierrez, Kameron Blair 2747
Gutierrez, Susan Margaret 2747
Guy, Delia 921
Guy, Dominic William 921
Guy, Laura Jade 2922
Guy, Robert Lincoln 2922
Guy, Rosemary Ann 2922
Guy, Susannah 921
Gwatkin, Amy Jean Stapleton 1000
Gwatkin, Frederick John Stapleton 1000
Gwatkin, Hannah Rosemary Theophila Stapleton 1000
Gwatkin, Martha Elspeth 1000
Gwatkin, Peter F S 1000
Gwatkin, Rosemary Jean 1000
Gwinnett, Adrian John 248
Gwinnett, Doreen Stella 248
Gwinnett, Giles Marcus 248
Gwinnett, Jane 248
Gwinnett, Verity Jane 248
Gwyn, Anna Elizabeth 1872
Gwyn, Charles A H 669
Gwyn, Charnisay Ann 669
Gwyn, Christina Alice 1872
Gwyn, Christopher Benedict 2167
Gwyn, Clare 2167
Gwyn, Jessica 669
Gwyn, Katharine Henrietta 1872
Gwyn, Philip Anthony 1872
Gwyn, Rebecca 669
Gwyn, Richard Hwfa 1872
Gwyn, Simon 669
Gwyn, Susan Alice Margaret 1872
Gwyn, Victoria 669
Gwynne, Angela Madeline 201
Gwynne, Belinda Judith 201
Gwynne, Chloe Patricia 1999
Gwynne, Christopher Howard 201
Gwynne, Deborah Judith 201
Gwynne, Frances Josephine 201
Gwynne, Frederica Rosana Gale Lennox 1999
Gwynne, John Howard 201
Gwynne, Katherine Anne 201
Gwynne, (Nevile) Martin 1999
Gwynne, Patrica Louisa 1999
Gwynne-Evans, Clelia Marie 1008
Gwynne-Evans, Francis Tristan 1008
Gwynne-Evans, Gloria Marie 1008
Gwynne-Evans, Melody Louise Bernadette 1008
Gwynne-Evans, Monica 1008
Gwynne-Evans, Richard William 1008
Gwynne-Evans, Soraya Charlotte 1008
Gwynne-Evans, Teo Leslie 1008
Gwynne Jones, Mona 539
Gybbon-Monypenny, Doronée Felicia 2266
Gybbon-Monypenny, Duncan Reginald 2266
Gybbon-Monypenny, Peter 2266
Gyle-Thompson, Camilla Kate 1079
Gyle-Thompson, David Courtenay Gladstone 1079
Gyle-Thompson, Penelope 1079
Gyle-Thompson, Sara Elizabeth Ninita 1079
Gyulai, Donald Leonard Trevor 2009
Gyulai, Edward Llewellyn Alexander 2009
Gyulai, Gwendolyn Grace 2009
Gyulai, Leonard Alexander 2009
Gyulai, Sandra Agnes Grace 2009
Gyulai, Sarah Teresa Marion 2009
Gyulai, Susan Julianne Gladys 2009

H

Haak, Annabella Edith 2830
Haak, Anoushka Lara 2830
Haak, Charlie 2830
Haak, Daniel Johannes 2830
Haak, Diana Margaret 2830
Haak, Jochen Daniel 2830
Haak, Jonathan Daniel 2830
Haak, Naomi Tara 2830
Haak, Nicola Jane 2830
Haak, Poppy Anna 2830
Haak, Roderick Johannes 2830
Haak, Sam Michael 2830
Haak, Toby Daniel 2830
Habdank-Kolaczkowski, Diana 2063
Habdank-Kolaczkowski, Ryszard 2063
Habgood, Adrian George Chetwynd 1260
Habgood, Elliott 1260
Habgood, Francis John Stapylton 1260
Habgood, John Stapylton 557
Habgood, Nicolette Tamsin 1260
Habgood, Rosalie Mary Anne 1260
Habgood, Sebastian 1260
Habouch, Christine Mary 988
Habouch, Samir 988
Hacking, Alexander Roland Harry 1261
Hacking, Belinda Anne 1261
Hacking, Christian Eric George 1261
Hacking, Daniel Robert 1261
Hacking, Douglas Francis 1261
Hacking, Douglas Percival Bolton 1261
Hacking, Edgar Bolton 1261
Hacking, Elizabeth 1261
Hacking, Evangeline Grace 1261
Hacking, Fiona Margaret 1261
Hacking, Geoffrey Edgar 1261
Hacking, Joanna 1261
Hacking, (Leslie) Bruce 1261
Hacking, Mary 1261
Hacking, Matthew Bruce 1261
Hacking, (Maxwell David) Leo 1261
Hacking, Susan Margaret 1261
Hackley, Bart 1488
Hackley, Sarah Victoria 1488
Hackney, David Samuel 24
Hackney, Frederick Molyneaux 24
Hackney, Gail Patricia 24
Hackney, Irene Gillbee 2818
Hackney, Joel Bruce 24
Hackney, Richard Antony 525
Hackney, Sibell Jeanne 24
Hackney, Sylvia Margaret 525
Hackney, Sylvia Norah Grace 24
Haddock, Bradley Graham Geoffrey 290
Haddock, Holly Rachelle 290
Haddock, John Graham 290
Haddock, Mandy 290
Haddock, Rogan Shane 2824
Haddon, Alice Mary 1359
Haddon, Claire Elizabeth 2479
Haddon, Clodagh 2479
Haddon, Denise 2479
Haddon, John Richard 2479
Haddon, Juliet Annabel 2479
Haddon, Laura Mary 2479
Haddon, Martin Thomas 2479
Haddon, Patrick Oliver 2479
Haddon, Paul Antony 2479
Haddon, Richard Deacon 1359
Haddon, Teresa Mary 1359
Haddrell, Annabel Louise 2752
Haddrell, David Henry 2752
Haden-Guest, Anne 1265
Haden-Guest, Anthony 1265
Haden-Guest, Elizabeth Ann 1265
Haden-Guest, Hadley 1265
Haden-Guest, Jamie Lee 1265
Haden-Guest, Jean Pauline 1265
Haden-Guest, Julia 1265
Haden-Guest, Marjorie 1265
Haden-Guest, Nicholas 1265

Haden-Guest, Pamela Ann 1265
Haden-Guest, Thomas 1265
Haden-Taylor, Annabella 765
Haden-Taylor, Anthony St John 765
Haden-Taylor, Susan Rosemary 765
Hadfield, Alastair David 2054
Hadfield, Christopher John 2054
Hadfield, David Carleton 1705
Hadfield, David Peter 2054
Hadfield, Mary Ellen 1705
Hadfield, Melissa Maisie 1705
Hadfield, Richard Henry 1705
Hadfield, Samuel Mark 1705
Hadfield, Susan Margaret Anne 2054
Hadland, Guy 1171
Hadland, Jane Evelyn 1171
Hadley, Arthur Twining 971
Hadley, Denis Bernard 669
Hadley, Paulina Mary Louise 669
Hadow, Angus John 3013
Hadow, George Louis 3013
Hadow, John Wigram 3013
Hadow, Lettice Margaret 3013
Hadow, Patrick William 3013
Hadow, Robert Edward 3013
Hadow, Susan Frances 3013
Hadwen, Debbie Anne 437
Hadwen, Georgina Frances 725
Hadwen, Grahame Robert 437
Hadwen, James Brian Mackenzie 725
Hadwen, Michael Robert 437
Hadwen, Sally Virginia 437
Hadwen, Susan Jane 437
Haeri, David 734
Haeri, Mina 734
Haeri, Sophia Helen 734
Haeri, Victoria 734
Hagar, Ailsa Joan 1550
Hagar, Joan Florence 1550
Hagar, John David 1550
Hagart-Alexander, Boyd John 1266
Hagart-Alexander, Claud 1266
Hagart-Alexander, Elaine Susan 1266
Hagart-Alexander, Hilda Etain 1266
Hagen, Gillian Barbara 1917
Hagen, Richard Llewellyn Whitley 1917
Hager, Dolores Freda 3054
Hager, Donald Benjamin 3054
Hager, Douglas Gordon 3054
Hager, Jamie Donald 3054
Hager, Jarret Benjamin 3054
Hager, Judith Frances 2103
Hager, Lesley Jane 3054
Hager, Nancy Anna 3054
Hager, Natalie 3054
Hager, Raymond Benjamin 3054
Hager, Richard Raymond 3054
Hager, Robert Stewart 2103
Haggerston, Joan Adeline 1886
Haggerston Gadsden, Belinda Ann 1885
Haggerston Gadsden, Elizabeth Ann 1886
Haggerston Gadsden, Peter Drury 1885
Haggerty, Gillian Ruth 1947
Haggerty, Susan 1947
Hague, Jane Olivia Marion 2812
Haguenauer, Elizabeth Cecilia Jane 677
Haguenauer, Olivier Philippe 677
Hahn, Harold Daniel 1665
Hahn, Mary Helen 1664
Hahn, Stuart Arthur 1665
Haig, (Adrienne) Raina 1267
Haig, Alexander Douglas Derrick 1267
Haig, Alexander Veitch 265
Haig, Anthony Oliver 265
Haig, Archie-Anne Rose 1828
Haig, Belinda Valerie 265
Haig, Catherine Rose Ingrid 2600
Haig, Christopher Edward (Kit) 1827
Haig, Daphne Margaret 1517
Haig, (Elizabeth) Vivienne Thérèse 1267
Haig, Georgiana Elizabeth 2600
Haig, Gerolama 1267
Haig, Hugh Kenneth 2106
Haig, Hugo Peter 265, 1827
Haig, Iona Frances 265
Haig, Janey Fiona 265, 1827
Haig, (Jean) Henrietta Rose 2106
Haig, Jonathan Peter Wolseley 1517
Haig, Katharine Jane 1517
Haig, Kirsty Louise 265
Haig, Nigel Geoffrey Wolseley 1517
Haig, Peter Ian 2600
Haig, Rachel Louisa 2600
Haig, Susan Anne Harriet 265
Haig, William Robin 2600
Haile, Emily Rebecca 1562
Haile, Jeremy Peter 1562
Haile, Maroulla Judith 1562
Haile, Peter 1562
Haile, Sarah 1562
Haile, Scott Matthew 1562
Haines, Elizabeth 288
Haines, Francis Christopher Minton 288
Haines, George Arthur 1229
Haines, Holly Nicola 1229
Haines, Joan Elizabeth 272
Haines, Mary 1229
Haines, Michael Geoffrey Minton 288
Haines, Richard David Eliot 1229
Haines, Richard Walter Minton 288
Haines, Rosalind Marion Minton 288
Haire, John Arthur 2703
Haire, John Stewart 2703
Haire, Rosemary 2703
Hakin, Jessica Katie 2412
Halagaza, Bonnie Mildred 672
Halagaza, Mark Leonard 672
Halagaza, Paul 672
Hale, Barbara Selina 2327
Hale, C Martin 1877
Hale, Claire Alexandra 1831
Hale, Deborah Sinclair 97
Hale, Emily Angela 2327
Hale, Frederick Clifford 1877
Hale, Gaynor 97
Hale, Georgina Sylvia 1877
Hale, Harriet Sarita 186
Hale, James George 1877
Hale, Jean 2445
Hale, Jennifer 3053
Hale, Johanna 3053
Hale, John Maitland 3053
Hale, John William Sanford 186
Hale, Jonathan Wilmot 97
Hale, Jonathon 3053
Hale, Lettice Evelyn 931
Hale, Marjorie 3053
Hale, Melanie Sarita 186
Hale, Nathan Alexander 2327
Hale, Penelope Ann 315
Hale, Philip William 2327
Hale, Robert Mathew 931
Hale, Roger William Stephen 186
Hale, Ruth Sinclair 97
Hale, Simon 1831
Hale, Veronica Ann Leslie 315
Hale, Victoria Madeline 97
Hale, William Edward 1877
Hales, Catherine Rose Mary 1111
Hales, Celestria Magdalen Mary 1111
Hales, Teresa Joan 2882
Hales, Timothy M 1111
Hales-Tooke, Ann Mary Margaret 2239
Hales-Tooke, Breda 2239
Hales-Tooke, Giles Anthony Raphael 2239
Hales-Tooke, Hugh Benedict Milton 2239
Hales-Tooke, Jonathan Petre Turner Paul 2239
Haley, Bertha Frances Grace 500
Haley, Damien Michael Douglas 500
Haley, Ian Richard 500
Haley, R P 934
Haley, Rose Elizabeth 500
Haley, Siobhan Geraldine 500
Haley, Valerie 934
Halfhead, Christopher Norman 1998
Halfhead, Daphne Veronica 1998
Halfhead, Francesca 1998
Halfhead, Lucy Christina 1998
Halfhead, Michael Christopher 1998
Halford, Caroline 3020
Halford, Edward David 3020
Halford, (John) Michael 3020
Halford, John Wallis Williams 3020
Halford, Lucy Alexandra 3020
Halford, Peter David 3020
Halford, Susan Mary 3020
Halford-Thompson, Guy 132
Halford-Thompson, Hugh Maximilian 132
Halford-Thompson, Jean Violet 132
Halford-Thompson, John Maximilian 132
Halford-Thompson, Ralph Mark 132
Halifax, Anne 1468
Halifax, Francesca Marjorie 2880
Halifax, Peter Kershaw 2880
Halkett, Hugh Dalzell 3055
Halkett, Patricia Jane 3055
Halkyard, Daphne Caroline 61
Hall, Albert Joseph 1696
Hall, Alexander Bullock 192
Hall, Alfred Robert Petrie 1740
Hall, Alison Elizabeth Vivienne 1240
Hall, Alison Judith 306
Hall, Allan John 2659
Hall, Amelia Rose 887
Hall, Andrew Bullock 192
Hall, Andrew Campbell 1403
Hall, Andrew Nicholas Francis William 543
Hall, Angela Margaret 1271
Hall, Anna Louise 1607
Hall, Annabel Barbara 192
Hall, Annabel Rose 549
Hall, Anne 887
Hall, Annie Madeline Renée 1272
Hall, Araminta Patricia 1529
Hall, Benjamin Charles Edward 2751
Hall, Bernard Neville 1271
Hall, Bill 41
Hall, Camilla Jane Kathleen 2587
Hall, Carolyn Rosemary 556
Hall, Catherine Elaine 1403, 2923
Hall, Catherine Jane 1699
Hall, Catherine Norah 543
Hall, Charlotte Louise 2587
Hall, Christopher 237
Hall, Christopher John 2751
Hall, Christopher Peter 1615
Hall, Clare Elisabeth Alexandra 543
Hall, David 1607
Hall, David Barnet 2594
Hall, David Bernard 1270
Hall, David Bullock 192
Hall, David Christopher 1272
Hall, David G 2845
Hall, Delphinia Frances Annie 1347
Hall, Denise 1237
Hall, Diane 192
Hall, Doriel Sybil 2546
Hall, Dorothy Maud 1271
Hall, Edith 2594
Hall, Edward Michael 277
Hall, Edward N 2594
Hall, Edward St John 887
Hall, Eliza Charlotte 887
Hall, Elizabeth 2068
Hall, (Elizabeth) Jane 2077
Hall, Elizabeth Katharine Favell 192
Hall, Elizabeth Marian 237
Hall, Ellen 192
Hall, Eric Peter 278
Hall, Felicity 1272
Hall, Francesca 1699
Hall, Frederick Amery Kynaston 2751
Hall, Geoffrey Richard 1099
Hall, George Howard 1615
Hall, Georgina Miranda Mary 549
Hall, Gillian Mary 2587
Hall, Hereward Ambrose Bertram 1347
Hall, Imogen Penelope Veronica 1347
Hall, Irene Anne 1740
Hall, Isobel Ellen Ruby 758
Hall, Isobel Wendy Anne 758
Hall, Jack Julian Bunke 556
Hall, James Henry 1615
Hall, James Martin Norman Aylmer 2068
Hall, James Stewart 1740
Hall, Jane Anastasia 2751
Hall, Janet Eleanor 306
Hall, Janet Vanessa 2845
Hall, Jennifer Margaret 1254
Hall, Jeremy Arnold 2587
Hall, Jeremy John 278
Hall, Jill Mary 116
Hall, Joan Beatrice Annie 1696
Hall, Jocelyn Dorothy Clervaux 549
Hall, John Anthony 887
Hall, John Christopher 1272
Hall, John Derek 556
Hall, John Douglas Hoste 1271
Hall, Jonathan 345
Hall, Jonathan Shawcross 2594
Hall, Julia Nancy 1270
Hall, Kate Louise 200
Hall, Katherine Louise 2077
Hall, Kathleen Dorothy 2587
Hall, Katrina Favell 192
Hall, Kenneth 2077
Hall, Kenneth John 71
Hall, Laurence Alexander 2587
Hall, Leander Arthur Caspar 1347
Hall, Louise Mary 1607
Hall, Lucinda 887
Hall, Lysbeth 71
Hall, Madeline Thomasina 237
Hall, Marie Antoinette ('Mariette') 887
Hall, Marion Ruth 117
Hall, Mark Bullock 192
Hall, Melissa Sarah 1607
Hall, Michael Fearon 549
Hall, Michael Stanley 306
Hall, Michael Timothy Chaytor 549
Hall, Nicholas 345
Hall, Nicholas Robert Stuart Arnold 2587
Hall, Nicholas William 543
Hall, Nicola 1272
Hall, Nina Diana 277
Hall, Oliver Charles 2213
Hall, Olwen Evelyn 1272
Hall, Pamela 2659
Hall, Patricia Margaret 345
Hall, Patrick Campbell 1403
Hall, Patrick Robert Aylmer 2068
Hall, Penelope Ann 2213
Hall, Peter 1615
Hall, Peter Arnold 2587
Hall, Peter John 1529
Hall, Philip Stephen 200
Hall, Phoebe Emma 887
Hall, Rachel Helen 2077
Hall, Rachel Katherine 41
Hall, Richard 345
Hall, Richard Alexander Bullock 192
Hall, Richard James Fairfax 1347
Hall, Richard John Nepean Aylmer 2068
Hall, Robert Hamilton 1615
Hall, Robert Hugh Bullock 192
Hall, Robin Michael 278
Hall, Rosalind Mary 192
Hall, Rosemary Megan 2659
Hall, Rosie Niamh 556
Hall, Rupert Dyson 887
Hall, Samantha Mary 1272
Hall, Sarah Jane 1615
Hall, Sheila Margaret 2594
Hall, Simon Leslie 2213
Hall, Simon Patrick Rawlings 1254
Hall, Simone Primrose 1099
Hall, Sophie 1699
Hall, Stephen Philip St John 306
Hall, Stuart 2213
Hall, Susan Cicely 2068
Hall, Susan 200
Hall, Susan Felicity 1254
Hall, Susan (Shoonan) Rosemary Lee 1254
Hall, Teresa Elisabeth 200
Hall, Theodore Thomas 887
Hall, Thomas Armitage 887
Hall, Thomas James 1271
Hall, Timothy Edward 277
Hall, Timothy Mark Lee 1254
Hall, Tracy-Jane 2068
Hall, Venetia Juliet Antonia 2587
Hall, Veronica Ann 2659
Hall, Victoria Joy 1272
Hall, William Tobias 1699
Hall, Winifred Jean 1615
Hall-Dare, Veronica Maud 1301
Hallam, Ann Margaret 2054
Hallam, Donna Adele 549
Hallam, Kathryn Marie 549
Hallam, Lynne Marie 549
Hallam, Richard Wayne 549
Hallett, Anthony 538
Hallett, Edward George 538
Hallett, Faith Mary 538
Hallett, James Anthony 538
Hallett, Thomas Alexander Pitfield 538
Halliday, Cher Odette 1858
Halliday, David Benedict 918
Halliday, Donnet Jane 918
Halliday, Linda 1858
Halliday, Martin John 918
Halliday, Mary 918
Halliday, Mary Kate 918
Halliday, Michael Sebastian 918
Halliday, Wayne 1858
Hallifax, Anne 288
Hallifax, Thomas Ronald 288
Halligan, Mary Ellen 242
Halligan, Michael Anthony 242
Halling, Natalie 2411
Halling, Simon 2411
Halls, Evelyn Marie 2481
Halls, Joanne Michelle 2481
Halls, Marjorie 2480
Halls, Peter John 2480
Halls, Robin 2481
Halls, Sadie Evelyn 2480
Hallward, Christopher Graham 1269
Hallward, Clare 1269
Hallward, Jennifer Rose 1269
Hallward, John Marsham 1269
Hallward, Julia Anne 1269
Hallward, Katherine Rosemary 1269
Hallward, Mary Clare 1269
Hallward, Peter Marsham 1269
Halpern, Barbara 2719
Halphen, Georges 2460
Halphen, Monique 2460
Halpin, David 1307
Halpin, Helen Mary 1307
Halse, Bernard Thomas 1234
Halse, John William 1878
Halse, Judith Joanna 1234
Halse, Norma Renee 2084
Halse, Rosemarie Julia 1878
Halse, Rosemary Joy 2084
Halse, Varney Marren 2084
Halsey, Daniel John 96, 1274
Halsey, Elizabeth Virginia 96, 1274
Halsey, Guy Francis Johnston 96, 1274
Halsey, Juliet Mary Gough 96, 1274
Halsey, Katherine Audrey 1274
Halsey, Nicholas Guy 96, 1274, 2208
Halsey, Robert Frederick (Robin) 96, 1274
Halsey, Ruth 1275
Halsey, Samuel Treve 96, 1274
Halsey, Viola Georgina Juliet 96, 1274, 2208
Halstead-Morton, Emily Victoria 436
Halstead-Morton, Hannah Elizabeth 436
Halsted, Peter Gordon 2239
Ham, Isobel Clare 549
Ham, William Gordon 549
Hamber, Geoffrey R 1213
Hamber, Jill Auriol 1213
Hambley, Keith Thomas 3020
Hambley, Kenneth Charles Claude 3020
Hambley, Kim Lee Ann 3020
Hamblin, Emma Louise 406
Hamblin, Kirsty Alexandra 406
Hambling, (Herbert) Peter Hugh 1276
Hambling, Austin Peter 1276
Hambling, Colin Hugh 1276
Hambling, Helen 1276
Hambling, Lorayn Louise 1276
Hambling, Rachel Veronica 1277
Hambro, Alexander Robert 1277
Hambro, Alissa Katherine 1277
Hambro, Anthony Everard George 1277
Hambro, Anthony Martin 1278
Hambro, Benjamin Jake Alexander 1277
Hambro, Carl Nigel Ivan 1278
Hambro, Charles Edward 1277
Hambro, Charles James 1277
Hambro, Charles Nigel 1278
Hambro, Cherry Felicity 1277
Hambro, Christiana 1277
Hambro, Clementine Silvia 1869
Hambro, Diana 1278
Hambro, Elizabeth Helen 1277
Hambro, Eric 1277
Hambro, Everard Nigel 1278
Hambro, Evy Piers George 1277
Hambro, George Jay 1277
Hambro, Gwen 1278
Hambro, Helen 1277
Hambro, James Daryl 1278
Hambro, Jemima Rose Amice 1277
Hambro, Jonathan Christopher 1278
Hambro, Leo Percival 1277
Hambro, Margaret Anne 1278
Hambro, Marina Isabella Kimberly 1277
Hambro, Marjorie Caroline 1278
Hambro, Martin Paul Otto 1277
Hambro, Mary 1278
Hambro, May 1278
Hambro, Maya 1277
Hambro, Nicole J 1277

Herbert, Alan Mervyn Edward Hugh 507
Herbert, Alice Mary 2217
Herbert, Amanda Colleen 2306
Herbert, Andrew Clive 2305
Herbert, Andrew Mark 1563
Herbert, Annabel Lillian Elfrida 2993
Herbert, Anthony James 1370
Herbert, Benson 2993
Herbert, Caroline 1370
Herbert, Caroline Kennedy 1563
Herbert, Caroline Mary Louis 1370
Herbert, (Caroline) Serena 1083
Herbert, Caspar David 760
Herbert, Catherine 760
Herbert, Catriona 760
Herbert, Charles (Charlie) Clive 2305
Herbert, Chloe Victoria 506
Herbert, Christopher Dennis Charles 1370
Herbert, David Andrew 2306
Herbert, David Neil 1563
Herbert, Diana Christine 2306
Herbert, Diana Mary 2219
Herbert, E Nicholas D 1083
Herbert, Edith Ann 2306
Herbert, Edward Alan Mervyn Molyneux 2023
Herbert, Edward David 2306
Herbert, Emma Letitia 3013
Herbert, Emma Louise 2217
Herbert, Erica Anne 1370
Herbert, Flora Katinka 2217
Herbert, Francesca (Chica) 506
Herbert, Francesca Jeanie 506
Herbert, George Kenneth Oliver Molyneux 506
Herbert, George (Geordie) Reginald Oliver Molyneux 506
Herbert, Graham Paul 3013
Herbert, Guy W C 2993
Herbert, Henry George Reginald Molyneux 2295
Herbert, Henry Malcolm 506
Herbert, Henry Myles 1370
Herbert, Janet 3011
Herbert, Jean Margaret 506, 2295
Herbert, Jemima Juliet 2217
Herbert, Jennifer Mary 1370
Herbert, Joanna Frances Clare 2306
Herbert, Jonathan Nicholas William 2304
Herbert, Joy Sarah 2306
Herbert, Julian David 1370
Herbert, Juliet Letitia 3013
Herbert, Katharine 2306
Herbert, Katie Ella 2217
Herbert, Kenneth Falkner 1370
Herbert, Lucy Alison Julia 2306
Herbert, Marijke 2304
Herbert, Mark Graham 3013
Herbert, Mark Jeremy 1370
Herbert, Mark Philip Clive 2306
Herbert, Mary Patricia 507
Herbert, Michael Clive 2306
Herbert, Miranda 760
Herbert, Miranda Juliet 2217
Herbert, (Monica) Brenda 2305
Herbert, Nicholas Mark 2305
Herbert, Oliver George Laurie 2306
Herbert, Oliver Hayley Dennis 1370
Herbert, Penelope Gabrielle Serena 507
Herbert, Peter James 2306
Herbert, Robin Clive 1370
Herbert, Rosanna Bethan 3013
Herbert, Samantha Julie Esther 2304
Herbert, Saoirse 506
Herbert, Sophia Elizabeth 2217
Herbert, Sophie Louise Mary 2306
Herbert, Stephanie Moira Christina 2304
Herbert, Susan Mary 2306
Herbert, Terri 2306
Herbert, Thomas Guy Clive 2306
Herbert, Timothy James 2306
Herbert, Timothy William Okes 1370
Herbert, Valentine Henry Okes 3011
Herbert, William Alexander Sidney 2217
Herberts, Alison Philippa 909
Herberts, Catherine Elizabeth 909
Herberts, Penelope Anne 909
Herbison, Cathleen Laura 2157
Herbison, D 2157
Herbison, Finnola Margaret 2157
Herbison, John Patrick Arthur 2157
Herbison, Virginia Maria 2157
Herd, John David Fyfe Monckton 1120
Herd, Meghan Alexandra 1120
Herd, Sheelagh Margaret 1120
Herd, William Arthur 1120
Herdman, Catherine Star Violetta 2725
Herdman, Emerson John 2654
Herdman, Giles 2725
Herdman, James Emerson 2654
Herdman, Katherine Louise 2654
Herdman, Penelope Ann 2654
Heriot-Maitland, Alexandra 1646
Heriot-Maitland, Beatrice Constance 489
Heriot-Maitland, Charles 1646
Heriot-Maitland, Eliza 1646
Heriot-Maitland, James Richard 1646
Heriot-Maitland, Joanna 1646
Heriot-Maitland, Katherine 1646
Heriot-Maitland, Lewis Dalgleish 1646
Heriot-Maitland, Lucia Jane 1646
Heriot-Maitland, Marilyn 1646
Heriot-Maitland, (Mary) Lorne 1646
Heriot-Maitland, Patricia 1646
Heriot-Maitland, Patrick Richard 1646
Heriot-Maitland, Prudence Jane 1646
Heriot-Maitland-Dougall, Hilda 1646
Hermann, Susan Mohr 1021
Herold, Alastair James Campbell 2266
Herold, Philippa Leslie 2266
Herold, Richard Anthony John 2266
Herold, Suzanne Jayne 2266
Herold, Timothy James Francis 2266
Herold, Valdene Rae 2266
Heron, (Antony) Giles 196
Heron, Jonathan Crawford 922
Heron, Marigold Wendy Maude 922
Heron, Mary Rosalie 196
Heron-Maxwell, Angela 1382
Heron-Maxwell, Claire Louise 1380
Heron-Maxwell, Colin Mellor 1382
Heron-Maxwell, David Mellor 1380
Heron-Maxwell, Dorothy Geraldine Emma 1382
Heron-Maxwell, Hayley Claudia 1382
Heron-Maxwell, Kirsten Diana 1382
Heron-Maxwell, Mary Elizabeth Angela 1380
Heron-Maxwell, Paul Mellor 1382
Herring, Alice Elizabeth 1489
Herring, Auriol Mary 136
Herring, Brian 999
Herring, Charles Thomas 999
Herring, Christopher John Murray 136
Herring, Frederick Ernest 136
Herring, John Roger Le Strange 1489
Herring, Jonathan James Auriol 136
Herring, Margaret Lucinda 999
Herring, (Mary) Elizabeth Magdalen 1489
Herring, Mary Grace 999
Herring, Monica Viola 2336
Herring, Norman Alexander John 2336
Herring, Rafe Henry Le Strange 1489
Herring, Roger Peter Le Strange 1489
Herring, Thomas Peter Le Strange 1489
Herring, Victoria Diana 999
Herschell, Heather Margaret Mary 771, 1386
Herschell, Rognvald Richard Farrer 771
Hersey, Angela Faye 597
Hersey, Benjamin Stuart 597
Hersey, Daniel Anthony James 2112
Hersey, John Paul 2112
Hersey, John Wharton 2112
Hersey, Justin Robert 597
Hersey, Katherine Viola 2112
Hersey, Mark Stuart 597
Hersey, Robert Christopher John 2112
Hersey, Susan Bernice 597
Hersfield, Gabriel Ian 913
Hersfield, Neil 913
Hersfield, Virginia Ann 913
Hersfield, Zach Dunmore 913
Hervé, Diana 2786
Hervé, Jacques Alois 2786
Hervey, Aileen Margaret 371
Hervey, Anthony Gerald 371
Hervey, Benjamin James William Peacham 371
Hervey, Christopher Symes 371
Hervey, Frederick William Augustus 372
Hervey, Gerald Edward 371
Hervey, Hannah Rachel Louisa 371
Hervey, Isabella Frederica Louisa 372
Hervey, Jeanne Patricia 371
Hervey, Kenneth William 371
Hervey, Lesley 371
Hervey, Mary Agnes 371
Hervey, Rebecca Maria 371
Hervey, Simon Anthony 371
Hervey, Susan Mary 371
Hervey, Tanya Maria 371
Hervey, Timothy Hugh 371
Hervey, Toby James Symes 371
Hervey, Victoria Frederica Isabella 372
Hervey, Yvonne Marie 372
Hervey-Bathurst, Annabel Peta 1392
Hervey-Bathurst, Anne 1392
Hervey-Bathurst, Caroline Myrtle 1392, 2695
Hervey-Bathurst, Eleanor Maryse 1392
Hervey-Bathurst, Frederick Benjamin Guy 1392
Hervey-Bathurst, (Frederick) John Charles Gordon 2695
Hervey-Bathurst, Frederick William John 1392
Hervey-Bathurst, George Arthur Somers 1392
Hervey-Bathurst, Imogen Elizabeth Somers 1392
Hervey-Bathurst, Isabella Katharine Somers 1392
Hervey-Bathurst, James Felton Somers 1392, 1504
Hervey-Bathurst, Nancy Rose Somers 1392
Hervey-Bathurst, Sarah Rachel 1392, 1504
Hervey-Talbot, Andrew 2924
Hervey-Talbot, Brian Harvey 2924
Hervey-Talbot, Mary Louise 2924
Hervey-Talbot, Wendy 2924
Herzig, Ana 454
Herzig, Andrew Michael 832
Herzig, Anita 454
Herzig, Catherine Jane 832
Herzig, Edmund Martin 454
Herzig, Francis Patrick 454
Herzig, Hugh J 1385
Herzig, Hugh John 454
Herzig, Isobel Oriane Clare 454, 1385
Herzig, Jessica Angelica Rachel 1385
Herzig, Martin Robert 832
Herzig, Michael Leopold 832
Herzig, Peter John 832
Herzig, Petra 454
Herzig, Rosemary 832
Herzig, Stephen Christopher 454
Hesketh, Anna Mary 2027
Hesketh, Catherine Ingrid 2027, 2560
Hesketh, Christian Mary 1894
Hesketh, Francis Roger Fleetwood 2027
Hesketh, Mary Olivia 2027
Hesketh, Rob(ert) (Fleetwood) 2027, 2560
Hesketh, Violet Ingrid 2027
Hesketh-Prichard, James Michael 2892
Hesketh-Prichard, Rebecca Sophie Venetia 2892
Hesketh-Prichard, Richard Michael 2892
Hesketh-Prichard, Thomas Richard Edward 2892
Hessener, Auriol Marion 1606
Hessey, Marilyn Joan 1379
Hessey, Rachel Ann 1379
Hessey, Robert Leslie 1379
Hessey, Steven James 1379
Hester, Gordon 2375
Hester, Laura Leticia 2375
Hetherington, Ann Margaret 237
Hetherington, Charles Hoste 237
Hetherington, Dinah Mary 2876
Hetherington, Emma Sarah Elizabeth 237
Hetherington, John Gabriel 237
Hetherington, Josephine Mary 2876
Hetherington, Mark 2876
Hetherington, Peter Hoste 237
Hetherington, Rebecca Clare 237
Hetherington, Teresa 2876
Hetherington, Virginia Mary 2876
Heusser, Christine 667
Heusser, Hilary Dawn 667
Heusser, Melinda Christine 667
Heusser, Noelle Pepys 667
Heusser, Ronald Vincent 667
Hewat, Angus Davidson 3020
Hewat, Harry William Davidson 3020
Hewat, Isabella Anne 3020
Hewat, Sophie Anne 3020
Hewetson, Edward Anthony 1873
Hewetson, Gillian Mary 1873
Hewetson, Richard Allan Webster 1873
Hewetson, Richard Tatton Wedderburn 1873, 2144
Hewett, Anita Noreen 1396
Hewett, Bridget Elizabeth Anne 1396
Hewett, Brind Nicholas Andrew 1396
Hewett, Carol Lavina Linley 1561
Hewett, David Patrick John 1395
Hewett, Davina Jane 1561
Hewett, Denis Neale 1396
Hewett, Dorothy 1395
Hewett, Felicity Sheena 1395
Hewett, Geoffrey Alexander 1396
Hewett, George Andrew Kendall 1396
Hewett, Georgia Isabel Davina 1561
Hewett, Jason Conrad Neale 1396
Hewett, Jennifer Ann 1395
Hewett, Jeremy Patrick Neale 1396
Hewett, Kari Denise 1396
Hewett, Kate Suzanne Elizabeth 1395
Hewett, Lara Jane Linley 1561
Hewett, Leucha Elizabeth Vivian 2319
Hewett, Margaret 1396
Hewett, Mary Elinor 1396
Hewett, Matthew Patrick George 1395
Hewett, Merri Bernard Neale 1395
Hewett, Neale Brind Stuart 1395
Hewett, Neale John Patrick 1395
Hewett, Richard Harald 1396
Hewett, Richard William 1395
Hewett, Rosemary 1395
Hewett, Sarah Margaret 1395
Hewett, Sharron-Rose 1396
Hewett, Shirley Norma 1396
Hewett, Vanessa Annabel 1395
Hewett, William George Lear 1561
Hewett, Yuilleen Maude 1396
Hewitt, Alice Mary 1704
Hewitt, Alison Mary 1704
Hewitt, Alison Mary Patricia 1706
Hewitt, Anna Charlotte 1705
Hewitt, Annabel Louise 1704
Hewitt, Anthony George 1035
Hewitt, Anthony James 1704
Hewitt, Antonia Julie 1704
Hewitt, Brian James Lifford 1704
Hewitt, Catherine Jane 1705
Hewitt, Charles Edward James 1396
Hewitt, Christopher 1704
Hewitt, Cushla Mary 1705
Hewitt, Danielle Margaret 1704
Hewitt, David Edward 719
Hewitt, David William 1965
Hewitt, Diana Faith 719
Hewitt, Edward Alexander 1705
Hewitt, Edward Michael George 719
Hewitt, Elizabeth Margaret 1396
Hewitt, Ellen 1704
Hewitt, Emily Kate 1704
Hewitt, Frances Meta 1705
Hewitt, Gemma Francis 719
Hewitt, George Geoffrey 1705
Hewitt, Hamish William 1705
Hewitt, Heather Jean 1705
Hewitt, Hugo George 357
Hewitt, James Donald 1705
Hewitt, James Thomas Wingfield 1704
Hewitt, Jean Hamilton 1705
Hewitt, Joan Millicent 1705
Hewitt, Jody Lee 1705
Hewitt, Judith 1704
Hewitt, Judith Clair 1705
Hewitt, Julie Margaret-Anne 1704
Hewitt, Lucy Eleanor Mary 1965
Hewitt, Margot Joan 1705
Hewitt, Marguerite 1396
Hewitt, Mary 1704
Hewitt, Michael Joseph 1396
Hewitt, Nicola Jane 1705
Hewitt, Oliver Michael James 1704
Hewitt, Pamela Margaret 1396
Hewitt, Patrick Francis 1704
Hewitt, Peter David 1705
Hewitt, Peter John 1705
Hewitt, Peter Lifford 1704
Hewitt, Rebecca Roie Cecilia 1704
Hewitt, Richard James 1705
Hewitt, Richard James Lifford 1704
Hewitt, Robert Johnson 1705
Hewitt, Rowena Edith Mabel 1704
Hewitt, Ruth Lifford 1705
Hewitt, Sarah Jane 357
Hewitt, Susan Elizabeth 1704
Hewitt, Susan Jean 1705
Hewitt, Terence John Lifford 1704
Hewitt, Theodore Denis 1704
Hewitt, Thomas Cameron 1705
Hewitt, Timothy Christopher 357
Hewitt, Timothy David 1705
Hewitt, Timothy George 1396
Hewitt, Timothy James 1705
Hewitt, Victoria Alexandra Margaret 1396
Hewitt, Victoria Louise 1704
Hewitt, William Ian Atkinson 1705
Hewlett, Adam James 627
Hewlett, Deborah Mary 627
Hewlett, Jacob (Jake) Robert 627
Hewlett, Megan Ruth 627
Hewlett, Steven H 627
Hewson, Annabel Mary 1215
Hewson, Anne Jennifer 1215
Hewson, Clare Louise 1215
Hewson, David Patrick Lewis 1215
Hewson, George Patrick David 1215
Hext-Fremlin, Ann Therese Margaret 3064
Hext-Fremlin, Robert 3064
Hext-Fremlin, Shelley Naomi 3064
Heycock, Bridget 1275
Heycock, Caroline Bridget 1275
Heycock, Edward Alfred 1275
Heycock, Eleanor Rachel 604
Heycock, Jennifer Lucy 1275
Heycock, Philip Henry Faudel 604
Heycock, Sarah Kerensa Faudel 604
Heycock, Thomas Henry Trefusis 604
Heycock, Thomasine Mary 604
Heyer, Amrik Frances 2197
Heyer, Daleep Andrew 2197
Heyer, Jasdev Philip 2197
Heyer, Judith Ursula 2197
Heyer, Malaika 2197
Heygate, Catherine 1398
Heygate, Eun-Hee Isobella Gage 1397
Heygate, Frederick Carysfort Gage 1397
Heygate, Hildegard Mathilde 1398
Heygate, Joanna 1398
Heygate, Joyce Marion 1398
Heygate, Robert George Liam 1397
Heygate, Susan Fiona 1397
Heyman, Benjamin Edward 2222
Heyman, Christian Philip 2222
Heyman, Emma Mary 2222
Heymanson, Antonina 201
Heymanson, Concetta Caratazzolo 201
Heymanson, Jonathan Simon 201
Heymanson, Kate Louise 201
Heymanson, Rebecca 201
Heymanson, Simon John 201
Heysen, David Hans 2951
Heysen, Marie Suzanne 2951
Heyward, Michael 491
Heyward, Yona Leslie 491
Heywood, Adrian Christopher Lempriere 1401
Heywood, Alice Ruth 1401
Heywood, Alison 1401
Heywood, Alizen 1403
Heywood, Anna Rose 1689
Heywood, Annabel Jane 1401
Heywood, Annabel Jane Louise 9
Heywood, Annabel Sarah 1400
Heywood, Anne Helen 1401
Heywood, Barnabus Timothy 1403
Heywood, Benjamin Coote 9
Heywood, Benjamin Michael 1402
Heywood, Benjamin Michael Lempriere 1402
Heywood, Carolyn Awdry 1403
Heywood, Charles Bernard Mark 1402
Heywood, Charles Michael Lempriere 1402
Heywood, Christopher David 1401
Heywood, Christopher Lempriere 1401
Heywood, Christopher Richard 1401
Heywood, Claude Geoffrey 1401
Heywood, Daniel Oliver 1403
Heywood, David Geoffrey 1401
Heywood, David Mark 1402
Heywood, Denise 1403
Heywood, Denys Guy Lempriere 1401
Heywood, Eileen Maud 1402
Heywood, Elisabeth Ann 1401

Hill, Ian Meyrick Cuthbertson 374
Hill, Ina Philpott 1408
Hill, Isabella Diana Juliet 871
Hill, Isobel 1158
Hill, Ivan 1655
Hill, Jacinta Bree 1858
Hill, James Carthew 1407
Hill, James Geoffrey 1407
Hill, James Herbert 1411
Hill, James Lawrence Ingram 1409
Hill, James Rowland Edward 1411
Hill, James Stuart 585
Hill, Jane Elizabeth 1405
Hill, Jane Margaret 2617
Hill, Janet 1411
Hill, Janet Elizabeth 1407
Hill, Jason James 1411
Hill, Jason Paul 1411
Hill, Jason Stirling 1627
Hill, Jean 1411
Hill, Jean Mary 3036
Hill, Jeanette Colla 1405
Hill, Jennifer Ann 2332
Hill, Jeremy Adrian 3038
Hill, Jeremy David Rhydian 1407
Hill, Jeremy John Maurice 2682
Hill, Jessie May 1412
Hill, Joan 374
Hill, Joan Rosemary 591
Hill, Joanne 1411
Hill, Jocelyn 1411
Hill, John Richard 1408
Hill, John Rowland Clement 1407
Hill, Jonathan Robert 125
Hill, Jonathan Rowland Vaisey 1407
Hill, Josephine Valerie 1409
Hill, Joshua Julian 1406
Hill, Joshua Mark 1411
Hill, Joyce Ann 1408
Hill, Judith 528
Hill, Judith Marianne 585
Hill, Julian 1406
Hill, Julie 1411
Hill, Katharine Martha 1407
Hill, Kathleen 1412
Hill, Katie 3036
Hill, Katriona Helen 1407
Hill, Keith Wynn 1366
Hill, Kelly Marie 1412
Hill, Kevin Leslie 1411
Hill, Krystal Moira 1412
Hill, Larry 1858
Hill, Leah 1412
Hill, Leanne Marie 1411
Hill, Leonard Graham 1412
Hill, Leonard James 1412
Hill, Lianne 1405
Hill, Linda 1412
Hill, Linda Elizabeth Anne 3036
Hill, Linda Joan 2581
Hill, Lindy Sue 585
Hill, Lorraine Margaret 1411
Hill, Lydia May 1411
Hill, Lynette Jean 1411
Hill, Maddison Hyde 585
Hill, Malcolm Ross 1412
Hill, Marcus Adam James 1411
Hill, Marcus Jeremy 3038
Hill, Marcus Robert Francis 871
Hill, Margaret 1411
Hill, Margaret Anne 1410
Hill, Margaret Clare 140
Hill, Margaret Elizabeth 1412
Hill, Margaret Lydia Faith 84, 656
Hill, Marion 1405
Hill, Marjorie Virginia 1408
Hill, Marjory 1410
Hill, Mark 1411
Hill, Marwyn Albert 1412
Hill, Mary Elizabeth 1407, 1411
Hill, Matthew 3036
Hill, Matthew Anthony 1407
Hill, Matthew Augustus Fremantle 676
Hill, Maude Monk 1412
Hill, Maximilian Alexander 125
Hill, Mervyn George 1411
Hill, Michael David 1412
Hill, Michael John 1411
Hill, Michael Mytton 1406
Hill, Michael Peter John 1412
Hill, Michelle Jane 1627
Hill, Michelle Lisa 1858
Hill, Molly 1408
Hill, Muriel Beatrice 1407
Hill, Murray Richard 1412
Hill, Naomi Juliet 676
Hill, Nesta Gwendolinel 1408
Hill, Nicholas Anthony Owen 1407
Hill, Nicholas Jeremy John 2682
Hill, Nicola Margaret 1407
Hill, Nigel John 1407
Hill, Noel Brian 1406
Hill, Noreen 872
Hill, Norman 729
Hill, Oliver Rowland Vaisey 1407
Hill, Orlando Harry Wills 871
Hill, Orlando William Eyre 84
Hill, Owen Patrick 1411
Hill, Patricia Ann 1411
Hill, Patricia Simpson 2552
Hill, Paul 1411
Hill, Paul Timothy 1411
Hill, Pearl Iris 1412
Hill, Percival Thomas 1412
Hill, Peter Brabant 1408
Hill, Peter Robert 1408
Hill, Peter William 140
Hill, Philip James 199
Hill, Philip William Adrian 1411
Hill, Phyllis 1411
Hill, Piers 1158
Hill, Priscilla 1406
Hill, Raewyn Alice 1412
Hill, Rebecca Ailsa 1412
Hill, Richard 3036
Hill, Richard Hebert 1407
Hill, Richard Lansley 830
Hill, Richard Stephen 1407
Hill, Robert George 1412
Hill, Robert Maxwell 1411
Hill, Robert Richard 578
Hill, Robyn 1411
Hill, Roderic 2998
Hill, Roger Babington 1191
Hill, Rory Nathan 1412
Hill, Rosanna Seymour 1407
Hill, Roslyn Anne Dimech 585
Hill, Rowena Jane Imogen 1407
Hill, Rowland David 1405
Hill, Rowland John 1406
Hill, Rowland Paul 1406
Hill, Rowland Robert 1405
Hill, Rowley Wilson 1412
Hill, Roy Ernest 1411
Hill, Ruby Alice 1411
Hill, Russell George 1412
Hill, Russell Sale 1412
Hill, Ruth Monica 1406
Hill, Sandra Elizabeth 1409
Hill, Sara Frances 1407
Hill, Sarah Loraine 3036
Hill, Sarah-Jane Frances 1412
Hill, Sebastian Martin Coote 84
Hill, Selwyn Wootton 528
Hill, Sharon 1412
Hill, Shirley Fay 1412
Hill, Simon Phillip 1408
Hill, Simon Sebastian 135
Hill, Sophie 84
Hill, Stacey 528
Hill, Stanley George 1411
Hill, Stanley Norman 1412
Hill, Stephen 2617
Hill, Stuart John 676
Hill, Susan 199, 1407
Hill, Susan Elizabeth 135
Hill, Susan Felicity 830
Hill, Susan Letitia 2998
Hill, Suzanne 1407
Hill, Tamsin Jean 585
Hill, Tania Marie 1412
Hill, Thelma 1411
Hill, Theodore Alexander 578
Hill, Thomas Colin Evelyn 2682
Hill, Tina-Jane 1411
Hill, Tobias Hunter 135
Hill, Tristram Darwin 3038
Hill, Valerie May 1412
Hill, Venetia Clare 729
Hill, Vera Maria 1411
Hill, Violet Alice Valentine 2245
Hill, Virginia Ann 3038
Hill, Virginia Mary Elizabeth 1191
Hill, Warren Stephen 1412
Hill, Wendy 1411
Hill, Wendy Helen 2682
Hill, Yvonne Aletta 830
Hill, Yvonne Clare 1411
Hill, Zia 498
Hill-Hottinger, Rory Alexander 1406
Hill-Norton, (Ann) Jennifer 1413
Hill-Norton, Margaret Eileen 1413
Hill-Norton, Nicholas John 1413
Hill-Norton, Peter Tom 1413
Hill-Norton, Simon Nicholas Sebastian 1413
Hill-Norton, Tamara 1413
Hill-Smith, Elizabeth Vere 2594
Hill-Smith, S R 2594
Hill-Trevor, Caroline Anne 2845
Hill-Trevor, Deborah Helen 2845
Hill-Trevor, Diana Rosemary 2845
Hill-Trevor, Iain Robert 2845
Hill-Trevor, Nevill Edward 2845
Hill-Trevor, Susan Janet Elizabeth 2845
Hill-Wood, Anne Katherine 1414
Hill-Wood, Charles Denis 1414
Hill-Wood, Edward Charles 1414
Hill-Wood, Emma Victoria 1414
Hill-Wood, Ian Charles 1414
Hill-Wood, Jennifer Anne 1414
Hill-Wood, Joan Louisa 753
Hill-Wood, Julian Peter 1414
Hill-Wood, Michael Kerrison 1414
Hill-Wood, Patricia Ann 1414
Hill-Wood, Peter 1278
Hill-Wood, Peter Denis 1414
Hill-Wood, Samuel Thomas 1414
Hill-Wood, Sarah Frances 1414
Hill-Wood, Sarah H (Sally) 1414
Hill-Wood, Steven Guy 1414
Hill-Wood, Susan Michelle 1414
Hilleary, Alasdair Malcolm Douglas Macleod 435
Hilleary, Angus Ewan MacLeod 1655
Hilleary, Edward Kenneth Macleod 3081
Hilleary, Ewan Iain MacLeod 1655
Hilleary, Fiona Mary 435
Hilleary, Flora Elizabeth 435
Hilleary, Geordie 435
Hilleary, Grace Janet Mary 3081
Hilleary, Rosannagh Catriona 435
Hilleary, Susanna Rose 1655
Hillgarth, Jocelyn Nigel Herbert Gardner Alan Aubrey 506
Hillgarth, Nina 506
Hilliard, Alexandra Carey 1290
Hilliard, Georgina Mary 1290
Hilliard, Melinda Mary 1290
Hilliard, Richard Guy 1290
Hillier, Alan John 970
Hillier, Anthony Edward 2820
Hillier, Brenda Frances 2820
Hillier, Brendan 970
Hillier, Damien John 970
Hillier, David 101
Hillier, Harriet 2820
Hillier, Jane 2820
Hillier, Nicholas Leofric 2820
Hillier, Patience Sarah 101
Hillier, Roy 2820
Hillier, Wendy Sue 970
Hills, Brenda 2687
Hills, Douglas 2423
Hills, Jennifer Claire 1256
Hills, John Evelyn Baring 726
Hills, John George Baring 726
Hills, Katherine Adrian 726
Hills, Matthew William 2894
Hills, Michael Anthony 1256
Hills, Philip Anthony 2894
Hills, Rachel Margaret 2894
Hills, Rosemary Caroline 1256
Hills, Rosemary Ethel 726
Hills, Susan Elisabeth 2423
Hills, Thomas Edmund 2894
Hills, Veronica Adrian Harriet 726
Hilton, Philip James 798
Hilton, Sarah 798
Hinchcliff-Mathew, Alexandra 2039
Hinchcliff-Mathew, Andrew 2039
Hinchcliff-Mathew, Carol 2039
Hinchcliff-Mathew, Daniel 2039
Hinchcliff-Mathew, David 2039
Hinchcliff-Mathew, Eileen Charmian 2039
Hinchcliff-Mathew, John Gervase 2039
Hinchcliff-Mathew, Marilyn Nazabal 2039
Hinchcliff-Mathew, Marjory Charlotte 2039
Hinchcliff-Mathew, Murray Alan 2039
Hinchcliff-Mathew, Rose Ann 2039
Hinchcliff-Mathew, Susan Penelope 2039
Hinchcliff-Mathew, Vanessa 2039
Hincks, Margaret Emily 2056
Hincks, Peter 2056
Hind, Jacqueline Mary 1660
Hind, Michael 1660
Hind, Sally Louise 1660
Hinde, Amanda 3015
Hinde, Craig Sydney 3015
Hinde, Darren 3015
Hinde, Douglas Patrick 3015
Hinde, Glen Richard 3015
Hinde, Jeanette 3015
Hinde, Noirin Fitzpatrick 3015
Hinde, Patrick Christopher 3015
Hinde, Richard Courtney Buckley 3015
Hinde, Stephen Ross 3015
Hinde, Tamsan 3015
Hindley, Alexander William Oliver (John) 130
Hindley, Anthony Talbot 2547
Hindley, Caroline Jane 130
Hindley, Douglas William John 130
Hindley, Jane Mary 130
Hindley, Lawrence Hugh John 130
Hindley, Michael Edward Oliver 130
Hindley, Olga Ann 130
Hindley, Sally 2547
Hindley, Thomas Henry Walter 130
Hindlip, Cecily Valentine Jane 322
Hindmarsh, Brigid 25
Hindmarsh, Christopher John 25
Hindmarsh, John Marcos 25
Hindmarsh, Mary Ann 25
Hinds, Amanda Gay 1370
Hindson, Camilla Sarah 1684
Hindson, Catherine 1684
Hindson, Christopher Eldred 1684
Hindson, John Francis 1684
Hindson, Margaret 1684
Hindson, Richard Charles 1684
Hine, Jonet Christian 2832
Hines, Benjamin Robert 2699
Hines, Constance Madeleine 965
Hines, Fiona Madeleine 965
Hines, Florence 2699
Hines, Godfrey Joseph 965
Hines, Laura Veronica 2699
Hines, Michael Robert 2699
Hines, Pamela Beatrice 2699
Hines, Peter John 2699
Hines, Robert Leslie 2699
Hines, Stuart Alan 2699
Hingle, Arthur Thomas 371
Hingle, Gillian Mary 371
Hingle, Margaret Mary Bridget 371
Hingle, Margery 371
Hingle, Margery Jane 371
Hingle, Peter John Benedict 371
Hingle, Veronica Anne 371
Hinks, Alexander John 2703
Hinks, Benjamin Stewart 2703
Hinks, Frank Peter 2703
Hinks, Julius James 2703
Hinks, Susan Mary 2703
Hinloopen, Claudine Emilie 317
Hinloopen, H M 317
Hinton, Barbara Ann 2182
Hinton, Bruce 2182
Hinton, Deborah Mary 2898
Hinton, Harriet Mary 2240
Hinton, Jennifer Ann 2182
Hinton, Jeremy Charles Dorsett 115
Hinton, John Dorsett Owen 115
Hinton, John Murray Raynor 115
Hinton, Josephine Mary Vivian 2898
Hinton, Mark William 2240
Hinton, Rosalind Ann 115
Hinton, Sarah Margaret 115
Hinton, Stuart Bruce 2182
Hinton, Wendy Lucille 2182
Hippisley, Antonia Frances Serena Olivia 1840
Hippisley, Caroline Ann 2146
Hippisley, Catherine Ann 2146
Hippisley, David John 2146
Hippisley, Elizabeth Anne 1840
Hippisley, Fiona Jane 2146
Hippisley, Lucinda Mary 2146
Hippisley, Michael John 2146
Hipwood, Camilla Diana 2991
Hipwood, Howard J 2991
Hipwood, Rosanna Charlotte 2991
Hipwood, Sebastian John 2991
Hird, David Ian 456
Hird, Jean Laura 456
Hiscocks, Antonia Mary 1151
Hiscocks, Nicholas Robin Thomas 1151
Hiscocks, Robert Henry Stallybrass 1151
Hiscocks, Sophie Jane Susannah 1151
Hiscox, Henry Charles 581
Hiscox, Julia Elizabeth 581
Hiscox, Milo Edmund 581
Hiscox, Robert Ralph Scrymgeour 581
Hiscox, Sidney John 581
Hitchings, Andrew Hope 1726
Hitchings, Charles Robin 1726
Hitchings, Guy Everingham 1726
Hitchings, Mark Alexander 1726
Hitchings, Rosemary Patricia 1726
Hives, Alice 1416
Hives, Annabelle 1416
Hives, David Benjamin 1416
Hives, Dinah 1416
Hives, Ellen 1416
Hives, Gladys Mary 1416
Hives, Helen Louise 1416
Hives, Imogen Jean 1416
Hives, Janet Rosemary 1416
Hives, Jeremy Robert 1416
Hives, Lawrence Ernest William 1416
Hives, Liza Joanna 1416
Hives, Michael Bruce 1416
Hives, Nigel Edward Ian 1416
Hives, Oscar 1416
Hives, Paul Michael 1416
Hives, Robert George 1416
Hives, Shirley 1416
Hives, Sophie Josephine 1416
Hives, Thomas Francis 1416
Hives, Victoria Jane 1416
Hives, William Duncan 1416
Hoah, Anthony Wayne 2928
Hoah, Christopher Henry 2928
Hoah, Evelyn May 2928
Hoah, Jason Henry 2928
Hoah, Lee 2928
Hoah, Selwyn Barton 2928
Hoare, Alexander Richard Quintin 1268
Hoare, Andrew James 1418
Hoare, Angela Francesca 1419
Hoare, Anne Violet 2923
Hoare, Arabella Jane 2541
Hoare, Arabella Peggy Marion 1590
Hoare, Arabella S 467
Hoare, Arthur Malortie 585
Hoare, Beverley Jean 1420
Hoare, Brioni 2923
Hoare, Camilla 855
Hoare, Caromy 467
Hoare, Caspar Michael Douro 1971
Hoare, Cecilia Violet 2283
Hoare, Cedric Hoare 392
Hoare, Charles Antony Richard 585, 2323
Hoare, Charles James 1417
Hoare, Charles Mark 1420
Hoare, Charles Martin Richard 1268
Hoare, Charles William Reginald 91
Hoare, Charlie Benjamin Douro 2541
Hoare, Christopher Henry St John (Toby) 855
Hoare, Clare Githa 1420
Hoare, David John 1421
Hoare, David O'Bryen 1418
Hoare, Diana Bridget 1590
Hoare, Dorothy Ann Katherine 585
Hoare, Dorothy Mary 2923
Hoare, Edith 2923
Hoare, Edward Bryan 1417
Hoare, Edward Eustace 1590
Hoare, Elizabeth Albinia 157
Hoare, Elizabeth Jean 2923
Hoare, Elizabeth Mary 1268
Hoare, Elizabeth McClean 1417
Hoare, Eric Reginald 1420
Hoare, Felicity Anne 1417
Hoare, Fiona Mary 1842
Hoare, Frances Evelyn 1268
Hoare, Francis 1590
Hoare, Geoffrey Charles Brodie 1420

Hoare, Georgiana Adeline 70
Hoare, Giles 855
Hoare, Gladys Margaret 1420
Hoare, Helen 1420
Hoare, Henry Cadogan 467
Hoare, Henry Ronald John 585
Hoare, Henry Samuel Malortie 585
Hoare, Henry Timothy 467
Hoare, Jacqueline 1419
Hoare, James Alexander 1590
Hoare, Jane Alice Patience 91
Hoare, Janet Frances Mary 585
Hoare, Jeremy Lachlan 392
Hoare, Jhansi 2323
Hoare, Jill 2323
Hoare, Jocelyn Charles Stewart 157
Hoare, John Michael 1420
Hoare, Joseph Andrew Christopher 91, 2288
Hoare, Kalwinder 2323
Hoare, Kate Annabella 1417
Hoare, Louisa 1417
Hoare, Lucy Mary Christina 91
Hoare, Marcelle 1418
Hoare, Margaret Edith 1420
Hoare, Marion Gertrude 1867
Hoare, Marjorie Francis 585
Hoare, Matthew James 1418
Hoare, Maxine 1418
Hoare, Melanie Louisa 2282
Hoare, Meriel Karen 1420
Hoare, Michael John 1420
Hoare, Morag 1420
Hoare, Natalie Kathleen 1421
Hoare, Nicholas 2923
Hoare, Nicholas Colt 467
Hoare, Nicholas David Douro 2541
Hoare, Nicola 2923
Hoare, Nicola Clare 157
Hoare, Nicole Suzanne 392
Hoare, Nigel 1420
Hoare, Oliver George David 2282
Hoare, Oscar 855
Hoare, Patrick Reginald Andrew Reid 2923
Hoare, Paul Reginald Richard 1420
Hoare, Peter Richard 1420
Hoare, Poppy 2923
Hoare, Reginald Arthur Reid 2923
Hoare, Reginald Merrick 1420
Hoare, Richard Charles 1420
Hoare, Richard Francis 1590
Hoare, Richard James O'Bryen 1418
Hoare, Richard Michael St George 1420
Hoare, Richard Quintin 1268
Hoare, Richard Sumner Anthony 1420
Hoare, Robert Patrick James 2282
Hoare, Robyn Joy 392
Hoare, Ronald James 157
Hoare, Rosemary Brodie Hallowell 1420
Hoare, Rosemary Jane 1418
Hoare, Sally Ann 1418
Hoare, Sam Patrick Douro 2456
Hoare, Sarah Jane 855
Hoare, Selina Albinia 157
Hoare, Simon Jonathan 2282
Hoare, Simon Merrick 1421
Hoare, Sorrel 2923
Hoare, Stewart John 1418
Hoare, Thomas Edward 2323
Hoare, Thomas Jame Douro 2541
Hoare, Timothy James 392
Hoare, Virginia Victoria 1421
Hobart, Andrew Hampden 422
Hobart, Anthony Hampden 1421
Hobart, Benedict Conrad William 422
Hobart, Caroline Fleur 1421
Hobart, Charles Hampden 1421
Hobart, Christopher Beauchamp 422
Hobart, Diana (Baba) 1421
Hobart, Edward Andrew Beauchamp 422
Hobart, George Hampden 1421
Hobart, Halina Zofia 422
Hobart, James Henry Miles 1421
Hobart, Jeremy Charles 422
Hobart, Jessica 1421
Hobart, Joanna Margaret 422
Hobart, John Hampden 422
Hobart, John Henry 422
Hobart, Kate 1421
Hobart, Katherine Anne 1421
Hobart, Leone 422
Hobart, Louise Gertrude 422
Hobart, Mark Michael 422
Hobart, Maureen 422
Hobart, Michael Wallace 422
Hobart, Patricia Mildred 422
Hobart, Phyllis Marion Rhoda 422
Hobart, Richard Hampden 422
Hobart, Robert Anthony 422
Hobart, Robert Henry 1421, 1798
Hobart, Simon Vere 422
Hobart, Sophie Camilla 1421
Hobart, (Una-Mary) Diana 1798
Hobart-Hampden, Alison 421
Hobart-Hampden, Gladys 423
Hobart-Hampden, Margot Macrae 423
Hobart-Topp, Annika Alexandra 422
Hobart-Topp, Matthew 422
Hobbs, Andrew Arthur Duncan 1880
Hobbs, Arabella Leonie 239
Hobbs, Caroline Anne 1154
Hobbs, David Andrew 1880
Hobbs, Francis 453
Hobbs, Jandy 1880
Hobbs, Joanna Rachel 453
Hobbs, John 3007
Hobbs, John Anthony 1154
Hobbs, Lola Dawn 3007
Hobbs, Sophie Louise Ann 239
Hobern, Andrew Robin 1413
Hobern, Clare Alyce 1413
Hobern, Kathleen Ann 1413
Hobern, Michael 1413
Hobern, Sean Maxwell 1413
Hobhouse, Alexander 1422
Hobhouse, Benjamin Alexander Cam 1422
Hobhouse, Charles John Spinney 2160
Hobhouse, Elspeth Jean (Jo) 1422
Hobhouse, George 1422
Hobhouse, Hugh 1422
Hobhouse, James Charles 1422
Hobhouse, John Cam 1422
Hobhouse, John Spencer 1422
Hobhouse, Judy Margaret 1422
Hobhouse, Julia Isobel 1422
Hobhouse, Katrina 1421, 2160
Hobhouse, Louise 1422
Hobhouse, Mark Cam 1422
Hobhouse, Martin Hugh John 1422
Hobhouse, Matthew Jack 1422
Hobhouse, Nicola 1422
Hobhouse, Rebecca Sarah 1422
Hobhouse, Sarah 1422
Hobhouse, Sophia 1422
Hobhouse, Stephanie 1422
Hobhouse, Thomasina 1422
Hobill-Cole, Flora Roma Maroa 1955
Hobill-Cole, Frank 1955
Hobill-Cole, Frank Molesworth 1955
Hobill-Cole, Robert Molesworth 1955
Hobill-Cole, Rowena Molesworth 1955
Hobson, Amanda Rosemary 593
Hobson, Amelia Rose 990
Hobson, Andrew James Alan 521
Hobson, Barnaby John 2063
Hobson, Bruce 990
Hobson, Dilys Richenda 2063
Hobson, Jake Timothy 2063
Hobson, Marian Rose 990
Hobson, Paul 1829
Hobson, Richenda Eveline 2063
Hobson, Samuel Jeffrey 2063
Hobson, Sophie 1829
Hobson, Timothy Hayward 2063
Hochschild, Augustin Emil 2229
Hochschild, Fabrizio Gerald Arturo 2229
Hochschild, Maurice Leo Robert 2229
Hocking, Gregory Francis 325
Hocking, Gwendalyn Jean 325
Hocknell, Anna Catherine 966
Hocknell, Catherine 966
Hocknell, Edward H 966
Hocknell, Elizabeth Anne 1406
Hocknell, Grizel Patience 966
Hocknell, Henrietta Jean 966
Hocknell, Richard Wilson 1406
Hocknell, Sarah Ann 1406
Hodari, Aaron 1137
Hodari, Juana 1137
Hodari, Veronica Roxana 1137
Hodder, Donald 2516
Hodder, Mary Veronica 2516
Hodge, Alexandra Albinia 1702
Hodge, Clara Albinia 1702
Hodge, Marcus A 1702
Hodge, Margaret Norma 1423
Hodge, Sally Joan 1423
Hodge, Vera Estelle 1423
Hodge, Vivienne 1423
Hodges, Alison Mary 2760
Hodges, Anne 2012
Hodges, Bruce 310
Hodges, Caroline Sheila 310
Hodges, David John 2012
Hodges, Elizabeth Mary 2760
Hodges, Gabrielle 279
Hodges, Gavin Cliff 279
Hodges, Jeremy George 668
Hodges, Jonathan Francis 668
Hodges, Katherine Mary 2760
Hodges, Linnea 279
Hodges, Marcus Birkett Adam 279
Hodges, Mary 668
Hodges, Michael Jeremy 2616
Hodges, Patrick Michael 2760
Hodges, Roy 668
Hodges, Rupert Henry 2760
Hodges, Veronica Mary 2616
Hodges, Victoria Françoise 279
Hodgetts, Charles Patrick 74
Hodgetts, Edward William 74
Hodgetts, George Harold 74
Hodgetts, Harold Patrick 74
Hodgetts, Mary 74
Hodgin, Daphne Roseabella Louise 1905
Hodgin, Wilfrid Rankin 1905
Hodgkin, Amy Beatrice 1971
Hodgkin, Barbara 1971
Hodgkin, Edward Eliot 1971
Hodgkin, George Harry 1971
Hodgkin, Harry John 1971
Hodgkin, John Eliot 1971
Hodgkin, Karen Aagot Georgina 1971
Hodgkin, Karen Lesley 1971
Hodgkin, Lucy Margaret 1971
Hodgkin, Polly Grace 1971
Hodgkin, Richard Eliot 1971
Hodgkinson, David John Tresilian 3012
Hodgkinson, Dominic Edward 2005
Hodgkinson, Edward 3012
Hodgkinson, Elizabeth Anne 1234
Hodgkinson, John 1234
Hodgkinson, John Francis Nicholas 3012
Hodgkinson, Laura 1234
Hodgkinson, Mark 3012
Hodgkinson, Patrick Francis 3012
Hodgkinson, Simon Nicholas 3012
Hodgkinson, Steven 1234
Hodgkinson, Thomas William 2005
Hodgson, Alan 2306
Hodgson, Alexandra Louise Pomeroy 1301
Hodgson, Camilla Rose 1723
Hodgson, Christopher James 1723
Hodgson, Christopher Prouty Sanford 1301
Hodgson, Clare Lucy 1723
Hodgson, Emily Barbarina 2306
Hodgson, Freda Violet 3015
Hodgson, Gabrielle Lavinia 1723
Hodgson, Geoffrey Peter Sanford 1301
Hodgson, (Helen) Mary Ursula 1301
Hodgson, Henry James 1723
Hodgson, Jean Margaret 1622
Hodgson, Jonathan Charles 1622
Hodgson, Matthew William 2306
Hodgson, Melissa 1301
Hodgson, Nicholas Pomeroy Sanford 1301
Hodgson, Olivia 1301
Hodgson, Robert John 1622
Hodgson, Sarah Barbarina 2306
Hodgson, Sarah Jane 1622
Hodgson, Sarah Rebecca 1723
Hodgson, Thomas Edward 1622, 2306
Hodgson, Ursula Virginia Sanford 1301
Hodgson, William Vere 3015
Hodson, Alexandra Mary 2442
Hodson, Anthony Edward 783
Hodson, Betty Estelle 1424
Hodson, Caroline Rose 307
Hodson, Catherine 1423
Hodson, Cecil George 1424
Hodson, Christopher James 783
Hodson, Elizabeth Charlotte Sarah 2863
Hodson, Fay Adah Rachel 1043
Hodson, Fiona Marion 1424, 1545
Hodson, Flora Anne 1424
Hodson, George Patrick 1424
Hodson, Hannah Rachel 1548
Hodson, James Patrick 1424, 1545
Hodson, James Roy Namani 1548
Hodson, Jane Katrina 1423
Hodson, Jennifer Alison 1548
Hodson, John Royden Cole 1043
Hodson, Joseph Patrick Luke 1548
Hodson, June 1424
Hodson, Kathleen (Kate) Mary Florence 1424, 2134
Hodson, Margaret-Anne 783
Hodson, Mark Adair 1424, 2134
Hodson, Patrick Douglas Gerard 1548
Hodson, Patrick Richard 1424
Hodson, Rita 2442
Hodson, Rupert Edward 1424
Hodson, Sophie Louise 307
Hodson, Tania Elizabeth 1423
Hodson, Texicia 307
Hodson, Tony 307
Hodson, Vera Constance Marjory 1424
Hoelter, Christopher Charles 2104
Hoelter, Georgia Helen 2104
Hoffen, Gillian Mary 698
Hoffen, Harry Michael Rogers 698
Hoffen, Lucy Gillian Mary 698
Hoffen, Roger 698
Hoffen, Rupert Peter Rogers 698
Hoffman, Bradney Stan Theodore 1229
Hoffman, Dahl Wendell Eduard 1229
Hoffman, Dennis 1663
Hoffman, Eileen Mary 195
Hoffman, Karen Kathleen 1663
Hoffman, Katrina Mary 195
Hoffman, Ken 195
Hoffman, Mandy Lee 195
Hoffmann, Gillian Lorna 1424
Hofmann, Heinrich 2835
Hofmann, Helen Mary 2835
Hofmann, Michael Leonhard 2835
Hogan, Anne Maree 686
Hogan, Gareth Michael Colin 2987
Hogan, Xavier 686
Hogarth-Scott, Janet 591
Hogarth-Scott, Robert Stirling 591
Hogben, Helen Abigail 2472
Hogben, Roger David 2472
Hogben, Sally Ann 2472
Hogg, Adam Charles 1424
Hogg, Adam Stewart 2699
Hogg, Alice Emily Geraldine 1426
Hogg, Alison Pauline 1424
Hogg, Amanda Elizabeth 2042
Hogg, Anthony Oliver Richard 1979
Hogg, Arabella Louisa Daphne 1979
Hogg, Barbara Elizabeth 468
Hogg, Barbara Mary Elisabeth 1426
Hogg, Camilla Adèle 1979
Hogg, Charlotte Katherine 1425
Hogg, Charlotte Mary 1268
Hogg, Colin Grant Ogilvie 1807
Hogg, Cynthia Rose 1807
Hogg, D Clare 1268
Hogg, Daniel Richard 1424
Hogg, Deborah 1425
Hogg, Deidre 1268
Hogg, Douglas 1424
Hogg, Douglas Martin 1267
Hogg, Elizabeth Anne Thérèse 1027, 1424
Hogg, George 2042
Hogg, James Edward 1424
Hogg, James Richard Martin 1268
Hogg, Jane Margaret 1425
Hogg, Joanna Wynfreda 2088
Hogg, John Goldsborough 2088
Hogg, John Nicholson 468, 1425
Hogg, Judith 1699
Hogg, Lucy Mary Arden 1426
Hogg, Madeleine Victoria 1424
Hogg, Malcolm David Nicholson 1426
Hogg, Mark Arthur Philip 1425
Hogg, Mark John 1699
Hogg, Mary Clare 1426
Hogg, Michael David 1027
Hogg, Nicola Frances 1425
Hogg, Oliver John 1424
Hogg, Patricia Isolda 1979
Hogg, Peter W A 1979
Hogg, Piers Michael James 1424
Hogg, Quinton John Neil Martin 1268
Hogg, Richard John Nicholson 1426
Hogg, Sandra Lea 1699
Hogg, Sarah Alice 1424
Hogg, Sarah Edith Noel 2088
Hogg, Sarah Elizabeth Mary 344, 1267
Hogg, Sarah Jane Ogilvie 1807
Hogg, Simon Charles 1425
Hogg, Stephen Mark 1425
Hogg, Vanessa Charlotte Ogilvie 1807
Hogg, Wilfred John 1699
Hoggard, Marie Tephea Diana 2131
Hoguet, Roland Henry 2459
Hohenzollern, Antonia 635
Hohler, Amanda Sophie 1867
Hohler, Camilla Clare 1867
Hohler, Clare Rosemary 1867
Hohler, Eveline Suzanne 1439
Hohler, Gerald Arthur 2750
Hohler, Harriet Valentine 1867
Hohler, Henry Arthur Frederick 1439
Hohler, Margaret Cynthia 2750
Hohler, Rio Tyrrell Arthur 1867
Hohler, Rupert John Frederick 1867
Hohler, Thomas Edward 2750
Holbarow, (Cynthia) Jane 1582
Holbarow, Simon D 1582
Holborow, Crispin David Jermyn 683
Holborow, Geoffrey Jermyn 683
Holborow, George Jermyn Maunsel 683
Holborow, Louise Cecilia 683
Holborow, Mary Christina 683
Holborrow, Anthea Kathleen 1404
Holborrow, Emma Katherine 1404
Holborrow, Richard 1404
Holbrook, Carolyn Anne 1786
Holbrook, Charles Philip Elston 1786
Holbrook, Hannah Claire 1821
Holbrook, Jonathan 1821
Holbrook, Miranda Carolyn 1786
Holbrook, Philip Norman Elston 1786
Holbrook, Rachel 1821
Holbrook, Ruth Helen 1821
Holcroft, Alexander James Culcheth 1426
Holcroft, Camilla 1426
Holcroft, Charles Anthony Culcheth 1426
Holcroft, Charmian Joy 1426
Holcroft, Christopher Nicholas 710
Holcroft, Elizabeth 1426
Holcroft, Harry Christopher Esmond 710
Holcroft, Harry St John 710
Holcroft, Michael William Culcheth 1427
Holcroft, Samara Elisabeth 1426
Holcroft, Sarah Jane 710
Holcroft, Tania Melanie 1426
Holcroft, Thomas Marcus Culcheth 1426
Holcroft, Timothy Gilbert Culcheth 1426
Holcroft, Toby David 1426
Holden, Andrew Charles 1428
Holden, Anthony Ivan 1428
Holden, Anthony Richard Norman 1427
Holden, Atie 1428
Holden, Benjamin John 1428
Holden, Bernadette Anne 1428
Holden, Brian Peter John 1428
Holden, Carl Temple 1428
Holden, Caroline Anne 1428
Holden, Caroline Jane 1427
Holden, Christopher Derek 1428
Holden, Christopher John 1427
Holden, Cynthia 1428
Holden, David Lawrence 1428
Holden, Deborah Elizabeth 1427
Holden, Derek John 1428
Holden, Dorothy 1428
Holden, Duncan Dudley 1427
Holden, Elizabeth Anne 1428
Holden, Elizabeth Barbarina 2306
Holden, Emma Jane 1428
Holden, Enid Natalie 1428
Holden, Ethel 1428
Holden, Frances Joan 1427
Holden, Golda 1428
Holden, Helen 1427
Holden, Hubert Joshua Robert 2306, 2462
Holden, Jacqueline Peta 1428
Holden, James Joseph 1428
Holden, James Temple 1428
Holden, Jonathan Robin 1428
Holden, Joseph Anthony 1428
Holden, Juliet 1427
Holden, Leslie 36
Holden, Lucia Hermione Sophia 2306, 2462
Holden, Margaret Susan 1428
Holden, Marjorie 1428

Holden, Mark Alan 2942
Holden, Matthew Keith 1427
Holden, Michael Peter 1427
Holden, Nancy 1428
Holden, Norman Michael 1428
Holden, Patricia Joan 1428
Holden, Patricia Kathleen 1428
Holden, Paul 1427
Holden, Peter James 1428
Holden, Peter Ritson 1427
Holden, Richard Ingham 1428
Holden, Richard John 1428
Holden, Rita 1428
Holden, Robert Arthur 1428
Holden, Robert David 2306, 2462
Holden, Robin John 1428
Holden, Ruth 1427
Holden, Samuel Ivan 1428
Holden, Sharon Joyce 1428
Holden, Sharon Leigh 2942
Holden, Susan 1428
Holden, (Susan) Emily Frances 2306, 2462
Holden, Suzanne 1428
Holden, Teresa 36
Holden, Vivien Mary 1427
Holden, William 1428
Holder, Alan 2456
Holder, Alexander John 1429
Holder, Barbara 1429
Holder, Caroline Margaret 1955
Holder, Hugo Richard 1429
Holder, Judith Mary 1429
Holder, (Linda) Kinvara 2456
Holder, Margaret 1429
Holder, Marjorie Emily 1429
Holder, Mary 1153
Holder, Meryl Evelyn 1429
Holder, Nigel John Charles 1429
Holder, Stephanie 1429
Holder, Stuart 1955
Holder, Toby Heyworth 1955
Holderness, Andrew James 1430
Holderness, Charlotte 1430
Holderness, Corinne Louisa Cassandra 2938
Holderness, Edward Thomas James 1430
Holderness, Elizabeth 1430
Holderness, Henrietta Emily Alice 1430
Holderness, (Joan Catherine) Cassandra 2938
Holderness, Marina Isabelle Cassandra 2938
Holderness, Martin William 1430
Holderness, Matthew William Thornton 1430
Holderness, Pamela Mary 1430
Holderness, Tessa Elizabeth Mary 1430
Holdsworth, Cecilia 586
Holdsworth, David Michael 586
Holford, Diana Sophia 652
Holford, Elizabeth Alice 1418
Holford, Frances Jane 1418
Holford, Graham Richard Desmond 652
Holford, Helena Rosalind Collette 652
Holford, John Edward 1418
Holford, Jonathan David 652
Holford, Melanie Sarah 1418
Holford, Rebecca Jane 1418
Holford-Walker, Bruce Edgar 1470
Holford-Walker, Cicely Patricia 1470
Holford-Walker, Michael O'Donnell Spencer 1470
Holford-Walker, Patrick Bruce Spencer 1470
Holford-Walker, Suzanne Patricia Spencer 1470
Holgate, Amy Louisa 158
Holgate, Anne Catherine 158
Holgate, Clare Susannah 158
Holgate, Mark Edward 158
Holgate, Timothy David 158
Holland, Aimee Grace 2698
Holland, (Alan) Simon Charles 2549
Holland, Alice Jane 139
Holland, André Sothern 3101
Holland, Anne Leonie 3101
Holland, Arabella Ann 1620
Holland, Bridget Mary 1620
Holland, Caitlin Frances 1620
Holland, Camilla Juliet 107
Holland, Catherine Jane 928
Holland, Charles Thurstan 928
Holland, Christian 2061
Holland, Claerwen Belinda 3101
Holland, David Charles 928
Holland, David Cuthbert Lyall 1620
Holland, Derek Simon 107
Holland, Elizabeth Hilda Margaret 3101
Holland, Elizabeth Joan Serena 1620
Holland, Fawn Skyla Madeleine 3101
Holland, Frederick Alistair Thurstan 1620
Holland, George David Bryant 2698
Holland, Guy Huntly 3101
Holland, Hannah Catharine 2549
Holland, Hereward Julian 2549
Holland, Jane Frances 3101
Holland, Jane Hart 928
Holland, Jane Mary 139
Holland, Jayne 1620
Holland, Jennifer Lisabeth Gwynllyn 3101
Holland, Joan Marian 3101
Holland, Jools Miles 1894
Holland, Joseph John 1620
Holland, Katherine (Kate) Angela Mary 2061
Holland, Lisa 3101

Holland, Lucy Elizabeth 139
Holland, Luke William Airey 2061
Holland, Mabel Ray Britannia 1894
Holland, Margaret Catharine 2549
Holland, Mary Verena Violet 1620
Holland, Matthew Francis 1620
Holland, Michael 139
Holland, Michael Sothern 3101
Holland, Rachael Margaret 928
Holland, Richard Oliver 928
Holland, Richard Thomas 107
Holland, Robert David 928
Holland, Rosemary Anne 1620
Holland, Samuel George William 139
Holland, Sarah Catherine 107
Holland, Siobhan Amanda 2698
Holland, Susan Jessica 3101
Holland, Thurstan James 1620
Holland, Toby Mark Andrew 2698
Holland, Toby Michael 107
Holland, Venetia Frances 2549
Holland-Hibbert, Henry Thurstan 1620, 2443
Holland-Hibbert, Isabel Katherine 1620
Holland-Hibbert, James Edward 1620
Holland-Hibbert, Katherine 1620, 2443
Holland-Hibbert, Michael 2292
Holland-Hibbert, Rosanna (Rosie) Sarah 1620
Holland-Hibbert, Sheila Constance 1620, 2292
Holland-Hibbert, Thomas Arthur 1620
Holland-Martin, Dominique 538
Holland-Martin, Emily Marie Charlotte 538
Holland-Martin, Robert George 538
Holland-Martin, Tamara Sophie 538
Holland-Martin, Timothy David 538
Holley, George Michael 2782
Holley, Scènie Gwendoline 2782
Hollick, Abigail Miranda 1431
Hollick, Caroline Daniela 1431
Hollick, Cecilia Ann Frederica 19
Hollick, Georgina Louise 1431
Hollick, Quinten Alexander 19
Hollick, Susan Mary 1431
Holliday, Celia Mary 2979
Holliday, Fiona Jane 2628
Holliday, James Robert Sinclair 2628
Holliday, Jane 2628
Holliday, (Lionel) Brook 2979
Holliday, Lucy 2979
Holliday, Robert Anthony John 2628
Holliday, Serena 2979
Hollingsworth, Lesley Mary Virginia 3070
Hollis, Charlie Buster 1379
Hollis, Christine Morley 97
Hollis, (James) Martin 1431
Hollis, Jennifer Marion 1379
Hollis, Lucy Anne 1379
Hollis, Marion Blanche 1379
Hollis, Matthew 1431
Hollis, Matthew Jonathon 97
Hollis, Michael Andrew Hollis 97
Hollis, Michaela 1379
Hollis, Nicholas Elkin 97
Hollis, Rebecca Anne 1379
Hollis, Ryan Arthur 1379
Hollis, Sarah Morley 97
Hollis, Simon 1431
Hollis, Timothy John Walter 1379
Hollis, Timothy Knowles 1379
Hollond, Beatrice Hannah Millicent 919
Hollond, James Nicholas 919
Hollond, John Ernle 919
Hollond, Lara Blaise 919
Hollond, Phoebe Natasha Lara 919
Hollond, Tom Robert 919
Holloway, Alexander Hugh George 777
Holloway, Alice Victoria 2722
Holloway, Benjamin Richard 1891
Holloway, Charles H W 2722
Holloway, Charlotte Anne 1377
Holloway, Christy 2336
Holloway, Deborah 2336
Holloway, Edward 1377
Holloway, Edward Charles 2722
Holloway, Emma Jane Caroline 777
Holloway, George Henry Rous 2722
Holloway, Georgina Alice 2722
Holloway, Graeme 2336
Holloway, Hilary Rose 1377
Holloway, James Oliver Pendrill 777
Holloway, Katharine Helen 1891
Holloway, Lavinia Sophie Olivia 777
Holloway, Lucinda Rose 2722
Holloway, Mark Graham 2719
Holloway, Nicholas Henniker 1377
Holloway, Rachel Sermonda 1377
Holloway, Sarah Margaret 1891
Holloway, Tatum 2336
Holloway, Thomas Henry Charles 777
Holloway, Timothy George 1891
Holloway, Victoria 2719
Holloway, William David 1377
Hollyoak, Caroline Peta 810
Hollyoak, Kevin Clive Arthur 810
Hollyoak, Liam 810
Hollyoak, Rory Clive Anthony 810
Holm, Póvi Frederich 2927
Holm, Shirley Norma 2927
Holman, Alice Elgiva Marie Gabrielle 798
Holman, Alva Grace 428
Holman, Anthony 2259
Holman, Catherine Rose 798
Holman, Charles Anthony 2259

Holman, Christopher Boot 798
Holman, Diana Elizabeth Virginia Sydney 1611
Holman, Edward Alexander 1611
Holman, Elizabeth Marjorie 2259
Holman, Emma Charlotte 1611
Holman, Georgiana Mary 1611
Holman, Jill Andrew 428
Holman, John Francis 1611
Holman, Richard Ian 1611
Holman, Sarah Charlotte 798
Holman, Serena Jane 798
Holman, Thomas Henry 2259
Holme, Caroline Elizabeth 1431
Holme, John Gordon 1431
Holme, Kathleen (Kay) Mary 1431
Holme, Richard Vincent 1431
Holmes, Andrew David 680
Holmes, Andrew Peter Geoffrey 280, 281
Holmes, Anthony Stephen 1150
Holmes, Benedict James 400
Holmes, Bridget Constantia 680
Holmes, Céleste 400
Holmes, Caroline 1892
Holmes, Cerise Elinor 1657
Holmes, Charlotte Clemency 129
Holmes, Christopher H M 680
Holmes, David 349, 1657
Holmes, Diana Hazel Susan 2521
Holmes, Edith Jane 657
Holmes, Elizabeth 1447
Holmes, Ewart John 2521
Holmes, Finella Harriet Rachel 1657
Holmes, Fiona Bridgid 349
Holmes, Genevieve Anne 2521
Holmes, Georgina 1447
Holmes, Gillian Sara Carolyn 712
Holmes, Gladys Mary 281
Holmes, Gloria Joan Mary 600
Holmes, Graham Francis 1150
Holmes, Guy Aladar 2946
Holmes, Helen Margaret 1447
Holmes, Hugh Clifford 600
Holmes, Jacquetta Noël Barbara 2947
Holmes, Jasper Stephen 129
Holmes, Jeremy Alan 400
Holmes, Jonathan Alistair 1150
Holmes, Joshua Thomas Cecil 400
Holmes, Loretta Anne 600
Holmes, Marcus 400
Holmes, Marion Jane 657
Holmes, Mark David 600
Holmes, Matilda Victoria 400
Holmes, Michèle Therese 600
Holmes, Michael Aristide 2947
Holmes, Michael John Wyndham 349
Holmes, Miranda Jane 129
Holmes, Oliver John 2521
Holmes, Philip Edward Knatchbull 349
Holmes, Polly Amanda 349
Holmes, Polly Bridget 400
Holmes, Priscilla Mary Caroline 2946
Holmes, Ralph Armatage 657
Holmes, Richard 1532
Holmes, Richard Mark 680
Holmes, Richard Michael 2946
Holmes, Richard Tilt 129
Holmes, Robert Hugh 600
Holmes, Rosamund 400
Holmes, Rosemary Jane 280
Holmes, Rosy 400
Holmes, Rowland St John 2521
Holmes, Serena Margaret 680
Holmes, Simon Brook 1892
Holmes, Susan 129
Holmes, Sylla 1532
Holmes, Thelma Heather 129
Holmes, Zenta Esther 400
Holmes à Court, Alan William 1399
Holmes à Court, Alison 1398
Holmes à Court, Bridget 1399
Holmes à Court, Campbell Worsley 1399
Holmes à Court, Catherine Elizabeth 1399
Holmes à Court, Constance Ann 1400
Holmes à Court, Deborah Anne 1399
Holmes à Court, Divonne 1399
Holmes à Court, Dorothy Kathleen 1400
Holmes à Court, Edith Clarice 1399
Holmes à Court, Eileen 1399
Holmes à Court, Elizabeth Ann 1399
Holmes à Court, Hilda Rose 1399
Holmes à Court, James William 1398
Holmes à Court, Janet Lee 1399
Holmes à Court, Juliet Helen 1399
Holmes à Court, Majorie Sophia 1399
Holmes à Court, Margaret 1399
Holmes à Court, Paul William 1399
Holmes à Court, Penelope 1399
Holmes à Court, Peter 1399
Holmes à Court, Peter Michael Hamilton 1399
Holmes à Court, Phillip John 1399
Holmes à Court, Robert Anthony Pierce 1399
Holmes à Court, Robert Leonard 1400
Holmes à Court, Simon Antony 1399
Holmes à Court, Simon Roger 1399
Holmes à Court, William Walter 1399
Holmes à Court, Astrid 1400
Holness, Edwin Peter 33
Holroyd, Alexander Ivor 468
Holroyd, Alistair Hugo 468
Holroyd, Amanda Jane 468, 1162
Holroyd, Annabel Juliette 468
Holroyd, (Charles) John 468, 1162

Holroyd, Charles Wilfrid 468
Holroyd, George Alexander James 468
Holroyd, Joanna Mary Ursula 468
Holroyd, Karine 468
Holroyd, Richard Norton 468
Holroyd, Sheila Mary 468
Holroyd, Susan Virginia 468
Holroyd, Wilfrid Andrew 468
Holstein, Alison Margaret 2058
Holstein, Christian 2058
Holt, Andrew 2252
Holt, Benjamin 998
Holt, Camilia Katherine 1414
Holt, Caroline Lucinda 1414
Holt, David Langford 998
Holt, Deborah Mary 998
Holt, Derek 622
Holt, (Dinah) Annabel 1669
Holt, Dorothy Elizabeth Vesey 2305
Holt, Elizabeth Jane 2305
Holt, Elizabeth Rebecca 1669
Holt, Georginia Sarah 1414
Holt, James 998
Holt, Luke 2252
Holt, M Jane R 1669
Holt, Michael Vernon Charles 1669
Holt, Nicholas James 1414
Holt, Nicholas James Vesey 1829
Holt, Peter John Vesey 2305
Holt, Philip James Harrison 1669
Holt, Richard Basil 1414
Holt, Sabina Orietta 2252
Holt, Sara Maria 998
Holt, Sarah Elizabeth 2305
Holt, Susannah Rachael 1414
Holt, Thor 2252
Holt, Trystan 2252
Holt, Vesey Martin Edward 2305
Holverson, Elizabeth Jean 2320
Holverson, Harry 2320
Holverson, Sarah Caroline 2320
Homan, Frances Mary 3072
Homan, John Richard Seymour 3072
Homan, Mary 3072
Homan, Robert Seymour 3072
Homan, Rosalind Claire 3072
Homburger, Avigail Esther 1527
Homburger, Elisheva 1527
Homburger, Isaac Aryeh 1527
Homburger, Meir 1527
Homburger, Pinchos Jacob 1527
Homburger, Yehoshua 1527
Home, Camilla Marian Isobel 907
Home, Catherine Mary 1435
Home, David McLaren 1435
Home, Dominique Meryl 1435
Home, Georgina Helen 1435
Home, Janet 1435
Home, Josephine Georgiana Janet 2041
Home, Marcus John Hepburn 907
Home, Mariota Eleanor 2041
Home, Nichola Anne Mary 2041
Home, Patrick 1435
Home, Thomas John 1435
Homer, Charles St John 776
Homer, David St John 776
Homer, Lucia Susan 776
Homer, Thomas David William 776
Homer, William Richard John 776
Homfray, John George Richards 125
Homfray, Josephine Dykes 125
Homfray, Matthew Anthony 125
Homfray, Serena Margaret 315
Homfray, Thomas Richards 125
Homfray, Virginia 125
Homrighausen, Amanda Anne 2928
Homrighausen, Darren Warren 2928
Homrighausen, Dennis 2928
Homrighausen, Eugenia Anne 2928
Homsi, Christian Chevallier 238
Hone, Adrian Michael Elliott 1302
Hone, Christopher Patrick George 1301
Hone, David Christopher 2951
Hone, J G E 1302
Hone, Judith 2951
Hone, Luke William 2951
Hone, Marcus John Elliott 1302
Hone, Margaret 1302
Hone, Mary 1301
Hone, Matthew Tom Elliott 1302
Hone, Timothy Raymond Patrick 1301
Hone, Valerie Edith 1301
Hone, Wendy Jane 2951
Honess, Rosemary Ann 944
Honess, Simon 944
Honey, Christopher Simon 3021
Honey, Rebecca Clare 3021
Honeybourne, Amanda Jane 277
Honeybourne, Robert N T 277
Honeybourne, Tamsin 277
Honeyman, Ailsa 1898
Honeyman, Dorothy Louisa 808
Honeyman, Morar 1898
Honeyman, Robert 808
Honnor, Julius Desmond 128
Honnor, Kerry Deborah 128
Honnor, Michael 128
Honnor, Seth Michael 128
Honsberger, Alison Michelle 2988
Honsberger, Eric Douglas 2988
Honsberger, Margaret Anne 2988
Honsberger, Penelope Anne 2988
Honsberger, Philip John Walter 2988
Honsberger, Stuart Douglas 2988
Honywood, Adriane 1437

I

Irby, Caroline Sarah 324
Irby, Charles Leonard Anthony 324
Irby, David John 325
Irby, Donna Elizabeth 325
Irby, Dorothy Mary 325
Irby, Douglas John 325
Irby, Edward Peter Anthony Wallace 324
Irby, Emma 324
Irby, Emma Mary 1775
Irby, Felica Lea 325
Irby, (George Anthony) Peter 324
Irby, George William Eustace Boteler 324
Irby, Ginger Kay Patricia Wanda May 324
Irby, Harry Robert Paul Anthony 324
Irby, Jacinta Elizabeth 325
Irby, Joanne Louise 325
Irby, John Charles 325
Irby, Jonathan Charles Timothy 324
Irby, Judith Ann 325
Irby, June Eve 325
Irby, Katharine Mary Louise 324
Irby, Kathleen 325
Irby, Kenneth Alan 325
Irby, Kenneth Francis 325
Irby, Leonard Edward 325
Irby, Mark Edward 325
Irby, Mary 325
Irby, Melissa Jan 325
Irby, Michael Anthony 325
Irby, Nicholas Charles Anthony 324
Irby, Nicholas Roland 325
Irby, Orene Ethel 325
Irby, Paul Anthony 324, 325, 1775
Irby, Paul Anthony Richard 325
Irby, Peggy May 325
Irby, Peter Brian Edward 325
Irby, Peter Richard 325
Irby, Philip Anthony Kenelm 325
Irby, Rachael Elizabeth 325
Irby, Rebecca Frances Anne 324
Irby, Rhonda A 324
Irby, Robyn 325
Irby, Robyn Joyce 325
Irby, Robyn M 325
Irby, Ross James 325
Irby, Rupert Paul Anthony 324
Irby, Ruth Helen 325
Irby, Sarah Jane 324
Irby, Stephen Victor 325
Irby, Suzanne Marie 325
Ireland, Blake Timothy Lawrence 2210
Ireland, Clare Margaret 2210
Ireland, Gemma Mary Clare 2210
Ireland, George Ian Kenneth 2277
Ireland, Jodi Hope 81
Ireland, Katherine Pepita 1415
Ireland, Kim Joanne 81

Ireland, Mark Peter Lawrence 2210
Ireland, Nicola Gwenllian 2210
Ireland, Sheila Marian 2277
Ireland, Timothy Lawrence 2210
Ireland, Timothy Scott 1415
Ironside, Alan Francklyn 1598
Ironside, Alice Octavia Louise 1517
Ironside, Andrew Philip 1598
Ironside, Audrey Marigold 1517, 1602
Ironside, Charles Edmund Grenville 623, 1517
Ironside, Dorothy Rosemary Joy 1598
Ironside, Edmund Oslac 1602
Ironside, Elizabeth Mary 623, 1517
Ironside, Emily Charlotte Olivia 1517
Ironside, Frederick Thomas Grenville 1517
Ironside, Margaret Joan 1517
Ironside, Philip Norman Jennings 1598
Irvin, Amy Hyacinthe 2282
Irvin, Emilie Jane 2282
Irvin, John 2282
Irvin, Luke Litchfield 2282
Irvine, Alastair 1518
Irvine, Alison Mary 1518
Irvine, Anne 1235
Irvine, Barbara 1173
Irvine, David 1518
Irvine, David Peter Gerard 1235
Irvine, Ian 1158
Irvine, James Eccles Malise 1235
Irvine, Jennifer Joan 1173
Irvine, Kate Dundas 1173
Irvine, Laura Hermione 1158
Irvine, Robert Andrew 1173
Irvine, Robert Brian 1173
Irvine, Susan Caroline Jane 1235
Irvine-Fortescue, Alexander Ramsay 1094
Irvine-Fortescue, Alexander Thomas 1094
Irvine-Fortescue, Brittany Avalon 1094
Irvine-Fortescue, Camilla 1094
Irvine-Fortescue, Caroline Ann Patricia 1094
Irvine-Fortescue, Clare 1094
Irvine-Fortescue, Drummond McLeod 1094
Irvine-Fortescue, Edith Caroline 1094
Irvine-Fortescue, Edmund William 1094
Irvine-Fortescue, Grenville Archer 1094
Irvine-Fortescue, Hazel J 1094
Irvine-Fortescue, Henry 1094
Irvine-Fortescue, Henry Boswell 1094
Irvine-Fortescue, Hugh William 1094
Irvine-Fortescue, Ian Henry 1094
Irvine-Fortescue, James Ramsay 1094
Irvine-Fortescue, James Robert 1094
Irvine-Fortescue, James William 1094
Irvine-Fortescue, John Hugh 1094
Irvine-Fortescue, Juliet 1094

Irvine-Fortescue, Kathryn 1094
Irvine-Fortescue, Margaret 1094
Irvine-Fortescue, Mark Paul 1094
Irvine-Fortescue, Nicholas Alexander 1094
Irvine-Fortescue, Patricia Anne Elizabeth 1094
Irvine-Fortescue, Rachel Sarah 1094
Irvine-Fortescue, Romney Foy 1094
Irvine-Fortescue, Simon Archer 1094
Irvine-Fortescue, Valerie Faith 1094
Irvine-Fortescue, Vanessa Louise Mary Marion 1094
Irvine-Fortescue, Virginia 1094
Irvine-Fortescue, Wendy Jayne 1094
Irvine-Fortescue, William Archer 1094
Irving-Bell, Raymond Gordon 1018
Irwin, Alexander Christian Stovin 1779
Irwin, Alice Catherine 417
Irwin, Alistair Stuart Hastings 2445
Irwin, Charles 2370
Irwin, Charlotte Christian 417
Irwin, Charlotte Theresa Stovin 1779
Irwin, David 417
Irwin, Diana Sarah 1132
Irwin, George Henry 417
Irwin, George Ronald Valentine Hastings 2445
Irwin, Gloria Anthea 249
Irwin, Jago 2370
Irwin, Ken 1189
Irwin, Laura Bridget 2445
Irwin, Luke 2370
Irwin, Lynn 1189
Irwin, Mary Rose Elizabeth 2445
Irwin, Michael Macfarlane 1132
Irwin, Mikaela 2370
Irwin, Nicola Valentine 2445
Irwin, Samson 2370
Irwin, Sophie Georgetta Kate 1779
Irwin-Clark, Benjamin John 1616
Irwin-Clark, Davina Mary 1616
Irwin-Clark, Jessamy Claire 1616
Irwin-Clark, Peter Elliot 1616
Isaac, Alexander 1855
Isaac, Beth Slater 1855
Isaac, David 238
Isaac, Felicity 1230
Isaac, Judith Margaret Anne 238
Isaac, Lionel Seymour John 1855
Isaac, Natasha 1855
Isaac, Pamela Bernadene 1855
Isaac, Philadelphia Jane 1855
Isaac-Cole, James Robert 1855
Isaac-Cole, Russell Jason 1855
Isaac-Cole, Suzanne Gaye 1855
Isaacs, Alexander Gerald 2376
Isaacs, Anthony Ian Michael 2376

Isaacs, Dorothea 2544
Isaacs, Heide 2376
Isaacs, Julian Michael 2376
Isaacs, Margot Irene 2376
Isaacs, Marjorie Frances 2376
Isaacs, Melinda Victoria 2376
Isaacs, Natasha Rose Eleanor 2376
Isaacs, Richard Marcel 2376
Isaacs, Ruby Jacqueline Kirsten 2376
Isaacs, Sybilla Alice 2376
Isaacs, Tallulah Elke Margot 2376
Isard, John David 1994
Isard, Katherine Patricia 1994
Isham, Angus David Vere 1519
Isham, Charles Vere Ian 1519
Isham, Joan 1519
Isham, Julia Claire Mary 1519
Isham, Lynne Janette 1519
Isham, Maximiliano Vere 1519
Isham, Norman Murray Crawford 1519
Isham, Oscar Howard Vere 1519
Isham, Richard Leonard Vere 1519
Isham, Vere Murray Gyles 1519
Isolani-Smyth, Paul H C T 2526
Isolani-Smyth, Teresa Philippa 2526
Issacson, Jane Elizabeth Catherine 1224
Issacson, John Alexander 1224
Issacson, Peter Gregory 1224
Issacson, Sophie Claire 1224
Istace, Craig Stephen 671
Istace, Dana 671
Istace, Drew 671
Istace, Edward 671
Istace, Linda Ann 671
Istace, Winnifred Alice 671
Ivens-Ferraz, Almary Bridget 1673
Ivens-Ferraz, Bronwen Mary 1673
Ivens-Ferraz, Caitlin Tessa 1673
Ivens-Ferraz, Penelope Kate 1673
Ivens-Ferraz, Peter 1673
Ivens-Ferraz, Robyn Ann 1673
Ivey, Kate Belinda 2070
Ivey, Rupert J 2070
Ivison, Danielle Barbara 1855
Ivison, Harry Ernest 1855
Ivison, Valentina Maria 1855
Ivor, Georgina Mancroft 1842
Ivor, Richard Alexander Burkhand 1842
Ivory, Anne Bernadette 2387
Ivory, Claire Louise 2387
Ivory, David Hugh 2387
Ivory, E J 2367
Ivory, Hugh 2387
Ivory, Martha Bridget 2367
Ivory, Ruth Marie 2387
Ivy, Betty Pamela 1528
Ivy, Thomas 1528

J

Jabbour, Charmaine 2337
Jabbour, Daniel 2337
Jabbour, George 2337
Jaboor, Douglas Ferris Hewat 149
Jack, Angus Gavin Lockhead 1505
Jack, Anne 2826
Jack, Anthea Audrey Charlotte 1517
Jack, Bridget Sarah 1505
Jack, Charles Watson Hamilton 1506
Jack, Christopher James Hamilton 1505
Jack, Daphne Carol 2164
Jack, Derek Robert 2164
Jack, Diana 2826
Jack, Fiona Georgina 1517
Jack, Geraldine Jennings 1505
Jack, Julia 2826
Jack, Kenneth Hamilton Muir 1505
Jack, Laetitia Mary 2740
Jack, Louise Diana 1505
Jack, Michael Anthony Gordon 2826
Jack, Oliver Edmund Maclean 1517
Jack, Richard Kenneth Hamilton 1505
Jack, Robert Logan 2740
Jack, Rosemary Ann 2740
Jack, William Logan 2740
Jacklin, Anthony 1310
Jacklin, Mary Anne 1310
Jackman, Caroline Lindsay 2921
Jackman, Charlotte Margaret 2921
Jackman, Connie Patricia 2921
Jackman, Eileen Jane 2062
Jackman, Richard William 2921
Jackman, Robert Arthur 2062
Jackman, Rosanna 2921
Jackman, Rose Ann 2062
Jackman, Scott Robert 2062
Jackson, Adam William Roland 1524
Jackson, Alan Hamilton 1521
Jackson, Alicia Sophie 1524
Jackson, Alison 2827
Jackson, Amelia Caroline 3072
Jackson, Andrew Conway 971
Jackson, Andrew Philip 1521
Jackson, Andros Vassilis 1522
Jackson, Ann Margaret 1525
Jackson, Anna Katharine 1162
Jackson, Anne Agnes 1521
Jackson, Anne-Marie 1524
Jackson, Anthony Lee 246
Jackson, Anthony Oliphant 1271

Jackson, Antony Percy 2826
Jackson, Ashley 2827
Jackson, Belinda Elizabeth 953
Jackson, Ben Philip Joseph 1524
Jackson, Bertha Mary 1520
Jackson, Brenden James 1521
Jackson, Bruce John 1521
Jackson, Carl Patrick Thomas 1524
Jackson, Carolyn Thelma 1522
Jackson, Catherine Ann Hungerford 1522
Jackson, Catherine Elizabeth 184
Jackson, Catherine Mary 2665
Jackson, Charles Desmond Bertram 1525
Jackson, Charlotte Dare 1523
Jackson, Colin Paul 1521
Jackson, Conrad Guy Frederick 936
Jackson, David Geoffrey 1525
Jackson, (David) Mark 2367
Jackson, David Murray James 1522
Jackson, David Rayney Montgomerie 953
Jackson, Dawn Nesta 1524
Jackson, Diana 953
Jackson, Dianna Jan 1522
Jackson, Edmund Robinson 1522
Jackson, Edward Hyde Rayney 953
Jackson, Eleni 1522
Jackson, (Elizabeth) Bridget 1525
Jackson, Elizabeth Katherine Marion 1271
Jackson, Emma Caroline 2359
Jackson, Ernest Cyril 1575
Jackson, Esme Ruth 1521
Jackson, Felix Mark 2367
Jackson, Flavia Anne 2774
Jackson, Flora Mary Margaret 1525, 1551
Jackson, Geoffrey Kendal 1522
Jackson, Geoffrey Laird 1525
Jackson, George Edward Stainton 280
Jackson, Georgina Mary 1525
Jackson, Georgina Victoria 1523
Jackson, Gillian Malise 1524
Jackson, Glenda Murdoch 1522
Jackson, Graham George 1522
Jackson, Guadalupe 1521
Jackson, Guy Nicholas Barrie 1525
Jackson, Harriet 1523
Jackson, Hayden Jesse Jones 1521
Jackson, Hazel May 1525
Jackson, Hilary Jennifer 2430
Jackson, Howard 2430
Jackson, Hugo Edward Stainton 280

Jackson, Igor 1521
Jackson, Ina 1526
Jackson, James 1271, 1521
Jackson, James Anthony Foljambe 1524
Jackson, James Hugo Stainton 280
Jackson, Jane Mary 1525
Jackson, Janet Elizabeth Naomi 184
Jackson, Jason Blair 3053
Jackson, Jean Cecilia Constance 971
Jackson, Jill Adrienne 1406
Jackson, Joanna Henrietta 1525
Jackson, John 1521
Jackson, John Guy Carmichael 1525, 1551
Jackson, Jolyon Thomas 1524
Jackson, Jonathan Guy Campion 1525
Jackson, Joyce Thomasina 1522
Jackson, Judith Rose 2367
Jackson, Juliet Mary Constance 1162
Jackson, Katharine Elizabeth 548
Jackson, Keith Arnold 1521
Jackson, Kenneth Grant 1521
Jackson, Kimiora Hikurangi Elijah 1437
Jackson, Kiro 1522
Jackson, Kirsten Renate 2430
Jackson, (Leslie) Andrew 2774
Jackson, Leslie Mackay 1521
Jackson, Lillian Jane 1521
Jackson, Louise Loftus 1523
Jackson, Louise Sarah 1525
Jackson, Luke Dominic Gregory 1524
Jackson, Luke Hadley 2367
Jackson, Lydia Ruth 2430
Jackson, Lynn 1521
Jackson, Margaret 1522
Jackson, Margaret Anne 1522
Jackson, Margaret Letitia 1525
Jackson, Margaret Ngaire Yoskyl 2826
Jackson, Margery Evelyn 1952
Jackson, Maria 1522
Jackson, Maria E 1520
Jackson, Mary Rose M 1525
Jackson, Matthew 3072
Jackson, Matthew Henry 2665
Jackson, Mitchell Lee Jones 1521
Jackson, Moana Maree 1437
Jackson, Murray Grant 1521
Jackson, Nadia Françoise Geneviève 1523
Jackson, Nancy 1522
Jackson, Nancy Laura 3053
Jackson, Nathan Dieter 2430

Jackson, Neil Keith 1521
Jackson, Ngaianne 2827
Jackson, Nicola Mary 1524
Jackson, Nikos Manolis 1522
Jackson, Olive 1522
Jackson, Oliver Thomas Peter 1524
Jackson, Olivia Susannah 548
Jackson, Patrick Huth 1525
Jackson, Paul Alan 1521
Jackson, Paul Murray 1522
Jackson, Pauline Mona 1521
Jackson, Peter 1521
Jackson, Peter Edmund 1522
Jackson, Peter Hungerford 1522
Jackson, Peter Lawrence 2827
Jackson, Phineas Arthur 1952
Jackson, Piers Anthony 1524
Jackson, Priscilla Rayney 953
Jackson, Quentin 1522
Jackson, Robert 2359
Jackson, Robert Humphrey 1525
Jackson, Robert John 1521
Jackson, Robert S 2145
Jackson, Roderick Edward 971
Jackson, Rosemary Frances 1271
Jackson, Rupert James 1525
Jackson, Russell Joseph 1522
Jackson, Ruth Clare 1525
Jackson, Ruth Helen Isobel 184
Jackson, Ruth Henrietta 1297
Jackson, Ruth Wynita 1521
Jackson, Sally Ann 1523
Jackson, Sandra 1521
Jackson, Sarah Jane Rayney 953
Jackson, Sean 9
Jackson, Sean D 1162
Jackson, Serena A 1524
Jackson, Serena Jane 280
Jackson, Shaun Lewis 1522
Jackson, Shelagh 1525
Jackson, Shirley 1521
Jackson, Stephen John 1521
Jackson, Stephen Keith 1521
Jackson, Stuart Harold 1522
Jackson, Stuart William 3053
Jackson, Susan 1522
Jackson, Susannah Elizabeth 3076
Jackson, Sybil Alexandra 953
Jackson, Thomas Archie Stainton 280
Jackson, Thomas Graham St George 1523

Jackson, Thomas Sebastian Esmé 1524
Jackson, Thomas St Felix 1523
Jackson, Timothy 2827, 3076
Jackson, Timothy Richard 1521
Jackson, Toni 1521
Jackson, Vanessa Jane 2145
Jackson, Verna Elizabeth 1522
Jackson, Violet Marguerite Loftus 1523, 2512
Jackson, Virginia Ida 936
Jackson, William David 1162
Jackson, William David Geoffrey 1525
Jackson, William Harry 3076
Jackson, William Lindsay 1521
Jackson, (William) Roland Cedric 1524
Jackson, William Wakatere 1437
Jackson-Taylor, Elizabeth Serena 650
Jacob, Alaric Justin 721
Jacob, Alice Mary 721
Jacob, Claudia Harriet 721
Jacob, Colin Andrew 2124
Jacob, Cyrilla Catherine 721
Jacob, David Keith 2124
Jacob, Esther Sybil 721
Jacob, John Anthony 721
Jacob, Karen 721
Jacob, Lynne 721
Jacob, Margaret Ann 1094
Jacob, Mark Robert 1094
Jacob, Michael Patrick 2124
Jacob, Naomi Margaret 2124
Jacob, Noeline Elizabeth 2124
Jacob, Peter Richard 1094
Jacob, Philip John 2124
Jacob, Rebecca Mary 2124
Jacob, Richard John 1094
Jacob, Robin 721
Jacob, Rosemary 721
Jacob, Rupert 721
Jacob, Thomas Alexander 721
Jacobs, Alice Enid 2100
Jacobs, Anne Imogen 612
Jacobs, Charles 2100
Jacobs, Clare Elizabeth 1249
Jacobs, David Lewis 1779
Jacobs, Evelyn Felicity 1526
Jacobs, Hugo Nicholas 1249
Jacobs, John Howard 612
Jacobs, Lindsay Alexandra 1779
Jacobs, Naomi Moira 612
Jacobs, Peter Howard 612
Jacobs, Roger Howard 612
Jacobsen, Susan Jane 1135
Jacoby, Charles John 2892
Jacoby, Cicely Elizabeth Theodosia 2892
Jacoby, Katherine Venetia 2892
Jacomb, Evelyn Helen 1363
Jacomb, Martin Wakefield 1363
Jacomb, Matthew Barnabas Wakefield 1363
Jacomb, Philippa A 1363
Jacomb, Saffron 1363
Jacomb, Tara 1363
Jacomb, Thomas Richard 1363
Jaeger, Catrina Louise 1357
Jaeger, Charlotte Louise 1357
Jaeger, Lars 1357
Jaffray, Alexandra Marina Ross 1526
Jaffray, Anne 1527
Jaffray, Jack Henry William 1526
Jaffray, Nicholas Gordon Alexander 1526
Jaffray, William Lawrence Paget 1526
Jager, Cindy Kay 1195
Jager, Lynne Elizabeth 1195
Jager, Marie Elizabeth 1195
Jager, Robert H 1195
Jagger, Brian Paul 1406
Jagger, Brigham Humphry 1406
Jagger, Christina Catherine 1406
Jagger, Ryan Selwyn 1406
Jagger, Sheila Elizabeth 1406
Jagger, Stephanie Elizabeth 1406
Jaik, Arthur G 2688
Jaik, Judith Cecily 2688
Jaik, Susan Christine 2688
Jain, Patricia Rose 1269
Jain, Sharad 1269
Jakins, Josephine Eugenie 2328
Jakins, Peter John 2328
Jakobovits, Amélie 1527
Jakobovits, David 1527
Jakobovits, Elie 1527
Jakobovits, Ester Gitel 1527
Jakobovits, Jeremy 1527
Jakobovits, Julian 1527
Jakobovits, Michelle 1527
Jakobovits, Nathan 1527
Jakobovits, Nechemya 1527
Jakobovits, Penina 1527
Jakobovits, Samuel 1527
Jakobovits, Shraga Feitel 1527
Jakobovits, Sima 1527
Jakobovits, Tzippora 1527
Jakobovits, Yaacov 1527
Jakobovits, Yehudit 1527
Jakobovits, Zipora 1527
Jaksch, Carmen Julia 2621
Jaksch, David Wenzel 2621
Jaksch, George Barrington 2621
Jaksch, Joan Edith Barrington 2621
Jaksch, Sandra Mary 2621
Jama, Alice Julia 2489
Jama, Ibrahim 2489
James, Alastair 2660
James, Alexander Oliver Charles 2110
James, Alexander Robert 2111

James, Aliki Louise Hélène Marie-Sygne 2110
James, Alison Mary 534
James, Anastasia 2110
James, Andrew Thurstan Trewartha 306
James, Andrew William 1162
James, Ann Barbara 444
James, Ann Rosemary 1401
James, Annabel Clare 2503
James, Annabel Louise 438
James, Anne Glover 438
James, Anne 873
James, Anthony Christopher Walter Paul 2110
James, Arthur Francis 2395
James, Belinda Anne Nonie 518
James, Caroline 2272
James, Caspar Lloyd 1151
James, Catherine Lucy 2110
James, Charles Henry Thomas 2111
James, Charles John 1162
James, Charles Quentin 306
James, Charles Richard Arthur 931
James, Charles Walter Henri 2110
James, Christopher Noel 1813
James, Christopher William 1401
James, Colin Prinsep 518
James, David Alistair 3012
James, David Lloyd 1151
James, David Matthew 1025
James, David Peter 2272
James, Deidre Elizabeth 518
James, Dorothy Kathryn 2584
James, Edward 1025
James, Edward Luke Daniel John 1162
James, Elizabeth Iona 918
James, Elizabeth Jane 2503
James, Emma Louise 518
James, Esmé Frances 1665
James, Fiona Martha Alison 931
James, Flora Emily 1512
James, Francesca Danielle 2111
James, Francis Bernard Wigram 3012
James, Gillian 2250
James, Grace Daisy 1512
James, Gregory 952
James, Gwynne Douglas 444
James, Helen 2395
James, Helen Mary 2597
James, Henry Christopher 2597
James, Henry Christopher William 2110
James, Henry Norman 2111
James, Hilary Jane 2657
James, Hugo 1512
James, Janice Alice 1025
James, Janine Patricia 2660
James, Jeremy 2250
James, John 2410
James, John Gwyn Mackworth 1813
James, John Henry 2111
James, John Nigel Courtenay 2503
James, Josephine Ann 1813
James, Julie Alice 1025
James, Karen Leslie 2111
James, Karen Linda 1025
James, Kenneth 2597
James, Kenneth M 2584
James, Kirsty Innes 534
James, Lindsay Mary 534
James, Lisa Maria 2111
James, Lucinda Sophie Rose 931
James, Madeline Gertrude 3012
James, Marjorie 2111
James, Marjorie Frederick 1104
James, Mark W 918
James, Mary 2111
James, Mary Victoria 2410
James, Michael John Frederick Lowry 989
James, Michelle Louise 438
James, Natasha 2395
James, Nicholas John 2111
James, Nicola Lesley 306
James, Nigel Antony 2111
James, Noel 1813
James, Oliver Francis Wintour 2395
James, Olivia Martha Alison 931
James, Ophelia Mary Katherine Christine 2111
James, Pamela Susan 1401
James, Patrick Esmond 2395
James, Pearl 2547
James, Peter Mansel Lloyd 1151
James, Philippa Helen 1512
James, R D C James 931
James, Raye V 989
James, Richard Lloyd 1151
James, Rosanna 2395
James, (Rose) Virginia 1162
James, Rosemary Monica 2597
James, Sebastian Richard Edward Cuthbert 2110
James, Serena Mary Barbara 2111, 2560
James, Simon Alan 438
James, Simon Charles Trewartha 306
James, Simon Drummond Courtenay 2503
James, Simon Stanley 1025
James, Siriol Anne 1651
James, Susan Alexandra Caroline 2272
James, Susan Kay 2584
James, Susan Mary 1151
James, Therese 2111
James, Thomas Egbert 1104
James, Thomas Strachan 1401
James, Timothy Robert 1401
James, Tracey Sharleen 952

James, Victoria Mary 1151
James-Duff, David R M 2657
James-Duff, Fiona Louise 2657
James-Duff, Monica Jean 2657
Jameson, Hilda Elizabeth 901
Jameson, James Leander 901
Jameson, Julius Pridden 901
Jameson, Linda Rose 901
Jameson, Melville Harry Stewart 2034
Jameson, Melville Stewart 2034
Jameson, Michael Andrew Stewart 2034
Jameson, Robert Julius Whitwell 901
Jameson, Sarah Amy 2034
Jamie, John Robert FitzHerbert 1069
Jamieson, Antonia Alexandra 1165
Jamieson, Catherine Nancy 1589
Jamieson, David Lawrence 1165
Jamieson, Diana Pauline 290
Jamieson, Emma Laura 1165
Jamieson, Francesca Catherine Sophie 510
Jamieson, Gillian 1997
Jamieson, Henry William Ashton 510
Jamieson, Hugh Alexander 2097
Jamieson, James Gerrard 2097
Jamieson, James Nicholas Rupert 510
Jamieson, Jerry Jocelyn 2097
Jamieson, June Hilary 510
Jamieson, Laura Margaret 1096, 2097
Jamieson, Leanda Georgina Hilary 510
Jamieson, Mariegold Magdalene 2097
Jamieson, Martin Clive 1589
Jamieson, Melanie Pamela 1165
Jamieson, Pamela Gwynedd Marie 1165
Jamieson, Simon 1096
Jamieson, Simon David 2097
Jamieson, William Magnus 510
Jamison, Penelope Jane 2575
Janner, Daniel 1528
Janner, Elsie Sybil 1528
Janner, Laura 1528
Janner, Marion 1528
Jans, Christopher Bramwell 2587
Jans, Danielle Frances 2587
Jans, Sarah Melody 2587
Jans, Zöe Rose 2587
Janson, Charles James 2771
Janson, Charles Noel 2771
Janson, Hugh Dearman 2169, 2651, 2771
Janson, Jonathan 2294
Janson, Martin Dearman Sutherland 176
Janson, Mary Ann 176
Janson, Mary Wallop 2294
Janson, Olwen Marcia Blanche 2169, 2651, 2771
Janson, Sara Arabella 2294
Janson, Sarah 2771
Jarboe, Alexander Christopher 2009
Jarboe, Christian Hunter 2009
Jarboe, (James) Patrick 2009
Jarboe, Jessica Rose 2009
Jarboe, Margaret Elizabeth 2009
Jarboe, Nicholas Killian 2009
Jarboe, Shannon K Smith 2009
Jarboe, Thomas Hughes 2009
Jardine, Adrian Douglas Francis 1530
Jardine, Alexander Maule 729
Jardine, Alice 1529
Jardine, Alma Glenise 1528
Jardine, Ann 1529
Jardine, Anne Romaine 1582
Jardine, Arthur John 3054
Jardine, Catherine 1529
Jardine, Catriona Louise 1529
Jardine, Charles Kenneth Herbert 1529
Jardine, Claire Vyvien 1529
Jardine, David Eric Cranswick 1529
Jardine, Donna Jean 3054
Jardine, Dorothea 1528
Jardine, Douglas 1582
Jardine, Edwin Jones 3054
Jardine, Emily 1529
Jardine, Gordon Samuel 3054
Jardine, Jacqueline Hannah 1529
Jardine, Jan Frances 1528
Jardine, Jean Maule 1528
Jardine, John Alexander 1529
Jardine, John Alexander Cross 1528
Jardine, Kathleen Hazel 3054
Jardine, Kirsty Sybil 1528
Jardine, (Maria) Milky 1530
Jardine, Mary Beatrice 729, 1528
Jardine, Mary Elizabeth 1528
Jardine, Michael Ian Christopher 1530
Jardine, Murray Hugh Lascelles 1528
Jardine, Naomi Kathleen 3054
Jardine, Oliver Michael Ian 1530
Jardine, Piers Leonard 1528
Jardine, Priscilla Daphne 1530
Jardine, Ruari John 1529
Jardine, William 1529
Jardine, William Murray 1528
Jarick, Michael Stephen 2163
Jarick, Sophie May 2163
Jarick, Stephen Arthur 2163
Jarick, Susan Louise 2163
Jarman, Anne Jennifer 136
Jarman, Elizabeth Caroline 136
Jarman, Ian 136
Jarman, Katherine Dorothy 2000
Jarman, Neil 136
Jarman, Peter 2000
Jarman, Stephen Andrew 136
Jarrett, Caroline Sarah 452
Jarrett, Nicholas M 452
Jarrey, Anthony Michael 1843

Jarrey, Hilary Nancy 1843
Jarvis, Allan 2546
Jarvis, Alton James 3058
Jarvis, Anthony George 580
Jarvis, Brenda 3058
Jarvis, Charles Alexander 3058
Jarvis, Claire Victoria 580
Jarvis, Frances Elizabeth 2546
Jarvis, Gertrude Minnie 3058
Jarvis, John David 968
Jarvis, Julia Simone 3058
Jarvis, Katherine Antonia 580
Jarvis, Michael 3058
Jarvis, Patricia English 3058
Jarvis, Sophia Camilla 580
Jarvis, Trevor 3058
Jarvis, Victoria Ena Mary 580
Jarvis, Vivien Mary 968
Jarvis, William Tom 968
Jascoll, Dorothy (Dorie) Ann 2063
Jascoll, Griselda Nancy 2063
Jascoll, Henry Feliks 2063
Jascoll, Jennifer Elizabeth 2063
Jascoll, John Henry David 2063
Jasiewicz, Charles Alexander Francis Beaumont 2137
Jasiewicz, Emma-Rose Everilde 2137
Jauncey, Anna Maria 1530
Jauncey, Aurora 1530
Jauncey, Charles Eliot 521
Jauncey, Cressida Jane 1530
Jauncey, Eleanor Fleur 1530
Jauncey, Jake Ludovic Dundas 1530
Jauncey, James Malise Dundas 704, 1530
Jauncey, Jeremy Cunninghame 1530
Jauncey, (Sarah) Camilla 521, 1530
Jauncey, Sarah Jacqueline 704, 1530
Jauncey, Simon Helias 1530
Jauncey, Sophie Jean Elizabeth 1530
Jauncey, Thomas Charles 1530
Jaworski, Anne Jean 864
Jaworski, Zbigniew Ernest 864
Jay, Adam 1946
Jay, Alice Katharine 1531
Jay, Christopher Laurence Monckton 1122
Jay, Ian 3060
Jay, Lucy 1946
Jay, Margaret Ann 474
Jay, Mary Margaret 1122
Jay, Patrick James Peter 1531
Jay, Raymonde 3060
Jayes, Andrew Patrick Harris 210
Jayes, Brian 210
Jayes, Clare Penelope 210
Jayes, Rosamund Sarah 210
Jayne, Alix Margaret Gray 2730
Jayne, Arthur Leonard 2730
Jazayeri, Ali 2357
Jazayeri, Griselda Mary 2357
Jeal, John Julian Timothy 2198
Jeal, Joyce 2198
Jean, Patrick John 2699
Jean, Valerie Elizabeth Grace 2699
Jeanes, Pamela Hanford 960
Jeans, Anthony Stanley Purcell 369
Jeans, Christine Anne 369
Jeans, Ellen Kathleen 369
Jeans, Michael Anthony Purcell 369
Jeay, Donald 2937
Jeay, Ramona Lee 2937
Jebb, Bernice Cruwys 1149
Jebb, David Gladwyn 1149
Jebb, Edwin Grancis 2692
Jebb, Henry Robert Gladwyn 1149
Jebb, Henry Walter Gladwyn 1149
Jebb, John Henry Desmond 1149
Jebb, Louis Bernard Alexander 2269
Jebb, Lucy Margaret 2269
Jebb, Magdalen Marianne Francesca 2269
Jebb, Matthew Hilary 2269, 2692
Jebb, Minette Caroline Mary 1149
Jebb, Minette Colleen Helen 1149
Jebb, Peter Cecil 1149
Jebb, Philip Nicholas Miles 1149
Jebb, Serena Emma Rose 2269, 2692
Jebb, Stephanie Dagmar 1149
Jebb, Susan Eve 1149
Jebb, Theodore Philip 2692
Jebb, Timothy Edward 1149
Jee, Colin Scott 1114
Jee, Daniel James 1114
Jee, Jonathan Noel 1114
Jee, Juliet Elizabeth 1114
Jee, Penelope Noel 1114
Jee, Rachel Clare 1114
Jee, Thomas Peter 1114
Jee, Timothy David 1114
Jeffcock, Cordelia Caroline 535
Jeffcock, David Philip 535
Jeffcock, John Philip Harold Patience 535
Jeffcock, Josephine Anne 535
Jeffcock, Venetia Mary 535
Jefferies, Christopher Ballantyne 2271
Jefferies, Doris Helen 678
Jefferies, Joel Bryan Heath 2271
Jefferies, Peter Kenneth 2271
Jefferies, Thomas Charles 678
Jefferies, Tiffany Anne 2271
Jefferson, Esmé Mai Lydia 1858
Jefferson, Fiona 1858
Jefferson, Ian David 1858
Jefferson, Kalena Ann 1858
Jefferson, Kay Leslie 1858
Jeffery, Mary Honor 650
Jeffes, Arthur William Phoenix Young 1564

Jones, Alan 207
Jones, Alan Peter 1514
Jones, Alan Roy 668
Jones, Alastair Frederick Martin 1551
Jones, Alex William 392
Jones, Alexander Daniel Mansel 1848
Jones, Alexander Roderick 601
Jones, Alexander Xenophon 1368
Jones, Alison Margaret 986
Jones, Alistair 1784
Jones, Amanda Jane 665
Jones, Amy Louise 2033
Jones, Andrew Julian Stuart 2319
Jones, Andrew Stewart 2699
Jones, (Andrew Stewart) Ross 394
Jones, Annabel Louise 394
Jones, Anne Jessie Alexandra 3061
Jones, Anne Wilga 392
Jones, Arnold Nelson 1259
Jones, Barbara Caroline 669
Jones, Benjamin Edward Webb 2439
Jones, Benjamin Robin Clavell 1848
Jones, Brian E 1016
Jones, Bruce Gordon 1259
Jones, Bryan Howard 2741
Jones, Carol Anne 802
Jones, Caroline Harriet 641
Jones, Catherine Eleanor 668
Jones, Catherine Leslie 207
Jones, Catherine Louise 2015
Jones, Catherine Margaret Mary 685
Jones, Celia Margaret 685
Jones, Charles Alan 668, 685
Jones, (Charles) Edward Webb 2439
Jones, Charles Mark 1259
Jones, Cherry Bronwen 1468
Jones, Christopher Bournes 1950
Jones, Christopher Bruce 654
Jones, Christopher John Peter 1259
Jones, Claire Patricia 812, 912
Jones, Colin David 1638
Jones, Craig 1339
Jones, David 1024
Jones, David Alan 2254
Jones, David Ian 390
Jones, David Ivor 1412
Jones, David Robert Ward 1551
Jones, David William Anthony 1551
Jones, Deborah Ann 1594
Jones, Derrice 1858
Jones, Dione Frances 654
Jones, Donaline Elizabeth 672
Jones, Doreen Patricia 682
Jones, Dorothy Mary Catherine 2656
Jones, Douglas 2875
Jones, Dympna Monica 1445
Jones, Edith Jane 722
Jones, Eileen Mary 2699
Jones, Elaine Beatrice 1259
Jones, Elizabeth Anne 2933
Jones, Elizabeth Davidson 2937
Jones, Elizabeth Lesley 207
Jones, Elizabeth Mary 371
Jones, Elonse Georgia 2731
Jones, Emlyn Donald 2015
Jones, Emma 1551
Jones, Emma Jennifer Lily 2265
Jones, Eulalie Jacqueline Patricia 3061
Jones, Euphemia 1368
Jones, Felicia Mary 2033
Jones, Felicity Ankaret 2610
Jones, Felix Maxwell 394
Jones, Flora Nancy Sarah 2306
Jones, Florence Anne 1024
Jones, Florence Maud 2131
Jones, Gary Carman 722
Jones, George Arthur 2741
Jones, George Marion 1259
Jones, George Sykes 2782
Jones, Gerald John 1514
Jones, Geraldine Ann 2015
Jones, Gillian Ann 2805
Jones, Glenn David 1412
Jones, Glenn Harold 672
Jones, Gordon 2610
Jones, Gypsy Gail 1468
Jones, Hamlyn (Lyn) Gordon 665
Jones, Harold 672
Jones, Harriet 1551
Jones, Herbert Alan 685
Jones, Heulwen 441
Jones, Howard Gilbert 2131
Jones, Hugo George Hearn 564
Jones, Hume Richard Webb 2439
Jones, Ian W 2810
Jones, Idina Maria 357
Jones, Imogen Margaux 394
Jones, (Inna) Veronica Adeline 2862
Jones, James Gethyn 2937
Jones, James Peter Martin 1551
Jones, Jane Amanda 2306
Jones, Jane Eulalie 3061
Jones, Janet Marie 3053
Jones, Jeffery Carman Blake 722
Jones, Jemma Suzanne 2439
Jones, Jennifer 3053
Jones, Joanna Catherine 1203
Jones, Joanna Elizabeth 2015
Jones, (John) Gilbert 1368
Jones, John Joseph 1858
Jones, John Lewis 3061
Jones, John Robert 2323
Jones, Judith Susanne 3053
Jones, Julia Patricia Gordon 665
Jones, Juliet Mary 812, 912
Jones, Justine Joanne 1412
Jones, Kate 641
Jones, Katherine Louise 2810
Jones, Katherine Myleta Gordon 665
Jones, Kathleen Edith 2805
Jones, Kathleen Elizabeth 2131
Jones, Kathleen Margaret 1259
Jones, Kathryn 1551
Jones, Kathryn Ann 1259
Jones, Kenneth Leslie 2805
Jones, Kerry Therese 392
Jones, Kiloran Imogen 2731
Jones, Kimberley Florence Delves 390
Jones, Larry Alexander 802
Jones, Laurence 1784
Jones, Laurence John 1858
Jones, Lavinia Lawrence 1654
Jones, Lorraine Elizabeth 2306
Jones, Lucy A 1551
Jones, Lucy Mary 2033
Jones, Lydia Iona 2731
Jones, Margaret 2937, 2966
Jones, Margaret Elizabeth Cowper 685
Jones, Margaret Fiona 1551
Jones, Marie June 1412
Jones, Mark 1858
Jones, Martin Edward 1784
Jones, Mary Joy 2741
Jones, Matthew 706, 1858
Jones, Maureen Grierson 2937
Jones, Michael Andronicus 1368
Jones, Michael O'Reilly 2131
Jones, Michael Robert 1259
Jones, Miranda Frances Louise 564
Jones, Nadine 1858
Jones, Natalie Carolyn 2741
Jones, Nicholas Alan 685
Jones, Nicholas David Richard 2810
Jones, Nicholas Houssemayne 346
Jones, Nicola Clare 2139
Jones, Nicola Marie 2805
Jones, Nicola Patricia 1638
Jones, Nicola Suzanne 207
Jones, Nigel Kenneth 2805
Jones, Norman 2131
Jones, Oliver David 2254
Jones, Oliver Mark 346
Jones, Oscar Joseph Lloyd 564
Jones, Owen Toby Rhys 1848
Jones, Pamela Anne 1784
Jones, Pamela Geraldine 1016
Jones, Pamela Mary 1368
Jones, Patricia Leslie 812, 912
Jones, Patricia Margaret 685
Jones, Peta Mary 2323
Jones, Peter Lindsay 1784
Jones, Philip Andrieus 357
Jones, Philip Charles 669
Jones, Richard 1445
Jones, Richard Edmund 1368
Jones, Richard Edward 2265
Jones, Richard Edwin Lewis 2015
Jones, Richard Eric Champion 2139
Jones, Richard Gethyn 2937
Jones, Richard Leslie 2323
Jones, Richard Michael Latham 2033
Jones, Robert Bernard 1594
Jones, Robert Gerald 1514
Jones, Robert Glyn 2306
Jones, Robert Hugh Dutton 392
Jones, Roger 986
Jones, Roger Samuel 2306
Jones, Romilly Arthur 1203
Jones, Ronald 2699
Jones, Rosemary Avril 2968
Jones, Rosemary de Courcy 1594
Jones, Rowena Rose 346
Jones, Sally 1551
Jones, Samuel Bruno 2306
Jones, Santiago Alexis Kanjuchi Sadiq 2875
Jones, Sara Katharine 2254
Jones, Sara Roberta Mary 2810
Jones, Sarah Catherine 2323
Jones, Sarah Louise 1784
Jones, Scott 1339
Jones, Scott Jeremy 392
Jones, Serena Clare 706
Jones, Shaari Horowitz 1784
Jones, Sheila 1339
Jones, Simon Maximian 1368
Jones, Sonia Margaret 1514
Jones, Sophia Venetia 2731
Jones, Stanley Oswald 2862
Jones, Stefan 2933
Jones, Stephen Buxton 2323
Jones, Susan 2323
Jones, Susan Kaye 2966
Jones, Susan Margaret 357
Jones, Suzanne Vere 2439
Jones, Tara Leigh 392
Jones, Taylah Marie 392
Jones, Theodora Serena Delves 390
Jones, Thomas Dunlop 912
Jones, Thomas Dunlop Bruce 812
Jones, Thomas Edmund 2265
Jones, Thomas Emlyn 641
Jones, Timothy Charles 685
Jones, Timothy Cresswell 2323
Jones, Trevor D 564
Jones, Veronica Anne 346
Jones, Veronica Margaret 812, 912
Jones, Victoria Leslie 812, 912
Jones, Warren Charles 2131
Jones, Wayne William Dutton 392
Jones, William Arthur 392
Jones, William David Studley 2033
Jones, William Edward Robert 2306
Jones, William Scott 2966
Jones-Davies, Frances Dorothy 452
Jones-Davies, Henry Ellis 452
Jones-Mortimer, Maurice Carstairs 171
Jones-Parry, David Anthony 1470
Jones-Parry, Gemma 1470
Jones-Parry, Gillian 1470
Jones-Parry, Jacqueline 1470
Jones-Parry, Matthew Nicholas 1470
Jones-Parry, Sarah Margaret 1470
Jones-Parry, Thomas Edward 1470
Jopling, Gail 1552
Jopling, Jeremy Michael Neal 1552
Jopling, Nicholas Mark Fletcher 1552
Jordan, Anthony Christopher 2213
Jordan, Carla Ann 952
Jordan, Caroline Claire 189
Jordan, Carrol Ann 952
Jordan, Christopher Wyndham 2213
Jordan, Clare Margaret 2798
Jordan, Dorothy Margaret 1729
Jordan, Elizabeth Mary 1729, 2213
Jordan, Gillian 2213
Jordan, Henry James Bourke 2798
Jordan, James Cass 189
Jordan, Oliver Charles d'Exeter 2798
Jordan, Peter E 2798
Jordan, Rhys Craig 952
Jordan, Richard 1729
Jordan, Terry Arthur 952
Jordan, Zalha Anne 2213
Jorgensen, Geraldine Frances 201
Jorgensen, I B 1924
Jorgensen, Jens Dalhoff 201
Jorgensen, Michael Dalhoff 201
Jorgensen, Pia Dalhoff 201
Jorgensen, Sonia Margery 1924
Jorgeson, Allen Edward 242
Jorgeson, Ellen Jean 242
Jorgeson, Gladys Dorothy 242
Jorgeson, Lynda Dorothy 242
Jorgeson, Robert Arthur 242
Joscelyn, Andrew Michael Hubert 1856
Joscelyn, Jean 1856
Joscelyne, Nigel Townshend 1980
Joscelyne, Ursula 1980
Josephs, Anna Frances 2618
Josephs, Charlotte Ann 2618
Josephs, Francis 2618
Josephs, Thomas Daniel 2618
Jost, Edward Peter 1800
Jost, Marylyn Jane 1800
Jost, Peter 1800
Jost, Thomas William 1800
Joughin, Jane 735
Jourdan, Mervyn Wingfield 2301
Jourdan, Phillip Montgomery 2301
Jourdier, Anthony Maxwell Kirkpatrick 1613
Jourdier, Cecilia Maye 1613
Jourdier, Hilda May 1613
Jourdier, Jessica Isobel 1613
Jourdier, Louise Caroline 1613
Jourdier, Peter Gilbert Kirkpatrick 1613
Jourdier, Sophie Maye 1613
Jowett, Benjamin 1413
Jowett, Kai 1413
Joya, Laura Caroline 1260
Joya, Virgilio Calderon 1260
Joyce, Barnaby 392
Joyce, Bridgette Maree 392
Joyce, David 2861
Joyce, Flora Tamsine 892
Joyce, Lily Philippa 892
Joyce, Natalie Terese 392
Joyce, Penelope Jillian 491
Joyce, Pollyanna Felicity Rose 892
Joyce, Tessa Margaret 2861
Joyce, Timothy James 491
Joynson, Alexander Timothy 1057
Joynson, Andrew Douglas Stuart 516
Joynson, Clare Katharine Grace Mary 1057
Joynson, Jeremy Duncan Stuart 516
Joynson, Linda Spencer 516
Joynson, Nicholas George Stuart 516
Joynson, Peter William 1057
Joynson, Timothy William Stuart 516
Joynson-Hicks, Amy Gillian 361
Joynson-Hicks, Emma Rosalie 361
Joynson-Hicks, Gillian Evelyn 361
Joynson-Hicks, Paul William 361
Juarez, Alicia Veronica 307
Juarez, Fanny de Valle 307
Juarez, Gustavo Alejandro 307
Juarez, Hugo Walter 307
Juarez, Juan Failla 307
Juarez, José Enrique 307
Juarez, Maria Cristina 307
Juarez, Maria Virginia 307
Juarez, Monica Alicia 307
Juarez, Ramon Bernardo 307
Juby, Elizabeth Ursula 277
Juby, Heather Susan 277
Juby, Herbert Bernard 277
Juby, Jonathan Birdwood 277
Juby, Nicholas Bernard 277
Juby, Penelope Jane 277
Judd, Anthony Hubert Scott 2829
Judd, Barbara Hersilia 2829
Judd, Christine Elizabeth Louise 1552
Judd, Christopher 1502
Judd, Christopher John Henry 2829
Judd, Diana Caroline 2829
Judd, Elizabeth 1552
Judd, Emma Mary 2829
Judd, George William 1218
Judd, Harry Mark Christopher 2829
Judd, Isabella Sarah Veronica 2829
Judd, Isabelle 1502
Judd, Jack 1218
Judd, James Hubert 1745
Judd, Kate Elisabeth 1218
Judd, Katherine Mary 2829
Judd, Philippa 1552
Judd, Sarah 2829
Judd, Stuart 1218
Judd, Thomas Jack Francis 2829
Judson, Amanda Clare 2901
Judson, B William 1870
Judson, Consuelo Sarah 1870
Judson, David John 2901
Judson, Ian 1870
Judson, Josiah Barclay 2901
Judson, Mariana 2901
Judson, Nicholas 1870
Juhre, Anne Selina Elizabeth 1409
Juhre, Janusz Maria Stanislaw Eugeniusz 1409
Juhre, Tadeusz Maria Gerald Alexander 1409
Julicher, Justin Peter Lloyd 1526
Julicher, Nikki Catherine Lloyd 1526
Julicher, Susan Hermine Lloyd 1526
Julicher, Wilhelmus 1526
Jurkiewicz, Ann Veronica 50
Jurkschat, Angus W Macgregor 579
Jurkschat, Katherine Emma Margaret 579
Justin, Darren 1411
Justin, Dawn Ann 1411
Justin, Glen 1411
Justin, John 1411
Justin, Kenneth 1411
Justofson, Lucy Christine 245
Justofson, Roy Arthur 245
Justofson, Vesper Grace 245

K

Kaberry, Andrew Murdoch Scott 1552
Kaberry, Angus George 1552
Kaberry, Claire Elizabeth 1552
Kaberry, Gaenor Elizabeth 1552
Kaberry, Imogen 1552
Kaberry, James Christopher 1552
Kaberry, Jonathan James Alexander 1552
Kaberry, Oliver George Henry 1552
Kaberry, Simon Edmund John 1552
Kacperek, Diana Elizabeth 2920
Kacperek, Jan Ryszard 2920
Kacperek, Paul Anthony 2920
Käfinger, Selma 864
Kain, Bernard B D 863
Kain, Jean Elena 863
Kalitinsky, Andrew 2426
Kalitinsky, Wendela Isabel 2426
Kalman, Caroline Rosemary 1121
Kalman, Lajos 1121
Kampel, Alison Jane 2850
Kampel, Ian Joseph 2850
Kampel, Maureen Hazel 2850
Kampel, Timothy Ian 2850
Kandasamy, Katharine 2962
Kandasamy, Krishna 2962
Kane, Alexander John Petre 2239
Kane, Clarinda Jane 1517
Kane, Eleanor Jane 2239
Kane, Eleanor Mary Petre 2239
Kane, Gregory 2400
Kane, John 2239
Kane, Jonathan S H A 1517
Kane, Paul 686
Kane, Robin Bunbury 2400
Kane, Sarah Anne 686
Kaplan, Edwina 1869
Kaplan, Felix Balthazar Inigo 2446
Kaplan, Jane Margaret Helen 2446
Kaplan, Michael S F 2446
Kaplan, Richard D 1869
Karlin, Hermione Mary 1941
Karlin, Marc 1941
Karron, Emily Sinclair 2358
Karron, Robert 2358

Karslake, Antony Edward Kent 1331
Karslake, Charlotte Cordelia Geraldine Leila 2095
Karslake, Claire Marie 2095
Karslake, Clare Laura 1332
Karslake, David Ian Howard 2095
Karslake, Eleanor Paget Musgrave 1331
Karslake, Eleanor Veldes 1332
Karslake, Emma Caroline Adeliza 2095
Karslake, Emma Kate 1332
Karslake, John Burgess 1332
Karslake, June Pauline 1331
Karslake, Lucy Olivia 1332
Karslake, Matthew 1332
Karslake, Naomi Celia 1332
Karslake, Pamela Evelyn 2094
Karslake, Samuel Kent 1332
Karslake, Sarah Ann 1332
Karslake, William Edward Kent 1332
Katz, Althea Patricia Dawes 2689
Katz, Antonia Jane 125
Katz, Barbara 2554
Katz, Howard R 2554
Katz, Jonathan 125
Katz, Stephen 2689
Kauffmann, Alejandro José 671
Kauffmann, Ana Elena 671
Kauffmann, José Manuel 671
Kauffmann, Leslie Cotter 671
Kaufmann, Augusta Jane 171
Kaufmann, Johanna 171
Kaufmann, Miranda Clare 171
Kaufmann, Olivia Katharine 171
Kaufmann, Peter Gerald Dorian 171
Kaulback, Bryan 2095
Kaulback, Bryan Henry 2095
Kaulback, Caroline Victoria Margaret 2095
Kaulback, Elizabeth Jane 2095
Kaulback, Jago 2095
Kaulback, Marcus Ronald Oliver 2095
Kaulback, Maria 2095
Kaulback, Peter John 2095
Kaulback, Simon Peter Howard 2095
Kavalieris, Laimonis 1123
Kavalieris, Winifred Jill 1123
Kavanagh, Cheyenne Vaire 2435
Kavanagh, Emma-Sarah Rosemarie Isabelle 72
Kavanagh, Gerard Martin 2435
Kavanagh, Helen Mary 2435
Kavanagh, Patrick J G 1928
Kavanagh, Robert 72
Kavanagh, Ryan Francis 2435
Kavanagh, Selina Ileene Suzanne Rosemarie 72
Kay, A M 2419
Kay, Alice Victoria Mary 1344
Kay, Amanda Mary 1385
Kay, Brodie 223
Kay, Charles John 1385
Kay, Courtney Eileen 223
Kay, Cynda 223
Kay, Danielle Elizabeth Josette 1344
Kay, George Nicholas Jemmett 1344
Kay, Jessie Catherine 223
Kay, Leo 3018
Kay, Sarah Kathleen 2419
Kay, Sarah Theresa Ceridwen 3018
Kay, Simon John Hervey 1344
Kay, William Douglas 223
Kay-Shuttleworth, Ann Mary 2614
Kay-Shuttleworth, David Charles 2614
Kay-Shuttleworth, Edward Roger Noël 2615
Kay-Shuttleworth, Ellen Anne 2615
Kay-Shuttleworth, (J) Claire 2615
Kay-Shuttleworth, Noemi 2615
Kay-Shuttleworth, Robert James 2615
Kay-Shuttleworth, Thomas Edward 2614
Kay-Shuttleworth, William James 2614
Kaye, Adelle Frances 1553
Kaye, Angus Frederick Gordon 1553
Kaye, Anne 1553
Kaye, Anthony Victor 704
Kaye, Charlotte Mary 704
Kaye, Denise Anne 1553
Kaye, Denys Michael 704
Kaye, Emma Lucy 704
Kaye, Eve 704
Kaye, Gabriel Fiona 704
Kaye, Hector Thomas Vernon 2886
Kaye, Margaret 2256
Kaye, Marita Margaret 1553
Kaye, Paul 2886
Kaye, Sally Ann Louise 1553
Kaye, Sandra Juliet 704
Kaye, Tobias John 704
Kaye, Yvonne Marie 1553
Kazantzis, Arthur Constantine 1751
Kazantzis, Judith Elizabeth 1751
Kazantzis, Miranda Elizabeth 1751
Keal, Catherine Isabel 617
Keal, Stephen Edward 617
Kean, Jennifer Mary Seton 2582
Kean, Quentin 2582
Kean, Reuben James Seton 2582
Keane, Amelia 1553
Keane, Camilla 1553
Keane, Christopher 1553
Keane, Corinne 1553
Keane, David Richard 1553
Keane, Gregory 1553
Keane, Henry 1553
Keane, Jessica 1553
Keane, Julia 1553
Keane, Olivia Dorothy 1553
Keane, Rosanna Emily 1553
Kearley, (Birgitta) Susanne 837
Kearley, Cecilia Laura Anthea 837
Kearley, Chester Dagley Hugh 837
Kearley, David 837
Kearley, Idonia Clare 836
Kearley, Josefa 837
Kearley, Marilyn 837
Kearley, Melanie 837
Kearley, Patrick Richard Hudson 837
Kearley, Selina Anna-Karin Georgiana 837
Kearley, Sheila Isabel 837
Kearley, Velvet Jane 836
Kearsley, Betty Rosamond 710
Kearsley, Nigel Steuart 710
Kearsley, Rosamond Joanna 710
Keast, Christopher John 301
Keast, Deborah Jane 301
Keast, Katherine Louise 301
Keast, Leslie 301
Keast, Vivienne Mary 301
Keating, Angela Isabel Mary 20
Keating, Clarissa Evelyn Georgette 564
Keating, Georgina Naomi 564
Keating, Keith James 564
Keating, Melissa Evelyn 564
Keating, Simon Keith 564
Keating, William 20
Keaveney, Catherine Ruth 2437
Keaveney, Deborah Maeve 2437
Keay, Alexander John Melville 2675
Keay, Anna Julia 2675
Keay, John Stanley Melville 2675
Keay, Julia Margaret 2675
Keay, Nell Christina 2675
Keay, Samuel Michael Cosmo 2675
Keays, Flora 2196
Keays, Sarah 2196
Kee, Catherine Mary 2843
Kee, Robert 2843
Keeble, Millicent Jessie Eleanor 164
Keelan, Andrew Piers 278
Keelan, George Douglas Birdwood 1980
Keelan, Gordon Douglas Birdwood 278
Keelan, Margaret Riddell 278
Keelan, Shandra Elizabeth 278
Keelan, Susan Katharine 1980
Keele, Stephanie Jane 107
Keeling, Dominique Elizabeth Priscilla 1722
Keeling, Jonathan Busil Maynard 1722
Keeman, Kris William Reginald 116
Keeman, Lauriely Elizabeth Wanda 116
Keeman, Marilyn Jane 116
Keeman, W B M 116
Keeman, Zane Basil Cornelius 116
Keen, Charles William Lyle 1465
Keen, Eleanor Margaret 1465
Keen, Julia 1202
Keen, (Priscilla) Mary Rose 1465
Keen, William Walter Maurice 1465
Keenan, Caroline Mary 2660
Keenan, David H 2798
Keenan, Katharine Victoria 236
Keenan, Lucinda Jane 236
Keenan, Nicholas Edward 2798
Keenan, Rosalind Jane 2798
Keenan, Sandra Christine 2660
Keenan, Thomas Desmond 2660
Keenan, Timothy James 2660
Keenan, Wendy Margaret 2798
Keene, Alexander Charles Edward 2567
Keene, Benjamin Charles Ruck 2567
Keene, Catharine 1950
Keene, Christine 1950
Keene, Dominic Nicholas John 2567
Keene, Frances Anne Marylee 2567
Keene, Harold Thomas 753
Keene, Hermione Katharine Mary 2567
Keene, Jason Robert 1560
Keene, Jessica Grace 1560
Keene, John Throckmorton 1950
Keene, Juliet Mary 1560
Keene, Justin Frederick 753
Keene, Justin Patrick 1560
Keene, Kathleen 1950
Keene, Lavinia Mary 1560
Keene, Mary Joan 2727
Keene, Oliver Stephen 753
Keene, Patrick Brian George 1560
Keene, Rachel Amanda 753
Keene, Richard Miles 753
Keene, Robert Michael John 2727
Keene, Tessa Emily 753
Keene, Vera 2652
Keetch, Andrew 1682
Keetch, Kirsty 1682
Keevil, Anne 686
Keevil, Caroline Elizabeth 2475
Keevil, Cordelia Jane 2475
Keevil, Katharine Elizabeth Adele 2475
Keevil, Richard James 2475
Keevil, Stanley Arnold Peter 686
Kehoe, Caroline Anne 1118
Kehoe, Catherine Frances 195
Kehoe, David 195
Kehoe, Joseph John 195
Kehoe, Monica Anne 195
Kehoe, Terence Michael 1118
Keighley, Alice Olivia Maureen 148
Keighley, Brenda Mary 143
Keighley, Francis Stephen 148
Keighley, John William 148
Keighley, Jonathan Eden 143
Keighley, Josephine Clare 148
Keighley, Pamela Jane 148
Keightley, Caroline Rosemary 449
Keightley, Richard Charles 449
Keightley, Victoria Rosemary 449
Keigwin, Michael Douglas 2160
Keigwin, Prudence Katharine Barbara 2160
Keigwin, Richard Skarratt 2160
Keigwin, Robin 2160
Keir, (Elizabeth) Sophia Rhiannon 71
Keir, James Alexander 2265
Keir, (James) Oliver Dewar 71
Keir, Lucille Dorothy 2265
Keir, (Owen) Samuel 71
Keir, Robert 71
Keir, Stuart Malcolm Forbes 2265
Keith, Alastair James 1555
Keith, Alexander David 1611
Keith, Alexander Lindsay 1555
Keith, Alexander Teagle 1555
Keith, Alicia Rose Juliet 1844
Keith, Alison Hope Alan 1555
Keith, Ariel Olivia Winifred 1611
Keith, Deborah Jane 1555
Keith, Delia Virginia 1611
Keith, Donald Murray 1739
Keith, Edward Michael 1844
Keith, Eleanor Mary 1555
Keith, Emily Margaret 1739
Keith, Flavia 1555
Keith, Frederick Donald David 1739
Keith, Geraldine Victoria 2166
Keith, Gillian Clare 1739
Keith, Hebe 2166
Keith, Hugo George 1555
Keith, Iona Delia Mary 1609
Keith, James Alan 1555
Keith, James Edward 1844
Keith, James William Falconer 1609
Keith, Jayne 1555
Keith, Marieluz (Muffet) 1555
Keith, Mary 350, 1609
Keith, Mildred Ann 2210
Keith, Nicholas Mark 2166
Keith, Penelope Jane 1555, 1844
Keith, Phoebe 1555
Keith, Ronald Leslie Keith 2210
Keith, Rosanna Victoria 1844
Keith, Sally 1555
Keith, Samuel Henry Michael 1555
Keith, Thomas Hamilton 1555
Keith, Victoria Rosemary 1844
Keith, William Richard 2166
Keith-Murray, Christopher Mark 2042
Keith-Murray, (David) Andrew 2042
Keith-Murray, (David) Mark 2042
Keith-Murray, David Wayne 2042
Keith-Murray, Deirdra 2042
Keith-Murray, Judith Anne 2042
Keith-Murray, Marnie 2042
Keith-Murray, Nancy May 2042
Keith-Murray, Peter 2042
Kellagher, Belinda Jane 622
Kellagher, Muara Ann 622
Kellagher, Richard Brian Bannerman 622
Keller, David B 1032
Keller, Dozmary Carolyn Claire 1032
Keller, Nicholas Francis David 1032
Kellett, Audrey Margaret 1556
Kellett, Bronwyn Jane 1556
Kellett, Bruce Lawrence 1556
Kellett, Catherine Lorna 1556
Kellett, Charles Rex 1556
Kellett, Christopher John 449
Kellett, Daisy Miriam 1556
Kellett, David John 1556
Kellett, Dianne 1556
Kellett, Florence 1556
Kellett, Graham Edward 1556
Kellett, Ida Mary 1556
Kellett, Jacqueline Ruth 1556
Kellett, James Andrew 1556
Kellett, Jane Maxine 1556
Kellett, Jennifer 1556
Kellett, John Raymond 1556
Kellett, Joshua Morgan 1556
Kellett, Katerina Deanne 449
Kellett, Lauren Ann 1556
Kellett, Leah Catherine Elizabeth 1556
Kellett, Leonie 1556
Kellett, Linda Darlene 449
Kellett, Maxwell 1556
Kellett, Michele Ruth 1556
Kellett, Nigel John 449
Kellett, Patricia Anne 449
Kellett, Peter Charles 1556
Kellett, Ray Weaver 1556
Kellett, Renée Helen 1556
Kellett, Rita Marjorie 1556
Kellett, Skye Emma 1556
Kellett, Susan 1556
Kellett, Tamara 1556
Kellett, William Andrew 1556
Kelley, Christopher Francis Valentine 867
Kelley, Elizabeth Louise Estelle 867
Kelley, Hélène Venetia Anne 867
Kelley, Kevin Francis Dormer 867
Kelley, Laura Anne 867
Kelley, Margaret Evelyn Venetia 867
Kelley, Matthew John Martin 867
Kelley, Patricia F 867
Kelley, Patrick David Christopher 867
Kelley, Peter John 867
Kelley, Peter John Dormer 867
Kellie, Diana Jane 1337
Kellie, Robert I W 1337
Kellie, Rupert Simon Chamier 1337
Kellie, Tara Margaret Joan 1337
Kellie, Toby Alastair Struan 1337
Kellie-Smith, David Anthony 549
Kellie-Smith, Griselda 549
Kellie-Smith, Lucy 1485
Kellie-Smith, (Margaret) Clare 549
Kellie-Smith, Owen William 549
Kellie-Smith, Samuel Anthony 549, 1485
Kellock, Christopher Charles 1373
Kellock, Clara Carys 1373
Kellock, Howard Nicholas 1373
Kellock, Jane Rebecca 1373
Kellock, Siân Louise 1373
Kellock, William Nicholas Russell 1373
Kellow, Janet 818
Kellow, Robert 818
Kellow, Robyn Tara 818
Kelly, Aidan John 1293
Kelly, Alana Mae 441
Kelly, Alexander 2097
Kelly, Alexander George 1413
Kelly, Alexandra Mary 1130
Kelly, Alexandra Mary Romana 1458, 2097
Kelly, Alice Beatrice Noëlle 2097
Kelly, (Alison) Linda 1330
Kelly, Allan Peter 1413
Kelly, Anna 1743
Kelly, Anthony Noël Francis 2097
Kelly, Archibald Clive 2565
Kelly, Arthur Edmund Campion 2269
Kelly, Beatrice Maeve 2269
Kelly, Benedict Bernard Noël d'Arenberg 2097
Kelly, Bernard 1256
Kelly, Bernard Noël David George Terrence 2097
Kelly, Caroline Anne 1130
Kelly, Catherine 2610
Kelly, Catherine Jane 1857
Kelly, Celina 2097
Kelly, Christopher James 241
Kelly, Crispin Bernard Noël 2097
Kelly, Crispin N 2247
Kelly, David 1130
Kelly, David John 1293
Kelly, David Mark Noël 1458, 2097
Kelly, Dermot Lindsay Patrick 1743
Kelly, Diane Marion 441
Kelly, Dominic Noël David Miles Charles 2097
Kelly, Donna Margaret 1413
Kelly, Doone 1743
Kelly, Dustin Philip 441
Kelly, Edward John 241
Kelly, Eleanor Louise 1857
Kelly, Elizabeth (Lisa) Georgiana Margaret 208
Kelly, Elizabeth A 2097
Kelly, Frances 2097, 2247
Kelly, Frederick David Joseph 2097
Kelly, Frederick George Bacon 157
Kelly, George Claude 2565
Kelly, Humphrey Martin Noël 2097
Kelly, Jack Alexander 1857
Kelly, James Charles 2565
Kelly, James Patrick Simeon 2269
Kelly, James Richard 2565
Kelly, Jason John 241
Kelly, Jemima Joanna 1130
Kelly, Jessica 2097
Kelly, John 2793
Kelly, John Laurence 31
Kelly, Joshua William 1413
Kelly, Julie Maree 241
Kelly, Justin Ghislain Octavius Noël 2097
Kelly, Karen Jean 1743
Kelly, Kim Edward 241
Kelly, Kylie Elizabeth 441
Kelly, Lauren Margaret 1413
Kelly, Laurence Charles Kevin 1330
Kelly, Lee Michael 241
Kelly, Louis Frederick Charles 208
Kelly, Lucy Anna Margaret 1130
Kelly, Marcus Benedict Noël 2097
Kelly, Margaret Hilary Vaughan 1293
Kelly, Margaret Mary Clare 2269
Kelly, Mehreen Saigol 1330
Kelly, Mirabel Magdalene 2097
Kelly, Miranda 2097
Kelly, Nadia 1330
Kelly, Natasha Mary Gabriella 2097
Kelly, Nathaniel David 1130
Kelly, Nicholas Tara 1330
Kelly, Patricia Margaret 157
Kelly, Patrick Dermot Stephen 1743
Kelly, Patrick Hyde 2269
Kelly, Paul 157
Kelly, Paulanne Mary 241
Kelly, Peter Richard 1293
Kelly, Sabine Mirabel Jemima Noëlle 2097
Kelly, Sebastian Charles Noël 2097
Kelly, Sonia Carol 1413
Kelly, Sophia Elizabeth 1944
Kelly, Stuart 1857
Kelly, Susannah Maria 2565
Kelly, Tabitha May 1130
Kelly, Tacy Avena 1256
Kelly, Thomas Alexander Noël 2097
Kelly, Thomas James Barttelot 208
Kelly, Vanessa Christina 2793
Kelly, William Gerald 1944
Kelsey, Elizabeth Anne 135
Kelsey, John Kneafsey 135
Kelway-Bamber, Ann Evelyn 839

Kelway-Bamber, Claude Glen 839
Kelway-Bamber, Emma Clare 839
Kelway-Bamber, Euan Glen 839, 1603
Kelway-Bamber, Laura Isabel Hester 839, 1603
Kelway-Bamber, Martin Charles 839
Kelway-Bamber, Roderick James 839
Kemmis, Bridget Mary Dean 2664
Kemp, Alexander George Munro 2637
Kemp, Annelise Audrey 2637
Kemp, Anthea Avice Yvonne 1704
Kemp, Carole Elizabeth 2688
Kemp, Christopher George 2428
Kemp, Elizabeth 2428
Kemp, Emma 2637
Kemp, Freda Sylvia 2213
Kemp, Joanna Victoria 2428
Kemp, Jonathan Hugo Durival 2428
Kemp, Malcolm Hugh David 355
Kemp, Ming Xian 2428
Kemp, Naomi Melicent 355
Kemp, Philip 2213
Kemp, Richard Geoffrey Horsford 1704
Kemp, Robin Middleton 2688
Kemp, Simon James 2637
Kemp, Susanna Jane 2428
Kemp-Gee, Henry Alfred 615
Kemp-Gee, John Andrew 615
Kemp-Gee, Lucy 615
Kemp-Gee, Mark 615
Kemp-Gee, Robert Arthur 615
Kemp-King, Andrew James de Courcy 1594
Kemp-King, Paul Robert 1594
Kemp-King, Stephen de Courcy 1594
Kemp Paterson, Margaret Carlina 2408
Kemp Paterson, William 2408
Kempster, Jade Michelle 39
Kempster, Karen Suzanne 39
Kempster, Rochelle 39
Kemys-Tynte, Eleanor Vanessa Rosabelle 2996
Kemys-Tynte, Nicholas Halswell 2996
Kenchington, Andrew Edward 549
Kenchington, Francesca Margaret 549
Kenchington, Heath Peter 549
Kenchington, Peter Harold 549
Kenchington, Robert John 549
Kendall, Andrew Christopher Barclay 453
Kendall, Andrew Thomas 1882
Kendall, Angela Josephine 453
Kendall, Benjamin Edward Buxton 453
Kendall, Charles Vyvyan 2902
Kendall, Claudia Daphne 643
Kendall, Edmund Andrew Fergus 1882
Kendall, Emily Lucy Page 2185
Kendall, Fiona Jean Lucia 1882
Kendall, Francesca Louise 643
Kendall, Jonathan Austrey 2902
Kendall, Josephine Louise 643
Kendall, Lucia Amelia Fiona 1882
Kendall, Matthew Simon Digby 453
Kendall, Miranda Elizabeth 2185
Kendall, Philip Henry 643
Kendall, Robert Bradley 2902
Kendall, Simon Christopher Edward 453
Kendall, Sophia Lucy Page 2185
Kendall, William B 2185
Kenhard, Amanda 2998
Kenhard, Robert Brindley 2998
Kenion, Robert Duncan 466
Kenion, Thomas Alexander Luckwell 466
Kenna, Justin 2883
Kenna, Lamorna Daisy 2883
Kenna, Nicholas Harry 2883
Kenna, Paul 2707
Kenna, Robyn Jane 2707
Kenna, Rosemary Janette 2883
Kennard, Alexander Mark 1560
Kennard, (Alice) Angelica 2883
Kennard, Angela Christine 1560
Kennard, Anthony 1560
Kennard, Arthur Norris 1559
Kennard, Brett Wingfield 2301
Kennard, Charles Robert 1559
Kennard, Charlotte Ann 1560
Kennard, Clare Mary Sophia 2301
Kennard, Colin David 1560
Kennard, Conan James Montrose 1560
Kennard, Cynthia Norma 2301
Kennard, Daniel James 1560
Kennard, David George 2301
Kennard, David James Risk 1559, 2883
Kennard, Desmond Richard 2301
Kennard, Edgar Robert 2883
Kennard, Fung Siu-Wan 1560
Kennard, Gaynor Bridget 1560
Kennard, Georgina 1559
Kennard, Gillian Rose 1559
Kennard, Grace Mary 1560
Kennard, Grant Richard 2301
Kennard, Heather Elizabeth Cates 1560
Kennard, Hector 2883
Kennard, Hester 1559
Kennard, Howard John 1559
Kennard, Isabella 2301
Kennard, Janet Ione Cates 1560
Kennard, Jennifer Caroline 1559
Kennard, (Jeremy) David 1560
Kennard, Joanna Frances 1559
Kennard, Joanna Gay 1560
Kennard, John Adrian Coleridge 1560
Kennard, John Michael 1560
Kennard, Kaline 1560
Kennard, Kate Ellen 2301
Kennard, Kathleen Margaret 1560
Kennard, Laura Jane 1560
Kennard, Lawrence Rochford 1560
Kennard, Leigh Mary 2301
Kennard, Lorna 1560
Kennard, Lucia Mary 1560
Kennard, Mark William 2301
Kennard, Martin Spencer 1560
Kennard, Martyn Astley 1560
Kennard, (Maurice) Nancy 1559
Kennard, Michele 1560
Kennard, Nichola 497
Kennard, Nicholas Birkbeck 1560
Kennard, Nigel Hugh 2301
Kennard, Olivia Ann 1560
Kennard, Paris Timothy 2883
Kennard, Patricia Ann Cates 1560
Kennard, Patricia Anne 1560
Kennard, Peggy 1560
Kennard, Penelope Ann 1560
Kennard, Robert Adam 1560
Kennard, Robert Jake Henry 1560
Kennard, Robert Jenner 1561
Kennard, Robert Nigel 1560
Kennard, Robert William 1559
Kennard, Roland Derek 2301
Kennard, Rosemary 1560
Kennard, Rowland Churchill Heyworth 1560
Kennard, Sheila 1560
Kennard, Simon John Vivian 1560
Kennard, Stephen Astley Martyn 1560
Kennard, Stephen Julian 1560
Kennard, Teresa C 1560
Kennard, Victoria Lindsay 1560
Kennard, Vivian Adam Mytton 1560
Kennard, Vivian Jan 1560
Kennaway, Alyson Clare Monica 1561
Kennaway, Anthony Francis 1561
Kennaway, Charles Lewis 1561
Kennaway, Christina Veronica 1561
Kennaway, Gabrielle Mary 1561
Kennaway, Hugh Edward 1561
Kennaway, Irma Annabelle 1561
Kennaway, Jessica 1561
Kennaway, John Michael 1561
Kennaway, Julia Frances 1561
Kennaway, Lucy Frances 1561
Kennaway, Mary Joyce 1562
Kennaway, Olivia Ursula 1561
Kennaway, Pamela Lavender 1561
Kennaway, Richard Noel 1562
Kennaway, (Roger) Ian 1561
Kennedy, Alastair Charles Coverley 41
Kennedy, Alexander I M 2536
Kennedy, Alicia-Jane Lesley 40
Kennedy, Amy Elizabeth 2547
Kennedy, Andrew Francis 1563
Kennedy, Angus Michael David 42
Kennedy, Annabel Deborah 1199
Kennedy, Annabel Margaret 1563
Kennedy, Anne 43
Kennedy, Archibald David 43
Kennedy, Benjamin James 1563
Kennedy, Beverley 1223
Kennedy, Brendan James 221
Kennedy, Brigid Madeline 2167
Kennedy, Caroline Anne 1199, 2547
Kennedy, Catherine Elizabeth 1123
Kennedy, Catherine Frances 1563
Kennedy, Catriona Anne 1123
Kennedy, Christopher Laurence Paul 2167
Kennedy, Christopher Patrick 1563
Kennedy, Christopher William 2279
Kennedy, Clare 2826
Kennedy, Clare Louise 253
Kennedy, Constance 1562
Kennedy, David Thomas 42
Kennedy, Diana Helen Marjorie 41
Kennedy, Edward Anthony Maxwell 2536
Kennedy, Edward Robert 1563
Kennedy, Elizabeth Lenore 2570
Kennedy, Emilia Jayne 1114
Kennedy, Emily Clare 1500
Kennedy, Emma Alexandra Elizabeth 1114
Kennedy, Evelyn Geraldine Margaret 1563
Kennedy, Fiona 42
Kennedy, Fiona Jane 41
Kennedy, George Gilbert 540
Kennedy, George Matthew Rae 1562
Kennedy, Gloria Patricia 221
Kennedy, Gordon Noel 1114
Kennedy, Graham John Clark 1563
Kennedy, Hamish Alexander Nigel 2279
Kennedy, Heather Catherine 1563
Kennedy, Helen Christine Jennifer 1562
Kennedy, Horace Charles 2570
Kennedy, Ian David 2620
Kennedy, Ian Michael Godfrey 42
Kennedy, James Edward 1114
Kennedy, James Stephen Bingham 253
Kennedy, James Titus Maxwell 2536
Kennedy, Jane Catherine 1563
Kennedy, Joan 1563
Kennedy, Joanna Mary 2167
Kennedy, John Edward 1563
Kennedy, John Hines 1852
Kennedy, John Ormiston 1563
Kennedy, John Patrick 2167
Kennedy, Josephine 1562
Kennedy, Josephine Osyth 2620
Kennedy, Judith Anne Vivian 253
Kennedy, Judith Patricia Wilhelmena 1563
Kennedy, Julia Susan 1563
Kennedy, Justin 1869
Kennedy, Katherine Fiona 2279
Kennedy, Katherine Jean 43
Kennedy, Lachlan Gene 221
Kennedy, Lisa 1390
Kennedy, Lou 1223
Kennedy, Lucy Joanne 2620
Kennedy, Ludovic Henry Coverley 41
Kennedy, Lyn Noel 1114
Kennedy, Malcolm Alistair Robert 2279
Kennedy, Margaret Lorna 1563
Kennedy, Margaret Mary 1563
Kennedy, Marion Beatrice 41
Kennedy, Marjorie Helen 41
Kennedy, Mark Edward Lucian 2160
Kennedy, Martin Charles 2620
Kennedy, Mary 42
Kennedy, Megan Anne 1563
Kennedy, Miles Thomas Pitt 540
Kennedy, Moira 41
Kennedy, Natalie Lisa 2570
Kennedy, Neil James 1390
Kennedy, Noelle Mona 1563
Kennedy, Patrick 1390
Kennedy, Paul Joseph Morrow 2167
Kennedy, Penelope Jane 1390
Kennedy, Percy William 1563
Kennedy, Peter Charles 2620
Kennedy, Peter Norman Bingham 1199
Kennedy, Priscilla Ann 1199
Kennedy, Rebecca 2167
Kennedy, Rebecca Jean 1123
Kennedy, Rebecca Madeleine Harris 2536
Kennedy, Richard Augustus 1563
Kennedy, Robert Edward 1563
Kennedy, Robert Francis 1563
Kennedy, Rosanna Jane 1199
Kennedy, Rosemary Margaret 40
Kennedy, Sally Anne 2279
Kennedy, Sally Mary 1563
Kennedy, Sandra Joan 1563
Kennedy, Sara Margaret 1199
Kennedy, Seamus Michael ffolliott 540
Kennedy, Shane Brett 2570
Kennedy, Shirley Angela Josephine 1852
Kennedy, Simon John 2547
Kennedy, Stewart Malcolm 1500
Kennedy, Suzanne Jayne 2620
Kennedy, Teresa Margaret 540
Kennedy, Thomas David Alexander 2620
Kennedy, Thomas James Peirse 253
Kennedy, Virginia 2167
Kennedy, Virginia Anne Nicola 42
Kennedy, Vivienne Gloria 1563
Kennedy, William Roger 1563
Kennerley, (Anne Marie) Ghislaine 2730
Kennerley, Peter Dilworth 2730
Kennerley, Samuel John Maximillian 2730
Kennerley, Sarah Marie Louise 2730
Kenneth, David 3011
Kenneth, Eileen Frances 3011
Kennett, Chantal Mary 2258
Kennett, Patience Vera 2258
Kennington, Benjamin Bruce James 1014
Kennington, Catherine Diana 1014
Kennington, Christopher John 1014
Kennington, David John 1014
Kennington, Elisabeth June 1014
Kennington, Eric Alasdair 1014
Kenny, Caroline Ann Florence 115
Kenny, Courtney 115
Kenny, Courtney Arthur Francis 115
Kensington, Patricia 3020
Kent, Alan 1821
Kent, Alice Vanessa 1821
Kent, Elfreda 2717
Kent, Elizabeth Audrey 1025
Kent, Emma ('Dizzy') Yseult 2717
Kent, Fiametta Maud 1119
Kent, Fiona Jane 1821
Kent, John Myles 1821
Kent, Judith Mary 1949
Kent, Lachlan Cameron 1025
Kent, Margaret Naomi Cameron 1025
Kent, Mary 1370
Kent, Miranda 2717
Kent, Olivia Mercedes 2717
Kent, P Sebastian 2717
Kent, Robin Margaret Cameron 1025
Kent, William Arnold 1025
Kent, William St John 1025
Kenton, Elizabeth Mary 937
Kenton, Geoffrey William 937
Kenworthy, Alwyn Jean Flack 2716
Kenworthy, Andrew David Whitley 2717
Kenworthy, Doreen Margaret 2715
Kenworthy, Duncan Alexander D'Isney 2716
Kenworthy, Kirsten Jane 2716
Kenworthy, Peggy Owtram 2717
Kenworthy, Stewart Alexander D'Isney 2716
Kenworthy, Victoria Hewitt 2717
Kenyon, Anne Judith 1567
Kenyon, Berenice Sofia 1568
Kenyon, Carol 1567
Kenyon, Carol Ann 1570
Kenyon, Carolyn Isabel 298
Kenyon, Christine Ann 1567
Kenyon, Clare Maria 1570
Kenyon, Crispin Simon Vicary 298
Kenyon, Eliza 2669
Kenyon, Eliza Hope 1568
Kenyon, (Eustace Allan) Michael 1568
Kenyon, Hugh 2813
Kenyon, (Hugh) Matthew 2813
Kenyon, Janet Mary 1567
Kenyon, Joan 1567
Kenyon, Joanna Louise Charlotte 1567
Kenyon, John Frederick 1567
Kenyon, John Robert 1567
Kenyon, Josephine Bridget Annette 298
Kenyon, Joyce Alma 1570
Kenyon, Judy Margaret 1567
Kenyon, Leila Mary 1570
Kenyon, Lloyd Douglas 1567
Kenyon, Marcia Joan 298
Kenyon, Martin Robert 1568, 2669
Kenyon, Mary Anne 1568, 2669
Kenyon, Mary Winifreds 2813
Kenyon, Natasha Vivien 1569
Kenyon, Nina Joan 1568
Kenyon, Peter Rowland 1568
Kenyon, Philippa Mary 1567
Kenyon, Rebecca Louise 1568
Kenyon, Richard Howard Trevor 1567
Kenyon, Robert Nicholas Andrew 1568
Kenyon, Robin George Blunden 298
Kenyon, Roger Lloyd 1570
Kenyon, Rowena Josette Caroline 298
Kenyon, Rupert David 1569
Kenyon, Rupert Peter 1568
Kenyon, Susanna 1568
Kenyon, Sylvia Elena 1569
Kenyon, Thomas Alexander 1569
Kenyon, Thomas David (Toby) 1568
Kenyon, Vanessa Zoe 1570
Kenyon, Venice 1569
Kenyon, Wendy Jean 1567
Kenyon, Wilma 1568
Kenyon-Slade, Lawrence 1260
Kenyon-Slade, Mark 1260
Kenyon-Slade, Ruth Barbara 1260
Kenyon-Slaney, Andrew William Orlando 1569
Kenyon-Slaney, Fenella 1569
Kenyon-Slaney, Francis Alan 1569
Kenyon-Slaney, Gerald Timothy Granville 1569
Kenyon-Slaney, Henry (Harry) James Rodolph 1569
Kenyon-Slaney, Jeremy Francis Gerald 1569
Kenyon-Slaney, Laura 1569
Kenyon-Slaney, Mary Helena 353, 1569
Kenyon-Slaney, Miles Christian Rodolph 1569
Kenyon-Slaney, Orlando Michael Philip 1569, 1659
Kenyon-Slaney, Philip Thomas Christopher 1569
Kenyon-Slaney, Philippa Margaret 1569, 1659
Kenyon-Slaney, (William) Simon Rodolph 353, 1569
Keown, Alice Belinda 24
Keown, David Nigel 24
Keown, Susan Caroline 24
Keown, Timothy Gordon 24
Keppel, Aline Lucy 49, 1317
Keppel, Christin Alexa 49
Keppel, Colin Rupert Harington 49
Keppel, Crispian Walter John 49
Keppel, Diana Cicely 49
Keppel, Frances May 49
Keppel, Isabel Frances Bridget 49
Keppel, Nancy Ethel 48
Keppel, Oliver George Rupert 49
Keppel, Tina 49
Keppel, Walter Arnold Crispian 1317
Keppel, William Richard Crispian 49
Ker, Alan Wemyss 372
Ker, Alexandra Mary 2763
Ker, Camilla Rosanna Gian 2763
Ker, Clare Rose 2763
Ker, David Humphry Rivers 2763
Ker, David John Richard 2763
Ker, David Peter James 2763
Ker, Desmond Agar-Ellis 2995
Ker, Priscilla Ann 2995
Ker, Sheila Hilary 372
Ker, Stephen Charles 2995
Ker, Veronica Hervey 372
Ker, Virginia Mary Eloïse 2763
Ker, William Wemyss 372
Ker-Lindsay, Adam Ronald 351
Ker-Lindsay, Alastair James 351
Ker-Lindsay, Anne 351
Ker-Lindsay, James 351
Ker-Lindsay, John Alexander 351
Ker-Lindsay, Laura 351
Ker-Lindsay, Mark 351
Kerby, David George 2512
Kerby, Margaret 2512
Kern, George 672
Kern, Joyce 672
Kerr, Adrian Oswald Wynn 1762
Kerr, Alisha Maree 1657
Kerr, Amabel Amy Antonella 1759
Kerr, Andrew Christopher 1763
Kerr, Andrew James 1761
Kerr, Andrew Peter Hugh 1763
Kerr, Andrew Philip 1763
Kerr, Andrew Robert Stephen Casamayor 1761
Kerr, Anne 1762
Kerr, Anne Frederica 1762
Kerr, Antonella 1759
Kerr, Barbara Helen 1763
Kerr, Benedict Blaise 1762
Kerr, Brian Lindsay 1582
Kerr, Britt Jean 1766

L

Lyle, David Archibald Evelyn 2547
Lyle, Edward Hugh 2547
Lyle, Ian Abram 1785
Lyle, Ian Alexander Douglas 2961
Lyle, Jake Archibald 1785
Lyle, James Robert Bryan 2547
Lyle, Joanna Mary 34
Lyle, Joshua 1785
Lyle, Matthew Alexander 1785
Lyle, Merry Claire 2547
Lyle, Rachel 1785
Lyle, Richard Charles Cecil 34
Lyle, Robert Giles 2547
Lyle, Robert John 34
Lyle, Rosemary 34
Lyle, Samuel 1785
Lynch, Alison Harriet 1641
Lynch, Amanda-Jayne Charlotte 3016
Lynch, Bahama Leslie Chandos 1449
Lynch, Charlotte 3016
Lynch, Francis Nicholas 1640
Lynch, Francis William Adrian 3016
Lynch, Harry John Renny 1963
Lynch, Hugh Arthur 1640
Lynch, Humphrey Gilbert Bohun 1640
Lynch, James Lawrence Francis 3016
Lynch, James Patrick Moncreiff 1963
Lynch, Julia Mary 3016
Lynch, Lewis Reedham 263
Lynch, Lindsay Marion 1640
Lynch, Mary Catherine 193
Lynch, Nicholas John Richard 3016
Lynch, Nicole 263
Lynch, Paul 1963
Lynch, Peter 193
Lynch, Prudence Jane 1963
Lynch, Susan 1640
Lynch, Tania 263
Lynch, William John Ivan 3016
Lynch-Blosse, Alannah Marie 1787
Lynch-Blosse, Andrew John 1787
Lynch-Blosse, Barbara Lorraine 1787
Lynch-Blosse, Blair Robert 1787
Lynch-Blosse, Brendon Scott 1787
Lynch-Blosse, Bridget Ruth 1788
Lynch-Blosse, Brittany Noel 1787
Lynch-Blosse, Cara Lynne 1786
Lynch-Blosse, Catherine Mary 1787
Lynch-Blosse, Christopher Andrew 1787
Lynch-Blosse, Craig Allan 1787
Lynch-Blosse, Danielle Bryann 1787
Lynch-Blosse, David Ian 1787
Lynch-Blosse, David Paul 1787
Lynch-Blosse, Elizabeth 1788
Lynch-Blosse, (Eric) Hugh 1787
Lynch-Blosse, Fiona Carol 1787
Lynch-Blosse, Gerald Bertram 1787
Lynch-Blosse, Hannah Victoria 1786
Lynch-Blosse, Heather Michelle 1787
Lynch-Blosse, Janice Marie 1787
Lynch-Blosse, Jean Evelyn 1787
Lynch-Blosse, Jennifer Sue 1787
Lynch-Blosse, Jessica Hannah 1787
Lynch-Blosse, Joan 1787
Lynch-Blosse, Joanne Maree 1787
Lynch-Blosse, Katherine Helen 1786
Lynch-Blosse, Marjorie Elizabeth 1787
Lynch-Blosse, Michael Anthony 1787
Lynch-Blosse, Moira Jean 1787
Lynch-Blosse, Nadine 1787
Lynch-Blosse, Oliver Daniel 1787
Lynch-Blosse, Richard Courtenay 1788
Lynch-Blosse, Robert Edward 1787
Lynch-Blosse, Robert Mark 1787
Lynch-Blosse, Sean James 1787
Lynch-Blosse, Shannon Elizabeth 1787
Lynch-Blosse, Stephen John 1787
Lynch-Blosse, Timothy Nigel 1787
Lynch-Blosse, Timothy Richard 1787
Lynch-Robinson, Anna Elizabeth 1788
Lynch-Robinson, Christopher Henry Jake 1788
Lynch-Robinson, Rosemary Seaton 1789
Lynch-Robinson, Victoria 1788
Lynch-Staunton, Charles H C 1777
Lynch-Staunton, George Henry 1777
Lynch-Staunton, Marcia Kaitilin 1777
Lynch-Staunton, Nicholas John 1777
Lynch-Staunton, Patrick Charles 1777
Lyndale, Denise Olivia 2371
Lynes, Diana Patricia 1160
Lynes, Richard A B 1160
Lynn, Carol Susan 865
Lynn, Frederick Graeme Stirling 2847
Lynn, Iain Patrick 865
Lynn, Joshua Alexander 865
Lynn, Julian Stirling Emmet 2847
Lynn, Patrick Howard 865
Lynn, Sarah Amy Janet 865
Lynn, Sophia Louise Mary 2847
Lyon, Bernadette Mary 1666
Lyon, Clare Winifred Mary 494
Lyon, Colin Arthur 2734
Lyon, Georgina Mary 622
Lyon, Giles Roderick 494
Lyon, Harry Dexter 494
Lyon, Heather 2183
Lyon, John Francis Stewart 2734
Lyon, Julian David Sinclair 622
Lyon, Kim Philip 1666
Lyon, Madeline Rosa Edith 1782
Lyon, Mary 2734
Lyon, Michèle Mary 622
Lyon, William 2183
Lyon-Dalberg-Acton, Daphne 30
Lyon-Dalberg-Acton, John Charles Ferdinand Harold 28
Lyon-Dalberg-Acton, Lucinda A F 28
Lyon-Dalberg-Acton, Patricia 28
Lyons, Alan Mark 439
Lyons, Amanda Kay 439
Lyons, Anthony Bruce 439
Lyons, Bridget Carol 1813
Lyons, Charlie John 439
Lyons, David 1035
Lyons, David Wayne 439
Lyons, Doris Mary 439
Lyons, Eleanor Amy 392
Lyons, Ernest Benjamin 439
Lyons, Georgia Anne 392
Lyons, Iella 1035
Lyons, Jai Douglas 439
Lyons, Jeremy Rhys 439
Lyons, Julie Christine 392
Lyons, Kenneth Brett 439
Lyons, Margaret Shirley 439
Lyons, Mary Annette 1813
Lyons, Megan Aimee 439
Lyons, Nathan John 439
Lyons, Rachel Jane 439
Lyons, Samantha Renee 439
Lyons, Sue 439
Lyons, Susan 1035
Lyons, Tamara Suzanne 392
Lyons, Valerie Anne 439
Lyons, Vanessa Lee 439
Lyons, Vivienne Lorna 439
Lyons, William 392
Lysaght, Anne Phyllis 1733
Lysaght, Christopher David Blandy 1732
Lysaght, Cornelius James Terence 1733
Lysaght, David James 1732
Lysaght, Deirdre Elizabeth Jane 1733
Lysaght, Dermot Edward 1733
Lysaght, Georgina Mary 1733
Lysaght, Gillian Mary 1732
Lysaght, Horace George 1733
Lysaght, Jennifer Mary 1733
Lysaght, John Daniel Blandy 1732
Lysaght, John Gareth 1733
Lysaght, John Nicholas Geoffrey 1732
Lysaght, John Patrick George 1733
Lysaght, Josephine 1733
Lysaght, Lawrence George 1733
Lysaght, Marie Helen 1733
Lysaght, Nicholas Richard Fettiplace 1732
Lysaght, Pauline Ann 1733
Lysaght, Pauline Anne 1733
Lysaght, Phyllis Jean 1732
Lysaght, Sarah Louise 1733
Lysaght, Stephen Henry 1733
Lysaght, Susan Anne 1733
Lysaght, Tessa Susan 1733
Lysaght, Vyrna 1733
Lysaght, Winifed Joyce 1732
Lysaght-Mason, Abigail Frances 1732
Lysaght-Mason, Charlotte Jennifer 1732
Lysaght-Mason, Elizabeth Anne 1732
Lysaght-Mason, Wayne Vernon 1732
Lysley, Dorothy Mary 1705
Lyster, Amanda Pamela 1609
Lyster, Anna Gillian 1208
Lyster, Gillian Barbara 1208
Lyster, Grania Mary 1208
Lyster, Julia Elizabeth 1609
Lyster, Lucy Caroline 1609
Lyster, Nicholas Charles 1609
Lyster, Peter Haggard 1208
Lyster, Rae Lionel Haggard 1609
Lyster, Thomas Henry 1208
Lythe, Edward Graeme 3078
Lythe, Graeme Allan 3078
Lythe, Henry Frederick 3078
Lythe, James Edgar 3078
Lythe, Letitia Marjorie 3078
Lyttelton, (Anthony) Stephen 615
Lyttelton, Arabella Sarah Lucy 541
Lyttelton, Benedict 541
Lyttelton, Caroline Mary 541
Lyttelton, Charles 615
Lyttelton, Christopher Charles 615, 746
Lyttelton, Cynthia Violet 614
Lyttelton, David Charles 615
Lyttelton, David George 615
Lyttelton, Deborah Claire 541
Lyttelton, Edward Gascoigne 614
Lyttelton, Elizabeth Hill 615
Lyttelton, Emma 615
Lyttelton, Francis Sebastian Jasper 541
Lyttelton, Georgina Pamela 615
Lyttelton, Henrietta Maria 615
Lyttelton, Humphrey Richard Adeane 615
Lyttelton, Laura Katherine 541
Lyttelton, Lisa Romaine 613
Lyttelton, Lucy Elizabeth Joanie 615
Lyttelton, Mary Viola 615
Lyttelton, Matthew Peregrine Antony 541
Lyttelton, (Nicholas) Adrian Oliver 541
Lyttelton, Nicholas Makeig 615
Lyttelton, Oliver Antony 541
Lyttelton, Oliver Christopher 615
Lyttelton, Oliver Stephen 615
Lyttelton, Phoebe Hermione 614
Lyttelton, Richard Cavendish 615
Lyttelton, Romilly 615
Lyttelton, Rosanna Mary 541
Lyttelton, Sophie Emma 615
Lyttelton, Teresa Mary 746
Lyttelton, (Teresa) Tessa Mary 615
Lyttelton, Thomas Charles Henry 615
Lyttelton, Thomas Glynne 615
Lyttle, Ronald Patrick Trevor 2272
Lyttle, Sonya 2272
Lytton, Caroline Mary Noel 1790
Lytton, Clarissa Mary 1790
Lytton, Eleanore 1790
Lytton, Katrina Mary Noel 1789
Lytton, Lucy Mary Frances 1790
Lytton, Madeleine Elizabeth 1790
Lytton, Philip Anthony Scawen 1789
Lytton, (Thomas) Roland Cyril Lawrence 1790
Lytton, Ursula Alexandra 1789
Lytton, Wilfrid Thomas Scawen 1789
Lytton Cobbold, Christine (Chryssie) Elizabeth 611, 2750
Lytton Cobbold, Edward 611
Lytton Cobbold, Frankie 612
Lytton Cobbold, Frederick Alexander 611
Lytton Cobbold, Ginette Elizabeth 611
Lytton Cobbold, Henry Fromanteel 611
Lytton Cobbold, Martha Frances 611
Lytton Cobbold, Morwenna Gray 611
Lytton Cobbold, Natasha Elizabeth 612
Lytton Cobbold, Peter Guy Fromanteel 611
Lytton Cobbold, Richard ('Freddie') Stucley Fromanteel 612
Lytton Cobbold, Rosina Kim 612

M

Maas, Deborah Anne 1297
Maas, Muller 1297
Mabberley, Elizabeth 1037
Maberly, Edward George Astley 2722
Maberly, Harry Robert Astley 2722
Maberly, James Harry Astley 2722
Maberly, Veronica Rose 2722
Mabin, Caroline Ruth 112
Mabin, Elizabeth 112
Mabin, Richard Peter 112
Mabin, Rosemary Kathleen 111
Mably, Sally Louise 2033
Mably, Stephen Bennett 2033
Maby, Keith Alan 1927
Maby, (Lilian) Mary 1927
Maby, Michael Robin Patrick 1927
Maby, Miranda Jane 1927
Macalister, Angus Charles 3080
Macalister, Duncan Joachim 3080
Macalister, Elke Maree 3080
Macalister, Fiona Anne 3080
MacAlister, Janice 526
Macalister, Jeanne 3080
Macalister, Kai-Donald 3080
MacAlister, Laurence Blair 526
MacAlister, Robert Kingsford 526
Macalister-Smith, Edward 2213
Macalister-Smith, Lynda Ann 2213
Macalister-Smith, Mathilda Rose 2213
Macalister-Smith, Sam Henry 2213
Macalpine, Alison Helen 2647
Macalpine, Arthur David 2647
Macalpine, Arthur Sydney 2647
Macalpine, Helen Eve 2647
Macalpine, Ian Christopher 2647
Macalpine, Jillian Elizabeth 2647
MacAndrew, Diana Sarah 1793
MacAndrew, Eileen May 1793
MacAndrew, Joy Meadows 1793
MacAndrew, Nicholas Rupert 1793
MacAndrew, Oliver Charles Julian 1793
MacAndrew, Rachel Emma 1793
MacAndrew, Robin Glen 1793
MacAndrew, Rose Clare 1793
MacAndrew, Sarah Helen 1793
MacAndrew, Tessa Deborah 1793
Macara, Rosalind Verena 1794
MacArthur-Onslow, Annette Rosemary 2160
MacArthur-Onslow, Benjamin George 2159
MacArthur-Onslow, Christina Helen 2159
MacArthur-Onslow, (Denzil) Ion 2159
MacArthur-Onslow, Dorothy 2160
MacArthur-Onslow, Duncan Reginald 2160
MacArthur-Onslow, Euan 2160
MacArthur-Onslow, Felicity Georgina 2159
MacArthur-Onslow, James William MacLeay 2159
MacArthur-Onslow, Jane Belinda 2159
MacArthur-Onslow, Jenifer Marie 2159
MacArthur-Onslow, John Walton 2159
MacArthur-Onslow, Julienne Elizabeth 2159
MacArthur-Onslow, Lachlan Robert Hugh 2159
MacArthur-Onslow, Lee 2160
MacArthur-Onslow, Lucienne Mary 2159
MacArthur-Onslow, Lucy Marie 2159
MacArthur-Onslow, Margaret Alice 2159
MacArthur-Onslow, Neil Gordon 2160
MacArthur-Onslow, Regina 2160
MacArthur-Onslow, Richard Bowring 2159
MacArthur-Onslow, Richard Matthew 2159
MacArthur-Onslow, Rohan James 2159
MacArthur-Onslow, Rupert Gordon 2159
MacArthur-Onslow, Sandra Ruth 2159
MacArthur-Onslow, Sarah 2159
MacArthur-Onslow, William Robert 2159
Macartney, Alexander Macdonald 1795
Macartney, Anita Louise 1794
Macartney, Anthony Craig 1795
Macartney, Beatrice 1795
Macartney, Belinda Lee 1795
Macartney, Benjamin Wallace 1794
Macartney, Betty Katrine 1795
Macartney, Christopher John 1794
Macartney, David Edwin 1795
Macartney, Diana Eileen 1795
Macartney, Donna Maree 1794
Macartney, Edward John 1794
Macartney, Elizabeth Lillias 1795
Macartney, Fenella Frances Dora 1154
Macartney, Geraldine 1794
Macartney, Harold Kenneth 1795
Macartney, Jack Hussey Burgh 1794
Macartney, John Alexander 1794, 1795
Macartney, John Hussey Burgh 1794
Macartney, John Ralph 1794
Macartney, Judith Anne 1795
Macartney, Karina Lee 1794
Macartney, Katharine Ann 1794
Macartney, Lynette Kathleen 1794
Macartney, Margaret 1794
Macartney, Penelope Ann 1795
Macartney, Robin Halliday 1154
Macartney, Robyn Judith 1795
Macartney, Robyn Mary 1795
Macartney, Sherryl 1794
Macartney, Suzanne Marie 1794
Macartney, Violet 1794
Macartney, Wallace Herbert 1795
Macartney, William James 1794
Macartney, William John 1795
Macartney-Snape, Susan 1794
Macartney-Snape, Tim 1794
Macaskill, Ben 2635
Macaskill, Bridget Anne 2635
Macaskill, John 2635
Macaulay, Mary 1795
Macauley, Alastair Mark Justin 1330
Macauley, Hamish Edward Dominic 1330
Macauley, Julie M 1330
Macauley, Mark Justin 1330
Macauley, Nico 1330
Macauley, Nicola Jane 1330
Macauley, Rupert Timothy 1330
Macauley, William Francis 1330
Macbain, (Andrew) Gillies 298
Macbain, Rowena Mary Phillida 298
MacBeath, Marianne Jean 3054
MacBeath, Roderick 3054
Maccabe, Fiona Marian 1172
Maccabe, Irvine J 1172
MacCaig, Alexander Stewart 2655
MacCaig, Anne Elizabeth 2655
MacCaig, Doris Mary 2655
MacCarthy, Christina Anne 457, 2910
MacCarthy, Desmond James 457, 2910
MacCarthy, Edmund Michael 457
MacCarthy, Isabel 457
MacCarthy, Mary Lisa 457
MacCarthy, Pamela Chloë 457
Maccelari, Angela Josephine Dodsworth 2650
Maccelari, Brian Carlo 2650
Maccelari, Douglas Charles Dodsworth 2650
Maccelari, Jeremy Christopher Dodsworth 2650
Maccelari, Julia Agnes 2650
Maccelari, Mary Frances Dodsworth 2650
Maccoy, Alan Harold 2211
Maccoy, Patricia Carlota 2211
Maccoy, Paul John Raymond 2211
MacDermot-Roe, Charles Alexander 2328
MacDermot-Roe, Katherine Emma 2328
Macdiarmid, Fergus Charles Ian 765
Macdiarmid, George Peter Robert 765
Macdiarmid, Lucinda Mary Joan 765
Macdiarmid, Philippa Rosemary Kate 765
Macdiarmid, Rory P A 765
Macdonald, Adrian Synge 2785
Macdonald, Alan Thomas 2785
Macdonald, Alastair Alan Graham 47
MacDonald, Alastair Ninian 489
Macdonald, Alexander Lachlan 2100
Macdonald, Alexander Lindsay 658
Macdonald, Alexandra Louisa 1799
Macdonald, (Alexandra) Ruth 2608
Macdonald, Alice 3040
Macdonald, Andrew Kenneth 2100
MacDonald, Angus Nelson 1404

Malyon, Mary Louise 2775
Malyon, Rodney Charles 389
Malyon, Tessa Margaret 2775
Mamone, Joanne Kaye 1450
Mamone, Joseph Anthony 1450
Mamone, Rachel 1450
Mamone, Rebecca 1450
Man, David Mortimer 1983
Man, Stephanie Jane 1983
Manassei di Collestate, Hugo Alexander 2616
Manassei di Collestate, Marina Catherine 2616
Mancroft, Arthur Louis Stormont 1841
Mancroft, Diana Elizabeth 1842
Mancroft, Emma 1841
Mancroft, Georgia Esmé 1841
Mander, Benedict Edward Arthur 1842
Mander, Catherine Daphne 1843
Mander, (Charles) Marcus Septimus Gustav 1842
Mander, (Charles) Nicholas 1842
Mander, Elizabeth Brehaut 1843
Mander, Fabian Edmund Quintin 1842
Mander, Fabienne H B 1843
Mander, Francis Peter 1842
Mander, Frederick George Arthur 1842
Mander, Gabrielle 1843
Mander, Georgina Jane 1842
Mander, Hannah Rachel 1843
Mander, Hugo Richard Theodore 1842
Mander, Janet 1843
Mander, Karin (Kasja) Margareta 1842
Mander, Luke Edward Charles 1842
Mander, Marcia Prudencia 1842
Mander, Maria Dolores Beatrice 1842
Mander, Martin Ian 1843
Mander, Melanie R 1843
Mander, (Mervyn) Nicholas 1842
Mander, Michael 1843
Mander, Priscilla Patricia 1843
Mander, Richard C 1843
Mander, Sarra Mary 1842
Mander, Simon Vivian 1843
Mander, Sophia Vivien 1842
Mander, Theodore 1843
Mander-Jones, Angela Margaret 914
Mander-Jones, Daisy 914
Mander-Jones, Geoffrey 914
Mander-Jones, Robert 914
Mander-Jones, Susan Elizabeth 914
Mander-Lahr, Anthea Loveday Veronica 1843
Mander-Lahr, Christopher David 1843
Manders, Isabel 195
Manders, Sandra Maree 195
Manders, Vaughan Edward 195
Manfredi, Manfredo 2861
Manfredi, Mary Grace Alexandra 2861
Manger, Gavin Robin Cunningham 1954
Manger, Rachel Jane 1954
Mangers, Johnny Pierre 143
Mangers, Margaret Joan 143
Mangnall, Anthony Derek Swift 2564
Mangnall, Mark John 1366
Mangnall, Paul Ian 1366
Mangnall, Susan Norah 1366
Mangnall, Terence André 1366
Mangriotis, Arthuros 1203
Mangriotis, Paraskevas 1203
Maniapoto, Bernadette Margaret 1437
Maniapoto, Maru John 1437
Maniapoto, Nepia 1437
Maniapoto, Niki Ann 1437
Manley, Anna Louise 429
Manley, Christopher Michael 548
Manley, Dorothy Anne 548
Manley, Edward John 429
Manley, Elaine Mary 548
Manley, George Egerton Lambert 548
Manley, John Patrick 429
Manley, Katherine Elizabeth 429
Manley, Peter George 548
Manley, Robert John Lambert 548
Manley, Susan Priscilla 429
Mann, Alexander Rupert 1844
Mann, Alison Catriona 1377
Mann, Andrew William 1844
Mann, Camilla Mary 1844
Mann, Charles Edward Lionel 1844
Mann, Charlotte Joanna 1844
Mann, D Clare de C 1844
Mann, Daisy Sarah 1844
Mann, Edgar 1844
Mann, Edward John 1844
Mann, Elizabeth Margaret 668
Mann, (Francis) George 1844
Mann, Frederick John 1844
Mann, Georgia 1844
Mann, Iain James Saddler 1377
Mann, Isabel 1844
Mann, Jack 1844
Mann, Jack Malcolm 1844
Mann, James John Francis 1844
Mann, Jane 1844
Mann, Jeffrey K 1606
Mann, Jessamy Robert 1377
Mann, John Pelham 1844
Mann, Lucy Clare 1844
Mann, Margaret Hildegarde 1844
Mann, Mary Rose 1844
Mann, Pamela Margaret 1844
Mann, Perdita 1844
Mann, Peter George 1844
Mann, Priscilla Margaret 1377
Mann, Rachel Poppy Jillian 1844
Mann, Richard William 1844
Mann, Selina Rose 1844
Mann, Simon Francis 1844
Mann, Sophie 1844
Mann, Thomas James 1844
Mann, William Edward 1844
Mannering, Alexia 3051
Mannering, Kenneth 3051
Mannering, Maximilian Timothy George 3051
Mannering, Miranda 3051
Mannering, Olivia 3051
Mannering, Stella Antoinette Jeanne 3051
Mannering, William 3051
Manners, Alice 2482
Manners, Anna 1845
Manners, Archie Thomas 1845
Manners, Arthur Roger 1845
Manners, Catherine 1845
Manners, Catherine Mary Patricia 1845
Manners, Charles Henry 1845
Manners, Charlotte Louisa 2482
Manners, David Charles Robert 2482
Manners, Edward John Francis 2482
Manners, Edward Preston 1845
Manners, Eliza Charlotte 2482
Manners, Emma L 2482
Manners, Finola St Lawrence 2487
Manners, Frances Helen 2482
Manners, Harriet Frances Mary 1845
Manners, Hugo 1845
Manners, John 2487
Manners, John Hugh Robert 1845
Manners, Joseph Peter 1845
Manners, Juliet Mary 1845, 2309
Manners, Lanya Mary Patricia 1845
Manners, Laura 1845
Manners, Lucy Rachel 2487
Manners, Mary 1845
Manners, Moira Violet Joanna 2487
Manners, Nichola E 1845
Manners, Olivia 1845
Manners, Orlando Douglas 1845
Manners, Philip 1845
Manners, Phoebe Constance Adeliza 2487
Manners, Richard John Peveril 2487
Manners, Richard Neville 1845, 2309
Manners, Robert Hugh 1845
Manners, Roger David 2487
Manners, Rupert Francis Henry 1845
Manners, Samantha S 1845
Manners, Sarah 1845
Manners, Stephen Francis 1845
Manners, Thomas Jasper 1845
Manners, Violet Diana Louise 2482
Manners, Wyn 1845
Manners, Zoe 1845
Manners-Sutton, Elizabeth Mary Gylda 2485
Manners-Sutton, John Frederick 2485
Manners-Sutton, John Lumley 2485
Manning, Allen 3044
Manning, Angela Ruth Alice 1726
Manning, Jennifer Mary 3015
Manning, Joanne 1726
Manning, John 3015
Manningham-Buller, Camilla Mary 848
Manningham-Buller, Edward John 848
Manningham-Buller, Elizabeth (Eliza) Lydia 848
Manningham-Buller, James Edward 848
Manningham-Buller, Lucy Meriel 848
Manningham-Buller, Mary Lilian 848
Manningham-Buller, Mervyn Reginald 848
Manningham-Buller, Nicola Marion 848
Manningham-Buller, Susanna Jane 848
Mannino, Meridee Francis 745
Mannion, Araminta Tanzy Ophelia 666
Mannion, Christopher Edward 666
Mannion, Elissa Jane 381
Mannion, Elizabeth Yda 666
Mannion, John Francis 381
Mannion, Kim Anabel 381
Mannion, Rebekah Anne 381
Mannion, Sassi Edward Paris 666
Mannion, Zacharia Ernest Gustave (Pingu) 666
Manns, Carolyn Mary 174
Manns, Emelia Jane 174
Mansel, Ann 1849
Mansel, Anthony Ranulf 1849
Mansel, Charlotte Elizabeth 1849
Mansel, Courtenay Robert John 1849
Mansel, Damaris Joan 1848
Mansel, Diana Theresa Violet 1848
Mansel, Elizabeth C 1849
Mansel, Frances 1849
Mansel, Hugh Clavell 1848
Mansel, Isabel Theresa 1849
Mansel, Isabella Maria 1848
Mansel, Joan Evans 1849
Mansel, Joanna Margaret 1849
Mansel, John Clavell 1848
Mansel, John Philip 1846
Mansel, Juliet Claire 1849
Mansel, Lavinia Sylvia 1848
Mansel, Margaret 1846
Mansel, Mary Germaine 1849
Mansel, Nicol 1846
Mansel, Philip Robert Rhys 1848
Mansel, Philippa Clare 1849
Mansel, Rhys Clavell 1848
Mansel, Rhys Edward Regnier 1849
Mansel, Richard James 1846
Mansel, Richard Mark 1849
Mansel, Robert Courtney 1849
Mansel, Robert Edward 1849
Mansel, Roderick Rhys 1849
Mansel, Timothy Mervyn Charles 1849
Mansel Lewis, Claire Mary 2777, 2993
Mansel Lewis, David Courtenay 2993
Mansel Lewis, Edward Vivian 2993
Mansel Lewis, John David 2993
Mansel Lewis, Mary Rosemary Marie-Gabrielle 2993
Mansel Lewis, Patrick Charles Archibald 2777, 2993
Mansel Lewis, Robert William 2993
Mansel-Pleydell, Charles David Luttrell Morton 1848
Mansel-Pleydell, Dagmar Rosalie 1848
Mansel-Pleydell, Elizabeth Susan 1848
Mansel-Pleydell, Harry Rupert Delalynde Morton 1848
Mansel-Pleydell, Jessica Gertrude 1848
Mansel-Pleydell, John Bowring Morton 1848
Mansel-Pleydell, Philip Morton 1848
Mansel-Pleydell, Rebecca 1848
Mansel-Pleydell, Rosanna Vivien 1848
Mansel-Pleydell, Rose Magdalen 1848
Mansel-Pleydell, Thomas Oliver Clavell Morton 1848
Mansel-Pleydell, Toby Edmund Luard Morton 1848
Mansell-Jones, Penelope Marion 1350
Mansell-Jones, Richard M 1350
Mansergh, Annabel Karenza 3020
Mansergh, Julia Karenza 3020
Mansergh, Michael Peter 3020
Mansergh, Philippa Louise 3020
Mansergh-Wallace, Henrietta Patricia 120
Mansergh-Wallace, Patrick 120
Mansfield, Alice Georgina 2550
Mansfield, Anthony Roderick 548
Mansfield, Charles James 548
Mansfield, Christopher John 2442
Mansfield, David William 549
Mansfield, Edward James 2549
Mansfield, Evelyn Cecil 2550
Mansfield, Guy Rhys John 2549
Mansfield, Janet Mary 2549
Mansfield, Jessica Helen 548
Mansfield, John Giles 1346
Mansfield, Margaretta Helena 1346
Mansfield, Philippa St Clair 2549
Mansfield, Ruth Sarah 549
Mansfield, Sophia Sally 2442
Manson, Christopher Spencer 1470
Manson, Frances Elspeth Luise 1203
Manson, Jane 1470
Manson, Joan Daphne 1470
Manson, Royston Edward Bindlos 1470
Manson, William Alastair Leslie 1203
Mant, Alexandra 2558
Mant, Alistair Donald 2546
Mant, Catherine Margaret 2546
Mant, Eleanor Frances 2546
Mant, Emma Lavinia 2558
Mant, Isabel Catherine 2546
Mant, Patrick Robert 2558
Mantel, Adolph S 1503
Mantel, Alison Margaret 1503
Manuel, Annabel Madeline Jane 2972
Manuel, Jessica 203
Manuel, Jonathan Reinier 2972
Manuel, Olivia Victoria Greta 2972
Manuel, Thomas 203
Manuel, Venetia Elizabeth Emily 2972
Mapp, Joel Dennis 2311
Mapp, Kate Miranda 2311
Mapp, Susan Joan Rose 2311
Mapp, Thomas Henry 2311
Mapplebeck, Althea Rosamund Louise 254
Mapplebeck, Anthony Peirse 254
Mapplebeck, Lilian Bridget 254
Mapplebeck, Selina Bridget Lucy 254
Mar, Elizabeth, of 1857
Mar, Janet Helen, of 1856
Marais, Charlotte Victoria 2732
Marais, Edward John 2732
Marais, John 2732
Marais, Maria-del-Mar 2732
Maran, Alicia 1881
Marble, Daniel Edward 2501
Marble, Harry Arthur 2501
Marble, Joseph Harry 2501
Marble, Karen Margaret 2501
Marble, Michael Stephen 2501
Marble, Nicola 2501
Marble, Sylvia 2501
Marble, Timothy John 2501
Marble, William Edward 2501
March, Maria 2402
March, Maxwell James 685
Marchant, Jennifer Margaret Felicity 407
Marchant, John 407
Marchbank, Anthea 1024
Marchbank, Joanna 1024
Marchbank, Jonathan Havelock 1024
Marchbank, Katharine Jane 1024
Marchbank, Michael Havelock 1024
Marckus, Melvyn 1592
Marckus, Rachel Mary Frances 1592
Marcow, Hannah Olive 1865
Mardones, Arturo 2672
Mardones, Diego 2672
Mardones, Magdalena 2672
Mardones, Maria Evelyn 2672
Mardones, Octavia 2672
Marendaz, Anne Elisabeth 3023
Marendaz, Arnaud Julien 3023
Marendaz, Aude Christelle 3023
Marendaz, Elizabeth-Anne 3023
Marendaz, Jean-Pierre Arnold Edmund 3023
Marendaz, Thierry Pierre 3023
Margesson, Agatha Hope 1863
Margesson, Agneta 1863
Margesson, (Charles) Philip 1863
Margesson, Franziska Anna Maria 1863
Margesson, Helena 1863
Margesson, Hugh David 1266
Margesson, Jane Henrietta 1863
Margesson, John Bertram 1266
Margesson, Lois 1863
Margesson, Lucy Emma Alexander 253
Margesson, Margaret 1863
Margesson, Michael Vere Hobart 1863
Margesson, Peter Reginald Hampden 1863
Margesson, Rhoda ('Rhodie') Frances 1863
Margesson, (Richard) David 1863
Margesson, Richard Francis David 1863
Margesson, Richard William 253, 1266, 1863
Margesson, Ruth Margaret 1863
Margesson, Sarah Helena 1863
Margesson, Susan Alice Prior 253
Margesson, Thomas Vere Hobart 1863
Margesson, Wendy Maree 1863
Margesson, (William) Robert Stanley 1863
Margolis, Dorothy Anne 1021
Margolis, Jack 1021
Marinori, Luigi 1520
Marinori, Sara 1520
Marion, Fabrice Gilles 22
Marion, Hélo 22
Marion, Kate Georgina 22
Marion, Oriane 22
Marion, Oscar 22
Marion, Tiphaine Jennifer 22
Maritz, Danielle Jeanne 967
Maritz, Terence 967
Marjoribanks-Egerton, Helen Elizabeth 1234
Marjoribanks-Egerton, John Caledon Richard 1234
Marjoribanks-Egerton, John Stephen 1234
Mark, Christopher Edward 2938
Mark, Jonathan Scott 2938
Mark, Michael Scott 2938
Mark, (Winifred) Anne 2938
Marker, Angela Nicole 2542
Marker, Joanna Petronela 2542
Marker, Karissa Ann 2542
Marker, Petronela Johana 2542
Marker, Richard John 2542
Marker, Stephanie Michelle 2542
Markes, Alice Olivia 1634
Markes, Araminta Victoria 554
Markes, Christopher John 1634
Markes, Dominic John 554
Markes, Edward Charles 554
Markes, Georgina Caroline 554
Markes, Gerard David 554
Markes, Louisa Meriel 1634
Markes, Miranda Grania 1634
Markeson, Juliana Diana 741
Markeson, Lucy Juliana 741
Markeson, Oliver James 741
Markeson, Stephen 741
Markgraf, Deidre Ann 1045
Markham, Allan N 63
Markham, Anne C 1864
Markham, Arthur David 1864
Markham, Carolyn L 1864
Markham, Christy Victoria 1864
Markham, Fleur 1864
Markham, (Frederica) Betty 1865
Markham, Geke 1864
Markham, Hanna Althea Marion 1864
Markham, Joanna Mary Hilda 1864
Markham, John 1864
Markham, John Lloyd 1864
Markham, Joy Elizabeth 1864
Markham, Julia Grace 1864
Markham, Lilly-Anne 63
Markham, Louise Christine Winsmore 63
Markham, Lyon Frederick 63
Markham, Matthew James 1864
Markham, Michael Arthur 1864
Markham, Moshe Arthur 1864
Markham, Natasha 1864
Markham, Nicholas Charles 1864
Markham, Richard Barry 1864
Markham, Tanya Valerie Helen 1864
Markham, Toby John 1864
Markham, Valerie 1864
Markiewicz, Davina Evelyn 1171
Markiewicz, James Josef 1171
Markiewicz, William David 1171
Markiewicz, Wojciech 1171
Markov, Alexandra Raina 850
Markov, Annabel Mary 850
Marks, Marina 1865
Marks, Marion 1865
Marks, Michael 1865
Marks, Miriam Ann 1865
Marks, Rebecca 1865
Marks, Simon Richard 1865
Marks, Susannah Elizabeth 1865
Markwick, Mary Beatrice 1726
Markwick, Michael 1726
Marland, Jonathan Hay 778
Marland, Penelope Margaret 778

Morton, Lavinia Elizabeth 2569
Morton, Louise Jean 2569
Morton, Peter Fergus 3086
Morton, Richard 1409
Morton, Richard M 2470
Morton, Roger Thomas 2569
Morton, Samuel Richard 2470
Morton, Stewart John 1548
Morton, Thomas Oliver 1548
Morton, William Roy 1548
Morton-Smith, Isabella Brenda Windham 340
Morton-Smith, Michael Braine 340
Morton-Stevens, Bernard 2947
Morton-Stevens, Charlotte Anne Esther 2947
Morton-Stevens, Dominic Peter 2947
Morton-Stevens, Lesley Anne 2947
Morton-Stevens, Robert Guy 2947
Morton-Stevens, Veronica Mary 2947
Mosby, Charlotte Elgitha Veronical 971
Moseley, Charlotte Elizabeth Anne 1180
Moseley, Christopher John Wallace 1180
Moseley, Dominic Richard Sheridan 1180
Moseley, Dorothy 3067
Moseley, Edward John Wallace 1180
Moseley, Emily Kathryn Louise 1180
Moseley, Isobel Mary Anne 1180
Moseley, James William Sheridan 1180
Moseley, Justin Robert Patrick 1180
Moseley, Kathryn Fiona 1180
Moseley, Laura Anne 1180
Moseley, Loretta Anna 1180
Moseley, Lucy Elizabeth Anne 1180
Moseley, Mary Teresa 1180
Moseley, Patricia 2056
Moseley, Robert Louis 2056
Moseley, Ursula Anne Marie 1180
Moseley, Walter Howard 3067
Moseling, Emma Jane 802
Moseling, Judy Mary 802
Moseling, Mark Christian 802
Moser, Anne 1166
Moser, Margaret Anne 1166
Moser, Nancy Jane 1166
Moser, William 1166
Mosey, Elizabeth 1235
Mosey, Frank 1235
Mosier, Frank 689
Mosier, Sarah 689
Mosley, Aidan 2362
Mosley, Alexander James 2365
Mosley, Amanda Wendy 2924
Mosley, Ana-Maria 2365
Mosley, Anne Marie 2365
Mosley, Anthony Noel 2364
Mosley, Caroline Rosalind 2365
Mosley, Charles Gordon 737
Mosley, Charlotte Diana 2365
Mosley, Charlotte Louise 2365
Mosley, Clare Imogen 2362
Mosley, Daniel Nicholas 2362
Mosley, Diana 2365, 2382
Mosley, Felix Harry 2362
Mosley, Frances Christine 737
Mosley, Francis 2362
Mosley, Gail 2924
Mosley, George Christopher 2365
Mosley, Gregory 2362
Mosley, Ivo Adam Rex 2167, 2362
Mosley, Jean Marjorie 2365
Mosley, John Ronald 2365
Mosley, Louis 2365
Mosley, Maria 2365
Mosley, Marius 2363
Mosley, Matthew 2362
Mosley, Max Alexander 2365
Mosley, Max Rufus 2365
Mosley, Michael 2366
Mosley, Monica 2362
Mosley, Nathaniel Inigo 2362
Mosley, Noah Billy 2362
Mosley, Olga Marie Noelle 2364
Mosley, Oliver Simon 2365
Mosley, Orson 2362
Mosley, (Oswald) Alexander 2365
Mosley, Patrick Max 2365
Mosley, Robert 2362
Mosley, Robert Anthony 2364
Mosley, Rosie 2362
Mosley, Scipio Louis 2362
Mosley, Shaun Nicholas 2362
Mosley, Simon James 2365
Mosley, Theresa 2362
Mosley, Thomas 2362
Mosley, Verity Elizabeth 2362
Mosley, Victoria 2362
Mosley, Vij 2362
Mosley, Xanthe Jennifer Grenville 2167, 2362
Moss, Alice Elinor 65
Moss, Annette Margaret 1067
Moss, Candida Rebecca 601
Moss, Edward Ian James Gray 65
Moss, Helen Jane 1067
Moss, James Robert 772
Moss, Jane Elizabeth 772
Moss, Jeremy Gilbert 831
Moss, Jo Ann 1067
Moss, Jonathan Mark 772
Moss, Julian Duncan 519
Moss, Juliet Mary 831
Moss, Linda 772
Moss, Mary Elizabeth Anne 772
Moss, Michael Duval 831
Moss, Nicola Ann 1067
Moss, Nigel Patrick Stringer 772
Moss, Pandora 601
Moss, Raymond Ernest 1067
Moss, Rebecca Alice 831
Moss, Susannah Elizabeth , 65
Moss, Theodora Katherine Rose 65
Moss, Tuckerman 831
Moss, Victoria Elizabeth 65
Mosse, Andrew David 2621
Mosse, Annabel Mary 843
Mosse, Barbara 2621
Mosse, Charles David Fairless 2157
Mosse, Charles Riou 2157
Mosse, Georgina Elaine 2621
Mosse, Jacob Sebastian Fairless 2157
Mosse, Julia 2157
Mosse, Martin Barrington 2621
Mosse, Oliver Benjamin 2157
Mosse, Patrick Tylden Rutherford 2621
Mosse, Peter John 2621
Mosse, Peter Vernon 843
Mosse, Sarah Francesca 2621
Mosse, Simon Rupert 2621
Mossman, John Vernon 2166
Mossman, Tessa Elizabeth 2166
Mostyn, Alexandra Stefanie 2005
Mostyn, Alice Mary 2010
Mostyn, Alison Mary Bridget 2011
Mostyn, Amy Clare 2875
Mostyn, Anna Teresa Joan 2010
Mostyn, Annette 2011
Mostyn, Anthony Damian 2874
Mostyn, Avice Louise Trevor 780
Mostyn, Casimira Anita Maria 2011
Mostyn, Catherine Sibylla 1620
Mostyn, Celia Mary 2010
Mostyn, Charles Francis Llewellyn 2009
Mostyn, Charles Gerard 2010
Mostyn, Chloe Mary 2011
Mostyn, Christopher Francis Joseph 2874
Mostyn, Clare Mary 2010
Mostyn, Cristina Beatrice Maria 2011
Mostyn, Daisy Catherine Mar Ghislaine 2010
Mostyn, (David) Mark Joseph 2010
Mostyn, (David) Pyers 2010
Mostyn, David Wallace 2010
Mostyn, Denise Suzanne 2005
Mostyn, Diana 2010
Mostyn, Dianna Lyn Carolyn 2009
Mostyn, Donald Mayne 2009
Mostyn, Doris 2009
Mostyn, Dorothy 2010
Mostyn, Douglas William Francis 2009
Mostyn, Edward John 2010
Mostyn, Elizabeth Catherine Bernadette 2011
Mostyn, Ella Aurora 2009
Mostyn, Francis Edward Terence 2010
Mostyn, Francis Llewellyn 2009
Mostyn, Freddy Joseph George 2011
Mostyn, Gay 2875
Mostyn, Georgia Mary 2010
Mostyn, Giles Patrick Joseph Ghislain 2010
Mostyn, Gregory Philip Roger 2005
Mostyn, Gregory Thomas Joseph Ghislain 2010
Mostyn, Harry Edward Llewelyn 2011
Mostyn, Helen Catharine Stewart 2010
Mostyn, Henry Francis Joseph Ghislain 2010
Mostyn, Hermione Mary Josephine 2011
Mostyn, Isobel Mary 2010
Mostyn, Jane Carolyn 2010
Mostyn, Jerome John Joseph 2010
Mostyn, Joan Elizabeth Verena 2875
Mostyn, Joanna Charlotte Mary Ghislaine 2010
Mostyn, (Joseph) David Frederick 2010
Mostyn, Joshua Marcus Joseph 2010
Mostyn, Katherine Mary 2010
Mostyn, Laurie Irene Grace 2009
Mostyn, Liam Alexander 2010
Mostyn, Llewellyn Roger Lloyd 2005
Mostyn, Lucy Joanna 2010
Mostyn, Margaret Claire 2011
Mostyn, Marion 2009
Mostyn, Mark Francis Joseph Ghislain 2010
Mostyn, Mary 2874
Mostyn, Matthew Anthony 2010
Mostyn, Meg Joan Elizabeth 2011
Mostyn, Melissa Bernadette 2011
Mostyn, Nicholas Anthony Joseph Ghislain 2010
Mostyn, Olivia Mary 2011
Mostyn, Patricia 2009
Mostyn, Paul 2011
Mostyn, Peter Llewellyn 2010
Mostyn, Philip Anthony Julio Jerome 2010
Mostyn, Philip Joseph 2010
Mostyn, Polly Elizabeth Hermione 2011
Mostyn, Rachel Joanna Maria 2011
Mostyn, Richard Anthony 2874
Mostyn, Richard Clive 2010
Mostyn, Richard Jan Joseph 2011
Mostyn, Richard Pyers 2010
Mostyn, Richard Thomas 2010
Mostyn, Rosanna Mary 2010
Mostyn, Rosemary Joy 2010
Mostyn, Rupert Joseph Sheridan 2010
Mostyn, Samuel John Savage 2011
Mostyn, Sarah Jane 2875
Mostyn, Sarah Katherine 2010
Mostyn, Shona Sugrue 2010
Mostyn, Simon Edward Basil 2011
Mostyn, Stephen John 2010
Mostyn, Suki Hermione 2011
Mostyn, Susan 2010
Mostyn, Theresa Antionette 2011
Mostyn, Toby Joseph 2011
Mostyn, Trevor Alexander Richard 2011
Mostyn, Trevor Angus 2009
Mostyn, Trevor Illtyd 2010
Mostyn, Ursula Anna 2010
Mostyn, Valentine Francis Damian 2875
Mostyn, Vaux Almond 2009
Mostyn, William Joseph 2010
Mostyn, Yvonne Brown 2009
Motion, Anthony David 2885
Motion, Georgina 2885
Motion, Penelope Mary 2885
Motion, Richard Peter 205
Motion, Sarah 205
Motion, Stephen Anthony 2885
Motl, Ann Lillian 1958
Motl, Julia 1958
Motl, Marion Ann 1958
Mott, Alison Mary 2011
Mott, Amanda Jane 2011
Mott, David Hugh 2011
Mott, Diana 2012
Mott, Elizabeth 2011
Mott, Jonathan William 2011
Mott, Martha 2012
Mott, Matthew David 2011
Mott, Peter Lewis 2012
Motteux, Helen 423
Motteux, Hugues Renier 423
Motteux, Jean-Paul 423
Motteux, Nicole 423
Motteux, Thierry 423
Mottram, David Leonard Garfit 1667
Mottram, Fiona Margaret 998
Mottram, Joe Neville 1667
Mottram, Moira Livingstone 1667
Mottram, Pamela Mary 1667
Mottram, Peter Hay 1667
Mottram, Richard 998
Mottram, Richard Neville Garfit 1667
Moubray, Anne Catherine Wilhelmina 2000
Moubray, Belinda Mary Claire 2000
Moubray, Charles John 107
Moubray, Claire Wilhelmina Maud 2000
Moubray, James 107
Moubray, John Robert Fitzroy 2000
Moubray, Lucinda Frances 107
Moule, Christopher Andrew Fenton 1949
Moule, Diana Elizabeth 2599
Moule, Henry 1949
Moule, John S 2599
Moule, Melita Frances 1949
Moule, Patrick Fenton 1949
Moule, Priscilla Joy 1949
Moule, Timothy James Neale 1949
Moulierac, Christophe Jean Philippe 584
Moulierac, Denise Catherine 584
Moulierac, Pascale Mireille Monique 584
Moulierac, Philippe 584
Moult, Adrian Thomas 223
Moult, Kathleen Dawn 223
Moult, Winifred Mary 223
Mounsey-Heysham, Anna 102
Mounsey-Heysham, Benjamin 102
Mounsey-Heysham, Giles H 102
Mounsey-Heysham, Penelope Auriol 102
Mounsey-Heysham, Rory 102
Mounsey-Heysham, Toby 102
Mount, Constance 2013
Mount, Deborah 2013
Mount, Frances Leone 2013
Mount, Henry Francis 2013
Mount, James Williams Spencer 992
Mount, John Richard Herbert Crichton 992
Mount, Julia Margaret 2013
Mount, Mark Donald Crichton 992
Mount, Martha 992
Mount, Mary Julia 2013
Mount, Patricia Jane 992
Mount, William Robert Horatio 2013
Mountain, Camilla 2016
Mountain, Charlotte Sarah 2016
Mountain, Denis 1205
Mountain, Doris Elsie 2016
Mountain, Edward Brian Stanford 2016
Mountain, Emma V G 2016
Mountain, Harry Brian Pownall 2016
Mountain, (Hélène) Fleur Mary Kirwan 1205, 2016
Mountain, Henry Nicholas 2016
Mountain, Nathalie Frances 2016
Mountain, Nicholas Brian Edward 2016
Mountain, Penelope 2016
Mountain, Thomas Denis Edward 2016
Mountain, William Denis Charles 2016
Mountbatten, Alexandra Noda Victoria 1931
Mountbatten, Clare 1928
Mountbatten, Ella Louise Georgina 1931
Mountbatten, Henry (Harry) David Louis 1928
Mountbatten, Ivar Alexander Michael 1931
Mountbatten, Janet Mercedes 1931
Mountbatten, Penelope A V 1931
Mountbatten, Tatiana Helen Georgia 1928
Mountier, Clifford Cedric 2698
Mountier, Phoebe Ethne 2698
Mountjoy, John Radforth 1366
Mountjoy, Winifred 1366
Mousley, Alda Mary 1420
Mousley, Gro Rieve 2203
Mousley, Jacqueline Frances 1420
Mousley, James Arthur 2203
Mousley, John Charles Allday 1420
Mousley, John Rieve 2203
Mousley, Karl Jane 2203
Mousley, Kristin Ethelwyn 2203
Mousley, Laura Frances 2203
Mousley, Peter John Hunter 1420
Mousley, Thomas Barnabas Hunter 1420
Mouzakitis, Sarah Rosemary Iris 2382
Mouzakitis, Spiros 2382
Mowatt, Christian Alexander 46
Mowatt, Marina Victoria Alexandra 46
Mowatt, Zenouska May 46
Mowbray, John Robert 2921
Mowbray, Lavinia Mary 2020, 2921
Mowbray, Teresa Jane 2020
Mowll, Carol Ann 1359
Mowll, Caroline Mary (Mollie) 1359
Mowll, Carolyn Frances 1359
Mowll, Nicholas Rothwell 1359
Mowll, Richard Finch 1359
Mowll, Richard Hanbury 1359
Moxon, Christian Frederick 815
Moxon, Matthew Sebastian 815
Moxon, Simon John 815
Moynihan, Antonita Maria Carmen 2029
Moynihan, Aurora Luzon Maria Dolores 2029
Moynihan, Daniel 2029
Moynihan, Editha Eduarda 2029
Moynihan, Gaynor(-Louise) 2028
Moynihan, George Edward Berkeley 2028
Moynihan, India Isabella 2028
Moynihan, Jinna 2029
Moynihan, Kathleen Maynila Helen Imogen Juliet 2029
Moynihan, Nicholas Ewen Berkeley 2028
Mrozowski, Isobel Catherine Joan 1126
Mrozowski, Joseph John Paul 1126
Mueller, Christa 2786
Mueller, Gerhard 2786
Mueller, Marcus Raymond George 2786
Mueller, Sharon Patricia 2786
Muende, Melanie Jane Ruth 84
Muende, Paul 84
Muers-Raby, Fiona Jane 2399
Muers-Raby, Nicholas Jonathan 2399
Muers-Raby, Nigel Andrew 2399
Muers-Raby, Oliver Henry 2399
Muers-Raby, Rosanna Louise 2399
Muers-Raby, Thomas Sebastian 2399
Muers-Raby, Victoria 2399
Muff, Andrew Raymond 474
Muff, Barbara Ann 474
Muff, Jonathan Edward 474
Muff, Mary 475
Muff, Peter Raymond 475
Muggeridge, Bryan 2933
Muggeridge, Sarah Jane 2933
Muir, Alastair James 973
Muir, Alexander Pepys 1870
Muir, Alexandra Julie 2030
Muir, Andrew Hugh John 2030
Muir, Andrew James 2030
Muir, Angela Cramp 2030
Muir, Ann Mary 2030
Muir, Anna Charlotte 2030
Muir, Bettine Clara 2030
Muir, C Neale 2550
Muir, Caroline Egeria Malise 1197
Muir, Catherine Elizabeth 2030
Muir, Daisy Mary 2030
Muir, Darcy Jane 1446
Muir, David Stuart 2030
Muir, Duncan Macpherson 1417
Muir, Duncan Russell 973
Muir, Elizabeth Mary 2030, 3098
Muir, Fiona Barbara Elspeth 2030
Muir, Griselda Catherine 2030
Muir, Hugh James Robin 2030
Muir, Ian Charles 2030
Muir, James 973
Muir, James Fergus Wemyss 1197
Muir, James Francis 2030
Muir, Jeremy Kim 2030
Muir, John Alexander Hector 2030
Muir, Juliet Sara Kirstie 2030
Muir, Linda Mary 990, 2030
Muir, Lisa Jane Fiona 2030
Muir, Louisa Jane 2030
Muir, Margaret Claire 2030
Muir, Margaret Wallis 1417
Muir, Maureen Yearsly 2030
Muir, Nicholas John 2030
Muir, Patricia Mary Braithwaite 1446
Muir, Penelope Jane 973
Muir, (Penelope) Sara Helene 2550
Muir, Philip John Fredrick 2030
Muir, Primrose Jean 2161
Muir, Raymond 1557
Muir, Richard Horsfall 1446
Muir, Robert William 2030
Muir, Robin Hugo 1870
Muir, Rosemary Mildred 1870
Muir, Sarah-Jane E 1870
Muir, Simon Huntly 1870
Muir, Sophie Alexander 1446
Muir, Sophie Amanda Nöel 2030
Muir, Thomas Sebastian 1870
Muir, Thomas Wemyss 1197
Muir, William Anthony Nathaniel 2030

N

Nugent, Laura Anne 2132
Nugent, Louise 2131
Nugent, Louise V 2131
Nugent, Lynette Ann 2131
Nugent, Margaret Anne 2131
Nugent, Margaret Mary Lavallin 2131
Nugent, Mark 2131
Nugent, Ngaire 2131
Nugent, Nicholas Myles John 2130
Nugent, Nigel Howard Clare 2133
Nugent, Okabe 2132
Nugent, Patrick Guy 2133
Nugent, Patrick Hulme 2131
Nugent, Patrick Mark Leonard 2980
Nugent, Penelope Anne 2130
Nugent, Peter James 2131
Nugent, Philippa Mary 2133
Nugent, Raewyn Gay 2131
Nugent, Rayna Joy 2131
Nugent, Rory David Neeld Lavallin 2131
Nugent, Rufus 2133
Nugent, Rupert Michael 2981
Nugent, Sandra May 2131
Nugent, Sean Charles Weston 2980
Nugent, Susanna Margaret 2980

Nugent, Sylvia Catherine 61
Nugent, Terence 2133
Nugent, Thomas Alexander 2981
Nugent, Trevor Charles 2131
Nugent, Valentine 2131
Nugent, Victoria Anna Irmgard 2133
Nugent, (Walter) Richard Middleton 2132
Nunneley, Catherine Elizabeth 3072
Nunneley, Clare Sabina 3072
Nunneley, Frances Mary 3072
Nunneley, Katherine Ruth 3072
Nunneley, Luke James Charles 3072
Nunneley, Rebecca 3072
Nutt, Jean Rosemary 2863
Nutt, John Allister 2863
Nuttall, Amber Louise 2134
Nuttall, Andrew John 75
Nuttall, Clive Patrick 2135
Nuttall, Edward James Stafford 75
Nuttall, Eileen Daphne Elizabeth 2135
Nuttall, Erin Rose 75
Nuttall, Eugenie Marie Alicia 2134
Nuttall, George Geoffrey 2134
Nuttall, Gytha Miranda 2134
Nuttall, Harry 2134

Nuttall, Heather 75
Nuttall, Kelly Marie 2134
Nuttall, Kenneth Mitchell 130
Nuttall, Mary 2134
Nuttall, Michael John Berkeley 75
Nuttall, Monica 2134
Nuttall, Nicholas Alexander David 2134
Nuttall, Olympia Jubilee 2134
Nuttall, Patricia Ann 128
Nuttall, Peggy Ellen Nan 128
Nuttall, Richard Francis 75
Nuttall, Roger A 128
Nuttall, Rose 75
Nuttall, Rosemary 2134
Nuttall, Serena Mary 130
Nuttall, Simon Dominic 2134
Nuttall, Tom Oliver 128
Nuttall, Valerie Doreen 75
Nutting, Alexandra 2135
Nutting, Annette Moira 2135
Nutting, Belinda 2135
Nutting, Cecilia Hester Marie-Louise Constance 69, 2135
Nutting, David Anthony 1995, 2135
Nutting, David Brin Charles 220

Nutting, Diane 2135
Nutting, James Edward Sebastian 2135
Nutting, John Grenfell 2135
Nutting, Laura Mary Catherine 220
Nutting, Margarita 2135
Nutting, Nicholas Duncan 220
Nutting, Nicholas Ronald 2135
Nutting, Patricia Elizabeth 2135
Nutting, Peter Robert 69, 2135
Nutting, Rupert Edward 2135
Nutting, Samantha Mary 2135
Nutting, Serena 2135
Nutting, Tessa Anne 1995, 2135
Nutting, Victoria Emily 2135
Nutting, William Frederick 2135
Nux, Anita Sofia 574
Nux, Rodolfo Juan Carlos 574
Nye, Alan 622
Nye, Alistair William James 622
Nye, Deborah Katherine Hildegrade 622
Nye, Lucy Elizabeth Katherine 622
Nye, Phyllis 57
Nyeland, Beverly Louise 1021
Nyeland, David Fairfax 1021
Nyeland, Sallie Virginia 1021

O

Oakeley, Andrew Gilbert 2137
Oakeley, Caroline Rachel 2137
Oakeley, Catherine Amanda 2136
Oakeley, Christopher Rowland 2137
Oakeley, Diana Margaret 2137
Oakeley, Edward James 2137
Oakeley, Henry Francis 2137
Oakeley, Margaret 2137
Oakeley, Matthew Thomas 2137
Oakeley, Maureen 2137
Oakeley, Maureen Frances 2136
Oakeley, Michael 2137
Oakeley, Olivia Kate 2136
Oakeley, Paul David 2137
Oakeley, Rachel Mary 2137
Oakeley, Robert John Atholl 2136
Oakeley, Rowland Henry 2137
Oakeley, Sara 2137
Oakeley, Shirley 2137
Oakeley, Timothy Christopher 2137
Oakeley, William 2136
Oakes, Alexander Waddington 1623
Oakes, Annette Christine 1623
Oakes, Bianca Eunice 2137
Oakes, Charlotte Anne 1623
Oakes, Christine 2137
Oakes, Gillian Walsham 2933
Oakes, Greta Anna Eunice 2137
Oakes, Harry Newell 2137
Oakes, Harry Philip 2137
Oakes, James Scudamore 2933
Oakes, John Waddington 1623
Oakes, Julie Dawn 2137
Oakes, Michael Lewis 2137
Oakes, Nigel John 1623
Oakes, Philip Gale 2137
Oakes, Victor 2137
Oakley, Edmund Ralph 556
Oakley, Elizabeth Grey 2599
Oakley, Elizavieta Mary 1151
Oakley, Emma Louise 1330
Oakley, Esther Amelia Blanche 556
Oakley, Frances Rachel 1151
Oakley, Georgia Alice 1330
Oakley, Jeremy N 1330
Oakley, Joshua 1330
Oakley, Laura Elizabeth 2599
Oakley, Mathew James 1151
Oakley, Michael Anthony Robert 1151
Oakley, Michael D R 2599
Oakley, Oliver Ronald 556
Oakley, Sylvia Dorothy 556
Oakshott, Alice 2139
Oakshott, Angus Withington 2139
Oakshott, Anne C 2139
Oakshott, Charles Michael 2139
Oakshott, Helen Clare 2139
Oakshott, Michael Arthur John 2139
Oakshott, Patrick Charles 2139
Oakshott, Roseanne 2139
Oakshott, Sarah 2139
Oakshott, Thomas Hendrie 2139
Oates, Catherine Jocelyn 2928
Oates, Georgina Rona 1695
Oates, Jillian Elizabeth 2928
Oates, Richard Allan 1695
Oates, Sandra Jocelyn 2928
Oatts, Andrew Robert Brydges 113
Oatts, (Evelyn) Mary 113
Oatts, Jeremy Roderick Henry 113
Oatts, Victoria Mary 113
O'Beirne, Bridgid Margaret 2239
O'Beirne, Catherine Mary 2239
O'Beirne, Cecil Hugh 2239
O'Beirne, Derek Francis 2239
O'Beirne, Helen Denise 2239
O'Beirne, Joseph Francis 2239
O'Beirne, Lynda Brynhild 2239
O'Beirne, Moana 2239
O'Beirne, Roderick William 2239

Obert de Thieusies, Fiona Jane 1501
Obert de Thieusies, Isabelle Stephanie 1501
Obert de Thieusies, Patrick Conor Alain 1501
Obert de Thieusies, Romano Louis Marie Joseph Ghislain 1501
Obert de Thieusies, Sophie Patricia 1501
O'Boyle, Dorothy Charlotte 2104
O'Boyle, Marlon Orion Sandford 2104
O'Brien, Alexander Kennedy 1498
O'Brien, Alice Louise 1498
O'Brien, Alison Ann 1499
O'Brien, Anastasia Grace Ailne 1499
O'Brien, Aubrey Martin 1498
O'Brien, Barbara Eileen 1499
O'Brien, Bartholomew Brendan 1498
O'Brien, Brenda 1498
O'Brien, Brian David 1499
O'Brien, Brian Dermod 1499
O'Brien, Brian Douglas Conor 1499
O'Brien, (Brian Edward) Nicholas 1499, 2271
O'Brien, Brian Murrough Fergus 1499
O'Brien, Caroline Louisa Maire 1500
O'Brien, Caroline Veronica Mary 1500
O'Brien, Catherine Lucy Bebhinn 1499
O'Brien, Charles Murrough 1499
O'Brien, Charlotte Elinor 1499
O'Brien, Christopher Keaton 1499
O'Brien, Christopher Michael 1499
O'Brien, Connie Alexandra 2880
O'Brien, Conor John Anthony 1501
O'Brien, Conor Michael 1498
O'Brien, David Donough 1499
O'Brien, David Nicholas 1498
O'Brien, Deborah Susan 2140
O'Brien, Deirdre 1499
O'Brien, Dermod Wilmer 1498
O'Brien, Donough Anthony 1500
O'Brien, Donough Patrick Vere 1499
O'Brien, Donough William 1498
O'Brien, Doon Veronica 2139
O'Brien, Edith Lawrie 1501
O'Brien, Edmond Mahon 1500
O'Brien, Edward Cecil 1501
O'Brien, Eleanor 111
O'Brien, Eleanor Minta 1498
O'Brien, Eliot Mary Brennagh 1499
O'Brien, Elizabeth 1500
O'Brien, Elizabeth Margaret 27
O'Brien, Felicity 111
O'Brien, Finola Clare 1499
O'Brien, Fionn Murrough 1501
O'Brien, Fionn Murrough Manning 1500
O'Brien, Florence Margaret Vere 1499
O'Brien, Frances Huband de Savoie 2139
O'Brien, George Lucius 1499
O'Brien, Gillian Ursula Helen 1501
O'Brien, Grania Catherine 1499
O'Brien, Helen 1495
O'Brien, (Horace) Donough 1498
O'Brien, Hugh Stephen Vere 1499
O'Brien, James Patrick 2139
O'Brien, Jane Elizabeth 350
O'Brien, Jason Errol 1353
O'Brien, Jennifer 1498
O'Brien, Jeremy William 1498
O'Brien, Joan 1501
O'Brien, John Michael 1501
O'Brien, Katherine 111
O'Brien, Katherine Abigail Thalia 1500
O'Brien, Katherine Elizabeth 1499
O'Brien, Katherine Jennifer Eileen 1499
O'Brien, Kathryn Ann 1499
O'Brien, Kirby 1498
O'Brien, Lauri Therese 1498
O'Brien, Leonora Thayne 1500
O'Brien, Lucia Josephine Mary 1495
O'Brien, Lucia Margaret 1498
O'Brien, Lucius Edward 1500
O'Brien, Lucy Ann 1498

O'Brien, Lucy Frances 2140
O'Brien, Lyndall Jane 2140
O'Brien, Margaret Clare 1499
O'Brien, Marjorie 1501
O'Brien, Mary Lockhart 1499
O'Brien, Melanie Frances Ann 2139
O'Brien, Michael David 1498
O'Brien, Michael George 1501
O'Brien, Miranda Penelope Gillian 1500, 2271
O'Brien, Monica 1500
O'Brien, Murrough 1498
O'Brien, Murrough Marinus Edward 1500
O'Brien, Murrough Martin Donough 1500
O'Brien, Murrough Richard 1501
O'Brien, Murrough Vere 1499
O'Brien, Nicholas Charles Donough 1499
O'Brien, Nigel Patrick Martin 1498
O'Brien, Olivia Alison Clare 1500
O'Brien, Patricia Angela 1353
O'Brien, Patricia Arlene 1498
O'Brien, Patrick Brian 1501
O'Brien, Patrick John 1499
O'Brien, Penelope Jayne 2880
O'Brien, Peter Thomond 1501
O'Brien, Phyllis Elsie Margaret 1501
O'Brien, Rachel Shirin 2140
O'Brien, Rebecca 1498, 1501
O'Brien, Rita 1498
O'Brien, Robert Murrough Vere 1499
O'Brien, Rosalind 1498
O'Brien, Sally Anne 350
O'Brien, Sarah Catherine 1499
O'Brien, Sarah Tsu Emily 1498
O'Brien, Seamus Timothy Lucius 1499
O'Brien, Selena Penelope Beatrice 1500
O'Brien, Sharon Mary 1353
O'Brien, Sheila Isobel 1499
O'Brien, Sheila Winifred 2139
O'Brien, Shirley 1498
O'Brien, Slaney Alexandra Anne 1495
O'Brien, Slaney Victoria 1501
O'Brien, Susan Anne 1499
O'Brien, Tasman David 1498
O'Brien, Teige Henry Patrick 1499
O'Brien, Thomas George 2880
O'Brien, Thomas P 350
O'Brien, Timothy Michael 2880
O'Brien, Vera Maud 1501
O'Brien, Violet Fairbrother 1499
O'Brien, Vivian 1501
O'Brien, William Thomas 1499
O'Brien, William Thomas Robin 350
O'Brien, Winifred Mary Sheila 1500
O'Brien, Xanthe Frances Henrietta 1500
O'Brien, Zoe 1500
O'Brien, Zsuzánna Eva Szeréna 1499
O'Burne, Patricia Kathleen 591
O'Callaghan, John Francis 3064
O'Callaghan, Sara-Jane 3064
O'Connell, Ann Marie 2140
O'Connell, Anna Elisa 3006
O'Connell, Anne Catherine 3006
O'Connell, Arabella Caroline 449
O'Connell, Brigid Emily Katharine 1573
O'Connell, Carlos Donal John 2140
O'Connell, Claire Helen Pauline MacCarthy 2141
O'Connell, Daniel Jose Emilio 3006
O'Connell, Daniel Wynne 1573
O'Connell, Elizabeth 2141
O'Connell, Ella Allison 2150
O'Connell, Emily Mary Frances 1454
O'Connell, Frances Susan 2140
O'Connell, Georgia Bard 2140
O'Connell, Georgina Rose 1454
O'Connell, James Alexander 1454
O'Connell, John Cardiff 2150
O'Connell, John Morgan Ross MacCarthy 2141

O'Connell, John V E F 1454
O'Connell, Katherine Lucila Jean MacCarthy 2141
O'Connell, Lucila Marie Valdemara Georgia 2140
O'Connell, Lucy Elizabeth 3006
O'Connell, Maria Thérèse 1573
O'Connell, Maurice Hugh Ricardo Ross 2140
O'Connell, Maurice William Hugh Rickard 2140
O'Connell, Morgan Basil Peter 2140
O'Connell, Patricia Elena 3006
O'Connell, Peter J 449
O'Connell, Ross John 2150
O'Connell, Ross Paul Francis 2140
O'Connell, Sarah Emily 2140
O'Connell, Seamus Morgan Basil Ross 2140
O'Connell, Simon David Sebastian 1454
O'Connor, Amanda Evelyn Alice 2642
O'Connor, Benedict 2069
O'Connor, Christopher Rupert 2069
O'Connor, Dominic Rupert 2069
O'Connor, Fergus Simon John 1482
O'Connor, Freya Laura Ellen 1482
O'Connor, Gregory 2069
O'Connor, John Morris 2642
O'Connor, Katharina Elizabeth Anne 1220
O'Connor, Marcus Michael Gerrard 1482
O'Connor, Mary Catharine 2069
O'Connor, Michael Villers Forbes 2069
O'Connor, Miranda Eleanor Phyllis 2642
O'Connor, Nadia 1482
O'Connor, Nichola Kate 1482
O'Connor, Patrick Haven 1220
O'Connor, Paul G 1482
O'Conor, Julia Mary Myfanwy 3018
O'Conor, Patrick Francis 146
O'Conor, Richard Shaun 3018
O'Conor, Virginia Elizabeth 146
Odasso, Christian 3044
Odasso, Diana Melody Christina 3044
Odasso, Fréderic Christian 3044
Odasso, (Lorraine) Aimée de Gaillard 3044
O'Day, Cheryl 440
O'Day, Cody Reeves 440
O'Day, Frederick Alan 440
O'Day, Lucas 440
O'Day, Ronald Patrick 440
O'Day, Shane Ronald 440
Odey, Felix Crispin 2203
Odey, Nichola 2203
Odey, R Crispin 2203
Odey, Sophia Anne 2203
O'Donaughy, Brenda Lynne 2010
O'Donaughy, Denise Margaret 2010
O'Donaughy, Kelly Corinne 2010
O'Donaughy, Kirby Michael 2010
O'Donaughy, Theresa Lynne 2010
O'Donel, Aodh 2151
O'Donnell, Abigail Kate 1963
O'Donnell, Alexa Caroline 1963
O'Donnell, Anthony John 1963
O'Donnell, Nicholas John Renny 1963
O'Donnell, Susan Miranda Fitzherbert 1963
O'Donoghue, Constance Anne 200
O'Donoghue, Michael John 200
O'Donovan, Anthony Derek 1498
O'Donovan, Charlotte Elizabeth 1498
O'Donovan, Cormac Brendan 1498
O'Donovan, Elinor Mary 1498
O'Donovan, Lucia Jane 1498
O'Donovan, Murrough Idries 1498
O'Donovan, Najma 1498
O'Donovan, Zahara Grace 1498
Odor, (Aileen) Pamela Hyacinthe 1340
Odor, Andreas 1340
Odor, Luciana 1340
Odor, Mervyn 1340
Odor, Roberto 1340
Odor, Roberto Padilla 1340
O'Dwyer, Hannah Charlotte 1168

O'Sullivan, Marney Darrell Owen 498
O'Sullivan, Œnone Venetia 498
O'Sullivan, Rowan John Amadeus 498
Oswald, Alice Priscilla Lyle 1465
Oswald, Angela Mary Rose 1015
Oswald, Arabella 1015
Oswald, Peter C P 1465
Oswald, William Alexander Michael 1015
Oswald, (William Richard) Michael 1015
O'Toole, George Bryan 2639
O'Toole, Howard Charles 2639
O'Toole, Laurence James 2639
O'Toole, Lucy Alicia 2639
O'Toole, Pamela Mary 2639
O'Toole, Stella Elizabeth 2639
Otter, Hilary Jane 455
Otter, James A 455
Ottewill, Angela 1972
Ottewill, Peter Alan Kirby 1972
Ouchterlony, Alison Stewart 1083
Ouchterlony, James Angus Heathcote 1083
Ouchterlony, Peter Anthony Heathcote 1083
Ouchterlony, Teresa Mary 1083
Outhwaite, Brian Robert 63
Outhwaite, Catherine Rossana 63
Outhwaite, Charles Cedric 63
Outhwaite, Diana 63
Outhwaite, James Edward 63
Outhwaite, Mark Robert Canning 63
Outhwaite, Sarah Elizabeth 63
Outram, Alison Catharine 2176
Outram, Anthony James 2318
Outram, Christopher James 2318
Outram, Colleen 2318
Outram, Douglas Benjamin James 2176
Outram, Eileen Grace 2176
Outram, Eleanor Mary 2177
Outram, (Francis) William 2177
Outram, Helen Lewis 2318
Outram, Johanna Catherine 2177
Outram, John Douglas 2176
Outram, Joshua Martin 2318
Outram, Katy Ann 2177
Outram, Keith Alastair 2177
Outram, Lucy Dora 2177
Outram, Nicholas Francis 2176
Outram, Oliver 2318
Outram, Philip Maxwell 2176
Outram, Rachel Helen 2176
Outram, Richard Graham 2177
Outram, Robin 2318
Outram, Ryan Stephen 2318
Outram, Sam 2318
Outram, Stefanie Gail 2318
Outram, Steven Jeremy 2318
Outram, Valerie Ann 2176
Outram, Victoria Jean 2176
Outwin, Christopher Dennis 237
Outwin, Dennis 237
Outwin, Ruth Margaret 237
Owbridge, Angela Alice 348
Owbridge, Anthony Wyndham 348
Owen, Ardyne Mary 1619
Owen, Astrid 1397
Owen, Barrie Miles 258
Owen, Charles Alexander Headon 1397
Owen, Charles William 1397
Owen, Christine Walker 1478
Owen, Clive Geoffrey 2505
Owen, David James 2505
Owen, Deborah 2177
Owen, Deirdre 2809
Owen, Delphine 2809
Owen, Diana Mary 1457
Owen, Eiddwen Sara 2505
Owen, Eric Cyril Coxon 2909
Owen, Felicity Cynthia June 1397
Owen, Gareth Schabert 2177
Owen, Georgina Hermione 2520
Owen, Glynn Meirion 26
Owen, Gwenllian Mary 2178
Owen, Henry Beaumont 1397
Owen, Hermione Patience 2520
Owen, Huw Algernon 2475
Owen, James Alexandre Dalziel 2572
Owen, John Arthur Dalziel 2572
Owen, John Maurice 2625
Owen, Josephine Camilla 2625
Owen, Lucy Mary 2177
Owen, Mary Celia Margaret 2909
Owen, Oliver Peter Stevens 1457
Owen, Penelope Jane 26
Owen, Philip Michael 2505
Owen, Rachel Elizabeth 1619
Owen, Robert Michael 2475
Owen, Robert Thomas 1478
Owen, Ronald James 1619
Owen, Rupert Charles 1397
Owen, Sally Faber 258
Owen, Sam Arthur Stanhope 2520
Owen, Sandra Mary 1619
Owen, Sarah Alexandra 2570
Owen, Sarah Ann 1478
Owen, Sarah Josephine 2475
Owen, Simon John 258
Owen, Simon Llewellyn 2570
Owen, Sophia Jane 2570
Owen, Thomas Llewellyn 2475
Owen, Tristan Llewellyn 2177
Owen, Valerie 2572
Owen, William Edward 26
Owen, William Francis Blundell 1457
Owen, William Stanhope 2520
Owen-George, Roland 1915
Owen-George, Susan Ethel 1915
Owen-Smith, Brian David 2277
Owen-Smith, Emma Elizabeth Jane 2277
Owen-Smith, Rose Magdalen 2277
Owen-Smith, Timothy Clive 2277
Owen-Taylor, Allan 2253, 2458
Owen-Taylor, Leslie H 2458
Owen-Taylor, Rosalind Phyllis Muriel 2253, 2458
Owen-Taylor, Vera 2458
Owens, Janet Cecilia Josephine 3092
Owrid, Emma 2196
Owrid, John 2196
Owston, Gavin Anthony 1313
Owston, Nicholas Adrian Fenton 379
Owston, Rosemary Sylvia 379
Owston, Vanessa Rosemary 379, 1313
Owston, Vivien Patricia 379, 1313
Owttrim, Denise 240
Owttrim, Mark William 240
Owttrim, Ryan Mark 240
Oxenford, Japh Alexander 964
Oxenham, Adèle Margaret 422
Oxenham, Anabel 422
Oxenham, Anthony Sydenham Charles 422
Oxenham, David George Henry 422
Oxenham, Diana Margaret 422
Oxenham, Gabrielle Ruth 422
Oxenham, James 422
Oxenham, Juliet 422
Oxenham, Madeleine Ruth 422
Oxenham, Mar David 422
Oxenham, Sharalee 422
Oxlade, Hilary Margaret 3013
Oxlade, Samantha Gay 3013
Oxlade, Stephen James Stuart 3013
Oxley, Peter John Reginald 98
Oxley, Rachel Mary 98
Oxley, Stephen David Richard 98
Oxley, Timothy Peter Charles 98
Oxley, Vania Joy 98
Ozanne, Julian Victor 2890
Ozanne, Nicola Rachel 2890
Ozanne, Rosalind Sylvia 2890
Ozanne, Ursula Winifred 2890
Ozarko, Audrey Lucille 3053
Ozarko, Catherine Lucille 3053
Ozarko, William 3053
Ozarko, William Edward 3053

P

Pace, Andrew Faviell 2480
Pace, Mark Faviell 2480
Packe, Aloïse Anne 2143
Packe, Andrew James 2143
Packe, Frederick Christopher William 2143
Packe, Katharine Olivia Mary 2143
Packe, Olivia Aloïse Hester 2143
Packe, Sally Margaret 2143
Packe, Thomas Gilbert 2143
Packe, William 2143
Packman, Camilla Jane 2102
Packman, Meriel Colleen 2102
Packman, Nicola Charlotte 2102
Packman, Theodore Cyril Vance 2102
Paddick, David Anthony 2315
Paddick, Jean Frances 2315
Padel, Adam Frederick 191
Padel, Felix John 191
Padel, Hilda Horatia 191
Padel, John Hunter 191
Padel, Nicola Mary 191
Padel, Oliver James 191
Padel, Ruth Sophia 191
Padgett, Christopher Stephen 1373
Padgett, Georgina Clementine 2382
Padgett, Henrietta Jane 2382
Padgett, Marilyn Anne 1373
Padgett, Patrick James 2382
Padgett, Richard Anthony 1373
Padgett, Stephen 1373
Padgett, Victoria Louise 2382
Padilla, Jimena 1187
Padilla, Marisol Manuela 1187
Padilla, Natalia 1187
Pagan, John Grant 2051
Pagan, Jonathan Edward 2051
Pagan, Peter Napier 2051
Page Croft, (Maria) Isabel 715
Page Croft, Mary Elizabeth 712
Page, A Geoffrey 405
Page, Alexia Frances 683
Page, Alice Mary 629
Page, Andrew 1310
Page, Andrew Frank Philip 1842
Page, Angela 2992
Page, Angela Fay 1411
Page, Angela Jean 1372
Page, Angela Mary 1244
Page, Angela Sybil Joan 2199
Page, Anita 1411
Page, Anne 137
Page, Anthea Deirdre Rosemary 982
Page, Antony Graham 2199
Page, Arabella Jennifer 1390
Page, Carol Ann 207
Page, Carole Mary 1244
Page, Cecilia Norah 683
Page, Christine Sheila 1372
Page, Christopher David 2199
Page, David 1310
Page, Deirdre Anne Elton 982
Page, Dermot Michael 1390
Page, Edward John Atholl 137
Page, Emma Rachel 147
Page, Gale Masterman 2992
Page, Harriet Constance Zenia 999
Page, Harry 207
Page, Henry Stewart Murray 137
Page, Ian 1411
Page, Jacqueline Frances 716
Page, James Douglas 716
Page, Jamie Douglas 405
Page, Jane Rosetta 1841
Page, John Keir 2992
Page, John Malcolm 2199
Page, (John) Nathaniel Micklem 2178
Page, Jonathan 1310
Page, Jonathan Richard 2199
Page, Katharine Rose Celestine 2178
Page, Leonie Frances 1173
Page, Lorna Lillianne Katrina 1310
Page, Michael 1310
Page, Michael Charles 147
Page, Natasha Diana 147
Page, Nicholas Leo Thomas 683
Page, Nigel Geoffrey 405
Page, Patricia Hannah 1390
Page, Pauline Margaret 405
Page, Pauline Shelley 405
Page, Philippa Shirley 716
Page, Rachelle Philippa 716
Page, Richard 1244
Page, Richard David O'Mahony 1390
Page, Robert James 716
Page, Sarah Jane 1390
Page, Sarah June 683
Page, Shane 1173
Page, Sophie Elizabeth 147
Page, Steven 1411
Page, Thomas 1310
Page, Thomas Leslie 683
Page, Thomas Patrick Murray 137
Page, Timothy A C 629
Page Wood, Betsann 2185
Page Wood, Evelyn Hazel Rosemary 2185
Page Wood, Matthew 2185
Paget, (Alexander) Lachlan John 2186
Paget, Ann 77
Paget, Annabelle Mary 75
Paget, (Anthony) Berkeley 75
Paget, Antonia 2186
Paget, Benedict Dashiel Thomas 71
Paget, Bernard Halfdan 2187
Paget, Betty May 75
Paget, Camilla Mary 2185
Paget, Caroline Elizabeth Astrid 76
Paget, Caspian James Alexander 1343
Paget, Catesby Langer 75
Paget, Catriona Isabel 2186
Paget, Cecily Innes 75
Paget, Charles Alexander Vaughan 71
Paget, Charles David 78
Paget, Charles John Leopold 76
Paget, Charlotte Patricia 75
Paget, Clara Elizabeth Isis 71
Paget, Cluny Patricia Maxine 2186
Paget, Daphne Ampuria 2187
Paget, David Arthur FitzRoy 76
Paget, David Vernon John 2186
Paget, Diana Frances 2187
Paget, Diana Jenefer 75
Paget, Edward Berkeley 75
Paget, Eleanor Mary 74
Paget, (Elizabeth) Shirley Vaughan 71
Paget, Emma Rachel 2185
Paget, Frances Catherine 74
Paget, Francis Andrew Edward 74
Paget, Gabriele Mathilde 75
Paget, Georganne Elizabeth Elliott 71
Paget, Georgina Elizabeth Beauclerk 1343
Paget, Gerardine Carol-Louise 75
Paget, Harry Arthur Westwood 1343
Paget, Henrietta Elizabeth 75
Paget, Henrietta Maria Elizabeth 1343
Paget, Henry Alexander Reginald 77
Paget, Henry James 2187
Paget, Hugh Charles Edward 74
Paget, Jack William Kyffin 71
Paget, James Nicholas 1775
Paget, Jane Bridget 77
Paget, John Byng Oswald Carleton 1775
Paget, John David 77
Paget, John Francis 76
Paget, Kim 76
Paget, Lily Florence Angharad 71
Paget, Louise Victoria 71
Paget, Lucy Caroline Eleanor 74
Paget, Margarete E Varvill 2187
Paget, Mark Sebastian Boye 76
Paget, Michael Robertson 75
Paget, Nancy Mary 2186
Paget, Nicholas David 77
Paget, Peter Jeremy Valentine 76
Paget, Richard Campbell 1343
Paget, (Richenda) Elizabeth 2185
Paget, Richenda Rachel 2185
Paget, Rodney Langer 75
Paget, Rory Edward 1775
Paget, Rupert Edward Llewellyn 71
Paget, Sara Veronica 76
Paget, Sarah Catherine 75
Paget, Selina Mary 74
Paget, Sheila Anne 1775
Paget, Sonia 77
Paget, Tessa Ann 77
Paget, Verily 401
Paget, Violet Gwendoline 75
Paget, William Berkeley 75
Paget, William Byng 1775
Paice, Edward Charles Richard 1098
Paice, Helen Amanda Catherine 1098
Paice, Rosemary Alison 1098
Paice, William Tasker 1098
Paige, Christopher David 2600
Paige, Cynthia Ann 2600
Paige, David Hugh 2600
Paige, Joanne Lesley 2600
Paige, Michael Robert 2600
Paige, Nicholas Robert 2600
Paige, Patricia Margaret 2600
Paige, Timothy John 2600
Pailthorpe, Jane Carleton 1430
Pailthorpe, Nicholas Richard Bruce 1430
Pailthorpe, Richard David Bruce 1430
Pailthorpe, Victoria Emma Carleton 1430
Pain, Anne Ward 1551
Pain, Charles Douglas 1551
Pain, Christina Elisabeth 1551
Pain, Michael Ward Eames 1551
Paine, Alice Sarah 2894
Paine, Christopher Hammon 2894
Paine, Edward Hammon 2894
Paine, Frances Margaret 1235
Paine, Lucy Hammon 2894
Paine, Simon John Hammon 2894
Paine, Susan 2894
Painter, Elizabeth Bridget Babington 238
Painter, Hilary Joanna 238
Painter, John Clifford 238
Painter, Philippa Jane 238
Painter, Stephen Langman 238
Pakenham, Adam Geoffrey 1754
Pakenham, Ailsa Jean 1753
Pakenham, Alexandra Clio 1751
Pakenham, Alice 1754
Pakenham, Angela Sarah Christine 1752
Pakenham, Anna Maria 1750
Pakenham, Anthony Edward 1755
Pakenham, Antonia Mary 1753
Pakenham, Arthur 1754
Pakenham, Arthur Godfrey 1752
Pakenham, Benjamin John 1751
Pakenham, Benjamin Thomas William 1753
Pakenham, Candace Debra Elaine 1752
Pakenham, Caroline 1753
Pakenham, Catherine Ruth 1751
Pakenham, Cheryl Owen 1752
Pakenham, Christine Catherine 1753
Pakenham, Claire Alexandra 1754
Pakenham, Claire Chatel 1751
Pakenham, Clio Isabelle Blaise 1751
Pakenham, Clive Sykes 1754
Pakenham, Daniel Nicholas 1754
Pakenham, Dermot Philip Michael 1754
Pakenham, Dominic Balthazar 1751
Pakenham, Edith 1752
Pakenham, Edward Charles Montague 1753
Pakenham, Edward Melchior 1750
Pakenham, Edward Michael 1752
Pakenham, Edwin Austin Westmoreland 1752
Pakenham, Eileen Isolde 1755
Pakenham, Elizabeth 1750
Pakenham, Elizabeth Ann 1753
Pakenham, Emma 1754
Pakenham, Frederick Augustus 1750
Pakenham, Frederick Edward 1752
Pakenham, Gaylynn Evon 1752
Pakenham, George Lawrence 1753
Pakenham, Guy 1751
Pakenham, Hannah 1753
Pakenham, Harry Michael 1751
Pakenham, Heidi 1753
Pakenham, (Henry) Desmond Verner 1755
Pakenham, Henry Francis Benjamin 1753
Pakenham, (Hercules) Michael Roland 1754
Pakenham, Hermione Clare 1751
Pakenham, Hilary Julia 1755
Pakenham, James Arthur 1752
Pakenham, James Edwin Helwell 1753
Pakenham, Jane 1754
Pakenham, Jeremy Edwin Montagu 1753
Pakenham, Johanna 1754
Pakenham, John Edwin 1752
Pakenham, John Hubert 1755
Pakenham, John Neville 1753
Pakenham, Jonathan Hugh Rust 1753

Q

R

Redmayne, Benjamin Hugh 2382
Redmayne, Caroline Mary 2383
Redmayne, Catherine 2383
Redmayne, Claire 2382
Redmayne, Doreen E 2383
Redmayne, Doreen Ellen 2382
Redmayne, Dorothy 2383
Redmayne, Elsa Harriet 2382
Redmayne, Geoffrey Brian 2382
Redmayne, Giles Martin 2382
Redmayne, Hannah Elizabeth 2382
Redmayne, John 2383
Redmayne, Katharine 2383
Redmayne, Oliver Stephen Tunstall 2382
Redmayne, Philippa 2383
Redmayne, Richard Hugh 2382
Redmayne, Roderick John 2383
Redmayne, Rosemary 2383
Redpath, Abdul Azis (George James) 695
Redpath, Abdul Razzaq 695
Redpath, Aisha Iman 695
Redpath, Hafidha 695
Redpath, Justin Abd'Allah 695
Redpath, Khyria 695
Redpath, Rabea (Lucy) 695
Redrup, Douglas Frederick 2901
Redrup, (Mary) Virginia 2901
Redshaw, Violet Mary 2639
Redwood, Charles Boverton 2384
Redwood, Colina Margaret Charlotte 2383
Redwood, Gaynor Elizabeth 2383
Redwood, Gillian 2383
Redwood, James Boverton 2384
Redwood, Mary Elizabeth 2384
Redwood, Morwenna Anne 2384
Redwood, Robert Boverton 2384
Redwood, Ursula 2384
Reed, Alice Bronwyn Diana 648
Reed, Andrew Laurence 1939
Reed, Andrew William Gadsden 2969
Reed, Anna Grant 2969
Reed, Anthony 1416
Reed, Catherine Anna 155
Reed, Charles Christian Thomas 1939
Reed, Christopher Stephen 1939
Reed, Clemintine Florence 1416
Reed, Darren Stafford 953
Reed, Denys Christian 1939
Reed, Dominic Wreford 155
Reed, Emma Sarah Annabel 648
Reed, Frederick Anthony Spencer 1416
Reed, Gabriel Olga Margaret 1939
Reed, Georgina 1939
Reed, Hilary Jane Stuart 272
Reed, Hugh William Bryan 648
Reed, Ian William 648
Reed, James Christian 1939
Reed, Jenifer Ann 155
Reed, Jeremy Matthew 1939
Reed, John 167
Reed, Laurence Cecil 1939
Reed, Lelda Sunday 167
Reed, Louisa Charlotte 2969
Reed, Mark 953
Reed, Martin David 1939
Reed, Mary Seton 953
Reed, Nichola Sarah Angénis 648
Reed, Nicholas William 1939
Reed, Rupert Wreford 155
Reed, Shirley 1939
Reed, Simon Francis 272
Reed, Stafford John 953
Rees, (Alice Alexandra) Constance 2147
Rees, Anthea Peronelle 2384
Rees, Elizabeth Stephanie 1951
Rees, Howard Alvine 2728
Rees, Margaret 1244
Rees, Martin C 1951
Rees, Mary Stewart 2728
Rees, Susan Enid 1844
Rees-Mogg, Annunziata Mary 2384
Rees-Mogg, Charlotte Louise 2384
Rees-Mogg, Gillian Shakespeare 2384
Rees-Mogg, Jacob William 2384
Rees-Mogg, Modwenna Vivien Hornby 1489, 2384
Rees-Mogg, Thomas 1489
Rees-Mogg, Thomas Fletcher 2384
Rees-Mogg, William Robert 2384
Rees-Williams, Beata 2147
Rees-Williams, Christine Ann 2147
Rees-Williams, Dylan 2147
Rees-Williams, Gillian Mavis 2147
Rees-Williams, Jennet Elizabeth 2147
Rees-Williams, Morgan Rees 2147
Rees-Williams, Tudor David 2147
Reese, Harry 2368
Reese, Sandra 2368
Reeve, Alice Eleanor 759, 1253
Reeve, Caroline Mary Louise 759, 1253, 3036
Reeve, Catherine Jane 759, 1253
Reeve, Christopher William 759, 1253
Reeve, Daphne Joan 971
Reeve, Eleanor Susan Katherine 759, 1253, 3036
Reeve, (Esmé) Jane 759, 1253
Reeve, Francesca Jane Briggs 759, 1253
Reeve, Frederick James 1800
Reeve, Harry William 759
Reeve, Harry William John Briggs 1253
Reeve, Henrietta Mary Louise 759, 1253, 3036
Reeve, James Edward 1800
Reeve, James Henry 759, 1253, 3036
Reeve, John 759, 1253
Reeve, Jonathan Sherard 759, 1253
Reeve, Laura Jane 1800
Reeve, Linda Patricia 759, 1253
Reeve, Lucy Harriet Isobel 759, 1253
Reeve, Matthew 759
Reeve, Matthew Welby 1253
Reeve, Merial 759
Reeve, Merial Elizabeth 1253
Reeve, Nicola Mary Clare 759, 1253
Reeve, Peter Richard 759, 1253, 3036
Reeve, Philip John 759, 1253
Reeve, William Francis 759, 1253, 3036
Reeve-Parker, Camilla 381
Reeve-Parker, Denise Beth 381
Reeve-Parker, Geoffrey John 381
Reeve-Parker, Parissa 381
Reeve-Tucker, Lalage Margarita 197
Reeve-Tucker, Stephen 197
Reevely, James Donald McGregor 434
Reevely, Lucy Elizabeth Constance 434
Reevely, Nicola Pamela Jane 434
Reevely, Timothy James McGregor 434
Reeves, Anne Elizabeth 2401
Reeves, Anne Elizabeth Gundry 58
Reeves, Diana Grace Angela 839
Reeves, Dudley William 2401
Reeves, (Frederick) John 839
Reeves, Georgina Caroline Angela 839
Reeves, Heather Jennifer 2401
Reeves, Henry Frederick Godfrey 839
Reeves, James 58
Reeves, Jessie Hilaria 2015
Reeves, Joshua Mark 1567
Reeves, Katharine Rebecca 551
Reeves, Michael David 58
Reeves, Myles Edward 2401
Reeves, Nicholas Mark Renny 2401
Reeves, Olivia Clare Lucy 839
Reeves, Peter 58
Reeves, Thomas Somerville Thesiger 551
Regester, Augusta Frances 107
Regester, Michael John Carr 107
Reid, Amanda 2924
Reid, Amelia Jane 2311
Reid, Amelia Louise Catherine 581
Reid, Andrew 2386
Reid, Angela Margaret 69
Reid, Angus Courtenay Daer 1522
Reid, Anna Louise 625
Reid, Antonia Elizabeth Tarn 1526
Reid, Ashley Louise 1204
Reid, Auriol Susan 687
Reid, Benjamin James Dundas 2385
Reid, Caroline Susan 2924
Reid, Caspar James Beauclerk 687
Reid, Catherine Fleetwood 1522
Reid, Charles Anthony Gilmore 2847
Reid, Charles Edward James 2385
Reid, Christina 2385
Reid, Christopher Robin James 2878
Reid, Clare 2878
Reid, Clementine Julia 581
Reid, Clodagh Mary 2479
Reid, Coleena Jane 2003
Reid, David 2311
Reid, David Lorne Dundas 2385
Reid, David Murray Arthur 2836
Reid, David William 2479
Reid, Duncan Andrew Daer 1522
Reid, Elizabeth 2311
Reid, Elizabeth Frances Catherine 587
Reid, Elizabeth Sarah 215
Reid, Emily Louise Mary 2847
Reid, Emily Patrica 1949
Reid, Frances Elizabeth 687
Reid, George Walter 2386
Reid, Georgina Charlotte Elizabeth 587
Reid, Hamish Ian Daer 1522
Reid, Heather Susan Daer 1522
Reid, Henry George Donald 587
Reid, Iain Malcolm Gordon 915
Reid, Ian Daer 1522
Reid, Ian Macpherson 2386
Reid, Imogen Elizabeth 215
Reid, Isabel Amy 2836
Reid, Isobel Laura 2173
Reid, Jack 1933
Reid, James Hugh 2386
Reid, James William 2173
Reid, Jennifer Laura 2173
Reid, Jennifer Tarn 1526
Reid, Jessica Mary 69
Reid, John 2924
Reid, Jonathan P Q 1646
Reid, Katharine Louise 625
Reid, Katrina 2924
Reid, Laura Louise 581
Reid, Leonora Emily Louise 2385
Reid, Lindsay Sutton 1204
Reid, Lorna Victoria 2385
Reid, Lucinda Jane Mary 2847
Reid, Lynette Moira 1646
Reid, Martin James 2311
Reid, Michael 1526
Reid, Michaela Ann 2385
Reid, Natalie Mills 1204
Reid, Nicholas 2311
Reid, Nicholas Andrew 69
Reid, Nicholas Hutson 2003
Reid, Nicholas James 587
Reid, Nicholas John Howard 581
Reid, Ogden Mills 1204
Reid, Olive Jean Courtenay 1522
Reid, Olivia Charlotte Mary 2847
Reid, P Malcolm G 2847
Reid, Pamela 2311
Reid, Patricia Howe 2386
Reid, Peter 2924
Reid, Peter Daer 1522
Reid, Philippa Susanna 915
Reid, Robert Wain 2173
Reid, Robyn 2311
Reid, Roxana Idonea 1204
Reid, Serena Madeleine 915
Reid, Simon Dale 215
Reid, Sophie Alexandra 2045
Reid, Stephen Douglas 2045
Reid, Susan 915
Reid, Susan Patricia 2045
Reid, Suzanne 2924
Reid, Tatiana 2385
Reid, Tedda Ann 2385
Reid, Timothy 2311
Reid, Toby John 2311
Reid, W Scott B 581
Reid, Wallace McMillan 687
Reid, William John 2311
Reid-Kay, Alexandra Esmé 1042
Reid-Kay, Angus Drummond 1042
Reid-Kay, Hamish George Strathern 1042
Reid-Kay, Robert Simon 1042
Reid-Kay, Simon James 1042
Reid-Smith, Pamela 371
Reidy, Evelyn Mary 2517
Reidy, Richard Daniel Kenneth 2517
Reignier, Bernard 2550
Reignier, Morley Rafael Kate 2550
Reignier, Sheldon Camille 2550
Reignier, Tom Samuel 2550
Reilly, Anna Marie 439
Reilly, Brian 1141
Reilly, Bruce 439
Reilly, Dennis John 1784
Reilly, Dominic 1141
Reilly, Fiona 1141
Reilly, Heather 439
Reilly, Jean Cynthia 1141
Reilly, Katharine 125
Reilly, Lesley 1141
Reilly, Margaret Amanda 1784
Reilly, Megan Jayne 439
Reilly, Michael Joseph 1784
Reilly, Nicola 1141
Reilly, Patrick Joseph 1784
Reilly, Rachel Dawn 439
Reilly, Sam 125
Reilly, Sophie 125
Reilly, Timothy 125
Reina, Louise Fenella 462
Reina, Massimo A 462
Reintjes, Lawrence Charles 1494
Reintjes, Nicola Catharine 1494
Reiss, Bryony 2077
Reiss, Charles 2077
Reiss, Holly Clare 2077
Reiss, Rowan Susannah Charlotte 2077
Reiss, Susan Rosemary 2077
Reitberg, Ethel Elisabeth Olga Mary 407
Reith, Anthony John 2387
Reith, Doreen Odell Mytton 1406
Reith, Douglas McNeill Mytton 1406
Reith, Hector McNeill Tytler 1406
Reith, James Harry John 2387
Reith, Julie Katharine 2387
Reith, (Penelope Margaret) Ann 2387
Reith, Sylvia Lucy 2387
Reitman, Robert Vernon Michael 1792
Reitman, Susan Diana Mary 1792
Reitman, Susan Theresa Maria 1792
Remak, Jacobus Antonius Ferdinand 1091
Remak, Jason William Johannes 1091
Remak, Lorena Joanne 1091
Rementer, Mildred Jane Elizabeth 1195
Remington-Hobbs, Alexander Charles 150
Remington-Hobbs, Clare Charlotte Rosemary 150
Remington-Hobbs, James 150
Remington-Hobbs, Jonathan Ian 150
Remington-Hobbs, Max Hugh 777, 1541
Remington-Hobbs, Susan Mary Sheila 2528
Remmick, Charles Gilbert 30
Remmick, Dorothy Elizabeth Mary Pelline 30
Remnant, Annabelle Rachel 2388
Remnant, Benjamin 2388
Remnant, Caroline Elizabeth Clare 839, 2388
Remnant, Christopher Michael 2388
Remnant, Edward James 2388
Remnant, Eleanor Clare 2388
Remnant, Erica 2388
Remnant, Gabrielle 2388
Remnant, Giles 2388
Remnant, Henrietta 2388
Remnant, Henry Frederick 2388
Remnant, Hugo Charles 2388
Remnant, Jack Preston 2388
Remnant, James Wogan 1329
Remnant, Judith 2388
Remnant, Patrick Tyrrell William 2388
Remnant, Philip John 839, 2388
Remnant, Robert James 2388
Remnant, Serena Jane 1329, 2388
Remnant, Shannon Lynn 2388
Remnant, Sophie Caroline 2388
Renals, Charles 2388
Renals, Frances Emma 2388
Renals, Jacqueline Ann 2388
Renals, Lloyd James 2388
Renals, Maria Dolores 2388
Renals, Marie 2388
Renals, Sheila Joyce 2388
Renals, Stanley Michael 2388
Rendall, Amelia Jane 143
Rendall, Angus Mark 143
Rendall, Edward Bertrand Montague 2490
Rendall, (Edward) Simon 2490
Rendall, Frederick Thomas Inigo 2490
Rendall, John Edward 143
Rendall, Rosemary Jane 143
Rendall, Sarah Elizabeth 2490
Rendall, Sophie Charlotte 143
Rendell, Donald 2389
Rendell, Hugo Anthony 804
Rendell, Imelda Jane 804
Rendell, Piers L 804
Rendell, Sebastian James 804
Rendell, Simon 2389
Renfrew, Alban 2390
Renfrew, Jane Margaret 2390
Renfrew, Magnus 2390
Renny, Abigail Eloise 1963
Renny, Alicia Nicola Rose 1963
Renny, Carol 1963
Renny, Emily Ellen Miranda 1963
Renny, Felicity Alice Prudence 1963
Renny, Nicholas Charles Moncreiff 1963
Renny, Nicola Gladys 1963
Renshaw, Andrew 565, 2392
Renshaw, Catherine 2392
Renshaw, Cherry Rose 565, 2392
Renshaw, Donna Lee 2392
Renshaw, Edward 2392
Renshaw, Edward Chichester 2392
Renshaw, Eloise Rose 2392
Renshaw, Harry John 2392
Renshaw, Joanna 2392
Renshaw, John David 2392
Renshaw, Mace Caroline 2392
Renshaw, Quintus 2392
Renshaw, Rory Andrew 2392
Renshaw, Thomas 2392
Renshaw, Winifred May 2392
Renton, Alan Edward Mayo 1313
Renton, Alexander James Torr 2393
Renton, Alice Blanche Helen 1048, 2393
Renton, Amanda Jane 1313
Renton, Caroline Mary 1313
Renton, Claudia Jessamine 1313
Renton, Daniel Charles Antony 2393
Renton, Davina Kathleen 2393
Renton, Henry James 2393
Renton, Julia Esther 1313
Renton, Katherine Chelsea 2393
Renton, Nicholas John 1313
Renton, Penelope Sally Rosita 2393
Renton, Simon Anthony 1313
Renton, Tim 1048
Renton, Zoë Eleanor 1313
Renwick, Alexandra Constance 2394
Renwick, Annie Colette 2394
Renwick, Aubrey 2394
Renwick, Barbara 2394
Renwick, Caroline Anne 1926, 2394
Renwick, Charles Richard 2394
Renwick, Diana Mary 2394
Renwick, Dorothy Forster 2394
Renwick, Dudley Cyril Deuchar 2394
Renwick, Eric Montague 2394
Renwick, George Charles Eustace 2394
Renwick, George Eustace 2394
Renwick, George Lionel 2394
Renwick, George Martin 589
Renwick, Guy Philip 2394
Renwick, Harry Timothy 2394
Renwick, Homayoun Mazandi 2393
Renwick, Jane ('Yorkie') Ann 2394
Renwick, (Janet) Melanie 2394
Renwick, Laura Laura 589
Renwick, Maxwell Mark 2394
Renwick, Michael David 2393
Renwick, Pamela Mary 2394
Renwick, Paul William 589
Renwick, Peter 2394
Renwick, Richard Eustace 1926
Renwick, Robert James 2393
Renwick, Rory Eustace Deuchar 2394
Renwick, Shaun Maurice 2394
Renwick, William Norman Hugh 589
Repard, James P 1869
Repard, Jennie Spencer 1869
Repard, (John) David Latimer 806
Repard, Peggy 806
Reppert, Helen Brooke 2040
Reppert, Ronald Grant 2040
Reppert, Stephen Harris 2040
Repucci, Arlene Doris 1223
Repucci, Doris Arlene 1223
Repucci, Louis Frederick 1223
Retson, Donald 2317
Retson, Jocelyn Elizabeth 2317
Retson, Serena Christine 2317
Reuter, Robert James 1787
Reuter, Sharon 1787
Revell, Flora Margaret 1118
Revell, Jennifer Mary 1118
Revell, Matthew James 1118
Revell, Melanie Louise 1118
Revell, Nicholas Stewart 1118
Revell, Rosemary Jean 1118
Revell, Stewart George 1118
Reviakin, Alexander Ronald 1330
Reviakin, Rosanna Mary 1330
Reviakin, Sergei 1330

Riddell, David John	2408
Riddell, David Ronald Carre	2409
Riddell, Eleanor Mary	2408
Riddell, Elizabeth Lyall	2408
Riddell, Emily	2407
Riddell, Frank Buchanan	2408
Riddell, Gail	2408
Riddell, Graham Samuel	2408
Riddell, Hugh Gordon	2406
Riddell, Jaki	2409
Riddell, James Walter	2409
Riddell, Jemma Jeannette	2408
Riddell, John Charles Buchanan	2399
Riddell, John Dalziel	1569
Riddell, John Gifford	2407
Riddell, John Walter	2409
Riddell, John Walter Rowland	2407
Riddell, Jonathan David	2407
Riddell, Judith Mary	2408
Riddell, Juliet Clare	2408
Riddell, Karen Anne	2407
Riddell, Kelly Jayne	2407
Riddell, Laura Virginia	2408
Riddell, Lynette Judith	2408
Riddell, Malcolm John Carre	2409
Riddell, Marion Gwyneth	2408
Riddell, Mary Frazer	2408
Riddell, Mary	2407
Riddell, Nicholas Peter	2408
Riddell, Oliver John	1569
Riddell, Patricia Maria	2407
Riddell, Peter James	2408
Riddell, Robert Balfour	2407
Riddell, Robert Henry	2406
Riddell, Robert James	2408
Riddell, Romayne	2407
Riddell, Sally Anne	2408
Riddell, Sandra Ngaire	2408
Riddell, Sarah	2399, 2406
Riddell, Stuart Edward	2407
Riddell, Taylor	2409
Riddell, Walter Gervase	2409
Riddell, Walter John Buchanan	2406
Riddell, William Grant	2408
Riddell, (William) James	2408
Riddell-Carre, David Alexander	2409
Riddell-Carre, John Timothy	2409
Riddell-Carre, Peter Thomas	2409
Riddell-Carre, Ralph John	2409
Riddell-Carre, Valerie Caroline	2409
Ridder Van Rosenthal, Eelco	2380
Ridder Van Rosenthal, Erica	2380
Ridder Van Rosenthal, Lodewijk Henrik Nicolaas	2380
Ridder Van Rosenthal, Maria Constantia	2380
Ridder Van Rosenthal, Saskia	2380
Riddett, Bridget Ursula Elaine (Jane)	1880
Riddett, Guy Edward West	1880
Riddett, John Villiers	1880
Riddett, Leo Patrick	1880
Riddett, Leonard Arthur Hammond	1880
Riddett, Linda Marie	1880
Riddett, Patrick Hammond	1880
Riddett, Paul James Massy	1880
Riddett, Philip Peel	1880
Riddick, Elspeth Marjorie	2474
Riddick, Graham Edward Galloway	2474
Riddick, Robert John Gurney	2474
Riddle, Dianne Roberta	893
Riddle, Peter	893
Riddle, Robert Adam	893
Rideout, Monica Winifred Mary	535
Ridge, Adeline Dyce Albinia Rose	52
Ridge, Angela Susan	2936
Ridge, Angus James Anderson	2936
Ridge, Edward Francis	52
Ridge, Iain Anderson	2936
Ridge, Marian Sophia	52
Ridge, Mary Blanche	52
Ridge, Rosemary Ann	2936
Ridge, Rupert Leander	52
Ridge, Thomas Leander	52
Ridgely, Joseph Vincent	2341
Ridgely, Julia Frances	2341
Ridgley, Martin Charles	275
Ridgley, Sylvia Anne	275
Ridgway, Amanda Jane	2546
Ridgway, Charlotte Rose	2546
Ridgway, Joanna Kate	2546
Ridgway, Peter Eric	2546
Ridgwell, Camilla Bridget	2736
Ridgwell, (David) Benjamin	2736
Ridley, Adam Nicholas	2412
Ridley, Alain Patrick	1889
Ridley, Annabel	1347
Ridley, Anne Katharine Gabrielle	2410, 2560
Ridley, Anya Christine	2410
Ridley, Caroline Lois	2411
Ridley, Caspar Charles	2
Ridley, Caspar Hawke Michael	1347
Ridley, Charles Walter Hayes	2
Ridley, Edward Alexander Keane	2411
Ridley, Elisa	2411
Ridley, Emily Marling	2411
Ridley, Emma Jane	2
Ridley, Emma Louise	1889
Ridley, Harriet Clare	1347
Ridley, Harriet Deirdre	2
Ridley, Henry Colborne	2411
Ridley, Isabel Susan	2674
Ridley, Jacqueline	1889
Ridley, Jacqueline Claire	2411
Ridley, Jasper	2412

Ridley, Jenifer Gaye	2411
Ridley, Jennifer Ann	1441
Ridley, Jo	2412
Ridley, Joan Elaine	2411
Ridley, Joan Madelina Marling	2411
Ridley, Johnathan Claude	1889
Ridley, Judith	2411
Ridley, Judith (Judy) Mary	2413
Ridley, Julia Harriet	2
Ridley, Julian Bowring	1441
Ridley, Lauretta Chinty	402, 2760
Ridley, Luke	2412
Ridley, Margaret Anne (Biddy)	2412
Ridley, Markham Hugh	1441
Ridley, Mary Randall	2411
Ridley, Matthew White	2410
Ridley, Michael James	2411
Ridley, (Nicholas) Adam	1347
Ridley, Nicholas Charles Philip Christison	2674
Ridley, Nicholas Charles Wetherill	402
Ridley, Nicholas John	2674
Ridley, Nicholas Mark	2411
Ridley, Nicolas Henry Sumner	2411
Ridley, Peter William Wake	2411
Ridley, Rebecca	1347
Ridley, (Richard) Nicholas	2411
Ridley, Robert Louis McAlpine	1889
Ridley, Serena Eloise	2411
Ridley, Susanna Mary	2674
Ridley, Timothy Jasper William	2411
Ridley, Valerie Susan	1889
Ridley, Wendy Ann	2411
Ridley, (William) Terence Colborne	2411
Ridlington, Brigid Mary	1491
Ridlington, Denise Mary	1491
Ridlington, Jack Harry	1491
Ridlington, Jacqueline Brigid	1491
Ridlington, Michael John	1491
Ridlington, Pauline Anne	1491
Ridlington, Peter Charles	1491
Ridlington, Peter Harold	1491
Ridlington, Rosemary Anne	516, 1491
Rietberg, Christopher Richard Francis	407
Rietberg, Gabrielle Catherine	407
Rietberg, Kathleen	407
Rietberg, Mark Andreas	407
Rifaat, Rashid Ali	2826
Rifaat, Samir	2826
Rifaat, Sasha Amy	2826
Rifaat, Sayyid	2826
Rifaat, Tariq Sayyid	2826
Rifaat, Victoria	2826
Rigby, Alexandrina	1469
Rigby, Alice Helen Elizabeth	2612
Rigby, Alice Olivia	2413
Rigby, Anthony John	2413
Rigby, Dominic John Vaughan	2612
Rigby, Eloise Jennifer	2612
Rigby, Emily Flora	2413
Rigby, Flora	2413
Rigby, Frances Evangeline	1469
Rigby, Gabriela	1469
Rigby, Hugh Macbeth	2413
Rigby, James Erskine	2413
Rigby, Janice Anita	1397
Rigby, Jennifer Mary	2612
Rigby, John Granville Beaumont	1469
Rigby, Kathleen Mary	2413
Rigby, Margaret	1397
Rigby, Martin Paul	2612
Rigby, Mary	2413
Rigby, Melissa Mary	2413
Rigby, Oliver Hugh	2413
Rigby, Peter Alexander Beaumont	1469
Rigby, Rachel Mary	2413
Rigby, Richard Arthur	1397
Rigby, Roger Macbeth	2413
Rigby, Rollo Macbeth	2413
Rigby, Sally Anne	2413
Rigby, Simon Henry Erskine	2413
Rigby, Simon William Granville	1469
Rigby, Stephen Leacock	2413
Rigby, Tom	2413
Rigby, Victoria Mary	2413
Rigby, Walter Oswald	1397
Rigby, William Peter	2413
Rigby, Yvonne Linda	1397
Rigby, Zachary John	2413
Righetti, Alessandra Mary	2232
Righetti, Franceso Montesi	2232
Righter, Ursula Rosemary	2326
Righton, Frederick	1041
Riley, Anita Joan	1410
Riley, Ankaret Tarn	1526
Riley, Christopher John	1410
Riley, David	2689
Riley, Deborah Susan	200
Riley, Eleanor Rose	2995
Riley, (Frances) Georgina	2549
Riley, Geoffrey Michael	200
Riley, Jacqueline Clare	2689
Riley, John Andrew	1417
Riley, Joseph Graham	1417
Riley, Michael Edward	1417
Riley, Nicola Ankaret Katherine	1526
Riley, Peter James Holland	2549
Riley, Peter James Wynne	1410
Riley, Ruth Margaret	1417
Riley, Suzanne	2689
Riley, Timothy Richard	1526
Riley, Wendy Jeanne	1410
Rimell, Amelia Sophie	1096
Rimell, Benjamin Charles Philip	1096
Rimell, Joanna Rosalind	1096

Rimell, Mark P R	1096
Rimell, Sybil Mary	1096
Rimington, Bridget Clare	2597
Rimington, Niel William	2597
Rimmer, Andrew Malcolm	1114
Rimmer, Christopher David	1114
Rimmer, James Edward	1114
Rimmer, Mary Penelope	1114
Rimmer, Rebecca Mary	1114
Rinagl, Celia Mary	1856
Rinagl, Marc Gerard Penn	1856
Rinagl, Nina Penn	1856
Rinaldi, Cecilia Pauline	560
Rinaldi, Helen Margaret	560
Rinaldi, Rinaldo G M	560
Ring, Charlotte Katharine	751
Ring, Gordon	751
Ringey, Bruce W	2966
Ringey, David Bruce	2966
Ringey, Diane Lea	2966
Ringey, Mary Elizabeth	2966
Ringrose, Amelia Angela Wendy	1561
Ringrose, Angela Margaret	1561
Ringrose, Basil John	329
Ringrose, Jean Alice	329
Ringrose, Nigel John Carter	1561
Ringrose, Simon Nigel Olav	1561
Ringrose, Timothy John	1561
Ringsell, Brett George Jervis	2529
Ringsell, Cassandra Phillida Anne	2529
Ringsell, Christopher Charles Robert	2529
Ripley, Dorothy Mary	912
Ripley, (Hilary) Susan	2413
Ripley, Katherine	2413
Ripley, Michael	2863
Ripley, Sarah Stella	2414
Ripley, William Hugh	2413
Ripper, Annabel Merry	2875
Ripper, Christopher James	2875
Ripper, Frances Mary Elizabeth	2875
Ripper, Georgina Louise	2875
Ripper, Harry James Hubert	2875
Ripper, Holly Charlton	2875
Ripper, Joan Mary Winefride	2875
Ripper, Stephen Louis Dudley	2875
Rischbieth, Amanda Mary	2952
Rischbieth, Briony Anne	2952
Rischbieth, Brooke Storm	2952
Rischbieth, Careena	2952
Rischbieth, Catherine Louise	2952
Rischbieth, Elaine	2952
Rischbieth, Emma Iles	2952
Rischbieth, Geoffrey John	2952
Rischbieth, Henry George	2952
Rischbieth, Henry Mark	2952
Rischbieth, Ian Harold	2952
Rischbieth, Jake Samuel David	2952
Rischbieth, James Henry John	2952
Rischbieth, Joan	2952
Rischbieth, John Beresford Wills	2952
Rischbieth, Judith Ann	2952
Rischbieth, Nancy	2952
Rischbieth, Peggy Jane	2952
Rischbieth, Peter Robert	2952
Rischbieth, Richard Harold Charles	2952
Rischbieth, Thomas James	2952
Rischbieth, Thomas John Hugh	2952
Rischbieth, William Hugh	2952
Riseley, Anne Catherine	1454
Riseley, David Michael	1454
Riseley, Mark James	1454
Riseley, Robert Sackville	1454
Risk, Diana	67
Risley, George Francis	1889
Risley, Jane Emma	1889
Risley, Rosemary Wendy Pamela	1889
Risley, Thomas Edward	1889
Ritchey, Emily Jane	1904
Ritchey, Jonathan Dale	1904
Ritchey, Kenneth Dale	1904
Ritchey, Sarah Nell	1904
Ritchie, Alastair D M	1903
Ritchie, Amy Helen	1568
Ritchie, Andrew William	2415
Ritchie, Angela Margaret	2519
Ritchie, Anne	2415
Ritchie, Barbara Ann	1568
Ritchie, Barbara Anne Lydia Janet	2414
Ritchie, Cecilia Elizabeth	2519
Ritchie, (Charles) Rupert Rendall	2415
Ritchie, Elspeth Jean	96
Ritchie, Fiona Mary	1275
Ritchie, Fiona Ruth	2414
Ritchie, Fionnah Alice Ellen	2415
Ritchie, Grant Phillip	2312
Ritchie, Harold Bruce	2415
Ritchie, Hermione Elizabeth	96
Ritchie, Ian Angus Dundas	2415
Ritchie, James Anthony Gregor	2415
Ritchie, James Henry Wood	1275
Ritchie, Jean Davina	263, 2744
Ritchie, Jeremy Kenyon Tod	1568
Ritchie, Kathryn Margaret	2312
Ritchie, Margaret Jean	1275
Ritchie, Mary Annabel	2519
Ritchie, Michael	263
Ritchie, Michael Denison	2744
Ritchie, Michael William	2519
Ritchie, Nancy Leith	2415
Ritchie, Nicholas William	96
Ritchie, Pamela Eveleen Elizabeth	2415
Ritchie, Peter Graham	2312
Ritchie, Philippa Jane	2415
Ritchie, Ruth Mary	1275
Ritchie, Sarah Ann	1903

Ritchie, Sibylla	2415
Ritchie, Simon John	1568
Ritchie, Wendy Lynne	2312
Ritchie, William Galloway Miller	96
Ritchie, William Harper	2312
Ritchie, William Nigel	2415
Ritson, Alice	197
Ritson, Harry William	197
Ritson, Verena April	197
Ritson, William A	197
Ritter, Martin Neill	811
Ritter, Michelle Clare	811
Ritter, Stanley	811
Ritter, Yvonne	811
Rittson-Thomas, Grace Mary	673
Rivero, Diego Pintado Caravita di Sirignano	2074
Rivero, Ricardo Pintado	2074
Rivero, Ricardo Pintado Caravita di Sirignano	2074
Rivero, Tazio Pintado Caravita di Sirignano	2074
Rivett-Carnac, Alexander John	2418
Rivett-Carnac, Alice Josephine	2418
Rivett-Carnac, Amanda	2418
Rivett-Carnac, April Sally	2419
Rivett-Carnac, Barbara Joyce	2418
Rivett-Carnac, Carol Ann	2418
Rivett-Carnac, Charles John Fergus	2418
Rivett-Carnac, Christopher Charles	2418
Rivett-Carnac, Cleone Patricia	2418
Rivett-Carnac, Clive Anthony Charles	2418
Rivett-Carnac, Eric Gordon	2418
Rivett-Carnac, Francesca Jane	2418
Rivett-Carnac, Gordon Seymour	2418
Rivett-Carnac, Jeremy Charles Percy	2417
Rivett-Carnac, Joan	2417
Rivett-Carnac, John Benedict	2418
Rivett-Carnac, John Charles Malcolm	2418
Rivett-Carnac, (John) Clive	2419
Rivett-Carnac, John Southey	2418
Rivett-Carnac, Jonathan James	2419
Rivett-Carnac, Lorna Isabel	2418
Rivett-Carnac, Louis Charles James	2418
Rivett-Carnac, Louise	2418
Rivett-Carnac, Marian Propert	2418
Rivett-Carnac, Marilyn	2418
Rivett-Carnac, Mary Rose	2418
Rivett-Carnac, Merlene Clare	2418
Rivett-Carnac, Michael Francis	2418
Rivett-Carnac, Michael James	2418
Rivett-Carnac, Michelle	2418
Rivett-Carnac, Miles James	2419
Rivett-Carnac, Monique Madeleine Marie	2417
Rivett-Carnac, Ora-Lee	2418
Rivett-Carnac, Paul Charles	2418
Rivett-Carnac, Percival Sydney	2417
Rivett-Carnac, Philippa Jane Mearns	2418
Rivett-Carnac, Roberta Grace	2418
Rivett-Carnac, Robyn Genevieve	2418
Rivett-Carnac, Sara Catherine	2418
Rivett-Carnac, Sarah	2419
Rivett-Carnac, Simon Miles	2419
Rivett-Carnac, Sophie Caroline	2418
Rivett-Carnac, Susan Marigold MacTier	2417
Rivett-Carnac, Tamara	2418
Rivett-Carnac, Thomas Charles	2418
Rivett-Carnac, Timothy Charles	2418
Rivett-Carnac, Tom Alexander Miles	2419
Rivett-Carnac, Valerie Kay	2418
Riviere, Amelia Sophie	2339
Riviere, Arabella Rose	2339
Riviere, Ellinor Eileen	2339
Riviere, Peter Gerard	2339
Riviere, Sara	2339
Rix, Benjamin	2419
Rix, Bernard Anthony	3094
Rix, Caroline	2419
Rix, Elspet Jeans	2419
Rix, (Elspet) Shelley	2419
Rix, Gideon	3094
Rix, Hannah	3094
Rix, Helen	2419
Rix, Jack	2419
Rix, Jacob	3094
Rix, James MacGregor	2419
Rix, Jonathan	3094
Rix, Jonathan Robert MacGregor	2419
Rix, Karen Debra	3094
Rix, Rachel Elsie	3094
Rizvi, Anver Jamal	458
Rizvi, Joanna Elisabeth	458
Roach, Brooke Normile	920
Roach, Chauncey Blane	920
Roach, Daisy	920
Roach, Dorothy Jane	920
Roach, Hal	920
Roach, Hillary Anne	920
Roach, Katie Elizabeth	920
Roach, Keegan Wade	920
Roach, Leigh Anne	920
Roach, Michael Todd	920
Roach, Sarah Savannah	920
Roach, Scott Evans	920
Roach, Susan Lynn	920
Roach, Todd Douglas	920
Roach, Zachary Cleveland	920
Road, Bonnie	1468
Road, Christopher Thorburn	1468
Road, Laurence Carrington	1468
Roads, Alex	2978
Roads, Nicola Jane	2978
Roane, Mary Lynette	1021

S

Shawcross, William Hartley Hume 1093
Shawe-Taylor, Desmond Edward Philip 1404
Shawe-Taylor, John Stewart 1404
Shawe-Taylor, Richard Arland 1404
Sheaffe, Alexandra Jane 1856
Sheaffe, Anthony John Lemprière 1856
Sheaffe, Jonathan Lemprière 1856
Sheaffe, Lucy Susan Elizabeth 1856
Sheaffe, Susan Elizabeth 1856
Shearer, George Brodie 1499
Shearer, James O'Brien 1499
Shearer, Joan Hilary 1499
Shearer, Margaret Kathleen 1499
Shearing, Philip T 121
Shearring, Camilla Gillian 2232
Shearring, Mark Ronald 2232
Shears, Mary Rose 2610
Shears, Peter George 2610
Shechterman, Abraham 1865
Shedden, (Kathleen) Patricia 2558
Shedden, Simon Rory Lindesay 2558
Sheehan, Patrick Timothy 1488
Sheehan, Phyllis 1135
Sheehan, Sarah Caroline Patricia 1488
Sheehan, Timothy Stafford 1488
Sheehy, Clare Ann 30
Sheehy, Jane Elizabeth 30
Sheehy, Mary Anne 30
Sheehy, Nicholas 1950
Sheehy, Sarah Jane 1950
Sheehy, Timothy John 30
Sheepshanks, Andrew Charles 2087
Sheepshanks, Christopher James 2087
Sheepshanks, David Richard 2087
Sheepshanks, Lilias 2087
Sheepshanks, Richard John 2087
Sheepshanks, Robin John 2087
Sheffield, Alexandra C 2598
Sheffield, Alice Daisy Victoria 2597
Sheffield, Andrew George 2598
Sheffield, Carolyn Alexandra 2598
Sheffield, Christine 2598
Sheffield, Edward John 2598
Sheffield, Emily Julia 2597
Sheffield, France Mary Agnes 2598
Sheffield, Frederick Arthur Digby 2598
Sheffield, George Henry Oliphant 2598
Sheffield, Helen Jane Ann 2598
Sheffield, Jean Ann 2598
Sheffield, John David 2598
Sheffield, (John) Julian Lionel George 2598
Sheffield, John Robert 2598
Sheffield, John Vincent 2598
Sheffield, Lionel Julian 2598
Sheffield, Lucy Mary 2597
Sheffield, Mary 2598
Sheffield, Nicola Elizabeth Anne 2598
Sheffield, Nigel Digby 2598
Sheffield, Richard Charles 2598
Sheffield, Robert Charles Berkeley 2597
Sheffield, Simon Robert Alexander 2598
Sheffield, Timothy John Digby 2598
Sheffield, Victoria Penelope 2597
Shelbourne, Arabella Frances 2625
Shelbourne, Catherine Elizabeth 143
Shelbourne, Charles Robin 143
Shelbourne, Frederick John Philip 2625
Shelbourne, Freya Anna 143
Shelbourne, India Lucie 2625
Shelbourne, Lucie 2625
Shelbourne, Richard John 2625
Shelbourne, Tatiana Francesca Sophia 2625
Shelburne, Frances Helen Mary 2514
Sheldon, Ann Gillian 721
Sheldon, Anthony Stewart 1025
Sheldon, Bryony Claire 1040
Sheldon, Camilla Frances 1040
Sheldon, Clare Helen Alexandra 721
Sheldon, Holly Samantha 1040
Sheldon, Jack Alan 1699
Sheldon, Jane Mary 457
Sheldon, Jane Stewart 1025
Sheldon, Jenifer 1040
Sheldon, Karim (Luis) Grunauer 721
Sheldon, Margaret Anne 1699
Sheldon, Mark Valentine D'Arcy 721
Sheldon, Martin Rothery 1040
Sheldon, Michael Alan 1699
Sheldon, Patricia 1025
Sheldon, Peter Goddard 1025
Sheldon, Peter Llewellyn 721
Sheldon, Robert Stewart 1025
Sheldon, Sharon Susan 1025
Sheldon, Ted William 1699
Sheldon, Timothy James 457
Shell, Barry 2063
Shell, David Spencer 573
Shell, Davina 2063
Shell, Dorinda May 2063
Shell, Geoffrey Norman 573
Shell, Joan Elizabeth 573
Shell, Jonathan Paul 573
Shell, Marianne Jane 573
Shell, Peter Geoffrey 573
Shell, Samuel 2063
Shell, Timothy Geoffrey 573
Shelley, Alexandra Margaret 2600
Shelley, Andrew Thomas Rupert 2600
Shelley, Anna 2599
Shelley, Benita Mary 2600
Shelley, Caroline Ruth 2599
Shelley, Charles Francis 2599
Shelley, Clare 2599
Shelley, David Robert 2600
Shelley, Dorothy Irvine 2600
Shelley, Elisabeth Rhoda 1275, 2600
Shelley, Elizabeth Shuna 1558
Shelley, Emma Jane 2600
Shelley, Florence 1304
Shelley, Frederick Norman 2599
Shelley, Genevieve Mary 2600
Shelley, Gillian Philippa 2600
Shelley, Guy William 2599
Shelley, Heidi 2599
Shelley, Jack Alexander Stewart 2600
Shelley, James Edward 2600
Shelley, James Spencer 2599
Shelley, James William 1558
Shelley, Jemima Louise 2600
Shelley, Joanna Margaret 2600
Shelley, Joanne Marie 2600
Shelley, Jonathan Rupert 2600
Shelley, Judith 2600
Shelley, Kirsten Rachel 2600
Shelley, Lynne Sharon 2600
Shelley, Malcolm Frederick 2600
Shelley, Marian Pamela 2600
Shelley, Mark Ian 1558
Shelley, Maureen 2599
Shelley, Nicholas Charles 2600
Shelley, Nigel Anthony 2600
Shelley, Nora Elizabeth 2600
Shelley, Pamela Mary 2600
Shelley, Penelope Sarah 2600
Shelley, Peter David 2600
Shelley, Philip John 2600
Shelley, Philip Norman 2599
Shelley, Philip Spencer 2600
Shelley, Rosamond Mary 2240
Shelley, Ruth Mary 2599
Shelley, Sarah Jane 2599
Shelley, Sarah Lucy 2600
Shelley, Spencer 2599
Shelley, Stephen Spencer 2599
Shelley, Thomas Henry 2600
Shelley, Thomas Joseph 2599
Shelley, Timothy James 2600
Shelley, Victoria Juliet 2600
Shelley, William Rowland 2599
Shellim, Alexander Brooke 2875
Shellim, Anne Mary Frances 2875
Shellim, Anton Brooke 2875
Shellim, Rebecca Frances 2875
Shelmerdine-Hare, Caroline Philippa W 2406
Shelmerdine-Hare, Roger John 2406
Shelton, David Patrick 815
Shelton, Fay Lilah 815
Shelton, Letitia Molesworth 1955
Shelton, Lucile Matheson 1955
Shelton, Peter Alfred 815
Shelton, Sarah 815
Shelton, Sophie Letitia 1955
Shelton, William Geoffrey 1955
Shenkman, Alexander Ivan Marcus 1811
Shenkman, Ivan Alexander 1811
Shenkman, Maximilian Ivan Michael 1811
Shenkman, Melissa Alexandra Mary 1811
Shenkman, Susan Mary 1811
Shennan, Malcolm Kenneth 2755
Shennan, Mark Douglas 2755
Shennan, Rosanna Mary 2755
Shepard, Carol Jean 1695
Shephard, Belinda Anne 2394
Shephard, William 2394
Shepherd, Andrew Charles 2480
Shepherd, Ann Catharine 1719
Shepherd, Anne Catherine 2146
Shepherd, Anthea Elizabeth Eve 1290
Shepherd, Christopher Patrick 1906
Shepherd, Clare Harriet Faviell 2480
Shepherd, Dennis John Dale 1290
Shepherd, Douglas Newton 2601
Shepherd, Edward James 2480
Shepherd, Eleanor 2601
Shepherd, Elizabeth Anne 263
Shepherd, Emma Gillian 2146
Shepherd, Gillian 2146
Shepherd, Graeme George 2601
Shepherd, Iris Anne Alayne 1906
Shepherd, Isobel Anthea 1290
Shepherd, Jack 1719
Shepherd, James 431
Shepherd, Janet Robina 2146
Shepherd, Jeremy Michael 1906
Shepherd, Jessica Kate 869
Shepherd, Justin Philip William 1290
Shepherd, Mary Mathilde 1906
Shepherd, Matthew 431
Shepherd, Melissa May 1290
Shepherd, Miranda Dorothy Emilia 1290
Shepherd, Patrick Malcolm 2601
Shepherd, Peter Andrew Dundas 1906
Shepherd, Philippa Ruth 869
Shepherd, Richard James 2480
Shepherd, Robert Beaumont 2146
Shepherd, Ronald Francis 1906
Shepherd, Samuel Elliot 869
Shepherd, Simon Beaumont 2146
Shepherd, Susan Clare 1906
Shepherd, Thomas Richard 2480
Shepherd, Timothy David 1906
Shepherd, Ulick Jacquelyn 431
Shepherd, Zoë Alexandra Denise 1290
Shepherd-Cross, David Benjamin 728
Shepherd-Cross, George Alexander 728
Shepherd-Cross, Max Peter 728
Shepherd-Cross, Rose Amabel 728
Sheppard, Catherine Christy 1972
Sheppard, Edward Noble 2061
Sheppard, Evelyn Frances 2698
Sheppard, Jocelyn Anne Sydney 2165
Sheppard, Mary 2601
Sheppard, Rachel Russell 340
Sheppard, Robert Arthur Byas 2214
Sheppard, Rosamund Malua 2061
Sheppard, Rosemary 2137
Shepperd, Grace 2601
Sherbrooke, Alexander 1384
Sherbrooke, Archie John 1383
Sherbrooke, Benedict 1383
Sherbrooke, Edmund 1384
Sherbrooke, Elizabeth 1384
Sherbrooke, Harry 1384
Sherbrooke, Hugh 890, 1384
Sherbrooke, John Penn 1383
Sherbrooke, Luke 1383
Sherbrooke, Madeleine Mary Josephine 1383
Sherbrooke, Miranda 1383
Sherbrooke, Nicola Mary 890, 1384
Sherbrooke, Rosanna 1384
Sherbrooke, Simon 1383
Sherbrooke, Tom 1384
Shere, Caleb Charles David 1067
Shere, Christine Gae 1067
Shere, Eileen Mildred 1067
Shere, Ian Geoffrey 1067
Shere, John Charles 1067
Shere, Katie Elisabeth 1067
Shere, Kelly Rose 1067
Sheridan, Howard Lewis Brinsley 1561
Sheridan, Lavina Mary 1561
Sheridan, Richard Brinsley 1561
Sheridan, Rollo Hugh Motley 1561
Sherlock, Charles Patrick 500
Sherlock, Francis Alexander Howard 500
Sherlock, Patrick John Howard 500
Sherlock, Sarah Elizabeth Agnes 500
Sherman, Alexandra Susan Anne 1060
Sherman, Charles Alexander Hoyt 1060
Sherman, Ian Andrew Henry 1060
Sherman, Peter Anthony Carnegie 1060
Sherriff, (Rosemary) June Christina 908
Sherston-Baker, Amy Margaret 2602
Sherston-Baker, David Arbuthnot George 2602
Sherston-Baker, Jane Magdalen 2602
Sherston-Baker, Vanessa R A 2602
Shervington, Caroline Faith 354
Shervington, Diana Clare 354
Shervington, Diana Elizabeth 354
Shervington, Evelyn Arthur 354
Shervington, Rupert Patrick 354
Sherwell, Francis Lloyd 2318
Sherwell, Isla Madeleine 2318
Sherwell, Madeleine Dawn 2318
Sherwell, Raynes Lloyd 2318
Sherwin, Amanda Kate 1669
Sherwin, Malcolm James 1669
Sherwin, Sarah Anthea 1669
Sherwin, Simon Patrick 1669
Sherwood, Andrew Godfrey Purvis 2162, 2275
Sherwood, Anna 347
Sherwood, Barbara 2162
Sherwood, Claire Margaret 2162
Sherwood, David Gerald 205
Sherwood, Diana 205
Sherwood, Diana Jane 378
Sherwood, Edward Godfrey DeWitt 2162
Sherwood, Edward Godfrey Purvis 2162
Sherwood, Gideon 2162
Sherwood, Jacalyn Anne 439
Sherwood, Jack Edward 347
Sherwood, Joanna Lisa 439
Sherwood, Joanna Ruth 2162
Sherwood, Julian George 378
Sherwood, Kathleen Theodosia 2162
Sherwood, Lucie 2162
Sherwood, Lucy Jane 347
Sherwood, Margaret Anne 2162
Sherwood, Mary Helen 2162, 2275
Sherwood, Nathan John 2162
Sherwood, Paul 378
Sherwood, Peter David Onslow 2162
Sherwood, Phoebe 2162
Sherwood, Robin Paul Austen 378
Sherwood, Samuel 2162
Sherwood, Simon E H 347
Sherwood, Susan Mary 439
Sherwood, Thomas James Mulso 2162
Shewell, Alda Evelyn 1420
Shewell, Alison Averil 1420
Shewell, Anthony Martin Edward 1420
Shewell, Christopher John Henry 1420
Shewell, Graham 2701
Shewell, Hugh Timothy 2701
Shewell, John Michael Henry 1420
Shewell, Sarah Jane Elinor 2701
Shewell, Teresa Elinor 2701
Shields, Anthony Hubert 200
Shields, Celia Catherine 3013
Shields, Graham Michael 199
Shields, Hester 199
Shields, Hubert Leake 199
Shields, Ian Cranston 3013
Shields, Joe 3013
Shields, Kellie Anne 200
Shields, Kerry Mohira 3013
Shields, Lynette 199
Shields, Marnie Jane 200
Shields, Mary Charm 200
Shields, Michael Graham 199
Shields, Peter William Hubert 200
Shields, Philippa Robin 200
Shields, Stuart Frederick 200
Shields, William Hubert 200
Shiffner, Caroline Mary Tilly 2603
Shiffner, Charles Tullis 2603
Shiffner, Dorothea Helena Cynthia 2603
Shiffner, Elizabeth Margaret Mary 2603
Shiffner, Elizabeth Marilyn 2603
Shiffner, George Frederick 2603
Shiffner, Henry Charles Alexander 2603
Shiffner, Joaquina 2603
Shiffner, John Edward 2603
Shiffner, John Robert 2603
Shiffner, Katherine 2603
Shiffner, Linda Mary 2603
Shiffner, Margaret Harriet 2603
Shiffner, Michael George Edward 2603
Shiffner, Penelope Ann Dorothy 2603
Shiffner, Priscilla Mary Scarlett 2603
Shiffner, Robin John Landon 2603
Shiffner, Rosamund Mary 2603
Shiffner, Rosemary Anne 2603
Shilling, George Frederick Alston 2942
Shilling, Vivienne Ellen 2942
Shillito, Christina Mary 2666
Shillito, Claire Patricia 2666
Shillito, Martin Lancelot 2666
Shillito, Richard Arthur 2666
Shine, Benjamin Griffith 1418
Shine, James Macquarie 1418
Shine, John 1418
Shine, Kathleen Mary 1418
Shine, Michael Patrick 1418
Shine, Molly Gertrude 1418
Shine, Rebecca Kathleen 1418
Shine, Richard 1418
Shine, Terri Sue 1418
Shinkman, Christopher Joseph 251
Shinkman, Elizabeth 251
Shinkman, Judith Kay 251
Shinkman, Marsha Ann 251
Shinkman, Paul Glanvill 251
Shipton, Harold William 140
Shipton, Janet Helen 140
Shirey, Frederick Elton 981
Shirey, Mary Melissa 981
Shirey, Richard Francis Elton 981
Shirey, Sandra 981
Shirey, Violet Mary Agnes 981
Shirkey, Christine 1449
Shirkey, Howard 1449
Shirkey, Joanne 1449
Shirkey, Julianne 1449
Shirkey, Marian 1449
Shirkey, Suzanne 1449
Shirley, Annabel Mary 1049
Shirley, Augusta 1052
Shirley, Edna Blodwen 1052
Shirley, Evelyn Robert 1052
Shirley, Frederick James Walter 1049
Shirley, Henry Benedict John 1050
Shirley, Hermione Mary Annabel 1049
Shirley, Horatio John 1052
Shirley, Hugh Sewallis 1052
Shirley, John Evelyn 889, 1052
Shirley, Judith Margaret 889, 1052
Shirley, Katherine Elizabeth 988
Shirley, Katherine Judith 988
Shirley, Mary Louisa Phyllis 1052
Shirley, Michael Bruce 988
Shirley, Nathaniel Guy 1052
Shirley, Perdita Rose 1052
Shirley, Philip Evelyn 1052
Shirley, Robert Hugh 988
Shirley, Robert William Saswalo 1049
Shirley, Sallyanne Margaret 1050
Shirley, Susannah Mary 1049
Shirley, Tamara 1050
Shirley, William Robert Charles 1049
Shirley-Beavan, Charles Michael 2895
Shirley-Beavan, George Ronald Benjamin 2895
Shirley-Beavan, Phillippa Margaret 2895
Shirley-Beavan, Simon Hamilton 2895
Shivarg, Alexander (Shura) 959
Shivarg, Camilla Gabrielle 959
Shivarg, Joan Olivia 959
Shlaim, Avi 1742
Shlaim, Gwyneth Roberta 1742
Shlaim, Tamar Megan 1742
Shober, Jennifer 1439
Shober, John Andrews Harris 1439
Shober, Margot Faye 1439
Shober, Martin Pemberton 1439
Shober, Stephanie 1439
Shocket, Godfrey S 968
Shocket, Susan 968
Shoesmith, Joanna 706
Shokoohy, Mehrdad 1652
Shokoohy, Natalia Honoria 1652
Sholdis, Christopher John 1893
Sholdis, Jennifer Elizabeth 1893
Sholdis, Joanne Christina 1893
Sholdis, Rachel Rosemary 1893
Sholdis, Richard 1893
Sholdis, Robert James 1893
Shone, Anthony Michael John 2695
Shone, Colin Henry Philip 2695
Shone, Henry Martin 2695
Shone, Jeremy Patrick Martin 2695
Shone, Jonathan 1418
Shone, Michael 1418
Shone, Patrick Douglas 2695

Smith, John Lindsay Eric 2115
Smith, Jonathan 113
Smith, Jonathan Christopher 2167
Smith, Joseph Henry 811
Smith, Joy Miriam 2204
Smith, Judith 1404
Smith, Judith Ann 2131
Smith, Judith Chaffey 2647
Smith, Judy Jennifer Constantine 636
Smith, Julia Bullock 2650
Smith, Julia Elizabeth 1904
Smith, Julia Mary 2882
Smith, (Julia Mary) Rona 435
Smith, Julian Arthur Vaughan 624
Smith, Julian David 1276
Smith, Julian G 79
Smith, Julian John Hamling 480
Smith, Julian Raymond Eric 435, 1096
Smith, Julie Louise 2828
Smith, Julie Stella Winwood 2647
Smith, Juliet Ann 879
Smith, Juliet Clare 2693
Smith, Justin William 113
Smith, Karen Rosanna 708
Smith, Karen Rose 1123
Smith, Katherine 960, 2115
Smith, Katherine Grace 1594
Smith, Kathleen Brigid 1498
Smith, Kathleen Mary Coningsby 811
Smith, Kathleen Wendy Elizabeth 810
Smith, Kathryn Rachel 200
Smith, Kenji 1276
Smith, Kim 2924
Smith, Kirsten Antonia 636
Smith, Kirsty Diana 2646
Smith, Laura Lillian 3054
Smith, Lawrence Alec 200
Smith, Lesa Kathleen 583
Smith, Lesley 1275
Smith, Leslie Gaye 2183
Smith, Lillemor Elizabeth 2818
Smith, Lorenzo Patrick Harold 1276
Smith, Louis Pottier 1253
Smith, Louisa Ann 2077
Smith, Louise Florence 2828
Smith, Lucia Jane 1501
Smith, Lucinda Rachael 1414
Smith, Lucinda Tranquilla 2648
Smith, Lucy Alexandra 435
Smith, Lucy Jane Mary 1041
Smith, Lucy Jennifer 2853
Smith, Lucy Marjorie Eileen 70
Smith, Lucy Patricia 683
Smith, Luke Alastair Robert 2809
Smith, Luke Eric 1414
Smith, Luke Robin Anthony 2464
Smith, Mabel 272
Smith, Madeleine Loveday 2649
Smith, Margaret Ann 1521
Smith, Margaret Bertha 182
Smith, Margaret Claire 143
Smith, Margaret Erica 2647
Smith, Marianne 2647
Smith, Marie Louise 333
Smith, Marie Therese 637
Smith, Mariza Joanna Phyllis 467
Smith, Mark Eric 1414
Smith, Mark V E 1982
Smith, Martin Roger 1218
Smith, Mary 1276
Smith, Mary Charlotte 2863
Smith, Mary Clare 1027
Smith, Mary Ellen 927
Smith, Mary Isiline 2349
Smith, Mary Kimbo 2183
Smith, Mary Lesley 1366
Smith, Mary Margaret 2653
Smith, Maryna Elizabeth 2653
Smith, Matilda Amelia 1006
Smith, Matthew Edward 2653
Smith, Matthew Eric 1414
Smith, Matthew Galbraith 182
Smith, Matthew John Patrick 2115
Smith, Matthew Roy Winwood 2647
Smith, Maureen Pamela Stewart 578
Smith, Megan Winwood 2647
Smith, Mervyn Nigel Bosworth 2653
Smith, Michael Clive Bowker 2077
Smith, Michael Constantine 636
Smith, Michael John Bosworth 2653
Smith, Michael L F 993
Smith, Michael R 683
Smith, Michael Simon 960
Smith, Michael Winwood 2647
Smith, Miles Stephen 1737
Smith, Milo Thomas Eric 435
Smith, Miranda 163
Smith, Moya Morvenna Irene 133
Smith, Myfanwy Ann 2505
Smith, Nancia Jean Margaret 2648
Smith, Nancy Margaret 2182
Smith, Nathanael Haden 1265
Smith, Neil Lindsay Vaughan 624
Smith, Nevil John Bosworth 2653
Smith, Nicholas Carey 1265
Smith, Nicholas Edward Peter 2464
Smith, Nicholas William Winwood 2648
Smith, Nicola Constantine 637
Smith, Nicola Elizabeth 2346
Smith, Nicola Henrietta 458
Smith, Nicola Jeanne 636
Smith, Nicolas Robin Bartolomeo 1276
Smith, Nigel Antony Carrington 1737
Smith, Nigel Peter 276
Smith, Nigel Thomas 2182
Smith, Nina Kakkar 2648
Smith, Oliver George Eric 435
Smith, Oliver James Coningsby 811
Smith, Ottoline Amelia 336
Smith, Patricia Christine 2649
Smith, Patrick Charles Gilbert 2649
Smith, Patrick Matthew Desmond 182
Smith, Paul Barry 1521
Smith, Paula Maria 1404
Smith, Pauline 1067
Smith, Penny 2134
Smith, Peter Anning 1774
Smith, Peter Henry 1276
Smith, Peter John 276
Smith, Peter Martin Stuart 1952
Smith, Peter Michael 2513
Smith, Peter Nigel Coningsby 811
Smith, Peter Randolph 1123
Smith, Peter Raymond 1521
Smith, Peter Selby 2204
Smith, Philip Anthony Medlycott 1904
Smith, Philip Henry 1276
Smith, Philip James Edward 578
Smith, Philip Reginald 1276
Smith, Philip Webster 960
Smith, Philippa Silvia 1008
Smith, Phillipa Anne 2346
Smith, Phinola Jane 1927
Smith, Phyllis Berenice 2647
Smith, (Phyllis) Jean 2253
Smith, Prescot, Alexandra Constance 336
Smith, Priscilla 163
Smith, Priscilla Anne Josephine 1041
Smith, Rachel Charlotte 1276
Smith, Rachel Hebe Philippa 2204
Smith, Raymond Shakespeare 2794
Smith, Reginald Alfred Henry Reardon 1404
Smith, Reginald Claude 2652
Smith, Reginald Claude Bosworth 2652
Smith, Renee Adrienne 2131
Smith, Rex 2747
Smith, Rhonda Jean 2647
Smith, Richard Charles Winwood 2647
Smith, Richard Edward 1276
Smith, Richard Michael 2649
Smith, Richard Michael Patrick 1041
Smith, Richard Orfeur Bateson 649
Smith, Richard Selby 2204
Smith, Robert Alexander 2647
Smith, Robert Chadwick 2131
Smith, Robert Hervé William de Montmorency 799
Smith, Robert Lee 2604
Smith, Robert Phillip Beresford 1067
Smith, Robert Russell Maunganui 1594
Smith, Robert Serge 2647
Smith, Robert Sydney Winwood 2647
Smith, Robert Vernon 799
Smith, Robert William 1067
Smith, Robyn Clare 2204
Smith, Robyn Louise 1123
Smith, Robyn Louise Winwood 2647
Smith, Rodney John 1521
Smith, Rona Kathleen 1404
Smith, Ronald James Thomas Winwood 2647
Smith, Rory Donal 2647
Smith, Rosalind Margaret 749
Smith, Rosanna Marcia 2220
Smith, Rosanna Tatiana 674
Smith, Rose 2183
Smith, Roslyn Nellie 2647
Smith, Rowena Jane 2134
Smith, Rupert Malise 2134
Smith, Rupert Timothy 2111
Smith, Rupert William Winwood 2648
Smith, Sabrina Mary Louise 993
Smith, Sadie Elizabeth 2653
Smith, Sally Anne 199
Smith, Sally Constantine 636
Smith, Samuel 1982
Smith, Samuel Gordon 2647
Smith, Sandra ('Sue') Dorothy 2167
Smith, Sandra Elizabeth 2346
Smith, Sandra Ellen 389
Smith, Sara Marie Celeste 1275
Smith, Sara Suzanne 1275
Smith, Sarah 2650
Smith, Sarah Anne 2809
Smith, Sarah Diana 2513
Smith, Sarah Helen 272
Smith, Sarah Jane 1737
Smith, Sarah Valentine 2065
Smith, Scilla Ann 1276
Smith, Scott Aaron 2877
Smith, Scott Vincent 927
Smith, Shamus Oliver Eric 1414
Smith, Shaun Thomas 2877
Smith, Sheila Margaret 1123
Smith, Sheila Marguerite Evelyn 799
Smith, Sheila Mary 960
Smith, Shona Joyce 2464
Smith, Sidney Edward 749
Smith, Simon Matthew 2863
Smith, Simon Winwood 2647
Smith, Sophia Gilliam 2863
Smith, Sophie Diana 435
Smith, Stanford 2924
Smith, Stephanie 2182
Smith, Stephanie Jane 749
Smith, Stephanie Sue 2648
Smith, Stephen Frederick John 2464
Smith, Stephen Hattersley 2314
Smith, Stephen John 2346
Smith, Stephen Neil 2863
Smith, Steven Winwood 2647
Smith, Susan 811
Smith, Susan Mary 272
Smith, Susan Muriel 637
Smith, Susan Patricia Mary 1290
Smith, Susanna 163
Smith, Susanna Mary 99
Smith, Suzanne 624
Smith, Sybil Mary 2924
Smith, Sylvia 1253
Smith, Sylvia Ada 1008
Smith, Tacy Susan 2604
Smith, Tanya Gwynne 2314
Smith, Tanya Nicole 636
Smith, Taro 1276
Smith, Terence John Winwood 2647
Smith, Terence William Devey 2621
Smith, Teresa Caroline 669
Smith, Terrick Elystan Scott 241
Smith, Tessa 2924
Smith, Thomas Arthur 2464
Smith, (Thomas) Edward 2182
Smith, Thomas William 199, 1276, 2699
Smith, Timothy 2853
Smith, Timothy Francis 2111
Smith, Timothy Hamilton 637
Smith, Timothy Ian 1123
Smith, Timothy John Medlycott 1904
Smith, Timothy Peter 336
Smith, Tina Georgina 1404
Smith, Titus Oliver 2853
Smith, Tobias Peter John 2505
Smith, Todd 2747
Smith, Tressa Rawhiti 2828
Smith, Ulrica Marjory 214
Smith, Ursula Susan Annette Mary 1737
Smith, Venetia Mary 2562
Smith, Victoria Clare Coningsby 811
Smith, Victoria Wendy 89
Smith, Vivien Dovey 649
Smith, Wayne Edward 2652
Smith, William Ernest 810
Smith, (William) Henry Bernard 1275
Smith, William Jeremy Reardon 1404
Smith, William Stewart 2699
Smith, Yasmine 241
Smith-Bingham, Alexander John 1623
Smith-Bingham, Alison Kate 1623
Smith-Bingham, Charles Arthur 567
Smith-Bingham, Guy Jeremy 1623
Smith-Bingham, Jennifer 567, 3008
Smith-Bingham, Jeremy 1623
Smith-Bingham, Priscilla Mary 1623
Smith-Bingham, Richard David 1623
Smith-Dodsworth, Cyrilla Denise 2650
Smith-Dodsworth, Daniel Leui'i 2650
Smith-Dodsworth, David John 2650
Smith-Dodsworth, Joanna Marie 2650
Smith-Dodsworth, Lolita 2650
Smith-Dorrien-Smith, Adam Robert Smith 2261
Smith-Dorrien-Smith, Frances Marcella 2261
Smith-Dorrien-Smith, Michael Horace 2261
Smith-Gordon, Eileen Laura 2651
Smith-Gordon, Kumi 2651
Smith-Gordon, Lionel George Eldred 2651
Smith-Gordon, Sandra Rosamund Ann 2651
Smith-Marriott, Barbara Mary 2655
Smith-Marriott, Ian Peter 2655
Smith-Marriott, Jean Graham Martin 2655
Smith-Marriott, Mark Nicholas 2655
Smith-Marriott, Martin Ralph 2655
Smith-Marriott, Neil Hugh 2655
Smith-Marriott, Paul Graham 2655
Smith-Marriott, Peter Francis 2655
Smith-Ryland, David James 696, 2827
Smith-Ryland, Hélène 2827
Smith-Ryland, Jeryl Marcia Sarah 696, 2827
Smith-Ryland, Joanna 696, 2827
Smith-Ryland, Petra 696
Smith-Ryland, Petra Louisa 2827
Smith-Ryland, Robin Charles 696, 2827
Smith-Ryland, Sarah Yoskyl 696
Smith-Wright, George Henry 1000
Smith-Wright, Jean Halcro 1000
Smithers, Christian Alexander Langley 2023
Smithers, Frances 1003
Smithers, Louisa Jane 1462
Smithers, Lucian James Angelo 2023
Smithers, Mary Frances (Mafra) 1462
Smithers, William Rupert John 1462
Smithies, Frances Mary Barbara 2100
Smithies, Helen Mary 2100
Smithies, Jeremy 2100
Smithies, Miranda Jean 1332
Smithies, Roland Jeremy Xavier Spruyt de Bay 2100
Smithson, Emilia 1512
Smithson, John Guthrie 1512
Smithson, Michael John 1512
Smithson, Robert Hugh 1512
Smithson, Sophia Marina 1512
Smithson, Susanna Loveday 1512
Smithyman, Margaret Ann 2015
Smithyman, William Kendrick 2015
Smitter, Caroline Allison Faith 971
Smitter, Leila Eliott 971
Smitter, Matthew Boswell Eliott Burton 971
Smitter, Victoria C 971
Smitter, Yvor Hyatt 971
Smitz, Carol Thew 1339
Smitz, Leigh-Ann Kimberley 1339
Smitz, Peter Gerard Littleton 1339
Smitz, Stephen Douglas 1339
Smutz, Margaret Lois 1011
Smutz, William 1011
Smyly, (Charmian) Miranda 2031
Smyly, George William Dennis 1243
Smyly, Harriet Lucy 1243
Smyly, (Henry) Richard 2031
Smyly, Hugo Richard Seymour 1243
Smyly, (Richard) Mark 1243
Smyly, Robert Dennis 2031
Smyth, Andrew 2656
Smyth, Annabel Mary 225
Smyth, Bernadette Mary 2655
Smyth, Brendan Julian 2655
Smyth, Bridget 3003
Smyth, Carolyn 3003
Smyth, Catriona Mary 1038
Smyth, Charles Henry Devaynes 142
Smyth, Christopher Charles 2656
Smyth, Clare Marie 2656
Smyth, Dominic 3003
Smyth, Elizabeth 1917
Smyth, Emily Margaret 225
Smyth, Emma Louise 2655
Smyth, Gerard Timothy 2655
Smyth, Joan 2656
Smyth, John George 2656
Smyth, John Julian 2656
Smyth, Kathryn Mary 2655
Smyth, Margaret Mary 2656
Smyth, Patrick Geoghegan 3003
Smyth, Peggy 2655
Smyth, Phyllis Philomena Mary 2656
Smyth, Robert Matthew 225
Smyth, Simon Gerard 2656
Smyth, Siobhan 3003
Smyth, Virginia Anne 142
Smyth-Osborn, Annabel Clare 2271
Smyth-Osborn, Michael 2271
Smyth-Osbourne, Annabel 2351
Smyth-Osbourne, Annabel Claire 2351
Smyth-Osbourne, Archie Alexander 2351
Smyth-Osbourne, Charles William 121, 2351
Smyth-Osbourne, Claudia A 2351
Smyth-Osbourne, Edward John 2351
Smyth-Osbourne, Joanna Mary 121, 2351
Smyth-Osbourne, Julian George 2351
Smyth-Osbourne, Luke John 2351
Smyth-Osbourne, Michael Alexander 2351
Smyth-Osbourne, Sophie Charlotte 2351
Smyth-Osbourne, William Hugh 2351
Smyth-Tyrrell, (Beaujolois) Katharine 839
Smyth-Tyrrell, Eleanor Katherine Beaujolois 839
Smyth-Tyrrell, Josephine Clare 839
Smyth-Tyrrell, Philip Charles 839
Smyth-Tyrrell, Stephen Charles 839
Snatt, Myra 848
Sneddon, Andrew Graham 100
Sneddon, Emily Fiona 100
Sneddon, Fiona 100
Sneddon, John Andrew 100
Sneddon, Laura Alice 100
Snell, Diana Mary Philippa 1732
Snell, Francesca 586
Snell, Francis Ivan 586
Snell, Graham Edward Frank 1732
Snell, Hugh 2070
Snell, Ivan Francis 586
Snell, Jessie 2070
Snell, Louise Jane 1732
Snell, Matthew Michael Charles 1732
Snellaert, Bernadette 2238
Snellaert, Catherine Elizabeth 2238
Snellaert, Claire Michelle 2238
Snellaert, Constance Elizabeth Mary 2238
Snellaert, Lambertus Jacobus Gerardus 2238
Snellaert, Michael John 2238
Snellaert, Peter William 2238
Snellaert, Philip Bernard 2238
Snellaert, Sarah Louise 2238
Snelson, Katherine Louise 86
Snelson, Michael John 86
Snelson, Rachel Mary 86
Snelson, William Lawrence 86
Snodgrass, Louise 1029
Snodgrass, Mark 1029
Snodin, Michael Robert 652
Snodin, Oliver Karl Astley 652
Snodin, Patricia Ann 652
Snook, Brian 1323
Snook, Deborah Ann 1323
Snook, Doris Emma 1323
Snook, Glen Townsend 1323
Snook, Lloyd Glen 1323
Snook, Mae 1323
Snow, Catriona Louisa 1157
Snow, Fiona 1157
Snow, Harriet Louise Julia 295
Snow, Jonathan Peter 1157
Snow, Justin Douglas Tennant 1157
Snow, Kirsten Fiona 1157
Snow, Neil Graham Douglas 1157
Snow, Rosemary 176
Snow, William Anthony 176
Snowball, Andrew M B 1618
Snowball, Clarinda Susan 1618
Snowball, Edward William George 1092

Standing, Michael Frederick Oliver 726
Standing, Paul 1325
Standing, Roderick Fremantle 676
Standing, Rosamund Beatrice 676
Standing, Rosemary Anne 726
Standish, Alexander Hugh 461
Standish, Ann Margaret 461
Standish, Anna Margaret 2222
Standish, Anthony Edward Byron 461
Standish, Diana Huguette 461
Standish, Edward Pery 461, 2222
Standish, Miles Anthony 461
Stanford, Anna Bethell 1606
Stanford, Annette Alistair 1606
Stanford, Barrie Robert 686
Stanford, Charlotte June 2899
Stanford, Charlotte Sylvia 1606
Stanford, David 1606
Stanford, Eleanor Ruth 454
Stanford, Emma 2566
Stanford, Giles Timothy 1606
Stanford, Giles William 1443
Stanford, Harriet 2566
Stanford, Hermione Mary 2566
Stanford, Jonathan David 1606
Stanford, Katherine Armorel 2899
Stanford, Lucinda Geraldine 1443
Stanford, Margaret Elaine 686
Stanford, Mark Peter 2899
Stanford, Matthew Bethell 1606
Stanford, Miles Richard 2566
Stanford, Olivia 2566
Stanford, Paul Hudson 454
Stangos, Alice Cristabel Ann 1112
Stangos, Ariadne 1112
Stangos, Asteris 1112
Stangos, Stavros 1112
Stanhope, Anita 1320
Stanhope, Aubrey Charles 1321
Stanhope, Ben 1320
Stanhope, Bonnie 1321
Stanhope, Charles Henry Leicester 1320
Stanhope, Christian 1321
Stanhope, Jean 1321
Stanhope, Jennifer 1321
Stanhope, John Seymour 1320
Stanhope, Jonathan 1321
Stanhope, Justin 1321
Stanhope, Leicester 1321
Stanhope, Leicester de Maclot 1321
Stanhope, Margot 1321
Stanhope, Maureen Elizabeth 1320
Stanhope, Muriel Grace 1321
Stanhope, Nina 1321
Stanhope, Noel 1321
Stanhope, Philip 1321
Stanhope, Priscilla 1321
Stanhope, Priscilla Margaret 1320
Stanhope, Russell Charles 1321
Stanhope, Sean 1321
Stanhope, Steven Francis Lincoln 1320
Stanhope, Tara 1320
Stanhope, Trina Maria 1320
Stanhope, William Henry Leicester 1320
Stanhope-White, J P 766
Stanhope-White, Katrina Jane 766
Stanier, Alexander James Sinnott 2690
Stanier, Dorothy 2690
Stanier, Henrietta Claire 2690
Stanier, Kathleen Gertrude Isobel 2690
Stanier, Philippa Mary 2690
Stanier, Sylvia Mary Finola 2690
Stanier, (Violet) Shelagh 2690
Staniland, Anna Patricia 1244
Staniland, Christopher John 1244
Staniland, Magdalene Cecilia 1244
Stanley, Adam 818
Stanley, Aidan 820
Stanley, (Aileen) Fortune Constance Hugh 819
Stanley, Alice 2040
Stanley, Andrew Mark 819
Stanley, Anita Jane 818
Stanley, Ann Jane 819
Stanley, Arabella Anne 2692
Stanley, Arthur Patrick 818
Stanley, Augusta 817
Stanley, Bernadette 819
Stanley, Beverley Ann 2691
Stanley, Carla Mary Angela 2691
Stanley, Caroline Emma 358, 815
Stanley, Catherine Anne Sheehan 818
Stanley, Charles Douglas Llewelyn 818
Stanley, Charles Ernest 2691
Stanley, Charles John Geoffrey 818
Stanley, Charles Orr Nicholas 1265
Stanley, Christopher Geoffrey Awdry 818
Stanley, Christopher John 818
Stanley, Clare Alexandra 819
Stanley, Clementine Masha 2692
Stanley, Daniel 819
Stanley, David Andrew 819
Stanley, David Patrick 819
Stanley, Deborah Rebecca 819
Stanley, Dominique 818
Stanley, Edward Murray 2040
Stanley, Edward Richard William 358
Stanley, Elinor Katherine Eve 52
Stanley, Eric William 818
Stanley, Fiona Anne 819
Stanley, Frances Ann (Fanny) 674, 1265
Stanley, Frances Caroline Burke 819, 1049
Stanley, Geoffrey Hugh Desmond 818
Stanley, George Edward 1125
Stanley, Georgina Mary Victoria 2692
Stanley, Grizel Sophie 819
Stanley, Harry John 2691
Stanley, Henrietta Mary Rose 815
Stanley, Henry Ferdinand 819
Stanley, Hermione Helena Rose 2691
Stanley, Hugh Richard Timothy 2692
Stanley, Imogen Alexandra Ruth 2691
Stanley, Isaac Martin 52
Stanley, Isabella 674
Stanley, Isabella Kate 2692
Stanley, Isobel Beauvais 818
Stanley, Jack William Oliver 820
Stanley, James Edward 1125
Stanley, Jane Barrett 2691
Stanley, Janet Elizabeth 2040
Stanley, Jessie Ernestine 818
Stanley, John Alexander 817
Stanley, John Michael 820
Stanley, John Orr 1265
Stanley, Joshua John 674
Stanley, Joy 818
Stanley, Julia Margaret 52
Stanley, Julian Alexander 52
Stanley, Katherine 818
Stanley, Kenneth William 2040
Stanley, Leslie Hugh 818
Stanley, Lorraine Elizabeth 2706
Stanley, Louisa Charlotte Ann 819
Stanley, Louise Melanie 1125
Stanley, Madeline Leah 52
Stanley, Margaret Jane 819
Stanley, Maria Elizabeth Jane 2691
Stanley, Marjorie 819
Stanley, Marjorie Laura Awdry 818
Stanley, Marjorie Mary 818
Stanley, Martin David Anthony 1265
Stanley, Martin John Llewelyn 818
Stanley, Martin Thomas Oliver 2692
Stanley, Mary 819
Stanley, Max Wilfred Southwell 818
Stanley, Maxine 818
Stanley, Mia 818
Stanley, Naomi Isabel 820
Stanley, Neil Raymond 2706
Stanley, Nicholas Charles 820
Stanley, Nicola Avory 819
Stanley, Nicole 819
Stanley, Norman Edward 818
Stanley, Oliver George 2692
Stanley, Oliver Hugh 819, 2692
Stanley, Olivia Marie 2691
Stanley, Peter Henry Arthur 819
Stanley, Peter Hugh Charles 819, 1049
Stanley, Peter Vivian 817
Stanley, Philip Thomas 1265
Stanley, Philippa Alison Beauvais 818
Stanley, Phoebe Elizabeth Mary 818
Stanley, Phyllida Mary Katherine 2692
Stanley, Phyllis 2040
Stanley, (Portia Ruth) Isobel 819
Stanley, Richard Hugh Edward 819
Stanley, Richard Morgan Oliver 2692
Stanley, Richard Oliver 2691
Stanley, Robin James Axel 819
Stanley, Ruth Mary Frances 818
Stanley, Sabrina Laura 2692
Stanley, Sally Ann 818
Stanley, Sally Avory 819
Stanley, Sarah Louise Gilroy 820
Stanley, Shaun Richard 674, 1265
Stanley, Shirim 2691
Stanley, Sophie Elizabeth 2692
Stanley, Stephen Patrick 818
Stanley, Susan 817
Stanley, Susannah Rose 2692
Stanley, Tessa 818
Stanley, Theo Peter 674
Stanley, Thomas Charles Edward 817
Stanley, Thomas Edward Christopher 818
Stanley, Thomas Michael Henry 820
Stanley, Venetia Jane 2691
Stanley, Violet Claire 818
Stanley, William Douglas 819
Stannard, Charles John William 1558
Stansfeld, Edward John Buxton 934
Stansfeld, John Raoul Wilmot 456, 934
Stansfeld, Martin Raymond Eardley 934
Stansfeld, Monica Ann Joseph 934
Stansfeld, Nicholas Desmond Morse 934
Stansfeld, Robert George Wilmot 934
Stansfeld, Rosalinde Rachel 456, 934
Stansfeld-Huelin, Alicia Antoinette 2453
Stansfeld-Huelin, Caroline Rose 2453
Stansfeld-Huelin, James Peter 2453
Stansfeld-Huelin, Rosanna Arlette 2453
Stansfield, Katharine Elizabeth 934
Stansfield, Mary Katharine Margaret 934
Stanton, Catharine Mary 1451
Stanton, Clare Marguerite 2107
Stanton, David John Nelson 1451
Stanton, Elizabeth Anne 1179
Stanton, Juliet Rose 1451
Stanton, Max George John 2107
Stanton, Richard 2107
Stanton, Rosemary Eleanor 1451
Stanworth, Kevin 291
Stanworth, Kirstie 291
Stanworth, Rebecca Joan 291
Stanworth, Siân Ayesha 291
Staples, Alice Henrietta 2694
Staples, Dwaine Grant van Euwen 2694
Staples, Eileen Patience 2694
Staples, Flora 2694
Staples, Heather Anne 2694
Staples, Henrietta Owen 2693
Staples, Isabel 2694
Staples, Noel Leslie 2694
Staples, Pamela June 2694
Staples, Priscilla Rosamunde 236
Staples, Richard Molesworth 2694
Staples, Sheila Elizabeth 2694
Staples, Sybell(a) 2694
Staples, Wilfred 236
Stapleton, Annabel Alison 1700
Stapleton, David Eric Cramer 1700
Stapleton, Delia Felicity Mary 2099
Stapleton, Edna Lyn 2099
Stapleton, Elizabeth 2100
Stapleton, Harry Edward John 1863
Stapleton, Lara Alexandra Mary-Rose 1700
Stapleton, Margarita 2099
Stapleton, Margarita Louisa 2099
Stapleton, Miles Gregory Rowland 2099
Stapleton, Sarah Jane 2100
Stapleton, Scarlett Margaret Laura 1863
Stapleton, Thomas 2099
Stapleton, Victoria Lucy Annabel 1700
Stapleton, Zoe Yvonne 2099
Stapleton-Cotton, David Peter Dudley 50, 642
Stapleton-Cotton, James Peter George 642
Stapleton-Cotton, Oliver Dudley 642
Stapleton-Cotton, Pamela Elizabeth (Jill) 639
Stapleton-Cotton, Simon 642
Stapleton-Cotton, Susan Nomakepu 50, 642
Stapleton-Cotton, Tessa 642
Stapleton-Cotton, Thomas Robert Wellington 639
Stapleton-Cotton, Toby James 642
Starkey, Ann Pauline 2695
Starkey, Edward Thomas William 2695
Starkey, Elizabeth Victoria 2694
Starkey, Gillian Mary 2695
Starkey, Henry John 2694
Starkey, Isabella Irené Marianne 2695
Starkey, Jane Victoria 2695
Starkey, John Philip 1106
Starkey, Katharine Alexandra 2694
Starkey, Lewis Stanton 2826
Starkey, Michael William 2695
Starkey, Victoria Henrietta Fleetwood 1106, 2694
Starling, Anna Letitia Mary 1500
Starling, Jonathan Walter David 1500
Starling, Lucinda Mary Sophia 1500
Starling, Sophia Rachel Xanthe 1500
Startin, Alan M 2541
Startin, Amanda Sarah 2541
Startin, Benjamin Marcus 2541
Startin, Hamish William 2542
Startin, Matthew Guy 2541
Startin, Pollyanna 2542
Statham, Caroline Rosemary 1065
Statham, Charles Reginald 1065
Statham, Christopher Desmond 1065
Statham, Donald 1170
Statham, Henrietta 1170
Statham, Michael Heathcote Wrey 3073
Statham, Philip 1065
Staveley, Anthony Arthur Merrik 2872
Staveley, Benjamin Richard 2872
Staveley, Claire Susan Meriel 2872
Staveley, Clive Lenox 2872
Staveley, Julia Caroline 2872
Staveley, Meriel Daphne Selina 2872
Staveley, Michael Peter 2872
Staveley, Nicola Anne 3081
Staveley, Peter Minet 2872
Staveley, Richard 3081
Staveley, Thomas Anthony 2872
Staves, Andrew 2919
Staves, Corinne Elizabeth 2919
Staves, Deborah Lesley 2919
Staves, Gregory 2919
Staves, Jane 2919
Staves, Philippa Dorothy Annora 2919
Staves, Rosemary Jane 2919
Staves, William Robert Anderson 2919
Stavrianou, Andrew Steven 1238
Stavrianou, Angela Eve 1238
Stavrianou, Christopher Andrew Steven 1238
Stavrianou, Winsome Mary 1238
Stead, Denise Frances 36
Steadman, Kevin Mark 2659
Steadman, Lynette Marguerite 2659
Steadman, Rachel Marguerite 2659
Steadman, Ryan David 2659
Steane, Caroline Anne 542
Steane, Christopher John 542
Steane, Isobel Sarah 542
Steane, Sebastian James David 542
Stebbings, Archie David 1662
Stebbings, Charles David Sandys 1662
Stebbings, Deborah Helen 1662
Stebbings, Eleanor Clemency 1662
Stebbings, Frederick Mortimer Lincolne 1662
Stebbings, Romily Paris 1662
Steel, Anthea Victoria 125
Steel, Anthony Nicholas Robert 1346
Steel, Arabella Rosemary Louise 587
Steel, Christopher Charles 125
Steel, Emily Susannah Letitia 1346
Steel, Fiennes William Strang 1034
Steel, Francis Gerard 125
Steel, Frederick James Edward 586
Steel, Isabella Ann Augusta 1346
Steel, Jacqueline E 586
Steel, James Alexander Drummond 2832
Steel, James Oliver 2111
Steel, James Thomas Jordan 586
Steel, Jean Eleanor 2832
Steel, Joan Ella 1034
Steel, Judith Mary 2695
Steel, Lesley 1197
Steel, Lindsay J 586
Steel, Lucinda Evelyn 2111
Steel, Oliver George Nigel 586
Steel, Oriel Sophia Rosamund 1346
Steel, Richard Hugh Jordan 586
Steel, Rosemary Verena Edith 586
Steel, (Rupert) Oliver 2111
Steel, Sheila Martin 2695
Steel, Sophia-Rose Eileen 1346
Steel, Sophie Mary Verena 586
Steel, Tim(othy) Michael 1346
Steele, Edna Frances 313
Steele, Graham Charles 2
Steele, John Stanley 113
Steele, Penelope 313
Steele, Richard Herbert Dennis 331
Steele, Ronald George Henry 313
Steele, Rosalind Jane 331
Steele, Terry Dee Sanborn 113
Steele, Timothy Edwar 113
Steele, Todd William 113
Steen, (David) Michael Cochrane Elsworth 617, 2893
Steen, Elizabeth Margaret 617
Steen, Jane Elizabeth Norah 617
Steen, Lucy Alannah Rosemary 617
Steen, Peter Robert Denis Elsworth 617
Steen, Rosalie Frances Elsworth 617
Steen, Rosemary Florence 2893
Steengracht van Moyland, Cecily 2341
Steengracht van Moyland, Henry Jan Berrington 2341
Steengracht van Moyland, Jan Tewdyr Patrick 2341
Steengracht van Moyland, Susanna Cecily 2341
Steer, Katharine ('Kash') Denise 2167
Steer, Nigel P 2167
Steere, Gordon Ernest 2252
Steere, Mary Kathrine 2252
Steere, Patience 2252
Steggall, Andrew Quinton 1856
Steggall, Edward Dicken 1856
Steggall, Sarah Jane Judith 1856
Steiger, Ben 2359
Steiger, Dodie Elfreda Noel 2867
Steiger, Jill Vivien 2359
Steiger, Max 2359
Steiger, Robert Stephen 2867
Steiger, Stephen Henry 2867
Steiger, Todd 2359
Steinberg, Clare 1729
Steinberg, Jack 3060
Steinberg, Michael Jefferey 1729
Steinschaden-Silver, Edwin 2999
Steinschaden-Silver, Sarah Margaret 2999
Stella, Ann Mary Elizabeth 2239
Stella, Daniel John 2239
Stella, Lucy Jane 2239
Stella, Nicholas James 2239
Stella, Robert Joseph 2239
Stene, Deborah 1562
Stene, Rebecca 1562
Stenhouse, Catriona Rose 1417
Stenhouse, Elizabeth 1417
Stenhouse, Jack M W 1417
Stenhouse, Sandra Dawn 1417
Stenning, Aisha 2488
Stenning, Alexander 2488
Stenning, Alison 2488
Stenning, Caroline 2488
Stenning, Christopher John William 2488
Stenning, Clare 2488
Stenning, Cynthia Margaret 2488
Stenning, Eliana Grace 2488
Stenning, Emily 2488
Stenning, Jonathan 2488
Stenning, Nicholas Julian Seymour 2488
Stenning, Philip Dives 2488
Stenning, Rachel 2488
Stenning, Richard Neil 2488
Stenning, Ruth 2488
Stenson, Renée Gavrelle 1819
Stepehnson, Madeleine Clare 2696
Stepehnson, Nicholas 2705
Stephen, Alexandra Montgomerie 1153
Stephen, Caroline Barbara 1244
Stephen, George 1244
Stephens, Alexandra Claire 2754
Stephens, Allan David 682
Stephens, Avril Rose 1230
Stephens, Brian Alexis Fenwick 1230
Stephens, Candida Imogen Every 1012
Stephens, Cecely Isobel 1230
Stephens, Charles Frederick Byng 2754
Stephens, Christine Louise 682
Stephens, Clare 1230
Stephens, Cynthia Mary Denise 1230
Stephens, D'Arcy Mark 2728
Stephens, David Allan 682
Stephens, David Paul 2587
Stephens, Georgina Kate 2754
Stephens, Helen Anne 2754
Stephens, Henry 1498
Stephens, Hugh Offley Prideaux 1230
Stephens, Jasper Roland Every 1012
Stephens, John Angelo 2587
Stephens, Katherine Alison 2728

T

Thistlethwayte, Elisabeth Anne 2294, 2715
Thistlethwayte, Emma 2294
Thistlethwayte, Harriet Cordelia Henrietta 2108
Thistlethwayte, Katharine 2294
Thistlethwayte, Oliver Seymour 2108
Thistlethwayte, Rupert Thomas Newton 2294, 2715
Thistlethwayte, (Seymour) Thomas 2108
Thistlethwayte, Thomas Noel 2294
Thomas, Adam 727
Thomas, Alison Edith 2049
Thomas, Ann Tresina 704
Thomas, Archie Charles 3007
Thomas, Barbara Anne 1634
Thomas, Benjamin Louis 2967
Thomas, Betty 2049
Thomas, Breanda 2106
Thomas, Brendan 2811
Thomas, Brian Hedley 211
Thomas, Byron 914
Thomas, Camilla Jean Amyse 2967
Thomas, Camilla Rose 3007
Thomas, Carinne 2809
Thomas, Carol Elisabeth 211
Thomas, (Charles) Inigo Gladwyn 2811
Thomas, Christopher James 403
Thomas, Clare Dorothy 403
Thomas, Clare Jeremy 2811
Thomas, Daniel 622
Thomas, Darren Paul de Courcy Dutton 392
Thomas, David 2272
Thomas, David Bruce 2049
Thomas, David Christian Charles 2106
Thomas, David Churchill 2811
Thomas, David John Godfrey 2809
Thomas, David Nigel Mitchell 2810
Thomas, David William Penrose 2811
Thomas, Dena 737
Thomas, Diana Lesley Kathryn 2883
Thomas, Edmund Christopher 403
Thomas, Edward 1195
Thomas, Elizabeth Mary 1397
Thomas, Elizabeth Penelope Kim 2809
Thomas, Emma Louise 823
Thomas, Frances Mary 1513
Thomas, Frederick Jacob Theseus 1000
Thomas, George Francis Maitland 704
Thomas, Georgiana Elaine Lindsay 704
Thomas, Georgina Lynne 439
Thomas, Geraldine 704
Thomas, Geraldine Dawn 2809
Thomas, Grace Vera 1113
Thomas, Guy Alexander 2967
Thomas, Harold Mostyn 1397
Thomas, (Henry) Isambard Tobias 2811
Thomas, Horatia Holly 1655, 2811
Thomas, Hugo Alistair Christian 2106
Thomas, Humphrey William 2810
Thomas, Huw Basil Maynard Mitchell 2810
Thomas, Ian 737
Thomas, Inigo 1655
Thomas, Ivo James 1427
Thomas, James William Grigg 439
Thomas, Jane 2413, 2810
Thomas, Jessica Nadine 1373
Thomas, Joan Mary 704
Thomas, Joseph Achilles Caleb 1000
Thomas, Judith Morag Sophie 2106
Thomas, June Denzilla Haidee 2272
Thomas, Justin 2811
Thomas, Kathleen Ada 1397
Thomas, Laurie 1195
Thomas, Letitia Juliette 2967
Thomas, Letitia Mary 1427
Thomas, Lisa 1195
Thomas, Lisa Michelle 2103
Thomas, Lucy Stephanie 403
Thomas, Luke 622
Thomas, Lynda 2811
Thomas, Margaret Greta 2809
Thomas, Marjory 1958
Thomas, Martin Nicholas Caleb 1000
Thomas, Mary 2810
Thomas, Mary Elizabeth 914
Thomas, Michael Charles 3007
Thomas, Michael David 915
Thomas, Michael Ewart 1634
Thomas, Miranda Cecilia 3004
Thomas, Miranda Jane 1000
Thomas, Mona 2106
Thomas, Morgan Adrian Maitland 704
Thomas, Nan Kerr 2810
Thomas, Neil 2811
Thomas, Nicholas J 1427
Thomas, Nicholas John 1382
Thomas, Nicholas Michael Guy 1634
Thomas, Nicola 211
Thomas, Nigel William 737
Thomas, Oliver 622
Thomas, Oliver Robert 823
Thomas, Patricia 2809
Thomas, Patricia Dorothy 2049
Thomas, Patricia Kathleen 2103
Thomas, Penelope Anne 1634
Thomas, Penelope Jane 439
Thomas, Peter 2067
Thomas, Peter Alexander 2106
Thomas, Peter William 1513
Thomas, Philip Stephen William 1373
Thomas, Phyllis 1195
Thomas, Pippa-Jane 2809
Thomas, Rachael Elizabeth Ann 2077
Thomas, Reginald Alexander 2106
Thomas, Renaud Louis Thomas 2967
Thomas, Reuben 3007
Thomas, Rhoda Mary 3004
Thomas, Richard 914
Thomas, Richard Edward 1397
Thomas, Robert Heriot Lindsay 704
Thomas, Robert John Paul 823
Thomas, Roger Harold 1397
Thomas, Roger Philip 2103
Thomas, Rosa Virginia 439
Thomas, Rose Ann Macdonald 2106
Thomas, Rosemary Douglas 2103
Thomas, Rupert Neil Dunbar 2106
Thomas, Sharon 1195
Thomas, Shona Ann 873
Thomas, Sidney Allen 1513
Thomas, Sophie Patricia 211
Thomas, Stephen Francis 2413, 2810
Thomas, Stephen George 622
Thomas, Tamara Mary Gabriel 727
Thomas, Toby James 2810
Thomas, Ursula Nancy 1373
Thomas, Valmai 2951
Thomas, Vanessa Mary 2811
Thomas, Victoria Mary 1427, 2103
Thomas, Virginia Murray 914
Thomas, William 1373, 2106
Thomas, William David 439
Thomas, William James Christian 2106
Thomas, William Lydston 2077
Thomas, William Michael 2810
Thomas, Isabella Pandora 2811
Thomasin-Foster, Christopher William 739
Thomasin-Foster, David James 739
Thomasin-Foster, Mark Treanor 739
Thomasin-Foster, Nicholai Charles 739
Thomasin-Foster, Valerie 739
Thomasson, Alan Mayfield 2731
Thomasson, Bryony Josephine Anne 2297
Thomasson, Charles 337
Thomasson, Christopher 1641
Thomasson, Christopher Lucas 337
Thomasson, Cicely Rose 1700
Thomasson, Clare 337
Thomasson, Eugenie Hope 2755
Thomasson, Jack James 1700
Thomasson, Julia Jane 1641
Thomasson, Kristina Cynthia 337
Thomasson, Laurie Francis 1700
Thomasson, Mary Elizabeth 2297
Thomasson, Patricia 2731
Thomasson, Robert Howard 2731
Thomasson, Samuel C 1700
Thomasson, Samuel Charles 2297
Thomasson, Sarah Anne Catriona 2731
Thomasson, Simon 2755
Thomasson, Sophy 337
Thomasson, Thomas 337
Thomasson, Virginia Mary 1700
Thompson, Alexandra Louise 1818
Thompson, Amicie Mary Bernadette 2237
Thompson, Andrew Hewlett 1568
Thompson, Andrew Theodore 1554
Thompson, Angela 2924
Thompson, Ann 758
Thompson, Ann Patricia 1554
Thompson, Anna Elizabeth 2812
Thompson, Anne 900
Thompson, Anne Christabel de Vere 2814, 2871
Thompson, Anthony Gordon 1010
Thompson, Anthony Seymour 1388
Thompson, Antony 2924
Thompson, Antony James Aird 2411
Thompson, Barbara Ann 758
Thompson, Barbara Anne 1554
Thompson, Benedict 2237
Thompson, Benjamin Charles 1545
Thompson, Benjamin John 1568, 1949
Thompson, Bentley Warrick James 2863
Thompson, Blyth Metcalf 2776
Thompson, Brian Henry 1818
Thompson, Bridget Clare 991
Thompson, Bruce Glen 1366
Thompson, Carol 900
Thompson, Carol Anne 900
Thompson, Carole Gail 1366
Thompson, Caroline Elizabeth 1818
Thompson, Catharine Joan 403
Thompson, Catherine 900
Thompson, Cecilia Frances 3092
Thompson, Charles C 382
Thompson, Charles Frederick 2814
Thompson, Charles Guy Martin 1882
Thompson, Charles Neil 2755
Thompson, Christina Elizabeth 2411
Thompson, Christopher Leslie 1554
Thompson, Christopher Mark 1554
Thompson, Claudia Rose 2383
Thompson, Columb 1568
Thompson, David 2237
Thompson, David Gordon 758
Thompson, David Harvey 722
Thompson, David Jonathan 2814
Thompson, David Paul Charles 2814
Thompson, David Robin Bibby 271
Thompson, Dawn 2383
Thompson, Dendy Martin Blyth 2776
Thompson, Donna Caron 1366
Thompson, Edward Martin Amphlett 1438
Thompson, Eleanor 1568
Thompson, Eleanor Clare Rucker 1949
Thompson, Eliot George 115
Thompson, Elisabeth Joy Fausitt 1568
Thompson, Elizabeth Angela Matilda 1882
Thompson, Elizabeth Frances 2411
Thompson, Elizabeth Joy 1010
Thompson, Emlyn Anna 1174
Thompson, Emma Joan 403
Thompson, Emma Louise 2814
Thompson, Emma Nancy 382
Thompson, Farleigh Taylor 1010
Thompson, Fiona Kate 1818
Thompson, Frances Margaret 991
Thompson, Francis Jonathan Longstreth 1995
Thompson, Gareth John Hunt 2416
Thompson, Geoffrey Hewlett 1568
Thompson, Georgina Helen Forbes 1078
Thompson, Glendyn Stephen Delamere 1366
Thompson, Grace Marian 213
Thompson, Grant Peter 2863
Thompson, Gwendolyn Patricia 722
Thompson, Hannah Yvonne 2776
Thompson, Harvey 722
Thompson, Helen Mary 1078
Thompson, Henry Swift 403
Thompson, Henry William Peter 85
Thompson, Hermione 1568
Thompson, Hermione Elizabeth Rucker 1949
Thompson, Howard Luke 85
Thompson, Humphrey 1568
Thompson, Humphrey John Rucker 1949
Thompson, Ian Forbes 1078
Thompson, Ian James Aird 2411
Thompson, Ivor 900
Thompson, Jack 1545
Thompson, Jack Peter 556
Thompson, James Angus Wilfred 321
Thompson, James Borthwick 321
Thompson, James Courtney 2755
Thompson, James Currie 321
Thompson, James Edwin Jerome 403
Thompson, James Harman 556
Thompson, James Marcus Crichton 991
Thompson, Jane Forbes 1078
Thompson, Jane Frances 2997
Thompson, Jean Pamela 1366
Thompson, Jennifer Ann 758
Thompson, Jennifer Anne Frances 2997
Thompson, Jeremy 1388
Thompson, Jessica 2237
Thompson, Joan 1388
Thompson, Joanna Janet Henrietta 403
Thompson, Joanna Mary 2755
Thompson, John 1174
Thompson, John Buckner 2383
Thompson, John Kenneth Glynne 2997
Thompson, Jonathan Michael Adrian 1554
Thompson, Joseph Andrew 2237
Thompson, Judith Mary 2813
Thompson, Julia Vanessa 2776
Thompson, Justin Joseph 1010
Thompson, Karena Melanie 2814
Thompson, Katharine (Kate) Jane 1545
Thompson, Katharine Sarah Tahlita 1308
Thompson, Keith 1545
Thompson, Kelly Charlton 1010
Thompson, Kenneth 900
Thompson, Kenneth Ross 2997
Thompson, Kenneth Taylor 213
Thompson, Lee Cameron 115
Thompson, Leonie Helen 1174
Thompson, Lucia 1568
Thompson, Lucy Jane 115
Thompson, Lucy Mary 1545
Thompson, Mack Ramsey 1010
Thompson, Mara Angela Matilda 1882
Thompson, Martin Thompson 1882
Thompson, Mary Jane 1438
Thompson, Mary Jessamine 115
Thompson, Matthew Harry William 3092
Thompson, Maureen Angela 321
Thompson, Michael Arthur George 1010
Thompson, Michael Thomas Redmayne 2383
Thompson, Millicent Francklyn 1598
Thompson, Miranda Jane 2416
Thompson, Monica Rambie 1010
Thompson, Moya Ann 2776
Thompson, Nancy Jane 1949
Thompson, Nancy-Jane 1568
Thompson, Neville 1366
Thompson, Nicholas Annesley Marler 2814
Thompson, Nicholas Austen 1388
Thompson, Nicola Robyn 2814
Thompson, Pamela 1078
Thompson, Patricia 1568
Thompson, Patrick Dowling 2383
Thompson, Patrick Lloyd Ker 991
Thompson, Paul David 85
Thompson, Paul Gregory 722
Thompson, Paul John 3092
Thompson, Pauline Dorothy 2814
Thompson, Peile Richard 2812
Thompson, Philip 2755
Thompson, Rachel Rebecca 115
Thompson, Richard Hilton Marler 2871
Thompson, Richard Kenneth Spencer 2814
Thompson, Robert Hugh 213
Thompson, Rosanna Patricia Mar 556
Thompson, Rosemary Claire 1438
Thompson, Sally Ann 758
Thompson, Sally Penelope 1438
Thompson, Sarah Ann 1438
Thompson, Sarah Catherine Elizabeth 2812
Thompson, Sarah Elizabeth 85
Thompson, Sarah Jane 271
Thompson, Shay Jean 1366
Thompson, Siana Camilla Elizabeth 1882
Thompson, Simon Patrick 1174
Thompson, Simon William 2814
Thompson, Sonya Suzanne 2776
Thompson, Stephen Peter 1438
Thompson, Susan Jane 2997
Thompson, Tanya Hilda 321
Thompson, Terence Dudley 1078
Thompson, Thomas D'Eyncourt John 2812
Thompson, Timothy John 2383
Thompson, Toby 2237
Thompson, Vanessa Eirene 2776
Thompson, Venetia Catherine 1995, 2814
Thompson, (Victoria) Mary Nevill 556
Thompson, Walter 900
Thompson, William Bethel 1598
Thompson, William James Richard 556
Thompson, William Rowland Blyth 2776
Thompson, Yvonne Irene Valerie 1818
Thompson-Butler-Lloyd, Mervyn 900
Thompson-Royds, Anne 2813
Thompson-Royds, Anne Penelope 2914
Thompson-Royds, Christopher 2813
Thompson-Royds, Gilbert 2577, 2813
Thompson-Royds, Katherine Louise 2813
Thompson-Royds, Laura Yolanda 2813
Thompson-Royds, Mark Christopher 2813
Thompson-Royds, Matthew 2813
Thompson-Royds, Susan Damaris 2813
Thompson-Royds, Timothy Christopher 2813, 2914
Thompson-Royds, Vanessa Maxine 2577, 2813
Thompson-Royds, Yolande Anne 2813
Thomson, Adam 1949
Thomson, Albert Mark Home 2815
Thomson, Alexa Catherine Home 2816
Thomson, Alexander Rory 465
Thomson, Alice Clara Margaret 1950
Thomson, Alison Monica 975
Thomson, Alix Rebecca 975
Thomson, Allan Priestley 2776
Thomson, Amy 294
Thomson, Andrew Brodie 2776
Thomson, Andrew John 975
Thomson, Andrew William Pollard 418
Thomson, Andrew Wilson 2671
Thomson, Anna Kathryn 2383
Thomson, Anna Marie 975
Thomson, Anna-Karina 465
Thomson, Anne 975
Thomson, Anthony Grant 1201
Thomson, Brenda Lynne 2816
Thomson, Bronwen Olivia 2547
Thomson, Camilla Rachel 975
Thomson, Carey Bruce 2816
Thomson, Carl Norman 2816
Thomson, Caroline Georgina 418
Thomson, Caroline Louise 2569
Thomson, Caroline Mary 2861
Thomson, Cecilia Bernadette 2815
Thomson, Charles David 2815
Thomson, Christopher Michael David 2815
Thomson, Christopher William Grant 1201
Thomson, Craig Ross 2816
Thomson, Daisy Jacqueline Carol 2815
Thomson, David 2519
Thomson, David Kenneth Roy 2816
Thomson, Dawn Marlene 2816
Thomson, Douglas Charles 2815
Thomson, Edward William 1949
Thomson, Eileen 1944
Thomson, Elizabeth Ann 294
Thomson, Evelyn Margaret Isabel (Bettina) 2815
Thomson, Gary Andrew 465
Thomson, Geoffrey Charles Byars 2610
Thomson, George Jolyon Hay 2861
Thomson, George Michael Mackinnon 2861
Thomson, Gerard Anthony 1201
Thomson, Gloria Alicia 2816
Thomson, Grace 2817
Thomson, Gregory Bruce 2816
Thomson, Hamish Andrew Buchan 418
Thomson, Harriet 1600
Thomson, Helen Joanna 2569
Thomson, Herbert Garrett 2816
Thomson, Hugh Lloyd 1950
Thomson, Iain James Speir 2569
Thomson, Ian 2902
Thomson, Ian Charles 1944
Thomson, Ian Clarence James 1411
Thomson, Ian Napier 1600
Thomson, Ian W 294
Thomson, Jack 2519
Thomson, Jacqueline Rosemary Margot 2376
Thomson, Jake Michael Alfred 2815
Thomson, James M D 2547
Thomson, Jane Myfanwy Mary 2902
Thomson, John 975
Thomson, John Elliot 1944
Thomson, Julia Margaret Clare 2815
Thomson, Julie Lynn 2816
Thomson, Karen Lynne 2816
Thomson, (Katharine) Margaret 294
Thomson, Katherine Claire 2547
Thomson, Kathleen Mary Prudence 2776
Thomson, Kathryn Helen 1487
Thomson, Keith Home 2816
Thomson, Lesley Lynne 2816
Thomson, Lorraine Gail 2816
Thomson, Lucinda Elisabeth 913
Thomson, Luke Ivo Charles 2815

U

Ulyate, Margaret Mary Anne 322
Ulyate, Raymond Grant 322
Ulyate, Shelley Diana 322
Ulyate, Stanley Robert Borwick 322
Ulyate, William Robert 322
Umney, Lydia Elisabeth Constantine 637
Umney, Michael David 637
Umney, Nicholas David 637
Underhill, (Moira) Isobel 1080
Underhill, Monica Anne 687
Underhill, Richard Walter 201
Underhill, William 1080
Underwood, Adrian Michael Campbell 203
Underwood, Alan Robert 153
Underwood, Ann Margot 2598
Underwood, Charles Edward Thomas 203
Underwood, Cherry 1258
Underwood, Denise 2858
Underwood, Fiona 153
Underwood, Harry Charles Gordon 2858
Underwood, James Michael Campbell 1034
Underwood, Janet 2858
Underwood, Jennifer Elizabeth 1259
Underwood, Joanne Lesley 1258
Underwood, John 2598
Underwood, John Benjamin Lionel 1258
Underwood, John Jeremy Campbell 1034
Underwood, Julie 153
Underwood, Katherine Anne 203
Underwood, Louis Hamilton 1258
Underwood, Margaret Susan 153
Underwood, Michael John Benjamin 1258
Underwood, Oliver Francis 1258
Underwood, Philip Lionel 2858
Underwood, Serena Henrietta 203
Underwood, Toby George Campbell 1034
Underwood, Victoria Angela 1034
Ungerman, Judith 266
Ungerman, Kenneth Armistead 266
Ungoed-Thomas, David Stephen Jerome 2179
Ungoed-Thomas, Harry Owen Nathaniel 2179
Ungoed-Thomas, Jasper R 2179
Ungoed-Thomas, Michael Fergus Jonathan 2179
Uniacke, Casper John 3031
Uniacke, Robie Jonjo 503
Unsworth, Amy Ruth 2430
Unsworth, Jodi Ann 2430
Unsworth, Joseph George 2430
Unsworth, Joseph Jonathan 2430
Unsworth, Mia Dawn 2430
Unsworth, Valerie Judith 2430
Unwin, Abrahm Arthur George 1635
Unwin, Arabella Helen Mary 1635
Unwin, Barry James 3055
Unwin, Carol John 3055
Unwin, Elizabeth Laura Dorothea 3055
Unwin, Guy Darell 3055
Unwin, Louise Rose 3055
Unwin, Patricia Ann 3055
Unwin, Patricia Rose 3055
Unwin, Phoebe Grace 3055
Unwin, Rosanna Helen 3055
Unwin, Rupert W H 1635
Unwin, Sally Victoria 3055
Unwin, Susan Louise 3055
Unwin, William Francis 3055
Unwin-Heathcote, Jane 1390
Unwin-Heathcote, Michael Arthur 1390
Upjohn, Marjorie Dorothy Bertha 1778
Upstone, Brenda Carey 748
Upstone, Malcolm Cecil 748
Upton, Jason Boaz 914
Upton, Maxwell Kevin 914
Upton, Natasha Ruby Marie 914
Upton, Wendy Lorraine 914
Urquhart, Alexander 1654
Urquhart, Annabel Harriet 1654
Urquhart, Anne Serena 1241
Urquhart, Duncan 1951
Urquhart, Elizabeth Anne 2549
Urquhart, Elizabeth Raphael 1951
Urquhart, Flora 1241
Urquhart, James 1241
Urquhart, Joanna 1951
Urquhart, Katherine 1241
Urquhart, Lorna Mary 1951
Urquhart, Mark Alexander 1951
Urquhart, Peter William Urquhart 1241
Urquhart, Roger David 1951
Urquhart, Serena 1241
Urwick, Beatrice Helen 1782
Urwick, Lyndall Fownes 1782
Usborne, Alice 2840
Usborne, Andrew Thornton 2840
Usborne, Anne Margaret Thornton 2840
Usborne, Diana 2840
Usborne, Eleanor Victoria Thornton 2840
Usborne, Harriet Georgina 2840
Usborne, Henrietta E M 2840
Usborne, Joanna Susan 2840
Usborne, John Edward 2840
Usborne, John Humphrey 2840
Usborne, Lamorna 2840
Usborne, Richard Thomas 2840
Usborne, Sarah Margaret 2840
Usborne, Thomas Masters 2840
Usher, Andrew John 2868
Usher, Callum 2868
Usher, Caroline Rosemary 2868
Usher, Charlotte Louise Alexandra 2868
Usher, Diana Katherine 2868
Usher, Dorothy Margaret 2868
Usher, Francis John 2868
Usher, Georgina Elizabeth 2868
Usher, Gillian Anne 2869
Usher, James Neil 2868
Usher, Katharine 2868
Usher, Katherine Anne 2869
Usher, Merilyn 2868
Usher, Michael William Reginald 2868
Usher, Peter James 2868
Usher, Randall Terrence 195
Usher, Richard William 2869
Usher, Rory James Andrew 2868
Usher, Rosanne Helen 2868
Usher, Rosemary Margaret 1456
Usher, Simon Francis 2868
Usher, Stuart Alexander 2869
Usher, Sylvia Marie Heather 2300
Usher, Valentine 2869
Usher, Valerie Clare 2300
Usherwood, Constance Hazel Kate 265
Usherwood, Henrietta Clare Elisabeth 265
Usherwood, Theodore Patrick John 265
Usill, David 2705
Usill, Judith Patricia 2705
Ussher, Patricia Somers 2660
Ussher, Simon Walter 2660
Ussher, Walter Percival 2660
Uttley, Alathea St John 2521
Uttley, Katherine Barbara 2521

V

Vacher, Michael 456
Vacher, Rosemary Anne 456
Vacquer, Judith Imogen 2961
Vacquer, Miguel de Serra 2961
Vajda, Frieda Dora Katherine Mary Josephine 1057
Vajda, Hans 1057
Vakharia, Comie 2233
Vakharia, Rustom F 2233
Valdambrini, Julia Louise 1544
Valdambrini, Richard Warren 1544
Valdambrini, Robert 1544
Valdambrini, Virginia 1544
Vale, Cyrilla Mary 242
Valentine, Annabel Lee Christine 2382
Valentine, Clare Rosemary 2382
Valentine, Debra Ellen 107
Valentine, E Massie 3044
Valentine, Francis Anthony Brinsley (James) 1629, 2965
Valentine, Hamish Guy 107
Valentine, Janet Sibella 2965
Valentine, Malcolm 2382
Valentine, Ranald Andrew 107
Valentine, Richard William 2382
Valentine, Robert Harris 2965
Valentine, Sheila Veronica Mary 2418
Valentine, Sibella Margaret 2965
Valentine, Virginia 3044
Valentine, (William) Danvers Oliphant 1629
Vallé, Elin Maria 2167
Vallé, Robert 2167
Vallance, Natasha A'Deane 2827
Vallat, Francis 1384
Valles, Fernanda 1187
Valttila, Barry Eric Antti 2105
Valttila, Christopher Tony 2105
Valttila, Daphne Margaret 2105
Valttila, Elina Carita 2105
Valttila, Emmanita Aleksandra 2105
Valttila, Eric Antti 2105
Valttila, Esa Christian 2105
Valttila, Gaye Helen 2105
Valttila, Jane Linda 2105
Valttila, Mirja Karina 2105
van Bastalaer, Carol Arthemise 1439
van Bastalaer, Sebastian 1439
van Bastalaer, Sophie 1439
van Bastalaer, Thierry 1439
Van Biervliet d'Overbroek, Emmie April Jessica 1699
Van Biervliet d'Overbroek, Jane 1699
Van Biervliet d'Overbroek, Malcolm 1699
Van Biervliet d'Overbroek, Oliver Robin 1699
van Blokland, Carola 1367
van Blokland, Jonkheer Alexander Gerard Beelaerts 1367
van Cortlandt Bailey, Herbert 1562
van Cortlandt Bailey, Kirsteen Susan 1562
van Cutsem, Edward Bernard Charles 2109
van Cutsem, Geoffrey Neil 2109
van Cutsem, Hugh Bernard Edward 2109
van Cutsem, Hugh Ralph 2109
van Cutsem, Jonkvrouwe Emilie 2109
van Cutsem, Nicholas Peter Geoffrey 2109
van Cutsem, Sally 2109
van Cutsem, Sophie 2109
van Cutsem, William Henry 2109
van Cutsem, Zara 2109
van de Kasteele, Mary Elizabeth 1787
van de Pol, Alexander 2368
van de Pol, Elizabeth Gay 2368
Van den Bergh, Ann Neale 362
van den Bogaerde, Alice Rosemary Patience Lucilla 849
van den Bogaerde, Gareth Ulric 849
van den Bogaerde, Jake 2804
van den Bogaerde, Jasmine 2804
van den Bogaerde, Lucilla Rose 849
van den Bogaerde, Rupert 2804
van den Bogaerde, Sophie Patricia 2804
van den Bogaerde, Ulric Michael Amadeus Landrover 849
van der Gucht, Benjamin Michael 2793
van der Gucht, Charles Graham 2793
van der Gucht, Guy Tristram 2740
van der Gucht, Henry Benjamin 2740
van der Gucht, Hugo Charles 2740
van der Gucht, (Juliet) Clare 2740
van der Gucht, Michael 2793
van der Gucht, Nicola Helen 2793
van der Gucht, Pamela Sabina 2740
van der Gucht, Sarah Celia 2793
van der Gucht, Victoria Anthea 2793
Van der Horst, Belinda Jane 1634
Van der Horst, Richard 1634
van der Merwe, Andries Johannes Stephanus 1385
van der Merwe, Marina 1367
van der Merwe, Maureen Cathrine 1367
van der Merwe, Megan Elizabeth 1385
van der Merwe, Pamela Jo 1385
van der Merwe, Petrus 1367
van der Merwe, Petrus Jacobus Alwyn 1367
van der Merwe, Randolph 1367
van der Merwe, Sheila Mary 1385
van der Merwe, Stephanie Ann 1385
van der Post, Ingaret Stella 1273
van der Schrieck, Marjorie Helen 94
van der Walt, Sarah Barbara 500
Van Der Walt, Susan Frances 1952
van der Woude, David Anthony 507
van der Woude, Esme Mary Gabriel 727, 2455
van der Woude, Michael Gerrit 507
van der Woude, Penelope Catherine Mary 507
van der Woude, (Reinier) Gerrit Anton 507, 2455
van der Wyck Bentinck, Brydgytte Blanche 2289
van der Zee, Evert 117
van der Zee, Julia 117
van der Zee, Matthew James 117
Van der Wyck, Douglas Roderick Arthur Duncan 2289
Van der Wyck, Evert Rein Robert Henry Van Der Walt, J J 1952
van Dongen, John Aubrey 1577
van Dongen, Lorraine Rosemary 1577
van Dongen, Robert Albert 1577
van Doorn, Agnès Madeleine Adélaide 2379
van Doorn, Antonius 2379
Van Emmenis, D 3015
Van Emmenis, Richardyne Megan 3015
van Fedyk, Christophe James 2928
van Fedyk, Ingrid 2928
van Gelder, Jacqueline 1165
van Gelder, Pamela Vivian 1165
van Gelder, Robert Herbert Smidt 1165
van Haersma Buma, Christiaan 2380
van Haersma Buma, Michiel 2380
van Haersma Buma, Robert 2380
van Haersma Buma, Roelina Gijsberta Gerardina 2380
van Harrenveld, Diederik Godard Adriaan Roelant 2289
van Harrenveld, H W 2289
van Harrenveld, Hugo Johannes Hendrik 2289
van Harrenveld, Reina Jeanne 2289
van Harrenveld, Wendela Blanche Catherine 2289
van Helden, Caroline 2400
van Helden, Hubert 2400
van Helden, Judith 2400
van Helden, Nichola 2400
van Helden, Vincent 2400
Van Houtte de la Chaise, Alexandra Constance Marie 1700
Van Houtte de la Chaise, Bertrand Maurice 1700
Van Houtte de la Chaise, Charlotte Jessica Louise 1700
Van Houtte de la Chaise, Edward Henri Cramer 1700
van Hove, Erik 2910
van Hove, Hannah Jean 2910
van Hove, Laura Iris 2910
van Hove, Rebecca Claire 2910
van Hove, Sarah Margaret 2910
van Koetsveld, Antony Guy Hans 1130
van Koetsveld, Christopher Dirk 1130
van Koetsveld, Margaret Ross 1130
van Koetsveld, Michael William 1130
van Koetsveld, Ralph Emilius Quintus 1130
van Laun, Emma 1824
van Laun, Samuel James 1824
van Laun, Susan Penelope Dora 1824
van Laun, Timothy Denzil 1824
van Laun, William 1824
van Lelyveld, Darren Richard 649
van Lelyveld, Jacobus Petrus 649
van Lelyveld, Sherryl Lyn 649
van Lelyveld, Susan Mary 649
van Lelyveld, Tracy Lee 649
Van Lieshout, David Thomas 86
Van Lieshout, Edward Henry 86
Van Lieshout, Robert 86
Van Lieshout, Sarah Elizabeth 86
Van Liew, Dennis John 2705
Van Liew, Elizabeth Patricia 2705
Van Liew, Lucy Janetta 2705
van Lynden, Anne 1367
van Lynden, Crel Diederic Aernout 1367
van Lynden, Diederic Wolter 1367
van Lynden, Jan Willem Alexander 1367
Van Oss, Anthony Tom Francis 218
Van Oss, Caroline Elizabeth 218
Van Oss, Celia Catherine 2374
Van Oss, Emily Atalanta 218
Van Oss, Francesca Camilla 218
Van Oss, Katharine Susanna 218
Van Oss, Mark Peter Anthony 218
Van Oss, Octavia Rose 218
Van Oss, Phoebe Herbert 2374
Van Oss, Richard Mark 2374
Van Oss, Thomas Richard 2374
van Raalte, Charles Henry 1557
van Raalte, Ghislaine Sara 1557
van Raalte, Kristina Beryl 1557
van Raalte, Marcus Lionel 1557
van Raalte, Mary Anne 1557
van Rensburg, Alida Jacoba 1366
van Rensburg, Anne Elizabeath 1366
van Rensburg, Emma Ida May 1366
van Rensburg, Jacobus Hendrikus 1366
van Rensburg, Jacobus Wessel 1366
van Rensburg, Jacobus Wessel Janse 1366
van Rensburg, Johanna Maria 1366
van Rensburg, Kathleen Mary 1366
van Rensburg, Luther Calvyn 1366
van Rensburg, Martin Luther 1366
van Rensburg, Martin Luther Janse 1366
van Schoor, Thora 1367
van Schoor, Willian Herbert 1367
van t'Hoff, Graham Robert 654
van t'Hoff, Hugh Colin 654
van t'Hoff, Rosemary Anne 654
van t'Hoff, Walter 654
van t'Hoff, William Gordon 654
van Tienen, Caroline Eleanor Kathleen 1818
van Tienen, Elizabet 1818
van Tienen, Emma 1818
van Tienen, Richard Mark 1818
van Tienen, Robbert Rudolf 1818
van Till, Caroline Anne 656
van Till, Lambert Frederick Casijn 656
Van Valkenburg, John 1937
Van Valkenburg, Josephine Helen 1937
van Veenen, Erica Maegan 593
van Veenen, Florence Nancy Thackeray 593
van Veenen, Hendrick Hubert Clayton 593
van Veenen, Vanessa 593
Van Wijngaarden, Louisa Carmen 1104
van Wyk, Wendy 1839
van Wyk, Werner Nicholas 1839
van Zuylen, Charles Tobias Edward 1848
van Zuylen, Edmond Marc Dominic 1848
Vance, Charles Ivan 2029
Vance, Imogen Anne Ierne 2029
Vance, Jacqueline Belinda Ierne 2029
Vanden-Bempdé-Johnstone, Cressida E 822
Vanden-Bempdé-Johnstone, Elsa Ann Zillah 823
Vanden-Bempdé-Johnstone, Eltis 823
Vanden-Bempdé-Johnstone, Frances Elizabeth 824
Vanden-Bempdé-Johnstone, Francis Patrick Harcourt 822
Vanden-Bempdé-Johnstone, Isabelle Catherine Sophie 822
Vanden-Bempdé-Johnstone, John Louis 823
Vanden-Bempdé-Johnstone, Louise Dorothy Ann 823
Vanden-Bempdé-Johnstone, Marie-Louise Henriette 824
Vanden-Bempdé-Johnstone, Nicholas Gilbert 824
Vanden-Bempdé-Johnstone, Robin Louise 823
Vanden-Bempdé-Johnstone, Sybille Marie Louise Marcelle 822
Vanden-Bempdé-Johnstone, Virginia Susan 823
Vandernoot, Barbara Mary 733
Vanderstegen-Drake, Carolyn Mary 2020
Vanderstegen-Drake, Charlotte Susannah 2020
Vanderstegen-Drake, John Peter 2020
Vanderstegen-Drake, John William 2020
Vanderstegen-Drake, Mark Stamford 2020
Vanderstegen-Drake, Stamford Robert Francis 2020

Vernon, Andrew Robert Richard 1792
Vernon, Andrew William 2890
Vernon, Annabel Elizabeth 2547
Vernon, Anne Cecilia 2889
Vernon, Benedicta Lucia 1451
Vernon, Beryl Eileen 2890
Vernon, Bryan Tom Jackson 2889
Vernon, Catherine Victoria 1792
Vernon, Charles Harry 2889
Vernon, Christopher Richard 1792
Vernon, Colin Ronald 1791
Vernon, Daniel Grant James 1791
Vernon, David Grierson 2889
Vernon, David Stewart Lyveden 1792
Vernon, Davina Elizabeth 2292, 2889
Vernon, Deborah Florence 2890
Vernon, Eliot Antony Stewart 2889
Vernon, Elizabeth 1326
Vernon, Elizabeth Jean 1326
Vernon, Elspeth Mary 2889
Vernon, Emma Mary 1326, 1792, 2542
Vernon, (Fiona) Dawn Cory 665, 1792
Vernon, Francesca 1792
Vernon, George Thornycroft 2889
Vernon, George William Howard 2889
Vernon, Georgina Amy 1792
Vernon, Grant 1791
Vernon, Greville Edward 665
Vernon, Greville Edward Mervyn 1792
Vernon, Greville Richard Eustace 1792
Vernon, Guy Alexander Howard 2889
Vernon, Hannah Emily 2889
Vernon, Harriet Laura 2058, 2890
Vernon, Harriet Lucy 2889
Vernon, Hilda Alice 2890
Vernon, Hugh Gowran 1792
Vernon, (Hugh) Richard Mervyn 1155, 1792
Vernon, Isobel Jennifer 1792
Vernon, Jack Leslie 1791
Vernon, James Fitzpatrick Greville 1792
Vernon, James John 1326
Vernon, James Loudon 2889
Vernon, James Michael 1326
Vernon, James Richard Alexander 2889
Vernon, James William 2292, 2889
Vernon, Jessica Rosheen 2890
Vernon, John Humphrey 2890
Vernon, Karen Marie 1791
Vernon, Karen Teresa Margaret 1791
Vernon, Kate Elizabeth 1326
Vernon, Kathryn 1791
Vernon, Louise Smith 1791
Vernon, Lucy Nicola 2889
Vernon, Lynette June 1791
Vernon, Margaret Ellen 2889
Vernon, Mark Thornycroft 2058, 2890
Vernon, Melissa Anne 2889
Vernon, Meredith Caroline 1792
Vernon, Mhairi Patricia 1326
Vernon, Michael R S 2547
Vernon, Mitchell Robert Allan 1791
Vernon, Nancy Grace 1792
Vernon, Nicola Jane 2890
Vernon, Pamela Violet 1241, 2889
Vernon, Patricia Jean 1326
Vernon, Patricia May 2889
Vernon, Peter John 1326
Vernon, Philippa Carolyn Nicol 1326
Vernon, Phoebe Rose 2890
Vernon, Queenie Constance 1791
Vernon, Rebecca Isobel 1792
Vernon, Richard Bagnall 2890
Vernon, Richard Wallace 1241, 2889
Vernon, Robert Andrew 1792
Vernon, Robert Courtenay John 1792
Vernon, Robert Howard 1791
Vernon, Rosemary Nicola 2889
Vernon, Rossanna 2889
Vernon, Russell Sydney 1791
Vernon, Sally June 2884
Vernon, Sarah Benedicta 1451
Vernon, Sasha Elizabeth 1792
Vernon, Sibyl Mason 2890
Vernon, Simon Richard 2889
Vernon, Stephanie Caroline 1792
Vernon, Sybil Mary 1829
Vernon, Tara Katharine Loudon 2889
Vernon, Tessa Hodgson 2889
Vernon, Thomas Andrew 2889
Vernon, Thomas Lisle Trelawney 1326
Vernon, Thomas Richard Adam 1451
Vernon, Timothy William 2889
Vernon, Tina Jeanette 2890
Vernon, Tobias Edward 2889
Vernon, Toby Richard 2890
Vernon, Vanessa Anne 2889
Vernon, Vicki Maree 1792
Vernon, Victoria 1155, 1792
Vernon, Wendy Caroline 1791
Vernon, Wilfred Allan 2890
Vernon, William Ernle Hardy 1326, 2542
Vernon, William Grierson 2889
Vernon, (William) Michael 2890
Vernon, Zara Caroline 1792
Vernon-Harcourt, Anne 2886
Vernon-Harcourt, Anthony William 2886
Vernon-Harcourt, Charlotte Lucy 2886
Vernon-Harcourt, Cherry 2886
Vernon-Harcourt, Edward William 2886
Vernon-Harcourt, Nancy 2886
Vernon-Harcourt, Oliver Thomas 2886
Vernon-Harcourt, Simon Anthony 2886
Vernon-Harcourt, Sylvia Jeannette (Jane) 2886
Vernon-Harcourt, William Ronald Denis 2886
Veron, Anne Grace 391
Veron, D'Hrie Sheree 391
Veron, Désirée D'Hrie Marie 391
Veron, Larissa Victoria 391
Veron, Zachery 391
Verrier, Charles Simpson 2863
Verrier, Frances Joan 2863
Versen, Cleone Lucinda 990
Versen, Frederick James 990
Versen, Richard F 990
Versluysen, Eugene 527
Versluysen, Jane 527
Verstraete, Jacques Michel Marie Ghislain 127
Verstraete, Lorraine Court 127
Verstraete, Maud 127
Verstraete, Patricia Anne 127
Verstraete, Philippe Jacques Marie Ghislain 127
Verstraete, Zoë 127
Vervuurt, Anita 849
Vervuurt, Gerard Michael 849
Vervuurt, Melvin Michael 849
Vervuurt, Norbert Calmon 849
Vervuurt, Otto Rene Gottleib 849
Vervuurt, Reinhardt James 849
Verwoerd, Anton 2228
Verwoerd, Clare 2228
Verwoerd, Olivia Margaret 2228
Vesey Holt, Margaret Jane Venetia 1829
Vesey, Alexander Thomas Ferdinand 829
Vesey, Cosima Frances 828
Vesey, Damian Brian John 828
Vesey, Marie-Christine Joaiane Renée 829
Vesey, Nicholas Ivo 829
Vesey, Oliver Ivo 828
Vesey, Olivia Denise Helen 829
Vesey, Sebastien Guillaume 829
Vesey, Sita-Maria Arabella 828
Vesey, Thomas Wilfrid 829
Vester, Annabel Sophia 1869
Vester, Emma 1869
Vester, Nicholas G S 1869
Vestey, Anne 2895
Vestey, Arthur George 2893
Vestey, Benjamin John 2894
Vestey, Carina Patricia 2894
Vestey, Caroline Louise 2894
Vestey, Celia Elizabeth 2893
Vestey, Christina Mary 2895
Vestey, Edmund Arthur Valentine 2895
Vestey, Edmund Hoyle 2895
Vestey, Flora Grace 2893
Vestey, George Moubray William 2895
Vestey, Georgina 2895
Vestey, Georgina Ann 2895
Vestey, Georgina Jane 2894
Vestey, Harry Robin Edmund 2895
Vestey, (Helen) Pamela Fullerton (Melba) 2894, 2895
Vestey, Jack Arthur 2895
Vestey, James Edmund McLean 2895
Vestey, James Patrick 2894
Vestey, Joanna Clare 2894
Vestey, John 2895
Vestey, Mark William 2894
Vestey, Mary Henrietta 2893
Vestey, Monica Hope 2894
Vestey, Nicola Jane 2894
Vestey, Paul Edmund 2894
Vestey, Penelope Jane 2894
Vestey, Phyllis Irene 2894
Vestey, Rachel 2895
Vestey, Richard George Archibald 2895
Vestey, Robin John Henry 2895
Vestey, Roger Edmund 2894
Vestey, Rose Amelia 2894
Vestey, Rose Elizabeth Jean 2895
Vestey, Ruby Constance 2895
Vestey, Tamara Pamela 2894
Vestey, Tessa 2895
Vestey, Thomas (Tom) Hector Moubray 2895
Vestey, Timothy Ronald Geoffry 2895
Vestey, Victoria Anne 2894
Vestey, Victoria Eileen 2895
Vestey, William Guy 2893
Vesty, Mark William 401
Vesty, Rose Amelia 401
Vetch, Amanda Jane 1766
Vetch, Annabel Susannah Clare 852
Vetch, James William Anderson 1766
Vetch, Patricia Eileen 1766
Vetch, Rachel Anne 1766
Veysey, Benjamin Stewart 229
Veysey, James William Philip 229
Veysey, Lesley Anne 229
Veysey, Philip 229
Veysey, Rachel Ruth 229
Vibraye, Honor Cecilia 77
Vicars, Claire Latham 168
Vicars, Robert James 168
Vicars-Miles, Anne Jacqueline 1240
Vicars-Miles, Anthony Edward 1240
Vicars-Miles, Katherine Julie 1240
Vicars-Miles, Sarah Elizabeth 1240
Vicary, Susan 1678
Vicary, Susan Antonia 218
Vicary, Timothy 1678
Vicary, William Sebastian 218
Vicat, Felix 649
Vicat, Giles 649
Vicat, Jane Anthea 649
Vicat, Theodore 649
Vick, Christabel Russell 3003
Vick, Mary 3003
Vickers, James 135
Vickers, Kathleen 516
Vickers, Mary Jennifer 135
Vickers, Robin Daniel Stuart 516
Vickers, Sandra 135
Vickery, Ian Lee 2043
Vidal, Carl Rudolf 798
Vidal, Jacqueline 798
Vidal, Martin Andreas 798
Vidigal, Serena Jane 915
Vigneron, Michael 669
Vigneron, Sarah Gay Lisette 669
Vigors, Charles Stewart Cliffe 1084
Vigors, Sarah Louise Rosemary 1084
Vigors, Thomas Ashmead Merton 601
Vijayaratnam, Emma Frances 802
Vijayaratnam, Logan 802
Villanueva Brandt, Alfredo Enrique 1502
Villanueva Brandt, Carlos Manuel 1502
Villanueva Brandt, Henrietta Julia 1502
Villanueva Brandt, Mateo Carlos 1502
Villiers, Alan Michael Hyde 586
Villiers, Alastair Michael Hyde 582
Villiers, Alice 583
Villiers, Annabel Jane 585
Villiers, Anne Virginia 583
Villiers, Anthony Henry Herbert 584
Villiers, (Anthony James) Valentine 584
Villiers, Antonia Aniela 585
Villiers, Barbara Béatrice 1538
Villiers, Barbara Clare 583
Villiers, Barbara Jane 583
Villiers, Betty Midelton 188, 584
Villiers, Bianca Maria Luciana Adriana 1538
Villiers, Birgitte 584
Villiers, Caroline Harriet 585
Villiers, Caroline Patricia 584
Villiers, Catherine Judith 584
Villiers, Catherine Mary 586, 797
Villiers, Catriona Sarah 584
Villiers, Charles Alastair Hyde 582
Villiers, Charles Churchill 582
Villiers, Charles James Hyde 586
Villiers, Charles Nigel 585
Villiers, Charles Russell 583
Villiers, Charles Sebastian 584
Villiers, Christine Joan 583
Villiers, Christopher Francis 584
Villiers, Christopher Frederick Pelham 585
Villiers, Christopher Nigel 583
Villiers, Clarissa Elizabeth Mairi 582
Villiers, Clive Matthew George 583
Villiers, Daniel James Hyde 586
Villiers, Deborah 584
Villiers, Delia Dorothy 584
Villiers, Derek Midelton Lister 584
Villiers, Edward Richard 583
Villiers, Eleanor Monica 1538
Villiers, Elizabeth Jill 584
Villiers, Elizabeth Mairi 49
Villiers, Ellen Margaret 582
Villiers, Emma Mary Jane 582
Villiers, Frederick George Edward 583
Villiers, Frederick James 584
Villiers, Frederick Montagu Hyde 585
Villiers, Geoffrey Richard 583
Villiers, George Alexander 584
Villiers, George Edward 583
Villiers, (George Francis) William 1538
Villiers, Geraldine Olive 584
Villiers, Harry Hyde 584
Villiers, Helen Fiona 583
Villiers, Helen Katherine Luisa 1538
Villiers, Henry Anthony Edward 584
Villiers, Henry Hyde 586
Villiers, Henry Raymond 583
Villiers, Hugo James 584
Villiers, (Irene) Mary 585
Villiers, Iris Patricia 188
Villiers, James 583
Villiers, James Lionel Edward 583
Villiers, Jamie Charles 1538
Villiers, Jane 582
Villiers, Janet Mary 583
Villiers, Janet Myra 583
Villiers, Jean 585
Villiers, Jean Annette Mary 585
Villiers, Joan 582
Villiers, John Francis Hyde 586
Villiers, Jonathan Paul 584
Villiers, Julia Helen 583
Villiers, Katherine 584
Villiers, Katherine Alexandra Hyde 2526
Villiers, Kirstie June 583
Villiers, Lamorne Jessica 582
Villiers, Lisa Alexandra 583
Villiers, Luciana Dorothea Sacha 1538
Villiers, Lucinda Claire 586
Villiers, Lucinda Victoria 584
Villiers, Marie José 586
Villiers, Mark Roger 583
Villiers, Mary Cecilia Georgina 587
Villiers, Mary Elizabeth 586
Villiers, (Mary) Jane 583
Villiers, Myee Miranda 49, 586
Villiers, Nancy 583
Villiers, Nicholas Christopher Lister 584
Villiers, Nicholas Hyde 585, 586, 797
Villiers, Nicholas Lister 188
Villiers, Nigel Richard 583
Villiers, Patricia de Lacey 583
Villiers, Peter William 583
Villiers, Robert Henry Hyde 586
Villiers, Robin Julian 584
Villiers, Roger Peter 583
Villiers, Rose Marie 585
Villiers, Rosemary 582
Villiers, Rosemary Elizabeth 584
Villiers, Sally Priscilla 585
Villiers, Sara 584
Villiers, Sarah Jane Amanda 585
Villiers, Sheila Joyce 585
Villiers, Simon William George 583
Villiers, Sophia Georgiana 1538
Villiers, Stephanie Louise 1538
Villiers, Stephen Hyde 584
Villiers, Susanna Sophia 586
Villiers, Theresa Anne 583
Villiers, Timothy Stewart 584
Villiers, Valerie Reeling 583
Villiers, (William) Nicholas Somers Laurence Hyde 587
Villiers-Stuart, Angus Theodore 444
Villiers-Stuart, Archie James 444
Villiers-Stuart, Bridget Mary 444
Villiers-Stuart, Caroline Mary 444
Villiers-Stuart, Charles Henry 443
Villiers-Stuart, Eileen Nora 444
Villiers-Stuart, Katherine Amelia 444
Villiers-Stuart, Michael Patrick 444
Vincent, Angela Carmen 1958
Vincent, Antonia Louise 1958
Vincent, Bruno Charles 1958
Vincent, Charles Michael Lacey 2895
Vincent, Christine 2895
Vincent, Edward Mark William 2895
Vincent, Helen 2895
Vincent, Helen Millicent 2423
Vincent, Jean Paterson 2896
Vincent, John James Robertson 2895
Vincent, John Russell 2717
Vincent, Katherine Eleanor 1958
Vincent, Leo Jonathan 2717
Vincent, Louisa Caroline Sarah 2777
Vincent, Nicolette Elizabeth 2717
Vincent, Patrick Henry Morse 1958
Vincent, Paul David 2777
Vincent, Philip Morse 1958
Vincent-Fosbery, Anthony 2055
Vincent-Fosbery, Napier 2055
Vind, Christian Tom 2961
Vind, Ivor Henrik 2961
Vind, Mogens Christian Christoph 2961
Vind, Susan Frances 2961
Vine, Anita Oonah 550
Vine, Antony Patrick Seton 2582
Vine, Catherine Rose 2824
Vine, Janet Rosalie 2824
Vine, Juliet Mary 550
Vine, Lydia Antoinette 2582
Vine, Norman Victor 2582
Vine, Oonah Caroline 550
Vine, Peter Gerald 550
Viner, Andrew John 1238
Viner, Belinda Jane 1238
Viner, Fleur Ruth 1238
Viner, Jack Randle 1238
Viner, Rosemary Jane 1238
Viney, Elliott Merriam 2216
Viney, Rosamund Ann 2216
Vinson, Antonia Charlotte 2896
Vinson, Bettina Claire 2896
Vinson, Rowena Ann 2896
Vinson, Yvonne Ann 2896
Visser, Christiaan 92
Visser, Christine 92
Visser, Jocelyn Mary 92
Visser, Richard 92
Vivian, Alastair Desmond 2897
Vivian, Alice Camilla 2897
Vivian, Alice Penelope 1348, 2897
Vivian, Amanda Mary 2897
Vivian, Anna 2777
Vivian, Anthony Chester 2302
Vivian, Arabella Victoria 2898
Vivian, Camilla Harriet 2896
Vivian, Carol 2896
Vivian, Charles Crespigny Hussey 2896
Vivian, Charles Eveyln 2897
Vivian, (Christopher) John Desmond 2897
Vivian, Claire Jennifer 2897
Vivian, Clare Veronica 2897
Vivian, Inger Johanne 2898
Vivian, (Isobel) Suzy 2897
Vivian, Jacqueline 2302
Vivian, Lucy 2777
Vivian, Mary Alice 319, 2898
Vivian, Natasha Sarah 2896
Vivian, Pamela Mary 2897
Vivian, Patrick Cyril 2897
Vivian, Richard Anthony Hussey 2777
Vivian, Robin Audley Clinton 1348, 2897
Vivian, Rupert James 2897
Vivian, Simon Paul Richard 2897
Vivian, Susan Caroline 2897
Vivian, Thomas Crespigny Brabazon 2898
Vivian, Vanda Rose 2897
Vivian, Victor Anthony Ralph Brabazon 2898
Vivian-Neal, (Elizabeth) Daphne 157
Vivian-Neal, Giles Arthur 157
Vivian-Neal, Gina Rosemary 157
Vivian-Neal, Henry Arthur 157
Vivian-Neal, James Francis 157
Vivian-Neal, Marianne Clare 157
Vlaanderen, Fiona Veronica 1522

W

Williams, Gillian Rachel 2030
Williams, Grace Amy May 1613
Williams, Grizel Margaretta 907
Williams, Guy Wordley 628
Williams, Gwenllian Elizabeth Anne 3016
Williams, Hannah Louise 3019
Williams, Harry John 1627
Williams, Hayley Michelle 3017
Williams, Helena Lucy 1329
Williams, Henrietta Cecilia 556
Williams, Henry Charles Ralph Fulford 1297
Williams, Henry John 1297
Williams, Hew Anthony John 1329
Williams, Hugh Edward 2747
Williams, Hugh Frederick 2030
Williams, Hugh Martyn 2520
Williams, Hugh Vincent 2303
Williams, Hugo Andrew Younger 982
Williams, Ian Maxwell 1385
Williams, Ian Muir 2030
Williams, Imogen 3021
Williams, Ingrid Louise 1251
Williams, Isabel Richenda Eileen 1764
Williams, (Isabel) Tara Mary 1330
Williams, Jacqueline 1870
Williams, Jake Peter Thomas 1385
Williams, James Frank 242
Williams, James Mark Edward 3018
Williams, James Matthew Thomas 2550
Williams, Jane 3016
Williams, Jane Charlotte 1627
Williams, Jane Gillian 3021
Williams, Janet 686
Williams, Janice Diana 229
Williams, Jasper Ambrose George 2849
Williams, Jennifer Elizabeth Mary 3098
Williams, Jennifer Lillian 1427
Williams, Jennifer Mary 856
Williams, Joanna Frances 1329
Williams, Joanna Susan 1385
Williams, John Charles 2641
Williams, John Morris 1427
Williams, John Philip Mackenzie 3017
Williams, John Robert Alexander 1788
Williams, John Warren 3098
Williams, Jonathan Frederick Matthew 556
Williams, Jonathan Mark 3017
Williams, Joshua John Ralph 556
Williams, Judith Jessie 325
Williams, Julia Margaret Frances 2303
Williams, Juliet Susan Harriet 3017
Williams, Karen Patricia 3020
Williams, Katharine Elizabeth 2303
Williams, Katherine Mary Elizabeth 556
Williams, Kathleen 1385
Williams, Kathleen Elizabeth 1613
Williams, Laura 2827
Williams, Leaerin Elizabeth 3020
Williams, Leslie Gaye 3020
Williams, Linda 136
Williams, Linda Jane Auriol 1193
Williams, Louise Beverly 3017
Williams, (Luke Edward) Timothy Hue 2827
Williams, Marcia 1576
Williams, Margaret 242, 2641
Williams, Margaret Ann 1613
Williams, Margaret Eryl 1800
Williams, (Margaret) Helen 884
Williams, Margaret Isabel 1339
Williams, Margaret Jane Louise 3017
Williams, Marie Jacqueline 1493
Williams, Marion Margaretta 1071
Williams, Mark 407, 1029
Williams, Martha 2520, 3021
Williams, Martyn Dennis Victor 3020
Williams, Mary Caroline 1297
Williams, Mary Jo 1385
Williams, Mary Rose 1193
Williams, Matthew 556
Williams, Matthew Stewart 3020
Williams, Maureen Elizabeth 2863
Williams, Merlin 2747
Williams, Merlin Anthony Baillie 2849
Williams, Michael 2161
Williams, Michael David 3020
Williams, Michael Duncan 1427
Williams, Michael Humphrey 1385
Williams, Michael Lodwig 856
Williams, Michael Montague 73
Williams, Michael Philip 3004
Williams, Michael Stuart 407
Williams, Michael Thomas Jerome Bate 1788
Williams, Michelle Ruth 3019
Williams, Natasha Elizabeth 3019
Williams, Nesta Rosemary 3017
Williams, Nigel David Blackstone 73
Williams, Olga Georgiana 2863
Williams, Oliver Brooks 628
Williams, Oliver Mervyn 1330
Williams, Olivia Rosemary 1648
Williams, Owain Anthony Mervyn 907
Williams, Patricia Helen 3098
Williams, Patricia Joan 2714
Williams, Patrick 2520
Williams, Paul 2714
Williams, Paul Arnold 1613
Williams, Paul Gerard Quentin 1329
Williams, Paul Joseph 1329
Williams, Penelope Helen 1029
Williams, Perdita 407
Williams, Peter Brinton 1627
Williams, Peter Duncan 1613
Williams, Peter Henry Bruce 2093
Williams, Peter Robert 3020
Williams, Philip John 1427
Williams, Phyllis June 3020
Williams, Rachael Mary 1603
Williams, Rachel 2641
Williams, Rachel J 3019
Williams, Rafe Thomas 959
Williams, Ray 2034
Williams, Raymond John 1777
Williams, Reginald 1339
Williams, Richard Charles 1330
Williams, Richard Gareth Macdonald 1800
Williams, Richard Murray 136
Williams, Robert Norrie 3017
Williams, Robin Lynn 3020
Williams, Roderic Greville David 73
Williams, Roger 1219
Williams, Rosemary Suzanne 1788
Williams, Ruth Emma 2641
Williams, Ruth Esther 2855
Williams, Ruth Margaret 3020
Williams, Sally Elizabeth 1071
Williams, (Samuel) Thomas Morgan 1330
Williams, Sandra Diana 3020
Williams, Sandra Victoria 2805
Williams, Sara Alexandra 2620
Williams, Sara Margaret Helen 3015
Williams, Sarah 2030
Williams, Sarah Catherine Anne 3017
Williams, Sarah Georgiana 2863
Williams, Sarah Jane 2161
Williams, Sarah Sophia Rhiannon 929
Williams, Sarah Yoskyl 2827
Williams, Shane Douglas 2660
Williams, Sheena 1765
Williams, Sheila Anne 686
Williams, Simon Bruce 2093
Williams, Simon Hilary 1339
Williams, Simon Roger 2534
Williams, Sophie 2827
Williams, Sophie Adeline 929
Williams, Stefan Orlando 929
Williams, Stephanie Gay 1219
Williams, Stephen Robin Alexander 3019
Williams, Steven John 2550
Williams, Susan 136
Williams, Susan Eileen Isabella 2303
Williams, Susan Margaret 73
Williams, Susan Venetia 1329
Williams, Tessa Emily Henrietta 2550
Williams, Thomas Alexander 407
Williams, Thomas Edward 2161
Williams, Thomas Joseph 1603
Williams, Thomas Wordley 628
Williams, Timothy John 3004
Williams, Timothy Nicholas Edward 73
Williams, Trelawny Michael 1648
Williams, Trevor 1385
Williams, Trevor Michael 2620
Williams, V M Russell 3021
Williams, Veronica 2520
Williams, Veronica Annabel 1777
Williams, Victoria Caroline 1603
Williams, Wanda Charlotte 3020
Williams, Wendy Adele Marguerite 3019
Williams, Wendy Amelia 2034
Williams, William Claude 3020
Williams, William Maurice 1493
Williams, Winston Guinness Andrew 1251
Williams, Yvonne Carole 2747
Williams-Bulkeley, David Haakon 3024
Williams-Bulkeley, Ellen-Marie 3024
Williams-Bulkeley, Harry David 3022
Williams-Bulkeley, Jacqueline 3022
Williams-Bulkeley, James 3024
Williams-Bulkeley, Michael 3024
Williams-Bulkeley, Oliver Hugh 3022
Williams-Bulkeley, Richard David Harry 3022
Williams-Bulkeley, Richard Hugh 3022
Williams-Bulkeley, Richard Thomas 2245
Williams-Bulkeley, Sarah Susan 2245, 3022
Williams-Bulkeley, Victoria Mary 3022
Williams-Ellis, David Hugo Martyn 1700
Williams-Ellis, Hugo John George 1700
Williams-Ellis, John Richard Baldwyn 2049
Williams-Ellis, Margaret Elizabeth 2049
Williams-Ellis, Phoebe Constance Mary 1700
Williams-Ellis, Serena Jane Clare 1700
Williams-Freeman, Andrew Frederick Peere 471
Williams-Freeman, David Peere 471
Williams-Freeman, Fiona 471
Williams-Freeman, Jean Elizabeth 471
Williams-Wynn, Alexandra June 3025
Williams-Wynn, Charles Edward Watkin 3025
Williams-Wynn, Gabrielle 3027
Williams-Wynn, Harry Watkin 3025
Williams-Wynn, Lucinda Jean 3025
Williams-Wynn, Nicholas Watkin 3025
Williams-Wynn, Robert Euan Watkin 3025
Williams-Wynn, Victoria Jane 3025
Williams-Wynne, Chloë Frances 3026
Williams-Wynne, Leonora Mary 3026
Williams-Wynne, Rose Margaret 3026
Williams-Wynne, Veronica Frances 459, 3026
Williams-Wynne, William Robert Charles 459, 3026
Williamson, Alexander Fergus Case 1092
Williamson, Alexandra 1092
Williamson, Amy 1092
Williamson, Ana 572
Williamson, Annabel Rosalind 3096
Williamson, Archibald 1091
Williamson, Ashlee Maree 195
Williamson, Aura Figueroa 572
Williamson, Catherine Ngaire 1092
Williamson, Charles Anthony 2237
Williamson, Charlotte Clara 1568
Williamson, Charlotte Mary 1092
Williamson, Christine 2237
Williamson, Claire Anne Helen 2258
Williamson, Clare Honor 1568
Williamson, Craig Kennedy 3096
Williamson, Daisy 1092
Williamson, Damian 572
Williamson, (David) Stephen Charles 1092
Williamson, Dermot Fergus 1092
Williamson, Desmond 2258
Williamson, Elizabeth Margaret 1528
Williamson, Elizabeth Wilbur 1092
Williamson, Emma Charlotte Mary 1568
Williamson, Emma Tian-Tian 1092
Williamson, Francis Charles FitzRoy 572
Williamson, George Archibald Mallam 1091
Williamson, Gilian 1568
Williamson, Guinevere Elsie 572
Williamson, Guthrie John 1091
Williamson, Hazel Maureen 3066
Williamson, Helen Camilla Mary 2258
Williamson, Hugh Thomas Saumarez 1568
Williamson, James Alec 2583
Williamson, James David Alexander 1092
Williamson, Jane 1091
Williamson, Jane Christian 1092
Williamson, Jayden Leigh 195
Williamson, Jean Suzanne 2583
Williamson, Joanna Mary 1092
Williamson, Leanne Maree 195
Williamson, Lily 1118
Williamson, Lucy Charlotte 2237
Williamson, Lydia 572
Williamson, Lynette Robyn 1092
Williamson, Malcolm Lindsay 195
Williamson, Marcus 2237
Williamson, Margaret Ann 1091
Williamson, Mark Herbert 1568
Williamson, Michael Anthony Wellesley 572
Williamson, Michael Paul 1568
Williamson, Mischa 572
Williamson, Pascale Eyre 572
Williamson, Patrick Alexander Campbell 572
Williamson, Paul Kenyon 1568
Williamson, Paula Jiao-Jiao 1092
Williamson, Penelope Jane 2258
Williamson, Peter Anstruther 1091
Williamson, Peter John 1568
Williamson, Philippa Marie-Theresa 2237
Williamson, Rachel 2237
Williamson, Richard Almeric Spencer 572
Williamson, Richard E 1118
Williamson, Robert Jerrard 2237
Williamson, Ronald 1528
Williamson, Ruaraidh James Stewart 1092
Williamson, Sabrina Ann 1092
Williamson, Sarah Frances 2258
Williamson, Sasha 572
Williamson, Sibyl Gladys 74
Williamson, Sophia Louisa Harriet 1568
Williamson, Yu Yu Su 1092
Willing, Arabella Jane 500
Willing, Edward John David 500
Willing, (Eva) Jane Agnes 500
Willing, Richard Hugh 500
Willink, Agnes Marjorie 3029
Willink, Annabella Mary Victoria 3029
Willink, Blanche Elsie Alice 3029
Willink, Daniel Patrick 3029
Willink, David Christopher 3029
Willink, Doris 3029
Willink, Edward Daniel 3028
Willink, Elizabeth 3028
Willink, Elizabeth Anne 3029
Willink, Henry Augustine 3029
Willink, Hester Anne 3029
Willink, James Christopher 3029
Willink, Jeanine Rebecca 3029
Willink, Jennifer Wendy 1873, 3029
Willink, John Dingle 3029
Willink, Judith Kate 3029
Willink, Judith Mary 3029
Willink, Katie 3029
Willink, Mary Louise 3029
Willink, Michael Derek 3029
Willink, Nicholas Warren 1873, 3029
Willink, Oliver Hal 3029
Willink, Patricia Janet 3029
Willink, Patricia Mary 3029
Willink, Patrick John 3029
Willink, Robin Daniel 3029
Willink, Simon Wakefield 3029
Willink, Stephen Henry 3029
Willink, Timothy Wakefield 3029
Willink, William Alfred 3029
Willis, Alexandra Rose 2570
Willis, Andrew James Scott 2879
Willis, Ann Catherine 2822
Willis, Anthony Brian 2570
Willis, Anthony Willis 1272
Willis, Barbara Joan 1561
Willis, Caroline Fiona 2822
Willis, Celia Kirstin 1347
Willis, Deborah Carol Jane 2879
Willis, Edward Tilea 2822
Willis, Francis Edmund Hugh 828
Willis, (Francis) Michael 828
Willis, Georgina Chloe Edwick 2879
Willis, Gillian 1877
Willis, Henry George 2822
Willis, Hilary Mary 369
Willis, Ian Henry 507, 2822
Willis, Jack Michael 1347
Willis, James Michael Billop 2879
Willis, John 369
Willis, John Douglas Charles 2879
Willis, Julian Charles d'Anyers 1877
Willis, Karen 2879
Willis, Linda 2879
Willis, Martin Atherton d'Anyers 1877
Willis, Mary Catherine Ileana Camilla 507, 2822
Willis, Matthew Henry Michael 828
Willis, Merrily Mary Susan 1272
Willis, Michael Philip Bruce 2879
Willis, Nancy Katharine 2822
Willis, Nicholas Henry David 2822
Willis, Nicholas John 1347
Willis, Nicholas Michael Thurlow 2822
Willis, Oenone Eileen Frances 2879
Willis, Olivia Grace 2570
Willis, Paula Carol 2879
Willis, Rebecca Margaret 2822
Willis, Robert Nigel Crum 2879
Willis, Robert William Peter 828
Willis, Robin Christopher Scott 2879
Willis, Rosalinda Mary 828
Willis, Rosemary Victoria 2570
Willis, Sean d'Anyers 1877
Willis, Simon Robert Crum 2879
Willis, Sophie Catherine Glory 2822
Willis, Stephanie Megan Edwick 2879
Willis, Stephen Mark 2570
Willis, Timothy Robert Crum 2879
Willison, Brendan Gregory Bruce 399
Willison, Gregory 399
Willison, Karen Elizabeth 399
Willison, Rachel 1340
Willison, Trecia 1340
Willmer, John Franklin 1483
Willmer, Margaret Lilian 1483
Willmott, Andrew Mark 262
Willmott, Colin Willmott 136
Willmott, Giles Benedict Paddington 136
Willmott, Jennifer Mary 136
Willmott, Victoria 136
Willmott, William Edward 262
Willoughby, (Anne) Leueen 3033
Willoughby, Anthony James Tweeddale 286
Willoughby, Bridget 1918
Willoughby, Caroline Rosemary 1919
Willoughby, Charles Edward Henry 1916
Willoughby, Charlotte Jacqueline Louise 1916
Willoughby, Christopher Ronald 1917
Willoughby, Colin James 1918
Willoughby, Emma Coralie Sarah 1916
Willoughby, Eritrea Isabella 1919
Willoughby, Fiona K 1919
Willoughby, Georgia Violet 1918
Willoughby, Guy Alexander 1918
Willoughby, Guy Nesbit John 1919
Willoughby, (Henry Ernest) Christopher 1919
Willoughby, Hugh Nesbit 1918
Willoughby, J Elizabeth 1919
Willoughby, James Lucas 286
Willoughby, James William Michael 1916
Willoughby, Jane Helen Veronica 992
Willoughby, Janet 1916
Willoughby, Jean 726
Willoughby, Joanna 286
Willoughby, (John) Hugh Francis 1916
Willoughby, Josephine Cicely Alice 1917
Willoughby, Lois Ann Mary 1918
Willoughby, Louisa Ariana Rose 1919
Willoughby, Lucy Corinna Agneta 797, 1916
Willoughby, Marie-Anne 1917
Willoughby, Michael Charles James 797, 1916
Willoughby, Nicholas 286
Willoughby, Olive 1918
Willoughby, Philip Mark Digby 1918
Willoughby, Rachel Joanna 286
Willoughby, Roger James 992
Willoughby, Rose Arabella Julia 1916
Willoughby, Ruth 1918
Willoughby, Sandra Evelyn 2694
Willoughby, Sean 2694
Willoughby, Thomas Henry Richard 1916
Willoughby, Veronica Anne 1918
Willoughby-Brown, Breanne 3033
Willoughby-Brown, Peregrine 3033
Wills, Alexander John 3037
Wills, Alice Elizabeth Vernon 3035
Wills, Alice Louise 3036
Wills, Alison Mary 891
Wills, Andrew Arnold Lyon 2431
Wills, Anna Rose Constance 3037
Wills, Anne Marie Frances 2183
Wills, Anthony John Vernon 3035
Wills, Benjamin James Hamilton 891
Wills, Camilla Jane Hamilton 890
Wills, Caryl Peter Melville 3035
Wills, Catherine Mary Hamilton 890
Wills, Charlotte Alexandra Hamilton 890
Wills, Charlotte Caroline 3037

Woodhouse, Teresa Anne 1703
Woodhouse, Thomas Duncan 2803
Woodin, Elizabeth Mary 1763
Woodin, Joanna 1763
Woodin, Mark Chandler 1763
Woodin, Walter Michael 1763
Wooding, David 936
Wooding, Jemima Tamsin 936
Wooding, Roland 936
Woodley, Christopher Benjamin 1406
Woodley, Daisy Anne 1406
Woodley, Juliet Priscilla Mary 1055
Woodley, Karin Lee 1055
Woodley, Nicola Anne 1406
Woodley, Paul Jonathan 1406
Woodley, Wilfred Trevor 1055
Woodman, Edward 2717
Woodman, Elizabeth Anne 2876
Woodman, Elizabeth Joan 2717
Woodman, Katherine 2717
Woodman, Lara 2876
Woodnutt, Colin George 2676
Woodnutt, Emily Sophie 504
Woodnutt, Martin 504
Woodnutt, Piers Mark 504
Woodnutt, Rosalind Muriel 2676
Woodnutt, Simon Edward 2676
Woodnutt, Susannah 504
Woodroffe, Amanda Aloysia Nicolette 2793
Woodroffe, Clifford Derry 2793
Woodroffe, Jean Frances 56, 977, 1278
Woodroffe, John 1278
Woodroffe, John William Richard 1278
Woodroffe, Justin Mackelean 2793
Woodroffe, Peter Mackelean 2793
Woodroffe, Ruth 339
Woodroffe, Simon 1278
Woodrow, Krystal Lee 1901
Woodrow, Megan Rose 1901
Woodrow, Rodney Hans 1901
Woodrow, Rowan Max 1901
Woodrow, Ryan Wayne 1901
Woodrow, Wendy Ann 1901
Woodruff, Deborah 2077
Woodruff, George M 2125
Woodruff, Peter Miles 2077
Woodruff, Stanley Thomas 2077
Woodruff, Susan Clare 2125
Woods, Adam Lindsay Broun 392
Woods, Andrew Kinderbee 1240
Woods, Ann Patricia 987
Woods, Caroline Elizabeth 1418
Woods, Caroline Susan 2319
Woods, Carrie Elizabeth Anne 1240
Woods, Christopher 988, 1461
Woods, Clare Marcello 1418
Woods, Craig Dennis 1366
Woods, Dorothy 392
Woods, Edward Harry Gridley 1240
Woods, Edward Richard 2317
Woods, Fiona 2921
Woods, Francis 1461
Woods, G Stephen 2319
Woods, Georgina Charlotte 2921
Woods, Georgina Rozelle 2319
Woods, (Gerald) Alexander William 2319
Woods, Guy Robert William 2453
Woods, Hannah Victoria 1418
Woods, Helen Lynette 392
Woods, Iona 2921
Woods, Isabella 1461
Woods, (Isobel) Ann 462
Woods, James Christopher 2317
Woods, James Douglas 2692
Woods, Jane Victoria 1418
Woods, Jessica Margaret 392
Woods, Joan Nancy 1346
Woods, Joanna Margaret 2317
Woods, John Francis Cornwall 987
Woods, Justin Thomas 392
Woods, Katherine Isabella 1461
Woods, Lucinda Ann 987
Woods, Lydia 1461
Woods, Madeline 1461
Woods, Margarita Henry 392
Woods, Marion Lester 1418
Woods, Melody Gaynor 1366
Woods, Michael William Frank 392
Woods, Nicola 988
Woods, Nicola Clare 987
Woods, Norman James 462
Woods, Oliver James 2921
Woods, Patricia Lindsay 2921
Woods, Robert Gerard Salisbury 2921
Woods, Robert Seton Rowan 987
Woods, Robert Tristram Rowan 987
Woods, Roland Francis 1366
Woods, Samuel Richard 2317
Woods, Sarah Dorothy 392
Woods, Serena Sylvia 2453
Woods, Susan Lesley 1240
Woods, Sylvia Claire 2453
Woods, Teresa Clare 2692
Woods, Thomas 1461
Woods, Timothy Michael 392
Woods, Victoria Venetia 2692
Woods, Wendy Frances 1366
Woods Ballard, Andrew James 1948
Woods Ballard, Basil 1948
Woods Ballard, Bridget Anne 1948
Woods Ballard, Helen Mary 1948
Woods Ballard, Hugh William 1948
Woods Ballard, Jennifer Clare 1948
Woods Ballard, Marianne Jean Elspeth 1948
Woods Ballard, Patrick Robert 1948
Woods Ballard, Timothy John 1948
Woods Ballard, William Richard 1948
Woodward, Andrew 1171
Woodward, Andrew St John 1820
Woodward, Angela Kay 1820
Woodward, Camilla Davan 2492
Woodward, Charlotte Jane 376
Woodward, Christopher Robert Dunbar 376
Woodward, David Thomas 484
Woodward, Deborah Diana 1171
Woodward, Eleanor Laura Davan 2492
Woodward, Elizabeth Bathurst 2665
Woodward, Elizabeth Deodata 2666
Woodward, Jessica Alice 131
Woodward, John 1820
Woodward, Katherine Matilda Rose 2492
Woodward, Lucy Elizabeth Campbell 484
Woodward, Margaret Rosemary 1468
Woodward, Nicholas Robert 376
Woodward, Olivia Mary Victoria 2492
Woodward, Rosamond Catherine 376
Woodward, Sarah Caroline 484
Woodward, Sarah Mary 1820
Woodward, Shaun Anthony 2492
Woodward, Stephanie Jane Campbell 484
Woodward, Thomas Rory George 2492
Woodward, William Lawrence 131
Woodworth, Carl Alexander 495
Woodworth, Carmon Marshall 495
Woodworth, Collin Matthew 495
Woodworth, Marion 495
Wooler, Alice Honor Lawrence 1651
Wooler, Harry Peter Lawrence 1651
Wooler, Pamela Jane 1651
Wooler, Stuart 1651
Woolerton, Colin Roy 1182
Woolerton, Elizabeth 1182
Woolerton, George Peter Christopher 1182
Woolf, Andrew James David 3067
Woolf, Benjamin 3067
Woolf, Benjamin Douglas 1937
Woolf, Bethia Fearne Milman 1937
Woolf, Christopher Patrick Milman 1937
Woolf, Eliot Charles Anthony 3067
Woolf, Inigo Rodney Milman 1937
Woolf, Jeremy Richard George 3067
Woolf, Jonathan Marcus 1937
Woolf, Linda 1937
Woolf, Lionel Noel 1937
Woolf, Marguerite 3067
Woolf, Nicholas David Milman 1937
Woolf, Patricia Freya 1937
Woolf, Robert James 3016
Woolf, Rosamond Alice 3016
Woolf, Simon Justin 1937
Woolf, Sophie Antonia 3016
Woolf, Soumhya Venkatesan 1937
Woolf, Susan Rebecca 1937
Woolf, Wendy 3067
Woolff, Catherine 2825
Woolff, Georgina Juliet 2825
Woolff, Malcolm 2825
Woolff, Nicholas Elliot 2825
Woolland, David Anthony Walter 665
Woolland, Peter Donald Cory 665
Woolley, Alice 2830
Woolley, Daniel 2830
Woolley, Emily Anne 832
Woolley, Giles Thomas 832
Woolley, Hugo C 832
Woolley, John Richard 2256
Woolley, Juliette Mary 606
Woolley, Michael 2830
Woolley, Peter 606
Woolley, Peter Melsome 2256
Woolley, Philippa June 832
Woolley, Rosemary Anne 2256
Woolley, Sara Jane 2830
Woolley, Yvonne Mary 2256
Woolliams, James Harvey 2400
Woolliams, Margaret Delves 2400
Woolliams, Richard Frank 2400
Woolls, Doreen Constance 1880
Woolls, John 1880
Woollven, Carol Frances Margaret 749
Woollven, Rowland Charles John 749
Woolven, Virginia Alexandra Frances 749
Woosnam, David Ralph William 109
Woosnam, Katharine Patricia Mary 109
Woosnam, Nicola Susan Katharine 109
Woosnam, Richard Bowen 109
Woosnam Mills, Alexander Ross Thomas 1886
Woosnam Mills, Antony Roland 1886
Woosnam Mills, Phyllida Angela de Marie 1886
Woosnam Mills, Victoria Ann Helen 1886
Worcester, David John 2679
Worcester, Monica Frances Mary 908
Worcester, Phyllida Margaret 2679
Wordsworth, Alexander Carlos 1035
Wordsworth, Andrew Guardino Theodore 2074
Wordsworth, Anne Lucy Susannah 2074
Wordsworth, Antony Christopher Curwen 1035
Wordsworth, Caroline Louise 1035
Wordsworth, Catherine Columbine Maria Annunziata 2074
Wordsworth, Charles William 1035
Wordsworth, Christine Stella 1035
Wordsworth, Cristina 1035
Wordsworth, Eleanor Margaret 1035
Wordsworth, Emma Harriet 1035
Wordsworth, Evelyn Mary 1035
Wordsworth, Giles Patrick John 1035
Wordsworth, Joan 1035
Wordsworth, Maria Reyes 1035
Wordsworth, Mark Edward Curwen 1035
Wordsworth, Michael 1035
Wordsworth, Peter John 1035
Wordsworth, Rosamond Anne 1035
Wordsworth, Sarah Elizabeth 1728
Wordsworth, Veronica 1035
Wordsworth, Zara Caroline 1035
Workman, Douglas Templeton 3093
Workman, Hugh Stewart Gray 3093
Workman, Katrina Margaret 3093
Workman, Robert Stewart Gray 3093
Wormald, Geoffrey John 2183
Wormald, Keith John Kingsford 2183
Wormald, Kirsten Anne 2183
Wormald, Marian Rose 2183
Wormser, Andrew Charles 2038
Wormser, Charles Mailert 2038
Wormser, Ivri Patricia 2038
Wormser, Nina Carolyn 2038
Worrall, Allister Stewart 2698
Worrall, Donald Rex 2698
Worrall, Elliot John 2698
Worrall, Jonathan Charles 2698
Worrall, Juliet Cynthia 2698
Worrall, Marcus James 2698
Worsley, Alice 3068
Worsley, Anne Penelope 3069
Worsley, Bridget 607, 3068
Worsley, Caroline Cicely 1097
Worsley, Caroline Patricia 2058
Worsley, Carolyn Mary Wynard 1304, 3069
Worsley, Charles Robert 3069
Worsley, Charles Roderick 2058
Worsley, Daniel 586
Worsley, David Christopher 3069
Worsley, Diana Rosalind 3069
Worsley, Dickon Carol 3069
Worsley, Elizabeth Frances 2058
Worsley, Francesca Sylvia 3068
Worsley, Giles Arthington 3068
Worsley, (George) Oliver 1106, 3069
Worsley, Henry John 3069
Worsley, Isabella Claire 3068
Worsley, James Jonathan 2058
Worsley, Jane Elizabeth 2058
Worsley, Jennifer Jane 2058
Worsley, Joanna 3068
Worsley, Joanna Rachel 2058
Worsley, John Arthington 1304, 3069
Worsley, John Bertrand 2058
Worsley, Jonathan Hugh 3069
Worsley, Joyce Marian 3069
Worsley, Juliet Anne 2058
Worsley, Justine Elizabeth Mary 84
Worsley, Katharine Margot 3069
Worsley, Marcus William Bernard 3068
Worsley, Marie-Noëlle 3068
Worsley, Marion 2058
Worsley, Michael Robert 2058
Worsley, Nicholas Richard 3069
Worsley, Nicolette Grace 84
Worsley, Penelope Suzanne Fleetwood 1106, 3069
Worsley, Peter Marcus 3068
Worsley, Philippa Jane 2058
Worsley, Richard Edward 1097
Worsley, Richard Henry Napier 2058
Worsley, Robert Napier 2058
Worsley, Rozanne Mary 84
Worsley, Sheila 3069
Worsley, Thomas Edward 3069
Worsley, Victoria Mary 2058
Worsley, Virginia Caroline 586
Worsley, Willa Victoria 3069
Worsley, (William) Marcus John 607
Worsley, William Ralph 3068
Worsthorne, Lucinda 922, 1722
Worsthorne, Peregrine Gerard 923, 1722
Worthington, Amber Chanelle 2183
Worthington, Anna 2750
Worthington, Blue 1462
Worthington, Camilla 143
Worthington, Charles William David 2750
Worthington, Greville 639
Worthington, Greville Thomas 1462
Worthington, Henrietta Mary 70
Worthington, Lance Noel 2183
Worthington, Nicholas R 70
Worthington, Raewyn Anne 2183
Worthington, Richard Philip 143
Worthington, Rosemary Claire 143
Worthington, Sara 143
Worthington, Sara Susan 2750
Worthington, Sophia Mary 639
Worthington, Sophie 1462
Worthington, Valerie Anne 1462
Worthington, Victoria Mary 70
Worthy, David Graham 175
Worthy, Henry Jonathan David Bruce 175
Worthy, Margaret 175
Wotton, Iona Victoria 1603
Wotton, Joanna Jane 1603
Wotton, John C L 1603
Wotton, Laura Elizabeth 1603
Wragg, Mary Ann Maud Sigrid 1222
Wragg, Thomas Henry 1222
Wrangel, Alexis 496
Wrangel, Diana Sylvia 496
Wratten, Edith Elizabeth 324
Wratten, Nigel Richard Irby 324
Wraxall, Irmgard Wilhelmina Maria 3071
Wraxall, Lesley Linda 3070
Wraxall, Lucy Rosemary Lascelles 3070
Wraxall, Peter Edward Lascelles 3071
Wraxall, Sylvia Laura 3071
Wraxall, William Nathaniel Lascelles 3070
Wreford-Brown, Amanda Jane 2255
Wreford-Brown, Christopher Louis 2255
Wreford-Brown, Jennifer 2255
Wreford-Brown, Paul Christopher 2255
Wrench, Laura Annette 2309
Wrench, Ruth Annette 2309
Wrench, Steven Walter 2309
Wrey, Alexander Mark Bourchier 3074
Wrey, Anne Christine Aubrey 3073
Wrey, Benjamin Harold Bourchier 3073
Wrey, Camilla Melusine 3073
Wrey, Caroline Janet 1718, 3072
Wrey, Catherine Margaret 2114, 3074
Wrey, Catriona Anne 3074
Wrey, Charles Bourchier 3074
Wrey, Charlotte Loveday 3074
Wrey, Edward Charles 3074
Wrey, (Edward) Sherard Bourchier 2114, 3074
Wrey, George Richard Bourchier 1718
Wrey, Harry David 3072
Wrey, Humphrey George 3072
Wrey, Katherine Frances Theodora 3074
Wrey, Loveday Elizabeth 3074
Wrey, Marcus Valerian Bourchier 3073
Wrey, Mark Eliot Bourchier 3074
Wrey, Maximilian George Bourchier 3074
Wrey, Rachel Pearl 3072
Wrey, Simon Sherard Bourchier 3074
Wrey, Susan Mary Bonita 3073
Wrey, Sybil Mabel Alice 3074
Wrey, Tallulah Kitty 3074
Wrey, Tanya Serena 3074
Wrey, Thomas Alexander 3074
Wrey, Timothy Christopher Bourchier 3073
Wright, Ada 1021
Wright, Alan Nigel 1071
Wright, Alexander Francis 2283
Wright, Alice Rosamund 2213
Wright, Andrew Firman 1071
Wright, Angus 3074
Wright, Ann Hilda 986
Wright, Anna 1444
Wright, (Arthur Robert) Donald 454
Wright, Atalanta Kathleen Ingeborg Elen 1320
Wright, Barnabas Mark 2328
Wright, Betty Millicent 2033
Wright, Brian Harry 2283
Wright, Brian Leslie 2033
Wright, Bryan Henry FitzHerbert 2304
Wright, Camilla 716
Wright, Carol Margaret 1413
Wright, Caroline Leslie 1071
Wright, Carolyn Sarah Louise 1725
Wright, Catherine Arundel 716
Wright, Catherine Frances 2987
Wright, Catriona Sarah 1623
Wright, Charles 1118
Wright, Charles Anthony 2003
Wright, Charles Piachaud 1340
Wright, Charlotte May 716
Wright, Christopher George 2161
Wright, Christopher John 1413
Wright, Christopher Jonathan Neave 2062
Wright, Daniel Leigh 194
Wright, Danny James Neave 2062
Wright, Daphne 1754
Wright, Darrell John 1413
Wright, David 2472
Wright, David Andrew 716
Wright, David Arundel 716
Wright, David James 2914
Wright, David Nathanael Beresford 1071
Wright, David William Benedict 1806
Wright, Deborah Jean 2859
Wright, Diana Margaret 1146
Wright, Douglas P W 1696
Wright, Edwina Primrose 1623
Wright, Eleanor Faith Rosina 1806
Wright, Emily Ann 595
Wright, Ernest George 2914
Wright, Flora Clemence Elizabeth 2541
Wright, Florence Cecilia 1408
Wright, Francis Gideon FitzWalter 1071
Wright, Francis Reuben 2328
Wright, Gail Louise 2033
Wright, Gareth Wickens 1725
Wright, George Stewart 2161
Wright, Gillian Diana 1806
Wright, Gladys Mary 1256
Wright, Graham Norman 1413
Wright, Harry Michael Ion 1623
Wright, Helen 1450
Wright, Helen Muryell 454
Wright, Henrietta Elizabeth 1454
Wright, Henry Joseph 2328
Wright, Henry Somerset 225
Wright, Isobel Artemis 2541
Wright, James Emanuel Shakespeare 1071
Wright, James Michael 986
Wright, Jane Anne Caroline 1340
Wright, Janice 1450
Wright, Jason 2859
Wright, Jemimah Alianore 1071
Wright, Jennifer Anne 2062
Wright, Joanna 1071
Wright, John 1450
Wright, John Desmond 1413
Wright, John Joseph Camplyon 1071
Wright, John Leslie FitzWalter 1071

Y

Z

Addenda and Corrigenda

General

For 'Ld Lt' *read* 'Ld-Lt' throughout

Max Craven, of the Derbyshire CC Record Office and a contributor of much valuable genealogical material concerning families with Derbyshire connections to this edition, was made an MBE in the 1998–99 New Year's Honours List

Royal Family

The last para. of the preliminary **Note**, specifically the mention of the 650 organisations of which HM THE QUEEN is Patron, should be amended in the light of the late-Feb 1999 announcement that HM would be be stepping down as Patron of over 80 during the following two years.

HRH THE PRINCE OF WALES became Patron of the Coll of Estate Management Aug 1998 and of Breakthrough (breast cancer research charity) Nov 1998; he was made a Maj-Gen, R-Adml and AVM 14 Nov 1998

HRH THE DUKE OF YORK was promoted Cdr RN 12 Jan 1999

HRH THE PRINCE EDWARD became engaged 6 Jan 1999 to *Sophie, dau of Chris Rhys-Jones, late geography master Sherborne; the wedding was scheduled to take place 19 June 1999

Volume I

ABERCONWAY: *for* '(1) *Susan Fiona Dorinthea [er dau of yr dau of 2nd Baron]; *b* 19 June 1955; *m* 1981 *Andrew Philip Drummond-Murray etc' *read* '(1) *Susan Fiona Dorinthea; *b* 19 June 1955; *m* 1981 (*divorce* 7 April 1997) Andrew Philip Drummond-Murray etc'

ABERCROMBY: Maria, *b* 10 Jan 1955 [not 1960], is the adopted dau of the present Bt not a blood dau

ACKROYD: *for* '**SIR TIMOTHY JOHN ROBERT WHYTE ACKROYD, 3RD BT**, of Dewsbury, W R Yorks [Sir Timothy Ackroyd Bt]' *read* '**SIR TIMOTHY JOHN ROBERT WHYTE ACKROYD, 3RD BT**, of Dewsbury, W R Yorks'

ACLAND, Bt, of Columb John: in entry for Richard Hugh Acland [3rd s of 4th s of Sir Hugh Thomas Dyke Acland, CMG, CBE, 4th s of 6th s of 6th Bt] *for* 'Greeson' *read* 'Gresson'

ACLAND, Bt, of Oxford: in entry for 6th and current Bt *for* 'educ All Hallows' *read* 'educ Allhallows'; in entry for Peter Edward Dyke Acland [3rd s of 2nd s of er s of 7th s of 1st Bt] *for* 'Hodge, (ret)' *read* 'Hodge'; in entry for Peter Acland [only s of Maj-Gen Sir John Hugh Bevil Acland, KCB, CBE, er s of yr s of 7th s of 1st Bt] *for* 'm 2nd *Cindy, dau of general Frederick Karsh, USME' *read* 'm 2nd 1991 *Cindy, dau of Gen Frederick Karsh, USMC'

ACTON: in entry for Stephen de Marffy von Versegh [6th s of est dau of 3rd Baron] *for* 'Dympha' *read* 'Dymphna'

ADAM: in entry for Charles David Adam [est s of 3rd s of 3rd s of 1st Bt] *for* 'm 1987' *read* 'm 1982'

AGNEW, Bt, of Great Stanhope Street: in entry for dau of s of er s of Sir Geoffrey William Gerald Agnew, CB [est s of 2nd s of 1st Bt] *for* '2d *Daisy Matilda' *read* '1d *Daisy Matilda'

AILESBURY: in entry for Stephen Taskova Zeese [listed as Kevin Bruce Zeese's 3rd s but actually Marc Charles Zeese's only s, both being sons of est dau of John Charles Brudenell-Bruce, MBE, 4th s of 4th s of 3rd Marquess] *for* '3c' *read* '1c'

for '**CHANDOS SYDNEY CEDRIC, 7th Marquess**' and 'CHANDOS SYDNEY CEDRIC BRUDENELL-BRUCE, **7th Marquess of Ailesbury**' *read* '(CHANDOS SYDNEY) CEDRIC, **7th Marquess**' and '(CHANDOS SYDNEY) CEDRIC BRUDENELL-BRUCE, **7th Marquess of Ailesbury**'

The 7th Marquess's 3rd w, Jean Frances Margaret, *d* 14 Feb 1999

AILSA: Angus Michael David Kennedy [s of s of yr s of er s of 5th s of Archibald Earl of Cassillis, er s of 1st Marquess] *m* 27 July 1996 *Dr Fiona Alexander, dau of James R Alexander, of Leigh-on-Sea, Essex

AIRD: in entry for Sir Alastair Sturgis Aird [2nd s of est s of 2nd s of 1st Bt] *for* 'KCVO 1984 CVO 1977 LVO 1969' *read* 'GCVO (1997, KCVO 1984, CVO 1977, LVO 1969'

ALDENHAM and HUNSDON OF HUNSDON: *for* '1a +David Charles Leslie [David Gibbs Esq etc' [est s of 1st Baron's 2nd s] *read* '1a +David Charles Leslie, AM (1993) [David Gibbs Esq AM etc'

Emily Jo [dau of Antony Richard Gibbs, est s of 2nd s of est s of yr bro of 1st Baron Aldenham] was *b* 26 July 1970

ALDINGTON: *for* '1(cont.) Maj Frederick Low *m* 2nd 1 Feb 1947 *Dorothy, dau of Arthur Hunter Denham Gillies, of Whitehall Court, London SW1, and by her had issue:
  (2) *George Stuart Hunter of Spain; *b* 6 March 1949; *educ* Harrow; *m* 1977 (*divorce* 1985)'

read '1 (cont.) Maj Frederick Low *m* 2nd 1 Feb 1947 *Dorothy, dau of Arthur Hunter Denham Gillies, of Whitehall Court, London SW1, and by her had:
  (2) *George Stuart Hunter; *b* 6 March 1949; *educ* Harrow; *m* 1977 (*divorce* 1985) Millicent Delmé-Radcliffe'

ALLENDALE: in entry for Anastasia [adopted dau of John Perowne, s of 4th dau of 1st Viscount] *for* 'Mouleton' *read* 'Monkton'

ALPORT: the Life Baron *d* 28 Oct 1998, when the title expired

AMHERST OF HACKNEY: in entry for George Henry Vanderbilt Cecil [er s of 3rd s of Baroness Amherst of Hackney, so *cr* in her own right] *for* '28813' *read* '28803'; the entry for William Robert Vanderbilt Cecil [s of s of yr s of 3rd s of Baroness Amherst of Hackney, so *cr* in her own right] should read 3b not 2b and come after his two er bros

AMPTHILL: the 2nd Baron's only dau, Phyllis, *d* early 1998; *for* '(3) *Angela Irene' [3rd dau of 3rd s of 1st Baron] *read* '(3) Angela Irene'; Sarah Caroline Villiers Wort [dau of Lt-Col (William) Rodney Villiers Russell, MC, er s of 4th s of 1st Baron] remarried her former husb Brian Roy Wort 10 June 1996

ANGLESEY: *for* 'Bayley' *read* 'Bayly' throughout

ANNESLEY: Melanie Jane Ruth [er dau of yr s of yr s of est s of est s of Hon Arthur Annesley later Grove-Annesley, 3rd s of 2nd Earl] *m* 1994

ANSON: in entry for Louisa Frances Anson [7th and present Bt's er dau] *for* 'Dr Michael' *read* '*Dr Michael'

ANSTRUTHER: *for* '**Sir Ralph Abercromby Anstuther, 4th Bt**; *b* 1 March 1804 etc' *read* '**Sir Ralph Abercromby Anstruther, 4th Bt**; *b* 1 March 1804 etc'

ARBUTHNOT, Bt, of Edinburgh: *for* '(2) Archibald Ernest' [3rd s of 4th s of 1st Bt] *read* '(3) Archibald Ernest'; in entry for Sarah Faith Madalyne Mackie [er dau of 2nd dau (but only one by his 2nd w) of Lt-Col Archibald Hugh Arbuthnot, est s of Archibald Ernest Arbuthnot (*see also* immediately above), 3rd (not 2nd) s of 4th s of 1st Bt] *for* 'Ian' *read* 'Iain'; in entry for issue of Elynth Mary, Countess Capponi [dau of est s of 2nd s of 2nd Bt] *for* 'Nicolo' *read* 'Niccolò', *for* 'Sebastiano Marca' *read* 'Sebastiano Maria', his w's name being Ginevra, dau of Count Gulinelli, also *for* 'Cosima Maria' *read* 'Cosima Tessa'; Deborah Sinclair Hale [yr dau of er dau of 2nd dau of 2nd s of 2nd s of 2nd Bt] has a 2nd s, Richard Geoffrey, *b* 1995, also presumably by John Martin Stew

ARBUTHNOTT: *for* '1c *Roy Ronald Montague-Jones [s of dau of 2nd sis of 15th Viscount]; *b* 21 July 1958; *m* 19– Henry Price' *read* '1c *Roy Ronald Montague-Jones; *b* 21 July 1958; *m* 19– *Alison, dau of Henry Price'; *for* '1b *Archibald Arbuthnott, DSC' [s of dau of next yr bro of f of 15th Viscount] *read* '1b Archibald Arbuthnott, DSC'

ARMSTRONG: the 6th Bt *d* 21 Dec 1997 and was *s* as 7th Bt by his only surv s

ASHBOURNE: *for* '1b *Anthony James [er s of 2nd s of middle sis of 3rd Baron]; *b* 1962; *m* *Arabella Sabina Lilian, only dau of Hon David Anthony Lawrence Caccia (*see* 1970 edn CACCIA , B), and has issue:
  1c *Olivia Sabina; *b* 1992
  2c *Ella Maria; *b* 1992'

read '1b *Anthony James; *b* 1962; *m* *Arabella Sabina Lilian, only dau of Hon David Anthony Lawrence Caccia (*see* 1970 edn CACCIA , B), and has:
  1c *Olivia Sabina; *b* 1992
  2c *Ella Maria; *b* 1992
  3c *Athene Isabella; *b* 1997'

ASHCOMBE: in entry for Victoria Jane [yr dau of only s of 2nd Baron's 6th s] *for* 'Hardinge-Rolls' *read* 'Harding-Rolls' throughout

ASHTOWN: in entry for Wallace Talbot TRENCH later WALDO TRENCH-FOX [er s of only s of 2nd s of Rev Frederic FitzJohn Trench, 7th s of Frederick Trench, of Moate and Woodlawn, f of 1st Baron] *for* 'TRENCH-FOX' *read* 'TRENCH FOX'; *for* 'Maximililan' [s of 2nd dau of s of est s of 2nd s of 3rd s of Most Rev Richard Chenevix Trench, PC, Archbp Dublin, 2nd s of 6th s of f of 1st Baron] *read* 'Maximilian'; in entry for Rev Francesca Dorothy Dixon [dau of yr dau of Col Arthur Henry Chenevix Trench, CIE, est s of 6th s of Most Rev Richard Chenevix Trench, PC, Archbp Dublin, 2nd s of s of f of 1st Baron] *for* 'DSC**' *read* 'DSC and two bars'

ASTOR OF HEVER: the 3rd and present Baron was apptd Dec 1998 a C Whip Ho Lds with responsibility for health and social security; his 4th dau's full names are Olivia Alexandra Elizabeth

for '[Lt-Col The Hon Hugh Astor JP etc' [postal address of 1st Baron's 2nd s] *read* '[The Hon Hugh Astor JP etc'

ATHOLL: in entry for Anne Jennifer Jarman [dau of 4th s of 2nd s of Sir Herbert Harley Murray, KCB, 4th s of Rt Rev Lord George Murray, 2nd s of 3rd Duke] *for* 'Shrubber' *read* 'Shrubbery'; *for* 'Georgina Patrica' [dau of yr dau of s of Maj

George Arthur Delmé Murray, DSO, est s of 3rd s (but 2nd by 2nd w) of s of 3rd s of Lord William Murray, 3rd s of 3rd Duke] *read* 'Georgina Patricia'; in entry for Hamish Douglas Murray [s of 3rd s of 6th s of s of s of Lord Henry Murray, 4th s of 3rd Duke] *for* 'Edwar' *read* 'Edward'

ATTLEE: in entry for 3rd and current Earl *for* 'educ Stowe; *m* etc' *read* 'educ Stowe; Capt (TA) REME, Jr Front-Bench Oppn (C) Spokesman Def, Environment and NI 1997–98, Oppn Front-Bench Spokesman NI 1998–; *m* etc'; in entry for Fergus Attlee [paternal ggs of 1st Earl's yr bro] *for* '1984' *read* '1994'; in entry for Paul Henry Attlee [2nd s of 1st Earl's yr bro] *for* 'Yew Tree Cottage etc' *read* 'Wheal Inde, Lanhydrock, Bodmin, Cornwall PL30 5AP'; *for* (3) *Theodore Mark [Theodore Attlee Esq, etc]' *read* '(3) *(Theodore) Mark [Mark Attlee Esq, Yew Tree Cottage etc (*i.e.*, address as for er bro prior to correction)]'

AVEBURY: in entry for issue of Joseph Lubbock [s of Brig-Gen Guy Lubbock, CMG, DSO, est s of 6th s of 3rd Bt] the Eve *b* 30 Sept 1996 is dau of Mr and Mrs Mark Jennings not of Elena and should be enumerated 1d not 2d; Elena has a s, Alexander, *b* 6 April 1998

BACKHOUSE: in entry for Poppy Skepper [3rd dau of yr dau of 3rd s of 5th s of 1st Bt] *for* '1998' *read* '1988'

BACON: *for* '2a +Edward Thomas Godfrey, OBE [Edward Bacon Esq OBE, 17 Abingdon Court, Abingdon Villas, London W8] [yr s of 2nd s of 4th s of 10th/11th Bt]; *b* 11 Dec 1939; *educ* Eton and Fitzwilliam Ho Cambridge (BA 1963, MA 1966); FRS *read* '2a +Edward Thomas Godfrey [Edward Bacon Esq, 17 Abingdon Court, Abingdon Villas, London W8]; *b* 11 Dec 1939; *educ* Eton and Fitzwilliam Ho Cambridge (BA 1963)'

BALFOUR OF INCHRYE: the 1st Baron's 2nd w, Mary Ainslie ('Maina'), *d* 6 Jan 1999

BALL: the 3rd Bt's widow Florine Isabel *d* 9 Nov 1992; his 2nd s Ronald Herbert *d* 4 Oct 1995

BANGOR: in entry for yst dau of 6th Viscount *for* 'Chesil Manor St' *read* 'Chelsea Manor St'

BARCLAY: in entry for issue of Margaret Elizabeth Gibbs [er dau of yr s of 4th s of 3rd s of 10th Bt] *for* '2c *b* 12 Feb 1961' *read* '2c *Hilary Eva; *b* 12 Feb 1961' and *for* '2c *Helen Dorothy' *read* '3c *Helen Dorothy'

BARLOW of Bradwall Hall: the 3rd and present Bt's yst s, Charles James Bulkeley, *m* 19 Sept 1998 *Michelle, dau of Michael Tory, of Hemsworth, Witchampton, Dorset

BARNARD: in entry for the 11th and present Baron's s *for* '1 +HENRY FRANCIS CECIL [The Hon Henry Vane, Selaby, Gainford, Co Durham]; *b* 11 March 1959 (HRH THE DUCHESS OF GLOUCESTER stood sponsor); *educ* Eton and Edinburgh U (BSc)' *read* '1 +HENRY (HARRY) FRANCIS CECIL [The Hon Henry Vane, Selaby, Gainford, Co Durham]; *b* 11 March 1959 (HRH THE DUCHESS OF GLOUCESTER stood sponsor); *educ* Eton and Edinburgh U (BSc); *m* 12 Dec 1998 *L Kate, yr dau of Christopher Robson, of Rudd Hall, Richmond, N Yorks'

BARRETT-LENNARD: *for* '1d *Deborah Susan . . . *m* . . . Riley' *read* '1d *Deborah Susan . . . *m* . . . Reilly'

BATH: *for* '1a *Ulrica Marjory [only dau of yst s of Lord Henry Frederick Thynne, 2nd s of 3rd Marquess]; *b* 5 May 1911, *m* 19 Feb 1936 (*divorce* 1961) Maj George Anthony Murray Smith, DL, MFH, RHG, of Gumley Hall, Market Harborough, s of Arthur Murray Smith, 2nd Life Gds' *read* '1a Ulrica Marjory; *b* 5 May 1911; Jt MFH Quorn 1959–85; author *The Magic of the Quorn* (1980); *m* 19 Feb 1936 (*divorce* 1961) Maj (George) (An)T(h)ony Murray Smith, DL, MFH, RHG (*m* 2nd 17 Nov 1961, as her 2nd husb, Sara Margaret, yr dau of Sir Henry Ralph Stanley Birkin, 3rd Bt, *qv*), of Gumley Hall, Market Harborough, s of Arthur Murray Smith, 2nd Life Gds, and *dsp* 22 Jan 1999'

BEAUFORT: *for* '1 +HENRY ('Bunter') JOHN FITZROY, *Marquess of Worcester*; *b* 22 May 1952; *educ* Eton; *m* 1987 *Tracy Louise, TV actress, yr dau of Hon Peter Alistair Ward (*see* DUDLEY, E), and has issue:

(1) +Robert (Bobby), *Earl of Glamorgan*; *b* 20 Jan 1989
(2) +Alexander; *b* 3 Sept 1995
(1) *Isabella Elsa; *b* 1991'

read '1 +HENRY ('Bunter') JOHN FitzROY, *Marquess of Worcester*; *b* 22 May 1952; *educ* Eton and RAC Cirencester; FRICS; with Morgan Grenfell Laurie Ltd then Franc Warwick; *m* 1987 *Tracy Louise, yr dau of Hon Peter Alistair Ward (*see* DUDLEY, E), and has:

(1) +Robert (Bobby), *Earl of Glamorgan*; *b* 20 Jan 1989
(2) +(Ale)Xan(der); *b* 3 Sept 1995
(1) *(Isa)Bella Elsa; *b* 1991'

also *see* below against DUDLEY, Earl

BEAVERBROOK: Jonathan Aitken's marriage to Lolicia Olivera Azucki was dissolved 1998

BERESFORD-PEIRSE: in entry for Raymond Windham de la Poer Beresford-Peirse [2nd s of Rev Windham de la Poer Beresford-Peirse, yst bro of 3rd Bt] *for* '*m* 2nd 28 Feb 1945 Suzanne Ashley (*d* 5 Oct 1967), widow of Sandys Stewart Macaskie etc' *read* '*m* 2nd 28 Feb 1945 Suzanne Ashley (*d* 5 Oct 1967), widow of Sandys Stewart Macaskie (*see also* LOWE, Bt) etc'

BERKELEY: *for* '1 Thomas (Sir)' [apparently est, but in reality only, s of 2nd Lord and 1st and last Marquess] *read* '(1) Thomas (Sir)'; *for* '1c +Janet Capel [Mrs Bryan Cleland, 450 Carrington, New Plymouth, NZ] [dau of dau of yr dau of s of 5th dau of 5th Earl of Berkeley]; *b* 1947; *m* 1969 *Bryan Alexander Cleland and has issue:

1d +Scott Law; *b* 1971
1d +Sarah Law; *b* 1971
2d +Sarah Jane Capel; *b* 1974'

read '1c +Janet Capel [Mrs Bryan Cleland, 450 Carrington, New Plymouth, New Zealand]; *b* 1947; *m* 1969 *Bryan Alexander Cleland and has:

1d +Scott Law; *b* 1971
1d +Sarah Jane Capel; *b* 1974'

BESSBOROUGH: *for* '3a *Nicholas (Nick) Ponsonby' [3rd s of 2nd dau of 4th s of 7th Earl] *read* '3a *Nicholas Ponsonby'

BETHELL: the 4th and present Baron's mother Ann Margaret Frances *d* 17 Aug 1996 not 1994

BICESTER: *see* ROSEBERY

BIRD: *for* '5a *Carol [Mrs Kenneth Rose, 6 Bibsworth Ave, Broadway, Hereford and Worcester] [yst dau of yr sis of 3rd Bt] *read* '5a *Carol [Mrs Kenneth Rose, 56 Elm Rd, Evesham, Worcs WR11 5DW]'

BIRDWOOD: Sarah-Jane Birdwood Muñoz-Gomez's dau Isabel Gwyneth [great-niece of 3rd and present Baron] was *b* 1992

BIRKIN: *for* '2a Sara Margaret; *m* 1st 1 June 1950 (*divorce* 1961), as his 2nd w of three, Maj James Robert Hanbury (*d* 4 March 1971), late Roy Scots Greys, Jt MFH Belvoir 1947–64, of Burley-on-the-Hill, Rutland, s of Maj Robert Evan Hanbury, and had issue:

1b *Evan ('Joss') Robert [Joss Hanbury Esq, Burley on the Hill, Oakham, Rutland]; *b* 18 March 1951; *educ* Eton and RAC Cirencester; sometime MFH Quorn and Cottesmore; *m* 1st 22 July 1974 (*divorce* 19–) Rosalind Jeanette (*m* 2nd 22 Dec 1997 Rodney Portman; *see* PORTMAN, V), dau of Derrick Allix Pease (*see* PEASE, Bt, of Hummersknott), and has issue; *m* 2nd 15 Jan 1995 *Nicky Rawlinson, of Stody, Norfolk, and has further issue:

1c *Sophie Rose; *b* 2 Oct 1996
2b *Timothy James [Timothy Hanbury Esq, Wembury House, Wembury, Plymouth PL9 0EF]; *b* 26 Sept 1952; *educ* Eton

2a (cont.) Mrs Sara Hanbury *m* 2nd 17 Nov 1961 Lt-Col George Anthony Murray Smith, s of Arthur George Murray Smith, of Gumley, Market Harborough, and *d* 1976'

read '2a Sara (Sally) Margaret; *m* 1st 1 June 1950 (*divorce* 1961), as his 2nd w of three, Maj James Robert Hanbury (*d* 4 March 1971), RSG, Jt MFH Belvoir 1947–64, of Burley-on-the-Hill, Rutland, s of Maj Robert Evan Hanbury, and had:

1b *Evan ('Joss') Robert [Joss Hanbury Esq, Burley-on-the-Hill, Oakham, Rutland]; *b* 18 March 1951; *educ* Eton and RAC Cirencester; sometime MFH Quorn and Cottesmore; *m* 1st 22 July 1974 (*divorce* 19–) Rosalind Jeanette (*m* 2nd 22 Dec 1997 Rodney Portman; *see* PORTMAN, V), dau of Derrick Allix Pease (*see* PEASE, Bt, of Hummersknott), and has issue; *m* 2nd 15 Jan 1995 *Nicky Rawlinson, of Stody, Norfolk, and by her has:

1c *Sophie Rose; *b* 2 Oct 1996
2b *Timothy James [Timothy Hanbury Esq, Wembury House, Wembury, Plymouth PL9 0EF]; *b* 26 Sept 1952; *educ* Eton

2a (cont.) Mrs Sara Hanbury *m* 2nd 17 Nov 1961, as his 2nd w, Lt-Col (George) (An)T(h)ony Murray Smith (*see* BATH, M) and *d* 1976'

BLAKE, Bt, of Menlough: the heir presumptive's address is 42 Higher Lane, Lymm, Cheshire WA13 0AZ

BLEDISLOE: in entry for Philip Charles Metcalfe Bathurst [yr s of 3rd s of yr bro of f of 1st Viscount] text should read '2a *Philip Charles Metcalfe [Philip Bathurst Esq, Appletree Cottage, Box, Glos GL9 9HH]; *b* 5 May 1922; Maj RE WW II; *m* 14 May 1953 *Winifrede Gillian, dau of Leonard Snowden Debenham, FRCS, and has:

1b *Nicholas Charles George; *b* 3 June 1954; FRCS, FRCR; *m* 24 Sept 1988 *Deborah Mary, dau of John Bernard Mitchell, MD, FRCP, and has:

1c *Alexander Philip David; *b* 10 Aug 1992
1c *Elizabeth Rosemary Anne; *b* 3 Feb 1990
2b *Robert Guy; *b* 22 Feb 1957; *m* 11 May 1985 *Caroline Victoria, dau of Richard Ian Threlfall, QC, and has:

1c *Matilda Charlotte Mora; *b* 14 Aug 1989
2c *Clemency Evelyn Anna; *b* 3 July 1991
3c *Oriel Alice; *b* 5 Jan 1994
4c *Honor Cecilia; *b* 10 Oct 1997
1b *Charlotte Mary; *b* 23 Sept 1961

BLUNT: the translation of the motto should read 'Thy [not 'The'] light is my life'

BOWMAN: three lines from end of article *for* 'Monymush' *read* 'Monymusk'

BOWNESS: *for* 'memb: Audit Commn 1983–, UK Delegn Cncl Europe 1990– and (for UK) Bureau and Transportn and Telecommunicns Commn EC Ctee Regns 1994–' *read* 'memb: Audit Commn 1983–, UK Delegn Cncl Europe 1990– and (for UK) Bureau and Transportn and Telecommunicns Commn EC Ctee Regns 1994–, C Spokesman Environment 1997–98'

BRABOURNE: *see* below against MOUNTBATTEN OF BURMA

BRAYBROOKE: the 10th and present Lord (Baron) *m* 3rd 2 Oct 1998 (the marriage with his 2nd w having been dissolved 1997 or 1998) *Perina, er dau of Baroness Butler of Saffron Walden (*see* 1970 edn) by her 1st husb Augustus Courtauld

BRIDGEMAN: *for* 'Caispar' *read* 'Caspar' and *for* '*b* 11 Jan 1995' *read* '*b* 16 Jan 1995'; in entry for issue of Daphne, the 3rd and present Viscount's sis, it is Frances Mary, the 2nd dau, not Rose Evelyn, the est, who *m* Mark Henry Leo Adams etc

BRISTOL: the 7th Marquess *d* 10 Jan 1999 and was *s* as 8th Marquess by his half-bro Lord Frederick Hervey

BROUGHSHANE: in entry for 2nd Baron's s Alexander *for* '*d* 1988, leaving by her' *read* '*d* 1988, leaving by his 2nd w'

BROUN: Peter James Dutton [2nd s of est dau of s of 9th Bt's 2nd s] has a 2nd dau, Emma Joan de Courcy, *b* 1987; in entry for his yst sis Miriam Lillian *for* 'Johannas Valks' *read* 'Johannes-Valk'

BRUCE, Bt, of Stenhouse: in entry for Louise Panette Bootes-Johns [yr dau of dau of s of er s of 3rd s of 7th Bt] *for* 'divorce' *read* 'separated'

BUCCLEUCH and QUEENSBERRY: the 7th/9th Duke's 3rd s's w, Lady George Montagu-Douglas-Scott, *d* 1 Nov 1998; in entry for Katharine Margaret [dau of yr s of 3rd s of 6th/8th Duke] *for* '[Mrs Robert Bernard etc' *read* '[Mrs Robert Spencer Bernard etc'

The 9th/11th (and present) Duke retired as Ld-Lt Roxburgh, Ettrick and Lauderdale 28 Sept 1998; his er gs by his est s (Richard John Walter, Earl of Dalkeith), Walter John Francis, Lord Eskdaill, ceased Jan 1999 to be a Page of Honour to HM THE QUEEN

BUCHAN-HEPBURN: *for* '**SIR (JOHN) ALASTAIR TRANT KIDD BUCHAN-HEPBURN**, of etc' *read* '**SIR (JOHN) ALASTAIR TRANT KIDD BUCHAN-HEPBURN, 7TH BT**, of etc'; a dau, Charlotte Mary, was *b* 30 Dec 1998 to the 7th and present Bt's only s

BURNETT: *for* 'Humphrey' *read* 'Humphery' throughout

BURNHAM: the 5th Baron's widow, Anne, *d* 3 Aug 1998

BURTON: *for* '**THE 3RD BARON BURTON OF BURTON-ON-TRENT AND OF RANGEMORE** . . . *m* 1st 28 April 1948 (*divorce* 1977) Elizabeth Ursula Forster (*d* 1993) etc' *read* '**THE 3RD BARON BURTON OF BURTON-ON-TRENT AND OF RANGEMORE** . . . *m* 1st 28 April 1948 (*divorce* 1977) (Elizabeth) Ursula Forster (*d* 1993) etc'

the 3rd and present Baron's 3rd dau, Georgina, *m* 30 Oct 1998, as his 3rd w, *Hugh Seymour, s of Leo Seymour (*see* HERTFORD, M)

BUTE: in entry for 5th Marquess's sis-in-law Helen *for* '[The Lady Helen Crichton-Stuart etc' *read* '[The Lady David Crichton-Stuart etc'; in her s's entry *for* '*b* 27 June' *read* '*b* 22 June'

BUTLER OF BROCKWELL: the Life Baron was apptd Feb 1999 a memb of the Royal Commission on Reform of the House of Lords

BUTT: the 2nd Bt *d* 10 Feb 1999, when the title expired; *for* '*m* 2nd 5 Aug 1948 *Marie Josephine [2nd Bt's 2nd w] etc' *read* '*m* 2nd 5 Aug 1948 *(Marie) Josephine (Joey) etc'

CABLE-ALEXANDER: the 8th and present Bt's er dau, Melanie Jane, gave birth 30 April 1998 to a s, Jasper, by the 1st Earl of Snowdon (*qv*)

CADOGAN: a yr s, Charles William Llewelyn, was *b* 2 Oct 1998 to Viscount and Viscountess Chelsea

CAIRNS: the 6th and present Earl's yst s, Alistair Benedict, *m* 26 Sept 1998 *Arabella, dau of Campbell Sim, of Four Elms, Kent, by Mrs Louisa Harmer, of Brook Green, London W6; the 6th and present Earl's only sis Elisabeth *d* 13 Oct 1998

CAITHNESS: in entry for 20th and present Earl's sis *for* '4 *Bridget Sarah [The Lady Bridget Oppenheim, 46 Lysia St, London SW6 6NG]; *b* 18 May 1947; *m* 1976 *Nicholas Anthony Oppenheim, son of Sir Duncan Oppenheim, and has issue:

  (1) *Christopher Duncan; *b* 1981
  (1) *Leonora Emily; *b* 1977
  (2) *Zerlina Gabrielle; *b* 1979'

read '4 *Bridget Sarah [The Lady Bridget Oppenheim, 46 Lysia St, London SW6 6NG]; *b* 18 May 1947; *m* 1976 *Nicholas Anthony Oppenheim, MA (Ch Ch Oxon), s of Sir Duncan Oppenheim (*see* MACNAGHTEN), and has:

  (1) *Christopher Duncan; *b* 29 April 1981
  (1) *Leonora Emily; *b* 4 July 1977
  (2) *Zerlina Gabrielle; *b* 8 June 1979'

CAREW: the 5th Baron's yst s's w, Barbara, *d* 18 Jan 1999

CARNARVON: Lord Porchester [the 7th and present Earl's er s and heir] *m* 2nd 18 Feb 1999 *Fiona, fashion designer, dau of Ronnie Aitken

CECIL OF ESSENDON: *for* 'Shadow Leader Ho Lds 1997–' *read* 'Shadow Leader Ho Lds 1997–98'

COLERAINE: the 2nd and present Baron *m* 12 Sept 1998 *Mrs Bobbie Smyth, of Sunderlandwick, Driffield, N Yorks

COPE OF BERKELEY: the Life Baron was appointed Front-Bench C Spokesman Home Affrs Ho Lds Nov 1998

CORY-WRIGHT: *for* '**SIR RICHARD MICHAEL CORY-WRIGHT, 4TH BT** . . . ; *m* 1976 *Veronica Mary, dau of James Harold Lucas Bolton, of Church Farm, Morningthorpe, Norwich, and has issue:

  1 +ROLAND ANTHONY; *b* 11 March 1979
  2 +Jonathan James; *b* 1981
. 3 +Felix Michael; *b* 1986'

read '**SIR RICHARD MICHAEL CORY-WRIGHT, 4TH BT** . . . ; *m* 1st 1976 Veronica Mary, dau of James Harold Lucas Bolton, of Church Farm, Morningthorpe, Norwich, and has:

  1 +ROLAND ANTHONY; *b* 11 March 1979
  2 +Jonathan James; *b* 1981
  3 +Felix Michael; *b* 1986

Sir MICHAEL *m* 2nd 11 Nov 1998 *Helga Wright, of Dorchester-on-Thames, Oxon'

CRATHORNE: *for* '**THE 2ND BARON CRATHORNE**, of Crathorne, N R Co York, and a **Baronet** (Sir (Charles) James Dugdale, Bt, DL (Cleveland 1983)) [The Rt Hon The Lord Crathorne DL, Crathorne House, Yarm, Cleveland TS15 0AT]; *b* 12 Sept 1939; s *f* 1977; *educ* Eton and Trin Coll Cambridge (MA); FRSA; consultant and lecturer in fine art, assist to Pres Parke-Bennet New York 1965–69, James Dugdale & Associates London, Independent Fine Art Consultancy Serv 1969–77, James Crathorne & Associates 1980–, memb: Yorks Regnl Ctee Nat Tst 1978–84 and 1988–, Court Leeds U 1985–, Conservative Advisory Gp Arts and Heritage 1988–; chm Georgian Gp 1990–, tstee: Georgian Theatre Royal Richmond 1970–, Capt Cook Tst 1978– (chm 1993–), Christian Inheritance 1989– and Nat Heritage Memorial Fund 1992–, dir: Blakeney Hotels Ltd 1981– and Woodhouse Securities Ltd 1989– etc'

read '**THE 2ND BARON CRATHORNE**, of Crathorne, N R Co York, and a **Baronet** (Sir (Charles) James Dugdale, Bt) [The Rt Hon The Lord Crathorne, Crathorne House, Yarm, N Yorks TS15 0AT]; *b* 12 Sept 1939; s *f* 1977; *educ* Eton and Trin Coll Cambridge (MA); FRSA; consultant and lecturer in fine art, assist to Pres Parke-Bennet New York 1965–69, James Dugdale & Associates London, Independent Fine Art Consultancy Serv 1969–77, James Crathorne & Associates 1980–, memb: Yorks Regnl Ctee Nat Tst 1978–84 and 1988–, Court Leeds U 1985–, Conservative Advisory Gp Arts and Heritage 1988–; Ld Lt N Yorks 1999– (DL 1983–99); chm Georgian Gp 1990–, tstee: Georgian Theatre Royal Richmond 1970–, Capt Cook Tst 1978– (chm 1993–), Christian Inheritance 1989– and Nat Heritage Memorial Fund 1992–, dir: Blakeney Hotels Ltd 1981– and Woodhouse Securities Ltd 1989– etc'

DACRE: *for* 'Robert ('Bertie') (Sir), GCB (1998, KCB 1991, CB 1987), KCVO (1989, LVO 1982), PC (1990) [er s of 2nd dau of Margaret, the 24th Lord's est dau]; *b* 1941; *educ* Eton; Assist Priv Sec to HM THE QUEEN 1977–85, Dep Priv Sec 1985–90, Priv Sec 1990–; *m* 1978 *Lady (Cynthia) Jane Spencer, 2nd dau of of 8th Earl Spencer (*qv*), and has issue:'

read 'Robert ('Bertie') (Sir), GCB (1998, KCB 1991, CB 1987), KCVO (1989, LVO 1982), PC (1990); *b* 11 Dec 1941; *educ* Eton; Scots Gds 1960–63, dir: Allen Harvey & Ross (discount brokers and bankers) 1968–77 and South African Breweries 1999–; Priv Sec to HM THE QUEEN 1990–99 (Assist Priv Sec 1977–85, Dep Priv Sec 1985–90), v-chm Barclays Private Banking 1999–; *m* 1978 *Lady (Cynthia) Jane Spencer, 2nd dau of of 8th Earl Spencer (*qv*), and has:'

DEAN OF THORNTON-LE-FYLDE: the Life Baroness was apptd Feb 1999 a memb of the Royal Commission on Reform of the House of Lords

DE MAULEY: in entry for only s of only s of Capt Victor Coope Ponsonby, MC [4th s of 4th s of 2nd Baron] *for* '+John Maurice Maynard; *b* 8 Aug 1955; S/Ldr RAF etc' *read* '+John Maurice Maynard, OBE (1998); *b* 8 Aug 1955; Gp Capt RAF etc'

DENNING: the Life Baron was made a Chev Legn Hon 1998

DENTON OF WAKEFIELD: *for* 'Oppn Spokesman NI 1997–' *read* 'C Spokesman NI 1997–98, Front Bench C Spokesman Trade and Industry 1998–'

DERBY: the 19th and present Earl was apptd Jan 1999 DL Merseyside

DEVON: the 17th Earl *d* 19 Nov 1998 and was s as 18th Earl by his only s

DEVONSHIRE: the 11th and present Duke's w, Deborah Vivien, was made DCVO in the 1998–99 New Year's Honours List

DERWENT: the 5th and present Baron's 3rd and yst dau, Isabella Catherine Sophie, *m* 19 Sept 1998 *Nikolai Tabain, only s of Hugo Tabain, of Wonthaggi, Australia

DIGBY: the 12th and present Baron was made a KCVO in the 1998–99 New Year's Honours List; also (against his entry) *for* 'V-Lt 196550' *read* 'V-Lt 1965–84, Ld-Lt 1984–'

DIXON-SMITH: the Life Baron was appointed Dec 1998 a Front-Bench C Spokesman on local govt

DOWNSHIRE: the 8th and present Marquess's 2nd w, Diana Marion, *d* 1 Aug 1998

DUDLEY, Earl: *for* '(2) *Tracy Louise [The Most Hon The Marchioness of Worcester, Badminton House, Glos GL9 1DB] [the 4th and present Earl's n]; *b* 22 Dec 1958; *m* 1987 *Henry John FitzRoy, Marquess of Worcester, est s of 11th Duke of Beaufort (*qv*), and has issue' *read* '(2) *Tracy Louise [Marchioness of Worcester, Badminton House, Glos GL9 1DB]; *b* 22 Dec 1958; actress (including part in TV series *Cats' Eyes* and (as Miss Scarlet) *Cluedo*); Tstee: Friends of the Earth, Soil Assoc and Transport 2000; assoc dir Internat Soc for for Ecology and Culture; pres: Community Action and Good Gardeners' Assoc; *m* 1987 *Henry John FitzRoy, Marquess of Worcester, est s of 11th Duke of Beaufort (*qv*), and has:'

DUNDONALD: *for* 'Lynette Joy Caites' *read* 'Lynette Joy Carter'

DUNSANY: the 19th Baron *d* 6 Feb 1999 and was s as 20th Baron by his only s

ECCLES: the 1st Viscount *d* 24 Feb 1999 and was s as 2nd Viscount by his er s; *see* also ECCLES OF MOULTON

ECCLES OF MOULTON: the Life Baroness's husb s his f 24 Feb 1999 as 2nd Viscount Eccles

EDWARDS, Bt, of Treforis: the 2nd Bt *d* 19 Feb 1999, when the title expired

EGLINTON and WINTON: the 18th/6th and present Earl's 3rd s, James David, *m* 26 Sept 1998 *Philippa, est dau of Dr N E Williams

ELGIN and KINCARDINE: the 11th/14th and present Earl's yst s, Alexander Victor, *m* 26 Sept 1998 *Victoria, er dau of David Bythell, of East Kirkland, Newton Stewart

ERROLL: the w of the 24th and present Earl's bro Peregrine gave birth 6 Nov 1998 to a 3rd dau

FALCONER OF THOROTON: the Life Baron was given part responsibility Jan 1999 for the Millennium Dome

FINLAY: the 2nd Bt *m* 5 Sept 1998 *Camilla, dau of Peter Acheson, of Castlecaulfield, Co Tyrone

FORBES ADAM: in entry for Carles David Adam [est s of 3rd s of 3rd s of 1st Bt] *for* '*m* 1987' *read* '*m* 1982'; in second part of entry for Nigel Colin Forbes Adam, JP, [3rd s of 3rd s of 1st Bt] *for* '(3) Nigel Adam *m* 2nd' *read* '(3) (cont.) Nigel Adam *m* 2nd'

FORESTER: the 8th and present Baron's est dau, Selina Lucy, *m* 11 July 1998 *Ian Graham, s of Michael Graham, of Raffingora, Zimbabwe

FRASER OF CARMYLLIE: *for* 'Min State: Scottish Off 1992–95 and DTI 1995–97' *read* 'Min State: Scottish Off 1992–95 and DTI 1995–97, Shadow Dep Leader Ho Lds 1997–98, Chm Internat Petroleum Exchange 1998–'

GEDDES: *for* '1 *Margaret Clair [3rd and present Baron's dau]; *b* 5 Oct 1967' *read* '1 *(Margaret) Clair; *b* 5 Oct 1967'

in entry for the Hon Mrs van Koetsveld [Margaret Ross, 2nd Baron's only dau] *for* '*m* 6 May 1961 *Ralph Emilius Quintus van Koetsveld, son of Johan Emilius van Koetsveld, of Rotterdam, and has issue:

(1) *Michael William, *b* 16 March 1963
(2) *Antony Guy Hans, *b* 30 July 1964
(3) *Christopher Dirk, *b* 11 Feb 1969'

read 'm 6 May 1961 *(Ralph Emilius) Quintus van Koetsveld, s of Johan Emilius van Koetsveld, of Rotterdam, and has:

(1) *Michael William; *b* 16 March 1963
(2) *(Antony) Guy Hans; *b* 30 July 1964
(3) *(Christopher) Dirk; *b* 11 Feb 1969'

the 2nd Baron's widow, Enid Mary, *d* 28 Jan 1999; the 3rd and present Baron's 1st w *d* 1995

GILBERT: *for* 'm 2nd 1963 *Jean Olive Ross Skinner' *read* 'm 2nd 23 March 1963 *Jean Olive, dau of William Milne Ross-Skinner (*see* PEASE, Bt, of Hummersknott)'

GLENCONNER: *for* '(3) *Stella [yr dau of Hon Tobias William Tennant, 3rd s (by his 1st w) of 2nd Baron]; *b* 17 Dec 1970; model' *read* '(3) *Stella; *b* 17 Dec 1970; *educ* Winchester Sch of Art; model (including 'Face of Chanel' 1996–98); has by *David Lasnet, photographer:

1a *Marcel; *b* Aug 1998'

GLENDEVON: in entry for the 2nd Baron *for* 'm 21 July 1948 *Elizabeth (Liz) Mary etc' *read* 'm 21 July 1948 Elizabeth (Liza) Mary (*d* 27 Dec 1998) etc'

GLYN: the 5th/9th Bt's widow Barbara *d* 15 June 1998

GORING: the 13th and present Bt *m* 3rd 5 Dec 1998 *Stephanie, dau of George Carter and formerly w of — Bullock

GRADE: the Life Baron *d* 13 Dec 1998, when the title expired

GRAHAM, Bt, of Norton Conyers: *for* 'Sir REGINALD *d* 2 June 1940; his est son,
Sir Richard Bellingham, 10th Bt, OBE'

read 'Sir REGINALD *d* 2 June 1940; his est s,
Sir Richard Bellingham Graham, 10th Bt, OBE'

GREEN: *for* '*Lucy Rose Lycett [est dau of 2nd s of 2nd s of 2nd Bt]; *b* 15 Dec 1964; *m* 1988 *Alexander Evelyn Giles Ward (*see* BANGOR, V)' *read* '*Lucy Rose Lycett; *b* 15 Dec 1964; *m* 1988 *Alexander Evelyn Giles Ward and has issue (*see* DUDLEY, E)'

GUINNESS: John Ralph Sidney Guinness, CB [yr s of Capt Edward (Ned) Guinness, 2nd s of Howard Rundell Guinness, 3rd s of Henry Guinness, of Burton Hall, Stillorgan, Co Dublin, yr s of Robert Rundell Guinness, also of Stillorgan, who was 2nd cousin of the 1st Bt] was made a Knight Bachelor in the 1998–99 New Year's Honours List

HACKING: the 3rd and present Baron's marriage to Tessa Margaret, *née* Hunt, was dissolved by 1998 and she subsequently *m* Antony Askew; the 3rd and present Baron's only dau, Dr Belinda Anne, *m* 19 Sept 1998 *Simon Holden, yr s of Maj Christopher Holden; the 2nd Baron's widow, Daphne, *d* June 1998

also *for* '1 *Elizabeth Margery, JP (Hants 1968) [The Hon Lady Waller, Hatchway, Hatch Lane, Kingsley Green, Haslemere, Surrey] [only dau of 1st Baron], late JP Newcastle-upon-Tyne; *b* 4 May 1916; *m* 2 April 1936 *Sir George Stanley Waller, OBE, WCdr RAFVR, BA Camb, Judge Queen's Bench, only s of James Stanley Waller, and has issue:

(1) *George Mark (Sir), QC (1979); *b* 13 Oct 1940, LLB; barrister Gray's Inn 1964, Recorder 1986, Judge Queen's Bench 1989, ktd 1989; *m* 29 April 1967 *Rachel Elizabeth, er dau of Judge Christopher Beaumont, MBE, and has:

1a *Charles James; *b* 4 Nov 1968
2a *Richard; *b* 1969
3a *Philip; *b* 1973'

read '1 *Elizabeth (Peg) Margery, JP (Hants 1968, formerly Newcastle) [The Hon Lady Waller, Hatchway, Hatch Lane, Kingsley Green, Surrey GU27 3LJ]; *b* 4 May 1916; *m* 2 April 1936 Sir George Stanley Waller, OBE, PC, WCdr RAFVR, BA Cantab, Ld Justice Appeal 1976–84 (*d* 5 Feb 1999), only s of James Stanley Waller, and has had:

(1) *(George) Mark (Sir), PC (1996); *b* 13 Oct 1940; *educ* Oundle and Durham U (LLB); barrister Gray's Inn 1964, Bencher 1988, QC 1979, Recorder 1986–89, High Court Judge Queen's Bench 1989–96, Presiding Judge NE Circuit 1992–95, Judge in charge Commercial List 1995–96, Ld Justice Appeal 1996–, ktd 1989; *m* 29 April 1967 *Rachel Elizabeth, er dau of Judge Christopher Beaumont, MBE, and has had:

1a Charles James; *b* 4 Nov 1968; *d* 8 Sept 1997
2a *Richard; *b* 1969
3a *Philip; *b* 1973'

HAILSHAM OF ST MARYLEBONE: the Life Baron's 3rd w, Deirdre Margaret, *d* 22 Dec 1998

HAMBRO: the Life Baron stepped down as chm GRE April 1999

HAMILTON and BRANDON: in entry for current Duke *for* '2 *Ann; *b* 14 May 1976

The 15th DUKE *m* 2nd 1988 *Jillian, dau of Noel Robertson, of Sydney, NSW, and formerly w of (a) Martin Page and (b) Edward, s of Sir Edward Hulton'

read '2 *Ann; *b* 14 May 1976; *m* 1 Aug 1998 *—

The 15th/12th DUKE *m* 2nd 1988 Jillian, dau of Noel Robertson, of Sydney, NSW, and formerly w of (a) Martin Page and (b) Edward, s of Sir Edward Hulton; *m* 3rd *c* 17 July 1998 *Kay, formerly w of — Carmichael'

HARLECH: the 6th and present Baron's marriage to Amanda Grieve was dissolved 31 Aug 1998

HASKEL: *for* 'Ld in Waiting (Govt Whip) 1997–' *read* 'Ld in Waiting (Govt Whip) 1997–98'

HAWARDEN: *for* '**THE 9TH VISCOUNT HARWARDEN**' *read* '**THE 9TH VISCOUNT HAWARDEN**';

in entry for 1st Bt, *for* '1727030' *read* '1727–30'

HAWKE: *for* '**THE 11TH BARON HAWKE OF TOWTON**, Co York (Edward George Hawke, TD) [The Rt Hon The Lord Hawke TD, Old Mill House, Cuddington, Northwich, Cheshire]; *b* 25 Jan 1950; *s f* 1992; *educ* Eton; 2nd Lt 1st Bn Coldstream Gds 1970–73, Maj QO Yeo 1973–93; FRICS; *m* 1993 *Bronwen M, dau of William T James, BVMS, MRCVS' *read* '**THE 11TH BARON HAWKE OF TOWTON**, Co York (Edward George Hawke, TD) [The Rt Hon The Lord Hawke TD, Old Mill House, Cuddington, Northwich, Cheshire]; *b* 25 Jan 1950; *s f* 1992; *educ* Eton; 2nd Lt 1st Bn Coldstream Gds 1970–73, Maj QO Yeo 1973–93; FRICS; *m* 1993 *Bronwen M, dau of William T James, BVMS, MRCVS, and has:

1 +WILLIAM MARTIN THEODORE; *b* 23 July 1995
1 *Alice Julia; *b* 8 Feb 1999'

for '1 EDWARD GEORGE HAWKE, **11th and present Baron Kawke of Towton**' *read* '1 EDWARD GEORGE HAWKE, **11th and present Baron Hawke of Towton**'

HAZLERIGG: the 2nd and present Baron's next yr bro, Thomas Heron Hazlerigg, *d* 31 July 1998

HENLEY: in entry for 8th and current Baron *for* 'Parly Under Sec: DSS 1989–93 and Employment 1993–94, MOD 1994–95, Min State Educn and Employment 1995–' *read* 'Parly U-Sec: DSS 1989–93 and Employment 1993–94, MOD 1994–95, Min State Educn and Employment 1995–97, C Spokesman Ho Lds 1997–98, C Ch Whip Ho Lds 1998–'

HEREFORD: *for* '**Hereford, previous creations:** It is possible that an Earldom of Hereford existed well before the Norman Conquest, although the putative holder, Ralph, a nephew of EDWARD THE CONFESSOR, seems on the balance of probability to have been Earl of the next door county of Worcester(shire) — at any rate so early as the late 1040s. (For the lack of distinction between county town and county names in assigning early medieval earldoms *see* in particular WINCHESTER, M, preliminary remarks.) By the mid-1050s the evidence for Ralph's possessing the Earldom of Hereford itself is stronger, though by no means conclusive.' *read* '**Hereford, previous creations:** It is possible that an Earldom of Hereford existed well before the Norman Conquest, although the putative holder, Ralph, a nephew of EDWARD THE CONFESSOR, seems on the balance of probability as it appeared to the 19th-century medievalist Professor Freeman to have been Earl of the next door county of Worcester(shire) — at any rate so early as the late 1040s. (For the lack of distinction between county town and county names in assigning early medieval earldoms *see* in particular WINCHESTER, M, preliminary remarks.) By the mid-1050s the evidence for Ralph's possessing the Earldom of Hereford itself is stronger, though by no means conclusive.'

HERTFORD: *for* '1d +Hugh Leopold [er s of er s of 2nd s of 2nd s of Rt Hon Sir George Seymour, only s of Lord George Seymour, 7th s of 1st Marquess) [Hugh Seymour Esq, Home Farm, Stobo, Peebles, Scotland]; *b* 2 July 1943; *educ* Eton and Magdalene Coll Cambridge (BA 1965, MA 1969); *m* 1st 6 Jan 1971 (*divorce* 1978) Emma Mary, only dau of Robert Henderson (*see* LOWTHER, Bt); *m* 2nd 31 May 1979 *Camilla Madelaine Gerard, yr dau of Col William Henry Gerard Leigh (*see* 1970 edn LESLIE, Bt, of Wardis), and by his 2nd w has issue:

1e *Molly Rose; *b* 3 Aug 1983'

read '1d +Hugh Leopold [Hugh Seymour Esq, Home Farm, Stobo, Peebles]; *b* 2 July 1943; *educ* Eton and Magdalene Coll Cambridge (BA 1965, MA 1969); *m* 1st 6 Jan 1971 (*divorce* 1978) Emma Mary, only dau of Robert Henderson (*see* LOWTHER, Bt); *m* 2nd 31 May 1979 Camilla Madelaine Gerard, yr dau of Col William Henry Gerard Leigh (*see* LESLIE, Bt), and by her has:

1e *Molly Rose; *b* 3 Aug 1983

1d (cont.) Hugh Seymour *m* 3rd 30 Oct 1998 *Hon Georgina Baillie, 3rd dau of 3rd Baron Burton (*qv*)'

HERVEY-BATHURST: the 6th Bt's half-bro's er s, James Felton Somers Hervey-Bathurst, was elected Nov 1998 Dep Pres HHA

HEWITT: the 3rd and current Bt's yr s, Michael Joseph, *m* 5 Sept 1998 *Lucinda, dau of Martin Dawson-Brown, of Low Askew, N Yorks

HOBHOUSE: in entry for 7th and current Bt *for* 'm 1993 *Katrina etc' *read* 'm 1993 (*divorce* 1997) Katrina etc'

HOFFMANN: the Life Baron is in addition to his other posts Chm Amnesty Internat Charity Ltd

HOLMPATRICK: the 3rd Baron's widow, Anne Loys Roche, *d* 23 Dec 1998

HOME: in entry for 15th and current Earl *for* 'chm Morgan Grenfell (Scotland) and Morgan Grenfell Internat' *read* 'chm Morgan Grenfell (Scotland) and Morgan Grenfell Internat, C Spokesman Trade and Industry Ho Lds 1997–98'

for '+(Alexander) Sholto [Sholto Douglas-Home Esq, 20 Redcliffe St, London SW10 9DT] [only s of er s of Hon Henry Montagu Douglas-Home, 2nd s of 13th Earl]; *b* 1 Sept 1962; author *Zayat Restaurant Guide to London* (1996); *m* 1992 *Alexandra, dau of Benjamin Miller, turf accountant (*see* also BRADFORD, E)' *read* '+(Alexander) Sholto [Sholto Douglas-Home Esq, 20 Redcliffe St, London SW10 9DT]; *b* 1 Sept 1962; mktg dir New Millennium Experience Co, author *Zayat Restaurant Guide to London* (1996); *m* 1992 *Alexandra, dau of Benjamin Miller, turf accountant (*see* also BRADFORD, E), and has:

1b +Louis Robin; *b* Jan 1999'

HOWARD-LAWSON: the 6th and current Bt's dau, Julia Frances Veronica (described as 'Julia Howard'), *m* 28 Nov 1998 *William A R Davie, er s of W F Davie and Mrs Ian Sinclair

HOWE OF ABERAVON: the Life Baron's w, Elspeth, was made CBE in the 1998–99 New Year Honours List

HUNT: the Life Baron *d* Nov 1998, when the title expired

HUNTINGDON: the 17th and present Earl gave up his career as a racehorse trainer, including the post of Trainer to HM THE QUEEN, at the end of the 1998 season; the 16th Earl's est dau, Lady Moorea Black, was made an MBE in the 1998–99 New Year's Honours List

HUNTINGFIELD: *for* '2c +William Prentice [William Vanneck, 521 Riversville Rd, Greenwich, CT 06831, USA] [yr s of only s of yr s of only s of 3rd s of 1st Baron]; *b* 15 Jan 1941; *m* 1st 4 Aug 1962 (*divorce* 1990) Nancy Walker, dau of

Lanphear Buck, of Rye, NY; *m* 2nd 19– *Rebbeca Heffington and by his 1st w has issue:

    1d +John Lanphear; *b* 2 Aug 1963

    2d +Richard Prentice; *b* 7 Jan 1966; *m* 1991 *Karen Elizabeth Bugniazet, and has issue:

        1e *Lindsay Bailey; *b* 1992'

read '2c +William Prentice [William P Vanneck, 217 West Indies Dve, Palm Beach, FL 33480, USA]; *b* 15 Jan 1941; v-pres Equitable Holding Corp, New York; *m* 1st 4 Aug 1962 (*divorce* 1990) Nancy Walker, dau of Lanphear Buck, of Rye, NY; *m* 2nd 28 June 1990 (*divorce* 1998) Rebecca Heffington and by his 1st w has:

    1d +John Lanphear; *b* 2 Aug 1963

    2d +Richard Prentice; *b* 7 Jan 1966; *m* 1991 *Karen Elizabeth Bugniazet and has:

        1e +William James; *b* 1994

        1e *Lindsay Bailey; *b* 1992'

HURD OF WESTWELL: the Life Baron was apptd July 1998 a memb of the Conservative Party constitutional commn to look at Ho Lds reform and Feb 1999 a memb of the Royal Commission on Reform of the House of Lords

HUSSEY OF NORTH BRADLEY: the Life Baron was apptd May 1998 pres Iris Fund for Prevention of Blindness

INCHCAPE: the 2nd Earl's 2nd s, Alan John Francis, *d* 1 Feb 1999

JACKSON, Bt, of Arlsey: *for* '1c *Peter Daer, CB (1981) [Maj-Gen Peter Reid CB, The Border House, Cholderton, nr Salisbury, Wilts][s of Maj-Gen Peter Reid, CB, er s of Dorothy Hungerford, *née* Jackson, only dau of Mountstuart Hungerford Jackson, est s of Elphinstone Jackson, er s by his 1st w of Judge Welby Brown Jackson, 3rd s of 1st Bt]; *b* 5 Aug 1925; Maj-Gen late Roy Dragoons; *m* 9 Aug 1958 *Catherine Fleetwood, yst dau of Wilfred Andrew Carmichael Boodle, and has:

    1d *Duncan Andrew Daer; *b* 1959'

read '1c *Peter Daer, CB (1981) [Maj-Gen Peter Reid CB, The Border House, Cholderton, Wilts SP4 0DU]; *b* 5 Aug 1925; *educ* Cheltenham and Wadham Coll Oxford; commissioned Coldstream Gds 1945, tfd Roy Dragoons 1947 (CO 1965–68), Staff Coll 1959, RCDS 1973, RAC: Cdr 3rd Div 1974–76 and Dir 1976–78, Ch Exec Main Battle Tank 80 Project 1979–80, Dir Armoured Warfare Studies 1981, def advsr GKN 1983–88, mil advsr Howden Airdynamics 1982–88, assoc memb Burdenshaw Assocs (USA) 1982–94, def consultant Vickers Defence Systems 1989–94; *m* 9 Aug 1958 *Catherine Fleetwood, yst dau of Wilfred Andrew Carmichael Boodle, and has:

    1d *Duncan Andrew Daer; *b* 1959

    2d *Jamie Douglas Daer; *m* 10 Aug 1998 *Diana Audrey Constance, er dau of Maj Robin David Oswald Petre (*see* PETRE, B)

        1d *A dau'

JERSEY: the 9th Earl *d* 9 Aug 1998 and was *s* as 10th Earl by his gs

KENNEDY OF THE SHAWS: *for* 'memb: Bar Cncl 1990–93, Ctee Assoc Women Barristers 1991–, Nat Bd Women's Legal Def Fund 1989–91, Cncl Howard League Penal Reform 1989– (Chm Commn on violence in penal institutions for children 1994–), CIBA Commn into Child Sexual Abuse 1981–83, Bd *City Limits* Magazine 1982–84, Exec Ctee NCCL 1983–85, Bd Minority Access to Legal Profession Project South Bank Poly 1984–85, Bd Hampstead Theatre 1989–, Bd *New Statesman* 1990–, Bd *Counsel* Magazine 1990–; Chm: Haldane Soc 1983–86 (V-Pres 1986–), Charter '88 1992–, Standing Ctee for Youth Justice NACRO 1993–, London Internat Festival of Theatre 1993' *read* 'memb: Bar Cncl 1990–93, Ctee Assoc Women Barristers 1991–, Nat Bd Women's Legal Def Fund 1989–91, Cncl Howard League Penal Reform 1989– (Chm Commn on violence in penal institutions for children 1994–), CIBA Commn into Child Sexual Abuse 1981–83, Bd *City Limits* Magazine 1982–84, Exec Ctee NCCL 1983–85, Bd Minority Access to Legal Profession Project South Bank Poly 1984–85, Bd Hampstead Theatre 1989–, Bd *New Statesman* 1990–, Bd *Counsel* Magazine 1990– and Internat Assoc of Democratic Lawyers; Chm: Haldane Soc 1983–86 (V-Pres 1986–), Charter '88 1992–, Standing Ctee for Youth Justice NACRO 1993–, London Internat Festival of Theatre 1993, Br Cncl 1998–'

KILMOREY: in entry for 6th and present Earl *for* 'author *Honourable Member* (1983)' *read* 'author: *Honourable Member* (1983) and *Battling for Peace: Northern Ireland's Longest-Serving British Minister* (1999)'

KINGSLAND: the Life Baron was apptd Shadow Ld Chllr 1997

KINLOSS: in entry for Roger Temple Morgan-Grenville [s of John Richard Bine Morgan-Grenville, 1st cousin of present Lady Kinloss] *for* '1a +Roger Temple etc' *read* '1a +Roger Temple [Roger Morgan-Grenville Esq, Park Cottage, Upperton, W Sussex GU28 9BL] etc'

KITCHENER: *for* '1a *Emma Joy [only dau of yr bro of 3rd and present Earl] [Mrs Julian Fellowes, 15 Moore St, London SW3 2QN]; *b* 18 Feb 1963; *m* 1990 *Julian Alexander Fellowes, yst s etc' *read* '1a *Emma Joy [Mrs Julian Kitchener-Fellowes, 15 Moore St, London SW3 2QN]; *b* 18 Feb 1963; Ldy-in-Waiting to HRH PRINCESS MICHAEL OF KENT; *m* 1990 *Julian Alexander FELLOWES later KITCHENER-FELLOWES, actor, yst s etc'

LANESBOROUGH: the 9th Earl *d* 21 Dec 1998, when all his titles expired

VOLUME II

LEICESTER: the 7th and current Earl was elected Pres HHA Nov 1998; Polly, w of his er s and heir, Thomas Edward, Viscount Coke, gave birth 29 Dec 1998 to a dau, Hermione Belinda

LEWIN: the Life Baron *d* 23 Jan 1999, when the title expired

LINLITHGOW: a yr dau, Georgina Anne, was *b* 30 Nov 1998 to the Earl and Countess of Hopetoun

LISBURNE: *for* '1 +DAVID JOHN FRANCIS MALET, *Viscount Vaughan* [Viscount Vaughan, 4 Porthmeor Studios, Porthmeor Sq, St Ives, Cornwall]; *b* 15 June 1945; *educ* Ampleforth; *m* 1973 *Jennifer Jane, only dau of James Desire John William Fraser Campbell, of Glengarry, Inverness-shire, and has issue:

    (1) +Digby Dylan; *b* 1973

    (1) *Lucy Bronwyn; *b* 1971

2 +Michael John Wilmot Malet [The Hon Michael Vaughan, 44 Pembroke Sq, London W8]; *b* 26 June 1948; *educ* Ampleforth and New Coll Oxford (MA); *m* 16 Sept 1978 *Lucinda, er dau of 7th Baron Ashburton (*qv*), and has issue:

    (1) *Emma Rose Nightingale; *b* 1983'

read '1 +DAVID JOHN FRANCIS MALET, *Viscount Vaughan* [Viscount Vaughan, 4 Porthmeor Studios, Porthmeor Sq, St Ives, Cornwall]; *b* 15 June 1945; *educ* Ampleforth; *m* 1973 *Jennifer Jane, only dau of James Desire John William Fraser Campbell, of Glengarry, Inverness-shire, and has:

    (1) *Digby Dylan; *b* 3 Jan 1973

    (1) *Lucy Bronwyn; *b* 1971

2 +Michael John Wilmot Malet [The Hon Michael Vaughan, 44 Tite St, London SW3 4JA]; *b* 26 June 1948; *educ* Ampleforth and New Coll Oxford (MA); *m* 16 Sept 1978 *Lucinda, er dau of 7th Baron Ashburton (*qv*), and has:

    (1) +Edward Wilmot Malet; *b* 1 Sept 1998

    (1) *Emma Rose Nightingale; *b* 1983'

LISLE: the 7th Baron's widow, Mary [not Marie] Helen, *d* 24 Jan 1999

LODER: the 3rd Bt *d* 24 Feb 1999 and was *s* as 4th Bt by his er s

LONDESBOROUGH: the 7th Baron's widow (his 3rd w), Jocelyn ('Josh') Helen, *d* 15 Dec 1998

LONGFORD: *for* '1 *(Margaret) Pansy Felicia [The Lady Pansy Lamb, via di Santo Stefano del Cacco 22, Rome, Italy] [est sis of 7th and present Earl]; *b* 18 May 1904; *m* 15 Aug 1928 Henry Taylor Lamb, MC, RA (*d* 8 Oct 1960), s of Prof Sir Horace Lamb, and has:' *read* '1 *(Margaret) Pansy Felicia; *b* 18 May 1904; author: *The Old Expedient, August* (1931) (novels) and a biography of Charles I (1936); *m* 15 Aug 1928 Henry Taylor Lamb, MC, RA (*d* 8 Oct 1960), s of Prof Sir Horace Lamb, and *d* 19 Feb 1999, leaving:

LOVAT: in entry for Mrs Paul Soros [2nd dau of Hon Sir Hugh Fraser, yr s of 14th Lord] *for* '*m* 1st 1980 (*divorce* 1992) Robert J Powell-Jones, barrister etc' *read* '*m* 1st 1980 (*divorce* 1992) Robert James Powell-Jones, barrister (*d* 17 Dec 1998) etc'

for '1 Simon Augustus, *Master of Lovat*; *b* 28 Aug 1939; *educ* Ampleforth; Lt Scots Gds; *m* 21 Feb 1972 *Virginia [The Hon Mrs Simon Fraser, Beaufort Lodge, Beauly, Inverness-shire], dau of David Grose, of Chelsea, and *d* 26 March 1994 while out hunting, leaving:

    (1) SIMON FRASER, **16th and present Lord (Fraser of) Lovat**'

read '1 Simon Augustus, *Master of Lovat*; *b* 28 Aug 1939; *educ* Ampleforth; Lt Scots Gds; *m* 21 Feb 1972 *Virginia (*m* 2nd 23 Dec 1998 Frank Robert Johnson, ed *Spectator* 1995–), dau of David Grose, of Chelsea, and *d* 26 March 1994 while out hunting, leaving:

    (1) SIMON FRASER, **16th and present Lord (Fraser of) Lovat**'

LOWE: in entry for 3rd Bt's 2nd w *for* 'yr dau of Sandys Mackaskie and Mrs R Beresford Pairse' *read* 'yr dau of Sandys Stewart Macaskie (*see* BERESFORD-PEIRSE, Bt)'

LOWRY: the Life Baron *d* 15 Jan 1999, when the title expired

MACANDREW: *for* '**THE 3RD BARON MacANDREW**, of the Firth of Clyde (Christopher Anthony Colin MacAndrew) [The Rt Hon The Lord MacAndrew, Hall Farm, Archdean Newton, Co Durham]' *read* '**THE 3RD BARON MacANDREW**, of the Firth of Clyde (Christopher Anthony Colin MacAndrew) [The Rt Hon The Lord MacAndrew, Hall Farm, Archdeacon Newton, Co Durham DL2 2YB]'

Mac GREGOR of Mac GREGOR: in entry for the 6th and present Bt's er s and heir *for* 'Archers, FRGS' *read* 'Archers'

MACKAY OF ARDBRECKNISH: the Life Baron was appointed Shadow Dep Leader Ho Lds Dec 1998

MACKAY OF CLASHFERN: the Life Baron was apptd July 1998 chm C Party constitutional commn to look at Ho Lds reform

MACKENZIE, Bt, of Coul: in entry for Kevin Roderick Mackenzie [er s of 2nd s (by his 2nd w) of Lt-Col Roderick Henry Turing Mackenzie, gf of the heir presumptive] *for* '*m* 1992 *Alexandra Mary Morton' *read* '*m* 1992 *Alexandra Jane Morton'; in entry for Angus Keith Turing Mackenzie [yr bro of heir presumptive] *for* 'Perseiner' *read* 'Persciner'

MACLEHOSE: the Life Baron was made KT [*i.e.*, Knight of the Thistle] 1983, not 'kt' [*i.e.*, knight bachelor]

MACNAGHTEN: *see* CAITHNESS above

MALET: a dau (Tabitha Louise) was *b* 31 Jan 1999 to Rachel and Charles Edward St Lo Malet, only s and heir of the 9th Bt

MALMESBURY: *for* '**THE 6TH EARL OF MALMESBURY, Viscount FitzHarris**, of Hurn Court, Co Southampton, and **6th Baron Malmesbury**, of Malmesbury, Co Wilts (William James Harris, TD (1944), JP (Hants 1950)) [The Right Hon The Earl of Malmesbury TD JP, The Coach House, Greywell, Hants RG25 1DB]; *b* 18 Nov 1907; *s* f 1950; *educ* Eton and Trin Coll Cambridge (BA 1930); CC Hants 1952, Ld Lt Hants and IoW 1973–74 (V-Lt 1960, DL 1957), Ld Lt Hants 1974–, Maj Hants Regt TA (ret), Gold Staff Offr Coronation 1937, ARICS 1937, Official Verderer New Forest 1966–, Min Ag's personal liaison offr Western Counties SE Regn 1959–64, chm: Hants Ag Exec Ctee 1960–67 (Dep Chm 1952–60), CLA (Hants Branch) 1954–55, Hants and IoW T&AFA 1960–68, Eastern Wessex TAVRA 1968–70, Master Skinners' Co 1953; *m* 1st 7 July 1932 Hon Diana Claudia Patricia Carleton (*d* 1990), er dau of 2nd Baron Dorchester (*see* 1897 edn); *m* 2nd 1991 Margaret Fleetwood, OBE (*d* 20 Dec 1994), yst dau of Col Robert William Pigott Clarke Campbell-Preston, of Ardchattan Priory, Argyllshire (*see also* COWDRAY, V), and widow of Capt Raymond Alexander Baring (*see* BARING, Bt), and has by his

1st w etc:' *read* '**THE 6TH EARL OF MALMESBURY**, **Viscount FitzHarris**, of Hurn Court, Co Southampton, and **Baron Malmesbury**, of Malmesbury, Co Wilts (William James Harris, TD (1944), JP (Hants 1950)) [The Right Hon The Earl of Malmesbury TD JP, The Ford, Greywell, Hants RG29 1BS]; *b* 18 Nov 1907; *s f* 1950; *educ* Eton and Trin Coll Cambridge (BA 1930); CC Hants 1952, Ld Lt Hants and IoW 1973–74 (V-Lt 1960–73, DL 1957), Ld Lt Hants 1974–82, Maj Hants Regt TA (ret), Gold Staff Offr Coronation 1937, ARICS 1937, Official Verderer New Forest 1966–74, Min Ag's personal liaison offr Western Counties SE Regn 1959–64, chm: Hants Ag Exec Ctee 1960–67 (Dep Chm 1952–60), CLA (Hants Branch) 1954–55, Hants and IoW T&AFA 1960–68, Eastern Wessex TAVRA 1968–70, Pres New Forest 9th Centenary Tst 1987–(Chm 1977–87), Master Skinners' Co 1953, KStJ 1973; *m* 1st 7 July 1932 Hon Diana Claudia Patricia Carleton (*d* 1990), er dau of 2nd Baron Dorchester (*see* 1897 edn); *m* 2nd 1991 Margaret Fleetwood, OBE (*d* 20 Dec 1994), yst dau of Col Robert William Pigott Clarke Campbell-Preston, of Ardchattan Priory, Argyllshire (*see also* COWDRAY, V), and widow of Capt Raymond Alexander Baring (*see* BARING, Bt); *m* 3rd 1996 Bridget (*d* 26 Jan 1999), formerly w of — Hawkings, and has his 1st w etc:'

MANCROFT: a yr s was *b* 3 Aug 1998 to the 3rd and current Baron

MARKS OF BROUGHTON: the 2nd Baron *d* 9 Sept 1998 and was *s* as 3rd Baron by his only s, who was by his 1st w

MEATH: the 14th Earl *d* 19 Dec 1998 and was *s* as 15th Earl by his er s

MONTGOMERY: the 9th and present Bt's yst dau, Laura, *m* 5 Sept 1998 *David Redvers, s of John Redvers, of Hartpury, Glos

MONTROSE: the 6th Duke's er dau, Mary Helen Alma, *d* 7 Feb 1999

MOON of Portman Sq: the 5th and present Bt has by *Noodaeng ('Mem'), dau of Loon Samingram, of Thailand, a dau, *Elana, *b c* Dec 1998

MORLEY: the 6th and present Earl's yr bro, Robin Michael, *d* 3 Jan 1999

MOUNTBATTEN OF BURMA: the present title-holder's yst s, Timothy Nicholas Sean, *m* 11 July 1998 *Isabella, dau of David Norman, of Burkham, Hants

MOWBRAY, SEGRAVE and STOURTON: the 26th/ 27th/23rd and present Baron *m* 2nd by 24 Feb 1999 *Joan Marian, widow of Sir Guy Hope Holland, 3rd and last Bt (*see* ZOUCHE, B)

MOYNE: the 2nd Baron's 2nd w, Elisabeth, *d* 19 Jan 1999

NEWBOROUGH: the 7th Baron *d* 11 Oct 1998 and was *s* as 8th Baron by his only s

NORFOLK: the 17th and present Duke's est gs by his er s (Edward William, Earl of Arundel), Henry Miles, Lord Maltravers, was apptd Jan 1999 a Page of Honour to HM THE QUEEN

for '2c +Michael, KCVO (1971), CB (1968), CBE (1962, MBE 1949), MVO (1952), MC (1944), DL Wilts 1974–93 [Maj-Gen The Lord Michael Fitzalan Howard KCVO CB CBE MVO MC DL, Fovant House, Fovant, Wilts SP3 5LA][the 17th and present Duke's next yr bro]; *b* 22 Oct 1916; *educ* Ampleforth and Trin Coll Cambridge (BA 1938); WW II (despatches) NW Europe, Palestine 1945–46, Malaya 1948–49, Maj-Gen late Scots Gds, Cdr Mobile Force Allied Cmd Europe 1964–66, Ch Staff Southern Cmd 1967–68, GOC London Dist and Maj-Gen cmdg Household Div 1968–71, Marshal Dip Corps 1972–81, Hon Col Cambridge U OTC 1968–71, Col Queen's Lancs Regt 1970–78, Col Life Gds and Gold Stick HM 1979–, Chm Cncl TA&VRA 1973–81, Pres 1981–84, Patron 1984–93, Hon Recorder Br Cwlth Ex-Serv League 1992–, chm Dow Valley Petroleum-UK 1980– etc' *read* '2c +Michael, KCVO (1971, MVO 1952), CB (1968), CBE (1962, MBE 1949), MC (1944) [Maj-Gen The Lord Michael Fitzalan Howard KCVO CB CBE MC, Fovant House, Fovant, Wilts SP3 5LA]; *b* 22 Oct 1916; *educ* Ampleforth and Trin Coll Cambridge (BA 1938); WW II (despatches) NW Europe, Palestine 1945–46, Malaya 1948–49, Maj-Gen late Scots Gds, Cdr Mobile Force Allied Cmd Europe 1964–66, Ch Staff Southern Cmd 1967–68, GOC London Dist and Maj-Gen cmdg Household Div 1968–71, Marshal Dip Corps 1972–81, Hon Col Cambridge U OTC 1968–71, Col Queen's Lancs Regt 1970–78, Col Life Gds and Gold Stick 1979–, TA&VRA: Chm Cncl 1973–81, Pres 1981–84, Patron 1984–93; DL Wilts 1974–93, Hon Recorder Br Cwlth Ex-Serv League 1992–, chm Dow Valley Petroleum-UK 1980–, Extra Equerry to HM THE QUEEN 1999– etc'

NUNBURNHOLME: the 4th Baron *d* 28 July 1998 and was *s* as 5th Baron by his yr bro Charles, who in Feb 1999 resigned the Conservative whip in the Ho Lds and though sitting as a cross-bencher became a spokesman for the Democratic Party (organisation promoting UK withdrawal from EU but retention of membership of European Common Market)

NUTTING: the 3rd Bt *d* 24 Feb 1999 and was *s* as 4th Bt by his er s; *for* '3 *Zara Nina [only dau of 3rd Bt]' *read* '1 *Zara Nina'

OXFORD AND ASQUITH: *for* '*Raymond Henry [The Hon Raymond Bonham Carter, 7 West Heath Ave, London NW11] [2nd s of Baroness Asquith of Yarnbury, only dau of 1st Earl by his 1st w]; *b* 19 June 1929; *educ* Winchester, Magdalen Coll Oxford (BA 1952) and Harvard (MBA 1954); 2nd Lt Irish Gds 1947–49, exec dir S G Warburg & Co 1967–77, ret 1975 following disability' *read* '*Raymond Henry [The Hon Raymond Bonham Carter, 7 West Heath Ave, London NW11]; *b* 19 June 1929; *educ* Winchester, Magdalen Coll Oxford (BA 1952) and Harvard Business Sch (MBA 1954); 2nd Lt Irish Gds 1947–49, with J Henry Schroder & Co 1954–58, actg advsr Bank of England 1958–63, alternate exec dir UK IMF and memb UK Treasury and Supply Delegn Washington 1961–63, with S G Warburg 1964–79 (exec dir 1967–77), dir: Tport Devpt Gp 1969–77, Banque de Paris et des Pays Bas NV 1973–77 and Mercury Securities 1974–77, seconded as Dir Industl Devpt DOI 1977–79, memb Cncl ISS (Hon Treas 1974–84)'

in entry for Helena Bonham-Carter [only dau of Raymond Henry above] *for* '*The Wings of the Dove* (1996, US National Board of Review of Motion Pictures best actress award 1997) (films)' *read* '*The Wings of the Dove* (1996, US National Board of Review of Motion Pictures best actress award 1997), *The Theory of Flight* (1997, Brussels Film Festival Crystal Star for best European feature 1999) (films)'

PAGET of Cranmore Hall: *for* '*John Wells' *read* 'John Wells (*d* 1997)'

PEEL: *for* '*Robert George [Robert Thorne Esq, Ovington House, Ovington, Hants] [er s of only dau of Hon (Arthur) George Villiers Peel, 2nd s of 1st Viscount Peel of Sandy]; *b* 7 Feb 1943; *educ* Eton and RAC Cirencester; with Barclays Bank 1964'; *m* 1990 *Sarah Veronica Bond, *née* Priestley' *read* '*Robert George [Robert Thorne Esq, Ovington House, Ovington, Hants]; *b* 7 Feb 1943; *educ* Eton and RAC Cirencester; with Barclays Bank 1964; *m* 1990 *Sarah Veronica, dau of Maj James Priestley, MC (*see* POLLOCK, Bt), and formerly w of Brian David Bond'

PELLY: *for* '**Lineage:** JOHN PELLYE etc' *read* '**Lineage:** The PELLYs may descend from a Norman family known to have originated at Au Peley, north of Coutances, one branch leaving just before the absorption of the mainland Duchy of Normandy territory by France in the early 13th century to settle in Guernsey, another to Dorset. (Three armigerous families called Le Pelley survived in Normandy into modern times; a Dumanoir Le Pelley was second in command of the French fleet at Trafalgar, hence a contemporary, and in the same branch of the armed services, as his putative distant cousin Capt Charles Pelly, the **1st Bt**'s brother.) A connection has been suggested but is unproven between the Norman-origin PELLYs and (a) John Pelley (*fl* 1383–1419), (b) William Pelley, gentleman, of Sturminster Marshall (*fl* 1431/2–40), (c) Sir John Pelley (*fl* 1454–86), Escheator (royal official implementing reversion to the Crown of certain lands) for Norfolk and Suffolk, and (d) William Pelley, of Sturminster Newton, between all of whom any family link is similarly conjectural. The last named was living in 1539 and was probably f of: JOHN PELLYE etc'

PERRING: the 1st Bt *d* 29 June 1998 and was *s* as 2nd Bt by his er surv s

PERTH: the 17th and present Earl, whose London address as printed is no longer operative, resigned as a Tstee Nat Library of Scotland 1995; his w, Nancy Seymour, *d* 7 June 1996;

also *for*   '6f Edward; *b* 11 March 1883; BCS; *m* 7 Aug 1862 Lucy Marion (*d* 5 April 1922), dau of Rev Charles J Barnard, and *d* 30 Nov 1916, leaving:

1g Edmund Berkeley; *b* 9 Jan 1867; *m* 6 June 1888 Mabel (*dsp* 29 Sept 1888), dau of Rev Francis Edward Tuke, Vicar Borden, and *d* 11 June 1961

2g Eustace Harvey; *b* 13 Aug 1870; *educ* Clifton; Lt RA Boer War; *d* 25 Aug 1954

1g Lilias Caroline; *b* 9 March 1868; *m* 1st 3 Aug 1897 (annulled 1905) John Cuthbert Eyre Leslie, yr s of Charles Stephen Leslie of Balquhain (for whose early ancestry *see* LESLIE, Bt); *m* 2nd 31 July 1906 Capt William Edward Murray (*ka* Sept 1914), Gordon Highrs, of The Manor House, Littlehampton, 3rd s and eventual heir of Lt-Col John Murray of Mastrick, and *d* 5 April 1959, having added her maiden name to his by deed poll 11 Jan 1919, leaving, with two daus:

1h Edward John MURRAY later DRUMMOND-MURRAY (roy licence 11 Jan 1919); *b* 17 June 1907; *educ* Beaumont; Capt Roy Sussex Regt WW II, memb Richmond Borough Cncl; *m* 1st 1 Dec 1928 (divorce 1936) Eulalia Ildefonsa Wilhelmina (*d* 1988), dau of William Anthony Raymond Heaven, of Ashfield, Queen's Co, and had:

1i *(William Edward) Peter Louis [Peter Drummond-Murray of Mastrick, 67 Dublin St, Edinburgh EH7 4RT]; *b* 24 Nov 1929; *educ* Beaumont; dir Utd and Gen Tst, Slains Pursuivant of Arms to Ld High Constable of Scotland (*see* ERROLL, E), SMO Malta: Kt Hon and Devotion 1971, Grand Cross Obedience 1984, Chllr Br Assoc 1977–89, Scottish Del 1989–; KStJ 1988; *m* 12 July 1954 *Hon Barbara Mary Hope, yst dau of 2nd Baron Rankeillour (qv), and has:

1j *Andrew Philip; *b* 3 July 1958; *educ* Worth; *m* 1981 *Susan Fiona Dorinthea, dau of Prof Donald Michie (*see* ABERCONWAY, B), and has:

1k *John Douglas; *b* 1986

1k *Jessica Catharine; *b* 1983

2k *Laura Catriona; *b* 1988

2j *James; *b* 25 Nov 1959; *m* 1989 *Namkhang, dau of Mak Tonwong, of Thailand

3j *Robert; *b* 4 March 1965

4j *Walter David; *b* 1973

1j *Isabel May; *b* 2 June 1966

2i *Ian Malcolm Gerard; *b* 17 Oct 1930; *educ* Beaumont; *m* 1st 25 July 1952 (divorce 1960) Marguerite Mary, dau of Dr Robert Robertson MacGibbon, of Huddersfield, and has:

1j *Hamish William Ian Algernon; *b* 14 March 1953

2j *Jasper Robert Ian Douglas; *b* 27 Feb 1954

3j *Ruaraidh Angus Ian Alastair; *b* 7 July 1955

4j *Alexander Sebastian Hugh Ian; *b* 14 June 1956

1h (cont.) Edward Drummond-Murray of Mastrick *m* 2nd 5 March 1936 Auriol Enid, dau of Cyril Broxholm, of Manchester, and *d* 1976, leaving by her:

3i *Anthony John; *b* 9 March 1944

4i *Niall Andrew; *b* 30 June 1947

5i *Richard Mark; *b* 4 Dec 1948

1f Hester Eliza; *b* 16 Oct 1820; *d* unm 1852

2f Georgina Charlotte; *b* 7 Nov 1822; *m* 12 June 1845 Alexander John Talbot EUSTACE MALPAS formerly EUSTACE, only s of Sir William Cornwallis Eustace (*d* 1870), and *d* 1887, leaving issue, who resumed the surname EUSTACE only

3f Henrietta Maria; *b* 14 June 1831; *m* 4 April 1853 Sir Campbell Munro, 3rd Bt, of Lindertis (qv), and *d* 28 Aug 1912, leaving issue

1e Charlotte; *b* 10 Nov 1791; *m* 27 Nov 1823 Robert Hibbert (*d* 17 Dec 1829), of Chalfont Lodge, Bucks, and *d* 15 Dec 1876

2e Harriet Anne; *b* 21 Dec 1795; *d* 6 July 1865

2d (cont) John Drummond *m* 2nd 1 May 1806 Barbara (*d* 9 Aug 1832)'

read '6f Edward; *b* 11 March 1883; BCS; *m* 7 Aug 1862 Lucy Marion (*d* 5 April 1922), dau of Rev Charles J Barnard, RN, and *d* 30 Nov 1916, leaving:

1g Edmund Berkeley; *b* 9 Jan 1867; *m* 6 June 1888 Mabel (*dsp* 29 Sept 1888), dau of Rev Francis Edward Tuke, Vicar Borden, and *d* 11 June 1961

2g Eustace Harvey; *b* 13 Aug 1870; *educ* Clifton; Lt RA Boer War; *d* 25 Aug 1954

1g Lilias Caroline; *b* 9 March 1868; *m* 1st 3 Aug 1897 (*annulled* 1905) John Cuthbert Eyre Leslie, yr s of Charles Stephen Leslie of Balquhain (for whose early ancestry *see* LESLIE, Bt); *m* 2nd 31 July 1906 Capt William Edward Murray (*ka* Sept 1914), Gordon Highrs, of The Manor House, Littlehampton, 3rd s and eventual heir of Lt-Col John Murray of Mastrick, and *d* 5 April 1959, having added her maiden name to his by deed poll 11 Jan 1919, leaving, with two daus:

1h Edward John MURRAY later DRUMMOND-MURRAY (11 Jan 1919); *b* 17 June 1907; *educ* Beaumont; Capt Roy Sussex Regt WW II, memb Richmond Borough Cncl; *m* 1st 1 Dec 1928 (*divorce* 1936) Eulalia Ildefonsa Wilhelmina (*d* 1988), dau of William Anthony Raymond Heaven, of Ashfield, Queen's Co, and had:

1i *(William Edward) Peter Louis [Peter Drummond-Murray of Mastrick, 6/2 Huntingdon Place, Edinburgh EH7 4RT]; *b* 24 Nov 1929; *educ* Beaumont; late dir Tyndall Ltd and N M Rothschild Asset Management; Slains Pursuivant of Arms to Ld High Constable of Scotland (*see* ERROLL, E), SMO Malta: Kt Hon and Devotion 1971, Grand Cross Obedience 1984, Chllr Br Assoc 1977–89, Scottish Del 1989–; KStJ 1988; *m* 12 July 1954 *Hon Barbara Mary Hope, yst dau of 2nd Baron Rankeillour (*qv*), and has:

1j *Andrew Philip [Andrew Drummond-Murray Esq, 115 Fortress Rd, London NW5 2HR]; *b* 3 July 1958; *educ* Worth; *m* 31 July 1981 (*divorce* 7 April 1997) Susan Fiona Dorinthea, dau of Prof Donald Michie (*see* ABERCONWAY, B), and has:

1k *John Douglas; *b* 29 July 1986
1k *Jessica Catharine; *b* 9 Sept 1983
2k *Laura Catriona; *b* 14 Dec 1988

2j *James [James Drummond-Murray Esq, Flat 2, City View Court, Overhill Rd, London SE22 0PZ]; *b* 25 Nov 1959; *educ* Worth and Sheffield and Bradford Us; archaeologist, Kt Hon and Devotion SMO Malta 1981; *m* 18 Feb 1989 *Namkang, dau of Mak Tonwong, of Thailand

3j *Robert [Robert Drummond-Murray Esq, 23 Lincoln Rd, Bolton BL1 4HR]; *b* 4 March 1965; *educ* Worth and Plumpton Ag Coll; with Customs and Excise, Kt Hon and Devotion SMO Malta 1990

4j *Walter David; *b* 2 Jan 1973; *educ* Edinburgh Acad and Strathclyde U; civil servant

1j *Isabel May [Miss Isabel Drummond-Murray, 54 Queen Charlotte St, Edinburgh EH6 7EX]; *b* 2 June 1966; *educ* Mayfield Convent, Alcester GS and St Andrews; civil servant

2i Ian Malcolm Gerard; *b* 17 Oct 1930; *educ* Beaumont; *m* 25 July 1952 (*divorce* 1960) Marguerite Mary (*d* 27/28 Oct 1990), dau of Dr Robert Robertson MacGibbon, of Huddersfield, and *d* 14 Oct 1989, having had:

1j Hamish William Ian Algernon; *b* 14 March 1953; *d* 4 Dec 1973

2j Jasper Robert Ian Douglas; *b* 27 Feb 1954; *m* 25 July 1984 *Edwina, dau of Geoffrey Barnes, of Bugbrooke, Northants, and *d* 12 March 1983

3j *Ruaraidh Angus Ian Alastair [Ruaraidh Drummond-Murray Esq, Hawthorn House, 32 Clarke Court, Earls Barton, Northants NN6 6LX]; *b* 7 July 1955; *m* 30 Sept 1978 *Susan, dau of W L Booth, of Bugbrooke, Northants, and has:

1k *David Ruaraidh; *b* 13 June 1979
1k *Tracey Mary; *b* 9 May 1981

4j Alexander Sebastian Hugh Ian; *b* 14 June 1956; *d* 31 Jan 1972

1h (cont) Edward Drummond-Murray of Mastrick *m* 2nd 5 March 1936 Auriol Enid (*d* 13 Aug 1973), dau of Cyril Broxholm, of Manchester, and *d* 30 June 1976, leaving by her:

3i *Anthony John [Anthony Drummond-Murray Esq, 8 Glamorgan Rd, Hampton Wick KT1 4HP]; *b* 9 March 1944; *m* 10 Aug 1968 Avril Sandra Joyce (*d* 14 March 1996), dau of Kenneth Tilford, of Norwich, and has:

1j *Justin Alexander; *b* 24 Dec 1969
2j *Dominick Giles; *b* 25 May 1978
4i *Niall Andrew; *b* 30 June 1947
5i *Richard Mark; *b* 4 Dec 1948

1f Hester Eliza; *b* 16 Oct 1820; *d* unm 1852

2f Georgina Charlotte; *b* 7 Nov 1822; *m* 12 June 1845 Alexander John Talbot EUSTACE MALPAS formerly EUSTACE, only s of Sir William Cornwallis Eustace (*d* 1870), and *d* 1887, leaving issue, who resumed the surname EUSTACE only

3f Henrietta Maria; *b* 14 June 1831; *m* 4 April 1853 Sir Campbell Munro, 3rd Bt, of Lindertis (*qv*), and *d* 28 Aug 1912, leaving issue

1e Charlotte; *b* 10 Nov 1791; *m* 27 Nov 1823 Robert Hibbert (*d* 17 Dec 1829), of Chalfont Lodge, Bucks, and *d* 15 Dec 1876

2e Harriet Anne; *b* 21 Dec 1795; *d* 6 July 1865

2d (cont) John Drummond *m* 2nd 1 May 1806 Hon Barbara (*d* 9 Aug 1832), Maid of Hon to QUEEN CHARLOTTE'

PETRE: Diana Audrey Constance Petre [er dau of Maj Robert David Oswald Petre, yr s of only s of yr s of Edward Henry Petre, JP, DL, of Whitley Abbey, Warwicks, er s by his 2nd w of Henry William Petre, n of 10th Baron] *m* 10 Aug 1998 *Jamie Douglas Daer Reid, yr s of Maj-Gen Peter Daer Reid, CB (*see* JACKSON, Bt, of Arlsey)

PHILLIPS OF ELLESMERE: the Life Baron *d* 23 Feb 1999, when the title expired

PORTMAN: the 8th Viscount's 2nd w, Nancy Maureen, *d* 31 Dec 1998

PORTSMOUTH: the 9th Earl's 2nd s's (by his 2nd w) w Lavinia was elected Jan 1999 an Hon Master Bench Gray's Inn

ROBSON OF KIDDINGTON: the Life Baroness *d* 9 Feb 1999, when the title expired

ROSEBERY: Helen Dorothy [the 6th Earl's er dau] *d* Oct 1998

ROTHERMERE: the 3rd Viscount *d* 1 Sept 1998 and was *s* as 4th Viscount by his only s

RUNCIMAN OF DOXFORD: the 1st Viscount's 3rd dau, Katherine, *d* July 1998

RUTLAND: the 10th Duke *d* 3 Jan 1999 and was *s* as 11th Duke by his est s

RYAN: *for* '1a +Barry Desmond [est s of heir presumptive]; *b* 30 June 1943; *m* 19–*— and has:

1b +Andrew; *b* 19–'

read '1a +Barry Desmond; *b* 30 June 1943; *m* 1975 *Evodia Masemola and has:

1b +Andrew Desmond; *b* 1986
1b *Lerato; *b* 1978'

SACKVILLE: in the section **Seat** the statement 'The first creator of Knole was apparently Thomas Bourchier etc' should be interpreted in the light of the statement in the article SAYE AND SELE, in the entry for the 1st Baron of the Feb 1446/7 creation, that he built Knole with spoils from the Hundred Years War. It seems on balance that a part at any rate of the fabric of the present mansion antedates Bourchier's proprietorship.

SAINSBURY: the Life Baron (*cr* 3 May 1962) *d* 21 Oct 1998, when the title expired

SAINT ALDWYN: *for* '1b +Edward Erick [er s of Edward Adryan Hicks-Beach, s of 4th s of William Frederick Hicks-Beach, yr bro of 1st Earl]; *b* 4 Sept 1941 etc' *read* '1b +Edward Erick [Edward Hicks-Beach, RR1 Box 60Y, Custer, SD 57730, USA]; *b* 4 Sept 1941; *m* 13 Aug 1991 *Betty May, dau of Henry C Snider, of Johnson Co, Iowa

2b +Frederick Howe [Frederick Hicks-Beach, 5181 Heil Ave, Huntington Beach, CA 92649, USA]; *b* 21 June 1944; *m* 12 Dec 1970 *Kathleen Mary, dau of Roy Edward Fincher, and has:

1c +Chad Edward; *b* 12 Dec 1977
1c *Cara; *b* 19 Jan 1983'

SALUSBURY-TRELAWNY: *for* '**SIR JOHN BARRY SALUSBURY-TRELAWNY, 13TH BT**, of Trelawny, Cornwall, JP (Kent 1973) [Sir John Trelawny Bt JP, Beavers Hill, Rectory Lane, Saltwood, Kent CT21 4QA]; *b* 4 Sept 1934; *s* f 1956; *educ* HMS *Worcester*; late 2nd Offr Merchant Navy, Sub-Lt RNVR, FInstM 1974, dir The Martin Walter Group Ltd 1971–74, jt dep md Korn Ferry Internat Inc 1981–83, dir Goddard Kay, Rogers Assoc 1984– (chm 1993–); *m* 4 Jan 1958 *Carol Knox, yr dau of Charles Frederick Knox Watson, of Saltwood, and has:

1 +JOHN WILLIAM RICHARD [John Salusbury-Trelawny Esq, 278 Seabrook Rd, Hythe, Kent]; *b* 30 March 1960; *m* 1st 1980 (*divorce* 1986) Anita, yr dau of Kenneth Snelgrove, and has:

(1) +Harry John; *b* 10 Dec 1982
(1) +Victoria Hayley; *b* 1981

1 (cont.) JOHN SALUSBURY-TRELAWNY *m* 2nd 1987 (*divorce* 1993) Sandra Patricia, dau of Joseph Thompson, of Hythe, and by her has:

(2) +Thomas Jonathon; *b* 1989

1 *Jane Louise; *b* 5 Sept 1958; *m* 1977 *Maj John R Martin, Parachute Regt, and has:

(1) *James Jonathan; *b* 1982
(1) *Emma Jane; *b* 1980

2 *Amanda Sarah; *b* 28 July 1961; *m* 1980 *Capt Alan M Startin, Devonshire and Dorset Regt, and has:

(1) *Matthew Guy; *b* 1982
(2) *Benjamin Marcus; *b* 1984
(3) *Hamish William; *b* 1988
(1) *Pollyanna Knox; *b* 1992

3 *Emma Mary; *b* 22 April 1966; *m* 1988 *William Ernle Hardy Vernon (*see* HARROWBY, E)

Lineage: HAMELIN; held Treloen or Trelawny, parish of Altarnun, Cornwall, from Robert Count of Mortain (half-bro of WILLIAM I (THE CONQUEROR)) 1086; had:

RICHARD; had:

WILLIAM; held a kt's fee from Reginald de Botrell; had

JOHN; *m* —, dau of his f's overlord Reginald de Botrell, and had:

WILLIAM; *m* Joan Trewynnick; had:

JOHN; living *temp* EDWARD I; *m* Laura, dau of Sir Richard Sergaux/Serjeaux, and had:

WILLIAM; MP Launceston *c* 1326; *m* Margery de Riparüs/Rivers, and had:

WILLIAM; *m* Joan Douggall and had:

Sir JOHN; living *c* 1367; *m* Matilda Mynwenyke and had:

Sir JOHN TRELAWNY; MP and Coroner Cornwall; granted pension of £20 (just under £500,000 in late–1990s terms) p.a. by HENRY V for mil servs in Hundred Years War, following which the TRELAWNYs long bore on their coat of arms an augmentation of three oak or laurel leaves; *m* Agnes Trogodeck and had, with an er s (Sir Richard, MP Liskeard 1422, *dspm*):

JOHN TRELAWNY; MP Truro 1449, Sheriff Cornwall *temp* EDWARD IV; *m* Joan, heiress of Heligan, and *d* after 1485, leaving:

Sir JOHN TRELAWNY; *m* Jane Powna and had, with a yr s (John, *m* Florence, sis of 1st Earl of Devon (*qv*) of the 1485 *cr*):

WALTER TRELAWNY; had:

JOHN TRELAWNY; MP Liskeard 1553; *m* 1st Margery Lamelion and had issue; *m* 2nd Lora Trecarrel and *d c* 1537, having had another s (John, *m* Beatrice Trevanion); his s by his 1st w:

JOHN TRELAWNY, DL (Cornwall); MP Lostwithiel and Cornwall; paid £6 (over £37,000 in late–1990s terms) to avoid being ktd; twice Sheriff *temp* ELIZABETH I; *m* Anne Reskymer and had a 2nd s:

Sir JONATHAN TRELAWNY; MP Liskeard *c* 1593 and Cornwall *c* 1597 and 1603, High Sheriff Cornwall *c* 1595, ktd 1597; *m* Elizabeth, 2nd dau of Sir Henry Killigrew, and *d* 21 June 1604, having had, with three daus and a yr s (Edward, of Coldrenick, Cornwall):

Sir John Trelawny, 1st Bt (E), so *cr* 1 July 1628, of Trelawny; *b* 24 April 1592; Sheriff Cornwall *c* 1631; *m* 1st Elizabeth, dau of Sir Reginald Mohun, 1st Bt, of Boconnock; *m* 2nd Douglas, widow of Sir William Courtenay and dau and coheir of Tristram Gorges, and was *bur* 16 Feb 1664, having had, with other issue, including a yr s (Francis, *m* Margaret, dau of Sir Edward Seymour, 2nd Bt; *see* SOMERSET, D) and a dau (Margaret, *m* Amos, s of Sir Francis Fulford), an est s:

Sir Jonathan Trelawny, 2nd Bt; MP Cornwall 1661–78 and E Looe 1678–79; *m* Mary, dau of Sir Edward Seymour, 2nd Bt (*see* SOMERSET, D), and was *bur* 5 March 1680/1, having had, with other issue (*d* unm):

1 John; *m* Catherine, 3rd dau of James Jenkyn, and *dsp & vp*'

read '**SIR JOHN BARRY SALUSBURY-TRELAWNY, 13TH BT**, of Trelawny, Cornwall [Sir John Trelawny Bt JP, Beavers Hill, Rectory Lane, Saltwood, Kent CT21 4QA]; *b* 4 Sept 1934; *s* f 1956; *educ* HMS *Worcester*; late 2nd Offr Merchant Navy, Sub-Lt RNVR, FInstM 1974, dir: The Martin Walter Group Ltd 1971–74 and Goddard Kay, Rogers Assoc 1984–95 (chm 1993–95), jt dep md Korn Ferry Internat Inc 1981–83, JP Kent 1973–78, Pres London Cornish Assoc 1997–; *m* 4 Jan 1958 *Carol Knox, yr dau of Charles Francis Knox Watson, of Saltwood, and has:

1 +JOHN WILLIAM RICHARD [John Salusbury-Trelawny Esq, 278 Seabrook Rd, Hythe, Kent]; *b* 30 March 1960; *m* 1st 1980 (*divorce* 1986) Anita, yr dau of Kenneth Snelgrove, and has:

  (1) +Harry John; *b* 10 Dec 1982

  (1) +Victoria Hayley; *b* 31 Aug 1981

1 (cont.) JOHN SALUSBURY-TRELAWNY *m* 2nd 1987 (*divorce* 1993) Sandra Patricia, dau of Joseph Thompson, of Hythe, and by her has:

  (2) +Thomas Jonathon; *b* 23 March 1989

1 *Jane Louise; *b* 5 Sept 1958; *m* 1977 *Maj John R Martin, Parachute Regt, and has:

  (1) *James Jonathan; *b* 12 Feb 1982

  (1) *Emma Jane; *b* 7 July 1980

2 *Amanda Sarah; *b* 28 July 1961; *m* 1980 *Capt Alan M Startin, Devonshire and Dorset Regt, and has:

  (1) *Matthew Guy; *b* 24 Aug 1982

  (2) *Benjamin Marcus; *b* 24 April 1984

  (3) *Hamish William; *b* 1 April 1988

  (1) *Pollyanna Knox; *b* 19 Aug 1992

3 *Emma Mary; *b* 22 April 1966; *m* 1988 *William Ernle Hardy Vernon and has issue (*see* HARROWBY, E)

Lineage: HAMELIN; held Treloen or Trelawny, parish of Altarnun, Cornwall, from Robert Count of Mortain (half-bro of WILLIAM I (THE CONQUEROR)) 1086; had:

RICHARD; had:

WILLIAM; held a kt's fee from Reginald de Botrell; had:

JOHN; *m* Joan, dau of his f's overlord Reginald de Botrell, and had:

WILLIAM; *m* Joan Trewynnick; had:

JOHN; living *temp* EDWARD I; *m* Laura, dau of Sir Richard Sergaux/Serjeaux, and had:

WILLIAM; MP Launceston *c* 1326; *m* Margery de Riparüs/Rivers, and had:

WILLIAM; *m* Joan Doyngnell and had:

Sir JOHN; living *c* 1367; ktd 1407/8; *m* Matilda Mynwenyke and had:

Sir JOHN TRELAWNY; MP and Coroner Cornwall; granted pension of £20 (just under £500,000 in late–1990s terms) p.a. by HENRY V 1420/1 for mil servs in Hundred Years War, following which the TRELAWNYs long bore on their coat of arms an augmentation of three oak or laurel leaves; *m* Agnes Trogodeck and had, with an er s (Sir Richard, MP Liskeard 1422, *dspm*):

JOHN TRELAWNY; MP Truro 1449, Sheriff Cornwall *temp* EDWARD IV; *m* Joan, heiress of Heligan, and *d* after 1485, leaving:

Sir JOHN TRELAWNY; *m* Jane Powna and had, with a yr s (John, *m* Florence, sis of 1st Earl of Devon (*qv*) of the 1485 *cr*):

WALTER TRELAWNY; Constable Plympton 1510; *m* Isabel Tawse and had:

JOHN TRELAWNY; MP Liskeard 1553; *m* 1st Margery Lamelion and had issue; *m* 2nd Lora Trecarrel and *d c* 1563, having had another s (John, *m* Beatrice Trevanion); his s by his 1st w:

JOHN TRELAWNY, DL (Cornwall); MP Lostwithiel and Cornwall; paid £6 (over £37,000 in late–1990s terms) to avoid being ktd; twice Sheriff *temp* ELIZABETH I; *m* Anne Reskymer and *d* Oct 1568, leaving a 2nd s:

Sir JONATHAN TRELAWNY; MP Liskeard *c* 1593 and Cornwall *c* 1597 and 1603, High Sheriff Cornwall *c* 1595, ktd 1597; *m* Elizabeth, 2nd dau of Sir Henry Killigrew, and *d* 21 June 1604 just after being apptd Amb Spain and with a warrant ordered creating him Baron Tiverton, having had, with three daus and a yr s (Edward, of Coldrenick, Cornwall):

Sir John Trelawny, 1st Bt (E), so *cr* 1 July 1628, of Trelawny; *b* 27 April 1592; Sheriff Cornwall *c* 1631; *m* 1st Elizabeth, dau of Sir Reginald Mohun, 1st Bt, of Boconnock; *m* 2nd Douglas, widow of Sir William Courtenay and dau and coheir of Tristram Gorges, and was *bur* 16 Feb 1664, having had, with other issue, including a yr s (Francis, *m* Margaret, dau of Sir Edward Seymour, 2nd Bt; *see* SOMERSET, D) and a dau (Margaret, *m* Amos, s of Sir Francis Fulford), an est s:

Sir Jonathan Trelawny, 2nd Bt; MP Cornwall 1661–78 and E Looe 1678–79; *m* Mary, dau of Sir Edward Seymour, 2nd Bt (*see* SOMERSET, D), and was *bur* 5 March 1680/1, having had, with other issue (*d* unm bar a 4th s, Charles, *b* 1654, MP E Looe 1685, Maj-Gen, Govr Plymouth 1698, *m* Ann, dau of Richard Lower, of Hengar, and *d* 1734):

1 John; *m* Catherine, 3rd dau of Peter Jenkyn, and *dsp & vp*'

for '**Sir William Trelawny, 6th Bt**; Offr RN, Govr Jamaica; *m* his cousin Letitia (*d* 24 Aug 1772; *see* above) and *d* 11 Dec 1772, having had, with a dau (Letitia Anne, *m* Paul Treby Treby, of Plympton, Devon, and *d* 1 Dec 1845, leaving issue)'

read '**Sir William Trelawny, 6th Bt**; Offr RN, Govr Jamaica 1768–72; *m* his cousin Letitia (*d* 24 Aug 1772; *see* above) and *d* 11 Dec 1772, having had, with a dau (Letitia Anne, *m* Paul Treby Treby, of Plympton, Devon, and *d* 12 Feb 1840, leaving issue)'

Mrs Christopher Bell [widow of the 12th Bt] lives not at Ditchling, E Sussex, but at 32 Harvest Vale, Lindfield, W Sussex RH16 2LW

SAYE AND SELE: *see* above against SACKVILLE

SIMPSON OF DUNKELD: the Life Baron resigned Feb 1999 as md GEC

SINHA: the 5th Baron *d* 18 Jan 1999 and was *s* as 6th Baron by his er s

SOPER: the Life Baron *d* 22 Dec 1998, when the title expired

STEWART, Bt, of Stewartby: the 2nd Bt *d* 26 Jan 1999, when the btcy expired

STEWART-CLARK: the 3rd and current Bt's 2nd dau Nadia had a 3rd dau, *Emily Rose, *b* 12 Aug 1998

TALBOT OF MALAHIDE: a s, Edward Benedict Richard, was *b* 2 Feb 1999 to Lt-Cdr Richard Paul Talbot RN [est s of 10th and present Baron's senior 1st cousin]

TREVOR: The Hon IAIN ROBERT HILL-TREVOR, yr bro and heir presumptive to the 5th and current Baron, *m* 22 Aug 1998 *Kate, yr dau of David Lord, of Deighton Hills, Norfolk

USHER: the 7th Bt *d* 25 July 1998 and was *s* as 8th Bt by his er s

VERNON, B: *for* 'Emily; *m* Algernon Charles PERCY later HEBER-PERCY (*see* NORTHUMBERLAND, D), whereby the Hodnet estate ultimately passed to the HERBER-PERCYs' *read* 'Emily; *m* Algernon Charles PERCY later HEBER-PERCY (*see* NORTHUMBERLAND, D), whereby the Hodnet estate ultimately passed to the HEBER-PERCYs'

in the section **Lineage (of Harcourt)** in entry for the Sir John Harcourt who *d* 19 Feb 1564/5, *for* 'Sir Wiliam barentyne' *read* 'Sir William Barentyne'

WHITAKER: the 3rd Bt *d* 13 Jan 1999 and was *s* as 4th Bt by his only s

WAKEHAM: the Life Baron was apptd Feb 1999 Chm of the Royal Commission on Reform of the House of Lords

WHARNCLIFFE: *for* '1b Elizabeth Anne [aunt of 5th and present Earl]; *b* 8 May 1925; BS, MS; *m* 27 Nov 1948 (*divorce* 1963) Chester Lyman Kingsbury Jr, s of Chester Lyman Kingsbury, of Middletown, Ohio, and had:

  1c *Chester Lyman; *b* 14 Feb 1950

  1c *Meredith Ellen; *b* 1 May 1952

  2c *Michelle Elizabeth; *b* 8 Oct 1957

  2b *Joan Isabella [Mrs Harry Bishop,18 Webber Ave, Bath, ME 04530, USA]; *b* 20 July 1928; *m* 1 Dec 1951 *Harry Atwater Bishop Jr, s of Harry Atwater Bishop, of Gorham, NH, and has:

    1c *Harry Atwater III [Harry Bishop III, 15 Burnside St, Lancaster, NH 03584, USA]; *b* 1 Feb 1957; *educ* U of NH, Plymouth; *m* 1982 *Julie Sayre, dau of Leonard Mulligan, and has:

      1d *Alex MacKenzie; *b* 1986

      1d *Erin Sayre; *b* 1984

    2c *Alan Stuart Wortley; *b* 3 June 1959; *educ* Syracuse U (BA)

    1c *Wendy Ann Isabella; *b* 16 June 1953; *educ* U of NH, Durham (BA); *m* 1975 *Dennis Charles Gillespie and has:

      1d *Kelly Anne Isabella; *b* 1977

      2d *Meghan Therese; *b* 1980

    2c *Linda Walters [Mrs Nicolo Bimbo, 76 Center St, Groveland, MA 10834, USA]; *b* 16 Oct 1954; *educ* Springfield Coll Mass. (BS, MSM); *m* 1981 *Nicolo Bimbo and has:

      1d *Katherine Anne; *b* 1985'

read '1b Elizabeth Anne; *b* 8 May 1925; BS, MS; *m* 27 Nov 1948 (*divorce* 1963) Chester Lyman Kingsbury Jr, s of Chester Lyman Kingsbury, of Middletown, Ohio, and *d* 19 June 1993, leaving:

  1c *Chester Lyman [Chester L Kingsbury III, 9430 N Bald Eagle Ave, Tucson, AZ 86742, USA]; *b* 14 Feb 1950; *m* 19– *Kimberley –

  1c *Meredith Ellen [Mrs James Lambert, 269 Williamsbury Circle, Idaho Falls, ID 83404, USA]; *b* 1 May 1952; *m* 19– *James Lambert and has:

    1d *Jessica; *b* 19–

2c *Michelle Elizabeth [Dr Michelle Kingsbury, 2404 Amigo Court, Virginia Beach, VA 23456, USA]; *b* 8 Oct 1957; MD; *m* 19– *John Walker and has:

    1d *Zeb; *b* 11 Dec 1996

2b *Joan Isabella [Mrs Harry Bishop,18 Webber Ave, Bath, ME 04530, USA]; *b* 20 July 1928; *m* 1 Dec 1951 *Harry Atwood Bishop Jr, s of Harry Atwood Bishop, of Gorham, NH, and has:

    1c *Harry Atwood [Harry A Bishop III, 9 Colony Dve, Turner, ME 04282, USA]; *b* 1 Feb 1957; *educ* U of NH, Plymouth; *m* 1982 *Julie Sayre, dau of Leonard Mulligan, and has:

        1d *Alex McKenzie; *b* 28 July 1986

        1d *Erin Sayre; *b* 5 April 1984

    2c *Alan Stuart Wortley [Alan Bishop, 25 Kerry Hill, Fairport, NY 14450, USA]; *b* 3 June 1959; *educ* Syracuse U (BA); radio station manager in Rochester, NY; *m* 19– *Lisa, dau of Anthony and Anne Marconi, of Waterloo, NY, and has:

        1d *Andrew Anthony; *b* 27 Dec 1992

        1d *Colleen Joan; *b* 4 Oct 1994

    1c *Wendy Ann Isabella [Mrs Dennis Gillespie, 19 Woodhaven Dve, Andover, MA 01810, USA]; *b* 16 June 1952; *educ* U of NH, Durham (BA); medical technologist; *m* 1975 *Dennis Charles Gillespie and has:

        1d *Kelly Isabella; *b* 2 Nov 1977

        2d *Meghan Therese; *b* 27 April 1980

    2c *Linda Walters [Mrs Nicolo Bimbo, 15b Orchard Ave, Haverhill, MA 10830, USA]; *b* 9 Oct 1953; *educ* Springfield Coll Mass. (BS, MSA, MBA); exec dir Mental Health Agy Malden, Mass.; *m* 1981 *Nicolo Bimbo and has:

        1d *Katherine Anne; *b* 11 Feb 1985'

WILLS of Blagdon: the 4th Bt *d* 26 Aug 1998 and was *s* as 5th Bt by his est s

NEW LIFE PEERS

The creation of the following as life peers was announced 13 June 1998 (Birthday Honours):

Burns, Sir Terence, GCB, Perm Sec Treasury: BARON BURNS, of Pitshanger, London Borough of Ealing

Laming, Sir William Herbert, CBE, DL (Herts 1999), Ch Inspr Soc Servs Inspectorate: BARON LAMING, of Tewin, Co Hertford

Marshall, Sir Colin Marsh, chm BA: BARON MARSHALL OF KNIGHTSBRIDGE, of Knightsbridge, City of Westminster

Richardson, Rev Dr Kathleen, OBE, Moderator Free Churches' Cncl: BARONESS RICHARDSON OF CALOW, of Calow, Co Derby

The creation of the following as life peers was announced 19 June 1998 (Working Peers):

Ahmed, Nazir, fndr Br Muslim Cncllrs Forum: BARON AHMED, of Rotherham, Co S Yorks

Alli, Waheed, md Planet 24 (TV company): BARON ALLI, of Norbury, London Borough of Croydon

Bach, William Stephen Goulden, barrister: BARON BACH, of Luterworth, Co Leicester

Bell, Sir Tim, PR executive: BARON BELL, of Belgravia, City of Westminster

Bragg, Melvyn, broadcaster: BARON BRAGG, of Wigton, Co Cumbria

Brookman, David, Gen Sec Iron and Steel Trades Confedn: BARON BROOKMAN, of Ebbw Vale, Co Gwent

Buscombe, Mrs Peta Jane, a V-Chm C Pty: BARONESS BUSCOMBE, of Goring, Co Oxford

Christopher, Anthony, CBE, Chm Trades Union Fund Managers: BARON CHRISTOPHER, of Leckhampton, Co Gloucester

Clarke, Tony, CBE, ex-Dep Gen Sec UPW, Chm Lab Pty 1992–93: BARON CLARKE OF HAMPSTEAD, of Hampstead, London Borough of Camden

Clement-Jones, Timothy Francis, management and corporate affrs consultant: BARON CLEMENT-JONES, of Clapham, London Borough of Lambeth

Crawley, Mrs Christine Mary, Lab MEP Birmingham E: BARONESS CRAWLEY, of Edgbaston, Co W Midlands

Evans, David, chm Centurion Press Gp: BARON EVANS OF WATFORD, of Chipperfield, Co Hertford

Goudie, Mrs Mary Theresa, Sec Lab Solidarity Campaign 1980–84: BARONESS GOUDIE, of Roundwood, London Borough of Brent

Harris, Toby, Lab Leader Haringey Cncl: BARON HARRIS OF HARINGEY, of Hornsey, London Borough of Haringey

Haskins, Christopher Robin, chm Northern Foods and Express Dairies: BARON HASKINS, of Skidby, County of E Yorks

Lamont, Norman Stewart Hughson, PC, ex-Chllr Exchequer: BARON LAMONT OF LERWICK, of Lerwick, Shetland Islands

Mackenzie, Brian, ex-Pres Police Superintendents' Assoc: BARON MACKENZIE OF FRAMWELLGATE, of Durham, Co Durham

Miller, Sue, ex-Lib Dem Leader S Somerset DC: BARONESS MILLER OF CHILTHORNE DOMER, of Chilthorne Domer, Co Somerset

Norton, Philip, Dir Centre Legislative Studies Hull U: BARON NORTON OF LOUTH, of Louth, Co Lincoln

Phillips, Andrew Wyndham, OBE, slr: BARON PHILLIPS OF SUDBURY, of Sudbury, Co Suffolk

Sawyer, Tom, Gen-Sec Lab Pty, dir Reed Executive 1999–: BARON SAWYER, of Darlington, Co Durham

Sharp, Margaret, fndr memb SDP: BARONESS SHARP OF GUILDFORD, of Guildford, Co Surrey

Thornton, Mrs (Dorothea) Glenys, Chm GLC Lab Pty 1986–91: BARONESS THORNTON, of Manningham, Co W Yorks

Tomlinson, John Edward, Lab MEP Birmingham W, MP Meriden 1974–79: BARON TOMLINSON, of Walsall, Co W Midlands

Uddin, Mrs Manzila Pola, ex-Dep Leader Tower Hamlets Cncl: BARONESS UDDIN, of Bethnal Green, London Borough of Tower Hamlets

Warner, Norman, Sr Policy Advsr to Home Sec, Dir Soc Servs Kent CC 1985–91: BARON WARNER, of Brockley, London Borough of Lewisham

White, Paul, ex-C Gp Leader Essex CC, ex-Dep Chm Local Govt Assoc: BARON HANNINGFIELD, of Chelmsford, Co Essex

The creation of the following as a life peer was announced 3 Aug 1998 (on being appointed Scottish Office Min for business and industry):

Macdonald, (An)Gus John, CBE, chm Scottish Media Gp, BARON MACDONALD OF TRADESTON, of Tradeston, City of Glasgow

The creation of the following as life peers was announced 1 Oct 1998 (on becoming Lds of Appeal in Ordinary):

Ld Justice Hobhouse (Rt Hon Sir John Stewart Hobhouse), BARON HOBHOUSE OF WOODBOROUGH, of Woodborough, Co Wilts

Ld Justice Millett (Rt Hon Sir Peter Julian Millett, PC), BARON MILLETT, of St Marylebone, City of Westminster

The creation of the following as life peers was announced 31 Dec 1998 (New Year Honours):

Imbert, Sir Peter Michael, QPM, JP, Ld-Lt Gtr London, Metropolitan Police Commr 1987–93, BARON IMBERT, of New Romney, Co Kent

Patel, Sir Naren(drakumar) Babubhai, consultant obstetrician Ninewells Hosp Dundee, formerly Pres RCOG and Chm Acad of Medical Roy Colls

O'Neill, Onora Sylvia, CBE (*see* RATHCAVAN, B)

Trotman, Sir Alexander, formerly chm and ch exec Ford Motor Co

Williamson, Sir David Francis, GCMG, CB, formerly Sec-Gen EC, BARON WILLIAMSON OF HORTON, of Horton, Co Somerset

The creation of the following as a life peer was announced 15 Jan 1999 (on becoming a Ld of Appeal in Ordinary):

Ld Justice Phillips (Rt Hon Sir Nicholas Addison Phillips, PC), BARON PHILLIPS OF WORTH MATRAVERS, of Belsize Park, London Borough of Camden